ISTRY ★ BIOLOGY ★ INVENTION
NATURE ★ INDUSTRY ★ SOCIOLOGY ★ ARCHEOLOGY
CROWN OF DISTINCTION
D1363546

THE
Consolidated-Webster
ENCYCLOPEDIC DICTIONARY

A LIBRARY OF
ESSENTIAL KNOWLEDGE

THE

Consolidated-Webster ENCYCLOPEDIC DICTIONARY

A Library of Essential Knowledge

Editor-in-Chief
FRANKLIN J. MEINE, Ph.B., M.A.

Associate Editors

DOROTHY O. ELLIOTT : FRITZ LEIBER, JR.
HAROLD LEE HITCHENS : CHARLES L. HOPKINS, JR.
GENEVRA D. DONOVAN : WILLIAM P. SCHENK
ORVILLE R. SNAPP : JACOB KOFFLER
LESTER M. STEARNS

Chicago : 1964

15

This dictionary is not published by the original publishers of WEBSTER'S DICTIONARY *or their successors*

The Consolidated-Webster Encyclopedic dictionary includes material contained in *Webster's Comprehensive Encyclopedic Dictionary*, copyright 1940, 1941, 1942; *Webster's Columbia Reference Dictionary; Webster's Columbia Concise Dictionary*, copyright 1939; by Columbia Educational Books, Inc.

Previous editions of this book have been published under the name of
WEBSTER'S COLUMBIA ENCYCLOPEDIC DICTIONARY *and*
WEBSTER'S ENCYCLOPEDIC DICTIONARY

Published by
CONSOLIDATED BOOK PUBLISHERS
DIVISION OF BOOK PRODUCTION INDUSTRIES, INC.

PRINTED IN THE UNITED STATES OF AMERICA

HINTS ON ENGLISH ETYMOLOGY

THE English language is one of a group of closely allied languages which are known by the general name of the Teutonic or Germanic tongues. The other languages of the group, some of which are more closely connected with English than the rest, are Dutch, German, Danish, Icelandic or Old Norse, Swedish, and Gothic; to which may be added, as of less importance and having more the character of dialects, Norwegian, Frisian, the Plattdeutsch or Low German of Northern Germany, and Flemish, which differs little from Dutch. The evidence that all these languages are closely akin is to be found in the great number of words that they possess in common, in the similarity of their structure, their inflections, their manner of compounding words—in short, in their family likeness. This likeness can only be accounted for by supposing that these languages are all descended from one common language, the primitive Teutonic, which must have been spoken at a remote period by the ancestors of the present Teutonic peoples, there being then only one Teutonic people as well as one Teutonic tongue. In their earliest form, therefore, and when they began to be differentiated, these languages must have had the character of mere dialects, and it is only in so far as each has had a history and literature of its own that they have attained the rank of independent languages. The rise of dialects is a well-known phenomenon, taking its origin in the perpetual change to which all languages are subject. A language that comes to be spoken over a considerable area and by a considerable number of persons—more especially when not yet to some extent fixed by writing and literature—is sure to develop dialects, and each of these may in course of time become unintelligible to the persons using the others, if the respective speakers have little intercourse with each other, being separated by mountain ranges, arms of the sea, or merely by distance. In this way is the existence of the different Teutonic tongues to be accounted for. A similar instance of several languages arising from one is seen in the case of Italian, French, Spanish, and Portuguese, all of which are descended from the Latin. Of the common origin of these we have, of course, direct and abundant evidence.

The Teutonic tongues are often divided into three sections, based on closeness of relationship: the *High German*, of which the modern classical German is the representative; the *Low German*, including English, Dutch, Frisian, and Gothic; and the *Scandinavian*, including Danish, Swedish, and Icelandic. Another division is into: *East Germanic*, which includes only the Gothic; *North Germanic*, which includes Danish, Swedish, and Icelandic; and *West Germanic*, which includes English, Dutch, and German. Some authorities again make only two divisions: *East Germanic*, including Gothic and Scandinavian; and *West Germanic*, including the others.

The Gothic language presents us with the earliest specimens of any Teutonic speech that we possess. This tongue, which has long been extinct, is known to us almost solely from fragments of a translation of the Bible made by Bishop Ulfilas or Wulfilas, about A.D. 360. These remains, scanty as they are, are of the highest importance to the student of Teutonic philology. Next to Gothic in the antiquity of its literary remains comes English. The earliest form of English, say English as used up to A.D. 1100, is usually called Anglo-Saxon, though many now call it Old English. In this dictionary Old English is applied to a later stage of the language than what belongs to the Anglo-Saxon period, yet it must never be forgotten that Anglo-Saxon is really Old English, and that there has been no break in the life of the English language since it was introduced into Britain by the Saxons, Angles, and Jutes. Anglo-Saxon, however, is very different from modern English. It possesses many inflections long since lost and many words long since gone out of use, and, indeed, has to be studied by a modern Englishman as if it were a foreign tongue. Old Saxon is the name given to the form of speech anciently in use among the Continental Saxons and preserved in a poem on our Saviour belonging to the ninth century.

The Teutonic tongues, with the primitive or parent Teutonic from which they are descended, have been proved by the investigations of philologists to belong to a wider group or family of tongues, which has received the name of the Aryan, Indo-European, or (especially in Germany) Indo-Germanic family. The chief members of this family are the Teutonic, Slavonic (Polish, Russian, Bohemian), Lithuanian, Celtic (Welsh, Irish, Gaelic, &c.), Latin (or Italic), Greek (or Hellenic), Armenian, Persian, and Sanskrit. Just as the Teutonic tongues are believed to be the offspring of one parent Teutonic tongue, so this parent Teutonic and the other members of the Aryan family are all believed to be descended from one primitive language, the Aryan or Indo-European parent-speech. The people who spoke this primeval Aryan language, the ancestors (linguistically at least) of the Aryan races of Europe and Asia, are believed by many to have had their seat in Central Asia to the eastward of the southern extremity of the Caspian Sea. This, however, is very problematical, and some philologists see reason to think that Europe may rather have been the original home of the Aryan race.

How remote the period may have been when the ancestors of the Teutons, the Celts, the Slavs, the Greeks, Romans, Persians, and Hindus were living together and speaking a common language is uncertain. Yet the general character of their language is approximately known, and philologists tell us with some confidence what consonant and what vowel sounds the Aryan parent-speech must have possessed, what were the forms of its inflections, and what, at the least, must have been the extent of its vocabulary, judging from the words that can still be traced as forming a common possession of the sister tongues of the family. In investigating and deciding on matters of this kind, however, hypothesis must always play a great part, and thus what has been accepted for fact at one time has been discarded as baseless at another. Hence it is not improbable that many of the so-called Aryan or Indo-European roots that modern philologists have established to account for the various words and forms in the Aryan tongues may have to be abandoned as a result of further investigations. Such roots have at best but a shadowy existence, since they can only be regarded as mere abstractions, having no life apart from the words in which they are presumed to exist.

The Aryan tongues, ancient and modern, are entitled to

claim the first rank among the languages of the globe, both for richness, harmony, and variety, and more especially as embodying a series of literatures to which no other family of tongues can show a parallel. Next in importance come the Semitic tongues—Hebrew, Chaldee, Syriac, Arabic, &c. These, like the Aryan tongues, form a well-marked family, one notable peculiarity of which is the possession of 'triliteral' roots, or roots of which three consonants form the basis and give the general meaning, while inflection or modification of meaning is indicated by internal vowel-change. Thus the vowels play a subordinate part to the consonants, and do not, as in the Aryan tongues, associate with them on equal terms. Other important linguistic families are the *Hamitic*, which includes the ancient Egyptian and the Coptic; the *Turanian* or *Ural-Altaic*, which includes Turkish, Finnish, Hungarian, Mongolian, &c.; and the *Monosyllabic* or *South-Eastern Asiatic*, which includes Chinese, Siamese, &c. All these families form groups, so far as is known, quite separate from and independent of each other; and attempts to connect any two of them, as Aryan and Semitic for instance, have met with no success. Formerly etymologists had no hesitation in deriving English words from Hebrew roots, but this was in the days when there was no science of comparative philology. That all languages are descendants of one original tongue, as is believed by many, linguistic science can neither affirm nor deny.

The exact relationship which the different Aryan languages bear to each other has been much discussed, and the question is not yet settled. It has been maintained, for instance, that Latin and Greek are more closely akin to each other than to any other languages of the family. Some, on the other hand, have insisted that Latin is more nearly akin to Celtic than to Greek. It is generally admitted that Sanskrit and Persian are closely akin. The following scheme, in the form of a genealogical table, exhibits the most commonly accepted theory as to their relationship:

verbs, the adjectives are compared after the native model, and the whole is welded together by the indispensable native particles *a*, *an*, *the*, *of*, *with*, *to*, *and*, &c., and by verbs and verbal forms that are peculiarly the property of the Teutonic tongues.

It is probably the fact of our language containing so many extraneous elements, combined with the idea of Anglo-Saxon being a separate language from English, that has led to the popular notion that all English words are 'derived' from some foreign source. It is to be feared there are too many persons who, when they learn, for example, that the German *haus* means the same as English *house*, think that in some mysterious way the English word is derived from the German. But this word, and the same of course is the case with a great many others, belongs to the earliest period of the language (Anglo-Saxon); and the reason why similar forms appear in the German and the rest of the Teutonic tongues is because they all have these slightly varying forms as a common inheritance from the primitive Teutonic. Even when the original of a modern English word cannot be found in Anglo-Saxon the word is not necessarily borrowed or derived from any other language. If it clearly has Teutonic relatives its absence from Anglo-Saxon may be accounted for by the imperfection of the records; for there can be little doubt that words were used in Anglo-Saxon times that we do not find in the literary remains of the period. The same must be the case also in regard to the other Teutonic tongues, and thus the history of some of our common words is very defective. In the etymologies of this dictionary the Anglo-Saxon original of any English word is always given when it is known, and the form the word assumes in the other Teutonic tongues is added for the sake of comparison, and to show how widely the word is spread. Sometimes only certain words supposed to be connected with the one in hand are all that can be given.

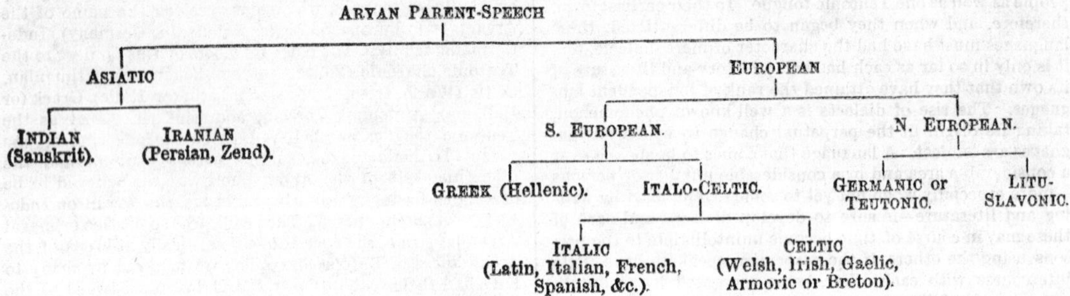

By those who have learned something vaguely of the antiquity and linguistic importance of Sanskrit, this language is sometimes supposed to be the parent-speech of English and other European tongues. The above table shows how erroneous such a notion is, Sanskrit being only a collateral relative.

Though English is a Teutonic language it has admitted into its vocabulary a vast number of non-Teutonic words—more especially words of Latin origin that have passed through the French. If we consider merely the vocabulary, therefore, English may be said to be a composite language. But in structure it is entirely Teutonic; in its grammar, its inflections, its formative elements, &c., it remains true to its origin. And we must remember that the Franco-Latin, or foreign portion of its vocabulary, has a very different character from the Teutonic. The latter is indispensable, the former is not. Without the Teutonic portion of our vocabulary communication is impossible; but a conversation of some length could be carried on, or a composition of some extent written, without the use of a single Franco-Latin word. The Lord's prayer, for example, is almost entirely Teutonic, and might easily be made wholly so. Even when the language, whether written or spoken, is made up to the largest possible extent of non-Teutonic elements, these are still forced into the Teutonic mould; the verbs are conjugated as English

The Teutonic portion of our vocabulary then is mainly of native origin and not derived from any foreign source. Certain Teutonic words, however, we must admit to have been borrowed into the English language. These are chiefly Dutch in origin, and are mostly connected with maritime or commercial affairs. A large number of distinctively Scandinavian words also exist in the language, but most of these are to be regarded as not, strictly speaking, borrowed, but as having been introduced by the Scandinavians (Danes) who settled in the country before the Norman Conquest, and formed an important element of the population, more especially in the northern districts.

In order to understand how it is that many words in the different Aryan tongues are really of the same origin, though superficially they may appear very different, it is necessary to know something of *Grimm's Law*. This law, which, like a natural law, is simply a statement of observed facts, is so named from the great German philologist who first definitely laid it down as the result of observation and comparison of the relative linguistic phenomena. It concerns the so-called 'mute' consonants and takes effect more especially when these are initial. According to it, in words and roots that form a common possession of the Aryan tongues, being inherited by them from the parent-speech, where in English (more especially

Anglo-Saxon) and in most of the Teutonic tongues we find *t*, *d*, or *th*, we find in Latin, Greek, and Sanskrit, not these letters, but respectively *d* instead of *t*, an aspirated sound instead of *d*, and *t* instead of *th*. That is, an English *t* corresponds to a Latin, Greek, and Sanskrit *d*, as is seen in *tame* compared with L. *domare*, Gr. *damaein*, Skr. *dam*, to tame; an English *d* corresponds to Latin *f*, Greek *th*, Sanskrit *dh*, as in E. *door*, L. *fores*, Gr. *thyra*, Skr. *dvāra* (for original *dhvāra*), a door; an English *th* corresponds to Latin, Greek, and Sanskrit *t*, as in *thin*, compared with L. *tenuis*, Gr. *tanaos* Skr. *tanu*, from root *tan*, to stretch. If we next take the gutturals we find that English *k* (or *c* hard), *g*, *h*, correspond respectively in the above languages to *g*, *h* (*ch*, *gh*), *k*, as is seen in E. *kin*, L. *genus*, Gr. *genos*, Skr. *janas* (where *j* is for original *g*); E. *goose* (modified from original *gans*), compared with L. *anser* (for older *hanser*), Gr. *chēn*, Skr. *hansa*; E. *head* (A.Sax. *heafod*), L. *caput*, Gr. *kephale*, Skr. *kapāla*. Similarly *b* in English corresponds to *f* in Latin, *ph* in Greek, and *bh* in Sanskrit, as in *brother*=L. *frater*, Gr. *phratēr*, Skr. *bhratri*, a brother; *f* in English to *p* in Latin, Greek, and Sanskrit, as in *father*=L. *pater*, Gr. *patēr*, Skr. *pitri*, father. German exhibits certain letter changes peculiar to itself, and for this reason is placed, in any full statement of Grimm's law, apart from the other Teutonic tongues. In German, for instance, *t* takes the place of an English *d*, as in G. *tag*, E. *day*, G. *teil*, E. *deal*; *d* the place of *th*, as in G. *ding*, E. *thing*, G. *drei*, E. *three*, &c. In some cases the law does not operate in consequence of the influence of other letters; thus the *s* of *stand* prevents the *t* from becoming *th*, as it ought to do to correspond with L. *stare*, to stand. Similarly *take* and L. *tango*, to touch, are believed to be allied words though both have the consonant *t*, because they are considered to be both from the root *stag* (the *n* in *tango* being inserted as is often the case). Certain exceptions to the law are accounted for by a subsidiary law of more recent discovery than Grimm's law, known as *Verner's Law*, and formulating certain facts connected with the original accentuation of Aryan words.

The correspondence of English words with cognate words is often fully seen only when we take them in their earliest or Anglo-Saxon form or when we note their spelling and know what their original pronunciation was. Thus the verb to *lean* corresponds to L. *clino* (in *incline*), Gr. *klinō*, but we might not have been sure of this had we not had the A.Sax. *hlinian*, to lean, in which the *h* (afterwards lost) represents the Latin and Gr. *k* as Grimm's law demands. Similarly *know*, which is now pronounced nō, duly corresponds (apart from the suffix) to L. *gnosco*, Gr. (*gi*)*gnōskō*; and *night* (nīt), A.Sax. *niht*, to the *noct* of L. *nox*, *noctis*. The older sounds are often better preserved in the dialects (as in that of Scotland) than in the modern pronunciation of the educated; thus, while in England *wright* is now pronounced as *rite*, in Scotland it is uttered so as to let the *w* and the guttural be very distinctly heard.

It may be useful here to give the Anglo-Saxon alphabet with the sounds of the various letters so far as can be ascertained.

The vowels are as follows:

a, like *a* in *far* or *father*.
á or â, similar but longer.
æ, like *a* in *glad* or *man*.
ǽ, æ̂, similar but long (printed *ae* in this dictionary).
e, like *e* in *met*.
é or ê, like *e* in *they*.
i, like *i* in *sin*.
í or î, like *ee* in *seem* or *i* in *machine*.
o, like *o* in *on* or *not*.
ó or ô, like *o* in *sore* or *oa* in *moan*.
u, like *u* in *full*.
ú or û, like *oo* in *fool* or *ou* in *route*.
y, like French *u*, German *ü*.
y or ŷ, the same sound lengthened.

The consonants are b, c, d, f, g, h, l, m, n, p, q, r, s, t, th (two characters for this), w, x. With regard to the pronunciation of these it must be noted that *c* was always sounded like *k* (which is used in some MS.), and was heard in such words as *cneów*, knee, *cnif*, knife; *cw*=*qu* (as in *queen*, A.Sax. *cwén*). *G* was always like *g* in *go*, or sometimes perhaps nearly like *y* consonant; it was sounded when initial before *n* (as in *gnagan*, to *gnaw*). *H* was always heard; when medial and final (as in *niht*, night, *burh*, city) it was strongly guttural like Scotch or German *ch*. It was common as an initial and distinctly pronounced before *l*, *n*, and *r*, a position from which it has since disappeared. *Hw* was written where we now write *wh* (*hwit*=white). In *wl*, *wr* initial, the *w* was pronounced, as also in such words as *sáwl*, soul, *treówth*, truth, *snáw*, snow, being then a semi-vowel.

In their transition to modern English Anglo-Saxon words undergo various changes, some of which take place with great regularity; thus *á* becomes *ō* or *oa*, as in A.Sax. *hám*, E. *home*, A.Sax. *ác*, E. *oak*, A.Sax. *bát*, E. *boat*; *æ* becomes *ee* or *ea* (with same sound), as *ǽl*, E. *eel*, *slǽpan*, E. to *sleep*, *sǽ*, E. *sea*; *é* becomes *ee* or *ea*, as in *félan*, to feel, *cépan*, to keep, *gréne*, green, *rédan*, to read; *ó* becomes *oo* or its equivalent, as A.Sax. *tó*, E. *to*, *too*, A.Sax. *dóm*, E. *doom*, A.Sax. *mód*, E. *mood*; *ú* becomes *ou*, as in A.Sax. *fúl*, E. *foul*, A.Sax. *múth*, E. *mouth*, A.Sax. *hús*, E. *house*, &c. Among consonantal changes may be noted the softening of the *k* sound to the palatal *ch*, as in *church*, *birch*, *watch*, *wretch*, &c.; and the softening of *g* into the *j* sound, *w* or *y*, as in A.Sax. *ecg*, E. *edge*, A.Sax. *hrycg*, E. *ridge*, A.Sax. *gnagan*, E. *gnaw*, A.Sax. *dæg*, E. *day*, A.Sax. *geár*, E. *year*.

Since there are so many words of French origin in English it may be as well to state that in early French there was a declension in substantives and adjectives based on the Latin declension, and with special forms for the nominative and accusative. Afterwards when only one form was retained for the noun as subject and as object it was the old accusative (based on the Latin accusative) that as a rule determined this general form; so that such a word as *motion*, for example, does not come from the Latin nominative *motio*, but from the accusative *motionem*; such a word as *favour* is not from L. *favor*, but from *favorem*. It is customary, however, in etymologies to give the nominative as the typical form of the noun, and to say that *motion* is from *motio*, *motionis*, the genitive being given to show the declensional character. Besides, many French words, being taken directly in modern times from the Latin dictionary, are not as a matter of fact based on the accusative though formed after the same model as those that are historically so.

PREFIXES AND SUFFIXES

PREFIXES

A-. This is a prefix of varying origin and meaning. (1) Having an intensive meaning, equivalent to up, from; from A.Sax. *á-* intensive; as in *arise, awake.* (2) From, off; from A.Sax. *of* (=E. *of, off*); as in *adown.* (3)=*on,* in *afoot, amid.* (4)=L. *ad,* to, in *ascend, achieve.* (5)=L. *ab,* from, in *avert.* (6)=L. *e* or *ex,* in *amend.* (7)=Gr. *a,* priv. or neg., in *amorphous.*

Ab-, from, away; as in *abduct, abjure.* From L. *ab,* from, prefix and preposition; allied to E. *of, off,* Gr. *apo,* from or away. Before *c* and *t* it generally assumes the lengthened form *abs,* it also appears as *a-* (see **A-**).

Abs-. See **Ab-.**

Ac-. A form of **Ad-.**

Ad-, to, towards, at or near; as in *adapt, admit,* &c. From L. *ad,* to, preposition and prefix; allied to E. *at.* Takes by assimilation the forms *ac-, af-, ag-, al-, an-, ap-, ar-, as-, at-;* as in *accede, affirm, aggregate, allude, annex, applaud, arrogant, assume, attribute.* It also appears as *a-* in *ascend.*

Af-, Ag-, Al-. Forms of **Ad-.**

Ambi-, Amb-, about, around; as in *ambition, amputate.* From L. *ambi-, amb-* on both sides, around; allied to Gr. *amphi,* about, L. *ambo,* both; A.Sax. *emb, ymb,* G. *um,* about.

Amphi-, about, around, on both or all sides; as in *amphibious, amphitheatre.* From Gr. *amphi,* about, around, prep. and prefix. See **Ambi-.**

An-. (1)=**Ad-.** (2) Not, negation or privation, from Gr. *an-* or *a-,* the negative prefix; as in *anarchy.* Allied to E. *un-,* L. *in-,* not. (3)=A.Sax. *and-,* against, opposite; as in *answer.* It appears as *a-* in *along.* Same as Goth. *and-,* G. *ant-, ent-,* Gr. *anti.*

Ana-, up, through, throughout; as in *analysis, anatomy, anabasis.* From Gr. *ana,* up, preposition and prefix; allied to E. *on.*

Ant-, against; as in *antagonist, antacid.* Same as **Anti-.**

Ante-, before; as in *antecedent, antedate,* &c. From L. *ante,* before, preposition and prefix. See **Anti-.**

Anti-, against, in opposition; as in *antichrist, anticlimax,* &c. From Gr. *anti,* against, preposition and prefix; allied to L. *ante,* before, and to the A.Sax. prefix *and-, an-,* seen in *answer.* See **An-.**

Ap-. A form of **Ad-.**

Apo-, Aph-, away, apart, off; as in *apostle, apostate, aphelion.* From Gr. *apo,* from, away, preposition and prefix; allied to L. *ab,* from, E. *off.* See **Ab-.**

Ar-. A form of **Ad-.**

Arch-, Archi-, chief, head, ruling; as in *archbishop, architect, archangel.* From Gr. *archi-,* chief, from *archē,* rule, beginning.

As-, At-. Forms of **Ad-.**

Auto-, self, of one's self; as in *autograph, automatic.* From Gr. *auto-,* from pronoun *autos,* self.

Be-. From A.Sax. *be-, bi-,* from *bi, big*=E. *by.* Has various meanings: by or near, or denoting locality, as in *beside, beneath, below;* with a causative or intensive force, as in *benumb, besprinkle, bemire;* with a privative force, in *behead;* upon or against, as in *befall.*

Bi-, twice, two ways, double, as in *bicycle, biennial, bisect.* From L. *bi-,* double, for older *dui-,* akin to *duo,* two (comp. *bellum,* war, for *duellum*), and to E. *two.*

Bis-, twice, double; as in *biscuit.* Longer form of **Bi-.**

Cata-, Cath-, Cat-, down, downward, through, according to; as in *cataract, cataclysm, catarrh, catholic, catechism.* From Gr. *kata,* down, through, &c., preposition and prefix.

Circum-, around, all round; as in *circumnavigate, circumspect, circumstance.* From L. *circum,* round, prep. and prefix, from *circus,* a circle. Seen also in *circuit.*

Cis-, on this side of; as in *cisalpine.* From L. *cis,* prep. and prefix.

Co-, Col-. Same as **Com-.**

Com-, with, together, altogether (intensively); as in *combine, compound, command,* &c. From L. *com-,* prefix, used for prep. *cum,* with, allied to Gr. *syn,* Skr. *sam,* with. Appears also as *co-, col-, con-, cor-,* as in *co-exist, collect, connect, correspond.*

Con-. Same as **Com-.**

Contra-, against; as in *contradict, contravene.* From L. *contra,* against, preposition and prefix, from *con-,* or *cum-* and *-tra* (as in *intra,* within, *extra,* beyond), akin to *trans,* across, Skr. *tar,* to pass.

Cor-. Same as **Com-.**

Counter-, against; same as **Contra,** but directly from Fr. *contre,* against.

De-, down, from, away; as in *descend, denude, depart, describe,* &c. From L. *de,* from, out of, prep. and prefix. In some cases **De-** represents O.Fr. *des-,* from L. *dis-,* apart, as in *decry, defeat.*

Demi-, half, semi-. From Fr. *demi.* See in Dict.

Di-, double, as in *dimorphous.* From Gr. *di-,* double, akin to *dis-, bis-.*

Dia-, through, between, double; as in *diameter, diagnosis, dialogue.* From Gr. *dia,* through, between, prep. and prefix; akin to *di-, dis-.*

Dif-. A form of **Dis-.**

Dis-, apart, asunder, in two; as in *disarm, discharge, distract;* also used negatively, as in *disbelief, disapprove.* From L. *dis,* asunder, preposition and prefix; allied to Gr. *dis, di-,* double, and to L. *bis,* twice.

Dys-, bad, ill, difficult; as in *dysentery, dyspepsia.* From Gr. *dys-,* prefix.

E. Same as **Ex-.** In *enough, e-* represents A.Sax. prefix *ge-,* in *esquire, estate,* &c., it is a mere euphonic element prefixed for ease in pronunciation.

Ec-, Ex-, out; as in *ecstasy, eclectic, exodus.* From Gr. *ek, ex,* out, prep. and prefix, akin to L. *ex.*

Ef-. A form of **Ex-.**

Em-, En-, in; as in *embrace, enclose, enlist;* or used with a causal force, as in *enable, enlarge.* From Fr. *em-, en-,* L. *im-, in-,* prep. and prefix. See **In-.**

En-, in; as in *encaustic, energy.* From Gr. *en,* in, prep. and prefix, akin to L. *in,* A.Sax. *in,* in.

Enter-, between, among; as in *enterprise.* From Fr. *entre,* L. *inter.* See **Inter-.**

Epi-, Eph-, Ep-, upon, over; as in *epitaph, epithet, epidermis, ephemeral.* From Gr. *epi,* upon; akin to Skr. *api.*

Es-, out, away; as in *escape, escheat.* From L. *ex* (which see).

Eu-, well; as in *eulogy, euphony.* From Gr. *eu-,* well, prefix, neuter of *eus,* good, for *esus,* from root *as,* to be (seen in E. *is*).

Ex-, out of, out, from; as in *exceed, exclude;* also used intensively, as in *exacerbate, exasperate.* From L. *ex,* out, akin to Gr. *ek, ex,* out. See **Ec-.** Appears also as *e-, ef-, es-.*

Extra-, beyond, without; as in *extraordinary, extrajudicial.* From L. *extra,* without, prep. and prefix, from *ex* and *-tra.* See **Contra-.**

For-. Used intensively or almost negatively; as in *forgive, forbid, forgo.* From A. Sax. *for-,* same as Icel. and Dan. *for-,* D. and G. *ver-,* Goth. *fra-;* allied to *far,* L. *per.*

Fore-, beforehand, in advance; as in *foretell, foreshow, foreground,* &c. See FORE, in Dict.

Hemi-, half; as in *hemisphere.* From Gr. prefix *hēmi-,* half, akin to L. *semi.*

Hetero-, other, different; as in *heterodox, heterogeneous.* From Gr. *heteros,* other.

Holo-, whole, entire; as in *holograph, holocaust.* From Gr. *holos,* whole.

Homo-, same; as in *homonym.* From Gr. *homos,* same; allied to E. *same.*

Hyper-, over, beyond, too; *hyperborean, hypercritical.* From Gr. *hyper,* above, over, prep. and prefix; allied to L. *super,* E. *over, up.*

Hypo-, under, beneath; as in *hypocaust, hypotenuse, hypothesis.* From Gr. *hypo,* under, prep. and prefix; allied to L. *sub,* under.

Il-. A form of **In-** (2 and 3).

Im-. A form of **In-.**

In-. (1) In, as in *inborn, insight,* &c. From A.Sax. and E. prep. *in,* cog. with L. *in,* in (whence next **In-**). It may become *im-*, as in *imbed, imbody.* (2) In, into; as in *include, inclose.* From L. *in*, in, prep. and prefix; cog. Gr. *en*, in, E. and Goth. *in*, Icel. *inn*, G. *ein*. Before *m, b, p*, it becomes *im-*, as in *immure, imbibe, implant;* before *l*, *il-*; before *r*, *ir-*. (3) Not—the negative prefix; as in *inactive, incapable*, &c. From L. *in-*, not, prefix; Gr. *an-*, E. *un-*, not (see **Un-**). Like the preceding it appears also as *il-, im-, ir-*; as in *illegitimate, immaculate, irrational.*

Inter-, between, among; as in *intercede, intermingle, interchange*, &c. From L. *inter*, between, among, prep. and prefix; a comparative form akin to *intra, intro*, within, *interior*, inner, *internus*, internal. See UNDER in Dict. It takes also the form **Intel-**, as in *intellect.*

Intra-, within; as in *intramural.* From L. *intra*, within. See **Inter-**.

Intro-, within, into; as in *introduce, introspection.* See **Inter-**.

Ir-. A form of **In-**.

Juxta-, near, nigh; as in *juxtaposition.* From L. prep. *juxta*, near.

Mal-, Male-, ill, badly; as in *maladministration, maladroit, malcontent, malefactor.* From Fr. *mal-*, L. *male*, badly, *malus*, evil.

Meta-, Met-, after, beyond, among, or denoting change as in *metaphysics, metaphor, metamorphosis, metathesis, metonymy.* From Gr. *meta*, with, among, prep. and prefix; cog. with A.Sax. *mid*, G. *mit*, Goth. *mith*, with.

Mis-. (1) Wrong, wrongly, bad, badly; as in *misdeed, mistake, misshapen, mishap, misinformed.* From A.Sax., Icel., Dan., and D. *mis-*, Sw. *miss-*, Goth. *missa-*, wrongly; akin to verb *miss.* (2) Ill, unfortunate; as in *misadventure, misalliance, mischance.* From. O.Fr. *mes-*, from L. *minus*, less. See Dict.

Mono-, Mon-, single, sole, having only one; as in *monarch, monody, monogram, monomaniac.* From Gr. *monos*, sole, single.

Multi-, Mult-, many; as in *multangular, multiform, multivalve.* From L. *multus*, many, much.

N-, negative element; as in *never, none.* From A.Sax. *ne*, not: cog. with L. *ne*, not, Skr. *na*, E. *no.* See NO in Dict.

Non-, not; often used as *in-*, negative, or as *un-*. From L. *non*, not, from *ne unum*, not one. See above.

Ob-, against, before, in the way of; as in *object, obstacle, obstruct.* From L. *ob*, against, prep. and prefix; allied to Gr. *epi*, upon, Skr. *api*, moreover. It appears also as *o-, oc-, of-, op-*, as in *omit, occur, offend, oppress.*

Oc-, Of-. Forms of **Ob-**.

Off-, from; as in *offshoot, offspring.* See OFF in Dict.

On-, on, against; as in *onset, onslaught.* See ON in Dict.

Op-. A form of **Ob-**

Out-, out, beyond; as in *outbid, outburst.* See OUT in Dict.

Over-, above, beyond, too much; as in *overhead, overhang, overburden, overcharge.* See OVER in Dict.

Pan-, Panto-, all; as in *panacea, pantheism, pantograph.* From Gr. *pan, pantos*, all.

Para-, Par-, beside, beyond or aside from; as in *parallel, paradox, parable, parody.* From Gr. *para*, beside, prep. and prefix; allied to *peri*, around, L. *per*, through; E. *for-*. See **For-**.

Pel-. A form of **Per-**.

Pen-, almost; as in *peninsula, penultimate.* From L. *pene, pœne*, almost.

Per-, through, throughout, thoroughly; as in *perforate, pervade, perfect, perdition.* It has sometimes the effect of E. *for-* (in *forswear, forget*), as in *perfidy, perjury.* From L. *per*, through, prep. and prefix; allied to Gr. *para*, E. *for-*. In *pellucid* it appears as *pel.*

Peri-, around, about; as in *periphery, peripatetic, periphrasis.* From Gr. *peri*, about, prep. and prefix; allied to Gr. *para*, L. *per.*

Pol-. A form of **Por-**.

Poly-, many; as in *polygamy, polygon, polysyllable.* From Gr. *polys*, many; same root as E. *full.*

Por-, Pol-, forward, forth; as in *portend, pollute.* From L. prefix *por-, pol-*, akin to *pro*, before, Gr. *pro*, Skr. *pra*, E. *forth.*

Post-, after, behind; as in *postdate, postpone.* From L. *post*, after, prep. and prefix.

Pre-, Præ-, before, beforehand, in advance; as in *predict, prefer, prefigure, preeminent.* From L. *præ*, before, prep. and prefix; akin to *pro, per, primus.* It is the *pr* of *prison*, the *pro* of *provost.*

Preter-, beyond, above, as in *preternatural, preterit.* From L. *præter*, beyond, a comparative form of *præ.* See **Præ**.

Pro-, before, forth, forward, as in *produce, project, profess, promise*: also instead of; as in *pronoun, proconsul.* From L. *pro*, before, for, prep. and prefix; akin to *præ* and to Gr. *pro*, before, Skr. *pra*, away, E. *for-* (which see). In some words *pro-* is the Gr. *pro*, as in *prologue, prophet.*

Pros-, towards, in addition; as in *proselyte, prosody.* From Gr. *pros*, towards, prep. and prefix; akin to Skr. *prati*, towards, E. *forth.*

Proto-, Prot-, first, original; as in *protocol, protoplasm, protagonist.* From Gr. *prōtos*, first, akin to *pro*, before.

Re-, Red-, back, again; as in *recall, regain, return, retract*; also change of place, as in *remove.* From L. *re-, red-*, prefix, the latter form being used before vowels, as in *redeem, redolent, redundant.*

Retro-, backward; as in *retroact, retrograde.* From L. prefix *retro-*, backwards, a comparative of **Re-** (comp. *intro* and *in*).

Se-, aside, apart; as in *secede, seduce, seclude*; also without, as in *secure.* From L. *se-*, originally *sed-*, only used as a prefix.

Semi-, half; as in *semicircle.* From L. prefix *semi-*, half; akin to Skr. *sāmi*, half, Gr. *hēmi-*. See **Hemi-**.

Sine-, without; as in *sinecure.* From L. *sine*, without, prep. and prefix, from *si*, if, and *ne*, not.

Sub-, under, beneath, inferior; as in *subject, subordinate, submarine, submerge, submit*), also slightly, as in *subacid, subobtuse.* From L. *sub*, under, prep. and prefix; allied to Gr. *hypo*, under, Skr. *upa*, near; and to E. *up, over.* It appears also as *su-, suc-, suf-, sug-, sum-, sup-, sur-*, as in *suspect, succeed, suffer, suggest, summon, suppress, surreptitious.*

Subter-, beneath, as in *subterfuge.* From L. *subter*, beneath, prep. and prefix, a comparative of *sub* (which see).

Suc-, Suf-, Sug-, Sum-, Sup-. Forms of **Sub-**.

Super-, above, over, more than; as in *superabound, superadd, supersede, superhuman.* From L. *super*, over, above, prep. and prefix; a comparative form akin to *sub*, and to Gr. *hyper*, over, E. *over.* See SUPER in Dict.

Supra-, above; as in *supracostal.* From L. *supra*, above, akin to *super.*

Sur-, over, above; as in *surface, surmount*, from Fr. *sur*, above, from L. *super* (which see).

Sur-. A form of **Sub-**.

Syn-, Sym-, Syl-, with, together with, in company; as in *synagogue, synclinal, symmetry, sympathy, syllable, syllogism.* From Gr. *syn*, with, prep. and prefix; allied to L. *cum.* See **Com-**.

To-, this, on this; as in *to-day, to-night, together, toward*, &c. From prep. *to.*

Trans-, Tra-, across, over, through, beyond; as in *transmit, transport, transfix, transgress, traverse, traduce.* From L. *trans*, across, prep. and prefix; same root as E. *through.* See THROUGH in Dict.

Tri-, three, thrice, threefold; as in *triangle, tricolour, trident, trilobite, trilogy.* From L. and Gr. *tri-*, prefix, three, thrice; allied to E. *three.*

Ultra-, beyond; as in *ultramarine, ultramontane.* From L. *ultra*, beyond, prep and prefix. See ULTRA in Dict.

Un-. (1) The negative prefix=not; as in *unavailing, unanswerable*, &c. From A.Sax. *un-*, not; allied to L. *in-*, not. (2) Denoting reversal of an action; as in *undo, untie*, &c. From A.Sax. *un-*, akin to G. *ent-*, Goth. *and-*, E. *an-* in *answer.* See UN- in Dict.

Under-, below, beneath; as in *undercurrent, underlie, underhand, undersell.* See UNDER in Dict.

Up-, up; as in *upheave.* See UP in Dict.

With-, against, back; as in *withstand, withdraw, withhold.* From A.Sax. *with*, against, same as prep. *with.* See Dict.

SUFFIXES

-able, that may be, capable of being; as in *lovable, affable.* L. *-abilis.*

-ac, pertaining to; as in *cardiac, demoniac.* Gr. *-akos.*

-aceous, partaking of the properties of; as in *arenaceous, herbaceous.* L. *-aceus.*

-acious, characterized by; as in *tenacious, pugnacious.* Fr. *-acieux*, L. *-ax, -acis.*

-age, abstract or collective, also locality; as in *advantage, foliage, parsonage.* Fr. *-age.* L.L. *-aticum*, L. *-aticus*, adj. termination.

-ain, giving adjectives and nouns; as in *certain, captain.* Fr. *-ain*, L. *-anus.*

-al, pertaining to; as in *annual, filial.* L. *-alis.*

-an, noun and adj. suffix; as in *pagan, Roman, human.* L. *-anus.*

-ance, -ancy, denoting state or action; as in *abundance, acceptance.* L. *-antia.* See **-nce.**

-ane, adj. suffix; as in *mundane, humane.* L. *-anus.*

-aneous, belonging to; as in *contemporaneous*, L. *-aneus.*

-ant, equivalent to E. suffix *-ing*; as in *abundant, accordant, pleasant.* L. *-ans, -antis*, term. of present participle.

-ar, pertaining to; as in *angular, familiar, polar.* L. *-aris.*

-ard, denoting disposition or character; as in *coward, niggard, sluggard.* Partly from A.Sax. *-heard*, lit. hard, partly from Fr. *-ard*, from G. *hart*, hard.

-ary, adj. and noun suffix; as in *auxiliary, contrary, library, secretary, antiquary, seminary.* L. *-arius, -arium.*

-asm. See **-ism.**

-aster, denoting contempt; as in *poetaster, criticaster.* O.Fr. *-astre*, L. *-aster*, having somewhat of, adj. termination.

-ate, seen in verbs, adjectives, and nouns; as *animate, agitate, delicate.* From L. *-atus*, term. of past participle.

-ble. See **-able, -ible.**

-ble, as in *treble.* See **-ple.**

-cle, -cule, dim. suffix; as in *article, particle, animalcule.* L. *-culus, -cula, -culum.*

-cy, state of, as in *idiocy.* Fr. *-cie*, L. *-tia.*

-d. See **-ed.**

-dom, power or jurisdiction, state; as in *kingdom, earldom, wisdom, martyrdom.* A.Sax. *dōm*, judgment, authority; akin G. *-thum.* See DOOM in Dict.

-ed, -d, suffix of past tense. A.Sax. *-de*, shortened for *-dide*, past tense of *dón*, E. to *do*.

-ed, -d, suffix of past participle and some adjectives and nouns; as in *loved, booted, horned*. Originally *-th*, and corresponding to L. *-tus*, of past participle; same as the *-d, -t, -th*, of *cold, dead, flight, height, death, health*, &c.

-ee, denoting one who is acted on, a recipient; as in *legatee, referee, trustee*. Fr. *-é, -ée*, from L. *-atus*, of past participle. See **-ate**.

-eer, -ier, denoting profession or employment; as in *brigadier, charioteer*. Fr. *-ier*, L. *-arius*.

-el, dim. See **-le**.

-en, -n, made of; as in *golden, waxen, leathern*; also pertaining to, as in *heathen*. A.Sax. *-en*, G. *-en*, Goth. *-ein*; akin to L. *-nus*, Gr. *-nos*, Skr. *-nas*.

-en, dim. as in *chicken, kitten*. A.Sax. *-en*.

-en, pl.; as in *oxen, kine, shoon*. A.Sax. *-an*.

-en, to make, verbal termination; as in *soften, whiten*. A.Sax. and Goth. infinitive *-nan*, originally an intransitive form.

-ence, -ency. Similar to **-ance, -ancy**.

-eous, pertaining to, containing; as in *aqueous*. L. *-eus*. [In *courteous*, *-eous* is from L. *-ensis*; in *righteous*, also of different origin.]

-er, one who does; as in *baker, singer, writer*. A.Sax. *-ere*, G. *-er*, Goth. *-areis*, allied to L. *-arius*. Sometimes takes *y* before it, as in *bowyer, lawyer, sawyer*; in *liar* takes form of *-ar*.

-er, frequentative; as in *flicker, sputter*. A.Sax. *-erian*, G. *-ern*.

-er, comparative suffix. A.Sax. *-er, -or*, G. *-er*, L. *-or*.

-erel, dim.; as in *cockerel, mongrel*. O.Fr. *-erel*.

-erly, to or from in direction; as in *northerly, easterly*. For *-ern-ly*.

-ern, expressing direction; as in *southern*. A.Sax. *-ern*.

-ery, business or place where it is carried on, also with collective force; as in *archery, brewery, cutlery, finery, soldiery*. From nouns in *-er* with Fr. *-ie*, L. *-ia*.

-es, -s, denoting plurals. A.Sax. *-as*; common to the Aryan languages.

-escent, becoming gradually; as in *convalescent, effervescent*. L. *-escens, -escentis*, pres. part. of inceptive verbs in *-esco*.

-ese, belonging to a country or city; as in *Siamese, Maltese*. Fr. *-ais, -ois*, It. *-ese*, from L. *-ensis*.

-esque, partaking of; as in *picturesque*. Fr. *-esque*, from L. *-iscus*, a form of *-icus*.

-ess, feminine suffix; as in *authoress, countess, giantess*. Fr. *-esse*, L. *-issa*, from Gr. *-issa*.

-est, suffix of superlatives. A.Sax. *-est, -ost*, G. *-est*; allied to Gr. *-istos*, Skr. *-ishthas*.

-et, -ette, dim. suffix; as in *billet, coronet, palette*. Fr. *-et, -ette*.

-ey, adjective suffix. See **-y**.

-ferous, bearing, producing; as in *auriferous, quartziferous*. L. *-fer*, from *fero*, to bear.

-fold, denoting multiplication; as in *threefold, manifold*. From *fold*, noun or verb.

-ful, full of; as in *fanciful, mournful*. A. Sax. *-ful*=E. *full*.

-fy, to make; as in *beautify*. Fr. *-fier*, L. *ficare*, from *facio*, to make.

-geneous, -genous, as in *homogeneous*. From Gr. and L. root *-gen*, to produce.

-graph, -graphy. From Gr. *-graphos, -graphia*, from *graphō*, to write.

-head, -hood, state, condition; as in *Godhead, widowhood*. A.Sax. *hád*, state, rank =G. *-heit*.

-ible, same meaning as **-able**, as in *accessible*.

-ic, pertaining to; as in *botanic, periodic, public*. L. *-icus*, Gr. *-ikos*, Skr. *-ikas*.

-ical, pertaining to; as in *logical*. From L. *-icus* and *-alis* combined.

-ics, properly plural, but used as a singular in names of branches of knowledge; as in *mathematics, ethics*. Gr. *-ika*, neut. pl. of *-ikos*, lit. things belonging to.

-id, adjective suffix; as in *arid, fluid, torpid*. L. *-idus*.

-id, -idæ, suffix of family names of animals. Gr. *-idēs*, denoting descent.

-ide, suffix of certain chemical compounds; as *chloride*. Gr. *-eidos*, form.

-ie, -y, dim. suffix; as in *wifie, Johnnie*. From *-ick*, weaker form of *-ock*.

-ier. Same as *-eer*.

-ile, capable of being; as in *docile, fragile*. L. *-ilis*.

-ile, belonging to; as in *puerile, senile, Gentile*. L. *-ilis*.

-ine, feminine suffix; as in *heroine*. Fr. *-ine*, L. *-ina*.

-ine, suffix of adjectives and nouns; as in *divine, iodine*. L. *-inus, -ina*.

-ing, noun suffix; as in *whiting, shilling*. A.Sax. *-ing*.

-ing, termination of present participles. Corrupted from A.Sax. *-ende*.

-ing, termination of verbal nouns. A.Sax. *-ung*.

-ion. See **-sion, -tion**.

-ique, adj. suffix; as in *antique, unique*. Fr. *-ique*, L. *-iquus*, a form of *-icus*.

-ise. See **-ize**.

-ish, pertaining to, having somewhat of; as in *childish, foolish, dwarfish, whitish, English*. A.Sax. *-isc*, G. *-isch*, Goth. *-isk*.

-ish, verbal suffix; as in *nourish, perish*. From forms in *-iss-* of French verbs, from L. *-esc-* of inceptive verbs (as *abolesco—abolish*).

-ism, -asm, suffix of nouns, often implying state, system, doctrines; as in *barbarism, atheism, organism, scepticism, pleonasm*. L. *-ismus, -asmus*, from Gr. *-ismos, -asmos*.

-ist, -ast, one who; suffix often corresponding to *-ism, -asm*; as in *atheist, gymnast*.

-ite, one of, a follower of; as in *Israelite, Spinozite*. L. *-ita*, Gr. *-itēs*.

-ite, a geological suffix = *-lite*. Also a chemical suffix, from L. adjective suffix *-itus*.

-itis, suffix denoting inflammation: used in medical terms; as in *laryngitis*. Gr. *-itis*.

-ity, state; as in *ability*. L. *-itas*. See **-ty**.

-ix. See **-trix**.

-ize, -ise, to make, to act; as in *civilize, economize*. Fr. *-iser*, O.Fr. *-izer*, L.L. *-izare*, from Gr. *-izein*.

-kin, dim. suffix; as in *lambkin*. Not in A. Sax.; same as D. *-ek-en*, Gr. *-ch-en*; equivalent to *-ock-en*, and thus a double diminutive.

-le, -el, a suffix in nouns denoting instrument, &c.; as in *needle, saddle, steeple, navel, weasel*. A.Sax. *-el, -ol, -ul, -ela*, G. *-el*, Aryan *-al, -ar*. Also in some adjectives, as *idle*.

-le, dim. and freq. suffix of verbs; as in *frizzle, nibble, sparkle*.

-lence, suffix in abstract nouns, corresponds to **-lent**.

-lent, full of; as in *violent, purulent*. L. *-lentus*.

-less, free from, without; as in *artless, fatherless*. A.Sax. *-leás*, G. *-los*; akin *lose, loss*.

-let, dim. suffix; as in *leaflet, streamlet*. From *-le* or *-el*, and *-et*.

-ling, dim. suffix; as in *darling, lordling, starveling*. From *-ing*, A.Sax. *-ing*, with prefixed *-le* or *-el*.

-ling, -long, adverbial suffix; as in *darkling, endlong*. A.Sax. *-linga, -lunga*, adverbial datives.

-lite, in mineralogical terms, &c., means stone; as in *aerolite*. Gr. *lithos*, a stone.

-logy, doctrine, science; as in *biology*. Gr. *-logia*, from *logos*, a word, speech.

-ly, like, an adjective and adverbial suffix; as in *lovely, truly*. A form of adj. *like*; A.Sax. *-lic*, adjective suffix, *-lice*, adverbial suffix.

-ment, act of, state of; as in *agreement, argument, experiment*. Fr. *-ment*, L. *-mentum*.

-meter, a measure; as in *hydrometer*. Gr. *metron*, a measure.

-mony, state; as in *matrimony, parsimony*. L. *-monium, -monia*.

-most, suffix in superlatives; as *foremost*. Not the same as *most*, superlative of *much*, but a double superlative composed of superlative suffixes *-ma* and *-est*. See FOREMOST in Dict.

-nce, -ncy, suffix of abstract nouns usually denoting state; as in *vigilance, brilliancy, abhorrence, excellency*. Fr. *-nce*, L. *-ntia*, from present participles in *-ans, -antis, -ens, -entis*, with suffix *-ia*.

-ness, denoting state of being; as in *barrenness, fulness, redness*. A.Sax. *-nes*, same as G. *-nis*, Goth. *-nassus*.

-ock, diminutive suffix; as in *hillock, bullock*. A.Sax. *-uca*.

-oid, -oidal, resembling; as in *elephantoid, spheroidal*. Gr. *-oeidēs*, from *eidos*, form.

-on, noun suffix, as in *dragon, falcon*. Fr. *-on*, L. *-onem*, accus. suffix of nouns in *-o, -onis*.

-or, one who; as in *emperor, sailor*. Fr. *-eur*, from L. *-torem*, accus. of nouns in *-tor*.

-ory. See **-tory**.

-our, -or, suffix of abstract nouns; as in *colour* or *color, favour, honour*. Fr. *-eur*, L. *-orem*, accus. of nouns in *-or, -oris*.

-ous, -ose, full of, abounding with; as in *copious, famous, operose, verbose*. Fr. *-eux*, L. *-osus*.

-pathy, state of feeling; as in *antipathy*. Gr. *-pathia*, from *pathos*, suffering.

-phorous, bearing, carrying; as in *phyllophorous*. Gr. *-phoros*, from *pherō*, to bear.

-ple, same sense as *-fold*; as in *triple, quadruple*. L. *-plus*, akin to *-pleo*, to fill.

-red, -ric. See HATRED, BISHOPRIC, in Dict.

-ry, collective noun suffix, an art; as in *nunnery, cookery, poetry*. Fr. *-rie*. L. *-ria*.

-'s, suffix of the possessive. A.Sax. *-es*=G. *-s, -es*, L. *-is*. The old notion that it stands for *his* is quite erroneous, though this may be the origin of the '.

-scope, -scopy, what assists sight, a seeing. Gr. *-skopos, -skopia*, from *skopeō*, to see.

-ship, state of, office of; as in *apprenticeship, censorship, rectorship*. A.Sax. *-scipe*, akin to *ship, shape*.

-sion, state or action abstractly; as in *explosion, tension*. L. *-sio, -sionis*, akin *-tion*.

-some, full of, abounding in; as in *gladsome, frolicsome, troublesome*. A.Sax. *-sum*, Icel. and G. *-sam*; akin to *same*.

-ster, one who; as in *gamester, maltster, songster*. A.Sax. *-estre*, originally a feminine suffix, as still in *spinster*.

-sy, state; as in *heresy, phantasy*. Gr. *-sis, -sia*.

-t, suffix of nouns; as in *height, flight*. Same as *-th*.

-teen, ten; as in *fifteen*. A.Sax. *-tyne*.

-ter, -ther, a comparative suffix; as in *after, other*. A.Sax. *-ter, -der, -ther*. See AFTER in Dict.

-th, suffix of abstract nouns; as in *breadth, death, health*. A.Sax. *-th*, allied to L. *-tus*, as in *juventus*, youth.

-th, suffix of ordinals; as *sixth*. A.Sax. *-tha*; allied to *-tus*, in L. *sextus*, sixth.

-ther, an agent; as in *father, mother, brother*. A.Sax. *-der, -dor, thor*; allied to L. *-tor* Skr. *-tar*, denoting an agent.

-tion, state or action abstractly; as in *conception, perception*. L. *-tio, -tionis*; akin *-sion*.

-tor, an agent; as in *actor*. See **-ther**.

-tory, adjective suffix; as in *amatory, confirmatory, explanatory*. L. *-torius*, corresponding to nouns in *-tor*. From the neuter

-torium comes the termination when signifying place, as in *dormitory, lavatory.*

-trix, feminine suffix corresponding to *-tor*; as in *testatrix.* L. *-trix.*

-tude, suffix of abstract nouns; as in *fortitude, gratitude.* L. *-tudo, -tudinis.*

-ture. See **-ure**.

-ty, suffix of abstract nouns; as in *gravity, levity.* Fr. *-té*, L. *-tas, -tatis.*

-ty, ten times; as in *fifty.* A.Sax. *-tig*; akin to *ten, -teen.*

-ule, dim. suffix; as in *globule, pilule.* L. *-ulus, -ula, -ulum.*

-ure, act, thing produced; as in *capture, gesture, creature, picture.* L. *-ura.*

-ward, -wards, suffix of direction; as in *homeward, homewards.* When with *-s* it is an adverbial genitive. A.Sax. *-weard, -weardes*; akin to *worth* (verb), L. *verto*, to turn.

-way, -ways, suffix of manner; as in *always, straightway.* From *way*, manner; *-ways* is an adverbial genitive.

-wise, suffix of manner; as in *lengthwise, likewise.* See WISE in Dict.

-y, -ey, adjective suffix; as in *bloody, clayey, dirty, filthy, skyey, woody.* A.Sax. *-ig*, G. *-ig*; allied to L. *-icus*, Gr. *-ikos.* In *hasty, jolly*, it represents Fr. *-if*, L. *-ivus.*

-y, noun suffix. Sometimes, as in *company, fallacy*, it represents Fr. *-ie*, L. *-ia*, or Gr. *-ia* (as in *apology*); sometimes it represents L. *-ium*, as in *remedy, subsidy*; sometimes L. *-ius*, as in *notary*; sometimes L. *-atus*, as in *deputy.*

KEY TO THE PRONUNCIATION

In showing the pronunciation the simplest and most easily understood method has been adopted, that of *re-writing* the word with a set of letters that have invariably the same *sound*, no matter by what letter or letters the sounds may be expressed in the word whose pronunciation is shown. The *key* by this means is greatly simplified, the reader having only to bear in mind one mark for each sound. Sounds and letters, it must be remembered, are often very different things. In English there are a great many more sounds than letters to represent them, so that some of the letters stand for more than one sound, the letter *a*, for instance, having at least six or seven, namely those given in the accompanying table and two more, as in the words *any* and *quality*, which may be better represented by *e* and *o* respectively. Our alphabet is therefore very far from being a perfect alphabet, which would have a distinct letter for each sound, and would always represent the same sound by the same letter. The following is a list of characters and key-words used to show the pronunciation in the dictionary.

Vowels

ā	as in	*fate.*	ō	as in	*note.*
ä	"	*far.*	o	"	*not.*
a	"	*fat.*	ö	"	*move.*
ạ	"	*fall.*	ū	"	*tube.*
ē	"	*me.*	u	"	*tub.*
e	"	*met.*	ụ	"	*bull.*
ė	"	*her.*	ů	"	Fr. *un.*
ë	"	Fr. *peur* = ė long.	ü	"	Fr. *dû.*
ī	as in	*pine.*	oi	"	*oil.*
i	"	*pin.*	ou	"	*pound.*

Consonants

ch	as in	*chain.*	ng	as in	*sing*
ch	"	Sc. *loch.* Ger. *nacht.*	TH	"	*then.*
j		*job.*	th	"	*thin.*
g	"	*go.*	w	"	*wig.*
ṅ	"	Fr. *ton.*	wh	"	*whig.*
			zh	"	*azure.*

The above system, it is believed, will be sufficient for all practical purposes, and the intelligent reader will not care for greater nicety, and will not be likely to cavi though the vowel sounds in *there* and *fate* (like those in *more* and *note*) are both represented by the same character. Consonants not in the list are used simply with their ordinary sounds.

Accent.—Words consisting of more than one syllable receive an accent, as the first syllable of the word *labor*, the second of *delay*, and the third of *comprehension.* The accented syllable is the most prominent part of the word, and is denoted by the mark ′, as in the words *la′bor, delay′*, and *comprehen′sion.*

Many polysyllabic words are pronounced with two accents, the primary and the secondary accent, as the word *excommunication*, in which the third as well as the fifth syllable is commonly accented. The accent on the fifth syllable is the primary accent, and when it requires to be indicated in the pronunciation it receives a double mark, thus ″, the secondary or inferior accent receiving only the single mark ′, as in *excŏmmu′nica″tion.*

THE ABBREVIATIONS AND SIGNS

USED IN THIS DICTIONARY

a. or adj. = adjective.
abbrev. .. abbreviation, abbreviated.
acc. .. accusative.
adv. .. adverb.
agri. .. agriculture.
alg. .. algebra.
Amer. .. American.
anat. .. anatomy.
anc. .. ancient.
antiq. .. antiquities.
aor. .. aorist, aoristic.
Ar. .. Arabic.
arch. .. architecture.
archæol. .. archæology.
arith. .. arithmetic.
Armor. .. Armoric.
art. .. article.
A.Sax. .. Anglo-Saxon.
astrol. .. astrology.
astron. .. astronomy.
at. wt. .. atomic weight.
aug. .. augmentative.
avi. .. aviation.
biol. .. biology.
bot. .. botany.
Bret. .. Breton (= Armoric).
Carl. .. Carlyle.
carp. .. carpentry.
caus. .. causative.
Celt. .. Celtic.
chem. .. chemistry.
chron. .. chronology.
Class. .. Classical (= Greek and Latin).
cog. .. cognate, cognate with.
colloq. .. colloquial.
com. .. commerce.
comp. .. compare.
compar. .. comparative.
conch. .. conchology.
conj. .. conjunction.
contr. .. contraction, contracted.
crystal. .. crystallography.
D. .. Dutch.
Dan. .. Danish.
dat. .. dative.
def. .. definite.
dial. .. dialect, dialectal.
dim. .. diminutive.
distrib. .. distributive.
dram. .. drama, dramatic.
dyn. .. dynamics.
E., *Eng.* .. English.
eccles. .. ecclesiastical, in ecclesiastical affairs.
elect. .. electricity.
engin. .. engineering.
engr. .. engraving.
entom. .. entomology.
ethn. .. ethnography, ethnology.
etym. .. etymology.
exclam. .. exclamation.
fem. .. feminine.
fig. .. figuratively.
Fl. .. Flemish.
fort. .. fortification.
Fr. .. French.
freq. .. frequentative.
Fris. .. Frisian.
fut. .. future.
G. .. German.
Gael. .. Gaelic.
galv. .. galvanism.
genit. .. genitive.
geog. .. geography.
geol. .. geology.
geom. .. geometry.
Goth. .. Gothic.
Gr. .. Greek.
gram. .. grammar.
gun. .. gunnery.
Heb. .. Hebrew.
her. .. heraldry.
Hind. .. Hindustani, or Hindi.
hist. .. history
hort. .. horticulture.
Hung. .. Hungarian.
hydros. .. hydrostatics.
Icel. .. Icelandic.
ich. .. ichthyology.
imper. .. imperative.
imperf. .. imperfect.
impers. .. impersonal.
incept. .. inceptive.
ind. .. indicative.
Ind. .. Indian.
indef. .. indefinite.
Indo-Eur. .. Indo-European.
inf. .. infinitive.
intens. .. intensive.
interj. .. interjection.
Ir. .. Irish.
It. .. Italian.
L. .. Latin.
L.G. .. Low German.
lit. .. literal, literally.
Lith. .. Lithuanian.
L.L. .. late Latin
mach. .. machinery.
manuf. .. manufactures.
masc. .. masculine.
math. .. mathematics.
mech. .. mechanics.
med. .. medicine.
Med.L. .. Medieval Latin.
mensur. .. mensuration.
metal. .. metallurgy.
metaph. .. metaphysics.
meteor. .. meteorology.
M.H.G. .. Middle High German.
Mil. .. Milton.
milit. .. military, in military affairs.
mineral. .. mineralogy.
Mod. Fr. .. Modern French.
mus. .. music.
myth. .. mythology.
N. .. Norse, Norwegian.
n. .. noun.
nat. hist. .. natural history.
nat. order .. natural order.
nat. phil. .. natural philosophy.
naut. .. nautical.
navig. .. navigation,
neg. .. negative.
neut. .. neuter.
N.H.G. .. New High German.
nom. .. nominative.
Norm. .. Norman.
North. E. .. Northern English.
N.T. .. New Testament.
numis. .. numismatics.
obj. .. objective.
obs. .. obsolete.
obsoles. .. obsolescent.
O.E. .. Old English (*i.e.* English between A. Saxon and Modern English).
O.Fr. .. Old French.
O.H.G. .. Old High German.
O.Sax. .. Old Saxon.
O.T. .. Old Testament.
ornith. .. ornithology.
p .. participle.
paint. .. painting.
palæon. .. palæontology.
part. .. participle.
pass. .. passive.
pathol. .. pathology.
pejor. .. pejorative.
Per. .. Persian.
perf. .. perfect.
pers. .. person.
persp. .. perspective.
Pg. .. Portuguese.
phar. .. pharmacy.
philol. .. philology.
philos. .. philosophy.
Phœn. .. Phœnician.
photog. .. photography.
phren. .. phrenology.
phys. .. physics.
phys. geog. .. physical geography.
physiol. .. physiology.
pl. .. plural.
pneum. .. pneumatics.
poet. .. poetical.
Pol. .. Polish.
pol. econ. .. political economy.
poss. .. possessive.
pp. .. past participle.
ppr. .. present participle.
Pr. .. Provencal.
prep. .. preposition.
pres. .. present.
pret. .. preterite.
print. .. printing.
priv. .. privative.
pron. .. pronunciation, pronounced.
pron. .. pronoun.
pros. .. prosody.
prov. .. provincial.
psych. .. psychology.
rail. .. railways.
refl. .. reflexively, with a reflexive pronoun.
R.Cath.Ch. Roman Catholic
rhet. .. rhetoric. [Church.
Rom. antiq. Roman antiquities
Rus. .. Russian.
Sax. .. Saxon.
Sc. .. Scotch.
Scand. .. Scandinavian.
Scrip. .. Scripture.
sculp. .. sculpture.
Shak. .. Shakespeare.
sing. .. singular.
Skr. .. Sanskrit.
Slav. .. Slavonic, Slavic.
Sp. .. Spanish.
sp. gr. .. specific gravity.
subj. .. subjunctive.
superl. .. superlative.
surg. .. surgery.
surv. .. surveying.
Sw. .. Swedish.
sym. .. symbol.
syn. .. synonym.
technol. .. technology.
tel. .. telegraphy and telephony.
teleg. .. telegraphy.
Tenn. .. Tennyson.
term. .. termination.
Teut. .. Teutonic.
Thack. .. Thackeray.
theol. .. theology.
trigon. .. trigonometry.
Turk. .. Turkish.
typog. .. typography.
v.i. .. verb intransitive.
v.n. .. verb neuter.
v.t. .. verb transitive.
W. .. Welsh.
zool. .. zoology.
† .. rare.
‡ .. obsolete.
= .. equivalent to.
∴ .. comparison of synonyms.

SUPPLEMENT

This supplement has been designed especially for the American reader and gives new words and new meanings of old words that have come into the American language. Special attention has been given to words stemming from regional colloquialisms, new scientific terms, and slang expressions which have come to be part of the American vocabulary.

Whenever possible, the derivation of the word and the part of speech has been indicated.

Words which appear in the main body of the dictionary but for which an additional meaning has been given are marked with an asterisk (*).

The following abbreviations which are used in this supplement are in addition to, or newer variations of, those used in the body of the dictionary. For abbreviations not listed below, see the abbreviations and signs in the forematter.

A system of simplified sound symbols has been used in respelling the words in this section in order to facilitate easy pronunciation. See FOREMATTER.

ABBREVIATIONS

abbr.	..abbreviation	cp.	..compound	Ital.	..Italian	pref.	..prefix
aeron.	..aeronautics	derog.	..derogatory	Jap.	..Japanese	psychiat.	..psychiatry
Afr.	..African	Dict.	..in the body of the dictionary	Lat.	..Latin	psychoanol.	..psychoanalysis
agric.	..agriculture			M. E.	..Middle English	psychol.	..psychology
anthropol.	..anthropology	Du.	..Dutch	mil.	..military	Russ.	..Russian
attrib.	..attributive	econ.	..economics	nav.	..naval	S.	..South
avn.	..aviation	educ.	..education	orig.	..originally	sociol.	..sociology
bacter.	..bacteriology	electr.	..electronics	obs.	..obsolescent	specif.	..specifically
biochem.	..biochemistry	esp.	..especially	phon.	..phonetic	suff.	..suffix
Brit.	..British	etymol.	..etymology	phr.	..phrase	theatr.	..theatrical
Calif.	..California	Ger.	..German	polit.	..political	transl.	..translation
caps.	..capitals	imit.	..imitative	Port.	..Portuguese	uncert.	..uncertain
Chin.	..Chinese						

A.A.A., Agricultural Adjustment Administration; American Anthropological Association; American Automobile Association; Antiaircraft Artillery.

A.A.A.S., American Association for the Advancement of Science.

Aberdeen Angus, ab-ẽr-dēn' angus, From **Aberdeen, Scotland.** A breed, or an animal of the breed, of black hornless beef cattle.

A-bomb, ā'-bäm, *n.* (*colloq.*) An atomic bomb.

Absolute*, *adj. aeron.* Of height, with reference to the ground rather than to sea level. **Absolute Altimeter,** an altimeter designed to measure this height, which is called **Absolute Altitude;** *phys.* Pertaining to, or based on, fundamental units of length, mass or time; pertaining to the scale of absolute temperature.

Absolute Temperature, *n.* Temperature measured in degrees from absolute zero, which is −273.16° centigrade. Symbol: *K.*

Abstraction*, *n.* From *abstract* and *–ion. art* An artistic composition intending to suggest an idea or emotion without imitating recognizable objects.

Abstractionism, ab-strak'shon-izm, *n.* From *abstraction* and *–ism.* The school of modern art devoted to the composition of abstractions. **—Abstractionist,** *n.* A member of this school.

Academician*, *n.* (derogatory) A scholar or other intellectual with no consideration for everyday values or the popular understanding of his subject.

Accelerator*, *n. chem.* A catalyst; *phys.* any device which increases the speed of charged particles.

Accelerometer, ak-sel'er-ä-met-ur, *n.* See ACCELERATE and METER in the Dict. A device for measuring acceleration.

Access road, *n.* A road providing access to raw materials.

Acclimate*, *v.t.* and *i.* back formation from *acclimatize.* See Dict. (U.S.) To accustom or become accustomed or inured to a foreign climate, or by extension to any new or different environment.

Ace*, *n.* Expert, champion; one proficient in a particular field of endeavor. *—adj.* Proficient, excelent.

Acetanilide, as'll-e-tan'ē-lid, *n.* A derivative, C_8H_9ON, of aniline and acetic acid, used to mitigate pain or fever.

Acetate*, *n.* A product made from cellulose acetate, e.g., acetate rayon.

Acidize, as'id-īz, *v.t.* From *acid* and *–ize.* To treat with acid.

Ack-Ack, ak-ak, *n.* and *adj.* From pronunciation of AA antiaircraft by British radio operators. (mil. slang) *adj.* Pertaining to antiaircraft. *n.* An antiaircraft gun; antiaircraft artillery; antiaircraft fire.

A.C.L.S., American Council of Learned Societies.

Acronym, ak'ru-nim, *n.* From *acro–* and Gr. *onoma,* name. Cp. *homonym* in the Dict. A noun formed from syllables or the initial letters of other words, such as radar from radio detecting and ranging.

Across*, (U.S. colloq.) to come across, to give what is expected of one.

Across the board, *adj. racing* Of a bet, divided into equal amounts, that a horse will win, place, and show; (by extension) equally touching or affecting all parts of a system, as an across the board wage increase.

ACTH, Abbreviation for adrenocorticotropic hormone, below.

Action station, *n.* (esp. Brit. Navy) One's place on shipboard during combat; pl. the signal to go to one's place for combat; the state of being ready for combat.

Activable, ak'tiv-u-bl, *adj.* From *activate,* below, and *–able.* Capable of being activated.

Activate, ak'tiv-āt, *v.t.* From *active* and *–ate. mil.* To remove the safety devices from, as a mine or other weapon; to organize for active duty, as a military unit; to put into execution, as a plan previously drawn up. *chem.* To treat charcoal so as to increase its adsorptive capacity. *phys.* To make radioactive.

Ad, *n.* From *advertisement.* (colloq.) Advertisement.

Additive, ad'i-tiv, *adj.* Something that adds to an existing element, or can itself be added to.

Addressograph, ad-dres'ō-graf, *n.* From *address* and *graph, trade-mark.* A machine using previously prepared stencils to address large quantities of mail.

Adjuster*, *n.* From *adjust* and *–er.* An employee charged with settling financial claims against a corporation, such as a railroad or an insurance company.

Ad lib, ad'lib, *v.i.* and *t. abbr.* of *ad libitum.* To say something not provided in the script of a play or radio broadcast; to vary from the text of a previously written speech; to introduce any improvisation, as in playing jazz music. —n. An improvisation.

Adrenocorticotropic hormone, *n.* From *adrenalin, cortex* and *trope.* A hormone, secreted by the anterior lobe of the pituitary gland, which stimulates the adrenal cortex to secrete cortisone. See CORTISONE, below.

Adsorb, ad sorb', *v.t.* From ad-and Lat. *sorbere,* to suck in. To condense and hold (as gas, liquid, or dissolved substance) on a surface. **—Adsorbent,** *adj.* and *n.* **—Adsorption,** *n.* **—Adsorptive,** *n.* and *adj.*

Adultoid, a-dult'oid, *n.* From *adult* and *–oid. biol.* An immature individual resembling an adult.

A.E.F., American Expeditionary Force or Forces.

Aerobatics, ā-ẽr'ō-bat''iks, *n.* From *aero–* and acro*bat* and *–ic.* The performance of feats of skill or of daring, in piloting aircraft through spectacular motions in the air; stunt flying. **—Aerobatic,** *adj.*

Aerobe, ā'ẽr-ōb, *n.* From *aero–* and Gr. *bios,* life. An organism, especially a microscopic organism, that can live only in the presence of oxygen. **—Aerobic,** *adj.*

Aeroembolism, ā-ẽr-ō-em'bol-izm, *n.* From *aero–* and *embolism.* Painful and dangerous development of nitrogen bubbles in the blood, resulting, in aviators, from too rapid ascent to high altitudes.

Aerographer, ā-ēr-og'ra-fēr, *n.* From *aero-* and *graph* and *-er. mil. avn.* One who makes or collates weather observations for the specific purpose of predicting flying conditions.

Aerosol, ā'ēr-o-sol', *n.* From *aero-* and *sol,* below. *phys. chem.* A colloidal suspension of particles in a gas, as smoke.

Aerosol bomb, *n.* A small bomb-shaped container, from which insecticides are sprayed under pressure in a fine mist.

Aerostatics*, *n.* Specifically, the study of lighter-than-air craft, such as airships and balloons.

Affect*, *n. psychol.* Feeling or emotion, especially as influencing behavior.

Afghan, af'gan, *n.* A native of Afghanistan; a kind of knit or loosely woven blanket or shawl, usually homemade, of various colors.

A.F.L., A.F. of L. American Federation of Labor.

Afrikaans, af-ri-kans', *n.* S. Afr. Du. var. of Du. *Afrikansch.* The variety of the Dutch language spoken in the Union of South Africa.

Afro-, afrō, *pref.* From Lat. *Afer,* African. Combining form denoting Negroes, with specific reference to their African descent and heritage.

Afro-American, afrō'-a-mer'i-kan, *n.* also Aframerican. An American Negro. *—adj.* Pertaining to American Negroes.

Afterimage*, *n. psych.* A sensation that continues or revives after the stimulus has been removed.

Aftosa, af-tō'sa, *n.* (S.W. U.S.) Foot-and-mouth disease.

Age*, *n.* To be or act one's age (colloq., orig. U.S.) to behave in a reasonable manner, as befits one's years.

Agitprop, aj'it-prop, *n.* From *agit*ation and *prop*aganda. Agitation and propaganda, esp. that of the Communist party. *—adj.* an agitprop novel, etc.

Agrobiology, agrō-bī-ol'o-ji, *n.* From Gr. *agros,* land and biology. The science of plant nutrition and growth. **—Agrobiological,** *adj.* **—Agrobiologically,** *adv.* **—Agrobiologist,** *n.*

Aide, *n.* An aide-de-camp. See Dict.

Air*, *n.* to be on the air 1. to be broadcasted 2. to be broadcasted from time to time.

Air alert, *n.* The state of readiness for an enemy air raid, characterized by defending aircraft being at combat altitude; the signal to initiate such a state.

Air bends, *n.* See AEROEMBOLISM, above.

Airborne, ār'bōrn, *adj.* many variant pronunciations, esp. in E. and S. See AIR and BORNE. *mil.* Off the ground, as of a plane after takeoff; designed to be transported by air, as airborne infantry or an airborne invasion.

Air brake*, *n. aeron.* Any device which lowers the speed of an airplane by being projected into the airstream and thus increasing the resistance.

Air-condition, ār-kon-dish'on, *v.t.* From *air* and *condition.* (orig. U.S.) To control the temperature and humidity, as of a theater, railroad car, or home; to supply with air-conditioning equipment. **—Air-conditioned,** *adj.*

Air conditioning, *n.* A system for controlling the temperature and humidity of the air supply, as in a building or a railroad car.

Air-cool, ār'-kōōl, *v.t.* back formation from *air-cooled,* in the Dict. To cool by air; to air-condition.

Airdrop, ār'-drop, *n.* Something dropped from an airplane, such as supplies; a system for dropping supplies by air, as to isolated bodies of troops or to communities cut off by flood, snow, etc. *—v.t.* To drop from an airplane.

Airfoil, ār'-foil, *n.* See *air* and *foil, aeron.* Any aircraft surface, such as an aileron, rudder, or wing, which receives a useful reaction from the windstream through which it moves.

Air force*, *n.* (U.S.) *mil. avn.* The largest strategic unit of air power, corresponding to an army.

Airframe, ār-frām, *n.* An airplane chassis without its engines.

Air letter, *n.* A letter sent by air mail; a postal device consisting of a single prestamped sheet of paper which can be sealed in envelope shape and air-mailed without additional postage.

Airlift, ār'-lift, *n.* A system of large-scale transportation, for military purposes or in an emergency, of passengers and freight by air. *—v.t.* To transport by such a system; e. g. the Berlin airlift.

Airline, *n.* A company operating a system of air transportation; straight, direct, as airline distances.

Airliner, ār'-lī'nėr, *n.* A plane designed to transport passengers.

Air mail*, *n.* A system of carrying mail by air. *—v.t.* To send mail by air.

Airmarker, ār'-märkėr *n.* A sign prominently placed to guide aircraft. **—Airmark,** *v.t.* To provide with airmarkers.

Air-raid shelter, *n.* A bomb-resistant shelter, affording protection during an air raid.

Air-raid warden, *n.* A local officer, ordinarily a deputized civilian, supervising protection of life and property during an air raid.

Airscrew, ār'-skrōō, *n.* (Brit.) An aircraft propeller.

Air speed, *n.* The speed of a plane relative to the air, as distinct from its speed relative to the ground.

Airstrip, ār'-strip, *n.* A strip of land for use by airplanes, often hurriedly leveled off in newly conquered territory and generally less well equipped than an airfield.

Airway, *n.* A channel for radio broadcasting.

Airworthy, ār''wėr'thi, *adj.* From *air* and *worthy,* prob. by analogy with seaworthy. (of aircraft) Fit to undertake a flight; sound in all parts, construction, etc. **—Airworthiness,** *n.*

Alert*, *n.* The signal to be in readiness for an enemy air raid; the period during which such a signal is in effect; to warn of an air raid; to signal troops to prepare for action.

Alibi*, *n.* (U.S. colloq.) Any excuse. *—v.i.* (slang) To attempt to excuse oneself.

All-American, *adj. athletics.* Nationally pre-eminent at a particular position in a particular sport. *—n.* an athlete so designated.

All-clear, *n.* The signal indicating the end of an enemy air raid.

Allele, al-lēl', *n. biol.* Short form of allelomorph, below. **—Allelic,** *adj.*

Allelomorph, al-lē'lo-morf, *n.* From Gr. *allelon,* reciprocally, mutually and *-morph. biol.* One of a pair of contrasting Mendelian characters; a gene giving rise to such a character.

Allergenic, al'ler-gen'ic, *adj.* From *allergy* and *-genic.* Causing allergy.

Allergy, *n. med.* Abnormal sensitivity to certain foods, pollens, etc., (colloq.) (By extension) any feeling of antipathy toward another person or thing. **—Allergic,** *adj.*

Alligator*, *n.* (slang) A motor-driven caterpillar-tread armored barge capable of operating on both land and water.

Allomorph, al'lo-morf, *n.* From *allo-* and *morph. linguistics* One of several varieties of forms, alternating freely or in automatically determined situations, that together constitute a morpheme. **—Allomorphic,** *adj.*

Allophone, al'lo-fōn, *n.* From *allo-* and *phone. linguistics* One of several varieties of sounds, alternating freely or in automatically determined situations, that together constitute a phoneme, below. **—Allophonic,** *adj.*

Allotment*, *n.* (U.S.) *mil.* A certain portion of a soldier's pay, voluntarily assigned by him to be paid to another person or institution.

All-out, *adj.* Prob. from motoring with all throttles out. (colloq.) Using all one's strength and resources unreservedly; to go all out, strive with all one's might.

Alnico, al'ni-kō, *n.* Coined from symbols for *al*uminum, *ni*ckel, and *co*balt. An alloy used for permanent magnets, containing aluminum, nickel, cobalt, and iron.

Alpha particle, *n. phys.* A positively charged particle of the same weight as a helium nucleus, emitted during some types of radioactive disintegration.

Alpha ray, *n. phys.* A stream of alpha particles.

Also-ran, *n.* (colloq.) A horse that finishes worse than third in a race (by extension) a contestant in any type of contest who wins no prize and furnishes no real competition to the winner.

Alternator, al'ter-nā'ter, *n.* See *alternate* and *-or. elect.* An alternating-current generator.

AM or **A.M.** Abbreviation for amplitude modulation, below.

Ambassador-at-large, *n.* A U.S. envoy assigned to study a particular international problem in several foreign countries.

Ambulatory*, *adj. med.* Of a patient, able to walk; *law* Alterable.

Americium, am'er-ish'ium, *n.* From *America* and *-ium. chem.* A transuranic element of atomic number 95, produced by nuclear bombardment. Symbol: *Am.*

Amerind, am'er-ind', *n.* Clipped form of Amerindian; an Eskimo or Indian native to America.

Amidol, am'i-dōl, *n.* trade-mark. A phenol salt used as a photographic developer.

Amigo, a-mē'go, *n.* Sp. friend. From Lat. *amare,* to love. Cp. AMICABLE, AMATIVE, in the Dict. A friend, esp. a friendly Spanish-speaking native.

Amino acid, a-mē'no, *n.* See *amine* and *ammonia* in the Dict. *chem.* Any of the acids containing the amino radical NH^2. They are the chief constituents of proteins.

Amoebic, a-mē'bik, *adj.* From *amoeba* and *-ic.* Pertaining to an amoeba; caused by amoebea.

Amoebic dysentery, *n.* A severe type of dysentery caused by an amoeba and characterized by ulceration.

Amoral, a-mor'al, *adj.* From *a-* and *moral.* Not concerned with moral value; lacking moral quality.

Amplitude modulation, *n. electronics.* A type of radio broadcasting characterized by modulation of the amplitude of the transmitting wave. Contrasted with frequency modulation below.

Anacrusis*, *n. mus.* By extension, introductory musical notes which are not accented.

Analysis*, *n.* Short form of psychoanalysis in the Dict. **—Analyst,** *n.* **—Analyze,** *v.t.*

Anchor*, *n.* Any device which serves to hold something fast. *mil.* A key military position in a given area.

Anchor leg, *n.* See ANCHOR in the Dict. and LEG, below. *sports* The final portion of a relay race.

Anchor man, *n. sports.* The person running the anchor leg, above.

Andric, an'drik, *adj.* From -ANDROUS in the Dict. Pertaining to a male contrasted with gynic, below.

Andro-, an'dro, Gr. combining form meaning male. Cp. ANDRIC, above, and -ANDROUS in the Dict. Male; *biol.* indicating the presence of a stamen.

Androgen, an'dro-jen, *n.* From ANDRO-, above, and *-gen. biochem.* Any substance which induces male characteristics.

Androsterone, an-dros'ter-ōn, *n.* From ANDRO-, above, and *ster*ol below and *-one. biochem.* A male sex hormone $C_{19}H_{30}O_2$, found in male urine.

Angel*, *n.* (slang) A financial backer of a person or venture esp. a stage play. *—v.t.* To underwrite a person or venture.

Angle*, *n.* (slang) A point of view. To get a new angle on something, to find a new way of thinking about it; an aspect; to look over all the angles, consider all aspects of a problem, etc. *—v.t.* To distort news, etc. so as to favor a particular point of view; to bend or move in angles.

Angle of attack, *n. aeron.* The angle at which the wind strikes the wing of an airplane.

Anglicist, ang'gli-sizt, *n.* From *Anglican* and *-ist.* A specialist in the study of English culture, esp. the English language.

Anglist, ang'lizt, *n.* A specialist in the study of English culture.

Angstrom unit or **Angstrom,** ang'strōm, *n.* Named after Swedish physicist A. J. Angström 1814–74. A unit equal to one ten-billionth of a meter, one tenth of a millimicron, used to measure intramolecular distances. Abbrev.: Å.,Å.U.

Anklet*, *n.* A sock reaching slightly above the ankle.

Annie Oakley, *n.* (theatrical slang) A free ticket to a stage performance, etc., from Annie Oakley Butler, famous marksman, whose ability to shoot holes in cards tossed in the air gave the name to passes perforated by punch marks.

Annulus, an'nū-lus, *n.* Pl. *-li* or *-luses.* From Lat. *annulus,* ring; cp. ANNULAR in Dict. A ring; a ringlike formation or shape.

Anodize, an'ōd-īz, *v.t.* From *anode* and *-ize.* To coat a piece of metal with a protective film by electrolysis.

Anoxia, an-ok'si-a, *n.* From *an-* and *oxygen* and *-ia. med.* Physical weakness from lack of oxygen. —**Anoxic,** *adj.* Pertaining to anoxia.

Anschluss, an'shloos, *n.* Ger. a joining. An accomplished political attachment, union; said esp. of the Nazi annexation of Austria in 1938.

Ante, an-tē, *n.* From Lat. *ante* before. *poker* A stake put up by a player before he draws new cards, or sometimes before he sees his hand. —*v.t.* and *i. poker* To put up one's stake; to ante up, to pay, esp. to pay one's share.

Antibiotic, anti-bī-ot'ik, *n.* From *anti—* and *biotic,* below. A chemical agent produced by living micro-organisms and medically useful against microbes.

Antifreeze, an'ti-frēz, *n.* A liquid possessing a low freezing point and noncorrosive qualities, used in the cooling systems of internal combustion motors to prevent freezing.

Antihistamine, -minic, anti-his'ta-min, *n.* See HISTAMINE, below. *biochem.* Any of several substances antagonistic to histamine, and believed to be medically useful for this reason. —**Antihistaminic,** *adj.*

Antiknock, an'ti-nok, *n.* A substance which limits detonation in internal-combustion engines during the combustion of fuel.

Antipersonnel, anti-pėr-son-el', *adj. mil.* Designed for use against troops, as an antipersonnel mine.

Antirachitic, anti-ra-kit'ik, *adj.* From *anti-* and *rachitic.* Tending to prevent or cure rickets. —*n.*

Anti-Semitism, anti-sem'ĭt-izm, *n.* See SEMITE in Dict. Hostility to Jews. —**Anti-Semitic,** *adj.* —**Anti-Semite,** *n.*

Antitank, anti-tangk', *adj. mil.* Designed for use against tanks.

Antivenin, anti-ven'in, *n.* From *anti-* and Lat *venenum,* poison. An antitoxin used to prevent poisoning from snakebite.

Aphid, a'fid, *n.* An aphis. —**Aphidian,** *adj.* and *n.*

APO Army Post Office.

Apple pie*, *n.* Easy as apple pie, something quite easily done.

Apple-polish, ap'l-polish, *v.t.* and *i.* To behave in a sycophantic manner. —**Apple-polisher,** *n.*

Applesauce, ap'l-sas, *n.* A sauce made from stewed apples; (slang) nonsense, esp. insincere flattery.

Apraxia, a-prak'si-a, *n.* From *a-* and Gr. *prāxis,* a doing, Fr. *prássein,* to do. *med.* Loss of co-ordination of voluntary movements.

Aptitude test, *n. psychol.* A test to determine one's aptitude for learning a certain type of work.

Aqua*, *n.* Lat. *aqua,* water. *pharm.* A solution of something dissolved in water.

Aquabelle, ak'wa-bel, *n.* From *aqua* and *belle.* A female performer in an aquacade.

Aquacade, ak'wa-kād, *n.* From *aqua* and suff. by analogy with caval*cade.* Commercial water exhibition, featuring swimming, diving, etc., of an unusual nature.

Aqualung, ak'wa-lung, *n.* From *aqua* and *lung.* A completely self-contained diving suit using compressed air.

Aquaplane, ak'wa-plān, *n.* From *aqua* and *plane.* A board gliding over the water when towed at high speed, so that a person may ride upon it. —*v.i.* To ride upon an aquaplane.

Aquavit, ak'wä-vit, *n. Scand.* A Scandinavian type of brandy.

Argyle or **Argyll,** är-gīl' *n.* Any design characterized by crisscrossing diamond shapes, patterned after the tartan of the Argyll family of the Campbell clan; socks knit in such a pattern.

Arm*, *v.t.* To make operative the fuse of a weapon, such as a bomb or torpedo, by removing the safety device.

Armchair*, *adj.* (derogatory) Removed from the reality pertaining to one's interests, as armchair philosophers, strategists, etc.

Arrivé or **Arriviste,** a'rē'vā', *n.* both mod. Fr. See ARRIVE in the Dict. (derogatory) One who has achieved success by unscrupulous means.

Arroyo, a-roi'ō, *n.* From Sp. A rivulet or small stream; the dry bed of a stream; a gully.

A.S.C.A.P., or **ASCAP,** American Society of Composers, Artists, and Publishers, an artist's union.

Ascorbic acid, a-skor'bik, *n.* See SCORBUTIC in the Dict. Vitamin C, used as a preventive of scurvy, found esp. in citrus fruits.

Ash can, *n.* A metal receptacle for ashes; (by extension) metal receptacle for any type of refuse; (U.S. Navy slang) A depth charge.

Assault*, *n.* and *v.t.* (Euphemism) esp. in newspapers for criminal assault.

Astatine, as'ta-tēn, *n.* From Gr. *ástatos,* unstable, Cp. STATIC in the Dict. *chem.* An unstable, naturally radioactive element of atomic number 85, first produced in nuclear experiments. Symbol: *At.*

Astrodome, as'trō-dōm, *n.* From *astro-* and *dome.* A transparent dome projecting from the upper surface of an aircraft.

Astronomic, -al*, *adj.* Like the large figures used in astronomy; immense, astoundingly big.

Atabrine, at'a-brin, *n. trade-mark* Quinacrine hydrochloride, an antimalarial drug developed in Germany, 1932.

Athlete's foot, *n.* A contagious ringworm of the feet.

Atomic bomb, *n.* Also Atom bomb, A-bomb. A bomb depending for its destructive effect on the energy released by nuclear fission.

Atomic clock, *n.* A clock of almost perfect accuracy regulated by the nitrogen atom of an ammonia molecule; the most precise method of determining the age of a mineral or the time at which a once-living organism died, based upon the constant rate of decay of radioactive isotopes.

Atomic energy, *n.* Energy released by nuclear fission or nuclear fusion.

Atomic pile. See PILE, below.

Atomistic*, *adj.* From *atom* and *-istic.* (fig.) A whole characterized by discrete, disorganized units, such as an atomistic society.

Audio, a'diō, *adj.* From Lat. base *audi-,* hearing. Cp. AUDIBLE in the Dict. *electronics* Pertaining to frequencies within the frequency range of audible sound waves, normally from 15,000 to 20,000 cycles per second, as distinguished from radio, below; pertaining to apparatus using such frequencies.

Audio-visual aids, audio-vizh'-ū-al āds, *n. educ.* Phonograph records, moving pictures, film strips, lantern slides, and similar devices used to supplement textbooks and lectures.

Audition*, *v.t.* (U.S. colloq.) To perform in an audition.

Aureomycin, ōrē-ō-mī'sin, *n.* From Lat. dim. *aureolus,* golden, and Gr. *mŭkēs,* fungus and *-in.* A yellow crystalline antibiotic, effective against a wide variety of disease-producing organisms.

Australian ballot, *n.* A ballot, originally used in South Australia, which lists the names of all candidates and which is cast and counted in complete secrecy.

Autarchy, a'tär-ki, *n,* From Ger. *Autarchie,* Fr. Gr. *autarkeia,* self-sufficiency. SEE AUTO- and ARCH-. Absolute power, autocracy; self-rule; —**Autarchic, -al,** *adj.*

Author*, *v.t.* (U.S. slang) To write or compose something as an author; to author a script or literary work.

Authoritarian, *adj.* Specif., of, pertaining to, a dictatorship; antidemocratic, nonparliamentary and oppressive toward civil liberties.—**Authoritarianism,** *n.*

Autobahn, o'tō-bän, *n.,* pl. *-bahnen;* From Ger., auto road. In Germany, a highway with no speed limit.

Autocade, o'tō-kād, *n.* From *auto* and *-cade,* by analogy with cavalcade. A procession of automobiles.

Auto court, *n.* (U.S.) A cluster of cabins around an administrative and service building, designed to furnish overnight accommodations for tourists traveling by automobile.

Automat, o'tō-mat, *n.* From *automaton.* See Dict. A restaurant in which service is automatically obtained by the use of coin-operated devices.

Automatic pilot, *n.* A gyroscopic device designed to hold an airplane on a set course.

Automatic rifle, *n.* A firearm which may be used either as a rifle or as a light machine gun, i. e. fired automatically.

Autotrophic, o'to-trof'ik, *adj.* From *auto-* and *trophic. plant physiol.* Of plants capable of producing their own nutrients, esp. by photosynthesis. **Autotroph,** *n.* A self-nourishing plant. **Autotrophy,** *n.*

Auxin, ok'sin, *n.* From Gr. *auxein,* to increase and *-in. bot.* and *chem.* Any one of a group of substances which promote plant growth.

A.W.O.L., (mil. slang) usage as one word, *mil.* Absent without official leave. *n.* Deserter.

Axe, Ax*, *n.* To give someone the axe, to dismiss from a post. —*v.t.* To trim with an axe.

Axenic, a-zen'ik, *adj.* From *a-* and *xenic,* From Gr. *xenos,* stranger. Coined by J. A. Baker and M. S. Ferguson, 1942. Of an organism having no demonstrable life apart from that produced by its own protoplasm; germ-free.

Axis*, *n.* An alliance of nations designed to further joint interests of foreign policy; specif., the Rome–Berlin axis, 1936.

Babbitt, bab'it, *n,* From main character of Sinclair Lewis's novel "Babbitt," 1922. derog. A person usually male who uncritically adheres to the values of the American upper middle class, esp. the value of business success. —**Babbitry,** *n.* This attitude.

Babbitt metal, From Isaac Babbitt 1799-1862, U.S. inventor. *metal.* An antifriction alloy composed of tin, antimony, copper, and sometimes lead.

Babushka, ba-boosh'ka, *n.* Rus. grandmother. A woman's triangular scarf, used as a head covering.

Baby sitter, *n.* One hired to care for children while the parents are away from home. —**Baby sit,** *v.i.* —**Baby sitting,** *n.*

Bacardi, ba-kar'de, *n.* From family name of manufacturers. *trade-mark* A brand of Cuban rum; a cocktail containing this brand of rum.

Bach, *v.i.* From *bachelor.* (slang) To live as a bachelor; to keep house alone. —(slang) A bachelor.

Bacillomycin, ba-sil'lo-mī'sin, *n.* From *bacillus* and Gr, *mukes,* fungus, Cp. *myco-* in the Dict. An antibiotic effective against fungi, esp. that causing athlete's foot.

Backfield, bak-fēld, *n. football.* Those players in back of the line who may receive a direct pass from the center.

Background*, *n.* The historical and environmental facts which are necessary to the understanding of a person or thing: the background of the revolution; his background is obscure; music or other sound effects accompanying any acting performance; unwanted sound accompanying a radio program, due to atmospheric interferences or circuit conditions.

Backlog, bak-log, *n.* From *back* and *log.* A large log at the back of a hearth fire; a reserve of work to be accomplished, esp. *commerce* unfilled orders.

Back number, *n.* (U.S.) An out-of-date issue of a periodical; (colloq.) anything which is no longer fashionable; a person holding antiquated notions.

Backstage, bak-stāj, *n.* In the wings or

dressing rooms of a theater, or on the portion of the stage behind the curtain; upstage; toward the rear of the stage. —*adj.* Located backstage; (by extension) concealed, covert.

Back talk, *n.* Impertinent or argumentative reply.

Badman, *n.* A gangster; a movie actor generally cast in unpopular roles.

Bailey bridge, *n.*, From its designer, Donald Bailey. *mil. engin.* A type of easily erected bridge, prefabricated in interlocking sections.

Bakelite, bā'ke-līt, *n.* Named after L. H. Baekland the inventor. *trade-mark* A thermosetting synthetic resin of the phenolaldehyde type, widely used instead of wood, pottery, etc.

BAL, *n.* From abbreviation of *B*ritish *A*nti-*L*ewisite. A chemical compound developed as an antidote for the poisonous gas lewisite, now used as the primary antidote for poisoning by mercury, arsenic, gold and other heavy metals.

Balding, bawl-ding, *adj.* Growing bald.

Balletomane, ba-let'o-mān, *n.* See BALLET and MANIA in the Dict. A devotee of ballet.

Ball-point pen, *n.* A pen whose point is a small ball bearing.

Ballyhoo, bal'i-hōō, *n.* Etymology obscure; term orig. circus cant. (slang) Noise, outcry to draw customers, as to a circus; by extension, any type of unrestrained advertising or publicity.

Banana republic, *n.* (derog.) Any of the republics of Central America.

Bandwagon, band-wa'gn, *n.* From *band* and *wagon.* A large, high wagon in which a band rides, esp. a circus band; (U.S. colloq.) sudden, widespread acclaim, as of a politician; esp. in the phrase to get on the bandwagon, to join in the current popular acclaim of someone.

Bang*, *n.* (U.S. slang) To get a bang out of, to be thrilled by something.

Bangalore torpedo, bang'ga-lōr, *n.* From Bangalore, city of S. India. A long pipe filled with TNT and exploded by means of a fuse, used esp. for cutting barbed wire.

Bang-up, *adj.* (Orig. Brit. slang) Excellent.

Bank*, *v.t. billiards.* To drive the cue ball into a cushion; *pool* to pocket an object ball by driving it into a cushion; to cover a fire and reduce the air supply, to make it burn more slowly.

Bank*, *n.* Any storage place for a reserve supply, as a blood bank or eye bank.

Bank night, *n.* A copyrighted type of lottery in which prizes are awarded to previously registered members of a movie audience; a night on which the drawing for such a lottery is made.

Banzai, ban'zī', *interj.* Japanese battle-cry. —*adj.* Reckless, suicidal; esp. of a Japanese infantry charge.

Barb*, *n.* From *barbarian.* (U.S. college slang) One who is not a member of a college fraternity.

Barbiturate, bar-bit'u-rāt, *n.* From *barbituric* acid and *uric,* named in 1863 by its discoverer, Adolph Baeyer, 1835–1917. One of a group of derivatives of barbituric acid, used as sedatives and hypnotics.

Bar fly, *n.* From *bar* and *fly.* (slang) A frequenter of public drinking places.

Barkeep, -er, *n.* The owner of a bar in which liquors are sold; a bartender.

Bar mitzva or **mizvah,** bar'mits'va, *n.* From Heb., son of law. *Jewish relig.* A boy of thirteen, the age at which he assumes religious duties; the religious ceremony marking this occasion.

Barne, *n. nuclear phys.* A unit of measurement equal to 10–24 sq. cm.

Barrel-house, *adj. jazz mus.* In a wild and crude manner, as the kind of music formerly played in a cheap drinking place; esp. of piano music. –*n.* This type of music; (obs.) A drinking place serving cheap liquor.

Barrel roll. *n. aeron.* The complete turn of an airplane on its longitudinal axis.

Bartender, *n.* (U.S.) A man who prepares and serves drinks at a bar.

Basal metabolism, *n. physiol.* The standard metabolism of the body after fasting and resting, expressed by the basic metabolic rate, the measurement of the rate of oxygen consumption.

Basic English or **Basic,** *n.* The English language systematically restricted to a vocabulary of 850 words together with compounds and combinations of these, not counting words that may be considered as technical or of international currency: Lamb's stories from Shakespeare in Basic; *attrib. n.* Of, or belonging to, rendered in Basic English: the Basic Rules of Reason, principles of logic expounded in Basic English.

Bassist, bās'ist, *n.* From *bass* and *-ist.* One who plays a bass instrument.

Bastion*, *n.* Any fortified place.

Bat*, A turn at batting; (slang) A spree; to go on a bat.

Bat boy, *n.* A young man who takes care of bats and other equipment used by baseball and softball players.

Bathinette, *n.* A portable, collapsible device of canvas and wood or steel, on which babies may be bathed and dressed.

Bathysphere*, *n.* See *bathos* and *sphere.* Hollow sphere constructed so that it can be let down to a considerable depth in the sea and e. g. bring up samples of water or aquatic life.

Battery*, *n. baseball* The pitcher and catcher together; any series of similar units in a group: a battery of tests, boilers, etc.

Batting average, *n. baseball* The ratio of a batter's hits to the total number of times at bat; (slang) A ratio expressing one's degree of success in any field of endeavor.

Battle fatigue, *n.* A neurotic breakdown occurring under the stress of combat conditions. Also called combat fatigue.

Battle wagon, *n.* (slang) A battleship.

Bawl*, *v.t.* (slang) To bawl someone out; to reprove, scold someone.

Bay*, *n.* A distinct compartment of an aircraft: bomb bay.

Bay seal, *n.* A simulated seal fur made from rabbit fur.

Bazooka, ba-zōō'ka, *n.* Coined word; orig. a type of musical instrument used by comedian Bob Burns. *milit.* A portable antitank rocket launcher.

Beachhead, bēch'hed', *n.* A position established and fortified on a shore by an invading force.

Beam*, *n. aeron.* A radio directional signal for guiding aircraft; off the beam, going in the wrong direction; (slang) crazy, erratic; on the beam, going in the right direction; (slang) sensible, alert; followed by *at* to direct a radio broadcast at receivers in a particular area.

Bean*, *n.* (slang) orig. U.S. The head. —*v.t.* To hit someone on the head with a thrown object, esp. with a baseball.

Beat-up, *adj.* From *beat,* —*v.t.* (slang). Badly damaged; worn out; *of persons* Tired, exhausted.

Beaut, būt, *n.* From *beauty.* (U.S. slang) Something beautiful; phrase That's a beaut.

Beauty parlor, shop or **salon,** *n.* Establishment for women's hairdressing, massage, etc.

Bedspread, bed'spred', *n.* The ornamental outer covering of a bed.

Beef*, *n.* (U.S. slang) A complaint. —*v.i.* To complain.

Beguine*, *n.* From Fr. dial. variation of *beguin,* flirtation. A type of Latin-American dance set to bolero rhythm.

Bell*, *n.* To ring the bell (slang) orig. U.S. to be successful, get good results; *fig.,* from a strength-testing mechanism which rings when heavily hit.

Bellboy, bel'boi', *n.* (U.S.) A hotel employee answering to the call of a bell, who carries guests' baggage and furnishes service to guests in their rooms.

Bellhop, bel'hop', *n.* (U.S. colloq.) A bellboy.

Bellyache, bel'lē-āk', *v.i.* From *n. bellyache,* in Dict. under BELLY. To complain. —*n.* A complaint. Cp. parallel development of meaning of GRIPE, below, and in the Dict.

Belly landing, *n.* From *belly* and *landing.* A crash landing of a plane on its belly, when its landing gear cannot be used. —**Bellyland,** *v.i.*

Bellylaugh, bel'lē-laf', *n.* From *belly* and *laugh.* A loud, hearty laugh; something funny; a joke.

Belt*, *n.* (U.S.) *ecology.* A region characterized by certain types of growth: corn belt, cotton belt, etc.; (slang) a region characterized by any peculiar condition: Bible belt.

Bends, benz, *n.* pl. (U.S. colloq.) Aeroembolism, esp. as affecting deep sea divers and workers in caissons.

Benelux, ben'e-luks, *n.* A customs union formed by *Be*lgium, the *Ne*therlands and *Lux*embourg after World War II. —*adj.* Pertaining to these three countries considered as a unit.

Bengaline, beng'ga-lēn, *n.* A type of heavily corded fabric.

Benzedrine, ben'zi-drēn, *n.* The trade name for amphetamine, a synthetic drug used as an inhalant and to prevent sleepiness.

Berkelium, burk'li-um, *n.* From *Berkeley, Calif.,* its place of discovery, and *-ium. chem.* A transuranic element of atomic number 97, first produced in 1949 by bombardment of Americium with alpha particles. Symbol: *Bk.*

Beta particle, *n. phys.* An electron emitted in certain types of radioactivity.

Beta ray, *n. phys.* A stream of beta particles.

Betatron, bē'ta-tron, *n.* From *beta* ray and elec*tron.* A machine, used in nuclear studies, that imparts extremely high velocities to electrons.

Bevatron, bev'a-tron, *n.* From *b*illion *e*lectric *v*olts and elec*tron. phys.* A device designed to accelerate protons and other charged particles to the level of several billion electron volts.

B film, B picture, *n.* A movie of relatively low quality, produced to enable theater owners to change their programs frequently.

Bibliofilm, bib'li-o-film, *n.* From *biblio-* and *film.* A microfilm used esp. for the reproduction of books.

Bibliotics, bib'li-ot'iks, *n.* From *biblio-* and *-otic.* The study of handwriting, esp. for determining authorship.

Bifocals, bī-fo'kals, *n.* pl. Eyeglasses with bifocal lenses, affording corrections for near and distant vision.

Big time, *n.* (U.S. colloq.) The highest level of achievement in an occupational field, as measured by status or income; esp. of professional entertainers. —*adj.* **Big-timer,** *n.*

Bill*, *n.* (U.S. slang) A piece of paper money; dollar bill. Phrase to sell someone a bill of goods, to cheat or take advantage of someone; to put someone into a disadvantageous position.

Billboard, bil'bōrd, *n.* From *bill* and *board.* A projection on the bow of a ship for the bill of an anchor to rest on; any large flat surface on which advertisements are posted.

Billing, *n.* From *bill* and *-ing.* The relative degree of prominence, measured by position and size of type, with which an actor or act is listed on posters, programs, etc; top billing, star billing, —*n.* The highest degree of prominence.

Bimester, bī-mes'ter, *n.* From Lat. *bimestris,* of two months. A period of two months. —**Bimestrial,** *adj.* Of two months duration; happening, appearing every two months.

Bindle, bindl, *n.* (slang) The roll of bedding and clothes carried by a hobo. —**Bindle-stiff,** *n.* (slang) A hobo who carries such a roll.

Bingle, bing'gl, *n.* (baseball slang) A base hit.

Bingo, bing'go, *n.* A type of gambling game, on the same principle as lotto.

Biological warfare, *n.* Warfare by means of toxins and disease-producing living organisms.

Biophysics, bī'ō-fis'iks, *n.* From *bio-* and *physics.* The study of biological phenomena by means of techniques and theory derived from the mathematico-physical sciences.

Biosynthesis, bī'ō-sin'tha-sis, *n.* From *bio-* and *synthesis.* The production of a chemical compound by a living organism.
Biotic, bī-ot'iks, *adj.* From Gr. *biotikos.* Pertaining to life.
Biotin, bī'ō-tin, *n.* From *bio-* and *-in.* A growth-promoting factor which is a member of the vitamin B complex.
Bird*, *n.* The shuttlecock used in badminton; (slang) a derisive sound; usually in phrase to get the bird, to give someone the bird. —*v.i.* To observe and identify birds in their natural surroundings.
Birder, one who observes or identifies wild birds.
Birdie, burd-ē. *n.* A small bird; *golf* a score on a hole of one stroke less than par.
Birth control, *n.* The limitation of the number of children born by preventing or lessening conception, as by the use of contraceptives.
Bizonia, bī-zo'ni-a, *n.* From *bi-* and *zone* and *-ia.* The British and American zones of occupation in Western Germany considered as a unit.
Black*, *n.* Phrase in the black, of a business enterprise showing a profit.
Black eye, *n.* A discolored bruise in the region of the eye; (colloq.) anything which discredits someone.
Blackjack*, *n. cards Vingt et un.* See Dict. Caramel or burnt sugar used for coloring wine, coffee, etc. The black pirate flag; an oak of the Eastern U.S., having a black bark. —*v.t.* To hit with a blackjack. (by extension) To coerce.
Black market, *n.* Illegal sale of goods, the distribution and prices of which are regulated by a government.
Black out, *v.i.* To switch off all stage lights during a theater performance; to lose consciousness, suddenly and usually temporarily; esp. in aviation; to suffer a temporary loss of memory. —*v.t.* To extinguish or cover all lights, as a military precaution; hence, to impose censorship. —**Blackout,** *n.* The act of blacking out or the condition of being blacked out.
Black Shirt, *n.* From the black shirt worn by the Italian Fascist militia. A member of a Fascist party, esp. a member of its militia.
Black widow, *n.* The female of a subtropical variety of American spider, whose bite is highly poisonous.
Blanket*, *v.t.* To silence a radio station by broadcasting on a more powerful station of the same frequency. —*adj.* Covering an entire class or group of things; blanket insurance, blanket indictment, etc.
Blankety-blank. Literary euphemism for profanity; indicated by the words "blankety-blank" or two dashes — —.
Bleachers, blēch'erz, *n.* pl. See BLEACH. A section of uncovered seats for spectators at outdoor games.
Bleed*, *v.t. print.* To trim the edge of a page too closely; to impose an illustration so that it will extend beyond the margins to which the page is to be trimmed in binding.
Blind alley, *n.* A road closed at one end; *fig.* a fruitless situation offering no hope of advancement or improvement.
Blind spot, *n. anat.* The part of the retina, at which the optic nerve enters the eye which is insensitive to light; a subject which one cannot fully understand, esp. because of prejudice; *radio* an area in which the reception of radio signals is poor.
Blinker tube, *n.* A tube used in Navy signaling equipped with shutters and a light and sighted like a gun.
Blister*, *n. mil. avn.* A blister-shaped transparent bulge on an airplane fuselage used for observation or gunnery.
Blitz, *n.* and *v.t.* (colloq.) Blitzkrieg.
Blitzkrieg, blits'krēg, *n.* Ger., lightning war. A technique of warfare consisting of swift strokes designed to pierce the enemy's lines, disrupt his communication and supply systems, and separate his forces; any swift, overwhelming attack. —*v.t.* To attack with a blitzkrieg.
Bloc, blok, *n.* From Fr., block. See BLOCK. A union of nations, parties, factions of parties, etc. to further a common interest or cause.
Blockbuster, blok'bust'er, *n.* (Orig. British) A high explosive bomb of two tons or more.
Blockhouse*, *n. mil.* Any small fortified structure having ports for machine guns or artillery.
Blood bank, *n.* A place for the storage of blood or blood plasma; a reserve supply of blood plasma.
Blood count, *n.* A count of the total number of corpuscles or the number of red and white corpuscles per cubic millimeter of blood.
Blood group, *n.* One of four types of blood distinguished by Landsteiner, and usually designated as O, A, B, and AB; erroneously, blood type.
Blood test, *n.* Any analysis of one's blood, esp. the Wassermann test for syphilis.
Blood type, *n.* One of several types of blood, including the four blood groups and other types; erroneously, blood group.
Blow*, *v.t.* (slang) To spend money on someone; to squander. —*v.i.* (slang) to leave, esp. to leave hurriedly; blowup *photog.* to make an enlarged reproduction of a photograph; blow in, to arrive, esp. to arrive unexpectedly.
Blowout*, *n.* The bursting of an automobile tire; the place where a tire has burst; (slang) a large, noisy, social affair.
Blue*, *adj.* Melancholy.
Blue law, *n.* Any law based upon a rigorous morality, esp. laws closing places of refreshment and amusement on Sundays.
Bluenose, *n.* (Amer.) Name applied to natives of New England and the Canadian Maritime Provinces; a Nova Scotian ship; a Nova Scotian potato; a puritanical, snobbish or inquisitive person; (obs.) a clam.
Blue notes, *n.* pl. See BLUES, below. Flatted thirds and sevenths characteristic of Afro-American blues, originating in the clash between the five whole-tone scale of West Africa and our diatonic major scale in which the third and seventh steps are half tones.
Blueprint*, *n.* The process of making a photographic print, white on a blue gound; (colloq.) a plan for anything. —*v.t.* To make a blue print of, a plan of.
Blues, bloōz, *n.* pl. short form of blue devils. Melancholy, despondency; a type of Afro-American folk song, sometimes classified as a branch of jazz music, characterized by flatted thirds and sevenths, twelve-bar form, duple time and melancholy lyrics.
Blurb, blerb, *n.* coined by Gelett Burgess in 1907. An advertisement praising a book, esp. if printed on the book's dust jacket; any laudatory advertisement.
Bobby pin, bobi'pin, *n.* From its orig. use with bobbed hair. A flat metal hairpin with prongs close together.
Bobby socks —sox, bobi'sox, *n.* pl. Ankle length socks for women, especially as worn by adolescent girls.
Bobby soxer, bobi'sox'er, *n.* An adolescent girl, especially one addicted to current fads.
Bobwhite, *n.* A quail of the genus *Colinus,* especially the game bird *C. virginianus,* so called from its distinctive call or whistle.
Boloney, Baloney, ba-lōn'ē, *n.* variant spelling of bologna. Bologna sausage; (U.S. slang) insincere talk; foolish talk, nonsense.
Bombardier*, *n.* A crew member of a bombing plane who releases the bombs.
Bomb bay, *n.* See BAY, above. The compartment in the interior of a bomber in which bombs are stored and from which they are dropped.
Bombsight, bom'sīt, *n.* A telescopic precision instrument for calculating the exact timing and aiming of a bomb released from an airplane.
Bonehead, bōn'hed, *n.* From *bone* and *head.* (U.S. slang) A blockhead, stupid person. Attrib. use: bonehead play.
Boner, bōn'er, *n.* One who bones; (U.S. slang) a foolish mistake. See BONEHEAD, above.
Boob, *n.* Clipped form of booby. (slang) A stupid person, booby.
Booby-trap, *n.* A hidden mine or other explosive, arranged to explode when some, apparently harmless object is moved.
Boogie-woogie, bōō'gē wōō'gē, *n.* From *boogie,* and imitative reduplication. *mus.* A percussive style of jazz piano playing, developed as a treatment of the blues, characterized by a heavily accented bass usually repetitive and eight notes to the bar and a freely improvised treble; piano music written in this manner; erroneously, band music played or written in this manner.
Bookmobile, book'mō-bēl, *n.* From *book* and auto*mobile.* A truck with shelves containing books, serving as a traveling library for small communities having no libraries of their own.
Book review, *n.* A critical estimate or summary of a book.
Boom-and-bust, *n.* (U.S. colloq.) An extreme cycle of great prosperity and severe depression.
Boondoggle, bōōn'dogl, *n.* coined by Robert Link, a Scoutmaster of Rochester, N. Y., 1925. A plaited leather cord made and worn by Boy Scouts; any simple article produced by handicraft; slang useless or impractical work. —*v.i.* To do useless or impractical work.
Borscht, borsch, bōrsht, *n.* Any of several varieties of Russian soup colored with beets.
Bottleneck, botl-nek, *n.* Always used figuratively. A narrow passageway, such as a road; any stage or point in a process which delays progress.
Bounce*, *v.t.* (U.S. slang) To dismiss from a post. —*n.* A dismissal from a post; Phr. to get the bounce, to be dismissed.
Bouncer*, *n.* From *bounce* and -er. (U.S. slang) One employed at a public place, such as a bar, to eject disorderly persons and maintain order.
Bound form, *n. linguistics* A speech form which is meaningful as a part of a larger construction, but which cannot be used alone with meaning. The *-ed* in cooked is a bound form
Boxcar, *n. railroad* An enclosed freight car. In the game of craps, a losing first throw of a pair of sixes.
Boysenberry, bois'en-ber-ē, *n.* From Rudolph H. Boysen, the originator, 1925. The largest bramble fruit known, obtained by crossing the blackberry, Youngberry and Cuthbert raspberry, having a flavor which is a blend of blackberry and red raspberry.
Bracer*, *n.* (U.S. colloq.) A stimulating drink.
Bracket*, Those players or teams in a particular section generally half of a tournament draw; persons or things grouped together on the basis of age, income, or price; an income level at which a particular surtax is imposed.
Brain storm, *n.* A sudden inspiration, bright idea.
Brain trust, *n.* Originally a group of advisers to President F. D. Roosevelt; (by extension) any group of experts.
Brain washing, *n.* (Korean war etym.) A process used by Communists in the Korean war, aimed at redirecting thoughts of prisoners along desired lines by psychological pressure.
Brain wave, *n.* An electric current generated by a brain cell.
Brass*, *n.* (U.S. slang) High-ranking military officers; by extension, any high-ranking executives.
Break*, *n.* (slang) An opportunity usually qualified by an adj.: a bad break; a lucky break; (slang) a breach of good manners or of social discretion; *mus.* a short solo improvisation in jazz music.
Breakdown*, *n.* An analysis of a program, job, etc. into its component parts. —*v.t.* To perform such an analysis.
Break-through, brāk-throō, *n.* A successful attack which breaks the foe's line of defense to a considerable depth.
Breather*, *n.* (U.S. slang) *sports* A contest against a weak opponent figuratively giving the stronger a pause for breath.
Bren gun, *n.* From *Br*no, city in Czechoslovakia, and *En*field, town in England. A type of light machine gun, originated in Czechoslovakia and adopted by the British.
Bridgehead, *n.* Any position seized and held deep in enemy territory.

Brief*, *v.t.* To give concise last-minute instructions and information, as about a military operation, to those designated to perform a particular task. —**Briefing,** *v.t.* and *n.*

Bromide*, *n.* Following figurative sense initiated by Gelett Burgess, 1906. (slang) A dull, uninventive person; a remark characteristic of such a person; a cliché.

Bronx cheer, bronks, *n.* From the Bronx, borough of N. Y. City. A noise expressing derision, made by placing the tongue between the lips and expressing air rapidly.

Brownian movement, *n.* From Robert Brown, who discovered the phenomenon in 1827. Rapid vibratory movement imposed on minute suspended particles by bombardment from the molecules of the suspending medium.

Brownie*, *n.* A small chocolate nut cake.

Brownout, *n.* From analogy with *blackout.* A partial dimout, usually adopted to save electricity.

Brown Shirt, *n.* From the brown shirt worn as a uniform. A member of the Nazi party, esp. of its militia.

Brunch, *n.* From *br*eakfast and *l*unch. A combination of breakfast and lunch eaten about noon.

Brush*, *v.t.* Phr. to brush someone off, to refuse or get rid of someone, summarily or with finality. Phr. to get the brush-off, be treated in this manner.

Buchmanism, buk'man-ism, *n.* From Rev. Frank Buchman, its founder. The so-called Oxford Group movement, an undenominational movement of the 1930's, emphasizing individual divine guidance, unselfish co-operation and sharing, and confession of sin. —**Buchmanite,** *n.*

Buffalo*, *v.t.* (U.S. slang) To mystify, impress, or bluff someone.

Build-up, Buildup, bild'up, *n. advertising jargon* Highly favorable notices of a person, product, etc. in the mass media of communication; a publicity campaign designed to secure such notices.

Bulldozer, *n.* (U.S. slang) One who intimidates; a type of tractor with a broad horizontal beam in front, for moving earth, etc. on construction projects.

Bum*, *n., adj.* and *v.i.* From M.E. bom. Origin uncertain. *n.*; (U.S. colloq.) a spree, drunken orgy. —*adj.* (U.S. slang) worthless, rotten: bum steer, worthless advice. —*v.i.* (U.S. slang) to live like a bum; esp. to sponge, get something for nothing.

Bumper*, *n.* Metal projection on the front or back of a motor vehicle to take the first shock of a collision.

Buna, bū'na, *n.* From *Bu*tadiene and *Na*, symbol for sodium. Synthetic rubber developed originally in Germany.

Bunker*, *n. mil.* A heavily protected small fortification.

Bunt*, *v.t.* and *i.* To push with the horns, to shove; —*n.* a push with the horns; *baseball* a ball which is bunted.

Burlesque*, *n.* (U.S.) A type of theatrical entertainment featuring erotic dances and low comedy.

Burp, *v.i.* imitative. (slang) To belch, eructate. —*v.t.* To cause to burp, as to burp a baby after feeding. —*n.* A belch.

Bursitis, bur-si'tis, *n. pathol.* See BURSA and *-itis.* A type of painful inflammation of a bursa.

Burst*, *n. mil.* A series of shots fired by an automatic weapon with one pressure on the trigger.

Bush league, *n.* See BUSH in the Dict. *baseball* (derogatory slang) A small minor league. —**Bush leaguer,** *n.* a player in such a league; a player lacking talent.

Buster, *n.* From *bust* and *-er.* One who or that which busts: bellybuster, trustbuster, blockbuster, etc; (slang) something unusually big; *Australia* a cold and violent southerly wind.

Butt*, *v.* Butt in, (colloq.) to intrude, to break in upon proceedings, conversation, etc.

Butyl, bū'til, *n.* From *buty*ric and *-yl. chem.* A univalent organic radical, C_4H_9.; (trade-mark) a type of synthetic rubber characterized by high elasticity and low permeability.

Buzz*, *v.t.* (colloq.) To call someone on the telephone; to fly spectacularly and dangerously low in airplane; to buzz the crowd.

Buzz bomb, *n.*, From its sound in flight. A jet-propelled, self-steering bomb, launched from ramps against distant targets.

By-line, *n.* (U.S.) *journalism* The line under the heading of an article, giving the name of the writer.

By-pass, *n. elect.* A shunt. —*v.t.* To avoid, circumvent, ignore.

Cabaña, ka-ba'nya, *n.* Sp. A cabin, small house; (U.S.) a small bathhouse; also cabana.

Cadé*, *adj.* Etym. unknown. Of young of animals abandoned by the mother and raised by hand: A cade lamb.

—cade, kād, *suff.* From caval*cade.* Signifying a long procession: motorcade, aquacade.

Café*, *n.* (U.S.) A barroom.

Cahoot, ka-hōōt', *n.* (U.S. slang) Usually pl., cahoots. Phr. in cahoots, in partnership or collusion; Phr. to go cahoots, to go shares, become partners.

Calciferol, kal-cif'er-ol, *n.* From *calcif*erous and st*erol. biochem.* The antirachitic vitamin D_2, an alcohol produced by irradiating ergosterol and found in fish-liver oils.

Californium, kal'i-for'ni-um, *n.* From *California* and -ium. *chem.* A transuranic element of atomic number 98, produced at the University of California by the bombardment of curium 242 with alpha particles.

Calypso, ka-lip'sō, *adj.* origin uncertain. A type of Negro folk music of the West Indies, characterized by African rhythmic style and irregularly accented lyrics about current events.

Camera*, *n. television* That part of the transmitting device in which the image of the subject to be televised is formed before being changed into electrical impulse.

Can*, *v.t.* fig., (U.S. slang) To cease, put a stop to anything; to fire, dismiss from a post.

Canasta, kan-as'ta, *n.* From Sp. See CANASTER in the Dict. A Uruguayan variety of rummy using two decks of cards popular in the U.S.

Capeskin, kāp'skin, *n.* From *Cape* of Good Hope and *skin.* A grade of washable leather especially adapted for glovemaking, similar to the leather originally obtained from the skins of South African goats.

Capital ship, *n.* Any warship which carries a gun of more than 8 inches in caliber.

Capsule*, *adj.* Brief, condensed, diminutive: a capsule comment.

Captive mine, *n.* A coal mine owned and operated by and for the sole benefit of a large commercial consumer, such as a railroad or steel mill.

Carcinogen, kar-sin'o-gin, *n.* From Gr. *karkínos*, crab, and *-gen. pathol.* Any substance which produces a cancer.

Caretaker, *adj.* Temporary or stopgap, as a caretaker government, one holding office pending an election or the ratification of a new constitution.

Carhop, kar'hop, *n.* (U.S. colloq.) An employee of a restaurant, usually female, who waits on customers in parked cars.

Carousel or **Carrousel,** *n.* From Ital. *carosello.* A merry-go-round.

Cartridge*, *n. photog.* A case protecting a roll of camera film from light, so that the camera may be loaded in daylight; a prefabricated unit containing the sensitive elements of a phonograph pickup.

Cash*, *v.t.* and *i.* (U.S. colloq.) Phr. to cash in: to realize one's assets, as to cash in one's chips in a poker game; to die; *followed by on* to gain from, as he cashed in on the price reduction.

Casket*, *n.* (U.S.) Euphemism for a coffin.

Catatonia, kat-a-tōn'ia, *n.* From Gr. *katá*, down from and *tónos*, tone, tension. *psychiat.* A syndrome occurring in schizophrenia, characterized by stupor and muscular rigidity, alternating with overactivity and stereotypy. —**Catatonic,** *adj.*

Cattalo, kat'a-lō, *n.* From cattle and buffalo. A hybrid of the male American bison and domestic cow.

Catty*, *adj.* From *cat* and *-y.* Like a cat; (by extension) slyly malicious, esp. by means of gossip.

Caucus*, *v.i.* From Algonquin *caucauasu*, one who advises. To hold a caucus or meet in a caucus.

Caudal anesthesia, *n. med.* A type of anesthesia, especially useful in childbirth, achieved by injections at the base of the spine.

Cauliflower ear, *n. boxing* An ear misshapen by blows.

Ceiling*, *n. aeron.* The maximum height from which the earth can be seen under given weather conditions; any upper limit: wage ceiling, price ceiling, etc.

Cell*, *n.* The smallest organizational unit within a larger political framework, esp. a unit devoted to radical activities.

Cellulose acetate, *n. chem.* An ester of cellulose, used in making rayon, artificial leather, photographic film, etc.

Cellulose nitrate, *n.* An ester formed by the action of nitric acid on cellulose, and used in making explosives, varnishes, etc.

Celtuce, sel'tis, *n.* From *ce*lery and let*tuce.* A vegetable whose stalks combine the flavors of celery and lettuce.

Centrist, sen'trist, *n.* From Fr. *centriste. polit.* One who holds the views of the center; a moderate.

Chain reaction, *n. phys.* and *chem.* A self-sustaining process in which a reaction causes other reactions of the same kind, as in nuclear fission; (by extension) any series of results, each one causing and caused by another.

Chair*, *v.t.* To enthrone, install in office; to act as chairman: he chaired the meeting.

Champ*, *n.* (slang) Clipped form of champion.

Chance*, *n. baseball* A reasonable opportunity to field the ball in time to make a put-out.

Chandelle, shan-del', *n.* From Fr., *candle. aeron.* An abrupt climbing turn.

Change-up, *n. baseball* A slow pitch thrown with the same motion as a fast ball, to confuse the batter's timing.

Charisma, *n.* From Gr. *kharisma*, gift *sociol.* That quality of leadership which consists of the ascription of extraordinary or supernatural powers to the leader by his followers. —**Charismatic,** *adj.*

Charley horse, *n.* Etym. uncertain, orig. used in baseball (U.S. colloq.) Painful stiffness of a limb due to muscular strain.

Checkoff, *n.* A practice in which the employer assumes the responsibility for collecting union dues, by deducting them from the workers' pay.

Checkrein, chek-rān, *n.* A short rein attached to the saddle to prevent a horse from lowering its head; a short rein connecting the bit of one of a pair of horses to the driving rein of the other.

Checkroom, *n.* A room in a restaurant hotel, etc. for the temporary safekeeping of outdoor clothing and packages.

Checkrow, chek-rō, *n.* From check in the sense of a *square* and *row. agric.* One of several rows, as of corn, dividing land into squares. —*v.t.* To plant in checkrows.

Checkup, *n.* A re-examination of something done, for the purpose of ascertaining its accuracy, truthfulness, etc; a complete medical examination.

Cheese*, *v.t.* Prob. from *cease.* (slang, orig. Brit.) To cease, stop; used esp. in phr. cheese it!, stop! look out!, run away!

Cheeseburger, chēz'ber-ger, *n.* From *cheese* and back formation *-burger*, based on false etymology of hamburger. See HAMBURGER, below. A sandwich of hamburger topped with melted cheese.

Chemo-, kemō', *pref.* also **chem.** Combining form representing chemical.

Chemoreception, kem'o-rē-sep'shun, *n.* From *chemo-* above, and *reception. physiol.* The reception of chemical stimuli. —**Chemoreceptor,** *n.*

Chemotherapy, kem'o-ther'-a-pē, *n.* From *chemo-*, above, and *therapy;* also chemotherapeutics. *med.* The treatment of disease by means of chemicals which have a toxic effect on the disease-producing micro-organisms.

Chemurgy, kem'ur-jē, *n.* See *chemo–*, above, and demi*urge* in the Dict. A branch of applied chemistry concerned with the industrial use of farm products as raw materials. —**Chemurgic, Chemurgical,** *adj.*
Chigger, *n.* A CHIGOE, in the Dict.
Chile con carne, chil'i kon kar'nē, *n.* From Sp. chili with flesh. A Mexican dish made with meat and minced red pepper.
Chin*, *v.t.* (colloq.) To bring up to, and hold with, the chin, as a violin; to bring one's chin above the level of a bar from which one is hanging with legs and arms fully extended; to talk to. —*v.i.* (colloq.) to talk.
Chinatown, *n.* The section of any large Occidental city, such as New York or San Francisco, in which its Chinese population is largely concentrated.
Chip or **Chip shot,** *n. golf* A short, lofted approach shot, usually with backspin.
Chipper, *adj.* (U.S. colloq.) Lively, in good spirits.
Chiropractic, kī'rō-prak'tic, *n.* From *cheiro–* and *practic*al. The practice of adjusting the joints, esp. of the spine, based upon the hypothesis that maladjustments of the joints are the cause of disease.
Chiropractor, *n.* From *chiropractic* and *–or.* One who practices chiropractic.
Chlordane, klor-dān, *n.* From *chlor*ine and *indane*, an indigo derivative. An insecticide produced by chlorination of hydrocarbons derived from coal tar, esp. effective against cockroaches and grasshoppers, also household pests.
Chloromycetin, klor-ō-mī'ci-tin, *n.* From *chlor*al and *mycet*oma and *–in. biochem.* Trade-name of the antibiotic chloramphenicol, effective against rickettsial and bacterial diseases.
Chloropicrin, klōr-ō-pik'rin, *n.* From *chlor*al and *picric* and *–in.* A heavy liquid used in chemical warfare because of its pungent vapor which causes vomiting.
Chloroquine, klor'ō-kwen, *n.* From *chlor*al and *quin*ine. A drug which cures falciparum malaria and is a suppressive agent in vivax malaria.
Chorine, kō'rēen, *n.* From *chor*us and *–ine.* A female member of the chorus of a musical comedy, etc. Also chorus girl.
Chow, *n.* (U.S. slang) Food.
Chow mein, —mān, *n.* From Chin., fried flour. A stew containing mushrooms, fish or meat, celery, onions, etc., served with fried noodles.
Christiania, kris'tē-an'ēa, *n.* From *Christiania*, former name of Oslo, Norway. *skiing* A type of fast turn used for changing direction, reducing speed or stopping. Also Christiania turn, Christy.
Chromoplast, krō'mō-plast, *n.* From *chromo–* and *plastic. bot.* A mass of protoplasm containing red or yellow pigment.
Chromous, krō'mus, *adj.* Pertaining to, derived from, or containing divalent chromium as distinguished from chromic, of trivalent chromium.
Chunky, *adj.* From *chunk* and *–y.* Of a person stocky, thickset; of things in chunks, lumpy.
Chute*, *n.* Clipped form of parachute.
Cinchophen, sin'kō fen, *n.* From *cinchona* and *phenyl*. A crystalline antipyretic and analgesic, $C_{16}H_{11}O_2N$, used in treating rheumatism and gout.
CinemaScope, *n.* (Trade name, motion pictures) A patented process owned by 20th Century Fox which utilizes a projector fitted with anamorphic lenses, which spreads the picture on a wide screen, thus giving it a slight three-dimensional effect.
Cinerama, *n.* (motion pictures) The process by which three synchronized projectors create a three dimensional effect by throwing the picture on an enlarged screen.
C.I.O. Congress of Industrial Organizations. Also CIO.
Circuit*, *n.* A series of theaters at which actors appear in turn.
Circuit breaker, *n. elect.* A device for temporarily interrupting an overloaded electric circuit.
Citrin, sit'rin, *n.* From Lat. *citrus*, citron tree and *–in.* Cp. CITRON in the Dict. *biochem.* Vitamin P for permeability, a substance isolated from citrus fruits, which promotes tissue and capillary permeability.
Civvies, *n.* pl. From *civilian. mil.* (slang) Civilian clothes; mufti.
Claiming race, *n.* A race in which any entered horse is subject to purchase, at a stated price, by anyone entering a horse in the same racing meet.
Clam*, *n. fig.* (slang) A silent, uncommunicative person; —*v.i.* to dig clams; (slang) to clam up, become uncommunicative, silent.
Clambake, *n.* (U.S.) A picnic, usually at the seashore, at which clams are baked; by extension (slang) a party.
Class consciousness, *n.* Of members of the same economic class. The awareness of belonging to the same class, of having common goals, etc. —**Class-conscious,** *adj.*
Class struggle, *n.* Any conflict of economic classes in a society; in Marxian theory of modern capitalism, the struggle between the bourgeoisie and the proletariat.
Clean*, *adj.* (U.S. slang) Phr. come clean, tell the whole truth, make a full confession.
Cleanup, *n.* (colloq.) Organized action to eradicate crime or corruption in a certain sphere or locality; (slang) a large profit; phr. to clean up, make a large profit.
Click*, *v.i.* (slang) To succeed in a performance esp. of an actor.
Cliff dweller, *n.* (Amer.) American Indian, member of tribes who lived in caves or pueblos high on the walls of canyons in S. W. U. S. or N. Mexico. (slang) Apartment house resident; one concerned or occupied chiefly with mental processes removed or unrelated to reality.
Cliff-hanger, *n.* A serialized movie or radio program with episodes usually ending at exciting or uncertain points.
Climate*, *n.* The general tendency of attitudes and beliefs in a given community or historical period; the climate of opinion, intellectual climate.
Clip*, *n.* A metal container for small-arms cartridges; a contraption to facilitate loading heavy shells into guns. —*v.t. football* To block a player not having the ball illegally across the back of the legs.
Close*, *adj.* Phr. close call, a narrow escape. Cp. close shave.
Closed corporation, *n.* A corporation whose stock is owned by few persons.
Closed shop, *n.* A business establishment in which only union members may be hired.
Close-up, clos'—, *n.* A movie sequence photographed at close range; hence, any detailed scrutiny.
Clothespress, kloz-pres, *n.* A receptacle for clothes, such as a wardrobe or closet.
Cloverleaf, klōv'er lēf, *n.* From its resemblance to a clover leaf. A complex arrangement of ramps and connecting roads in order to permit the uninterrupted flow of traffic on two major intersecting highways.
Club car, *n.* A railway car equipped with lounge chairs, writing facilities, a bar, food service, etc.
Club sandwich, *n.* A sandwich consisting of three slices of toast, cold chicken or turkey, lettuce, tomato, bacon or ham, and mayonnaise.
Club steak, *n.* A steak cut from the loin.
Clutch*, *n.* (baseball slang) A critical moment. Phr. in the clutch, in an emergency. —**Clutch-hitter,** *n.* Baseball player noted for hitting safely in crucial situations.
C.O. Commanding officer; conscientious objector.
Coaxial*, *adj.* Of a cable having an insulated central conductor surrounded by a tubular conductor; of a loud-speaker having a bass cone and treble cone with a common axis.
Cocoon*, *n. fig.* A protective plastic covering sprayed on inactive airplanes, parts of warships, etc.
Coffee shop, *n.* A restaurant, usually small and with a relatively informal atmosphere. Also coffee room.
Coffee table, *n.* A very low table used in a living-room to hold coffee service and light refreshments
Coffin corner, *n. football* One of the corners made by a goal line and a side line.
Coke*, *n.* (slang) Short form of cocaine; trade-mark coca-cola.
Cold sore, *n.* An eruption on the face often accompanying a cold or fever.
Cold war, *n.* Intense international economic and political rivalry without actual resort to arms.
Cold wave, *n. meteor.* A sudden sharp drop in temperature in a particular area; a type of permanent wave employing a chemical agent on the hair.
Collaborate*, *v.i.* To assist the representative of an occupying country in keeping one's homeland subservient. —**Collaborationist,** *n.*
Collage, ko-lazh', *n.* From Fr. gluing. *art* A type of abstraction consisting of materials such as newspaper clippings, playing cards, etc., pasted together and with lines and color added. —**Collagist,** *n.* One who makes collages.
Collective*, *n.* A governmental unit organized on the principle of collectivism.
Collectivity, kol-lek'tiv'i-tē, *n.* From *collective* and *–ity.* Quality of being collective; a collective whole; esp. the people collectively.
Collectivize, *v.t.* From *collective* and *–ize.* To organize according to the principles of collectivism.
Column*, *n.* A feature or department of a newspaper, appearing regularly under a permanent title. —**Columnist,** *n.* The editor or writer of such a column.
Combat*, *adj.* Engaged in or designed for combat: combat troops, car, team, etc.
Combat fatigue, *n.* See BATTLE FATIGUE, above.
Combust, kom-bust', *adj.* See COMBUSTION. *astrol.* Of a planet or star near enough to the sun to be obscured by it.
Combustor, *n.* From *combustion* and *–or.* The combustion chamber of a jet engine.
Come-on*, *n.* (U.S. slang) A lure, enticement, esp. to buy something.
Comer*, *n.* (colloq.) One who shows promise, is progressing rapidly.
Comeuppance, kum-up'ans, *n.* (colloq.) Deserved punishment, esp. invited by arrogance and callousness.
Comic*, *n.* (colloq.) pl. The comic strips; the humorous element in art or nature; a booklet of comic strips; also comic book.
Comic strip, *n.* A series of drawings in panels portraying a comic incident, adventurous story, etc.
Cominform, kom'in-form, *n.* Abbr. for *Com*munist *Inform*ation Bureau. An international Communist organization, founded in 1947 for the purpose of co-ordinating activities of European Communist parties, esp. in eastern Europe.
Comintern, kom'in-tern, *n.* Abbr. of *Com*munist *Intern*ational. The Third Communist International, dissolved in 1943. See INTERNATIONAL in the Dict. and below.
Commando*, *n.* A unit of troops, esp. British, specially trained to carry out small-scale but highly important raids; a member of such a unit; —*adj.* pertaining to such a unit: commando training, tactics.
Commentator*, *n. radio* One who broadcasts his analysis and interpretation of the news.
Commercial*, *n. radio* A commercial radio or television program, one having a sponsor; an advertisement which is broadcast or televised.
Commie, komē, *n.* (colloq.) A member or follower of the Communist party.
Commissariat*, n. Any of the departments of the Soviet government.
Compact*, *n.* A small case for a woman's purse, containing face powder, a puff, a mirror, and often rouge.
Company union, *n.* A labor union comprised of the employees of a single company, sometimes organized by and always dominated by the employer.
Compass card, *n.* A circular card attached to a mariner's compass, on which the points of direction are marked.
Compensate*, To stabilize the purchasing power of a monetary unit in the face of price fluctuations by varying its gold content.

Compensation*, *n. psychoanal.* Cultivation of some trait or accomplishment as an offset to a feeling of inferiority.
Complected*, *adj.* (U.S. dial. or colloq.) Complexioned: dark-complected, etc.
Complex*, *adj. gram.* Of a word having at least one bound form.
Compound*, *n.* A temporary place for keeping prisoners of war, prior to their more permanent distribution.
Compression wave, *n. phys.* a wave forming against the side of an object approaching the speed of sound.
Con*, *adj.* (U.S. slang) Short for confidence: con man, con game; —*v.t.* to swindle, defraud; —*n.* a confidence game.
Concentration camp*, *n.* Place for the temporary concentration of troops.
Concertize, kon'ser-tīz, *v.i.* From *concert* and *-ize.* To perform in a series of concerts.
Conchie, kon'shē, *n.* (slang) Short for conscientious objector to military service.
Condition*, *v.t.* To adopt measures for keeping, e.g., merchandise, air in a state of freshness; *psych.* to induce by association of stimuli to behave in a predetermined way in given circumstances; conditioned reflex, capacity to act in a familiar way to new stimulus.
Conditioning, kon-dish'on-ing, *n.* From *condition* and *-ing.* Process, effect, of being conditioned.
Conductance, kon-duk'tans, *n.* From *conduct* and *-ance. elect.* The capacity to conduct a current.
Confect*, *v.t.* See CONFECTION in the Dict. To compound, make from several ingredients; esp. to make into a preserve or confection.
Conference*, *n.* (U.S.) An intercollegiate organization of athletic teams.
Conga, kong'ga, *n.* From Sp. A Cuban dance originating in Africa, performed by a group in one or more files, recently adapted to the ballroom in the U.S.
Conk, *v.i.* Imitative word. (slang) To cease functioning; to become suddenly exhausted and inert; also conk out.
Con-man, *n.* Short form of confidence man; one who betrays trust, usually financial, placed in him.
Conservationist, *n.* From *conservation* and *-ist.* One who supports conservation, esp. of natural resources.
Consist*, *n. railroads* The scheduled make-up of a train.
Console*, *n.* The structure containing the keyboards, pedals, etc., of an organ, and from which the organ is played; a large radio cabinet.
Construct*, *n.* Something constructed, esp. an intellectual synthesis.
Consumer subsidy, *n.* A government plan enabling low-income groups to purchase surplus foods at reduced prices.
Contact*, *v.t.* and *i. v.t.* to bring into contact; (U.S. colloq.) to get in touch with a person.
Contact flying, *n.* Flying an aircraft by means of visual observation of known landmarks.
Contact lens, *n.* A type of plastic lens worn under the eyelid and conforming to the contours of the eyeball.
Contact mine, *n. mil.* A mine designed to be exploded by contact with an external object.
Contact print, *n. photog.* A photographic print made with the negative in contact with sensitized paper.
Continuance*, *n. law* Postponement of proceedings to a specified future day.
Continuity*, *n.* Special captions inserted between sections of a film to bridge over and explain, e.g., an imaginary interval of time; *also attrib.:* continuity writer, clerk; a movie scenario; a script for the spoken parts of a radio program.
Contour*, *n. Attrib. use:* contour plowing, a system of plowing designed to reduce erosion by having the furrows follow contour lines.
Contraindicate*, *v.t. med.* Of a condition to indicate the inadvisability of a certain treatment. —**Contraindication,** *n.*
Contraprop, *n.* From *contra-* and *prop,* below. *aeron.* A combination of two propellers turning in opposite directions.
Control*, *n.* In airplane and auto racing that portion of the course not counted in the timing.
Control column, *n.* The lever and/or wheel which operates the elevator and ailerons of an airplane.
Conventioneer, kon-vent'shun-ēer, *n.* From *convention* and *-eer.* One addicted to attending conventions.
Convertible*, *n.* An automobile whose top can be lowered for fair-weather driving.
Cookbook, *n.* (U.S.) A book of recipes and other instructions for preparing food.
Coolant, kōōl'ant, *n.* From *cool* and *-ant.* A liquid used for cooling a mechanical or electrical device or a nuclear reactor.
Cooler*, *n.* A refrigerant; (slang) a jail.
Cooling-off period, *n.* A period provided by law or contract to allow violent emotions to subside, as between the taking of a strike vote and the actual beginning of a strike.
Coop*, *n.* (slang) A jail. Phr. to fly the coop, escape from jail.
Co-op, kō-op, *n.* (slang) Abbr. of consumers' co-operative society or store. See CO-OPERATIVE in the Dict.
Cootie, kōōt'i, *n.* (slang) A body louse.
Copilot, *n.* An associate aviator at the plane's control.
Copperhead*, *n.* (caps.) A northerner who sympathized with the Confederate cause during the Civil War.
Copter, *n.* Short form of HELICOPTER.
Copycat, kop'i-kat, *n.* (*colloq.*) A mimic.
Cords, *n.* pl. (colloq.) Corduroy trousers.
Corn*, *n.* (colloq.) Whisky made from corn; corny music, etc. See corny, below.
Cornfed, *adj.* (slang) Of a person unsophisticated, rustic.
Corn pone, *n.* (Southern U.S.) Corn bread.
Corny*, *adj.* Pertaining to, abounding in, or producing corn; slang of something esp. a performance of popular music having a banal, trite quality.
Coronary*, *adj.* See CORONA. *anat.* Like a crown, esp. of the two arteries which supply the heart tissues and which issue from the aorta. Coronary thrombosis, a clot in the coronary arteries.
Corporate*, *adj.* Corporate state, one with supreme authority officially established in one body of representatives of corporations. Also corporative state.
Corpsman, korz-, *n.* (U.S.) *mil.* An enlisted man working as a medical assistant.
Correspondence course, *n.* A course of study taken by mail.
Correspondence school, *n.* A profit-making school offering correspondence courses.
Corridor*, *n.* A lane for air traffic.
Corticosterone, kor'ti-cos'ter-ōn, *n.* See CORTICAL in the Dict. and STEROL, below. A hormone secreted in the suprarenal cortex.
Cortisone, kor'ti-sōn, *n.* Coined by its discoverer, Dr. E. Kendall, 1949. From *cortex* and *-one.* A hormone, secreted in the suprarenal cortex, which has a profound effect on the body's reaction to stress and shock.
Cortone, kor-tōn, *n. trade-mark* Cortisone.
Corvette*, *n.* A vessel considerably smaller than a destroyer, used to provide anti-aircraft and antisubmarine protection for convoys.
Cosmetician, koz'met-ish'en, *n.* From *cosmetic* and *-ian;* pseudo-elegant U.S. coinage. One engaged in the business of giving cosmetic treatments.
Cosmic dust, *n. astron.* Fine particles which fall upon the earth from interstellar space.
Cottage cheese, *n.* (U.S.) A soft cheese consisting of the curd of sour milk.
Cottage pudding, *n.* A pudding which consists of a piece of plain cake covered with a sweet sauce.
Counterattack, *n.* An attack upon an enemy, made shortly after he has delivered an attack. —*v.t.* and *i.*
Counterintelligence, *n. mil.* Activity to keep an enemy from gaining military information; the organization by which this activity is performed.
Counteroffensive, *n.* A military offensive launched by defending forces immediately following the successful repulse of an enemy attack; a counterattack on a large scale.
Counterword, *n.* A word which tends, due to its increasing use in a variety of situations, to lose its original specific meaning and serve merely as a substitute for a word of more precise meaning.
Couturier, kōō'tu'ryā', *n.* From Fr. *couture,* sewing. A male dressmaker. —**Couturière,** —air, *n.* A female dressmaker.
Covalence, kō-vā'lens, *n.* The number of electron pairs an atom can share with surrounding atoms; the bond formed between two atoms by the sharing of a pair of electrons. —**Covalent,** *adj.*
Coverage, kov'er-ij, *n.* From *cover* and *-age. insurance.* The total number of risks covered by an insurance policy; *finance* the amount of reserve funds available to meet liabilities; *advertising* the area or the number of people covered by a communication medium, such as a newspaper.
Cover charge, *n.* A service charge made by a restaurant. Also cover.
Cover crop, *n.* A crop grown to protect the soil during the winter and to increase its fertility.
Cowbell, *n.* A bell hung about a cow's neck to indicate her whereabouts.
Cow hand, *n.* A cowboy.
Cowlick, *n.* An unruly, turned up tuft of hair usually over the forehead.
Cowling, *n.* From *cowl* and *-ing. aeron.* An engine covering, usually stream-lined.
Cowman, *n.* (U.S.) A cattle owner; (Brit.) A workman who takes care of cattle.
Crab*, *v.i. avn.* To counteract drift by flying into a cross wind.
Crack*, *n.* (slang) A witticism; a sententious, often a sarcastic, remark: a wise crack.
Crackerjack, krak'er-jak, *n.* etym. unknown. (U.S. slang) A person or thing of marked ability or excellence; a confection made from molasses, popcorn and sometimes peanuts; —*adj.* (U.S. slang) of marked ability or excellence.
Cracking, *n.* From CRACK in the Dict. The process of breaking down hydrocarbons e.g. in petroleum by destructive distillation.
Crackup, *n.* A crash or collision, as of an airplane; a collapse, as of an army; *colloq.* a breakdown of one's health, esp. a mental breakdown.
Cradlesong, *n.* A lullaby.
Craft union, *n.* A union whose members all practice the same trade.
Cramp*, *v.t. fig.* (colloq.) Phr. to cramp one's style, put one ill at ease, hinder one, etc.
Craniate, kra'ni-at, *adj.* From *cranium* and *-ate.* Having a skull or cranium of the Craniata, consisting of the mammals, birds, reptiles, amphibians and fishes; —*n.* a craniate animal.
Crash*, *v.t.* (colloq.) To intrude into a party, etc. without an invitation; crash the gate, to enter a public performance, etc. without paying the admission charge.
Crash landing, *n. avn.* A landing in which a plane cannot make full or effective use of its landing gear or controls. —**Crashland,** *v.t.* and *i.*
Crate*, *v.t.* To pack in a crate.
Crazy bone, *n.* (U.S.) Funny bone. See Dict.
Crazy quilt, *n.* (U.S.) A patchwork quilt. See Dict.
Crease*, *n. ice hockey* A rectangular area in front of each goal cage, which attacking players may not enter except under certain conditions; *lacrosse* a lined area containing the goal, which attacking players may not enter except under certain specified conditions.
Crease*, *v.t.* (U.S.) To wound by a grazing shot.
Credit*, *n. educ.* Official certification of the completion of a course of study; a unit of academic study; an acknowledgment of the source of material used in a publication, radio program, etc.
Crème de cacao, krem'di ka'ka'ō', *n.* A liqueur flavored with cacao.
Crème de la crème, krem' di la krem', *n.* From cream of the cream. The best, choicest.

Crescive, kres'iv, *adj.* From L. *crescere,* to grow. Increasing, growing.

Critical*, *adj.* Of commodities and raw materials essential for an undertaking e.g. waging war, and in such short supply as to require stringent rationing.

Critter, *n.* (dial.) Creature.

Cross-fertilization*, *n. bot.* Fertilization by means of cross-pollination; *biol.* the fertilization of the egg of one organism by the sperm of another organism. —**Cross-fertilize,** *v.t.* and *i.*

Cross hairs, *n.* pl. The fine wires or threads crossing in the focal plane of an optical instrument, for the purpose of defining the line of sight.

Crosspiece, kros-pēc, *n.* A piece placed across something.

Cross section*, *n.* A representative sample: a cross section of voters; *phys.* the area of an atomic nucleus as measured statistically by a type of bombardment experiment.

Crouton, kroo-ton', *n.* From Fr. *croûton.* See CRUST in the Dict. A small piece of fried or toasted bread, used chiefly in soups.

Crow*, *n.* Phr. to eat crow, be humbled, humiliated, forced to recant.

Crush*, *n.* Drink made of the juice of crushed fruit; chiefly in compounds: orange crush, etc.; (U.S. slang) Phr. to have a crush on a person, to become suddenly enamored of.

Crux ansata, kruks on-sā'ta, *n.* L. cross with a handle. The ankh or tau cross, looped at the top, sacred symbol of life.

Cryptanalysis, krip'tan-al'is-us, *n.* From *crypto* and *analysis.* The technique of deciphering cryptograms. —**Cryptanalyst,** *n.*

Cryptographer*, *n.* One who deciphers cryptograms.

Cub*, *n.* A young and inexperienced reporter. Also cub reporter; a member of a division of the Boy Scouts for boys aged 8 to 11.

Cue ball, *n. billiards* The ball struck with the cue.

Cuff*, *n.* (slang) Phr. off the cuff, informally, unofficially, unrehearsed; (slang) Phr. on the cuff, on credit.

Cui bono, kī bō'nō, Lat. For whose benefit? Of what use?

Culch, kulch, *n.* From O.Fr. *culche,* bed. (dial.) Rubbish; debris spread over oyster beds for the spawn of the oyster to grow on. Also Cultch, Cuch.

Culottes, ku-lots', *n.* pl. A garment similar to a skirt, but separated and seamed like trousers.

Culture*, A specific stage of a civilization: Greek culture; *anthropol.* and *sociol.* the transmissible complex of the ways of life which are characteristic of a human group, as manifested in types of social action, artifacts, etc.

Cure-all, *n.* A cure for all ailments; a panacea.

Curie, kū'rē, *n.* named after French chemist Marie Curie, 1867–1934. *phys.* A unit expressing the amount of radioactivity of a substance, equal to 37 billion disintegrations per second.

Curium, kū're-um, *n.* From Pierre and Marie *Curie* and *–ium.* A transuranic element of atomic number 96, produced by the bombardment of uranium and plutonium with helium ions. Symbol: *Cm.*

Curvaceous, kur-va'shus, *adj.* From *curve* and *–aceous.* (colloq.) Characterized by curves, specif. of a female figure.

Curve*, *n. baseball* A pitched ball having a curved course other than that caused by gravity; the course itself.

Curvesome, kurv'sum, *adj.* From *curve* and *–some.* Same as CURVACEOUS, above.

Custom*, *adj.* Made to individual order: custom clothes; dealing in things made to individual order: custom tailor.

Custom-made, *adj.* Made to individual order: custom-made clothes. Also custom-built.

Cutback, *n. movies* same as a flash-back, below; a reduction, esp. in the size of an order for goods.

Cybernetics, sī'ber-net'iks, *n.* From Gr. *kybernān,* to steer, to govern. Cp. GOVERN in the Dict. Coined by mathematician Norbert Wiener, 1947. The study of control of communication devices, both in machines and animals.

Cyclotron, sī'klo-tron, *n.* From *cyclo–* and *electron;* term orig. slang used 1935 in laboratory of E. O. Lawrence, the inventor. *phys.* A machine used in nuclear experiments to impart very high speeds to electrified particles.

Dark horse, *n. racing* A horse whose ability is not known; hence, such a horse that unexpectedly wins; (by extension) a person unexpectedly nominated for political office.

Day*, *n.* (colloq.) Phr. call it a day, reckon the day's work or main occupation finished, i.e., leave off anything.

D-day, *n.* From D for day; hence this is a type of reduplication. *milit.* The day, concealed until the last possible moment, on which a previously planned military operation is to begin.

DDT, *n.* Abbr. of *d*ichloro-*d*iphenyl-*t*richloroethane, a powerful insecticide developed during World War II.

Deactivate, dē-ak'ti-vāt, *v.t.* To break up, disband a military unit.

Dead beat, *n.* (U.S. slang) A sponger, esp. a person who avoids paying bills.

Deadline, ded-līn, *n.* A line which must not be crossed; a limit which it is very dangerous to exceed; the time at which copy goes to press, after which no material can be inserted; hence, the latest time for finishing any operation.

Dead pan, *n.* (slang) An expressionless face. —**Deadpan,** *v.i.* and *adj.*

Deadwood, *n.* Dead branches of a tree; by extension a person or thing no longer useful; bowling pins which have been knocked down but have not been cleared from the alley or gutters.

Deal*, *n.* A raw deal, grossly unfair treatment; cp. RAW in the Dict; The New Deal, President Franklin D. Roosevelt's attempted liberal reconstruction of the administrative and economic system in the U.S.A.; (by extension) any similar or comparable attempt at reconstruction; The Fair Deal, the domestic economic and social program of President Truman's administration.

Decibel, des'i-bel, *n.* From *deci–* and bel, after Alexander Graham Bell. *phys.* A unit of power ratio, used to measure the relative loudness of sounds.

Decontaminate, dee'kon-tam'i-nāt, *v.t.* From *de–* and *contaminate.* To rid of, purify from, contamination; specif., to rid of poison gas in warfare, or to eliminate dangerous radioactivity.

Deep*, *adj.* Phr. to go in off the deep end: (U.S.) To overdo something; (Brit.) to become overly excited, esp. to become very angry.

Deepfreeze, *n. trade-mark* A food locker in which temperatures of about 0° F can be maintained; (by extension) any piece of refrigerating equipment designed for preserving food at subfreezing temperatures. Also deepfreezer.

Defenestration, dee-fen'es-trā'shun, *n.* From *de–* and L. *fenestra,* window, opening, and *–ation.* The throwing of a person or thing out of a window.

Defense mechanism, *n.* The activity of an organism for defense, as against toxins; *psychiat.* one of various defensive means by which the psychic structure deals with instincts.

Deficiency disease, *n. med.* A disease due to lack of vitamins or minerals in the diet.

Definition*, *n. electronics* The degree of fidelity with which a radio receiver reproduces sound; the degree of fidelity with which a television receiver reproduces an image.

Defrost, *v.t.* To rid of frost. —**Defroster,** *n.* A device which removes or prevents frost, specif., on a windshield.

Degauss, dē-gos', *v.t.* From *de'–* and *gauss,* in the Dict. To neutralize the magnetic field of a ship, so that it will not detonate magnetic mines.

Deicer, dē-īs'er, *n.* From *de–* and *ice* and *–er.* A device to melt ice or prevent it from forming, esp. on an airplane. —*Deice, v.t.*

Delicatessen, *n.* From Fr. *délicat,* agreeable to taste. See DELICATE. A store dealing in prepared foods; pl. the foods themselves.

Delouse, *v.t.* To rid of lice.

Demilitarize, *v.t.* To rid of military character.

Demitasse, dem'i-tas', *n.* From Fr., half cup. A small cup of black coffee, served at the end of a meal; the cup itself.

Denazify, de-nats'i-fī, *v.t.* To remove Nazi influence from. —**Denazification,** *n.*

Démodé, dā'mo'dā', *adj.* From Fr. See MODE in the Dict. Gone out of fashion. Also demoded.

Dendrite*, *n. anat.* and *physiol.* The branching twig of a nerve cell.

Dendrochronology, den'drō-krō'nol'o-ji, *n.* From *dendro–* and *chronology.* The fixing of dates of past events by the study of tree rings.

Depress*, *v.t.* To lower the pitch of musical sound; (Brit.) to deprive of trade and prosperity.

Depression*, *n. psychiat.* A pathological state characterized by emotional dejection, loss of interest in the outside world, inhibition of activity and loss of self-esteem, esp. as occurring in manic-depressive psychosis; *surv.* the angle formed by a line from the observer to an object below him and a line from the observer to the horizon.

Depressor*, *n. anat.* Depressor nerve, one which decreases the activity of an organ; *surg.* an instrument for depressing a part, such as the tongue.

Derby, dur'bi, *n.* Any of various well-known races: Kentucky Derby; (not cap.) a stiff felt hat with a rounded crown; a bowler.

Desensitize, *v.t.* From *de–* and *sensitize.* To reduce or eliminate sensitivity to anything.

Desterilize, *v.t.* From *de–* and *sterilize.* To remove from disuse, as gold for the basis of additional paper currency.

Desynchronized, dē sin'krō-nīz, *adj.* Not synchronized, as the engines in German multimotored aircraft; a practice adopted to thwart acoustic systems of detection and range finding.

Deuce*, *v.t.* To bring the score of a tennis game or set to deuce.

Deuteride, dū'ter īd, *n.* See DEUTERIUM, below, and *–ide.* A compound containing deuterium.

Deuterium, doo-tēr'ē-um, *n.* See *deutero–* and *–ium. chem.* A hydrogen isotope of twice the mass of ordinary hydrogen. Symbol: *D.* Also heavy hydrogen.

Deuteron, dū'ter-on, *n.* See *deutero–. phys.* The deuterium nucleus, formed of a proton and a neutron.

Deva, dā'vā, *n.* Cp. DEITY. *Hinduism* and *Buddhism* A deity or divine spirit.

Diagram*, *v.t.* To make a diagram of.

Dick, *n.* (U.S. slang) A detective.

Dickey, *n.* A front panel of a woman's blouse, for wear with a dress or suit.

Dicoumarin, dī-koo'ma-rin, *n.* From *di–* and *coumarin.* A compound found in spoiled clover and also synthesized, used to delay the coagulation of blood.

Dictaphone, dik'ta-fōn, *n. trade-mark* A type of low-fidelity sound recording and reproducing apparatus, designed for use in business offices.

—Diene, *suff.,* From *di–* and *–ene. chem.* Denoting a compound having two double bonds.

Digenesis, dī-jen'e-sis, *n.* From *di–* and *genesis. biol.* The alternation of sexual and asexual reproduction.

Digestant, dī-jes'tant, *n.* and *adj.* From *digest* and *–ant.* Digestive.

Dim*, *adj.* Phr. to take a dim view of, have an unfavorable or pessimistic opinion of a subject.

Dimout, *n.* Cp. BLACKOUT, above. A decrease in outdoor illumination, usually to obscure potential targets.

Dinky, *adj.* (derog.) Small in size.

Diplex, dī'pleks, *adj.* From *di–* and *–plex,* by analogy with DUPLEX in the Dict. Pertaining to electronic communication of two signals simultaneously.

Diploid, dip'loid, *adj.* From *dipl–* and *–oid.*

biol. Having double the normal number of chromosomes. —*n.* See HAPLOID, below.

Dipole, dĭ'pōl', *n.* From *di-* and *pole.* A dipolar object.

Dipso, *n.* (U.S. colloq.) Clipped form of dipsomaniac, in the Dict.

Direction finder, *n. radio* A device for determining the direction from which radio waves are coming.

Directive*, *n.* esp. *mil.* An order.

Director*, *movies* Person having control of the actual making of a film; assistant director, person responsible for assembling actors at the right time and for all details connected with the floor.

Dirndl, durn'dl, *n.* From Ger., girl. A dress fashioned after central European peasant costume, having a tight waist and full skirt.

Disc or **disk jockey,** *n.* (colloq.) *radio* The announcer in charge of a program of recorded popular music.

Discography, dis-kog'ra-fē, *n.* From *disc* and *-o* and *-graphy.* The study or account of the history of phonograph records; descriptive list of phonograph records arranged according to some principle such as type of music, performer, etc.

Discophile, dis'ko-fil, *n.* From *disc* and *-o* and *-phile.* An avid collector or student of phonograph records.

Disnature, *v.t.* To make unnatural.

Dispersion*, *n. physical chem.* A system in which one component consists of discrete particles usually of colloidal dimensions dispersed in the other component, which is a continuous medium called the vehicle.

Displaced person, Abbr. DP, *n.* A person forcibly removed from his homeland, esp. as by the Nazis or Communists, usually for the purpose of slave labor.

Disqualify*, *v.t. sports.* To prohibit from participation in a match because of violation of the rules.

Dissolve*, *n. movies.* The device, effect, in which one shot fades away while a new shot becomes more distinct. —*v.i.* To produce such an effect.

Distributor, *n. distribute* and *-or.* In engines, a device which determines the order in which the plugs shall spark; *commerce.* one engaged in the marketing of a specific type of merchandise.

District attorney, *n.* (U.S.) The prosecuting attorney for a judicial subdivision. (Slang) abbr.: D.A.

Ditch*, *v.t.* (U.S.) To throw into a ditch; (slang) to abandon, get rid of a person or thing.

Dither, *n.* Origin uncertain. A trembling or shaking; a state of flustered over-excitement; —*v.i.* to be in a dither.

Dive bomber, *n.* A plane from which bombs are dropped while diving toward the target. —**Dive-bomb,** *v.t.* and *i.*

Diversionary, di-vur'shun-er-i, *adj.* From *diversion* and *-ary. esp. mil.* Having the character of a diversion; diversionary tactics.

Divvy, *v.* and *n.* See DIVIDE. (colloq.) *v.t.* and *i.* To divide, share usually followed by up; a share, division.

Dixie also **Dixie Land,** *n.* Origin uncertain. The southern states of the United States; a popular minstrel song composed in 1859 by D. D. Emmett.

Dixiecrat, *n.* From *Dixie* and Demo*crat.* A southern member of the national Democratic party who is opposed to the national party platform; specif., one of those southerners who in 1948 nominated their own candidates for president and vice-president.

D layer, *n.* The lowest layer of the ionosphere.

Documentary*, *adj.* Treating artistically but factually an economic or other social problem, as in a movie. —*n.* A documentary movie.

Doggy, *adj.* (Ostentatious) Cp. Phr. to put on the dog, behave pretentiously.

Doghouse, *n. dog* and *house.* A shelter for a dog; phr. to be in the doghouse, be in disfavor.

Do-gooder, *n.* (colloq.) A person who interferes in other people's lives out of altruistic motives, a derogatory term applied esp. to social workers.

Dog tag, *n. mil.* (slang) A metal identification disc or rectangular plaque worn by a member of the armed forces.

Doll*, *v.t.* and *i.* followed by *up* To dress up, put on one's best clothes.

Dolly, *n.* A platform mounted on wheels, for moving heavy objects, such as a movie camera.

Dominant*, *adj.* and *n. biol.* A Mendelian character that prevails over a recessive and wholly or partially determines some feature of the organism.

Dominie*, *n.* From Scot. (U.S.) A minister.

Doodad, *n.* Arbitrary coinage. (U.S. colloq.) Any ornamental trifle, frill, etc., not having a specific name.

Doodle, *n.* Origin uncertain. An idle scrawl. —*v.i.* to draw a doodle. —*v.t.* to cover with doodles.

Doodlebug, *n.* From obs. *doodle,* a foolish person, and *bug.* The larva of a beetle; a divining rod.

Dope*, *n.* (slang) Information. Phr. inside dope, confidential information, e.g. a tip from racing stables; to spill the dope, give inside information; to upset the dope, turn out disconcertingly otherwise than as forecasted; —*v.t.* usually followed by *out* to solve, as a problem; to predict the result of, as a race; to work out, as a plan of action.

Double*, *n.* A linked bet on two separate events, receiving heavier odds because of the greater risk to the backer; baseball a two-base hit; movies one who substitutes for an actor or actress, esp. in dangerous situations.

Double feature, *n.* A movie program in which two full-length pictures are shown.

Double-header, dubl-hed'er, *n.* A train pulled by two engines; *sports* two games played in succession on the same day and for a single admission price. In baseball two teams play each other twice; double-headers in basketball or ice hockey involve different pairs of teams.

Double-jointed, *adj.* Of a person having unusually limber joints.

Double-park, *v.i.* To park on a street outside the area in which parking is legally allowed, generally when all designated parking spaces are occupied.

Double take, *n.* Orig. U.S. vaudeville comedy. (slang) A second glance or scrutiny, involving surprised recognition of the true significance of something which was misunderstood at first.

Double talk, *n.* Any ostensibly intelligible speech or writing, actually a mixture of sense and nonsense; any high-sounding public pronouncement, such as by a politician, in which the illusion of taking a definite position is given but the responsibility for such a position is carefully avoided.

Double-tongue, *v.i.* To vibrate the tongue rapidly in playing a staccato passage, as on a trumpet.

Downtown, *n.* The central business district of a city. —*adv.* to or in this district. —*adj.* of or pertaining to this district.

Down under, *n.* (colloq.) Australia, Tasmania, and New Zealand.

DP, abbr. Displaced person.

Draftee, *n.* From *draft* and *-ee.* A person drafted for military service.

Drag*, *n.* The total resistance to air of the wings and body of an aircraft along its line of flight; (slang) influence.

Drain*, Phr. to go down the drain, to be wasted.

Dramamine, dram'a-min, *n.* A proprietary drug which is used in the treatment of motion sickness, such as seasickness.

Dramatics, dram-at'iks, *n.* and *n. pl.* The study of the acting and production of dramas; dramatic performances, esp. by amateurs.

Dream*, *v.t.* To dream up, to make up or work out in one's mind, often without taking sufficient account of reality.

Dressage, *n.* Fr. training of horses. In manège, the maeuvering of a horse without use of the aids.

Dressing room*, *n.* Specif., a backstage room for changing costume in a theater.

Dress rehearsal, *n.* A full-scale rehearsal of a play, with use of costumes, lights, etc., exactly as if it were a public performance; (by extension) any full-scale rehearsal; the Commando raids were a dress-rehearsal for the invasion.

Drip*, *n.* (slang) An unattractive, socially undesirable person.

Drive-in, *n.* Any roadside business serving customers in their automobiles; —*adj.* having such a character, as drive-in restaurant, drive-in theater.

Driveway, *n.* Road along which vehicles may be driven. Specif. an approach from the street to a house; a depressed portion of a sidewalk providing access to a garage, delivery entrance of a commercial establishment, etc.

Drone*, *n. avn.* A pilotless plane, generally used for experimental or target purposes, directed by remote control.

Drop*, *n.* Phr. to get have the drop on: (colloq.) to cover an opponent, have him covered with a gun before he can draw and aim; to get have an advantage over someone. Phr. at the drop of a hat, to act immediately, upon slight provocation.

Drop-forge, —forj, *v.t.* To forge a piece of metal placed between dies by means of a drop hammer.

Drop leaf, *n.* An extension hinged to a table and folded down when not used.

Dropping zone, *n. mil.* The area designated for the landing of paratroops.

Drugstore, *n.* Place where drugs, toilet articles, etc. are sold.

Drum major*, *n.* Any male leader of a marching band or drum corps; the comparable female is a drum majorette.

Dry*, *adj.* (colloq.) Dry run, a practice maneuver.

Dual purpose, *adj.* Having two uses: dual-purpose cattle, dual-purpose gun, etc.

Dub*, *n.* An unskilled novice.

Dub*, *v.t.* Clipped form of double. To provide a movie, radio program, etc. with added music or sound effects; to make a recorded copy of another phonograph record. —**Dubbing,** *n.* this process; a copy of a phonograph record.

Duck*, *n. mil.* An amphibious truck, specifically and originally of 2½ tons.

Duck soup, *n.* (slang) Something extremely easy to do.

Duckpin, *n.* A type of relatively short bowling pin; pl. the bowling game with such pins and small balls.

Dumbbell, *n.* (U S. slang) A stupid person.

Dummy*, *n. print.* Blank sheets arranged to show the features of sequence of pages, size, etc. of a forthcoming piece of printing. —*v.i.* followed by up print. To indicate on a dummy the layout of the copy.

Dump*, *n.* (U.S. slang) A house, town, etc. in poor condition.

Dungaree*, *n.* pl. Work clothes made of this fabric.

Dunk, *v.t.* and *i.* From Ger. *tunken,* to dip. To dip doughnuts, cookies, etc. into coffee, tea, etc. —**Dunker,** *n.* One who dunks.

Dunkirk, *n.* A severe military defeat and evacuation under fire, such as that suffered by the British at Dunkirk, France, in June, 1940.

Dunker*, *n.* From Ger. *tunker.* One of the German Baptist Brethren, practicing baptism by immersion and refusing oaths or military service. Also dunkard.

Duplicate*, *n.* A kind of tournament bridge in which the same hands are played at all tables.

Dural, du-ral', *n.* Clipped form of DURALUMIN in the Dict.

Dust*, *v.t.* Also dust off. *baseball* (slang) To pitch a ball deliberately at the batter.

Dust bowl, *n.* Any region in which a series of unexpected drought years produces crop failures, wind erosion, and dust storms, esp. (cap.) the U.S. Western Plains in the late 1930's.

Duster*, *n.* Cp. DUST, above. *baseball* (slang) A pitched ball thrown deliberately at or needlessly close to a batter.

Dutch uncle, *n.* (U.S. colloq.) A severe critic; one who reproves with great frankness.

Dynamo*, *n.* (U.S. slang) An extremely energetic person.

Dysgenic, dis-gen'ik, *adj.* From *dys-* and

genic. Having undesirable hereditary effects. Contrasted with eugenic.

Dysphoria, dis-fō'ri-a, *n.* From Gr. *dusphoría*, anguish. *psychiat.* State of restless dissatisfaction, anxiety.

Dysprosium, dis-prō'shi-um, *n.* From Gr. *dusprósitos*, hard to get at. A metallic element, one of the rare earths, of atomic number 66. Symbol: *Dy*.

Earmuff, *n.* (U.S.) One of a pair of warm coverings for the ears.

Earphone, ēr-fōn, *n.* A headphone.

Easy*, *adj.* (slang) Phr. easy on the eyes, pleasant to look at; (slang) Phr. on Easy Street, finacially well off.

Eatery, *n.* (U.S. slang) A restaurant.

Eburnation, ē'ber-nā'shun, *n.* See EBURNINE in the Dict. *pathol.* A morbid condition in which the bone becomes hard like ivory.

Ecdysiast, ek-diz'i-ast, *n.* From ecdysis. Mock-refined word coined by H. L. Mencken, 1940. A strip-teaser.

Echelon*, *n. mil.* A subdivision of command or authority.

Echo ranging, *n.* A method of determining the position and nature of objects by means of transmitting large quantities of energy and measuring the minute quantities which are reflected from the object in the form of echoes.

Econometrics, ē-kon'ō-met'riks, *n.* From *economy* and *–ics*. A method of testing economic theory by means of statistical analysis of large masses of data.

—Ectomy, *suff.* From *ex–* and *–tomy*. Combining form denoting a surgical excision, as in tonsillectomy.

Edit*, *v.t.* Specif., to edit a film, piece it together, cutting out superfluous strips, revising montage, etc.

Editorialize, *v.i.* From *editorial* and *–ize*. To pronounce one's views in the manner of an editorial; esp. to introduce value judgments where they are out of place, as in a piece of objective research.

Egg*, *n.* (U.S. slang) Phr. to lay an egg, to do something which completely fails to produce the desired results; originally, in vaudeville, to tell a joke at which no one laughs.

Ego*, *n. psychoanal.* That organization of the psyche which, in reacting to perceptual stimuli, mediates between the demands of the primitive drives of the Id and the demands of the external reality; (colloq.) egotism; conceit.

Ego-ideal, *n. psychoanal.* The individual's modifiable criteria of personal worth, derived from identifications with parental substitutes.

Eidetic, *adj.* From Ger. *psych.* Of remembered images characterized by a pseudo-perceptual quality and extraordinary clarity, brilliance and accuracy.

Eikon, *n.* Icon.

Ejecta, e-jek'ta, *n.* pl. From Lat. *ejectus*, cast out. See EJECT. Matter which has been ejected, as from a volcano.

El, *n.* The letter L; something having this shape; (colloq.) an elevated railroad.

Elastomer, ē-las'to-mer, *n.* From *elastic* and *–o* and Gr. *méros*, part. *chem.* An elastic substance.

E layer or **region,** *n.* An ionospheric layer which reflects radio waves.

Electra complex, *n.* So named from Electra's love for her father. *psychoanal.* A complex characterized chiefly by a daughter's sexual attachment to her father.

Electric blanket, *n.* A blanket with automatically controlled electric heating.

Electric chair, *n.* An electrified chair used to put criminals to death; the sentence of death by electrocution; often shortened to chair, as in to get the chair.

Electric eye, *n.* A photoelectric cell.

Electric organ, *n.* A type of organ using electrically induced vibrations rather than wind resonance in pipes.

Electrocardiogram, e-lek'trō-kar'di-o-gram', *n.* From *electro–* and *cardio–* and *–gram*. A photographic record of heart activity, produced by an electrocardiograph.

Electrocardiograph, e-lek'trō-kar'di-o-graf', *n.* From *electro–* and *cardio–* and *–graph*. An apparatus for recording heart activity. **—Electrocardiography,** *n.*

Electrodeposit, *n. electro–* and *deposit*. A deposit, such as metal, made electrically; *—v.t.* to deposit metal, etc. electrically.

Electroencephalogram, e-lek'trō-en-sef'-a-lō-gram, *n.* The record of brain waves detected by an electroencephalograph.

Electroencephalograph, e-lek'trō-en-sef'-a-lō-graf', *n.* See ENCEPHALIC in the Dict. An instrument for detecting the electric waves produced by the brain, used in the diagnosis of epilepsy, brain tumors, etc.

Electrograph, e-lek'trō-graf', *n.* From *electro–* and *–graph*. A record of the measurements made by an electrometer; an apparatus for tracing etching designs; an apparatus for the electric transmission of pictures, etc.

Electron gun, *n. television* The apparatus in the neck of a cathoderay tube, consisting of an electron-emitting cathode and other electrodes which concentrate and focus the emitted electrons into a spot of desired size on the screen.

Electronics, e-lek'tron'iks, *n.* The study of the movements of free electrons, esp. as applied to technology of radio, television, etc.

Electron microscope, *n.* A high-power microscope using beams of electrons focused by election lenses to produce a magnified image on a flourescent screen or photographic plate.

Electronography, e-lek'tron'og'raf-e, *n.* See *electron* and *–graphy*. *print.* A method of printing without contact between plate and paper, in which the electrically charged particles of ink migrate from the plate to the oppositely charged printing surface. **—Electronographic,** *adj.*

Element*, *n. math.* An infinitesimal part of a given magnitude; *elect.* either of the two substances constituting a voltaic couple; one of the electrodes in a vacuum tube; *mil. avn.* a small flight formation, usually consisting of two or three aircraft.

Elementary particle, *n. phys.* One of the particles hypothesized to be the basic constituents of matter, such as the electron, the mesons, etc.

Elevation*, *n. ballet* The ability of a dancer to attain height in a leap.

Elevator*, *n. aeron.* A hinged surface or flap usually attached to the tail plane of an airplane, for controlling the airplane's longitudinal inclination.

Embolic, em-bol'ik, *adj.* See EMBOLISM. *pathol.* Pertaining to an embolus or embolism; embryology growing inwardly; a form of invagination.

Embolus, *n.*, pl. **–li.** From Gr. *émbolos*, wedge. Any abnormal particle in the blood stream.

Emcee, *n.* Spelling of pronunciation of M.C. for master of ceremonies. A master of ceremonies; *—v.t.* and *i.* to act as master of ceremonies.

—Emia, —Aemia, *suff.* From Gr. *haima*, blood. *med.* Pertaining to a condition of the blood, as in anemia.

Empathy, em'pa-thi, *n.* From *en*, in, and *pathos*, suffering, passion. *psych.* The intellectual recognition and understanding of the feelings of another as opposed to affective recognition and identification, sympathy. **—Empathic,** em-path'ic, *adj.*

Emulsion*, *n. physical chem.* Colloidal suspension of a liquid in a liquid; *photog.* a light-sensitive suspension of silver salts in gelatin, used for coating plates, films and paper.

Encephalo—, Encephal—, *pref.* From Gr. *egképhalos*, the brain. Combining form meaning the brain, as in encephalograph.

Encrypt, en-kript', *v.t.* and *i.* From *–en* and *crypt*. To put into code.

Endocrinology, en'do-krī-nol'o-ji, *n.* From *endocrine* and *–ology*. *physiol.* The theory and experimental study of the internal secretions of the ductless glands. **—Endocrinologist,** *n.*

Engram*, From Gr. *eggraphein*, to inscribe, incise, engrave. *psych.* Presumed pattern of nerve paths, due partly to heredity and partly to previous experience of the individual, and tending to cause specific behavior; the physiological basis of a habit.

Enrich*, *v.t. of foods* To supply, as flour, with added food value, esp. with vitamins and minerals.

Enzymology, en'zī-mol'o-ji, *n.* From *enzyme* and *–ology*. The study of the nature and effects of enzymes.

Epicritic, ep-i-krit'ik, *adj.* From Gr. *epikerinein*, to decide, determine. *physiol.* and *psychol.* Pertaining to cutaneous receptors capable of fine discriminations of sensation; pertaining to such discrimination itself. Opposed to PROTOPATHIC, below.

Epigone, *n.*, pl. **–ni.** From *epi–* and Gr. *–gonos*, root of *gignesthai*, to be born. One of the descendants of the seven heroes who unsuccessfully attacked Thebes; one of any later, less distinguished, generation; an inferior imitator of an artist, political theorist, etc.

Equal-area, *adj. of a map projection* All of those parts give a correct representation of area.

Equalitarian, e-qwal'i-tār-i-an, *adj.* From *equality* and *–arian*. Pertaining to the belief that all men are equal; *–n.* one who holds this belief.

Er, *interj.* A purely literary indication of the sound denoting hesitation in speech, the spelling originating with those who did not sound the *r*. Cp. FELLER, below.

Ergosterol, er-gos'ter-ōl, *n.* From ERGOT, in the Dict., and STEROL. *biochem.* A yeast derivative, originally obtained from ergot, which is exposed to ultraviolet rays to form vitamin D.

Erotism, e-rot'izm, *n.* From *erotic* and *–ism*. Eroticism.

Ersatz, er-zats', *adj.* Ger. *substitute*. Used as a substitute, as ersatz gasoline. *—n.* A substitute.

Erythrism, e-rith'rizm, *n.* From Gr. *eruthrós*, red and *–ism*. Unusual redness of the hair.

Erythroblast, e-rith'ro-blast, *n.* From Gr. *eruthrós*, red and *blástos*, bud, sprout, growth. *anat.* A nucleated cell from which red blood corpuscles develop.

Erythrocyte, e-rith'ro-sīt, *n.* From Gr. *eruthrós*, red and *–cyte*. A red blood corpuscle.

Escalator, *n.* Escalator clause, a clause in a treaty or contract permitting the adjustment of quantities, prices or wages to suit unforeseen conditions. Specif., a clause in a contract between labor and management providing for adjustment of wages on the basis of fluctuations in the cost of living.

Escape*, *adj.* Tending to avoid the problems of reality by attracting the mind to something more pleasing and fanciful: escape movie, escape mechanism, etc.

Escapement*, *n.* A mechanism which controls the motion of a typewriter carriage.

Escapism, es-kāp'izm, *n.* From *escape* and *–ism*. The mind's avoidance of the problems of reality by habitual indulgence in diversions, particularly that of fantasy. **—Escapist,** *adj.* and *n.*

ESP. Extrasensory perception.

Esterase, es'ter-ās, *n.* See ESTER. Any of the enzymes that split esters.

Esthesia, or **Aesthesia,** es-thē'zhi-a, *n.* From Gr. *aísthesis*, perception by the senses, feeling. Sensibility, perception of sensation. Frequently used as a combining form.

Estrogen, es'trō-jen, *n.* From *oestrus* and *–gen*. *biochem.* Any of the female hormones which promote oestrus.

Estrogenic, es'trō-jen-ik, *adj.* See ESTROGEN, above. *biochem.* Promoting oestrus; pertaining to estrogen.

Estrone, es'trōn, *n.* From *oestrus* and *–one*. A female hormone, $C_{18}H_{22}O_2$, having estrogenic properties.

Estrus, es-trus, *n.* Oestrus.

Ethanol, eth'a-nōl, *n.* From *ethane* and *–ol*. *chem.* Ethyl alcohol.

Ethical*, *adj.* Ethical pharmacy, one which supposedly sells only drugs, but which also sells cosmetics and other toilet articles; its distinguishing feature is the lack of a soda fountain; *Ethical drug*: one advertised only to physicians contrasted w. PROPRIETARY DRUG, below; mistakenly, a drug which cannot be purchased without a doctor's prescription.

Ethnarch, eth'nark, *n.* From *ethnic* and *arch–*. The ruler of a people or province.

Ethylene*, *n.* From *ethyl* and *–ene.* A colorless gas, C_2H_4, forming an explosive mixture with air.

Ethylene glycol, eth'i-lēn glī'kol, *n.* A nonevaporating antifreeze preparation, sold under a variety of trade-names.

Europium, u-rō'pi-um, *n.* From *Europe* and *–ium. chem.* A metallic rare-earth element, of atomic weight 152. Symbol: *Eu.*

Euthenics, u-then'iks, *n.* From Gr. *euthēnein,* to thrive and *–ics* by analogy w. EUGENICS. The science of improving the human race by betterment of environmental condition. Contrasted with eugenics, in the Dict.

Euxenite, ūk'se-nīt, *n.* From Gr. *eúxenos,* hospitable and *–ite.* A complex mineral of brownish black hue, containing titanium, uranium, yttrium, columbrium, etc.

Evacueé, e-vak'u-ē,' *n.* Fr. A person removed from a zone of war or disaster.

Evocable, ev'o-ka-bl, *adj.* From *evoke* and *–able.* Capable of being evoked.

Exclosure, eks-klō'zher, *n.* From *ex–* and *closure,* by analogy w. enclosure. An area surrounded by a barrier designed to keep out insects, rodents, etc.

Exhibitionism, ek-si-bi'shon-izm, *n.* From *exhibition* and *–ism.* Propensity for focusing the attention of others on oneself; showing-off. —**Exhibitionist,** *n.*

Existential*, *adj.* Pertaining to existentialism.

Existentialism, eg-zis-ten'shal-izm, *n. philos.* The doctrine which maintains that existence precedes essence, and stresses contingency and personal freedom of decision. —**Existentialist,** *n.*

Exocrine, ek'so-krīn, *adj.* From Gr. *éxo,* outside and *krīnein,* to separate. *physiol.* Secreting externally; of glands whose secretion is discharged through a duct.

Expansionism, ek-span'shun-izm, *n.* The belief in expansion, as of a country's territory. —**Expansionist,** *n.*

Expedite*, *v.t.* To issue officially. —**Expediter,** *n.*

Expendable, *adj.* From *expend* and *–able.* Designed to be used up without regard to cost, esp. of men or materials sacrificed or about to be sacrificed to gain a military objective. —**Expendables,** *n.* pl. Expendable men or supplies.

Explant, *v.t.* From *ex–* and *plant.* To place and cultivate living tissue in a new medium.

Exploded sketch, Exploded view, *n.* A drawing of a piece of machinery with the parts shown slightly spread apart, so that their interrelationship may be more clearly seen.

Exponible, eks-pō'ni-bl, *adj.* See EXPONENT. *log.* of an obscure proposition Requiring restatement or explanation.

Exposure meter, *n. photog.* Any device which indicates the proper exposure for photographing a scene under given lighting conditions.

Expressionism, *n.* From *expression* and *–ism.* An artistic theory, originally developed in painting, emphasizing the artist's emotional reaction to a subject rather than objective appearance of the subject.

Expressman, *n.* (U.S.) A person employed by an express company, usually one who makes deliveries.

Extend*, *v.t.* To make a scarce or expensive article esp. a food go farther by mixing it with something cheaper or more plentiful.

Extensometer, eks'ten-som'e-ter, *n.* From *extension* and *meter.* An instrument for measuring the amount of deformation of a sample piece of metal, as caused by twisting compression, etc.

Extractant, *n.* From *extract* and *–ant. chem.* A solvent used in extraction.

Extrasensory perception, *n. psych.* Perception not explicable in terms of the ordinary operation of the senses.

Extracurricular, *adj.* From *extra* and *curriculum* and *–ar.* Not connected with the regular curriculum; esp. of student activities such as athletics, debates, etc. which are outside the classroom but more or less supervised by the school. Also extracurriculum.

Extraversion, *n.* Extroversion. —**Extravert,** *n.* Extrovert.

Eye*, *n.* Phr. easy on the eye, (slang) goodlooking, of pleasing appearance.

Eyebright*, *n.* The scarlet pimpernel.

Eyecup, *n.* A cup whose rim is designed to fit the orbit of the eye, used in applying liquid medication to the eye.

Eye rhyme, *n.* A rhyme which appears to be exact because the syllables in question are spelled the same: mead, head, finger, ginger, etc.

Eyestrain, *n.* Feeling of fatigue of the eyes due to excessive use, lack of needed glasses, etc.

Eyetooth*, *n.* (colloq.) Phr. to cut one's eyeteeth, become sophisticated by experience, mature in judgment.

Fabrikoid, *n. trade-mark* A type of imitation leather.

Face card, *n. playing cards* The king, queen or jack.

Face-harden, *v.t.* To harden the face of steel and other metals.

Face-lifting, *n.* (colloq.) Plastic surgery to remove facial blemishes, such as those due to age.

Face value, *n.* The value indicated on the face of a bond, etc.; (by extension) the apparent value: His promises were not doubted, but taken at their face value.

Facial index, *n. anthropol.* Ratio of a face's breadth to its height.

Facsimile*, *n.* A system of transmission and reproduction of photographs, printed matter, etc., by means of radio or telegraph.

Fact-finder, *n.* A person selected, as in a labor dispute, to report the facts of the case, presumably as a basis for further negotiation.

Fade-in, *n. movies* The gradual appearance of a new shot on the screen out of darkness into full intensity; *radio* the gradual increase in loudness of a sound.

Fade-out, *n, movies* The gradual disappearance of a shot on the screen from full intensity into darkness; *radio* the gradual diminishing of the loudness of a sound; (slang) and *fig.* a gradual withdrawal from publicity as of a person.

Fading*, *n.* See FADE, *radio* The periodical weakening of tone experienced in reception, esp. on medium wave lengths.

Fair ball, *n. baseball* Any batted ball that is not a foul.

Fair catch, *n.* (U.S.) *football* A catch of any kick in which the catcher raises one hand above his head, thus indicating that he will not advance the ball and cannot be tackled.

Fairground, *n.* usually pl. An area, including its facilities such as buildings, in which fairs and other public events are held.

Fair-haired, *adj.* Favorite; esp. in phr. to be someone's fair-haired boy.

Fairing, *n.* From *fair* and *–ing. aeron, engin.* A part of an airplane's structure which is designed to reduce drag.

Fair-lead, fār'lēd, *n.* From *fair* and *lead v. naut.* A guide, such as a block or ring, through which running rigging is passed to avoid chafing.

Fair-minded, *adj.* From *fair* and *minded.* Impartial; unbiased; just.

Fair-traded, *adj. of merchandise* Subject to a fair-trade agreement between a manufacturer and a distributor, which provides that certain trade-marked merchandise may not be sold below a fixed price.

Fake*, *n.* One who fakes.

Faker, *n.* One who fakes; (colloq.) a swindler; (colloq.) a peddler.

Falangist, fa-lan'jist, *n.* A member of the Falange, the Spanish Fascist political organization which came to power in the Civil War of 1936–39 under General Franco.

Fall*, *v.i.* Fall for, (slang) to fall a victim to, be captivated by, the charm of a person or thing.

Falstaffian, fal-staf'i-an, *adj.* Like Shakespeare's character Sir John Falstaff, a fat, jovial braggart and likeable rogue.

Faltboat, fawlt'bōt, *n,* From Ger. *faltboot,* folding boat. A collapsible boat similar to a kayak.

Family*, *n.* used attrib. Family skeleton, an embarrassing incident in the history of a family which is kept secret.

Fan*, *n.* Used attrib.; Fan club, an organization whose chief object is the worship of a movie star, etc.; Fan mail, mail received by a figure of public adulation from his devotees.

Fancy-free, *adj.* Free from emotional influence, esp. that of love.

Fantail*, *n. naut.* The after overhang of a ship.

Farm*, *n.* A minor league baseball club, affiliated with and usually owned by a major league club, for which it trains promising young players. *v.t.* and *i.* Farm out: *manuf.* To subcontract parts of a job to someone else; *baseball* to assign a player to a minor league club for further experience before calling him to active duty with the major league club with which he has a contract.

Farmerette, *n.* From *farmer* and from fem. suff. *–ette.* (colloq.) A female farmer.

Farm hand, *n.* A hired laborer on a farm.

Fashion-plate, *n.* (usually derogatory) One dressed in the latest fashion.

Fast*, *adj. of a timepiece* Registering a time in advance of that which is correct; *photog.* adapted to short exposure of a film or lens; dishonest or deceptive. Phr. a fast shuffle from cards and to pull or put over a fast one both denote an action which is intended to cheat or deceive the victim by not allowing him sufficient time to reflect.

Fathead, *n.* A stupid person.

Fathometer, fa-thom'e-ter, *n.* From *fathom* and *meter.* trade-mark A type of sonic depth finder.

Fatigue clothes, Fatigues, *n.* pl. *mil.* Work clothes.

Fat-soluble, fat'sol'u-bl, *adj. chem.* Not soluble in water of certain vitamins.

Fatuitous, fa-tū'i-tus, *n.* From *fatuity* and *–ous.* Characterized by fatuity.

Favonian*, *adj.* From Lat. *favōnius,* the west wind. Favoring; mild.

F.B.I., Federal Bureau of Investigation.

Feather*, *v.t. avn.* To turn the propeller blades, as those on a dead engine, so that they provide the least possible air resistance or drag.

Featherbed, *v.i.* To make work last by limiting output, or to force an employer to hire more workers than are necessary. —*adj.* of union rules Designed to accomplish this purpose. —**Featherbedding,** *n.*

Feather cut, *n.* A style of cutting women's hair short, with the ends of uneven length.

Feature*, *n.* Double feature, a movie program containing two full-length pictures; *U. S. journalism* Feature story, one specially written and printed for reasons other than its value as news.

Federalese, fed'er-al-ēz, *n.* From *federal* and *–ese.* (slang) The awkward and unnecessarily difficult style in which official federal documents and correspondence are written.

Fedora, fedō'ra, *n.* From *Fedora,* title of a play by Sardou. (U.S.) A low soft felt hat with its crown creased lengthwise.

Feeder*, *n.* A branch line of any transportation system.

Feller, *n.* A purely literary indication of the pronunciation of fellow with a wholly unaccented vowel in the final syllable, the spelling originating with those who did not sound the *r.* See *–er,* above. Feller is a spelling pronunciation, though perhaps influenced by intrusive *r.*

Fellow traveler, *n.* Literal transl. of Russ. *popuchiki.* A person who supports the beliefs, aims and activities of the Communist party, but who is not a party member; (by extension) one who supports the program of an organized group but is not officially a member of the group.

Feminize, *v.t. biol,* Specif., to induce female characteristics in a male by the use of an estrogen.

Ferry*, *v.t.* To fly military aircraft from the factory to the combat zone in which they are to be used; to transport goods esp. milit. by an organized air service.

Ferry*, *n.* An organized system of flying military airplanes from the factory to the zone in which they are to be used. Also attrib: ferry command, ferry pilot.
Festschrift, fest'shrift, *n.* From Ger., festival writing. A collection of papers published in honor of a scholar, written by his colleagues or former students and presented to him on an anniversary occasion.
Fever*, *n.* Attrib: fever therapy, the medical treatment of disease by means of artificially induced fever.
Fiberglas, *n. trade-mark* A material made from glass drawn into fine fibers, suitable for use in fabrics or as insulation.
Fibrinogen, fī-brin'ō-jen, *n.* From *fibrin* and *-gen. biochem.* A protein in the blood which produces coagulation by yielding fibrin.
Fieldball, *n.* A game played by two teams of eleven members and combining certain features of basketball, soccer and field hockey; a score is made by putting the ball through the opponents' goal posts.
Fifth*, *n.* One fifth of a U.S. gallon a measure of alcoholic beverages.
Fifth column, *n.* Coined by fascist Gen. Mola, who led four columns against Madrid during the Spanish Civil War, to describe the fascist sympathizers within the city. (by extension) Individuals in one country secretly engaged in sabotage, espionage, and other activities on behalf of another country.
Fighter*, *n.* A type of small, fast, easily maneuvered military aircraft used as a pursuit ship to fight enemy planes. Also fighter plane.
Fighter bomber, *n. mil. avn.* A fighter plane equipped for light bombing operations.
Fighting cock. *n.* A pugnacious person.
Filled gold, *n.* A base metal, such as brass, mechanically covered with a thick layer of gold.
Filled milk, *n.* Skim milk with vegetable oils added.
Filling station, *n.* A retail establishment where motorists can obtain gasoline, oil, and miscellaneous minor parts, repairs, and services.
Film strip, *n.* A series of individual pictures and explanatory text on film, illustrating a text or lecture.
Fink, *n.* Etymol. unknown. (U. S. labor slang) A company spy; a strikebreaker.
Fin keel, *n. naut.* A finlike piece of metal affixed to the keel of a sailboat, to prevent lateral motion and increase stability.
Firepower, *n. mil.* The amount of shells which a unit or piece of equipment is capable of firing.
Fireproof*, *v.t.* To render fireproof.
Fire sale, *n. U.S.* The sale at reduced prices of goods supposedly damaged by fire.
Fireworks*, *n.* Usually pl. in U.S.
Firn, fern', *n.* From Ger. *firn*, of last year. Névé. Granular snow.
Fishpound, *n.* (U.S.) An underwater net attached to stakes, used to catch fish.
Fish story, *n.* (colloq.) orig. U.S. An exaggerated or incredible story.
Fissile*, *adj.* Fissionable. See below.
Fission*, *n.* Specif. *phys.* and *chem.* the splitting of an atomic nucleus.
Fissionable, fish'un-a-bl, *adj.* From *fission* and *-able.* Capable of undergoing nuclear fission.
Fit*, *n.* Phr. to throw a fit, to be, become, outraged, infuriated.
Fit*, *adj.* Phrs. fit to be tied, exasperated; fit to kill, excessively, in an overdone manner.
Five-and-ten, *n.* A store selling low-priced goods, originally at prices not exceeding ten cents. Also five-and-dime, store, ten cent store.
Fix*, *v.t.* (U.S. slang) To tamper dishonestly with the normal progress of law, a sports event, etc. —*n.* Such as tampering.
Flagwaving, *n.* (derogatory) Exaggerated and aggressive patriotism; jingoism. —**Flagwaver**, *n.*
Flak, *n.* Acronym of Ger. *fliegergabwehrkanone*, aircraft defense gun. Shells fired by antiaircraft artillery. Also used attrib.
Flame cultivation, *n. agric.* The use of flame throwers to destroy weeds without harming the crop.
Flammable, *n.* Inflammable.
Flap*, *n.* A hinged control surface of an airplane, parallel with the aileron on the trailing edge of the wing, and acting as a brake in controlling the speed and distance of the landing glide.
Flash*, *adj.* Occurring suddenly often unexpectedly, briefly, and violently, as a flash flood.
Flashback, *n. movies* Episode beginning with a sudden change to an earlier point of time.
Flashbulb, *n. photog.* A bulb producing a sudden bright light, used esp. for taking pictures in darkened surroundings.
Flashgun, *n. photog.* A device which sets off the flashbulb and opens the shutter simultaneously.
Flashlamp, *n.* A flashbulb.
Flatfoot, *n.* (slang) A policeman.
Flatfooted, *adj.* (colloq.) Firm, unyielding; unprepared or without proper defenses: to be caught flatfooted.
Flattop, *n.* U.S. Navy (slang) an aircraft carrier.
Fletcherism, flech'er-izm, *n.* From its advocate Horace Fletcher 1849-1919. The practice of thoroughly chewing one's food. —**Fletcherize**, *v.i.* and *t.*
Flight analyzer, *n.* A machine automatically recording such details of a flight as altitude, speed, and gasoline consumption.
Flight crew, *n.* The group assigned to man a plane in flight.
Flight deck, *n. navy* The deck of an aircraft carrier used for takeoffs and landings.
Flint*, *n.* Any material used for producing fire, as an alloy used in cigarette lighters.
Float*, *n.* The buoyant boat-shaped watertight support fitted to the undercarriage of a seaplane or amphibian.
Floater*, *n.* (U.S. colloq.) A vagrant; one who changes his residence and place of work frequently; (U.S.) one who illegally votes in different polling places, esp. for pay.
Floating stock, *n.* Stock held for speculation rather than investment.
Floodlight, flud'līt, *n.* An artificial light from a wide bright beam; a floodlight projector, a lamp with a reflector designed to produce such a light; —*v.t.* to illuminate with floodlight.
Floor*, *n. movies* The part of the studio where the actors perform; *industry* a minimum limit on wages, hours, or prices.
Floor show, *n.* A program of entertainment at a night club.
Flop*, *v.i. fig.* (slang) To fail dismally.
Flophouse, *n.* (U.S. slang), A place where a bed for the night can be obtained cheaply.
Florivorous, *adj.* From Lat. *flori-* combining form of *flos*, flower and *-vorus*, eating. *of certain insects* Flower-eating.
Flow Sheet, Flowsheet, *n, manuf.* A diagram or outline showing, in order, the operations and machines through which material passes.
Fluid coal, *n.* A mixture of finely divided coal with air, which can be transported through pipes under pressure.
Fluidextract, *n. phar.* An alcoholic solution of a vegetable drug, one cubic centimeter of which is equal in activity to one gram of the drug in dry form.
Flunk, *v.i.* and *t.* Etymol. uncertain. (colloq.) *v.i.* To fail, as in an examination; to shrink from, back out, as through cowardice followed by out; *v.t.* to fail a course of studies, etc.; to give a student a failing grade; —*n.* a failure.
Fluorescent lamp, *n.* An electric lamp in which an electrically-conducting vapor, such as that from mercury, replaces the incandescent filament.
Fluorosis, flōō'or-ō'sis, *n.* From *fluor-* and *-osis. med.* An abnormal condition resulting from an excess of fluorine.
Flush*, *adj. print.* Even with the margin of the type face; not indented.
Flying boat, *n.* A seaplane with a hull fit for floating and designed for long overseas flights.
Flying bomb, *n.* A jet-propelled bomb, shaped like an airplane, launched from a ramp against distant targets.
Flying colors, *n.* Phr. to come off with flying colors, emerge victorious, be completely successful.
Flying laboratory, *n.* An airplane used to test flight phenomena; an airplane of new design used primarily for experimental purposes.
Flying saucer, *n.* A mythical saucer-shaped high-speed aerial object, often reported sighted over various parts of the United States.
Flying squad, *n.* A small, highly mobile unit of an organization designed for quick and effective action, as in holding political rallies or suppressing riots.
Flying Wing, *n. trade-mark* An airplane with a specially designed wing, no fuselage, and pusher-type engines.
Flyway, *n.* The route regularly flown by migratory birds.
Flyweight, flī'wāt', *n.* A boxer weighing 112 pounds or less.
FM, *n., radio* Frequency modulation.
F number, *n., focal.* The focal length of a lens divided by the effective aperture, used to indicate the speed of a lens.
Fold*, *v.i.* (slang) usually with *up* To fail, as a play; to collapse.
Foldboat, *n.* See faltboat, above.
Folic acid, fō'lik, *n.* From Lat. *folium*, leaf and *-ic. biochem.* A vitamin of the B complex, found in leaves and prepared synthetically, used in treating anemia.
Folkway, *n.*, usually pl. *sociol.* The ways of living peculiar to members of a social group. Cp. Mores, below.
Fool's gold, *n.* Iron pyrites, mistaken for gold because of the resemblance in color.
Fool's paradise, *n.* An illusory condition of happiness.
Footage, foot'ij, *n.* From *foot* and *-age.* Length as measured in feet, as lumber or motion picture film.
Foot-candle, *n. photometry* A unit of illumination, equivalent to the direct illumination given by a standard candle at a distance of one foot.
Footloose, *adj.* Free, not burdened with responsibilities.
For*, *prep.* (Phr. colloq.) to be in for trouble, etc., to be in for it (slang) have trouble, punishment, a reprimand, in store for one; to be out for trouble, for a row, etc., (colloq.) be intending to cause it; to be out for anything, (colloq.) have it as one's aim.
Forint, fo'rint, *n.* See Florin. The monetary unit of Hungary.
Fork*, *v.t.* and *i.* (slang) Fork over, to hand over esp. money.
Form letter, *n.* A letter having standardized contents, copies of which are sent to large numbers of individuals.
Fortify*, *v.t.* To increase the nutritive qualities of a food product by adding vitamins and minerals.
Forty-niner, *n.* (U.S. colloq.) One who participated in the California gold rush of 1849.
Fotosetter, *n. trade-mark* A printing machine which reduces steps in plate-making by composition of copy on film and direct transference of the copy from the film to the printing surface.
Foundation garment or **foundation**, *n.* Any woman's undergarment, such as a corset or girdle, designed to control body contours.
Foxhole, *n.* A small skirmisher's trench, dug by the soldier for protection while under fire.
Fragmentation bomb, *n.* From *fragment* and *-ation. mil.* A bomb designed to scatter metal fragments over a wide area.
Francium, fran'si-um, *n.* From *France*, where discovered in 1939, and *-ium.* Coined by its discoverer, Mme Perey. A radioactive element of atomic number 87. Symbol: *Fr.*
Frank*, *n.* (colloq.) Clipped form of Frankfurter, below.
Frankfurter, *n.* Ger., pert. to Frankfurt. A linked sausage made from beef and pork. Also frankfurt.
Fraternize*, *v.i. mil.* To have friendly social relationships with inhabitants of an occupied territory.

Free form, *n. linguistics* A linguistic form which has meaning when used alone: boy, girl. Contrasted with bound form, above.
Freeway, *n.* An express automobile highway.
Freeze*, *v.t.* To prohibit withdrawal, as of funds belonging to enemy nations and their nationals to halt prices of goods at certain levels by governmental action; to cease making changes in the model of a plane, tank, etc., and so make possible its quick mass production; —*n.* an order imposing such restrictions.
Freezer*, *n.* A machine for freezing ice cream.
Freight yard, *n.* Yard in which freight trains are broken up and reformed. Brit. marshalling yard.
French dressing, *n.* Salad dressing made from oil and vinegar seasoned with salt and spices.
French fried, *adj.* Usually of potatoes cut into strips and fried in deep fat.
French toast, *n.* Bread soaked in a mixture of egg and milk and sautéed.
Freon, frē'on, *n. trade-mark.* Any of the fluorochloro derivatives of low molecular weight hydrocarbons, used as refrigerants; popularly, one of these, the gas CCl_2F_2.
Frequency modulation, *n. electronics* Radio transmission, virtually static-free, based on varying the frequency of the carrier wave in accordance with the sound waves impressed upon it. Contrasted with amplitude modulation, above. Abbr: FM, F.M.
Frigate*, *n.* A British war vessel, larger than a corvette but smaller than a destroyer, used to provide antisubmarine and antiaircraft protection for convoys during wartime.
Frisk*, *v.t.* (slang) To search a person by feeling his clothing; hence, to steal from someone in this manner.
Front*, *n.* Any sphere of conflict; a coalition of political forces: united front, popular front from Fr. front *populaire*; (colloq.) a person who allows his name to be used to lend prestige to an organization; a figurehead; outward appearance of wealth or status with the implication that this is simulated; (colloq.) an organization ostensibly formed for legitimate purposes but used chiefly to further the aims of groups in political disfavor: Communist front, Nazi front; meteor. the forward edge of a discrete air mass; cold front. *v.i.* To act as a front for a person or organization.
Front matter, *n. print.* All printed matter in a book which precedes the actual text.
Frontolysis, frun-tol'e-sis, *n.* From FRONT above, and -LYSIS. *meteorol.* The destruction of a front.
Frosted, *adj. of food* Quickly frozen for preservation.
Frostflower, *n.* A plant, *Milla biflora*, of Mexico and the southwestern U.S.; its white star-shaped flower.
Froufrou, frōō'frōō', *n.* From a rustling, esp. of a silk dress.
Frozen*, *adj. of food* Subjected to rapid freezing so that its chemical composition, taste, and food value are preserved.
Fruit cup, *n.* A dessert or appetizer consisting of various fruits.
Fry*, *v.i.* (U.S. slang) To be electrocuted.
Fuchsin, Fuchsine, fook'sin, *n.* From *fuchsia*, which it resembles in color, and *-ine.* A dye derived from the oxidation of a mixture of aniline and toluidines, having a deep red color in solution.
Fuddy-duddy, fud'i-dud'i, *n.* Perhaps from *fuddle* and imit. reduplication. A meddlesome, ineffectual old person. Also attrib: fuddy-duddy ways; —*v.i.* to act ineffectually.
Führer, Fuehrer, fu'rer, *n.* Ger. In Germany, a leader or chief; specif., der führer, Adolph Hitler, chancellor of the Third Reich.
Functionalism, fungk'shun-al-izm, *n.* A doctrine, esp. in architecture, which stresses the adaptation of form to function or use.
Funnies, *n.* pl. See FUNNY. Comic strips; a book or section of a newspaper containing them.
Fusion, *n. polit.* A local political party formed by a coalition of other parties or interest groups.
Fuze*, *n.* Fuse; *mil.* any noncombustible device for exploding a charge. Contrasted with a fuse, which is combustible.
Gabfest, *n.* From *gab* and *fest*, party, festival. A prolonged conversation among several persons.
Gag*, *n.* A joke.
Gagman, *n.* One who writes jokes for radio or television performers.
Gag rule, *n. polit.* A rule prescribing ways of shutting off debate in order to come to a vote on a measure; cloture.
Gal, *n.* (U.S. slang) Girl.
Gallus, gal'us, *n.*, usually pl. From gallows in the sense of trouser braces. (U.S. dial.) A suspender or brace.
Galoot, *n.* Origin unknown. (U.S. slang) An awkward person.
Game room, *n.* A room with equipment for indoor games, such as table tennis, shuffleboard, etc.
Game theory, *n.* The application of mathematical statistics to the expectation of gain in any game or conflict situation which can be made mathematically equivalent to a game. —Game-theoretic, *adj.*
Gangsterism, *n.* From *gangster* and *-ism.* Gangster-like behavior.
Garand rifle, gar'and, *n.* From its inventor, John Garand. A semiautomatic rifle of rapid fire, the basic U.S. infantry firearm.
Gargoylism, gar'goil-ism, *n.* From *gargoyle* and *-ism. genetics* A genetic condition in man involving severe skeletal and mental defects.
Gas black, *n.* Fine carbon, obtained as soot from a natural gas flame.
Gas chamber, *n.* A training and testing room where gas is used for experimental purposes to train soldiers in chemical warfare and to test gas masks before they are given to troops; a room in which criminals or political prisoners are put to death by gas.
Gastrin, gas'trin, *n. gastric* and *-in. biochem.* A stomach hormone which promotes the secretion of gastric juice.
Gastroentero—, From *gastro-* and *entero-*. A combining form meaning "pertaining to the stomach and intestine," as in gastroenterology.
Gastroscope, gas'tro-skōp, *n.* From *gastro-* and *-scope. med.* An instrument for viewing the interior of the stomach. **—Gastroscopic,** *adj.*
Gat*, *n.* From abbr. of Gatling gun. (slang) A gun, esp. a pistol or revolver.
Gauleiter, gau'lī-ter, *n.* Ger. District leader; specif. the governor of a political district in Nazi Germany.
Gauntlet*, *n.* In modern warfare, a cross fire of batteries which an attacking or retreating force must run through before reaching its objective.
G.C.A., abbr. for *ground controlled approach*, a radar-operated system by which a ground operator directs a pilot making a blind landing.
Gear*, *v.t.* To plan or direct something with relation to something else: wages were geared to the cost of living.
Geiger counter, gī'ger, *n.* From physicist Hans Geiger. A device for detecting and measuring radioactivity.
Gel, jel, *n.* Abbr. from gelatine. *chem.* A colloid which, under suitable conditions, has set or formed a jelly.
General-purpose, *adj.* Of broad utility, as an animal or implement.
—Genic, jen'ik, suff. From *-gen* and *-ic.* Combining form used to form adjectives corresponding to nouns ending in *-gen;* combining form meaning: 'highly appropriate for reproduction by a communication medium': photogenic, telegenic.
Genocide, jen'ō-sīd, *n.* From Gr. *gênos*, race and *-cids.* Coined by Prof. Raphael Lemkin, 1944. The systematic extermination of a particular racial, religious, or cultural group.
Genome, jēn'ōm, *n.* From *gene* and chromos*ome. genetics* A haploid of chromosomes with its genes.
Genotype, jen' ō-tīp, *n.* Gr. *gênos*, birth, breed, etc.; see GENUS and TYPE. *biol.* Hereditary genetic constitution of an organism; a group of organisms with a common heredity.
Gentleman*, *n.* Phr. gentlemen's agreement, a mutual understanding with no guarantee but the honor of those entering into it; euphemistically with a more or less dishonest aim.
Geopolitics, gē'ō-pol'i-tiks, *n.* From *geo-* and *politics.* The application of political and economic geography to the policies and problems of states, especially as related to territorial expansion.
Geriatrics, jer-i-at'riks, *n.* From Gr. *geras, old age* and *-iatric. med.* The study of the diseases of old age. **—Geriatrician,** *n.*
Gestalt, ge-shtalt, *n.* Ger., form. *psychol.* An organized whole in experience; chiefly used attrib.: *gestalt psychology*, a theory which explains psychological phenomena by their relation to organized wholes, at least some of which are immediately given in experience.
Gestapo, ge-sta'pō, *n.* Ger. *geheime Staats polizei*, secret state police. The secret police organization of the Nazi regime in Germany; (by extension) any system of informers and secret terror as might be used.
Gesundheit, ge-zoont'hīt, *n.* Ger. health. Used as meaning 'to your health, may you be healthy,' as a toast, or after someone has sneezed.
Get*, *v.t.* and *i.* Phr. to get religion, socialism, etc., (colloq.) become preoccupied with; get! *imperat.*, (slang) abbr. for 'get along!' Get an idea, etc. across, trans. (colloq.) orig. U.S., get the public to accept it.
Getaway, *n.* (slang) Escape: to make a getaway.
Geyserite, gī'zer-īt, *n.* From *geyser* and *-ite.* A type of silica deposited around the openings of geysers and hot springs.
Ghetto*, *n.* A section of a city in which any minority racial group is segregated, esp. in slum conditions.
Ghost*, *n.* An undesired duplicate image, as on a television screen; —*v.t.* to act as a ghost writer: he ghosted the book.
Ghost writer, *n.* One who executes literary work for someone else who takes public credit. **—Ghostwrite,** *v.t.* and *i.*
Ghost town, *n.* A town that has lost its economic basis for existence and is therefore deserted.
G.I., *adj.* Abbr. Government issue of anything supplied members of the military by the government: G.I. beer; according to military standards or regulations: G.I. haircuts; —*n.* any present or former enlisted man of any of the U.S. armed services.
Gigolo, jig'o-lō, *n.* Fr. formed from *gigole*, loose woman. A professional male escort or dancing partner.
Gila monster, hē'la, *n.* From *Gila* River in Arizona. A venomous lizard, *Heloderma suspectum*, having orange and black tubercles and inhabiting the southwestern U.S.
Gilly, *n.* See GILLIE in the Dict.
Gimmick, gim'ik, *n.* Etymol. uncertain. (U.S. slang) A device secretly used to control a prize wheel at a carnival, or to work a magician's trick; anything tricky; a catch.
Gin rummy, *n.* Orig. unknown. A variety of rummy in which a player may end the hand when he holds ten or less unmatched points. Also gin.
Giveaway, giv'a-wā, *n.* (slang) A betrayal usually unintentional of something intended to be kept hidden from observation or knowledge; an act of giving, or throwing, away an opportunity or something which should have been retained; a giveaway, giveaway show, giveaway program, an audience-participation radio program in which successful contestants receive prizes; a premium given for the purchase of certain goods.
Glad hand, *n.* (U.S. colloq.) A hearty welcome.
Glamorous, glam'er-us, *adj.* From *glamour* and *-ous.* Possessing glamor. Also glamourous. **—Glamorously,** *adv.*
Glass*, *v.t.* To pack in air-tight glass containers, as preserves.

Glassine, glas-ēn', *n.* From *glass* and *-ine.* A thin semitransparent paper similar to cellophane.

Glider*, *n.* A swing with an upholstered seat suspended by links from a metal framework.

G man, jē' man, *n.* Abbr. of government man. An agent of the F.B.I.

Go*, *v.i.* (slang) Phr. to go to town: of a public performer, esp. a jazz musician. To be inspired; (by extension) proceeding rapidly and successfully toward one's objective.

Gobbledygook, gob'l-di-gook' *n.* Coined by Maury Maverick. The obscure and tortured language in which government documents are written; hence, any pompous and meaningless verbiage.

Gold-brick, *v.i.* U.S. *mil.* (slang) To evade or shirk work. —**Goldbricker,** *n.*

Gold exchange standard, *n.* A modified gold standard whereby a central bank is permitted to base part of its note issue, not on its own gold reserves, but on foreign exchange of a country that is on the gold standard.

Gold reserve, *n.* A reserve fund of gold, as held by the treasury or central bank of a country; the gold held by the U. S. Treasury to redeem promissory notes.

Gold standard, *n.* The monetary system by which a unit of currency is based strictly on gold, a central bank is obliged to exchange its names for gold on demand, and there is no restriction on the flow of gold into and out of a country.

Gonadotropic, gon'a-do-trop'ik, *adj.* From Gonad, and -Tropic, below. *biochem.* Of substances influencing the growth and activity of the gonads.

Goo, *n.* From *burgoo,* a thick soup or porridge. (U.S. slang) Any sticky substance; *fig.* sentimentality.

Goober, *n.* From Angolan *nguba.* (Southern U.S.) The peanut.

Goods, *n.* Phr. caught with the goods, caught with evidence of guilt.

Gooey, *adj.* (U.S. slang) Sticky; like goo.

Goofy, *adj.* goof, *n.* (slang) Stupid.

Googol, *n.* Arbitrary coinage by U.S. mathematician Edward Kasner. The figure 1 followed by 100 zeros.

Gook, *n.* Etymol. uncertain. U.S. *mil.* (slang) A nonwhite native, as of the Pacific Islands.

Goon, *n.* Origin obscure; popularized by E. C. Segar's comic strip "Popeye the Sailor." A ruffian hired to terrorize workers or employers in a labor dispute.

Grab bag, *n.* (U.S.) Receptacle containing various objects from which an individual takes one without knowing what he will get.

Gradus, *n. mus.* A work composed of exercises.

Gram atom, Gram atomic weight, *n. chem.* The amount of an element whose weight in grams is numerically equivalent to its atomic weight.

Grand mal, grahn mahl, *n.* Fr. lit. great sickness. A pronounced form of epileptic attack, characterized by complete loss of consciousness and convulsions.

Granger, *n.* From *grange* and *-er.* A farmer; (U.S.) a member of a Grange.

Grasshopper*, *n.* A scouting plane used for directing artillery fire.

Grass roots, *n.* pl. The small town and rural U.S., especially in the Middle West. Also attrib.: grass roots politics; *fig.* the true source, fountainhead of anything: the grass roots of art.

Graveyard shift, *n.* (U.S. colloq.) In a factory or mine, the working hours between midnight and 8 a.m.

Gravimetric, grav'i-met'ric, *adj.* See Gravimeter. Pertaining to measurement by weight, esp. *chem.* as a technique for analyzing compound bodies.

Gravimetry, gra-vim'e-tri, *n.* See Gravimeter. The measurement of weight or density.

Gravy train, *n.* (U.S. slang) Phr. on the gravy train, in a job or situation which requires little work but is extremely profitable. Also gravy boat.

Gray market, *n.* Formed by analogy with Black Market, above. A market which violates the spirit while conforming to the letter of price and rationing regulations; a barely legal type of profiteering.

Grease monkey, *n.* (slang) A mechanic or mechanic's helper, especially employed at airports.

Green light, *n.* (colloq.) Permission to proceed with something: to give someone the green light.

Green thumb, *n.* The ability to stimulate plant growth; a person who has this ability.

Greisen, grī'zen, *n.* Ger. A rock, found esp. in Saxony, composed of quartz and mica.

Gremlin, grem'lin, *n.* Etymol. uncertain. One of a race of mythical, spiteful creatures to whose machinations airmen's folklore attributes all unexpected trouble involving aircraft.

Grill*, *v.t.* (slang) To subject to harsh and intimidating questioning, esp. of suspected criminals.

Grilling, *n.* From Grill above and *-ing.* (slang) A severe questioning.

Grind*, *n.* (U.S. college slang) A student who studies a great deal.

Gripe*, *v.i.* (U.S. slang) To complain, whine; —*n.* a complaint. Cp. Bellyache, above.

Groove*, *n.* Phr. in the groove (slang): *Of swing music,* truly inspired; (by extension), of anyone following the right policy, etc.

Gross*, *adj. biol.* Able to be seen without the aid of a microscope.

Ground-controlled approach, *n.* A radar-operated system by which a person on the ground directs a pilot making a blind landing. Abbr.: G.C.A.

Ground crew, *n.* Mechanics, radiomen, and other specialists who service a plane before and after its flight.

Ground loop, *n. avn.* A sharp loop on the ground, when landing or taking off.

Ground sheet, *n.* A waterproof sheet used as the floor of a tent.

Growing, *adj.* Growing pains, difficulties encountered in any new undertaking.

G-string, *n. mus.* A string tuned to G; a breechcloth worn by certain primitive tribes.

Guayule, gwa-yōō'lā, *n.* Sp., from native name. A rubber-yielding shrub, *Parthenium argentatum,* growing in northern Mexico and the southwestern United States; the rubber produced by this plant.

Guided missile, *n.* A missile, such as a rocket or pilotless plane, directed by remote control, such as radio.

Guinea pig*, *n.* (colloq.) Any person or animal used as the subject of an experiment.

Gumshoe, *n.* From *gum* and *shoe.* A shoe made of rubber or other elastic substance. Specif.: a rubber overshoe; pl. sneakers; (U.S. slang) a detective; —*v.i.* to go softly, stealthily.

Gun*, *v.t.* To accelerate an engine by opening the throttle.

Guppy, *n.* From R. J. Lechmere Guppy, who gave specimens to the British Museum. A small minnow, *Lebistes reticulatus,* often kept in home aquaria.

Gutter*, *n.* One of the channels at either side of a bowling alley; *philately* the space left for perforation between stamps on a printed sheet; *printing* The inside margin of the page.

Gym, jim, *n.* (colloq.) Clipped form of gymnasium in the Dict.

Gynic, jin'ic, *adj.* From Gr. *gune,* woman. Pertaining to a female. Contrasted with Andric, above.

Gyrene, *n.* From *G.I.* and *marine.* (U.S. mil. slang) A member of the U.S. Marine Corps.

Gyromagnetic, jī'rō-mag-net'ik, *adj.* From *gyro-* and *magnetic. phys.* Pertaining to the magnetic properties of a rotating charged particle, esp. the electron.

Gyropilot, jī'rō-pī'lut, *n.* From *gyro*scope and *pilot. aeron.* The automatic pilot of an airplane, consisting of two gyroscopes arranged to keep the plane on a set course.

Gyrostabilizer, jī'rō-sta-bil-īz'er, *n.* From *gyro*scope and *stabilizer.* A gyroscopically controlled stabilizer, used to maintain the equilibrium of a ship or airplane.

Habanera, a-ba-nā'ra, *n.* Sp. of Habana. A Cuban dance of Spanish origin, in slow to moderate duple time; the music for this dance.

Habile, hab'il, *adj.* Fr., from Lat. *habilis,* fit, suitable. Skillful, adroit.

Hair-do, *n.* A woman's hair as arranged in any style.

Half-cocked, *adj.* See Half-Cock in the Dict. (colloq.), fig. Not fully ready. Phr. to go off half-cocked, to act rashly, without adequate preparation.

Half life, *n. phys.* and *chem.* The time taken by a given amount of a radioactive isotope to lose one half of its radioactivity, i.e. for one half of its atoms to disintegrate.

Half-pint, *n.* (U.S. slang) A short person.

Half sole, *n.* A shoe sole extending from the toe to the instep; —*v.t.* to put such a sole on a shoe.

Half-track, *n.* An army motor vehicle with tractor treads in place of rear wheels.

Halter*, *n.* The bodice of a woman's abbreviated costume, such as a swimming suit or play suit, tied with straps about the neck and across the back, so that the arms and back are exposed.

Ham*, *n.* Clipped form of hamfatter. (slang) A very poor actor, esp. one given to overacting emotional scenes; a licensed amateur radio operator; —*v.i.* (slang) to overact.

Hamburger, ham'ber-ger, *n.* From *hamburg* steak after the Ger. city and *-er.* The false etymology *ham* and *-burger,* has given rise to cheeseburger, muleburger, etc. A cake of ground or chopped beef, usually served on a roll.

Hand-me-down, *n.* (U.S. colloq.) A second-hand garment; one handed down; a cheap, ready-made garment.

Handout, *n.* (U.S. slang) A dole; something given free, as to a beggar.

Handset, *n.* A telephone mouthpiece and receiver joined in one piece.

Hangout, *n.* (U.S. slang) Any place frequently visited by a person or group.

Hang-over, *n.* (U.S. colloq.) A survival from a previous period, as a custom; unpleasant after-effects of drinking too much liquor.

Hansen's disease, *n.* After physician Armauer Hansen, who described the micro-organism which causes it, 1871. *med.* Leprosy.

Haploid, hap'loid, *adj.* From *haplo-* and *-oid.* Single; *biol.* having only one set of chromosomes, half of the diploid number.

Hard-boiled, *adj. of persons* Shrewd, hard-headed, exacting; of schemes, etc. practical, esp. in a financial sense.

Hard coal, *n.* Anthracite coal.

Hard currency, *n.* Currency easily converted into other currencies.

Hard sauce, *n.* A creamed mixture of butter and confectioners' sugar, often with flavoring and cream added, used on various desserts.

Hard-spun, *adj. of yarn.* Firmly twisted in spinning.

Harness*, *n. avn.* Combination of straps for attaching a parachute to the users; combination of straps for holding an occupant of a plane to his seat.

Hasenpfeffer, ha'zen-fef'er, *n.* Ger., from *hase,* hare and *pfeffer,* pepper. A highly seasoned rabbit stew.

Hash mark, *n* (U.S. mil. slang) A stripe sewn on the sleeve of a uniform, denoting a period of service.

Hatchet man, *n.* (obs.) A member of the Chinese settlement in a U.S. city who may be hired as an assassin; *fig.* a journalist or demagogue who specializes in aggressive and ruthless attempts to besmirch the character of his opponent.

Haulaway, *n.* A large truck trailer used for transporting automobiles.

Hay*, *n.* To hit the hay (slang) retire to bed.

Haymaker, *n. boxing* A blow powerful enough to cause a knockout.

Haymow, *n.* A place, as the loft of a barn, where hay is stored.

Haywire, hā'wīr', *n.* Wire used to bind hay, straw, etc. into bales. —*adj.*; (slang) tangled, out of order; usually in phr. to go haywire, become disordered, tangled.

From action of haywire when a bale is cut open; (slang) crazy, mad.
H-bomb, *n.* (colloq.) A hydrogen bomb, one utilizing for destructive effects the energy released by the fusion of hydrogen nuclei.
Headcheese, hed'chēz', *n.* (U.S.) A cooked preparation of cut-up meat from the head and feet of hogs.
Headliner, *n. theatr.* (slang) A principal performer; one whose name heads the bill; journalism one who writes headlines for newspapers, etc.
Headlock, *n.* From *head* and *lock. wrestling* A hold in which the head of one wrestler is locked in the arm or arms of his opponent.
Head resistance, *n.* Air resistance of an airplane which does not aid in its support; dead resistance.
Headset, *n. radio* A set of headphones.
Headway*, *n.* The time interval between two trains traveling over the same route.
Heartland, *n.* From *heart* and *land. In geopolitics,* a self-sufficient, dominating land area.
Heat*, *n.* (slang) Period of ardent law enforcement: the heat's on; (slang) coercion; phr. to turn on the heat, to coerce, intimidate.
Heatronic, hē-tron'ic, *adj.* From *heat* and elec*tronic.* Pertaining to a method of uniform heating by the application of high-frequency radio waves.
Heavy*, *n. movie* (slang.) An actor usually cast as the villain, or in some other unpopular role.
Heavy cruiser, *n. naval* A cruiser mounting guns of more than 6.1″ caliber.
Heavy-duty, *adj.* Able to stand unusual wear, strain, and exposure; subject to a high tariff rate.
Heavy hydrogen, *n. phys.* One of the heavy isotopes of hydrogen, deuterium or tritium.
Heavy water, *n.* Water in which the ordinary hydrogen is replaced by deuterium. Formula: D_2O.
Heavyweight*, *n.* (colloq.) Person very influential in any field of endeavor.
Hebephrenia, hē'be-fren'ia, *n.* From Gr. *hebe,* youth and *-phrenia,* combining form from Gr. *phren,* mind. A type of dementia praecox schizophrenia, characterized by almost complete withdrawal from reality, delusions concerning omniscience and omnipotence, and feelings of cosmic identification.
Hedgehog*, *n. mil.* A position strongly furnished with both active and passive means of defense.
Heeby-jeebies, hē-be jē'bez, *n.* pl. Etymol. unknown. (slang) orig. U.S. State of alarm and trepidation.
Heel*, *n.* (slang) A contemptible person.
Heldentenor, hel'den-te-nor', *n.* Ger. hero tenor. A tenor suited to heroic or other dramatic roles.
Helmet*, *n.* Protective head covering, usually of leather, worn in certain sports such as U.S. football.
He-man, *n. he* and *man* pleonastic emphasis. (slang) orig. U.S. A sturdy and virile man.
Hematology, Haematology, *n.* From *haemal* and *-ology med.* The scientific study of the blood.
Hematosis, Haematosis*, *n.* From Gr. *haimatosis,* from *haimatoun,* to make into blood. *physiol.* The purification of blood in the lungs.
Hep*, *adj.* Origin unknown. (U.S. slang) Well informed, having thorough knowledge; usually followed by *to.*
Hepcat, *n.* From *hep,* above, and *cat.* (U.S. slang) *swing music* A swing musician or an ardent admirer of swing music.
Herrenvolk, her'en-folk, *n.* Ger. From *herren,* masters and *volk,* people. The master-race. Specif., in Nazi ideology, the Germans.
Het up, *adj.* P.P. of *heat* and *up.* (slang) orig. U.S. Emotionally disturbed, agitated; esp. annoyed: all het up, thoroughly so.
Hex, *n.* From Ger. *hexe,* witch. (U.S. dial.) A witch; a witch's spell or curse; —*v.t.* to practice witchcraft on; to put under a spell.
H-hour, *n.* From *H* for hour; hence this is a type of reduplication. *mil.* The scheduled hour for the start of an attack on the enemy.
Hideout, hīd'owt', *n.* (criminal slang) A place where one may safely hide from the police.
Highball*, *n. R.R.* A signal permitting full speed; a fast train especially a freight; —*v.i.* to go or work at high speed.
High-fidelity, hī'fī-del'i-ti, *adj. electronics* Reproducing sound, esp. the highest and lowest frequencies, with relatively little distortion: high-fidelity amplifier, etc. Also abbrev. hi-fi.
High-hat*, *n.* From the high hat seen as a symbol of aristocracy or wealth. (U.S. slang.) —*adj.,* Snobbish, supercilious.
Highjack, *n.* and *v.t.* Variant spelling of hijack, below.
High jinks, *n.* pl. See Jinks in the Dict.
Highlight, *v.t.* Usually fig. To give prominence to, emphasize. —*n.* A prominent or striking part.
High-tail, *v.i.* (colloq.) To move rapidly; esp. to leave quickly, flee.
High tea, *n.* (Brit.) Light meal, taken in the afternoon or early evening, at which tea is drunk.
High-test, *adj.* of gasoline. Having a low boiling point.
Hijack, hī'jak, *v.t.* To steal illegal liquor shipments; (by extension) to steal any goods in transit, on a large scale and usually with the threat of force.
Hiker, hīk'er, *n.* From *hike* and *-er.* (colloq.) One who hikes, or is hiking.
Hip*, *v.t.* (U.S. sports slang) To hinder an opponent illegally by bumping him with one's hip, as in ice hockey.
Hispanic, his-pan'ic, *adj.* From Lat. *Hispania,* ancient name of the Spanish peninsula including Portugal; Spanish.
Hispanidad, ēs'pan-ē-thath', *n.* From Sp. See Hispanic, above. A movement emphasizing the unity of Spanish culture and the goal of Spanish control of Latin America.
Histaminase, *n.* See Histamine, below. *biochem.* An enzyme which inactivates histamine.
Histamine, his'ta-mēn, *n.* From *histo-* and *amine* in the Dict. An allergy-provoking by-product of proteins.
Hit*, *v.t.* Phr. hit the ceiling or roof, become very angry. Phr. hit the dirt: *In baseball,* to slide into a base; to dodge or duck something by falling to the ground.
Hit-and-run, *adj. baseball* Pertaining to a play in which a base runner starts for the next base on a certain pitch which the batter has been instructed to swing at; pertaining to an automobile accident in which the driver flees the scene; pertaining to the driver of the automobile.
Hitlerism, *n.* From *Hitler* and *-ism.* See Nazism, in the Dict.
Hock shop, *n.* (U.S. slang) Pawn-shop.
—Hog*, element of abuse in slang compounds: road-hog, speed-hog, *n.,* one who selfishly and regardlessly drives a car at high speed.
Hokum, hocum*, *n.* From *hocus-pocus* and *bunkum.* (slang) Stale, outworn conventional situations and recipes for a plot, etc., in plays, novels, and the like.
Holding company, *n. finance* A company formed to hold stocks in other companies.
Holdover, *n.* (U.S. colloq.) Something remaining from a previous period; a person who remains in office longer than his colleagues, as in the U.S. Senate, where ⅔ of the members are holdovers in any election year.
Holmium, *n.* From *Stockholm,* Sweden. A metallic element of the rare-earth group. Atomic weight: 164.94 Atomic no.: 67 Symbol: *Ho.*
Home*, *v.i.* To return to one's home. —*v.t.* To send to or provide with a home.
Homeostasis, hō'mē-ō-stā'sis, *n.* From Gr. *homos,* same and *stasis. physiol.* The maintenance of relatively stable conditions by a living organism, through mechanisms compensating for disturbances; the similar process in a social group.
Home stretch*, *n.* The last portion of any race course; the last portion of any process or operation.
Homogenate, hō-moj'e-nāt, *n.* From Homogenize, below, and *-ate* in the Dict. That which has been homogenized.
Homogenize, ho-moj'en-īz, *v.t.* From *homogenous* and *-ize.* To make homogenous by mixing and emulsifying: homogenized milk.
Honky-tonk, hongk'i-tongk', *n.* Origin uncert. (U.S. slang) A low, cheap place for drinking and dancing.
Hood*, *n.* The covering over an automobile engine; (local U.S. slang) Short form of hoodlum in the Dict.
Hoofer, *n.* From *hoof* and *-er.* (slang) A professional dancer, as in a night club.
Hook*, *n. baseball* A curve.
Hookup, *n.* An arrangement of apparatus for a particular purpose, such as a special radio hookup for a presidential speech; (colloq.) an alliance or connection, as a hookup between former enemies.
Hooky, *n.* Always in Phr. to play hooky, to absent oneself from school without permission, to play truant.
Hoopla, *n.* From *hoop.* A game at a carnival in which prizes are won by tossing rings over them.
Hooverville, hoo'ver-vil, *n.* Named after President Herbert Hoover. (U.S. colloq.) Any group of dilapidated shacks in which the unemployed lived during the depression of the 1930's.
Horizon*, *n.* A distinct soil layer.
Horn*, *v.i.* Horn in, (colloq.) orig. U.S. to intrude, interfere, butt in.
Hornswoggle, horn'swog'l, *v.t.* Etymol. unknown. (U.S. slang) To bamboozle; to cheat, swindle.
Horse opera, *n.* (U.S. slang) Any movie based on outdoor action, especially one dealing with frontier conditions in the Western U.S.
Horse trade, *n.* A trade of horses; any agreement, esp. political, arrived at by negotiation and mutual compromise.
Hospitalize, hos'pit-l-īz, *v.t.* From *hospital* and *-ize.* To place in a hospital for treatment. —**Hospitalization,** *n.*
Hostel*, *n.* Lodging place for young people who are hiking or traveling by bicycle.
Hot*, *adj. mus.* Having a stimulating jazz rhythm; (slang) orig. U.S. Dangerous because wanted by the law, as a fugitive, a stolen car, or counterfeit money; charged with electricity; contaminated with radio-activity.
Hot air, *n.* Boastful exaggeration or lying; baloney.
Hotbox, *n.* A journal box which has over-heated due to friction.
Hot plate, *n.* A portable gas or electric appliance for cooking; a dish of warm food.
Hot-rod, *n.* An automobile, stripped of extra weight and provided with extra power, used by adolescents as a source of thrills.
Houdry process, *n.* From engineer E. Houdry, its discoverer. A method of cracking gas, oil in order to produce high-octane gasoline.
Hound*, *n.* In compounds, (U.S. slang) an uncomplimentary term for one who habitually hunts after a certain thing: news-hound, hunter after newspaper 'copy'; publicity hound, one who is always trying to get himself into the news; smut-hound, self-appointed investigator and censor of public morals; sin-hound.
House coat, *n.* A woman's loose long outer garment, worn instead of a dress while at home.
House detective, *n.* Resident private detective employed by a hotel. Also (slang) house dick.
House dress, *n.* A dress more loosely fitting, less well made, and cheaper than a dress for street wear, worn while working in the house or yard.
House physician, *n.* A resident physician in a hospital or other public institution.
Huckster*, *n.* (U.S. colloq.) An advertising broker, especially one handling radio advertising.
Huddle*, *n.* Any secret conference.
Hula, hoo'la, *n. Hawaiian.* A pantomimic Hawaiian dance, emphasizing movements of the torso. Also hula-hula.
Hump*, *n. railroad.* The elevated structure

in a freight yard, used for sorting cars into trains; the most difficult, crucial stage of a process; esp. in phr. over the hump, past this stage; The Hump, the Himalaya Mountains (World War II avn. slang.)

Hundred-percenter, *n.* A fervent patriot, jingoist esp. of an American.

Hush-hush, *adj.* (colloq.) Kept secret and so sometimes intentionally rather mysterious.

Hutment, *n.* From *hut* and *-ment. mil.* A camp of huts.

Hydrobomb, hī'drō-bom, *n.* From *hydro-* and *bomb.* A self-propelled torpedo, dropped into the water from an airplane.

Hydrofoil, *n.* From *hydro-* and *foil.* A streamlined fin designed to guide water craft.

Hydrogenate, hī-dro'jen-āt, *v.t.* See HYDROGENIZE in the Dict. *chem.* To treat or combine with hydrogen.

Hydrogen bomb, *n.* A bomb depending for its destructive effect on the energy released by the fusion of hydrogen nuclei. Also (colloq.) H-bomb.

Hydromechanics, hī'dro-me-kan'iks, *n.* From HYDRO and *mechanics.* The study of the principles of equilibrium and motion in fluids; hydrostatics and hydrokinetics.

Hydroponics, hī'dro-pon'iks, *n.* From *hydro-* and Gr. *pónos,* labor. Soilless gardening or agriculture, using tanks of chemical solution as the media in which plants are grown.

Hypersonic, hī'per-son'ik, *adj.* From HYPER and SONIC, below. Having a speed greater than five times the speed of sound.

Hypertension, hī'per-ten'shun, *n.* From *hyper-*and *tension. med.* Abnormally high blood pressure; the arterial condition involving this symptom.

Hypertensive, hī-per-ten'siv, *adj.* From *hyper-* and *tensive.* Of or characterized by high blood pressure. —*n.* A person who has high blood pressure.

Hypnoanalysis, hip'nō-a-nal'i-sis, *n.* From *hypno-* and *analysis. psychiat.* The use of hypnosis to facilitate the securing of data from psychoanalytic patients.

Hypnotherapy, *n.* From *hypno-* and *therapy. med.* The treatment of disease by the use of hypnotism.

Hypoplasia, hī'po-plā'zhi-a, *n.* From *hypo-* and *plasma* and *-ia. anat.* Underdeveloped condition of any part of an organism.

Hypospray, hī'pō-sprā', *n.* From *hypo-* and *spray.* An airgun used to inject drugs hypodermically without breaking the skin.

Ice, *n.* (slang) jewelry.

Icebox, īs'boks, *n.* A box with a compartment in which ice is placed, for preserving food; a box which produces its own ice, as by electrical means, used for preserving food.

Icebreaker*, *n.* A structure for protection against floating ice.

Iceman, *n.* (U.S.) One who manufactures or delivers ice.

Ice needle, *n. meteor.* A slender particle of ice floating in the air on clear, cold days.

Iconoscope, ī-kon'ō-skōp, *n. trade-mark* A cathode-ray tube which converts optical images into electrical impulses for television transmission.

Id*, *n. psychoanal.* The part of the unconscious psyche which is the source of instinctive energy.

Idiosyncrasy*, *n. med.* Individual hypersensitivity to drugs.

Iffy, *adj.* lit. 'full of ifs'. (colloq.) Highly debatable or uncertain. Also iffish.

Igloo, *n.* A type of mound shelter, resembling an igloo, used for storing ammunition.

Illiquid, il-lik'wid, *adj.* From *il-* and *liquid. finance* Of assets not liquid, i.e., not readily convertible into cash.

Imagist, im'ij-ist, *n.* See IMAGE. One of a school of early 20th-century poets emphasizing use of precise imagery and freedom from conventional metrical forms. **—Imagism,** *n.*

Imago*, *n. psychoanal.* A childhood image of a person, usually a parent, formed and retained in the unconscious.

Immelmann turn, im'el-man, *n.* From Ger. aviator Max Immelmann. *avn.* A maneuver in which an airplane changes its direction 180° and at the same time gains altitude by means of a half loop, which is followed by a roll to level position.

Immunology, im'ū-nol'ō-ji, *n.* From *immune* and *-logy.* The study of immunity from disease, infection, etc., and the conditions governing it.

Implant*, *n. med.* That which is implanted in the body, as a tube of radio-active substance for the treatment of cancer.

Impreg, *n.* From IMPREGNATE. A type of plywood impregnated with a resin to increase its durability and weather resistance.

Inactivate, in-ak'tiv-āt, *v.t.* From *inactive* and *-ate.* To render inactive, as a mine; *biol.* to destroy the usefulness of, as of a serum by heat.

Incendiary*, *n.* An incendiary bomb.

Incentive pay or **wage,** *n.* Extra pay according to a system by which production over a certain fixed standard is rewarded.

Incident*, *n.* An encounter, usually on a small scale, between the armed forces of two countries unwilling to declare open war.

Incommunicado, in'ko-mū'ni-ka'dō, *adj.* From Sp. *incommunicado,* without communication. Deprived of means of communication, esp. of a prisoner.

Indian-giver, *n.* (U.S. colloq.) A person who, having given a thing, demands its return.

Indian pudding, *n.* A pudding composed chiefly of corn meal.

Indicator*, *n. chem.* A compound which by means of a change in color indicates a chemical change.

Induct*, *v.t.* (U.S.) To enroll in the armed forces.

Inductee, *n.* From *induct* and *-ee.* Anyone inducted into the armed forces.

Induction heating or **Inductive heating,** *n.* Heating produced by induced electric currents.

Industrial union, *n.* A union whose members all work in the same type of industry, generally one employing mass-production technology.

Infestant, in-fes'tant, *n.* From *infest* and *-ant.* Any organism that attacks fabrics or preserved foods.

Infiltration*, *n. mil.* Operation against enemy lines by advancing troops through relatively undefended areas with a minimum of outright combat; (by extension) any similar attempt to quietly take over and exploit for one's own purposes an organization designed for something else, as a political group's infiltration of a labor union.

Inflationary, in-flā'shun-er'i, *adj.* From *inflation* and *-ary.* Of, pertaining to, tending to produce inflation: inflationary prices, spiral, etc.

Informant*, *n.* A person interviewed for the purpose of obtaining information bearing on the topic of research; esp. a native speaker supplying material for linguistic analysis.

Inhalant*, *adj.* From *inhale* and *-ant.* Used for inhaling. —*n.* An inhaler, device for inhaling; the drug inhaled.

Initiative*, *n.* A procedure by which legislation may be introduced or enacted by direct popular vote.

In-migrate, in-mī'grāt, *v.i.* From *in-* and *migrate.* To move to a new community within a country, esp. as a result of the community's industrial growth. **—In-migration,** *n.*

Instar, *v.t.* From *in-* and *star.* To place as a star; to make into a star; to adorn or set with stars.

Institution*, *n.* Euphemism for a mental hospital.

Institutional*, *adj. advertising jargon* of advertising. Intended to create a favorable impression of a company rather than to sell specific products.

Institutionalism, in'sti-tū'shun-al-izm, *n.* From *institutional* and *-ism.* Belief in the positive value of established institutions, such as the family.

Institutionalize, in'sti-tu'shun-al-īz, *v.t.* From *institutional* and *-ize.* To transform into the nature of an institution; (euphemism) to commit to a mental hospital, home for the senile, etc.

Integration*, *n. psychol.* The co-ordination of the structures and functions of the psyche into a well-organized, integrated personality.

Intelligence quotient, *n.* A number indicating the comparative intelligence of a person, obtained by dividing his mental age by his actual age and multiplying the result by 100. Abbr.: IQ.

Intercept*, *n. math.* A part of a line that is intercepted.

Interceptor, *n.* From *intercept* and *-or.* A heavily armed fighter plane, capable of rapid ascent and designed for use against enemy aircraft.

Intercom, *n.* Short form of intercommunication. *mil. slang.* A telephone system designed for carrying messages over very short distances, as in an airplane or office.

International*, *n.* Fourth International, a revolutionary Marxist organization opposed to the Stalinist regime, founded in 1936 by Leon Trotsky.

Internationale, *n.* Fr. See INTERNATIONAL. A song originating in France in 1871 and since used by revolutionary workers' movements.

Interphone, *n.* Same as INTERCOM, above.

Interventionism, in'ter-ven'shun-izm, *n.* From *intervention* and *-ism.* A political policy of intercession or interference in the affairs of another country esp. as applied to U.S. foreign policy.

Intocostrin, in-tō-kos'trin, *n. trade-mark* A purified and standardized extract of curare, used in control of spastic conditions.

Introjection, in-trō-jek'shun, *n.* From *intro-* and Lat. *jactus,* P.P. of *jacere,* to throw, cast and *-ion. psychoanal.* The incorporation into one's ego of the image of an object or other person, and the transfer of psychic energy from the object to its image. **—Introject,** *v.t.* and *i.*

Inviability, *n.* From *in-* and *viability.* Condition of being unable to live; said esp. of a child whose constitution dooms it to certain death.

In vitro, in-vē'trō, *adj.* Lat. In glass; i.e., in a test tube or beaker, Cp. IN VIVO, below.

In vivo, in-vē'vō, *adj.* Lat. In a living organism. Cp. IN VITRO, above.

Ionone, ī'on-ōn, *n.* From Gr. *ion,* violet and *ketone.* Either of two unsaturated ketones, $C_{13}H_{20}O$, having a violet scent and used in the manufacture of perfumes.

Ionosphere, ī-on'o-sfēr', *n.* From *ion* and *sphere.* The ionized region of air above the earth, consisting of several layers, from which radio waves are reflected; the heaviside layer. **—Ionospheric,** *adj.*

IQ or **I.Q.,** abbr. Intelligence quotient, above.

Iron*, *v.t.* Phr. to iron out, to set in order, make something function smoothly.

Ironclad, *adj.* (colloq.) Rigorous, having no loopholes: ironclad contract.

Iron curtain, *n.* Coined by novelist H. G. Wells in 1904, but popularized by Winston Churchill in 1946. Any privacy enforced by a rigid system of censorship and secrecy; specif., the system thus setting off Russia and her satellites.

Iron lung, *n.* A pressure chamber surrounding a patient's chest, used to produce artificial respiration, esp. in cases of infantile paralysis.

Iron rations, *n. mil.* An emergency food ration, in small and nourishing, but unappetizing, portions.

—Ish, *adv.* suff. of time, (colloq.) Approximately: 4:30–ish.

Ishihara test, ish'i-ha'ra, *n.* From Japanese opthalmologist S. Ishihara. A test for the determination of color blindness.

Island*, *n.* The superstructure of an aircraft carrier; a raised safety zone in the middle of a street.

Isobar*, *n. chem.* One of two atoms having the same atomic weights but different atomic numbers.

Isobaric*, *adj.* From *isobar* and *-ic.* Of or pertaining to isobars.

Isoelectronic, ī'sō-e-lek'trik, *adj.* From *iso-* and *electronic. phys.* Having the same number of electrons outside the nucleus.

Isogloss, ī'sō-glos, *n.* From *iso-* and Gr. *glossa,* tongue, speech. A heuristic device consisting of a line, drawn on a map, which delimits with more or less accuracy the area in which a speech form is used.

Isogram, *n.* From *iso-* and *-gram.* A line on a map or chart drawn through places which are equal with respect to a certain variable, such as temperature.

Isolating language, *n.* A language characterized by a lack of bound forms.

Isolationism, *n.* From *isolation* and *-ism.* A national policy of avoiding participation in international affairs.

Isolationist, *n.* From *isolation* and *-ist.* One who advocates or adopts a policy of isolationism. Often attrib.: isolationist sentiments.

Isoleucine, ī'sō-lū'sēn, *n.* From *iso-* and *leuco-* and *-ine.* One of the amino acids, $C_6H_{13}NO_2$, which are essential for human nutrition.

Isomer, ī'sō-mer, *n.* From ISOMERIC, below. *chem.* and *phys.* A substance which is isomeric with one or more other substances.

Isomeric*, *adj.* From *iso-* and Gr. *méros,* part and *-ic. phys.* Having the same atomic weight and atomic number, but differing in energy content.

Isomerism, ī-sŏ'mer-izm, *n.* From *isomer* and *-ism. chem.* State or condition of being isomeric.

Isomerous*, *adj.* From *iso-* and Gr. *méros,* part and *-ous.* Having the same number of parts, markings, etc.

Isostasy, ī-sos'ta-si, *n.* From *iso-* and *stasis. geol.* The hypothesis that between the land or water surface and the center of the earth there is the same amount of matter under every unit of surface area.

Isostatic, ī'sō-stat'ik, *adj.* See ISOSTASY, above. Of or characterized by isostasy.

Isotope, ī'sō-tōp, *n.* From *iso-* and Gr. *tópos,* place. *chem.* and *phys.* Any of two or more forms of one element, having the same atomic number but different atomic weights. **-Isotopic,** *adj.*

Isotropic*, *adj.* From *iso-* and Gr. *trópos,* turn, direction. *biol.* Not having axes which are predetermined, as some eggs.

Issei, ēs-sā, *n.* Jap. first generation. A Japanese born in Japan, residing in the U.S., but ineligible for citizenship.

Ivory tower, *n.* Transl. of Fr. *tour d'ivoire,* coined in poem by Sainte-Beuve, 1837. An intellectual retreat. Also used attrib. in sense of unrealistic or impractical: ivory tower attitudes.

Ivy League, *n.* (U.S. colloq.) A group of eastern U.S. universities with relatively long traditions and high social prestige, esp. as referring to their intercollegiate athletic relationships. Also attrib. Ivy League school, student.

Ivy Leaguer, *n.* See IVY LEAGUE, above, and *-er.* (U.S. colloq.) A student, esp. an athlete, at one of the schools of the Ivy League.

Jack*, *v.t.* (colloq.) Usually jack up, to increase prices, wages, etc.; *n.* (slang) money.

Jack-in-the-pulpit, *n.* (U.S) A North American herb, *Arisaema atrorubens,* distinguished by an upright spadix with a spathe arching over it.

Jackpot*, *n.* (by extension) Any large sum of money. Phr. to hit the jackpot, to win a large sum of money, esp. from a slot machine.

Jacksonian, jak-sōn'i-an, *adj.* Of or pertaining to Andrew Jackson. —*n.* A supporter or disciple of Andrew Jackson.

Jalopy, *n.* Origin uncert. (U.S. colloq.) An old or battered automobile.

Jam*, *v.t. radio.* To prevent the reception of a broadcast from station usually an enemy station by broadcasting on the same frequency.

Jam session, *n. jazz music.* An experimental or unrehearsed performance of jazz musicians, characterized esp. by free improvisation. —**jam,** *v.i.* To play in this fashion.

Jam-pack, *v.t.* From *jam* and *pack.* To crowd together, cram: the crowd jampacked the theater.

Jato, jā'to, *n.* acronym of jet-assisted takeoff. The use of rockets attached to the wing to enable a plane to gain flying speed after a short take-off run.

Jaw-breaker, *n.* (slang) A piece of hard candy.

Jazz, *v.* and *n.* Etymol. uncert.; word first used by Louisiana Negroes, and perhaps of African origin. *n.* (by extension) the Afro-American music played in New Orleans; loosely, any of several types of popular or nonclassical music, esp. if characterized by rapid tempo.

Jazzy, *adj. jazz* and -y. (slang) Pertaining to or like jazz music; lively, full of vigor and energy.

Jeep, jēp', *n.* From pronunciation of G.P. for general purpose as influenced by jeep, a word used in E. C. Segar's comic strip "Popeye." A light, durable, and highly maneuverable military automobile.

Jell, *v.i.* back formation from *jelly.* (colloq.) To turn into jelly; (colloq.) *fig.* to become settled, well-defined: the negotiations have jelled.

Jerk*, *n.* (slang) A stupid, naive, or clumsy person.

Jerk*, *v.t.* To prepare and serve sodas.

Jerkwater, *n.* From *jerk* and *water.* (colloq.) A train on a branch line of a railroad. Now most commonly used attrib., meaning 'minor' or 'rural and unsophisticated': jerkwater town.

Jerry, *n.* From Ger. (slang, chiefly Brit.) A German or the Germans collectively. Also capitalized.

Jet*, *n.* Short for jet engine or jet plane.

Jet engine, *n.* An engine operated by jet propulsion.

Jet plane, *n.* A plane moved by jet propulsion.

Jet propulsion, *n.* A type of propulsion utilizing the rearward thrush of gases formed when fuel is sucked into an engine, heated, and partially compressed. —**Jet-propelled,** *adj.*

Jig*, *n. mach.* A device to guide a tool, esp. a drill; a device for separating ores by agitation in water; (slang) Phr. the jig's up, the situation is hopeless.

Jigger*, *n.* origin U. S. Any appliance or mechanical device; a contraption; a 1½ ounce measure for alcoholic beverages.

Jigsaw puzzle, *n.* A puzzle made by cutting a picture into irregular pieces with a jigsaw.

Jim Crow, *n.* The institutionalized segregation of, and discrimination against, the Negro race, esp. as practised in the southern U.S.

Jimmy, *n.* From Jimmy, familiar form of James. Burglar's crowbar. —*v.t.* To force open a locked door or window by use of a jimmy.

Jimson weed, *n.* From Jamestown, Va. A poisonous, foul-smelling weed, *Datura stramonium,* having large white flowers.

Jitterbug, *n.* From *jitter* and *bug.* —*v.i.* to dance wildly.

Jittery, *adj.* From *jitter,* and *-y.* (U.S. slang) Nervous, fearful.

Job*, *n.* Phr. on the job, busily at work; (slang) a criminal act: to pull a job, commit a crime; (slang) any manufactured article, as an automobile. Usually qualified by an adjective: nice job, custom job, etc.

Job holder, *n.* A public office holder, esp. an employee of the federal government.

Judge advocate, *n. U.S. mil.* The prosecuting officer at a trial by court-martial.

Juke box, jōōk, *n.* The term juke is of West African origin. (U.S. colloq.) An automatic, coin-operated record player usually found in taverns.

Juke joint, *n.* See JUKE BOX, above.(U.S. slang) A cheap, rowdy drinking resort. Also jook joint.

Jump bid, *n. bridge* Any bid more than necessary to overcall the previous bid.

Jump pass, *n. football* A forward pass, usually short, thrown to a designated spot as the passer jumps into the air.

Juncture*, *n. linguistics.* The phenomena characterizing the linkages between the segments of an utterance.

Jungle*, *n.* (U.S. slang) A hobo camp, usually found near railroads.

Jungle rot, *n.* Any of several tropical skin diseases; any of several tropical fungi attacking clothes or equipment.

Junk*, *n. cant.* Dope, narcotics.

Junk*, *v.t.* (slang) To discard as useless.

Junkie or **Junker,** *n.* From JUNK, above. *cant* A dope peddler.

Juvenile*, *n. theater.* An actor of youthful roles.

Kamerad, *n.* Ger. Comrade; used to indicate surrender.

Kamikaze, ka'mi-ka'zē, *n.* Jap. divine wind. The pilot of a suicidal attack, esp. against a ship, in which he deliberately crashes a bomb-laden plane into a target; the plane involved in a suicidal attack.

Kangaroo court, *n.* (U.S. colloq.) An unauthorized or irregular court in which principles of justice and legal procedure are flagrantly violated.

Kaputt or **Kaput,** ka-poot', *adj.* Ger. Ruined, spoiled, done for.

Kasbah or **Casbah,** kaz'ba, *n. Ar.* fortress. The native section of a city in North Africa; specif., the native section of Algiers.

Kayo, *n.* From respelling of abbr. K.O. for knockout; (slang) Knockout.

Kegler, *n.* Ger. (colloq.) A bowler.

Kenny method, *n.* A technique of treating poliomyelitis by massage, etc., developed by Sister Elizabeth Kenny, an Australian nurse.

Keno, kē'nō, *n.* See FIVE in the Dict. A form of lotto, closely resembling bingo, used for small-scale gambling.

Kewpie, kū'pē, *n.* From *cupid. trade-mark.* A doll representing a very fat baby.

Keynoter, *n.* From *keynote* and *-er.* One who announces the essential policy of a political party, esp. with respect to a particular campaign.

Kibei, kē'bā, *n. Jap.* A native-born American of Japanese ancestry who has received all or part of his education in Japan.

Kibitz, kib'itz, *v.i.* See KIBITZER, in the Dict. (colloq.) To act as a kibitzer.

Kick*, *n.* Phr. to get a kick out of something, to find it stimulating, amusing, enjoyable.

Kickback, *n.* (colloq.) A violent response or reaction; (slang) a rebate or return of a part of money received, usually under pressure but sometimes by free agreement: the company gives a kickback to its biggest customers, the workers give a kickback to the foreman, etc.; a forced contribution from a public office holder to a political machine.

Kickoff, *n. football* A method of commencing play by kicking the ball from a point on or behind the kicking team's 40-yard line; slang, *fig.* the start of anything.

Kilter, *n.* Origin uncertain. (U.S. dial.) Order, good condition usually in Phr. out of kilter, out of order.

Kinescope, kin'e-skōp, *n.* See *kin-* and *-scope. trade-mark.* A cathode-ray tube, used in television receivers to convert electrical values into light values and having a luminescent screen on which the image is produced.

Kingpin*, *n.* A kingbolt.

King's English, *n. fig.* Perfectly correct English usage.

King snake, *n.* A large harmless snake, *Lampropeltus getulus,* inhabiting the southern U.S.

Kit*, *n.* (colloq.) Any collection or group of things or persons.

Kitchen police, *n. mil.* Work assisting the cooks; men assigned to this work. Abbr., K.P.

Kiva, kē'va, *n. Hopi.* An underground chamber used by the Pueblo Indians for religious ceremonies.

Kleenex, *n. trade-mark.* A soft facial tissue also used as a handkerchief.

Klieg light, klēg, *n.* From Kliegl brothers, the inventors. An arc light used in taking motion pictures.

Klister, klis'ter, *n. N.* A soft wax used on skis.

Klystron, klis'tron, *n.* From Gr. *kluster,* syringe and *electron.* A device which generates ultrahigh frequency current by operating on a continuous stream of electrons with electric field so as to segregate the electrons into discrete bunches.

Knee-high, *adj.* Phr. knee-high to a grasshopper, of a very short child.

Knockout drops, *n.* pl. (U.S. colloq.) A drug, esp. chloral hydrate, producing stupor or unconsciousness; the essential ingredient of a Mickey Finn.

Know-how, *n.* Proficiency and expert knowledge in a particular field of endeavor.

Know-nothing, *n.* An ignoramus; an agnostic; *caps.* member of a secret political party (American party), fl. 1853-1856, whose chief aim was to restrict the political power of immigrants.

Knuckle ball, *n. baseball.* A slow pitched ball, gripped with the knuckles instead of the finger tips. Also Knuckler.

K.O., abbr. Knockout.

Koine, koi'nē, *n.* From Gr. *koine(diálektos,)* common language. The type of Greek language common in the Roman period and used in the New Testament.

Kolkhos, kŏl-kōz', *n. Russ.*, abbr. of *kollektivii*, collective and *khos*, base of *khozyaistvo*, household, etc. *U.S.S.R.* Collective farm organized, esp. under Five-Year Plan, by pooling of peasant holdings.

Komintern, *n.* See COMINTERN, above.

Koroseal, *n. trade-mark.* A plastic used in various manufactured articles as a substitute for rubber or leather.

Kosher*, *adj.* (slang) (By extension) anything legitimate, genuine, ethically correct.

K ration, *n. U.S. Army.* A type of emergency ration for individual soldiers.

Kulak, k(y)ōō'lak, *n.* Russ. fist, grasper. *U.S.S.R.* Rich peasant or farmer, esp. one considered as anti-Bolshevik and an exploiter of labor.

Kyack, kī'ak, *n.* Origin unknown. Western U.S. A packsack hung on either side of a packsaddle.

Lab, *n.* Orig. an abbreviation spelled, now a clipped form pronounced. (U.S. colloq.) Laboratory.

Laborite*, *n.* From *labor* and *-ite.* Member or supporter of a party representing the interests of labor; specif., member or supporter of the British Labour Party.

Lactoflavin, lak'tō-flā'vin, *n.* See LACTEAL and FLAVIN in the Dict. Riboflavin.

Lagniappe*, län-yäp', *n.* By extension, anything given in addition to merchandise paid for during a transaction.

Lagomorph, lag'ō-morf, *n.* From Gr. *lagos*, hare and *-morph*, below. *zool.* Any of the order *Lagomorpha*, rodent-like mammals having two pairs of upper incisors, including rabbits, hares, and pikas.

Lam, *v.i.* (slang) To run away, esp. from the police. —*n.* To beat soundly; Phr. on the lam, fleeing from the police; take it on the lam, to flee.

Lambaste, *v.t.* LAM above and BASTE. (slang) To beat severely.

Lame*, *adj.* (U.S. slang) Lame duck, a legislator who has been defeated for reelection and is nearing the end of his term.

Laminate*, *v.t.* To make by fusing or binding several layers together: laminated wood.

Land mine, *n.* An excavation filled with an explosive charge to destroy personnel, equipment, or defenses.

Landing craft, *n. mil.* Any of several types of ships especially designed to put ashore troops and equipment under enemy fire.

Landing field, *n.* An airfield, an airport, an air station; any place where an airplane lands.

Landing party, *n.* A detachment of soldiers, marines or sailors sent ashore for a specific task.

Landing strip, *n.* A hard surfaced runway for the take-off and landing of airplanes; a portable runway constructed of linked steel mats.

Land-office business, *n.* (U.S. colloq.) A heavy, rapid business.

Landsman*, *n.* From *land* and *man. naut.* A sailor on his first voyage; an inexperienced sailor, rated below an ordinary seaman.

Langlauf, *n.* Ger. long course. Skiing, esp. in a race, cross-country.

Lanital, lan'i-tal, *n.* From Ital. *lana* wool and *Italia*, Italy. A substance derived from casein, resembling wool in its physical and chemical properties.

Laryngectomy, lar'inj-ek'tō-mē, *n.* See LARYNX, in the Dict., and *-ectomy*, above. Surgical removal of the larynx.

Lastex, *n. trade-mark* An elastic yarn made by winding textile threads around a latex core.

Lateral*, *adj. football.* Lateral pass, one thrown backwards approximately parallel to the goal-line; a pass thrown in any direction other than toward an opponent's goal line.

Latitude*, *n. photog.* The range of exposure time within which a film will produce a satisfactory image.

Launcher, *n.* From *launch* and *-er.* One who or that which launches. Specif., *mil.* any of several devices for launching grenades or rockets.

Laundromat, *n.* From *laundry* and *automat.* An establishment in which customers may do their own laundry, renting the use of automatic washing machines on the premises.

Lay*, *v.t.* and *i.* Lay off; to dismiss an employee temporarily, through slackness of business, etc.; (slang) to desist, cease; (slang) Phr. lay an egg: to tell a joke at which no one laughs; (by extension) to fail completely in any undertaking.

Lay-away plan, *n.* A form of merchandising in which the customer pays in installments for goods retained in the dealer's possession until the full amount is paid.

Layover, *n.* A temporary stay at a place during the course of a journey.

Layup*, *n. basketball.* A one-handed shot taken when close to the basket, the ball being rebounded from the backboard into the basket.

Lazy Susan, *n.* A revolving tray holding foodstuffs placed on a dining table.

Leaf*, *v.t.* To rapidly turn the pages of: to leaf through a book.

Lebensraum, lā'bens-roum, *n.* Ger. space for living. In Nazi ideology, territory which must be dominated because it is considered vital to the national economic welfare.

Leftist, *n.* See LEFT in the Dict. A person holding radical political views. —*adj.* Holding radical political views.

Leftover, *n.* usually pl. Something remaining; specif., food left over from a meal, eaten or used in the preparation of new dishes.

Left wing, *n.* See LEFT in the Dict. A political party or group advocating liberal or radical reforms, Often attrib.: left wing views.

Leg*, *n. sports.* An event won, when others must be won for ultimate victory; the part of a course run by one member of a relay team.

Legionnaire, *n.* Fr. A legionary; (esp. U.S.) a member of the American Legion; also a member of the French Foreign legion.

Legit, le-jit', *adj.* (slang) Legitimate.

Lend-lease, *n.* and *adj.* Aid in munitions, food and other supplies extended (World War II) by the United States to countries at war with Germany and Italy.

Leopardine, lep'er-dēn, *n.* From *leopard* and *-ine.* Fur processed to simulate leopard.

Leotard, lē'ō-tard, *n.* From *Leotard*, Fr. aerialist. A close-fitting, sleeveless garment, worn by dancers, acrobats, etc.

Leptosome, lep'to-sōm, *n.* From *lepto-* and *-some. anthropol.* A body type of slender and delicate structure.

Leucine*, lū'sēn, *n.* From *leuco-* and *-ine.* One of the amino acids, $C_6H_{13}NO_2$, which are essential for human nutrition.

Leucotomy, lū-kot'om-ē, *n.* From *leuco-* and *-tomy. med.* A prefrontal brain incision for the relief of certain psychiatric disorders.

Level*, *n.* (colloq.) Phr. on the level, honest.

Levis, lē'vīz', *n.* pl. *trade-mark.* From the manufacturer Levi Strauss. Overalls or jeans made of heavy blue denim reinforced with copper rivets.

Lewisite, *n.* From U.S. chemist W. Lee Lewis, 1878-1943. A colorless, poisonous gas, $C_2H_2AsCl_3$, used in chemical warfare.

Lex, *n.* pl. *leges*, Lat. Law.

Lexicon*, *n.* The total vocabulary belonging to a particular language, subject, etc.

Lex loci, leks-lō'sī, *n.* Lat. The law of the place.

Lex non scripta, non-skrip'ta, *n.* Lat. Unwritten law; common law.

Lex scripta, *n.* Lat. Written law; statute law.

Lex talionis, tal'i-ō'nis, *n.* Lat. Law of retaliation.

Libido, li-bī'dō, *n.* From Lat. *libido*, pleasure, desire, longing. *psychoanal.* Instinctual, specifically energy; the totality of psychic energy or life force.—**Libidinal,** *adj.*

Lick*, *n. swing music cant.* An improvised musical figure.

Liederkranz, lē'der-krantz', *n.* From Ger. *lieder*, songs and *kranz*, wreath. *trade-mark.* A soft cheese somewhat milder than Limburger in flavor; not cap. a German male singing society.

Life jacket, *n.* A life preserver fashioned in the form of a sleeveless coat.

Lifeline*, *n.* A route which is vital for reaching isolated areas.

Life net, *n.* A net or similar device held by firemen to catch persons jumping from burning buildings.

Life preserver*, *n.* Any buoyant device to prevent persons from sinking in the water.

Lifer, *n.* From *life* and *-er.* (slang) One sentenced to life imprisonment.

Life raft, *n.* A strong, floating wooden platform, specially constructed to hold several people, carried by ships for an emergency.

Lift*, *v.t.* To lift someone's face, when facial muscles have sagged, to restore the face to more normal shape by surgical treatment.

Lift*, *n.* The force exerted on the wing surfaces of a plane by the air in a direction perpendicular, or nearly so, to its motion; the total buoyancy in a lighter-than-air craft; an airlift.

Light*, *v.i.* Phr. to light out, to leave quickly, at great speed.

Light heavyweight, *n. boxing.* A boxer weighing between 160 and 175 pounds.

Lightning war, *n.* See BLITZKRIEG, above.

Light-struck, *adj. photog.* Of film fogged by inadvertent exposure to light.

Light trap, *n.* A trap for insects which attracts them by means of a strong light.

Lillibullero, lil'i-bu-lēr'ō, *n.* Part of the refrain of a song deriding the Irish Catholics, popular among the English at the time of the revolution of 1688; the song itself.

Lily pad, *n.* One of the floating leaves of a water lily.

Lima bean, *n.* A variety of bean, *Phaseolus limensis*, having a flat, edible seed; the seed itself, much used for food.

Line*, *n.* A scanning line in television; (U.S. slang) information, special or inside information: to get a line on, obtain information about; glib, slightly dishonest talk; don't hand me that line.

Linear accelerator, *n. phys.* A machine used in nuclear experiments to impart very high speeds to electrified particles.

Line-backer, *n. U.S. football.* A member of the backfield who plays very close to the line when his team is on defense.

Line drive, *n. baseball.* A hard hit ball traveling nearly parallel to the ground.

Liner*, *n. baseball.* A line drive; one who or that which makes lines; that which serves as a lining.

Line-up, Lineup, *n.* See LINE. An alignment of persons. Specif.: a group of suspected criminals, arranged so as to be easily viewed by police; the arrangement of football players before the start of a play; hence, the disposition of players in various other games; any organization of persons for a common purpose.

Linguistic form, *n.* Any meaningful unit of speech, as a sentence, word, phoneme, etc.

Linkage, *n. biol.* The association of certain hereditary characters because their genes are located in the same chromosome. Such linked genes are called a linkage group.

Lipo, pref. from Gr. *lipos*, fat. *chem.* Word element denoting fat, as in lipotropic, 'fat producing'.

Lipstick, *v.t.* To color the lips with a lipstick.

Liquidate*, *v.t.* To abolish, to do away with; (euphemistic) to kill ruthlessly, esp. political prisoners.
Liquid fire, *n. mil.* A burning liquid, such as petroleum, for use against enemy troops and fortifications.
Listening post*, *n.* (by extension) Any position used for the purpose of gathering information.
Lister bag, lis'ter, *n.* From British surgeon Joseph Lister, 1827–1912. A large, portable canvas bag for the purification and dispensing of drinking water.
Lithoprint, lith'ō-print, *v.t.* and *i.* From *litho-* and *print.* To lithograph. —*n.* Printed matter produced by this process. See LITHOGRAPH.
Lithosphere, lith'ō-sfēr, *n.* From *litho-* and *sphere.* The solid crust of the earth.
Live*, *adj. radio.* Of a program in which the performers appear in the studio as contrasted with a recorded or transcribed program; *television.* Of a program in which the performers appear in the studio as contrasted with a program recorded on movie film.
Liver sausage, *n.* Liverwurst.
Liverwurst, *n.* Partial translation of Ger. *leberwurst,* liver sausage. A sausage whose chief ingredient is liver.
Live wire, *n.* (slang) An energetic, forceful person.
Loafer*, *n.* An informal shoe resembling a moccasin.
Loan shark, *n.* (U.S. colloq.) A usurer.
Lobbyist, *n.* From *lobby* and *-ist.* One who attempts to influence the votes of legislators.
Lobo, lō'bō', *n.* From Sp., wolf. Western U.S. A large gray wolf.
Lobotomy, lō-bot'o-mi, *n.* From *lobe* and *-tomy.* Leucotomy.
Lobster*, *n.* (U.S. newspaper slang) Attrib., pertaining to members of a newspaper staff who work from late at night until morning. Lobster trick, this shift or period of work.
Lobster thermidor, *n.* A preparation of lobster meat, mushrooms, etc., browned and served in a lobster shell.
Location*, *n. movies.* Any place outside of a studio where a movie is filmed. Phr. on location, of a movie crew encamped, taking pictures at some place away from the studio. Also attrib.: location scene.
Locker*, *n.* An insulated compartment for storing frozen food.
Loco, lō'cō, *adj.* Sp. (U.S. slang) Crazy.
Locoweed, *n.* From Sp. *loco,* crazy, and *-weed.* Any of various herbs of the southwestern U.S., which produce brain disease in cattle, sheep, and horses.
Loge, lōzh, *n.* Fr. See LODGE. A box in a theater or opera house.
Logger, *n.* From *log* and *-er.* A lumberman; a machine for hauling or loading logs.
Logography*, *n.* From *logo* and *-graphy.* Printing by means of logotypes; a technique of recording speeches in longhand, several reporters each taking down a few words in succession.
Logorrhoea, log'o-rē'a, *n. logo-* and Gr. *rhoia,* a flow, flowing. Excessive flow of words; wordiness, verbosity, prolixity.
Log-rolling*, *n.* Also logrolling. The process in which two or more legislators each agree to assist the others, interests in return for similar help. Also attrib.: logrolling legislation; the rotation of floating logs by treading on them; a sport in which two men treading on a floating log try to dislodge each other.
Long-distance, *n.* Communication, via the telephone, between points far apart, esp. between two cities. Often attrib.: long distance call, operator, etc.
Long house, *n. U.S. hist.* A communal dwelling place of certain U.S. Indian tribes, esp. the Iroquois.
Long-playing, *adj.* Of phonograph records composed of a great many small grooves (microgrooves) and designed to be played at 33⅓ revolutions per minute.
Long-standing, *adj.* Having been in existence for a long time: longstanding disagreement.
Loon, *n.* Any of the diving, fish-eating birds comprising the genus *Gavia.*
Loran, lō'ran, *n.* Acronym of *long range navigation.* A device for determining the position of a ship or aircraft by measuring the time intervals between signals from two pairs of known radio stations.
Loss leader, *n. commerce.* Article sold at a price below cost in order to draw customers to a store.
Lovers' lane, *n.* Any secluded road, path, etc. frequented by lovers.
Love seat, *n.* A seat, esp. a sofa, for two persons.
Lowdown, *n.* (slang) facts, correct information: I'm giving you the lowdown.
LP, *trade-mark.* Abbreviation for LONG-PLAYING, above.
Lube, *n. mach.* Short for lubricating oil.
Lucite, lū'sīt, *n.* From Lat. base *luc-,* light, shine and *-ite. trade-mark* The resin polymethyl methacrylate, a transparent plastic used as a substitute for glass.
Luftwaffe, lōōft'va-fe, *n.* Ger. air weapon. The Nazi air force.
Lulu, *n.* Origin unknown. (slang) An exceptionally pleasing person or thing: the play was a lulu.
Luncheonette, *n. luncheon* and *-ette.* A place where light lunches are served.
Lunkhead, *n.* Origin uncert. U.S. (colloq.) A stupid person; blockhead.
Lutecium, lų-tē'shi-um, *n.* From Lat. *Lutetia,* Paris. One of the rare-earth elements, having an atomic number of 71 and an atomic weight of 174.99. Symbol: *Lu.*
Lyre*, *n.* cap., *astron.* The constellation Lyra.
Lysine, lī'sēn, *n.* From Gr. *lúsis,* a loosening and *-ine.* One of the amino acids, $C_6H_{14}N_2O_2$, essential for human nutrition.
Machine shop*, *n.* A workshop in which material is worked on by machine tools.
Mach number, *n.* From Austrian physicist Ernst Mach, 1838–1916. The ratio of the speed of an object traveling through air to the speed of sound at the same altitude.
Mackinaw or **Mackinaw coat**, *n.* From Canadian Fr. place name, ultimate origin uncert. A heavy, woolen, short coat, of plaid design.
Macroclimate, mak'rō-klī'mit, *n. macro-* and *climate.* The over-all climate of a large geographic area contrasted with microclimate, below.
Macrocyte, mak'rō-sīt, *n. macro-* and *-cyte. med.* An abnormally large red blood cell, esp. as found in pernicious anemia. —**Macrocytic**, *adj.*
Macrogamete, mak'rō-ga-mēt', *n. macro-* and *gamete. biol.* The larger, female gamete of an organism having unlike gametes.
Macrograph, mak'rō-graf, *n. macro-* and *-graph.* A photograph or other graphic reproduction of an object equal to or larger than the object.
Mae West, *n. mil.* A life preserver in the form of an inflatable vest, worn by aviators flying over the sea.
Maginot line, mazh'i-nō, *n.* From Fr. minister of war André Maginot, 1877–1932. A series of fortifications erected along the eastern border of France.
Magnetic mine, *n.* A submarine mine so constructed that the magnetic field set up by the near-by passing of a steel ship is sufficient to actuate the trigger of the mine.
Magneton, mag'ne-ton, *n. phys.* The elementary unit of magnetic property.
Magnetron, mag'ne-tron, *n.* From *magnet* and *electron.* A vacuum tube, containing an anode and cathode, in which the electronic flow is controlled by an external magnetic field.
Magnum*, *n.* A type of extremely high powered fire-arm or cartridge load.
Mailbox, *n.* A box, in a public place, where letters may be posted; a box, attached to or near a private residence, for the delivery of mail.
Mail-order house, *n.* A commercial establishment which sells goods primarily by mail.
Major*, *n.* (U.S.) The primary field of study chosen by a college student. —*v.i.* (colloq.) To devote most of one's attention to a chosen field of study followed by in: he majored in chemistry.
Majorette, *n.* From *major* and *-ette.* (U.S. colloq.) Female leader of a marching band or drum corps. Also drum majorette.
Major league, *n.* (U.S.) Either of the two principal professional baseball leagues in the U.S.
Make-believe*, *n.* One who pretends; *adj.* unreal.
Make-up*, *n.* General appearance of anything, way in which it is put together; (colloq.) a test taken to make up for absence or other deficiency.
Making, *n.*pl. Makings, specif., material for making a cigarette.
Malaguena, mal'a-gwā'nya, *n.* Sp. *malaguena.* A type of southern Spanish folk song or dance, similar to the fandango.
Malocclusion, mal'a-klōō'zhun, *n.* From *mal-* and *occlusion.* A faulty relationship between the upper and lower teeth which prevents their proper meeting; an offset bite.
Malodorant, *n.* From *mal-* and *odorant.* An ill-smelling substance.
Malonic acid, ma-lō'nik, *n.* Fr. *malonique.* A derivative of malic acid, CH_2 $COOH_2$, yielding an ester used in organic syntheses.
Malted milk, *n.* Coined, orig. as a trademark, by William Horlick. A powder of dehydrated milk and malted cereals; a drink made from this powder, usually with the addition of milk and ice cream. Also malted.
Mañana, ma-nya'na, *n.* Sp. Tomorrow; the indefinite future.
Manhattan, *n.* name of island in New York City. A cocktail made of whiskey, sweet vermouth, and bitters. Also Manhattan cocktail.
Man-hour, *n.* An industrial time unit signifying the output of one worker in one hour.
Manic-depressive, *adj. psychiat.* Characterized by states of mania or melancholia or both in alternation: manic-depressive psychosis. —*n.* A person having this disorder.
Man power, Manpower, *n.* Power derived from the physical efforts of man; usually (second spelling) the over-all strength of a nation, army, etc. as indicated by the total number of persons available for service.
Manqué, man'kā, *adj.* Fr. Defective, falling short of one's expectations.
Man-sized, *adj.* (slang) Large, difficult enough to occupy or tax a man's energies: a man-sized job.
Man-tailored, *adj.* Of women's suits or other tailored garments designed to copy or imitate the lines of men's clothing.
Maquis, ma'kē', *n.* sing. and pl. From Fr. *maquis* or *makis,* piece of wild, bushy land. often cap. A member of the French underground during World War II.
Maraca, ma-ra'ka, *n.* Port. A gourd rattle used in pairs for rhythmic effects in Latin-American music.
Marble cake, *n.* A cake having a marble-like appearance due to the use of light and dark batter.
Marginal*, *adj. sociol.* Of a person who lives on the fringes of two or more cultural groups, not identifying with, nor being fully accepted by, any one of them: marginal man. —**Marginality**, *adv.*
Marimba, ma-rim'ba, *n. Bantu.* A type of xylophone originating in Africa.
Marijuana, Marihuana, ma'ri-hwa'na, *n.* Amer. Sp. Etymol. uncertain. A hemp plant, *Cannabis sativa,* the leaves and flowers of which are smoked as a narcotic.
Mark*, *n. criminal slang.* A victim or potential victim, esp. of a confidence game; an easy mark. *track.* The point at the starting line assigned to a contestant: on your marks!
Mark*, *v.t.* Mark down, to reduce the price of merchandise; markup, to fix a selling price by adding a certain amount to the cost price of merchandise.
Mark, *n.* From Ger. *marke,* brand. *mil.* A label, used with a following numeral, for a particular model of a piece of military equipment: Mark VI tank.
Markdown, *n.* See MARK, above. A reduction in the usual selling price of an article.
Markup, *n.* See MARK, above. The difference between the cost price and the selling

-counter, *adj. of stocks, bonds,* other than through an exchange.
nask, *n.* A device worn over the connected to an oxygen supply; aviators flying at high altitudes.
ent, *n.* A canopy or tent used to patients with supplementary

rab, *n.* A crab, *Pinnotheres os-* ving as a commensal in oysters.
racker, *n.* A small round cracker ith soups, oyster stew, etc.
hite, *adj.* Very pale grey with a yellow or green.
***,** *n.* A merchandising unit con- different items, services, or a com- of both offered for sale at one ten attrib.: package deal.
store, *n.* A store which sells of liquor only for consumption off nises.
ennis, *n.* A game similar to tennis, yed on a smaller court and using paddles and a sponge rubber ball.
wagon, *n.* From Paddy, Irish ne. (U.S. colloq.) A police vehicle transport prisoners to and from

t. To locate a person by calling out ne, as by a public address system cel.
n. (western U.S.) A spotted horse.
guard, *n.* (derogatory) The circle close to the head of a state.
n. A small portable platform used ing or transporting goods.
e, pāl'et-īz, *v.t.* PALLET, above, and o place, store, or transport on a

no, pal'ō-mē'nō, *n.* Sp. Amer. A tan or cream colored horse with mane and tail.
a, pa-lōō'ka, *n.* Origin unknown. ang) An inferior prizefighter; a lout.
ine, pal'ū-drēn, *n.* From *paludal ine.* An antimalarial drug derived oal tar.
t. (colloq.) To criticize severely; to

t. and *i.* From *pan*orama. *movies* To a camera in order to keep an object v or secure a panoramic effect.
romatic, pan'krō-mat'ik, *adj.* From and *chromatic. photog.* Sensitive to of all colors: panchromatic film.
wdy, *n.* Origin obscure. (U.S.) A dish apple pie or pudding, often ened with molasses.
***,** *n.* A list or group of persons en- in public discussion.
discussion, *n.* A prearranged public ssion by a selected group of speakers, y experts.
heating, *n.* Heating of a house, etc. e use of heat radiated from preheated surfaces such as floors or walls.
andler, *n.* From *pan* and *handler.* g) A beggar.
***,** *n.* (slang) Something or someone mely laughable. —*v.t.* (slang) To e extreme amusement in: he panicked udience.
ing, *v.n.* From PAN, above. *movies* ping horizontally with the camera to panoramic effect; the visual effect so uced.
er, pan'zer, *adj.* From Ger., armor. ored: panzer division.
eg, *n.* From *pa*per and impr*eg*nated. naterial made by binding together ts of resin-impregnated paper, and acterized by high tensile strength.
n. golf The number of strokes re- ed for a hole or course played well.
—*, *pref. mil.* Combining form repre- ing parachute, as in paratroop.
chute spinnaker, *n.* An unusually spinnaker.
de rest, *n.* The formal rest position ch a soldier assumes in drill.
llel bars, *n.* A pair of bars on up- ts and parallel to each other, used for ous gymnastic exercises.
mecium, Paramecia, pār'a-mē'sē- *n.,* pl. From Gr. *paramekes,* oblong. of a genus, *Paramecium,* of ciliate in- rians, having an oval body and a long ove on the oral surface.

Paraplegic, *n.* One affected by paraplegia. See Dict.
Parapsychology, par'a-sī-kol'ō-jē, *n.* From *para-* and *psychology.* The branch of psychology which investigates phenomena such as clairvoyance, extrasensory perception, etc.
Paratroop, *n.* See PARA–, above, and *troop.* A group of soldiers trained to reach battle by parachuting from aircraft.
Paratrooper, *n.* See PARA–, above, and *trooper.* A member of a paratroop.
Parity*, *n.* Specif., an equivalence between the income of a farmer and the income standards of other areas of the national economy. Often attrib.: parity price.
Park*, *v.t.* (slang) To place a thing on one side or in some spot chosen for safety or convenience; facet., pretending that a person is an inanimate object; to leave e.g. a child in someone's charge.
Parka, *n. Eskimo.* A loose outer garment, usually made of wool, with an attached hood; used esp. in arctic climates.
Parking meter, *n.* A coin-operated device used to charge a fee for automobile parking space.
Part-time, *adj.* Employed for, taking up, only part of the working day: a part-time worker, a part-time job.
Part-timer, *n.* (colloq.) Part-time worker.
Party line*, *n.* The authoritative doctrine of a group, especially of the Communist party.
Pass*, *v.t.* Phr. to pass the buck, to shift responsibility or blame from oneself to another; *baseball* to fail to catch a pitched ball; —*v.i.* of light-colored Negroes to be accepted as a white person; (colloq.) Phr. to pass out: to faint, become unconscious; to become dead drunk.
Pass*, *n.* (slang) An embrace or other amatory gesture: he made a pass at her; *craps* a winning throw of the dice.
Pastrami, pas-tra'mē, *n. Yiddish.* A shoulder cut of beef, smoked and highly seasoned.
P.A. system, *n.* PUBLIC-ADDRESS SYSTEM which see, below.
Patch pocket, *n.* A pocket consisting of a piece of material sewed to the outside of a garment.
Patrolman, *n.* A policeman who patrols a certain district; anyone who patrols.
Patrol wagon, *n.* A vehicle used by the police to transport prisoners.
Pay dirt, *n.* Soil containing enough of a mineral so as to make mining profitable.
Payoff, *n.* A payment of a bribe; the time when a payment is made; (colloq.) a climax, decisive fact: his home run was the payoff.
Payroll, *n.* The total amount of money required to pay those on the paymaster's list.
Peach*, *n.* (slang) Anything greatly admired: a peach of a car.
Peak year, *n.* A year for which statistics recording some selected data reach a maximum point as compared with surrounding years.
Peanut brittle, *n.* A candy made from roasted peanuts and melted sugar.
Peanut butter, *n.* A food paste made from finely ground roasted peanuts.
Peart, *adj.* Variant of PERT in the Dict.
Pecksniffian, pek-snif'i-an, *adj.* From *Pecksniff* and *–ian.* Hypocritical, insincere show of high-mindedness and benevolence.
Pedal pushers, *n.* Knee-length trousers worn by women and girls.
Pedicure*, *n.* From I at. *ped–,* stem of *pes,* foot and *cura,* care, healing. The care of the feet; chiropody.
Pedology, ped-ol'ō-ji, *n.* From Gr. *pédon,* soil and *–logy.* The scientific study of soils.
Pedology, *n.* From Gr. *paido–* stem of *pais,* boy, child and *–logy.* The study of the development of children.
Peel*, *v.t.* and *i.* (colloq.) Phr. to keep one's eyes peeled, keep a sharp lookout; *avn.* to peel off, to separate one's plane from a flying formation.
Peg*, *v.t.* (colloq.) To throw a ball. —*n.* A throw of a ball.
Pen*, *n.* From PEN or clipped form of *penitentiary.* (slang) A prison.

Penicillin, *n.* See PENICILLIUM, below. A potent antibacterial agent derived from *Penicillium* molds.
Penicillium, pen'i-sil'i-um, *n.* From Lat. *penicillum,* brush and *–ium.* A member of the genus of fungi *Penicillium,* species of which are used in cheesemaking and in the production of penicillin.
Pennant*, *n.* A flag symbolizing a championship in sports, esp. baseball.
Penny ante, *n.* A poker game in which the ante is one penny.
Penny arcade, *n.* An arcade containing a number of amusement devices operated by a penny.
Pentagon*, *n.* See PENTAGON in the Dict. by extension, the five-sided office building in Arlington, Va., which houses the Department of Defense.
Pentaquine, pen'ta-kwēn, *n.* From PENTA- and QUININE. An antimalarial substance prepared synthetically.
Pentose, pen'tōs, *n.* From *penta* and *–ose.* chem. Any of several simple sugars containing five atoms of oxygen, produced by hydrolysis from complex sugars found in plants.
Pentothal Sodium, pen'tō-thal sō'di-um, *n. trade-mark* An anaesthetic and hypnotic, used with partial success as a "truth drug."
Pep talk, *n.* A speech, as by a coach to an athletic team, designed to stimulate enthusiasm.
Percentage*, *n.* (slang) Profit; advantage: there's no percentage in it.
Perchloric acid, per-klō'rik, *n.* From *per–* and *chloric.* A colorless acid of chlorine, $HClO_4$.
Percussionist, per-kush'un-ist, *n.* From *percussion* and *–ist.* One who plays percussion instruments.
Perimeter*, *n. mil.* The outer boundary of a military position.
Permafrost, per'ma-frost, *n.* From *permanent* and *frost.* Subsoil which is permanently frozen, as in arctic regions.
Permanent*, *n.* A permanent wave.
Permanent wave, *n.* A hair wave lasting for several months, set by a special technique.
Personal*, *n.* A short newspaper or magazine item about a person or persons, esp. an advertisement of this nature.
Pessimal, pes'i-mal, *adj.* From Lat. *pessimus,* worst. Cp. PESSIMISM in the Dict. *of conditions.* Most disadvantageous, unfavorable.
Pessimum, pes'i-mum, *n.* From Lat. *pessimus,* worst. The most disadvantageous circumstance for a given end; worst possible condition.
Pesticide, pes'ti-sīd, *n.* From *pest* and *–cide.* Any chemical used to kill pests such as vermin, insects, etc.
Petrolatum, pet'rō-lā'tum, *n.* From *petrol* and *–ate.* A jelly-like substance derived from petroleum, used in ointments.
Peyotl, Peyote, pā-yō't'l –tā, *n.* Sp. Amer., from Nahuatl *peyotl,* caterpillar. The mescal cactus, *Lophophora williamsi,* which contains a powerful narcotic; the narcotic obtained from mescal buttons.
Phase*, *n. physical chem.* One component of a heterogeneous mixture.
Phenobarbital, fē'nō-bar'bi-tol, *n.* From PHENO, and BARBITURATE, above. A white powder, $C_{12}H_{12}O_3N_2$, used as a hypnotic.
Phenolic, fē-nol'ik, *adj.* From *phenol* and *–ic.* Pertaining to, derived from, phenol. —*n.* Any of several synthetic thermosetting resins derived from phenol.
Phenolphthalein, fē'nōl-thal'ēn, *n.* From *phenol* and *naphthalene.* A crystalline compound, $C_4H_{14}O_{20}$, used as a laxative and as an acid-base indicator.
Phenomenology, fē-nom'ē-nol'ō-ji, *n.* From *phenomenon* and *–logy.* A school of philosophical thought originating from Husserl, which claims to reject rational judgments and concepts and to start from reality as it appears in pure intuition.
Phenotype, fē'nō-tīp, *n.* From *phenomenon* and *type. biol.* The part of its hereditary constitution that an organism actually displays.
Phenylene, fen'i-lēn, *n.* From *phenyl* and *–ene. chem.* A bivalent radical, C_6H_4, derived from benzene.

price of an article: a markup of 40 per cent on books.
Martini, mar-tē'nē, *n.* Origin uncertain. A cocktail made of gin and vermouth, served with an olive, cocktail onion, or twist of lemon peel.
Marxian, marks'i-an, *adj.* Of, pertaining to, Karl Marx or his political and economic theories. —*n.* A Marxist.
Marxism, marks'ism, *n.* From Karl Marx, 1818–1883, and *–ism.* The doctrine of Karl Marx concerning the materialistic i.e. economic interpretation of history, the class struggle caused by capitalistic appropriation of 'surplus-value,' and the ultimate triumph of the proletariat, leading to a system of communism.
Marxist, *n.* A follower of the political and economic theories of Karl Marx. —*adj.* Of, pertaining to, the theories of Karl Marx.
Mascara, *n.* Sp. mask, pretext. A substance for darkening the color of the eyelashes.
Masculinize, *v.t. masculine* and *–ize. biol.* To produce male characteristics in a female by administration of an androgen.
Mask*, *n.* A device, covering the nose and mouth, to aid in the inhalation of a substance: oxygen mask.
Masonite, mā'son-īt, *n. trade-mark.* A pressed wood fiber board, used for paneling and insulation.
Mass-energy equivalence, *n. phys.* The theory of the interconvertibility of mass and energy, propounded by Albert Einstein in 1905. It is expressed as $E=MC^2$, in which E is the energy, M is the mass, and C is a constant, the velocity of light.
Massive*, *adj. med.* Unusually large: a massive dose; unusually extensive or severe, as a disease.
Mass number, *n. phys.* An integer expressing the mass of an isotope.
Mass observation, *n.* (Brit.) A technique of determining public opinion.
Mass production, *n.* Production of goods in large quantities, esp. by means of machinery, division of labor and standardized procedures.
Mass spectograph, *n. phys.* A device which separates electrified particles having different masses.
Mastermind*, *v.t.* (U.S. slang) To plan something astutely.
Masthead*, *n.* The statement, printed in every issue of a newspaper or other periodical, giving the title of the publication, staff, advertising rates, etc.
Matchbook, *n.* A folder containing two rows of paper safety matches and a prepared surface for igniting them.
Materia medica, ma-tēr'i-a med'i-ka, *n.* Lat. medical material. Substances used in medical remedies; the branch of medicine devoted to the study of these substances.
Matronymic, mat'rō-nim'ik, *n.* Same as METRONYMIC, in the Dict.
Maverick, mav'er-ik, *n.* From Samuel Maverick, 1803–1870, a Texas cattle owner who neglected to brand his calves. (U.S.) A stray, unbranded animal, formerly belonging to the one who found it; (colloq. by extension) a nonconformist or dissenting member of a group.
Mayoress*, *n.* (U.S.) A woman mayor.
Mazuma, ma-zoo'ma, *n.* Yiddish, from Chaldean *m'zumon,* lit. the ready necessary. (U.S. slang) Money.
McCoy, *n.* Origin uncertain. (slang) Usually in phr. the real McCoy, the genuine article.
Measure*, *v.t.* Phr. measure up to, fulfill the requirements of.
Mechanization, mek'a-ni-zā'shun, *n. mechanize* and *–ation.* Technical transformation, for the sake of increased efficiency, by substituting machinery for direct human effort; specif. the transformation of military units, redesigning them for mobility and resistance to gunfire.
Medium frequency, *n.* Any wave frequency between 3,000 and 30,000 cycles per second.
Megagamete, meg'a-ga-mēt', *n.* From *mega–* and *gamete. bot.* A macrogamete.
Megasporangium, meg'a-spō'ran'ji-um, *n.* From MEGASPORE, below, and SPORANGIUM. A sporangium which develops megaspores.
Megaspore, meg'a-spōr', *n.* In seed plants and some ferns, a type of asexual spore which produces the female prothallium.
Megasporophyll, meg'a-spōr'ō-fil, *n.* See MEGASPORE, above, and SPOROPHYLL, below. A spore-bearing leaf which produces only megasporangia.
Melanin, mel'a-nin, *n.* See MELANISM. *biochem.* A dark pigment, the degree of concentration of which determines the color of skin or hair.
Melba toast, *n.* Named after Madame Melba, Mrs. Nellie Mitchell Armstrong, 1861-1931. Thin, narrow slices of crisp toast.
Meld, *v.t.* and *i.* From Ger. *melden,* to announce. In pinochle and other card games to declare a partial score. —*n.* Act of melding; a score so declared.
Memo, *n.* (colloq.) Clipped form of memorandum.
Menopausal, *adj.* Of, pertaining to, the menopause. Also menopausic.
Mental age, *n. psychol.* The mental development of a person, as measured by intelligence tests and compared with the norm for various chronological age groups.
Merchandise, *v.t.* and *i.* To trade, esp. to sell by means of publicity.
Merchant marine*, *n.* The officers and crews of the commercial vessels of a nation.
Mercy killing, *n.* The killing of a person incurably ill to spare him further suffering; euthanasia.
Mesoderm*, *n.* From *meso–* and *derm. embryology* and *zool.* The middle germ layer of the embryo.
Meson, mēs'on, *n.* Orig. called mesotron, from *meso–* and *–tron* as in electron; abbreviated form meson suggested by Indian physicist H. J. Bhabba and officially adopted in 1947. *phys.* Any of several nuclear particles, charged or neutral, having weights between those of the electron and the proton.
Mess hall, *n.* A large dining hall, esp. in camps and military establishments.
Mess kit, *n.* A soldier's cooking and eating utensils, carried in the field.
Metabolite, met-ab'ō-līt, *n,* See METABOLISM and *–ite.* A product of metabolism.
Metagalaxy, met'a-gal'ak-si, *n.* From *meta–* and *galaxy.* The entire system of nebulae or galaxies outside the Milky Way.
Methadon, meth'a-dōn, *n. trade-mark.* A synthetic drug, developed in Germany, used as a substitute for morphine in the relief of pain.
Methionine, me-thī'ō-nēn, *n.* From *methyl* and *thio–* and *–ine.* One of the amino acids, $C_5H_{11}NO_2S$, which are essential for human nutrition.
Methylate, *n.* A derivative of methyl alcohol obtained by substituting a metal for the hydrogen of the hydroxyl group.
Methylene, meth'il-ēn, *n.* From Fr. *methylene,* from Gr. *methu,* wine and *hule,* wood. The methane derivative CH_2, a bivalent hydrocarbon radical not found in its free form.
Methylene blue, *n.* A thiazine dye.
Metol, mē'tol, *n. trade-mark.* A soluble white powder used as a photographic developer.
Metonym, met'ō-nim, *n.* A word used in metonymy.
Metrazol, met'ra-zōl, *n. trade-mark.* A heart and lung stimulant, $C_6H_{10}N_4$, used for psychotherapeutic shock.
Mickey Finn, *n.* Origin unknown. A drink of liquor to which a drug, such as chloral hydrate, has been added.
Microanalysis, *n.* From *micro–* and *analysis. chem.* The analysis of minute quantities of substances.
Microbarograph, *n.* From *micro–* and *barograph. meteor.* A barograph designed to record small changes in atmospheric pressure.
Microcard, *n.* From *micro–* and *card.* A card 3″ x 5″ containing a reduced photographic reproduction of printed matter, used in libraries to conserve space.
Microchemistry, *n.* From *micro–* and *chemistry.* A branch of chemistry dealing with minute quantities.
Microclimate, *n.* From *micro–* and *climate.* The climate, usually uniform, of a small local area.
Microclimatology, mī'krō-klī'ma-tol'ō-ji, *n.* From *micro–* and *climatology.* The study of microclimates.
Microcline, mī'krō-klīn, *n.* From *micro–* and Gr. *klinein,* incline. Potassium aluminum silicate, a mineral of the feldspar group, used in making porcelain.
Micrococcus*, *n.* pl. –cocci, From *micro–* and *coccus.* Any of the genus *Micrococcus,* globular bacteria living as parasites or on dead matter.
Microcopy, *n.* From *micro–* and *copy.* A reduced photographic copy of printed matter, ready by means of an enlarging device.
Microcrystalline, *adj.* From *micro–* and *crystalline.* Of a substance having its crystalline structure visible under a microscope.
Microcyte, mī'krō-sīt, *n.* From *micro–* and *cyte. anat.* A very small red blood cell, esp. as occurring pathologically in anemia.
Microdont, mī'krō-dont, *adj.* From *micro–* and *–odont.* Having small teeth. —Microdontous, *adj.*
Microelement, mīk-rō-el'e-ment, *n.* From *micro–* and *element. chem.* An element which occurs only in very small quantities.
Microfilm, *n.* From *micro–* and *film.* A film strip of small size, used for reduced photographic copies of printed matter. —*v.t.* To record printed matter on microfilm to preserve it.
Microgamete, mīk'rō-ga-mēt', *n.* From *micro–* and *gamete. biol.* The smaller, usually male, gamete of an organism having unlike gametes.
Microgram, *n.* From *micro–* and *gram. chem.* and *phys.* A millionth part of a gram. Also microgramme.
Micrograph, *n.* An instrument for making minute writing or engraving.
Micrography*, *n.* From *micro–* and *graphy.* The art of producing minute writing; examination with the microscope.
Microgroove, *adj.* From *micro–* and *groove.* Of a long-playing phonograph record, cut with very narrow grooves 200–275 per inch. —*n.* Such a groove.
Micronutrient, mī'krō-nū'tri-ent, *n.* From *micro–* and *nutrient. biol.* An element or compound which is essential, in very small amounts, for human nutrition.
Microphonics*, *n.* pl. From *micro–* and *phonic.* Undesirable noise in the loudspeaker of an audio system, as from mechanical vibration of tubes.
Microphotograph, *n.* A very small photograph, not clearly visible unless enlarged.
Microprint, *n.* From *micro–* and *print.* A greatly reduced photographic print of printed matter, read by means of a magnifying device.
Microtone, *n.* From *micro–* and *tone. mus.* Any interval smaller than a semitone.
Microwave, *n.* From *micro–* and *wave. radio.* An electromagnetic wave of high frequency, having a wave length of less than one meter.
Middlebrow, *n.* by anal. with HIGHBROW and LOWBROW in the Dict. (slang) A person of average intellectual achievements, neither a lowbrow nor a highbrow. Also attrib.: middlebrow magazine.
Middleweight, *n.* A boxer weighing between 147 and 160 pounds.
Middy blouse, *n.* A full, loose, hip-length blouse with a sailor collar, worn esp. by young girls.
Midriff*, *n.* A woman's garment which exposes the midriff section of the body.
Mike, mīk, *n.* (Slang) abbr. of microphone.
Milk Shake, *n.* (U.S.) A drink made of cold milk, flavoring and usually ice cream beaten together.
Mill*, *n.* (colloq.) Phr. to be put through the mill, to be severely disciplined or tested.
Milpa, mil'pa, *n.* Sp. southwestern U.S. A small cultivated field.
Milquetoast, milk'tōst', *n.* From comic-strip character Caspar Milquetoast. An extremely timid person.
Mind reading, *n.* Discerning another's thoughts without apparent aid of ordinary communication. —**Mind reader,** *n.*
Mind-set, *n.* A relatively fixed, unyielding state of the mind, as a strongly held value.

Miniature camera, *n.* A small camera using film of 35 mm. width or smaller, used esp. for candid photography.
Minicam, min'i-cam, *n.* Short for miniature camera.
Minimax principle, min'i-maks, *n.* From *mini*mum and *max*imum. A game-theoretic principle which correlates one player's strategy for maximizing his return with his opponent's strategy for minimizing the same return.
Minor*, *n.* (U.S.) The secondary field of study chosen by a college student. Contrasted with MAJOR, above.—*v.i.* To devote one's attention to a secondary field of study followed by in: he minored in physics.
Minority group, *n.* A racial or religious group finding itself a minority within a nation.
Minor league, *n.* (U.S.) Any professional sports league other than the recognized major ones.
Minuteman, min'it'man, *n.* *U.S. hist.* During the Revolutionary War period, one of a group of American militia who pledged themselves to be ready for instant military action.
Miscue*, *n.* (slang) A mistake. —*v.i.* To make a mistake; specif. *theater* to answer a wrong cue or not answer one's own cue.
Mishmash, *n.* Ger. *misch-masch.* A confused mixture; a jumble.
Missile*, *n.* A jet-propelled projectile.
Mission*, *n. mil.* An operation against the enemy, esp. by aircraft.
Mixer*, *n.* (U.S. colloq.) A social gathering for acquainting people with one another.
Mixing, *v.n. movies, radio.* Recording such as to mix in, e. g., music with the actors' voices.
Mobile*, *n.* Sculpture which moves when blown upon or touched, constructed of wire, metal, etc., in various combinations.
Mobster, *n.* From *mob* and *–ster.* (slang) A member of a gang of criminals.
Mocha, *n.* not cap. A flavoring derived from coffee or a combination of coffee and chocolate.
Mock-up, *n.* See mock. A fullscale model of a machine or weapon, used for teaching and experimental purposes.
Model*, *v.i.* To pose as a model, as for an artist.
Moire*, *adj.* Of stamps having a wavy pattern printed on the back.
Moll, *n.* From Molly, variant of Mary (slang) A female companion of a criminal; gun moll.
Mom, *n.* Clipped form of mama. familiar Mother, esp. as a mode of address.
Mongolian*, *adj.* Mongolian idiocy, Mongolism.
Monitor*, *v.t.* To listen to radio broadcasts in order to check on signal quality; to listen to foreign broadcasts for the purpose of censorship, gaining information, hearing propaganda, etc.
Monoculture, mon'ō-kul'tur, *n.* From *mono–* and *culture. agric.* The use of land for the growing of a single crop.
Monolithic*, *adj.* Displaying complete uniformity, sameness: a monolithic organization, state, etc.
Monomolecular, mon'ō-mō-lek'ū-ler, *adj.* From *mono–* and *molecular.* Referring to a layer one molecule in thickness.
Monopitch, *n.* From *mono–* and *pitch.* Sameness of pitch of the voice.
Monoplegia, mon'ō-plē'jē-a, *n.* From *mono–* and Gr. *plege,* a blow. *med.* The paralysis of a single arm or leg. —Monoplegic, *adj.*
Monosaccharide, mon'ō-sak'a-rīd, *n.* From *mono–* and *sacchar–* and *–ide.* A simple sugar, such as fructose or glucose, which cannot be decomposed by hydrolysis.
Monovalent*, *adj.* From *mono–* and *–valent. chem.* Having a valence of one; univalent; *bacter.* having the antibodies or antigens necessary to resist a specific disease organism.
Monovular, mon-ov'ū-ler, *adj.* From *mono–* and *ovular. bot.* Having one ovule; of identical twins derived from one ovum.
Montage*, *n.* A picture which is a composite of several pictures, superimposed or otherwise blended; the process or technique of making such a picture.
Mooch, *v.i.* and *t.* (slang) To engage in petty borrowing without intent of repayment; to "bum." —**Moocher,** *n.*
Moppet*, *n.* A disheveled child.
Morbid*, *adj.* (colloq.) Gruesome, as in morbid details.
Mores, mō'rēz, *n.* pl. Lat. customs. *sociol.* Those folkways which have come to be regarded as sacred and inviolable; "unwritten law."
—Morph, suff. From Gr. *morphe,* shape, used to form nouns corresponding to adjective ending in –morphic.
Morpheme, mōr'fēm, *n.* From Gr. *morphe,* shape and *–eme* by analogy with PHONEME, below. *linguistics.* A minimum unit of meaningful linguistic form, either free, as dog, or bound, as the *s* in dogs.
Morphemics, *n.* From *morpheme* and *–ics.* The branch of descriptive linguistics concerned with the study of morphemes.
Mosey, *v.i.* Origin obscure. (U.S. slang) To depart; to stroll along, shuffle.
Mosquito boat, *n.* A motorboat, armed with torpedoes and small guns, used for sudden attacks on enemy craft.
Mossback, *n.* (U.S. slang) A person holding antiquated views, esp. political ones; an extreme conservative.
Motel, mō-tel', *n.* From *mot*orist and hot*el.* U. S. A highway hotel with special facilities for motorists.
Motion sickness, *n. med.* General term for sickness due to motion while traveling, as airsickness or seasickness.
Motorcade, *n.* From *motor* and *–cade,* by anology with cavalcade. An automobile procession.
Motorize*, *v.t.* From *motor* and *–ize.* esp. military units. To transform by substituting motor for horse transport.
Motorized force, *n.* A fighting unit usually infantry or artillery transported by truck, or truck drawn, to the site of action, where it dismounts to fight on the ground while most of the vehicles are sent to the rear.
Motor pool, *n.* The place at an army post where automobiles and other motor vehicles are kept and dispatched for official duty.
Motor torpedo boat, *n.* See MOSQUITO BOAT, above.
Mouthful*, *n. fig.* and sometimes ironical, (colloq.) To say a mouthful, say something striking, important.
Mouton, mōō'ton', *n.* Fr., sheep. Cp. MUTTON in the Dict. The skin of sheep, processed to imitate beaver or seal.
Mucin, mū'sin, *n.* From *mu*cus and *–in. biochem.* Any of several proteins contained in mucous secretions.
Mucluc, Muckluck, *n.* See MUKLUK, below.
Mucoid, mu'koid, *n.* From *mu*cin and *–oid. biochem.* Any of several substances resembling mucin.
Mud*, *n.* Charges which discredit someone: to throw mud at someone; (colloq.) Phr. someone's name is mud, he has lost any prestige, good name, credit, he once had.
Mug*, *v.t.* From MUG in the Dict. (slang) To photograph someone; to attack, esp. for the purpose of robbery, by garroting. —*v.i.* to overact by means of facial expressions.
Mugger, *n.* One who attacks victims by garroting; an actor, esp. a comedian, who depends primarily on facial expressions for his effects.
Mukluk, muk'luk, *n.* From Alaskan Eskimo *muklok,* large seal. A soft sealskin boot worn by Eskimos; any similar boot, having a soft leather or imitation leather sole and a textile covering for the foot and leg.
Mulready, mul-red'i, *n.* From British artist William Mulready, 1786–1863. Any of the first postal envelopes ever issued, put into use by Great Britain in 1840.
Multiflash, mul'ti-flash, *adj.* From *multi–* and *flash* as in flashbulb. *photog.* Using, photographed by means of, several flashbulbs synchronized with the camera shutter.
Multiplex*, *adj. electr.* Pertaining to the simultaneous transmission of several signals over the same wire or carrier wave.
Mumbo Jumbo*, *n.* not cap. Jargon, gibberish.
Muscle*, *v.* (U.S. slang) Muscle in, to force oneself into a situation, business, etc., against opposition.
Museum piece, *n.* Valuable object in, suitable for, a museum.
Mushroom*, *v.i.* To spread out quickly, as a bullet or fire; used esp. of the atomic bomb.
Must*, *adj.* Necessary, mandatory: a must book.—*n.* That which is necessary, cannot be neglected: the book is a must.
Mutant, mū'tant, *adj.* From Lat. *mutans,* Pres. Part. of *mutare,* change. Undergoing or resulting from mutation. —*n.* An organism which is a result of mutation.
Mutt, *n.* (slang) A mongrel dog.
Myocardiograph, mī'ō-kar'di-o-graf', *n.* From *myocardium,* and *–graph.* A device which makes a record of the heart action.
Myocarditis, mi'ō-kar-dī'tis, *n.* From *myocardium,* and *itis. pathol.* Inflammation of the heart muscles.
Myoma, mī-ō'ma, *n.* From *myo–* and *–oma. pathol.* A tumor made up of muscular tissue.
Myotic, mī-ot'ik, *adj.* See MYOSIS. Pertaining to or affecting excessive contraction of the pupil of the eye. *–n.* A myotic drug.
Napalm, nā'pam, *n.* Acronym of napthenic and palmitic acids. A substance which converts fuels into jelly form, used in incendiary warfare.
Narcohypnosis, nar'cō-hip-nō'sis, *n.* From *narco*sis and *hypnosis.* A hypnotic-like state produced by narcotics.
Narcosynthesis, nar'kō-sin'thē-sis, *n.* From *narco*sis and *synthesis. psychiat.* The treatment of neurotic conditions by the use of narcotics, enabling the patient to talk about and synthesize previously repressed memories.
Narcotherapy, *n.* From *narco*sis and *therapy.* Psychotherapy in which drugs are used as an aid.
National park, *n.* A land area owned and maintained by the federal government, equipped esp. for recreational use by the public.
Natural*, *n.* (colloq.) A person or thing naturally suitable and highly successful in a particular endeavor.
Natural gas, *n.* Gas formed in the earth, esp. in petroleum regions, suitable for fuel.
Naval Stores, *n.* Supplies used on merchant vessels, or in the Navy; by extension (comm.) hemp, pitch, tar, turpentine and other resinous products.
Navicert, nav'i-surt, *n.* Acronym of navigation certificate. A document issued by British blockade authorities, testifying that a ship carries no contraband goods.
Navy yard, *n.* A naval station on shore with facilities to construct, repair, and equip war vessels.
Needle*, *v.t.* (colloq.) To irritate, prod someone, especially in order to bring about a desired action.
Negatron, *n.* See *neg*ative and elec*tron. phys.* and *chem.* The ordinary electron as contrasted with a POSITRON, which sees below.
Nembutal, nem'bū-tol, *n. trade-mark.* A barbiturate drug used as a sedative.
Neomycin, nē'ō-mī'sin, *n.* From *neo–* and Gr. *mūkes,* fungus. An antibiotic isolated from a soil micro-organism.
Neoprene, nē'ō-prēn, *n.* From *neo–* and chloro*prene.* A synthetic plastic similar to rubber, formed by polymerizing chloroprene.
Nephrotomy, nef-rot'ō-mē, *n.* From *nephro–* and *–tomy. med.* Surgical incision in the kidney, as for the removal of kidney stones.
Neptunium*, *n.* From the planet Neptune. A radioactive element produced by neutron bombardment of U-238. It exists freely for a short time only, losing an electron to form plutonium. Abbr. *Np;* atomic number 93, atomic weight 239.
Nerve center, *n. fig.* A vital, controlling part of any system.

Nesselrode pudding, *n.* From Russ. statesman Count K. R. Nesselrode, 1780–1862. A dessert containing preserved chestnuts, fruit, etc.
Nest*, *n.* Machine gun nest, a camouflaged emplacement for one or several machine guns.
Neuropsychiatry, nū'rō-sī-kī'a-trē, *n.* From *neuro–* and *psychiatry.* The branch of medicine combining neurology and psychiatry, dealing with diseases of both the mind and the nervous system.
Neuropsychosis, *n.* From *neuro–* and *psychosis. med.* Psychosis, esp. that associated with nerve disease.
Neurotomy*, *n.* From *neuro–* and *–tomy.* Cutting of a nerve, as to relieve pain.
Neutralize*, *v.t. elect.* To make electrically neutral.
Neutrino, nū-trē'nō, *n.* Ital. small neutral one, coined by physicist Enrico Fermi. *phys.* A hypothetical chargeless particle with a mass less than the electron.
Neutron, nū'tron, *n.* From *neu*ter and *–tron* on the analogy of electron. Coined by U.S. physicist William Draper Harkins 1873–1951, on April 12, 1920. *phys.* A particle of slightly larger mass than the proton, but without electrical charge.
New Deal, *n.* The policies of the administration of President Franklin D. Roosevelt.
News*, *n.* pl. Anything that the public can be induced to read about in newspapers.
Newscast, *n.* From *news* and broad*cast.* A radio news broadcast. —**Newscaster,** *n.*
Newsworthy, *adj.* Suitable for publication in newspapers.
N.G., abbrev. (colloq.) No good.
Niacin, nī'a-sin, *n.* From *ni*cotinic *ac*id and *–in.* Nicotinic acid.
Nickelodeon, *n.* See NICKEL and ODIUM in the Dict. U.S. Any early movie theater, charging five cents for admission; a juke box.
Nicotinic acid, nik'ō-tin'ik, *n.* See NICOTINE. A member of the vitamin B complex, derived from nicotine, found in fresh meat, yeast, etc.
Night clerk, *n.* A person on duty during the night at a hotel reception desk.
Night owl, *n.* An owl of nocturnal habits; (colloq.) a person who habitually stays up late at night.
Night stick, *n.* A policeman's weighted stick, often carried in the daytime as well as at night.
Nimbostratus, nim'bō-strā'tus, *n.* From *nimbo–,* combining form of nimbus, and *stratus.* A dark, low, rain cloud.
Nine*, *n.* (colloq.) A baseball team.
Nipponese, nip'o-nēz', *n.* sing. and pl. From Nippon, Japanese name of Japan. A Japanese; the Japanese collectively; —*adj.* Japanese.
Nisei, nē'sā, *n.* Jap. second generation. A native of the United States having Japanese immigrant parents. Also used as pl.
Nissen hut, nis'n, *n.* From Brit. designer Lieut. Col. P. N. Nissen, 1871–1830. A prefabricated, semicylindrical military shelter, usually made of corrugated iron on a cement floor. Cp. QUONSET HUT, below.
Nite, *n.* Pseudo-phonetic spelling for night.
Nitrogen mustard, *n.* Any of several compounds similar in effect to mustard gas.
No-account, *adj.* (slang) Of persons shiftless, irresponsible.
No-good, *n.* (slang) A worthless person.
No-hitter, *n.* (colloq.) A baseball game in which one side makes no hits. Also no-hit game.
Nonobjective, *adj. art* Not representing any real object.
Nonrepresentational, *adj. art.* Not representing an object of physical reality.
Nonstop, *adj.* and *adv.* Without a stop: the plane flew nonstop to New Orleans.
Normal curve, *n.* A graphic representation of statistical distribution, always bell-shaped.
Normative, nor'ma-tiv, *adj.* From *norm* and *–ative.* Pertaining to, concerned with, norms; specif., *linguistics.* concerned with a standard of usage: a normative grammar.
Nosedive*, *n.* Any debacle, sudden downward trend in fortune, etc. —*v.i.* To take such a downward trend.
Nostalgia*, *n.* Intense longing for any aspect of a previous state of existence.
Nostology, nos-tol'ō-ji, *n.* From Gr. *nóstos,* return home, and *–logy.* The study of the phenomena of old age in organisms; geriatrics.
Novocain*, *n.* *trade-mark.* Procaine. A pain-killing drug.
Nuclear*, *adj. chem.* and *phys.* Of or pertaining to atomic nuclei; nuclear physics.
Nuclear energy, *n.* See ATOMIC ENERGY, above.
Nuclear fission, *n.* See FISSION, above.
Nuclear isomer, *n.* Coined by physicist L. Meitner, 1936, *phys.* One of two or more nuclear species having identical atomic numbers and atomic weights, but differing in energy content.
Nuclear physics, *n.* The branch of physics that deals with atomic nuclei.
Nuclear reactor, *n.* See REACTOR, below.
Nucleon, nū'klē-on, *n.* Coined by Danish physicist C. Moller in 1941, from nucleus. *phys.* A proton or neutron in the nucleus of an atom.
Nucleonics, *n.* From *nucleon,* above, and *–ics;* proposed by Z. Jeffries in 1944. *phys.* The study of the structure, motion and effects of atomic nuclei.
Nucleus*, *n. phys.* The positively charged central core of an atom.
Nuclide, nū'klīd, *n.* From *nucle*us and *–ide. phys.* A species of atomic nucleus, as identified by the nucleons it contains.
Nudism, *n.* From *nude* and *–ism.* The practice or belief in going naked.
Nudist, *n.* One who advocates or practices nudism.
Nuisance tax, *n.* A tax paid in small amounts by consumers.
Numbers game or **pool,** *n.* An illegal daily lottery in which small sums may be wagered on the appearance of a certain number, as in the last digits of the total of stock transactions for the day.
Nursery school, *n.* A school for children too young to attend kindergarten.
Nut*, *n.* (slang) An eccentric or crazy person.
Nuts, *interj.* (slang) Expression of contempt, defiance, etc. —*adj.* (slang) Crazy.
Nylon*, *n.* Orig. a coined trade-mark. A synthetic derivative of coal, air and water made into threads, bristles and sheets and having qualities of durability and elasticity; pl. stockings made from nylon.
Occupational, *adj.* From *occupation* and *–al.* Pertaining to or chacteristic of a given occupation or trade: occupational disease, occupational hazard.
Occupational therapy, *n.* A technique making use of handicraft skills to divert or retrain a medical patient.
Octane, ok'tān, *n.* From *oct–* and *–ane.* chem. Any of a group of hydrocarbons, C_8H_{18}, obtained primarily from petroleum;
Octane number or **rating,** *n.* A designation of the antiknock qualities of a motor fuel, a high octane number indicating little likelihood of knocking.
Ofay, ō'fā, *n.* Origin uncert. (U.S. Negro slang) A white person.
Off-chance, *n.* An unlikely chance or possibility.
Off-color*, *adj.* Risqué or obscene: off-color story.
Offset*, *n.* A method of indirect printing by transferring the design from a flat surface to a cylinder and thence to the paper; an impression produced by this method.
Off-the-record, *adj.* Not for publication; confidential.
Off-year, *n.* (U.S.) An election year in which there is no presidential election. Also attrib.: off-year election.
Okay or **Okeh,** *adv.* and *adj.* Synonym for all right, yes, etc.
Old-fashioned*, *n.* A cocktail made of whisky or brandy, sugar, and bitters.
Old hat, *adj.* Trite, dated.
Omnibus*, *n.* A volume of collected works by one author or an anthology of literary pieces all dealing with the same subject.
Omnirange, om'ni-rānj, *n.* From *omni–* and *range. aeron.* A system of navigation in which two signals in different phases sent out from a central station are compared by an aircraft within range to de-

termine its bea
station which b
On*, *prep.* At t
have this one
on him; th
to me, i.e
Once-o
hasty e
the onc
One-ar
of slot r
by pull
One-ste
dance; r
One-tra
only a s
a one-tr
One way
directio
Onionsk
paper.
Open-an
open-and
Open ch
atoms in
structura
join to fo
Open cit
tified and
internatio
bombardi
Operation
–ism. phil
by physic
cept is n
possible o
determine
Order of t
military
situation,
task, or g
matters.
Organza, o
like organd
Orlon, or'l
plastic resi
ized by res
Orthicon, c
vision cam
electrons fo
Orthodonti
ortho– and
dentistry w
ing of teeth
Orthogenic,
ortho– and
cational and
disorders in
Orthopsychi
From *ortho–*
psychiatry c
prevention c
especially in
Oscar, os'ker
proper name
given annual
performance,
the Academy
Sciences.
Osteotomy*,
Surgical cutti
Ostosis, os-tō'
physiol. The r
body.
Ouch*, *interj.*
sion of sudder
Out*, *n.* (collo
Outboard mo
with steering
fastened to th
Outgoing*, *a*
personality.
Outing flanne
having a slight
Out-of-date,
fashionable.
Outride*, *v.t.*
storm; —*n.* a r
Outsized, *adj.*
mon size, esp. l
Overcompensa
TION, above. *p*
striving for po
duced by an
inferiority.
Overstuffed, *adj.*
framework heav

Over-th
etc. Sol
Oxygen
face an
worn b
Oxygen
furnish
oxygen
Oyster
treum,
Oyster
served
Oyster
tinge c
Packag
taining
binatic
price.
Packag
bottles
the pr
Paddle
but pl
woode
Paddy
nickna
used
jail.
Page*,
his na
in a h
Paint*
Palace
of the
Pallet
for st
Pallet
–ize.
pallet
Palom
(U.S.
a whi
Paloo
U.S.
Palud
and
from
Pan*,
derid
Pan,
move
in vi
Panc
pan–
light
Pand
deep
swee
Pane
gage
Pane
disc
usua
Pane
by
larg
Pan
(sla
Pan
ext
ind
the
Pan
Sw
get
pro
Pan
Ar
Pap
A
she
cha
Par
qu
Par
ser
Par
lar
Par
wh
Pa
rig
va
Pa
u
O
fu
gı

Philadelphia lawyer, *n.* Origin uncertain; perhaps, orig. an allusion to the diplomatic skill of Benjamin Franklin. (colloq.) A shrewd lawyer, esp. one versed in legal trickery and technicalities.
Phon—, pref. Variant of PHONO in the Dict.
Phoneme, fō'nēm', *n.* From Gr. *phonema,* a sound. The smallest class of sounds in a language forming a unit which functions to differentiate meaning. In *tip* and *hip* the sounds represented by *t* and *h* belong to different phonemes, since they distinguish words otherwise alike; the aspirated *t* in *tone* and the unaspirated *t* in *stone* belong to the same phoneme because, even though phonetically different, they never distinguish words otherwise alike.
Phonemics, fō-nē'miks, *n.* See PHONEME, above, and *–ics.* The branch of linguistics which deals with the study of phonemes.
Phonevision, *n.* telephone television. (trade-mark) A commercial system by which motion pictures are transmitted over telephone wires to a specially equipped television set.
Phoney, *adj.* Variant of PHONY, below.
Phonics, *n.* From *phono–* and *–ics.* A technique for teaching reading by making use of the regularity of ordinary spelling.
Phonophobia, fōn'ō-fō'bi-a, *n.* From *phono–* and *phobia.* Morbid fear of sounds, esp. of speaking aloud.
Phony, fō'nē, *adj.* From Irish *fawney,* thieves cant, a gilt brass ring used in swindling. (slang) Sham, counterfeit, fake. —*n.* (slang) A fake person or thing.
Phosphor, fos'fōr, *n. phys.* A substance which emits light when irradiated by light of a different wave length, usually ultraviolet.
Photodisintegration, fo'tō-dis-in'te-grā'-shun, *n. phys.* Nuclear disintegration as a result of the absorption of radiant energy.
Photoelectric, *adj. phys.* Pertaining to, characterized by, electrical effects produced by exposure to light. Also photoelectrical.
Photoemission, fō'tō-ē-mish'un, *n.* From *photo–* and *emission. phys.* The emission of electrons upon exposure to light of a suitable wave length. **—Photoemissive,** *adj.*
Photo finish, *n. racing.* The termination of a very close race in which the victor must be determined by a high-speed photograph of the contestants as they cross the finish line.
Photoflash lamp, *n.* A lamp used in photography, giving a brilliant light of extremely short duration.
Photoflood lamp, *n.* A lamp used in photography giving a steady, intense light.
Photogenic*, *adj.* Pertaining to a person whose beauty, etc. is especially suitable for photographic purposes.
Photogrammetry, fō'tō-gram'e-tri, *n.* From *photo–* and *–gram* and *–metry.* The making of surveys and maps by means of photographs, esp. aerial photographs.
Photokinesis, fō'to-ki-nē'sis, *n.* From *photo* and *kinesis. physiol.* Movement induced by light
Photolysis, fō'tŏl'i-sis, *n.* From *photo–* and *–lysis. physical chem.* Decomposition due to the action of light. **—Photolytic,** *adj.*
Photomap, *n.* A map made of assembled aerial photographs.
Photometry, fō-tom'et-ri, *n.* See *photometer,* in the Dict. The measurement of the intensity of light; the branch of science concerned with this measurement.
Photomontage, fō'tō-mon-tazh', *n.* From *photo–* and *montage.* A series of photographs made into a single picture.
Photomural, fō'tō-mū'ral, *n.* A photograph of greatly enlarged size used as a wall decoration.
Photon, fō'ton, *n.* From Gr. *phot–,* stem of *phos,* light and *–on* by analogy w. electron. *phys.* A quantum of light energy.
Photoneutron, *n.* fo'to-nū'tron *phys.* A neutron released in photodisintegration.
Phototaxis, fō'tō-taks'is, *n.* From *photo–* and *–taxis. biol.* Movement of organisms toward or away from light. Also phototaxy.
Phototelegraphy, fō'tō-te-leg'ra-fi, *n.* From *photo–* and *telegraphy.* The transmission of a photographic image by telegraphic means.
Phototherapy, fō'tō-ther'a-pi, *n.* From *photo–* and *therapy. med.* The treatment of disease esp. of the skin by the application of light.
Photo-timer, *n.* An electrical device which photographs the finish of a race and records the elapsed time.
Photothermic, *adj.* From *photo–* and *thermic.* Pertaining to both light and heat.
Phototropism, fō-tot'rō-pizm, *n.* See TROPE in the Dict. *bot.* The growing of a plant in a particular direction because of the stimulus of light.
Physical chemistry, *n.* The branch of chemistry concerned with the interrelation of the physical and chemical properties of substances.
Physiotherapy, fiz'i-ō-ther'a-pi, *n.* From *physio–* and *therapy. med.* The treatment of disease by physical means, such as massage.
Phytocidal, fī'to-sīd'al, *adj.* From *phyto–* and *–cide.* Plant-killing.
Pick*, *v.t.* pick up*, (slang) to take into custody, arrest; pick on, to single someone out and pester, badger him.
Picked, *adj.* From PICK, above, and *ed.* Cleaned, stripped by picking; specially chosen; choice: a picked crew.
Picket boat, *n.* A Coast Guard patrol boat.
Pickup, *n.* See PICK in the Dict. (slang) Improvement; (slang) a stimulant, esp. an alcoholic drink; *automobiles* acceleration: the car has a fast pickup; a small, light truck; *radio* the receiving of sound in the transmitting set for conversion to electrical impulses; a receiving device; the place where a broadcast originates; device on a phonograph which converts the variations impressed on a record into electrical impulses; (slang) a person, esp. female, with whom one strikes up a casual acquaintance.
Picture window, *n.* A very large window affording a pleasing outside view.
Pig bed, *n.* A sand bed in which metal is cast into pigs.
Piggy-back, *adv.* Variant of PICKABACK, in the Dict.
Piggy bank, *n.* A small savings bank for a child, often shaped like a pig.
Pigskin*, *n.* (colloq.) A football.
Piker, *n.* Orig. uncertain. (U.S. slang) A small-time gambler, cautious investor, etc., (U.S. slang) a cheapskate; a shirker.
Pile*, *n. phys.* A type of nuclear reactor, consisting of a lattice arrangement of uranium and moderating materials used to make plutonium.
Pilot*, *attrib. n.* Serving as a small scale experimental unit, as a pilot model or pilot plant.
Pilot light, *n.* A small burner which burns continuously and serves to light a gas stove or water heater.
Pinball, *n.* A mechanical game played on a slanting board, usually with a spring arrangement to drive balls into numbered holes which are partially obstructed by pins or other obstacles. Also attrib.: pinball machine.
Pincers*, *n. mil.* Pincers movement, a striking at enemy lines from two widely divergent points, the two attacking columns attempting to converge like the jaws of a pincers and thus encircle the enemy.
Pinch-hit, *v.i. baseball* To serve as a pinch-hitter; to act as a substitute for someone; —*n.* a safe hit made by a pinch-hitter.
Pinch-hitter, *n. baseball* One who bats for another, esp. at a critical point in the game; one who substitutes for another in an emergency.
Pineapple*, *n.* (mil. slang) A hand grenade or dynamite bomb.
Pink*, *n.* A person slightly inclined to radical political views. Parlor pink, One who advocates radicalism in theory but not in practice.
Pinpoint, *v.t.* To make something specific or precise; esp. *mil.* to locate a target precisely for the purpose of bombing. —*adj.* Very precise; pinpoint bombing.
Pinto, pin'tō, *adj.* Sp. painted. western U.S. of a horse Spotted; piebald, —*n.* A pinto horse.
Pinup, *n.* An unframed picture of a sexually attractive person, especially a scantily dressed woman. —*adj.* Of, appearing in, such a picture: pinup girl.
Pip*, *n.* (slang) Something or someone greatly esteemed.
Pipe*, *v.i.* (colloq.) Phr. to pipe down, become less cock-sure, less exorbitant; to become quiet.
Pipe dream, *n.* An unrealistic hope, illusion likened to the visions produced by smoking opium.
Pipeline, *n.* A line of pipe for transporting liquids and gas; a source of information, esp. information of a confidential nature.
Pip-squeak, pip-skwēk, *n.* From the sound made by a Ger. high velocity shell used in World War I; by extension, (derog.) A futile person.
Pitch*, *n.* (slang) A sales talk; *aeron.* the distance a propeller advances in one revolution.
Pitchman, *n.* See PITCH, above. A salesman, specif. one who gives a sales talk to a group of people in the street, at a fair, etc.
Pix, *n.* pl. From pictures. (slang) Photographs, esp. for newspapers or magazines; moving pictures.
Pixilated, pik'si-lāt'ed, *adj.* From *pixy* and *led.* Orig. a dialect word of Marblehead, Mass., meaning bewildered, confused; current use for movie "Mr. Deeds Goes to Town," 1936. Eccentric in an amusing way.
Pizza, pēt'sa, *n.* Ital. A kind of pie made of baked bread dough covered with tomatoes, cheese, spices and often bits of meat, mushrooms, etc.
Pizzeria, pēt'se-rē'a, *n.* Ital. A bakery or restaurant where pizzas are sold.
Placatory, plā'ka-tō'ri, *adj.* From *placate* and *–ory.* Intended to placate; conciliatory.
Plane table, *n.* From *plane* and *table.* Drawing board mounted on a tripod and used, e.g., by surveyors.
Planetarium*, *n.* A machine which projects a representation of the solar system on a dome-shaped ceiling; a building which contains his machine.
Planner, *n.* From *plan* and *–er.* One who plans; esp., one who plans social and economic systems.
—Plast, suff. Combining form, from Gr. *plastós,* formed, meaning formed, molded.
Plastid, *n.* See –PLAST, above. *biol.* A cell; a specialized unit of protoplasm within certain cells.
Plasterboard, *n.* A kind of wallboard made of plaster and felt, with a paper covering used in place of plaster.
Plastic*, *n.* Any synthetic or processed organic compound that is capable of being molded; used in lacquers, as substitutes for wood, metal, etc.
Plate*, *n.* Phr. to hand someone something on a plate, *fig.* surrender something gratuitously.
Plateau*, *n.* A stage, indicated by a level stretch on a graph, in which there is little fluctuation: prices have reached a plateau.
Platform shoe, *n.* A woman's dress shoe with an extremely thick sole and a high heel.
Platter*, (slang) A phonograph record.
Playback machine or **playback,** *n.* See TURNTABLE, below.
Playhouse*, *n.* A house for children to play in.
Playoff, *n. sports* A contest to determine the winner among teams that have tied.
Playpen, *n.* A small rectangular enclosure in which a baby may play safely while unsupervised.
Playroom, *n.* A room in a home which has been fitted out for recreational purposes.
Playsuit, *n.* An informal summer ensemble for women, consisting of several pieces such as shorts, blouse, skirt, etc. which may be worn in various combinations.
Plebe, plēb, *n.* From *plebeian.* A member of the lowest class in the military academies at West Point or Annapolis.
Pledge*, *n.* A person who has pledged his intention of joining a fraternity and has entered a probationary period pending final acceptance.

Plein-air, plăn'ar', *adj.* Fr. open air. Pertaining to a school of painting concerned with representing effects, esp. of light, that are observable out of doors and not in the studio.

Plexiglass, pleks'i-glas, *n. trade-mark* A transparent, easily molded plastic, methyl methacrylate.

Pliofilm, plī-ō-film', *n. trade-mark* A nonporous material made from rubber; used in packaging, raincoats, etc.

Plottage, *n.* From *plot* and *-age.* The area of a plot of land.

Plug*, *n.* (U.S. colloq.) A short advertisement inserted into a radio program, etc.

Plummet*, *v.i.* To fall swiftly.

Plushy, *adj.* (slang) Luxurious, opulent. Also plush.

Plutonium, *n.* From Gr. *Ploúton,* Pluto, and *-ium. chem.* A radioactive element obtained from neptunium. Symbol: *Pu.* At. no.: 94. At wt.: 239.

—Ply, *suff.* Combining form of PLY, as in three-ply, four-ply, etc.

Pocket battleship, *n.* A small battleship, so built in order to keep within limits set by treaty.

Pocket veto, *n.* A method by which the president of the United States may prevent a bill passed within ten days of legislative adjournment from becoming law, by retaining it unsigned.

Podunk, pō'dunk, *n.* Orig. an Indian Algonquian place-name. (U.S.) Any small, insignificant town, esp. as characterized by dullness and backwardness.

Point*, *n. craps,* Any of the numbers 4–6 or 8–10 when turned up by a player on his first throw; he must throw that number again, before throwing a seven, in order to win.

Point, *n.* Slang for West Point, usu. with the.

Pointe, pwant' *n.* Fr. *dancing* A balancing position on the very tip of the toe.

Pointer*, *n.* (U.S. colloq.) A hint; piece of advice.

Poker face, *n.* From *poker.* (Colloq.) An expressionless face; orig. and esp., a face which does not betray the quality of one's poker hand.

Polarograph, pō-lar'ō-graf, *n.* From *polar* and *graph.* An instrument which automatically records the degree of electrical polarization in an electrolytic solution.

Polaroid, pō'ler-oid, *n. trade-mark* A material which polarizes light in such a way as to reduce glare; used in sunglasses, etc.

Police*, *v.t.* (usu. *mil.*) To clean up an encampment.

Police dog, *n.* A sheep dog of wolflike appearance, trained to assist the police.

Polio, pō'li-ō, *n.* (colloq.) Abbr. of poliomyelitis.

Poll*, *n.* An investigation of public opinion on a question. *—v.t.* To register the opinions of a sample of the public, etc.: he polled the audience on the question.

Pollster, *n.* From POLL, above and depreciatory suff. -STER in the Dict. (colloq.) sometimes derogatory. One who conducts public opinion polls.

Pollyanna, *n.* From the heroine in stories of Eleanor Porter, 1868–1920. An excessively optimistic, good-natured girl; any person characterized by these qualities. **—Pollyannaish,** *adj.*

Polo coat, *n.* A topcoat made of genuine or imitation camel's hair.

Polo shirt, *n.* A pull-over shirt of knit cotton, having short sleeves and no collar; a T-shirt.

Polyester, pol'i-es'ter, *n.* From *poly-* and *ester. chem.* A complex ester produced by polymerization.

Polymer, pol'i-mer, *n.* From Gr. *polumeres,* of many parts. *chem.* One of two or more polymeric compounds, esp. one produced by polymerization.

Polymerism*, *n. bot.* The state of being polymerous.

Polymerize, *v.t.* and *i.* From POLYMER, above, and *-ize.* To change into a polymer. **—Polymerization,** *n.*

Polymerous*, *adj.* From Gr. *polús,* many and *méros,* part. *bot.* Having many parts in each whorl.

Polyphyletic, pol-i-fī-let'ik, *adj.* From Gr. *polus,* many, and *phuletik-ós,* tribal. Descended from more than one ancestral type or family.

Polyploid, pol'i-ploid, *adj.* From *poly-* and Gr. *-plóos,* fold and *-oid. biol.* Having more than twice the haploid number of chromosomes. *—n.* An organism so characterized.

Polysaccharide, pol-i-sak'a-rīd, *n.* From *poly-* and *sacchar-* and *-ide. chem.* Any of several carbohydrates capable of hydrolysis into two or more molecules of monosaccharides.

Polystyrene, ——stī-rēn, *n.* See POLYMER, above, and STYRENE, below. *chem.* A transparent, easily molded plastic; a polymer of styrene.

Polyvalent, pol-i-va'lent, *adj.* From *poly-* and *-valent. chem.* Having more than one valence.

Ponderator, pon'der-ā-ter, *n. phys.* A particle accelerator in which particles approach the velocity of light so that, in accordance with Einstein's equations, the mass rather than the speed is increased as further energy is added.

Pony*, *n.* (colloq.) The amount of liquor a small liquor glass will hold; *—v.t.* and *i.* (U.S. slang) to pay money, as in settling a bill followed by up.

Pony express, *n.* A postal system in the western U.S. using relays of ponies 1860–61.

Pooch, *n.* Orig. uncertain. (slang) A dog, esp. an inferior one.

Poop*, *v.t.* (slang) To exhaust, cause to be out of breath.

Pop*, *n.* Clipped form of papa. *familiar* Father esp. as a mode of address.

Popular front, *n.* Fr. Front Populaire. A coalition against rightist or dictatorial parties by all other parties.

Pork*, *n.* (U.S. slang) Federal money or other favors granted primarily for reasons of political patronage.

Pork barrel, *n.* See PORK, above. (U.S. slang) A government appropriation for local improvements given primarily as political patronage. Also attrib.: pork barrel legislation.

Pork-chopper, *n.* See PORK, above. (U.S. labor slang) A union member holding a nonelective post and primarily interested in personal gain.

Pork-pie hat*, *n.* A felt hat for men, having a low crown relatively flat on top.

Posh, *n.* Prob. variant of BOSH, in the Dict. (slang) Nonsense: baloney.

Posh, *adj.* Prob. from poshed up, from polished up. (slang, orig. Brit.) Chic; swanky.

Positron, pos'i-tron, *n.* From *positive* and *electron;* coined by C. D. Anderson, who discovered it in 1932. *phys.* A positively charged particle having a mass equal to that of the electron.

Postdoctoral, *adj.* Pertaining to advanced study or research by one holding a doctor's degree, as a post-doctorial fellowship.

Post exchange, *n.* (U.S. mil.) A retail store on a military post. Abbr.: PX.

Postfix*, *v.t.* To affix at the end; suffix.

Post office*, *n.* (U.S.) A type of kissing game played esp. at children's parties.

Potato chip, *n.* A very thin slice of potato fried crisp in deep fat and served cold.

Pot-bound, *adj. of a plant* Suffering from insufficiency of space for its roots in a pot; *fig.* suffering from lack of room to expand.

Potlatch, *n.* From metathesis of Chinook *patschatl,* gift, giving. Northwestern U.S. Indians; *anthropol.* A festival or other occasion involving the ceremonial distribution of gifts.

POW, PW, *abbr.* Prisoner of war.

Powder*, *n.* Phr. take a powder criminal cant, to scram, beat it.

Power dive, *n.* In aviation, a steep descent using power of the plane's motor or motors.

Powerhouse*, *n. fig.* (slang) Someone or something of unusual strength.

Power politics, *n.* Tautological expression referring to international diplomacy in which the threat of ultimate resort to arms is particularly apparent.

Precondition, prē-con-dish'un, *v.t.* From *pre-* and *condition.* To put a person or thing in a desired condition beforehand.

Predate*, *n. journalism* A newspaper dated ahead of time, intended for distribution to outlying towns.

Predictor, *n.* A device for guiding anti-aircraft fire that predicts the position of the plane on the arrival of a shell.

Prefab, *n.* Abbr. of PREFABRICATED, below. (colloq.) Something prefabricated, esp. a house.

Prefabricate, —fab'ri-cāt, *v.t.* To manufacture parts according to established patterns for ease in assembly as in houses, etc. **—Prefabricated,** *adj.* **—Prefabrication,** *n.*

Preferential shop, *n.* A shop which gives preference in hiring to union members; nonunionists hired are often required to join the union.

Première*, *n.* The leading lady, esp. in a play. *—v.t.* To perform something in public for the first time: the play was premièred in Philadelphia.

Presell, *v.t. advertising* To pre-dispose customers for eventual purchase of an item, as by certain types of advertising.

Preshrink, *v.t.* To shrink fabrics before they are cut. **—Preshrunk,** *adj.*

Press*, *v.t.* To produce phonograph records from a master.

Press*, *n.* A device used to keep tennis rackets from warping when not in use.

Pressing*, *n.* A group of phonograph records issued from a master record.

Pressure cabin, *n.* A sealed airplane cabin which maintains an atmospheric pressure comparable to that at sea level.

Pressure group, *n.* A combination of persons or interests which seeks to influence legislation.

Pressurize, *v.t.* From *pressure* and *-ize.* To maintain in a sealed aircraft cabin atmospheric pressure comparable to that at sea level.

Preview, *n.* From *pre-* and *view.* An advance showing, esp. of a motion picture. *—v.t.* To show or view in advance. Also prevue.

Primary group, *n. sociol.* A social group characterized by intimate, face-to-face relationships.

Prize crew, *n.* Seamen and their officers, detailed from the crew of a victorious warship to man a captured vessel until it is brought into the victor's port.

Probable*, *n. mil.* An enemy plane retiring from battle in a badly damaged state, hence reported by the victorious flier as "a probable" loss to the enemy.

Procaine, pro-cān', *n.* From *pro-* and *cocaine.* A local anaesthetic, $C_{13}H_{20}N_2O_2$-HC_1, used as a substitute for cocaine because it is less toxic.

Process*, *v.t.* To put someone through a set of procedures, as in military examination, training program, etc.

Processing tax, *n.* A tax imposed on the process of preparing goods for the market.

Prod*, *n.* Phr. (colloq.) on the prod, angry.

Prof, *n.* Orig. an abbreviation spelled; now a clipped form pronouced. (slang) Professor.

Profile*, *n.* A concise biographical sketch of an individual; *psychol.* a graphic representation of personality factors of an individual.

Progesterone, pro-jes'ter-ōn, *n.* From *pro-* and *gestation* and *sterol* and *-one. biochem.* A hormone, $C_{21}H_{30}O_2$, which prepares the lining of the uterus for the fertilized ovum.

Projection*, *n. psychoanalysis* The attribution of qualities within oneself to the external environment. Cp. INTROJECTION, above.

Projectionist, *n.* An operator of a motion picture projector.

Prom, *n.* (colloq.) Clipped form of PROMENADE, in sense below.

Promenade*, *n.* An opening of a formal ball, in which the guests march into the ballroom; a formal dance or ball.

Promethium, pro-mē'thē-um, *n.* From Gr. *Prometheus,* Titan who gave fire to man, and *-ium.* Coined by J. A. Marinsky and L. E. Glendenin. A rare-earth element of atomic number 61. Symbol: *Pm.* At. wt.: approx. 147.

Pronto, *adv.* Sp. (U.S. colloq.) Quickly; promptly.
Prop*, *n. theatrical* (slang) Short for property See Dict. Often attrib.: prop man.
Prop, *n. avn.* (slang) Short for propeller.
Propellant*, *n.* The fuel and oxidizing agent for a rocket engine.
Proprietary*, *adj. phar.* Of a drug sold only by one company which has exclusive rights to its manufacture. Cp. ETHICAL, above.
Prosateur, prōs'a-tur, *n.* Fr. A writer of prose only.
Prospect*, *n.* (colloq.) A prospective buyer or client.
Protactinium, prō-tak-tin'i-um, *n.* Formerly protoactinium. *chem.* A radioactive element yielding actinium upon disintegration. Symbol: *Pa.* At. no.: 91. At. wt.: 231.
Protium, prō'ti-um, *n.* From *proto–* and *–ium. chem.* The usual isotype of hydrogen. At. wt.: 1.008. Symbol: H^0.
Protocol*, *n.* The rules of etiquette pertaining to diplomatic functions, esp. rules concerning order of precedence.
Protolithic, prō-tō-lith'ic, *adj.* From *proto–* and *lith–* and *–ic.* Pertaining to the earliest portion of the stone age; eolithic.
Protopathic, —path'ik, *adj.* From *proto* and *pathos* and *–ic physiol. of sensations* Not accurately localized nor accurately estimated. Contrasted with EPICRITIC, above.
Prowl car, *n.* A police car assigned to patrol a designated area.
Proximity fuse, *n.* A radio device which causes a projectile to detonate when near the target.
Psychodrama, sī'ko-dram-a, *n.* From *–psycho–* and drama. A psychotherapeutic technique involving spontaneous roletaking by the patients.
Psychogenesis*, *n.* From *psycho–* and *genesis.* Origination within the psyche.
Psychogenic, sī-ko-jen'ik, *adj.* See PSYCHOGENESIS, above, and *–ic.* Originating within the psyche, as a mental disorder.
Psychograph, sī'ko-graf, *n.* From *psycho–* and *–graph. psychol.* A chart or other record of a person's personality traits.
Psychoneurosis, sī-ko-nu-rō'sis, *n.* From *psycho–* and neurosis. A mental disorder having its origin in the psyche. —**Psychoneurotic,** *adj.* and *n.*
Psychosis*, *n. psychiat.* A severe type of mental disorder, which may or may not involve organic disease, characterized by extensive or total disruption of normal psychic functioning. —**Psychotic,** *adj.* and *n.*
Psychosomatic, —sō-mat'ik, *adj.* From *psycho–* and *somatic.* Involving both mind and body; specif., of physical disorders caused at least in part by mental disturbances.
Psychosurgery, —surj'eri, *n.* From *psycho–* and *surgery.* A type of brain surgery used in the treatment of mental disorders.
PT boat, *n.* abbr. of patrol torpedo *boat.* A small, very fast U.S. Navy torpedo boat.
Public-address system, *n.* An arrangement for broadcasting sound over a wide area, composed of a microphone, amplifier, and one or more loud-speakers. Often abbrev. **P.A. system.**
Public domain, *n.* Property to which there is no private patent or copyright.
Pull*, *v.t.* (slang) To carry out, execute. Phr. to pull a fast one, do something tricky and unfair.
Pull*, *n.* (slang) Influence with those in authority.
Pulp*, *n.* (colloq.) A magazine printed on cheap, coarse paper, the contents being sensational in character and of poor literary quality. Cp. SLICK, below.
Pulse-jet engine, *n. aeron.* A jet engine having an intermittent or pulsating thrust.
Punch*, *v.t.* (Western U.S.) To drive, prod cattle.
Punch board, *n.* A gambling device consisting of a board containing holes which are punched through to reveal various numbers, etc.
Punch drunk, *adj.* esp. of professional boxers. Mentally incapacitated, in the manner of a drunken person, by repeated blows about the head.
Punching bag, *n.* An inflated or stuffed bag, usually suspended, punched for exercise.
Punch line, *n.* The climactic, usually final, line of a joke, story, etc.
Punk*, *adj.* (slang) Rotten, worthless, no good at all.
Punk*, *n.* Fr. underworld slang. A trigger man.
Pup tent, *n.* (U.S.) Army shelter tent issued to a team of two soldiers, each man responsible for his half-tent until the two halves are put together to provide shelter for the pair.
Purism, *n.* The artistic theory and practice emphasizing the use of familiar and recognizable objects in painting.
Pursuit plane, *n. mil.* A small, fast fighter of great maneuverability, with heavy fire power and capable of good performance at high altitudes.
Push button, *n.* A small button which closes an electric circuit when pushed. Often attrib.: push-button warfare.
Pushover, *n.* (slang) A person easily defeated; a task easily performed; a gullible person, one easily taken in: he's a pushover for a sob-story.
Pussyfoot, *n.* A timid person; one who is wary of committing himself.
Put*, *v.t.* (U.S. slang) Put over, to get the public to accept an idea, etc.
P.X., abbr. Post exchange.
Pyrex, *n. trade mark* A heat-resistant glass used to make cooking utensils.
Pyridoxine, pir-i-dok'sēn, *n.* From *pyridine* and *oxy–.* Vitamin B_6, $C_8H_{11}NO_3$, essential to human nutrition, found in eggs, wheat, fish, etc.
Q-fever, *n.* From *Queensland, Australia,* where first noted. A disease caused by rickettsia, characterized by fever, chills and muscle pains.
Quadrivalent*, *adj.* From *quadri–* and *–valent. chem.* Having a valence of four; exhibiting four different valences.
Quarantine*, *v.t.* To cut off a country from ordinary business or political relations.
Quick-freeze, *v.t.* To freeze food rapidly at very low temperatures so that natural flavor is retained.
Quickie, *n.* From *quick* (slang) Anything hastily and cheaply produced, as certain movies.
Quint*, *n.* (colloq.) A quintuplet.
Quisle, quiz'l, *v.i.* Back-formation from QUISLING, below. To betray one's country by collaborating with a conquering enemy.
Quisling, *n.* From Vidkun *Quisling,* Norwegian collaborator with the Nazi invaders. One who betrays his country by collaborating with the conquering enemy.
Quiz*, *v.t.* To examine a class of students, etc.
Quonset hut, qwan'sit, *n.* From Quonset, R. I., orig. place of manufacture. A semicylindrical building made of corrugated metal, used by armed forces, in World War II; later used extensively for other purposes.
Rabble-rouser, *n.* One who makes inflammatory speeches; a demagogue.
Racism, rā'sizm, *n.* From *race* and *–ism.* A doctrine of the physical, mental, or moral superiority of certain races.
Racist, *n.* From *race* and *–ist.* One who advocates, believes in, racism. —*adj.* Pertaining to, characterized by, racism.
Racket*, *n.* (U.S. slang) Any illegal or dishonest activity.
Racon, rā-con, *n.* Acronym of *ra*dar bea*con.* A system of navigation in which a ship or aircraft receives a coded signal from a radar beacon by sending a proper radar signal of its own.
Radar, rā'dar, *n.* Acronym of *ra*dio *d*etecting *a*nd *r*anging. A device which locates objects at a distance by the use of ultra high-frequency radio waves.
Radial engine, *n.* An internal combustion engine with cylinders arranged radially around the crankshaft.
Radiation sickness, *n.* A condition resulting from overexposure to radioactivity, characterized by internal bleeding, nausea, etc.
Radio—*, *pref. chem.* Referring to radioactive isotopes, as radiocarbon.
Radio*, *n.* A wireless receiving set. —*adj.* Pertaining to, employed in, radio; pertaining to, using, radiant energy.
Radioastronomy, *n.* From *radio–* and *astronomy.* The use of high-frequency radio waves to study the movements of the sun, meteors, and stars.
Radioautograph, rā-di-ō-o'to-graf, *n.* From *radio–* and *autograph.* A picture produced on a sensitized surface by radioactive emanation from the object.
Radio beam, *n.* A continuous radio signal transmitted along a narrow path, used esp. for the guidance of aircraft.
Radiofrequency*, *n.* Any frequency above 15,000 cycles per second. Also attrib.
Radiogenic, rā-dē-ō-jēn'ik, *adj.* From *radio* and *genesis. of certain elements* Produced by radioactivity.
Radioisotope, rā-di-ō-ī'sō-tōp, *n.* From *radio* and *isotope. phys. and chem.* A radioactive isotope.
Radiology*, *n.* Specif. the study of the medical applications of X rays and rays from radioactive substances in general.
Radiometeorograph, rā-di-ō-mē'tē-or-o-graf', *n.* RADIOSONDE, below.
Radionics, rā-dē-oniks, *n.* From *radio–* and electr*onics.* Electronics.
Radiophonograph, *n.* A combination radio receiver and phonograph.
Radiosonde, rā-dē-ō-sond', *n.* Fr. *meteor.* A device which, carried aloft by a balloon, automatically registers and broadcasts information on atmospheric temperature, pressure and humidity.
Radiothermy, *n.* From *radio–* and Gr. *therme,* heat. A medical treatment which makes use of the heat generated by a short-wave radio apparatus.
Radiothorium*, rā-di-ō-thor'ium, *n.* From RADIO, above, and *thorium. chem.* A radioactive isotope of thorium.
Radon, rā'don, *n.* From radium and *–on* by analogy w. neon, argon, etc. *chem.* A radioactive but chemically inert gas, element 86. Symbol: *Rn.* Atomic wt.: 222.
Raffinose, raf'i-nōs, *n.* From *raffiner,* to refine and *–ose. chem.* A colorless, crystalline sugar, $C_{18}H_{32}O_{16}$, having a slightly sweet taste, occurring in the sugar beet, cottonseed, etc.
Railhead*, *n. mil.* Point on a railroad where supplies are distributed or transferred to other means of transport.
Railroad gun, *n.* An eight-inch or other caliber gun moved about on specially built railroad-train platforms.
Rain check, *n.* A check given to spectators at an outdoor sporting event, etc., to be used at a future date in the event the performance is stopped by rain; *fig.* an assurance of being able to accept an invitation at a future date: I can't come tonight, but I'll take a rain check on the invitation.
Raise*, *n.* (U.S.) An increase in amount, esp. in wages. Cp. RISE in the Dict.
Rake-off, rāk'of, *n.* (slang) Pecuniary profit made illegitimately by one or more persons concerned in a transaction; also, middleman's profit.
Rambunctious, ram-bunk'shus, *adj.* Orig. uncertain. (colloq.) Unrestrained; boisterous.
Ramjet, *n.* From *ram* and *jet. aeron.* An aviation engine with no moving parts, depending for its power on the thrust developed by exhaust gases from a burner in combination with oxygen from the atmosphere.
Range computer, *n.* A large boxlike field instrument, working in conjunction with the range finder, for automatic timing and directing of gunfire.
Range-finder, *n. photog.* A device used to determine the distance between the camera and an object, so as to assure proper focusing.
Ranger*, *n. cap.* During World War II, member of a special U.S. military unit trained for sudden raids on enemy installations; comparable to the British Commando.

Rank-and-file, *n. mil.* The body of a military unit, as distinct from its officers; hence, the majority of members, as of a labor union, not holding important offices.
Rathskeller, *n.* Ger., from *ratskeller,* town-hall cellar. A cellar restaurant serving beer, similar in function to the cellar of a German town hall.
Raticide, rat-i-sīd, *n.* From *rat* and *-cide.* Any substance used to exterminate rats.
Ravioli, rav-i-ō'li, *n.* Ital. pl. A cooked dish of small pieces of dough enclosing minced and seasoned meat or vegetables.
Ray*, *n.* Cosmic rays, penetrating rays producing ionization and coming from an extraterrestrial source.
Razz, *v.t.* From RASPBERRY, in the Dict. (U.S. slang) To deride; to give a raspberry to. —*n.* Derision; a raspberry.
R-colored, *adj. phon.* of a vowel Pronounced with an *r* quality, as the vowels in murmur.
Reach*, *v.t.* To communicate with.
Reaction*, *n. chem.* and *phys.* Nuclear reaction, one involving change in the nucleus of the atom.
Reactivate, rē-ak'ti-vāt, *v.t.* From *re-* and *active* and *-ate.* To restore a military unit to active service; to change an organization or condition from a dormant state to an active one.
Reactor, re-ak'tor, *n.* From *react* and *-or.* That which reacts; *elect.* a device for promoting reactance in a circuit; *phys.* any of several types of devices for producing controlled nuclear fission.
Readership, *n.* The total number of actual readers of a magazine, newspaper, etc.
Real McCoy, *n.* See McCOY, above.
Recap, *v.t.* From *re-* and *cap.* To renovate used motor tires by refurbishing the worn tread with prepared strips of rubber. —*n.* A tire so renovated.
Recap, *n.* (slang) Clipped form of recapitulation.
Receptionist, *n.* From *reception* and *-ist.* An employee, as in a business office, who receives callers.
Recession*, *n.* A mild economic depression.
Reconstructed, rē-kon-strukt'ed, *adj.* From *reconstruct* and *-ed.* Rebuilt; *of persons* converted to more liberal political views. Contrasted with UNRECONSTRUCTED, below.
Reconvert*, *v.t.* Specif., to adapt an industrial plant for producing civilian goods again, after termination of production of war materials.
Record*, *n.* Phr. off the record, not for publication.
Record player, *n.* A machine for playing phonograph records, consisting essentially of a turntable, amplifier, and loudspeaker.
Recreation room, *n.* A room, esp. in a home, set aside and fitted out for indoor games.
Rectification*, *n. elect.* The process of converting an alternating current into a direct current.
Redbait, *v.t.* and *i.* From *red* and *bait.* (colloq.) To attack, denounce publicly as a radical.
Red-blooded, *adj.* Virile; courageous.
Redcap, *n.* (U.S.) A porter in a railroad station; (Brit. colloq.) a military policeman; the European goldfinch.
Red-eye*, *n.* (slang) Inferior whiskey.
Red light, *n.* A red lamp used as a signal of danger, esp. as a traffic signal to stop.
Reefer*, *n.* (U.S. slang) A marijuana cigarette.
Reform school, *n.* Reformatory.
Refresher*, attrib. Serving to refresh one's mind on a subject previously studied: refresher course.
Register*, *v.t. movie acting* To depict, express usually some emotion; (by extension) (colloq.) to express, represent.
Reject*, *n.* That which has been rejected, esp. a defective manufactured article.
Relativistic, *adj.* From *relativist* and *-ic.* In accordance with the principles of, accepting the postulates of, relativity: relativistic, as opposed to Newtonian, mechanics.
Relocate, rē-lō-cāt', *v.t.* From *re-* and *locate.* To locate again; to locate elsewhere.
Relocation, *n.* From RELOCATE, above, and *-ion.* (U.S. mil.); *euphemism* Forcible removal from coastal areas and internment inland; specif., of Americans of Japanese descent during World War II.
Renegotiate, rē-nē-gō'shi-āt', *v.t.* and *i.* From *re-* and *negotiate.* To negotiate again; esp. to adjust a war contract to make the contracted price of a product conform more closely to production costs.
Renin, rē-nin, *n.* From L. *ren,* kidney, and *-in. biochem.* A protein which increases blood pressure, found in the kidney.
Rental*, *adj.* Pertaining to rent. Rental library, one lending books for a small fee.
Rent party, *n.* (U.S., esp. urban Negro) A party at which guests give a small fee in order to help pay the rent.
Reprint*, *n. philately* An impression of a stamp from an old plate, no longer used for postage.
Re-recording, *n. movies* Changing the sound-track by mixing or by adding a voice or voices to it.
Resinoid, rez'i-noid, *adj.* From *resin* and *-oid.* Resinlike; —*n.* gum resin; a synthetic resin.
Resinol, res'i-nol, *n.* From *resin* and *-ol. chem.* Any of several alcohols occuring as esters in resins.
Resistance*, *n.* usually w. *the; often cap.* The various underground groups in countries conquered by the Axis in World War II, organized to carry out sabotage against the enemy.
Resnatron, res'na-tron, *n.* From *resona*tor and elec*tron. milit.* A powerful type of electron tube used to jam enemy radar.
Rest mass, *n. phys.* The mass of a body at rest, *i.e.* exclusive of the mass gained in motion by the transformation of energy into mass in accordance with the theory of relativity.
Retread, rē'tred', *n.* From *re-* and *tread.* A motor tire, the original tread of which has been removed and replaced by new rubber. —*v.t.* To furnish with new treads.
Rev, *n.* (colloq.) Abbrev. of revolution of a motor. —*v.t.* and *i. avn.* (slang) Rev up, to increase, or rev down, to decrease, the number of revolutions per minute of an airplane motor.
Revisionism, rē-vizh'on-ism, *n.* From *revision* and *-ism.* Policy, advocacy, of revising something; specif., *of revision* the Versailles and associated treaties; Marxism.
Revisionist, *n.* and *adj.* One who works, or is in favor of, revisionism.
Rewrite*, *v.t.* (U.S.) *journalism* To write the news submitted by a reporter in a form suitable for publication. —*n.* The article so written.
R.F.D., *abbr.* Rural free delivery.
Rh factor, *n.* A substance found in red blood cells; named from rhesus monkey in which it was first discovered. Rh positive: blood containing this factor; Rh negative: blood from which the factor is absent. Also Rhesus factor.
Rheology, *n.* From *rheo-* and *-logy.* The scientific study of the flow of liquids, gases and plastic substances.
Rheometer*, *n.* From *rheo-* and *-meter.* An instrument for measuring rate of flow, as of blood.
Rhubarb*, *n. baseball* (slang) A lively altercation, especially one involving several players and an umpire.
Rhumba, *n.* Variant of rumba, below.
Rib*, *v.t.* (slang) To ridicule, make fun of.
Ribbing*, *n.* See RIB, above. An instance of being ridiculed; he took a ribbing for his error.
Ribbon building or **development,** *n.* (Brit.) The building of homes and stores in lines along roads, esp. roads leading from cities into the country.
Riboflavin, *n.* From FLAVIN, and RIBOSE, below. *biochem.* Vitamin B_2, $C_{17}H_{20}N_4O_6$, promoting growth and found in eggs, green vegetables, etc.
Ribose, rī'bōs, *n.* From *ribonic* a pentose sugar, and *-ose.* A pentose, $C_5H_{10}O_5$, derived esp. from certain nucleic acids.
Rickettsia, rik-ket'sea, *n.* See RICKETS in the Dict. A micro-organism of the genus *Rickettsia,* causing certain fever diseases in man. —**Rickettsial,** *adj.*
Rickey, *n.* Said to be named after a Colonel Rickey. A drink made of lime juice, carbonated water and a spirituous liquor, esp. gin; a carbonated lime drink, without liquor.
Ride*, *v.t.* (slang) To tease, harass.
Riff, *n.* From *refrain.* (colloq.) *music* A brief melodic figure, repeated in the background of a piece of swing music.
Rigger*, *n.* See RIG in the Dict. A person skilled in structural work on airplanes, with hoisting apparatus, or in fitting ships' rigging; a protective scaffold around a building on which work is being done.
Rightist, *n.* From *right* and *-ist.* A person holding reactionary or conservative political views. —*adj.* Having such views.
Right-of-way, *n.* The land acquired for railroad tracks, power lines, etc.
Rimland, *n.* From *rim* and *land.* In geopolitics, an area on the boundary of the heartland.
Ringer*, *n.* (slang) An athlete or horse fraudulently entered in a contest misrepresented as to identity or ability; (slang) one who closely resembles another.
Rip cord, *n.* The release cord on a parachute, withdrawing the parachute from its pack; in a balloon, a cord by which the gas bag may be opened to cause a quick descent.
Rip current or **tide,** *n.* Cp. RIPPLE in Dict. A rough water current, as that caused by passage over a shoal.
Riprap*, *n.* ablaut reduplication of *rap.* —*v.t.* To strengthen with a riprap.
Rip-roaring, *adj.* (slang) Hilarious; tumultuous: a rip-roaring party.
Risk capital, *n.* Same as VENTURE CAPITAL, below.
Ritzy, *adj.* From various elegant hotels named after builder César Ritz. (slang) Ostentatiously elegant; smart.
River novel, *n.* See ROMAN-FLEUVE, below.
Road agent, *n.* (Western U.S.) A highwayman.
Roadblock, rōd-blok, *n.* A barricade across a highway to stop traffic for military or law-enforcement purposes.
Roadhouse*, *n.* A roadside hotel, tavern, or dance hall.
Robot bomb, *n.* A jet- or rocket-propelled bomb.
Robot plane, *n.* An airplane guided by remote radio control.
Rock candy, *n.* Sugar in the form of large, hard crystals.
Rocket*, *n.* A jet engine based on the principles of the rocket firework.
Rocket bomb, *n.* A bomb propelled by rocket power, either launched from a plane or from the ground.
Rocket launcher, *n. mil.* Any type of tubular weapon used to launch rocket shells, as the bazooka.
Rocketry, *n.* The study of rockets.
Rock wool, *n.* A fluffy, wool-like material made from molten rock and used in insulating.
Rod*, *n.* (U.S. slang) A pistol.
Rodenticide, rō-den'ti-cīd, *n.* From *rodent* and *-cide.* A rat or mouse poison.
Roger, *interj.* (slang) All right; OK.
Roll*, *n.* (U.S. slang) A large wad of paper money; hence, money in general.
Roll*, *v.i. Roll in*; slang to pay a casual or unexpected visit, to arrive. *Roll up*; to keep a rendezvous, put in an appearance; to arrive in large numbers. *Roll back*; to reduce the amount of anything to a previous level.
Rollback, *n.* An instance of rolling back, as of prices.
Roller bearing, *n. mach.* A bearing in which the journal rotates on steel rollers.
Roller coaster, *n.* A circular railway with several slopes, designed for amusement purposes.
Rollway, *n.* A road where logs are rolled into a river, or where objects are moved on rollers.
Romaine, rō-mān', *n.* Fr., fem. of *romain,* Roman. A type of lettuce with long, narrow leaves.
Roman à clef, ro-man'na-klā *n.* Fr., novel with a key. A novel with real persons and events disguised as fiction.
Roman-fleuve, ro-man'fluv', *n.* Fr.,

stream-novel. A type of novel, esp. French, consisting of a long, detailed social history of the generations of a family or other social group. Also called saga novel.

Room clerk, *n.* Clerk in charge of assigning rooms to guests at a hotel.

Roomette, *n.* From *room* and *-ette.* (U.S.) *railroads* A small combination bedroom and living room on a railroad car.

Root*, *v.i.* From rout, to shout. (U.S. slang) To applaud, encourage, a contestant.

Rooter, *n.* Root, above, and *-er.* (U.S. slang) One who roots in sense above.

Rorschach test, rōr'shak, *n.* Named after Swiss psychiatrist Hermann Rorschach, 1884–1922. A psychological test analyzing the subject's interpretations of ten inkblots, used to obtain a picture of the subject's personality and for diagnostic purposes.

Rotisserie, rō'tēs'rē', *n.* From Fr. *rotir,* to roast. (U.S.) A restaurant where patrons may select meat and watch it be roasted; an oven fitted with a spit for broiling meat.

Rotogravure, —gra-vūr', *n.* From Lat. *rota,* wheel and *gravure.* A type of photogravure using etched copper cylinders on a rotary press; a picture so printed; (U.S.) *journalism* the section of a newspaper devoted to such pictures. Also roto section.

Rotor*, *n.* A group of rotating blades used to provide lift for an aircraft, as in a helicopter.

Rotor plane, *n.* An airplane supported by rotating horizontal blades, as a helicopter.

Roughage, ruf'aj', *n.* From *rough* and *-age.* Rough or course material; specif., food of low nutritive value.

Rough-house, *v.i.* From Phr. a rough house, see under Rough. To behave rowdily; to brawl.

Roundabout*, *n.* (Brit.) Arrangement of the roadways, at a junction, such that traffic circulates in one direction round a central object or space.

Round table, *n.* A group of persons meet for the purpose of discussion; the meeting itself.

Round-the-clock, *adj.* Continuously for over twenty-four hours: round-the-clock bombing.

Round trip, *n.* A trip to a place and back. —**Round-trip,** *adj.*

Rove-over, *adj. prosody* In sprung rhythm, a metrical foot consisting of the end of one line and the beginning of the next.

Rube, *n.* From personal name *Reuben.* (U.S. slang) A rustic; country bumpkin.

Rugged*, *adj.* Difficult; trying: hockey is a rugged sport.

Rumba, *n.* Sp. A complex Afro-Cuban dance; modified version of it as danced elsewhere. Also rhumba.

Rumble*, *n.* In full, rumble-seat. A small folding seat behind the covered part of an automobile.

Rumpus room, *n.* A room, usually in the basement of a home, set aside for recreational purposes.

Runaround, *n.* From *run* and *around.* (slang) Evasion.

Run-in, *n.* (U.S. slang) A quarrel.

Runoff, *n.* Water which is drained off land surface; a decisive final contest to determine a single winner.

Run-through, *n.* (colloq.) A quick rehearsal, as of a play or radio script.

Runway, *n.* A specially prepared level lane for airplane landings and take-offs; any similar lane, as for automobiles, etc.; the channel of a stream.

Rural free delivery, *n.* Free delivery of mail to isolated country districts. Abbrev.: R. F. D.

Rurban, rur'ban, *adj.* From *rural* and *urban.* Partaking of both rural and urban characteristics, as a town.

Rush*, *n. movies.* A preliminary print of a scene just filmed usually pl.

Sabotage*, *v.t.* To commit sabotage upon.

Saboteur, sab'o-tur', *n.* Fr. One who engages in sabotage.

Saddle shoe, *n.* An oxford reinforced over the instep with a wide band or "saddle" of leather, the saddle being of a darker color than the rest of the shoe.

Saddle soap, *n.* A mild, oily soap used especially to clean leather.

Sadism, *n.* Loosely, any form of cruelty.

Sadist, sad'ist, *n.* From Sadism and *-ist.* Person who displays sadism.

Sadistic, *adj.* From *sadism* and *-ic.* Characteristic of, pertaining to, a sadist.

Sad sack, *n.* (U.S. slang) An inept person; esp. a clumsy soldier.

Safecracker, *n.* A person who felonously opens a safe by using tools or explosives; a burglar who specializes in opening safes.

Safety belt*, *n. avn.* A belt, attached to the seat of an airplane, for securing the wearer during turns, landings, etc.

Safety glass, *n.* A shatterproof glass consisting of two layers of glass separated by a layer of polyvinyl acetate.

Saga novel, *n.* See Roman-Fleuve, above.

Salariat, sa-lar'i-at, *n.* From Salary and *-ate.* Salaried workers as a class.

Salesclerk, *n.* From *sales* and *clerk.* A salesman at a store counter.

Salesresistance, *n.* Resistance to salesmanship, refusal to buy or order goods, etc.

Sales tax, *n.* A tax imposed on the selling price of goods, usually at retail.

Salty*, *adj.* Saucy; provocative; racy: salty humor, remarks, etc.

Salvo*, *n.* A group of bombs released together from an airplane.

Samba, *n.* Port., of African origin. A lively Brazilian dance, in duple time.

Sanction*, *n.* Measure adopted by several countries to coerce a nation into compliance with international law.

Sand lot, *n.* An improvised playing field for baseball and similar games. Also attrib.: sand lot baseball.

Sanforized, *adj. trade-mark of cotton and linen fabrics* Mechanically shrunk by a patented process, so as to reduce shrinkage in the finished produce.

Sansei, San'sā, *n.* Jap., third generation. An American of Japanese descent whose grandparents were immigrants to the U.S.

Sarge, sarj, *n. mil.* (colloq.) Abbr. of sergeant.

Sashay, *v.i.* From Fr. *chassé,* a gliding dance step. (U.S. colloq.) To perform a gliding dance step; hence, to go; to glide as in dancing.

Sass, *n.* Dialect variant of sauce.

Satellite*, *n.* A state subordinated to a larger state and completely dominated by it. Also attrib.: satellite country.

Scalp*, *v. t.* To buy esp. tickets and resell them for more than the official prices.

Scan*, *v.t.* and *i. television.* To analyze an optical image, as by an electron beam, for the purpose of reproduction.

Scat*, *n.* (slang) Nonsense-words used as the lyrics of a song. Also attrib.: scat singer.

Scene*, *n.* In movies, a shot, which see below.

Schedule*, *v.t.* (colloq.) To plan to do something at a fixed future date.

Schizoid, skiz'oid, *adj.* See *schizo-* and *-oid. psychiat.* Resembling, tending toward, schizophrenia. —*n.* A person so characterized.

Schizophrenia, skiz-o-frēn-ia, *n.* Coined by psychiatrist Eugen Bleuler, 1857–1939. *psychiat.* The commonest type of psychosis, characterized esp. by withdrawal from the world of reality, also delusions and hallucinations.

Schizophrenic, *adj.* Suffering from, characterized by, schizophrenia. —*n.* A person suffering from schizophrenia.

Schmaltz, *n.* Yiddish, from Ger. *schmalz,* fat. (slang) Extreme sentimentalism, esp. as occurring in music. —**Schmaltzy,** *adj.*

Schnörkel, *n.* See Snorkel, below.

Schwa, *n.* Ger. from Heb. *sh'wa. phonetics.* The vowel sound in wholly unaccented syllables, as the a of sofa or the e of soften; the phonetic symbol used to represent this sound.

Scope*, *n.* Short for periscope, oscilloscope, etc.

Scorched earth, *n.* A military policy of destroying everything useful to the enemy before retreating.

Score*, *n.* (colloq.) The unvarnished facts of a situation: he knows what the score is.

Scotch tape, *n. trade mark.* An adhesive cellulose tape.

Scram, *v.i.* From *scramble.* (U.S. slang) To depart hastily; esp. imperat.: Scram! off with you.

Scrappy*, *adj.* (colloq.) Aggressive; always willing to fight.

Scratch hit, *n. baseball.* A safe hit due to an accident; a hit which ordinarily should have been an out.

Scratch test, *n. med.* A test for allergy made by scratching various irritating substances into the skin.

Screen*, *v.t. movies.* To make a moving picture of a play, etc.

Screen*, *v.t. esp. mil.* To weigh, test the qualifications of a person, as for military service.

Screenwriter, *n.* One who writes stories in form suitable for motion picture production, or adapts others' stories to this form.

Screwball, *n.* (U.S. slang) A person who behaves eccentrically. —*adj.* Eccentric; unorthodox.

Screwy, *adj.* (U.S. slang) Not quite right in the head; slightly mad. See Phr. a screw loose, under Screw in the Dict.

Scrip*, *n.* Paper or token money issued not by a bank or by a state treasury, but by a municipality or by some organization for production and exchange, and backed not by gold but by goods. Also attrib.: scrip money: scrip group, group of persons using this medium of exchange.

Scuff, *n.* A lounging slipper without heel or quarter.

Scuttle*, *v.t.* To wreck or spoil: he scuttled our plans.

Scuttlebutt, *n.* From *scuttle* and *butt.* (U.S. Navy slang) Rumor; gossip.

Seabees, se'bēs', *n.* pl. Respelling of C.B., abbr. for construction battalion. The construction battalions of the U.S. Navy.

Sea cock, *n.* A valve opening and closing a pipe crossing a ship's hull and leading to the sea.

Sea food, *n.* Any edible salt-water fish or shellfish.

Sealant, sēl'ant, *n.* From *seal* and *-ant.* Any substance used for sealing.

Seaway*, *n.* An inland water route connecting to the sea and capable of receiving ocean vessels.

Second lieutenant, *n.* A commissioned officer of the lowest grade in the U.S. Army and Marine Corps.

Section*, *n. railroads* A section of railroad track maintained by a single crew; a division of a sleeping car including an upper and a lower berth.

Section*, *n. railroads.* A section of railroad section crew.

Seed*, *v.t.* To drop pellets of dry ice, etc. into clouds to produce rain.

Seeing Eye, *n.* An organization which trains dogs as guides for the blind.

Seersucker*, *n.* A cotton material with rough surface.

Selectee, *n.* From *select* and *-ee.* (U.S.) One drafted into the armed forces.

Self-addressed, *adj.* of an envelope, etc. Addressed by and to oneself.

Self-service, *adj.* Pertaining to a restaurant, store, etc. in which the customers serve themselves. —*n.* The serving of oneself.

Sellout, *n.* (colloq.) A performance, as of a play or sports event, for which all the available seats have been sold.

Seminary*, *n.* A seminar; original research done by students, under faculty direction, and the exposition of this research by discussion, lectures, etc.

Separation center, *n.* A station at which armed forces personnel are discharged from the service.

Sequence*, *n. movies.* Succession of shots together forming a main division of a film.

Serigraph, ser'i-graf, *n.* A color print made by serigraphy.

Serigraphy, *n.* sē-rig'ra-fi See Sericeous and -graphy. A process in which an artist makes color reproductions of his work by squeezing pigments through stencils prepared on silk screens, one stencil being used for each color.

Serology, *n.* From *sero-* and *-logy.* The scientific study of the nature and use of various types of serums.

Service*, *v.t.* To repair; put in condition for service.
Service club, *n.* A place offering recreational facilities to military personnel; an organization devoted to civic welfare.
Serviceman, *n.* A member of the armed forces; one whose trade is the repair and maintenance of something: radio serviceman.
Service station, *n.* An establishment that sells gasoline, oil and other supplies to motorists.
Set, *adj.* (slang) Ready to begin; ready to start away: esp., all set, quite ready.
Set-aside, *n.* Something, esp. a portion of total goods produced, set aside or reserved for special use.
Settle*, *v.t.* and *i.* Settle for, be content with: he settled for a fraction of what he had originally demanded.
Setup, *n.* The way in which something is organized or set up: the school has a good research setup; (U.S.) carriage of the body; (U.S. slang) a task or contest deliberately made easy; (U.S. slang) a contest with an opponent whom it is easy to defeat.
Sex hormone, *n. biochem.* Any of several hormones which affect the sexual functions, usually by having a stimulatory effect.
Shadowboxing, *n.* Boxing against an imaginary opponent, esp. for training purposes.
Shadowgraph, —graf, *n.* From *shadow* and *-graph.* A picture produced by a shadow, esp. of the hands, on a screen; a radioautograph.
Shakedown cruise, *n.* (U.S. Navy) A trial cruise of a newly commissioned ship, made to condition the ship and to familiarize the crew with it.
Shangri-La, *n.* Name of utopian city in James Hilton's novel Lost Horizon, 1933. An idealized place of retreat, hidden from the rest of the world.
Sharkskin*, *n.* A smooth, hard-finished fabric, made of cotton or rayon.
Shebang, *n.* (slang) Affair; thing: usually in Phr. the whole shebang.
Sheet*, *n.* A flat, tin-plated baking utensil used for cookies, cakes, etc.
Shellac*, *v.t.* (U.S. slang) To beat, thrash; hence, to defeat decisively.
Shellacking, *n.* From SHELLAC, above. and *-ing.* (U.S. slang) A severe beating; hence, a decisive defeat.
Shell game, *n.* A swindling game at carnivals, etc., resembling thimblerig; hence, any swindling game.
Shelter half, *n.* Half of a shelter tent, carried by an individual soldier.
Shelter tent, *n.* A small tent of waterproof material, constructed by fastening two halves together with buttons, etc.
Shenanigan, *n.* Origin unknown. (colloq.) often pl. Trickery; nonsense.
Shivaree, *n.* Variant of *charivari.* (U.S.) A mock serenade with pans, horns, etc., esp. as given to newlyweds. —*v.t.* To serenade, annoy, in this manner.
Shock absorber, *n. mach.* Any device for reducing the effects of vibration, sudden blows, etc., especially in an automobile.
Shock therapy, *n. psychiat.* The treatment of certain psychotic conditions by use of shock, artificially induced by means of electrical impulses or drugs such as insulin.
Shock troops, *n.* pl. *mil.* Troops specially selected and trained for use in an initial assault.
Shoestring*, *n.* (U.S. colloq.) Phr. to start a business on a shoestring, to start with a very small amount of capital; *baseball* shoestring catch, a catch of a ball just before it hits the ground.
Shooting iron, *n.* (U.S. slang) A firearm.
Shooting star*, *n.* A flower, the American cowslip *Dodecatheon meadia.*
Shoran, *n.* Acronym of short range navigation. A method for computing the position of an aircraft by timing radar signals from two known radio stations.
Shore patrol, *n.* The military police of the U.S. Navy. Abbr.: SP.
Short*, *n. elect.* A short circuit; a short motion picture; also, short subject; *baseball* (colloq.) shortstop.
Shortstop, *n.* The infielder who plays between second and third base in baseball; a photographic chemical solution to stop the action of the developer.
Short wave, *n.* A radio wave of a length of 60 meters or less.
Shot*, *n.* An example, short continuous piece, of cinema photography: an unusually interesting shot. Long shot, shot taken from long distance; mid-shot, shot taken from medium distance; crane shot, zoom shot, shot taken while the camera is moved by a crane; model shot, shot taken, not of the subject represented, but of a small-scale model of it; (U.S. colloq.) big shot, an important person; (slang) a drink of liquor.
Shot glass, *n.* See SHOT, above. A small glass for a drink of liquor.
Shotput, *n.* An athletic event consisting of the putting of a shot, an iron ball held in the hand and propelled by extending the arm from the shoulder.
Show, *v.i.* (racing slang) To finish third or better in a horse race.
Show bill, *n.* A poster containing an advertisement.
Show business, *n.* The vaudeville segment of the entertainment field.
Showdown*, *n.* From the showing down i.e. showing face-upwards on the table of the cards after bidding, etc., in certain card games. A frank avowal of, or exchange of confidences about, personal motives.
Show-through, *n.* A condition in which the printing on one side of a sheet of paper shows through on the other side, caused by using paper of poor quality.
Shroud, *n. avn.* One of the set of cords attaching the harness of a parachute to the canopy. Also, shroud line.
Shut*, *v.t.* and *i.* Shut out*, sports to prevent the opposing side from scoring.
Shuttle*, *n.* Any transportation system involving moving back and forth between two near points, as by trains, airplanes, etc. Also attrib., as in shuttle service.
Sibling, *n.* One of two or more children of the same parentage.
Sideburns, *n.* pl. variant of burnsides, type of whiskers orig. worn by Gen. A. E. Burnside Side whiskers.
Siderosis, sid-er-ō'sis, *n.* From Gr. *sideros,* iron and *-osis.* A lung disease produced by inhaling particles of iron or other metals.
Sidesplitting, *adj.* Extremely funny; producing uproarious laughter.
Sideswipe, *v.t.* (U.S. colloq.) To strike a glancing blow with or along the side. —*n.* Such a blow.
Side-wheel, *adj.* Of a steamboat having a paddle wheel on each side. —**Side-wheeler,** *n.*
Sidewinder, *n.* (U.S.) Any of several rattlesnakes, so called due to their lateral method of movement; (U.S. slang) a swinging blow from the side.
Signature*, *n. radio* A song or sound effect which regularly introduces or closes a program.
Silent butler, *n.* A container with a hinged lid used to collect litter such as cigarette ashes, etc.
Silent film, *n.* A motion picture without an accompanying sound track.
Silex, *n.* Lat. flint, hard stone. Heat-resistant glass; cap.; *trade-mark* a coffee maker constructed of this glass.
Silica gel, *n. chem.* A colloidal, highly absorbent form of silica.
Silicified wood, *n.* See SILICIFY in the Dict. Wood turned to quartz by the replacement of the wood structure with a silica solution which crystallizes.
Silicone, sil'i-cōn, *n.* From *silicon* and *-one. chem.* Any of a number of organic silicon compounds, characterized esp. by resistance to heat, produced as oils, greases and resins.
Silicosis, *n.* From *silicon* and *-osis. med.* A respiratory infection caused by breathing siliceous dust, as by miners.
Silk-screen, *n.* A process of color printing using silk stencils one for each color through which pigment is forced onto the printing surface. —*v.t.* and *i.* To print by this process.
Simon Legree, *n.* Name of brutal slave dealer in Harriet Beecher Stowe's "Uncle Tom's Cabin." Hence, any severe or difficult master.
Simon-pure, *adj.* Real, genuine.
Simp, *n.* (slang) Abbr. of simpleton.
Single file, *n.* A line of persons one behind the other.
Single tax*, *n. econ.* A tax on only one object; esp. the theory of Henry George that only land should be taxed.
Sinker*, *n. baseball* (slang) A pitched ball which drops suddenly as it nears the plate.
Sissy, *n.* From *sister.* (colloq.) An effeminate boy or man.
Sit-down strike, *n.* A strike in which workers remain in continuous occupation of a plant, etc., preventing work from continuing. Also sit-down.
Sitter*, *n.* A baby sitter.
Sitzmark, sits'mark, *n.* Ger., seat mark. *skiing* A depression made in the snow by a skier falling on his rump.
Skate*, *n.* (U.S. slang) An old, broken-down horse.
Skeet*, *n.* A kind of trap-shooting with different firing stations and shooting aisles designed to simulate actual hunting conditions.
Skid row, —rō, *n.* prob. from skid road, a road along which logs are dragged. A poor section of a city frequented by social outcasts such as drunkards, beggars and drug addicts.
Skin game, *n.* Cp. SKIN. (slang) A fraud, deception, swindling.
Ski suit, *n.* A suit of outer clothing intended esp. for use in winter sports, consisting of a jacket and trousers with snug-fitting ankles.
Skit*, *n.* Scottish A joke; hoax.
Ski troops, *n.* pl. *mil.* White-clad units on skis, armed with rifles or other light arms and especially trained for action in snowy hills or mountains.
Skitter, *v.i.* To skim along a surface. —*v.t.* To cause to skitter.
Skivvies, skiv'ēz, *n.* pl. (U.S. Navy) Underwear.
Skunk*, *v.t.* (U.S. slang) To defeat so thoroughly that the opponent does not score.
Slack*, *n. prosody.* In sprung rhythm, the unstressed syllable or syllables in a foot.
Slam*, *v.t.* (U.S. slang) To criticize, censure severely. —*n.* A severe criticism, often sarcastic.
Slant*, *n.* A point of view; personal bias. —*v.t.* To distort so as to conform to a personal bias: that paper slants the news.
Slapjack, *n.* A card game; (U.S.) a griddle-cake, flapjack.
Slash*, *v.t.* To reduce drastically in amount: relief funds were slashed.
Sleeper*, *n.* Something not much thought of that suddenly attains importance or success, as a poorly regarded horse which wins a race.
Sleeping bag, *n.* A bag, well insulated against cold and water, designed esp. for sleeping in out of doors.
Slenderize, *v.t.* From *slender* and *-ize.* To make slender; reduce the weight of the body.
Slick*, *adj.* (slang) of persons or things Smart but unsound; specious; —*n.* a smooth portion of a surface, esp. a water area covered with oil; (colloq.) a magazine printed on expensive, glossy paper, with contents catering to urbane, upper-class tastes; —*v.t.* to make smooth; (colloq.) to make smart or elegant followed by up.
Slicker, *n.* See SLICK in the Dict. (U.S.) A long, loose waterproof coat, usu. of oilskin; (colloq.) a sly person; a swindler.
Slide fastener, *n.* A fastener, used instead of buttons, etc., consisting of two rows of teeth mounted on strips of cloth, which are drawn together or separated by a piece sliding between them.
Slide knot, *n.* A type of slipknot.
Slider*, *n. baseball.* A pitched ball having a mild curve.
Slide trombone, *n.* See TROMBONE in the Dict.
Slim*, *v.t.* and *i.* To make or become slim.
Slingshot, *n.* From *sling* and *shot.* A forked stick with an elastic band fastened to the prongs, used to propel small stones, etc.

Slipnoose, *n.* A knot that slides easily along the rope as it is pulled.
Slip-on*, *n.* A piece of clothing, as a sweater or blouse, designed to be slipped on quickly, esp. by pulling over the head.
Slipover, *adj.* Designed to be slipped over the body, a piece of furniture, etc. —*n.* Something which slips over, as a sweater.
Slippage, *n.* From *slip* and *-age.* Act or extent of slipping; *mach.* extent of work lost, as by slipping of parts.
Slipsheet, *v.t.* and *i. print.* to insert blank pages between newly printed sheets so as to prevent offset.
Slip stream, *n. avn.* A stream of air forced back by a propeller and having a speed greater than the surrounding air.
Slip-up, *n.* (colloq.) A mistake; a minor error.
Slit trench, *n. mil.* A short, narrow trench similar to a foxhole.
Slivovitz, sliv'ō-vits, *n.* Serbo-Croatian, from *sliva,* plum. Cp. sloe in the Dict. A powerful plum brandy, made in Yugoslavia, Hungary, etc.
Slowdown, *n.* (colloq.) A slowing down. Specif., a deliberate slowing down of production by workers as a means of enforcing wage demands, etc. Also called slowdown strike.
Slow-motion, *adj. Of a motion picture* taken with the film moving at greater than usual speed, so that when projected at normal speed the movement on the screen appears slower than usual.
Slug*, *n.* (colloq.) A counterfeit coin.
Slugger, *n.* From Slug, above, and *-er.* (colloq.) One who hits hard; specif., of a prizefighter or baseball player.
Slush fund, *n. naut.* A fund from the sale of refuse, used for small luxuries; (U.S. slang) a fund for use in propaganda, bribery, etc., as in a political campaign.
Small change, *n.* Coins of low denomination; U.S. hence, a trifle; an unimportant person or thing.
Small potatoes, *n.* pl. construed as sing. (U.S. colloq.) A paltry, insignificant person or thing.
Smalltime, *adj.* Minor; insignificant.
Smart alec, *n.* second element from proper name. (U.S. colloq.) A conceited person; a know-it-all.
Smear*, *n.* Something smeared on a slide, for microscopic examination; a vilification.
Smear*, *v.t.* To besmirch an opponent's reputation, as in a political campaign; (U.S. slang) to defeat decisively.
Smoker*, *n.* A gathering of men for smoking and social purposes.
Smoke-screen, *n. fig.* Anything done or put forward as a blind, to conceal one's real aims and activities.
Smoke tree, *n.* A shrub of the European species *Cotinus coggygria* or the American species *Cotinus americanus,* bearing clusters of small flowers suggestive of smoke.
Snack-bar, *n.* Bar or counter at which light refreshments are sold.
Snafu, snaf-ōō', *adj.* Acronym of phr. *s*ituation *n*ormal—*a*ll *f*ouled *u*p. (U.S. mil. slang) Muddled; characterized by red tape and bureaucratic inefficiency. —*v.t.* To muddle.
Snap*, *v.t.* and *i.* Phr. snap into it, (slang) to make a vigorous start, act with decision, enthusiasm.
Snap*, *n.* (slang) Something easy to do; a cinch.
Snapback, *n. football.* The snapping back of the ball; the center, the one who snaps back the ball.
Snap bean, *n.* The string bean.
Snapper-back, *n.* (U.S.) *football.* The center, who snaps back the ball to put it in play.
Snap roll, *n. avn.* A quick revolution of a plane on its horizontal axis while keeping a nearly level line of flight.
Sneaker*, *n.* From *sneak* and *-er.* (U.S.) A soft canvas shoe with a rubber sole, used esp. in sports.
Sniperscope, snīp-er-scōp, *n.* From *sniper* and *-scope.* A device similar to a periscope attached to a rifle, permitting a rifleman to aim and fire without exposing himself; a snooperscope adapted for use on a rifle.
Snood*, *n.* A coarse net for holding women's hair in place, sometimes attached to a hat.
Snooperscope, *n.* From *snooper* and *scope.* A device permitting one to see in the dark, by means of infrared rays transmitted to the object and reflected back onto a flourescent screen.
Snoot, *n.* variant of *snout.* (slang) The nose; the face, esp. if expressing contempt.
Snooty, *adj.* From Snoot, above and *-y.* (U.S. colloq.) Haughty; snobbish.
Snorkel, *n.* From Ger. *schnorkel,* spiral. A tubelike breathing apparatus used on submarines to permit the intake of fresh air without resurfacing.
Snort*, *n.* A drink of straight liquor, swallowed in one gulp.
Snowball*, *v.i.* To increase rapidly in number: the complaints snowballed.
Snowsuit, *n.* A ski suit, esp. one for a child.
Soapbox, *n.* A box used for packing soap, esp. a box of this type used as a platform by a street orator. Also attrib.: soapbox speech, etc.
Soap opera, *n.* Apparently from sponsorship of such a program by a soap manufacturer. (U.S.) A daytime radio serial of poor quality, having a romantic, highly emotional character and intended primarily for housewives.
Sob sister, *n.* (U.S. slang) A female journalist who writes excessively sentimental newspaper articles.
Sob story, *n.* (U.S. slang) An overly sentimental story, tale of woe.
Social control, *n. sociol.* The exercise of power by society over its members, as by law or moral disapproval, in order to maintain conformity.
Social disease, *n. euphemism.* Syphilis or gonorrhea.
Socialite, sō'shal-īt, *n.* Coined by magazine *Time,* 1929; From *social* and *-ite,* punning on "social light." (U.S. colloq.) A person of high social status, prominent in "society."
Social register, *n.* A directory of members of the social élite.
Social security, *n.* A type of insurance set up by the government to provide old-age pensions.
Social work, *n.* Work, as carried on by organized groups, designed to improve human welfare.
Socio—, *pref.* Combining form, from Lat *socius,* companion, denoting social or sociological.
Soda jerk or **jerker,** *n.* (U.S. colloq.) One who dispenses drinks or refreshments at a soda fountain.
Sodium-vapor lamp, *n. elect.* A lamp filled with sodium vapor which produces a yellow light upon passage of a current between electrodes, used esp. for lighting highways.
Sofa bed, *n.* A sofa having a back which can be lowered to form a double bed. Cp. Studio Couch, below.
Softball, *n.* A game similar to baseball, played with a larger and softer ball; the ball used in this game.
Soft currency, *n.* A national currency subject to great fluctuations in value, and not easily converted into foreign currencies.
Soft pedal, *n. mus.* A lever on a piano used to soften the tone; (slang) a restraint, as on speech.
Soft-pedal, *v.i.* To play with use of the soft pedal; —*v.t.* to soften the sound of by using the soft pedal; (slang) to tone down; make less prominent.
Softy, *n.* From *soft* and *-y.* (colloq.) A sentimental person, easily taken advantage of; a sissy or weakling.
Soilage, *n.* From *soil* and *-age. agric.* Green plants grown as feed for fenced-in animals.
Solarize, *v.t. photog.* To overexpose to light, either accidentally or for deliberate effect, as during the developing of film.
Solar still, *n.* A device, utilizing the heat of the sun's rays, which converts impure water into water fit for drinking.
Somatotype, sō-mat'o-tīp, *n.* From *somato-* and *type. Anthropol.* Tupe of body structure.
Sonar, sōn'ar, *n.* Acronym of *so*und *na*vigation *r*anging. A device for locating underwater objects, such as submarines, by means of echoes reflected from the objects.
Song*, *n.* Phr. song and dance. Vaudeville routine of singing and dancing; (slang) a long explanation or story, often deceitful.
Sonic, son'ik, *adj.* From Lat. *sonus,* sound and *-ic.* Pertaining to sound or the speed of sound.
Sonic barrier, *n.* The obstruction set up by the atmosphere when an airplane approaches the speed of sound.
Sooner, *n.* From *soon* and *-er.* (U.S. slang) One who settles on government land before it is legally permitted, in order to gain advantage over other settlers; (U.S. slang) one who takes unfair advantage by premature action; *cap.* a native of Oklahoma.
Sortie, *n. mil. avn.* A raid made by a single plane.
Sound-boom, *n.* From *sound* and *boom. movies* Apparatus for moving a microphone about as required during a shot.
Soundproof, *adj.* Impervious to sound. —*v.t.* To make impervious to sound, as a ceiling.
Soundproofing, *n.* From *soundproof,* above, and *-ing.* The activity of making something soundproof; the material used to make something soundproof.
Sound track, *n.* That part of a sound film on which accompanying sounds are recorded.
Soup*, *n. avn.* (slang) Fog or rain.
Soup, *v.t.* From supercharger. *avn.* and *automotive* (slang) Soup up, to increase the horsepower of a motor, as by supercharging.
Sour*, *v.i. fig.* to sour on, (slang) to change from liking to disliking a person or thing.
Sourdough, sawr'dō, *n.* (Western U.S., Canada, Alaska) A fermented dough used as a leaven; (Western U.S., Canada, Alaska) a prospector from habit of carrying this dough.
Sour grapes, *n.* pl. Things a person pretends to despise because he cannot have them.
Southpaw, *n. sports* (slang). A left-handed player, esp. a baseball pitcher who throws left handed. —*adj.* Left-handed.
Sowbelly, *n.* From *sow* and *belly.* (U.S. colloq.) Salt pork or bacon.
Sow bug, *n.* From *sow.* A wood louse.
Sox, *n.* pl. Variant spelling of socks, pl. of Socks.
Spaceship, *n.* A hypothetical aircraft capable of flight between the earth and other planets.
Spall, *v.i. phys.* of a target of nuclear bombardment To split into fragments. —**Spallation,** *n.*
Span*, *n.* The transverse dimension, from wing tip to wing tip, of an aircraft.
Spare*, *n. bowling.* The knocking down of all ten pins with two successive bowls; also, the score obtained by this.
Spark*, *v.t.* (slang) To motivate, make lively: the catcher sparked the team to victory.
Sparkler*, *n.* A firework emitting bright sparks.
Spark plug, *n.* (slang) A person who is the motive force in a group.
Sparks, *n.* From Spark. *naut.* (slang) A radioman on a ship.
Spasmolytic, spaz-mō-lit'ik, *adj.* From *spasm* and *-lytic.* of a drug, etc. Alleviating spasms.
Speaker*, *n.* A loud speaker.
Spearfish, *n.* A marlin or any of several ocean fishes related to it.
Spearhead*, *n.* The leading person or thing in an attack or other enterprise — used esp. of military troops.
Specs, spex, *n.* pl. (colloq.) Abbrev. of spectacles.
Speech Community, *n.* A group speaking a given language or dialect.
Speedboat, *n.* A motorboat designed to attain high speeds.
Speed-up, *n.* An increase of speed, as on a factory production line.
Spell*, *v.t.* and *i.* Spell out*, to explain simply and in detail.
Spelunker, *n.* From Lat. *spelunca,* cave, hole. One whose hobby is the exploration and study of caves.
Spherics, sfĕr'iks, *n.* From *sphere* and *-ics. mat.* Spherical geometry and spherical trigonometry.

Spindle*, *v. t.* To impale on a spike or spindle, as in filing receipts, etc.
Spinet*, *n.* A very small upright piano.
Spiral*, *n. avn.* A steeply banked, continuous gliding turn, with the engine throttled; *football* a pass or kick in which the ball spins on its longitudinal axis; *econ.* a steady and accelerating rise or fall in wages, the price of goods, etc.
Spiv, *n.* Origin uncertain. (Brit. slang) One who lives by his wits, without working. **—Spivery**, *n.* This way of life.
Sponge rubber, *n.* Foamed latex used for making such articles as cushions and mattresses.
Sponson, *n.* A small float attached to the hull of a hydroplane, increasing its stability in water.
Sporophyll, spŏr'ō-fil, *n.* From *sporo–* and Gr. *phullon*, leaf; *bot.* A leaf, somewhat modified in structure, which bears sporangia.
Sport shirt, *n.* A shirt designed to be worn on informal occasions.
Spot*, *n.* Phr. to be on the spot*, (U.S. slang) to be in great peril.
Spot check, *n.* A rapid, unmethodical survey used to obtain a general idea of some specific situation.
Spotlight, *n.* An automobile light which can be turned in various directions; *fig.* public prominence. Cp. LIMELIGHT in the Dict.
Spotted*, *adj.* Sullied.
Spotter, *n.* From *spot* and *–er.* (U.S.) One employed to watch others, esp. for detecting dishonesty; *mil.* one who supplies a gun crew with the position of an enemy target; one who keeps a lookout for enemy aircraft.
Spring*, *v.t.* (slang) To release from prison.
Springer*, *n.* A young frying chicken hatched in the spring.
Sprung rhythm, *n.* A kind of verse meter in which the foot always begins with a stressed syllable, the number of unaccented syllables being variable.
Spumone, spew-mō'nē, *n.* (Ital.) Italian ice cream, usually containing fruit and chopped nuts.
Spun*, *adj.* Spun rayon, yarn or fabric made from rayon threads.
Squad car, *n.* A police patrol car, able to communicate with headquarters by radio telephone.
Squadron*, *n. mil.* An air force unit composed of two or more flights.
Square, *v.t. sports.* To even the score of a contest.
Squeeze*, *n.* (colloq.) Tight squeeze, difficult situation.
Squeeze play, *n. baseball.* A play used with a runner on third base and less than two out in which the batter bunts a previously agreed on ball, the runner starting for home plate on the pitching motion.
Stab*, *n.* (colloq.) An attempt: to have a stab at something.
Stabile, stā'bl, *adj.* From Lat. *stabilis* firm. See STABLE. Fixed; stationary. Specif., *med.* of electrodes used in therapy.
Stable*, *n.* (slang) Group of artists, writers, etc. under contract to one organization, as a motion picture company.
Stack*, *v.t.* (slang) To cheat by previously arranging a deck of playing cards; hence, to have the outcome of any situation determined in advance.
Staffer, *n.* From *staff* and *-er.* (colloq.) A member of a staff.
Stakhanovism, *n.* From A. G. Stakhanov, a Russian miner who, in 1935, succeeded in increasing his output prodigiously. A method of increasing industrial output in Russia, via the encouragement of rationalization and competition among workers, rewarding individual initiative, etc. **—Stakhanovite**, *n.* and *adj.*
Stalinism, *n.* From Russ. leader Joseph Stalin, born 1879, and *–ism.* The Russian political and social system as developed since the coming of Joseph Stalin to power, 1928.
Stalking-horse*, *n. politics.* A candidate used to conceal someone else's candidacy, or to divide and weaken the vote of the opposition.
Stall*, *v.t.* and *i.* To evade, deceive, delay in order to gain time esp. in a sports contest.
Stand-in, *n. movies.* Someone whose job is to stand in place of an actor, as in a dangerous scene; hence, any substitute.
Standing army, *n.* A permanent army of paid soldiers as distinguished from a conscripted army.
Starch*, *n.* (U.S. slang) Energy; vigor.
Stardom, *n.* From *star* and *–dom.* Eminence, as in acting.
Starlet, *n.* A promising young movie actress.
Star sapphire, *n.* A sapphire which, when properly cut, gives a starlike reflection of light.
Stateless, *adj.* From *state* and *–less.* usually *of a person* Having no nationality.
States' evidence, *n.* (U.S.) Evidence for the state, esp. as voluntarily given by a criminal against his accomplices. Usually in phr. to turn states' evidence.
Station wagon, *n.* A motor car usually having a paneled wooden body and removable seats, designed to carry passengers and luggage.
Statism, *n.* From *state* and *–ism.* Belief in, condition of, highly centralized governmental control.
Statist*, *n.* One who supports statism.
Steam fitter, *n.* One who installs or repairs steampipes and their fittings.
Steam-roller, *n.* (colloq.) *fig.* Any overwhelming force, ruthlessly overcoming opposition. Also attrib.: steam-roller tactics. *—v.t.* To crush as with a steam-roller.
Steam shovel, *n.* Large digging machine powered by its own steam unit.
Stellar*, *adj.* Pertaining to the leading roles or performances in a play or motion picture; excellent.
Stereotype*, *n.* Something seen as conventional, undistinguished.
Stereotypy*, *n. psychiat.* Constant repetition of an action, posture, etc., esp. as found in the catatonic form of schizophrenia.
Sterol, ster'ōl, *n.* From Gr. *stereós*, firm, solid. Any of a group of solid alcohols obtained from plants and animals.
Stew*, *v.i.* (colloq.) To worry.
Stewed, *adj.* From *stew* and *-ed.* Cooked by stewing; (slang) intoxicated.
Stick*, *n.* The control lever in an airplane.
Sticker*, *n.* An adhesive label.
Stiff*, *n.* A stupid or clumsy person; esp. big stiff, an utter fool or bungler; (slang) a corpse.
Still*, *n.* A single photograph abstracted from a motion film or shot separately and, in many cases, displayed as film advertisement.
Sting*, *v.t.* (slang) To make a person pay an exorbitant price, to fleece.
Stirrup pump, *n.* A water-pumping device attached to a rubber hose and operated on the principle of a bicycle pump.
Stockpile, stok'pīl, *n.* An accumulated reserve of materials essential to war industries. *—v.t.* and *i.* To build up such a reserve.
Stomp, *n.* and *v.* Variant of stamp.
Stooge, *n.* Orig. uncertain. (slang) A comedian's helper; one who sets up humorous situations for a comedian; a "straight man;" a servile subordinate; *—v.i.* to act as a stooge.
Stool pigeon, *n.* A pigeon used as a decoy to trap others; (slang) one who betrays others; specif. a spy for the police.
Stop*, *n. photog.* The size of a lens opening as regulated by the diaphragm.
Stopover, *n.* From *stop* and *over.* A stopping during the course of a journey; a place where one stops during the course of a journey.
Straight man, *n.* Entertainer who acts as a foil for another.
Strategic*, *adj.* Needed for strategy, and in short supply; strategic materials.
Stratification*, *n.* Social stratification, the division of a society into class and status groups.
Strato—, *pref. aeron.* Combining form of stratosphere, as in stratochamber.
Stratosphere, strā'tō-sfēr, *n.* See STRATUM and SPHERE. The upper and more rarefied part of the atmosphere above the tropo pause.
Streamliner, *n.* From *streamline* and *–er.* A streamlined railroad train.
Strep throat, *n.* (colloq.) A severe streptococcal infection of the throat.
Streptomycin, strep-tō-mī'sin, *n.* From Gr. *streptós*, pliant, and *múkes*, fungus. An antibiotic extremely effective against certain types of bacteria.
Strikebreaker, *n.* From *strike* and *breaker.* One hired by employers to break up a strike, as by providing workers or intimidating strikers; one who works in place of a striking worker. **—Strikebreaking**, *n.*
Striker*, *n.* (U.S. Army) An enlisted man employed for odd jobs by a commissioned officer.
String bean, *n.* Any of various beans having edible pods, so called from strings attached to the pods; (slang) a tall skinny person.
Strip*, *n.* An airstrip, which see above.
Strip tease, *n.* A burlesque dance in which a woman removes her clothing piece by piece.
Stroller*, *n.* A type of light baby carriage.
Struck*, *adj.* of a factory, etc. Closed or otherwise affected by a workers' strike.
Strut*, *n. aeron.* A brace between airplane wings, or between wing and fuselage.
Studio couch, *n.* A couch, with a cot underneath it which can be pulled out to form a double bed, having large detached pillows instead of a back.
Stuff*, *n.* (slang) In the Phr. to do one's stuff, special accomplishment or subject; prearranged performance or harangue: Now then, do your stuff!
Stymie*, *n.* To block, impede, as with a stymie.
Styrene, stī'rēn', *n.* From *styrax* and *–ene.* A fragrant liquid hydrocarbon. $C_6H_5CH{:}CH_2$, used esp. in the preparation of plastics.
Sub*, *n.* (slang) Abbr. of substitute. *—v.i.* (slang) To act as a substitute.
Sub chaser, *n.* See SUB in Dict. A light, fast vessel equipped esp. for use against submarines.
Subclinical, *adj.* From *sub–* and *clinical. med.* of a physical state not seriously abnormal; not observable by usual clinical procedures.
Subdeb, *n.* (colloq.) Abbr. of SUBDEBUTANTE, below.
Subdebutante, *n.* From *sub–* and *debutante.* A teen-aged girl, not yet a debutante; a girl preparing for her formal introduction to "society."
Submachine gun, *n.* A light-weight weapon similar to the automatic rifle but firing pistol ammunition.
Subsonic, sub-son'ik, *adj.* Of a speed less than 550 m.p.h.
Substandard, *adj.* (U.S.) *statute law.* Of foods, etc. below the standards set by the Federal Food and Drugs Act and not labeled as such; *linguistics* below the standards of cultivated speech.
Substratosphere, *n. avn.* Atmospheric region below the stratosphere but high enough so that oxygen masks, pressurized cabins, etc. are necessary for flying.
Subtitle, *n. movies.* Explanatory printed matter in a movie, esp. as introducing a scene.
Sucker*, *n.* (colloq.) A lollipop. All-day sucker, large lollipop.
Sugarcoat, *v.t.* To coat with sugar, as medicine having a bad taste; *fig.* hence, to make any unattractive thing seem attractive.
Sukiyaki, *n.* (Jap.) A Japanese dinner dish consisting of strips of beef, green onions, sake, etc. fried together.
Sulfa, *adj.* See SULFUR in the Dict. Pertaining to any of the various antibacterial drugs related to sulfanilamide.
Sulfadiazine, sul'fa-dī'a-zen, *n.* From *sulfa*nilamide and *di–* and *azote* and *–ine.* A sulfa drug, $C_{10}H_{10}N_4O_2S$, used in the treatment of various infections.
Sulfanilamide, —nil'a-mīd, *n.* From *sul* phur and *anil*ine and *amide.* A white crystalline compound, $NH_2C_6H_4SO_2NH_2$, effective against infections.

Sulfonamide, sul-fon'a-mīd, *n.* From *sulpho* and *amide.* Any amide of a sulfonic acid.
Sunglass, *n.* A burning glass.
Sunglasses, *n.* pl. Spectacles using colored or specially constructed lenses to reduce harmful glare from the sun.
Sunk*, *adj.* (slang) Utterly frustrated, in a desperate situation or fix, now we're sunk, that finishes our chances.
Sunlamp, *n.* An electric lamp producing ultraviolet radiation, used therapeutically and to induce artificial sunburn.
Sun parlor, *n.* Room or enclosed porch exposed to the sun.
Suntan, *n.* Tanning of the skin due to sunburn; *pl.* tan cotton uniform worn by U.S. Army.
Super, *adj.* From the prefix *super–.* (slang) Excellent; unusually good.
Superego, soo'per-e-go, *n.* From *super–* and *ego. psychoanalysis.* A part of the psyche, largely unconscious, which functions primarily as a conscience.
Superhighway, *n.* A highway for use at high speeds, having four or more lanes.
Supermarket, *n.* A large self-service food store.
Supernova, *n. astron.* An extremely brilliant new star.
Supersensory, *adj.* Supersensible; beyond the range of the senses.
Supersonic, *adj. phys.* Having a speed faster than that of sound in air preferred meaning; ultrasonic.
Supporter*, *n.* Elastic device for holding up some part of the body.
Supraconductivity, su-pra-con'duc-tiv'-i-tē, *n.* From *supra–* and *conductivity.* Increased electrical conductivity at exceptionally low temperatures.
Sure-fire, *adj.* (U.S. slang) Certain to be successful.
Surface*, *v.i.* To come up to the surface of the water, as a submarine; *mining* to work at or on the surface.
Surface plate, *n.* A flat steel plate used to test the flatness of other surfaces.
Surface raider, *n.* A warship raiding the enemy's shipping as distinct from a submarine raider.
Surrealism, sir-rē'al-ism, *n.* From Fr. *surrealisme;* see SUR– and REALISM. An artistic and literary movement originating in France, having as its chief subject matter material of dreams and the unconscious, and emphasizing immediacy and spontaneity with a minimum of conscious elaboration.
Surrealist, *n.* See SURREALISM, above, and *–ist.* A exponent or adherent of surrealism. *—adj.* Of, pertaining to, or exemplifying, surrealism.
Suspension point, *n.* In punctuation, one of a series of successive dots usually three used to indicate omission or pause.
Suspensoid, sus-pen'soid, *n.* From *suspension,* and *–oid. phys. chem.* A colloidal solution containing dispersed solid particles.
Sustaining program, *n.* A radio program having no commercial sponsor.
Swagger stick, *n. mil.* A short cane or stick, sometimes carried by officers.
Swan dive, *n.* A dive with arms outstretched at the sides, and with the legs together.
Swastika, *n.* A Greek cross, with four arms the ends of which are bent clockwise, used as the official symbol of the Nazi party and the Third Reich.
Sweat*, *v.t.* Phr. to sweat out*, (slang) To endure, await in a distressed manner, the culmination of an unpleasant situation: he sweated out the results of the examination.
Sweat shirt, *n.* A warm pull-over worn by athletes to absorb perspiration.
Sweatshop, swet'shop, *n.* A shop employing workers at low pay, for long hours, and under generally unhealthful working conditions.
Sweet-potato*, *n.* (slang) An ocarina.
Sweet tooth, *n.* (U.S. colloq.) A craving for candy and sweet foods.
Swimsuit, *n.* (colloq.) A bathing suit.
Swing*, *n.* A kind of modern dance music with a prominent rhythm and individual variations of the melody.
Swing shift, *n.* (U.S.) In factories operating day and night, the shift from mid-afternoon until midnight.
Symbiot, sim'bē-ot, *n.* See SYMBIOSIS in the Dict. *biol.* One of the organisms living in symbiosis.
Synchrocyclotron, sin-krō-sī'klō-tron, *n.* From *synchronize* and *cyclotron. phys.* A cyclotron in which the frequency of the electric field may be synchronized with the rotating particles.
Synchroflash, *n.* From *synchronize* and *flash. photog.* A mechanical device which simultaneously opens the camera shutter and fires a flash bulb. Also attrib.
Synchrotron, sin'krō-tron, *n.* From *synchronize* and *–tron* as in ELECTRON. Coined by U.S. physicist E. M. McMillan, 1946. *phys.* An apparatus using features of the cyclotron and betatron to impart high speeds to charged particles.
Tab, *n.* Clipped form of tabulation. A check or notation of money owed, as for a meal in a restaurant.
Table tennis, *n.* Ping-pong; a game resembling tennis played with paddles and a very light ball on a table.
Tabloid, *n.* A newspaper of small page size, containing scanty news accounts and many photographs.
Tactical*, *adj.* Skillful in the use of tactics.
Tailor*, *v.t.* To modify or make suitable for a specific purpose: the play was tailored for the leading lady.
Tailor-made, *adj.* specif. of women's clothing cut with severe lines, like men's clothing; made specially to order.
Tail plane, *n. avn.* A horizontal, fixed surface to which the elevator of an aircraft is attached, and which assists in maintaining longitudinal stability in flight.
Take-home pay, *n.* The portion of a salary actually taken home; i.e., the salary less various deductions made for tax, insurance, etc.
Takedown, *adj.* Made so as to be easily taken apart. —*n.* Act of taking down.
Talking book, *n.* A recording of a piece of literature, made for the use of the blind.
Tangelo, tan'je-lō, *n.* From *tangerine* and *pomelo.* A hybrid of the tangerine and the grapefruit.
Tank destroyer, *n.* A speedy military vehicle equipped with special antitank weapons.
Tank farming, *n.* Hydroponics; growing plants without soil.
Tank trap, *n.* A mine field or, more often, a barricade of concrete pillars, felled trees, or camouflaged ditches designed to explode, hold up, or cripple enemy tanks.
Tape*, *v.t.* To measure with a tapeline; to record sound on magnetic tape.
Tape recorder, *n.* Device for recording and reproducing sound, using magnetic tape instead of a phonograph record.
Taps, *n.* pl. *mil.* Signal for lights out in soldiers' barracks.
Task force, *n. mil., nav.* A number of naval vessels detailed to stage a raid on enemy shores, or to execute some other definite assignment.
Tass, *n.* Russ. abbr. from *T*elegraphnoye *A*gentstvo *S*ovyetskovo *S*oyuza. News agency of the Soviet Union.
Taxi dancer, *n.* A woman who is paid to dance with customers at a public dance hall.
Tear-jerker, tēr'——, *n.* (slang) An overly sentimental tale of woe, etc., designed to move the audience to tears.
Tear sheet, tār'shēt, *n.* A sheet torn from a book or magazine, esp. for sending to an advertiser to show him how his advertisement looks in print.
Technetium, tek-nē'shi-um, *n.* From Gr. *tekhne,* art, skill, and *–ium.* Formerly called masurium. *chem.* A metallic element of atomic number 43. Symbol: *Tc.*
Technicolor, tek'nē-kul-er, *n. trade-mark.* A process of making colored motion pictures.
Technocracy, tek-nok'ras-e, *n.* From *technic* and *–cracy.* A proposed type of social organization in which engineers and technicians would exercise a decisive control of industry.
Technocrat, tek'nō-krat, *n.* See TECHNIC and *–crat.* An advocate of technocracy; an engineer or technician, as controller of production in such a régime.
Teen-ager, *n.* (colloq.) A person in the age range of 13 to 19; an adolescent.
Telecast, *v.t.* and *i.* From *tele*vision and broad*cast.* To transmit by television. —*n.* A television program.
Telegenic, tel-a-jēn'ik, *adj.* From *tele*vision and *–genic,* above. *of a person.* Suitable as to voice and appearance for television broadcasting.
Telephoto, tel-a-fō'to, *adj.* See TELEPHOTOGRAPH, TELEPHOTO LENS in Dict.
Teleprinter, *n.* From *tele–* and *printer.* A teletypewriter.
Teleran, tel'er-an, *n.* Acronym of *tele*vision *r*adar *a*ir *n*avigation. A system of aerial navigation combining the use of radar and television.
Teletypewriter, *n.* A typewriter-like telegraphic device, automatically printing messages received.
Teleview, tel'a-vū, *v.t.* and *i.* Fr. TELE-, above, and *view.* To view by means of a television receiver.
Televise, *v.t.* From *television.* To transmit or receive by television.
Telford pavement, *n.* From Scottish engineer T. Telford, 1757–1834. A type of pavement made of rolled stone.
Tell*, *v.t.* Phr. you're telling me! (slang) don't, or there's no need to, tell me that!
Tendency*, *n.* From Ger. *tendenz.* Used attrib. of writings favoring a particular interpretation of society: tendency novel.
Ten-strike, *n. bowling.* A strike; knocking down of all ten pins with one bowl; (U.S. colloq.) any very successful act.
Terminal leave, *n.* Accrued leave granted to a member of the armed forces before final separation from the service.
Term insurance, *n.* A type of life insurance which protects the policy holder for a specific period of time only.
Terramycin, ter-a-mī'sin, *n.* From Lat. *terra,* soil, and Gr. *mūkes,* fungus, and *–in.* An antibiotic of low toxicity, isolated from the soil fungus *Streptomyces rimosus,* effective against a wide variety of infections.
Terrarium, ter-ra'rē-um, *n.* From Lat. *terra,* earth, and *–arium* as in *aquarium.* See —ARY in the Dict. A vivarium for land animals.
Terry*, *n.* Also terry cloth. A soft fabric with pile formed by uncut loops, used in making towels, beach robes, etc.
Testosterone, tes-tos'ter-ōn, *n.* From *test*is and *ster*ol and *–one.* A male sex hormone, $C_{19}H_{28}O_2$, extracted from animal testes and also synthesized.
Test paper*, *n.* (U.S.) Paper containing printed examination questions or student's answers to them.
Test pilot, *n.* Aviator who tries out planes of new design before they are approved for mass production.
Test-tube*, *n.* Also attrib., as in test-tube baby, one produced by artificial insemination.
Thanatos, than'a-tōs, *n.* Gr. death. Death personified; *psychoanalysis* death instincts.
Theme*, *n. radio* Song, phrase or sound effect which regularly opens or closes a radio program.
Theme song, *n.* Melody used often enough in a musical drama so as to identify it; melody regularly used on a radio program and identifying the program; melody identifying a popular orchestra.
Thermal*, *n. aeron.* A rising current of warm air.
Thermoplastic, ther-mo-plas'tik, *adj.* From *thermo–* and *plastic.* Easily molded when heated, as certain plastic material. —*n.* A substance of this nature.
Thermosetting, *adj.* From *thermo–* and *setting.* Becoming permanently hard when heated, as certain plastics.
Thiamine, thī'a-mēn, *n.* From *thio* and *amine. chem.* A chemical compound whose chloride, vitamin B_1, is a preventative of beriberi.
Thiazine, thī'a-zēn, *n.* From *thio* and *azo–* and *–ine. chem.* Any of a class of organic compounds having a ring composed of four atoms of carbon, one atom of sulfur and one atom of nitrogen.

Third rail, *n.* A rail laid parallel to the two rails of an electric railway, carrying the motive electric current.

Thoro, *adj.* Pseudo-phonetic spelling of thorough.

Thought control, *n.* Strict state censorship. Named after former Japanese practice of arresting persons for having "dangerous thoughts" against the state.

Three-D, *n.* (motion pictures) A three-dimensional illusion created when the picture is viewed through kaleidoscopic glasses.

Thrombin, throm'bin, *n.* From Gr. *thrómbos,* a clot, and *-in. biochem.* The substance in the blood which causes clotting.

Thrombophenia, throm-bo-pē'nya, *n.* From *thrombin* and Gr. *penia,* poverty. *pathol.* Deficiency of thrombin in the blood.

Throw*, *v.t.* (U.S. colloq.) To deliberately lose a game or contest; (U.S. slang) to give as a social gesture: he threw a cocktail party yesterday.

Throwaway, *n.* (colloq.) An advertising circular, leaflet, etc., esp. one distributed to people in the streets.

Throw-out, *n.* Article thrown aside, esp. in the factory where it is made, as defective or useless.

Thru, *prep.* and *adv.* Pseudo-phonetic spelling of through.

Thrust*, *n. engin.* The force or push generated by a propeller or jet engine.

Thumb*, *v.t.* (slang) To hitch-hike a ride by signaling with the thumb.

Thumbnail, *n.* The nail of the thumb; something very small or brief. —*adj.* Very small or brief: thumbnail biography.

Thumbtack, *n.* A tack with a broad, flat head, easily pushed into a surface with the thumb.

Thunderbird, *n.* N. Am. Indian mythol. A gigantic bird able to produce thunder and lightning.

Thunder stick, *n.* Ab. Bull-roarer.

Thyroidectomy, thī'roy-dek'to-mē, *n.* From *thyroid* and *-ectomy.* Surgical cutting or removal of the thyroid gland.

Thyroiditis, *n.* From *thyroid* and *itēs. pathol.* Inflammation of the thyroid gland.

Thyroxine, thī-roks'ēn, *n.* From *thyroid* and *oxy-* and *-ine. biochem.* A hormone, $C_{15}H_{11}I_4NO_4$, secreted by the thyroid gland and also obtained synthetically, used in treatment of thyroid deficiency.

Tie-in sale, *n.* Sale in which the purchaser, in order to obtain an item he wants, must purchase in addition an undesired item.

Tightfisted, *adj.* From *tight* and *fist* and *-ed.* Miserly; stingy.

Tightwad, *n.* From *tight* and *wad* (U.S. slang) A miserly person.

Tilt*, *n.* Any sports contest; a dispute.

Timberline, *n.* The altitude above which timber does not grow.

Timecard, *n.* A card showing the time an employee spends at his work.

Time clock, *n.* A clock with a recording device for stamping an employee's arrival and departure time on a card.

Time exposure, *n. photog.* An exposure in which the camera shutter is left open for several seconds or minutes before being released.

Time-lag, *n.* Interval of time between one phenomenon and another which is associated with it or caused by it.

Time out, *n.* An intermission; *sports* an official suspension of play during a game, as to care for an injured player.

Tinhorn gambler, *n.* From a metal device in which dice are shaken. (slang) A small-time, pretentious gambler.

Tin-pan alley, *n.* District, esp. of New York City, which is the center of the composition and publication of popular music; composers and publishers of popular music considered collectively.

Tintype, *n. photog.* A ferrotype.

Tissue culture, *n. biol.* The growing of animal body tissue in a culture medium.

Title*, *n. sports.* The championship.

Titlist, *n.* See Title, above, and *-ist. sports* The holder of a championship.

Tizzy, *n.* (slang) Over-excited state: she flew into a tizzy.

T-man, *n.* From U.S. *Treasury.* (U.S. colloq.) An agent of the U.S. Treasury Department.

T.N.T., *abbr.* See Trinitrotoluene in the Dict.

Toggle switch, *n. elect.* A switch opening or closing a circuit by means of a projecting lever moving through a small arc.

Toluidine, to-loo'i-dēn, *n.* From *toluene* and *-ide* and *-ine. chem.* Any of three isomeric amines, $CH_3C_6H_4NH_2$, obtained from toluene.

Tone poem, *n. mus.* A musical composition, usually in one movement, which is a symphonic type of program music.

Tool*, *v.i.* To equip a factory with necessary tools; usually followed by *up.*

Topflight, *adj. colloq.* Excellent, of highest quality.

Top kick, *n. mil.* (slang) First sergeant.

Topper*, *n.* A woman's loose topcoat.

Top-secret, *adj.* Usually *mil.* Most highly secret.

Top sergeant, *n. mil.* (colloq.) The first, the highest ranking sergeant of a company, troop, or battery.

Topsoil, *n.* Surface soil. —*v.t.* To remove topsoil from land.

Torsade, tor-säd', *n.* From Lat. *torquēre,* to twist. A twisted cord or other ornament of twisted form.

Tortoise shell*, *n.* Also attrib. Having a mottled color like tortoise shell; made of tortoise shell: tortoise-shell eyeglasses.

Tossed salad, *n.* A combination of various salad greens served with a dressing made of oil, vinegar and condiments and mixed by tossing lightly with a fork and spoon.

Totalitarian*, *adj.* From *totality* and *-arian.* Conscripting a country's entire resources in population and material.

Totem pole, *n.* A pole, usually placed in front of an Indian house, covered with carved and painted representations of totems.

Towboat, tō'bōt, *n.* A tugboat.

Towhead, tō'hed, *n.* From *tow* and *head.* A person having light-colored hair; a head of such hair.

Toxicity, toks-i'sit-ē, *n.* From *toxic* and *-ity.* Poisonous quality.

Trace element, *n. biol.* An element found in small quantities in plants or animals, but believed necessary for their growth.

Tracer*, *n. Chem.* A substance used to follow the course of some process, as in the human body; esp., a radioactive element so used.

Tracking, *v.n.* From *track. movies.* Moving the camera nearer and nearer to, or farther away from, the subject; the visual effect so produced.

Trackwalker, *n.* (U.S.) *railroads.* Man hired to walk over a section of railroad tracks and inspect them.

Trade-in, *n.* Something given in trade, usually as partial payment for the purchase of similar goods.

Trailer*, *n.* Parts of a forthcoming film shown on the screen at a public performance, to advertise the film.

Trainee, *n.* From *train* and *-ee.* One who is being trained.

Transcendentalist*, *n.* (U.S.) *hist.* A believer in the transcendentalism of Emerson.

Transcribe*, *v.t. radio.* To make a phonograph record of, for later radio broadcast.

Transcription*, *n.* A recording of a radio program; *mus.* see Arrangement in the Dict.

Transducer, tranz-dōō'ser, *n, phys.* A device transforming energy from one system to another.

Transference*, *n. psychoanalysis.* During the course of psychoanalytic treatment, the reactivation of repressed emotional experiences of early childhood and their displacement upon the physician.

Transient*, *n.* One who stays for a short while only, as a guest at a hotel.

Transonic, trans-son'ik, *adj.* From *trans-* and *sonic. aeron.* Of a speed between 550 and 900 miles per hour.

Transuranic, tranz-ur-an'ik, *adj.* From *trans-* and *uranic.* Of elements heavier than uranium.

Tray agriculture, *n.* Hydroponics.

Trench knife, *n.* Long knife used in hand-to-hand combat.

Trench mouth, *n.* So called from its occurrence among soldiers in the trenches. *pathol.* Inflammatory disease of the mouth.

Trial balloon, *n.* A balloon sent aloft to determine wind currents, etc.; an announcement of plans in a tentative or cautious manner, in order to determine public opinion.

Trifocal, trī-fō-kal, *adj.* From *tri-* and *focal.* Of lenses, esp. in eyeglass, having three foci. **—Trifocals,** *n.* pl. Eyeglasses having such lenses.

Trigger*, *v.t.* To release, set off.

Tritium, trit'i-um, *n.* From Gr. *tritos,* third, and *-ium.* Cp. Deuterium above. *chem.* A hydrogen isotope of mass number 3.

Trivia, *n.* pl. See Trivial in the Dict. Unimportant things; trifles.

Trooper*, *n.* (U.S.) A member of a state police force.

—Tropic, *suff.* Combining form used in adjectives to denote turning.

Tropical fish, *n.* Any of various fishes kept in an aquarium and requiring water maintained at a certain temperature.

Tropopause, trō-pō-paws, *n.* From *tropo-*sphere and *pause.* A belt of atmosphere, about two miles thick, between the troposphere and the stratosphere, i.e. from seven to twelve miles above sea level.

Troposphere, trō'pō-sfēr', *n.* From *trope* and *sphere.* That part of the atmosphere which immediately surrounds the earth reaching up as far as the tropopause, and in which increase of height is associated with decrease of temperature.

Trotskyite, *n.* From Russ. revolutionary leader Leon *Trotsky,* 1879–1940, and *-ite.* An adherent of Leon Trotsky's program of Marxist communism, opposed to both capitalism and Stalinism. **Trotskyism,** *n.*

Trouble-shooter, *n.* One skilled in detecting and removing the source of trouble in the operation of something, as communications equipment.

Truck*, *n.* (U.S.) Vegetables raised for sale.

Truck farm, *n.* (U.S.) A farm raising vegetables for the market.

Trucker*, *n.* From Truck, above, and *-er.* (U.S.) One who raises or sells truck.

Trucker*, *n.* From *truck* and *-er.* The driver of a truck; one in the business of transporting goods on trucks.

Trust*, *n.* Investment trust, a joint stock company whose profits are drawn from investments distributed among a number of other companies and from the judicious buying and selling of investments; fixed trust, investment trust whose capital is permanently invested in a few securities.

Trusteeship*, *n.* The supervision and control of the affairs of a territory, granted to a country by the United Nations.

Trusty*, *n.* One who is trustworthy; specif., (U.S.) a trustworthy convict allowed special privileges.

Truth serum, *n.* A drug, esp. sodium pentothal, used to make subjects more talkative.

Tryout, *n.* (U.S. colloq.) An instance of trying out someone or something; a test of the fitness of some person or thing.

T shirt or tee shirt, *n.* From its shape. A man's undershirt having short sleeves and no collar; a similar shirt or jersey for outer wear.

T square, *n.* A ruler having a crosspiece at one end, used on a drawing board for making parallel lines.

Tubocurarine, tū'bo-cu-ra'rēn, *n.* From *tube* and *curare* and *-ine.* First element from the fact that natives distinguish three different types of curare by storing them in tubes, pots, or calabashes; the drug is from the tube type. An alkaloid derived from curare, used as a muscle relaxant in spastic paralysis, etc.

Tucker*, *v.t.* To tire, exhaust; usually in phr. tuckered out, exhausted.

Turbo—, *pref.* Combining form for turbine.

Turbojet, *n.* From Turbo-, above, and *jet.* An aviation engine of the jet type which employs turbines to compress the air used in generating power.

Turkey*, *n. theatr.* (slang) A play or motion picture that is a failure.

Turkish towel, *n.* A heavy towel having a thick, rough surface.
Turnabout, *n.* A reversal or change of belief, allegiance, etc.; (U.S.) a merry-go-round.
Turntable*, *n.* A machine for reproducing sound from radio transcriptions and records; the rotating disk of a phonograph, on which the record is carried.
Turret*, *n. mil.* A tower-like structure for guns in an airplane or tank.
Tutu, too'too', *n.* Fr. A short skirt worn by a ballet dancer.
TV, *abbr.* Short for television.
Tweedy, *adj.* From *tweed* and *-y.* Like tweed; of a man wearing tweeds; having an informal manner.
Tweet, *n.* Imitative. A bird's chirp or a similar sound. —*v.i.* To utter a tweet.
Tweeter, *n.* From TWEET, above, and *-er.* A loudspeaker, or component of a loudspeaker, designed to reproduce high tones.
Twelve-tone, *adj. mus.* Constructed on an arbitrary pattern of twelve chromatic tones and disregarding ordinary tonal principles.
Twenty-one, *n.* See VINGT-UN in the Dict.
Twin*, *n.* Identical twins, twins developed from the same fertilized ovum and therefore of identically the same genotype; fraternal twins, twins developed from different genotypes, though from the same pregnancy.
2-4-D, *n. chem.* A powerful weed killer causing abnormal growth.
Two-platoon system, *n. football.* The use of two teams, one specializing in offense and the other in defense.
Tycoon*, *n.* Introduced in following sense by Time magazine, 1928 (U.S. colloq.) A powerful and wealthy businessman.
—Type, *n.* (U.S. colloq.) Used to form adjectives from nouns and adjectives: a nice-type girl.
Typecast, *v.t.* To cast an actor for a role which is similar to his appearance, etc. in real life.
Typescript, *n.* A typewritten copy of anything, as distinguished from a manuscript or printed copy.
Typewriter*, *n. print.* A type style which looks like typewriting.
Typhlology, tif-lol'o-ji, *n.* From Gr. *tuphlós,* blind, and *-ology.* The scientific study of blindness.
Udo, *n. Jap.* A Japanese plant, Aralia cordata, having edible shoots.
Ugly duckling, *n.* From a fairy tale by Hans Christian Andersen. An ugly or awkward child who becomes a handsome adult.
Ultrasonic, *adj.* From *ultra-* and SONIC, above. Pertaining to a wave of soundlike nature which is of higher frequency than audible sound.
Ultravirus, *n.* From *ultra-* and *virus.* A filtrable, ultramicroscopic virus.
Umbrella*, *n. mil.* Protective covering afforded ground forces by a strong force of fighter planes.
U.N., *abbr.* The United Nations.
Uncle Tom, *n.* From name of hero in Harriet Beecher Stowe's "Uncle Tom's Cabin," 1852. (U.S. Negro slang) A negro who is servile to whites.
Underground*, *n.* Any secret group or groups outlawed by a political regime, but maintaining its organization and actively fighting the regime.
Underpass, *n.* A passage going underneath; esp. such a passage for traffic going under a railway.
Underpinning*, *n.* (slang) Someone's legs.
UNESCO, *n. abbr.* United Nations Educational, Scientific and Cultural Organization.
Unionize*, *v.t.* From *union* and *-ize.* To make subject to the rules of a labor union: the plant was unionized last year; —*v.i.* to form a union.
Union shop, *n.* A factory or business establishment whose employment and working practices are subject to trade union approval.
Unipod, ū'ni-pod, *n.* From *uni-* and *-pod* by analogy with tripod. A support having one leg.
Unit character, *n. biol.* A trait inherited according to Mendel's law.
United Nations, *n.* pl. The official organization for the promotion of international harmony, embracing most of the nations of the world.
Unit factor, *n. biol.* A gene; factor responsible for inheritance of a single character.
Unknown Soldier, *n.* The unidentified body of a soldier chosen by a nation to represent all the soldiers of that nation who died in World War I, and honored at special ceremonies.
Unreconstructed, *adj.* See RECONSTRUCTED, above. *Of a southerner* Maintaining the secessionist point of view and unwilling to accept the changes brought about by the Civil War; (by extension) clinging to outmoded social beliefs; unwilling to accept accomplished social change.
Unsaddle, *v.t.* To cause to be thrown from a horse; to unhorse.
Up-and-up, *n.* (slang) Phr. to be on the up-and-up, to be open, honest.
Update, *v.t.* To make up-to-date.
Upend, *v.t.* and *i.* To stand on end.
Upgrade, *n.* An upward slope.
Upset*, *n.* (colloq.) In a sports contest, the loss of a favored competitor.
Upstage, up'staj, *adv.* From the fact that the rear of the stage was originally higher than the front. On or toward the back of the stage. —*adj.* Of or pertaining to the back of the stage; (slang) supercilious, stand-offish; —*v.t. theatr.* (slang) to deflect the attention of an audience from one's fellow actors to oneself, by standing farther upstage than other actors and thus making them turn away from the audience in order to speak to you.
Upstairs*, *adv. avn.* At high altitude.
Upsweep, *n.* A sweeping upward, specif.: the upward curve of the lower jaw of certain animals; a coiffure in which the hair is brushed up from the nape of the neck and arranged in curls, etc. on top of the head.
Uptake*, *n.* A pipe or shaft conducting air, etc. upward, as for ventilation purposes.
Uptown, *adv.* To or in the upper part of a town, usually the part far from the business district. —*adj.* In or pertaining to the upper part of town.
Urea resin, *n.* Any of the thermosetting resins formed by the condensation of urea with formaldehyde.
V*, *n.* Symbol for Victory, used esp. by the Allies in World War II.
Valedictorian, val-e-dik-tōr'ian, *n.* (U.S.) The student in a graduating class who is chosen, usually because he or she ranks first in scholarship, to deliver the farewell address at graduation exercises.
Vapor tension or **pressure,** *n. phys.* The pressure exerted by a confined quantity of vapor.
Variable time fuse, *n.* Same as PROXIMITY FUSE, above.
Varsity, *n.* A team, in any competitive activity, which officially represents a university or other school.
Vaseline, vas-a-lēn', *n. trade-mark.* Petroleum jelly.
V.D., *abbr.* Venereal disease.
Vector*, *n. biol.* An organism, esp. an insect, transmitting micro-organisms which cause disease.
V-E Day, *n.* May 8, 1945; date of Allied victory in Europe, World War II.
Venin, ven'in, *n.* From Lat. *venēnum,* a drug. *biochem.* Any of several toxic substances found in snake venom.
Venture capital, *n. econ.* Capital invested in an enterprise involving a considerable risk, as in the founding of a new business.
Vernalize, *v.t.* From *vernal* and *-ize.* To speed up the growing time of plants by subjecting the seed or bulbs to low temperatures.
Very lights*, *n.* pl. From Lt. Very, the inventor. A signal system using a pistol which fires balls of red and green fire in certain coded groups.
Victrola, *n. trade-mark.* A type of phonograph.
Video, vid'e-o, *adj.* From Lat. *vidēre,* to see. *television* Pertaining to television. —*n.* Television.
Videogenic, vid'e-ō-jen'ik, *adj.* See VIDEO, above, and GENIC, above. Telegenic.
Vigilante, vij'i-lan'tē, *n.* Sp., vigilant. (U.S.) A member of a vigilance committee.
Vigilantism, vij-i-lan'tizm, *n.* From VIGILANTE, above, and *-ism.* The action of vigilantes.
Vinyl, vī'nil, *n.* From Lat. *vinum,* wine, and *-yl, chem.* A radical, CH_2:CH whose compounds are widely used in making plastics.
Vinylite, vī'ni-līte, *n. trade-mark.* A vinyl plastic used for making unbreakable phonograph records, etc.
VIP, *n.*; Acronym of *v*ery *i*mportant *p*erson. *avn.* (slang) A "big shot" airplane passenger, especially one traveling under an assumed name.
Viral, vī'rul, *adj.* From *virus* and *-al.* Pertaining to or caused by a virus.
Virgin wool, *n.* Wool not previously used in manufacturing.
Virology, vī-rol'ō-ji, *n.* From *virus* and *-ology.* The scientific study of the parasitic viruses.
Virgule*, *n. print.* A short, slanting stroke separating two words, indicating that either may be used in interpreting the meaning: invite Mark and/or Richard.
Virosis, vī-ro'sis, *n.* From *virus* and *-osis.* Any disease caused by a virus.
Virus pneumonia, *n.* A type of pneumonia caused by a filtrable virus.
Visual aid, *n.* Any device or technique using vision as an aid to instruction: the filmstrip is a good visual aid.
Vitamer, vī'ta-mer, *n.* From *vit*amin and *isomer. biochem.* Any compound removing a specific vitamin deficiency.
Vitascope, *n.* From Lat. *vita,* life, and *-scope.* A motion-picture projector.
Vivax, *n.* From Lat. *vivax,* tenacious of life, lively, vigorous. A malarial parasite, *Plasmodium vivax.* Also attrib.: vivax malaria.
V-J Day, *n.* The date of the Allied victory over Japan in World War II, Sept. 2, 1945.
V-mail, *n.* See V, above. A method used in World War II of transmitting letters by photographing them; designed to save space on ships, planes, etc.
Volleyball, *n.* A team sport in which a large ball is hit back and forth over a high net.
Volt-ampere, *n. elect.* A unit of measurement of electricity, equal to the product of one volt and one ampere.
Voluntarism*, *n. philos.* Any theory in which the will is postulated to be the basic life principle.
WAC, *abbr.* (U.S.) The Women's Army Corps of the U.S. Army; a member of the Women's Army Corps.
Wad*, (slang) Money.
Wainwright, *n.* From *wain* and *wright.* A wagon builder.
Waistline, *n.* The line surrounding the waist where it is smallest; the line of meeting between the skirt and waist of a dress.
Waldorf salad, *n.* From the Waldorf-Astoria Hotel, New York City. A salad made of diced apples, nuts, celery, and mayonnaise.
Walk*, *v.t.* Walk out of an assembly, walk out ostentatiously to show strong disapproval or contempt. Walk out on, (slang) decamp, clear off, leaving person in the lurch.
Walkie-talkie, *n.* From *walk* and *talk.* A radio receiver and transmitter small enough to be carried about by a man.
Walkout, *n.* (U.S. colloq.) A labor strike.
Wallboard, *n.* A building material made by compressing fiber into heavy sheets, used for interior paneling of walls, etc.
Wampum*, (slang) Money.
Want ad, *n.* (colloq.) An advertisement in a newspaper classified section for employment, real estate, miscellaneous items for sale, etc.
Warfarin, *n.* Named from initials of Wisconsin Alumni Research Foundation. *trade mark* A potent rat poison, causing internal hemorrhage.
War game, *n. mil.* A game played with pins and blocks representing troops, equipment, etc.; *usually pl.* maneuvers simulating wartime conditions.
War machine, *n.* The total governmental mechanism for the mobilization and utilization of the nation's manpower, weapons, and other resources in time of war.

Watercraft, *n.* Skill in sailing, swimming, etc.; a boat or vessel; boats or vessels collectively.

Water front, *n.* A section of land, esp. a part of a city, fronting on a body of water.

Water-wagon, *n.* Wheeled vehicle for carrying water. Phr. on the water-wagon, (U.S. slang) having forsworn all alcoholic drinks.

Wave, *n.* A member of the WAVES, below.

Waves, *n.* Acronym of Women Appointed for Volunteer Emergency Service. The women's branch of the U. S. Navy.

Wave guide, *n. radio* A metal tube used to conduct waves of ultra high frequency.

Wave mechanics, *n. phys.* A development of quantum mechanics in which matter is treated as a wave motion.

Wave recorder, *n.* A device which measures the force and oscillation of ocean waves.

Wax*, *v.t.* (slang) To make a phonograph record of.

Weak sister, *n.* (U.S. slang) A person who is a hindrance to an enterprise; one undependable in emergencies.

Weatherman, *n.* (colloq.) One who predicts the weather; a member of the U.S. Weather Bureau who releases reports on the weather.

Weatherstrip, *v.t.* To fit out with weatherstrips.

Wedgie, wej'i, *n.* From *wedge.* A woman's shoe having the heel and sole constructed in one piece shaped like a wedge.

Wehrmacht, vār'makt, *n.* From Ger. *wehr,* defense, and *macht,* force. The German armed forces.

Weight*, *v.t.* To assign relative importance to, as by different numerical values: the parts of the test were not equally weighted.

Weldment, *n.* From *weld* and *-ment.* The act of welding; something composed of several pieces welded together.

Welfare state, *n.* A state which actively concerns itself with the welfare of its citizens, esp. by means of economic legislation.

Welterweight, wel'ter-wāt' *n.* From *welter* and *weight.* A boxer weighing between 135 and 147 pounds.

Wet*, *adj.* (slang) Distasteful, unacceptable; foolish, crazy. Phr. you're all wet, completely off the track.

Wetback, *n.* (southwestern U.S. colloq.) A Mexican who illegally enters the United States by swimming or wading across the Rio Grande.

Wetting agent, *n.* A chemical which causes a substance to have a greater affinity for water.

Whale*, *n.* (slang) Phr. a whale of a —, a very big —, that's a whale of a car; phr. a whale of a lot, a great deal.

Wheelbase, *n.* In automobiles the distance between the front and rear axles, measured in inches.

Wheel-horse*, *n.* A person who is a steady, thorough worker.

White book, *n.* A collection of state papers, bound in white and issued by a government.

White-collar, *adj.* (U.S.) Pertaining to employment, such as office work, which permits wearing of conventional clothing: white-collar workers' jobs.

White noise, *n.* Noise produced by sounding all audible frequencies. By analogy with white light, composed of all the rays of the spectrum.

White primary, *n.* A primary election restricted to members of the white race, as in parts of the southern U.S.

Whiz*, *n.* Prob. punning on *whizz* and *wizard.* (slang) An expert.

Whodunit, *n.* From vulg. *who done it.* Coined by Donald Gordon, 1930. A mystery story.

Whole-wheat, *adj.* Referring to flour made from the entire wheat grain: whole-wheat bread.

Whoopee, *interj.* From whoop. (slang interj.) Expressing gaiety and exhilaration. —*n.* Riotous gaiety. Phr. to make whoopee, act with wild abandon.

Wide-angle, *adj. photog.* Having a wider angle, covering a wider area, than usual: wide-angle lens.

Widow*, *n. print.* A word or short line carried over from the foot of one column or page to the head of the next.

Wigwag, *v.t.* and *i.* To wave to and fro; to signal, using flags or lamps waved according to a code, as in a naval service; —*n.* the process or art of wigwagging; the message so sent.

Wildcat strike, *n.* A labor strike not authorized by union officials.

Wildcatter, *n.* One who promotes risky enterprises; specif., one who prospects for oil in territory not believed to contain oil.

Win*, *v.i.* Win back (colloq.) to recover lost ground by strenuous efforts.

Windbreaker, *n. trade-mark.* A short sportsjacket made of material relatively impervious to wind, such as leather.

Windmill*, *n.* An imaginary opposition, wrong, etc. in allusion to the hero of Cervantes' "Don Quixote."

Window-shopping, *v.n.* Gazing at what is displayed in shop windows, without entering the store to buy.

Windshield, *n.* A glass pane in front of the driver of an automobile, etc. to protect him from the wind.

Wind sock, *n.* A tapered cloth sleeve hung on a pole; used at airports to indicate wind direction at ground level.

Windup, *n.* The conclusion or outcome of any action; (colloq.) the final act or attraction of an entertainment; *baseball* the preliminary, rotary motion of the pitcher's arm before the ball is thrown.

Wings, *n.* pl. Any of various insignia, in the form of an outstretched pair of bird's wings, awarded to certain military aviation personnel upon completion of their training.

Winterize, *v.t.* From *winter* and *-ize.* To protect against the effects of winter weather, as an automobile.

Wipe*, *n. movies.* The effect of making one shot appear to be peeled off revealing another as if it had been underneath it.

Wire recorder, *n.* A machine in which sound is recorded on magnetized wire.

Wire tapper, *n.* One who secretly taps communication lines, as telephone wires, to obtain information. —**Wire-tapping,** *n.*

Wise*, *adj.* (U.S. slang) Wise guy, a disconcertingly, irritatingly well-informed or conceited person, one who 'knows it all'; an iconoclast, would-be exposer of frauds.

Wisecrack, *n.* (slang) A witticism; a sententious, esp. a sarcastic, remark; —*v.i.* to make such remarks. —**Wisecracker,** *n.*

Wish*, *n. psychoanal.* An unconscious desire which is tending to translate itself into action through some bodily mechanism, but which may be diverted or inhibited.

Wish-fulfillment, *n. psychoanal.* Fulfillment of a desire, either in a dream or in fantasy as expressed, e. g., in some inadvertent gesture or verbal error.

Witch-hunt, *n.* (U.S. colloq.) A search for those alleged to engage in disloyal or radical political activities, when accompanied by irresponsible persecution and defamation of political opponents.

Withholding tax, *n.* An income tax collected by deductions from salary or wages.

Wiz, *n.* Clipped form of wizard. (slang) An expert; highly skilled person.

Wobbly, *n.* Origin uncertain. (U.S. slang) A member of the Industrial Workers of the World.

Wolf pack *n.* A group of submarines, attacking enemy shipping in concert.

Wolfram*, *n.* By international agreement 1949 the official name for the metallic element 74, formerly called tungsten.

Wonder drug, *n.* (colloq.) Any of a number of drugs with extraordinary healing powers such as the sulfa drugs, penicillin, etc.

Woodsy, *adj,* From *woods* and *-y.* (U.S.) Of, pertaining to the woods.

Woofer, *n.* From *woof-* and *-er.* A loudspeaker, or component of a loudspeaker, which is designed to produce low tones.

Workbook, *n.* A book of rules of procedure, as for operating a machine; an instructional textbook; a book for recording work done or planned.

Workout, *n.* (colloq.) A session of exercise, as in preparation for a boxing contest; a practice performance, esp. of sports.

Workup, *n. print.* A mark on printed matter caused by the rising of spacing material.

World*, *n.* (slang) Phr. out of this world, amazingly good, of the highest quality.

Worrisome, *adj,* From *worry* and *-some. of persons* Given to worrying.

Worry wart, *n.* (slang) A gloomy, pessimistic person; a 'wet blanket.'

Wrangle*, *v.t.* (western U.S.) To tend livestock.

Wrap*, *n.* Phr. remove the wraps from, take the wraps off, to exhibit something previously hidden: the navy took the wraps off its new submarine.

Wrecker*, *n.* A vehicle equipped with a crane or derrick, used to remove wreckage from highways, railroads, etc.

Wrist watch, *n.* A small timepiece fastened about the wrist with a strap or bracelet.

Write-up, *n.* (slang) A newspaper or magazine story, esp. laudatory; U.S. *finance* a false statement of the assets of a corporation, in excess of the actual assets.

Xenophobia, zĕn'ō-fō'bi-a, *n.* From Gr. *xenos,* stranger, guest, and *phobia.* Fear or hatred of strangers.

Xeric, zē'rik, *adj.* From Gr. *xeros,* dry, and *-ic.* Containing or requiring little moisture, as a desert.

Xylene*, *n.* From Gr. *xulon,* wood. *chem.* Any of three isomeric hydrocarbons, $C_6H_4(CH_3)_2$, derived from benzene and used in making dyes, etc.

Yam*, *n.* (southwestern U.S.) The sweet potato.

Yardstick*, *n.* An arbitrary standard for determining cost of production, excellence, etc.

Yarn-dyed, *adj.* Woven from yarn which has been previously dyed.

Yegg, *n.* Origin uncertain. (U.S. slang) A burglar. Also yeggman.

Yellow dog contract, *n.* Fr. use of yellow dog as symbol of contempt, worthlessness. (U.S. colloq.) A contract between employer and worker stipulating that the latter may not join a labor union.

Yeoman*, *n.* (U.S. navy) A petty officer performing chiefly clerical duties.

Yes man, *n.* (U.S. colloq.) A sycophantic underling who always agrees with his superior.

Yoghurt, Yogurt, *n.* Turk. A curdled and fermented milk product, used as a food.

Youngberry, *n.* From B. M. Young, fruitgrower. A kind of blackberry developed by crossing several varieties.

Yoyo, *n. trade-mark.* A round, flat, wooden toy deeply grooved on the circumference; a string which is wound in the groove reels the toy in and out from the hand.

Zaibatsu, zī-bat'sōō, *n. sing. and pl.* Jap., from *zai,* property, and *batsu,* family. The combine of wealthy families dominating the economic life of Japan before and during World War II.

Zero hour, *n. mil.* The time appointed for an attack to start. Time appointed for the start of anything.

Zero-zero, *adj.* A weather condition in which the vision is limited vertically to less than 50 ft. and horizontally to 165 ft.

Zinc ointment, *n. pharm.* A soothing salve made of petroleum jelly and 20 per cent of zinc oxide.

Zip, *n.* (colloq.) Energy; vigor. —*v.i.* To move with a whizzing sound; (colloq.) to move energetically.

Zipper*, *n. trade-mark.* A type of boot using a slide fastener.

Zombi, Zombie, *n.* West African. The snake god of voodoo cults in West Africa, Haiti and the southern U.S.; a supernatural force which is believed to reanimate a corpse; a corpse brought back to life in this way; a potent drink made by mixing various kinds of rum.

Zwitterion, tsvit'er-ī'on, *n.* From Ger. *zwitter,* hybrid, and *-ion. physical chem.* An ion having both a positive and negative charge.

A, the first letter in the English and other alphabets derived from the Latin and Greek alphabets. In *music*, it designates the sixth note of the model or diatonic scale of C, the note sounded by the open second string of the violin.

A, the indefinite article, a contraction of *an*, used before nouns singular beginning with a consonant. AN.

A 1, a character attached to a ship of the first-class in Lloyd's register of shipping.

Aam, äm, *n.* [D., from L. *hama*, a bucket.] Liquid measure in Holland=about 30 gals.

Aardvark, ärd'värk, *n.* [D.=earth pig.] The ground-hog of South Africa, a burrowing, insectivorous, edentate animal.

Aardwolf, ärd'wulf, *n.* [D.=earth wolf.] The earth wolf of South Africa, an animal allied to the hyænas and civets.

Aaronic, Aaronical, ā-ron'ik, ā-ron'-ik-al, *a.* Pertaining to Aaron, or to his priesthood.

Abaca, ab'a-ka, *n.* Native name of the plant which yields Manilla-hemp.

Aback, a-bak', *adv.* [Prefix *a*, on, and *back*.] Backwards: *naut.* catching the wind so as to urge a vessel backwards (of sails); *fig.* by surprise; unexpectedly: as, to take a person *aback*.

Abacus, ab'a-kus, *n.* [L.] A slab or board for reckoning on; the Pythagorean multiplication table; *arch.* a slab or table forming the crowning of a column and its capital.

Abaddon, a-bad'on, *n.* [Heb. *abad*, he perished.] Hell. Rev. ix. 11.

Abaft, a-bäft', *adv.* or *prep.* [Prefix *a*, and A. Sax. *be-æftan*, *bæftan*. AFT.] On or towards the aft or hinder part of a ship.

Abalone, ab-a-lō'nē, *n.* [Spanish, of unknown origin.] A name in California for a marine mollusc, a species of ear-shell which furnishes mother-of-pearl.

Abandon, a-ban'dun, *v.t.* [Fr. *abandonner*, from *a*, to, and O.Fr. *bandon*, control, liberty; to leave at liberty. BAN.] To detach or withdraw one's self from; desert; forsake; give up; resign; yield up; *refl.* to yield one's self up without attempt at restraint; as, to *abandon one's self* to grief. —*n.* Abandonment†; heartiness; frank, unrestrained demeanour (a French usage). —**Abandoned**, a-ban'dund, *a.* Given up to vice; shamelessly and recklessly wicked; profligate; depraved; vicious. —**Abandonedly**, a-ban'dund-li, *adv.* In an abandoned manner.—**Abandonee**, a-ban'dun-ē", *n. Law*, one to whom anything is abandoned. —**Abandoner**, a-ban'dun-ėr, *n.* One who abandons.—**Abandonment**, a-ban'dun-ment, *n.* The act of abandoning or state of being abandoned; relinquishment; desertion; giving up.

Abarticulation, ab-är-tik'ū-lā"shon, *n.* [L. *ab*, from, and *articulus*, a joint.] *Anat.* an immovable articulation.

Abase, a-bās', *v.t.*—*abased, abasing.* [Fr. *abaisser*—*a*, to, and *baisser*, to lower, from L.L. *bassus*, low. BASE.] To lower or depress (of material objects)‡; to reduce lower, as in rank; humble; degrade.—**Abasement**, a-bās'ment, *n.* The act of abasing; a state of depression, degradation, or humiliation.—**Abaser**, a-bās'ėr, *n.* One who abases.

Abash, a-bash', *v.t.* [O.Fr. *esbahir*, ppr. *esbahissant*, from *es*=*ex*, intens., *bair*, *baer*, to gape; Mod.Fr. *s'ébahir*, to be astonished; probably from *bah!* exclamation of astonishment.] To confuse or confound, as by consciousness of guilt, inferiority, &c.; make ashamed; put to confusion. *Abash* is a stronger word than *confuse*, but not so strong as *confound*.—**Abashment**, a-bash'ment, *n.* Act of; state of being.

Abate, a-bāt', *v.t.*—*abated, abating.* [Fr. *abattre*, to beat down, from L. *batere*, a form of *batuere*, to beat. BATTER.] To beat down‡; to lessen; diminish; remit; moderate (zeal, a demand, a tax); *law*, to annul; put an end to.—*v.i.* To decrease or become less in strength or violence. —**Abatable**. a-bāt'a-bl, *a.* Capable of being abated.—**Abatement**, a-bāt'ment, *n.* The act of or state of being; decrease; decline; mitigation; amount or sum deducted; deduction; decrease.—**Abater**, a-bāt'ėr, *n.* One who or that.

Abatis, ab'a-tis, *Brit.* **Abattis**, a-bat'ē, *n.* [Fr. *abatis*, *abattis*, from *abattre*, to beat down. ABATE.] *Fort.* a collection of felled trees, from which the smaller branches have been cut off, and which are laid side by side, with the branched ends towards assailants, forming an obstruction to their progress.—**Abatised**, ab'a-tist, *a.* Provided with an abatis.

Abattoir, a-bat-wạr, *n.* [Fr., from *abattre*, to beat or knock down. ABATE.] A public slaughter-house.

Abaxial, Abaxile, ab-ak'si-al, ab-aks'il, *a.* [Prefix *ab*, from, and *axis*.] Not in the axis.

Abb, ab, *n.* [A.Sax. *ab* or *ob*, the woof.] Yarn for the warp in weaving; two qualities of wool, called respectively coarse *abb* and fine *abb*.

Abbacinate,† ab-ba'sin-āt, *v.t.* [It. *abbacinare*—*ab* for *ad*, to, and *bacino*, a basin.] To deprive of sight by applying a red-hot copper basin close to the eyes; a mode of punishment employed in the middle ages.

Abbacy, ab'ba-si, *n.* The dignity, rights, and privileges of an abbot.—**Abbat**, ab'bat, *n.* Same as *Abbot*.—**Abbatical, Abbatial**, ab-bat'ik-al, ab-bā'shi-al, *a.* Belonging to an abbey.

Abbé, ab-bā, *n.* [Fr., an abbot.] In France, especially before the revolution, one who devoted himself to divinity, or who had pursued a course of study in a theological seminary; many of them became tutors, professors, and men of letters.

Abbess, ab'bes, *n.* [Fr. *abbesse*, L.L. *abbatissa*.] A female superior of an abbey, possessing, in general, the same dignity and authority as an abbot, except that she cannot exercise the spiritual functions appertaining to the priesthood.—**Abbey**, ab'bi, *n.* [Fr. *abbaye*, from L.L. *abbatia*, an abbey. ABBOT.] A monastery or monastic establishment of the highest rank; a society of persons of either sex, secluded from the world, and devoted to religion and celibacy, governed by an *abbot* or *abbess*.—**Abbot**, ab'but, *n.* [Formerly *abbat*, L.L. *abbas*, *abbatis*, from Syr. and Chal. *abba*, father.] The male head or superior of an abbey or monastery. Some abbots were *mitred* abbots, almost equal in rank with bishops. Laymen were sometimes abbots, enjoying the abbey revenues.—*Abbot of Misrule*, of unreason; burlesque figure in mediæval mystery plays and revels. —**Abbotship**, ab'butship, *n.* The state or office of an abbot.

Abbreviate, ab-brē'vi-āt, *v.t.*—*abbreviated, abbreviating.* [L. *abbrevio*, *abbreviatum*, to shorten—*ab* for *ad*, and *brevis*, short. BRIEF, ABRIDGE (which is really the same word).] To make briefer; shorten; abridge; reduce to smaller compass.—**Abbreviation**, ab-brē'vi-ā"shon, *n.* Act of abbreviating, shortening, or contracting; that which is abbreviated; a syllable, letter, or series of letters, standing for a word or words; as, *esq.* for *esquire*; *F.R.S.* for *Fellow of the Royal Society*.—**Abbreviator**, ab-brē'vi-ā-tėr, *n.* One who abbreviates.—**Abbreviatory**, ab-brē'vi-a-to-ri, *a.* Abbreviating or tending to abbreviate; shortening.

Abdest, ab'dest, *n.* [Per. *ābdast*—*āb*, water, and *dast*, hand.] Purification or ablution before prayer; a Mohammedan rite.

Abdicate, ab'di-kāt, *v.t.*—*abdicated, abdicating.* [L. *abdico*, *abdicatum*—*ab*, from, and *dico*, *dicatum*, to declare publicly.] To give up, renounce, lay down, or withdraw from in a voluntary, public, or formal manner, as a throne, duties, &c.; vacate; resign.—*v.i.* To renounce or give up power voluntarily. —**Abdicant**, ab'di-kant, *n.* One who abdicates.—*a.* Renouncing.—**Abdication**, ab-di-kā'shon, *n.* The act of abdicating an office, especially the kingly office.—**Abdicator**, ab'di-kāt-ėr, *n.* One who abdicates.

Abdiel, ab'di-el, *n.* **Faithful Angel**, type of fidelity. (*Mil.*)

Abdomen, ab-dō'men or ab'do-men, *n.* [L.] That part of the human body which lies between the thorax and the pelvis, containing the stomach, liver, spleen, pancreas, kidneys, bladder, and intestines; the posterior of the three parts of a perfect insect. —**Abdominal**, ab-dom'in-al, *a.* Pertaining to the abdomen or belly.—*Abdominal regions*, certain regions into which the abdomen in men is arbitrarily divided for convenience in anatomical or medical descriptions.—**Abdominous**,† ab-dom'in-us, *a.* Abdominal; pot-bellied.

Abduce, ab-dūs', *v.t.*—*abduced, abducing.* [L. *abduco*, to lead away—*ab*, and *duco*, to lead, to draw. DUKE.] To draw or conduct away.—**Abducent**, ab-dū'sent, *a.* Drawing away; pulling back.—*Abducent muscles*, muscles which pull back certain parts of the body from the mesial line.—**Abduct**, ab-dukt', *v.t.* To draw or lead away; to take away surreptitiously and by force.—**Abduction**, ab-duk'shon, *n.* The act of abducting; *anat.* the action by which muscles withdraw a limb or other part from the axis of the body; *law*, the unlawful leading away of a person, as a young woman, by fraud, persuasion, or open violence.—**Abductor**, ab-duk'tėr, *n.* One who or that which abducts; *anat.* a muscle which moves certain parts from the axis of the body.

Abeam, a-bēm', *adv.* *Naut.* in the direction of the beams, that is, at right angles to the keel of a ship.

Abecedarian,† ā'bē-sē-dā"ri-an, *n.* [From the letters *a, b, c, d.*] One who teaches the letters of the alphabet, or a learner of the letters.—**Abecedary**,† ā-bē-sē'da-ri, *a.* Pertaining to or formed by the letters of the alphabet.—*n.* A first principle or element; rudiment.

Abed, a-bed', *adv.* In bed; gone to bed.

Abele, a-bēl', *n.* [D. *abeel*, G. *albele*, L. *albus*, white.] The white poplar.

Aberdevine, a-bėr'de-vīn, *n.* The siskin, a well-known song-bird.

Aberr,† ab-er', *v.i.* [L. *aberro, aberratum*—*ab*, from, and *erro*, to wander, to err.] To wander; to err.—**Aberrance**,† **Aberrancy**,† ab-er'rans, ab-er'ran-si, *n.* A wandering; aberration.—**Aberrant**, ab-er'rant, *a.* Characterized by aberration; wandering; straying from the right way; differing from a common type.—**Aberrate**,† ab-er'rāt, *v.i.* To wander or deviate from the right way.—**Aberration**, ab-er-rā'shon, *n.* [L. *aberratio.*] The act of wandering from the right way; deviation from truth or rectitude, or from a type or standard; partial alienation of mind; mental wandering; the difference between the true and the observed position of a heavenly body.

Aberuncator, ab-ē-rung'kāt-ėr, *n.* [L. *ab*, from, *e*, out, and *runco*, to weed.] An implement for extirpating weeds.

Abet, a-bet', *v.t.*—*abetted, abetting.* [O.Fr. *abetter, abeter*, to incite, to lure; *abet*, a bait—prefix *a*, and word=*bait*, to incite, set on. BAIT, BITE.] To encourage by aid, countenance, or approval: used chiefly in a bad sense; incite; support; encourage; back up.—**Abetment**, **Abettal**, a-bet'ment, a-bet'al, *n.* The act of abetting; aid.—**Abetter**, **Abettor**, a-bet'ėr, *n.* One who abets or incites; a supporter or encourager, generally of something bad.

Abeyance, a-bā'ans, *n.* [O.Fr. *abbaiaunce*, expectation, from *abbayer*, to listen with the mouth open, from *bayer, baer*, to gape, as in crying *bah!* ABASH.] A state of expectation, or waiting for an occupant or holder: said of lands, honours, or dignities; a state of temporary suspension.—**Abeyant**, a-bā'ant, *a.* Being in abeyance.

Abhor, ab-hor', *v.t.*—*abhorred, abhorring.* [L. *abhorreo*, to shrink back—*ab*, from, and *horreo*, to feel horror. HORRIBLE.] To hate extremely or with loathing; loathe, detest, or abominate; shrink from with horror; fill with horror and loathing (*Shak.*)†.—**Abhorrence**, ab-hor'rens, *n.* Extreme hatred; detestation; great aversion.—**Abhorrent**, ab-hor'rent, *a.* Struck with abhorrence; hating; detesting; utterly repugnant: in the last sense used formerly with *from*, now with *to*.—**Abhorrently**, ab-hor'rent-li, *adv.* With abhorrence.—**Abhorrer**, ab-hor'ėr, *n.* One who abhors; petitioner to Charles II in 1680 against the change of succession.—**Abhorring**, ab-hor'ing, *n.* Feeling of abhorrence; object of abhorrence. [O.T.]

Abib, ā'bib, *n.* The first month of the Jewish ecclesiastical year, called also Nisan, answering to the latter part of March and beginning of April.

Abide, a-bīd', *v.i.*—*abode* (pret. and pp.), *abiding.* [A. Sax. *abīdan, gebīdan*, to abide, from *bīdan*, to bide. See BIDE.] To take up one's abode; dwell; stay; not to depart.—*To abide by*, to remain beside; to adhere to; to maintain; to remain satisfied with.—*v.t.* To be prepared for; to await; be able to endure or sustain; remain firm under; to put up with; to tolerate.—**Abider**, a-bīd'ėr, *n.* One who abides.—**Abiding**, a-bīd'ing, *a.* Continuing; permanent; steadfast; as an *abiding* faith.—**Abidingly**, a-bīd'ing-li, *adv.* In such a manner as to continue; permanently.

Abies, ab'i-es, *n.* [L.] The genus of trees to which the fir belongs; a tree of this genus.—**Abietic**, ab-i-et'ik, *a.* Of or pertaining to trees of the genus Abies.

Abigail, ab'i-gāl, *n.* [From the title of *handmaid* assumed to herself by *Abigail*, wife of Nabal. See 1 Sam. xx. 5.] A general name for a waiting woman or lady's-maid. [Colloq.]

Ability, a-bil'i-ti, *n.* [Fr. *habilité*, L. *habilitas*, ableness. ABLE.] The state or condition of being able; power, whether bodily or mental; *pl.* talents; powers of the mind; mental gifts or endowments.

Abiogenesis, **Abiogeny**, a-bī'ō-jen"e-sis, a-bī-oj'en-i, *n.* [Gr. *a*, priv., *bios*, life, and *genesis*, generation.] The doctrine that living matter may be produced by not-living matter. BIOGENESIS, HETEROGENESIS.—**Abiogenesist**, **Abiogenist**, a-bī'ō-jen"e-sist, a-bī-oj'en-ist, *n.* A believer in the doctrine of abiogenesis.—**Abiogenetic**, a-bī'ō-jen-et"ik, *a.* Of, pertaining to, or produced by abiogenesis.—**Abiogenetically**, a-bī'ō-jen-et'ik-al-li, *adv.* In an abiogenetic manner.

Abject, ab'jekt, *a.* [L. *abjectus*, from *abjicio*, to throw away—*ab*, and *jacio*, to throw.] Sunk to a low condition; worthless, mean, despicable; low, grovelling.—*n.* A person in a low or abject condition.—**Abjection**, ab-jek'shon, *n.* A low state; meanness of spirit; abjectness.—**Abjectly**, ab'jekt-li, *adv.* In an abject or contemptible manner; meanly; servilely.—**Abjectness**, ab'jekt-nes, *n.* The state of being abject; meanness; servility.

Abjunctive,† abjungk'tiv, *a.* [L. *abjungo, abjunctum*—*ab*, from, and *jungo*, to join.] Isolated; exceptional.

Abjure, ab-jūr', *v.t.*—*abjured, abjuring.* [L. *abjuro*, to deny upon oath—*ab*, and *juro*, to swear. JURY.] To renounce upon oath; to reject or withdraw from with solemnity; abandon (as allegiance, errors); to recant or retract.—**Abjurement**, ab-jūr'ment, *n.* The act of abjuring; renunciation.—**Abjurer**, ab-jū'rėr, *n.* One who abjures.—**Abjuration**, ab-jū-rā'shon, *n.* The act of abjuring; a renunciation upon oath; a rejection or denial with solemnity; a total abandonment.—**Abjuratory**, ab-jū'ra-to-ri, *a.* Pertaining to abjuration.

Ablactate, ab-lak'tāt, *v.t.* [L. *ablacto*, to wean—*ab*, from, and *lac*, milk.] To wean from the breast.—**Ablactation**, ab-lak-tā'shon), *n.* The weaning of a child from the breast; *hort.* same as *Inarching.*

Ablative, ab'la-tiv, *a.* [L. *ablativus*, from *ablatus*, carried away—*ab*, away, and *latus*, carried.] Taking or tending to take away†: applied to a case of nouns in Sanskrit, Latin, and some other languages, originally given to the case in Latin because separation from was considered to be one of the chief ideas expressed by it.—**Ablation**,† ab-lā'shon, *n.* A carrying or taking away.

Ablaut, ab'lout, *n.* [G., from *ab*, off, and *laut*, sound.] *Philol.* a substitution of one vowel for another in the body of a word, to indicate a corresponding modification of use or meaning; as, *bind, band, bound, bond*; especially the change of a vowel to indicate tense-change in verbs, instead of the addition of a syllable (*-ed*); as, *sink, sank, sunk.*

Ablaze, a-blāz', *adv.* or *a.* In a blaze; in a state of eager excitement or desire.

Able, ā'bl, *a.* [O.Fr. *able, hable, habile*, skilful, fit, from L. *habilis*, suitable, fit, from *habeo*, to have; akin are *ability, habilament, habit*, suffix *-able.*] Having the power, means, or qualification sufficient; competent; qualified; having strong or unusual powers of mind, or intellectual qualifications; gifted; vigorous; active.—**Able**,† ā'bl, *v.t.* To make able; to enable; to warrant or answer for. [*Shak.*]—**Able-bodied**, *a.* Having a sound, strong body; having strength sufficient for work; often applied to a seaman who is well skilled in seamanship, and classed in the ship's books as A.B.—**Ableness**, ā'bl-nes, *n.* Ability of body or mind; force; vigour.—**Ably**, ā'bli, *adv.* In an able manner; with ability.

Ablepsia,† **Ablepsy**,† a-blep'si-a, a-blep'si, *n.* [Gr. *ablepsia*—*a*, not, and *blepō*, to see.] Want of sight; blindness.

Ablet, ab'let, *n.* [Fr. *ablette*, from L. *albus, albulus*, white, whitish, from its colour. The name *bleak* is given it for the same reason.] A small fresh-water fish, the bleak. Called also *Ablen.*

Ablocate, ab'lo-kāt, *v.t.*—*ablocated, ablocating.* [L. *abloco*—*ab*, away, and *locare*, to let out, from *locus*, a place.] To let out; to lease.—**Ablocation**, ab-lo-kā'shon, *n.* A letting to hire.

Abloom, a-blöm', *a.* or *adv.* In a blooming state.

Abluent, ab'lū-ent, *a.* [L. *abluens, abluentis*, ppr. of *abluo*, to wash off—*ab*, from, and *luo*, to wash.] Washing clean; cleansing by water or liquids.—*n.* That which washes or carries off impurities; a detergent.—**Ablution**, ab-lū'shon, *n.* The act of washing; cleansing or purification by water or other liquid; specifically, a washing of the body preparatory to religious rites.—**Ablutionary**, ab-lū'shon-a-ri, *a.* Pertaining to ablution.

Abnegate, ab'nē-gāt, *v.t.*—*abnegated, abnegating.* [L. *abnego, abnegatum*—*ab*, from, and *nego*, to deny. NEGATIVE, DENY.] To deny; to renounce.—**Abnegation**, ab-nē-gā'shon, *n.* [L. *abnegatio.*] The act of abnegating; denial; renunciation.—**Abnegative**, ab-neg'a-tiv, *a.* Denying; negative.—**Abnegator**, ab'nē-gā-tėr, *n.* One who abnegates, denies, or renounces.

Abnormal, ab-nor'mal, *a.* [L. *abnormis*—*ab*, from, and *norma*, a rule. NORMAL.] Not conformed or conforming to rule; deviating from a type or standard; irregular; contrary to system or law.—**Abnormality**, ab-nor-mal'i-ti, *n.* The state or quality of being abnormal; deviation from a standard, rule, or type; irregularity; that which is abnormal.—**Abnormity**,† ab-nor'mi-ti, *n.* Abnormality.

Aboard, a-bōrd', *adv.* On board; within a ship or boat.—*prep.* On board; into (to go *aboard* a ship).

Abode, a-bōd', pret. of *abide.*—**Abode**, a-bōd', *n.* [From *abide.*] Residence or place of residence; a place where a person abides, a dwelling; habitation.—*To make abode*, to dwell or reside.

Abolish, a-bol'ish, *v.t.* [Fr. *abolir*; L. *abolere*, to annul, abolish—*ab*, from, and *oleo*, to grow. ADULT.] To do away with; to put an end to; to destroy; to efface or obliterate; to make void; to annul; to put out of existence.—**Abolishable**, a-bol'ish-a-bl, *a.* Capable of being abolished.—**Abolisher**, a-bol'ish-ėr, *n.* One who or that which abolishes.—**Abolishment**,† a-bol'ish-ment, *n.* Abolition.—**Abolition**, ab-ō-li'shon, *n.* The act of abolishing, or the state of being abolished.—**Abolitionism**, ab-ō-li'shon-izm, *n.* The principles of an abolitionist.—**Abolitionist**, ab-ō-li'shon-ist, *n.* A person who favours the abolition of anything; applied especially to those who favoured the abolition of slavery in the United States.

Abomasus, **Abomasum**, ab-ō-mā'sus, ab-ō-mā'sum, *n.* [L. prefix *ab*, from, and *omasum.*] The fourth stomach of ruminating animals, lying next to the omasum or third stomach.

Abominate, a-bom'in-āt, *v.t.*—*abomin-*

ated, abominating. [L. *abominor, abominatus*, to deprecate, as of ill omen—*ab*, from, and *omen*, an omen.] To hate extremely; to abhor; to detest.—**Abominable**, a-bom'in-a-bl, *a.* Deserving or liable to be abominated; detestable; loathsome; odious in the utmost degree; execrable.—**Abominableness**, a-bom'in-a-bl-nes, *n.* The quality or state of being abominable, detestable, or odious.—**Abominably**, a-bom'in-a-bli, *adv.* In an abominable manner or degree.—**Abomination**, a-bom'-in-ā''shon, *n.* The act of abominating or state of being abominated; detestation; that which is abominated or abominable; hence, hateful or shameful vice.

Aboral, ab-ō'ral, *a.* [L. *ab*, from, and *os, oris*, a mouth.] *Anat.* away from or at the opposite extremity from the mouth.

Aboriginal, ab-o-rij'in-al, *a.* [L. *ab*, from, and *origo*, origin.] Inhabiting a country from the earliest known times; as, *aboriginal* tribes.—*n.* An original inhabitant; one of an aboriginal race.—**Aboriginally**, ab-o-rij'in-al-li, *adv.* In or at first origin; originally; from the very first.—**Aborigines**, ab-o-rij'in-ēz, *n. pl.* [L.] The people found in a country at the time of the earliest known settlement.

Abort, a-bort', *v.i.* [L. *aborior, abortus*, to miscarry—*ab*, and *orior, ortus*, to arise. ORIENT.] To miscarry in giving birth; to appear in a rudimentary or undeveloped state.—**Aborted**, a-bort'ed, *a.* Imperfectly developed.—**Abortient**, a-bor'shi-ent, *a.* *Bot.* sterile; barren.—**Abortion**, a-bor'shon, *n.* The act of miscarrying, or producing young before the natural time, or before the fetus is perfectly formed; the product of untimely birth; a misshapen being; a monster; anything which fails before it is matured or perfect, as a design.—**Abortive**, a-bort'iv, *a.* Brought forth in an immature state; rudimentary; imperfectly formed or developed; producing or intended to produce abortion; not brought to completion or to a successful issue; coming to nought.—**Abortive**, a-bort'iv, *n.* A drug causing or thought to cause abortion.—**Abortively**, a-bort'iv-li, *adv.* In an abortive manner; immaturely.—**Abortiveness**, a-bort'iv-nes, *n.* The state of being abortive.—**Abortment**,† a-bort'ment, *n.* An untimely birth; abortion.

Abound, a-bound', *v.i.* [Fr. *abonder*, from L. *abundare*, to overflow—*ab*, and *unda*, a wave. UNDULATE, WATER.] To be in great plenty; be very prevalent; have or possess in great quantity; be copiously supplied: in the latter sense followed by *with* or *in*.

About, a-bout', *prep.* [A.Sax. *âbûtan, onbûtan*, about, around—prefixes *â, on*, on, and *bûtan*, without. BUT.] Around; on the outside or surface of; in a circle surrounding; round (two yards *about* the stem); near to in place, time, size, number, quantity, &c.; near to in action; on the point of (to be *about* to speak): in this sense followed by the infinitive; concerned in; engaged in (what is he *about*?) concerning; relating to; respecting.—*adv.* Around the outside; in circuit; in a circle; near to in number, time, place, quality, or degree (*about* as high); here and there; around; in one place and another; in different directions.—*To bring about*, to cause to happen; to effect or accomplish.—*To come about*, to come to pass; to happen.—*To go about*, to prepare to do.—*Turn about, week about*, &c., alternately, on each alternate week, and the like.

Above, a-buv', *prep.* [A.Sax. *âbûfan*, above: a triple compound of *â*, on, at, *be*, by, and *ûfan*, upwards, akin to E. *over*, L. *super*, Gr. *hyper*, above.] In or to a higher place than; superior to in any respect; too high for (*above* mean actions); more in number, quantity, or degree than; in excess of (*above* a ton).—*Above all*, above or before everything else; before every other consideration.—*adv.* In or to a higher place; overhead; before, in rank or order, especially in a book or writing (what has been said *above*); besides, in the expression *over and above*. *Above* is often used elliptically as a noun, meaning (1) heaven; (2) the aforesaid; as, from the *above* you will learn. It is equal to an adjective in such phrases as, the *above* particulars, in which *cited* or *mentioned* is understood.—**Above-board**, *adv.* [Said to mean lit. above the table, not with hands below the table, as one trying to cheat at cards.] In open sight; without tricks or disguise.—**Above-ground**, *adv.* Alive; not buried.

Abracadabra, ab'ra-ka-dab''ra, *n.* A word of eastern origin used in incantations. When written on paper so as to form a triangle, the first line containing the word in full, the one below it omitting the last letter, and so on each time until only one letter remained, and worn as an amulet, it was supposed to be an antidote against certain diseases.

Abrade, a-brād', *v.t.*—*abraded, abrading.* [L. *abrado*, to scrape off—*ab*, away, and *rado*, to scrape, whence *raze, razor*, &c.] To rub or wear down; to rub or grate off.—**Abradant**, a-brād'ant, *n.* A material for grinding, usually in powder, such as emery, sand, glass, &c.—**Abrasion**, ab-rā'zhon, *n.* The act of abrading, wearing, or rubbing off; an injury of the skin by removal of cuticle.—**Abrasive**, ab-rā'ziv, *a.* and *n.* Serving to abrade; an abradant.

Abrahamic, ā-bra-ham'ik, *a.* Pertaining to Abraham, the patriarch.

Abranchiate, a-brang'ki-āt, *a.* [Gr. *a*, without, and *branchia*, gills.] Devoid of branchiæ or gills.—*n.* A vertebrate animal (mammal, bird, reptile) that at no period of its existence possesses gills.

Abrasion. See ABRADE.

Abrazitic, ab-ra-zit'ik, *a.* [Gr. *a*, not, *brazō*, to bubble.] *Mineral.* not effervescing when melted before the blow-pipe.

Abreast, a-brest', *adv.* Side by side, with the breasts in a line; hence, up to a level or standard (to keep *abreast* of science).

Abreption, ab-rep'shon, *n.* [L. *abripio, abreptum*, to snatch away—*ab*, from, and *rapio*, to snatch.] A carrying away, or state of being seized and carried away.

Abridge, a-brij', *v.t.*—*abridged, abridging.* [Fr. *abréger*, from L. *abbreviare*, to shorten. ABBREVIATE.] To make shorter; to curtail; to epitomize; to shorten by using fewer words; to condense; to lessen; to diminish; to deprive or cut off from: in the last sense followed by *of* (to *abridge* one *of* his rights).—**Abridger**, a-brij'ėr, *n.* One who or that which abridges.—**Abridgment**, a-brij'-ment, *n.* The act of abridging or state of being; that which is abridged; an epitome; a summary, as of a book; an abstract. ∴ An *abridgment* is a larger work shortened; a *compendium* is a condensed view of a particular subject regarded as complete in itself; an *epitome* has more reference to the selection of essential facts than an *abridgment*; an *abstract* is a bare statement of facts contained in, or of the leading features of a work.

Abroach, a-brōch', *a.* or *adv.* Broached; in a position for letting out liquor: said of a cask.

Abroad, a-brąd', *adv.* At large; without being confined to narrow limits; with expansion (to spread its branches *abroad*); beyond or out of the walls of a house or other inclosure; beyond the bounds of a country; in foreign countries.

Abrogate, ab'rō-gāt, *v.t.*—*abrogated, abrogating.* [L. *abrogo*, to repeal—*ab*, from, and *rogo*, to ask, propose as a law.] To repeal; to make void; to do away with; to annul by an authoritative act.—**Abrogable**, ab'rō-ga-bl, *a.* Capable of being abrogated.—**Abrogation**, ab-rō-gā'shon, *n.* The act of abrogating; repeal by authority.—**Abrogative**, ab'rō-gā-tiv, *a.* Capable of abrogating; tending to abrogate.

Abrupt, ab-rupt', *a.* [L. *abruptus*, from *abrumpo*, to break off—*ab*, off, from, and *rumpo, ruptum*, to break, whence *rupture*, &c.] Steep; craggy (of rocks, precipices, &c.); sudden; without notice to prepare the mind for the event (an *abrupt* entrance); disconnected; having sudden transitions (an *abrupt* style).—*Abrupt leaf, root, bot.*, one terminating suddenly as if the end were cut off.—**Abruption**, ab-rup'shon, *n.* A sudden and violent breaking off.—**Abruptly**, ab-rupt'li, *adv.* In an abrupt manner; suddenly; without any notice or warning; precipitously.—**Abruptness**, ab-rupt'nes, *n.* The state or quality of being abrupt; precipitousness; suddenness; unceremonious haste or vehemence.

Abscess, ab'ses, *n.* [L. *abscessus*, from *abscedere*, to separate, to gather into an abscess—*abs*, away, and *cedo, cessum*, to go, whence *cession, cede*, &c.] A collection of purulent matter in the tissue of an organ or part, with pain and heat.

Abscind, ab-sind', *v.t.* L. *abscindo, abscissum*, to cut off—*ab*, from, and *scindo*, to cut.] To cut off.—**Abscissa**, ab-sis'sa, *n.* pl. **Abscissæ**, ab-sis'sē. Any part of the diameter or transverse axis of a conic section (as an ellipse), intercepted between the vertex and a line at right angles to the axis; the x-co-ordinate of a point.—**Abscission**, ab-si'zhon, *n.* The act of cutting off; severance; removal.

Abscond, ab-skond', *v.i.* [L. *abscondo*, to hide—*abs*, from, and *condo*, to hide.] To withdraw or absent one's self in a private manner; run away in order to avoid a legal process; decamp.—**Absconder**, ab-skond'-ėr, *n.* One who absconds.

Absence, ab'sens, *n.* L. *absentia*, from *absens, absentis*, absent, pres. part. of *absum*, to be absent—*ab* or *abs*, away, and *sum, esse*, to be.] The state of being absent; opposite of *presence*; the state of being at a distance in place; the state of being awanting; non-existence within a certain sphere (*absence* of evidence); inattention.—*Absence of mind*, attention not to things or objects present, but to others distant or foreign.—**Absent**, ab'sent, *a.* Not present; away; somewhere else; awanting; having the mind withdrawn from what is passing characterized by absence of mind (an *absent* man).—**Absent**, ab-sent', *v.t.* To keep away intentionally: used *refl.*; as, to *absent* one's self from a meeting.—**Absentee**, ab-sen-tē', *n.* One who is absent; one who absents himself: often applied to landlords who, deriving their income from one country, reside and spend it in another.—**Absenteeism**, ab-sen-tē'izm, *n.* The practice or habit of an absentee.—**Absenter**, ab-sent'ėr, *n.* One who absents himself.—**Absently**, ab'sent-li, *adv.* In an absent or inattentive manner.—**Absentment**, ab-sent'ment, *n.* The act of absenting.

Absinthe, ab-sant or ab'sinth, *n.* [Fr., from L. *absinthium*, wormwood.] A popular French liqueur or cordial consisting of brandy flavoured with wormwood.—**Absinthian, Absinthic**, ab-sin'thi-an, ab-sin'thik, *a.* Pertaining to wormwood or obtained from it.—**Absinthiate**, ab-sin'-thi-āt, *v.t.* To impregnate with wormwood.

Absolute, ab'sō-lūt, *a.* [L. *absolutus*. ABSOLVE.] Freed from limitation or condition; unconditional (an *absolute* promise); unlimited by extraneous power or control (an *absolute* government or prince); complete in itself; finished; perfect (*absolute* beauty); free from mixture (*absolute* alcohol); positive; decided; peremptory (now rare); *metaph.* (*a*) not relative; considered without reference to other things; (*absolute* knowledge); (*b*) existing independent of any other cause; self-existing; unconditioned; *gram.* applied to the case which is not determined by any other word in the sentence.—**Absolute Units**. *Dynam.* units of force, such as the poundal and dyne, which are independent of the acceleration due to gravity; *electric.* electrostatic and electro-magnetic units derived immediately from the fundamental centimetre-gramme-second system of units.—**Absolutely**, ab'sō-lūt-li, *adv.* In an absolute manner; completely; without restriction, limitation, or qualification; unconditionally; positively.—**Absoluteness**, ab'sō-lūt-nes, *n.* The state of being.—**Absolutism**, ab'sō-lūt-izm, *n.* State of being absolute, or principles of absolute government.—**Absolutist**, ab'sō-lūt-ist, *n.* An advocate for absolute government.—**Absolutistic, Absolutist**, ab'sō-lūt-ist"ik, ab'sō-lūt-ist, *a.* Pertaining to absolutism.

Absolution, ab-sō-lū'shon, *n.* The act of absolving or state of being absolved; specifically, in the Roman Catholic and some other churches, a remission of sins pronounced by a priest in favour of a penitent. —**Absolutory**, ab-sol'ū-to-ri, *a.* Absolving or capable of absolving.

Absolve, ab-solv', *v.t.—absolved, absolving.* [L. *absolvo, absolutum*, to set free—*ab*, from, and *solvo*, to loose. SOLVE.] To set free or release from some duty, obligation, or responsibility (to *absolve* a person *from* a promise; acquit; to forgive or grant remission of sins to; pronounce forgiveness of sins to (with *from*).—**Absolvable**, ab-solv'a-bl, *a.* Capable of being absolved.—**Absolvatory**, ab-solv'a-to-ri, *a.* Conferring or having power to absolve. — **Absolver**, ab-solv'ėr, *n.* One who absolves.

Absorb, ab-sorb', *v.t.* [L. *absorbeo—ab*, from, and *sorbeo*, to suck in.] To drink in; suck up; imbibe, as a sponge; take in by capillarity; swallow up; engross or engage wholly.—**Absorbability**, ab-sorb'a-bil"i-ti, *n.* The state or quality of being absorbable.—**Absorbable**, ab-sorb'a-bl, *a.* Capable of being absorbed or imbibed.—**Absorbent**, ab-sorb'ent, *a.* Capable of absorbing fluids; performing the function of absorption.—**Absorbent**, ab-sorb'ent, *n.* Anything which absorbs; a vessel in an animal body which takes in nutritive matters into the system; a substance applied to a wound to stanch or arrest the flow of blood. — **Absorption**, ab-sorp'shon, *n.* The act or process of absorbing; state of being absorbed or engrossed.—**Absorptive**, ab-sorp'tiv, *a.* Having power to absorb or imbibe.—**Absorptivity**, ab-sorp-tiv'i-ti, *n.* The power or capacity of absorption.

Abstain, ab-stān', *v.i.* [O.Fr. *abstener*, Mod.Fr. *abstenir*, from L. *abstineo*, to keep from—*abs*, from, and *teneo*, to hold, whence *contain, tenant, tenacious*, &c.] To forbear or refrain voluntarily; to withhold.—**Abstainer**, ab-stān'ėr, *n.* One who abstains; specifically, one who abstains from the use of intoxicating liquors.—**Abstention**, ab-sten'shon, *n.* The act of holding off or abstaining; abstinence. — **Abstinence**, ab'sti-nens, *n.* The act or practice of voluntarily refraining from the use of anything within our reach, especially from some bodily indulgence; partaking sparingly of food or drink.—**Abstinent**, ab'sti-nent, *a.* Practising abstinence.—**Abstinently**, ab'sti-nent-li, *adv.* In an abstinent manner.

Abstemious, ab-stē'mi-us, *a.* [L. *abstemius—abs*, and root seen in *temetum*, strong drink, *temulentus*, drunken; Skr. *tim*, to be wet.] Sparing in diet; refraining from a free use of food and strong drinks; temperate; devoted to or spent in abstemiousness or abstinence (an *abstemious* life); very moderate and plain; very sparing (*abstemious* diet). — **Abstemiously**, ab-stē'mi-us-li, *adv.* In an abstemious manner.—**Abstemiousness**, ab-stē'mi-us-nes, *n.*

Abstention. ABSTAIN.

Absterge, ab-stėrj', *v.t.—absterged, absterging.* [L. *abstergeo*, to wipe off—*abs*, and *tergeo, tersum*, to wipe, whence *terse.*] To wipe, or make clean by wiping; to wash away; to deterge.—**Abstergent**, ab-stėrj'ent, *a.* Having cleansing or purgative properties.—**Abstergent**, ab-stėrj'ent, *n.* Whatever aids in scouring or cleansing; a detergent. — **Absterse**,† ab-stėrs', *v.t.* To absterge; to cleanse; to purify.—**Abstersion**, ab-stėr'shon, *n.* The act of absterging or cleansing.—**Abstersive**, ab-stėrs'iv, *a.* Cleansing; abstergent. **Abstersive**, ab-stėrs'iv, *n.* That which effects abstersion. — **Abstersiveness**, ab-stėrs'iv-nes, *n.* Quality of being abstersive or abstergent.

Abstinence, Abstinent, Abstinently. See ABSTAIN.

Abstract, ab-strakt', *v.t.* [From L. *abstraho, abstractum*, to draw away—*abs*, and *traho, tractum*, to draw, seen also in *trace, contract, detract, retract*, &c.] To draw or take away; to withdraw; to purloin; to take away mentally; consider separately; epitomize or reduce to a summary.—**Abstract**, ab'strakt, *a.* Considered or thought of in itself; not concrete; considered and treated apart from any particular object (*abstract* mathematics; *abstract* logic). In *gram.* and *logic, abstract nouns* or *terms* are names of qualities, in opposition to *concrete*, which are names of things.—*n.* A summary or epitome containing the substance; a bare or brief statement of facts detailed elsewhere. *Syn.* under ABRIDGMENT. — **Abstracted**, ab-strakt'ed, *a.* Absent in mind; inattentive. — **Abstractedly**, ab-strakt'ed-li, *adv.* In an abstracted or absent manner.—**Abstractedness**, ab-strakt'ed-nes, *n.*—**Abstracter**, ab-strakt'ėr. *n.* One who abstracts or purloins.—**Abstraction**, ab-strak'shon, *n.* The act of abstracting or separating; the act of withdrawing; the act of considering separately what is united in a complex object; something abstract; an idea or notion of an abstract character; absence of mind; the state of being entirely engrossed in thought.—**Abstractive**, ab-strakt'iv, *a.* Having the power or quality of abstracting. — **Abstractively**, ab-strakt'iv-li, *adv.* In an abstractive manner. —**Abstractly**, ab-strakt'li, *adv.* In an abstract manner or state.—**Abstractness**, ab'strakt-nes, *n.* The state or quality of being abstract.

Abstriction,† ab-strik'shon, *n.* [L. *ab*, from, and *stringo, strictum*, to bind.] The act of unbinding.—**Abstringe**,† ab-strinj', *v.t.* To unbind.

Abstruse, ab-strūs', *a.* [L. *abstrusus*, pp. of *abstrudo*, to thrust away.] Remote from ordinary minds or notions; difficult to be comprehended or understood; profound; recondite.—**Abstrusely**, ab-strūs'li, *adv.* In an abstruse manner; profoundly; with terms or notions remote from such as are obvious.—**Abstruseness**, ab-strūs'nes, *n.* The quality of being abstruse.

Absurd, ab-sėrd', *a.* [L. *absurdus—ab*, and *surdus*, deaf, insensible. SURD.] Inconsistent with reason or common sense; ridiculous; nonsensical; logically contradictory. —**Absurdity**, ab-sėrd'i-ti, *n.* The state or quality of being absurd; that which is absurd; an absurd action, statement, &c. —**Absurdly**, ab-sėrd'li, *adv.* In an absurd manner. — **Absurdness**, ab-sėrd'nes, *n.* The quality of being absurd.

Abundance, a-bun'dans, *n.* [L. *abundantia*, abundance, from *abundo*, to abound (which see).] A fulness or plenteousness great to overflowing; ample sufficiency; plenteousness; copiousness.—**Abundant**, a-bun'dant, *a.* Plentiful; ample; fully sufficient; abounding; overflowing. — **Abundantly**, a-bun'dant-li, *adv.* In a plentiful or sufficient degree; amply; plentifully.

Abuse, a-būz', *v.t.—abused, abusing.* [Fr. *abuser*; L. *abutor, abusus—ab*, and *utor*, to use. USE.] To misuse; to put to a wrong or bad use; to do wrong to; injure; dishonor; violate; deceive; impose on; take undue advantage of.—**Abusable**, a-būz'a-bl, *a.* Capable of being abused. — **Abuse**, a-būs', *n.* Improper treatment or employment; improper use or application; misuse; a corrupt practice or custom (the *abuses* of government); injury; scurrilous or contumelious language.—**Abuser**, a-būz'ėr, *n.* One who abuses, in speech or behaviour.—**Abusive**, a-būs'iv, *a.* Practising abuse; offering harsh words or ill-treatment; scurrilous; opprobrious; insulting.—**Abusively**, a-būs'iv-li, *adv.* In an abusive manner.—**Abusiveness**, a-būs'iv-nes, *n.* The quality of being abusive; rudeness of language.

Abut, a-but', *v.i.—abutted, abutting.* [Fr. *aboutir*, to meet at the end, to border on—*a*, at, and *bout*, extremity. BUTT.] To be contiguous; to join at a border or boundary; to form a point or line of contact: with *on, upon, against.*—**Abutment**, a-but'ment, *n.* The condition of abutting; the part abutting; the solid part of a pier or wall against which an arch abuts, or from which it springs. — **Abuttal**, a-but'al, *n.* The abutting part of a piece of land.—**Abutter**, a-but'ėr, *n.*—That which abuts.

Aby, a-bī', *v.t.—abied.* [=prefix *a*, and *buy*: A.Sax. *âbicgan*, to pay a penalty.] To atone for; to suffer for; to pay the penalty for.

Abyss, a-bis', *n.* [L. *abyssus*, Gr. *abyssos*, bottomless—*a*, priv., and *byssos*, bottom.] A bottomless gulf; anything profound and unfathomable, literally or figuratively. — **Abysmal**, a-biz'mal, *a.* Pertaining to an abyss; profound; immeasurable. — **Abyssal**, a-bis'al, *a.* Relating to or like an abyss; pertaining to the deeper parts of the sea.

Abyssinian, ab-is-sin'i-an, *a.* Belonging to Abyssinia or its inhabitants.—*n.* A native or inhabitant of Abyssinia; a member of the Abyssinian Church.

Acacia, a-kā'shi-a, *n.* [L. *acacia*, Gr. *akakia*, from *akē*, a point.] A genus of ornamental plants, some species of which produce catechu, and some exude gum-arabic. *Acacia-tree*, a name sometimes given to the locust-tree [*Robinia pseudacacia*).

Acacio, a-kā'shi-ō, *n.* A heavy durable wood of the red-mahogany character, but darker and plainer. Called also *Acajou*.

Academy, a-kad'e-mi, *n.* [L. *academia*, Gr. *akadēmeia*, the Academy, from the hero *Akadēmus*, to whom the ground originally belonged which formed the garden in which Plato taught.] The members of the philosophical school founded by the Greek philosopher Plato; a school holding a rank between a college and an elementary school; a seminary of learning of the higher class; an association for the promotion of literature, science, or art, established sometimes by government, and sometimes by the voluntary union of private individuals, the members of which are called *Academicians*.—**Academe**, *n.* An academy. [Poet.]—**Academic, Academical**, ak-a-dem'ik, ak-a-dem'ik-al, *a.* Belonging to the school or philosophy of Plato; belonging to an academy, or to a college or university; as, *academic* studies.—**Academic**, ak-a-dem'-ik, *n.* A disciple of Plato; a student in a college or university.—**Academical**, ak-a-dem'i-kal, *n.* A member of an academy; *pl.* the costume proper to the officers and students of a school or college.—**Academically**, ak'a-dem"ik-al-li, *adv.* In an academical manner.—**Academician**, ak'a-dē-mi"shan, *n.* A member of an academy or society for promoting arts and sciences. — **Academics, Academism**, ak-a-dem'iks, a-kad'em-izm, *n.* The doctrines of the Academic philosophy; Platonism. — **Academist**, a-kad'em-ist, *n.* An Academic philosopher.—**Academicism**, ak-a-dem'i-sizm, *n.* The system or mode of teaching at an academy; an academical mannerism.

Acadian, a-kā'di-an, *a.* Belonging to Acadia, a former name of Nova Scotia.—*n.* A native or inhabitant of Acadia.

Acajou, ak'a-jö, *n.* [Fr. *acajou*, mahogany, probably from Malay *kāyu*, a tree.] A kind of heavy red mahogany; acacio; gum and resin from the stem of the mahogany tree.

Acalephæ, a-ka-lē'fē, *n. pl.* [Gr. *akalēphē*, a nettle.] A name sometimes applied to the marine animals commonly known as sea-nettles, jelly-fish, &c.—**Acaleph, Acalephan**, ak'a-lef, ak-a-lē'fan, *n.* A member of the Acalephæ.—**Acalephoid**, a-ka-lē'foid, *a.* Like an acaleph or medusa; medusoid.

Acalycine, Acalycinous, a-kal'i-sin, ak-a-lis'in-us, *a.* [Gr. *a*, not, and *kalyx*, a cup.] *Bot.* without a calyx or flower-cup.

Acanaceous, ak-a-nā'shus, *a.* [Gr. *akanos*, a prickly shrub.] *Bot.* armed with prickles.

Acantha, a-kan'tha, *n.* [Gr. *akantha*, a spine or thorn.] A prickle of a plant; a spine of an animal; one of the acute processes of the vertebræ of animals.—**Acanthaceous**, ak-an-thā'shus, *a.* Armed with prickles, as a plant.—**Acanthine**, a-kan'thin, *a.* Pertaining to or resembling the plant Acanthus; prickly. — **Acanthocephalous**, a-kan-thō-sef'a-lus, *a.* [Gr.

akantha, thorn, *kephalē*, head.] *Zool.* having spines or hooks on the head, as certain intestinal worms (the Acanthokephala), which are thus attached within the bodies of animals.—**Acanthoid, Acanthous**, a-kan′thoid, a-kan′thus, *a.* Spiny.—**Acanthophorous**, ak-an-tho′for-us, *a.* Having or producing spines or prickles.—**Acanthus**, a-kan′thus, *n.* [Gr. *akanthos*, from its prickly leaves.] The plant bear's-breech or brankursine; an architectural ornament used in capitals of the Corinthian and Composite orders, and resembling somewhat the foliage of this plant.

Acanthopterygii, a-kan′thop-te-rij″i-ī, *n. pl.* [Gr. *akantha*, a thorn, and *pterygion*, the fin of a fish, from *pteryx*, a wing.] One of the two primary divisions of the osseous fishes, characterized by having one or more of the first rays of the fins in the form of spines. — **Acanthopterygian, Acanthopterygious**, a-kan′thop-te-rij″i-an, a-kan′thop-te-rij″i-us, *a.* Of or pertaining to the Acanthopterygii. — **Acanthopterygian**, a-kan′thop-te-rij″i-an, *n.* An Acanthopterygian fish.

Acanthus, a-kan′thus, *n.* ACANTHA.

Acardia, a-kär′di-a, *n.* [Gr. *a*, priv., and *kardia*, the heart.] The state of being without a heart, as is the case in some monstrous births.

Acarida, a-kar′i-da, *n. pl.* [Gr. *akarēs*, too short to be cut, small, tiny—*a*, priv., and *keirō*, to cut.] A division of Arachnida, including the mites, ticks, and water-mites. The mouth in all is formed for suction.—**Acaridan, Acarid**, a-kar′i-dan, ak′a-rid, *n.* One of the Acarida. — **Acaricide**, a-kär′i-sīd, *n.* A substance that destroys mites.

Acaroid, ak′a-roid, *n.* A resin that exudes from the grass-trees of Australia, used in varnishes.

Acarpous, a-kär′pus, *a.* [Gr. *akarpos*, unfruitful—*a*, priv., and *karpos*, fruit.] *Bot.* not producing fruit; sterile; barren.

Acarus, ak′a-rus, *n.* [ACARIDA.] The genus to which the true mites belong; a mite or tick generally.

Acatalectic, a′kat-a-lek″tik, *a.* [Gr. *akatalēktos*.] Having the complete number of syllables (an *acatalectic* verse).

Acataleptic, a′kat-a-lep″tik, *a.* [Gr. *a*, priv., *kata*, down, and *lēpsis*, a taking.] Incomprehensible; not to be known with certainty. — *n.* One who believes that we can know nothing with certainty.

Acaulous, Acaulescent, a-kal′us, a-kales′ent, *a.* [Gr. *a*, priv., and *kaulos*, a stalk.] *Bot.* without a conspicuous stem; stemless. *Acauline*, *Acaulose*, are also used in same sense.

Accad, Accadian, ak′ad, ak-kā′di-an, *n.* A member of one of the primitive races of Babylonia, a non-Semitic race the existence of which has been shown by the cuneiform inscriptions; the language of this race.—**Accadian**, ak-kā′di-an, *a.* Belonging to the Accads or their language.

Accede, ak-sēd′, *v.i.* — *acceded*, *acceding*. [Fr. *accéder*, to assent, from L. *accedo*—*ad*, to, and *cedo*, to move, to give place. CEDE.] To agree or assent, as to a proposition, or to terms proposed by another; to become a party by agreeing to terms; to join or be added; to succeed, as an heir; come to by inheritance: said especially of a sovereign. —**Accession**, ak-se′shon, *n.* The act of acceding; the act of agreeing or assenting; increase by something added; that which is added; the act of succeeding to a throne, office, or dignity; the attack or commencement of a disease.

Accelerate, ak-sel′ėr-āt, *v.t.*—*accelerated*, *accelerating*. [L. *accelero*, *acceleratum*, to hasten—*ad*, to, and *celer*, swift. CELERITY.] To make quicker; to cause to move or advance faster; hasten; add to the velocity of; bring about or help to bring about more speedily. — **Acceleration**, ak′sel-ėr-ā″shon, *n.* The act of accelerating or state of being accelerated; increase of velocity.—**Accelerative**, ak-sel′ėr-āt-iv, *a.* Tending to accelerate; adding to velocity.—**Accelerator**, ak-sel′ėr-āt-ėr, *n.* One who or that which accelerates; a hastener.—**Acceleratory**, ak-sel′ėr-a-to-ri, *a.* Accelerating or tending to accelerate.

Accend,† ak-send′, *v.t.* [L. *accendo*, *accensum*, to kindle; root seen in *candle*, *candid*, &c.] To set on fire; to kindle.—**Accendent**, ak-sen′dent, *n.* An accensor. **Accendible**, ak-send′i-bl, *a.* Capable of being inflamed or kindled.—**Accension**, ak-sen′shon, *n.* The act of kindling or setting on fire. — **Accensor**, ak-sen′sėr, *n.* *R. Cath. Ch.* one whose business it is to light and trim the candles and tapers.

Accent, ak′sent, *n.* [L. *accentus*, an accent —*ad*, to, and *cano*, *cantum*, to sing. CHANT.] A superior stress or force of voice upon certain syllables of words, which distinguishes them from the other syllables, and forms an element in correct pronunciation; a mark or character used in writing to direct the stress of the voice in pronunciation, or to mark a particular tone, length of vowel sound, or the like; a peculiar or characteristic modulation or modification of the voice, such as that found in a given district; *pl.* words or expressions; *music*, stress or emphasis on particular notes.—*v.t.* ak-sent′. To give an accent or accents to in speaking; mark with an accent or accents.—**Accentor**, ak-sent′ėr, *n.* The hedge-warbler, dunnock, or hedge-sparrow.—**Accentual**, ak-sent′ū-al, *a.* Pertaining to accent.—**Accentuate**, ak-sent′ū-āt, *v.t.*—*accentuated*, *accentuating*. To mark or pronounce with an accent or with accents; to emphasize or give prominence to.—**Accentuation**, ak-sent′ū-ā″shon, *n.* The act of accentuating or state of being accentuated.

Accept, ak-sept′, *v.t.* [L. *acceptare*, freq. of *accipio*, *acceptum*, to accept—*ad*, to, and *capio*, to take. CAPABLE, HAVE.] To take or receive, as something offered; receive with approbation or favour; take as it comes; accede or assent to (a treaty, a proposal); to acknowledge, especially by signature, and thus to promise to pay (a bill of exchange).—**Acceptable**, ak-sep′ta-bl, *a.* Capable, worthy, or sure of being accepted or received; pleasing to a receiver; gratifying; agreeable; welcome.—**Acceptableness, Acceptability**, ak-sep′ta-bl-nes, ak-sep′ta-bil″i-ti, *n.* The quality of being acceptable. — **Acceptably**, ak-sep′ta-bli, *adv.* In an acceptable manner; in a manner to please. — **Acceptance**, aksep′tans, *n.* The act of accepting; a taking or receiving; favourable reception; an agreeing to terms; a written engagement to pay money, made by a person signing his name across or at the end of a bill of exchange; an accepted bill, or the amount contained in it.—**Acceptant**,† ak-sep′tant, *n.* One who accepts. — **Acceptation**, ak-sep-tā′shon, *n.* The act of accepting or receiving; kind or favourable reception; the meaning or sense in which a word or expression is understood, or generally received. — **Accepter, Acceptor**, ak-sept′ėr, ak-sept′or, *n.* A person who accepts; specifically, the person who accepts a bill of exchange.—**Acceptress**,† ak-sep′tres, *n.* A female who accepts.

Access, ak′ses, *n.* [L. *accessus*, from *accedo*, to come near, to approach. ACCEDE.] A coming to; near approach; admittance; admission; the means or way of approach; passage allowing communication; increase or accession; attack or return fit of a disease. — **Accessibility**, ak′ses-si-bil″i-ti, *n.* The condition or quality of being accessible or of admitting approach.—**Accessible**, ak-ses′si-bl, *a.* Capable of being approached or reached; easy of access; approachable; attainable.—**Accessibly**, akses′si-bli, *adv.* So as to be accessible.—**Accession**, ak-se′shon, *n.* ACCEDE.—**Accessional, Accessive**, ak-se′shon-al, ak-ses′iv, *a.* Additional.

Accessory, Accessary, ak′ses-so-ri, ak′ses-sa-ri, *a.* [L. *accessorius*, from *accessus*, *accedo*. ACCEDE.] Contributing; aiding in producing some effect, or acting in subordination to the principal agent; contributing to a general effect; belonging to something else as principal; accompanying. — *n.* One who aids or gives countenance to a crime; that which belongs to something else, as its principal; that which contributes to the effect of something more important; an accompaniment. — **Accessorial**, ak-ses-sō′ri-al, *a.* Pertaining to an accessory. —**Accessorily, Accessarily**, ak′ses-so-ri-li, ak′ses-sa-ri-li, *adv.* In the manner of an accessory; not as principal but as a subordinate agent.—**Accessoriness, Accessariness**, ak′ses-so-ri-nes, ak′ses-sa-rines, *n.* The state of being accessory, or of being or acting in a secondary character.

Accident, ak′si-dent, *n.* [L. *accidens*, falling—*ad*, and *cado*, to fall, whence *case*, *cadence*, *casual*, *decadence*, &c.] Chance or what happens by chance; an event that happens when quite unlooked for; an unforeseen and undesigned injury to a person; casualty; mishap; a property or quality of a thing which is not essential to it nor is one of its invariable signs (as whiteness in paper).—**Accidence**, ak′si-dens, *n.* [A corruption of *accidents* in the old sense of inflections of words.] That part of grammar which treats of the inflection of words, or the declension of nouns, adjectives, &c., and the conjugation of verbs; a small book containing the rudiments of grammar.—**Accidental**, ak-si-dent′al, *a.* Happening by chance or accident, or unexpectedly; casual; fortuitous; non-essential; not necessarily belonging; adventitious.—*n.* A casualty; a property not essential; *music*, a sharp, flat, or natural which does not occur in the clef, and which implies some change of key or modulation different from that in which the piece began.—**Accidentalism, Accidentality**, ak-si-dent′al-izm, ak′si-dental″i-ti, *n.* The condition or quality of being accidental; accidental character; that which is accidental.—**Accidentally**, ak-si-dent′al-li, *adv.* In an accidental manner; by chance; fortuitously; not essentially.

Accipiter, ak-sip′i-tėr, *n.* [L. *accipiter*, a bird of prey, from root *ak*, signifying sharpness and swiftness, and *pet*, to fly, like Gr. *ōkypteros*, swift-winged.] One of the order of birds Accipitres or Raptores.—**Accipitres**, ak-sip′i-trēz, *n. pl.* An order of rapacious birds, now usually called Raptores.—**Accipitral, Accipitrine**, ak-sip′i-tral, ak-sip″i-trin, *a.* Of or pertaining to the Accipitres; having the character of a bird of prey; rapacious.

Accite,† ak-sīt′, *v.t.* To call or summon. [*Shak.*]

Acclaim,† ak-klām′, *v.t.* [L. *acclamo*—*ac* for *ad*, and *clamo*, to cry out, whence *claim*, *clamour*, &c.] To applaud; to declare or salute by acclamation. — **Acclaim**, akklām′, *n.* A shout of joy; acclamation.—**Acclamation**, ak-kla-mā′shon, *n.* A shout or other demonstration of applause made by a multitude, indicating joy, hearty assent, approbation, or good wishes.—**Acclamatory**, ak-klam′a-to-ri, *a.* Expressing joy or applause by acclamation.

Acclimate, Acclimatize, ak-klī′māt, ak-klī′mat-īz, *v.t.*—*acclimated*, *acclimating*; *acclimatized*, *acclimatizing*. [Fr. *acclimater*, to acclimate. CLIMATE.] To habituate to a foreign climate; to render proof against the prejudicial influences of a foreign climate; to adopt for permanent existence and propagation in a foreign climate. **Acclimatation, Acclimation, Acclimatization**, ak-klī′ma-tā″shon, ak-klī-mā′shon, ak′klī-mat-iz-ā″shon, *n.* The act or process of acclimating or acclimatizing, or state of being acclimatized.

Acclinal, ak-klī′nal, *a.* [L. *acclino*, to bend up. ACCLIVITY.] *Geol.* leaning or bending up, as the slopes of a stratum towards an anticlinal axis.

Acclivity, ak-kliv′i-ti, *n.* [L. *acclivitas*, an acclivity—*ac* for *ad*, to, and *clivus*, a slope, from root *cli* seen in *clino*, *inclino*, to incline, Gr. *klinō*, to bend, incline; akin E. to *lean*.] A slope or inclination of the earth, as the side of a hill, considered as *ascending*, in opposition to *declivity*.—**Acclivitous, Acclivous**, ak-kliv′i-tus, akkliv′us, *a.* Rising, as a hill with a slope; sloping upwards.

Accolade, ak-kō-lād′, *n.* Fr. *accolade*, the accolade, lit. an embracing of the neck—L. *ad*, to, and *collum*, the neck; Fr. *accoler*, to embrace, *donner l'accolade*, to dub a knight. COLLAR.] A ceremony used in conferring knighthood, anciently consisting in putting the hand on the knight's neck, now usually a blow over the neck or shoulder with the flat of a sword.

Accommodate, ak-kom′mō-dāt, *v.t.*—*accommodated, accommodating.* [L. *accommodo*, to apply or suit—*ac* for *ad*, to, and *commodo*, to profit or help, from *con*, with, and *modus*, measure, proportion, limit, or manner. MODE.] To make suitable, correspondent, or consistent; to fit; adapt; conform; adjust; reconcile (with *to* after the object); to supply or furnish with required conveniences (with *with* after the object, as a friend *with* money). **Accommodating**, ak-kom′mō-dāt-ing, *a.* Obliging; yielding to the desires of others; disposed to comply and to oblige another.—**Accommodation**, ak-kom′mō-dā″shon, *n.* The act of accommodating; adjustment; adaptation; adjustment of differences; anything which supplies a want, as in respect of ease, refreshment, and the like; a convenience; lodgings; a loan of money.—*Accommodation bill*, a bill of exchange not given like a genuine bill of exchange in payment of a debt, but merely intended to accommodate the drawer.—*Accommodation ladder*, a light ladder hung over the side of a ship to facilitate ascending from, or descending to, boats. —**Accommodative**, ak-kom′mō-dāt-iv, *a.* Furnishing accommodation.—**Accommodator**, ak-kom′mō-dāt-ėr, *n.* One who accommodates or adjusts.—**Accommodable**, ak-kom′mō-da-bl, *a.* Capable of being accommodated, made suitable, or made to agree; adaptable.—**Accommodableness**, ak-kom′mō-da-bl-nes, *n.* The state or condition of being accommodable.

Accompany, ak-kum′pa-ni, *v.t.*—*accompanied, accompanying.* [Fr. *accompagner*, to accompany—*ac* for *ad*, to, and *compagnon*, a companion. COMPANION.] To go with or attend as a companion or associate; to go together; to be associated or connected with; to play a subordinate musical part to, as to a singer or other performer of a musical composition.—**Accompanier**, ak-kum′pa-ni-ėr, *n.* One who accompanies. —**Accompaniment**, ak-kum′pa-ni-ment, *n.* Something that attends as a circumstance, or which is added by way of ornament to the principal thing, or for the sake of symmetry; the subordinate part or parts performed by instruments accompanying a voice, or several voices, or a principal instrument.—**Accompanist**, ak-kum′pan-ist, *n.* The performer in music who plays the accompaniment.

Accomplice, ak-kom′plis, *n.* [Prefix *ac* for *ad*, to, and the older E. *complice*, Fr. *complice*, L. *complex, complicis*, confederate, participant—*con*, with, and *plico*, to fold, *plica*, a fold, a stem which appears also in E. *comply, ply, triple*, &c. PLY, &c.] An associate or confederate, especially in a crime, a partner or partaker in guilt.—**Accompliceship**,† ak-kom′plis-ship, *n.* State of being an accomplice.—**Accomplicity**,† ak-kom-plis′i-ti, *n.* The state of being an accomplice.

Accomplish, ak-kom′plish, *v.t.* [Fr. *accomplir*, to finish—prefix *ac* for *ad*, to, and L. *compleo*, to complete. COMPLETE.] To complete; to finish entirely; to execute; to carry out; to fulfil or bring to pass.—**Accomplishable**, ak-kom′plish-a-bl, *a.* Capable of accomplishment.—**Accomplished**, ak-kom′plisht, *a.* Perfected; finished; consummate; having the attainments and graces regarded as necessary for cultivated or fashionable society.—**Accomplisher**, ak-kom′plish-ėr, *n.* One who accomplishes.—**Accomplishment**, ak-kom′plish-ment, *n.* The act of accomplishing or carrying into effect; fulfilment; acquirement; attainment, especially such as belongs to cultivated or fashionable society.

Accompt, ak-kount′, *n.* An account.—**Accomptant**, ak-kount′ant, *n.* A reckoner; a computer; an accountant. *Accompt* and *accomptant* are obsolete or nearly so (*account, accountant*, being now generally written), though they may still be used in the formal or legal style.

Accord, ak-kord′, *n.* [Fr. *accord*, agreement—prefix *ac* for *ad*, to, and L. *cor, cordis*, the heart, formed like L. *concors, discors*, E. *concord, discord.*] Agreement; harmony of minds; as, to do a thing with one *accord*; just correspondence of things; concord; harmony of sound; voluntary or spontaneous impulse or act: in this sense in such phrases as *of my, of his, of its, of their own accord.*—*v.t.* To make to agree or correspond†; to grant; to give; to concede; as, to *accord* to one due praise.—*v.i.* To be in correspondence or harmony.—**Accordance, Accordancy**, ak-kord′ans, ak-kord′an-si, *n.* The state of being in accord; agreement with a person; conformity with a thing.—**Accordant**, ak-kord′ant, *a.* Corresponding; consonant; agreeable; of the same mind.—**Accordantly**, ak-kord′ant-li, *adv.* In accordance or agreement.—**According**, ak-kord′ing, *a.* Agreeing; agreeable; in accordance.—*According as*, agreeably, conformably, or proportionately as.—*According to*, agreeably to or in accordance with (zeal *according to* knowledge): followed by a personal object it refers to a statement of the person (*according to him* you are wrong).—**Accordingly**, ak-kord′ing-li, *adv.* Agreeably; suitably; in a manner conformable; consequently.

Accordion, ak-kord′i-on, *n.* [From *accord.*] A small keyed wind-instrument, whose tones are generated by the play of wind upon metallic reeds.—**Accordionist**, ak-kord′i-on-ist, *n.* A player on the accordion.

Accost, ak-kost′, *v.t.* [Fr. *accoster*, L.L. *accostare*—*ac* for *ad*, to, and L. *costa* (Fr. *côte*), a rib, a side. COAST.] To speak first to; to address, before oneself is addressed.

Accoucheur, ak-kō-shėr, *n.* [Fr., a man-midwife—*ac* for *ad*, and *coucher*, to lie or lay down. COUCH.] A surgeon who attends women in child-birth.—**Accoucheuse**, ak-kō-shėz, *n.* A midwife.—**Accouchement**, ak-kösh-män, *n.* Child-birth.

Account, ak-kount′, *n.* [O.E. *accompt*—*ac* for *ad*, and O.Fr. *compte*, a calculation, from L. *computo*, to compute, reckon. The Mod.Fr. *conte, conter*, present the same change of *m* into *n* as our own word.] A reckoning, enumeration, or computation; a list of debts and credits, or charges; a statement of things bought or sold, of payments, services, &c.; an explanatory statement of particulars, facts, or events; narrative; relation, description; reason or consideration; ground (on all *accounts*); profit; advantage (to turn to *account*); regard; behalf; sake (trouble incurred on one's *account*); *stockbroking*, the operations on the stock-exchange performed during the period before the ordinary settling-day. —*To make account of*, to hold in estimation or esteem; to value: with an adjective of quantity, as *much, little, no*, &c.—*Account current*, the statement of the successive mercantile transactions of one person with another, drawn out in the form of debtor and creditor, and in the order of their dates. —**Account**, ak-kount′, *v.t.* To deem, judge, think, or hold in opinion.—*v.i.* To render an account or relation of particulars; to answer in a responsible character; to give reasons; to explain: followed by *to* before a person, *for* before a thing.—**Accountability**, ak-kount′a-bil″i-ti, *n.* The state of being accountable or answerable.—**Accountable**, ak-kount′a-bl, *a.* Liable to pay or make good in case of loss; responsible for a trust; liable to be called to account; answerable to a superior.—**Accountableness**, ak-kount′a-bl-nes, *n.* The state of being accountable; accountability.—**Accountably**, ak-kount′a-bli, *adv.* In an accountable manner.—**Accountant**, ak-kount′ant, *n.* One who makes the keeping or examination of accounts his profession; an officer in a public office who has charge of the accounts.—**Accountantship**, ak-kount′ant-ship, *n.* The office or employment of an accountant. —**Account-book**, ak-kount′buk, *n.* A book in which accounts are kept.

Accouter, Accoutre, ak-kö′tėr, *v.t.*—*accoutred, accoutring.* [Fr. *accoutrer*—prefix *ac* for *ad*, to, and *couture*, a seam, from L. *consutura*, a stitching together, from *con*, together, and *suo, sutum*, to sew.] To equip or furnish with personal trappings; especially, to array in a military dress and arms; to equip for military service.—**Accouterments**, ak-kö′tėr-ments, *n. pl.* Military dress and arms; fighting array.

Accredit ak-kred′it, *v.t.* [Fr. *accréditer*, to accredit—L. *ad*, to, and *credo, creditum*, to trust.] To repose confidence in; to trust (a person); to give credit to; to believe (a story); to confer credit or authority on; to send with credentials, as an envoy.—**Accreditation**, ak-kred′it-ā″shon, *n.* The act of accrediting.

Accresce, ak-kres′, *v.i.* [L. *accresco, accretum*, to increase, to grow to—*ad*, to, and *cresco*, to grow, increase.] To accrue (which see).—**Accrescence**, ak-kres′ens, *n.* Act of increasing; gradual growth or increase; accretion.—**Accrescent**, ak-kres′ent, *a.* Increasing; growing.—**Accrete**,† ak-krēt′, *v.i.* To grow by accretion; to be added by growth.—**Accretion**, ak-krē′shon, *n.* The act of accreting or accrescing; a growing to; an increase by natural growth; an increase by an accession of parts externally; *med.* the growing together of parts naturally separate, as the fingers or toes; the thing added by growth; an accession.—**Accretive**, ak-krēt′iv, *a.* Of or pertaining to accretion.—**Accrementitial**, ak-krē-men-ti″shal, *a.* Of or pertaining to accrementition.—**Accrementition**, ak′krē-men-ti″shon, *n.* The process in the lower animals of producing a new individual by the growth and separation of a part of the parent; gemmation.

Accriminate, ak-krim′in-āt, *v.t.* [Prefix *ac*, and *criminate.*] To charge with a crime; to accuse.

Accrue, ak-krö′, *v.i.*—*accrued, accruing.* [Fr. *accrue*, increase, from *accrû*, pp. of *accroître*, to increase, from L. *accrescere*—*ac* for *ad*, to, and *cresco*, to grow, seen also in *crescent, decrease, increase.*] To be gained or obtained; to proceed, arise, or spring; as, a profit or a loss *accrues* from a commercial transaction.—**Accrument**,† ak-krö′ment, *n.* That which accrues; addition; increase.

Accumbent, ak-kum′bent, *a.* [L. *accumbens*, ppr. of *accumbo*, from *ad*, to, and *cumbo*, to lie down.] Leaning or reclining; lying against anything.—**Accumbency**, ak-kum′ben-si, *n.* State of being accumbent.

Accumulate, ak-kū′mū-lāt, *v.t.*—*accumulated, accumulating.* [L. *accumulo, accumulatum*, to heap up—*ad*, to, and *cumulus*, a heap.] To heap or pile up; to amass; to collect or bring together.—*v.i.* To grow to be extensive in number or quantity; to increase greatly.—**Accumulation**, ak-kū′mū-lā″shon, *n.* The act of accumulating; a collecting or being heaped up; that which has accumulated; a mass that has been collected.—**Accumulative**, ak-kū′mū-lāt-iv, *a.* Causing accumulation; heaping up.—**Accumulatively**, ak-kū′mū-lāt-iv-li, *adv.* In an accumulative manner; in heaps.—**Accumulator**, ak-kū′mū-lāt-ėr, *n.* One who or that which accumulates; a contrivance, such as a spring, that by being coiled up serves as a store of force; a kind of electric battery by which electric energy may be kept in store.

Accurate, ak′kū-rāt, *a.* [L. *accuratus*, prepared with care—*ac* for *ad*, to, and *cura*, care. CURE.] In exact conformity to truth, or to a standard or rule, or to a model; free from error or defect; exact; precise; strictly correct; adhering to exactness or correctness.—**Accuracy, Accurateness**, ak′kū-ra-si, ak′kū-rāt-nes, *n.* The condition or quality of being accurate; extreme precision or exactness; exact conformity to truth, or to a rule or model; correctness.—**Accurately**, ak′kū-rāt-li, *adv.* In an accurate manner.

Accurse, ak-kėrs′, *v.t.* [Prefix *ac* for *ad*,

or A. Sax. *ā*, intens., and *curse.*] To call down curses on; to curse.—**Accursed, Accurst**, ak-kėrst′ or ak-kėrs′ed, ak-kėrst′, *a.* Lying under a curse; blasted; ruined; execrable; cursed.

Accuse, ak-kūz′, *v.t.*—*accused, accusing.* [L. *accuso*, to call to account, blame, indict—*ad*, to, and *causa*, cause, process. CAUSE.] To charge with a crime, offence, or fault; to blame (with *of* before the crime or offence). ∴*Accuse* is both a legal and a general term, and commonly expresses something more formal than *charge.* The construction of the two verbs is also different: *accuse of, charge with.*—**Accusable**, ak-kūz′a-bl, *a.* Liable to be accused; chargeable with a crime.—**Accusant**, ak-kūz′ant, *n.* One who accuses.—**Accusation**, ak-kū-zā′shon, *n.* The act of accusing; that of which one is accused; a charge brought against one.—**Accusative**, ak-kūz′at-iv, *a.* Accusatory.—**Accusative**, ak-kūz′-at-iv, *n.* The fourth case of nouns and other declinable words in Latin, Greek, &c., corresponding to the *objective* in English.—**Accusatively**, ak-kūz′at-iv-li, *adv.* By way of accusation; in the position or relation of an accusative case.—**Accusatory, Accusatorial**, ak-kūz′a-to-ri, ak-kūz′a-tō″ri-al, *a.* Accusing; containing an accusation; as, an *accusatory* libel.—**Accusatorially**, ak-kūz′a-tō″ri-al-li, *adv.* By way of accusation.—**Accused**, ak-kūzd′, *pp.* used as a *noun.* A person or persons charged with a crime.—**Accuser**, ak-kūz′ėr, *n.* One who accuses; one who formally brings a charge.

Accustom, ak-kus′tum, *v.t.* [O.Fr. *accoustumer*, to accustom—*ac* for L. *ad*, to, and O.Fr. *coustume*, custom. CUSTOM.] To familiarize by use or habit; to habituate or inure.—**Accustomarily**,† ak-kus′tum-a-ri-li, *adv.* According to custom; customarily.—**Accustomary**,† ak-kus′tum-a-ri, *a.* Usual; customary.—**Accustomed**, ak-kus′tumd, *a.* Often practised; customary; habitual; wonted; familiar; as, in their *accustomed* manner.

Ace, ās, *n.* [Fr. *as*, ace at dice or cards; L. *as*, a unit, a pound, a foot, &c., from Doric Gr. *as, ais*, Attic Gr. *heis*, one.] A unit; a single pip on a card or die, or the card or face of a die so marked; a trifle or insignificant quantity or distance (within an *ace* of it). In *aviation*, the name given to a flying-man who has brought down ten machines, the ace in certain card-games counting as ten. (French and American.)

Aceldama, a-kel′da-ma, *n.* [Heb.] Field of blood. Acts, i. 19.

Acentric, a-sen′trik, *a.* [Prefix *a*, neg., and *centre.*] Not centric; away from a centre.—*n.* An aeroplane so designed that the line of the propeller thrust does not pass through the centre of gravity.

Acephala, a-sef′a-la, *n. pl.* [Gr. *akephalos*, headless—*a*, priv., and *kephalē*, head.] Molluscous animals, like the oyster and scallop, that have not a distinct head.—**Acephalan**, a-sef′a-lan, *n.* One of the Acephala; a lamellibranchiate mollusc.—**Acephalist, Acephalite**, a-sef′al-ist, a-sef′al-it, *n.* One who acknowledges no head or superior.—**Acephalous**, a-sef′al-us, *a.* Without a head; headless.

Acerb, a-sėrb′, *a.* [L. *acerbus*, unripe, harsh, sour, from *acer*, sharp; same root as in *acid.*] Sour, bitter, and harsh to the taste; sour with astringency and roughness.—**Acerbity**, a-sėrb′it-i, *n.* Sourness, with roughness or astringency of taste; poignancy or severity; painfulness; sharpness; harshness or severity of temper; sourness.

Aceric, a-ser′ik, *a.* [L. *acer*, a maple-tree.] Pertaining to the maple; obtained from the maple.

Acerous, Acerose, as′ėr-us, as′ėr-ōz, *a.* [L. *acerosus*, chaffy, from *acus, aceris*, chaff.] *Bot.* resembling chaff; narrow and slender, with a sharp point.

Acervate,† a-sėrv′āt, *v.t.* [L. *acervo*, to heap up, from *acervus*, a heap.] To heap up.—**Acervation**,† as-ėr-vā′shon, *n.* The act of heaping together.

Acescent, a-ses′ent, *a.* [L. *acescens*, turning sour. ACID.] Turning sour; becoming tart or acid; slightly sour; acidulous; subacid.—**Acescence, Acescency**, a-ses′-ens, a-ses′en-si, *n.* The act or process of becoming acescent.

Acetabulum, as-ē-tab′ū-lum, *n.* pl. **Acetabula**, as-ē-tab′ū-la. [L., vinegar cruet, a cup-shaped vessel, from *acetum*, vinegar. ACID.] The cavity which receives the head of the thigh-bone; the socket in which the leg of an insect is inserted; the cup-like sucker with which the arms of the cuttle-fish are provided; the cup- or saucer-like fructification of many lichens; the receptacle of certain fungi.—**Acetabuliferous**, as-ē-tab′ū-lif″ėr-us, *a.* Having acetabula or cup-like suckers.—**Acetabuliform**, as′ē-ta-bū″li-form, *a.* Cup-shaped.

Acetary, as′ē-ta-ri, *n.* [L. *acetaria*, herbs eaten raw with vinegar and oil, from *acetum*, vinegar. ACID.] An acid pulpy substance in certain fruits, as the pear.—**Acetarious**, as-ē-tā′ri-us, *a.* A term applied to plants used in making salads; such as lettuce, mustard and cress, endive, &c.

Acetic, a-set′ik, *a.* [L. *acetum*, vinegar.] Having the properties of vinegar; sour.—*Acetic acid*, an acid often prepared by the oxidation of alcohol (acetous fermentation), and along with water forming the chief ingredient of vinegar.—**Acetate**, as′ē-tāt, *n.* A salt formed by the union of acetic acid with a base.—**Acetification**, a-set′i-fi-kā″shon, *n.* The act of acetifying or making acetous or sour; the process of becoming acetous; the operation of making vinegar.—**Acetifier**, a-set′i-fī-ėr, *n.* An apparatus used in making vinegar.—**Acetify**, a-set′i-fī, *v.t.*—*acetified, acetifying.* To convert into acid or vinegar.—*v.i.* To become acid; to be converted into vinegar.—**Acetimeter, Acetometer**, as-et-im′et-ėr, as-et-om′et-ėr, *n.* An instrument for ascertaining the strength or purity of acids; an acidimeter.—**Acetimetry**, as-et-im′et-ri, *n.* The act or method of ascertaining the strength or purity of acids.—**Acetopathy**, as-et-op′a-thi, *n.* A method of treating ailments by applying dilute acetic acid to the surface of the body.—**Acetous, Acetose**, a-sē′tus, as-et-ōs′, *a.* Having a sour taste; having the character of vinegar; acid; causing or connected with acetification.

Acetylene, a-set′i-lēn, *n.* [From *acetic*, and Gr. *hylē*, matter.] An inflammable gas made with calcium carbide and water, and used as an illuminant.

Ache, āk, *n.* [A.Sax, *ace, æce, ece*, ache, pain; *acan*, to ache; akin to Icel. *aka*, to drive, press hard; cog. L. *ago*, to drive.] Pain, or continued pain, in opposition to sudden twinges, or spasmodic pain; a continued gnawing pain as in toothache or earache; feeling of distress (heartache).—*v.i.*—*ached, aching.* To suffer from an ache or pain; to be distressed.—**Acheweed**, āk′wēd, *n.* Same as *Goutwort.*

Achene, Achenium, a-kēn′, a-kē′ni-um, *n.* [Gr. *a*, priv., and *chainō*, to yawn, to gape.] *Bot.* a small dry carpel, containing a single seed, which does not open when ripe.

Achieve, a-chēv′, *v.t.*—*achieved, achieving.* [Fr. *achever*, to finish—*a*, to, and O.Fr. *cheve*, Fr. *chef*, the head or end, from L. *caput*, the head. CHIEF.] To perform or execute; to finish or carry on to a final and prosperous close; to obtain or bring about, as by effort.—**Achievable**, a-chēv′a-bl, *a.* Capable of being achieved or performed.—**Achievance**,† a-chēv′ans, *n.* Achievement.—**Achievement**, a-chēv′ment, *n.* The act of achieving or performing; accomplishment; an exploit; a great or heroic deed; an escutcheon or ensign armorial; a hatchment.—**Achiever**, a-chēv′ėr, *n.* One who achieves or accomplishes.

Achlamydate, a-klam′id-āt, *a.* [Gr. *a*, priv., and *chlamys, chlamydos*, a cloak.] *Zool.* not possessing a mantle, as certain molluscs.—**Achlamydeous**, a-kla-mid′ē-us, *a.* *Bot.* having neither calyx nor corolla, the flowers being without floral envelope.

Acholia, a-kō′li-a, *n.* [Gr. *a*, not, *cholē*, bile.] *Med.* absence of bile.

Achor, ā′kor, *n.* [Gr. *achōr*, dandruff.] Scald-head, a skin disease.

Achromatic, ak-rō-mat′ik, *a.* [Gr. *a*, priv., and *chrōma, chrōmatos*, colour.] Destitute of colour; transmitting light without decomposing it into its primary colours; as, an *achromatic* lens or telescope.—**Achromaticity, Achromatism**, ak′rō-ma-tis″i-ti, ak-rō′ma-tizm, *n.* The state of being achromatic; want of colour.—**Achromatize**, a-krō′ma-tīz, *v.t.* To deprive of colour; to render achromatic.—**Achromatopsy**, a-krō′ma-top-si, *n.* [-*opsy*, from Gr. *opsis*, sight.] Colour blindness.

Achronic, Achronical, a-kron′ik, a-kron′ik-al, *a.* ACRONYC.

Acicula, a-sik′ū-la, *n.* pl. **Aciculæ**, a-sik′ū-lē. [L., dim. of *acus*, a needle. ACID.] A name given by naturalists to a spine or prickle of an animal or plant.—**Acicular, Aciculate, Aciculiform, Aciform**, a-sik′ū-lėr, a-sik′ū-lāt, a-sik′ū-li-form, as′i-form, *a.* Having the shape of a needle; having sharp points like needles; needle-shaped.—**Acicularly**, a-sik′ū-lėr-li, *adv.* In an acicular manner.

Acid, as′id, *a.* [L. *acidus*, sour, from root *ac, ak*, a point, seen in *acus*, a needle; *acuo*, to sharpen; *acer*, sharp; *aceo*, to be sour; *acetum*, vinegar; giving such English words as *acrid, acumen, acute, ague, eager*, &c.] Sour, sharp, or biting to the taste; not sweet; not alkaline.—**Acid**, as′id, *n.* A sour substance; specifically, in *chem.* a compound of which hydrogen is an essential constituent. Acids possess a sour taste, change blue vegetable colours to red, and combine with bases to form salts.—**Acidic**, a-sid′ik, *a.* *Chem.* pertaining to acid; containing a large amount of an acid constituent.—**Acidiferous**, as-id-if′ėr-us, *a.* Bearing, producing, or containing acids, or an acid.—**Acidify**, a-sid′i-fī, *v.t.*—*acidified, acidifying.* To make acid; to convert into an acid.—**Acidifiable**, a-sid′i-fī-a-bl, *a.* Capable of being acidified or converted into an acid.—**Acidific**, as-id-if′ik, *a.* Producing acidity or an acid.—**Acidification**, a-sid′i-fi-kā″shon, *n.* The act or process of acidifying.—**Acidifier**, a-sid′i-fī-ėr, *n.* One who or that which acidifies; an acetifier.—**Acidimeter, Acidimetry**, as-id-im′et-ėr, as-id-im′et-ri, *n.* Same as *Acetimeter, Acetimetry.*—**Acidity, Acidness**, a-sid′i-ti, as′id-nes, *n.* The quality of being acid or sour; sourness; tartness.—**Acidulate**, a-sid′ū-lāt, *v.t.*—*acidulated, acidulating.* [Pr. *aciduler*, to make slightly sour; L. *acidulus*, slightly sour.] To make acid in a moderate degree.—**Acidulent**, a-sid′ū-lent, *a.* Somewhat acid or sour; tart; peevish.—**Acidulous**, a-sid′ū-lus, *a.* Slightly sour; sub-acid; as cream of tartar, oranges, &c.

Acierage, ā′sē-ėr-āj, *n.* [Fr. *acier*, steel, L. *acies*, sharp edge.] Process by which an engraved copper-plate, or an electrotype from an engraved plate, has a film of iron deposited over its surface by electricity, to protect the engraving from wear in printing.

Aciform, as′i-form, *a.* ACICULA.

Acinaceous, as-in-ā′shus, *a.* [L. *acinus*, a grape-stone or kernel.] Full of kernels.—**Acinarious**, as-in-ā′ri-us, *a.* *Bot.* covered with little spherical stalked vesicles resembling grape seeds, as in some algæ.—**Aciniform**, a-sin′i-form, *a.* Having the form of grapes, or being in clusters like grapes.—**Acinose, Acinous**, as′in-ōs, as′in-us, *a.* Consisting of minute, granular concretions.

Acinaciform, as-in-as′i-form, *a.* [L. *acinaces*, Gr. *akinakēs*, a scimitar.] Formed like or resembling a scimitar; as, an *acinaciform* leaf.

Acknowledge, ak-nol′ej, *v.t.*—*acknowledged, acknowledging.* [Prefix *a*, on, and *knowledge.*] To own or recognize by avowal or by some act; to assent to the truth or claims of; to admit to be; to own or confess; to avow receiving. ∴We *acknowledge* what is in some way brought or set before our notice; when we *confess* we make known, and often of our own free will.—**Acknowledger**, ak-nol′ej-ėr, *n.* One who acknowledges.—**Acknowledgment**, ak-nol′ej-ment, *n.* The act of acknowledging; owning; recognition; avowal; confession; expression of thanks; something given or done in return for a favour; a receipt for money received.

Acme, ak′mē, *n.* [Gr. *akmē*, a point. Root *ak.* ACID.] The top or highest point; the furthest point attained; maturity or perfection; the height or crisis of a disease.

Acne, ak′nē, *n.* [Origin unknown.] An eruption of hard, inflamed tubercles or pimples on the face. Called also *Sycosis.*

Acolyte, ak′o-līt, *n.* [Fr. from L.L. *acolythus*, an acolyte; Gr. *akolouthos*, a follower.] An attendant; in the *R. Cath. Ch.* one of an inferior order of clergy, who attends during service on the superior orders; a lay attendant so employed.

Acondylous, Acondylose, a-kon′di-lus, a-kon′di-lōs, *a.* [Gr. neg. prefix *a*, and *kondylos*, a joint.] Jointless.

Aconite, ak′on-īt, *n.* L. *aconitum*, Gr. *akoniton*, a poisonous plant, like monk's-hood.] The plant wolf's-bane or monk's-hood, *Aconitum Napellus.*—**Aconitic**, ak-on-it′ik, *a.* Of or pertaining to aconite.—**Aconitin, Aconitine**, ak-on′it-in, *n.* A highly poisonous narcotic alkaloid, got from the roots and leaves of aconite.

Acopic, a-kop′ik, *a.* [Gr. *akopos*, prefix *a*, priv., and *kopos*, toil, weariness.] *Med.* fitted to relieve weariness; restorative.

Acorn, ā′korn, *n.* [A. Sax. *æceren, æcern*, an acorn; Goth. *akram*, fruit; Icel. *akarn*, Dan. *agern*, O.H.G. *ackeran*, an acorn; the word originally meant simply fruit, fruit of the field, being allied to *acre.*] The fruit of the oak; a one-celled, one-seeded, oval nut, which grows in a permanent cup.—**Acorned**, ā′kornd, *a.* Furnished or loaded with acorns.—**Acorn-cup**, *n.* The capsule of the acorn.—**Acorn-oil**, *n.* An oil expressed from acorns.—**Acorn-shell**, *n.* The shell of the acorn; a marine molluscous animal, one of the cirripeds.

Acosmism, a-koz′mizm, *n.* [Gr. neg. prefix *a*, and *kosmos*, the world.] The denial of the existence of an eternal world.—**Acosmist**, a-koz′mist, *n.* One who holds the doctrine of acosmism.—**Acosmistic**, a-koz-mist′ik, *a.* Pertaining to the doctrine of acosmism.

Acotyledon, a-kot′il-ē″don, *n.* [Gr. *a*, priv., and *kotylēdōn*, any cup-shaped cavity, from *kotylē*, a hollow.] *Bot.* a plant whose seeds, called spores, are not furnished with cotyledons or seed-lobes.—**Acotyledonous**, a-kot′il-ē″don-us, *a.* Having no seed lobes.

Acouchy, a-kösh′i, *n.* [Fr. *acouchi, agouchi*, name in Guiana.] An animal belonging to the guinea-pig family, the olive cavy or Surinam rat, inhabiting Guiana.

Acoustic, Acoustical, a-kous′tik, a-kous′tik-al, *a.* [Gr. *akoustikos*, from *akouō*, to hear.] Pertaining to the sense or organs of hearing, or to the science of acoustics.—**Acoustic**, *n.* A remedy for deafness or imperfect hearing.—**Acoustically**, a-kous′tik-al-li, *adv.* In relation to or in a manner adapted to acoustics.—**Acoustician**, a-kous-ti′shan, *n.* One skilled in the science of acoustics.—**Acoustics**, a-kous′tiks, *n.* The science of sound, teaching the cause, nature, and phenomena of the vibrations of elastic bodies which affect the organ of hearing.

Acquaint, ak-kwānt′, *v.t.* [O.Fr. *accointer*; L.L. *accognitare*, to make known, from L. *ad*, to, and *cognitus*, known, from *cognosco, cognitum*, to know; same root as in *know.*] To make to know; to make aware of; to apprise; to make familiar; inform: *with* is used before the subject of information, if a noun (*acquaint* a person *with* facts).—**Acquaintance**, ak-kwānt′ans, *n.* A state of being acquainted, or of having more or less intimate knowledge; knowledge; familiarity (followed by *with*): a person known to one; the whole body of those with whom one is acquainted.—**Acquaintanceship**, ak-kwānt′ans-ship, *n.* State of being acquainted.—**Acquainted**, ak-kwānt′ed, *a.* Having acquaintance; knowing, but not a close or intimate friend.

Acquiesce, ak-kwi-es′, *v.i.*—*acquiesced, acquiescing.* [Fr. *acquiescer*, L. *acquiesco*, to rest, to acquiesce—*ad*, to, and *quiesco*, to be quiet. QUIET.] To rest satisfied, or apparently satisfied, or to rest without opposition and discontent; to assent quietly; to agree.—**Acquiescence, Acquiescency**, ak-kwi-es′ens, ak-kwi-es′en-si, *n.* The act of acquiescing or giving a quiet assent.—**Acquiescent**, ak-kwi-es′ent, *a.* Disposed to acquiesce; disposed to submit; quietly assenting.—**Acquiescently**, ak-kwi-es′ent-li, *adv.* In an acquiescent manner.

Acquire, ak-kwīr′, *v.t.*—*acquired, acquiring.* [L. *acquiro*, to get—*ad*, to, and *quæro*, to look or search for. QUEST.] To get or gain, the object being something which is more or less permanent (as fortune, title, habits, &c.). A mere temporary possession is not expressed by *acquire*, but by *obtain, procure*, &c.; as, to *obtain* (not *acquire*) a book on loan.—**Acquirability**, ak-kwīr′a-bil″i-ti, *n.* State of being acquirable.—**Acquirable**, ak-kwīr′a-bl, *a.* Capable of being acquired.—**Acquirement**, ak-kwīr′ment, *n.* The act of acquiring, or of making acquisition; that which is acquired; attainment, especially personal attainment (as contrasted with a natural *gift* or *endowment*).—**Acquirer**, ak-kwīr′ėr, *n.* A person who acquires.—**Acquisition**, ak-kwi-zi′shon, *n.* The act of acquiring; the thing acquired or gained: generally applied to material gains.—**Acquisitive**, ak-kwiz′-it-iv, *a.* Disposed to make acquisitions; having a propensity to acquire property.—**Acquisitively**, ak-kwiz′it-iv-li, *adv.* In an acquisitive manner; by way of acquisition.—**Acquisitiveness**, ak-kwiz′it-iv-nes, *n.* Quality of being acquisitive; a propensity to acquire property; *phren.* the organ which is said to produce the desire to acquire and possess.

Acquit, ak-kwit′, *v.t.*—*acquitted, acquitting.* [Fr. *acquitter*, to discharge, to set at rest with respect to a claim—L. *ad*, to, and *quietus*, at rest, quiet. QUIET.] To release or discharge from an obligation, accusation, or the like; to pronounce not guilty (with *of* before the thing; *refl.* to behave; to bear or conduct one's self.—**Acquittal**, ak-kwit′al, *n.* The act of acquitting; a judicial setting free from the charge of an offence.—**Acquittance**, ak-kwit′ans, *n.* An acquitting or discharging from a debt or any other liability; the writing which is evidence of such a discharge.

Acre, ā′kėr, *n.* [A.Sax. *acer, æcer*, a field = D. *akker*, Icel. *akr*, Dan. *ager*, G. *acker*, Goth. *akrs*, arable land, a field; L. *ager*, Gr. *agros*, Skr. *ajra*, a field. From root, *ag, ak*, as in L. *ago*. Icel. *aka*, to drive; the word probably meaning originally the place to or over which cattle were driven; a pasture. *Acorn* is from this root.] A definite quantity of land. The United States and British statute acre contains 160 square rods or perches, or 4840 square yards.—**Acreable**, ā′kėr-a-bl, *a.* According to the acre; measured or estimated in acres or by the acre.—**Acreage**, ā′kėr-āj, *n.* The number of acres in a piece of land; acres taken collectively.—**Acred**, ā′kėrd, *a.* Possessing acres or landed property.

Acreophagy, ak-rē-of′a-ji, *n.* [Gr. *a*, not, *kreas*, flesh.] See AKREOPHAGY. The practice of abstaining from flesh. **Acreophagist**, ak-rē-of′a-jist, *n.* One who abstains from flesh.

Acrid, ak′rid, *a.* [From L. *acer, acris, acre*, sharp: with *id*, from the common L. adjective termination *-idus.* ACID.] Sharp or biting to the taste; pungent; bitter; virulent; bitter (as in temper or disposition).—**Acrid**, ak′rid, *n.* An acrid or irritant poison.—**Acridity, Acridness**, a-krid′i-ti, ak′-rid-nes, *n.* The quality of being acrid or pungent.

Acrimony, ak′ri-mo-ni, *n.* [L. *acrimonia*, from *acris*, sharp.] Acridity; pungency; sharpness or severity of temper; bitterness of expression; acerbity; asperity.—**Acrimonious**, ak-ri-mō′ni-us, *a.* Abounding in acrimony; severe; bitter; virulent; caustic; stinging.—**Acrimoniously**, ak-ri-mō′ni-us-li, *adv.* In an acrimonious manner; sharply; bitterly; pungently.—**Acrimoniousness**, ak-ri-mō′ni-us-nes, *n.* The quality of being.

Acrisia, a-kris′i-a, *n.* [Gr. neg. prefix *a*, and *krisis*, judgment.] A condition of disease in which no judgment can be formed.—**Acritical**, a-krit′ik-al, *a.* Having or giving no indications of a crisis.

Acrita, ak′ri-ta, *n.* [Gr. *a*, not, *krinō*, I distinguish.] *Zool.* animals with no distinct nervous system.

Acritude,† ak′ri-tūd, *n.* [L. *acritudo*, ACRID.] An acrid quality; acridity.

Acroamatic, Acroamatical, Acroatic, ak′rō-a-mat″ik, ak′rō-a-mat″ik-al, ak-rō-at′ik, *a.* [Gr. *akroamatikos*, from *akroaomai*, to hear.] Designed for being heard only by a select audience; hence, abstruse; pertaining to deep learning; esoteric.

Acrobat, ak′rō-bat, *n.* [Gr. *akrobatos*—*akros*, high, and *bainō*, to go.] A rope-dancer; also, one who practises vaulting, tumbling, throwing somersaults, &c.—**Acrobatic**, ak′rō-bat-ik, *a.* Of or pertaining to an acrobat or his performance.

Acrocarpous, ak-rō-kärp′us, *a.* [Gr. *akros*, highest, and *karpos*, fruit.] *Bot.* applied to mosses whose flower terminates the growth of a primary axis.

Acrocephalic, ak′rō-sē-fal″ik, *a.* [Gr. *akros*, high, and *kephalē*, the head.] High-skulled; having the top of the skull high or pyramidal.

Acroceraunian, ak′rō-sē-ra̤″ni-an, *a.* [Gr. *akron*, a summit, and *keraunos*, thunder.] Thunder-smitten: applied to certain mountains in Greece, from being often struck with lightning. [Poetical.]

Acrogen, ak′rō-jen, *n.* [Gr. *akros*, high, on the top, and root *gen*, to produce.] A plant (as a moss, fern, horse-tail) increasing by extension of the stem or axis of growth at the top.—**Acrogenous**, a-kroj′en-us, *a.* Increasing by growth at the summit, as the tree-ferns; pertaining to the acrogens.

Acrolith, ak′rō-lith, *n.* [Gr. *akros*, high, extreme, and *lithos*, a stone.] In *arch.* and *sculp.* a statue, of which only the extremities are stone.—**Acrolithan**, a-krol′ith-an, *a.* Pertaining to or formed like an acrolith.

Acromion, a-krō′mi-on, *n.* [Gr. *akros*, high, extreme, and *ōmos*, shoulder.] A process of the shoulder-blade which receives the collar-bone.

Acronarcotic, ak′rō-när-kot″ik, *n.* [Gr. *akros*, extreme, and E. *narcotic.*] A narcotic poison which irritates and inflames the alimentary canal, and acts on the brain and spinal cord.

Acronyc, Acronycal, Acronyctous, a-kron′ik, a-kron′ik-al, ak-ro-nik′tus, *a.* [Gr. *akros*, extreme, and *nyx*, night.] *Astron.* culminating at midnight: said of a star which rises as the sun sets, and sets as the sun rises.—**Acronycally**, a-kron′ik-al-li, *adv* In an acronycal manner.

Acropolis, a-krop′o-lis, *n.* [Gr. *akros*, high, and *polis*, a city.] The citadel or highest part of a Grecian city, usually situated on an eminence commanding the town.

Acrospire, ak′rō-spīr, *n.* [Gr. *akros*, highest, and *speira*, a spire, or spiral line.] The first leaf which rises above the ground when corn germinates; also the rudimentary stem or first leaf which appears in malted grain.—**Acrospired**, ak′rō-spīrd, *a.* Having or exhibiting the acrospire.

Across, a-kros′, *prep.* and *adv.* [Prefix *a*, and *cross.*] From side to side; opposed to *along*; athwart; quite over; intersecting; passing over at any angle; from one side to another; crosswise.

Acrostic, a-kros′tik, *n.* [Gr. *akrostichion*, an acrostic—*akros*, extreme, and *stichos*, order or verse.] A composition in verse, in which the first, or the first and last, or certain other letters of the lines, taken in order, form a name, title, motto, &c.,

which is the subject of the poem.—*a.* Relating to or containing an acrostic.—**Acrostically**, a-kros'tik-al-li, *adv.* In the manner of an acrostic.

Acroterium, ak-rō-tē'ri-um, *n.* pl. **Acroteria**, ak-rō-tē'ri-a. [Gr. *akrotērion*, a summit, apex, from *akros*, highest.] *Arch.* an angle of a pediment, or a small pedestal resting on the angle.

Acrotic, a-krot'ik, *a.* [L.L. *acroticus*, from Gr. *akros*, extreme.] *Med.* belonging to or affecting external surfaces.

Acrotism, ak'rō-tizm, *n.* [Gr. *a*, priv., and *krotos*, a beating.] An absence or weakness of the pulse.

Act, akt, *v.i.* [L. *ago*, *actum*, to exert power, to put in motion, to do; Gr. *agō*, to lead; allied to Icel. *aka*, to drive, and to E. *acre* (which see).] To exert power; to produce effects; to be in action or motion; to carry into effect a purpose or determination of the mind; to behave, demean, or conduct one's self; to perform, as an actor.—*v.t.* To transact; to do or perform; to represent as real; to perform on or as on the stage; to play; hence, to feign or counterfeit.—**Act**, akt, *n.* That which is being done or which has been done; a deed; an exploit; the exertion of power; the effect of which power exerted is the cause; a state of reality or real existence, as opposed to a possibility; actuality; a part or division of a play, generally subdivided into smaller portions called *scenes*; a decree, edict, or law, especially one proceeding from a legislative body. ACTION.—*In the act*, in the actual performance or commission of some misdeed.—*In act to*, prepared or ready to, by being in a suitable posture. —**Actable**, akt'a-bl, *a.* Capable of being acted or performed; practically possible.—**Acting**, akt'ing, *a.* Performing duty, service, or functions; doing the real work of an office for a nominal or honorary holder of the post.—*n.* A playing on the stage.—**Actor**, ak'tėr, *n.* One who acts or performs; one who represents a character or acts a part in a play.—**Actress**, ak'tres, *n.* A female actor.

Actinia, ak-tin'i-a, *n.* pl. **Actiniæ**. [Gr. *aktis*, *aktinos*, a ray; from their tentacles being ray-like.] A sea-anemone; a polyp having the mouth surrounded by tentacles in concentric circles, which when spread resemble the petals of a flower: often of brilliant colours.

Actinic, ak-tin'ik, *a.* [Gr. *aktis*, *aktinos*, a ray.] Pertaining to rays; pertaining to the chemical rays of the sun. —**Actinism**, ak'tin-izm, *n.* The radiation of heat or light; the property of the chemical part of the sun's rays, which, as seen in photography, produces chemical combinations and decompositions.—**Actinium**, ak-tin'i-um, *n.* A radio-active substance taken to be a chemical element; found in pitchblende.—**Actinoid**, ak'tin-oid, *a.* Resembling a ray or rays; radiated.—**Actinograph**, ak-tin'ō-graf, *n.* An instrument for measuring and registering the variations of actinic or chemical influence in the solar rays.—**Actinology**, ak-ti-nol'ō-ji, *n.* The science which investigates the power of sunlight to cause chemical action.—**Actinolite**, ak-tin'ō-līt, *n.* [*-lite* = Gr. *lithos*, a stone.] A radiated mineral, nearly allied to hornblende, and consisting chiefly of silica, calcium, magnesium, and iron.—**Actinolitic**, ak-tin'ō-lit"ik, *a.* Like or pertaining to actinolite.—**Actinometer**, ak-tin-om'et-ėr, *n.* An instrument for measuring the intensity of the sun's actinic rays.—**Actinometric**, ak-tin'ō-met"rik, *a.* Of or belonging to the actinometer or its use.—**Actinozoa**, ak-tin'ō-zō"a, *n. pl.* [*-zoa*, from Gr. *zōon*, an animal.] A class of radiated, soft marine zoophytes, embracing the sea-anemones, corals, sea-pens, &c. With the Hydrozoa they constitute the sub-kingdom Cœlenterata.—**Actinozoon**, ak-tin'ō-zō"on, *n.* An individual member of the Actinozoa.

Action, ak'shon, *n.* [L. *actio*. ACT.] The state or manner of acting or being active, as opposed to *rest*; activity; an act or thing done; the performance of a function; a deed; an exploit; a battle or engagement; the mechanism or movement of a compound instrument, or the like; agency; operation; impulse; the connected series of events on which the interest of a drama or work of fiction depends; gesture or gesticulation; a suit or process at law. ∴ *Action* and *Act* have some meanings in common, but others are peculiar to each. Thus, the meanings battle, lawsuit, mechanism, belong only to the former; those of law, part of a play, to the latter. So we speak of a *course of action*. But we may speak of performing a noble *action* or a noble *act*.—**Actionable**, ak'shon-a-bl, *a.* Furnishing ground for an action at law.—**Actionably**, ak'shon-a-bli, *adv.* In an actionable manner.

Active, ak'tiv, *a.* [Fr. *actif*, *active*; L. *activus*. ACT.] Having the power or property of acting; exerting or having the power to exert an influence (as opposed to *passive*); performing actions quickly; quick; nimble; brisk; agile; constantly engaged in action; busy; assiduous; accompanied or characterized by action, work, or by the performance of business (an *active* demand for goods); actually proceeding (*active* hostilities); *gram.* expressing action, especially action affecting an object; transitive.—**Actively**, ak'tiv-li, *adv.* In an active manner.—**Activity**, ak-tiv'i-ti, *n.* The state or quality of being active; the active faculty; active force; nimbleness; agility; briskness. —**Activeness**, ak'tiv-nes, *n.* State of being active.

Acton, ak'ton, *n.* [O.Fr. *acoton*, *auqueton*, Sp. *al-coton*, Ar. *al-q'oton*, from being originally padded with cotton.] A kind of vest or tunic made of taffeta or leather quilted, formerly worn to protect the body from wounds.

Actor, **Actress**. ACT.

Actual, ak'tū-al, *a.* Acting or existing really and objectively; real; effectively operative; effectual: opposed to *potential* or *nominal*: now existing; present.—*n.* Something actual or real.—**Actualist**, ak'tū-al-ist, *n.* One who deals with actualities: opposed to *idealist*.—**Actualness**, ak'tū-al-nes, *n.* The quality of being actual.—**Actuality**, ak-tū-al'i-ti, *n.* The state of being actual; that which is real or actual.—**Actualization**, ak'tū-al-iz-ā"shon, *n.* A making real or actual.—**Actualize**, ak'tū-al-iz, *v.t.*—*actualized*, *actualizing*. To make actual.—**Actually**, ak'tū-al-li, *adv.* In fact; really; with active manifestation.

Actuary, ak'tū-a-ri, *n.* [L. *actuarius*, a clerk, a registrar, from *acta*, records, acts.] A registrar or clerk; an official in a joint-stock company, particularly an insurance company, whose duty it is to make the necessary computations, especially computations of some complexity.—**Actuarial**, ak-tū-ā'ri-al, *a.* Of or pertaining to an actuary or to his business.

Actuate, ak'tū-āt, *v.t*—*actuated*, *actuating*. [From *act*.] To put into action; to move or incite to action.—**Actuation**, ak-tū-ā'shon, *n.* The state of being put in action. —**Actuator**, ak'tū-āt-ėr, *n.* One who actuates or puts in action.

Aculeate, **Aculeated**, a-kū'lē-āt, a-kū'lē-āt-ed, *a.* [L. *aculeus*, a spine, a prickle, dim. of *acus*, a needle. ACID.] *Bot.* having prickles or sharp points; *zool.* having a sting. — **Aculeiform**, a-kū'lē-i-form, *a.* Formed like a prickle.—**Aculeolate**, a-kū'lē-ō-lāt, *a.* *Bot.* having small prickles or sharp points.

Acumen, a-kū'men, *n.* [L. *acumen*, from *acuo*, to sharpen. ACID.] Quickness of perception; mental acuteness or penetration; keenness of insight; sagacity.—**Acuminate**, **Acuminated**, a-kū'min-āt, a-kū'min-āt-ed, *a.* [L. *acuminatus*, sharpened.] Pointed; acute.—**Acuminate**, a-kū'min-āt, *v.t.* — *acuminated*, *acuminating*. To render sharp or keen.—*v.i.*† To taper to a point.—**Acumination**, a-kū'min-ā"shon, *n.* Act of acuminating or sharpening; a pointed extremity; a sharp point or jag.

Acupressure, **Acupression**, ak-ū-pre'shūr, ak-ū-pre'shon, *n.* [L. *acus*, a needle, and E. *press*.] *Surg.* a method of stopping hæmorrhage in arteries in amputations, &c., by means of needles or wires instead of ligatures to keep the wound closed.—**Acupress**, ak'ū-pres, *v.t.* To stop arterial hemorrhage by means of acupressure.

Acupuncture, ak-ū-pungk'tūr, *n.* [L. *acus*, a needle, and *punctura*, a pricking. PUNCTURE.] A surgical operation resorted to in certain complaints, as in headaches, neuralgia, rheumatism, &c., and consisting in the insertion of a delicate needle or set of needles beneath the tissues. —**Acupuncturator**, ak-ū-pungk'tū-rāt-ėr, *n.* An instrument for performing the operation of acupuncture.

Acuru, ak'ō-rō, *n.* The name in India of a fragrant aloe-wood.

Acute, a-kūt', *a.* [L. *acutus*, sharp-pointed, from *acuo*, to sharpen. From root, *ac*, *ak*, a point. ACID.] Sharp at the end; ending in a sharp point: opposed to *blunt* or *obtuse*; intellectually sharp; perceiving minute distinctions, or characterized by the use of such; characterized by keenness of insight: opposed to *dull* or *stupid*; having nice or quick sensibility; susceptible of slight impressions (*acute* hearing); keen; sharp; said of pain; high in pitch; shrill: said of sound; *med.* a term applied to a disease which is attended with more or less violent symptoms, and comes speedily to a crisis; *geom.* less than a right angle.—**Acutely**, a-kūt'li, *adv.* In an acute manner; sharply; keenly; with nice discrimination.—**Acuteness**, a-kūt'nes, *n.* The quality of being acute; sharpness; keenness; sagacity; acumen.

Adage, ad'āj, *n.* [Fr. *adage*, L. *adagium*, a proverb.] A proverb; an old saying, which has obtained credit by long use.

Adagio, a-dä'jō, *a.* and *adv.* [It.] *Music*, slow; slowly, leisurely, and with grace.—*n.* A slow movement.

Adam, ad'am, *n.* The name of the first man; hence, the frailty inherent in human nature.—*Adam's apple*, the prominence on the fore part of the throat.—*Adam's needle*, the popular name of the plants otherwise called *Yucca*. — **Adamic**, a-dam'ik, *a.* Pertaining to Adam.—**Adamite**, ad'am-īt, *n.* One of an ancient religious sect who aimed at establishing a state of innocence, and went naked.—**Adamitic**, ad-am-it'ik, *a.* Pertaining to the Adamites or to Adam.

Adamant, ad'a-mant, *n.* [L. *adamas*, *adamantis*, Gr. *adamas*, the hardest iron or steel, anything inflexibly hard, the diamond; lit. the unconquerable—Gr. *a*, priv., and *damaō*, to tame. TAME, DIAMOND.] Any substance of impenetrable hardness: chiefly a rhetorical or poetical word. (Formerly it sometimes meant the diamond, sometimes loadstone, from confusion with L. *adamantem*, through the loving-attractive quality.)—**Adamantean**, **Adamantine**, ad'a-mant-ē"an, ad-a-mant'īn, *a.* Made of adamant; having the qualities of adamant; impenetrable.

Adapt, a-dapt', *v.t.* [L. *adapto*—*ad*, to, and *apto*, to fit. APT.] To make suitable; to make to correspond; to fit or suit; to proportion; to remodel, work up, and render fit for representation on the stage, as a play from a foreign language or a novel.—**Adaptability**, **Adaptableness**, a-dapt'a-bil"i-ti, a-dapt'a-bl-nes, *n.* The quality of being capable of adaptation.—**Adaptable**, a-dapt'a-bl, *a.* Capable of being adapted.—**Adaptation**, ad-ap-tā'shon, *n.* The act of adapting or making suitable; the state of being suitable or fit; that which is adapted.—**Adaptedness**, a-dapt'ed-nes, *n.* State of being adapted; suitableness.—**Adapter**, a-dapt'ėr, *n.* One who or that which adapts.—**Adaptive**,† a-dapt'iv, *a.* Tending to adapt; suitable.

Adar, ā'där, *n.* A Hebrew month, answering to the latter part of February and the beginning of March, the twelfth of the sacred and sixth of the civil year.

Add, ad, *v.t.* [L. *addo*, to add—*ad*, to, and *do*, to put, to place, to give.] To set or put together; to join or unite; to put into one sum; to annex; subjoin; say further. —*v.i.* To be or serve as an addition (with *to*); also, to perform the arithmetical operation of addition.—**Addability, Addibility**, ad-a-bil'i-ti, ad-i-bil'i-ti, *n.* The condition of being addable; the capability of being added.—**Addable, Addible**, ad'-a-bl, ad'i-bl, *a.* Capable of being added.—**Addition**, ad-di'shon, *n.* The act or process of adding; the uniting of two or more numbers in one sum; the rule or branch of arithmetic which treats of adding numbers; an increase; something added; a title coming after a personal name (*Shak.*).—**Additional**, ad-di'shon-al, *a.* Added; supplementary.—**Additionally**, ad-di'shon-al-li, *adv.* By way of addition.—**Additive**, ad'it-iv, *a.* Falling to be added; additional; helping to increase.

Addax, ad'aks, *n.* A species of large antelope inhabiting Africa, with long and beautifully twisted horns.

Addendum, ad-den'dum, *n.* pl. **Addenda**, ad-den'da. [L.] A thing to be added; an addition; an appendix to a work.

Adder, ad'ėr, *n.* [O.E. *addre, addere*, by loss of initial *n* from A.Sax. *nædre, næddre*, O. and Prov. E. *nedder*, Icel. *nadr*, Goth. *nadrs*, G. *natter*.] A variety of venomous serpents, as the common viper, found in America and over Europe.—**Adder-fly**, *n.* A name for the dragon fly.—**Adder-pike**, *n.* A small fish, the lesser weever or sting-fish.—**Adder-stone**, *n.* A name given to certain rounded perforated stones, popularly supposed to have a kind of supernatural efficacy in curing the bites of adders.—**Adder's-tongue**, *n.* A species of fern.—**Adder's-wort**, *n.* Snake-weed, a kind of plant.

Addible. See under ADD.

Addict, ad-dikt', *v.t.* [L. *addico, addictum*, to devote—*ad*, to, and *dico*, to dedicate.] To apply habitually; to habituate: generally with a reflexive pronoun, and usually in a bad sense (followed by *to*; as, to *addict* one's self to intemperance.—*n.* (ad'-dikt). One who is addicted.—**Addicted**, ad-dikt'ed, *a.* Habitually practicing; given up; devoted; habituated (followed by *to*).—**Addiction**, ad-dik'shon, *n.* The act of devoting or giving up one's self to a practice; the state of being devoted; devotion.

Addition, Additional, &c. ADD.

Addle, ad'l, *a.* [From A.Sax. *adela*, filth; Sw. *adel* (seen in *ko adel*, cow urine), urine; Sc. *addle*, putrid water, urine.] Having lost the power of development and become rotten; putrid: applied to eggs; hence, barren; producing nothing.—*v.t.—addled, addling.* To make rotten, as eggs.—**Addle-headed, Addle-pated**, *a.* Stupid; muddled.

Address, ad-dres', *v.t.* [Fr. *adresser*. DRESS.] To direct or aim words; to pronounce; to apply to by words or writings; to accost; to speak to; to direct in writing; to write an address on; to court or make suit to.—*To address one's self to*, to speak to; to address.—*n.* The act of addressing one's self to a person; a speaking to; any speech or writing in which one person or set of persons makes a communication to another person or set of persons; manner of speaking to another; a person's bearing in conversation; courtship (in this sense generally in the plural); skill; dexterity; adroitness; direction of a letter.—**Addressee**, ad-dres'ē, *n.* One who is addressed.—**Addresser**, ad-dres'ėr, *n.* One who addresses or petitions.

Adduce, ad-dūs', *v.t.—adduced, adducing.* [L. *adduco*, to lead or bring to—*ad*, to, and *duco*, to lead. DUKE.] To cite; to name or instance as authority or evidence; to bring to notice as bearing on a subject.—**Adducent**, ad-dūs'ent, *a.* Bringing forward or together (an *adducent* muscle).—**Adducer**, ad-dūs'ėr, *n.* One that adduces.—**Adducible**, ad-dūs'i-bl, *a.* Capable of being adduced.—**Adduction**, ad-duk'shon, *n.* The act of adducing; *anat.* the action by which a part of the body is drawn towards the bodily axis.—**Adductive**, ad-dukt'iv, *a.* Adducing or bringing forward.—**Adductor**, ad-dukt'ėr, *n.* A muscle which draws one part to another.

Adenalgy, ad-en-al'ji, *n.* [Gr. *adēn*, a gland, and *algos*, pain.] Pain in a gland.—**Adeniform, Adenoid**, a-den'i-form, ad'en-oid, *a.* Of a gland-like shape or character; glandular.—**Adenitis**, ad-e-nī'tis, *n.* Inflammation of one or more of the lymphatic glands.—**Adenoids**, ad'e-noidz, *n. pl.* Glandlike morbid growths in the throat behind the soft palate.—**Adenological**, ad'en-ō-loj''ik-al, *a.* Pertaining to adenology.—**Adenology**, ad-en-ol'o-ji, *n.* The doctrine of glands, their nature, and their uses.—**Adenoma**, ad-e-nō'ma, *n.* A tumour originating in a gland.—**Adenophorous**, ad-e-nof'or-us, *a.* Bearing glands.—**Adenose, Adenous**, ad'en-ōs, ad'en-us, *a.* Like or appertaining to a gland; glandular.—**Adenotomy**, ad-en-ot'o-mi, *n.* [Gr. *tomē*, a cutting.] A cutting or incision of a gland.

Adephagia, ad-ē-fā'ji-a, *n.* [Gr. *adēn*, abundantly, and *phagō*, to eat.] Morbidly voracious appetite.

Adept, a-dept', *n.* [L. *adeptus*, pp. of *adipiscor*, to obtain. Alchemists who were reputed to have *obtained* the philosopher's stone were termed *adepts*; hence *adept*, a proficient.] One fully skilled or well versed in any art; a proficient.—*a.* Well skilled.

Adequate, ad'ē-kwāt, *a.* [L. *adæquatus*, made equal, pp. of *adæquo—ad*, to, and *æquus*, equal.] Equal; proportionate; exactly correspondent; fully sufficient.—**Adequacy**, ad'ē-kwa-si, *n.* The state of being adequate; a sufficiency for a particular purpose.—**Adequately**, ad'ē-kwāt-li, *adv.* In an adequate manner; sufficiently.—**Adequateness**, ad'ē-kwāt-nes, *n.* The state of being adequate; sufficiency.

Adhere, ad-hēr', *v.i.—adhered, adhering.* [L. *adhæreo—ad*, to, and *hæreo*, to stick, whence *hesitate*.] To stick together; to cleave; to become closely joined or united; to be fixed in attachment or devotion.—**Adherence**, ad-hēr'ens, *n.* The quality or state of adhering; fidelity; steady attachment.—**Adherent**, ad-hēr'ent, *a.* Sticking fast to something; clinging; attached.—**Adherent, Adherer**, ad-hēr'ent, ad-hēr'ėr, *n.* One who adheres; one who follows a leader, party, or profession; a follower or partisan.—**Adherently**, ad-hēr'ent-li, *adv.* In an adherent manner.—**Adhesion**, ad-hē'zhon, *n.* L. *adhæsio*, from *adhæreo*, to adhere.] The act or state of adhering, or being united and attached; a sticking together of the surface of bodies; close connection or association; steady attachment of the mind or feelings; assent; concurrence (*adhesion* to a treaty).—**Adhesive**, ad-hē'siv, *a.* Sticky; tenacious.—**Adhesively**, ad-hē'siv-li, *adv.* In an adhesive manner.—**Adhesiveness**, ad-hē'siv-nes, *n.* The state or quality of being adhesive; *phren.* an organ which is said to promote attachment to objects.

Adhibit, ad-hib'it, *v.t.* [L. *adhibeo, adhibitum—ad*, to, and *habeo*, to hold.] To apply†; to attach (one's signature).—**Adhibition**, ad-hi-bi'shon, *n.* The act of adhibiting.

Adiabatic, a-di-a-bat'ik, *n.* [Gr. *a*, not, *diabainō*, pass through.] Of physical changes without gain or loss of heat; *adiabatic curve*, curve showing relation between the volume and the pressure of a fluid which changes its volume without gain or loss of heat.

Adiactinic, a'dī-ak-tin''ik, *a.* [Gr. *a*, priv., *dia*, through, and E. *actinic*.] Impervious to the actinic or chemical rays of light.

Adiaphorous, a-dī-af'or-us, *a.* [Gr. *a*, priv., and *diaphoros*, different.] Indifferent; neutral; neither right nor wrong morally.

Adiathermic, a'dī-a-thėr''mik, *a.* [Gr. *a*, priv., *dia*, through, and *thermē*, heat.] Impervious to heat.

Adieu, a-dū'. [Fr. *à*, to, and *Dieu*, God, It. *addio*, Span. *a dios*, all forms of L. *ad*, to, and *Deus*, God.] *Lit.* to God: an ellipsis for I commend you to God; farewell; an expression of kind wishes at the parting of friends.—*n.* pl. **Adieus** or **Adieux**, a-dūz'. A farewell or commendation to the care of God.

Adipic, a-dip'ik, *a.* [L. *adeps, adipis*, fat.] Of or belonging to fat.

Adipocere, ad'i-pō-sēr, *n.* [L. *adeps*, fat, and *cera*, wax.] A soft, unctuous, or waxy substance, into which the flesh of dead animals is converted when protected from atmospheric air, and under certain circumstances of temperature and humidity.—**Adipocerate**, ad-i-pos'ėr-āt, *v.t.* To convert into adipocere.—**Adipocerous**, ad-i-pos'ėr-us, *a.* Relating to adipocere; containing adipocere.

Adipose, ad'i-pōs, *a.* [From L. *adeps, adipis*, fat.] Fatty; consisting of or resembling fat.—*n.* Fat; the fat on the kidneys.

Adipsia, Adipsy, a-dip'si-a, a-dip'si, *n.* [Gr. *a*, priv., and *dipsa*, thirst.] *Med.* the total absence of thirst.—**Adipsous**, a-dip'-sus, *a.* Tending to quench thirst.

Adit, ad'it, *n.* [L. *aditus—ad*, to, and *eo*, *itum*, to go.] Approach; access; passage; a more or less horizontal passage into a mine.

Adjacent, ad-jā'sent, *a.* [L. *adjacens, adjacentis*, pp. of *adjaceo*, to lie contiguous—*ad*, to, and *jaceo*, to lie.] Lying near or close; bordering upon; neighbouring; adjoining.—**Adjacence, Adjacency**, ad-jā'sens, ad-jā'sen-si, *n.* The state of being adjacent.—**Adjacently**, ad-jā'sent-li, *adv.* So as to be adjacent.

Adjective, ad'jek-tiv, *n.* [L. *adjectivum, adjectivus*, added—*ad*, to, and *jacio*, to throw.] *Gram.* a word used with a noun to express a quality of the thing named, or something attributed to it, or to specify or describe a thing as distinct from something else, and so to limit and define it.—**Adjectival**, ad-jek-tī'val, *a.* Belonging to or like an adjective; having the import of an adjective.—**Adjectivally, Adjectively**, ad-jek-tī'val-li, ad'jek-tiv-li, *adv.* By way of, or as, an adjective.

Adjoin, ad-join', *v.t.* [Fr. *adjoindre*; L. *adjungo—ad*, to, and *jungo*, to join. JOIN.] To join or add; to unite; to annex or append.—*v.i.* To lie or be next or in contact; to be contiguous.—**Adjoining**, ad-join'ing, *a.* Adjacent; contiguous; neighbouring.

Adjourn, ad-jėrn', *v.t.* [Fr. *ajourner*, O.Fr. *ajorner, adjorner*—prefix *a*, *ad*, to, and O.Fr. *jorn* (now *jour*), a day, L. *diurnus*, diurnal, from *dies*, a day. DIURNAL.] To put off or defer to another day or till a later period; to suspend the meeting of, as of a public or private body, to a future day; to postpone to a future meeting of the same body.—*v.i.* To cease sitting and carrying on business for a time.—**Adjournment**, ad-jėrn'ment, *n.* The act of adjourning; the period during which a public body adjourns its sittings.

Adjudge, ad-juj', *v.t.—adjudged, adjudging.* [Prefix *ad*, and *judge*. JUDGE.] To award judicially; to adjudicate upon; to settle.—**Adjudgment**, ad-juj'ment, *n.* The act of adjudging; adjudication; sentence.

Adjudicate, ad-jū'di-kāt, *v.t.—adjudicated, adjudicating.* [L. *adjudico*, to give sentence—*ad*, to, and *judico*, to judge. JUDGE.] To adjudge; to award judicially.—*v.i.* To sit in judgment; to give a judicial decision.—**Adjudication**, ad-jū'di-kā''shon, *n.* The act of adjudicating; the act or process of trying and determining judicially; judgment or decision of a court.—**Adjudicator**, ad-jū'di-kāt-ėr, *n.* One who adjudicates.

Adjunct, ad'jungkt, *n.* [L. *adjunctus*, joined, from *adjungo—ad*, to, and *jungo*, *junctum*, to join. JOIN.] Something added to another, but not essentially a part of it.—*a.* United with in office or in action of any kind; conjoined with.—**Adjunction**, ad-jungk'shon, *n.* The act of joining; the thing joined.—**Adjunctive**, ad-jungk'tiv, *a.* Joining; having the quality of joining.—*n.* One who or that which is joined.—**Adjunctively**, ad-jungk'tiv-li, *adv.* In an adjunctive manner.—**Adjunctly**, ad-jungkt'li, *adv.* In connection with; by way of addition or adjunct.

Adjure, ad-jūr', *v.t.—adjured, adjuring.* [L. *adjuro—ad*, to, and *juro*, to swear.] To charge, bind, or command, earnestly and solemnly.—**Adjuration**, ad-jū-rā'shon, *n.* The act of adjuring; a solemn charging on oath; a solemn oath.—**Adjuratory**, ad-jūr'a-to-ri, *a.* Containing an adjuration, or characterized by adjurations. — **Adjurer**, ad-jūr'ėr, *n.* One who adjures.

Adjust, ad-just', *v.t.* [Fr. *ajuster*, Mod.Fr. *adjouter*, L.L. *adjuxtare*, to bring together —*ad* and *juxta.*] To fit; to make correspondent; to adapt; to accommodate; to put in order; to regulate or reduce to system; to settle or bring to a satisfactory state, so that parties are agreed in the result. — **Adjustable**, ad-just'a-bl, *a.* Capable of being adjusted.—**Adjuster**, ad-just'ėr, *n.* One who or that which adjusts.—**Adjustive**, ad-just'iv, *a.* Tending or serving to adjust.—**Adjustment**, ad-just'ment, *n.* The act of adjusting.

Adjutant, ad'jū-tant, *n.* [L. *adjutans*, ppr. of *adjuto*, to assist—*ad*, and *juvo*, *jutum*, to help.] *Milit.* an officer whose business is to assist a commanding officer by receiving and communicating orders.—**Adjutancy**, ad'jū-tan-si, *n.* The office of an adjutant. —**Adjutant-bird, Adjutant-crane, Adjutant-stork**, *n.* A very large grallatorial bird allied to the storks, a native of the warmer parts of India. It feeds on carrion, and is most voracious.

Adjutor,† ad-jūt'ėr, *n.* A helper; a coadjutor. — **Adjutrix**,† ad-jū'triks, *n.* A female assistant.—**Adjuvant**, ad'jū-vant or ad-jū'vant, *n.* An assistant; *med.* a substance added to a prescription to aid the operation of the principal ingredient or basis.

Admeasure, ad-me'zhūr, *v.t.* — *admeasured, admeasuring.* [L. *ad*, to, and E. *measure.* MEASURE.] To ascertain the dimensions, size, or capacity of; to measure. —**Admeasurement**, ad-me'zhūr-ment, *n.* The act of admeasuring; the measure of a thing, or dimensions ascertained.— **Admeasurer**, ad-me'zhūr-ėr, *n.* One who.

Adminicular, Adminiculary, ad-min-ik'ū-lėr, ad-min-ik'ū-la-ri, *a.* [L. *adminiculum*, a prop, stay, or support.] Supplying help; helpful; lending aid or support.

Administer, ad-min'is-tėr, *v.t.* [L. *administro*—*ad*, to, and *ministro*, to serve. MINISTER.] To manage or conduct as chief agent or directing and controlling official; to direct or superintend the execution of, as of laws; to afford, give, furnish, or supply; to give, as a dose of medicine; to dispense or distribute; to tender, as an oath; *law*, to manage, as the estate of a deceased person, collecting debts, paying legacies, &c. —*v.i.* To contribute assistance; to bring aid or supplies: with *to*; as, to *administer to* one's necessities; *law*, to perform the office of administrator. — **Administerial**, ad-min'is-tē"ri-al, *a.* Pertaining to administration or to the executive part of government.—**Administrable**, ad-min'is-tra-bl, *a.* Capable of being administered. —**Administration**, ad-min'is-trā"shon, *n.* The act of administering; direction; management; government of public affairs; the executive functions of government; the persons, collectively, who are intrusted with such functions; the executive; *law*, the management of the estate of a deceased person, consisting in collecting debts, paying debts and legacies, and distributing the property among the heirs.—**Administrative**, ad-min'is-trāt-iv, *a.* Pertaining to administration. — **Administrator**, ad-min'is-trāt-ėr, *n.* One who administers, or who directs, manages, distributes, or dispenses; one who has the charge of the goods and estate of a person dying without a will.—**Administratorship**, ad-min'is-trāt-ėr-ship, *n.* The office of an administrator. — **Administratrix**, ad-min'is-trāt-riks, *n.* A female administrator.

Admirable, &c. ADMIRE.

Admiral, ad'mi-ral, *n.* [O.E. *amiral*, Fr. *amiral*, from Ar. *amir*, *emir*, a prince, chief, with the Ar. article suffixed.] A naval officer of the highest rank; a commander-in-chief of a fleet or navy; there being three degrees of this rank, namely, admiral, vice-admiral, and rear-admiral; the ship which carries the admiral; also, the most considerable ship of any fleet; a name given to two species of butterflies, *Vanessa atalanta*, or red admiral, and *Limenitis camilla*, or white admiral.—**Admiralship**, ad'mi-ral-ship, *n.* The office or power of an admiral. — **Admiralty**, ad'mi-ral-ti, *n.* The office and jurisdiction of the officials appointed to take the general management of the naval affairs of a state; the officials collectively; the building in which they transact business.—**Admiral-shell**, *n.* The popular name of a sub-genus of magnificent molluscous shells.

Admire, ad-mīr', *v.t.*—*admired, admiring.* [Fr. *admirer*, L. *admiror*—*ad*, and *miror*, to wonder.] To wonder at‡; to regard with wonder mingled with approbation, esteem, reverence, or affection; to take pleasure in the beauty of; to look on or contemplate with pleasure.—*v.i.* To feel or express admiration.—**Admirer**, ad-mīr'ėr, *n.* One who admires; one who esteems greatly; one who openly shows his admiration of a woman; a lover.—**Admiringly**, ad-mīr'ing-li, *adv.* In an admiring manner; with admiration. — **Admiration**, ad-mi-rā'shon, *n.* Wonder‡; wonder mingled with pleasing emotions, as approbation, esteem, love, or veneration; an emotion excited by something beautiful or excellent. — **Admirable**, ad'mi-ra-bl, *a.* Worthy of admiration; most excellent.—**Admirableness**, ad'mi-ra-bl-nes, *n.*—**Admirably**, ad'mi-ra-bli, *adv.* In an admirable manner; excellently; exceedingly well.

Admissible, &c. Under ADMIT.

Admit, ad-mit', *v.t.*—*admitted, admitting.* [L. *admitto*—*ad*, to, and *mitto*, *missum*, to send, seen also in *commit*, *submit*, *mission*, &c.] To suffer to enter; to grant entrance to; to give right of entrance to; to grant in argument; to receive as true; to permit, grant, or allow, or to be capable of; to acknowledge; to own; to confess.—*v.i.* To give warrant or allowance; to grant opportunity; to permit: with *of* (the words do not *admit of* this interpretation).—**Admittable**, ad-mit'a-bl, *a.* Capable of being admitted. — **Admittability**, ad-mit'a-bil"i-ti, *n.* Capability of.—**Admittance**, ad-mit'ans, *n.* The act of admitting; permission to enter; entrance. — **Admittedly**, ad-mit'ed-li, *adv.* By admission, acknowledgment, or concession.—**Admitter**, ad-mit'ėr, *n.* One who admits. — **Admissible**, ad-mis'i-bl, *a.* [Fr. *admissible*, L.L. *admissibilis*, from *admitto*, *admissum*, to admit.] Capable of being admitted, allowed, or conceded. — **Admissibility**, ad-mis'i-bil"i-ti, *n.* The quality of being admissible. — **Admissibly**, ad-mis'i-bli, *adv.* In an admissible manner; so as to be admitted. — **Admission**, ad-mi'shon, *n.* [L. *admissio.*] The act of admitting; power or permission to enter; entrance; access; power to approach; the granting of an argument or position not fully proved; a point or statement admitted; acknowledgment; confession of a charge, error, or crime. —**Admissory**, ad-mis'so-ri, *a.* Granting admission; admitting.—**Admissive**, ad-mis'iv, *a.* Having the nature of an admission.

Admix, ad-miks', *v.t.* [Prefix *ad*, to, and *mix.*] To mingle with something else.— **Admixture**, ad-miks'tūr, *n.* The act of mingling or mixing; that which is formed by mingling.

Admonish, ad-mon'ish, *v.t.* [O.E. *amoneste*, O.Fr. *amonester*, to admonish—prefix *a*, *ad*, and L.L. *monestum*, for L. *monitum*, pp. of *moneo*, to warn. MONITION.] To warn or notify of a fault; to reprove with mildness; to counsel against wrong practices; to caution or advise; to instruct or direct; to remind; to recall or incite to duty.—**Admonisher**, ad-mon'ish-ėr, *n.* One who admonishes. — **Admonishment**,† ad-mon'ish-ment, *n.* Admonition. —**Admonition**, ad-mō-ni'shon, *n.* The act of admonishing; counsel or advice; gentle reproof; instruction in duties; caution; direction.—**Admonitive**, ad-mon'it-iv, *a.* Containing admonition. — **Admonitively**, ad-mon'it-iv-li, *adv.* By admonition.—**Admonitor**, ad-mon'it-ėr, *n.* An admonisher; a monitor.—**Admonitorial**, ad-mon'i-tō"ri-al, *a.* Admonitory. —**Admonitory**, ad-mon'i-to-ri, *a.* Containing admonition; tending or serving to admonish.

Adnascent,† ad-nas'ent, *a.* [L. *ad*, to, *nascens*, growing.] Growing on something else.—**Adnate**, ad'nāt, *a.* [L. *adnatus*—*ad*, to, and *natus*, grown.] Growing attached: chiefly a term in *bot.*

Adnominal, ad-nom'in-al, *a.* *Gram.* relating to an adnoun or adjective; adjectival.—**Adnoun**, ad'noun, *n.* *Gram.* an adjective or attribute, so called because going with a noun.

Ado, a-dö', *n.* [Prefix *a* for *at*, and *do*, that is, to do; *at* being here the sign of the infinitive, as in Icelandic.] Bustle; trouble; labour; difficulty.

Adobe, a-dō'be, *n.* [Sp.] A sun-dried brick.

Adolescence, Adolescency, ad-ō-les'ens, ad-ō-les'en-si, *n.* [L. *adolescentia*—*ad*, and *olesco*, to grow.] The state of growing: applied almost exclusively to the young of the human race; youth, or the period of life between childhood and the full development of the frame.—**Adolescent**, ad-ō-les'ent, *a.* Growing up; advancing from childhood to manhood.

Adonic, Adonean, a-don'ik, ad-ō-nē'an, *a.* [From *Adonis*, a mythical personage among the Greeks, originally the Phœnician sun-god.] Of or pertaining to Adonis.— *Adonic verse*, in Greek and Latin poetry, a verse consisting of a dactyl and a spondee or trochee.—**Adonis**, a-dōn'is, *n.* Beautiful person; a beau.—**Adonise**,†**Adonize**,† ad'on-īz, *v.t.* To make an Adonis of one's self with the view of attracting admiration.

Adopt, a-dopt', *v.t.* [L. *adopto*—*ad*, and *opto*, to desire or choose. OPTION.] To take into one's family and treat as one's own child; to take to one's self by choice or approval, as principles, opinions, a course of conduct, &c.—**Adoptability**, a-dopt'a-bil"i-ti, *n.* The state of being adoptable. —**Adoptable**, a-dopt'a-bl, *a.* Capable of, fit for, or worthy of being adopted.— **Adoptedly**, a-dopt'ed-li, *adv.* In the manner of something adopted.—**Adopter**, a-dopt'ėr, *n.* One who adopts.—**Adoption**, a-dop'shon, *n.* [L. *adoptio.*] The act of adopting, or the state of being adopted.— **Adoptive**, a-dopt'iv, *a.* [L. *adoptivus.*] Constituted by adoption; adopting or adopted; assumed.

Adore, a-dōr', *v.t.*—*adored, adoring.* [L. *adoro*, to pray, to adore—*ad*, to, and *oro*, to ask. ORACLE.] To worship with profound reverence; to pay divine honours to; to regard with the utmost esteem, love, and respect; to love in the highest degree, as a man a woman.—**Adorability**, a-dōr'a-bil"i-ti, *n.* Quality of being adorable.— **Adorable**, a-dōr'a-bl, *a.* Demanding adoration; worthy of being adored.—**Adorableness**, a-dōr'a-bl-nes, *n.*—**Adorably**, a-dōr'a-bli, *adv.* In a manner worthy of adoration.—**Adoration**, ad-ō-rā'shon, *n.* The act of adoring; the act of paying honours, as to a divine being; worship addressed to a deity; the highest degree of love, as of a man for a woman.—**Adorer**, a-dōr'ėr, *n.* One who adores; one who worships or honours as divine; a lover; an admirer.— **Adoringly**, a-dōr'ing-li, *adv.* With adoration.

Adorn, a-dorn', *v.t.* [L. *adorno*—*ad*, to, and *orno*, to deck or beautify.] To deck or decorate; to add to the attractiveness of by dress or ornaments; to set off to advantage; beautify; embellish.—**Adorner**, a-dorn'ėr, *n.* One who adorns.—**Adorning**, a-dorn'ing, *n.* Ornament; decoration. [N.T.] —**Adorningly**, a-dorn'ing-li, *adv.* By adorning.—**Adornment**, a-dorn'ment, *n.* An ornament or decoration.

Adosculation, ad-os'kū-lā"shon, *n.* [L. *ad*, to, and *osculatio*, a kissing, from *osculum*, a kiss, *os*, *oris*, the mouth.] The impregnation of plants; impregnation of animals by external contact merely.

Adown, a-doun′, *prep.* [A.Sax. *of-dûne*, off or from the down or hill.] From a higher to a lower situation; down; along the length of; downwards; all along.—*adv.* Downward; down.

Adpressed, ad-prest′, *a.* *Bot.* growing parallel to and in contact with a stem but not adhering to it.

Adrift, a-drift′, *a.* or *adv.* [Prefix *a*, on, and *drift*, a driving or floating. DRIVE.] Floating at random; impelled or moving without direction; at the mercy of winds and currents; swayed by any chance impulse; at sea; at a loss.

Adroit, a-droit′, *a.* [Fr. *adroit*, dexterous —*a*, to, and *droit*, right, as opposed to left (comp. *dexterous*, from L. *dexter*, right); from L. *directus*, straight, direct.] Dexterous; skilful; expert; active in the use of the hand, and, figuratively, in the exercise of the mental faculties; ready in invention or execution.—**Adroitly**, a-droit′li, *adv.* In an adroit manner; with dexterity; readily; skilfully.—**Adroitness**, a-droit′nes, *n.* The quality of being adroit; dexterity; readiness.

Adry, a-drī′, *a.* or *adv.* [Prefix *a* for *of*, intens., and *dry*.] Thirsty; in want of drink; athirst.

Adscititious, ad-si-ti′shus, *a.* [L. *adscisco*, to take knowingly, to appropriate.] Added; taken as supplemental; additional; not requisite.—**Adscititiously**, ad-si-ti′shus-li, *adv.* In an adscititious manner.

Adscript, ad′skript, *n.* [L. *adscriptus*, pp. of *adscribo*, to enroll—*ad*, to, and *scribo*, to write.] One who is held to service as attached to some object or place; a serf.—**Adscriptive**, ad-skript′iv, *a.* Pertaining to an adscript.

Adstriction, ad-strik′shon, *n.* [L. *adstrictio*—*ad*, to, and *stringo*. STRICT.] A binding fast together; costiveness; constipation.

Adularia, ad-ū-lā′ri-a, *n.* [From *Adula*, the summit of the St. Gothard, where fine specimens are got.] A very pure, limpid, translucent variety of the common felspar, called also *Moonstone*.

Adulation, ad-ū-lā′shon, *n.* [L. *adulatio*, *adulationis*, a fawning, *adulor*, *adulatus*, to flatter.] Servile flattery; praise in excess, or beyond what is merited; high compliment.—**Adulate**, ad′ū-lāt, *v.t.* To show feigned devotion to; to flatter servilely.—**Adulator**, ad′ū-lāt-ėr, *n.* A flatterer.—**Adulatory**, ad′ū-lāt-o-ri, *a.* Flattering.

Adult, a-dult′, *a.* [L. *adultus*, grown to maturity, from *ad*, to, *oleo*, to grow. ADOLESCENCE.] Having arrived at mature years, or to full size and strength; pertaining or relating to full strength; suitable for an adult.—**Adult**, a-dult′, *n.* A person grown to full size and strength.—**Adultness**, a-dult′nes, *n.* The state of being adult.

Adulterate, a-dul′tėr-āt, *v.t.*—*adulterated*, *adulterating*. [L. *adultero*, from *adulter*, mixed, an adulterer—*ad*, to, and *alter*, other.] To debase or deteriorate by an admixture of foreign or baser materials.—**Adulterant**, a-dul′tėr-ant, *n.* The person or thing that adulterates.—**Adulteration**, a-dul′tėr-ā″shon, *n.* The act of adulterating, or the state of being adulterated or debased by foreign mixture.—**Adulterator**, a-dul′tėr-āt-ėr, *n.* One who.

Adultery, a-dul′tėr-i, *n.* [L. *adulterium*, from *adulter*, an adulterer. ADULTERATE.] Violation of the marriage-bed; sexual commerce by a married person with one who is not his or her wife or husband.—**Adulterer**, a-dul′tėr-ėr, *n.* A man guilty of adultery.—**Adulteress**, a-dul′tėr-es, *n.* A woman guilty of adultery.—**Adulterine**, a-dul′tėr-īn, *a.* Proceeding from adulterous commerce.—**Adulterous**, a-dul′tėr-us, *a.* Guilty of adultery; pertaining to adultery; illicit.—**Adulterously**, a-dul′tėr-us-li, *adv.* In an adulterous manner.

Adumbrate, ad-um′brāt, *v.t.*—*adumbrated*, *adumbrating*. [L. *adumbro*, to shade—*ad*, and *umbra*, a shade.] To give a faint shadow of; to exhibit a faint resemblance of, like a shadow; to shadow forth.—**Adumbrant**, ad-um′brant, *a.* Giving a faint shadow, or showing a slight resemblance.—**Adumbration**, ad-um-brā′shon, *n.* The act of adumbrating or shadowing forth; a faint or imperfect representation of a thing.—**Adumbrative**, ad-um′bra-tiv, *a.* Shadowing forth; faintly resembling.—**Adumbratively**, ad-um′bra-tiv-li, *adv.* In an adumbrative manner.

Aduncous, ad-ungk′us, *a.* [L. *aduncus*, hooked—*ad*, to, and *uncus*, a hook.] Hooked; bent or made in the form of a hook.—**Aduncity**, ad-un′si-ti, *n.* Hookedness.

Adust, a-dust′, *a.* [L. *adustus*, burned—*ad*, to, and *uro*, *ustum*, to burn.] Burned; scorched; parched up; looking as if burned or scorched.

Advance, ad-vans′, *v.t.*—*advanced*, *advancing*. [Fr. *avancer*, from *avant*, forward (whence also E. *van*), L. *abante*, from before, in front—*ab*, from, *ante*, before.] To bring forward; to move further in front; to promote; to raise to a higher rank; to forward or further; to encourage the progress of; to enhance (price); to accelerate the growth of; to offer or propose; to bring to view or notice, as something one is prepared to abide by; to allege; to supply beforehand; to furnish on credit, or before goods are delivered, or work done.—*v.i.* To move or go forward; to proceed; to make progress; to grow better, greater, wiser, or older; to rise in rank, office, or consequence.—*n.* A moving forward or towards the front; a march forward; gradual progression; improvement; advancement; promotion; a proposal; a first step towards; addition to price; rise in price; a giving beforehand; that which is given beforehand, especially money.—*In advance*, in front, before; beforehand; before an equivalent is received.—**Advancement**, ad-vans′ment, *n.* The act of advancing; the state of being advanced; the act of promoting; preferment; promotion; improvement; furtherance.—**Advancer**, ad-vans′ėr, *n.* One who advances.—**Advance-note**, *n.* A draft on the owner or agent of a vessel, generally for one month's wages, given by the master to a sailor on his signing the articles of agreement.

Advantage, ad-van′tāj, *n.* [O.Fr. *advantage*, Fr. *avantage*, from *avant*, before. ADVANCE.] Any state, condition, circumstance, opportunity, or means specially favourable to success, prosperity, or any desired end (the *advantage* of a good constitution, of an excellent education); superiority; benefit; gain; profit.—*v.t.*—*advantaged*, *advantaging*. To bring advantage to; to be of service to; to benefit; to yield profit or gain to.—**Advantageous**, ad-van-tā′jus, *a.* Being of advantage; profitable; useful; beneficial.—**Advantageously**, ad-van-tā′jus-li, *adv.* In an advantageous manner.—**Advantageousness**, ad-van-tā′jus-nes, *n.*

Advene, ad-vēn′, *v.i.* [L. *advenio*, to come to—*ad*, to, and *venio*, to come. VENTURE.] To accede or be superadded; to become a part, though not essential.—**Advent**, ad′vent, *n.* [L. *adventus*, an arrival.] A coming; approach; visitation; the coming of our Saviour; an ecclesiastical division of the year embracing the four weeks before Christmas.—**Adventitious**, ad-ven-tish′us, *a.* [L. *adventitius*.] Added extrinsically; not essentially inherent; accidentally or casually acquired.—**Adventitiously**, ad-ven-tish′us-li, *adv.*—**Adventitiousness**, ad-ven-tish′us-nes, *n.*

Adventure, ad-ven′tūr, *n.* [O.Fr. *adventure*, Fr. *aventure*, L.L. *adventura*, *aventura*, from L. *adventurus*, about to arrive, fut. part. of *advenio*, to arrive. ADVENE.] Hazard; risk; chance; a hazardous enterprise; a bold and dangerous undertaking of uncertain issue; a commercial speculation; a speculation in goods sent abroad; a remarkable occurrence in one's personal history; a noteworthy event or experience in one's life.—*v.t.*—*adventured*, *adventuring*. To risk or hazard; to venture on; to attempt.—**Adventurer**, ad-ven′tūr-ėr, *n.* One who engages in an adventure or speculation; one who attempts or takes part in bold, novel, or extraordinary enterprises; one who lives by underhand means, or by a system of imposition.—**Adventuress**, ad-ven′tūr-es, *n.* A female adventurer.—**Adventurous**, ad-ven′tūr-us, *a.* Bold to encounter danger; daring; courageous; enterprising; full of hazard; attended with risk.—**Adventurously**, ad-ven′tūr-us-li, *adv.* In an adventurous manner.—**Adventurousness**, ad-ven′tūr-us-nes, *n.*

Adverb, ad′vėrb, *n.* [L. *adverbium*—*ad*, to, and *verbum*, a word, a verb.] *Gram.* one of the indeclinable parts of speech, so called from being frequently joined to verbs for the purpose of limiting or extending their signification.—**Adverbial**, ad-vėrb′i-al, *a.* Pertaining to or having the character or structure of an adverb—**Adverbialize**, ad-vėrb′i-al-īz, *v.t.* To give the form or force of an adverb to; to use as an adverb.—**Adverbially**, ad-vėrb′i-al-li, *adv.* In the manner or with the force or character of an adverb.

Adversary, ad′vėr-sa-ri, *n.* [L. *adversarius*. ADVERSE.] An enemy; a foe; an antagonist; an opponent... An *adversary* is one who is opposed to another, without necessarily having hostile feelings; an *antagonist* is one who strives personally against another for victory; an *enemy* is one who entertains feelings of personal hostility.

Adversative, ad-vėrs′at-iv, *a.* Expressing difference, contrariety, or opposition (an *adversative* conjunction).—*n.* A word denoting contrariety or opposition.

Adverse, ad′vėrs, *a.* [L. *adversus*, opposite—*ad*, to, and *versus*, turned, from *verto*, to turn.] Acting in a contrary direction; counteracting; opposing (*adverse* winds); hostile; inimical (a party, criticism); unfortunate; calamitous; unprosperous (fate or circumstances).—**Adversely**, ad′vėrs-li, *adv.* In an adverse manner.—**Adverseness**, ad′vėrs-nes, *n.* The state or quality of being adverse.—**Adversity**, ad-vėrs′i-ti, *n.* An event, or series of events, which oppose success or desire; misfortune; calamity; affliction; distress; state of unhappiness.

Advert, ad-vėrt′, *v.i.* [L. *advert*—*ad*, to, and *verto*, to turn.] To turn the mind or attention; to regard, observe, or notice; to refer or allude: followed by *to*. ∴ *Advert* is to turn directly, and it may be abruptly; *allude* is to touch slightly, and it may be in a very vague and uncertain manner; *refer*, lit. to carry back, is to bring a thing already well known into notice; to mention or speak of directly.—**Advertence**, **Advertency**, ad-vėrt′ens, ad-vėrt′en-si, *n.* Attention; notice; regard; heedfulness.—**Advertent**, ad-vėrt′ent, *a.* Attentive; heedful.—**Advertently**, ad-vėrt′ent-li, *adv.* In an advertent manner.

Advertise, ad-vėr-tīz′, *v.t.*—*advertised*, *advertising*. [Fr. *avertir*, *avertissant*, to warn, inform, from L. *adverto*, to turn towards—*ad*, *verto*, to turn.] To inform or give notice; to make public intimation of, especially by printed notice.—*v.i.* To announce one's wishes or intentions by a public and usually a printed notice.—**Advertisement**, ad-vėr′tiz-ment, *n.* Warning, advice, or admonition (*Shak.*); a written or printed notice intended to make something known to the public; especially a printed and paid notice in a newspaper or other public print.—**Advertiser**, ad-vėr-tīz′ėr, *n.* One who advertises

Advice, ad-vīs′, *n.* [O.Fr. *advis*, opinion, counsel—L. *ad*, to, and *visum*, what is seen or judged proper. VISION.] An opinion recommended, or offered, as worthy to be followed; counsel; suggestion; information; notice; intelligence; a notification in respect of a business transaction.—*To take advice*, to consult with others; specifically, to take the opinion of a professional or skilful man, as a physician or lawyer.—**Advisability**, ad-vīz′a-bil″i-ti, *n.* Advisableness; expediency.—**Advisable**, ad-vīz′a-bl, *a.* Proper to be advised; expedient; proper to be done or practised; open to advice.—**Advisable-**

ness, ad-vīz'a-bl-nes, *n.* The quality of being advisable or expedient.—**Advisably**, ad-vīz'a-bli, *adv.* With advice.—**Advise**, ad-vīz', *v.t.*—*advised, advising.* [Fr. *aviser.* ADVICE.] To give counsel to; to counsel; to give information to; to inform; to acquaint.—*v.i.* To consider; to reflect; to take counsel.—**Advised**, ad-vīzd', *a.* Cautious; prudent; done, formed, or taken with advice or deliberation (an *advised* act).—**Advisedly**, ad-vīz'ed-li, *adv.* With deliberation or advice; heedfully; purposely; by design.—**Advisedness**, ad-vīz'-ed-nes, *n.* The state of being advised; prudent procedure.—**Adviser**, ad-vīz'ėr, *n.* One who gives advice or admonition; a counsellor.—**Advisership**, ad-vīz'ėr-ship, *n.* The office of an adviser.—**Advisory**, ad-vīz'o-ri, *a.* Having power to advise; containing advice.

Advocate, ad'vō-kāt, *n.* [L. *advocatus*, one summoned to aid—*ad*, to, and *voco, vocatum*, to call. VOICE, VOCAL.] One who pleads the cause of another in a court of law; one who defends, vindicates, or espouses a cause by argument; a pleader in favour of something; an upholder; a defender.—*v.t. advocated, advocating.* To plead in favour of (a thing, not a person); to defend by argument before a tribunal; to support or vindicate.—**Lord Advocate**, the highest law-officer of the Crown in Scotland.—**Advocates**. *Faculty of Advocates*, Scottish bar.—**Advocacy**, ad'vō-ka-si, *n.* The act of pleading for; intercession; defence.—**Advocateship**, ad'vō-kāt-ship, *n.* The office or duty of an advocate.—**Advocation**, ad-vō-kā'shon, *n.* The act of advocating; a pleading for.

Advowson, ad-vou'sn, *n.* [O.Fr. *advoeson, advouson*, protection, patronage; L. *advocatio, advocationis*, a calling to one for help. ADVOCATE.] The right of presentation to a vacant benefice in the Established Church of England.—**Advowee**, ad-vou-ē', *n.* One who has the right of advowson.

Adynamia, ad″-i-nā'mi-a, *n.* [Gr. *a*, priv., and *dynamis*, power.] Weakness; want of strength occasioned by disease; a deficiency of vital power.—**Adynamic; Adynamical**, a-di-nam'ik, a-di-nam'ik-al, *a.* Weak; destitute of strength.

Adytum, ad'i-tum, *n.* pl. **Adyta**, ad'i-ta. [L. *adytum*, Gr. *adyton*, lit. a place not to be entered—*a*, priv., and *dyō*, to enter.] An innermost sanctuary or shrine; the chancel or altar-end of a church.

Adz, Adze, adz, *n.* [O.E. *addice*, A.Sax. *adese*, an adze.] An instrument of the axe kind used for chipping the surface of timber, the cutting edge being at right angles to the handle.—*v.t.* To chip or shape with an adz.

Ædile. Same as *Edile*.

Ægagrus, ē-gag'rus, *n.* [Gr. *aigagros*—*aix, aigos*, a goat, and *agros*, a field.] A wild species of ibex found in troops on the Caucasus, and many Asiatic mountains.

Ægis, ē'jis, *n.* [Gr. *aigis.*] Among the ancient Greeks the shield of Zeus; in later times part of the armour of Pallas Athena, a kind of breastplate; hence, anything that protects or shields; protecting power or influence.

Ægophony, ē-gof'o-ni, *n.* [Gr. *aix, aigos*, goat, *phōnē*, voice.] A sound heard by auscultation in certain chest diseases.

Ægrotat, ē-grō'tat, *n.* [L., he is sick.] A medical certificate showing that a person is unable to attend to his duties.

Æolian. Same as *Eolian*.

Æolotropic, ē'ol-ō-trop″ik, *a.* [Gr. *aiolos*, varied, *tropē*, a turn.] Applied to bodies unequally elastic in different directions: opposed to *isotropic*.

Æon, *n.* Same as *Eon*.

Æpyornis, ē-pi-or'nis, *n.* [Gr. *aipys, aipyos*, high, and *ornis*, a bird.] A genus of gigantic birds found fossil in Madagascar.

Ærarian, ē-rā'ri-an, *n.* [L. *ærarius*, from *æs, æris*, bronze, bronze money.] A Roman citizen of the lowest class of freeman.

Aerate, ā'ėr-āt, *v.t.*—*aerated, aerating.* [L. *aer*, air, AIR.] To combine with carbonic acid or other gas, or with air.—*Aerated waters*, acidulous and alkaline beverages more or less impregnated with carbonic acid, including lemonade, soda-water, &c.—**Aeration**, ā-ėr-ā'shon, *n.* The act or operation of aerating.—**Aerator**, ā'ėr-āt-ėr, *n.* A blower; an apparatus for making aerated waters.—**Aerial**, ā-ē'ri-al, *a.* [L. *aerius.*] Belonging or pertaining to the air or atmosphere; inhabiting or frequenting the air; produced by or in the air; reaching far into the air; high; lofty; possessed of a light and graceful beauty.—**Aerially**, ā-ē'-ri-al-li, *adv.* In an aerial manner.—**Aeriferous**, ā-ėr-if'ėr-us, *a.* Conveying air.—**Aeriform**, ā'ėr-i-form, *a.* Having the form or nature of air.—**Aerify**, ā'ėr-i-fī, *v.t.*—*aerified, aerifying.* To infuse air into; to fill with air, or to combine air with; to change into an aeriform state.—**Aerification**, ā'ėr-i-fi-kā″shon, *n.* The act of aerifying.

Aerie, ē'rē or ā'ėr-i, *n.* [Fr. and Pr. *aire*, L.L. *aeria, aerea, area*, an aerie; origin doubtful.] The nest of a bird of prey, as of an eagle or hawk; a brood of eagles or hawks. Written also *Eyrie.*

Aerify. AERATE.

Aerobic, ā-ėr-ob'ik, *a.* [Gr. *aēr*, air, *bios*, life.] Requiring air or free oxygen in order to live and thrive, as certain bacteria.

Aeroclinoscope, ā'ėr-ō-klin″ō-skōp, *n.* [Gr. *aēr*, air, *klinō*, to bend or incline, *skopeō*, to view.] An apparatus for showing the direction of the wind in connection with the barometric pressure.

Aerocyst, ā'ėr-ō-sist, *n.* [Gr. *aēr*, air, *kystis*, a bladder.] An air-vesicle.

Aerodrome, ā'ėr-o-drōm, *n.* [Gr. *aēr*, air, *dromos*, a course.] A course or area for experiments in flying; shed for housing machines.

Aerodynamics, ā'ėr-ō-di-nam″iks, *n.* [Gr. *aēr, dynamis*, power.] The science treating of the motion of the air and gases, and of their effects when in motion.

Aerolite, Aerolith, ā'ėr-ō-līt, ā'ėr-ō-lith, *n.* [Gr. *aēr*, air, and *lithos*, a stone.] A meteoric stone; a meteorite.—**Aerolithology**, ā'ėr-ō-lith-ol″o-ji, *n.* The science of aerolites.—**Aerolitic**, ā'ėr-ō-lit″ik, *a.* Relating to aerolites.

Aerology, Aerognosy, ā-ėr-ol'o-ji, ā-ėr-og'no-si, *n.* [Gr. *aēr, aeros*, air, *logos*, description, *gnōsis*, knowledge.] That branch of physics which treats of the air, its constituent parts, properties, and phenomena.—**Aerologic, Aerological**, ā'ėr-ō-loj″-ik, ā'ėr-ō-loj″ik-al, *a.* Pertaining to aerology.—**Aerologist**, ā-ėr-ol'o-jist, *n.* One who is versed in aerology.

Aeromancy, ā'ėr-ō-man″si, *n.* [Gr. *aēr*, air, and *manteia*, divination.] Divination by means of the air and winds or atmospheric phenomena.

Aerometer, ā-ėr-om'et-ėr, *n.* [Gr. *aēr*, air, and *metron*, measure.] An instrument for weighing air, or for ascertaining the density of air and gases.—**Aerometric**, ā'ėr-ō-met″rik, *a.* Pertaining to aerometry.—**Aerometry**, ā-ėr-om'et-ri, *n.* The science of measuring the weight or density of air and gases.

Aeronaut, ā'ėr-ō-nąt, *n.* [Gr. *aēr*, air, and *nautēs*, a sailor, from *naus*, a ship.] An aerial navigator; a balloonist.—**Aeronautic, Aeronautical**, ā'ėr-ō-nąt″ik, ā'ėr-ō-nąt″ik-al, *a.* Pertaining to aeronautics or aerial sailing.—**Aeronautics**, ā'ėr-ō-nąt″-iks, *n.* The doctrine, science, or art of floating in the air, as by means of a balloon.—**Aeronautism**, ā'ėr-ō-nąt-izm, *n.* The practice of an aeronaut.

Aerophobia, ā'ėr-ō-fō″bi-a, *n.* [Gr. *aēr*, air, and *phobos*, fear.] A dread of air, that is, of a current of air.

Aerophore, ā'ėr-o-for, *n.* [Gr. *aēr, pherō*, to bring.] A kind of ventilating apparatus; a portable receptacle by which air is supplied artificially under water or elsewhere.

Aerophyte, ā'ėr-o-fīt, *n.* [Gr. *aēr*, air, and *phyton*, a plant.] A plant which lives exclusively in air; an air-plant.

Aeroplane, ā'ėr-ō-plān, *n.* [Gr. *aēr*, air, and E. *plane.*] Any flying machine in which the carrying or supporting surfaces are of the nature of planes, depending on the kite principle, and driven through the air by one or more screw propellers and petrol engine.

Aeroscopy, ā-ėr-os'ko-pi, *n.* [Gr. *aēr*, air, and *skopeō*, to explore.] The investigation or observation of the state and variations of the atmosphere.

Ærose, ē'rōs, *a.* [L. *ærosus*, from *æs*, copper.] Containing copper or brass; coppery.

Aerosiderite, ā'ėr-ō-sid″ėr-īt, *n.* [Gr. *aēr*, air, and *sidēros*, iron.] An iron meteorite.—**Aerosiderolite**, ā'ėr-ō-sid″ėr-o-līt, *n.* [*-lite* = Gr. *lithos*, a stone.] A meteor containing both stone and iron.

Aerostat, ā'ėr-ō-stat, *n.* [Fr. *aérostat*, a balloon—Gr. *aēr*, air, and *statos*, standing, from *histēmi*, to stand.] A machine or vessel sustaining weights in the air; a name given to air-balloons.—**Aerostatic, Aerostatical**, ā'ėr-ō-stat″ik, ā'ėr-ō-stat″ik-al, *a.* Pertaining to aerostatics; pertaining to aerostation, or aerial navigation.—**Aerostatics**, ā'ėr-ō-stat″iks, *n.* The science which treats of the weight, pressure, and equilibrium of air and other elastic fluids, and of the equilibrium of bodies sustained in them.—**Aerostation**, ā'ėr-ō-stā″shon, *n.* Aerial navigation.

Æruginous, Ærugineous, ē-rö'jin-us, ē-rö-jin'ē-us, *a.* [L. *æruginosus*, from *ærugo*, rust of copper, verdigris.] Partaking of, pertaining to, or resembling verdigris or the rust of copper.

Aery, ā'ėr-i, *a.* Airy; breezy; aerial. [Poetic.]

Aesculapian, ēs-kul-āp'i-an, *a. Med.* of or pertaining to Aesculapius, the ancient healing god.

Æsthematology, ēs-thē'ma-tol″o-ji, *n.* [Gr. *aisthēma*, a perception, and *logos*, discourse.] The doctrine of the senses, or the apparatus of the senses; that part of physiology which treats of the senses.

Æsthesia, ēs-thē'si-a, *n.* [Gr. *aisthēsis*, perception, sensibility.] Perception; feeling; sensibility.—**Æsthesiology**, ēs-thē'si-ol″-o-ji, *n.* The doctrine or branch of knowledge concerned with the sensations.

Æsthesiometer, ēs-thē'si-om″et-ėr, *n.* [Gr. *aisthēsis*, perception, and *metron*, a measure.] An instrument for testing the tactile sensibility of the human body in health and disease.

Æsthesodic, ēs-thē-sod'ik, *a.* [Gr. *aisthēsis*, and *hodos*, a path.] Capable of conducting sensation.

Æsthete, ēs'thēt, *n.* [From *æsthetic.*] One devoted to the principles or doctrines of æsthetics; a lover of the beautiful.—**Æsthetic, Æsthetical**, ēs-thet'ik, ēs-thet'-ik-al, *a.* [Gr. *aisthētikos*, from *aisthanomai*, to perceive by the senses.] Pertaining to the science of taste or beauty; pertaining to the sense of the beautiful.—**Æsthetically**, ēs-thet'ik-al-li, *adv.* According to the principles of æsthetics; with reference to the sense of the beautiful.—**Æstheticism**, ēs-thet'i-sizm, *n.* The principles or doctrines of æsthetics; attachment to æsthetics.—**Æsthetics**, ēs-thet'iks, *n.* The theory of the fine arts; the science or that branch of philosophy which deals with the beautiful; the doctrines of taste.

Æstho-physiology, ēs'thō-fiz-i-ol″o-ji, *n.* [Gr. *aisthanomai*, to perceive, and E. *physiology.*] The physiology of sensation.

Æstiferous, ēs-tif'ėr-us, *a.* [L. *æstus*, heat, and *fero*, to bear.] Producing heat.

Æstivation. ESTIVATION.

Æther. ETHER.

Æthrioscope, ēth'ri-ō-skōp, *n.* [Gr. *aithrios*, clear, pertaining to the open air, and *skopeō*, to see.] An instrument for measuring the minute variations of temperature due to different conditions of the sky.

Ætiology. ETIOLOGY.

Afar, a-fär′, *adv.* At a distance in place; to or from a distance: often with *from* preceding or *off* following, or both.

Affable, af′fa-bl, *a.* [L. *affabilis*, affable—*af* for *ad*, to, *fari*, to speak.] Easy of conversation; admitting others to free conversation without reserve; courteous; complaisant, of easy manners; condescending.—**Affability, Affableness**, af-fa-bil′i-ti, af′fa-bl-nes, *n.* The quality of being affable.—**Affably**, af′fa-bli, *adv.* In an affable manner; courteously.

Affair, af-fär′, *n.* [Fr. *affaire*—*a*, to, and *faire*, to do, L. *facere*, to make, to do.] Business of any kind; that which is done, or is to be done; matter; concern; sometimes used by itself in the plural with the specific sense of public affairs or pecuniary affairs; special business; personal concern; a rencontre; a skirmish.—*Affair of honour*, a duel.

Affect, af-fekt′, *v.t.* [L. *affecto*, to desire, to strive after, freq. of *afficio*, *affectum*, to affect the mind or body—*af* for *ad*, to, and *facio*, to do.] To act upon; to produce an effect or change upon; to influence; to move or touch by exciting the feelings; to aspire to; to endeavour after; to choose commonly; to habitually follow after; make a show of; to assume the appearance of; to pretend.—**Affectation, Affectedness**, af-fek-tā′shon, af-fekt′ed-nes, *n.* [L. *affectatio*.] An attempt to assume or exhibit what is not natural or real; false pretence, especially of what is praiseworthy or uncommon; artificial appearance or show.—**Affected**, af-fekt′ed, *a.* Inclined or disposed (especially with *well*, *ill*, &c.); given to affectation; assuming or pretending to possess what is not natural or real; assumed artificially; not natural.—**Affectedly**, af-fekt′ed-li, *adv.* In an affected or assumed manner; with affectation.—**Affecter**, af-fekt′ėr, *n.* One who affects, pretends, or assumes.—**Affecting**, af-fekt′ing, *a.* Having power to excite emotion; suited to affect; pathetic.—**Affectingly**, af-fekt′ing-li, *adv.* In an affecting or impressive manner.

Affection, af-fek′shon, *n.* [L. *affectio*, *affectionis*, the being affected or touched. AFFECT.] The state of having one's feelings affected in some way; bent or disposition of mind; sentiment or moral feeling (as esteem, envy, jealousy); appetite; inclination; a settled good-will, love, or zealous attachment; a property or attribute inseparable from its object (as figure from bodies); any particular morbid state of the body (a gouty *affection*).—**Affectionate**, af-fek′shon-āt, *a.* Having great love or affection; warmly attached; fond; kind; loving; proceeding from affection; tender.—**Affectionately**, af-fek′shon-āt-li, *adv.* In an affectionate manner; fondly; tenderly; kindly.—**Affectionateness**, af-fek′shon-āt-nes, *n.* The quality of being affectionate; fondness; affection.—**Affectioned**, af-fek′shond, *a.* Having a certain disposition of feeling; disposed.

Affeer, af-fēr′, *v.t.* [O.Fr. *afferer*, *afforer*, to assess or value, from L. *forum*, a market.] *Law*, to assess or settle, as an arbitrary fine.

Afferent, af′fėr-ent, *a.* [L. *afferens*, *afferentis*, ppr. of *affero*—*af* for *ad*, to, and *fero*, to carry. Carrying to or inwards (of vessels or nerves in animals).

Affiance, af-fī′ans, *n.* [O.Fr., from *af* for *ad*, to, and *fiancer*, to betroth, L. *fidans*, *fidantis*, ppr. of *fido*, to pledge one's faith, *fides*, faith.] Marriage contract or promise; faith pledged; confidence; reliance.—*v.t.*—*affianced*, *affiancing*. To betroth; to bind by promise of marriage.—**Affianced**, af-fī′anst, *n.* One bound by a promise of marriage; a betrothed wife.—**Affiancer**, af-fī′ans-ėr, *n.* One who affiances.

Affidavit, af-fi-dā′vit, *n.* [3rd pers. sing. perf. ind. of L.L. *affido*, to pledge one's faith—L. *af* for *ad*, to, and *fides*, faith.] A written declaration upon oath; a statement of facts in writing signed by the party, and sworn to or confirmed by declaration before an authorized magistrate.

Affiliate, af-fil′i-āt, *v.t.*—*affiliated*, *affiliating*. [L.L. *adfiliare*, to adopt as a son—L. *ad*, to, and *filius*, a son.] To adopt; to receive into a family as a son; to establish the paternity of, as of a bastard child, to connect in the way of descent; to receive into a society as a member.—**Affiliation**, af-fil′i-ā″shon, *n.* The act of one who affiliates; the settlement of the paternity of a child on its true father.—**Affiliable**, af-fil′i-a-bl, *a.* Capable of being affiliated.

Affined,† af-fīnd′, *a.* [O.Fr. *affiner*, to unite. AFFINITY.] Joined in affinity, akin, bound or impelled by any kind of affinity. [*Shak.*]

Affinity, af-fin′i-ti, *n.* [L. *affinitas*, from *affinis*, adjacent, related—*af* for *ad*, to, and *finis*, boundary.] The relation contracted by marriage, in contradistinction from *consanguinity*, or relation by blood; relation, connection, or alliance in general (as of languages, sounds, &c.); similarity in kind or nature; *chem.* that force by which bodies of dissimilar nature unite in certain definite proportions to form a compound, different in its nature from any of its constituents.—**Affinitatively**, af-fin′i-tāt-iv-li, *adv.* By means of affinity.

Affirm, af-fėrm′, *v.t.* [L. *affirmo*—*af* for *ad*, to, and *firmo*, to make firm.] To assert positively, to tell with confidence, to aver; declare; allege: opposed to *deny*, to confirm or ratify.—*v.i.* To make a solemn assertion or declaration; to make a legal affirmation.—**Affirmable**, af-fėrm′a-bl, *a.* Capable of being affirmed, asserted, or declared.—**Affirmably**, af-fėrm′a-bli, *adv.* In a way capable of affirmation.—**Affirmance**,† af-fėrm′ans, *n.* Confirmation; ratification; affirmation.—**Affirmant**, **Affirmer**, af-fėrm′ant, af-fėrm′ėr, *n.* One who affirms or asserts; one who makes affirmation instead of an oath.—**Affirmation**, af-fėr-mā′shon, *n.* The act of affirming or asserting as true; that which is asserted; averment; confirmation; ratification; a solemn declaration made in lieu of an oath by one who has scruples about taking the oath.—**Affirmative**, af-fėrm′at-iv, *a.* Affirming or asserting: opposed to *negative*.—*n.* A word or phrase expressing assent or affirmation or answering a question affirmatively; the opposite of a negative.—*The affirmative*, that side of a debated question which maintains the truth of the affirmative proposition.—**Affirmatively**, af-fėrm′at-iv-li, *adv.* In an affirmative manner; positively.

Affix, af-fiks′, *v.t.* [L. *affigo*, *affixum*—*af* for *ad*, to, and *figo*, *fixum*, to fix.] To subjoin, annex, unite, or add at the close or end; to append; to attach.—**Affix**, af′fiks, *n.* A syllable or letter added to the end of a word; a suffix; a post-fix.—**Affixal**, af-fiks′al, *a.* Pertaining to an affix; having the character of an affix.—**Affixion**,† af-fik′shon, *n.* The act of affixing.

Afflation, af-flā′shon, *n.* [L. *afflo*, *afflatum*—*af* for *ad*, to, and *flo*, to blow.] A blowing or breathing on.—**Afflatus**, af-flā′tus, *n.* [L.] A breath or blast of wind; inspiration; the inspiration of the poet.

Afflict, af-flikt′, *v.t.* [L. *afflicto*, intens. of *affligo*, to dash down—*af* for *ad*, to, and *fligo*, to strike.] To give (to the body or mind) pain which is continued or of some permanence; to trouble, grieve, harass, or distress.—**Afflicter**, af-flikt′ėr, *n.* One who afflicts.—**Afflicting**, af-flikt′ing, *a.* Grievous; distressing (an *afflicting* event).—**Afflictingly**, af-flikt′ing-li, *adv.* In an afflicting manner.—**Affliction**, af-flik′shon, *n.* The state of being afflicted; a state of acute pain or distress of body or mind; the cause of continued pain of body or mind. ∴ *Affliction* is stronger than *grief*, and *grief* than *sorrow*. *Affliction* is acute mental suffering caused by the loss of something cherished, as friends, health, or fortune.—**Afflictive**, af-flikt′iv, *a.* Painful; distressing.—**Afflictively**, af-flikt′iv-li, *adv.*

Affluence, af′flu-ens, *n.* [L. *affluentia*, from *affluo*, to flow to—*ad*, to, and *fluo*, to flow. FLUENT.] A flowing to or concourse; an abundant supply; great plenty of worldly goods; wealth. Also **Affluency**, af′flu-en-si.—**Affluent**, af′flu-ent, *a.* Flowing to; wealthy; abundant.—*n.* A tributary stream.—**Affluently**, af′flu-ent-li, *adv.*

Afflux, af′fluks, *n.* [From L. *affluo*, *affluxum*. AFFLUENCE.] The act of flowing to; a flowing to, or that which flows to.

Afford, af-förd′, *v.t.* [O.E. *aforth*, to afford, from prefix *a*, and *forth*; A. Sax. *forthian*, to further.] To give forth; to yield, supply, or produce (fruit, profit); to grant or confer (as consolation, gratification); to buy, sell, expend, &c., from having a sufficiency of means; to bear the expense of (with *can*, *could*, *may*, *might*, &c.).

Afforest, af-for′est, *v.t.* [Prefix *af* for *ad*, to, and *forest*.] To convert into a forest; to turn into forest land.—**Afforestation**, af-for′es-tā″shon, *n.* The act of.

Afformative, af-form′a-tiv, *n.* [Prefix *af* for *ad*, to, and *formative*.] An affix.

Affranchise, af-fran′chiz, *v.t.* [Prefix *af*, and *franchise*.] To make free; to liberate from servitude.—**Affranchisement**, af-fran′chiz-ment, *n.* The act of.

Affray, af-frā′, *v.t.* [O or Prov. Fr. *affraier*, *effroyer*, Fr. *effrayer*, to frighten; from L.L. *exfrediare*—L. *ex*, intens., and O.H.G. *fridu*, G. *friede*, peace. AFRAID.] To frighten; to terrify.—*n.* Fear†; a noisy quarrel; a brawl; a tumult; disturbance.

Affreight, af-frāt′, *v.t.* [Prefix *af* for *ad*, to, and *freight*.] To hire for the transportation of freight; to freight.

Affright, af-frīt′, *v.t.* [A.Sax. *afyrhtian*, *afyrhtan*—prefix *a*, intens., and *fyrhtan*, to frighten. FRIGHT.] To impress with sudden fear; to frighten.—*n.* Sudden or great fear; terror.—**Affrightedly**, af-frīt′ed-li, *adv.* With fright.—**Affrighten**,† af-frīt′n, *v.t.* To terrify; to affright.—**Affrightment**, af-frīt′ment, *n.* The act of terrifying, affright; terror.

Affront, af-frunt′, *v.t.* [Fr. *affronter*, to encounter face to face—*af* for *ad*, to, and L. *frons*, *frontis*, front, face.] To confront (*Shak.*)†; to offend by an open manifestation of disrespect; to insult; to put out of countenance.—*n.* An open manifestation of disrespect or contumely; an outrage to the feelings; an insult; anything producing a feeling of shame or disgrace.—**Affronter**, af-frunt′ėr, *n.* One who affronts.

Affuse, af-fūz′, *v.t.*—*affused*, *affusing*. [L. *affundo*, *affusum*—*af* for *ad*, to, and *fundo*, *fusum*, to pour out.] To pour upon; to sprinkle, as with a liquid.—**Affusion**, af-fū′zhon, *n.* The act of pouring or sprinkling liquid upon; *med.* the act of pouring water on the body as a curative means.

Affy,† af-fī′, *v.t.*—*affied*, *affying*. [AFFIANCE.] To betroth; to affiance.—*v.i.* To trust or confide.

Afield, a-fēld′, *adv.* To the field; in the field; astray.

Afire, a-fīr′, *a.* or *adv.* On fire.

Aflame, a-flām′, *a.* or *adv.* Flaming; glowing.

Aflat, a-flat′, *a.* or *adv.* On a level with the ground.

Aflaunt, a-flant′, *a.* or *adv.* In a flaunting manner; with showy equipage or dress.

Afloat, a-flōt′, *a.* or *adv.* Borne on the water; floating; passing from one person to another; in circulation (as a rumour).

Afoam, a-fōm′, *a.* or *adv.* In a foaming state; foaming.

Afoot, a-fut′, *a.* or *adv.* On foot; borne by the feet; walking; in a state of being planned for execution (as a plan or plot).

Afore, a-fōr′, *adv.* [Prefix *a*, at, and *fore*; A.Sax. *onforan*.] Before in time or place: now mainly a nautical term; in the fore part of a vessel.—*prep.* Before in time, position, rank, &c.; in presence of: now a *naut.* term.; more toward the head of a ship than; nearer the stem than.—*A′ore the mast*, applied to a common sailor.—**Aforegoing**, a-fōr′gō-ing, *a.* Going before.—**Aforehand**, a-fōr′hand, *adv.* In time previous; by previous provision; not behindhand.—**Aforementioned, Aforenamed, Aforesaid**, a-fōr′men-shond, a-fōr′nāmd, a-fōr′sed, *a.* Mentioned before in the same writing or discourse.—**Aforethought**, a-fōr′that, *a.* Thought of beforehand; premeditated; prepense.—**Afore-**

time, a-fōr'tīm, *adv.* In time past; formerly. [N.T.]

Afraid, a-frād', *a.* or *pp.* [O.E. *affrayd*, *afrayde*, &c., pp. of *affray*. AFFRAY.] Impressed with fear or apprehension; fearful: not used attributively. [Colloquially, *I am afraid* is often nearly equivalent to I suspect, I am inclined to think, or the like.]

Afresh, a-fresh', *adv.* Anew; again; after intermission.

African, af'rik-an, *a.* Pertaining to Africa. —*n.* A native of Africa.—**Africander**, af'rik-an-dėr, *n.* [African-Dutch *Afrikander*; modelled on analogy of England-er, Holland-er.] A native of South Africa born of white parents.—**Africanize**, af'rik-an-īz, *v.t.* To give an African or negro character to.

Afrit, **Afreet**, af-rit', af-rēt', *n.* *Mohammedan myth.* a powerful evil jinnee or demon. Written also *Efreet*, *Afrite*.

Afront, a-frunt', *adv.* In front. [*Shak.*]

Aft, aft, *a.* or *adv.* [A.Sax. *æft*, *eft*, after, behind; Goth. *afta*; from A.Sax. *af*, *æf*, Goth. *af*, E. *of*, *off*.] *Naut.* a word used to denote position at or near, or direction towards the stern of a ship.

After, aft'ėr, *a.* [A.Sax. *æfter*, a compar. from *af*, E. *of*, *off*, *-ter* being the compar. syllable, seen as *-ther* in *whether*, *hither*, as *-der* in *under*. OF.] Later in time; subsequent, succeeding; as, an *after* period of life in this sense often combined with the following noun.—*prep.* Behind in place; later in time; in pursuit of; in search of; with or in desire for; in imitation of, or in imitation of the style of (*after* a model); according to; in proportion to (*after* our deserts); below in rank or excellence; next to; concerning (inquire *after*).—*After all*, at last, upon the whole; at the most; notwithstanding.—*adv.* Later in time; afterwards, behind; in pursuit.—**Afterings**, aft'ėr-ingz, *n.pl.* The last milk drawn in milking; strokings.

After-age, *n.* A later age or time; posterity.—**After-birth**, *n.* That which is expelled from the uterus after the birth of a child: called also *Secundines*.—**After-body** *n.* That part of a ship's hull which is abaft the midships.—**After-cost**, *n.* Expense after the execution of the main design.—**After-crop**, *n.* The second crop in the same year.—**After-damp**, *n.* Choke-damp or carbonic acid, found in coal-mines after an explosion of 'fire-damp'.—**After-glow**, *n.* The glow in the west after sunset.—**After-grass**, *n.* The grass which again springs up from land previously mowed the same year.—**After-growth**, *n.* A second growth or crop springing up after a previous one has been removed.—**After-hold**, *n.* That portion of a ship's hold lying behind the mainmast.—**After-hours**, *n pl* Hours that follow business; time following.—**After-image**, *n.* The image of a bright object left for a time on the retina.—**After-life**, *n.* Future life; remainder of life; the life after death.—**After-math**, *n.* A second mowing of grass from the same land in the same season. —**After-mentioned**, *a.* Mentioned or to be mentioned afterwards.—**Afternoon**, *n.* The part of the day which follows noon, between noon and evening.—**After-pains**, *n. pl.* The pains which succeed childbirth.—**After-part**, *n.* The latter part, the part of a ship towards the stern. —**After-piece**, *n.* A short dramatic entertainment performed after the principal performance.—**After-sail**, *n.* One of a vessel's sails on the main and mizzen masts. —**After-taste**, *n.* A taste which succeeds eating or drinking.—**After-thought**, *n.* Reflection after an act, some consideration that occurs to one's mind too late or after the performance of the act to which it refers.—**After-time**, *n.* Succeeding time: more commonly in the plural.—**After-wise**, *a.* Wise after the event; wise when it is too late.—**After-wit**, *n.* Wisdom that comes too late.

Aftermost, aft'ėr-mōst, *a. superl.* [A.Sax. *æftemest*, a double superlative, *mest* being from *ma* + *st*, two superlative suffixes.] Hindmost: opposed to *foremost*.

Afterward, **Afterwards**, aft'ėr-wėrd, aft'ėr-wėrdz, *adv.* [A.Sax. *æfterweard*. *Afterwards* is an adverbial genitive. WARD.] In later or subsequent time.

Aga, ā'ga, *n.* In the Turkish dominions, a commander or chief officer.

Again, a-gen' or a-gān', *adv.* [A.Sax. *ongeán*, again; *geán*, against. AGAINST.] A second time; once more; on another occasion; on the other hand; moreover; besides; further; in return; back; in answer.

Against, a-genst', *prep.* [O.E. *agayns*, *ongaenes*, A.Sax. *ongeán*, against. The *es* is an adverbial or genit. termination and the *t* has been added, like that in *amidst*, *betwixt*. A.Sax. *geán*, again or against, is the same as *gain* in *gainsay*; G. *gegen*, against.] Opposite in place (often preceded by *over*); in opposition to; adverse or hostile to (*against* law or public opinion); towards or upon; so as to meet (to strike *against* a rock); bearing or resting upon (to lean *against*); in preparation for (an event).

Agallochum, a-gal'lok-um, *n.* [Gr. *agallochon*.] A fragrant wood used by the Orientals as supplying a perfume.

Agalmatolite, a-gal-mat'ō-līt, *n.* [Gr. *agalma*, image, and *lithos*, stone.] A kind of soft stone found in China and resembling steatite, often cut into images.

Agami, ag'a-mi, *n.* [Native name.] The golden-breasted trumpeter, a bird of the crane family, a native of South America.

Agamic, a-gam'ik, *a.* [Gr. *a*, priv., and *gamos*, marriage.] Reproduced without the congress of individuals of the opposite sex. —**Agamist**, ag'am-ist, *n.* One who refuses or rejects marriage.

Agamogenesis, a-gam'ō-jen"e-sis, *n.* [Gr. *a*, priv., *gamos*, marriage, and *genesis*, reproduction.] The production of young without the congress of the sexes.—**Agamogenetic**, a-gam'ō-jen-et"ik, *a.* Of or pertaining to agamogenesis.

Agape, a-gāp', *adv.* or *a.* Gaping as with wonder; having the mouth wide open.

Agape, ag'a-pē, *n.* [Gr. *agapē*, love.] Among the primitive Christians a love-feast or feast of charity, held before or after the communion, when contributions were made for the poor.

Agar-agar, āgar-ā'gar, *n.* The native name of a dried sea-weed much used in the East for soups and jellies.

Agaric, a-gar'ik, *n.* [Gr. *agarikon*.] A name of various fungi. Many of the species are edible like the common mushroom, while others are deleterious and even poisonous. —*Agaric mineral*, *mountain-milk*, or *mountain-meal*, a native carbonate of lime, resembling a fungus; a stone of which bricks may be made so light as to float in water.

Agast. AGHAST.

Agastric, a-gas'trik, *a.* [Gr. *a*, without, and *gastēr*, *gastros*, belly.] Without a stomach, or proper intestinal canal, as the tape-worm.

Agate, ag'āt, *n.* [Fr. *agate*, from L. *achates*, so called because found near a river of that name in Sicily.] A semipellucid mineral, consisting of bands or layers of various colours blended together, the base generally being chalcedony, and this mixed with jasper, amethyst, quartz, opal, &c.: used for rings, seals, cups, beads, &c.; an instrument used by gold-wire drawers, so called from the agate in the middle of it; a gilder's tool; a kind of type, called also *Ruby*.—**Agatiferous**, ag-ā-tif'ėr-us, *a.* Containing or producing agates.—**Agatine**, ag'āt-īn, *a.* Pertaining to or resembling agate.—**Agatize**, ag'āt-īz, *v.t.* To change into agate.—*Agatized wood*, a kind of hornstone formed by petrifaction.—**Agaty**, ag'āt-i, *a.* Of the nature of agate.

Agave, a-gā'vē, *n.* [Gr. *agauos*, noble. A genus of plants, comprehending the American aloe. They live for many years—ten to seventy—before flowering.

Age, āj, *n.* [Fr. *âge*, O.Fr. *eage*, L.L. *ætaticum*, from L. *ætas*, *ætatis*, abbrev. of *ævitas*, from *ævum*, an age. EVER.] A period of time representing the whole or a part of the duration of any individual thing or being; the time during which an individual has lived; the latter part of life; the state of being old; oldness; old people collectively; the state of having arrived at legal maturity (the completion of the first twenty-one years of one's life); great length of time; a long or protracted period, sometimes definitely a century; a historical epoch; an epoch having a particular character; the people who live at a particular period.—*The age*, the times we live in.—*v.i.*—*aged* (ājd), *aging*. To grow old; to assume the appearance of old age.—*v.t.* To give the character of age or ripeness to (to *age* wine).—**Aged**, āj'ed, *a.* Old; having lived long; having a certain age (*aged* forty years); in this sense often ājd).—**Agedly**, āj'ed-li, *adv.* Like an aged person.—**Agedness**, āj'ed-nes, *n.* The state or condition of being aged; oldness.

Agenda, a-jen'da, *n. pl.* [L., things to be done.] Memoranda; a memorandum-book; a church service; a ritual or liturgy.

Agent, ā'jent, *n.* [L. *agens*, *agentis*, acting. ACT.] One who or that which acts; an actor; one that exerts power or has the power to act; an active power or cause; a body or substance that causes a certain action to begin; a person entrusted with the business of another.—**Agency**, ā'jen-si, *n.* The state of being in action or of exerting power; operation; instrumentality; the office or business of an agent or factor.—**Agential**, ā-jen'shal, *a.* Pertaining to an agent or agency.

Ageustia, a-gūs'ti-a, *n.* [Gr. *a*, priv., and *geuomai*, to taste.] *Med.* a defect or loss of taste.

Agglomerate, ag-glom'ėr-āt, *v.t.*—*agglomerated*, *agglomerating*. [L. *agglomero*—*ad*, and *glomus*, *glomeris*, a ball of yarn.] To collect or gather into a mass.—*v.i.* To become collected into a ball or mass.—*n.* *Geol.* a collective name for masses consisting of angular fragments ejected from volcanoes.—**Agglomeration**, ag-glom'-ėr-ā"shon, *n.* The act of agglomerating; a collection; a heap.—**Agglomerative**, ag-glom'ėr-āt-iv, *a.* Disposed to agglomerate.

Agglutinate, ag-glū'tin-āt, *v.t.*—*agglutinated*, *agglutinating*. [L. *agglutino*—*ad*, and *glutino*, from *gluten*, glue. GLUE.] To unite or cause to adhere, as with glue or other viscous substance; to glue together. —*a.* United as by glue; joined.—*Agglutinate* or *Agglutinating languages*, in *philol.* those languages in which the suffixes for inflection retain a kind of independence, and are felt to be distinct from the root or main significant element of the word.—**Agglutinant**, ag-glū'tin-ant, *a.* Uniting as glue; tending to cause adhesion.—*n.* Any viscous substance which agglutinates or unites other substances.—**Agglutination**, ag-glū'tin-ā"shon, *n.* The act of agglutinating or the state; adhesion of parts; the marked feature of agglutinate languages.—**Agglutinative**, ag-glū'tin-āt-iv, *a.* Tending or having power to agglutinate.

Aggrandize, ag'gran-dīz, *v.t.*—*aggrandized*, *aggrandizing*. [Fr. *agrandir*—L. prefix *a* for *ad*, to, and *grandis*, grand.] To make great or greater: especially to make greater in power, wealth, rank, or honour; to exalt; to elevate; extend; enlarge.—**Aggrandizement**, ag'gran-dīz-ment or ag-gran'dīz-ment, *n.* The act of aggrandizing; the act of increasing one's own power, rank, or honour; advancement.—**Aggrandizer**, ag'gran-dīz-ėr, *n.* One that aggrandizes.—**Aggrandizable**, ag'gran-dīz-a-bl, *a.* Capable of being.—**Aggrandization**, ag'gran-dīz-ā"shon, *n.* The act of.

Aggravate, ag'gra-vāt, *v.t.*—*aggravated*, *aggravating*. [L. *aggravo*—*ad*, to, and *gravis*, heavy. whence *grave*, *grief*, &c.] To make worse, more severe, or less tolerable; to make more enormous, or less excusable; to intensify; to exaggerate; to provoke; irritate; tease.—**Aggravating**, ag'gra-vāt-ing, *a.* Provoking; annoying.—**Aggravatingly**, ag'gra-vāt-ing-li, *adv.* In an aggravating manner.—**Aggravation**, ag-gra-vā″shon, *n.* The act of aggravating or making worse; addition to that which is evil or improper; provocation; irritation.

Aggregate, ag′grē-gāt, *v.t.—aggregated, aggregating.* [L. *aggrego, aggregatum—ad*, and *grex, gregis*, a herd or band.] To bring together; to collect into a sum, mass, or body.—*a.* Formed by the conjunction or collection of particulars into a whole mass or sum; total.—*n.* A sum, mass, or assemblage of particulars; a whole or total.—*In the aggregate*, taken altogether; considered as a whole; collectively.—**Aggregately**, ag′grē-gāt-li, *adv.* Collectively; taken in a sum or mass.—**Aggregation**, ag-grē-gā′shon, *n.* The act of aggregating; the state of; an aggregate.—**Aggregative**, ag′grē-gāt-iv, *a.* Tending to aggregate; collective.—**Aggregator**, ag′grē-gāt-ėr, *n.* One who collects into a whole or mass.

Aggress, ag-gres′, *v.i.* [L. *aggredior, aggressus—ad*, and *gradior*, to go.] To make a first attack; to commit the first act of hostility or offence.—*v.t.*† To attack.—**Aggression**, ag-gre′shon, *n.* The first attack or act of hostility; the first act leading to a war or controversy.—**Aggressive**, aggres′iv, *a.* Characterized by aggression; tending to aggress.—**Aggressiveness**, ag-gres′iv-nes, *n.* The quality of being aggressive.—**Aggressor**, ag-gres′ėr, *n.* The person who aggresses; an assaulter; an invader.

Aggrieve, ag-grēv′, *v.t.—aggrieved, aggrieving.* [O.Fr. *agrever*, to weigh down, from *grever*, to oppress, from L. *gravis*, heavy, whence also *grief, grave*, &c.] To give pain or sorrow; to afflict; to grieve; to bear hard upon; to oppress or injure in one's rights.—**Aggrievance**,† ag-grēv′ans, *n.* Oppression; hardship; grievance.

Aghast, a-gast′, *a.* or *p.* [A participial form from O.E. *agasten, agesten*, to terrify—prefix *a*, intens., and A.Sax. *gaestan*, to terrify: allied to Goth. *gaisjan; usgaisjan*, to terrify; comp. Prov. E. *gast*, to terrify, *gast*, fear, *gastful.*] Struck with amazement; stupefied with sudden fright or horror. Written also *agast*, which is etymologically the better spelling.

Agile, aj′il, *a.* [Fr. *agile*; L. *agilis*, from *ago*. ACT.] Nimble; quick in movement; brisk; active.—**Agilely**, aj′il-li, *adv.* In an agile or nimble manner.—**Agility**, **Agileness**, a-jil′i-ti, aj′il-nes, *n.* The state or quality of being agile; nimbleness; briskness; activity.

Agio, ā-ji-ō, *n.* [It.] The difference in value between one sort of money and another, especially between paper-money and metallic coin.—**Agiotage**, ā-ji-ot-āj, *n.* The manœuvres by which speculators in stocks contrive to lower or enhance their price; stock-jobbing.

Agist, a-jist′, *v.t.* [O.Fr. *agister*, from *giste* (Fr. *gîte*), a lodging; L. *jacitum*, from *jacere*, to lie.] *Law*, to take the cattle of others to graze at a certain sum.—**Agistage**, **Agistment**, a-jist′āj, a-jist′ment, *n.* The taking and feeding of other men's cattle; the price paid for such feeding.

Agitate, aj′it-āt, *v.t.—agitated, agitating.* [L. *agito, agitatum*, freq. from *ago*. ACT.] To move or force into violent irregular action; to shake or move briskly; to disturb; to perturb; to discuss; debate; arouse public attention to, as by speeches, pamphlets, &c.—*v.i.* To engage in agitation.—**Agitable**, aj′it-a-bl, *a.* Capable of being agitated.—**Agitated**, aj′it-āt-ed, *a.* Disturbed; perturbed; excited; expressing agitation (countenance, manner).—**Agitation**, aj-it-ā′shon, *n.* The act of agitating, or state of being agitated; perturbation of mind or feelings; commotion; disturbance.—**Agitative**, aj′it-āt-iv, *a.* Having a tendency to agitate.—**Agitator**, aj′it-āt-ėr, *n.* One who or that which agitates, rouses, or stirs up.

Aglet, ag′let, *n.* [Fr. *aiguillette*, a point, from *aiguille*, a needle; L. *acus*, a needle.] A metal tag at the end of a lace or point, formerly worn on dresses.

Aglow, a-glō′, *a.* In a glow; glowing.

Aglutition, ag-glū-ti′shon, *n.* [Gr. *a*, priv., and L. *glutio*, to swallow.] Inability to swallow.

Agminate, **Agminated**, ag′min-āt, ag′min-āt-ed, *a.* [L. *agmen, agminis*, a crowd, a band.] Crowded; closely packed; *anat.* applied to certain glands or follicles in the small intestines.

Agnail, ag′nāl, *n.* [A.Sax. *angnægl=ange*, pain, and *nægl*, nail.] A sore hard as a nail; a corn; corrupted to *hangnail*, from false idea of sore on finger-nail.

Agnate, ag′nāt, *n.* [L. *agnatus—ad*, and *nascor, natus*, to be born.] Any male relation by the father's side.—*a.* Related or akin by the father's side.—**Agnatic**, agnat′ik, *a.* Pertaining to descent by the male line of ancestors.—**Agnation**, ag-nā′shon, *n.* Relation by the father's side only, or descent in the male line.

Agnomen, ag-nō′men, *n.* [L.—*ag* for *ad*, to, and *nomen*, a name.] An additional name or epithet conferred on a person.—**Agnomination**,† ag-nom′in-ā″shon, *n.* An additional name or title.

Agnostic, ag-nos′tik, *n.* [Gr. *agnōstos*, unknowing, unknown, from *a*, priv., and stem of *gignōskō*, to know. Same root as *know.*] One of those persons who disclaim any knowledge of God or of the origin of the universe or of anything but material phenomena, holding that with regard to such matters nothing can be known.—*a.* Pertaining to the agnostics or their doctrines.—**Agnosticism**, ag-nos′ti-sizm, *n.* The doctrines or belief of agnostics.

Agnus, ag′nus, *n.* [L., a lamb.] An image of a lamb as emblematical of our Saviour; an agnus Dei.—*Agnus Dei.* [L., Lamb of God.] A medal, or more frequently a cake of wax, consecrated by the pope, stamped with the figure of a lamb supporting the banner of the cross; supposed to possess great virtues, such as preserving those who carry it in faith from accidents, &c.

Agnus Castus, ag′nus kas′tus, *n.* [Gr. *agnos*, name of the shrub, and *castus*, L. chaste; it was supposed to be preservative of chastity.] A shrub of the verbena family, a native of the Mediterranean countries, with white flowers and acrid, aromatic fruits.

Ago, a-gō′, *a.* or *adv.* [Really a *pp.*, being shortened form of *agone*, formerly used in same sense; A.Sax. *āgān*, gone by—*ā*, away, *gān*, to go.] Past; gone; as, a year ago.

Agog, a-gog′, *adv.* [Prefix *a*, on, and W. *gog*, activity, *gogi*, to shake.] In eager excitement; highly excited by eagerness after an object.

Agoing, a-gō′ing, *adv.* [Prefix *a* for *on*, and verbal noun *going.*] In motion (to set a machine *agoing*).

Agone,‡ a-gon′, *adv.* Ago. [O.T.]

Agonic, a-gon′ik, *a.* [Gr. *a*, priv., and *gōnia*, an angle.] Not forming an angle.—*Agonic lines*, two lines on the earth's surface, on which the magnetic needle points to the true north, or where the magnetic meridian coincides with the geographical.—**Agone**, ag′ōn, *n.* An agonic line.

Agonist,† ag′ō-nist, *n.* [Gr. *agōnistēs*. AGONY.] One who contends for the prize in public games; a combatant; a champion.—**Agonistics**, ag-ō-nist′iks, *n.* The art of contending in public games.

Agony, ag′ō-ni, *n.* [Gr. *agōnia*, struggle, anguish, from *agōn*, a contest or struggle, from *agō*, to lead, to bring together.] A violent contest or striving‡; the struggle, frequently unconscious, that precedes natural death; the death throe or pang (often in plural); extreme bodily or mental pain; intense suffering; anguish; torment. ∴ *Agony* is extreme bodily pain; *anguish* is mental pain or the effect of extreme distress on the mind.—**Agony column**. Column of advertisements in newspapers, anxiously requesting information about absent relatives, &c.—**Agonize**, ag′ō-nīz, *v.i.*—*agonized, agonizing.* To writhe with agony or extreme pain.—*v.t.* To distress with extreme pain; to torture.—**Agonizing**, ag′ō-nīz-ing, *a.* Giving extreme pain.—**Agonizingly**, ag′ō-nīz-ing-li, *adv.*

Agouta, a-gö′ta, *n.* [W. Indian name.] An insectivorous animal peculiar to Hayti, of the tanrec family, and rather larger than a rat.

Agouti, a-gö′ti, *n.* The native American name of several species of rodent mammals allied to the guinea pig.

Agraffe, **Agraff**, a-graf′, *n.* [Fr. *agrafe.*] A sort of hook or clasp, often jewelled.

Agraphia, a-graf′i-a, *n.* [Gr. *a*, priv., and *graphō*, to write.] A form of aphasia, in which the patient is unable to express ideas by written signs.

Agrarian, a-grā′ri-an, *a.* [L. *agrarius*, from *ager*, a field. ACRE.] Relating to lands, especially public lands; growing wild in fields†.—*Agrarian laws*, in ancient Rome, laws for regulating the distribution of the public lands among the citizens.—*n.* One in favour of an equal division of landed property.—**Agrarianism**, a-grā′ri-an-izm, *n.* The upholding of an equal division of lands and property; the principles of one who does so.—**Agrarianize**, a-grā′ri-an-īz, *v.t.* To distribute among the people, as land.

Agree, a-grē′, *v.i.—agreed, agreeing.* [Fr. *agréer—a*, to, and *gré*, O.Fr. *gret*, good-will, favour, from L. *gratus*, pleasant, whence *gratitude, grateful*, &c.] To be of one mind; to harmonize in opinion; to live in concord or without contention; to come to an arrangement or understanding; to arrive at a settlement (*agree to* a proposal; *agree with* a person); to be consistent; to harmonize; not to contradict or be repugnant (stories *agree with* each other); to tally; to match; to correspond; to suit; to be accommodated or adapted (food *agrees with* a person); *gram.* to correspond in number, case, gender, or person.—**Agreeability**, a-grē′a-bil″i-ti, *n.* Agreeableness.—**Agreeable**, a-grē′a-bl, *a.* Suitable; conformable; correspondent; pleasing, either to the mind or senses (*agreeable* manners; *agreeable* to the taste); willing or ready to agree or consent; giving consent: with *to*.—**Agreeableness**, a-grē′a-bl-nes, *n.* The state or quality of being agreeable; the quality of pleasing.—**Agreeably**, a-grē′a-bli, *adv.* In an agreeable manner; suitably; consistently; conformably; in a manner to give pleasure; pleasingly.—**Agreement**, a-grē′ment, *n.* The state of agreeing or being agreed; harmony; conformity; union of opinions or sentiments; bargain; compact; contract.

Agrestial,† **Agrestic**,† a-gres′ti-al, a-gres′tik, *a.* [L. *agrestis*, from *ager*, a field.] Rural; rustic.

Agriculture, ag′ri-kul-tūr, *n.* [L. *agricultura—ager*, a field, and *cultura*, cultivation. ACRE and CULTURE.] The cultivation of the ground, more especially with the plough and in large areas or fields; it may include also the raising and feeding of cattle or other live stock; husbandry; tillage; farming.—**Agricultural**, ag-ri-kul′tūr-al, *a.* Pertaining to, connected with, or engaged in agriculture.—**Agriculturist**, **Agriculturalist**, ag-ri-kul′tūr-ist, ag-ri-kul′tūr-al-ist, *n.* One engaged or skilled in agriculture; a husbandman.

Agrimony, ag′ri-mon-i, *n.* [L. *argemonia*, from Gr. *argema*, a whitish ulceration on the eye (which this plant was supposed to cure), from *argos*, white.] A British plant formerly of much repute as a medicine. Its leaves and root-stock are astringent, and the latter yields a yellow dye.

Agrin, a-grin′, *a.* or *adv.* In the act or state of grinning; on the grin.

Agriology, ag-ri-ol′o-ji, *n.* [Gr. *agrios*, pertaining to a wild state, and *logos*, a discourse.] The comparative study of human customs, especially of the customs of man in a rude or uncivilized state.—**Agriologist**, ag-ri-ol′o-jist, *n.* A student of agriology.

Agronomy, a-gron′ō-mi, *n.* [Gr. *agronomos*, rural, from *agros*, a field.] Agriculture and other rural pursuits.—**Agronomic**, **Agronomical**, ag-rō-nom′ik, ag-rō-nom'ik-al, *a.* Relating to agronomy.—**Agronomist**, a-gron'ō-mist, *n.* One who studies agronomy.

Agrostography, a-gros-tog'ra-fi, *n.* [Gr. *agrōstis*, a grass.] A description of grasses.—**Agrostology**, a-gros-tol'o-ji, *n.* That part of botany which relates to grasses.

Aground, a-ground', *adv.* or *a.* On the ground; run ashore; stranded.

Agroupment, a-gröp'ment, *n.* [Fr. *agrouper*, to group.] The arrangement of a group in a picture or in statuary; grouping.

Agrypnotic, ag-rip-not'ik, *n.* [Gr. *agrypnos*, sleepless.] Something which tends to drive away sleep.

Aguardiente, ä'gwär-dē-ent"ā, *n.* [Sp., contr. for *agua ardiente*, burning water.] A second-class brandy made from the red wines of Spain and Portugal.

Ague, ā'gū, *n.* [Fr. *aigu*, acute; *fièvre aiguë* (L.L. *febris acuta*), acute fever; L. *acutus*, sharp.] The cold fit or rigor which precedes a fever or a paroxysm of fever in intermittents; a fever coming in periodical fits accompanied by shivering; a chill or state of shaking not resulting from disease.—**Agued**, ā'gūd, *a.* Having a fit of ague; shivering with cold or fear.—**Aguish**, ā'gū-ish, *a.* Having the qualities of an ague; productive of agues; chilly, shivering.—**Aguishness**, ā'gū-ish-nes, *n.* The quality of being aguish; chilliness.—**Ague-cake**, *n.* The tumour caused by enlargement and hardening of the spleen.—**Ague-tree**, *n.* A name sometimes applied to sassafras on account of its febrifuge qualities.

Agynous, a'jin-us, *a.* [Gr. *a*, without, and *gynē*, a female.] *Bot.* applied to plants having no female organs.

Ah, ä. [A natural cry expressive of sudden emotion; comp. G. *ach*, L. *ah*, Skr. *ā*, *āh*, ah.] An exclamation expressive of pain, surprise, pity, compassion, complaint, contempt, dislike, joy, exultation, &c., according to the manner of utterance. **Aha**, ä-hä'. [A lengthened form of *ah*, or formed of *ah* and *ha*; comp. G. *aha*, Skr. *ahō*, *ahaha*.] An exclamation expressing triumph, contempt, surprise, &c.

Ahead, a-hed', *adv.* Headlong; head foremost‡; in or to the front; in advance; before; further on (to walk *ahead of* a person; *naut.* opposite to *astern*.

Aheap, a-hēp', *adv.* Huddled or heaped together.

Ahoy, a-hoi', *exclam.* [Longer form of *hoy!*] A word used chiefly at sea in hailing.

Ai, ä'ē, *n.* The three-toed sloth, so called from its cry.

Aid, ād, *v.t.* [Fr. *aider*, O. Fr. *ajuder*, from L. *adjutare*, freq. of *adjuvo*, *adjutum*, to help—*ad*, to, and *juvo*, *jutum*, to help.] To help; to assist; to come to the support or relief of; to succour.—**Aid**, ād, *n.* [Fr. *aide*.] Help; succour; support; assistance; the person or thing that aids or yields assistance; a helper; an auxiliary; an assistant; a subsidy or tax formerly granted by parliament to the crown; a tax paid by a feudal tenant to his lord.—**Aidance**,† ād'ans, *n.* Aid; help; assistance.—**Aidant**,‡ ād'ant, *a.* Helping; helpful; supplying aid. [*Shak.*]—**Aider**, ād'ėr, *n.* One who aids; an assistant.—**Aidful**,† ād'fųl, *a.* Giving aid; helpful.—**Aidless**, ād'les, *a.* Without aid or succour.

Aide-de-camp, ād-de-koṅ, *n.* pl. **Aides-de-camp**, ād-de-koṅ. [Fr., lit. field assistant.] *Milit.* an officer whose duty is to receive and communicate the orders of a general officer, to act as his secretary, &c.

Aigret, Aigrette, ā'gret, ā-gret', *n.* [EGRET.] A plume or ornament for the head composed of feathers or precious stones.

Aiguille, ā'gwil, *n.* [Fr., a needle.] A name given to the needle-like points or tops of rocks and mountain masses, or to sharp-pointed masses of ice on glaciers, &c.

Ail, āl, *v.t.* [O.E. *eylen*, A. Sax. *eglian*, to feel pain; to ail; *eglan*, to give pain; *egle*, trouble, grief; comp. Goth. *aglo*, affliction, Sw. *agg*, a prick.] To affect with pain or uneasiness, either of body or mind; to trouble; to be the matter with (with *what*, *nothing*, *something*, &c., as nom.).—*v.i.* To be in pain or trouble.—**Ailment**, āl'ment, *n.* Disease; indisposition; morbid affection of the body.

Ailanthus, ā-lan'thus, *n.* [From *ailanto*, the Malacca name.] A handsome tree of India and China, now planted in France and Germany to shade public walks, &c.

Aileron, ā'ler-ŏn, *n.* [Fr. *aile*, wing.] Any one of certain small movable planes fixed to the main planes of an aeroplane and used as balancing flaps, or to give stability, being actuated by suitable leverage.

Aim, ām, *v.i.* [O. Fr. *esmer*, *aesmer*—L. *ad*, to, and *æstimare*, to estimate.] To direct a missile towards an object; to direct the mind or intention; to make an attempt; to endeavour (followed by *at* before the object).—*v.t.* To direct or point to a particular object with the intention of hitting it; to level at.—*n.* The pointing or directing of a missile; the point intended to be hit, or object intended to be effected; the mark; a purpose; intention; design; scheme.—**Aimer**, ām'ėr, *n.* One that aims.—**Aimless**, ām'les, *a.* Without aim; purposeless.—**Aimlessly**, ām'les-li, *adv.* Purposely.

Air, âr, *n.* [Fr. *air*, L. *aër*, from Gr. *aēr*, *air*.] A heterogeneous mixture of tasteless, odorless, colorless, and invisible gases surrounding the earth, which consists of 78.03% nitrogen, 20.99% oxygen, 0.94% argon, 0.03% carbon dioxide, 0.01% hydrogen, and traces of krypton, neon, helium, and xenon; that which we breathe and which is essential to all plant and animal life; a breeze; air in motion; a tune; a melody; the principal melody part in a harmonized piece of music; outward appearance, mien, bearing, manner of a person or thing as, an *air of importance*; semblance; an affected manner as, *to put on airs*.—*v.t.* To expose to, put out in, the air; to let air into, to ventilate, as *to air a room*; to state publicly, as *to air one's views, one's grievances*, &c.—**Air base**, *n.* The base of operations for aircraft.—**Air bladder**, *n.* A sac or vesicle filled with air located under the backbone of most fishes, and responsible for their buoyancy.—**Air brake**, *n.* A mechanical brake worked by air pressure.—**Airbrush**, *n.* A device attached to a compressed-air hose, for the spraying of paint.—**Air castle**, *n.* A daydream; an unrealizable scheme.—**Air cell**, *n.* A minute cavity containing air; one of the cells of the lungs.—**Air chamber**, *n.* Any cavity filled with air.—**Air compressor**, *n.* A device used for compressing air.—**Air conditioner**, *n.* A ventilating device that filters, washes and cools or warms the air.—**Air-cooled**, *a.* Cooled by air, as in an engine motor cooled by a current of air.—**Aircraft**, *n.* Any kind of flying machine.—**Aircraft carrier**, *n.* A ship designed to carry naval airplanes, with special decks for taking-off and landing.—**Air drill**, *n.* A device for drilling, powered by compressed air.—**Airdrome**, *n.* An airfield; a hangar.—**Air duct**, *n.* A tube, especially used in mines, through which fresh air is pumped in, and impure air expelled.—**Air engine**, *n.* An engine worked by heated or compressed air.—**Airfield**, *n.* A landing and taking-off field for airplanes; an airport.—**Air fleet**, *n.* The military and naval aircraft of a nation.—**Air force**, *n.* That branch of the armed forces which fights in the air.—**Air gauge**, *n.* An instrument for measuring air pressure.—**Air hole**, *n.* A hole made to allow air to pass in or out; an *air pocket*; an artificial hole in ice or one kept open by warm running water.—**Airily**, *adv.* In an airy manner; in a light, gay manner.—**Airing**, *n.* An exposure to air as, *to give clothes an airing*; a short walk or drive out of doors.—**Air lane**, *n.* A particular route through the air traversed by aircraft.—**Air line**, *n.* A transportation system of airplanes making regularly scheduled flights and transporting passengers and freight between its points of flight.—**Air mail**, *n.* Mail carried by airplanes.—**Airman**, *n.* A flier; an aviator.—**Air meter, Airo-meter**, *n.* A device that measures the rate of flow of air.—**Air-minded**, *a.* Interested in, and approving of, air-travel or things aeronautic.—**Airplane**, *n.* Any one of the different kinds of flying machines which are heavier than air and which are supported in the air by planes or wings, propelled forward by a screw propeller.—**Air plant**, *n.* A general name for plants that grow upon others and derive all their food from the atmosphere; an epiphyte.—**Air pocket**, *n.* A disturbance of the atmosphere that causes aircraft to drop suddenly for a considerable distance; an air hole.—**Airport**, *n.* An airfield; a field, with a hangar or hangars, for the landing, taking-off, and servicing of aircraft.—**Air pump**, *n.* A machine for the purpose of compressing air, or of exhausting air from a vessel to create a vacuum.—**Air raid**, *n.* A hostile destructive incursion by enemy aircraft.—**Air route**, *n.* An established route followed by commercial aircraft.—**Air shaft**, *n.* A passage for admitting fresh air into a mine or tunnel; a passage in a building which affords ventilation and light.—**Airship**, *n.* A machine for navigating the air, capable of being steered, supported by gas bags, and propelled by an engine or engines; a dirigible.—**Airsickness**, *n.* Illness experienced in flying at altitudes.—**Airtight**, *a.* Impermeable to air; hermetically sealed.—**Airy**, *a.* Consisting of or having the character of air; ethereal; exposed to air; gay and sprightly; lively.

Aisle, īl, *n.* [O.Fr. *aisle*, Fr. *aile*, a wing, an aisle; L. *ala*, a wing; the *s* does not properly belong to the word.] A lateral division of a cathedral or other church, separated from the central part, called the nave, by pillars or piers.—**Aisled**, īld, *a.* Furnished with aisles.

Ait, āt, *n.* [A form of *eyot*, an islet.] A small island in a river or lake.

Aitchbone, āch'bōn, *n.* [For *natch-bone* (by loss of initial *n* as in *apron*), from Fr. *nache*, L.L. *naticæ*, L. *nates*, the rump.] The rump-bone of an ox. Called also *Edgebone* (by false etymology).

Ajar, a-jär', *adv.* [O.E. *achar*, *onchar*, lit. on the turn—prefix *a*, on, *jar*, *char*, A. Sax. *cerre*, a turn, seen also in *chare*, *charwoman*.] On the turn; neither quite open nor shut; partly opened: said of a door.

Ajutage, a'jūt-āj, *n.* [Fr. *ajoutage*, from *ajouter*, to join—L. *ad*, to, *juxta*, nigh.] A sort of tube fitted to the aperture of a vessel through which water is played.

Akee, a-kē', *n.* The fruit of a tree (*Blighia sapida*) belonging to W. Africa, now common in the W. Indies and S. America.

Akimbo, a-kim'bō, *a.* or *adv.* [Prefix *a*, on, and *kimbo*, from Icel. *keng-boginn*, lit. crook-bowed, *kengr*, a crook.] With the elbow pointing outwards and the hand resting on the hip: said of the arm.

Akin, a-kin', *a.* or *adv.* [Prefix *a*, of, and *kin*.] Related by blood; allied by nature; partaking of the same properties.

Alabandine, al-a-ban'din, *n.* [From *Alabanda*, in Asia Minor.] Manganese glance or blende, a sulphide of manganese.

Alabaster, al'a-bas-tėr, *n.* [L. *alabaster*, Gr. *alabastros*, from Alabastron, a village in Egypt where it was got.] A soft, semi transparent, marble-like mineral of which there are two well-known varieties—the gypseous and the calcareous. Small works of art are often made of it.—**Alabastrine**, al-a-bas'trin, *a.* Of or pertaining to.

Alack, a-lak', *interj.* [Probably a corruption of *alas*; but comp. *lauk!* euphemism for Lord.] An explanation expressive of sorrow.—**Alackaday**, a-lak'a-dā, *interj.* [Comp. *Well-a-day!*] An exclamation uttered to express regret or sorrow.

Alacrity, a-lak'ri-ti, *n.* [L. *alacritas*, from *alacer*, *alacris*, cheerful.] A cheerful readiness or promptitude to do some act; cheerful willingness; briskness.

Alactaga, a-lak′ta-ga, *n.* A rodent allied to the jerboa, inhabiting South Russia and Asia.

Alalia, a-lā′li-a, *n.* [Gr. *alalos*, not speaking—*a*, not, *laleō*, I speak.] *Med.* loss of the power of speaking from paralysis of the muscles concerned.

A-la-mode, Alamode, a-la-mōd′, *adv.* [Fr. *à la mode*, after the fashion.] According to the fashion or prevailing mode: sometimes used as an adjective.

Alar, ā′lėr, *a.* [L. *ala*, a wing.] Pertaining to wings; having the character of a wing.

Alarm, a-lärm′, *n.* [Fr. *alarme*, alarm, from It. *all'arme* = L. *ad arma*, to arms.] A summons to arms; an outcry or other notice of approaching danger; a tumult; a disturbance; a sudden fear or painful suspense excited by an apprehension of danger; apprehension; terror; a mechanical contrivance for awakening persons from sleep or rousing their attention.—*v.t.* To call to arms for defence; to give notice of danger; to rouse to vigilance; to disturb with terror; to fill with anxiety by the prospect of evil.—**Alarmed**, a-lärmd′, *a.* Indicating or expressive of alarm (look, countenance).—**Alarming**, a-lärm′ing, *a.* Calculated to rouse alarm; causing apprehension.—**Alarmingly**, a-lärm′ing-li, *adv.* In an alarming manner.—**Alarmist**, a-lärm′ist, *n.* One that excites alarm; one who is prone to take alarm, and to circulate and exaggerate any sort of bad news.

Alarum, a-lär′um, *n.* [A corruption of *alarm*.] An alarm; a watchword or signal indicating danger; any loud noise or disturbance. [Now only poetical.]

Alary, ā′la-ri, *a.* Alar.

Alas, a-las′, *exclam.* [O.Fr. *alas*, from interj. *a*, *ah*, L. *lassus*, weary.] An exclamation expressive of sorrow, grief, pity, concern, or apprehension of evil.

Alate, ā′lāt, *a.* [L. *alatus*, winged, *ala*, a wing.] Winged; having membranous expansions like wings.

Alb, Albe, alb, *n.* [L. *alba*, white (*vestis*, garment, understood).] A clerical vestment worn by priests, a long robe of white linen bound with a girdle.

Albacore, Albicore, al′ba-kōr, al′bē-kōr, *n.* [Sp. *albacora*, Fr. *albicore*, from Ar. *al*, the, *bakr*, a young cow or heifer.] A name given to several fishes of the tunny kind, especially to the Pacific tunny.

Albata, al-bā′ta, *n.* [L. *albus*, white.] An alloy consisting of a combination of nickel, zinc, tin, and copper, often with antimony and silver; German silver.

Albatros, Albatross, al′ba-tros, *n.* [Fr. *albatros*, a corruption of Sp. and Pg. *alcatraz*, a pelican, from Ar. *al-qādūs*, the bucket of a water-wheel, the pelican being supposed to carry water to its young ones in the pouch below its bill.] An aquatic bird, the largest sea-bird known, some measuring 17½ feet from tip to tip of the wings, met with at immense distances from land.

Albeit, al-bē′it, *conj.* [*Al* in old sense of though, *be*, and *it*, and equivalent to *be it so*.] Be it so; admit all that; although; notwithstanding.

Albert, al′bėrt, *n.* [After the Prince Consort, *Albert*.] A short chain attaching the watch to a waistcoat button-hole.

Albescent, al-bes′ent, *a.* [L. *albesco*, to grow white, an incept. from *albus*, white.] Becoming white or rather whitish; moderately white; of a pale, hoary aspect.

Albicore, al′bē-kōr, *n.* ALBACORE.

Albigenses, al-bi-jens′ez, *n.pl.* A party of religious reformers in the twelfth century, who were ruthlessly persecuted: so called from *Albi*, a town of Languedoc in France, where they resided

Albino, al-bī′nō, *n.* pl. **Albinos** or **Albinoes**, al-bī′nōz. [Pg., from L. *albus*, white.] A person of abnormally pale, milky complexion, with light hair and pink eyes; an animal characterized by the same peculiarity in physical constitution.—**Albinism, Albinoism**, al′bin-izm, al-bī′nō-izm, *n.* The state or condition of an albino; leucopathy.

Albite, al′bīt, *n.* [L. *albus*, white.] A name given to felspar whose alkali is soda instead of potash; it is a constituent in Aberdeen granite.

Albuginea, al-bū-jin′ē-a, *n.* [L. *albugo*, *albuginis*, whiteness, from *albus*, white.] The white fibrous coating of the eye; the white.—**Albugineous**, al-bū-jin′ē-us, *a.* Pertaining to or resembling the white of the eye or of an egg.

Albugo, al-bū′gō, *n.* [L., from *albus*, white.] An affection of the eye, consisting in a white opacity of the cornea; also called *leucoma*.

Album, al′bum, *n.* [L., from *albus*, white.] A book, originally blank, in which may be inserted autographs of celebrated persons or favourite pieces of poetry or prose, generally contributed by friends; a book for preserving photographic or other views, portraits, &c.—**Album Græcum**, *n.* [Lit. Greek white.] The dung of dogs, wolves, &c., whitened by exposure to the air, used by tanners to soften leather.

Albumen, al-bū′men, *n.* [L., from *albus*, white.] A substance entering largely into the composition of the animal and vegetable fluids and solids: so named from the Latin for the white of an egg, in which it abounds in its purest natural state.—**Albumenize**, al-bū′men-īz, *v.t.*—*albumenized*, *albumenizing*. To convert into albumen; to cover or impregnate with albumen.—**Albumin**, al-bū′min, *n.* Same as *Albumen*, but used more strictly as a chemical term.—**Albuminoid**, al-bū′min-oid, *a.* Like albumen.—*n.* A substance resembling albumen; proteid.—**Albuminose, Albuminous**, al-bū′min-ōs, al-bū′min-us, *a.* Pertaining to or having the properties of albumen: applied to plants whose seeds have a store of albumen, as all kinds of grain, palms, &c.—**Albuminousness**, al-bū′min-us-nes, *n.*—**Albuminuria**, al-bū′mi-nū″ri-a. [*Albumen* and Gr. *ouron*, urine.] *Pathol.* a condition in which the urine contains albumen, evidencing a diseased state of the kidneys.

Alburnum, al-bėr′num, *n.* [L. *alburnum*, sapwood, from *albus*, white.] The white and softer part of the wood of exogenous plants between the inner bark and the heart-wood; the sapwood.—**Alburnous**, al-bėr′nus, *a.* Relating to alburnum.

Alcahest, al′ka-hest, *n.* Same as *Alkahest*.

Alcaic, al-kā′ik, *a.* [L. *alcaicus*.] Pertaining to *Alcæus*, a lyric poet of Mitylene.—*Alcaic verse*, a variety of verse used in Greek and Latin poetry, consisting of five feet, a spondee or iambus, an iambus, a long syllable, and two dactyls.

Alcalde, Alcaide, äl-käl′dā, äl-kä′i-dā, *n.* [Sp. and Pg. from Ar.] In Spain, Portugal, &c., a commander of a fortress; the chief civil magistrate of a town; also, a jailer.

Alchemy, Alchymy, al′ke-mi, al′ki-mi, *n.* [O.F. *alquimie*, L.L. *alchimia*, from Ar. *al-Kimia*—*al*, the, and *Khemia*, the name of Egypt; confusion with Gr. *kheō*, I pour, *khumeia*, gives alchymy. CHEMISTRY.] The art which had for its main objects the transmuting of the baser metals into gold or silver, the discovery of an elixir of life, a universal solvent, &c.—**Alchemic, Alchemical, Alchemistic, Alchemistical**, al-kem′ik, al-kem′ik-al, al-kem-ist′ik, al-kem-ist′ik-al, *a.* Relating to, produced by, or practising alchemy. Also spelt with *y* for *e*.—**Alchemically, Alchymically**, al-kem′ik-al-li, al-kim′ik-al-li, *adv.* In the manner of alchemy.—**Alchemist, Alchymist**, al′kem-ist, al′kim-ist, *n.* One who practises alchemy.—**Alchemise**,† al′kem-īz, *v.t.* To change by alchemy; to transmute, as metals.—**Alchymy**. A mixed metal (Mil.).

Alco, al′kō, *n.* A small variety of dog found wild in Mexico and Peru, and now domesticated.

Alcohol, al′kō-hol, *n.* [Sp. Pg. *alcohol*—Ar. *al*, the, and *kohl*, a fine powder of antimony, hence anything very fine or purified, as rectified spirits.] A liquid forming the intoxicating principle of all vinous and spirituous liquors, and obtained by distillation. Having been first procured from wine, the name of *spirit of wine* is given to the strongest alcohol used in commerce, containing about 90 per cent of pure alcohol.—**Alcoholate, Alcohate**, al′kō-hol-āt, al′ko-hāt, *n.* A salt in which alcohol appears to replace the water of crystallization.—**Alcoholic**, al-kō-hol′ik, *a.* Pertaining to alcohol, or partaking of its qualities.—*n.* An alcoholic liquid.—**Alcoholism**, al′kō-hol-izm, *n.* The condition of habitual drunkards, whose tissues are saturated with spirits.—**Alcoholize**, al′kō-hol-īz, *v.t.* To convert into alcohol; to rectify (spirit) till it is wholly purified.—**Alcoholmeter, Alcoholometer**, al-kō-hol′mē-tėr, al′kō-hol-om″ēt-ėr, *n.* An instrument for determining the quantity of pure alcohol in any liquid.—**Alcoholometrical**, al′kō-ho-lo-met″rik-al, *a.* Relating to the alcoholometer.—**Alcoholometry**, al′kō-hol-om″et-ri, *n.* The determination of the percentage of absolute alcohol in a liquid.

Alcoran. ALKORAN.

Alcove, al′kōv, *n.* [Fr. *alcove*, Sp. *alcoba*—Ar. *al*, the, and *kubbeh*, an alcove, a little chamber.] A wide and deep recess in a room, intended for the reception of a bed or seats, &c.; any natural recess.

Alcyonium, al-si-ō′ni-um, *n.* [L.] The generic name of various polyps, some of which grow grouped together so as to form fleshy bodies, familiarly known as 'deadman's fingers' and 'cow's paps'. They are akin to the animals that produce coral.

Aldehyde, al′dē-hīd, *n.* [*Al*, first syllable of *alcohol*, and *dehyd*, the first two of *dehydrogenatus*, deprived of hydrogen.] A transparent colourless liquid produced by the oxidation of pure alcohol; one of a class of organic compounds, derived from alcohol by the abstraction of two atoms of hydrogen, and converted into acids by the addition of one atom of oxygen.—**Aldehydic**, al-dē-hīd′ik, *a.* Of or pertaining to or containing aldehyde.

Alder, al′dėr, *n.* [O.E. *aller* (the *d* being a more modern insertion), A. Sax. *aler*, *alr*; Icel. *ölr*, G. *eller*; allied to L. *alnus*, an alder.] The popular name of plants of the genus Alnus. *A. glutinosa* is the common alder, usually growing in moist land.—**Alder-buckthorn**, *n.* *Rhamnus Frangula*, a British plant, a shrub 3 to 10 feet high.

Alderman, al′dėr-man, *n.* pl. **Aldermen**, al′dėr-men. [A.Sax. *aldorman*, *ealdorman*—*ealdor*, an elder, from *eald*, old, and *man*.] Anciently, an Anglo-Saxon nobleman, often a governor of a shire; now a magistrate or officer of a town corporate, next in rank below the mayor.—**Aldermanic**, al-dėr-man′ik, *a.* Relating to or becoming an alderman.—**Aldermanly**, al′dėr-man-li, *a.* Pertaining to or like an alderman.—**Aldermancy, Aldermanry, Aldermanship**, al′dėr-man-si, al′dėr-man-ri, al′dėr-man-ship, *n.* The office, quality, or condition of an alderman.

Aldine, al′dīn, *a.* Proceeding from the printing-press of *Aldus* Manutius, of Venice, and his family, from 1490 to 1597.—**Aldine type** = Italic type invented by the printer for his 1501 edition of Virgil.

Ale, āl, *n.* [A. Sax. *ealu*, Dan. Sw. and Icel. *öl*, ale.] A liquor made from an infusion of malt by fermentation; beer, or a kind of beer; a merry meeting in English country places, so called from the liquor drunk.—**Ale-berry**, *n.* A beverage made by boiling ale with spice, sugar, and sops of bread.—**Ale-conner**, *n.* [*Con*, to know or see.] An officer appointed to assay ale and beer, or to inspect the measures used in public-houses.—**Ale-cost**, *n.* Costmary, a plant put into ale to give it an aromatic flavour.—**Ale-gill** (-jil), *n.* A kind of medicated liquor from the infusion of ground-ivy in malt liquor.—**Ale-hoof**, *n.* [D. *eiloof*, ivy.] Ground-ivy. The word assumed this form because its leaves were used in making ale before the use of hops.—**Ale-house**, *n.* A house where ale is retailed; a beer-shop.—**Ale-wife**, *n.* A woman who keeps an ale-house.—**Ale-yard**, *n.* A very elongated form of drinking-glass and measure for ale formerly used.

Aleatory, al'ē-a-to-ri, *a.* [L. *alea*, a die, chance.] Pertaining to chance or contingency; depending on a contingency.

Alee, a-lē', *adv.* *Naut.* on the lee side; on the side opposite to that on which the wind strikes: opposite of *a-weather*.

Alegar, äl'ē-gėr, *n.* [*Ale*, and *eager*, Fr. *aigre*, sour.] Sour ale; vinegar made of ale.

Alembic, a-lem'bik, *n.* [L.L. *alembicum*; Sp. *alambique*—Ar. *al*, the, *ambik*, an alembic, from Gr. *ambix*, a cup.] A chemical vessel formerly used in distillation, usually made of glass or copper.

Alepidote, a-lep'i-dōt, *a.* [Gr. *a*, priv., and *lepis*, *lepidos*, a scale.] Not having scales.—*n.* Any fish whose skin is not covered with scales.

Alert, a-lėrt', *a.* [Fr. *alerte*, alert, and (as noun) alarm or notice of danger, formerly *allerte*, and *a l'erte*, from It. *all'erta*, to the watch-tower, the look-out—*erta*, fem. p.p. of L. *erigere*, erect.] Active in vigilance; watchful; vigilant; brisk; nimble.—*On* or *upon the alert*, upon the watch; on the look-out; guarding against surprise or danger.—**Alertness**, a-lėrt'nes, *n.* The state or quality of being alert.

Alethiology,† a-lē'thī-ol''o-ji, *n.* [Gr. *aletheia*, truth, and *logos*, discourse.] The doctrine of truth and error in logic.

Aleurone, a-lū'rōn, *n.* [Gr. *aleuron*, fine flour.] Albuminoid granules found in seeds.

Alewife, āl'wīf, *n.* A fish of the shad genus, caught in the Severn; also a similar N. American fish much used as food.

Alexanders, al-egz-an'dėrz, *n.* A plant of the carrot family formerly eaten.

Alexandrian, al-egz-an'dri-an, *a.* Pertaining to *Alexandria* in Egypt, more especially ancient Alexandria.—**Alexandrine**, al-egz-an'drīn, *n.* A kind of verse consisting of twelve syllables in English poetry, or in French of twelve and thirteen in alternate couplets: so called from a poem written in French on the life of *Alexander the Great*.

Alexipharmic, Alexipharmical, a-lek'si-färm''ik, a-lek'si-färm''ik-al, *a.* [Gr. *alexō*, to ward off, *pharmakon*, a drug, remedy, poison.] Acting as a means of warding off disease or the effects of poison; acting as a remedy.—**Alexipharmic**, *n.* A remedy; an antidote.—**Alexiteric, Alexiterical**, a-lek'si-ter''ik, a-lek'si-ter''-ik-al, *a.* Resisting poison; obviating the effects of venom.—*n.* A medicine of this kind.

Alfa, Alfa-grass, al'fa, al'fa-gras, *a.* A North African name for one of the varieties of esparto and its fibre.

Alfalfa, alf-al'fa, *n.* [Sp.] A common name in the United States for the fodder plant lucerne.

Alfenid, al'fe-nid, *n.* [Origin doubtful.] An alloy of nickel plated with silver, used for spoons, tea-services, &c.

Alga, al'ga, *n.* pl. **Algæ**, al'jē, [L.] A seaweed; one of an order of cryptogamic plants found for the most part in the sea and fresh water, comprising sea-weeds.—**Algal**, al'gal, *n.* One of the Algæ.—**Algine**, al'jin, *n.* [From L. *alga*, seaweed.] A substance obtained from sea-weeds and used for such substances as horn is used for.—**Algist**, al'jist, *n.* One who scientifically studies Algæ.—**Algal, Algous**, al'gal, al'gus, *a.* Of or pertaining to the Algæ; having the nature of the Algæ.—**Algology**, al-gol'o-ji, *n.* The study or science of Algæ.

Algebra, al'je-bra, *n.* [Sp. *algebra*, from Ar. *al-jabr*, the putting together of broken things, reduction of fractions to whole numbers, from Ar. *jabara*, to bind together, to consolidate.] That branch of mathematical analysis in which signs are employed to denote arithmetical operations, and letters are used to represent numbers and quantities; a kind of universal arithmetic.—**Algebraic, Algebraical**, al-je-brā'ik, al-je-brā'ik-al, *a.* Pertaining to algebra; containing an operation of algebra.—**Algebraically**, al-je-brā'ik-al-li, *adv.* By algebraic process.—**Algebraist**, al-je-brā'-ist, *n.* One versed in the science of algebra.

Algerian, Algerine, al-jē'ri-an, al-je-rēn', *a.* Pertaining to Algeria or its inhabitants.—*n.* A person belonging to Algiers or Algeria.

Algid, al'jid, *a.* [L. *algidus*, cold, *algeo*, to be cold.] Cold.—*Algid cholera*, Asiatic cholera.—**Algidity, Algidness**, al-jid'i-ti, al'jid-nes, *n.* The state of being algid; chilliness; coldness.—**Algific**, al-jif'ik, *a.* [L. *algificus*.] Producing cold.—**Algor**, al'-gor, *n.* [L.] An unusual coldness in the human system.—**Algose**, al'gōs, *a.* [L. *algosus*.] Cold in a high degree.

Algology. ALGA.

Algorithm, Algorism, al'gō-rithm, al'-gō-rizm, *n.* [O.F. *augorisme*, L. *algorismus*, Ar. *al-khowarazmi*, the man of Khiva, name of a mathematician; confused with Gr. *arithmos*, number.] Arabic decimal notation; the art of computing or reckoning in reference to some particular subject, or in some particular way (the *algorithm* of the differential calculus).

Algous. ALGA.

Alhambraic, Alhambresque, äl-äm-brā'ik, äl-äm'bresk, *a.* Of or pertaining to the *Alhambra* (lit. red house), a Moorish palace near Granada in Spain; built or decorated after the fanciful manner of the Alhambra, in which arabesques are a notable feature.

Alias, ā'li-as, *adv.* [L.] Otherwise; used especially of persons who assume various names (John Smith *alias* Thomas Jones).—*n.* pl. **Aliases**, ā'li-as-ez. An assumed name; another name.

Alibi, al'i-bī, *n.* [L., elsewhere.] *Law*, a plea which avers that the accused was in another place at the time of the commission of the offence, and therefore cannot be guilty.

Alien, āl'yen, *a.* [L. *alienus*, alien, from *alius*, another. The same root appears in E. *else*.] Not belonging to the same country, land, or government; foreign; different in nature; estranged; adverse: with *to* or *from*.—*n.* A foreigner; one born in or belonging to another country; one who is not a denizen, or entitled to the privileges of a citizen.—**Alienability**, āl'yen-a-bil''-i-ti, *n.* The state or quality of being alienable.—**Alienable**, āl'yen-a-bl, *a.* Capable of being alienated, sold, or transferred to another.—**Alienage**, āl'yen-āj, *n.* The state of being an alien.—**Alienate**, āl'yen-āt, *v.t.*—*alienated*, *alienating*. [L. *alieno*, *alienatum*, to alienate.] To transfer or convey, as title, property, or other right, to another; to withdraw, as the affections; to make indifferent or averse, where love or friendship before subsisted; to estrange; to wean: with *from*.—**Alienation**, āl-yen-ā'shon, *n.* [L. *alienatio*.] The act of alienating or the state of being alienated.—**Alienator**, āl-yen-ā'tėr, *n.* One who alienates.—**Alienee**, āl-yen-ē', *n.* One to whom the title of property is transferred.—**Alienism**, āl'yen-izm, *n.* The state of being an alien; the scientific study and treatment of mental alienation or insanity.—**Alienist**, āl'yen-ist, *n.* One who studies or practises alienism.—**Alienor**, āl'yen-or, *n.* One who transfers property.

Aliferous, Aligerous, a-lif'ėr-us, a-lij'-ėr-us, *a.* [L. *ala*, wing, and *fero*, *gero*, to bear.] Having wings.—**Aliform**, ā'li-form, *a.* [L. *ala*, wing, and *forma*, shape.] Having the shape of a wing or wings.

Alight, a-līt', *v.i.* [A.Sax. *âlihtan*, *gelihtan*, to alight or light. See LIGHT in this sense.] To get down or descend, as from horseback or from a carriage; to settle or lodge, as a bird on a tree; to light down.

Alight, a-līt', *a.* or *adv.* Lighted; kindled; made to burn by having a light applied.

Align, a-līn', *v.t.* [Fr. *aligner*, to align—*a*, to, and *ligne*, L. *linea*, a line.] To lay out or regulate by a line; to form in line, as troops.—**Alignment**, a-līn'ment, *n.* The act of aligning; an adjusting to a line; the line of adjustment; the ground-plan of a railway or other road, in distinction from the gradients or profile; a row of things.

Alike, a-līk', *a.* [Prefix *a*, and *like*; A.Sax. *gelic*, alike. LIKE.] Having resemblance or similitude; similar; without difference (always used as a predicate).—**Alike**, a-līk', *adv.* In the same manner, form, or degree; in common (all have erred *alike*).

Aliment, al'i-ment, *n.* [L. *alimentum*, nourishment—*alo*, to nourish.] That which nourishes; food; nutriment.—**Alimental**, al-i-ment'al, *a.* Of or pertaining to aliment; supplying food; having the quality of nourishing.—**Alimentally**, al-i-ment'-al-li, *adv.* In an alimental manner.—**Alimentariness**, al-i-ment'a-ri-nes, *n.* The quality of being alimentary.—**Alimentary**, al-i-ment'a-ri, *a.* Pertaining to aliment or food; having the quality of nourishing.—**Alimentation**, al'i-ment-ā''shon, *n.* The act or power of affording nutriment; the state of being nourished.—**Alimentiveness**, al-i-ment'iv-nes, *n.* *Phren.* the organ that is said to communicate the pleasure which arises from eating and drinking.—**Alimony**, al'i-mo-ni, *n.* [L. *alimonia*.] An allowance out of her husband's estate made for the support of a woman legally separated from him.

Alineation, a lin'ē-ā''shon, *n.* [L. *a*, by or from, and *linea*, a line.] The determination of the position of a more remote object, by following a line drawn through one or more intermediate and more easily recognizable objects.

Aliped, al'i-ped, *a.* [L. *ala*, wing, and *pes*, *pedis*, a foot.] Wing-footed; having the toes connected by a membrane, which serves as a wing, as the bats.—*n.* An animal whose toes are so connected.

Aliquant, al'i-kwant, *a.* [L. *aliquantum*, somewhat.] *Arith.* applied to a number which does not measure another without a remainder.—**Aliquot**, al'i-kwot, *a.* [L. *aliquot*, some, several.] *Arith.* applied to a part of a number or quantity which will measure it without a remainder.

Alive, a-līv', *a.* [Prefix *a* for *on*, and *life*; in old English it was written *on live*, *on lyve*, where *live*, *lyve* is a dat. form of *life*.] Having life; living; not dead; in a state of action; in force or operation (keep an agitation *alive*); full of alacrity; sprightly (*alive* with excitement); easily impressed; sensitive to; susceptible (*alive* to the beauties of nature): used always after its noun.

Alizarine, al'i-za-rin, *n.* [Fr. *alizarine*, from *alizari*, an Eastern name of madder, from the (Ar.) root of *azure*, with the article prefixed.] A red colouring matter obtained from madder, but made for commercial purposes from coal-tar products, and now largely used instead of madder.

Alkahest, al'ka-hest, *n.* [Etym. unknown.] The pretended universal solvent or menstruum of the alchemists.—**Alkahestic**, al-ka-hest'ik, *a.* Pertaining to the alkahest.

Alkali, al'ka-li, *n.* pl. **Alkalies** or **Alkalis**, al'ka-liz. [Sp. Fr. *alcali*, Ar. *al-qali*, the plant from which soda was first obtained.] A term applied to an important class of bases which combine with acids to form salts, turn vegetable yellows to red and vegetable blues to green, and unite with oil or fat to form soap. The proper alkalies are hydroxide of potassium (potash), hydroxide of sodium (soda), hydroxide of lithium (lithia), and hydroxide of ammonium (an aqueous solution of ammonia).—**Alkalescent**, al-ka-les'ent, *a.* Tending to the properties of an alkali; slightly alkaline.—**Alkalescence, Alkalescency**, al-ka-les'ens, al-ka-les'en-si, *n.* A tendency to become alkaline.—**Alkalifiable**, al'ka-li-fī-a-bl or al-kal'i-fī-a-bl, *a.* Capable of being alkalified.—**Alkalify**, al'ka-li-fī or al-kal'-i-fī, *v.t.*—*alkalified*, *alkalifying*; **Alkalize**, al'ka-līz, *v.t.*—*alkalized*, *alkalizing*. To form or to convert into an alkali; to make alkaline.—*v.i.* To become an alkali.—**Alkaligenous**, al-ka-lij'en-us, *a.* Producing or generating alkali.—**Alkalimeter**, al-ka-lim′et-ėr, *n.* An instrument for ascertaining the strength of alkalies.—**Alkalimetric, Alkalimetrical**, al′ka-li-met″rik, al′ka-li-met″rik-al, *a.* Relating to alkalimetry.—**Alkalimetry**, al-ka-lim′et-ri, *n.* The finding of the amount of real alkali in an alkaline mixture or liquid.—**Alkaline**, al′ka-lin, *a.* Having the properties of an alkali.—*Alkaline earths*, lime, magnesia, baryta, strontia.—**Alkalinity**, al-ka-lin′i-ti, *n.* The state of being alkaline; the quality which constitutes an alkali.—**Alkalization**, al′ka-liz-ā″shon, *n.* The act or process of rendering alkaline.—**Alkaloid**, al′-ka-loid, *n.* A term applied to a class of nitrogenized compounds found in living plants, and containing their active principles, such as *morphine, quinine, aconitine, caffeine*, &c.—*a.* Relating to or containing alkali.

Alkanet, al′ka-net, *n.* [Sp. *alcaneta*, dim. of *alcana, alcanna*, from Ar. *al-hinna*, henna.] A plant, *Alkanna* (*Anchusa tinctoria*) whose root yields a red dye.

Alkoran, al-kō-rạn′ or al′kō-ran, *n.* [Ar. —*al*, the, *qurân*, book.] The book which contains the religious and moral code of the Mohammedans, and by which indeed all their transactions, civil, legal, military, &c., are regulated; the Koran.

All, ạl, *a.* [A.Sax. *eal* (sing.), *ealle* (pl.); Icel. *allr*, Goth. *alls*, G. *all*, all. Common to all the Teutonic tongues; also in Celtic.] Every one of; the whole number or quantity of. It goes before an article or adj. belonging to the same noun: *all the* men, *all good* men, *all my* labour, &c. With nouns of time it is equivalent to during the whole (*all* day, *all* night).—*adv.* Wholly; completely; entirely; altogether; quite (*all* alone, *all* unarmed).—*All but*, nearly; almost; not quite.—*All one*, the same thing in effect; quite the same.—*n.* The whole number; the entire thing; the aggregate; the total.—*At all*, in the least degree; to the least extent; under any circumstances.—*In all*, everything reckoned or taken into account; all included.—*All*, in composition, has often the force of an adverb; as in *almighty, all-powerful, all-perfect, all-important*; sometimes of a noun in the objective case; as, *all-seeing*.—**All-along**, *adv.* Throughout; from the beginning onwards.—**All-fools' Day**, *n.* The first day of April.—**All-fours**, *n.* A game at cards, so called from the four chances of which it consists, for each of which a point is scored.—*On all-fours*, on four legs, or on two legs and two arms or hands; hence, *fig.* even or evenly; as a parallel case.—**All-hail**, *exclam.* and *n.* All-health: a phrase of salutation.—**All-hallows**, *n.* All-saints' Day.—**All-hallowmas, All-hallowtide**, *n.* The time near All-saints, or first of November.—**All-heal**, *n.* A plant, cat's or common wild valerian; so called from its medicinal virtues.—**All-Highest**, *n.* The self-assumed designation of the German Emperor, as War Lord (*Archaic*).—**All-in-all**. Used as a *noun*, everything to a person; everything in all respects; used as an *adverb*, altogether; as a whole.—**All-saints' Day**. A church festival held on first November; Hallowmas. —**All-souls' Day**. A church festival held on 2d November, when prayers are offered up for the dead.—**All-spice**, *n.* A spice of a mildly pungent taste, the fruit of a West Indian tree, so called from being regarded as combining many different flavours; pimento.

Allah, al′la, *n.* The Arabic name of the Supreme Being.

Allantois, Allantoid, al-lan′tois, al-lan′toid, *n.* [Gr. *allas, allantos*, a sausage, and *eidos*, form.] A sac developed from the posterior end of the abdominal cavity in vertebrate embryos.—**Allantoic, Allantoid, Allantoidal**, al-lan-tō′ik, al-lan′-toid, al-lan-toid′al, *a.* Pertaining to or contained in the allantois.

Allay, al-lā′, *v.t.* [A.Sax. *âlecgan*, to lay down, suppress, tranquillize, from prefix *â*, and *lecgan*, to lay. LAY.] To make quiet; to pacify or appease (a tumult); to abate, mitigate, or subdue; to relieve or alleviate (grief, thirst).—*v.i.* To subside; to grow calm.—**Allayer**, al-lā′ėr, *n.* One who or that which allays.—**Allayment**, al-lā′-ment, *n.* The act of allaying; the state of being.

Allege, al-lej′, *v.t.*—*alleged, alleging.* [O.F. *esligier*, L.L. *exlitigare*, to clear at law (confused with L.L. *allegare*).] To assert, with idea of false statement; to pronounce with positiveness; to declare; to affirm; to assert; to produce as an argument, plea, or excuse; cite; quote; bring forward.—**Allegation**, al-lē-gā′shon, *n.* The act of alleging; affirmation; declaration; that which is affirmed or asserted.—**Allegeable**, al-lej′-a-bl, *a.* Capable of being alleged or affirmed.

Allegiance, al-lē′jans, *n.* [Prefix *a*, to, and O.Fr. *ligence*, allegiance, loyalty, from *lige*, loyal. LIEGE.] The tie or obligation of a subject to his sovereign or government; the duty of fidelity to a king, government, or state.

Allegory, al′lē-go-ri, *n.* [Gr. *allēgoria*—*allos*, other, and *agoreuō*, to speak, from *agora*, a forum, an oration.] A figurative discourse, in which the principal subject is described by another subject resembling it in its properties and circumstances; a narrative in which abstract ideas are personified; a continued metaphor.—**Allegoric, Allegorical**, al-lē-gor′ik, al-lē-gor′ik-al, *a.* Pertaining to allegory; in the manner of allegory.—**Allegorically**, al-lē-gor′ik-al-li, *adv.* In an allegorical manner; by way of allegory.—**Allegoricalness**, al-lē-gor′-ik-al-nes, *n.*—**Allegorist, Allegorizer**, al′lē-go-rist, al′lē-go-rīz-ėr, *n.* One who allegorizes; a writer of allegory.—**Allegorize**, al′lē-go-rīz, *v.t.*—*allegorized, allegorizing.* To turn into allegory; to narrate in allegory; to explain in an allegorical sense.—*v.i.* To use allegory.—**Allegorization**, al′lē-gor-ī-zā″shon, *n.* The act of turning into allegory.

Allegro, äl-lā′grō, *a.* and *n.* [It., merry, cheerful.] *Music*, a word denoting a brisk movement; a sprightly part or strain.—**Allegretto**, äl-lē-gret′to. Time quicker than *andante*, but not so quick as *allegro*.

Alleluia, Alleluiah, al-lē-lū′ya, *n.* [Heb. *halelû-yâh*, praise to Jah—*halal*, to praise, and *Yâh*, Jehovah.] Praise Jehovah; a word used to denote pious joy and exultation, chiefly in hymns and anthems. Written also *Halleluiah, Hallelujah.*

Alleviate, al-lē′vi-āt, *v.t.*—*alleviated, alleviating.* [L.L. *alleviare, alleviatus*, L. *allevare, allevatus*—*ad*, to, and *levo*, to ease, from *levis*, light. LEVITY.] To make light, in a figurative sense; to lessen, mitigate, or make easier to be endured (sorrow, pain, distress).—**Alleviation**, al-lē′vi-ā″shon, *n.* The act of alleviating; that which lessens, mitigates, or makes more tolerable.—**Alleviative**, al-lē′vi-āt-iv, *a.* Tending to alleviate; mitigative.—*n.* That which alleviates or mitigates.—**Alleviator**, al-lē′vi-āt-ėr, *n.* One who or that which alleviates.

Alley, al′li, *n.* [Fr. *allée*, from *aller*, to go, from O.Fr. *aner*, from L. *adnare*, lit. to swim to—*ad*, to, and *nare*, to swim.] A passage; especially, a narrow passage or way in a town.

Alliaceous, al-li-ā′shus, *a.* [L. *allium*, garlic.] Pertaining to garlic and allied plants; having the properties of garlic.

Alliance. ALLY.

Alligation, al-li-gā′shon, *n.* [L. *alligatio*, a binding together—*ad*, to, and *ligo*, to bind.] The act of tying together; the state of being tied; a rule of arithmetic for finding the price of a compound of ingredients of different values.

Alligator, al′li-gā-tėr, *n.* [A corruption of Sp. *el lagarto*, lit. the lizard—*el*, the, and *lagarto*, a lizard, from L. *lacertus*, whence E. *lizard*.] A large reptile of the crocodile family found in tropical America. The alligators differ from the true crocodiles in having a shorter and flatter head, in having cavities or pits in the upper jaw, into which the long canine teeth of the under jaw fit, and in having the feet much less webbed.

Allision,† al-li′zhon, *n.* [L. *allisio, allisionis*, from *allido*, to dash against—*ad*, and *lædo, læsum*, to hurt by striking.] A striking against.

Alliteration, al-lit-ėr-ā′shon, *n.* [L. *al* for *ad*, to, and *litera*, a letter.] The repetition of the same letter at the beginning of two or more words immediately succeeding each other, or at short intervals (as in '*apt alliteration's* artful aid').—**Alliterative, Alliteral**, al-lit′ėr-āt-iv, al-lit′ėr-al, *a.* Pertaining to or consisting in alliteration; characterized by alliteration.—**Alliterativeness**, al-lit′ėr-āt-iv-nes, *n.* Quality of being alliterative.—**Alliterator**, al-lit′ėr-āt-ėr, *n.* One who uses alliteration.

Allocate, al′lō-kāt, *v.t.*—*allocated, allocating.* [L. *ad*, to, and *loco, locatum*, to place, from *locus*, a place.] To assign or allot to a person or persons; to set apart for a particular purpose; to apportion or distribute (shares in a public company or the like).—**Allocation**, al-lō-kā′shon, *n.* The act of allocating, allotting, or assigning; allotment; assignment; apportionment.

Allochrous, al-lok′rus, *a.* [Gr. *allochroos, allochrous*—*allos*, other, and *chroa*, colour.] Of various colours: generally applied to minerals.—**Allochroite**, al-lō-krō′īt, *n.* A massive, fine-grained variety of iron garnet, showing changes of colour before the blow-pipe.

Allocution, al-lō-kū′shon, *n.* [L. *allocutio* —*ad*, to, and *loquor*, to speak.] A speaking to; an address, especially a formal address.

Allodium, al-lō′di-um, *n.* [L.L. *allodium*, of Ger. or Scand. origin; *allod*, all, *od*, estate. UDAL. Comp. Icel. *ódal*, Dan. and Sw. *odel*, a patrimonial estate.] Freehold estate; real estate held in absolute independence, without being subject to any rent, service, or acknowledgment to a superior.—**Allodial**, al-lō′di-al, *a.* Pertaining to allodium or freehold; held independent of a lord paramount: opposed to *feudal*.—**Allodially**, al-lō′di-al-li, *adv.* In an allodial manner.

Allomorphism, al-lō-mor′fizm, *n.* [Gr. *allos*, other, and *morphē*, form.] That property of certain substances of assuming a different form, the substance remaining otherwise unchanged.—**Allomorphic**, al-lō-mor′fik, *a.* Pertaining to, or possessing the qualities of allomorphism.

Allopathy, al-lop′a-thi, *n.* [Gr. *allos*, other, and *pathos*, morbid condition.] That method of treating disease by which it is endeavoured to produce a condition of the system either different from, opposite to, or incompatible with the condition essential to the disease: it is opposed to *homœopathy*, and is the common method of treatment.—**Allopathic**, al-lo-path′ik, *a.* Pertaining to allopathy.—**Allopathically**, al-lo-path′ik-al-li, *adv.* In a manner conformable to allopathy.—**Allopathist**, al-lop′a-thist, *n.* One who practises allopathy.

Allophane, al′lō-fān, *n.* [Gr. *allos*, other, and *phainō*, to appear.] A mineral of a pale blue, or sometimes of a green or brown colour.

Allophylian, al-lō-fil′i-an, *n.* [Gr. *allophylos*—*allos*, other, and *phylē*, a tribe.] One of another tribe or race; specifically, one of the pre-Aryan inhabitants of Europe.

Allot, al-lot′, *v.t.*—*allotted, allotting.* [O.Fr. *allotir, alloter*, to divide, part—*al* for *ad*, to, and *lotir*, to cast lots for, from *lot*, a share, which itself is a Teutonic word=A. Sax. *hlot*. LOT.] To distribute or parcel out in parts or portions; to assign; to set apart; to destine.—**Allotable**, al-lot′a-bl, *a.* Capable of being allotted.—**Allotment**, al-lot′ment, *n.* The act of allotting; that which is allotted; a share, part, or portion granted or distributed; a place or piece of ground appropriated.—*Allotment-system*, the system of allotting small portions of land to farm labourers or others, to be cultivated, after regular work, by themselves and families.—**Allottee**, al-lot′tē, *n.* One to whom anything is allotted.

Allotropy, Allotropism, al-lot′ro-pi, al-lot′ro-pizm, *n.* [Gr. *allos*, another, and *tropos*, condition.] The capability exhibited by some substances of existing in more than one form, and with different characteristics (thus carbon forms both the diamond and charcoal).—**Allotropic**, al-lō-trop′ik, *a.* Of or pertaining to.

Allow, al-lou′, *v.t.* [Fr. *allouer*, to grant, settle, L.L. *allocare*—*ad*, to, and *locare*, to place. (ALLOCATE.) O.Fr. *allouer*, to approve or praise, from L. *ad*, and *laudare*, to praise, from *laus, laudis*, praise, has also influenced the meaning.] To grant, give, or make over; to assign (to *allow* him £300 a year); to admit; to own or acknowledge (*allow* a claim); to abate or deduct; to set apart (*allow* so much for loss); to grant permission to; to permit.—*v.i.* To concede; to make abatement or concession.—**Allowable**, al-lou′a-bl, *a.* Proper to be or capable of being allowed or permitted; not forbidden; permissible.—**Allowableness**, al-lou′a-bl-nes, *n.*—**Allowably**, al-lou′a-bli, *adv.* In an allowable manner; with propriety.—**Allowance**, al-lou′ans, *n.* Permission; licence; sanction; a quantity allowed or granted; relaxation of severity in censure; a deduction or abatement.—**Allowance**, al-lou′ans, *v.t.* To put upon allowance.—**Allowedly**,† al-lou′ed-li, *adv.* Admittedly.—**Allower**, al-lou′ėr, *n.* One who allows, permits, grants, or authorizes.

Alloy, al-loi′, *n.* [Originally *allay*, O.F. *aley*, L. *alligare*, bind, with confusion of Fr. *aloi*, legal standard of coin, *a*, according, and *loi*, law.] A baser metal mixed with a finer; a mixture of different metals; any metallic compound; *fig.* evil mixed with good.—**Alloy**, al-loi′, *v.t.* To reduce the purity of (a metal) by mixing with it a portion of less valuable metal; to reduce, abate, or impair by mixture.—**Alloyage**, al-loi′āj, *n.* The act of alloying metals.

Allspice, al′spīs, *n.* ALL.

Allude, al-lūd′, *v.i.*—*alluded, alluding.* [L. *alludo*, to play upon, to allude—*ad*, and *ludo*, to play.] To refer to something not directly mentioned; to hint at by remote suggestions (followed by *to*). *Syn.* under ADVERT.—**Allusion**, al-lū′zhon, *n.* The act of alluding; a reference to something not explicitly mentioned; an indirect or incidental suggestion; a hint.—**Allusive, Allusory**, al-lū′siv, al-lū′so-ri, *a.* Having allusion or reference to something not fully expressed; containing allusions.—**Allusively**, al-lū′siv-li, *adv.* In an allusive manner; by way of allusion.—**Allusiveness** al-lū′siv-nes, *n.*

Allure, al-lūr′, *v.t.*—*allured, alluring.* [Prefix *al* for *ad*, to, and *lure*, Fr. *leurrer*, to decoy. LURE.] To tempt by the offer of some good, real or apparent; to draw or try to draw by some proposed pleasure or advantage; to entice, decoy, tempt, attract.—**Allurement**, al-lūr′ment, *n.* The act of alluring, or that which allures.—**Allurer**, al-lūr′ėr, *n.* One who, or that which, allures.—**Alluring**, al-lūr′ing, *a.* Inviting; having the quality of attracting or tempting.—**Alluringly**, al-lūr′ing-li, *adv.* In an alluring manner; enticingly.

Alluvium, al-lū′vi-um, *n.* [L. *alluvius*, alluvial—*ad*, to, and *luo* = Gr. *louō*, L. *lavo*, to wash; akin *deluge, lotion, dilute*, &c.] Soil deposited by means of the action of water, often washed down from mountains or high grounds.—**Alluvial**, al-lū′vi-al, *a.* Pertaining to or having the character of alluvium; deposited by the action of waves or currents of water.

Ally, al-lī′, *v.t.*—*allied, allying.* [Fr. *allier*, to join, to unite, *s'allier*, to confederate or become allied—*al* for *ad*, to, and *lier*, to tie or unite; L. *ligare*, to bind, whence *league, ligament.*] To unite by marriage, treaty, league, or confederacy; to connect by formal agreement; to bind together or connect (as by friendship or pursuits).—*v.i.* To be closely united.—*n.* A prince or state united by treaty or league: a confederate.—**Alliance**, al-lī′ans, *n.* [O.Fr. *alliance.*] The state of being allied or connected; the relation or union between families, contracted by marriage; a union between nations, contracted by compact, treaty, or league; any union or connection of interests; a compact or treaty; the persons or parties allied.

Almagest, al′ma-jest, *n.* [Ar. *al*, the, Gr. *megistē*, greatest.] The great geographical compilation of Ptolemy; great books on astrology and kindred arts.

Almagra, al-mā′gra, *n.* [Sp., from Ar. *almaghrat*, red clay or earth.] A fine deep red ochre; Indian red.

Alma-Mater, al′ma-mā′tėr. [L., benign mother, fostering mother.] An epithet applied by students to the university where they have been trained.

Almanac, Almanack, al′ma-nak, *n.* [Fr. *almanach*, Sp. *almanaque*, Ar. *al-manakh*, probably from a root meaning to reckon; Heb. *manah.*] A table, book, or publication of some kind, generally annual, comprising a calendar of days, weeks, and months, with the times of the rising of the sun and moon, changes of the moon, eclipses, stated festivals of churches, &c., for a certain year or years.

Almandine, Almondine, al′man-dīn, al′mun-dīn, *n.* [Fr. *almandine*, L.L. *alamandina, alavandina, alabandina*, a gem brought from *Alabanda*, a city in Asia Minor.] A name given to the violet or violet-red varieties of the spinel ruby, and also to precious or noble garnet.

Alme, Almeh, al′mē, *n.* The name given in some parts of the East, and especially in Egypt, to singing and dancing girls.

Almighty, al-mī′ti, *a.* [*All* and *mighty.*] Possessing all power; omnipotent; being of unlimited might.—*The Almighty*, the omnipotent God.—**Almightily**,† al-mī′ti-li, *adv.* In an almighty manner; with almighty power.—**Almightiness**, al-mī′ti-nes, *n.* The quality of being almighty; omnipotence.

Almond, ä′mund, *n.* [O.Fr. *almandre*, Fr. *amande*, It. *amandola*, corrupted from L. *amygdala*, Gr. *amygdalē*, an almond.] The seed or kernel of a tree allied to the peach; the tree itself. There are two varieties, *sweet* and *bitter*. The name is also given to the seeds of some other species of plants; also to a tonsil or gland of the throat.—**Almond-cake**, *n.* The cake left after expressing the oil from almonds.—**Almond-oil**, *n.* A bland, fixed oil obtained from almonds.—**Almond-paste**, *n.* A cosmetic to soften the skin and prevent chaps.—**Almond-willow**, *n.* *Salix amygdalina*, a British species of willow.

Almondine. ALMANDINE.

Almoner, al′mon-ėr, *n.* [O.Fr. *almosnier*, L.L. *eleemosynarius*, from Gr. *eleēmosynē* = E. *alms.*] A dispenser of alms or charity; more especially an officer who directs or carries out the distribution of charitable doles in connection with religious communities, hospitals, or alms-houses, or on behalf of some superior.—**Almonry**, al′mon-ri, *n.* The place where an almoner resides, or where alms are distributed.

Almost, al′mōst, *adv.* [*All* and *most.*] Nearly; well nigh; for the greatest part.

Alms, ämz, *n.* [O.E. *almesse, almes*, A. Sax. *almes, ælmesse*, borrowed from L. *eleemosyna*, alms, from Gr. *eleēmosynē*, pity.] Anything given gratuitously to relieve the poor; a charitable dole; charity. [This word (like *riches*) is strictly a singular, but its form has caused it to be often regarded as grammatically plural.]—**Alms-deed**, *n.* An act of charity; a charitable gift.—**Alms-folk**, *n.* Persons supported by alms.—**Alms-gate**, *n.* The gate of religious or great houses, at which alms were distributed to the poor.—**Alms-giver**, *n.* One who gives alms.—**Alms-giving**, *n.* The act of giving alms.—**Alms-house**, *n.* A house appropriated for the use of the poor who are supported by the public or by a revenue derived from public endowment; a poor-house.—**Alms-man**, *n.* pl. **Alms-men**. A person supported by charity or by public provision.

Almug, Algum, al′mug, al′gum, *n.* A tree or wood of unknown species mentioned in the Old Testament.

Alnage, al′nāj, *n.* [Fr. *aulnage*, from O.Fr. *alne*, L. *ulna*, an *ell.*] A measuring by the ell.—**Alnager**, al′nā-jėr, *n.* Formerly an official whose duty was to inspect and measure woollen cloth, and fix upon it a seal.

Aloe, al′ō, *n.* [Gr. *aloē.*] The common name of the plants of the genus Aloë, of the same order as the lily. They are natives of warm climates, and especially abundant in Africa. Several species yield *aloes*, the well-known bitter purgative medicine.—**Aloes-wood**, *n.* Same as *Agallochum*.—**Aloetic, Aloetical**, al-ō-et′ik, al-ō-et′-ik-al, *a.* Pertaining to or obtained from the aloe or aloes; partaking of the qualities of aloes.

Aloft, a-loft′, *adv.* [Icel. *á lopt* (pron. loft). LOFT.] On high; in the air; high above the ground; *naut.* on the higher yards or rigging.

Alone, a-lōn′, *a*, or *adv.* [*All* and *one*—the *all* and *one* being formerly printed as separate words; G. *allein*, Dan. *allene*, D. *alleen*, alone, are formed in the same way.] Apart from another or others; single; solitary (to remain *alone*, to walk *alone*); only; to the exclusion of other persons or things; solely (he *alone* remained, two men *alone* returned). Rarely used before a noun, as one *alone* verse.—*To let alone*, to leave untouched or not meddled with.—**Aloneness**,† a-lōn′-nes, *n.* The state of being.

Along, a-long′, *adv.* [A.Sax. *andlang*, *an-long*—prefix *and*, *an* (in answer), and *lang*, *long.*] By the length; lengthwise; in a line with the length (stretched *along*); in a line or with a progressive motion; onward (to walk *along*); in company; together (followed by *with*).—*prep.* By the length of, as distinguished from *across*; in a longitudinal direction over or near.—**Alongshore**, a-long′shōr, *adv.* By the shore or coast; lengthwise and near the shore.—*Alongshore man*, a labourer employed about shipping.—**Alongside**, a-long′sīd, *adv.* Along or by the side; beside each other (to lie *alongside* or *alongside of*).—*prep.* Beside; by the side of.

Along, a-long′, *prep.* [A.Sax. *gelang*, owing to, from *gelingan*, to happen.] Owing to; on account of: followed by *of*, and now used mainly by the vulgar or uneducated.

Aloof, a-löf′, *adv.* (O.E. *a-lofe*—prefix *a*, on, and *loof* or *luff*, windward.] At a distance, but within view; apart; separated.—*prep.*‡ Away or apart from. [*Mil.*]

Alopecy, al′ō-pe-si, *n.* [L. *alopecia*, Gr. *alōpekia*, from *alōpēx*, a fox, because foxes are said to be subject to this disease.] A disease called the fox-evil or scurf, accompanied by a falling off of the hair.

Aloud, a-loud′, *adv.* With a loud voice or great noise; loudly.

Alow, a-lō′, *adv.* In a low place, or a lower part: opposed to *aloft*.

Alp, alp, *n.* [From the *Alps*, well-known mountains in Central Europe.] A high mountain.—**Alpenhorn**, al′pen-horn, *n.* [G. *Alpen*, the Alps, and *horn*, a horn.] A very long, powerful, nearly straight horn, but curving slightly and widening towards its extremity, used on the Alps to convey signals. Called also *Alphorn*.—**Alpenstock**, al′pen-stok, *n.* [G. *Alpen*, the Alps, and *stock*, a stick.] A strong tall stick shod with iron, pointed at the end, used in climbing the Alps and other high mountains.—**Alpine**, al′pīn, *a.* Of, pertaining to, or connected with the Alps, or any lofty mountain; mountainous.—*n.* An Alpine plant.—**Alpinery**, al-pīn′ėr-i, *n.* A place in a garden or elsewhere set apart for the cultivation of Alpine plants.

Alpaca, al-pak′a, *n.* [Peruv. *alpaco.*] A ruminant mammal, of the camel tribe, a native of the Andes, valued for its long, soft, and silky wool, which is woven into fabrics of great beauty; a fabric manufactured from the wool of the alpaca.

Alpha, al′fa, *n.* The first letter in the Greek alphabet, answering to A, sometimes used to denote what is first or a beginning.—*Alpha and Omega*. The first and last letters of the Greek alphabet; the end of all things, the consummation of all.—**Alphabet**, al'fa-bet, *n.* [Gr. *alpha* and *bēta*, A and B.] The letters of a language arranged in the customary order; any series of elementary signs or symbols used for a similar purpose; hence, first elements; simplest rudiments.—**Alphabetarian**, al'fa-bet-ā"ri-an, *n.* A learner of the alphabet.—**Alphabetic, Alphabetical**, al-fa-bet'ik, al-fa-bet'ik-al, *a.* Pertaining to an alphabet; furnished with an alphabet; expressed by an alphabet; in the order of an alphabet.—**Alphabetically**, al-fa-bet'ik-al-li, *adv.* In an alphabetical manner; in the customary order of the letters.—**Alphabetize**, al'fa-bet-īz, *v.t.* To arrange alphabetically.

Alquifou, Alquifore, al'ki-fö, al'ki-fōr, *n.* [Fr. *alquifoux*, Sp. *alquifol*: of Arabic origin.] A sort of lead ore found in Cornwall, used by potters to give a green varnish to their wares, and called potter's ore.

Already, al-red'i, *adv.* [*All* and *ready*.] Before the present time; before some specified time.

Alsatia. Formerly a sanctuary for criminals and law-breakers, Whitefriars in London. From Alsace, a French province which lies between the Vosges and the Rhine.

Alsatian, al-sā'shi-an, *a.* Of or pertaining to Alsace in France.—*n.* A native of Alsatia.

Also, al'so, *adv.* and *conj.* [*All* and *so*; A. Sax. *eall-swā, ealswā, alswā*, from *eall, eal*, all, quite, and *swā*, so. *As* is this word contracted.] In like manner; likewise; in addition; too; further.

Altaic, Altaian, al-tā'ik, al-tā'yan, *a.* Pertaining to the Altai, a vast range of mountains in Eastern Asia.—*Altaic* or *Altaian family of languages*, a family of languages which includes Hungarian, Finnish, Turkish, &c. Also called *Scythian* and *Turanian*.

Altar, al'tėr, *n.* [L. *altare*, from a root seen in L. *altus*, high.] An elevated place on which sacrifices were offered or incense burned to a deity; a table in a church for the celebration of the eucharist.—**Altarage**, al'tėr-āj, *n.* Offerings made upon an altar or to a church; the profits arising to priests from oblations, gifts, or dues on account of the altar; the small tithes. Called also *Altar-dues*.—**Altar-bread**, *n.* Bread prepared for the eucharist.—**Altar-card**, *n.* A printed or written transcript of certain portions of the communion service for the use of the priest officiating at the altar.—**Altar-cloth**, *n.* The cloth that covers the altar, and hangs down in front.—**Altar-piece**, *n.* A painting or piece of sculpture placed behind or above an altar in a church.—**Altar-table**, *n.* The flat portion of an altar; a communion table.—**Altar-tomb**, *n.* A tomb having a general resemblance to an altar.

Altazimuth, alt-az'i-muth, *n.* [From *altitude* and *azimuth*.] An astronomical instrument for determining the altitude and azimuth of heavenly bodies, consisting of a vertical circle and attached telescope, the two having both a vertical and a horizontal motion.

Alter, al'tėr, *v.t.* [L.L. *altero*, to change, from L. *alter*, another of two—root *al*, another (seen in *alius*, Gr. *allos*, another, E. *else*), and compar. suffix *-ter* = E. *-ther* in *other*, &c.] To make other or different; to make some change in; to vary in some degree, without an entire change.—*v.i.* To become, in some respects, different; to vary; to change.—**Alterability**, al'tėr-a-bil"i-ti, *n.* The quality of being susceptible of alteration.—**Alterable**, al'tėr-a-bl, *a.* Capable of being altered, varied, or made different.—**Alterableness**, al'tėr-a-bl-nes, *n.* The quality of being alterable.—**Alterably**, al-tėr-a-bli, *adv.* In an alterable manner; so as to be altered or varied.—**Alteration**, al-tėr-ā'shon, *n.* The act of altering; the state of being altered; also, the change made.—**Alterative**, al'tėr-āt-iv, *a.* Causing alteration; having the power to alter; *med.* having the power to restore the healthy functions of the body without sensible evacuations.—*n.* A medicine having this character.

Altercate, al'tėr-kāt, *v.i.* [L. *altercor, altercatus*, to wrangle, from *alter*, another. ALTER.] To contend in words; to wrangle.—**Altercation**, al-tėr-kā'shon, *n.* The act of altercating; warm contention in words; heated argument; a wrangle.

Altern,† al'tėrn, *a.* [L. *alternus*, from *alter*, another. ALTER.] Acting by turns; alternate. [*Mil.*]—**Alternacy**,† al-tėr'na-si, *n.* The state of being alternate.—**Alternant**, al-tėr'nant, *a.* Alternating.—**Alternate**, al-tėr'nāt, *a.* [L. *alternatus*, pp. of *alterno*, to do by turns.] Being by turns; following one another in time or place by turns; first one, then another successively; reciprocal; having one intervening between each pair; occupying every second place; consisting of parts or members proceeding in this way (an *alternate* series).—*Alternate generation*, that species of generation among animals by which the young do not resemble their parent, but their grand-parent or some remote ancestor; heterogenesis.—**Alternate**, al'tėr-nāt or al-tėr'nāt, *v.t.*—*alternated, alternating*. To perform by turns or in succession; to cause to succeed or follow by turns.—*v.i.* To follow one another in time or place by turns.—**Alternately**, al-tėr'nāt-li, *adv.* In an alternate manner.—**Alternateness**, al-tėr'nāt-nes, *n.* The state or quality of being alternate.—**Alternation**, al-tėr-nā'shon, *n.* The act of alternating, or state of being alternate; the act of following and being followed in turn.—**Alternative**, al-tėr'na-tiv, *a.* Offering a choice or possibility of one of two things.—*n.* A choice between two things, so that if one is taken the other must be left; a possibility of one of two things, so that if one is false the other must be true.—**Alternatively**, al-tėr'na-tiv-li, *adv.* In an alternative manner.—**Alternativeness**, al-tėr'na-tiv-nes, *n.*

Although, al-THŌ', *conj.* [*All*, if, even, and *though*; comp. *albeit*.] Grant all this; be it so; suppose that; admit all that. *Although* differs very little from *though*, but is perhaps rather stronger.

Altimeter, al-tim'et-ėr, *n.* [L. *altus*, high, and Gr. *metron*, measure.] An instrument for taking altitudes by geometrical principles, as a quadrant.—**Altimetry**, al-tim'et-ri, *n.* The art of ascertaining altitudes.

Altiscope, al'ti-skōp, *n.* [L. *altus*, high, and Gr. *skopeō*, to look at.] An instrument of a telescopic character with lenses and mirrors, enabling a person to overlook objects intervening between himself and another object.

Altitude, al'ti-tūd, *n.* [L. *altitudo*, from *altus*, high (whence *exalt, haughty*).] Height; amount of space to a point above from one below; measure of elevation; *pl.* haughty airs (colloq.).

Alto al'tō or äl'tō, *n.* [It., from L. *altus*, high, being above the tenor.] *Mus.* contralto; the deepest voice among women and boys, and the highest among men, a special voice above the tenor; a singer in this voice.—*a.* Pertaining to this voice.—**Alto-clef**, *n.* *Mus.* the C clef.—**Alto-rilievo**, äl'tō-rē-lyā"vo, *n.* High relief; sculpture in which the figures stand out prominently from the background.

Altogether, al-tu-geTH'ėr, *adv.* [*All*, quite, and *together*.] Wholly; entirely; completely; quite.

Altruism, al'trö-izm, *n.* [It. *altrui*, others, from L. *alter*, another.] Devotion to others or to humanity: the opposite of *selfishness*.—**Altruist**, al'trö-ist, *n.* One who practises altruism.—**Altruistic**, al-trö-ist'ik, *a.* Pertaining to altruism; regardful of others.

Alum, al'um, *n.* [L. *alumen*.] A general name for a class of double sulphates containing aluminium and such metals as potassium, ammonium, iron, &c. Common or potash alum is used medicinally as an astringent and a styptic; in dyeing, as a mordant; in tanning, for restoring the cohesion of skins.—*v.t.* To steep in or impregnate with a solution of alum.—**Alumina, Alumine**, al-ū'min-a, al'ū-min, *n.* The oxide of aluminium, the most abundant of the earths, widely diffused in the shape of clay, loam, &c.—**Aluminiferous**, al-ū'-min-if"ėr-us, *a.* Containing alum or alumina.—**Aluminiform**, al-ū-min'i-form, *a.* Having the form of alum, alumina, or aluminium.—**Aluminite**, al-ū'min-īt, *n.* Hydrous sulphate of alumina.—**Aluminium, Aluminum**, al-ū-min'i-um, al-ū'-min-um, *n.* Chemical sym. Al; atomic weight = 27·5; sp. gr. 2·6 nearly. The metallic base of alumina; a white metal with a bluish tinge, and a lustre somewhat resembling, but far inferior to, that of silver.—*Aluminium bronze*, an alloy of aluminium and copper, possessed of great tenacity, for industrial purposes.—*Aluminium gold*, an alloy of 10 parts of aluminium to 90 of copper.—**Aluminous**, al-ū'min-us, *a.* Pertaining to or containing alum or alumina.—**Alum-rock, Alum-stone**, *n.* A mineral of a grayish or yellowish-white colour, containing alumina and potash.—**Alum-root**, *n.* A name given to the astringent root of several plants.—**Alum-schist, Alum-slate**, *n.* A thin-bedded fissile rock chiefly composed of silica and alumina.

Alumnus, a-lum'nus, *n.* pl. **Alumni**, a-lum'nī. [L. a disciple, from *alo*, to nourish.] Formerly a pupil; now a graduate of an educational institution.

Alveary, al'vē-a-ri, *n.* [L. *alvearium*, a bee-hive.] A bee-hive, or something resembling a bee-hive; the hollow of the external ear.—**Alveated**, al'vē-āt-ed, *a.* Formed or vaulted like a bee-hive.—**Alveolar, Alveolary**, al'vē-o-lėr, al'vē-o-la-ri, *a.* Containing sockets, hollow cells, or pits; pertaining to sockets, specifically the sockets of the teeth.—**Alveolate**, al'vē-o-lāt, *a.* Deeply pitted, so as to resemble a honey-comb.—**Alveolus**, al-vē'o-lus, *n.* pl. **Alveoli**, al-vē'o-lī. [L., a little hollow, dim. of *alveus*.] A cell, as in a honey-comb or in a fossil; the socket of a tooth.—**Alveus**, al'vē-us, *n.* [L., a hollow vessel, a channel.] *Anat.* a tube or canal through which some fluid flows.

Alvine, al'vīn, *a.* [From L. *alvus*, the belly.] Belonging to the belly or intestines; relating to the intestinal excrements.

Always, al'wāz, *adv.* [*All* and *way, -ways* being an adverbial genitive.] Perpetually; uninterruptedly; continually (*always* the same); as often as occasion recurs (he is *always* late).

Am, am. [For hypothetical *arm, asm*; comp. Goth. *im* for *ism*, Icel. *em* for *erm, esm*, Lith. *esmi*, L. *sum*, Skr. *asmi*, made up of root *as*, to breathe, exist, be, and *mi*, cognate with E. *me*. In the conjugation of this verb three different roots are employed; seen in *am, was, be*. BE, WAS.] The first person of the verb *to be*, in the indicative mood, present tense.

Amadavat, am-a-da-vat', *n.* [East Indian name.] A small granivorous bird of India, having a red conical beak and red and black plumage, often imported as a cage bird.

Amadou, am'a-dö, *n.* [Fr. *amadou*, a word of Scandinavian origin.] A soft leathery substance used for tinder, prepared from a fungus growing on trees; German tinder.

Amain, a-mān', *adv.* [Prefix *a*, in, on, and *main*, force.] With force, strength, or violence; suddenly; at once.

Amalgam, a-mal'gam, *n.* [Fr. *amalgame*, Gr. *malagma*, a soft mass.] A compound of mercury or quicksilver with another metal; any metallic alloy of which mercury forms an essential constituent part; a mixture or compound of different things.—**Amalgamate**, a-mal'gam-āt, *v.t.*—*amalgamated, amalgamating*. To compound or mix (a metal) with quicksilver; commonly, to blend, unite, or combine generally into one mass or whole.—*v.i.* To combine to form an amalgam; to unite or coalesce generally; to become mixed or blended together.—**Amalgamation**, a-mal'ga-mā"shon, *n.* The act or operation of amalgamating; the state of being amalgamated;

union or junction into one body or whole; the process of separating gold and silver from their ores by combining them with mercury, which dissolves and separates the other metal, and is afterwards driven off by heat.—**Amalgamator**, a-mal'ga-mā-tėr, *n.* One who or that which amalgamates.

Amandine, a-man'din, *n.* [Fr. *amande*, an almond.] A kind of paste for chapped hands prepared from almonds.

Amandola, a-man'dō-la, *n.* [It., an almond.] A green marble with white spots.

Amanuensis, a-man'ū-en"sis, *n.* pl. **Amanuenses**, a-man'ū-en"sēz. [L. *a*, by, and *manus*, the hand.] A person whose employment is to write what another dictates, or to copy what has been written by another.

Amaracus, a-mar'a-kus, *n.* [L.] Marjoram.

Amaranth, am'a-ranth, *n.* [Gr. *amarantos*, unfading—*a*, neg., and *marainō*, to wither.] A poetical name loosely used to signify a flower supposed never to fade; a colour inclining to purple.—**Amaranthine**, am-a-ranth'in, *a.* Belonging to, consisting of, or resembling amaranth; never-fading; of a purplish colour.

Amaryllis, am-a-ril'lis, *n.* [Greek female name.] A genus of bulbous-rooted plants with fine flowers. Some of them, called lilies, forming the type of a natural order of plants, the Amaryllidaceæ.

Amass, a-mas', *v.t.* [Fr. *amasser*—*a*, to, and *masse*, L. *massa*, a mass.] To collect into a heap; to gather a great quantity or number of; to accumulate.—**Amassment**, a-mas'ment, *n.* The act of amassing.

Amateur, am'a-tūr, am-a-tėr (ė long), *n.* [Fr., from L. *amator*, *amatoris*, a lover, from *amo*, to love.] One who cultivates any study or art from taste or attachment without pursuing it professionally or with a view to gain; one who has a taste for the arts.—**Amateurish**, am-a-tūr'ish, *a.* Pertaining to or characteristic of an amateur; wanting the skill, finish, or other faculties of a professional.

Amative, am'at-iv, *a.* [L. *amo*, *amatum*, to love.] Full of love; amorous; amatory.—**Amativeness**, am'at-iv-nes, *n.* *Phren.* that propensity which impels to sexual passion.—**Amatorial**,† **Amatorian**,† **Amatorious**,† am-a-tō'ri-al, am-a-tō'ri-an, am-a-tō'ri-us, *a.* Pertaining to love; amatory.—**Amatory**, am'a-to-ri, *a.* Pertaining to or producing love; expressive of love (verses, sighs, &c.).

Amaurosis, am-ą-rō'sis, *n.* [Gr. *amaurōsis*, from *amauros*, obscure.] A partial or complete loss of sight from loss of power in the optic nerve or retina, without any visible defect in the eye except an immovable pupil; gutta serena.—**Amaurotic**, a-mą-rot'ik, *a.* Pertaining to or affected with amaurosis.

Amaze, a-māz', *v.t.* [Prefix *a*, on or in, and *maze* (which see).] To confound with fear, sudden surprise, or wonder; to confuse utterly; to perplex; to astound; to astonish; to surprise.—*n.* Astonishment; confusion; amazement: used chiefly in poetry.—**Amazedly**, a-māz'ed-li, *adv.* With amazement.—**Amazedness**, a-māz'ed-nes, *n.* The state of being amazed; amazement.—**Amazeful**,‡ a-māz'fụl, *a.* Full of amazement; amazing.—**Amazement**, a-māz'-ment, *n.* The state of being amazed or astounded; astonishment; great surprise.—**Amazing**, a-māz'ing, *a.* Very wonderful; exciting astonishment.—**Amazingly**, a-māz'ing-li, *adv.* In an amazing manner or degree.

Amazon, am'a-zon, *n.* [Gr. *amazōn*: of unknown origin.] One of a fabled race of female warriors who are mentioned by the ancient Greek writers; hence, a warlike or masculine woman; a virago.—**Amazonian**, am-a-zō'ni-an, *a.* Pertaining to or resembling an Amazon; of masculine manners; also, belonging to the river Amazon in South America.

Ambages,† am-bā'jēz, *n.pl.* [L.] Windings or turnings; hence, circumlocution; subterfuges; evasions.—**Ambagious**,† **Ambagitory**,† am-bā'jus, am-baj'i-to-ri, *a.* Circumlocutory; roundabout.

Ambassador, am-bas'sa-dor, *n.* [Fr. *ambassadeur*, from *ambassade*, an embassy, from L. *ambactus*, a vassal, a dependant, from a Teutonic word = Goth. *andbahts*, A.Sax. *ambiht*, *ambeht*, a servant, from prefix *and* (the *an* in *an*swer), and a root allied to Skr. *bhaj*, to serve or honour.] A minister of the highest rank employed by one prince or state at the court of another to transact state affairs. [The spelling *Embassador* is obsolete, though *Embassy*, not *Ambassy* is used.]—**Ambassadorial**, am-bas'sa-dō"ri-al, *a.* Belonging to an ambassador.—**Ambassadress**, am-bas'sa-dres, *n.* The wife of an ambassador; a female ambassador.

Ambatch, am'bach, *n.* [African name.] A thorny leguminous shrub with yellow flowers, growing in tropical African rivers, with light spongy wood, often made into rafts.

Amber, am'bėr, *n.* [Fr. *ambre*, It. *ambra*, Sp. *ambar*, from Ar. *ambar*, ambergris, from its resemblance to this.] A mineralized pale-yellow, and sometimes reddish or brownish, resin of extinct pine-trees, found most abundantly on the shores of the Baltic.—**Amber-seed**, *n.* The seed of *Abelmoschus moschatus*, an Asiatic plant, used as a perfume, having a musky smell.—**Amber-tree**, *n.* An African shrub, the leaves of which, when bruised, emit a fragrant odour.

Ambergris, am'bėr-grēs, *n.* [Fr. *ambre gris* (*gris*, gray), gray amber.] A solid, opaque, ash-coloured inflammable substance used in perfumery. It is a morbid secretion obtained from the spermaceti whale.

Ambidexter,† am-bi-deks'tėr, *n.* [L. *ambo*, both, and *dexter*, the right hand.] A person who uses both hands with equal facility; one equally ready to act on either side.—**Ambidexterity**,† **Ambidextrousness**,† am'bi-deks-ter"i-ti, am-bi-deks'trus-nes, *n.* The quality of being ambidextrous; double-dealing.—**Ambidextrous**,† am-bi-deks'trus, *a.* Having the faculty of using both hands with equal ease; double-dealing.

Ambient, am'bi-ent, *a.* [L. *ambiens*, *ambientis*—*amb*, around, and *iens*, ppr. of *ire*, to go.] Surrounding; encompassing on all sides: applied to fluids or diffusible substances (the *ambient* air).

Ambiguous, am-big'ū-us, *a.* [L. *ambiguus*, from *ambigo*, to go about—*ambi*, about, and *ago*, to drive.] Doubtful or uncertain, especially in respect to signification; liable to be interpreted two ways; equivocal; indefinite.—**Ambiguously**, am-big'ū-us-li, *adv.* In an ambiguous manner; with doubtful meaning.—**Ambiguity**, **Ambiguousness**, am-bi-gū'i-ti, am-big'ū-us-nes, *n.* The state or quality of being ambiguous; doubtfulness or uncertainty, particularly of signification.

Ambiloquous,† am-bil'o-kwus, *a.* [L. *ambo*, both, and *loquor*, to speak.] Using ambiguous expressions.

Ambit, am'bit, *n.* [L. *ambitus*, a circuit. AMBIENT.] Compass or circuit; circumference; scope; sphere; extent.

Ambition, am-bi'shon, *n.* [L. *ambitio*, *ambitionis*, the going about of candidates for office in Rome, hence flattery, ambition—*amb*, around, round about, and *eo*, *itum*, to go, from L. Gr. and Skr. root *i*, to go.] An eager and sometimes inordinate desire after honour, power, fame, or whatever confers distinction; desire to distinguish one's self among others.—*v.t.*† To seek after ambitiously.—**Ambitionless**, am-bi'shon-les, *a.* Devoid of ambition.—**Ambitious**, am-bi'shus, *a.* [L. *ambitiosus*.] Possessing ambition; eagerly or inordinately desirous of power, honour, fame, office, superiority, or distinction; strongly desirous (with *of* or *after*); springing from, indicating, or characterized by ambition; showy; pretentious (*ambitious* ornament).—**Ambitiously**, am-bi'shus-li, *adv.* In an ambitious manner.—**Ambitiousness**, am-bi'shus-nes, *n.* The quality of being ambitious; ambition.

Amble, am'bl, *v.i.*—*ambled*, *ambling*. [O.Fr. *ambler*, to amble, from L. *ambulo*, to walk, from *amb*, about.] To move by lifting both legs on each side alternately: said of horses, &c.; hence, to move easily and gently.—*n.* The pace of a horse or like animal when ambling; easy motion; gentle pace.—**Ambler**, am'blėr, *n.* One who ambles.—**Amblingly**, am'bling-li, *adv.* With an ambling gait.

Amblotic, am-blō'tik, *a.* [Gr. *amblōsis*, abortion.] Having the power to cause abortion.

Amblygon, am'bli-gon, *n.* [Gr. *amblys*, obtuse. and *gōnia*, an angle.] An obtuse-angled triangle.—**Amblygonal**, am-blig'-on-al, *a.* Having an obtuse angle; obtuse.—**Amblygonite**, am-blig'on-īt, *n.* A greenish-coloured mineral, of different pale shades, marked with reddish and yellowish brown spots.

Amblyopia, **Amblyopy**, am-bli-ō'pi-a, am'bli-o-pi, *n.* [From Gr. *amblys*, dull, and *ōps*, *ōpos*, the eye.] Dulness or dimness of eyesight without any apparent defect in the organs—the first stage in amaurosis.

Ambo, **Ambon**, am'bo, am'bon, *n.* [Gr. *ambōn*, a stage, a pulpit.] In early Christian churches a raised desk or pulpit.

Amboyna-wood, am-boi'na-wụd, *n.* [*Amboyna*, one of the Molucca Islands.] A beautifully mottled and curled wood employed in cabinet-work.

Ambreada, am-bre-ā'da, *n.* [From *amber*.] A kind of fictitious amber.

Ambrosia, am-brō'zhi-a, *n.* [Gr. *ambrosia*, from *ambrotos*, immortal—*a*, priv., and same root as L. *mors*, death, E. *murder*.] The fabled food of the ancient Greek gods, which conferred immortality on those who partook of it; hence, anything pleasing to the taste or smell, as a perfumed draught, unguent, or the like.—**Ambrosial**, am-brō'zhi-al, *a.* Of or pertaining to ambrosia; anointed or fragrant with ambrosia; delicious; fragrant.—**Ambrosially**, am-brō'zhi-al-li, *adv.* In an ambrosial manner; with an ambrosial odour.

Ambry, am'bri, *n.* [From L. *armarium*, tool chest. Scottish *aumry*, through French.] An almonry‡; a niche or recess in the wall of ancient churches near the altar in which the sacred utensils were deposited; a cupboard†.

Ambsace, āmz'ās, *n.* [O.F. *ambes ace*.] Amesace; complete bad luck, the two aces being the lowest throw at dice.

Ambulacrum, am-bū-lā'krum, *n.* pl. **Ambulacra**, am-bū-lā'kra. [L. *ambulacrum*, an alley.] One of the perforated spaces or avenues through which are protruded the tube feet, by means of which locomotion is effected in the sea-urchins, &c.—**Ambulacral**, am-bū-lā'kral, *a.* Pertaining to ambulacra.

Ambulance, am'bū-lans, *n.* [Fr. AMBULATE.] A vehicle fitted with suitable appliances for conveying the injured and sick. Also a mobile hospital unit which accompanies an army in its movements in the field.—**Ambulance-company**, *n.* A group of hospital corps.

Ambulate,† am'bū-lāt, *v.i.*—*ambulated*, *ambulating*. [L. *ambulo*, *ambulatum*, to go about. AMBLE.] To move backward and forward; to walk.—**Ambulant**, am'bū-lant, *a.* Walking; moving from place to place.—**Ambulation**, am-bū-lā'shon, *n.* The act of ambulating or walking about.—**Ambulator**, am'bū-lāt-ėr, *n.* One who walks about; an instrument for measuring distances travelled.—**Ambulatory**, am'-bū-la-to-ri, *a.* Having the power or faculty of walking; adapted for walking; pertaining to a walk; accustomed to move from place to place; not stationary (an *ambulatory* court).—*n.* Any part of a building intended for walking in.

Ambury, am'bu-ri, *n.* Same as *Anberry*.

Ambuscade, am-bus-kād', *n.* [Fr. *embuscade*, from It. *imboscare*, to lie in bushes-

in, in, and *bosco*, a wood, the same word as E. *bush*.] A lying in wait and concealed for the purpose of attacking an enemy by surprise; a place where one party lies concealed with a view to attack another by surprise; those lying so concealed; ambush. —*v.t.* and *i.*—*ambuscaded, ambuscading.* To lie in wait in order to attack from a concealed position.—**Ambush**, am'bush, *n.* [O.Fr. *embusche*, verb *embuscher*, to lie in wait.] Same as *Ambuscade.*—*v.t.* To post or place in ambush.—*v.i.* To lie or be posted in ambush.—**Ambushment**, am'bush-ment, *n.* An ambush. [O.T.]

Ameer, Amir, a-mēr', *n.* [Ar.] A nobleman; a chief; a ruler; an emir.

Amelancier, a-me-lan'shi-ėr, *n.* [Fr.] A genus of small trees allied to the medlar, natives of Europe and N. America, cultivated for both flowers and fruit.

Ameliorate, a-mēl'yor-āt, *v.t.*—*ameliorated, ameliorating.* [Fr. *améliorer*, from L. *ad*, to, and *melioro, melioratum*, to make better, from *melior*, better.] To make better; to improve; to meliorate.—*v.i.* To grow better; to meliorate.—**Ameliorable**, a-mēl'yor-a-bl, *a.* Capable of being ameliorated.—**Amelioration**, a-mēl'yor-ā"shon, *n.* The act of ameliorating; improvement; melioration.—**Ameliorative**, a-mēl'yor-āt-iv, *a.* Producing, or having a tendency to produce, amelioration.—**Ameliorator**, a-mēl'yor-āt-ėr, *n.* One who ameliorates.

Amen, ā-men. [Heb. *āmen*, verily, firm, established.] A term occurring generally at the end of a prayer, and meaning So be it. In the N. T. it is used as a noun to denote Christ as being one who is true and faithful, and as an adjective to signify made true, verified, fulfilled.

Amenable, a-mē'na-bl, *a.* [Fr. *amener*, to bring or lead to—*a*, to, and *mener*, to lead. DEMEAN.] Liable to answer or be called to account; responsible; ready to yield or submit, as to advice; submissive.—**Amenableness, Amenability**, a-mē'na-bl-nes, a-mē'na-bil"i-ti, *n.* The state of being amenable.—**Amenably**, a-mē'na-bli, *adv.* In an amenable manner.

Amend, a-mend', *v.t.* [Fr. *amender*, for *emender*, to correct, from L. *emendo*, to free from faults—*e*, out, out of, and *menda*, a fault. MEND.] To make better, or change for the better, by removing what is faulty; to correct; to improve; to reform.—*v.i.* To grow or become better by reformation or rectifying something wrong in manners or morals. ∴ *Amend* differs from *improve* in this, that to *amend* implies something previously wrong, while to *improve* does not necessarily do so.—**Amendable**, a-mend'a-bl, *a.* Capable of being amended or corrected.—**Amendatory**, a-mend'a-to-ri, *a.* Supplying amendment; corrective.—**Amender**, a-mend'ėr, *n.* One who amends.—**Amendment**, a-mend'ment, *n.* The act of amending, or changing for the better, in any way; the act of becoming better, or state of having become better; an alteration proposed to be made in the draft of a parliamentary bill, or in the terms of any motion under discussion before a meeting.—**Amends**, a-mendz', *n.pl.* Compensation for a loss or injury; recompense; satisfaction; equivalent.

Amende, ä-mänd, *n.* [Fr. *amende*, L.L. *amenda*, a penalty, reparation. AMEND.] A pecuniary punishment or fine; a recantation or reparation.—*Amende honorable*, a public or open recantation and reparation to an injured party.

Amenity, a-men'i-ti, *n.* [Fr. *aménité*, L. *amœnitas, amœnus*, pleasant.] The quality of being pleasant or agreeable, in respect of situation, prospect, climate, &c., as also of temper, disposition, or manners.

Amenorrhœa, a-men-o-rē'a, *n.* [Gr. *a*, priv., *mēn*, month, *rheō*, to flow.] *Med.* a morbid or unnatural suppression of menstruation.

Amentia, a-men'shi-a, *n.* [L., want of reason—*a*, from, and *mens, mentis*, mind.] Imbecility of mind; idiocy or dotage.

Amentum, a-men'tum, *n.* pl. **Amenta**, a-men'ta. *Bot.* a kind of inflorescence consisting of unisexual apetalous flowers in the axils of scales or bracts ranged along a stalk or axis; a catkin.—**Amentaceous**, a-men-tā'shus, *a.* Consisting of, resembling, or furnished with an amentum or amenta.

Amerce, a-mėrs', *v.t.*—*amerced, amercing.* [Fr. *amercié*, fined at the mercy of the court —*a*, at, and *merci*, mercy.] To punish by a pecuniary penalty, the amount of which is left to the discretion of the court; hence, to punish by deprivation of any kind†.—**Amerceable**, a-mėrs'a-bl, *a.* Liable to amercement.—**Amercement**, a-mėrs'-ment, *n.* The act of amercing; a pecuniary penalty inflicted on an offender at the discretion of the court.—**Amercer**, a-mėrs'ėr, *n.* One who amerces.

American, a-mer'i-kan, *a.* Pertaining to America; often, in a restricted sense, pertaining to the United States.—*n.* A native of America; in a restricted sense, one of the inhabitants of the United States.—**Americanism**, a-mer'i-kan-izm, *n.* The feelings of nationality which distinguish American citizens; the exhibition of national prejudice by Americans; a word, phrase, or idiom peculiar to Americans.—**Americanize**, a-mer'i-kan-īz, *v.t.*—*americanized, americanizing.* To render American or like what prevails in or is characteristic of America (especially the United States); to naturalize in America.

Ametabola, a-me-tab'o-la, *n.pl.* [Gr. *ametabolos*, unchangeable.] A division of insects, including such as do not undergo any metamorphosis (lice, &c.).—**Ametabolic**, a-met'a-bol"ik, *a.* Of or belonging to the Ametabola.

Amethyst, am'ē-thist, *n.* [Gr. *amethystos* —*a*, neg., and *methyō*, to inebriate, from its supposed power of preventing or curing intoxication.] A violet-blue or purple variety of quartz which is wrought into various articles of jewelry.—*Oriental Amethyst*, a rare violet-coloured gem, a variety of corundum, of extraordinary brilliancy and beauty. —**Amethystine**, a-mē-thist'īn, *a.* Pertaining to, composed of, or resembling amethyst.

Amiable, ā'mi-a-bl, *a.* [Partly from Fr. *aimable*, lovely, amiable, from L. *amabilis*, from *amo*, to love, partly from Fr. *amiable*, amicable, L. *amicabilis*.] Worthy of love; delightful or pleasing (said of things)‡; possessing agreeable moral qualities; having an excellent and attractive disposition; lovable.—**Amiability, Amiableness**, ā'mi-a-bil"i-ti, ā'mi-a-bl-nes, *n.* The quality of being amiable or lovable; sweetness of temper.—**Amiably**, ā'mi-a-bli, *adv.* In an amiable manner.

Amianth, Amianthus, am'i-anth, am-i-an'thus, *n.* [Gr. *amiantos*—*a*, neg., and *miainō*, to pollute or vitiate: so called from its incombustibility.] Flexible asbestos, earth-flax, or mountain-flax; an incombustible mineral composed of delicate filaments, very flexible, and somewhat elastic, often long and resembling threads of silk.—**Amianthiform**, am-i-an'thi-form, *a.* Having the form or likeness of amianth.—**Amianthoid**, am-i-an'thoid, *n.* A mineral which resembles amianth or asbestos.

Amicable, am'ik-a-bl, *a.* [L. *amicabilis*, from *amicus*, a friend, from *amo*, to love.] Characterized by or exhibiting friendship, peaceableness, or harmony; friendly; peaceable; harmonious in social or mutual transactions. *Amicable* is a weaker word than *friendly*. *Friendly* is active and positive; *amicable* simply implies a degree of friendship such as makes us unwilling to disagree with those with whom we are on harmonious terms.—**Amicability, Amicableness**, am'ik-a-bil"i-ti, am'ik-a-bl-nes, *n.* Quality of being amicable.—**Amicably**, am'ik-a-bli, *adv.* In an amicable or friendly manner; with harmony.

Amice, am'is, *n.* [Confusion of O.F. *amit*, L. *amictus*, garment, with O.F. *amusse*, cap, mutch.] A flowing cloak formerly worn by priests and pilgrims; an oblong embroidered piece or strip of fine linen, falling down the shoulders like a cope, worn under the alb by priests in the service of the mass.

Amid, Amidst, a-mid', a-midst', *prep.* [Prefix *a*, on, in, and *mid, midst*, O.E. *amidde, amiddes* (the latter a genitive form); A. Sax. *on-middan*; the *t* has been tacked on as in *against*.] In the midst or middle of; surrounded or encompassed by; mingled with; among.—**Amidships**, a-mid'ships, *adv.* In or towards the middle or the middle line of a ship.

Amide, Amine, am'id, am'in, *n.* [From *am-* of *ammonia*.] *Chem.* names given to a series of salts produced by the substitution of elements or radicals for the hydrogen atoms of ammonia: often used as terminations of the names of such salts.—**Amidine**, am'id-in, *n.* A peculiar substance procured from wheat or potato starch, the soluble or gelatinous part.

Amiss, a-mis', *a.* [Prefix *a*, on, and *miss*.] Wrong; faulty; out of time or order; improper.—*adv.* In a faulty manner.—*To be not amiss*, to be passable or suitable; to be pretty fair. [Colloq.]

Amission,† a-mi'shon, *n.* [L. *amissio, amissionis*, from *amitto*—*a*, away, and *mitto*, to send.] Loss.—**Amissibility**,† a-mis'-i-bil"i-ti, *n.* The capability or possibility of being lost.—**Amissible**,† a-mis'i-bl, *a.* Capable of being or liable to be lost.

Amity, am'i-ti, *n.* [Fr. *amitié*, from L.L. *amicitas*, friendship; L. *amicus*, a friend, from *amo*, to love.] Friendship; harmony; good understanding, especially between nations.

Ammonia, am-mō'ni-a, *n.* [Gr. *ammoniakon*, sal-ammoniac, from being first obtained near the Temple of *Ammon* in Libya.] The modern name of the *volatile alkali*, formerly so called to distinguish it from the more fixed alkalies. It is a pungent gas, and may be procured artificially from organic matter (except fat) by subjecting it to heat in iron cylinders. It is used for many purposes, both in medicine and chemistry, most frequently in solution in water, under the names of *liquid ammonia* or *spirits of hartshorn*.—**Ammoniac, Ammoniacal**, am-mō'ni-ak, am-mō-nī'ak-al, *a.* Pertaining to ammonia, or possessing its properties.—**Ammoniacum, Ammoniac**, am-mō-nī'a-kum, am-mō'ni-ak, *n.* An exudation of an umbelliferous plant with a fetid smell, used as an antispasmodic and expectorant, and in plasters.—**Ammoniaphone**, am-mō'ni-a-fōn, *n.* [From *ammonia* and Gr. *phōnē*, voice.] A contrivance by means of which ammonia is inhaled, in order to make the voice fuller and clearer.—**Ammonium**, am-mō'ni-um, *n.* A name given to the hypothetical base of ammonia, not obtained separately.

Ammonite, am'mon-īt, *n.* [Resembling the horns with which Jupiter *Ammon* was furnished when represented by statues.] One of the fossil shells of an extensive genus of extinct cuttle-fishes, coiled in a plane spiral, and chambered within like that of the nautilus, to which the ammonites were allied.—**Ammonitiferous**, am'mon-īt-if"ėr-us, *a.* Containing the remains of ammonites.

Ammunition, am-mū-ni'shon, *n.* [Fr. *amunition*, L. *munitio*, defence, from *munio*, to fortify.] Military stores, especially such articles as are used in the discharge of firearms and ordnance of all kinds, as powder, balls, shells, shot, &c.

Amnesia, am-nē'si-a, *n.* [Gr. *a*. priv., and *mnēsis*, memory.] Loss of memory.

Amnesty, am'nes-ti, *n.* [L. *amnestia*, from Gr. *amnēstia*, oblivion—*a*, not, and root *mna*, to remember.] An act of oblivion; a general pardon of the offences of subjects against the government, or the proclamation of such pardon.—*v.t.*—*amnestied, amnestying.* To grant an amnesty to; to pardon.

Amnion, Amnios, am'ni-on, am'ni-os, *n.* [Gr.] The innermost membrane surrounding the fetus of mammals, birds, and reptiles; also a thin, semi-transparent, gelatinous fluid, in which the embryo of a seed is suspended when it first appears.—**Amniotic**, am-ni-ot'ik, *a.* Pertaining to the amnion; possessing an amnion.

Amœba, a-mē'ba, *n.* [Gr. *amoibē*, change.] The generic name of various microscopic Protozoa, one of which is common in our fresh-water ponds and ditches. It consists of a gelatinous mass, and from continually altering its shape it received this as well as its former name of *proteus-animalcule.*—**Amœboid, Amœbous**, a-mē'boid, a-mē'bus, *a.* Of or pertaining to or resembling the amœba.

Amœbean, am-ē-bē'an, *a.* [L. *amœbæus*, from Gr. *amoibaios*, alternate, *amoibē*, answer.] Alternately answering or responsive; exhibiting persons speaking alternately (an *amœbæan* poem).

Amok, a-mok', *n.* Same as *Amuck*.

Among, Amongst, a-mung', a-mungst', *prep.* [O.E. *amonge, amonges, amongest*, A. Sax. *amang, onmang*, from *mengan*, to mingle; the *es* being an adverbial genitive termination, and the *t* tacked on, as in *amidst.* MINGLE.] Mixed or mingled with (implying a number); in or into the midst of; in or into the number of (one *among* a thousand); jointly or with a reference to some one or other (they killed him *among* them).

Amontillado, a-mon'til-ä"dō, *n.* [Sp.] A dry kind of sherry of a light colour.

Amorce, a-mors', *n.* [Fr. *amorce*, from L. *ad*, to, *mordeo*, to bite.] A sort of percussion cap, a toy detonator consisting of a small quantity of explosive matter between two bits of gummed paper.

Amoretto, am-o-ret'tō (pl. **Amoretti**); **Amorino**, am-o-rē'nō (pl. **Amorini**), *n.* [It. from *amor*, love.] Terms in art for loves or cupids.

Amorous, am'or-us, *a.* [Fr. *amoureux*, L.L. *amorosus*, L. *amor*, love; akin *amity*, *amiable*, &c.] Inclined to love persons of the opposite sex; having a propensity to love, or to sexual enjoyment; loving; fond; pertaining or relating to love; produced by love; indicating love; enamoured (in this sense with *of*).—**Amorously**, am'or-us-li, *adv.* In an amorous manner; fondly, lovingly.—**Amorousness**, am'or-us-nes, *n.* The quality of being amorous.

Amorphous, a-mor'fus, *a.* [Gr. *amorphos*—*a*, neg., and *morphē*, form.] Having no determinate form; of irregular shape; not having the regular forms exhibited by the crystals of minerals; being without crystallization; formless; characterless.—**Amorphism**, a-mor'fizm, *n.* State of being amorphous or without shape.—**Amorphy**,† a-mor'fi, *n.* Irregularity of form.

Amortize, a-mor'tiz, *v.t.*—*amortized, amortizing.* [L.L. *amortisare*, to sell in mortmain—L. *ad*, to, and *mors, mortis*, death.] To alienate in mortmain; to extinguish (a debt) by means of a sinking fund.—**Amortization, Amortizement**, a-mor'tiz-ā"shon, a-mor'tiz-ment, *n.* The act or right of alienating lands or tenements in mortmain; the extinction of debt, especially by a sinking fund.

Amount, amount', *v.i.* [O.Fr. *amonter*, to advance, increase, *amont*, upwards—*a*, to, and *mont*, L. *mons, montis*, a hill.] To mount upwards ‡; to reach a certain total by an accumulation of particulars; to come in the aggregate or whole; to result in; to be equivalent: followed by *to*.—*n.* The sum total of two or more particular sums or quantities; the aggregate; the effect, substance, or result.

Amour, a-mör', *n.* [Fr., from L. *amour*, love.] A love intrigue; an affair of gallantry.

Ampere, am-pār', *n.* [From *Ampère*, name of a French electrician.] *Elect.* the unit employed in measuring the strength of an electric current.

Amphibia, am-fib'i-a, *n. pl.* [Gr. *amphibios*, living a double life—*amphi*, both, and *bios*, life.] A term strictly applied to such few animals as have both gills and lungs at once; but ordinarily extended so as to include all animals which possess both gills and lungs, whether at different stages of their existence or simultaneously, thus including the frogs and toads, which have gills in the tadpole stage.—**Amphibious**, am-fib'i-us, *a.* Having the power of living in two elements, air and water; having the characters of the Amphibia: applied in popular usage to any lung-breathing animal which can exist for a considerable time under water, as the crocodile, whale, seal, &c.; adapted for living on land or at sea.—**Amphibial, Amphibian**, am-fib'i-al, am-fib'i-an, *a.* Amphibious.—*n.* One of the Amphibia.—**Amphibiousness**, am-fib'i-us-nes, *n.*

Amphiblastic, am-fi-blas'tik, *a.* A term applied to ova intermediate between the holoblastic or mammalian ova, and the meroblastic, or ova of birds or reptiles.

Amphibole, am'fi-bōl, *n.* [Gr. *amphibolos*, doubtful, equivocal.] A name given to hornblende, from its resemblance to augite, for which it may readily be mistaken.—**Amphibolic**, am-fi-bol'ik, *a.* Pertaining to or resembling amphibole.—**Amphibolite**, am-fib'o-līt, *n.* A rock with a base of amphibole or hornblende; trap or greenstone.

Amphibology, am-fi-bol'o-ji, *n.* Gr. *amphibologia*—*amphi*, in two ways, *ballō*. to throw, and *logos*, discourse.] A phrase or discourse susceptible of two interpretations; and hence, a phrase of uncertain meaning.—**Amphibolous**, am-fib'ol-us, *a.* [Gr. *amphibolos.*] Susceptible of two meanings; ambiguous; equivocal.—**Amphiboly**,† am-fib'o-li, *n.* Ambiguity of meaning.—**Amphibological**, am-fib'o-loj"ik-al, *a.* Of or pertaining to amphibology; of doubtful meaning; ambiguous.—**Amphibologically**, am-fib'o-loj"ik-al-li, *adv.* With a doubtful meaning.

Amphibrach, Amphibrachys, am'fi-brak, am-fib'ra-kis, *n.* [Gr.—*amphi*, on both sides, and *brachys*, short.] *Pros.* a foot of three syllables, the middle one long, the first and last short.

Amphicarpic, Amphicarpous, am-fi-kär'pik, am-fi-kär'pus, *a.* [Gr. *amphi*, in two ways, and *karpos*, fruit.] *Bot.* possessing two kinds of fruit, either in respect of form or time of ripening.

Amphicœlous, Amphicœlian, am-fi-sē'lus, am-fi-sē'li-an, *a.* [Gr. *amphi*, at both ends, and *koilos*, hollow.] Applied to vertebræ which are doubly concave or hollow at both ends (as in fishes).

Amphictyonic, am-fikt'i-ōn-ik, *a.* Of or belonging to the Amphictyonic Council, or council of amphictyones or neighbours, meeting in spring at Thermopylæ, in autumn at Delphi.

Amphigean, am-fi-jē'an, *a.* [Gr. *amphi*, around, and *gē*. the earth.] Extending over all the zones of the globe.

Amphigen, am'fi-jen, *n.* [Gr. *amphi*, around, and root *gen*, to produce.] A plant which has no distinct axis, but increases by the growth or development of its cellular tissue on all sides, as the lichens.

Amphigory, am'fi-gōr-i, *n.* [Fr. *amphigouri.*] A meaningless rigmarole; a nonsensical parody.—**Amphigoric**, am-fi-gor'ik, *a.* Of, relating to, or consisting of amphigory; absurd; nonsensical.

Amphihexahedral, am-fi-heks'a-hē"-dral, *a.* Doubly hexahedral; six-sided in both directions: said of crystals.

Amphilogy, am-fil'o-ji, *n.* [Gr. *amphi*, in two ways, and *logos*, discourse.] Equivocation; amphibology.

Amphimacer, am-fim'a-sėr, *a.* [Gr. *amphimakros*, long on both sides.] *Pros.* a foot of three syllables, the middle one short and the others long.

Amphioxus, am-fi-oks'us, *n.* [Gr. *amphi*, on both sides, and *oxus* or *oxys*, sharp, because sharp at both ends.] A kind of fish of a very rudimentary type, the lancelet.

Amphipneust, am'fip-nūst, *n.* [Gr. *amphi*, in two ways, and *pneō*, to breathe.] An animal strictly amphibious, or having both gills and lungs.

Amphipod, am'fi-pod, *n.* [Gr. *amphi*, on both sides, and *pous, podos*, a foot.] One of an order (Amphipoda) of small crustaceous animals common in fresh and salt water, including such as the sand-hopper.

Amphiprostyle, am-fip'ro-stīl, *a.* [Gr. *amphi*, on both sides, *pro*, before, and *stylē*, a column.] Having a prostyle or portico on both ends or fronts, but with no columns on the sides.

Amphirhine, am'fi-rīn, *a.* [Gr. *amphi*, and *rhis, rhinos*, nose.] *Zool.* having the nostrils double.

Amphisbæna, am-fis-bē'na, *n.* [Gr. *amphisbaina*—*amphis*, on both sides, and *bainō*, to go, from the belief that it moved with either end foremost.] The generic name of small serpent-like reptiles, formerly but erroneously deemed poisonous.

Amphiscii, Amphiscians, am-fish'i-ī, am-fish'i-anz, *n. pl.* [Gr. *amphi*, on both sides, and *skia*, shadow.] The inhabitants of the intertropical regions, whose shadows at noon in one part of the year are cast to the north and in the other to the south.

Amphistomous, am-fis'to-mus, *a.* [Gr. *amphi*, on both sides, *stoma*, mouth.] *Zool.* having a mouth or equivalent orifice at either end of body: said of certain parasitic worms.

Amphitheater, am-fi-thē'a-tėr, *n.* [Gr. *amphitheatron*—*amphi*, on both sides, and *theatron*, theater.] An ancient edifice of an oval form, having a central area encompassed with rows of seats, rising higher as they receded from the center, on which people used to sit to view some spectacle or performance; a similar modern edifice; anything, as a natural hollow among hills, resembling an amphitheater in form.—**Amphitheatral, Amphitheatric, Amphitheatrical**, am-fi-thē'a-tral, am'-fi-thē-at"rik, am'fi-thē-at"rik-al, *a.* Pertaining to or resembling an amphitheater; exhibited in an amphitheater.

Amphitropal, Amphitropous, am-fit'rop-al, am-fit'rop-us, *a.* [Gr. *amphi*, round, and *trepō*, to turn.] *Bot.* applied to an ovule curved upon itself so that both ends are brought near to each other, with the hilum in the middle.

Amphitryon, am-fit'ri-ōn, *n.* King of Thebes, used for host, the man who provides dinner, from Molière's play of that name.

Amphiuma, am-fi-ū'ma, *n.* [Gr. *amphi*, both, and *huō*, to wet.] A North American animal belonging to the Amphibia, 2 or 3 feet in length.

Amphora, am'fo-ra, *n.* pl. **Amphoræ**, am'fo-rē. [L. *amphora*, Gr. *amphoreus*—*amphi*, on both sides, and *phoreō*, to carry, from its two handles.] Among the Greeks and Romans, a vessel, usually tall and narrow, with two handles or ears and a narrow neck, used for holding wine, oil, honey, and the like.—**Amphoral**, am'fo-ral, *a.* Pertaining to or resembling an amphora.

Ample, am'pl, *a.* [Fr. *ample*, L. *amplus*—prefix *am, amb*, round, about, and root of *pleo*, to fill; akin *double.*] Large in dimensions; of great size, extent, capacity, or bulk; wide; spacious; extended (*ample* room); fully sufficient for some purpose intended; abundant; copious; plentiful (an *ample* supply; *ample* justice).—**Ampleness**, am'pl-nes, *n.* The state of being ample; largeness; sufficiency; abundance.—**Ampliative**, am'pli-āt-iv, *a.* Enlarging; increasing; *philos.* adding to what is involved in the meaning of the subject of a proposition.—**Amplification**, am'pli-fi-kā"shon, *n.* The act of amplifying; an enlargement; extension; diffusive description or discussion.—**Amplificative, Amplificatory**, am'pli-fi-kāt-iv, am'pli-fi-kā-to-ri, *a.* Serving or tending to amplify.—**Amplifier**, am'pli-fi-ėr, *n.* One who amplifies or enlarges.—**Amplify**, am'pli-fī, *v.t.*—*amplified, amplifying.* [Fr. *amplifier*, to enlarge—L. *amplus*, ample, and *facio*, to make.] To make more ample, larger, more extended, more copious, and the like. *v.i.*—To grow or become ample or more ample; to be diffuse in argument or description.—**Amplitude**, am'pli-tūd, *n.* [L. *amplitudo.*] State of being ample; largeness of dimensions; extent of surface or space; greatness; *astron.* an arc of the horizon intercepted between the east or west point and the centre of the sun or star at its rising or setting.—**Amply**, am'pli, *adv.* In an ample manner; largely; sufficiently; copiously.

Amplectant, am-plek'tant, *a.* [L. *amplectens, amplectentis*, ppr. of *amplector*, to embrace.] *Bot.* embracing; clasping.—**Amplexicaul**, am-plek'si-kal, *a.* [L. *amplexus*, embracing, and *caulis*, a stem.] *Bot.* nearly surrounding or embracing the stem, as the base of a leaf.

Ampulla, am-pul'la, *n.* pl. **Ampullæ**, am-pul'lē. [L.] A more or less globular bottle, used by the Romans for holding oil; a vessel for holding the consecrated oil used in various church rites and at the coronation of kings; a small sac or bag-like appendage of a plant; a hollow flask-shaped leaf.—**Ampullaceous**, am-pul-lā'shus, *a.* Of or pertaining to or like an ampulla.

Amputate, am'pū-tāt, *v.t.*—*amputated, amputating.* [L. *amputo, amputatum—amb*, about, and *puto*, to prune.] To cut off, especially a human limb or that of an animal.—**Amputation**, am-pū-tā'shon, *n.* The act of amputating; the operation of cutting off a limb or other projecting part of the body.

Amuck, a-muk', *n.* [Malay or Javanese.] A furious, reckless onset; a term used in the Eastern Archipelago by Malays, who are occasionally seen to rush out in a frantic state with daggers in their hands, yelling 'Amuck, amuck,' and attacking all that come in their way.—*To run amuck*, to rush about frantically, attacking all that come in the way; to attack all and sundry.

Amulet, am'ū-let, *n.* [L. *amuletum*, Fr. *amulette*, from Ar. *hamâlat*, anything worn, from *hamala*, to carry, to wear.] Something worn or carried about the person, intended to act as a charm or preservative against evils or mischief, such as diseases and witchcraft.—**Amuletic**, am-ū-let'ik, *a.* Pertaining to an amulet.

Amurcous,† a-mėrk'us, *a.* [L. *amurca*, the dregs or lees of olives.] Full of dregs or lees; foul.—**Amurcosity**,† a-mėr-kos'i-ti, *n.* The quality of being amurcous.

Amuse, a-mūz', *v.t.*—*amused, amusing.* [Fr. *amuser*, to amuse, to divert, to hold in play—*a*, to, and O.Fr. *muser*, to muse. Muse, *v.*] To entertain the mind of agreeably: to occupy or detain the attention of in a pleasant manner or with agreeable objects; to divert; entertain: often *refl.*; to keep in expectation, as by flattery, plausible pretences, and the like; to keep in play. ∴ *Amuse* is to occupy lightly and pleasantly; *divert* generally implies something absolutely lively or sportive; *entertain*, to keep in a continuous state of interest, often by something instructive.—**Amusable**, a-mūz'a-bl, *a.* Capable of being amused.—**Amusement**, a-mūz'ment, *n.* The act of amusing, or state of being amused; a slight amount of mirth or tendency towards merriment; that which amuses; entertainment; sport; pastime.—**Amuser**, a-mūz'ėr, *n.* One who amuses.—**Amusing**, a-mūz'ing, *a.* Giving amusement; pleasing; diverting.—**Amusingly**, a-mūz'ing-li, *adv.* In an amusing manner.—**Amusive**,† a-mū'ziv, *a.* Having power to amuse.

Amygdalate, a-mig'da-lāt, *n.* [L. *amygdalus*, an almond.] An emulsion made of almonds; milk of almonds.—**Amygdaline**, a-mig'da-lin, *a.* Pertaining to, resembling, or made of almonds.—**Amygdalic**, a-mig-dal'ik, *a.* Obtained from almonds.—**Amygdaloid**, a-mig'da-loid. *n.* A term applied to igneous rock, especially trap, containing round or almond-shaped vesicles or cavities partly or wholly filled with crystalline nodules of various minerals.—**Amygdaloidal**, a-mig'da-loid"al, *a.* Pertaining to amygdaloid; almond-shaped.

Amyl, am'il, *n.* [Gr. *amylon*, starch.] *Chem* a hypothetical radical said to exist in many compounds, as amylic alcohol, &c.—*Nitrite of amyl*, an amber-coloured fluid with a pleasant odour, having the property when inhaled of quickening the heart's action.—**Amylaceous**, am-il-ā'shus, *a.* Pertaining to starch, or the farinaceous part of grain; resembling starch.—**Amylate**, am'il-āt, *n.* A compound of starch with a base.—**Amylene**, am'il-ēn, *n.* A hydrocarbon obtained from amylic alcohol, and possessing anæsthetic properties.—**Amylic**, am-il'ik, *a.* Pertaining to amyl.—**Amyloid**, am'il-oid, *a.* Resembling or being of the nature of amyl.—*n.* A semi-gelatinous substance, analogous to starch, met with in some seeds.

An, A, an, a, *indef. art.* [A.Sax. *án*, one, an, the former being the original, the latter a developed meaning; the same word as *one*. One.] A word used before nouns in the singular number to denote an individual as one among more belonging to the same class, and not marking singleness like *one*, nor pointing to something known and definite like *the*. In such phrases as 'once *an* hour,' 'a shilling *an* ounce,' *an* has a distributive force, being equivalent to *each, every*. The form *a* is used before consonants (including the name sound of *u* as in *unit, European* = *yu*); *an* is used before words beginning with a vowel sound, or the sound of *h* when the accent falls on any syllable except the first; as, *an inn, an umpire, an heir, an historian* (but also *a historian*).

Ana, ā'na, *n. pl.* [The neuter plural termination of Latin adjectives in *-anus*, often forming an affix to the names of eminent men to denote a collection of their memorable sayings—thus *Scaligeriana, Johnsoniana.*] The sayings of notable men; personal gossip or anecdotes.

Anabaptist, an-a-bap'tist, *n.* [Gr. *ana*, again, and *baptistēs*, a baptist.] One who holds the invalidity of infant baptism, and the necessity of rebaptism, generally by immersion, at an adult age.—**Anabaptistic, Anabaptistical**, an'a-bap-tis"tik, an'a-bap-tis"tik-al, *a.* Relating to the Anabaptists or to their doctrines.—**Anabaptism**, an-a-bap'tizm, *n.* The doctrine or practices of the Anabaptists.

Anabasis, an-ab'a-sis, *n.* [Gr.—*ana*, up, and *basis*, a going, from *bainō*, to go.] A going up; an expedition from the coast inland; the expedition of Cyrus the Younger against Persia in B.C. 401, described by Xenophon.

Anacamptic, an-a-kam'tik, *a.* [Gr. *ana*, back, and *kamptō*, to bend.] Pertaining to the reflection of light or sound; reflecting or reflected.—**Anacamptically**, an-a-kam'tik-al-li, *adv.* By reflection.—**Anacamptics**, an-a-kam'tiks, *n.* The doctrine of reflected light or sound.

Anacanthous, an-a-kan'thus, *a.* [Gr. neg. prefix *an*, and *akantha*, a spine.] Spineless; a term applied to fishes with spineless fins, such as the cod, plaice, &c.; malacopterygious.

Anacatharsis, an'a-ka-thär"sis, *n.* [Gr. *ana*, upward, and *kathairō*, to cleanse.] *Med.* purgation upward; also cough, attended by expectoration.—**Anacathartic**, an'a-ka-thär"tik, *a.* Pertaining to or of the nature of anacatharsis.—*n.* A medicine which excites discharges by the mouth or nose, as expectorants, emetics, &c.

Anacharis, an-ak'a-ris, *n.* [*Ana*, for Gr. neg. prefix *an*, and *charis*, favour, from being often a nuisance.] A water-plant introduced from North America into British rivers and ponds, which by its rapid growth tends to choke them up; water-thyme or water-weed.

Anachronism, an-ak'ron-izm, *n.* [Gr. *ana*, implying inversion, error, and *chronos*, time.] An error in computing historical time; any error which implies the misplacing of persons or events in time; anything foreign to or out of keeping with a specified epoch (as where Shakespeare makes Hector quote Aristotle).—**Anachronous, Anachronic, Anachronical, Anachronistic, Anachronistical**, an-ak'ron-us, an-a-kron'ik, an-a-kron'ik-al, an-ak'ron-ist"ik, an-ak'ron-ist"ik-al, *a.* Erroneous in date; containing an anachronism.

Anaclastic, an-a-klas'tik, *a.* [Gr. *anaklasis*, a bending back—Gr. *ana*, back, and *klasis*, a breaking, from *klaō*, to break.] Pertaining to or produced by the refraction of light; bending back; flexible.—**Anaclastics**, an-a-klas'tiks, *n.* A term equivalent to *Dioptrics*.

Anacoluthon, an'a-kol-ū"thon, *n.* [Gr. *anakolouthos*, wanting sequence—neg. prefix *an*, and *akolouthos*, following.] *Gram.* want of sequence in a sentence, owing to the latter member of it belonging to a different grammatical construction from the preceding; as, 'He that curseth father or mother, let him die the death.'—Mat. xv. 4.—**Anacoluthic**, an'a-kol-ū"thik, *a.* Wanting sequence; containing an anacoluthon.

Anaconda, an-a-kon'da, *n.* The popular name of two of the largest species of the serpent tribe, namely, a Ceylonese species and a South American species, both growing to the length of over 30 feet.

Anacreontic, a-nak'rē-on"tik, *a.* Pertaining to or after the manner of *Anacreon*; relating to the praise of love and wine; convivial; amatory.—**Anacreontic**, a-nak'rē-on"tik, *n.* A poem by Anacreon, or composed in the manner of Anacreon; a little poem in praise of love or wine.

Anacrusis, an'a-krū-sis, *n.* [Gr. *anakrousis*, striking up.] The unstressed syllable at the beginning of a verse.

Anadem, Anademe, an'a-dem, an'a-dēm, *n.* [Gr. *anadēma*, a head-band or fillet—*ana*, up, and *deō*, to bind.] A band, fillet, garland, or wreath.

Anadromous, a-nad'rom-us, *a.* [Gr. *ana*, up, and *dromos*, course.] Passing from the sea into fresh waters at stated seasons, as the salmon.

Anæmia, a-nē'mi-a, *n.* [Gr.—*an*, priv., and *haima*, blood.] *Med.* a deficiency of blood; a state of the system marked by a deficiency in certain constituents of the blood.—**Anæmic**, a-nē'mik, *a.* Pertaining to or affected with anæmia.

Anæsthesia, Anæsthesis, an-es-thē'si-a, an-es-thē'sis, *n.* [Gr. *anaisthēsia, anaisthēsis*—*an*, priv., and *aisthanomai*, to feel.] Diminished or lost sense of feeling; an artificially produced state of insensibility, especially to the sense of pain.—**Anæsthetic**, an-es-thet'ik, *a.* Of or belonging to anæsthesia; having the power of depriving of feeling or sensation.—*n.* A substance which has the power of depriving of feeling or sensation, as chloroform when its vapour is inhaled.—**Anæsthetize**, an-es'thē-tiz, *v.t.*—*anæsthetized, anæsthetizing.* To bring under the influence of an anæsthetic agent; to render insensible to the feeling of pain.

Anaglyph, an'a-glif, *n.* [Gr. *anaglyphon*, embossed work—*ana*, up, and *glyphō*, to engrave.] An ornament in relief chased or embossed.—**Anaglyphic, Anaglyphical**, an-a-glif'ik, an-a-glif'ik-al, *a.* Pertaining to anaglyphs or to the art of chasing and embossing in relief.—**Anaglyphy**, an-ag'li-fi, *n.* The act of chasing or embossing in relief.—**Anaglyptic, Anaglyptical**, an-a-glip'tik, an-a-glip'tik-al. Same as *Anaglyphic*.—**Anaglyptograph**, an-a-glip'to-graf, *n.* An instrument for making a medallion engraving of an object in relief, such as a medal or cameo.—**Anaglyptography**, an'a-glip-tog"ra-fi, *n.* The art of copying works in relief.

Anagoge, Anagogy, an'a-gō-jē, an'a-go-ji, *n.* [Gr. *anagōgē—ana*, upward, and *agōgē*, a leading, from *agō*, to lead.] An elevation of mind to things celestial; the spiritual meaning or application of words; a mysterious or allegorical interpretation, especially of Scripture.—**Anagogic, Anagogical**, an-a-goj'ik, an-a-goj'ik-al, *a.* Of or pertaining to anagoge; mysterious; elevated; spiritual.—**Anagogically**, an-a-goj'ik-al-li, *adv.* In an anagogic manner.

Anagram, an'a-gram, *n.* [Gr. *ana*, up, again, and *gramma*, a letter.] A transposition of the letters of a word or sentence, to form a new word or sentence.—**Anagrammatic, Anagrammatical**, an′a-gram-mat″ik, an′a-gram-mat″ik-al, *a.* Pertaining to or forming an anagram.—**Anagrammatically**, an′a-gram-mat″ik-al-li, *adv.* In the manner of an anagram.—**Anagrammatism**, an-a-gram′mat-izm, *n.* The act or practice of making anagrams.—**Anagrammatist**, an-a-gram′mat-ist, *n.* A maker of anagrams.—**Anagrammatize**, an-a-gram′mat-īz, *v.t.* To transpose, as the letters of a word, so as to form an anagram. —*v.i.* To make anagrams.

Anal, ā′nal, *a.* [L. *anus*, the fundament.] Pertaining to or situated near the anus.

Analcime, a-nal′sim, *n.* [Gr. *an*, priv., and *alkimos*, strong, from *alkē*, strength.] A mineral of frequent occurrence in trap-rocks, especially in the cavities of amygdaloids. By friction it acquires a *weak* electricity; hence its name.

Analecta, an-a-lek′ta, *n.pl.* [Gr. neut. pl. of *analektos*, select—*ana*, up, and *legō*, to gather.] Extracts or small pieces selected from different authors.—**Analect**, an′a-lekt, *n.* A selected piece; an extract.—**Analectic**, an-a-lek′tik, *a.* Relating to analecta; made up of selections.

Analepsis, an-a-lep′sis, *n.* [Gr., from *ana*, up or again, and *lēpsis*, a taking, from *lambanō*, to take.] *Med.* recovery of strength after disease.—**Analeptic**, an-a-lep′tik, *a.* Invigorating; giving strength after disease.

Analgesia, an-al-jē′zi-a, *n.* [Gr. *analgesia* —*an*, priv., and *algos*, pain.] *Pathol.* incapacity for feeling pain in some part of the body.—**Analgetic**, an-al-jet′ik, *a.* Pertaining to analgesia, insensible to pain.

Anallantoic, an′al-lan-tō′ik, *a.* [Prefix *an*, not, *allantois*.] Not possessing an allantois, *q.v.*

Analogy, an-al′o-ji, *n.* [Gr. *analogia*—*ana*, according to, and *logos*, ratio, proportion.] An agreement or likeness between things in some circumstances or effects, when the things are otherwise entirely different; relationship; conformity; parallelism; likeness. ∴ *Analogy* is sometimes confounded with *similarity*, but the latter properly denotes general likeness or resemblance; the former implies general difference, with identity or sameness in one or more relations. Thus there is *analogy*, but no *similarity* between the wing of a bird and that of a bat. [We say analogy *between* things, one thing has an analogy *to* or *with* another.]—**Analogical**, an-a-loj′ik-al, *a.* Having analogy; analogous; used by way of analogy; expressing or implying analogy.—**Analogically**, an-a-loj′ik-al-li, *adv.* In an analogical manner.—**Analogicalness**, an-a-loj′ik-al-nes, *n.* The quality of being analogical.—**Analogism**, an-al′o-jizm, *n.* An argument from the cause to the effect; an a priori argument; investigation of things by the analogy they bear to each other.—**Analogist**, an-al′o-jist, *n.* One who adheres to analogy.—**Analogize**, an-al′o-jīz, *v.t.*—*analogized*, *analogizing*. To explain by analogy; to consider with regard to its analogy to something else.—**Analogous**, an-al′og-us, *a.* Having analogy; bearing some resemblance in the midst of differences (followed by *to* or *with*).—**Analogously**, an-al′og-us-li, *adv.* In an analogous manner.—**Analogue**, an′a-log, *n.* Something having analogy with something else.

Analysis, an-al′i-sis, *n.* pl. **Analyses**, an-al′i-sēz. [Gr.—prefix *ana*, implying distribution, and *lysis*, a loosing, resolving, from *lyō*, to loosen.] The resolution of a compound object whether of the senses or the intellect into its constituent elements or component parts; a consideration of anything in its separate parts and their relation to each other: opposed to *synthesis*; the process of subjecting to chemical tests to determine ingredients; a syllabus or table of the principal heads of a discourse or treatise.—**Analyzable**, an-a-līz′a-bl, *a.* Capable of being analyzed.—**Analyzation**, an′a-līz-ā″shon, *n.* The act of analyzing.—**Analyze**, an′a-līz, *v.t.*—*analyzed*, *analyzing*. [Fr. *analyser*.] To resolve into its elements; to separate, as a compound subject into its parts or propositions.—**Analyzer**, an′a-līz-ėr, *n.* One who or that which analyzes.—**Analyst**, an′a-list, *n.* One who analyzes or is versed in analysis; one who subjects articles to chemical tests to find out their ingredients.—**Analytic, Analytical**, an-a-lit′ik, an-a-lit′ik-al, *a.* Pertaining to analysis; resolving into first principles or elements.—**Analytically**, an-a-lit′ik-al-li, *adv.* In an analytical manner; in the manner of analysis.—**Analytics**, an-a-lit′iks, *n.* The science of analysis.

Anamorphosis, Anamorphism, an-a-mor′fō-sis or an′a-mor-fō″sis, an-a-mor′fizm, *n.* [Gr. *ana*, again, and *morphōsis*, formation, from *morphē*, a form.] A drawing presenting a distorted image of the object, unless when viewed from a certain point, or reflected by a curved mirror; an anomalous development of any part of a plant.

Ananas, a-nä′na, *n.* [Peruvian *nanas*.] Pine-apple, with intrusive *s*, as if a plural.

Anandrous, an-an′drus, *a.* [Gr. *an*, priv., and *anēr*, *andros*, a male or stamen.] *Bot.* applied to flowers that are destitute of a stamen (female flowers).

Anantherous, an-an′thėr-us, *a.* [Gr. *an*, priv., and E. *anther*.] *Bot.* destitute of anthers.

Ananthous, an-an′thus, *a.* [Gr. *an*, priv., and *anthos*, a flower.] Destitute of flowers.

Anapest, Anapæst, an′a-pest, *n.* [L. *anapæstus*, from Gr. *anapaistos*.] A poetical foot consisting of three syllables, the first two short or unaccented, the last long or accented.—**Anapestic**, an-a-pes′tik, *a.* Pertaining to an anapest; consisting of anapests.—**Anapestically**, an-a-pes′tik-al-li, *adv.* In an anapestic manner.

Anaphrodisiac, an-af′ro-diz″i-ak, *n.* [Gr. neg. prefix *an*, and *aphrodisiakos*, venereal.] A substance capable of dulling sexual appetite.

Anaplasty, an′a-plas-ti, *n.* [Gr. *ana*, again, and *plassō*, to fashion.] *Surg.* an operation to supply by the employment of adjacent healthy structure the loss of small portions of flesh.—**Anaplastic**, an-a-plas′tik, *a.* Of or pertaining to anaplasty.

Anaplerotic, an′a-plē-rot″ik, *a.* [Gr. *ana*, up, and *plēroō*, to fill.] *Med.* filling up; promoting granulation of wounds or ulcers. —*n.* A remedy which promotes the granulation of wounds and ulcers.

Anapodeictic, an-ap′o-dik″tik, *a.* [Gr. *an*, priv., and *apodeiktikos*, demonstrable.] Incapable of being demonstrated.

Anaptotic, an-ap-tot′ik, *a.* [Gr. *ana*, back, and *ptōsis*, inflection.] *Philol.* applied to languages which have a tendency to lose the use of inflections.

Anarchy, an′är-ki, *n.* [Gr. *anarchia*, lawlessness—*an*, priv., and *archē*, rule.] Want of government; a state of society when there is no law or supreme power; political confusion.—**Anarchic, Anarchical**, an-ärk′ik, an-ärk′ik-al, *a.* Of or pertaining to anarchy or anarchism; in a state of anarchy or confusion; lawless. Also **Anarchal**, an-ärk′al.—**Anarchism**, an′ärk-izm, *n.* The doctrine of the abolition of formal government, free action for the individual, land and other resources being common property.—**Anarchist, Anarch**, an′ärk-ist, an′ärk, *n.* One who excites disorder in a state; an advocate of anarchy or anarchism.—**Anarchize**,† an′är-kīz, *v.t.* To put into a state of anarchy.

Anarthropoda, an-är-throp′o-da, *n. pl.* [Gr. *an*, priv., *arthros*, joint, and *pous*, *podos*, foot.] Annulose animals without jointed limbs, as leeches, &c.—**Anarthropodous**, an-är-throp′o-dus, *a.* Pertaining to.

Anarthrous, an-är′thrus, *a.* [Gr. *an*, priv., and *arthron*, a joint or article.] *Gram.* without the article; *zool.* without joints or jointed appendages.

Anasarca, an-a-sär′ka, *n.* [Gr. *ana*, through, and *sarx*, flesh.] *Med.* dropsy of the cellular tissue; general dropsy.—**Anasarcous**, an-a-sär′kus, *a.* Dropsical.

Anastaltic, an-a-stal′tik, *a.* [Gr. *anastaltikos*, fitted for checking.] *Med.* astringent; styptic.

Anastatic, an-a-stat′ik, *a.* [Gr. *ana*, up, and *histanai*, to stand.] Consisting of or furnished with raised characters: applied to a mode of printing from zinc plates etched so that the design or what else is to be shown is left in relief.

Anastomose, a-nas′tō-mōz, *v.i.*—*anastomosed*, *anastomosing*. [Fr. *anastomoser*, Gr. *anastomoō*—*ana*, again, anew, and *stoma*, a mouth.] *Anat.* and *bot.* to inosculate or run into each other, to communicate with each other by minute branches or ramifications, as the arteries and veins.—**Anastomosis**, a-nas′tō-mō′sis, *n.* The inosculation of vessels in vegetable or animal bodies.—**Anastomotic**, a-nas′tō-mot″ik, *a.* Pertaining to anastomosis.

Anastrophe, Anastrophy, a-nas′tro-fe, *n.* [Gr.—*ana*, back, *strephō*, to turn.] An inversion of the natural order of words.

Anathema, a-nath′ē-ma, *n.* [Gr. *anathema*, a thing devoted to evil, from *anatithēmi*, to dedicate—*ana*, up, and *tithēmi*, to place.] A curse or denunciation pronounced with religious solemnity by ecclesiastical authority, and accompanied by excommunication; execration generally; curse.—**Anathematic, Anathematical**, a-nath′ē-mat″ik, a-nath′ē-mat″ik-al, *a.* Pertaining to or having the nature of an anathema.—**Anathematically**, a-nath′ē-mat″ik-al-li, *adv.* In the manner of anathema.—**Anathematization**, a-nath′ē-mat′iz-ā″shon, *n.* The act of anathematizing.—**Anathematize**, a-nath′ē-mat-īz, *v.t.*—*anathematized*, *anathematizing*. To pronounce an anathema against.—*v.i.* To pronounce anathemas; to curse.—**Anathematizer**, a-nath′ē-mat-īz-ėr, *n.* One who.

Anatomy, a-nat′o-mi, *n.* [Gr. *anatomē*—*ana*, up, and *tomē*, a cutting.] The art of dissecting or artificially separating the different parts of an organized body, to discover their situation, structure, and economy; the science which treats of the internal structure of organized bodies, as elucidated by dissection: when used alone it refers to the human body, *vegetable anatomy* being the anatomy of plants, *zootomy* that of the lower animals; the act of taking to pieces something for the purpose of examining in detail (the *anatomy* of a discourse); a skeleton (colloq.); hence, a thin meagre person. —**Anatomic, Anatomical**, an-a-tom′ik, an-a-tom′ik-al, *a.* Belonging to anatomy or dissection.—**Anatomically**, an-a-tom′ik-al-li, *adv.* In an anatomical manner; by means of dissection.—**Anatomism**. Anatomical analysis; explanation of vital phenomena by anatomical structure.—**Anatomist**, a-nat′o-mist, *n.* One who is skilled in dissection, or in the doctrine and principles of anatomy.—**Anatomization**, a-nat′o-miz-ā″shon, *n.* The act of anatomizing.—**Anatomize**, a-nat′o-mīz, *v.t.*—*anatomized*, *anatomizing*. To cut up or dissect for the purpose of displaying or examining the structure; *fig.* to lay open or expose minutely; to analyse (to *anatomize* an argument).

Anatropal, Anatropous, a-nat′rop-al, a-nat′rop-us, *a.* [Gr. *ana*, denoting inversion, and *trepō*, to turn.] *Bot.* having the ovule inverted, so that the chalaza is at its apparent apex.

Anberry, an′be-ri, *n.* [A.Sax. *an*=on, and *berry*.] A kind of warty protuberance or growth on a horse or ox, sometimes hanging quite loosely; a kind of gall or excrescence on a turnip.

Ancestor, an′ses-tėr, *n.* [O.Fr. *ancestre*, *ancessor*, Fr. *ancêtre*, an ancestor, from L. *antecessor*, a predecessor—*ante*, before, and *cedo*, *cessum*, to go. CEDE.] One from whom a person descends, either by the father or mother, at any distance of time; a progenitor; a forefather; one from whom an inheritance is derived.—**Ancestral, Ancestorial**, an-ses′tral, an-ses-tō′ri-al, *a.* Pertaining to ancestors; claimed or descending from ancestors.—**Ancestress**,† an′ses-tres, *n.* A female ancestor.—**An-**

cestry, an'ses-tri, *n.* A series of ancestors; lineage; honourable descent; high birth.

Anchor, ang'kėr, *n.* [A.Sax. *ancor*, borrowed from L. *ancora*, Gr. *angkyra*, an anchor. From a root meaning crooked, bent, seen in L. *angulus*, a corner, E. *ankle*, *angle*, a fish-hook.] An iron implement, consisting usually of a straight bar called the shank, at the upper end of which is a transverse piece called the stock, and of two curved arms at the lower end of the shank, each of which arms terminates in a triangular plate called a fluke, and used for holding a ship or other vessel at rest in comparatively shallow water; something serving a purpose analogous to that of a ship's anchor; *fig.* that which gives stability or security; that on which we place dependence for safety.—*At anchor*, floating attached to an anchor; anchored.—*v.t.* To hold at rest by lowering the anchor; to place at anchor; *fig.* to fix or fasten on; to fix in a stable condition.—*v.i.* To cast anchor; to come to anchor.—**Anchorable**, ang'kėr-a-bl, *a.* Capable of being anchored; fit for anchoring.—**Anchorage**, ang'kėr-āj, *n.* Anchoring ground; a place where a ship can anchor; a duty imposed on ships for anchoring in a harbour.

Anchoret, **Anchorite**, ang'kō-ret, ang'kō-rīt, *n.* [L. *anachoreta*; Gr. *anachōrētēs*—*ana*, back, and *chōreō*, to retire, from *chōros*, a place.] A hermit; a recluse; one who retires from society to avoid the temptations of the world and devote himself to religious duties. — **Anchoritess**, **Anchoress**, ang'kō-rīt-es, ang'kō-res, *n.* A female anchoret.—**Anchoretic**, **Anchoretical**, **Anchoritical**, ang-kō-ret'ik, ang-kō-ret'-ik-al, ang-kō-rit'ik-al, *a.* Pertaining to a hermit, or his mode of life.

Anchovy, an-chō'vi, *n.* [Pg. and Sp. *anchova*, an anchovy, from Basque *anchua*, *anchuva*, dry.] A small fish belonging to the herring family, caught in vast numbers in the Mediterranean, and pickled for exportation. An esteemed sauce is also made from them.

Anchovy-pear, an-chō'vi-pār, *n.* A fruit of Jamaica, which is pickled and eaten.

Anchylose, ang'ki-lōs. A common but erroneous spelling of *Ankylose*.

Ancient, ān'shent, *a.* [Fr. *ancien*, L.L. *antianus*, from L. prep. *ante*, before. The final *t* has no right to its place in this word.] That happened or existed in former times, usually at a great distance of time; associated with, or bearing marks of the times of long ago (*ancient* authors); of long standing; having lasted from a remote period; of great age; old (an *ancient* city); having lived long (an *ancient* man—poetical). ∴ *Old* refers to the duration of the thing itself; *ancient*, to the period with which it is associated. *Ancient* is opposed to *modern*; *old* to *young*, *new*, *fresh*. An *old* dress, custom, &c., is one which has lasted a long time, and which still exists; an *ancient* dress, custom, &c., is one which prevailed in former ages.—*n.* A person living at an early period of history (generally in plural, and opposed to *moderns*); a very old man; an elder or person of influence.—**Anciently**, ān'shent-li, *adv.* In old times; in times long past.—**Ancientness**, ān'shent-nes, *n.* The state or character of being ancient; antiquity.

Ancient,† ān'shent, *n.* [Corrupted from *ensign*.] A flag; an ensign; also, a standard-bearer. [*Shak.*]

Ancillary, an'sil-la-ri, *a.* [L. *ancillaris*, from *ancilla*, a maid-servant.] Subservient; aiding; auxiliary; subordinate.

Ancipital, **Ancipitous**, an-sip'it-al, an-sip'it-us, *a.* [L. *anceps*, *ancipitis*, two-headed, ambiguous—*an* for *amb*, on both sides, and *caput*, the head.] Doubtful or double; ambiguous; *bot.* two-edged.

Ancon, an'kon, *n.* pl. **Ancones**, an-kō'nēz. [L. *ancon*, Gr. *angkōn*, the elbow.] *Anat.* the upper end of the ulna or elbow; *arch.* a console, cantilever, corbel, or other stone projection.—**Anconal**, an-kō'nal, *a.* Pertaining to the ancon or elbow.—**Anconoid**, an'kon-oid, *a.* Elbow-like: applied to a process of the forearm.

And, and, *conj.* [A.Sax. *and*, D. *en*, *ende*, G. *und*, O.H.G. *anti*, all signifying and; Icel. *enda*, and yet, and if.] A particle joining words and sentences, and expressing the relations of connection or addition; sometimes used to introduce interrogative and other clauses. In old writers *and*, *an*, has often the sense of if; hence 'but *and if*' in the Bible = but if if.

Andalusite, an-da-lū'sīt, *n.* A pellucid mineral of the garnet family, of a gray, green, bluish, flesh or rose-red colour: so called from *Andalusia* in Spain, where it was first discovered.

Andante, an-dän'tā, *a.* [It. *andante*, walking moderately, from *andare*, to go.] *Music*, moving with a moderate, even, graceful, onward progression.—*n.* A movement or piece composed in *andante* time.—**Andantino**, an-dan-tē'no, *a.* Applied to a movement quicker than *andante*.

Andean, an-dē'an, *a.* Pertaining to the Andes, the great mountain chain of South America. — **Andesin**, an'dez-in, *n.* A mineral resembling felspar originally obtained from the Andes.

Andiron, and'ī-ėrn, *n.* [O.E. *andiren*, *aundirin*, *aundire*, O.F. *andier*; origin unknown.] A horizontal iron bar raised on short legs, with an upright standard at one end, used to support pieces of wood when burning on an open hearth, one being placed on each side; a fire-dog.

Andranatomy, an-dra-nat'o-mi, *n.* [Gr. *anēr*, *andros*, a man, and *anatomē*, dissection.] The dissection of a human body, especially of a male; androtomy.

Andrœcium, an-drē'si-um, *n.* [Gr. *anēr*, *andros*, a man, a male, and *oikos*, a house.] *Bot.* the male system of a flower; the assemblage of the stamens.

Androgynal, **Androgynous**, an-droj'-in-al, an-droj'in-us, *a.* [Gr. *androgynos*—*anēr*, *andros*, a man, and *gynē*, woman.] Having two sexes; being male and female; hermaphroditical; having or partaking of the mental characteristics of both sexes.—**Androgynally**, an-droj'in-al-li, *adv.* With the parts of both sexes.

Andropetalous, an-drō-pet'al-us, *a.* [Gr. *anēr*, *andros*, a male, and *petalon*, a petal.] *Bot.* applied to double flowers produced by the conversion of the stamens into petals.

Androphagi, an-drof'a-jī, *n. pl.* [Gr. *anēr*, *andros*, a man, and *phagō*, to eat.] Man-eaters; anthropophagi. — **Androphagous**, an-drof'a-gus, *a.* Pertaining or addicted to cannibalism.

Androphore, an'dro-fōr, *n.* [Gr. *anēr*, *andros*, a male, and *pherō*, to bear.] *Bot.* a stalk supporting the stamens.

Androsphinx, an'dro-sfingks, *n.* [Gr. *anēr*, *andros*, a man, and *sphingx*, a sphinx.] A sphinx with a human head.

Androtomy, an-drot'o-mi, *n.* [Gr. *anēr*, *andros*, a man, and *tomē*, a cutting.] Same as *Andranatomy*.

Androus, an'drus, *a.* [Gr. *anēr*, *andros*, a male.] *Bot.* producing stamens only; staminate; male.

Anecdote, an'ek-dōt, *n.* [Gr. *anekdotos*, not published—*a*, neg., *ek*, out, and *dotos*, given, from *didōmi*, to give.] A short story, narrating a detached incident or fact of an interesting nature; a biographical incident; a single passage of private life.—**Anecdotage**. The garrulity of dotage, or old age.—**Anecdotic**, **Anecdotal**, **Anecdotical**, an-ek-dot'ik, an'ek-dōt-al, an-ek-dot'ik-al, *a.* Pertaining to anecdotes; consisting of or of the nature of anecdotes.—**Anecdotist**, **Anecdotarian**, an'ek-dōt-ist, an'ek-dō-tā"ri-an, *n.* One who deals in anecdotes.

Anele, an-ēl', *v.t.* [O.E. *ele*, L. *oleum*, oil.] Anoint, with extreme unction. [*Shak.*]

Anelectric, an-ē-lek'trik, *a.* [Gr. *an*, priv., and E. *electric*.] Having no electric properties; non-electric.

Anelectrode, an-ē-lek'trōd, *n.* [Prefix *ana*, up, and *electrode*.] The positive pole of a galvanic battery: opposed to *catelectrode*.

Anemograph, a-nem'o-graf, *n.* [Gr. *anemos*, the wind.] An instrument for measuring and recording the force and direction of the wind.—**Anemography**, an-e-mog'ra-fi, *n.* The use of the anemograph. — **Anemology**, an-e-mol'o-ji, *n.* The doctrine of or a treatise on winds.—**Anemometer**, an-e-mom'et-ėr, *n.* An instrument for measuring the force and velocity of the wind.—**Anemometry**, an-e-mom'et-ri, *n.* The process of determining the pressure or force of the wind.

Anemone, a-nem'o-ne, *n.* [Gr. *anemōnē*, the wind-flower, from *anemos*, the wind, being easily stripped of its petals by the wind.] Wind-flower, a genus of plants. Three species occur in Britain, but only one, the wood-anemone, is truly a native.—*Sea-anemone*. Actinia.—**Anemonic**, an-e-mon'ik, *a.* Of or pertaining to anemone.

Anemophilous, an-e-mof'i-lus, *a.* [Gr. *anemos*, wind, *philos*, loving.] *Bot.* having the pollen conveyed and fertilization effected by the wind.

Anemoscope, a-nem'o-skōp, *n.* [Gr. *anemos*, wind, and *skopeō*, to view.] A contrivance which shows the direction of the wind; a weathercock; a wind-vane.

Anemosis, an-ē-mō'sis, *n.* [Gr. *anemos*, the wind.] A condition of the timber of trees in which the annual layers are separated from each other, sometimes regarded as the result of strong gales.

Anent, a-nent', *prep.* [A.Sax. *on efn*, *on emn*, on a level, near, lit. on even. The *t*, as in *ancient*, is superfluous.] About; respecting; regarding.

Anenterous, an-en'tėr-us, *a.* [Gr. *an*, priv., and *entera*, bowels.] Destitute of intestines; having no alimentary canal.

Anergy, an'ėr-ji, *n.* [Gr. *an*, not, *ergon*, work.] *Pathol.* morbid loss of energy.

Aneroid, an'ē-roid, *a.* [Gr. *a*, priv., *nēros*, moisture, and *eidos*, form.] Dispensing with fluid, as with quicksilver.—*Aneroid barometer*, a barometer the action of which depends on the pressure of the atmosphere on a circular metallic box exhausted of air, hermetically sealed, and having a slightly elastic top, the vacuum serving the purpose of the column of mercury in the ordinary barometer.

Anesthesia, an-es-thē'si-a, *n.* Same as *Anæsthesia*.—**Anesthetic**, an-es-thet'ik, *a.* Same as *Anæsthetic*.

Aneurism, an'ū-rizm, *n.* [Gr. *aneurysmos*, a widening—*ana*, up, and *eurys*, wide.] *Med.* the swelling of an artery, or the dilatation and expansion of some part of an artery, often a very dangerous ailment.—**Aneurismal**, an-ū-riz'mal, *a.* Pertaining to an aneurism.

Anew, a-nū', *adv.* [Prefix *a*, of or on, and *new*.] Over again; in a new form; afresh.

Anfractuous, an-frak'tū-us, *a.* [Fr. *anfractueux*, L. *anfractus*, winding—*frango*, *fractum*, to break.] Winding; full of windings and turnings; sinuous.—**Anfractuose**, an-frak'tū-ōs, *a.* *Bot.* twisted or sinuous.—**Anfractuosity**, an-frak'tū-os"i-ti, *n.* A state of being anfractuous; *anat.* a sinuous depression. — **Anfractuousness**, an-frak'tū-us-nes, *n.* Anfractuosity.

Angel, ān'jel, *n.* [L. *angelus*, Gr. *anggelos*, a messenger.] A divine messenger; a spiritual being employed in the service of God; also applied to an evil being of similar powers; a gold coin, formerly current in England, varying in value from 6*s.* 8*d.* to 10*s.*, bearing the figure of the archangel Michael.—**Angelhood**, ān'jel-hụd, *n.* The state or condition of an angel; the angelic nature or character.—**Angelic**, **Angelical**, an-jel'ik, an-jel'ik-al, *a.* Resembling or belonging to, or partaking of the nature and dignity of angels.—*Angelic doctor*, Thomas Aquinas.—**Angelica**, an-jel'ik-a, *n.* [From possessing what were regarded as *angelic* powers or virtues.] The name of two umbelliferous plants. One (*Angelica sylvestris*) is common in Britain and used in preparing gin and bitters, &c.; the other, garden angelica (*Archangelica officinalis*), possesses carminative and tonic properties.—**Angelically**, an-jel'ik-al-li, *adv.* In an angelic manner.—**Angelicalness**, an-jel'ik-al-nes, *n.*—**Angelicize, Angelify, Angelize**, an-jel'i-sīz, an-jel'i-fī, ān'jel-īz, *v.t.* To make angelic or like an angel.—**Angelolatry**, ān-jel-ol-a-tri, *n.* [E. *angel* and Gr. *latreia*, worship.] The worship of angels.—**Angelology**, ān-jel-ol'o-ji, *n.* A discourse on angels, or the doctrine of angelic beings.—**Angelophany**, ān-jel-of'a-ni, *n.* [*Angel* and Gr. *phainō*, to appear.] The appearance of an angel or angels to man.—**Angelus**, an'jel-us, *n.* *R. Cath. Ch.* a solemn devotion in memory of the incarnation; the bell tolled to indicate the time when the angelus is to be recited.—**Angel-fish**, ān'-jel-fish, *n.* A fish nearly allied to the sharks: so called from its pectoral fins, which are so large as to spread like wings.

Anger, ang'gėr, *n.* [Originally grief, from Icel. *angr*, grief, sorrow, *angra*, to grieve, annoy; Dan. *anger*, sorrow; same root as in A.Sax. *ange*, vexed, narrow, G. *enge*, narrow; L. *ango*, to trouble, *angor*, vexation, Gr. *anchō*, to choke.] A violent passion or emotion of the mind, excited by a real or supposed injury to one's self or others; passion; ire; choler; rage; wrath. ∴ *Anger* is more general and expresses a less strong feeling than *wrath* and *rage*, both of which imply a certain outward manifestation, and the latter violence and want of self-command.—*v.t.* To excite to anger; to rouse resentment in; to make angry; to exasperate.—**Angerly**,† ang'gėr-li, *adv.* **Angrily**. [*Tenn.*]—**Angrily**, ang'gri-li, *adv.* In an angry manner.—**Angriness**, ang'gri-nes, *n.* The state of being angry.—**Angry**, ang'gri, *a.* Feeling resentment; provoked; showing anger; caused by anger; raging; tumultuous.

Angevin, an'jē-vin, *a.* Of or pertaining to *Anjou*, a former province of France.

Angina, an-jī'na, *n.* [L., from *ango*, to choke. ANGER.] *Med.* an inflammatory affection of the throat or fauces.—*Angina pectoris*, a fatal disease characterized by paroxysms of intense pain and a feeling of constriction in the chest. (Also pron. an'-ji-na.)

Angiocarpous, an'ji-ō-kär″pus, *a.* [Gr. *angeion*, a capsule, and *karpos*, fruit.] *Bot.* having a fruit whose seed-vessels are inclosed within a covering that does not form a part of themselves, as the acorn.

Angiography, Angiology, an-ji-og'ra-fi, an-ji-ol'o-ji, *n.* [Gr. *angeion*, a vessel.] *Med.* a description of the vessels of the body.

Angioma, an-ji-ō'ma, *n.* [Gr. *angeion*, a vessel.] *Med.* a tumour produced by the enlargement of a blood-vessel.

Angiosperm, an'ji-ō-spėrm, *n.* [Gr. *angeion*, a vessel, and *sperma*, seed.] *Bot.* a plant which has its seeds inclosed in a seed-vessel.—**Angiospermous**, an'ji-ō-spėrm″us, *a.* *Bot.* having seeds inclosed in a seed-vessel.

Angle, ang'gl, *n.* [L. *angulus*, a corner. ANCHOR.] The point where two lines or planes meet that do not run in the same straight line; a corner; the degree of opening or divergence of two straight lines which meet one another.—**Angle of repose**. The angle of inclination to the horizontal of an inclined plane when the force of gravity is just sufficient to overcome friction.—**Angled**, ang'gld, *a.* Having angles: used chiefly in compounds.—**Anglemeter**, ang'gl-mē-tėr, *n.* Any instrument for measuring angles.—**Angular**, ang'gū-lėr, *a.* Having an angle or angles; having corners; pointed; consisting of or forming an angle.—*Angular motion, angular velocity*, the motion or velocity of a body or a point moving circularly.—**Angularity**, ang-gū-lar'i-ti, *n.* The quality of being angular.—**Angularly**, ang'gū-lėr-li, *adv.* In an angular manner.—**Angularness**, ang'gū-lėr-nes, *n.* The quality of being angular.—**Angulate, Angulated**, ang'gū-lāt, ang'gū-lāt-ed, *a.* Angled; cornered.—**Angulation**, ang-gū-lā'shon, *n.* The state of being angulated; that which is angulated.—**Angulosity**, ang-gū-los'i-ti, *n.* A state of being angulous or angular.—**Angulose**, ang'gū-lōs, *a.* Angular.—**Angle-bar**, *n.* A bar fitting into an angle or corner to connect the side pieces.—**Angle-iron**, *n.* A piece of rolled iron in the shape of the letter L, used for forming the joints of iron plates in girders, boilers, &c., to which it is riveted.

Angle, ang'gl, *n.* [A.Sax. *angel*, a fish-hook; G. *angel*, Icel. *öngull*, a hook; from a root meaning crooked, seen also in ANCHOR.] A fish-hook.—**Angle**, ang'gl, *v.i.*—*angled, angling*. To fish with an angle, or with line and hook.—**Angler**, ang'glėr, *n.* One who fishes with an angle; a fish having long filamentous appendages in its head, which attract the smaller fishes and thus provide it with prey.—**Angling**, ang'-gling, *n.* The act or art of fishing with a rod and line; rod-fishing.

Angles, ang'glz, *n. pl.* [A.Sax. *Angle*, *Engle*, the Angles.] A Low German tribe who in the fifth century and subsequently crossed over to Britain along with bands of Saxons, Jutes, and others, and colonized a great part of what from them has received the name of England.—**Anglian**, ang'gli-an, *a.* Of or pertaining to the tribe of the Angles.—*n.* A member of the tribe of the Angles.

Anglican, ang'glik-an, *a.* [L.L. *anglicus*, English.] English; pertaining to the English Church.—*Anglican Church*, the Church of England and the Protestant Episcopal churches in Ireland, Scotland, and the colonies; sometimes including also the Episcopal churches of the United States.—*n.* A member of the Anglican Church.—**Anglicanism**, ang'glik-an-izm, *n.* The principles of or adherence to the Established Church of England.—**Anglice**, ang'-gli-sē, *adv.* [L.] In English; in the English manner.—**Anglicism**, ang'gli-sizm, *n.* The quality of being English; an English idiom.—**Anglicize, Anglify**, ang'-gli-sīz, ang'gli-fī, *v.t.*—*anglicized, anglicizing*. To make English; to render conformable to the English idiom or to English analogies.—**Anglification**, ang'gli-fi-kā″shon, *n.* The act of converting into English.

Anglo-, ang'glō, prefix. [L.L. *Anglus*, an Englishman.] A prefix signifying *English*, or connected with England.—**Anglo-American**, *n.* A descendant from English ancestors born in America or the United States: used also as an adj.—**Anglo-Catholic**, *n.* A member of the Church of England who lays stress on the claim that his church is historically a part of the Catholic Church: used also as an adj.—**Anglo-Catholicism**, *n.* The principles or doctrines of the Anglo-Catholics.—**Anglo-Indian**, *n.* One of the English race born or resident in the East Indies. Also as an adj.—**Anglo-Irish**, *n. pl.* English people born or resident in Ireland; descendants of parents English on the one side and Irish on the other. Also as an adj.—**Anglomania**, ang-glō-mā'ni-a, *n.* [Gr. *mania*, madness.] An excessive or undue attachment to, respect for, or imitation of Englishmen or English institutions and customs by a foreigner.—**Anglophobia**, ang-glō-fō'bi-a, *n.* [Gr. *phobos*, fear.] An excessive hatred to or dread of English people, customs, or institutions.—**Anglo-Saxon**, *n.* [ANGLES, SAXON.] One of the nation formed by the union of the Angles, Saxons, and other early Teutonic settlers in Britain, or one of their descendants; one belonging to the English race; the language of the Anglo-Saxons, or the English language in its first stage.—*a.* Pertaining to the Anglo-Saxons or to the oldest form of English.

Angola, an-gō'la, *n.* A light cloth, made from the wool or long silky hair of the Angora goat, a native of Asia Minor.—**Angola-cat**. A large variety of the domestic cat originally from Angora, with beautiful long silky hair.

Angostura, ang-gos-tū'ra, *a.* Belonging to or brought from the town of Angostura in Venezuela—an epithet of a kind of bark having febrifugal properties and of a kind of bitters made from it.

Angrily, Angriness, Angry. ANGER.

Anguilliform, an-gwil'li-form, *a.* [L. *anguilla*, an eel, and *forma*, shape.] Having the form of an eel or of a serpent.

Anguine, Anguineal, an'gwin, an-gwin'ē-al, *a.* [L. *anguineus*, from *anguis*, a snake.] Pertaining to or resembling a snake; snake-like.

Anguish, ang'gwish, *n.* [O.E. *anguis, angoise*, Fr. *angoisse*, from L. *angustia*, a strait, perplexity, from *angustus*, narrow; root *ang* as in E. *anger*.] Extreme pain, either of body or mind; any keen affection of the emotions or feelings ('an *anguish* of delight.' *Thack.*)—**Anguish**,† ang'gwish, *v.t.* To distress extremely.

Angular, Angularity, &c. ANGLE.

Angustifoliate, ang-gus'ti-fō'li-āt, *a.* [L. *angustus*, narrow, and *folium*, a leaf.] *Bot.* having narrow leaves.

Anhelation, an-hē-lā'shon, *n.* [L. *anhelatio, anhelationis*, from *anhelo*, to pant.] Shortness of breath; a panting; also, eager desire or aspiration.

Anhydrous, an-hī'drus, *a.* [Gr. *anydros*, dry—neg. prefix *an*, and *hydōr*, water.] Destitute of water; specifically, *chem.* destitute of the water of crystallization.—**Anhydride**, an-hī'drid, *n.* One of a class of oxygen compounds in which there is no water.—**Anhydrite**, an-hī'drit, *n.* Anhydrous sulphate of calcium, a mineral resembling a coarse-grained granite.

Anicut, an'i-kut, *n.* ANNICUT.

Anidiomatical, an-id'i-o-mat″ik-al, *a.* [Gr. neg. prefix *an*, and E. *idiomatical*.] Contrary to the idiom of a language.

Anil, an'il, *n.* [Sp. *anil*, Ar. *neel*, Skr. *nīlam*, indigo, *nīlī*, the indigo-plant.] A shrub from whose leaves and stalks the West Indian indigo is made.—**Anilla**, an-il'la, *n.* A commercial term for West Indian indigo.—**Aniline**, an'i-lin, *n.* A substance obtained from indigo and other organic substances, though the aniline of commerce is obtained from benzole, a product of coal-tar. It furnishes a number of brilliant dyes.

Anile, an'īl, *a.* [L. *anilis*, from *anus*, an old woman.] Old-womanish; aged; imbecile.—**Anility, Anileness**, a-nil'i-ti, an'-īl-nes, *n.* The state of being anile.

Animadvert, an'i-mad-vėrt″, *v.i.* [L. *animadverto*—*animus*, mind, and *adverto*, to turn to.] To perceive or take cognizance; usually, to make remark by way of criticism; to pass strictures or criticisms (followed by *on, upon*).—**Animadverter**, an'i-mad-vėrt″ėr, *n.* One who animadverts.—**Animadversion**, an'i-mad-vėr'-shon, *n.* The act of one who animadverts; a remark by way of criticism or censure; stricture; censure.—**Animadversive**,† an'i-mad-vėr″siv, *a.* Perceiving; percipient.

Animal, an'i-mal, *n.* [L. *animal*, a living being, from *anima*, air, breath, life, the soul, from a root *an*, to breathe or blow.] A living being characterized by sensation and voluntary motion; an inferior or irrational being, in contradistinction to man; also often popularly used to signify a quadruped.—*a.* Belonging or relating to animals (*animal* functions); pertaining to the merely sentient part of a living being, as distinguished from the intellectual or spiritual part (*animal* passions); of or pertaining to, or consisting of, the flesh of animals.—**Animalish**,† an'i-mal-ish, *a.* Of or pertaining to or like an animal; brutish.—**Animalism**, an'i-mal-izm, *n.* The state of a mere animal; the state of being actuated by sensual appetites only; sensuality.—**Animality**, an-i-mal'i-ti, *n.* The state of being an animal; *physiol.* those vital phenomena which, superadded to vegetality, constitute animal existence.—**Animalization**, an'i-mal-iz-ā″shon, *n.* The act of animalizing; conversion into animal matter by the process of assimilation.—**Animalize**, an'i-mal-īz, *v.t.*—*animalized, animalizing*. To give animal life to; to convert into animal matter; to bring under the sway of animal appetites.—**Animalness**, an'i-mal-nes, *n.* Animality.

Animalcule, an-i-mal'kūl, *n.* [L.L. *animalculum*, dim. of L. *animal*, an animal.] A minute animal, especially one that is microscopic or invisible to the naked eye. —**Animalcular, Animalculine**, an-i-mal'kū-lėr, an-i-mal'kū-līn, *a.* Pertaining to or resembling animalcules.—**Animalculum**, an-i-mal'kū-lum, *n.* pl. **Animalcula**, an-i-mal'kū-la. An animalcule.

Animate, an'i-māt, *v.t.—animated, animating.* [L. *animatus*, animated, pp. of *animo*, to fill with breath. ANIMAL.] To give natural life to; to quicken; to make alive; to give life, spirit, or liveliness to; to heighten the powers or effect of; to stimulate or incite; to inspirit; rouse.—**Animate**, an'i-māt, *a.* Alive; possessing animal life.—**Animated**, an'i-māt-ed, *a.* Endowed with animal life; lively; vigorous; full of spirit (an *animated* discourse).—**Animater, Animator**, an'i-māt-ėr, *n.* One who animates.—**Animating**, an'i-māt-ing, *a.* Giving life; infusing spirit; enlivening; rousing.—**Animatingly**, an'i-māt-ing-li, *adv.* So as to animate.—**Animation**, an-i-mā'shon, *n.* The act of animating or state of being animated; state of having life; liveliness; briskness; vivacity. —**Animative**, an'i-māt-iv, *a.* Giving life or spirit.

Anime, an'i-me, *n.* [Sp.] A resin exuding from a large American tree, called in the West Indies *locust-tree.* It produces a fine varnish. The name is also given to Indian copal.

Animism, an'i-mizm, *n.* [L. *anima*, the soul.] The old hypothesis of a force (*Anima mundi*, soul of the world) immaterial but inseparable from matter, and giving to matter its form and movements; the attribution of spirit or soul to inanimate things. —**Animist**, an'i-mist, *n.* One who holds to or believes in animism.—**Animistic**, an-i-mist'ik, *a.* Pertaining to, or founded on, animism.

Animosity, an-i-mos'i-ti, *n.* [L. *animositas*, from *animosus*, full of courage, ardent, from *animus*, the mind, courage, pride.] Courage†; rancorous feeling; bitter and active enmity.

Animus, an'i-mus, *n.* [L., spirit, temper.] Intention; purpose; spirit; temper; especially, hostile spirit or angry temper.

Anion, an'i-on, *n.* [Gr. *ana*, upward, and *iōn*, going.] *Elect.* the element of an electrolyte which is evolved at the positive pole or *anode.*

Anise, an'is, *n.* [Fr., from L. *anisum.*] An annual umbelliferous plant (*Pimpinella Anisum*), the seeds of which have an aromatic smell and a pleasant warm taste, and are employed in the manufacture of liqueurs.—**Aniseed**, an'i-sēd, *n.* The seed of the anise.—**Anisette**, an-i-set, *n.* [Fr.] A liqueur flavoured with anise.—**Anisic**, a-nis'ik, *a.* Of or pertaining to anise.

Anisomeric, an-ī'so-mer"ik, *a.* [Gr. *anisos*, unequal, and *meros*, a part.] Not consisting of symmetrical or corresponding parts; unsymmetrical.

Anisostemonous, an-ī'so-stem"on-us, *a.* [Gr. *anisos*, unequal, and *stēmōn* = *stamen.*] *Bot.* having the number of the stamens not corresponding with the number of the petals or the sepals.

Anisotrope, Anisotropic, an'i-sō-trōp, an'i-sō-trōp'ik, *a.* Same as *Æolotropic.*

Anitrogenous, a-nī-troj'en-us, *a.* Not containing or supplying nitrogen; non-nitrogenous.

Anker, ang'kėr, *n.* A Dutch liquid measure, formerly used in England, containing 10 wine gallons.

Ankle, ang'kl, *n.* [A.Sax. *ancleow*, O.Fris. *ankel*, Dan. and Sw. *ankel*, G. *enkel*; from a root *ang*, meaning crooked. ANCHOR.] The joint which connects the foot with the leg.—**Ankled**, ang'kld, *a.* Having ankles: used in composition.—**Anklet**, ang'klet, *n.* An ornament, support, or protection for the ankle.

Ankyloblepharon, an'ki-lō-blef"a-ron, *n.* [Gr. *ankylōsis*, and *blepharon*, eyelid.] Adhesion of the eyelids to one another.

Ankylosis, ang-ki-lō'sis, *n.* [Gr., from *angkylos*, crooked.] Stiffness and immovability of a joint; morbid adhesion of the articular ends of contiguous bones.—**Ankylose**, ang'ki-lōs, *v.t.—ankylosed, ankylosing.* To affect with ankylosis.—*v.i.* To become ankylosed.—**Ankylotic**, ang-ki-lot'ik, *a.* Pertaining to ankylosis.

Anna, an'na, *n.* In the East Indies, the sixteenth part of a rupee, or about 1*d.*

Annals, an'nalz, *n. pl.* [L. *annales* (*libri*, books, understood), *annalis*, pertaining to a year, from *annus*, a year.] A history or relation of events in chronological order, each event being recorded under the year in which it happened.—**Annalist**, an'nal-ist, *n.* A writer of annals.—**Annalistic**, an-nal-ist'ik, *a.* Pertaining or peculiar to an annalist.

Annats, Annates, an'nats, an'nāts, *n.pl.* [L.L. *annata*, from L. *annus*, a year.] The first year's income of a spiritual living, formerly vested in the sovereign, but in the reign of Queen Anne appropriated to the augmentation of poor livings.

Annatto, an-nat'tō, *n.* ARNOTTO.

Anneal, an-nēl', *v.t.* [A. Sax. *anaelan*, *onaelan*, to set on fire, to anneal—*an* or *on*, on, and *œlan*, to kindle.] To heat, as glass or iron vessels, in an oven or furnace, and then cool slowly, for the purpose of rendering less brittle; to temper by a gradually diminishing heat; to heat in order to fix colours; to bake.

Annelid, Annelidan, an'ne-lid, an-nel'i-dan, *n.* [L. *annellus*, a little ring, and Gr. *eidos*, form.] One of an extensive division or class of annulose animals, so called because their bodies are formed of a great number of small rings, as in the earthworm.—**Annelida**, an-nel'i-da, *n.pl.* The anneiids.

Annex, an-neks', *v.t.* [L. *annecto, annexum*, to bind to—*ad*, to, and *necto, nexum*, to bind.] To unite at the end; to subjoin; to unite, as a smaller thing to a greater; to connect, especially as a consequence (to *annex* a penalty).—*n.* Something annexed. —**Annexation**, an-neks-ā'shon, *n.* The act of annexing; what is annexed; addition; union.—**Annexationist**, an-neks-ā'shon-ist, *n.* One favourable to annexation, as of a portion of another country to his own.—**Annexe**, an-neks', *n.* [Fr.] A wing or subsidiary building communicating with the main edifice.—**Annexion**,† an-nek'shon, *n.* The act of annexing or thing annexed; annexation. [*Shak.*]

Annicut, an'ni-kut, *n.* In the East Indies, a dam.

Annihilate, an-nī'hil-āt, *v.t.—annihilated, annihilating.* [L. *annihilo*—*ad*, to, and *nihil*, nothing.] To reduce to nothing; to destroy the existence of; to cause to cease to be; to destroy the form or peculiar distinctive properties of.—**Annihilable**, an-nī'hil-a-bl, *a.* Capable of being annihilated.—**Annihilation**, an-nī'hil-ā'shon, *n.* The act of annihilating or the state of being annihilated.—**Annihilationist**, an-nī'hil-ā"shon-ist, *n.* One who believes that annihilation by way of punishment is the fate of the wicked after death.—**Annihilator**, an-nī'hil-āt-ėr, *n.* One who or that which annihilates.

Anniversary, an-ni-vėrs'a-ri, *a.* [L. *anniversarius*—*annus*, a year, and *verto, versum*, to turn.] Returning with the year at a stated time; annual; yearly.—*n.* A stated day on which some event is annually celebrated; the annual celebration in honour of an event.

Annomination, an-nom'in-ā"shon, *n.* [L. *ad*, to, *nomen*, a name.] The use of words nearly alike in sound but of different meanings; a pun; a paronomasia.

Annotate, an'nō-tāt, *v.t.—annotated, annotating.* [L. *annoto, annotatum*—*ad*, to, and *noto*, to note.] To comment upon; to make remarks on by notes.—*v.i.* To act as an annotator; to make annotations or notes (with *on*).—**Annotation**, an-nō-tā'shon, *n.* The act of annotating or making notes on; an illustrative note on some passage of a book.—**Annotator**, an'nō-tāt-ėr, *n.* A writer of annotations or notes; a commentator.—**Annotatory**, an-nōt'a-to-ri, *a.* Relating to or containing annotations.

Annotinous, an-not'in-us, *a.* [L. *annotinus*, from *annus*, a year.] *Bot.* being a year old; lasting from the previous year.

Annotto, Annotta, an-not'tō, an-not'ta, *n.* ARNOTTO.

Announce, an-nouns', *v.t.—announced, announcing.* [Fr. *annoncer*, from L. *annuncio*—*ad*, and *nuncio*, to tell, from *nuncius*, a messenger.] To publish; to proclaim; to give notice or first notice of.—**Announcement**, an-nouns'ment, *n.* The act of announcing or giving notice; proclamation; publication.—**Announcer**, an-nouns'ėr, *n.* One that announces; a proclaimer.

Annoy, an-noi', *v.t.* [O.Fr. *anoier*, from *anoi*, annoyance, vexation, from L. *in odio*, in hatred, common in such phrases as *est mihi in odio*, it is hateful to me. ODIUM.] To torment or disturb, especially by continued or repeated acts; to tease, vex, pester, or molest.—*n.* Molestation; annoyance (chiefly a poetical word).—**Annoyance**, an-noi'ans, *n.* The act of annoying; the state of being annoyed; that which annoys; trouble.—**Annoyer**, an-noi'ėr, *n.* One that annoys.—**Annoying**, an-noi'ing, *a.* Vexatious; troublesome.

Annual, an'nū-al, *a.* [L.L. *annualis*, from L. *annus*, a year.] Returning every year; coming yearly; lasting or continuing only one year or one yearly season; performed in a year; reckoned by the year.—*n.* A plant that grows from seed, flowers, and perishes in the course of the same season; a literary production published annually.—**Annually**, an'nū-al-li, *adv.* Yearly; returning every year; year by year.

Annuity, an-nū'i-ti, *n.* [Fr. *annuité*, from *annus*, a year.] A yearly payment of money which a person receives for life or for a term of years, the person being usually entitled to such payment in consideration of money advanced to those who pay.—**Annuitant**, an-nū'it-ant, *n.* One receiving an annuity.

Annul, an-nul', *v.t.—annulled, annulling.* [Fr. *annuler*, from L. *ad nullum*, to nothing.] To reduce to nothing or annihilate (*Mil.*)†; to make void; to nullify; to abrogate; cancel (laws, decrees, compacts, &c.). —**Annuller**, an-nul'ėr, *n.* One who annuls. —**Annulment**, an-nul'ment, *n.* The act of.

Annular, Annulary,† an'nū-lėr, an'nū-la-ri, *a.* [L. *annularis*, from *annulus*, *anulus*, dim. of *anus*, a ring, akin to *annus*, a year, ANNUAL.] Having the form of a ring; pertaining to a ring.—*Annular eclipse*, an eclipse of the sun in which a ring of light formed by the sun's disc is visible around the dark shadow of the moon.—**Annularly**, an'nū-lėr-li, *adv.* In the manner of a ring.—**Annulata**, an-nū-lā'ta, *n.pl.* Same as *Annelida.*—**Annulate, Annulated**, an'nū-lāt, an'nū-lāt-ed, *a.* Furnished with rings, or circles like rings; having belts.—**Annulation**, an-nū-lā'shon, *n.* A circular or ring-like formation.—**Annulet**, an'nū-let, *n.* [A dim. from L. *annulus*, a ring.] A little ring or ring-like body.—**Annuloida**, an-nū-loi'da, *n.pl.* A division of animals made up of the sea-urchins, tape-worms, &c.—**Annulose**, an'-nū-lōs, *a.* Furnished with rings; having a body composed of rings: a term applied to animals forming a sub-kingdom which embraces the worms, leeches, crabs, spiders, insects.—**Annulosa**, an-nū-lō'sa, *n. pl.* The annulose animals.

Annumerate,† an-nū'mėr-āt, *v.t.—annumerated, annumerating.* [L. *annumero*—*ad*, and *numerus*, number.] To add to a former number.—**Annumeration**, an-nū'mėr-ā"shon, *n.* Addition to a former number.

Annunciate, an-nun'shi-āt, *v.t.—annunciated, annunciating.* [ANNOUNCE.] To bring tidings of; to announce.—**Annunciation**, an-nun'shi-ā"shon, *n.* The act of announcing; announcement; the tidings brought by the angel to Mary of the incarnation of Christ; the church festival in memory of this announcement, falling on 25th March.—**Annunciative, Annunciatory**, an-nun'shi-āt-iv, an-nun'shi-a-to-ri, *a.* Having the character of an annunciation. — **Annunciator**, an-nun'shi-āt-ėr, *n.* One who announces.

Anode, an'ōd, *n.* [Gr. *ana*, upwards, and *hodos*, a way.] The part of the surface of an electrolyte which the electric current enters: opposed to *cathode*.

Anodyne, an'ō-dīn, *n.* [Gr. neg. prefix *an*, and *odynē*, pain.] Any medicine which allays pain.—*a.* Assuaging pain. — **Anodynous**, an'ō-dīn-us, *a.* Having the qualities of an anodyne.

Anoint, a-noint', *v.t.* [O.E. *anointen, enointen*; O.Fr. *enoindre*, part. *enoint*, from L. *inungere, inunctum*, from *in*, in, on, and *ungo, unctum*, to anoint. UNGUENT.] To pour oil upon; to smear or rub with oil or unctuous substances; to consecrate by unction, or the use of oil.—**Anointer**, a-noint'-ėr, *n.* One who anoints.—**Anointment**, a-noint'ment, *n.* The act of anointing.

Anomaly, a-nom'a-li, *n.* [Fr. *anomalie*; L. *anomalia*, Gr. *anōmalia*, inequality, neg. prefix *an*, and *homalos*, equal, similar, from *homos*, the same. SAME.] Deviation from the common rule; something abnormal; irregularity; *astron.* the angular distance of a planet from its perihelion, as seen from the sun; also the angle measuring apparent irregularities in the motion of a planet.—**Anomalism**, a-nom'al-izm, *n.* An anomaly; a deviation from rule.—**Anomalistic**, a-nom'a-list"ik, *a.* Pertaining to an anomaly.—*Anomalistic year*, the interval between two occasions when the earth is in perihelion, rather longer than the civil year.—**Anomalous**, a-nom'a-lus, *a.* [L. *anomalus*, Gr. *anōmalos*.] Forming an anomaly; deviating from a general rule, method, or analogy; irregular; abnormal.—**Anomalously**, a-nom'a-lus-li, *adv.*—**Anomalousness**, a-nom'a-lus-nes, *n.*

Anon, a-non', *adv.* [O.E. *anan, anoon*, A.Sax. *on ân, an ân*=on one, that is, without break.] Forthwith; immediately; quickly; at another time; thereafter; sometimes.—*Ever and anon*, every now and then.

Anonymous, a-non'im-us, *a.* [Gr. *anōnymos*—neg. prefix *an*, and *onoma*, name. NAME.] Wanting a name; without any name acknowledged as that of author, contributor, and the like.—**Anonymously**, a-non'im-us-li, *adv.* In an anonymous manner; without a name.—**Anonyme**, an'on-īm, *n.* An assumed or false name.—**Anonymity, Anonymousness**, a-non-im'i-ti, a-non'im-us-nes, *n.* The state of being anonymous.

Anopisthographic, an-op'is-tho-graf"ik, *a.* [Gr. *an*, priv., *opisthen*, behind, *graphō*, to write.] Not having writing on the reverse side.

Anoplotherium, an'op-lo-thē"ri-um, *n.* [Gr. neg. prefix *an*, *hoplon*, armour, and *thērion*, a beast.] The generic name of certain extinct hoofed animals, discovered in the gypsum quarries of Paris and fresh-water deposits of the Isle of Wight.

Anorexy, an'o-rek-si, *n.* [Gr. neg. prefix *an*, and *orexis*, desire, appetite.] Want of appetite without a loathing of food.

Anorthic, an-or'thik, *a.* [Gr. neg. prefix *an*, and *orthos*, straight, right.] Without right angles; *mineral.* having unequal oblique axes.—**Anorthite**, a-nor'thīt, *n.* A mineral of the felspar family.

Anosmia, an-os'mi-a, *n.* [Gr. neg. prefix *an*, and *osmē*, smell.] *Med.* a loss of the sense of smell.

Another, an-uTH'ėr, *a.* [*An*, indefinite art., and *other*.] Not the same; different; one more, in addition to a former number; any other; any one else. Often used without a noun, as a substitute for the name of a person or thing, and much used in opposition to *one*; as, *one* went *one* way, *another another*. Also frequently used with *one* in a reciprocal sense; as, 'Love *one another*'.

Anotta, Anotto, a-not'ta, a-not'tō, *n.* Same as *Arnotto*.

Anserine, an'sėr-īn, *a.* [L. *anserinus*, from *anser*, a goose.] Relating to or resembling a goose, or the skin of a goose: applied to the skin when roughened by cold or disease.

Anschluss, ăn'shlus, *n.* [G.] Political annexation of territory; political union.

Answer, an'sėr, *v.t.* [A.Sax. *andswerian*, to answer—*and*, a prefix meaning against (=*a* in *along*, L. *ante*, before, Gr. *anti*, against), and *swerian*, to swear.] To speak or write in return to; to reply to; to refute; to say or do in reply; to act in compliance with, or in fulfilment or satisfaction of; to render account to or for; to be security for (*Shak.*); to be equivalent or adequate to; to serve; to suit.—*v.i.* To reply; to speak or write by way of return; to respond to some call; to be fit or suitable.—*To answer for*, to be accountable for; to guarantee.—*To answer to*, to be known by; to correspond to, in the way of resemblance, fitness, or correlation.—**Answer**, an'sėr, *n.* A reply; that which is said, written, or done, in return to a call, question, argument, challenge, allegation, petition, prayer, or address; the result of an arithmetical or mathematical operation; a solution; something done in return for, or in consequence of, something else; *law*, a counter-statement of facts in a course of pleadings.—**Answerable**, an'sėr-a-bl, *a.* Capable of being answered: obliged to give an account; amenable; responsible; correspondent.—**Answerableness**, an'sėr-a-bl-nes, *n.* The quality of being answerable.—**Answerably**, an'sėr-a-bli, *adv.* In due proportion, correspondence, or conformity; suitably.—**Answerer**, an'sėr-ėr, *n.* One who answers.—**Answerless**, an'sėr-les, *a.* Having no answer, or incapable of being answered.—**Answerlessly**, an'sėr-les-li, *adv.*

Ant, ant, *n.* [From A.Sax. *aemete*, an emmet (like *aunt*, from L. *amita*). EMMET.] An emmet; a pismire; a hymenopterous insect living in communities which consist of males, females, and neuters. The name is also given to the neuropterous insects more correctly called *Termites*.—**Ant-bear**, *n.* A kind of large ant-eater.—**Ant-eater**, *n.* A quadruped that eats ants, especially an edentate animal (genus Myrmecophaga) which feeds on ants and other insects, catching them by thrusting among them the long tongue covered with a viscid saliva.—**Ant-egg**, *n.* One of the small white bodies found in the hillocks of ants, popularly supposed to be their eggs, but really their larvæ.—**Ant-hill, Ant-hillock**, *n.* A little tumulus or hillock formed by ants for their habitation, and composed of earth, leaves, twigs, &c.—**Ant-lion**, *n.* The larva of a neuropterous insect which prepares a kind of pit-fall for the destruction of ants, &c.

Antacid, ant-as'id, *n.* [*Anti*, against, and *acid*.] An alkali, or a remedy for acidity in the stomach.—*a.* Counteracting acidity.

Antacrid, ant-ak'rid, *n.* [*Anti*, against, and *acrid*.] That which corrects acridity of the secretions.

Antagonist, an-tag'ō-nist, *n.* [Gr. *antagōnistēs*—*anti*, against, and *agōnistēs*, a champion, a combatant, from *agōn*, a contest (whence *agony*).] One who contends with another; an opponent; a competitor; an adversary. ∴ *Syn.* under ADVERSARY.—*a.* Counteracting; opposing (said of muscles).—**Antagonistic, Antagonistical**, an-tag'ō-nist"ik, an-tag'ō-nist"ik-al, *a.* Contending against; acting in opposition; opposing.—**Antagonistic**, *n.* A muscle whose action counteracts that of another.—**Antagonistically**, an-tag'ō-nis"tik-al-li, *adv.* In an antagonistical manner.—**Antagonize**, an-tag'ō-nīz, *v.i.*—*antagonized, antagonizing.* To contend against; to act in opposition.—**Antagonism**, an-tag'ō-nizm, *n.* Character of being an antagonist or antagonistic; counteraction or contrariety of things or principles.

Antalgic, an-tal'jik, *n.* [Gr. *anti*, against, and *algos*, pain.] A medicine to alleviate pain; an anodyne.—*a.* Alleviating pain.

Antalkali, ant-al'ka-li, *n.* [*Anti*, against, and *alkali*.] A substance which neutralizes an alkali.—**Antalkaline**, ant-al'ka-līn, *a.* Having the property of neutralizing alkalies.

Antaphrodisiac, Antaphroditic, ant-af'ro-diz"i-ak, ant-af'ro-dit"ik, *a.* [Gr. *anti*, against, and *aphrodisios*, venereal.] Antivenereal; having the quality of extinguishing or lessening venereal desire.—*n.* A medicine with this property.

Antarchism,† ant-är'kizm, *n.* [Gr. *anti*, and *archē*, government.] Opposition to all government.—**Antarchist**,† ant-är'kist, *n.* One who opposes all social government, or control of individuals by law.—**Antarchistic**,† ant-är-kis'tik, *a.* Pertaining to antarchism.

Antarctic, ant-ärk'tik, *a.* [L. *antarcticus*, Gr. *antarktikos*—*anti*, against, and *arktos*, the north. ARCTIC.] Opposite to the northern or arctic pole; relating to the southern pole or to the region near it, and applied to a circle parallel to the equator and distant from the pole 23° 28'.

Antarthritic, ant-är-thrit'ik, *a.* [Gr. *anti*, against, and *arthritis*, gout.] Counteracting the gout.—*n.* A remedy which cures or alleviates the gout.

Antasthmatic, ant-ast-mat'ik, *a.* [Gr. *anti*, against, and *asthma*, asthma.] Fitted to relieve asthma.—*n.* A remedy for asthma.

Antatrophic, an-ta-trof'ik, *a.* [Gr. *anti*, against, and *atrophia*, a wasting away.] Efficacious against atrophy or consumption.—*n.* A medicine for the cure of atrophy.

Antebrachial, an-tē-brā'ki-al, *a.* [L. *ante*, before, and *brachium*, the arm.] *Anat.* of or pertaining to the fore-arm.

Antecede, an-tē-sēd', *v.t.*—*anteceded, anteceding.* [L. *ante*, before, and *cedo*, to go. CEDE.] To go before in time; to precede.—**Antecedence, Antecedency**, an-tē-sē'dens, an-tē-sē'den-si, *n.* The act or state of going before in time; precedence.—**Antecedent**, an-tē-sē'dent, *a.* Going before; prior; anterior; preceding.—*n.* One who or that which goes before in time or place; *gram.* the noun to which a relative or other pronoun refers; *pl.* the earlier events of a man's life; previous course, conduct, or avowed principles.—**Antecedently**, an-tē-sē'dent-li, *adv.* Previously; at a time preceding.—**Antecessor**, an-tē-ses'ėr, *n.* One who goes before; a leader; *law*, an ancestor.

Ante-chamber, Anteroom, an'tē-chām-bėr, an'tē-röm, *n.* A chamber or room before or leading to another apartment.

Ante-chapel, an'tē-chap-el, *n.* The part of the chapel through which is the passage to the choir or body of it.

Antecians, Antœci, an-tē'shi-anz, an-tē'si, *n.pl.* [Gr. *anti*, against, and *oikos*, a house.] Those living in the same latitude, but on different sides of the equator.

Antedate, an'tē-dāt, *n.* [Prefix *ante*, before, and *date*.] Prior date; a date antecedent to another.—*v.t. antedated, antedating.* To date before the true time or beforehand; to give an earlier date than the real one to; to anticipate or give effect to before the due time.

Antediluvian, an'tē-di-lū"vi-an, *a.* [L. *ante*, before, and *diluvium*, a flood.] Existing, happening, or relating to what happened before the deluge.—*n.* One who lived before the deluge.

Antelope, an'tē-lōp, *n.* [Doubtfully derived from a Gr. *antholōps*, an antelope, supposed to be compounded of *anthos*, a flower, and *ōps*, an eye.] A name applied to many species of ruminant mammals resembling the deer in general appearance, but essentially different in nature from them, having hollow, unbranched horns that are not deciduous.

Antelucan, an-tē-lū'kan, *a.* [L. *antelucanus*—*ante*, before, and *lux*, light.] Being before light; preceding the dawn.

Antemeridian, an'tē-mē-rid"i-an, *a.* [L.

ante, before, and *meridies*, noon.] Being before noon; pertaining to the forenoon.

Antemetic, ant-ē-met'ik, *a.* [Prefix *anti*, against, and *emetic*.] Restraining or allaying vomiting.—*n.* A medicine which checks vomiting.

Antemundane, an-tē-mun'dān, *a.* [L. *ante*, before, and *mundus*, the world.] Being before the creation of the world.

Antenatal, an-tē-nā'tal, *a.* [L. *ante*, before, and *natalis*, pertaining to birth.] Existing or happening previous to birth.

Antenna, an-ten'na, *n.* pl. **Antennæ**, an-ten'nē. [L. *antenna*, a sail-yard.] One of the hornlike filaments that project from the head in insects, crustacea, and myriapods, and are considered as organs of touch and hearing; a feeler.—**Antennal**, an-ten'nal, *a.* Belonging to the antennæ.—**Antenniferous**, an-ten-nif'ėr-us, *a.* Bearing antennæ.—**Antenniform**, an-ten'ni-form, *a.* Shaped like antennæ.

Antenuptial, an-tē-nup'shal, *a.* [Prefix *ante*, before, and *nuptial*.] Occurring or done before marriage; preceding marriage.

Antepaschal, an-tē-pas'kal, *a.* [Prefix *ante*, before, and *paschal*.] Pertaining to the time before Easter.

Antepast, an'tē-past, *n.* [L. *ante*, before, *pastus*, food.] A foretaste.

Antependium, an-tē-pen'di-um, *n.* [L. *ante*, before, and *pendo*, to hang.] The hanging with which the front of an altar is covered.

Antepenult, Antepenultima, an"tē-pē-nult, an'tē-pē-nul"ti-ma, *n.* [L. *ante*, before, *pene*, almost, and *ultimus*, last.] The last syllable of a word except two.—**Antepenultimate**, an'tē-pē-nul"ti-māt, *a.* Pertaining to the last syllable but two. —*n.* The antepenult.

Antepileptic, ant-ep'i-lep"tik, *a.* [*Anti*, against, and *epileptic*.] Resisting or curing epilepsy.—*n.* A remedy for epilepsy.

Anteposition, an'tē-pō-zi"shon, *n.* [Prefix *ante*, before, and *position*.] A placing before; *gram.* the placing of a word before another which ought to follow it.

Anteprandial, an-tē-pran'di-al, *a.* [L. *ante*, before, and *prandium*, a meal, a dinner.] Relating to the time before dinner; occurring before dinner.

Anterior, an-tē'ri-ėr, *a.* [L., a comparative from *ante*, before.] Before in time; prior; antecedent; before in place; in front. —**Anteriority**, an-tē'ri-or"i-ti, *n.* The state of being anterior in time or place.—**Anteriorly**, an-tē'ri-ėr-li, *adv.* In an anterior manner; before.

Anteroom, an'tē-röm, *n.* ANTE-CHAMBER.

Antero-posterior, an'tē-rō-pos-tē"ri-ėr, *a.* [L. *anterior*, from *ante*, before, and *posterior*, from *post*, behind.] Lying in a direction from behind forward.

Anthelion, ant-hē'li-on, *n.* pl. **Anthelia**, ant-hē'li-a. [Gr. *anti*, opposite to, and *hēlios*, the sun.] A luminous ring, or rings, caused by the diffraction of light, seen in alpine and polar regions opposite the sun when rising or setting.

Anthelminthic, Anthelmintic, an-thel-min'thik, an-thel-min'tik, *a.* [Gr. *anti*, against, and *helmins*, *helminthos*, a worm.] *Med.* destroying or expelling worms in the intestines.—*n.* A vermifuge; a remedy for worms in the intestines.

Anthem, an'them, *n.* [O.E. *antempne*, *antemne*, *antefne*, &c., A.Sax. *antefen*, an anthem; from L.L. *antiphona*, from Gr. *antiphōnon*, an antiphon—*anti*, against, and *phōnē*, sound, the voice.] A hymn sung in alternate parts; in modern usage, a sacred tune or piece of music set to words taken from the Psalms or other parts of the Scriptures.

Anther, an'thėr, *n* [Gr. *antheros*, flowery, from *anthos*, a flower.] The essential part of the stamen of a plant containing the pollen or fertilizing dust.—**Antheral**, an'-thėr-al, *a.* Pertaining to anthers.—**Antheriferous**, an-thėr-if'ėr-us, *a.* Producing or supporting anthers. — **Antheriform**, an-thėr'i-form, *a.* Having the form of an anther.—**Antheroid**, an'thėr-oid, *a.* Resembling an anther.

Anthesis, an-thē'sis, *n.* [Gr., from *antheō*, to bloom, from *anthos*, a flower.] The period when flowers expand; expansion into a flower.

Anthocarpous, an-tho-kär'pus, *a.* [Gr. *anthos*, a flower, and *karpos*, fruit.] *Bot.* said of a fruit formed by masses of inflorescence adhering to each other, as the fir-cone, pine-apple, &c.

Anthocyanin, an-tho-sī'an-in, *n.* [Gr. *anthos*, a flower, and *kyanos*, blue.] The blue colouring matter of plants.

Anthodium, an-thō'di-um, *n.* [Gr. *anthōdēs*, from *anthos*, a flower.] *Bot.* the head of flowers of composite plants, as of a thistle or daisy.

Anthography, an-thog'ra-fi, *a.* [Gr. *anthos*, a flower, and *graphē*, description.] That branch of botany which treats of flowers; a description of flowers.

Anthoid, an'thoid, *a.* [Gr. *anthos*, a flower, and *eidos*, form.] Having the form of a flower; resembling a flower.

Antholite, an'tho-līt, *n.* [Gr. *anthos*, flower, *lithos*, stone.] *Geol.* the impress of the inflorescence of plants on rocks.

Anthology, an-thol'o-ji, *n.* [Gr. *anthologia*, from *anthologos*, flower-gathering—*anthos*, a flower, and *legō*, to gather.] A collection of beautiful passages from authors; a collection of selected poems.—**Anthological**, an-tho-loj'ik-al, *a.* Pertaining to anthology.

Anthophore, an'tho-fōr, *n.* [Gr. *anthos*, a flower, and *pherein*, to bear.] *Bot.* a columnar process arising from the bottom of the calyx, and having at its apex the petals, stamens, and pistil.

Anthophyllite, an-thof'il-īt, *n.* [L.L. *anthophyllum*, a clove.] A clove-brown variety of hornblende, occurring in radiating columnar aggregates.

Anthotaxis, an-tho-taks'is, *n.* [Gr. *anthos*, a flower, and *taxis*, order.] *Bot.* the arrangement of flowers on the axis of growth; the inflorescence.

Anthoxanthin, an-tho-zan'thin, *n.* [Gr. *anthos*, a flower, and *zanthos*, yellow.] The yellow colouring matter of plants.

Anthracene, an'thra-sēn, *n.* [ANTHRACITE.] A hydrocarbon obtained from coal-tar and furnishing alizarine.

Anthracite, an'thra-sīt, *n.* [Gr. *anthrax*, *anthrakos*, coal.] Glance or blind coal, a non-bituminous coal of a shining lustre, approaching to metallic, and which burns without smoke, with a weak or no flame, and with intense heat.—**Anthracitic**, an-thra-sit'ik, *a.* Pertaining to anthracite.—**Anthraconite**, an-thrak'on-īt, *n.* A variety of marble of a coal-black lustre, occurring at Kilkenny: stinkstone.

Anthrax, an'thraks, *n.* [Gr.] *Med.* a carbuncle; a malignant ulcer.

Anthropic, an-throp'ik, *a.* [Gr. *anthrōpos*, a man.] Belonging to man; man-like; sprung from man.

Anthropogeny, an-thrō-poj'en-i, *n.* [Gr. *anthrōpos*, a man, and root *gen*, to beget.] the science of the origin and development of man.—**Anthropogenic**, an-thrō'pō-je"nik, *a.* Of or pertaining to anthropogeny.

Anthropoglot, an-thrō'po-glot, *n.* [Gr. *anthrōpos*, man, *glōtta*, tongue.] An animal with a tongue like that of a man, as the parrot.

Anthropography, an-thrō-pog'ra-fi, *n.* [Gr. *anthrōpos*, a man, and *graphē*, a description.] A description of man or of the human race; ethnography.

Anthropoid, an'thrō-poid, *a.* [Gr. *anthrōpos*, a man, and *eidos*, resemblance.] Resembling man; specifically applied to such apes as most closely approach the human race.

Anthropolatry, an-thrō-pol'a-tri, *n.* [Gr. *anthrōpos*, a man, and *latreia*, service, worship.] The worship of man.

Anthropolite, an-thrō'pō-līt, *n.* [Gr. *anthrōpos*, a man, and *lithos*, a stone.] A petrifaction of the human body or skeleton.

Anthropology, an-thrō-pol'o-ji, *n.* [Gr. *anthrōpos*, a man, and *logos*, discourse.] The science of man and mankind, including the study of the physical and mental constitution of man, or his whole nature, as exhibited both in the present and the past. —**Anthropologic, Anthropological**, an-thrō'pō-loj"ik, an-thrō'pō-loj"ik-al, *a.* Pertaining to anthropology.—**Anthropologist**, an-thrō-pol'o-jist, *n.* One who writes on or studies anthropology.

Anthropometry, an-thrō-pom'et-ri, *n.* [Gr. *anthrōpos*, a man, and *metron*, measure.] The measurement of the human body.

Anthropomorphism, an-thrō'pō-morf"-izm, *n.* [Gr. *anthrōpos*, a man, and *morphē*, form.] The representation or conception of the Deity under a human form, or with human attributes and affections. — **Anthropomorphic**, an'thrō-pō-mor"fik, *a.* Relating to or characterized by anthropomorphism; resembling man.—**Anthropomorphist, Anthropomorphite**, an-thrō'pō-morf"ist, an-thrō'pō-morf"īt, *n.* One who believes that the Supreme Being has a human form and human attributes.—**Anthropomorphitic, Anthropomorphitical**, an-thrō'pō-morf-it"ik, an-thrō'pō-morf-it"ik-al, *a.* Pertaining to anthropomorphism. — **Anthropomorphitism**, an-thrō'pō-morf"it-izm, *n.* The doctrines of anthropomorphites. — **Anthropomorphous**, an-thrō'pō-morf"us, *a.* Having the figure of or resemblance to a man.

Anthropopathism, Anthropopathy, an-thrō-pop'ath-izm, an-thrō-pop'a-thi, *n.* [Gr. *anthrōpos*, a man, and *pathos*, passion.] The affections or passions of man; the ascription of human passions to the Supreme Being.—**Anthropopathic, Anthropopathical**, an-thrō'pō-path"ik, an-thrō'pō-path"ik-al, *a.* Pertaining to anthropopathism. — **Anthropopathically**, an-thrō'pō-path"ik-al-li, *adv.*

Anthropophagi, an-thrō-pof'a-jī, *n. pl.* [Gr. *anthrōpos*, a man, and *phagō*, to eat.] Man-eaters; cannibals; men that eat human flesh.—**Anthropophagical**, an-thrō'pō-faj"ik-al, *a.* Relating to cannibalism.—**Anthropophagite**, an-thrō-pof'a-jīt, *n.* A cannibal. — **Anthropophagous**, an-thrō-pof'a-gus, *a.* Feeding on human flesh. —**Anthropophagy**, an-thrō-pof'a-ji, *n.* Cannibalism.

Anthropotomy, an-thrō-pot'o-mi, *n.* [Gr. *anthrōpos*, a man, and *tomē*, a cutting.] The anatomy or dissection of the human body; human anatomy.

Antianarchic, an'ti-an-är"kik, *a.* Opposed to anarchy or confusion.

Antiar, an'ti-är, *n.* [Javanese.] The milky juice which exudes from wounds made in the upas-tree, and which is one of the most acrid and virulent vegetable poisons.

Antiarthritic, an'ti-är-thrit"ik, *a.* Efficacious against the gout (arthritis).

Antiasthmatic, an'ti-ast-mat"ik, *n.* A remedy for the asthma.

Antibacchius, an'ti-bak-kī"us, *n.* [Gr.] *Pros.* a foot the opposite of the bacchius, containing three syllables, the two first long and the last short.

Antibilious, an-ti-bil'yus, *a.* Counteractive of bilious complaints.

Antic, an'tik, *a.* [A form of *antique*, L. *antiquus*, ancient. The modern sense of this word is derived from the grotesque figures seen in the antique sculpture of the middle ages. ANTIQUE.] Odd; fanciful; grotesque; fantastic (tricks, postures).—*n.* A buffoon or merry-andrew (*Shak.*); a grotesque or fantastic figure (*Shak.*); an absurd or ridiculous gesture, an odd gesticulation; a piece of buffoonery; a caper.—**Anticly**, an'tik-li, *adv.* In an antic manner.—**Anticness**, an'tik-nes, *n.*

Anticardium, an-ti-kär′di-um, *n.* [Gr. *anti*, opposite to, and *kardia*, the heart.] The hollow at the bottom of the breast or epigastrium; the pit of the stomach.

Antichlor, an′ti-klōr, *n.* [Gr. *anti*, against, and the *chlor-* of *chlorine*.] A substance employed to remove, or neutralize the effects of, the free chlorine left in goods bleached by means of chloride of lime, &c.

Antichrist, an′ti-krīst, *n.* An opponent of Christ; a person or power antagonistic to Christ.—**Antichristian**, an-ti-kris′tyan, *a.* Opposite to or opposing the Christian religion.

Anticipate, an-tis′i-pāt, *v.t.*—*anticipated, anticipating.* [L. *anticipo* for *antecipo*, to take beforehand—*ante*, before, and *capio*, to take.] To be before in doing something; to prevent or preclude by prior action; to forestall; to realize beforehand; to foretaste or foresee; to look forward to; to expect.—*v.i.* To treat of something, as in a narrative, before the proper time.—**Anticipant**, an-tis′i-pant, *a.* Anticipating; anticipative.—**Anticipation**, an-tis′i-pā″shon, *n.* The act of anticipating; expectation; foretaste; realization beforehand; previous notion; preconceived opinion.—**Anticipative**, an-tis′i-pāt-iv, *a.* Anticipating or tending to anticipate; containing anticipation.—**Anticipatively**, an-tis′i-pāt-iv-li, *adv.* By anticipation.—**Anticipator**, an-tis′i-pāt-ėr, *n.* One who anticipates.—**Anticipatory**, an-tis′i-pā-to-ri, *a.* Anticipative.

Anticlimax, an-ti-klī′maks, *n.* A sentence in which the ideas first increase in force, and then terminate in something less important and striking: opposed to *climax*.

Anticlinal, an-ti-klī′nal, *a.* [Gr. *anti*, opposite, and *klinō*, to incline.] Inclining in opposite directions.—*Anticlinal axis, geol.* a line from which strata dip on either side as from the ridge of a house: opposed to *synclinal*.—*n.* An anticlinal line or axis.—**Anticlinic**, an-ti-klin′ik, *a.* Anticlinal.

Anticonstitutional, an-ti-kon′sti-tū″shon-al, *a.* Opposed to the constitution of a state; unconstitutional.

Anticontagious, an′ti-kon-tā″jus, *a.* Opposing or destroying contagion.

Anti-convulsive, an′ti-kon-vul″siv, *a.* Efficacious against convulsions.

Anticous, an-tī′kus, *a.* [L. *anticus*, in front, from *ante*, before.] *Bot.* placed in front of a flower or organ, as the lip in orchids.

Anticyclone, an-ti′sī-klōn, *n.* A meteorological phenomenon consisting of a region of high barometric pressure, the pressure being greatest in the centre, with light winds flowing outwards from the centre, and not inwards as in the cyclone.

Antidactyl, an-ti-dak′til, *n.* A dactyl reversed; an anapest.

Antidemocrat, an-ti-dem′ō-krat, *n.* One who is opposed to democrats or democracy.—**Antidemocratic, Antidemocratical**, an-ti-dem′ō-krat″ik, an-ti-dem′ō-krat″-ik-al, *a.* Opposing or contrary to democracy.

Antidote, an′ti-dōt, *n.* [L. *antidotum*, from Gr. *antidoton*, an antidote—*anti*, against, and *dotos*, given, from *didōmi*, to give.] A medicine to counteract the effects of poison, or of anything noxious taken into the stomach; *fig.* anything that prevents or counteracts evil.—**Antidotal, Antidotical**, an-ti-dōt′al, an-ti-dot′ik-al, *a.* Having the qualities of an antidote; serving as an antidote.—**Antidotally, Antidotically**, an′ti-dōt-al-li, an-ti-dot′ik-al-li, *adv.* In the manner of an antidote; by way of antidote.

Antidysenteric, an′ti-dis-en-ter″ik, *a.* Efficacious against dysentery.—*n.* A remedy for dysentery.

Antiemetic, an′ti-ē-met″ik, *a.* Acting in the opposite manner of an emetic; checking vomiting.—*n.* A substance with this property.

Antienthusiastic, an′ti-en-thū′zi-as″tik, *a.* Opposed to enthusiasm.

Antiephialtic, an′ti-ef′i-al″tik, *a.* [Gr. *anti*, against, and *ephialtēs*, nightmare.] Curative of nightmare.—*n.* A remedy for nightmare.

Antiepileptic, an′ti-ep′i-lep″tik, *a.* and *n.* Same as *Antepileptic*.

Antiepiscopal, an′ti-ē-pis″kop-al, *a.* Opposed to Episcopacy.

Antievangelical, an′ti-ē-van-jel″ik-al, *a.* Opposed to evangelical principles.

Antifebrile, an-ti-feb′ril or an-ti-fē′bril, *a.* Having the quality of abating fever; opposing or tending to cure fever.

Antifederal, an-ti-fed′ėr-al, *a.* Opposed to or opposing federalism or a federal constitution.—**Antifederalism**, an-ti-fed′-ėr-al-izm, *n.* Opposition to federalism.—**Antifederalist**, an-ti-fed′ėr-al-ist, *n.* One who is averse to federalism.

Antifriction, an-ti-frik′shon, *a.* Obviating or lessening friction.

Antigraph, an′ti-graf, *n.* [Gr. *anti*, equal to, and *graphō*, to write.] *Law*, a copy or counterpart of a deed.

Antiguggler, an-ti-gug′lėr, *n.* A small tube admitting air into a vessel from which liquid is poured, to prevent a guggling sound.

Antihypnotic, an′ti-hip-not″ik, *a.* [Gr. *anti*, and *hypnos*, sleep.] Counteracting sleep; tending to prevent sleep or lethargy.

Antihypochondriac, an-ti-hip′ō-kon″-dri-ak, *a.* Counteracting or tending to cure hypochondriac affections.

Antihysteric, an′ti-his-ter″ik, *a.* Preventing or curing hysterics.—*n.* A remedy for hysterics.

Antilegomena, an′ti-le-gom″e-na, *n. pl.* [Gr.—*anti*, against, and *legomena*, things spoken, from *legō*, to speak.] *Lit.* things spoken against; specifically, applied to certain books of the New Testament whose inspiration was not at first universally acknowledged by the church.

Antilibration, an′ti-lī-brā″shon, *n.* The act of counterbalancing, or state of being counterbalanced; equipoise.

Antilithic, an-ti-lith′ik, *a.* [Gr. *anti*, against, and *lithos*, a stone.] *Med.* tending to destroy or prevent the formation of urinary calculi.—*n.* A medicine with this property.

Antilogy, an-til′o-ji, *n.* [Gr. *antilogia*—*anti*, against, and *legō*, to speak.] A contradiction between any words or passages in an author, or between members of the same body.—**Antilogous**, an-til′o-gus, *a.* Contradictory; *elect.* applied to that pole of a crystal which is negative when being electrified by heat, and afterwards, when cooling, positive.

Anti-macassar, an′ti-ma-kas″är, *n.* [Gr. *anti*, against, and E. *macassar*-oil.] A covering for chairs, sofas, couches, &c., made of open cotton or worsted work, to preserve them from being soiled.

Antimere, an′ti-mēr, *n.* [Gr. *anti*, opposite, *meros*, part.] *Biol.* one of two or more corresponding parts on opposite sides of animals.

Antimeter, an-tim′et-ėr, *n.* [Gr. *anti*, and *metron*, measure.] An optical instrument for measuring angles under 10°. Called also the *Reflecting Sector*.

Antimonarchic, Antimonarchical, an′ti-mon-ärk″ik, an′ti-mon-ärk″ik-al, *a.* Opposed to monarchy; opposing a kingly government.—**Antimonarchist**, an-ti-mon′ärk-ist, *n.* An enemy to monarchy.

Antimony, an′ti-mo-ni, *n.* [L. of twelfth century *antimonium*; origin doubtful.] Chemical sym. Sb, from L. *stibium*; sp. gr. 6·7. A brittle metal of a bluish-white or silver-white colour and laminated or scaly texture, much used in the arts in the construction of alloys, and also in medicine.—**Antimonial**, an-ti-mō′ni-al, *a.* Pertaining to antimony, or partaking of its qualities; composed of or containing antimony.—*Antimonial wine, med.* solution of tartar emetic in sherry wine.—*n.* A preparation of antimony; a medicine in which antimony is a principal ingredient.—**Antimoniated**, an-ti-mō′ni-āt-ed, *a.* Partaking of antimony; mixed or prepared with antimony.—**Antimonic, Antimonious**, an-ti-mon′ik, an-ti-mō′ni-us, *a.* Applied to acids derived from antimony.

Antinatural, an-ti-na′tūr-al, *a.* Opposed to what is natural; non-natural.

Antinephritic, an′ti-ne-frit″ik, *a.* *Med.* counteracting diseases of the kidneys.

Antinomy, an-tin′om-i, *n.* [Gr. *anti*, against, and *nomos*, a law.] The opposition of one law or rule to another law or rule; anything, as a law, statement, &c., opposite or contrary.—**Antinomian**, an-ti-nō′-mi-an, *a.* Opposed to law; pertaining to the Antinomians.—*n.* One of a sect who maintain that, under the gospel dispensation, the moral law is of no use or obligation.—**Antinomianism**, an-ti-nō′mi-an-izm, *n.* The tenets of the Antinomians.

Antipapal, Antipapistical, an-ti-pā′-pal, an′ti-pa-pis″tik-al, *a.* Opposed to the pope or to Roman Catholicism.

Antiparalytic, an′ti-pa-ra-lit″ik, *a.* *Med.* effective against paralysis.—*n.* A remedy for paralysis.

Antipathy, an-tip′a-thi, *n.* [Gr. *antipatheia*—*anti*, against, and *pathos*, feeling. PATHOS.] Natural aversion; instinctive contrariety or opposition in feeling; an aversion felt at the presence of an object; repugnance; contrariety in nature: commonly with *to* before the object.—**Antipathetic, Antipathetical**, an′ti-pa-thet″ik, an′ti-pa-thet″ik-al, *a.* Having antipathy.—**Antipathist**,† an-tip′a-thist, *n.* A direct opposite. [*Coleridge*.]

Antiphlogistic, an′ti-flo-jis″tik, *a.* Opposed to the theory of phlogiston; counteracting inflammation, or an excited state of the system.—*n.* A medicine which checks inflammation.

Antiphon, Antiphony, an′ti-fon, an-tif′o-ni, *n.* [Gr. *anti*, in response to, and *phōnē*, voice. *Anthem* is the same word.] The answer of one choir or one portion of a congregation to another when an anthem or psalm is sung alternately; alternate singing; a short versicle sung before and after the psalms.—**Antiphonal, Antiphonary**, an-tif′o-nal, an-tif′o-na-ri, *n.* A book of antiphons or anthems.—**Antiphonal, Antiphonic, Antiphonical**, an-tif′-on-al, an-ti-fon′ik, an-ti-fon′ik-al, *a.* Pertaining to antiphony or alternate singing.

Antiphrasis, an-tif′ra-sis, *n.* [Gr. *anti*, against, and *phrasis*, a form of speech.] *Rhet.* the use of words in a sense opposite to their proper meaning.—**Antiphrastic**, an-ti-fras′tik, *a.* Pertaining to antiphrasis.—**Antiphrastically**, an-ti-fras′tik-al-li, *adv.* In the manner of antiphrasis.

Antipodes, an-tip′o-dēz, *n. pl.* [Gr.—*anti*, opposite, and *pous*, *podos*, foot.] Those who live on the opposite side of the globe; the region directly on the opposite side of the globe; *fig.* anything diametrically opposite or opposed to another; a contrary.—**Antipodal, Antipodean**, an-tip′o-dal, an-tip′o-dē″an, *a.* Pertaining to antipodes.—**Antipode**, an′ti-pōd, *n.* One who or that which is in opposition or opposite.

Antipoison, an-ti-poi′zn, *n.* An antidote for a poison; a counter-poison.

Antipole, an′ti-pōl, *n.* The opposite pole.

Antipope, an′ti-pōp, *n.* One who usurps the papal power in opposition to the pope; a pretender to the papacy.

Antiputrefactive, Antiputrescent, an′ti-pū-tre-fak″tiv, an′ti-pū-tres″sent, *a.* Counteracting or preventing putrefaction; antiseptic.

Antipyretic, an′ti-pi-ret″ik, *n.* [Gr. *anti*, against, and *pyretos*, fever.] *Med.* a remedy efficacious against fever.

Antipyrin, an-ti-pī′rin, *n.* [Gr. *anti*, against, *pyr*, fire, referring to the heat in fevers. PYRETIC.] A drug obtained from coal-tar products, valuable in reducing fever and relieving pain, much used in nervous headache and neuralgia.

Antiquary, an′ti-kwa-ri, *n.* [L. *antiqua-*

rius, from *antiquus*, old, ancient, from *ante*, before.] One devoted to the study of ancient times through their relics; one versed in antiquity: an archæologist.—**Antiquarian**, an-ti-kwā'ri-an, *a*. Pertaining to antiquaries or to antiquity.—*n*. An antiquary.—**Antiquarianism**, an-ti-kwā'ri-an-izm, *n*. Character of an antiquarian; love or study of antiquities.—**Antiquated**, an'ti-kwāt-ed, *a*. Grown old-fashioned; obsolete; out of use; behind the times.—**Antiquatedness**, an'ti-kwāt-ed-nes, *n*.—**Antique**, an-tēk', *a*. [Fr., from L. *antiquus*, ancient. *Antic* is a form of this word.] Having existed in ancient times; belonging to or having come down from antiquity; ancient (an *antique* statue); having the characteristics of an earlier day; smacking of bygone days; of old fashion (an *antique* robe).—*n*. Anything very old; specifically, a term applied to the remains of ancient art, more especially to the works of Grecian and Roman antiquity.—**Antiquely**, an-tēk'li, *adv*.—**Antiqueness**, an-tēk'nes, *n*.—**Antiquity**, an-tik'wi-ti, *n*. [L. *antiquitas*, from *antiquus*, ancient.] The quality of being ancient; ancientness; great age; ancient times; former ages; the people of ancient times; *pl*. the remains of ancient times; institutions, customs, &c., belonging to ancient nations.

Antirrhinum, an-ti-rī'num, *n*. [Gr. *anti*, like, and *rhin*, a nose. The flowers of most of the species bear a resemblance to the snout of some animal.] Snap-dragon, the generic name of various plants with showy flowers, much cultivated in gardens.

Antisabbatarian, an-ti-sab'ba-tā"ri-an, *n*. One averse to observing the Christian Sabbath with the strictness of the Jewish Sabbath.

Antiscii, Antiscians, an-tish'i-ī, an-tish'i-anz, *n.pl*. [L. *antiscii*—Gr. *anti*, opposite, and *skia*, shadow.] The inhabitants of either side of the equator, as contrasted with those of the other side, whose shadow is cast in a contrary direction.

Antiscorbutic, an'ti-skor-bū'tik, *a*. *Med*. counteracting scurvy or a scorbutic tendency.—*n*. A remedy for or preventive of scurvy.

Antiscriptural, an-ti-skrip'tūr-al, *a*. Opposed to the principles or doctrines of Scripture.—**Antiscripturist**,† an-ti-skrip'tūr-ist, *n*. One who opposes the truth of Scripture.

Anti-Semite, an-ti-sem'īt, *n*. One opposed to the Semitic or Jewish race, leading opposition to the Jews in Germany and Russia.

Antiseptic, Antiseptical, an-ti-sep'tik, an-ti-sep'tik-al, *a*. [Gr. *anti*, against, and *sēptos*, putrid, from *sēpō*, to putrefy.] Opposing or counteracting putrefaction, or a putrescent tendency.—*n*. A substance which resists or corrects putrefaction.

Antisocialist, an-ti-sō'shal'ist, *a*. Opposed to the doctrine and practice of socialism.

Antispasmodic, an'ti-spaz-mod"ik, *a*. *Med*. opposing spasm; resisting convulsions.—*n*. A remedy for spasm.

Antispast, an'ti-spast, *n*. [Gr. *antispastos*.] *Pros*. a foot, in which the first and last syllables are short and the two middle syllables long.

Antisplenetic, an'ti-sple-net"ik, *a*. Good as a remedy in diseases of the spleen.

Antistrophe, an-tis'tro-fe, *n*. [Gr.—*anti*, opposite, and *strophē*, a turning.] A part of an ancient Greek choral ode alternating with the strophe.—**Antistrophic**, an-ti-strof'ik, *a*. Relating to the antistrophe.

Antistrumatic, Antistrumous, an'-ti-strō-mat"ik, an-ti-strō'mus, *a*. Good against struma or scrofulous disorders.

Antisyphilitic, an-ti-sif'il-it"ik, *a*. Efficacious against syphilis, or the venereal poison.—*n*. A medicine of this kind.

Antitheism, an-ti-thē'izm, *n*. Opposition to theism.—**Antitheist**, an-ti-thē'ist, *n*. An opponent of theism.—**Antitheistic**, an'ti-thē-is"tik, *a*. Pertaining to antitheism.

Antithesis, an-tith'e-sis, *n*. pl. **Antitheses**, an-tith'e-sēz. [Gr. *antithesis*—*anti*, against, and *thesis*, a setting, from *tithēmi*, to place.] Opposition; contrast; *rhet*. a figure by which contraries are opposed to contraries; a contrast or opposition of words or sentiments; as, the prodigal *robs his heir*, the miser *robs himself*.—**Antithetic, Antithetical**, an-ti-thet'ik, an-ti-thet'ik-al, *a*. Pertaining to or characterized by antithesis.—**Antithetically**, an-ti-thet'ik-al-li, *adv*. In an antithetical manner.

Antitoxin, an-ti-tok'sin, *n*. [Gr. *anti*, against. TOXIC.] *Med*. a fluid introduced into the blood to counteract the poison of a disease.

Anti-trade, an'ti-trād, *n*. A tropical wind blowing above a trade-wind and in the opposite direction.

Antitrinitarian, an-ti-trin'i-tā"ri-an, *n*. One who denies the doctrine of the Trinity, or the existence of three persons in the Godhead.—*a*. Opposing the doctrine of the Trinity.—**Antitrinitarianism**, an-ti-trin'i-tā"ri-an-izm, *n*. Opposition to the doctrine of the Trinity.

Antitype, an'ti-tīp, *n*. That which is correlative to a type; that which is prefigured or represented by the type.—**Antitypical**, an-ti-tip'ik-al, *a*. Pertaining to an antitype; explaining the type.—**Antitypically**, an-ti-tip'ik-al-li, *adv*. By way of antitype.

Antivaccinist, an-ti-vak'sin-ist, *n*. One who is opposed to vaccination.

Antivariolous, an'ti-va-rī"ol-us, *a*. Preventing the contagion of small-pox (variola).

Antivenereal, an'ti-vē-nē"rē-al, *a*. Resisting or efficacious against the venereal poison.

Antler, ant'lėr, *n*. [O.Fr. *antoillier*, *entoillier*; origin doubtful.] A branch of the horn of a deer, particularly of a stag; one of the horns of the cervine animals.—**Antlered**, ant'lėrd, *a*. Furnished with antlers.

Antlia, ant'li-a, *n*. pl. **Antliæ**, ant'li-ē. [Gr. *antlia*, a pump.] The spiral tongue or proboscis of butterflies and moths, by which they suck the juices of plants.

Antonomasia, Antonomasy, an-ton'-o-mā"zi-a, an-ton'o-ma-zi, *n*. [Gr. *antonomasia*—*anti*, instead, *onoma*, a name.] *Rhet*. the use of the name of some office, dignity, profession, &c., instead of the name of the person; or, conversely, the use of a proper noun instead of a common noun (as 'a *Solomon*', for a wise man).—**Antonomastic, Antonomastical**, an-ton'o-mas"-tik, an-ton'o-mas"tik-al, *a*. Of or pertaining to antonomasia.—**Antonomastically**, an-ton'o-mas"tik-al-li, *adv*. With use of antonomasia.

Antonym, ant'ō-nim, *n*. [Gr. *anti*, against, *onoma*, name.] A word of directly contrary signification to another: the opposite of a synonym.

Antorbital, ant-or'bit-al, *a*. [L. *ante*, before, and *orbitus*, an orbit.] Anterior to the orbit.

Antre,‡ an'tėr, *n*. [Fr. *antre*, L. *antrum*, a cave.] A cavern; a cave. [*Shak.*]

Antrorse, an-trors', *a*. [From L. *ante*, before, and *versus*, turned.] *Bot*. forward or upward in direction.

Anura, a-nū'ra, *n.pl*. [Gr. *an*, priv., and *oura*, a tail.] An order of batrachians which lose the tail when they reach maturity, as the toad and frog. Written also *Anoura*.—**Anuran**, a-nū'ran, *n*. One of the Anura.—**Anurous**, a-nū'rus, *a*. Of or pertaining to the Anura.

Anus, ā'nus, *n*. [L.] *Anat*. the inferior opening of the alimentary canal; the fundament.

Anvil, an'vil, *n*. [A.Sax. *anfilt*, O.H.G. *anafalz*—*an*, on, and A.Sax. *fealdan*, G. *falten*, *falzen*, to *fold*.] An iron block with a smooth, usually steel, face, and often a projecting horn, on which metals are hammered and shaped.—*v.t.*† To form or shape on an anvil.

Anxiety, ang-zī'e-ti, *n*. [L. *anxietas*, from *anxius*, solicitous, from *ango*, to vex. ANGER.] Pain or uneasiness of mind respecting some event, future or uncertain; concern; solicitude; care; disquietude.—**Anxious**, angk'shus, *a*. Full of anxiety or solicitude respecting something future or unknown; being in painful suspense (of persons); attended with or proceeding from solicitude or uneasiness (of things): followed often by *for*, *about*, *on account of*.—**Anxiously**, angk'shus-li, *adv*. In an anxious manner; solicitously.—**Anxiousness**, angk'shus-nes, *n*. Anxiety.

Any, en'ni, *a*. [A.Sax. *aenig*, from *ân*, one, and term. *ig* (parallel to *naenig*, none); like G. *einig*, D. *eenig*, any.] One out of many indefinitely (*any* man); some; an indefinite number or quantity (*any* men, *any* money): often used as a pronoun, the noun being understood.—*adv*. In any degree; to any extent; at all (*any* better).—**Anybody**, en'ni-bo-di, *n*. Any one person.—**Anyhow**, en'ni-hou, *adv*. In any manner, at any rate; in any event; on any account.—**Anywhere**, en'ni-whār, *adv*. In any place.—**Anywise**, en'ni-wīz, *adv*. [-*wise*=*guise*.] In any way.

Anzac, an'zak, *n*. The *A*ustralian—*N*ew *Z*ealand *A*rmy *C*orps, at Gallipoli during the war of 1915: from the initial letters.

Aorist, ā'or-ist, *n*. [Gr. *aoristos*, indefinite —*a*, priv., and *horos*, limit.] *Gram*. a tense in the Greek verb which expresses past time indefinitely (like E. *did* or *saw*).—**Aoristic, Aoristical**, ā-or-ist'ik, ā-or-ist'ik-al, *a*. Pertaining to or having the character of an aorist.

Aorta, ā-or'ta, *n*. [Gr. *aortē*, from *aeirō*, to lift, to heave.] *Anat*. the great artery or trunk of the arterial system, proceeding from the left ventricle of the heart, and giving origin to all the arteries except the pulmonary.—**Aortal, Aortic**, ā-or'tal, ā-or'tik, *a*. Pertaining to the aorta.—**Aortitis**, ā-ort-ī'tis, *n*. Inflammation of the aorta.

Apace, a-pās', *adv*. With a quick pace; fast; speedily; with haste.

Apache, a-pash', *n*. [American Indian tribe.] A French street-ruffian or desperado.

Apagynous, a-paj'in-us, *a*. [Gr. *hapax*, once, and *gynē*, a female.] *Bot*. fructifying but once, perishing thereafter.

Apanthropy, ap-an'thrō-pi, *n*. [Gr. *apanthrōpia*—*apo*, from, and *anthrōpos*, man.] An aversion to the company of men; a love of solitude.

Apart, a-pärt', *adv*. [Fr. *à part*, aside, separate—*à*, from L. *ad*, to, *part*=E. *part*, side.] Separately; in a state of separation; distinct or away from others; at some distance.—**Apartment**, a-pärt'ment, *n*. [Fr. *appartement*.] A room in a building; a division in a house separated from others by partitions; *pl*. a suite, or set, of rooms; lodgings (a French usage).

Apathy, ap'a-thi, *n*. [L. *apathia*, Gr. *apatheia*—*a*, priv., and *pathos*, suffering.] Want of feeling; privation of passion, emotion, or excitement; insensibility; indifference.—**Apathetic, Apathetical**, ap-a-thet'ik, ap-a-thet'ik-al, *a*. Affected with or proceeding from apathy; devoid of feeling; insensible.—**Apathist**, ap'a-thist, *n*. One affected with apathy, or destitute of feeling.

Apatite, ap'a-tīt, *n*. [From Gr. *apatē*, deceit, it having been mistaken for other minerals.] A mineral consisting chiefly of phosphate of lime, used as manure.

Ape, āp, *n*. [A.Sax. *apa*, Icel. *api*, D. *aap*, Dan. *abe*, G. *affe*, O.H.G. *affo*, Ir. and Gael *apa*: an initial guttural has been lost, seen in Gr. *kēpos*, Skr. *kapi*, an ape.] One of a family of quadrumanous animals found in both continents, having the teeth of the same number and form as in man, and possessing neither tails nor cheek-pouches; *fig*. one who imitates servilely.—*v.t*. *aped*, *aping*. To imitate servilely; to mimic.—**Aper**, āp'ėr, *n*. One who apes.—**Apery**, āp'ėr-i, *n*. A collection of apes; tricks of apes; the practice of aping.—**Apish**, āp'ish, *a*. Having the qualities of an ape; inclined to imitate superiors; affected.—**Apishly**, ăp'ish-li, *adv.* In an apish manner.—**Apishness**, ăp'ish-nes, *n.*

Apeak, a-pēk', *adv.* [Fr. *à-pic*, to the summit.] On the point; in a posture to pierce; *naut.* perpendicular, or inclining to the perpendicular: said of the anchor or yards.

Apellous, a-pel'lus, *a.* [Gr. *a*, without, and L. *pellis*, a skin.] Destitute of skin.

Apepsia, **Apepsy**, a-pep'si-a, a-pep'si, *n.* [Gr. *a*, priv., and *peptō*, to digest.] Defective digestion; indigestion; dyspepsia.

Aperient, a-pē-ri-ent, *a.* [L. *aperiens*, *aperientis*, part. of *aperio*, to open.] *Med.* gently purgative; having the quality of opening; deobstruent; laxative.—*n.* A medicine which gently opens the bowels; a laxative.—**Aperitive**, a-per'it-iv, *a.* Aperient.

Apert, a-pėrt', *a.* [L. *apertus*, open.] Open; evident. — **Aperture**, ap'ėr-tūr, *n.* [L. *apertura*, from *aperio*, *apertum*, to open.] An opening; a mouth, entrance, gap, cleft, &c.; a passage; a perforation; the diameter of the exposed part of the object-glass of a telescope or other optical instrument.

Apetalous, a-pet'al-us, *a.* [Gr. *a*, neg., and *petalon*, a petal.] *Bot.* having no petals or corolla.—**Apetalousness**, a-pet'al-us-nes, *n.*

Apex, ā'peks, *n.* pl. **Apices**, **Apexes**, ā'pi-sēz, ā'peks-ez. [L. *apex*, pl. *apices*.] The tip, point, or summit of anything.

Aphæresis, **Apheresis**, a-fē're-sis, *n.* [Gr. *aphairesis*, a taking away—*apo*, from, and *haireō*, to take.] *Gram.* the taking of a letter or syllable from the beginning of a word; *med.* the removal of anything noxious; *surg.* amputation.

Aphanipterous, af-an-ip'tėr-us, *a.* [Gr. *aphanēs*, indistinct (*a*, priv., *phainō*, to appear), and *pteron*, a wing.] Destitute of conspicuous wings: said of insects.

Aphanite, af'an-īt, *n.* [Gr. *aphanēs*, indistinct—*a*, priv., and *phainō*, to appear.] A name of fine-grained minerals whose structure cannot be detected by the naked eye.—**Aphanitic**, af-an-it'ik, *a.* Pertaining to aphanite or of similar character.

Aphasia, a-fā'zi-a, *n.* [Gr. *a*, not, *phasis*, speech.] Loss of the faculty of speech, or of connecting words and ideas, owing to morbid conditions of brain, while the speech-organs and general intelligence remain unaffected.

Aphelion, a-fē'li-on, *n.* pl. **Aphelia**, a-fē'li-a. [Gr. *apo*, from, and *hēlios*, the sun.] That point of a planet's or comet's orbit which is most distant from the sun: opposed to *perihelion*.

Aphesis, af'e-sis, *n.* [Gr. *aphesis*, a letting go.] Loss of a short unaccented syllable at the beginning of a word; as *squire* for *esquire*.—**Aphetic**, a-fet'ik, *a.* Pertaining to.—**Aphetize**, af'e-tīz, *v.t.* To shorten by aphesis.

Aphilanthropy, a-fil-an'thrō-pi, *n.* [Prefix *a*, neg., and *philanthropy*.] Want of love to mankind; want of benevolence; dislike to society.

Aphis, ā'fis, *n.* pl. **Aphides**, af'i-dēz. [A term of modern origin, perhaps from Gr. *aphyssō*, to draw or drink up liquids.] A plant-louse; a puceron or vine-fretter. The aphides are small insects, some of them wingless; they are very numerous and destructive, almost every species of plant supporting a different variety.—**Aphidian**, a-fid'i-an, *a.* Pertaining to the aphides.—**Aphidivorous**, af-i-div'ō-rus, *a.* [-*vorous*, from L. *voro*, to eat.] Eating or subsisting on aphides.

Aphnology, af-nol'o-ji, *n.* [Gr. *aphnos*, wealth, and *logos*, a discourse.] The science of wealth; plutology.

Aphonia, **Aphony**, a-fō'ni-a, af'ō-ni, *n.* [Gr. *a*, priv., and *phōnē*, voice.] A loss of voice; dumbness; speechlessness.—**Aphonous**, af'ō-nus, *a.* Destitute of voice.

Aphorism, af'or-izm, *n.* [Gr. *aphorismos*, from *aphorizō*, to mark out, to define—*apo*, from, and *horos*, a boundary.] A precept or principle expressed in a few words; a brief sentence containing some important truth; a maxim. ∴ *Aphorism* is the brief statement of a doctrine. *Axiom*, a statement claiming to be considered as a self-evident truth. *Maxim*, a formula referring rather to practical than to abstract truth; a rule of conduct. *Apophthegm*, a terse sententious saying. — **Aphorismatic**, **Aphorismic**, af'or-iz-mat"ik, af-or-iz'mik, *a.* Relating to or containing aphorisms.—**Aphorist**, af'or-ist, *n.* A writer of aphorisms.—**Aphoristic**, **Aphoristical**, af-or-ist'ik, af-or-ist'ik-al, *a.* Pertaining to, resembling, or containing aphorisms; in the form of an aphorism.—**Aphoristically**, af-or-ist'ik-al-li, *adv.* In the form or manner of aphorisms.—**Aphorize**, af'or-īz, *v.i.* To make aphorisms.

Aphrite, af'rīt, *n.* [Gr. *aphros*, froth.] A variety of carbonate of lime or calc-spar of a pearly lustre.

Aphrodisiac, **Aphrodisiacal**, af-ro-diz'i-ak, af-ro-diz'i-ak-al, *a.* [Gr. *aphrodisios*, *aphrodisiakos*, from *Aphrodite*, goddess of love.] Exciting venereal desire.—**Aphrodisiac**, *n.* Food or a medicine exciting sexual desire.

Aphthæ, af'thē, *n.pl.* [Gr. *aphthai.*] In *med.* small white ulcers upon the tongue and inside of the mouth; thrush.—**Aphthous**, af'thus, *a.* Pertaining to aphthæ or thrush.

Aphyllose, **Aphyllous**, af'il-ōs or a-fil'ōs, af'il-us or a-fil'us, *a.* [Gr. *a*, neg., and *phyllon*, a leaf.] *Bot.* destitute of leaves.

Apiary, ā'pi-a-ri, *n.* [L. *apiarium*, from *apis*, a bee.] The place where bees are kept; a stand or shed for bees.—**Apiarian**, ā-pi-ā'ri-an, *a.* Relating to bees. —*n.* A bee-keeper; an apiarist.—**Apiarist**, ā'pi-a-rist, *n.* One who keeps bees; a bee-master. —**Apiculture**, āp-i-kul'tūr, *n.* The art of managing bees in hives; bee-keeping.

Apical, ap'ik-al, *a.* [L. *apex*, an apex, a sharp point or peak.] Relating to the apex or top; belonging to the pointed end of a cone-shaped body.—**Apices**, **Apexes**, pl. of *apex*.—**Apicillary**, ap-i-sil'a-ri, *a.* Situated at or near the apex.—**Apiculate**, **Apiculated**, a-pik'ū-lāt, a-pik'ū-lāt-ed, *a.* *Bot.* tipped with a short and abrupt point.

Apician, a-pi'shan, *a.* [From *Apicius*, a celebrated Roman gourmand.] Relating to or resembling Apicius; relating to cookery or delicate viands.

Apiece, a-pēs', *adv.* To each; as the share of each; each by itself; by the individual.

Apish, **Apishly**. Ape.

Aplacental, ap-la-sen'tal, *a.* [Prefix *a*, priv., and *placental.*] Applied to those mammals in which the young are destitute of a placenta (as the kangaroo, duck-mole, &c.).

Aplanatic, ap-la-nat'ik, *a.* [Gr. *a*, priv., and *planaō*, to wander.] *Optics*, corrective of the defect by which rays of light diverge and do not come to a focus (an *aplanatic* lens). — **Aplanatism**, a-plan'a-tizm, *n.* *Optics*, the condition of being aplanatic.

Aplastic, a-plas'tik, *a.* [Prefix *a*, priv., and *plastic.*] Not plastic; not easily moulded.

Aplomb, a-plon, *n.* [Fr., lit the state of being perpendicular, or true to the *plumb*-line.] Self-possession springing from perfect self-confidence; assurance.

Apocalypse, a-pok'a-lips, *n.* [Gr. *apokalypsis*, from *apokalyptō*, to disclose—prefix *apo*, and *kalyptō*, to cover.] Revelation; discovery; disclosure; specifically, applied as the name of the last book of the New Testament.—**Apocalyptic**, **Apocalyptical**, a-pok'a-lip"tik, a-pok'a-lip"tik-al, *a.* Containing or pertaining to revelation; pertaining to the Revelation of St. John.—**Apocalyptic**, **Apocalyptist**, a-pok'a-lip"tik, a-pok'a-lip"tist, *n.* A writer on the Apocalypse.—**Apocalyptically**, a-pok'a-lip"tik-al-li, *adv.* In an apocalyptic manner; by revelation.

Apocarpous, ap-o-kär'pus, *a.* [Gr. *apo*, denoting separation, and *karpos*, fruit.] In *bot.* having the carpels, or at least their styles, disunited.

Apocope, a-pok'o-pe, *n.* [Gr. *apokopē*, a cutting off—*apo*, and *kopē*, a cutting.] The cutting off or omission of the last letter or syllable of a word, as *th'* for *the*.—**Apocopate**, a-pok'ō-pāt, *v.t.*—*apocopated*, *apocopating.* To cut off or drop the last letter or syllable of.

Apocrustic, ap-o-krus'tik, *a.* [Gr. *apokroustikos*—*apo*, away, and *krouō*, to drive.] *Med.* repelling; astringent.—*n.* An astringent and repellent medicine.

Apocrypha, a-pok'ri-fa, *n.* [Gr. *apokryphos*, hidden, spurious — *apo*, away, and *kryptō*, to conceal. Crypt.] The collective name of certain books admitted by the R. Catholics into the Old Testament canon, but whose authenticity as inspired writings is not generally admitted.—**Apocryphal**, a-pok'ri-fal, *a.* Pertaining to the Apocrypha; not canonical; of uncertain authority or credit; fictitious. — **Apocryphally**, a-pok'ri-fal-li, *adv.* In an apocryphal manner; equivocally; doubtfully. — **Apocryphalness**, a-pok'ri-fal-nes, *n.*

Apodal, **Apodous**, ap'o-dal, ap'o-dus, *a.* Having no feet: also said of fishes having no ventral fins, as the eel, sword-fish, &c.

Apodeictic, **Apodeictical**, ap-o-dīk'tik, ap-o-dīk'tik-al, *a.* [Gr. *apodeiktikos*—*apo*, forth, and *deiknymi*, to show.] Demonstrative; evident beyond contradiction. Spelled also *Apodictic*, *Apodictical*.—**Apodeictically**, ap-o-dīk'tik-al-li, *adv.* Demonstratively.

Apodosis, a-pod'o-sis, *n.* [Gr. *apodosis*, a giving back—*apo*, from, and *didōmi*, to give.] *Gram.* the latter part of a conditional sentence (or one beginning with *if*, *though*, &c.), dependent on the *protasis* or condition.

Apogee, ap'o-jē, *n.* [Gr. *apo*, from, and *gē*, the earth.] That point in the orbit of a planet or other heavenly body which is at the greatest distance from the earth; properly this particular point of the moon's orbit.—**Apogean**, ap-o-jē-an, *a.* Pertaining to or connected with the apogee.

Apograph, ap'o-graf, *n.* [Gr. *apo*, from, and *graphō*, to write.] A copy or transcript.

Apollyon, apol'yon, *n.* [Gr. *apollūmi*, to destroy.] The Devil.

Apologue, ap'o-log, *n.* [Gr. *apologos*, an apologue, a fable—*apo*, from, and *logos*, discourse.] A moral fable; a relation of fictitious events intended to convey useful truths, such as the fables of Æsop.

Apology, a-pol'o-ji, *n.* [Gr. *apologia*, a speech in defence—*apo*, away from, and *logos*, a discourse.] Something said or written in defence; justification; vindication; an acknowledgment, usually accompanied by an expression of regret, for some improper remark or act; a temporary substitute or make-shift (colloq.). — **Apologetic**, **Apologetical**, a-pol'o-jet"ik, a-pol'o-jet"ik-al, *a.* Of or pertaining to or containing apology; defending by words or arguments. — **Apologetically**, a-pol'o-jet"ik-al-li, *adv.* In an apologetic manner; by way of apology.—**Apologetics**, a-pol'o-jet"iks, *n.* That branch of theology by which Christians are enabled scientifically to justify and defend the peculiarities of their faith, and to answer its opponents.—**Apologist**, **Apologizer**, a-pol'o-jist, a-pol'o-jīz-ėr, *n.* One who makes an apology. — **Apologize**, a-pol'o-jīz, *v.i.* — *apologized*, *apologizing.* To make an apology.

Apomecometer, ap'o-mē-kom"et-ėr, *n.* [Gr. *apo*, away, *mēkos*, distance, *metron*, measure.] An instrument used in measuring distances on the principle of the sextant.

Aponeurosis, ap'o-nū-rō"sis, *n.* pl. **Aponeuroses**, ap'o-nū-rō"sēz. [Gr. *aponeurōsis*—*apo*, from, and *neuron*, a nerve, because formerly supposed to be an expansion of a nerve or nerves.] A white, shining, and very resisting membrane, composed of interlaced fibres, found surrounding the voluntary muscles, large arteries, and other parts of the body.—**Aponeurotic**, ap'o-nū-rot"ik, *a.* Relating to the aponeuroses.

Apophthegm, ap'o-them, *n.* [Gr. *apo*, from, and *phthegma*, word.] A short, pithy.

and instructive saying; a sententious precept or maxim. Written also *Apothegm.* *Syn.* under APHORISM. — **Apophthegmatic, Apophthegmatical,** ap'o-theg-mat''ik, ap'o-theg-mat''ik-al, *a.* Pertaining to or having the character of an apophthegm; sententious.—**Apophthegmatize,** ap-o-theg'mat-īz, *v.i.* To utter apophthegms.

Apophyllite, a-pof'i-līt, *n.* [Gr. *apo,* from, and *phyllon,* a leaf, from its tendency to exfoliate.] A mineral of a foliated structure, and readily separating into thin laminæ, with a peculiar lustre.

Apophysis, a-pof'i-sis, *n.* pl. **Apophyses,** a-pof'i-sēz. [Gr.—*apo,* from, and *physis,* growth.] *Anat.* a prominence; a prominent part of a bone.

Apoplexy, ap'o-plek-si, *n.* [Gr. *apoplēxia,* apoplexy—*apo,* from, and *plēssō, plēxō,* to strike.] Abolition or sudden diminution of sensation and voluntary motion, resulting from congestion or rupture of the blood-vessels of the brain.—**Apoplectic, Apoplectical,** ap-o-plek'tik, ap-o-plek'tik-al, *a.* Pertaining to or consisting in apoplexy; predisposed to apoplexy. — **Apoplectic,** ap-o-plek'tik, *n.* A person affected with apoplexy.

Aposiopesis, ap'o-sī-ō-pē''sis, *n.* [Gr.—*apo,* from, and *siopaō,* to be silent.] *Rhet.* sudden stopping short and leaving a statement unfinished for the sake of effect.

Apostasy, a-pos'ta-si, *n.* [Gr. *apostasia,* a standing away from, a defection—*apo,* from, and root *sta,* to stand.] An abandonment of what one has professed; a total desertion or departure from one's faith, principles, or party.—**Apostate,** a-pos'tāt, *n.* One who has forsaken his faith, principles, or party.—*a.* False, traitorous.—**Apostatize,** a-pos'ta-tīz, *v.i.*—*apostatized, apostatizing.* To turn apostate; to abandon principles, faith, or party.

Aposteme, ap'os-tēm, *n.* [Gr. *apostēma*—*apo,* from, and *histēmi,* to stand.] An abscess; a swelling filled with purulent matter. —**Apostemate,** a-pos'tē-māt, *v.i.* To form into an abscess; to swell and fill with pus. —**Apostemation,** a-pos'tē-mā''shon, *n.* The formation of an aposteme.—**Apostematous,** ap-os-tem'at-us, *a.* Pertaining to an abscess.

A posteriori, a pos-tē'ri-ō''ri. [L. *posterior,* after.] A phrase applied to a mode of reasoning founded on observation of effects, consequences, or facts, whereby we reach the causes; inductive: opposed to *a priori.*

Apostle, a-pos'l, *n.* [Gr. *apostolos, lit.* one sent forth, a messenger—*apo,* forth, and *stellō,* to send.] One of the twelve disciples of Christ, who were commissioned to preach the gospel; one regarded as having a similar mission.—**Apostleship,** a-pos'l-ship, *n.* The office or dignity of an apostle.—**Apostolate,** a-pos'tol-āt, *n.* The dignity or office of an apostle, a mission; the dignity or office of the pope, the holder of the apostolic see.—**Apostolic, Apostolical,** ap-os-tol'ik, ap-os-tol'ik-al, *a.* Pertaining or relating to or characteristic of an apostle, more especially of the twelve apostles; according to the doctrines of the apostles; proceeding from an apostle.—*Apostolic see,* the see of the bishop of Rome, as directly founded by the apostle Peter.—*Apostolic succession,* the uninterrupted succession of bishops, and, through them, of priests and deacons, in the church by regular ordination from the first apostles down to the present day.—**Apostolically,** ap-os-tol'ik-al-li, *adv.* In an apostolical manner. —**Apostolicalness, Apostolicism, Apostolicity,**† ap-os-tol'ik-al-nes, ap-os-tol'i-sizm, ap-os'tol-is''i-ti, *n.* The character of being apostolical.

Apostrophe, a-pos'tro-fe, *n.* [Gr. *apo,* from, and *strophē,* a turning.] A sudden change in discourse; a sudden and direct address to a person or thing in the course of a speech; *gram.* the omission of a letter or letters from a word marked by a sign ('); the sign used to mark the omission, or merely as the sign of the possessive case in nouns.—**Apostrophic,** ap-os-trof'ik, *a.* Pertaining to an apostrophe. — **Apostrophize,** a-pos'trof-īz, *v.t.*—*apostrophized, apostrophizing.* To address by apostrophe; to make a direct address to in course of a speech; to mark with an apostrophe.—*v.i.* To make an apostrophe in speaking.

Apothecary, a-poth'e-ka-ri, *n.* [L.L. *apothecarius,* a shopkeeper, from Gr. *apothēkē,* a repository—*apo,* away, and *thēkē,* a chest, from *tithēmi,* to place.] One who practises pharmacy; a skilled person who prepares drugs for medicinal uses, and keeps them for sale.

Apothecium, ap-o-thē'si-um, *n.* pl. **Apothecia,** ap-o-thē'si-a. [APOTHECARY.] *Bot.* the receptacle of lichens, the spore-case.

Apothegm, Apothegmatic, ap'o-them, ap'o-theg-mat''ik. Same as *Apophthegm, Apophthegmatic.*

Apotheosis, ap'o-thē-ō'sis or -thē'o-sis, *n.* [Gr. *apo,* away, and *theos,* God.] Deification; the placing or ranking of a person among deities.—**Apotheosize,** ap-o-thē'ō-sīz, *v.t.* To exalt to the dignity of a deity; to deify.

Apozem, ap'o-zem, *n.* [Gr. *apozema*—*apo,* off, and *zeō,* to boil.] *Med.* a decoction.—**Apozemical,** ap-o-zem'ik-al, *a.* Pertaining to or resembling an apozem.

Appall, Appal, ap-pal', *v.t.*—*appalled, appalling.* [O.Fr. *appalir,* to make pale, from prefix *ap* for *ad,* and *palle,* pale, from L. *pallidus,* pallid.] To impress with overpowering fear; to confound with terror; to dismay.—*n.* Terror; affright; dismay. [*Cowper.*]—**Appalling,** ap-pal'ing, *a.* Calculated to cause dismay or horror. — **Appallingly,** ap-pal'ing-li, *adv.* In a manner to appall.—**Appallment,** ap-pal'ment, *n.* State of being appalled.

Appanage, ap'pan-āj, *n.* [Fr. *appanage, apanage,* from O.Fr. *apaner,* L.L. *apanare,* to furnish with bread—L. *ad,* to, and *panis,* bread.] An allowance to the younger branches of a sovereign house out of the revenues of the country, generally together with a grant of public domains; whatever belongs or falls to one from rank or station in life.—**Appanagist,** ap'pan-āj-ist, *n.* A prince having an appanage.

Apparatus, ap-pa-rā'tus, *n. sing.* and *pl.*; pl. rarely **Apparatuses,** ap-pa-rā'tus-ez. [L., from *apparo,* to prepare—*ad,* and *paro,* to make ready.] Things provided as means to some end; a collection or combination of articles or materials for the accomplishment of some purpose, operation, or experiment; *physiol.* a collection of organs all ministering to the same function.

Apparel, ap-par'el, *n.* (no pl.). [Fr. *appareil,* dress, *appareiller,* to match, to fit, to suit—*a,* to, and *pareil,* like, L.L. *pariculus,* from L. *par,* equal.] Clothing; vesture; garments; dress; external array; the furniture of a ship.—*v.t.*—*apparelled, apparelling.* To dress or clothe; to cover as with garments.

Apparent, ap-pā'rent, *a.* [L. *apparens, apparentis,* ppr. of *appareo.* APPEAR.] Visible to the eye; within sight or view; appearing to the eye or to the judgment; seeming (often in distinction to *real*); obvious; plain; evident: in the latter sense now used only as a predicate.—*Heir apparent,* the heir who is certain to inherit if he survive the present holder.—*n.*† Heir apparent; one who has a claim. [*Shak.*]—**Apparently,** ap-pā'rent-li, *adv.* Openly; evidently; seemingly; in appearance.—**Apparentness,** ap-pā'rent-nes, *n.*

Apparition, ap-pa-ri'shon, *n.* [APPEAR.] The act of appearing; appearance; the thing appearing; especially, a ghost; a spectre; a visible spirit.—**Apparitional,** ap-pa-ri'shon-al, *a.* Pertaining to an apparition.

Apparitor, ap-par'it-or, *n.* [L., from *appareo,* to attend. APPEAR.] A messenger or officer who serves the process of a spiritual court; the beadle in a university.

Appeal, ap-pēl', *v.i.* [Fr. *appeler,* from L. *appellare,* to call, address, appeal to.] To call, as for aid, mercy, sympathy, and the like; to refer to another person or authority for the decision of a question controverted; to refer to a superior judge or court for a final settlement. — *v.t.* To summon or to challenge†; to remove (a cause) from an inferior to a superior judge or court; to charge with a crime; to accuse.—*n.* A call for sympathy, mercy, aid, and the like; a supplication; an entreaty; the removal of a cause or suit from an inferior to a superior tribunal, that the latter may, if needful, amend the decision of the former; a challenge; a reference to another for proof or decision; resort; recourse (*appeal* to arms). —**Appealable,** ap-pēl'a-bl, *a.* Liable to be appealed; removable to a higher tribunal for decision.—**Appealer,** ap-pēl'ėr, *n.* One who appeals; an appellant.—**Appellancy,** ap-pel'an-si, *n.* Appeal; capability of appeal.—**Appellant,** ap-pel'ant, *n.* One who appeals; one who removes a cause from a lower to a higher tribunal.—**Appellate,** ap-pel'āt, *a.* Relating to appeals; having cognizance of appeals. — **Appellee,** ap-pel-lē', *n.* One against whom an appeal is brought. — **Appellor,** ap-pel'or, *n.* One who appeals.

Appear, ap-pēr', *v.i.* [O.Fr. *apparoir,* L. *appareo*—*ad,* to, and *pareo,* to show one's self.] To come or be in sight; to be or become visible to the eye; to stand in presence of some one; to be obvious; to be clear or made clear by evidence; to seem; to look like.—**Appearance,** ap-pēr'ans, *n.* The act of appearing or coming into sight; a coming into the presence of a person or persons; the thing seen; a phenomenon; an apparition; external show; semblance, in opposition to reality or substance; mien; build and carriage; figure.—**Appearer,** ap-pēr'ėr, *n.* One who appears.

Appease, ap-pēz', *v.t.*—*appeased, appeasing.* [Fr. *appaiser,* to pacify—*a,* from L. *ad,* to, and O.Fr. *pais* (Fr. *paix*), L. *pax, pacis,* peace.] To make quiet; to still; to assuage (hunger); to tranquillize; to calm or pacify (a person, anger).—**Appeasable,** ap-pēz'a-bl, *a.* Capable of being appeased.—**Appeasableness,** ap-pēz'a-bl-nes, *n.*—**Appeasement,** ap-pēz'ment, *n.* Act of appeasing; appeased state.—**Appeaser,** ap-pēz'ėr, *n.* One who appeases.—**Appeasive,** ap-pēz'iv, *a.* Appeasing; quieting.

Appellant, Appellate, &c. APPEAL.

Appellation, ap-pel-ā'shon, *n.* [L. *appellatio,* from *appellare,* to address, accost, appeal to. APPEAL.] The word by which a thing or person is known; name; title.—**Appellative,** ap-pel'a-tiv, *a.* Serving as an appellation; naming or marking out; denominative.—*n.* An appellation; a general name. — **Appellatively,** ap-pel'a-tiv-li, *adv.* In an appellative manner; as an appellation. — **Appellativeness,** ap-pel'a-tiv-nes, *n.*

Append, ap-pend', *v.t.* [L. *appendo*—*ad,* to, and *pendo,* to hang. PENDANT.] To hang on or attach; to add, as accessory or adjunct to a thing; to subjoin; to annex.—**Appendage,** ap-pend'āj, *n.* Something appended or attached; what is attached to a greater thing.—**Appendant,** ap-pend'ant, *a.* Hanging to; annexed; attached.—*n.* That which is appendant.—**Appendicle,** ap-pend'i-kl, *n.* A small appendage.—**Appendicular,** ap-pen-dik'ū-lėr, *a.* Having the character of an appendage.—**Appendiculate,** ap-pen-dik'ū-lāt, *a.* Provided with appendages; appendicular.—**Appendix,** ap-pen'diks, *n.* pl. **Appendixes** and **Appendices,** ap-pen'di-sēz. [L. *appendix, appendicis,* from *appendo.*] Something appended or added; an addition appended to a book relating, but not essential, to the main work; *anat.* an appendage, process, or projecting part. — **Appendicatory,** ap-pend'i-ka-to-ri, *a.* Pertaining to or of the nature of an appendix.—**Appendicitis,** ap-pen'di-sī''tis, *n.* Inflammation of the vermiform appendix, a small hollow blind process attached to the cæcum in man and some animals, an ailment often fatal.

Apperception, ap-pėr-sep'shon, *n.* [Prefix *ap* for *ad,* and *perception.*] Perception that reflects upon itself; consciousness; spontaneous thought.

Appertain, ap-pėr-tān′, *v.i.* [Fr. *appartenir*—L. *ad*, and *pertineo*, to pertain.] To belong or pertain: with *to*.—**Appertaining**, **Appertainment**,† ap-pėr-tān′ing, ap-pėr-tān′ment, *n*. That which appertains or belongs. [*Shak.*]—**Appertinent**,‡ ap-pėr′tin-ent, *a*. Belonging; appurtenant. Also as *n*. [*Shak.*]

Appetence, Appetency, ap′pē-tens, ap′pē-ten-si, *n*. [L. *appetentia*, from *appetens*, *appetentis*, ppr. of *appeto*, to desire—*ad*, and *peto*, to desire. PETITION.] Desire; inclination; propensity; strong natural craving or tendency; appetite.—**Appetent**, ap′pē-tent, *a*. Desiring; very desirous.—**Appetible**,† ap′pet-i-bl, *a*. Desirable; capable of being the object of appetite.—**Appetite**, ap′pē-tīt, *n*. [L. *appetitus*, desire.] The natural desire of pleasure or good; taste; inclination; a desire to supply a bodily want or craving; a desire for food or drink; eagerness or longing.—**Appetitive**, ap′pē-tīt-iv, *a*. Having the quality of desiring.—**Appetize**, ap′pē-tīz, *v.t.*—*appetized*, *appetizing*. To give an appetite to; to increase or whet the appetite of.—**Appetizer**, ap′pē-tīz-ėr, *n*. That which appetizes or whets the appetite.—**Appetizing**, ap′pē-tīz-ing, *a*. Whetting the appetite.

Applaud, ap-plad′, *v.t.* [L. *applaudo*, *applausum*—*ad*, and *plaudo*, to make a noise by clapping the hands.] To show approbation of by clapping the hands, acclamation, or other significant sign; to praise highly; to extol.—*v.i.* To give praise; to express approbation.—**Applause**, ap-plaz′, *n*. Praise loudly expressed; approbation expressed by clapping the hands or shouting; commendation; approval.—**Applausive**, ap-plaz′iv, *a*. Applauding; containing applause.

Apple, ap′l, *n*. [A. Sax. *æppel*, *æpl*, a word common to the Teutonic, Celtic, Slavonic, and Lithuanian tongues; root unknown.] A fruit of a well-known fruit-tree, or the tree itself; also a name popularly given to various exotic fruits or trees having little or nothing in common with the apple, as the pine-apple, &c.—*Apple of the eye*, the pupil.—*Apple of Sodom*, a fruit described by old writers as externally of fair appearance, but turning to ashes when plucked.—*Adam's apple*, a prominence on the throat.—**Apple-blight**, *n*. A species of aphis.—**Apple-john**, *n*. A kind of apple, considered to be in perfection when shrivelled and withered. [*Shak.*]—**Apple-moth**, *n*. A moth, the larvæ of which take up their abode in apples.—**Apple-pie**, *n*. A pie made of apples, covered with paste.—*Apple-pie order*, perfect order. [Colloq.]

Apply, ap-plī′, *v.t.*—*applied*, *applying*. [O. Fr. *applier*, from L. *applicare*, to fasten to—*ad*, to, and *plico*, to fold. PLY.] To lay on (the hand to a table); to put or place on another thing; to use or employ for a particular purpose or in a particular case (a remedy, a sum of money); to put, refer, or use as suitable or relative to some person or thing (a proverb, &c.); to engage and employ with attention; to occupy (the mind, or *refl.*).—*v.i.* To suit; to agree; to have some connection, agreement, analogy, or reference; to make request; to solicit; to have recourse with a view to gain something: followed by *to*.—**Appliable**,† ap-plī′a-bl, *a*. Applicable.—**Appliance**, ap-plī′ans, *n*. The act of applying; the thing applied; means to an end; a device; an application; a remedy (*Shak.*).—**Applicability**, ap′pli-ka-bil″i-ti, *n*. The quality of being applicable.—**Applicable**, ap′pli-ka-bl, *a*. Capable of being applied; fit to be applied; having relevance.—**Applicableness**, ap′pli-ka-bl-nes, *n*. The state or quality of being applicable.—**Applicably**, ap′pli-ka-bli, *adv*. In an applicable manner.—**Applicancy**, ap′pli-kan-si, *n*. The state of being applicable.—**Applicant**, ap′pli-kant, *n*. One who applies; a petitioner; a candidate.—**Applicate**,† ap′pli-kāt, *a*. Applied or put to some use.—**Application**, ap-pli-kā′shon, *n*. The act of applying or putting to; the thing applied; the act of making request or soliciting; the employment of means; close study; attention; the testing of something theoretical by applying it in practice.—**Applicative, Applicatory**, ap′pli-kāt-iv, ap′pli-ka-to-ri, *a*. Having an application; that may be applied.—**Applier**, ap-plī′ėr, *n*. One that applies.

Appoggiatura, ap-poj′a-tö″ra, *n*. [It.] *Mus*. a grace-note: an added note of embellishment to an original passage.

Appoint, ap-point′, *v.t.* [Fr. *appointer*, from L.L. *appunctare*, to bring to the point—L. *ad*, to, and *punctum*, a point. POINT.] To make firm, establish, or secure (O.T.)‡; to constitute, ordain, or decree; to allot, set apart, or designate; to nominate, as to an office; to settle; to fix, name, or determine by authority or upon agreement; to equip.—*v.i.* To ordain; to determine.—**Appointable**, ap-point′a-bl, *a*. Capable of being appointed or constituted.—**Appointer**, ap-point′ėr, *n*. One who appoints.—**Appointment**, ap-point′ment, *n*. The act of appointing; designation to office; an office held; the act of fixing by mutual agreement; arrangement; decree; direction; command; equipment, furniture, &c. (*Shak.*); an allowance; a salary or pension.

Apportion, ap-pōr′shon, *v.t.* [O.Fr. *apportioner*—L. *ad*, and *portio*, portion.] To divide and assign in just proportion; to distribute in proper shares; to allot.—**Apportioner**, ap-pōr′shon-ėr, *n*. One that apportions.—**Apportionment**, ap-pōr′shon-ment, *n*. The act of apportioning.

Apposite, ap′pō-zit, *a*. [L. *appositus*, set or put to, from *appono*, *appositum*—*ad*, and *pono*, to put or place.] Suitable; fit; appropriate; very applicable; well adapted: followed by *to*, and said of answers, arguments, &c.—**Appositely**, ap′pō-zit-li, *adv*. In an apposite manner; suitably; fitly.—**Appositeness**, ap′pō-zit-nes, *n*. The state or quality of being apposite; fitness.—**Apposition**, ap-pō-zi′shon, *n*. The act of adding to; addition; a setting to; *gram*. the relation in which a noun or a substantive phrase or clause stands to a noun or pronoun when it explains without being predicated of it, at the same time agreeing in case; as, Cicero, the orator, was there.—**Appositional**, ap-pō-zi′shon-al, *a*. Pertaining to apposition.—**Appositive**, ap-poz′it-iv, *a*. Placed in apposition.

Appraise, ap-prāz′, *v.t.*—*appraised*, *appraising*. [O.Fr. *appreiser*; L. *appretiare*, to set a price on—*ad*, to, and *pretium*, a price. PRAISE, PRICE, PRECIOUS.] To set a price upon; to estimate the value of under the direction of a competent authority; to estimate generally.—**Appraisement**, ap-prāz′ment, *n*. The act of appraising; the value fixed; the valuation.—**Appraiser**, ap-prāz′ėr, *n*. One who appraises; a person licensed and sworn to estimate and fix the value of goods and estate.

Appreciate, ap-prē′shi-āt, *v.t.*—*appreciated*, *appreciating*. [Fr. *apprécier*, to set a value, L. *appretio*, *appreciatum*. APPRAISE.] To set a just price, value, or estimate on; to estimate or value properly.—*v.i.* To rise in value; to become of more value.—**Appreciable**, ap-prē′shi-a-bl, *a*. Capable of being appreciated or estimated; sufficiently great to be capable of estimation.—**Appreciably**, ap-prē′shi-a-bli, *adv*. To a degree that may be appreciated or estimated; perceptibly.—**Appreciation**, ap-prē′shi-ā″shon, *n*. The act of appreciating; the act of valuing or estimating; the act of setting a due price or value on.—**Appreciative**, ap-prē′shi-ā-tiv, *a*. Capable of appreciating; manifesting due appreciation.—**Appreciatory**, ap-prē′shi-a-to-ri, *a*. Pertaining to appreciation.

Apprehend, ap-prē-hend′, *v.t.* [L. *apprehendo*—*ad*, and *prehendo*, to take or seize, *præ*, before, and *hendo* (not used), to seize.] To take or seize (a person); to arrest; to take or lay hold of by the mind; to become cognizant of; to understand; to entertain suspicion or fear of; to dread or be apprehensive of.—*v.t.* To form a conception; to conceive; to believe or be of opinion without positive certainty; to be apprehensive; to be in fear of a future evil.—**Apprehender**, ap-prē-hend′ėr, *n*. One who apprehends.—**Apprehensible**, ap-prē-hen′si-bl, *a*. Capable of being apprehended or conceived.—**Apprehension**, ap-prē-hen′shon, *n*. The act of apprehending; a seizing or arresting by legal process; the operation of the mind in contemplating ideas, or merely taking them into the mind; opinion; belief; the power of perceiving and understanding; distrust or fear at the prospect of future evil, accompanied with uneasiness of mind.—**Apprehensive**, ap-prē-hen′siv, *a*. Quick of apprehension (*Shak.*); inclined to believe, fear, or dread; anticipating, or in expectation of evil (*apprehensive of* evil; *apprehensive for* our lives).—**Apprehensively**, ap-prē-hen′siv-li, *adv*. In an apprehensive manner.—**Apprehensiveness**, ap-prē-hen′siv-nes, *n*. The character of being apprehensive.

Apprentice, ap-pren′tis, *n*. [L.L. *apprenticius*, from L. *apprehendo*, *apprendo*, to seize, to apprehend. APPREHEND.] One bound, often by legal document, to learn some art, trade, or profession; a learner in any subject; one not well versed in a subject.—*v.t.* *apprenticed*, *apprenticing*. To make an apprentice of; to put under the care of a master, for the purpose of learning a trade or profession.—**Apprenticeship**, ap-pren′tis-ship, *n*. The state or condition of an apprentice; the term during which one is an apprentice.

Apprise, ap-prīz′, *v.t.*—*apprised*, *apprising*. [O.E. *apprise*, notice, information, from Fr. *appris*, *apprise*, pp. of *apprendre*, to inform, to learn, L. *apprehendo*. APPREHEND.] To give notice, verbal or written; to inform: followed by *of* before that of which notice is given.

Approach, ap-prōch′, *v.i.* [Fr. *approcher*, from L.L. *appropiare*, to approach—L. *ad*, to, and *prope*, near. PROPINQUITY.] To come or go near in place or time; to draw near; to advance nearer; to approximate.—*v.t.* To bring near; to advance or put near; to come or draw near to, either literally or figuratively; to come near to, so as to be compared with.—*n*. The act of approaching or drawing near; a coming or advancing near; access; a passage or avenue by which buildings are approached.—**Approachable**, ap-prōch′a-bl, *a*. Capable of being approached; accessible.—**Approachableness**, ap-prōch′a-bl-nes, *n*.—**Approacher**, ap-prōch′ėr, *n*. One who approaches or draws near.—**Approachless**, ap-prōch′les, *a*. That cannot be approached.—**Approachment**,† ap-prōch′ment, *n*. The act of approaching; approach.

Approbate,† ap′prō-bāt, *v.t.* [L. *approbo*, *approbatum*, to approve. APPROVE.] To express satisfaction with; to express approval of; to approve.—**Approbation**, ap-prō-bā′shon, *n*. [L. *approbatio*.] The act of approving; that state or disposition of the mind in which we assent to the propriety of a thing with some degree of pleasure or satisfaction; approval.—**Approbative**, ap′prō-bāt-iv, *a*. Approving; implying approbation.

Appropriate, ap-prō′pri-āt, *v.t.*—*appropriated*, *appropriating*. [L. *approprio*, *appropriatum*, to make one's own—*ad*, to, *proprius*, one's own. PROPER, PROPRIETY.] To claim or take to one's self in exclusion of others; to claim or use as by an exclusive right; to set apart for or assign to a particular purpose.—*a*. Set apart for a particular use or person; hence, belonging peculiarly; peculiar; suitable; fit; proper.—**Appropriable**, ap-prō′pri-a-bl, *a*. Capable of being appropriated, set apart, or assigned to a particular use.—**Appropriately**, ap-prō′pri-āt-li, *adv*. In an appropriate manner.—**Appropriateness**, ap-prō′pri-āt-nes, *n*. The quality of being appropriate.—**Appropriation**, ap-prō′pri-ā″shon, *n*. The act of appropriating; application to a special use or purpose; the act of making one's own; anything appropriated or set apart.—**Appropriative**, ap-prō′pri-āt-iv, *a*. Appropriating; making appropriation.—**Appropriator**, ap-prō′pri-āt-ėr, *n*. One who appropriates.

Approve, ap-pröv′, *v.t.*—*approved*, *approving*. [Fr. *approuver*, *approver*, from L. *approbo*, to approve, to find good—*ad*, to, and *probare*, to try, test, prove, from *probus*, good.] To admit the propriety or excellence of; to think or judge well or favourably of; to find to be satisfactory; to show to be real or true (to *approve* one's bravery); to prove by trial (*Shak.*)†.—*v.i.* To be pleased; to feel or express approbation; to think or judge well or favourably: followed by *of*.—**Approvable**, ap-pröv'a-bl, *a.* Capable of being approved.—**Approvableness**, ap-pröv'a-bl-nes, *n.*—**Approval**, ap-pröv'al, *n.* The act of approving; approbation; commendation; sanction; ratification.—**Approver**, ap-pröv'ėr, *n.* One who approves; one who confesses a crime and accuses another.—**Approvingly**, ap-pröv'ing-li, *adv.* In an approving manner.

Approximate, ap-prok'si-māt, *v.t.*—*approximated, approximating.* [L.L. *approximo, approximatum*, to bring or come near —L. *ad*, to, and *proximus*, nearest. PROXIMATE, APPROACH.] To carry or advance near; to cause to approach (especially said of amount, state, or degree).—*v.i.* To come near; to approach (especially as regards amount, state, or character).—*a.* Being near in state, place, or quantity; approaching; nearly equal or like.—**Approximately**, ap-prok'si-māt-li, *adv.* In an approximate manner; by approximation.—**Approximation**, ap-prok'si-mā"shon, *n.* The act of approximating; an approximate estimate or amount; approach.—**Approximative**, ap-prok'si-māt-iv, *a.* Coming near, as to some state or result.

Appulse, Appulsion, ap-puls', ap-pul'-shon, *n.* [L. *appulsus*—*ad*, to, and *pello, pulsum*, to drive.] The act of striking against; a sudden contact; *astron.* the approach of a planet to a conjunction with the sun.—**Appulsive**, ap-puls'iv, *a.* Striking against; impinging.—**Appulsively**, ap-puls'iv-li, *adv.* By appulsion.

Appurtenance, ap-pėr'ten-ans, *n.* [Fr. *appartenance*. APPERTAIN.] That which appertains or belongs to something else; something belonging to another thing as principal; an adjunct; an appendage.—**Appurtenant**, ap-pėr'ten-ant, *a.* Appertaining or belonging; pertaining; being an appurtenance.

Apricot, ā'pri-kot, *n.* [O.E. *apricock, abricot*, Fr. *abricot*, Sp. *albarcoque*, from Ar. *alburqūq*, from *al*, the article, and L. Gr. *praikokkion*, from L. *præcox, præcoquus*, early ripe. PRECOCIOUS.] A roundish fruit of a delicious flavour, the produce of a tree of the plum kind.

April, ā'pril, *n.* [L. *aprilis*, the month in which the earth opens for the growth of plants, from *aperio*, to open.] The fourth month of the year.—*April fool*, one who is sportively imposed upon by others on the 1st of April, as by being sent on some absurd errand.

A priori, ā pri-ō'ri. [L., from something prior or going before.] A phrase applied to a mode of reasoning by which we proceed from the cause to the effect, as opposed to *a posteriori* reasoning, by which we proceed from the effect to the cause; also a term applied to knowledge independent of all experience.

Apron, ā'prun, *n.* [O.E. *napron*, Fr. *napperon*, from *nape, nappe*, a table-cloth, &c. (whence E. *napkin*), *nappe* being another form of *mappe*, E. *map*. *Apron*, like *adder, auger*, has lost the initial *n*.] A piece of cloth or leather worn on the fore-part of the body to keep the clothes clean or defend them from injury; a covering for the front part of a body.—*v.t.* To put an apron on; to furnish with an apron.

Apropos, ap-ro-po, *a.* [Fr.—*à*, to, according to, and *propos*, purpose, L. *propositum*, a thing proposed.] Opportune; seasonable; to the purpose (an *apropos* remark).

Apse, aps, *n.* [Gr. (*h*)*apsis*, (*h*)*apsidos*, an arch, vault, joining, from (*h*)*aptō*, to join.] A portion of any building forming a termination or projection semicircular or polygonal in plan, and having a dome or vaulted roof; especially such a structure at the east end of a church.—**Apsidal**, ap-sī'dal, *a.* Pertaining to or resembling an apse; pertaining to apsides.—**Apsis**, ap'sis, *n.* pl. **Apsides**, ap-sī'dēz. *Arch.* an apse; *astron.* one of the two points in the orbit of a heavenly body which mark its greatest and its least distance from the primary round which it revolves.

Apt, apt, *a.* [L. *aptus*, fitted, fit.] Fit; suitable; apposite; pertinent; appropriate; having a tendency; liable; inclined; disposed; ready; prompt.—**Aptitude**, ap'ti-tūd, *n.* The state or quality of being apt; disposition; tendency; fitness; suitableness; readiness in learning; docility.—**Aptly**, apt'li, *adv.* In an apt or suitable manner; justly; pertinently; readily; quickly; cleverly.—**Aptness**, apt'nes, *n.* The state or quality of being apt; fitness; tendency; quickness of apprehension; readiness in learning; docility.

Aptera, ap'tėr-a, *n.pl.* [Gr. *apteros*, without wings—*a*, priv., and *pteron*, a wing.] An order of insects which have no wings.—**Apteral, Apterous**, ap'tėr-al, ap'tėr-us, *a.* Destitute of wings.—**Apteran**, ap'tėr-an, *n.* One of the aptera; a wingless insect.

Apteryx, ap'tėr-iks, *n.* [Gr. *a*, priv., and *pteryx*, a wing.] A bird peculiar to but now nearly extinct in New Zealand, having no tail and very short rudimentary wings.

Aptote, ap'tōt, *n.* [Gr. *aptōtos*, indeclinable.] *Gram.* a noun which has no variation of termination or distinction of cases; an indeclinable noun.—**Aptotic**, ap-tot'ik, *a.* Of or pertaining to an aptote; having no declensional forms, &c.

Apyretic, ap-i-ret'ik, *a.* [Gr. *a*, without, and *pyretos*, fever, from *pyr*, fire.] Without fever; marked by the absence of fever.—**Apyrexia, Apyrexy**, ap-i-rek'si-a, ap'i-rek-si, *n.* The absence or intermission of fever.—**Apyrous**, a-pī'rus, *a.* Incombustible, or capable of sustaining a strong heat without alteration.

Aqua, ak'wa, *n.* [L.] Water: a word forming an element in various terms; also used by itself as a commercial name of whisky.—*Aqua fortis* (= strong water), a name given to weak and impure nitric acid.—*Aqua regia* (= royal water), a mixture of nitric and hydrochloric acids, so called from its power of dissolving gold and other noble metals.—*Aqua vitæ* (= water of life), ardent spirits, as whisky, brandy, &c.—**Aquarium**, a-kwā'ri-um, *n.* A case, vessel, tank, or the like, in which aquatic plants and animals are kept; a place containing a collection of such vessels or tanks.—**Aquarius**, a-kwā'ri-us, *n.* [L.] The Water-bearer; a sign in the zodiac which the sun enters about the 21st of January.—**Aquatic**, a-kwat'ik, *a.* Pertaining to water; living in or frequenting water.—*n.* A plant which grows in water; *pl.* sports or exercises practised on or in water, as rowing or swimming.—**Aquatile**, ak'wa-til, *a.* Inhabiting the water.—**Aqueous**, ak'wē-us, *a.* Partaking of the nature of water, or abounding with or formed by it; watery.—**Aqueousness**, ak'wē-us-nes, *n.* The quality or state of being aqueous.

Aquamarine, ak'wa-ma-rēn, *n.* [L. *aqua*, water, and *marinus*, pertaining to the sea.] The finest beryl, so called from its bluish or sea-green tint.

Aquarelle, ak-wa-rel', *n.* [Fr., from L. *aqua*, water.] Water-colour painting, a painting in water-colour.

Aquatint, Aquatinta, ak'wa-tint, ak-wa-tin'ta, *n.* [L. *aqua*, water, and It. *tinta*, dye, tint.] A method of etching on copper by which a beautiful effect is produced, resembling a fine drawing in water-colours or Indian ink.—**Aquatinter**, ak-wa-tint'-ėr, *n.* One who practises the art of aquatinting.—**Aquatinting**, ak-wa-tint'ing, *n.* The art or process of engraving in the aquatint method.

Aqueduct, ak'wē-dukt, *n.* [L. *aquæductus*—*aqua*, water, and *ductus*, a pipe or canal, from *duco*, to lead.] A conduit or channel for conveying water from one place to another; a structure for conveying water for the supply of a town.

Aqueous. See AQUA.

Aquiferous, a-kwif'ėr-us, *a.* [L. *aqua*, water, and *fero*, to bear.] Conducting water or watery fluid (*aquiferous* system of the sponges).—**Aquiform**, ak'wi-form, *a.* [L. *aqua*, water, and *forma*, form.] In the form of water.

Aquiline, ak'wil-īn, *a.* [L. *aquilinus*, from *aquila*, an eagle.] Of or belonging to the eagle; resembling an eagle's beak; curving; hooked.

Arab, ar'ab, *n.* A native of Arabia; a neglected outcast boy or girl of the streets.—*a.* Of or pertaining to the Arabs or Arabia.—**Arabesque**, ar'ab-esk, *n.* [Fr., from the *Arabs*, who brought the style to high perfection.] A species of architectural ornamentation for enriching flat surfaces, either painted, inlaid, or wrought in low relief, often consisting of fanciful figures, human or animal, combined with floral forms.—**Arabian**, a-rā'bi-an, *a.* Pertaining to Arabia.—*n.* A native of Arabia; an Arab.—**Arabian bird**. The phœnix.—**Arabian Nights**. Oriental collection of tales.—**Arabic**, ar'ab-ik, *a.* Belonging to Arabia or the language of its inhabitants.—*n.* The language of the Arabians.

Arable, ar'a-bl, *a.* [Fr. *arable*, L. *arabilis*, from *aro*, to plough, from root seen also in A.Sax. *erian*, E. to *ear*, Icel. *erja*, Goth. *erjan*, Lith. *arti*, Rus. *orati*, to plough, to till; Ir. and W. *ar*, tillage; W. *aru*, to plough.] Fit for ploughing or tillage.

Arachis, ar'a-kis, *n.* The generic name of the ground-nut (*A. hypogæa*).—*Arachis oil*, the oil expressed from the seeds of the ground-nut, the nut-oil of commerce.

Arachnida, a-rak'ni-da, *n. pl.* [Gr. *arachnē*, a spider.] A class of annulose, wingless animals, intermediate between the insects and the Crustacea, including spiders, mites, and scorpions.—**Arachnidan**, a-rak'ni-dan, *n.* One of the Arachnida.—**Arachnoid**, a-rak'noid, *a.* Resembling a spider's web; *anat.* applied to a semi-transparent thin membrane which is spread over the brain and pia mater; *bot.* having hair that gives an appearance of being covered with cobweb.—**Arachnology**, ar-ak-nol'o-ji, *n.* That branch of natural history which treats of spiders.—**Arachnologist**, ar-ak-nol'o-jist, *n.* One versed in arachnology.

Arack, ar'ak, *n.* Same as *Arrack*.

Aramaic, ar-a-mā'ik, *n.* [From *Aram*, a son of Shem, the supposed ancestor of the Chaldeans and Syrians.] A language or group of languages anciently spoken in Syria, the earliest specimens being the Chaldee passages in the Old Testament and Apocrypha; Chaldaic; Chaldee.

Araneid, a-rā'nē-id, *n.* [L. *aranea*, a spider.] An animal of the spider family.—**Araneiform**, a-rā'nē-i-form, *a.* Resembling a spider.—**Araneous, Araneose**, a-rā'nē-us, a-rā'nē-ōs, *a.* Resembling a cobweb; arachnoid.

Araucaria, ar-ą-kā'ri-a, *n.* [From the *Araucanos*, a tribe of Indians in Chili.] The generic name of some fine coniferous trees found chiefly in South America, but now also commonly grown in Britain.—**Araucarian**, ar-ą-kā'ri-an, *a.* Relating to the araucarias.—**Araucarite**, a-rą'ka-rīt, *n.* A fossil plant allied to the araucarias.

Arbalist, Arbalest, är'bal-ist, är'bal-est, *n.* [O.Fr. *arbaleste*, from L. *arcus*, a bow, and *ballista, balista*, an engine to throw stones.] A kind of powerful cross-bow formerly used.—**Arbalister**, är'bal-ist-ėr, *n.* A cross-bow-man.

Arbiter, är'bit-ėr, *n.* [L., an arbiter, umpire, judge.] A person appointed or chosen by parties in controversy to decide their differences; one who judges and determines without control; one whose power of deciding and governing is not limited; an arbitrator.—**Arbitrage**, är'bi-trāj, *n.* The calculation of the best mode by which advantage may be taken of differences in the value of money, stocks, &c., at different places in the same time; the dealing in bills of exchange, stocks, &c., for the purpose of making profit by such calculations.—**Arbitrageur**, är'bi-trä-zhėr, *n.* One whose business it is to make such calculations.—**Arbitrament**, är-bit'ra-ment, *n.* Determination; decision; settlement; award (the *arbitrament* of the sword). —**Arbitrary**, är'bi-tra-ri, *a.* [L. *arbitrarius.*] Given, adjudged, or done according to one's will or discretion; exercised according to one's will or discretion; capricious; despotic; imperious; tyrannical; uncontrolled.—**Arbitrarily**, är'bi-tra-ri-li, *adv.* In an arbitrary manner; capriciously.—**Arbitrariness**, är'bi-tra-ri-nes, *n.* The quality of being arbitrary. —**Arbitrate**, är'bi-trāt, *v.i. arbitrated, arbitrating.* [L. *arbitror, arbitratus.*] To act as an arbiter or umpire; to hear and decide in a dispute.—*v.t.* To hear and decide on.—**Arbitration**, är-bi-trā'shon, *n.* The act of arbitrating; the hearing and determination of a cause between parties in controversy, by a person or persons chosen by the parties. —**Arbitrator**, är'bi-trāt-ėr, *n.* One who arbitrates; an arbiter. —**Arbitrement**, är-bit're-ment, *n.* Same as *Arbitrament.*

Arblast, är'blast, *n.* A cross-bow; an arbalist.

Arbor, är'bor, *n.* [L., a tree, a wooden bar, &c.] The principal spindle or axis of a machine, communicating motion to the other moving parts.—**Arboreous, Arboreal**, är-bō'rē-us, är-bō'rē-al, *a.* Pertaining to trees; living on or among trees; having the character of a tree.—**Arborescence**, är-bor-es'ens, *n.* The state of being arborescent; an arborescent form or growth. —**Arborescent**, är-bor-es'ent, *a.* [L. *arborescens*, pp. of *arboresco*, to grow to a tree.] Resembling a tree; *bot.* partaking of the nature and habits of a tree; dendritic.—**Arboretum**, är-bo-rē'tum, *n.* [L.] A place in which a collection of different trees and shrubs is cultivated for scientific or educational purposes. —**Arborization**, är'bor-i-zā''shon, *n.* A mineral or other body with a tree-like form.

Arboriculture, är'bo-ri-kul''tūr, *n.* [L. *arbor*, a tree, and *cultura*, cultivation. CULTURE.] The cultivation of trees; the art of planting, dressing, and managing trees and shrubs.—**Arboricultural**, är-bor'i-kul''tūr-al, *a.* Relating to arboriculture. —**Arboriculturist**, är'bo-ri-kul''-tūr-ist, *n.* One who practises arboriculture.

Arbor-vitæ, är'bor-vī'tē, *n.* [L., the tree of life.] A common name of certain coniferous trees; a tree-like arrangement which appears in the medullary substance of the brain when the cerebellum is cut vertically.

Arbor, Arbour, är'bėr, *n.* [O.E. *herber*, O.Fr. *herbier*, L. *herba*, herb; the spelling influenced by L. *arbor*, tree.] A seat in the open air sheltered by intertwining branches or climbing plants; a bower.—**Arborous**, är'bor-us, *a.* Having the appearance or nature of an arbor. (*Mil.*)

Arbuscular, är-bus'ku-ler, *a.* [From L. *arbuscula*, dim. of *arbor*, a tree.] Resembling a shrub or small tree.

Arbutus, är'bū-tus, *n.* [L., the strawberry-tree.] The generic name of an evergreen tree or shrub, with bright red or yellow berries, somewhat like the strawberry, having an unpleasant taste and narcotic properties.—Also called **Arbute**, är'-būt.—**Arbutean**, är-bū-tē'an, *a.* Pertaining to the arbutus.

Arc, ärk, *n.* [L. *arcus*, a bow. ARCH.] *Geom.* a curve line forming or that might form part of the circumference of a circle; formerly also an arch.—**Arcade**, är-kād', *n.* [Fr., L.L. *arcata*, L. *arcus*, an arch.] A series of arches supported on pillars, often used as a roof support or as an ornamental dressing to a wall; a covered-in passage containing shops or stalls.

Arcadian, är-kā'di-an, *a.* Pertaining to Arcadia, a mountainous district in southern Greece; hence, rustic; rural; pastoral.

Arcanum, är-kā'num, *n.* pl. **Arcana**, är-kā'na. [L.] A secret; a mystery: generally used in the plural (the *arcana* of nature).

Arch, ärch, *n.* [Fr. *arche*, L.L. *archia*, from L. *arcus*, a bow, arch, arc.] A structure composed of separate wedge-shaped pieces, arranged on a curved line, so as to retain their position by mutual pressure; a covering, or structure, of a bow shape; a vault. —*Court of arches*, an ecclesiastical court of appeal pertaining to the archbishopric of Canterbury, anciently held in the church of St. Mary-le-bow, called also St. Mary-of-the-arches.—*v.t.* To cover or span with an arch; to curve or form into the shape of an arch.—**Archway**, ärch'wā, *n.* A passage under an arch.

Arch, ärch, *a.* [From next word, from being often used in such phrases as *arch* wag, *arch* rogue.] Cunning, sly, shrewd; waggish; mischievous for sport; roguish.—**Archly**, ärch'li, *adv.* In an arch or roguish manner.—**Archness**, ärch'nes, *n.*

Arch, ärch, *a.* [From Gr. *archi*, in compound words, from stem of *archē*, power or rule.] Chief; of the first class or rank: principally used in composition as the first part of many words; as, *arch*bishop, *arch*-priest, &c.—*n.*‡ A leader; a chief. (*Shak.*)

Archæan, är-kē'an, *a.* [Gr. *archaios*, ancient.] *Geol.* applied to the oldest rocks of the earth's crust, crystalline in character, and embracing granite, syenite, gneiss.—**Archæolithic**, pertaining to the early stone period, palæolithic.

Archæology, är-kē-ol'o-ji, *n.* [Gr. *archaios*, ancient, and *logos*, discourse.] The science of antiquities, especially prehistoric antiquities, which investigates the history of peoples by the remains belonging to the earlier periods of their existence.—**Archæological, Archæologic**, är'kē-o-loj''ik-al, är'kē-o-loj''ik, *a.* Pertaining to archæology. —**Archæologist, Archæologian**, är-kē-ol'o-jist, är'kē-o-lō''ji-an, *n.* One skilled in archæology.

Archæopteryx, är-kē-op'tėr-iks, *n.* [Gr. [*archaios*, ancient, and *pteryx*, wing.] A fossil bird of the size of a rook, having two claws representing the thumb and fore-finger projecting from the wing, and about twenty tail vertebræ prolonged as in mammals.

Archaic, Archaical, är-kā'ik, är-kā'ik-al, *a.* [Gr. *archaïkos*, old-fashioned, from *archaios*, ancient.] Old-fashioned; obsolete; antiquated. —**Archaism**, är'kā-izm, *n* An ancient or obsolete word or idiom; antiquity of style or use; obsoleteness.

Archangel, ärk-ān'jel, *n.* An angel of the highest order in the celestial hierarchy.—**Archangelic**, ärk-an-jel'ik, *a.* Of or pertaining to archangels.

Archbishop, ärch-bish'up, *n.* A bishop who has the supervision of other bishops (the sees of whom form his province), and also exercises episcopal authority in his own diocese.—**Archbishopric**, ärch-bish'up-rik, *n.* The jurisdiction, office, or see of an archbishop.

Archdeacon, ärch-dē'kn, *n.* In England, an ecclesiastical dignitary, next in rank below a bishop, who has jurisdiction either over a part of or over the whole diocese. —**Archdeaconate, Archdeaconry**, ärch-dē'kn-āt, ärch-dē'kn-ri, *n.* The office, jurisdiction, or residence of an archdeacon.

Archduke, ärch-dūk', *n.* A prince belonging to the reigning family of the Austrian empire.—**Archducal**, ärch-dūk'al, *a.* Pertaining to an archduke. —**Archduchess**, ärch-duch'es, *n.* The wife of an archduke. —**Archduchy, Archdukedom**, ärch-duch'i, ärch-dūk'dum, *n.* The territory or rank of an archduke or arch-duchess.

Archebiosis, är'kē-bi-o''sis, *n.* [Gr. *archē*, beginning, *bios*, life.] The origin of life; the origin of living from non-living matter.

Archegony, är-keg'o-ni, *n.* [Gr. *archē*, beginning, and *gonos*, offspring.] The doctrine of the origin of life.

Archenemy, ärch-en'ē-mi, *n.* A principal enemy; Satan.

Archer, ärch'ėr, *n.* [Fr. *archer*, from *arc*, L. *arcus*, a bow. ARCH.] One who uses, or is skilled in the use of the bow and arrow; a bowman.—**Archery**, ärch'ėr-i, *n.* The practice, art, or skill of shooting with a bow and arrow. —**Archer-fish**, *n.* A small fish of Asia which shoots drops of water at insects, causing them to fall into the water and become its prey.

Archetype, är'kē-tīp, *n.* [Gr. *archetypon* —*archē*, beginning, and *typos*, form.] A model or first form; the original pattern after which a thing is made, or to which it corresponds. —**Archetypal**, är'kē-tīp-al, *a.* Of or pertaining to an archetype.

Archidiaconal, är'ki-dī-ak''on-al, *a.* [Gr. *archi*, chief, *diakonos*, deacon.] Pertaining to an archdeacon.

Archiepiscopacy, Archiepiscopate, är'ki-ē-pis''kō-pa-si, är-ki-ē-pis'kō-pāt, *n.* The dignity, office, or province of an archbishop. —**Archiepiscopal**, är'ki-ē-pis''-kō-pal, *a.* Belonging to an archbishop.

Archil, är'kil, *n.* A violet, mauve, or purple colouring matter obtained from lichens growing on rocks in the Canary and Cape de Verd Islands.

Archimandrite, är-ki-man'drīt, *n.* [Gr. *archi*, chief, *mandra*, a monastery.] *Greek Ch.* an abbot, or abbot-general, who has the superintendence of other abbots and convents.

Archimedean, är'ki-mē-dē''an, *a.* Pertaining to Archimedes, the Greek philosopher.—*Archimedean screw*, an instrument for raising water, formed by winding a flexible tube round a cylinder in the form of a screw; being placed in an inclined position, and the lower end immersed in water, by causing the screw to revolve the water is raised to the upper end.

Archipelago, är-ki-pel'a-gō, *n.* [Gr. *archi*, chief, and *pelagos*, the sea.] Originally the Egean Sea, which is studded with a number of small islands; hence any water space interspersed with many islands; a group of many islands.—**Archipelagic**, är'ki-pe-laj''ik, *a.* Relating to an archipelago.

Architect, är'ki-tekt, *n.* [Fr. *architecte*, L. *architectus*, Gr. prefix *archi*, chief, and *tektōn*, a workman.] A person skilled in the art and science of building; one who makes it his occupation to form plans and designs of buildings, and superintend their erection; a former or maker. **Architectonic, Architectonical**, är'ki-tek-ton''-ik; är'ki-tek-ton''ik-al, *a.* Pertaining to or skilled in architecture.—**Architectonics**, är'ki-tek-ton''iks, *n.* The science of architecture. —**Architectural**, är-ki-tek'tūr-al, *a.* Pertaining to architecture or the art of building. —**Architecture**, är'ki-tek-tūr, *n.* [L. *architectura.*] The art or science of building; that branch of the fine arts which has for its object the production of edifices pleasing to a cultivated and artistic taste; construction.

Architrave, är'ki-trāv, *n.* [It. *architrave* —prefix *archi*, chief, and *trave*, from L. *trabs*, a beam.] *Arch.* the lower division of an entablature, or that part which rests immediately on the column.

Archive, är'kīv, *n.* [L.L. *archivum*, a place for keeping public records, from Gr. *archeion*, a government building, from *archē*, rule, government.] A record or document preserved in evidence of something; almost always in plural and signifying documents or records relating to the affairs of a family, corporation, community, city, or kingdom. —**Archival**, är'kīv-al, *a.* Pertaining to or contained in archives or records.—**Archivist**, är'kīv-ist or är'ki-vist, *n.* The keeper of archives or records.

Archlute, ärch'lūt, *n.* A kind of large lute; a theorbo.

Archon, är'kon, *n.* [Gr.] One of the chief magistrates of ancient Athens chosen to superintend civil and religious concerns.

Arctation, ärk-tā'shon, *n.* [L. *arctus*, tight.] Narrowness or constriction; *med.* unnatural contraction of any natural opening, as of the anus.

Arctic, ärk'tik, *a.* [L. *arcticus*; Gr. *arktikos*, from *arctos*, a bear, the northern constellation Ursa Major.] Northern; surrounding or lying near the north pole. The *arctic* circle is a circle parallel to the equator, 23° 28′ from the north pole.

Arctitude, ärk'ti-tūd, *n.* Arctation.

Arcturus, ärk-tū'rus, *n.* [Gr. *arktos*, a bear, and *oura*, tail.] A fixed star of the first magnitude near the tail of the Great Bear.

Arcuate, ärk'ū-āt, *a.* [L. *arcuatus*, from *arcus*, a bow.] Bent or curved in the form of a bow.—**Arcuation**, ärk-ū-ā'shon, *n.* The act of bending; incurvation; curvity.

Arcubalist, ärk'ū-bal-ist, *n.* An arbalist.

Ardent, är'dent, *a.* [L. *ardens, ardentis*, pp. of *ardeo*, to burn, to be eager.] Burning; causing a sensation of burning; warm: applied to the passions and affections; vehement; passionate; eager; fervent; fervid; zealous.—*Ardent spirits*, alcoholic drinks, as brandy, whisky, rum, &c.—**Ardently**, är'dent-li, *adv.* In an ardent manner; with warmth.—**Ardentness**, är'dent-nes, *n.* The state or quality of being ardent; ardency.—**Ardency**, är'den-si, *n.* The quality of being ardent; warmth; ardor; eagerness.—**Ardor**, är'dėr, *n.* [L. *ardor*.] Heat in a literal sense; warmth or heat, as of the passions and affections; eagerness.

Arduous, är'dū-us, *a.* [L. *arduus*; allied to Ir. and Gael. *ard*, high.] Steep, and therefore difficult of ascent; hard to climb; attended with great labor; difficult; hard (task or employment).—**Arduously**, är'dū-us-li, *adv.* In an arduous manner.—**Arduousness**, är'dū-us-nes, *n.*

Are, är. [O. Northumbrian *aron, arn*, we (you, they) are; the A. Sax. form proper is *sind* or *sindon*. The *r* is changed from *s*, the root being *as*. AM.] The present tense plural of the verb *to be, art* being the second pers. sing.

Are, ār or är, *n.* [L. *area*.] The unit of French superficial or square measure, containing 100 square metres or 1076·44 English square feet.

Area, ā'rē-a, *n.* [L. *area*, a thrashing-floor, then any level open piece of land.] Any plain surface within boundaries, as the floor of a hall, &c.; a space sunk below the general surface of the ground before windows in the basement story of a building; a yard; the superficial contents of any space; a surface, as given in square inches, feet, yards, &c.—**Areal**, ā'rē-al, *a.* Pertaining to an area.

Areca, a-rē'ka, *n.* [The Malabar name.] A genus of palms, including the betel-nut and cabbage-trees.

Areed,† a-rēd', *v.t.* [A. Sax. *araedan*.] To advise or counsel. (*Mil.*)

Arefaction, ar-ē-fak'shon, *n.* [L. *arefacio*, to dry, *areo*, to be dry, *facio*, to make.] The act of drying; the state of growing dry.—**Arefy**, ar'ē-fī, *v.t.* To dry or make dry.

Arena, a-rē'na, *n.* [L. *arena*, lit. sand, a sandy place.] The inclosed space (usually covered with sand) in the central part of the Roman amphitheatres; hence, the scene or theatre of exertion or contest of any kind.—**Arenaceous**, ar-ē-nā'shus, *a.* Abounding with sand; having the properties of sand; sandy; granular.—**Arenarious**, **Arenose**, ar-ē-nā'ri-us, a-rē'nōs, *a.* Sandy.

Areng, a-reng', *n.* The sago-palm.

Arenilitic, a-rē'ni-lit"ik, *a.* [L. *arena*, sand, and Gr. *lithos*, a stone.] Of or pertaining to sandstone.

Areola, a-rē'ō-la, *n.* pl. **Areolæ**, a-rē'ō-lē. [L., dim. of *area* (which see).] A small area or space; a small interstice; the coloured circle or halo surrounding the nipple or surrounding a pustule.—**Areolar**, a-rē'ō-lėr, *a.* Pertaining to an areola.—**Areolate**, a-rē'ō-lāt, *a.* Marked by areolæ or small spots.—**Areolation**, a-rē'ō-lā"shon, *n.* Any small space or spot differing from the rest of a surface in colour, texture, &c.

Areometer, ar-ē-om'et-ėr, *n.* [Gr. *araios*, rare, thin, and *metron*, a measure.] An instrument for measuring the specific gravity of liquids; a hydrometer.—**Areometric**, **Areometrical**, a-rē'ō-met"rik, a-rē'ō-met"rik-al, *a.* Pertaining to an areometer.—**Areometry**, ar-ē-om'et-ri, *n.* The measuring of the specific gravity of fluids.

Areopagus, ar-ē-op'a-gus, *n.* [Gr., lit. hill of Ares or Mars.] A tribunal at ancient Athens, so called because held on a hill of this name.—**Areopagist**, **Areopagite**, ar-ē-op'a-jist, ar-ē-op'a-jīt, *n.* A member of the Areopagus.—**Areopagitic**, ar-ē-op'a-jit"ik, *a.* Pertaining to the Areopagus.

Aretalogy, **Aretology**, ar-e-tal'o-ji, ar-e-tol'o-ji, *n.* [Gr. *aretē*, virtue, and *logos*, discourse.] That part of ethics which treats of virtue.

Argal, **Argol**, är'gal, är'gol, *n.* Unrefined or crude tartar; a hard crust formed on the sides of vessels in which wine has been kept.

Argali, är'ga-li, *n.* [Mongolian name.] A species of wild Asiatic sheep with very large horns, nearly as bulky as a moderately sized ox.

Argand-lamp, är'gand-lamp, *n.* [From name of inventor.] A lamp with a circular hollow wick, allowing an outside and inside current of air, which greatly increases the brilliancy of the flame.—*Argand burner*, a gas-burner in a similar form.

Argent, är'jent, *n.* [Fr., from L. *argentum*, silver; cog. Gr. *argyros*, silver, *argos*, white; Ir. *arg*, white, *airgiod*, silver, money.] Silver†; whiteness, like that of silver; *her.* the white colour in coats of arms, intended to represent silver, &c.—*a.* Resembling silver; bright like silver; silvery.—**Argental**, **Argentic**, är-jent'al, är-jent'ik, *a.* Pertaining to, like, or containing silver.—**Argentation**, är-jen-tā'shon, *n.* An overlaying with silver.—**Argentiferous**, är-jen-tif'ėr-us, *a.* Producing or containing silver (*argentiferous* ore).—**Argentine**, är'jen-tīn, *a.* Pertaining to, resembling, or sounding like silver; silvery.—*n.* A silvery-white slaty variety of calc-spar; white metal coated with silver; the Argentine Republic, S. America.—**Argentite**, är'jen-tīt, *n.* Sulphide of silver, a valuable ore of this metal, a blackish, lead-gray mineral.

Argil, är'jil, *n.* [L. *argilla*, white clay, allied to *argentum*, silver. ARGENT.] Clay or potter's earth; sometimes, pure clay or alumina.—**Argillaceous**, är-jil-lā'shus, *a.* Partaking of the nature of argil or clay; clayey.—**Argilliferous**, är-jil-lif'ėr-us, *a.* Producing or containing clay or argil.—**Argillite**, är'jil-līt, *n.* Clay-slate.—**Argillitic**, är-jil-lit'ik, *a.* Pertaining to argillite.

Argive, är'jīv, *n.* A native or inhabitant of Argos, in ancient Greece; an ancient Greek. [Poetical.]

Argon, är'gon, *n.* [Gr. *argos*, inert.] A gas existing in the atmosphere in very small quantities; an inert chemical element.

Argonaut, är'gō-nąt, *n.* [Gr. *Argō*, and *nautēs*, a sailor.] One of the persons who, in the Greek legend, sailed with Jason, in the ship Argo, in quest of the golden fleece; a kind of cuttle-fish, the paper-nautilus or paper-sailor of the Mediterranean, the female having a boat-like shell, in which its eggs are received. It was fabled to float with its arms extended to catch the breeze, and with other arms as oars.—**Argonautic**, är-gō-ną'tik, *a.*

Argosy, är'go-si, *n.* [From *Ragusa*.] A large merchantman or other ship, especially if richly laden. [Poetical.]

Argot, är-gō, *n.* [Fr.] Slang.

Argue, är'gū, *v.i.*—*argued, arguing.* [L. *arguo*, to show, argue, to make clear.] To offer reasons to support or overthrow a proposition, opinion, or measure; to reason; to discuss; to debate; to dispute.—*v.t.* To debate or discuss (*argue* a cause in court); to prove, show, or evince; to cause to be inferred (his conduct *argued* suspicion).—**Arguable**, är'gū-a-bl, *a.* Capable of being argued.—**Arguer**, är'gū-ėr, *n.* One who.—**Argument**, är'gū-ment, *n.* [L. *argumentum*, proof, theme, subject-matter.] The subject of a discourse or writing; an abstract or summary of a book or section of a book; a reason offered for or against something; a debate, controversy, or discussion; a process of reasoning.—*Argumentum ad hominem*, an argument which presses a man with consequences drawn from his own principles and concessions, or his own conduct.—**Argumental**, är-gū-ment'al, *a.* Belonging to or consisting in argument.—**Argumentation**, är'gū-men-tā"shon, *n.* The act of arguing, discussing, or debating; reasoning.—**Argumentative**, är-gū-ment'a-tiv, *a.* Consisting of argument; addicted to argument, disputing, or debating.—**Argumentatively**, är-gū-ment'a-tiv-li, *adv.*—**Argumentativeness**, är-gū-ment'a-tiv-nes, *n.*

Argus, är'gus, *n.* A being in Greek mythology having a hundred watchful eyes; hence, any watchful person; a species of pheasant having its plumage marked with eye-like spots.—**Argus-eyed**, *a.* Vigilant; watchful; extremely observant.

Argute, är-gūt', *a.* [L. *argutus*.] Subtle; ingenious; sagacious; shrewd.—**Argutely**, är-gūt'li, *adv.* In an argute or subtle manner.—**Arguteness**, är-gūt'nes, *n.*

Argyria, **Argyrism**, är-jir'i-a, är'jir-izm, *n.* [Gr. *argyros*, silver.] Discoloration of the skin from the use of preparations of silver as medicine.

Aria, ä'ri-a, *n.* [It. *aria*.] A song; an air; a tune.—**Arietta**, ä-ri-et'ta. A short song or air.

Arian, ā'ri-an, *n.* One maintaining the doctrines of *Arius* (fourth century A.D.), who held Christ to be a created being inferior to God.—**Arian**, ā'ri-an, *a.* Pertaining to Arius or to his doctrines.—**Arianism**, ā'ri-an-izm, *n.* The doctrines of the Arians.

Arid, ar'id, *a.* [L. *aridus*.] Dry; exhausted of moisture; parched with heat.—**Aridity**, **Aridness**, a-rid'i-ti, ar'id-nes, *n.* The state of being arid; dryness; want of interest.

Aries, ā'ri-ēz, *n.* [L. *aries*, a ram.] The Ram, a northern constellation, the first of the twelve signs in the zodiac, which the sun enters at the vernal equinox.

Aright, a-rīt', *adv.* In a right way or form; properly; correctly; rightly.

Aril, ar'il, *n.* [L. *areo*, to be dry, because it falls off when dry.] An extra covering of the seed of some plants (as the nutmeg) outside of the true seed-coats, falling off spontaneously.—**Arillated**, **Arilled**, a-ril'lāt-ed, ar'ild, *a.* Furnished with an aril.

Arise, a-rīz', *v.i.*—*arose* (pret.), *arisen* (pp.), *arising.* [Prefix *a*, and *rise*; A.Sax. *árisan*. RISE.] To move to a higher place; to mount up; to ascend; to come into view; to get out of bed, or quit a sitting or lying posture; to spring; to originate; to start into action; to rise.

Arista, a-ris'ta, *n.* [L.] *Bot.* an awn or beard.—**Aristate**, a-ris'tāt, *a.* Awned.

Aristarch, ar'is-tärk, *n.* A severe critic, from the ancient critic Aristarchus.

Aristocracy, ar-is-tok'ra-si, *n.* [Gr. *aristokratia*—*aristos*, best, and *kratos*, rule.] Government by the nobility or persons of rank in the state; the nobility or chief persons in a state.—**Aristocrat**, a-ris'to-krat, *n.* A member of the aristocracy; one who favours an aristocracy; one who apes the aristocracy.—**Aristocratic**, **Aristocratical**, a-ris'to-krat"ik, a-ris'to-krat"ik-al, *a.* Pertaining or belonging to the aristocracy or to the rule of aristocrats; resembling the aristocracy.—**Aristocratically**, a-ris'to-krat"ik-al-li, *adv.*—**Aristocraticalness**, a-ris-to-krat"ik-al-nes, *n.*—**Aristocratism**, a-ris'to-krat-izm, *n.* The condition of belonging to an aristocracy; support of an aristocracy.

Aristotelian, a-ris'to-tē"li-an, *a.* Pertaining to *Aristotle* (born B.C. 384), the celebrated Greek philosopher, and founder of the Peripatetic school.—*n.* A follower of Aristotle; a peripatetic.—**Aristotelianism**, a-ris'to-tē"li-an-izm, *n.* The philosophy or doctrines of Aristotle.

Arithmetic, a-rith'met-ik, *n.* [Gr. *arithmētikē*, from *arithmos*, number.] The science of numbers or the art of computation by figures or numerals.—**Arithmetical**, ar-ith-met'ik-al, *a.* Pertaining to arithmetic; according to the rules or methods used in arithmetic.—*Arithmetical progression*, series of numbers showing increase or decrease by a constant quantity, as 1, 2, 3, 4, &c.—9, 7, 5, 3; opposed to *geometrical progression*, *q.v.* —**Arithmetically**, ar-ith-met′ik-al-li, *adv.* By the rules or methods of arithmetic. —**Arithmetician**, a-rith′me-ti″shan, *n.* One skilled in arithmetic.

Ark, ärk, *n.* [A.Sax. *arc*, from L. *arca*, a chest.] A small chest or coffer‡; *Scrip.* the repository of the covenant or tables of the law, over which was placed the golden covering or mercy-seat; the large floating vessel in which Noah and his family were preserved during the deluge; hence, a place of safety or shelter.

Arkose, är′kōs, *n.* A sandstone formed from the disintegration of granite.

Arm, ärm, *n.* [A.Sax. *arm*, *earm* = Goth. *arms*, Icel. *armr*, G. Fris. D. Dan. and Sw. *arm*; cog. L. *armus*, the shoulder; Gr. *armos*, a fitting, from *arō*, to fit.] The limb of the human body which extends from the shoulder to the hand; an anterior limb; anything projecting from a main body, as a branch of a tree, a narrow inlet of waters from the sea; *fig.* power, might, strength.—**Armful**, ärm′ful, *n.* As much as the arms can hold; that which is embraced by the arms.—**Armless**, ärm′les, *a.* Without arms.—**Armlet**, ärm′let, *n.* A little arm; a piece of armour for defending the arm; an ornament worn on the arm; a bracelet.—**Arm-chair**, *n.* A chair with arms to support the elbows.—**Arm-hole**, *n.* The arm-pit‡; a hole for the arm in a garment.—**Arm-pit**, *n.* The cavity under the shoulder or upper arm.

Arm, ärm, *n.* [Fr. *arme*, a weapon, from L. *arma*, arms.] A weapon; a branch of the military service; *pl.* war; the military profession; armour; armorial bearings.—*Small arms*, arms that can be carried by those who use them.—*A stand of arms*, a complete set of arms for one soldier.—*v.t.* To furnish or equip with arms or weapons; to cover or provide with whatever will add strength, force, or security; to fortify.—*v.i.* To provide one's self with arms; to take arms. —**Armada**, är-mā′da, *n.* [Sp.] A fleet of armed ships; a squadron: usually applied to the Spanish fleet intended to act against England in the reign of Queen Elizabeth, A.D. 1588.—**Armadillo**, är-ma-dil′lō, *n.* [Sp. dim. of *armado*, one who is armed, so called from its bony shell.] A mammal peculiar to South America, covered with a hard bony shell, divided into belts, composed of small separate plates like a coat of mail. —**Armament**, är′ma-ment, *n.* A body of forces equipped for war; a land force or a naval force.—**Armature**, är′ma-tūr, *n.* Armour; hence, anything serving as a defence, as the prickles and spines of plants; a piece of iron connecting the two poles of a magnet.

Armageddon, ar′ma-ged″on, *n.* [Possibly from Plain of Megiddo.] The scene of the final conflict of nations. *Rev.* xvi. 16.

Armenian, är-mē′ni-an, *a.* Pertaining to Armenia, a country in Asia.—*n.* A native of Armenia; the language of the country; an adherent of the Christian Church of Armenia.

Armilla, är-mil′la, *n.* [L., from *armus*, the shoulder.] An armlet; a bracelet; an iron ring, hoop, or brace, in which the gudgeons of a wheel move; a circular ligament of the wrist binding the tendons of the whole hand. —**Armillary**, är′mil-la-ri, *a.* Resembling an armilla; consisting of rings or circles.—*Armillary sphere*, an arrangement of rings, all circles of one sphere, intended to show the relative positions of the principal circles of the heavens.

Arminian, är-min′i-an, *n.* A member of the Protestant sect who follows the teaching of *Arminius*, a Dutch theologian (died 1609), specially opposed to the Calvinistic doctrine of predestination.—*a.* Pertaining to Arminius or his principles.—**Arminianism**, är-min′i-an-izm, *n.* The peculiar doctrines or tenets of the Arminians.

Armipotent, är-mip′ō-tent, *a.* [L. *armipotens*, *armipotentis*—*arma*, arms, and *potens*, powerful.] Powerful in arms; mighty in battle.—**Armipotence**, är-mip′ō-tens, *n.* Power in arms.

Armistice, är′mis-tis, *n.* [L. *arma*, arms, *sisto*, to stand still.] A temporary suspension of hostilities by agreement of the parties; a truce.

Armoric, **Armorican**, är-mor′ik, är-mor′ik-an, *a.* [Celt. *ar*, upon, and *mor*, the sea.] Pertaining to the north-western part of France, formerly called *Armorica*, now Brittany. — *n.* The language of the Celtic inhabitants of Brittany, allied to the Welsh.

Armor, **Armour**, är′mėr, *n.* [O.E. *armure*, O.Fr. *armeure*, from L. *armatura*, armor, from *armare*, to arm.] Defensive arms; any covering worn to protect the body in battle: also called *Harness*; the steel or iron covering intended as a protection for a ship of war.—**Armorial**, är-mō′ri-al, *a.* Belonging to armor, or to the arms or escutcheon of a family.—**Armorer**, är′mėr-ėr, *n.* A maker of armor or arms, or one who keeps them in repair; one who has the care of arms and armor.—**Armory**, **Armoury**, är′mėr-i, *n.* A place where arms and instruments of war are made or deposited for safe-keeping; a collection of arms.— **Armor-bearer**, *n.* One who carries the armor of another.—**Armor-plate**, *n.* An iron or steel plate of great thickness attached to the side of a ship, or the outer wall of a fort, with the view of rendering them shot-proof.—**Armor-plated**, **Armored**, är′mėrd, *a.* Covered or protected by armor-plates; iron-clad.

Armstrong-gun, ärm′strong-gun, *n.* [After the inventor, Sir William *Armstrong*.] A rifled cannon of wrought-iron, constructed principally of spirally coiled bars, and occasionally having an inner tube, or core of steel.

Army, är′mi, *n.* [Fr. *armée*, an armed force or army, from *armer*, to arm. ARM, a weapon.] A collection or body of men armed for war, and organized in regiments, brigades, or similar divisions, under proper officers; a host; a vast multitude; a great number.—**Army corps**, *n.* Section of army, complete in itself, embracing infantry, cavalry, artillery.—**Army List and Directory**, *n.* A periodical of the War Department in which are stated the location of units, and officer's stations and promotions; also the relative rank of officers in various branches of the U. S. Army.— **Army War College**, *n.* An advanced school of military science and tactics located in Washington, D. C., and open to senior officers of the U. S. Army. It is under the supervision of the Secretary of War.—**Army-worm**, *n.* The larva of a moth, so called from its marching in compact and enormous bodies, devouring green things; destructive particularly in N. America.

Arnica, är′ni-ka, *n.* A composite plant, otherwise called mountain-tobacco. The roots yield tannin, and a tincture of the plant is used as an application to wounds and bruises.

Arnotto, **Annotto**, är-not′tō, än-not′tō, *n.* A small tropical American tree, the seeds of which yield an orange-red dye-stuff, also called arnotto. Called also *Annotta*, *Annatto*, *Arnatto*.

Arnut, är′nut, *n.* [A corruption of *earth nut*.] The nut or tuber of the earth-nut plant. EARTH-NUT.

Aroint, *v.t.* AROYNT.

Aroma, a-rō′ma, *n.* [Gr. *arōma*, spice, sweet herb.] An agreeable odour; fragrance; perfume; *fig.* delicate intellectual quality; flavour. — **Aromatic**, ar-ō-mat′ik, *a.* Giving out an aroma; fragrant; sweet-scented; odoriferous. Also **Aromatical**, ar-ō-mat′ik-al. — *Aromatic vinegar*, a perfume made by adding oil of lavender, cloves, &c., to acetic acid.—**Aromatic**, ar-ō-mat′-ik, *n.* A plant or drug which yields a fragrant smell, and often a warm, pungent taste. — **Aromatization**, a-rō′mat-i-zā″-shon, *n.* The act of rendering aromatic.— **Aromatize**, a-rō′mat-īz, *v.t.*—*aromatized*, *aromatizing*. To impregnate with aroma; to render fragrant; to perfume.—**Aromatizer**, a-rō′mat-īz-ėr, *n.* One who or that which.

Arose, a-rōz′, pret. of *arise*.

Around, a-round′, *prep.* About; on all sides; encircling; encompassing.—*adv.* In a circle; on every side.

Arouse, a-rouz′, *v.t.*—*aroused*, *arousing*. [Prefix *a*, with intens. force, and *rouse*.] To excite into action that which is at rest; to stir or put in motion or exertion; to rouse; to animate; to awaken.—**Arousal**, a-rouz′al, *n.* The act of arousing.

Arow, a-rō′, *adv.* In a row; successively; one after the other.

Aroynt, **Aroint**, a-roint′, *interj.* [From imperat. of A.Sax. *rýman*, *gerýman*, to make room, to give place, from *rûm*, room.] An interjection equivalent to begone! avaunt! away! (*Shak.*)

Arpeggio, är-ped′jē-ō, *n.* [It., from *arpa*, a harp.] The distinct sound of the notes of a chord, heard when the notes are struck in rapid succession.

Arquebuse, **Arquebus**, är′kwē-bus, *n.* [Fr. *arquebuse*, corrupted from D. *haakbus*, a gun fired from a rest, from *haak*, a hook, a forked rest, and *bus*, a gun = E. *hagbut*, *hackbut*.] An old-fashioned hand-gun fired from a rest. Spelled also *Harquebuse*, &c. —**Arquebusier**, är′kwē-bus-ēr″, *n.* A soldier armed with an arquebuse.—**Arquebusade**, är′kwē-bus-ād″, *n.* An aromatic spirituous liquor applied to sprains or bruises.

Arquerite, är′ke-rīt, *n.* A rich silver ore found in the silver mines of *Arqueros*, near Coquimbo, Chili.

Arrack, ar′ak, *n.* [Ar. *araq*, juice, spirits, from *araqa*, to sweat.] A spirituous liquor distilled in the East Indies from rice, the juice of the cocoa-nut, and other palms, &c.

Arraign, a-rān′, *v.t.* [O.Fr. *arraigner*, *aresner*, &c., to arraign—L. *ad*, to, and *ratio*, *rationis*, account, a pleading in a suit. REASON.] To call or set at the bar of a court of justice; to call before the bar of reason or taste; to accuse or charge; to censure publicly; to impeach.—**Arraigner**, a-rān′ėr, *n.* One who arraigns.—**Arraignment**, a-rān′ment, *n.* The act of arraigning.

Arrange, a-rānj′, *v.t.*—*arranged*, *arranging*. [Fr. *arranger*—*ar* = L. *ad*, and *ranger*, to range, from *rang*, a rank. RANGE, RANK.] To put in proper order; to dispose or set out; to give a certain collocation to; to adjust; to settle; to come to an agreement or understanding regarding.—*v.i.* To make or come to terms; to come to a settlement or agreement.—**Arrangement**, a-rānj′-ment, *n.* The act of arranging; disposition in suitable form; that which is arranged; preparatory measure; preparation; settlement; adjustment.—**Arranger**, a-rānj′ėr, *n.* One that arranges or puts in order.

Arrant, ar′ant, *a.* [A form of *errant*, wandering, hence vagrant, vagabond, thorough, in a bad sense.] Wandering‡; vagrant‡; shameless; notorious; thorough; out-and-out; downright.—**Arrantly**, ar′ant-li, *adv.* In an arrant manner.

Arras, ar′as, *n.* [From *Arras*, in France, where this article was manufactured.] Tapestry; hangings, consisting of woven stuffs ornamented with figures.

Array, a-rā′, *n.* [O.Fr. *arrai*, order, arrangement, dress—prefix *ar-* (L. *ad*, to), and *rai*, order, from the Teutonic root seen in E. *ready*.] A collection or assemblage of men or things disposed in regular order, as an army in order of battle; raiment; dress; apparel.—*v.t.* To place or dispose in order, as troops for battle; to marshal; to deck or dress; to attire.—**Arrayer**, a-rā′ėr, *n.* One who.—**Arrayment**, a-rā′ment, *n.* The act of.

Arrear, a-rēr′, *n.* [Fr. *arrière*, behind—L. *ad*, to, and *retro*, behind.] The state of being behindhand; that which remains unpaid or undone when the due time is past: usually in the plural.

Arrect, a-rekt′, *v.t.* [L. *arrigo*, *arrectum*, to raise or erect—*ad*, to, *rego*, to direct.] To raise or lift up; to prick up (the ears).—*a.* Erect; pricked up: said of the ears; hence, attentively listening.

Arrest, a-rest′, *v.t.* [O.Fr. *arrester*, Fr. *arrêter*—L. *ad*, to, and *restare*, to remain. REST.] To check or hinder the motion or action of; to stop; to seize or apprehend by virtue of a warrant from authority; to seize and fix (attention); to engage; to secure; to catch.—*n.* The act of arresting; apprehension; stoppage; stay; restraint.—**Arrestation**,† a-rest-ā′shon, *n.* The act of arresting.—**Arrester**, **Arrestor**, a-rest′ėr, a-rest′or, *n.* One who arrests.—**Arrestment**, a-rest′ment, *n.* The act of arresting; detention; arrest.

Arride, a-rīd′, *v.t.* [L. *arrideo*—*ad*, and *rideo*, to smile.] To please or gratify. (*C. Lamb.*)

Arris, ar′is, *n.* [O.Fr. *areste*, an arris.] The line in which two meeting surfaces of a body form an angle.

Arrive, a-rīv′, *v.i.*—*arrived*, *arriving*. [Fr. *arriver*, from L.L. *adripare*, to come to shore—L. *ad*, to, and *ripa*, Fr. *rive*, the shore or bank.] To come to a certain place or point; to get to a destination; to reach a point or stage; to attain to a certain result or state: followed by *at*.—*v.t.*† To reach or arrive at. (*Mil.*)—**Arrival**, a-rī′val, *n.* The act of arriving; a coming to or reaching; attainment; the person or thing which arrives.

Arrogance, a′rō-gans, *n.* [L. *arrogantia*, *arrogo*, *arrogatum*—*ad*, to, and *rogo*, to ask or desire.] The character of being arrogant; the disposition to make exorbitant claims of rank, dignity, or estimation; the pride which exalts one's own importance; pride with contempt of others; presumption; haughtiness; disdain.—**Arrogant**, a′rō-gant, *a.* Making exorbitant claims on account of one's rank, power, worth; presumptuous; haughty; overbearing; proud and assuming.—**Arrogantly**, a′rō-gant-li, *adv.* In an arrogant manner.—**Arrogate**, a′rō-gāt, *v.t.*—*arrogated*, *arrogating*. To claim or demand unduly or presumptuously; to lay claim to in an overbearing manner.—**Arrogation**, a-rō-gā′shon, *n.* The act of arrogating; the claiming of superior consideration or privileges.

Arrondissement, ä-roṅ-dēs-mäṅ, *n.* [Fr.] In France, an administrative district forming a subdivision of a department.

Arrow, a′rō, *n.* [A.Sax. *arewe*, *aruwe*, *arwe*; allied to A.Sax. *earu*, swift, Icel. *ör*, pl. *örvar*, an arrow, *örr*, swift.] A missile weapon, straight, slender, pointed, and barbed, to be shot with a bow; anything resembling this.—**Arrowy**, a′rō-i, *a.* Resembling an arrow in shape, in rapidity of flight, or the like.—**Arrow-headed**, *a.* Shaped like the head of an arrow: said of alphabetic characters used in ancient Assyria; cuneiform.—**Arrow-root**, *n.* A flour or starch obtained from the rootstocks of several West Indian reed-like plants, and much used as an article of food.

Arsenal, är′se-nal, *n.* [Fr. *arsenal*, Sp. *arsenal*, from an Ar. word.] A repository or magazine of arms and military stores for land or naval service; a public establishment where arms or warlike equipments are manufactured or stored.

Arsenic, är′sen-ik, *n.* [From Ar. *az-zernikh*, the orpiment (q.v.).] A chemical element of a steel-blue colour, quite brittle. Combined with oxygen it forms arsenious oxide, which is the *white arsenic*, or simply *arsenic*, of the shops, a well-known virulent poison.—**Arsenical**, är-sen′ik-al, *a.* Of or pertaining to arsenic; containing arsenic.—**Arsenicate**, är-sen′ik-āt, *v.t.* To combine with arsenic.—**Arsenious**, är-sē′ni-us, *a.* Pertaining to or containing arsenic.

Arsis, är′sis, *n.* [Gr. *arsis*, from *airō*, to elevate.] Elevation of the voice at a word or syllable, in distinction from *thesis*, or its depression; *pros.* a greater stress or force on a syllable.

Arson, är′son, *n.* [O.Fr. *arson*, from L. *ardeo*, *arsum*, to burn.] The malicious burning of a house, shop, church, or other building, agricultural produce, ship, &c., which by the common law is felony.

Art, ärt. Second pers. sing. ARE.

Art, ärt, *n.* [L. *ars*, *artis*, art, from same root as Gr. *arō*, to join, to fit. ARM.] The use or employment of things to answer some special purpose; the employment of means to accomplish some end: opposed to *nature*; a system of rules to facilitate the performance of certain actions; skill in applying such rules (the *art* of building or of engraving; the fine *arts*): opposed to *science*; one of the fine arts or the fine arts collectively, that is those that appeal to the taste or sense of beauty, as painting, sculpture, music; the profession of a painter or sculptor; the special skill required by those who practise these arts; artistic faculty; skill; dexterity; knack; artfulness; cunning; duplicity.—*Art union*, an association for encouraging art, an object which it mainly pursues by disposing of pictures, sculptures, &c., by lottery among subscribers.—**Artful**, ärt′fųl, *a.* Cunning; sly; deceitful; crafty.—**Artfully**, ärt′fųl-li, *adv.* In an artful manner; cunningly; craftily.—**Artfulness**, ärt′fųl-nes, *n.* The quality of being artful.—**Artless**, ärt′les, *a.* Devoid of art, skill, or cunning; natural; simple.—**Artlessly**, ärt′les-li, *adv.* In an artless manner; naturally; simply.—**Artlessness**, ärt′les-nes, *n.* Naturalness; simplicity; ingenuousness.

Artery, är′tėr-i, *n.* [L. *arteria*, Gr. *artēria*.] One of a system of cylindrical vessels or tubes, which convey the blood from the heart to all parts of the body, to be brought back again by the veins.—**Arterial**, är-tē′ri-al, *a.* Pertaining to or contained in an artery or the arteries.—**Arterialization**, är-tē′ri-al-iz-ā″shon, *n.* The conversion of the venous into the arterial blood.—**Arterialize**, är-tē′ri-al-īz, *v.t.*—*arterialized*, *arterializing*. To communicate, as to venous blood, the qualities of arterial blood, a result effected by the oxygen of the air taken into the lungs.—**Arteriotomy**, är-tē′ri-ot″o-mi, *n.* [-*tomy*=Gr. *tomē*, a cutting.] *Anat.* the opening of an artery by the lancet or other instrument, for the purpose of letting blood.

Artesian, är-tē′zi-an, *a.* [Fr. *artésien*, lit. pertaining to *Artois*.] Term descriptive of a kind of well formed by a perpendicular boring into the ground, often of great depth, through which water rises to the surface of the soil by natural gravitation, producing a constant flow or stream.

Artful, &c. Under ART.

Arthritis, är-thrī′tis, *n.* [Gr., from *arthron*, a joint.] Any inflammation of the joints; the gout.—**Arthritic**, **Arthritical**, är-thrit′ik, är-thrit′ik-al, *a.* Pertaining to or affecting the joints; pertaining to the gout.—**Arthrodia**, är-thrō′di-a, *n.* A ball-and-socket joint.—**Arthrodial**, **Arthrodic**, är-thrō′di-al, är-throd′ik, *a.* Pertaining to an arthrodia.

Artichoke, är′ti-chōk, *n.* [It. *articiocco*, probably of Ar. origin.] A composite plant somewhat resembling a thistle, cultivated in gardens for the thick and fleshy receptacle (or part supporting the flower), which is eaten. The *Jerusalem artichoke* is quite different, being a species of sunflower whose roots are used like potatoes. See GIRASOLE.

Article, är′ti-kl, *n.* [L. *articulus*, a joint, division, part, or member, dim. of *artus*, a joint.] A single clause, item, point, or particular; a point of faith, doctrine, or duty; a prose contribution to a newspaper, magazine, or other periodical; a particular commodity or substance; a part of speech used before nouns to limit or define their application—in English *a* or *an* and *the*.—*Articles of war*, the regulations for the government and discipline of the British army and navy, embodied in the Mutiny Act passed each year.—*v.t.*—*articled*, *articling*. To draw up under distinct heads or particulars; to bind, as an apprentice; to indenture.—**Articular**, är-tik′ū-lėr, *a.* [L. *articularis*.] Belonging to the joints or to a joint.—**Articularly**, är-tik′ū-lėr-li, *adv.*—**Articulata**, är-tik′ū-lā″ta, *n.pl.* According to the arrangement of Cuvier, all the invertebrate animals with an external skeleton forming a series of rings articulated together and enveloping the body, such as the crustaceans, insects, worms, &c.—**Articulate**, är-tik′ū-lāt, *a.* [L. *articulatus*, jointed, distinct.] Jointed; formed with joints (an *articulate* animal); formed by the distinct and intelligent movement of the organs of speech; pronounced distinctly; expressed clearly; distinct (*articulate* speech or utterance).—*n.* One of the Articulata.—*v.t.* *articulated*, *articulating*. To joint; to unite by means of a joint; to utter by intelligent and appropriate movement of the vocal organs; to enunciate, pronounce, or speak; to draw up or write in separate particulars or in articles (*Shak.*)‡.—*v.i.* To utter articulate sounds; to utter distinct syllables or words; to treat or stipulate (*Shak.*)‡.—**Articulately**, är-tik′ū-lāt-li, *adv.* In an articulate manner; with distinct utterance.—**Articulateness**, är-tik′ū-lāt-nes, *n.* The quality of being articulate.—**Articulation**, är-tik′ū-lā″shon, *n.* The act or manner of articulating or being articulated; a joining or juncture, as of the bones; a joint; a part between two joints.—**Articulator**, är-tik′ū-lāt-ėr, *n.* One who articulates.

Artifice, är′ti-fis, *n.* [L. *artificium*—*ars*, *artis*, art, and *facio*, to make.] Artful, skilful, or ingenious contrivance; a crafty device; trick; shift; stratagem; deception; cunning; guile; fraud.—**Artificer**, är-tif′-is-ėr, *n.* A skilful or artistic worker; a constructor; a maker; a contriver; an inventor; a mechanic or handicraftsman.—**Artificial**, är-ti-fish′al, *a.* Made or contrived by art, or by human skill and labour; feigned; fictitious; assumed; affected; not genuine or natural.—**Artificiality**, är-ti-fish′al′i-ti, *n.* The quality of being artificial.—**Artificialize**,† är-ti-fish′al-īz, *v.t.* To render artificial.—**Artificially**, är-ti-fish′al-li, *adv.* In an artificial manner; by human skill and contrivance.—**Artificialness**, är-ti-fish′al-nes, *n.* Artificiality.

Artillery, är-til′lėr-i, *n.* (No pl.) [Fr. *artillerie*, from *artiller*, to work with art, to fortify, from L. *ars*, *artis*, art.] Formerly offensive weapons of war in general whether large or small (see 1 *Sa.* xx. 40); now, cannon; great guns; ordnance; ordnance and its equipment both in men and material; the men and officers that manage the guns; the science which treats of the use and management of great guns.—**Artillerist**, är-til′lėr-ist, *n.* A person skilled in gunnery.—**Artillery-man**, *n.* A man engaged in the management of large guns.

Artiodactyle, är′ti-ō-dak″til, *n.* [Gr. *artios*, even-numbered, and *daktylos*, a toe.] A hoofed mammal in which the number of toes is even (two or four), as the ox and other ruminants, the pig, &c.

Artisan, är′ti-zan, *n.* [Fr. *artisan*, It. *artigiano*, L.L. *artitianus*, from L. *ars*, *artis*, art.] One skilled in any art or trade; a handicraftsman; a mechanic.

Artist, ärt′ist, *n.* [Fr. *artiste*, It. *artista*, from L. *ars*, *artis*, art.] One skilled in an art or profession, especially, one who professes and practises one of the fine arts, as painting, sculpture, engraving, and architecture; specifically, and most frequently, a painter.—**Artiste**, är-tēst, *n.* [Fr.] One who is peculiarly skilful in almost any art, as a public singer, an opera-dancer, and even a cook.—**Artistic**, **Artistical**, är-tist′ik, är-tist′ik-al, *a.* Pertaining to art or artists; trained in art; conformable to or characterized by art.—**Artistically**, är-tist′ik-al-li, *adv.* In an artistic manner.

Artless, &c. Under ART.

Arum, ā′rum, *n.* [L. *arum*, Gr. *aron*.] The generic name of certain plants, one of which, the common arum, wake-robin, or lords-and-ladies, is abundant in woods and hedges in England and Ireland.

Arundinaceous, a-run′di-nā″shus, *a.* [L. *arundo*, a reed.] Pertaining to reeds; resembling a reed.—**Arundineous**, **Arundinose**, ar-un-din′ē-us, a-run′din-ōs, *a.* Abounding with reeds.

Aruspex, Aruspice, a-rus'peks, a-rus'-pis, *n.* [L. *aruspex* or *haruspex.*] One of a class of priests in ancient Rome whose business was to inspect the entrails of victims killed in sacrifice, and by them to foretell future events.—**Aruspicy**, a-rus'pi-si, *n.* The art of an aruspex; augury; prognostication.

Aryan, är'i-an or ā'ri-an, *n.* [Skr. *ârya*, noble, eminent.] An Indo-European; a member of that division of the human race which includes the Hindus and Persians and most Europeans (except Turks, Hungarians, Finns, &c.).—*a.* Pertaining or belonging to the Aryans; Indo-European.

As, az, *adv.* and *conj.* [Contr. from A.Sax. *eallswâ*, that is, *all so*, through the forms *alswa, also, alse, als, ase*; similarly G. *als, also*, as.] A word expressing equality, similarity of manner or character, likeness, proportion, accordance; in the same manner in which (ye shall be *as* gods; I live *as* I did); while; when (he whistled *as* he went); for example; for instance; thus; because; since (*as* the wind was fair we set sail); often equivalent to the relative *that* after *such* (give us *such* things *as* you please).

As, as, *n.* pl. **Asses**, as'ez. A Roman weight of 12 oz.; also, a Roman copper or bronze coin, latterly weighing ½ oz.

Asafetida, Asafœtida, as-a-fē'tid-a, *n.* [Per. *aza*, gum, and L. *fœtidus*, fetid.] A fetid inspissated sap from a large umbelliferous plant found in Central Asia, used in medicine as an antispasmodic, in flatulency, hysteric paroxysms, &c.

Asbestos, Asbestus, as-bes'tos, as-bes'-tus, *n.* [Gr. *asbestos*, inextinguishable—*a*, neg., and *sbennymi*, to extinguish.] A fibrous variety of several members of the hornblende family, having fine, elastic, flexible, flaxy-like filaments, which are incombustible, and are made into fire-proof cloth, paper, &c.—**Asbestic**, as-bes'tik, *a.* Relating to or containing asbestos.—**Asbestiform**, as-bes'ti-form, *a.* Having the structure of asbestos.—**Asbestine**, as-bes'-tin, *a.* Pertaining to asbestos, or partaking of its nature and qualities.

Ascend, as-send', *v.i.* [L. *ascendo*—*ad*, to, and *scando*, to climb. SCAN.] To move upwards; to mount; to go up from a lower to a higher place; to rise; to proceed from an inferior to a superior degree, from mean to noble objects, from particulars to generals, &c.; to pass from a grave tone to one more acute.—*v.t.* To go or move upwards upon; to climb; to move upwards along; to go towards the source of (a river).—**Ascendable, Ascendible**, as-send'a-bl, as-send'-i-bl, *a.* Capable of being ascended.—**Ascendant**, as-send'ant, *n.* An ancestor, or one who precedes in genealogy or degrees of kindred; superiority or commanding influence; predominance.—**Ascendant, Ascendent**, as-send'ant, as-send'ent, *a.* Directed upward; rising; superior; predominant; surpassing.—**Ascendency**, as-send'en-si, *n.* Governing or controlling influence; power; sway; control.—**Ascension**, as-sen'shon, *n.* [L. *ascensio.*] The act of ascending; a rising; *the ascension*, the visible elevation of our Saviour to heaven.—*Ascension Day*, the day on which the ascension of the Saviour is commemorated, falling on the Thursday but one before Whitsuntide.—*Right ascension* of the sun or of a star, the arc of the equator intercepted between the first point of Aries and that point of the equator which comes to the meridian at the same instant with the star.—**Ascensional**, as-sen'shon-al, *a.* Relating to ascension; ascending or rising up.—**Ascent**, as-sent', *n.* The act of rising; motion upwards; rise; the way by which one ascends; acclivity; an upward slope; the act of proceeding from an inferior to a superior degree, from particulars to generals, &c.

Ascertain, as-sėr-tān', *v.t.* [O.Fr. *acertainer*—*as* for *ad*, to, *certain*, from L. *certus*, sure. CERTAIN.] To make certain; to make sure or find out by trial or examination; to establish; to determine with certainty.—**Ascertainable**, as-sėr-tān'a-bl, *a.* Capable of being ascertained.—**Ascertainer**, as-sėr-tān'ėr, *n.* One who ascertains.—**Ascertainment**, as-sėr-tān'ment, *n.* The act of ascertaining.

Ascetic, as-set'ik, *a.* [Gr. *askētos*, exercised, disciplined, from *askeō*, to exercise.] Excessively strict or rigid in devotions or mortifications; severe; austere.—**Ascetic**, as-set'ik, *n.* One who retires from the world and devotes himself to a strictly devout life; one who practises excessive rigour and self-denial; a hermit; a recluse.—**Asceticism**, as-set'i-sizm, *n.* The condition or practice of ascetics.

Ascian, as'si-an, *n.* [L. *ascius*, Gr. *askios*—*a*, priv., and *skia*, a shadow.] One who has no shadow; an inhabitant of the torrid zone when the sun is in the zenith.

Ascidian, as-sid'i-an, *n.* [Gr. *askidion*, a little bottle.] One of certain marine molluscous animals of a low type, having frequently the shape of a double-necked bottle, often found on the beach at low water or attached to rocks, shells, &c.; a sea-squirt; a tunicate animal.—**Ascidiform**, as-sid'-i-form, *a.* Shaped like an ascidian; bottle-shaped.—**Ascidium**, as-sid'i-um, *n.* *Bot.* a pitcher-like appendage found in some plants and formed by a modified leaf.

Ascites, as-sī'tēz, *n.* [Gr. *askos*, a bladder.] *Med.* dropsy of the abdomen, or of the peritoneal cavity.—**Ascitic, Ascitical**, as-sit'ik, as-sit'ik-al, *a.* Relating to ascites; dropsical.

Ascititious, as-si-tish'us, *a.* Same as *Adscititious.*

Asclepiadic, as-klē'pi-ad"ik, *a.* [From *Asclēpiadēs*, a Greek poet, who invented this metre.] *Pros.* consisting of four feet, a spondee, two choriambi, and an iambus.

Ascribe, as-krīb', *v.t.*—*ascribed, ascribing.* [L. *ascribo*—*ad*, to, and *scribo*, to write. SCRIBE.] To attribute, impute, or refer, as to a cause; to assign; to set down; to attribute, as a quality or appurtenance.—**Ascribable**, as-krīb'a-bl, *a.* Capable of being ascribed or attributed.—**Ascription**, as-krip'shon, *n.* The act of ascribing.—**Ascriptitious**, as-krip-tish'us, *a.* [L. *ascriptitius*, enrolled as a soldier, bound.] Bound or attached to the soil: applied to serfs or villeins annexed to the freehold and transferable with it.

Ascus, as'kus, *n.* pl. **Asci**, as'kī. [Gr. *askos*, a leather bottle.] *Bot.* one of the little membranous bags or cells in which the spores of lichens, some fungi, and some other cryptogams are produced.

Asexual, a-seks'ū-al, *a.* [Prefix *a*, neg., *sexual.*] Not sexual; having no distinctive organs of sex, or imperfect organs; performed without the union of males and females.—**Asexually**, a-seks'ū-al-li, *adv.* In an asexual manner.

Ash, ash, *n.* [A.Sax. *æsc* = Icel. *askr*, Sw. and Dan. *ask*, D. *esch*, G. *esche.*] A well-known tree cultivated extensively for its hard and tough timber; the timber of this tree.—**Ash, Ashen**, ash, ash'en, *a.* Pertaining to or like the ash; made of ash.

Ash, ash, *n.* [A.Sax. *æsce*, *asce*—a word common to the Teutonic tongues.] What remains of a body that is burnt; the dust or powdery substance to which a body is reduced by the action of fire: generally used in the plural; incombustible residue; the remains of a human body when burnt or otherwise decayed; *fig.* a corpse.—*Ash Wednesday*, the first day of Lent, so called from the ancient custom of sprinkling ashes on the heads of penitents on that day.—**Ashery**, ash'ėr-i, *n.* A pit or hole for ashes.—**Ashy**, ash'i, *a.* Composed of or resembling ashes; lifeless and pale.—**Ashy-pale**, *a.* Pale or white as ashes.—**Ash-pit**, *n.* Pit for ashes.

Ashame, a-shām', *v.t.*—*ashamed, ashaming.* [Prefix *a*, intens., for *of*, and *shame.*] To make ashamed; to shame.—**Ashamed**, a-shāmd', *p.* and *a.* Affected or touched by shame; feeling shame; exhibiting shame (an *ashamed* look): with *of* before the object.—**Ashamedly**, a-shām'ed-li, *adv.* In a shamefaced manner.

Ashlar, Ashler, ash'lėr, *n.* [O.Fr. *aisselle, aissil*, a shingle, from L. *assula*, a small board, a chip or splinter.] Common freestones rough from the quarry; a facing made of squared stones on the front of buildings; hewn stone for such facing.

Ashore, a-shōr', *adv* On the shore, bank, or beach; on the land adjacent to water; to the shore.

Asian, ā'shi-an, *a.* Pertaining to Asia, one of the continents of the globe.—**Asiatic**, ā-shi-at'ik, *a.* Belonging to Asia or its inhabitants.—*n.* A native of Asia.

Aside, a-sīd', *adv.* On or to one side; to or at a short distance off; apart; away from some normal direction; out of one's thoughts, consideration, or regard; away; off (to lay cares *aside*); so as not to be heard, or supposed not to be heard, by some one present.—**Aside**, a-sīd', *n.* Something spoken and not heard, or supposed not to be heard, by some one present, as something uttered by an actor on the stage.

Asinine. Under Ass.

Ask, ask, *v.t.* [A.Sax. *ascian, acsian, axian*, = Dan. *æske*, D. *eischen*, O.Fris. *askia*, O.G. *eiscôn.*] To request; to seek to obtain by words; to petition (with *of* before the person); to require, expect or claim; to demand; to interrogate or inquire of; to question; to inquire concerning; to seek to be informed about (to *ask* the way); to invite. [This verb may take two objectives; as, to *ask* a person the time.]—*v.i.* To make a request or petition (with *for* before an object); to inquire or seek by request (often followed by *after*).—**Asker**, ask'ėr, *n.* One who asks; a questioner, inquirer, petitioner.

Askance, a-skans', *adv.* [Etymology doubtful; perhaps It. *scansare*, to slip aside.] Sideways; obliquely; out of one corner of the eye.—**Askant**, a-skant', *adv.* A less common form of *Askance.*

Askew, a-skū', *adv.* In an oblique or skew position; obliquely; awry.

Aslant, a-slant', *a.* or *adv.* Slantwise; on one side; obliquely; not perpendicularly or at right angles.

Asleep, a-slēp', *a.* or *adv.* In or into a state of sleep; at rest.

Aslope, a-slōp', *a.* or *adv.* Sloping; deflected from the perpendicular.

Asp, Aspic, asp, as'pik, *n.* [L. and Gr. *aspis*, an asp.] A deadly species of viper found in Egypt; also, a species of viper found on the continent of Europe.

Asparagus, as-par'a-gus, *n.* [Gr. *asparagos.*] A perennial herb of the lily family cultivated in gardens, the young shoots being used at table.

Aspect, as'pekt, *n.* [L. *aspectus*, from *aspicio*, to look on—*ad*, to, and *specio*, to see or look.] Look; view; appearance to the eye or the mind (to present a subject in its true *aspect*); countenance; look or particular appearance of the face; mien; air (a severe *aspect*); view commanded; prospect; outlook (a house with a southern *aspect*); *astrol.* the situation of one planet with respect to another.

Aspen, asp'en, *n.* [A.Sax. *aspen, æspe*, the aspen; D. *esp*, Icel. *ösp*, Sw. and Dan. *asp*, G. *espe*, the aspen-tree.] A species of poplar that has become proverbial for the trembling of its leaves, which move with the slightest impulse of the air.

Asperate,† as'pėr-āt, *v.t.*—*asperated, asperating.* [L. *aspero*, from *asper*, rough.] To make rough or uneven.—**Asperation**,† as-pėr-ā'shon, *n.* A making or becoming rough.

Aspergill, Aspergillus, as'pėr-jil, as-pėr-jil'lus, *n.* [Dim. from L. *aspergo*, to sprinkle—*ad*, to, and *spargo*, to sprinkle.] *R. Cath. Ch.* the brush used for sprinkling holy water on the people, said to have been originally made of hyssop.

Asperity, as-per'i-ti, *n.* [L. *asperitas*, from *asper*, rough.] The quality or state of being rough; roughness or harshness to the touch, taste, hearing, or feelings; tartness; crabbedness; severity; acrimony.

Aspermous, Aspermatous, a-spėrm'us,

a-spérm'a-tus, *a.* [Gr. *a*, without, and *sperma*, seed.] *Bot.* destitute of seed.

Asperse, as-pėrs', *v.t.* — *aspersed, aspersing.* [L. *aspergo, aspersus*—*ad*, and *spargo*, to scatter or sprinkle.] To bespatter with foul reports or false and injurious charges; to slander or calumniate. — **Asperser**, as-pėrs'ėr, *n.* One that asperses or vilifies another. — **Aspersion**, as-pėr'shon, *n.* A sprinkling, as of water (*Shak.*)†; the spread of calumnious reports or charges; calumny; censure.—**Aspersive, Aspersory**, as-pėrs'iv, as-pėr'so-ri, *a.* Tending to asperse; defamatory; calumnious; slanderous.

Asphalt, as-falt', *n.* [Gr. *asphaltos*, from the Phœnician.] The most common variety of bitumen; mineral pitch; a black or brown substance which melts readily and has a strong pitchy odour; a mixture of asphalt or bitumen and sand or other substances, used for pavements, floors, the lining of tanks, &c.—*Asphalt rock* or *stone*, a dark-coloured bituminous limestone found in Switzerland and elsewhere.—**Asphaltic**, as-falt'ik, *a.* Pertaining to or containing asphalt; bituminous.

Asphodel, as'fō-del, *n.* [Gr. *asphodelos.*] The name given to various species of plants of the lily family: the asphodel of the older English poets is the daffodil.

Asphyxia, Asphyxy, as-fik'si-a, as-fik'si, *n.* [Gr. *asphyxia*—*a*, priv., and *sphyxis*, the pulse, from *sphyzō*, to throb.] Suspended animation or loss of consciousness, with temporary stoppage of the heart's action, caused by interrupted respiration, particularly from suffocation or drowning, or the inhalation of irrespirable gases. — **Asphyxial**, as-fik'si-al, *a.* Relating to asphyxia; resulting from or indicating asphyxia. — **Asphyxiate**, as-fik'si-āt, *v.t.* To bring to a state of asphyxia; to cause asphyxia in. — **Asphyxiation**, as-fik'si-ā"shon, *n.* The act of causing asphyxia; a state of asphyxia.

Aspic, Aspick. See ASP.

Aspic, as'pik, *n.* [Fr.; origin unknown.] A dish consisting of a clear, savoury, meat jelly, and containing fowl, game, fish, &c.

Aspick, as'pik, *n.* [Fr., from L. *spica*, a spike or ear of corn.] A species of lavender growing in France, and yielding a white, aromatic, and very inflammable oil, used by painters, &c.

Aspire, as-pīr', *v.i.*—*aspired, aspiring.* [L. *aspiro*, to breathe—*ad*, to, and *spiro*, to breathe, to endeavour after (in *expire, respire*, &c.). SPIRIT.] To desire with eagerness; to pant after a great or noble object; to aim at something elevated or above one; to be ambitious: followed by *to* or *after*; to ascend; to tower; to point upward; to soar.—**Aspirant**, as-pīr'ant, *n.* One who aspires or seeks with eagerness; a candidate.—**Aspirate**, as'pi-rāt, *v.t.*—*aspirated, aspirating.* To pronounce with a breathing or audible emission of breath; to pronounce with such a sound as our letter *h* has; to add an *h*-sound to (the word *horse* is aspirated, but not the word *hour*). —*n.* An aspirated sound like that of *h*; the letter *h* itself, or any mark of aspiration.—**Aspiration**, as-pi-rā'shon, *n.* The act of aspirating; an aspirated sound; the act of aspiring or of ardently desiring; an ardent wish or desire chiefly after what is great and good.—**Aspiratory**, as-pīr'a-to-ri, *a.* Pertaining to breathing; suited to the inhaling of air.—**Aspirer**, as-pīr'ėr, *n.* One who aspires; an aspirant.—**Aspiring**, as-pīr'ing, *a.* Having an ardent desire of power, importance, or excellence; ambitious.—**Aspiringly**, as-pīr'ing-li, *adv.* In an aspiring or ambitious manner. — **Aspiringness**, as-pīr'ing-nes, *n.*

Aspirin, as'pi-rēn, *n.* A recent chemical preparation for the expulsion of uric acid from the human system.

Asportation, as-pōr-tā'shon, *n.* [L. *asportatio*—*abs*, from, and *porto*, to carry.] A carrying away; specifically, the felonious removal of goods from the place where they were deposited.

Asquint, a-skwint', *adv.* In a squinting manner; not in the straight line of vision; obliquely.

Ass, as, *n.* [A.Sax. *assa*, a male ass, *assen*, the female, also *esol, asal*; Goth. *asilus*, D. *ezel*, G. *esel*, Icel. *asni, asna*, Dan. *asen*, Lith. *asilas*, Gael. *asal*, W. *asyn*, L. *asinus*; ultimate origin unknown.] A well-known quadruped of the horse family, supposed to be a native of Asia, in parts of which vast troops roam in a wild state; from the slowness and want of spirit of the domestic ass, the type of obstinacy and stupidity; hence, a dull, stupid fellow; a dolt; a blockhead.—**Asinine**, as'i-nīn, *a.* [L. *asininus*, from *asinus*, an ass.] Belonging to or having the qualities of an ass; absurdly stupid or obstinate.—Also **Assish**, as'ish.

Assafœtida, *n.* Same as *Asafetida.*

Assagai, as'sa-gā, *n.* [Pg. *azagaia*, Ar. *al-zagāya*—*al*, the, and *zagaya*, a Berber word for a kind of weapon.] An instrument of warfare among the Kaffirs; a throwing spear; a species of javelin.

Assail, as-sāl', *v.t.* [Fr. *assaillir*, from L. *assilio*, to leap or rush upon—*ad*, to, and *salio*, to leap, to rise. ASSAULT.] To fall upon with violence; to set upon; assault; attack, with actual weapons or with arguments, censure, abuse, criticism, entreaties, or the like. ∴ *Assail* is not so strong as *assault*, which implies more violence, and is more frequently used in a figurative sense. —**Assailable**, as-sāl'a-bl, *a.* Capable of being assailed.—**Assailant**, as-sāl'ant, *n.* One who assails, attacks, or assaults.—*a.* Assaulting; attacking.—**Assailer**, as-sāl'ėr, *n.* One who assails.

Assapan, Assapanic, as-sa-pan', as-sa-pan'ik, *n.* [American Indian.] A North American species of flying-squirrel.

Assassin, as-sas'sin, *n.* [Ar. *hashāshin, hashishin*, one who murders when infuriated by *hashish*, a maddening drink made from hemp.] One of a strange sect in Palestine in the time of the Crusades, the followers of the Old Man of the Mountains, distinguished for their secret murders; one who kills or attempts to kill by surprise or secret assault; a secret murderer; a cut-throat.—**Assassinate**, as-sas'sin-āt, *v.t.*—*assassinated, assassinating.* To kill or attempt to kill by surprise or secret assault; to murder by sudden violence.—*n.*‡ [Fr. *assassinat.*] An assassin; assassination.—**Assassination**, as-sas'sin-ā"shon, *n.* The act of assassinating; a killing or murdering by surprise or secret assault.—**Assassinator**, as-sas'sin-āt-ėr, *n.* An assassin.

Assault, as-sạlt', *n.* [O.Fr. *assault* (Fr. *assaut*), from L.L. *assaltus*, from L. *ad*, to, and *saltus*, a leap, from *salio*, to leap. *Assail, insult, result*, &c., are akin.] An attack or violent onset; an onslaught; a violent attack with the intention of injuring a person; specifically, a sudden and vigorous attack on a fortified post; a storm.—*Assault at arms*, a name sometimes given to an exhibition of fencing or similar military exercises.—*v.t.* To fall upon by violence or with a hostile intention; to fall on with force; to assail. ASSAIL.—**Assaulter**, as-sạlt'ėr, *n.* One who assaults.

Assay, as-sā', *n.* [O.Fr. *assai, essay*, a trial, examination, *essayer*, to test, from L. *exagium*, Gr. *exagion*, a weighing—*ex*, out, *agō*, to bring. *Essay* is the same word.] Examination; trial; the trial of the goodness, purity, weight, value, &c., of metals or metallic substances, especially gold and silver, their ores and alloys.—**Assay**, as-sā', *v.t.* To make any assay of; to examine by trial; to test the purity or metallic constituents of; to attempt, endeavour, essay (*Shak.*)†.—**Assayer**, as-sā'ėr, *n.* One who assays.

Assegai, *n.* Same as *Assagai.*

Assemble, as-sem'bl, *v.t.*—*assembled, assembling.* [Fr. *assembler*, from L.L. *assimulo*, to assemble—L. *ad*, to, and *simul*, together; akin, *similar, simulate, assimilate*, &c.; same root as E. *same*.] To collect into one place or body; to bring or call together; to convene; to congregate; to fit together (pieces of mechanism).—*v.i.* To meet or come together; to gather; to convene.—**Assemblage**, as-sem'blāj, *n.* The act of assembling, or state of being assembled; a collection of individuals or of particular things; a gathering or company. — **Assembler**, as-sem'bl-ėr, *n.* One who assembles.—**Assembly**, as-sem'bli, *n.* [Fr. *assemblée.*] A company or collection of human beings in the same place, usually for the same purpose; the name given to the legislative body or one of the divisions of it in various states; a ball, especially a subscription ball.—*General Assembly*, the chief ecclesiastical court of the Established and of the United Free Church of Scotland.

Assent, as-sent', *n.* [O.Fr. *assent*—L. *ad*, and *sentio*, to think (also in *consent, dissent, sense*, &c.).] The act of the mind in admitting or agreeing to the truth of a proposition; consent; concurrence; acquiescence; agreement to a proposal; accord; agreement; approval.—*Royal assent*, the approbation given by the British sovereign in parliament to a bill which has passed both houses, after which it becomes law.—*v.i.* To express an agreement of the mind to what is alleged or proposed; to concur; to acquiesce.—**Assentation**, as-sen-tā'shon, *n.* [L. *assentatio*, flattery; from *assentor*, to assent from interested motives, to flatter.] Flattery; adulation.—**Assenter, Assentient**, as-sent'ėr, as-sen'shi-ent, *n.* One who assents.—**Assentient, Assentive**, as-sent'iv, *a.* Yielding assent; complying.

Assert, as-sėrt', *v.t.* [L. *assero, assertum*—*ad*, to, and *sero, sertum*, to join, connect, bind, from root of *series.*] To support the cause or claims of (rights, liberties); to vindicate a claim or title to; to affirm positively; to asseverate; to aver; *refl.* to come forward and assume one's rights, claims, &c.—**Assertion**, as-sėr'shon, *n.* The act of affirming; the maintaining of a claim; a positive declaration or averment; an affirmation. — **Assertional**,† as-sėr'shon-al, *a.* Containing an assertion.—**Assertive, Assertory**, as-sėrt'iv, as-sėrt'o-ri, *a.* Positive; affirming confidently; peremptory; declaratory.—**Assertively**, as-sėrt'iv-li, *adv.* In an assertive manner; affirmatively. — **Assertor, Asserter**, as-sėrt'ėr, *n.* One who asserts; one who affirms positively; one who maintains or vindicates.

Assess, as-ses', *v.t.* [O.Fr. *assesser*, L.L. *assessare*, from L. *assideo, assessum*, to sit beside, and hence to act as assessor—*ad*, to, and *sedeo*, to sit; akin *assiduous, reside, sedentary*, &c.] To set, fix, or charge a certain sum upon (a person), by way of tax; to value, as property or the amount of yearly income, for the purpose of being taxed; to settle or determine the amount of (damages). —**Assessable**, as-ses'a-bl, *a.* Capable of being assessed; liable to be assessed.—**Assessably**, as-ses'a-bli, *adv.* By assessment. —**Assessment**, as-ses'ment, *n.* The act of assessing; a valuation of property, profits, or income, for the purpose of taxation; a tax or specific sum charged on a person or property. — **Assessor**, as-ses'ėr, *n.* One appointed to make assessments; an officer of justice who sits to assist a judge.—**Assessorial**, as-ses-sō'ri-al, *a.* Pertaining to an assessor or assessors.

Asset, as'set, *n.* [O.Fr. *aset, assetz*, Fr. *assez*, enough, from L. *ad.* to, and *satis*, enough.] An article of goods or property available for the payment of a person's obligations or debts: generally used in the plural; any portion of the entire effects belonging to a person.

Asseverate, as-sev'ėr-āt, *v.t.*—*asseverated, asseverating.* [L. *assevero, asseveratum*—*ad*, to, and *severus*, serious, severe.] To affirm or aver positively, or with solemnity. **Asseveration**, as-sev'ėr-ā"shon, *n.* The act of asseverating; positive affirmation or assertion.—**Asseveratory**, as-sev'ėr-a-to-ri, *a.* Of the nature of an asseveration; solemnly or positively affirming.

Assibilate, as-sib'i-lāt, *v.t.*—*assibilated, assibilating.* To make sibilant, as a letter. —**Assibilation**, as-sib'i-lā"shon, *n.* The act of assibilating.

Assident, as'si-dent, *a.* [L. *assidens*—*ad*, and *sedeo*, to sit.] Accompanying; concomitant: applied to signs or symptoms in *med.*

Assiduous, as-sid'ū-us, *a.* [L. *assiduus*, from *assideo*, to sit close—*ad*, and *sedeo*, to sit. ASSESS.] Constant in application; attentive; devoted; unremitting; performed with constant diligence or attention.—**Assiduously**, as-sid'ū-us-li, *adv.* In an assiduous manner.—**Assiduousness, Assiduity**, as-sid'ū-us-nes, as-si-dū'i-ti, *n.* The quality of being assiduous; constant or diligent application to any business or enterprise; diligence.

Assign, as-sīn', *v.t.* [Fr. *assigner*, L. *assigno*, —*ad*, and *signo*, to allot, mark out, from *signum*, a mark (whence *sign*, *consign*, &c.).] To mark out as a portion allotted; to apportion; to allot; to fix or specify; *law*, to transfer or make over to another.—*n.* A person to whom property or an interest is transferred; an assignee.—**Assignable**, as-sīn'a-bl, *a.* Capable of being assigned.—**Assignation**, as-sig-nā-shon, *n.* The act of assigning or allotting; the act of fixing or specifying; a making over by transfer of title; an appointment of time and place for meeting: used chiefly of love-meetings.—**Assignee**, as-sin-ē', *n.* A person to whom an assignment is made; a person appointed or deputed to perform some act or business, or enjoy some right.—**Assigner, Assignor**, as-sīn'ėr, as-sīn'or, *n.* One who assigns or appoints.—**Assignment**, as-sīn'ment, *n.* The act of assigning, fixing, or specifying; the writing by which an interest is transferred.—**Assignat**, as'sig-nat or as-sin-yä, *n.* [Fr., from L. *assignatus*, assigned.] A public note or bill in France during the first revolution.

Assimilate, as-sim'il-āt, *v.t.*—*assimilated*, *assimilating*. [L. *assimilo*—*ad*, to, and *similis*, like. ASSEMBLE.] To make alike; to cause to resemble; to absorb and incorporate (food) into the system; to incorporate with organic tissues; to liken or compare†.—*v.i.* To become similar; to harmonize; to become incorporated with the body; to perform the act of converting food to the substance of the body.—**Assimilability**, as-sim'il-a-bil"i-ti, *n.* The quality of being assimilable.—**Assimilable**, as-sim'il-a-bl, *a.* Capable of being assimilated.—**Assimilation**, as-sim'il-ā"shon, *n.* The act or process of assimilating or being assimilated; the process by which animals and plants convert and absorb nutriment so that it becomes part of the substances composing them.—**Assimilative, Assimilatory**, as-sim'il-āt-iv, as-sim'il-a-to-ri, *a.* Having the power of assimilating; tending to assimilate; producing assimilation.

Assist, as-sist', *v.t.* [Fr. *assister*, to stand by, help; L. *assisto*—*ad*, to, and *sisto*, to stand.] To help; to aid; to succour.—*v.i.* To lend aid; to be present; to take part in a ceremony or discussion.—**Assistance**, as-sist'ans, *n.* Help; aid; succour; a contribution in aid.—**Assistant**, as-sist'ant, *a.* Helping; lending aid or support; auxiliary.—*n.* One who aids or assists another; one engaged to work along with another; an auxiliary.—**Assister**, as-sist'ėr, *n.* An assistant.

Assize, Assise, as-sīz', *n.* [Fr. *assises*, assizes, *assise*, a fixed rate, a tax, from L. *assideo*, to be an assessor. ASSESS.] A jury or similar assembly†; the periodical sessions held at stated intervals by at least two judges in each of the counties of England and Wales (except Middlesex), for the purpose of trying criminal and certain other cases before a jury: generally in the plural; an ordinance; a decree; an assessment; particularly, an ordinance formerly fixing the weight, measure, and price of articles (hence the word *size*).—*v.t.*—*assized*, *assizing*; *assised*, *assising*. To fix the weight, measure, or price of; to fix the rate of; to assess†.—**Assizer**, as-sīz'ėr, *n.* An officer who has the care or inspection of weights and measures.

Associate, as-sō'shi-āt, *v.t.*—*associated*, *associating*. [L. *associo*, *associatum*—*ad*, to, and *socius*, a companion. SOCIAL.] To join in company (another with ourselves); to adopt as a partner, companion, and the like; to join or connect intimately (things together); to unite; to combine.—*v.i.* To unite in company; to join in a confederacy or association.—*a.* Joined in interest, object, office, &c.; combined together; joined with another or others.—*n.* A companion; a mate; a fellow; a partner; a confederate; an accomplice; an ally.—**Associable**, as-sō'shi-a-bl, *a.* Capable of being associated; companionable; social.—**Associability, Associableness**, as-sō'shi-a-bil"i-ti, as-sō'shi-a-bl-nes, *n.* The quality of being associable.—**Associateship**, as-sō'shi-āt-ship, *n.* The state or office of an associate.—**Association**, as-sō'shi-ā"shon, *n.* The act of associating or state of being associated; connection; union; a society, the members of which are united by mutual interests or for a common purpose; *philos.* the tendency which one idea, feeling, &c., has for one reason or another to recall another.—**Associational**, as-sō'shi-ā"shon-al, *a.* Pertaining to association.—**Associative**, as-sō'shi-āt-iv, *a.* Capable of associating; tending to associate or unite; leading to association.

Assoil,† as-soil', *v.t.* [O.Fr. *assoiler*, from L. *absolvo*, to absolve.] To solve; to release; to acquit.—**Assoilzie**, as-soil'yē, *v.t.* *Scots law*, to acquit; to pronounce innocent; to absolve.

Assonant, as'sō-nant, *a.* [L. *assonans*, ppr. of *assono*—*ad*, to, and *sono*, to sound.] Having a resemblance of sounds; *pros.* rhyming only so far as the vowels are concerned.—**Assonance**, as'sō-nans, *n.* Resemblance of sounds; *pros.* a species of imperfect rhyme which consists in using the same vowel with different consonants.

Assort, as-sort', *v.t.* [Fr. *assortir*, to sort, to assort—*as* for L. *ad*, to, and *sors*, *sortis*, a lot. SORT.] To separate and distribute into sorts, classes, or kinds; to furnish with a suitable variety of goods (to *assort* a cargo); to adapt or suit.—*v.i.* To agree; to suit together; to associate; to keep company.—**Assortment**, as-sort'ment, *n.* The act of assorting; a collection of things assorted.

Assuage, as-swāj', *v.t.*—*assuaged*, *assuaging*. [O.Fr. *assouager*, *assouagier*, from L. *ad*, to, and *suavis*, sweet.] To allay, mitigate, ease, or lessen (pain or grief); to moderate; to appease or pacify (passion or tumult).—**Assuagement**, as-swāj'ment, *n.* The act of assuaging; mitigation; abatement.—**Assuager**, as-swāj'ėr, *n.* One who or that which assuages or allays.—**Assuasive**,† as-swā'siv, *a.*—Softening; mitigating; tranquillizing.

Assuetude,† as'swē-tūd, *n.* [L. *assuetudo*, from *assuetus*, part. of *assuesco*, to accustom.] Custom; habit; habitual use.

Assume, as-sūm', *v.t.*—*assumed*, *assuming*. [L. *assumo*—*ad*, to, and *sumo*, to take, also seen in *concume*, *presume*, *sumptuous*, &c.] To take upon one's self; to take on; to appear in (*assume* a figure or shape); to appropriate; to take for granted; suppose as a fact; to pretend to possess; to put on (*assume* a wise air).—*v.i.* To be arrogant; to claim more than is due; *law*, to undertake or promise.—**Assumer**, as-sūm'ėr, *n.* One who assumes.—**Assuming**, as-sūm'ing, *a.* Putting on airs of superiority; haughty; arrogant; overbearing.—**Assumption**, as-sum'shon, *n.* [L. *assumptio*.] The act of assuming; a taking upon one's self; the act of taking for granted; supposition; the thing supposed; a postulate or proposition assumed; a church festival in honour of the miraculous ascent to heaven of the Virgin Mary's body after death, celebrated 15th August.—**Assumptive**, as-sum'tiv, *a.* Capable of being assumed; assumed.—**Assumptively**, as-sum'tiv-li, *adv.* In an assumptive manner; by way of assumption.

Assure, a-shör', *v.t.*—*assured*, *assuring*. [Fr. *assurer*, O.Fr. *asseürer*, L.L. *assecurare*—L. *ad*, to, and *securus*, secure.] To make (a person) sure or certain; to convince (to *assure* a person of a thing); to declare or affirm solemnly to; to confirm; to ensure; to secure (to *assure* success to a person); to insure (one's life or property); to embolden or make confident (N.T.); to affiance or betroth (*Shak.*).—**Assurable**, a-shör'a-bl, *a.* Capable of being assured; suitable for insurance.—**Assurance**, a-shör'ans, *n.* The act of assuring; a pledge furnishing ground of full confidence; firm persuasion; certain expectation; undoubting steadiness; intrepidity; excess of boldness; impudence; laudable confidence; self-reliance; insurance.—**Assured**, a-shörd', *a.* Certain; convinced; not doubting or doubtful; bold to excess; confident; having life or goods insured (in this sense often a noun, sing. or pl.).—**Assuredly**, a-shör'ed-li, *adv.* Certainly; indubitably.—**Assuredness**, a-shör'ed-nes, *n.* The state of being assured; certainty; full confidence.—**Assurer**, a-shör'ėr, *n.* One who assures; an insurer or underwriter.—**Assuringly**, a-shör'ing-li, *adv.* In an assuring manner; in a way to create assurance.

Assurgent, as-sėr'jent, *a.* [L. *assurgens*, *assurgentis*, ppr. of *assurgo*—*ad*, to, and *surgo*, to rise. SURGE.] Rising or directed upward.—**Assurgency**,† as-sėr'jen-si, *n.* The act of rising upward.

Assyrian, as-sir'i-an, *a.* Pertaining or relating to Assyria or to its inhabitants.—*n.* A native or inhabitant of Assyria; the language of the Assyrians.—**Assyriologist**, as-sir'i-ol"o-jist, *n.* One skilled in the antiquities, language (as exhibited in the cuneiform inscriptions), &c., of ancient Assyria.

Astatic, a-stat'ik, *a.* [Gr. *a*, priv., and root *sta*, to stand.] Being without polarity.—*Astatic needle*, a magnetic needle having its directive property destroyed by the proximity of another needle of the same intensity fixed parallel to it, but with the poles reversed.—**Astatically**, a-stat'ik-al-li, *adv.* In an astatic manner.

Astel, as'tl, *n.* [O.Fr. *astelle*, L. *astula*, a splint or chip.] *Mining*, a board or plank; an arch or ceiling of boards over the men's head in a mine, to protect them from any portion of the roof falling.

Aster, as'tėr, *n.* [Gr. *astēr*, a star.] A large genus of composite plants, the flowers of which somewhat resemble stars.—**Asteria**, as-tē'ri-a, *n.* A variety of sapphire, showing a star-like opalescence in the direction of the axis, if cut round.—**Asteriated**, as-tē'ri-āt-ed, *a.* Radiated; presenting diverging rays, like a star.—**Asterid, Asteridan**, as'tėr-id, as-tėr'i-dan, *n.* A star-fish.—**Asterisk**, as'tėr-isk, *n.* [Gr. *asteriskos*, a little star.] The figure of a star, thus *, used in printing and writing, as a reference to a note or to fill the space where something is omitted.—**Asterism**, as'tėr-izm, *n.* [Gr. *asterismos*.] A small collection of stars; an asterisk, or several asterisks together†.

Astern, a-stėrn', *adv.* In or at or toward the stern of a ship; behind a ship; backward; with the stern foremost.

Asteroid, as'tėr-oid, *n.* [Gr. *astēr*, a star, and *eidos*, form.] One of the small planets between the orbits of Mars and Jupiter, more accurately called *planetoids*.—**Asteroid, Asteroidal**, as'tėr-oid, as-tėr-oid'al, *a.* Resembling a star; pertaining to the asteroids, or to the star-fishes.

Asterolepis, as-tėr-ol'e-pis, *n.* [Gr. *astēr*, a star, and *lepis*, a scale.] A genus of gigantic ganoid fishes which sometimes attained the length of 18 or 20 feet, found fossil in the old red sandstone.

Asthenia, Astheny, as-thē-nī'a, as'the-ni, *n.* [Gr. *astheneia*—*a*, priv., and *sthenos*, strength.] Debility; want of strength.—**Asthenic**, as-then'ik, *a.* Characterized by asthenia or debility.—**Asthenology**, as-then-ol'o-ji, *n.* The doctrine of diseases connected with debility.

Asthma, as'ma, *n.* [Gr. *asthma*, short-drawn breath.] A chronic disorder of respiration, characterized by difficulty of breathing, a cough, and expectoration.—**Asthmatic, Asthmatical**, ast-mat'ik, ast-mat'ik-al, *a.* Pertaining to asthma; affected by asthma.—*n.* A person troubled with asthma.—**Asthmatically**, ast-mat'ik-al-li, *adv.* In an asthmatical manner.

Astigmatism, a-stig'mat-izm, *n.* [Gr. *a*,

neg., and *stigma*, *stigmatos*, a mark.] A malformation of the lens of the eye, such that rays of light are not brought to converge in the same point.

Astir, a-stėr′, *adv.* or *a.* On the stir; on the move; stirring; active; not used attributively.

Astomatous, **Astomous**, as-tom′a-tus, as′tō-mus, *a.* [Gr. *a*, without, and *stoma*, a mouth.] Without a mouth.

Astonish, as-ton′ish, *v.t.* [Partly from O.Fr. *estonner*, L.L. *extonare*, lit. to make thunder-struck, from *ex*, intens., and *tono*, to thunder; partly from A.Sax. *āstunian*—*ā*, intensive, and *stunian*, to stun.] To strike or impress with wonder, surprise, or admiration; to surprise; to amaze; to stun†; to confound‡.—**Astonishedly**,† as-ton′ish-ed-li, *adv.* In an astonished manner. —**Astonishing**, as-ton′ish-ing, *a.* Calculated to astonish; amazing; wonderful.—**Astonishingly**, as-ton′ish-ing-li, *adv.* In an astonishing manner.—**Astonishingness**,† as-ton′ish-ing-nes, *n.*—**Astonishment**, as-ton′ish-ment, *n.* The state or feeling of being astonished; amazement; great surprise; a cause or matter of astonishment (O.T.).—**Astony**, as-tō′ni, *v.t.* [A. Sax. *āstunian.*] To astonish; to terrify; to confound. [Obs. or poet.]—**Astound**, astound′, *v.t.* [For old *astoune*, A.Sax. *āstunian*, with *d* added, as in *sound*, *expound.*] To astonish; to strike dumb with amazement. —**Astounding**, as-tound′ing, *a.* Fitted or calculated to astound; causing terror; astonishing. —**Astoundment**,† as-tound′ment, *n.* Amazement.

Astraddle, a-strad′l, *adv.* Straddling; with one leg on either side; astride.

Astragal, as′tra-gal, *n.* [Gr. *astragalos*, a huckle-bone, a moulding.] A small semicircular moulding separating the shaft of a column from the capital; one of the bars which hold the panes of a window; the huckle or ankle bone; the upper bone of the foot.

Astrakhan, as′tra-kan, *n.* [From *Astrakhan* in Russia.] A rough kind of cloth with a curled pile.

Astral, as′tral, *a.* [L. *astralis*, from *astrum*, a star.] Belonging to the stars; starry.

Astray, a-strā′, *adv.* Having strayed; out of the right way or proper place.

Astrict,† as-trikt′, *v.t.* [L. *astrictum*. ASTRINGE.] To constrict; to contract; to limit.—**Astriction**, as-trik′shon, *n.* The act of binding close, contracting, or restricting; limitation. —**Astrictive**, as-trikt′iv, *a.* Binding; compressing.

Astride, a-strīd′, *adv.* With one leg on each side; with the legs wide apart.

Astringe,† as-trinj′, *v.t.* —*astringed*, *astringing.* [L. *astringo*—*ad*, to, and *stringo*, to strain STRAIN.] To compress; to bind together.—**Astringency**, as-trin′jen-si, *n.* The quality of being astringent.—**Astringent**, as-trin′jent, *a.* Contracting; especially contracting the organic tissues and canals of the body, and thereby checking or diminishing excessive discharges.—*n.* An astringent substance, as alum, catechu, &c. —**Astringently**, as-trin′jent-li, *adv.* In an astringent manner.

Astrogeny, as-troj′e-ni, *n.* [Gr. *astron*, a star, and root *gen*, to produce.] The creation or evolution of the celestial bodies.—**Astrognosy**, as-trog′nō-si, *n.* [-*gnosy*, from Gr. *gnōsis*, knowledge.] Knowledge of the stars.—**Astrography**, as-trog′ra-fi, *n.* A description of, or the art of describing, the stars.

Astrolabe, as′trō-lāb, *n.* [Gr. *astēr*, a star, and root *lab*, seen in *lambanō*, to take.] An instrument formerly used for taking the altitude of the sun or stars at sea, now superseded by the quadrant and sextant.

Astrolatry, as-trol′a-tri, *n.* [Gr. *astēr*, star, *latreia*, worship.] The worship of the stars.

Astrolithology, as′trō-li-thol″o-ji, *n.* [Gr. *astēr*, star, *lithos*, stone, *logos*, discourse.] The science of aerolites.

Astrology, as-trol′o-ji, *n.* [Gr. *astron*, a star, and *logos*, discourse, theory.] The pseudo-science which pretends to enable men to discover effects and influences of the heavenly bodies on human and other mundane affairs and to foretell the future; astronomy‡. —**Astrologer**, **Astrologian**, as-trol′o-jėr, as-trō-lō′ji-an, *n.* One who practises astrology; an astronomer‡.—**Astrologic**, **Astrological**, as-trō-loj′ik, as-trō-loj′ik-al, *a.* Pertaining to astrology. —**Astrologically**, as-trō-loj′ik-al-li, *adv.* In an astrological manner. —**Astrologize**, as-trol′o-jīz, *v.i.* To practise astrology.

Astrometer, as-trom′et-ėr, *n.* [Gr. *astron*, a star, and *metron*, a measure.] An instrument which measures the stars or the light of the stars.—**Astrometry**, as-trom′et-ri, *n.* The art of determining by measurement the relative distances, magnitudes, &c., of the stars.

Astronomy, as-tron′o-mi, *n.* [Gr. *astron*, a star, and *nomos*, a law or rule.] The science which treats of the celestial bodies, their nature, magnitudes, motions, distances, periods of revolution, &c.; astrology (*Shak.*)‡. —**Astronomer**, as-tron′o-mėr, *n.* One who is versed in astronomy; an astrologer (*Shak.*)‡.—**Astronomic**, **Astronomical**, as-trō-nom′ik, as-trō-nom′ik-al, *a.* Pertaining to astronomy.—**Astronomically**, as-trō-nom′ik-al-li, *adv.* In an astronomical manner; by the principles of astronomy.—**Astronomize**, as-tron′o-mīz, *v.i.* To study astronomy.

Astucious, as-tū′shus, *a.* [Fr. *astucieux*, L. *astus*, craft.] Astute; crafty.—**Astucity**, as-tū′si-ti, *n.* Astuteness; craftiness.

Astute, as-tūt′, *a.* [L. *astutus*, from *astus*, craft, subtlety.] Of a shrewd and penetrating turn; cunning; sagacious; keen.—**Astutely**, as-tūt′li, *adv.* In an astute manner; shrewdly; sharply, cunningly.—**Astuteness**, as-tūt′nes, *n.* The quality of being astute; cunning; shrewdness.

Astylar, a-stī′lėr, *a.* [Gr. *a*, priv., and *stylos*, a column.] *Arch.* having no columns.

Asunder, a-sun′dėr, *adv.* In sunder; apart; into parts; separately.

Asylum, a-sī′lum, *n.* [L. *asylum*, Gr. *asylon*—*a*, priv., and *sylaō*, to strip, plunder.] A sanctuary or place of refuge; any place of retreat and security; an institution for receiving and maintaining persons labouring under certain bodily defects or mental maladies; a refuge for the unfortunate.

Asymmetry, a-sim′met-ri, *n.* [Gr. *a*, priv., and *symmetria*, symmetry.] The want of symmetry or proportion between the parts of a thing. —**Asymmetrical**, a-sim-met′rik-al, *a.* Not having symmetry; inharmonious; not reconcilable.

Asymptote, as′im-tōt, *n.* [Gr. *asymptōtos*, not falling together—*a*, priv., *syn*, with, and *piptō*, to fall.] *Math.* a line which approaches nearer and nearer to some curve, but though infinitely extended would never meet it.—**Asymptotic**, **Asymptotical**, as-im-tot′ik, as-im-tot′ik-al, *a.* Belonging to or having the character of an asymptote. —**Asymptotically**, as-im-tot′ik-al-li, *adv.* In an asymptotic manner.

Asynartete, a-sin′är-tēt, *a.* [Gr. *asynartētos*—*a*, not, *syn*, with, *artaō*, to fasten.] Disconnected; not fitted or adjusted.

Asyndeton, a-sin′de-ton, *n.* [Gr. *a*, priv., *syn*, together, *deō*, to bind.] A figure of speech by which connectives are omitted; as, *veni, vidi, vici*; I came, I saw, I conquered.—**Asyndetic**, as-in-det′ik, *a.* Pertaining to or characterized by the use of asyndeton.

At, at, *prep.* [A.Sax. *æt*, Goth. O.Sax. Icel. *at*, Dan. *ad*, O.H.G. *az*; allied to L. *ad*, to, Skr. *adhi*, upon.] Denoting coincidence or contiguity: *in time* (*at* first); *in space* (*at* home, *at* church); *in occupation* or *condition* (*at* work, *at* prayer); *in degree* or *condition* (*at* best, *at* the worst); *in effect*, as coincident with the cause (*at* the sight); *in relation*, as existing between two objects (*at* your command); *in value* (*at* a shilling a head); also, direction towards (fire *at* the target).—*At large*, at liberty; unconfined; also, generally; as a whole (the country *at large*).

Atacamite, at-a-kä′mīt, *n.* [From *Atacama*, in Chili.] A copper ore occurring abundantly in some parts of S. America.

Ataghan, at′a-gan, *n.* YATAGHAN.

Atavism, at′a-vizm, *n.* [L. *atavus*, an ancestor.] The resemblance of offspring to a remote ancestor; the return or reversion among animals to the original type; *med.* the recurrence of any peculiarity or disease of an ancestor.

Ataxia, **Ataxy**, a-tak′si-a, at′ak-si, *n.* [Gr. *a*, priv., and *taxis*, order.] Want of order; disturbance; *med.* irregularity in the functions of the body or in the crisis and paroxysms of disease.—**Ataxic**, a-tak′sik, *a.* Irregular; disorderly; characterized by irregularity.

Atchievement, at-chēv′ment, *n.* A hatchment.

Ate, āt. The preterit of *eat* (which see).

Atechnic,† a-tek′nik, *n.* [Gr. *a*, priv., and *technē*, art.] A person unacquainted with art, especially with its technology. —*a.* Destitute of a knowledge of art.

Atelier, at-lē-ā, *n.* [Fr., a workshop.] A workshop; specifically, the workroom of sculptors and painters.

A tempo, ä tem′pō. [It.] *Music*, a direction that, after any change of movement, the original movement be restored.

Athalamous, a-thal′a-mus, *a.* [Gr. *a*, priv., *thalamos*, bed.] *Bot.* not furnished with shields or beds for the spores.

Athanasian, ath-a-nā′si-an, *a.* Pertaining to *Athanasius*, bishop of Alexandria, in the fourth century.—*Athanasian creed*, a creed of the Christian church, erroneously attributed to Athanasius, and also ascribed to Hilary, bishop of Arles (about A.D. 430). It defines the doctrines of the trinity and the incarnation in very precise and emphatic language, declaring damnation to be the lot of those who do not hold the right faith.

Atheism, ā′thē-izm, *n.* [Gr. *atheos*, an atheist—*a*, priv., and *theos*, God.] The disbelief of the existence of a God or Supreme intelligent Being.—**Atheist**, ā′thē-ist, *n.* One who professes atheism or disbelief in God. —**Atheistic**, **Atheistical**, ā-thē-ist′ik, ā-thē-ist′ik-al, *a.* Pertaining to, implying, or containing atheism; disbelieving the existence of a God.—**Atheistically**, ā-thē-ist′ik-al-li, *adv.* In an atheistic manner. —**Atheisticalness**, ā-thē-ist′ik-al-nes, *n.*—**Atheize**, ā′thē-īz, *v.i.* To discourse as an atheist.—*v.t.* To render atheistic.

Atheling, **Ætheling**, ath′el-ing, eth′el-ing. [A.Sax. *ætheling*, from *æthele*, noble=G. *edel*, noble.] In Anglo-Saxon times, a prince; one of the royal family; a nobleman.

Athenæum, **Atheneum**, ath-e-nē′um, *n.* [L. from Gr. *Athēnē*, the goddess of wisdom.] An institution for the encouragement of literature and art, where a library, periodicals, &c., are kept for the use of the members.

Athenian, a-thē′ni-an, *a.* Pertaining to *Athens*, in Greece.—*n.* A native or inhabitant of Athens.

Atheous,‡ ā′thē-us, *a.* Atheistic; impious. (*Mil.*)

Athermanous, a-thėr′man-us, *a.* [Gr. *a*, priv., and *thermainō*, to heat, from *thermē*, heat.] A term applied to those substances which have the power of absorbing radiant heat. —**Athermancy**, a-thėr′man-si, *n.* The power or property of absorbing radiant heat.

Atheroma, **Atherome**, ath-ē-rō′ma, ath′ē-rōm, *n.* [Gr., from *athērē*, pap.] A species of wen or encysted tumour, whose contents resemble bread-sauce. —**Atheromatous**, ath-ē-rō′mat-us, *a.* Pertaining to an atheroma.

Athirst, a-thėrst′, *a.* or *adv.* Thirsty; wanting drink; having a keen appetite or desire (with *for*).

Athlete, ath′lēt, *n.* [Gr. *athlētēs*, from *athlon*, a contest.] One trained to exercises of agility and strength. —**Athletic**, ath-let′ik, *a.* Pertaining to athletes or such exercises as are practised by athletes; strong; robust; vigorous.—**Athletics**, ath-let′iks, *n.pl.* Athletic exercises.—**Athletically**, ath-let′ik-al-li, *adv.* In an athletic manner. —**Athleticism, Athletism**, ath-let′i-sizm, ath′lēt-izm, *n.* The practice of athletics; the profession of an athlete.

Athwart, a-thwąrt′, *prep.* Across; from side to side of; *naut.* across the line of a ship's course.—*adv.* In a manner to cross and perplex; crossly; wrong. (*Shak.*)

Atilt, a-tilt′, *adv.* In the manner of a tilter; in the manner of a cask tilted up.

Atlas, at′las, *n.* [Gr. *Atlas*, one of the Titans, who, according to the legend, bore the earth on his shoulders.] A collection of maps in a volume; a volume of plates or tables illustrative or explanatory of some subject; the first vertebra of the neck (so named because it supports the head).—**Atlantean**, at-lan-tē′an, *a.* Pertaining to Atlas; resembling Atlas.—**Atlantes**, at-lan′tēz, *n.pl.* [Gr., pl. of *Atlas.*] Sculptured figures or half figures of men used in the place of columns or pilasters in buildings, supporting or seeming to support some mass above them.—**Atlantic**, at-lan′tik, *a.* Pertaining to or descended from Atlas (*Mil.*); pertaining to that division of the ocean which lies between Europe and Africa on the east and America on the west (named from *Mt. Atlas*).

Atmidometer, at-mi-dom′et-ėr, *n.* [Gr. *atmis, atmidos*, vapour, *metron*, measure.] An instrument for measuring the evaporation from water, ice, or snow.

Atmology, at-mol′o-ji, *n.* [Gr. *atmos*, vapour, *logos*, discourse.] That branch of science which treats of the laws and phenomena of aqueous vapour.—**Atmological**, at-mō-loj′ik-al, *a.* Pertaining to atmology. —**Atmologist**, at-mol′o-jist, *n.* One who studies atmology.

Atmolysis, at-mol′i-sis, *n.* [Gr. *atmos*, vapour, *lysis*, a loosing, from *lyō*, to loose.] A method of separating the constituent elements of a compound gas, by causing it to pass through a vessel of porous material.

Atmometer, at-mom′et-ėr, *n.* [Gr. *atmos*, vapour, *metron*, measure.] An instrument for measuring the quantity of exhalation from a humid surface in a given time; an evaporometer.

Atmosphere, at′mos-fēr, *n.* [Gr. *atmos*, vapour, and *sphaira*, a sphere.] The whole mass of aeriform fluid surrounding the earth, and generally supposed to extend to the height of 40 or 50 miles above its surface; any similar gaseous envelope or medium; the amount of pressure of a column of the atmosphere on a square inch (= 15 lbs.); *fig.* pervading influence (to live in an *atmosphere* of doubt).—**Atmospheric, Atmospherical**, at-mos-fer′ik, at-mos-fer′ik-al, *a.* Pertaining to, existing in, or consisting of the atmosphere; caused, produced, or operated on by the atmosphere.—*Atmospheric railway*, a railway, the motive power of which is derived from the pressure of the atmosphere, brought to act when air is exhausted from a tube of uniform bore, laid from one place to another.

Atoll, a-tol′, *n.* [Name in the Maldive group.] A coral island, consisting of a strip or ring of coral surrounding a central lagoon or lake: such islands are very common in the Pacific Ocean.

Atom, at′om, *n.* [L. *atomus*, Gr. *atomos*, an atom, lit. what is indivisible—*a*, not, and *temnō*, to cut.] An extremely minute particle of matter; a molecule; a particle of matter so minute as to admit of no division either mechanical or chemical; hence, anything extremely small; a minute quantity (not an *atom* of sense).—**Atomic**, a-tom′ik, *a.* Pertaining to atoms; consisting of atoms; extremely minute.—*Atomic philosophy*, a system of philosophy which taught that atoms, by virtue of their own properties, brought all things into being without the aid of a Creator.—*Atomic theory*, the theory that all chemical combinations take place in a definite manner between the ultimate particles or atoms of bodies.—**Atomical**, a-tom′ik-al, *a.* Atomic.—**Atomician**, **Atomist**, at-om-i′shan, at′om-ist, *n.* An adherent of the atomic philosophy or theory. —**Atomism**, at′om-izm, *n.* The doctrine of atoms; atomic philosophy.—**Atomistic**, at-om-ist′ik, *a.* Pertaining to atomism.—**Atomization**, at′om-iz-ā″shon, *n.* The process of atomizing or state of being atomized.—**Atomize**, at′om-iz, *v.t.*—*atomized, atomizing.* To reduce to atoms.—**Atomizer**, at′om-iz-ėr, *n.* One who or that which atomizes or reduces to atoms; an apparatus for reducing a liquid into spray for disinfecting, cooling, perfuming, &c.—**Atomy**, at′om-i, *n.* An atom; a minute creature. (*Shak.*)

Atone, a-tōn′, *v.i.*—*atoned, atoning.* [Compounded of *at* and *one*, often found together in such phrases as 'to be *at one*,' 'to set *at one*.'] To be at one‡; to agree or accord (*Shak.*)‡; to make reparation, amends, or satisfaction, as for an offence or a crime.—*v.t.* To expiate; to answer or make satisfaction for; to reconcile, as parties at variance.‡ —**Atonable**, a-tōn′a-bl, *a.* Capable of being atoned for; reconcilable.—**Atonement**, a-tōn′ment, *n.* The act of atoning, reconciling, or making reparation; reconciliation after enmity or controversy; specifically, the reconciliation of God with man through Christ; satisfaction; expiation.—**Atoner**, a-tōn′ėr, *n.* One who makes atonement.

Atony, at′o-ni, *n.* [Gr. *atonia*—*a*, priv., *tonos*, tone.] *Med.* a want of tone; defect of muscular power; weakness of every organ; debility.—**Atonic**, a-ton′ik, *a.* *Med.* characterized by atony.

Atop, a-top′, *adv.* On or at the top.

Atrabiliarian, Atrabiliarious at′ra-bi-lā″ri-an, at′ra-bi-lā″ri-us, *a.* [L. *atra bilis*, black bile.] Affected with melancholy, which the ancients attributed to black bile; very bilious.—**Atrabilarian**, at′ra-bi-lā″ri-an, *n.* A person of an atrabiliar temperament; a hypochondriac. — **Atrabiliariousness**, at′ra-bi-lā″ri-us-nes, *n.* The state of being atrabilious.—**Atrabiliar, Atrabiliary, Atrabilious**, at-ra-bil′i-ar, at-ra-bil′i-a-ri, at-ra-bil′i-us, *a.* Melancholic or hypochondriacal; atrabilarian.

Atramental, Atramentarious, Atramentous, at-ra-men′tal, at′ra-men-tā″-ri-us, at-ra-men′tus, *a.* [L. *atramentum*, ink.] Inky; black as ink.

Atrip, a-trip′, *a.* Of anchor loosed from bottom by means of a cable; of sails turned from horizontal to vertical position.

Atrium, ā′tri-um, *n.* [L.] The entrance-hall and usually the most splendid apartment of an ancient Roman house; *zool.* the chamber into which the intestine opens in ascidians.

Atrocious, a-trō′shus, *a.* [L. *atrox, atrocis*, fierce, cruel.] Extremely heinous, criminal, or cruel; enormously or outrageously wicked; enormous; horrible.—**Atrociously**, a-trō′shus-li, *adv.* In an atrocious manner.—**Atrociousness**, a-trō′shus-nes, *n.* The quality of being atrocious.—**Atrocity**, a-tros′i-ti, *n.* The state or quality of being atrocious; enormous wickedness or cruelty; a specific act of extreme heinousness or cruelty.

Atropal, Atropous, at′ro-pal, at′ro-pus, *a.* [Gr. *a*, priv., and *trepō*, to turn.] *Bot.* erect: said of an ovule.

Atrophy, at′ro-fi, *n.* [Gr. *atrophia*—*a*, priv., and *trephō*, to nourish.[A wasting of the flesh with loss of strength; emaciation.

Atropin, Atropine, at′rō-pin, *n.* A very poisonous substance obtained from the deadly nightshade (*Atrŏpa belladonna*).

Attach, at-tach′, *v.t.* [Fr. *attacher*, same word as *attaquer*, to attack, from Arm. *tach*, Ir. *taca*, a peg, a nail=E. *tack*, a small nail.] To make to adhere; to tie, bind, or fasten; to connect or associate; to gain over, win, charm, or attract; to arrest or seize (a person or goods) by lawful authority, as in case of debt, &c.—*v.i.* To be attached or connected; to be joined or bound up with; to belong: with *to* (interest *attaches* to a subject).—**Attachable**, at-tach′a-bl, *a.* Capable of being attached.—**Attache**, ă-tä-shā, *n.* [Fr.] One attached to an embassy or legation to a foreign court. — **Attachment**, at-tach′ment, *n.* The act of attaching; the state of being attached; close adherence or affection; any passion or liking which binds one person to another or to a place, &c.; love; regard; that which attaches one object to another; the object attached; an adjunct; *law*, a taking of a person or goods by legal means to secure a debt.

Attack, at-tak′, *v.t.* [Fr. *attaquer*. ATTACH.] To assault; to fall upon with force or violence; to make a hostile onset on; to assail; to endeavour to injure by any act, speech, or writing; to come or fall upon; to seize, as a disease.—*v.i.* To make an attack or onset; to begin an assault.—*n.* A falling on, with force or violence, or with calumny, satire, &c.; an onset; an assault; a seizure by a disease.—**Attackable**, at-tak′a-bl, *a.* Capable of being attacked; assailable.—**Attacker**, at-tak′ėr, *n.* One who attacks.

Attaghan, at′ta-gan, *n.* YATAGHAN.

Attain, at-tān′, *v.t.* [O.Fr. *ataindre*, Fr. *atteindre*, L. *attingere*—*ad*, to, and *tango*, to touch. Akin *attaint, attainder, tact, tangent*, &c.] To reach by effort; to achieve or accomplish; to acquire; to gain: said of an end or object; to come to; to arrive at; to reach: said of a place.—*v.i.* To reach; to come or arrive: followed by *to*.—**Attainable**, at-tān′a-bl, *a.* Capable of being attained, reached, achieved, or accomplished. —**Attainability, Attainableness**, at-tān′a-bil″i-ti, at-tān′a-bl-nes, *n.* The quality of being attainable. — **Attainment**, at-tān′ment, *n.* The act of attaining; that which is attained; an acquisition; an acquirement.

Attainder, at-tān′dėr, *n.* [O.Fr. *atteindre, attaindre*, to touch or reach, as with law; to attaint, from L. *attingo*. ATTAIN, *v.t.*] The act or legal process of subjecting a person to the consequences of judgment of death or outlawry pronounced in respect of treason or felony; forfeiture of civil privileges; a bringing under some disgrace or dishonour (*Shak.*).—**Attaint**, at-tānt′, *v.t.* [O.Fr. *attaint*, pp. of *attaindre, ataindre.*] To affect with attainder; to find guilty of a crime, as of felony or treason, involving forfeiture of civil privileges

Attaint,‡ at-tānt′, *n.* [Prefix *at*, from L. *ad*, to, and *taint*, from L. *tinctus*, pp. of *tingo*, to dye. TAINT.] A spot, taint, stain, disgrace. (*Shak.*)—*a.*‡ Tainted; corrupted; infected. (*Shak.*)

Attar, at′tär, *n.* [Ar. *atr*, perfume.] A perfume from flowers.—*Attar* or *otto of roses*, an essential oil made from various species of roses, which forms a valuable perfume.

Attemper, at-tem′pėr, *v.t.* [L. *attempero*—*ad*, and *tempero*, to temper, mix, or moderate. TEMPER.] To reduce, mollify, or moderate by mixture; to soften, modify, or regulate; to accommodate or make fit.—**Attemperation**, at-tem′pėr-ā″shon, *n.* The act of regulating temperature.—**Attemperator**, at-tem′pėr-āt-ėr, *n.* A contrivance for regulating temperature, as in brewing.

Attempt, at-temt′, *v.t.* [O.Fr. *attempter*, from L. *attemptare*—*ad*, to, and *tempto*, to try.] To make an effort to effect; to endeavour to perform; to undertake; to try; to attack; to make an effort upon (a person's life); to try to win or seduce.—*n.* An essay, trial, or endeavour; an effort to gain a point; an attack, onset, or assault.—**Attemptability**, at-temt′a-bil″i-ti, *n.* The state or condition of being attemptable. — **Attemptable**, at-temt′a-bl, *a.* Capable of being attempted.—**Attempter**, at-temt′ėr, *n.* One who attempts.

Attend, at-tend′, *v.t.* [Fr. *attendre*, L. *attendo*, to turn one's mind to, to turn to—*ad*, to, and *tendo*, to stretch. TEND.] To accompany or be present with, as a companion or servant; to be present at or in for some purpose (church, a concert, &c.); to accompany or follow in immediate sequence, especially from a causal connection (a cold *attended* with fever); to wait for‡.—*v.i.* To pay regard or heed; to be present, in pursuance of duty; to act as an attendant;

to be concomitant: by itself or followed by *on* or *upon*.—**Attendance**, at-tend'ans, *n.* The act of attending or attending on; the act of waiting on or serving; service; ministry; the persons attending for any purpose; a train; a retinue.—**Attendant**, at-tend'ant, *a.* Accompanying; being present or in attendance upon; connected with, or immediately following.—*n.* One who attends or accompanies another; one who belongs to a person's retinue; a follower; one who is present or regularly present; that which accompanies or is consequent on.—**Attender**, at-tend'ėr, *n.* One who attends; a companion; an associate.—**Attention**, at-ten'shon, *n.* [L. *attentio, attentionis*, from *attendo.*] The act of attending or heeding; the application of the ear to sounds, or of the mind to objects presented to its contemplation; heedfulness; observation; an act of civility or courtesy.—**Attentive**, at-tent'iv, *a.* Paying or giving attention; heedful; intent; observant; regarding with care; mindful; habitually heedful or mindful; sedulous.—**Attentively**, at-tent'iv-li, *adv.* In an attentive manner.—**Attentiveness**, at-tent'iv-nes, *n.* The state of being attentive; attention.

Attenuate, at-ten'ū-āt, *v.t.*—*attenuated, attenuating.* [L. *attenuo, attenuatum*—*ad*, and *tenuo*, to make thin; *tenuis*, thin; same root as in E. *thin, tender.*] To make thin, fine, or slender; to reduce the thickness of either liquids or solid bodies; to reduce the strength of; to render meagre or jejune.—*v.i.* To become thin, slender, or fine; to diminish; to lessen.—**Attenuation**, at-ten'ū-ā"shon, *n.* The act of attenuating or making thin, as fluids, or slender and fine, as solid bodies.—**Attenuant**, at-ten'ū-ant, *a.* Attenuating; making thin, as fluids; diluting.—*n.* A medicine which increases the fluidity of the humours; a diluent.

Attest, at-test', *v.t.* [Fr. *attester*, L. *attestor*—*ad*, and *testor*, to witness. TESTAMENT, DETEST.] To bear witness to; to certify; to affirm to be true or genuine; to declare the truth of; to manifest (one's joy, &c.).—**Attestation**, at-test-ā'shon, *n.* The act of attesting; a solemn declaration, verbal or written, in support of a fact; evidence; testimony.—**Attester**, **Attestor**, at-test'ėr, *n.* One who attests.

Attic, at'tik, *a.* [L. *Atticus*, Gr. *Attikos.*] Pertaining to *Attica*, in Greece, or to its principal city, Athens; marked by the qualities characteristic of the Athenians; as, *Attic wit, Attic salt*, a delicate wit for which the Athenians were famous.—*n.* The dialect spoken in Attica or Athens; the chief literary and most elegant language of ancient Greece; *arch.* a low story erected over a principal; an apartment in the uppermost part of a house, with windows in the cornice or the roof; a garret.—**Atticism**, at'ti-sizm, *n.* A peculiarity or characteristic of the Attic dialect of Greek; elegance of diction.—**Atticize**, at'ti-sīz, *v.t.* and *i.* To conform to the Attic dialect.

Attire, at-tīr', *v.t.*—*attired, attiring.* [O.Fr. *attirer*, to array, from prefix *at*, L. *ad*, to, and same word as G. *zier*, ornament, A.Sax. *tir*, splendour, Dan. *ziir*, ornament.] To dress; to deck; to array; to adorn with elegant or splendid garments.—*n.* (no pl.). Dress; clothes; garb; apparel.

Attitude, at'ti-tūd, *n.* [Fr., from It. *attitudine*, fitness, posture, L.L. *aptitudo*, fitness, L. *aptus*, fit. APT.] Posture or position of a person, or the manner in which the parts of his body are disposed; state, condition, or conjuncture, as likely to have a certain result; aspect (the *attitude* of affairs).—**Attitudinal**, at-ti-tūd'in-al, *a.* Pertaining to attitude.—**Attitudinarian**, at-ti-tūd'in-ā"ri-an, *n.* One who studies or practises attitudes.—**Attitudinize**, at-ti-tūd'in-īz, *v.i.*—*attitudinized, attitudinizing.* To assume affected attitudes, airs, or postures.

Attollent, at-tol'lent, *a.* [L. *attollens, attollentis*, ppr. of *attollo*—*ad*, and *tollo*, to lift.] Lifting up; raising (an *attolent* muscle).

Attorney, at-tėr'ni, *n.* [O.Fr. *attorné*, pp. of *attorner*, to transfer—*at*, L. *ad*, to, and *torner*, to turn. TURN.] One who is appointed or admitted in the place of another to transact any business for him.—*Letter* or *power of attorney*, a formal instrument by which one person authorizes another to do some act or acts for him.—*v.t.*†—**District attorney**, the prosecuting officer of a Federal judicial district, or of a state, or any district thereof.—**Attorney in fact**, *n.* A person authorized to act for another, with or without letter or power of attorney, in any matters outside of court.—**Attorney general**, *n.* Head of the Federal Department of Justice; also the chief officer of a Federal judicial district; also legal adviser to the state legislature.

Attract, at-trakt', *v.t.* [L. *attraho, attractum*—*ad*, to, and *traho*, to draw, whence *tract, treat, trace*, &c.] To draw to or toward, either in a physical or mental sense; to cause to draw near or close to by some influence; to invite or allure; to entice; to win.—*v.i.* To possess or exert the power of attraction; to be attractive or winning.—**Attractability**, at-trakt'a-bil"i-ti, *n.* The quality of being attractable.—**Attractable**, at-trakt'a-bl, *a.* Capable of being attracted; subject to attraction.—**Attracter**, **Attractor**, at-trakt'ėr, *n.* One who or that which attracts.—**Attractile**,† at-trakt'il, *a.* Having the power to attract; attractive.—**Attraction**, at-trak'shon, *n.* The act, power, or property of attracting; *physics*, the tendency, force, or forces through which all particles of matter, as well as all individual masses of matter, are attracted or drawn towards each other; the inherent tendency in bodies to approach each other, to unite and to remain united; the power or act of alluring, drawing to, inviting, or engaging; allurement; enticement; that which attracts; a charm; an allurement.—**Attractive**, at-trakt'iv, *a.* [Fr. *attractif.*] Having the quality of attracting; having the power of charming or alluring; inviting; engaging; enticing.—*n.* That which attracts; a charm or allurement.—**Attractively**, at-trakt'iv-li, *adv.* In an attractive manner.—**Attractiveness**, at-trakt'iv-nes, *n.* The quality of being attractive or engaging.

Attrahent,† at'tra-hent, *a.* [L. *attrahens, attrahentis*, ppr. of *attraho*. ATTRACT.] Drawing to; attracting; dragging or pulling.

Attribute, at-trib'ūt, *v.t.*—*attributed, attributing.* [L. *attribuo, attributum*—*ad*, and *tribuo*, to assign.] To ascribe; to impute; to consider as belonging or as due; to assign.—**Attribute**, at'tri-būt, *n.* Any property, quality, or characteristic that can be ascribed to a person or thing; *fine arts*, a symbol of office or character added to any figure (thus the eagle is the *attribute* of Jupiter).—**Attributable**, at-trib'ūt-a-bl, *a.* Capable of being, or liable to be attributed; ascribable; imputable.—**Attribution**, at-tri-bū'shon, *n.* The act of attributing; that which is ascribed; attribute.—**Attributive**, at-trib'ū-tiv, *a.* Pertaining to or expressing an attribute; *gram.* coming before the noun it qualifies.—*n.* *Gram.* a word expressive of an attribute; an adjective.—**Attributively**, at-trib'ū-tiv-li, *adv.* *Gram.* in an attributive manner; used before the noun.

Attrition, at-tri'shon, *n.* [L. *attritio*, from *attero, attritum*, to rub down—*ad*, to, and *tero, tritum*, to rub.] The act of wearing or rubbing down; the state of being worn down or smoothed by friction; abrasion.

Attune, at-tūn', *v.t.*—*attuned, attuning.* [Prefix *at* for *ad*, to, and tune.] To tune or put in tune; to adjust one sound to another; to make accordant; *fig.* to arrange fitly; to bring into harmony, concord, or agreement.

Atween, a-twēn', *adv.* Between. [*Tenn.*]

Atypic, a-tip'ik, *a.* [Gr. *a*, priv., and *typos*, a type.] Devoid of typical character; irregular.

Auburn, ą'bėrn, *a.* [L.L. *alburnus*, whitish, from L. *albus*, white.] Originally, whitish or flaxen-coloured; now reddish brown or rich chestnut: generally applied to hair.

Auction, ąk'shon, *n.* [L. *auctio*, from *augeo, auctum*, to increase (from the rising in successive bids); allied to Icel. *auka*, Goth. *aukan*, E. *eke*, to increase. AUGMENT, AUXILIARY.] A public sale of property to the highest bidder.—*v.t.* To sell by auction.—**Auctionary**, ąk'shon-a-ri, *a.* Belonging to an auction or public sale.—**Auctioneer**, ąk-shon-ēr', *n.* One whose business it is to sell things by auction.—*v.t.*† To sell by auction.

Audacious, ą-dā'shus, *a.* [L. *audax, audacis*, from *audeo*, to dare.] Over bold or daring; bold in wickedness; insolent; impudent; shameless; unabashed.—**Audaciously**, ą-dā'shus-li, *adv.* In an audacious manner.—**Audaciousness**, **Audacity**, ą-dā'shus-nes, ą-das'i-ti, *n.* The quality of being audacious; impudence; effrontery; insolence.

Audible, ą'di-bl, *a.* [L. *audibilis*, from *audio*, to hear; same root as in E. *ear.*] Capable of being heard; perceivable by the ear; loud enough to be heard.—**Audibleness**, **Audibility**, ą'di-bl-nes, ą-di-bil'i-ti, *n.* The quality of being audible.—**Audibly**, ą'di-bli, *adv.* In an audible manner.—**Audience**, ą'di-ens, *n.* [L. *audientia.*] The act of listening; a hearing; liberty or opportunity of being heard before a person or assembly; an assembly of hearers.

Audiometer, ą-di-om'et-ėr, *n.* [L. *audio*, to hear, and Gr. *metron*, measure.] An instrument for testing the sense of hearing.

Audiphone, ą'di-fōn, *n.* [L. *audio*, to hear, and Gr. *phōnē*, voice.] An instrument for enabling the deaf to hear, essentially consisting of a fan-shaped vibratory plate of caoutchouc which is applied to the upper teeth, through which the sound vibrations are conveyed to the auditory nerve.

Audit, ą'dit, *n.* [L. *audit*, he hears, or *auditus*, a hearing, from *audio*, to hear. AUDIBLE.] An examination into accounts or dealings with money or property by proper officers, or persons appointed for that purpose, hence, a calling to account; an examination into one's actions; also, an audience or hearing†.—*v.t.* To make audit of; to examine, as an account or accounts.—**Audition**, ą-di'shon, *n.* [L. *auditio*, a hearing.] The act of hearing; a hearing or listening.—**Auditor**, ą'dit-ėr, *n.* [L.] A hearer; a listener; a person appointed and authorized to audit or examine an account or accounts.—**Auditorium**, ą-di-tō'ri-um, *n.* [L.] In an opera-house, public hall, &c., the space allotted to the hearers.—**Auditory**, ą'di-to-ri, *a.* [L. *auditorius.*] Relating to hearing or to the sense or organs of hearing.—*n.* [L. *auditorium.*] An audience; an assembly of hearers; a place for hearing or for the accommodation of hearers; an auditorium.—**Auditress**,† ą'di-tres, *n.* A female hearer. (*Mil.*)

Augean, ą-jē'an, *a.* Of or pertaining to the mythical *Augeas*, King of Elis, in Greece.—*Augean stable*, the stable of this king, in which he kept 3000 oxen, and the cleaning out of which, after it had remained uncleaned for thirty years, was assigned as a task to Hercules, who accomplished it in a single day. Hence cleaning the Augean stables became a synonym for the removal of accumulated nuisances, abuses, &c.

Auger, ą'gėr, *n.* [For *nauger*, initial *n* having been lost (as in *adder, apron*), this word being from A.Sax. *nafe-gār, nafugār*, from *nafu, nafa*. the nave of a wheel; and *gār*, a sharp-pointed thing, a dart or javelin. NAVE, GORE, to pierce.] An instrument for boring holes larger than those bored by a gimlet, chiefly used by carpenters, joiners, &c., and made in a great many forms; instruments on the same plan are used for boring into the soil.

Aught, ąt, *n.* [A.Sax. *áwiht*, from *á* for *án*, one, and *wiht*=E. *whit, wight*; lit. a whit, its negative being *naught*, not a whit.] Anything, indefinitely; any part or quantity; anywhit.

Augite, ą'jīt, *n.* [Gr. *augē*, brightness.] The name given to a class of minerals, greenish-black, pitch or velvet black, or leek-green in colour, and consisting of silicates of lime, magnesia, and iron, with alumina in the darker varieties.—**Augitic**, a̤-jit′ik, *a.* Pertaining to, consisting of, resembling, or containing augite.

Augment, a̤g-ment′, *v.t.* [Fr. *augmenter*, L. *augmento*, from *augmentum*, increase, from *augeo*, to increase. AUCTION.] To increase; to enlarge in size or extent; to swell; to make bigger.—*v.i.* To increase; to grow larger.—**Augment**, ag′ment, *n.* Increase; enlargement by addition†; *gram.* an increase at the beginning of certain inflectional forms of a verb, as the *e* prefixed in certain tenses of the Greek verb, and the *ge* in the past participle of the German verb.—**Augmentable**, a̤g-ment′a-bl, *a.* Capable of being augmented or increased. —**Augmentation**, a̤g-men-tā′shon, *n.* The act of augmenting; the act of adding to or enlarging; the state or condition of being made larger; increase; enlargement; accession; the thing added by way of enlargement; addition.—**Augmentative**, a̤g-ment′a-tiv, *a.* Having the quality or power of augmenting.—*n.* A word formed to express greatness: opposed to a *diminutive*.—**Augmentatively**, a̤g-ment′a-tiv-li, *adv.* In an augmentative manner; in a manner to augment.—**Augmenter**, a̤g-ment′ėr, *n.* One who or that which augments.

Augur, a̤′gėr, *n.* [L. *augur*, from *avis*, a bird, and L. *garrio*, to chatter.] Among the ancient Romans a functionary whose duty was to derive signs concerning future events from the flight or other actions of birds, from certain appearances in quadrupeds, from lightning and other unusual occurrences; hence, one who foretells future events by omens; a soothsayer; a prophet. —*v.i.* To guess; to conjecture, as from signs or omens; to be a sign; to bode (to *augur* well or ill for a project).—*v.t.* To guess or conjecture; to predict; to anticipate: said of persons; to betoken; to forebode: said of things.—**Augural**, a̤′gū-ral, *a.* Pertaining to an augur, or the duties or profession of an augur; pertaining to divination.—**Augurate**,† a̤′gū-rāt, *v.t.* or *i.* To conjecture or foretell by augury; to predict.—**Augurer**, a̤′gėr-ėr, *n.* One who augurs; an augur. (*Shak.*)—**Augurize**,† a̤′gėr-īz, *v.t.* or *i.* To augur; to act as an augur.—**Augurship**, a̤′gėr-ship, *n.* The office or period of office of an augur.—**Augury**, a̤′gū-ri or a̤′gėr-i, *n.* The art or practice of an augur; that which forebodes; that from which a prediction is drawn; a prognostication.

August, a̤-gust′, *a.* [L. *augustus*, from *augeo*, to increase, the same word as the name *Augustus*. AUGMENT, AUCTION.] Grand; magnificent; majestic; impressing awe; inspiring reverence.—**Augustly**, a̤-gust′li, *adv.* In an august manner.—**Augustness**, a̤-gust′nes, *n.* The quality of being august.

August, a̤′gust, *n.* [L. *Augustus*, from the Roman Emperor Augustus.] The eighth month of the year, containing thirty-one days.—**Augustan**, a̤-gust′an, *a.* Pertaining to the Emperor *Augustus*; as, the *Augustan* age, which was the most brilliant period in Roman literature; hence, any brilliant period in the literary history of other countries.

Augustin, Augustine, a̤-gust′in, *n.* A member of one of the fraternities who follow rules framed by St. Augustine or deduced from his writings. Also *Augustinian*.

Auk, a̤k, *n.* [Dan. *alke*, Icel. *alka*, *álka*, an auk.] The name of one or two swimming birds found in the British seas, having their legs placed so far back as to cause them to stand nearly upright, and with very short wings more useful for swimming and diving than for flight.

Aulic, a̤′lik, *a.* [L. *aulicus*, from *aula*, Gr. *aulē*, a court.] Pertaining to a royal court.

Aunt, änt, *n.* [O.Fr. *ante*, from L. *amita*, contracted in the same way as *emmet* is contracted into *ant*.] The sister of one's father or mother, a term correlative to nephew or niece.

Aura, a̤′ra, *n.* [L. *aura*, a breath of air.] An air; an effluvium or odour; an exhalation.—**Aural**, a̤′ral, *a.* Pertaining to an aura.

Aural, a̤′ral, *a.* [L. *auris*, the ear.] Relating to the ear (*aural* surgery).—**Auriform**, a̤′ri-form, *a.* Ear-shaped; having the form of the human ear.—**Aurist**, a̤′rist, *n.* One skilled in disorders of the ear, or who professes to cure them.—**Aurited**, a̤′rit-ed, *a.* [L. *auritus*.] *Bot.* and *zool.* eared; auriculate; having lobes or appendages like an ear.

Aurated,† a̤′rāt-ed, *a.* [L. *auratus*, pp. of *auro*, to gild, from *aurum*, gold.] Resembling gold; golden-coloured; gilded.—**Aureate**, a̤′rē-āt, *a.* [L. *aureatus*.] Golden; gilded.

Aurelia, a̤-rē′li-a, *n.* [From L. *aurum*, gold, from its colour.] The nymph, chrysalis, or pupa of a butterfly or other lepidopterous insect.—**Aurelian**, a̤-rē′li-an, *a.* Like or pertaining to the aurelia.

Aureola, Aureole, a̤-rē′ō-la, a̤′rē-ōl, *n.* [Fr. *auréole*, from L. *aureolus*, dim. of *aureus*, golden, from *aurum*, gold.] *Painting*, an illumination surrounding a holy person, as Christ, a saint, &c.; anything resembling an aureola; a halo.

Auricle, a̤′ri-kl, *n.* [L. *auricula*, dim. from *auris*, the ear.] The external ear, or that part which is prominent from the head; either of the two cavities in the mammalian heart, placed above the two ventricles, and resembling in shape the external ear.—**Auricled**, a̤′ri-kld, *a.* Having ears or auricles; having appendages resembling ears.—**Auricula**, a̤-rik′ū-la, *n.* A garden flower of the primrose family, found native in the Swiss Alps, and sometimes called bear's-ear from the shape of its leaves.—**Auricular**, a̤-rik′ū-lėr, *a.* Pertaining to the ear or the sense of hearing, or to an auricle; confided to one's ear, especially privately confided to the ear of a priest (*auricular* confession).—**Auricularly**, a̤-rik′ū-lėr-li, *adv.* In an auricular manner; by words privately addressed to the ear.—**Auriculate**, a̤-rik′ū-lāt, *a.* Shaped like the ear; having ears or some kind of expansions resembling ears; eared, as a leaf.

Auriferous, a̤-rif′ėr-us, *a.* [L. *aurifer*—*aurum*, gold, and *fero*, to produce.] Yielding or producing gold; containing gold.

Auriform, Aurist. Under AURAL.

Aurochs, a̤′roks, *n.* [G.] A species of wild bull or buffalo, once abundant on the continent of Europe, but now reduced to a few herds inhabiting the forests of Lithuania.

Aurora, a̤-rō′ra, *n.* [L., the goddess of morning, the dawn; same root as L. *uro*, to burn, *aurum*, gold.] The dawn, or morning twilight; the goddess of the morning, or dawn deified; the aurora borealis (in this sense with the plural *auroræ*).—*Aurora borealis*, the northern lights or streamers, a luminous meteoric phenomenon of varying brilliancy seen in the northern heavens, and in greatest magnificence in the arctic regions, believed to be electric in origin.—*Aurora australis*, the aurora of the southern hemisphere, quite a similar phenomenon to that of the north.—**Auroral**, a̤-rō′ral, *a.* Belonging to or resembling the dawn; belonging to or resembling the polar lights; roseate; rosy.

Auscultation, a̤s-kul-tā′shon, *n.* [L. *auscultatio*, a listening, from *ausculto*, to listen, from *auris*, the ear.] *Med.* a method of distinguishing the state of the internal parts of the body, particularly of the chest, by observing the sounds arising there either through the application of the ear or by the stethoscope.—**Auscultator**, a̤s′kul-tāt-ėr, *n.* One who practises auscultation.—**Auscultatory**, a̤s-kul′ta-to-ri, *a.* Pertaining to auscultation.

Auspice, a̤′spis, *n.* [L. *auspicium*, from *auspex*, an augur—*avis*, a bird, and *specio*, to view.] An augury from birds; an omen or sign in general; protection; favourable influence.—**Auspicate**,† a̤′spi-kāt, *v.t.* [L. *auspicor*, to take the auspices.] To initiate with pomp or ceremony; to inaugurate.—**Auspicatory**, a̤′spi-ka-to-ri, *a.* Of or belonging to auspices or omens.—**Auspicious**, a̤-spi′shus, *a.* Having omens of success, or favourable appearances; propitious; favourable; prosperous; happy.—**Auspiciously**, a̤-spi′shus-li, *adv.* In an auspicious manner.—**Auspiciousness**, a̤-spi′shus-nes, *n.*

Austere, a̤-stēr′, *a.* [L. *austerus*, Gr. *austēros*, harsh.] Harsh; tart; sour; rough to the taste; *fig.* severe; harsh; rigid; rigorous; stern.—**Austerely**, a̤-stēr′li, *adv.* In an austere manner; severely; rigidly; harshly. —**Austereness, Austerity**, a̤-stēr′nes, a̤-ste′ri-ti, *n.* The state or quality of being austere; severity; rigour; strictness; harshness.

Austral, a̤s′tral, *a.* [L. *australis*, from *auster*, the south wind, or south.] Southern; lying or being in the south.—**Australasian**, a̤s-tral-ā′shi-an, *a.* [From *austral* and *Asia*.] Relating to Australasia, that is, to Australia, New Zealand, and the adjacent islands.—*n.* A native of Australasia. —**Australian**, a̤s-trā′li-an, *a.* Pertaining to Australia.—*n.* A native or inhabitant of Australia.

Authentic, a̤-then′tik, *a.* [L. *authenticus*, from Gr. *authentikos*, original, genuine, from *authentēs*, one who does anything with his own hand.] Being what it purports to be; not false or fictitious; genuine; valid; authoritative; reliable. ∴ *Authentic*, applied to a document or book, indicates that it can be relied on as narrating real facts; *genuine*, that we have it as it left its author's hands.—**Authentically**, a̤-then′tik-al-li, *adv.* In an authentic manner.—**Authenticate**, a̤-then′ti-kāt, *v.t.*—*authenticated*, *authenticating*. To render authentic: to give authority to by proof, attestation, &c.; to prove authentic; to determine as genuine.—**Authentication**, a̤-then′ti-kā″shon, *n.* The act of authenticating; the giving of proof or authority.—**Authenticity**, a̤-then-tis′i-ti, *n.* The quality of being authentic; the quality of being genuine; genuineness.

Author, a̤′thor, *n.* [O.F. *autheur*, L. *auctor*, improperly written *autor*, *author*, from *augeo*, *auctum*, to increase, to produce. AUGMENT.] The beginner, former, or first mover of anything (*author* of our being): the originator or creator; efficient cause; the original composer of a literary work; the writer of a book or other literary production.—**Authoress**, a̤′thor-es, *n.* A female author.—**Authoritative**, a̤-thor′i-tā-tiv, *a.* Having authority; having the sanction or appearance of authority; positive; peremptory; dictatorial.—**Authoritatively**, a̤-thor′i-tā-tiv-li, *adv.* In an authoritative manner; with a show of authority.—**Authoritativeness**, a̤-thor′i-tā-tiv-nes, *n.* The quality of being authoritative.—**Authority**, a̤-thor′i-ti, *n.* [O.Fr. *authorité*.] Power or right to command or act; dominion; control; the power derived from opinion, respect, or esteem; influence conferred by character, station, mental superiority, &c.; a person or persons exercising power or command: generally in the plural (the civil and military *authorities*); that to which or one to whom reference may be made in support of any fact, opinion, action, &c. (a person's *authority* for a statement); credit or credibility (a work of no *authority*).—**Authorize**, a̤′thor-īz, *v.t.* —*authorized*, *authorizing*. To give authority, warrant, or legal power to; to give a right to act; to empower; to make legal; to establish by authority or by usage or public opinion (an *authorized* idiom); to warrant; to sanction; to justify.—**Authorization**, a̤′thor-iz-ā″shon, *n.* The act of authorizing. —**Authorship**, a̤′thor-ship, *n.* The character or state of being an author; the source from which a work proceeds.

Autobiography, a̤′tō-bī-og″ra-fi, *n.* [Gr. *autos*, self, and E. *biography*.] Biography or memoirs of a person written by himself.—**Autobiographer, Autobiographist**, a̤′tō-bī-og″ra-fėr, a̤′tō-bī-og″ra-fist, *n.* One who writes an autobiography.—**Autobiographic, Autobiographical**, a̤-tō-bī′o-graf″ik, a̤-tō-bī′o-graf″ik-al, *a.*

Pertaining to, consisting of, or containing autobiography.—**Autobiographically**, a̤-tō-bī′o-graf″ik-al-li, *adv.* In an autobiographical manner.

Auto-car, a̤′tō-kär, *n.* [Gr. *autos*, self.] A carriage driven by a motor carried with it.

Autochthon, a̤-tok′thōn, *n.* pl. **Autochthones**, a̤-tok′thon-ēz. [Gr. *autochthōn*—*autos*, self, and *chthōn*, the earth.] One of the primitive inhabitants of a country; an aboriginal inhabitant; that which is original to a particular country.—**Autochthonal**, **Autochthonous**, **Autochthonic**, a̤-tok′thon-al, a̤-tok′thon-us, a̤-tok′thon-ik, *a.* Aboriginal; primitive; indigenous.

Autocracy, a̤-tok′ra-si, *n.* [Gr. *autokrateia*—*autos*, self, and *kratos*, power.] Supreme power invested in a single person; the government or power of an absolute monarch.—**Autocrat**, a̤′tō-krat, *n.* [Gr. *autokratēs*.] An absolute sovereign; a monarch who governs without being subject to restriction: a title assumed by the emperors of Russia; hence, one who is invested with or assumes unlimited authority in any relation.—**Autocratic**, **Autocratical**, a̤-tō-krat′ik, a̤-tō-krat′ik-al, *a.* Pertaining to autocracy; absolute; holding unlimited powers of government.—**Autocratically**, *adv.* In an autocratic manner.—**Autocratrix**,† a̤-tok′ra-triks, *n.* A female autocrat.

Auto-de-fe, ou′tō-de-fā″, *n.* pl. **Autos-de-fe**, ou′tōs-de-fā″. [Sp., lit. act (in sense of decree, judgment, sentence) of faith—*auto* = L. *actum*, an act, *de*, of, and *fe* = L. *fides*, faith.] A public solemnity, formerly held by the courts of the Inquisition in Spain and Portugal and their dependencies at the execution of heretics condemned to the stake. **Auto-da-fe**, ou′tō-dä-fā″, is the Portuguese form.

Autogenous, a̤-toj′en-us, *a.* [Gr. *autos*, self, and root *gen*, to generate.] Self-produced; self-generated; produced independently.

Autograph, a̤′tō-graf, *n.* [Gr. *autos*, self, and *graphē*, writing.] A person's own handwriting; an original manuscript or signature.—**Autographic**, **Autographical**, a̤-tō-graf′ik, a̤-tō-graf′ik-al, *a.* Pertaining or relating to an autograph, or one's own handwriting; relating to or used in the process of autography.—**Autography**, a̤-tog′ra-fi, *n.* A person's own handwriting; a process in lithography by which a writing or drawing is transferred from paper to stone.

Automatic, **Automatical**, a̤-tō-mat′ik, a̤-tō-mat′ik-al, *a.* [Gr. *automatos*, self-acting—*autos*, self, and root *ma*, to strive.] Belonging to or proceeding by spontaneous movement; having the power of self-motion; self-acting: said especially of mechanism; not depending on the will; instinctive: applied to actions.—**Automatic guns**. Guns that after the first shot fire others in rapid succession.—**Automatism**, a̤-tom′a-tizm, *n.* Automatic action; theory regarding automatic actions.—**Automaton**, a̤-tom′a-ton, *n.* pl. **Automata**, **Automatons**, a̤-tom′a-ta, a̤-tom′a-tonz. That which is self-moving; a self-acting machine; a mechanical contrivance which imitates the arbitrary or voluntary motions of living beings; a person who acts mechanically.

Automedon, a̤-tom′e-dōn, *n.* Coachman, from the name of Achilles' charioteer.

Automobile, a̤′tō-mō-bil, *n.* [Gr. *autos*, self. MOBILE.] An auto-car or similar vehicle.

Automorphic,† a̤-tō-mor′fik, *a.* [Gr. *autos*, self, and *morphē*, form.] Framed or conceived after the form of one's self.

Autonomy, a̤-ton′o-mi, *n.* [Gr. *autonomia*—*autos*, self, and *nomos*, law, rule.] The power or right of self-government.—**Autonomic**, **Autonomous**, a̤-tō-nom′ik, a̤-ton′o-mus, *a.* Relating to autonomy; independent in government; having the right of self-government.

Autophagi, a̤-tof′a-jī, *n. pl.* [Gr. *autos*, self, and *phagein*, to eat.] Birds which have the power of feeding themselves as soon as they are hatched.

Autoplasty, a̤′tō-plas-ti, *n.* [Gr. *autos*, self, and *plassō*, to form.] *Surg.* same as *Anaplasty*.

Autopsy, a̤′top-si, *n.* [Gr., from *autos*, self, and *opsis*, sight.] Personal observation; ocular view; *med.* post-mortem examination.—**Autoptic**, **Autoptical**, a̤-top′tik, a̤-top′tik-al, *a.* Relating to or based on autopsy or personal observation.—**Autoptically**, a̤-top′tik-al-li, *adv.* In an autoptical manner.

Autotype, a̤′tō-tīp, *n.* [Gr. *autos*, self, *typos*, a stamp.] A photographic process resembling heliotype; a picture produced by the process.

Autotypography, a̤′tō-tī-pog″ra-fi, *n.* [Gr. prefix *autos*, self, and E. *typography*.] A process by which designs are impressed on a metal plate, from which copies may be taken for printing.

Autumn, a̤′tum, *n.* [L. *autumnus*, for *auctumnus*, the season of increase, from *augeo*, *auctum*, to increase. AUGMENT.] The third season of the year, or the season between summer and winter, popularly regarded as comprising Aug., Sept., and Oct., but astronomically beginning at the autumnal equinox, 23d Sept., and ending at the winter solstice, 21st December.—**Autumnal**, a̤-tum′nal, *a.* Belonging to autumn; produced or gathered in autumn; *fig.* belonging to the period past the middle stage of life.

Auxiliary, a̤g-zil′i-a-ri, *a.* [L. *auxiliaris*, from *auxilium*, aid, from *augeo*, to increase, whence also *auction*, *augment*, *autumn*, &c.] Conferring aid or support; helping; aiding; assisting; subsidiary.—**Auxiliary**, a̤g-zil′i-a-ri, *n.* A helper; an assistant; an associate in some undertaking; *pl.* foreign troops in the service of a nation at war; *gram.* a verb which helps to form the moods and tenses of other verbs; as, *have*, *may*, *shall*, and *will*.

Avail, a-vāl′, *v.t.* [O.Fr. *valeir*, to be worth, from L. *valeo*, to be strong, with prefix *a* for L. *ad*.] To be for the advantage of; to assist or profit; to benefit.—*To avail one's self of*, to turn to one's profit or advantage; to take advantage of.—*v.i.* To be of use, benefit, or advantage; to answer a purpose; to have strength, force, or efficacy sufficient.—*n.* Advantage tending to promote success; benefit; service; utility; efficacy: used in such phrases as, of little *avail*; of much *avail*.—**Available**, a-vāl′a-bl, *a.* Advantageous; having efficacy: capable of being used; attainable; accessible.—**Availableness**, **Availability**, a-vāl′a-bl-nes, a-vāl′a-bil″i-ti, *n.* State of being available; power or efficacy; legal force; validity.—**Availably**, a-vāl′a-bli, *adv.* In an available manner.

Avalanche, av′a-lansh, *n.* [Fr. *avalanche*, from *avaler*, to descend—*a*, to, *val*, a valley.] A vast body of snow or ice sliding down a mountain, or over a precipice.

Avant-courier, a-väṅ-kö-rēr, *n.* [Fr. *avant*, before, from L. *ab*, from *ante*, before.] A person despatched before another person or a company, to give notice of their approach.—**Avant-guard**, a-väṅ-gärd, *n.* [Fr. *avant-garde*.] The van or advanced body of an army; the vanguard.

Avanturine, **Aventurine**, a-van′tū-rin, a-ven′tū-rin, *n.* [Fr. *aventure*, chance.] A variety of artificial gem consisting of glass, oxide of copper, and oxide of iron: a compound discovered accidentally (*par aventure*); also, a variety of quartz rock containing spangles of mica or quartz.

Avarice, av′a-ris, *n.* [L. *avaritia*, from *avarus*, greedy, from *aveo*, to covet.] An inordinate desire of gaining and possessing wealth; covetousness; cupidity; greediness.—**Avaricious**, av-a-ri′shus, *a.* Characterized by avarice; greedy of gain; miserly; covetous.—**Avariciously**, av-a-ri′shus-li, *adv.* In an avaricious manner; covetously; greedily.—**Avariciousness**, av-a-ri′shus-nes, *n.* The quality of being avaricious.

Avast, a-vast′, *exclam.* [From D. *houd vast*, hold fast, stop.] *Naut.* the order to stop, hold, cease, or stay in any operation: sometimes used colloquially, without reference to ships.

Avatar, **Avatara**, av-a-tär′, av-a-tä′ra, *n.* [Skr. *avatāra*—*ava*, down, and root *tri*, to go.] A descent from heaven; the incarnation of the Hindu deities, or their appearance in some manifest shape upon earth.

Avaunt, a-va̤nt′, *interj.* [Fr. *avant*, *en avant*, forward, march!—from L. *ab*, from *ante*, before. *Van* is the same word.] Begone; depart: an exclamation of contempt or abhorrence.

Ave, ā′vē, *interj.* [L.] Hail! farewell! God bless you! Sometimes used as a noun for an Ave-Maria.—**Ave-Maria**, ā′vē-ma-rī′a, *n.* [L. = hail Mary!—the first words of Gabriel's salutation to the Virgin Mary.] Devotional words often repeated in the Roman Catholic Church, chaplets and rosaries being divided into a certain number of ave-marias and paternosters.

Avenaceous, av-e-nā′shus, *a.* [L. *avena*, oats.] Belonging to or partaking of the nature of oats.

Avenge, a-venj′, *v.t.*—*avenged*, *avenging*. [O.Fr. *avengier*—prefix *a*, and L. *vindicare*, to avenge, vindicate.] To vindicate by inflicting pain or evil on the wrong-doer; to deal punishment for injury done to: with a person as object; to take satisfaction for, by pain or punishment inflicted on the injuring party; to deal punishment on account of: with a thing as object.—**Avengement**, a-venj′ment, *n.* The act of avenging.—**Avenger**, a-venj′ėr, *n.* One who avenges; one who takes vengeance.

Avens, av′enz, *n.* The popular name of several species of rosaceous plants growing wild: common avens is also called herb-bennet.

Aventurine, *n.* and *a.* AVANTURINE.

Avenue, av′e-nū, *n.* [Fr., from *avenir*, to arrive, L. *advenio*. ADVENE, ADVENT.] A passage; a way or opening for entrance; a wide straight roadway or street; an alley or walk planted on each side with trees; *fig.* means of access or attainment.

Aver, a-vėr′, *v.t.*—*averred*, *averring*. [Fr. *averer*, from L. *ad*, to, and *verus*, true.] To affirm with confidence; to declare in a positive or peremptory manner; to assert.—**Averment**, a-vėr′ment, *n.* The act of averring; affirmation; a positive assertion or declaration.

Average, av′ėr-āj, *n.* [Fr. *avarie*, Sp. *averia*, damage sustained by goods at sea; from Ar. *awār*, defect, flaw, modified by the influence of L.L. *averagium*, the carriage of goods by *averia* or draught-cattle, a contribution towards loss of things carried, from O.Fr. *aver*, a work-horse, from L. *habere*, to have.] A contribution falling on the owners of a ship's freight and cargo, in proportion to their several interests, to make good a loss that has been sustained; a sum or quantity intermediate to a number of different sums or quantities; a mean or medial amount; a general estimate based on comparison of a number of diverse cases; a medium.—*a.* Exhibiting a mean proportion or mean quality; forming an average; medium; not extreme; ordinary; *com.* estimated in accordance with the rules of average.—*v.t.*—*averaged*, *averaging*. To find the average of; to reduce to a mean sum or quantity; to show or have as an average or mean (trees average 50 feet in height).—**Averagely**, av′ėr-āj-li, *adv.* In an average way or manner; by taking an average.

Avernian, a-vėr′ni-an, *a.* Pertaining to *Avernus*, a lake of Campania, in Italy, represented by classical poets as the entrance to hell.

Averruncate, av-e-rung′kāt, *v.t.* [L. *averrunco*, to avert—*a*, from, and *verrunco*, to turn.] To avert.—**Averruncation**, av′e-rung-kā″shon, *n.* The act of averting; eradication; extirpation; removal.—**Averruncator**, av-e-rung′kāt-ėr, *n.* An implement for pruning trees when their branches are beyond easy reach of the hand.

Avert, a-vėrt′, *v.t.* [L. *averto*, *aversum*, to

turn away—*a*, from, and *verto, versum*, to turn, whence *verse, convert, converse, diverse*, &c.] To turn or direct away from; to turn or to cause to turn off or away (the eyes, calamity, &c.).—**Averter**, a-vėrt′ėr, *n*. One who or that which averts or turns away. —**Averse**, a-vėrs′, *a*. [L. *aversus*, turned from, pp. of *averto*.] Turned away from; averted (*Mil.*); unwilling; having repugnance: now regularly followed by *to*, not by *from*.—**Aversely**, a-vėrs′li, *adv*. In an averse manner; with repugnance; unwillingly.—**Averseness**, a-vėrs′nes, *n*. The state of being averse.—**Aversion**, a-vėr′-shon, *n*. Opposition or repugnance of mind; dislike; disinclination; reluctance; hatred: used absolutely or with *to*; the cause of dislike; the object of repugnance.

Avesta, a-ves′ta, *n*. The sacred writings attributed to Zoroaster; the Zend-avesta.—**Avestan**, a-ves′tan, *n*. The language of the Avesta; Zend.

Avian, ā′vi-an, *a*. [L. *avis*, a bird.] Pertaining to birds.—**Aviary**, ā′vi-a-ri, *n*. [L. *aviarium*.] A building or inclosure for the breeding, rearing, and keeping of birds.—**Aviation**, ā-vi-ā′shon, *n*. Aerial navigation by machines heavier than air.—**Aviator**, ā′vi-ā-tėr, *n*. One who engages in aviation.—**Aviculture**, ā′vi-kul′tūr, *n*. The breeding and rearing of birds.—**Avifauna**, ā′vi-fa̤-na, *n*. A collective name for the birds or avian fauna of a district.—**Aviform**, ā′vi-form, *a*. Bird-shaped.

Avid, av′id, *a*. [L. *avidus*, from *aveo*, to desire; akin *avarice*.] Eager; greedy: with *of*.—**Avidity**, a-vid′i-ti, *n*. [L. *aviditas*.] Greediness; strong appetite; eagerness; intenseness of desire.

Avizandum, av-i-zan′dum. In Scotland, the private consideration by a judge of a case that has been heard in court.

Avocado-pear, av-ō-kä′dō-pār, *n*. [Corrupted from Mexican name.] The fruit of a small tree of the laurel family, common in tropical America and the West Indies: also called *Alligator-pear*.

Avocate,† av′ō-kāt, *v.t*. [L. *avoco, avocatum*—*a*, from, and *voco*, to call.] To call off or away; to remove from an inferior to a superior court.—**Avocation**, av-ō-kā′shon, *n*. The act of calling aside or diverting from some object or employment; the authoritative removal of a case from an inferior to a superior court; that which calls a man away from his proper business; a distraction; a hinderance; a man's business, pursuit, or occupation; vocation or calling.—**Avocative**, a-vok′a-tiv, *a*. Calling off.

Avocet, av′ō-set, *n*. Same as *Avoset*.

Avoid, a-void′, *v.t*. [Originally to empty; from prefix *a*, and *void*.] To make void (in legal phraseology); to shun; to keep away from; to eschew; to evade; to elude (expense, danger, bad company).—*v.i*. To become void or vacant; to retire†; to withdraw†.—**Avoidable**, a-void′a-bl, *a*. That may be vacated or annulled; capable of being avoided, shunned, or escaped.—**Avoidance**, a-void′ans, *n*. The act of annulling or making void; the act of avoiding or shunning.—**Avoider**, a-void′ėr, *n*. One who avoids.—**Avoidless**,† a-void′les, *a*. Inevitable; certain; unavoidable.

Avoirdupois, av-ėr′dū-poiz″, *n*. [O.Fr. *avoir du pois*, to have weight—L. *habeo*, to have, *pensum*, something weighed out. POISE.] A system of weight of which 1 lb. contains 16 oz., in distinction to troy weight, which has only 12—the system by which commodities in general are weighed.

Avoset, av′ō-set, *n*. [Fr. *avocette*, It. *avocetta*.] A wading-bird of the size of a lapwing, with very long legs, feathers variegated with black and white, and a long slender bill bent upwards toward the tip.

Avouch, a-vouch′, *v.t*. [Prefix *a* (= L. *ad*, to), and *vouch*; O.Fr. *avochier, avocher*.] To affirm openly; to avow; to maintain, vindicate, or justify (a statement); to establish; guarantee; substantiate.—*n*.‡ Evidence; testimony. (*Shak.*)—**Avouchable**, a-vouch′a-bl, *a*. Capable of being avouched.—**Avoucher**, a-vouch′ėr, *n*. One who avouches.—**Avouchment**, a-vouch′ment, *n*. The act of avouching; declaration; avowal.

Avow, a-vou′, *v.t*. [Fr. *avouer*—*a* (from L. *ad*, to), and *vouer*, to vow. VOW.] To declare openly, with a view to justify, maintain, or defend (sentiments, &c.); to acknowledge; to own.—**Avowable**, a-vou′-a-bl, *a*. Capable of being avowed or openly acknowledged.—**Avowably**, a-vou′a-bli, *adv*. In an avowable manner.—**Avowal**, a-vou′al, *n*. An open declaration; frank acknowledgment.—**Avowance**, a-vou′-ans, *n*. The act of avowing; avowal.—**Avowed**, a-voud′, *a*. Declared; open (an *avowed* enemy).—**Avowedly**, a-vou′-ed-li, *adv*. In an avowed or open manner; with frank acknowledgment.—**Avower**, a-vou′ėr, *n*. One who avows, owns, or asserts.

Avulsion, a-vul′shon, *n*. [L. *avulsio*, from *avello*—*a*, from, away, and *vello, vulsum*, to pull.] A pulling or tearing asunder or off.

Avuncular, a-vung′kū-lėr, *a*. [L. *avunculus*, an uncle.] Of or pertaining to an uncle.

Await, a-wāt′, *v.t*. To wait for; to look for or expect; to be in store for; to be ready for (a reward *awaits* him).

Awake, a-wāk′, *v.t*.—*awoke* or *awaked* (pret. & pp.), *awaking*. [Prefix *a*, intens., and *wake*; A.Sax. *áwacan*, pret. *áwóc*, also *áwacian*, to awake. WAKE.] To rouse from sleep or from a state resembling sleep; to put into action or new life.—*v.i*. To cease to sleep; to bestir or rouse one's self from a state resembling sleep.—*a*. [A.Sax. *áwacen*, pp. of *áwacan*.] Not sleeping; in a state of vigilance or action.—**Awakement**, a-wāk′ment, *n*. Act of awakening, or state of being awake; revival.—**Awaken**, a-wāk′n, *v.i*. [A.Sax. *áwacnan, áwacnian*, to awake (intrans.).] To become awake; to awake.—*v.t*. To rouse from sleep; to awake. —**Awakener**, a-wāk′n-ėr, *n*. One who or that which awakens.—**Awakening**, a-wāk′n-ing, *n*. Act of awaking from sleep; a revival of religion.—*a*. Rousing; alarming.—**Awakeningly**, a-wāk′n-ing-li, *adv*. In a manner to awaken.—**Awakenment**, a-wāk′n-ment, *n*. The act of awakening, or state of being awakened.

Awanting, a-wont′ing, *a*. Wanting; absent; missing. [Not used attributively.]

Award, a-wa̤rd′, *v.t*. [O.Fr. *awarder*, to have under *ward*, to inspect, to pronounce as to the sufficiency of. WARD.] To adjudge; to assign judicially or by sentence (as an arbitrator pronouncing upon the rights of parties).—*v.i*. To make an award. —*n*. Judgment; decision; the decision of arbitrators on points submitted to them.—**Awarder**, a-wa̤rd′ėr, *n*. One that awards or makes an award.

Aware, a-wãr′, *a*. [Prefix *a*, and *ware* (as in be*ware*); A.Sax. *gewær*, wary, cautious; G. *gewahr*, aware. WARE, WARY.] Apprised; cognizant; informed; conscious: followed by *of*. [Not used attributively.]

Away, a-wā′, *adv*. [A.Sax. *onweg*—*on*. on, and *weg*, way.] Absent; at a distance; apart; to a distance (to go *away*). It is often used elliptically (whither *away* so fast?). With many verbs it conveys a notion of using up or consuming (to squander *away*, to idle or loiter *away*); it has also merely an intensive force (eat *away*, laugh *away*).—*int*. Begone! depart! go away.

Awe, a̤, *n*. [O.E. *aghe, eghe*, A.Sax. *ege*, fear, dread; Icel. *agi*, awe, terror; Goth. *agis*, fear; allied to Gael. *agh*, fear; Gr. *achos*, anguish—from root seen in *anguish, anger*, &c. ANGER.] Dread or great fear; fear mingled with admiration or reverence; reverential fear; feeling inspired by something sublime.—*v.t*.—*awed, awing*. To strike with awe; to influence by fear, reverence, or respect.—**Aweless**, **Awless**, a̤′les, *a*. Devoid of awe; wanting the power of inspiring reverence or awe.—**Awful**, a̤′fu̇l, *a*. Striking or inspiring with awe; filling with dread, or dread mingled with profound reverence; proceeding from awe; extraordinary or highly remarkable (colloq.). —**Awfully**, a̤′fu̇l-li, *adv*. In an awful manner; in a manner to fill with awe; terribly; excessively.—**Awfulness**, a̤′fu̇l-nes, *n*. The quality of being awful, or of striking with awe, reverence, or terror.

Aweary, a-wē′ri, *a*. Weary. [Poetical.]

Aweather, a-weTH′ėr, *a*. or *adv*. On or to the weather side of a ship: opposed to *alee*.

Awhile, a-whīl′, *adv*. [O.E. *ane hwile*, a while.] For a space of time; for some time.

Awkward, a̤k′wėrd, *a*. [O.E. *awk, awke*, wrong, backwards, reverse, and term. *-ward*. *Awk* corresponds to Icel. *öfigr, öfugr*, Sw. *afvig*, turned the wrong way, from *af* = E. *off*.] Wanting dexterity in the use of the hands or of instruments; bungling; clumsy; ungraceful in manners; uncouth.—**Awkwardly**, a̤k′wėrd-li, *adv*. In an awkward manner; clumsily.—**Awkwardness**, a̤k′wėrd-nes, *n*. The quality of being awkward.

Awl, a̤l, *n*. [A.Sax. *awul, ael, ǽl*; Icel. *alr*, G. *ahle*.] A pointed instrument for piercing small holes in leather, wood, &c.

Awn, a̤n, *n*. [Icel. *ögn*, Dan. *avne*, Sw. *agne*, chaff, husk; akin to Gr. *achnē*, chaff.] The bristle or beard of corn or grass, or any similar bristle-like appendage.—**Awned**, *a*. Having awns.—**Awner**, a̤n′ėr, *n*. One who or that which removes awns from grain: a hummeller.—**Awny**, a̤n′i, *a*. Having awns.

Awning, a̤n′ing, *n*. [L.G. *havenung*, a shelter, from *haven*, a haven.] A covering of canvas or other cloth spread over any place as a protection from the sun's rays.

Awry, a-rī′, *a*. or *adv*. In a wry position; turned or twisted toward one side; asquint; crooked; perverse.

Axe, **Ax**, aks, *n*. [A.Sax. *ax, æx*, Icel. *öx*, Dan. *öxe*, D. *aakse*, G. *ax, axt*; allied to Gr. *axinē*, L. *ascia* for *acsia*—an axe. From root *ac, ak*, a point. ACID.] An instrument, consisting of a head, with an arching edge of steel in the plane of the sweep of the tool, attached to a handle, and used for hewing timber and chopping wood.—**Axe-head**, *n*. The head or iron of an axe.—**Axe-stone**, *n*. The mineral nephrite or jade.

Axial, **Axially**, &c. See AXIS.

Axil, **Axilla**, aks′il, aks-il′la, *n*. [L. *axilla*, the arm-pit.] The arm-pit; a cavity under the upper part of the arm or shoulder; *bot*. the angle on the upper side between an axis and any organ growing from it.—**Axillar**, **Axillary**, aks′il-lėr, aks′il-la-ri, *a*. Pertaining to the arm-pit or to the axil of plants.

Axiom, aks′i-om, *n*. [Gr. *axiōma*.] A self-evident truth or proposition; a proposition whose truth is so evident at first sight that no process of reasoning or demonstration can make it plainer; an established principle in some art or science; a principle universally received.—*Syn*. under APHORISM.—**Axiomatic**, **Axiomatical**, aks′-i-ō-mat″ik, aks′i-ō-mat″ik-al, *a*. Pertaining to, consisting of, or having the character of an axiom.—**Axiomatically**, aks′i-ō-mat″ik-al-li, *adv*. In an axiomatic manner.

Axis, aks′is, *n*. pl. **Axes**, aks′ēz. [L.] The straight line, real or imaginary, passing through a body or magnitude, on which it revolves, or may be supposed to revolve; an agreement between two or more leading powers by which lesser powers may align themselves for or against the general principles set forth; specifically the Rome-Berlin axis; *bot*. the central line or column about which other parts are arranged; *anat*. the second vertebra of the neck.—**Axial**, aks′i-al, *a*. Pertaining to an axis.—**Axially**, aks′i-al-li, *adv*. According to or in line with the axis.—**Axiform**, aks′i-form, *a*. In the form of an axis.

Axle, **Axle-tree**, aks′l, aks′l-trē, *n*. [A dim. from A.Sax. *eax, ex*, an axle; same root as L. *axis*, namely, *ag*, to drive. ACRE.] A piece of timber or bar of iron on which the wheels of a vehicle, &c., turn.—**Axled**, aks′ld, *a*. Furnished with an axle.—**Axle-nut**, *n*. A screw-nut on the end of an axle to keep the wheel in place.—**Axle-pin**, *n.* Same as *Linch-pin.*

Axolotl, aks'o-lotl, *n.* [Mexican name.] A remarkable member of the tailed amphibians found in Mexican lakes, possessing four limbs resembling those of a frog, and usually having throughout life both lungs and gills, but sometimes losing the latter.

Axunge, aks'unj, *n.* [L. *axungia*—*axis*, an axle, and *ungo*, to grease.] Hog's lard.

Ay, Aye, ī, *adv.* [Of doubtful origin.] Yes; yea; a word expressing assent or affirmation; truly; certainly; indeed.—*n.* The word by which assent is expressed in Parliament; hence, an affirmative vote.—*The ayes have it*, the affirmative votes are in a majority.

Ayah, ä'yä, *n.* In the East Indies, a native waiting-woman or lady's-maid.

Aye, ā, *adv.* [Icel. *ei*, aye, ever; A.Sax. *á*, always; allied to L. *ævum*, Gr. *aiōn*, age, *aiei*, ever.] Always; for ever; continually; for an indefinite time: used mostly in poetry.

Aye-aye, ī-ī, *n.* [From its cry.] A nocturnal quadruped, about the size of a hare, found in Madagascar, allied to the lemurs, and in its habits resembling the sloth.

Azalea, a-zā'lē-a, *n.* [Gr. *azaleos*, dry, from inhabiting dry localities.] The generic name of certain plants belonging to the heath family, remarkable for the beauty and fragrance of their flowers, and distinguished from the rhododendrons chiefly by the flowers having five stamens instead of ten.

Azedarach, a-zed'a-rak, *n.* [Fr. *azedarac*, Persian *āzād*, noble, and *dirakht*, tree.] An Asiatic tree and a drug therefrom, used as a vermifuge, emetic, and purgative.

Azimuth, az'i-muth, *n.* [Ar. *as-sumuth*, pl. of *as-samt*, a way, a path. *Zenith* has the same origin.] *Astron.* an arc of the horizon intercepted between the meridian of a place and the vertical circle passing through the centre of a celestial object and the zenith.—*Azimuth circle*, a circle passing through the zenith and cutting the horizon perpendicularly.—*Azimuth compass*, a kind of compass used for finding the azimuth of a heavenly object.—**Azimuthal**, az'i-muth-al, *a.* Pertaining to the azimuth.

Azoic, a-zō'ik, *a.* [Gr. *a*, priv., and *zōē*, life.] Destitute of any vestige of organic life: applied to rocks, especially some very old rocks, in which no fossils have as yet been found.

Azote, az'ōt, *n.* [Gr. *a*, priv., and *zōē*, life.] A name formerly given to nitrogen because it is unfit for respiration.—**Azotic**, a-zot'ik, *a.* Pertaining to azote; fatal to animal life.—**Azotide**, az'ō-tid, *n.* An azotized body.—**Azotize**, az'ō-tīz, *v.t.*—*azotized*, *azotizing.* To imbue with nitrogen; to deprive of life.—**Azotous**, a-zō'tus, *a.* Nitrous.

Aztec, az'tek, *n.* and *a.* One of or pertaining to the Aztecs, the ruling tribe in Mexico at the time of the Spanish invasion.

Azure, ā'zhūr, *a.* [Fr. *azur*, L.L. *azurrum*, *lazurum*, &c., from Arab. *lazwerd*, blue.] Resembling the clear blue colour of the sky; sky-blue.—*n.* The fine blue colour of the sky; a name common to several sky-coloured or blue pigments, as ultramarine or smalt; the sky or vault of heaven.—*v.t.* To colour blue.—**Azurite**, ā'zhūr-īt, *n.* A blue mineral, an ore of copper, composed chiefly of hydrous carbonate: called also *Azure-stone.*

Azygous, az'i-gus, *a.* [Gr. *azygos*—*a*, priv., and *zygon*, a yoke.] Not one of a pair; single: applied to certain muscles, &c.

Azymous,† az'im-us, *a.* [Gr. *a*, priv., and *zymē*, leaven.] Unleavened; unfermented.

B

B, the second letter and the first consonant in the English and most other alphabets; *mus.* the seventh note of the model diatonic scale or scale of C.

Baa, bä, *v.i.* [Imitation of the sound.] Bleating of a sheep.

Baal, bā'al, *n.* [Heb. *ba'al*, lord.] A deity worshipped among the Canaanites, Phœnicians, &c., and supposed to represent the sun.—**Baalism**, bā'al-izm, *n.* The worship of Baal; gross idolatry.—**Baalite**, bā'al-īt, *n.* A worshipper of Baal; a grovelling idolizer.

Babbitt-metal, bab'it-met-al, *n.* [From the name of the inventor.] An alloy of copper, zinc, and tin, used for obviating friction in the bearing of cranks, axles, &c.

Babble, bab'bl, *v.i.* [From *ba*, a sound uttered by an infant; D. and G. *babbeln*, Icel. *babbla*, Dan. *bable*, Fr. *babiller.*] To utter words imperfectly or indistinctly; to talk idly or irrationally; to make a continuous murmuring sound; to prate; to tell secrets.—*v.t.* To utter idly or irrationally.—*n.* Idle talk; senseless prattle; murmur as of a stream.—**Babblement**,† bab'bl-ment, *n.* Idle talk; babble. (*Mil.*)—**Babbler**, bab'blėr, *n.* One who babbles; a teller of secrets.

Babe, Baby, bāb, bā'bi, *n.* [From the Celtic; W. Ir. and Gael. *baban*, Gael. and Ir. *bab*, child, infant.] An infant; a young child of either sex.—**Babish, Babyish**, bā'bish, bā'bi-ish, *a.* Like a babe; childish.—**Babishly**, bāb'ish-li, *adv.* Childishly.—**Babishness, Babyishness**, bāb'ish-nes, bā'bi-ish-nes, *n.*—**Babyhood**, bā'bi-hųd, *n.* The state of being a baby; infancy.—**Babyism**, bā'bi-izm, *n.* The condition of a baby; babyhood.—**Baby-farm**, *n.* The establishment of a baby-farmer.—**Baby-farmer**, *n.* One who receives infants, generally illegitimate, along with a sum of money for their bringing up, and whose object is to get rid of the children, by neglect or ill usage, as soon as possible.—**Baby-farming**, *n.* The system or practices of a baby-farmer.

Babel, bā'bel, *n.* The city mentioned in Scripture where the confusion of tongues took place; any great city where confusion may be supposed to prevail; a confused mixture of sounds; confusion; disorder.

Babiroussa, bab-i-rös'sa, *n.* Same as *Babyrussa.*

Bablah, bab'la, *n.* The pod of several species of acacia sometimes used in dyeing, to produce a drab colour.

Baboo, Babu, ba-bö', *n.* A Hindu title of respect paid to gentlemen, equivalent to master, sir.—**Babu.** *Babu-English.* The broken English of Bengal.

Baboon, ba-bön', *n.* [Fr. *babouin.*] A term applied to certain quadrumanous animals of the Old World having elongated muzzles like a dog, strong canine teeth, short tails, cheek-pouches, small deep eyes with huge eyebrows, and naked callosities on the hips.

Baby, &c. Babe.

Babylon, bab'i-lōn, *n.* Type of any great or evil city; capital of Chaldæan Empire.—**Babylonian, Babylonish, Babylonic**, bab-i-lō'ni-an, bab-i-lō'nish, bab-i-lon'ik, *a.* Pertaining to Babylon; like the confusion of tongues at Babel; mixed; confused.

Babyrussa, Babyroussa, bab-i-rös'sa, *n.* A species of the swine family with long curved tusks in the upper jaw, inhabiting the islands of the Eastern Archipelago and the Malayan Peninsula, and allied to the wild boars of Europe.

Bacca, bak'ka, *n.* [L.] *Bot.* a berry; a one-celled fruit, with several naked seeds immersed in a pulpy mass.—**Baccate**, bak'kāt, *a.* *Bot.* having a pulpy texture like a berry; bearing berries; berried.—**Baccated**, bak'kāt-ed, *a.* Having many berries; set or adorned with pearls.—**Bacciferous**, bak-sif'ėr-us, *a.* [L. *bacca*, and *fero*, to bear.] Bearing or producing berries.—**Baccivorous**, bak-siv'ō-rus, *a.* [L. *bacca*, and *voro*, to devour.] Eating or subsisting on berries.

Baccalaureate, bak-ka-la̧'rē-āt, *n.* [L.L. *baccalaureatus*, from *baccalaureus*, a corrupted form, through *bacca lauri*, laurel berry, of L.L. *baccalarius*, Fr. *bachelier*, a *bachelor*, or one who has attained the lowest degree in a university. Bachelor, Laureate.] The degree of Bachelor of Arts.—*a.* Pertaining to a Bachelor of Arts.

Baccarat, bak'ka-rat or bak-ka-rä, *n.* [Fr.] A game of cards played by any number of players or rather bettors.

Bacchanal, Bacchanalian, bak'a-nal, bak-a-nā'li-an, *a.* [L. *bacchanalis*, from *Bacchus*, the god of wine.] Revelling in or characterized by intemperate drinking; riotous; noisy.—*n.* A votary of Bacchus; one who indulges in drunken revels; a drunken feast.—**Bacchanalia**, bak-a-nā'li-a, *n.pl.* [L.] Feasts or festive rites in honour of Bacchus.—**Bacchanalianism**, bak-a-nā'li-an-izm, *n.* The practice of bacchanalian rites; drunken revelry.—**Bacchanalianly**,† bak-a-nā'li-an-li, *adv.* In a bacchanalian manner.—**Bacchant**, ba-kant', *n.* [L. *bacchans*, ppr. of *bacchor*, to celebrate the feast of Bacchus.] A priest of Bacchus; a bacchanal.—**Bacchante**, ba-kan'tē, *n.* [It. *baccante.*] A priestess of Bacchus, or one who joined in the feasts of Bacchus, one in a state of Bacchic frenzy; a female bacchanal.—**Bacchic, Bacchical**, bak'ik, bak'ik-al, *a.* Relating to Bacchus; jovial; drunken; mad with intoxication.

Bacchius, ba-kī'us. *n.* *Pros.* a foot composed of a short syllable and two long ones, the opposite of the *antibacchius.*

Bachelor, bach'el-ėr, *n.* [O.Fr. *bacheler*, *bachiler*, Fr. *bachelier*, from L.L. *baccalarius*, the owner of a small farm or a herd of cows, a vassal, from *bacca*, for L. *vacca*, a cow.] Formerly, a young man in the first or probationary stage of knighthood; hence, a man who has not been married; one who has taken the degree below that of Master or Doctor in Arts, Science, or other subjects at a university.—*Knight bachelor*, a man who has been knighted without being made a member of any of the orders of knighthood, as the Bath.—**Bachelorhood, Bachelorism, Bachelorship**, bach'el-ėr-hųd, bach'el-ėr-izm, bach'el-ėr-ship, *n.* The state of being a bachelor.

Bacillary, ba-sil'a-ri, *a.* Relating to bacilli.—**Bacillus**, ba-sil'us, *n.* pl. **Bacilli**, ba-sil'ī. [L., a little rod.] A microscopic organ that often swarms in the blood of animals in morbid states; a bacterium.

Back, bak, *n.* [A.Sax. *bæc*, Icel. Sw. and L.G. *bak.*] The posterior part of the trunk; the region of the spine; the hinder part of the body in man and the upper in other animals; that which is behind or furthest from the face or front; the rear (the *back* of a house); that which is behind or in the furthest distance; the part which comes behind in the ordinary movements of a thing, or when it is used (the *back* of the hand, a knife, saw, &c.); a reserve or secondary resource; a support or second; *pl.* among leather dealers the thickest and best-tanned hides.—*Behind one's back*, in secret, or when one is absent.—*adv.* [Short for *aback*, A.Sax. *on bæc*, back.] To or toward a former place, state, or condition; not advancing; in a state of restraint or hinderance (to keep *back*); toward times or things past (to look *back*); again; in return (to give *back*); away from contact; by reverse movement; in withdrawal or resilement from an undertaking or engagement (to draw *back*).—*To* *go or give back*, to retreat, to recede; to give way; to succumb.—*a.* Belonging to the back; lying in the rear; remote; in a backward direction: chiefly in compounds.—*v.t.* to furnish with a back or backing; to support; to second or strengthen by aid (often with *up*); to bet or wager in favour of; to get upon the back of; to mount; to write something on the back of; to endorse; to put backward; to cause to move backwards or recede.—*v.i.* To move or go back; to move with the back foremost.—**Backed**, bakt, *a.* Having a back: used chiefly in composition.—**Backer**, bak'ėr, *n.* One who backs or gets on the back; one who supports another; one who bets in favour of a particular party in a contest.—**Backing**, bak'-ing, *n.* Something put at or attached to the back of something else by way of support or finish.

Back, bak, *n.* [Fr. *bac*, a back or ferry-boat, a brewer's or distiller's back; Armor. *bac*, a boat; D. *bak*, a bowl; Dan. *bakke*, a tray. The word may be originally Celtic. *Basin* is akin to this word.] A ferry-boat, especially one adapted for carrying vehicles, and worked by a chain or rope fastened on each side of the ferry; *brewing* and *distilling*, a large tub or vessel into which the wort, &c., is drawn for the purpose of cooling, straining, mixing, &c.

Backbite, bak'bīt, *v.t.* — *backbit* (pret.), *backbit* or *backbitten* (pp.), *backbiting*. To censure, slander, or speak evil of, in the absence of the person traduced.—**Backbiter**, bak'bīt-ėr, *n.* One who backbites; a calumniator of the absent.—**Backbiting**, bak'bīt-ing, *n.* Secret calumny.—**Backbitingly**, bak'bīt-ing-li, *adv.* With secret slander.

Backboard, bak'bōrd, *n.* A board for the back; a board used to support the back and give erectness to the figure.

Backbone, bak'bōn, *n.* The bone of the back; the spine; the vertebral column; *fig.* firmness; decision of character; resolution. —*To the backbone*, to the utmost extent; out and out; all through or over (a soldier *to the backbone*).

Backdoor, bak'dōr, *n.* A door in the back part of a building.

Backgammon, bak-gam'mon, *n.* [Dan. *bakke*, a tray, *gammen*, mirth.] A game played by two persons upon a table or board made for the purpose, with pieces or men, dice-boxes, and dice.

Background, bak'ground, *n.* The part of a picture represented as farthest from the spectator; *fig.* a situation little seen or noticed; a state of being out of view (to keep a fact in the *background*).

Backhand, bak'hand, *n.* Writing sloping backwards or to the left.—**Backhand**, **Backhanded**, bak'hand, bak'hand-ed, *a.* With the hand turned backward (a *backhanded* blow); unfair; oblique; indirect; sloping back or to the left (of writing).—**Backhandedness**, bak'hand-ed-nes, *n.* —**Backhander**, bak'hand-ėr, *n.* A blow with the back of the hand. [Colloq.]

Back-settlement, *n.* An outlying and unreclaimed or only partially reclaimed district of a country beginning to be occupied for cultivation.—**Back-settler**, *n.* One inhabiting the back-settlements of a country.

Backshish, **Backsheesh**, bak'shēsh, *n.* Same as BAKSHISH.

Backside, bak'sīd, *n.* The back part of anything; the side opposite to the front or behind that which is presented to the spectator.

Back-sight, *n.* The rear sight of a gun.

Backslide, bak'slīd, *v.i.* (conjugated as *slide*). To slide back; to fall off or turn away from religion or morality; to apostatize.—**Backslider**, bak'slīd-ėr, *n.* One who backslides; one who falls away from religion or morality.—**Backsliding**, bak'-slīd-ing, *a.* Apostatizing from faith or practice. — **Backslidingness**, bak'sliding-nes, *n.*

Backstair, **Backstairs**, bak'stār, bak'-stārz, *n.* A stair or stairs in the back part of a house; private stairs.—*a.* Of or pertaining to backstairs; hence, indirect; underhand: secret and unfair (*backstairs* influence).

Back-stay, *n.* A long rope or stay, extending from the top of a mast backwards to the side of a ship to assist the shrouds in supporting the mast.

Backward, **Backwards**, bak'wėrd, bak'wėrdz, *adv.* [*Back* and *ward*, denoting direction.] With the back in advance; toward the back; in a direction opposite to forward: toward past times or events; from a better to a worse state; in a contrary or reverse manner, way, or direction.—**Backward**, *a.* Being in the back or at the back; turned or directed back (a *backward* look); unwilling; reluctant; slow; dull; not quick of apprehension; late; behind in time. — **Backwardation**, bak-wėrd-ā'-shon, *n.* A consideration paid to purchasers for an extension of time by speculators on the Stock Exchange unable to supply the stock or shares they have contracted to deliver. CONTANGO. — **Backwardly**, bak'wėrd-li, *adv.* Unwillingly; reluctantly; aversely; perversely†.—**Backwardness**, bak'wėrd-nes, *n.* The state or quality of being backward.—**Backwater**, *n.* Ebb-tide.—*v.i.* To fall back in the boat-course.

Backwoods, bak'wụdz, *n. pl.* Woody or forest districts of a country situated back or away from the more thickly settled parts: more especially used in regard to the United States and Canada.—**Backwoodsman**, bak'wụdz-man, *n.* An inhabitant of the backwoods.

Bacon, bā'kn, *n.* [O.Fr. *bacon*, from O.D. *baken*, bacon, from *bak*, *bake*, a pig; G. *bache*, a wild sow.] Swine's flesh salted or pickled and dried, usually in smoke.

Baconian, ba-kō'ni-an, *a.* Pertaining to Francis *Bacon*, or his system of philosophy.

Bacteriology, bak-tē'ri-ol"o-ji, *n.* The doctrine or study of bacteria.—**Bacteriologist**, bak-tē'ri-ol"o-jist, *n.* One who investigates the phenomena of bacteria, especially in relation to disease.—**Bacterium**, bak-tē'ri-um, *n. pl.*—**Bacteria**, bak-tē'ri-a. [Gr. *baktērion*, a stick.] A name applied to certain very minute organisms which appear in infusions of organic matter, in fluids exposed to the air, in diseased animal tissues, for instance, typhoid fever or malaria bacilli are disease-producing while others as acetic or lactic acid microbes are useful to bring about fermentation in many industrial processes.

Bactrian, bak'tri-an, *a.* Of or pertaining to Bactria, an ancient province of the Persian empire (the *Bactrian* camel).

Bactris, bak'tris, *n.* [Gr. *baktron*, a staff.] A fine species of palm found about rivers and in marshy places in America within the tropics.

Baculite, bak'ū-līt, *n.* [L. *baculum*, a staff.] A fossil cephalopod with a shell straight, conical, and very much elongated.

Bad, bad, *a.* compar. (from quite a different root) *worse*, superl. *worst*. [Perhaps of Celtic origin; comp. Corn. *bad*, Gael. *baodh*, *baoth*, vain, foolish, &c.] The opposite of good; wanting good qualities, physical or moral; not coming up to a certain type or standard or the average of individuals of the particular class; wicked, unprincipled, depraved, immoral, vicious; pernicious, debasing, corrupting (influence, habits); ill, infirm (health); unwholesome, noxious (air, climate, food); defective, insufficient (work, crop); infertile, sterile (soil); unfortunate or unhappy (result, marriage); incompetent (workman), &c. &c.—*n.* That which is bad.—*To go to the bad*, to fall into bad company, bad ways, or bad circumstances; to fall into vicious courses and ruin one's life.—**Baddish**, bad'ish, *a.* Somewhat bad; indifferent. [Colloq.]—**Badly**, bad'li, *adv.* In a bad manner; not well; unskilfully.—**Badness**, bad'nes, *n.* The state of being bad; want of good qualities, physical or moral.

Bad, **Bade**, bad, pret. of *bid*.

Baddam, bad'dam, *n.* A species of bitter almond imported into some parts of India from Persia and used as money: worth about one farthing.

Badderlocks, bad'ėr-loks, *n.* A common name for a sea-weed found on the shores of the north of Europe, the midrib of which is edible.

Badge, baj, *n.* [L.L. *bagia*, a sign, probably from O.Sax. *bāg*, A.Sax. *beag*, Icel. *baugr*, a bracelet, ring, garland.] A mark, sign, token, or cognizance worn to show the relation of the wearer to any person, occupation, or order.—*v.t.*† To mark or distinguish with a badge or as with a badge. (*Shak.*)—**Badgeman**, baj'man, *n.* A man who wears a badge; an alms-house man.

Badger, baj'ėr, *n.* [For *bladger*, from O.Fr. *blaage*, store of corn (the animal being supposed to steal corn), from L.L. *bladum*, wheat (Fr. *blé*), lit. grain carried off the field; L. *ablatum*—*ab*, from, and *latum*, carried.] A plantigrade carnivorous mammal belonging to a family intermediate between the bears and the weasels, living in a burrow, nocturnal in habits, and feeding on vegetables, small quadrupeds, &c.—*v.t.* To attack (a person), as the badger is attacked when being drawn or baited; to assail (as with importunities, commands, &c.): to worry; to pester. — **Badger-legged**, *a.* Having a leg or legs shorter on one side than on the other, as the badger's are erroneously supposed to be.

Badiane, **Badian**, bā'di-ān, bad'i-an, *n.* The fruit of the Chinese anise tree used as a condiment.

Badigeon, ba-dij'on, *n.* [Fr.] A mixture compounded in various ways (with plaster, whiting, or other substances), and used to fill up small holes in joiners' or other work.

Badinage, bad'i-nāj or bä-dē-näzh, *n.* [Fr., from *badin*, facetious.] Light or playful discourse.

Badminton, bad'min-ton, *n.* [From a residence of the Dukes of Beaufort.] An outdoor game, the same as lawn-tennis but played with shuttlecocks; a kind of claret-cup or summer beverage.

Baffle, baf'fl, *v.t.*—*baffled*, *baffling*. [Origin unknown.] To elude; to foil; to frustrate; to defeat; to thwart; to subject to indignities‡ (*Shak.*).—*v.i.*† To struggle ineffectually (as a ship in a storm).—**Baffler**, baf'-flėr, *n.* One who or that which baffles.—**Bafflingly**, baf'fling-li, *adv.* In a baffling manner.—**Bafflingness**, baf'fling-nes, *n.*

Bag, bag, *n.* [Icel. *baggi*, *bōggr*, a bag, a bundle; comp. O.Fr. *bague*, a bundle, Gael. *bag*, a bag.] A sack; a wallet; a pouch; what is contained in a bag (as the animals shot by a sportsman); a definite quantity of certain commodities. — *v.t.* — *bagged*, *bagging*. To put into a bag; to distend; to swell; to shoot or otherwise lay hold of (game).—*v.i.* To swell or hang like a bag.—**Bagging**, bag'ing, *n* The cloth or other materials for bags.—**Baggy**, bag'i, *a.* Having the appearance of a bag; puffy.—**Bagginess**, bag'i-nes, *n.* Character of being baggy.—**Bagman**, bag'man, *n.* A name sometimes given to a commercial traveller. —**Bagpipe**, bag'pīp, *n.* A musical wind-instrument consisting of a leathern bag which receives the air from the mouth or from a bellows; and of pipes into which the air is pressed from the bag by the performer's elbow.—**Bagpiper**, bag'pīp-ėr, *n.* One who plays on a bagpipe.—**Bag-wig**, *n.* A wig with a sort of purse attached to it.

Bagasse, ba-gas', *n.* [Fr.] The sugar-cane in its dry crushed state as delivered from the sugar-mill.

Bagatelle, bag-a-tel', *n.* [Fr., from It. *bagatella*, a dim. of *bagata*, a trifle, L.L. *baga*, a bundle, a bag.] A trifle; a thing of no importance; a game played on a board having at the end nine holes, into which balls are to be struck with a cue or mace.—**Bagatelle-board**, *n.* The board or table on which to play at bagatelle.

Baggage, bag'āj, *n.* [Fr. *bagage*, baggage, O.Fr. *bague*, a bundle. BAG.] The necessaries of an army, or other body of men on the move; luggage; things required for a journey.

Baggage, bag'āj, *n.* [Fr. *bagasse*, It. *bagascia*, Sp. *bagazo*, a strumpet.] A low worthless woman; a strumpet: now usually a playful epithet applied familiarly to any young woman.

Bagnio, bän'yo, *n.* [It. *bagno*, from L. *balneum*, a bath.] A bath; a brothel; a stew.

Bah, bä, *interj.* An exclamation expressing contempt, disgust, or incredulity.

Bahadur, ba-hä'dur, *n.* [Hindu, gallant.] Title of officers in Indian army.

Bail, bāl, *v.t.* [O.Fr. *bailler*, to bail, to guard, from L. *bajulus*, a bearer, later a tutor or governor. Hence *bailiff*.] To liberate from arrest and imprisonment, upon security that the person liberated shall appear and answer in court.—*n.* The person or persons who procure the release of a prisoner from custody by becoming surety for his appearance in court; the security given for the release: not used with a plural termination (we were his *bail*).—**Bailable**, bāl'a-bl, *a.* Capable of being admitted to bail; admitting of bail (a *bailable* offence).—**Bailer**, bāl'ėr, *n.* One who or that which bails.—**Bail-bond**, *n.* A bond given for the appearance in court of a person who is bailed.

Bail, bāl, *n.* [O.Fr. *baille*, a palisade, from L. *baculum*, a rod or staff.] A little stick laid on the tops of the stumps in playing cricket.

Bail, bāl, *v.t.* [Fr. *baille*, a bucket, Armor. *bal*, a tub.] To free (a boat) from water with a bucket or other utensil.

Bailiff, bā'lif, *n.* [O.Fr. *baillif*, *bailli*, from *baillir*, *bailler*, to hold, to govern, L. *bajulare*, to bear, *bajulus*, a porter. Bail, to liberate.] A civil officer or functionary, a sheriff's deputy, a court officer who executes writs, processes, distraints, and arrests; who also acts as a messenger or usher in court. — **Baille, Baillie**, bā'li, *n.* A magistrate in Scotland corresponding to an *alderman* in England. — **Bailiwick**, bā'li-wik, *n.* [-*wick* from A.Sax. *wic*, dwelling, station, L. *vicus*, a village.] The precincts in which a bailiff has jurisdiction.

Bailment, bāl'ment, *n.* The act of bailing an arrested person.

Bairam, Beiram, bā'ram, bī'ram, *n.* The name of two Mohammedan festivals, one held at the close of the fast Ramazan, the other seventy days after.

Bairn, bārn, *n.* [A.Sax. *bearn*, Icel. and Goth. *barn*; from *bear*, to bring forth.] A child. [Prov. E. and Sc.]

Bait, bāt, *v.t.* [From Icel. *beita*, to make to eat, to feed, to bait a hook—a causative of *bíta*, E. *bite*.] To give a portion of food and drink to a beast when travelling; to furnish with a piece of flesh or other substance which acts as a lure to fish or other animals (to *bait* a hook); to provoke and harass by dogs (as a bull, badger, or bear); to annoy.—*v.i.* To take a portion of food and drink for refreshment on a journey.—*n.* A portion of food and drink, or a refreshment taken on a journey; any substance used as a lure to catch fish or other animals; an allurement; enticement.

Bait, bāt, *v.i.* [Fr. *battre*, to beat. Bate.] To clap the wings; to hover above prey. (*Shak.*)

Baize, bāz, *n.* [A modified plural; O.E. *bayes*, Fr. *baie*, coarse woollen cloth, originally of a bay colour; from L. *badius*, bay-coloured.] A coarse woollen stuff with a long nap, sometimes friezed on one side.

Bajan, bā-jan, *n.* [Fr. *bec jaune*, yellow beak. G. *Gelbschnabel*.] A first-year student at mediæval universities, still used at Paris, Aberdeen, St. Andrews.

Bake, bāk, *v.t.*—*baked*, *baking* (old pp. *baken*). [A.Sax. *bacan* = Icel. and Sw. *baka*, Dan. *bage*, D. *bakken*, G. *backen*.] To dry and harden by heat, in an oven, kiln, or furnace, or by the solar rays (as bread, bricks, pottery); to prepare in an oven.—*v.i.* To do the work of baking; to dry and harden in heat.—**Baker**, bāk'ėr, *n.* One whose occupation is to bake bread, biscuit, &c.—**Baker's dozen**. Thirteen, the extra as retailer's profit.—**Bakery**, bāk'ėr-i, *n.* A place used for the business of baking bread, &c.; a bake-house.—**Baking**, bāk'-ing, *n.* A quantity baked at once.—**Baked-meat, Bake-meat**, *n.* Meat cooked in an oven; a meat-pie.—**Bake-house**, *n.* A house or building for baking.

Bakshish, Bukshish, bak'shēsh, buk'-shēsh, *n.* [Per., from *bakkshidan*, to give.] A present or gratuity of money: used in Eastern countries.

Balaam, bā-lam, *n.* [*Numbers*, xxii. 28.] A half-hearted or poor ally; odd matter kept in Balaam box for padding vacant spaces in newspapers.

Balachong, bä'la-chong, *n.* [Malay.] A substance composed of small fishes or shrimps pounded up with salt and spices and then dried: used in the East as a condiment.

Balance, bal'ans, *n.* [Fr., from L. *bilanx*—*bis*, double, and *lanx*, a dish, the scale of a balance.) An instrument for ascertaining the weight of bodies, consisting in its common form of a beam or lever suspended exactly at the middle, and having a scale or basin hung to each extremity of exactly the same weight, so that the beam rests horizontally when nothing is in either scale or when they are loaded with equal weights; the excess by which one thing is greater than another; surplus; the difference of two sums; the sum due on an account; an equality of weight, power, advantage, and the like; the part of a clock or watch which regulates the beats; the balance-wheel.—*v.t.*—*balanced*, *balancing*. To bring to an equipoise; to keep in equilibrium on a small support; to poise; to compare by estimating the relative importance or value of; to weigh; to serve as a counterpoise to; to settle (an account) by paying what remains due; to examine (a merchant's books) by summations and show how debits and credits stand.—*v.i.* To be in equipoise; to have equal weight or importance; to be employed in finding balances on accounts.—**Balancement**, bal'ans-ment, *n.* The act of balancing, or state of being balanced.—**Balancer**, bal'ans-ėr, *n.* One who or that which balances; an organ of an insect useful in balancing the body.—**Balance-electrometer**, *n.* An instrment on the principle of the common balance and weights to estimate the mutual attraction of oppositely electrified surfaces.—**Balance-sheet**, *n.* A statement of the assets and liabilities of a trading concern.—**Balance-wheel**, *n.* That part of a watch or chronometer which, like a pendulum, regulates the beat or strike.

Balaniferous, bal-a-nif'ėr-us, *a.* [L. *balanus*, an acorn, and *fero*, to bear.] Yielding or producing acorns.—**Balanoid**, bal'-a-noid, *a.* Having the form or appearance of an acorn.—*n.* One of the acorn-shells.

Balas, bal'as, ba-las', *n.* [From Ar. *balakhsh*, from *Badakhshan*, in Central Asia.] A variety of spinel ruby, of a pale rose-red colour, sometimes inclining to orange.

Balata, ba-lä'ta, *n.* A gum obtained from a S. American tree, used for similar purposes to india-rubber, and in the United States as a chewing-gum. Bullet Tree.

Balaustine, ba-las'tin, *n.* [Gr. *balaustion*, a wild-pomegranate flower.] Pertaining to the pomegranate.—*Balaustine flowers*, the dried flowers of the pomegranate, used in medicine as astringents.

Balbuties, bal-bū'ti-ēz, *n.* [L. *balbutio*, to stammer, *balbus*, stammering.] The defect of speech known as stammering.

Balcony, bal'kō-ni (nineteenth century), bal-kō'ni (previously), *n.* [It. *balcone*, from *balco*, a scaffold, from O.H.G. *balcho*, G. *balken* = E. *balk*, a beam.] A platform projecting from the front of a building, supported by columns, pillars, or consoles, and encompassed with a balustrade, railing, or parapet; a projecting gallery in the interior of a building, as of a theatre.—**Balconet**, bal'kō-net, *n.* A low ornamental railing to a door or window, projecting but slightly beyond the threshold or sill.—**Balconied**, bal'kō-nid, *a.* Having balconies.

Bald, bald, *a.* [O.E. *balled*, lit. marked with a white spot; of Celtic origin, comp. Armor. *bal*, a white mark on an animal's face; Ir. and Gael. *bal*, a spot.] Having white on the face (said of animals); destitute of hair, especially on the top and back of the head; destitute of the natural or usual covering of the head or top; destitute of appropriate ornament; unadorned (said of style or language); *bot.* destitute of beard or awn.—**Baldly**, bald'li, *adv.* Nakedly; meanly; inelegantly. — **Baldness**, bald'-nes, *n.* The state or quality of being bald. —**Bald eagle**, the white-headed eagle of America. — **Bald-faced**, *a.* Having a white face or white on the face: said of animals.—**Bald head**, *n.* A person bald on the head. [O.T.] — **Bald-headed**, *a.* (*to go*). Having a bald head. In a wild, reckless manner.

Baldachin, Baldachino, Baldaquin, bal'da-kin, bal-da-kē'nō, bal'da-kin, *n.* [It. *baldacchino*, Sp. *baldaquino*, from *Baldacco*, Italian form of *Bagdad*, where the cloth was manufactured.] A canopy or covering; a canopy on four poles held over the pope; a canopy on four columns over an altar; a canopy over a throne.

Balderdash, bal'dėr-dash, *n.* [W. *baldordus*, prattling, *baldordd*, prattle.] Senseless prate; a jargon of words; noisy nonsense.

Baldpate, *n.* Same as *Bald-head*.

Baldrick, Baldric, bald'rik, *n.* [O.E. *baudric*, *baldric*, &c., O.Fr. *baudric*, from O.G. *balderich*, from *balz*, a belt. Belt.] A broad belt, stretching from the right or left shoulder diagonally across the body, either as an ornament or to suspend a sword, dagger, or horn.

Bale, bāl, *n.* [O.Fr. *bale*, the same word as *ball*, meaning originally a round package.] A bundle or package of goods.—*v.t.*—*baled*, *baling*. To make up into a bale or bundle.

Bale, bāl, *v.t.*—*baled*, *baling*. To free from water by laving; to bail.

Bale, bāl, *n.* [A.Sax. *bealu*, O.Sax. *balu*, Icel. *böl*, calamity, sorrow.] Misery; calamity; that which causes ruin, destruction, or sorrow.—**Baleful**, bāl'ful, *a.* Full of bale, destruction, or mischief; destructive; pernicious; calamitous; deadly. — **Balefully**, bāl'ful-li, *adv.* In a baleful or calamitous manner. — **Balefulness**, bāl'ful-nes, *n.* The state or quality of being baleful.

Baleen, ba-lēn', *n.* [Fr. *baleine*, from L. *balæna*, a whale.] The whalebone of commerce.

Bale-fire, bāl'fīr, *n.* [A.Sax. *bael*, fire, flame, a funeral pile; Icel. *bál*, flame, a funeral pile.] A signal-fire; an alarm-fire.

Balk, bak, *n.* [A.Sax. *balca*, a balk or ridge, a beam; Icel. *bálkr*, Sw. *balk*, a balk, a partition; Dan. *bjelke*, G. *balken*, a beam.] A ridge of land left unploughed; an uncultivated strip of land serving as a boundary; a beam or piece of timber of considerable length and thickness; a barrier or check; a disappointment.—*v.t.* To bar the way of; to disappoint; to frustrate.—*v.i.* To turn aside or stop in one's course (as a horse).—**Balker**, bak'ėr, *n.* One who balks.—**Balkingly**, bak'ing-li, *adv.* In a manner to balk or frustrate.

Ball, bal, *n.* [Fr. *balle*, from O.H.G. *balla*, G. *ball*, Icel. *böllr*, ball. *Bale*, a package, is another form, and *balloon*, *ballot* are derivatives.] A round body; a small spherical body often covered with leather and used in many games; any part of a thing that is rounded or protuberant; *farriery*, a form of medicine, corresponding to the term *bolus* in pharmacy; *metal.* a mass of half-melted iron; a loop; the projectile of a firearm; a bullet (in this sense also used collectively).—*Ball-and-socket joint*, a joint (as in the human hip) formed by a ball or rounded end playing within a socket so as to admit of motion in all directions.—**Ball**, bal, *v.t.* To make into a ball.—*v.i.* To form or gather into a ball.—**Ball-cartridge**, *n.*

A cartridge containing a ball, in contradistinction to *blank-cartridge*. — **Ball-cock**, *n.* A kind of self-acting stop-cock opened and shut by means of a hollow sphere or ball of metal floating on the surface of a liquid, and attached to the end of a lever connected with the cock.—**Ball-proof**, *a.* Impenetrable by balls from firearms.

Ball, bąl, *n.* [Fr. *bal*, L.L. *ballare*, to dance, to shake, from Gr. *ballizō*, to dance. Akin *ballad*, *ballet*.] A social assembly of persons of both sexes for the purpose of dancing.

Ballad, bal'lad, *n.* [Fr. *ballade*, from L.L. (and It.) *ballare*, to dance. BALL, a dance, BALLET]. A short narrative poem, especially such as is adapted for singing; a poem partaking of the nature both of the epic and the lyric.—**Ballad**,† bal'lad, *v.t.* To celebrate in a ballad. (*Shak.*)—**Ballade**, ba-läd, *n.* [Fr. *ballade.*] Poem consisting in its normal form of three stanzas of eight lines each, with a closing stanza or envoy of four lines, the rhymes throughout being not more than three.—**Balladist**, bal'lad-ist, *n.* A writer or singer of ballads.—**Balladize**,† bal'lad-īz, *v.t.* To convert into the form of a ballad.—**Ballad-monger**, *n.* A dealer in ballads; an inferior poet; a poetaster.—**Ballad-opera**, *n.* An opera in which only ballads are sung.

Ballan-wrasse, bal'lan-ras, *n.* [Lit. spotted-wrasse; Ir. *bal*, *ball*, a spot, Gael. *ballach*, spotted.] A fish of no great value taken all along the British coasts.

Ballast, bal'ast, *n.* [D. *ballast*, ballast, literally worthless load (being worthless in itself), from *bal* (akin to E. *bale*, misery, bad, and *last*, a load. (LAST.) In Danish it was modified to *baglast*, lit. a back-load—*bag*, back, after, and *last*, load.] Heavy matter, as stone, sand, or iron, carried in the bottom of a ship or other vessel, to prevent it from being readily overset (the vessel being said to be in *ballast* when she sails without a cargo); sand carried in bags in the car of a balloon to steady it, and enable the aeronaut to lighten the balloon by throwing part of it out; material filling up the space between the rails on a railway in order to make it firm and solid; *fig.* that which confers steadiness on a person.—*v.t.* To place ballast in or on (a ship, a railway track); *fig.* to steady; to counterbalance.—**Ballasting**, bal'last-ing, *n.* Materials for ballast; ballast. — **Ballast-heaver**, *n.* One who is employed in putting ballast on board ships.

Ballet, bal-lā or bal'let, *n.* [Fr. *ballet*, It. *balletto*. BALL, a dance.] A dance, more or less elaborate, in which several persons take part; a theatrical representation, in which a story is told by gesture, accompanied with dancing, scenery, &c.

Ballista, **Balista**, bal-lis'ta, ba-lis'ta, *n.* pl. **Ballistæ**, **Balistæ**, bal-lis'tē, ba-lis'tē. [L., from Gr. *ballō*, to throw.] A military engine used by the ancients for discharging heavy stones or other missiles especially against a besieged place.—**Ballistic**, bal-lis'tik, *a.* Pertaining to the ballista or its use.—*Ballistic pendulum*, a kind of pendulum made to vibrate by the impact of a shot for ascertaining the velocity of military projectiles, and consequently the force of fired gunpowder.

Balloon, bal-lön', *n.* [Fr. *ballon*, an aug. of *balle*, a ball. BALL.] A large hollow spherical body; a very large bag, usually made of silk or other light fabric, varnished with caoutchouc, and filled with hydrogen gas or heated air, or any other gaseous fluid lighter than common air, the contained gas causing it to rise and float in the atmosphere.—**Ballonet**, bäl'o-net, *n.* The name of the separate bags, or small balloons, that contain the gas within the envelope of a dirigible; used in pairs, deflated or inflated as desired, to give the balloon the necessary position in its flight. **Ballooning**, bal-lön'ing, *n.* The art or practice of managing balloons; of testing public opinion, with 'kite-flying'; inflated puffery of candidates by exaggerated certificates.—**Balloonist**, bal-lön'ist, *n.* One who manages or ascends in a balloon; an aeronaut.—**Balloon-fish**, *n.* A curious tropical fish, having the power of distending itself by swallowing air and making it pass into cavities beneath the skin, causing its spines to erect themselves.

Ballot, bal'lot, *n.* [Fr. *ballotte*, a ball used in voting, dim. of *balle*, a ball. BALL.] A ball, ticket, paper, or the like, by which one votes, and which gives no indication of who the voter is; the system of voting by means of this kind.—*v.i.* To vote or decide by ballot: frequently with *for*.—**Balloter**, bal'lot-ėr, *n.* One who ballots or votes by ballot.—**Ballot-box**, *n.* A box for receiving ballots.

Balm, bäm, *n.* [O.Fr. *baulme*, Fr. *baume*; a contr. of *balsam*.] A name common to several species of odoriferous or aromatic trees or shrubs, and to the fragrant medicinal exudations from them; any fragrant or valuable ointment; anything which heals, soothes, or mitigates pain.—**Balm**, bäm, *v.t.* To anoint as with balm or with anything fragrant or medicinal; to soothe; to mitigate; to assuage; to heal.—**Balmily**, bäm'i-li, *adv.* In a balmy manner.—**Balminess**, bäm'i-nes, *n.* The state or quality of being balmy.—**Balmy**, bäm'i, *a.* Having the qualities of balm; aromatic; fragrant; healing; soothing; assuaging; refreshing.

Balsam bąl'sam, *n.* [L. *balsamum*, Gr. *balsamon*, a fragrant gum.] An oily, aromatic, resinous substance, flowing spontaneously or by incision from certain plants and used in medicine and perfumery; balm. —**Balsamic**, bąl-sam'ik, *a.* Having the qualities of balsam, stimulating; unctuous; soft; mitigating; mild.—*n.* A warm, stimulating, demulcent medicine, of a smooth and oily consistence. — **Balsamically**, bąl-sam'ik-al-li, *adv.* In a balsamic manner. —**Balsamiferous**, bąl-sam-if'ėr-us, *a.* Producing or yielding balm or balsam.

Baluster, bal'us-tėr, *n.* [Fr. *balustre*, It. *balaustro*, a baluster, from L. *balaustium*, Gr. *balaustion*, the flower of the wild pomegranate, being so called from some resemblance of form.] A small column or pilaster, of various forms and dimensions, used for balustrades. — **Balustrade**, bal-us-trād', *n.* [Fr. *balustrade.*] A row of small columns or pilasters, joined by a rail, serving as an inclosure for altars, balconies, staircases, terraces, &c., or used merely as an ornament.

Bambino, bäm-bē'nō, *n.* [It., a child.] In Catholic countries, the figure of our Saviour represented as an infant in swaddling-clothes, often surrounded by a halo, and watched over by angels.

Bamboo, bam-bö', *n.* [Malay.] A tropical plant of the family of the grasses, with large jointed stems, the thickest being much used in India, China, &c., for building purposes, and the slenderest for walking-canes.

Bamboozle, bam-bö'zl, *v.t.* [Origin doubtful.] To impose or practise upon; to hoax; to humbug; to deceive.—**Bamboozler**, bam-bö'zl-ėr, *n.* One who bamboozles.

Ban, ban, *n.* [A.Sax. *ban*, *gebann*, interdict, proclamation, edict; D. *ban*, excommunication; Icel. and Sw. *bann*, proclamation; Dan. *band*, a ban, *bande*, to curse. Akin *bandit*, *banish*, *abandon*, &c.] An edict or proclamation in general; an edict of interdiction or proscription; interdiction; prohibition; curse; excommunication; anathema; *pl.* proclamation of marriage (BANNS).—*v.t.*—*banned*, *banning*. To curse; to execrate; to prohibit; to interdict.—*v.i.* To curse.

Ban, ban, *n.* [Serv. *ban*, a lord.] A Croatian or Hungarian military chief or ruler.

Banal, ban'al, *a.* [Fr.] Hackneyed; commonplace; vulgar; properly, a *bannal mill* was by feudal custom the mill common by *ban* or order to *all* the vassals.—**Banality**, ban-al'i-ti, *n.* Banal character; what is banal.

Banana, ba-nä'na, *n.* [Sp., from the native name.] A herbaceous plant closely allied to the plantain, and extensively cultivated in tropical countries for its soft luscious fruit, which is the staple food of millions of people; an Australian from Queensland. CORN-STALK.

Banco, bang'kō, *n.* [It., a bank. BANK.] *Com.* bank money or value; the money standard in which banks in some countries keep or kept their accounts, in contradistinction to the current money of the place; *law*, a seat or bench of justice.

Band, band, *n.* [A.Sax. *bend*, a band, from *bindan*, to bind; D. Icel. Sw. and G. *band*. In sense of body of men, from Fr. *bande*, G. *bande*, from same root.] BIND.] That which binds together; a bond or means of attachment in general; a fetter or similar fastening; a narrow strip or ribbon-shaped ligature, tie, or connection; a fillet; a border or strip on an article of dress; that which resembles a band, tie, or ligature; *pl.* the linen ornament about the neck of a clergyman, with the ends hanging down in front; a company of persons united together by some common bond, especially a body of armed men; a company of soldiers; an organized body of instrumental musicians; an orchestra.—*v.t.* To bind with a band; to mark with a band; to unite in a troop, company, or confederacy.—*v.i.* To associate or unite for some common purpose.—**Bandage**, band'āj, *n.* A fillet, roller, or swathe used in dressing and binding up wounds, restraining hemorrhages, &c.; a band or ligature in general; that which is bound over something else.—*v.t. bandaged*, *bandaging*.—To put a bandage on.—**Bandbox**, band'box, *n.* A box made of pasteboard, or thin flexible pieces of wood and paper, for holding bands, bonnets, or other light articles.—**Band-fish**, *n.* A long thin flat fish; ribbon-fish or snake-fish.—**Banded**, band'ed, *a.* Marked by bands or stripes; striped. — **Band-master**, *n.* The conductor and trainer of a band of musicians. —**Band-saw**, *n.* A saw formed of a long flexible belt of steel revolving on pulleys.—**Bandsman**, bandz'man, *n.* A player in a band of musicians.

Bandala, ban-dä'la, *n.* [Native name.] The strong outer fibre of the plant yielding Manilla-hemp, made into cordage, especially into the well-known Manilla white rope.

Bandana, **Bandanna**, ban-dan'a, *n.* [Hind. *bāndhnū*, to tie.]. An Indian silk handkerchief having a pattern formed by tying little bits so as to keep them from being dyed; hence, a silk or cotton handkerchief having a somewhat similar pattern, that is, a uniform ground, usually of bright red or blue, with white or yellow figures of simple form.

Bandeau, ban'dō, *n.* pl. **Bandeaux**, ban'dō. [Fr., dim. from *bande*, a band.] A fillet worn round the head; a head-band.

Banderole, ban'de-rōl, *n.* [Fr. *banderole*, Sp. *banderola*, a little banner, from *bandera*, a banner, from G. *band*. BAND.] A little flag or streamer affixed to a mast, a military weapon, or a trumpet; a pennon; a bandrol. *Arch.* stone band with inscription.

Bandicoot, ban'di-kųt, *n.* [Corruption of the Telinga name *pandikoku*, lit. pig-rat.] A large species of rat, attaining the weight of 2 or 3 lbs., a native of India and Ceylon, where its flesh is a favourite article of food among the coolies.

Bandit, ban'dit, *n.* pl. **Bandits**, **Banditti**, ban'dits, ban'dit-ti. [It. *bandito*, pp. of *bandire*, L.L. *bannire*, to banish. BAN, BANISH.] An outlaw; more commonly a robber; a highwayman.

Bandlet, **Bandelet**, band'let, band'e-let, *n.* [Fr. *bandelette*, dim. of *bande*, a band.] A small band or fillet or something similar in shape.

Bandog, ban'dog, *n.* [*Band* and *dog*, lit. bound-dog.] A large, fierce kind of dog, in England generally a mastiff, usually kept chained.

Bandoleer, ban-dō-lēr', *n.* [Sp. *bandolera*, Fr. *bandoulière*, from Sp. *banda*, a sash.] A large leathern belt carrying a bag for balls and a number of charges of gunpowder, worn by musketeers; a shoulder-belt carrying ball-cartridges.

Bandoline, ban'dō-lēn, *n.* A gummy

perfumed substance used to impart a glossiness and stiffness to the hair.

Bandore, ban'dōr, *n.* [Fr., from It. *pandora*, L. *pandura*, Gr. *pandoura*, a musical instrument ascribed to *Pan.*] A musical stringed instrument like a lute.

Bandrol, band'rōl, *n.* Same as *Banderole.*

Bandy, ban'di, *n.* [Fr. *bandé*, bent, from *bander*, to bend a bow, to bind, to swathe, from G. *band*, a band. BAND.] A club bent at the end for striking a ball at play; a game played with such clubs.—*v.t.*—*bandied, bandying.* To beat to and fro, as a ball in play; to toss from one to another; to exchange contentiously; to give and receive reciprocally (words, compliments).—*v.i.* To contend; to strive. (*Shak.*)—**Bandy**, ban'di, *a.* Bent, especially having a bend or crook outwards: said of a person's legs. —**Bandy-legged**, *a.* Having bandy or crooked legs.

Bane, bān, *n.* [A.Sax. *bana*, destruction, death, bane; Icel. *bani*, Dan. and Sw. *bane*, O.H.G. *bana*; allied to Gr. *phonos*, murder.] Any fatal cause of mischief, injury, or destruction; ruin; destruction; deadly poison.—**Baneful**, bān'ful, *a.* Destructive; pernicious; poisonous.—**Banefully**, bān'ful-li, *adv.* In a baneful manner.—**Banefulness**, bān'ful-nes, *n.* The quality of being baneful.—**Bane-wort**, *n.* A poisonous plant; belladonna or deadly-nightshade.

Bang, bang, *v.t.* [Comp. Icel. *bang*, a knocking; G. *bängel*, a club, the clapper of a bell; D. *bangel*, a bell.] To beat, as with a club or cudgel; to thump; to cudgel; to beat or handle roughly or with violence (*Shak.*); to bring a loud noise from or by, as in slamming a door, and the like.—*v.i.* To resound with a loud noise; to produce a loud noise; to thump violently.—*n.* A loud, sudden, resonant sound; a blow as with a club; a heavy blow.

Bang, *n.* BHANG.

Bangle, bang'gl, *n.* [Hind. *bangri.*] An ornamental ring worn upon the arms or ankles in India, Africa, and elsewhere.

Banian, **Banyan**, ban'yan, *n.* [Hind. *banyá*, a merchant.] An Indian trader or merchant; a Hindu trader strict in regard to food.—*Banian days*, days in which sailors get no flesh-meat; days of poor fare.

Banian, ban'yan, *n.* A tree, the banyan.

Banish, ban'ish, *v.t.* [Fr. *bannir*, ppr. *bannissant*, to banish, from L.L. *bannire*, to proclaim, denounce, from O.H.G. *bannan*, to proclaim. BAN.] To condemn to exile; to send (a person) from a country as a punishment; to drive away; to exile; to cast from the mind (thoughts, care, business).—**Banisher**, ban'ish-ér, *n.* One who banishes.—**Banishment**, ban'ish-ment, *n.* The act of banishing; the state of being banished; enforced absence; exile.

Banister, **Bannister**, ban'is-tér, *n.* [Form of *baluster.*] A baluster; an upright in a stair rail.

Banjo, ban'jō, *n.* [Negro corruption of *bandore.*] A musical instrument having six strings, a body like a tambourine, and a neck like a guitar.

Bank, bangk, *n.* [A.Sax. *banc*, a bank, a hillock, also *benc*, a bench; Sw. and Dan. *bank*, *bänk*, Icel. *bakki* (for *banki*), D. and G. *bank*, a bank, a bench. In sense of establishment dealing in money the word is directly from the Fr. *banque*, a banking establishment; It. *banco*, a bench, counter, a bank, this being from the German. *Bench* is the same word.] A mound or heap of earth; any steep acclivity, as one rising from a river, the sea, or forming the side of a ravine or the like; a rising ground in the sea, partly above water or covered everywhere with shoal water; a shoal; the face of coal at which miners are working; a bench or seat for the rowers in a galley; one of the rows of oars; an establishment which trades in money; an establishment for the deposit, custody, remittance, and issue of money; the office in which the transactions of a banking company are conducted; the funds of a gaming establishment; a fund in certain games at cards.—*v.t.* To inclose, defend, or fortify with a bank; to embank; to lay up or deposit in a bank.—*v.i.* To deposit money in a bank.—*To bank (upon)*, to stake or rest hopes upon an event (recent use).—**Bankable**, bangk'a-bl, *a.* Receivable or discountable at a bank.—**Banker**, bangk'ér, *n.* One who keeps a bank; one who traffics in money, receives and remits money, negotiates bills of exchange, &c.—**Banking**, bangk'ing, *n.* The business or profession of a banker; the system followed by banks in carrying on their business; the tilting up of an aeroplane at a sharp angle sideways when flying swiftly round a curve, on the same principle as that on which a cycle track is 'banked' steeply at corners rounded at high speed.—**Bank-agent**, *n.* A person employed by a bank to conduct its banking operations in a branch office.—**Bank-book**, *n.* The book given to a customer, in which the officers of the bank enter his debits and credits.—**Bank-note**, *n.* A promissory note issued by a banking company payable in gold or silver at the bank on demand.—**Bank-stock**, a share or shares in the capital stock of a bank.

Bankrupt, bangk'rupt, *n.* [*Bank*, a bench, and L. *ruptus*, broken, lit. one whose bench has been broken, the bench or table which a merchant or banker formerly used in the exchange having been broken on his bankruptcy.] A person declared by legal authority unable to pay his debts; popularly, one who has wholly or partially failed to pay his debts; one who has compounded with his creditors; an insolvent.—*a.* Insolvent; unable to meet one's obligations.—**Bankruptcy**, bangk'rupt-si, *n.* The state of being a bankrupt; inability to pay all debts; failure in trade.

Banlieue, ban'lū, *n.* [Fr. *ban*, jurisdiction, and *lieue*, a league, a district of indeterminate extent.] The territory without the walls, but within the legal limits of a town or city.

Banner, ban'ér, *n.* [Fr. *bannière*, L.L. *banderia*, from *bandum*, banner, standard, from G. *band*, a band or strip of cloth, from *binden*, to bind.] A piece of cloth usually bearing some warlike or heraldic device or national emblem, attached to the upper part of a pole or staff; an ensign; a standard; a square flag.—**Bannerol**, ban'ér-ol, *n.* A little flag; a banderole.—**Bannered**, ban'érd, *a.* Having a banner; displaying banners.—**Banneret**, ban'ér-et, *n.* A knight of a rank between a baron and an ordinary knight, raised to this rank for bravery on the field.

Bannock, ban'ok, *n.* [A.Sax. *bannuc*, Gael. *bannach.*] An unleavened cake of oatmeal or other meal baked at an open fire, and generally on an iron plate. [Scotch.]

Banns, banz, *n.pl.* [See BAN.] The proclamation in church previous to a marriage, made by calling over the names of the parties intending matrimony.

Banquet, bang'kwet, *n.* [Fr. *banquet*, dim. of *banque*, a bench, a seat, and hence a feast. BANK.] A feast; a rich entertainment of meat and drink; *fig.* something specially delicious or enjoyable.—*v.t.* To treat with a feast or rich entertainment. —*v.i.* To feast; to regale one's self; to fare daintily.—**Banqueter**, bang'kwet-ér, *n.* A feaster; one who provides feasts or rich entertainments.

Banquette, baṅ-ket, *n.* [Fr., from *banc*, a bench, a bank.] *Fort.* a little raised way or bank running along the inside of a parapet, on which musketeers or riflemen stand to fire upon the enemy in the moat or covered-way; the footway of a bridge when raised above the carriage-way.

Banshee, **Benshi**, ban'shē, ben'shi, *n.* Ir. *bean-sith*, Gael. *ban-sith*, from Ir. and Gael. *bean*, *ban*, woman, and *sith*, fairy.] A kind of female fairy believed in Ireland and some parts of Scotland to attach herself to a particular house, and to appear before the death of one of the family.

Bantam, ban'tam, *n.* A small but spirited breed of domestic fowl with feathered shanks, first brought from the East Indies, and supposed to derive its name from *Bantam* in Java; a soldier under the regulation height (recent term).—*a.* Pertaining to or resembling the bantam; of the breed of the bantam; hence, diminutive; puny.

Banter, ban'tėr, *v.t.* [Origin unknown.] To address humorous raillery to; to attack with jokes or jests; to make fun of; to rally.—*n.* (no pl.) A joking or jesting; humorous raillery: pleasantry with which a person is attacked.—**Banterer**, ban'tér-ér, *n.* One who banters.

Banting, bant'ing, *n.* Method for treating or reducing obesity, from William Banting, 1796-1878.

Bantling, bant'ling, *n.* [Probably from *band*, a wrapping, and the dim. suffix *-ling*, meaning properly a child in swaddling clothes.] A young child; an infant: a term carrying with it a shade of contempt.

Banxring, bangks'ring, *n.* [Native name.] The popular name of certain squirrel-like insectivorous mammals of the East.

Banyan, **Banyan-tree**, ban'yan, *n.* [From the connection of one such tree with certain *banians* or Indian merchants.] An Indian tree of the fig genus, remarkable for its horizontal branches sending down shoots which take root when they reach the ground and enlarge into trunks, which in their turn send out branches; the tree in this manner covering a prodigious extent of ground.

Banyan, ban'yan, *n.* A native Indian merchant. BANIAN.

Baobab, bā'ō-bab, *n.* [The name in Senegal.] A large African tree usually from 40 to 70 feet high, and often 30 feet in diameter, having an oblong pulpy fruit called monkey-bread; the sour-gourd or calabash-tree.

Baphomet, baf'ō-met, *n.* [A corruption of *Mahomet.*] The imaginary idol or symbol which the Templars were accused of employing in their mysterious rites.—**Baphometic**, baf-ō-met'ik, *a.* Of or pertaining to Baphomet or to the rites in which it was supposed to be employed. (*Carl.*)

Baptism, bap'tizm, *n.* [Gr. *baptisma*, from *baptizō*, to baptize, from *baptō*, to dip in water.] The application of water by sprinkling or immersion to a person, as a sacrament or religious ceremony.—**Baptismal**, bap-tiz'mal, *a.* Pertaining to baptism.—**Baptismally**, bap-tiz'mal-li, *adv.* In a baptismal manner.—**Baptist**, bap'tist, *n.* [Gr. *baptistēs.*] One who administers baptism: specifically applied to John, the forerunner of Christ; as a contraction of *Anabaptist*, one who objects to infant baptism.—**Baptistery**, bap'tis-tér-i, *n.* A building or a portion of a building in which is administered the rite of baptism.—**Baptistic**, **Baptistical**,† bap-tis'tik, bap-tis'tik-al, *a.* Pertaining to baptism.—**Baptistically**,† bap-tis'tik-al-li, *adv.* In a baptistical manner.—**Baptizable**, bap-tīz'a-bl, *a.* Capable of being baptized.—**Baptize**, bap-tīz', *v.t.*—*baptized, baptizing.* [Gr. *baptizō.*] To administer the sacrament of baptism to; to christen.—**Baptizer**, bap-tīz'ér, *n.* One who baptizes.

Bar, bär, *n.* [Fr. *barre*; from the Celtic; W. and Armor. *bar*, the top branch of a tree, a rail, a bar. *Barrier, barrister, barricade, embarrass*, &c., are derivatives.] A piece of wood, metal, or other solid matter, long in proportion to its thickness; a pole; a connecting piece in various positions and structures, often for a hinderance or obstruction; anything which obstructs, hinders, or impedes; an obstruction; an obstacle; a barrier; a bank of sand, gravel, or earth forming an obstruction at the mouth of a river or harbour; the railing inclosing the place which counsel occupy in courts of justice; the place in court where prisoners are stationed for arraignment, trial, or sentence; all those who can plead in a court; barristers in general; the profession of barrister; the railing or partition which separates a space near the door from the body of either house of parliament; a tribunal in general; the inclosed place of a tavern, inn, or other establishment where liquors, &c., are served out; the counter over which such articles are served out; military mark of distinction, stripe added to medal; *music*, a line drawn perpendicularly across the staff dividing it into equal measures of time; the space and notes included between two such lines.—*v.t.*—*barred, barring.* To fasten with a bar or as with a bar; to hinder; to obstruct; to prevent; to prohibit; to restrain; to except; to exclude by exception; to provide with a bar or bars; to mark with bars; to cross with one or more stripes or lines.—**Bar-maid**, *n.* A maid or woman who serves at the bar of an inn or other place of refreshment.—**Bar-room**, *n.* The room in a public-house, hotel, &c., containing the bar or counter where refreshments are served out.—**Bar-shot**, *n.* A double shot, consisting of two round-shot united by a bar.—**Bar-wood**, *n.* A kind of red dyewood from Africa.

Barb, bärb, *n.* [Fr. *barbe*, L. *barba*, beard.] The sharp point projecting backwards from the penetrating extremity of an arrow, fish-hook, or other instrument for piercing, intended to prevent its being extracted; a barbel; a beard.—*v.t.* To shave or dress the beard‡; to furnish with barbs, as an arrow.

Barb, bärb, *n.* [Contr. from *Barbary.*] A horse of the Barbary breed, remarkable for speed, endurance, and docility.

Barbacan, Barbican, bär′ba-kan, bär′-bi-kan, *n.* [Fr. *barbacane*, It. *barbacane*, from Ar. *bāb-khānah*, a gateway or gatehouse.] A kind of watch-tower; an advanced work defending the entrance to a castle or fortified town, as before the gate or drawbridge.

Barbadoes Tar, bär-bā′dōz, *n.* Petroleum or mineral tar found in some of the West Indian islands.

Barbarian, bär-bā′ri-an, *n.* [L. *barbarus*, from Gr. *barbaros*, one whose language is unintelligible, a foreigner.] A foreigner‡ (N.T.); a man in his rude savage state; an uncivilized person; a cruel, savage, brutal man; one destitute of pity or humanity.—*a.* Of or pertaining to savages; rude; uncivilized; cruel; inhuman. — **Barbaric**, bär-bar′ik, *a.* Of or pertaining to, or characteristic of a barbarian; uncivilized; savage; wild; ornate without being in accordance with sound taste.—**Barbarism**, bär′bär-izm, *n.* An uncivilized state; want of civilization; rudeness of manners; an act of barbarity, cruelty, or brutality; an outrage; an offence against purity of style or language; any form of speech contrary to correct idiom.—**Barbarity**, bär-bar′i-ti, *n.* The state of being barbarous; barbarousness; savageness; ferociousness; inhumanity; a barbarous act.—**Barbarization**, bär′bär-iz-ā″shon, *n.* The act or process of rendering barbarous or of becoming barbarous.—**Barbarize**, bär′bär-īz, *v.i.* To become barbarous.—*v.t.* To make barbarous.—**Barbarous**, bär′ba-rus, *a.* Unacquainted with arts and civilization; uncivilized; rude and ignorant; pertaining to or characteristic of barbarians; adapted to the taste of barbarians; barbaric; cruel; ferocious; inhuman.—**Barbarously**, bär′ba-rus-li, *adv.* In a barbarous manner; without knowledge or arts; savagely; cruelly; ferociously; inhumanly. — **Barbarousness**, bar′ba-rus-nes, *n.* The state or quality of being barbarous; barbarity.

Barbe, Barb, bärb, *n.* [For *barde*, Fr. *barde*, Sp. *albarda*, from Ar. *barda′a*, a pad, a covering for a horse's back.] One of the ornaments and housings of a horse; one of the pieces of defensive armour with which the war-horses of knights were anciently clad.—**Barbed**, bärbd, *p.* and *a.* Furnished with or clad in barbes or armour.

Barbecue,† bär′bē-kū, *n.* [Conjectured to be from Fr. *barbe-à-queue*, from beard to tail; more probably from Carib *barbacoa*, a kind of large gridiron.] A crate on posts; a hog or other large animal dressed whole; a terrace partly or wholly surrounding a house. — *v.t.* — *barbecued, barbecuing.* To dress and cook whole by splitting to the backbone and roasting on a gridiron.

Barbel, bär′bel, *n.* [O.Fr. *barbel*, from L. *barbus*, a barbel (the fish), from *barba*, a beard. In sense of appendage it is rather for *barbule.*] A fresh-water fish having four beard-like appendages on its upper jaw; a vermiform process appended to the mouth of certain fishes, serving as an organ of touch.

Barber, bär′bėr, *n.* [Fr. *barbier*, from *barbe*, L. *barba*, a beard.] One whose occupation is to shave the beard or to cut and dress hair. — *v.t.* To shave and dress the hair of. (*Shak.*)

Barberry, bär′be-ri, *n.* [Fr. *berberis*, from Ar. *barbāris*, the barberry, but the spelling has been modified so as to give the word an English appearance.] A shrubby plant bearing small acid and astringent, red berries, common in hedges.

Barbet, bär′bet, *a.* [Fr. *barbet*, from L. *barba*, a beard.] A variety of dog having long curly hair; a poodle; one of a group of climbing birds, approaching the cuckoos, having a large conical beak, and at its base tufts of stiff bristles.

Barbette, bär-bet′, *n.* [Fr. *barbette.*] A fixed armoured shelter on a warship, inside which a gun revolves on a turn-table.

Barbican, *n.* BARBACAN.

Barbule, bär′būl, *n.* [L. *barbula*, dim. of *barba*, a beard.] A small barb; a little beard.

Barcarolle, bär′ka-rōl, *n.* [Fr., from It. *barcarolo*, a boatman, from *barca*, a boat or barge.] A simple song or melody sung by Venetian gondoliers; a piece of instrumental music composed in imitation of such a song.

Bard, bärd, *n.* [Celtic.] A poet and singer among the ancient Celts; a poet generally. —**Bardic**, bärd′ik, *a.* Pertaining to bards or to their poetry.—**Bardish**, bärd′ish, *a.* Pertaining to bards; written by a bard.—**Bardism**, bärd′izm, *n.* The learning and maxims of bards.—**Bardling**, bärd′ling, *n.* An inferior bard; a mediocre poet.—**Bardship**, bärd′ship, *n.* The state or quality of being a bard.

Bare, bār. Old pret. of *bear*, now *Bore.*

Bare, bār, *a.* [A. Sax. *bær*, Icel. *ber*, Sw. Dan. *bar*, D. *baar*, G. *bar*, *baar*, probably from root meaning shining seen in Skr. *bhās*, to shine.] Naked; without covering; laid open to view; detected; no longer concealed; poor; destitute; indigent; ill-supplied; empty; unfurnished; unprovided: often followed by *of* (*bare of* money); threadbare; much worn.—*v.t.*—*bared, baring.* To strip off the covering from; to make naked. —**Barely**, bār′li, *adv.* In a bare manner; nakedly; poorly; without decoration; scarcely; hardly.—**Bareness**, bār′nes, *n.* The state of being bare; want of clothing or covering; nakedness; deficiency of appropriate covering, ornament, and the like; poverty; indigence.—**Barebacked**, bār′-bakt, *a.* Having the back uncovered; unsaddled.—**Areboned**, bār′bōnd, *a.* Having the bones scantly covered with flesh; very lean.—**Barefaced**, bār′fāst, *a.* Having the face uncovered; hence undisguised; unreserved; shameless; impudent; audacious (*barefaced* robbery).—**Barefacedly**, bār′fāst-li, *adv.* In a barefaced manner; openly; shamelessly; impudently.—**Barefacedness**, bār′fāst-nes, *n.* Effrontery; assurance. — **Barefoot, Barefooted**, bār′fụt, bār′fụt-ed, *a.* and *adv.* With the feet bare; without shoes or stockings.

Barege, ba-rāzh′, *n.* [From *Baréges*, a village of the Pyrenees.] A thin gauze-like fabric for ladies' dresses, usually made of silk and worsted, but, in the inferior sorts, with cotton instead of silk.

Bargain, bär′gin, *n.* [O.Fr. *bargaine*, L.L. *barcania*, a bargain, traffic; believed to be from L.L. *barca*, a bark.] A contract or agreement between two or more parties; a compact settling that something shall be done, sold, transferred, &c.; the thing purchased or stipulated for; what is obtained by an agreement; something bought or sold at a low price.—*v.i.* To make a bargain or agreement; to make an agreement about the transfer of property.—*v.t.* To sell; to transfer for a consideration: generally followed by *away.*—**Bargainer**, bär′gin-ėr, *n.* One who bargains or stipulates.

Barge, bärj, *n.* [O.Fr. *barge*, L.L. *bargia*, *barga*, *barca*, bark. BARQUE.] A vessel or boat elegantly fitted up and decorated, used on occasions of state and pomp; a flat-bottomed vessel for loading and unloading ships or conveying goods from one place to another.—*v.i.* Barge (*about*), to sail idly up and down (recent use).—**Bargee**, bärj′ē, *n.* One of the crew of a barge or canal-boat.—**Bargeman**, bärj′man, *n.* The man who manages a barge.

Barilla, ba-ril′la, *n.* [Sp.] An impure soda or carbonate and sulphate of soda obtained in Spain and elsewhere by burning several species of plants; a kind of kelp; Spanish soda.

Baritone, bar′i-tōn, *n.* and *a.* Same as *Barytone.*

Barium, bā′ri-um, *n.* [Gr. *barys*, heavy. BARYTA.] The metallic basis of baryta (which is an oxide of *barium*); a metal as yet obtained in very small quantities.

Bark, bärk, *n.* [Dan. and Sw. *bark*, Icel. *börkr*, G. *borke*, bark.] The outer rind of a tree, shrub, &c.; the exterior covering of exogenous plants, composed of cellular and vascular tissue.—*v.i.* To strip bark off; to peel; to apply bark to; to treat with bark in tanning.—**Barker**, bärk′ėr, *n.* One who barks; one who removes the bark from trees.—**Barkery**, bärk′ėr-i, *n.* A tan-house, or place where bark is kept.—**Bark-bed, Bark-stove**, *n.* A bed formed of the spent bark used by tanners, which is placed in the inside of a brick pit in a glazed house, constructed for forcing or for the growth of tender plants.—**Bark-mill**, *n.* A mill for crushing bark for the use of tanners and dyers.

Bark, bärk, *n.* Same as *Barque.*

Bark, bärk, *v.i.* [A.Sax. *beorcan.*] To emit the cry of a dog, or a similar sound.—*n.* The cry of the domestic dog; a cry resembling that of the dog.—**Barker**, bärk′-ėr, *n.* An animal that barks; a person who clamours unreasonably.

Barkantine, bärk′an-tīn, *n.* Same as *Barquantine* (which see).

Barker's Mill, *n.* A machine driven by water; a kind of simple turbine.

Barley, bär′li, *n.* [O.E. *barlic*, *berlic*, from A.Sax. *bere* (= Sc. *bear*), barley, and *leac*, a plant (also a *leek*); comp. *garlic.*] A kind of grain commonly grown and used especially for making malt; the plant yielding the grain.—**Barleycorn**, bär′li-korn, *n.* A grain of barley; a measure equal to the third part of an inch.—John Barleycorn, a surname of malted drink. — **Barley-sugar**, *n.* Sugar boiled till it is brittle (formerly with a decoction of barley), and candied.—**Barley-water**, *n.* A decoction of pearl barley used in medicine as an emollient.

Barm, bärm, *n.* [A.Sax. *beorma* = Sw. *bärma*, Dan. *bärme*, L. G. *barme*, G. *bärme*, barm; from root of *brew.*] Yeast.—**Barmy**, bärm′i, *a.* Containing or consisting of barm; frothy, as beer.

Barmecide, bar′me-sīd, *a.* Disappointing, fallacious. — **Barmecide feast.** Rich apparent feast given in the *Arabian Nights*, by prince to guest, with nothing but names for the dishes.

Barn, bärn, *n.* [A.Sax. *berern*—*bere*, barley, and *ern*, a house.] A covered building for securing grain, hay, or other farm produce.—*v.t.* To store up in a barn.—**Barn-owl**, *n.* The common white owl often found in barns, where it proves very useful by destroying mice.

Barnacle, bär′na-kl, *n.* [Fr. *bernacle*, *barnacle*, L.L. *bernacula*, for *pernacula*, dim. of L. *perna*, a ham, a kind of shell-fish. In sense of goose origin doubtful.] A stalked cirriped, often found on the bottoms of ships, on timber fixed below the surface of the sea, &c.; a species of goose found in the northern seas, but visiting more southern climates in winter.

Barnacles, bär'na-klz, *n. pl.* [Origin unknown.] An instrument to put upon a horse's nose, to confine him for shoeing, bleeding, or dressing; a cant name for a pair of spectacles.

Barograph, bar'ō-graf, *n.* [Gr. *baros*, weight, and *graphō*, to write.] A self-registering barometric instrument for recording the variations in the pressure of the atmosphere.

Barometer, ba-rom'et-ėr, *n.* [Gr. *baros*, weight, and *metron*, measure.] An instrument for measuring the weight or pressure of the atmosphere, consisting ordinarily of a glass tube containing a column of mercury, its lower end dipping into a cup containing the same metal; the mercury in the tube, having a vacuum above it, rises and falls according to the varying pressure of the air on the mercury in the cup. In the aneroid barometer no fluid is used.—**Barometric, Barometrical**, bar-ō-met'rik, bar-ō-met'rik-al, *a.* Pertaining or relating to the barometer; made by a barometer.—**Barometrically**, bar-ō-met'rik-al-li, *adv.* By means of a barometer.

Baron, bar'on, *n.* [Fr. *baron*, from O.H.G. *bar*, a man, from *beran* = E. to *bear*, the original sense being probably that of one who could *bear*, as being strong and robust.] In Great Britain, a title or degree of nobility; one who holds the lowest rank in the peerage; a title of certain judges or officers; as, *barons of the exchequer*, the judges of the court of exchequer.—*Baron of beef*, two sirloins not cut asunder. — **Baronage**, bar'on-āj, *n.* The whole body of barons or peers; the dignity or condition of a baron. —**Baroness**, bar'on-es, *n.* A baron's wife or lady; a holder of the title in her own right.—**Baronet**, bar'on-et, *n.* [Dim. of *baron*.] One who possesses a hereditary rank or degree of honour next below a baron, and therefore not a member of the peerage; one belonging to an order founded by James I. in 1611.—**Baronetage**, bar'on-et-āj, *n.* The baronets as a body; the dignity of a baronet.—**Baronetcy**, bar-on-et-si, *n.* The title and dignity of a baronet. — **Baronial**, ba-rō'ni-al, *a.* Pertaining to a baron or a barony.—**Barony**, bar'on-i, *n.* The title or honour of a baron; also the territory or lordship of a baron; in Ireland, a territorial division, corresponding nearly to the English hundred.

Baroscope, bar'o-skōp, *n.* [Gr. *baros*, weight, *skopeō*, to view.] An instrument for exhibiting changes of atmospheric pressure; a kind of weather-glass.

Barouche, ba-rösh', *n.* [From G. *barutsche*, from It. *baroccio*, *biroccio*, from L. *birotus*, two-wheeled—*bis*, double, and *rota*, a wheel.] A four-wheeled carriage with a falling top.

Barque, bärk, *n.* [Fr. *barque*, L.L. *barca*, a barque, through a dim. form *barica*, from Gr. *baris*, a skiff. *Barge* is a form of this word.] A sailing vessel of any kind; *naut.* a three-masted vessel with only fore-and-aft sails on the mizzen-mast, the other two masts being square-rigged. — **Barquantine**, bärk'an-tīn, *n.* [From *barque*, in imitation of *brigantine*.] A three-masted vessel square-rigged in the foremast and fore-and-aft rigged in the main and mizzen masts.

Barrack, bar'ak, *n.* [Fr. *baraque*, It. *baracca*, from L.L. *bárra*, a bar, from the Celtic; comp. Ir. *barrachad*, a hut or booth.] A hut or house for soldiers, especially in garrison; permanent buildings in which both officers and men are lodged; a large building, or a collection of huts for a body of work-people: generally in pl.—**Barrack-master**, *n.* The officer who superintends the barracks of soldiers. — **Barracoon**, bar-a-kön', *n.* A negro-barrack; a slave depot or bazaar.

Barrage, bar'āj, *n.* [Fr. *barre*.] Damming-up, chiefly on the Nile.—**Barrage-fire**, *n.* The discharge of artillery in such a manner as to keep a selected zone under continuous fire, with a view to preventing the passage of reinforcements through the line. Also called *curtain-fire*.

Barranca, bar-ran'ka, *n.* [Sp.] A deep gully or ravine.

Barrator, bar'a-tor, *n.* [O.Fr. *barateur*, a cheater, *barate*, deceit. Barter.] One who frequently excites suits at law; an encourager of litigation; the master or one of the crew of a ship who commits any fraud in the management of the ship or cargo, by which the owner, freighters, or insurers are injured. — **Barratrous**, bar'a-trus, *a.* Characterized by or tainted with barratry. — **Barratrously**, bar'a-trus-li, *adv.* — **Barratry**, bar'a-tri, *n.* The act or practice of a barrator; the exciting and encouraging of lawsuits and quarrels; fraud in a shipmaster to the injury of the owners, freighters, or insurers, as by running away with the ship, sinking, or deserting her.

Barrel, bar'el, *n.* [O.Fr. *bareil*, Fr. *baril*, from Celt; comp. W. *baril*, Gael. *baraill*, a barrel; so called because made of *bars* or staves. Bar.] A somewhat cylindrical wooden vessel made of staves and bound with hoops; a cask; anything resembling a barrel in shape; a hollow cylinder or tube (as the *barrel* of a gun).—*v.t.*—*barreled*, *barreling*. To put in a barrel.—**Barreled**, bar'eld, *a.* Having a barrel or barrels: generally used in composition. — **Barrel-bellied**, *a.* Having a round and protuberant or barrel-shaped belly. — **Barrel-bulk**, *n.* *Naut*, a measure of capacity for freight, equal to 5 cubic feet. — **Barrel-organ**, *n.* An organ in which a barrel or cylinder furnished with pegs or staples, when turned round, opens a series of valves to admit a current of air to a set of pipes, or acts on wires, so as to produce a tune.

Barren, bar'en, *a.* [From O.Fr. *baraigne*, *brehaine*, *brehaigne*, sterile, possibly from Armor. *brec'han*, sterile.] Incapable of producing its kind; not prolific: applied to animals and vegetables; unproductive; unfruitful; sterile: applied to land; *fig.* not producing or leading to anything (*barren* speculation, *barren* of ideas); unsuggestive; uninstructive.—*n.* A barren or unproductive tract of land.—**Barrenly**, bar'en-li, *adv.* Unfruitfully.—**Barrenness**, bar'en-nes, *n.* The state or quality of being barren; sterility; want of fertility, instructiveness, interest, or the like (*barrenness* of invention).

Barret cap, bar'et, *a.* [Fr. *barrette*.] Flat cap, or biretta.

Barretor, Barretry, bar'et-or, bar'et-ri, *n.* Same as *Barrator*, *Barratry*.

Barricade, bar-i-kād', *n.* [From Sp. *barricada*, blocking with *barricas* or casks.] A temporary fortification made of trees, earth, stones, or anything that will obstruct the progress of an enemy or serve for defence or security against his shot; a fence around or along the side of a space to be kept clear; any barrier or obstruction. — *v.t.* — *barricaded*, *barricading*. To stop up by a barricade; to erect a barricade across; to obstruct.—**Barricader**, bar-i-kād'ėr, *n.* One who erects barricades.

Barrier, bar'i-ėr, *n.* [Fr. *barrière*, a barrier, from *barre*, a bar. Bar.] A fence; a railing; any obstruction; what hinders approach, attack, or progress; what stands in the way; an obstacle; a limit or boundary of any kind; a line of separation.—*Barrier reef*, a coral-reef rising from a great depth to the level of low tide, encircling an island like a barrier, or running parallel to a coast, with a navigable channel inside, as on the north-east coast of Australia.

Barring, bär'ing, *part.* of verb to *bar*, used as *prep.* Excepting; leaving out of account. (Colloq.)—**Barring-out**, *n.* The act of excluding a schoolmaster from school by barricading the doors and windows; a boyish sport at Christmas.

Barrister, bar'is-tėr, *n.* [From *bar*.] A counsellor or advocate admitted to plead at the bar of a court of law in protection and defence of clients: a term more especially used in England and Ireland, the corresponding term in Scotland being *advocate*, in the United States *counsellor*.

Barrow, bar'ō, *n.* [A.Sax. *berewe*, a barrow, from *beran*, E. to *bear*, to carry; comp. *bier*.] A light small carriage, moved or carried by hand: when having a wheel it is a *wheel*-barrow.

Barrow, bar'ō, *n.* [A.Sax. *beorg*, *beorh*, *berg*, a hill or funeral mound; Dan. Sw. G. *berg*, a hill; allied to *burgh*.] A prehistoric or at least ancient sepulchral mound formed of earth or stones, found in Britain and elsewhere, and met with in various forms: often containing remains of the dead, implements, &c.

Barter, bär'tėr, *v.i.* [O.Fr. *bareter*, *barater*, to cheat, to barter, *barat*, *barate*, deceit, barter; origin doubtful.] To traffic or trade by exchanging one commodity for another (and not for money).—*v.t.* To give in exchange; to exchange, as one commodity for another. — *n.* The act of exchanging commodities; the thing given in exchange. —**Barterer**, bär'tėr-ėr, *n.* One who barters or traffics by exchanging commodities.

Bartizan, bär'ti-zan, *n.* [Comp. O.Fr. *bretesche*, a fortification of timber; G. *bret*, a board.] A small turret projecting from the top part of a tower or wall, with apertures for archers to shoot through.

Barton, bar'ton, *n.* [O.E. *bere tun*; *bere*, barley, *tun*, enclosure.] That part of the farm retained by the owner and not let to the tenant.

Barwood, bär'wud, *n.* A red dye-wood brought from Africa; camwood.

Baryta, ba-rī'ta, *n.* [Gr. *barys*, heavy, *barytēs*, weight.] Oxide of barium, called sometimes *heavy-earth*, generally found in combination with sulphuric and carbonic acids, forming sulphate and carbonate of baryta, the former of which is called *heavy-spar*. Baryta is a gray powder with a sharp caustic alkaline taste.—**Barytes**, ba-rī'tēz, *n.* A name of baryta or its sulphate (heavy-spar).—**Barytic**, ba-rī'tik, *a.* Of or containing baryta.

Barytone, Baryton, bar'i-tōn, *a.* [Gr. *barys*, heavy, and *tonos*, tone.] Ranging between tenor and bass; having a voice ranging between tenor and bass; *Greek gram.* having no accent marked on the last syllable, the grave being understood.—*n.* A male voice, the compass of which partakes of the bass and the tenor, but which does not descend so low as the one nor rise as high as the other; a person with a voice of this quality; a deep brass instrument.

Basalt, ba-sạlt', *n.* [Gr. *basaltēs*, of unknown origin.] A well-known igneous dark-gray or black rock occurring in the ancient trap and the recent volcanic series, and remarkable as often assuming the form of regularly prismatic columns, such as are to be seen at Fingal's Cave in Staffa, or the Giant's Causeway in the north of Ireland.—**Basaltic**, ba-sạlt'ik, *a.* Pertaining to basalt; formed of or containing basalt.—**Basaltiform**, ba-sạlt'i-form, *a.* In the form of basalt; columnar.

Basanite, baz'an-īt, *n.* [Gr. *basanos*, the touchstone.] Touchstone.

Bascinet, bas'i-net, *n.* [O.Fr. *bassinet*, *bacinet*, dim. of *bassin*, *bacin*, a helmet in the form of a basin.] A light helmet, originally without a vizor.

Bascule, bas'kūl, *n.* [Fr.] An arrangement in bridges by which one portion balances another.—*Bascule bridge*, a kind of drawbridge in which the roadway may be raised at will and kept in an upright position by means of weights or otherwise.

Base, bās, *a.* [Fr. *bas*, low, from L.L. *bassus*, low, short, allied to Ir. *bass*, W. *bas*, Armor. *baz*, shallow.] Of little or no value; coarse in comparison (the *base* metals); worthless; fraudulently debased in value; spurious (*base* coin); of or pertaining to humble or illegitimate birth; of low station; lowly; of mean spirit; morally low; showing or proceeding from a mean spirit; deep; grave: applied to sounds.—*n.pl.* An old name for a skirt or something similar worn by knights, &c. (*Mil.*)—**Basely**, bās'li, *adv.* In a base manner or condition; meanly; humbly; vilely.—**Baseness**, bās'nes. *n.* The state or quality of being base; meanness; lowness; vileness; worthlessness.—**Base-born**, *a.* Born in a base condition; of illegitimate birth.—**Base-court**, *n.* The court or yard at the back of a house.

Base, bās, *n.* [Fr. *base*, L. *basis*, a base, a pedestal, from Gr. *basis*, a going, a foot, a base, from *bainō*, to go.] The bottom of anything, considered as its support, or the part of a thing on which it stands or rests; the opposite extremity to the apex; *arch.* the part between the bottom of a column and the pedestal or the floor; *chem.* one of those compound substances which unite with acids to form salts; *dyeing*, a mordant; *geom.* the line or surface forming that part of a figure on which it is supposed to stand; *mus.* the bass; *milit.* a tract of country protected by fortifications, or strong by natural advantages, from which the operations of an army proceed; the place from which racers or tilters start; a starting-post; the game of base-ball or prisoner's base, or an old game somewhat similar.—*v.t.*—*based*, *basing.* To lay the base or foundation of; to place on a basis; to found.—**Basal**, **Basilar**, **Basilary**, bās'al, baz'il-ér, baz'-il-a-ri, *a.* Of or pertaining to a base: situated at the base.—**Baseless**, bās'les, *a.* Without a base; without grounds or foundation (a *baseless* rumour).—**Basement**, bas'ment, *n.* *Arch.* the lowest story of a building, whether above or below the ground.—**Basic**, bās'ik, *a.* Relating to a base; *chem.* performing the place of a base in a salt, or having the base in excess.—**Basic-slag**, *n.* The slag or refuse matter got in making basic-steel, a valuable fertilizer from the phosphate of lime it contains.—**Basic-steel**, *n.* Steel made in a Bessemer converter, which is lined with lime or other substance to absorb the phosphorus in the iron.—**Basicity**, bās-is'i-ti, *n.* *Chem.* the state of being a base; the power of an acid to unite with one or more atoms of a base.

Baseball, *n.* The national American game or sport played with bat and ball, four bases indicating the points of the diamond marking the course each player takes in making a run (scoring), played by two teams of nine players each, one team being at bat while the other is in the field alternately; a horsehide-covered ball used in the game of baseball

Bash, bash, *v.t.* [Scand.: Dan. *bask*, a slap, *baske*, to slap; akin to *box*, to fight.] To beat violently; to knock out of shape. (Colloq.)

Bashaw, ba-shą', *n.* [Per. *bâshâ*, *pâshâh.*] A pasha.

Bashful, bash'fụl, *a.* [For *abashful.*] Easily put to confusion; modest to excess; diffident; shy.—**Bashfully**, bash'fụl-li, *adv.* In a bashful manner; very modestly.—**Bashfulness**, bash'fụl-nes, *n.* The quality of being bashful; excessive modesty; timorous shyness.

Bashi-bazouk, bash'ē-ba-zök″, *n.* [Turk.] A kind of irregular soldier in the Turkish army, a member of a corps collected hastily in a time of emergency.

Basial,† bā'si-al, *a.* [L. *basium*, a kiss.] Relating to or consisting of a kiss.

Basic, **Basicity.** Under BASE, *n.*

Basidium, ba-sid'i-um, *n.* pl. **Basidia**, ba-sid'i-a. [Gr. *basis*, a base, and *eidos*, likeness.] *Bot.* the cell to which the spores of some fungi are attached.

Basil, baz'il, *n.* [O.Fr. *bisel*, perhaps from L. *bis*, denoting doubleness. *Bezel* is the same word.] The slope at the edge of a cutting tool, as of a chisel or plane.—*v.t.* To grind the edge (of a tool) to an angle.

Basil, baz'il, *n.* [Shortened from O.Fr. *basilic*, from Gr. *basilikos*, royal, *basileus*, a king.] A plant, a native of India, cultivated in Europe as an aromatic pot-herb, and used for flavouring dishes.—**Basil-thyme**, *n.* A British plant with bluish-purple flowers and a fragrant aromatic smell.—**Basil-weed**, *n.* Wild basil or field-basil, a plant common in woods and copses.

Basilar. Under BASE, *n.*

Basilian, ba-zil'i-an, *a.* Belonging to the order of St. *Basil*, an order of monks founded in the fourth century in Cappadocia by a saint of that name.—*n.* A monk of the order of St. Basil.

Basilica, ba-zil'ik-a, *n.* [L., from Gr. *basilikē*, a colonnade; lit. a royal colonnade or porch, from *basileus*, a king.] Originally, the name applied by the Romans to their public halls: usually of rectangular form, with a middle and two side aisles and an apse at the end. The ground-plan of these was followed in the early Christian churches, and the name is now applied to some of the churches in Rome by way of distinction, or to other churches built in imitation of the Roman basilicas.—**Basilical**, **Basilican**, ba-zil'ik-al, ba-zil'ik-an, *a.* In the manner of or pertaining to a basilica; *anat.* applied to the middle vein of the right arm and the interior branch of the axillary vein (= royal vein).

Basilicon, ba-zil'ik-on, *n.* [L. *basilicon*, from Gr. *basilikos*, royal.] An ointment composed of yellow wax, black pitch, and resin.

Basilisk, baz'il-isk, *n.* [Gr. *basiliskos*, lit. little king, from *basileus*, king.] A fabulous creature formerly believed in, and variously regarded as a kind of serpent, lizard, or dragon, and sometimes identified with the cockatrice; a name of several reptiles of the lizard tribe with a crest or hood; a large piece of ordnance formerly used.

Basin, bā'sn, *n.* [Fr. *bassin*, O.Fr. *bacin*, a dim. of *bac*, a wide open vessel, same as E. *back*, a brewer's vat. BACK.] A vessel or dish of some size, usually circular, rather broad and not very deep, used to hold water for washing, and for various other purposes; any reservoir for water, natural or artificial; the whole tract of country drained by a river and its tributaries; *geol.* an aggregate of strata dipping towards a common axis or centre; strata or deposits lying in a depression in older rocks.

Basis, bās'is, *n.* pl. **Bases**, bās'ēz. [L. and Gr. *basis*, the foundation. BASE.] A base; a foundation or part on which something rests; *fig.* grounds or foundation. BASE.

Bask, bask, *v.i.* [Formerly to bathe, a word of Scandinavian origin = Icel. *batha sik*, to bathe one's self—*sik* being the reflexive pronoun. *Busk* is a similar form.] To lie in warmth; to be exposed to genial heat; *fig.* to be at ease and thriving under benign influences.—*v.t.* To warm by continued exposure to heat; to warm with genial heat.—**Basking-shark**, *n.* A species of shark, so called from its habit of lying on the surface of the water basking in the sun.

Basket, bas'ket, *n.* [Possibly of Celtic origin; comp. W. *basged* or *basgawd*, Ir. *bascaid*, a basket; W. *basg*, a netting or piece of wickerwork.] A vessel made of twigs, rushes, thin strips of wood, or other flexible materials interwoven; as much as a basket will hold.—*v.t.* To put in a basket.—**Basket-carriage**, *n.* A light carriage made of wickerwork.—**Basket-hilt**, *n.* A hilt, as of a sword or rapier, which covers the hand, and defends it from injury.

Basque, bäsk, *n.* A language of unknown affinities spoken in parts of France and Spain on both sides of the Pyrenees at the angle of the Bay of Biscay, supposed to represent the tongue of the ancient Iberians, the primitive inhabitants of Spain; Biscayan or Euskarian.—*a.* Pertaining to the people or language of Biscay.

Bas-relief, **Basso-rilievo**, bas' or bä'-rē-lēf, bäs'sō-rē-lyā'vō, *n.* [Fr. *bas*, It. *basso*, low, and *relief*, It. *rilievo*, relief.] A sculpture in low relief; a mode of sculpturing figures on a flat surface, the figures being raised above the surface, but not so much as in high relief or *alto-rilievo.*

Bass, **Basse**, bäs, *n.* [A corruption of *barse*, A.Sax. *bærs*, G. *bars*, D. *baars*, a perch.] The name of various British and American sea-fishes allied to the perch, some of them of considerable size and used as food.

Bass, bäs, *n.* [Same as *bast*, the *t* being dropped or changed to *s.* BAST.] The American linden or lime tree; a mat made of bast; a hassock.—**Bass-wood**, *n.* The American lime-tree or its timber.

Bass, bās, *n.* [It. *basso*, deep, low. BASE, *a.*] *Mus.* the lowest part in the harmony of a musical composition, whether vocal or instrumental; the lowest male voice.—*a.* *Mus.* low; deep; grave.—*v.t.*† To sound in a deep tone. (*Shak.*)—*v.i.* To sing a bass part.—**Bass-clef**, *n.* The character shaped like an inverted C put at the beginning of the bass-staff.—**Bass-staff**, *n.* The staff on which are written the notes belonging to the bass of a harmonized composition.—**Bass-viol**, *n.* A violoncello.

Bass, bas, *n.* A variety of bitter pale ale brewed by the firm *Bass* & Co. of Burton-on-Trent.

Basselisse, bäs'lis, *a.* [Fr. *basse-lisse*, low warp.] Wrought with a horizontal warp: said of a kind of tapestry, as distinguished from *hautelisse* tapestry, or that wrought with a perpendicular warp.

Basset, bas'set or bas-set', *n.* [Fr. *bassette*; It. *bassetta.*] An old game at cards, resembling modern faro.

Basset, bas'set, *n.* A miner's term for the outcrop or surface edge of any inclined stratum.—*v.i.* *Mining*, to incline upwards, so as to appear at the surface; to crop out.

Basset-horn, bas'set-horn, *n.* [It. *bassetto*, somewhat low, and E. *horn.*] A musical instrument, a sort of clarinet of enlarged dimensions and extended compass.

Bassinet, bas'i-net, *n.* [Probably a dim. from Fr. *berceau*, a cradle.] A wicker-basket with a covering or hood over one end, in which young children are placed by way of cradle.

Bassoon, bas-sön', *n.* [Fr. *basson*; It. *bassone*, aug. of *basso*, low.] A musical wind-instrument of the reed order, blown with a bent metal mouthpiece, and holed and keyed like the clarinet. It serves for the bass among wood wind-instruments, as hautboys, flutes, &c.—**Bassoonist**, bas-sön'ist, *n.* A performer on the bassoon.

Bassorine, bas'sō-rin, *n.* A substance extracted from gum-tragacanth and gum of *Bassora* (which is almost entirely composed of it), by treating these gums successively with water, alcohol, and ether.

Bass-relief, bas'rē-lēf, *n.* BAS-RELIEF.

Bast, bast, *n.* [A.Sax. *bæst* = Icel. Sw. D. Dan. and G. *bast*, bark, perhaps from root of *bind.*] The inner bark of exogenous trees, especially of the lime, consisting of several layers of fibres; rope or matting made of this.

Basta, bäs'tä, *interj.* [It.] Enough! stop! (*Shak.*)

Bastard, bas'tėrd, *n.* [O.Fr. *bastard*, from *bast* (Fr. *bât*), a pack-saddle, with the common termination *-ard* added to it, referring to the old locution *fils de bast*, son of a pack-saddle, the old saddles being often used by way of beds or to serve as pillows.] A natural child; a child begotten and born out of wedlock; an illegitimate or spurious child; what is spurious or inferior in quality; a kind of impure, soft, brown sugar; a kind of sweet, heady Spanish wine (*Shak.*).—*a.* Begotten and born out of lawful matrimony; illegitimate; spurious; not genuine; false; adulterate; impure; not of the first or usual order or character.—**Bastardism**,† bas'tėrd-izm, *n.* Bastardy.—**Bastardize**, bas'tėrd-īz, *v.t.*—*bastardized*, *bastardizing.* To make or prove to be a bastard.—**Bastardly**, bas'tėrd-li, *a.* Bastard; spurious.—**Bastardy**, bas'tėrd-i, *n.* The state of being a bastard, or begotten and born out of lawful wedlock.—**Bastard-wing**, *n.* A group of stiff feathers attached to the bone of a bird's wing that represents the thumb.

Baste, bāst, *v.t.*—*basted*, *basting.* [Allied to Icel. *beysta*, to strike, to beat, Dan. *böste*, to beat. As term in cookery the origin may be different.] To beat with a stick; to cudgel; to give a beating to; to drip butter or fat upon meat in roasting it.

Baste, bāst, *v.t.* [O.Fr. *bastir*, lit. to sew with *bast*, the fibres of bast having been used as thread. BAST.] To sew with long stitches, and usually to keep parts together temporarily; to sew slightly.—**Basting**, bāst'ing, *n.* The long stitches by which pieces of garments are loosely attached to each other.

Bastille, Bastile, bas-tēl', *n.* [Fr. *bastille*, a fortress, O.Fr. *bastir*, to build.] A tower or fortification.—*The Bastille*, an old castle in Paris used as a state prison, demolished by the enraged populace in 1789.

Bastinado, bas-ti-nā'dō, *n.* [Sp. *bastonada*, from *baston*, a stick, a baton.] A sound beating with a stick or cudgel; a mode of punishment in oriental countries, especially Mohammedan, by beating the soles of the feet with a rod.—*v.t.* To beat with a stick or cudgel; to beat on the soles of the feet, as a judicial punishment.

Bastion, bas'ti-on, *n.* [Fr. and Sp. *bastion*, from O.Fr. and Sp. *bastir*, Fr. *bâtir*, to build.] *Fort.* a huge mass of earth, faced with sods, brick, or stones, standing out with an angular form from the rampart at the angles of a fortification.—**Bastionary**, bas'ti-on-a-ri, *a.* Pertaining to or consisting of bastions.—**Bastioned**, bas'ti-ond, *a.* Provided with bastions.

Basyle, bās'il, *n.* [Gr. *basis*, base, and *hylē*, matter.] A body that unites with oxygen to form a base.

Bat, bat, *n.* [A Celtic word: Ir. and Armor. *bat*, a stick.] A heavy stick or club; a piece of wood shaped somewhat like the broad end of an oar, and provided with a round handle, used in driving the ball in cricket and similar games; a batsman or batter; a piece of a brick; a brickbat.—*v.i.* —*batted, batting.* To manage a bat or play with one at baseball.—**Batlet, Batler**, bat'let, bat'lėr, *n.* [Dim. of *bat.*] A small bat or square piece of wood with a handle for beating linen when taken out of the buck.—**Batsman, Batter**, bats'man, bat'ėr, *n.* The player who wields the bat in baseball.

Bat, bat, *n.* [Corruption of O.E. *back*, *bak*; Sc. *bak*, *bakie-bird*, a bat. Dan. *bakke* (in *aften-bakke*, a bat, lit. evening-bird), the word having lost an *l*, seen in Icel. *lethrblaka*, 'leather-flapper', a bat, from *blaka*, to flutter.] One of a group of mammals possessing a pair of leathery wings which extend between the fore and the posterior limbs, the former being specially modified for flying, the bones of the fore-feet being extremely elongated.—**Batty**, bat'i, *a.* Pertaining to or resembling a bat. (*Shak.*)—**Bat-fowling**, *n.* A mode of catching birds at night by means of a light and nets; the birds being roused fly towards the light and are entangled in the nets.

Batavian, ba-tā'vi-an, *a.* [From L. *Batavi*, a people anciently inhabiting an island at the mouth of the Rhine.] Pertaining to Holland or its inhabitants, or to Batavia in Java, the capital of the Dutch East Indies.—*n.* A Dutchman or inhabitant of Batavia.

Batch, bach, *n.* [From the verb to *bake.*] The quantity of bread baked at one time; any quantity of a thing made at once; a number of individuals or articles similar to each other.

Bate,‡ bāt, *n.* [Abbrev. of *debate.*] Strife; contention. (*Shak.*)

Bate, bāt, *v.t.*—*bated, bating.* [Abbrev. of *abate.*] To abate, lessen, or reduce; to leave out; to take away; to weaken, dull, or blunt (*Shak.*)‡.—*v.i.*‡ To grow or become less; to lessen.—**Bating**, bāt'ing, *ppr.* used as *prep.* Abating; taking away; deducting; excepting.—**Batement**, bāt'ment, *n.* Abatement.

Bateau, bä-tō', *n.* [Fr.] A light broad and flat boat used in Canada; also the pontoon of a floating bridge.

Bath, bäth, *n.* [A.Sax. *bæth*, a bath=Icel. *bath*, Dan. D. G. *bad*; from root of *bake*; *bask* is akin.] The immersion of the body or a part of it in water or other fluid or medium; a vessel for holding water in which to plunge, or wash the body; an apparatus or contrivance for exposing the surface of the body to water or other diffusible body (as oil, medicated fluids, steam, &c.); a building in which people may bathe; an apparatus for regulating the heat in chemical processes, by interposing a quantity of sand, water, &c., between the fire and the vessel to be heated.—*Knights of the Bath*, a British order of knighthood instituted at the coronation of Henry IV in 1399, and revived by George I in 1725. It received this name from the candidates for the honour being put into a bath the preceding evening, to denote a purification or absolution from evil deeds.—**Bathe**, bāTH, *v.t.*—*bathed, bathing.* [A.Sax. *bathian*, from *bæth*, a bath=Icel. *batha*, Dan. *bade*, D. and G. *baden.* BATH.] To subject to a bath; to immerse in water, for pleasure, health, or cleanliness; to wash, moisten, or suffuse with any liquid; to immerse in or surround with anything analogous to water.—*v.i.* To take a bath; to be or lie in a bath; to be in water or in other liquid; to be immersed or surrounded as if with water.—**Bather**, bāTH'ėr, *n.* One who bathes.—**Bathing-box**, *n.* A fixed covered shed in which bathers dress and undress.—**Bathing-machine**, *n.* A covered vehicle, driven into the water, in which bathers dress and undress.—**Bath-room**, *n.* A room for bathing in.

Bath, bäth, *n.* [Heb.] A Hebrew liquid measure, the tenth part of a homer.

Bath-brick, bäth'brik, *n.* [From the town of *Bath*, in Somersetshire.] A preparation of siliceous earth in the form of a brick, used for cleaning knives, &c.—**Bath-bun**, *n.* A sort of light sweet roll or bun, generally mixed with currants, &c.—**Bath-chair**, *n.* A small carriage capable of being pushed along by an attendant: used by invalids.—**Bath-metal**, *n.* An alloy of copper and zinc in nearly equal proportions.

Bathometer, ba-thom'et-ėr, *n.* [Gr. *bathos*, depth, and *metron*, a measure.] An apparatus for taking soundings, especially one in which a sounding-line is dispensed with.—**Bathymetrical**, bath-i-met'ri-kal, *a.* [Gr. *bathys*, deep, and *metron.*] Pertaining to bathymetry, or to depth under water.—**Bathymetry**, ba-thim'et-ri, *n.* The art of sounding or of measuring depths in the sea.—**Bathysphere**, bath'i-sfēr, *n.* A diving sphere for deep-sea observation and study developed by William Beebe.

Bat-horse, bat'hors, *n.* [Fr. *bât*, a pack-saddle.] A pack-horse; a baggage-horse. BATMAN.

Bathos, bā'thos, *n.* [Gr. *bathos*, from *bathys*, deep.] A ludicrous descent from the elevated to the mean in writing or speech; a sinking; anti-climax.—**Bathetic**,† ba-thet'ik, *a.* [Formed on type of *pathetic* from *pathos.*] Relating to bathos; sinking; from the lofty to the mean.

Bathybius, ba-thib'i-us, *n.* [Gr. *bathys*, deep, and *bios*, life.] A name for masses of animal matter (or what appears to be so) found covering the sea-bottom at great depths, and similar to protoplasm.

Bating. Under BATE.

Batist, Batiste, bä-tēst', *n.* [Fr. *batiste*, from its inventor *Baptiste.*] A fine linen cloth made in Flanders and Picardy, a kind of cambric.

Batman, ba'man, *n.* [Fr. *bât*, a pack-saddle.] A person having charge of the cooking utensils of each company of a regiment of soldiers on foreign service, and of the horse (bat-horse) that carries them.—**Bat-money**, ba'mun-i, *n.* Money paid to a batman.

Baton, bat'on, *n.* [Fr. *bâton*, O.Fr. *baston*; akin *baste*, to beat.] A staff or club; a truncheon, the official badge of various officials of widely different rank; the stick with which a conductor of music beats time.

Batrachia, ba-trā'ki-a, *n.pl.* [Gr. *batrachos*, a frog.] Frog-like animals; a group of amphibious animals, otherwise known as the tailless Amphibia, or frogs, toads, &c. When young they breathe by gills.—**Batrachian**, ba-trā'ki-an, *a.* Pertaining to the Batrachia.—*n.* One of the Batrachia.—**Batrachoid**, bat'ra-koid, *a.* Having the form of a frog; pertaining to the Batrachia.

Batta, bat'ta, *n.* An allowance made to British officers serving in the East Indies over and above their pay.

Battalion, bat-tal'yon, *n.* [Fr. *bataillon*, It. *battaglione*, aug. of *battaglia*, a battle or body of soldiers. BATTLE.] A body of infantry comprising about 600 men, and usually forming a third part of a regiment.—**Battalioned**, bat-tal'yond, *a.* Formed into battalions.

Battels, bat'elz, *n.* [Of unknown origin.] Oxford weekly college bills.

Batten, bat'n, *v.t.* [Icel. *batna*, to grow better, from root *bat*, *bet* in *better.*] To fatten; to make fat; to make plump by plenteous feeding.—*v.i.* To grow or become fat; to feed greedily; to gorge.

Batten, bat'n, *n.* [Fr. *bâton*, a stick.] A long piece of wood from 1 inch to 7 inches broad, and from ½ in. to 2½ in. thick; a plank; *naut.* one of the slips of wood used to keep a tarpaulin close over a hatchway; *weav.* a lathe.—*v.t.* To fasten with battens (to *batten* down the hatches).

Batter, bat'ėr, *v.t.* [Fr. *battre*, It. *battere*, from L.L. *batere*, a form of L. *batuere*, to beat, whence also *battle.*] To beat with successive blows; to beat with violence, so as to bruise or dent; to assail by a battering-ram or ordnance; to wear or impair, as by beating, long service, or the like (usually in pp.).—*v.i.* To make attacks, as by a battering-ram or ordnance.—**Batter**, bat'ėr, *n.* A mixture of several ingredients, as flour, eggs, &c., beaten together with some liquor into a paste, and used in cookery.—**Battering-ram**, *n.* An engine formerly used to beat down the walls of besieged places, consisting of a large beam, with a head of iron somewhat resembling the head of a ram, whence its name.—**Battery**, bat'ėr-i, *n.* [Fr. *batterie.*] The act of battering‡; a small body of cannon for field operations, with complement of wagons, artillerymen, &c.; a parapet thrown up to cover a gun or guns and the men employed in loading, &c.; a number of guns placed near each other and intended to act in concert; *elect.* an apparatus for originating an electric current; a series of connected Leyden jars that may be discharged together; *law*, the unlawful beating of a person.

Battle, bat'l, *n.* [Fr. *bataille*, from L.L. *batalia*, *batualia*, a fight; from L. *batuere*, to beat, to fence. BATTER.] A fight or encounter between enemies or opposing armies; an engagement; more especially a general engagement between large bodies of troops; a combat, conflict, or struggle; a division of an army‡.—*To give battle*, to attack; *to join battle*, to meet in hostile encounter. ∴*Battle* is the appropriate word for great engagements. *Fight* has reference to actual conflict; a man may take part in a *battle*, and have no share in the *fighting*. *Combat* is a word of greater dignity than *fight*, but agrees with it in denoting close encounter.—*v.i.*—*battled, battling.* To join in battle; to contend; to struggle; to strive or exert one's self.—**Battle-axe**, *n.* An axe anciently used as a weapon of war.—**Battle-field**, *n.* The field or scene of a battle.—**Battlement**, bat'l-ment, *n.* [Perhaps from O.Fr. *bastille*, a fortress, *bastiller*, to fortify, to embattle, modified by the influence of E. *battle.*] A notched or indented parapet, originally constructed for defence, afterwards for ornament, formed by a series of rising parts called cops or merlons, separated by openings called crenelles or embrasures, the latter intended to be fired through.—**Battled**, bat'ld, *a.* Furnished or strengthened with battlements.

Battledore, Battledoor, bat'l-dōr, *n.* [From Sp. *batidor*, a beater, from *batir*, to beat.] An instrument with a handle and a flat board or palm, used to strike a ball or shuttlecock; a racket.

Battology, bat-tol'o-ji, *n.* [Gr. *battologia*, from *battos*, a stammerer, and *logos*, discourse.] Idle talk or babbling; a needless repetition of words.

Battue, bat-tū, *n.* [Fr., from *battre*, to beat.] A kind of sport in which the game is driven by a body of beaters from under cover into a limited area where the animals may be easily shot.

Bauble, ba̤'bl, *n.* [O.Fr. *babole*, a toy or baby-thing; from same Celtic root as *babe*.] A short stick with a fool's head, anciently carried by the fools attached to great houses; a trifling piece of finery; something showy without real value; a gewgaw; a trifle.

Baulk, ba̤k. Same as *Balk*.

Bavin, bav'in, *n.* [Perhaps connected with O.Fr. *baffe*, a faggot.] A faggot of brushwood: light and combustible wood used for lighting fires.

Bawbee, ba̤-bē, *n.* [Fr. *bas billon*.] A halfpenny in Scottish money. BILLON.

Bawble, ba̤'bl, *n.* Same as *Bauble*.

Bawd, ba̤d, *n.* [O.Fr. *baud*, bold, wanton, from G. *bald*=E. *bold*.] A person who keeps a house of prostitution or acts as a go-between in illicit amours.—**Bawdry**, ba̤d'ri, *n.* Lewdness; obscenity; fornication. (*Shak.*) —**Bawdy**, ba̤'di, *a.* Obscene; lewd; indecent; smutty; unchaste. Hence **Bawdily**, **Bawdiness**.

Bawl, ba̤l, *v.i.* A word imitative of sound; akin, *bell*, *bellow*; L. *balo*, to bleat.] To cry out with a loud full sound; to make vehement or clamorous outcries; to shout.—*v.t.* To proclaim by outcry; to shout out.—*n.* A vehement cry or clamour.—**Bawler**, ba̤l'ėr, *n.* One who bawls.

Bay, bā, *n.* [Fr. *baie*, L.L. *baia*, a bay; of doubtful origin.] A rather wide recess in the shore of a sea or lake; the expanse of water between two capes or headlands; a gulf; any recess resembling a bay.—**Bay-rum**, bā-rum', *n.* A spirituous liquor containing the oil of the bayberry of Jamaica, a species of pimento, and used for the hair.—**Bay-salt**, *n.* Coarse-grained salt; salt obtained by the natural evaporation of seawater. — **Bay-window**, *n.* A window forming a recess or bay in a room, and projecting outwards on a generally polygonal plan. — **Bay-wood**, *n.* A variety of mahogany exported from Honduras, or the Bay of Honduras.

Bay, bā, *n.* [Fr. *baie*, L. *bacca*, a berry.] The laurel-tree, noble laurel, or sweet-bay; a garland or crown bestowed as a prize for victory or excellence, consisting of branches of the laurel; hence, fame or renown; laurels: in this sense chiefly in plural.

Bay, bā, *n.* [O.Fr. *abai*, *abbai*, a barking, *abbayer*, to bark; Mod. Fr. *aboi*, a barking, *aux abois*, at bay; comp. Fr. *bayer*, to gape, or stand gaping. ABASH.] The bark of a dog; especially, a deep-toned bark. — *At bay*, so hard pressed by enemies as to be compelled to turn round and face them from impossibility of escape.—*v.i.* To bark; to bark with a deep sound.—*v.t.* To bark at; to follow with barking (*Shak.*); to express by barking.

Bay, bā, *n.* [Fr. *bai*, L. *badius*, brown or chestnut coloured; akin *baize*.] Red or reddish, inclining to a chestnut colour.—**Bayard**, bā'yard, *n.* A brave man, from the Chevalier Bayard; also, a horse, from *Bayard*, the horse given by Charlemagne to Renaud.

Baya, bā'ya, *n.* [Hind.] The weaver-bird, an East Indian bird somewhat like the bullfinch which weaves a pendulous nest.

Bayadeer, **Bayadere**, bā-ya-dēr', *n.* [Pg. *bailadeira*, from *bailar*, to dance.] In the East Indies, a professional dancing girl.

Bayberry, bā'be-ri, *n.* The fruit of the bay-tree; also the wax-myrtle and its fruit.

Bayonet, bā'on-et, *n.* [O.Fr. *bayonnette*, Fr. *baïonnette*, usually derived from *Bayonne* in France, because bayonets are said to have been first made there.] A short triangular sword or dagger, made so that it may be fixed upon the muzzle of a rifle or musket.—*v.t.* To stab with a bayonet; to compel or drive by the bayonet.

Bayou, bī'ö, *n.* [Fr. *boyau*, a gut, a long narrow passage.] A channel proceeding from a lake or a river.

Bazaar, **Bazar**, ba-zär', *n.* [Per. *bāzār*.] In the East, a place where goods are exposed for sale, usually consisting of small shops or stalls in a narrow street or series of streets; a series of connected shops or stalls in a European town; a sale of miscellaneous articles in furtherance of some charitable or other purpose; a fancy fair.

Bdellium, del'li-um, *n.* [L. *bdellium*, Gr. *bdellion*, from Heb.] An aromatic gum-resin brought chiefly from Africa and India, in pieces of different sizes and figures, used as a perfume and a medicine, externally of a dark reddish brown, internally clear, and not unlike glue.

Be, bē, *v.i. substantive verb*, pres. *am*, *art*, *is*, *are*; pret. *was*, *wast* or *wert*, *were*; subj. pres. *be*; pret. *were*; imper. *be*; pp. *been*; ppr. *being*. [One of the three verbal roots required in the conjugation of the substantive verb, the others being *am* and *was*. A.Sax. *beó*, I am, *beón* to be; G. *bin*, I am; allied to L. *fui*, I was, Skr. *bhû*, to be. It is now chiefly used in the subjunctive, imperative, infinitive, and participles, being seldom used in the present tense. AM and WAS.] To have a real state or existence; to exist in the world of fact, whether physical or mental; to exist in or have a certain state or quality; to become: to remain. ∴ The most common use of the verb to *be* is to assert connection between a subject and a predicate, forming what is called the copula; as, he *is* good; John *was* at home; or to form the compound tenses of other verbs.— **Being**, bē'ing, *n.* Existence, whether real or only in the mind; that which has life; a living existence; a creature. —**Be-all**, *n.* All that is to be. (*Shak.*)

Beach, bēch, *n.* [Origin doubtful; comp. Icel. *bakki*, Sw. *backe*, Dan. *bakke*, a bank, the shore; or from old *bealch*, to belch, alluding to the washing up of pebbles, &c.] That part of the shore of a sea or lake which is washed by the tide and waves; the strand. —*Raised beaches*, in *geol.* a term applied to those long terraced level pieces of land, consisting of sand and gravel, and containing marine shells, now, it may be, a considerable distance above and away from the sea.—*v.t.* To run (a vessel) on a beach.—**Beachcomber**, bēch-komb-ėr, *n.* Pacific islands inhabitant; a long rolling wave breaking on beach.—**Beached**, bēcht, *a.* Having a beach; bordered by a beach; formed by, or consisting of, a beach. (*Shak.*) —**Beachy**, bēch'i, *a.* Having a beach or beaches; consisting of a beach or beaches. (*Shak.*)

Beacon, bē'kn, *n.* [A.Sax. *bēcn*, *beácen*, a beacon; hence *beck*, *beckon*.] An object visible to some distance, and serving to denote the presence of danger, as a light or signal shown to signify the approach of an enemy, or to warn seamen of the presence of rocks, shoals, &c.; hence, anything used for a kindred purpose. A revolving light supported by a structure for the guidance of aviators.—*v.t.* To light up by a beacon; to illuminate; to signal.—*v.i.*† To serve as a beacon.

Bead, bēd, *n.* [A.Sax. *bed*, *bead*, a prayer, from *biddan*, to pray. From beads being used to count prayers (as in the rosary), the word which originally meant prayer came to mean what counted the prayers. BID.] A little perforated ball of gold, amber, glass, &c., strung with others on a thread, and often worn round the neck as an ornament, or used to form a rosary; any small globular body, as a drop of liquid and the like; *arch.* and *joinery*, a small round moulding sometimes cut so as to resemble a series of beads or pearls; an astragal.—*v.t.* To mark or ornament with beads.— **Beaded**, bēd'ed, *a.* Furnished with beads; beady.—**Beady**, bēd'i, *a.* Consisting of or containing beads; bead-like. —**Bead-proof**, *a.* Carrying bubbles on the surface after being shaken: said of spirituous liquors.—**Bead-roll**, *n.* A list of persons for the repose of whose souls a certain number of prayers is to be said; hence, any list or catalogue. — **Beadsman**, *n.* A man employed in praying, generally in praying for another; one privileged to claim certain alms or charities.—**Beads-woman**, *n.* The feminine equivalent of *Beads-man*.

Beadle, bē'dl, *n.* [A.Sax. *bydel*, a herald, a beadle, from *beódan*, to bid. BID.] A messenger or crier of a court; a parish officer whose business is to punish petty offenders; a church officer with various subordinate duties.—**Beadleship**, bē'dl-ship, *n.* The office of a beadle.

Beagle, bē'gl, *n.* [Comp. Ir. and Gael. *beag*, little.] A small smooth-haired, hanging-eared hound, formerly kept to hunt hares.

Beak, bēk, *n.* [Fr. *bec*, from the Celtic—Armor. *bek*, *beg*, Ir. and Gael. *bec*, a beak.] The bill or neb of a bird; anything in some way resembling a bird's bill; the bill-like mouth of some fishes, reptiles, &c.; a pointed piece of wood fortified with brass, fastened to the prow of ancient galleys, and intended to pierce the vessels of an enemy; a similar, but infinitely more powerful appendage of iron or steel in modern war-ships; a magistrate. (Colloq.) —**Beaked**, bēkt, *a.* Having a beak or something resembling a beak; beak-shaped; rostrate.

Beaker, bēk'ėr, *n.* [Icel. *bikarr*, D. *beker*, G. *becher*, from L.L. *bicarium*, a cup, from Gr. *bikos*, a wine-jar.] A large drinking cup or glass.

Beam, bēm, *n.* [A.Sax. *beám*, a beam, a post, a tree, a ray of light; D. *boom*, G. *baum*, a tree.] A long straight and strong piece of wood or iron, especially when holding an important place in some structure, and serving for support or consolidation; a horizontal piece of timber in a structure; the part of a balance from the ends of which the scales are suspended; the pole of a carriage which runs between the horses; a cylindrical piece of wood, making part of a loom, on which the warp is wound before weaving; one of the strong timbers stretching across a ship from one side to the other to support the decks and retain the sides at their proper distance; the oscillating lever of a steam-engine forming the communication between the piston-rod and the crank-shaft; a ray of light, or more strictly a collection of parallel rays emitted from the sun or other body.—*v.i.* To emit rays of light or beams; to give out radiance; to shine.—**Beamful**, bēm'-ful, *a.* Beaming; bright. — **Beamless**, bēm'les, *a.* Emitting no rays of light; rayless. — **Beamy**, bēm'i, *a.* Like a beam; heavy or massive; emitting beams or rays of light; radiant.—**Beam-compass**, *n.* An instrument consisting of a wooden or brass beam, having sliding sockets that carry steel or pencil points: used for describing large circles. — **Beam-tree**, *n.* *White-beam tree*, that is *White tree*, from the white under-surface of the leaves. A British tree of the same genus as the mountain ash and apple, having scarlet edible berries.

Bean, bēn, *n.* [A.Sax. *beán* = Icel. *baun*, Sw. *böna*, Dan. *bönne*, D. *boon*, G. *bohne*.] A name given to several kinds of valuable leguminous seeds contained in a bivalve pod, and to the plants producing them, as the common bean, cultivated both in fields and gardens for man and beast, the French bean, the kidney-bean, &c.—**Bean-caper**, *n.* A small tree growing in warm climates, the flower-buds of which are used as capers. —**Bean-feast**, *n.* Employer's annual feast to workpeople. — **Bean-fly**, *n.* A beautiful fly of a pale purple colour found on bean flowers. — **Bean-goose**, *n.* A species of wild goose which winters in Britain.—**Bean-king**, *n.* The person who presided as king over the Twelfth-night festivities, attaining this dignity through getting the bean buried in the Twelfth-night cake.

Bear, bār, *v.t.* pret. *bore* (formerly *bare*); pp. *borne*; ppr. *bearing*. [A.Sax. *beran*= Icel. *bera*, Dan. *bære*, to bear, to carry, to bring forth; D. *baren*, G. (*ge*)*bären*, to bring forth; cog. L. *ferre*, Gr. *pherein*, Skr. *bhri*, to bear, to support. Akin are *birth, burden, bairn, barrow.*] To support, hold up, or sustain, as a weight; to suffer, endure, undergo, or tolerate, as pain, loss, blame, &c.; to carry or convey; to have, possess, have on, or contain; to bring forth or produce, as the fruit of plants or the young of animals. [*Born* is the passive participle in the sense of brought forth by a female, as the child was *born*; but we say actively, she has *borne* a child. *Born* is also used attributively, *borne* not.]—*To bear down*, to overcome by force.—*To bear out*, to give support or countenance to (a person or thing); to uphold, corroborate, establish, justify.—*To bear up*, to support; to keep from sinking.—*To bear a hand*, to lend aid; to give assistance.—*To bear in mind*, to remember.—*v.i.* To suffer, as with pain, to be patient; to endure; to produce (fruit); to be fruitful; to lean, weigh, or rest burdensomely; to tend; to be directed or move in a certain way (to *bear* back, to *bear* out to sea, to *bear* down upon the enemy); to relate; to refer: with *upon*; to be situated as to some point of the compass, with respect to something else.—*To bear up*, to have fortitude; to be firm; not to sink.—*To bear with*, to tolerate; to be indulgent; to forbear to resent, oppose, or punish.—**Bearable**, bār′a-bl, *a.* Capable of being borne, endured, or tolerated.—**Bearably**, bār′a-bli, *adv.* In a bearable manner.—**Bearer**, bār′ėr, *n.* One who or that which bears, sustains, supports, carries, conveys, &c.—**Bearing**, bār′ing, *n.* The act of one who bears; manner in which a person comports himself; carriage, mien, or behaviour; import, effect, or force (of words); that part of a shaft or axle which is in connection with its support; the direction or point of the compass in which an object is seen; relative position or direction; a figure on a heraldic shield.—**Bearing-rein**, *n.* The rein by which the head of a horse is held up in driving.

Bear, bār, *n.* [A.Sax. *bera*, a bear=D. *beer*, G. *bär*, Icel. *bera.*] A name common to various quadrupeds of the carnivorous order and of the plantigrade group, having shaggy hair and a very short tail, the most notable being the brown or black bear of Europe, the grisly bear of the Rocky Mountains, the white or Polar bear, &c.; the name of two constellations in the northern hemisphere, called the Greater and Lesser Bear; *fig.* a rude or uncouth man; in stock-exchange slang, a person who does all he can to bring down the price of stock in order that he may buy cheap: opposed to a *bull*, who tries to raise the price that he may sell dear.—**Bearish**, bār′ish, *a.* Resembling a bear; rude; violent in conduct; surly.—**Bear-baiting**, *n.* The sport of baiting bears with dogs.—**Bear-bine**, **Bear-bind**, *n.* A climbing plant of the convolvulus family, with a milky juice and large beautiful flowers.—**Bear-garden**, *n.* A place in which bears are kept for sport, as bear-baiting, &c.; *fig.* a place of disorder or tumult.—**Bear-leader**, *n.* One who leads about a trained bear; an eighteenth-century travelling tutor with backward or titled pupil.—**Bear-berry**, bār′ber-i, *n.* An evergreen shrub of the heath family, growing on barren moors in the colder parts of the northern hemisphere, the leaves being used as an astringent and tonic under the name *uva-ursi*.—**Bear-pit**, *n.* A pit or sunk area in a zoological garden for keeping bears.—**Bear's-ear**, *n.* A species of primrose, so called from the shape of the leaf.—**Bear's-foot**, *n.* A herbaceous plant of the hellebore genus, having a rank smell and purgative and emetic properties.—**Bear's-grease**, *n.* The fat of the bear, but often the fat of some other animal substituted, used for promoting the growth of the hair.

Bear, bēr, *n.* Same as *Bere*.

Beard, bērd, *n.* [A.Sax. *beard*, a beard=D. *baard*, G. *bart*; L. *barba*, W. and Armor. *barf*—beard.] The hair that grows on the chin, lips, and adjacent parts of the face of male adults; anything resembling this; a hairy, bristly, or thread-like appendage of various kinds, such as the filaments by which some shell-fish attach themselves to foreign bodies, &c.; the awn on the ears of grain; a barb, as of an arrow.—*v.t.* To take by the beard; to oppose to the face; to set at defiance.—**Bearded**, bērd′ed, *a.* Having a beard in any of the senses of that word.—**Beardless**, bērd′les, *a.* Without a beard; hence, of persons of the male sex, young; not having arrived at manhood.—**Beard-grass**, *n.* The name given to two well-known British grasses, from the bearded appearance of the panicle.—**Beard-moss**, *n.* A lichen which clothes trees with a shaggy gray growth.

Beast, bēst, *n.* [O.Fr. *beste*, from L. *bestia*, a beast.] Any four-footed animal, as distinguished from birds, insects, fishes, and man; as opposed to *man*, any irrational animal; a brutal man; a disgusting person.—**Beastish**, bēst′ish, *a.* Like a beast; brutal. (*Mil.*)—**Beastliness**, bēst′li-nes, *n.* The state or quality of being beastly; brutality; filthiness.—**Beastly**, bēst′li, *a.* Like a beast; brutish; brutal; filthy; contrary to the nature and dignity of man.

Beat, bēt, *v.t.* pret. *beat*; pp. *beat, beaten*; ppr. *beating*. [A.Sax. *beátan*=Icel. *bauta*, *bjáta*, O.H.G. *pózan*, to beat; akin *butt*, *abut*, *beetle* (a mallet).] To strike repeatedly; to lay repeated blows upon; to knock, rap, or dash against often; to pound; to strike for the purpose of producing sound (a drum); to shape by hammer; to scour with bustle and outcry in order to raise game; to overcome, vanquish, or conquer in a battle, contest, competition, &c.; to surpass or excel; to be too difficult for; to be beyond the power or skill of; to baffle; to fatigue utterly; to prostrate; to flutter (the wings).—*To beat back*, to compel to retire or return.—*To beat down*, to dash down by beating or battering, as a wall; to lay flat; to cause to lower a price by importunity or argument; to lessen the price or value of; to depress or crush.—*To beat off*, to repel or drive back.—*To beat out*, to extend by hammering.—*To beat up*, to attack suddenly; to alarm or disturb, as an enemy's quarters.—*To beat time*, to regulate time in music by the motion of the hand or foot.—*To beat a retreat*, to give a signal to retreat by a drum; hence, generally, to retreat or retire.—*v.i.* To strike or knock repeatedly; to move with pulsation; to throb (as the pulse, heart, &c.); to dash or fall with force or violence (as a storm, flood, &c.); to summon or signal by beating a drum; *naut.* to make progress against the direction of the wind by sailing in a zigzag.—*To beat about*, to make search by various means or ways.—*To beat up for*, to go about in quest of (recruits); to search earnestly or carefully for.—*n.* A stroke; a blow; a pulsation; a throb; a footfall; a round or course which is frequently gone over, as by a policeman, &c.; *music*, the beating or pulsation resulting from the joint vibrations of two sounds of the same strength, and all but in unison.—**Beaten**, bēt′n, *p.* and *a.* Made smooth by beating or treading; worn by use; conquered; vanquished; exhausted; baffled. [*Beat* is so far synonymous with *beaten*, but is less of an adjective, not being used attributively as the latter is; thus we do not say *beat* gold.]—**Beater**, bēt′ėr, *n.* One who or that which beats; an instrument for pounding or comminuting substances; the striking part in various machines.

Beatify, bē-at′i-fī, *v.t.*—*beatified, beatifying*. [Fr. *beatifier*, L. *beatificare*—*beatus*, blessed, and *facere*, to make.] To make happy; to bless with the completion of celestial enjoyment; *R. Cath. Ch.* to declare that a person is to be reverenced as blessed, though not canonized.—**Beatific**, **Beatifical**, bē-a-tif′ik, bē-a-tif′ik-al, *a.* Blessing or making happy; imparting bliss.—**Beatifically**, bē-a-tif′ik-al-li, *adv.* In a beatific manner.—**Beatification**, bē-at′i-fi-kā″shon, *n.* The act of beatifying; the state of being blessed; blessedness; *R. Cath. Ch.* an act of the pope by which he declares a person beatified; an inferior kind of canonization.—**Beatitude**, bē-at′i-tūd, *n.* [L. *beatitudo*.] Blessedness; felicity of the highest kind; consummate bliss; felicity; one of the declarations of blessedness to particular virtues, made by our Saviour in the sermon on the mount.

Beau, bō, *n.* pl. **Beaux**, bōz. [Fr. *beau*, O.Fr. *bel*, from L. *bellus*, beautiful.] One whose great care is to deck his person according to the first fashion of the times; a fop; a dandy; a man who attends or is suitor to a lady; a male sweetheart or lover.—**Beauish**, bō′ish, *a.* Like a beau; foppish; fine.—**Beau Ideal**, bō ī-dē′al or ē-dā-al, *n.* [Fr. *beau idéal*, beautiful ideal.] A conception of any object in its perfect typical form; a model of excellence in the mind or fancy.—**Beau Monde**, bō moṅd, *n.* [Fr. *beau*, fine, and *monde*, world.] The fashionable world; people of fashion and gaiety.

Beauty, bū′ti, *n.* [O.Fr. *biaute*, Fr. *beauté*, beauty, from L.L. *bellitas, bellitatis*, beauty, from L. *bellus*, beautiful.] An assemblage of perfections through which an object is rendered pleasing to the eye; those qualities in the aggregate that give pleasure to the aesthetic sense; qualities that delight the eye, the ear, or the mind; loveliness; elegance; grace; a particular grace or ornament; that which is beautiful; a part which surpasses in beauty that with which it is united; a beautiful person, especially, a beautiful woman.—**Beauty-shop**, an establishment where a woman may receive a hairdress, manicure, and other beauty treatments.—**Beauteous**, bū′tē-us, *a.* Possessing beauty; beautiful.—**Beauteously**, bū′tē-us-li, *adv.*—**Beautician**, bū-tish′an, one whose business is to improve the appearance of women's hair, nails, complexion, &c.—**Beautification**, bū′ti-fi-kā″shon, *n.* The act of beautifying or rendering beautiful; decoration; adornment; embellishment.—**Beautiful**, bū′ti-ful, *a.* Having the qualities that constitute beauty; highly pleasing to the eye, the ear, or the mind (a *beautiful* scene, melody, poem, character, but not a *beautiful* taste or smell); beauteous; lovely; handsome; fair; charming; comely.—*The beautiful*, all that possess beauty; beauty in the abstract.—**Beautifully**, bū′ti-ful-li, *adv.* In a beautiful manner.—**Beautifulness**, bū′ti-ful-nes, *n.* The quality of being beautiful; beauty.—**Beautify**, bū′ti-fī, *v.t.*—*beautified, beautifying*. To make or render beautiful; to adorn; to deck; to decorate.

Beaver, bē′vėr, *n.* [A.Sax. *befer*=D. *bever*, Dan. *bæver*, Sw. *bäfver*, Icel. *bjórr*, G. *biber*, L. *fiber*.] A rodent quadruped valued for its fur, about 2 feet in length, haunting streams and lakes, now found in considerable numbers only in North America, and generally living in colonies, with large webbed hind-feet and a flat tail covered with scales on its upper surface; beaver-fur; a hat or cap made of beaver-fur.—**Beaverteen**, bē′vėr-tēn, *n.* [Erroneously formed from *beaver*, on the model of *velveteen*.] A species of fustian cloth.—**Beaver-rat**, *n.* A rodent animal of Tasmania, an excellent swimmer and diver; also the musk-rat.

Beaver, bē′vėr, *n.* [O.Fr. *baviere*, a child's bib, a beaver, *bave*, slaver.] The face-guard of a helmet, so constructed with joints or otherwise that the wearer could raise or lower it to eat and drink; a visor.—**Beavered**, bē′vėrd, *a.* Having a beaver or visor.

Bebeeru, bē-bē′rö, *n.* [Native name.] A tree of British Guiana of the laurel family, the timber of which, known as *green-heart*, is used for building ships and submarine structures.—**Bebeerine**, bē-bē′rin, *n.* The active principle of the bark of the *bebeeru*, analogous to quinine, and highly febrifuge.

Becalm, bē-käm′, *v.t.* To render calm, still, or quiet (the sea, passions, &c.)†; to keep from motion for want of wind (as a ship); to delay (a person) by a calm.

Became, bē-kām′, pret. of *become*.

Because, bē-kaz′, *conj.* [*Be* for *by*, and *cause*; O.E. *bicause, bycause*=by or for the cause that.] By cause, or by the cause that; on this account that; for the cause or reason next explained; as, he fled *because* (as the reason given) he was afraid.

Beccafico, bek-a-fē'kō, *n.* [It., lit. fig-pecker.] A bird resembling the nightingale; the greater petty-chaps or garden-warbler, a summer visitant to England.

Bechamel, besh'a-mel, *n.* [Named after its inventor.] A fine white broth or sauce thickened with cream.

Bechance,† bē-chans', *v.t.* To befall; to happen to. (*Shak.*)

Bêche-de-mer, bāsh-de-mer, *n.* [Fr., lit. sea-spade, from its shape when dried and pressed.] The trepang, a species of sea-slug or sea-cucumber obtained in Eastern seas, and eaten by the Chinese.

Beck, bek, *n.* [Icel. *bekkr*, Dan. *bæk*, Sw. *bäck*, D. *beek*, G. *bach*, a brook—the *beck* in Wel*beck*, Trout*beck*, &c.] A small stream; a brook.

Beck, bek, *v.i.* [Shortened form of *beckon*.] To nod or make a significant gesture.—*v.t.* To call by a nod; to intimate a command or desire to by gesture.—*n.* A nod of the head or other significant gesture intended as a sign or signal.

Becket, bek'et, *n.* A contrivance in ships for confining loose ropes, &c.

Beckon, bek'n, *v.i.* [A.Sax. *beácnian*, *bécnian*, to beckon, from *beácn*, *bécn*, a beacon.] To make a sign to another by a motion of the hand or finger, &c., intended as a hint or intimation.—*v.t.* To make a significant sign to; to direct by making signs (*beckon* him to us).

Become, bē-kum', *v.i.*—*became* (pret.), *become* (pp.), *becoming*. [A.Sax. *becuman*, *bicuman*, to arrive, happen, turn out—prefix *be* = *by*, and *cuman*, to come, to happen.] To pass from one state to another; to change, grow, or develop into (the boy *becomes* a man). — *To become of* (usually with *what* preceding), to be the fate of; to be the end of; to be the final or subsequent condition. —*v.t.* To suit or to be suitable to (anger *becomes* him not); to befit; to accord with, in character or circumstances; to be worthy of, or proper to; to grace or suit as regards outward appearance (a garment *becomes* a person).—**Becoming**, bē-kum'ing, *a.* Suitable; meet; proper; appropriate; befitting; seemly. — **Becomingly**, bē-kum'ing-li, *adv.* After a becoming or proper manner.

Bed, bed, *n.* [A.Sax. *bed* = D. *bed*, *bedde*, Dan. *bed*, Goth. *badi*, G. *bett*.] That on or in which one sleeps, or which is specially intended to give ease to the body at night; especially, a large flat bag filled with feathers or other soft materials: the word may include or even be used for the bedstead; a plat or piece of tilled ground in a garden; the bottom of a river or other stream, or of any body of water; a layer; a stratum; an extended mass of anything, whether upon the earth or within it; that on which anything lies, rests, or is supported.—*v.t.*—*bedded*, *bedding*. To place in, or as in, a bed; to plant, as flowers, in beds.—**Bedding**, bed'ing, *n.* A bed and its furniture; materials of a bed.—**Bedfast**, bed'fast, *a.* Confined to one's bed by illness, &c.—**Bedrid**, **Bedridden**, bed'rid, bed'rid-n, *a.* [A.Sax. *bed-rida*, lit. a bedrider.] Long confined to bed by age or infirmity.—**Bedstead**, bed'sted, *n.* The framework of a bed.—**Bedstraw**, bed'stra, *n.* Straw for packing into a bed; also, a herbaceous perennial plant bearing yellow or white flowers growing in waste places in Britain.—**Bed-chair**, *n.* A chair with a back so constructed as to be folded down and constitute a bed.—**Bed-chamber**, *n.* An apartment intended for sleeping in, or in which there is a bed; a bed-room.—**Bed-clothes**, *n.pl.* Blankets, coverlets, &c., for beds.—**Bed-fellow**, *n.* One who occupies the same bed with another.—**Bed-key**, *n.* An instrument for fitting the parts of a bedstead tightly together. — **Bed-linen**, *n.* Sheets, pillow-covers, &c., for beds.—**Bed-pan**, *n.* A pan for warming a bed; also a necessary utensil for bedridden persons.—**Bed-plate**. The sole-plate or foundation-plate of an engine, &c.—**Bed-post**, *n.* One of the posts forming part of the framework and often supporting the canopy of a bed. —**Bed-room**, *n.* A room intended for sleeping in; a sleeping-room or bed-chamber.—**Bed-sore**, *n.* A sore liable to occur on bedridden persons on the parts of the body subjected to most pressure.—**Bed-tick**, *n.* A tick or stout linen or cotton bag for containing the feathers or other packing material of a bed.—**Bed-time**, *n.* The time to go to bed; the usual hour of retiring to rest.

Bedabble, bē-dab'l, *v.t.*—*bedabbled*, *bedabbling*. To wet; to sprinkle. (*Shak.*)

Bedaub, bē-dąb', *v.t.* To daub over; to soil with anything thick, slimy, and dirty.

Bedazzle, bē-daz'l, *v.t.*—*bedazzled*, *bedazzling*. To dazzle; to blind by excess of light.

Bedeck, bē-dek', *v.t.* To deck; to adorn; to grace.

Bedegar, **Bedeguar**, bed'ē-gär, *n.* [Fr. *bédegar*, *bédeguar*, from Per.] A spongy excrescence or gall found on roses, especially the sweet-brier, produced by insects.

Bedell, **Bedel**, bē'dl, *n.* [L.L. *bedellus*= E. *beadle*.] A beadle in a university or connected with a law-court.

Bedesman, bēdz'man, *n.* A beads-man; formerly, in Scotland, a privileged beggar.

Bedevil, bē-dev'il, *v.t.* To throw into utter disorder and confusion; spoil or corrupt, as by evil spirits.

Bedew, bē-dū', *v.t.* To moisten with or as with dew.

Bedim, bē-dim', *v.t.* — *bedimmed*, *bedimming*. To make dim; to obscure or darken.

Bedizen, bē-diz'n, *v.t.* [DIZEN.] To deck or trick out; especially, to deck in a tawdry manner or with false taste.

Bedlam, bed'lam, *n.* [Corrupted from *Bethlehem*, the name of a religious house in London, afterwards converted into an hospital for lunatics.] A mad-house; a place appropriated for lunatics; hence, any scene of wild uproar and madness.—**Bedlamite**, bed'lam-īt, *n.* A madman.

Bedouin, bed'ö-in, *n.* [Ar. *bedâwî*, dwellers in the desert.] A nomadic Arab living in tents in Arabia, Syria, Egypt, and elsewhere.

Bedraggle, bē-drag'l, *v.t.*—*bedraggled*, *bedraggling*. To soil by draggling; to soil by drawing along on mud.

Bedrop, bē-drop', *v.t.* To sprinkle, as with drops; to speckle.

Bee, bē, *n.* [A.Sax. *beó*, *bí* = Icel. *bý*, Sw. Dan. *bi*, D. *bij*, *bije*, O. and Prov. G. *beie*, Ir. and Gael. *beach*, a bee.] An insect, of which there are numerous species, the honey or hive bee being the most familiar and typical species, having been kept in hives from the earliest periods for its wax and honey. — **Bee-bread**, *n.* A brown substance, the pollen of flowers, collected by bees as food for their young. — **Bee-eater**, *n.* A bird of several species that feeds on bees.—**Bee-hive**, *n.* A case or box intended as a habitation for bees, and in which they may store honey for the use of their owners.—**Bee-line**, *n.* The direct line or nearest distance between two places. —**Bee-master**, *n.* One who keeps bees. —**Bee-orchis**, **Bee-flower**, *n.* An orchid with a bee-like flower.—**Bee-moth**, *n.* A moth that produces caterpillars which infest bee-hives. — **Bees'-wax**, *n.* The wax secreted by bees, and of which their cells are constructed. — **Bees'-wing**, *n.* A gauzy film in port-wines indicative of age, and much esteemed by connoisseurs.

Beech, bēch, *n.* [A.Sax. *béce*, from *bóc*, a beech, a book=Icel. *bók*, Dan. *bög*, D. *beuk*, G. *buche*, a beech; cog. L. *fagus*, a beech; Gr. *phēgos*, the esculent oak, from root seen in Gr. *phagein*, Skr. *bhag*, to eat, from its nuts being eaten. BOOK.] A large-sized tree with a smooth bark yielding a hard timber made into tools, &c., and nuts from which an oil is expressed. — **Beechen**, bēch'en, *a.* Consisting of the wood of the beech; belonging to the beech.—**Beech-mast**, *n.* The mast or nuts of the beech-tree.—**Beech-nut**, *n.* One of the nuts or fruits of the beech.—**Beech-oil**, *n.* A bland, fixed oil expressed from beech-mast.

Beef, bēf, *n.* [Fr. *bœuf*, from L. *bos*, *bovis*, an ox; cog. Ir. and Gael. *bo*, W. *buw*, Skr. *go*, a cow.] Originally an animal of the ox kind in the full-grown state (in this sense with the plural *beeves*, but the singular is no longer used); the flesh of an ox, bull, or cow when killed.—**Beef-eater**, bēf'ēt-ėr, *n.* [Fr. *buffetier*.] A yeoman of the royal guard (of England), a body of men who attend the sovereign at state banquets and on other occasions; an African bird that picks the larvæ of insects from the hides of oxen.—**Beef-steak**, *n.* A steak or slice of beef for broiling.—**Beef-tea**, *n.* A nutritious soup made from the flesh of the ox which, from being easy of digestion, is recommended for invalids and convalescents.—**Beef-witted**, *a.* With no more wit than an ox; dull; stupid. (*Shak.*)—**Beef-wood**, *n.* The timber of some Australian trees of a reddish colour, hard, and with dark and whitish streaks, chiefly used in ornamental work.

Beelzebub, bē-el'zē-bub, *n.* [Heb. *baal*, lord, and *zebub*, a fly.] A god of the Philistines; in the N.T. the prince of devils.

Beer, bēr, *n.* [A.Sax. *beór*=D. and G. *bier*; origin doubtful.] A fermented alcoholic liquor made from any farinaceous grain, but generally from malted barley flavoured with hops, and yielding a spirit on being distilled; a fermented drink prepared with various substances, as ginger, molasses, &c. —**Beery**, bē'ri, *a.* Pertaining to beer; soiled or stained with beer; affected by beer; intoxicated. — **Beer-engine**, *n.* A hydraulic machine for raising beer out of a cask in a cellar.—**Beer-house**, **Beer-shop**, *n.* A house or shop where malt-liquors are sold; an ale-house. — **Beer-money**, *n.* A pecuniary allowance made to soldiers, servants, &c., as an equivalent for a supply of beer.—**Beer-pump**, *n.* A pump for raising beer from the cellar to the bar in a beer-shop.

Beestie, bēs'ti, *n.* [Hind. *bihishti*.] An East Indian water-carrier, who supplies domestic establishments with water, fills the baths of the house, &c.

Beestings, bēst'ingz, *n.pl.* [A.Sax. *býsting*, *býst*, *beóst*, D. *biest*, *biestemelk*, G. *biestmilch*.] The first milk given by a cow after calving.

Beet, bēt, *n.* [A.Sax. *béte*, D. *biet*, G. *beeta*, from L. *beta*, beet.] A plant of various species cultivated for its thick fleshy roots, the red varieties of which are much used as a kitchen vegetable, while the white varieties yield a large portion of sugar, and are now extensively cultivated.—**Beet-root**, *n.* The root of the beet plant; the plant itself.

Beetle, bē'tl, *n.* [A.Sax. *bytl*, *bitel*, a mallet from *beátan*, to beat; L.G. *betel*, *bötel*.] A heavy wooden mallet used to drive wedges, consolidate earth, &c.—*v.t.* To use a beetle on; to beat with a heavy wooden mallet as a substitute for mangling.—**Beetle-headed**, *a.* Having a head like a beetle or mallet; dull; stupid. (*Shak.*)

Beetle, bē'tl, *n.* [A.Sax. *bitel*, from *bitan*, to bite.] A general name of many insects having four wings, the anterior pair of which are of a horny nature and form a sheath or protection to the posterior pair; a coleopterous insect.

Beetle, bē'tl, *v.i.* [From A.Sax. *bítel*, sharp, hence prominent, from *bitan*, to bite.] To be prominent (as a cliff, a battlement); to hang or extend out; to overhang; to jut.—**Beetling**, bē'tl-ing, *a.* Standing out from the main body; jutting; overhanging: said of cliffs, &c.—**Beetle-brow**, *n.* A prominent brow.—**Beetle-browed**, *a.* Having prominent brows.

Beeve,† bēv, *n.* A bovine animal, as an ox. BEEF.

Befall, bē-fąl', *v.t.*—*befell*, *befallen*, *befalling*. [A.Sax. *befeallan*—prefix *be*, and *feallan*, to fall.] To happen to; to occur to.—*v.i.* To happen; to come to pass.

Befit, bē-fit', *v.t.*—*befitted*, *befitting*. [Prefix *be*, and *fit*.] To be fitting for; to suit; to be suitable or proper to.

Befog, bē-fog′, *v.t.—befogged, befogging.* To involve in fog; hence, to confuse.

Befool, bē-föl′, *v.t.* To fool; to make a fool of; to delude or lead into error.

Before, bē-fōr′, *prep.* [A.Sax. *beforan*—prefix *be*, and *foran*, fore.] In front of; preceding in space; in presence of; in sight of; under the cognizance or consideration of (a court, a meeting); preceding in time; earlier than; ere; in preference to; prior to; having precedence of in rank, dignity, &c.—*Before the mast*, in or into the condition of a common sailor, the portion of a ship behind the main-mast being reserved for the officers.—*adv.* Further onward in place; in front; in the forepart; in time preceding; previously; formerly; already.—**Beforehand**, bē-fōr′hand, *a.* In good pecuniary circumstances; having enough to meet one's obligations and something over.—*adv.* In anticipation; in advance.—**Beforetime**,‡ bē-fōr′tīm, *adv.* Formerly; of old time. (O.T.)

Befoul, bē-foul′, *v.t.* To make foul; to soil.

Befriend, bē-frend′, *v.t.* To act as a friend to; to aid, benefit, or assist.

Beg, beg. Same as *Bey*, a Turkish title.

Beg, beg, *v.t.—begged, begging.* [Contr. it is believed from A.Sax. *bedegian* or *bedecian*, to beg; from stem of *bid*, A.Sax. *biddan*, to beg, to ask; comp. Goth. *bidagwa*, a beggar, from same root.] To ask or supplicate in charity; to ask for earnestly (alms); to ask earnestly (a person); to beseech; to implore; to entreat or supplicate with humility; to take for granted; to assume without proof. [The phrase *I beg to* is often used as a polite formula for introducing a question or communication; as, *I beg* to inquire, *I beg* to state. It may be regarded as elliptical for *I beg leave to*.]—*v.i.* To ask alms or charity; to live by asking alms.—**Beggar**, beg′ėr, *n.* One that begs; a person who lives by asking alms; one who supplicates with humility; a petitioner.—*v.t.* To reduce to beggary; to impoverish; to exhaust the resources of (to *beggar* description); to exhaust.—**Beggarliness**, beg-ėr-li-nes, *n.* The character of being beggarly; meanness; extreme poverty.—**Beggarly**, beg′ėr-li, *a.* Like or belonging to a beggar; poor; mean; contemptible.—**Beggary**, beg′ėr-i, *n.* The state of a beggar; a state of extreme indigence.—**Beggar-my-neighbor**, *n.* A child's game at cards.

Began, bē-gan′, pret. of *begin.*

Beget, bē-get′, *v.t.—begot, begat* (pret., the latter now almost obsolete), *begot, begotten* (pp.), *begetting.* [A.Sax. *begitan, bigitan*—prefix *be*, and *gitan*, to get.] To procreate, as a father or sire; to produce, as an effect; to cause to exist; to generate.—**Begetter**, bē-get-ėr, *n.* One who begets or procreates; a father.

Begin, bē-gin′, *v.i.—began* (pret.), *begun* (pp.), *beginning.* [A.Sax. *beginnan*, to begin—prefix *be*, and *ginnan*, to begin.] To take rise; to originate; to commence; to do the first act; to enter upon something new; to take the first step.—**Begin**, bē-gin′, *v.t.* To do the first act of; to enter on; to commence.—**Beginner**, bē-gin′ėr, *n.* A person who begins or originates; the agent who is the cause; one who first enters upon any art, science, or business; a young practitioner; a novice; a tyro.—**Beginning**, bē-gin′ing, *n.* The first cause; origin; the first state; commencement; entrance into being; that from which a greater thing proceeds or grows.—**Beginningless**, bē-gin′ing-les, *a.* Having no beginning.

Begird, bē-gėrd′, *v.t.—begirt* (pret. & pp.), *begirding.* [A.Sax. *begyrdan.*] To gird or bind with a band or girdle; to surround; to encompass.

Beglerbeg, beg′lėr-beg, *n.* [Turk. *beglerbegi*, beg of begs.] The governor of a province in the Turkish Empire, next in dignity to the grand vizier.

Begone, bē-gon′, *interj.* Go away; hence! —the imperative *be* and pp. *gone* combined.

Begonia, bē-gō′ni-a, *n.* [From M. *Begon*, a French botanist.] The generic name of tropical plants much cultivated in hothouses for the beauty of their leaves and flowers.

Begot, bē-got′(pret. & pp.). **Begotten**, bē-got′n, pp. of *beget.*

Begrudge, bē-gruj′, *v.t.—begrudged, begrudging.* To grudge; to envy the possession of: with two objects (to *begrudge* a person something).

Beguile, bē-gīl′, *vt.—beguiled, beguiling.* To practice guile upon; to delude; to deceive; to cheat; to trick; to dupe; to impose on by artifice or craft; to dispel or render unfelt by diverting the mind (cares); to while away (time).—**Beguilement**, bē-gīl′ment, *n.* The act or state of beguiling.—**Beguiler**, bē-gīl′ėr, *n.* One who beguiles.—**Beguilingly**, bē-gīl′ing-li, *adv.* In a manner to beguile or deceive.

Beguine, bā-gēn′, *n.* [Fr. *béguine*; from founder's name, Lambert Begue, 1180.] One of an order of females in Holland, Belgium, and Germany, who, without taking the monastic vows, form societies for the purposes of devotion and charity.

Begum, bē′gum, *n.* In the East Indies, a princess or lady of high rank.

Begun, bē-gun′, pp. of *begin.*

Behalf, bē-häf′, *n.* [Prefix *be*, and *half*, in old sense of side.] Interest; profit; support; defence: always in such phrases as in or on *behalf* of, in my, his, some person's *behalf.*

Behave, bē-hāv′, *v.t.—behaved, behaving.* [Prefix *be*, and *have.*] To conduct one's self; to demean one's self: used *refl.*—*v.i.* To act; to conduct one's self.—**Behaved**, bē-hāvd′, *a.* Having or being of a certain behavior.—**Behavior**, bē-hāv′yėr, *n.* Manner of behaving; conduct; deportment; mode of acting (of a person, a machine, &c.).

Behead, bē-hed′, *v.t.* To cut off the head of; to sever the head from the body of.

Beheld, bē-held′, pret. and pp. of *behold.*

Behemoth, bē′hē-moth, *n.* [Heb.] An animal described in Job xl. 15-24, and which some suppose to be an elephant, others a hippopotamus, crocodile, &c.

Behen, Ben, bē′hen, ben, *n.* [Per. and Ar.] A plant, the bladder-campion; the root of one or two plants used in medicine.

Behest, bē-hest′, *n.* [Prefix *be*, and *hest*; A.Sax. *behaes.* HEST.] A command; precept; mandate. [Poetical.]

Behind, bē-hīnd′, *prep.* [A.Sax. *behindan*, behind—prefix *be*, and *hindan*, behind. HIND.] On the side opposite the front or nearest part of, or opposite to that which fronts a person; at the back of; towards the back or back part of; remaining after; later in point of time than; farther back than; in an inferior position to.—*adv.* At the back; in the rear; out of sight; not exhibited; remaining; towards the back part; backward; remaining after one's departure.—**Behindhand**, bē-hīnd′hand, *adv.* or *a.* In a state in which means are not adequate to the supply of wants in arrear; in a backward state; not sufficiently advanced; not equally advanced with another; tardy.

Behold, bē-hōld′, *v.t.—beheld* (pret. & pp.), *beholding.* [A.Sax. *behealdan*—prefix *be*, and *healdan*, to hold.] To fix the eyes upon; to look at with attention; to observe with care; to contemplate, view, survey, regard, or see.—*v.i.* To look; to direct the eyes to an object; to fix the attention upon an object; to attend or fix the mind: in this sense chiefly in the imperative, and used interjectionally.—**Beholden**, bē-hōld′n, *a.* Under obligation; bound in gratitude; obliged; indebted.—**Beholder**, bē-hōld′ėr, *n.* One who beholds; a spectator.

Behoof, bē-höf′, *n.* [A.Sax. *behóf* = D. *behoef*, G. *behuf*—prefix *be*, and word equivalent to Icel. *hóf*, measure, moderation.] That which is advantageous to a person; behalf; interest; advantage; profit; benefit: always in such phrases as in or for *behoof* of, for a person's *behoof.*—**Behoove**, bē-höv′, *v.t.—behoved, behoving.* [A.Sax. *behôfian*, from the noun.] To be fit or meet for, with respect to necessity, duty, or convenience; to be necessary for: used impersonally (*it behooves* us, or the like).

Beiram, bī′ram, *n.* Same as *Bairam.*

Beistings, bēst′ingz. Same as *Beestings.*

Belabor, bē-lā′bėr, *v.t.* [Prefix *be*, and *labor*; comp. G. *bearbeiten*, to labor, and to beat soundly—prefix *be*, and *arbeit*, work.] To beat soundly; to deal blows to; to thump.

Belace, bē-lās′, *v.t.—belaced, belacing.* To fasten, as with a lace or cord; to adorn with lace.

Beladle, bē-lā′dl, *v.t.* To pour out with a ladle; to ladle out. (*Thack.*)

Belate, bē-lāt′, *v.t.* [Prefix *be*, and *late.*] To make too late; to benight: generally used in pp. *belated*, with sense of having lingered or remained till late; being out late; overtaken by darkness; benighted.

Belaud, bē-lad′, *v.t.* [Prefix *be*, and *laud.*] To laud; to praise highly.

Belay, bē-lā′, *v.t.* [Prefix *be*, and *lay.*] *Naut.* to make fast by winding round something.—**Belaying-pin**, *n. Naut.* a pin for belaying ropes to.

Belch, belsh, *v.t.* [O.E. *belken, belke*, A. Sax. *bealcian*, to belch.] To throw out or eject with violence, as from the stomach or from a deep hollow place; to cast forth (a volcano *belches* flames or ashes).—*v.i.* To eject wind from the stomach; to issue out, as with eructation.—*n.* The act of one who or that which belches; eructation.

Belcher, belsh′ėr, *n.* Blue-and-white spotted neckcloth, affected by the pugilist Jem Belcher.

Beldam, Beldame, bel′dam, bel′dām, *n.* [Fr. *belle*, fine, handsome, and *dame*, lady; it was at one time applied respectfully to elderly females.] A grandmother (*Shak.*)‡; an old woman in general, especially an ugly old woman; a hag.

Beleaguer, bē-lē′gėr, *v.t.* [Prefix *be*, and *leaguer.*] To besiege; to surround with an army so as to preclude escape; to blockade.—**Beleaguerer**, bē-lē′gėr-ėr, *n.* One who.

Belemnite, bel′em-nīt, *n.* [Gr. *belemnon*, a dart or arrow, from *belos*, a dart, from the root of *ballō*, to throw.] A straight, tapering, dart-shaped fossil, the internal bone or shell of animals allied to the cuttle-fishes, common in the chalk formation; the animal to which such a bone belonged.

Bel Esprit, bel es-prē, *n.* pl. **Beaux Esprits**, bōz es-prē. [Fr.] A fine genius or man of wit.

Belfry, bel′fri, *n.* [O.Fr. *belfroi, beffroit*, &c., a watch-tower, from O.G. *bervrit, bercvrit*, a tower or castle for defence, from *bergen*, to protect, and *frid*, a strong place (Mod. G. *friede*, peace). False etymology connected the word with *bell*, hence its modern English meaning.] A bell-tower, generally attached to a church or other building; that part of a building in which a bell is hung.

Belgian, bel′ji-an, *a.* Pertaining to Belgium.—*n.* A native of Belgium.

Belgravian, bel-grā′vi-an, *a.* Belonging to *Belgravia*, an aristocratic portion of London; aristocratic; fashionable.—*n.* An inhabitant of Belgravia; a member of the upper classes. (*Thack.*)

Belial, bē′li-al, *n.* [Heb. *belial*—*beli*, not, without, and *yaal*, use, profit.] Wickedness; a wicked and unprincipled person; an evil spirit; Satan.

Belie, bē-lī′, *v.t.—belied, belying.* [Prefix *be*, and *lie*, to speak falsely; like G. *belügan*, to belie. LIE.] To tell lies concerning; to calumniate by false reports; to show to be false; to be in contradiction to (his terror *belies* his words); to fail to equal or come up to; to disappoint (*belie* one's hopes).

Believe bē-lēv′, *v.t.—believed, believing.* [O.E. *bileve, beleve*, from A.Sax. *gelyfan, gelēfan*, to believe, the initial particle being changed; *-lieve* is akin to *lief* and *leave, n.*] To credit upon the ground of authority, testimony, argument, or any other circumstances than personal knowledge; to expect or hope with confidence.—*v.i.* To be more or less firmly persuaded of the truth of anything.—*To believe in*, to hold as an object of faith; to have belief of.—**Belief**, bē-lēf′, *n.* An assent of the mind to the truth of a declaration, proposition, or alleged fact, on the ground of evidence, distinct from personal knowledge; *theol.* faith, or a firm persuasion of the truths of religion; the thing believed; the object of belief; the body of tenets held by the professors of any faith; a creed.—**Believability**, bē-lēv′a-bil″i-ti, *n.* Credibility; capability of being believed.—**Believable**, bē-lēv′a-bl, *a.* Capable of being believed; credible.—**Believableness**, bē-lēv′a-bl-nes, *n.* Credibility.—**Believer**, bē-lēv′ėr, *n.* One who believes; an adherent of a religious faith; a professor of Christianity.—**Believing**, bē-lēv′ing, *a.* Having faith or belief.—**Believingly**, bē-lēv′ing-li, *adv.* In a believing manner.

Belike, bē-līk′, *adv.* [Prefix *be* for *by*, and *like.*] Perhaps; probably.

Belittle, bē-lit′l, *v.t.* To make smaller; to lower; speak disparagingly of.

Bell, bel, *n.* [A.Sax. *belle*; allied to *bellan*, to bellow, E. to *bell*, as a deer; akin *bellow*, and G. *bellen*, to bark.] A metallic vessel which gives forth a clear, musical, ringing sound on being struck, generally cup-shaped; anything in form of a bell; *pl.* the phrase employed on shipboard to denote the divisions of daily time, from their being marked by strokes on a bell each half-hour.—*To bear the bell*, to be the first or leader, in allusion to the bell-wether of a flock.—*Passing bell*, a bell which used to be rung when a person was on the point of death.—*v.i.* To flower; to put out bell-shaped blossoms.—*v.t.* To put a bell on.—**Bell-bird**, *n.* A South American passerine bird, and also an Australian insessorial bird: so named from their bell-like notes.—**Bell-buoy**, *n.* A buoy on which is fixed a bell, which is rung by the heaving of the sea.—**Bell-crank**, *n.* *Mach.* a rectangular lever by which the direction of motion is changed through an angle of 90°.—**Bell-flower**, *n.* A common name of plants of the genus Campanula, from the shape of the flower.—**Bell-gable**, *n.* The gable of a church or other building having its apex surmounted by a small turret for the reception of one or more bells.—**Bell-glass**, *n.* A glass covering for flowers or vegetables in the shape of a bell.—**Bell-hanger**, *n.* One who fixes up bells in houses.—**Bell-man**, *n.* A public crier who uses a bell.—**Bell-metal**, *n.* An alloy of copper and tin, used for making bells.—**Bell-mouthed**, *a.* Gradually expanded at the mouth in the form of a bell.—**Bell-pull**, *n.* That by which a bell is made to ring; a bell-rope.—**Bell-punch**, *n.* A small punch fitted to the jaws of a pincers-shaped instrument, combined with a little bell which sounds when the punch makes a perforation, used as a check on tramway-car conductors, &c.—**Bell-ringer**, *n.* One who rings a bell; a ringer of church bells.—**Bell-rope**, *n.* A rope for ringing a bell.—**Bell-tower**, **Bell-turret**, *n.* A belfry.—**Bel-wether**, *n.* A wether or sheep which leads the flock, with a bell on his neck.

Bell, bel, *v.i.* [A.Sax. *bellan*, Icel. *belja*, to bellow. Bellow.] To roar; to bellow, as a bull or a deer in rutting-time.

Belladonna, bel-la-don′na, *n.* [It., beautiful lady.] A plant of the nightshade family, found throughout Europe. The whole plant is poisonous, containing atropin, but it yields a useful medicine.

Belle, bel, *n.* [Fr., from L. *bellus*, beautiful.] A young lady; a lady of superior beauty and much admired.

Belleric, bel-ler′ik, *n.* An astringent fruit imported from India under the name of myrobalans for the use of calico-printers.

Belles-lettres, bel-let-tr, *n.pl.* [Fr. Belle and Letter.] Polite or elegant literature, a term including rhetoric, poetry, history, criticism, with the languages in which the literature is written.—**Belletrist**, bel-let′rist, *n.* One given to belles-lettres.

Belleter,† bel′e-tėr, *n.* A bell-founder.

Bellicose, bel′li-kōs, *a.* [L. *bellicosus*, from *bellum*, war.] Inclined to war; warlike; pugnacious; indicating warlike feelings.

Belligerent, bel-lij′ėr-ent, *a.* [L. *bellum*, war, and *gerens, gerentis*, carrying on.] Waging war; carrying on war; pertaining to war or warfare.—*n.* A nation, power, or state carrying on war; one engaged in fighting.—**Belligerence**,† bel-lij′ėr-ens, *n.* The act of carrying on war; warfare.

Bellite, bel′īt, *n.* [From the name *Bell.*] An explosive substance recently introduced, and fired by means of a detonator, its chief ingredient being ammonium nitrate.

Bellon, bel′lon, *n.* [Fr. *bellon.*] That variety of colic produced by the action of lead on the system; painter's colic.

Bellow, bel′lō, *v.i.* [A. Sax. *bylgean*, to bellow, allied to *bellan*, to bell, Icel. *belja*, to bellow. Bell.] To utter a hollow, loud sound, as a bull; to make a loud noise or outcry; to roar.—*n.* A loud outcry; roar.—**Bellower**, bel′lō-ėr, *n.* One who bellows.

Bellows, bel′lōz, *n. sing.* and *pl.* [Really a plural form of the word *belly*, A.Sax. *bælg, belg, bælig*, a bag, a belly, bellows. Belly.] An instrument for producing a strong current of air, and principally used for blowing fire, either in private dwellings or in forges, furnaces, mines, &c., or for supplying the pipes of an organ with wind.—**Bellows-fish**, *n.* The trumpet-fish, *Centriscus scolopax*, having an oval body and a tubular elongated snout; *also called snipe-fish.*

Belly, bel′li, *n.* [A.Sax. *bælg, belg, bælig*, bag, belly=Icel. *belgr*, D. *balg*, Dan. *bælg*, G. *balg*, the belly; akin to *bulge*; comp. Gael. and Ir. *bolg, balg*, the belly, a bag, bellows. *Bellows* is a plural form of this word.] That part of the human body which extends from the breast to the thighs, containing the bowels; the abdomen; the corresponding part of a beast; the part of anything which resembles the human belly in protuberance or cavity.—*v.t. bellied, bellying.* To fill; to swell out.—*v.i.* To swell and become protuberant like the belly.—**Bellied**, bel′lid, *a.* Having a belly: used generally in composition; also swelling out in the middle; protuberant.—**Bellyful**, bel′li-fụl, *n.* As much as satisfies the appetite.—**Belly-band**, *n.* A band that goes round the belly of a horse as part of its harness.—**Belly-god**, *n.* One who makes a god of his belly; a glutton or epicure.

Belong, bē-long′, *v.i.* [Prefix *be*, and O.E. *long*, to belong (to extend in length to), from the adjective *long*; comp. D. and G. *belangen*, to concern, from *lang*, long.] To be the property of; to appertain; to be the concern or affair; to be appendant or connected; to be suitable; to be due; to have a settled residence; to be domiciliated; to be a native of a place; to have original residence: in all senses followed by *to.*—**Belonging**, bē-long′ing, *n.* That which belongs to one: used generally in plural; qualities, endowments, property, possessions, appendages.

Beloochee, bel-ụ′chē, *n.* A native or inhabitant of Beloochistan.

Belopteron, be-lop′tėr-on, *n.* [Gr. *belos*, a dart, and *pteron*, a wing.] The fossil internal bone of an extinct cephalopod somewhat like a belemnite, but having a wing-like projection on each side.

Beloved, bē-luv′ed, *a.* Loved; greatly loved; dear to the heart.

Below, bē-lō′, *prep.* [Prefix *be*, and *low.*] Under, in place; beneath; not so high as; inferior to in rank, excellence, or dignity.—*adv.* In a lower place, with respect to any object; beneath; on the earth, as opposed to the heavens; in hell, or the regions of the dead; in a court of inferior jurisdiction.

Belt, belt, *n.* [A.Sax. *belt*=Dan. *bælte*, Icel. *belti*, a belt, a girdle, from L. *balteus*, a belt. Comp. Ir. and Gael. *balt*, a border, a welt.] A girdle; a band, usually of leather, in which a sword or other weapon is hung; anything resembling a belt; a strip; a stripe; a band; a band passing round two wheels, and communicating motion from one to the other.—**Belt**, Greater and Less. Passages into the Baltic from the Cattegat.—*v.t.* To encircle; to surround.—**Belted**, belt′ed, *a.* Wearing a belt; marked or distinguished with a belt.—**Belted-cruiser**, *n.* Ship of war protected by a belt of armour at the water-line and with an armoured deck.—**Belting**, belt′ing, *n.* Belts taken generally; the material of which the belts used in machinery are made.—**Belt-saw**, *n.* A saw of a belt-shape running on pulleys.

Beltane, bel′tān, *n.* [A Celtic word: Gael. *bealltainn*, Ir. *bealltaine*; the first of May; origin unknown.] The name of a sort of festival formerly observed among all the Celtic tribes of Europe. It was celebrated in Scotland on the first day of May (o.s.), and in Ireland on 21st June, by kindling fires on the hills and eminences.

Beluga, bē-lū′ga, *n.* [Rus. *bieluga*, from *bielyi*, white.] A kind of whale found in northern seas, the white whale or white fish, from 12 to 18 feet in length, killed for its oil and skin.

Belvedere, bel′ve-dēr, *n.* [It., lit. a beautiful view—*bello, bel*, beautiful, and *vedere*, to see.] In Italy an open erection on the top of a house for the purpose of obtaining a view of the country; in France, a summer-house on an eminence.

Belvidere, bel′vi-dēr, *n.* [L. *bellus*, fine, and *videre*, to see.] A plant, broom-cypress or summer-cypress, cultivated as an ornamental annual.

Bema, bē′ma, *n.* [Gr.] A stage or platform for an orator; part of a church raised above the rest and reserved for the higher clergy.

Bemaul, bē-mạl′, *v.t.* To maul or beat severely.

Bemaze, bē-māz′, *v.t.* To bewilder.

Bemire, bē-mīr′, *v.t.—bemired, bemiring.* To drag or stall in the mire; to soil by mud or mire.

Bemoan, bē-mōn′, *v.t.* To moan or mourn for; to lament; to bewail; to express sorrow for.—**Bemoanable**, bē-mōn′a-bl, *a.* Capable or worthy of being lamented.—**Bemoaner**, bē-mōn′ėr, *n.* One who bemoans.

Bemock, bē-mok′, *v.t.* To treat with mockery; to mock.

Bemused, bē-mūzd′, *a.* Originally, overcome with musing; sunk in reverie; hence, muddled; stupefied.

Ben, ben, *n.* A tree of India, called also horse-radish tree, having seeds or nuts that yield an oil (*oil of ben*) which keeps without becoming rancid for many years.

Bench, bensh, *n.* [A.Sax. *benc*, a bench= Dan. *bænk*, a parallel form with *bank*. Bank.] A long seat; a strong table on which carpenters or other mechanics prepare their work; the seat on which judges sit in court; the seat of justice; the persons who sit as judges; the court.—*Bench of bishops*, or *episcopal bench*, a collective designation of the bishops who have seats in the House of Lords.—*King's* (or *Queen's*) *Bench*, a superior English court of civil and criminal jurisdiction, now incorporated in the High Court of Justice.—*v.t.* To furnish with benches; to seat on a bench or seat of honour (*Shak.*)‡.—*v.i.*‡ To sit on a seat of justice. (*Shak.*)—**Bencher**, bensh′ėr, *n.* One of the senior barristers in an inn of court, who have the government of the society.—**Benchership**, bensh′ėr-ship, *n.* Office or condition of a bencher.

Bend, bend, *v.t.—bended* or *bent* (pret. & pp.), *bending.* [A. Sax. *bendan*, to bend, lit. to bend and keep bent by the string, from *bend*, a band; comp. Fr. *bander un arc*, to bend a bow, from *bande*, a string.] To curve or make crooked; to deflect from a normal condition of straightness; to direct to a certain point (one's mind, course, steps); to subdue; to cause to yield.—*v.i.* To be or become curved or crooked; to incline; to lean or turn; to be directed; to bow or be submissive.—*n.* A curve; a crook; a turn;

flexure; incurvation.—**Bender**, bend'ėr, *n.* Sixpence. (Colloq.)

Bene, ben'ē, *n.* BENNE.

Beneath, bē-nēth', *prep.* [A.Sax. *beneoth*, *beneothan*—prefix *be*, and *neothan*, below. NETHER.] Under; lower in place than something which rests above; burdened or overburdened with; lower than in rank, dignity, or excellence; below the level of.—*adv.* In a lower place; below.

Benedicite, ben-e-dis'i-tē, *n.* [L., lit. bless ye, the first word of the hymn.] A canticle or hymn in the Book of Common Prayer, as old as the time of St. Chrysostom.

Benedick, **Benedict**, ben'e-dik, ben'e-dikt, *n.* A sportive name for a married man, especially one who has been long a bachelor: from one of the characters (*Benedick*) in Shakspere's *Much Ado about Nothing.*

Benedictine, ben-e-dik'tin, *a.* Pertaining to the monks of St. Benedict.—*n.* A Blackfriar; a member of the order of monks founded at Monte Casino about the year 530 by St. Benedict, and wearing a loose black gown with large wide sleeves, and a cowl on the head; a liqueur made by the Benedictine monks at Fécamp, in Normandy, consisting of spirits containing juices of certain plants. CHARTREUSE.

Benediction, ben-e-dik'shon, *n.* [L. *benedictio*—*bene*, well, and *dictio*, speaking.] The act of invoking a blessing; blessing, prayer, or kind wishes uttered in favour of any person or thing; a solemn or affectionate invocation of happiness.—**Benedictive**, **Benedictory**, ben-e-dik'tiv, ben-e-dik'to-ri, *a.* Giving a blessing; expressing a benediction, or wishes for good.

Benedictus, ben-e-dik'tus, *n.* [L., blessed —'Blessed be the Lord God of Israel', &c.] The song of Zacharias in *Luke* i, used in the service of the Roman Catholic Church and introduced with English words into the morning prayer of the English Church.

Benefaction, ben-e-fak'shon, *n.* [L. *benefactio*, from *benefacio*, to do good to one. BENEFICE.] The act of conferring a benefit; a benefit conferred, especially a charitable donation.—**Benefactor**, ben-e-fak'tėr, *n.* One who confers a benefit.—**Benefactress**, ben-e-fak'tres, *n.* A female who confers a benefit.

Benefice, ben'e-fis, *n.* [Fr. *bénéfice*, a benefice, from L. *beneficium*, a kindness, in late L. an estate granted for life—*bene*, well, and *facio*, to do.] An ecclesiastical living; a church endowed with a revenue for the maintenance of divine service, or the revenue itself.—**Beneficed**, ben'e-fist, *a.* Possessed of a benefice or church preferment.—**Beneficence**, be-nef'i-sens, *n.* [L. *beneficentia.*] The practice of doing good; active goodness, kindness, or charity. ∴ *Beneficence*, lit. well-doing, is the outcome and visible expression of *benevolence*, or well-willing. *Benevolence* may exist without *beneficence*, but *beneficence* always presupposes *benevolence*.—**Beneficent**, **Beneficient**,‡ be-nef'i-sent, ben-e-fi'shent, *a.* Doing good; performing acts of kindness and charity.—**Beneficently**, be-nef'i-sent-li, *adv.* In a beneficent manner.—**Beneficial**, ben-e-fi'shal, *a.* Contributing to a valuable end; conferring benefit; advantageous; useful; profitable; helpful.—**Beneficially**, ben-e-fi'shal-li, *adv.* In a beneficial manner; advantageously; profitably; helpfully.—**Beneficialness**, ben-e-fi'shal-nes, *n.*—**Beneficiary**, ben-e-fi'shi-a-ri, *a.* Connected with the receipt of benefits, profits, or advantages.—*n.* One who holds a benefice; one who is in the receipt of benefits, profits, or advantages; one who receives something as a free gift.

Benefit, ben'e-fit, *n.* [O.E. *benfite*, *bienfete*, O.Fr. *bienfet*, from L. *benefactum*, a benefit. BENEFICE.] An act of kindness; a favour conferred; whatever is for the good or advantage of a person or thing; advantage; profit; a performance at a theatre or other place of public entertainment, the proceeds of which go to one of the actors, or towards some charitable object.—*v.t.* To do good to; to be of service to; to advantage.—*v.i.* To gain advantage; to make improvement.

Benevolence, bē-nev'ō-lens, *n.* [L. *benevolentia*—*bene*, well, and *volens*, *volentis*, ppr. of *volo*, to will or wish.] The disposition to do good; the love of mankind, accompanied with a desire to promote their happiness; good-will; kindness; charitableness; an act of kindness; a contribution or tax illegally exacted by arbitrary kings of England. ∴ BENEFICENCE.—**Benevolent**, bē-nev'ō-lent, *a.* Possessing love to mankind, and a desire to promote their prosperity and happiness; inclined to charitable actions.—**Benevolently**, bē-nev'ō-lent-li, *adv.* In a benevolent manner.

Bengalee, **Bengali**, ben-gạl-ē', *n.* The language or dialect spoken in Bengal.—**Bengalese**, ben-gạl-ēz', *a.* Of or pertaining to Bengal.—*n.sing.* and *pl.* A native or natives of Bengal.—**Bengal-light**, *n.* A species of fireworks used as signals by night or otherwise, producing a steady and vivid blue-coloured fire.

Benight, bē-nīt', *v.t.* To shroud with the shades of night; to shroud or involve in gloom; to overtake with night: in this sense usually in past participle; *fig.* to involve in moral darkness or ignorance (the *benighted* heathen).

Benign, bē-nīn', *a.* [L. *benignus* for *benigenus*, kind-hearted—*benus* for *bonus*, good, and *genus*, kind, race.] Of a kind disposition; gracious; kind (our *benign* sovereign); proceeding from or expressive of gentleness, kindness, or benignity; salutary (*benign* influences); *med.* mild; not severe or violent.—**Benignant**, bē-nig'nant, *a.* Kind; gracious; favourable: frequently, like *benign*, used of the kindness of superiors; but *benign* is more a poetical word.—**Benignantly**, bē-nig'nant-li, *adv.* In a benignant manner.—**Benignity**, bē-nig'ni-ti, *n.* The state or quality of being benign or benignant; kindness of nature; graciousness; beneficence.—**Benignly**, bē-nīn'li, *adv.* In a benign manner; favourably; kindly; graciously.

Benison, ben'i-zn, *n.* [O.Fr. *beneison*, from L. *benedictio*, a benediction. *Benediction* is thus the same word.] A blessing uttered by a person; a benediction.

Benjamin, ben'ja-min, *n.* [Proper name. O.T.] The youngest son of family.

Benjamin, ben'ja-min, *n.* [Fr. *benjoin*, benzoin.] A common form of the name of the gum *benzoin.*

Benne, ben'e, *n.* [Malay.] Sesame, an East Indian annual herbaceous plant, from the seeds of which a valuable oil is expressed, used, like olive-oil, as an article of diet and for other purposes.

Bent, bent, pret. & pp. of *bend.*—*n.* Originally, a condition of being bent (as a bow); flexure; hence, *fig.* turn; inclination; disposition; natural tendency; leaning or bias of the mind.

Bent, **Bent-grass**, bent, bent'gras, *n.* [A.Sax. *beonet* = G. *binse*, a rush.] A wiry grass, such as grows on commons or neglected ground; any wild piece of land.—**Benty**, ben'ti, *a.* Abounding in or resembling bent.

Benthamism, ben'tham-izm, *n.* The doctrine according to Jeremy Bentham, by which man's actions are regulated purely by utilitarian considerations; profit-and-loss morality.

Benumb, bē-num', *v.t.* [NUMB.] To make numb or torpid; to deprive of sensation; to stupefy; to render inactive.—**Benumber**, bē-num'ėr, *n.* One who or that which benumbs.—**Benumbment**, bē-num'ment, *n.* Act of benumbing; torpidity.

Benzoin, **Benzoine**, ben-zō'in or ben'zoin, *n.* [Of Ar. origin = Fr. *benjoin*, Pg. *beijoim.*] Gum benjamin; a concrete resinous juice or balsam flowing from incisions made in the stem of a tree of Sumatra, &c., chiefly used in cosmetics and perfumes, and in incense, having a fragrant and agreeable smell.—**Benzoic**, ben-zō'ik, *a.* Pertaining to or obtained from benzoin.—**Benzole**, **Benzoline**, ben'zōl, ben'zō-lin, *n.* A clear colourless liquid, of a peculiar ethereal agreeable odour, obtained from coal-tar, much used as a solvent for removing grease spots, &c. Called also **Benzine** (ben'zin).

Bepraise, bē-prāz', *v.t.*—*bepraised*, *bepraising.* To praise greatly or extravagantly; to puff.

Bequeath, bē-kwēTH', *v.t.* [A.Sax. *becwethan* — prefix *be*, and *cwethan*, to say. QUOTH.] To give or leave by will; to devise by testament; to hand down; to transmit.—**Bequeathable**, bē-kwēTH'a-bl, *a.* Capable of being bequeathed.—**Bequeather**, bē-kwēTH'ėr, *n.* One who.—**Bequest**, bē-kwest', *n.* The act of bequeathing or leaving by will; something left by will; a legacy.

Berate, bē-rāt', *v.t.*—*berated*, *berating* To rate or chide vehemently; to scold.

Berber, bėr'bėr, *n.* A person belonging to, or the language spoken by, certain tribes of North Africa (Barbary).

Berberine, bėr'bėr-in, *n.* A substance obtained from the root of the barberry-tree, used in dyeing yellow.

Bere, bēr, *n.* [A.Sax. *bere*, barley. BARLEY.] A species of barley having six rows in the ear.

Bereave, bē-rēv', *v.t.*—*bereaved* or *bereft* (pret. & pp.), *bereaving.* [Prefix *be*, and *reave*; A.Sax. *bereáfian.* REAVE.] To deprive of something that is prized; to make destitute; to rob; to strip: with *of* before the thing taken away.—**Bereavement**, bē-rēv'ment, *n.* The act of bereaving, or state of being bereaved; deprivation, particularly the loss of a friend by death.—**Bereaver**, bē-rēv'ėr, *n.* One who or that which bereaves.

Berg, bėrg, *n.* [A.Sax. and G. *berg*, a hill.] A large mass or mountain, as of ice; an iceberg.—**Bergmehl**, bėrg'māl, *n.* [G. *berg*, mountain, and *mehl*, meal.] Mountain-meal, a geological deposit in the form of an extremely fine powder, consisting almost entirely of the minute siliceous portions of diatoms.

Bergamot, bėr'ga-mot, *n.* [Fr. *bergamote*, It. *bergamotta*, from *Bergamo*, in Italy.] A variety of pear; the lime or its fruit, the rind of which yields a fragrant oil; an essence or perfume from the fruit of the lime; a coarse tapestry manufactured originally at *Bergamo*, in Italy.

Bergomask, bėr'gō-mask, *n.* [It. *bergamasco*, from *Bergamo* in N. Italy.] A kind of rustic dance. (*Shak.*)

Bergylt, bėr'gilt, *n.* The Norwegian haddock, a fish found in the northern seas.

Beri-beri, ber'i-ber'i, *n.* [Singhalese, *beri*, weakness.] A dangerous disease endemic in parts of India and Ceylon, characterized by paralysis, difficult breathing, and other symptoms.

Berlin, bėr'lin or bėr-lin', *n.* A four-wheeled vehicle of the chariot kind, first made at Berlin; Berlin wool; a knitted glove.—*Berlin blue*, Prussian blue.—*Berlin wool*, a kind of fine dyed wool used for tapestry, knitting, &c.—*Berlin work*, fancy work in Berlin wools or worsted.

Berm, **Berme**, bėrm, *n.* [O.Fr. *barme*, from G. *brame*, *brāme* = E. *brim*, border.] *Fort.* a space of ground of 3, 4, or 5 feet in width, between the rampart and the moat or fosse; the bank or side of a canal which is opposite to the towing-path.

Bernese, ber'nēz, *n.sing.* and *pl.* A citizen or citizens of *Berne.* — *a.* Pertaining to *Berne* or its inhabitants.

Beroe, ber'ō-ē, *n.* [Gr. *Beroe*, one of the ocean nymphs.] A marine cœlenterate animal gelatinous and transparent, resembling a globe of jelly, shining at night while floating in the sea.

Berry, be'ri, *n.* [A.Sax. *berie*, a berry; Icel. *ber*, Sw. and D. *bär*, G. *beere*, Goth. *basi*; root seen in Skr. *bhas*, to eat.] A succulent or pulpy fruit, containing many seeds, and usually of no great size, such as the gooseberry, the strawberry, &c.; what resembles a berry, as one of the eggs of the lobster.—*v.i.* To bear or produce berries.—**Berried**, be'rid, *a.* Furnished with berries.

Bersaglieri, ber-säl'yē-ā-rē, *n.pl.* The riflemen or sharp-shooters in the Italian army.

Berserk, Berserker, bėr'sėrk, bėr'sėr-kėr, *n.* [Icel. *berserkr*, lit. 'bear-sark', or bear-shirt.] A kind of wild warrior or champion of heathen times in Scandinavia; a person of extreme violence and fury.

Berth, bėrth, *n.* [From the root of *bear.*] A station in which a ship lies or can lie; a small room in a ship set apart for one or more persons; a box or place for sleeping in a ship or railway-carriage; a post or appointment; a situation.—*v.t.* To assign a berth or anchoring ground to; to allot a berth or berths to.—**Berthage**, bėrth'āj, *n.* A charge made on vessels occupying a berth in a dock or harbour.

Beryl, ber'il, *n.* [L. *beryllus*, Gr. *bēryllos*, of Eastern origin.] A colourless, yellowish, bluish, or less brilliant green variety of emerald, the prevailing hue being green.—**Berylline**, ber'il-lin, *a.* Like a beryl; of a light or bluish green.—**Beryllium**, be-ril'li-um, *n.* Glucinum.

Beseech, bē-sēch', *v.t. besought* (pret. & pp.), *beseeching*. [O.E. *beseke*, *biseke*—prefix *be*, and *seek.*] To entreat; to supplicate; to implore; to beg eagerly for; to solicit.—**Beseecher**, bē-sēch'ėr, *n.* One who beseeches.—**Beseechingly**, bē-sēch'ing-li, *adv.* In a beseeching manner.

Beseem, bē-sēm', *v.t.* [Prefix *be*, and *seem*, in old sense of become, be seemly.] To become; to be fit for or worthy of.—**Beseeming**, bē-sēm'ing, *a.* Becoming; fit; worthy of.—**Beseemingly**, bē-sēm'ing-li, *adv.* In a beseeming manner.—**Beseemingness**, bē-sēm'ing-nes, *n.*

Beset, bē-set', *v.t.*—*beset*, *besetting*. [A.Sax. *besettan*, to set near, to surround—prefix *be*, and *settan*, to set.] To distribute over; to intersperse through or among; to surround; to inclose; to hem in (*beset* with enemies, a city *beset* with troops; to press on all sides, so as to perplex (temptations that *beset* us); to press hard upon.—**Besetment**, bē-set'ment, *n.* The condition of being beset; the sin or failing to which one is most liable; a besetting sin.—**Besetting**, bē-set'ing, *a.* Habitually attending or assailing us (a *besetting* sin).

Beshrew, bē-shrö', *v.t.* [Prefix *be*, and *shrew*. SHREWD.] To wish a curse to; to execrate: generally used impersonally in phrases intended as mild imprecations or maledictions (*beshrew* me! *beshrew* the fellow!).

Beshroud, bē-shroud', *v.t.* To cover with or as with a shroud; to hide in darkness.

Beside, bē-sīd', *prep.* [Prefix *be*, by, and *side.*] At the side of a person or thing; near to; apart from; not connected with (*beside* the present subject).—*To be beside one's self*, to be out of one's wits or senses.—**Beside, Besides**, bē-sīdz', *adv.* Moreover; over and above; not included in the number, or in what has been mentioned. [*Besides* is now the commoner form.]—**Besides**, *prep.* Over and above; separate or distinct from; in addition to.

Besiege, bē-sēj', *v.t.*—*besieged*, *besieging*. To lay siege to; to beset or surround with armed forces for the purpose of compelling to surrender; to beset; to harass (*besieged* with applications).—**Besieger**, bē-sēj'ėr, *n.* One who besieges.

Beslobber, Beslubber, bē-slob'ėr, bē-slub'ėr, *v.t.* To soil or smear; to besmear.

Besmear, bē-smēr', *v.t.* To smear all over; to bedaub; to overspread with some viscous, glutinous, or soft substance that adheres; to foul; to soil.

Besom, bē'zum, *n.* [A.Sax. *besema*, *besma*, a besom=D. *bezem*, G. *besem*, *besen*: root unknown.] A broom; a brush of twigs or other materials for sweeping.—*v.t.*† To sweep, as with a besom. (*Cowper.*)

Besot, bē-sot', *v.t.*—*besotted*, *besotting*. To make sottish, as with drink; to infatuate; to stupefy; to make dull, stupid, or senseless.—**Besotment**, bē-sot'ment, *n.* The act of besotting; the state of being besotted; stupidity; infatuation.—**Besotted**, bē-sot'ed, *a.* Made sottish by drink; indicating or proceeding from gross stupidity; stupid; infatuated.—**Besottedly**, bē-sot'ed-li, *adv.* In a besotted manner.—**Besottedness**, bē-sot'ed-nes, *n.*

Besought, bē-sạt', pret. and pp. of *beseech*.

Bespangle, bē-spang'gl, *v.t.*—*bespangled*, *bespangling*. To adorn with spangles; to dot or sprinkle with something brilliant.

Bespatter, bē-spat'ėr, *v.t.* To soil by spattering; *fig.* to asperse with calumny or reproach.

Bespeak, bē-spēk', *v.t.*—*bespoke* (pret.), *bespoke*, *bespoken* (pp.), *bespeaking*. To speak for (something wanted) beforehand; to order or engage against a future time; to betoken; to indicate by outward appearance (an action that *bespoke* a kind heart).—*n.* Among actors, a benefit.

Bespice, bē-spīs', *v.t.* To season with spices; to mingle drugs with; to drug. (*Shak.*)

Bespread, bē-spred', *v.t.* To spread over; to cover or form a coating over.

Besprent, bē-sprent', pp. [A participle of the obsolete verb *besprenge*, to besprinkle.] Sprinkled or scattered. [Poetical.]

Besprinkle, bē-spring'kl, *v.t.* To sprinkle over; to cover by scattering or being scattered over.

Bessemer-steel, bes'e-mėr-stēl, *n.* [From Sir H. *Bessemer*, the inventor of the process.] Steel made directly from molten cast-iron by driving through it currents of air so as to oxidize and carry off the carbon and impurities, the proper quantity of carbon for making steel being then introduced.

Best, best, *a. superl.* [A.Sax. *betest*, *betst*, *best*, serving as the superl. of *gód*, good=D. and G. *best*, Dan. *beste*, Icel. *bestr*, Sw. *bästa*. The root is *bat*, *bet*, seen also in *better*, Goth. *batista*, best. BETTER.] Most good; having good qualities or attainments in the highest degree; possessing the highest advantages.—*Best man*, the right-hand man or supporter of the bridegroom at a wedding.—*adv.* In the highest degree.—*n.* Highest possible state of excellence (*Shak.*); all that one can do, or show in one's self: often used in this sense with the possessive pronouns *my*, *thy*, *his*, *their*, &c.—*At best*, considered or looked at in the most favourable light.—*To make the best of*, to use to the best advantage; to get all that one can out of; to put up with as well as one can.

Bestead, bē-sted', pp. of an obs. verb. Prefix *be*, and *stead*, place.] Placed, disposed, or circumstanced as to convenience, benefit, and the like; situated: now always with *ill*, *well*, *sore*, &c.

Bestial, bes'ti-al, *a.* [L. *bestialis*, from *bestia*, a beast.] Belonging to a beast or to the class of beasts; animal; having the qualities of a beast; brutal; brutish.—**Bestiality**, bes-ti-al'i-ti, *n.* The quality of a beast; beastliness.—**Bestialize**, bes'ti-al-īz, *v.t.*—*bestialized*, *bestializing*. To make like a beast; to bring or reduce to the condition of a beast.—**Bestially**, bes'ti-al-li, *adv.* In a bestial manner.—**Bestiarian**, bes-ti-ā'ri-an, *n.* One who takes an interest in the kind treatment of beasts; one who opposes vivisection.

Bestir, bē-stėr', *v.t.* To stir; to put into brisk or vigorous action: usually *refl.*

Bestow, bē-stō', *v.t.* To stow away; to lay up in store: to deposit; to lodge; to place (often *refl.*); to give; to confer; to impart; followed by *on* or *upon* before the recipient.—**Bestower**, bē-stō'ėr, *n.* One who bestows; a giver; a disposer.—**Bestowment, Bestowal**, bē-stō'ment, bē-stō'al, *n.* The act of bestowing.

Bestrew, bē-strö' or bē-strō', *v.t.* To scatter over; to besprinkle; to strew.

Bestride, bē-strīd', *v.t.*—*bestrid*, *bestrode* (pret.), *bestrid*, *bestridden* (pp.), *bestriding*. To stride over; to stand or sit on with the legs on either side; to step over; to cross by stepping (*Shak.*).

Bet, bet, *v.t.* and *i.*—*bet* or *betted*, *betting*. [A contraction of *abet*, to encourage, back up.] To lay or stake in wagering; to stake or pledge something upon the event of a contest; to wager.—*n.* A wager; that which is laid, staked, or pledged on any uncertain question or event; the terms on which a bet is laid.—**Better, Bettor**, bet'ėr, bet'or, *n.* One who lays bets or wagers.

Betake, bē-tāk', *v.t.*—*betook* (pret.), *betaken* (pp.), *betaking*. [Prefix *be*, and *take.*] To repair; to resort; to have recourse: with the reflexive pronouns.

Betel, Betle, bē'tl, *n.* [An Oriental word.] A species of pepper, a creeping or climbing plant, cultivated throughout India, the Malayan Peninsula and Islands, for the sake of its leaf, which is chewed with the betel-nut and lime.—**Betel-nut**, *n.* The kernel of the fruit of a beautiful palm-tree found in India and the East, which is eaten both in its unripe and mature state.

Bethink, bē-thingk', *v.t.* [Prefix *be*, and *think.*] To call or recall to mind; to bring to consideration: always with a reflexive pronoun (to *bethink* one's self *of* a thing).—*v.i.*† To have in recollection; to consider.

Betide, bē-tīd', *v.t.*—*betid*, *betided* (pret.), *betid* (pp.), *betiding*. [Prefix *be*, and *tide*, from A.Sax. *tidan*, to happen. TIDE.] To happen to; to befall; to come to.—*v.i.* To come to pass; to happen.

Betimes, bē-tīmz', *adv.* [Prefix *be* for *by*, and *time*, with adverbial genitive termination.] Seasonably; in good season or time; early; at an early hour; soon; in a short time.

Betoken, bē-tō'kn, *v.t.* To be or serve as a token of; to foreshow; to indicate as future by that which is seen.

Beton, bet'on or bā-toṅ, *n.* [Fr. *béton*, from O.Fr. *beter*, to harden.] A mixture of lime and gravel, which grows into a compact mass; concrete.

Betongue, bē-tung', *v.t.* To scold; to attack with the tongue.

Betony, bet'o-ni, *n.* [L. *betonica.*] A British plant formerly much employed in medicine, and sometimes used to dye wool of a fine dark yellow.

Betook, bē-tụk, pret. of *betake*.

Betray, bē-trā', *v.t.* [Prefix *be*, and O.Fr. *trair*, Fr. *trahir*, to betray, from L. *tradere*, to give up or over. TRADITION.] To deliver into the hands of an enemy by treachery in violation of trust; to violate by fraud or unfaithfulness (to *betray* a cause or trust); to play false to; to reveal or disclose (secrets, designs); to let appear or be seen inadvertently (to *betray* ignorance).—**Betrayal**, bē-trā'al, *n.* Act of betraying.—**Betrayer**, bē-trā'ėr, *n.* One who betrays; a traitor.

Betroth, bē-trōth', *v.t.* [Prefix *be*, and *troth*. TROTH.] To contract to any one in order to a future marriage; to affiance; to pledge one's troth to (O. T.).—**Betrothal, Betrothment**, bē-trōth'al, bē-trōth'-ment, *n.* The act of betrothing.

Better, bet'ėr, *a.* serving as the compar. of *good*. [A.Sax. *betera*, *betra*, with corresponding forms in the other Teutonic languages. BEST.] Having good qualities in a greater degree than another; preferable, in regard to use, fitness, or the like; improved in health.—*To be better off*, to be in improved or in superior circumstances.—*adv.* In a more excellent or superior manner; more correctly or fully; in a higher or greater degree; with greater advantage; more, in extent or amount (*better* than a mile).—*v.t.* To make better; to improve; to ameliorate; to increase the good qualities of (soil, &c.); to advance the interest or worldly position of; to surpass; to exceed; to improve on (as a previous effort).—*v.i.* To grow better; to become better; to improve.—*n.* A superior; one who has a claim to precedence: generally in the plural, and with possessive pronouns.—*The better*, a state of improvement; generally in adverbial phrase *for the better* (to alter a thing *for the better*); advantage; superiority; victory (to have or get *the better* of). — **Betterment**, bet'ér-ment, *n.* A making better; improvement; value added to property from public improvements.—**Betterness**, bet'ér-nes, *n.* The quality of being better; superiority. — **Better-half**, *n.* A colloquial term for wife.

Bettong, bet'tong, *n.* [Native name.] A kind of small kangaroo.

Between, bē-twēn', *prep.* [A.Sax. *betweó-num*, *betweónan*—prefix *be*, and dat. pl. of *tweon*, twain, from *twá*, two; akin *twain*, *twin.*] In the space, place, or interval of any kind separating; in intermediate relation to; from one to another of (letters passing *between* them); in partnership among (shared *between* them); so as to affect both of; pertaining to one or other of two (the blame lies *between* you). — **Betwixt**, bē-twikst', *prep.* [A.Sax. *betweox*, *betweohs*—prefix *be*, and *tweoh*, from *twá*, two. The *t* is excrescent as in *amidst*, &c.] Between; passing between; from one to another.

Bevel, bev'el, *n.* [O.Fr. *bevel*; origin unknown.] The obliquity or inclination of one surface of a solid body to another surface of the same body; an instrument for drawing or measuring angles.—*a.* Having the form of a bevel; slant; not upright, (*Shak.*).—*v.t.*—*beveled, beveling.* To cut to a bevel.—*v.i.* To slant or incline off to a bevel-angle.—**Bevel-angle**, *n.* Any angle except a right angle.—**Bevel-gear**, *n.*—A species of wheel-work in which the axis or shaft of the driving-wheel forms an angle with the axis or shaft of the wheel driven.—**Beveled**, bev'eld, *a.* Having a bevel; formed with a bevel-angle.—**Beveling**, bev'el-ing, *a.* Inclining from a right line; slanting towards a bevel-angle.

Beverage, bev'ėr āj, *n.* [O.Fr. *beuvrage*, from *boivre*, *bevre*, L. *bibere*, to drink.] Drink; liquor for drinking.

Bevy, bev'i, *n.* [Perhaps of similar origin with *beverage*, and originally a drinking company, or animals collected at a watering-place.] A flock of birds; a company of females.

Bewail, bē-wāl', *v.t.* To wail or weep aloud for; to lament.—**Bewailable**, bē-wāl'a-bl. *a.* Capable or worthy of being bewailed.—**Bewailer**, bē-wāl'ér, *n.* One who bewails or laments.—**Bewailing**, bē-wāl'-ing, *n.* Lamentation. — **Bewailingly**, bē-wāl'ing-li, *adv.* In a bewailing manner.—**Bewailment**, bē-wāl'ment, *n.* The act of bewailing.

Beware, bē-wār', *v.i.* [*Be*, imperative of verb to *be*, and *ware* = wary. WARE, WARY.] To be wary or cautious; to be suspicious of danger; to take care: now used only in imperative and infinitive, with *of* before the noun denoting what is to be avoided.

Bewilder, bē-wil'dėr, *v.t.* [Prefix *be*, and old *wilder*, to lead astray. WILD.] To lead into perplexity or confusion; to perplex; to puzzle; to confuse.—**Bewilderingly**, bē-wil'dėr-ing-li, *adv.* So as to bewilder. — **Bewilderment**, bē-wil'dėr-ment, *n.* State of being bewildered.

Bewitch, bē-wich', *v.t.* To subject to the influence of witchcraft; to throw a charm or spell over; to please to such a degree as to take away the power of resistance.—**Bewitcher**, bē-wich'ér, *n.* One that bewitches or fascinates.—**Bewitchery**, bē-wich'ér-i, *n.* Witchery; fascination; charm.—**Bewitching**, bē-wich'ing, *a.* Having power to bewitch or to control by the arts of pleasing.—**Bewitchingly**, bē-wich'ing-li, *adv.* — **Bewitchingness**, bē-wich'ing-nes, *n.*—**Bewitchment**, bē-wich'ment, *n.* Fascination; power of charming.

Bewray,‡ bē-rā', *v.t.* [Prefix *be*, and A. Sax. *wregan*, to disclose, accuse.] To disclose perfidiously; to betray; to divulge. (N.T.).

Bey, bā, *n.* [Turk. *beg*, pron. as *bey.*] A governor of a town or district in the Turkish dominions; also, a prince; a beg.

Beyond, bē-yond', *prep.* [A.Sax. *begeond*, *begeondan* — prefix *be*, and *geond*, yond, yonder. YON.] On the further side of; out of reach of; further than the scope or extent of; above; in a degree exceeding or surpassing.

Bezant, bez'ant, *n.* [From *Byzantium.*] A gold coin of Byzantium; a coin current in England from the tenth century till the time of Edward III.

Bezel, bez'el, *n.* [A form of *basil*, Fr. *beseau*, a slope. BASIL.] The part of a finger ring which surrounds and holds fast the stone; the groove in which the glass of a watch is set.

Bezetta, bē-zet'ta, *n.* Coarse linen rags or sacking soaked in certain pigments, which are thus prepared for exportation; such pigment itself. Red bezetta is coloured with cochineal.

Bezique, be-zēk', *n.* [Fr.] A simple game at cards, played by two, three, or four persons.

Bezoar, bē'zōr, *n.* [O.Fr. *bezoar*, from Per. *pâdzahr*—*pâd*, dispelling, and *zâhr*, poison.] A name for certain concretions found in the intestines of some animals (especially ruminants), formerly (and still in some places) supposed to be an antidote to poison.

Bhang, bang, *n.* An Indian variety of the common hemp, having highly narcotic and intoxicant properties; a drug prepared from the plant used as a narcotic, an anodyne, &c.

Biangular, Biangulate, bī-ang'gū-lėr, bī-ang'gū-lāt, *a.* Having two angles or corners.

Biarticulate, bī-är-tik'ū-lāt, *a.* Having two joints.

Bias, bī'as, *n.* [Fr. *biais*, from L.L. *bifax*, *bifacis*, two-faced—L. *bi*, double, and *facies*, the face.] A weight on the side of a bowl which turns it from a straight line; that which causes the mind to incline towards a particular object or course; inclination; bent; prepossession.—*v.t.*—*biassed* or *biased*, *biassing* or *biasing.* To give a bias or particular direction to; to prejudice; to prepossess.—*adv.* In a slanting manner; obliquely.

Biaxial, bī-aks'i-al, *a.* Having two axes, as in biaxial polarization.

Bib, bib, *n.* A fish of the cod family, about a foot in length, found in the British seas.

Bib,‡ bib, *v.t.* and *i.*—*bibbed, bibbing.* [L. *bibo*, *bibere*, to drink.] To sip; to tipple; to drink frequently.—*n.* [So called because protective of the child's dress when drinking.] A small piece of linen or other cloth worn by children over the breast.—**Bibacious**,† bī-bā'shus, *a.* [L. *bibax*, *bibacis.*] Addicted to drinking. — **Bibacity**,† bī-bas'i-ti, *n.* The quality of being bibacious.—**Bibber**, bib'ér, *n.* A tippler; a man given to drinking.—**Bibulous**, bib'ū-lus, *a.* [L. *bibulus.*] Having the quality of imbibing fluids; spongy; addicted to drinking intoxicants; pertaining to the drinking of intoxicants (*bibulous* propensities).

Bibble-babble, bib'l-bab'l, *n.* [Reduplication of *babble.*] Babble; chatter.

Bibelot, bib'lō, *n.* [Fr., origin doubtful.] A small object of vertu; a knick-knack.

Biberine, bi-bē'rin, *n.* Same as *Bebeerine.*

Bible, bī'bl, *n.* [Fr. *bible*, Gr. *biblia*, the books, pl. of *biblion*, dim. from *biblos*, papyrus, paper, a book.] Originally a book, but specifically restricted now to THE BOOK, by way of eminence; the sacred Scriptures, consisting of two parts, the Old Testament, originally written in Hebrew, the New Testament in Greek.—**Biblical**, bib'lik-al, *a.* Pertaining to the Bible or to the sacred writings.—**Biblically**, bib'lik-al-li, *adv.* In a biblical manner; according to the Bible.—**Biblicist**, bib'li-sist, *n.* One skilled in the knowledge and interpretation of the Bible.—**Biblist**, bī'blist, *n.* One conversant with the Bible; one who makes the Bible the sole rule of faith.

Bibliography, bib-li-og'ra-fi, *n.* [Gr. *biblion*, a book, and *graphō*, to write.] A history or description of books or manuscripts, with notices of the different editions, the times when they were printed, &c.—**Bibliographer**, bib-li-og'ra-fér, *n.* One versed in bibliography; one who composes or compiles the history of books.—**Bibliographic, Bibliographical**, bib'li-ō-graf''ik, bib'li-ō-graf''ik-al, *a.* Pertaining to bibliography.

Bibliolatry, bib-li-ol'a-tri, *n.* [Gr. *biblion*, a book, and *latreia*, worship.] Worship or homage paid to books; excessive reverence for any book, especially the Scriptures.—**Bibliolatrist**, bib-li-ol'a-trist, *n.* A book-worshipper; a worshipper of the Bible.

Bibliology, bib-li-ol'o-ji, *n.* [Gr. *biblion*, a book, and *logos*, discourse.] Biblical literature, doctrine, or theology; a treatise on books; bibliography. — **Bibliological**, bib'li-ō-loj''ik-al, *a.* Relating to bibliology.

Bibliomancy, bib'li-ō-man-si, *n.* [Gr. *biblion*, a book, and *manteia*, divination.] Divination performed by means of a book; divination by means of the Bible, consisting in selecting passages of Scripture at hazard and drawing from them indications concerning things future.

Bibliomania, bib'li-ō-mā''ni-a, *n.* [Gr. *biblion*, a book, and *mania*, madness.] Book-madness; a rage for possessing rare and curious books.—**Bibliomaniac**, bib'li-ō-mā''ni-ak, *n.* One affected with bibliomania.—**Bibliomaniacal**, bib'li-ō-ma-nī''-ak-al, *a.* Pertaining to bibliomania.—**Bibliomanist**,† bib-li-om'an-ist, *n.* A bibliomaniac.

Bibliopegy, bib-li-op'e-ji, *n.* [Gr. *biblion*, a book, and *pēgnymi*, to make firm.] The art of bookbinding.

Bibliophile, bib'li-ō-fīl, *n.* [Gr. *biblion*, book, and *phileō*, to love.] A lover of books.—**Bibliophilism**, bib-li-of'il-izm, *n.* Love of bibliography or of books.—**Bibliophilist**, bib-li-of'il-ist, *n.* A bibliophile.

Bibliopole, bib'li-ō-pōl, *n.* [Gr. *biblion*, a book, and *pōleō*, to sell.] A bookseller.—**Bibliopolic, Bibliopolical**, bib'li-ō-pol''ik, bib'li-ō-pol''ik-al, *a.* Relating to bookselling or booksellers. — **Bibliopolist**, bib-li-op'ol-ist, *n.* A bibliopole.

Bibliotheca, bib'li-ō-thē''ka, *n.* [L., from Gr. *biblion*, a book, and *thēkē*, a repository.] A library.—**Bibliothecal**, bib'li-ō-thē''-kal, *a.* Belonging to a library.

Bibulous. BIB.

Bicameral, bī-kam'ér-al, *a.* [L. prefix *bi*, twice, and *camera*, a chamber.] Pertaining to or consisting of two legislative or other chambers.

Bicarbonate, bī-kär'bon-āt, *n.* A carbonate containing two equivalents of carbonic acid to one of a base.

Bice, Bise, bīs, *n.* [Fr. *bis*; etymology unknown.] A name given to two colours used in painting, one blue, the other green, and both native carbonates of copper.

Bicentenary, bī-sen'te-na-ri, *n.* [L. *bi*, twice, and E. *centenary.*] The period of two hundred years; the commemoration of an event that happened two hundred years before.—*a.* Relating to a bicentenary; occurring once in two hundred years.

Biceps, bī'seps, *n.* [L., from *bi*, double, and *caput*, the head.] A muscle having two heads or origins; the name of two muscles, one of the arm the other of the thigh.—**Bicipital, Bicipitous**, bī-sip'it-al, bī-sip'it-us, *a.* Having two heads; two-headed; pertaining to a biceps.

Bicker, bik'ėr, *v.i.* [W. *bicra*, to fight, *bicre*, conflict.] To skirmish; to quarrel; to contend in words; to scold; to run rapidly; to move quickly with some noise, as a stream; to quiver; to be tremulous, like flame or water; to make a confused noise; to clatter.—*n.* A fight, especially a confused fight.

Biconcave, bī-kon'kāv, *a.* Hollow or concave on both sides.

Biconjugate, bī-kon'jū-gāt, *a.* In pairs; placed side by side; *bot.* twice paired, as when a petiole forks twice.

Bicorn, Bicornous, bī'korn, bī-kor'nus, *a.* [L. *bi*, double, and *cornu*, a horn.] Having two horns or antlers; crescent-shaped.

Bicorporal, bī-kor′po-ral, *a.* Having two bodies; double-bodied.

Bicuspid, bī-kus′pid, *a.* [L. prefix *bi*, two, and *cuspis*, a prong.] With two cusps or points; two-fanged: often applied to teeth, as to the two first pairs of grinders in each jaw.

Bicycle, bī′si-kl, *n.* [L. prefix *bi*, two, and Gr. *kyklos*, a circle or wheel.] A two-wheeled velocipede; a vehicle consisting of two wheels, one behind the other, connected by a light metal frame carrying a seat, the vehicle being propelled by the feet of the rider pressing on treadles which act directly or through gearing.—**Bicyclist**, bī′sik-list, *n.* One who rides on a bicycle.

Bid, bid, *v.t.*—*bid* or *bade* (pret.), *bid*, *bidden* (pp.), *bidding*. [Partly from A. Sax. *biddan*, to pray, ask, declare, command = Icel. *bidja*, G. *bitten*, Goth. *bidjan*, to ask, to pray; partly from A. Sax. *beódan*, to offer, to bid = Goth. *biudan*, G. *bieten*, to offer, command.] To ask, request, or invite (a person); to pray; to wish; to say to by way of greeting or benediction (to *bid* good-day, farewell); to command; to order or direct; to enjoin: followed by an objective and infinitive without *to* (*bid* him come); to offer; to propose, as a price at an auction.—*n.* An offer of a price, especially at an auction.—**Bidder**, bid′ėr, *n.* One who bids or offers a price.—**Bidding-prayer**, *n.* An old form of prayer used before sermon exhorting the people to pray for men of all conditions.

Bide, bīd, *v.i.* [A. Sax. *bidan* = Icel. *bída*, D. *beiden*, Goth. *beidan*. Hence *abide*.] To be or remain in a place or state; to dwell; to inhabit.—*v.t.* To endure; to suffer; to bear; to wait for (chiefly in phrase *to bide one's time*).

Bidental, Bidentate, bī-den′tal, bī-den′tāt, *a.* [L. *bidens*—prefix *bi*, and *dens*, a tooth.] Having two teeth, or processes like teeth; two-toothed.

Bidery, bid′ėr-i, *n.* [From *Bidar*, a town in India.] An alloy of copper, lead, tin, and zinc, used in India for making many elegant and artistic articles.

Bidet, bi-det′ or bē-dā, *n.* [Fr.] A horse for carrying a trooper's baggage; a chamber-pot mounted on a stand; a sort of small portable bath.

Biennial, bī-en′ni-al, *a.* [L. *biennium*, a space of two years—prefix *bi*, twice, *annus*, a year.] Happening or taking place once in two years; *bot.* continuing for two years and then perishing; taking two years to produce its flowers and fruit.—*n.* A biennial plant.—**Biennially**, bī-en′ni-al-li, *adv.* Once in two years; at the return of two years.

Bier, bēr, *n.* [O.E. *beere*, *bere*, A. Sax. *baer*, a bier; from the root of *bear*, to carry.] A carriage or frame of wood for conveying a corpse to the grave.

Biestings, bēst′ingz. See BEESTINGS.

Bifacial, bī-fā′shi-al, *a.* [L. prefix *bi*, twice, *facies*, a face.] Having the opposite surfaces alike.

Bifarious, bī-fā′ri-us, *a.* [L. *bifarius*, twofold.] Divided into two parts; double; twofold.—**Bifariously**, bī-fā′ri-us-li, *adv.* In a bifarious manner.

Biferous, bif′ėr-us, *a.* [L. prefix *bi*, twice, and *fero*, to bear.] *Bot.* bearing flowers or fruit twice a year.

Biffin, bif′in, *n.* [From the resemblance of its flesh to *beef*.] An excellent kitchen apple cultivated in England and often sold in a dried and flattened condition.

Bifid, bī′fid, *a.* [L. *bifidus*—prefix *bi*, twice, *findo*, *fidi*, to split.] Cleft or divided into two parts; forked; *bot.* divided half-way down into two parts; opening with a cleft.

Bifilar, bī-fī′lėr, *a.* [L. prefix *bi*, twice, and *filum*, a thread.] Two-threaded; fitted or furnished with two threads (a *bifilar* micrometer).

Bifold, bī′fōld, *a.* [Prefix *bi*, twice, and *fold*.] Twofold; double; of two kinds, degrees, &c. (*Shak.*)

Bifoliate, bī-fō′li-āt, *a.* [L. *bi*, twice, two, and *folium*, a leaf.] In *bot.* having two leaves.

Biform, Biformed, bī′form, bī′formd, *a.* [L. *biformis*, double-formed—*bi*, twice, and *forma*, form.] Having two forms, bodies, or shapes; double-bodied.—**Biformity**, bi-for′mi-ti, *n.* The state of being biform; a doubleness of form.

Bifurcate, bī-fėr′kāt, *a.* [L. *bi*, twice, and *furca*, a fork.] Forked; divided into two branches.—**Bifurcation**, bī-fėr-kā′shon, *n.* A forking or division into two branches.

Big, big, *a.* [Etymology doubtful; perhaps connected with Sc. or North. E. to *big*, Icel. *byggja*, Dan. *bygge*, to build.] Having size, whether large or small; more especially, great; large; bulky; great with young; pregnant; hence, *fig.* full of something important; teeming; distended; full, as with grief or passion; tumid; haughty in air or mien; pompous; proud.—**Bigness**, big′nes, *n.* The state or quality of being big; size; bulk.—**Big-horn**, *n.* A large and very wild species of sheep with horns 3½ feet long found in the western mountains of N. America; the Rocky Mountain sheep.—**Big-wig**, *n.* A person of great importance, consequence, or dignity; a great or notable personage. [Colloq.]

Bigamy, big′a-mi, *n.* [Prefix *bi*, twice, and Gr. *gamos*, marriage.] The crime, fact, or state of having two wives or husbands at once.—**Bigamist**, big′a-mist, *n.* One who has committed bigamy.—**Bigamous**, big′a-mus, *a.* Of or pertaining to bigamy; guilty of bigamy.

Bigg, big, *n.* [Icel. *bygg*, Dan. *byg*, barley.] A variety of barley having six rows of grains; bere.

Biggin, Biggen, big′in, **Bigonet**, big′o-net, *n.* [Fr. *beguin*, the cap of the *Beguines*.] A child's cap; a night-cap; a coif. (*Shak.*)

Biggin, big′in, *n.* [A form of *piggin*, from *pig*, a small earthen vessel.] A can; a contrivance for straining the grounds from coffee.

Bight, bīt, *n.* [A.Sax. *byht*, from *bigan*, *bugan*, to *bow* or bend = L.G. Dan. Icel. *bugt*, a bending, a bay. BOW.] A bend in a coast-line; a bay; the double of a rope when folded; a bend anywhere except at the ends; a loop.

Bignonia, big-nō′ni-a, *n.* [After M. *Bignon*, librarian to Louis XIV.] The generic name of a number of plants, inhabitants of hot climates, usually climbing shrubs with beautiful trumpet-shaped flowers, hence their name of *trumpet-flower*.

Bigot, big′ot, *n.* [Fr. *bigot*, a bigot; It. *bigotto*, *bigozzo*. Etymology uncertain; Some suppose it a corruption of *Visigoth*, as intolerant Arians, persecuting in Spain, others refer it to the oath *bi Gott* (by God) common among the Norse settlers in Normandy.] A person obstinately and unreasonably wedded to a particular religious creed, opinion, or practice; a person blindly attached to any opinion, system, or party.—**Bigoted, Bigotted**, big′ot-ed, *a.* Having the character of a bigot; belonging to a bigot; showing blind attachment to opinions.—**Bigotedly**, big′ot-ed-li, *adv.* In a bigoted manner.—**Bigotry**, big′ot-ri, *n.* The practice or tenets of a bigot; obstinate or blind attachment to a particular creed or to certain tenets; unreasoning zeal; intolerance.

Bijou, bē-zhö, *n.* [Fr.] A jewel; something small and pretty.—**Bijouterie**, bē-zhö-trē, *n.* Jewelry; trinkets.

Bijugous, Bijugate, bī′jū-gus, bī′jū-gāt, *a.* [L. *bijugus*—*bi*, two, *jugum*, a yoke.] Having two pairs of leaflets.

Bike, bīk, *n.* A bicycle. [Colloq.]

Bilabiate, bī-lā′bi-āt, *a.* [L. *bi*, twice, and *labium*, a lip.] *Bot.* applied to a corolla having two lips, the one placed over the other.

Bilaminar, bī-lam-i-nėr, *a.* [L. *bi*, twice, two, and *lamina*, a lamina.] Having or consisting of two thin plates or laminæ.

Bilander, bī′lan-dėr, *n.* [D. *bijlander*—*bij*, by, near, and *land*, land.] A small merchant vessel with two masts, used chiefly in the Dutch canals; a kind of hoy.

Bilateral, bī-lat′ėr-al, *a.* [L. *bi*, twice, and *latus*, *lateris*, a side.] Having two sides; of or pertaining to two sides; two-sided.

Bilberry, bil′be-ri, *n.* [Dan. *böllebær*, bilberry—*bölle*, of doubtful meaning, and *bær*, a berry.] A dark blue or almost black berry, the fruit of a small shrub belonging to the cranberry family (akin to the heaths) growing on moors and woods in Britain; the shrub itself.

Bilbo,‡ bil′bō, *n.* [From *Bilbao* in Spain, famous for their manufacture.] A rapier; a sword.—**Bilboes**, bil′bōz, *n.pl.* A contrivance for confining the feet of prisoners—a long bar or bolt of iron with shackles sliding on it and a lock at the end.

Bile, bīl, *n.* [Fr. *bile*, L. *bilis*, bile, also anger, spleen.] A yellow bitter liquid, separated from the blood by the action of the liver, and discharged into the gall-bladder, its most obvious use being to assist in the process of digestion; ill-nature; bitterness of feeling; spleen.—**Biliary**, bil′i-a-ri, *n.* Pertaining to or containing bile.—**Bilious**, bil′i-us, *a.* Consisting of, or affected by bile; having an excess of bile; having the health deranged from excess of bile in the system.—**Biliousness**, bil′i-us-nes, *n.* The state or quality of being bilious, or of suffering from an excessive secretion of bile.

Bilge, bilj, *n.* [A different orthography of *bulge*.] The protuberant part of a cask; the breadth of a ship's bottom, or that part of her floor which approaches to a horizontal direction.—*v.i.* *Naut.* to spring a leak in the bilge.—**Bilge-pump**, *n.* A pump to draw the bilge-water from a ship.—**Bilge-water**, *n.* A water which enters a ship and lies upon her bilge or bottom.

Bilingual, bī-ling′gwal, *a.* [L. *bilinguis*—*bi*, double, and *lingua*, a tongue, a language.] Containing, or expressed in, two languages (a *bilingual* dictionary).—**Bilinguous**, bī-ling′gwus, *a.* Speaking two languages; bilingual.

Biliteral, bī-lit′ėr-al, *a.* [L. *bi*, twice, and *litera*, a letter.] Consisting of two letters.

Bilk, bilk, *v.t.* [Probably a form of *balk*.] To deceive or defraud by non-fulfilment of engagement; to leave in the lurch; to decamp without paying (a person).

Bill, bil, *n.* [A.Sax. *bile*, a beak.] The beak of a fowl.—*v.t.* To join bills or beaks, as doves; to caress fondly.—**Billed**, bild, *a.* Having a bill: usually in composition.

Bill, bil, *n.* [A.Sax. *bil*, *bill*, a bill, a sword, &c.; D. and G. *bille*, a pick; Dan. *biil*, D. *bijl*, G. *beil*, a hatchet; root in Skr. *bhil*, to split.] A cutting instrument hook-shaped towards the point, or with a concave cutting edge, used in pruning, &c.; a bill-hook; an ancient military weapon, consisting of a broad hook-shaped blade, having a short pike at the back and another at the summit, attached to a long handle.—**Bill-hook**, *n.* A small variety of hatchet with a hook at the end of the cutting edge.

Bill, bil, *n.* [O.Fr. *bille*, a label or note, from L.L. *billa*, *bulla*, a seal, a letter, a roll, from L. *bulla*, a boss, a stud, whence *bull*, a papal edict.] A sheet or piece of paper containing a statement of certain particulars; a sheet containing a public notice or advertisement; a note of charges for goods supplied, work done, or the like, with the amount due on each item; a declaration of certain facts in legal proceedings; a written promise to pay or document binding one to pay a specified sum at a certain date; a bill of exchange (see below); a draft of a law presented to a legislature to be passed into an act: also applied to various measures that are really acts.—*Bill of divorce*, a writing given by a husband to his wife among the Jews by which their marriage was dissolved.—*Bill of entry*, a written account of goods entered at the custom-house.—*Bill of exchange*, an order drawn by one person (the drawer) on another (the drawee) who is either in the same or in some distant country, requesting or directing him to pay money at a specified time to some person assigned (the payee), who may either be the drawer himself or some other person. The person on whom the bill is drawn becomes the 'acceptor' by writing his name on it as such.—*Bill of fare*, in a hotel, restaurant, &c., a list of refreshments ready to be supplied.—*Bill of health*, a certificate signed by consuls or other authorities as to the health of a ship's company at the time of her clearing any port, a *clean bill* being given when no disorder is supposed to exist, and a *foul bill* when it is known to exist.—*Bill of lading*, a memorandum of goods shipped on board of a vessel, signed by way of receipt by the master of the vessel.—*Bill of mortality*, an official return of the number of deaths occurring in a place within a certain time.—*Bill of sale*, a formal instrument for the transfer of personal property (as furniture, the stock in a shop), often given in security for a debt, empowering the receiver to sell the goods if the money is not repaid at the appointed time.—**Bill-broker**, *n.* One who buys, negotiates, or discounts bills of exchange, promissory notes, and the like.—**Bill-poster, Bill-sticker**, *n.* One who posts or sticks up bills or placards in public places.

Billet, bil'et, *n.* [A dim of *bill* = Fr. *billet*. BILL.] A small paper or note in writing; a short letter; a ticket directing soldiers at what house to lodge.—**Billet**, bil'et, *v.t.* To quarter or place in lodgings, as soldiers in private houses.—*v.i.* To be quartered; to lodge: specifically applied to soldiers.

Billet, bil'et, *n.* [Fr. *billot*, a log, from *bille*, the stock of a tree, from the Celtic.] A small stick or round piece of wood used for various purposes; *arch.* an imitation of a wooden billet placed in a hollow moulding at intervals apart, usually equal to its own length.

Billet-doux, bil-le-dö, *n.* pl. **Billets-doux**, bil-le-dö. [Fr., lit. sweet billet or note.] A love note or short love-letter.

Billiards, bil'yėrdz, *n.* [Fr. *billard*, the game of billiards, a billiard-cue, from *bille*, a piece of wood] A game played on a long rectangular, cloth-covered table, without pockets, with three ivory balls. Scoring is made by the use of a cue to cause one ball to strike the other two. Pocket billiards are played on the same kind of table but having six pockets and fifteen numbered balls and one cue ball, the object being to drive the numbered balls into pockets with the cue ball.

Billingsgate, bil'ingz-gāt, *n.* [From a fish-market of this name in London, celebrated for the use of foul language.] Profane or foul language; ribaldry.

Billion, bil'yon, *n.* [Fr., contr. from L. *bis*, twice, and *million*.] A thousand millions

Billon, bil'on, *n.* [Fr.] An alloy of copper and silver, used in some countries for coins of low value.

Billow, bil'ō, *n.* [Icel. *bylgja*, Dan. *bölge*, Sw. *bölja*, a swell, a billow, from root of *bulge, belly, bellows*.] A great wave or surge of the sea.—*v.i.* To swell; to rise and roll in large waves or surges.—**Billowy**, bil'lō-i, *a.* Swelling into large waves; full of surges; belonging to billows; wavy.

Billy-boy, bil'i-boi, *n.* A one- or two-masted, bluff-bowed vessel of light draught, especially built for the navigation of the Humber and its tributaries.—**Billycock**, bil'i-kok, *n.* Hat with round crown, cocked in the fashion of a *bully*.—**Billygoat**, bil'i-gōt, *n.* A he-goat, after the man's name.

Bilobate, bī-lō'bāt, *a.* [Prefix *bi*, and *lobate*.] Divided into two lobes (a *bilobate* leaf).

Bilocular, bī-lok-ū-lėr, *a.* [L. *bi*, twice, and *loculus*, a cell, from *locus*, a place.] Divided into two cells or small compartments.

Bilophodont, bī-lof'ō-dont, *a.* [Prefix *bi*, double, Gr. *lophos*, crest, *odous, odontos*, tooth.] Double-crested, said of teeth.

Biltong, bil'tong, *n.* An African name for lean meat cut in strips and dried.

Bimaculate, bī-mak'ū-lāt, *a.* [L. *bi*, twice, *macula*, a spot.] Marked with two spots.

Bimanous, bī'ma-nus, *a.* [L. *bi*, twice, two, and *manus*, a hand.] Having two hands; pertaining to the Bimana.—**Bimana**, bī'ma-na, *n.pl.* Animals having two hands: a term applied to the highest order of Mammalia, of which man is the type and sole genus.

Bimensal, bī-men'sal, *a.* [L. *bi*, two, twice, and *mensis*, a month.] Occurring once in two months.

Bimetallic, bī-me-tal'ik, *a.* [Prefix *bi*, twice, and *metallic*.] Of or pertaining to two metals; pertaining to the use of a double metallic standard in currency.—**Bimetallism**, bī-met'al-izm, *n.* That system of currency which recognizes coins of two metals, as silver and gold, as legal tender to any amount.—**Bimetallist**, bī-met'al-ist, *n.* One who favours bimetallism.

Bimonthly, bī-munth'li, *a.* [Prefix *bi*, twice, and *monthly*.] Occurring every two months.

Bin, bin, *n.* [A.Sax. *bin, binn*, a bin, a hutch; D. *ben*, G. *benne, binne*, a basket.] A box or inclosed place used as a repository of any commodity; one of the subdivisions of a cellar for wine-bottles.

Binacle, bin'a-kl, *n.* Same as *Binnacle*.

Binary, bī'na-ri, *a.* [L. *binus*, double. two and two.] Consisting or composed of two or of two parts; double; twofold; dual—*Binary compound, chem.* a compound of two elements, or of an element and a compound equivalent to an element, or of two such compounds, according to the laws of combination.—*Binary star*, a double star, one of two stars associated together so as to form a system, the one revolving round the other, or both round their common centre of gravity.—**Binate**, bī'nāt, *a. Bot.* being double or in couples; growing in pairs.

Bind, bīnd, *v.t.*—*bound* (pret. & pp.), *binding*. [A. Sax. *bindan*, pret. *band*, pp. *bunden*=Icel. Sw. *binda*, Dan. *binde*, D. and G. *binden*, same root as Skr. *bandh*, to bind.] To tie or confine with a cord, or anything that is flexible; to fasten or encircle, as with a band or ligature; to put a ligature or bandage on; to put in bonds or fetters; to hold in, confine, or restrain; to engage by a promise, agreement, vow, law, duty, or any other moral or legal tie; to form a border on, or strengthen by a border; to sew together and cover (a book).—*v.i.* To exercise an obligatory influence; to be obligatory; to tie up; to tie sheaves up; to grow hard or stiff (of soil).—**Binder**, bīnd'ėr, *n.* A person who binds; one whose occupation is to bind books; one who binds sheaves; anything that binds, as a fillet, cord, rope, or band; a bandage.—**Bindery**, bīnd'ėr-i, *n.* A place where books are bound.—**Binding**, bīnd'ing, *a.* Serving to bind; having power to bind or oblige; obligatory; making fast; astringent.—*n.* The act of one who binds; anything which binds; the cover of a book, with the sewing and accompanying work; something that secures the edges of cloth.—**Bindingly**, bīnd'ing-li, *adv.* In a binding manner; so as to bind.—**Bindingness**, bīnd'ing-nes, *n.* The character of being binding or obligatory.—**Bind-weed**, *n.* The common name for twining or trailing plants of the convolvulus family, common in cornfields and waste places and overrunning hedges.

Bine, bīn, *n.* [From the verb to *bind*.] The slender stem of a climbing plant: sometimes written *Bind*.

Bing, bing, *n.* [Dan. *binge*, Icel. *bingr*, a heap.] A large heap, as of corn, coal, ore, &c.

Binn, bin, *n.* Same as *Bin*.

Binnacle, bin'a-kl, *n.* [Formerly, *bittacle*, from Fr. *habitacle*, a little house for pilot and steersman, from L. *habitaculum*, an abode, from *habito*, to dwell. HABITATION.] A box on the deck of a vessel, near the helm, containing the compass and lights by which it can be read at night.

Binocle, bī'nō-kl or bin'o-kl, *n.* [L. *binus*, double, and *oculus*, an eye.] A telescope with two tubes, for the use of both eyes at once; a field-glass.—**Binocular**, bī-nok'-ū-lėr, *a.* Having two eyes; pertaining to both eyes; suited for the simultaneous use of both eyes.—*n.* A binocle.

Binomial, bī-nō'mi-al, *n.* [L. *bi*, two, twice, and *nomen*, a name.] *Alg.* an expression or quantity consisting of two terms connected by the sign *plus* (+) or *minus* (−).—*a.* Pertaining to binomials.—*Binomial theorem*, a celebrated theorem by Sir Isaac Newton, for raising a binomial to any power, or for extracting any root of it.—**Binominal**, bī-nom'i-nal, *a.* Consisting of or pertaining to two names; pertaining to the scientific naming of plants and animals by a Latin or Latinized generic and specific name, a system introduced by Linnæus; as *Elephas Indicus*, the Indian elephant.

Binturong, bin'tū-rong, *n.* [Native name.] An ursine animal allied to the racoon, found in the Malay Archipelago.

Biocellate, bī-os'el-lāt, *a.* [L. *bi*, two, and *ocellus*, an eyelet.] Marked with two eye-like spots, as an insect's wing.

Biodynamics, bī'ō-di-nam"iks, *n.* [Gr. *bios*, life, and E. *dynamics* (which see).] The doctrine of vital forces or energy.

Biogenesis, bī-ō-jen'e-sis, *n.* [Gr. *bios*, life, and *genesis*, generation.] The origin of what has life (vegetable or animal) from living matter; the doctrine which holds that living organisms can spring only from living parents: as opposed to *abiogenesis*; the history of the life development of organized existences.—**Biogenetic**, bī-ō-je-net'ik, *a.* Of or pertaining to biogenesis.

Biography, bī-og'ra-fi, *n.* [Gr. *bios*, life, and *graphō*, to write.] The history of the life and character of a particular person; a life; a memoir; biographical writings in general, or as a department of literature.—**Biographer**, bī-og'ra-fėr, *n.* One who writes a biography; a writer of lives.—**Biographic, Biographical**, bī-ō-graf'-ik, bī-ō-graf'ik-al, *a.* Pertaining to biography; containing biography.—**Biographically**, bī-ō-graf'ik-al-li, *adv.* In the manner of a biography.—**Biographize**, bī-og'ra-fīz, *v.t.* To write the biography of.—**Biograph**, bī'ō-graf, *n.* A kind of cinematograph: also *Bioscope*.

Biology, bī-ol'o-ji, *n.* [Gr. *bios*, life, and *logos*, a discourse.] The science of life, or which treats generally of the life of animals and plants, including their morphology, physiology, origin, development, and distribution.—**Biologic, Biological**, bī-ō-loj'ik, bī-ō-loj'ik-al, *a.* Pertaining to biology.—**Biologist**, bī-ol'o-jist, *n.* One skilled in or who studies biology.

Bioplasm, bī'ō-plazm, *n.* [Gr. *bios*, life, and *plasma*, anything formed, from *plassō*, to form.] The albuminoid substance constituting the living matter of the elementary part or cell in plants and animals; germinal matter.—**Bioplasmic**, bī-ō-plaz'mik, *a.* Consisting of or pertaining to bioplasm.

Bioscope, bī'ō-skōp, *n.* [Gr. *bios*, life, *skopeō*, to view.] A kind of cinematograph.

Biotaxy, bī'ō-tak-si, *n.* [Gr. *bios*, life, and *taxis*, arrangement.] The scientific classification of animals and plants.

Biparous, bip'a-rus, *a.* [L. *bi*, twice, and *pario*, to bear.] Bringing forth two at a birth.

Bipartible, Bipartile, bī-pär'ti-bl, bī-pär'til, *a.* [L. prefix *bi*, twice, and *partio*, to divide.] Capable of being divided into two parts.—**Bipartite**, bī-pär'tīt, *a.* In two parts; having two correspondent parts; double; *bot.* divided into two parts nearly to the base, as leaves.—**Bipartition**, bī-pär-ti'shon, *n.* The act of making bipartite.

Biped, bī'ped, *n.* [L. *bipes*—*bi*, twice, and *pes, pedis*, a foot.] An animal having two feet, as man.—**Bipedal**, bī'ped-al, *a.* [L. *bipedalis*.] Having two feet.

Bipennate, bī-pen'nāt, *a.* [L. *bi*, double, and *penna*, a wing.] Having two wings or organs resembling wings.

Bipinnate, bī-pin′nāt, *a.* [L. *bi*, double, and *pinnatus*, winged.] *Bot.* doubly pinnate; having pinnæ which are pinnate.

Biplane, bī′plān, *n.* [Prefix *bi*, and *plane.*] A flying machine with an upper and an under plane or carrying surface.

Biplicate, bī′pli-kāt, *a.* [L. *bi*, twice, and *plico*, to fold.] Doubly folded; twice folded together.—**Biplicity**, bī-plis′i-ti, *n.* State of being biplicate; doubleness.

Biquadratic, bī-kwod-rat′ik, *n.* [L. *bi*, double, twice, and *quadratus*, squared.] *Math.* the fourth power, arising from the multiplication of a square by itself; the square of the square.—*a.* Pertaining to this power.

Birch, bėrch, *n.* [A. Sax. *byrc*, *beorc*=Icel. and Sw. *björk*, Dan. and Sc. *birk* (comp. Sc. *kirk*, E. *church*), D. *berk*, G. *birke*, Rus. *bereza*, Lith. *berzas*, Skr. *bhurja*—a birch.] A graceful tree having small leaves, slender, often drooping branches, and a smooth whitish bark; a kind of wine is made from its spring sap, its bark is much used in tanning, and its timber is employed in turnery; an instrument of punishment used by schoolmasters, generally made of the tough, slender twigs of the common birch.—**Birchen**, bėrch′en, *a.* Made of birch; consisting of birch.

Bird, bėrd, *n.* [A. Sax. *brid*, a young bird, from the root of *brood*, *breed*. *Fowl* was originally the word for bird in general.] A feathered, warm-blooded animal, with two legs and two wings, producing young from eggs; one of the feathered class (Aves) of the vertebrate animals.—*v.i.* To catch birds.—**Bird-bolt**, *n.* An arrow, broad at the end, for shooting birds.—**Bird-call**, *n.* An instrument for imitating the cry of birds in order to attract or decoy them.—**Bird-cherry**, *n.* A species of cherry having the flowers in racemes and fruit only fit for birds.—**Bird-lime**, *n.* A viscous substance prepared from holly-bark, &c., used for entangling birds, twigs being for this purpose smeared with it at places where birds resort.—*v.t.* To besmear with bird-lime.—**Bird-of-Paradise**, *n.* One of a family of conirostral birds found in the islands of the Indian Archipelago, the male birds being celebrated for their gorgeous plumage.—**Bird-organ**, *n.* A small barrel-organ used in teaching birds to whistle tunes.—**Bird's-eye**, *n.* The popular name of a species of primrose or wild germander and several other plants; a kind of cut tobacco, the minute slices of the stems of which are marked somewhat like a bird's eye.—*Bird's-eye maple*, the wood of the sugar-maple, which is marked by little knotty spots resembling birds' eyes, and is much used in cabinet-making.—*Bird's-eye view*, a view or landscape shown as it might appear to a flying bird; hence, a rapid and comprehensive view of a subject.—**Bird's-foot**, *n.* A common name for several plants, having legumes somewhat resembling the claws of a bird.—**Bird's-nest**, *n.* A name of several plants, especially a British orchid having a root resembling a nest.—**Bird-spider**, *n.* A Brazilian species of spider large enough to prey on small birds.—**Bird-witted**, *a.* Not having the faculty of attention; flighty.

Bireme, bī′rēm, *n.* [L. *biremis*—*bi*, two, and *remus*, an oar.] An ancient Greek or Roman vessel with two banks or tiers of oars.

Biretta, **Beretta**, bē-ret′ta, bā-ret′ta, *n.* [It. *berretta*, L.L. *birettum*, *birretum*, dim. of *birrus*, a hood.] A square cap worn by ecclesiastics; priests have it black, bishops purple, cardinals red: written also *Birretta*.

Birostrate, bī-ros′trāt, *a.* [L. *bi*, twice, and *rostrum*, a beak.] Having a double beak, or process resembling a beak.

Birr, bir, *n.* [Imitative of the sound.] A whirring noise.—*v.i.* To make a whirring noise.

Birth, bėrth, *n.* [A.Sax. *beorth*, *byrth*, from *beran*, to bear; Goth. *gabaurths*, G. *geburt.*] The act or process of being born; the occasion of an individual's coming into life; the act of bearing or bringing forth; parturition; the condition in which a person is born; lineage; extraction; descent; that which is born or produced; origin; beginning.—**Birthday**, *n.* The day on which any person is born, or the anniversary of the day; day or time of origin.—**Birthmark**, *n.* Some congenital mark or blemish on a person's body.—**Birthnight**, *n.* The night in which a person is born; the anniversary of that night.—**Birthplace**, *n.* The place of one's birth; place of origin.—**Birthright**, *n.* Any right or privilege to which a person is entitled by birth; right of primogeniture.—**Birth-root**, *n.* A North American plant, the roots of which are esteemed as astringent, tonic, and antiseptic.

Biscotin, bis′kot-in, *n.* [Fr.; It. *biscotino*. BISCUIT.] A confection made of flour, sugar, marmalade, and eggs; sweet biscuit.

Biscuit, bis′ket, *n.* [Fr. *bis*, twice, and *cuit* (L. *coctus*), cooked. COOK.] A kind of unraised bread, plain, sweet, or fancy, formed into flat cakes, and baked hard;—commonly called *cracker* in the United States; porcelain or earthenware after being first fired, and before the application of the glazing and embellishments; unglazed porcelain, of which small articles of statuary are made.

Biscutate, bī-skū′tāt, *a.* [L. prefix *bi*, double, and *scutum*, a shield.] *Bot.* resembling or having two shield-like parts.

Bisect, bī-sekt′, *v.t.* [L. *bi*, two, and *seco*, *sectum*, to cut.] To cut or divide into two parts, more especially into two equal parts, as a line, &c.—**Bisection**, bī-sek′shon, *n.* The act of bisecting; the division of a line, angle, &c., into two equal parts.—**Bisegment**, bī-seg′ment, *n.* One of the parts of a bisected line.

Biserial, **Biseriate**, bī-sē′ri-al, bī-sē′ri-āt, *a.* Arranged in two series or rows.

Bisexual, bī-seks′ū-al, *a.* Having the organs of both sexes in one individual; of two sexes; hermaphrodite; *bot.* having both stamen and pistil within the same envelope.

Bishop, bish′up, *n.* [A. Sax. *biscop*, a bishop, from Gr. *episcopos*, an overseer—*epi*, over, and *skopeō*, to look. *Bishop* is the same word as Fr. *évêque* (a bishop), though they have not a letter in common.] A member of the highest order of the Christian ministry; a prelate having the spiritual direction and government of a diocese, the oversight of the clergy within it, and with whom rests the power of ordination, confirmation, and consecration; a piece in the game of chess having its upper section cleft in the form of a bishop's mitre.—**Bishopric**, bish′up-rik, *n.* [*Bishop*, and *ric*, jurisdiction = A. Sax. *rice*, D. *rijk*, G. *reich*, realm, dominion.] The office or dignity of a bishop; the district over which the jurisdiction of a bishop extends; a diocese.

Bisk, bisk, *n.* [Fr. *bisque*, probably from L. *biscoctus*, twice cooked or boiled. BISCUIT.] Soup or broth made by boiling several sorts of meats together.

Bismuth, bis′muth or biz′muth, *n.* [G. *bismuth*, *wismuth.*] Chemical sym. Bi; sp. gr. 9·8. A metal of a yellowish or reddish white colour and a lamellar texture, somewhat harder than lead and not malleable, used in the composition of pewter, in the fabrication of printers' types, and in various other metallic mixtures.—*Bismuth glance*, the name of one or two ores of bismuth.—**Bismuthal**, **Bismuthic**, bis′(biz′)-muth-al, bis′(biz′)muth-ik, *a.* Pertaining to or composed of bismuth.—**Bismuthin**, **Bismuthine**, bis′(biz′)muth-in, *n.* A native sulphuret of bismuth.—**Bismuthite**, bis′(biz′)muth-īt, *n.* Native carbonate of bismuth; a white, dull green, or yellowish mineral.

Bison, bī′son, *n.* [L. *bison*, Gr. *bisōn*, a name borrowed from the ancient Germans.] The name of two bovine quadrupeds, the European bison or aurochs, and the American bison, usually called the buffalo, having short, black, rounded, horns, and on the shoulders a large hunch, consisting of a fleshy substance.

Bisque, bisk, *n.* [Fr.] Unglazed white porcelain for making statuettes; biscuit.

Bissextile, bis-seks′til, *n.* [L. *bisextilis* (*annus*), leap-year, from *bi*, twice, and *sextus*, sixth, because the sixth day before the calends of March (= our 24th Feb.) was reckoned twice every fourth year, a day (the *bisextus*) being intercalated.] Leap-year.—*a.* Pertaining to leap-year.

Bistort, bis′tort, *n.* [L. *bistorta*—*bis*, twice, and *tortus*, twisted.] A plant, so called because of its twisted roots: called also *Snakeweed* and *Adder's-wort*.

Bistoury, bis′tu̧-ri, *n.* [Fr. *bistouri.*] A surgical instrument for making incisions, shaped in various ways.

Bistre, **Bister**, bis′tėr, *n.* [Fr. *bistre.*] A brown pigment prepared from the soot of wood, especially of the beech.

Bisulcate, bī-sul′kāt, *a.* [L. *bi*, double, and *sulcus*, a furrow.] Cloven-footed, or having two-hoofed digits, as oxen or swine.

Bisulphate, bī-sul′fāt, *n.* In *chem.* a salt of sulphuric acid, in which one-half of the hydrogen of the acid is replaced by a metal.—**Bisulphite**, bī-sul′fīt, *n.* A salt of sulphurous acid, in which one-half of the hydrogen of the acid is replaced by a metal.

Bit, bit, prep. & pp. of *bite*.

Bit, bit, *n.* [From the verbal stem *bite*. In sense of piece it is the A.Sax. *bita*, *bite*, Icel. *biti*, a bite, a morsel; in sense of part of a bridle it corresponds to A.Sax. *bitol*, D. *bit*, Icel. *bitill*, G. *gebiss.*] A small piece of anything; a piece, morsel, fragment, or part; any small coin (a threepenny-*bit*); the metal part of a bridle which is inserted in the mouth of a horse, and its appendages, to which the reins are fastened; a boring tool for wood or metal, fixed in a stock, brace, lathe, or the like; the part of a key which enters the lock and acts on the bolts and tumblers; the cutting blade of a plane. ∴ In certain phrases *a bit* often means somewhat, a little, a whit; as, he is *a bit* of a painter; not *a bit* better.—*A bit of one's mind*, one's candid opinions expressed in clear and unflattering terms.—*v.t.*—*bitted*, *bitting*. To put a horse's bit into the mouth of.

Bitch, bich, *n.* [A.Sax. *bicce*=Sc. *bick*, Icel. *bikkja*, Dan. *bikke.*] The female of canine animals, as of the dog, wolf, and fox; a term of reproach for a woman.

Bite, bīt, *v.t.* *bit* (pret.), *bit*, *bitten* (pp.), *biting*. [A.Sax. *bītan*=Icel. *bíta*, D. *bijten*, Goth. *beitan*, G. *beiszen*; allied to L. *findo*, *fidi*, Skr. *bhid*, to split. *Bit*, *bitter*, *beetle* are from this stem.] To cut, break, or crush with the teeth; to penetrate or seize with the teeth; to cause a sharp or smarting pain to (pepper *bites* the mouth); to pinch or nip as with frost; to blast or blight; to grip or catch into or on, so as to act with effect (as an anchor, a file, &c.); to corrode or eat into, by aqua fortis or other acid.—*v.i.* To have a habit of biting persons; to seize a bait with the mouth; to grip or catch into another object, so as to act on it with effect (the anchor *bites*).—*n.* The seizure of anything by the teeth or with the mouth; a wound made by the mouth; a mouthful; a bit; a cheat, trick, fraud‡; catch or hold of one object on another.—**Biter**, bīt′ėr, *n.* One who or that which bites; an animal given to biting; one who cheats or deceives‡ (in phrase now, 'the *biter* bit').—**Biting**, bīt′ing, *a.* Sharp; severe; cutting; pungent; sarcastic.—**Bitingly**, bīt′ing-li, *adv.* In a biting manner; sarcastically; sneeringly.

Bitt, bit, *n.* [Comp. Icel. *biti*, a cross-beam or girder.] *Naut.* a piece of wood or frame secured to the deck, on which to make fast the cables.

Bittacle,‡ bit′a-kl, *n.* A binnacle.

Bitter, bit′ėr, *a.* [A.Sax. *biter*, from *bītan*, to bite, from causing the tongue to smart = D. G. Dan. and Sw. *bitter*, Icel. *bitr.*] Acrid, biting, pungent to taste; keen, cruel, poignant, severe, sharp, harsh, painful, distressing, piercing to the feelings or to the mind; reproachful, sarcastic, or cutting, as words.—**Bitterish**, bit′ėr-ish, *a.* Somewhat bitter, especially to the taste.—**Bitterishness**, bit′ėr-ish-nes, *n.*—**Bitterly**, bit′ėr-li, *adv.* In a bitter manner; keenly, sharply, severely, intensely.—**Bittern,** bit′ėrn, *n.* The residual brine in salt-works, used for making Epsom salts.—**Bitterness,** bit′ėr-nes, *n.* The state or quality of being bitter in all its senses, whether to the taste, feelings, or mind.—**Bitters,** bit′ėrz, *n.pl.* A liquor prepared with bitter herbs or roots, and used as a stomachic, &c. —**Bitter-apple, Bitter-gourd,** *n.* A plant the fruit of which is a many-seeded gourd; colocynth.—**Bitter-sweet,** *n.* The woody nightshade, a trailing plant with small scarlet berries and strongly narcotic leaves, common in hedges in Britain, so called because the root and branches when chewed produce first a bitter, then a sweet taste.—**Bitter-sweeting,** *n.* A variety of apple which has supplied many allusions to the poets.—**Bitterwort,** bit′ėr-wėrt, *n.* Yellow gentian, so called from its remarkably bitter taste.

Bittern, bit′ėrn, *n.* [O.E. *bitore, bittor, bittour*; Fr. *butor*, Sp. *bitor*; origin uncertain.] A name given to several grallatorial or wading birds of the heron family: the common British species is celebrated for the singular booming or drumming noise it makes.

Bitumen, bi-tū′men, *n.* [L.] A mineral substance of a resinous nature and highly inflammable, appearing in a variety of forms which are known by different names, *naphtha* being the most fluid, *petroleum* and *mineral tar* less so, and *asphalt* being solid. —**Bituminate,** bi-tū′min-āt, *v.t.*—*bituminated, bituminating.* To impregnate with bitumen.—**Bituminiferous,** bi-tū′mi-nif″ėr-us, *a.* Producing bitumen.—**Bituminization,** bi-tū′min-iz-ā″shon, *n.* Transformation into a bituminous substance.—**Bituminize,** bi-tū′min-īz, *v.t.*—*bituminized, bituminizing.* To form into or impregnate with bitumen; to convert (as wood) into a bituminous body.—**Bituminous,** bi-tū′min-us, *a.* Having the qualities of bitumen; containing or yielding bitumen.

Bivalve, bī′valv, *n.* [L. prefix *bi*, double, and *valva*, a valve.] An animal of the molluscous class, having two valves, or a shell consisting of two parts which open by an elastic hinge and are closed by muscles, as the oyster, cockle, mussel, &c.; *bot.* a pericarp in which the seed-case opens or splits into two parts.—**Bivalve, Bivalvular,** bī′valv, bī-val′vū-lėr, *a.* Having two valves: said especially of the shells of molluscs.

Biventral, bī-ven′tral, *a.* [Prefix *bi*, and L. *venter*, belly.] With two bellies, as a muscle at the back of the neck.

Bivouac, biv′ö-ak, *n.* [Fr. *bivouac, bivac*, from G. *beiwache*; lit. by- or near-watch. WAKE, WATCH.] An encampment of soldiers in the open air without tents, each remaining dressed and with his weapons by him; a similar encampment of travellers, hunters, &c.—*v.i. bivouacked, bivouacking.* To encamp in bivouac; to pass the night in the open air without tents or covering.

Biweekly, bī-wēk′li, *a.* Occurring or appearing every two weeks (a *biweekly* magazine).

Bizarre, bi-zär′, *a.* [Fr., from Sp. *bizarro*, gallant, of Basque origin.] Old in appearance; fanciful; fantastical; formed of incongruous parts.

Blab, blab, *v.t.*—*blabbed, blabbing.* [Allied to L.G. *blabben*, Dan. *blabbre*, G. *plappern*, to gabble; Gael. *blabaran*, a stutterer; *blubber*-lipped, *blob*, &c.] To utter or tell in a thoughtless or unnecessary manner what ought to be kept secret; to let out (secrets).—*v.i.* To talk indiscreetly; to tattle; to tell tales.—*n.* One who blabs; a telltale. (*Mil.*)—**Blabber,** blab′ėr, *n.* A blab; a tattler; a tell-tale.

Black, blak, *a.* [A.Sax. *blæc, blac*, black= Icel. *blakkr*, O.H.G. *plak*, black; comp D. and L.G. *blaken*, to burn or scorch, Gr. *phlegō*, to burn, the original meaning perhaps referring to blackness caused by fire.] Of the darkest colour; the opposite of white; very dark in hue (though not absolutely incapable of reflecting light; destitute of light, or nearly so; dismal, gloomy, sullen, forbidding, or the like; destitute of moral light or goodness; mournful; calamitous; evil; wicked; atrocious.—*Black art*, the art of performing wonderful feats by supernatural means, or aided by evil spirits; necromancy; magic.—*Black beer*, a kind of beer of a black colour and syrupy consistence manufactured at Dantzic.—*Black cattle*, oxen, cows, &c., reared for slaughter, as distinguished from dairy cattle: used without reference to colour.—*Black death*, an oriental plague which first visited Europe in the fourteenth century, characterized by inflammatory boils and black spots all over the skin.—*Black flag*, the flag formerly assumed by pirates.—*Black list*, a printed list circulated among commercial men, containing the names of persons who have become bankrupt or unable to meet their bills, &c.—*Black snake*, a name given to some snakes of a black colour, such as a large non-venomous North American snake which feeds on birds and small quadrupeds. —*Black spruce*, a spruce tree belonging to North America, which furnishes the spruce deals of commerce.—*n.* The opposite of white; a black dye or pigment or a hue produced by such; a black part of something, as of the eye; a black dress or mourning: frequently in plural; a small flake of soot; a member of one of the dark-coloured races; a negro or other dark-skinned person.—*v.t.* To make black; to apply blacking to (shoes); to blacken; to soil.—**Blacken,** blak′n, *v.t.* To make black; to polish with blacking; to sully; to stain; to defame; to vilify; to slander.—*v.i.* To become black or dark.—**Blacking,** blak′ing, *n.* A composition for polishing boots, shoes, harness, &c., consisting usually of a mixture of lamp-black, oil, vinegar, &c.—**Blackish,** blak′ish, *a.* Somewhat black.—**Blackly,** blak′li, *adv.* In a black manner; darkly; gloomily; threateningly; angrily; atrociously.—**Blackness,** blak′nes, *n.* The state or quality of being black; black colour; darkness; gloominess; sombreness; sullen or severe aspect; atrocity.—**Blacky,** blak′i, *n.* A colloquial term for a negro or person of the dark-coloured races.—**Blackamoor,** blak′a-mör, *a.* [*Black*, and *Moor*, in the old sense of black man or negro, formerly written also *blackmoor*.] A negro; a black man or woman.—**Black-ball,** *v.t.* To reject, as a proposed member of a club; to exclude by vote.—**Black-band,** *n.* The most valuable kind of clay-ironstone (clay-carbonate) from which most of the Scotch iron is manufactured.—**Black-beetle,** *n.* A cockroach.—**Black-berry,** *n.* The berry of the bramble.—**Blackbird,** blak′bėrd, *n.* An insessorial bird of the thrush family, the male bird being characterized by its black plumage and its rich mellow note; the merle.—**Black-board,** *n.* A board painted black, used in schools and lecture-rooms for writing or drawing lines on for instruction.—**Black-cap,** *n.* A dentirostral British bird of the warbler family, noted for the sweetness of its song, and so called from its black tufted crown; a species of raspberry having black fruit, native to North America.—**Black-chalk,** *n.* A mineral of a bluish-black color, also a preparation of ivory-black and fine clay, used for drawing.—**Black-coat,** *n.* A colloquial name for a clergyman, as *red-coat* is for a soldier.—**Black-cock,** *n.* A bird of the grouse family, so called from the glossy black plumage of the male; the heath-cock or black grouse.—**Black-currant,** *n.* A well-known garden plant and its fruit, so called from its black berries.—**Black-draught,** *n.* A purgative medicine, consisting of the infusion of senna with sulphate of magnesia.—**Black-fisher,** *n.* Poacher.—**Black-flux,** *n.* A mixture of carbonate of potash and charcoal, used in melting metallic substances.—**Black-friar,** *n.* A friar of the Dominican order, so called from the colour of the dress; a Dominican.—**Blackguard,** blak′gärd or bla′gärd, *n.* [Formerly a name given to the scullions and lowest menials connected with a great household, who attended to the pots, coals, &c.] A man of coarse and offensive manners; a fellow of low character; a scamp; a scoundrel.—*v.t.* To revile in low or scurrilous language.—**Blackguardism,** blak′gärd-izm or bla′gärd-izm, *n.* The conduct or language of a blackguard. —**Blackguardly,** blak′gärd-li or bla′-gärd-li, *a.* Characteristic of a blackguard; rascally; villainous.—**Black-hearted,** *a.* Having a black or malignant heart.—**Black-hole,** *n.* Formerly a dungeon or dark cell in a prison; now more specifically applied to a place of confinement for soldiers. —**Black-jack,** *n.* A capacious can, now made of tin, but formerly of waxed leather; the flag or ensign of a pirate; a small leather-covered club or billy weighted at the head and having an elastic shaft; a card game.—**Black-lead,** *n.* Amorphous graphite; plumbago. GRAPHITE.—**Blackleg,** *n.* [Origin undecided.] One who systematically tries to win money by cheating in connection with races, or with cards, billiards, or other game; a rook; a swindler; also same as *Black-quarter*, a disease of cattle; anti-striker ('scab'), one who works for employer during a strike.—**Black-letter,** *n.* The old English or Gothic type used in early printed books, being an imitation of the written character in use before the art of printing, still in general use in German books.—**Black-mail,** *n.* [*-mail* is from Icel. *mál*, stipulation, agreement, *mæla*, to stipulate.] Money or an equivalent, anciently paid, in the north of England and in Scotland, to certain men allied with robbers, to be protected by them from pillage; hence, the act of demanding payment by means of intimidation; also extortion of money from a person by threats of public accusation, exposure, or censure.—**Black-out,** *a.* Pertaining to the dimming of a city's lights as a precaution against air raids.—*n.* The condition obtaining when lights have been dimmed.—**Black-quarter,** *n.* An apoplectic disease peculiar to cattle, indicated by lameness of the fore-foot and blackness of the flesh.—**Black-rod,** *n.* In England, the usher belonging to the order of the Garter, usher of parliament, and one of the official messengers of the House of Lords, so called from the black rod which he carries.—**Black-sheep,** *n.* A member of a family or society distinguished from his fellows by low habits or loose conduct.—**Blacksmith,** blak′smith, *n.* A smith who works in iron and makes iron utensils; an ironsmith: opposed to a *whitesmith* or tinsmith.—**Black-thorn,** *n.* The sloe.—**Black-tin,** *n.* Tin ore when dressed, stamped, and washed, ready for smelting.—**Black-vomit,** *n.* A blackish substance vomited in yellow fever; the fever itself.—**Black-wad,** *n.* An ore of manganese used as a dryer in paints.—**Black Watch,** *n.* [From their dark tartan.] The 42nd Regiment, raised to protect the Highlands.—**Black-water,** *n.* An African fever in which the urine is dark-coloured.

Bladder, blad′ėr, *n.* [A.Sax. *blǽdr, blǽddre*, a bladder, pustule, blister = Icel. *blathra*, Sw. *blåddra*, L.G. *bladere, bledder*, O.H.G. *plâtara*, a bladder, G. *blatter*, a pustule; the root is probably in E. to *blow*.] A thin membranous bag in animals, which serves as the receptacle of some secreted fluid, as the urine, the gall, &c.; any vesicle, blister, or pustule, especially if filled with air or a thin watery liquor; a hollow appendage in some plants.—*v.t.* To put up in a bladder, as lard; to puff up; to fill with windt.—**Bladdery,** blad′ėr-i, *a.* Resembling or containing bladders.

Blade, blād, *n.* [A.Sax. *blæd*, a leaf=D. Dan. Sw. *blad*, Icel. *blath*, G. *blatt*, a leaf; from root of to *blow*, and allied to *bloom*, *blossom*.] The leaf of a plant, especially the leaf or the young stalk or spire of grass or corn plants; a thing resembling a blade in shape, &c., as the cutting part of an instrument; the broad part of an oar; a dashing or rollicking fellow; a swaggerer; a rakish fellow.—*v.t.* To furnish with a blade.—*v.i.* To come into blade; to produce blades. —**Bladed,** blād′ed, *a.* Having a blade or blades.—**Blade-bone**, *n.* The scapula or upper-bone in the shoulder; the shoulder-blade.

Blaeberry, blā-ber'i, *n.* Blue berry.

Blain, blān, *n.* [A.Sax. *blegen*=D. *blein*, Dan. *blegn*, a blain, a blister: probably from root of to *blow*, and allied to *bladder*.] A pustule; a botch; a blister.

Blame, blām, *v.t.*—*blamed, blaming.* [Fr. *blâmer*, O.Fr. *blasmer*, from L.L. *blasphemare*, from Gr. *blasphemein*, to calumniate. *Blaspheme* is the same word.] To express disapprobation of (a person or thing); to find fault with; to censure; to reproach; to chide; to condemn; to upbraid. ∴ In such phrases as 'he is *to blame*,' *to blame* has the passive meaning = to be blamed, like 'a house to let,' &c.—*n.* An expression of disapprobation for something deemed to be wrong; imputation of a fault; censure; reproach; reprehension; that which is deserving of censure (the *blame* is yours); fault; crime; sin.—**Blamable**, blām'a-bl, *a.* Deserving of blame or censure; faulty; culpable; reprehensible; censurable. —**Blamableness**, blām'a-bl-nes, *n.* The state or quality of being blamable.—**Blamably**, blām'a-bli, *adv.* In a blamable manner; culpably.—**Blameful**, blām'fụl, *a.* Meriting blame; reprehensible; faulty; guilty; criminal.—**Blamefully**, blām'fụl-li, *adv.* In a blameful manner.—**Blamefulness**, blām'fụl-nes, *n.*—**Blameless**, blām'les, *a.* Not meriting blame or censure; without fault; undeserving of reproof; innocent; guiltless.—**Blamelessly**, blām'les-li, *adv.* In a blameless manner.—**Blamelessness**, blām'les-nes, *n.* —**Blamer**, blām'ėr, *n.* One who blames, finds fault, or censures.—**Blameworthy**, blām-wėr-ᴛʜi, *a.* Deserving blame; censurable, culpable; reprehensible.—**Blameworthiness**, blām'wėr-ᴛʜi-nes, *n.*

Blanch, blansh, *v.t.* [Fr. *blanchir*, to whiten, from *blanc*, white. Blank.] To whiten by depriving of colour; to render white, pale, or colourless (fear *blanches* the cheek); *hort.* to whiten or prevent from turning green by excluding the light, a process applied to kitchen vegetables, such as celery, lettuce, sea-kale, &c.; to whiten or make lustrous, as metals, by acids or other means.—*v.i.* To become white; to bleach. —**Blancher**, blansh'ėr, *n.* One who blanches or whitens.

Blanc-mange, Blanc-manger, bla-manzh', blan̄-man̄-zhā, *n.* [Fr. *blanc*, white, and *manger*, food.] *Cookery*, a preparation of the consistency of a jelly, variously composed of dissolved isinglass, arrow-root, maize-flour, &c., with milk and flavouring substances.

Bland, bland, *a.* [L. *blandus*, mild.] Mild; soft; gentle (*bland* zephyrs); affable; suave (his manner is very *bland*); soothing; kindly. —**Blandness**, bland'nes, *n.* State of being bland; mildness; gentleness.—**Blandiloquence**,† blan-dil'ō-kwens, *n.* [L. *blandiloquentia*—*blandus*, mild, and *loquor*, to speak.] Fair, mild, flattering speech; compliment.

Blandish, blan'dish, *v.t.* & *i.* [O.Fr. *blandir*, *blandissant*, L. *blandior*, to flatter, from *blandus*, bland.] To render pleasing, alluring, or enticing; to caress, soothe, fawn, or flatter. — **Blandisher**, blan'dish-ėr, *n.* One that blandishes; one that flatters with soft words.—**Blandishment**, blan'dish-ment, *n.* Words or actions expressive of affection or kindness, and tending to win the heart; artful caresses; flattering attention; cajolery; endearment.

Blank, blangk, *a.* [Fr. *blanc*, white, blank, from G. *blank*, white, lustrous, blank, from *blinken*, to *blink*, to glimmer; cog. D. Dan. and Sw. *blank*, white. Blink.] White or pale†; void of written or printed characters, as paper; wanting something necessary to completeness; vacant; unoccupied; void; empty; pale from fear or terror; hence, confused; confounded; dispirited; dejected; unrhymed: applied to verse.—*n.* A piece of paper without writing or printed matter on it; a void space on paper or in any written or printed document; a document remaining incomplete till something essential is filled in; any void space; a void; a vacancy; a ticket in a lottery on which no prize is indicated; a lot by which nothing is gained; *archery*, the white mark in the centre of a butt or target to which an arrow is directed; hence, the object to which anything is directed; aim; a piece of metal prepared to be formed into something useful by a further operation; a plate, or piece of gold or silver, cut and shaped, but not stamped into a coin.—*v.t.*‡ To make white or pale; confuse, confound, dispirit. (*Shak.*) —**Blankly**, blangk'li, *adv.* In a blank manner; with paleness or confusion. — **Blankness**, blangk'nes, *n.* State of being blank. — **Blank-cartridge**, *n.* A cartridge filled with powder but having no ball.

Blanket, blang'ket, *n.* [O.Fr. *blanket*, dim. from *blanc*, white. Blank.] A soft thick cloth made of wool loosely woven, and used as a covering in beds; any similar fabric used as covering, &c.—*v.t.* To toss in a blanket by way of punishment; to cover or clothe with a blanket (*Shak.*).

Blare, blār, *v.i.*—*blared, blaring.* [Probably an imitative word; comp. D. *blaren*, L.G. *blarren*, *blaren*, G. *blarren*, *blärren*, to bellow, bleat, blare.] To give forth a loud sound like a trumpet; to give out a brazen sound; to bellow.—*v.t.* To sound loudly; to proclaim noisily.—*n.* Sound like that of a trumpet; noise; roar.

Blarney, blär'ni, *n.* [From Castle *Blarney*, near Cork, in the wall of which is a stone said to endow any one who kisses it with skill in the use of flattery.] Excessively complimentary language; gross flattery; smooth, deceitful talk; gammon. (Colloq.)—*v.t.* To talk over by soft delusive speeches; to flatter; to humbug with talk. (Colloq.)

Blasé, blä-zā. [Fr.] Lost to the power of enjoyment; used up; having the healthy energies exhausted.

Blaspheme, blas-fēm', *v.t.*—*blasphemed, blaspheming.* [L. *blasphemare*, Gr. *blasphēmein*, to calumniate—from *blapsis*, injury, and *phēmi*, to speak. *Blame* is a shortened form of this word.] To speak in terms of impious irreverence of; to revile or speak reproachfully of instead of reverentially: used of speaking against God or things sacred.—*v.i.* To utter blasphemy; to use blasphemous language. — **Blasphemer**, blas-fēm'ėr, *n.* One who blasphemes; one who speaks of God in impious and irreverent terms.—**Blasphemous**, blas'fē-mus, *a.* Containing or exhibiting blasphemy; impiously irreverent or reproachful toward God. — **Blasphemously**, blas'fē-mus-li, *adv.* In a blasphemous manner.— **Blasphemy**, blas'fē-mi, *n.* The language of one who blasphemes; words uttered impiously against God; grossly irreverent or outrageous language.

Blast, blast, *n.* [A.Sax. *blaest*, a puff of wind, from *blaesan*, to blow = Icel. *blástr*, Dan. *blæst*, a blowing; Icel. *blása*, Dan. *blæse*, G. *blasen*, to blow; same root as E. *blow*, *blase*.] A gust or puff of wind; a sudden gust of wind; the sound made by blowing a wind-instrument, as a horn or trumpet; the sound produced by one breath; a blight or sudden pernicious influence on animals or plants; a forcible stream of air from the mouth, bellows, &c.; a violent explosion of gunpowder or other explosive in splitting rocks, &c. — *v.t.* To injure by a blast; to cause to fade, shrivel, or wither; to blight or cause to come to nothing; to ruin; to split by an explosion. — *v.i.* To wither or be blighted. (*Shak.*) — **Blast-engine**, *n.* A ventilating machine used to draw off foul air; a machine for producing a blast by compressing air.—**Blast-furnace**, *n.* The smelting furnace used for obtaining iron from its ores with the aid of a powerful blast of air, usually a lofty furnace of masonry, in which the iron is smelted from its ore by being mixed with coal and the whole mass kept burning, the melted metal being run off at the bottom. —**Blasting-powder**, *n.* A coarse kind of gunpowder for mining and quarrying purposes.—**Blast-pipe**, *n.* The pipe of a locomotive steam-engine which carries the waste steam up the chimney, and thus induces a stronger draught.

Blastema, blas-tē'ma, *n.* [Gr. *blastēma*, a shoot, growth, from *blastano*, to bud.] *Bot.* the axis of growth of an embryo; that part of the embryo comprising the radicle and plumule, with the intervening portion.— **Blastemal**, blas-tē'mal, *a.* Relating to blastema; rudimentary.

Blastocarpous, blas-tō-kär'pus, *a.* [Gr. *blastos*, a germ, and *karpos*, fruit.] Having the germ beginning to grow inside the pericarp of the fruit.—**Blastoderm**, blas'tō-dėrm, *n.* [Gr. *derma*, a skin.] *Anat.* the germinal skin or membrane; the superficial layer of the embryo in its earliest condition.—**Blastodermic**, blas-tō-dėr'mik, *a.* Relating to the blastoderm.—**Blastogenesis**, blas-tō-jen'e-sis, *n.* *Biol.* reproduction by germination or budding.

Blastula, blas'tū-la, *n.* [From Gr. *blastos*, a germ.] An embryo so far developed from a germ or ovum as to consist of a sack formed of a single layer of cells.—**Blastulation**, blas-tū-lā'shon, *n.* The process by which a germ becomes a blastula.

Blatant, blā'tant, *a.* [From Prov. E. *blate*, to *bleat*, with suffix *-ant*, as in *errant*, &c.] Bellowing; bawling; noisy.

Blaze, blāz, *n.* [A. Sax. *blæse*, a blaze, a torch, from root of *blow*; comp. Icel. *blys*, Dan. *blus*, a torch; akin to *blast*.] The stream of light and heat from any body when burning; a flame; brilliant sunlight; effulgence; brilliance; a bursting out; an active or violent display (a *blaze* of wrath). —*v.i.*—*blazed, blazing.* To flame; to send forth or show a bright and expanded light. —**Blazer**, blāz'ėr, *n.* That which blazes; a bright-coloured jacket or short coat suited for sports, &c.—**Blazing**, blāz'ing, *a.* Emitting a blaze; flaming.

Blaze, blāz, *v.t.*—*blazed, blazing.* [A. Sax. *blaesan*, to blow=Icel. *blása*, Dan. *blæse*, G. *blasen*, to blow, to sound as a trumpet. Blast, Blow.] To make known to all; to noise or bruit abroad; to proclaim.

Blaze, blāz, *n.* [D. *bles*, Icel. *blesi*, Dan. *blis*, a white spot or streak on the forehead.] A white spot on the forehead or face of a horse or other quadruped; a white spot on a tree by removing the bark with a hatchet. —*v.t.* To set a blaze on, by paring off part of the bark; to indicate or mark out, as a path, by paring off the bark of a number of trees in succession.

Blazon, blā'zn, *n.* [O.E. *blasoun*, *blason*, Fr. *blason*, heraldry, *blasonner*, to blazon, from a G. word equivalent to E. *blaze*, to spread abroad or make known.] The drawing or representation on coats of arms; a heraldic figure; show; pompous display, by words or other means (*Shak.*).—*v.t.* To explain, in proper terms, the figures on ensigns armorial; to deck; to embellish; to adorn; to display; to publish; to celebrate.— **Blazoner**, blā'zn-ėr, *n.* One that blazons; a herald; one prone to spread reports; a propagator of scandal. — **Blazonment**, blā'zn-ment, *n.* The act of blazoning; emblazonment.—**Blazonry**, blā'zn-ri, *n.* The art of describing or explaining coats of arms in proper heraldic terms and method; emblazonry.

Bleach, blēch, *v.t.* [A. Sax. *blaecan*, from *blaec*, pale, white. Bleak.] To make white or whiter by taking out colour; to whiten; to blanch; to whiten by exposure to the action of the air and sunlight or of chemical preparations.—*v.i.* To grow white in any manner.—**Bleacher**, blēch'ėr, *n.* One who bleaches; one whose occupation is to whiten cloth. — **Bleachery**, blēch'ėr-i, *n.* An establishment where bleaching textile fabrics or the like is carried on.— **Bleachfield**, blēch'fēld, *n.* A piece of ground where cloth or yarn is bleached, often connected with a bleachery.—**Bleaching**, blēch'ing, *n.* The act or art of freeing textile fibres and fabrics and various other substances from their natural colour, and rendering them white. — **Bleaching-powder**, *n.* Chloride of lime made by exposing slaked lime to the action of chlorine.

Bleak, blēk, *a.* [A. Sax. *blaec*=Icel. *bleikr*, D. *bleek*, G. *bleich*, pale, pallid, white; allied to A. Sax. *blícan*, Icel. *blíkja*, G. *blicken*, to shine, to gleam, E. to *blink*. *Bleach* is from this word.] Exposed to cold and winds (situation, tract of land); desolate; ungenial; cheerless; dreary; cold; chill (*bleak* winds).—**Bleakish**, blēk'ish, *a.* Moderately bleak.—**Bleakly**, blēk'li, *adv.* In a bleak manner; coldly.—**Bleakness**, blēk'nes, *n.* State of being bleak; coldness; desolation.—**Bleaky**,† blēk'i, *a.* Bleak; unsheltered; cold; chill.

Bleak, blēk, *n.* [So called from the *bleak* or pale colour of its scales.] A small river fish, 5 or 6 inches long, belonging to the carp family, occurring in many European and English rivers.

Blear, blēr, *a.* [L.G. *blarr*, *bleer*, blear; Sw. *blira*, Dan. *blire*, *plire*, to twinkle, to wink; Dan. *pliiröiet*, blear-eyed.] Sore, with a watery rheum: said of the eyes.—*v.t.* To make sore so that the sight is indistinct; to affect with soreness of eyes; to make rheumy and dim; *fig.* to hoodwink or deceive. — **Blearedness**, blēr'ed-nes, *n.* The state of being bleared or dimmed with rheum. — **Blear-eyed**, *a.* Having sore eyes; having the eyes dim with rheum; dim-sighted; wanting in perception or understanding.

Bleat, blēt, *v.i.* [A. Sax. *blaetan*=D. *blaten*, *bleeten*, L.G. *blaten*, *bleten*, to bleat, probably an imitative word.] To utter the cry of a sheep or a similar cry.—**Bleat**, **Bleating**, blēt'ing, *n.* The cry of a sheep. —**Bleater**, blēt'ėr, *n.* One who bleats; a sheep.

Bleed, blēd, *v.i.*—*bled* (pret. & pp.), *bleeding*. [A. Sax. *blēdan*, from *blód*, blood=D. *bloeden*, Icel. *blœtha*, Dan. *blöde*, to bleed.] To lose blood; to be drained of blood; to run with blood; to let sap or other moisture flow from itself; to trickle or flow, as from an incision; to have money extorted, or to part with it freely to some wheedling or unworthy party (colloq.).—*v.t.* To take blood from by opening a vein; to emit or distil (a tree *bleeds* juice, sap, or gum); to extort or extract money from (colloq.).—**Bleeding**, blēd'ing, *n.* A running or issuing of blood; a hemorrhage; the operation of letting blood, as in surgery; the drawing of sap from a tree or plant.

Bleek-bok, blāk'bok, *n.* [D. *bleek*, pale, *bok*, buck.] The pale-buck, a South African species of antelope.

Blemish, blem'ish, *v.t.* [O.Fr. *blemir*, *blemissant*, to spot, to beat one blue, from Icel. *blāman*, the livid colour of a wound, from *blár*, blue, livid. BLUE.] To injure or impair; to mar or make defective; to deface; to sully; to tarnish, as reputation or character; to defame.—*n.* A defect, flaw, or imperfection; something that mars beauty, completeness, perfection, or reputation.

Blench, blensh, *v.i.* [Probably a softened form of *blink*, in old sense to wink; hence, to turn aside, to flinch; *blanch* seems to have been partly confounded with it.] To shrink; to start back; to give way; to flinch; to turn aside, as from pain, fear, repugnance, &c.—*n.* A start back; a deviation; aberration.

Blend, blend, *v.t.*—*blended* (pret.), *blended* or *blent* (pp.), *blending*. [A. Sax. *blandan*, to mix=Icel. and Sw. *blanda*, Dan. *blande*, to mix; allied to *blind*, originally turbid. BLIND.] To mix or mingle together; to confound so that the separate things mixed cannot be distinguished.—*v.i.* To be mixed; to become united; to merge insensibly the one into the other (as colours).—*n.* A mixture, as of liquids, colours, &c.; a mixture of spirits from different distilleries.—**Blending**, blend'ing, *n.* The act of one who blends; *painting*, a process by which the pigments are made to melt or blend together; the effect or result of such process.

Blende, blend, *n.* [G. *blende*, blend, from *blenden*, to blind, to dazzle.] An ore of zinc, of which there are several varieties; a native sulphide of zinc. This word is also employed in such compound terms as manganese blende, zinc blende, ruby blende.

Blenheim, blen'em, *n.* One of a breed of dogs of the spaniel kind, preserved in perfection at Blenheim Palace in Oxfordshire, the seat of the Dukes of Marlborough.

Blennogenous, blen-noj'en-us, *a.* [Gr. *blennos*, mucus, and root *gen*, to produce.] *Med.* producing or generating mucus. —**Blennorrhœa**, blen-no-rē'a, *n.* [Gr. *rheō*, to flow.] A flow of mucus; gonorrhœa.

Blenny, blen'i, *n.* [L. *blennius*, from Gr. *blennos*, slime.] The name of several small fishes frequenting rocky coasts.

Blepharitis, blef-a-rī'tis, *n.* [Gr. *blepharon*, eyelid.] Inflammation of the eyelids.

Bles-bok, bles'bok, *n.* [D. *bles*, a blaze or spot on the forehead, and *bok*, a buck.] An antelope of Cape Colony, with a white face.

Bless, bles, *v.t.*—*blessed* or *blest*, *blessing*. [A. Sax. *bletsian*, *bledsian*, to bless, from *blód*, blood; originally perhaps to consecrate by sprinkling blood.] To invoke the divine favour on; to express a wish for the good fortune or happiness of; to bestow happiness, prosperity, or good things of any kind upon (*blest* with peace and plenty); to make and pronounce holy; to consecrate; to glorify for benefits received; to extol for excellencies (to *bless* the Lord; to esteem or account happy: with the reflexive pronoun.—*Bless me! bless my soul!* expressions of surprise.—**Blessed**, bles'ed, *a.* [As pret. and pp. *blessed* is now commonly pronounced *blest*, and is also so written.] Enjoying happiness; favoured with blessings; highly favoured; happy; fortunate; enjoying spiritual blessings and the favour of God; fraught with or imparting blessings; sacred; hallowed; holy.—**Blessedly**, bles'ed-li, *adv.* In a blessed or fortunate manner; joyfully. —**Blessedness**, bles'ed-nes, *n.* The state of being blessed; happiness; felicity; heavenly joys; the favour of God.—*Single blessedness*, the unmarried state; celibacy.—**Blesser**, bles'ėr, *n.* One that blesses.—**Blessing**, bles'ing, *n.* The act of one who blesses; a prayer or solemn wish imploring happiness upon another; a benediction; the act of pronouncing a benediction or blessing; that which promotes temporal prosperity and welfare or secures immortal felicity; any good thing falling to one's lot; a mercy.

Blew, blö, pret. of *blow*.

Blewits, blū'its, *n.* [Corruption of *blue hats*.] The popular name in England of a purplish mushroom common in meadows in autumn.

Blight, blīt, *n.* [Possibly from prefix *be*, and *light*, the original meaning being perhaps to scorch or blast as by lightning.] Something that nips, blasts, or destroys plants; a diseased state of plants; smut, mildew, or other plant disease; *fig.* something that frustrates, blasts, destroys, brings to nought, &c.—*v.t.* To affect with blight; to cause to wither or decay; to blast; to frustrate.—*v.i.* To injure or blast as blight does.—**Blighted**, blīt'ed, *a.* Smitten with blight; blasted (*blighted* hopes).—**Blighting**, blīt'ing, *a.* Producing the effects of blight; blasting; destroying.—**Blightingly**, blīt'ing-li, *adv.* By blighting.

Blighty, blī'ti, *n.* [Ar. *viláyat*, a foreign country, more particularly Britain. Soldier-Hindustani, *blatty*, by Cockney pronunciation *blighty*.] Home, *going home to Blighty*, word and phrase in the Indian army, extended to home generally.

Blimp, blimp, *n.* A non-rigid costal airship of the smallest size, with fuselage similar to aeroplane.

Blind, blīnd, *a.* [A. Sax. D. Icel. Sw. Dan. G. *blind*; originally meaning turbid or cloudy, and allied to *blend*, to mix.] Destitute of the sense of sight; not having sight; not having the faculty of discernment; destitute of intellectual, moral, or spiritual light; not easily discernible; dark; obscure (*blind* paths, *blind* mazes); indiscriminate; heedless (*blind* wrath); without openings for admitting light (*blind* window), or otherwise wanting something ordinarily essential; closed at one end; having no outlet (a *blind* alley).—*v.t.* To make physically, morally, or intellectually blind; to render incapable of clear vision (*blinded* by passion); to darken; to obscure to the eye or to the mind; to conceal ('to *blind* the truth'. *Tenn.*); to eclipse.—*n.* Something to hinder sight, to intercept a view, or keep out light; a screen of some sort to prevent too strong a light from shining in at a window, or to keep people from seeing in; something ostensible to conceal a covert design; a cover; a pretext. — **Blindage**, blīn'dāj, *n.* *Milit.* a kind of screen made of timber and earth, used to protect men in fortresses.—**Blind-beetle**, *n.* A name for the cockchafer.—**Blinder**, blīnd'ėr, *n.* One who or that which blinds; a blinker on a horse's bridle. —**Blindfold**, blīnd'fōld, *a.* Having the eyes covered, as with a bandage; having the mental eye darkened (*Shak.*).—*v.t.* To cover the eyes of; to hinder from seeing by binding something round the eyes.—**Blinding**, blīnd'ing, *a.* Making blind; preventing from seeing clearly; depriving of sight or of understanding.—**Blindingly**, blīnd'ing-li, *adv.* In a blinding manner; so as to blind.—**Blindly**, blīnd'li, *adv.* In a blind manner; without sight or understanding; without examination; regardlessly; recklessly.—**Blindman's-buff**, **Blind-Harry**, *n.* A play in which one person is blindfolded and tries to catch some one of the company and tell who it is.—**Blindness**, blīnd'nes, *n.* State of being blind; want of bodily sight; mental darkness; ignorance.—**Blind-tooling**, *n.* In *bookbinding*, the ornamental impressions of heated tools upon leather without the interposition of gold-leaf, ink, &c. — **Blind-worm**, *n.* [So called because, its eyes being very minute, it has popularly been supposed to be blind.] A small harmless worm-like reptile, called also slow-worm, connecting the serpents and lizards.

Blink, blingk, *v.i.* [Same word as D. *blinken*, Dan. *blinke*, Sw. *blinka*, G. *blinken*, to shine, glance, twinkle; allied to A.Sax *blícan*, to gleam, D. *blikken*, Dan. *blikke*, G. *blicken*, to glance, to glimpse. Akin *blank*, *blench*, *bleach*.] To wink; to twinkle; to see with the eyes half shut or with frequent winking; to get a glimpse; to peep (*Shak.*); to intermit light; to glimmer.—*v.t.* To shut one's eyes to; to avoid or purposely evade (to *blink* a question or topic).—*n.* A glance of the eye; a glimpse; a gleam; a glimmer; the gleam or glimmer reflected from ice in the Arctic regions.—**Blinkard**, bling'kėrd, *n.* A person who blinks or has bad eyes.—**Blinker**, bling'kėr, *n.* One who blinks; a leather flap placed on either side of a horse's head, to prevent him from seeing sideways or backwards.—**Blinky**,† bling'ki, *a.* Prone to blink or wink.

Bliss, blis, *n.* [A.Sax. *blis*, *bliss*, joy, alacrity, exultation, from *blithe*, blithe. BLITHE.] The highest degree of happiness; blessedness; felicity; often specifically heavenly felicity.—**Blissful**, blis'fụl, *a.* Full of, abounding in, enjoying, or conferring bliss.—**Blissfully**, blis'fụl-li, *adv.* In a blissful manner. — **Blissfulness**, blis'fụl-nes, *n.* Exalted happiness; felicity; fulness of joy.

Blister, blis'tėr, *n.* [Connected with *blast*, to blow or puff, from same root as to *blow*; comp. G. *blase*, a blister, a bladder.] A thin vesicle on the skin, containing watery matter or serum; a pustule; an elevation made by the separation of an external film or skin, as on plants; something applied to the skin to raise a blister; a vesicatory.—*v.t.* To raise a blister or blisters on.—*v.i.* To rise in blisters or become blistered.—**Blister-beetle**, **Blister-fly**, *n.* A beetle used to raise a blister on the skin; the Spanish-fly.—**Blistering**, blis'tėr-ing, *a.* Causing or tending to cause blisters.—**Blister-plaster**, *n.* A plaster of cantharides or Spanish-flies designed to raise a blister.—**Blister-steel**, *n.* Iron bars which, when converted into steel, have their surface covered with blisters.—**Blistery**, blis'tėr-i, *a.* Full of blisters.

Blithe, blīth, *a.* [A.Sax. *blíthe*, blithe, joyful; O.Sax. *blíthi*, clear, joyful; Goth. *bleiths*, merciful; Icel. *blíthr*, Dan. *blid*, bland; D. *blijde*, blithe. Hence *bliss*.] Gay; merry; joyous; sprightly; mirthful; characterized by blitheness or joy.—**Blithely**, blīᴛʜ'li, *adv.* In a blithe, gay, or joyful manner.—**Blitheness**, blīᴛʜ'nes, *n.* The quality of being blithe; gaiety; sprightliness.—**Blithesome**, blīᴛʜ'sum, *a.* Full of blitheness or gaiety; gay; merry; cheerful.

Blitzkrieg, blits'krēg, *n.* [G. *Blitz*, lightning, and *Krieg*, war.] A technique of warfare developed by German strategists, consisting of swift strokes designed to pierce the enemy's lines, disrupt his communications and supply systems, and separate his forces so that they can be destroyed piecemeal.

Blizzard, bliz'ard, *n.* [Akin to *blaze, blast.* Originally provincial English, but general in American literature since 1880.] A biting-cold snow-storm.

Bloat, blōt, *v.t.* [Allied to Icel. *blautr* soaked and soft; Sw. *blōt*, soaked, *blōta*, to soak, to cure fish by soaking.] To make turgid or swollen, as with air, water, &c.; to cause to swell, as in adenia; to inflate; to make vain; to cure by smoking, as herrings.—*v.i.* To become swollen; to dilate.

Blob, blob, *n.* [Also in form *bleb*, and allied to *blab, blubber*.] A small globe of liquid; a dewdrop; a blister; a bubble.

Block, blok, *n.* [Same word as D. and Dan. *blok*, G. and Sw. *block*, a block, a log, a lump; Ir. *blog*, a fragment.] Any solid mass of matter, usually with one or more plane or approximately plane faces; a lump; a stock or stupid person; the mass of wood on which criminals lay their necks when they are beheaded; any obstruction or cause of obstruction; a stop; the state of being blocked or stopped up; a casing or shell containing one or more pulleys over which a rope or chain works; a connected mass of buildings; a portion of a city inclosed by streets; a mold or piece on which something is shaped, or placed to make it keep in shape; a piece of wood on which an engraving is cut.—*v.t.* To hinder egress or passage from or to; to stop up or barricade; to obstruct; to act in opposition or by interference, as in boxing, football, cricket; to mold, shape, or stretch on a block.—*To block out*, to begin to reduce to the required shape; to shape out.—**Blockade**, blok-ād', *n.* [Comp. such words as *barricade, stockade, palisade*, &c.] The shutting up of a place by surrounding it with hostile troops or ships with a view to compel a surrender, by hunger and want, without regular attacks.—*To raise a blockade*, to remove or break up a blockade.—*v.t. blockaded, blockading.* To subject to a blockade; to prevent ingress to or egress from by warlike means; to shut up or in by obstacles of any kind; to obstruct.—**Blockader**, blok-ād'ėr, *n.* One who blockades; a vessel employed in blockading. **Blockhead**, blok'hed, *n.* A stupid fellow; a dolt; a stock; a person deficient in understanding.—**Block-house**, *n. Milit.* a strong building of one or more stories, so named because constructed chiefly of logs or beams of timber, having loopholes for musketry.—**Blocking-course**, *n.* The course of stones or bricks erected on the upper part of a cornice to make a termination.—**Blockish**, blok'ish, *a.* Like a block; stupid; dull; deficient in understanding. (*Shak.*)—**Block-printing**, *n.* The process or art of printing from engraved blocks of wood.—**Block-system**, *n.* The system of working the traffic on a railway, according to which the line is divided into short sections, and no train is allowed to enter upon any one section till it is signalled wholly clear, so that between two successive trains there is an interval of time as well as one of space.—**Block-tin**, *n.* Tin cast into ingots or blocks.

Blond, Blonde, blond, *a.* [Fr. *blond, blonde*, a word of Teutonic origin; comp. D. and G. *blond*, fair, flaxen; A.Sax. *blonden*, grayish or grizzled; allied to *blend*.] Of a fair colour or complexion.—*n.* A person (especially a woman) of very fair complexion, with light hair and light-blue eyes.—**Blondness**, blond'nes, *n.* The state of being blond; fairness.—**Blond-lace**, *n.* Lace made of silk, originally of unbleached silk, from the yellowish colour of which the name was given, now of white, black, or coloured silk. Also called *Blond.*

Blood, blud, *n.* [O.E. *blod, blode*, &c., A.Sax. *blód*=Goth. *bloth*, Icel. *blóth*, Dan. Sw. *blod*, L.G. *blood*, D. *bloed*, G. *blut*; root probably seen in to *blow* (as a flower), *bloom*, from the brightness of its colour.] The fluid which circulates through the arteries and veins of the human body and that of other animals, and which is essential to life and nutrition—in man and the higher animals of a more or less red colour; relationship by descent from a common ancestor (allied by *blood*); consanguinity; lineage; kindred; family; birth; extraction; often high birth; good extraction; natural disposition; temper; spirit (to do a thing in hot *blood* or cold *blood*, that is in anger or deliberately); mettle; passion; anger (his *blood* was up).—*The blood*, the royal family or royal lineage; thus it is common to speak of princes of *the blood.*—*Flesh and blood*, human nature; mortal man.—*v.t.* To let blood; to bleed; to stain with blood; to inure to blood; to give a taste of blood.—**Blood-bought**, *a.* Bought or obtained at the expense of life or by the shedding of blood.—**Blood-guiltiness**, *n.* The state of being blood-guilty; the guilt or crime of shedding blood.—**Blood-guilty**, *a.* Guilty of murder.—**Blood-horse**, *n.* A horse of a breed derived originally from a cross with the Arabian horse, combining lightness, strength, swiftness, and endurance.—**Blood-hound**, *n.* A large variety of dog with long smooth and pendulous ears, remarkable for the acuteness of its smell, and employed to recover game or prey by scent.—**Bloodily**, blud'i-li, *adv.* In a bloody manner; cruelly.—**Bloodiness**, blud'i-nes, *n.* The state of being bloody; disposition to shed blood; murderousness.—**Bloodless**, blud'les, *a.* Without blood; drained of blood; dead; without shedding of blood or slaughter (a *bloodless* victory); without spirit or activity.—**Bloodlessly**, blud'les-li, *adv.* In a bloodless manner; without bloodshed.—**Blood-letting**, blud'let-ing, *n.* The act of letting blood by opening a vein.—**Blood-money**, *n.* Money earned by the shedding of blood or by laying, or supporting, a charge implying peril to the life of an accused person.—**Blood-relation**, *n.* One related by blood or descent.—**Bloodshed**, blud'shed, *n.* The shedding or spilling of blood; slaughter; waste of life.—**Bloodshedder**, blud'shed-ėr, *n.* One who sheds blood; a murderer.—**Bloodshedding**, blud'shed-ing, *n.* The crime of shedding blood or taking human life.—**Bloodshot**, blud'-shot, *a.* Red and inflamed by a turgid state of the blood-vessels: said of the eye.—**Blood-spavin**, *n.* A dilatation of the vein that runs along the inside of the hock of a horse, forming a soft swelling.—**Blood-stained**, *a.* Stained with blood; guilty of slaughter.—**Blood-stone**, *n.* A stone worn as an amulet, to prevent bleeding at the nose; red hematite; a species of heliotrope dotted with spots of jasper.—**Blood-sucker**, *n.* Any animal that sucks blood, as a leech, a fly, &c.; a hard niggardly man; an extortioner.—**Bloodthirstiness**, blud'thėrs-ti-nes, *n.* Thirst for shedding blood.—**Bloodthirsty**, blud'thėrs-ti, *a.* Desirous to shed blood; murderous.—**Blood-vessel**, *n.* Any vessel in which blood circulates in an animal body; an artery or a vein.—**Blood-warm**, *a.* Warm as blood; lukewarm.—**Bloody**, blud'i, *a.* Of or pertaining to blood; consisting of, containing, or exhibiting blood; blood-stained; cruel; murderous; given to the shedding of blood; attended with much bloodshed.—**Bloody-flux**, *n.* The dysentery, a disease in which the discharges from the bowels have a mixture of blood.—**Bloody-minded**, *a.* Having a cruel, ferocious disposition; barbarous; inclined to shed blood.

Bloom, blōm, *n.* [Same word as Icel. *blóm*, Sw. *blomma*, Dan. *blomme*, Goth. *bloma*, D. *bloem*, G. *blume*, a flower, from stem of *blow*, to blossom; akin *blossom*.] A blossom; the flower of a plant; the act or state of blossoming; fulness of life and vigour; a period of high success; a flourishing condition; the delicate rose hue on the cheek indicative of youth and health; a glow; a flush; a superficial coating or appearance upon certain things, as the delicate powdery coating upon certain fruits when newly gathered.—*v.i.* To produce or yield blossoms; to blossom; to flower; to show the beauty of youth; to glow.—*v.t.*‡ To put forth, as blossoms. (O.T.)—**Blooming**, blōm'ing, *a.* Showing blooms; glowing as with youthful vigour.—**Bloomingly**, blōm'ing-li, *adv.* In a blooming manner.—**Bloomingness**, blōm'ing-nes, *n.*—**Bloomy**, blō'mi, *a.* Full of bloom or blossoms; flowery; having freshness or vigour as of youth; having a delicate powdery appearance, as fresh fruit.

Bloom, blōm, *n.* [A.Sax. *blóma*, a mass or lump of metal.] A lump of puddled iron, which leaves the furnace in a rough state, to be subsequently rolled into the bars or other material into which it may be desired to convert the metal.—**Bloomary, Bloomery**, blōm'a-ri, blōm'ėr-i, *n.* The first forge through which iron passes after it is melted from the ore.

Bloomer, blōm'ėr, *n.* [After Mrs. *Bloomer*, an American lady, who originated the style of dress in 1849.] Loose trousers gathered about the knees and worn by women engaged in athletics; also a woman's undergarment of similar design.

Blossom, blos'om, *n.* [A.Sax. *blóstma*, a blossom, from same root as *bloom* (which see).] The flower of a plant, consisting of one or more coloured leaflets, generally of more delicate texture than the leaves; the bloom; blooming state or period (the plant is in *bloom*).—*v.i.* To put forth blossoms or flowers; to bloom; to flourish.—**Blossomed**, blos'omd, *a.* Covered with blossoms; in bloom.—**Blossomy**,† blos'om-i, *a.* Full of or covered with blossoms.

Blot, blot, *n.* [Same word as Icel. *blettr*, Dan. *plet*, a blot; Dan. dial. *blat*, a drop, a spot of something wet.] A spot or stain, as of ink on paper; a blur; an obliteration of something written or printed; a spot in reputation; a blemish.—*v.t.*—*blotted, blotting.* To spot, to stain, as with ink; to stain with infamy; to tarnish; to obliterate or efface: in this sense generally with *out*; to dry by means of blotting-paper or the like.—**Blotter**, blot'ėr, *n.* One who or that which blots.—**Blotting-paper**, *n.* A species of unsized paper, serving to imbibe the superfluous ink from newly written manuscript, &c.

Blotch, bloch, *n.* [For *blatch, blach*, a softened form of *black* (comp. *bleak, bleach*), the meaning being influenced by *botch*, a pustule.] A pustule or eruption on the skin; an irregular spot.—*v.t.* To mark with blotches.—**Blotched, Blotchy**, blocht, bloch'i, *a.* Marked with blotches.

Blouse, blouz or blös, *n.* [Fr.] A light loose upper garment, resembling a smock-frock, made of linen or cotton, and worn by men as a protection from dust or in place of a coat; also, a dress of nearly the same form and of various materials worn by women and children.—**Bloused**, bloust, *a.* Wearing a blouse.

Blow, blō, *v.i.*—*blew, blown, blowing.* [A.Sax. *bláwan*; allied to G. *blähen*, to blow, Icel. *blása*, Goth. *blésan*, G. *blasen*, to blow, to blow a wind-instrument; also to E. *blow*, to bloom, *bladder, blast*, &c., and L. *flo, flare*, to breathe or blow.] To make a current of air, as with the mouth, a bellows, &c.; to constitute or form a current of air; to be a wind: often used with an indefinite *it* for the subject (*it blew* strongly yesterday); to pant; to puff; to breathe hard or quick; to give out sound by being blown, as a horn or trumpet; to boast; to brag: in this sense colloq.—*To blow over*, to pass away after having spent its force (the storm *blew over*).—*To blow up*, to be broken and scattered by an explosion.—*To blow upon*, to bring into disfavour or discredit; to render stale, unsavoury, or worthless; also to inform upon.—*v.t.* To throw or drive a current of air upon; to drive by a current of air; to sound by the breath (a wind-instrument); to form by inflation (to *blow* a glass bottle); to swell by injecting air into; to put out of breath by fatigue; to scatter or shatter by explosives (to *blow* up, to *blow* to pieces).—*To blow out*, to extinguish by a current of air; to scatter (one's brains) by firearms.—*To blow up*, to fill with air; to swell; to inflate; to puff up; to blow into a blaze; to burst in pieces and scatter by explosion; to scold: in this sense colloq.—*n.* A gale of wind; a blast; the breathing or spouting of a whale.—**Blower**, blō'ėr, *n.* One who or that which blows; a blowing-engine.—**Blowy**, blō'i, *a.* Windy; gusty.—**Blow-fly**, *n.* A name of various species of flies (dipterous insects) which deposit their eggs on flesh, and thus taint it.—**Blow-hole**, *n.* The nostril of a cetacean, situated on the highest part of the head; a hole in the ice to which whales and seals come to breathe.—**Blowing-engine**, **Blowing-machine**, *n.* Any contrivance for supplying a current of air, as for blowing glass, smelting iron, renewing the air in confined spaces, and the like. —**Blow-pipe**, *n.* An instrument by which a current of air or gas is driven through a flame so as to direct it upon a substance, an intense heat being created by the rapid supply of oxygen and the concentration of the flame; a pipe or tube through which poisoned arrows are blown by the breath, used by South American Indians and natives of Borneo.

Blow, blō, *v.i.*—*blew, blown.* [A. Sax. *blōwan*, to bloom or blossom; D. *bloeijen*, G. *blühen*; allied to the other verb *to blow*, and to L. *florere*, to bloom.] To flower; to blossom; to bloom, as plants.—*v.t.*‡ To make to blow or blossom.—*n.* A mass of blossoms; the state or condition of blossoming or flowering; the highest state of anything; bloom; an ovum or egg deposited by a fly; a fly-blow.—**Blown**, blōn, *p.* and *a.* Fully expanded or opened, as a flower.

Blow, blō, *n.* [Akin to O.D. *blauwen*, to strike; D. *blouwen*, to beat flax; G. *bleuen*, to cudgel; and perhaps also with *blue*. BLUE.] A stroke with the hand or fist, or a weapon; a knock; an act of hostility; a sudden calamity; a sudden or severe evil; mischief or damage received.—*At a blow*, by one single action; at one effort; suddenly.

Blowze, blouz, *n.* [From the same root as *blush*.] A ruddy fat-faced woman; a blowzy woman.—**Blowzed**, **Blouzy**, blouzd, blou'zi, *a.* Ruddy-faced; fat and ruddy; high-coloured.

Blubber, blub'ėr, *n.* [A lengthened form of *blub, blob, bleb*; perhaps from same root as that of *blow, bladder*.] The fat of whales and other large sea animals, from which train-oil is obtained; a gelatinous mass of various kinds; the sea-nettle; a jelly-fish.—*v.i.* To weep, especially in such a manner as to swell the cheeks or disfigure the face. —*v.t.* To disfigure with weeping.—**Blubber-lip**, *n.* A swollen lip; a thick lip, such as that of a negro.—**Blubber-lipped**, *a.* Having blubber-lips.

Blucher, bluch'ėr, *n.* A strong leather half boot or high shoe, named after Field-marshal von *Blücher*.

Bludgeon, bluj'on, *n.* [Origin unknown; perhaps allied to G. *blotzen*, to strike, D. *blutsen*, to bruise.] A short stick, with one end loaded or thicker and heavier than the other, and used as an offensive weapon.

Blue, blū, *n.* [Same as Sc. *blae*, Icel. *blár*, livid; Dan. *blaa*, D. *blaauw*, G. *blau*, blue; connected with *blow*, a blow producing a blue colour. Akin *blemish*.] One of the primary colours; the colour of the clear sky or deep sea; azure; what is blue; a dye or pigment of this hue.—*a.* Of the colour of blue; sky-coloured; azure.—*v.t.*—*blued, bluing.* To make blue; to dye of a blue colour.—**Blueing**, **Bluing**, blū'ing, *n.* A material used to impart a blue colour, as indigo used by washerwomen.—**Bluely**, blū'li, *adv.* With a blue hue or shade.—**Blueness**, blū'nes, *n.* The quality of being blue; a blue hue or colour.—**Bluish**, blū'ish, *a.* Blue in a slight degree; somewhat blue.—**Bluishness**, blū'ish-nes, *n.* —**Blue-Beard**, *n.* Personage in mediæval tale, synonymous with wife-murderer.—**Blue-bell**, *n.* The popular name given in England to the wild hyacinth, and in Scotland to the harebell.—**Blue-bird**, *n.* A small bluish bird with a red breast very common in the United States; the blue robin.—**Blue-bonnets**, *n.* The Scottish nation.—**Blue-book**, *n.* In the U. S. a directory of persons of social prominence. In colleges, a blue-covered booklet for writing examinations.—**Blue-bottle**, *n.* A composite plant found frequently in cornfields; a fly with a large blue belly.—**Blue-cap**, *n.* A fish of the salmon kind, with blue spots on its head; the blue titmouse.—**Blue-coat**, *n.* A person wearing a blue coat as a special dress.—*Blue-coat boy*, a boy attending Christ's Hospital School, dressed in long, blue coat with yellow stockings.—**Blue-fish**, *n.* A name of certain American fishes, one of them a food fish allied to the mackerel, common on the Atlantic coast of N. America.—**Blue-devils**, *n. pl.* A colloquial phrase for dejection, hypochondria, or lowness of spirits; also for delirium tremens. Often called simply *the blues*.—**Blue-gown**, *n.* The name of Scottish bedesmen, or licensed beggars.—**Blue-grass**, *n.* A name of several grasses, more especially a grass of Kentucky, highly valued for pasturage and hay. —**Blue-gum**, *n.* A species of Eucalyptus or gum-tree with valuable medicinal properties, and now planted in malarious localities with beneficial results. It yields the drug Eucalyptol.—**Blue-jacket**, *n.* A sailor, from the colour of his jacket.—**Blue-mould**, *n.* A name of a thread-like fungus growing on cheese, as also on dried sausages and rolled bacon.—**Blue-ointment**, *n.* Mercurial ointment.—**Blueprint**, *n.* A photographic printing method using sensitized paper for the reproduction of engineering drawings; the print itself.—**Blue-pill**, *n.* Mercurial pill.—**Blue-ribbon**, *n.* The broad, dark-blue ribbon, worn by members of the order of the Garter over the left shoulder, and hanging down to the hip; hence, a member of this order; a piece of blue ribbon, usually with suitable words or markings, awarded as evidence of the winning of a highest award; hence a prize, a distinction.—**Blue-ribbon stock**, stock or cattle that won highest awards at stock shows.—**Blue-stone**, **Blue-vitriol**, *n.* Sulphate of copper.—**Blue-verditer**, *n.* A blue oxide of copper, or a precipitate of the nitrate of copper by lime.—

Bluing, blū'ing, *n.* A blue liquid used in laundering to offset the yellow tinge of linen or cotton.

Bluff, bluf, *a.* [Perhaps from or allied to O.D. *blaf*, applied to a broad full face, also to a forehead rising straight up.] Broad and full: specially applied to a full countenance, indicative of frankness and good humour; rough and hearty; somewhat boisterous and unconventional; having a steep front (a *bluff* bank).—*v.t.* To deceive or impose upon, by boisterous talk or action. —*n.* A high bank with a steep front; a bold headland; bold words or acts intended to daunt or test an opponent.—**Bluffy**, bluf'i, *a.* Having bluffs or bold projecting banks.

Blunder, blun'dėr, *v.i.* [Allied to Icel. *blunda*, to doze, *blundr*, slumber, Dan. and Sw. *blund*, a nap, also to *blind, blend*.] To make a gross mistake, especially through mental confusion; to err stupidly; to move without direction or steady guidance; to flounder; to stumble, literally or figuratively.—*n.* A mistake through precipitance or mental confusion; a gross and stupid mistake.—**Blunderer**, blun'dėr-ėr, *n.* One who is apt to blunder or to make gross mistakes.—**Blunderingly**, blun'dėr-ing-li, *adv.* In a blundering manner.

Blunderbuss, blun'dėr-bus, *n.* [A humorous corruption of D. *donderbus*, a blunderbuss—*donder*, thunder, and *bus*, a tube, gun, originally a box.] A short gun or firearm, with a large bore.

Blunt, blunt, *a.* [Akin to Prov. G. *bludde*, a dull or blunt knife; Dan. *blunde*, Sw. and Icel. *blunda*, to doze, E. *blunder*.] Having a thick edge or point, as an instrument; dull; not sharp; dull in understanding; slow of discernment; abrupt in address; plain; unceremonious.—*v.t.* To dull the edge or point of, by making it thicker; to impair the force, keenness, or susceptibility of.—**Bluntish**, blunt'ish, *a.* Somewhat blunt.—**Bluntishness**, blunt'ish-nes, *n.* —**Bluntly**, blunt'li, *adv.* In a blunt manner; plainly; abruptly; without delicacy or the usual forms of civility.—**Bluntness**, blunt'nes, *n.* The state or quality of being blunt.

Blur, blėr, *n.* [Probably a form of *blear*.] Something that obscures or soils; a blot; a stain; confused appearance, as produced by indistinct vision.—*v.t.*—*blurred, blurring.* To obscure without quite effacing; to render indistinct; to confuse and bedim; to cause imperfection of vision in; to dim; to sully; to stain; to blemish (reputation).

Blurt, blėrt, *v.t.* [Perhaps imitative of abrupt sound made by the lips.] To utter suddenly or inadvertently; to divulge unadvisedly: commonly with *out*.

Blush, blush, *v.i.* [A.Sax. *blisian, blysian*, allied to Dan. *blusse*, to blaze, to blush, D. *blos*, a blush, *blozen*, to blush; akin *blaze, blow*.] To redden in the cheeks or over the face, as from a sense of guilt, shame, confusion, or modesty; to exhibit a red or rosy colour; to bloom.—*n.* The act of blushing; the suffusion of the cheeks or the face generally with a red colour through confusion, shame, diffidence, or the like; a red or reddish colour; a rosy tint.—*At the first blush*, at the first review or consideration of a matter.—**Blushful**, blush'fụl, *a.* Full of blushes.—**Blushfully**, blush'fụl-li, *adv.* With many blushes.—**Blushing**, blush'ing, *a.* Exhibiting blushes or a rosy tint; blooming.—**Blushingly**, blush'ing-li, *adv.* In a blushing manner; with blushes.

Bluster, blus'tėr, *v.i.* [A kind of intens. of *blow*; akin to *blast, blister*.] To roar and be tumultuous, as wind; to be boisterous; to be loud, noisy, or swaggering; to bully; to swagger.—*v.t.* To utter or effect in a blustering manner or with noise and violence: with *out*, or other prep.—*n.* A violent blast of wind; a gust; noisy talk; swaggering; boisterousness.—**Blusterer**, blus'tėr-ėr, *n.* One who blusters; a swaggerer; a bully.—**Blustering**, blus'tėr-ing, *a.* Stormy; windy; noisy; tumultuous; swaggering.—**Blusteringly**, blus'tėr-ing-li, *adv.* In a blustering manner.—**Blusterous**, **Blustrous**, **Blustery**, blus'tėr-us, blus'trus, blus'tėr-i, *a.* Noisy; tumultuous; tempestuous.

Boa, bō'a, *n.* [L., a water-serpent.] The generic and common name of certain serpents destitute of fangs and venom, having a prehensile tail, and including some of the largest species of serpents, the constrictor being 30 or 40 feet long; a long round article of dress for the neck, made of fur.

Boar, bōr, *n.* [A.Sax. *bár*=D. *beer*, O.H.G. *pēr*, M.H.G. *ber*, a boar; perhaps akin to *bear* (the animal).] The male of swine: when applied to the wild species the term is used without reference to sex.—**Boarish**, bōr'ish, *a.* Pertaining to or resembling a boar; swinish; brutal.

Board, bōrd, *n.* [A.Sax. *bord*, table, plank, deck or side of a ship=Icel. Dan. G. *bord*, Goth. *baurd*, D. *boord*; allied probably to verb *bear*. *Border, broider*, are akin.] A piece of timber sawed thin, and of considerable length and breadth compared with the thickness; a table; hence, what is served on a board or table; food; diet; specifically, daily food obtained for a stipulated sum at the table of another; a council table; a number of persons having the management, direction, or superintendence of some public or private office or trust; the deck or side of a ship or boat, or its interior part (on *board*, to fall over *board*); a table or frame for a game, as chess, draughts, &c.; a kind of thick stiff paper; a sheet of substance formed by layers of paper pasted together, usually in compounds (as, card-*board*, mill-*board*); one of the two stiff covers on the sides of a book.—*The boards*, the stage of a theater.—*v.t.* To lay or spread with boards; to cover with boards; to place at board, or where food or food and lodging are to be had; to furnish with food, or food and lodging, for a compensation; to go on board a vessel; to enter a vessel by force in combat. —*v.i.* To live at board; to live as a boarder. —**Boardable**, bōrd'a-bl, *a.* Capable of being boarded, as a ship.—**Boarder**, bōrd'-ėr, *n.* One furnished with food or food and lodging at another's house at a stated charge; one who boards a ship in action.—**Boarding-house**, *n.* A house where board or board and lodging is furnished.—**Boarding-pike**, *n.* A weapon used by sailors in boarding an enemy's ship.—**Boarding-school**, *n.* A school in which pupils are boarded and lodged as well as taught. **Board-school**, *n.* A school under the management of a school-board.—**Board-wages**, *n.* Wages allowed to servants.

Boast, bōst, *v.i.* [Probably of Celtic origin; comp. W. *bost*, a boast, *bostio*, to boast, Corn. *bostye*, to boast.] To speak in high praise of one's self or belongings; to use exulting, pompous, or pretentious language; to brag; to exult; to glory; to vaunt; to bluster. — *v.t.* To display in ostentatious language; to speak of with pride, vanity, or exultation; to magnify or exalt (strength, genius); to vaunt: often *refl.*—*n.* A statement expressive of ostentation, pride, or vanity; a vaunting or bragging; a brag; the cause of boasting; occasion of pride, vanity, or laudable exultation.—**Boaster**, bōst'ėr, *n.* One who boasts, glories, or vaunts with exaggeration or ostentatiously; a bragger. —**Boastful**, bōst'ful, *a.* Given to boasting.—**Boastfully**, bōst'ful-li, *adv.* In a boastful manner.—**Boastfulness**, bōst'-ful-nes, *n.*—**Boastingly**, bōst'ing-li, *adv.* Boastfully; with boasting.

Boat, bōt, *n.* [A.Sax. *bát*=Icel. *bátr*, D. L.G. and G. *boot*, a boat. Similar forms occur also in Celtic, as Ir. W. *bad*, Gael. *bata.*] A small open vessel or water-craft, usually moved by oars or rowing; any sailing vessel, but usually described by another word denoting its use or mode of propulsion; as, a packet-*boat*, steam-*boat*, &c.—*v.t.* To transport in a boat.—*v.i.* To go or sail in a boat.—**Boat-bill**, *n.* A bird of the heron family, inhabiting South America, and named from having a bill resembling a boat with the keel uppermost.—**Boat-fly**, *n.* An aquatic insect whose hind-legs resemble a pair of oars, the body resembling a boat. —**Boat-hook**, *n.* An iron hook with a point on the back, fixed to a long pole, to pull or push a boat. — **Boat-house**, *n.* A house or shed for protecting boats from the weather.—**Boatman**, bōt'man, *n.* A man who manages a boat; a rower of a boat. —**Boatswain**, bōt'swān or bō'sn, *n.* [A. Sax. *bátswán*—*bát*, boat, and *swán*, swain.] A ship's officer who has charge of the sails, rigging, anchors, cables, &c., and who pipes or summons the crew to their duty.

Bob, bob, *n.* [Perhaps imitative or suggestive of abrupt, jerky motion; in some of its senses allied to Gael. *babag*, *baban*, a tassel.] A general name for any small round object playing loosely at the end of a cord, line, chain, &c., as a knot of worms on a string used in fishing for eels, the ball or weight at the end of a pendulum, plumb-line, and the like; a short jerking action or motion; a shake or jog; a blow.—**Bob**, bob, *n.* A shilling. [Colloq.] *Bell-ringing*, a peal of courses or sets of changes.—*v.t.* *bobbed, bobbing.* To move in a short, jerking manner; to perform with a jerky movement; to cut short, as a horse's tail; to beat or strike; to deceive; to defraud of (*Shak.*)‡.— *v.i.* To play backward and forward; to play loosely against anything; to make a quick, jerky motion, as a rapid bow or obeisance; to angle or fish with a bob, or by giving the hook a jerking motion in the water.—**Bob-tail**, bob'tāl, *n.* A short tail or a tail cut short; the rabble: used in contempt, as in the phrase *ragtag and bobtail.* — **Bob-tailed**, bob'tāld, *a.* Having the tail cut short.—**Bob-wig**, *n.* A wig of short hair.

Bobbin, bob'in, *n.* [Fr. *bobine*, from L. *bombus*, a humming sound, or more probably connected with E. *bob.*] A small cylindrical piece of wood with a head or flange at one or both ends, on which thread or yarn is wound for use in sewing, weaving, &c.— **Bobbinet**, bob'in-et, *n.* A machine-made cotton net, originally imitated from the lace made by means of a pillow and bobbins.

Bobby, bob'i, *n.* Policeman, from the London force established by Sir Robert Peel when Home Secretary. Also called *Peelers.* So *Charlies*, the London police attributed to Charles I.

Bobolink, Boblink, bob'ō-lingk, bob'-lingk, *n.* The rice-bird or reed-bird of the United States: so called from its cry.

Bocasine, bok'a-sēn, *n.* [Fr.] A kind of calamanco or woollen stuff.

Boche, Bosche, bosh, *n.* [Fr. of disputed origin. Perhaps short form of *Alboche*, slang for *Allemand*, a German.] A term of opprobrium for a German.

Bode, bōd, *v.t.*—*boded, boding.* [A.Sax. *bodian*, to announce, to proclaim, from *bod*, an edict, a message; Icel. *botha*, to proclaim; to bode; A.Sax. *boda*, D. *bode*, G. *bote*, a messenger; allied to *bid.*] To portend; to foreshow; to presage; to indicate something future by signs; to be the omen of.—*v.i.* To be ominous. — **Bodeful**, bōd'ful, *a.* Ominous; threatening; foreboding.—**Bodement**, bōd'ment, *n.* An omen; portent; prognostic. — **Boding**, bōd'ing, *a.* Portentous; ominous.—*n.* A portent; an omen. —**Bodingly**, bōd'ing-li, *adv.* Ominously; forebodingly; portentously.

Bode, bōd, pret. of *bide.*

Bodega, bod'ē-ga, *n.* [Sp. from Gr. *apothékē.*] A wine cellar or shop.

Bodice, bod'is, *n.* [Formerly *bodies*, pl. of *body*, being originally in two pieces.] The body part of a woman's dress; a kind of waistcoat; stays; a corset.

Bodkin, bod'kin, *n.* [From W. *bidogyn*, a dagger, dim. of *bidog*, Gael. *biodag*, a short sword.] Originally a dagger; now a pointed pin of steel, ivory, or the like, for piercing holes in cloth; a blunted needle for drawing a ribbon, cord, or string through a loop, or a pin for keeping up the hair; to sit *bodkin*, to sit squeezed between two persons.

Bodle, bod'l, *n.* [Supposed to be from *Bothwell*, a mint-master.] A copper coin formerly current in Scotland, of the value of two pennies Scots, or the sixth part of an English penny.

Body, bod'i, *n.* [A.Sax. *bodig*, a body— O.H.G. *potach*, later *botech*, *bodech*, body; comp. Gael. *bodhaig*, the body.] The frame or material organized substance of an animal, in distinction from the soul, spirit, or vital principle; the main central or principal part of anything, as distinguished from subordinate parts, such as the extremities, branches, wings, &c.; a person; a human being: now generally forming a compound with *some* or *no* preceding; a number of individuals spoken of collectively, united by some common tie or by some occupation; a corporation; any extended solid substance; matter; any substance or mass distinct from others; a united mass; a general collection; a code; a system; a certain consistency or density; substance; strength (as of liquors, paper, &c.).—*v.t.* —*bodied, bodying.* To produce in some form; to embody; to invest with a body.— **Bodiless**, bod'i-les, *a.* Having no body or material form; incorporeal. — **Bodily**, bod'i-li, *a.* Pertaining to or concerning the body; of or belonging to the body or to the physical constitution; not mental; corporeal. ∴ *Bodily*, relating to or connected with the body as a whole: opposed to *mental*; *corporal*, relating to the body as regards outward bearings; *corporeal*, relating to its nature; opposed to *spiritual.* Hence *bodily* form, *corporal* punishment, *corporeal* existence. — *adv.* Corporeally; united with a body or matter; entirely; completely (to remove a thing *bodily*). — **Body-color**, *n.* *Painting*, a pigment that imparts opacity or hiding power to a paint; the predominant color of a house as contrasted with the color of the trim.—**Body-guard**, *n.* The guard that protects or defends one's person; life-guard.—**Body-servant**, *n.* A servant that waits upon or accompanies his employer; a valet; a personal attendant.—**Body-snatcher**, *n.* One who robs burying-places of dead bodies.

Bœotian, bā-ō'shun, *a.* Of or relating to Bœotia, thick-witted, dull, in distinction from *Attic*, the inhabitants of Attica.

Boer, bör or bō'ėr, *n.* [D., a peasant, farmer.] The name applied to the Dutch colonists of South Africa engaged in agriculture or cattle-breeding.

Bog, bog, *n.* [Gael. and Ir. *bog*, soft, moist, *bogan*, *bogach*, a quagmire.] A piece of wet, soft, and spongy ground, where the soil is composed mainly of decaying and decayed vegetable matter; a piece of mossy ground or where peat is found; a quagmire or morass.—*v.t.*—*bogged, bogging.* To whelm or plunge in mud or mire.—**Boggy**, bog'i, *a.* Pertaining to or resembling a bog; full of bogs; marshy; swampy; miry. — **Bog-butter**, *n.* A fatty spermaceti-like mineral resin found in masses in peat-bogs, composed of carbon, oxygen, and hydrogen.— **Bog-earth**, *n.* An earth or soil composed of light siliceous sand and a considerable portion of vegetable fibre in a half-decomposed state.—**Bog-iron-ore**, *n.* A loose porous earthy ore of iron found in thin layers in the subsoil of many bogs and swamps.—**Bog-oak**, *n.* Trunks or large branches of oak-trees found in peat-bogs, the timber being of a shining black colour and often manufactured into ornamental articles.—**Bog-spavin**, *n.* An encysted tumour on the inside of the hough of a horse.—**Bog-trotter**, *n.* A derisive term for an inhabitant of a boggy country, applied especially to the Irish peasantry, whose ability in traversing bogs has often enabled them to escape when pursued by the officers of justice.

Bogey, Bogy, bō'gi, *n.* [W. *bwg*, *bwgan*, a hobgoblin, scarecrow, *bug*bear.] A hobgoblin; a wicked spirit. — *Old Bogey*, the devil.

Boggle, bog'l, *v.i.*—*boggled, boggling.* [Probably connected with *bogey*, Prov.E. *bogle*, a goblin.] To doubt; to hesitate; to stop, as if afraid to proceed or as if impeded by unforeseen difficulties; to waver; to shrink; to play fast and loose; to shilly-shally.— **Boggler**, bog'lėr, *n.* A doubter; a timorous man; a waverer; an inconstant person.

Bogie, Bogey, bō'gi, *n.* [Perhaps from inventor's or maker's name.] Originally a coal-wagon or truck so constructed as to turn readily in little room; now, generally, a four-wheeled truck supporting the front part of a locomotive, and turning beneath it by means of a central pivot.—**Bogie-roll**, *n.* A coarse kind of twisted tobacco.

Bogus, bō'gus, *a.* [A word of uncertain origin. It first appeared in America, having been originally applied, it is said, in 1827, to an apparatus for coining spurious money.] Counterfeit; spurious; sham; pretended. [Originally Amer.]

Bohea, bō-hē', *n.* [Said to be from a mountain in China called *Voo-y.*] An inferior kind of black tea: sometimes applied to black teas in general.

Bohemian, bō-hē'mi-an, *n.* [Fr. *Bohémien*, a gypsy, because the first of that wandering race that entered France were believed to be Hussites driven from Bohemia, their native country.] A person, especially an artist or literary man, who leads a free, often somewhat dissipated life, despising conventionalities generally.—**Bohemianism**, bō-hē'mi-an-izm, *n.* The life or habits of a Bohemian.

Boiar, Boyar, boi'är, *n.* A member of a peculiar order of the old Russian aristocracy next in rank to the ruling princes.

Boil, boil, *v.i.* [O.Fr. *boiller*, Fr. *bouillir*, L. *bullare*, *bullire*, to boil, to bubble, from *bulla*, a bubble. *Bill* (a paper), *billet*, *bullet*, are of same origin.] To be in a state of ebullition; to bubble by the action of heat, as water or other fluids; to exibit a swirling or swelling motion; to seethe, as waves; to be violently agitated or excited, as the blood; to be subjected to the action of boiling water in cooking, &c., as meat.—*v.t.* To put into a state of ebullition; to cause to be agitated or bubble by the application of heat; to collect, form, or separate by the application of heat, as sugar, salt; to subject to the action of heat in a boiling liquid, as meat in cooking; to prepare in a boiling liquid; to seethe.—**Boiler**, boil'ėr, *n.* A person who boils; a vessel, generally a large vessel of iron, copper, &c., in which anything is boiled in great quantities; a strong metallic vessel, usually of wrought-iron or steel plates riveted together, in which steam is generated for driving engines or other purposes.—**Boilery**, boil'ėr-i, *n.* A place and apparatus for boiling.—**Boilingly**, boil'-ing-li, *adv.* In a boiling manner.—*Boiling point*, the degree of heat at which a fluid is converted into vapour with ebullition, as water at 212° Fahr., mercury at 662°, &c.—*Boiling springs*, springs or fountains which give out water at the boiling point or at a high temperature, as the geysers of Iceland and in the Yellowstone region in the United States.

Boil, boil, *n.* [O.E. *bile*, *byle*, A.Sax. *byl*, a blotch, a sore; D. *buil*, G. *beule*, a boil; Icel. *bóla*, a blain or blister; Dan. *byld*, a boil.] An inflamed and painful suppurating tumour.

Boisterous, bois'tėr-us, *a.* [Probably from W. *bwystus*, brutal, ferocious, *bwyst*, wildness, ferocity; perhaps connected with *boast.*] Violent; stormy; turbulent; furious; tumultuous; noisy.—**Boisterously**, bois'-tėr-us-li, *adv.* In a boisterous manner.—**Boisterousness**, bois'tėr-us-nes, *n.* The state or quality of being boisterous.

Bolary,† bō'la-ri, *a.* Pertaining to bole or clay, or partaking of its nature and qualities.

Bold, bōld, *a.* [A. Sax. *beald*, *bald*, bold, courageous = Icel. *ballr*, D. *bout*, O.H.G. *bald*, bold.] Daring; courageous; brave; intrepid; fearless, as a man; requiring or exhibiting courage in execution; executed with courage and spirit, as a deed; rude; forward; impudent; overstepping usual bounds; presuming upon sympathy or forbearance; showing liberty or licence; striking to the eye; markedly conspicuous; steep; abrupt; prominent.—**Boldly**, bōld'-li, *adv.* In a bold manner; courageously; intrepidly; forwardly; insolently; abruptly, &c.—**Boldness**, bōld'nes, *n.* The quality of being bold, in all the senses of the word; courage; bravery; confidence; assurance; forwardness; steepness; abruptness.—**Bold-faced**, *a.* Impudent.

Bole, bōl, *n.* [From Icel. *bolr*, *bulr*, Dan. *bul*, trunk, stem of a tree; probably of same root as *bowl*, *bulge*, &c.] The body or stem of a tree.

Bole, bōl, *n.* [Fr. *bol*, bole, a bolus, L. *bolus*, from Gr. *bōlŏs*, a clod of earth.] A friable clayey shale or earth of various kinds used as a pigment, generally yellow, or yellowish-red, or brownish-black, from the presence of iron oxide. These earths were formerly employed as astringent, absorbent, and tonic medicines, and they are still in repute in the East; they are also used occasionally as veterinary medicines in Europe. Armenian bole is used as a coarse red pigment.

Bolero, bō-ler'ō, *n.* [Sp., from *bola*, a ball.] A favourite dance in Spain.

Boletus, bō-lē'tus, *n.* [L., from *bolus*, Gr. *bōlos*, a mass, from its massive globular form.] A fungus or mushroom of various species, some of which are eaten, and from one of which German tinder is obtained, this species being also used as a styptic.—**Boletic**, bō-let'ik, *a.* Pertaining to or obtained from the Boletus, a genus of mushrooms.

Bolide, bō'līd, *n.* [Fr., from L. *bolis*, *bolidis*, a fiery meteor, from Gr. *bolis*, a missile, from *ballō*, to throw.] A meteoric stone or aerolite which explodes on coming in contact with our atmosphere; a fire-ball.

Boll, bōl, *n.* [G. *bolle*, a seed-vessel of flax, D. *bol*, a round body; same root as *bole*, a stem.] The pod or capsule of a plant, as of flax.—*v.i.* To form into or produce seed-vessels.

Boll, bōl, *n.* [A form of *bowl*, A. Sax. *bolla*, a bowl, cup, measure.] An old Scotch dry measure still often used, varying according to locality and article measured, the potato, barley, oats, &c., boll, containing six bushels.

Bollandist, bol'land-ist, *n.* One of a series of Jesuit writers who published the *Acta Sanctorum*, a well-known collection of the traditions of the saints of the Roman Catholic Church: so called from John Bollandus, who edited the first five or six vols. Also used adjectively.

Bollard, bol'lärd, *n.* [Allied to *bole*, the stem of a tree.] A strong post fixed vertically into the ground on a wharf or quay; a kind of stanchion in a ship or boat.

Bologna-phial, bō-lō'nya, *n.* [From *Bologna* in Italy.] A small phial of unannealed glass, which flies in pieces when its surface is scratched by a hard body, as by dropping into it an angular fragment of flint, whereas a lead bullet, or other smooth body, may be dropped into it without causing injury.—**Bologna-sausage**, *n.* A large sausage made of bacon, veal, and pork-suet, chopped fine, and inclosed in a skin.

Bolo-ism, bol'o-izm. [From Paul Bolo, French adventurer in high finance, condemned to death 14th February, 1918.] Treachery in high places.

Bolshevik, bōl-she'vik, *n.* The Russian name for the majority party, as opposed to the minority (*mensheviki*), in the 1903 split of the Social Democrats; revolutionists, extreme Socialists.

Bolster. bōl'stėr, *n.* [A. Sax. D. Dan. and Sw. *bolster*, Icel. *bólstr*, G. *polster*, a cushion, a bolster; root *bol*, *bul*, as in *bulge*, &c., and term. *-ster*, as in *holster*.] A long pillow or cushion used to support the head of persons lying on a bed; something resembling a bolster more or less in form or application, as a pad or quilt used to prevent pressure; a compress, a cushioned or padded part of a saddle; the part of a cutting tool which joins the end of the handle; a hollow tool for punching holes, &c.—*v.t.* To furnish or support with a bolster, pillow, or any soft pad; to pad; to stuff; *fig.* to support; to maintain: usually implying support of an unworthy cause or object and generally with *up* (to *bolster up* his pretentions with lies).—**Bolsterer**, bōl'stėr-ėr, *n.* One who bolsters; a supporter.

Bolt, bōlt, *n.* [A. Sax. *bolt*, an arrow, a bolt; Dan. *bolt*, a bolt, an iron peg, a fetter, G. *bolz*, *bolzen*, an arrow, a bolt or large nail.] An arrow; a thunderbolt; a stream of lightning; a stout metallic pin used for holding objects together, frequently screw-threaded at one extremity to receive a nut; a movable bar for fastening a door, gate, window-sash, or the like; especially that portion of a lock which is protruded from or retracted within the case by the action of the key; an iron to fasten the legs of a prisoner; a shackle.—*v.t.* To fasten or secure with a bolt or iron pin, as a door, a plank, fetters, &c.; to swallow hurriedly or without chewing, as food (colloq.); to start or spring game.—*v.i.* To shoot forth suddenly; to spring out with speed and suddenness; to start forth like a bolt; to run out of the regular path; to start and run off; to take flight; to make one's escape (colloq.).—*adv.* As straight as a bolt; suddenly; with sudden meeting or collision (to come *bolt* against a person).—**Bolter**, bōlt'ėr, *n.* One who fastens with a bolt; one who makes his escape or runs away; a horse given to starting off or running away.—**Bolt-upright**, *a.* or *adv.* As straight or upright as a bolt; erect or erectly.

Bolt, bōlt, *v.t.* [O.Fr. *buleter*, *bulter* (Mod. Fr. *bluter*), with change of *r* into *l*, from an older form *bureter*, from *bure*, the thick woollen cloth of which bolting-sieves are made, from L. *burra*, coarse cloth.] To sift or pass through a sieve so as to separate the coarser from the finer particles, as bran from flour; *fig.* to sift or separate good from bad, or the like.—**Bolter**, bōlt'ėr, *n.* One who bolts; a sieve or apparatus for bolting.—**Bolt-head**, *n.* A long straight-necked glass vessel for chemical distillations; a matrass or receiver.—**Bolting-house**, *n.* A house where meal is sifted.—**Bolting-hutch**, *n.* A tub for bolted flour.—**Bolting-mill**, *n.* A mill or machine for sifting meal.—**Bolting-tub**, *n.* A tub to sift meal in.—**Bolt-rope**, *n.* A rope to which the edges of sails are sewed to strengthen them.

Bolus, bō'lus, *n.* [L. *bolus*, a bit, a morsel, a lump, Gr. *bōlos*, a clod, a lump.] A soft round mass of anything medicinal to be swallowed at once, larger and less solid than an ordinary pill.

Bomb, bom, *n.* [Fr. *bombe*, a bomb, from L. *bombus*, Gr. *bombos*, a hollow deep sound. Probably imitative, like E. *bum*, *boom*, to make a deep hollow sound.] A destructive projectile, consisting of a hollow ball or spherical shell, generally of cast-iron, filled with explosive materials, fired from a mortar, and usually exploded by means of a fuse or tube filled with a slow-burning compound, which is ignited by the discharge of the mortar.—**Bomb-ketch**, **Bomb-vessel**, *n.* A small ship or vessel of very strong build, for throwing bombs into a fortress from the sea.—**Bomb-proof**, *a.* Secure against the force of bombs; capable of resisting the shock or explosion of shells.—**Bomb-shell**, *n.* A spherical shell; a bomb.—**Bombard**, bom'bärd, *n.* [Fr. *bombarde*, a piece of ordnance.] A piece of short thick ordnance with a large mouth, formerly used; a barrel; a drinking vessel (*Shak.*).—*v.t.*, bom-bärd'. To attack with bombs; to fire shells at or into; to shell: sometimes used somewhat loosely for to assault with artillery of any kind.—**Bombardier**, bom-bär-dēr', *n.* A person employed in throwing bombs or shells; specifically, in the British army, a non-commissioned artillery officer whose duty is to load shells, &c., and to fix the fuses, and who is particularly appointed to the service of mortars and howitzers.—*Bombardier beetle*, the common name of many coleopterous insects, possessing a remarkable power of violently expelling from the anus a pungent, acrid fluid, accompanied by a smart report.—**Bombardment**, bom-bärd'ment, *n.* The act of bombarding; the act of throwing shells and shot into a town, fortress, &c.—**Bombardon**, bom-bär'don, *n.* [Fr., ultimately from L. *bombus*, a hollow sound.] A large-sized and grave-toned musical instrument of the trumpet kind, in sound not unlike the ophicleide.

Bombasine, **Bombazine**, bom-ba-zēn', *n.* [Fr. *bombasin*, *bombasine*, It. *bombicina*, bombasin, L. *bombycinus*, made of silk or cotton, from Gr. *bombyx*, *bombykos*, a silkworm, silk.] A slight twilled fabric, of which the warp is silk (or cotton) and the weft worsted.—**Bombazette**, bom-ba-zet', *n.* A sort of thin woollen cloth.

Bombast, bom'bast, *n.* [Originally padding made of cotton, of same origin as *bombasine.*] Cotton or other stuff of soft, loose texture used to stuff garments‡; hence, high-sounding words; inflated or turgid language; fustian; words too big and high-sounding for the occasion.—**Bombastic**, bom-bas'tik, *a.* Characterized by bombast; high-sounding; turgid; inflated.—**Bombastically**, bom-bas'tik-al-li, *adv.* In a bombastic or inflated manner or style.

Bombyx, bom'biks. [L. silkworm.] A genus of moths of which the common silkworm moth (*Bombyx mori*) is the type. The larva feeds on the leaves of the mulberry tree and spins a large amount of strong silk in constructing its cocoon before changing to a pupa. In America efforts have been made to use the silk of imported worms.

Bona fide, bō'na fī'dē. [L.] With good faith; without fraud or deception: frequently used as a sort of adjective.

Bonanza, bo-nan'zä, *n.* [Sp. good weather, L. *bonus*.] Good luck, good output of farms, mines, stocks.

Bonapartist, bon'a-pärt-ist, *n.* One attached to the policy or the dynasty of the Bonapartes; one who favours the claims of the Bonaparte family to the throne of France.

Bonassus, bō-nas'us, *n.* A wild ox, aurochs, or wild bison of Europe.

Bon-bon, boṅ-boṅ, *n.* [Fr.] Some article of sugar-confectionery; a sugar-plum.

Bond, bond, *n.* [A form of *band*. BAND, BIND.] Anything that binds, fastens, confines, or holds things together, as a cord, a chain, a rope; hence, *pl.* fetters, chains, and so imprisonment, captivity; a binding power or influence; a uniting tie (the *bond* of affection); an obligation imposing a moral duty, as by a vow or promise; an obligation or deed by which a person binds himself, his heirs, &c., to do or not to do a certain act, usually to pay a certain sum on or before a certain day; *masonry*, the connection of one stone or brick with another by lapping them over each other in building so that an inseparable mass may be formed, which could not be the case if every vertical joint were over that below it; the state of being bonded, as goods in bond, that is stored in a bonded warehouse until customs or excise duties have been paid on them.—*a.* [For *bound*.] In a state of servitude or slavery; captive.—*v.t.* To put in bond or into a bonded warehouse, as goods liable for customs or excise duties, the duties remaining unpaid till the goods are taken out. —*Bonded warehouse*, a licensed warehouse or store in which goods liable to government duties may be lodged after bond has been given on behalf of the owners of the goods, for the payment of such duty on their removal for home consumption.—**Bondage**, bon'dāj, *n.* Slavery or involuntary servitude; thraldom; captivity; imprisonment; restraint of a person's liberty by compulsion.—**Bonder**, bon'dėr, *n.* One who bonds; one who deposits goods in a bonded warehouse; one of the stones which reach a considerable distance into or entirely through a wall for the purpose of binding it together.—**Bondholder**, *n.* A person who holds a bond for money lent. —**Bondmaid**, bond'mād, *n.* A female slave, or one bound to service without wages, in opposition to a hired servant.—**Bondman, Bondsman**, bond'man, bondz'man, *n.* [Dan. *bonde*, pl. *bönder*, yeoman, peasant. Same as A.S. *bonda*, a householder, the *-band* of *husband*.] Serf, with mistaken meaning of one bound by bond. At the Norman Conquest the yeoman sank to a serf, and the meaning changed to suit. A man slave, or one bound to service without wages.—**Bond-servant**, *n.* A slave; a bondman or bond-woman.—**Bond-service**, *n.* The condition of a bond-servant; slavery.—**Bond-slave**, *n.* A person in a state of slavery.—**Bond-store**, *n.* A bonded warehouse. — **Bonds-woman, Bond-woman**, *n.* A woman slave.

Bone, bōn, *n.* [A.Sax. *bān*, a bone; cog. D. and Dan. *been*, Icel. and G. *bein*, a bone, the lower part of the leg.] One of the pieces of which the skeleton of an animal is composed; the substance of which the skeleton of vertebrate animals is composed; a firm hard substance of a dull white colour, more or less hollow or cellular internally, and consisting of earthy matters (chiefly phosphate of lime and some carbonate of lime) about 67 per cent, and animal matter 33 per cent; *pl.* pieces of bone held between the fingers somewhat after the manner of castanets, and struck together in time to music of the negro minstrel type.—*Bone of contention*, a subject of dispute and rivalry, probably from the manner in which dogs quarrel over a bone.—*To make no bones*, to make no scruple: a metaphor taken from a dog, which greedily swallows meat, bones included.—*v.t.—boned, boning.* To take out the bones from, as in cookery; to put whalebone into (stays).—**Bony**, bō'ni, *a.* Pertaining to, consisting of, or resembling bone; having prominent bones.—**Bone-bed**, *n.* *Geol.* a bed or deposit composed of fragments of teeth and small bones, scales, coprolites, &c., of extinct animals, especially fishes and saurians.—**Bone-black**, *n.* Animal charcoal; the black carbonaceous substance into which bones are converted by charring in close vessels.—**Bone-breccia**, *n.* *Geol.* a conglomerate of fragments of bones and limestone cemented into a rock by a red calcareous concretion.—**Bone-brown**, *n.* A brown pigment produced by roasting bones of ivory till they become of a brown colour throughout.—**Bone-dust**, *n.* Bones ground to dust for manure.—**Bone-earth, Bone-ash**, *n.* The white, porous, earthy or mineral residue of bones which have been calcined so as to destroy the animal matter and carbon. —**Bone-mill**, *n.* A mill for grinding or bruising bones.—**Bone-setter**, *n.* One whose occupation is to set broken and dislocated bones.—**Bone-setting**, *n.* The art or practice of setting bones.—**Bone-spavin**, *n.* A bony excrescence or hard swelling on the inside of the hock of a horse's leg.

Bonfire, bon'fīr, *n.* [From Dan. *baun*, a beacon, and E. *fire*; or from W. *bàn*, conspicuous, lofty, whence *ban-ffagl*, a lofty blaze, a bonfire.] A fire made as an expression of public joy and exultation.

Boniface, bon'i-fās, *n.* [The name of the landlord in Farquhar's *Beaux' Stratagem*.] A sleek, jolly, good-natured landlord or innkeeper.

Bonito, bō-nē-to, *n.* [Sp.] A fish of several species, one of which is the striped-bellied tunny common in tropical seas, one of the fishes which pursue the flying-fish.

Bon-mot, boṅ-mō, *n.* [Fr. *bon*, good, and *mot*, a word.] A witticism; a witty repartee.

Bonne, bon, *n.* [Fr.] A nurse; a nursery governess.

Bonnet, bon'et, *n.* [Fr. *bonnet*, Sp. and Pg. *bonete*, L.L. *bonetus*, *boneta*, originally a sort of stuff so called; perhaps of Oriental origin.] A covering for the head worn by men; a cap; a covering for the head worn by women, and distinguished from a hat by details which vary according to the fashion; anything that covers the head or top of an object, as the cowl or wind-cap of a chimney, &c.—*v.t.* To force the hat over the eyes of, with the view of mobbing or hustling.—*v.i.* To pull off the bonnet; to make obeisance. (*Shak.*)—**Bonneted**, bon'et-ed, *a.* Wearing a bonnet, or furnished with a bonnet. —**Bonnet-piece**, *n.* A gold piece with the head of James V of Scotland.—**Bonnet-rouge**, bon-e-rözh, *n.* [Fr., lit. red cap.] A red or fervid republican: so named because a red cap was assumed as a distinguishing mark by the leaders of the first French revolution.

Bonny, bon'i, *a.* [Doubtfully derived from Fr. *bonne*, good.] Handsome; beautiful; fair or pleasant to look upon; pretty; fine.

Bonspiel, bon'spēl, *n.* [Dan. *bondespil*, a rustic game, from *bonde*, a rustic (A.Sax. *bonda*), and *spil*, G. *spiel*, a game.] In Scotland, a match in the game of curling between parties belonging to different districts.

Bon-ton, boṅ-toṅ, *n.* [Fr. 'good tone'.] The style of persons in high life; high mode or fashion; fashionable society.

Bonus, bō'nus, *n.* [L. *bonus*, good.] A sum given or paid over and above what is required to be paid, as a premium given for a loan, or for a charter or other privilege granted to a company; an extra dividend or allowance to the shareholders of a joint-stock company, holders of insurance policies, &c., out of accumulated profits; a sum paid to an employé over and above his stated pay in recognition of successful exertions.

Bon-vivant, boṅ-vē-väṅ, *n.* [Fr. *bon*, good, and *vivant*, ppr. of *vivre*, L. *vivere*, to live.] A generous liver; a jovial companion.

Bony, *a.* Under BONE.

Bonze, bonz, *n.* [Pg., a corruption of Japanese *busso*, a pious man.] The European name for a priest or monk of the religion of Fo or Buddha in China, Burmah, Japan, &c.; there are both male and female bonzes living in monasteries.

Booby, bö'bi, *n.* [Sp. *bobo*, a fool, the bird called the booby.] A dunce; a stupid fellow; a lubber; a bird allied to the gannet, and included in the pelican family, apparently so stupid as to allow itself to be knocked on the head by a stick or caught by the hand. — **Boobyish**, bö'bi-ish, *a.* Like or pertaining to a booby; stupid.

Boodhism, Boodhist, *n* BUDDHISM, BUDDHIST.

Boodle, bö'dl, *n.* [D. *boedel*, goods, lumber.] Goods fraudulently obtained; gain made by cheating in public office; lot, crowd, or pack.

Book, bu̦k, *n.* [A.Sax. *boc*, a book, originally a beech-tree; Icel. *bók*, a book, a beech; D. *boek*, a book, a beech; G. *buch*, a book, *buche*, a beech; Slav. *bukva*, a book, *buk*, a beech. The words *book* and *beech* are closely akin, beechen tablets or pieces of beech bark having probably formed the early books.] A number of sheets of paper or other material folded, stitched, and bound together on edge, blank, written, or printed; a volume; a particular part (generally including several chapters or sections) of a literary composition; a division of a subject in the same volume; a register or record; a register containing commercial transactions or facts in proper form.—*v.t.* To enter, write, or register in a book; to secure the carriage or transmission of by purchasing a ticket for coach, rail, or steamer.—**Bookful**,† bu̦k'-fu̦l, *a.* Full of notions gleaned from books; bookish. — **Bookish**, bu̦k'ish, *a.* Given to reading or study; more acquainted with books than with the world; pertaining to, contained in, or learned from books; theoretical.—**Bookishness**, bu̦k'ish-nes, *n.* Addictedness to books; fondness for study.—**Bookless**,† bu̦k'les, *a.* Without books unlearned; ignorant.—**Booklet**, bu̦k'let, *n.* A little book.—**Bookbinder**, bu̦k'-bīnd-ėr, *n.* One whose occupation is to bind books.—**Bookbindery**, bu̦k'bīnd-ėr-i, *n.* A place where books are bound.—**Bookbinding**, bu̦k'bīnd-ing, *n.* The act or practice of binding books; or of sewing the sheets and covering them with leather or other material.—**Book-case**, *n.* An upright case with shelves for holding books.

—**Book-collector**, *n.* One who collects books, especially rare and fine editions; a bibliophile.—**Book-debt**, *n.* A debt standing against a person in an account-book.—**Book-hunter**, *n.* An eager collector of books; especially one who frequents old book-shops, stalls, book-sales, in search of old and rare books and editions; a bibliomaniac.—**Booking-office**, *n.* In the United States an agency where theatrical people and musicians may procure employment.—**Book-keeper**, *n.* One who keeps accounts; a person who has the charge of entering or recording business transactions or items of debit and credit in the regular set of books belonging to business houses.—**Book-keeping**, *n.* The art of recording mercantile transactions by keeping accounts in a book or set of books in such a manner as to give a permanent record of business transactions, so that at any time the true state of one's pecuniary affairs and mercantile dealings may be exhibited.

—**Book-learned**, *a.* Versed in books and literature: sometimes implying an ignorance of men or of the common concerns of life.—**Book-learning**, *n.* Learning acquired by reading; acquaintance merely with books and literature.—**Book-louse**, *n.* pl. **Book-lice**. One of a small family of minute insects very destructive to old books. — **Book-maker**, *n.* One who writes and publishes books; especially, a compiler; in betting phraseology, a person, generally a professional betting man, who wagers on the defeat of a specified horse or other competitor in a race; a layer as opposed to a backer.—**Book-making**, *n.* The occupation of a book-maker.—**Bookman**, *n.* A studious or learned man; a scholar. (*Shak.*)—**Book-muslin**, *n.* A kind of fine transparent muslin having a stiff or elastic finish: so called from being folded in book form. — **Book-post**, *n.* That arrangement in the post-office by which books, printed matter, and manuscripts left open at the ends are conveyed at a reduced rate of payment.—**Bookseller**, buk'sel-ėr, *n.* One whose occupation is to sell books.—**Bookselling**, buk'sel-ing, *n.* The business of selling books.—**Book-stall**, *n.* A stall on which books are placed which are offered for sale.—**Book-stand**, *n.* A stand or support to hold books for reading or reference.—**Book-worm**, *n.* A worm or mite that eats holes in books; a person too much addicted to books or study.

Boom, böm, *n.* [Akin to *beam*, from D. *boom*, a tree, a pole, a beam, Dan. *bom*, a rail or bar.] A long pole or spar run out from various parts of a vessel for extending the bottom of particular sails, as the jib-*boom*, main-*boom*, &c.; a strong beam, or an iron chain or cable, extended across a river or harbour to prevent ships from passing.

Boom, böm, *v.i.* [An imitative word; comp. D. *bomme*, a drum; *bommen*, to drum; L. *bombus*, a humming sound. BOMB.] To make a sonorous, hollow, humming, or droning sound.—*n.* A deep hollow noise, as the roar of waves or the sound of distant guns: applied also to the cry of the bittern and the buzz of the beetle; a sudden briskness or rise in prices. [American.]

Boomerang, böm'e-rang, *n.* A missile formed generally of a piece of hard wood, parabolic in shape, used by the Australian aborigines, and remarkable from the fact that when thrown to a distance it rises into the air, then returns to hit an object behind the thrower if skilfully handled.

Boon, bön, *n.* [Icel. *bón*, a request, a boon, Dan. and Sw. *bön* = A.Sax. *bén*, Icel. *bœn*, a prayer.] Originally a prayer, petition, or request; hence, that which is asked; a petition, favour; a grant; a benefaction; a benefit; a blessing; a great privilege.

Boon, bön, *a.* [Norm. Fr. *boon*, Fr. *bon*, from L. *bonus*, good.] Gay; jovial; merry (a *boon* companion).

Boon, bön, *n.* [Gael. and Ir. *bunach*, coarse tow, from *bun*, stubble.] The useless vegetable matter from dressed flax.

Boor, bör, *n.* [A.Sax. (*ge*)*búr*, a countryman or farmer = D. *boer*, G. *bauer*; from A.Sax. *buan*, Icel. *búa*, to dwell, to inhabit, to cultivate; D. *bouwen*, G. *bauen*, to cultivate.] A countryman; a peasant; a rustic; a clown; hence, one who is rude in manners and illiterate.—**Boorish**, bör'ish, *a.* Clownish; rustic; awkward in manners, illiterate.—**Boorishly**, bör'ish-li, *adv.* In a clownish manner.—**Boorishness**, bör'ish-nes, *n.* The state of being boorish.

Boost, böst, *n.* A push that helps one over an obstacle; any help given; an increase in price, etc.—*v.t.* To give a boost to.—**Booster**, böst'ér, *n.* A person who enthusiastically promotes the welfare of another person or thing; a device that increases pressure or force.

Boot, böt, *n.* [A.Sax. *bót*, reparation, amends; Icel. *bót*, remedy, amends; same root as in *better*.] Profit; gain; advantage; that which is given to supply the deficiency of value in one of the things exchanged.—*To boot* [A.Sax. *to-bóte*], in addition to; over and above; into the bargain.—*v.t.* To profit; to advantage; to avail: used impersonally (it *boots* us little; what *boots* it?).—**Bootless**, böt'les, *a.* Without boot, profit, or advantage; unprofitable; unavailing; useless.—**Bootlessly**, böt'les-li, *adv.* In a bootless or unprofitable manner.—**Bootlessness**, böt'les-nes, *n.*

Boot, böt, *n.* [Fr. *botte*, a butt, and also a boot, from resemblance in shape. BUTT.] An article of dress, generally of leather, covering the foot and extending to a greater or less distance up the leg; an instrument of torture fastened on to the leg, between which and the boot wedges were introduced and hammered in, often crushing both muscles and bones; the luggage-box in a stage-coach, either on the front or the hind part; *pl.*, used as a singular noun, the servant in hotels who cleans the boots of the guests, or part of whose work was originally to do so.—*v.t.* To put boots on.—**Booted**, böt'ed, *a.* Equipped with boots; having boots on.—**Bootee**, böt'ē, *n.* A half or short boot; also a child's knitted boot.—**Boot-hook**, *n.* A sort of holdfast with which long boots are pulled on.—**Boot-hose**, *n.* Stocking-hose or spatter-dashes, in lieu of boots.—**Boot-jack**, *n.* An instrument for drawing off boots.—**Boot-lace**, *n.* The string or cord for fastening a boot.—**Boot-maker**, *n.* One whose occupation is to make boots.—**Boot-rack**, *n.* A frame or stand to hold boots, especially with their tops downwards.—**Boot-tree**, **Boot-last**, *n.* A shoe tree: an instrument for blocking or stretching boots or shoes.

Bootes, bo-ō'tēz, *n.* [Gr. *boōtēs*, a herdsman, from *bous*, an ox or cow.] A northern constellation, containing the star Arcturus.

Booth, böth, *n.* [Icel. *búth*, Dan. and Sw. *bod*, G. *bude*, a booth; allied to Gael. *buth*, Slav. *bauda*, *buda*, Lith. *buda*, a booth, a hut.] A covered stall at a fair, market, exposition or polling place; a closed stall for privacy when telephoning.

Booty, bö'ti, *n.* [Same as Icel. *bytt*, Dan. *bytte*, exchange, barter, booty, from *byta*, to divide into portions, to deal out.] Spoil taken from an enemy in war; that which is seized by violence and robbery; plunder; pillage.

Booze, böz, *v.i.* **Boozy**, bö'zi, *n.* Intoxicating liquor, generally of inferior quality.—*v.i.* To drink intoxicating liquor, especially excessively.—**Boozer**, böz'ér, *n.* One who boozes; a drunkard.

Bo-peep, bō-pēp', *n.* [*Bo*, an exclamation, and *peep*.] A game among children in which one suddenly appears from behind something, cries 'bo!' and as suddenly disappears, for the purpose of startling its companions.

Borachio,‡ bō-rach'i-ō, *n.* [Sp. *borracha*, a leather wine-vessel, from *borra*, a lamb or ewe; *borracho*, drunk.] The dressed skin of a goat or pig used for holding wine or other liquid; a skin or leather bottle; hence a drunkard.

Borage, bor'āj, *n.* [L.L. *borrago*, *borago*, from *borra*, hair, from its hairy leaves.] A plant allied to the forget-me-not, having very rough hairy leaves and pretty blue flowers, which were supposed to be cordial and were infused in drinks.

Borax, bō'raks, *n.* [Sp. *borrax*, Ar. *búraq*, saltpetre, from *barak*, to shine.] A salt formed by the combination of boracic acid with soda occurring in a crude state (tincal) in India, Persia, China, Peru, Chili, &c., or prepared from a solution of boracic acid and of carbonate of soda combined and crystallized: used as a flux in soldering metals, and in making glass and artificial gems.—**Boracic**, bō-ras'ik, *a.* Of, pertaining to, or produced from borax.—*Boracic acid*, a compound of boron with oxygen and hydrogen.—**Boracite**, bō'ra-sīt, *n.* A mineral consisting of borate and chloride of magnesium.—**Borate**, bō'rāt, *n.* A salt formed by a combination of boracic acid with any base.

Borborygmus, **Borborygm**, bor-bor-ig'mus, bor'bor-im, *n.* [Gr. *borborygmos*, from *borboryzō*, to have a rumbling in the bowels.] The rumbling noise caused by wind within the intestines.

Borcer, bōrs'ér, *n.* A steel-pointed iron instrument for boring holes in rocks preparatory to blasting.

Bord, bōrd, *n.* [Fr., border, edge.] *Mining*, the face of coal parallel to the natural fissures.

Bordelais, bor-de-lā, *a.* Belonging to the Bordeaux district of France, a term applied to a class of fine red wines.

Border, bor'dėr, *n.* [Fr. *bordure*, *bord*, a border, *border*, to border, from the German. BOARD.] The outer part or edge of anything, as of a garment, piece of cloth, a country, &c.; margin; verge; brink; boundary; confine; frontier.—*v.i.* To have the edge or boundary adjoining; to be contiguous or adjacent; to approach; to come near: with *on* or *upon*.—*v.t.* To make a border to; to adorn with a border of ornaments; to form a border to; to touch at the edge or end; to be contiguous to; to limit.—**Borderer**, bor'dėr-ėr, *n.* One who dwells on a border, or at the extreme part or confines of a country, region, or tract of land.—**Border-land**, *n.* Land forming a border or frontier; an uncertain intermediate district.

Bore, bōr, *v.t.*—*bored*, *boring*. [A.Sax. *borian*; Icel. *bora*, Sw. *borra*, Dan. *bore*, D. *boren*, G. *bohren*, to bore; of same root with L. *foro*, to bore.] To pierce or perforate and make a round hole in; to drill a hole in; to form by piercing or drilling (to *bore* a hole); to force a narrow and difficult passage through; to weary by tedious iteration or repetition; to tire by insufferable dulness; to tease; to annoy; to pester.—*v.i.* To pierce or enter by drilling, &c.; to push forward toward a certain point.—*n.* The hole made by boring; hence, the cavity or hollow of a gun, cannon, pistol, or other firearm; the calibre, whether formed by boring or not; a person that tires or wearies, especially by trying the patience; a dull person who forces his company and conversation upon us; anything troublesome or annoying.—**Boredom**, bōr'dum, *n.* The domain of bores; bores collectively; the state of being bored or of being a bore.—**Borer**, bōr'ėr, *n.* One who or that which bores; a term sometimes applied to certain worms, insects, fishes, which penetrate foreign bodies.

Bore, bōr, *n.* [Icel. *bára*, a wave or swell.] A sudden influx of the tide into the estuary of a river from the sea, the inflowing water rising and advancing like a wall, rushing with tremendous noise against the current for a considerable distance.

Bore, bōr, pret. of *bear* (which see).

Boreal, bō'rē-al, *a.* [L. *borealis*, from *boreas*, the north wind.] Northern; pertaining to the north or the north wind.

Borecole, bōr'kōl, *n.* A variety of hardy winter cabbage with the leaves curled or wrinkled, and not forming into a hard head.

Boric, bō'rik, *a.* Same as *Boracic*.—**Boride**, bō'rīd, *n.* A compound of boron with an element.

Born, born, pp. of *bear*, to bring forth.

Borne, bōrn, pp. of *bear*, to carry, &c.

Borne, bōrn, *n.* BOURN.

Boroglyceride, bō-rō-glis'ėr-id, *n.* [From *boron* and *glycerine*.] A substance composed of boric acid and glycerine, used as an antiseptic.

Boron, bō'ron, *n.* [From *borax*.] Sym. B. *Chem.* the characteristic element contained in borax, forming dark-coloured brilliant crystals, or sometimes a dark-brown powder.

Borough, bur'ō, *n.* [A.Sax. *burg*, *burh*, a fort, town, city; Icel. Sw. Dan. *borg*, Goth. *baurgo*, G. D. *burg*; root in A.Sax. *beorgan*, Goth. *bairgan*, G. *bergen*, to protect. From same root are *bury*, *borrow*, *burrow*, *barrow* (grave mound), &c.] A corporate town or township; a town with a properly organized municipal government.—**Borough-English**, *n.* *Law*, a customary descent of estates to the youngest son instead of the eldest, or, if the owner leaves no son, to the youngest brother.—**Borough-monger**, *n.* One who buys or sells the parliamentary representation of a borough.

Borrow, bor'rō, *v.t.* [A.Sax. *borgian*, properly to take on security, from *borg*, *borh*, security, from *beorgan*, to protect; G. and D. *borgen*, to borrow. BOROUGH.] To ask and obtain on loan, trust, or on credit, with the intention of returning or giving an equivalent for; to take or adopt from another or from a foreign source and use as one's own; to adopt; to appropriate; to imitate; to copy.—**Borrower**, bor'rō-ėr, *n.* One who borrows; one who takes what belongs to another and uses it as his own; a copier; an imitator; a plagiarist.

Borstal, bor'stal, *n.* [From Borstal in Kent.] A system of imprisonment for criminals, chiefly young, based on indeterminate sentences.

Bort, bort, *n.* Diamonds too coarse for ornamental setting, or small fragments of pure diamonds, used, when reduced to a powder, for polishing and grinding.

Boscage, **Boskage**, bos'kāj, *n.* [O.Fr. *boscage*, from the German. BUSH.] A mass of growing trees or shrubs; woods; groves or thickets; sylvan foliage.

Bosch-vark, **Bosh-vark**, bosh'värk, *n.* [D. *bosch*, wood, and *vark*, hog.] The bush-hog or bush-pig of South Africa, one of the most formidable members of the swine family.

Bosh, bosh, *n.* [Turk., empty, vain, useless.] Nonsense; absurdity; trash.

Bosk,† bosk, *n.* [An old form of *bush.*] A thicket; a small close natural wood, especially of bushes. (*Tenn.*) — **Boskage**, *n.* BOSCAGE. — **Bosky**, bos'ki, *a.* Bushy; covered with groves or thickets. (*Mil.*)

Bosom, bö'zum, *n.* [A.Sax. *bósm*, D. *boezem*, G. *busen*, probably from root of *bow*, meaning literally a swelling or protruding part.] The breast of a human being; the folds of the dress about the breast; the seat of the tender affections, passions, inmost thoughts, wishes, secrets, &c.; embrace or compass (the *bosom* of the church); something likened to the human bosom (the *bosom* of the earth, of a lake, &c.).—*a.* Intimate; familiar; close; dear. — *v.t.* To inclose or harbour in the bosom; to embrace; to keep with care; to cherish intimately; to conceal; to embosom.

Boss, bos, *n.* [Fr. *bosse*, a swelling, from O.H.G. *bôzo*, a bunch or bundle, same root as G. *boszen*, to beat; E. *beat.*] A protuberant part; a round, swelling body; a projecting mass; a stud or knob; a protuberant ornament of silver, ivory, or other material, used on bridles, harness, &c.; *arch.* an ornament placed at the intersection of the ribs or groins in vaulted or flat roofs.—*v.t.* To ornament with bosses; to bestud; to emboss. (*Shak.*)—**Bossy**, bos'i, *a.* Containing a boss; ornamented with bosses.

Boss, bos, *n.* [D. *baas*, a master.] An employer; a master; a superintendent; a chief man.

Bostangi, bos-tan'jē, *n. pl.* [Turk., from *bostan*, a garden.] A class of men in Turkey, originally the sultan's gardeners, but now also employed in various capacities more closely connected with his person.

Bot, **Bot-fly**. BOTT.

Botany, bot'a-ni, *n.* [As if from a form *botaneia*, from Gr. *botanē*, herbage, a plant, from *boskō*, to feed.] The science which treats of the vegetable kingdom, dealing with the forms, structure, and tissues of plants, the laws or conditions which regulate their growth or development, the functions of their various organs, the classification of the various specific forms of plants, their distribution over the face of the globe, and their condition at various geological epochs. — *Botany Bay*, Sydney, N.S.W., from its botanical richness when discovered by Captain Cook, 1770; as a penal settlement, in 1787.—**Botanic**, **Botanical**, bō-tan'ik, bō-tan'ik-al, *a.* Pertaining to botany; relating to plants in general.—**Botanically**, bō-tan'ik-al-li, *adv.* In a botanical manner; after the manner of a botanist; according to a system of botany.—**Botanist**, bot'an-ist, *n.* One skilled in botany; one versed in the knowledge of plants or vegetables, their structure, and generic and specific differences. — **Botanize**, bot'an-īz, *v.i.*—*botanized, botanizing.* To study plants; to investigate the vegetable kingdom; to seek for plants with a view to study them.

Botargo, **Botarga**, bō-tär'gō, bō-tär'ga, *n.* [Sp.] A relishing sort of food, made of the roes of the mullet or tunny strongly salted after they have become putrid, much used on the coast of the Mediterranean.

Botch, boch, *n.* [O.E. *bocche*, *botche*, a sore, a swelling, from O.Fr. *boce*, a boss, a botch, a boil, a parallel form of *boss*; comp. O.D. *butse*, a boil, a swelling.] A swelling on the skin; a large ulcerous affection; a boil or blotch; a patch, or the part of a garment patched or mended in a clumsy manner; a part in any work bungled or ill-finished; bungled work generally.—*v.t.* To mark or cover with botches or boils†; to mend or patch in a clumsy manner; to perform or express in a bungling manner.—**Botcher**, boch'ėr, *n.* One who botches; a clumsy workman at mending; a mender of old clothes; a bungler.—**Botchery**,† boch'ėr-i, *n.* A botching, or that which is done by botching; clumsy workmanship.—**Botchy**, boch'i, *a.* Marked with botches; full of botches.

Both, bōth, *a.* and *pron.* [A Scandinavian word=Icel. *báthir*, *bœthi*, Sc. *baith*, Dan. *baade*, Goth. *bajoths*, G. *beide*, both. The first element is seen in A. Sax. *bátwá*, both-two, both, Goth. *bai*, both, L. *ambo*, G. *amphō*, Skr. *ubha*, both.] The one and the other; the two; the pair or the couple. In such a sentence as '*both* men were there', it is an adjective; in 'he invited James and John, and *both* went', it is a pronoun; in 'the men *both* went', 'he took them *both*', it is a pronoun in apposition to *men*, *them*. It is often used as a conjunction in connection with *and*—*both* . . . *and* being equivalent to as well the one as the other; not only this but also that; equally the former and the latter.

Bother, boᴛʜ'ėr, *v.t.* [Probably a word of Irish origin; comp. Ir. *buaidhirt*, trouble, affliction; *buaidhrim*, I vex, disturb; Ir. and Gael. *buair*, to vex, trouble.] To perplex; to perturb; to tease; to annoy.—*v.i.* To trouble or worry one's self; to make many words or much ado.—*n.* A trouble, vexation, or plague.—**Botheration**, boᴛʜ-ėr-ā'shon, *n.* The act of bothering, or state of being bothered; annoyance; trouble; vexation; perplexity.—**Botherer**, boᴛʜ'ėr-ėr, *n.* One who bothers, vexes, or annoys.

Bothie, **Bothy**, both'i, *n.* [Gael. *bothag*, a cot, from same root as *booth.*] In Scotland a house for the accommodation of workpeople engaged in the same employment; a farm building in which the unmarried male or female servants or labourers are lodged.

Bothrenchyma, both-ren'ki-ma, *n.* [Gr. *bothros*, a pit, and *engchyma*, a tissue.] *Bot.* a term applied to the pitted tissue or dotted ducts of plants; cellular tissue, the sides of which are marked by pits sunk in the substance of the membrane.

Botryoid, **Botryoidal**, bot'ri-oid, bot-ri-oi'dal, *a.* [Gr. *botrys*, a bunch of grapes, and *eidos*, form.] Having the form of a bunch of grapes; like grapes, as a mineral presenting an aggregation of small globes.

Bott, **Bot**, bot, *n.* [Gael. *botus*, a bott, *boiteag*, a maggot.] A name given to the larvæ or maggots of several species of gadfly when found in the intestines of horses, under the hides of oxen, in the nostrils of sheep, &c.: generally in plural.—**Bot-fly**, *n.* A fly that produces botts.

Bottine, bot-ēn, *n.* [Fr., dim. of *botte*, a boot.] A half-boot; a lady's boot; also, an appliance resembling a boot, with straps, springs, buckles, &c., to obviate distortion in the lower extremities of children.

Bottle, bot'l, *n.* [Fr. *bouteille*, from L.L. *buticula*, a dim. from *butica*, a kind of vessel, from Gr. *boutis*, a flask.] A hollow vessel of glass, leather, or other material, with a narrow mouth, for holding and carrying liquors; the contents of a bottle; as much as a bottle contains; hence, *fig.* *the bottle* is used as equivalent to strong drink in general; the practice of drinking (to be fond of *the bottle*). — *v.t.* — *bottled, bottling.* To put into bottles.—**Bottler**, bot'lėr, *n.* One whose occupation it is to bottle wines, spirits, beer, or the like.—**Bottle-fish**, *n.* A fish of the eel family with a long whip-like tail and a body capable of being inflated like a sack or leathern bottle from 4 to 6 feet long.—**Bottle-glass**, *n.* A coarse green glass used in the manufacture of bottles.—**Bottle-green**, *a.* Of a dark green colour like common bottle-glass.—**Bottle-head**, *n.* The whale called also the *Bottle-nose.* — **Bottle-holder**, *n.* One who waits upon another in a prize-fight, administering refreshment, wiping off blood, &c.; hence, a backer; a second; a supporter in a conflict of any kind.—**Bottle-nose**, *n.* A whale measuring from 22 to 28 feet long, and having a beaked snout, occurring in high north latitudes; also, the caaing-whale. — **Bottle-nosed**, *a.* Having a nose bottle-shaped; with a nose full and swollen about the wings and end.—**Bottle-tit**, *n.* The long-tailed titmouse, so called from its bottle-shaped nest.—**Bottle-tree**, *n.* An Australian tree allied to the baobab, with a stem which bulges out enormously in the middle, and contains much sap.

Bottle, bot'l, *n.* [O.Fr. *botel*, dim. of *botte*, a bundle, from O.H.G. *bôzo*, a bundle. BOSS.] A quantity of hay or grass tied or bundled up for fodder.

Bottom, bot'om, *n.* [A. Sax. *botm*, bottom = D. *bodem*, Icel. *botn*, O.H.G. *podam*, Mod.G. *boden*, from same root as L. *fundus*, Gr. *pythmēn*, base, bottom.] The lowest or deepest part of anything, as distinguished from the top; that on which anything rests or is founded; utmost depth either literally or figuratively; base; foundation; the ground under any body of water; the lower or hinder extremity of the trunk of an animal; the buttocks; the portion of a chair for sitting on; the seat; low land formed by alluvial deposits along a river; a dale; a valley; the part of a ship below the wales; hence, the ship itself; power of endurance; stamina; native strength.—*a.* At the bottom; lowest; undermost; having a low situation; alluvial. —*v.t.* To found or build upon; to base; to furnish with a bottom.—**Bottomed**, bot'omd, *a.* Having a bottom of this or that kind: used in composition.—**Bottomless**, bot'om-les, *a.* Without a bottom; hence, fathomless; whose bottom cannot be found by sounding. — **Bottomry**, bot'om-ri, *n.* The act of borrowing money, and pledging the *bottom* of the ship, that is, the ship itself, as security for the repayment of the money.

Bottom, bot'om, *n.* [W. *botwm*, a boss, a bud, a button.] A ball or skein of thread; a cocoon.—*v.t.* To wind round something, as in making a ball of thread.

Botulism, bot'ū-lizm, *n.* [L. *botulus.*] A disease, of a contagious character, producing the effects of paralysis without facial distortion. Originally, but erroneously, connected with the theory of its origin in bad sausages.

Bouche, **Bouch**, bösh, *v.t.* [Fr. *bouche*, mouth.] To form or drill a new mouth or vent in, as a gun which has been spiked.

Boudoir, bö-dwar, *n.* [Fr., from *bouder*, to pout, to sulk.] A small room to which a lady may retire to be alone, or in which she may receive her intimate friends.

Bough, bou, *n.* [A. Sax. *bóg*, *bóh*, an arm, a shoulder, a bough; Icel. *bógr*, Dan. *boug*, *bov*, the shoulder, a vessel's bow; allied to Gr. *pēchys*, the fore-arm, Skr. *bâhus*, the arm. *Bow* (of a ship) is the same word.] An arm or large branch of a tree.

Bought, bąt, pret. & pp. of *buy* (which see).

Bougie, bö-zhē, *n.* [Fr., a wax-candle, from Sp. *bugia*, from *Bugia*, in North Africa, whence wax-candles were first brought. A wax taper; *surg.* a slender flexible cylinder made of waxed linen or silk cord, or of caoutchouc, steel, German silver, &c., intended for introduction into the urethra, œsophagus, or rectum, when those passages are obstructed, as by stricture.

Bouilli, bö-yē, *n.* [Fr., from *bouillir*, to boil.] Meat stewed with vegetables; boiled or stewed meat of any kind.—**Bouillon**, bö-yoṅ, *n.* [Fr.] Broth; soup.

Boulder, bōl'dėr, *n.* From Dan. *buldre*, E. dial. *bolder*, Sw. *bullra*, to make a loud noise, to thunder; Sw. dial. *bullersten* (*sten* =stone), a large pebble; lit. a stone that makes a thundering noise.] A water-worn roundish stone of considerable size, and larger than a pebble; *geol.* applied to ice-worn and smoothed blocks lying on the surface of the soil, or imbedded in the clays and gravels of the drift formation.—**Boulder-clay**, *n.* The stiff, unlaminated, tenacious clay of the glacial or drift epoch or ice-age.

Boule, **Boule-work**, böl, böl'wėrk, *n.* Same as *Buhl.*

Boulevard, böl-vär, *n.* [Fr., older forms

boulevert, boulevere, borrowed and altered from G. *bollwerk*. BULWARK.] Originally, a bulwark or rampart of a fortification or fortified town; hence a public walk or street occupying the site of demolished fortifications: now sometimes extended to any wide street or walk encircling a town.

Bounce, bouns, *v.i.*—*bounced, bouncing*. [O.E. *bounsen, bunsen*, to strike suddenly; L.G. *bunsen*, to knock; D. *bonzen*, to strike, bounce; *bons*, a bounce; imitative of the noise of a blow.] To make a sudden leap or spring; to jump or rush suddenly; to knock or thump; to boast or bluster; to brag.—*v.t.* To drive against anything suddenly and violently.—*n.* A heavy blow, thrust, or thump; a loud heavy sound; a sudden crack or noise; a boast; a piece of brag or bluster; boastful language; exaggeration; a bold or impudent lie.—*adv.* With a bounce or abrupt movement; abruptly (to come *bounce* into a room).—**Bouncer**, bouns'ėr, *n.* One that bounces; a boaster) a bully; a bragging liar; a barefaced lie; something big or large of its kind.—**Bouncing**, bouns'ing, *a.* Vigorous; strong; stout: exaggerated; excessive; big.—**Bouncingly**, bouns'ing-li, *adv.* In a bouncing manner.

Bound, bound, *n.* [O.Fr. *bodne, bonne*, a bound, limit (Fr. *borne*), from L.L. *bodina, bonna*, a boundary, from Armor. *boden*, a cluster of trees serving as a boundary.] That which limits or circumscribes; the external or limiting line of any object or of space (to pass beyond the *bounds*); hence, that which keeps in or restrains; limit (to set *bounds* to ambition).—*v.t.* To set bounds or limits to; to act as a bound or limit to; to limit; to terminate; to restrain or confine; to circumscribe.—**Boundary**, boun'-da-ri, *n.* [From *bound*, with a Latin termination.] That which marks a bound or limit; a limit; a bound.—**Bounded**, boun'-ded, *a.* Limited; circumscribed; cramped; narrow (a man of *bounded* views).—**Bounder**, boun'dėr, *n.* One who or that which bounds; assertive, unduly forceful person. [Colloq.]—**Boundless**, bound'les, *a.* Without bounds or limits; unlimited; limitless; immeasurable; illimitable; infinite.—**Boundlessly**, bound'les-li, *adv.* In a boundless manner; infinitely.—**Boundlessness**, bound'les-nes, *n.* The state or quality of being boundless or without limits.

Bound, bound, *v.i.* [Fr. *bondir*, to leap, O.Fr. to ring, to echo; from L.L. *bombitare*, to resound, from L. *bombus*, a humming. BOMB.] To leap; to jump; to spring; to move forward by leaps; to rebound.—*n.* A leap; a spring; a jump; a rebound.

Bound, bound, pp. of *bind* (also pret.). Made fast by a band or by chains, fetters, &c.; hemmed in; kept back; tied; having a binding; obliged by moral ties; confined; restrained. Colloquially the word is often used as equivalent to certain, sure; as, he is *bound* to succeed; the town is *bound* to increase.

Bound, bound, *a.* [Formerly *boun*, from Icel. *búinn*, pp. of *búa*, to till, prepare, get ready. The *d* is parasitic, as in *sound*, from L. *sonus*. Same root as *boor, bower*.] Prepared; ready, hence, going or intending to go (outward *bound*); destined: often with *to* or *for* (a ship *bound for* London).

Bounden, boun'den, *a.* [An old participle of *bind*.] Obliged or beholden†; appointed; indispensable; obligatory (our *bounden* duty).

Bounty, boun'ti, *n.* [O.Fr. *bonteit*, Fr. *bonte*, goodness, favour, from L. *bonitas*, goodness, from *bonus*, good.] Liberality in bestowing gifts and favours; generosity; munificence; a favour bestowed from a benevolent disposition; that which is given bounteously; a free gift; a premium offered to induce men to enlist into the public service, or to encourage some branch of industry.—**Bounteous**, boun'tē-us, *a.* Disposed to give freely; free in bestowing gifts; bountiful; liberal; generous; munificent.—**Bounteously**, boun'tē-us-li, *adv.* In a bounteous manner; liberally.—**Bounteousness**, boun'tē-us-nes, *n.* The quality of being bounteous.—**Bountiful**, boun'ti-fu̧l, *a.* Liberal in bestowing gifts, favours, or bounties; munificent; generous.—**Bountifully**, boun'ti-fu̧l-li, *adv.* In a bountiful manner; liberally.—**Bountifulness**, boun'ti-fu̧l-nes, *n.*

Bouquet, bö-kā, *n.* [Fr., O.Fr. *bousquet, bosquet*, a little wood, dim. of *bosc*, a wood. BUSH.] A nosegay; a bunch of flowers; something resembling a bunch of flowers; an agreeable aromatic odour, such as that of the finer wines.

Bourdon, bör-doṅ, *n.* [Fr.] The drone of the bagpipe; a bass stop in the organ or harmonium having a drone-like quality of tone.

Bourg,† börg, *n.* [The French form of *borough, burgh*.] A town; a borough. (*Tenn.*)

Bourgeois, börzh-wą, *n.* [Fr., sing. & pl.] A citizen; a burgher; a man of middle rank.—**Bourgeois, Burgeois**, bur-jō', bur-jois', *n.* [Perhaps from a type-founder of the name.] A small kind of printing type, larger than brevier and smaller than longprimer.—**Bourgeoisie**, börzh-wą-zē, *n.* [Fr.] The middle classes of a country, especially those dependent on trade.

Bourgeon, bör'jon, *n.* [Fr. *bourgeon*, a bud.] A bud.—*v.i.* To sprout; to put forth buds.

Bourn, Borne, börn, bōrn, *n.* [Fr. *borne*, a limit, corruption of *bonne*, a boundary. BOUND.] A bound; a limit.

Bourn,‡ börn, *n.* [Prov. E. and Sc. *burn*, A.Sax. *burna*, a stream = D. *born*, Icel. *brunnr*, Sw. *brunn*, Goth. *brunna*, G. *brunnen*, a spring, a well.] A brook; a torrent; a rivulet; a burn. (*Shak.*)

Bourse, börs, *n.* [Fr., a purse, an exchange, from L. *bursa*, a hide, leather.] An exchange; a place where merchants assemble for general business.

Bouse, Bousy, böz, bö'zi. BOOSE, BOOSY.

Bout, bout, *n.* [Older form *bought*; same word as Dan. *bugt*, a bend, a bight; closely akin to E. *bight*, and verb to *bow*.] A twist or turn; a bend or flexure; a going and returning, as in ploughing, reaping, &c.; as much as is performed at one time; a trial; a set-to; a contest; a debauch.

Bouts-rimes, bö-rē-mā, *n. pl.* [Fr. *bout*, an end, and *rimé*, rhymed.] Words that rhyme given as the ends of a stanza, the other parts of the lines to be supplied by the ingenuity of another person.

Bouze. Same as *Boose*.

Bovine, bō'vīn, *a.* [L.L. *bovinus*, from L. *bos, bovis*, an ox.] Pertaining to oxen and cows, or the quadrupeds of the same family.

Bovril, bō'vril, *n.* [By the Company, derived from L. *bos, bovis*, and *ril*, an unknown force. Bulwer Lytton (*Coming Race*) gives it *vril*.] Trade name for beef-tea extract.

Bow, bou, *v.t.* [A.Sax. *búgan*, to bend (trans. and intrans.) = D. *buigen*, Dan. *böie*, Goth. *biugan*, G. *beugen*; cog. L. *fugio*, Gr. *pheugō*, to flee; Skr. *bhuj*, to bend. From same stem are *bow* (for arrows), *bight, bout*.] To make crooked or curved; to bend; to bend or incline, as the head or the body, in token of respect or civility; to bend or cause to yield; to subdue (to *bow* the will); to make a bow to (to *bow* a person out, &c.).—*v.i.* To bend in token of reverence, respect, or civility; to be bent or inflected; to curve.—*n.* An inclination of the head, or a bending of the body, in token of reverence, respect, or submission.—**Bower**, bou'ėr, *n.* One who bows.

Bow, bou, *n.* [Icel. *bógr*, Dan. *bov, boug*, a shoulder, the bow of a vessel; same word as *bough*.] *Naut.* the rounding part of a ship's side forward, on either side, terminating at the stem or prow.—**Bower**, bou'ėr, *n.* One of two anchors at the bow of a vessel, which are both kept in constant working use: called also *Bower-anchor*.—**Bowline**, bō'-lin, *n.* A rope fastened near the middle of the perpendicular edge of the square sails, and used to keep the weather edge of the sails tight forward towards the bow.—**Bowsprit**, bō'sprit, *n.* The large spar or boom projecting over the bow or stem of a vessel.

Bow, bō, *n.* [A.Sax. *boga*, Icel. *bogi*, Dan. *bue*, D. *boog*; from root of verb to *bow*.] A missile weapon made of a strip of wood or other elastic material, which, being bent by means of a string fastened to its two ends, can discharge an arrow placed endwise on the string by the latter being drawn back and suddenly let go; anything bent or in form of a curve, as the rain*bow*; an implement strung with horse-hair, by means of which the tone is produced from instruments of the violin kind; an instrument in use among smiths for turning a drill, with turners for turning wood, with hatters for breaking fur and wool, and consisting of a piece of wood more or less curved, and having a string extending from one extremity to the other; a kind of ornamental knot of ribbon or other material.—*v.t.* or *i.* *Mus.* to perform or play with the *bow*.—**Bowman**, bō'man, *n.* One who shoots with or is skilled in the use of the bow; an archer.—**Bowyer**, bō'yėr, *n.* An archer or bowman; a maker of bows.—**Bow-knot**, *n.* A slip-knot made by a ribbon or other material.—**Bow-leg**, *n.* A crooked or bandy leg.—**Bow-legged**, *a.* Having crooked or bandy legs.—**Bow-pen**, *n.* A metallic pen having the part which holds the ink bent out towards the middle.—**Bow-saw**, *n.* A flexible saw consisting of a very narrow blade fixed in a bow-shaped frame, used for cutting curves.—**Bow-shot**, *n.* The distance a bow can propel an arrow.—**Bow-string**, *n.* The string with which a bow is bent; a similar string used by the Turks for strangling offenders.—*v.t.* To strangle with a bow-string.—**Bow-window**, *n.* A window built so as to project from a wall, properly one that forms a segment of a circle.—**Bow-compass, Bow-compasses**, *n.* A pair of compasses of various forms for describing arcs, as a small instrument furnished with a bow-pen for describing circles with ink; a beam of wood or brass with three long screws to bend a lath or steel to any arc, used for drawing curves of large radius.

Bowdlerize, boud'lėr-īz, *v.t.* To abbreviate, or expunge texts of objectionable matter, on moral grounds. From Thomas Bowdler, who expurgated Shakespeare in 1818, in which "those words and expressions are omitted which cannot with propriety be read aloud in a family".

Bowel, bou'el, *n.* [O.Fr. *boel*, from L. *botellus*, a small sausage, an intestine.] One of the intestines of an animal; a gut, especially of man; *pl.* the supposed seat of pity or tenderness; hence kindness, compassion, or affection; the interior part of anything (the *bowels* of the earth).—*v.t.*—*bowelled, bowelling*. To take out the bowels of; to eviscerate.

Bower, bou'ėr, *n.* [A.Sax. *búr*, a chamber, from *búan*, to dwell; Icel. *búr*, a chamber, from *búa*, to live; akin *boor, bound* (ready).] A woman's private apartment; any room in a house except the hall (in these senses now only poetical); a shelter made with boughs or twining plants; an arbour; a shady recess.—**Bower-bird**, *n.* A name of certain Australian birds of the oriole family, about the size of a large starling, and remarkable for erecting bowers and adorning them with gay feathers, shells, and other bright-coloured objects, these bowers being used as places of resort, but not as nests.—**Bowered**, bou'ėrd, *a.* Furnished with bowers.

Bower, bou'ėr, *n.* [G. *bauer*, peasant, knave.] One of two cards at Euchre. The right bower is the knave of trumps, the left is the knave of same colour.

Bowie-knife, bō'i, *n.* [After its inventor, Colonel James *Bowie*.] A knife from 10 to 15 inches long and about 2 inches broad, worn as a weapon in the United States.

Bowl, bōl, *n.* [O.E. *bolle*, A.Sax. *bolla*, a bowl; Icel. *bolli*, M.H.G. *bolle*, a bowl; allied to *ball*.] A concave vessel of a somewhat semi-globular shape; a large cup with roundish outlines; a goblet: often used as the emblem of festivity; the hollow part of anything, as of a spoon or of a tobacco-pipe.

Bowl, bōl, *n.* [O.E. *bowle*, Fr. *boule*, from L. *bulla*, a bubble (whence verb to *boil*).] A ball of wood or other material used for rolling on a level surface at play; a ball of wood loaded on one side used in a game played on a level plat of green-sward; *pl.* the game played with such balls.—*v.i.* To play with bowls or at bowling; to roll a bowl, as in the game of bowls; to deliver the ball to be played by the batsman at cricket; to move rapidly and like a ball (*bowl* along).—*v.t.* To roll in the manner of a bowl; to pelt with or as with bowls.—**Bowler**, bōl′ėr, *n.* One who plays at bowls; *cricket*, the player who delivers the ball in order to be played by the batsman.—**Bowling-alley**, *n.* A covered place for the game of bowls.—**Bowling-green**, *n.* A level piece of green-sward kept smooth for bowling.

Bowlder, bōl′dėr, *n.* Same as *Boulder*.

Bowler, bō′lėr, *n.* A round-shaped felt hat. [Colloq.]

Bowse, bouz, *v.i.* To boose (which see); *naut.* to haul or pull hard.

Bow-wow, bou-wou′, *n.* A dog, from sound of bark; *a.* in a big, high, lofty strain or style.

Box, boks, *n.* [A.Sax. *box*, a box, from L. *buxus*, *buxum*, the box-tree, and something made of its wood.] A case or receptacle of any size and made of any material; the driver's seat on a carriage; a present, especially a Christmas present; a compartment for the accommodation of a small number of people, as in a theatre; a narrow confined inclosed place; a place of shelter for one or two men engaged in certain duties, as sentries, signalmen, &c.; a small house for sportsmen during the shooting season or the like.—*v.t.* To inclose, as in a box; to confine.—*To box the compass*, to repeat or go over the points of the compass in order, or to answer any questions regarding the divisions of the compass; to perform a swift change in politics.—**Boxing-day**, **Boxing-night**, *n.* The day and night after Christmas-day when Christmas-boxes and presents are given [in England].

Box, boks, *n.* [Corresponding by metathesis to Dan. *bask*, a slap, *baske*, to beat; akin *bash*.] A blow with the fist.—*v.t.* To strike with the fist or hand.—*v.i.* To fight with the fists; to practise fighting with the fists.—**Boxer**, bok′sėr, *n.* One who fights with his fists; a pugilist; member of Chinese anti-foreign society.—**Boxing-glove**, *n.* A large padded glove used for sparring.

Box, boks, *n.* [L. *buxus*, Gr. *pyxos*, the box-tree. Box, a case.] The name given to several species of trees or shrubs, the most important being a small evergreen tree with small shining leaves, and yielding a hard close-grained wood, and the dwarf variety used as edgings of garden walks.—**Boxen**, bok′sen, *a.* Made of box-wood; resembling box†.—**Box-wood**, *n.* The fine hard-grained timber of the box-tree, much used by wood-engravers and in the manufacture of musical and mathematical instruments, &c.

Boy, boi, *n.* [Fris. *boi*, *boy*, a boy; allied to D. *boef*, G. *bube*, Sw. *bue*, a boy.] A male child from birth to the age of puberty; a lad; a man wanting in vigour, experience, judgment; a familiar term applied in addressing or speaking of grown persons, especially one's associates; in compounds sometimes applied to grown men without any idea of youth or contempt; as, a post*boy*, a pot*boy*.—**Boyhood**, boi′hụd, *n.* The state of being a boy or of immature age.—**Boyish**, boi′ish, *a.* Belonging to a boy; pertaining to boyhood; in a disparaging sense; childish; trifling; puerile.—**Boyishly**, boi′ish-li, *adv.* In a boyish manner.—**Boyishness**, boi′ish-nes, *n.* The quality of being boyish.

Boycott, boi′kot, *v.t.* [From Capt. *Boycott*, an Irish landlord, the first prominent victim of the system in 1880.] To combine in refusing to work for, to buy from or sell to, or to have any dealings with, on account of difference of opinion on social and political questions or the like.

Boza, bō′za, *n.* [Of Oriental origin.] An intoxicating fermented drink made in Egypt from millet-seed or from darnel and hemp-seed.

Brabançonne, bra-bañ′son, *n.* The national air of Belgium, from Brabant.

Brabble, brab′l, *n.* [D. *brabbelen*, to confound, to stammer.] A broil; a wrangle.—*v.i.*—*brabbled*, *brabbling*. To dispute or quarrel noisily.—**Brabblement**, brab′l-ment, *n.* A clamorous contest; a brabble.—**Brabbler**, brab′lėr, *n.* A quarrelsome noisy fellow.

Brace, brās, *n.* [O.Fr. *brace*, *brasse*, &c., from L. *brachia*, the arms, pl. of *brachium*, an arm; allied to Gael. *brac*, W. *braic*, the arm.] That which holds anything tight, tense, firm, or secure, or which supports, binds, or strengthens, as a piece of timber placed near and across the angles in the frame of a building; a thick strap which supports a carriage on wheels; suspenders passing over a man's shoulders for supporting his trousers; the crank-shaped stock in which boring-tools, &c., are held, serving as a lever for turning them, &c.; a mark (⏟) used in written or printed matter connecting two or more words or lines; a couple or pair (not of persons unless in contempt).—*v.t.*—*braced*, *bracing*. To bind or tie closely; to make tense; to strain up; to increase the tension, tone, or vigor of (the nerves, the system); to strengthen; to invigorate.—**Bracer**, bras′ėr, *n.* One who or that which braces; an archery guard for the left fore-arm.—**Bracing**, brās′ing, *a.* Giving vigor or tone to the bodily system.

Bracelet, brās′let, *n.* [Fr. *bracelet*, a dim. of O.Fr. *bracel*, *brachel*, an armlet, from L. *brachile*, from *brachium*, the arm. BRACE.] An ornament encircling the wrist, now worn mostly by ladies.

Brach, brach, *n.* [O.Fr. *brache*, Fr. *braque*, from O.H.G. *bracke*, *bracco*, G. *brack*, a kind of hunting dog.] A bitch of the hound kind; a species of scenting hound; a pointer or setter.

Brachial, brā′ki-al, *a.* [L. *brachium*, the arm.] Belonging to the arm; of the nature of an arm; resembling an arm.—**Brachiate**, brā′ki-āt, *a.* *Bot.* having branches in pairs, nearly horizontal, and each pair at right angles with the next.

Brachiopoda, brā-ki-op′o-da, *n.pl.* [Gr. *brachiōn*, an arm, and *pous*, a foot.] A class of marine, bivalve, molluscoid animals, including the lamp-shells, &c., so named from the development of a long spirally-coiled fringed respiratory appendage or arm on either side of the mouth.—**Brachiopod**, brā′ki-o-pod, *n.* One of the Brachiopoda.—**Brachiopodous**, brā-ki-op′o-dus, *a.* Belonging to the class Brachiopoda.

Brachistochrone, bra-kis′to-krōn, *n.* [Gr. *brachistos*, shortest, *chronos*, time.] *Math.* the curve of shortest descent, or that along which a body will move in the least possible time from point to point.

Brachycephalic, **Brachycephalous**, brak′i-se-fal″ik, brak-i-sef′al-us, *a.* [Gr. *brachys*, short, and *kephalē*, the head.] In *ethn.* terms applied to heads (or races possessing such heads) whose diameter from side to side is not much less than that from front to back, their ratio being as 0·8 to 1, as those of the Mongolian type.

Brachygraphy, bra-kig′ra-fi, *n.* [Gr. *brachys*, short, and *graphē*, a writing.] The art or practice of writing in shorthand; stenography.—**Brachygrapher**, bra-kig′ra-fėr, *n.* A writer in shorthand.

Brachyura, **Brachyoura**, brak-i-ū′ra, brak-i-ou′ra, *n.pl.* [Gr. *brachys*, short, and *oura*, tail.] A section of ten-footed crustaceans (Decapoda), with the abdomen forming a very short, jointed tail, folded forwards closely under the thorax, as in the common edible crab.—**Brachyural**, **Brachyurous**, brak-i-ū′ral, brak-i-ū-rus, *a.* Short-tailed: applied to certain Crustacea, as the crab, to distinguish them from the macrurous or long-tailed crustaceans, as the lobster.—Also **Brachyoural**, brak-i-ou′ral.—**Brachyuran**, brak-i-ū′ran, *n.* One of the Brachyura.

Bracken, brak′en, *n.* [A Scandinavian word; same as Sw. *bräken*, Dan. *bregne*, fern; closely allied to *brake*.] Fern. BRAKE.

Bracket, brak′et, *n.* [Ultimately perhaps from L. *brachium*, an arm.] A kind of short supporting piece projecting from a perpendicular surface, either plain or ornamentally carved, as an ornamental projection from the face of a wall to support a statue; a triangular wooden support for a shelf or the like; an ornamental piece supporting a hammer-beam; one of two projecting pieces attached to a wall, beam, &c., for carrying or supporting a line of shafting; *printing*, one of two marks [ ], used to inclose a reference, note, or explanation, to indicate an interpolation, rectify a mistake, &c.; a gas-pipe projecting from a wall, usually more or less ornamental.—*v.t.* To furnish with a bracket or with brackets; *printing*, to place within brackets; to connect by brackets.

Brackish, brak′ish, *a.* [D. and L.G. *brak*, G. *brack*, brackish.] Possessing a salt or somewhat salt taste; salt in a moderate degree; applied to water.—**Brackishness**, brak′ish-nes, *n.* The quality of being brackish.

Bract, brakt, *n.* [L. *bractea*, a thin plate of metal.] *Bot.* a modified leaf differing from other leaves in shape or colour, and generally situated on the peduncle near the flower.—**Bracteate**, brak′tē-āt, *a.* Furnished with bracts.—**Bracteated**, brak′tē-āt-ed, *a.* A term applied to coins or medals covered over with a thin plate of some richer metal.—**Bracteole**, **Bractlet**, brak′tē-ōl, brakt′let, *n.* A little bract on a partial flower-stalk or pedicel in a many-flowered inflorescence.

Brad, brad, *n.* [Same word as Icel. *broddr*, a spike, a nail; Dan. *brodde*, a frost-nail; A.Sax. *brord*, a prick, a spire of grass; comp. Gael. and Ir. *brod*, goad, sting.] A finishing nail with little or no head used where it is deemed proper to drive nails entirely into the wood.—**Brad-awl**, *n.* An awl to make holes for brads or other nails.

Bradypod, brad′i-pod, *n.* [Gr. *bradys*, slow, *pous*, *podos*, a foot.] A slow-moving animal; a sloth.

Brae, brā, *n.* [Icel. *brá*, eyelid, akin to G. *braue*, eyebrow.] A sloping bank, acclivity. [Scottish.]

Brag, brag, *v.i.*—*bragged*, *bragging*. [From the Celtic; W. *bragiaw*, Ir. *braghaim*, to boast; Gael. *bragaireachd*, boasting; Armor. *braga*, to make a display; from root of *break*.] To use boastful language; to speak vaingloriously; to boast; to vaunt; to swagger; to bluster.—*n.* A boast or boasting; a vaunt; the thing boasted of; a game at cards: so called because one player *brags* he has a better hand than the others, staking a sum of money on the issue.—**Braggadocio**, brag-a-dō′shi-ō, *n.* [From *Braggadochio*, a boastful character in Spenser's 'Faery Queen', from the verb to *brag*.] A boasting fellow; a braggart; empty boasting; brag.—**Braggardism**,† brag′ärd-izm, *n.* Boastfulness; vain ostentation. (*Shak.*)—**Braggart**, brag′ärt, *n.* [*Brag*, and suffix *-art*, *-ard*.] A boaster; a vain fellow.—*a.* Boastful; vainly ostentatious.—**Bragger**, brag′ėr, *n.* One who brags.—**Braggingly**, brag′ing-li, *adv.* In a bragging manner; boastingly.

Brahman, brä′man, *n.* Among the Hindus a member of the sacred or sacerdotal caste, who claim to have proceeded from the mouth of Brahmā (the Creator, one of the deities of the Hindu triad or trinity), and who are noted for their many minute religious observances, their abstemiousness, and their severe penances.—**Brahmanic**, **Brahmanical**, brä-man′ik, brä-man′ik-al, *a.* Of or pertaining to the Brahmans or their doctrines and worship.—**Brahmanism**, brä′man-izm, *n.* The religion or system of doctrines of the Brahmans.—

Brahmanist, brä'man-ist, *n.* An adherent of Brahmanism. These words are also spelled *Brahmin, Braminic*, &c.

Braid, brād, *v.t.* [A.Sax. *bredan, bregdan*, to weave, to braid; Icel. *bregtha*, to braid, *bragth*, a sudden movement; O.H.G. *brettan*, to braid.] To weave or intertwine, as hair, by forming three or more strands into one; to plait.—*n.* A sort of narrow textile band formed by plaiting or weaving several strands of silk, cotton, woollen, &c., together; a plait or plaited tress of hair.—**Braiding**, brād'ing, *n.* Braid, or trimming made of braid collectively.

Brail, brāl, *n.* [O.Fr. *braiel, braieul*, &c., a trouser-band, from *braies*, breeches, from L. *braccæ*, breeches.] BREECHES.] *Naut.* a rope attached to a fore-and-aft sail, or a jib to assist in taking in the sail.—*v.t.* To haul in by means of the brails: followed by *up*.

Braille, brāl, *n.* [Fr. *Braille*, inventor's name.] A system of reading with raised letters for the blind.

Brain, brān, *n.* [A.Sax. *brægen, bregen*, D. and O.Fris. *brein*.] The soft whitish mass inclosed in the skull in man and other vertebrate animals, forming the centre of the nervous system, and the seat of consciousness and volition, and in which the nerves and spinal marrow terminate; the cerebrum: sometimes used to include also the cerebellum; the understanding; the fancy; the imagination.—*v.t.* To dash out the brains of; to kill by beating out the brains.—**Brained**, brānd, *a.* Furnished with brains; used chiefly in composition.—**Brainish**, brān'ish, *a.* Hot-headed; furious (*Shak.*).—**Brainless**, brān'les, *a.* Without understanding or judgment; silly; stupid.—**Brainy**, brān'i, *a.* Provided with brains, intellectual. — **Brain-fever**, *n.* Inflammation of the brain.—**Brain-pan**, *n.* The skull which incloses the brain. (*Shak.*)—**Brain-sick**, *a.* Disordered in the understanding; fantastic; crotchety; crazed. — **Brain-sickly**, *adv.* Weakly; madly. (*Shak.*) — **Brain-sickness**, *n.* Disorder of the understanding.

Braise, Braize, brāz, *v.t.* [Fr. *baiser*, to braise, from Dan. *brase*, to fry; Sw. *brasa*, to flame. BRASS.] To bake, broil, or stew with herbs, spices, &c., in a closely-covered pan.—**Braising-pan**, *n.* A small covered pan or air-tight oven for braising meat in.

Braize, brāz, *n.* [By metathesis from A.Sax. *bærs*, a perch; D. *baars*, G. *barsch*.] A spiny-finned fish of an ovate shape and uniformly red colour, allied to the sea-bream, found on the British coasts.

Brake, brāk, *n.* [A.Sax. *bracce*, fern, bracken; L.G. *brake*, brushwood; allied to D. *braak*, Dan. *brak*, G. *brach*, fallow.] A fern; bracken; a place overgrown with brakes or brushwood, shrubs, and brambles; a thicket, as of canes, &c.—**Braky**, brā'ki, *a.* Full of brakes, ferns, brambles, shrubs, &c.; thorny; rough.

Brake, brāk, *n.* [From the verb to *break*; comp. L.G. *brake*, G. *breche*, an instrument for breaking flax; O.D. *brake*, a fetter for the neck, *braake*, an instrument for holding an animal by the nose.] An instrument or machine to break flax or hemp; a pump-handle; a kneading-trough; a sharp bit or snaffle; a frame for confining refractory horses while shoeing; a large heavy harrow for breaking clods; a kind of wagonette; a strong heavy vehicle with a seat only for the driver, used for breaking in young horses to harness; an appliance used to stop or retard the motion of a machine or vehicle by friction, and generally consisting of a simple or compound lever which can be pressed forcibly against the rim of a wheel on one of the axles of the machine or carriage.—**Brakeman, Brakesman**, brāk'man, brāks'man, *n.* The man whose business is to stop a railway train by applying the brake; *mining*, the man in charge of a winding-engine.—**Brake-van**, *n.* The van or car in a railway train to whose wheels the brake is applied.

Bramble, bram'bl, *n.* [A. Sax. *bremel, brembel*, from stem *bram, brem* (seen also in *broom*), *el* being simply a termination and *b* inserted as in *number*, &c., comp. L.G. *brummel*beere, Dan. *brambär*, G. *brombeere*, Sw. *brom*-bär, a blackberry.] A prickly trailing shrub of the rose family growing in hedges and waste places, and bearing a black berry somewhat like a raspberry; the berry itself; the blackberry.—**Brambled**, bram'bld, *a.* Overgrown with brambles.—**Brambly**, bram'bli, *adv.* Full of brambles.—**Brambling**, bram'bling, *n.* A finch inhabiting Britain, very like the chaffinch but larger.

Bramin, brä'min, *n.* BRAHMAN.

Bran, bran, *n.* [A Celtic word = W. Ir. Gael. *bran*, bran, chaff; Armor. *brenn*, bran, whence O.Fr. *bren*.] The outer coat of wheat, rye, or other farinaceous grain, separated from the flour by grinding.—**Branny**, bran'i, *a.* Resembling bran; consisting of bran.

Branch, bransh, *n.* [From Fr. *branche*, a branch, from Armor. *branc*, an arm; connected with L.L. *branca*, a claw, W. *braich*, L. *brachium*, an arm.] A portion of a tree, shrub, or other plant springing from the stem, or from a part ultimately supported by the stem; a bough; a shoot; something resembling a branch; an offshoot or part extending from the main body of a thing; any member or part of a body or system; a department, section, or subdivision; a line of family descent, in distinction from some other line or lines from the same stock.—*v.i.* To spread in branches; to send out branches as a plant; to divide into separate parts or subdivisions; to diverge (a road *branches* off); to ramify.—*v.t.*† To divide, as into branches; to adorn, as with needle-work, representing branches, flowers, or twigs.—**Branchless**, bransh'les, *a.* Without branches; bare; naked; barren.—**Branchlet**, bransh'let, *n.* A small branch; a twig; a shoot.—**Branchy**, bran'shi, *a.* Full of or consisting of branches, or having wide-spreading branches; covered or shaded with branches.—**Branchiness**, bran'shines, *n.*

Branchiæ, brang'ki-ē, *n. pl.* [L.] The respiratory organs of fishes, &c.; the gills.—**Branchial**, brang'ki-al, *a.* Relating to the branchiæ or gills; performed by means of branchiæ.

Branchiopoda, brang-ki-op'o-da, *n. pl.* [Gr. *branchia*, gills, and *pous, podos*, a foot.] An order of crustaceous animals, so called because their branchiæ, or gills, are situated on the feet, as in the water-fleas, brine-shrimps, &c.—**Branchiopod**, brang'ki-o-pod, *n.* An animal belonging to the order Branchiopoda. — **Branchiopodous**, brang-ki-op'o-dus, *a.* Gill-footed; belonging to the order Branchiopoda.

Branchiostegal, Branchiostegous, brang-ki-os'te-gal, brang-ki-os'te-gus, *a.* [Gr. *branchia*, gills, and *stegos*, a covering.] Having gill-covers, or covered gills; having a membrane covering the gills below the operculum; covering the gills (the *branchiostegal* membrane).

Brand, brand, *n.* [A. Sax. *brand*, a burning, a sword = Icel. *brandr*, fire-brand, sword; Dan. D. and G. *brand*, a burning. The sword is so called from its gleaming. Akin to verb *burn*.] A piece of wood burning or partly burned; a sword; a mark made by burning with a hot iron or by other means, as on commodities to indicate the quality or manufacturer, on sheep to indicate the owner, or on criminals to indicate their crime or for identification; a trade-mark; hence, kind or quality; a mark of infamy; a stigma; a disease in vegetables by which their leaves and tender bark are partially destroyed as if they had been burned.—*v.t.* To burn or impress a mark upon with a hot iron, or to distinguish by a similar mark; to fix a mark or character of infamy upon; to stigmatize as infamous.—**Brander**, brand'ėr, *n.* One who brands.—**Brand-iron, Branding-iron**, *n.* An iron to brand with.—**Brand-new**, *a.* A more correct form of *Bran-new* (which see).

Brandish, bran'dish, *v.t.* [From Fr. *brandir, brandissant*, from Teut. *brand*, a sword. BRAND.] To move or wave, as a weapon; to raise and move in various directions; to shake or flourish.—**Brandisher**, bran'dish-ėr, *n.* One who brandishes.

Brandling, brand'ling, *n.* The parr or young of the salmon, so named from having, as it were, branded markings; also, a small red worm used for bait in fresh-water fishing.

Brandy, bran'di, *n.* [O.E. *brandywine*, D. *brandewijn*, lit. burnt wine—D. *branden*, to burn, to distil, and *wijn*, wine, like G. *branntwein—brennen*, to burn, and *wein*, wine. BRAND.] A spirituous liquor obtained by the distillation of wine, or of the refuse of the wine-press; a name now also given to spirit distilled from other liquors or fruit juices.

Brangle, brang'gl, *n.* [Perhaps for *braggle*, from *brag*.] A wrangle; a squabble; a noisy contest or dispute.—*v.i.* To wrangle; to dispute contentiously, to squabble.

Brank, brangk, *n.* [L. *brance*, properly an ancient Gallic word.] Buckwheat.

Branks, brangks, *n.* [From the Celtic: Gael. *brangas*, a kind of pillory; Ir. *brancas*, a halter.] An instrument of the nature of a bridle formerly used for correcting scolding women; a scolding-bridle.

Bran-new, bran'nū, *a.* [For *brand-new*, the original form, from *brand*, a burning, and *new*.] *Lit.* glowing like metal newly out of the fire or forge; hence, quite new.

Brash, brash, *n.* [From Fr. *brèche*, a breach, broken stuff, breccia.] A confused heap of fragments, as masses of loose, broken, or angular fragments of rocks; small fragments of crushed ice, collected by winds or currents, near the shore; refuse boughs of trees.

Brasier, brā'zi-ėr, *n.* [Fr. *brasier, braisier*, from *braise*, embers, live coals; same origin as *braze, brass*.] An open pan for burning wood or coal.

Brasier, brā'zi-ėr, *n.* [From *brass* or from *braze*.] An artificer who works in brass.

Brasil, bra-zil', *n.* Same as *Brazil*.

Brass, bras, *n.* [A. Sax. *bræs*, brass = Icel. *bras*, solder; from verbal stem seen in Icel. *brasa*, to harden by fire; Sw. *brasa*, to blaze; Dan. *brase*, to fry (whence Fr. *braise*, live embers, *braser*, to braze, *braiser*, to braise).] A malleable and fusible alloy of copper and zinc, of a yellow colour, usually containing about one-third of its weight of zinc; a utensil, ornament, or other article made of brass, as a monumental plate bearing effigies, coats of arms, &c., inlaid in a slab of stone, common in the pavements of mediæval churches; *pl.* musical instruments of the trumpet kind; brazenness or impudence (colloq.); money (colloq.). — *v.t.* To cover or coat over with brass.—**Brassy**, bras'i, *a.* Resembling or composed of brass; brazen.—*n.* A golf-club shod with brass.—**Brassiness**, bras'i-nes, *n.* — **Brass-band**, *n.* A company of musicians who perform on instruments of brass.—**Brass-finisher**, *n.* A workman who perfects and polishes articles made of brass. — **Brass-founder**, *n.* A founder or maker of articles in cast brass.

Brassard, bras'ėrd, *n.* [Fr., from *bras*, arm.] A protecting piece, or a badge, for the arm. Also *Brassart*.

Brat, brat, *n.* [Ir. and Gael. *brat*, a rag, an apron.] A child: so called in contempt.

Brattice, brat'is, *n.* [O.Fr. *bretesche*, a bartizan; probably from G. *bret*, a board, a plank.] A partition which divides a mining shaft into two chambers, serving as the upcast and downcast shafts for ventilation, or placed across a gallery to keep back noxious gases, or prevent the escape of water; a fence put round dangerous machinery.

Bravado, bra-vā'dō, *n.* [Sp. *bravada*, Fr. *bravade*. BRAVE.] An arrogant menace, intended to intimidate; a boast; a brag.

Brave, brāv, *a.* [Fr. *brave*, brave, gay, proud, braggard; Sp. and It. *bravo*, brave, courageous; perhaps from the Celtic; comp. Armor. *brao, brav*, gaily dressed, fine, handsome; also O.Sw. *braf*, good.] Courageous; bold; daring; intrepid; high-spirited; valiant; fearless; making a fine display in bearing, dress, or appearance generally; excellent‡; capital‡.—*n.* A brave, bold, or daring person; a man daring beyond discretion; a North American Indian or other savage warrior. —*v.t.*—*braved, braving.* To encounter with courage and fortitude, or without being moved; to defy; to dare.—**Bravely**, brāv'li, *adv.* In a brave manner; courageously; gallantly; prosperously. —**Braveness**, brāv'nes, *n.* The quality of being brave.—**Bravery**, brāv'ėr-i, *n.* The quality of being brave; courage; undaunted spirit; intrepidity; gallantry; splendour‡; show‡; bravado‡.

Bravo, brä'vō, *interj.* [It. BRAVE.] Well done! The word being an Italian adjective, the correct usage is to say *bravo* to a male singer or actor, *brava* to a female, and *bravi* to a company.

Bravo, brä'vō, *n.* pl. **Bravoes**, brä'vōz. [It. and Sp., lit. a daring man.] A daring villain; an assassin or murderer for hire.

Bravura, brä-vö'ra, *a.* [It., bravery, spirit.] *Mus.* applied to a florid air, serving to display a performer's flexibility of voice and distinctness of articulation.

Brawl, bral, *v.i.* [Perhaps from W. *brawl*, a boast, *broliaw*, to boast, *bragal*, to vociferate; or akin to D. *brallen*, to boast, Dan. *bralle*, to jabber, to prate, *brölle*, to roar.] To be clamorous or noisy; to quarrel noisily; to make the noise of rushing or running water; to flow with a noise (a brook *brawls* along).—*n.* A noisy quarrel; loud angry contention; an uproar, row, or squabble; a kind of dance‡.—**Brawler**, bral'ėr, *n.* One who brawls; a noisy fellow; a wrangler.—**Brawling**, bral'ing, *a.* Given to indulge in brawls; contentious; quarrelsome; making the noise of rushing water; purling; rippling. —**Brawlingly**, bral'ing-li, *adv.* In a brawling or quarrelsome manner.

Brawn, bran, *n.* [O.Fr. *braon*, the muscular parts of the body, from O.H.G. *brato*, *braton*, meat for roasting, from *braten*, to roast.] Boar's flesh; the flesh of the boar or swine, collared so as to squeeze out much of the fat, boiled, and pickled; the flesh of a pig's head and ox feet cut in pieces and boiled, pickled, and pressed into a shape; a fleshy, protuberant, muscular part of the body, as on the thigh or the arm; muscular strength; muscle; the arm‡.—**Brawniness**, bra'ni-nes, *n.* The quality of being brawny; strength, hardiness.—**Brawny**, bra'ni, *a.* Having large strong muscles; muscular; fleshy; bulky; strong.

Braxy, brak'si, *n.* [Perhaps from the verb to *break*; comp. G. *brechen*, vomiting, *brechen*, to break; or from Gael. *bragsaidh*, a disease of sheep.] The name given to several diseases of sheep; a sheep having the braxy; the mutton of such a sheep.—*a.* Affected or tainted with braxy.

Bray, brā, *v.t.* [O.Fr. *brayer* (Fr. *broyer*), to pound, from G. *brechen*, to break.] To pound, beat, or grind small.

Bray, brā, *v.i.* [Fr. *braire*, to bray; L.L. *bragire*, *bragare*, to bray, from Celtic root seen in *brag*.] To utter a harsh cry: said especially of the ass; to make a loud, harsh, disagreeable sound.—*v.t.* To utter with a loud harsh sound: sometimes with *out*.—*n.* The harsh sound or roar of an ass; a harsh or grating sound.—**Brayer**, brā'ėr, *n.* One that brays like an ass.

Braze, brāz, *v.t.*—*brazed, brazing.* [Fr. *braser*, to braze, from the Scandinavian. BRASS.] To solder with hard solder, such as an alloy of brass and zinc; to cover or ornament with brass; to harden; to harden to impudence (*Shak.*)‡.—**Brazen**, brā'zn, *a.* Made of brass; also, from brass often serving as a type of strength or impenetrability, extremely strong; impenetrable; pertaining to brass; proceeding from *brass* (a *brazen* sound); impudent; having a front like brass.—*v.t.* To behave with insolence or effrontery: with an indefinite *it*.—*To brazen out*, to persevere in treating with effrontery: with an indefinite *it*, or a noun like *matter*, *affair*, *business*.—**Brazenly**, brā'zn-li, *adv.* In a brazen manner; boldly; impudently.—**Brazenness**, brā'zn-nes, *n.* Appearance like brass; brassiness; impudence.—**Brazier**, brā'zi-ėr, *n.* Same as *Brasier*.—**Brazen-face**, *n.* An impudent person; one remarkable for effrontery.—**Brazen-faced**, *a.* Impudent; bold to excess.

Brazil, **Brazil-wood**, bra-zil', *n.* [Pg. *brasil*, from *braza*, a live coal, the name being given to the wood from its colour, and the country being called after the wood.] A very heavy wood of a red colour, growing in Brazil and other tropical countries, used for dyeing red.—**Brazilletto**, braz-i-let'to, *n.* An inferior species of Brazil-wood brought from Jamaica.—**Brazilin**, braz'il-in, *n.* The red colouring matter of Brazil-wood.—**Brazil-nut**, *n.* The seeds of a very lofty tree growing throughout tropical America. The fruit is nearly round and about 6 inches in diameter, having an extremely hard shell, and containing from eighteen to twenty-four triangular wrinkled seeds, which, besides being eaten, yield an oil, used by watchmakers and others.

Breach, brēch, *n.* [From A.Sax. *brece*, *brice*, a breach or breaking, from *brecan*, to break; partly also from Fr. *brèche*, a breach, from the same stem, but directly from the German.] The act of breaking in a figurative sense; the act of violating or neglecting some law, contract, obligation, or custom; the space between the several parts of a mass parted by violence; a rupture; a break; a gap (a *breach* in a wall); separation between persons through ill feeling; difference; quarrel; injury; wound (O.T.); the breaking of waves; the surf (*Shak.*).—*v.t.* To make a breach or opening in.

Bread, bred, *n.* [A.Sax. *bredd* = D. *brood*, Sw. and Dan. *bröd*, G. *brod*, *brot*. Root doubtful; perhaps *brew*.] A kind of food made by moistening and kneading the flour or meal of some species of grain, or that prepared from other plants, and baking it, the dough being often caused to ferment; food or sustenance in general.—**Bread-corn**, *n.* Corn or grain of which bread is made, as wheat, rye, oats, maize, &c.—**Bread-fruit**, *n.* The fruit of a tree which grows in the islands of the Pacific Ocean, producing a large round fruit used as a substitute for bread, and forming the principal food of a considerable population.—**Bread-nut**, *n.* The fruit of a tree common in the woods of Jamaica, which, when roasted, is used as bread.—**Breadstuff**, bred'stuf, *n.* Bread-corn: used frequently in the plural to signify all the different varieties of grain and flour from which bread is made collectively.—**Bread-winner**, *n.* One who works for the support of himself or of himself and a family.

Breadth, bredth, *n.* [O.E. *brede*, with *th* added, from A.Sax. *braedu*, breadth, from *brád*, broad; comp. *length*, *width*. BROAD.] The measure or extent of any plane surface from side to side; width; *fig.* largeness of mind; liberality; wide intellectual grasp; *fine arts*, an impression of largeness, freedom, and space produced by bold or simple touches and strokes of the pencil.—**Breadthways**, bredth'wāz, *adv.* In the direction of the breadth.

Break, brāk, *v.t.*—*broke* (pret. *brake* is still used in archaic style); *broken* or *broke* (pp.); *breaking*. A.Sax. *brecan*, to break, weaken, vanquish, &c. = D. *breken*, Dan. *brække*, G. *brechen*, Goth. *brikan*, to break, to crush, &c.; Icel. *braka*, to creak; same root as L. *frango*, Gr. (*f*)*rēgnymi*, to break.] To part or divide by force and violence (as a stick, a rope); *fig.* to sever or interrupt (connection, friendship); to cause to give way (to *break* an enemy's lines); to destroy, weaken, or impair (health, constitution); to subdue; to quell (to *break* one's spirit); to train to obedience; to make tractable (to *break* a horse); to dismiss or cashier; pay off (troops); to reduce in rank or condition (an officer); to give a superficial wound to so as to lacerate (the skin); to violate, as a contract, law, or promise; to stop; to interrupt (sleep); to cause to discontinue (to *break* a person *of* a habit); to check; to lessen the force of (a fall or a blow); to make a first and partial disclosure of; to impart or tell cautiously so as not to startle or shock (to *break* unwelcome news); to destroy the completeness of; to remove a part from (a sum of money, a set of things).—*To break off*, to sever by breaking; to put a sudden stop to (a marriage); to discontinue; to leave off (intimacy, a conversation).—*To break up*, to open forcibly (a door); to lay open (to *break up* ground); to dissolve or put an end to (a meeting); to separate; to disband.—*To break ground*, to begin to plough or dig; to commence excavation; *fig.* to begin to execute any plan.—*To break the heart*, to afflict grievously; to cause to die of grief.—*To break one's mind to*, to reveal one's thoughts to.—*To break the ice*, to overcome obstacles and make a beginning; to get over the feeling of restraint incident to a new acquaintanceship.—*v.i.* To become broken; to burst forth violently (a storm, a deluge); to open spontaneously or by force from within; to burst (a bubble, a tumour); to show the first light of morning; to dawn (the day, the morning *breaks*); to become bankrupt; to decline or fail in health and strength; to fail, change in tone, or falter, as the voice.—*To break away*, to disengage one's self abruptly; to rush off.—*To break down*, to come down by breaking; to fail and be unable to proceed in an undertaking.—*To break forth*, to burst out; to be suddenly manifested (rage, light, noise); to rush or issue out; to give vent to one's feelings.—*To break from*, to disengage one's self from; to leave abruptly or violently.—*To break in* or *into*, to enter by force; to start into suddenly (*break* into a gallop).—*To break loose*, to get free by force; to shake off restraint.—*To break off*, to part; to become separated; to desist suddenly.—*To break out*, to issue forth; to arise or spring up (fire, fever, sedition); to appear in eruptions.—*To break up*, to dissolve and separate (as a company).—*To break with*, to cease to be friends with; to quarrel; to broach a subject to (*Shak.*)‡.—*n.* An opening made by force; a rupture; a breach; an interruption of continuity (five years without a *break*); a line in writing or printing, noting a suspension of the sense or a stop in the sentence; a contrivance to check the velocity of a wheeled carriage; a brake; a contrivance for interrupting or changing the direction of electric currents; a large high-set four-wheeled vehicle; a brake; in *cricket*, a sudden swerve of the ball after pitching, in direction of the batsman; in *billiards*, a continuous score of points.—*Break of day*, the dawn.—**Breakable**, brāk'a-bl, *a.* Capable of being broken.—**Breakage**, brāk'āj, *n.* The act of breaking; allowance for what is accidentally broken.—**Breakdown**, *n.* An overthrow, as of a carriage; a downfall; a crash; a failure; a collapse; a lively, noisy dance.—**Breaker**, brāk'ėr, *n.* The person who or that which breaks anything; a violator or transgressor; a wave broken into foam against the shore, a sand-bank, or a rock near the surface; a small flat water-cask (in this sense perhaps a corruption of Sp. *barrica*, a keg).—**Breakfast**, brek'-fast, *n.* The first meal in the day; the meal which enables one to break the fast lasting from the previous day; the food eaten at the first meal.—*v.t.* To furnish with breakfast.—*v.i.* To eat breakfast.—**Break-neck**,† brāk'nek, *n.* A fall that breaks the neck; a dangerous business (*Shak.*).—*a.* Endangering the neck or life; extremely hazardous.—**Break-up**, *n.* A disruption; a dissolution of connection; a separation of a mass into parts; a disintegration; a disbandment.—**Breakwater**, brāk'wa-tėr, *n.* Any structure or contrivance serving to break the force of waves and protect a harbour or anything exposed to the force of the waves.

Bream, brēm, *n.* [Fr. *brème*, O.Fr. *bresme*, from O.H.G. *brahsema*, G. *bressem*, the bream.] The name of several fresh-water soft-finned fishes belonging to the carp family; the name is also given to some spiny-finned sea-fishes resembling the perches.

Bream, brēm, *v.t.* [D. *brem*, broom, furze,

from the materials commonly used; the verb *broom* is also used in same sense.] *Naut.* to clear of shells, sea-weed, ooze, &c., by fire—an operation applied to a ship's bottom.

Breast, brest, *n.* [A.Sax. *breóst* = Icel. *brjóst*, Sw. *bröst*, Dan. *bryst*, D. *borst*, Goth. *brusts*, G. *brust*; allied to E. *burst*, and primarily signifying a protuberance, a swelling.] The soft protuberant body adhering to the thorax in females, in which the milk is secreted for the nourishment of infants; the fore-part of the thorax, or the fore-part of the body between the neck and the belly in man or animals; *fig.* the seat of the affections and emotions; the repository of consciousness, designs, and secrets; anything resembling or likened to the breast.—*To make a clean breast*, to make full confession. —*v.t.* To meet in front boldly or openly; to oppose with the breast; to bear the breast against (a current); to stem.—**Breasted**, brest'ed, *a.* In compounds, having a breast (of this or that kind).—**Breast-bone**, *n.* The bone of the breast; the sternum.—**Breast-deep**, **Breast-high**, *a.* Deep as from the breast to the feet; as high as the breast. —**Breast-knot**, *n.* A kind of ribbon worn on the breast.—**Breast-pang**, *n.* Angina pectoris.—**Breast-pin**, *n.* A pin worn for a fastening or for ornament on the breast; a brooch.—**Breastplate**, brest'plāt, *n.* A plate worn on the breast as a part of defensive armour; *Jewish antiq.* a part of the vestment of the high-priest; a plate or piece which receives the butt end of a boring tool, and is held against the breast when the tool is in use.—**Breast-plough**, *n.* A kind of spade propelled by the hands placed upon a cross-bar held opposite the breast, used to cut or pare turf. —**Breast-wall**, *n.* A retaining wall at the foot of a slope.—**Breast-wheel**, *n.* A kind of water-wheel, in which the water is delivered to the float-board at a point somewhere between the bottom and top, generally a very little below the level of the axis.—**Breast-work**, *n.* *Fort.* a hastily-constructed work thrown up breast-high for defence; the parapet of a building.

Breath, breth, *n.* [A.Sax. *braeth*, odour, scent, breath; allied to G. *bradem*, *brodem*, steam, vapour, breath, *brod*, vapour, a bubble; same root as E. *broth* and *brew*.] The air inhaled and expelled in the respiration of animals; the power of breathing; life; the state or power of breathing freely (to be out of *breath* from violent exercise); a pause; time to breathe; a single respiration; the time of a single respiration; a very slight breeze; air in gentle motion; an exhalation; an odour; a perfume.—*Out of breath*, breathless.—**Breathable**, brēᴛʜ'a-bl, *a.* Capable of being breathed.—**Breathableness**, brēᴛʜ'a-bl-nes, *n.* State of being breathable.—**Breathe**, brēᴛʜ, *v.i.*—*breathed*, *breathing.* To respire; to inspire and expire air; to live; to make a single respiration; to take breath; to rest from action; to pass or blow gently, as air; to exhale, as odour; to emanate; *fig.* to be instinct with life; to be alive.—*v.t.* To inhale and exhale in respiration; to inspire or infuse (*breathe* life into); to exhale; to send out; to utter; to speak; to whisper (vows, &c.); to suffer to take or recover breath (a horse); to put out of breath; to exhaust.—**Breathed**, bretht, *a.* Endowed with breath; *philol.* uttered with breath as distinguished from *voice*; surd or mute. —**Breather**, brēᴛʜ'ėr, *n.* One who breathes; one who lives (*Shak.*); a sharp spell of exercise.—**Breathing**, brēᴛʜ'-ing, *n.* Respiration; the act of inhaling and exhaling air; a gentle breeze; *fig.* a gentle influence or operation; inspiration; soft or secret utterance (*Shak.*); time taken to recover breath; a stop; a delay; *gram.* an aspiration; an aspirate.—**Breathless**, breth'les, *a.* Being out of breath; spent with labour or violent action; without breath; dead; incapable of breathing, as with wonder or admiration.—**Breathlessness**, breth'les-nes, *n.* The state of being breathless.

Breccia, brech'i-a, *n.* [It., a breach, a breccia.] *Geol.* an aggregate composed of angular fragments of the same rock or of different rocks united by a matrix or cement. —**Brecciated**, brech'i-āt-ed, *a.* Consisting of angular fragments cemented together.

Bred, bred, pp. of *breed.*

Breech, brēch, *n.* [A singular developed from a plural. Breeches.] The lower part of the body behind; the hinder part of anything: the large thick end of a cannon or other firearm.—*v.t.* To put into breeches; to whip on the breech; to fit or furnish with a breech; to fasten by a breeching.—**Breech-block**, *n.* A movable piece at the breech of a breech-loading gun which is withdrawn for the insertion of the charge, and closed before firing.—**Breeches**, brēch'ez, *n.pl.* [A double plural, from A.Sax. *bréc*, breeches, pl. of *bróc*, as *feet* is the pl. of *foot*=Fris. *brôk*, pl. *brêk*, breehes; D. *broek*, breeches; Dan. *brog*, breeches, the breeching of a gun; Icel. *brók*, pl. *brœkr*, breeches; Ir. *brog*, Gael. *briogais*, Armor. *brœges*—breeches.] A garment worn by men, covering the hips and thighs; less properly used in the sense of trousers.—*To wear the breeches*, to usurp the authority of the husband: said of a wife.—**Breeching**, brēch'ing, *n.* A whipping on the breech; a strong rope to prevent a cannon from recoiling too much when fired; that part of a horse's harness attached to the saddle and hooked on the shafts, which enables him to push back the vehicle to which he is harnessed; a bifurcated smoke-pipe of a furnace.—**Breech-loader**, *n.* A cannon or smaller firearm loaded at the breech instead of the muzzle. —**Breech-loading**, *a.* Receiving the charge at the breech instead of the muzzle: applied to firearms.

Breed, brēd, *v.t.*—*bred*, *breeding.* [A.Sax. *brédan*, to nourish, cherich, keep warm; allied to D. *broeden*, G. *brüten*, to brood, hatch, and to E. *brew*, W. *brwd*, warm.] To procreate; to beget; to engender; to hatch; to cause; to occasion; to produce; to originate (to *breed* dissension); to produce; to yield or give birth to; to bring up; to nurse and foster; to train; to rear, as live stock.—*v.i.* To beget or bear a child or children; to be fruitful; to be produced; to take rise (dissensions *breed* among them); to engage in rearing live stock.—*n.* A race or progeny from the same parents or stock; kind or sort in a general sense.—**Breeder**, brēd'ėr, *n.* One who breeds, procreates, or produces young; one who or that which rears or brings up; one who or that which produces, causes, brings about; one who takes care to raise a particular breed or breeds, as of horses or cattle.—**Breeding**, brēd'ing, *n.* The act of generating or producing; the rearing of cattle or live stock of different kinds; upbringing; nurture; education; deportment or behaviour in social life; manners, especially good manners.—*Cross breeding*, breeding from individuals of two different offsprings or varieties.—*In-and-in breeding*, breeding from animals of the same parentage.

Breeze, brēz, *n.* [Fr. *brise*, Sp. *brisa*, a breeze.] A wind, generally a light or not very strong wind; a gentle gale.—**Breezeless**, brēz'les, *a.* Motionless; destitute of breezes.—**Breezy**, brē'zi, *a.* Fanned with gentle winds or breezes; subject to frequent breezes; vivacious; hilarious.

Breeze, **Breeze-fly**, brēz, *n.* [A.Sax. *briosa*, *breosa*, a gadfly; comp. A.Sax. *brimse*, a gadfly, a horsefly; D. *brems*, G. *bremse*; O.H.G. *bremen*, to hum.] A name given to flies of various species, the most noted of which is the great horsefly, which sucks the blood of horses.

Breeze, brēz, *n.* [Fr. *bris*, *débris*, rubbish, fragments, from *briser*, to break.] House sweepings, as fluff, dust, ashes, &c.; small ashes and cinders used for burning bricks.

Brehon, brech'on, *a.* [Irish *brithem*, a judge.] Brehon Law, old Irish law-code.

Brent-goose, **Brant-goose**, brent'gös, brant'gös, *n.* [D. and G. *brent-gans*, Icel. *brand-gás*, probably from its colour being likened to that caused by burning. Brand.] A species of goose much smaller than the common goose, which breeds in the far north, but migrates for the winter as low down as the middle of France.

Brequet-chain, brek'et, *n.* [After a French watchmaker named *Brequet.*] A short watch-guard or chain; a fob-chain.

Bressomer, **Bressummer**, **Brest-summer**, **Breast-summer**, bres'om-ėr, bres'um-ėr, brest'sum-ėr, *n.* A summer (*q.v.*) or beam placed horizontally to support an upper wall or partition; a lintel.

Breteche, **Bretesche**, bret'āsh, *n.* [Fr. *bretèche*, O.Fr. *bretesche*. Brattice, Buttress.] A name common to several wooden, crenellated, and roofed erections, used in the middle ages for military purposes.

Brethren, breᴛʜ'ren, *n.* pl. of *brother.*

Breton, bret'on, *a.* Relating to Brittany, or Bretagne in France, or the language of its people.—*n.* The native language of Brittany; Armoric.

Brettice, bret'is, *n.* Same as *Brattice.*

Bretwalda, bret'wal-da, *n.* [A.Sax. *bretwalda*, *bryten-walda*—*bret*, *bryten*, wide, powerful, and *walda*, ruler.] A title for such of the Anglo-Saxon kings as had some sort of supremacy among the others his contemporaries.

Breve, brēv, *n.* [From L. *brevis*, short.] *Music*, a note or character of time, 𝅜, equivalent to two semibreves or four minims; *printing*, a mark (˘) used to indicate that the syllable over which it is placed is short.

Brevet, bre-vet', *n.* [Fr., commission, licence. Brief.] A commission to an officer which entitles him to a rank in the army above that which he holds in his regiment, without, however, conferring a right to receive corresponding advance in pay; a patent; a warrant; a licence.—*a.* Taking rank by brevet.—*v.t.* To confer brevet rank upon.

Breviary, brē'vi-a-ri, *n.* [Fr. *breviaire*, L. *breviarium*, from *brevis*, short. Brief.] *R. Cath. Ch.* a book containing the daily offices which all who are in orders are bound to read. It consists of prayers or offices to be used at the canonical hours, and is an abridgment (whence the name) of the services of the early church.

Brevier, bre-vēr', *n.* [G. *brevier*, Fr. *breviaire*: so called from being originally used in printing breviaries.] A kind of printing type in size between bourgeois and minion.

Breviloquence,† bre-vil'o-kwens, *n.* [L. *breviloquentia*—*brevis*, short, and *loquor*, to speak.] A brief or laconic mode of speaking.

Breviped, brev'i-ped, *a.* [L. *brevis*, short, and *pes*, foot.] Having short legs, as certain birds.—*n.* A bird having short legs.

Brevipennate, brev'i-pen-āt, *a.* [L. *brevis*, short, and *penna*, a feather, a wing.] Having short wings: said of such birds as the ostrich, emu, cassowary, dodo, &c.—*n.* A bird having short wings.

Brevirostrate, brev-i-ros'trāt, *a.* [L. *brevis*, short, and *rostrum*, a beak.] Having a short beak or bill.

Brevity, brev'i-ti, *n.* [L. *brevitas*, from *brevis*, short. Brief.] The state or character of being brief; shortness; conciseness; fewness of words.

Brew, brö, *v.t.* [A.Sax. *breówan*, to brew; D. *brouwen*, Icel. *brugga*, Dan. *brygge*, G. *brauen*, to brew; akin *broth.*] To prepare, as beer, ale, or other similar liquor is prepared, from malt or other materials, by steeping, boiling, and fermentation; to mingle; to mix; to concoct (a bowl of punch, a philtre); to contrive; to plot.—*v.i.* To perform the business of brewing or making beer; to be mixing, forming, or collecting (a storm *brews*).—*n.* The mixture formed by brewing; that which is brewed.—**Brewage**, brö'āj, *n.* A mixed drink; drink brewed or prepared in any way.—**Brewer**, brö'ėr, *n.* One who brews; one whose occupation is to brew malt liquors.—**Brewery**, brö'ėr-i, *n.* The establishment and apparatus where brewing is carried on.—**Brewing**, brö'ing, *n.* The act or process of making ale, beer, or other fermented liquor; the quantity brewed at a time.—**Brewster**, brö'stėr, *n.* One who brews; a brewer; more especially, a female who brews.

Brewster-Sessions, *n.* Assizes in England when licences are granted for the retail of beer and spirits; licensing court.

Breziline, brē-zil'in, *n.* [Fr. *brésiline.*] Same as *Brazilin.*

Briar, Briary, &c. BRIER, BRIERY.

Briarean, bri-ā'rē-an, *a.* Pertaining to or resembling *Briareus*, a giant with a hundred hands.

Briar-root, brī'ėr-röt, *n.* [The first part of this word is a corruption of Fr. *bruyère*, heath.] The root of the white heath, extensively used in the manufacture of tobacco pipes.

Bribe, brīb, *n.* [Fr. *bribe*, Prov. Fr. *brife*, broken victuals, such as are given to beggars, something given away; from root seen in Armor. *breva*, to break; W. *briw*, a fragment.] A price, reward, gift, or favour bestowed or promised with a view to pervert the judgment or corrupt the conduct.—*v.t.* —*bribed, bribing.* To induce to a certain course of action, especially a wrong course, by the gift or offer of something valued; to gain over by a bribe.—*v.i.* To practise bribery; to give a bribe to a person.—**Bribable**, brī'ba-bl, *a.* Capable of being bribed; liable to be bribed.—**Briber**, brī'bėr, *n.* One who bribes or pays for corrupt practices. — **Bribery**, brī'bėr-i, *n.* The act or practice of giving or taking a bribe or bribes; the giving or receiving of money by which one's conduct in some public capacity is influenced.

Bric-à-brac, brik-a-brak, *n.* [Fr. Origin doubtful.] Articles of vertu; a collection of objects having a certain interest or value from their rarity, antiquity, or the like.

Brick, brik, *n.* [Fr. *brique*, a brick, also a piece, a fragment, from O.D. *brick*, a piece, a fragment, a brick or tile, from *breken*, to *break.*] A kind of artificial stone made principally of clay moistened and made fine by kneading, formed usually into a rectangular shape in a mould and hardened by being burned in a kiln; bricks collectively or as designating the material of which any structure is composed; a mass or object resembling a brick; a jolly good fellow (colloq. or slang).—*a.* Made of brick; resembling brick.—*v.t.* To lay or pave with bricks, or to surround, close, or wall in with bricks. —**Brickbat**, brik'bat, *n.* A piece or fragment of a brick.—**Brick-clay**, *n.* Clay used or suitable for making bricks and tiles; *geol.* a finely laminated clay immediately overlying and evidently derived from the boulder-clay.—**Brick-dust**, *n.* Dust of pounded bricks.—**Brick-duster**. Inhabitant of Adelaide, Australia, from the grains of desert sand from the interior sweeping over the district.—**Brick-field**, *n.* A field or yard where bricks are made.—**Brick-kiln**, *n.* A kiln or furnace in which bricks are baked or burned; or a pile of bricks, laid loose, with arches underneath to receive the fuel.—**Bricklayer**, brik'lā-ėr, *n.* One whose occupation is to build with bricks.—**Bricklaying**, brik'lā-ing, *n.* The art of building with bricks.—**Brick-nogging**, *n.* Brickwork carried up and filled in between timber framing. — **Brick-tea**, *n.* The larger leaves and young shoots of the tea-plant softened by steam and moulded into a brick-shaped mass.—**Brickwork**, brik'wėrk, *n.* The laying of bricks; masonry consisting of bricks; a place where bricks are made.

Bricole, brē-kōl', *n.* [Fr.] *Milit.* harness worn by men for dragging guns where it is impossible to use horses.

Bride, brīd, *n.* [A.Sax. *brýd, brid*; cog. D. *bruid*, Icel. *brúthr*, Dan. *brud*, Goth. *bruths*, G. *braut*—a bride.] A woman newly married, or on the eve of being married.—**Bridal**, brī'dal, *n.* [Formerly *bride-ale*, from *bride*, and *ale*, in the sense of a feast; comp. *church-ale*, &c.] A nuptial festival; a marriage; a wedding.—*a.* Belonging to a bride or to a wedding.—**Bride-chamber**, *n.* A nuptial apartment.—**Bridegroom**, brīd'gröm, *n.* [A.Sax. *brydguma*, from *bryd*, a bride, and *guma*, a man—D. *bruidegom*, Icel. *brúthgumi*, Dan. *brudgom*, G. *bräutigam.* A.Sax. is cognate with L. *homo*, a man.] A man newly married, or just about to be married. — **Bridecake, Bridescake**, brīd'kāk, brīdz'kāk, *n.* The cake which is made for the guests at a wedding, and pieces of which are sent to friends after the festival.— **Bridesmaid, Bridemaid**, brīdz'mād, brīd'mād, *n.* A woman or girl who attends on or accompanies a bride at her wedding.—**Bridesman**, brīdz'man, *n.* A man who accompanies a bridegroom at his wedding; a groomsman.

Bridewell, brīd'wel, *n.* A house of correction for the confinement of disorderly persons: so called from the palace of King John, 1210, built near *St. Bride's* or *Bridget's Well*, in London, which was turned into a penal workhouse by Edward VI in 1553.

Bridge, brij, *n.* [O.E. *brig, brigge*, Sc. *brig*, A. Sax. *bricg, brycg*, Icel. *bryggja*, Dan. *brygge*, a pier, D. *brug*, G. *brücke*, a bridge; akin to Icel. *brú*, Dan. *bro*, a bridge.] Any structure of wood, stone, brick, or iron, raised over a river, pond, lake, road, valley, or the like, for the purpose of a convenient passage; in *furnaces*, a low wall or vertical partition for compelling the flame and heated vapour to ascend; the part of a stringed instrument over which the strings are stretched, and by which they are raised above the sounding-board; a range of planks which forms a communication between the paddle-boxes of a steam-vessel; the upper and bony part of the nose; a modern card game based on whist.—*Electric bridge*, a contrivance for determining the resistance of an electric circuit.—*v.t.*— *bridged, bridging.* To build a bridge or bridges on or over; to make a bridge or bridges for (a road); *fig.* to find a way of overcoming or getting over: generally with *over* (to *bridge over* a difficulty).—**Bridge-deck**, *n.* A partial deck, common in paddle-steamers, extending from side to side of a vessel amidships.

Bridle, brī'dl, *n.* [A. Sax. *bridel*, a bridle =D. *bridel*, O.H.G. *bridel.* Probably from A. Sax. *bredan*, to braid.] The portion of gear or harness fitted to the head of a horse (or animal similarly used), and by which he is governed and restrained; a restraint; a curb; a check.—*v.t.*—*bridled, bridling.* To put a bridle on; to restrain, guide, or govern; to check, curb, or control.—*v.i.* To hold the head up and backwards; to assume a lofty manner so as to assert one's dignity or express indignation at its being offended; to toss the head: generally with *up.*—**Bridle-hand**, *n.* The hand which holds the bridle in riding; the left hand. — **Bridle-path, Bridle-road**, *n.* A path or road which can be travelled on horseback but not by wheeled carriages.

Bridoon, bri-dön', *n.* [Fr. *bridon*, from *bride*, a bridle.] A light snaffle or bit of a bridle in addition to the principal bit, and having a distinct rein.

Brief, brēf, *a.* [O.Fr. *brief*, Fr. *bref*, from L. *brevis*, short, seen also in *brevity, breve, abbreviate, abridge.*] Short in duration; lasting a short time; short in expression; using few words; concise; succinct.—*In brief*, in few words; in short.—*n.* An epitome; a short or concise writing (*Shak.*); an abridged relation of the facts of a litigated case drawn up for the instruction of an advocate or barrister in conducting proceedings in a court of justice; a formal letter from the pope on some matter of discipline.—*v.t.* To furnish (a barrister) with a brief.—**Briefless**, brēf'les, *a.* Receiving or having received no briefs (a *briefless* barrister).—**Briefly**, brēf'li, *adv.* In a brief manner; concisely; in few words.—**Briefness**, brēf'nes, *n.* The state or quality of being brief; shortness; conciseness; brevity.

Brier, Briar, brī'ėr, *n.* [A. Sax. *braer*, *brér*, a brier; probably borrowed from the Celtic; comp. Ir. *briar*, a thorn, a pin, a brier; Gael. *preas*, a bush, a brier.] A prickly plant or shrub in general; the sweet-brier and the wild-brier, species of the rose; the wild-rose. — **Briered**, brī'ėrd, *a.* Set with briers. — **Briery, Briary**, brī'ėr-i, *a.* Full of briers; rough; thorny.

Brig, brig, *n.* [An abbrev. of *brigantine.*] A vessel with two masts, square rigged nearly like a ship's mainmast and foremast.

Brigade, bri-gād', *n.* [Fr. *brigade*, from It. *brigata*, a brigade, from *brigare*, to fight. BRIGAND.] A party or division of troops, consisting of several regiments, squadrons, or battalions; in the U. S. army formation, three regiments ordinarily constitute a *brigade*, and three *brigades* a division; an organized body of individuals, usually wearing a uniform, and acting under an authorized head (a fire *brigade*).—**Brigade-major**, *n.* The officer who assists a brigadier.—**Brigadier**, brig-a-dēr', **Brigadier-general**, *n.* The general officer next in rank below a major-general.

Brigand, brig'and, *n.* [Fr. *brigand*, from It. *brigante*, a pirate, a brigand, from *brigare*, to intrigue, to quarrel (whence also *brigade*), from *briga*, an intrigue, a quarrel.] A robber; a freebooter; a highwayman; especially, one of those robbers who live in gangs in secret retreats in mountains or forests.—**Brigandage**, brig'an-dāj, *n.* The life and practices of a brigand; highway-robbery.

Brigandine, Brigantine, brig'an-dīn, brig'an-tīn, *n.* [Fr. *brigandine*, from *brigand*, in old sense of foot-soldier. BRIGAND.] Body armour composed of iron rings or small thin iron plates sewed upon canvas, linen, or leather, and covered over with similar materials.

Brigantine, brig'an-tīn, *n.* [Fr. *brigantin*, from It. *brigantino*, a pirate vessel, from *brigante*, a pirate. BRIGAND. *Brig* is an abbrev. of this word.] A kind of light sailing vessel formerly much used by corsairs; a two-masted vessel partly square-rigged and resembling a brig.

Bright, brīt, *a.* [A. Sax. *beorht, bryht*, clear, shining=Goth. *bairhts*, O.H.G. *berht*, bright; same root as L. *flagro* (anciently *fragro*), to flame, *flamma* (*flagma*), flame, Skr. *bhraj*, to shine.] Radiating or reflecting light; blazing with light; brilliant; shining; luminous; resplendent; sparkling; illustrious; glorious (name, period); quick in wit; witty; clever; not dull; lively; vivacious; animated; cheerful. — **Brighten**, brīt'n, *v.t.* To make bright or brighter; to shed light on; to make to shine; to cheer; to make gay or cheerful; to heighten the splendour of; to add lustre to; to make acute or witty; to sharpen the faculties of. —*v.i.* To grow bright or more bright; to clear up; to become less dark or gloomy.—**Brightly**, brīt'li, *adv.* In a bright manner; splendidly; with lustre.—**Brightness**, brīt'nes, *n.* The state or quality of being bright; splendour; lustre; acuteness of mental faculties; sharpness of wit.—**Brightsome**,† brīt'sum, *a.* Bright; brilliant.—**Bright's disease** (Dr. Bright). Granular kidney-degeneration.

Brill, bril, *n.* [Probably from Corn. *brithel*, a mackerel, pl. *brithelli, brilli*, from *brith*, streaked, variegated.] A kind of flat-fish resembling the turbot, but inferior to it both in size and quality.

Brilliant, bril'yant, *a.* [Fr. *brillant*, sparkling, from *briller*, to shine or sparkle, L.L. *beryllare*, to shine like a beryl, from L. *beryllus*, a beryl.] Sparkling or gleaming with lustre; glittering; bright; distinguished by such qualities as command admiration; splendid; shining (a *brilliant* achievement, a *brilliant* writer).—*n.* A diamond of the finest cut, formed into faces and facets so as to reflect and refract the light in the most vivid manner possible; *printing*, a very small type, a size less than diamond.—**Brilliance, Brilliancy**, bril'yans, bril'yan-si, *n.* Great brightness; splendour; lustre.—**Brilliantly**, bril'yant-li, *adv.* In a brilliant manner; splendidly. — **Brilliantness**, bril'yant-nes, *n.*

Brills, brilz, *n. pl.* The hair on the eyelids of a horse.

Brim, brim, *n.* [A. Sax. *brim*, the surf, the sea=Icel. *brim*, the surf; akin Dan. *brœmme*, G. *bräme*, the edge, border; from root seen in L. *fremere*, to roar, Skr. *bhram*, to whirl, *bhrimi*, a whirlpool, *brim* being thus the part where the surf roars or rages.] The brink, edge, or margin of a river or sheet of water; the upper edge of anything hollow, as a cup; a projecting edge, border, or rim round anything hollow, as a hat.—*v.t.*—*brimmed, brimming.* To fill to the brim, upper edge, or top; to furnish with a brim, as a hat.—*v.i.* To be full to the brim; to be full to overflowing.—*To brim over*, to run over the brim; to be so full as to overflow.—**Brimful**, brim'fu̥l, *a.* Full to the top; completely full: used predicatively.—**Brimless**, brim'les, *a.* Having no brim, as a hat.—**Brimmer**, brim'ėr, *n.* A bowl or glass full to the top.—**Brimming**, brim'ing, *a.* Full to the top or brim (a *brimming* pail).

Brimstone, brim'stōn, *n.* [O.E. *bremstone, brenston*, &c., Sc. *bruntstane, brunstane*; lit. *burn-stone*, or *burning-stone*, like Icel. *brennisteinn*, brimstone.] Sulphur.—**Brimstone-butterfly**, *n.* A species of butterfly, so called from its yellow colour.

Brinded, brin'ded, *a.* [Equivalent to Prov. E. and Sc. *branded*, of a reddish-brown colour with darker markings; lit. of a burnt colour, the root being in *burn, brand*, &c.] Of a gray or tawny colour with bars or streaks of a darker hue; having a hide variegated by streaks or blotches lighter and darker in hue.—**Brindled**, brin'dld, *a.* Same as *Brinded*, and now the more commonly used word.

Brine, brīn, *n.* [A. Sax. *bryne*, brine, so called from its burning taste = A. Sax. *bryne*, a burning. BURN.] Water saturated or strongly impregnated with salt, like the water of the ocean; salt water; hence used for tears, and for the sea or ocean.—*v.t.*—*brined, brining.* To steep in brine.—**Brinish**, brī'nish, *a.* Like brine; somewhat salt; saltish.—**Briny**, brī'ni, *a.* Consisting of or resembling brine; of the nature of brine; salt.—**Brine-pan**, *n.* A pit of salt water, where, by the action of the sun, salt is formed by crystallization.—**Brine-pit**, *n.* A salt spring or well from which water is taken to be boiled or evaporated for making salt.—**Brine-shrimp**, *n.* A branchiopodous crustacean, ½ inch in length, found in salt-pans and in the Great Salt Lake, Utah.

Bring bring, *v.t.*—*brought, bringing.* [A. Sax. *bringan, brang, brungen*, later *brengan, brohte, broht* = D. *brengen*, Goth. *briggan* (pron. *bringan*), G. *bringen*; same root as *bear*, to carry.] To bear or convey from a distant to a nearer place, or to a person; to fetch; to carry; to make to come (honour, wisdom, strength, sleep); to procure; to conduct or attend in going; to accompany; to change in state or condition (*bring* to nought, &c.); to persuade (*bring* to reason, to terms).—*To bring about*, to effect; to accomplish.—*To bring down*, to cause to come down; to lower; to humiliate; to abase.—*To bring forth*, to produce, as young or fruit; to beget; to cause.—*To bring forward*, to produce to view or notice (*bring forward* arguments).—*To bring in*, to introduce; to supply; to furnish (income, rent).—*To bring off*, to bear or convey from a place; to procure to be acquitted; to clear from condemnation.—*To bring on*, to cause to begin (a battle, &c.); to originate (*bring on* a disease).—*To bring over*, to convey over; to convert by persuasion or other means; to cause to change sides or an opinion.—*To bring (a ship) to*, to check the course of (a ship) by making the sails counteract each other and keep her nearly stationary.—*To bring to light*, to reveal.—*To bring to mind*, to recall what has been forgotten or out of the thoughts.—*To bring to pass*, to effect.—*To bring under*, to subdue; to reduce to obedience.—*To bring up*, to nurse, feed, and tend; to rear; to educate; to introduce to notice (to *bring up* a subject); to cause to advance near (troops); to cause to stop (a horse); to pull up.—*To bring up the rear*, to move onwards in the rear; to form the rear portion.—**Bringer**, bring'ėr, *n.* One who brings or conveys.

Brink, bringk, *n.* [A Scandinavian word; Dan. and Sw. *brink*, a hill, declivity; allied to W. *bryncyn*, a hillock, from *bryn*, a hill.] The edge, margin, or border of a steep place, as of a precipice or the bank of a river; verge; hence, close proximity to danger.

Briony, brī'o-ni, *n.* Same as *Bryony*.

Briquette, bri-ket', *n.* [Dim. of Fr. *brique*, a brick.] A lump of fuel, in the form of a brick, made from coal-dust, with some binding material such as coal tar.

Brise, brēz, *n.* Same as *Breeze*, an insect.

Brisk, brisk, *a.* [From the Celtic: W. *brysg*, Ir. *brisg*, quick, lively.] Lively; active; nimble; gay; sprightly; vivacious; effervescing vigorously; sparkling (liquor); burning freely; rapid; quick (movement, pace).—*v.t.* To make brisk.—*v.i.* To become brisk, lively, or alert: often with *up*.—**Briskly**, brisk'li, *adv.* In a brisk manner; actively; vigorously; with life and spirit.—**Briskness**, brisk'nes, *n.* The state or quality of being brisk.

Brisket, bris'ket, *n.* [O.Fr. *brischet* or *bruschet* (Fr. *bréchet*), from Armor. *brusk*, the breast.] The breast of an animal, or that part of the breast that lies next to the ribs; in a horse, the fore-part of the neck at the shoulder down to the fore-legs.

Bristle, bris'l, *n.* [A diminutive from A. Sax. *byrst*, a bristle = D. *borstel*, a bristle; akin Icel. *burst*, Dan. *börste*, G. *borste*, a bristle.] One of the stiff, coarse, glossy hairs of the hog and the wild boar, especially one of the hairs growing on the back; a stiff roundish hair or similar appendage.—*v.t.*—*bristled, bristling.* To erect in bristles; to make bristly; to erect in defiance or anger, like a swine; to furnish with bristles or stiff hairs.—*v.i.* To rise up or stand on end like bristles; to appear as if covered with bristles; to show anger, resentment, or defiance: generally followed by *up*.—**Bristled**, bris'ld, *a.* Having bristles; bristly.—**Bristliness**, bris'li-nes, *n.* The quality of being bristly.—**Bristly**, bris'li, *a.* Thick set with bristles, or with hairs like bristles; rough; resembling a bristle or bristles.

Bristol-board, *n.* [From the city of *Bristol*, in England.] A fine kind of pasteboard, smooth, and sometimes glazed on the surface.—**Bristol-brick**, *n.* A sort of brick of a siliceous material, and used for cleaning cutlery.—**Bristol-paper**, *n.* Stout paper for drawing.—**Bristol-diamond, Bristol-stone**, *n.* Quartz in the form of small, round crystals, found in the Clifton limestone, near Bristol; rock-crystal.

Britannia-metal, *n.* A metallic compound or alloy of tin, with a little copper and antimony, used chiefly for tea-pots, spoons, &c.

Britannic, bri-tan'ik, *a.* Pertaining to Britain.—**British**, brit'ish, *a.* Pertaining to Great Britain or its inhabitants; sometimes applied distinctively to the original Celtic inhabitants.—**Britisher**, brit'ish-ėr, *n.* A patriotic or typical British subject.—**Briton**, brit'on, *n.* A native of Briton or the British islands.

Brittle, brit'l, *a.* [O.E. *britel*, from A.Sax. *brytan, breótan*, to break=Icel. *brjóta*, Dan. *bryde*, to break.] Easily broken, or easily breaking short, without splinters or loose parts rent from the substance; fragile; not tough or tenacious.—*v.t.* [Same origin as adj. *brittle*.] To cut up a deer: old hunting term.—**Brittleness**, brit'l-nes, *n.* Aptness to break; fragility.

Britzska, brits'ka, *n.* [A Polish word.] An open carriage with a calash top, and space for reclining when used for a journey.

Brize, brēz, *n.* The breeze-fly. BREEZE.

Broach, brōch, *n.* [Fr. *broche*, from L.L. *brocca*, a spit, a point; allied to Gael. *brog*, to goad, *brog*, an awl.] A spit†; a spire, especially a spire springing directly from a tower; a general name for all tapered boring-bits or drills.—*v.t.* To pierce with or as with a spit†; to open for the first time for the purpose of taking out something; more especially to tap; to pierce, as a cask in order to draw the liquor; to begin conversation or discussion about; to open up (a topic or subject).—*To broach to* (*naut.*), to incline suddenly to windward, so as to lay the sails aback and expose the vessel to the danger of oversetting; to overset, by death.—**Broacher**, broch'ėr, *n.* One who broaches, opens, or utters.

Broad, bra̤d, *n.* [A.Sax. *brád* = D. *breed*, Icel. *breithr*, Dan. and Sw. *bred*, Goth. *braids*, G. *breit*, broad; root unknown.] Having extent from side to side, as distinguished from *long*, or extended from end to end; having breadth; having a great extent from side to side, as opposed to *narrow*; wide; extensive; vast; *fig.* not limited or narrow; liberal; comprehensive; enlarged; widely diffused; open: full (*broad* daylight); plain or unmistakable; free; unrestrained (*broad* humour); somewhat gross, coarse, or unpolished; indelicate; indecent; bold; unreserved; characterized by vigour, boldness, or freedom of style, as in art, so that strong and striking effects or impressions are produced by simple unelaborate means.—*Broad Church*, a section of the Church of England contrasted with the High Church and the Low Church; a section of any church holding moderate or not very rigid views.—**Broaden**, bra̤d'n, *v.t.* To make broad or broader; to increase the width of; to render more comprehensive, extensive, or open.—*v.i.* To become broad or broader.—**Broadish**, bra̤d'ish, *a.* Somewhat or rather broad.—**Broadly**, bra̤d'li, *adv.* In a broad manner; widely; comprehensively; fully; openly; plainly.—**Broadness**, bra̤d'nes, *n.* The state or quality of being broad; breadth.—**Broadwise**, bra̤d'wīz, *adv.* In the direction of the breadth.—**Broad-arrow**, *n.* A stamp resembling the barbed head of an arrow put upon stores, &c., belonging to the British government.—**Broad-brim**, *n.* A hat with a very broad brim, such as is worn by members of the Society of Friends; hence, a member of said society; a Quaker. (Colloq.)—**Broad-brimmed**, *a.* Having a broad brim; wearing a hat with a broad brim.—**Broadcast**, bra̤d'kast, *n.* *Agri.* a casting or throwing seed from the hand for dispersion in sowing.—*a.* Effected by casting the seed on the ground with the hand.—*adv.* By scattering or throwing at large from the hand; in a widely disseminated manner.—**Broadcast**, *v.t.*—in radio, the transmission of sound; the performance broadcast; also a single program of such material.—**Broad-cloth**, *n.* A kind of fine woolen cloth woven about twice the usual breadth, and dyed in the piece.—**Broads**, *n.* Wide spaces of water formed on Norfolk coast by the expansion of a river.—**Broad-shouldered**, *a.* Having the back broad across the shoulders.—**Broadside**, bra̤d'sīd, *n.* The side of a ship above the water from the bow to the quarter; a simultaneous discharge of all the guns on one side of a ship; a sheet of paper, one side of which is covered by printed matter, often of a popular character.—**Broadsword**, bra̤d'sōrd, *n.* A sword with a broad blade and cutting edges.

Brobdingnagian, brob-ding-nag'i-an, *a.* Gigantic, like an inhabitant of the fabled region of Brobdingnag in Swift's *Gulliver's Travels*.

Brocade, brō-kād', *n.* [Sp. *brocado*, from an old *brocar*, equivalent to Fr. *brocher*, to pick, emboss. BROACH.] Silk stuff variegated with gold and silver, or having raised flowers, foliage, and other ornaments; also applied to other stuffs wrought and enriched in like manner.—**Brocaded**, brō-kād'ed, *a.* Woven or worked into a brocade; dressed in brocade.

Brocage, **Brokage**, brō'kāj, *n.* The premium or commission of a broker.

Brocard, bro-kärd', *n.* [Origin doubtful.] A law maxim founded on inveterate custom; an elementary principle or maxim; a short proverbial rule; a canon.

Brocatel, **Brocatello**, brō'ka-tel, brō-ka-tel'lo, *n.* [Sp. *brocatel*, Fr. *brocatelle*, It.

brocatello, from root of *brocade*.] Sienna marble, a species of brecciated marble composed of fragments of various colours; a kind of light thin woollen cloth of silky surface used for linings, &c.; linsey-woolsey. Spelled also *Brocatelle*.

Broccoli, brok'o-li, *n.* [It. *broccoli*, pl. of *broccolo*, sprout, cabbage-sprout, dim. of *brocco*, a skewer, a shoot. BROACH.] One of the many varieties of the common cabbage, closely resembling the cauliflower.

Brochure, brō-shör', *n.* [Fr., from *brocher*, to stitch.] A pamphlet, especially a slight pamphlet, or one on a matter of transitory interest.

Brock, brok, *n.* [A.Sax. *broc*=Dan. *brok*, Ir. and Gael. *broc*, W. *broch*, a badger, from the white-streaked face of the animal; comp. Gael. *brocach*, speckled; Dan. *broget*, Sw. *brokug*, party-coloured.] A badger.

Brocket, brok'et, *n.* [Fr. *brocart*, because it has one *broche* or snag to its antler.] A red-deer two years old; a pricket.

Brogue, brōg, *n.* [Ir. and Gael. *brog*, a shoe of rough hide. From this shoe being used by the wilder Irish the word came to designate their manner of speaking English.] A kind of shoe made of raw or half-tanned leather, of one entire piece; a stout, coarse shoe; a dialectical manner of pronunciation; especially the pronunciation peculiar to the Irish.

Broider, broi'dėr, *v.t.* [Fr. *broder*, from Armor. *broud*, a needle, *brouder*, to broider; comp. Ir. and Gael. *brod*, a point, a prickle.] To adorn with figures of needlework, or by sewing on pearls, or the like; to embroider. —**Broiderer**, broi'dėr-ėr, *n.* One that embroiders. — **Broidery**, broi'dėr-i, *n.* Embroidery. (*Tenn.*)

Broil, broil, *n.* [Fr. *brouiller*, to jumble or mix up, to throw into bustle or confusion; origin doubtful.] A tumult; a noisy quarrel; contention; discord; a brawl.—**Broiler**, broil'ėr, *n.* One who excites broils or quarrels, or who readily takes part in tumults or contentions.

Broil, broil, *v.t.* O.Fr. *bruiller*; origin doubtful.] To dress or cook over a fire, generally upon a gridiron; to subject to a strong heat.—*v.i.* To be subjected to the action of heat, like meat over the fire; to be greatly heated or to sweat with heat.—**Broiler**, broil'ėr, *n.* One who or that which dresses by broiling; a gridiron.

Broke, brōk. Pret. and obsolescent or poetical pp. of *break*.—**Broken**, brō'kn, pp. of *break*, often used as an *a.* Parted by violence; separated into fragments, as by a blow; nor integral or entire; fractional, as numbers; humble; contrite; violated; transgressed (a *broken* vow); interrupted by sobs or imperfect utterance.—**Brokenly**, brō'kn-li, *adv.* In a broken interrupted manner. — **Brokenness**, brō'kn-nes, *n.* The state of being broken. — **Brokenhearted**, *a.* Having the spirits quite crushed by grief or despair.—**Brokenwind**, *n.* A disease in horses, characterized by a difficult expiration of the air from the lungs, and often accompanied with an enlargement of the lungs and heart.—**Broken-winded**, *a.* Affected with broken wind.

Broker, brō'kėr, *n.* [O.Fr. *brokeor*, *brokiere*, from a verb meaning to tap or *broach*; originally a retailer of liquor.] An agent who buys and sells goods or shares or transacts other business for others, being generally paid at a rate per cent on the value of the transaction, such as exchange-brokers, ship-brokers, stock-brokers, &c.; one who deals in second-hand household goods, clothes, and the like.—**Brokerage**, brō'kėr-āj, *n.* The fee, reward, or commission given or charged for transacting business as a broker; the business or employment of a broker.—**Broking**,† brōk'ing, *a.* Pertaining to the business of a broker. (*Shak.*)

Brom, brōm, *n.* [Gr. *bromos*, oats.] A name of several oat-like species of grass.

Bromelia, brō-mē'li-a, *n.* [After *Bromel*, a Swedish botanist.] The generic name of tropical plants some species of which are cultivated for their beautiful flowers.

Bromine, brō'min or brō'min, *n.* [Gr. *brōmos*, a fetid odour.] A simple non-metallic element (symbol Br) much resembling chlorine and iodine): at common temperatures it is a very dark reddish liquid of a powerful and suffocating odour, and emitting red vapour.—**Bromal**, brō'mal, *n.* A colourless oily fluid of a penetrating odour, obtained by the action of bromine on alcohol.—**Bromate**, brō'māt, *n.* A salt formed of bromic acid.—**Bromic**, brō'mik, *a.* Pertaining to or obtained from bromine, as *bromic* acid, a compound of oxygen and bromine.—**Bromide**, brō'mid, *n.* A compound formed by the union of bromine with another element.—**Bromite**, **Bromyrite**, brō'mīt, brō'mi-rīt, *n.* Native bromide of silver, consisting of 57·5 parts silver and 42·5 bromine, of a yellowish-green colour.

Bronchia, brong'ki-a, *n.pl.* [Gr. and L.] The two tubes, with their ramifications, arising from the bifurcation of the windpipe in the lungs, and conveying air to the latter; the bronchi.—**Bronchial**, brong'ki-al, *a.* Belonging to the bronchia.—*Bronchial tubes*, the ramifications of the bronchia, terminating in the bronchial cells, or air-cells of the lungs.—**Bronchic**, brong'kik, *a.* Same as *Bronchial*.—**Bronchitis**, brong-kī'tis, *n.* [The term. *-itis* signifies inflammation.] An inflammation of the lining membrane of the bronchi or bronchia, often a troublesome ailment.—**Bronchocele**, brong'kō-sēl, *n.* [Gr. *kēlē*, a tumour.] Same as *Goitre*.—**Bronchotomy**, brong-kot'o-mi, *n.* [Gr. *tomē*, a cutting.] *Surg.* an incision into the windpipe or larynx between the rings, to afford a passage for the air into and out of the lungs when respiration in the usual way is prevented. — **Bronchus**, brong'kus, *n.* pl. **Bronchi**, brong'kī. [Gr. *bronchos*, the windpipe.] One of the two bronchia or bifurcations of the trachea.

Brontosaurus, bron-tō-sa̤'rus, *n.* [Gr. *brontē*, thunder, *sauros*, a lizard.] A fossil reptile with a remarkably small skull.

Bronze, bronz, *n.* [Fr. *bronze*, from It. *bronzo*, bronze, L. *Aes Brundusinum*, the brass of Brundusium.] A compound or alloy of from 2 to 20 parts of copper to 1 of tin, to which other metallic substances are sometimes added, especially zinc, used for statues, bells, cannon, coins, &c.; any statue, bust, urn, medal, or other work of art, cast of bronze; a brown colour resembling bronze; a pigment prepared for the purpose of imitating bronze.—*v.t.*—*bronzed*, *bronzing*. To give the appearance or colour of bronze to, by covering with bronze leaf, copper dust, &c.; to make brown or tan, as the skin by exposure to the sun.—**Bronzine**, bron'zīn, *a.* Resembling bronze; bronze-coloured.—**Bronzite**, bron'zīt, *n.* A mineral, a variety of diallage, having a yellowish-brown colour, and semi-metallic lustre approaching to that of bronze. — **Bronzy**, bron'zi, *a.* Belonging to or resembling bronze.—**Bronze-steel**, *n.* Bronze condensed and hardened, as in the making of cannon by forcing in steel cylinders into the bore of the piece.

Brooch, brōch, *n.* [A form of *broach* (which see).] An ornamental pin or clasp used for fastening the dress or merely for display.

Brood, bröd, *n.* [A.Sax. *bród*, a brood=D. *broed*, G. *brut*, a brood; from root of *breed*.] Offspring; progeny; the young birds hatched at once; that which is bred or produced.—**Brood-parasitism**, par'a-sīt-izm, *n.* Evasion of parental responsibility by certain animals, e.g. the cuckoo.—*v.i.* To sit upon eggs or upon young, as a hen for the purpose of hatching, warming, or protecting them; hence, to remain steadfastly settled over something; to have the mind dwelling for a long time uninterruptedly on a subject: with *on* or *over*.—*v.t.* To sit over, cover, and cherish; to nourish; to foster.—**Brooding**, bröd'ing, *a.* Pondering; disposed to ponder or think deeply (a *brooding* disposition).

Brook, bru̥k, *n.* [A.Sax. *bróc*, a spring, a brook, from *brecan*, to burst forth; comp. D. *brock*, G. *bruch*, a marsh. A brook is a breaking forth of water; comp. *spring*.] A small natural stream of water, or a current flowing from a spring or fountain less than a river. —**Brooklet**, bru̥k'let, *n.* A small brook. — **Brooklime**, bru̥k'līm, *n.* [*Brook*, stream, and A.Sax. *hleomoc*, brooklime.] A water-loving species of speedwell with small blue flowers.—**Brooky**, bru̥'ki, *a.* Abounding with brooks.

Brook, bru̥k, *v.t.* [A.Sax. *brúcan*, to use, enjoy = D. *gebruiken*, Icel. *brúka*, Goth. *brukjan*, to use; allied to L. *frui*, to enjoy (whence *fruition*).] To bear; to endure; to support: usually in negative or interrogative sentences (they cannot *brook* restraint).

Broom, bröm, *n.* [A.Sax. *bróm* = L.G. *brâm*, D. *brem*, broom; allied to *bramble*. BRAMBLE, BRIM.] A leguminous shrub growing abundantly on sandy pastures and heaths, distinguished by having large, yellow, papilionaceous flowers, leaves in threes, and single, and the branches angular; a besom or brush with a long handle for sweeping floors: so called from being originally made of the broom-plant.—**Broomy**, brö'mi, *a.* Full of broom; containing broom; pertaining to or consisting of broom.—**Broom-corn**, **Broom-grass**, *n.* The common millet or guinea-corn, a cereal plant so called from its branched panicles being made into carpet-brooms.—**Broom-rape**, *n.* A parasitic plant growing on the roots of broom, furze, &c.—**Broomstick**, **Broomstaff**, bröm'stik, bröm'staf, *n.* The stick or handle of a broom.

Brose, brōz, *n.* [Gael. *brothas*, brose; same root as *brew*, *broth*, &c.] A Scotch dish, made by pouring boiling water, boiling milk, the liquor in which meat has been boiled, or the like, on oatmeal, or other meal, and immediately mixing the ingredients by stirring.

Broth, broth, *n.* [A.Sax. *broth*, from root of *brew*.] Liquor in which flesh is boiled and macerated, usually with certain vegetables to give it a better relish.

Brothel, broth'el, *n.* [O.E. *brothel*, a wretch, from *brothen*, ruined, destroyed, from *breóthan*, to destroy.] A house appropriated to the purposes of prostitution; a bawdy-house.

Brother, bruᴛʜ'ėr, *n.* pl. **Brothers**, bruᴛʜ'ėrz, or **Brethren**, breᴛʜ'ren. [A. Sax. *bróthor*=D. *broeder*, Icel. *bróthir*, Dan. and Sw. *broder*, Goth. *brothar*, G. *bruder*, Ir. and Gael. *brathair*, W. *brawd*, Rus. *brat'*, Bohem. *brâtr*, L. *frater*, Gr. *phratēr*, Skr. *bhratr*, brother; the root meaning of the word is unknown.] Strictly a human male born of the same father and mother (also used of animals); a male born of the same father or mother (more strictly called a *half*-brother); a relation or kinsman; an associate; one of the same rank, profession, or occupation; or more generally, a fellow-creature; specifically, a member of a religious order; one that resembles another in manners or disposition. [The plural *brethren* is now used only in the wider meanings of the word.]—**Brotherhood**, bruᴛʜ'ėr-hu̥d, *n.* The state of being a brother or brotherly; an association of men for any purpose; a class of individuals of the same kind, profession, or occupation; a fraternity. —**Brotherless**, bruᴛʜ'ėr-les, *a.* Without a brother.—**Brotherly**, bruᴛʜ'ėr-li, *a.* Pertaining to brothers; such as is natural for brothers; becoming brothers (*brotherly* love).—**Brotherliness**, bruᴛʜ'ėr-li-nes, *n.* State of being brotherly.—**Brother-in-law**, *n.* The brother of one's husband or wife; also, a sister's husband.

Brougham, brö'am or bröm, *n.* [After the first Lord *Brougham*.] A one-horse close carriage, either two or four wheeled, and adapted to carry either two or four persons.

Brought, bra̤t, pret. & pp. of *bring*.

Brow, brou, *n.* [A.Sax. *brú*, the eyebrow =D. *braauw*, Icel. *brún*, G. *braue*, the eyebrow; cog. with Gr. *ophrys*, Per. *abru*, Skr. *bhrû*, the eyebrow.] The prominent ridge over the eye, forming an arch above the orbit; the arch of hair over the eye; the eyebrow; the forehead; the edge of a steep place; the upper portion of a slope.—**Browbeat**, brou'bēt, *v.t.* To abash or bear down with haughty, stern looks, or with arrogant speech and dogmatic assertions.—**Browbeater**, brou'bēt-ėr, *n.* One who browbeats; a bully.

Brown, broun, *a.* [A.Sax. *brún* = Icel. *brúnn*, Dan. *bruun*, Sw. *brun*, D. *bruin*, G. *braun*, brown; lit. of a *burnt* colour, from root of *burn*, *bronze*, &c.] Of a dark or dusky colour, inclining to redness.—*n.* A dark colour inclining to red or yellow of various degrees of depth, and resulting from a mixture of red, black, and yellow.—*Brown bread*, wheaten bread made from unbolted flour, which thus includes the bran, and hence is of a brown colour.—*Brown coal*, lignite.—*Brown study*, a fit of mental abstraction or meditation; a reverie.—*v.t.* To make brown or dusky; to give a brown colour to.—*v.i.* To become brown.—**Brownie**, *n.* Household servant of a fairy or goblin nature, in Scottish mythology. Milton's 'drudging-goblin', 'lubber-fiend'.—**Browning**, broun'ing, *n.* The act of making brown; a preparation of sugar, port-wine, spices, &c., for colouring and flavouring meat and made dishes.—**Brownish**, broun'ish, *a.* Somewhat brown; inclined to brown.—**Brownness**, broun'nes, *n.* The quality of being brown.

Brownist, broun'ist, *n.* A follower of Robert *Brown*, a Puritan or dissenter from the Church of England in the sixteenth century.

Browse, brouz, *v.t.*—*browsed*, *browsing*. [O.Fr. *brouster* (Fr. *brouter*), to browse, from *brost*, *broust*, a sprout, a shoot, from O.H.G. *broz*, G. *bross*, sprout.] To feed on: said of cattle, deer, &c.; to pasture on; to graze.—*v.i.* To feed on pasture or on the leaves, shoots, &c., of shrubs and trees: said of cattle, deer, &c.—*n.* The tender shoots or twigs of trees and shrubs, such as cattle may eat; green food fit for cattle, deer, &c.

Brucine, brö'sin, *n.* [From name *Bruce*.] A vegetable alkaloid akin to strychnine, bitter and acid, but less powerful in its action.

Bruin, brö'in, *n.* [The bear's name in the celebrated fable Reynard the Fox; from the D. *bruin*, brown.] A name given to the bear.

Bruise, bröz, *v.t.*—*bruised*, *bruising*. [O.Fr. *bruiser*, *bruser*, *briser*, to break, to shiver, from O.G. *brestan*, to break, to burst.] To injure by a blow without laceration; to contuse; to crush by beating or pounding; to pound; to bray, as drugs or articles of food; to make a dent or dint in.—*v.i.* To fight with the fists; to box (colloq.).—*n.* A contusion; a hurt upon the flesh of animals, upon plants or other bodies, with a blunt or heavy object.—**Bruiser**, bröz'ėr, *n.* The person or thing that bruises; an instrument or machine for bruising substances; a pugilist, boxer, or prize-fighter (colloq.).

Bruit, bröt, *n.* [Fr. *bruit*, noise, uproar, rumour, from *bruire*, to make a noise.] Something noised abroad; report; rumour; fame; brwē, *n.*—Abnormal sounds heard on auscultation.—*v.t.* To announce with noise; to report; to noise abroad.

Brumal, **Brumous**, brö'mal, brö'mus, *a.* [L. *brumalis*, from *bruma*, winter.] Belonging to the winter.

Brunette, brö-net', *n.* [Fr., a dim. from *brun*, brown. BROWN.] A woman with a brown or dark complexion.

Brunt, brunt, *n.* [From the root or stem of to *burn*; comp. Sc. *brunt*, burnt; Icel. *bruni*, a burning; Dan. *brynde* and *brunst*, ardour, ardency, burning heat. BURN.] The heat or utmost violence of an onset; the first or severest shock of a battle or struggle; the force of a blow; violence; shock of any kind.

Brush, brush, *n.* [O.Fr. *broche*, *brosse*, brushwood; Mod.Fr. *brosse*, a brush; from O.H.G. *broz*, a sprout. BROWSE.] An instrument made of bristles or other similar material bound together, used for various purposes, as for dressing the hair, removing dust from clothes, laying on colours, whitewash, and the like; the small trees and shrubs of a wood, or a thicket of small trees; electricity issuing in a diverging manner from a point; the bushy tail of some animals, as the fox, squirrel, &c.; the act of using a brush, or of applying a brush to; a slight encounter; a skirmish.—*v.t.* To sweep or rub with a brush; to strike lightly by passing over the surface; to pass lightly over; to remove by brushing or by lightly passing over.—*To brush up*, to furbish; to polish; to improve; especially, to improve the appearance of.—*v.i.* To move nimbly in haste; to move so lightly as scarcely to be perceived; to move over lightly.—**Brusher**, brush'ėr, *n.* One who brushes.—**Brushiness**, brush'i-nes, *n.* The quality of being brushy.—**Brushy**, brush'i, *a.* Resembling a brush; rough; shaggy; having long hair.—**Brush-turkey**, *n.* A large gregarious rasorial bird of Australia, somewhat resembling the turkey, laying its eggs in a heap of vegetable matter to be hatched by the heat arising from fermentation.—**Brush-wood**, *n.* Small trees or shrubs forming a thicket or coppice; branches of trees cut off.

Brusque, **Brusk**, brusk, *a.* [Fr. *brusque*, from It. *brusco*, brusque, sharp, sour.] Abrupt in manner; blunt; rude.—**Brusqueness**, **Bruskness**, brusk'nes, *n.* A rude, abrupt, or blunt manner.—**Brusquerie**, brüsk-rē, *n.* [Fr.] Bruskness; a hasty or blunt expression.

Brussels-carpet, *n.* A carpet having a heavy linen web inclosing worsted yarns of different colours, which are raised in loops to form the patterns.—**Brussels-sprouts**, *n. pl.* A variety of cabbage, characterized by little clusters of leaves which form miniature heads of cabbage.

Brute, bröt, *n.* [L. *brutus*, stupid, insensible, irrational.] A beast; any animal destitute of reason; a brutal person; a savage in disposition or manners; a low-bred, unfeeling human being.—*a.* Insensible, irrational, or unintelligent; not proceeding from or inspired by reason and intelligence (*brute* force, the *brute* earth).—**Brutal**, brö'tal, *a.* Pertaining to a brute; like a brute; savage; cruel; inhuman; brutish.—**Brutality**, brö-tal'i-ti, *n.* The quality of being brutal; inhumanity; savageness; gross cruelty; insensibility to pity or shame; a savage, shameless, or inhuman act.—**Brutalize**, brö'tal-īz, *v.t.*—*brutalized*, *brutalizing*. To make brutal, coarse, gross, or inhuman; to degrade to the level of a brute.—**Brutally**, brö'tal-li, *adv.* In a brutal manner; cruelly; inhumanly; in a coarse, gross, or unfeeling manner.—**Brutify**, brö'ti-fī, *v.t.*—*brutified*, *brutifying*. To make a person a brute; to make senseless, stupid, or unfeeling.—**Brutish**, brö'tish, *a.* Pertaining to or resembling a brute; uncultured; ignorant; stupid; unfeeling; savage; brutal; gross; carnal; bestial.—**Brutishly**, brö'tish-li, *adv.* In a brutish manner.—**Brutishness**, brö'tish-nes, *n.* The quality of being brutish.

Bryology, brī-ol'o-ji, *n.* [Gr. *bryon*, moss, and *logos*, discourse.] The science of mosses, their structure, affinities, classification, &c.—**Bryological**, brī-ō-loj'ik-al, *a.* Pertaining to bryology, or to the mosses.

Bryony, brī'ō-ni, *n.* [L. *bryonia*, Gr. *bryōnia*, bryony, from *bryō*, to swell, to sprout, from the quick growth of the stems.] A climbing plant of various species; *white bryony*, found in the hedgerows of England, has small red berries and abounds in an acrid fetid juice, which acts as a cathartic and emetic; *black bryony* is a plant of the yam family, and has a tuberous root-stalk, also with cathartic and emetic properties.—**Bryonine**, brī'ō-nin, *n.* The bitter, cathartic, and somewhat poisonous principle extracted from several species of bryony.

Bryozoa, brī-ō-zō'a, *n.pl.* [Gr. *bryon*, moss, and *zōon*, animal.] A group of minute molluscoid animals living together in moss-like masses; now commonly called *Polyzoa* (which see).—**Bryozoan**, brī-ō-zō'an, *n.* One of the Bryozoa.

Bubble, bub'l, *n.* [Dan. *boble*, Sw. *bubbla*, D. *bobbel*, a bubble; akin to *blob*.] A small vesicle of water or other fluid inflated with air; a blob of air in a fluid; *fig.* something that wants firmness or solidity; a vain project; a false show; a delusive or fraudulent scheme of speculation; a fraud.—*v.i. bubbled*, *bubbling*. To rise in bubbles, as liquors when boiling or agitated; to run with a gurgling noise; to gurgle.—*v.t.* To cause to bubble; to cheat; to deceive; to trick.—**Bubbly**, bub'li, *a.* Full of bubbles.

Bubo, bū'bō, *n.* [Gr. *boubōn*, the groin, a swelling in the groin.] A tumour or abscess, with inflammation, which rises in certain glandular parts of the body, as in the groin or armpit.—**Bubonocele**, bū-bon'ō-sēl, *n.* [Gr. *kēlē*, a tumour.] Rupture or hernia in the groin.

Buccal, buk'al, *a.* [L. *bucca*, the cheek.] Pertaining to the cheek.—*Buccal glands*, the small glands of the mouth which secrete a viscous fluid that mixes with the saliva.

Buccaneer, **Bucaneer**, buk-a-nēr', *n.* [Fr. *boucanier*, a pirate, originally a hunter who smoked the flesh of the animals killed, from *boucaner*, to smoke meat, from *boucan*, a place for smoking meat, a Carib word.] A pirate; a sea-robber; more especially, one of the piratical adventurers, English and French, who combined to make depredations on the Spaniards in America in the 17th and 18th centuries.—*v.i.* To act the part of a pirate or sea-robber.

Buccinator, buk'sin-ā-tėr, *n.* [L., a trumpeter, from *buccina*, a trumpet, from *bucca*, the cheek.] The trumpeter's muscle, a flat thin muscle forming the wall of the cheek, assisting in mastication, and also in blowing wind-instruments.

Bucentaur, bū-sen'tar, *n.* [Gr. *bous*, an ox, and *kentauros*, a centaur.] A mythological monster, half man and half ox; the state barge of Venice, in which the doge and senate went to wed the Adriatic.

Bucephalus, bū-sef'a-lus, *n.* A war horse, the steed of Alexander the Great.

Buck, buk, *n.* [Ir. and Gael. *buac*, cow-dung used in bleaching, bleaching liquor, lye; from W. *bu*, *buw*, Gael. *bo*, a cow.] Lye or suds in which clothes are soaked in the operation of bleaching.—*v.t.* To soak or wash in lye, a process in bleaching; to break up and pulverize, as ores.—**Buck-basket**, *n.* A basket in which clothes are carried to the wash.

Buck, buk, *n.* [A.Sax. *bucca*, a he-goat, a buck = D. *bok*, Icel. *bokkr*, a he-goat; Dan. *buk*, a buck, a he-goat, a ram; G. *bock*, a he-goat, a buck; W. *bwch*, a buck, Ir. *boc*, a he-goat.] The male of the fallow-deer, of the goat, the rabbit and hare: often used specifically of the male of the fallow-deer; a roe-buck; a dashing fellow; a fop, swell, or dandy.—**Buckish**, buk'ish, *a.* Pertaining to a buck or dashing fellow; foppish.—**Buckishness**, buk'ish-nes, *n.*—**Buck-eye**, *n.* A name for several species of American horse-chestnut.—**Buck-hound**, *n.* A kind of hound, less than the stag-hound, for hunting bucks or fallow-deer.—**Buck-skin**, buk'skin, *n.* A kind of soft, yellowish or grayish leather originally made of the skin of the deer, but now of that of the sheep; *pl.* breeches made of this leather.—**Buck-shot**, *n.* A large kind of shot used for killing deer or other large game.—**Buck-thorn**, *n.* A somewhat spiny shrub of various species; as the purging-buck-thorn, a native of Britain, having small shining black berries with powerful cathartic properties; another species yields the Persian or yellow berries of commerce.—**Buck-tooth**, *n.* A projecting tooth in a person's jaw, a prominent canine tooth.

Bucket, buk'et, *n.* [A.Sax. *buc*, a bucket, a flagon, a pitcher, with dim. term. added. Probably allied to *back*, a vessel.] A vessel made of wood, leather, metal, or other material, for drawing or holding water or other liquids; one of the cavities on the circumference of a water-wheel, into which the water is delivered to move the wheel; the scoop of a dredging-machine or of a grain-elevator.—**Bucketful**, buk'et-fụl, *n.* As much as a bucket will hold.—**Bucket-wheel**, *n.* A water-wheel containing cavities on its circumference to catch the water that drives it; a wheel for raising water, having a rope passing round it with buckets which dip into a well and discharge at the surface.

Buckle, buk'l, *n.* [Fr. *boucle*, buckle, from L.L. *buccula*, the central part of the buckler, the boss, dim. of L. *bucca*, a cheek.] An instrument, usually made of some kind of metal, and consisting of a rim with a chape and tongue, used for fastening harness, belts, or parts of dress together; a curl of hair; a state of being curled or crisped (as a wig).—*v.t. buckled, buckling.* To fasten with a buckle or buckles; *refl.* to set vigorously to work at anything; to join together, as in marriage (colloq.).—*v.i.* To bend or bow (*Shak.*)‡; to apply with vigour; to engage with zeal: followed by *to*.

Buckler, buk'lėr, *n.* [O.Fr. *bocler*, Fr. *bouclier*, a protuberance, a boss on the shield. BUCKLE.] A kind of shield, a piece of defensive armour anciently used in war, and worn on the left arm.—*v.t.*† To be a buckler or shield to; to shield; to defend.

Buckra, buk'ra, *n.* [W. African word meaning supernatural being or demon.] A negro term for a white man.

Buckram, buk'ram, *n.* [O.E. *bokeram*, from O.Fr. *boucaran*, *boqueran*, M.H.G. *buckeram*, *buckeran*, L.L. *boquerannus*, &c.; perhaps stuff made originally of goat's hair (G. *bock*, a goat). BUCK.] A coarse linen cloth, stiffened with glue, used in garments to keep them in the form intended, and for wrappers to some kinds of merchandise; imaginary or phantom foemen; *men in buckram* (Shak. 1 *Henry IV*).—*a.* Made of buckram or resembling buckram; hence, stiff, precise, formal.

Buckshish, Bucksheish, buk'shēsh, Same as *Bakshish.*

Buckshot, buk'shot, *n.* A coarse leaden pellet used as a projectile for killing large game.

Buckwheat, buk'whēt, *n.* [From Prov. E. *buck*, beech, and *wheat*; D. *boek-weit*, G. *buchweizen* (D. *boek*, G. *buche*, a beech); from the resemblance of its triangular seeds to beech-nuts.] A plant with a branched and jointed herbaceous stem, somewhat arrow-shaped leaves, purplish-white flowers, and bearing small triangular seeds, which are ground into flour.—**Buckwheat cakes**, a batter cake of buckwheat flour, prepared by frying thoroughly.

Bucolic, bū-kol'ik, *a.* [L. *bucolicus*, from Gr. *boukolikos*, pertaining to cattle, pastoral, from *bous*, an ox.] Pastoral; relating to country affairs and to a herdsman's life and occupation.—*n.* A pastoral poem.

Bud, bud, *n.* [Allied to D. *bot*, a bud; O.Fr. *boter*, to bud; Fr. *bouton*, a bud; E. *button*.] A small, generally more or less ovoid, protuberance on the stem or branches of a plant, being the form in which leaves or flowers exist before expanding; a prominence on or in certain animals of low organization, as polyps, which becomes developed into an independent being, which may or may not remain permanently attached to the parent organism.—*v.i.—budded, budding.* To put forth or produce buds; to sprout; to begin to grow from a stock like a bud, as a horn; *fig.* to be in an early stage of development.—*v.t.* To graft by inserting a bud under the bark of another tree.—**Budding**, bud'ing, *n.* *Hort.* a mode of grafting, in which a leaf-bud is inserted as a graft instead of a young shoot, the bud sending out a stem which has all the properties of its parent; *zool.* same as *Gemmation.*—**Budlet**, bud'let, *n.* A little bud springing from another bud.

Buddhism, böd'izm, *n.* [*Buddha*, from Skr. *buddh*; pp. from Skr. *budh*, to awake, the Enlightened, known otherwise as Sakyamuni, Gautama: the sacred name of the founder of the system, who appears to have lived in the 6th cent. B.C.] The religious system founded by Buddha, one of the most prominent doctrines of which is that *nirvâna*, or an absolute release from existence, is the chief good; it prevails in China, Japan, Cashmere, Thibet, Burmah, Ceylon, &c., its adherents comprising about a third of the human race.—**Buddhist**, böd'ist, *n.* A worshipper of Buddha; one who adheres to the system of Buddhism.—**Buddhistic**, böd-ist'ik, *a.* Relating to Buddha or to Buddhism.

Buddle, bud'l, *n.* [Comp. G. *butteln*, to shake.] *Mining*, a large square frame of boards used in washing metalliferous ore. —*v.t.* or *i.* To wash ore in a buddle.

Budge, buj, *v.i.* [Fr. *bouger*, to stir, to move = Pr. *bolegar*, to be agitated, It. *bolicare*, to bubble, from L. *bullire*, to boil. BOIL.] To move off; to stir; to remove from a spot a little; to flinch; to take one's self off.—**Budger**, buj'ėr, *n.* One who moves or stirs from his place. (*Shak.*)

Budge, buj, *n.* [O.Fr. *bouge*, L. *bulga*, a leather bag, from a Gallic word seen in Ir. and Gael. *balg*, *bolg*, a bag; akin *bellows*, *belly*.] Lamb-skin with the wool dressed outwards, formerly used as an ornamental border for scholastic habits.—*a.*‡ Trimmed or adorned with budge; scholastic; pedantic; austere; stiff; formal. (*Mil.*)

Budget, buj'et, *n.* [O.E. *boget*, *bouget*, from Fr. *bougette*, dim. of *bouge*, a leather bag. BUDGE, *n.*] A little sack, with its contents; hence, a stock or store; a financial statement of estimated income and expenditures of a country for a fiscal year; a plan of financing a government, based on such a statement; in general, the *weekly budget* of a family, estimating costs of living.

Buff, buf, *n.* [Abbrev. of *buffalo*, O.E. *buffle*, Fr. *buffle*, a buffalo.] A sort of leather prepared from the skin of the buffalo, ox, &c., dressed with oil, like shammy; the colour of buff; a light yellow.—*a.* Made of buff; of the colour of buff.—**Buffy**, buf'i, *a.* Resembling buff; buff-coloured.—*Buffy coat*, the coat which appears on a clot of blood drawn from a vein in cases of inflammation, pleurisy, &c.—**Buff-stick**, *n.* A stick covered with leather, velveteen, &c., and powdered with emery, used in polishing.—**Buff-wheel**, *n.* A wheel for a similar purpose with the buff-stick.

Buffalo, buf'fa-lō, *n.* [From Sp. *bufalo*, Fr. *buffle*, L. *bubalus*, *bufalus*, from Gr. *boubalos*, from *bous*, an ox.] A ruminant mammal of the ox family somewhat larger than the common ox and with stouter limbs; in North America, it is called the *bison*, while in India it is named *water buffalo*, in Africa, the *cape buffalo*.—*v.t.* To bewilder; to bamboozle; to get one *buffaloed*. [*American Slang.*]—**Buffalo clover**, *n.* An American species of short clover which covers the vast prairies on which bisons fed.—**Buffalo grass**, *n.* A species of short grass growing on the prairies of North America.—**Buffalo robe**, *n.* The skin of the bison of North America prepared with the hair on, whether used for covering the person or not.

Buffer, buf'ėr, *n.* [O.E. *buff*, to strike; *buffet*, a blow.] Any apparatus for deadening the concussion between a moving body and the one on which it strikes; an apparatus with powerful springs attached to railway-carriages to prevent injury from violent contact.—**Buffer-state**, *n.* [Name invented by Archibald Forbes to express the position of Afghanistan in relation to India.] A state between two rival nations.

Buffer, buf'ėr, *n.* [From O.E. *buffe*, to stammer, Fr. *bufer*, to puff out the cheeks; comp. Sc. *buff*, nonsense.] A foolish fellow; a fellow: a term expressive of extreme familiarity, and generally having a flavour of contempt.

Buffet, buf'et, *n.* [Fr. *buffet*, a sideboard, a cupboard.] A cupboard, sideboard, or closet, to hold china, crystal, plate, and other like articles; the space set apart for refreshments in public places.

Buffet, buf'et, *n.* [O.Fr. *buffet*, *bufet*, a slap, a blow, dim. from *buffe*, *bufe*, a blow.] A blow with the fist; a box; a cuff; a slap; hence, hard usage of any kind suggestive of blows (Fortune's *buffets*).—*v.t.* To strike with the hand or fist; to box; to beat; to beat in contention; to contend against (*buffet* the billows).—*v.i.* To deal blows or buffets; to make one's way by buffeting.

Buffo, buf'fō, *n.* [It.] The comic actor in an opera; a comic singer.—*a.* Comic.

Buffoon, buf-fön', *n.* [Fr. *bouffon*, from It. *buffone*, from *buffare*, to jest or sport, from *buffa*, a trick, a piece of sport.] A man who makes a practice of amusing others by low tricks, odd gestures and postures, jokes, &c.; a merry-andrew; a clown; a jester.—*v.t.* To make ridiculous.—*v.i.* To play the buffoon.—*a.* Characteristic of a buffoon.—**Buffoonery**, buf-fön'ėr-i, *n.* The arts and practices of a buffoon; low jests; ridiculous pranks.—**Buffoonish**, buf-fön'ish, *a.* Like a buffoon; consisting in low jests or gestures.—**Buffoonism**, buf-fön'izm, *n.* The practices of a buffoon.

Bufonite, bū'fon-īt, *n.* [From L. *bufo*, *bufonis*, a toad.] Toadstone; a fossil consisting of the petrified teeth of fishes, formerly much esteemed for its imaginary virtues.

Bug, bug, *n.* [W. *bwg*, a hobgoblin, a scarecrow; akin to E. *bogey*, Sc. *bogle*.] A hobgoblin, specter, or bugbear (*Shak.*)‡; a name applied to insects of various kinds, as the may-*bug*, the lady-*bug*; particularly applied to an annoying insect of a flat shape and rusty color, which infests the furniture, beds, and walls of houses, emits an offensive smell, and inflicts severe bites on persons.—**Bugaboo**, bug'ä-bö, *n.* An imagined object of fright; a bogeyman; a bugbear.—**Bugbear**, bug'bãr, *n.* [Lit. a *bug* or hobgoblin in the shape of a *bear*.] Something real or imaginary that causes terror.—**Buggy**, bug'i, *a.* Abounding with bugs.—**Bugginess**, bug'i-nes, *n.*

Buggy, bug'i, *n.* A name given to several species of light one-horse carriages or gigs.

Bugle, Bugle-horn, bū'gl, bū'gl-horn, *n.* [Lit. a buffalo-horn, from O.E. *bugle*, a buffalo, from L. *buculus*, a young bullock.] A hunting-horn; a military musical brass wind-instrument, now frequently furnished with keys so as to be capable of producing all the notes of the scale.—**Bugler**, bū'glėr, *n.* One who plays a bugle; a soldier whose duty is to convey the commands of the officers by sounding a bugle.

Bugle, bū'gl, *n.* [L.L. *bugulus*, a female ornament, from root seen in A.Sax. *būgan*, to bend, to *bow*, G. *bügel*, a bent piece of metal.] A shining elongated glass bead, usually black, used in decorating female apparel, &c.—*a.*‡ Black as a bugle or bead; jet-black. (*Shak.*)

Bugloss, bū'glos, *n.* [L. *buglossus*, Gr. *bouglōssos*—*bous*, an ox, and *glōssa*, tongue.] A bristly plant of several species, with narrow oblong leaves and deep purple flowers, a common weed, and so called from the shape and roughness of its leaves; ox-tongue.

Buhl, būl, *n.* [From *Boule*, an Italian wood-carver, who introduced this style of work into France in the reign of Louis XIV.] Unburnished gold, brass, or mother-of-pearl worked into complicated and ornamental patterns, used for inlaying; articles ornamented in this style.—**Buhlwork**, būl'wėrk, *n.* Work in which wood, tortoise-shell, &c., is inlaid with buhl.

Buhrstone, bėr'stōn, *n.* Same as *Burrstone.*

Build, bild, *v.i.*—*built*, *building*. The pret. & pp. *builded* are now confined to poetry. [Of obscure origin, but connected with A.Sax. *bold*, a house, a building; Icel. *ból*, Dan. *bol*, a house, a dwelling, from same root as Icel. *búa*, to dwell, G. *bauen*, to build or cultivate.] To frame, construct, and raise, as an edifice or fabric of almost any kind; to construct; to frame; to raise on a support or foundation; to rear; to erect; to settle or establish (fame, hopes, &c.).—*v.i.* To exercise the art or practise the business of building; to rest or depend (to *build* on another's foundation); to base; to rely.—*n.* Construction; make; form.—**Builder**, bil'dėr, *n.* One who builds; one whose occupation is to build, as an architect, ship-wright, mason, &c.—**Building**,

bild'ing, *n.* The act of one who builds; the thing built, as a house, a church, &c.; fabric; edifice.—**Built**, bilt, *p.* and *a.* Formed; shaped (of the human body, &c.): frequently in composition; constructed of different pieces instead of one, as a mast, beam, &c.

Bukshish, buk'shēsh, *n.* Same as *Bakshish.*

Bulb, bulb, *n.* [L. *bulbus*, a bulbous root.] The rounded part or head of an onion or similar plant; strictly, a modified leaf-bud, consisting of imbricated scales or concentric coats or layers, formed on a plant usually beneath the surface of the ground, emitting roots from its base, and producing a stem from its centre, as in the onion, lily, hyacinth, &c.; any protuberance or expansion resembling a bulb, especially an expansion at the end of a stalk or long and slender body, as in the tube of a thermometer.—*v.i.* To project or be protuberant: with *out.*—**Bulbed**, bulbd, *a.* Having a bulb or having the form of a bulb.—**Bulbel, Bulbil**, bul'bel, bul'bil, *n. Bot.* a separable bulb formed on certain flowering plants; a small axillary bulb.—**Bulbiferous**, bul-bif'ėr-us, *a.* Producing bulbs.—**Bulblet**, bulb'let, *n. Bot.* a bulb which separates spontaneously from the stem of a plant.—**Bulbose, Bulbous**, bul'bōs, bul'bus, *a.* Having or pertaining to bulbs or a bulb; growing from bulbs; resembling a bulb in shape; swelling out.

Bulbul, bụl'bụl, *n.* The Persian name of the nightingale, or a species of nightingale; an Eastern name of other singing birds.

Bulgarian, bul-gā'ri-an, *a.* Pertaining to Bulgaria.—*n.* A member of the Bulgarian race; the language of the Bulgarians, a Slavonic tongue.

Bulge, bulj, *v.i.*—*bulged, bulging.* [From the Scandinavian; O.Sw. *bulgja*, to swell; Icel. *bólginn*, swollen: the same word as A.Sax. *belgan*, to swell, in sense of be angry; akin, *belly, bellows, bowl, billow, bulk*, &c. *Bilge* is another spelling.] To swell out; to be protuberant; to bilge, as a ship.—**Bulgy**,† bul'ji, *a.* Bending outward.

Bulimia, Bulimy, bū-lim'i-a, bū'li-mi, *n.* [Gr. *boulimia*—*bous*, an ox, in composition, huge, great, and *limos*, hunger.] Morbidly voracious, insatiable appetite.

Bulk, bulk, *n.* [Same root as *bulge*; Icel. *bulki*, a heap, the freight of a vessel; Dan. *bulk*, a lump, a clod; O.Sw. *bolk*, a crowd, a mass.] Magnitude of material substance; whole dimensions; size; the gross; the majority; the main mass or body (the *bulk* of a nation); the whole contents of a ship's hold.—*In bulk*, loose or open, that is not packed in bags, boxes, &c.—*v.i.* To grow large; to swell; to appear large or important.—**Bulky**, bul'ki, *a.* Of great bulk or dimensions; of great size; large.—**Bulkiness**, bul'ki-nes, *n.* The state or quality of being bulky.—**Bulk-head**, *n.* A partition in a ship made with boards, to form separate apartments.

Bull, bụl, *n.* [A.Sax. *bull* (only found in dim. *bulluca*, a bullock); L.G. *bulle, bolle*, D. *bul*, Icel. *boli*, a bull. The root may be in A.Sax. *bellan*, to bellow.] The male of any bovine quadruped or animal of the ox or cow kind; an old male whale; *stock-exchange slang*, one who operates in order to effect a rise in the price of stock in order to sell out at a profit: the opposite of a *bear*; **bull in a china shop**, one who from complete lack of judgment commits great havoc, usually in a delicate situation.—*a.* Male, or of large size; characteristic of a bull, as coarse, loud, obstinate, or the like: used in composition; as, a *bull*-trout, *bull*-head, *bul*rush, &c.—**Bullock**, bụl'ok, *n.* [A.Sax. *bulluca*, dim. of *bull.*] An ox or castrated bull; a full-grown steer.—**Bull-baiting**, *n.* The practice of baiting or attacking bulls with trained dogs.—**Bull-calf**, *n.* A male calf; a stupid fellow (*Shak.*).—**Bull-dog**, *n.* A very strong muscular variety of dog, with large head, broad muzzle, short hair, and of remarkable courage and ferocity: formerly much used in bull-baiting.—**Bull-fight**, *n.* A combat between armed men and bulls in a closed arena; a popular amusement in Spain, Portugal, and Latin America.—**Bull-fighter**, *n.* A man who engages in bull-fights.—**Bull-finch**, *n.* A species of finch, distinguished by the large size of the head, the stoutness of the bill, and by having the beak and crown of the head black; a European song-bird.—**Bull-fly**, *n.* The gadfly (which see).—**Bull-frog**, *n.* A large species of frog living in marshy places, having a loud bass voice which resembles the bellowing of a bull.—**Bull-head**, *n.* A name given to several species of fish with wide and flattened heads, as the *catfish*; **Bull-headed**, *a.* Headstrong; obstinate; opinionated.—**Bull's-eye**, *n. Arch.* any circular opening for the admission of light or air: a round piece of thick glass convex on one side let into the deck, port, or skylight of a vessel for the purpose of admitting light: a small lantern with a lens on one side to concentrate the light in a given direction; the center of a target of a different color from the rest of it, and usually round, also a shot that hits the bull's-eye.—**Bull-terrier**, *n.* Breed of dog with characteristics of terrier and bull-dog.

Bull, bụl, *n.* [L. *bulla*, a boss, an ornament worn on a child's neck, later a leaden seal.] Originally the seal appended to the edicts and briefs of the pope, hence, a letter, edict, or rescript of the pope, published or transmitted to the churches over which he is head, containing some decree, order, or decision.

Bull, bụl, *n.* [Origin doubtful.] A gross inconsistency in language; a ludicrous blunder involving a contradiction in terms.

Bullace, bụl'ās, *n.* [A Celtic word; W. *bwlas*, Ir. *bulos*, Fr. *buloce*, Armor. *bolos.*] The wild plum, a native of Asia Minor, yielding two varieties of fruit, red and white, used like damsons.

Bullate, bụl'lāt, *a.* [L. *bullatus*, from *bulla*, a bubble.] In *bot.* having elevations like bubbles or blisters, as a leaf whose membranous part rises between the veins in elevations like blisters.

Bullet, bụl'et, *n.* [Fr. *boulet*, a dim. from *boule*, a ball, from L. *bulla*, a bubble, a boss, a seal. Akin *bullion, bulletin*, to *boil*, a papal *bull.*] A small ball; a projectile generally of lead intended to be discharged from small-arms, as rifles, muskets, pistols, &c.—**Bullet-mould**, *n.* A mould for casting bullets.—**Bullet-proof**, *a.* Capable of resisting the force of a bullet.—**Bullet-tree**, *n.* [Corruption of native name.] The name of several tropical American trees, one of which yields balata gum.

Bulletin, bụl'e-tin, *n.* [Fr., from It. *bulletino*, dim. of *bulla*, an edict of the pope.] An official report concerning some public event, such as military operations, the health of the sovereign, &c., issued for the information of the public; any public announcement, especially of news recently received.

Bullion, bụl'yon, *n.* [From L.L. *bullio, bulliona*, a mass of gold or silver, from L. *bulla*, a boss, a stud, a seal. BULLET.] Uncoined gold or silver in the mass; gold or silver not in the form of current coin; the precious metals in bars, ingots, or in any uncoined form; foreign or uncurrent coins; a kind of heavy twisted fringe frequently made of silk and covered with fine gold or silver wire.—**Bullioner**, bụl'yon-ėr, *n.* A dealer in bullion.—**Bullionist**, bụl'yon-ist, *n.* An advocate of an exclusive metallic currency.

Bullock. Under BULL.

Bully, bụl'i, *n.* [From root of *bull, bellow*; originally the first element in compounds such as *bully-rook, bully-Jack*, and other old terms; comp. Sw. *bullerbas*, a noisy person, from *bullra*, to make a noise.] A blustering, quarrelsome, overbearing fellow, more distinguished for insolence than for courage; a swaggerer; one who domineers or browbeats; a brisk, dashing fellow: a familiar term of address (*Shak.*)†.—*v.t.*—*bullied, bullying.* To act the bully towards; to overbear with bluster or menaces.—*v.i.* To be loudly arrogant and overbearing; to be noisy and quarrelsome; to bluster, swagger, hector, or domineer.

Bully, bụl'i, *n.* [Fr. *bouilli.*] Tinned beef. (Army slang.)

Bulrush, bụl'rush, *n.* [From *bull*, implying largeness, and *rush.*] A name given to large rush-like plants, of various genera, growing in marshes.—**Bulrushy**, bụl'rush-i, *a.* Abounding in bulrushes, resembling or pertaining to bulrushes.

Bulse, buls, *n.* [Pg. *bolsa*, a purse; same word as *burse, bourse.*] In the East Indies, a bag or purse to carry or measure valuables; a certain quantity of diamonds or other valuables.

Bulwark, bụl'wėrk, *n.* [Lit. a *work* built of the *boles* or trunks of trees, from Dan. *bulværk*, D. *bolwerk*, G. *bollwerk*, rampart; hence by corruption Fr. *boulevard.*] A mound of earth round a place, capable of resisting cannon shot, and formed with bastions, curtains, &c.; a rampart; a fortification; that which protects or secures against attack; means of protection and safety; the boarding round the sides of a ship, above the level of the decks, to prevent them being swept by the waves, &c.—*v.t.* To fortify with a bulwark or rampart; to protect.

Bum,† bum, *v.i.* [A different spelling of *boom*, D. *bommen*, to boom or sound hollow.] To make a hollow noise; to boom.—*n.* A droning or humming sound, as that made by the bee; a hum.

Bum, bum, *n.* An inebriate; a mendicant; a loafer; one who prefers charity to work; a panhandler.—*v.i.* To travel without expense to oneself, by begging or stealing food and lodging.

Bumble-bee, bum'bl-bē, *n.* [From *bum*, to hum or boom.] A large bee; a humble-bee: so named from its sound.

Bumbledom, bum'bl-dum, *n.* [From *Bumble*, the beadle, a character in Dickens' *Oliver Twist.*] A sarcastic term applied to fussy official pomposity and incapacity, especially in the case of the members of petty corporations, as vestries.

Bumboat, bum'bōt, *n.* [D. *bumboot*, a wide fishing-boat, from *bun*, a tank in a boat in which fish are kept alive, and *boot*, a boat.] A boat for carrying provisions to a ship at a distance from shore.

Bump, bump, *v.t.* [Perhaps imitative of sound; comp. L.G. *bumsen*, to strike or fall on with a hollow noise; also W. *pwmp*, a round mass; *pwmpiaw*, to thump.] To make to come in violent contact; to give a shock to; to strike; to thump.—*v.i.* To come in collision; to strike against something.—*n.* A swelling or protuberance (especially on the body); *phren.* one of the natural protuberances on the surface of the skull regarded as indicative of distinct qualities, affections, propensities, &c., of the mind; a shock from a collision.

Bumper, bum'pėr, *n.* [Corrupted from older *bumbard, bombard.*] A cup or glass filled to the brim; something well or completely filled.—**Bumper-house**, *n.* A crowded house.

Bumpkin, bump'kin, *n.* [For *bumkin*, a short boom, a bumpkin being a blockish fellow, a blockhead.] An awkward, clumsy rustic; a clown or country lout.—**Bumpkinly**, bump'kin-li, *a.* Of or pertaining to a bumpkin or clown.

Bumptious, bump'shus, *a.* [For *bumpish*, from *bump*, apt to strike against or come in contact with others.] Offensively self-assertive; disposed to quarrel; domineering. (Colloq.)—**Bumptiousness**, bump'shus-nes, *n.* (Colloq.)

Bun, bun, *n.* [O.Fr. *bugne*, a swelling; Fr. *bugnet*, a little puffed loaf.] A kind of cake; a kind of sweet bread.

Bunch, bunsh, *n.* [From O.Sw. and Dan. *bunke*, Icel. *bunki*, a heap. BUNK.] A protuberance; a bunch; a knob or lump; a collection, cluster, or tuft of things of the same kind connected together in growth or tied together; any cluster or aggregate. —*v.i.* To swell out in a protuberance; to cluster, as into bunches.—*v.t.* To form or tie in a bunch.—**Bunch-backed**, *a.* Having a bunch on the back; crooked. (*Shak.*) —**Bunchy**, bunsh'i, *a.* Having a bunch or bunch; having knobs or protuberances; growing in a bunch; like a bunch.—**Bunchiness**, bunsh'i-nes, *n.*

Bund, bund, *n.* A confederation of states; the German-American bund.

Bundle, bun'dl, *n.* [A dim. from *bind*; equivalent to D. *bondel*, G. *bündel*, bundle.] A number of things bound or rolled into a convenient form for conveyance or handling; a package.—*v.t.*—*bundled*, *bundling*. To tie or bind in a bundle or roll: often followed by *up*; to place or dispose of in a hurried unceremonious manner.—*To bundle off*, to send a person off in a hurry; to send off unceremoniously.—*To bundle out*, to expel summarily.—*v.i.* To depart in a hurry or unceremoniously: often with *off*.

Bung, bung, *n.* [Allied to D. *bom*, O.D. *bonne*, a bung; Ir. *buinne*, a tap, a spigot; W. *bwng*, a bung-hole.] A large cork or stopper for closing the hole in a cask through which it is filled.—*v.t.* To stop the orifice of with a bung; to close up.—**Bung-hole**, *n.* The hole or orifice in a cask through which it is filled, and which is closed by a bung.

Bungalow, bung'ga-lō, *n.* [Per. *bangalah*, from *Bengal*; lit. a Bengalese house.] A house or residence, generally of a single floor, and surrounded by a veranda.

Bungle, bung'gl, *v.i.*—*bungled*, *bungling*. [Akin to *bang*, G. dial. *bungen*, O.Sw. *bunga*, to beat, to bang.] To perform in a clumsy awkward manner.—*v.t.* To make or mend clumsily; to botch; to manage awkwardly; to perform inefficiently.—*n.* A clumsy performance; a piece of awkward work; a botch.—**Bungler**, bung'glėr, *n.* One who bungles; one who performs without skill.—**Bungling**, bung'gling, *a.* Prone to bungle; clumsy; characterized by bungling.—**Bunglingly**, bung'gling-li, *adv.* In a bungling manner; clumsily; awkwardly.

Bunion. BUNYON.

Bunk, bungk, *n.* [Sw. *bunke*, a wooden vessel, a coop, in O.Sw. also part of a vessel's deck.] A wooden box or case, serving as a seat during the day and a bed at night; one of a series of sleeping berths arranged above each other.—**Bunker**, bung'kėr, *n.* A sort of fixed chest or box; a large bin or receptacle (a coal-*bunker*).

Bunker, *n.* A sandy hollow in golf links. —**Bunker**, *v.t.* To block, to check.

Bunkum, **Buncombe**, bung'kum, *n.* [From *Buncombe*, in N. Carolina, whose member of Congress had on one occasion admitted that he was talking simply 'for Buncombe', that is, to please his constituents.] Talking for talking's sake; bombastic speech-making; mere words.

Bunny, bun'i, *n.* [Ir. and Gael. *bun*, root, stump; lit. the short-tailed animal.] A sort of pet name for the rabbit.

Bunsen, bun-sen, *n.* [From inventor, Baron *Bunsen*.] A kind of lamp or gas-burner producing an intensely hot flame.

Bunt, bunt, *v.t.* To tap a baseball lightly with a loosely-held bat.—**Buntline**, bunt'lin, *n.* *Naut.* one of the ropes fastened on the bottoms of square sails, to draw them up to their yards.

Bunt, bunt, *n.* [Supposed to be a corruption of *burnt*.] A disease of wheat; smut; also, the fungus producing the disease.

Bunter-sandstein, bun'tėr-sand'stin, *n.* [G., lit., variegated sandstone.] *Geol.* a German name for the New Red Sandstone.

Bunting, bun'ting, *n.* [O.E. *bunting*, *bounting*, *buntel*, Sc. *buntlin*; origin unknown.] The popular name of a number of insessorial birds closely allied to finches and sparrows; such as the English or common bunting; the rice bunting, &c.

Bunting, **Buntine**, bun'ting, bun'tin, *n.* [Probably from G. *bunt*, D. *bont*, party-coloured, of different colours. Comp. next art.] A thin woollen stuff, of which the colours, or flags and signals, of ships are made; a vessel's flags collectively.

Bunting-crow, bun'ting-krō, *n.* [D. *bontekraai*—*bont*, party-coloured, and *kraai*, a crow.] The hooded crow.

Bunyon, **Bunion**, bun'yon, *n.* [From It. *bugnone*, a round knot or bunch, a boil. *Bun* is of the same origin.] An excrescence or knob on some of the joints of the feet, generally at the side of the ball of the great toe, which causes an inflammation of the small membranous sac called *bursa mucosa*.

Buoy, boi, *n.* [D. *boei*, a buoy, a fetter, O.Fr. *boye*, from L. *boiæ*, a kind of fetter or shackle; a buoy being fettered at a fixed point.] A floating object fixed at a certain place to show the position of objects beneath the water, as shoals, rocks, &c., or to mark out the course a ship is to follow, &c.; a floating object used to throw overboard for a person who has fallen into the water to lay hold of, and to keep him afloat till he can be taken out; more particularly called a *life-buoy*.—*v.t.* To keep afloat in a fluid, as in water or air: generally with *up*; *fig.* to keep from sinking into despondency; to fix buoys in as a direction to mariners.—**Buoyage**, boi'āj, *n.* A series of buoys or floating beacons, for the guidance of vessels into or out of port, &c.—**Buoyancy**, **Buoyance**, boi'an-si, boi'ans, *n.* The quality of being buoyant, that is of floating on the surface of water or in the atmosphere; *fig.* lightheartedness; cheerfulness; hopefulness; elasticity of spirit.—**Buoyant**, boi'ant, *a.* Floating; light; having the quality of rising or floating in a fluid; *fig.* cheerful; hopeful; not easily depressed.—**Buoyantly**, boi'ant-li, *adv.* In a buoyant manner.

Bur, **Burr**, bėr, *n.* [A.Sax. *burr*, a bur, a burdock; Dan. *borre*, Sw. *kardborre*, a burdock; the root is probably seen in Ir. *borr*, a knob, *borraim*, to swell.] A rough prickly covering of the seeds of certain plants, as of the chestnut and burdock; the plant burdock; *engr.* a slight ridge of metal left by the graver on the edges of a line, and which is removed by a scraper; the guttural pronunciation of the rough *r* common in some of the northern counties of England. —**Burry**, bėr'i, *a.* Full of burs; resembling burs.

Burberry, bur'bėr-i, *n.* [Maker's name.] Waterproof overcoat of material specially treated by Burberry process.

Burbot, bėr'bot, *n.* [Fr. *barbote*, from *barbe* L. *barba*, a beard.] A fish of the cod family, shaped like an eel but shorter, with a flat head and two small beards on the nose and another on the chin, found in several English rivers and lakes.

Burden, **Burthen**, bėr'dn, bėr'THn, *n.* [A.Sax. *byrthen*, from *beran*, to bear, like Icel. *byrthr*, *byrthi*, Dan. *byrde*, Goth. *baurthei*, G. *bürde*, a burden. BEAR.] That which is borne or carried; a load; that which is grievous, wearisome, or oppressive; the quantity or number of tons a vessel will carry.—*v.t.* To load; to lay a heavy load on; to encumber with weight; to oppress with anything grievous; to surcharge. —**Burdensome**, **Burthensome**, bėr'dn-sum, bėr'THn-sum, *a.* Weighing like a heavy burden; grievous to be borne; causing uneasiness or fatigue; oppressive; heavy; wearisome.—**Burdensomely**, **Burthensomely**, bėr'dn-sum-li, bėr'THn-sum-li, *adv.* In a burdensome manner.—**Burdensomeness**, bėr'dn-sum-nes, *n.* The quality of being burdensome; heaviness; oppressiveness.

Burden, bėr'dn, *n.* [Fr. *bourdon*, a drone or bass, the humble-bee, from L.L. *burdo*, a drone.] The part in a song which is repeated at the end of each verse; the chorus or refrain; a subject on which one dwells.

Burdock, bėr'dok, *n.* [*Bur* and *dock*.] The popular name of a large rough-leaved perennial plant belonging to the composite family, common on roadsides and waste places, and a troublesome weed in cultivated grounds.

Bureau, bū-rō', pl. **Bureaux** or **Bureaus**, bū-rōz', *n.* [Fr. *bureau*, an office, a desk or writing-table, originally a kind of russet stuff with which writing-tables were covered, from L. *burrus*, red or reddish.] A desk or writing-table, with drawers for papers; an escritoire; an office or place where business is transacted; a department for the transaction of public business; a chest of drawers for clothes, &c.—**Bureaucracy**, bū-rō'kra-si, *n.* The system of centralizing the administration of a country, through regularly graded series of government officials; such officials collectively.—**Bureaucrat**, **Bureaucratist**, bū-rō'krat, bū-rō'krat-ist, *n.* An advocate for or supporter of bureaucracy.—**Bureaucratic**, **Bureaucratical**, bū-rō-krat'ik, bū-rō-krat'ik-al, *a.* Relating to bureaucracy.

Burette, bū-ret', *n.* [Fr. from *buire*, a flagon, L. *bibere*, to drink.] A tube used in chemistry for accurately measuring out quantities of fluids.

Burgamot, bėr'ga-mot, *n.* Same as *Bergamot*.

Burganet, **Burgonet**, bėr'ga-net, bėr'gō-net, *n.* [Fr. *bourguignotte*, properly a Burgundian helmet.] A kind of helmet with a small visor formerly worn.

Burgee, bėr'jē, *n.* A flag or pennant which ends in two points; a kind of small coal suited for burning in furnaces.

Burgeois, bur-jō', *n.* A printing type. BOURGEOIS.

Burgeon, bėr'jon, *n.* and *v.i.* Same as *Bourgeon*.

Burgh, bu'rė, *n.* [BOROUGH.] A corporate town or borough; the Scotch term corresponding to the English *borough*, applied to several different kinds of corporations. —**Burghal**, bėr'gal, *a.* Belonging to a burgh.—**Burgher**, bėr'gėr, *n.* An inhabitant of a burgh or borough, who enjoys the privileges of the borough of which he is a freeman.—**Burgess**, bėr'jes, *n.* [O.Fr. *burgeis*, Fr. *bourgeois*, from *bourg*, L.L. *burgus*, a borough.] An inhabitant of a borough or walled town, especially one who possesses a tenement therein; a citizen or freeman of a borough; a parliamentary representative of a borough.—**Burgess-ship**, bėr'jes-ship, *n.* The state or condition of a burgess.

Burglar, bėrg'lėr, *n.* [From Fr. *bourg*, a town, and O.Fr. *laire*, Pr. *lairo*, L. *latro*, a thief.] One guilty of nocturnal house-breaking.—**Burglarious**, bėrg-lā'ri-us, *a.* Pertaining to burglary; constituting the crime of burglary.—**Burglariously**, bėrg-lā'ri-us-li, *adv.* With an intent to commit burglary; in the manner of a burglar.—**Burglary**, bėrg'la-ri, *n.* The act or crime of nocturnal housebreaking, with an intent to commit a felony.

Burgomaster, bėr'gō-mas-tėr, *n.* [D. *burgemeester* = E. *borough-master*.] The chief magistrate of a municipal town in Holland, Flanders, and Germany, nearly corresponding to *mayor* in England and the United States.

Burgoo, bėr'gō, *n.* A kind of oatmeal porridge, a dish used at sea; contemptuous Russian anarchist expression for middle-class or bourgeois politics.

Burgrave, bėr'grāv, *n.* [L.L. *burggravius*, from G. *burggraf*—*burg*, a town, and *graf*, a count, an earl.] In some European countries an hereditary governor of a town or castle.

Burgundy, bėr'gun-di, *n.* A kind of wine, so called from Burgundy, in France.—*Burgundy pitch*, a pitch obtained from the Norway spruce, used in plasters.

Burial, be'ri-al, *n.* Under BURY.

Burin, bū'rin, *n.* [Fr. *burin*, from root of *bore*.] A graver; an instrument for engraving made of tempered steel, of a prismatic form, and with the graving end ground off obliquely so as to produce a sharp point.

Burke, bėrk, *v.t.* [From the name of an Irishman who first committed the crime, in 1829, in Edinburgh, with the view of selling the dead bodies for dissection.] To murder by suffocation; *fig.* to smother; to shelve (a question or discussion); to get rid of by some indirect manœuvre.—**Burker**, bėr′kėr, *n.* One who burks.

Burl, bėrl, *n.* [Fr. *bourre*, a flock of wool as for stuffing, L.L. *burra*, a flock of wool.] A small knot or lump in thread, whether woven into cloth or not.—*v.t.* To pick knots, loose threads, &c., from, as in finishing cloth.—**Burler**, bėr′lėr, *n.* One who burls cloth.—**Burling-iron**, *n.* A kind of pincer or tweezer used in burling cloth.

Burlesque, bėr-lesk′, *a.* [Fr. *burlesque*, from It. *burlesco*, ridiculous, from *burlare*, to ridicule, *burla*, mockery.] Tending to excite laughter by ludicrous images, or by a contrast between the subject and the manner of treating it.—*n.* That kind of literary composition which exhibits a contrast between the subject and the manner of treating it so as to excite laughter or ridicule; travesty; caricature; a kind of dramatic extravaganza with more or less singing in it; a ludicrous or debasing caricature of any kind; a gross perversion.—*v.t.*—*burlesqued, burlesquing.* To make ridiculous by burlesque representation; to turn into a burlesque.—*v.i.*† To use burlesque.—**Burlesquer**, bėr-lesk′ėr, *n.* One who burlesques or turns to ridicule.—**Burletta**, bėr-let′a, *n.* [It., dim. of *burla*, mockery.] A comic opera; a musical farce.

Burly, bėr′li, *a.* [Of same origin as *bur*, *burr*, Ir. and Gael. *borr*, a knob, with term. *-ly*.] Great in bodily size; bulky; lusty: the word, now used only of persons, includes the idea of some degree of coarseness.—**Burliness**, bėr′li-nes, *n.* The state or quality of being burly.

Burmese, bur′mēz, *a.* Of or pertaining to Burmah.—*n.* An inhabitant or inhabitants of Burmah; the language of the people of Burmah.

Burn, bėrn, *v.t.*—*burned* or *burnt, burning.* [A.Sax. *bernan, byrnan, beornan, brinnan*, to burn=Icel. *brenna*, Dan. *brænde*, O.D. *bernen*, Goth. *brinnan*, G. *brennen*, to burn. *Brand, brown, brine, brim*stone, &c., are akin.] To consume with fire; to reduce to ashes; to injure by fire; to scorch; to act on with fire; to expose to the action of fire (limestone, bricks); to make into by means of fire (to *burn* charcoal); to affect with a burning sensation; to apply a cautery to; to cauterize.—*To burn daylight*, to use artificial light before it is dark; to waste time. (*Shak.*)—*v.i.* To be on fire; to flame; to suffer from or be injured by an excess of heat; to shine; to sparkle; to glow; to gleam; to be inflamed with passion or desire; to be affected with strong emotion; to rage; to be affected with a sensation of heat (the cheeks *burn*); in certain games, to be near a concealed object which is sought; hence, to be nearly right in guessing (colloq.).—*n.* A hurt or injury of the flesh caused by the action of fire.—**Burnable**, bėr′na-bl, *a.* Capable of being burnt.—**Burner**, bėr′nėr, *n.* A person who burns or sets fire to anything; the part of a lamp from which the flame issues; the part that holds the wick; the jet-piece from which a gas-flame issues.—**Burning**, bėr′ning, *a.* Much heated; flaming; scorching; vehement; powerful; causing excitement, ardour, or enthusiasm (a *burning* question).—**Burning-glass**, *n.* A double-convex lens of glass, which, when exposed to the direct rays of the sun, collects them into a focus, where an intense heat is produced, so that combustible matter may be set on fire.—**Burning-house**, *n.* The furnace in which tin ores are calcined to sublime the sulphur from the pyrites.—**Burning-mirror**, *n.* A concave mirror, usually made of metal, which reflects the rays of the sun in such a way as to make them converge to a focus, where their whole heat is concentrated.—**Burnt-ear**, *n.* A disease in corn caused by the minute germs or seeds of a parasitic mushroom, in which the fructification of the plant is destroyed, and, as it were, burnt up.—**Burnt-offering, Burnt-sacrifice**, *n.* Something offered and burnt on an altar as an atonement for sin; a sacrifice.—**Burnt-sienna**, sī-en′na, *n.* Earth of Sienna submitted to the action of fire, by which it is converted into a fine orange-red pigment, used both in oil and water-colour painting.

Burn, burn, *n.* [A.Sax. *burna*, a stream, a well; Icel. *brunnr*, D. *born*, Goth. *brunna*, G. *brunnen*, akin to verb to *burn*; comp. *torrent*, from L. *torreo*, to burn.] A rivulet; a brook. [Prov. E. and Sc.]

Burnish, bėr′nish, *v.t.* [O.Fr. *burnir, burnissant*, to polish, to embrown, from *brun*, O.H.G. *brun*, brown. BROWN.] To cause to glow or become resplendent; to polish and make shining by friction; to make smooth and lustrous.—*v.i.*† To grow bright or brilliant; to show conspicuously.—*n.*† Gloss; brightness; lustre.—**Burnisher**, bėr′nish-ėr, *n.* One who or that which burnishes or makes glossy.

Burnoose, bėr-nös′, *n.* [Fr. *burnous, bournous*, from Sp. *al-bornoz*, a kind of Moorish cloak. An Ar. word.] A white woollen mantle, with hood, woven in one piece, worn by the Arabs.

Burrel, bur′el, *n.* [O.Fr. *burel*, reddish, from L. *burrus*, red.] A sort of pear, called also the red butter pear, from its smooth, delicious soft pulp.—**Burrel-fly**, *n.* A kind of reddish-colored gadfly, or breeze.

Burrel-shot, bur′el-shot, *n.* [Fr. *bourreler*, to torment.] Small shot, nails, stones, pieces of old iron, &c., put into cases, to be discharged from a cannon at short range; an emergency shot.

Burrh, Burr-stone, ber, bėr′stōn, *n.* A name given to certain siliceous or siliceo-calcareous stones, whose dressed surfaces present a burr or keen-cutting texture, whence they are much used for millstones.

Burro, bur′o, *n.* A small donkey, used as a pack-animal.

Burrock, bur′ok, *n.* [A.Sax. *burg, burh*, a hill, and dim. *-ock*.] A small weir or dam in a river to direct the stream to gaps where fish-traps are placed.

Burrow, bur′ō, *n.* [The same word with *burgh, borough*, from A.Sax. *beorgan*, to protect, shelter.] A hole in the ground excavated by rabbits, hares, and some other animals, as a refuge and habitation.—*v.i.* To make a hole or burrow to lodge in; to work a way into or under something; to lodge in a burrow or in any deep or concealed place; to hide.—**Burrower**, bur′ō-ėr, *n.* One who burrows; an animal which excavates and inhabits burrows.—**Burrow-duck**, *n.* The sheldrake: so called because it makes its nest in holes in soft soil.—**Burrowing-owl**, *n.* An American species of owl which dwells in holes in the ground.

Burry, bėr′i, *a.* BUR.

Bursa, bėr′sa, *n.* [L.] *Anat.* a kind of sack.—*Bursa mucosa*, a sack situated at a joint and containing the synovial fluid.

Bursar, bėr′sėr, *n.* [BURSE.] A treasurer or cash-keeper of a college or of a monastery; a purser; a student to whom a bursary is paid.—**Bursarship**, bėrs′ėr-ship, *n.* The office of a bursar.—**Bursary**, bėr′sa-ri, *n.* The treasurer of a college or monastery; an exhibition or scholarship in a Scottish academy or university.

Burse, bėrs, *n.* [Fr. *bourse*, a purse, bursary, exchange, from L.L. *bursa*, a purse, a skin, leather. PURSE.] A purse to hold something valuable; one of the official insignia of the lord high chancellor of England; an exchange; a bourse†.—**Bursiform**, bėr′si-form, *a.* Shaped like a purse; sub-spherical.

Burst, bėrst, *v.i.*—*burst, bursting.* [A.Sax. *berstan* = Icel. *bersta*, Dan. *briste, bröste*, D. *bersten*, O.G. *bresten*, Mod.G. *bersten*, to burst; same root in Ir. *brisaim*, Gael. *bris, brisd*, to break.] To fly or break open from internal force and with sudden violence; to suffer a violent disruption; to explode; to become suddenly manifest; to rush: with prepositions, adverbs, and adverbial phrases (to *burst* out, to *burst* into life).—*v.t.* To break or rend by force or violence; to open suddenly (to *burst* one's bonds, to *burst* a cannon).—*n.* A sudden disruption; a violent rending; a sudden explosion or shooting forth; a rush; an outburst.—**Bursting-charge**, *n.* *Mining*, a small charge of fine powder, placed in contact with a charge of coarse powder to ensure the ignition of the latter; *ordnance*, the charge of powder required for bursting a shell or case-shot.

Burthen. BURDEN.

Burton, bėr′ton, *n.* A small tackle formed by two blocks or pulleys, used in ships to set up or tighten the topmost shrouds and for various other purposes.

Bury, ber′i, *v.t.*—*buried, burying.* [A.Sax. *byrgan, byrigan*, to bury; allied to *beorgan*, to protect, and thus to *burgh, borough, burrow, barrow*, &c.] To cover with earth or other matter; to deposit in a grave when dead; to inter; to entomb; to hide; to conceal; to withdraw or conceal in retirement: used *refl.*; to hide in oblivion (to *bury* injuries, &c.).—**Burying**, ber′i-ing, *n.* Burial; sepulture. (N.T.)—**Burial**, ber′i-al, *n.* The act of burying, especially the act of burying a deceased person; sepulture; interment; the act of depositing a dead body in the earth, in a tomb or vault, or in the water.—**Buried**, ber′id, *p.* and *a.* Interred; hidden by the lapse of time; forgotten.—**Burier**, ber′i-ėr, *n.* One who buries; that which buries or covers.

Bus, bus, *n.* An abbreviation of *omnibus*, a public vehicle; a motor coach.

Busby, buz′bi, *n.* A military head-dress consisting of a fur hat with a bag, of the same colour as the facings of the regiment, hanging from the top over the right side.

Bush, bush, *n.* [Scandinavian: Dan. *busk*, Sw. *buske*, a bush = D. *bosch*, a grove; G. *busch*, a bush. The word passed from the Teutonic into the Romance languages, and *ambush, ambuscade, bosky, bouquet*, &c., are akin.] A shrub with branches; a thick shrub; a branch of a tree, properly of ivy, fixed or hung out as a tavern sign (*Shak.*); a stretch of shrubby vegetation; a district covered with brush-wood, or shrubs, trees, &c.—*To beat about the bush*, to use circumlocution; to dilly-dally.—*v.i.* To grow thick or bushy.—*v.t.* To set bushes about; to support with bushes; to use a bush-harrow on.—**Bushiness**, bush′i-nes, *n.* The quality of being bushy.—**Bushy**, bush′i, *a.* Full of bushes; overgrown with shrubs; resembling a bush; thick and spreading, like a bush.—**Bush-buck**, bush′buk, *n.* [D. *bosch-bok*.] The name given to several species of South African antelopes.—**Bush-cat**, *n.* The serval.—**Bush-fighting**, *n.* A mode of fighting in which the combatants scatter, and fire from behind the shelter of trees and bushes.—**Bush-harrow**, *n.* An implement of husbandry for harrowing, consisting of a frame with three or more bars, in which bushes are interwoven.—**Bushman**, bush′man, *n.* A woodsman; a settler in the bush or forest districts of a new country, as Australia; an aboriginal of Bushmanland, near the Cape of Good Hope; a Bosjesman.—**Bushranger**, *n.* In Australia, one who takes to the 'bush', or woods, and lives by robbery.—**Bush-shrike**, *n.* A species of ant-bird found in the hotter latitudes of America.

Bush, bush, *n.* [Parallel form of *box*, from D. *bus*, a box, a bush; G. *büchse*, a box, the bush of a wheel.] A lining of harder material let into an orifice (as for an axle) to guard against wearing by friction.—*v.t.* To furnish with a bush.—**Bush-metal**, *n.* Hard brass; gun-metal; a composition of copper and tin, used for journals, bearings of shafts, &c.

Bushel, bush′el, *n.* [O.Fr. *bussel*, L.L. *bussellus*, a dim. form from *bussida*, for *buxida, pyxida*, from Gr. *pyxis*, a box.] A dry measure containing 8 gallons or 4 pecks. The imperial bushel has a capacity of 2218·192 cubic inches, and holds 80 lbs. avoirdupois of distilled water at the temperature of 62° Fahr. with the barometer at 30 inches; a vessel of the capacity of a bushel.

Business, biz'nes, *n.* [This word, though with the form of an ordinary abstract noun from *busy*, has lost the meaning of state of being busy, *busy-ness*.] A matter or affair that engages a person's time, care, and attention; that which one does for a livelihood; occupation; employment; mercantile concerns, or traffic in general; the proper duty; what belongs to one to do; task or object undertaken; concern; right of action or interposing; affair; point; matter.—*a.* Relating to or connected with business, traffic, trade, &c.

Busk, busk, *n.* [Fr. *busc, busque*, probably from It. *busto*, bust, boddice, by change of letter.] A piece of steel, whalebone, or wood, somewhat elastic, worn by women to stiffen or support their stays.

Busk, busk, *v.t. i.* & *r.* [From Icel. *búask*, to get one's self ready, a contraction of *búa sik*, from *búa*, to prepare, and *sik* (=G. *sich*), one's self. *Bask* is similarly formed. *Bound*, on the point of going, is from same verb. Old English and Scotch.] To prepare; equip; dress.

Buskin, bus'kin, *n.* [For *broskin, bruskin*, a dim. from D. *broos*, a buskin, akin to *brogue*.] A kind of half-boot or high shoe covering the foot and leg to the middle of the calf; the high shoe worn by ancient tragic actors; the tragic drama as opposed to comedy. — **Buskined**, bus'kind, *a.* Wearing buskins; pertaining to tragedy; tragic.

Buss, bus, *n.* [Same as G. *bus*, Sw. *puss*, a kiss; comp. also Ir. and Gael. *bus*, a mouth, a lip.] A kiss; a salute with the lips.—*v.t.* [Comp. O. and Prov. G. *bussen*, Sw. *pussa*, to kiss.] To kiss; to salute with the lips.

Buss, bus, *n.* [O.Fr. *busse*, L.L. *bussa*, a kind of boat; really the same word as *box*.] A small vessel, from 50 to 70 tons burden, and carrying two masts, used in herring-fishing.

Bussu-palm, bụs'sö-päm, *n.* A palm found in the swamps of the Amazon, 10 to 15 feet high, and having leaves often 30 feet long by 4 to 5 feet in breadth.

Bust, bust, *n.* [Fr. *buste*, It. and Sp. *busto*, L.L. *bustum*, from *busta*, a small box, L. *buxida*. Box.] A sculptured figure of a person showing only the head, shoulders, and breast; the chest or thorax.

Bustard, bus'tėrd, *n.* [O.Fr. *bistarde*, a corruption of L. *avis tarda*; lit. slow bird.] A bird belonging to the order of the runners, but approaching the waders. The great bustard is the largest European bird, the male often weighing 30 lbs.

Bustle, bus'l, *v.i.*—*bustled, bustling*. [Same word as Icel. *bustla*, to bustle, to splash in water; *bustl*, bustle, a splash.] To display activity with a certain amount of noise or agitation; to be active and stirring.—*n.* Activity with noise and agitation; stir; hurry-scurry; tumult. —**Bustler**, bus'lėr, *n.* One who bustles; an active stirring person.—**Bustling**, bus'ling, *a.* Moving actively with noise or agitation; active; busy; stirring.

Bustle, bus'l, *n.* [Perhaps for *buskle*, a dim. of *busk*, a support for a lady's stays.] A pad, cushion, or wire framework worn at one time, about 1880, beneath the skirt of a woman's dress, expanding and supporting it behind.

Busy, biz'i, *a.* [O.E. *bisy*, A.Sax. *bysig*, *bisig* = D. *bezig*, L.G. *besig*, busy; further affinities doubtful.] Employed with constant attention; engaged about something that renders interruption inconvenient; occupied without cessation; constantly in motion; meddling with or prying into the affairs of others; officious; causing or spent in much employment (a *busy* day).—*v.t.*—*busied, busying*. To employ with constant attention; to keep engaged; to make or keep busy: often *refl.*—**Busybody**, biz'i-bod-i, *n.* One who officiously concerns himself or herself with the affairs of others.—**Busybodyism**, biz'i-bod-i-izm, *n.* The habit of busying one's self about other people's affairs.—**Busily**, biz'i-li, *adv.* In a busy manner; with constant occupation; importunately; officiously. — **Business**. See separate art.

But, but. Originally a prep. and still often to be so regarded, though also an adv. and frequently a conj. [A.Sax. *bútan*, without, out of, unless—*be*, by, and *útan*, out, without.] Except; besides; unless (all, none *but* one); save or excepting that; were it not (commonly followed by *that*); only; merely; simply (I do *but* jest); sometimes equivalent to, that . . . not (who knows *but* or *but that* he may); as an adversative conj. equivalent to, on the contrary; on the other hand; yet; still; however; nevertheless.

Butcher, bụch'ėr, *n.* [Fr. *boucher*, from *bouc*, a he-goat (from G. *bock*, a goat = E. *buck*), the males being killed for food, the females kept for milk.] One whose trade is to kill beasts for food; one who deals in meat; one who kills in a cruel or bloody manner.—*v.t.* To kill or slaughter for food or for market; to murder in a bloody or barbarous manner.—**Butcherly**,‡ bụch'ėr-li, *a.* Cruel; savage; murderous. (*Shak.*) — **Butchery**, bụch'ėr-i, *n.* The business of slaughtering cattle for the table or for market; murder committed with unusual barbarity; great slaughter. —**Butcher-bird**, *n.* A name given to the shrikes from their habit of suspending their prey, as a butcher does his meat, and then pulling it to pieces and devouring it at their leisure.—**Butcher-meat**, *n.* The flesh of animals slaughtered by the butcher for food.—**Butcher's-broom**, *n.* A stiff erect spiny-leaved shrub belonging to the lily family, often made into brooms for sweeping butchers' blocks.

Butler, but'lėr, *n.* [O.E. *boteler*, from L.L. *botellarius*, a butler, from *botellus*, a bottle. Bottle.] A servant or officer in a household whose principal business is to take charge of the liquors, plate, &c.—**Butlership**, but'lėr-ship, *n.* The office of a butler.

Butt, but, *n.* [O.Fr. *bot, bout*, the end or extremity of a thing, Fr. *but*, an end, aim, goal, also *butte*, a butt used in shooting; from M.H.G. *bózen*, to strike, to beat, a word akin to E. *beat*.] The end or extremity of a thing, particularly the larger end of a thing, as of a piece of timber or of a felled tree; the thick end of a musket, fishing-rod, whip-handle, &c.; an irregularly shaped piece of land, as an outlying piece left unploughed at the end of a field; the end of a plank or piece of timber which unites with another endways in a ship's side or bottom, also, the joining of two such pieces; the thickest and stoutest part of tanned ox-hides; a mark to be shot at, the point where a mark is set or fixed to be shot at; the object of aim; the person at whom ridicule, jests, or contempt is directed; a goal; a bound (*Shak.*); *rifle-practice*, the hut, embankment, or other protection in which the marker sits. —**Butt-end**, *n.* The largest, thickest, or blunt end of anything.—**Butt-shaft**,‡ *n.* An arrow. (*Shak.*)

Butt, but, *v.t.* & *i.* [Fr. *bouter*, O.Fr. *boter*, to push, to butt. Butt, an end.] To strike by thrusting the head against, as an ox or a ram; to have a habit of so striking.—*n.* [In the first sense directly from the verb; in second from Fr. *botte*, a pass or thrust in fencing.] A push or thrust given by the head of an animal; a thrust in fencing.—**Butter**, but'ėr, *n.* An animal that butts.

Butt, but, *n.* [O.Fr. *boute*, Fr. *botte*, a boot, a butt, the two having a considerable resemblance. Boot.] A large cask; a measure of 126 gallons of wine or 2 hogsheads, or 108 gallons of beer.

Butte, büt, *n.* [Fr.] A term applied to a detached hill or ridge of no great height rising abruptly in the Rocky Mountain region of America.

Butter, but'ėr, *n.* [A.Sax. *buter, butor*, from L. *butyrum*, from Gr. *boutyron*, butter, from *bous*, an ox, and *tyros*, cheese.] An oily or unctuous substance obtained from cream or milk by churning; *old chem.* a term applied to certain anhydrous, metallic chlorides of buttery consistency and fusibility.—*Vegetable butters*, a name given to certain vegetable oils, from their resemblance to butter.—*Rock butter*, a peculiar mineral composed of alum combined with iron, of the consistence and appearance of soft butter, appearing as a pasty exudation from aluminiferous rocks.—*v.t.* To smear with butter; to flatter grossly (vulgar).—**Butter-bird**, *n.* A name given to the rice-bunting.—**Butter-boat**, *n.* A vessel for the table in which melted butter, intended to be used as a sauce, is contained.—**Buttercup**, but'ėr-kup, *n.* A name given to several species of Ranunculus, a common field-plant with bright yellow flowers.—**Butterfly**, but'ėr-flī, *n.* [The reason for the name is doubtful; probably it was originally given to a common yellow species.] The common English name of all the diurnal lepidopterous insects (the nocturnal ones being moths), in their last and fully developed state, having four wings often decked with the most beautiful colours, and a suctorial mouth; *fig.* a person whose attention is given up to a variety of trifles of any kind; a showily dressed, vain and giddy person. — **Butterine**, but'ėr-in, *n.* An artificial butter made from animal fat, churned with milk and water, or from milk churned with some sweet butter and the yolks of eggs, the whole of the contents of the churn in the latter case being converted into butterine. — **Butter-knife**, *n.* A blunt, and generally ornamented, knife used for cutting butter at table.—**Butterman**, *n.* A man who sells butter.—**Buttermilk**, *n.* The milk that remains after the butter is separated from it. — **Butter-mould**, *n.* A mould in which pats of butter are shaped and stamped.—**Butternut**, *n.* The fruit of a North American tree akin to the walnut, so called from the oil it contains; also the fruit of one or two lofty hard-wood trees growing in Guiana.—**Butter-Scotch**, but'ėr-skoch, *n.* The name given to a kind of toffee containing a considerable admixture of butter. —**Butter-tongs**, *n. pl.* A kind of tongs with flat blades for slicing and lifting butter. **Butter-tooth**, *n.* A broad fore-tooth.—**Butter-tree**, *n.* A species of African tree, the seeds of which yield a substance like butter, called shea-butter.—**Butterwort**, but'ėr-wėrt, *n.* A European plant growing in bogs or soft grounds, the leaves of which are covered with soft, pellucid, glandular hairs, which secrete a glutinous liquor that catches small insects.—**Buttery**, but'ėr-i, *a.* Having the qualities or appearance of butter.

Buttery, but'ėr-i, *n.* [Originally *botelerie*, a place for bottles, but altered to *buttery* from butter being also kept in it.] An apartment in a household, in which wines, liquors and provisions are kept; in some colleges, a room where refreshments are kept for sale to the students.—**Buttery-bar**, *n.* A ledge on the top of the buttery-hatch on which to rest tankards. (*Shak.*) —**Buttery-hatch**, *n.* A hatch or half-door giving entrance to the buttery.

Buttock, but'ok, *n.* [Dim. of *butt*.] The rump, or the protuberant part of an animal behind.

Button, but'n, *n.* [Fr. *bouton*, a button, a bud, from *bouter*, to push. Butt, to thrust, Butt, an end.] A small round or roundish object of bone, ivory, metal, wood, mother-of-pearl, &c., used for fastening the parts of dress, by being passed into a hole, slit, or loop, or sometimes attached as mere ornament; something resembling a button; a round knob or protuberance; the small disc at the end of fencing foils, &c. The plural used as a singular is a colloquial or slang term for a page boy, from the buttons on his jacket.—*v.t.* To attach a button or buttons to; to fasten with a button or buttons; to inclose or make secure with buttons. —*v.i.* To be capable of being buttoned (his coat will not *button*).—**Button-bush**, *n.* A North American shrub of the cinchona family, so called on account of its globular flower-heads. — **Button-hole**, *n.* The hole or loop in which a button, or flower, is fastened.—*v.t.* To seize a man by the button or button-hole and detain him in conversation against his will.—**Button-**

wood, *n.* A common name in America for the western plane-tree; also the same as *button-bush.*

Buttress, but'res, *n.* [O.E. *butrasse, boterase*, &c., from Fr. *bouter*, to thrust (BUTT), or a modification of *brattice, bretèche.*] A projecting support of masonry built on to the exterior of a wall, especially common in churches in the Gothic style; *fig.* any prop or support (a *buttress* of the constitution). —*v.t.* To support by a buttress; to prop.

Butty, but'i, *n.* A person who raises coal or ore by contract at a stated price per ton, employing men to do the work.

Butyraceous, Butyrous, bū-ti-rā'shus, bū'ti-rus, *a.* [From L. *butyrum*, butter. BUTTER.] Having the qualities of butter; resembling butter.—**Butyric**, bū-tir'ik, *a.* Pertaining to or derived from butter; a term applied to an acid obtained from butter, and also occurring in perspiration, flesh-juice, &c.

Buxeous, buk'sē-us, *a.* [L. *buxeus*, from *buxus*, the box-tree.] Pertaining to the box-tree or resembling it.

Buxom, buk'sum, *a.* [A.Sax. *buhsom*, compliant, obedient, from *búgan*, to bend, to *bow*, and term. *-som, -some*, as in *blithesome*, &c.: D. *buigzaam*, G. *biegsam*, flexible, tractable, are exactly similar.] Yielding to pressure‡; flexible or elastic (*Mil.*)‡; obedient‡; healthy and cheerful; brisk; jolly; lively and vigorous: applied especially to women.—**Buxomly**, buk'sum-li, *adv.* In a buxom manner; briskly; vigorously. —**Buxomness**, buk'sum-nes, *n.*

Buy, bī, *v.t.*—*bought* (pret. & pp.), *buying.* [O.E. *bygge, bugge*, A.Sax. *bicgan, bycgan*, to buy; Goth. *bugjan*, to buy. Hence *aby.*] To acquire by paying a price to the satisfaction of the seller; to purchase: opposed to *sell*; to get, acquire, or procure for any kind of equivalent (to *buy* favour with flattery); to bribe; to corrupt or pervert by paying a consideration.—*To buy in*, to buy for the owner at a public sale, especially when an insufficient price is offered.—*To buy off*, to release from military service by a payment; to get rid of the opposition of by paying; to purchase the non-intervention of.—*To buy out*, to purchase the share or shares of a person in a commercial concern, the purchaser thus taking the place of the seller.—*To buy over*, to detach by a bribe or consideration from one party and attach to the opposite party.—**Buyer**, bī'ėr, *n.* One who buys; a purchaser.

Buzz, buz, *v.i.* [Purely imitative of the sound. Comp. It. *buzzicare*, to buzz, whisper.] To make a low hissing sound, as that of bees; to whisper; to speak with a low hissing voice.—*v.t.* To whisper; to spread or report by whispers; to spread secretly.—*n.* A continuous humming sound, as of bees; a low whispering hum; a report circulated secretly and cautiously; a general confused conversation.—**Buzzer**, buz'ėr, *n.* One who buzzes; a whisperer; one who is busy in telling tales secretly. (*Shak.*)—**Buzzingly**, buz'ing-li, *adv.* With a low humming sound.

Buzzard, buz'ėrd, *n.* [Fr. *buzard, busard*, from *buse*, a buzzard, and term. *-ard*, *buse* being from L.L. *busio*, for L. *buteo*, a buzzard.] A name for several large raptorial birds of the falcon family, with short weak toes; a blockhead; a dunce.

By, bī, *prep.* [A.Sax. *bī, big*, by; O.Sax. O.Fris. *bi*, D. *bij*, G. *bei*, Goth. *bi*. Often as a prefix in form *be.*] Near; close to; near along with motion past; through or with, denoting the author, producer, or agent, means, instrument, or cause; according to; by direction, authority; or example of (*by* his own account, ten *by* the clock, a rule to live *by*); at the rate of; in the ratio or proportion of (*by* the yard, *by* the dozen); to the amount or number of (larger *by* half, older *by* ten years); during the course of; within the compass or period of (*by* day); not later than (*by* this time, *by* two o'clock). In oaths or adjurations it comes before what is invoked or appealed to (*by* heaven).—*Two by two, day by day, piece by piece*, &c., each two, each day, each piece, taken separately or singly. —*Five feet by four*, measuring five feet one way and four the other.—*a.* Side; secondary: used only in composition, as *by*-path, *by*-play, *by*-street, &c.—*adv.* Near; in the same place with; at hand; aside (to stand *by*, to lay a thing *by*); so as to pass (to run *by*); so as to be past or over (the time went *by*).—*By and by*, in the near future; soon; presently.—**By, Bye**, bī, *n.* A thing not directly aimed at; something not the immediate object of regard; as, by the *by*, or by the *bye*, that is, by the way, in passing; an odd or side run gained at cricket.—**By-blow**, *n.* A side or accidental blow (*Mil.*); an illegitimate child (vulgar).—**By-end**, *n.* Private end; secret purpose or advantage.—**By-gone**, bī'gon, *a.* Past; gone by.—**By-gones**, bī'gonz, *n. pl.* What is gone by and past.—**By-lane**, *n.* A private lane, or one out of the usual road.—**By-name**,‡ *n.* Nick-name.—**By-past**, bī'past, *a.* Past; gone by. (*Shak.*)—**By-path, By-road, By-street, By-way**, *n.* A path, road, street, or way which is secondary to a main road, street, &c.; a lesser, private, or obscure way.—**By-play**, *n.* Action carried on aside, and commonly in dumb-show, while the main action proceeds; action not intended to be observed by some of the persons present.—**By-product**, *n.* A secondary product; something obtained, as in a manufacturing process, in addition to the principal product or material.—**By-stander**, *n.* One who stands by or near; an onlooker or spectator: one present but taking no part in what is going on.—**By-word**, *n.* A common saying; a proverb.

By-law, Bye-law, bī'la, *n.* [From the Scand. *by*, a town, the termination in Whit*by* and other names, and *law*; Dan. *by-lov*, a municipal law; Sw. *by-lag*, a by-law.] A local or private law; a law made by an incorporated body, as a railway company, for the regulation of its own affairs, or the affairs intrusted to its care.

Byre, bīr, *n.* [A Scandinavian word = E. *bower.*] A cow-house. [Scotch.]

Byssus, bis'us, *n.* pl. **Byssi**, bis'ī. [L. *byssus*, Gr. *byssos*, fine linen or cotton.] *Zool.* a long, lustrous, and silky bunch of filaments by which certain bivalve molluscs, as the oyster, are attached to fixed objects; *bot.* the stipe of certain fungi.—**Byssaceous**, bis-sā'shus, *a.* Resembling a byssus; consisting of fine silky filaments.—**Byssiferous**, bis-sif'ėr-us, *a.* Producing a byssus. —**Byssine**, bis'in, *a.* Made of byssus; having a silky or flax-like appearance.—**Byssoid**, bis'oid, *a.* Having the appearance of byssi; *bot.* exhibiting a fringed structure with threads of unequal lengths. —**Byssolite**, bis'o-līt, *n.* [*-lite*=Gr. *lithos*, stone.] A name given to the finer fibrous varieties of filamentous minerals, as amianthus, tremolite, actinolite, &c.

Byzant, Byzantine, biz'ant, biz-an'tīn, *n.* Same as *Bezant* (which see).

Byzantine, Byzantian, biz-an'tīn or biz'an-tīn, biz-an'shi-an, *a.* Pertaining to *Byzantium*, at one time the capital of the Eastern Roman Empire, now, under the name of Istanbul, the largest city and seaport of the Turkish Republic.

C

C, the third letter in the English alphabet and the second of the consonants, originally having the sound of *k*, now having also the sharp sound of *s* (before *e, i*, and *y*); *music*, the name of the first or key note of the modern normal scale, answering to the *do* of the Italians and the *ut* of the French.

Caaba, kä'a-ba, *n.* [Ar. from *ka'b*, a cube.] An oblong stone building forming the great temple at Mecca, containing at the north-west corner the famous black stone (an aërolite), presented in Arab tradition by the angel Gabriel to Abraham.

Caaing-whale, kä'ing-whāl, *n.* [A Scotch name, from the verb *to ca'*, that is, to drive, because these whales can be driven like cattle.] The round-headed porpoise, a cetaceous animal of the dolphin family, of a black colour, and attaining the length of 24 feet.

Cab, kab, *n.* [Heb.] A Hebrew dry measure containing according to one estimate 2 pints, according to another 4.

Cab, kab, *n.* [Abbrev. of *cabriolet.*] A closed four-wheel vehicle, usually for public hire; a taxicab. The covered part of a locomotive.—**Cab-stand**, *n.* A place where cabs stand for hire.

Cabal, ka-bal', *n.* [Fr. *cabale*, the *cabala*, an intrigue, a cabal. CABALA.] Intrigue; secret artifices of a few persons united in some design; a number of persons united in some close design, usually to promote their private views in church or state by intrigue; a junto; specifically, a name given to a ministry of Charles II., consisting of Clifford, Ashley, Buckingham, Arlington, and Lauderdale, the initials of whose names happened to compose the word. — *v.i.*—*caballed, caballing.* To form a cabal; to intrigue; to unite in secret artifices to effect some design.—**Caballer**, ka-bal'ėr, *n.* One who cabals.

Cabala, Cabbala, kab'a-la, *n.* [Heb. *qabbâlâ*, reception, the cabala or mysterious doctrine received traditionally, from *qâbal*, to take or receive.] A mysterious kind of science or learning among Jewish rabbins, transmitted by oral tradition, serving for the interpretation of difficult passages of Scripture.—**Cabalism**, kab'al-izm, *n.* The science of the cabalists.—**Cabalist**, kab'al-ist, *n.* A Jewish doctor who professes the study of the cabala.—**Cabalistic, Cabalistical**, kab-al-ist'ik, kab-al-ist'ik-al, *a.* Pertaining to the cabala; containing an occult meaning.—**Cabalistically**, kab-al-ist'ik-al-li, *adv.* In the manner of the cabalists.

Caballine, kab'al-līn, *a.* [L. *caballinus*, from *caballus*, a horse.] Pertaining to or suited for a horse (*caballine* aloes).—*n.* A coarse kind of aloes used as a medicine for horses.

Cabaret, kab'a-rā, *n.* [Fr.] A restaurant where dancers and singers entertain.

Cabas, ka-bä', *n.* [Fr., of Ar. origin.] A lady's flat work-basket or reticule.

Cabbage, kab'āj, *n.* [O.E. *cabbish, cabage*, from Fr. *cabus*, O.Fr. *choux cabus*, a large-headed cabbage—*cabus, cabuce*, large-headed, from L. *caput*, a head.] A well-known vegetable of several varieties, the kinds most cultivated being the common cabbage, the savoy, the broccoli, and the cauliflower; the common cabbage forms its leaves into dense rounded heads, the inner leaves being blanched. — *v.i.* To form a head like that of a cabbage in growing.—**Cabbage-butterfly**, *n.* A large white butterfly, the larvæ of which destroy cruciferous plants, especially of the cabbage tribe.—**Cabbage-moth**, *n.* A large dusky-coloured moth having a greenish-black caterpillar which feeds on cabbages. —**Cabbage-palm, Cabbage-tree**, *n.* A West Indian palm, having a simple unbranched slender stem growing to a great height, and so called from the young unexpanded leaves being eaten as a vegetable.

—**Cabbage-rose**, *n.* A very fragrant species of rose of many varieties, having a large, rounded, and compact flower.—**Cabbage-worm**, *n.* The larva or caterpillar of a butterfly or moth infesting cabbages.

Cabbage, kab'āj, *v.t.*—*cabbaged*, *cabbaging*. [Fr. *cabasser*, to put in a *cabas* or basket; hence, to hoard, steal. CABAS.] To purloin, especially to purloin pieces of cloth after cutting out a garment.—*n.* A cant name for anything filched, more particularly, cloth purloined by one who cuts out garments.

Cabbala, **Cabbalism**, &c., *n.* CABALA, CABALISM, &c.

Cabble, kab'l, *v.t.* or *i.*—*cabbled*, *cabbling*. *Metal.* to break the masses of partially finished iron into pieces, to be again heated in a furnace and wrought or hammered into bar-iron.—**Cabbler**, kab'lėr, *n.* One who cabbles.

Cabby, kab'i, *n.* Driver of cab. (Colloq.)

Cabeca, ka-bā'sa, *n.* [Pg., lit. a head.] A fine kind of Indian silk; a money of account on the west coast of Africa.

Caber, kā'ber, *n.* [Gael. *cabar*, a pole, a stake, a rafter.] In Highland games, a long undressed stem of a tree, used for tossing as a feat of strength.

Cabin, kab'in, *n.* [From W. *caban*, a cabin, dim. of *cab*, a kind of hut; Ir. and Gael. *caban*, a cabin.] A small room or inclosed place; a cottage; a hut or small house or habitation, especially one that is poorly constructed; an apartment in a ship for officers or passengers.—*v.i.* To live in a cabin; to lodge. (*Shak.*)—*v.t.* To confine as in a cabin. (*Shak.*)—**Cabin-boy**, *n.* A boy whose duty is to wait on the officers and passengers on board of a ship.

Cabinet, kab'in-et, *n.* [Fr. *cabinet*, a closet, receptacle of curiosities, &c., a dim. form, ultimately from the Celtic. CABIN.] A small room, closet, or retired apartment; a private room in which consultations are held; hence, the select or secret counsel of a prince or executive government; the collective body of ministers who direct the government of a nation or country: so called from the apartment in which the meetings were originally held; a piece of furniture consisting of a chest or box, with drawers and doors.—**Cabinet-council**, *n.* The confidential council of a prince or executive magistrate; a council of cabinet ministers held with privacy to deliberate upon public affairs; a select number of confidential counsellors.—**Cabinet Edition**. Size of book between library and popular style.—**Cabinet-maker**, *n.* A man whose occupation is to make household furniture, such as cabinets, side-boards, tables, &c.

Cable, kā'bl, *n.* [Fr. *câble*, a rope, from L.L. *capulum*, *caplum*, a rope, a halter, from L. *capio*, to take.] A large strong rope, usually of 3 or 4 strands of hemp, or a chain, such as is used to retain a vessel at anchor; a cablegram; *arch.* a moulding with its surface cut in imitation of the twisting of a rope; also, a cylindrical moulding in the flute of a column and partly filling it.—*Cable's length*, a nautical measure, one tenth of a sea mile, or about 100 fathoms.—*Submarine* or *electric telegraph cable*, a cable by which telegraphic messages are conveyed through the ocean, usually composed of a single wire of pure copper, or of several wires, embedded in a compound of gutta-percha and resinous substances, so as to be compacted into one solid strand, encircled by layers of gutta-percha or india-rubber, hemp or jute padding, and coils of iron wire.—*v.t.*—*cabled*, *cabling*. To fasten with a cable; to send a message by electric cable; *arch.* to fill (the flutes of columns) with cables or cylindrical pieces.—**Cablegram**, kā'bl-gram, *n.* A message by cable.—**Cable-moulding**, *n.* See above.

Cabob, ka-bob', *n.* [Per.] An oriental dish, consisting generally of a neck or loin of mutton cut in pieces and roasted, dressed with onions, eggs, spices, &c.

Caboose, ka-bös', *n.* [From D. *kabuis*, a caboose or ship's galley; Dan. *kabys*, Sw. *kabysa*, *kabyssa*, a caboose, L.G. *kabuse*, *kabüse*, a little room or hut; probably from same root as *cabin*.] The cook-room or kitchen of a ship; last car of a freight train.

Cabriole, kab'ri-ōl, *n.* [Fr. *cabriole*, a goat-leap; L.L. *capriolus*, a goat, from L. *caper*, a goat.] A leap or curvet of a horse; a capriole.—**Cabriolet**, kab-rē-ō-lā, *n.* [Fr. *cabriolet*, dim. from *cabriole*, a goat-leap.] A one-horse carriage; a cab.

Cabrit, kab'rit, *n.* The prong-horned antelope of North America.

Cacao, ka-kā'ō, *n.* [Fr. Sp. Pg. *cacao*, from Mexican *cacauatl*, cacao.] The chocolate-tree, a small tree 16 to 18 feet high, a native of the West Indies, and much cultivated in the tropics of both hemispheres on account of its seeds, from which cocoa (a corruption of the word *cacao*) and chocolate are prepared.

Cachalot, kash'a-lot or kash-a-lō, *n.* [Fr. *cachalot*, from Catalan *quichal*, a tooth, lit. therefore toothed whale.] A very large cetaceous mammal, tho blunt-headed sperm-whale, having a head of enormous size, containing a large receptacle filled with spermaceti; sperm-oil and ambergris are also obtained from this animal.

Cache, kash, *n.* [Fr.] A hole in the ground in which travellers hide and preserve provisions which it is inconvenient to carry.

Cachet, ka-shā, *n.* [Fr., from *cacher*, to conceal.] A seal.—*Lettre de cachet*, a private letter of state; a name given especially to letters bearing the private seal of the French kings, often employed as arbitrary warrants of imprisonment for an indefinite period.

Cachexy, **Cachexia**, ka-kek'si, ka-kek'-si-a, *n.* [Gr. *kachexia*, from *kakos*, ill, and *hexis*, habit, from *echō*, to have.] A morbid state of the bodily system, the result of disease or of intemperate habits.—**Cachectic**, **Cachectical**, ka-kek'tik, ka-kek'tik-al, *a.* Having or pertaining to cachexy.

Cachinnation, kak-in-nā'shon, *n.* [L. *cachinnatio*, from *cachinno*, to laugh; imitative of the sound.] Loud or immoderate laughter.—**Cachinnatory**, ka-kin'a-to-ri, *a.* Of or pertaining to cachinnation; laughing loudly.

Cacholong, kash'o-long, *n.* [*Cach*, the name of a river in Bucharia, and *cholong*, a Calmuc word for stone.] A mineral of the quartz family, a variety of opal, and so often called *Pearl-opal*, usually milk-white, sometimes grayish or yellowish-white, opaque or slightly translucent at the edges.

Cachou, ka-shö, *n.* [Fr. Same as *cashew*.] A sweetmeat generally in the form of a pill, and made of the extract of liquorice, cashew-nut, gum, &c., used to remove an offensive breath.

Cachucha, ka-chö'cha, *n.* [Sp.] A Spanish dance similar to the bolero, a piece of music for it.

Cacique, ka-sēk', *n.* CAZIQUE.

Cackle, kak'l, *v.i.*—*cackled*, *cackling*. [D. and L.G. *kakelen*, Sw. *kackla*, Dan. *kagle*; of imitative origin like *giggle*, *cachinnation*, &c.] To utter a noisy cry such as that often made by a goose or a hen; to laugh with a broken noise, like the cackling of a goose; to giggle; to prate; to prattle; to tattle.—*n.* The broken cry of a goose or hen; idle talk; silly prattle.—**Cackler**, kak'lėr, *n.* A fowl that cackles; a tell-tale; a tattler.

Cacodemon, **Cacodæmon**, kak-ō-dē'-mon, *n.* [Gr. *kakos*, evil, and *daimōn*, a demon.] An evil spirit; a devil. (*Shak.*)

Cacodyle, kak'ō-dil, *n.* [Gr. *kakos*, bad, *odōdē*, smell, and *hylē*, matter.] A compound of hydrocarbon and arsenic; a clear liquid of an insupportably offensive smell and poisonous vapour.

Cacoethes, kak-ō-ē'thēz, *n.* [L. *cacoethes*, from Gr. *kakoēthes*, a bad habit, an itch for doing something—*kakos*, vicious, and *ēthos*, custom, habit.] A bad custom or habit.—*Cacoethes scribendi*, a diseased propensity for writing; an itch for authorship.

Cacography, ka-kog'ra-fi, *n.* [Gr. *kakos*, bad, and *graphō*, to write.] Bad spelling or writing.—**Cacographic**, kak-ō-graf'ik, *a.* Of, pertaining to, or characterized by cacography or bad writing or spelling; ill-written.

Cacolet, kak-o-lā, *n.* [Fr.] A kind of chair fixed on the back of a mule or horse for carrying travellers in mountainous districts, or sick or wounded persons.

Cacology, ka-kol'o-ji, *n.* [Gr. *kakologia*—*kakos*, bad, and *logos*, word.] Bad speaking; bad choice of words.

Cacoon, ka-kön', *n.* [African.] The large seeds of a climbing tropical leguminous plant, often made into scent-boxes, &c.

Cacophony, ka-kof'o-ni, *n.* [Gr. *kakophōnia*—*kakos*, bad, and *phōnē*, sound, voice.] A disagreeable vocal sound; discord.—**Cacophonic**, **Cacophonous**, kak-ō-fō'-nik, ka-kof'o-nus, *a.* Sounding harshly.

Cactus, kak'tus, *n.* [L., from Gr. *kaktos*, a prickly plant.] A succulent, spiny, and usually leafless shrub of numerous species, natives of tropical America, the fruit of some being edible, and many being cultivated in conservatories for their showy flowers and curious stems.—**Cactaceous**, kak-tā'shus, *a.* Relating to or resembling the cactus.

Cad, kad, *n.* [An abbreviation of *cadet*.] A slang term applied originally to various classes of persons of a low grade, as hangers-on about inn-yards, messengers or errand-boys, &c.; now extended to any mean, vulgar fellow of whatever social rank.

Cadastre, ka-das'tėr, *n.* [Fr. *cadastre*, a survey and valuation of property, from L.L. *capitastrum*, register for a poll-tax, from L. *caput*, the head.] A detailed survey of a country, as the basis of an assessment for fiscal purposes, &c.—**Cadastral**, ka-das'-tral, *a.* Pertaining to or having the character of a cadastre.

Cadaverous, ka-dav'ėr-us, *a.* [L. *cadaverosus*, from *cadaver*, a dead body, from *cado*, to fall.] Pertaining to a dead body; especially, having the appearance or color of a dead human body; pale; wan; ghastly.—**Cadaverously**, ka-dav'ėr-us-li, *adv.* In a cadaverous manner.—**Cadaverousness**, ka-dav'ėr-us-nes, *n.*

Caddice, **Caddis**, kad'is, *n.* [From W. *cadach*, a rag, *cadas*, a kind of cloth, from the rough or ragged covering of the larva.] The larva of the caddice-fly.—**Caddice-fly**, **Caddis-fly**, *n.* A neuropterous insect, called also the *May-fly*, the larva or grub of which forms for itself a case of small roots, stalks, stones, shells, &c., and lives under water till ready to emerge from the pupa state.

Caddie, **Caddy**, kad'i, *n.* One who carries clubs for a golfer.—*v.i.* to serve as a caddie.—**Caddie-master**, a man who supervises caddies.—**Caddy**, *n.* A small box for keeping tea.

Cade, kād, *n.* [L. *cadus*, a cask.] A barrel or cask; a *cade* of herrings = 500.

Cadence, kā'dens, *n.* [L.L. *cadentia*, a falling, from L. *cado*, to fall. *Chance* is the same word.] A decline; a state of falling or sinking; the general tone or modulation of the voice in reading or reciting; tone; sound; rhythm; measure; *mus.* a short succession of notes or chords at the close of a musical passage or phrase; also a shake or trill, run, or division, introduced as an ending or as a means of return to the first subject.—**Cadent**,‡ kā'dent, *a.* Falling down; sinking. (*Shak.*)—**Cadenza**, ka-den'za, *n.* [It.] *Mus.* an embellishment made at the end of a melody, either actually extempore or of an impromptu character; also, a running passage at the conclusion of a vocal piece.

Cadet, ka-det', *n.* [Fr. *cadet*, O.Fr. *capdet*, contr. from L.L. *capitettum*, dim. of L. *caput*, the head; lit. little head or chief.] A younger or youngest son; a junior male member of a noble family; a young man in training for the rank of an officer in the army or navy; cadets of the U. S. Naval Academy at Annapolis are officially called *midshipmen*. — **Cadetship**, ka-det'-

ship, *n.* The state of being a cadet; the rank or office of a cadet.

Cadge, kaj, *v.t.* and *i.* [Perhaps from noun *cadger.*] To carry about for sale; to hawk, go about begging.

Cadger, kaj'ėr, *n.* [Perhaps from O.Fr. *cagier*, one who carried about falcons or other birds in a *cage* for sale.] An itinerant huckster or hawker.

Cadi, kad'i or kā'di, *n.* [Turk.] A judge in civil affairs among the Turks; usually the judge of a town or village.

Cadmean, Cadmian, kad-mē'an, kad'-mi-an, *a.* Relating to *Cadmus*, a legendary prince of ancient Greece, who is said to have introduced the sixteen simple letters of the Greek alphabet, thence called *Cadmean* letters. — *Cadmean victory*, a victory in which the victors suffer as much as the vanquished.

Cadmium, kad'mi-um, *n.* [L. *cadmia*, Gr. *kadmia, kadmeia*, calamine.] A ductile, malleable, and fusible metal, of a fine white colour with a shade of bluish gray, resembling that of tin; it is very scarce, is in all its relations very analogous to zinc, and is almost invariably associated with it. —**Cadmium-yellow**, *n.* A pigment of an intense yellow colour and much body, prepared from the sulphide of cadmium.

Cadre, kä'dr, *n.* [Fr. from L. *quadra*, a square.] The permanent skeleton or framework of a regiment, which may be filled up as need requires.

Caduceus, ka-dū'sē-us, *n.* [L.] Mercury's rod represented as a winged rod entwisted by two serpents, in modern times used as a symbol of commerce.—**Caducean**, ka-dū'sē-an, *a.* Belonging to the caduceus or wand of Mercury.

Caducibranchiate, ka-dū'si-brang"ki-āt, *a.* [L. *caducus*, falling, and *branchiæ*, gills.] A term applied to animals such as the newts, which lose the gills before attaining maturity.

Caducous, ka-dū'kus, *a.* [L. *caducus*, from *cado*, to fall.] Having a tendency to fail or decay; specifically applied to organs of animals and plants that early drop off, as branchiæ, floral envelopes, &c.

Cæcum, sē'kum, *n.* pl. **Cæca**, sē'ka. [L. *cæcus*, blind.] The blind gut or intestine; a branch of an intestine with one end closed; mammals have generally only one cæcum, birds usually two cæca, while in fishes they are often numerous.—**Cæcal**, sē'kal, *a.* Of or belonging to the cæcum; having the form of a cæcum; bag-shaped.—**Cæcally**, sē'kal-li, *adv.* In the form or manner of a cæcum.

Cænozoic, sē-nō-zō'ik, *a.* CAINOZOIC.

Caen-stone, kä'en or kon, *n.* A cream-coloured building-stone of excellent quality, got near Caen in Normandy, the material of which many English buildings are constructed.

Cærulean. CERULEAN.

Cæsar, sē'zėr, *n.* A title, originally a surname of the Julian family at Rome, which, after being dignified in the person of the dictator C. Julius Cæsar, was adopted by successive Roman emperors, and latterly came to be applied to the heir presumptive to the throne; personification of the civil power, the State.—**Cæsarean, Cæsarian**, sē-zā'rē-an, sē-zā'ri-an, *a.* Of or pertaining to Cæsar.—*Cæsarean operation*, the operation by which the fetus is taken out of the uterus by an incision through the abdomen and uterus, when delivery of a living child is otherwise impossible: said to be so named because Julius Cæsar was brought into the world in this way.—**Cæsarism**, sē'zėr-izm, *n.* Despotic sway exercised by one who has been raised to power by popular will; imperialism.

Cæsium, sē'zi-um, *n.* [L. *cæsius*, blue.] A rare metal originally discovered in mineral waters, and so named because its spectrum exhibits two characteristic blue lines. It is always found in connection with rubidium.

Cæspitose, Cæspitous, ses'pi-tōs, ses'pi-tus, *a.* CESPITOSE.

Cæsura, sē-zū'ra, *n.* [L. *cæsura*, a cutting, from *cædere, cæsum*, to cut.] A pause or division in a verse; a separation, by the ending of a word or by a pause in the sense, of syllables rhythmically connected.—**Cæsural**, sē-zū'ral, *a.* Pertaining to the cæsura.

Café, kaf-ā, *n.* [Fr., coffee, a coffee-house.] A coffee-house; a restaurant.

Caffeic, ka-fē'ik, *a.* Of or pertaining to coffee.—**Caffeine**, ka-fē'in, *n.* A slightly bitter alkaloid found in coffee, tea, &c., which, when taken in large doses, is poisonous.

Caffre, kaf'ėr, *n.* KAFIR.

Caftan. KAFTAN.

Cage, kāj, *n.* [Fr. *cage*, from L. *cavea*, a hollow, from *cavus*, hollow (whence E. *cave*).] A box, or inclosure, a large part of which consists of lattice-work of wood, wicker, wire, or iron bars, for confining birds or beasts; a prison or place of confinement for petty malefactors†; a skeleton framework of various kinds; the framework of a hoisting apparatus, as the framework in which miners ascend and descend the shaft, and by which hutches are raised and lowered.—*v.t.*—*caged, caging.* To confine in a cage; to shut up or confine.—**Cageling**, kāj'ling, *n.* A bird kept in a cage; a cage bird.

Caimacam, kā-ma-kam', *n.* A lieutenant or lieutenant-general in the Turkish service; the governor of Constantinople.

Caiman, *n.* CAYMAN.

Cain, kān, *n.* [Biblical.] Murderer, fratricide. **Cain-coloured**, *a.* The yellow beard of the character in the mediæval mystery plays.

Cainozoic, kā-nō-zō'ik, *a.* [Gr. *kainos*, recent, and *zōē*, life.] *Geol.* a term applied to the latest of the three divisions into which strata have been arranged, with reference to the age of the fossils they include, embracing the tertiary and post-tertiary systems.

Caique, ka-ēk', *n.* [Fr. from Turk. *kaik.*] A light skiff used in the Bosporus, where it almost monopolizes the boat traffic.

Cairn, kärn, *n.* [Gael. Ir. W. *carn*, a heap, a cairn.] A heap of stones; one of those large heaps of stones common in Great Britain, particularly in Scotland and Wales, and generally of a conical form, erected as sepulchral monuments, to commemorate some events, as landmarks, &c.

Cairngorm, Cairngorm-stone, kärn'-gorm, *n.* A yellow or brown variety of rock-crystal, found in great perfection on *Cairngorm* and the neighbouring mountains in Scotland, and much used for brooches, seals, and other ornaments.

Caisson, kās'son, *n.* [Fr., *caisson*, from *caisse*, a chest, a case, from L. *capsa*, a chest.] A wooden chest filled with explosives to be fired when approached by an enemy; also, an ammunition wagon, or an ammunition chest; a vessel in the form of a boat used as a flood-gate in docks; a water-tight structure or case filled with air and placed under sunken vessels to raise them; a kind of floating dock; a water-tight box or cylindrical casing used in founding and building structures in water too deep for the coffer-dam, such as piers of bridges, quays, &c.

Caitiff, kā'tif, *n.* [O.Fr. *caitif*, captive, unfortunate; from L. *captivus*, a captive, from *capere*, to take.] A mean villain; a despicable knave; one who is both wicked and mean.—*a.* Belonging to a caitiff; servile; base.

Cajeput, Cajuput, kaj'i-put, kaj'u-put, *n.* [Malay *kāyū*, a tree, and *putih*, white.] A pungent, volatile oil, having stimulant and antispasmodic properties, obtained from the cajeput-tree of the Moluccas.

Cajole, ka-jōl', *v.t.*—*cajoled, cajoling.* [Fr. *cajoler*, to cajole; O.Fr. *cageoler*, to sing or chatter like a bird in a cage, from *cage.*] To deceive or delude by flattery, specious promises, &c.; to wheedle; to coax.—**Cajoler**, ka-jōl'ėr, *n.* One who cajoles; a wheedler.—**Cajolery**, ka-jōl'ėr-i, *n.* The act of cajoling; coaxing language or tricks; a wheedling to delude.

Cake, kāk, *n.* [Icel. and Sw. *kaka*, Dan. *kage*, D. *koeck*, G. *kuchen*, cake; probably from L. *coquere*, to cook. COOK.] A mass of fine light dough baked, and generally sweetened or flavoured with various ingredients; something made or concreted in the form of a cake; a mass of matter in a solid form relatively thin and extended.—*To take the cake*, complete the victory, to surpass. (Colloq.)—*v.t.*—*caked, caking.* To form into a cake or mass.—*v.i.* To concrete or become formed into a hard mass, as dough in an oven, &c.

Calabash, kal'a-bash, *n.* [Pg. *calabaça*, Sp. *calabaza*, from Ar. *qar*, a gourd, and *aibas*, dry.] A gourd shell dried; the fruit of the calabash-tree; a vessel made of a dried gourd shell or of a similar shell, used for containing liquors or goods, as pitch, resin, and the like.—**Calabash-tree**, *n.* A name of several American trees bearing large gourd-like fruits, the hard shells of which are made into numerous domestic utensils, as basins, cups, spoons, bottles, &c.

Calamanco, kal-a-mang'ko, *n.* [Sp. *calamanco, calamaco*, L.L. *calamancus, calamaucum.*] A woollen stuff of a fine gloss and checkered in the warp.

Calamander Wood, kal-a-man'dėr, *n.* [Supposed to be a corruption of *Coromandel.*] A beautiful species of wood, a kind of ebony obtained from a Ceylonese tree resembling rosewood, and so hard that it is worked with great difficulty.

Calamary, kal'a-ma-ri, *n.* [Sp. *calamar*, a calamary, from L. *calamus*, a reed, pen, from their pen-shaped internal shell.] A decapod cuttle-fish, having the body oblong, fleshy, tapering, flanked behind by two triangular fins, and containing a pen-shaped internal horny shell. Called also *Squid, Sea-sleeve.*

Calambac, kal'am-bak, *n.* [Per.] A fragrant wood; agallochum.

Calambour, kal'am-bör, *n.* [Akin to *calambac.*] A species of aloes-wood of a dusky or mottled colour, used by cabinet-makers.

Calamine, kal'a-min, *n.* [L.L. *calamina*, from L. *cadmia* (*d* being changed into *l*), calamine.] The native siliceous oxide of zinc, an important British ore of zinc, from which the metal is got chiefly by distillation.

Calamint, kal'a-mint, *n.* [Gr. *kalaminthē, kalaminthos.*] A name for labiate plants akin to mint.

Calamite, kal'a-mīt, *n.* [L. *calamus*, a reed.] A kind of fossil plants, common in the carboniferous rocks, having the habit of the modern equisetums, but with woody stems, and growing to the size of trees.

Calamity, ka-lam'i-ti, *n.* [L. *calamitas, calamitatis.*] Any great misfortune or cause of misery; a disaster accompanied with extensive evils; misfortune; mishap; affliction; adversity.—**Calamitous**, ka-lam'i-tus, *a.* [Fr. *calamiteux*, L. *calamitosus.*] Producing or resulting from calamity; making wretched; distressful; disastrous; miserable; baleful.—**Calamitously**, ka-lam'i-tus-li, *adv.* In a calamitous manner. —**Calamitousness**, ka-lam'i-tus-nes, *n.*

Calamus, kal'a-mus, *n.* [L. *calamus*, a reed, a reed-pen; same root as in E. *haulm.*] A reed or reed-like plant; a perennial tufted Indian grass, called also sweet-scented lemon-grass, yielding an aromatic oil used in perfumery; the root of the sweet-rush; the generic name of the palms yielding rattans.—**Calamiferous**, kal-a-mif'ėr-us, *a.* Producing reeds.

Calash, ka-lash', *n.* [Fr. *calèche*, from G. *kalesche*, a word of Slavonic origin; Bohem. *kolesa*, Pol. *koluska.*] A light carriage with very low wheels and a folding top; the folding hood or top fitted to such a carriage; a kind of head-dress worn by ladies, and consisting of a frame of cane or whalebone covered with silk.

Calathiform, kal'a-thi-form, *a.* [L. *calathus*, a work-basket, a bowl, and *forma.*

form.] *Bot.* hemispherical or concave, like a bowl or cup.

Calcaneum, kal-kā'nē-um, *n.* [L., the heel.] *Anat.* the largest bone of the tarsus; the bone that forms the heel.

Calcar, kal'kär, *n.* [L. *calcar*, a spur, from *calx, calcis*, the heel.] *Bot.* a spur; a hollow projection from the base of a petal.—**Calcarate**, kal'ka-rāt, *a.* *Bot.* furnished with a spur, as the corolla of larkspur.

Calcar, kal'kär, *n.* [L. *calcaria*, a lime-kiln, from *calx*, lime.] A kind of oven or reverberating furnace, used in glass-works for the calcination of sand and salt of potash, and converting them into frit.

Calcareous, kal-kā'rē-us, *a.* [L. *calcarius*, from *calx*, lime.] Partaking of the nature of lime; having the qualities of lime; containing lime.—**Calcareousness**, kal-kā'rē-us-nes, *n.* Quality of being calcareous.

Calcedonic, Calcedony, kal-si-don'ik, kal-sed'o-ni. CHALCEDONIC, CHALCEDONY.

Calceolaria, kal-sē-ō-lā'ri-a, *n.* [L. *calceolus*, a slipper, from the shape of the inflated corolla resembling a shoe or slipper.] The generic name of a number of ornamental herbaceous or shrubby plants, natives of South America, and now very common in gardens, most having yellow flowers, some puce-coloured, and some with the two colours intermixed, while others are white.

Calcic, kal'sik, *a.* [L. *calx, calcis*, lime.] Of or pertaining to lime; containing calcium.—**Calciferous**, kal-sif'ėr-us, *a.* [L. *calx*, and *fero*, to produce.] Producing or containing lime, especially when in considerable quantity (*calciferous* strata).—**Calcification**, kal'si-fi-kā"shon, *n.* A changing into lime; the process of changing into a stony substance by the deposition of lime.—**Calciform**, kal'si-form, *a.* In the form of chalk or lime.—**Calcify**, kal'si-fī, *v.i.*—*calcified, calcifying.* [L. *calx*, and *facio*, to make.] To become gradually changed into a stony condition by the deposition or secretion of lime.—*v.t.* To make stony by depositing lime.—**Calcimine**, kal'si-mīn, *n.* [From L. *calx*.] A superior kind of white or coloured wash for the walls of rooms, ceilings, &c.—**Calcine**, kal-sīn', *v.t.*—*calcined, calcining.* [Fr. *calciner*, from L. *calx*.] To reduce to a powder or to a friable state by the action of heat; to free from volatile matter by the action of heat, as limestone from carbonic acid, iron ore from sulphur; to oxidize or reduce to a metallic calx.—*v.i.* To be converted into a powder or friable substance by the action of heat.—**Calcinable**, kal-sī'na-bl, *a.* Capable of being calcined.—**Calcination**, kal-si-nā'shon, *n.* The act or operation of calcining.—**Calciner**, kal-sīn'ėr, *n.* One who calcines; a calcining or roasting furnace.—**Calcite**, kal'sīt, *n.* A term applied to various minerals, including limestone, all the white and most of the coloured marbles, chalk, Iceland-spar, &c.—**Calcium**, kal'si-um, *n.* [From L. *calx*.] Sym. Ca. The metallic basis of lime, and the most widely diffused of the alkaline metals; it is a light yellow metal, about as hard as gold, very ductile and malleable, and burns in chlorine with a most brilliant flame.

Calcography, kal-kog'ra-fi, *n.* [L. *calx*, chalk, and Gr. *graphō*, to engrave.] The art of drawing with black or coloured chalks.—**Calcographer**, kal-kog'ra-fėr, *n.* One who practises calcography.—**Calcographical**, kal-kō-graf'ik-al, *a.* Pertaining to calcography.

Calc-sinter, kalk'sin-tėr, *n.* [L. *calx*, lime, and G. *sinter*, a stalactite.] A stalactitic carbonate of lime, a variety of calcite, consisting of deposits from springs holding carbonate of lime in solution.—**Calc-spar**, kalk'spär, *n.* Calcareous spar, or crystallized carbonate of lime.—**Calc-tuff**, kalk'tuf, *n.* An alluvial formation of carbonate of lime.

Calculary. Under CALCULUS.

Calculate, kal'kū-lāt, *v.t.*—*calculated, calculating.* [L. *calculo, calculatum*, from *calculus*, a counter or pebble used in calculations, from *calx*, a small stone, a counter.] To ascertain by computation; to compute; to reckon up; to estimate (value, cost); to make the necessary or usual computations regarding (an eclipse, &c.); to fit or prepare by the adaptation of means to an end; to make suitable: generally in pp. in this sense = suited or suitable; adapted (a scheme *calculated* to do much mischief).—*v.i.* To make a computation; to weigh all the circumstances; to deliberate.—**Calculable**, kal'kū-la-bl, *a.* Capable of being calculated or ascertained by calculation.—**Calculating**, kal'kū-lāt-ing, *a.* Having the power or habit of making arithmetical calculations; quick at arithmetical calculations; given to forethought and calculation; deliberate and selfish; scheming (a *calculating* disposition).—**Calculation**, kal-kū-lā'shon, *n.* The act of calculating; the art or practice of computing by numbers; reckoning; computation; a series of arithmetical processes set down in figures and bringing out a certain result; estimate formed by comparing the circumstances bearing on the matter in hand.—**Calculative**, kal'kū-lā-tiv, *a.* Pertaining to calculation; tending to calculate.—**Calculator**, kal'kū-lā-tėr, *n.* One who calculates.

Calculus, kal'kū-lus, *n.* pl. **Calculi**, kal'kū-lī. [L., a pebble used for calculating, from *calx*, a small stone, a counter.] A general term for hard concretions of various kinds formed in various parts of the body, the more important being those formed in the gall-bladder, called *biliary calculi* or gall-stones, and those formed by a deposition from the urine in the kidney or bladder, called *urinary calculi*; the stone; gravel; a method of mathematical computation using algebraic symbols.—**Calculous, Calculose**, kal'kū-lus, kal'kū-lōs, *a.* Stony; gritty; hard like stone; arising from calculi, or stones in the bladder.

Caldron, Cauldron, kal'dron, *n.* [O.Fr. *caldron* = Sp. *calderon*, It. *calderone*, from L. *caldus, calidus*, hot.] A large kettle or boiler of copper or other metal.

Caledonian, kal-i-dō'ni-an, *a.* Pertaining to Caledonia, an ancient name of Scotland; Scottish; Scotch.—*n.* A native of Caledonia, now Scotland; a Scotchman.

Calefacient, kal-i-fā'shi-ent, *a.* [L. *calefacio*, to make warm, from *caleo*, to be warm, and *facio*, to make.] Warming; heating.—*n.* That which warms or heats; *med.* a substance which excites a degree of warmth in the part to which it is applied, as mustard, pepper, &c.—**Calefaction**, kal-i-fak'shon, *n.* The act or operation of warming or heating; the state of being heated.—**Calefactive, Calefactory**, kal-i-fak'tiv, kal-i-fak'to-ri, *a.* Adapted to make warm or hot; communicating heat.—**Calefy**, kal'i-fī, *v.t.*—*calefied, calefying.* To make warm or hot.

Calendar, kal'en-dėr, *n.* [L. *calendarium*, an account-book, a calendar, from *calendæ*, the first day of each month, the calends; root in *calo*, Gr. *kalein*, to call.] A register of the year, in which the months, weeks, and days are set down in order, with the feasts observed by the church, &c.; an orderly table or enumeration of persons or things, as a list of criminal causes which stand for trial; a list; a catalogue; a register.—*v.t.* To enter or write in a calendar; to register.—**Calends**, kal'endz, *n. pl.* [L. *calendæ*.] Among the Romans the first day of each month.—*The Greek calends*, a time that never occurred or never will occur, a phrase which originated in the fact that the Greeks had nothing corresponding to the Roman calends.

Calender, kal'en-dėr, *n.* [Fr. *calandre*, L.L. *celendra*, a calender, from L. *cylindrus*, Gr. *kylindros*, a cylinder.] A machine consisting of two or more cylinders revolving so nearly in contact with each other that cloth passing through between them is smoothed and glazed by their pressure; an establishment in which woven fabrics are calendered, starched, stretched, and otherwise finished for the market; one engaged in calendering; a calendrer].—*v.t.* To press or finish in a calender.—**Calendrer, Calenderer**, kal'en-drėr, kal'en-dėr-ėr, *n.* A person who calenders cloth.

Calender, kal'en-dėr, *n.* [From the founder of the order.] One of an order of dervishes in Turkey and Persia, of not very strict morals, nor held in very high esteem by the Mohammedans.

Calenduline, ka-len'dū-lin, *n.* A mucilaginous substance or gum obtained from the marigold, the Calendula of botanists.

Calenture, kal'en-tūr, *n.* [Fr. *calenture*, Sp. *calentura*, heat, a calenture, from *calentar*, to heat, from L. *caleo*, to be hot.] A kind of delirium caused within the tropics, especially on board ship, by exposure to excessive heat.

Calescence, ka-les'ens, *n.* [From L. *calesco*, to grow warm, incept. of *caleo*, to be hot.] Growing warmth; growing heat.

Calf, käf, *n.* pl. **Calves**, kävz. [A.Sax. *cealf* = D. *kalf*, Icel. *kálfr*, Sw. *kalf*, Dan. *kalv*, G. *kalb*, a calf.] Properly the young of the cow or the bovine genus of quadrupeds, but applied also to the young of the marine mammalia, as the whale; an ignorant, stupid person; a dolt; a weak or cowardly man; leather made from the skin of a calf.—**Calf-love**, *n.* A youthful romantic passion or affection.—**Calf-skin, Calf's-skin**, *n.* The hide or skin of a calf; leather made of the skin.

Calf, käf, *n.* [Icel. *kálfi*, the calf of the leg.] The thick fleshy part of the leg behind, below the knee.

Caliber, Calibre, kal'i-bėr, *n.* [Fr. *calibre*, possibly from Ar. *kâlib*, Pers. *kâlab*, a mould.] The diameter of a body, as of a column or a bullet; usually the diameter of the bore of a firearm; *fig.* compass or capacity of mind; the extent of one's intellectual endowments.—*Caliber-compasses, calibers*, or *callipers*, compasses made either with arched legs to measure the diameters of cylinders or globular bodies, or with straight legs and points turned outwards to measure the interior diameter or bore of anything.—**Calibrate**, kal'i-brāt, *v.t.* To ascertain the calibre of.—**Calibration**, kal-i-brā'shon, *n.* The act or process of calibrating, especially of ascertaining the calibre of a thermometer-tube, with the view of graduating it to a scale of degrees.

Calice, kal'is, *n.* [Fr. *calice*, L. *calix*, a cup.] *Zool.* the little cup in which the polyp of a coral-producing zoophyte is contained.

Calico, kal'i-kō, *n.* [From *Calicut* in India, whence the cloth was first introduced.] A term for any white or unprinted cotton cloth.—**Calico-printer**, *n.* One whose occupation is to print calicoes.—**Calico-printing**, *n.* The art of printing or impressing calicoes with variegated figures and colours, more or less permanent.

Calid, kal'id, *a.* [L. *calidus*, from *caleo*, to be hot.] Hot; burning; warm.—**Calidity**, ka-lid'i-ti, *n.* Heat; warmth.—**Caliduct**, kal'i-dukt, *n.* [L. *caleo*, and *duco, ductum*, to lead.] A pipe or canal used to convey hot air or steam from a furnace to the apartments of a house.

Calif, Caliph, kā'lif, *n.* [Fr. *calife*, from Ar. *khalifa*, successor, from *khalafa*, to succeed.] A title given to the acknowledged successors of Mohammed, regarded among Mohammedans as being vested with supreme dignity and power in all matters relating to religion and civil policy. Written also *Kalif, Khalif*, &c.—**Califate**, kal'i-fāt, *n.* The office or dignity of a calif; the government of a calif. Written also *Kalifate, Caliphate.*

Caliginous, ka-lij'i-nus, *a.* [L. *caliginosus*, from *caligo, caliginis*, darkness.] Dim; obscure; dark.—**Caliginously**, ka-lij'i-nus-li, *adv.* Obscurely; darkly.—**Caliginousness**, ka-lij'i-nus-nes, *n.*

Caligraphic, Caligraphist, Caligraphy. CALLIGRAPHIC, &c.

Calipash, kal'i-pash, *n.* [A form of *calabash*, with sense of *carapace*, the upper shell of the tortoise.] That part of a turtle which belongs to the upper shield, consisting of a fatty, gelatinous substance of a dull, greenish colour: spelled also *Callipash*.—**Calipee**, kal'i-pē, *n.* That part of a turtle which belongs to the lower shield, of a light yellow colour: spelled also *Callipee*.

Caliph, Caliphate, *n.* CALIF, CALIFATE.

Calisaya, kal-i-sä'a, *a.* A name for the yellow, or orange yellow, febrifugal barks of several species of cinchona trees, consisting of the inner bark.—**Calisayine**, kal-i-sä'in, *n.* An alkaline substance obtained from calisaya bark, now used in making a kind of bitters.

Calisthenics, kal-is-then'iks, *n.* [Gr *kalos*, beautiful, and *sthenos*, strength.] The art or practice of taking exercise for health, strength, or grace of movement. —**Calisthenic**, kal-is-then'ik, *a.* Relating to calisthenics.

Calk, kąk, *v.t.* Same as *Caulk*.

Calk, kąk, *v.t.* [Fr. *calquer*, It. *calcare*, from L. *calx*, lime.] To copy (a print or design) by covering the back with chalk, a pencil, or crayon, and tracing lines through on a piece of paper by passing lightly over each stroke of the design with a point.

Calker, Calkin, kąk'ėr, kąk'in, *n.* [Perhaps from L. *calcar*, a spur, from L. *calx*, the heel.] The prominent part of either extremity of a horse-shoe, bent downwards and brought to a sort of point; the semicircular ring of iron nailed on to the heel of a strong shoe or boot. Also **Calk**, kąk, in same sense.—**Calk**, kąk, *v.t.* To furnish with a calker or calkin.

Call, kąl, *v.t.* [A.Sax. *ceallian*=Icel. and Sw. *kalla*, Dan. *kalde*, to call; D. *kallen*, to talk, to prattle; same root as Gr. *gēryō*, to cry; Skr. *gar*, to call.] To name; to denominate: with the name or appellation as well as the person or thing named; to pronounce the name of; to designate or characterize as; to affirm to be; to invite or command to come or assemble (a person, a cab, a meeting); to summon; to select or appoint, as for an office, duty, or employment; to invoke or appeal to; to arouse, as from sleep; to awaken; to proclaim or utter loudly.—*To call back*, to recall; to summon or bring back.—*To call forth*, to bring or summon to action (one's energies).—*To call in*, to collect (as debts or money); to draw from circulation (coin).—*To call names*, to use opprobrious epithets to.—*To call out*, to challenge to a duel; to summon into service or action (the military).—*To call over*, to go over by reading aloud name by name.—*To call to mind*, to recollect; to revive in memory.—*To call to the bar*, to admit to the rank of barrister or advocate.—*To call up*, to bring into view or recollection; to recall; to require payment of.—*v.i.* To utter a loud sound; or to draw a person's attention by name: often with *to*; to make a short stop or pay a short visit: often followed by *at*, *for*, or *on*.—*To call at*, to visit a place in passing; *to call for* (a person or thing) is to visit in order to obtain the company of the person to some other place, or to get the thing; also, to demand, require, claim (crime *calls for* punishment).—*To call on* or *upon*, to visit (a person); to demand from or appeal to; to invoke.—*To call out*, to utter in a loud voice; to bawl.—*n.* A summons or invitation made vocally or by an instrument; a demand; requisition; claim (the *calls* of justice or humanity; *calls* on one's time); divine vocation or summons; invitation or request to a clergyman by a congregation to become their minister; a short or passing visit paid to a person; the cry of a bird to its mate or young; a whistle or pipe used by a boatswain and his mate to summon sailors to their duty; a pipe to call birds by imitating their voice.—**Call-bell**, *n.* A small hand-bell on a stand or frame.—**Call-bird**, *n.* A bird taught to allure others into a snare.—**Call-boy**, *n.* A boy whose duty it is to call actors on to the stage at the proper moment.—**Caller**, kąl'ėr, *n.* One who calls.—**Calling**, kąl'ing, *n.* A vocation; profession; trade; usual occupation or employment; a collective name for persons following any profession; state of being divinely called (N.T.).—**Calling-crab**, *n.* The popular name for tropical crabs which, when disturbed, hold up a claw before them, as if beckoning or calling upon some one.—**Calling-hare**, *n.* PIKA.—**Call-note**, *n.* The note or sound produced by the male of birds and some other animals to call the female.

Callet, kal'et, *n.* [Fr. *caillette*, a frivolous babbling woman, dim. from *caille*, a quail.] A tattling or talkative woman; a scold; a gossip; a trull; a drab.

Callid,† kal'id, *a.* [L. *callidus*, expert, shrewd, from *callum*, the hardened skin of the hands caused by labor.] Skilled; expert; shrewd. — **Callidity, Callidness**, kal-lid'i-ti, kal'id-nes, *n.* [L. *calliditas*.] Skill; discernment; shrewdness.

Calligraphy, kal-lig'ra-fi, *n.* [Gr. *kalligraphia*—*kalos*, beautiful, and *graphō*, to write.] The art of beautiful writing; fair or elegant writing or penmanship. — **Calligrapher, Calligraphist**, kal-lig'ra-fėr, kal-lig'ra-fist, *n.* One skilled in calligraphy. — **Calligraphic, Calligraphical**, kal-li-graf'ik, kal-i-graf'ik-al, *a.* Relating to calligraphy.

Callimanco, kal-i-mang'kō, *n.* CALAMANCO.

Calliope, ka-lī'ō-pē, *n.* A set of musical whistles, played like an organ.

Callipash, Callipee, kal'i-pash, kal'i-pē CALIPASH, CALIPEE.

Callipers, kal'i-pėrz, *n. pl.* CALIBER.

Callipeva, kal-i-pē'va, *n.* A much-prized river mullet of the West Indies. Its scales are used for ornaments, &c., and its roes form an excellent caviar.

Callisthenic, Callisthenics. CALISTHENIC, &c.

Callotechnics,† kal-o-tek'niks, *n. pl.* [Gr. *kalos*, beautiful, and *technē*, art.] The fine or ornamental arts.

Callous, Callose, kal'us, kal'ōs, *a.* [L. *callosus*, from *callus*, *callum*, hard thick skin. CALLID.] Hardened or thickened from continuous pressure or friction; said of the skin; having a hardened skin; hence, hardened in mind or feelings; insensible; unfeeling. — **Callosity**, kal-los'i-ti, *n.* [L. *callositas*.] The state or quality of being hardened or indurated; any thickened or hardened part on the surface of the human body or that of any other animal; any part of a plant unusually hard.—**Callously**, kal'us-li, *adv.* In a callous, hardened, or unfeeling manner.—**Callousness**, kal'us-nes, *n.* The state or character of being callous; insensibility; apathy; indifference.—**Callus**, kal'us, *n.* A callosity; a new growth of osseous matter between the extremities of fractured bones; any part of a plant unusually hard; the new formation over the end of a cutting before it sends forth rootlets.

Callow, kal'ō, *a.* [A.Sax. *calu*, bald=D. *kaal*, Sw. *kal*, G. *kahl*, bald; cog. L. *calvus*, bald.] Destitute of feathers, as a young bird; naked; unfledged; pertaining to the condition of a young bird.

Callum, kal'um, *n.* [L. for hard skin.] (1) *Bot.* a healing tissue by which wounds are closed. (2) *Surg.* growth of bone by which fractures are mended.

Calm, käm, *a.* [Fr. *calme*, calm, from L.L. *cauma*, the heat of the sun, hence the hot part of the day, the time for rest; from Gr. *kauma*, heat, from *kaiō*, to burn.] Still; quiet; undisturbed; not agitated; not stormy: said of the weather, the sea, &c.; undisturbed by passion; not agitated or excited in feeling; tranquil, as the mind, temper, &c.—*n.* Freedom from motion, agitation, or disturbance; stillness; tranquillity; quiet; especially, a state or period at sea when there is neither wind nor waves. —*Region of calms* or *calm latitudes*, the tracts in the Atlantic and Pacific Oceans on the confines of the trade-winds, where calms of long duration prevail.—*v.t.* To make calm; to still; to quiet; to appease, allay, or pacify (grief, anger, anxiety, &c.); to becalm (*Shak.*).—*v.i.* To become calm or serene.—**Calmer**, käm'ėr, *n.* One who or that which calms.—**Calmly**, käm'li, *adv.* In a calm manner; without agitation; quietly.—**Calmness**, käm'nes, *n.* The state of being calm, quiet, or unruffled; quietness; stillness; tranquillity.

Calmuck, Calmuc, kal'muk, *n.* A member of a branch of the Mongol race, now spread over a large portion of Asia; the language spoken by the Calmucks.

Calomel, kal'o-mel, *n.* [Gr. *kalos*, fair, good, and *melas*, black, perhaps because it was good for black bile.] A preparation of mercury, a compound of this metal and chlorine, usually in the form of a whitish powder, much used in medicine.

Caloric, ka-lor'ik, *n.* [L. *calor*, heat.] The name given to a supposed subtle imponderable fluid to which the sensation and phenomena of heat were formerly attributed.—*a.* Pertaining to caloric.—*Caloric engine*, an engine similar in principle to the steam-engine, the motive power being the expansive force of heated air.—**Caloricity**, kal-o-ris'i-ti, *n.* That faculty in animals of developing a quantity of heat necessary to life.—**Calorifere**, ka-lor'i-fār, *n.* [Fr., from L. *calor*, heat, and *fero*, to bear.] An apparatus for heating conservatories, &c., by means of hot water circulating in tubes.—**Calorific**, kal-o-rif'ik, *a.* Capable of producing heat; causing heat; heating. —*Calorific rays*, certain invisible rays emanating from the sun, and which are only manifested by their effects on the thermometer. — **Calorification**, ka-lor'i-fi-kā''shon, *n.* The production of heat, especially animal heat.—**Calorificient, Calorifient, Calorifacient**, ka-lor'i-fish''-eut, ka-lor'i-fī''ent, ka-lor'i-fā''shi-ent, *n.* [L. *calor*, heat, and *facio*, to make.] Heat-producing; producing heat in the bodily system.—**Calorescence**, kal-o-res'ens, *n.* *Physics*, the transmutation of heat rays into others of higher refrangibility.—**Calorist**, kal'or-ist, *n.* A believer in the fluid called caloric.—**Calorie**, kal'o-rē, *n.* The quantity of heat required to raise a *Kg.* of water from 0° to 1° C.; or the quantity required to raise a *gm.* of water through the same range; used as the unit of heat.

Calorimeter, kal-o-rim'e-tėr, *n.* [L. *calor*, heat, and Gr. *metron*, measure.] An apparatus for measuring absolute quantities of heat.—**Calorimetric**, ka-lor'i-met''rik, *a.* Of or belonging to the use of the calorimeter.—**Calorimetry**, kal-o-rim'et ri, *n.* The art or process of using the calorimeter.

Calotte, ka-lot', *n.* [Fr. *calotte*, a skull-cap, dim. of *cale*. CAUL.] A skull-cap worn by ecclesiastics, &c.

Calotype, kal'o-tīp, *n.* [Gr. *kalos*, beautiful, and *typos*, figure, impression.] The name given to the process of producing photographs by the action of light upon nitrate of silver.

Caloyer, kal'o-yėr, *n.* [Fr. from Mod. Gr. *kalogeros*, from Gr. *kalos*, beautiful, and *gerōn*, Mod. Gr. *geros*, an old man.] One of a sect of monks of the Greek Church.

Calp, kalp, *n.* Soft limestone found in Ireland, of a bluish-black, or gray color.

Caltrop, kal'trop, *n.* [L.L. *calcitrapa*, from L. *calx*, *calcis*, a heel, and L.L. *trappa*, a snare.] *Milit.* an instrument with four iron points disposed in such a manner that any three of them being on the ground the other points upward, used as an obstacle to the advance of troops; *bot.* a term applied to several plants from the resemblance of their heads or fruits to the military instrument.

Calumba, Calumbo, ka-lum'ba, ka-lum'bō, *n.* [From a mistaken notion that the plant came from *Colombo*, Ceylon.] A plant indigenous to the forests of Mozambique, the roots of which are used as a bitter tonic in cases of indigestion.

Calumet, kal'ū-met, *n.* [Fr. *calumet*, from L. *calamus*, a reed.] The North American Indians' pipe of peace, the smoking of which was a pledge of amity and good faith.—**Calumet River**, at Chicago, Ill., connects by a drainage canal the Great Lakes with the Gulf of Mexico.

Calumniate, ka-lum′ni-āt, *v.t.*—*calumniated, calumniating.* [L. *calumnior, calumniatus*, to calumniate, from *calumnia*, calumny.] To speak evil of falsely; to cast aspersions on; to charge falsely and knowingly with some crime, offence, or something disreputable; to slander.—*v.i.* To propagate evil reports with a design to injure the reputation of another.—**Calumniation**, ka-lum′ni-ā″shon, *n.* The act of calumniating; calumny.—**Calumniator**, ka-lum′ni-ā″tėr, *n.* One who calumniates or slanders.—**Calumniatory, Calumnious**, ka-lum′ni-a″to-ri, ka-lum′ni-us, *a.* Using calumny; containing or implying calumny; injurious to reputation; slanderous.—**Calumniously**, ka-lum′ni-us-li, *adv.* In a calumnious manner; slanderously.—**Calumniousness**, ka-lum′ni-us-nes, *n.*—**Calumny**, kal′um-ni, *n.* [L. *calumnia.*] False accusation of a crime or offence, knowingly or maliciously made or reported, to the injury of another; a defamatory or slanderous report; slander; defamation.

Calvary, kal′va-ri, *n.* [L. *calvaria*, a skull, from *calva*, a bare scalp.] Golgotha, the place where Christ was crucified, west of Jerusalem; in R. Cath. countries a place of devotion, often on the top of a hill, in memory of the place where our Saviour suffered.

Calve, käv, *v.i.*—*calved, calving.* [From *calf* = D. *kalven*, Dan. *kalve*, to calve.] To bring forth a calf or calves: used specifically of cows, whales, and seals.—**Calvish**, käv′ish, *a.* Like a calf.

Calvinism, kal′vin-izm, *n.* The theological tenets or doctrines of *Calvin*, the celebrated reformer, and his followers, among the distinguishing doctrines of whose system are, predestination, original sin, the irresponsible sovereignty of God, &c.—**Calvinist**, kal′vin-ist, *n.* A follower of Calvin; one who embraces the theological doctrines of Calvin.—**Calvinistic, Calvinistical**, kal-vin-ist′ik, kal-vin-ist′ik-al, *a.* Pertaining to Calvin or to his opinions in theology.—**Calvinize**, kal′vin-īz, *v.t.* To convert to Calvinism.

Calvities, kal-vish′i-ēz, *n.* [L., from *calvus*, bald.] Diffused or general baldness, appearing generally first on the crown or on the forehead and temples.

Calx, kalks, *n.* pl. **Calxes, Calces**, kalk′sēz, kal′sēz. [L. *calx*, limestone.] Lime or chalk; an old term for the substance of a metal or mineral which remains after being subjected to violent heat or calcination; an oxide; lime recently prepared by calcination; broken and refuse glass, which is restored to the pots in glass-making.

Calyptra, ka-lip′tra, *n.* [Gr. *kalyptra*, a veil or covering.] *Bot.* the hood of the theca or capsule of mosses.—**Calyptrate**, ka-lip′trāt, *a. Bot.* furnished with a calyptra; also applied to the calyx when it comes off like a lid or extinguisher.—**Calyptriform**, ka-lip′tri-form, *a.* Having the form of a calyptra.

Calyx, kā′liks, *n.* pl. **Calyces, Calyxes**, kā′li-sēz, kā′lik-sez. [L. *calyx*, from Gr. *kalyx*, a calyx, a covering.] *Bot.* the exterior covering of a flower within the bracts and external to the corolla, which it incloses and supports, and consisting of several verticillate leaves called sepals, either united or distinct, usually of a green colour and of a less delicate texture than the corolla.—**Calycanthemous**, kal-i-kan′the-mus, *a.* [Gr. *kalyx*, a calyx, and *anthos*, a flower.] *Bot.* a term applied to plants having the corolla and stamens inserted in the calyx.—**Calycifloral**, ka-lis′i-flō″ral, *a.* [L. *calyx*, and *flos, floris*, a flower.] *Bot.* having the petals and stamens springing from the tube of the calyx.—**Calyciform**, ka-lis′i-form, *a. Bot.* having the form of a calyx.—**Calycinal, Calycine**, ka-lis′i-nal, kal′i-sin, *a. Bot.* pertaining to a calyx; situated on a calyx.—**Calycle, Calycule**, kal′i-kl, kal′i-kūl, *n.* [L. *calyculus*, dim. of *calyx.*] *Bot.* an outer accessory calyx, or set of leaflets or bracts looking like a calyx; *zool.* same as *Calice.*—**Calycoid**, kā′li-koid, *a. Bot.* like a calyx; cup-shaped.—**Calycled, Calyculate**, kal′i-kld, ka-lik′ū-lāt, *a. Bot.* having bracts which resemble an additional external calyx.

Cam, kam, *n.* [O.E. *camb*, a comb, a crest; comp. Dan. *kam-hiul*, G. *kamm-rad*, a cog-wheel, from *kam, kamm*, a comb.] *Mach.* a projecting part of a wheel or other revolving piece so placed as to give an alternating motion, especially in a rectilinear direction, to another piece (often a rod) that comes in contact with it and is free to move only in a certain direction. The eccentric is a kind of cam.

Camaieu, Camayeu, ka-mā′ū, *n.* [Fr. *camaieu*, a form equivalent to *cameo.*] A stone engraved in relief; a cameo; also monochrome painting or painting with a single colour, varied only by the effect of chiaroscuro.

Camaraderie, kam′a-räd-ėr-ē, *n.* [Fr.] Mutual good fellowship as comrades.

Camarilla, kam-a-ril′a, Sp. pron. ka-ma-rēl′ya, *n.* [Sp., a small room, a dim. from *camara*, L. *camera, camara*, a vault. CHAMBER.] A company of secret counsellors or advisers; a cabal; a clique.

Camata, kam′a-ta, *n.* The commercial name for the half-grown acorns of a kind of oak, dried and imported for tanning.

Camber, kam′bėr, *n.* [Fr. *cambrer*, to arch, to vault, from L. *camera*, a vault.] A convexity upon an upper surface, as a ship's deck, a bridge, a beam, a lintel; the curve of a ship's plank.—*Camber window*, a window arched at the top.—*v.t.* To arch; to bend; to curve ship-planks.

Cambist, kam′bist, *n.* [Fr. *cambiste*, from L. *cambio*, to exchange. CHANGE.] One who has to do with exchange, or is skilled in the science of exchange; one who deals in notes and bills of exchange; a banker.—**Cambistry**, kam′bis-tri, *n.* The science of exchange, weights, measures, &c.—**Cambial**,† kam′bi-al, *a.* Belonging to exchanges in commerce.

Cambium, kam′bi-um, *n.* [L. *cambio*, to exchange, from the alterations occurring in it.] *Bot.* a mucilaginous viscid substance interspersed between the wood and bark of exogenous trees, and particularly abundant in spring.

Cambrian, kam′bri-an, *a.* Relating or pertaining to Wales or *Cambria.*—*n.* A Welshman; a series of strata on the base of the PALÆOZOIC (which see).

Cambric, kām′brik, *n.* A species of fine white linen fabric, said to be named from *Cambray* in Flanders, where it was first manufactured.

Came, kām, pret. of *come.*

Camel, kam′el, *n.* [L. *camelus*, from Gr. *kamēlos*, from Heb. *gāmāl*, camel.] A large hoofed quadruped of the ruminant class, with one or two humps on its back, used in Asia and Africa for carrying burdens, and for riding on; a water-tight structure placed beneath a vessel in the water, being first filled with water and sunk, after which the water is pumped out, when the camel gradually rises, lifting the vessel with it.—**Camelry**, kam′el-ri, *n.* Troops mounted on camels; a camel corps.—**Camel's-thorn**, *n.* A spiny leguminous shrub on which camels browse, and which yields a kind of manna.

Cameleon, ka-mē′lē-on, *n.* Same as *Chameleon.*

Camellia, ka-mel′i-a or ka-mēl′ya, *n.* [After George Joseph *Kamel*, a Moravian Jesuit.] A genus of beautiful trees or shrubs belonging to the tea family, with showy flowers somewhat resembling the rose, and elegant dark-green, shining, laurel-like leaves.

Camelopard, ka-mel′o-pärd or kam′el-o-pärd, *n.* [L. *camelus*, a camel, and *pardalis*, a leopard.] The giraffe.

Cameo, kam′ē-ō, *n.* [It. *cameo, cammeo*, from L.L. *cammæus*, a word of uncertain origin.] A stone or shell composed of several different coloured layers having a subject in relief cut upon one or more of the upper layers, an under layer of a different colour forming the ground.

Camera, kam′ėr-a, *n.* [L., a vault, a chamber, from Gr. *kamara*, anything arched. CHAMBER.] *Anc. arch.* an arched roof, ceiling, or covering; a vault.—*Camera lucida* [L., lit. clear chamber], an optical instrument for facilitating the delineation of distant objects, by producing a reflected picture of them upon paper by means of a glass prism suitably mounted, and also for copying or reducing drawings.—*Camera obscura* [L., dark chamber], an apparatus in which the images of external objects, received through a double-convex lens, are exhibited in their natural colours, on a white surface placed at the focus of the lens.—*Photographic camera*, a form of camera obscura in which a sensitized surface is exposed to the actinic action of light.

Camerate,† kam′ėr-āt, *v.t.*—*camerated, camerating.* [L. *camero, cameratum.*] To build in the form of an arch or vault.—**Camerated**, kam′ėr-āt-ed, *a. Arch.* arched; vaulted; *conch.* divided by partitions into a series of chambers; chambered.—**Cameration**,† kam-ėr-ā′shon, *n.* An arching or vaulting.

Cameralistics,† kam′ėr-a-lis″tiks, *n.* [G. *cameralist*, a financier, from It. *camerale*, pertaining to a camera or treasury, from L. *camera*, a chamber.] The science of state finance.—**Cameralistic**,† kam′ėr-a-lis″tik, *a.* Pertaining to finance and public revenue.

Camerlingo, kä-mėr-lēn′gō, *n.* [It., a chamberlain, from L. *camera*, a chamber.] The highest officer in the papal household; the chamberlain.

Cameronian, kam-ėr-ō′ni-an, *n.* A follower of Richard *Cameron*, one of a sect of Scotch Presbyterians who refused to accept the indulgence granted to the Presbyterian clergy by Charles II., lest they should be understood to recognize his ecclesiastical authority.

Camisade, Camisado, kam-i-sād′, kam-i-sā′do, *n.* [Fr. *camisade*, Sp. *camisado*, O.Fr. *camise*, a shirt. CHEMISE.] A shirt worn by soldiers over their armor in a night attack to enable them to recognize each other; an attack by soldiers wearing the camisade; an attack made in the dark.

Camisards, kam′i-zärds, *n.* [As above.] Huguenots in the Cevennes, so disguised in their risings after the revocation of the Edict of Nantes in 1685.

Camisole, kam′i-sōl, *n.* [Fr. dim. of O.Fr. *camise*, L.L. *camisa*, a chemise.] A short light garment worn by ladies when dressed in *negligée*: a straight-jacket for lunatics or criminals condemned to the guillotine.

Camlet, kam′let, *n.* [Fr. *camelot*, from *camel.*] A stuff originally made of camel's hair, now made sometimes of wool, sometimes of silk, sometimes of hair, especially that of goats, with wool or silk.

Cammas, kam′as, *n.* Quamash.

Camomile, kam′ō-mīl, *n.* Any plant of the genus *Anthemis*, especially *Matricaria chamomilla.* Foliage and flowers are strong-scented and contain essential oils of medicinal value.

Camouflage, kam-ö-fläzh, *n.* [Fr.] The art of disguising; especially the art of disguising material in warfare.—*v.* To alter the appearance so as to mislead or render difficult to recognize.

Camp, kamp, *n.* [Fr. *camp*, a camp, formerly a field, from L. *campus*, a plain. *Campaign, champion, decamp, scamper*, are from same source.] The place where an army or other body of men is or has been encamped; the collection of tents or other erections for the accommodation of a number of men, particularly troops in a temporary station; an encampment.—*v.t.*† To put into or lodge in a camp, as an army; to encamp; to afford camping ground for (*Shak.*).—*v.i.* To live in a camp, as an army; to encamp.—**Camp-bedstead**, *n.* A bedstead made to fold up within a narrow space.—**Camp-ceiling**, *n.* A ceiling formed by an inclination of the wall on each side toward the plane surface in the middle, frequently used in garrets.—**Camp-follower**, *n.* One who follows or attaches himself or herself to a camp or army without serving.—**Camp-kettle**, *n.* An iron pot for the use of soldiers and others in camp.—**Camp-meeting**, *n.* In *Amer.* a religious meeting in the open air, where the frequenters encamp for some days for continuous devotion.—**Camp-stool**, *n.* A stool with crossed legs, so made as to fold up when not used.

Camp, kamp, *n.* [A.Sax. *camp*, from L. *campus*, a plain, in late times a battle.] An ancient English form of the game of football.

Campagnol, kam'pan-yol, *n.* [Fr. name, from *campagne*, open country.] A species of field-rat or vole, with a short tail.

Campaign, kam-pān', *n.* [Fr. *campagne* country, open country, campaign, from L. *campania*, a level country, *campus*, a plain. CAMP.] An open field or open plain‡; the time, or the operations of an army during the time it keeps the field in one season.—*v.i.* To serve in a campaign; a political, commercial or other contest.—**Campaigner**, kam-pān'ėr, *n.* One who has served in an army several campaigns.

Campanero, kam-pa-ner'ō, *n.* [Sp., a bellman, from L.L. *campana*, a bell.] The bell-bird, a white-plumaged bird of South America, so called from the bell-like sound of its voice.

Campanile, kam-pa-nē'lā or kam'pa-nīl, *n.* pl. **Campanili**, kam-pa-nē'lē [It. *campanile*, from It. and L.L. *campana*, a bell.] *Arch.* a clock or bell tower; a term applied especially to detached buildings in some parts of Italy, erected for the purpose of containing bells.

Campanology, kam-pa-nol'o-ji, *n.* [L.L. *campana*, a bell, and Gr. *logos*, discourse.] The art or principles of bell-ringing; a treatise on the art.—**Campanologist**, kam-pa-nol'o-jist, *n.* One skilled in the art of bell-ringing or campanology.

Campanula, kam-pan'ū-la, *n.* [L.L., a dim. of *campana*, a bell, from form of the corolla.] The bell-flowers, a large genus of herbaceous plants, with bell-shaped flowers usually of a blue or white colour.—**Campanulate**, kam-pan'ū-lāt, *a.* In the form of a bell: applied to many parts of plants, particularly to the corolla.

Campeachy-wood, kam'pē-chi, *n.* [From the Bay of *Campeachy*, in Mexico.] Logwood.

Campestral, Campestrian, kam-pes'tral, kam-pes'tri-an, *a.* [L. *campestris*, from *campus*, a field.] Pertaining to an open field; growing in a field or open ground.

Camphine, kam'fēn, *n.* The commercial term for purified oil of turpentine, obtained by distilling the oil over quicklime to free it from resin, and used in lamps.

Camphor, kam'fėr, *n.* [L.L. *camphora*, L.Gr. *kaphoura*, from Ar. *kāfūr*, camphor, said to be from a Malay word signifying chalk.] A whitish translucent substance belonging to the class of vegetable oils, with a bitterish aromatic taste and a strong characteristic smell, found in many plants and sometimes secreted naturally in masses, obtained also by distillation of the wood, and used in medicine as a diaphoretic, antispasmodic, &c.—**Camphoraceous**, kam-fėr-ā'shus, *a.* Of the nature of camphor; partaking of camphor.—**Camphorate**, kam'fėr-āt, *v.t.* To impregnate with camphor.—**Camphoric**, kam-for'ik, *a.* Pertaining to or obtained from camphor, or partaking of its qualities.—**Camphor-oil**, *n.* A fragrant, limpid, colourless oil obtained from a camphor-producing tree of the Indian Archipelago.—**Camphor-tree**, *n.* A species of laurel from which common camphor is obtained by distillation of the wood.

Campion, kam'pi-on, *n.* [Probably from L. *campus*, a field.] The popular name of certain English plants belonging to the genera Lychnis and Silene, such as bladder campion, sea-campion, rose-campion, &c.

Campylospermous, kam'pi-lō-spėr''mus, *a.* [Gr. *kampylos*, crooked, *sperma*, seed.] *Bot.* having the albumen curved so as to present a longitudinous furrow said of seeds.—**Campylotropal**, kam-pi-lot'ro-pal, *a.* *Bot.* curved so that the ends of an ovule or seed are brought close together.

Camwood, kam'wụd, *n.* [Probably for *Campeachy-wood*, from a notion that it came from *Campeachy*.] A red dye-wood imported from Sierra Leone.

Can, kan, *v.i.*—pret. *could*. [A.Sax. *can*, pres. ind. of *cunnan*, to know, to know how to do, to be able; *could* = O.E. *coude* (with *l* erroneously inserted), A.Sax. *cúthe*, pret. of *cunnan*. Akin D. *kunnen*, to be able; Sw. *kunna*, Dan. *kunde*, Icel. *kunna*, to know, to be able; G. *können*, to be able. The root is the same as that of *ken* and *know*. KNOW.] (A verb now used only as an auxiliary and in the indicative mood.) To be able, physically, mentally, morally, legally, or the like; to possess the qualities, qualifications, or resources necessary for the attainment of any end or the accomplishment of any purpose, the specific end or purpose being indicated by the verb with which *can* is joined.—*Can but*, can do no more than; can only (we *can but* fail).—*Cannot but*, cannot help doing or being; cannot refrain from (*cannot but* remember, *cannot but* acknowledge).

Can, kan, *n.* [A.Sax. *canne*=D. *kan*, Icel. *kanna*, G. *kanne*, a can.] A rather indefinite term applied to various vessels of no great size, now more especially to vessels made of sheet metal, for containing liquids, preserves, &c.—*v.t.*—*canned*, *canning*. To put into a can (to *can* preserved meat, fruit, &c.).—**Canakin**, kan'a-kin, *n.* A little can or cup. (*Shak.*)—**Cannery**, kan'ėr-i, *n.* An establishment at which provisions are canned.

Canaanite, kā'nan-īt, *n.* An inhabitant of the land of *Canaan*; specifically, one of the inhabitants before the return of the Israelites from Egypt.—**Canaanitish**, kā-nan-īt'ish, *a.* Of or pertaining to Canaan or the Canaanites.

Canadian, ka-nā'di-an, *a.* Pertaining to Canada.—*n.* An inhabitant or native of Canada.—*Canadian balsam*, *Canada balsam*, a fluid resin mixed with a volatile oil, obtained from fir-trees, and much valued for optical purposes on account of its perfect transparency and its refractive power.—*Canada rice*, a plant growing in deep water in the northern states of America and Canada, the seeds of which form much of the food of the American Indians, and of the great flocks of water-fowl.

Canaille, ka-nāl' or ka-nä-ya, *n.* [Fr., from It. *canaglia*, a pack of dogs, from L. *canis*, a dog.] The lowest orders of the people; the rabble; the vulgar.

Canal, ka-nal', *n.* [Fr. *canal*, from L. *canalis*, a channel, from the same root as Skr. *khan*, to dig.] An artificial watercourse, particularly one constructed for the passage of boats or ships; *arch.* a channel; a groove or a flute; *anat.* any cylindrical or tubular cavity in the body through which solids, liquids, or certain organs pass; a duct; *zool.* a groove observed in different parts of certain univalve shells.—**Canaliculate, Canaliculated**, kan-a-lik'ū-lāt, kan-a-lik'ū-lāt-ed, *a.* [L. *canaliculatus*, from *canaliculus*, a little pipe, from *canalis*.] Channelled; furrowed; grooved.—**Canalize**, ka-nal'īz, *v.t.* To make a canal through (to *canalize* an isthmus); to make like a canal, to *canalize* a river.—**Canalization**, ka-nal'i-zā''shon, *n.* The act of canalizing.

Canard, kä-när or ka-närd', *n.* [Fr., a duck, from L.L. *canardus*, a kind of boat, from G. *kahn*, a boat or skiff.] An absurd story which one attempts to impose on his hearers or readers; a false rumour set afloat by way of news.

Canary, ka-nā'ri, *n.* Wine made in the Canary Islands; an old dance introduced from the Canary Islands into Europe; a singing bird, belonging to the finch family, a native of those islands, and which has long been very common as a cage-bird in various countries.—**Canary-grass**, *n.* A kind of grass, a native of the Canary Isles, the seeds of which are much used under the name of *Canary-seed*, as food for cage-birds.—**Canary-wood**, *n.* [From its colour resembling that of a *canary*.] A wood of a light orange colour brought from South America, and used in cabinet-work.

Canaster, ka-nas'tėr, *n.* [Fr. *canastre*, Sp. *canastro*, a basket; same word as *Canister*.] The rush basket in which tobacco is packed in South America; a kind of tobacco for smoking, consisting of the dried leaves coarsely broken.

Cancan, kan'kan, *n.* A kind of French dance performed by men and women, who indulge in extravagant postures and lascivious gestures.

Cancel, kan'sel, *v.t.*—*cancelled*, *cancelling*. [Fr. *canceller*, to cancel; L.L. *cancellare*, to cancel by drawing lines across in the form of lattice-work, from L. *cancelli*, a lattice, whence also *chancel*, *chancellor*.] To draw lines across (something written) so as to deface; to blot out or obliterate; to annul or destroy (an obligation, a debt); to throw aside as no longer useful (sheets of a printed book, &c.).—*n.* Lattice-work‡; that which is cancelled or thrown aside.—**Cancellation**, kan-sel-lā'shon. The act of cancelling.—**Cancellareate, Cancellarian**, kan-sel-lā'rē-āt, kan-sel-lā'ri-an, *a.* Belonging to a chancellor.—**Cancellate, Cancellated, Cancellous**, kan'sel-lāt, kan'sel-lāt-ed, kan'sel-lus, *a.* Separated into spaces or divisions, as by lattice-work; formed of or resembling a lattice-work or cancelli.—**Cancelli**, kan-sel'li, *n. pl.* [L.] Lattice-work; a lattice-work partition in a church; a lattice-like tissue of animals or plants.

Cancer, kan'sėr, *n.* [L., a crab, a cancer.] A genus of crustaceans, including some edible species of crabs; one of the twelve signs of the zodiac, represented by the form of a crab; the sign of the summer solstice; a malignant growth or structure on the body or on some internal part which can extend itself and form again after removal, arising from a vitiated constitution and usually ending in death.—**Cancerate**, kan'sėr-āt, *v.i.* To grow into a cancer; to become cancerous.—**Canceration**, kan-sėr-ā'shon, *n.* A growing cancerous, or into a cancer.—**Cancerous**, kan'sėr-us, *a.* Like a cancer; having the qualities of a cancer; virulent.—**Cancerously**, kan'sėr-us-li, *adv.* In the manner of a cancer.—**Cancerousness**, kan'sėr-us-nes, *n.* The state of being cancerous.—**Canceriform**, kang'kri-form, *a.* Cancerous; having the form of a cancer or crab.—**Cancrine**, kang'krīn, *a.* Having the qualities of a crab.—**Cancroid**, kang'kroid, *a.* Like cancer: applied to morbid growths somewhat like cancer, but not really cancerous.—*n.* A skin disease approaching in its nature to cancer.

Candelabrum, kan-de-lā'brum, *n.* pl. **Candelabra**, kan-de-lā'bra. [L., from *candela*, a candle.] A tall candlestick; a stand by which lamps were supported; a branched highly ornamental candlestick; a chandelier.

Candent, kan'dent, *a.* [L. *candens*, *candentis*, from *candeo*, to be white or hot. CANDID.] Heated to whiteness; glowing with white heat.—**Candescence**, kan-des'ens, *n.* [L. *candesco*, incept. of *candeo*.] A state of glowing; incandescence.

Canderos, kan'de-ros, *n.* An East Indian gum, sometimes turned into toys of various kinds, which are very light and of a good polish.

Candid, kan'did, *a.* [L. *candidus*, white, bright, frank, sincere, from *candeo*, to be white; akin *candle*, *incense*, *incendiary*, &c.] White‡; honest and frank; open and sincere; ingenuous; outspoken; fair; just; impartial.—*A candid friend*, a person disposed to tell unpleasant truths or to say ill-natured things under the guise of candor.—**Candid camera**, a small camera of hand-size with powerful lens and quick shutter that permits the photographing of unposed pictures.—**Candidly**, kan'did-li, *adv.* Openly; frankly.—**Candidness**, kan'did-nes, *n.* Candor.—**Candor, Candour**, kan'dėr, *n.* The quality or trait of being candid; readiness to make known anything relating to one's self; openness of heart; frankness; sincerity.

Candidate, kan'di-dāt, *n.* [L. *candidatus*, from *candidus*, white; those who sought offices in Rome wearing a white robe during their candidature.] A person who aspires or is put forward by others as an aspirant to an office or honour.—**Candidature, Candidateship, Candidacy**, kan'di-dā-tūr, kan'di-dāt-ship, kan'di-da-si, *n.* The state of being, or act of standing as, a candidate.

Candle, kan'dl, *n.* [L. *candela*, a candle, from *candere*, to shine. CANDID.] A taper; a cylindrical body of tallow, wax, spermaceti, or other fatty material, formed on a wick, and used for a portable light.—*Not fit to hold the candle to one*, not fit to act as a mere attendant; to be very inferior.—*The game is not worth the candle*, a phrase of French origin, indicating that an object is not worth the pains requisite for its attainment.—**Candle-berry, Candle-nut**, *n.* The fruit of the candle-berry tree, a name given to several species of myrtle, especially the wax-myrtle, a shrub common in North America, the berries of which are covered with a greenish-white wax, of which candles are made.—**Candle-coal**, *n.* CANNEL-COAL.—**Candle-fish**, *n.* A small sea-fish of the salmon family, frequenting the north-western shores of America, so extremely oily that it is used for making oil, and as a natural candle whence its name.—**Candle-power**, *n.* The illuminating power of a candle, taken as a unit in estimating the luminosity of any illuminating agent (as gas), the standard usually employed being a spermaceti candle burning at the rate of 120 grains of sperm per hour.—**Candlemas**, kan'dl-mas, *n.* [So named from the blessing or consecration of candles on this day, in the Roman Church.] An ecclesiastical festival held on the second day of February in honour of the purification of the Virgin Mary; in *Scot.* a quarterly money term.—**Candlestick**, kan'dl-stik, *n.* An instrument to hold a candle when burning, made in different forms and of different materials.—**Candle-wood**, *n.* The wood of a West Indian resinous tree.

Candor, Under CANDID

Candy, kan'di, *n.* [It *candi*, candy, from Ar. *qandi*, made of sugar, from *qand*, sugar.] A solid preparation of sugar or molasses, either alone or in combination with other substances, to flavour, colour, or give it the desired consistency.—*v.t.*—*candied, candying.* To conserve with sugar so as to form a thick mass; to boil in sugar; to form into congelations or crystals.—*v.i.* To become incrusted by candied sugar; to become crystallized or congealed.—**Candied**, kan'did, *p.* and *a.* Preserved or incrusted with sugar; *fig.* honeyed, flattering glozing.—**Candify**, kan'di-fī, *v.t.* or *i.*—*candified, candifying.* To make or become candied, to candy.—**Candy-sugar**, *n.* Crystallized sugar formed upon threads by repeated boiling and clarifying, and suffered to crystallize slowly.

Candytuft, kan'di-tuft, *n.* [From *Candia*, the ancient Crete.] The popular name of a tufted flower brought from the island of Candia.

Cane, kān, *n.* [Old spelling also *canne*, from L. *canna*, Gr. *kanna*, a reed.] A term applied to the stems of some palms, grasses, and other plants, such as the bamboo, rattan, and sugar-cane; a cane used as a walking-stick.—*v.t.*—*caned, caning.* To beat with a cane or walking-stick; to furnish or complete with cane (as chairs).—**Cane-brake**, *n.* A thicket of canes.—**Cane-chair**, *n.* A chair with a platted cane seat or bottom, or one framed with bamboo or other cane.—**Cane-mill**, *n.* A mill for grinding sugar-canes for the manufacture of sugar.—**Cane-sugar**, *n.* Sugar obtained from the sugar-cane, as distinguished from beet-root sugar, grape-sugar, maple-sugar, &c.

Canella, ka-nel'la, *n.* [Dim. of L. *canna*, a reed, from the cylindrical form of the bark when peeled off.] A kind of aromatic bark, also called white cinnamon, brought from the West Indies and used as a tonic.

Canephorus, ka-nef'o-rus, *n.* [Gr. *kanēphoros*, a basket-bearer.] *Arch.* a term applied to figures bearing baskets on their heads.

Canescent, ka-nes'ent, *a.* [L. *canescens*, *canescentis*, ppr. of *canesco*, to grow white, from *caneo*, to be white.] Growing white or hoary; tending or approaching to white; whitish.

Canine, ka-nīn', *a.* [L. *caninus*, from *canis*, a dog.] Pertaining to dogs; having the properties or qualities of a dog.—*Canine teeth*, or *canines*, two sharp pointed teeth in both jaws of man and other mammalia, one on each side, between the incisors and grinders, most highly developed in the Carnivora.

Canister, kan'is-tėr, *n.* [L *canistrum*, Gr. *kanastron*, from *kanna*, a reed.] A small basket†; a small box or case, usually of tin, for tea, coffee, &c.; a case containing shot which bursts on being discharged; case-shot.

Canker, kang'kėr, *n.* [From L. *cancer*, properly pronounced *canker*, a crab, a cancer.] A kind of cancerous, gangrenous, or ulcerous sore or disease, whether in animals or plants; an eating, corroding, or other noxious agency producing ulceration, gangrene, rot, decay, and the like; anything that insidiously or persistently destroys, corrupts, or irritates, as care, trouble, annoyance, grief, pain, &c.; a kind of wild, worthless rose; the dog-rose (*Shak.*).—*v.t.* To infect with canker either literally or figuratively; to eat into, corrode, or corrupt; to render ill-conditioned, crabbed, or ill-natured.—*v.i.* To grow corrupt; to be infected with some poisonous or pernicious influence; to be or become malignant.—**Cankerous**, kang'kėr-us, *a.* Corroding, destroying, or irritating like a cancer; cancerous.—**Canker-bit**, *a.* Bitten with a cankered or envenomed tooth. (*Shak.*)—**Canker-bloom, Canker-blossom**, *n.* A bloom, blossom, or flower eaten by canker; a bloom or flower of the dog-rose. (*Shak.*)—**Canker-fly**, *n.* A fly that preys on fruit.—**Canker-rash**, *n.* A variety of scarlet-fever.—**Canker-worm**, *n.* A worm or larva destructive to trees or plants.

Cannel-coal, Candle-coal, kan'el-kōl, kan'dl-kōl, *n.* A glistening grayish-black hard bituminous coal, so called because it burns with a bright flame like a candle; it is chiefly used in making gas.

Cannelure, kan'ne-lūr, *n.* [Fr., lit. channelling, fluting. CANAL. CHANNEL.] A groove or channel on the surface of anything, as the fluting on Doric columns.

Cannery, kan'ėr-i, *n.* An establishment for canning or preserving meat, fish, or fruit in tins hermetically sealed.

Cannibal, kan'i-bal, *n.* [Sp. *canibal*, a cannibal, a corruption of *Caribal*, a Carib, the Caribs being reputed cannibals.] A human being that eats human flesh; a man-eater or anthropophagite; an animal that eats the flesh of its own or kindred species.—**Cannibalism**, kan'i-bal-izm, *n.* The act or practice of eating human flesh by mankind; anthropophagy; murderous cruelty.—**Cannibally**, kan'i-bal-li, *adv.* In the manner of a cannibal. (*Shak.*)

Cannon, kan'un, *n.* pl. **Cannons** or **Cannon.** [Fr. *canon*, a tube, barrel, cannon, from L. *canna*, Gr. *kanna*, a cane or reed. Akin *canister, canon, cane.*] A large military firearm for throwing balls and other missiles by the force of gunpowder; a big gun or piece of ordnance; *billiards*, the act of hitting your adversary's ball with your own, so that your ball flies off and strikes the red, or vice versa.—*v.i.* To make a cannon at billiards; to fly off or asunder from the force of collision.—**Cannonade**, kan-un-ād', *n.* The act of discharging cannon and throwing balls, for the purpose of destroying an army or battering a town, ship, or fort.—*v.t.* and *i.*—*cannonaded, cannonading.* To attack with ordnance or artillery; to batter with cannon.—**Cannoneer, Cannonier**, kan-un-ēr', *n.* A man who manages cannon.—**Cannoneering, Cannoniering**, kan-un-ēr'ing, *n.* The act or art of using cannons; practice with cannons.—**Cannon-bone**, *n.* (1) In horses, &c., the large metacarpal or metatarsal of the single digit. (2) In ruminants, the bone formed by fusion of third and fourth metacarpals or metatarsals.—**Cannon-proof**, *a.* Proof against cannon-shot.—**Cannon-shot**, *n.* A ball or shot for cannon; the range or distance a cannon will throw a ball.—**Cannon-ball, Cannon-bullet**, *n.* A ball or solid projectile to be thrown from cannon.

Cannot, kan'ot. *Can* and *not.* [These words are usually written as one word, being colloquially so pronounced.]

Cannula, kan'ū-la, *n.* [L., dim. of *canna*, a reed.] A small tube used by surgeons for various purposes.—**Cannular**, kan'ū-lėr, *a.* Having the form of a cannula or small tube.

Canny, Cannie, kän'i, *a.* [Akin to *can*, *ken.*] Cautious; prudent; wary; watchful; expert; not extortionate or severe; gentle; quiet in disposition; tractable; easy; comfortable. [Prov. E. and Sc.]

Canoe, ka-nö', *n.* [Sp. *canoa*, from the native West Indian name.] A light narrow boat made by hollowing out and shaping the trunk of a tree, such as is used by savage tribes; any light boat narrow in the beam, and propelled by paddles.—**Canoeist**, ka-nö'ist, *n.* One who uses a canoe.

Canon, kan'on, *n.* [A.Sax. *canon*, from L. *canon*, Gr. *kanōn*, a straight rod, a rule or standard—from *kanē*, a form of *kanna*, *kannē*, a reed, a cane, whence also *cannon.*] A law or rule in general; a law or rule regarding ecclesiastical doctrine or discipline, especially one enacted by a council and duly confirmed; the books of the Holy Scriptures universally received as genuine by Christian churches; the rules of a religious order; a dignitary who possesses a prebend or revenue allotted for the performance of divine service in a cathedral or collegiate church; the catalogue of saints acknowledged in the Roman Catholic Church; *mus.* a kind of perpetual fugue, in which the different parts, beginning one after another, repeat incessantly the same air; *printing*, one of the largest kinds of type or letter, supposed to be so named because it was used in the printing of canons.—**Canoness**, kan'on-es, *n.* A female canon; a woman who enjoys a prebend without having to make religious vows.—**Canonic, Canonical**, ka-non'ik, ka-non'ik-al, *a.* Pertaining or according to a canon or rule, especially according to ecclesiastical canons or rules; belonging to the canon of Scripture.—*Canonical books*, those books of the Bible which are admitted to be of divine origin.—*Canonical hours*, hours appointed in Roman Catholic Church by canon law for the celebration of marriage, 8 a.m. to 3 p.m. Also the times, from midnight onwards, at which certain parts of the daily service are recited. They are matins, prime, tierce, sext, nones, vespers, and compline (*Ps.* cxix. 164: 'Seven times a day do I praise thee').—**Canonically**, ka-non'ik-al-li, *adv.* In a canonical manner; in accordance with a canon or canons.—**Canonicalness**, ka-non'ik-al-nes, *n.* The quality of being canonical.—**Canonicals**, ka-non'ik-alz, *n.pl.* The dress or habit prescribed by canon to be worn by the clergy when they officiate; certain articles or appurtenances of dress sometimes worn by university men, barristers, &c.—**Canonicity**, kan-o-nis'i-ti, *n.* The quality of being canonical; the state of belonging to the canon or genuine books of Scripture.—**Canonist**, kan'on-ist, *n.* A professor of canon law; one skilled in the study and practice of ecclesiastical law.—**Canonistic**, kan-o-nis'tik, *a.* Pertaining to the canonists.—**Canonization**, kan'on-iz-ā"-shon, *a.* The act of canonizing a person; the act of ranking a deceased person in the catalogue of saints, called a canon.—**Canonize**, kan'on-īz, *v.t.*—*canonized, canonizing.* To declare a man a saint, and rank him in the catalogue or canon of saints, this act being in the power of the popes.—**Canonizer**, kan′on-iz-ėr, *n.* One who canonizes.—**Canonry**, **Canonship**, kan′on-ri, kan′on-ship, *n.* The benefice filled by a canon.—**Canon-law**, *n.* A collection of ecclesiastical constitutions for the regulation of a church; specifically those of the Roman Catholic Church.

Cañon, **Canyon**, kä-nyon′, kan′yun, *n.* [Sp. *cañon*, a canon, a tube, a canyon.] A long and narrow mountain gorge or deep ravine with precipitous sides occurring in the Rocky Mountains and the great western plateaus of North America.

Canopy, kan′ō-pi, *n.* [Fr. *canapé*, O.Fr. *conopé*, L. *conopeum*, Gr. *kōnōpeion*, lit. a net to keep off gnats, from *kōnōpos*, a gnat.] A covering fixed at some distance above a throne or a bed; any somewhat similar covering; a covering held over a person's head in a procession or public ceremony; *arch.* a decoration, often richly sculptured, above a tomb, niche, pulpit, &c.—*v.t.*—*canopied*, *canopying*. To cover with a canopy, or as with a canopy.

Canorous, ka-nō′rus, *a.* [L. *canorus*, from *cano*, to sing.] Musical; tuneful.—**Canorousness**, ka-nō′rus-nes, *n.*

Cant, kant, *v.i.* [From L. *canto*, freq. of *cano*, to sing.] To speak with a whining voice or in an affected, assumed, or supplicating tone (as a beggar); to make whining pretensions to goodness; to affect piety without sincerity; to sham holiness.—*n.* A whining manner of speech; the whining speech of beggars, as in asking alms; the language or jargon spoken by gypsies, thieves, professional beggars, &c.; a kind of slang; the words and phrases peculiar to or characteristic of a sect, party, or profession; a pretentious assumption of a religious character; a hypocritical addiction to the use of religious phrases, &c.; religious phrases hypocritically used.—*a.* Of the nature of cant or slang.—**Canter**, kan′tėr, *n.* One who cants, whines, or uses an affected hypocritical style of speech.—**Canting**, kant′ing, *a.* Given to the use of hypocritical phraseology or whining talk.—**Cantingly**, kant′ing-li, *adv.* In a canting manner.

Cant, kant, *n.* [Same word as Dan. Sw. and D. *kant*, edge, border, margin, &c.; G. *kante*, a side, a border or brim; O.Fr. *cant*, corner, angle.] An external or salient angle; an inclination from a perpendicular or horizontal line; a toss, thrust, or push with a sudden jerk.—*v.t.* To turn about or over by a sudden push or thrust; to cause to assume an inclining position; to tilt; to toss; to cut off an angle from (a square block).

Can't, känt. A colloquial contraction of *can not*.

Cantab, kan-tab′. An abbreviation of *Cantabrigian*.—**Cantabrigian**, kan-ta-brij′i-an, *n.* [L.L. *Cantabrigiensis*, pertaining to Cambridge.] A student or graduate of Cambridge University.

Cantaliver, **Cantilever**, kan′ta-liv-ėr, kan′ti-lev-ėr, *n.* O.Fr. *cant*, an angle, and *lever*, to raise.] A wooden or iron bracket projecting from a wall, to carry mouldings, eaves, balconies, &c.; a long projecting arm to support the roadway of a bridge.

Cantaloupe, **Canteloupe**, kan″ta-löp, kan′te-löp, *n.* [Gr. *kanthos*.] The angle formed by the meeting of the upper and under eyelids; a variety of muskmelon.

Cantankerous, kan-tang′kėr-us, *a.* [Comp. O.E. *contek*, *contak*, debate, strife.] Ill-natured; ill-conditioned; cross; waspish; contentious; disputatious. [Colloq.]—**Cantankerously**, kan-tang′kėr-us-li, *adv.* In a cantankerous manner.—**Cantankerousness**, kan-tang′kėr-us-nes, *n.*

Cantata, kan-tä′tä, *n.* [It., from *cantare*, L. *cantare*, freq. of *cano*, to sing.] *Mus.* a short composition in the form of an oratorio, but without *dramatis personæ*.

Cantatrice, kän-tä-trē′chā (It.), kan-tä-trēs (Fr.), *n.* [It. and Fr.] A female singer.

Canteen, kan-tēn′, *n.* [Fr. *cantine*, from It. *cantina*, a wine-cellar, a vault, from *canto*, an angle, a corner. CANT, an angle.] A shop in barracks, camps, garrisons, &c., where provisions, liquors, &c., are sold to non-commissioned officers and privates; a vessel used by soldiers, when on the march or in the field, for carrying liquor for drink; a box, fitted up with compartments, in which officers on foreign service pack spirit-bottles, knives, forks, &c.

Canter, kan′tėr, *v.i.* [An abbrev. of *Canterbury Gallop*, the gallop of pilgrims in olden times riding to Canterbury.] To move in a moderate gallop, raising the two fore-feet nearly at the same time, with a leap or spring: said of horses.—*n.* A moderate gallop; a gallop by a winner at the end of an easy race.

Canterbury, kan′tėr-be-ri, *n.* A stand with divisions for holding music, portfolios, loose papers, &c.—**Canterbury-bell**, *n.* A species of Campanula, so named because it is abundant around Canterbury.

Cantharides, kan-thar′i-dēz, *n. pl.* [Gr. *kantharis*, *kantharidis*, a blistering fly.] Coleopterous insects of several species, the best known being the Spanish or blistering fly, which is, when bruised, extensively used as the active element in blistering plasters, having a very powerful effect.—**Cantharidin**, **Cantharidine**, kan-thar′i-din, kan-thar′i-dīn, *n.* A peculiar substance which causes vesication or blistering, existing in the Spanish fly or other insects, and when taken internally acting as a violent irritant poison.

Canticle, kan′ti-kl, *n.* [L. *canticulum*, a little song, from *canto*, to sing. CANT.] A song, especially a little song; an unmetrical hymn taken from Scripture, arranged for chanting, and used in church service; *pl.* The Song of Songs or Song of Solomon, one of the books of the Old Testament.

Cantilever, kan′ti-lev-ėr, *n.* CANTALIVER.

Cantle, kan′tl, *n.* [O.Fr. *cantel*, corner-piece, dim. of *cant*. CANT, an angle.] A corner; a fragment; a piece; a portion (*Shak.*); the protuberant part of a saddle behind; the hind-bow.—*v.t.*—*cantled*, *cantling*. To cut into pieces; to cut a piece out of.

Canto, kan′tō, *n.* pl. **Cantos**, kan′tōz. [It. *canto*, a song: L. *cantus*. CHANT, CANT.] A part or division of a poem of some length; *mus.* the highest voice part in concerted music; soprano.

Canton, kan-ton′, *n.* [Fr. *canton*; It. *cantone*, aug. of *canto*, a corner. CANT, CANTLE.] A distinct or separate portion or district of territory; one of the states of the Swiss republic; a distinct part or division, as of a painting or of a flag.—*v.t.* To divide into cantons or distinct portions; to separate off; to allot separate quarters to each regiment of.—**Cantonal**, kan′ton-al, *a.* Pertaining to a canton or cantons.—**Cantonment**, kan-ton′ment, *n.* A part or division of a town or village assigned to a particular regiment of troops; a permanent military station of a slighter character than barracks; military towns at some distance from any city, such as are formed in India.

Cantor, kän′tor, *n.* [L. *cantor*, singer.] A leader of the singing in a cathedral or other church.

Canty, kan′ti, *a.* [Comp. Ir. *cainteach*, talkative.] Lively; sprightly; cheerful. [Prov. E. and S.]

Canvas, kan′vas, *n.* [Fr. *canevas*, Pr. *canabas*, It. *canavaccio*, L.L. *canabacius*, from L. *cannabis*, hemp.] A coarse cloth made of hemp or flax, used for tents, sails of ships, painting on, and other purposes; hence sails in general; a painting.—*Under canvas*, in a tent or tents; with sails spread.—**Canvas-back**, *n.* A sea duck of North America, with delicate flesh: so called from the colour of its back.—**Canvased**, kan′vast, *a.* Fitted with canvas.

Canvass, kan′vas, *v.t.* [From *canvas*, canvas, and formerly also a sieve, a strainer, because sieves were made of canvas; like O.Fr. *canabasser*, to examine, search, sift.] To examine; to scrutinize; to sift or examine by way of discussion; to discuss; to debate; to visit or apply to in order to obtain orders for goods, votes, or support for a candidate for an office or appointment, &c.—*v.i.* To seek or go about to solicit votes or interest, or to obtain mercantile orders.—*n.* The act of canvassing; close inspection; scrutiny; discussion; debate; a seeking; solicitation of votes, orders for goods, &c.—**Canvasser**, kan′vas-ėr, *n.* One who canvasses or solicits votes, mercantile orders, &c.

Canyon, **Cañon**, kan′yun, kä-nyon′, *n.* [Sp. *cañon*, a canon, a tube, a canyon.] A narrow chasm with steep sides, formed by erosion.

Canzonet, kan-zō-net′, *n.* [It. *canzonetta*.] *Mus.* a little or short song, shorter and less elaborate than the airs of oratorio or opera; a short concerted air; a madrigal.

Caoutchouc, kö′chök, *n.* [A South American word.] An elastic gummy substance, which is the inspissated juice of several tropical plants, much used in the industrial arts for covering fabrics to render them waterproof, making elastic webbing, flexible tubes, &c.; india-rubber, gum-elastic.—**Caoutchine**, **Caoutchoucine**, kö′chin, kö′chö-sin, *n.* An inflammable volatile oil produced by distillation of caoutchouc at a high temperature.

Cap, kap, *n.* [A.Sax. *cæppe*, a cap, cope, cape, hood, from L.L. *capa*, *cappa* (of unknown origin), a cape, whence Sp. *capa*, It. *cappa*, Fr. *chape*, a cloak, cape, cover. *Cape* and *cope* are forms of the same word.] A part of dress made to cover the head, generally of softer material than a hat, and without a brim; an act of respect made by uncovering the head; the summit, top, or crown; anything resembling a cap in appearance, position, or use, as the inner case which covers the movement of some kinds of watches, &c.; a percussion-cap (which see).—*v.t.*—*capped*, *capping*. To put a cap on; to cover with a cap or as with a cap; to cover the top or end of; to place a cap on the head of, when conferring official distinction, admitting to professional honours, &c.; to complete; to consummate; to crown; to follow up with something more remarkable than what has previously been done.—*To cap verses*, *texts*, or *proverbs*, to quote verses, texts, or proverbs alternately in emulation or contest.—*To set one's cap at*, to use measures to gain the affections of a man with a view to matrimony.—**Capful**, kap′ful, *n.* As much as a cap will hold; a small quantity; specifically, a light flaw of wind; a passing gust.

Capable, kā′pa-bl, *a.* [Fr. *capable*, capable, able, sufficient, L.L. *capabilis*, from L. *capio*, to take, which appears also in *captious*, *captive*, *accept*, *except*, *conception*, *susceptible*, *recipient*, *occupy*, &c.] Able to receive; open to influences; impressible; susceptible; admitting: with *of* (*capable of* pain, *of* being broken); having sufficient power, skill, ability: with *of* (*capable of* judging); able; competent; fit; duly qualified (a *capable* instructor).—**Capability**, **Capableness**, kā-pa-bil′i-ti, kā′pa-bl-nes, *n.* The state or quality of being capable.

Capacious, ka-pā′shus, *a.* [L. *capax*, *capacis*, able to take in or contain, spacious, capable, from *capio*, to take. CAPABLE.] Capable of containing much, either in a physical or mental sense; large; wide; spacious; extensive; comprehensive.—**Capaciously**, ka-pā′shus-li, *adv.* In a capacious manner or degree.—**Capaciousness**, ka-pā′shus-nes, *n.* The state or quality of being capacious.—**Capacitate**, ka-pas′i-tāt, *v.t.*—*capacitated*, *capacitating*. To make capable; to enable; to qualify.—**Capacity**, ka-pas′i-ti, *n.* [L. *capacitas*, from *capax*, capacious.] The power of receiving or containing; specifically, the power of containing a certain quantity exactly; cubic contents; the extent or comprehensiveness of the mind; the power of receiving ideas or knowledge; the receptive faculty; active power; ability (a man with the *capacity* of judging); ability in a moral or legal sense; legal qualification (to attend a meeting in the *capacity* of an elector); character (to give advice in the *capacity* of a friend); used in *phys.* in various ways with the general notion of power of containing or receiving; in *electrostatics*, the capacity of a conductor is the quantity of electricity required to charge it to unit potential; in *heat*, the mean thermal capacity of a body between t°_1 and t°_2 is Q/t_2-t_1, where Q is the quantity of heat required to raise the temperature from t°_1 to t°_2.

Cap-a-pie, kap-a-pē′, *adv.* [O.Fr., lit. head to foot.] From head to foot; all over.

Caparison, ka-par′i-son, *n.* [O.Fr. *caparasson*, from Sp. *caparazon*, a cover for a saddle, aug. of *capa*, a cover. CAP, CAPE.] A cloth or covering, more or less ornamented, laid over the saddle or furniture of a horse, especially a sumpter horse, or horse of state; hence, clothing, especially gay clothing.—*v.t.* To cover with a caparison; to adorn with rich dress.

Cape, kāp, *n.* [O.Fr. *cape*, L.L. *capa*, a kind of covering for the shoulders. CAP.] The part of a garment hanging from the neck behind and over the shoulders; a loose cloak or garment, hung from the shoulders, and worn as a protection against rain, cold weather, &c.

Cape, kāp, *n.* [Fr. *cap*, It. *capo*, a cape, from L. *caput*, the head.] A piece of land jutting into the sea or a lake beyond the rest of the coast-line; a headland; a promontory; by pre-eminence, the Cape of Good Hope, Cape Colony.

Capeline, Capelline, kap′e-lin, *n.* [Fr. *capeline*, hood, dim. from L. *capa*.] A kind of hood worn by ladies going to evening entertainments; a surgical bandage for the head.

Caper, kā′pėr, *n.* [O.Fr. *capriole*, It. *capriola*, a caper, from L. *caper*, *capra*, a goat. Akin *caprice*, *cab*.] A leap; a skip; a spring, as in dancing or mirth, or in the frolic of a goat or lamb; a sportive or capricious action; a prank.—*To cut capers*, to leap or dance in a frolicsome manner; to act sportively or capriciously. —*v.i.* To cut capers; to skip or jump; to prance; to spring.—**Caperer**, kā′pėr-ėr, *n.* One who capers.

Caper, kā′pėr, *n.* [Fr. *câpre*, O.Fr. *cappre*, L. *capparis*, Gr. *kapparis*, from Per. *kabar*, the caper.] The bud of a bush (the caper-bush), pickled and used as a condiment; the plant itself, a low prickly shrub, growing in rocky or stony places in the countries bordering on the Mediterranean.—**Caper-tea**, *n.* A kind of black tea with a knotted curled leaf regarded as resembling the caper.

Capercailzie, Capercaillie, kā-pėr-kāl′yi, kā-pėr-kāl′ē, *n.* [Gael. *capull-choille*—*capull*, a horse, and *coille*, a wood—so named from its great size.] The Scotch name for the wood-grouse or cock of the woods, the largest of the gallinaceous birds of Europe, most frequently found in the northern parts of the Continent, and reintroduced into Scotland after having become extinct there.

Capetian, ka-pē′ti-an, *a.* Pertaining to the dynasty of the *Capets*, founded about the close of the tenth century, when Hugo *Capet* ascended the French throne.

Capias, kā′pi-as, *n.* [L., you may take.] *Law*, a writ of various kinds authorizing a person or his goods to be laid hold of.

Capibara, kap-i-bä′ra, *n.* CAPYBARA.

Capillaire, ka-pil-lār′, *n.* [Fr.] A simple syrup, as of sugar or honey, flavoured with orange flowers, or orange-flower water.

Capillament. Under CAPILLARY.

Capillary, kap′il-la-ri or ka-pil′la-ri, *a.* [L. *capillaris*, from *capillus*, hair, from root of *caput*, the head.] Resembling a hair; fine, minute, small in diameter though long; filiform; as, a *capillary* tube, that is, a tube with a very minute bore; a *capillary* vessel in animal bodies (see the *n.*); pertaining to capillary tubes, or to the capillary vessels or capillaries in organic structures.—*Capillary action*, the spontaneous elevation or depression of liquids in fine hair-like tubes, or in bodies of a porous structure, when these are dipped in the liquid; the term *capillary attraction* being applied when the liquid rises, as the sap in trees, water in a sponge, &c.; and *capillary repulsion* when it sinks, as mercury does in a fine glass tube.—*n.* A tube with a small bore; a minute blood-vessel constituting the termination of an artery or vein; one of the minute vessels which intervene between the terminal arteries and veins.—**Capillarity**, kap-il-lar′i-ti, *n.* The state or condition of being capillary; capillary action.—**Capillament**, ka-pil′la-ment, *n.* A very fine filament or fibre.—**Capilliform**, ka-pil′li-form, *a.* In the shape or form of a hair or of hairs (a *capilliform* fibre).—**Capillose**, kap′il-lōs, *a.* Hairy; abounding with hair.

Capital, kap′i-tal, *a.* [L. *capitalis*, capital, deadly, also pre-eminent, from *caput*, *capitis*, the head, seen also in *captain*, *chapter*, *chief*, *cadet*, &c.] First in importance; chief; principal; notable; affecting the head or life (*capital* punishment); incurring the forfeiture of life (a *capital* offence); punishable with death; excellent; very good; first-class; splendid; a term applied to a type or letter of a certain form and a larger size than that generally used in the body of written or printed matter.—*n.* The uppermost part of a column, pillar, or pilaster, serving as the head or crowning, and placed immediately over the shaft and under the entablature; the chief city or town in a kingdom or state; a metropolis; a type or letter of a certain form, and of a larger size than that commonly used in the body of a piece of writing or printing; a capital letter; money or wealth in some shape employed in trade, in manufactures, or in any business; stock in trade, in money, goods, property, &c.; *fig.* stock of any kind, whether physical or moral; means of influence or of increasing one's power.—**Capitalist**, kap′i-tal-ist, *n.* A man who has a large capital or stock in trade; a man of large property, which is or may be employed in business.—**Capitalization**, kap′i-tal-iz-ā″shon, *n.* The act of converting anything into capital; the act of computing or realizing the present value of a periodical payment.—**Capitalize**, kap′i-tal-īz, *v.t.*—*capitalized*, *capitalizing*. To convert into capital; to apply as capital to the purposes of trade; to compute or realize the present value of (a periodical payment) for a definite or indefinite length of time.—**Capitally**, kap′i-tal-li, *adv.* In a capital manner; so as to involve life; in a pre-eminent degree; excellently; finely.—**Capitalness**†, kap′i-tal-nes, *n.* State or quality of being capital.—**Capitate**, kap′i-tāt, *a.* [L. *capitatus*.] *Bot.* growing in a head; having a rounded head: applied to a flower, &c.—**Capitation**, kap-i-tā′shon, *n.* [L. *capitatio*.] Numeration by the head; a numbering of persons.—*Capitation grant*, a grant given to a certain number of persons, a certain amount being allowed for each individual among the number.—*Capitation tax*, a tax levied on each head or person; a poll-tax.

Capitol, kap′i-tol, *n.* [L. *capitolium*, from *caput*, the head.] In ancient Rome, the name of a hill crowned by a temple dedicated to Jupiter; the temple itself, in which the senate assembled; the edifice occupied by the United States Congress in their deliberations at Washington; also, in some states the state-house or house in which the legislature holds its sessions; a government house.—**Capitolian**, kap-i-tō′li-an, *a.* Pertaining to the Capitol in Rome.—**Capitoline**, kap′i-tol-īn, *a.* Pertaining to the Capitol in Rome.

Capitular, Capitulary, ka-pit′ū-lėr, ka-pit′ū-la-ri, *n.* [L.L. *capitulare*, from L. *capitulum*, a chapter, a capital. CAPITAL.] An act passed in a chapter, as of knights or canons; the body of laws or statutes of a chapter or of an ecclesiastical council; the member of a chapter.—**Capitular**, ka-pit′ū-lėr, *a.* Belonging to a chapter; capitulary; *bot.* growing in a capitulum or head, as composite plants.—**Capitularly**, ka-pit′ū-lėr-li, *adv.* In the form of an ecclesiastical chapter.—**Capitulary**, ka-pit′ū-la-ri, *a.* Relating to the chapter of a cathedral.

Capitulate, ka-pit′ū-lāt, *v.i.*—*capitulated*, *capitulating*. [L.L. *capitulo*, *capitulatum*, to arrange in heads or chapters, from L. *capitulum*, a chapter, dim. of *caput*, the head.] To draw up articles of agreement; to arrange terms of agreement; to treat (*Shak.*); more usually to surrender, as an army or garrison, to an enemy on certain stipulated conditions. — **Capitulation**, ka-pit′ū-lā″shon, *n.* The act of capitulating or surrendering to an enemy upon stipulated terms or conditions; the treaty or instrument containing the conditions of surrender; an article of agreement; formal agreement†. — **Capitulator**, ka-pit′ū-lā-tėr, *n.* One who capitulates.

Capitulum, ka-pit′ū-lum, *n.* *Bot.* a close head of sessile flowers.

Capivi, ka-pē′vi, *n.* COPAIBA.

Caplin, kap′lin, *n.* [Fr. *caplan*, *capelan*.] A small fish, a kind of salmon, which frequents the shores of Greenland, Iceland, Newfoundland, and Labrador in immense shoals.

Capnomancy, kap′no-man-si, *n.* [Gr. *kapnos*, smoke, and *manteia*, divination.] Divination by the ascent or motion of smoke.

Capon, kā′pon, *n.* [L. *capo*, Gr. *kapōn*—a capon, from a root seen in Gr. *koptō*, to cut.] A castrated cock; a cock-chicken castrated for the purpose of improving the flesh for table.—**Caponize**, kā′pon-īz, *v.t.*—*caponized*, *caponizing*. To make a capon of.

Caponiere, Caponniere, kap-o-nēr′, *n.* [Fr. *caponnière*, Sp. *caponera*, It. *capponiera*.] *Fort.* a passage from one part of a work to another, protected on the right and left by a wall or parapet, and sometimes covered overhead; also the wall or parapet protecting such a passage.

Capot, ka-pot′, *n.* [Fr., from *cape*, a hood or cape, a person that is capotted having, as it were, a hood thrown over his head.] A winning of all the tricks of cards at the game of piquet.—*v.t.*—*capotted*, *capotting*. To win all the tricks from at piquet.

Capote, ka-pōt′, *n.* [Fr. *capote*, from *cape*, a hood or cape, L.L. *capa*. CAP.] A kind of long cloak. (*Byron.*)

Cappagh-brown, kap′pach-broun, *n.* [From *Cappagh*, near Cork.] A bituminous earth, coloured by oxide of manganese and iron, yielding pigments of various rich brown colours.

Capreolate, kap′rē-ō-lāt, *a.* [From L. *capreolus*, a wild goat, a tendril of a vine, from *caper*, a goat.] *Bot.* having tendrils, or filiform spiral claspers, by which plants fasten themselves to other bodies, as in vines, &c.

Capric, kap′rik, *a.* [L. *caper*, a goat.] Of or pertaining to a goat.—*Capric acid*, a peculiar acid in the butter of cow's milk, as well as in the milk and fat of the goat.

Capriccio, ka-prē′chō, *n.* [It., a caprice.] A caprice; a whim (*Shak.*); a musical piece in which the composer is guided more by fancy than by strict rule.

Caprice, ka-prēs′, *n.* [Fr. *caprice*, It. *capriccio*, whim, freak, originally a fantastical goat-leap, from L. *caper*, *capra*, a goat; akin *caper*, *capriole*.] A sudden start of the mind; a sudden change of opinion or humour; a whim or freak; capriciousness; fickleness. — **Capricious**, ka-prish′us, *a.* Characterized by caprice; apt to change opinions suddenly, or to start from one's purpose; unsteady; changeable; fickle; subject to change or irregularity. — **Capriciously**, ka-prish′us-li, *adv.* In a capricious manner. — **Capriciousness**, ka-prish′us-nes, *n.* The quality of being capricious.

Capricorn, kap′ri-korn, *n.* [L. *capricornus*—*caper*, a goat, and *cornu*, a horn.] One of the twelve signs of the zodiac; the tenth sign, marking the winter solstice.

Caprification, kap′ri-fi-kā″shon, *n.* [L. *caprificatio*, from *caprificus*, the wild fig-tree—*caper*, a goat, and *ficus*, a fig, from goats feeding on it.] A process intended to accelerate the ripening of the fig by causing a species of gall-insect to spread over the plant, the supposed beneficial effect being produced by the insects either distributing the pollen of the male flowers or by puncturing the fruit.—**Caprificate**, kap'ri-fi-kāt, *v.t.*—*caprificated, caprificating.* To perform the operation of caprification on.

Capriform, kap'ri-form, *a.* [L. *caper*, a goat, and *forma*, form.] Having the form of a goat, or of something belonging to a goat (*capriform* horns).—**Caprine**, kap'-rin, *a.* [L. *caprinus.*] Like a goat; pertaining to a goat.

Capriole, kap'ri-ōl, *n.* [O.Fr. *capriole*, now *cabriole*, lit. a goat-leap, from L. *capriolus*, a wild goat, from *caper*, a goat.] A caper or leap, as in dancing; an active bound; a spring; a leap, accompanied with a jerking out of the hind legs, which a horse makes without advancing. — *v.i.* To execute a capriole.

Capsicum, kap'si-kum, *n.* [From L. *capsa*, a box, from the shape of the fruit.] The generic name of some South American and Asiatic plants, many species of which are cultivated for their pods, used in cookery under the name of chillies, and when dried and ground called Cayenne pepper, to which the name capsicum is also sometimes given. —**Capsicine**, kap'si-sin, *n.* An alkaloid, the active principle of the capsules of Cayenne pepper.

Capsize, kap-sīz', *v.t.*—*capsized, capsizing.* [Origin doubtful; probably the first syllable means head or top, ultimately from L. *caput.*] To upset or overturn.—*v.i.* To be upset or overturned.

Capstan, kap'stan, *n.* [Fr. *cabestan*, from Sp. *cabestante*, *cabrestante*; of unknown origin.] An apparatus working on the principle of the wheel and axle, and consisting of a cylinder or barrel adjusted on an upright axis, the barrel being made to turn round by means of horizontal bars or levers, the ends of which are inserted in holes near the top of the barrel, so that a rope is thus wound round it and a weight, such as an anchor, raised or moved.

Capsule, kap'sūl, *n.* [L. *capsula*, a little chest, dim. of *capsa*, a chest, from *capio*, to take.] *Bot.* a dry fruit, containing seeds, and opening of itself by valves or pores when mature; *chem.* a small saucer used for roasting or melting ores, for evaporations, solutions, &c.; *anat.* a membranous body covering a part like a bag; a gummy envelope for a nauseous drug; a metallic seal or cover for going over the cork or stopper of a bottle. — **Capsular, Capsulary**, kap'sū-lėr, kap'sū-la-ri, *a.* Hollow like a capsule; pertaining to a capsule.—**Capsulate, Capsulated**, kap'sū-lāt, kap'sū-lāt-ed, *a.* Inclosed in a capsule.

Captain, kap'tin, *n.* [Fr. *capitaine*, O.Fr. *capitain*, from L.L. *capitanus*, from L. *caput*, the head.] One who is at the head of or has authority over others; a chief; a leader; a commander, especially in military affairs; more specifically, the military officer who commands a company, whether of infantry, cavalry, or artillery; an officer in the navy commanding a ship of war; the commander or master of a merchant vessel. —**Captaincy**, kap'tin-si, *n.* The rank, post, or commission of a captain.—**Captainship**, kap'tin-ship, *n.* The condition or post of a captain or chief commander; skill in military affairs.—**Captain-general**, *n.* A commander-in-chief.

Caption, kap'shon, *n.* [L. *captio*, a taking, fraud, deceit, from *capio*, to seize.] The act of taking or arresting‡; the act of taking any one unawares by some trick or imposition‡; the act of urging captious objections; cavilling. — **Captious**, kap'shus, *a.* [L. *captiosus*, from *captio*, a taking.] Apt to catch at faults; disposed to find fault or raise objections; apt to cavil; difficult to please; carping; cavilling; proceeding from a captious or cavilling disposition; fitted to insnare or perplex (a *captious* question).—**Captiously**, kap'shus-li, *adv.* In a captious manner.—**Captiousness**, kap'shus-nes, *n.* The quality of being captious.

Captive, kap'tiv, *n.* [From L. *captivus*, a captive, from *capio, captus*, to seize. *Caitiff* is the same word derived through the French.] One who is taken prisoner, especially a prisoner taken in war; one who is charmed or subdued by beauty or excellence; one whose affections are seized, or who is held by strong ties of love.—*a.* Made prisoner in war; kept in bondage or confinement; bound by the ties of love or admiration; captivated.—**Captivate**, kap'ti-vāt, *v.t.*—*captivated, captivating.* [L. *captivo, captivatum.*] To capture or make prisoner‡; to overpower and gain with excellence or beauty; to charm; to engage the affections of; to fascinate, enslave, subdue, enchant. —**Captivating**, kap'ti-vāt-ing, *a.* Having power to engage the affections; winning.—**Captivation**, kap-ti-vā'shon, *n.* The act of captivating; the act of gaining over or winning one's affections.—**Captivity**, kap-tiv'i-ti, *n.* [L. *captivitas.*] The state of being a captive; subjection; a state of being under control; bondage; servitude.—**Captor**, kap'tėr, *n.* [L. *captor.*] One who captures or takes by force, stratagem, &c.—**Capture**, kap'tūr, *n.* [L. *captura.*] The act of one who captures; the act of making prize of something; seizure; arrest; the thing taken; a prize.—*v.t.*—*captured, capturing.* To take or seize by force, surprise, or stratagem, as an enemy or his property; to make a prize or prisoner of.

Capuchin, kap-ū-shēn', *n.* [Fr. *capuchon*, *capucine*, from *capuce*, a hood or cowl, from *cape*, a cape.] A monk of the order of St. Francis, so called from the *capuchon*, a stuff cap or cowl, the distinguishing badge of the order; a garment for females, consisting of a cloak and hood in imitation of the dress of Capuchin monks.

Capybara, Capibara, kap-i-bä'ra, *n.* [The native Brazilian name.] A rodent quadruped, allied to the guinea-pig, abounding in rivers of South America, feeding on vegetables and fish, over 3 feet in length, tailless, with a large head and blunted muzzle, and toes imperfectly webbed.

Car, kär, *n.* [O.Fr. *car* (Mod.Fr. *char*), from L. *carrus*, a four-wheeled vehicle, from the Celtic; Armor. *carr*, a chariot, W. *car*, Ir. and Gael. *carr*, a dray, wagon, &c. Akin *carry, charge, cargo*, &c.] A name applied to various kinds of wheeled vehicles, as railroad cars, freight cars, passenger cars, dining cars, sleeping cars, street cars, motor cars.

Carbine, Carabine, kär'bīn, kar'a-bīn, *n.* [Fr. *carabine*, a carabine; O.Fr. *carabin*, *calabrin*, a musqueteer, from *calabre*, an engine of war, from L.L. *chadabula*, an engine for throwing stones, from Gr. *katabolē*, a throwing down—*kata*, down, and *ballō*, to throw.] A gun or firearm commonly used by cavalry, shorter in the barrel than the infantry musket or rifle.—**Carbineer, Carabineer**, kär-bin-ēr, kar'a-bin-er", *n.* One armed with a carbine or carabine.

Caracal, kar'a-kal, *n.* [From a Turkish word signifying black-eared.] A species of lynx, about the size of a fox and of a deep brown colour, a native of Northern Africa and South-western Asia.

Caracara, kä-ra-kä'ra, *n.* [From its hoarse cry.] A South American bird of prey of several species, akin to the eagles and vultures, and feeding on carrion.

Carack, kar'ak, *n.* [Fr. *caraque, carraque*, from L.L. *carraca, carrica*, a ship of burden, from L. *carrus*, a car.] A large round-built vessel of great depth, fitted for fight as well as burden, such as were used by the Portuguese and Spaniards in trading with America and the East Indies.

Caracole, kar'a-kōl, *n.* [Fr., from Sp. and Pg. *caracol*, a winding staircase, a caracole.] A half-turn which a horseman makes, either to the right or left; *arch.* a spiral staircase. —*v.i.*—*caracoled, caracoling.* To move in a caracole; to wheel.

Carafe, kar'af or ka-raf', *n.* [Fr.] A glass water-bottle or decanter.

Carageen, Caragheen, kar'a-gēn, *n.* CARRAGEEN.

Carambole, ka'ram-bōl, *n.* [Fr., of unknown origin.] In billiards, the stroke otherwise called a cannon. Also as *v.i.*

Caramel, kar'a-mel, *n.* [Fr. *caramel*, caramel, from Sp. *caramelo*, a lozenge, of Ar. origin.] Anhydrous or burnt sugar, a product of the action of heat upon sugar; it dissolves readily in water, is of a brown colour, and is used to colour spirits and wines.

Carapace, kar'a-pās, *n.* [Fr., from Sp. *carapacho*, a carapace or shell.] The shell which protects the body of chelonian reptiles; also the covering of the anterior upper surface of the crustaceans.

Carap-oil, kar'ap-oil, *n.* Oil obtained from the crab-wood tree of South America, used for lamps.

Carat, kar'at, *n.* [Fr. *carat*, Ar. *qirrât*, a carat, from Gr. *keration*, lit. a little horn, also the seed of the carob-tree, used for a weight, a carat.] A weight, about 3¼ grains, used in weighing precious stones and pearls; a term used to express the proportionate fineness of gold, gold of twenty-four carats being pure gold, gold of sixteen (for instance) having eight parts of alloy.

Caravan, kar'a-van, *n.* [Fr. *caravane*, from Sp. *caravana*, Ar. *qairawân*, Per. *kârwân*, a caravan.] A company of travellers who associate together in many parts of Asia and Africa that they may travel with greater security; a large close carriage for conveying travelling exhibitions or the like from place to place.—**Caravaneer**, kar'-a-van-ēr", *n.* The person who leads the camels, &c., of a caravan.—**Caravansary, Caravansera**, kar-a-van'sa-ri, kar-a-van'-se-ra, *n.* [Per. *kârwân*, a caravan, and *sarâi*, an inn.] In the East, a place appointed for receiving and lodging travellers.

Caravel, Carvel, kar'a-vel, kär'vel, *n.* [Sp. and It. *caravela*, a caravel, dim. of L. *carabus*, Gr. *karabos*, a light ship, a boat, also a crab.] A small galley-rigged ship formerly used by the Spanish and Portuguese; also a small fishing vessel.

Caraway, kar'a-wā, *n.* [Sp. *al-carahueya*, from Ar. *karwiyâ, karawiyâ*, caraway; probably from Gr. *karon*, L. *careum*, caraway.] A biennial plant, with a taper root like a parsnip, the seeds of which are used to flavour cakes, and also in comfits, a volatile oil being obtained by distilling them in spirits.

Carbazotic, kär-ba-zot'ik, *n.* [*Carbon* and *azote.*] The term applied to a kind of acid, obtained by the action of nitric acid on indigo and some other substances, dyeing silk of a fine yellow colour, with a mordant of alum or cream of tartar. PICRIC.

Carbide, kär'bīd, *n.* A compound of carbon with a metal; a carburet.

Carbine, Carbineer. CARABINE.

Carbohydrate, kär-bō-hī'drāt, *n.* [L. *carbo*, charcoal, Gr. *hydōr*, water.] A chemical compound made of carbon, hydrogen, and oxygen, the two latter being commonly in the same proportion as in water (H_2O).

Carbolic, kär-bol'ik, *a.* [*Carbon* and *oil.*] A term applied to an acid obtained from the distillation of coal-tar, an oily, colourless liquid, with a burning taste, now much employed as an antiseptic and disinfectant.

Carbon, kär'bon, *n.* [L. *carbo, carbonis*, a coal.] Sym. C. Pure charcoal; one of the chemical elements, a black, brittle, light, and inodorous substance existing in three distinct allotropic forms, viz. diamond, graphite, and amorphous carbon—the last including lampblack, coal, animal charcoal, &c.—**Carbonaceous**, kär-bo-nā'shus, *a.* Pertaining to carbon or charcoal.—**Carbonate**, kär'bon-āt, *n.* *Chem.* a compound formed by the union of carbonic acid with a base.—**Carbonated**, kär'bon-āt-ed, *a.* Containing or saturated with carbonic acid. —**Carbonic**, kär-bon'ik, *a.* Pertaining to carbon, or obtained from it.—*Carbonic acid*, a gaseous compound of 12 parts by weight of carbon and 32 of oxygen, incapable of maintaining flame or animal life, and acting as a narcotic poison when present in the air to the extent of only 4 or 5 per cent.—**Carboniferous**, kär-bo-nif′ėr-us, *a.* Containing or yielding carbon or coal.—*Carboniferous system*, *geol.* the great group of strata which lie between the old red sandstone below and the Permian or new red sandstone above, and are the chief source of coal.—**Carbonize**, kär′bon-īz, *v.t.*—*carbonized*, *carbonizing.* To convert into carbon by combustion, or the action of fire.—**Carbonization**, kär′bon-iz-ā″shon, *n.* The act or process of carbonizing.

Carbonado, kär-bo-nā′dō, *n.* [From L. *carbo*, a coal.] An old name for a piece of meat, fowl, or game, cut across, seasoned, and broiled; a chop. (*Shak.*)—*v.t.*‡ To make a carbonado of; to cut or slash.

Carbonari, kar-bon-ä′rē, *n.* Members of a Neapolitan secret revolutionary society who took their name from the charcoal-burners of the Abruzzi, amongst whom many of them were obliged to take refuge, and with whom they identified themselves.

Carborundum, kär-bo-run′dum, *n.* [*Carbon* and *corundum.*] Silicon carbide, a very hard substance used as a substitute for emery, and made by fusing together coke, sand, sawdust, and a little common salt.

Carboxyl, karb-oks′il, *n.* [L. *carbo*, charcoal, Gr. *oxys*, acid.] The group CO . OH, typical of organic acids.

Carboy, kär′boi, *n.* [Per. *karabā*, a large vessel for containing wine.] A large, strong, glass bottle, protected by an outside covering, and used chiefly for corrosive liquids, as vitriol.

Carbuncle, kär′bung-kl, *n.* [L. *carbunculus*, a little coal, from *carbo*, a coal.] A beautiful gem of a deep red colour, with a mixture of scarlet, found in the East Indies; an inflammatory tumour, or malignant gangrenous boil or ulcer. — **Carbuncled**, kär′bung-kld, *a.* Set with carbuncles; afflicted with carbuncle; pimpled and blotched. — **Carbuncular**, **Carbunculate**, kär-bung′kū-lėr, kär-bung′kū-lāt, *a.* Belonging to a carbuncle; resembling a carbuncle; inflamed.

Carburet, kär′bū-ret, *n.* Same as *Carbide.* —**Carbureted**, kär′bū-ret-ed, *a.* Combined with carbon like a carburet. *Light carbureted hydrogen*, a kind of gas, the fire-damp of coal-mines.—**Carburation**, *n.* The process of mixing thoroughly gasoline and air ready for combustion.—**Carburetor**, kär′bū-ret-ėr, *n.* In an internal combustion engine the device for vaporizing gasoline or other fuel.—**Carburize**, kär′bū-rīz, *v.t.* To combine with carbon or a compound of it.

Carcajou, kär′ka-jö, *n.* [Fr. *carcajou*, from native name.] An American name for the wolverine or glutton, and erroneously for the badger and lynx.

Carcanet, kär′ka-net, *n.* [Fr. *carcan*, a carcanet, from Armor. *kerchen*, the neck or bosom.] A necklace or collar of jewels.

Carcass, **Carcase**, kär′kas, *n.* [Fr. *carcasse*, the carcass, a framework, a kind of bomb, same word as *carquois*, a quiver, from L.L. *tarcasius*, a quiver, from Ar. and Per. *tarkash*, a quiver.] The body, usually the dead body, of an animal; a corpse; the decaying remains of a bulky thing; the frame or main parts of a thing unfinished; a kind of bomb or shell filled with combustible matter, and having apertures for the emission of flame, so as to set fire to buildings, &c.

Carcinology, kär-si-nol′o-ji, *n.* [Gr. *karkinos*, a crab, and *logos*, discourse.] That department of zoology which interests itself with crustaceans, or crabs, shrimps, &c.—**Carcinological**, kär-sin-ō-loj″ik-al, *a.* Pertaining to carcinology.

Carcinoma, kär-si-nō′ma, *n.* [Gr. *karkinōma*, from *karkinos*, a cancer.] A kind of cancer or cancerous growth.

Card, kärd, *n.* [From Fr. *carte*, a card, from L. *charta*, paper, from Gr. *chartē*, *chartēs*, a layer of papyrus bark.] A rectangular piece of thick paper or pasteboard; such a piece with certain devices, marks, or figures, used for playing games; a piece having one's name, &c., written or printed on it, used in visiting; a larger piece written or printed, and conveying an invitation, or some intimation or statement; the dial or face of the mariner's compass. — **Cardboard**, kärd′bōrd, *n.* A stiff kind of paper or pasteboard for making cards, &c.—**Card-case**, *n.* A small pocket case, generally of an ornamental kind, for holding visiting-cards.—**Card-rack**, *n.* A rack or frame for holding visiting, business, &c., cards.—**Card-sharper**, *n.* One who cheats in playing cards; one who makes it a trade to fleece the unwary in games of cards.

Card, kärd, *n.* [Fr. *carde*, from L.L. *cardus*, L. *carduus*, a thistle, from *carere*, to card —thistles having been used as cards.] An instrument for combing, opening, and breaking wool or flax, freeing it from the coarser parts and from extraneous matter. —*v.t.* or *i.* To comb or open wool, flax, hemp, &c., with a card.—**Carder**, kär′dėr, *n.* One who cards; the machine employed in carding.

Cardamom, kär′da-mum, *n.* [L. *cardamomum*, Gr. *kardamōmon.*] The aromatic capsule of various plants of the ginger family, employed in medicine as well as an ingredient in sauces and curries.

Cardiac, **Cardiacal**, kär′di-ak, kär-dī′ak-al, *a.* [L. *cardiacus*, Gr. *kardiakos*, from *kardia*, the heart.] Pertaining to the heart; exciting action in the heart through the medium of the stomach; having the quality of stimulating action in the system, invigorating the spirits, and giving strength and cheerfulness.—**Cardiac**, *n.* A medicine which excites action in the stomach and animates the spirits; a cordial.—**Cardiagraphy**, **Cardiography**, kär-di-ag′ra-fi, kär-di-og′ra-fi, *n.* An anatomical description of the heart.—**Cardialgia**, **Cardialgy**, kär-di-al′ji-a, kär′di-al-ji, *n.* [Gr. *algos*, pain.] *Med.* heart-burn.

Cardigan, kär′di-gan, *n.* [After Earl of *Cardigan.*] A kind of knitted waistcoat worn over or instead of the waistcoat.

Cardinal, kär′di-nal, *a.* [L. *cardinalis*, from *cardo*, a hinge.] Chief, principal, pre-eminent, or fundamental.—*Cardinal numbers*, the numbers *one*, *two*, *three*, &c., in distinction from *first*, *second*, *third*, &c., called ordinal numbers.—*Cardinal points*, north and south, east and west.—*Cardinal virtues*, justice, prudence, temperance, and fortitude.—*n.* An ecclesiastical prince in the Roman Catholic Church, next in rank to the pope, and having a distinguishing dress of a red colour. — **Cardinalate**, **Cardinalship**, kär′di-nal-āt, kär′di-nal-ship, *n.* The office, rank, or dignity of a cardinal. — **Cardinalitial**, kär′di-nal-ish″al, *a.* Of or pertaining to a cardinal; of the rank of a cardinal.—**Cardinalize**†, kär′di-nal-īz, *v.t.* To make a cardinal.—**Cardinal-bird**, *n.* A North American bird, with a fine red plumage, and a crest on the head.—**Cardinal-flower**, *n.* The name commonly given to a species of lobelia because of its large, very showy, and intensely red flowers.

Cardiograph, kär′di-o-graf, *n.* [Gr. *kardia*, heart, and *graphō*, to write.] An instrument tracing and recording the movements of the heart.

Cardioid, kär′di-oid, *n.* A curve of a heart shape.

Cardiology, kär-di-ol′o-ji, *n.* [Gr. *kardia*, the heart, and *logos*, discourse.] A discourse or treatise on the heart; scientific facts relating to the heart.—**Carditis**, kär-dī′tis, *n.* [The term. *-itis*, denotes inflammation.] Inflammation of the muscular substance of the heart.

Cardol, kär′dol, *n.* [From *card* in *Anacardium*, the genus to which belongs the cashew, and L. *oleum*, oil.] An oily liquid contained in the pericarp of the cashew-nut, used as a blistering agent.

Cardoon, kär-dön′, *n.* [Sp. *cardon*, from L. *carduus*, a thistle.] A plant akin to the artichoke, and somewhat resembling it, used as an esculent vegetable in Spain and France.

Care, kãr, *n.* [A.Sax. *caru*, *cearu*, care, sorrow = O.Sax. *cara*, Icel. *kæri*, complaint, Goth. *kara*, sorrow, O.H.G. *chara*, lamentation; from a root signifying to cry, seen also in E. *call.*] Some degree of pain in the mind from apprehension of evil; a painful load of thought; mental trouble; concern; anxiety; solicitude; attention or heed; a looking to; caution; regard; watchfulness; charge or oversight, implying concern for safety and prosperity; the object of care or watchful regard and attention. ∴ *Care* denotes mental trouble regarding the present, the future, or even the past; *solicitude* and *concern* denote affections of the mind of a more active kind than *care*, and relate to the present and the future, while the latter may also be excited by something past. — *v.i.* — *cared*, *caring.* To be anxious or solicitous; to be concerned; to be inclined or disposed; to like.—**Careful**, kãr′ful, *a.* Full of care; anxious; solicitous; attentive to support and protect; giving good heed; watchful, cautious; showing or done with care or attention: generally with *of* before the object.—**Carefully**, kãr′ful-li, *adv.* In a careful manner.—**Carefulness**, kãr′ful-nes, *n.* The state or quality of being careful.—**Careless**, kãr′les, *a.* Free from care or anxiety; heedless; negligent, unthinking, inattentive; regardless, unmindful: with *of* or *about* before an object; done or said without care; unconsidered.—**Carelessly**, kãr′les-li, *adv.* In a careless manner or way. — **Carelessness**, kãr′les-nes, *n.* The state or quality of being careless.—**Careworn**, *a.* Worn, oppressed or burdened with care; showing marks of care or anxiety.

Careen, ka-rēn′, *v.t.* [Fr. *carener*, from *carène*, the side and keel of a ship, L. *carina*, a keel.] To heave or bring (a ship) to lie on one side for caulking, repairing, cleansing, or the like.—*v.i.* To incline to one side, as a ship under a press of sail, or a motor car turning a corner on two wheels.

Career, ka-rēr′, *n.* [Fr. *carrière*, O.Fr. *cariere*, road, race-course, course, career, from L. *carrus*, a car. CAR.] A race or running; course of proceeding; a specific course of action or occupation forming the object of one's life.—*v.i.* To move or run rapidly (as a horse, a ship, &c.).

Caress, ka-res′, *n.* [Fr. *caresse*, from It. *carezza*, L.L. *caritia*, from L. *carus*, dear.] An act of endearment; any act or expression of affection.—*v.t.* To treat with caresses; to fondle; to embrace with tender affection. — **Caressingly**, ka-res′ing-li, *adv.* In a caressing manner.

Caret, kā′ret, *n.* [L. *caret*, there is (something) wanting, from *careo*, to want.] In *writing*, a mark made thus, ‸, which shows that something, omitted in the line, is interlined above or inserted in the margin, and should be read in that place.

Cargo, kär′gō, *n.* [Sp., from *cargar*, to load, L.L. *carricare*, to load, from L. *carrus*, a car. CAR, CHARGE.] The lading or freight of a ship.

Cariacou, kar′i-a-kö, *n.* [Probably an Indian name.] The Virginian deer of North America, an elegant species, somewhat smaller than the common stag.

Cariatid, kar′i-at-id. CARYATID.

Carib, **Caribbee**, kar′ib, kar′ib-bē, *n.* One of a native race inhabiting certain portions of Central America, and formerly also the Caribbean Islands.

Caribou, **Cariboo**, kar′i-bö, *n.* [Probably of Indian origin.] A North American variety of the reindeer.

Caricature, kar′i-ka-tūr″, *n.* [It. *caricatura*, an overloaded representation, from *caricare*, to load. CHARGE.] A representation, pictorial or descriptive, in which beauties are concealed and peculiarities or defects exaggerated so as to make the person or thing ridiculous, while a general likeness is retained.—*v.t.*—*caricatured*, *caricaturing.* To make or draw a caricature of; to represent in a ridiculous and exaggerated fashion.—**Caricaturist**, kar′i-ka-tūr″ist, *n.* One who caricatures others. (*Malone.*)

Caries, kā'ri-ēz, *n.* [L.] Ulceration of bony substance; the gangrenous eating away of a bone.—**Cariosity**, kā-ri-os'i-ti, *n.* The state of being carious.—**Carious**, kā'ri-us, *a.* Affected with caries; ulcerated: said of a bone.

Carillon, kar'il-lon, *n.* [Fr., from L.L. *quadrilio*, from L. *quatuor*, four, because *carillons* were played formerly on four bells.] A chime of bells, properly tuned, and rung by means of finger-keys like those of the pianoforte; a simple air adapted to be performed on a set of bells.

Carina, ka-rī'na, *n.* [L., the keel of a boat.] *Bot.* the two partially united lower petals of papilionaceous flowers; *zool.* a prominent median ridge or keel in the sternum or breast-bone of all existing birds except the runners (ostrich, &c.).—**Carinate, Carinated**, kar'i-nāt, kar'i-nāt-ed, *a.* [L. *carinatus.*] Shaped like a keel; having a carina or keel; keeled; *bot.* having a longitudinal ridge like a keel; *zool.* applied to those birds whose sternum is keeled, or to their sternum.

Cariole, kar'i-ōl, *n.* [Fr., from L. *carrus*, a car.] A small open carriage; a kind of calash; a covered cart.

Carious. Under CARIES.

Carjacou, kär'ja-kö, *n.* See CARIACOU.

Cark, kärk, *n.* [O.Fr. *cark*, *kark*, load, *karkir*, to load = E. *charge*; comp. also W. *carc*, care; Gael. *carc*, care.] Care; anxiety; concern; solicitude; distress.—*v.i.* To be careful, anxious, solicitous, concerned.—*v.t.*† To oppress with grief, anxiety, or care; to worry; to perplex; to vex.—**Carking**, kärk'ing, *a.* Distressing; giving anxiety.

Carl, Carle, kärl, *n.* [A Scandinavian word = Icel. Dan. Sw. *karl*, a man; A.Sax. *carl*, male, as in *carl-catt*, a he-cat.] A man; a robust, strong, or hardy man; an old man. [O.E. and Sc.] Hence **Carline**, a woman.

Carline, Carling, kär'lin, kär'ling, *n.* Fr. *carlingue* or *escarlingue.*] One of the fore-and-aft deck timbers in a ship.

Carline-thistle kär-lin-this-l, *n.* [Fr. *carline*, after the Emperor Charlemagne.] The popular name of a thistle common in dry fields and pastures throughout Britain and the Continent.

Carlist, kär'list, *n.* A follower of Don *Carlos* of Spain, the heir to the crown but for the repeal of the Salic law; an adherent and supporter of the family of Don Carlos.—**Carlism**, kär'lizm, *n.* The principles of the Carlists.

Carlock, kär'lok, *n.* [Rus. *karlŭk.*] A sort of isinglass from Russia, made of the sturgeon's bladder, and used in clarifying wine.

Carlovingian, kär-lō-vin'ji-an, *a.* Pertaining to or descended from Charlemagne.

Carmagnole, kär-ma-nyōl, *n.* [Fr. *Carmagnole* in Piedmont.] A revolutionary dance and song in France during 1789-93 Revolution, from the street-dancing Savoyards; any bombastic harangue.

Carman, kär'man, *n.* A man whose employment is to drive a car or cart, or to convey goods and other things in a cart or car.

Carmelite, kär'mel-īt, *n.* A mendicant friar of the order of our Lady of Mount *Carmel*; a sort of pear; the White Friars founded at Mount Carmel; gray woollen stuff.

Carminative, kär'mi-nā-tiv or kär-min'a-tiv, *n.* [L. *carmino*, *carminatum*, to card wool (hence to make fine or thin), from *carmen*, a card.] A medicine which tends to expel wind from the stomach and remedy flatulency.—*a.* Expelling wind from the stomach; anti-spasmodic.

Carmine, kär'mīn, *n.* [Sp. *carmin*, from *carmesino*, carmine, crimson, from *carmes*, kermes (which see). *Crimson* has the same origin.] The pure colouring matter or principle of cochineal; a red or crimson pigment made from cochineal.—**Carminated**, kär-mi-nāt'ed, *a.* Mixed with or made of carmine.—**Carminic**, kär-min'ik, *a.* Of or pertaining to carmine.

Carnage, kär'nāj, *n.* [Fr. *carnage*, slaughter, from L.L. *carnaticum*, from L. *caro*, *carnis*, flesh.] Slaughter; great destruction of men; butchery; massacre.

Carnal, kär'nal, *a.* [L. *carnalis*, carnal, from *caro*, *carnis*, flesh.] Pertaining to the body, its passions and appetites; not spiritual; fleshly; sensual; lustful; impure.—**Carnalism, Carnality**, kär'nal-izm, kär-nal'i-ti, *n.* The state of being carnal; want of spirituality; fleshliness; fleshly lusts or desires, or the indulgence of those lusts; sensuality.—**Carnalist**, kär'nal-ist, *n.* One given to the indulgence of sensual appetites.—**Carnalize**,† kär'nal-īz, *v.t.*—*carnalized, carnalizing.* To make carnal; to debase to carnality.—**Carnally**, kär'-nal-li, *adv.* In a carnal manner; according to the flesh; not spiritually.

Carnallite, kär'nal-līt, *n.* [After a German called Von *Carnall.*] A pink-coloured mineral obtained from the Stassfurt salt mines.

Carnassials, kar-nas'i-als, *n.* [L. *carnosus*, relating to flesh.] Flesh teeth, in carnivores, four large cheek-teeth which act like scissors.

Carnation, kär-nā'shon, *n.* [Fr. *carnation*, the naked part of a picture, flesh colour; from L. *caro*, *carnis*, flesh.] Flesh colour; the parts of a picture which exhibit the natural colour of the flesh; the representation of flesh; a perennial plant found in many varieties, much prized for the beautiful colours of their sweet-scented double flowers.—**Carnationed**, kär-nā'shond, *a.* Having a colour like carnation; pink.

Carnauba, kär-na-ö'ba *n.* The Brazilian name of a tall South American palm which has its leaves coated with small waxy scales, yielding a straw-coloured wax by boiling. Also written *Carnahuba.*

Carnelian, kär-nē'li-an, *n.* [More correctly *cornelian*, from Fr. *cornaline*, a carnelian, from L. *cornu*, a horn, from its horny appearance.] A variety of chalcedony, of a deep red, flesh-red, or reddish-white colour, tolerably hard, capable of a good polish, and used for seals, &c.

Carneous, kär'nē-us, *a.* [L. *carneus*, from *caro*, *carnis*, flesh.] Fleshy; having the appearance, consistence, or qualities of flesh.—Also **Carnose, Carnous**, kär'nōs, kär'nus.

Carnival, kär'ni-val, *n.* [Fr. *carnaval*, It. *carnovale*, from L.L. *carnelevamen*, for *carnis levamen*, solace of the body, permitted in anticipation of any fast—L. *caro*, flesh, and *levare*, to solace, to lighten.] The feast or season of rejoicing before Lent; feasting or revelry in general.

Carnivorous, kär-niv'o-rus, *a.* [L. *caro*, *carnis*, flesh, and *voro*, to devour.] Eating or feeding on flesh: an epithet applied to animals which naturally seek flesh for food, as the lion, tiger, wolf, dog, &c.; also applied to some plants that can assimilate animal substances.—**Carnivora**, kär-niv'-ō-ra, *n. pl.* [L.] A term applicable to any creatures that feed on flesh or animal substances, but generally denoting an order of mammals which prey upon other animals.—**Carnivore**, kär'ni-vōr, *n.* A carnivorous animal; one of the Carnivora.

Carnose. Under CARNEOUS.

Carob, Carob-tree, kar'ob, kar'ob-trē, *n.* [O.Fr. *carobe*, from Ar. *kharrūb*, bean-pods.] A tree growing in the countries skirting the Mediterranean, the pods of which, known as locust-beans, contain a sweet nutritious pulp.

Carol, kar'ol, *n.* [O.Fr. *carole*, a kind of dance, also a Christmas song or carol; from the Celtic: Armor. *koroll*, a dance; W *carol*, a carol, a song.] A song, especially one expressive of joy; a religious song or ballad in celebration of Christmas.—*v.i.*—*carolled, carolling.* To sing; to warble; to sing in joy or festivity.—*v.t.*—To praise or celebrate in song.

Carolingian, kar-ō-lin'ji-an, *a.* Same as *Carlovingian.*

Carolitic, Carolytic, kar-ō-lit'ik, *a.* *Arch.* decorated with branches and leaves, as a column.

Carolus, kar'ō-lus, *n.* A gold coin struck in the reign of *Charles* I and originally 20*s.* in value, afterwards 23*s.* The name was given also to various other coins.

Caromel, kar'o-mel, *n.* Same as *Caramel.*

Carosse, ka-ros', *n.* A garment of fur worn by the natives of South Africa.

Carotic, ka-rot'ik, *a.* [Gr. *karos*, torpor, stupor.] Relating to stupor or carus; also same as carotid.—**Carotid**, ka-rot'id, *a.* [Gr. pl. *karōtides*, the carotids, said to be from *karos*, a deep sleep, because the ancients believed that sleep was caused by an increased flow of blood to the head through these arteries, or by the compression of these arteries.] Of or pertaining to the two great arteries, one on either side of the neck, which convey the blood from the aorta to the head and brain.—*n.* One of these arteries.

Carouse, ka-rouz', *v.i.*—*caroused, carousing.* [O.Fr. *carousser*, to quaff, to carouse, from *carous*, a carouse, a bumper, from G. *garaus!* quite out! that is, empty your glasses! an old German drinking exclamation.] To drink freely and with jollity; to quaff; to revel.—**Carousal, Carouse**, ka-rou'zal, ka-rouz', *n.* A feast or festival; a noisy drinking bout or revelling.—**Carouser**, ka-rouz'ėr, *n.* One who carouses; a drinker; a toper; a noisy reveller or bacchanalian.—**Carousingly**, ka-rouz'ing-li, *adv.* In a carousing manner.

Carp, kärp, *v.i.* [Formerly to speak, tell, from Icel. *karpa*, to boast, its modern sense being due to L. *carpo*, to seize, catch, pick.] To censure, cavil, or find fault, particularly without reason or petulantly: used absolutely or followed by *at.*—**Carper**, kärp'ėr, *n.* One who carps; a caviller.—**Carping**, kärp'ing, *a.* Cavilling; captious; censorious.—**Carpingly**, kärp'ing-li, *adv.* In a carping manner; captiously.

Carp, kärp, *n.* [Same as D. *karper*, Dan. *karpe*, Sw. *karp*, a carp.] A fresh-water fish found in lakes, rivers, ponds, &c. The most noted species are the common carp and the gold fish. The carp has been introduced in America, where it has become so numerous as to be a pest.

Carpal. Under CARPUS.

Carpel, Carpellum, kär'pel, kär-pel'-lum, *n.* [Mod.L. *carpellum*, dim. from Gr. *karpos*, fruit.] *Bot.* a single-celled ovary or seed-vessel, or a single cell of an ovary or seed-vessel together with what belongs to that cell.—**Carpellary**, kär'pel-la-ri, *a.* Belonging to a carpel or carpels.

Carpenter, kär'pen-tėr, *n.* [O.Fr. *carpentier* (Mod.Fr. *charpentier*); L.L. *carpentarius*, a carpenter, from L. *carpentum*, a chariot, a word of Celtic origin.] An artificer who works in timber; a framer and builder of houses and of ships.—**Carpenter-bee**, *n.* The common name of different species of bees, so called from their habit of excavating nests in decaying wood.—**Carpentry**, kär'pen-tri, *n.* The art of cutting, framing, and joining timber; an assemblage of pieces of timber connected by framing or letting them into each other.

Carpet, kär'pet, *n.* [O.Fr. *carpite*, a carpet, from It. and L.L. *carpita*, a woolly cloth, from *carpere*, to tease wool, L. *carpo*, to pluck, to pull in pieces, &c.] A thick fabric used for covering floors, stairs, &c.; a covering resembling a carpet (a *carpet* of moss).—*To be on the carpet*, is to be under consideration; to be the subject of deliberation.—*Carpet knight*, a knight who has not known the hardships of the field.—*v.t.* To cover with or as with a carpet; to spread with carpets.—**Carpeting**, kär'pet-ing, *n.* Cloth for carpets; carpets in general.—**Carpet-bag**, *n.* A travelling bag made of the same material as carpets.—**Carpet-bagger**, *n.* A new-comer to a place, having all his property in a carpet-bag; a new-comer or political candidate, without possessing property in a community.—**Carpet-bedding**, *n.* *Hort.* a system of bedding in which neat and dwarf-growing foliage plants alone are used in the form of mosaic, geometrical, or other designs.—**Carpet-rod**, *n.* One of the rods used to keep a stair carpet in its place.

Carpolite, kär'po-līt, *n.* [Gr. *karpos*, fruit, and *lithos*, stone.] A fossil fruit.

Carpology, kär-pol'o-ji, *n.* [Gr. *karpos*, fruit, *logos*, discourse.] The division of botany relating to the structure of seeds and seed-vessels.—**Carpological**, kär-po-loj'i-kal, *a.* Pertaining to carpology.—**Carpologist**, kär-pol'o-jist, *n.* One who studies or treats of carpology.

Carpophore, kär'po-fōr, *n.* [L. *carpophorum*, from Gr. *karpos*, fruit, and *pherō*, to bear.] *Bot.* the prolongation of the floral axis which bears the pistil beyond the stamens.

Carpus, kär'pus, *n.* [L., the wrist.] *Anat.* that part of the skeleton between the fore-arm and hand; the *wrist* in man and the corresponding bones in other animals.—**Carpal**, kär'pal, *a.* Pertaining to the carpus.

Carrageen, Carragheen, kar'ra-gēn, *n.* [From *Carragaheen*, near Waterford, Ireland, where it abounds.] A sea-weed very common on rocks and stones on every part of the coast of Britain, which, when dried, becomes whitish, and in this condition is known as Irish moss, being used for making soups, jellies, &c.

Carriage, kar'ij, *n.* [O.Fr. *cariage*, from *carier*, to carry. CARRY.] The act of carrying, bearing, transporting, or conveying; the price or expense of carrying; the manner of carrying one's self; behaviour; conduct; deportment; a wheeled vehicle for persons, especially a four-wheeled vehicle supported on springs and with a cover, belonging to a private person and not used for hire; in composition, a wheeled stand or support; as, a gun-*carriage*; *print.* the frame on rollers by which the bed carrying the types is run in and out from under the platen.—**Carriageable**, kar'ij-a-bl, *a.* Capable of being conveyed in carriages; passable by carriages.—**Carriage-dog**, *n.* A Dalmatian dog (q.v.).—**Carriage-free**, *a.* Free of charge for carriage.—**Carriage-spring**, *n.* An elastic contrivance adapted to carriages to lessen the shocks caused by the inequalities of the road in driving.—

Carrick bend, kär'ik, a kind of knot.—**Carrick bitts**, supports for the windlass of a ship.

Carrier. Under CARRY.

Carrion, kar'ri-on, *n.* [O.Fr. *caroigne*, from L.L. *caronia*, from L. *caro*, *carnis*, flesh.] The dead and putrefying body or flesh of animals; flesh so corrupted as to be unfit for food.—*a.* Pertaining to carrion; feeding on carrion.—**Carrion-crow**, *n.* The common crow, so called because it often feeds on carrion.

Carronade, kar-on-ād', *n.* [From *Carron* in Scotland, where it was first made.] A short piece of ordnance of confined range, formerly used in the navy.—**Carron-oil**, *n.* A liniment composed of linseed-oil and lime-water: so called from being first used, in the case of burns, at the Carron Iron-works.

Carrot, kar'ot, *n.* [Fr. *carotte*; L.L. *carota*.] A plant having a long esculent root of a reddish colour much used as a culinary vegetable and also for feeding cattle.—**Carroty**, kar'ot-i, *a.* Like a carrot in colour.—**Carrotiness**, kar'ot-i-nes, *n.*

Carry, kar'i, *v.t.*—*carried, carrying.* [O.E. *carie*, from O.Fr. *carier*, to convey in a car, from O.Fr. *car*, a cart or car. CAR.] To bear, convey, or transport by sustaining and moving with the thing carried; to drive, drag, or fetch (*carry* a person off prisoner); to transfer, as from one column, page, book, &c., to another; to convey or take with one generally (as a message, news, &c.); to urge, impel, lead, or draw, in a moral sense (anger *carried* him too far); to effect, accomplish, achieve, bring to a successful issue (a purpose, &c.); to gain; *milit.* to gain possession of by force; to capture (to *carry* a fortress); to extend or continue in any direction, in time, in space, or otherwise: commonly with such words as *up, back, forward*, &c. (to *carry* a history on to the present, to *carry* improvements far); to bear; to have in or on; to bear or bring as a result (words *carry* conviction); to import, contain, or comprise (the words *carry* a promise); to manage; to conduct (matters or affairs).—*To carry off*, to remove to a distance; to kill or cause to die (to be *carried off* by sickness or poison).—*To carry on*, to manage or prosecute; to continue to pursue (a business).—*To carry out, to carry through*, to sustain to the end; to continue to the end; to accomplish; to finish; to execute (a purpose, an undertaking).—*v.i.* To act as a bearer; to bear; to convey; to propel, as a gun.—*Carrying trade* or *traffic*, the trade which consists in the transportation of goods, especially by water, &c., from country to country, or place to place.—**Carriable**, kar'i-a-bl, *a.* Capable of being carried.—**Carrier**, kar'i-ėr, *n.* One who or that which carries or conveys; one who for hire undertakes the conveyance of goods or persons for any one who employs him; the name of a particular part in various machines.—**Carrier-pigeon**, *n.* A variety of pigeon noted for its faculty of finding its way home from great distances, often used to carry letters, &c.

Carse, kärs, *n.* [O.Sc. *kers, kerss*, probably a plural form from Sw. *kærr*, Icel. *kiörr*, a marsh or marshy place; Dan. *kær*, a pool.] In Scotland, a stretch of fertile, alluvial land along the side of a stream; the low-lying part of a valley that is watered by a river.

Cart, kärt, *n.* [From W. *cart*, a cart or wagon, Ir. *cairt*. CAR.] A carriage usually without springs for the conveyance of heavy goods.—*v.t.* To carry or convey on a cart.—**Cartage**, kär'tāj, *n.* The act of carrying in a cart; the price paid for carting.—**Carter**, kär'tėr, *n.* One who drives a cart; one whose occupation is to drive a cart.—**Cart-horse**, *n.* A horse that draws a cart, or is intended for such work.—**Cart-load**, *n.* A load borne on a cart; as much as is usually carried at once on a cart.—**Cart-wright**, *n.* An artificer who makes carts.

Carte, kärt, *n.* [Fr., a card.] A card; a bill of fare at a tavern; a carte-de-visite photograph. — **Carte-blanche**, kärt-blänsh, *n.* [Fr., white paper.] A blank paper; a paper duly authenticated with signature, &c., and intrusted to a person to be filled up as he pleases; hence, unconditional terms; unlimited power to decide.—**Carte-de-visite**, kärt'de-vi-zēt", *n.* pl. **Cartes-de-visite** (same pron.). [Fr.] A visiting card; a photographic likeness on a small card.

Cartel, kär'tel, *n.* [Fr., from L. *chartula*, dim. of *charta*, paper, a paper.] A writing or agreement between states at war, for the exchange of prisoners or for some mutual advantage. In Europe, an organization controlling the commercial policy of a number of independent companies, the equivalent of the American pool or trust.

Cartesian, kär-tē'zi-an, *a.* Pertaining to the philosopher René *Descartes*, or to his philosophy.—*n.* One who adopts the philosophy of Descartes.—**Cartesianism**, kär-tē'zi-an-izm, *n.* The philosophy of Descartes.

Carthaginian, kär-tha-jin'i-an, *a.* Pertaining to ancient Carthage, a celebrated city on the northern coast of Africa.—*n.* An inhabitant or native of Carthage.

Carthusian, kär-thū'zi-an, *n.* One of an order of monks, founded in 1086, under Benedictine rule, by St. Bruno, so called from *Chartreuse*, in France, the place of their institution; pupil of the Charterhouse School, founded on the site of the London monastery.

Cartilage, kär'ti-lāj, *n.* [Fr. *cartilage*, L. *cartilago*.] An elastic tissue occurring in vertebrate animals, and forming the tissue from which bone is formed by a process of calcification; gristle. — **Cartilaginous**, kär-ti-laj'i-nus, *a.* Pertaining to or resembling a cartilage; gristly; consisting of cartilage; having cartilage only and not true bones (as many fishes).

Cartographer, Cartographic, Cartography. CHARTOGRAPHY, &c.

Carton, a box with cover made of various kinds of board, as pasteboard, fiberboard, for shipping light articles.

Cartoon, kär-tön', *n.* [Fr. *carton*, pasteboard, a cartoon, from It. *cartone* (same sense), aug. of *carta*, L. *charta*, paper.] A pictorial design drawn on strong paper as a study for a picture intended to be painted of same size, and more especially for a picture to be painted in fresco; a caricature, often satirical, representing important events in politics, &c., on the front page of the daily papers or in the comic strips.

Cartouch, Cartouche, kär'tösh, *n.* [Fr. *cartouche*, O.Fr. *cartoche*, from It. *cartoccio*, a cartridge, a roll of paper, from *carta*, L. *charta*, paper. *Cartridge* is a corruption of this.] A case of wood filled with shot to be fired from a cannon; a cartridge; a portable box for charges for firearms; on Egyptian monuments, papyri, &c., a group of hieroglyphics in a small oblong area; *arch.* a sculptured ornament in the form of a scroll unrolled.

Cartridge, kär'trij, *n.* [Formerly also *cartrage*, a corruption of *cartouch*.] A case of pasteboard, parchment, copper, tin, &c., holding the exact charge of any firearm.—*Blank cartridge*, a cartridge without ball or shot. — **Cartridge-box, Cartridge-case**, *n.* A portable case or box for carrying cartridges. — **Cartridge-paper**, *n.* A thick sort of paper originally manufactured for soldiers' cartridges, but extensively used in the arts.

Cartulary, kär'tū-la-ri, *n.* Same as *Chartulary*.

Carucate, kar'ụ-kāt, *n.* [L.L. *carruca*, a plough, from L. *carrus*, a car.] Formerly as much land as one team could plough in the year. Spelled also *Carrucate*.

Caruncle, Caruncula, kar'ung-kl, ka-rung'kū-la, *n.* [L. *caruncula*, dim. from *caro*, flesh.] A small fleshy excrescence; a fleshy excrescence on the head of a fowl, as a wattle or the like; *bot.* a protuberance surrounding the hilum of a seed.—**Caruncular, Carunculous**, ka-rung'kū-lėr, ka-rung'kū-lus, *a.* Pertaining to or in the form of a caruncle. — **Carunculate, Carunculated**, ka-rung'kū-lāt, ka-rung'kū-lāt-ed, *a.* Having a fleshy excrescence.

Carve, kärv, *v.t.*—*carved, carving.* [A.Sax. *ceorfan* = D. *kerven*, Icel. *kyrfa*, to carve; Dan. *karve*, G. *kerven*, to notch or indent; same root as *grave*.] To cut (some solid material) in order to produce the representation of an object or some decorative design; to make or shape by cutting; to form by cutting or hewing; to cut into, hew, or slash; to cut into small pieces or slices, as meat at table. — *v.i.* To exercise the trade of a carver; to engrave or cut figures; to cut up meat at table.—**Carver**, kär'vėr, *n.* One who carves, as one who cuts ivory, wood, or the like, in a decorative way; one who cuts meat for use at table; a large table-knife for carving.—**Carving**, kär'ving, *n.* A branch of sculpture usually limited to works in wood, ivory, &c.; the device or figure carved.

Carvel, kär'vel, *n.* Same as *Caravel*.—**Carvel-built**, *a.* A term applied to a ship or boat the planks of which are all flush and not overlapping, as in clincher-built boats.

Caryatid, kar'i-at-id, *n.* pl. **Caryatids, Caryatides**, kar'i-at-idz, kar-i-at'i-dēz. [Perhaps from *Caryæ*, a city in the Peloponnesus.] *Arch.* a figure of a woman dressed in long robes, serving to support entablatures.—**Caryatic**, kar-i-at'ik, *a.* Pertaining to the inhabitants of Caryæ, or to caryatids.

Caryophyllaceous, Caryophyllous, kar'i-ō-fil-lā"shus, kar-i-of'i-lus, *a.* [Gr. *karyophyllon*, the clove-tree.] Pertaining or similar to the plants known as pinks, and their allies; applied to flowers having five petals with long claws in a tubular calyx.

Caryopsis, kar-i-op'sis, *n.* [Gr. *karyon*, a nut, and *opsis*, an appearance.] *Bot.* a small, one-seeded, dry, indehiscent fruit, in which the seed adheres to the thin pericarp throughout, as in wheat and other grains.

Casava, ka-sä'va, *n.* Same as *Cassava*.

Cascade, kas-kād', *n.* [Fr. *cascade*, It. *cascata*, from *cascare*, to fall, from L. *cado*, *casum*, to fall.] A fall or flowing of water over a precipice in a river or other stream; a waterfall.

Cascara sagrada, kas-ka'ra sag-ra'da, *n.* [Sp. sacred bark.] A purgative medicine obtained from the bark of an American tree.

Cascarilla, kas-ka-ril'la, *n.* [Sp. dim. of *cascara*, peel, bark.] The aromatic bitter bark of a small tree of the Cinchona family, cultivated chiefly in Eleuthera, one of the Bahamas, employed as a substitute for cinchona.

Case, kās, *n.* [O.Fr. *casse* (now *caisse*), from *capio*, to take, receive, contain. *Cash* is really the same word.] A covering, envelope, box, frame, or sheath; that which incloses or contains; the skin of an animal‡; a case with its contents; hence, a certain quantity; *print.* a partitioned tray for types, from which the compositor gathers them and arranges them in lines and pages to print from.—*v.t.*—*cased, casing.* To cover with a case; to surround with any material that shall inclose or defend; to coat or cover over; to put in a case or box; to skin (*Shak.*)‡. —**Casing**, kās'ing, *n.* The act of putting a case on, or of putting into a case; a case or covering —**Case-bottle**, *n.* A bottle made so as to readily fit into a case with others often square.—**Case-harden**, *v.t.* To harden the outer part or surface of (iron tools, &c.) by converting it into steel.—**Case-hardened**, *a.* Having the surface hardened by being converted into steel; *fig.* shameless; abandoned; brazen-faced.—**Case-history**, *n.* A record of facts of an individual's personal history for use in analyzing his case for treatment, compensation, &c.—**Case-knife**, *n.* A long knife kept in a case or sheath; a large table-knife.—**Case-law**, *n.* Law made by decided cases that serve as precedents; judge-made laws. —**Case-shot**, *n.* A collection of shot or small projectiles inclosed in cases to be discharged from cannon; an iron case holding a number of bullets. —**Case worker**, *n.* A social-service worker soliciting information about persons in need of social assistance.

Case, kās, *n.* [Fr. *cas*, a case, L. *casus*, a falling, from *cado*, *casum*, to fall.] The particular state, condition, or circumstances that befall a person, or in which he is placed; an individual occurrence or specific instance, as of disease; a question or group of facts involving a question for discussion or decision; a cause or suit in court; a cause; one of the forms in the declension of a noun, pronoun, or adjective.—*In case*, in the event or contingency; if it should so fall out or happen, supposing. —**Casal**, kā'sal, *a. Gram.* of or belonging to case.

Casein, kā'sē-in, *n.* A white amorphous phosphoprotein contained in the milk of all mammals. Acids precipitate it as in souring milk. It is used for paints and glues, the coating of paper and, after treatment with formaldehyde, as artificial ivory; it is likewise the raw material in the manufacture of synthetic wool.

Casemate, kās'māt, *n* [Fr *casemate*, from It. *casamatta*, a casemate, from *casa*, a house, and *matto*, dim, dark = G. *matt*, feeble, E. *mate* in *checkmate*.] *Fort.* a bomb-proof vault for the protection of the garrison, and sometimes used as a barrack or hospital; a loopholed gallery excavated in a bastion, from which the garrison could fire on an enemy in possession of the ditch.

Casement, kās'ment, *n.* [From *case*, in the sense of a frame, as of a door, &c.] A window frame, or portion of one made to turn and open on hinges; a compartment between the mullions of a window.

Cash, kash, *n.* [O.Fr *casse*, Mod.Fr. *caisse*, It. *cassa*, a chest, box, coffer, from L. *capsa*, a box or case. CASE.] A receptacle for money‡; a money-box‡; money, primarily, ready money; money in chest or on hand, in bank or at command; Chinese copper coin, 22 of which equal 2 cents U. S. currency.—*v.t.* To turn into money, or to exchange for money (to *cash* a bank-note). —**Cashier**, kash-ēr', *n.* One who has charge of cash; one who keeps an account of the monetary transactions of a commercial or trading establishment.—**Cashier's check**, in the United States a check drawn by a bank upon itself and signed by its cashier. —**Cash-book**, *n.* A book in which is kept a register or account of money received and paid.—**Cash-register**, *n.* A device recording the amount of cash received. It contains an automatic adding machine and a money drawer.

Cashew, ka-shö', *n.* [From native name.] The tree which produces cashew-nuts, a native of tropical America.—**Cashew-nut**, *n.* The kidney-shaped fruit of an American tree, having a kernel abounding in a sweet milky juice; the inner layer of the shell contains a black acrid caustic oil.

Cashew, ka-shö', *n.* Same as *Cachou*.

Cashier, kash-ēr', *v.t.* [O.E. *casseere*, G. *cassiren*, from O.Fr. *casser*, to break, to cashier, from L. *cassare*, to annul, from *cassus*, void, empty.] To dismiss from an office, place of trust, or service for bad conduct; to discharge; to discard.—**Cashierer**, kash-ēr'ėr, *n.* One who cashiers.

Cashmere, kash'mēr, *n.* A fine costly shawl made of the downy wool of the Cashmere goat and the wild goat of Tibet, and so called from the country where first made.

Casino, ka-sē'nō, *n.* [It., a small house, from L. *casa*, a cottage.] A building used for social meetings or public amusements, for dancing, gambling, &c.

Cask, kask, *n.* [Sp. *casco*, helmet, wine-cask, skull, potsherd, peel or rind, from a L.L. *quassicare*, to break or burst, from L. *quassare*, to break, whence E. *quash*.] A closed vessel for containing liquors, formed by staves, heading, and hoops; a general term comprehending the pipe, hogshead, butt, barrel, &c.—*v.t.* To put into a cask.

Casket, **Casquet**, kas'ket, *n.* [In form a dim. of *cask*, but in meaning from Fr. *cassette*, a coffer or casket, dim. of *casse*, a box. CASH.] A small chest or box for jewels or other small articles.—*v.t.* To put in a casket.

Casque, kask, *n.* [Fr., from Sp. *casco*, a helmet. CASK.] A helmet generally, but more precisely a head-piece wanting a vizor, but furnished with cheek-pieces and ear-pieces, and frequently elaborately ornamented and embossed.

Cassareep, **Cassireepe**, kas'sa-rēp, kas'si-rēp, *n.* [South American name.] The boiled and concentrated juice of the roots of the bitter cassava used as a relish in cookery.

Cassava, kas-sä'va or kas-sä'va, *n.* [Pg. *cassave*, Sp. *casabe*, *cazabe*, from Haytian name *kasabi*.] A slender erect shrub belonging to the spurge family extensively cultivated in tropical America and the West Indies on account of the nutritious starch obtained from the root, and formed into cakes (cassava-bread) and into tapioca.

Casserole, kas'e-rōl, *n.* [Fr., of same origin as *kettle*.] A kind of stewpan or saucepan; a kind of stew; rice, potatoes, &c., formed into a cup to hold some other kind of food; a small dish with a handle, used for chemical operations.

Cassia, kash'i-a, *n.* [L. *cassia*, Gr. *kasia*, *kassia*, from the Hebrew or Phoenician name.] A tropical leguminous plant of many species, consisting of trees, shrubs, or herbs, the leaflets of several of which constitute the drug called senna, while the pulp from the legumes of another species is used as a purgative.—**Cassia-bark**, *n.* The bark of a species of cinnamon, used as a substitute for the true cinnamon. Called also **Cassia-lignea** (-lig'nē-a).—**Cassia-buds**, *n.* The flower-buds of a kind of cinnamon used in cookery.

Cassideous, kas-sid'ē-us, *a.* [L. *cassis*, a helmet.] *Bot.* helmet-shaped, like the upper sepal of the flower of the aconite.

Cassimere, kas'si-mēr, *n.* [Fr. *cassimir*, same word as *cashmere*.] A twilled woolen cloth woven in imitation of Cashmere shawls; kerseymere.

Cassiopeia, kas'si-ō-pē"ya, *n.* A constellation in the northern hemisphere with five of its stars forming a kind of W.

Cassiterite, kas'si-tėr-it, *n.* [Gr. *kassiteros*, tin.] The most common ore of tin; it is a peroxide, consisting of tin 79, and oxygen 21.

Cassock, kas'ok, *n.* [Fr. *casaque*, from It. *casacca*, from *casa*, a house, L. *casa*, a cottage.] A sort of long coat or tight-fitting garment worn by clergymen.

Cassolette, kas-o-let', *n.* [Fr., akin to *casserole*.] A small box for holding perfumes, with a perforated lid for exhalation.

Cassowary, kas'sō-wa-ri, *n.* [Malay *casuwaris*.] A large cursorial bird inhabiting the islands of the Indian Archipelago, nearly as large as the ostrich, which it resembles; but its legs are thicker and stronger in proportion, and it has three toes on the foot; its head is surmounted by a large horny crest.

Cast, kast, *v.t.*—*cast, casting.* [Dan. *kaste*, Sw. and Icel. *kasta*, to throw: a Scandinavian word.] To throw, fling, or send; to hurl; to shed or throw off (leaves, the skin); to discard, dismiss, or reject; to shed or impart (*cast* light); to turn or direct (a look, the eyes); to throw down (as in wrestling); to decide against at law; to condemn; to bring forth abortively (young); to form by pouring liquid metal, &c., into a mold; to compute, reckon, or calculate; to distribute (the parts of a drama) among the actors; to assign a part to, the work of the casting director in the movies.—*To cast aside*, to dismiss or reject.—*To cast away*, to reject; to lavish or waste by profusion; to wreck (a ship).—*To cast down*, to throw down; *fig.* to deject or depress.—*To cast forth*, to throw out or reject; to emit or send out.—*To cast a vote*, to enter a check-mark in the ballot for the candidate of one's choice.—*To cast off*, to discard or reject; to drive away; *naut.* to loosen from or let go.—*To cast out*, to reject or turn out.—*To cast up*, to compute; to reckon; to calculate; to eject; to vomit; to twit or upbraid with.—*To cast one's self on* or *upon*, to resign or yield one's self to the disposal of.—*To cast in one's lot with*, to share the fate or fortune of.—*To cast* (something) *in the teeth*, to upbraid (with something); to charge; to twit.—*v.i.* To throw or fling; to throw the line in angling, especially one with a fly; to work arithmetical calculations; to turn or revolve in the mind; to calculate; to consider; to warp or twist.—*n.* The act of casting; a throw; the distance passed by a thing thrown; motion or turn of the eye; direction, look, or glance; a throw of dice; the form or shape into which something is cast; anything formed in a mold, as a figure in bronze, plaster, &c.; *fig.* shape; mold; impression generally; a tinge or slight coloring or slight degree of a color (a *cast* of green); manner; air; mien; style; the company of actors to whom the parts of a play are assigned.—*Cast in the eye*, squint.—**Castaway**, kast'a-wā, *n.* One who or that which is cast away or ship-wrecked; one ruined in fortune or character.—*a.* Thrown away; rejected; useless; abandoned.—**Caster**, kas'tėr, *n.* One who or that which casts; specifically, one who makes castings; a founder; a small cruet or bottle for holding sauce, pepper, &c., for the table; spelled also *Castor*; a small wheel attached by a vertical pivot to the legs of a chair, sofa, table, &c., to facilitate their being moved without lifting: spelled also *Castor*.—**Casting**, kas'ting, *n.* The act of one who casts; that which is cast; especially, something cast or formed in a mold; something formed of cast-metal.—*a.* Throwing; sending; computing; turning; deciding; determining.—*Casting-vote*, a vote given by a president or chairman which decides when the votes are equally divided.—**Cast-iron**, **Cast-metal**, **Cast-steel**, *n.* Iron, metal, and steel melted and cast into pigs, ingots, or molds, which renders the metal hard and non-malleable.—**Cast-off**, *a.* Laid aside as worn out or useless; rejected.

Castalian, kas-tā'li-an, *a.* Pertaining to

Castalia; the spring on Mount Parnassus, sacred to the Muses.

Castanet, kas'ta-net, *n.* [Sp. *castañeta*, from L. *castanea*, a chestnut, from resembling that fruit.] One of a pair of small concave pieces of ivory or hard wood, shaped like spoons, fastened to the thumb, and beat with the middle finger in certain Spanish dances.

Caste, kast, *n.* [Fr. *caste*, Pg. *casta*, breed, race, caste.] One of the classes or distinct hereditary orders into which the Hindus are divided according to the religious law of Brahmanism; a class or order of the same kind prevailing in other countries; a rank or order of society; social position; in social insects, a set of similar individuals, e.g. the 'workers' in ants, bees, &c.

Castellan, kas'tel-lan, *n.* [L.L. *castellanus*, from L. *castellum*, a castle. CASTLE.] A governor or constable of a castle.—**Castellated**, kas'tel-lāt-ed, *a.* Furnished with turrets and battlements like a castle; built in the style of a castle.

Castigate, kas'ti-gāt, *v.t.*—*castigated*, *castigating.* [L. *castigo*, *castigatum*, from *castus*, pure.] To chastise; to punish; to correct; to criticise for the purpose of correcting; to emend.—**Castigation**, kas-ti-gā'shon, *n.* The act of castigating; punishment by whipping; correction; chastisement; discipline; critical scrutiny and emendation; correction of textual errors.—**Castigator**, kas'ti-gā-tėr, *n.* One who castigates or corrects.—**Castigatory**, kas'ti-ga-to-ri, *a.* Serving to castigate; tending to correction. —*n.* Something that serves to castigate; particularly a ducking-stool or trebuchet.

Castile-soap, kas-tēl', *n.* A kind of fine hard, white or mottled soap, originally from Castile, made with olive-oil and a solution of caustic soda.—**Castilian**, kas-til'i-an, *a.* Pertaining to Castile in Spain.—*n.* An inhabitant or native of Castile; the language of Castile, the classic or literary language of Spain.

Castle, kas'l, *n.* [L. *castellum*, dim. of *castrum*, a fort.] A building, or series of connected buildings, fortified for defence against an enemy; a house with towers, often surrounded by a wall and moat, and having a donjon or keep in the centre; a fortified residence; a fortress; the house or mansion of a person of rank or wealth: somewhat vaguely applied, but usually to a large and more or less imposing building; a piece made in the form of a castle, used in the game of chess; the rook.—*Castle in the air*, a visionary project; a scheme that has no solid foundation.—*v.t.* or *i. Chess*, to move the king two squares to the right or left and bring up the castle to the square the king has passed over.—**Castled**, cas'ld, *a.* Furnished with a castle or castles.—**Castle-builder**, *n.* One who builds castles in the air; one who forms visionary schemes.—**Castle-building**, *n.* The act of building castles in the air.

Castner-Kellner process, *n.* An electrical method of manufacturing caustic soda.

Castor, kas'tėr, *n.* [L. *castor*; Gr. *kastōr*, a beaver.] A substance of a strong penetrating smell, secreted by special glands of the beaver, and used in medicine and perfumery; a beaver hat.—**Castor-oil**, *n.* [Probably from some resemblance to the substance *castor*.] The oil, used in medicine as a purgative, obtained from the seeds of the tropical Palma Christi tree.

Castrametation, kas'tra-mē-tā"shon, *n.* [L. *castrametor*, to encamp—*castra*, camp, and *metior*, to measure.] The art or act of encamping; the marking or laying out of a camp.

Castrate, kas'trāt, *v.t.*—*castrated*, *castrating.* [L. *castro*, *castratum*, to castrate.] To deprive of the testicles; to geld; to take the vigour or strength from; to emasculate; to remove something objectionable from, as obscene parts from a writing; to expurgate.—*n.* A man (as a eunuch) or male animal (as an ox) that has been castrated. —**Castration**, kas-trā'shon, *n.* The act of castrating.

Casual, kazh'ū-al, *a.* [L. *casualis*, from *casus*, a chance or accident, from *cado*, *casum*, to fall; akin *case*, *chance*, *accident*, &c.] Happening or coming to pass, without design in the person or persons affected, and without being foreseen or expected; accidental; fortuitous; coming by chance; not happening or coming regularly; occasional; incidental.—*n.* A person who receives relief and shelter for one night at the most in the workhouse of a parish or union to which he does not belong.—**Casualism**, kazh'ū-al-izm, *n.* The doctrine that all things happen by chance, or without an intelligent cause or design.—**Casualist**, kazh'ū-al-ist, *n.* A believer in casualism.—**Casually**, kazh'ū-al-li, *adv.* In a casual manner; accidentally; fortuitously.—**Casualness**, kazh'ū-al-nes, *n.* The fact of being casual.—**Casualty**, kazh'ū-al-ti, *n.* Chance, or what happens by chance; accident; contingency; an unfortunate chance or accident, especially one resulting in death or bodily injury; loss suffered by a body of men from death, wounds, &c.

Casuist, kaz'ū-ist, *n.* [Fr. *casuiste*, from L. *casus*, a case.] One versed in or using casuistry; one who studies and resolves cases of conscience, or nice points regarding conduct.—**Casuistic**, **Casuistical**, kaz-ū-is'tik, kaz-ū-is'tik-al, *a.* Pertaining to casuists or casuistry; partaking of casuistry.—**Casuistically**, kaz-ū-is'tik-al-li, *adv.* In a casuistic manner.—**Casuistry**, kaz'ū-ist-ri, *n.* The science, doctrine, or department of ethics dealing with cases of conscience; frequently used in a bad sense for quibbling in matters of morality, or making too nice moral distinctions.

Cat, kat, *n.* [A.Sax. *cat*, *catt*=D. and Dan. *kat*, Sw. *katt*, Icel. *köttr*, G. *katze*, *kater*, O.Fr. *cat*, Mod. Fr. *chat*, Ir. *cat*, W. *cath*, Rus. and Pol. *kot*, Tur. *kedi*, Ar. *qitt*—a cat; origin unknown.] A name applied to certain species of carnivorous quadrupeds of the feline tribe, many varieties of which have long been tamed and kept in houses for catching mice, &c., and are proverbial for their stealthiness and cunning; a strong tackle or combination of pulleys, to hook and draw an anchor perpendicularly up to the cat-head of a ship; a double tripod having six feet: so called because it always lands on its feet as a cat is proverbially said to do; an abbreviation of cat-o'-nine-tails (which see).—*To let the cat out of the bag*, to disclose a trick; to let out a secret.—**Catamount**, **Catamountain**, kat'a-mount, kat'a-moun-tān, *n.* The cat of the mountain; the wild cat; the North American puma or cougar.—**Cat-bird**, *n.* A North American singing-bird, a species of thrush which utters a cry of alarm like the mew of a cat.—**Catcall**, kat'kal, *n.* A sound like the cry of a cat, such as that made by a dissatisfied audience in a theatre; a small squeaking instrument for producing such a sound.—**Catgut**, kat'gut, *n.* The intestines of sheep (sometimes of the horse or the ass) dried and twisted into strings for the violin and for other purposes: so called from a notion that the material was the gut or intestines of the cat.—**Catkin**, kat'kin, *n.* The blossom of the willow, birch, hazel, &c., which resembles a kitten or cat's tail.—**Catling**, kat'ling, *n.* A kitten; a surgeon's dismembering knife.—**Catmint**, **Catnip**, kat'mint, kat'nip, *n.* A plant resembling mint, having a strong odour and taste, and which cats are said to be fond of.—**Cattish**, kat'ish, *a.* Like or pertaining to a cat; feline.—**Cat-head**, *n.* A strong beam projecting over a ship's bows, and furnished with a block and tackle to lift an anchor.—**Cat-o'-nine-tails**, *n.* An instrument consisting generally of nine pieces of knotted cord, used to flog offenders on the bare back.—**Cat's-eye**, *n.* A hard and semi-transparent variety of quartz, having an opalescent radiation or play of colours like a cat's eye.—**Cat-silver**, *n.* A variety of mica.—**Cat's-paw**, *n.* The instrument used by a person to accomplish his designs; a tool; a dupe: so called from the story of the monkey which, instead of using his own paw, used that of the cat to draw nuts from the fire.

Cat, kat, *n.* [Icel. *kati*, a kind of small ship.] A trading ship built on the Norwegian model with narrow stern, projecting quarters, and a deep waist.

Catacaustic, kat-a-kas'tik, *a.* [Gr. *katakausis*, a burning.] A term applied to a species of caustic curves formed by reflection of light.—*n.* A curve formed by the reflection of rays of light.

Catachresis, kat-a-krē'sis, *n.* [Gr. *katachrēsis*, abuse—*kata*, against, and *chraomai*, to use.] The wresting of a word from its true signification; the employment of a word under a false form through misapprehension in regard to its origin (*crayfish* for example).—**Catachrestic**, **Catachrestical**, kat-a-kres'tik, kat-a-kres'tik-al, *a.* Belonging to catachresis; wrested from its natural sense, use, or form.—**Catachrestically**, kat-a-kres'tik-al-li, *adv.* In a catachrestical manner.

Cataclysm, kat'a-klizm, *n.* [Gr. *kataklysmos*, a deluge, from *kataklyzō*, to inundate—*kata*, down, and *klyzō*, to wash.] A deluge. flood, or inundation sweeping over a territory.—**Cataclysmal**, **Cataclysmic**, kat-a-kliz'mal, kat-a-kliz'mik, *a.* Of or belonging to a cataclysm.

Catacomb, kat'a-kōm, *n.* [It. *catacomba*, L.L. *catacumba*, from Gr. *kata*, down, and *kumbe*, *kumbos*, a hollow or recess.] A cave or subterranean place for the burial of the dead, in which the bodies are deposited in recesses hollowed out of the sides of the cave, the most notable being those near Rome, supposed to be the cells and caves in which the primitive Christians concealed themselves, and in which were deposited the bodies of the martyrs.

Catacoustics, kat-a-kous'tiks, *n.* [Prefix *cata*, and *acoustics*.] That part of acoustics which treats of reflected sounds, or of the properties of echoes; cataphonics.

Catadioptric, **Catadioptrical**, kat'a-dī-op"trik, kat'a-dī-op"trik-al, *a.* [Prefix *cata*, and *dioptric*.] Pertaining to or involving both the refraction and reflection of light.

Catafalque, kat'a-falk, *n.* [Fr. *catafalque*, from It. *catafalco*, from *falco*, for O.H.G. *palcho* (G. *balke*), a beam, with *cata* (as in Sp. *catar*, to view) prefixed. *Scaffold* is the same word with French prefix *es*.] A temporary structure representing a tomb placed over the coffin of a distinguished person in churches or over the grave.

Catalan,‡ ka-tā'an, *n.* A native of Cathay or China; a foreigner generally; hence, an indiscriminate term of reproach. (*Shak.*)

Catalan, kat'a-lan, *a.* Pertaining to Catalonia, a province of Spain.—*n.* A native of Catalonia; the language of Catalonia; an old Spanish literary dialect early cultivated.

Catalectic, kat-a-lek'tik, *a.* [Gr. *katalēktikos*, from *katalēgo*, to leave off, to stop.] *Pros.* having the measure incomplete; ending abruptly, as a verse wanting a syllable of its proper length.

Catalepsy, **Catalepsis**, kat'a-lep-si, kat-a-lep'sis, *n.* [Gr. *katalēpsis*, a seizing, from *katalambanō*, to seize.] A nervous affection characterized by a more or less complete but temporary suspension of the senses and volition with rigidity of the muscles; trance; mental apprehension or perception.—**Cataleptic**, kat-a-lep'tik, *a.* Pertaining to catalepsy.

Catalogue, kat'a-log, *n.* [Fr. *catalogue*, from Gr. *katalogos*, a counting up—*kata*, thoroughly, and *logos*, a reckoning.] A list or enumeration of the names of men or things disposed in a certain order, often in alphabetical order; a list; a register.—*v.t.*—*catalogued*, *cataloguing.* To make a catalogue of.—*Catalogue raisonné*, a catalogue of books, paintings, &c., classed according to their subjects.

Catalysis, ka-tal'i-sis, *n.* [Gr. *kata*, down, and *lyō*, to loose.] Dissolution; destruction; *chem.* a decomposition and new combination produced by the mere presence of substances which do not of themselves enter into combination.—**Catalytic**, kat-a-lit'ik, *a.* Relating to catalysis.

Catamaran, kat'a-ma-ran', *n.* [Said to be from a Tamil word signifying 'tied logs'.] A kind of float or raft used as a substitute for a surf-boat, particularly in the East and West Indies, and consisting usually of three pieces of wood lashed together, the middle piece being longer than the others, and having one end turned up in the form of a bow.

Catamenia, kat-a-mē'ni-a, *n. pl.* [Gr. *katamēnios—kata*, down, and *mēn*, a month.] The menstrual discharge of females.—**Catamenial**, kat-a-mē'ni-al, *a.* Pertaining to the catamenia or menstrual discharges.

Catamite, kat'a-mīt, *n.* [L. *catamitus.*] Immoral minion, from *Ganymede*, cupbearer to Jupiter.

Catamount. Under CAT.

Catapetalous, kat-a-pet'al-us, *a.* [Gr. *kata*, against, and *petalon*, a petal.] *Bot.* having the petals held together by stamens which grow to their bases, as in the mallow.

Cataphonics, kat-a-fon'iks, *n.* [Gr. *kata*, against, and *phōnē*, sound.] The doctrine of reflected sounds; catacoustics.—**Cataphonic**, kat-a-fon'ik, *a.* Relating to cataphonics.

Cataphract, kat'a-frakt, *n.* [L. *cataphractes*, Gr. *kataphraktēs*, from *kataphrassō*, to cover.] Defensive armour formerly in use formed of cloth or leather strengthened with scales or links; the armour of plates or strong scales protecting some animals.—**Cataphracted**, kat'a-frak-ted, *a.* *Zool.* covered with horny or bony plates or scales closely joined together, or with a thick hardened skin. — **Cataphractic**, kat-a-frak'tik, *a.* Pertaining to a cataphract; resembling a cataphract.

Cataplasm, kat'a-plazm, *n.* [Gr. *kataplasma*, from *kataplassō*, to anoint or to spread as a plaster.] *Med.* a soft and moist substance to be applied to some part of the body; a poultice.

Catapult, kat'a-pult, *n.* [L. *catapulta*, from Gr. *katapeltēs* — *kata*, against, and *pallō*, to brandish, hurl.] A military engine anciently used for discharging missiles against a besieged place; originally an engine of the nature of a powerful bow: a toy from which small missiles are thrown by the elastic force of india-rubber.

Cataract, kat'a-rakt, *n.* [L. *cataracta*, Gr. *katarraktēs*, from *kata*, down, and *rhēgnymi*, to break.] A great fall of water over a precipice; a waterfall; any furious rush or downpour of water; a disease of the eye consisting in an opacity of the crystalline lens or its capsule, by which the pupil seems closed by an opaque body, usually whitish, vision being thus impaired or destroyed.—**Cataractous**, kat-a-rak'tus, *a.* Partaking of the nature of a cataract in the eye.

Catarrh, ka-tär', *n.* [From Gr. *katarrheō*, to flow down.] A discharge or increased secretion of mucus from the membranes of the nose, fauces, and bronchia, characteristic of the ailment commonly called a *cold* in the head.—**Catarrhal**, **Catarrhous**, ka-tär'ral, ka-tär'rus, *a.* Pertaining to catarrh, produced by it, or attending it (a *catarrhal* fever).

Catarrhine, **Catarhine**, kat'a-rīn, *a.* [Gr. *kata*, down, and *rhis, rhinos*, the nose.] Of or pertaining to the section of monkeys characterized by having the nostrils approximated, and the aperture pointing downward, as in the gorilla, chimpanzee, and other Old World apes.

Catastrophe, ka-tas'trō-fe, *n.* [Gr. *katastrophē*, an overthrowing, a sudden turn, from *katastrephō*, to subvert—*kata*, down, and *strephō*, to turn.] The unfolding and winding up of the plot, clearing up of difficulties, and closing of a dramatic piece; the dénouement; a notable event terminating a series; a finishing stroke or wind-up; an unfortunate conclusion; a calamity or disaster; a supposed change in the crust of the earth from sudden physical violence, causing elevation or subsidence of the solid parts; a cataclysm.—**Catastrophic**, kat-as-trof'ik, *a.* Pertaining to a catastrophe or catastrophes; pertaining to the theory of great changes on the globe being due to violent and sudden physical action.—**Catastrophism**, ka-tas'trō-fizm, *n.* The theory that all geological changes are due to catastrophes or sudden violent physical causes. — **Catastrophist**, ka-tas'trō-fist, *n.* One who believes in catastrophism.

Catawba, ka-ta'ba, *n.* A variety of grape much cultivated in Ohio, United States, discovered on the *Catawba* river, Carolina; the wine made from the grape.

Catch, kach, *v.t.* pret. & pp. *caught* (*catched* is obsolete or vulgar). [O.E. *cacche*, O.Fr. *cachier, chacier*, &c., to hunt (Mod. Fr. *chasser*), from L.L. *captiare*, from L. *captare*, from *capere*, to take (whence *capable*, *captious*, &c.). *Chase* is the same word.] To lay sudden hold on; to seize, especially with the hand; to grasp; to snatch; to perceive or apprehend; to seize, as in a snare or trap; to ensnare; to entangle; to get entangled with, or to come into contact or collision with (the branch *caught* his hat); to get; to receive (to *catch* the sunlight; especially, to take or receive as by sympathy, contagion, or infection; to take hold of; to communicate to; to fasten on (the flames *caught* the woodwork); to seize the affections of; to engage and attach; to charm; to captivate.—*To catch it*, to get a scolding, a beating, or other unpleasant treatment. (Colloq.)—*To catch hold of*, to take or lay hold of.—*To catch up*, to snatch; to take up suddenly; to lay hold suddenly of something said.—*v.i.* To take or receive something; to be entangled or impeded; to spread by or as by infection; to be eager to get, use, or adopt: with *at*.—*n.* The act of seizing; seizure; anything that seizes or takes hold, that checks motion or the like, as a hook, a ratchet, a pawl, a spring bolt for a door or lid, &c.; a choking or stoppage of the breath; something caught or to be caught, especially anything valuable or desirable obtained or to be obtained; a gain or advantage; one desirable from wealth as a husband or wife (*colloq.*); *mus.* a kind of canon or round for three or four voices, the words written to which are so contrived that by the union of the voices a different meaning is given by the singers *catching* at each other's words.—**Catchable**, kach'a-bl, *a.* Capable of being caught.—**Catcher**, kach'ėr, *n.* One who or that which catches. —**Catching**, kach'ing, *a.* Communicating, or liable to be communicated, by contagion; infectious; captivating; charming; attracting.—**Catchment**, kach'ment, *n.* A surface of ground of which the drainage is capable of being directed into a common reservoir.—**Catch-penny**, *n.* Something of little value got up to hit the popular taste, and thereby catch the popular penny; anything got up merely to sell.—**Catchpoll**, *n.* [Med. L. *cacepollus*, Fr. *chacepol.*] A *chaser* of *fowls*. (L. *pullus.*) A sheriff's officer, bailiff, constable, or other person whose duty is to arrest persons.—**Catchword**, *n.* The word formerly often, now rarely placed at the bottom of each page, on the right hand under the last line, and forming the first word on the following page; in a play the last word of one actor to be caught up by another as a reminder that he is to speak next; cue; a word caught up and repeated for effect.—**Catchy**, *a.* Attractive, infectious, easily picked up, of tunes and songs.

Catchup, kach'up, *n.* Same as *Ketchup.*

Cate, kāt, *n.* [O.E. *acates*, provisions purchased, from O.Fr. *acat*, buying. CATER.] Food, more particularly rich, luxuriant, or dainty food; a delicacy; a dainty: commonly used in the plural.

Catechetic, **Catechetical**, kat-ē-ket'ik, kat-ē-ket'ik-al, *a.* [CATECHISE.] Relating to catechising, or one who catechises; consisting in asking questions and receiving answers, as in teaching pupils. — **Catechetically**, kat-ē-ket'ik-al-li, *adv.* In a catechetical manner.—**Catechetics**, kat-ē-ket'iks, *n.* The art or practice of teaching by question and answer.

Catechise, **Catechize**, kat'ē-kīz, *v.t.*—*catechised, catechized, catechising, catechizing.* [Gr. *katēchisō*, to catechize, from *katēcheō*, to utter sound, to teach by the voice — *kata*, down, and *ēcheō*, to sound, whence *echo.*] To instruct by asking questions, receiving answers, and offering explanations and corrections; to question; to interrogate; to examine or try by questions, especially such questions as would implicate the answerer.—**Catechiser**, **Catechizer**, kat'ē-kīz-ėr, *n.* One who catechises.—**Catechism**, kat'ē-kizm, *n.* [Gr. *katēchismos*, instruction.] A book containing a summary of principles in any science or art, but especially in religion, reduced to the form of questions and answers. — **Catechismal**, kat'ē-kiz-mal, *a.* Pertaining to or after the manner of a catechism.—**Catechist**, kat'ē-kist, *n.* One who instructs by question and answer; a catechiser. —**Catechistic**, **Catechistical**, kat-ē-kist'ik, kat-ē-kist'ik-al, *a.* Pertaining to a catechist or catechism.—**Catechistically**, kat-ē-kist'ik-al-li, *adv.* In a catechistical manner.

Catechu, kat'ē-shū, *n.* [Tamil *katti*, tree, and *shu*, juice.] A name common to several astringent extracts prepared from the wood, bark, and fruits of various plants, especially from some species of acacia, and used in dyeing, tanning, and medicine. — **Catechuic**, kat-ē-shū'ik, *a.* Of or pertaining to catechu.

Catechumen, kat-ē-kū'men, *n.* [Gr. *katēchoumenos*, instructed. CATECHISE.] One who is under instruction in the first rudiments of Christianity; a neophyte.—**Catechumenical**, kat'ē-kū-men"ik-al, *a.* Belonging to catechumens.

Category, kat'ē-gor-i, *n.* [Gr. *katēgoria*, a class or category, from *katēgoreō*, to accuse, show, demonstrate—*kata*, down, &c., and *agoreō*, to speak in an assembly, from *agora*, a forum or market.] One of the highest classes to which objects of thought can be referred; one of the most general heads under which everything that can be asserted of any subject may be arranged; in a popular sense, any class or order in which certain things are embraced.—**Categorematic**, kat'ē-gor'ē-mat"ik, *a.* [Gr. *katēgorēma*, a predicate.] *Logic*, conveying a whole term, *i.e.* either the subject or predicate of a proposition, in a single word.—*n.* A word which is capable of being employed by itself as a term.—**Categorematically**, kat'ē-gor'ē-mat"ik-al-li, *adv.* In a categorematic manner.—**Categorical**, kat-ē-gor'ik-al, *a.* Pertaining to a category; absolute; positive; express; not relative or hypothetical (statement, answer). — **Categorically**, kat-ē-gor'ik-al-li, *adv.* In a categorical manner; absolutely; directly; expressly; positively.—**Categoricalness**, kat-ē-gor'ik-al-nes, *n.*

Catelectrode, kat-ē-lek'trōd, *n.* [Prefix *kata*, down, and *electrode.*] The negative electrode or pole of a voltaic battery, the positive electrode being the *anelectrode.*

Catenary, **Catenarian**, ka-tē'na-ri or kat'ē-na-ri, kat-ē-nā'ri-an, *a.* [L. *catenarius*, from *catena*, a chain.] Relating to a chain; like a chain.—*Catenary curve*, that variety of curve which is formed by a rope or chain, of uniform density and thickness, when allowed to hang freely with its ends attached to two fixed points.—**Catenate**,‡ kat'ē-nāt, *v.t.* To connect in a series of links or ties; to concatenate.—**Catenation**,‡ kat-ē-nā'shon, *n.* Connection of links; union of parts, as in a chain; regular connection; concatenation.

Cater, kā'tėr, *v.i.* [From obs. *cater*, a caterer, O.Fr. *acateur, acator*, from *acater*, L.L. *accaptare*, to buy, from L. *ad*, to, and L. *captare*, intens. of *capere*, to take.] To buy or provide something for use, enjoyment, or entertainment; to purvey food, provisions, amusement, &c.: followed by *for*. — **Caterer**, kā'tėr-ėr, *n.* One who caters; a provider or purveyor of provisions; one who provides for any want or desire.—**Cateress**, kā'tėr-es, *n.* A woman who caters; a female provider. (*Mil.*)

Cateran, kat'ėr-an, *n.* [Gael. and Ir. *ceatharnach*, a soldier.] A kern; a Highland or Irish irregular soldier; a Highland freebooter.

Cater-cousin,† kā′tėr-kuz-n, *n.* [*Cater* = Fr. *quatre*, four.] A distant cousin; a remote relation. (*Shak.*)

Caterpillar, kat′ėr-pil-lėr, *n.* [O.E. *catyrpel* (comp. *caterwaul*); from *cat*, and *pill*, from rolling themselves up in a ball.] Properly, the hairy, worm-like larva or grub of the lepidopterous insects (butterflies and moths), but also sometimes applied to the larvæ of other insects.

Caterwaul, kat′ėr-wal, *v.i.* [From *cat*, and *waul*, in imitation of the sound made by a cat; O.E. *caterwawe*.] To utter noisy and disagreeable cries: said of cats; to make a disagreeable howling or screeching.

Catharist, kath′a-rist, *n.* [Gr. *katharos*, pure.] One who pretends to more purity than others possess; a puritan: a term applied to various ancient religious sects or bodies.

Cathartic, ka-thär′tik, *a.* [Gr. *kathartikos*, from *kathairō*, to purge, *katharos*, clean.] Purgative; cleansing the bowels.—*n.* A medicine that cleanses the stomach and bowels by purging; a purge; a purgative.—**Cathartine,** ka-thär′tin, *n.* The active principle of cathartics, such as senna, rhubarb, &c.

Cathedra, ka-thed′ra, *n.* [L. *cathedra*, a teacher's or professor's chair, a bishop's chair, Gr. *kathedra*, a chair or seat—*kata*, down, and *hedra*, a seat.] The throne or seat of a bishop in the cathedral or episcopal church of his diocese.—**Cathedral,** ka-thē′dral, *n.* The principal church in a diocese, that which is specially the church of the bishop: so called from possessing the episcopal chair called *cathedra*.—*a.* Pertaining to the bishop's or head church of a diocese (a *cathedral* church).

Catherine-wheel, kath′ėr-in-whēl, *n.* [*St. Catherine* was tortured by toothed wheels.] A wheel-shaped firework which rotates as the fire issues from the aperture; *arch.* a circular window, or compartment of a window, with radiating divisions or spokes.

Catheter, kath′e-tėr, *n.* [Gr. *kathetēr*, from *kathiēmi*, to thrust in—*kata*, down, and *hiēmi*, to send.] In *surg.* a tubular instrument, usually made of silver, to be introduced through the urethra into the bladder to draw off the urine when the natural discharge is arrested.—**Catheterize,** kath′e-tėr-īz, *v.t.* To operate on with a catheter.

Cathode, kath′ōd, *n.* [Gr. *kata*, down, and *hodos*, a way.] The negative pole of an electric current, or that by which the current leaves: opposed to *anode*.

Catholic, kath′o-lik, *a.* [Gr. *katholikos*—*kata*, down, throughout, and *holos*, the whole; L. *catholicus*, Fr. *catholique*.] Universal or general; embracing all true Christians (the *catholic* church or faith); not narrow-minded, partial, or bigoted; free from prejudice; liberal (*catholic* tastes or sympathies); pertaining to or affecting the Roman Catholics.—*Catholic epistles*, the epistles of the apostles which are addressed to all the faithful, and not to a particular church; the epistles general.—*Catholic king*, King of Spain, opposed to the *Most Christian* of France, *Most Apostolic* of Hungary.—*n.* A member of the universal Christian church; often restricted to members of the Church of Rome.—**Catholicism,** ka-thol′i-sizm, *n.* The state of being catholic or universal; catholicity; adherence to the Roman Catholic Church; the Roman Catholic faith.—**Catholicity,** kath-o-lis′i-ti, *n.* The state or quality of being catholic or universal; catholic character or position; universality; the quality of being catholic or liberal-minded.—**Catholicize,** ka-thol′i-sīz, *v.i.* To become a Catholic.—**Catholicly,** kath′o-lik-li, *adv.* In a catholic manner; universally; generally.—**Catholicon,**† ka-thol′i-kon, *n.* [Gr. *katholikon iama*, universal remedy.] A remedy for all diseases; a panacea.

Cation, kat′i-on, *n.* [Gr. *kata*, down, and *ion*, going.] The element or elements of an electrolyte which in electro-chemical decompositions appear at the negative pole or cathode.

Catkin, *n.* Under **Cat.**

Catonian, ka-tō′ni-an, *a.* Pertaining to or resembling either of the Romans, *Cato* the censor or *Cato* Uticensis, both remarkable for severity of manners; hence, grave; severe; inflexible.

Catoptric, ka-top′trik, *a.* [Gr. *katoptrikos*, from *katoptron*, a mirror—*kata*, against, and *optomai*, to see.] Pertaining to incident and reflected light; pertaining to catoptrics.—**Catoptrics,** ka-top′triks, *n.* That branch of optics which explains the properties of incident and reflected light, and particularly that which is reflected from mirrors or polished bodies.

Catsup, *n.* **Ketchup.**

Cattle, kat′l, *n. pl.* [O.E. *catel*, goods, cattle, from O.Fr. *catel*, *chatel*, property in general, from L.L. *capitale*, *captale*, property, capital, from L. *capitalis*, chief, capital, from *caput*, the head. *Cattle*=*chattel*, *capital*.] A term applied collectively to domestic quadrupeds, such as serve for tillage or other labour, or for food to man, including camels, horses, asses, cows, sheep, goats, and perhaps swine, but now chiefly restricted to domestic beasts of the cow kind.—**Cattle-pen,** *n.* A pen or inclosure for cattle.—**Cattle-plague,** *n.* A virulently contagious disease affecting cattle; rinderpest.—**Cattle-show,** *n.* An exhibition of domestic animals for prizes with a view to the encouragement of agriculture.

Catty, kat′i, *n.* A Chinese weight of 1⅓ lbs.

Caucasian, ka-kā′zi-an or ka-kā′zhi-an, *a.* Pertaining to Mount *Caucasus* in Asia; specifically, a term appellative of one of the races into which the human family has been divided.—*n.* An ethnological term applied to the highest type of the human family, including nearly all Europeans, the Circassians, Armenians, Persians, Indians, Jews, &c., being invented by Blumenbach, who regarded a skull he had got from Caucasus as representing the standard of perfection.

Caucus, ka′kus, *n.* [Originally American: a term of doubtful origin.] A private meeting of citizens to agree upon candidates to be proposed for election to offices, or to concert measures for supporting a party.

Caudal, ka′dal, *a.* [L. *cauda*, a tail.] Pertaining to a tail; of the nature of a tail; having the appearance of a tail.—**Caudate, Caudated,** ka′dāt, ka′dāt-ed, *a.* Having a tail: a term applied in *bot.* to seeds which have a tail-like appendage.—**Caudicle,** ka′di-kl, *n.* In *bot.* the process supporting the pollen masses of orchideous plants.

Caudex, ka′deks, *n.* L. pl. **Caudices,** ka′di-sēz, E. pl. **Caudexes,** ka′deks-ez. [L.] In *bot.* the stem of a tree; specially the scaly trunk of palms and tree-ferns.

Caudle, ka′dl, *n.* [O.Fr. *caudel*, *chaudel*, a dim. form from L.L. *calidum*, *caldum*, a kind of hot drink, from L. *calidus*, warm.] A kind of warm drink made of spiced and sugared wine or ale, given to sick persons, women in childbed, or the like.—*v.t.* To make into caudle; to refresh or make warm, as with caudle (*Shak.*).—**Caudle-cup,** *n.* A vessel or cup for holding caudle.

Cauf, kaf, *n.* [Perhaps for *corf*, or akin to *coffer*; comp. also W. *caf*, a hollow, a cave.] A chest with holes for keeping fish alive in water; a vessel of sheet-iron employed to raise coal from the bottom of a shaft; a corb or corf.

Caught, kat, pret. & pp. of *catch*.

Cauk, kak, *n.* [Akin *chalk*.] A kind of nodular siliceous ironstone, also sulphate of baryta or heavy-spar.

Cauker, ka′kėr, *n.* A calker or projecting piece of iron on a horse's shoe.

Caul, kal, *n.* [From O.Fr. *cale*, a kind of little cap; from the Celtic; comp. Ir. *calla*, Gael. *call*, a veil, a hood.] A kind of head-covering worn by females; a net inclosing the hair; the hinder part of a cap; a membrane investing some part of the viscera (O.T.); a portion of the amnion or membrane enveloping the fetus, sometimes encompassing the head of a child when born, and superstitiously supposed to be a preservative against drowning.

Cauldron, kal′dron. Same as *Caldron*.

Caulescent, ka-les′ent, *a.* [L. *caulis*, a stalk.] *Bot.* having a caulis or obvious stem rising above the ground.—**Caulicle,** ka′li-kl, *n.* [L. *cauliculus*.] *Bot.* a little or rudimentary stem.—**Caulicule, Cauliculus,** ka′li-kūl, ka-lik′ū-lus, *n. Arch.* the little twists or volutes under the flower on the abacus in the Corinthian capital; *bot.* same as *Caulicle*.—**Cauliferous,** ka-lif′ėr-us, *a. Bot.* same as *Caulescent*.—**Cauliform,** ka-li-form, *a. Bot.* having the form of a caulis.—**Cauline,** ka′līn, *a. Bot.* of or belonging to a stem (*cauline* leaves).—**Caulis,** ka′lis, *n. Bot.* the stem of a plant rising above the ground.

Cauliflower, ka′li-flou-ėr, *n.* [Lit. cabbage-flower, from its appearance, from L. *caulis*, colewort, cabbage, and E. *flower*; comp. Fr. *choufleur* (*chou*, cabbage, *fleur*, flower), cauliflower.] A garden variety of cabbage, the inflorescence of which is condensed while young into a depressed fleshy head, which is highly esteemed as a table vegetable.

Caulk, kak, *v.t.* [O.E. *cauke*, O.Fr. *cauquer*, to tread, from L. *calcare*, to tread, to tread on, from *calx*, *calcis*, a heel.] To drive oakum into the seams of (a ship or other vessel), to prevent leaking, the seams being then smeared with melted pitch.—**Caulker,** ka′kėr, *n.* One who caulks.—**Caulking-iron,** *n.* A chisel used for caulking or driving oakum into the seams of ships or other vessels.

Caulome, kal′ōm, *n.* [L. *caulis*, a stalk.] The stem of a plant.

Cause, kaz, *n.* [Fr. *cause*, L. *causa*, a cause.] That which produces an effect; that which brings about a change; that from which anything proceeds, and without which it would not exist; the reason or motive that urges, moves, or impels the mind to act or decide; a suit or action in court; any legal process which a party institutes to obtain his demand, or by which he seeks his right; any subject of question or debate; case; interest; matter; affair; that object or side of a question to which the efforts of a person or party are directed.—*v.t.*—*caused*, *causing*. To be the cause of; to effect by agency; to bring about; to be the occasion of; to produce.—**Causable,** ka′za-bl, *a.* Capable of being caused, produced, or effected.—**Causal,** ka′zal, *a.* [L. *causalis*.] Relating to a cause or causes; implying, containing, or expressing a cause or causes.—*n.* A verb signifying to make to do something; as *fell*, to make to fall.—**Causality,** ka-zal′i-ti, *n.* The state of being causal; the fact of acting as a cause; the action or power of a cause, in producing its effect; the doctrine or principle that every change implies the operation of a cause.—**Causally,** ka′zal-li, *adv.* In a causal manner; by tracing effects to causes; by acting as a cause.—**Causation,** ka-zā′shon, *n.* The act of causing or producing; the doctrine as to the connection of causes and effects.—**Causationism,** ka-zā′shon-izm, *n.* The doctrine that every event or phenomenon is the result of some previous event or phenomenon, without which it could not have taken place.—**Causationist,** ka-zā′shon-ist, *n.* A believer in causationism.—**Causative,** ka′za-tiv, *a.* Effective as a cause or agent: often followed by *of*; *gram.* expressing a cause or reason; causal.—*n.* A word expressing a cause.—**Causatively,** ka′za-tiv-li, *adv.* In a causative manner.—**Causeless,** kaz′les, *a.* Having no cause or producing agent; self-originated; uncreated; without just ground, reason, or motive.—**Causelessly,** kaz′les-li, *adv.* In a causeless manner; without cause or reason.—**Causer,** kaz′ėr, *n.* One who or that which causes.

Causerie, kōz-rē, *n.* [Fr.] Newspaper light talk; literary conversation; an informal lecture.

Causeway, kąz'wā, *n.* [Original spelling *causey*, from O.Fr. *cauoie* (Mod.Fr. *chaussée*), from L.L. *calciata* (*via*, understood), a road in making which lime or mortar is used, from L. *calx*, *calcis*, lime (whence *chalk*, *calcareous*).] A road or path raised above the natural level of the ground by stones, earth, timber, &c., serving as a passage over wet or marshy ground or the like; a raised and paved roadway.—*v.t.* To provide with a causeway; to pave, as a road or street, with blocks of stone.—**Causey**, ką'zi, *v.* and *n.* Causeway: a less common but more correct spelling.

Caustic, kąs'tik, *a.* [Gr. *kaustikos*, from *kaiō*, *kausō*, to burn.] Capable of burning, corroding, or destroying the texture of animal substances; *fig.* severe; cutting; stinging; pungent; sarcastic.—*n. Med.* any substance which burns, corrodes, or disintegrates the textures of animal structures; an escharotic; sometimes popularly restricted to lunar caustic or nitrate of silver when cast into sticks for surgeons' use; *math* the name given to the curve to which the rays of light reflected or refracted by another curve are tangents.—**Caustically**, kąs'ti-kal-li, *adv.* In a caustic or severe manner.—**Causticity**, kąs-tis'i-ti, *n.* The quality of being caustic or corrosive; *fig.* severity of language; pungency; sarcasm.—**Causticness**, kąs'tik-nes, *n.* Causticity.

Cautel,‡ ką'tel, *n.* [L. *cautela*, from *caveo*, to take care.] Caution; prudence; craftiness; cunning. (*Shak.*)—**Cautelous**,‡ ką'tel-us, *a.* [Fr. *cauteleux*.] Cautious; wary; provident; cunning; treacherous; wily.

Cauterize, ką'tér-īz, *v.t.*—*cauterised*, *cauterizing*. [L.L. *cauterizo*, from Gr. *kautēriazō*, from *kautērion*, *kautēr*, a burning or branding iron, from *kaiō*, to burn.] To burn or sear with fire or a hot iron or with caustics, as morbid flesh.—**Cauterant**, ką'tér-ant, *n.* A cauterizing substance.—**Cauterization**, ką'tér-īz-ā"shon, *n. Surg.* the act or the effect of cauterizing.—**Cautery**, ką'tér-i, *n.* [L. *cauterium*, Gr. *kautērion*.] A burning or searing, as of morbid flesh, by a hot iron or by caustic substances; the instrument or drug employed in cauterizing.

Caution, ką'shon, *n.* [L. *cautio*, from *caveo*, *cautum*, to be on one's guard, beware.] Provident care; prudence in regard to danger; wariness; watchfulness, forethought, or vigilance; a measure taken for security; a security or guarantee‡; a warning or admonition.—*v.t.* To give notice of danger to; to warn; to exhort to take heed.—**Cautionary**, ką'shon-ar-i, *a.* Containing caution, or warning to avoid danger; given as a pledge or in security.—**Cautioner**, ką'shon-ér, *n.* One who cautions.—**Cautious**, ką'shus, *a.* Possessing or exhibiting caution; attentive to examine probable effects and consequences of actions with a view to avoid danger or misfortune; prudent; circumspect, wary, watchful; vigilant; careful.—**Cautiously**, ką'shus-li, *adv.* In a cautious manner.—**Cautiousness**, ką'shus-nes, *n.* The quality of being cautious; caution.

Caval veins, kā'val, *n.* [L., hollow.] In air-breathing vertebrates, the large veins returning impure blood to the heart.

Cavalcade, kav'al-kād, *n.* [Fr. *cavalcade*, It. *cavalcata*, from L. *caballus*, a horse. CAVALIER, CAVALRY.] A procession of persons on horseback, or consisting mostly of persons on horseback.

Cavalier, kav-a-lēr', *n.* [Fr. *cavalier*, L.L. *caballarius*, from L. *caballus*, a horse, whence also *cavalry*, *chivalry*, *cavalcade*, &c. *Chevalier* is a parallel form.] A horseman, especially an armed horseman; a knight; a partisan of Charles I, as opposed to a Roundhead or adherent to the Parliament; a gentleman attending on or escorting a lady; a beau; the gentleman acting as partner to a lady in dancing; *fort.* a work commonly situated within the bastion, and raised higher than the other works so as to command all the adjacent works and the surrounding country.—*a.* Gay; sprightly; easy; off-hand; haughty; disdainful; supercilious (a *cavalier* answer).—**Cavalierly**, kav-a-lēr'li, *adv.* In a cavalier manner; haughtily; arrogantly; disdainfully.—**Cavalierness**, kav-a-lēr'nes, *n.*—**Cavalry**, kav'al-ri, *n.* [Fr. *cavalerie*, from It. *cavalleria*, from *cavallo*, L. *caballus*, a horse. *Chivalry* is a parallel form.] A body of troops, or soldiers, that serve on horseback; horse soldiers.

Cavass, Cawass, ka-vas', ka-was', *n.* A Turkish police-officer; a messenger; an orderly.

Cavatina, kav-a-tē'na, *n.* [It.] *Music*, a melody of short simple character, and without a second part and a return part.

Cave, kāv, *n.* [Fr. *cave*, from L. *cavus*, hollow, whence also *cavity*, *cavern*, and *cage*.] A hollow place in the earth; a subterranean cavern; a den.—**Cave**, *n.* A political party-desertion; seceders; applied by John Bright in 1866 to deserters, with reference to the Cave of Adullam, 1 *Sam.* xxii. 1-2.—*v.t.* To make hollow.—*v.i.*† To dwell in a cave.—*To cave in*, to fall in and leave a hollow, as earth on the side of a well or pit or the roof of a subterranean passage.—**Cave-dweller, Cave-man**, *n.* One who dwells in caves, a name given to such of the earliest races of prehistoric man as dwelt in natural caves, subsisting on shell-fish and wild animals.

Caveat, kā'vē-at, *n.* [L. *caveat*, let him beware, from *caveo*, to beware.] In *law*, a process in a court to stop proceedings; hence, an intimation of caution; hint; warning; admonition.—*v.i.* To enter a caveat.—**Caveat emptor**. [L., let the buyer beware.] At the buyer's risk.—**Caveator**, kā'vē-āt-ér, *n.* One who enters a caveat.

Cavendish, kav'en-dish, *n.* Tobacco which has been softened and pressed into quadrangular cakes; the authority on Whist.

Cavern, kav'érn, *n.* [L. *caverna*, from *cavus*, hollow. CAVE.] A deep hollow place in the earth; a cave.—**Caverned**, kav'érnd, *a.* Full of caverns or deep chasms; having caverns; inhabiting a cavern.—**Cavernous**, kav'érn-us, *a.* [L. *cavernosus*.] Hollow, or containing a cavern or caverns; filled with small cavities.—**Cavernulous**, ka-vér'nū-lus, *a.* [L. *cavernula*, dim. of *caverna*, a cavern.] Full of little cavities (*cavernulous* metal).

Cavetto, ka-vet'tō, *n.* [It., from *cavo*, hollow, L. *cavus*.] *Arch.* a hollow member, or round concave moulding, containing the quadrant of a circle.

Cavezon, kav'e-zon, *n.* [Fr. *caveçon*, from It. *cavezzone*, from *cavezza*, a halter, from L. *caput*, head.] A kind of nose-band used in breaking horses.

Caviar, Caviare, kav-i-är' or kav-ē-är', *n.* [Fr. *caviar*, Turk. *haviār*.] The roes of certain large fish, as the sturgeon, prepared and salted, and chiefly caught in the lakes or rivers of Russia.—*Caviar to the general*, a delicacy beyond the reach of most; a reasoning beyond the popular grasp.

Cavicorn, kav'i-korn, *a.* [L. *cavus*, hollow, and *cornu*, a horn.] Applied to a family of ruminants, as the ox, antelope, and goat, with persistent horns (thus differing from the deer), consisting of a bony core and a horny sheath, in both sexes or in males only.—*n.* One of the above animals.

Cavil, kav'il, *v.i.*—*cavilled*, *cavilling*. [O.Fr. *caviller*, from L. *cavillor*, to cavil, *cavilla*, a quibble, trick, shuffle.] To raise captious and frivolous objections; to find fault without good reason: frequently followed by *at*.—*n.* A captious or frivolous objection; captious or specious argument.—**Caviller**, kav'il-ér, *n.* One who cavils; one who is apt to raise captious objections; a captious disputant.—**Cavilling**, kav'il-ing, *a.* Given to cavil or make captious objections.—**Cavillingly**, kav'il-ing-li, *adv.* In a cavilling manner.—**Cavillous**,† kav'il-us, *a.* Cavilling.

Cavil, kav'il, *n.* A stone-mason's axe, with a flat face and a pointed peen.

Cavity, kav'i-ti, *n.* [Fr. *cavité*, L. *cavitas*, from L. *cavus*, hollow. CAVE.] A hollow place; a hollow; a void or empty space in a body; an opening; a hollow part of the human body.—**Cavitied**, kav'i-tid, *a.* Having cavities.

Cavo-relievo, kä'vō-rē-lē-ā'vō, *n.* [It.] *Sculp.* a kind of relief in which the highest surface is only level with the plane of the original stone.

Cavy, kā'vi, *n.* The name common to certain South American rodent animals, the most familiar species being the well-known guinea-pig.

Caw, ką, *v.i.* [Imitative of the sound; comp. Sc. *kae*, D. *kaauw*, Dan. *kaa*, a jackdaw.] To cry like a crow, rook, or raven.—*n.* The cry of the rook or crow.

Cawquaw, ką'kwą, *n.* The urson or Canadian porcupine, whose spines are often used as ornaments by the Indians.

Cay, kā, *n.* [Sp. *cayo*, a rock, a shoal, an islet.] An islet; a range or reef of rocks lying near the surface of the water: used especially in the West Indies and sometimes written *Key*.

Cayenne, kī-en' or kā-en', *n.* [From *Cayenne* in South America.] A kind of pepper, a powder made from the dried and ground fruits, and more especially the seeds, of various species of Capsicum.

Cayman, Caiman, kā'man, *n.* [Native Guiana name.] A name applied popularly to the alligator of the West Indies and South America.

Cayuse, kī-ūs', *n.* A small horse; an Indian pony; a bronco.

Cazique, ka-zēk', *n.* The native name of the princes or head chiefs of Hayti, Cuba, Peru, Mexico, and other regions of America, who were found reigning there when these countries were discovered.

Cease, sēs, *v.i.*—*ceased*, *ceasing*. [Fr. *cesser*, L. *cesso*, *cessare*, to cease, a freq. from *cedere*, to yield, to *cede*. CEDE] To stop moving, acting, or speaking; to leave off; to give over; to desist: followed by *from* before a noun; to come to an end; to terminate; to become extinct; to pass away (the storm *ceases*).—*v.t.* To put a stop to; to put an end to; to desist from.—**Ceaseless**, sēs'les, *a.* Without a stop or pause; incessant; continual; without intermission; enduring for ever; endless.—**Ceaselessly**, sēs'les-li, *adv.* Incessantly; perpetually.—**Ceaselessness**, sēs'les-nes, *n.*

Cebadilla, seb-a-dil'la, *n.* The Spanish American name for the seeds of a bulbous plant used in medicine.

Cebyura, seb-i-ū'ra, *n.* A Brazilian tree, the bark of which is used in decoctions for baths and fomentations in rheumatism and cutaneous diseases.

Cedar, sē'dér, *n.* [L. *cedrus*, Gr. *kedros*, a kind of juniper.] A coniferous evergreen tree which grows to a great size, and is remarkable for its durability, forming fine woods on the mountains of Syria and Asia Minor, and often called distinctively the cedar of Lebanon. The deodar cedar is closely akin to it, and the name is also given to various other trees.—*a.* Made of cedar; belonging to cedar.—**Cedared**, sē'dérd, *a.* Covered or furnished with cedars.—**Cedarn**, sē'dérn, *a.* Pertaining to the cedar; made of cedar. (*Tenn.*)—**Cedrine**, sēd'rin, *a.* Of or pertaining to cedar.

Cede, sēd, *v.t.*—*ceded*, *ceding*. [L. *cedo*, *cessum*, to retire, yield, grant, give up, a word which appears also in *accede*, *concede*, *exceed*, *precede*, *recede*, *decease*, *abscess*, *antecedent*, *ancestor*, *predecessor*, *cease*, &c.] To yield; to surrender; to give up; to resign; to relinquish.—*v.i.* To yield; to submit; to pass over; to be transferred; to fall to; to lapse.—**Cedent**†, sēd'ent, *a.* Yielding; giving way.

Cedilla, sē-dil'la, *n.* [Fr. *cédille*, It. *zediglia*, a dim. of *zeta*, the name of *z* in Greek; because formerly, in order to give *c* the sound of *s*, it was customary to write *cz*: thus *leczon*, for modern *leçon*.] A mark placed under the letter *c*, especially in French (thus *ç*), to show that it is to be sounded like *s*.

Cedrate, Cedrat, sē′drāt, sē′drat, *n.* [Fr. *cédrat.*] A variety of the citron-tree; also, the fruit of the tree.

Ceil, sēl, *v.t.* [O.E. *seile*, a canopy, from Fr. *ciel*, It. *cielo*, a canopy, heaven, from L. *cœlum*, heaven, same root as Gr. *koilos*, hollow, and E. *hollow*.] To overlay or cover the inner roof of a room or building; to provide with a ceiling.—**Ceiling**, sēl′ing, *n.* The inside lining or surface of an apartment above; the horizontal or curved surface of an apartment opposite the floor, usually finished with plastered work; maximum height to which an aeroplane can climb.

Celadon, sel′a-don, *n.* [French romance.] A soft, pale, sea-green color.

Celandine, sel′an-dīn, *n.* [O. Fr. *celidoine*, Fr. *chélidoine*, from L. *chelidonium*, Gr. *chelidonion*, swallow-wort, from *chelidōn*, a swallow.] A name given to two British plants belonging to the poppy family, which yield an acrid juice used in medicine.

Celanese, sel′an-ēz, *n.* A trade-marked name for a type of rayon material.

Celebrate, sel′ē-brāt, *v.t.*—*celebrated*, *celebrating.* [L. *celebrare*, *celebratum*, to celebrate, from *celeber*, famous, frequented, populous.] To make known or mention often, especially with honour or praise; to extol; to distinguish by any kind of observance or ceremony (to *celebrate* a birthday).—**Celebrant**, sel′ē-brant, *n.* One who celebrates; one who performs a public religious rite.—**Celebrated**, sel′ē-brāt-ed, *a.* Having celebrity; distinguished; well-known; famous.—**Celebratedness**,† sel′ē-brā-ted-nes, *n.*—**Celebrater**, sel′ē-brā-tėr, *n.* One who celebrates.—**Celebration**, sel-ē-brā′shon, *n.* The act of celebrating; the act of praising or extolling; honour or distinction bestowed; the act of observing with appropriate rites or ceremonies.—**Celebrity**, sē-leb′ri-ti, *n.* [L. *celebritas.*] The condition of being celebrated; fame; renown (the *celebrity* of the Duke of Wellington, of Homer, or of the Iliad); a person of distinction.

Celerity, sē-ler′i-ti, *n.* [L. *celeritas*, from *celer*, swift.] Rapidity of motion; swiftness; quickness; speed. As distinguished from *velocity*, *celerity* is now generally applied to the motions or actions of living beings, *velocity* to inanimate objects.

Celery, sel′e-ri, *n.* [Fr. *céleri*, It. *seleri*, from Gr. *selinon*, parsley.] A plant indigenous to the ditches and marshy places near the sea-coast in England and Ireland, and long cultivated in gardens as a salad and culinary vegetable.

Celestial, sē-les′ti-al, *a.* [O.Fr. *celestial*, *celestiel*, L. *cœlestis*, from *cœlum*, heaven, whence also *ceiling.*] Heavenly; belonging or relating to heaven; dwelling in heaven; supremely excellent or delightful; belonging to the upper regions or visible heaven; pertaining to the heavens.—*Celestial Empire*, China, so called because the first emperors are fabled to have been deities.—*n.* An inhabitant of heaven; a native of China, the so-called Celestial Empire.—**Celestialize**,† sē-les′ti-al-īz, *v.t.*—*celestialized*, *celestializing.* To make celestial.—**Celestially**, sē-les′ti-al-li, *adv.* In a celestial or heavenly manner.—**Celestialness**, sē-les′ti-al-nes, *n.*

Celestine, sel′es-tīn, *n.* One of a religious order founded by pope *Celestine* V. in the thirteenth century.

Celiac, *a.* Cœliac.

Celibacy, sel′i-ba-si, *n.* [L. *cœlibatus*, a single life, celibacy, from *cœlebs*, unmarried.] The state of being celibate or unmarried; a single life.—**Celibate, Celibatist**, sel′i-bāt, se-lib′a-tist, *n.* One who adheres to or practises celibacy.—*a.* Unmarried; single. —*v.i.* To lead a single life.—**Celibite**,† sel′i-bīt, *n.* A monk.

Cell, sel, *n.* [L. *cella*, a cell, a small room, a hut, from same root as *celare*, whence *concelare*, to conceal. *Hole* and *hollow* are from same root.] A small apartment, as in a convent or a prison; a small or mean place of residence, such as a cave or hermitage; a small cavity or hollow place: variously applied (the *cells* of the brain, the *cells* of a honey-comb, the *cells* of a galvanic battery); *eccles.* a lesser religious house, especially one subordinate to a greater; *arch.* the part of the interior of a temple where the image of a god stood; *biol.* a small, usually microscopic, mass of contractile protoplasm with a membranous envelope forming the most elementary constituent or the structural unit in the tissues of animals and plants.—**Cellophane**, sel′lō-fān, *n.* A trade-marked name denoting transparent moisture-proof cellulose sheets or film, used extensively as coverings and wrappings for cigarettes, cigars, foodstuffs, and other kinds of merchandise.—**Cellular**, sel′lū-lėr, *a.* [L. *cellula*, a little cell.] Consisting of cells, or containing cells.—**Cellulares**, sel-lū-lā′rēz, *n. pl.* One of the grand divisions of the vegetable kingdom, consisting of plants the tissues of which are cellular.—**Cellulated**, sel′lū-lāt-ed, *a.* Having a cellular structure.—**Celluliferous**, sel-lū-lif′ėr-us, *a.* Bearing or producing little cells.—**Celluloid**, sel′lū-loid, *n.* An artificial substance, chiefly composed of cellulose or vegetable fibrine, used as a substitute for ivory, bone, coral, &c.—**Cellulose, Celluline**, sel′lū-lōs, sel′lū-lin, *a.* Containing cells.—*n. Bot.* the substance of which the permanent cell membranes of plants are always composed, in many respects allied to starch.

Cellar, sel′lėr, *n.* [L. *cellarium.* Cell.] A room in a house or other building, either wholly or partly under ground, used for storage purposes.—**Cellarage**, sel′lėr-āj, *n.* The space occupied by cellars; cellars collectively; charge for storage in a cellar. —**Cellarer**, sel′lėr-ėr, *n.* An officer in a monastery who has the care of the cellar; a butler; one who keeps wine or spirit cellars; a spirit-dealer.—**Cellaret**, sel-lėr-et′, *n.* [Dim. of *cellar.*] A case of cabinet work for holding bottles of liquors.—**Cellaring**, sel′lėr-ing, *n.* A range or system of cellars; cellarage.—**Cellarman**, sel′lėr-man, *n.* A person who is employed in a wine-cellar; a cellarer; a butler.

Celo, sē′lō, *n.* [L. *celero*, I hasten.] The unit of acceleration, one ft. per sec.

Celt, selt, *n.* [L. *Celtæ*, Gr. *Keltoi*, *Keltai*, connected with W. *celt*, a covert or shade; Gael. *ceiltach*, an inhabitant of the forest.] One of a distinct race of men inhabiting the south and west of Europe; the Celts now speaking a distinctive language are the Bretons, Welsh, Scotch Highlanders, and a portion of the Irish. [The word with its derivatives is frequently written with an initial K—*Kelt*, *Keltic*, &c.]—**Celtic, Celtish**,† sel′tik, sel′tish, *a.* Pertaining to the Celts, or to their language.—*n.* The language or group of dialects spoken by the Celts.—**Celticism**, sel′ti-sizm, *n.* The manners and customs of the Celts; a Celtic expression or mode of expression.

Celt, selt, *n.* [L.L. *celtis*, a chisel, a celt.] A cutting implement resembling an axe-head, made of stone or metal, found in ancient tumuli and barrows.

Cement, sē-ment′, *n.* [O.Fr. *cement*, L. *cæmentum*, chips of stone made into cement, contr. from *cædimentum*, from *cædo*, to cut.] Any glutinous or other substance capable of uniting bodies in close cohesion; a kind of mortar consisting of those hydraulic limes which contain silica and therefore set quickly; *fig.* bond of union; that which unites persons firmly together.—*v.t.* To unite by cement or other matter that produces cohesion of bodies; *fig.* to unite firmly or closely.—*v.i.* To unite or become solid; to unite and cohere.—**Cementation**, sē-men-tā′shon, *n.* The act of cementing; the conversion of iron into steel by heating the iron in a mass of ground charcoal, and thus causing it to absorb a certain quantity of the latter.—**Cementatory**, sē-men′ta-to-ri, *a.* Cementing; having the quality of uniting firmly.—**Cementer**, sē-men′tėr, *n.* The person or thing that cements.—**Cementite**, se-ment′īt, *n.* [From *cement.*] Iron carbide (Fe_3C).—**Cementitious**, sē-men-ti′shus, *a.* Pertaining to cement; having the quality of cementing; of the nature of cement.

Cemetery, sem′ē-te-ri, *n.* [L. *cœmeterium*, a burying-place, from Gr. *koimētērion*, a sleeping-place, afterwards a burying-place, from *koimaō*, to sleep.] A place set apart for interment; a graveyard; a necropolis.

Cenatory, Cenatical,† sē′na-to-ri, sē-nat′ik-al, *a.* [L. *cœnatorius*, from *cœnare*, *cœnatum*, to sup, *cœna*, supper.] Pertaining to dinner or supper.—**Cenation, Cœnation**, se-nā′shon, *n.* The act of dining or supping.

Cenobite, sen′ō-bīt, *n.* [L. *cœnobita*, from Gr. *koinobios*, living in common, from *koinos*, common, and *bios*, life.] One of a religious order living in a convent or in community; in opposition to an anchorite or hermit, who lives in solitude.—**Cenobitic, Cenobitical**, sen-ō-bit′ik, sen-ō-bit′ik-al, *a.* Living in community, as men belonging to a convent.—**Cenobitism**, sen′ō-bīt-izm, *n.* The state of being a cenobite; the principles or practice of a cenobite.

Cenogamy, sē-nog′a-mi, *n.* Same as *Cœnogamy.*

Cenotaph, sen′ō-taf, *n.* [Gr. *kenotaphion*—*kenos*, empty, and *taphos*, a tomb.] A sepulchral monument erected to one who is buried elsewhere.

Cense,† sens, *v.t.*—*censed*, *censing.* [Fr. *encenser.* Incense.] To perfume with incense.—*v.i.* To scatter incense.—**Censer**, sen′sėr, *n.* [A shortened form for *incenser*; Fr. *encensoir.*] A vase or pan in which incense is burned; a vessel for burning and wafting incense; a thurible.

Censor, sen′sėr, *n.* [L. *censor*, from *censeo*, to value, enrol, tax.] An officer in ancient Rome whose business was to draw up a register of the citizens, to keep watch over their morals, and to superintend the finances of the state; one empowered to examine all manuscripts, pamphlets, newspapers, and books before they are published, and to see that they contain nothing obnoxious; a war official employed to open, destroy, or revise correspondence, or sources of information calculated to instruct the enemy.—**Censor**, *v.t.* To revise in this sense; one who censures, blames, or reproves.—**Censorial**, sen-sō′ri-al, *a.* Belonging to a censor or to the correction of public morals; censorious. —**Censorious**, sen-sō′ri-us, *a.* Addicted to censure; apt to blame or condemn; ready to pass severe remarks on a person's conduct; implying or expressing censure.—**Censoriously**, sen-sō′ri-us-li, *adv.* In a censorious manner.—**Censoriousness**, sen-sō′ri-us-nes, *n.* The quality of being censorious; disposition to blame and condemn.—**Censorship**, sen′sėr-ship, *n.* The office or dignity of a censor; the period of his office.

Censure, sen′shör, *n.* [Fr. *censure*; L. *censura*, an opinion or judgment; from *censere*, to value, to estimate, whence *censor*, *census.*] Judgment or opinion†; the act of blaming or finding fault and condemning as wrong; expression of blame or disapprobation; fault-finding; condemnation; animadversion.—*v.t.*—*censured*, *censuring.* To find fault with and condemn as wrong; to blame; to express disapprobation of.—*v.i.*† To pass an opinion, especially a severe opinion. (*Shak.*)—**Censurable**, sen′shör-a-bl, *a.* Worthy of censure; blamable; culpable; reprehensible; blameworthy.—**Censurableness**, sen′shör-a-bl-nes, *n.* The quality of being censurable.—**Censurably**, sen′shör-a-bli, *adv.* In a censurable manner; in a manner worthy of blame.—**Censurer**, sen′shör-ėr, *n.* One who censures or expresses blame.

Census, sen′sus, *n.* [L., from *censere*, to register, enrol, whence *censure*, *censor.*] In ancient Rome a registered statement of the particulars of a person's property for taxation purposes; an enumeration and register of the Roman citizens and their property; in modern times, an enumeration of the inhabitants of a state or part of it, taken by order of its legislature; any official enumeration of population. — **Censual,** sen'shō-al, *a.* [L. *censualis.*] Relating to or containing a census.

Cent, sent, *n.* [Contr. of L. *centum,* a hundred.] A hundred, commonly used with *per;* as, ten *per cent,* that is in the proportion of ten to the hundred; in various countries a coin equal to the hundredth part of the monetary unit; in the United States the hundredth part of the dollar.— **Cental,** sen'tal, *n.* A weight of 100 lbs.— *a.* Pertaining to or consisting of a hundred; reckoned or proceeding by the hundred.— **Centesimal,** sen-tes'i-mal, *a.* [L. *centesimus,* from *centum.*] Hundredth; by the hundred. — *n.* Hundredth part; the next step of progression after decimal.

Centaur, sen'tạr, *n.* [L. *centaurus;* Gr. *kentauros,* lit. bull-pricker; the Centaurs probably represented some race that hunted wild cattle and lived almost constantly on horseback.] *Greek myth.* a member of a race of fabulous beings supposed to be half man and half horse; the name given to a constellation in the southern hemisphere.— **Centaurize,**† sen'tạr-īz, *v.i.* To perform the acts of, or to be like a centaur.—**Centaury,** sen'tạ-ri, *n.* [L. *centaurea,* Gr. *kentaurion,* after the *Centaur* Cheiron, because said to have cured a wound in his foot.] The popular name of various plants. Common centaury is an annual herb of the gentian family in high repute among the old herbalists for its medicinal properties.

Centenary, sen'te-na-ri, *n.* [L. *centenarius,* consisting of a hundred, relating to a hundred, from *centum,* a hundred.] What consists of or comprehends a hundred; the space of a hundred years; the commemoration of any event which occurred a hundred years before.—*a.* Relating to or consisting of a hundred; relating to a hundred years.—**Centenarian,** sen-te-nā'ri-an, *n.* A person a hundred years old or upwards. —*a.* Of or pertaining to a centenary or centenarian.—**Centennial,** sen-ten'ni-al, *a.* [L. *centum,* and *annus,* a year.] Consisting of or lasting a hundred years; aged a hundred years or upwards; happening every hundred years.—*n.* The commemoration or celebration of any event which occurred a hundred years before.—**Centennially,** sen-ten'ni-al-li, *adv.* Once in every hundred years.

Centering, sen'tėr-ing, *n.* [From Fr. *cintre,* centering, an arch, from L. *cingo, cinctum,* to gird, whence *cincture.*] The framing of timber by which the arch of a bridge or other structure is supported during its erection.

Centesimal, sen-tes'i-mal, *a.* [L. *centesimus,* hundredth.] Pertaining to division into a hundred parts.—**Centesimally,** *adv.* By division into hundreds. — **Centesimate,** *v.t.* To punish every hundredth man.

Centicipitous,† sen-ti-sip'i-tus, *a.* [L. *centiceps, centicipitis—centum,* a hundred, *caput,* the head.] Having a hundred heads.

Centifidous,† sen-tif'i-dus, *a.* [L. *centum,* a hundred, and *findo,* to split.] Divided into a hundred parts.

Centifolious, sen-ti-fō'li-us, *a.* [L. *centifolius—centum,* a hundred, *folium,* a leaf.] Having a hundred leaves.

Centigrade, sen'ti-grād, *a.* [From L. *centum,* a hundred, *gradus,* a degree.] Consisting of a hundred degrees; graduated into a hundred divisions or equal parts; pertaining to the scale which is divided into a hundred degrees.—*Centigrade thermometer,* a thermometer which divides the interval between the freezing and boiling points of water into 100 degrees, while in Fahrenheit's thermometer the same interval is divided into 180 degrees.

Centime, sen-tēm' or sän-tēm, *n.* [Fr.] The hundredth part of a franc.

Centimeter, sen'ti-mē-tr or sän-tē-mā-tr, *n.* [Fr. *centimètre,* from L. *centum,* a hundred, and Gr. *metron,* measure.] A French measure of length, the hundredth part of a meter; rather more than .39 of an inch.

Centipede, sen'ti-pēd, *n.* [L. *centipeda—centum,* a hundred, and *pes, pedis,* a foot.] A term applied to various long, flat-bodied animals having many feet, popularly called insects, but belonging to the Myriapoda.—**Centipedal,** sen'ti-pē-dal, *a.* Pertaining or belonging to the centipedes.

Centner, sent'nėr, *n.* [G., from L. *centenarius,* from *centum,* a hundred.] A name in several European countries for a weight nearly equivalent to a hundredweight.

Cento, sen'tō, *n.* [L. *cento,* patchwork, a poem made up of selections from different poems.] A composition (whether literary or musical) made up of selections from the works of various authors or composers.— **Centoist,** sen'tō-ist, *n.* One who compiles centos; a compiler. — **Centonism,**† sen'tō-nizm, *n.* The act of constructing centos. — **Centonize,**† sen'tō-nīz, *v.t.* and *i.* To make a cento or centos; to work up into a cento.

Center, sen'tėr, *n.* [Fr., from L. *centrum,* Gr. *kentron,* a prick or point, from *kenteō,* to prick.] That point of a line, plane figure, or solid body which is equally distant from the extremities; the middle point, portion, or place; the middle or central object; a point of concentration; the nucleus around which or into which things are collected (a *center* of attraction); the part of a target next the bull's-eye; the men of the moderate party in Parliament.—*Center of buoyancy,* in hydrostatics, the center of gravity of the liquid displaced by a floating body. It is the point through which the upward thrust of the liquid may be conceived to act.—*Center of gravity,* the point of a body about which all the parts of the body exactly balance each other, and which being supported the whole body will remain at rest though acted on by gravity.—*Center of magnitude,* that point in a body which is equally distant from all the similar external parts of it. In the regular solids this point coincides with the center of gravity.—*Center of mass,* that point in a body through which the resultant of absolutely parallel forces exerted on its particles always acts, whatever the direction of the forces.—*Center of motion,* the point which remains at rest while all the other parts of a body move round it.—*Center of oscillation,* the point of a body suspended, at which, if all the matter were concentrated, the oscillations would be performed in the same time.— *Center of pressure,* the point in a submerged plane area through which the resultant of the fluid-pressures upon it acts.—*v.t.—centered, centering.* To place on a center; to fix on a central point; to collect to a point.— *v.i.* To be placed in a center or in the middle; to be collected to one point; to be concentrated or united in one.—**Central,** sen'tral, *a.* [L. *centralis.*] Relating or pertaining to the center; placed in the center or middle; constituting or containing the center; originating or proceeding from the center.—**Centralism,** sen'tral-izm, *n.* The quality of being central; the combination of several parts into one whole; centralization. — **Centralist,** sen'tral-ist, *n.* One who promotes centralization.—**Centrality, Centralness,** sen-tral'i-ti, sen'tral-nes, *n.* The state of being central.—**Centralization, Centralisation,** sen'tral-iz-ā"shon, *n.* The act of centralizing or bringing to one center.—**Centralize, Centralise,** sen'tral-īz, *v.t.—centralized, centralizing.* To draw to a central point; to bring to a center; to render central; to concentrate in some particular part: often applied to the process of transferring local administration to the capital or seat of government of a country. — **Centrally,** sen'tral-li, *adv.* In a central manner or position; with regard to the center. — **Center-bit,** *n.* A carpenter's tool for boring large circular holes, which turns on an axis or central point when in operation. — **Center-board,** *n.* A kind of movable keel in American yachts, capable of being raised and lowered in a well extending longitudinally amidships, to prevent lee-way.— **Centerpiece,** *n.* An ornament intended to be placed in the middle or center of something, as of a table. — **Centric,** sen'trik, *n.* In *anc. astron.* a circle the center of which was the same as that of the earth. (*Mil.*) — **Centric, Centrical,** sen'trik-al, *a.* Placed in the center or middle; central. — **Centrically,** sen'trik-al-li, *adv.* In a central position; centrally. — **Centricalness,** sen'trik-al-nes, *n.* Situation in the center. — **Centricity,** sen-tris'i-ti, *n.* The state of being centric.— **Centring,** sen'tring, *n.* CENTERING.

Centrifugal, sen-trif'ū-gal, *a.* [L. *centrum,* a center, and *fugio,* to flee.] Tending to recede from the center; acting by or depending on centrifugal force or action; *bot.* expanding first at the summit and later at the base, as an inflorescence.—*Centrifugal force,* that force by which all bodies moving round another body in a curve tend to fly off at any point of their motion in the direction of a tangent to the curve. — **Centrifugence,** sen-trif'ū-jens, *n.* Centrifugal force or tendency. — **Centripetal,** sen-trip'e-tal, *a.* [L. *centrum,* a center, and *peto,* to seek.] Tending toward the center; progressing by changes from the exterior of an object to its center.—*Centripetal force* is that force which draws a body towards a center, and thereby acts as a counterpoise to the centrifugal force in circular motion.—**Centripetency,** sen-trip'e-ten-si, *n.* Tendency to the center.

Centrobaric, sen'trō-bar"ik, *a.* [Gr. *kentron,* the centre, and *baros,* weight.] Relating to the centre of gravity or method of finding it.

Centrosome, sen'trō-sōm, *n.* [L. *centrum,* centre, *sōma,* a body.] In cells, a minute particle outside the nucleus which plays an active part in indirect division.

Centumvir, sen-tum'vir, *n.* pl. **Centumviri,** sen-tum'vi-rī. [L. *centum,* a hundred, and *vir,* a man.] One of a hundred and five judges in ancient Rome appointed to decide common causes among the people.— **Centumvirate,** sen-tum'vi-rāt, *n.* The office or dignity of the centumviri; a body of a hundred men.

Centuple, sen'tū-pl, *a.* [L. *centuplus—centum,* a hundred, and root of *plica,* a fold.] Multiplied or increased a hundred-fold.— *v.t.—centupled, centupling.* To multiply a hundred-fold. — **Centuplicate,** sen-tū'pli-kāt, *v.t.—centuplicated, centuplicating.* [L. *centum,* and *plicatus,* folded.] To make a hundred-fold; to repeat a hundred times.

Century, sen'tū-ri, *n.* [L. *centuria,* from *centum,* a hundred.] An aggregate of a hundred; anything consisting of a hundred in number; a period of a hundred years; often such a period reckoned from the birth of Christ. — **Centurial,**† sen-tū'ri-al, *a.* [L. *centurialis.*] Relating to or occurring once in a century.—**Centurion,** sen-tū'ri-on, *n.* [L. *centurio,* from *centum,* a hundred.] In ancient Rome a military officer who commanded a century or company of infantry consisting of a hundred men.

Cephalalgy, sef'al-al-ji, *n.* [Gr. *kephalalgia—kephalē,* the head, and *algos,* pain.] Headache.—**Cephalalgic,** sef-a-lal'jik, *a.* Relating to cephalalgy or headache.—*n.* A medicine for the headache.

Cephalaspis, sef-a-las'pis, *n.* [Gr. *kephalē,* the head, and *aspis,* a shield.] A fossil fish with a large head, resembling a saddler's knife in shape, and protected by a large buckler-shaped plate.

Cephalata, sef-a-lā'ta, *n.pl.* [Gr. *kephalē,* the head.] A division of molluscs which have a distinct head, with eyes, as the gasteropods, cuttle-fishes, &c. — **Cephalate,** sef'al-āt, *n.* A mollusc of the division Cephalata.

Cephalic, sē-fal'ik, *a.* [Gr. *kephalikos,* from *kephalē,* the head.] Pertaining to the head.—*n.* A medicine for headache or other disorder in the head.—**Cephalic index,** *n.* A number denoting the ratio of the transverse to the longitudinal (front to back) diameter of the skull, and according to which skulls and races of people are called brachycephalic or dolichocephalic.— **Cephalistic,**† sef-a-list'ik, *a.* Cephalic. —**Cephalitis,** sef-a-lī'tis, *n.* [The term.

-*itis* signifies inflammation.] Inflammation of the brain.—**Cephaloid**, sef'a-loid, *a.* Shaped like the head; spherical.—**Cephalous**, sef'a-lus, *a.* Having a head: applied specifically to the cephalates.

Cephalopod, sef'a-lō-pod, *n.* [Gr. *kephalē*, a head, and *pous, podos*, a foot.] Any member of the class Cephalopoda.—**Cephalopoda**, sef-a-lop'o-da, *n. pl.* A class of the mollusca, the highest in organization, characterized by having the organs of prehension and locomotion, called tentacles or arms, attached to the head, and including the cuttle-fishes, squids, ammonites, &c.—**Cephalopodous**, sef-a-lop'o-dus, *a.* Relating or belonging to the Cephalopoda.

Cephalo-thorax, sef'a-lō-thō"raks, *n.* [Gr. *kephalē*, the head, and *thōrax*, the thorax.] The anterior division of the body in crustaceans, spiders, scorpions, &c., which consists of the head and thorax blended together.

Cephalotomy, sef-a-lot'o-mi, *n.* [Gr. *kephalē*, the head, and *tomē*, a cutting.] The dissection or opening of the head.

Ceraceous, sē-rā'shus, *a.* [L. *ceraceus*, waxy, from *cera*, wax.] *Bot.* waxy: a term applied to bodies which have the texture and colour of new wax.—**Cerago**, sē-rā'go, *n.* A substance consisting chiefly of the pollen of flowers, used by bees for aliment; bee-bread.

Ceramic, se-ram'ik, *a.* [Gr. *keramikos*, from *keramos*, potter's-clay, a piece of pottery.] Of or belonging to the fictile arts or pottery; pertaining to the manufacture of porcelain and earthenware.—**Ceramics**, se-ram'iks, *n.* The art of the potter; pottery.

Cerasin, Cerasine, sėr'a-sin, *n.* [L. *cerasus*, a cherry-tree.] A gum which exudes from the cherry and plum tree.—**Cerasinous**, se-ras'i-nus, *a.* Pertaining to or containing cerasin; cherry-coloured; deep red.

Cerate, sē'rāt, *n.* [L. *ceratum*, from *cera*, wax.] A thick kind of ointment composed of wax, lard, or oil, with other ingredients, applied externally in various diseases.—**Cerated**, sē'rāt-ed, *a.* Covered with wax.

Ceratite, sėr'a-tīt, *n.* [Gr. *keras, keratos*, a horn.] A genus of fossil cephalopods, allied to and resembling the ammonites.—**Ceratitis**, ser-a-tī'tis, *n.* [Gr. *keras*, horn, alluding to the horny cornea.] *Pathol.* inflammation of the cornea of the eye.—**Ceratium**, sē-rā'shi-um, *n.* [Gr. *keration*, dim. of *keras*.] *Bot.* a slender horn-shaped many-seeded fruit resembling a siliqua; a kind of pod.—**Ceratodus**, se-rat'ō-dus, *n.* [Gr. *keras*, horn, *odous*, tooth.] A fish of Australia, one of the few that have lungs, said to be able to leave the water for some time.—**Ceratose**, sėr'a-tōz, *a.* Like horn; having the texture and consistence of horn; horny.

Ceraunics,† se-ra̤'niks, *n.* [Gr. *keraunos*, thunder.] That branch of physics which treats of heat and electricity.—**Ceraunite**, se-ra̤'nīt, *n.* A thunder-stone; a belemnite.

Cerberus, sėr'bėr-us, *n.* [L.] *Class. myth.* the three-headed watch-dog of the infernal regions; hence, any watchful and dreaded guardian. — **Cerberean, Cerberian**, sėr-bē'rē-an, sėr-bē'ri-an, *a.* Relating to Cerberus.

Cerca, sėr'ka, *n.* pl. **Cercæ**, sėr'sē. [Gr. *kerkos*, a tail.] One of the feelers projecting from the hind parts of the bodies of some insects.—**Cercarian**, sėr-kā'ri-an, *n.* A trematode worm or fluke in one of its stages when it has a tadpole form.

Cere, sēr, *n.* [L. *cera*, wax; from its appearance.] The term applied to the space destitute of feathers, and having a waxy appearance, generally observed at the base of the bill in birds.

Cereal, sē'rē-al, *a.* [From *Ceres*, the goddess of corn.] Pertaining to edible grain, as wheat, rye, barley, oats, maize, rice, millet.—*n.* A grain plant, such as wheat, oats, barley, &c.

Cerebellum, sėr-ē-bel'lum, *n.* [L., dim. of *cerebrum*, the brain.] The little brain; that portion of the brain in vertebrate animals which is posterior to and underlies the great cerebral mass or cerebrum.—**Cerebellar, Cerebellous**, sėr-ē-bel'lėr, sėr-ē-bel'lus, *a.* Relating to the cerebellum.—**Cerebral, Cerebrine, Cerebric**, sėr'-ē-bral, sėr'ē-brīn, se-rē'brik, *a.* Pertaining to the cerebrum or brain.—*Cerebral letters*, in *philol.* certain consonants in the Sanskrit alphabet, formed by bringing the tip of the tongue backward and applying its under surface against the roof of the mouth.—**Cerebralism**, sėr'ē-bral-izm, *n Psychol.* the theory or doctrine that all mental operations arise from the activity of the cerebrum or brain.—**Cerebralist**, sėr'ē-bral-ist, *n.* One who holds the doctrine or theory of cerebralism.—**Cerebrate**, sėr'ē-brāt, *v.i.* To have the brain in action; to exhibit brain action.—**Cerebration**, sėr-ē-brā'shon, *n.* Exertion or action of the brain, conscious or unconscious.—**Cerebriform**, se-rē'bri-form, *a.* Brain-shaped.—**Cerebrin, Cerebrine**, sėr'ē-brin, *n.* A name given to several substances obtained chemically from the brain.—**Cerebritis**, sėr-ē-brī'tis, *n.* [L. *cerebrum*, brain.] Brain inflammation.—**Cerebrose**,† sėr-ē-bros, *a.* [L. *cerebrosus*.] Brain-sick; mad; passionate.—**Cerebro-spinal**, se-rē'brō-spī"nal, *a.* Pertaining to the brain and spinal cord together; consisting in the brain and spinal cord.—**Cerebro-spinal meningitis**, men'in-jīt"is, *n.* [Gr. *meninx, meningos*, a membrane, -*itis*, inflammation.] Spotted fever; a virulent bacterial disease, associated with inflammation of the membranes covering the brain and spinal cord.—**Cerebrum**, sėr'ē-brum, *n.* [L.] The superior and chief portion of the brain, occupying the whole upper cavity of the skull.

Cerecloth, Cerement, sēr'kloth, sēr'-ment, *n.* [L. *cera*, wax.] Cloth dipped in melted wax, with which dead bodies are enfolded when embalmed; hence, *pl.* grave-clothes (poetical).

Ceremony, sėr'ē-mo-ni, *n.* [Fr. *cérémonie*, from L. *cærimonia*, a rite or ceremony, veneration, sanctity; probably from same root as Skr. *kri, kar*, to do.] A religious or other rite or observance; a solemn or formal display or performance; a solemnity; a usage of politeness, or such usages collectively; formality; punctilio; punctiliousness.—*Master of ceremonies*, a person who regulates the forms to be observed by the company or attendants on a public occasion.—**Ceremonial**, sėr-ē-mō'ni-al, *a.* [L. *cærimonialis*.] Relating to ceremonies or external forms or rites; ritual; pertaining to the forms and rites of the Jewish religion (the *ceremonial* law).—*n.* A system of rites; ceremonies or formalities to be observed on any occasion.—**Ceremonialism**, sėr-ē-mō'ni-al-izm, *n.* Adherence to or fondness for ceremony.—**Ceremoniality**, sėr-ē-mō'ni-al"i-ti, *n.* Ceremonial character.—**Ceremonially**, sėr-ē-mō'ni-al-li, *adv.* In a ceremonial manner; according to rites and ceremonies.—**Ceremonialness**, sėr-ē-mō'ni-al-nes, *n.*—**Ceremonious**, sėr-ē-mō'ni-us, *a.* Full of ceremony; accompanied with rites; according to prescribed or customary formalities or punctilios; formally respectful or polite; observant of conventional forms; fond of using ceremony.—**Ceremoniously**, sėr-ē-mō'ni-ous-li, *adv.* In a ceremonious manner; formally; with due forms.—**Ceremoniousness**, sėr-ē-mō'ni-us-nes, *n.* The quality of being ceremonious; the practice of much ceremony; formality.

Ceres, sē'rēz, *n.* A Roman goddess watching over the growth of grain and other plants; hence, grain; also a name of one of the asteroids or planetoids.

Ceriph, sėr'if, *n.* One of the fine lines of a type for printing, especially one of the fine cross lines at the top or bottom, as of I.

Cerise, se-rēz', *n.* [Fr., a cherry.] Cherry-colour.—*a.* Of the colour of cerise; cherry-coloured.

Cerium, sē'ri-um, *a.* [From the planet *Ceres*, discovered a year or two before.] A rare metal discovered in 1803, of a colour between that of iron and that of lead; specific gravity 6·9.—**Cerite**, sē'rīt, *n.* A rare mineral, of a pale rose-red colour, from which cerium was first obtained.

Cernuous, sėr'nū-us, *a.* [L. *cernuus*.] *Bot.* drooping; pendulous.

Cerograph, sē'rō-graf, *n.* [L. *cera*, wax, and Gr. *graphō*, to write.] A writing or engraving on wax; a painting in wax-colours; an encaustic painting.—**Cerographic, Cerographical**, sē-rō-graf'ik, sē-rō-graf'-ik-al, *a.* Pertaining to cerography.—**Cerographist**, sē-rog'raf-ist, *n.* One who is versed in or who practises cerography.—**Cerography**, sē-rog'ra-fi, *n.* The act of writing or engraving on wax; the art of painting in wax-colours; encaustic painting.

Ceroon, sē-rön', *n.* SEROON.

Ceroplastic, sē-rō-plas'tik, *a.* [Gr. *kēros*, wax, and *plastikē* (*technē*), the art of the modeller or carver.] Pertaining to the art of modelling in wax; modelled in wax.—*n.* The art of modelling or of forming models in wax.

Certain, sėr'tin, *a.* [Fr. *certain*, as if from a L. adjective *certanus*, formed from *certus*, certain, by adding suffix -*anus*. *Certus* is connected with *cerno, cretum*, to distinguish, dis*cern*.] Sure; undoubtedly true; established as a fact; undoubtedly existing or impending (death, danger); capable of being counted or depended on; unfailing; infallible: of things (a sign, a remedy); capable of being counted upon or able to count on: of persons (he is *certain* to be there, you are *certain* to find him); assured in mind; free from doubt; having no doubt or suspicion regarding: often with *of*; stated; fixed; determinate; definite (a *certain* rate); not specifically named; indefinite; one or some (a *certain* person, a *certain* pleasure in something).—*For certain*, certainly.—**Certainly**, sėr'tin-li, *adv.* Without doubt or question; in truth and fact; without fail; assuredly; of a certainty.—**Certainness**, sėr'tin-nes, *n.* The state of being certain; certainty.—**Certainty**, sėr'tin-ti, *n.* The fact of being certain; exemption from failure to happen or produce the natural result; a fact or truth certainly established; that which cannot be questioned; full assurance of mind; exemption from doubt.—**Certes**,† sėr'tēz, *adv.* [Fr.] Certainly; in truth; verily.—**Certify**, sėr'ti-fī, *v.t.*—*certified, certifying*. [Fr. *certifier*, from L.L. *certifico*, to certify—L. *certus*, certain, and *facio*, to make.] To assure or make certain; to give certain information *to* (a person); to give certain information *of*; to make clear or definite; to testify to in writing; to make known or establish as a fact.—**Certificate**, sėr-tif'i-kāt, *n.* [Fr. *certificat*.] A written testimony to the truth of a certain fact or facts; a testimonial; a legally authenticated voucher or testimony of certain facts; sometimes a kind of licence.—*v.t.* To give a certificate to, as to one who has passed an examination; to attest or certify by certificate.—**Certification**, sėr'ti-fi-kā"shon, *n.* The act of certifying.—**Certifier**, sėr'ti-fī-ėr, *n.* One who certifies.—**Certiorari**, sėr'shi-ō-rā"rī, *n.* [Lit. to be informed of, L.L. *certioro*, to inform, from L. *certus*, certain.] *Law*, a writ to call up the records of an inferior court or remove a cause there depending, that it may be tried in a superior court.—**Certitude**, sėr'ti-tūd, *n.* [L.L. *certitudo*.] Certainty; assurance; freedom from doubt.

Cerulean, sē-rṳ'lē-an, *a.* [L. *cæruleus*, azure, for *cæluleus*, sky-coloured, from *cælum*, the sky.] Sky-coloured; azure; blue.—**Ceruleum**, sē-rṳ'lē-um, *n.* A blue pigment.—**Cerulific**, sėr-ṳ-lif'ik, *a.* Producing a blue or sky-colour.

Cerumen, sē-rṳ'men, *n.* [From L. *cera*, wax.] The wax or yellow matter secreted by certain glands lying in the external canal of the ear.—**Ceruminous**, sē-rṳ'mi-nus, *a.* Relating to or containing cerumen.

Ceruse, sē'rṳs, *n.* [Fr., from L. *cerussa*, white-lead, from *cera*, wax.] White-lead, composed of hydroxide and carbonate of lead, produced by exposing the metal in thin plates to the vapour of vinegar. It is much used in painting, and a cosmetic is prepared from it.—*v.t.* To wash with ceruse; to apply ceruse to as a cosmetic.—**Cerusite, Cerussite**, sē′rụ-sīt, sē-rụs′īt, *n.* A native carbonate of lead; a common lead-ore.

Cervical, sėr′vi-kal, *a.* [L. *cervix, cervicis*, the neck.] Belonging to the neck.

Cervine, sėr′vīn, *a.* [L. *cervinus*, from *cervus*, a deer.] Pertaining to the deer family.

Cesarean, Cesarian, sē-zā′rē-an, sē-zā′ri-an, *n.* CÆSAREAN.

Cesarewitch, sē-zar′e-vich, *n.* Same as *Czarowitz.*

Cespitose, Cespitous, ses′pi-tōs, ses′pi-tus, *a.* [L. *cæspes, cespitis*, turf.] Pertaining to turf; turfy; *bot.* growing in tufts.

Cess, ses, *v.t.* [Shortened and corrupted from *assess.*] To impose a tax; to assess.—*n.* A rate or tax. (Colloq.)

Cessation, ses-sā′shon, *n.* [L. *cessatio*, from *cesso*, from *cedo, cessum*, to cease. CEDE.] A ceasing; a stop; a rest; the act of discontinuing motion or action of any kind, whether temporary or final.

Cession, se′shon, *n.* [L. *cessio*, from L. *cedo, cessum.* CEDE.] The act of ceding, yielding, or surrendering, as of territory, property, or rights; a giving up, resignation, or surrender.—**Cessionary**, se′shon-a-ri, *a.* [Fr. *cessionaire.*] Giving up; yielding.

Cess-pool, ses′pöl, *n.* [The better spelling seems to be *sess-pool*, the word being from A.Sax. *sessian*, to settle; or from prov. *soss, suss*, a mess, filth; Gael. *sos.*] A cavity or well in a drain or privy to receive the sediment or filth.

Cestoid, ses′toid, *a.* [L. *cestus*, a girdle, from their shape.] A term used to characterize certain intestinal worms, such as tape-worms.—**Cestoidean**, ses-toi′dē-an, *n.* A cestoid worm; a tape-worm.

Cestracion, ses-trā′si-on, *n.* [Gr. *kestra*, a kind of fish.] A kind of shark found on the coast of Australia.

Cestus, ses′tus, *n.* [L. *cestus, cæstus*, from *cædo, cæsum*, to strike.] Among the Greeks and Romans, a kind of boxing-glove, loaded with lead or iron, which boxers fastened on their hands and arms by leather thongs.

Cesura. CÆSURA.

Cetacea, sē-tā′shē-a, *n. pl.* [L. *cetus*, Gr. *kētos*, any large sea-monster, a whale.] An order of marine mammals comprising the whales and dolphins.—**Cetacean**, sē-tā′shan, *n.* An animal of the order Cetacea.—**Cetaceous**, sē-tā′shus, *a.* Pertaining to the whale; belonging to the Cetacea or whale kind.—**Cetology**, sē-tol′o-ji, *n.* The description or natural history of cetaceous animals.—**Cetological**, sē-tō-loj′i-kal, *a.* Pertaining to cetology.—**Cetologist**, sē-tol′o-jist, *n.* One who is versed in cetology.

Cetiosaurus, Cetiosaur, sē′ti-ō-sạ″rus, sē′ti-ō-sạr, *n.* [Gr. *keteios*, belonging to a whale, and *sauros*, a lizard.] A kind of gigantic fossil saurian or lizard, 50 to 70 feet long, probably an inhabitant of marshes or river sides.

Cevadilla, sev-a-dil′la, *n.* Same as *Cebadilla.*

Ceylanite, sē′lan-īt, *n.* [From *Ceylon.*] A ferruginous variety of spinel from Ceylon.

C.G.S. The standard contraction for the centimetre-gramme-second system of units now in universal use for scientific purposes: named from the fundamental units of length, mass, and time.

Chablis, shab′lē, *n.* A celebrated white French wine, having good body and an exquisite perfume, so called from the town of that name near which it is produced.

Chabouk, Chabuk, cha-bụk′, *n.* [Hind. *chabuk*, a horse-whip.] A long whip; the whip used in the East for inflicting corporal punishment.

Chace, chās, *n.* and *v.* See CHASE.

Chacma, chak′ma, *n.* A baboon found in South Africa.

Chaco, chä′kō, *n.* An unctuous earth found at La Paz, South America, which is made into pats and eaten with chocolate.

Chad, chad, *n.* A kind of fish, the shad.

Chætopod, kē′to-pod, *n.* [Gr. *chaitē*, mane, *pous*, foot.] The name for many annelids, a kind of marine worms having feet provided with bristles.

Chafe, chāf, *v.t.*—*chafed, chafing.* [O.E. *chaufe*, Fr. *chauffer*, O.Fr. *chaufer*, to warm, from L. *calefacere*, to warm, from *caleo*, to grow warm, and *facere*, to make.] To excite heat in (some part of the body) by friction; to stimulate to warmth by rubbing; to excite the passions of; to inflame; to anger; to excite violent action in; to cause to rage (the wind *chafes* the ocean); to fret and wear by rubbing (the rope was *chafed*).—*v.i.* To be excited or heated; to rage; to fret; to dash, as in anger; to rage or boil (as the sea); to be fretted and worn by rubbing.—*n.* A state of being angry or annoyed; heat; fret.—**Chafer**, chā′fėr, *n.* One who or that which chafes; a chafing-dish.—**Chafing-dish**, *n.* A dish or vessel to hold coals for heating anything set on it; a portable grate for coals.

Chafer, chā′fėr, *n.* [A.Sax. *ceafor*, a chafer: D. *kever*, G. *käfer*, a beetle.] A beetle; especially applied to such as are destructive to plants, and generally in compounds; as, cock-*chafer*, rose-*chafer*, bark-*chafer*, &c.

Chaff, chaf, *n.* [A.Sax. *ceaf* = D. *kaf*, G. *kaff*, chaff.] The glumes or husks of corn and grasses, but more commonly restricted to the husks when separated from the corn by thrashing, sifting, or winnowing; worthless matter, especially that which is light and apt to be driven by the wind; refuse.—**Chaffless**, chaf′les, *a.* Without chaff; free from worthless matter or rubbish. (*Shak.*)—**Chaffy**, chaf′i, *a.* Like chaff; full of chaff; light; frivolous; worthless.

Chaff, chaf, *v.t.* and *i.* [A corruption of *chafe*, to irritate or annoy.] To assail with sarcastic banter or raillery; to banter; to make game of. (Colloq.)—*n.* Banter, especially slangy banter; sarcastic raillery. (Colloq.)—**Chaffer**, chaf′ėr, *n.* One who employs chaff or slangy banter. (Colloq.)

Chaffer, chaf′ėr, *v.i.* [O.E. *chapfare, chaffare*, bargaining, merchandise, from *chap*, A.Sax. *ceáp*, a bargain, and *fare*, procedure, journey, A. Sax. *faru*, a journey. Akin *cheap, cheapen.* CHEAP.] To treat about a purchase; to bargain; to haggle; to talk much and idly.—**Chafferer**, chaf′ėr-ėr, *n.* One who chaffers; a bargainer; a buyer.

Chaffinch, chaf′finsh, *n.* [Perhaps from its note; comp. *chiff-chaff*, the name of a British bird, from its cry.] A common British bird of the finch family, whose pleasant song is heard from early spring to the middle of summer.

Chagrin, sha-grēn′, *n.* [Fr., said to be another form of *shagreen*, which, from being used to polish wood, has come to be employed as a type of grinding or gnawing care.] Ill humour, as from disappointment, wounded vanity, &c.; vexation; peevishness; mortification; fretfulness.—*v.t.* To excite ill humour in; to vex; to mortify.

Chain, chān, *n.* [Fr. *chaîne*, O.Fr. *chaene, cadene*, from L. *catena*, a chain.] A series of links or rings connected or fitted into one another, generally of some kind of metal, and used for various purposes; *fig.* that which binds, restrains, confines, or fetters; a bond; a fetter; bondage; slavery: in this sense often in the plural (the *chains* of evil habit); a series of things linked together; a series, line, or range of things connected or following in succession (*chain* of causes, events, &c.); *weaving*, the warp threads of a web, so called because they form a long series of links or loops; *pl. naut.* strong links or plates of iron bolted to a ship's sides, and forming part of the attachments of the shrouds; *surv.* a measuring instrument, generally consisting of 100 links, and having a total length of 66 feet.—*v.t.* To fasten, bind, restrain, or fetter with a chain or chains; to put in chains; to restrain; to hold in control; to unite firmly; to link.—**Chainless**, chān′les, *a.* Without chains or fetters; fetterless; free; unconfined.—**Chain-bridge**. A kind of suspension bridge in which the roadway is supported by strong chains.—**Chain-cable**, *n.* A cable composed of iron links.—**Chain-gang**, *n.* A gang or number of convicts chained together.—**Chain-moulding**, *n.* *Arch.* a species of moulding cut in imitation of a chain.—**Chain-pier**, *n.* A pier running into the sea, supported by chains like a suspension bridge.—**Chain-pump**, *n.* A pump consisting, in one of its simplest forms, of an endless chain equipped with a series of discs or buckets, passing downward into the water, and returning upwards through a tube.—**Chain-shot**, *n.* Two cannon-balls or half-balls connected by a chain, formerly much used in naval warfare for carrying away rigging.—**Chain-stitch, Chain-work**, *n.* Sewing consisting of threads or cords linked together in the form of a chain; also, a kind of machine-sewing, which consists in looping the upper thread into itself on the under side of the fabric, or in using a second thread to engage the loop of the upper thread: in contradistinction to *lock-stitch.*—**Chain-wheel**, *n.* An inversion of the chain-pump, by which it is converted into a recipient of water-power.

Chair, chār, *n.* [Fr. *chaire*, O.Fr. *chayere*, L. *cathedra*, Gr. *kathedra*, a seat. CATHEDRAL. *Chaise* is a corruption of *chaire.*] A movable seat, with a back, for one person; a seat of office or authority; hence, the office itself, especially the office of a professor, and sometimes the person occupying the chair; a chairman or president; a sedan-chair; one of the iron blocks which support and secure the rails in a railway.—*v.t.* To place or carry in a chair; to carry publicly in a chair in triumph.—**Chairman**, chār′man, *n.* The presiding officer of an assembly, association, or company, committee or public meeting; one whose business is to carry a sedan-chair.—**Chairmanship**, chār′man-ship, *n.* The office of a chairman or presiding officer of a meeting.—**Chair-bed**, *n.* A bed-chair.

Chaise, shāz, *n.* [Fr., a corruption of *chaire*, a chair.] A two-wheeled carriage drawn by one or more horses, and generally furnished with a hood or top that may be let down.

Chalaza, ka-lā′za, *n.* [Gr. *chalaza*, a pimple.] *Bot.* that part of the ovule or seed where the integuments cohere with each other and with the nucleus; *zool.* one of the two membranous twisted cords which bind the yolk-bag of an egg to the lining membrane at the two ends of the shell.—**Chalazal**, ka-lā′zal, *a.* Of or relating to a chalaza.

Chalcedony, kal-sed′ō-ni, *n.* [From *Chalcedon*, an ancient Greek town in Asia Minor.] A kind of quartz, resembling milk diluted with water, and more or less clouded or opaque, with veins, circles, and spots.—**Chalcedonic**, kal-sē-don′ik, *a.* Pertaining to chalcedony.—**Chalcedonyx**, kal-sed′ō-niks, *n.* [From *chalcedony* and *onyx.*] A variety of agate, in which white and gray layers alternate.

Chalcography, kal-kog′ra-fi, *n.* [Gr. *chalkos*, copper, brass, and *graphō*, to engrave.] The art of engraving on copper or brass.—**Chalcographer, Chalcographist**, kal-kog′raf-ėr, kal-kog′raf-ist, *n.* An engraver on brass or copper.—**Chalcographic**, kal-ko-graf′ik, *a.* Pertaining to chalcography.

Chaldaic, Chaldean, Chaldee, kal-dā′ik, kal-dē′an, kal′dē, *a.* Pertaining to Chaldea or Chaldæa, anciently a country on the Euphrates in Asia.—*n.* The language or dialect of the Chaldeans; Aramaic.—**Chaldaism**, kal-dā′izm, *n.* An idiom or peculiarity of the Chaldee dialect.

Chalder, chạl′dėr, *n.* [Same as *chaldron.*] A Scotch dry measure for grain consisting of 16 bolls, or nearly 8 quarters.

Chaldron, chäl′dron, *n.* [The same word as *caldron.*] A measure of coals consisting of 36 bushels, or 25½ cwt.

Chalet, shä-lā, *n.* [Fr.; properly a Swiss word.] A cottage, cabin, or hut for sheltering the herdsmen and their cattle in the Swiss mountains; a small dwelling-house built in a similar style.

Chalice, chal'is, *n.* [Fr. *calice*, from L. *calix*, *calicis*, a cup or goblet.] A drinking cup or bowl; a cup used to administer the wine in the celebration of the Lord's supper.

Chalk, chak, *n.* [A.Sax. *cealc*, from L. *calx*, lime, limestone.] A well known earthy limestone, an impure carbonate of lime of an opaque white colour, soft, and admitting no polish.—*v.t.* To rub with chalk; to mark with chalk; to trace out; to describe: from the use of chalk in marking lines.—*Black chalk.* See under BLACK.—*Brown chalk*, a name for umber.—*Red chalk*, a natural clay containing 15 to 20 per cent of protoxide and carbonate of iron.—*French chalk*, steatite or soap-stone.—**Chalky**, chak'i, *a.* Resembling chalk; consisting of or containing chalk.—**Chalkiness**, chak'i-nes, *n.* The state of being chalky.—**Chalk-stones**, *n.* Certain concretions in the joints of persons violently affected by the gout.

Challenge, chal'lenj, *n.* [O.Fr. *chalenge*, *calenge*, *calonge*, &c., claim, accusation, dispute, from L. *calumnia*, a false accusation, a calumny. *Calumny* is thus the same word.] An invitation to a contest or trial of any kind, a calling or summons to fight in a single combat; the letter or message containing the summons to a contest; the calling in question or taking exception to something; the act of a sentry in demanding the countersign from any one who appears near his post; the claim of a party that certain jurors shall not sit in trial upon him or his cause, a right given both in civil and criminal trials when the impartiality of the jurors may be reasonably questioned.—*v.t.*—*challenged*, *challenging*. To address a challenge to; to call to a contest, to summon to fight, or to a duel, to demand the countersign or password from: said of a sentry; to claim as due, to demand as a right; *law*, to demand the removal of from among the jurymen; to object to (a person or thing); to take exception to; to call in question (a statement).—**Challengeable**, chal'len-ja-bl, *a.* Capable of being challenged or called to an account.—**Challenger**, chal'len-jer, *n.* One who challenges; one who defies another to a contest; an objector; one who calls in question.

Chalybeate, ka-lib'ē-āt, *a.* [From Gr. *chalyps*, *chalybos*, steel.] Impregnated with iron: applied to medicines containing iron, and especially to springs and waters impregnated with iron, or holding iron in solution.—*n.* Any water or other liquid into which iron enters. **Chalybite**, kal'i-bīt, *n.* An important iron ore occurring abundantly in connection with the carboniferous system, and yielding large quantities of iron.

Cham,‡ kam, *n.* The sovereign prince of Tartary: now written *Khan*.

Chamade, sha-mäd' or sha-mäd', *n.* [Fr., from It. *chiamata*, a calling, *chiamare*, to call, from L. *clamare*, to call = E. *claim*.] The beat of a drum or sound of a trumpet inviting an enemy to a parley.

Chamber, chām'bėr, *n.* [Fr. *chambre*, from L. *camera*, Gr. *kamara*, a vault or arched roof.] A room of a dwelling-house; an apartment; a room where professional men, as lawyers, conduct their business; especially, the room in which judges sit for the disposing of matters not sufficiently important to be heard in court; a hall or place where an assembly, association, or body of men meets; the assembly or body itself, as a *chamber* of commerce or of agriculture; a hollow or cavity in a thing, especially when of definite form and use; the part of a pump in which the bucket or plunger works; that part of a firearm where the powder lies.—*v.i.* To reside in or occupy as a chamber; to indulge in wantonness‡.—*v.t.* To shut up in, or as in, a chamber. (*Shak.*)—**Chambered**, chām'bėrd, *a.* Having or divided into a number of chambers or compartments.—**Chamberer**,‡ chām'bėr-ėr, *n.* One who intrigues or indulges in wantonness; a gallant. (*Shak.*).—**Chamberlain**, chām'bėr-lin, *n.* [O.Fr. *chamberlain*, from O.H.G. *chamarling*, *chamarlinc*—*chamar*, chamber, and suffix *-ling*.] A person charged with the direction and management of a chamber or chambers; specifically, an officer charged with the direction and management of the private apartments of a monarch or nobleman; the treasurer of a city, corporation, or the like.—**Chamberlainship**, chām'bėr-lin-ship, *n.* The office of a chamberlain.—**Chamber-maid**, *n.* A woman who has the care of chambers, making the beds and cleaning the rooms.—**Chamber-pot**, *n.* A vessel for containing slops, used in bedrooms.—**Chamber-practice**, *n.* The practice of a counsel, a barrister, or advocate who gives his opinions in private or at his chambers, but does not advocate cases in court.

Chambertin, shon-ber-taṅ, *n.* A superior sort of red Burgundy wine, named after the place where it is made.

Chameleon, ka-mē'le-on, *n.* [Gr. *chamaileōn*—*chamai*, on the ground, and *leōn*, lion; lit. ground-lion.] An insectivorous lizard, having a naked body, a prehensile tail, four feet suited for grasping branches, and the eye covered by a single circular eyelid with an aperture in the centre. It has long been remarkable for its faculty of changing its colour; and its powers of fasting and inflating itself gave rise to the notion that it lived on air.

Chamfer, cham'fėr, *n.* [Fr. *chanfrein*, a chamfer.] A small gutter or furrow cut in wood or other hard material; a bevel or slope; the corner of anything originally right-angled cut aslope equally on the two sides which form it.—*v.t.* To cut a chamfer in or on; to flute; to channel; to cut or grind so as to form a bevel.

Chamfron, cham'fron, *n.* [O.Fr. *chamfrein*, from *champ*, field, battle-field, and *frein*, L. *frenum*, a bridle.] The defensive armour for the fore part of the head of a war-horse.

Chamiso, **Chamise**, chä-mē'sō, chä-mēs', *n.* [Sp. *chamiza*.] A California shrub, that forms a dense thicket called **chamisal**, typical of parts of the Sierra Nevada.

Chamois, sham'oi or sham'i, *n.* [Fr.] A species of goat-like antelope inhabiting high inaccessible mountains in Europe and Western Asia, about the size of a well-grown goat, and extremely agile; a kind of soft leather made from various skins dressed with fish-oil; so called because first prepared from the skin of the chamois: in this sense often written *Shammy*.

Champ, champ, *v.t.* [From O.Fr. *champayer*, to graze, from *champ*, L. *campus*, a field, or a modification of obsolete *cham*, to chew.] To bite with repeated action of the teeth and with a snapping noise; to bite into small pieces; to chew; to munch; to craunch.

Champagne, sham-pān', *n.* A kind of light sparkling wine made chiefly in the department of Marne, in the former province of *Champagne*, in France.

Champaign, **Champain**, sham-pān', *n.* [O.Fr. *champaigne*, from *champ*, L. *campus*, a field. CAMPAIGN.] A flat open country.—*a.* Level; open; having the character of a plain.

Champ de Mars, shän de märs, the Campus Martius of the Romans, an open space, parade grounds, on the left bank of the Seine in Paris, the scene of innumerable historic events.

Champignon, sham-pin'yon, *n.* [Fr., a mushroom, from L.L. *campinio*, what grows in fields, from L. *campus*, a field.] A name for two edible mushrooms growing in Britain, one the common mushroom, the other a species growing in fairy rings.

Champion, cham'pi-on, *n.* [Fr. *champion*, L.L. *campio*, *campionis*, a champion, from L. *campus*, a field, later a combat, duel.] One who comes forward in defence of any cause; especially one who engages in single combat in the cause of another; more generally, a hero; a brave warrior; one who has acknowledged superiority in certain matters decided by public contest or competition; one open to contend with all comers, or otherwise requiring to resign the title.—*v.t.* To challenge to a combat; to come forward and maintain or support (a cause or a person).—**Championship**, cham'pi-on-ship, *n.* State of being a champion; support or maintenance of a cause.

Chance, chans, *n.* [Fr. *chance*, chance, hazard, from L.L. *cadentia*, a falling (E. *cadence*), from L. *cadere*, to fall; in allusion to the falling of the dice.] A casual or fortuitous event; an accident; that which is regarded as determining the course of events in the absence of law, ordinary causation, or providence (to happen by *chance*); accident; what fortune may bring; fortune; possibility of an occurrence; opportunity (to lose a *chance*).—*v.i.* To happen; to fall out; to come or arrive without design or expectation.—*v.t.* To put under the influence of chance; to risk; to hazard.—*a.* Happening by chance; casual.—**Chanceful**,† chans'ful, *a.* Full of chances or accidents; hazardous.—**Chance-medley**, *n.* Originally, a casual affray or riot, without deliberate or premeditated malice; now, the killing of another in self-defence upon a sudden and unpremeditated encounter.

Chancel, chan'sel, *n.* [So named from being railed off from the rest of the church by lattice-work—L. *cancelli*. CANCEL.] That part of the choir of a church between the altar or communion table and the balustrade or railing that incloses it, or that part where the altar is placed.—**Chancel-screen**, *n.* The screen or railing, often richly carved and ornamented, which separates the chancel from the body of the church.—**Chancellor**, chan'sel-ėr, *n.* [L.L. *cancellarius*, from L. *cancelli*, a lattice-work railing, from the chancellor formerly standing *ad cancellos* (at the latticed railing), to receive petitions, &c.] A state official in various European states, invested with judicial powers, and particularly with the superintendence of charters, letters, and other official writings of the government, varying in degree of political importance and responsibility. In the ecclesiastical sense, the chancellor of a cathedral is an official who superintends arrangements for religious ceremonies and services. The head of some universities; as the **chancellor** of McGill University, or of the University of Kansas. The usual title of university heads in the United States is **president**. In U. S. law courts, a judge in a court of chancery or equity; especially the presiding judge as distinguished from the vice-chancellors.—**Chancellorship**, chan'sel-ėr-ship, *n.* The office of a chancellor.

Chancery, chan'se-ri, *n.* [Modified from older *chancelry*, from Fr. *chancellerie*. CHANCELLOR.] A court or department of public affairs at the head of which is a chancellor; in England, formerly the highest court of justice next to parliament, but since 1873 a division of the High Court of Justice, which is itself one of the two departments of the Supreme Court of Judicature.

Chancre, shang'kėr, *n.* [Fr. = *canker*.] A sore or ulcer which arises from the direct application of the venereal virus.—**Chancrous**, shangk'rus, *a.* Having the qualities of a chancre; ulcerous.

Chandelier, shan-de-lēr', *n.* [Fr. *chandelier*, a chandelier, from L. *candela*, a candle. CANDLE.] A stand with branches to hold a number of candles, to light up a room.

Chandler, chand'lėr, *n.* [Fr. *chandelier*, a dealer in candles, from L. *candela*, a candle.] One who makes or sells candles; a dealer in general: the particular meaning of the term being determined by a prefix; as, tallow-*chandler*; ship-*chandler*, &c.—**Chandlery**, chand'lėr-i, *n.* The commodities sold by a chandler; a chandler's warehouse; a store-room for candlest.

Change, chānj, *v.t.—changed, changing.* [Fr. *changer*, to change, from L.L. *cambiare*, from L. *cambire*, to change, to barter.] To cause to turn or pass from one state to another; to vary in form or essence; to alter or make different; to substitute another thing or things for (to *change* the clothes); to shift; to give or procure another kind of money for (to *change* a bank-note); to give away for a money equivalent of a different kind; to exchange (to *change* places with a person).—*v.i.* To suffer change; to be altered; to undergo variation; to be partially or wholly transformed; to begin a new revolution, or to pass from one phase to another, as the moon.—*n.* Any variation or alteration in form, state, quality, or essence; a passing from one state or form to another; a succession of one thing in the place of another (*change* of seasons); the passing from one phase of the moon to another; alteration in the order of a series; permutation; that which makes a variety or may be substituted for another (two *changes* of clothes); small money, which may be given for larger pieces; the balance of a sum of money returned when the price of goods is deducted; a place where merchants and others meet to transact business: in this sense an abbreviation for *Exchange*, and often written '*Change*.—**Changeable**, chān'ja-bl, *a.* Liable to change; subject to alteration; fickle; inconstant; mutable; variable. — **Changeableness, Changeability**, chān'ja-bl-nes, chān-ja-bil'i-ti, *n.* The quality of being changeable.—**Changeably**, chān'ja-bli, *adv.* In a changeable manner.—**Changeful**, chānj'ful, *a.* Full of change; inconstant; mutable; fickle; uncertain; subject to alteration.—**Changefully**, chānj'ful-li, *adv.* In a changeful manner. — **Changefulness**, chānj'ful-nes, *n.*—**Changeless**, chānj'les, *a.* Constant; not admitting alteration.—**Changeling**, chānj'ling, *n.* One apt to change; a waverer (*Shak.*); a child, often a deformed or stupid child supposed to be substituted by fairies for another; hence, an idiot; a fool.—**Changer**, chānj'ėr, *n.* One who changes or alters the form of anything; one that is employed in changing and discounting money; a money-changer; one given to change; one who is inconstant or fickle.

Chank, Chank-shell, changk, *n.* [Skr. *çankha.*] The common conch-shell which is fished up by divers in the Indian seas.

Channel, chan'el, *n.* [From O.Fr. *chanel*, *canel*, L. *canalis*, a water-pipe; whence also *canal* and *kennel*, a gutter.] The bed of a stream of water; the hollow or course in which a stream flows; the deeper part of an estuary, bay, &c., where the current flows, or which is most convenient for the track of a ship; a strait or narrow sea between two islands, two continents, or a continent and an island; that by which something passes or is transmitted (as news, information); means of passing, conveying, or transmitting; a furrow or groove.—*v.t.—channelled, channelling.* To form a channel in; to cut channels in; to groove. (*Shak.*)

Channel, chan'el, *n.* [A corruption of *chain-wale.*] One of the pieces of plank projecting edgewise from a ship's sides and over which the shrouds are extended to keep them clear of the gunwale.

Chant, chänt, *v.t.* [Fr. *chanter*, from L. *cantare*, aug. of *cano*, *cantum*, to sing. Akin *cant.*] To utter with a melodious voice; to warble; to sing; to celebrate in song; to repeat the words of, in a kind of intoning voice or in a style between air and recitative. —*v.i.* To sing; to make melody with the voice; to intone, or perform a chant. —*n.* A song or singing; melody; specifically, a short musical composition consisting generally of a long reciting note, on which an indefinite number of words may be intoned, and a melodic phrase or cadence.—**Chanter**, chän'tėr, *n.* One who chants; a singer or songster; in bagpipes, the tube with finger-holes for playing the melody.—**Chanticleer**, chan'ti-klēr, *n.* [From *chant* and *clear.*] A cock, so called from the clearness or loudness of his voice in crowing.—**Chantress**,† chänt'res, *n.* A female singer. (*Mil.*)—**Chantry**, chän'tri, *n.* [O.Fr. *chanterie*, from *chant.*] A church or chapel endowed for the maintenance of one or more priests daily to sing or say mass for the souls of the donors or such as they appoint.

Chanterelle, shan-trel' or shan-tėr-el', *n.* [Fr., perhaps from O.Fr. *chanterelle*, a small bell, from its shape, from *chanter*, to sing.] An English edible mushroom, having a bright orange colour, a fragrant fruity smell, and being found frequently in woods under trees.

Chaos, kā'os, *n.* [Gr. *chaos*, from a root *cha*, to gape, to yawn, whence also *chasm.*] That confusion or confused mass out of which the universe was created; a confused mixture of parts or elements; a scene of extreme confusion; disorder.—**Chaotic**, kā-ot'ik, *a.* Resembling chaos; confused. —**Chaotically**, kā-ot'ik-al-li, *adv.* In a chaotic state.

Chap, chap or chop, *v.t.—chapped, chapping.* [Same word as *chop*, to cut.] To cause to cleave, split, crack, or open longitudinally, as the surface of the earth or the skin and flesh of the hand.—*v.i.* To crack; to open in long slits; to have the skin become cracked and sore, as from frost. —*n.* A crack in the surface of the hands or feet.

Chap, Chop, chop, *n.* [A form standing for *chaf* or *chof*, and equivalent to Sc. *chaft*, Icel. *kjaptr*, Dan. *kjæft*, Sw. *käft*, a jaw, without the *t.*] The upper or lower part of the mouth; the jaw; either of the two planes or flat parts of a vice or pair of tongs or pliers, for holding anything fast.—**Chapfallen**, chop'fąln, *a.* Having the lower chap or jaw depressed; hence, dejected or dispirited; silenced.—**Chapless**, chop'les, *a.* Without a chap or lower jaw. (*Shak.*)

Chap, chap, *n.* [An abbrev. of *chapman*; as regards its modern use compare *customer*, in senses of regular purchaser and fellow or chap.] A buyer‡; a chapman (*Steele*)‡; a man or a boy; a youth: used familiarly and laxly, much as the word *fellow* is.—**Chapman**, chap'man, *n.* [A.Sax. *ceápman*, a buyer or seller, from *ceáp*, a bargain, trade, and *mann*, a man.] Originally, a buyer and seller, a merchant; now, a hawker, pedlar, or travelling dealer. — **Chap-book**, *n.* A kind of small book or tract formerly much sold among the people by chapmen, containing generally lives of heroes, giants, &c., fairy-lore, ghost and witch stories, ballads, songs, and the like.

Chape, chāp, *n.* [Fr. *chape*, a catch, hook, chape, also a *cope*; same origin as *cape*, *cap.*] The part by which an object is attached, as the back-piece by which a buckle is fixed on the article or garment; the transverse guard of a sword for a protection to the hand; the metal tip at the end of a scabbard, or at the end of a belt or girdle.—**Chapeless**, chāp'les, *a.* Without a chape.

Chapel, chap'el, *n.* [Fr. *chapelle*, from L.L. *capella*, dim. of *capa*, a cape, hood, canopy, covering of the altar, a recess or chapel attached to the altar. CAP, CAPE, CHAPLET.] A subordinate place of worship usually attached to a large church or cathedral, connected with a palace or private residence, or subsidiary to a parish church; a place of worship used by dissenters from the Church of England; a meeting-house; a union or society formed by the workmen in a printing-office; printing-office, from Caxton's establishment in Westminster Abbey.—**Chapelry**, chap'el-ri, *n.* The territorial district assigned to a chapel dependent on a mother church.—**Chapel-cart**, *n.* A contraction of *Whitechapel-cart.*

Chaperon, shap'ėr-ōn or shap-roṅ, *n.* [Fr. *chaperon*, from *chape*, a cope. CHAPEL.] A kind of ancient hood or cap; a lady, especially a married lady, who attends a young lady to public places as a guide or protector. —*v.t.* To attend on as chaperon, guide, or the like.—**Chaperonage**, shap'ėr-ōn-āj, *n.* The protection or countenance of a chaperon.

Chapiter,‡ chap'i-tėr, *n.* [From O.Fr. *chapitel*, from L.L. *capitellum*, L. *capitulum*, dim. of *caput*, a head; *chapter* is the same word.] The upper part or capital of a column or pillar. (*O.T.*)

Chaplain, chap'lin, *n.* [Fr. *chapelain*; L.L. *capellanus*, from *capella*, a chapel. CHAPEL.] An ecclesiastic who performs divine service in a chapel; more generally, an ecclesiastic who officiates at court, in the household of a nobleman, or in an army, garrison, ship, institution, &c.—**Chaplaincy, Chaplainship**, chap'lin-si, chap'lin-ship, *n.* The office or post of a chaplain.

Chaplet, chap'let, *n.* [Fr. *chapelet*, a dim. of O.Fr. *chapel*, Mod.Fr. *chapeau*, a hat, from *chape*, L.L. *capa*, a hood, a cape; akin *chapel*, *chape*, &c.] A garland or wreath to be worn on the head; a string of beads used by Roman Catholics, by which they count their prayers; a small rosary; *arch.* a small round moulding, carved into beads, pearls, olives, or the like.

Chapman. Under CHAP, a buyer.

Chapter, chap'tėr, *n.* [Fr. *chapitre*, formerly *chapitle*, *capitel*, from L. *capitulum*, dim. of *caput*, the head, whence also *capital*, *cattle*, &c.] A division of a book or treatise; the council of a bishop, consisting of the canons or prebends and other clergymen attached to a collegiate or cathedral church, and presided over by a dean; the place in which the business of the chapter is conducted; a chapter-house; the meeting of certain organized orders and societies; a branch of some society or brotherhood.—**Chapter-house**, *n.* The building in which a chapter meets for the transaction of business.

Chaptrel, chap'trel, *n.* [A dim. from *chapiter.*] The capital of a pillar or a pilaster, which supports arches.

Char, Charr, chär, *n.* [Ir. and Gael. *cear*, red: from its having a red belly.] A name given to at least two species of the salmon family, inhabiting lakes in many parts of the north of Europe.

Char, Chare, chär, chār, *n.* [From A.Sax. *cerr*, *cyrr*, a turn, time, occasion; *cerran*, *cyrran*, to turn = D. *keeren*, G. *kehren*, to turn or move about. Hence *charcoal.*] A turn of work; a single job or piece of work; household work.—*v.i.* To work at others' houses by the day without being a hired servant; to do small jobs.—**Char-woman**, chär- or chār-, *n.* A woman employed by the day on odd jobs about a house; one employed in the house of another to do occasional or miscellaneous work.

Char, chär, *v.t.—charred, charring.* [O.E. *char*, to turn, from A.Sax. *cerran*, to turn; to *char* wood is to turn or change it; *charcoal* is wood turned into coal. CHAR, a turn.] To burn with slight admission of air; to reduce to charcoal; to burn (wood) slightly or partially, and on the surface. —**Charcoal**, chär'kōl, *n.* Coal made by charring wood; or more generally, the carbonaceous residue of vegetable, animal, or combustible mineral matter when they undergo smothered combustion. Wood-charcoal is much employed in the manufacture of gunpowder, and, like coke or *mineral charcoal*, as a more or less smokeless fuel; while *animal charcoal* from oils, fats, and bones, is the basis of lampblack and printer's-ink.

Character, kar'ak-tėr, *n.* [L. *character*, an engraved mark, from Gr. *charaktēr*, from *charattō*, *charaxō*, to cut, engrave.] A distinctive mark made by cutting, stamping, or engraving, as on stone, metal, or other hard material; a mark or figure, written or printed, and used to form words and communicate ideas; a letter, figure, or sign, the peculiar form of letters, written or printed, used by a particular person or people (the Greek *character*); the peculiar qualities impressed by nature or habit on a person, which distinguish him from others; a distinctive quality assigned to a person by repute; reputation: sometimes restricted to good qualities or reputation; strongly marked distinctive qualities of any kind; an account or statement of qualities or peculiarities; especially, an oral or written account of a servant's or employee's character or qualifications; a person; a personage; especially applied to individuals represented in fiction or history, to persons of eminence, and to persons marked by some prominent trait.—*v.t.* To mark with or as with characters; to engrave; to inscribe.—**Characteristic**, kar′ak-tėr-is″tik, *a.* [Gr. *charaktēristikos.*] Pertaining to or serving to constitute the character; exhibiting the peculiar qualities of a person or thing; peculiar; distinctive.—*n.* That which serves to constitute a character; that which characterizes; that which distinguishes a person or thing from another.—**Characteristical**, kar′ak-tėr-is″tik-al, *a.* Characteristic. —**Characteristically**, kar′ak-tėr-is″tik-al-li, *adv.* In a characteristic manner.—**Characteristicalness**, kar′ak-tėr-is″-tik-al-nes, *n.*—**Characterization**, kar′-ak-tėr-iz-ā″shon, *n.* Act of characterizing. —**Characterize**, kar′ak-tėr-īz, *v.t.* [Gr. *charaktērizō.*] To give a special stamp or character to; to constitute a peculiar characteristic or the peculiar characteristics of; to stamp or distinguish (*characterized* by benevolence); to give a character or an account of the personal qualities of a man; to describe by peculiar qualities.—**Characterless**, kar′ak-tėr-les, *a.* Destitute of any peculiar character.

Charade, sha-räd′ or sha-rād′, *n.* [Fr. Etymology unknown.] An enigma the solution of which is a word of two or more syllables each of which is separately significant, the word and its syllables being intended to be discovered from description, or in other cases from representation, when it is called an *acting charade.*

Charcoal, *n.* Under CHAR, to burn.

Chard, chärd, *n.* [Fr. *charde*, from L. *carduus*, a thistle or artichoke.] The leaves of artichoke, covered with straw in order to blanch them, and to make them less bitter; the vegetable, Swiss chard.

Chare, chār, *n.* and *v.* CHAR, work.

Charge, chärj, *v.t.*—*charged, charging.* [Fr. *charger*, from L.L. *carricare*, from L. *carrus*, a car, whence also *carry, cargo, caricature.*] To lay a load or burden on; to burden; to load; to fill; to occupy (to *charge* the memory); to impute or register as a debt; to put down to the debt of; to register as indebted or as forming a debt (to *charge* a person *for* a thing; to *charge* a thing *to* or *against* a person); to fix the price of: with *at* before the price or rate; to accuse; to impeach (to *charge* a person *with* a crime); to lay to one's charge; to impute; to ascribe the responsibility of (to *charge* guilt *on* a person); to intrust; to commission (a person *with*); to command; to enjoin; to instruct; to urge earnestly; to exhort; to adjure; to give directions to (a jury, &c.); to instruct authoritatively; to make an onset on; to attack by rushing against violently. ∴ Syn. under ACCUSE.—*v.i.* To make an onset; to rush to an attack; to place the price of a thing to one's debit.—*n.* That which is laid on or in; in a general sense, any load or burden; the quantity of anything which an apparatus, as a gun, an electric battery, &c., is intended to receive and fitted to hold, or what is actually in as a load; an attack, onset, or rush; an order, injunction, mandate, or command; hence, a duty enjoined on or intrusted to one; care, custody, or oversight; the person or thing committed to another's custody, care, or management; a trust; instructions given by a judge to a jury, or an exhortation given by a bishop to his clergy; what is alleged or brought forward by way of accusation; accusation; the sum payable as the price of anything bought; cost; expense; rent, tax, or whatever constitutes a burden or duty.—**Chargeable**, chärj′a-bl, *a.* Capable of being charged; falling to be set, laid, or imposed, as a tax or duty; subject to a charge or tax, as goods; capable of being laid to one's charge; capable of being imputed to one; subject to accusation; liable to be accused; causing expense, and hence burdensome.—**Chargeableness, Chargeability**, chärj′a-bl-nes, chärj-a-bil′i-ti, *n.* The quality of being chargeable. —**Charger**, chärj′ėr, *n.* One who or that which charges; a large dish (N.T.); a war-horse.

Chargé d'Affaires, shär-zhā dä-fär, *n.* [Fr., lit. charged with affairs.] One who transacts diplomatic business at a foreign court during the absence of his superior the ambassador, or at a court where no functionary so high as an ambassador is appointed.

Charily, Chariness. Under CHARY.

Chariot, char′i-ot, *n.* [Fr. *chariot*, from *char*, a car. CAR.] A stately four-wheeled pleasure or state carriage having one seat; a car or vehicle formerly used in war, in processions, and for racing, drawn by two or more horses.—*v.t.*† To convey in a chariot. (*Mil.*)—**Charioteer**, char′i-o-tēr″, *n.* The person who drives or conducts a chariot.—**Charioteering**, char′i-o-tēr″-ing, *n.* The act or art of driving a chariot.

Charity, char′i-ti, *n.* [Fr. *charité*, O.Fr. *charitet, cariteit*, from L. *caritas, caritatis*, from *carus*, dear, whence also *caress.*] The good affection, love, or tenderness which men should feel towards their fellows, and which should induce them to do good to and think favourably of others; benevolence; liberality in thinking or judging; liberality in giving to the poor; whatever is bestowed gratuitously on the poor for their relief; alms; any act of kindness or benevolence; a charitable institution; an hospital.—**Charitable**, char′it-a-bl, *a.* Pertaining to or characterized by charity; full of good-will or tenderness; benevolent and kind; liberal in benefactions to the poor and in relieving them in distress; pertaining to almsgiving or relief to the poor; springing from charity or intended for charity; lenient in judging of others; not harsh; favourable.—**Charitableness**, char-it-a-bl-nes, *n.* The quality of being charitable.—**Charitably**, char′it-a-bli, *adv.* In a charitable manner.

Charlatan, shär′la-tan, *n.* [Fr., from It. *ciarlatano*, a quack, from *ciarlare*, to prate, to chatter like birds.] One who prates much in his own favour and makes unwarrantable pretensions to skill; a quack; an empiric; a mountebank.—**Charlatanic, Charlatanical**, shär-la-tan′ik, shär-la-tan′ik-al, *a.* Pertaining to or resembling a charlatan; quackish.—**Charlatanically**, shär-la-tan′ik-al-li, *adv.* In a charlatanic manner.—**Charlatanism, Charlatanry**, shär′la-tan-izm, shär′la-tan-ri, *n.* The behaviour of a charlatan; undue pretensions to skill; quackery.

Charles's Law. The law that equal increments of temperature add equal amounts to the product of the volume and pressure of a given mass of gas: the law that volume is proportional to absolute temperature when pressure is constant.

Charles's-wain, chärlz′iz-wān, *n.* [A corruption of *churl's* (that is farmer's or peasant's) *wain.*] The seven brightest stars in the constellation called Ursa Major or the Great Bear: known also as the *Plough.*

Charlock, chär′lok, *n.* [A.Sax. *cerlic*; the termination is the same as in *garlic, hemlock*, and meant properly *leek.*] A weedy annual of the mustard family, with bright yellow flowers, occurring in cornfields.

Charm, chärm, *n.* [Fr. *charme*, a charm, an enchantment, from L. *carmen*, a song, a verse, a charm.] A melody‡; a song‡ (*Mil.*); anything believed to possess some occult or supernatural power, such as an amulet or spell or some mystic observance; something which exerts an irresistible power to please and attract; fascination; allurement; attraction; a trinket, such as a locket, seal, &c., worn on a watch-guard.—*v.t.* To subdue or control by incantation or magical or supernatural influence; to fortify or make invulnerable with charms; to subdue or soothe as if by magic; to allay or appease by what gives delight; to give exquisite pleasure to; to fascinate; to enchant.—*v.i.* To act as a charm or spell; to produce the effect of a charm.—**Charmer**, chär′mėr, *n.* One who charms, fascinates, enchants, allures, or attracts.—**Charming**, chär′ming, *a.* Pleasing in the highest degree; delighting; fascinating; enchanting; alluring.—**Charmingly**, chär′-ming-li, *adv.* In a charming manner.—**Charmingness**, chär′ming-nes, *n.*—**Charmless**,† chärm′les, *a.* Destitute of charms.

Charnel, chär′nel, *a.* [Fr. *charnel*, O.Fr. *carnel*, carnal, from L. *carnalis*, from *caro, carnis*, flesh.] Containing dead bodies.—**Charnel-house**, *n.* A place under or near churches where the bones of the dead are deposited.

Charpie, shär-pē, *n.* [Fr. *charpir*, to tease out, from L. *carpo*, to pluck, to pull.] Lint for dressing a wound.

Charqui, chär′kē, *n.* [The Chilian name, of which the term *jerked* beef is a corruption.] Jerked beef; beef cut into strips of about an inch thick and dried by exposure to the sun.

Charr, *n.* A kind of fish, the char.

Chart, chärt, *n.* [L. *charta*, paper, a leaf of paper. *Card* is the same word.] A sheet of any kind on which information is exhibited in a methodical or tabulated form; specifically, a marine map, with the coasts, islands, rocks, soundings, &c., to regulate the courses of ships.—*v.t.* To delineate, as on a chart; to map out.—**Chartaceous**, kär-tā′shus, *a. Bot.* papery; resembling paper: applied to the paper-like texture of leaves, bark, &c.—**Charter**, chär′tėr, *n.* [O.Fr. *chartre*, from L. *chartarius*, from *charta*, paper.] A writing given as evidence of a grant, contract, &c.; any instrument executed with form and solemnity bestowing or granting powers, rights, and privileges; privilege; immunity; exemption.—*v.t.* To hire or let (a ship) by charter or contract; to establish by charter; to grant; to privilege.—**Charterable**, chär′tėr-a-bl, *a.* Capable of being, or in a condition to be, chartered or hired, as a ship.—**Chartered**, chär′tėrd, *a.* Granted by charter; permitted by charter; privileged.—**Charterer**, chär′tėr-ėr, *n.* One who charters.—**Charter-party**, *n.* [Fr. *charte-partie*, a divided charter, from the practice of cutting the instrument in two, and giving one part to each of the contractors.] *Com.* an agreement respecting the hire of a vessel and the freight, signed by the proprietor or master of the ship, and by the merchant who hires or freights it.—**Chartism**, chär′tizm, *n.* The political principles or opinions of the Chartists. —**Chartist**, chär′tist, *n.* One of a body of political reformers in England that sprung up about the year 1838, and advocated as their leading principles universal suffrage, no property qualification for a seat in parliament, annual parliaments, equal representation, payment of members, and vote by ballot, all which privileges they demanded as constituting the people's charter.

Chartography, kär-tog′ra-fi, *n.* [E. *chart*, L. *charta*, paper, and Gr. *graphē*, writing, description.] The art or practice of drawing up maps or charts.—**Chartographer**, kär-tog′raf-ėr, *n.* One who prepares or publishes maps or charts; a maker of maps or charts.—**Chartographic**, kär-to-graf′-ik, *a.* Pertaining to chartography.—**Chartographically**, kär-to-graf′ik-al-li, *adv.* In a chartographic manner; by chartography.

Chartreuse, shär′tröz, *n.* A highly esteemed liqueur made with fine spirits and aromatic plants growing on the Alps, and so called from the monastery of the same name, where it used to be made.

Chartulary, kär′tū-la-ri, *n.* [Fr. *cartulaire*, L.L. *cartularius*, from *chartula*, dim. of L. *charta*, paper.] A record or register, as of a monastery.

Char-woman, *n.* CHAR, work.

Chary, chā′ri, *a.* [A.Sax. *cearig*, full of care, sad, from *cearu, caru*, care. CARE.] Careful; cautious; frugal; sparing: with *of* before an object.—**Charily**, chā′ri-li, *a.* In a chary manner; carefully; sparingly. —**Chariness**, chā′ri-nes, *n.*

Chase, chās, *v.t.*—*chased, chasing.* [Also written *chace*, from O.Fr. *chacier*, Mod.Fr. *chasser*, to chase, a parallel form with *catch*, being like it from L.L. *captiare*. CATCH.] To pursue for the purpose of taking, as game; to hunt; to follow after or search for with eagerness; to pursue for any purpose; to follow with hostility; to drive off. —*n.* Pursuit; hunting; ardent search for or following after; that which is pursued or hunted; specifically, a vessel pursued by another; an open piece of ground or place well stored with game, and belonging to a private proprietor.—**Chasable**, chās'a-bl, *a.* Capable of being chased; fit for the chase.—**Chaser**, chās'ėr, *n.* One who or that which chases; a pursuer or hunter; a ship that pursues another; a chase-gun.—**Chase-gun**, *n.* In war-ships, a gun used in chasing an enemy or in defending a ship when chased.

Chase, chās, *n.* [Fr. *châsse*, from L. *capsa*, box, case. *Case*, for holding things, is a form of the same word.] An iron frame used by printers to confine types when set in columns or pages; the part of a gun between the trunnions and the muzzle; a wide groove.

Chase, chās, *v.t.* [Shortened from *enchase*.] To enchase; to cut a thread on, so as to make a screw.—**Chaser**, chās'ėr, *n.* One who chases or enchases; an enchaser; a steel tool used for cutting or finishing the threads of screws.

Chasm, kazm, *n.* [Gr. *chasma*, from root *cha*, as in *chaos*.] A gaping or yawning opening, as in the earth; an abyss; a wide and deep cleft; a fissure; a void space.—**Chasmy**, kaz'mi, *a.* Abounding with chasms.

Chasseur, shas-sėr, *n.* [Fr., a huntsman.] One of a body of soldiers, light and active, both mounted and on foot, trained for rapid movements; a person dressed in a sort of military style in attendance upon persons of rank.

Chassis, shä-sē, *n.* [Fr.] The framework of a motor car, carrying the body and other parts.

Chaste, chāst, *a.* [Fr. *chaste*, from L. *castus*, chaste.] Pure from all unlawful sexual commerce; free from libidinous desires; continent; virtuous; free from obscenity or impurity in thought and language; as applied to literary style, free from barbarous words and phrases, affected or extravagant expressions, or the like; in art, free from meretricious ornament or affectation; not gaudy.—**Chastely**, chāst'li, *adv.* In a chaste manner.—**Chasteness**, chāst'nes *n.* The state or quality of being chaste.—**Chastity**, chas'ti-ti, *n.* The state or property of being chaste, pure, or undefiled; sexual purity; continence.

Chasten, chās'n, *v.t.* [O.Fr. *chastier*, from L. *castigare*, to castigate or chastise, from *castus*, pure, whence *chaste*; comp. *chastise*.] To inflict pain, trouble, or affliction on for the purpose of reclaiming from evil; to correct; to chastise; to punish: not now used of corporal punishment, which is expressed by *chastise*; to purify, as the taste; to refine.—**Chastener**, chās'n-ėr, *n.* One who chastens.

Chastise, chas-tīz', *v.t.*—*chastised*, *chastising*. [Same word as *chasten*, but with a different verbal termination; O.E. *chastie*, *chasty*, from O.Fr. *chastier*. CHASTEN.] To inflict pain on by stripes or in any other manner, for the purpose of punishing and recalling to duty; to correct by punishment; to free from faults or excesses; to correct; to restrain.—**Chastisable**, chas-tīz'a-bl, *a.* Deserving of chastisement.—**Chastisement**, chas'tiz-ment, *n.* The act of chastising; pain inflicted for punishment and correction, either by stripes or otherwise.—**Chastiser**, chas-tīz'ėr, *n.* One who chastises; a punisher; a corrector.

Chasuble, chas'ū-bl, *n.* [Fr. *chasuble*, from L.L. *casubula*, from L. *casula*, a little cottage, a hooded garment, dim. of *casa*, a cottage.] A rich vestment or garment worn uppermost by a priest at the celebration of the eucharist.

Chat, chat, *v.i.*—*chatted*, *chatting*. [An abbreviated form of *chatter*.] To talk idly or in a familiar manner; to talk without form or ceremony.—*n.* Free, familiar talk; idle talk; prate.—**Chatty**, chat'i, *a.* Inclined to chat; talkative.

Chat, chat, *n.* [From the chattering sound of its voice.] A name of several small, lively birds of the warbler family, three species of which are found in Britain, namely, the stone-chat, the whin-chat, and the wheat-ear.

Château, shä-tō', *n.* pl. **Châteaux**, shä-tōz', Fr. tō. [Fr. *château*, O.Fr. *chastel*, a castle, from L. *castellum*. CASTLE.] A castle; a mansion in the country; a country-seat.—**Chatelaine**, shat'ė-lān, *n.* [Fr. *châtelaine*, lit. a female castellan or castle-keeper.] A female castellan; a bunch of chains worn at a lady's waist, having attached such articles as a key, thimble-case, penknife, cork-screw, &c.—**Chatelet**, shat-lā, *n.* [Fr. *châtelet*, dim. of *château*.] A little castle.

Chatoyant, sha-toi'ant, *a.* [Fr., pp. of *chatoyer*, to change lustre like the eye of a cat, from *chat*, a cat.] Having a changeable, undulating lustre or colour, like that of a cat's eye in the dark.

Chattel, chat'el, *n.* [O.E. *chatel*, also *catel*, really the same word as *cattle* (which see).] An item or article of goods, specifically applied in law to goods movable or immovable, except such as have the nature of freehold.

Chatter, chat'ėr, *v.i.* [Probably an imitative word, allied to D. *kwetteren*, Dan. *kviddre*, Sw. *kvittra*, to chirp, to chatter.] To utter sounds rapidly and indistinctly, as a magpie or a monkey; to make a noise by repeated rapid collisions of the teeth; to talk idly, carelessly, or rapidly; to jabber. —*v.t.* To utter as one who chatters.—*n.* Sounds like those of a magpie or monkey; idle talk.—**Chatter-box**, *n.* One that talks incessantly: applied chiefly to children. (Colloq.)—**Chatterer**, chat'ėr-ėr, *n.* One who chatters; a prater; an idle talker; the popular name of sundry insessorial birds, one of which is the waxwing, or Bohemian chatterer.

Chaud-medley, shōd'med-li, *n.* [Fr. *chaud*, hot (L. *calidus*), and E. *medley*.] *Law*, the killing of a man in an affray in the heat of blood or passion.

Chaufer, Chauffer, cha̤'fėr, *n.* [Fr. *chauffer*, to heat. CHAFE.] A small portable furnace, usually of sheet-iron, with a grating near the bottom.—**Chauffeur**, shō'fėr, *n.* [Fr.] The driver of a heat motor vehicle.

Chaunt, chänt. CHANT.

Chauvin, shō-vaṅ, *n.* [From Nich. *Chauvin*, an enthusiastic military adherent of Napoleon I.] Originally, one of the veterans of the first French Empire who professed, after the fall of Napoleon, a sort of adoration for his person and his acts; hence, any one possessed by an absurdly exaggerated patriotism or military enthusiasm.—**Chauvinism**, shō'vin-izm, *n.* The sentiments of a chauvin; absurdly exaggerated patriotism or military enthusiasm.

Chaw, cha̤, *v.t.* To chew: an old form now vulgar.—**Chaw-bacon**, *n.* A country lout; a bumpkin.

Chay, Chaya-root, chā, chā'a, *n.* An Indian root yielding a red dye.

Cheap, chēp, *a.* [Strictly a noun, being = A.Sax. *ceáp*, price, bargain; from the use of the phrase *good cheap*, as to buy a thing *good cheap*, that is a good bargain, the noun came to be used as an adjective. Cog. D. *koop*, a purchase, *koopen*, to buy; Icel. *kaup*, a bargain; *kaupa*, to buy; G. *kaufen*, to buy; Goth. *kaufon*, to traffic. *Cheapen*, *chop*, *chaffer*, *chapman*, are akin.] Bearing a low price in market; capable of being purchased at a low price, either as compared with the usual price of the commodity, or with the real value, or more vaguely with the price of other commodities; being of small value; common; not respected.—**Cheapen**, chē'pn, *v.t.* To ask the price of; to chaffer or bargain for; to beat down the price of; to lessen the value of; to depreciate.—**Cheapener**, chē'pn-ėr, *n.* One who cheapens or bargains.—**Cheaply**, chēp'li, *adv.* At a small price; at a low rate.—**Cheapness**, chēp'nes, *n.* The state or quality of being cheap.—**Cheap-Jack, Cheap-John**, *n.* A travelling hawker professing to give wonderful bargains; a seller of cheap articles.

Cheat, chēt, *v.t.* [Abbrev. of *escheat*, to act like an escheater, who held an office giving great opportunities of fraud. ESCHEAT.] To deceive and defraud; to impose upon; to trick (to *cheat* a person *of* or *out of* something); to illude; to deceive; to mislead.—*v.i.* To act dishonestly; to practise fraud or trickery.—*n.* A fraud committed by deception; a trick, imposition, or imposture; a person who cheats; a fraudulent person; a swindler.—**Cheatable**, chēt'a-bl, *a.* Capable of being cheated; easily cheated.—**Cheatableness**, chēt'a-bl-nes, *n.*—**Cheater**, chēt'ėr, *n.* One who cheats; an escheater (*Shak.*).—**Cheating**, chēt'ing, *a.* Given to cheat or associated with cheating; fraudulent.—**Cheatingly**, chēt'ing-li, *adv.* In a cheating manner.

Check, chek, *n.* [Fr. *échec*, O.Fr. *eschec*, a check, a check at chess, lit. king, the call of king! in chess, from Per. *shâh*, king, the chief piece at chess. CHESS, CHEQUE, CHEQUER.] The act of suddenly stopping or restraining; a stop; hindrance; restraint; obstruction; a term or word of warning in chess when one party obliges the other either to move or guard his king; a reprimand; rebuke; censure; slight; a species of cloth, in which coloured lines or stripes cross each other rectangularly, making a pattern resembling the squares of a chess-board; the pattern of such cloth; a mark put against names or items on going over a list; a duplicate, or counterpart, used for security or verification; a counterfoil; a ticket or token given for identification; a cheque (which see).—*v.t.* To stop or moderate the motion of; to restrain in action; to hinder; to curb; to rebuke; to chide or reprove; *chess*, to make a move which puts the adversary's king in check; to compare with a counterfoil or something similar, with a view to ascertain authenticity or accuracy.—*v.i.* To make a stop; to stop; to pause.—*a.* Made of check; chequered.—**Checker**, chek'ėr, *n.* One who checks. For *Checker* in other senses see CHEQUER.—**Checkmate**, chek'māt, *n.* [From Per. *shâh mât*, the king is dead (*shâh*, the king, *mât*, he is dead).] *Chess*, the position of a king when he is in check, and cannot release himself, which brings the game to a close; hence, defeat; overthrow.—*v.t.*—*checkmated*, *checkmating*. To put in check, as an opponent's king in chess-playing, so that he cannot be released; hence, to defeat; to thwart: to frustrate.—**Check-string**, *n.* A string in a coach by pulling which the occupant may call the attention of the coachman.

Cheddar, ched'ėr, *n.* A rich fine-flavoured cheese made at *Cheddar* in Somersetshire, England; any cheese of similar character.

Cheek, chēk, *n.* [A.Sax. *ceáce*, cheek; cog. D. *kaak*, Sw. *kek*, the jaw, *käk*, the cheek; probably same root as *chaw*, *jaw*, *chaps*.] The side of the face below the eyes on each side; something regarded as resembling the human cheek in position or otherwise; one of two pieces, as of an instrument, apparatus, framework, &c., which form corresponding sides or which are double and alike, as the *cheeks* of a vice, of a lathe, of a door, &c.; cool confidence; brazen-faced impudence; impudent or insulting talk (in these senses rather vulgar).—**Cheek-bone**, *n.* The bone of the cheek.—**Cheek-pouch**, *n.* A bag situated in the cheek of a monkey, by means of which it is enabled to stow away and carry off food for future consumption.—**Cheek-tooth**, *n.* A molar tooth or grinder. (*O.T.*)

Cheep, chēp, *v.i.* & *t.* [Imitative.] To pule or peep, as a chicken; to chirp; to squeak. —*n.* A chirp; a squeak.

Cheer, chēr, *n.* [O.E. *chere*, face, look, mien, from O.Fr. *chere*, *chiere*, face, countenance, from L.L. *cara*, the face, from Gr. *kara*, the head.] Expression of countenance, as noting a greater or less degree of good spirits (*Shak.*); state or temper of the mind; state of feeling or spirits; a state of gladness or joy; gaiety; animation; that which makes cheerful or promotes good spirits; provisions for a feast; viands; fare; a shout of joy, encouragement, applause, or acclamation.—*v.t.* To gladden; to make cheerful; to encourage; to salute with shouts of joy or cheers; to applaud.—*v.i.* To grow cheerful; to become gladsome or joyous: often with *up*; to utter a cheer or shout of acclamation or joy.—**Cheerer**, chēr′ėr, *n.* One who or that which cheers.—**Cheerful**, chēr′ful, *a.* Of good cheer; having good spirits; gay; moderately joyful; associated with or expressive of agreeable feelings; lively; animated; promoting or causing cheerfulness; gladdening; animating; genial. —**Cheerfully**, chēr′ful-li, *adv.* In a cheerful manner; with alacrity or willingness; readily; with life, animation, or good spirits. —**Cheerfulness**, chēr′ful-nes, *n.* The state or quality of being cheerful.—**Cheerily**, chē′ri-li, *adv.* In a cheery manner.—**Cheeriness**, chēr′i-nes, *n.* Quality or state of being cheery.—**Cheering**, chēr′ing, *a.* Giving joy or gladness; enlivening; encouraging; animating. — **Cheeringly**, chēr′ing-li, *adv.* In a cheering manner.—**Cheerless**, chēr′les, *a.* Without joy, gladness, or comfort; gloomy; destitute of anything to enliven or animate the spirits.—**Cheerlessly**, chēr′les-li, *adv.* In a cheerless manner; dolefully.—**Cheerlessness**, chēr′les-nes, *n.* State of being cheerless.—**Cheerly**, chēr′li, *adv.* Cheerily; cheerfully; heartily; briskly. (*Shak.*)—**Cheery**, chē′ri, *a.* Showing cheerfulness or good spirits; blithe; hearty; gay; sprightly; promoting cheerfulness.

Cheese, chēz, *n.* [A.Sax. *cése*, *cyse*, cheese; derived like G. *käse*, D. *kaas*, from L. *caseus*, cheese.] An article of food consisting of the curd or caseine of milk, coagulated by rennet or some acid, separated from the whey, and usually pressed into a solid mass in a mould.—**Cheesy**, chē′zi, *a.* Having the qualities, taste, odour, or form of cheese; resembling or pertaining to cheese.—**Cheesiness**, chē′zi-nes, *n.* The quality of being cheesy.—**Cheese-cake**, *n.* A cake filled with a jelly made of soft curds, sugar, and butter; a small cake made in various ways and with a variety of different ingredients.—**Cheese-fly**, *n.* A small black fly which lays its eggs in the cracks of cheese, producing a maggot known as the *cheese-hopper*.—**Cheesemonger**, chēz′mung-gėr, *n.* One who deals in or sells cheese.—**Cheese-paring**, *a.* Meanly economical; parsimonious. — **Cheese-press**, *n.* A press or apparatus for pressing curd in the making of cheese.—**Cheese-vat**, *n.* The vat or case in which curds are confined for pressing.

Cheetah, chē′ta, *n.* Same as *Chetah*.

Chef, shef, *n.* [Fr., lit. head, from L. *caput*.] Head or chief; specifically, the head cook of a great establishment, as a nobleman's household, a club, &c.—**Chef-d'œuvre**, shā-dö-vr, *n.* pl. **Chefs-d'œuvre**, shā-dö-vr. [Fr.] A master-piece; a fine work in art, literature, &c.

Chegoe, Chegre, cheg′ō, cheg′ėr, *n.* Same as *Chigoe*.

Cheirognomy, kī-rog′no-mi, *n.* Same as *Chirognomy*.—**Cheirology**, kī-rol′o-ji, *n.* Same as *Chirology*.—**Cheiropodist**, kī-rop′o-dist, *n.* Same as *Chiropodist*.

Cheiropter, kī-rop′tėr, *n.* [Gr. *cheir*, a hand, and *pteron*, a wing.] A bat. Bat.—**Cheiropterous**, kī-rop′tėr-us, *a.* Belonging to the Cheiroptera or bat tribe.

Cheirotherium, kī-rō-thē′ri-um, *n.* [Gr. *cheir*, the hand, and *therion*, a wild beast.] *Geol.* a name given to an animal known by its footprints, and supposed to be identical with the labyrinthodon.

Chela, kē′la, *n.* pl. **Chelæ**, kē′lē. [Gr. *chēlē*, a claw.] One of the prehensile claws possessed by certain crustacea, as the crab, lobster, &c.—**Chelate, Cheliferous**, kē′lāt, kē-lif′ėr-us, *a.* Furnished with chelæ. —**Cheliform**, kē′li-form, *a.* Having the form of a chela or prehensile claw.

Chelicera, pl. -æ, kē-lis′ėr-a, *n.* [Gr. *chēlē*, a claw, *keros*, a horn.] In arachnids, each of first pair of head-limbs.

Chelonian, kē-lō′ni-an, *a.* [Gr. *chelōnē*, a tortoise.] Pertaining to or designating animals of the tortoise kind.—*n.* A tortoise or turtle.

Chemise, she-mēz′, *n.* [Fr. *chemise*, L.L. *camisia*, a shirt, from Ar. *qamis*, a shirt, an under-garment of linen.] A shift or smock worn by females; a wall that lines the face of an earthwork; a breast-wall.—**Chemisette**, shem-i-zet′, *n.* [Fr.] A short under-garment worn on the breast over the chemise.

Chemist, kem′ist, *n.* [Shortened from *alchemist*, from *alchemy*, O.Fr. *alchemie*, from Ar. *al*, the, and *qimīā*, chemistry, from L. Gr. *chēmeia*, chemistry, from Gr. *cheō*, to pour, to drop.] A person versed in chemistry; one whose business is to make chemical examinations or investigations; one who deals in drugs and medicines.—**Chemistry**, kem′ist-ri, *n.* The science which seeks to discover the different kinds of matter of which the globe is composed, and treats of the nature, laws of combination, and mutual actions of the particles of matter, and the properties of the compounds they form. *Theoretical* or *pure chemistry* deals chiefly with the laws and principles underlying chemical actions, while *practical* (or *applied*) *chemistry* is more concerned with the modes of preparing chemical substances, of analysing these, or of finding useful applications for them in the arts.—*Organic chemistry*, the chemistry of the carbon compounds; in older sense, the chemistry of organized bodies (animals and plants). — *Inorganic chemistry*, the chemistry of the elements and of compounds other than those of carbon.—**Chemical**, kem′i-kal, *a.* Pertaining to chemistry. — *Chemical combination*, that intimate union of two substances, whether fluid or solid, by which is produced a compound differing in one or more of its essential qualities from either of the constituents. -*n.* A substance used to produce chemical effects; a chemical agent.—**Chemically**, kem′i-kal-li, *adv.* In a chemical manner; according to chemical principles; by chemical process or operation. —**Chemico-electric**, kem′i-kō-ē-lek″-trik, *a.* Pertaining or relating to electricity resulting from chemical action; also, pertaining to chemical action resulting from electricity.

Chemitype, Chemitypy, kem′i-tīp, kem′i-tī-pi, *n.* [*Chemi-* in *chemistry*, and *type*.] A process by which an impression from an engraved plate is obtained in relief, so as to be printed on an ordinary printing-press.

Chemosmosis, kem-os-mō′sis, *n.* [*Chem-* in *chemistry*, and *osmosis*.] Chemical action acting through an intervening membrane, as parchment, &c.—**Chemosmotic**, kem-os-mot′ik, *a.* Pertaining or relating to chemosmosis.

Chenille, she-nēl′, *n.* [Fr., a caterpillar.] A tufted cord of silk or worsted, somewhat resembling a caterpillar, used for making rugs, bedspreads, &c.

Chenomorph, ke′no-morf, *n.* [Gr. *chēn*, goose, *morphē*, form.] *Ornith.* any bird of the duck tribe.

Check, chek, *n.* [From *chequer*, or *exchequer*, in old sense of banker's or money-changer's office or counter; or from *check*, in sense of counterfoil.] An order for money drawn on a banker or bank, payable to the bearer.—**Check-book**, *n.* A book containing blank bank-checks.

Checker, Chequer, chek′ėr, *n.* [O.Fr. *eschequier*, Mod.Fr. *échiquier*, a chess-board, an exchequer, from O.Fr. *eschecs*, chess. Check, Chess.] A chess or draught board‡; *pl.* the game of draughts; one of the divisions of a pattern that consists of squares; the pattern itself; an exchequer or treasury‡.—*v.t.* To mark with little squares, like a chess-board, by lines or stripes of different colors; to mark with different colors; *fig.* to variegate with different qualities, scenes, or events; to diversify; to impart variety to (events that *checker* one's career).—**Checkered, Chequered**, chek′ėrd, *a.* Marked with or exhibiting squares of different colors; varied with a play of different colors; *fig.* variegated with different qualities, scenes, or events; crossed with good and bad fortune (a *checkered* life or narrative).—**Checker-board**, *n.* A board on which checkers or draughts are played.—**Checker-work**, *n.* Work exhibiting checkers or squares of varied color or materials; work consisting of cross lines; *fig.* an aggregate of vicissitudes.

Cherimoyer, cher′i-moi-ėr, *n.* [Peruvian name.] A fruit of South America allied to the custard-apple.

Cherish, cher′ish, *v.t.* [O.Fr. *cherir*, *cherissant* (Fr. *chérir*), to hold dear, from *cher*, L. *carus*, dear, whence also *caress*.] To treat with tenderness and affection; to take care of; to foster; to hold as dear; to indulge and encourage in the mind; to harbour; to cling to.—**Cherisher**, cher′ish-ėr, *n.* One who cherishes; an encourager; a supporter.—**Cherishingly**, cher′ish-ing-li, *adv.* In an affectionate or cherishing manner.

Cheroot, she-röt′, *n.* [Tamil *shuruttu*, a roll.] A kind of cigar of a cylindrical or often somewhat tapering shape, with both ends cut square off.

Cherry, cher′i, *n.* [O.E. *cheri*, *chiri*, from Fr. *cerise*, L. *cerasus*, from Gr. *kerasos*, a cherry.] The fruit of a tree belonging to the plum family, consisting of a pulpy drupe inclosing a one-seeded smooth stone; the tree itself; also the name of other fruits.—*a.* Like a red cherry in colour; red; ruddy; blooming.—**Cherry-brandy**, *n.* Brandy in which cherries have been steeped.—**Cherry-laurel**, *n.* An evergreen shrub of the cherry genus, a native of Asia Minor. —**Cherry-pepper**, *n.* A species of capsicum, whose fruit is small and cherry-shaped.—**Cherry-pit**, *n.* A child's play, in which cherry-stones are thrown into a hole.—**Cherry-stone**, *n.* The seed of the cherry.

Chersonese, kėr′sō-nēz, *n.* [Gr. *chersonēsos*—*chersos*, land, and *nēsos*, an isle.] A peninsula.

Chert, chėrt, *n.* [Probably Celtic; comp. Ir. *ceart*, a pebble.] A variety of quartz, more or less translucent, less hard than common quartz, with a fracture usually conchoidal and dull, sometimes splintery. —**Cherty**, chėr′ti, *a.* Like chert; full of chert; flinty.

Cherub, cher′ub, *n.* pl. **Cherubs**; Hebrew pl. **Cherubim**, cher′ub-im. [Heb. *kerub*.] One of an order of angels; a beautiful child. [In the latter sense the plural is always *cherubs*.]—**Cherubic, Cherubical**, che-rū′bik, che-rū′bik-al, *a.* Pertaining to or resembling cherubs; angelic.—**Cherubimic**, cher-ū-bim′ik, *a.* Of or belonging to cherubim.

Chervil, chėr′vil, *n.* [A.Sax. *cerfille*, from L. *chærophyllum*, from Gr. *chairephyllon*—*chairō*, to rejoice, and *phyllon*, leaf, from their agreeable odour.] A hairy herb of the carrot family, with longish grooved fruits, common in fields and waste places throughout Britain.—*Garden chervil*, an annual plant cultivated as an aromatic pot-herb.

Chesnut. Chestnut.

Chess, ches, *n.* [O.Fr. *eschecs*, Fr. *échecs*, chess, really a plural, meaning lit. kings, from Per. *shāh*, a king, the principal figure in the game, whence also *check*.] An ingenious game played by two persons or parties with different pieces on a checkered board, divided into sixty-four squares.—**Chess-board**, *n.* The board used in the game of chess.—**Chess-man**, *n.* A piece used in playing the game of chess.

Chessel, ches′el, *n.* [From *cheese*.] A mould or vat in which cheese is formed.

Chest, chest, *n.* [A.Sax. *cyste*, from L. *cista*, Gr. *kistē*, a chest, a box.] A box of considerable size; *com.* a case in which certain kinds of goods, as tea, indigo, &c., are packed for transit; hence, the quantity such a chest contains; the trunk of the body from the neck to the belly; the thorax.—*Chest of drawers*, a piece of furniture with sliding boxes or drawers for holding various articles of dress, linen, &c.—*v.t.* To deposit in a chest; to hoard.—**Chested**, ches'ted, *a.* Having a chest of this or that kind: used chiefly in composition (broad-*chested*).

Chestnut, ches'nut, *n.* [For *chesten-nut*, O.E. *chesteine*, *chesteyne*, from O.Fr. *chastaigne*, from L. *castanea*, the chestnut-tree, from Gr. *kastanon*, from *Castana* in Pontus, where this tree abounded.] The seed or nut of a forest tree allied to the beech, inclosed in a prickly pericarp, containing two or more edible seeds; the tree itself or its timber; the colour of the husk of a chestnut; a reddish-brown colour; an old joke (colloq.).—*a.* Of the colour of a chestnut; reddish-brown.

Chetah, chē'ta, *n.* [Native name, meaning spotted.] The hunting leopard, trained in India to hunt such game as deer, &c.

Chetvert, chet'vėrt, *n.* A Russian grain measure, equal to 5·77 bushels.

Cheval-de frise, she-val'de-frēz, *n.* pl. **Chevaux-de-frise**, she-vō'de-frēz. [Fr. *cheval*, a horse, pl. *chevaux*, and *Frise*, Friesland, where first employed.] A horizontal piece of timber or iron with long spikes transversely through it, set on the ground to bar a passage, form an obstacle to the advance of cavalry, &c.

Cheval-glass, *n.* A swing looking-glass mounted on a frame, and large enough to reflect the whole figure.

Chevalier, shev-a-lēr', *n.* [Fr., from *cheval*, a horse. CAVALRY, CAVALIER.] A horseman; a cavalier; a member of certain orders of knighthood.—*Chevalier d'industrie*, one who gains a living by dishonest means; a sharper; a swindler; a thief.

Cheveril,† shev'ėr-il, *n.* [O.Fr. *chevrel*, a kid, dim. of *chèvre*, L. *capra*, a goat.] A soft pliable leather made of kid-skin.

Cheviot, chē'vi-ot, *n.* and *a.* A name for a variety of sheep, noted for their large carcass and valuable wool, so called from the Cheviot Hills between Scotland and England.

Chevrette, shev-ret', *n.* [Fr., from *chèvre*, L. *capra*, a goat.] An old machine for raising guns or mortars into their carriages; thin goat-skin leather for gloves.

Chevron, shev'run, *n.* [Fr., a rafter, from *chèvre*, L. *capra*, a goat, because rafters are reared on end like butting goats.] *Her.* a figure on a shield representing two rafters of a house meeting at the top; *arch.* a variety of fret ornament; a zigzag; *milit.* the distinguishing marks on the sleeves of non-commissioned officers' coats, to mark the rank of the bearer.—**Chevroned**, shev'rund, *a.* Bearing a chevron; resembling a chevron.

Chew, chö, *v.t.* [From A.Sax. *ceówan*, to chew = D. *kaauwen*, G. *kauen*, to chew. *Jaw*, *jowl*, *chaps*, *chops* are from the same root.] To bite and grind with the teeth; to masticate.—*To chew the cud*, to ruminate, and *fig.* to ruminate or meditate on something.—*v.i.* To perform the act of chewing; to champ.—*n.* That which is chewed; a quid of tobacco.

Chian, kī'an, *a.* Pertaining to *Chios*, an isle in the Levant.—*Chian earth*, a kind of earth used anciently as an astringent and a cosmetic.

Chiaroscuro, **Chiaro-oscuro**, ki-ä'rō-skö''rō, ki-ä'rō-os-kö''rō, *n.* [It., lit. clear-obscure, from L. *clarus*, clear, and *obscurus*, obscure; Fr. *clair-obscur*.] That department of painting which relates to light and shade; the art of judiciously distributing the lights and shadows in a picture.

Chiasma, kī-az'ma, *n.* [Gr. *chiasma*, from the Greek letter χ.] *Anat.* the central body of nervous matter, where the optic nerves cross each other proceeding from the brain to the eyes; a cross arrangement [X] of clauses e.g. *I cannot sing, to laugh I would be ashamed.*

Chibouque, **Chibouk**, shi-bųk', *n.* [Turk.] A Turkish tobacco-pipe.

Chic, shik, *n.* [Fr., from G. *schick*, due order, tact.] Easy elegance; smartness; adroitness; knowingness.—*a.* Smart.

Chica, chē'ka, *n.* [Sp.] A red colour extracted from the leaves of a species of Bignonia in tropical South America.

Chicane, **Chicanery**, shi-kān', shi-kān'ėr-i, *n.* [Fr. *chicane*, *chicanerie*, originally a kind of game and the manœuvres in playing it, from Per. *chaugān*, the game of golf played on horseback, polo.] The art of protracting a contest or discussion by the use of evasive stratagems or mean and unfair tricks and artifices; trickery; sophistry; artifice.—*v.i.* To use chicane.—**Chicaner**, shi-kān'ėr, *n.* One who uses chicane or chicanery.

Chicken, chik'en, *n.* [A.Sax. *cicen*, *cycen*, a chicken; cog. L.G. *kiken*, *küken*, Prov. G. *küchen*.] A young fowl; particularly a young domestic fowl; a person of tender years: generally used of females, as in the phrase, she is no *chicken*.—**Chick**, chik, *n.* A chicken.—**Chickling**, chik'ling, *n.* [Dim. of *chick*.] A small chick or chicken.—**Chicken-hearted**, *a.* Having no more courage than a chicken; timid; cowardly.—**Chicken-pox**, *n.* A mild contagious eruptive disease generally appearing in children.—**Chick-weed**, *n.* A common weed with small white blossoms much used for feeding cage-birds.

Chickling, **Chickling-vetch**, chik'ling, *n.* [From Fr. *chiche*, It. *cece*, from L. *cicer*, the chick-pea.] A vetch or pea extensively cultivated in the south of Europe for its seed.—**Chick-pea**, *n.* A plant cultivated for its seeds, which form an important article in French cookery.

Chicory, chik'o-ri, *n.* [Fr. *chicorée*, L. *cichorium*, from Gr. *kichōrion*, chicory.] The popular name of a composite plant common in England, with a fleshy tapering root which is extensively employed as a substitute for coffee, or to mix with coffee.—**Chicoraceous**, chik-o-rā'shus, *a.* Pertaining to chicory; cichoraceous.

Chide, chīd, *v.t.*—*chid* (pret.), *chid* or *chidden*, *chiding*. [A.Sax. *cīdan*, to chide; connections unknown.] To scold; to reprove; to rebuke; to find fault with or take exception to (a thing); to strike by way of punishment or admonition (*Tenn.*).—*v.i.* To scold; to find fault; to contend in words of anger.—**Chider**, chīd'ėr, *n.* One who chides, reproves, or rebukes.—**Chiding**, chīd'ing, *n.* A scolding; a rebuke; reproof.—**Chidingly**, chīd'ing-li, *adv.* In a scolding or reproving manner.

Chief, chēf, *a.* [O.Fr. *chef*, *chief* (Fr. *chef*), the head, top, chief; from L. *caput*, the head, whence also *capital*, *cattle*, *captain*, &c.] Highest in office, authority, or rank; principal or most eminent, in any quality or action; most important; at the head; leading; main.—*n.* The person highest in authority, the head or head man; a military commander; the person who heads an army; the principal person of a clan, tribe, family, &c.—**Chiefdom**, chēf'dum, *n.* The rank or office of a chief; sovereignty.—**Chiefly**, chēf'li, *adv.* Principally; above all; in the first place; for the most part; mostly.—**Chief-justice**, *n.* The justice who is the official head of a judicial body; a high legal functionary.—**Chief-justiceship**, *n.* The office of chief-justice.

Chieftain, chēf'tān, *n.* [O.Fr. *chevetaine*, *chieftaine*, &c.; from L.L. *capitaneus*, from *caput*, the head: really the same word as *captain*.] A leader or commander; a chief; the head of a clan or family.—**Chieftaincy**, **Chieftainship**, chēf'tān-si, chēf'tān-ship, *n.* The rank, dignity, or office of a chieftain.

Chiffonnier, shif'o-nēr, *n.* [Fr., a chiffonnier, a rag-picker, from *chiffon*, a rag.] A kind of small sideboard; a wooden stand with shelves.

Chignon, shē-nyoṅ, *n.* [Fr., the nape of the neck, a chignon.] The term applied to ladies' back hair when raised and folded up, usually round a pad of artificial hair.

Chigoe, **Chigre**, **Chiggre**, chig'ō, chig'ėr, *n.* [Of West Indian or South American origin.] An insect closely resembling the common flea, but of more minute size, found in the West Indies and South America, which burrows beneath the skin of the foot, and becoming distended with eggs produces a troublesome ulcer.

Chikara, chi-kä'ra, *n.* A species of goat-like antelope found in Bengal, of which the male is furnished with four horns.

Chilblain, chil'blān, *n.* [*Chill*, cold, and *blain*.] A blain or inflamed sore on the hands or feet produced by cold.—*v.t.* To afflict with chilblains; to produce chilblains in.

Child, chīld, *n.* pl. **Children**, chil'dren. [A.Sax. *cild*, a child, pl. *cildru*, afterwards *cildre*, *childre*, to which *r* or *en* another plural termination was added. The root is the same as that of *kin*, *kind*, &c., G. *kind*, a child.] A son or a daughter of any age; a male or female descendant in the first degree; a very young person of either sex; one of crude or immature knowledge, experience, judgment, or attainments; *pl.* descendants; offspring.—*Child's play*, a trivial matter of any kind; anything easily accomplished or surmounted.—*With child*, pregnant.—**Child-crowing**, *n.* A nervous disease of children, consisting in a spasm of the larynx, causing a peculiar crowing sound.—**Childhood**, chīld'hųd, *n.* The state of a child; the time in which persons are still classed as children.—**Childing**,† chīld'ing, *a.* Bearing children; productive; fruitful.—**Childish**, chīld'ish, *a.* Of or belonging to a child or to childhood; like a child, or what is proper to childhood; with the disparaging senses of trifling, puerile, ignorant, silly, weak.—**Childishly**, chīld'ish-li, *adv.* In a childish manner.—**Childishness**, chīld'ish-nes, *n.* The state or quality of being childish.—**Childless**, chīld'les, *a.* Destitute of children or offspring.—**Childlessness**, chīld'les-nes, *n.* State of being without children.—**Childlike**, chīld'līk, *a.* Resembling a child or that which belongs to children; meek; submissive; dutiful: never used in a disparaging sense.—**Childly**,† chīld'li, *a.* Like a child; acquired or learned when a child. (*Tenn.*).—**Child-bearing**, *n.* The act of producing or bringing forth children; parturition.—**Child-bed**, *n.* The state of a woman who is lying-in or in labour.—**Child-birth**, *n.* The act of bringing forth a child; travail; labour. **Childermas-day**, chil'dėr-mas-dā, *n.* [*Childer*, pl. of *child*, *mass*, and *day*.] An anniversary of the Church of England, held on the 28th of December; Innocents'-day.

Childe, chīld, *n.* A noble youth; a youth, especially one of high birth, before he was advanced to the honour of knighthood; a squire.

Chiliad, kil'i-ad, *n.* [Gr. *chilias*, from *chilioi*, a thousand.] A thousand; a collection or sum containing a thousand individuals or particulars; the period of a thousand years.—**Chiliaedron**, **Chiliahedron**,† kil'i-a-ē''dron, kil'i-a-hē''dron, *n.* [Gr. *hedra*, a seat, a side.] *Geom.* a figure of a thousand sides.—**Chiliagon**, kil'i-a-gon, *n.* [Gr. *gōnia*, a corner.] A plane figure of a thousand angles and sides.—**Chiliarch**, kil'i-ärk, *n.* [Gr. *archos*, a chief.] The military commander or chief of a thousand men.—**Chiliarchy**, kil'i-är-ki, *n.* A body consisting of a thousand men.—**Chiliasm**, kil'i-azm, *n.* A millennium.—**Chiliast**, kil'i-ast, *n.* A millenarian.—**Chiliastic**, kil-i-as'tik, *a.* Relating to the millennium; millenarian.

Chill, chil, *n.* [A.Sax. *cele*, *cyle*, a cold, chill, from *cōl*, cool; akin D. *kill*, chill, *killen*, to chill; Sw. *kyla*, to chill; same root as in L. *gelidus*, gelid. COOL.] A shivering with cold; a cold fit; sensation of cold in an animal body; chilliness; coldness or absence of heat in a substance; *fig.* the feeling of being damped or discouraged; a depressing influence. *a.* Cold; tending to cause shivering (*chill* winds); experiencing cold; shivering with cold; *fig.* depressing; discouraging, distant; formal; not warm (a *chill* reception).—*v.t.* To affect with chill; to make chilly; *fig.* to check in enthusiasm or warmth; to discourage; to dispirit; to depress; *metal.* to reduce suddenly the temperature of (a piece of cast-iron), with the view of hardening (a *chilled* shot).—**Chiller**, chil'ėr, *n.* One who or that which chills.—**Chilling**, chil'ing, *a.* Cooling; causing to shiver; *fig.* tending to repress enthusiasm or warmth; cold; distant (a *chilling* manner or address).—**Chillingly**, chil'ing-li, *adv.* In a chilling manner; coldly.—**Chillness**, chil'nes, *n.* The state or quality of being chill.—**Chilly**, chil'i, *a.* [*Chill*, and term. *-y.*] Experiencing or causing the sensation of chillness; disagreeably cold; chilling.—*adv.* chil'li. [*Chill*, and term. *-ly.*] In a chill or chilly manner. **Chilliness**, chil'i-nes, *n.* The state or quality of being chilly.

Chilli, Chilly, chil'i, *n.* [Sp. *chile.*] A kind of guinea-pepper or capsicum.

Chillum, chil'um, *n.* [Hind.] A hookah.

Chiltern Hundreds, chil'tėrn hun'dredz, *n.* A hilly district of Buckinghamshire belonging to the British crown, the stewardship of which is accepted by a member of parliament who wishes to resign his seat, this being regarded as an office of profit under the crown, and so compelling resignation.

Chimera, Chimaera, kī-mē'ra, *n.* [L. *chimæra*, from Gr. *chimaira*, a chimaera.] *Class. myth.* a fire-breathing monster, the fore parts of whose body were those of a lion, the middle of a goat, and the hinder of a dragon; *ornamental art*, a fantastic assemblage of animal forms so combined as to produce one complete but unnatural design; hence, a vain or idle fancy; a mere phantasm of the imagination; also the name of a cartilaginous fish of extraordinary appearance inhabiting the northern seas, and sometimes called king of the herrings.—**Chimeric, Chimerical**, ki-mer'ik, ki-mer'ik-al, *a.* Merely imaginary; fanciful; fantastic; wildly or vainly conceived.—**Chimerically**, ki-mer'-ik-al-li, *adv.* In a chimerical manner.

Chime, chīm, *n.* [O.E. *chimbe*, *chymbe*, a cymbal, a shortening of *chymbale*, A.Sax. *cimbal*, from L. *cymbalum*, a cymbal.] The harmonious sound of bells or musical instruments; a set of bells (properly five or more) tuned to a musical scale, and struck by hammers, not by the tongues.—*v.i.* To sound in consonance, rhythm, or harmony; to give out harmonious sounds; hence, to accord; to agree; to suit; to harmonize; to express agreement: often with *in with* (to *chime in with* one's sentiments or humour).—*v.t.* To cause to sound harmoniously, as a set of bells.—**Chimer**, chīm'ėr, *n.* One who chimes.

Chime, Chimb, chīm, *n.* [D. *kim*, Sw. *kim*, *kimb*, the edge of a cask, G. *kimme*, edge, brim.] The edge or brim of a cask or tub, formed by the ends of the staves projecting beyond the head.

Chimere, shi-mēr', *n.* [Fr. *simarre*, It. *zimarra.*] The upper robe, to which the lawn sleeves of a bishop are attached.

Chimney, chim'ni, *n.* [Fr. *cheminée*, L.L. *caminata*, a chimney, from L. *caminus*, a furnace, a flue, from Gr. *kaminos*, an oven.] An erection, generally of stone or brick, containing a passage by which the smoke of a fire or furnace escapes to the open air; a chimney-stack; a flue; the funnel of a steam-engine; a tall glass to surround the flame of a lamp to protect it and promote combustion.—**Chimney-can, Chimney-pot**, *n.* A pipe of earthenware or sheet-metal placed on the top of chimneys to prevent smoking.—**Chimney-corner**, *n.* The corner of a fireplace; the fireside, or a place near the fire.—**Chimney-piece**, *n.* The assemblage of architectural dressings around the open recess constituting the fireplace in a room.—**Chimney-stack**, *n.* A group of chimneys carried up together.—**Chimney-stalk**, *n.* A long chimney, such as that connected with manufactories.—**Chimney-swallow**, *n.* A common European swallow with long and very deeply forked tail.—**Chimney-sweep, Chimney-sweeper**, *n.* One whose occupation is to clean chimneys of the soot that adheres to their sides.

Chimpanzee, Chimpansee, chim-pan'zē or chim'pan-zē, *n.* [The native Guinea name.] A large West African ape belonging to the anthropoid or man-like monkeys, and most nearly related to the gorilla.

Chin, chin, *n.* [A.Sax. *cin* = D. *kin*, G. *kinn*, the chin; Icel. *kinn*, Dan. *kind*, Goth. *kinnus*, the cheek; Cog. Armor. *gen*, the cheek; W. *gen*, the chin; L. *genæ*, the cheek; Gr. *genys*, the jaw, the chin; Skr. *hanu*, the jaw.] The lower extremity of the face below the mouth; the point of the under jaw in man or a corresponding part in other animals.—**Chinned**, chind, *a.* Having a chin of this or that kind.

China, Chinaware, chī'na, chī'na-wār, *n.* A species of earthenware made in *China*, or in imitation of that made there, and so called from the country; porcelain.—**China-aster**, *n.* The common name of a hardy and free-flowering composite plant.—**China-clay**, *n.* Kaolin.—**China-ink**, *n.* A kind of fine black pigment used in water-colour drawing, made of lamp-black and gum: also called Indian ink.—**China-orange**, *n.* The sweet orange, said to have been originally brought from China.—**China-root**, *n.* The root or rhizome of a plant closely allied to sarsaparilla, formerly much esteemed as a medicine.—**China-rose**, *n.* The name given to a number of varieties of garden rose, natives of China.—**China-shop**, *n.* A shop in which china, crockery, glassware, &c., are sold.

Chinch, chinch, *n.* [Sp. *chinche*, a bug, from L. *cimex.*] The common bed-bug; also the popular name of certain fetid American insects resembling the bed-bug, very destructive to wheat, maize, &c.

Chinchilla, chin-chil'la, *n.* [Spanish name.] A genus of rodent animals peculiar to the South American continent, one species of which produces the fine pearly-gray fur which has been so much prized in Europe for many years; the fur of the chinchilla.

Chinchona, chin-chō'na, *n.* Same as *Cinchona.*

Chin-cough, chin'kof, *n.* [For *chink-cough*, *chink* being for *kink*, as in Sc. *kink-host* (*host*, a cough), D. *kink-hoest.*] Hooping-cough.

Chine, chīn, *n.* [Fr. *échine*, O.Fr. *eschine*, the spine.] The backbone or spine of an animal; a piece of the backbone of an animal, with the adjoining parts, cut for cooking.—*v.t.* To cut through the backbone, or into chine pieces.

Chine, chīn, *n.* [A.Sax. *cine*, a chink, fissure.] A rocky ravine on a coast: used in south of England.

Chinese, chī-nēz', *a.* Pertaining to China.—*Chinese fire*, a composition used in fireworks.—*Chinese lantern*, a lantern made of coloured paper used in illuminations.—*Chinese white*, the white oxide of zinc.—*n. sing.* and *pl.* A native or natives of China; the language of China.

Chink, chingk, *n.* [Akin to O.E. *chine*, A. Sax. *cinu*, a chink, a fissure, *cinan*, to gape.] A narrow aperture; a cleft, rent, or fissure of greater length than breadth; a cranny, gap, or crack.—*v.t.* To cause to open or part and form a fissure; to make chinks in; to fill up chinks in.—*v.i.* To crack; to open.—**Chinky**, ching'ki, *a.* Full of chinks or fissures; opening in narrow clefts.

Chink, chingk, *v.i.* [Imitative; comp. *jingle.*] To make a small sharp metallic sound.—*v.t.* To cause to sound as by shaking coins or small pieces of metal.—*n.* A short, sharp, clear, metallic sound; a term for money (vulgar); the reed-bunting.

Chinkapin, ching'ka-pin, *n.* [Of Amer.-Indian origin.] The dwarf chestnut of the U. States, yielding edible nuts; also an American tree allied to the oak.

Chintz, Chints, chints, *n.* [Hind. *chint*, Per. *chinz*, spotted, stained.] Cotton cloth of calico printed with flowers or other devices in at least five different colours, and now generally glazed.

Chip, chip, *v.t.*—*chipped*, *chipping.* [Closely connected with *chop* and *chap*; O.D. *kippen*, to knock to pieces; O.Sw. *kippa*, to chop; G. *kippen*, to clip or cut money.] To cut into small pieces; to diminish by cutting away a little at a time or in small pieces.—*v.i.* To break or fly off in small pieces.—*n.* A piece of wood, stone, or other substance separated from a body by a blow of an instrument; wood split into thin slips for the manufacture of hats and bonnets.—**Chippy**, chip'i, *a.* Abounding in chips; produced by chips.—**Chip-axe**, *n.* An axe for chipping.—**Chip-bonnet, Chip-hat**, *n.* A bonnet or hat made of wood split into small slips.

Chipmunk, Chipmuck, chip'mungk, chip'muk, *n.* The popular name of the ground-squirrel, a rodent animal very common in the United States.

Chippendale, chip'en-dāl, *a.* [Inventor's name.] A slight style of drawing-room furniture.

Chiragra, kī-rag'ra, *n.* [L. *chiragra*, from Gr. *cheiragra*, hand-gout—*cheir*, the hand, and *agra*, seizure.] Gout in the hand.—**Chiragric, Chiragrical**, kī-rag'rik, kī-rag'rik-al, *a.* Having or pertaining to the gout in the hand.

Chirognomy, kī-rog'no-mi, *n.* [Gr. *cheir*, *cheiros*, the hand, and *gnōmē*, knowledge.] A so-called art or science which professes to judge of mental character from the form and appearance of the hand.

Chirographer, Chirographist, kī-rog'ra-fėr, kī-rog'ra-fist, *n.* [Gr. *cheir*, the hand, *graphō*, to write.] One who exercises or professes the art of writing; one who tells fortunes by examining the hand.—**Chirographic, Chirographical**, kī-rō-graf'ik, kī-rō-graf'ik-al, *a.* Pertaining to chirography.—**Chirography**, kī-rog'ra-fi, *n.* The art of writing; hand-writing; the art of telling fortunes by examining the hand.

Chirologist, kī-rol'o-jist, *n.* [Gr. *cheir*, the hand, and *logos*, discourse.] One who communicates thoughts by signs made with the hands and fingers.—**Chirology**, kī-rol'o-ji, *n.* The art or practice of communicating thoughts by signs made by the hands and fingers, much used by deaf-mutes.—**Chirological**, kī-rō-loj'ik-al, *a.* Pertaining to chirology.

Chiromancy, kī'rō-man-si, *n.* [Gr. *cheir*, the hand, and *manteia*, divination.] Divination by the hand; the art or practice of foretelling one's fortune by inspecting the lines and lineaments of his hand; palmistry.—**Chiromancer, Chiromanist, Chiromantist**, kī'rō-man-sėr, kī-rom'an-ist, kī'rō-man-tist, *n.* One who practises chiromancy.—**Chiromantic, Chiromantical**, kī-rō-man'tik, kī-rō-man'tik-al, *a.* Pertaining to chiromancy.

Chiropodist, kī-rop'od-ist, *n.* [Gr. *cheir*, the hand, and *pous*, *podos*, the foot.] One who treats diseases of the feet; a surgeon for the feet.

Chiropractic, kī-rō-prak'tik, *n.* [Gr. *cheir*, hand, and *praktikos*, practice.] Manipulation of the spine to cure disease.—**Chiropractor**, kī'rō-prak-tėr, *n.* One who practices chiropractic.

Chirp, chėrp, *v.i.* [Akin to G. *zirpen*, *tschirpen*, *schirpen*, to chirp, *chirrup* being a lengthened form; the same root is in D. *kirren*, to coo, L. *garrio*, to chatter.] To make a short sharp shrill sound, as is done by small birds or certain insects; to cheep.—*n.* A short, shrill note, as of certain birds or insects.

Chirrup, chir'up, *v.i.* [A lengthened form of *chirp.*] To chirp.—*n.* A chirp.

Chirurgeon,† kī-rėr'jon, *n.* [Fr. *chirurgien*; same word as *surgeon.*] A surgeon.—**Chirurgeonly**,† kī-rėr'jon-li, *adv.* In the manner of a surgeon. (*Shak.*)—**Chirurgery**,† kī-rėr'jėr-i, *n.* Surgery.—**Chirurgic**,† **Chirurgical**, kī-rėr'jik, kī-rėr'jik-al, *a.* Surgical.

Chisel, chiz′el, *n.* [O.Fr. *cisel* (Fr. *ciseau*), L.L. *cisellus*, from L. *cædo*, *cæsum*, to cut.] An instrument of iron or steel, used in carpentry, joinery, cabinet work, masonry, sculpture, &c., for paring, hewing, or gouging.—*v.t.*—*chiseled, chiseling.* To cut, pare, gouge, or engrave with a chisel (a statue *chiseled* out of marble); *fig.* to cut close, as in a bargain; to cheat (slang).—**Chiseled**, chiz′eld, *a.* Worked with a chisel or as with a chisel; clear-cut; statuesque.—**Chisel-tooth**, *n.* A tooth like a chisel, a name given to the incisor teeth of rodent animals from their form.

Chisleu, kis′lū, *n.* [Heb. *kisleu.*] The ninth month of the Jewish year, answering to a part of November and a part of December.

Chisley, chiz′li, *a.* [A.Sax. *ceosel*, *ceosl*, gravel, sand.] Having a sandy and clayey character; containing a large admixture of gravel and small pebbles.

Chit, chit, *n.* [A.Sax. *cíth*, a shoot or twig.] A shoot or sprout; the first shoot of a seed or plant; a child or babe; a young and insignificant person.—**Chitty**, chit′i, *a.* Full of chits or sprouts.

Chit-chat, chit′chat, *n.* [A reduplication of *chat.*] Prattle; familiar or trifling talk.

Chitin, Chitine, kī′tin, *n.* [Gr. *chitōn*, a tunic.] The organic substance which forms the wing-covers and integuments of insects and the carapaces of crustacea, having a somewhat horny character.—**Chitinous**, kī′tin-us, *a.* Consisting of, or having the nature of chitin.

Chiton, kī′ton, *n.* [Gr. *chitōn*, a tunic, a cuirass, a coat of mail.] The name of certain molluscs, the shell of which is formed of successive portions, often in contact and overlapping each other, but never truly articulated.

Chitterling, chit′ėr-ling, *n.* *Cookery*, part of the small intestines, as of swine, fried for food: generally used in the plural.

Chivalry, shiv′al-ri, *n.* [Fr. *chevalerie*, from *chevalier*, a knight or horseman, from *cheval*, a horse. CAVALRY.] Knighthood; the system to which knighthood with all its laws and usages belonged; the qualifications of a knight, as courtesy, valour, and dexterity in arms; knights or warriors collectively; any body of illustrious warriors, especially cavalry.—**Chivalric, Chivalrous**, shiv′al-rik, shiv′al-rus, *a.* Pertaining to chivalry or knight-errantry; warlike; bold; gallant.—**Chivalrously**, shiv′al-rus-li, *adv.* In a chivalrous manner or spirit.—**Chivalrousness**, shiv′al-rus-nes, *n.* The quality of being chivalrous.

Chive, chīv, *n.* CIVE.

Chlamydospore, klam′i-dō-spōr. [Gr. *chlamys*, a cloak, *sporos*, seed.] In some fungi, a thick-walled resting spore.

Chlamys, klam′is, *n.* [Gr. *chlamys, chlamydos.*] A light and freely-flowing scarf or plaid worn by the ancients as an outer garment; *bot.* the floral envelope of a plant.—**Chlamydate**, klam′i-dāt, *a.* Having a mantle; said of molluscs.—**Chlamydeous**, kla-mid′ē-us, *a.* Pertaining to the chlamys or floral envelope.

Chloasma, klō-az′ma, *n.* [Gr. *chloē*, yellowish grass.] An affection of the skin showing yellowish or brownish spots.

Chloral, klō′ral, *n.* [From *chlor*, the first part of *chlorine*, and *al*, the first syllable of *alcohol.*] An oily liquid with a pungent odour and slightly astringent taste, produced from chlorine and alcohol; also the name popularly applied to chloral hydrate, a white crystalline substance used in medicine for producing sleep.—**Chloralism**, klō′ral-izm, *n.* A morbid state of the system arising from an incautious or habitual use of chloral.

Chlorine, klō′rin, *n.* [Gr. *chlōros*, greenish-yellow, from its colour.] An elementary gaseous substance (symbol Cl) of a greenish-yellow colour, contained in common salt, from which it is chiefly obtained, being used as a bleaching agent and disinfectant, especially in the form of chloride of lime.—**Chlorate**, klō′rāt, *n.* A salt of chloric acid.—**Chloric**, klō′rik, *a.* Pertaining to or containing chlorine; specifically, containing chlorine in smaller proportion than chlorous compounds.—**Chloride**, klō′rīd, *n.* A compound of chlorine with another element.—*Chloride of lime*, a compound of chlorine and lime, used as a bleaching agent and as a disinfectant.—**Chloridize**, klō′rid-īz, *v.t.* *Photog.* to cover with chloride of silver, for the purpose of rendering sensitive to the actinic rays of the sun.—**Chlorite**, klō′rīt, *n.* A mineral of a grass-green colour, closely allied in character to mica and talc; also, a salt of chlorous acid.—**Chloritic**, klō-rit′ik, *a.* Pertaining to or containing chlorite.—**Chlorous**, klō′rus, *a.* Pertaining to or containing chlorine; specifically, containing chlorine in larger proportion than chloric compounds.

Chlorodyne, klō′rō-dīn or klō′rō-din, *n.* [*Chlor-*, from *chloroform*, and Gr. *odynē*, pain.] A popular anodyne remedy, the active elements of which are morphia, chloroform, prussic acid, and extract of Indian hemp.

Chloroform, klō′rō-form, *n.* [*Chlor-*, from *chloride* or *chlorine*, and *-form*, from *formic* acid, from chemical connection.] A volatile colourless liquid, of an agreeable, fragrant, sweetish apple taste and smell, prepared by distilling together a mixture of alcohol, water, and chloride of lime, and much used as an anæsthetic, for which purpose its vapour is inhaled.—*v.t.* To put under the influence of chloroform; to treat with chloroform.

Chlorometer, klō-rom′et-ėr, *n.* [*Chlor-*, from *chloride*, and Gr. *metron*, a measure.] An instrument for testing the bleaching powers of chloride of lime, &c.—**Chlorometry**, klō′rom-et-ri, *n.* The process for testing the decolouring power of any combination of chlorine, especially of the commercial articles, the chlorides of lime, potash, and soda.

Chlorophane, klō′rō-fān, *n.* [Gr. *chlōros*, greenish-yellow, and *phainō*, to show.] A variety of fluor-spar which exhibits a bright-green phosphorescent light when heated.

Chlorophyll, klō′rō-fil, *n.* [Gr. *chlōros*, green, and *phyllon*, a leaf.] The green colouring matter of plants, which is developed by the influence of light; hence arises the etiolation or blanching of plants by privation of light.

Chlorosis, klō-rō′sis, *n.* [Gr. *chlōros*, greenish-yellow.] The green-sickness, a peculiar form of anæmia or bloodlessness which affects young females, and is characterized by a pale greenish hue of the skin.—**Chlorotic**, klō-rot′ik, *a.* Pertaining to chlorosis; affected by chlorosis.

Chlorous. Under CHLORINE.

Chock-full, chok′fụl, *a.* Same as *Choke-full.*

Chocolate, chok′ō-lāt, *n.* [Sp. *chocolate*; Mex. *chocolatl*—*choco*, cocoa, and *latl*, water.] A paste or cake composed of the kernels of the cacao-nut ground and combined with sugar and vanilla, cinnamon, cloves, or other flavouring substance; the beverage made by dissolving chocolate in boiling water or milk.—*a.* Having the colour of chocolate; of a dark, glossy brown.

Choice, chois, *n.* [O.Fr. *chois*, a choice, from *choisir*, to choose; from the German. CHOOSE.] The act or power of choosing; a selecting or separating from two or more things that which is preferred; selection; election; option; preference; the thing chosen; the best part of anything.—*a.* Carefully selected; worthy of being preferred; select; precious.—**Choiceless**,† chois′les, *a.* Not having the power of choosing.—**Choicely**, chois′li, *adv.* In a choice manner or degree.—**Choiceness**, chois′nes, *n.* The quality of being choice or select; excellence; value.

Choir, kwīr, *n.* [O.Fr. *choeur*, L. *chorus*, Gr. *choros*, a dance in a ring, a band; same word as *chorus*, *quire.*] A band of dancers‡; a collection of singers, especially in a church; that part of a church appropriated for the singers in cruciform churches; that part eastward of the nave, and separated from it usually by a screen of open work; a chancel.—*v.t.* and *i.* To sing in company.—**Choir-screen**, *n.* An ornamental open screen of wood or stone between the choir or chancel and the nave.

Choke, chōk, *v.t.*—*choked, choking.* [Akin to *cough*, and to Icel. *koka*, to gulp, *kyka*, to swallow; perhaps imitative of the convulsive sound made when the throat is impeded.] To deprive of the power of breathing by stopping the passage of the breath through the windpipe; to compress the windpipe of; to strangle; to stop by filling (any passage); to obstruct; to block up; to hinder by obstruction or impediments (as plants from growing).—*v.i.* To have the windpipe stopped; to have something stick in the throat.—**Choker**, chō′kėr, *n.* One who or that which chokes.—**Choky, Chokey**, chō′ki, *a.* Tending to choke; interrupted or indistinct as if by choking; gasping, as the voice.—**Choke-damp**, *n.* Same as *After-damp.*—**Choke-full**, *n.* Full as possible; quite full. Written also *Chock-full.*

Cholæmia, ko-lē′mi-a, *n.* [Gr. *cholē*, bile, *haima*, blood.] A morbid accumulation of bile in the blood.

Cholagogue, kol′a-gog, *n.* [Gr. *cholagōgos*—*cholē*, bile, and *agōgos*, leading, from *agō*, to lead.] A medicine that has the quality of carrying off the bile.

Choler, kol′ėr, *n.* [O.Fr. *cholere* (Fr. *colère*), choler, anger, L. *cholera*, a bilious ailment, from Gr. *cholera*, from *cholē*, bile, anger.] The bile, the excess of which was formerly supposed to produce anger, &c.; hence, anger, wrath, irascibility.—**Choleric**, kol′ėr-ik, *a.* Abounding with choler or bile; easily irritated; irascible; inclined to anger; proceeding from anger.

Cholera, kol′ėr-a, *n.* [L. bile, a bilious complaint. CHOLER.] A disease characterized by copious vomiting and purging of bilious matter, followed by great prostration, and in severe cases often by death; it is of two varieties, common or English cholera, which is generally of a mild character; and malignant or Asiatic cholera, which is far more fatal.—**Choleraic**, kol-ėr-ā′ik, *a.* Pertaining to cholera.

Cholesterine, ko-les′tėr-in, *n.* [Gr. *cholē*, bile, and *stereos*, solid.] A substance occurring in biliary calculi, yolk of egg, beans, peas, wheat, and other plants.

Choliambus, kō-li-am′bus, *n.* [Gr. *chōliambos*, that is, lame or limping iambus—*chōlos*, lame.] An iambic verse (line) in poetry having a spondee or trochee in the sixth or last foot.

Chomer, kō′mėr, *n.* A Hebrew measure; a homer.

Chondrify, kon′dri-fī, *v.t.* and *i.* [Gr. *chondros*, cartilage, and L. *facere*, to make.] To convert or be converted into cartilage.—**Chondrification**, kon′dri-fi-kā″shon, *n.* The act of making or state of becoming cartilage.—**Chondrography**, kon-drog′ra-fi, *n.* A description of cartilages.—**Chondrology**, kon-drol′o-ji, *n.* The science or knowledge of cartilages.

Chondrite, kon′drīt, *n.* [L. *chondrus*, a species of sea-weed.] A fossil marine plant of the chalk and other formations resembling Irish-moss.

Chondropterygian, Chondropterygious, kon′drop-te-rij″i-an, kon′drop-te-rij″i-us, *a.* [Gr. *chondros*, cartilage, and *pteryx*, *pterygos*, a wing or fin.] Pertaining to the Chondropterygii, that is, to the section of fishes having a cartilaginous skeleton and gristly fins.—**Chondropterygian**, *n.* One of the Chondropterygii.—**Chondropterygii**, kon′drop-te-rij″i-ī, *n. pl.* The cartilaginous fishes.

Chondrotomy, kon-drot′o-mi, *n.* [Gr. *chondros*, cartilage, and *tomē*, a cutting.] A dissection of cartilages.

Choose, chöz, *v.t.*—*chose* (pret.), *chosen*, *choosing.* [A.Sax. *ceósan* = D. *kiezen*, Icel. *kjósa*, G. *kiesen*, to choose, Goth. *kiusan*, to choose, to prove; from root seen in L. *gustare*, Gr. *geuomai*, to taste.] To take by preference; to make choice or selection of; to pick out; to select; to prefer; to wish; to be inclined or have an inclination for (colloq.). —*v.i.* To make a choice.—**Chooser**, chöz'ėr, *n.* One that chooses; one that has the power or right of choosing.

Chop, chop, *v.t.*—*chopped, chopping.* [Same word as *chap*, to split, with a slightly different form and meaning = D. and G. *kappen*, to chop, to mince, to cut; Dan. *kappe*, to cut, to lop.] To cut into pieces; to mince; to sever or separate by striking with a sharp instrument: usually with *off*.—*v.i.* To chap or crack, as the skin.—*n.* A piece chopped off; a slice, particularly of meat.—**Chopper**, chop'ėr, *n.* One who or that which chops; a tool for chopping or mincing meat; a cleaver.—**Chop-house**, *n.* A house where meat chops are dressed ready for eating; an eating-house.

Chop, chop, *v.t.*—*chopped, chopping.* [Same origin as *cheap.*] To buy, or rather to barter; to truck or exchange.—*To chop logic*, to dispute or argue in a sophistical manner or with an affectation of logical terms or methods.—*v.i.* To bargain‡; to bandy words or dispute‡; to turn, vary, change, or shift suddenly: said of the wind.—*n.* A turn of fortune; change; vicissitude, especially in the phrase *chops and changes*.

Chop, chop, *n.* The chap; the jaw; *pl.* the mouth or entrance to a channel. CHAP.—**Chop-fallen**, *a.* Dejected; chap-fallen.

Chop, chop, *n.* [Hind. *chhap*, stamp, print.] An eastern custom-house or other stamp on goods; hence, quality or brand (silk or tea of the first *chop*).

Chopin, chop'in, *n.* [Fr. *chopine.*] An old English measure equal to half a pint; in Scotland equal to a quart.

Chopine, Chioppine, cho-pēn', *n.* [From Sp. *chapin*, a clog or chopine.] A sort of very lofty clog or patten formerly worn.

Choppy, chop'i, *a.* [From *chop*, change.] Showing short broken waves.

Chopstick, chop'stik, *n.* One of two small sticks of wood, ivory, &c., used by the Chinese and Japanese for conveying food to the mouth.

Choragus, kō-rā'gus, *n.* [Gr. *choragos*—*choros*, a chorus, and *agō*, to lead.] The leader or superintendent of a chorus or of a theatrical representation in ancient Greece; the person who had to provide at his own expense the choruses for dramatic representations and religious festivals.—**Choragic**, kō-rā'jik, *a.* Pertaining to or connected with a choragus.

Choral, &c. Under CHORUS.

Chord, kord, *n.* [L. *chorda*, from Gr. *chordē*, an intestine, of which strings were made. *Cord* is the same word.] The string of a musical instrument; *mus.* the simultaneous combination of different sounds, consonant or dissonant; *geom.* a straight line drawn or supposed to extend from one end of an arc of a circle to the other.—*v.t.* To furnish with chords or musical strings.

Chorea, kō'rē-a or ko-rē'a, *n.* [Gr. *choreia*, a dance.] *Med.* St. Vitus's dance; convulsive motions of the limbs, and strange and involuntary gesticulations.

Chorepiscopal, kō-rē-pis'ko-pal, *a.* [Gr. *chōra*, place, locality, and *episkopos*, a bishop.] Pertaining to the power of a chorepiscopus, that is, a suffragan or local bishop.

Choriambus, kō-ri-am'bus, *n.* [Gr. *choreios*, a trochee, and *iambos*, iambus.] *Pros.* a foot consisting of four syllables, the first two forming a trochee and the second two an iambus.—**Choriambic**, kō-ri-am'bik, *a.* Pertaining to a choriambus.

Chorion, kō'ri-on, *n.* [Gr.] *Anat.* the external vascular membrane which invests the fetus in the womb; *bot.* the external membrane of the seeds of plants.—**Choroid**, kor'oid, *a.* and *n.* A term applied to a membrane resembling the chorion, especially to one of the membranes of the eye of a very dark colour.

Chorisis, kō'ri-sis, *n.* [Gr. *chorizō*, to separate, to sever.] *Bot.* the separation of a lamina from one part of an organ, so as to form a scale, or a doubling of the organ.

Chorister, &c. CHORUS.

Chorography, kō-rog'ra-fi, *n.* [Gr. *chōros*, a place or region, and *graphō*, to describe.] The art or practice of making maps of or of describing particular regions, countries, or districts.—**Chorographer**, kō-rog'ra-fėr, *n.* One skilled in chorography.—**Chorographic, Chorographical**, kō-rō-graf'ik, kō-rō-graf'ik-al, *a.* Pertaining to chorography; descriptive of particular regions or countries.

Choroid. Under CHORION.

Chorus, kō'rus, *n.* [L. *chorus*, from Gr. *choros*, a dance in a ring, a chorus.] Originally a band of dancers accompanied by their own singing or that of others; the performers in a Greek play who were supposed to behold what passed in the acts, and sing their sentiments between the acts; the song between the acts; now, usually, verses of a song in which the company join the singer, or the singing of the company with the singer; a union or chiming of voices in general (a *chorus* of laughter or ridicule); *mus.* a composition in parts sung by many voices; the whole body of vocalists other than soloists, whether in an oratorio, opera, or concert.—*v.t.* To sing or join in the chorus of; to exclaim or call out in concert.—**Choral**, kō'ral, *a.* Belonging, relating, or pertaining to a chorus, choir, or concert.—**Choral, Chorale**, kō-ral', kō-rä'le, *n.* A psalm or hymn tune, often sung in unison by the congregation, the organ supplying the harmony.—**Choric**, kō'rik, *a.* Pertaining to a chorus; choral. (*Tenn.*)—**Chorister**, kor'ist-ėr, *n.* A singer in a choir or chorus; a singer generally.

Chose, chōz, pret. of *choose*.—**Chosen**, chō'zn, pp. of *choose*. As an adjective, choice; select.

Chough, chuf, *n.* [A.Sax. *ceó*, a chough or jackdaw; D. *haauw*, Dan. *kaa.*] A British bird of the crow family, which frequents chiefly the coasts of Cornwall, of a black colour with red beak, legs, and toes.

Choultry, chōl'tri, *n.* In the East Indies, a place of rest and shelter for travellers; a caravansary.

Chouse, chous, *v.t.*—*choused, chousing.* [Formerly spelled also *chiaus, chiaous*, from Turk. *chiaus, chaush*, a messenger, interpreter, &c., from the notorious swindling of a Turkish interpreter in London, in 1609.] To cheat, trick, defraud: followed by *of* or *out of* (to *chouse* one *out of* his money).

Chow-chow, chou'chou, *n.* A Chinese term for any mixture, but in trade circles confined generally to mixed pickles.

Chowry, chou'ri, *n.* In the East Indies, a whisk to keep off flies.

Chrematistics, krē-ma-tis'tiks, *n.* [Gr. *chrēmata*, wealth.] The science of wealth; a name sometimes given to political economy.

Chrestomathy, kres-tom'a-thi, *n.* [Gr. *chrēstos*, useful, and *mathein*, to learn.] A book of extracts from a foreign language, with notes, intended to be used in acquiring the language.—**Chrestomathic, Chrestomathical**, kres-tō-math'ik, kres-tō-math'ik-al, *a.* Relating to a chrestomathy.

Chrism, krizm, *n.* [Gr. *chrisma*, an unguent, from *chriō*, to anoint, whence also *Christ.*] Holy or consecrated oil or unguent used in the administration of baptism, confirmation, ordination, and extreme unction, more especially in the Latin and Greek churches; the baptismal cloth laid upon the head of a child newly baptized; the baptismal vesture; the chrisom.—**Chrismal**, kriz'mal, *a.* Pertaining to chrism.—*n.* The vessel holding the consecrated oil or chrism; the white cloth laid over the head of one newly baptized, after the unction with chrism.—**Chrismation**, kriz-mā'shon, *n.* The act of applying the chrism or consecrated oil.—**Chrismatory**, kriz'ma-to-ri, *n.* [L.L. *chrismatorium.*] A receptacle for the chrism or holy oil used in the services of the Greek and Roman churches.—**Chrisom, Chrisome**, kris'um, *n.* [A form of *chrism.*] A cloth anointed with chrism laid on a child's face at baptism; the white consecrated vesture put about a child when christened.—*Chrisom child*, a newly baptized infant; a child that dies within a month after christening.

Christ, krīst, *n.* [L. *Christus*, Gr. *Christos*, lit. anointed, from *chriō*, to anoint.] THE ANOINTED: an appellation given to the Saviour of the World, and synonymous with the Hebrew MESSIAH.—**Christen**, kris'n, *v.t.* [A.Sax. *cristnian*, to christen, from *Cristen*, a Christian, from *Crist*, Christ.] To initiate into the visible church of Christ by the application of water; to name and baptize; to baptize; to name or denominate generally.—**Christendom**, kris'n-dum, *n.* [A.Sax. *cristendóm*—*Cristen*, Christian, and term. *-dom.*] The territories, countries, or regions chiefly inhabited by Christians or those who profess to believe in the Christian religion; the whole body of Christians.—**Christian**, kris'tyan, *n.* [L. *christianus*, from *Christus*, Christ.] One who believes, professes to believe, or who is assumed to believe, in the religion of Christ; a believer in Christ who is characterized by real piety.—*a.* Pertaining to Christ or to Christianity.—*Christian name*, the name given or announced at baptism, as distinguished from the family name.—*Christian era* or *period*, the period from the birth of Christ to the present time.—**Christianity**, kris-ti-an'i-ti, *n.* The religion of Christians, or the system of doctrines and precepts taught by Christ; conformity to the laws and precepts of the Christian religion.—**Christianization**, kris'tyan-iz-ā"shon, *n.* The act or process of converting to Christianity.—**Christianize**, kris'tyan-īz, *v.t.*—*christianized, christianizing.* To make Christian; to convert to Christianity.—**Christianly**, kris'tyan-li, *adv.* In a Christian manner; in a manner becoming the principles of a Christian.—*a.* Christianlike; becoming a Christian.—**Christless**, krīst'les, *a.* Having no interest in Christ; without the spirit of Christ.—**Christmas**, kris'mas, *n.* [*Christ*, and *mass*, A.Sax. *mæssa*, a holy day or feast.] The festival of the Christian church observed annually on the 25th day of December, in memory of the birth of Christ; Christmas-day or Christmas-tide.—**Christmas-day**, *n.* The 25th day of December, when Christmas is celebrated.—**Christmas-eve**, *n.* The evening of the day before Christmas.—**Christmas-rose**, *n.* A plant of the hellebore genus, so called from its open rose-like flower, which blossoms during winter.—**Christmas-tide, Christmas-time**, *n.* The season of Christmas.—**Christmas-tree**, *n.* A small evergreen tree set up in a family, &c., at Christmas, from which are hung presents, generally with the names of the recipients inscribed on them.—**Christology**, kris-tol'o-ji, *n.* [Gr. *Christos*, Christ, and *logos*, discourse.] A discourse or treatise concerning Christ; that branch of divinity that deals directly with Christ.—**Christ's-thorn**, *n.* A deciduous shrub with large hooked spines, a native of Palestine and the south of Europe: so named from a belief that it supplied the crown of thorns for Christ.

Chromatic, krō-mat'ik, *a.* [Gr. *chrōmatikos*, from *chrōma*, colour.] Relating to colour, or to coloured inks or pigments; *mus.* including notes not belonging to the diatonic scale.—*Chromatic scale*, a scale made up of thirteen successive semitones, that is, the eight diatonic tones and the five intermediate tones.—**Chromatically**, krō-mat'ik-al-li, *adv.* In a chromatic manner.—**Chromatics**, krō-mat'iks, *n.* The science of colours; that part of optics which treats of the properties of the colours of light and of natural bodies.—**Chromatography**, krō-ma-tog'ra-fi, *n.* A treatise on colours; printing in colours.—**Chromatology**, krō-ma-tol'o-ji, *n.* The doctrine of or a treatise on colours.—**Chromatometer**, krō-ma-tom'et-ėr, *n.* A scale for measuring colours.—**Chromatophore**, krō-mat'ō-fōr, *n.* [Gr. *chrōma*, and *pherein*, to bear.] One of the pigment cells in animals, well seen in the chameleons and cuttle-fishes.—**Chromatrope**, krō'ma-trōp, *n.* [Gr. *chrōma*, and *trepō*, to turn.] An arrangement in a magic lantern in which brilliant effects are produced by designs being painted on two circular glasses and the glasses being made to rotate in opposite directions.

Chromatin, krō'ma-tin, *n.* [Gr. *chrōma*, *-atos*, colour.] In cells, that part of the nucleus which can be deeply stained.

Chrome, Chromium, krōm, krō'mi-um, *n.* [Gr. *chrōma*, color.] A metal which forms very hard steel-gray masses: so called from the various and beautiful colors—green, orange, yellow, red, &c.—which its oxide and acid communicate to minerals into whose composition they enter, yielding such pigments as *chrome-green*, *chrome-yellow*, &c. An admixture of less than 3 per cent of chromium to steel produces an extremely hard alloy used for ball and roller bearings and machine parts subject to wear. It is used also for plating metals that easily corrode.—**Chromate**, krō'māt, *n.* A salt of chromic acid.—**Chromic**, krōm'ik, *a.* Pertaining to chrome or obtained from it.—*Chromic acid*, or *chromic oxide*, destroys the color produced by indigo and many other matters, and hence is used in calico-printing.—**Chromite**, krō'mit, *n.* A mineral containing chromium.

Chromogene, krō'mō-jēn, *n.* [Gr. *chrōma*, color, and root *gen*, to produce.] A chemical compound containing CHROMOPHORES (which see).

Chromo-lithography, *n.* A method of producing colored lithographic pictures by using stones having different portions of the picture drawn upon them with inks of different colors, and so arranged as to blend into a complete picture.—**Chromo-lithograph**, *n.* A picture obtained by means of chromo-lithography.—**Chromo-lithographer**, *n.* One who practices chromo-lithography.—**Chromo-lithographic**, *a.* Pertaining to chromo-lithography.

Chromosome, krō'mō-som, *n.* A part of the reproductive cell that is believed to carry the determination of inheritable characteristics; one of the small bodies of the cell into which the chromatin of a cell nucleus resolves itself previous to the mitotic division of the cell.

Chromosphere, krō'mō-sfēr, *n.* [Gr. *chrōma*, color, and *sphaira*, a sphere.] The gaseous envelope supposed to exist round the body of the sun, through which the light of the photosphere passes.—**Chromo-spheric**, krō-mō-sfer'ik, *a.* Pertaining or relating to a chromosphere.

Chromotrope, *n.* CHROMATROPE.

Chronic, kron'ik, *a.* [Gr. *chronikos*, from *chronos*, time, duration.] Pertaining to time; having reference to time; continuing a long time, as a disease.—**Chronicle**, kron'i-kl, *n.* [Fr. *chronique*, a chronicle.] An account of facts or events disposed in the order of time; a history, more especially one of a simple unpretentious character; *pl.* the title of two books of the Old Testament consisting mainly of the annals of the kingdom of Judah.—*v.t. chronicled*, *chronicling.* To record in history or chronicle; to record; to register.—**Chronicler**, kron'i-klėr, *n.* One who chronicles; a writer of a chronicle.

Chronogram, kron'ō-gram, *n.* [Gr. *chronos*, time, and *gramma*, a letter or writing.] A word or words in which a date is expressed by the numeral letters occurring therein.—**Chronogrammatic, Chronogrammatical**, kron'ō-gram-mat″ik, kron'ō-gram-mat″ik-al, *a.* Belonging to a chronogram; containing a chronogram.—**Chronogrammatically**, kron'ō-gram-mat″ik-al-li, *adv.* In the manner of a chronogram. — **Chronogrammatist**, kron-ō-gram'mat-ist, *n.* A writer of chronograms.

Chronograph, kron'ō-graf, *n.* [Gr. *chronos*, time, and *graphō*, to write.] A chronogram; a device of various kinds for measuring and registering very minute portions of time with extreme precision, generally consisting of a revolving hand, disc, or cylinder, moved by clockwork, the time of the event being indicated by a point or pen marking the disc or cylinder, such marking being controlled either by the observer himself or by electricity.—**Chronographer**, kro-nog'raf-ėr, *n.* One who writes concerning time or the events of time; a chronologer.

Chronology, kro-nol'o-ji, *n.* [Gr. *chronologia*—*chronos*, time, and *logos*, discourse or doctrine.] The science of ascertaining the true periods or years when past events or transactions took place, and arranging them in their proper order according to their dates. — **Chronologic, Chronological**, kron-o-loj'ik, kron-o-loj'ik-al, *a.* Relating to chronology; containing an account of events in the order of time; according to the order of time.—**Chronologically**, kron-o-loj'ik-al-li, *adv.* In a chronological manner. — **Chronologist, Chronologer**, kro-nol'o-jist, kro-nol'o-jėr. *n.* One versed in chronology; a person who investigates the dates of past events and transactions.

Chronometer, kro-nom'et-ėr, *n.* [Gr. *chronos*, time, and *metron*, measure.] Any instrument that measures time, as a clock, watch, or dial; specifically, a time-keeper of great perfection of workmanship, made much on the principle of a watch, but rather larger, used (in conjunction with observations of the heavenly bodies) in determining the longitude at sea. **Chronometric, Chronometrical**, kron-o-met'rik, kron-o-met'rik-al, *a.* Pertaining to a chronometer; measured by a chronometer.—**Chronometry**, kro-nom'et-ri, *n.* The art of measuring time; the measuring of time by periods or divisions.

Chronoscope, kron'ō-skōp, *n.* [Gr. *chronos*, time, and *skopeō*, to observe.] An instrument for measuring the duration of extremely short-lived phenomena; more especially, the name given to instruments of various forms for measuring the velocity of projectiles.

Chrysalis, Chrysalid, kris'a-lis, kris'a-lid, *n.* [Gr. *chrysallis*, a grub, from *chrysos*, gold, from its golden colour.] The form which butterflies, moths, and most other insects assume when they change from the state of larva or caterpillar and before they arrive at their winged or perfect state. Called also *Aurelia* and *Pupa.*

Chrysanthemum, kri-san'thē-mum, *n.* [Gr. *chrysos*, gold, and *anthemon*, a flower.] The generic and common name of numerous species of composite plants, two of which are common weeds in Britain, the ox-eye daisy and the corn-marigold, while the Chinese chrysanthemum, in its numerous varieties, is equally well known. — **Chryselephantine**, kris'el-ē-fan″tin, *a.* [Gr. *elephas*, *elephantos*, ivory.] Composed or partly composed of gold and ivory: a term specially applied to statues overlaid with gold and ivory, as made among the ancient Greeks. — **Chrysoberyl**, kris'ō-ber-il, *n.* Gr. *beryllion*, beryl.] A gem of a yellowish-green colour, next to the sapphire in hardness, and employed in jewelry, being found in Ceylon, Peru, Siberia, Brazil, &c. — **Chrysochlore**, kris'ō-klōr, *n.* [Gr. *chrysos*, gold, *chlōros*, greenish-yellow.] A mole-like animal of South Africa, having fur with a gold and green lustre; the golden mole.—**Chrysocolla**, kris'ō-kol-la, *n.* [Gr. *kolla*, glue.] A silicate of the protoxide of copper of a fine emerald-green colour, apparently produced from the decomposition of copper ores, which it usually accompanies. —**Chrysography**, kri-sog'ra-fi, *n.* [Gr. *graphein*, to write.] The art of writing in letters of gold; the writing itself.—**Chrysolite**, kris'ō-lit, *n.* [Gr. *lithos*, stone.] A greenish, sometimes transparent, gem, composed of silica, magnesium, and iron, not of great value. — **Chrysophanic acid**, kris-o-fan'ik, *n.* [Gr. *chrysos*, gold, *phainein*, to shine.] A yellow substance of vegetable origin used as an ointment in skin diseases. — **Chrysoprase**, kris'ō-prāz, *n.* [Gr. *prason*, a leek.] A translucent mineral of an apple-green colour, a variety of chalcedony much esteemed as a gem.

Chthonian, kthōn'i-an. — **Chthonic**, kthōn'ik, *a.* [Gr. *chthonios*, from *chthōn*, the earth.] Pertaining to the earth; belonging to the underworld or divinities of subterraneous regions, preceding the Olympian system.

Chub, chub, *n.* [So called probably from its *chubbiness* or plumpness.] A river fish of the carp family, having the body oblong, nearly round; the head and back green, the sides silvery, and the belly white.

Chubb-lock, chub'lok, *n.* [From the name of its inventor, a London locksmith.] An intricate lock having in addition to its several tumblers a lever called a detector, which on the application of a false key moves and fixes the bolt so securely that further attempts at picking are useless.

Chubby, chub'i, *a.* [Akin to E. *chump*; Sw. dial. *kubbug*, plump, *kubb*, a lump, a block.] Having a round plump face or plump body; round and fat; plump. — **Chubbiness**, chub'i-nes, *n.* The state of being chubby.—**Chub-faced**, *a.* Having a plump round face.

Chuck, chuk, *n.* [Imitative; comp. *cluck.*] The voice or call of a hen and some other birds, or a sound resembling that.—*v.i.* To make the noise which a hen and some other birds make when they call their chickens.

Chuck, chuk, *n.* [Corrupted from *chick.*] A chicken. (*Shak.*)

Chuck, chuk, *v.t.* [A modification of *shock*, Fr. *choquer*, and formerly written *chock.*] To strike, tap, or give a gentle blow; to throw, with quick motion, a short distance; to pitch.—*n.* A slight blow or tap under the chin; a toss; a short throw.—**Chuck-farthing**, *n.* A play in which a farthing is pitched or chucked into a hole.

Chuckle, chuk'l, *v.t.*—*chuckled*, *chuckling.* [A freq. and dim. from *chuck*, to cry like a hen; or connected with *choke.*] To call, as a hen her chickens.—*v.i.* To cackle, as a hen or other fowl; to laugh in a suppressed or broken manner; to feel inward triumph or exultation.—*n.* The call of a hen and some other birds to their young; a short suppressed laugh, expressive of satisfaction, exultation, and the like.

Chuff,† chuf, *n.* [Perhaps from W. *cyff*, a stock or stump.] A coarse, heavy, dull, or surly fellow; a niggard; an old miser.

Chum, chum, *n.* [Perhaps an abbrev. of *chamber-fellow*; or, a rather more probable suggestion, of *chimney-fellow.*] One who lodges or resides in the same room or rooms; hence, a close companion; a bosom-friend; an intimate. — *v.i.* To occupy the same room or rooms with another; to be the chum of some one.

Chump, chump, *n.* [Same as Icel. *kumbr*, a log, akin to *kubba*, to chop, and therefore allied to E. *chop*, *chub*, *chubby.*] A short, thick, heavy piece of wood; a block-head.—**Chump-end**, *n.* The thick end of a loin of veal or mutton next the tail.

Chunk, tshungk, *n.* Lump of bread, cheese, wood; a short, heavy-set person.

Church, chėrch, *n.* [O.E. *chirche*, *cherche*, &c., A.Sax. *circe*, *cirice*, *cyrice* (the *c*'s all hard), from Gr. *kyriakon*, a church, the Lord's house, from *Kyrios*, the Lord = Sc. *kirk*, D. *kerk*, Dan. *kirke*, G. *kirche.*] A house consecrated to the worship of God among Christians; in England often restricted to a place of public worship belonging to the Established Church (as opposed to *chapel* and *meeting-house*); the collective body of Christians; a particular body of Christians united under one form of ecclesiastical government, in one creed, and using the same ritual and ceremonies; ecclesiastical power or authority.—*v.t.* To perform with or for any one the office of returning thanks in the church, as a mother after childbirth. — **Churchism**, chėrch'izm, *n.* Strict adherence to the forms or principles of some church, especially a state church. — **Church-court**, *n.* A court connected with a church for hearing and deciding ecclesiastical causes.—**Church-goer**, *n.* One who habitually attends church.—**Church-going**, *a.* Usually attending church; summoning to church, as a bell.—**Churchman**, chėrch′man, *n.* An ecclesiastic or clergyman; in England, a member of the Established Church.—**Churchmanship**, chėrch′man-ship, *n.* State of being a churchman.—**Church-rate**, *n.* A rate raised for the purpose of repairing and maintaining the church, churchyard, &c., in England.—**Church-service**, *n.* The religious service performed in a church; the Book of Common Prayer, with the addition of the Sunday and proper lessons.—**Church-warden**, *n.* A functionary appointed by the minister, or elected by the parishioners, to superintend a church and its concerns, to represent the interests of the parish, &c.—**Churchyard**, chėrch′yärd, *n.* The ground in which the dead are buried, adjoining a church.

Churl, chėrl, *n.* [A.Sax. *ceorl*, a countryman of the lowest rank; Icel. Dan. Sw. *karl*, a man, a male; G. *kerl*, a fellow.] A rustic; a peasant; a countryman or labourer; a rude, surly, sullen, selfish, or rough-tempered man.—**Churlish**, chėr′lish, *a.* Like or pertaining to a churl; rude; surly; sullen; unfeeling; uncivil; selfish; narrow-minded; avaricious.—**Churlishly**, chėr′lish-li, *adv.* In a churlish manner.—**Churlishness**, chėr′lish-nes, *n.* The quality of being churlish.

Churn, chėrn, *n.* [A.Sax. *cyrn*, Sc. *kirn*, Icel. *kirna*, Dan. *kierne*, a churn; probably from same root as *corn*, *kernel*, butter being as it were the kernel or best portion of the milk.] A vessel in which cream or milk is agitated for separating the oily parts from the caseous and serous parts, to make butter. —*v.t.* To stir or agitate (milk or cream) in order to make into butter; to make (butter) by the agitation of milk or cream; to shake or agitate with violence or continued motion. —**Churn-staff**, *n.* The staff or plunger which is worked in a churn.

Chute, shöt, *n.* [Fr., a fall.] A river-fall or rapid over which timber is floated; an inclined trough or tube through which articles are passed from a higher to a lower level.

Chutney, **Chutnee**, chut′ni, chut′nē, *n.* An East Indian condiment compounded of ripe fruit, spices, sour herbs, cayenne, lemon-juice, pounded and boiled together and bottled for use.

Chyle, kīl, *n.* [Gr. *chylos*, juice, chyle, from *cheō*, to flow, whence also *chyme*.] A white or milky fluid separated from aliments while in the intestines, taken up by the lacteal vessels and finally entering the blood. —**Chylaceous**, kī-lā′shus, *a.* Belonging to chyle; consisting of chyle.—**Chylifaction**, **Chylification**, kī-li-fak′shon, kī′li-fi-kā″shon, *n.* The act or process by which chyle is formed from food in animal bodies. —**Chylifactive**, **Chylificatory**, kī-li-fak′tiv, kī-lif′i-ka-to-ri, *a.* Forming or changing into chyle; having the power to make chyle.—**Chylific**, kī-lif′ik, *a.* Chylifactive. —**Chylify**, kī′li-fī, *v.t.* and *i.* To convert or be converted into chyle. — **Chylopoetic**, kī′lō-pō-et″ik, *a.* [Gr. *poieō*, to make.] Pertaining to or concerned in the formation of chyle; chylifactive.—**Chylous**, kī′lus, *a.* Consisting of, pertaining to, or resembling chyle.

Chyluria, kī-lū′ri-a, *n.* [Gr. *chylē*, matter, *ouron*, urine.] The presence of chyle in the urine.

Chyme, kīm, *n.* [Gr. *chymos*, juice. CHYLE.] The pulpy mass of partially digested food before the chyle is extracted from it.—**Chymification**, kī′mi-fi-kā″shon, *n.* The process of becoming or of forming chyme. —**Chymify**, kī′mi-fī, *v.t.* and *i.* To form or be formed into chyme. — **Chymous**, kīm′us, *a.* Pertaining to chyme.

Chymical, **Chymist**, **Chymistry**, kim′ik-al, kim′ist, kim′ist-ri. CHEMICAL, &c.

Cibol, sib′ol, *n.* [Fr. *ciboule*, from L. *cepula*, dim. of *cepa*, an onion.] A plant of the onion genus without a bulb, and the leaves of which are used for culinary purposes.

Cicada, si-kā′da, *n.* pl. **Cicadæ** or **Cicadas**, si-kā′dē, si-kā′daz. [L.] The popular and generic name of certain insects, the males of which have on each side of the body an organ with which they can make a considerable noise.—**Cicala**, si-kä′la; It. pron. chi-kä′la, *n.* [It., from L. *cicada*.] A cicada.

Cicatrice, sik′a-tris, *n.* [Fr. *cicatrice*, L. *cicatrix*.] A scar; a little seam or elevation of flesh remaining after a wound or ulcer is healed. Also **Cicatrix**, si-kā′triks, pl. **Cicatrices**, sik-a-trī′sēz.—**Cicatricula**, **Cicatricle**, sik-a-trik′ū-la, sik′a-tri-kl, *n.* [L. *cicatricula*, dim. of *cicatrix*.] The germinating point in the embryo of a seed; the point in the yolk of an egg at which development is first seen.—**Cicatrisive**, sik′-a-trī-siv, *a.* Tending to promote the formation of a cicatrice.—**Cicatrize**, sik′a-trīz, *v.t.*—*cicatrized*, *cicatrizing*. To induce the formation of a cicatrice on; to heal up (a wound).—*v.i.* To become healed leaving a cicatrice; to skin over.—**Cicatrizant**, sik′a-trī-zant, *n.* That which cicatrizes; a medicine or application that promotes the formation of a cicatrice.—**Cicatrization**, sik′a-trī-zā″shon, *n.* The process of healing or forming a cicatrice.—**Cicatrose**, sik′a-trōs, *a.* Full of scars; scarry.

Cicely, sis′e-li, *n.* [L. *seseli*, Gr. *seseli*.] Popular name applied to several umbelliferous plants, *sweet cicely*, or sweet chevril, being an aromatic plant with fine, fern-like foliage.

Cicerone, sis-e-rō′ne; It. pron. chē-chā-rō′nā, *n.* [It., from *Cicero*, the Roman orator.] A name given by the Italians to the guides who show travellers the antiquities of the country; hence, in a general sense, one who explains the curiosities of a place; a guide.—**Ciceronian**, sis-e-rō′ni-an, *a.* Resembling the style of Cicero; eloquent. —**Ciceronianism**, sis-e-rō′ni-an-izm, *n.* The manner or style of Cicero; a Ciceronian phrase or form of expression.

Cichoraceous, sik-ō-rā′shus, *a.* [L. *cichorium*, chicory.] Having the qualities of or belonging to plants of the succory or chicory family.

Cider, sī′dėr, *n.* [Fr. *cidre*, from L. *sicera*, Gr. *sikera*, strong drink, from Heb. *shakar*, to intoxicate.] A fermented, slightly alcoholic drink prepared from the juice of apples.—**Ciderkin**, sī′dėr-kin, *n.* An inferior beverage made from apples after the juice has been pressed out for cider.—**Cider-mill**, *n.* A mill for crushing apples for making cider.

Ci-devant, sē-dė-voṅ, *a.* [Fr. from *ci*=*ici* (from L. *hicce*), here, and *devant*, representing L. *de ab ante*, lit. of from before.] Previous; former; at a former period.

Ciel, **Cieling**, sēl, sēl′ing, *n.* Same as *Ceil*, *Ceiling*.

Cierge, sėrj, *n.* [Fr., from L. *cera*, wax.] A candle carried in religious processions.

Cigar, si-gär′, *n.* [Fr. *cigare*, Sp. *cigarro*, originally the name of a kind of tobacco in Cuba.] A small roll of tobacco-leaf, with a pointed end for putting into the mouth, used for smoking.—**Cigarette**, sig-a-ret′, *n.* [Fr. dim. of *cigare*.] A little cut tobacco rolled up in tissue paper, used for smoking.

Cilia, sil′i-a, *n. pl.* [L. *cilium*, an eyelash.] The hairs which grow from the margin of the eyelids; eyelashes; hairs or bristes situated on the margin of a vegetable body; small, generally microscopic, hair-like vibratile processes which project from animal membranes, and have usually important functions.—**Ciliary**, sil′i-a-ri, *a.* Belonging to the eyelids or eyelashes; pertaining to or performed by vibratile cilia (*ciliary* motion).—**Ciliate**, **Ciliated**, sil′i-āt, sil′i-āt-ed, *a.* Furnished with cilia; bearing cilia.—**Ciliiform**, sil′i-i-form, *a.* Having the form of cilia; very fine or slender.

Cimbric, sim′brik, *a.* Pertaining to the *Cimbri*, an ancient people of Europe, generally considered a North German race.

Cimeter,‡ **Cimiter**,‡ sim′e-tėr, sim′i-tėr, *n.* A scimitar.

Cimmerian, sim-mē′ri-an, *a.* Pertaining to the *Cimmerii* or *Cimmerians*, a mythical people described as dwelling where the sun never shines, and perpetual darkness reigns; hence, very dark (*Mil.*).

Cimolite, sim′ō-līt, *n.* [Fr. *cimolite*, from *Cimolus*, *Cimoli*, or Argentiera, one of the Cyclades.] A white, soft variety of clay, used by the ancients as a remedy for erysipelas and other inflammations, by the moderns as a fuller's earth.

Cinch, sinch, *n.* [Sp. *cincha*, same as *cincture*.] A saddle-girth, in United States; firm hold, a sure thing.

Cinchona, sin-kō′na, *n.* [From the Countess of *Chinchon*, vice-queen of Peru, who was cured of fever by it in 1638, and assisted in spreading the remedy.] The name of a number of South American trees and shrubs, some of which yield the bark whence quinine is obtained; the bark of such trees, called also *Peruvian bark*.—**Cinchonaceous**, sin-kō-nā′shus, *a.* Pertaining to cinchona or plants of allied genera.—**Cinchonic**, sin-kon′ik, *a.* Of or belonging to cinchona; derived from cinchona; having the properties of cinchona.—**Cinchonin**, **Cinchonine**, sin′ko-nin, *n.* An alkaloid obtained from the bark of several species of cinchona, along with quinine, and one of the medicinal active principles of this bark, being valuable as a febrifuge.—**Cinchonism**, sin′kon-izm, *n.* A disturbed condition of the system, the result of overdoses of cinchona or quinine.

Cincture, singk′tūr, *n.* [L. *cinctura*, from *cingo*, *cinctum*, to gird, seen also in *precinct*, *succinct*.] A belt, girdle, or something similar; that which rings, encircles, or incloses; inclosure; *arch.* a ring round a column.—**Cinctured**, singk′tūrd, *a.* Girt with a cincture.

Cinder, sin′dėr, *n.* [A.Sax. *sinder*, dross, cinder=Icel. *sindr*, Sw. *sinder*, Dan. *sinder*, *sinner*, a cinder; D. *sintel*, G. *sinter*.] A solid piece of matter remaining after having been subjected to combustion; especially, a piece of coal more or less completely burnt, but not reduced to ashes.—**Cinderella**, *n.* A dance ending at twelve at night, from the French fairy-tale of that name; a household drudge. — **Cindery**, sin′dėr-i, *a.* Resembling cinders; containing cinders, or composed of them.

Cinematograph, sin-e-mat′o-graf, *n.* [Gr. *kinēma*, motion, and-*graph*.] *Brit.* A motion-picture camera and projector taking a large series of instantaneous pictures, at least sixteen images per second, to obtain consecutive and uninterrupted movement.

Cinenchyma, si-nen′ki-ma, *n.* [Gr. *kineō*, to move, and *enchyma*, infusion—*en*, in, *cheō*, to pour.] *Bot.* a tissue containing elaborated sap or latex.—**Cinenchymatous**, si-nen-kim′at-us, *a.* Pertaining to cinenchyma; laticiferous.

Cineraceous, **Cinereous**, sin-e-rā′shus, si-nē′rē-us, *a.* [L. *cineraceus*, *cinereus*, from *cinis*, *cineris*, ashes.] Like ashes; having the color of the ashes of wood.—**Cineraria**, sin-e-rā′ri-a, *n.* [From the soft ashy white down on the surface of the leaves.] The common and generic name of several species of composite plants (chiefly South African) many varieties of which are cultivated in our gardens.—**Cinerary**, sin′e-ra-ri, *a.* [L. *cinerarius*.] Pertaining to ashes; a term applied to the urns in which the ashes of bodies which had been burned were deposited. — **Cineration**, sin-e-rā′-shon, *n.* The reducing of anything to ashes by combustion. — **Cineritious**, sin-e-ri′-shus, *a.* [L. *cineritius*.] Having the color or consistence of ashes; ash-gray; *anat.* a term applied to the exterior or cortical part of the brain.

Cingalese, sing′ga-lēz, *a.* *Brit.* Pertaining to the primitive inhabitants of Ceylon, or to the island itself. Also used as a noun, *sing.* and *pl.* SINGHALESE.

Cinnabar, sin′na-bär, *n.* [L. *cinnabaris*, Gr. *kinnabari*, a word of Eastern origin; Per. *quinbār*.] Red sulphide of mercury, which, when sublimed and used as a pigment, is called *vermilion*; a red resinous juice obtained from an East Indian tree formerly used as an astringent: called also *Dragon's-blood*.—**Cinnabaric, Cinnabarine**, sin'na-bar'ik, sin'na-bar-in, *a.* Pertaining to cinnabar; consisting of cinnabar or containing it.

Cinnamon, sin'na-mon, *n.* [L. *cinnamomum*; from Gr. *kinnamōmon*, through Phœn. from Heb. *kinnamon*.] The inner bark of a tree of the laurel family, a native of Ceylon and other parts of tropical Asia, dried and having a fragrant smell, moderately pungent taste, with some degree of sweetness and astringency, being one of the best cordial, carminative, and restorative spices.—*White cinnamon*. CANELLA.—**Cinnamic, Cinnamomic**, sin-nam'ik, sin-na-mom'ik, *a.* Pertaining to or obtained from cinnamon.—**Cinnamon-stone**, *n.* A variety of garnet of a cinnamon colour.

Cinque, singk, *n.* [Fr., L. *quinque*, five.] A five: a word used in certain games.—**Cinque-foil**, *n.* [L. *folium*, a leaf.] An ornament in the pointed style of architecture somewhat resembling five leaves about a common centre, the apertures of circular windows being often in this form; the name of various plants having quinate leaves, as the five-bladed clover, &c.—**Cinque-pace**, *n.* A kind of dance, the steps of which were regulated by the number five. (*Shak.*)—**Cinque-ports**, *n. pl.* Five ports or havens on the southern shore of England, towards France, viz. Hastings, Romney, Hythe, Dover, and Sandwich, to which were afterwards added Winchelsea, Rye, and Seaford, all having royal grants of particular privileges, on condition of providing a certain number of ships in war at their own expense.

Cipher, sī'fėr, *n.* [O.Fr. *cifre*, Mod.Fr. *chiffre*, It. *cifra*, Ar. *sifr*, cipher, from Ar. *sifr*, empty.] The numerical character or figure 0 or nothing; any numerical character; some person or thing of no consequence, importance, or value; a monogram or literal device formed of the intertwined initials of a name; a kind of secret writing.—*v.i.* To use figures; to practise arithmetic.—*v.t.* To write in occult or secret characters.

Cipolin, sip'ol-in, *n.* [It. *cipollino*, from *cipolla*, an onion, from its being veined or stratified like an onion.] A green marble from Rome, containing white zones.

Cippus, sip'pus, *n.* pl. **Cippi**, sip'pī. [L.] In *Rom. antiq.* a low column, generally rectangular and sculptured, and often bearing an inscription, serving as a sepulchral monument, and occasionally as a landmark, milestone, &c.

Circ, sėrk, *n.* [L. *circus*, a circle.] A prehistoric stone circle.

Circar, sėr'kär, *n.* [Per. *sarkār*.] In India, a large portion of a province.

Circean, sėr-sē'an, *a.* Pertaining to *Circe*, in Greek mythology a celebrated sorceress, who transformed the companions of Ulysses into swine by a magical beverage; hence, fascinating but brutifying or poisonous; magical.

Circensian, sėr-sen'shi-an, *a.* [L. *circenses*, games of the *circus*.] Pertaining to the circus in Rome, or the games practised there.

Circinate, sėr'si-nāt, *a.* [From L. *circinus*, a compass, a circle, from *circus*, a circle.] *Bot.* rolled up on itself like a shepherd's crook or bishop's crosier, as the fronds of ferns in a young state.

Circle, sėr'kl, *n.* [L. *circulus*, dim. of *circus*, a circle.] A plane figure, comprehended by a single curve line, called its circumference, every part of which is equally distant from a point within it called the centre; the line bounding or forming such a figure, or something in a similar form; a ring; a round body; compass; circuit; a series (as of actions) ending where it begins; an ending where one began; a number of particulars regarded as having a central point; a number of persons associated by some tie; a coterie; a set.—*v.t.*—*circled, circling*. To encircle; to encompass; to surround; to inclose; to move round; to revolve round.—*v.i.* To move circularly; to circulate; to revolve.—*Great circle*, a circle on a sphere having as its centre the centre of the sphere: opposed to a *small* or *lesser circle*. The equator is a great circle; any parallel of latitude a small circle.—*Great circle sailing*, the manner of conducting a vessel between one place and another so that her track may always be along or nearly along the arc of a great circle.—*Polar circles*, the Arctic and the Antarctic circles 23½° from the respective poles.—**Circled**, sėr'kld, *a.* Circular; round. (*Shak.*)—**Circlet**, sėr'klet, *n.* A little circle; a ring-shaped ornament for the head; a chaplet; a headband.

Circuit, sėr'kit or sėr'kūt, *n.* [Fr. *circuit*, L. *circuitus*—*circum*, round, and *eo*, *itum*, to go.] The act of moving or passing round; a circular journey; a revolution; the distance round any space whether circular or otherwise; a boundary line encompassing an object; circumference; the journey of judges or other persons through certain appointed places for the purpose of holding courts or performing other stated duties; the district or portion of country in which a particular judge or judges hold courts and administer justice; the arrangement by which a current of electricity is kept up between the two poles of a galvanic battery; the path of a voltaic current.—**Circuitous**, sėr-kū'it-us, *a.* Having a roundabout or devious course; not direct; roundabout.—**Circuitously**, sėr-kū'it-us-li, *adv.* In a circuitous manner.—**Circuitousness, Circuity**, sėr-kū'it-us-nes, sėr-kū'i-ti, *n.* The character or condition of being circuitous.

Circular, sėr'kū-lėr, *a.* [L. *circularis*. CIRCLE.] In the form of a circle; round; circumscribed by a circle; passing over or forming a circle, circuit, or round; addressed to a number of persons having a common interest (a *circular* letter).—*Circular note*, a note or letter of credit furnished by bankers to persons about to travel abroad, and which is payable at any one of a number of places.—*Circular numbers*, those whose powers terminate in the roots themselves, as 5 and 6, whose squares are 25 and 36.—*n.* A letter, notice, or intimation, generally printed or multiplied by some other rapid process, of which a copy is sent to several persons on some common business.—**Circularity**, sėr-kū-lar'i-ti, *n.* The state or quality of being circular; a circular form.—**Circulate**, sėr'kū-lāt, *v.i.*—*circulated, circulating*. [L. *circulo*, *circulatum*.] To move in a circle; to move round and return to the same point; to flow in the veins or channels of an organism; to pass from one person or place to another; to be diffused.—*v.t.* To cause to pass from place to place or from person to person; to put about; to spread.—*Circulating* or *recurring decimals*, interminate decimals in which two or more figures are continually repeated.—*Circulating library*, a library the books of which circulate among the subscribers.—**Circulation**, sėr-kū-lā'shon, *n.* The act of circulating or moving in a course which brings or tends to bring the moving body to the point where its motion began; the act of flowing through the veins or channels of an organism; recurrence in a certain order or series; the act of passing from place to place or from person to person (as of money, news, &c.); the extent to which anything is circulated (a newspaper with a large *circulation*); currency; circulating coin, or notes, bills, &c., current and representing coin.—**Circulative**, sėr'kū-lā-tiv, *a.* Circulating; causing circulation.—**Circulator**, sėr'kū-lā-tėr, *n.* One who or that which circulates: specifically applied to a circulating decimal fraction.—**Circulatory**,‡ sėr'kū-la-to-ri, *a.* Passing round a certain circuit; circular.—**Circulable**, sėr'kū-la-bl, *a.* Capable of being circulated, or put in circulation, as coins, bank-notes, &c.

Circumambient, sėr-kum-am'bi-ent, *a.* [L. *circum*, around, and *ambio*, to go about.] Surrounding; encompassing; inclosing or being on all sides, as the air about the earth.—**Circumambiency**, sėr-kum-am'bi-en-si, *n.* The state or quality of being circumambient.

Circumambulate, sėr-kum-am'bū-lāt, *v.i.* [L. *circum*, around, and *ambulo*, to walk.] To walk round about.—**Circumambulation**, sėr-kum-am'bū-lā"shon, *n.* The act of circumambulating.

Circumcise, sėr-kum-sīz, *v.t.*—*circumcised, circumcising*. [L. *circumcido*, *circumcisum*—*circum*, about, and *cædo*, to cut.] To cut off the prepuce or foreskin of, a ceremony or rite among the Jews, Mohammedans, and others.—**Circumciser**, sėr'kum-sīz-ėr, *n.* One who performs circumcision.—**Circumcision**, sėr-kum-si'zhon, *n.* The act of circumcising.

Circumference, sėr-kum'fėr-ens, *n.* [L. *circumferentia*—*circum*, round, and *fero*, to carry.] The line that bounds a circle or any regular curvilinear figure; periphery; measure round a circular or spherical body.—**Circumferential**, sėr-kum'fėr-en"shal, *a.* Pertaining to the circumference.—**Circumferentor**, sėr-kum'fėr-en-tėr, *n.* An instrument used by surveyors for taking angles, now almost superseded by the theodolite.

Circumflect, sėr'kum-flekt, *v.t.* [L. *circum*, round, and *flecto*, *flexum*, to bend.] To bend round; to circumflex.—**Circumflex**, sėr'kum-fleks, *n.* A wave of the voice, embracing both a rise and a fall on the same syllable; an accent placed only on long vowels, and indicating different things in different languages. In Greek it is marked by the signs ~ and ^, in French and some other languages by the sign ^.—*a.* Term for the above accent; *anat.* applied to several curved parts in the body.—*v.t.* To mark or pronounce with the circumflex.

Circumfluence, sėr-kum'flu̇-ens, *n.* [L. *circumfluens*—*circum*, round, and *fluo*, to flow.] A flowing round on all sides; an inclosure of waters.—**Circumfluent, Circumfluous**, sėr-kum'flu̇-ens, sėr-kum'flu̇-us, *a.* Flowing round; surrounding as a fluid.

Circumfuse, sėr-kum-fūz', *v.t.*—*circumfused, circumfusing*. [L. *circumfundo*, *circumfusus*—*circum*, round, and *fundo*, *fusus*, to pour.] To pour round; to spread round (*Mil.*)—**Circumfusile**, sėr-kum-fū'zil, *a.* Capable of being poured or spread round.—**Circumfusion**, sėr-kum-fū'zhon, *n.* The act of circumfusing.

Circumgyrate, sėr-kum-jī'rāt, *v.t.* and *i.* [L. *circum*, round, and *gyro*, to turn, from *gyrus*, a circle.] To roll or turn round.—**Circumgyration**, sėr-kum'jī-rā"shon, *n.* The act of circumgyrating; a circular motion.

Circumjacent, sėr-kum-jā'sent, *a.* [L. *circumjacens*—*circum*, round, and *jaceo*, to lie.] Lying round; bordering on every side.—**Circumjacence, Circumjacency**, sėr-kum-jā'sens, sėr-kum-jā'sen-si, *n.* State or condition of being circumjacent.

Circumlittoral, sėr-kum-lit'o-ral, *a.* [L. *circum*, round, and *littus*, *littoris*, the shore.] About or adjoining the shore.

Circumlocution, sėr'kum-lō-kū"shon, *n.* [L. *circum*, round, and *locutio*, a speaking, *loquor*, to speak.] A roundabout way of speaking; the use of more words than necessary to express an idea; a periphrasis.—**Circumlocutory**, sėr-kum-lok'ū-to-ri, *a.* Exhibiting circumlocution; periphrastic.

Circummure, sėr-kum-mūr', *v.t.* [L. *circum*, round, and *murus*, a wall.] To wall round; to encompass with a wall. (*Shak.*)

Circumnavigate, sėr-kum-nav'i-gāt, *v.t.*—*circumnavigated, circumnavigating*. [L. *circumnavigo*—*circum*, round, and *navigo*, to sail, from *navis*, a ship.] To sail round; to pass round by water (the globe, an island, &c.)—**Circumnavigable**, sėr-kum-nav'i-ga-bl, *a.* Capable of being circumnavigated or sailed round.—**Circumnavigation**, sėr-kum-nav'i-gā"shon, *n.* The act of sailing round.—**Circumnavigator**, sėr-kum-nav'i-gā-tėr, *n.* One who circumnavigates: generally applied to one who has sailed round the globe.

Circumpolar, sėr-kum-pō'lėr, *a.* Surrounding either pole of the earth or heavens.

Circumscissile, sėr-kum-sis'sil, *n.* [L. *circum*, round, and *scindo*, *scissum*, to cut.]

Bot. opening or divided by a transverse circular line: a term applied to a mode of dehiscence in some fruits, as in the henbane, monkey-pot, &c.

Circumscribe, sėr'kum-skrīb, *v.t.*—*circumscribed, circumscribing.* [L. *circumscribo*—*circum*, round, and *scribo*, to write.] To inscribe or draw a line round; to mark out certain bounds or limits for; to inclose within certain limits; to limit, bound, confine, restrain (authority, &c.).—**Circumscribable**, sėr-kum-skrīb'a-bl, *a.* Capable of being circumscribed.—**Circumscriber**, sėr-kum-skrīb'ėr, *n.* One who or that which circumscribes.—**Circumscription**, sėr-kum-skrip'shon, *n.* The act of circumscribing or state of being circumscribed; limitation; restriction; also a periphery or circumference. — **Circumscriptive**, sėr-kum-skrip'tiv, *a.* Circumscribing or tending to circumscribe; limiting; restricting. (*Mil.*)

Circumspect, sėr'kum-spekt, *a.* [L. *circumspectus*—*circum*, round, and *specio*, to look.] Examining carefully all the circumstances that may affect a determination; watchful on all sides; wary; vigilant; prudent; cautious.—**Circumspection**, sėr-kum-spek'shon, *n.* The quality of being circumspect; observation of the true position of circumstances; watchfulness; vigilance; wariness; caution.—**Circumspective**,† sėr-kum-spek'tiv, *a.* Circumspect; cautious. — **Circumspectly**, sėr'kum-spekt-li, *adv.* In a circumspect manner; cautiously; watchfully.—**Circumspectness**, sėr'kum-spekt-nes, *n.* Circumspection.

Circumstance, sėr'kum-stans, *n.* [L. *circumstantia*, from *circumstans*, standing about—*circum*, round, and *sto*, to stand.] Something attending, appendant, or relative to a fact or case; something incidental; some fact giving rise to a certain presumption, or tending to afford some evidence; detail; incident; event; *pl.* situation; surroundings; state of things; especially, condition in regard to worldly estate.—*v.t. circumstanced, circumstancing.* To place in a particular situation or in certain surroundings: usually in pp.—**Circumstantial**, sėr-kum-stan'shal, *a.* Consisting in or pertaining to circumstances; attending; incidental; relating to, but not essential; exhibiting all the circumstances (account or recital); minute; particular; obtained or inferred from the circumstances of the case; not direct or positive (*circumstantial* evidence).—*n.* Something incidental and of subordinate importance: opposed to *essential.* — **Circumstantiality**, sėr-kum-stan'shi-al"i-ti, *n.* The quality of being circumstantial; minuteness; fulness of detail; — **Circumstantially**, sėr-kum-stan'-shal-li, *adv.* In a circumstantial manner; minutely; in full detail; indirectly; not positively.—**Circumstantiate**, sėr-kum-stan'shi-āt, *v.t.* To confirm by circumstances; to describe circumstantially or in full detail.

Circumvallate,† sėr-kum-val'lāt, *v.t.* [L. *circum*, round, and *vallum*, a rampart.] To surround with a rampart.—**Circumvallation**, sėr-kum'val-lā"shon, *n.* The act of surrounding with a rampart; a line of field fortifications consisting of a rampart or parapet with a trench, surrounding a besieged place or a camp.

Circumvent, sėr-kum-vent', *v.t.* [L. *circumvenio, circumventum* — *circum*, about, and *venio*, to come.] To gain advantage over by artfulness, stratagem, or deception; to defeat or get the better of by cunning; to outwit; to overreach.—**Circumvention**, sėr-kum-ven'shon, *n.* The act of circumventing; outwitting or overreaching; stratagem. — **Circumventive**, sėr-kum-vent'iv, *a.* Tending or designed to circumvent.—**Circumventor**, sėr-kum-vent'ėr, *n.* One who circumvents.

Circumvolve, sėr-kum-volv', *v.t.*—*circumvolved, circumvolving.* [L. *circum*, round, and *volvo, volutum*, to roll.] To turn or cause to roll round; to cause to revolve.—**Circumvolution**, sėr-kum'vō-lū"shon, *n.* A rolling or being rolled round; one of the windings of a thing wound or twisted; a convolution; a roundabout procedure.

Circus, sėr'kus, *n.* pl. **Circuses**, sėr'kus-ez. [L.] Among the ancient Romans a kind of theater or amphitheater adapted for horse-races, the exhibition of athletic exercises, contests with wild beasts, &c.; in modern times, a place of amusement where feats of horsemanship and acrobatic displays form the principal entertainment.

Cirque, sėrk, *n.* [Fr., a circle, a circus.] A circus; a kind of circular valley among mountains; an amphitheatre.

Cirrhosis, sir-rō'sis, *n.* [Gr. *kirrhos*, orange-tawny, from the appearance of the diseased liver.] A disease consisting of diminution and deformity of the liver, often seen in drunkards.—**Cirrhotic**, sir-rot'ik, *a.* Affected with or having the character of cirrhosis.

Cirribranch, Cirribranchiate, sir'ri-brangk, sir-ri-brang'ki-āt, *a.* [L. *cirrus*, a tendril, and *branchiæ*, gills.] Having tendril-like gills: a term applied to certain molluscs.—**Cirriferous, Cirrigerous**, sir-rif'ėr-us, sir-rij'ėr-us, *a.* Possessing cirri.—**Cirriform**, sir'ri-form, *a.* Formed like a tendril.—**Cirrigrade**, sir'ri-grād, *a.* [L. *gradior*, to go.] Moving by means of tendril like appendages.—**Cirriped**, sir'ri-ped, *n.* [L. *cirrus*, and *pes, pedis*, the foot. [A member of an order of lower crustaceous animals, so called from the cirri or filaments with which their transformed feet are fringed.—**Cirrose, Cirrous**, sir'rōs, sir'rus, *a. Bot.* having a cirrus or tendril; resembling tendrils or coiling like them. Written also *Cirrhose, Cirrhous.*—**Cirrus**, sir'rus, *n.* pl. **Cirri**, sir'rī. A tendril; a long thread-like organ by which a plant climbs; a soft curled filamentary appendage to parts serving as the feet of certain lower animals, as barnacles, and the jaws of certain fishes; one of the forms which clouds assume; a light fleecy cloud at a high elevation, *cirro-cumulus* and *cirro-stratus* being intermediate forms partaking partly of this character, partly of that of the cumulus and stratus.

Cisalpine, sis-al'pīn, *a.* [L. *cis*, on this side, and *Alpes*, Alps.] On this side of the Alps, with regard to Rome; that is, on the south of the Alps.—**Cisatlantic**, sis-at-lan'tik, *a.* Being on this side of the Atlantic Ocean.—**Cismontane**, sis-mon'tān, *a.* Existing on this side of the mountains; specifically, on this side of the Alps: opposed to *Ultramontane.* —**Cispadane**, sis'pa-dān, *a.* [L. *Padus*, the river Po.] On this side of the Po, with regard to Rome; that is, on the south side.

Ciselure, sēz'lūr, *n.* [Fr., from *ciseler*, to carve or engrave with a chisel.] The art or operation of chasing; chased metal work.

Cisleu, sis'lē-ū, *n.* Same as *Chisleu.*

Cissoid, sis'soid, *n.* [Gr. *kissos*, ivy.] *Geom.* a particular variety of curve invented by the Greek geometer Diocles.—**Cissoidal**, sis-soid'al, *a.* Pertaining to the cissoid.

Cist, sist, *n.* [L. *cista*, Gr. *kistē*, a chest. *Chest* is another form of this word.] A place of interment of an early or prehistoric period, consisting of a stone chest formed of two parallel rows of stones fixed on their ends, and covered by similar flat stones. — **Cistella**, sis-tel'la, *n.* [L., a casket, dim. of *cista*, a box.] *Bot.* the capsular shield of some lichens.

Cistercian, sis-tėr'shi-an, *n.* A member of a religious order, which takes its name from its original convent, *Cistercium* or Citeaux, near Dijon, where the society was founded in 1098.

Cistern, sis'tėrn, *n.* [L. *cisterna*, from *cista*, a chest.] An artificial reservoir or receptacle for holding water, beer, or other liquor.

Cistus, sis'tus, *n.* [Gr. *kistos.*] The rock-rose, the name of European plants of various species, some of them beautiful evergreen flowering shrubs, ornamental in gardens.

Citadel, sit'a-del, *n.* [Fr. *citadelle.* Same origin as *city.*] A fortress or castle in or near a city, intended to keep the inhabitants in subjection, or, in case of a siege, to form a final point of defence.

Cite, sīt, *v.t.*—*cited, citing.* [Fr. *citer*, from L. *cito, citare*, freq. of *cieo*, to call, to summon; seen also in *excite, incite, recite.*] To call upon officially or authoritatively to appear; to summon before a person or tribunal; to quote, adduce, or bring forward; to refer to in support, proof, or confirmation (to *cite* an authority).—**Citable**, sīt'-a-bl, *a.* Capable of being cited or quoted. —**Cital**, sī'tal, *n.* The act of citing to appear; a summons; mention; quotation†; citation†. — **Citation**, sī-tā'shon, *n.* A summons; an official call or notice given to a person to appear, as in a court; the act of citing a passage from a book or person; the passage or words quoted; quotation.—**Citatory**, sī'ta-to-ri, *a.* Having the power or form of citation.—**Citer**, sīt'ėr, *n.* One who cites.

Cithara, sith'a-ra, *n.* [L., from Gr. *kithara*, whence *gittern, guitar.*] An ancient stringed instrument resembling the more modern cittern or guitar. — **Citharist**, sith'ar-ist, *n.* A player on the cithara.—**Citharistic**, sith-ar-ist'ik, *a.* Pertaining to the cithara.—**Cithern, Cittern**, sith'-ėrn, sit'tėrn, *n.* An old instrument of the guitar kind, strung with wire instead of gut.

Citizen, &c. CITY.

Citron, sit'ron, *n.* [Fr. *citron*, from L. *citreum*, from *citrus*, the lemon or citron.] The fruit of the citron-tree, a large species of lemon; the tree itself.—**Citric**, sit'rik, *a.* Belonging to or derived from lemons or citrons.—*Citric acid*, the acid of lemons, used for making cooling drinks, and as a discharge in calico-printing.—**Citrine**, sit'-rin, *a.* [L. *citrinus*, from *citrus*, a lemon or citron.] Like a citron or lemon; of a lemon colour; yellow or greenish-yellow.—*Citrine ointment*, the ointment of nitrate of mercury.—*n.* Lemon colour; a yellow pellucid variety of quartz.

Cittern, sit'tėrn, *n.* CITHARA.

City, sit'i, *n.* [Fr. *cité*, from L. *civitas, civitatis*, a city, state, from *civis*, a citizen, whence also *civil.*] In a general sense, a large and important town; in a narrower sense and as regards Great Britain, a town corporate that is or has been the seat of a bishop and of a cathedral church; in the United States an incorporated town governed by a mayor and aldermen; the inhabitants of a city collectively.—*a.* Pertaining to a city.—**Citied**, sit'id, *a.* Belonging to a city; having the qualities of a city; covered with cities.—**Citizen**, sit'i-zen, *n.* [O.E. *citezein*, from O.Fr. *citeain, citeien*, &c. (Mod. Fr. *citoyen*), from *cité*, a city. The *z* is a corruption of the old symbol used for *y.*] The native of a city, or an inhabitant who enjoys the freedom and privileges of the city in which he resides; a member of a state with full political privileges. — *a.* Having the qualities of a citizen; town-bred. — **Citizenize**, sit'i-zen-īz, *v.t.* To make a citizen; to admit to the rights and privileges of a citizen. — **Citizenship**, sit'i-zen-ship, *n.* The state or principles of a citizen.

Cive, sīv, *n.* [Fr. *cive*, L. *cepa*, an onion.] A small perennial plant of the same genus as the leek and onion, cultivated in kitchen-gardens as a pot-herb.

Civet, siv'et, *n.* [Fr. *civette*, It. *zibetto*, from Ar. *zabad*, the substance civet.] A strong-smelling substance taken from the anal glands of the civet-cats, and yielding a perfume; the animal that yields this substance. —*v.t.* To scent with civet.—**Civet-cat**, *n.* The name of several carnivorous mammals natives of North Africa and Asia, having a gland near the anus containing the odoriferous substance civet.

Civic, siv'ik, *a.* [L. *civicus*, from *civis*, a citizen; whence also *city.*] Pertaining to a city or citizen; relating to civil affairs or honours.—*Civic crown, Rom. antiq.* a crown of oak leaves given to a soldier who saved the life of a citizen in battle.—**Civics**, siv'iks, *n.* The science of the rights and duties of citizens.—**Civil**, siv'il, *a.* [L. *civilis*, from *civis.*] Relating to the community, or to the policy and government of the citizens and subjects of a state (*civil* rights, government, &c.); political; municipal or private, as opposed to criminal; not ecclesiastical or military; exhibiting some refinement of manners; civilized; courteous; obliging; well bred; affable; polite.—*Civil engineering*, that branch of engineering which relates to the forming of roads, bridges, railroads, canals, aqueducts, harbours, &c.—*Civil law*, the law of a state, city, or country; more specifically, the Roman law, the system of law which prevailed in the Roman Empire, and has largely influenced modern systems.—*Civil list*, a yearly sum of money allotted to the sovereign of Britain, mainly for the expenses of the royal household, pensions, &c.—*Civil service*, that branch of the public service in which the non-military employees of a government are engaged, or those persons collectively.—*Civil war*, a war between the people of the same state.—*Civil year*, the tropical or solar year.—**Civilly**, siv'il-li, *adv.* In a civil manner; as regards civil rights or privileges; politely; courteously; in a well-bred manner.—**Civilian**, si-vil'i-an, *n.* One skilled in the Roman or civil law; one whose pursuits are those of civil life, not military or clerical.—**Civility**, si-vil'i-ti, *n.* [L. *civilitas*, from *civilis.*] The state of being civilized‡; good breeding; politeness, or an act of politeness; courtesy; kind attention.—**Civilizable**, siv'il-īz-a-bl, *a.* Capable of being civilized.—**Civilization**, siv'il-iz-ā"shon, *n.* The act of civilizing, or state of being civilized; the state of being refined in manners from the rudeness of savage life, and improved in arts and learning.—**Civilize**, siv'il-īz, *v.t.*—*civilized, civilizing.* [Fr. *civiliser*, formerly also *civilizer.*] To reclaim from a savage state; to introduce order and civic organization among; to refine and enlighten; to elevate in social life.—**Civilized**, siv'il-īzd, *p.* and *a.* Possessing some culture or refinement; refined; cultivated.—**Civilizer**, siv'il-īz-ėr, *n.* One who or that which civilizes or tends to civilize.

Clachan, klach'an, *n.* [Gael. from *clach*, a stone.] In Scotland, a small village or hamlet.

Clack, klak, *v.i.* [An imitative word; comp. Fr. *claque*, a clap or clack; D. *klakken*, to clap; E. *clap, crack.*] To make a sudden sharp noise, as by striking or cracking; to rattle; to utter sounds or words rapidly and continually, or with sharpness and abruptness.—*v.t.* To cause to make a sharp, short sound; to clap; to speak without thought; to rattle out.—*n.* A sharp, abrupt sound, continually repeated; a kind of small windmill for frightening birds; continual talk; prattle.—**Clacker**, klak'ėr, *n.* One who or that which clacks.—**Clack-dish**, *n.* A dish formerly used by mendicants, with a cover, which they *clacked* to excite notice. (*Shak.*)—**Clack-valve**, *n.* A valve in pumps with a single flap, hinged at one edge.

Clad, klad, *pp.* Clothed.

Cladode, klad'ōd, *n.* [Gr. *kladŏs*, a young branch.] A leaf-like branch.

Claim, klām, *v.t.* [O.Fr. *claimer*, from L. *clamo, clamare*, to shout, whence also *clamour, acclaim, acclamation, exclaim, reclaim, &c.*] To ask or seek to obtain by virtue of authority, right, or supposed right; to assert a right to; to demand as due.—*v.i.* To be entitled to a thing; to have a right; to derive a right; to assert claims; to put forward claims.—*n.* A demand of a right or supposed right; a calling on another for something due or supposed to be due; a right to claim or demand; a title to anything; the thing claimed or demanded; specifically, in America, Australia, &c., a piece of land allotted to one.—**Claimable**, klām'a-bl, *a.* Capable of being claimed or demanded as due.—**Claimant, Claimer**, klām'ant, klām'ėr, *n.* A person who claims; one who demands anything as his right.—**Claimless**,† klām'les, *a.* Having no claim.

Clairvoyance, klãr-voi'ans, *n.* [Fr. *clair*, clear, and *voyant*, seeing, ppr. of *voir* (L. *videre*), to see.] A power attributed to persons in the mesmeric state, by which the person (called a clairvoyant or clairvoyante) discerns objects concealed from sight, tells what is happening at a distance, &c.—**Clairvoyant**, klãr-voi'ant, *a.* Of or pertaining to clairvoyance.—**Clairvoyant, Clairvoyante**, klãr-voi'ant, *n.* A man or woman in a certain stage of mesmerism, in which state the subject is said to see things not present to the senses.

Clam,† klam, *v.t.*—*clammed, clamming.* [A. Sax. *clam*, mud, clay, that which is clammy; Dan. *klam*, clammy, *klamme*, to clog.] To clog with glutinous or viscous matter.—*v.i.*† To be glutinous or moist; to stick like clammy matter or moisture.—**Clammy**, klam'mi, *a.* Viscous; adhesive; soft and sticky; glutinous; tenacious.—**Clammily**, klam'mi-li, *adv.* In a clammy manner.—**Clamminess**, klam'mi-nes, *n.* The state of being clammy or viscous; viscosity; stickiness.

Clam, klam, *n.* [Shortened from *clamp*, the former name, given from the firmness with which some of these animals adhere to rocks. CLAMP.] The popular name of certain bivalvular shell-fish, of several genera and many species.—**Clam-shell**, *n.* The shell of a clam.

Clamant, klam'ant, *a.* [CLAIM.] Clamorous; beseeching; pressing; urgent; crying.

Clamber, klam'bėr, *v.i.* [O.E. *clamer, clammer*, akin to *clam*, to adhere, *clamp*, and *climb.*] To climb with difficulty or with hands and feet; to rise up steeply (*Tenn.*)†.—*v.t.*† To ascend by climbing; to climb with difficulty. (*Shak.*)—*n.* The act of clambering or climbing with difficulty.

Clamor, klam'ėr, *n.* [L. *clamor*, an outcry, from *clamo*, to cry out, whence E. *claim.*] A great outcry; vociferation made by a loud human voice continued or repeated, or by a number of voices; loud complaint; urgent demand; loud and continued noise.—*v.t.* To utter in a loud voice; to shout.—*v.i.* To make a clamor; to utter loud sounds or outcries; to vociferate; to make importunate complaints or demands.—**Clamorer**, klam'ėr-ėr, *n.* One who clamors.—**Clamorous**, klam'ėr-us, *a.* Making a clamor or outcry; noisy; vociferous; loud.—**Clamorously**, klam'ėr-us-li, *adv.* In a clamorous manner; with loud noise or words.—**Clamorousness**, klam'-ėr-us-nes, *n.* State of being clamorous.

Clamp, klamp, *n.* [Most closely connected with L.G. and D. *klamp*, Dan. *klampe*, G. *klampe*, a clamp; from root seen in E. *climb, clamber, clem* (to pinch with hunger), *clam.*] Something rigid that fastens or binds; a piece of wood or metal fastening two pieces together, or strengthening any framework; an instrument of wood or metal used by joiners, &c., for holding pieces of timber closely together until the glue hardens.—*v.t.* To fasten with clamps; to fix a clamp on.

Clamp, klamp, *n.* [Imitative; comp. *clank, clink.*] A heavy footstep or tread; a tramp; a heap of turnips, potatoes, &c., covered over with straw and earth for winter keeping; pile of bricks for burning.—*v.i.* To tread heavily. (*Thack.*)

Clan, klan, *n.* [Gael. and Ir. *clann*, family, tribe.] A race; a family; a tribe; the common descendants of the same progenitor, under the patriarchal control of a chief; a clique, sect, society, or body of persons closely united by some common interest or pursuit.—**Clannish**, klan'ish, *a.* Imbued with the feelings, sentiments, and prejudices peculiar to clans; blindly devoted to those of one's own clan, set, or locality, and illiberal towards others.—**Clannishly**, klan'ish-li, *adv.* In a clannish manner.—**Clannishness**, klan'ish-nes, *n.* The state or quality of being clannish.—**Clanship**, klan'ship, *n.* A state of union, as in a family or clan; an association under a chieftain.—**Clansman**, klanz'man, *n.* A member of a clan.

Clandestine, klan-des'tin, *a.* [L. *clandestinus*, from *clam*, in secret.] Secret; private; hidden; withdrawn from public view; generally implying craft, deception, or evil design.—**Clandestinely**, klan-des'tin-li, *adv.* In a clandestine manner; secretly; privately; in secret.—**Clandestineness, Clandestinity**,† klan-des'tin-nes, klan-des-tin'i-ti, *n.* The state or quality of being clandestine.

Clang, klang, *n.* [Imitative of sound, and akin to *clank, clink, clack*; G. *klingen*, to sound; Dan. Sw. G. *klang*, D. *klank*, a sound; L. *clangor*, Gr. *klanggē.*] A loud sound produced from solid bodies, especially that produced by the collision of metallic bodies; a clank; clangor.—*v.i.* To give out a clang; to clank; to resound—*v.t.* To cause to sound with a clang.—**Clangorous**, klang'gėr-us, *a.* Making a clangor; having a hard or ringing sound.—**Clangor**, klang'gėr, *n.* [Directly from L. *clangor.*] A sharp, hard, ringing sound as of a trumpet.

Clank, klangk, *n.* [CLANG.] The loud sound made by collision of metallic or other similarly sounding bodies (as chains, iron armour, &c.): generally expressing a less resounding sound than *clang*, and a deeper and stronger sound than *clink.*—*v.t.* To cause to sound with a clank.—*v.i.* To sound with or give out a clank.

Clap, klap, *v.t.*—*clapped* or *clapt* (pret. & pp.), *clapping.* [Same as Icel. and Sw. *klappa*, Dan. *klappe*, D. and L.G. *klappen*, to clap, to pat, &c.; perhaps imitative of sound.] To strike with a quick motion; to slap; to thrust; to drive together; to shut hastily: followed by *to* (to *clap to* the door); to place or put by a hasty or sudden motion (to *clap* the hand to the mouth, to *clap* spurs to a horse).—*To clap hands*, to strike the palms of the hands together, as a mark of applause or delight.—*To clap the wings*, to flap them, or to strike them together so as to make a noise.—*To clap hold of*, to seize roughly and suddenly.—*v.i.* To come together suddenly with noise; to clack; to strike the hands together in applause.—*n.* A collision of bodies with noise; a bang; a slap; a sudden act or motion (in phrase *at a clap*, that is at a blow, all at once); a burst or peal of thunder; a striking of hands to express approbation.—**Clapper**, klap'ėr, *n.* A person who claps or applauds by clapping; that which claps or strikes, as the tongue of a bell; a kind of small noisy windmill to scare birds.—**Clap-net**, *n.* A net for taking larks and other small birds, which is made to fold smartly over on itself by the pulling of a string.—**Clap-sill**, *n.* The bottom part of the frame on which the lock-gates of docks, &c., shut.—**Clap-trap**, *n.* An artifice or device to elicit applause or gain popularity; high-flown sentiments or other rhetorical device by which a person panders to an audience; bunkum.—*a.* Designing or designed merely to catch applause.

Claque, klak, *n.* [Fr., from *claquer*, to clap the hands, to applaud.] A name applied collectively to a set of men who in theatres (as in those of Paris) are regularly hired to applaud the piece or the actors.—**Claquer**, klak-ėr, *n.* [Fr.] A member of the claque; one hired to publicly applaud a theatrical piece.

Clare, klar, *n.* A nun belonging to the order of St. Clare.

Clarence, klar'ens, *n.* [After the Duke of *Clarence*, William IV.] A closed four-wheeled carriage, with inside seats for four.

Clara-bella, klarā-bel'a, *n.* An 8-foot organ stop with open wooden pipes, giving a soft sweet tone.

Clarendon type, klar'en-don, *n.* In printing, a style of type.

Clare-obscure,† klãr'ob-skūr, *n.* [L. *clarus*, clear, and *obscurus*, obscure.] *Paint.* light and shade; chiaroscuro.

Claret, klar'et, *n.* [Fr. *clairet*, from *clair*, clear; It. *claretto.*] The name given in England to the red wines of the Bordeaux district.—*a.* Having the colour of claret wine.—**Claret-cup**, *n.* A summer beverage, composed of iced claret, a little brandy, and a slice or two of lemon or other flavouring ingredients.—**Claret-jug**, *n.* A fancy glass or silver decanter, with lip and handle, for holding claret.

Clarify, klar'i-fī, *v.t.*—*clarified, clarifying.* [Fr. *clarifier*, from L. *clarificare—clarus*, clear, *facio*, to make.] To make clear; to purify from feculent matter; to defecate; to fine (liquor).—*v.i.* To grow or become clear or free from feculent matter; to become pure, as liquors.—**Clarifier**, klar'i-fī-ėr, *n.* One who or that which clarifies or purifies; a vessel in which liquor is clarified. —**Clarification**, klar'i-fi-kā"shon, *n.* The act of clarifying; particularly the clearing or fining of liquid substances from all feculent matter.

Clarinet, Clarionet, klar'i-net, klar'i-on-et, *n.* [Fr. *clarinette*—L. *clarus*, clear.] A wind-instrument of music, made of wood, having finger-holes and keys, and a fixed mouthpiece, containing a reed, forming the upper joint of the instrument.—**Clarion**, klar'i-on, *n.* [L.L. *clario, clarionis*, a clarion, Fr. *clairon*, from L. *clarus*, clear, from its clear sound.] A kind of trumpet whose tube is narrower and tone more acute and shrill than that of the common trumpet.

Clash, klash, *v.i.* [An imitative word; comp. D. *kletsen*, G. *klatschen*, Dan. *klatsche*, to clap.] To make a loud, harsh noise, as from violent or sudden collision; to dash against an object with a loud noise; to come into violent collision; *fig.* to act with opposite power or in a contrary direction; to meet in opposition (their opinions and their interests *clash* together).—*v.t.* To strike against with sound; to strike noisily together.—*n.* The noise made by the meeting of bodies with violence; a striking together with noise; collision or noisy collision of bodies; *fig.* opposition; contradiction, as between differing or contending interests.

Clasp, klasp, *n.* [By metathesis for O.E. *clapse*, to clasp, *claps*, a clasp: allied to O.E. *clip*, to embrace, in the same way as *grasp*, to *grip*, and *gripe*.] A catch to hold something together; a hook for fastening, or for holding together the covers of a book, or the different parts of a garment, of a belt, &c.; a clinging, grasping, or embracing; a close embrace; bar on medal-ribbon for additional service in a campaign.—*v.t.* To shut or fasten together with a clasp; to catch and hold by twining or embracing; to surround and cling to; to embrace closely; to catch with the arms or hands; to grasp.—*v.i.*† To cling. (*Shak.*)—**Clasper**, klas'pėr, *n.* One who or that which clasps.—**Clasp-knife**, *n.* A knife the blade of which folds into the handle.

Class, klas, *n.* [L. *classis*, a class.] An order or rank of persons; a number of persons in society supposed to have some resemblance or equality in rank, education, property, talents, and the like; a number of pupils in a school, or students in a college, of the same standing or pursuing the same studies; *nat. hist.* a large group of plants or animals formed by the union or association of several orders.—*v.t.* To arrange in a class or classes; to rank together; to refer to a class or group; to classify.—*v.i.* To be arranged or classed.—**Classible**, klas'i-bl, *a.* Capable of being classed. —**Classic**, klas'ik, *n.* [L. *classicus*, pertaining to the first or highest of the classes or political divisions into which the Roman people were anciently divided, hence the use of the word in reference to writers.] An author of the first rank; a writer whose style is pure, correct, and refined: primarily, a Greek or Roman author of this character; a literary production of the first class or rank; *the classics*, specifically, the literature of ancient Greece and Rome.—*a.* Same as *Classical*.—**Classical**, klas'ik-al, *a.* Pertaining to writers of the first rank; being of the first order; more specifically relating to Greek and Roman authors of the first rank or estimation; pertaining to ancient Greece or Rome; relating to localities associated with great ancient or modern authors, or to scenes of great historical events; pure, chaste, correct, or refined (taste, style, &c.).—*Classic orders*, *arch.* the Doric, Ionic, and Corinthian orders.—**Classicalism**, klas'ik-al-izm, *n.* A classic idiom or style; classicism; *art*, close adherence to the rules of Greek or Roman art.—**Classicalist**, klas'ik-al-ist, *n.* A devoted admirer of classicalism; one who scrupulously adheres to the canons of Greek or Roman art.—**Classicality, Classicalness**, klas-i-kal'i-ti, klas'ik-al-nes, *n.* The quality of being classical.—**Classically**, klas'ik-al-li, *adv.* In a classical manner; according to the manner of classical authors. —**Classicism**, klas'i-sizm, *n.* A classic idiom or style.—**Classicist**, klas'i-sist, *n.* One versed in the classics.—**Classify**, klas'i-fī, *v.t.*—*classified, classifying.* [L. *classis*, a class, and *facio*, to make.] To arrange in a class or classes; to arrange in sets or ranks according to some method founded on common characteristics in the objects so arranged.—**Classifiable**, klas'i-fī-a-bl, *a.* Capable of being classified.—**Classification**, klas'i-fi-kā"shon, *n.* The act of classifying or forming into a class or classes, so as to bring together those beings or things which most resemble each other, and to separate those that differ; distribution into sets, sorts, or ranks.—**Classificatory**, klas'i-fi-kā-to-ri, *a.* Belonging to classification; concerned with classifying. —**Classifier**, klas'i-fī-ėr, *n.* One who classifies.—**Class-fellow, Class-mate**, *n.* One of the same class at school or college.

Clathrate, klath'rāt, *a.* [L. *clathrus*, a lattice.] *Bot.* and *zool.* latticed; divided like lattice-work.

Clatter, klat'ėr, *v.i.* [From the sound. A. Sax. *clatrung*, a clattering, a rattle; D. *klater*, a rattle; *klateren*, to rattle.] To make rattling sounds; to make repeated sharp sounds, as when sonorous bodies strike or are struck rapidly together; to rattle.—*v.t.* To strike so as to produce a rattling noise from.—*n.* A rapid succession of abrupt, sharp sounds; rattling sounds; tumultuous and confused noise.—**Clatterer**, klat'ėr-ėr, *n.* One who clatters; a babbler.—**Clatteringly**, klat'ėr-ing-li, *adv.* With clattering.

Clause, klaz, *n.* [Fr. *clause*, from L.L. *clausa*, for L. *clausula*, a conclusion, a clause, from *claudo, clausum*, to close, whence *close, exclude*, &c.]. A member of a compound sentence containing both a subject and its predicate; a distinct part of a contract, will, agreement, charter, commission, or the like; a distinct stipulation, condition, proviso, &c.—**Clausular**, klaz'ū-lėr, *a.* Consisting of or having clauses.—**Clausule**, klaz'ūl, *n.* A little clause.

Claustral, klas'tral, *a.* [L.L. *claustralis*, from L. *claustrum*, an inclosure, a cloister, from *claudo*, to shut.] Relating to a cloister; cloister-like; secluded.

Claustrophobia, klas'trō-fō'bē-a, *n.* [L. *claustrum*, an enclosure, Gr. *phobos*, fear.] Morbid fear of confined spaces.

Clavate, Clavated, Claviform, klā-vāt, klā'vāt-ed, klav'i-form, *a.* [L. *clava*, a club.] *Bot.* and *zool.* club-shaped; having the form of a club; growing gradually thicker toward the top, as certain parts of a plant.

Clave, klāv, pret. of *cleave*.

Clavecin, klav'e-sin, *n.* [Fr. *clavecin*, from It. *clavicembalo*, L. *clavis*, a key, and *cymbalum*, a cymbal.] A harpsichord; one of the keys by means of which a player of carillons performs on the bells.

Clavellated, klav'el-lāt-ed, *a.* [L.L. *clavella*, dim. of L. *clava*, a club, a billet of wood.] Relating to billets of wood.—*Clavellated ashes*, potash and pearl-ash, so termed from the billets from which they are obtained by burning.

Clavichord, klav'i-kord, *n.* [L. *clavis*, a key, and *chorda*, a string.] An old stringed instrument, a precursor of the spinet and harpsichord.

Clavicle, klav'i-kl, *n.* [L. *clavicula*, a little key or fastener, from *clavis*, a key.] The collar-bone.—**Clavicular**, kla-vik'ū-lėr, *a.* Pertaining to the collar-bone or clavicle.

Clavicorn, klav'i-korn, *n.* [L. *clava*, a club, and *cornu*, a horn.] A member of a family of beetles, so named from the antennæ being thickened at the apex so as to terminate in a club-shaped enlargement.

Clavier, klav'i-ėr, *n.* [Fr. *clavier*, from L. *clavis*, a key.] The key-board of a pianoforte or other instrument whose keys are arranged similarly; the instrument itself.

Claw, kla, *n.* [A.Sax. *clāwu, clā*, a claw = D. *klaauw*, Icel. *klō*, Dan. and Sw. *klo*, G. *klaue*, a claw; allied to *cleave*, to adhere.] The sharp hooked nail of a quadruped, bird, or other animal; the whole foot of an animal with hooked nails; a hooked extremity belonging to any animal member or appendage; anything shaped like the claw of an animal, as the crooked forked end of a hammer used for drawing nails; *bot.* the narrow base of a petal.—*v.t.* To tear, scratch, pull, or seize with claws or nails; to scratch.—**Clawed**, klad, *a.* Furnished with claws.—**Claw-hammer**, *n.* A hammer furnished with two claws, for convenience of drawing nails out of wood; evening-dress coat, or coat with tails.

Clay, klā, *n.* [A.Sax. *clæg* = Dan. *klæg*, L.G. *klei*, D. *klai, klei*, G. *klei*, clay; same root as in *cleave, clog, glue*.] The name common to various earths, compounds of silica and alumina; earth which is stiff, viscid, and ductile when moistened, and many kinds of which are used in the arts, as pipe-*clay*, porcelain *clay*, &c.; earth in general, especially as the material of the human body.—*a.* Formed or consisting of clay.—*v.t.* To cover or mingle with clay; to purify and whiten (sugar) with clay.—**Clayey**, klā'i, *a.* Consisting of clay; abounding with clay; partaking of clay; like clay; bedaubed or besmeared with clay.—**Clay-marl**, *n.* A whitish, smooth, chalky clay.—**Clay-mill**, *n.* A mill for mixing and tempering clay; a pug-mill.—**Clay-pit**, *n.* A pit where clay is dug.—**Clay-slate**, *n.* A kind of rock consisting of clay which has been hardened and otherwise changed, for the most part extremely fissile and often affording good roofing slate.—**Clay-stone**, *n.* An earthy felstone or felspathic rock of the igneous group.

Claymore, klā'mōr, *n.* [Gael. *claidheam-mor—claidheam*, a sword, and *mor*, great.] Formerly the large two-handed sword of the Scotch Highlanders; now a basket-hilted, double-edged broadsword.

Clean, klēn, *a.* [A.Sax. *claene*, clean, pure, bright; cog. with W. *glain, glan*, Ir. and Gael. *glan*, clean, pure, radiant.] Clear of dirt or filth; having all impurities or foreign matter removed; pure; without fault, imperfection, or defect (timber, a copy); well-proportioned; shapely (*clean* limbs); not bungling; dexterous; adroit (a *clean* leap); complete or thorough; free from moral impurity, guilt, or blame; among the Jews, not defiled or polluted; not forbidden by the ceremonial law for use in sacrifice and for food.—*adv.* Quite; perfectly; wholly; entirely; fully.—*v.t.* To make clean; to remove all foreign matter from; to purify; to cleanse.—*To clean out*, to exhaust the pecuniary resources of. (Colloq.)—**Cleaner**, klēn'ėr, *n.* One who or that which cleans. —**Cleanly**, klen'li, *a.* Free from dirt, filth, or any foul matter; neat; carefully avoiding filth.—**Cleanlily**,† klen'li-li, *adv.* In a cleanly manner.—**Cleanliness**, klen'li-nes, *n.* The state or quality of being cleanly.—**Cleanly**, klēn'li, *adv.* In a clean manner; neatly; without filth; adroitly; dexterously.—**Cleanness**, klēn'-nes, *n.* The state or quality of being clean. —**Clean-handed**, *a.* Having clean hands; *fig.* free from moral taint or suspicion.—**Clean-limbed**, *a.* Having well-proportioned limbs.

Cleanse, klenz, *v.t.*—*cleansed, cleansing.* [A.Sax. *claensian*, from *claene*, clean.] To make clean; to free from filth, or whatever is unseemly, noxious, or offensive; to purify.—**Cleanser**, klen'zėr, *n.* One who or that which cleanses.—**Cleansing**, klen'-zing, *a.* Adapted to cleanse and purify.

Clear, klēr, *a.* [O.Fr. *cleir* (Fr. *clair*), from L. *clarus*, clear; akin *claret, clarify, clari-*

net.] Free from darkness or opacity; brilliant; light; luminous; unclouded; not obscured; free from what would dim transparency or bright colour (*clear* water); free from anything that confuses or obscures; acute, sagacious, or discriminating (intellect, head); perspicuous; lucid (statement); evident; manifest; indisputable; undeniable; free from accusation, imputation, distress, imprisonment, or the like: followed by *of* or *from*; free from impediment or obstruction; unobstructed (a *clear* view); sounding distinctly; distinctly audible; in full; net (*clear* profit or gain).—*Clear days* (preceded by a numeral), days reckoned exclusively of those on which any proceeding is commenced or completed.—*adv.* Clearly; quite; entirely; clean; indicating entire separation.—*v.t.* To make or render clear; to free from whatever diminishes brightness, transparency, or purity of colour; to free from obscurity, perplexity, or ambiguity: often followed by *up*; to free from any impediment or encumbrance, or from anything noxious or injurious; to remove; with *off, away*, &c.; to free from the imputation of guilt; to acquit; to make by way of gain or profit beyond all expenses and charges; to leap over or pass without touching or failure; *naut.* to pay the customs on or connected with; to obtain permission to sail for (a cargo, a ship).—*v.i.* To become free from clouds or fog; to become fair or serene; to pass away or disappear from the sky; often followed by *up, off*, or *away*; to exchange cheques and bills and settle balances, as is done in clearing-houses; *naut.* to leave a port: often followed by *out* or *outwards*.—**Clearance**, klē′rans, *n.* The act of clearing.—**Clear-cole**, klēr-kōl, *n.* and *v.t.* [Fr. *claire colle*, clearglue.] Paint with size and white-lead as the first coat in house-painter work.—**Clearer**, klē′rėr, *n.* One who or that which clears.—**Clearing**, klēr′ing, *n.* The act of one who clears; among *bankers*, the act of exchanging drafts on each other's houses and settling the differences; among *railways*, the act of distributing among the different companies the proceeds of the through traffic passing over several railways; a place or tract of land cleared of wood or cultivation.—

Clearing-house, *n.* An institution through which the claims of banks against one another are settled. These claims are represented in the form of bank checks in the case of bank clearing houses. At the Stock Exchange and the Board of Trade similar clearing houses exist for the facilitation of trading in stocks and in grain. —**Clearing-nut**, *n.* A tree of the nux vomica genus, the seeds of which are said to clear turbid water.—**Clearly**, klēr′li, *adv.* In a clear manner; brightly; luminously; plainly; evidently.—**Clearness**, klēr′nes, *n.* The state or quality of being clear.—

Clear-headed, *a.* Having a clear head or understanding; having acute discernment or keen intelligence.—**Clear-sighted**, *a.* Seeing with clearness; having acuteness of mental discernment; discerning; perspicacious.—**Clear-sightedness**, *n.*—**Clear-starch**, *v.t.* To stiffen and dress with clear or colorless starch.—

Clear-starcher, *n.* One who clear-starches.

Cleat, klēt, *n.* [Allied to G. *klate, klatte*, a claw.] A piece of wood or iron used in a ship to fasten ropes upon; a piece of iron worn on a shoe; a piece of wood nailed on transversely to a piece of joinery for the purpose of securing it in its proper position, or for strengthening.—*v.t.* To strengthen with a cleat or cleats.

Cleave, klēv, *v.i.*—pret. *clave* or *cleaved*; pp. *cleaved*; ppr. *cleaving*. [A.Sax. *clifian, cleofian*, pret. *clifode*, pp. *clifod* (*cleaved* is therefore historically the correct pret. & pp.); cog. D. and L.G. *kleven*, Dan. *klæbe*, G. *kleben*, to adhere, to cleave. *Climb* is akin.] To stick; to adhere; to be attached physically, or by affection or other tie.

Cleave, klēv, *v.t.*—pret. *clove*, or *clave* (the latter antiquated), also *cleft*; pp. *cloven*, *cleft* or *cleaved*; ppr. *cleaving*. [A.Sax. *cleófan*, pret. *cleáf*, pp. *clofen*, (the historically correct conjugation is therefore *cleave, clave* or *clove, cloven*), to cleave or split; cog. D. *kloven*, Icel. *kljúfa*, Dan. *klöve*, G. *klieben*.] To part or divide by force; to split or rive; to sever forcibly; to hew; to cut.—*v.i.* To divide; to split; to open.—**Cleavable**, klē′va-bl, *a.* Capable of being cleaved or divided.—**Cleavage**, klē′vāj, *n.* The act of cleaving or splitting; the manner in which rocks or mineral substances regularly cleave or split according to their natural joints, or regular structure; in animals, early divisions of fertilized egg-cell.—**Cleaver**, klē′vėr, *n.* One who or that which cleaves; a butcher's instrument for cutting carcasses into joints or pieces.

Cleek, klēk, *n.* An iron club with a narrow face and a long shaft used as a golf club.

Clef, klef, *n.* [Fr. *clef*, L. *clavis*, a key.] A character in music, placed at the beginning of a staff, to determine the degree of elevation to be given to the notes belonging to it as a whole.

Cleft, kleft, pret. & pp. of *cleave*, to divide. —*n.* A space or opening made by splitting; a crack; a crevice.—**Cleft-footed**, *a.* Having cleft or cloven feet.—**Cleft-palate**, *n.* A malformation in which more or less of the palate is wanting, so as to leave a longitudinal gap in the upper jaw, often an accompaniment of harelip.

Cleg, kleg, *n.* [Icel. *kleggi*, Dan. *klæg*, a cleg.] A blood-sucking fly of a gray color, troublesome to horses, cattle, and even man; a horse-fly or breeze.

Cleistogamic, Cleistogamous, klīs-to-gam′ik, klīs-tog′a-mus, *a.* [Gr. *kleiō*, to close or shut up, and *gamos*, marriage.] *Bot.* having minute, bud-like, self-fertilizing flowers as well as other flowers conspicuously coloured.

Cleithral, klīth′ral, *a.* [Gr. *kleiō*, to shut in.] Having a roof that forms a complete covering: said of ancient Greek temples.

Clematis, klem′a-tis, *n.* [Gr. *klēmatis*.] The generic name of woody climbing plants, the only British species of which, the common traveller's-joy, runs over hedges, walls, &c., in many parts of England, having clusters of white blossoms.

Clemency, klem′en-si, *n.* [L. *clementia*, from *clemens, clementis*, merciful.] Mildness of temper as shown by a superior to an inferior; disposition to spare or forgive; mercy; leniency; softness or mildness of the elements. — **Clement**, klem′ent, *a.* Mild in temper and disposition; gentle; lenient; merciful; kind; tender; compassionate. — **Clemently**, klem′ent-li, *adv.* With mildness of temperature; mercifully.

Clench, klench, *v.t.* [Shortened form=Sc. *clink*, Dan. *klinke*, Sw. *klinka*, to clinch, to rivet; akin *clink*.] To secure or fasten, as a nail, by beating down the point when it is driven through anything; to rivet; to establish, settle, or confirm (a denial, argument, &c.); to bring together and set firmly; to double up tightly (the teeth or the hands); to grasp firmly.—*n.* A catch; a grip; a persistent clutch; a clinch.—**Clencher**, klen′sher, *n.* That which clenches; a retort or reply so decisive as to close a controversy; a clincher.

Clepe,‡ klēp, *v.t.*—pp. *yclept*. [A.Sax. *clipian, cleopian*.] To call or name. (*Shak.*)

Clepsydra, klep′si-dra, *n.* [Gr. *klepsydra* —*kleptō*, to steal, to hide, and *hydōr*, water.] A name common to devices of various kinds for measuring time by the discharge of water; a water-clock.

Cleptomania, klep-tō-mā′ni-a, *n.* KLEPTOMANIA.

Clere-story, klēr′stō-ri, *n.* Under CLEAR.

Clergy, klėr′ji, *n.* [O.Fr. *clergie*, from L. *clericus*, Gr. *klērikos*, clerical, from *klēros*, a lot, an allotment, the clergy. Akin *clerical, clerk*.] The body of men set apart and consecrated, by due ordination, to the service of God in the Christian church; the body of ecclesiastics, in distinction from the laity; *law*, benefit of clergy. — *Benefit of clergy, law*, the exemption of clergymen from criminal process before a secular judge; in cases of felony, an immunity latterly extended to any person who could read, though laymen could only claim it once: abolished in 1827. — **Clergyable**, klėr′ji-a-bl, *a.* Entitled to or admitting the benefit of clergy (*clergyable* offence). — **Clergyman**, klėr′ji-man, *n.* A man in holy orders; the minister of a Christian church.

Clerical, kler′ik-al, *a.* [L. *clericus*, Gr. *klērikos*. CLERGY, CLERK.] Relating or pertaining to the clergy; relating to a writer or copyist.—*Clerical error*, an error in the text of a document made by carelessness or inadvertence on the part of the writer or transcriber. — **Cleric**, kler′ik, *n.* A clergyman or scholar. — **Clericalism**, kler′ik-al-izm, *n.* Clerical power or influence; undue influence of the clergy; sacerdotalism.—**Clericity**,† kle-ris′i-ti, *n.* The state of being a clergyman. — **Clerisy**,† kler′i-si, *n.* A body of clerks or learned men; the literati; the clergy, as opposed to the laity.

Clerk, klėrk, *n.* [A.Sax. *clerc*, a priest; O.Fr. *clerc*; from L. *clericus*, Gr. *klērikos*. CLERGY.] A clergyman or ecclesiastic; a man in holy orders, especially in the Church of England; formerly also any man of education; the layman who leads in reading the responses in the service of the Anglican Church; one who is employed in keeping records or accounts; an officer attached to courts, municipal and other corporations, associations, &c., whose duty generally is to keep records of proceedings, and transact business under direction of the court, body, &c., by whom he is employed; in America, an assistant in a shop; a shopman.—*St. Nicholas' clerk*, a thief. (*Shak.*)—**Clerkess**, klėrk′es, *n.* A female clerk.—**Clerkly**, klėrk′li, *a.* Pertaining to a clerk or to penmanship; scholarly.—*adv.*† In a scholarly manner. (*Shak.*)—**Clerkship**, klėrk′ship, *n.* The office or business of a clerk or writer.

Clever, klev′ėr, *a.* [Connected with O.E. *cliver*, a claw, and with *cleave*, to adhere.] Performing or acting with skill or address; possessing ability of any kind, especially such as involves quickness of intellect or mechanical dexterity; indicative of or exhibiting cleverness; dexterous; adroit; able. —**Cleverish**, klev′ėr-ish, *a.* Tolerably clever.—**Cleverly**, klev′ėr-li, *adv.* In a clever manner; dexterously; skilfully; ably. —**Cleverness**, klev′ėr-nes, *n.* The quality of being clever; dexterity; adroitness; skill; ingenuity; smartness.

Clew, *n.* or *v.t.* CLUE.

Cliché, klē-shā, *n.* [Fr., from *clicher*, to stereotype, from older *cliquer*, to fasten, make firm, from root of *clinch, clench* (omitting the nasal).] Hackneyed jest or stereotyped phrase. A stereotype plate, especially one derived from an engraving.

Click, klik, *v.i.* [An imitative word expressing a slighter sound than *clack*; comp. *clack, cluck, clink, clank*; D. *klikken*, Fr. *cliquer*, to click.] To make a small sharp sound, or a succession of small sharp sounds, as by a gentle striking; to tick.—*v.t.* To move with a clicking sound.—*n.* A small sharp sound; the cluck of the natives of South Africa; the piece that enters the teeth of a ratchet-wheel; a detent or ratchet; the latch of a door.

Client, klī′ent, *n.* [L. *cliens, clientis*, a client, from O.L. *cluo*, to hear.] An ancient Roman citizen who put himself under the protection of a man of distinction and influence (his *patron*); one whose interests are represented by any professional man: especially one who applies to a lawyer, or commits his cause to his management.—**Cliency**, klī′en-si, *n.* The state or condition of a client.—**Clientage**, klī′en-tāj, *n.* The state or condition of being a client; a body of clients.—**Cliental**, klī′en-tal, *a.* Pertaining to a client or clients.—**Clientelary**, klī-en′tel-a-ri, *a.* Pertaining to clients.—**Clientele, Clientelage**, klī′-en-tēl, klī-en′tel-āj, *n.* [L. *clientela*.] A body of clients or dependents; one's clients collectively.—**Clientship**, klī′ent-ship, *n.* The condition of being a client.

Cliff, klif, *n.* [A.Sax. *clif*, a rock, a cliff = D. *klif*, Icel. *klif*, a cliff; comp. also Dan.

klippe, Sw. *klippa*, G. *klippe*, a crag.] A precipice; the steep and rugged face of a rocky mass; a steep rock; a headland.—**Cliffy**, klif'i, *a.* Having cliffs; precipitous; craggy.

Climacteric, klī-mak'tėr-ik, *n.* [Gr. *klimaktēr*, the step of a ladder, from *klimax*, a ladder or scale. CLIMAX.] A critical period in human life, or a period in which some great change is supposed to take place in the human constitution; the *grand* or *great climacteric* being the 63d year.—*a.* Pertaining to a climacteric.

Climate, klī'māt, *n.* [L. *clima*, Gr. *klima*, *klimatos*, a slope, a zone of the earth, a clime, from *klinō*, to bend, referring to the inclination of the earth from the equator to the pole.] The condition of a tract or region in relation to the various phenomena of the atmosphere, as temperature, wind, moisture, miasmata, &c., especially as they affect the life of animals or man.—**Climatic, Climatical, Climatal**, klī-mat'ik, klī-mat'ik-al, klī'mat-al, *a.* Pertaining to a climate or climates; limited by a climate.—**Climatize**, klī'mat-īz, *v.t.*—*climatized, climatizing.* To accustom to a new climate, as a plant; to acclimatize.—*v.i.* To become accustomed to a new climate.—**Climatography**, klī-ma-tog'ra-fi, *n.* A description of climates.—**Climatographical**, klī'mat-ō-graf''ik-al, *a.* Belonging to climatography or the study of the variations of climate.—**Climatology**, klī-ma-tol'o-ji, *n.* The science of climates; an investigation of the causes on which the climate of a place depends.—**Climatological**, klī'-mat-ō-loj''ik-al, *a.* Pertaining to climatology.—**Clime**, klīm, *n.* A tract or region of the earth. (Poetical.)

Climax, klī'maks, *n.* [L., from Gr. *klimax*, a ladder, from *klinō*, to slope. CLIMATE, CLIMACTERIC.] A figure of speech or rhetorical device in which the language rises step by step in dignity, importance, and force; the highest point of anything; the culmination; acme.

Climb, klīm, *v.i.*—(*clomb* for pret. & pp. *climbed* is now only poetical). [A.Sax. *climban*, G. and D. *klimmen*; from same root as *cleave*, to adhere, *clip*, to embrace.] To mount or ascend anything steep with labour and difficulty; especially, to ascend by means of the hands and feet; of things, to rise with a slow motion; to ascend, as certain plants, by means of tendrils, &c.—*v.t.* To climb up.—**Climbable**, klīm'a-bl, *a.* Capable of being climbed.—**Climber**, klīm'ėr, *n.* One who climbs; a plant that rises by attaching itself to some support; one of an order of birds, including the parrots, woodpeckers, &c., so called from their climbing habits.—**Climbing**, klīm'-ing, *a.* Possessing the power or character of climbing; assisting to climb (a *climbing* plant).

Clime. Under CLIMATE.

Clinanthium, klī-nan'thi-um, *n.* [Gr. *klinē*, a bed, *anthos*, a flower.] *Bot.* a term for the receptacle of a composite plant.

Clinch, klinsh, *n.* A position in boxing in which the contestants hold each other around the body with one or both arms.

Clincher-built, Clinker-built, klinsh'ėr, klingk'ėr, *a.* *Naut.* built with the planks of the side so disposed that the lower edge of each overlies the upper edge of the next below it, like slates on a roof.

Cling, kling, *v.t.*—*clung, clinging.* [A.Sax. *clingan*, to adhere, to dry up or wither; Dan. *klynge*, to grow in clusters; *klynge*, a heap, a cluster.] To adhere closely; to stick; to hold fast, especially by winding round or embracing.—**Clinger**, kling'ėr, *n.* One who or that which clings.

Clinic, klin'ik, *n.* [Gr. *klinikos*, from *klinē*, a bed, from *klinō*, to recline.] A medical institution in which a group of physicians jointly examine and treat patients; also, the examination and treatment of patients in the presence of medical students.—**Clinical**, klin'i-kal, *adj.* Pertaining to the clinic; in medicine, the study of patients as opposed to study by laboratory experiment.—**Clinically**, klin'ik-al-li, *adv.*

Clinician, kli-nish'an, *n.* A qualified clinical physician; one who practices in a clinic; a clinical instructor.

Clink, klingk, *v.i.* [An imitative word, akin to *click* and *clank*; comp. D. *klinken*, to tinkle; Dan. *klinge*, to jingle; Icel. *klingja*, G. *klingen*, to ring, to chink.] To ring or jingle; to give out a small sharp sound or a succession of such sounds, as by striking small metallic bodies together; to rhyme.—*v.t.* To cause to produce a small sharp ringing sound.—*n.* A sharp sound made by the collision of sonorous bodies.—**Clinker**, klingk'ėr, *a.* A partially vitrified brick; a kind of hard brick used for paving; a mass of incombustible slag which forms in grates and furnaces.—**Clink-stone**, *n.* [From its sonorousness.] A felspathic rock of the trachytic group with a slaty structure, sometimes used as roofing slates.

Clinker-built, *a.* CLINCHER-BUILT.

Clinometer, klī-nom'et-ėr, *n.* [Gr. *klinō*, to lean, and *metron*, measure.] An instrument for measuring the dip of rock strata.—**Clinometric, Clinometrical**, klī-nō-met'rik, klī-nō-met'rik-al, *a.* Of or pertaining to a clinometer; ascertained or determined by a clinometer; pertaining to crystals which have oblique angles between the axes.—**Clinometry**, klī-nom'et-ri, *n.* The method or art of measuring the dip of rock strata.

Clio, klī'ō, *n.* The muse who was supposed to preside over history; the name of an asteroid; a genus of pteropodous molluscs.

Clip, klip, *v.t.*—*clipped, clipt; clipping.* [Icel. *klippa*, to clip, to cut the hair; Dan. *klippe*, Sw. *klippa*, to clip or shear.] To cut off or sever with shears or scissors; to trim or make shorter (the hair) with scissors; to diminish (coin) by paring the edge; to curtail; to cut short (words); to pronounce shortly and indistinctly.—*n.* The quantity of wool shorn at a single shearing of sheep; a season's shearing; a clasp or spring-holder for letters or papers.—**Clipper**, klip'ėr, *n.* A full-rigged ship of a type developed in America about 1840 characterized by a sharp bow, graceful lines, tall masts and a large sail area; a giant airship of the Pan-American Airways.—**Clipper-built**, *a.* Built after the type of a clipper.

Clipp-fish, klip'fish, *n.* [Dan. *klipfisk*.] Fish, chiefly cod, split open, salted, and dried.

Clique, klēk, *n.* [Fr. *clique*, probably a mere variant of *claque*, with a somewhat different sense. CLAQUE.] A party; a set; a coterie: used generally in a bad sense.—**Cliquish**, klēk'ish, *a.* Relating to a clique or party; disposed to form cliques; having a petty party spirit.—**Cliquishness**, klēk'ish-nes, *n.* The state or quality of being cliquish.—**Cliquism**, klēk'izm, *n.* The principles or spirit of a clique; cliquishness.

Clitellum, klī-tel'lum, *n.* [L. *clitellæ*, a pack-saddle.] In earthworms and leeches, a glandular thickening of skin secreting material for egg capsules.

Cloaca, klō-ā'ka, *n.* [L., a common sewer.] An underground conduit for drainage; a common sewer; the excrementory cavity in birds, reptiles, many fishes, and lower mammalia, formed by the extremity of the intestinal canal and the outlet of the urinary organs.—**Cloacal**, klō-ā'kal, *a.* Pertaining to a cloaca.

Cloak, klōk, *n.* [O. and Prov.Fr. *cloque*, L.L. *cloca*, *clocca*, a bell, a kind of horseman's cape of a bell-shape; same word as *clock*.] A loose outer garment worn over other clothes; *fig.* that which conceals; a disguise or pretext; an excuse.—*v.t.* To cover with a cloak; to hide; to conceal.—**Cloak-room**, *n.* A room attached to any place of general resort, as railway-station, opera-house, &c., where ladies' cloaks, &c., are deposited.

Clock, klok, *n.* [Originally a bell. A.Sax. *clucga*, Icel. *klukka*, Dan. *klokke*, Sw. *klocka*, D. *klok*, G. *glocke*, a bell or clock; Ir. and Gael. *clog*, a bell or clock. *Cloak* is the same word.] A machine for measuring time, indicating the hours, minutes, and often seconds by means of hands moving over a dial-plate, and generally marking the hours by the strokes of a hammer on a bell, the motion being kept up by weights or springs, and regulated by a pendulum or a balance-wheel. ∴ *O'clock*, in such phrases as, 'it is one *o'clock*', is contracted from *of the clock*.—**Clock-work**, *n.* The machinery of a clock; a complex mechanism of wheels producing regularity of movement.

Clock, klok, *n.* [Possibly originally applied to a bell-shaped ornament or flower.] A figure or figured work embroidered on the ankle of a stocking.

Clock, klok, *n.* [Origin unknown.] A general name for a beetle.

Clod, klod, *n.* [A slightly modified form of *clot*; comp. Dan. *klode*, a globe or ball, *klods*, a block or lump.] A lump or mass in general†; a lump of earth, or earth and turf; a lump of clay; a dull, gross, stupid fellow; a dolt.—**Cloddish**, klod'ish, *a.* Clownish; boorish; doltish; uncouth; ungainly.—**Cloddy**, klod'i, *a.* Consisting of clods; abounding with clods; earthy; gross in sentiments or thoughts.—**Clodhopper**, klod'hop-ėr, *n.* A clown; a dolt; a boor.—**Clodpoll**, klod'pōl, *n.* [*Poll* = head.] A stupid fellow; a dolt; a blockhead.

Cloff, klof, *n.* [Perhaps originally a portion *cleft*, or split off, from *cleave*.] A certain deduction or allowance formerly made on the net weight of some kinds of goods, that the weight might hold out in retailing.

Clog, klog, *n.* [Comp. Sc. *clag*, a clog, an impediment, *clag*, to clog, as with something viscous or sticky, from A.Sax. *clæg*, clay. CLAY.] An encumbrance that hinders motion, or renders it difficult, as a piece of wood fastened to an animal's leg; hinderance; encumbrance; impediment; a sort of shoe with a wooden sole; a wooden shoe; a sabot; a patten.—*v.t.*—*clogged, clogging.* To impede the movements of by a weight, or by something that sticks or adheres; to encumber, restrain, or hamper; to choke up (a tube, &c.); to obstruct so as to hinder passage through; to throw obstacles in the way of; to hinder; to burden; to trammel.—*v.i.* To become loaded or encumbered with extraneous matter.—**Cloggy**, klog'i, *a.* Clogging or having power to clog; adhesive; viscous.—**Clogginess**, klog'i-nes, *n.*—**Clog-almanac**, *n.* An ancient kind of almanac or calendar, made by cutting notches or characters on a *clog* or block of wood, horn, bone, or brass.—**Clog-dance**, *n.* A dance in which the feet, shod with clogs, are made to perform a noisy accompaniment to the music.

Cloister, klois'tėr, *n.* [O.Fr. *cloistre*, Fr. *cloître*; from L. *claustrum*, a bolt, inclosed place, from *claudo*, *clausum*, to shut. CLOSE.] An arched way or covered walk running round the walls of certain portions of monastic and collegiate buildings; a place of religious retirement; a monastery; a convent; any arcade or colonnade round an open court; a piazza.—*v.t.* To confine in a cloister or convent; to shut up in retirement from the world; to furnish with a cloister or cloisters.—**Cloisterer**, klois'tėr-ėr, *n.* One belonging to a cloister.—**Cloistral**, klois'tral, *a.* Of or pertaining to a cloister.—**Cloistress**,† klois'tres, *n.* A nun; a woman who has vowed religious retirement. (*Shak.*)

Cloke, klōk, *n.* and *v.* Same as *Cloak*.

Clonic, klon'ik, *a.* [From Gr. *klonos*, a shaking.] *Pathol.* convulsive, with alternate relaxation.—*Clonic spasm*, a spasm in which the muscles or muscular fibres rapidly contract and relax alternately, as in epilepsy: used in contradistinction to *tonic spasm*.

Close, klōz, *v.t.*—*closed, closing.* [Fr. *clos*, pp. of *clore*, to shut up; from L. *claudo*, *clausum*, to shut; seen also in *conclude*, *exclude*, *include*, *seclude*, *cloister*, &c.] To bring together the parts of; to shut (a door, window, book, eyes, hands); make fast; to end, finish, conclude, complete; to fill or stop up; to consolidate: often followed by *up*; to encompass or inclose; to shut in.—*v.i.* To come together; to unite; to coalesce; to end, terminate, or come to a period; to engage in close encounter; to grapple; to accede or consent to (to *close with* terms); to come to an agreement (to *close with* a person).—*n.* Conclusion; termination; end; pause; cessation; a grapple, as in wrestling.—**Closer**, klō'zėr, *n.* One who or that which closes.—**Closure**, klō'zūr, *n.* The act of closing; an end or conclusion; the act of bringing a parliamentary debate to an end, by special vote or otherwise, when a question or measure has been fairly discussed.

Close, klōs, *a.* [Fr. *clos*, L. *clausus*, shut. CLOSE, *v.t.*] Shut fast; made fast so as to leave no opening; strictly confined; strictly watched (a *close* prisoner); retired; secluded; hidden; private; secret; having the habit or disposition to keep secrets; secretive; reticent; confined within narrow limits; narrow; without motion or ventilation; difficult to breathe; oppressive: of the air or weather; in direct contact or nearly so; adjoining; with little or no intervening distance in place or time; with little difference, as between antagonists or rival parties; almost evenly balanced (*close* contest); having the parts near each other; compact; dense; firmly attached; intimate; trusty; confidential (*close* friends); firmly fixed on a given object (*close* attention); keen and steady; not deviating from a model or original (a *close* translation); niggardly; stingy; penurious.—*n.* [Fr. *clos*, an inclosed place.] An inclosed place; any place surrounded by a fence; specifically, the precinct of a cathedral or abbey; a narrow passage or entry leading off a street.—*adv.* Tightly, so as to leave no opening; in strict confinement; in contact, or very near in space or time.—**Closely**, klōs'li, *adv.* In a close manner; so as to be close; compactly; nearly; intimately; intently; rigidly; narrowly; strictly; with strict adherence to an original.—**Closeness**, klōs'nes, *n.* The state or quality of being close, in the various senses of the word.—**Close-fisted**, *a.* Miserly; niggardly; penurious. — **Close-hauled**, *a.* *Naut.* sailing as nearly against the wind as possible. — **Close-stool**, *n.* A chamber utensil; a night-stool.

Closet, kloz'et, *n.* [O.Fr. *closet*, dim. of *clos*, an inclosure. CLOSE, *n.*] A small room or apartment for retirement; any room for privacy; a small side-room or recess for storing utensils, furniture, provisions, &c.—*v.t.* To put in or admit into a closet, as for concealment or for private consultation: usually in pp. *closeted*.

Closure, *n.* Under CLOSE, *v.t.*

Clot, klot, *n.* [Older form of *clod*, and formerly used in same sense: A.Sax. *clot*, a mass; D. *kloot*, a ball or globe; Sw. *klot*, a sphere; *klots*, a block; G. *kloss*, a clod, a lump, *klotz*, a block; akin *cloud*.] A coagulated mass of soft or fluid matter, as of blood, cream, &c.—*v.i.*—*clotted, clotting*. To coagulate, as soft or fluid matter, into a thick, inspissated mass.—*v.t.* To cause to coagulate; to make or form into clots.—**Clotty**, klot'i, *a.* Full of clots; resembling a clot; coagulated.

Cloth, kloth, *n.* [A.Sax. *cláth* = D. *cleed*, Icel. *klæthi*, Dan. and Sw. *klæde*, G. *kleid*, cloth.] A fabric of wool or hair, or of cotton, flax, hemp, or other vegetable filaments, formed by weaving; frequently, a fabric of wool in contradistinction to that made of other material; a piece of linen for covering a table at meals; a table-cloth; a professional dress, specifically that of a clergyman; hence, with the definite article or other defining word, the office of a clergyman; the members of the clerical profession.—**Clothe**, klōᴛʜ, *v.t.*—*clothed* or *clad*; *clothing*. To put garments on; to dress; to furnish or supply with clothes or raiment; *fig.* to cover or spread over with anything; to invest; to put on or over.—**Clothes**, klōᴛʜz, *n. pl.* [A plural of *cloth*, though it cannot now be said to have a singular.] Garments for the human body; dress; vestments; vesture; the covering of a bed; bed-clothes. — **Clothes-horse**, *n.* A frame to hang clothes on.—**Clothes-moth**, *n.* A name for several moths whose larvæ are destructive to woollen fabrics, furs, &c.—**Cloth-hall**, *n.* A hall at the great woollen-cloth marts, where producers and buyers meet periodically.—**Clothier**, klōᴛʜ'i-ėr, *n.* A seller of cloth or of clothes.—**Clothing**, klōᴛʜ'ing, *n.* Garments in general; clothes.—**Cloth-worker**, *n.* A maker of cloth. — **Cloth-yard**, *n.* A measure for cloth which differed somewhat in length from the modern yard.—*Cloth-yard shaft*, an arrow a cloth-yard long.

Clotpoll, klot'pōl, *n.* Same as *Clodpoll*.

Cloud, kloud, *n.* [Originally a mass or rounded mass in general; A.Sax. *clúd*, a rock, a hillock, the root being that seen in *clod*; so in O.D. *klot*, a clod, and *klote*, a cloud.] A collection of visible vapour or watery particles suspended in the atmosphere at some altitude, the principal forms being designated as the *cirrus*, the *cumulus*, and the *stratus* (see these words); something resembling a cloud, as a body of smoke or flying dust; a dark area of colour in a lighter material; that which obscures, darkens, sullies, threatens, or the like; a multitude; a collection; a mass.—*v.t.* To overspread with a cloud or clouds; hence, to obscure; to darken; to render gloomy or sullen; to darken in spots; to variegate with colours.—*v.i.* To grow cloudy; to become obscured with clouds.—**Cloudberry**, kloud'be-ri, *n.* A plant of the bramble family, with large and white flowers and orange-red berries of an agreeable taste.—**Cloudy**, kloud'i, *a.* Overcast with clouds; obscured with clouds, as the sky; consisting of a cloud or clouds; obscure; dark; not easily understood; having the appearance of gloom; indicating gloom, anxiety, sullenness, or ill-nature; not open or cheerful; marked with spots or areas of dark or various hues.—**Cloudily**, kloud'i-li, *adv.* In a cloudy manner; with clouds; darkly; obscurely.—**Cloudiness**, kloud'i-nes, *n.* The state of being cloudy.—**Cloudless**, kloud'les, *a.* Being without a cloud; unclouded; clear; bright.—**Cloudlessly**, kloud'les-li, *adv.* In a cloudless manner; without clouds.—**Cloudlet**, kloud'let, *n.* A small cloud.—**Cloud-built**, *a.* Built up of clouds; fanciful; imaginary; chimerical.—**Cloud-burst**, *n.* A tremendous downpour of rain over a limited area.—**Cloud-capped**, **Cloud-capt**, *a.* Capped with clouds; touching the clouds; lofty. (*Shak.*)—**Cloud-kissing**, *a.* Touching the clouds; lofty. (*Shak.*)

Clough, kluf, *n.* [A.Sax. *cleófa*, a cleft, ravine, from *cleófan*, to cleave; D. *kloof*, a ravine.] A cleft, ravine, or valley in a hillside; a kind of sluice for letting off water gently, employed in flooding fields.

Clout, klout, *n.* [A.Sax. *clút*, a clout, a patch; Dan. *klud*, Sw. *klut*, a clout: also W. *clwt*, Ir. and Gael. *clud*, a clout.] A patch or rag; a piece of cloth or the like used to mend something; any piece of cloth, especially a worthless piece; *archery*, the mark fixed in the center of a target; a hard blow, struck usually with the fist, in baseball, a long hard-hit ball; a dull or stupid person.

Clout, **Clout-nail**, klout, klout'nal, *n.* [Fr. *clouet*, a dim. of *clou*, a nail.] A short, large-headed nail worn in the soles of shoes; also, a nail for securing small patches of iron, as on axle-trees, &c.—*v.t.* To stud or fasten with nails.

Clove, klōv, pret. of *cleave*.

Clove, klōv, *n.* [Sp. *clavo*, a clove, a nail, from L. *clavus*, a nail, from its resemblance to a nail in shape.] The dried flower-bud of an evergreen tree of the myrtle tribe, a native of the Molucca Islands, such buds forming a very pungent aromatic spice: the tree yielding cloves.—**Clove-bark**, *n.* An aromatic pungent bark, the product of a kind of cinnamon, used in medicine.—**Clove-gillyflower**, **Clove-pink**, *n.* Names popularly given to the clove-scented, double-flowered, whole-coloured varieties of the pink family of flowers.

Clove, klōv, *n.* [A.Sax. *clufe*, a bulb.] One of the small bulbs formed in the axils of the scales of a mother bulb, as in garlic; a denomination of weight; one of the divisions of a wey of cheese, &c., being about 8 lbs.

Cloven, klōv'n, pp. of *cleave*. Divided; parted. — **Cloven-footed**, **Cloven-hoofed**, *a.* Having the hoof divided into two parts, as the ox; bisulcate.

Clover, klō'vėr, *n.* [A.Sax. *clæfre* = D. *klaver*, L.G. *klever*, Dan. *klöver*, Sw. *klöfver*, perhaps from root of *cleave*, from its trifid leaves.] A herbaceous leguminous plant of numerous species bearing three-lobed leaves and roundish heads or oblong spikes of small flowers, several species being widely cultivated for fodder.—*To be* or *to live in clover*, to be in most enjoyable circumstances; to live luxuriously or in abundance.—**Clovered**, klō'vėrd, *a.* Covered with clover.—**Clover-grass**, *n.* Clover.

Clown, kloun, *n.* [Icel. *klunni*, a clumsy, boorish fellow; Fris. *klönne*, a bumpkin; allied to Sw. *klunn*, a block.] An awkward country-fellow; a peasant; a rustic; a man of coarse manners; a person without refinement; a boor; a lout; a churl; a jester, merryman, or buffoon, as in a theatre, circus, or other place of entertainment.—*v.i.* To act as a clown; to play the clown.—**Clownish**, kloun'ish, *a.* Of or pertaining to clowns or rustics; rude; coarse; awkward; ungainly; abounding in clowns.—**Clownishly**, kloun'ish-li, *adv.* In a clownish manner.—**Clownishness**, kloun'ish-nes, *n.* Boorishness; rusticity.

Cloy, kloi, *v.t.* [O.Fr. *cloyer*, to stop up, equivalent to *clouer*, *cloer*, originally to fasten with a nail, O.Fr. *clo*, Fr. *clou*, from L. *clavus*, a nail.] To gratify to excess so as to cause loathing; to surfeit, satiate, or glut.—**Cloyless**, kloi'les, *a.* Not causing satiety. (*Shak.*)

Club, klub, *n.* [A Scandinavian word: Icel. *klubba*, *klumba*, Sw. *klubba*, Dan. *klub*, a club.] A stick or piece of wood, with one end thicker and heavier than the other, suitable for being wielded with the hand; a thick heavy stick used as a weapon; a cudgel; a staff with a crooked and heavy head for driving the ball in the game of golf, &c.; a card of the suit that is marked with trefoils; *pl.* the suit so marked; a select number of persons in the habit of meeting for the promotion of some common object, as social intercourse, literature, science, politics; a club-house. — *v.i.* *clubbed, clubbing*. To form a club or combination for a common purpose; to combine to raise a sum of money: often with *for* before the object; to combine generally.—*v.t.* To beat with a club; to convert into a club; to use as a club by brandishing with the small end; to add together, each contributing a certain sum.—**Clubbable**, klub'a-bl, *a.* Having the qualities that make a man fit to be a member of a club; social. — **Clubbist**, klub'ist, *n.* One who belongs to a party, club, or association; one fond of clubs.—**Club-foot**, *n.* A short, distorted foot, generally of congenital origin. — **Club-footed**, *a.* Having a club-foot or club-feet.—**Club-house**, *n.* A house occupied by a club or in which a club assembles.—**Club-law**, *n.* Government by clubs or violence; anarchy. — **Club-moss**, *n.* A moss-like plant; a lycopod.

Cluck, kluk, *v.i.* [A.Sax. *cloccian* = D. *klokken*, Dan. *klukke*, an imitative word like *clack*, *click*, &c.] To utter the call or cry of a brooding hen.—*n.* A sound uttered by a hen; a similar sound, or click, characteristic of the languages of South Africa, especially the Kaffir and Hottentot.

Clue, **Clew**, klū, *n.* [A.Sax. *cliwe*, *cliwen*, a ball of thread = D. *kluwen*, a clue; akin to L. *globus*, *glomus*, a mass.] A ball of thread; the thread that forms a ball; *fig.* anything that guides or directs one in an intricate case (there being sundry stories of persons being guided in intricate mazes or labyrinths by a clue of thread); *naut.* the lower corner of a square sail.—**Clue-line**, *n.* *Naut.* a rope for hauling up the lower corner of a square sail.

Clump, klump, *n.* [Same as D. *klomp*, Dan. Sw. and G. *klump*, a lump, a clod: from same root as *clumsy*, *club*, &c.] A shapeless mass; a lump; a cluster of trees or shrubs. —**Clumpy**, klump'i, *a.* Consisting of clumps; shapeless.

Clumsy, klum'zi, *a.* [From old *clumsen*, *clomsen*, to benumb or stupefy; allied to Sw. *klummsen*, benumbed, Icel. *klumsa*, lockjaw, D. *kleumen*, to be benumbed; the root being same as in *clump*, &c.] Awkward; ungainly; without readiness, dexterity, or grace; ill-made; badly constructed; awkwardly done; unskilfully performed.—**Clumsily**, klum'zi-li, *adv.* In a clumsy manner.—**Clumsiness**, klum'zi-nes, *n.* The quality of being clumsy.

Clung, klung, pret. & pp. of *cling*.

Cluniac, klö'ni-ak, *n.* One of a reformed order of Benedictine monks so called from *Cluny* in France.

Cluster, klus'tėr, *n.* [A.Sax. *cluster*; same root as Sw. and Dan. *klase*, Icel. *klasi*, a cluster.] A number of things, as fruits, growing naturally together; a bunch; a number of individuals of any kind collected or gathered into a body; an assemblage; a group; a swarm; a crowd.—*v.i.* To grow or be assembled in clusters or groups.—*v.t.* To collect into a cluster or group; to produce in a cluster or clusters.—*Clustered column*, *arch.* a column or pier which appears to consist of several columns or shafts clustered together.

Clutch, kluch, *v.t.* [O.E. *clucche*, *cloche*, from *cloche*, a claw, a softened form of older *cloke*, a claw, Sc. *cluik*, *cluke*, a claw; allied to *claw*.] To seize, clasp, or grip with the hand; to close tightly; to clench.—*n.* A griping or pinching with the fingers; seizure; grasp; a paw, talon, or grasping merciless hand; hence such phrases as, to fall into a person's *clutches*; *mach.* a contrivance for connecting shafts with each other or with wheels, so as that they may be disengaged at pleasure.

Clutch, klutch, *n.* [A form of *cluck*, cry of a brooding hen.] The eggs laid and hatched by a bird at one time.

Clutter, klut'tėr, *n.* [A modification of *clatter*.] Confused noise; bustle; confusion; litter.—*v.t.* To put in a clutter; to crowd together in disorder.—*v.i.* To make a bustle or disturbance.

Clypeate, Clypeiform, klip'ē-āt, klip'ē-i-form, *a.* [L. *clypeus*, a shield.] Shaped like a round buckler; shield-shaped; scutate.

Clyster, klis'tėr, *n.* [Gr. *klystēr*, from *klyzō*, to wash or cleanse.] A liquid substance injected into the lower intestines to purge or cleanse them, or to relieve from costiveness; an injection.

Cnida, nī'da, *n.* pl. **Cnidæ**. [Gr. *knidē*, a nettle.] One of the cells by which the jellyfishes cause a stinging sensation.

Coach, kōch, *n.* [Fr. *coche*, from Hung. *kocsi* (pron. ko-chi), from *Kocs*, in Hungary.] A vehicle drawn by horses and intended to carry passengers; more particularly a four-wheeled, closed vehicle of considerable size; a two-door automobile; a railroad passenger car; a private tutor, often one employed to prepare pupils for examination; an instructor in athletics, especially an adviser and trainer for contests.—*v.t.* To carry in a coach; to prepare for an examination by private instruction; to train for an athletic contest; to direct the actions of a player (*Baseball*).—**Coach-box**, *n.* The seat on which the driver of a coach sits.—**Coach-dog**, *n.* A dog of Dalmatian breed, generally white spotted with black, kept to accompany carriages.—**Coachman**, kōch'man, *n.* The person who drives a coach.—**Coachmanship**, kōch'man-ship, *n.* Skill in coaching.

Coact, kō-akt', *v.t.* [Prefix *co*, and *act*.] To act together.—**Coactive**, kō-ak'tiv, *a.* Acting in concurrence; also forcing or compelling; compulsory (in this sense from L. *cogo*, *coactum*, to compel).—**Coactively**, kō-ak'tiv-li, *adv.* In a coactive manner.

Coadjutor, kō-ad-jū'tėr, *n.* [L. *coadjutor*—prefix *co*, *ad*, to, and *juvo*, *jutum*, to help.] One who aids another; an assistant; a fellow-helper; an associate; a fellow-worker; a colleague; the assistant of a bishop or other prelate.—**Coadjutorship**, kō-ad-jūt'ėr-ship, *n.* The state of being a coadjutor; assistance.—**Coadjutress, Coadjutrix**, kō-ad-jū'tres, kō-ad-jū'triks, *n.* A female assistant or fellow-helper.

Coadunate, kō-ad'ū-nāt, *a.* [L. *coadunatus*—prefix *co*, *ad*, to, *unus*, one.] United or joined together: especially used in *bot.* and applied to leaves united at the base.

Coagulate, kō-ag'ū-lāt, *v.t.*—*coagulated*, *coagulating*. [L. *coagulo*, *coagulatum*, from *coagulum*, rennet—*con*, together, and *ago*, to bring, drive, &c.] To change from a fluid into a curd-like or inspissated solid mass; to curdle, congeal, or clot.—*v.i.* To curdle or congeal.—**Coagulability**, kō-ag'ū-la-bil"i-ti, *n.* The capacity of being coagulated.—**Coagulable**, kō-ag'ū-la-bl, *a.* Capable of becoming coagulated.—**Coagulant**, kō-ag'ū-lant, *n.* That which produces coagulation.—**Coagulation**, kō-ag'ū-lā"shon, *n.* The act of coagulating or clotting; the state of being coagulated; the substance formed by coagulation.—**Coagulative, Coagulatory**, kō-ag'ū-lā-tiv, kō-ag'ū-la-to-ri, *a.* Causing coagulation.—**Coagulator**, kō-ag'ū-lā-tėr, *n.* That which causes coagulation.—**Coagulum**, kō-ag'ū-lum, *n.* A coagulated mass, as curd, &c.; *med.* a blood-clot.

Coaita, kō-ī'ta, *n.* [Native name.] A South American monkey, about 18 inches in length.

Coal, kōl, *n.* [A.Sax. *col* = D. *kool*, Dan. *kul*, Icel. and Sw. *kol*, G. *kohle*.] A piece of wood or other combustible substance burning or charred; charcoal; a cinder; now, usually, a solid black substance found in the earth, largely employed as fuel, and formed from vast masses of vegetable matter deposited through the luxurious growth of plants in former epochs of the earth's history.—*v.t.* To supply with coal, as a steam-vessel or locomotive engine.—*v.i.* To take in coals.—*To haul*, (*take*, &c.) *over the coals*, to call to a strict or severe account; to reprimand.—*To carry coals to Newcastle*, to take things where there are already plenty; to perform unnecessary labour.—**coalite**, kōl'īt, *n.* [From *coal*.] A substance claimed to be superior to coal in heat production.—**Coaly**, kō'li, *a.* Pertaining to, resembling, or containing coal.—**Coal-bed**, *n.* A formation in which there are one or more strata of coals; the stratum or strata of coal themselves.—**Coal-black**, *a.* Black as a coal; very black.—**Coal-brass**, *n.* The iron pyrites found in the coal-measures, and employed in the manufacture of copperas, and in alkali works for the sulphur it contains.—**Coal-field**, *n.* An extensive deposit or bed of coal; a district where coal abounds.—**Coal-fish**, *n.* A species of cod, growing to the length of 2 feet or more, found on the northern coasts of Britain, and so named from the colour of its back.—**Coal-gas**, *n.* A variety of carburetted hydrogen which produces the ordinary gas-light. GAS.—**Coal-heaver**, *n.* One who is employed in carrying coal, and especially in discharging it from coal-ships.—**Coal-master**, *n.* The owner or lessee of a coal-field who works it and disposes of its produce.—**Coal-measures**, *n. pl.* *Geol.* the upper division of the carboniferous system, consisting of alternate layers of sandstone with thinly laminated beds of clay, between which the coal-seams occur.—**Coal-meter**, *n.* One appointed to superintend the measuring of coals.—**Coal-mine**, *n.* A mine or pit in which coal is dug.—**Coal-pit**, *n.* A pit where coal is dug.—**Coal-plant**, *n.* Any of the plants which are found fossil in the coal-measures.—**Coal-tar**, *n.* A thick, black, viscid, opaque liquid which condenses in the pipes when gas is distilled from coal.—**Coal-tit**, *n.* One of the titmice: so called from its glossy black head and neck.—**Coal-trimmer**, *n.* One who is employed to stow and trim the fuel for the fires of the boilers of marine steam-engines.—**Coal-whipper**, *n.* One who raises coal from the hold of a ship.

Coalesce, kō-a-les', *v.t.*—*coalesced*, *coalescing*. [L. *coalesco*—prefix *co*, and *alesco*, to grow up, from *alo*, to nourish.] To unite by growth into one body; to grow together physically; to combine or be collected into one body or mass; to join or unite into one body, party, society, or the like.—**Coalescence**, kō-a-les'ens, *n.* The act of coalescing or uniting; the state of being united or combined.—**Coalescent**, kō-a-les'ent, *a.* Growing together; uniting.—**Coalition**, kō-a-li'shon, *n.* Union in a body or mass; voluntary union of individual persons, parties, or states for a common object or cause.—**Coalitionist**, kō-a-li'shon-ist, *n.* One who favours or joins a coalition.

Coaming, kōm'ing, *n.* [For *combing*, from *comb*.] *Naut.* a raised border or edge round the hatches to keep out water.

Coarse, kōrs, *a.* [The same word as *course*, a thing *of course*, or *in course*, being what is natural, ordinary, common.] Of ordinary or inferior quality; wanting in fineness of texture or structure, or in elegance of form; rude; rough; unrefined; gross; indelicate (*coarse* language).—**Coarsely**, kōrs'li, *adv.* In a coarse manner; rudely; uncivilly; without art or polish; grossly.—**Coarsen**,† kōr'sn, *v.t.* To render coarse or wanting in refinement; to make vulgar.—**Coarseness**, kōrs'nes, *n.* The state or quality of being coarse.—**Coarse-grained**, *a.* Consisting of large particles or constituent elements; wanting in refinement or delicacy; vulgar.

Coast, kōst, *n.* [O.Fr. *coste*, Fr. *côte*, rib, hill, shore, coast, from L. *costa*, a rib, side.] The exterior line, limit, or border of a country (O.T.); the edge or margin of the land next to the sea; the sea-shore.—*The coast is clear*, a phrase equivalent to danger is over; the enemies have gone.—*v.i.* To sail near a coast; to sail by or near the shore, or in sight of land; to sail or trade from port to port in the same country.—*v.t.* To sail by or near to.—**Coaster**, kōs'tėr, *n.* A vessel that is employed in sailing along a coast, or in trading from port to port in the same country.—**Coastwards**, kōst'wėrdz, *adv.* Toward the coast.—**Coastways, Coastwise**, kōst'wāz, kōst'wīz, *adv.* By way of or along the coast.—**Coast-guard**, *n.* That branch of the U. S. naval service detailed to ice patrol, life-saving, and enforcement of customs, navigation and immigration laws.

Coat, kōt, *n.* [O.Fr. *cote*, Fr. *cotte*, a coat, from L.L. *cota*, a coat, from O.G. *cotte*, a coarse mantle, G. *kutte*, a cowl: allied to *cot*.] An upper garment, in modern times generally applied to the outer garment worn by men on the upper part of the body; an external covering; a layer of one substance covering another; a coating.—*Coat of arms*, a representation of the armorial insignia which used to be depicted on a coat worn by knights over their armour; an escutcheon or shield of arms.—*Coat of mail*, armour worn on the upper part of the body, and consisting of a net-work of iron or steel rings, or of small plates, usually of tempered iron, laid over each other like the scales of a fish, and fastened to a strong linen or leather jacket.—*v.t.* To cover with a coat; to spread over with a coating or layer of any substance.—**Coat-armour**, *n.* A coat of arms; armorial ensigns.—**Coat-card**, *n.* A card bearing a coated figure, as the king, queen, or knave: now corrupted into *Court-card*.—**Coatee**, kō-tē', *n.* A close-fitting coat with short tails.—**Coating**, kōt'ing, *n.* Any substance spread over for cover or protection; a thin external layer, as of paint or varnish; cloth for coats.—**Coat-link**, *n.* A pair of buttons held together by a link, or a loop and button used for fastening a coat over the breast.

Coati, kō'a-ti, *n.* [A native name.] A plantigrade carnivorous mammal, belonging to the bear family, but recalling in appearance the civets.

Coax, kōks, *v.t.* [From O.E. *cokes*, a fool; to *coax* one being thus to make a *cokes*, or fool, of him.] To soothe, appease, or persuade by flattery and fondling; to wheedle; to cajole.—**Coaxer**, kōk'sėr, *n.* One who coaxes; a wheedler.—**Coaxingly**, kōk'-sing-li, *adv.* In a coaxing manner.

Co-axial, kō-ak'si-al, *a.* Having a common axis.

Cob, kob, *n.* [Probably, in some of the meanings, from W. *cob*, a top, a tuft.] A roundish lump of anything; the receptacle on which the grains of maize grow in rows; a short-legged stout horse or pony; clay mixed with straw.—**Cob-coal**, *n.* A large round piece of coal.—**Cob-loaf**, *n.* A loaf that is irregular, uneven, or crusty.—**Cob-stone**, *n.* COBBLE.

Cobalt, kō'balt, *n.* [G. *kobalt*, *kobolt*, the same word as *kobold*, a goblin, the demon of the mines.] A mineral of a reddish-gray or grayish-white colour (specific gravity 8·5), very brittle, never found in a pure state, but usually as an oxide, or combined with arsenic or its acid, with sulphur, iron, &c. —**Cobaltic**, kō-bal'tik, *a.* Pertaining to cobalt, or consisting of it; resembling cobalt or containing it.—**Cobalt-blue**, *n.* A compound of alumina and oxide of cobalt, forming a beautiful pigment.—**Cobalt-green**, *n.* A permanent green pigment.

Cobble, kob'l, *n.* [From *cob*, a lump.] A roundish stone; a stone rounded by the attrition of water; a boulder; a cobstone.

Cobble, kob'l, *v.t.*—*cobbled*, *cobbling*. [O.Fr. *cobler*, to join or knit together, from L. *copulare*, to couple.] To make or mend coarsely (shoes); to botch; to make or do clumsily or unhandily.—*v.i.* To work as a cobbler; to do work badly.—**Cobbler**, kob'lėr, *n.* One who cobbles; a mender of boots and shoes; a clumsy workman; a cooling beverage, composed of wine, sugar, lemon, and finely pounded ice.

Co-belligerent, kō-bel-lij'ėr-ent, *a.* Carrying on war in conjunction with another power.—*n.* One that carries on war in connection with another.

Coble, **Cobble**, kob'l, *n.* [W. *ceubal*, a coble.] A flattish-bottomed boat, clincher-built, with a square stern.

Cobra, **Cobra-de-Capello**, kob'ra, kob'-ra-de-ka-pel'lō, *n.* [Pg., snake of the hood.] The hooded or spectacle snake, a reptile of the most venomous nature, found in different hot countries of the old continent, especially in India.

Cobres, kob'rez, *n.* [Sp.] A superior kind of indigo, prepared in South America.

Coburg, **Cobourg**, kō'bėrg, *n.* [From *Coburg* in Germany.] A thin fabric of worsted and cotton, or worsted and silk, twilled on one side.

Cobweb, kob'web, *n.* [O.E. also *copweb*, A.Sax. *coppe*, a spider, seen in *attor-coppe*, a spider.] The net-work spun by a spider to catch its prey; something to entangle the weak or unwary; something flimsy and worthless; old musty rubbish.—**Cobwebbed**, **Cobwebby**, kob'webd, kob'-web-i, *a.* Covered with cobwebs; *bot.* covered with a thick interwoven pubescence.

Coca, kō'ka, *n.* [Native name.] The dried leaf of a South American plant which is chewed by the inhabitants of countries on the Pacific side of South America, giving great power of enduring fatigue; the plant itself.

Cocaine, kō'ka-in, *n.* The active principle of coca, which has invigorating properties, and is also used as a local anæsthetic in minor surgical operations.

Cocciferous, kok-sif'ėr-us, *a.* [L. *coccum*, a berry, and *fero*, to bear.] Bearing or producing berries.

Coccolite, kok'kō-līt, *n.* [Gr. *kokkos*, a berry, and *lithos*, a stone.] A variety of augite or pyroxene.

Coccosteous, kok-os'tē-us, *n.* [Gr. *kokkos*, berry, *osteon*, bone.] A fossil fish with berry-like tubercules on the bony plates covering its body.

Cocculus, kok'kū-lus, *n.* [Dim. of L. *coccus*, Gr. *kokkos*, a berry.] A genus of Eastern plants.—*Cocculus Indicus* (in'di-kus), the berry-like fruit of an East Indian climbing shrub, sometimes employed in medicine as a narcotic, and sometimes added to malt liquors to give bitterness and increase their stupefying qualities.

Coccus, kok'us, *n.* [Gr. *kokkos*, a berry.] In bacteria, a spheroidal type.

Coccyx, kok'siks, *n.* [Gr. *kokkyx*.] An assemblage of small bones attached to the lower extremity of the backbone; the rump.—**Coccygeal**, kok-sij'ē-al, *a.* Of or belonging to the coccyx.

Cochin-China, koch'in-chī-na, *n.* and *a.* A term applied to a large variety of the domestic fowl, which was imported from Cochin-China.

Cochineal, koch'i-nēl, *n.* [Fr. *cochenille*, from Sp. *cochinilla*, a wood-louse, cochineal, dim. of *cochina*, a sow.] A dye-stuff consisting of the dried bodies of a species of insect, a native of the warmer climates of America, found on the cochineal-fig tree.—**Cochineal-fig**, *n.* A tree-like cactaceous plant, a native of America, cultivated for the sake of the cochineal insect.

Cochlea, kok'lē-a, *n.* [L., a snail or snail's shell.] A bony structure in the internal ear, so called from resembling a snail-shell. —**Cochlean**, kok'lē-an, *a.* Pertaining to the cochlea.—**Cochleariform**, kok-lē-a'-ri-form, *a.* [L. *cochlear*, a spoon for eating snails.] Shaped like a spoon.—**Cochleary**, kok'lē-a-ri, *a.* Cochleate.—**Cochleate**, **Cochleated**, kok'lē-āt, kok'lē-āt-ed, *a.* Having a form like the spiral of a snail-shell; spiral. Also *Cochleous*, kok'lē-us.

Cock, kok, *n.* [A.Sax. *coc*, *cocc*; comp. O.Fr. *coc*, Fr. *coq*, a cock; probably like *cuckoo*, a word of onomatopoetic origin.] The male of birds, particularly of the gallinaceous, domestic or barn-door fowls: often used adjectively and occasionally to signify the male of certain animals other than birds (a *cock* lobster); a kind of faucet or turn-valve, for permitting or arresting the flow of fluids through a pipe; a prominent portion of the lock of a firearm, the hammer; the act of cocking or setting up, or the effect or form produced by such an act (a *cock* of the head, nose, &c.).—*Cock of the wood*, the capercailzie.—*v.t.* [Probably from the strutting of the animal.] To set erect (the ears); to turn up with an air of pertness; to set or draw back the cock in order to fire (to *cock* a gun).—*v.i.* To hold up the head; to look big, pert, or menacing.—**Cockerel**, kok'ėr-el, *n.* A young cock.—**Cock-a-hoop**, kok'a-hup, *a.* [Fr. *coq à huppe*, lit. cock with crest.] Strutting like a cock; triumphant.—**Cock-and-bull**, *a.* [From some old tale about a cock and a bull; comp. Fr. *coq-à-l'âne* (cock-and-ass), a cock-and-bull story.] A term applied to idle or silly fictions, stories having no foundation, canards. (Colloq.)—**Cock-crow**, **Cock-crowing**, *n.* The time at which cocks crow; early morning.—**Cock-eye**, *n.* A squinting eye.—**Cock-eyed**, *a.* Having a squinting eye.—**Cock-fight**, **Cock-fighting**, *n.* A fight between game-cocks; the practice of fighting game-cocks. —**Cock-horse**, *n.* A child's rocking-horse: now commonly used in the adverbial phrase, *a-cock-horse*, on horseback; in an elevated position; on the high horse.—**Cock-loft**, *n.* [Lit. a loft for cocks to roost in.] A small loft in the top of a house; a small garret immediately under the roof.—**Cock-pit**, *n.* A pit or area where game-cocks fight; an apartment under the lower gun-deck of a ship of war.—**Cockscomb**, koks'kōm, *n.* The caruncle or comb of a cock; an annual branching plant bearing loose spikes of flowers; a coxcomb.—**Cock's-foot**, **Cock's-foot Grass**, *n.* A perennial pasture grass of a coarse, harsh, wiry texture.

Cock, kok, *n.* [Dan. *kok*, a heap, a pile; Icel. *kökkr*, a lump.] A small conical pile of hay, so shaped for shedding rain.—*v.t.* To put into cocks or piles.

Cock, kok, *n.* [O.Fr. *coque*, a kind of boat; Sp. *coca*, It. *cocca*, from L. *concha*, a kind of shell, a vessel.] A small boat. (*Shak.*)

Cock, kok, *n.* [It. *cocca*, Fr. *coche*, a notch.] The notch of an arrow or cross-bow.

Cockade, ko-kād', *n.* [Fr. *cocarde*, O.Fr. *coquarde*, from *coq*, a cock, from its resemblance to the comb of the cock.] A ribbon or knot of ribbon worn in the hat; a rosette of leather worn on the hat by gentlemen's servants; the badge of the House of Hanover.—*White Cockade*, white rosette, the emblem of the French and English Jacobites.—**Cockaded**, ko-kā'ded, *a.* Wearing a cockade.

Cock-a-leekie, *n.* Scottish broth of cock boiled with leeks.

Cockatoo, kok-a-tö', *n.* [Malay *kakatûa*, from its cry.] A name common to numerous beautiful birds of the parrot kind, chiefly inhabiting Australia and the Indian islands, having crests composed of a tuft of elegant feathers, which they can raise or depress at pleasure.

Cockatrice, kok'a-tris, *n.* [O.Fr. *cocatrice*, L.L. *cocatrix*, a crocodile, a cockatrice, a corrupted form of L. *crocodilus*, crocodile. In time the first syllable was thought = *cock*.] A fabulous monster said to be hatched by a serpent from a cock's egg, and represented as possessing characters belonging to both animals; a basilisk.

Cockchafer, kok'chā-fėr, *n.* [*Cock* is probably for *clock*, Prov. E. and Sc. for a beetle.] A lamellicorn beetle, the larvæ or caterpillars of which feed on the roots of corn, &c., and the insects in their winged state do much injury to trees.

Cocker, kok'ėr, *v.t.* [Probably from W. *cocru*, to fondle, *cocr*, a coaxing.] To fondle; to indulge; to treat with tenderness; to pamper.

Cocker, kok'ėr, *n.* A dog of the spaniel kind, used for raising woodcocks (whence probably the name) and snipes from their haunts.

Cocket, kok'et, *n.* [Supposed to be a corruption of '*quo quietus*', two words which occurred in the Latin form of the document.] A document delivered by the custom-house officers to merchants as a warrant that their merchandise is entered.

Cockle, kok'l, *n.* [A.Sax. *coccel*, tares; comp. Gael. *cogal*, Fr. *coquiole*, cockle.] A plant that grows among corn, the corn-cockle.

Cockle, kok'l, *n.* [Dim. from Fr. *coque*, a cockle, a shell, from L. *concha*, Gr. *kongchē*, a mussel or cockle.] A heart-shaped mollusc with wrinkled shells, common on the sandy shores of Britain, and much used as food; a kind of stove, a stove in which the fuel-chamber is surrounded by an open space.—*v.t.* and *i.*—*cockled*, *cockling*. [Perhaps from *cockle*, the shell, marked with wrinkles.] To wrinkle or ridge; to give or assume a wrinkled or ridged surface (as a piece of paper).—**Cockled**, kok'ld, *a.* Having a shell. (*Shak.*)—**Cockle-hat**, *n.* A hat bearing a shell, the badge of a pilgrim.

Cockney, kok'ni, *n.* [Usually connected with the old term *Cockaigne*, land of abundance, perhaps from L. *coquo*, to cook.] A native or resident of London: used slightingly or by way of contempt.—*a.* Related to or like cockneys.—**Cockneydom**, kok'-ni-dum, *n.* The region or home of cockneys, a contemptuous or humorous name for London and its suburbs.—**Cockneyfy**, kok'ni-fi, *v.t.* To make like a cockney.—**Cockneyish**, kok'ni-ish, *a.* Relating to or like cockneys.—**Cockneyism**, kok'ni-izm, *n.* The condition, qualities, manner, or dialect of the cockneys; a peculiarity of the dialect of the Londoners.

Cockroach, kok'rōch, *n.* [Sp. *cucaracha*, a wood-louse, a cockroach.] An orthopterous insect, the so-called black-beetle, very troublesome in houses, where they often multiply to a great extent, infesting kitchens and pantries.

Cocksure, kok'shör, *a.* [Said to be derived from the *cock* of a musket, as being much more reliable than the match of the old matchlock.] Perfectly secure (*Shak.*)‡; confidently certain. (Colloq.)

Cockswain, kok'swān or kok'sn, *n.* [*Cock*, a boat, and *swain*.] The person who steers a boat; a person on board of a ship who has the care of a boat and its crew under an officer.

Cocoa, kō′kō, *n.* [Pg. *coco*, from *coco*, a bugbear, a distorted mask, from the monkey-like face at the base of the nut.] A palm to be found in most tropical regions growing on coasts, and producing the cocoa-nut.—**Cocoa-nut, Coco-nut**, *n.* The nut or fruit of the cocoa palm, twelve inches long and covered with a fibrous rind.—*Cocoa-nut oil, cocoa-oil*, an orange-coloured oil obtained from the nuts of the cocoa palm.—**Cocoa-plum**, *n.* The fruit of a small West Indian tree, about the size of a plum, with a sweet and pleasant pulp.

Cocoa, kō′kō, *n.* [Corruption of *cacao.*] The kernels of the cacao or chocolate tree prepared for making a beverage, or the beverage itself.

Cocoon, kō-kön′, *n.* [Fr. *cocon*, from *coque*, a shell, from L. *concha*, a shell-fish.] The silky tissue or envelope which the larvæ of many insects spin as a covering for themselves while they are in the chrysalis state.—**Cocoonery**, kō-kön′ér-i, *n.* A building or apartment for silkworms when feeding and forming cocoons.

Coction, kok′shon, *n.* [L. *coctio*, from *coquo*, to cook.] The act of boiling or exposing to heat in liquor; *med.* that alteration in morbific matter which fits it for elimination; digestion.—**Coctible**, kok′ti-bl, *a.* Capable of being boiled or baked.—**Coctile**, kok′tīl, *a.* Made by baking or exposing to heat, as a brick.

Cocum-butter, Cocum-oil, kō′kum, *n.* A greenish-yellow solid oil got from the seeds of trees that yield gamboge.

Cod, Codfish, kod, kod′fish, *n.* [D. *kodde*, a club, from its large club-shaped head.] A species of fish of great commercial importance, inhabiting northern seas; used as food either fresh, salted, or dried, and yielding cod-liver oil.—**Cod-fisher**, *n.* A person or vessel employed in the cod-fishery.—**Cod-fishery**, *n.* The business or operation of fishing for cod.—**Codling**, kod′ling, *n.* A young cod.—**Cod-liver Oil**, *n.* An important medical oil obtained from the liver of the common cod.

Cod, kod, *n.* [A.Sax. *cod*, *codd*, a small bag; Icel. *koddi*, a pillow; Sw. *kudde*, a cushion.] Any husk, envelope, or case containing the seeds of a plant; a pod.—*v.t.* To inclose in a cod.—**Codling**, kod′ling, *n.* A term applied to several cultivated varieties of kitchen apple.—**Codling-moth**, *n.* A small moth the larva of which feeds on the apple.

Coda, kō′da, *n.* [It., from L. *cauda*, a tail.] *Music*, an adjunct to the close of a composition, for the purpose of enforcing the final character of the movement.

Coddle, kod′l, *v.t.*—*coddled, coddling.* [O.Fr. *cadeler*, to cocker, pamper, make much of, *cadel*, an animal cast or born out of time, from L. *cado*, to fall.] To make effeminate by pampering; to make much of; to treat tenderly like an invalid; to pamper; to cocker.—*n.* An over-indulged, pampered being.

Code, kōd, *n.* [Fr., from L. *codex*, the trunk of a tree, a tablet, a book.] A systematic collection or digest of laws; any system or body of rules or laws relating to one subject; a system of signals or the like agreed upon; *teleg.* a set of words representing others for purposes of secrecy.—**Codify**, kod′i-fī, *v.t.* To reduce to a code or digest, as laws.—**Codification**, kod′i-fi-kā″shon, *n.* The act or process of codifying.—**Codifier, Codist**, kod′i-fī-ér, kō′dist, *n.* One who codifies.—**Codex**, kō′deks, *n.* pl. **Codices**, kō′di-sēz. A manuscript volume, as of a Greek or Latin classic, or of the Scriptures.

Codger, koj′ér, *n.* [Probably a form of *cadger* (which see).] A mean miserly man; a curious old fellow; an odd fish; a character; a familiar term of address. (Slang.)

Codical, kod′i-kal, *a.* Relating to a codex or to a code.—**Codicil**, kod′i-sil, *n.* [L. *codicillus*, dim. of *codex.*] A writing by way of supplement to a will, containing anything which the testator wishes to add, or any revocation or explanation of what the will contains.—**Codicillary**, kod-i-sil′la-ri, *a.* Of the nature of a codicil.

Codilla, ko-dil′la, *n.* [A dim. form from It. *coda*, L. *cauda*, a tail.] The coarsest part of hemp or flax, sorted out by itself.

Cœcum, sē′kum, *n.* CÆCUM.

Coefficacy, kō-ef′fi-ka-si, *n.* Joint efficacy.

Coefficient, kō-ef-fish′ent, *a.* Co-operating, acting in union to the same end.—*n.* That which unites in action with something else to produce the same effect; *alg.* a number or known quantity put before letters or quantities, known or unknown, into which it is supposed to be multiplied.—*Coefficient of expansion*, in heat, for a given material a small fraction denoting the portion of its size by which it increases when heated through one degree of temperature.—*Coefficient of friction*, the constant ratio of the retarding force of friction between two surfaces to the mutual pressure between them.—*Coefficient of performance* (marine engineering), coefficient involving the efficiency of the engine and the efficiency of the screw, required in obtaining the speed of a ship in terms of engine-power.—*Coefficient of restitution*, the ratio of the relative velocity of two bodies after impact to their relative velocity before impact.—**Coefficiency**, kō-ef-fish′en-si, *n.* State of being coefficient; co-operation.—**Coefficiently**, kō-ef-fish′ent-li, *adv.* In a coefficient manner; by co-operation.

Coed, kō′ĕd, *n.* A female student in a co-educational institution, college or university.

Cœlacanth, Cœlacanthous, sē′la-kanth, sē-la-kan′thus, *a.* [Gr. *koilos*, hollow, and *akantha*, a thorn.] Having hollow spines: said of certain fossil fishes.

Cœlebs, sē′lebz, *n.* [L.] A name given to a bachelor.

Cœlenterate, sē-len′tér-āt, *a.* [Gr. *koilos*, hollow, *enteron*, an intestine.] Of or pertaining to a sub-kingdom of animals (the Cœlenterata), including those whose alimentary canal communicates freely with the general cavity of the body. The Cœlenterata are divided into two sections, the Actinozoa and Hydrozoa, and comprise the corals, sea-anemones, medusæ, &c.—**Cœlenterata**, sē-len′tér-a″ta, *n. pl.* The cœlenterate animals.

Coelestine, sē-les′tin, *n.* [L. *coelestis*, heavenly, from *coelum*, the sky, from its occasional delicate blue hue.] Native sulphate of strontium, a mineral often forming beautiful crystals.

Cœliac, Celiac, sē′li-ak, *a.* [Gr. *koiliakos*, from *koilia*, the belly, *koilos*, hollow.] Pertaining to the cavity of the abdomen.

Cœlodont, sē′lō-dont, *a.* [Gr. *koilos*, hollow, *odous*, *odontos*, a tooth.] Having hollow teeth: said of certain lizard-like reptiles.—**Cœlom**, sē′lom, *n.* [Gr. *koilōma*, a cavity.] In animals, a body-cavity that does not contain blood.

Cœlosperm, sē′lō-sperm, *n.* [Gr. *koilos*, hollow, and *sperma*, seed.] *Bot.* a seed in which the albumen is curved so that the base and apex approach, as in coriander.—**Cœlospermous**, sē-lō-spér′mus, *a.* Hollow-seeded.

Coemption, kō-em′shon, *n.* [L. *coemptio*—*con*, and *emo*, *emptum*, to buy.] The buying up of the whole quantity of a commodity.

Coendoo, kō-en′dö, *n.* [Native name.] A tree-climbing Brazilian porcupine with a prehensile tail.

Cœnesthesis, sē-nes-thē′sis, *n.* [Gr. *koinos*, common, and *aisthēsis*, perception.] The general sensibility of the system, as distinguished from the special sensations (sight, smell, &c.).

Cœnobite, sē′nō-bīt. Same as *Cenobite.*

Cœnœcium, sē-nē′si-um, *n.* [Gr. *koinos*, common, and *oikos*, dwelling.] The common dermal system or plant-like structure of the Polyzoa or 'sea-mosses'.

Cœnogamy, sē-nog′a-mi, *n.* [Gr. *koinos*, common, and *gamos*, marriage.] The state of having husbands or wives in common; a community of husbands and wives.

Cœnosarc, sē′nō-särk, *n.* [Gr. *koinos*, common, and *sarx*, *sarkos*, flesh.] The common living basis by which the several beings included in a composite zoophyte are connected with one another.

Cœnure, Cœnurus, sē′nūr, sē-nū′rus, *n.* [Gr. *koinos*, common, *oura*, a tail.] The larval form of a tape-worm, producing staggers in sheep.

Coequal, kō-ē′kwal, *a.* Equal with another person or thing; of the same rank, dignity, or power.—*n.* One who is equal to another.—**Coequality**, kō-ē-kwal′i-ti, *n.* The state of being coequal.—**Coequally**, kō-ē′kwal-li, *adv.* With joint equality.

Coerce, kō-ėrs′, *v.t.* [L. *coerceo*—prefix *co*, and *arceo*, to drive or press.] To restrain by force, particularly by moral force, as by law or authority; to repress; to compel to compliance; to constrain.—**Coercible**, kō-ėr′si-bl, *a.* Capable of being coerced.—**Coercibleness**, kō-ėr′si-bl-nes, *n.* The state of being coercible.—**Coercion**, kō-ėr′shon, *n.* The act of coercing; restraint; compulsion; constraint.—**Coercive, Coercitive**, kō-ėr′siv, kō-ėr′si-tiv, *a.* Capable of coercing; restrictive; able to force into compliance.—*n.* That which coerces; that which constrains or restrains.—**Coercively**, kō-ėr′siv-li, *adv.* By constraint or coercion.

Coessential, kō-es-sen′shal, *a.* Having the same essence.—**Coessentiality**, kō-es-sen′shi-al″i-ti, *n.* The fact of having the same essence.—**Coessentially**, kō-es-sen′shal-li, *adv.* In a coessential manner.

Coetaneous,† kō-ē-tā′nē-us, *a.* [L. *coætaneus*—prefix *co*, and *ætas*, age.] Of the same age with another; beginning to exist at the same time; coeval.—**Coetaneously**,† kō-ē-tā′nē-us-li, *adv.* Of or from the same age or beginning.—**Coetanean**,† kō-ē-tā′nē-an, *n.* One of the same age with another.

Coeternal, kō-ē-tér′nal, *a.* Equally eternal with another.—**Coeternally**, kō-ē-tér′nal-li, *adv.* With coeternity or equal eternity.—**Coeternity**, kō-ē-tér′ni-ti, *n.* Existence from eternity equal with another eternal being; equal eternity.

Coeval, kō-ē′val, *a.* [L. *coævus*—*con*, and *ævum*, age.] Of the same age; having lived for an equal period; existing at the same time, or of equal antiquity in general (*coeval with* a person).—*n.* One who is coeval; one who lives at the same time.

Coexecutor, kō-eg-zek′ū-tėr, *n.* A joint executor.—**Coexecutrix**, kō-eg-zek′ū-triks, *n.* A joint executrix.

Coexist, kō-eg-zist′, *v.i.* To exist at the same time with another (to *coexist with*).—**Coexistence**, kō-eg-zis′tens, *n.* Existence at the same time with another; contemporary existence.—**Coexistency**, kō-eg-zis′ten-si, *n.* Coexistence.—**Coexistent**, kō-eg-zis′tent, *a.* Existing at the same time with another.

Coexpand, kō-eks-pand′, *v.i.* To expand together equally; to expand over the same space or to the same extent.

Coextend, kō-eks-tend′, *v.t.* and *i.* To extend through the same space or duration with another; to extend equally.—**Coextension**, kō-eks-ten′shon, *n.* The fact or state of being equally extended with something else.—**Coextensive**, kō-eks-ten′siv, *a.* Equally extensive; having equal scope or extent.—**Coextensively**, kō-eks-ten′siv-li, *adv.* So as to exhibit coextension.—**Coextensiveness**, kō-eks-ten′siv-nes, *n.*

Coffee, kof′i, *n.* [Fr. *café*, from Turk. *qahveh*, coffee.] The berries or the ground seeds of a tree a native of Arabia and Abyssinia, but now extensively cultivated throughout tropical countries, each berry containing two seeds, commonly called coffee-beans; a drink made from the roasted and ground seeds of the coffee-tree, by infusion or decoction.—**Coffee-bean, Coffee-nib**, *n.* A coffee-seed.—**Coffee-berry**, *n.* The fruit of the coffee-tree.—**Coffee-bug**, *n.* An insect which lives on the coffee-tree, and is very destructive to coffee-plantations. — **Coffee-cup**, *n.* A cup from which coffee is drunk.—**Coffee-house**, *n.* A house of entertainment where guests are supplied with coffee and other refreshments.—**Coffee-mill**, *n.* A small machine or mill for grinding coffee.—**Coffee-pot**, *n.* A covered pot in which the decoction or infusion of coffee is made, or in which it is brought upon the table for drinking.—**Coffee-roaster**, *n.* The utensil in which the coffee-beans are roasted before being ground.—**Coffee-room**, *n.* A public room in an inn or hotel where guests are supplied with refreshments.—**Coffee-tree**, *n.* The tree which produces coffee.—**Coffein**, **Coffeine**, kof-fē′in, *n.* Same as *Caffeine.*

Coffer, kof′ėr, *n.* [Fr. *coffre*, O.Fr. *cofre*, *cofin*, a coffer, from L. *cophinus*, Gr. *kophinos*, a basket. *Coffin* is the same word.] A chest, trunk, or casket for holding jewels, money, or other valuables; a sunk panel or compartment in a ceiling of an ornamental character; a kind of caisson or floating dock.—*v.t.* To deposit or lay up in a coffer. —**Coffer-dam**, *n.* A wooden inclosure formed in a river, &c., by driving two or more rows of piles close together, with clay packed in between the rows to exclude the water, and so obtain a firm and dry foundation for bridges, piers, &c.—**Coffered**, kof′ėrd, *a.* Furnished or ornamented with coffers (a *coffered* ceiling).

Coffin, kof′in, *n.* [O.Fr. *cofin*, a chest, L. *cophinus*, a basket. COFFER.] The chest or box in which a dead human body is buried or deposited in a vault; a casing of paste for a pie (*Shak.*)‡; the hollow part of a horse's hoof.—*v.t.* To put or inclose in a coffin.—**Coffin-bone**, *n.* A small spongy bone inclosed in the hoof of a horse.

Cog, kog, *v.t.*—*cogged, cogging.* [W. *coegio*, *coegiaw*, to trick, from *coeg*, empty, vain.] To flatter; to wheedle; to draw from by flattery; to foist or palm: now hardly used except in regard to dice, *to cog a die* being to load it so as to direct its fall, for the purpose of cheating.—*v.i.* To cheat; to wheedle; to lie.—*n.* A trick or deception.

Cog, kog, *n.* [Sw. *kugg*, *kugge*, a cog.] The tooth of a wheel, by which it drives another wheel or body, or any similar mechanical contrivance.—**Cog-wheel**, *n.* A wheel with cogs or teeth.—*v.t.*—*cogged, cogging.* To furnish with cogs.

Cogent, kō′jent, *a.* [L. *cogens*, *cogentis*, forcing, compelling, from *cogo*—*con*, together, or intens., and *ago*, to lead or drive.] Compelling in a physical sense†; resistless†; convincing; having the power to compel conviction; powerful; not easily resisted; forcible; irresistible: of arguments, proofs, reasoning, &c.—**Cogently**, kō′jent-li, *adv.* In a cogent manner; powerfully; forcibly. —**Cogency**, **Cogence**,† kō′jens-si, kō′-jens, *n.* The quality of being cogent; power of moving the will or reason; power of compelling conviction; force; conclusiveness.

Cogitate, koj′i-tāt, *v.i.*—*cogitated, cogitating.* [L. *cogito*, *cogitatum*—*co* for *con*, together, and *agito*, to shake, to agitate. AGITATE.] To think; to meditate; to ponder. — **Cogitation**, koj-i-tā′shon, *n.* The act of cogitating or thinking; thought; meditation; contemplation.—**Cogitative**, koj′i-tā-tiv, *a.* Thinking; having the power of cogitating; meditative; given to thought. —**Cogitatively**, koj′i-tā-tiv-li, *adv.* In a cogitative or thinking manner.—**Cogitativity**,† koj′i-tā-tiv″i-ti, *n.* Power of thinking.—**Cogitability**, koj′i-ta-bil″i-ti, *n.* The state or quality of being cogitable; conceivableness. — **Cogitable**, koj′i-ta-bl, *a.* Capable of being thought; capable of being conceived.—*n.* Anything capable of being the subject of thought.

Cognac, kō-nyak, *n.* [Fr.] A kind of French brandy, so called from the town of the same name, where large quantities are made.

Cognate, kog′nāt, *a.* [L. *cognatus*—prefix *co* for *con*, with, and *gnatus*, old form of *natus*, born.] Allied by blood; kindred by birth; *law*, connected by the mother's side; related in origin generally; proceeding from the same stock or root; of the same family (words, roots, languages); allied in nature; having affinity of any kind (*cognate* sounds). —*n.* One connected with another by ties of kindred; *law*, a relation connected by the mother's side; anything related to another by origin or nature.—**Cognateness**, kog′nāt-nes, *n.* State of being cognate.—**Cognation**, kog-nā′shon, *n.* [L. *cognatio.*] Relationship by descent from the same original; affinity; resemblance in nature or character.

Cognition, kog-ni′shon, *n.* [L. *cognitio*; *cognosco*, *cognitus*—*co* for *con*, and *nosco*, anciently *gnosco*, to know.] Knowledge from personal view or experience; perception; a thing known.—**Cognitive**, kog′-ni-tiv, *a.* Knowing or apprehending by the understanding.—**Cognizable**, **Cognisable**, kog′niz-a-bl or kon′, *a.* Capable of falling under notice or observation; capable of being known, perceived, or apprehended; capable of falling under judicial notice. — **Cognizably**, **Cognisably**, kog′niz-a-bli or kon′, *adv.* In a cognizable manner. — **Cognizance**, kog′ni-zans or kon′, *n.* [O.Fr. *cognoissance*, *connoissance.*] Knowledge or notice; perception; observation; *law*, judicial or authoritative notice or knowledge, also right to try and determine causes; a crest; a badge; a badge worn by a retainer, soldier, &c., to indicate the person or party to which he belongs.—**Cognizant**, **Cognisant**, kog′ni-zant or kon′, *a.* Acquainted with; having obtained knowledge of; competent to take legal or judicial notice.—**Cognize**, **Cognise**, kog-nīz′, *v.t.* —*cognized, cognised; cognizing, cognising.* To recognize as an object of thought; to perceive; to become conscious of; to know.

Cognomen, kog-nō′men, *n.* [L. *cognomen* —prefix *co* for *con*, and *nomen*, formerly *gnomen*, a name.] Strictly the last of the three names by which a Roman of good family was known, indicating the family to which he belonged; hence a surname or distinguishing name in general.—**Cognominal**, kog-nom′i-nal, *a.* Pertaining to a cognomen or surname. — **Cognomination**, kog-nom′i-nā″shon, *n.* A surname; a cognomen.

Cognoscible, kog-nos′i-bl, *a.* [From L. *cognosco.* COGNITION.] Capable of being known; subject to judicial investigation.—**Cognoscibility**, kog-nos′i-bil″i-ti, *n.* The quality of being cognoscible.

Cognovit, kog-nō′vit, *n.* [L., he has acknowledged.] A written acknowledgment in law by defendant that the action of the plaintiff is just, thus allowing judgment to be given against him.

Cohabit, kō-hab′it, *v.i.* [L. *cohabito*, from *co*, with, and *habito*, to dwell.] To dwell or live together as husband and wife: often applied to persons not legally married, and suggesting sexual intercourse. — **Cohabitation**, kō-hab′i-tā″shon, *n.* The state of living together as man and wife.

Coheir, kō-ār′, *n.* A joint-heir; one who succeeds to a share of an inheritance divided among two or more.—**Coheiress**, kō′ār-es, *n.* A joint-heiress.

Cohere, kō-hēr′, *v.i.* — *cohered, cohering.* [L. *cohæro*—*co* for *con*, and *hæro*, to stick together.] To stick or cleave together; to be united; to keep in close contact as parts of the same mass, or as two substances that attract each other; to hang well together; to agree or be consistent (as parts of a discourse or an argument). — **Coherence**, **Coherency**, kō-hē′rens, kō-hē′ren-si, *n.* The state of cohering; a cleaving together of bodies by means of attraction; suitable connection or dependence; due agreement as of ideas; consistency.—**Coherent**, kō-hē′rent, *a.* Cohering or sticking together; united; having a due agreement of parts; hanging well together; consecutive; observing due agreement; consistent (a *coherent* argument or discourse, a *coherent* speaker).—**Coherently**, kō-hē′rent-li, *adv.* In a coherent manner.—**Coherer**, kō-hēr-ėr, *n.* In wireless telegraphy, the essential part of the receiving instrument.—**Cohesibility**, kō-hē′zi-bil″i-ti, *n.* The tendency to unite by cohesion; cohesiveness.—**Cohesible**, kō-hē′zi-bl, *a.* Capable of cohesion.—**Cohesion**, kō-hē′-zhon, *n.* [Fr. *cohésion.*] The act or state of cohering, uniting, or sticking together; logical connection; *physics*, the state in which, or the force by which, the particles of bodies of the same nature are kept in contact so as to form a continuous mass.—**Cohesion**, kō-hē′zhun, *n.* [L. *cohæro*, *cohesum*, I stick to.] In flowers, the union of like parts, e.g. petals.—**Cohesive**, kō-hē′-siv, *a.* Causing cohesion.—**Cohesively**, kō-hē′siv-li, *adv.* In a cohesive manner; with cohesion.—**Cohesiveness**, kō-hē′siv-nes, *n.* The quality of being cohesive; the tendency to unite by cohesion.

Cohibit, kō-hib′it, *v.t.* [L. *cohibeo*, *cohibitum*, from *co*, together, and *habeo*, to hold.] To restrain.—**Cohibition**, kō-hi-bi′shon, *n.* Restraint.—**Cohibitor**, kō-hib′it-ėr, *n.* One who restrains.

Cohobate, kō′ho-bāt, *v.t.* [Fr. *cohober*, of Arabic origin.] To redistil or subject to several distillations.

Cohorn, kō′horn, *n.* Same as *Coehorn.*

Cohort, kō′hort, *n.* [L. *cohors*, *cohortis.*] In Roman armies, the tenth part of a legion, a body of about 500 or 600 men; a band or body of warriors in general.

Coif, koif, *n.* [Fr. *coiffe*, L.L. *cofia*, *cufia*, from M.H.G. *kuffe*, *kupfe*, a kind of cap.] A close-fitting cap or head-dress worn usually by nuns, a hood without a cape; a kind of close-fitting cap of mail; a kind of caul or cap.—*v.t.* To cover or dress with, or as with a coif.—**Coiffure**, koif′ūr, *n.* [Fr.] A head-dress, especially the head-dress of a lady.

Coign,‡ koin, *n.* A corner; a coin or quoin. (*Shak.*)

Coil, koil, *v.t.* [O.Fr. *coillir*, *cueillir*, from L. *colligere*, to collect. COLLECT.] To gather (a rope, chain, &c.) into a series of rings above one another; to twist or wind spirally.—*v.i.* To form rings or spirals; to wind. —*n.* A ring or series of rings or spirals into which a rope or other pliant body is wound.

Coil, koil, *n.* [Comp. Ir. and Gael. *goill*, war, battle; *goil*, to rage.] Perplexities; tumult; bustle; turmoil. (*Shak.*)

Coin, koin, *n.* [Fr. *coin*, a wedge, the die with which money is stamped, a coin, a corner, from L. *cuneus*, a wedge.] A piece of metal, as gold, silver, copper, or some alloy, converted into money by impressing some stamp on it; such pieces collectively; metallic currency; money; also, a quoin.—*v.t.* To stamp and convert into money; to mint; to make, fabricate, or invent.—**Coinage**, koi′nāj, *n.* The stamping of money; coin; money coined; the act of inventing, forming, or producing; invention; fabrication; what is fabricated or produced.—**Coiner**, koi′nėr, *n.* One who coins; a maker of money: often a maker of base or counterfeit coin; an inventor or maker, as of words.

Coincide, kō-in-sīd′, *v.i.*—*coincided, coinciding.* [L.L. *coincido*, from L. prefix *co*, with, and *incido*, to fall in—*in*, and *cado*, to fall.] To occupy the same place in space, or the same position in a scale or series; to happen at the same point of time; to be exactly contemporaneous; to correspond exactly; to concur; to agree (to *coincide with* a person *in* an opinion).—**Coincidence**, **Coincidency**,† kō-in′si-dens, kō-in′si-den-si, *n.* The fact of coinciding; exact correspondence in position; a happening or agreeing in time; contemporaneousness; agreement in circumstance, character, &c.; exact correspondence generally, or a case of exact correspondence.—**Coincident**, **Coincidental**, kō-in′si-dent, kō-in-si-den′-tal, *a.* Coinciding; happening at the same time; concurrent; exactly corresponding.—**Coincidently**, kō-in′si-dent-li, *adv.* In a coincident manner; with coincidence.—**Coincider**, kō-in-sīd′ėr, *n.* One who coincides with another, as in an opinion, course of action, &c.

Coindication, kō-in′di-kā″shon, *n.* A concurrent indication, sign, or symptom.

Co-inhere, kō-in-hēr′, *v.i.* To inhere together; to be included or exist together in the same thing.

Coinheritance, kō-in-her′it-ans, *n.* Joint inheritance.—**Coinheritor**, kō-in-her′it-ėr, *n.* A joint-heir; a coheir.

Cointense, kō-in-tens′, *a.* Of equal intensity with another object.—**Cointension**, **Cointensity**, kō-in-ten′shon, kō-in-ten′si-ti, *n.* The condition of being of equal intension or intensity.

Co-interest, kō-in′tėr-est, *n.* A joint interest.

Coir, **Coire**, koir, *n.* A species of yarn manufactured from the husk of cocoa-nuts, and formed into cordage, sailcloth, matting, &c.

Coition, kō-i′shon, *n.* [L. *coitio*—*con*, and *eo*, *itum*, to go.] A coming together; copulation.

Coke, kōk, *n.* [Probably from *cook* or *cake*; comp. *caking* coal.] Coal deprived of its bitumen, sulphur, or other extraneous or volatile matter by fire.—*v.t.*—*coked*, *coking*. To convert into coke; to deprive of volatile matter, as coal.

Col, kol, *n.* [Fr., neck.] An elevated mountain pass between two higher summits; the most elevated part of a mountain pass.

Colander, kul′an-dėr or kol′an-dėr, *n.* [From L. *colans*, *colantis*, ppr. of *colo*, to strain, from *colum*, a colander.] A vessel with a bottom perforated with little holes for straining liquors; a strainer.

Cola-nut, **Cola-seed**, kō′la, *n.* A brownish bitter seed, about the size of a chestnut, produced by an African tree, containing much caffeine and highly valued as yielding a refreshing and invigorating beverage. —**Cola-tree**, *n.* The tree which produces the cola-nut.

Co-latitude, kō-lat′i-tūd, *n.* [Abbrev. of *complement* and *latitude*.] The complement of the latitude, or what it wants of 90°.

Colchicum, kol′chi-kum, *n.* [L., a plant with a poisonous root, from *Colchis*, the native country of Medea, the famous sorceress.] A genus of liliaceous plants, the most familiar species being the meadow-saffron, a plant with a solid bulb-like root-stock and purple, crocus-like flowers, found in England and various parts of the Continent.—**Colchicine**, kol′chi-sin, *n.* An alkaloid obtained from colchicum bulbs, and used for the alleviation or cure of gout and rheumatism.

Colcothar, kol′ko-thär, *n.* [Probably of Ar. origin.] The brownish-red peroxide of iron, used for polishing glass and other substances.

Cold, kōld, *a.* [A.Sax. *cald*, *ceald*, *a.* and *n.* = Dan. *kold*, Icel. *kaldr*, Sw. *kall*, D. *koud*, Goth. *kaldo*, G. *kalt*; from root of *cool*, *chill*, which also appears in L. *gelidus*, gelid.] Not warm or hot; gelid; frigid; chilling; cooling; having the sensation of coolness; wanting warmth or animal heat; chill; wanting passion, zeal, or ardour; insensible; not animated or easily excited into action; not affectionate, cordial, or friendly; unaffecting; not animated or animating; not able to excite feeling or interest; spiritless.—*In cold blood*, without excitement, emotion, or passion.—*To give*, *show*, or *turn the cold shoulder*, to treat a person with studied coldness, neglect, or contempt.—*n.* The relative absence or want of heat; the cause of the sensation of coolness; the sensation produced in animal bodies by the escape of heat; an indisposition occasioned by cold; a catarrh.—**Coldish**, kōl′dish, *a.* Somewhat cold.—**Coldly**, kōld′li, *adv.* In a cold manner; without warmth; without concern; without apparent passion, emotion, or feeling; with indifference or negligence; dispassionately; calmly.—**Coldness**, kōld′nes, *n.* The state or quality of being cold; frigidity; indifference.—**Cold-blast**, *n.* A blast or current of cold air; *metal.* the name given to air at its natural temperature forced through furnaces for smelting iron.—**Cold-blooded**, *a.* Having cold blood; without sensibility or feeling; *zool.* a term applied to those animals the temperature of whose blood is a very little higher than that of their habitat.—**Cold-chisel**, *n.* A chisel for cutting metal in its cold state.—**Cold-cream**, *n.* A kind of cooling unguent for the skin, variously prepared.—**Cold-hearted**, *a.* Wanting passion or feeling; indifferent.—**Cold-heartedness**, *n.*—**Cold-short**, *n.* [*Short*, Scand. *skjör*. See SHORT-BREAD.] Brittle iron in the cold state.

Cole, kōl, *n.* [From L. *colis*, *caulis*, a cabbage-stalk, a cabbage.] The general name of all sorts of cabbage.—**Cole-rape**, *n.* The common turnip.—**Cole-seed**, *n.* The seed of the winter rape from which oil-cake is prepared for feeding cattle.—**Coleslaw**, kōl′sla. A salad made of sliced cabbage leaves.

Co-legatee, kō′leg-a-tē″, *n.* One who is a legatee along with another or others.

Colemanite, kōl′man-īt, *n.* A mineral.

Coleophyll, **Coleophyllum**, kol′ē-ō-fil, kol′ē-ō-fil″um, *n.* [Gr. *koleos*, a sheath, and *phyllon*, a leaf.] *Bot.* the first leaf which follows the cotyledon in endogens, and ensheaths the succeeding leaves.—**Coleophyllous**, kol′ē-ō-fil″lus, *a.* *Bot.* having the leaves inclosed in a sheath.

Coleoptera, kol-ē-op′tėr-a, *n. pl.* [Gr. *koleos*, a sheath, and *pteron*, a wing.] An order of insects commonly known by the name of *beetles*, and characterized by having four wings, of which the two anterior, called elytra, are not suited for flight, but form a covering and protection to the two posterior, and are of a hard and horny or parchment-like nature.—**Coleopter**, **Coleopteran**, kol-ē-op′tėr, kol-ē-op′tėr-an, *n.* A member of the order Coleoptera. —**Coleopterist**, kol-ē-op′tėr-ist, *n.* One versed in the natural history of the Coleoptera.—**Coleopterous**, kol-ē-op′tėr-us, *a.* Pertaining or belonging to the Coleoptera.

Coleorhiza, kol′ē-ō-rī″za, *n.* [Gr. *koleos*, a sheath, and *rhiza*, a root.] *Bot.* the sheath which covers the young radicle of monocotyledonous plants.

Colestaff, kōl′staf. Same as *Colstaff*.

Cole-tit, *n.* COAL-TIT.

Colic, kol′ik, *n.* [L. *colicus*, Gr. *kōlikos*, from *kōlon*, the colon.] A painful spasmodic affection of the intestines, especially of the colon, attended with fever or inflammation.—**Colic**, **Colical**, kol′ik, kol′ik-al, *a.* Affecting the bowels.—**Colicked**, kol′ikt, *a.* Affected with colic; griped.—**Colicky**, kol′ik-i, *a.* Pertaining to colic.

Colin, kol′in, *n.* [Fr.] The Virginian quail or American partridge.

Collaborator, **Collaborateur**, kol-lab′ō-rā-tėr, kol-lab′o-ra-tėr, *n.* [Fr. *collaborateur*—L. *col* for *con*. together, and *laboro*, to labor.] An assistant; an associate in labor, especially in literary or scientific pursuits.—**Collaboration**, kol-lab′ō-rā″shon, *n.* The act of working together; united labor.

Collapse, kol-laps′, *v.i.*—*collapsed*, *collapsing*. [L. *collabor*, *collapsus*—*col* for *con*, and *labor*, *lapsus*, to slide or fall (whence *lapse*).] To fall in or together, as the two sides of a vessel; to close by falling together; hence, to come to nothing; to break down.—*n.* A falling in or together, as of the sides of a hollow vessel; a more or less sudden failure of the vital powers; a sudden and complete failure of any kind; a breakdown.—**Collapsable**, kol-lap′sa-bl, *a.* Capable of collapsing or being made to collapse.—**Collapsion**, kol-lap′shon, *n.* A state of collapsing.

Collar, kol′ėr, *n.* [L. *collare*, Fr. *collier*, a collar, from L. *collum*, the neck.] Something worn round the neck, whether for use or ornament or both, or it may be for restraint; the necklace or chain worn by knights, and having the badge of the order appended to it; part of the harness of an animal used for draught; an article of dress or part of a garment going round the neck; something resembling a collar; something in the form of a ring, especially at or near the end of something else.—*To slip the collar*, to escape or get free; to disentangle one's self.—*v.t.* To seize by the collar; to put a collar on; to roll up and bind with cord (a piece of meat) for keeping for a time.—**Collar-beam**, *n.* A piece of timber extending between two opposite rafters, at some height above their base.—**Collar-bone**, *n.* The clavicle; one of the two bones of the thorax in man and many quadrupeds joined at one end to the shoulder-bone and at the other to the breast-bone.—**Collaret**, kol′ėr-et, *n.* A small collar of linen, fur, or the like, worn by women.

Collate, kol-lāt′, *v.t.*—*collated*, *collating*. [L. *confero*, *collatum*, to bring together, compare, bestow—*col* for *con*, and *fero*, *latum*, to carry.] To bring together and compare; to examine critically, noting points of agreement and disagreement (manuscripts and books); to confer or bestow (a benefice) on (to *collate* a person *to* a church); to gather and place in order, as the sheets of a book for binding.—**Collatable**, kol-lā′ta-bl, *n.* Capable of being collated.—**Collation**, kol-lā′shon, *n.* The act of collating; a comparison, especially the comparison of manuscripts or editions of books; the presentation of a clergyman to a benefice by a bishop who has the benefice in his own gift, or by neglect of the patron has acquired the patron's rights; the reading of passages in Scripture and in the Fathers, in Benedictine monasteries, followed by a discussion and light repast.—**Collationer**, kol-lā′shon-ėr, *n.* One who examines the sheets or pages of a book, after printing, to ascertain whether they are correctly printed, paged, &c.—**Collative**, kol-lā′tiv, *a.* *Eccles.* presented by collation; having the bishop as patron.—**Collator**, kol-lā′tėr, *n.* One who collates.

Collateral, kol-lat′ėr-al, *a.* [L.L. *collateralis*—*col* for *con*, and L. *lateralis*, from *latus*, a side.] At the side; belonging to the side or what is at the side; acting indirectly; acting through side channels; accompanying but subordinate; auxiliary; subsidiary; descending from the same ancestor, but not in a direct line, as distinguished from *lineal*.—*n.* Pertaining to an obligation or security attached to another to secure its performance: hence, guaranteed by security as in a loan.

Colleague, kol′lēg, *n.* [L. *collega*, a colleague—*col* for *con*, and stem of *lego*, *legatum*, to send on a mission.] A partner or associate in the same office, employment, or commission, civil or ecclesiastical: never used of partners in trade or manufactures. —**Colleagueship**, kol′lēg-ship, *n.* The state of being a colleague.

Collect, kol-lekt′, *v.t.* [L. *colligo*, *collectum*—*col* for *con*, and *lego*, to gather, which appears also in *neglect*, *select*, *lecture*, &c., also *coil*, *cull*.] To gather into one body or place; to assemble or bring together; to gather; to infer or conclude (in this sense now rare).—*To collect one's self*, to recover from surprise or a disconcerted state.—*v.i.* To run together; to accumulate.—*n.* (kol′lekt). A short comprehensive prayer; a form of prayer adapted to a particular day or occasion.—**Collectanea**, kol-lek-tā′nē-a, *n. pl.* [L., things collected.] A selection of passages from various authors, usually made for the purpose of instruction; a miscellany.—**Collected**, kol-lek′ted, *p.* and *a.* Gathered together; not disconcerted; cool; firm; prepared; self-possessed.—**Collectedly**, kol-lek′ted-li, *adv.* In one view; together; in a cool, firm, or self-possessed manner.—**Collectedness**, kol-lek′ted-nes, *n.* The state of being collected.—**Collectible**, kol-lek′ti-bl, *a.* Capable of being collected.—**Collection**, kol-lek′shon, *n.* The act or practice of collecting or of gathering; that which is collected or gathered together (as pictures or objects of interest); that which is collected for a charitable, religious, or other purpose; the jurisdiction of a collector; a collectorship; the act of deducing from premises, or that which is deduced (*Mil.*)†.—**Collective**, kol-lek′tiv, *a.* [L. *collectivus*, Fr. *collectif*.] Formed by collecting; gathered into a mass, sum, or body; aggregate; *gram.* expressing a number or multitude united, though in the singular number (a *collective noun*).—*Collective note*, in *diplomacy*, an official communication signed by the representatives of several governments.—*n. Gram.* a noun with a singular form comprehending in its meaning several individuals, such as *people*, *infantry*, *crowd*.—**Collectively**, kol-lek′tiv-li, *adv.* In a collective manner; in a mass or body; in the aggregate; unitedly.—**Collectivism**, kol-lek′tiv-izm, *n.* The socialistic doctrine that the land and means of production should belong to the people collectively. So also **Collectivist**.—**Collector**, kol-lek′tėr, *n.* One who collects; especially, one who collects objects of interest; an officer appointed to collect and receive customs, duties, taxes, &c., within a certain district.—**Collectorate**, kol-lek′tėr-āt, *n.* The district of a collector; a collectorship.—**Collectorship**, kol-lek′tėr-ship, *n.* The office or jurisdiction of a collector.

College, kol′ej, *n.* [L. *collegium*, a society, guild, or fraternity, from *collega*, a colleague. COLLEAGUE.] A society of men invested with certain powers and rights, performing certain duties, or engaged in some common pursuit; a guild; a corporation; especially, a society or institution for purposes of instruction and scientific research in the higher branches of knowledge; the edifice belonging to a college.—**Collegial**,† kol-lē′ji-al, *a.* Pertaining to a college; collegiate.—**Collegian**, kol-lē′ji-an, *n.* A member of a college, particularly of a literary institution so called; a student.—**Collegiate**, kol-lē′ji-āt, *a.* Pertaining to a college (*collegiate* studies); constituted after the manner of a college.—*Collegiate church*, a church that has no cathedral, but does have a college of canons, or a dean, as Westminster Abbey; in the U. S., a church or an association of churches.

Collenchyma, kol-len′ki-ma, *n.* [Gr. *kolla*, glue, and *enchyma*, an infusion.] *Bot.* the cellular matter in which pollen is generated.

Collet, kol′et, *n.* [Fr. *collet*, a collar or necklace, from *col*, L. *collum*, the neck.] A band or collar; among jewellers, the horizontal face or plane at the bottom of brilliants, and the part of a ring containing the bezel in which the stone is set; *bot.* the neck or part of a plant from which spring the ascending and descending axes.

Colletic, kol-let′ik, *a.* [Gr. *kollētikos*, from *kolla*, glue.] Having the property of gluing; agglutinant.—*n.* An agglutinant.—**Colleterium**, kol-le-tē′ri-um, *n.* An organ in the females of certain insects, containing a glutinous substance by which the ova are cemented together.—**Colleterial**, kol-le-tē′ri-al, *a.* Pertaining to the colleterium.

Collide, kol-līd′, *v.i.*—*collided*, *colliding*. [L. *collido*—*col* for *con*, and *lædo*, to strike.] To strike or dash against each other; to meet in shock; to meet in opposition or antagonism.—**Collision**, kol-li′zhon, *n.* [L. *collisio*.] The act of striking or dashing together; the meeting and mutual striking of two or more moving bodies, or of a moving body with a stationary one; opposition; antagonism; interference.—**Collisive**, kol-lī′siv, *a.* Causing collision; clashing.

Collie, Colly, kol′i, *n.* [Origin doubtful.] A variety of dog especially common in Scotland, and much esteemed as a sheep-dog.

Collier, kol′yėr, *n.* [From *coal*; comp. *lawyer*, *sawyer*.] A digger of coal; one who works in a coal-mine; a vessel employed in the coal trade.—**Colliery**, kol′yėr-i, *n.* The place where coal is dug; a coal-mine or pit.

Colligate, kol′li-gāt, *v.t.*—*colligated*, *colligating*. [L. *colligo*—*col* for *con*, and *ligo*, to bind.] To bind or fasten together; to connect by observing a certain relationship or similarity (to *colligate* phenomena).—**Colligation**, kol-li-gā′shon, *n.* The act of colligating; that process by which many isolated facts are brought together under one general conception or observation.

Collimation, kol-li-mā′shon, *n.* [From a fancied L. verb *collimare*, really a false reading for *collineare*—*col*, together, and *linea*, a line.] The act of levelling or of directing the sight to a fixed object.—*Line of collimation*, in an astronomical instrument, the straight line which passes through the centre of the object-glass, and intersects at right angles the fine wires which are fixed in the focus.—*Error of collimation*, the deviation of the actual line of sight in a telescope from the focus and centre of the object-glass, or from the proper position.—**Collimate**, kol′li-māt, *v.t.* To adjust the line of collimation in.—**Collimating**, kol′li-māt-ing, *a.* Pertaining to collimation; correcting the error of collimating.—**Collimator**, kol-lim′ā-tėr, *n.* A small telescope used for adjusting the line of collimation.

Collinear, kol-lin′ē-ėr, *a.* [L. *col* for *con*, and *linea*, a line.] Pertaining to or situated in a corresponding line.—**Collineate**, kol-lin′ē-āt, *v.t.* and *i.* To aim or direct in a line corresponding with another.—**Collineation**, kol-lin′ē-ā″shon, *n.* The act of collineating.

Collingual, kol-ling′gwal, *a.* [L. *col* for *con*, with, and *lingua*, a tongue.] Speaking the same language.

Colliquate, kol′li-kwāt, *v.t.* or *i.* [L. *col* for *con*, and *liquo*, *liquatum*, to melt.] To melt; to dissolve; to change from solid to fluid; to make or become liquid.—**Colliquable**, kol-lik′wa-bl, *a.* Capable of being or liable to become liquefied.—**Colliquant**, kol′li-kwant, *a.* Having the power of dissolving or melting.—**Colliquation**, kol-li-kwā′shon, *n.* The act of melting; a melting or fusing together.—**Colliquative**, kol-lik′wa-tiv, *a.* Melting; dissolving; *med.* profuse or excessive, so as to cause exhaustion: said of discharges.—**Colliquefaction**, kol-lik′wē-fak″shon, *n.* A melting together.

Collision. Under COLLIDE.

Collocate, kol′lō-kāt, *v.t.*—*collocated*, *collocating*. [L. *colloco*—*col* for *con*, together, and *loco*, to place, *locus*, a place.] To set or place; to set; to station.—**Collocation**, kol-lō-kā′shon, *n.* [L. *collocatio*.] The act of collocating, placing, disposing, or arranging along with something else; the manner in which a thing is placed with regard to something else; disposition; arrangement.

Collocution, kol-lō-kū′shon, *n.* [L. *collocutio*—*col* for *con*, together, and *locutio*, from *loquor*, to speak.] A speaking or conversing together; a colloquy; mutual discourse.—**Collocutor**, kol-lo-kū′tėr or kol-lok′ū-tėr, *n.* One of the speakers in a dialogue.—**Collocutory**, kol-lok′ū-to-ri, *a.* Pertaining to or having the form of a colloquy; colloquial.

Collodion, kol-lō′di-on, *n.* [Gr. *kolla*, glue, and *eidos*, resemblance.] A substance prepared by dissolving gun-cotton in ether, or in a mixture of ether and alcohol, used as a substitute for adhesive plaster in the case of slight wounds, and as the basis of a photographic process.—**Collodionize**, kol-lō′di-on-īz, *v.t.*—*collodionized*, *collodionizing*. To prepare (a plate) with collodion; to treat with collodion.—**Colloid**, kol′loid, *a.* Like glue or jelly; *chem.* applied to uncrystallizable liquids; *geol.* applied to partly amorphous minerals.—*n.* The name given to a transparent, viscid, yellowish, structureless or slightly granular matter, resembling liquid gelatine. CRYSTALLOID.—**Colloidal**, kol-loi′dal, *a.* Of or pertaining to or of the nature of colloids.—**Colloidality**, kol-loi-dal′i-ti, *n.* Colloidal nature or character.

Collogue, kō-log′, *v.i.* To plot together. (Colloq.)

Collop, kol′op, *n.* [Perhaps lit. a piece of meat made tender by beating; Sw. *kollops*, G. *klopps*, meat that has been beaten; D. *kloppen*, G. *klopfen*, to beat; E. to *clap*.] A slice or lump of flesh.

Colloquy, kol′lō-kwi, *n.* [L. *colloquium*—*col*, together, and *loquor*, to speak.] The mutual discourse of two or more; a conference; a dialogue; a conversation.—**Colloquial**, kol-lō′kwi-al, *a.* Pertaining to conversation; peculiar to the language of common conversation.—**Colloquialism**, kol-lō′kwi-al-izm, *n.* A word or phrase peculiar to the language of common conversation.—**Colloquiality**, kol-lō′kwi-al″i-ti, *n.* The state of being colloquial.—**Colloquialize**, kol-lō′kwi-al-īz, *v.t.* To make colloquial.—**Colloquially**, kol-lō′kwi-al-li, *adv.* In a colloquial or conversational manner; in colloquial language.—**Colloquist**, kol′lō-kwist, *n.* A speaker in a dialogue.—**Colloquize**, kol′lō-kwīz, *v.i.* To take part in a colloquy or conversation; to converse.

Collotype, ko′lō-tīp, *n.* [Gr. *kolla*, glue.] Thin gelatinous plate etched by actinic rays and then printed from.

Collude, kol-lūd′, *v.i.*—*colluded*, *colluding*. [L. *colludo*—*col*, together, and *ludo*, to play, as in *allude*, *delude*.] To play into the hands of each other; to conspire in a fraud; to act in concert; to connive.—**Colluder**, kol′lūd′ėr, *n.* One who colludes.—**Collusion**, kol-lū′zhon, *n.* Secret agreement for a fraudulent purpose.—**Collusive**, kol-lū′siv, *a.* Fraudulently concerted between two or more.—**Collusively**, kol-lū′siv-li, *adv.* In a collusive manner; by collusion.—**Collusiveness**, kol-lū′siv-nes, *n.* The quality of being collusive.—**Collusory**, kol-lū′so-ri, *a.* Collusive.

Colly,† kol′i, *v.t.* [A.Sax. *col*, coal.] To make foul; to blacken. (*Shak.*)

Collyrium, kol-lir′i-um, *n.* [L.] Eye-salve; eye-wash.

Colocynth, kol′ō-sinth, *n.* [Gr. *kolokynthis*, a gourd or pumpkin.] A kind of cucumber, the fruit of the wild gourd, indigenous in the warmer parts of Asia, but now widely cultivated on account of its medicinal properties, being a purgative.

Cologne-earth, kō-lōn′, *n.* A kind of ochre of a deep-brown colour, used in water-colour painting.—**Cologne-water**, *n.* Eau de Cologne.

Cololite, kō′lō-līt, *n.* [Gr. *kōlon*, the colon, and *lithos*, a stone.] *Geol.* the name given to what appears to be the petrified intestines of fishes or their contents, but more probably consists of worm-casts.

Colomba, Columba, ko-lom′ba, ko-lum′-ba, *n.* CALUMBA.

Colombier, kō-lom′bi-ėr, *n.* *Columbier.*

Colon, kō′lon, *n.* [Gr. *kōlon*, the colon, a member or limb, a clause.] The largest portion of the human intestine, forming the middle section of the large intestine, and terminating in the rectum; a punctuation mark formed thus [:], used to mark a pause greater than that of a semicolon, but less than that of a period.

Colonel, kėr′nel, *n.* [Formerly also *coronel*, which is an old French form and has given the modern pronunciation; Fr. *colonel*, O.Fr. *colonnel*, from It. *colonello*, a colonel, a little column, dim. of *colonna*, L. *columna*, a column; the name was originally given to the leading company in a regiment.] The chief commander of a regiment of troops, in any branch of service.—**Colonelcy, Colonelship**, kėr′nel-si, kėr′nel-ship, *n.* The office, rank, or commission of a colonel.

Colonial, ko-lō′ni-al, *n.* A person belonging to a colony.—**Colonialize**, *v.t.* To invest with a colonial character or attributes.

Colonnade, kol-on-nād′, *n.* [It *colonnata*, from *colonna*, a column. COLUMN.] *Arch.* any series or range of columns placed at certain intervals from each other, such intervals varying according to the rules of art and the order employed.

Colony, kol′o-ni, *n.* [L. *colonia*, from *colo*, *cultum*, to till (hence *cultivate*, *culture*).] A body of people transplanted from their mother-country to a remote province or country, and remaining subject to the jurisdiction of the parent state; a body of settlers or their descendants; the country planted or colonized; a number of animals or plants living or growing together.—**Colonial**, ko-lō′ni-al, *a.* Pertaining to a colony.—**Colonialism**, ko-lō′ni-al-izm, *n.* A phrase, idiom, or practice peculiar to a colony.—**Colonist**, kol'on-ist, *n.* An inhabitant of or settler in a colony; a member of a colonizing expedition.—**Colonize**, kol'on-īz, *v.t.*—*colonized, colonizing.* To plant or establish a colony in; to send a colony to; to migrate and settle in.—*v.i.* To remove and settle in a distant country.—**Colonization**, kol'on-iz-ā″shon, *n.* The act of colonizing or state of being colonized.—**Colonizationist**, kol'on-iz-ā″shon-ist, *n.* An advocate for colonization.—**Colonizer**, kol'on-īz-ėr, *n.* One who colonizes; one who establishes colonies.

Colophon, kol'o-fōn, *n.* [Gr. *kolophōn*, a summit, top, finishing.] A device, or printer's name, place of publication, and date, formerly put at the conclusion of a book; from the acme or finish of horsemanship displayed by the Ionians of Colophon.—**Colophonian**, kol-o-fō'ni-an, *a.* Relating to a colophon or the conclusion of a book.

Colophony, Colophany, kol'o-fo-ni, kol'o-fa-ni, *n.* [Gr. *kolophōnia*, from *Colophōn*, a city of Ionia, whence the Greeks obtained it.] Black resin or turpentine boiled in water and dried.—**Colophonic**, kol-o-fon'ik, *a* Pertaining to colophony.

Coloquintida, kol-o-kwin'ti-da, *n.* The colocynth or bitter-apple.

Color, kul'ėr, *n.* [L. *color*, color.] That in respect of which bodies have a different appearance to the eye independently of their form; any tint or hue distinguished from white; that which is used for coloring; a pigment; paint; the blood-red hue of the face; redness, complexion; false show; pretense; guise; *pl.* a flag, ensign, or standard borne in an army or fleet; a color used as a badge.—*Complementary colors*, colors which together make white; thus, any of the three primary colors is complementary to the other two.—*Primary colors*, red, green, and violet (or blue); or in a looser sense the colors into which white light is divided by a glass prism.—viz. red, orange, yellow, green, blue, indigo, and violet.—*Persons of color*, members of the darker varieties of mankind, as negroes, mulattoes, &c.—*v.t.* To impart color to; to dye; to tinge; to paint; to stain; *fig.* to clothe with an appearance different from the real; to give a specious appearance to; to make plausible.—*v.i.* To blush.—**Colorable**, kul'ėr-a-bl, *a.* Specious; plausible; giving an appearance of right or justice (pretense, grounds); intended to deceive (a *colorable* imitation of a trademark). ∴ *Colorable*, having such an appearance as would not lead to the suspicion of anything underhand; *specious*, having a fair outside show, and likely to mislead thereby; *plausible*, apparently reasonable or satisfactory, though not convincing; *ostensible*, put forward as having a certain character but not really having it.—**Colorableness**, kul'ėr-a-bl-nes, *n.* Speciousness.—**Colorably**, kul'ėr-a-bli, *adv.* In a colorable manner.—**Colored**, kul'ėrd, *p.* and *a.* Having a color; dyed, painted, or stained; having some other color than white or black; having a specious appearance; a term applied to the darker varieties of mankind; *bot.* applied to a leaf, calyx, seed, &c., to express any color except green.—**Coloring**, kul'ėr-ing, *n.* The act or art of applying colors; color applied; tints or hues collectively, as in a picture; a specious appearance; show.—**Colorist**, kul'ėr-ist, *n.* One who colors; a painter whose works are remarkable for beauty of color.—**Colorless**, kul'ėr-les, *a.* Destitute of color.—**Colorman**, kul'ėr-man, *n.* One who prepares and sells colors.—**Color-blind**, *a.* Incapable of accurately distinguishing colors; having an imperfect perception of colors.—**Color-blindness**, *n.* Total or partial incapability of distinguishing colors, arising from some defect in the eye, though otherwise vision may be quite perfect.—**Color-box**, *n.* A portable box for holding artists colors, brushes, &c.—**Color-printing**, *n.* The art or process of printing in colors.—**Color-sergeant**, *n.* A non-commissioned officer who ranks higher than an ordinary sergeant, and who attends the colors in the field or near headquarters.

Colorate,† kul'ėr-āt, *a.* [L. *coloratus*.] Colored; dyed or tinged with some color.—**Coloration**, kul-ėr-ā'shon, *n.* Coloring; the state of being colored; the tints of an object.—**Colorific**, kul-ėr-if'ik, *a.* Having the quality of tingeing; able to give color or tint to other bodies.—**Colorimeter**, kol-ō-rim'et-ėr, *n.* An instrument for measuring the depth of color in a liquid by comparison with a standard liquid of the same tint.

Colorado Beetle, kol-ō-rä'dō, *n.* A coleopterous insect, a native of south-western United States (Colorado), which works great havoc among the potato crops.

Colossus, kō-los'sus, *n.* pl. **Colossi**, kō-los'sī, or rarely **Colossuses**, kō-los'sus-ez. [Gr. *kolossos*, a colossal statue.] A statue of a gigantic size or of size much greater than the natural, such as the statue of Apollo which anciently stood at the entrance to the port of Rhodes.—**Colossal**, kō-los'sal, *a.* Like a colossus; much exceeding the size of nature; very large; huge; gigantic.

Colostrum, kō-los'trum, *n.* [L.] The first milk secreted in the breasts after childbirth.

Colporteur, kol-por-tėr, ė long, *n.* [Fr.—*col*, from L. *collum*, the neck, and *porteur*, a carrier, from L. *porto*, to carry.] A hawker of wares; a hawker of books and pamphlets, particularly a hawker of religious books and pamphlets.—**Colportage**, kol'pōr-tāj, *n.* The system of distributing religious books, tracts, &c., by colporteurs.

Colstaff, kol'staf, *n.* [Fr. *col*, the neck, and E. *staff*.] A staff for enabling two persons to carry a burden between them, each resting one end of the staff on his shoulder.

Colt, kōlt, *n.* [A.Sax. *colt*, a young ass, a young camel; comp. Sw. *kult*, a young boar, a stout boy.] A young horse, or a young animal of the horse genus; commonly and distinctively applied to the male, *filly* being the female; a young camel or a young ass (O.T.)‡.—**Coltish**, kōl'tish, *a.* Like a colt; wanton; frisky; gay.—**Coltishly**, kōl'tish-li, *adv.* In the manner of a colt; wantonly.—**Coltishness**, kōl'tish-nes, *n.* Wantonness; friskiness.—**Colt's-foot**, *n.* The popular name of a composite plant whose leaves were once much employed in medicine; tussilago.

Colubrine, kol'ū-brīn, *a.* [L. *colubrinus*, from *coluber*, a serpent.] Relating to serpents; cunning; crafty.

Columba, ko-lum'ba, *n.* CALUMBA.

Columbarium, kol-um-ba'ri-um, *n.* [L. *columba*, pigeon.] An ancient sepulchre with recesses for urns containing the ashes of the dead.

Columbian, ko-lum'bi-an, *a.* [From *Columbia*, a name sometimes given to the United States, after Christopher *Columbus*.] Pertaining to the United States or to America.

Columbier, ko-lum'bi-ėr, *n.* A size of drawing-paper measuring 34½ by 23 inches.

Columbine, kol'um-bīn, *a.* [L. *columbinus*, from *columba*, a pigeon.] Like or pertaining to a pigeon or dove; of a dove-colour; resembling the neck of a dove in colour.—*n* [L. *columbina*.] A plant of the buttercup family, so called from the curved petals being in shape somewhat like pigeons, the sepals forming the wings; the name of the mistress of Harlequin in our pantomimes.

Columbium, ko-lum'bi-um, *n.* [From *Columbia*, America.] A rare metal; niobium.—**Columbite**, ko-lum'bīt, *n.* The ore of columbium.

Columbo, ko-lum'bō, *n.* CALUMBA.

Columella, kol-ū-mel'a, *n.* [L. dim. of *columna*, column.] A name for various plants having the appearance of such.

Column, kol'um, *n.* [L. *columna*, a column, from root which appears in *collis*, a hill, *culmen*, a summit.] A solid body of considerably greater length than thickness, standing upright, and generally serving as a support to something resting on its top; a pillar; anything resembling a column in shape (a *column* of water, air, or mercury); *bot.* the united stamens and styles of plants when they form a solid central body, as in orchids; *milit.* a formation of troops, narrow in front, and deep from front to rear; *naut.* a body of ships following each other; *printing* and *writing*, a division of a page; a perpendicular set of lines separated from another set by a line or blank space.—**Columel, Columella**, kol'ū-mel, kol-ū-mel'la, *n.* [L. *columella*, dim. of *columen* or *columna*, a column.] *Bot.* the central column in the capsule of mosses, from which the spores separate; the axis round which the parts of a fruit are arranged; *conch.* the upright pillar in the centre of most of the univalve shells.—**Columelliform**, kol-ū-mel'li-form, *a.* Shaped like a columella or little column.—**Columnar**, ko-lum'nėr, *a.* Formed in columns; like the shaft of a column.—**Columnarity**, kol-um-nar'i-ti, *n.* The quality of being columnar.—**Columnated**, ko-lum'nāt-ed, *a.* Ornamented with columns.—**Columned**, kol'umd, *a.* Furnished with columns; supported on or adorned by columns.—**Columniation**, ko-lum'ni-ā″shon, *n.* *Arch.* the employment of columns in a design.

Colure, kol'ūr, *n.* [Gr. *kolo*[illegible]*ros*, dock-tailed (with *grammē*, a line, understood)—*kolos*, stunted, and *oura*, a tail, because a part is always beneath the horizon.] Either of the two great circles supposed to intersect each other at right angles in the poles of the world, one of them passing through the solstitial and the other through the equinoctial points of the ecliptic, the points where they intercept the ecliptic being called cardinal points.

Colza, kol'za, *n.* [Fr. *colza*, O.Fr. *colzat*, from D. *koolzaad*, lit. cabbage-seed—*kool*, cabbage, and *zaad*, seed.] A variety of cabbage whose seeds afford an oil much employed for burning in lamps, and for many other purposes.

Coma, kō'ma, *n.* [Gr. *kōma*, lethargy.] A state of more or less complete insensibility and loss of power of thought or motion; lethargy.—**Comatose, Comatous**, kō'ma-tōs, kō'ma-tus, *a.* Pertaining to coma; drowsy; lethargic.

Coma, kō'ma, *n.* [L., the hair.] *Bot.* the empty leaf or bract terminating the flowering stem of a plant, in a tuft or bush; also, the silky hairs at the end of some seeds; *astron.* the nebulous hair-like envelope surrounding the nucleus of a comet.—**Comate**, kō'māt, *a.* [L. *comatus*.] Hairy; furnished with a coma.

Comb, kōm, *n.* [A.Sax. *camb*, a comb, a crest = D. *kam*, Icel. *kambr*, a comb, a crest; Dan. *kam*, a comb, a cam; G. *kamm*, a comb.] An instrument with teeth for separating, cleansing, and adjusting hair, wool, or flax; also, an instrument used by women for keeping the hair in its place when dressed; the crest, caruncle, or red fleshy tuft growing on a cock's head; the top or crest of a wave; honey-comb.—*v.t.* To dress with a comb.—*v.i.* To roll over, as the top of a wave, or to break with a white foam.—**Combed**, kōmd, *a.* Having a comb or crest.—**Comber**, kōm'ėr, *n.* One who combs; one whose occupation is to comb wool, &c.—**Combing**, kōm'ing, *n.* The act of using a comb; that which is removed by combing: in the latter sense, generally in the plural.

Comb, Combe, kōm, *n.* [W. *cwm*, a hollow; or A.Sax. *comb*, *cumb*, a vessel, a valley. COOMB.] A valley between hills or mountains; specifically, that portion of a valley which forms its continuation above the most elevated spring.

Combat, kom'bat or kum'bat, *v.i.* [Fr. *combattre*—*com*, and *battre*, to beat. BATTER.] To fight; to struggle or contend.—*v.t.* To fight with; to oppose by force; to contend against; to resist: now chiefly *fig.* (he *combated* their scruples).—*n.* A fight; a struggle to resist, overthrow, or conquer; contest; engagement; battle.—*Single combat*, a fight between two individuals; a duel.

∴ Syn. under BATTLE.—**Combatable**, kom'ba-ta-bl, *a.* Capable of being combated, disputed, or opposed. — **Combatant**, kom'ba-tant, *a.* Contending; disposed to combat or contend.—*n.* A person who combats; any person engaged in active war; a person who contends with another in argument or controversy. — **Combative**, kom'ba-tive, *a.* Disposed to combat; showing such a disposition; pugnacious.—**Combatively**, kom'ba-tiv-li, *adv.* In a combative manner; pugnaciously.—**Combativeness**, kom'ba-tiv-nes, *n.* State of being combative; disposition to contend or fight.

Comber, kom'bėr, *n.* A name given to a fish of the perch family, and also to a species of wrasse.

Combine, kom-bīn', *v.t.*—*combined*, *combining.* [Fr. *combiner*, from the L.L. *combino*—*com*, and L. *binus*, two and two, or double.] To unite or join; to link closely together.—*v.i.* To unite, agree, or coalesce; to league together; to unite by affinity or chemical attraction.—kom'bīn, *n.* Group of persons or associations leagued together in a joint undertaking; a harvesting machine which cuts and threshes grain while traveling across a field.—**Combinable**, kom-bī'na-bl, *a.*—**Combination**, kom-bi-nā'shon, *n.* The act of combining; the act of joining, coming together, or uniting; union of particulars; concurrence; meeting; union or association of persons or things for effecting some object by joint operation; commixture; union of bodies or qualities in a mass or compound; chemical union; *math.* the union of a number of individuals in different groups, each containing a certain number of the individuals.—**Combinatory**, **Combinative**,† kom-bī'na-to-ri, kom-bī'nā-tiv, *a.* Tending to combine; uniting.—**Combined**, kom-bīnd', *p.* and *a.* United; associated; leagued; conjoined.—**Combinedly**, kom-bī'ned-li, *adv.* In a combined manner; unitedly; jointly.—**Combiner**, kom-bī'nėr, *n.* One who or that which combines.

Combustible, kom-bus'ti-bl, *a.* [Fr. *combustible*, from L. *comburo*, *combustum*, to consume—*comb*, for *cum* or *con*, and *uro*, to burn; same root as Gr. *auein*, to kindle; Skr. *ush*, to burn.] Capable of taking fire and burning; inflammable; *fig.* fiery or irascible; hot-tempered.—*n.* A substance that will take fire and burn. — **Combustibility**, **Combustibleness**, kom-bus'ti-bil''i-ti, kom-bus'ti-bl-nes, *n.* The state or quality of being combustible.—**Combustion**, kom-bust'yon, *n.* The operation of fire on inflammable substances; burning; or, in chemical language, the union of an inflammable substance with oxygen or some other supporter of combustion, attended with heat, and in most instances with light. —*Spontaneous combustion*, the ignition of a body by the internal development of heat without the application of an external flame.

Come, kum, *v.i.*—*came* (pret.), *come* (pp.); *coming.* [A.Sax. *cuman* or *cwiman* = D. *komen*, Icel. *koma*, Dan. *komme*, Sw. *komma*, G. *kommen*, Goth. *kwiman*: also from same root, L. *venio*, to come; Gr. *bainō*, to go.] To move hitherward; to advance nearer in any manner and from any distance; to approach the person speaking or writing, or the person addressed: opposed to *go*; to arrive; to take place; to reach a certain stage or point of progress; to arrive at: followed by an infinitive (I now *come* to consider the next subject); to get into a certain state or condition: especially followed by *to be*; to happen or fall out; to befal (*come what* will); to advance or move into view; to appear (colour *comes* into the face); to accrue or result; to be formed (knowledge *comes*): frequently with *of* (this *comes* of not taking heed). *Come*, in the imperative, is used to excite attention, or to invite to motion or joint action; or it expresses earnestness, or haste, impatience, remonstrance, &c.—*To come and go*, to alternate; to appear and disappear.—*To come about*, to happen; to fall out (how did these things *come about*?). — *To come at*, to reach; to arrive within reach of; to gain.—*To come away*, to leave; to germinate; to sprout.—*To come by*, to pass near; to obtain, gain, acquire.—*To come down*, to descend; to be humbled or abased.—*To come home*, to come to one's dwelling; to touch nearly; to touch the feelings, interest, or reason.—*To come in*, to enter, as into an inclosure or a port; to become fashionable; to be brought into use.—*To come in for*, to get a share of; to get; to obtain.—*To come into*, to acquire by inheritance or bequest.—*To come near* or *nigh*, to approach in place; to approach in quality; to arrive at nearly the same degree. —*To come off*, to escape; to get free; to emerge (to *come off* with honour); to happen; to take place.—*To come on*, to advance; to progress; to thrive.—*To come out*, to remove from within; to become public; to be introduced to general society: said of a young lady; to appear after being obscured by clouds (the sun has *come out*); to result from calculation.—*To come out of*, to issue forth; to get clear of (he has *come out of* that affair very well).—*To come out with*, to give publicity to; to let out or disclose.—*To come over*, to pass above or across, or from one side to another.—*To come round*, to recover; to revive; to regain one's former state of health.—*To come short*, to fail; not to reach; to be inadequate.—*To come to*, to fall or be allotted to; to amount to.—*To come to one's self*, to get back one's consciousness; to recover.—*To come to pass*, to happen.—*To come true*, to be verified.—*To come up*, to ascend; to rise; to spring; to shoot or rise above the earth.—*To come up to*, to attain to; to equal; to amount to.—*To come up with*, to overtake in following or pursuit.—*Come your ways*, come along; come hither.—*To come*, future; in future (time *to come*).—**Comeatable**, kum-at'a-bl, *n.* [*Come*, *at*, and suffix *-able*.] Capable of being come at; capable of being reached or obtained. (Colloq.)—**Comer**, kum'ėr, *n.* One that comes; one who has arrived and is present.—*All comers*, any one that may come; everybody, without exclusion. —**Coming**, kum'ing, *p.* and *a.* Drawing nearer or nigh; approaching; moving toward; advancing; future; next in the future.—**Coming-in**, *n.* (pl. **Comings-in**). Entrance; arrival; introduction; income‡; revenue (*Shak.*)‡.

Comedy, kom'e-di, *n.* [L. *comœdia*, Gr. *kōmōdia*, a comedy, from *kōmos*, a revel or feast, and *ōdē*, a song.] A dramatic composition of a light and amusing class, its characters being represented as in the circumstances or meeting with the incidents of ordinary life.—**Comedian**, ko-mē'di-an, *n.* An actor or player in comedy; a player in general; a writer of comedy. — **Comedic**, ko-mē'dik, *a.* Pertaining to or having the nature of comedy.—**Comedietta**, ko-mē'di-et''ta, *n.* A dramatic composition of the comedy class, in one or at most two acts and not so much elaborated as a regular comedy.

Comely, kum'li, *a.* [A.Sax. *cymlic*, comely, from *cyme*, suitable, from *cuman*, to *come*.] Handsome; graceful; symmetrical; well-proportioned; decent; suitable; proper; becoming. — **Comeliness**, kum'li-nes, *n.* The quality of being comely.

Comestible, ko-mes'ti-bl, *n.* [Fr. *comestible*, from L. *comedo*, *comesum* or *comestum*, to eat up—*com*, and *edo*, to eat.] An eatable; an article of solid food.

Comet, kom'et, *n.* [L. *cometa*, from Gr. *komētēs*, long-haired, a comet, from *komē*, hair: from the appearance of its tail.] The name given to certain celestial bodies consisting of a star-like nucleus, surrounded by a luminous envelope, called the *coma*, and usually accompanied with a tail or train of light, appearing at irregular intervals, moving through the heavens in paths which seem to correspond with parabolic curves, or in a few instances in elliptical orbits of great eccentricity. — **Cometic**, **Cometary**, ko-met'ik, kom'et-a-ri, *a.* Pertaining to a comet.—**Comet-finder**, *n.* A telescope of low power, but with a wide field, used to discover comets.—**Cometographer**, kom-e-tog'raf-ėr, *n.* One who writes about comets.—**Cometography**, kom-e-tog'ra-fi, *n.* A description of, or treatise on, comets.—**Cometology**, kom-e-tol'o-ji, *n.* A discourse on comets; that branch of astronomy which investigates comets.

Comfit, kum'fit, *n.* [Fr. *confit*, pp. of *confire*, to preserve, to make into a sweetmeat, from L. *conficere*—*con*, together, and *facio*, to make.] A dry sweetmeat; any kind of fruit or root preserved with sugar and dried; a bon-bon; a lollipop.

Comfort, kum'fėrt, *v.t.* [O.E. *confort*, from O.Fr. *conforter*, to comfort, from L.L. *confortare*, to strengthen—*con*, intens., and L. *fortis*, brave.] To raise from depression; to soothe when in grief or trouble; to bring solace or consolation to; to console; to cheer; to hearten; to solace; to enliven.—*n.* Relief from affliction, sorrow, or trouble of any kind; solace; consolation; a state of quiet or moderate enjoyment, resulting from the possession of what satisfies bodily wants and freedom from all care or anxiety; a feeling or state of well-being, satisfaction, or content; that which furnishes moderate enjoyment or content. — **Comfortable**, kum'fėrt-a-bl, *a.* Being in comfort or in a state of ease or moderate enjoyment; giving comfort; affording help, ease, or consolation.—**Comfortableness**, kum'fėrt-a-bl-nes, *n.* The state of being comfortable.—**Comfortably**, kum'fėrt-a-bli, *adv.* In a comfortable manner; in a manner to give comfort or consolation. — **Comforter**, kum'fėrt-ėr, *n.* One who comforts; a knit woollen fabric for tying round the neck in cold weather.—**Comfortless**, kum'fėrt-les, *a.* Without comfort; without affording or without being attended by any comfort. —**Comfortlessly**, kum'fėrt-les-li, *adv.*—**Comfortlessness**, kum'fėrt-les-nes, *n.*

Comfrey, **Comfry**, kum'fri, *n.* [Fr. *conferve*, L. *conferva*, from *conferveo*, to heal, to grow together, from prefix *con*, and *ferveo*, to boil, from the plant's supposed healing power.] A name given to several species of rough herbaceous European and Asiatic plants, one species of which, the common comfrey, found in Britain on the banks of rivers and ditches, was formerly in high repute as a vulnerary.

Comic, kom'ik, *a.* [L. *comicus*, Gr. *kōmikos*. COMEDY.] Relating or belonging to comedy, as distinct from tragedy; also comical.—*n.* A comic actor or singer.—**Comical**, kom'ik-al, *a.* Exciting mirth; ludicrous; laughable; diverting; sportive; droll.—**Comicality**, kom-i-kal'i-ti, *n.* The quality of being comical; ludicrousness; that which is comical or ludicrous.—**Comically**, kom'ik-al-li, *adv.* In a comical manner; in a manner to raise mirth; laughably; ludicrously.—**Comicalness**, kom'ik-al-nes, *n.* The quality of being comical; comicality.—**Comique**, kom-ēk, *n.* [Fr.] A comic actor or singer.

Comitia, kō-mish'i-a, *n. pl.* [L.] Legislative assemblies or meetings among the ancient Romans.—**Comitial**, kō-mish'i-al, *a.* Pertaining to the comitia.

Comity, kom'i-ti, *n.* [L. *comitas*, from *comis*, mild, affable.] Mildness and suavity of manners; courtesy; civility; good breeding.—*Comity of nations* (*comitas gentium*), that kind of courtesy by which the laws and institutions of one state or country are recognized and to some extent given effect to by the government of another within its territory.

Comma, kom'ma, *n.* [Gr. *komma*, a segment, from *koptō*, to cut off.] A punctuation mark [,] denoting the shortest pause in reading, and separating a sentence into divisions or members, according to the construction; *mus.* an enharmonic interval, being the difference between a major and a minor tone.

Command, kom-mand' or kom-mänd', *v.t.* [Fr. *commander*, L. *commendo*, to intrust, later to enjoin, to command—*com* for *con*, and *mando*, to commit to, to command.] To order with authority; to lay injunction upon; to direct; to charge; to have or to exercise supreme authority, especially military authority, over; to have control over;

to dominate through position, often specifically military position; to have within the range of the eye; to overlook; to exact or compel by moral influence; to challenge (to *command* respect); to have at one's disposal and service (to *command* assistance).—*v.i.* To act as or have the authority of a commander; to exercise influence or power.—*n.* The power of governing with chief authority; supreme power; control; exercise of authority; a commandment; mandate; order; power or control, as from holding an advantageous military position; the power of overlooking from elevated position; a force under the command of a particular officer. **Commandable**, kom-man'da-bl, *a.* Capable of being commanded.—**Commandant**, kom-man-dant', *n.* [Fr.] A commander. — **Commander**, kom-man'dėr, *n.* One who commands; a chief; one who has supreme authority; a leader; the chief officer of an army or of any division of it; a naval officer next in rank above lieutenant and under the captain; one on whom is bestowed a commandery.—*Commander-in-chief*, a supreme military commander; the highest staff appointment in the British army. — **Commandeer**, kom-mand-ēr', *v.t.* [African-Dutch.] To impress or force men or stores for military purposes.—**Commandership**, kom-man'dėr-ship, *n.* The office of a commander.—**Commandery**, kom-man'dėr-i, *n.* [Fr. *commanderie.*] Among several orders of knights, and in certain religious orders, a district under the control of a member of the order called a commander or preceptor; the office of such a member; the official building of a commandery. — **Commanding**, kom-man'ding, *a.* Governing; bearing rule; exercising supreme authority; controlling by influence, authority, or dignity (*commanding* eloquence); dominating; overlooking a wide region without obstruction (a *commanding* eminence). — **Commandingly**, kom-man'ding-li, *adv.* In a commanding manner. — **Commandment**, kom-mand'ment, *n.* A command; a mandate; an order or injunction given by authority; charge; precept; a precept of the decalogue; authority; power of commanding.—**Commando**, kom-man'dō, *n.* [D. *commando*, lit. a command.] A body of armed men raised for military service among the Boers or other whites of South Africa; a military expedition undertaken by such a body of men.

Commeasure,† kom-mezh'ūr, *v.t.* To coincide with; to be co-extensive with.—**Commeasurable**,† kom-mezh'ūr-a-bl, *a.* Commensurate; equal.

Commemorate, kom-mem'or-āt, *v.t.*—*commemorated, commemorating.* [L. *commemoro — com*, and *memoro*, to mention. MEMORY.] To preserve the memory of by a solemn act; to celebrate with honour and solemnity. — **Commemoration**, kom-mem'o-rā"shon, *n.* The act of commemorating or calling to remembrance by some solemnity; the act of honouring the memory of some person or event by solemn celebration. — **Commemorable**, kom-mem'or-a-bl, *a.* Worthy to be commemorated.—**Commemorative**, kom-mem'or-āt-iv, *a.* Tending to commemorate or preserve the remembrance of something.—**Commemorator**, kom-mem'or-āt-ėr, *n.* One who commemorates. — **Commemoratory**, kom-mem'o-ra-to-ri, *a.* Serving to commemorate.

Commence, kom-mens', *v.t.*—*commenced, commencing.* [Fr. *commencer*, from a (hypothetical) L.L. *cominitiare*—L. prefix *com*, and *initiare*, to begin. INITIATE.] To begin; to take rise or origin; to have first existence; to begin to be, as in a new state or character.—*v.t.* To begin; to enter upon; to perform the first act of.—**Commencement**, kom-mens'ment, *n.* The act or fact of commencing; beginning; rise; origin; first existence; the day when, or the ceremonies at which, degrees are conferred.

Commend, kom-mend', *v.t.* [L. *commendo*, to commit, to commend—*com*, and *mando*, to commit to; the same word as *command* with a different signification.] To commit, deliver, intrust, or give in charge (N.T.); to represent as worthy of confidence, notice, regard, or kindness; to recommend; with reflexive pronoun sometimes to call for notice or attention (this subject *commends itself* to our attention); to mention with approbation; to mention by way of keeping in memory; to send greetings or compliments from (*Shak.*).—*v.i.* To approve; to praise.—**Commendable**, kom-men'da-bl, *a.* Capable or worthy of being commended or praised; praiseworthy; laudable. — **Commendableness**, kom-men'da-bl-nes, *n.* State of being commendable.—**Commendably**, kom-men'da-bli, *adv.* In a commendable or praiseworthy manner.—**Commendam**, kom-men'dam, *n.* [L.L.] An ecclesiastical benefice or living commended to the care of a qualified person to hold till a proper pastor is provided. When a beneficed parson was made a bishop, and was empowered to retain his benefice, he was said to hold it *in commendam.*—**Commendatary**, kom-men'da-ta-ri, *a.* Holding *in commendam.*—*n.* One who holds a living *in commendam.*—**Commendator**, kom-men'da-tėr, *n.* One who holds a benefice *in commendam.*—**Commendatory**, kom-men'da-to-ri, *a.* Serving to commend; presenting to favourable notice or reception; containing praise; holding a benefice *in commendam.* — **Commendation**, kom-men-dā'shon, *n.* [L. *commendatio.*] The act of commending; praise; favourable representation in words; declaration of esteem; respects; greeting; message of love. —**Commender**, kom-men'dėr, *n.* One who commends or praises.

Commensal, kom-men'sal, *n.* [L. *com*, with, and *mensa*, table.] One that eats at the same table‡; one of two animals or plants that are always found together; an animal which lives on or in another without being parasitic.—*a.* Having the character of a commensal. — **Commensalism**, kom-men'sal-izm, *n.* The state of being commensal.

Commensurable, kom-men'sū-ra-bl, *a.* [L. prefix *com*, and *mensura*, measure. MEASURE.] Having a common measure; reducible to a common measure.—**Commensurability**, **Commensurableness**, kom-men'sū-ra-bil"i-ti, kom-men'sū-ra-bl-nes, *n.* The state of being commensurable, or of having a common measure.—**Commensurably**, kom-men'sū-ra-bli, *adv.* In a commensurable manner.—**Commensurate**, kom-men'sū-rāt, *a.* Reducible to a common measure; of equal size; having the same boundaries; corresponding in amount, degree, or magnitude; adequate.—**Commensurately**, kom-men'sū-rāt-li, *adv.* In a commensurate manner; so as to be commensurate; correspondingly; adequately. — **Commensurateness**, kom-men'sū-rāt-nes, *n.* State or quality of being commensurate. — **Commensuration**, kom-men'sū-rā"shon, *n.* Proportion; a state of being commensurate.

Comment, kom-ment', *v.i.* [L. *commentor*, from *commentus*, pp. of *comminiscor*, to reflect on—*com*, with, together with, and stem *min*, seen in *memini*, to remember, and in E. *mind.*] To make remarks or observations, either on a book or writing, or on actions, events, or opinions; to write notes on the works of an author, with a view to illustrate his meaning, or to explain particular passages; to make annotations. —*n.* (kom'ment). A remark or observation; a note intended to illustrate a difficult passage in an author; annotation; exposition; talk; discourse. — **Commentary**, kom'men-ta-ri, *n.* A series or collection of comments or annotations; a historical narrative; a memoir of particular transactions (the *Commentaries* of Cæsar).—**Commentate**,† kom-men'tāt, *v.i.* To make comments; to write a commentary or annotations. (*Lamb.*) — **Commentation**, kom-men-tā'shon, *n.* The act of one who comments; annotation. — **Commentative**, kom-men'ta-tiv, *a.* Making or containing comments. — **Commentator**, kom'men-tā-tėr, *n.* One who writes a commentary; one who writes annotations; an annotator.—**Commentatorial**, kom-men'ta-tō"ri-al, *a.* Relating to or characteristic of commentators.—**Commenter**, kom'men-tėr, *n.* One who comments.

Commerce, kom'mėrs, *n.* [Fr. *commerce*, L. *commercium*—*com*, together with, and *merx, mercis*, merchandise.] An interchange of goods, merchandise, or property of any kind between countries or communities; mercantile pursuits; trade; traffic; mutual dealings in common life; intercourse.—*v.t.* To carry on trade‡; to hold intercourse; to commune.— **Commercial**, kom-mėr'shal, *a.* Pertaining to commerce or trade; dealing with or depending on commerce; carrying on commerce.—*Commercial announcement*, an announcement made over the radio concerning the product of the advertiser who sponsors the program.—**Commercialism**, kom-mėr'shal-izm, *n.* The doctrines, tenets, or practices of commerce or of commercial men.

Commination, kom-mi-nā'shon *n.* [L. *comminatio—com*, and *minatio*, a threatening, from *minor*, to threaten. MENACE.] A threat or threatening; a denunciation of punishment or vengeance; an office in the liturgy of the Church of England, appointed to be read on Ash Wednesday or on the first day of Lent.—**Comminatory**, kom-min'a-to-ri, *a.* Threatening; denouncing punishment.

Commingle, kom-ming'gl, *v.t.* or *i.*—*commingled, commingling.* [Prefix *com*, and *mingle.*] To mix together; to mingle in one mass or intimately; to blend.

Comminute, kom'mi-nūt, *v.t.* — *comminuted, comminuting.* [L. *comminuo, comminutum*, to make small—*com*, with, and *minuo*, to lessen; root *min*, as in *minor*, less.] To make small or fine; to reduce to minute particles or to a fine powder; to pulverize; to triturate; to levigate. — *a.* Divided into very small parts or particles.—**Comminution**, kom-mi-nū'shon, *n.* The act of comminuting or reducing to a fine powder or to small particles; pulverization.

Commiserate, kom-miz'ėr-āt, *v.t.*—*commiserated, commiserating.* [L. *commiseror —com*, and *miseror*, to pity. MISERABLE.] To feel sorrow, pain, or regret for, through sympathy; to compassionate; to pity.—**Commiseration**, kom-miz'ėr-ā"shon, *n.* The act of commiserating: a sympathetic suffering of pain or sorrow for the afflictions or distresses of another; pity; compassion.—**Commiserative**, kom-miz'ėr-ā-tiv, *a.* Compassionate.—**Commiseratively**, kom-miz'ėr-ā-tiv-li, *adv.* In a compassionate manner; with compassion.—**Commiserator**, kom-miz'ėr-ā-tėr, *n.* One who commiserates or pities.

Commissary, kom'mis-a-ri, *n.* [Fr. *commissaire*, L.L. *commissarius*, one to whom any trust or duty is delegated; L. *committo, commissum*, to commit.] In a general sense, a commissioner; one to whom is committed some charge, duty, or office by a superior power; *eccles.* an officer of a bishop exercising spiritual jurisdiction in remote parts of a diocese, or one intrusted with the performance of the duties in the bishop's absence; *Scots law*, the judge in a commissary-court; *milit.* a name given to officers or officials of various kinds, especially to officers of the commissariat department —**Commissarial**, kom-mis-sā'ri-al, *a.* Pertaining to a commissary.—**Commissariat**, kom-mis-sā'ri-at, *n.* The department of an army whose duties consist in supplying transport, provisions, forage, camp equipage, &c., to the troops; also, the body of officers in that department; the office or employment of a commissary; the district of country over which the authority or jurisdiction of a commissary extends.—Any of the departments of government within the Union of Soviet Socialist Republics; a body of commissars.

Commission, kom-mish'on, *n.* [L. *commissio, commissionis.* COMMIT.] The act of committing; the act of doing something wrong; the act of perpetrating (the *com-*

mission of a crime); the act of intrusting, as a charge or duty; the thing committed, intrusted, or delivered: a duty, office, charge, or piece of work intrusted to any one; the warrant by which any trust is held, or any authority exercised (as that of an officer in an army); mandate; authority given; a number of persons joined in an office or trust; commissioners; the state of acting in the purchase and sale of goods for another; position or business of an agent; agency; the allowance made to an agent for transacting business.—*Commission of the Justice of the Peace*, a warrant of authority issued by the state for the granting of certain powers to, and the appointment of, Justices of the Peace.—*To put a ship into commission*, to equip and man a vessel, and place it in service after it has been in dry dock for repairs—*v.t.* To give a commission to: to give special powers and instructions for the accomplishment of an act; to empower or authorize by special commission: to send with a mandate or authority.—**Commission-agent, Commission-merchant**, *n.* One who buys or sells goods for another on commission.—**Commissionaire**, kom-mēs-yōn-ār, *n.* [Fr.] At European hotels and terminals, a kind of messenger or light porter.—**Commissional,**† **Commissionary,**† kom-mish′on-al, kom-mish′on-a-ri, *a.* Pertaining to a commission.—**Commissioned**, kom-mish′ond, *p.* and *a.* Furnished with a commission, holding a commission; empowered, authorized.—**Commissioner**, kom-mish′on-ér, *n.* One who commissions: a person who has a commission or warrant from proper authority to perform some office or execute some business; an officer having charge of some department of the public service, which is put into commission; a steward or agent who manages affairs on a large estate; one of the persons elected to manage the affairs of a police burgh or non-corporate town in Scotland.

Commissure, kom′mis-sūr, *n.* [Fr. *commissure*, from L. *commissura*, a joining together, joint, seam—*com*, together, and *mitto*, *missum*, to send.] A joint or seam; the place where two parts of a body meet and unite; a juncture; a suture: used chiefly in *anat.*—**Commissural**, kom-mis-sū′ral, *a.* Belonging to a commissure.

Commit, kom-mit′, *v.t.*—*committed, committing.* [L. *committo*, to make over in trust, to set to work, do wrong—*com*, together, and *mitto*, to send, whence also *admit, permit, dismiss, mission, missile*, &c.] To give in trust; to put into charge or keeping: to intrust; to surrender, give up, consign: with *to*; *refl.* to bind to a certain line of conduct, or to expose or endanger by a preliminary step or decision which cannot be recalled; to compromise; to order or send into confinement; to imprison (the magistrate *commits* a guilty person); to refer or intrust to a committee or select number of persons for their consideration and report; to do (generally something wrong); to perpetrate.—*To commit to memory*, to learn by heart.—**Committable, Committible**, kom-mit′a-bl, kom-mit′i-bl, *a.* Capable of being committed.—**Commitment, Committal**, kom-mit′ment, kom-mit′al, *n.* The act of committing; commission (but we do not say the *committal* or *commitment* of crimes, but the *commission*).—**Committee**, kom-mit′tē, *n.* A body of persons elected or appointed to attend to any matter or business referred to them, often a section of a larger body.—*Committee of the whole house*, an arrangement by which matters are discussed in a particular manner in congress, the chair being occupied by the chairman of committee, and members being allowed to speak more than once on a question.—**Committee-man**, *n.* A member of a committee, as of the national, state, county, and city district.—**Committee-room**, *n.* A room in which a committee holds its meetings.—**Committer**, kom-mit′ér, *n.*

Commix, kom-miks′, *v.t.* or *i.* [L. *commisceo, commixtus—com*, together, and *misceo*, to mix. MIX.] To mix or mingle; to blend.—**Commixtion**, kom-miks′tyon, *n.* Mixture; a blending together.—**Commixture**, kom-miks′tūr, *n.* The act of mixing; the state of being mingled; the mass formed by mingling; a compound.

Commode, kom-mōd′, *n.* [Fr., from L. *commodus*, convenient. COMMODIOUS.] A kind of head-dress formerly worn by ladies; a chest of drawers, often with shelves and other conveniences added; a night-stool.

Commodious, kom-mō′di-us, *a.* [L.L. *commodiosus*, from L. *commodus*, useful—*com*, together, and *modus*, measure, mode.] Roomy and convenient; spacious and suitable; serviceable.—**Commodiously**, kom-mō′di-us-li, *adv.* So as to be commodious.—**Commodiousness**, kom-mō′di-us-nes, *n.* The state or quality of being commodious.—**Commodity**, kom-mod′i-ti, *n.* [Fr. *commodité*, convenience, commodity; L. *commoditas*, fitness, convenience.] Suitableness or convenience†; what is useful; specifically, an article of merchandise; anything movable that is bought and sold, as goods, wares, produce of land and manufactures.

Commodore, kom′mō-dōr, *n.* [From Sp. *commendador*, a commander, or from Pg. *capitao mor*, superior captain.] An officer who commands a detachment of ships in the absence of an admiral; a title given by courtesy to the senior captain when three or more ships of war are cruising in company, to the senior captain of a line of merchant vessels, and to the president of a yachting club; the leading ship in a fleet of merchantmen.

Common, kom′on, *a.* [Fr. *commun*, L. *communis—com*, together, and *munis*, ready to be of service, obliging.] Belonging or pertaining equally to more than one, or to many indefinitely; belonging to all; general; universal; public; of frequent or usual occurrence; not extraordinary; frequent; usual; ordinary; habitual; not distinguished by rank or character; not of superior excellence; of low or mean rank or character; *gram.* applied to such nouns as are both masculine and feminine, and to those that are the names of all the objects possessing the attributes denoted by the noun (river, &c.).—*Common council*, the council of a city or corporate town, empowered to make bylaws for the government of the citizens.—*Common law*, the unwritten law, the law that receives its binding force from immemorial usage and universal reception, in distinction from the written or statute law.—*Common measure*, a number or quantity that divides two or more numbers or quantities without leaving a remainder.—*Common Pleas*, formerly one of the three superior courts of common law in England, now a division of the High Court of Justice.—*Common Prayer*, the liturgy or public form of prayer prescribed by the Church of England to be used in all churches and chapels.—*Common seal*, a seal used by a corporation as the symbol of their incorporation.—*Common sense*, sound practical judgment; the natural sagacity or understanding of mankind in general.—*Common time*, musical time or rhythm with two, four, or eight beats to a bar.—*In common*, equally with another or with others.—*n.* A tract of ground, the use of which is not appropriated to an individual, but belongs to the public or to a number; in all other senses *pl.*: the common people; the untitled; the vulgar, the lower house of the British Parliament, consisting of the representatives of cities, boroughs, and counties; food provided at a common table, as at colleges; food or fare in general.—*Short commons*, stinted allowance.—*Extra commons*, increased allowance.—**Commonage**, kom′on-āj, *n.* The right of pasturing on a common; the joint right of using anything in common with others.—**Commonalty**, kom′on-al-ti, *n.* The common people; all below the rank of nobility.—**Commoner**, kom′on-ér, *n.* A person under the degree of nobility; a student of the second rank in the University of Oxford, not dependent on the foundation for support.—**Commonly**, kom′on-li, *adv.* In a common manner; usually; generally; ordinarily; frequently; for the most part.—**Commonness**, kom′on-nes, *n.* The state or fact of being common.—**Commonplace**, kom′on-plās, *a.* Not new or extraordinary; common; trite.—*n.* A memorandum of something that is likely to be frequently referred to; a well-known or customary remark; a trite saying; a platitude.—**Commonplace-book**, *n.* A book in which things to be remembered are recorded.—**Commonweal**, kom′on-wēl, *n.* A commonwealth; the body politic; a state.—**Commonwealth**, kom′on-welth, *n.* [Here *wealth* means strictly well-being.] The body politic; the public; a republican state; the form of government which existed in England from the death of Charles I in 1649 to the abdication of Richard Cromwell in 1659.

Commotion, kom-mō′shon, *n.* [L. *commotio*, from *commoveo, commotum—com*, with, and *moveo*, to move. MOVE.] Agitation; tumult of people; disturbance; perturbation; disorder of mind; excitement.—**Commove**,† kom-möv′, *v.t.*—*commoved, commoving.* [L. *commoveo*.] To put in motion; to disturb; to agitate; to unsettle.

Commune, kom-mūn′, *v.i.*—*communed, communing.* [Fr. *communier*; L. *communico*, to communicate, from *communis*, common. COMMON.] To converse; to talk together familiarly; to impart sentiments mutually; to interchange ideas or feelings.—*n.* (kom′mūn). Familiar interchange of ideas or sentiments; communion; intercourse; friendly conversation (to hold *commune*, to be in *commune*).

Commune, kom′mūn, *n.* [Fr., from *commun*, common.] A small territorial district in France and in some other countries, under the government of a mayor; the inhabitants of a commune; the members of a communal council.—*The commune of Paris*, a revolutionary committee which took the place of the municipality of Paris in the French revolution of 1789; also, a committee or body of communalists who in 1871 for a brief period ruled over Paris after the evacuation of the German troops.—**Communal**, kom′mū-nal, *a.* Pertaining to a commune or to communalism.—**Communalism**, kom′mū-nal-izm, *n.* The theory of government by communes or other local self-governing bodies.—**Communalist**, kom′mū-na-list, *n.* One who adheres to communalism.—**Communalistic**, kom′mū-na-lis″tik, *a.* Pertaining to communalism.—**Communism**, kom′mūn-izm, *n.* [Fr. *communisme*.] The system or theory which upholds the absorption of all proprietary rights in a common interest; the doctrine of a community of property.—**Communist**, kom′mūn-ist, *n.* One who holds the doctrines of communism.—**Communistic**, kom-mū-nis′tik, *a.* Relating to communists or communism, according to the principles of communism.—**Communistically**, kom-mū-nis′tik-al-li, *adv.* In accordance with communism; in a communistic way or form.

Communicate, kom-mū′ni-kāt, *v.t.*—*communicated, communicating.* [L. *communico*, from *communis*, common.] To impart to another or others; to bestow or confer for joint possession, generally or always something intangible, as intelligence, news, opinions, or disease: with *to* before the receiver.—*v.i.* To share; to participate; followed by *in*; to have a communication or passage from one to another (one room *communicates with* another); to have or hold intercourse or interchange of thoughts; to partake of the Lord's supper or communion.—**Communicability**, kom-mū′ni-ka-bil″i-ti, *n.* The quality of being communicable; capability of being imparted.—**Communicable**, kom-mū′ni-ka-bl, *a.* Capable of being communicated or imparted from one to another; capable of being recounted; communicative; ready to impart information, news, &c.—**Communicableness**, kom-mū′ni-ka-bl-nes, *n.*—**Communicant**, kom-mū′ni-kant, *n.* One who communicates or partakes of the sacrament at the celebration of the Lord's supper.—**Communication**, kom-mū′ni-kā″shon, *n.* The act of communicating; means of communicating; connecting passage; means of passing from place to place; that which is communicated or imparted; information or intelligence imparted by word or writing; a document or message imparting information.—**Communicative**, kom-mū'ni-kā-tiv, *a.* Inclined to communicate; ready to impart to others; free in communicating; not reserved; open.—**Communicatively**, kom-mū'ni-kā-tiv-li, *adv.* In a communicative manner; by communication.—**Communicativeness**, kom-mū'ni-kā-tiv-nes, *n.* The state or quality of being communicative; readiness to impart to others; freedom from reserve.—**Communicator**, kom-mū'ni-kā-tėr, *n.* One who or that which communicates.—**Communicatory**, kom-mū'ni-kā-to-ri, *a.* Imparting knowledge.

Communion, kom-mūn'yon, *n.* [L. *communio, communionis*, participation.] Participation of something in common; fellowship; concord; bond or association; intercourse between two or more persons; interchange of thoughts or acts; union in religious worship, or in doctrine and discipline; union with a church; a body of Christians who have one common faith and discipline; the act of partaking in the sacrament of the eucharist; the celebration of the Lord's supper.—*Communion elements*, the bread and wine used in the sacrament of the Lord's supper.—**Communionable**, kom-mūn'yon-a-bl, *a.* Admission to communion.

Communique, *n.* [Fr.] An official communication, a statement given to the Press.

Communism, &c. Under COMMUNE, *n.*

Community, kom-mū'ni-ti, *n.* [L. *communitas*. COMMON.] Common possession or enjoyment (a *community* of goods); a society of people having common rights and privileges; a society of individuals of any kind; the body of people in a state; the public, or people in general: used in this sense always with the definite article; common character (individuals distinguished by *community* of descent).

Commute, kom-mūt', *v.t.*—*commuted, commuting*. [L. *commuto*—prefix *com*, and *muto*, to change. MUTABLE, MUTATION.] To exchange; to put one thing in the place of another; to give or receive one thing for another; to exchange, as one penalty or punishment for one of less severity; to pay in money instead of in kind or in duty; to travel back and forth daily between places, as to and from a city.—**Commuter**, one who travels to and from a city, daily.—**Commutability, Commutableness**, kom-mūt'a-bil"i-ti, kom-mūt'a-bl-nes, *n.* The quality of being commutable; interchangeableness.—**Commutation**, kom-mū-tā'shon, *n.* [L. *commutatio*.] The act of commuting; the act of substituting one thing for another; the change of a penalty or punishment from a greater to a less.—*Commutation ticket*. A railroad ticket at a reduced rate for a number of trips, between stations.—**Commutative**, kom-mūt'a-tiv, *a.* Relating to exchange; interchangeable; mutual.—**Commutatively**, kom-mūt'a-tiv-li, *adv.* By way of exchange.—**Commutator**, kom'-mū-tā-tėr, *n.* [L. *commutatio*, a change] *Elect.* A device for converting an alternating current into a direct one; the rotating terminal of the armature of an electric motor or generator.

Comose, kō-mōs', *a.* [L. *coma*, hair.] Hairy; comate.

Compact, kom-pakt', *a.* [L. *compactus*, pp. of *compingo, compactum*, to join or unite together—*com*, together, and *pango*, to fix.] Closely and firmly united, as the parts or particles of solid bodies; having the parts or particles close; solid; dense; not diffuse; not verbose; concise; composed; made up: with *of* (*Shak.*).—*v.t.* To thrust, drive, or press closely together; to join firmly; to consolidate; to make close; to unite or connect firmly, as in a system.—**Compactly**, kom-pakt'li, *adv.* In a compact or condensed manner; closely; concisely; briefly; tersely; neat.—**Compactness**, kom-pakt'nes, *n.* State of being compact.

Compact, kom'pakt, *n.* [L. *compactum*, a compact, from *compaciscor, compactus*, to make an agreement—*com*, together, and *paciscor*, to fix, settle, covenant.] An agreement; a contract, covenant, bargain, or settlement between parties.—**Compacter**, kom-pak'tėr, *n.* One who makes a compact.

Compages,† **Compage**,† kom-pā'jēz, kom-pāj', *n.* [L. *compages*, from *compingo*. COMPACT, close.] A system or structure of many parts united.

Companion, kom-pan'yon, *n.* [O.Fr. *compainon, companion*; Fr. *compagnon*—L. *com*, together, and *panis*, bread; lit. a sharer of one's bread; a mess-fellow.] One with whom a person frequently associates and converses; a mate; a comrade; one who accompanies another; a person holding the lowest rank in an order of knighthood (as of the Bath).—*a.* Accompanying; united with.—*v.t.* To be a companion to; to accompany; to put on the same level (*Shak.*)‡.—**Companionable**, kom-pan'yon-a-bl, *a.* Fit for good fellowship; qualified to be agreeable in company; sociable.—**Companionableness**, kom-pan'yon-a-bl-nes, *n.* The quality of being companionable; sociableness.—**Companionably**, kom-pan'yon-a-bli, *adv.* In a companionable manner.—**Companionless**, kom-pan'yonles, *a.* Having no companion.—**Companionship**, kom-pan'yon-ship, *n.* The state or fact of being a companion; fellowship; association.—**Company**, kum'pa-ni, *n.* [Fr. *compagnie*; O.Fr. also *companie*.] The state of being along with; companionship; fellowship; society; any assemblage of persons; a collection of men or other animals, in a very indefinite sense; guests at a person's house; a number of persons united for performing or carrying on anything jointly, as some commercial enterprise, the term being applicable to private partnerships or to incorporated bodies; a firm (but this word usually implies fewer partners than *company*); the members of a firm whose names do not appear in the style or title of the firm: usually contracted when written (Messrs. Smith & *Co.*); a subdivision of an infantry regiment or battalion commanded by a captain; the crew of a ship, including the officers.—*To bear* or *keep* (a person) *company*, to accompany; to attend; to go with; to associate with.—*To be good company*, to be an entertaining companion.—*v.t.* and *i.*† To associate or associate with; to frequent the company of.

Companion, kom-pan'yon, *n.* [Comp. O.Sp. *compaña*, an outhouse.] *Naut.* the framing and sash-lights upon a quarter-deck, through which light passes to the cabins below; a raised cover to the cabin stair of a merchant vessel.—*Companion ladder*, the steps or ladder between the main-deck and the quarter-deck.—*Companion way*, the staircase at the entrance to the cabin of a vessel.

Compare, kom-pār', *v.t.*—*compared, comparing*. [L. *compaño*, to put together, unite, match, compare—*com*, together, and *par*, equal, whence *peer, pair, parity*. PAIR.] To set or bring together in fact or in contemplation, and examine the relations they bear to each other, especially with a view to ascertain agreement or disagreement, resemblances or differences (to *compare* one thing *with* another); to liken; to represent as similar for the purpose of illustration (to *compare* one thing *to* another); *gram.* to inflect by the degrees of comparison.—*v.i.* To hold or stand comparison; to contrast favourably.—*n.* Comparison; scope or room for comparison (rich beyond *compare*).—**Comparable**, kom'pa-ra-bl, *a.* [L. *comparabilis*.] Capable of being compared; worthy of comparison; being of equal regard.—**Comparableness**, kom'pa-ra-bl-nes, *n.* State of being comparable.—**Comparably**, kom'pa-ra-bli, *adv.* By comparison; so as to be compared.—**Comparative**, kom-par'a-tiv, *a.* (L. *comparativus*.] Estimated by comparison; not positive or absolute; proceeding by comparison; founded on comparison, especially founded on the comparison of different things belonging to the same science or study (*comparative* anatomy, &c.); having the power of comparing different things (the *comparative* faculty; *gram.* expressing a greater degree; expressing more than the positive but less than the superlative: applied to forms of adjectives and adverbs.—*n.* *Gram.* the comparative degree.—**Comparatively**, kom-par'a-tiv-li, *adv.* By comparison; according to estimate made by comparison; not positively, absolutely, or in itself.—**Comparer**, kom-pā'rėr, *n.* One who compares.—**Comparison**, kom-par'i-son, *n.* [Fr. *comparaison*, L. *comparatio*.] The act of comparing; the act of examining in order to discover how one thing stands with regard to another; the state of being compared; relation between things such as admits of their being compared; something with which another thing is compared; a similitude, or illustration by similitude; a parallel; *gram.* the inflection of an adjective or adverb to express degrees of the original quality.

Compartment, kom-pärt'ment, *n.* [Fr. *compartiment*, L.L. *compartimentum*, from L. *compartior*, to divide, share, from *pars, partis*, a part.] A division or separate part of a general design, as of a building, railroad car, picture, plan, or the like.

Compass, kum'pas, *n.* [Fr. *compas*, from L.L. *compassus*, a circuit—L. *com*, and *passus*, a step. PACE.] A passing round; a circular course; a circuit (to fetch a *compass*, that is, to make a circuit or round); limit or boundary; extent; range: applied to time, space, sound, &c.; moderate estimate; moderation; due limits (to keep within *compass*); an instrument consisting essentially of a magnet suspended so as to have as complete freedom of motion as possible, and used to indicate the magnetic meridian or the position of objects with respect to that meridian; a mathematical instrument for describing circles, measuring figures, distances between two points, &c.: often with the plural designation *compasses*, or a *pair of compasses*.—*v.t.* To stretch round; to encompass; to inclose, encircle, environ, surround; to go or walk about or round; to obtain; to attain to; to accomplish (to *compass* one's purposes); *law*, to plot; to contrive (a person's death).—**Compassable**, kum'pas-a-bl, *a.* Capable of being compassed.—**Compass-needle**, *n.* The magnetized needle of a compass.—**Compass-plant**, *n.* A composite plant, common on the prairies of North America: so called from being disposed to present the edges of its leaves north and south.—**Compass-saw**, *n.* A saw with a narrow blade, so that it may be made to cut round in a circle of moderate radius.—**Compass-window**, *n.* *Arch.* a circular bay-window or oriel.

Compassion, kom-pa'shon, *n.* [Fr. *compassion*, L. *compassio*. PASSION.] A suffering with another; sympathy; pity; commiseration; an act of mercy (O.T.)‡.—**Compassionable**,† kom-pa'shon-a-bl, *a.* Deserving of pity.—**Compassionate**, kom-pa'shon-āt, *a.* Characterized by compassion; full of pity; tender-hearted.—*v.t.*—*compassionated, compassionating*. To pity; to commiserate; to have compassion for.—**Compassionately**, kom-pa'shon-āt-li, *adv.* In a compassionate manner; with compassion; mercifully.—**Compassionateness**, kom-pa'shon-āt-nes, *n.* The quality of being compassionate.

Compatible, kom-pat'i-bl, *a.* [Fr. *compatible*, L.L. *compatibilis*—L. *com*, together, and *patior*, to suffer.] Capable of coexisting or being found together in the same subject; capable of existing together in harmony; suitable; agreeable; not incongruous (things *compatible* with one another).—**Compatibility, Compatibleness**, kom-pat'i-bil"i-ti, kom-pat'i-bl-nes, *n.* The quality of being compatible; consistency; suitableness.—**Compatibly**, kom-pat'i-bli, *adv.* In a compatible manner; fitly; suitably; consistently.

Compatriot, kom-pā'tri-ot, *n.* [Fr. *com-*

patriote.] One of the same country.—*a.*† Of the same country; patriotic.—**Compatriotism,**† kom-pā′tri-ot-izm, *n.* The state of being a compatriot.

Compeer, kom-pēr′, *n.* [L. *com*, and *par*, equal. PEER.] An equal; a companion; an associate; a mate.—*v.t.*‡ To equal; to match. (*Shak.*)

Compel, kom-pel′, *v.t.*—*compelled, compelling.* [L. *compello, compulsum*, to drive together—*com*, and *pello*, to drive; hence *compulsion, compulsory*, &c.] To drive or urge with force or irresistibly; to constrain; to oblige; to necessitate; to subject; to cause to submit; to take by force or violence (*Shak.*)—**Compellable,** kom-pel′a-bl, *a.* Capable of being compelled or constrained.—**Compellable witness,** kom-pel′a-bl, *n.* usually in the United States, one who can claim no exemption from testifying in a legal proceeding.—**Compellably,** kom-pel′a-bli, *adv.* By compulsion.—**Compellatory,**† kom-pel′a-to-ri, *a.* Tending to compel; compulsory.—**Compeller,** kom-pel′ėr, *n.* One who compels or constrains.—**Compellingly,**—kom-pel′ing-li, *adv.* In a compelling or constraining manner; compulsively; in a way to force attention or obedience.

Compellation, kom-pel-lā′shon, *n.* [L. *compellatio*, the act of accosting, from *compello, compellare*, to address.] Style or manner of address; word of salutation.—**Compellative,** kom-pel′a-tiv, *n.* *Gram.* a term sometimes given to the name by which a person is addressed.

Compendium, kom-pen′di-um, *n.* [L. *compendium*, a shortening, abbreviating—*com*, with, and *pendo*, to weigh.] A brief compilation or composition containing the principal heads or general principles of a larger work or system; an abridgment; a summary; an epitome. ∴ Syn. under ABRIDGMENT. — **Compendious,** kom-pen′di-us, *a.* [L. *compendiosus.*] Containing the substance or general principles of a subject or work in a narrow compass; succinct; concise.—**Compendiously,** kom-pen′di-us-li, *adv.* In a compendious manner; summarily; concisely; in epitome.—**Compendiousness,** kom-pen′di-us-nes, *n.* The state of being compendious.

Compensate, kom-pen′sāt or kom′pen-sāt, *v.t.*—*compensated, compensating.* [L. *compenso, compensatum*—*com*, together, and *penso*, freq. of *pendo, pensum*, to weigh; lit. to weigh together, hence to balance, give an equivalent for.] To give equal value to; to recompense; to give an equivalent to (to *compensate* a laborer for his work); to make up for; to counterbalance; to make amends for (losses, defects, &c.).—*v.i.* To supply or serve as an equivalent; followed by *for*; to make amends.—**Compensation,** kom-pen-sā′shon, *n.* The act of compensating; that which is given or serves as an equivalent for services, debt, want, loss, or suffering; amends; indemnity; recompense; that which supplies the place of something else or makes good a deficiency.—*Compensation Act for Workmen*, any of a number of state laws providing for the compensation of a workman by his employer in case of accident.—**Compensative,** kom-pen′sa-tiv, *a.* Making amends or compensation.—*n.*† That which compensates; compensation.—**Compensator,** kom′pen-sā-tėr, *n.* One who or that which compensates.—**Compensatory,** kom-pen′sa-to-ri, *a.* Serving for compensation; making amends.

Compesce, kom-pes′, *v.t.* [L. *compesco.*] To hold in check; to restrain; to curb. (*Carl.*)

Compete, kom-pēt′, *v.i.*—*competed, competing.* [L. *competo*, to strive after—*com*, together, and *peto*, to seek.] To seek or strive for the same thing as another; to carry on a contest or rivalry for a common object; to vie (to *compete with* a person *for* a thing).—**Competition,** kom-pē-ti′shon, *n.* [L.L. *competitio.*] The act of competing; mutual contest or striving for the same object; rivalry; a trial of skill proposed as a test of superiority or comparative fitness. ∴ In a *competition* the persons strive to attain a common end, and may have the most friendly feelings towards each other; in *rivalry* there is rather the desire of one to supplant or get before another, and usually a certain hostility.—**Competitive,** kom-pet′i-tiv, *a.* Relating to competition; carried out by competition.—**Competitor,** kom-pet′i-tėr, *n.* [L. *competitor* (*i* long).] One who competes; one who endeavours to obtain what another seeks; one who claims what another claims; a rival.—**Competitory,**† kom-pet′i-to-ri, *a.* Acting in competition; rival.

Competent, kom′pē-tent, *a.* [Fr. *compétent*, from *competer*, to be sufficient; L. *competo*, to be meet or suitable—*com*, together, and *peto*, to seek.] Answering all requirements; suitable; fit; sufficient or fit for the purpose; adequate; having legal capacity or power; rightfully or lawfully belonging.—**Competently,** kom′pē-tent-li, *adv.* In a competent manner; sufficiently; adequately; suitably. — **Competence, Competency,** kom′pē-tens, kom′pē-ten-si, *n.* State of being competent; fitness; suitableness; adequateness; ability; sufficiency; such a quantity as is sufficient; especially, property or means of subsistence sufficient to furnish the necessaries and conveniences of life, without superfluity.

Compile, kom-pīl′, *v.t.*—*compiled, compiling.* [L. *compilo*, to plunder, pillage—*com*, together, and *pilo*, to pillage.] To draw up, write out, or compose by collecting materials from various sources; to collect or put together by utilizing the writings of others.—**Compilation,** kom-pi-lā′shon, *n.* The act of compiling or collecting from written or printed documents or books; that which is compiled; a book or treatise drawn up by compiling. — **Compiler,** kom-pīl′ėr, *n.* One who compiles.

Complacent, kom-plā′sent, *a.* [L. *complacens, complacentis*, pleasing, ppr. of *complaceo*, to please—*com*, and *placeo*, to please (whence *pleasure*).] Accompanied with a sense of quiet enjoyment; displaying complacency; gratified; satisfied. — **Complacence, Complacency,** kom-plā′sens, kom-plā′sen-si, *n.* A feeling of quiet pleasure; satisfaction; gratification; complaisance or civility‡.—**Complacently,** kom-plā′sent-li, *adv.* In a complacent manner.

Complain, kom-plān′, *v.i.* [Fr. *complaindre*, from L.L. *complangere*—L. *com*, together, and *plango*, to beat the breast in sorrow. PLAINT.] To utter expressions of grief, pain, uneasiness, censure, resentment, or the like; to lament; to murmur; to bewail; to make a formal accusation against a person; to make a charge: now regularly followed by *of* before the cause of grief or censure.—**Complainant,** kom-plā′nant, *n.* One who complains or makes a complaint; a complainer; *law*, one who prosecutes by complaint, or commences a legal process against an offender; a plaintiff; a prosecutor.—**Complainer,** kom-plā′nėr, *n.* One who complains; one who finds fault; a murmurer.—**Complaining,** kom-plā′ning, *n.* The expression of regret, sorrow; or injury; a complaint.—*a.* Expressive of complaint.—**Complainingly,** kom-plā′ning-li, *adv.* In a complaining manner; murmuringly.—**Complaint,** kom-plānt′, *n.* [Fr. *complainte.*] Expression of grief, regret, pain, censure, or resentment; lamentation; murmuring; a finding fault; the cause or subject of complaint or murmuring; a malady; an ailment; a disease: usually applied to disorders not violent; a charge; a representation of injuries suffered; accusation.

Complaisance, kom′plā-zans, *n.* [Fr. *complaisance*, from *complaisant*, ppr. of *complaire*, to please = L. *complacere.* COMPLACENT.] A pleasing deportment; affability; civility; courtesy; desire of pleasing; disposition to oblige. — **Complaisant,** kom′plā-zant, *a.* Pleasing in manners; courteous; obliging; desirous to please; proceeding from an obliging disposition.—**Complaisantly,** kom′plā-zant-li, *adv.* In a complaisant manner. — **Complaisantness,**† kom′plā-zant-nes, *n.* Complaisance.

Complected, kom-plek′ted, *a.* [L. prefix *com*, and *plecto*, to weave.] Woven together; interwoven.

Complement, kom′plē-ment, *n.* [L. *complementum*, that which fills up or completes, from *compleo*, to complete. COMPLETE. *Compliment* is the same word.] Full quantity or number; full amount; what is wanted to complete or fill up some quantity or thing; difference; *math.* what is wanted in an arc or angle to make it up to 90°; outward show (*Shak.*)‡; courtesy or compliment (*Shak.*)‡. — **Complemental,** kom-plē-men′tal, *a.* Forming a complement; completing; complementary.—**Complementary,** kom-plē-men′ta-ri, *a.* Completing; supplying a deficiency; complemental.—*Complementary colours.* COLOUR.

Complete, kom-plēt′, *a.* [L. *completus*, pp. of *compleo, completum*, to fill up — *com*, intens., and *pleo*, to fill; same root as E. *fill.*] Having no deficiency; wanting no part or element; perfect; thorough; consummate; in every respect; finished; ended; concluded. ∴ 'Nothing is *whole* that has anything taken from it; nothing is *entire* that is divided; nothing is *complete* that has not all its parts and those parts fully developed. *Complete* refers to the perfection of parts; *entire* to their unity; *whole* to their junction; *total* to their aggregate' (*Angus*).—*v.t.*—*completed, completing.* To make complete; to finish; to end; to perfect; to fulfil; to accomplish; to realize.—**Completely,** kom-plēt′li, *adv.* In a complete manner; fully; perfectly; entirely; wholly; totally; utterly; thoroughly; quite.—**Completeness,** kom-plēt′nes, *n.* The state of being complete.—**Completion,** kom-plē′shon, *n.* Act of completing, finishing, or perfecting; state of being complete or completed; perfect state; fulfilment; accomplishment. — **Completive,** kom-plē′tiv, *a.* Completing or tending to complete; making complete. — **Completory,** kom-plē′to-ri, *a.* Fulfilling; accomplishing.

Complex, kom′pleks, *a.* [L. *complexus*, pp. of *complector, complexus*, to fold or twine together—*com*, together, and stem *plec, plic*, to fold; seen also in *ply, apply, complicate, display*, &c.] Composed of various parts or things; including sundry particulars connected; composite; not simple (being, idea); involved; intricate; complicated; perplexed (process).—*n.* Assemblage of things related as parts of a system; *Psychoanalysis* (which see), a series of emotionally accentuated ideas in a repressed state. — **Complexity, Complexness,** kom-plek′si-ti, kom′pleks-nes, *n.* The state of being complex; anything complex; intricacy; involvement; entanglement.—**Complexly,** kom′pleks-li, *adv.* In a complex manner; not simply.—**Complexus,** kom-plek′sus, *n.* [L.] An aggregation of involutions or complications; *anat.* a broad and pretty long muscle, lying along the back part and side of the neck.

Complexion, kom-plek′shon, *n.* [L. *complexio, complexionis*, a combination, in L.L. physical constitution, from *complector, complexus.* COMPLEX.] The temperament, habitude, or natural disposition of the body or mind‡; physical character or nature‡; the colour or hue of the skin, particularly of the face; the general appearance of anything; aspect (*Shak.*).—**Complexional,** kom-plek′shon-al, *a.* Pertaining to or depending on the disposition or temperament‡; pertaining to the complexion.—**Complexionary,** kom-plek′shon-a-ri, *a.* Pertaining to the complexion, or to the care of it.—**Complexioned,** kom-plek′shond, *a.* Having a complexion of this or that kind; having a certain hue, especially of the skin: used in composition.

Compliance, &c. COMPLY.

Complicate, kom′pli-kāt, *v.t.* — *complicated, complicating.* [L. *complico*—*com*, and *plico*, to fold, weave, or knit. COMPLEX, PLY.] To intertwine; to interweave; to render complex or intricate; to involve.—*a.* Composed of various parts intimately united; complex; involved; intricate; *bot.* folded together, as the valves of the glume or chaff in some grasses.—**Complicated,** kom'pli-kāt-ed, *p.* and *a.* Complicate; involved; intricate.—**Complicacy,** kom'-pli-ka-si, *n.* A state of being complex or intricate.—**Complicately,** kom'pli-kāt-li, *adv.* In a complicated manner.—**Complicateness,** kom'pli-kāt-nes, *n.* The state of being complicated.—**Complication,** kom-pli-kā'shon, *n.* The act of complicating or state of being complicated; entanglement; complexity; something complicated; an aggregate of things involved, mixed up, or mutually united; what complicates or causes complication.—**Complicative,** kom'pli-kā-tiv, *a.* Tending or adapted to involve or complicate.

Complice,‡ kom'plis, *n.* [Fr. *complice.* ACCOMPLICE.] An accomplice. (*Shak.*)—**Complicity,** kom-plis'i-ti, *n.* The state of being an accomplice; partnership in crime.

Compliment, kom'pli-ment, *n.* [Fr. *compliment,* It. *complimento,* from *complire,* to fill up, to satisfy, L. *compleo, complere,* to complete: same word as *complement,* which formerly was used in this sense.] An act or expression of civility, respect, or regard; delicate flattery; expression of commendation or admiration; praise.—*v.t.* To pay a compliment to; to flatter or gratify by expressions of approbation, esteem, or respect, or by acts implying the like.—**Complimentary,** kom-pli-men'ta-ri, *a.* Full of or using compliments; intended to express or convey a compliment or compliments; expressive of civility, regard, or praise.—**Complimentarily,** kom-pli-men'ta-ri-li, *adv.* In a complimentary manner.—**Complimenter,** kom'pli-men-tėr, *n.* One who compliments.

Compline, kom'plin, *n.* [From Fr. *complie,* from L. *completæ* (*horæ*), 'complete hours': so called because this service completes the religious exercises of the day.] The last of the seven canonical hours in the Roman Catholic breviary; the last prayer at night, to be recited after sunset.

Complot, kom'plot, *n.* [Fr. *complot,* a plot, from L. *complicitum.* COMPLICATE.] A plotting together; a plot; a conspiracy. (*Shak.*)—*v.t.* To plan together; to contrive; to plot.—*v.i.*—*complotted, complotting.* To plot together; to conspire; to form a plot.—**Complotter,** kom-plot'ėr, *n.* One joined in a plot; a conspirator.

Comply, kom-plī', *v.i.*—*complied, complying.* [From L. *complere,* to fill up, satisfy (whence *complete, compliment*), like *supply* from *supplere*—*com,* with, and *plere,* to fill. The meaning has been affected by *ply* and *pliant.*] To adopt a certain course of action at the desire of another; to yield; to acquiesce; to consent; to agree: used alone or followed by *with.*—**Compliable,**‡ kom-plī'a-bl, *a.* Compliant. (*Mil.*)—**Compliance,** kom-plī'ans, *n.* The act of complying; a yielding as to a request, wish, desire, &c.; a disposition to yield to others; complaisance.—**Compliancy,** kom-plī'an-si, *n.* A disposition to yield, or a habit of yielding to others.—**Compliant,** kom-plī'ant, *a.* Given to comply; yielding to request or desire; ready to accommodate; obliging.—**Compliantly,** kom-plī'ant-li, *adv.* In a compliant or yielding manner.—**Complier,** kom-plī'ėr, *n.* One who complies or yields.

Component, kom-pō'nent, *a.* [L. *componens*—*com,* together, and *pono,* to place.] Composing; constituting; entering into as a part.—*n.* A constituent part.—**Component,** kom-pō'nent, *n.* [L. *compono,* I construct.] The effective part of a force, velocity, &c., in a given direction; one of any number of constituent forces, velocities, &c., of which the given force, velocity, &c., is the resultant.—**Componency,** kom-pō'-nen-si, *n.* Composition; structure; nature.

Comport, kom-pōrt', *v.i.* [Fr. *comporter,* to admit of, allow, endure, from L. *comportare,* to bear or carry together—*com,* and *porto,* to carry.] To be suitable; agree; accord; fit; suit: with *with* (pride *comports* ill *with* poverty).—*v.t.* To behave; to conduct: used *refl.*—**Comportment,** kom-pōrt'ment, *n.* Behaviour; demeanour; deportment.

Composant, kom'pō-zant, *n.* Same as *Corposant.*

Compose, kom-pōz', *v.t.*—*composed, composing.* [From Fr. *composer,* to compose, from prefix *com,* and *poser,* to place, L. *pausare* (see POSE), but early identified with L. *compono, compositum,* to compound, from *com,* and *pono,* to place; so also *dispose, expose.*] To form by uniting two or more things; to form, frame, or fashion; to form by being combined or united; to constitute; to make; to write, as an author; to become the author of (a book, a piece of music); to calm; to quiet; to appease; to settle; to adjust (differences, &c.); to place in proper form; to dispose; *fine arts,* to arrange the leading features of; *printing,* to set in proper order for printing, as types in a composing-stick.—*v.i.* To practise literary, musical, or artistic composition.—**Composed,** kom-pōzd', *a.* Free from disturbance or agitation; calm; sedate; quiet; tranquil.—**Composedly,** kom-pō'zed-li, *adv.* In a composed manner; calmly; without agitation; sedately.—**Composure, Composedness,** kom-pō'zhūr, kom-pō'-zed-nes, *n.* The state of being composed; a settled state of mind; sedateness; calmness; tranquillity.—**Composer,** kom-pō'-zėr, *n.* One who or that which composes; one who writes an original work; most commonly, one who composes musical pieces.—**Composite,** kom'po-zit, *a.* [L. *compositus,* from *compono, compositum,* to compound.] Made up of distinct parts, elements, or substances; compounded; *arch.* a term applied to one of the orders because the capital belonging to it is *composed* out of those of the other orders, exhibiting leaves, volutes, &c.; *bot.* applied to plants forming a vast order, and having flowers forming dense heads composed of many florets, as in the daisy, dandelion, &c.—*Composite number*—A product of two or more integers each greater than 1.—*Composite ship,* a ship having a wooden skin on an iron frame-work.—*n.* Anything made up of parts or of different elements; a compound; a composition.—**Composition,** kom-pō-zi'shon, *n.* [L. *compositio,* Fr. *composition,* in meaning akin partly to *compose,* partly to the verb *compound.*] The act of composing or compounding, or the state of being composed or compounded; the act of producing some literary or musical piece; what is composed, as a literary, musical, or artistic production; the act of writing for practice in English or a foreign language; the act of making a mutual agreement for the discharge of a debt, or the agreement itself; the amount or rate paid in compounding with creditors; *gram.* the act of forming compound words; the arrangement of parts in a whole; mode of arrangement; a material compounded of two or more ingredients; a compound; *printing,* the act of setting types or characters in the composing-stick, to form lines, and of arranging the lines in a galley to make a column or page, and from this to make a form.—**Compositive,** kom-poz'i-tiv, *a.* Having the power of compounding or composing; proceeding by composition.—**Compositor,** kom-poz'i-tėr, *n.* *Printing,* one who sets types and makes up the pages and forms.—**Composing-stick,** *n.* A printer's instrument in which types are arranged into words and lines.

Compost, kom'post, *n.* [O.Fr. *composte,* It. *composta,* a mixture, from L. *compositum,* from *compono.* COMPOUND.] A mixture or composition of various manuring substances for fertilizing land; a composition for plastering the exterior of houses.—*v.t.* To manure with compost; to plaster.

Composure. Under COMPOSE.

Compotation, kom-pō-tā'shon, *n.* [L. *compotatio*—*com,* with, and *potatio,* from *poto,* to drink.] The act of drinking or tippling together.—**Compotator,** kom-pō-tā'tėr, *n.* One who drinks with another.

Compote, kom'pōt, *n.* [Fr.] Fruit, generally stone-fruit, stewed or preserved in syrup.

Compound, kom'pound, *a.* [Originally a participle of O.E. *compoune, compone,* to compound. See the verb.] Composed of two or more elements, parts, or ingredients; not simple; *bot.* made up of smaller parts of like kind with or similar to the whole.—*Compound animals,* animals, such as coral polyps, in which individuals, distinct as regards many of the functions of life, are yet connected by some part of their frame so as to form a united whole.—*Compound fracture, surg.* a fracture in which a bone is broken and there is also laceration of the tissues.—*Compound interest,* that interest which arises from the principal with the interest added.—*Compound quantities, alg.* such quantities as are joined by the signs + and —, plus and minus; *arith.* quantities which consist of more than one denomination (as of dollars and cents); hence the operations of adding, subtracting, multiplying, and dividing such quantities are termed *compound addition, subtraction, multiplication,* and *division.*—*Compound word,* a word composed of two or more words.—*n.* Something produced by compounding two or more ingredients, parts, or elements, as a substance or a word.—*v.t.* (kom-pound'). [O.E. *compone, compoune,* with *d* added (as in *expound, propound, sound,* vulgar *drownd,* &c.), from L. *compono*—*com,* together, and *pono, positum,* to set or put, whence *position.* COMPOSE.] To mix up or mingle together; to form by mingling two or more ingredients or elements into one; to combine; to settle amicably; to adjust by agreement (a controversy); to fail to prosecute (an offense) for a consideration; to discharge (a debt) by paying a part.—*v.i.* To agree upon concession; to come to terms of agreement; to arrange or make a settlement by compromise; especially, to settle with creditors by agreement, and discharge a debt by paying a part of its amount; or to make an agreement to pay a debt by means or in a manner different from that stipulated or required by law (to *compound with* a person, and *for* a debt).—**Compoundable,** kom-poun'da-bl, *a.* Capable of being compounded.—**Compounder,** kom-poun'dėr, *n.* One who compounds.

Compound, kom'pound, *n.* [From Malay *kampong,* a yard or court.] In the East Indies, the inclosure in which isolated houses stand, or surrounding a dwelling-house, garden, &c.

Comprehend, kom-prē-hend', *v.t.* [L. *comprehendo*—*com,* together, *præ,* before, and an obs. *hendere,* to catch.] To take in or include within a certain scope; to include by implication or signification; to embrace; to comprise; to take into the mind; to grasp by the understanding; to possess or have in idea; to understand.—**Comprehender,** kom-prē-hen'dėr, *n.* One who comprehends; one who understands thoroughly.—**Comprehensible,** kom-prē-hen'si-bl, *a.* [L. *comprehensibilis.*] Capable of being comprehended; capable of being understood; conceivable by the mind; intelligible: also **Comprehendible,** kom-prē-hen'di-bl.—**Comprehensibility, Comprehensibleness,** kom-prē-hen'si-bil''i-ti, kom-prē-hen'si-bl-nes, *n.* The quality of being comprehensible; the capability of being understood.—**Comprehensibly,** kom-prē-hen'si-bli, *adv.* In a comprehensible manner; conceivably.—**Comprehension,** kom-prē-hen'shon, *n.* [L. *comprehensio.*] The act of comprehending, including, or embracing; a comprising; inclusion; capacity of the mind to understand; power of the understanding to receive and contain ideas; capacity of knowing.—**Comprehensive,** kom-prē-hen'siv, *a.* Having the quality of comprehending or embracing a great number or a wide extent; of extensive application; wide in scope; comprehending much in a comparatively small compass; having the power to comprehend or understand.—**Comprehensively,** kom-prē-hen'siv-li, *adv.* In a comprehensive manner; with great extent of scope; so as to contain much in small compass.—**Comprehensiveness**, kom-prē-hen′siv-nes, *n.* The quality of being comprehensive.

Compress, kom-pres′, *v.t.* [L. *comprimo, compressum—com*, together, and *premo, pressum*, to press.] To press together; to force, urge, or drive into a smaller compass; to condense.—*n.* (kom′pres). In *surg.* a soft mass formed of tow, lint, or soft linen cloth, so contrived as by the aid of a bandage to make due pressure on any part.—**Compressed**, kom-prest′, *p.* and *a.* Pressed into narrow compass; condensed; *bot.* and *zool.* flattened laterally or lengthwise.—**Compressibility, Compressibleness**, kom-pres′i-bil″i-ti, kom-pres′i-bl-nes, *n.* The quality of being compressible, or yielding to pressure.—**Compressible**, kom-pres′i-bl, *a.* Capable of being compressed or forced into a narrower compass, yielding to pressure; condensable.—**Compression**, kom-presh′on, *n.* The act of compressing; the act of forcing into closer union or density; the state of being compressed; condensation.—**Compressive**, kom-pres′iv, *a.* Having power to compress; tending to compress.—**Compressor**, kom-pres′ėr, *n.* [L.] One who or that which compresses.

Comprise, kom-prīz′, *v.t.*—*comprised, comprising.* [Fr. *compris*, part. of *comprendre*, L. *comprehendo*, to comprehend. COMPREHEND.] To comprehend; to contain; to include (the United States *comprises* various states).—**Comprisal**,† kom-prī′zal, *n.* The act of comprising; inclusion.

Compromise, kom′prō-mīz, *n.* [Fr. *compromis*, a compromise, originally a mutual promise to refer to arbitration, from *compromettre*, L. *compromitto—com*, and *promitto, promissum*, to promise. PROMISE.] A settlement of differences by mutual concessions; a combination of two rival systems, principles, &c., in which a part of each is sacrificed to make the combination possible; what results from, or is founded on, such an agreement; a mutual concession.—*v.t.*—*compromised, compromising.* To adjust or combine by a compromise; to settle by mutual concessions; to put to risk or hazard, or expose to serious consequences, by some act or declaration which cannot be recalled; to put in jeopardy; to endanger the interests of: often *refl.* (he *compromised himself* by his rash statements).—*v.i.* To make a compromise.

Compsognathus, komp-sog′na-thus, *n.* [Gr. *kompsos*, elegant, and *gnathos*, the jaw.] An extinct reptile having very close affinities to the birds.

Comptometer, komp-tom′ē-tėr, *n.* A name applied to a kind of calculating machine; hence, a machine bearing this trade-mark.

Comptroller, kon-trōl′ėr, *n.* A controller; an officer who examines expenditures.—**Comptrollership**, kon-trōl′ėr-ship, *n.* The office of comptroller.

Compulsion, kom-pul′shon, *n.* [L. *compulsio, compulsionis*, constraint, compulsion, from *compello, compulsum*, to compel. COMPEL.] The act of compelling or driving by force, physical or moral; constraint of the will.—**Compulsative**,† **Compulsatory**,† kom-pul′sa-tiv, kom-pul′sa-to-ri, *a.* Compelling; constraining.—**Compulsatively**,† kom-pul′sa-tiv-li, *adv.* By constraint or compulsion.—**Compulsive**, kom-pul′siv, *a.* Exercising compulsion; compulsory.—**Compulsively**, kom-pul′siv-li, *adv.* By or under compulsion; by force.—**Compulsiveness**, kom-pul′siv-nes, *n.* Force; compulsion.—**Compulsorily**, kom-pul′so-ri-li, *adv.* In a compulsory manner; by force or constraint.—**Compulsory**, kom-pul′so-ri, *a.* Exercising compulsion; compelling; constraining; enforced; due to compulsion; obligatory (a *compulsory* contribution).

Compunction, kom-pungk′shon, *n.* [L. *compunctio, compungo—com*, and *pungo*, to prick or sting. PUNGENT.] The stinging or pricking of the conscience; regret, as for wrong-doing or for causing pain to some one; contrition; remorse.—**Compunctious**, kom-pungk′shus, *a.* Causing compunction; stinging the conscience; remorseful.—**Compunctiously**, kom-pungk′shus-li, *adv.* With compunction.

Compurgation, kom-pėr-gā′shon, *n.* [L. *compurgo—com*, and *purgo*, to purge or purify.] An ancient mode of trial in England, where the accused was permitted to call a certain number of persons who joined their oaths to his in testimony to his innocence.—**Compurgator**, kom′pėr-gā-tėr, *n.* One who by oath testified to another's innocence.—**Compurgatorial**, kom′pėr-gā-tō″ri-al, *a.* Relating to compurgation.

Compute, kom-pūt′, *v.t.*—*computed, computing.* [L. *computo*, to calculate—*com*, together, and *puto*, to reckon, esteem, whence also *dispute, impute.* To *count* is really the same as this word.] To determine by calculation; to count; to reckon; to calculate; to estimate.—*v.i.* To reckon.—**Computability**, kom-pū′ta-bil″i-ti, *n.* The quality of being computable.—**Computable**, kom-pū′ta-bl, *a.* Capable of being computed, numbered, or reckoned.—**Computation**, kom-pū-tā′shon, *n.* [L. *computatio.*] The act or process of computing, reckoning, or estimating; calculation; the result of a computation.—**Computator**, kom-pū-tā′tėr, *n.* A computer; a calculator.—**Computer**, kom-pū′tėr, *n.* One who computes; a reckoner; a calculator.

Comrade, kom′rād, *n.* [O.E. *camarade, camerade*, from Sp. *camarada*, Fr. *camarade*, one who occupies the same chamber, from L. *camera*, a chamber.] An associate in occupation or friendship; a close companion; a mate.—**Comradeship, Comradery**, kom′rād-ship, kom′rād-ri, *n.* The state or feeling of being a comrade; companionship; fellowship.

Comtism, kom′tizm, *n.* The philosophical system founded by Auguste *Comte*; positivism.—**Comtist**, kom′tist, *n.* A disciple of Comte; a positivist. Used also adjectively.

Con, kon, *adv.* and *n.* [Abbrev. from L. *contra*, against.] Against, in the phrase *pro and con*, for and against, as a noun, a statement, argument, point, or consideration supporting the negative side of a question (to discuss the *pros* and *cons*).

Con, kon, *v.t.*—*conned, conning.* [A form of *can.*] To peruse carefully and attentively; to study over; to learn; to direct the steering of (a ship).—**Conning-tower**, a turret on a ship from which the vessel's movements are directed.

Conacre, kon′ā-kėr, *n.* [For *corn-acre.*] In Ireland, the subletting of tilled land in small portions for a single crop.

Conation, ko-nā′shon, *n.* [L. *conor, conatus*, to attempt.] *Metaph.* the faculty of voluntary agency, embracing desire and volition.—**Conative**, kon′a-tiv, *a.* Relating to the faculty of conation.

Concamerate,† kon-kam′ėr-āt, *v.t.* [L. *concamero*, to arch—*con*, and *camera*, an arch (whence *chamber*).] To arch over; to vault.—**Concameration**,† kon-kam′ėr-ā″shon, *n.* An arching; an arch or vault.

Concatenate, kon-kat′e-nāt, *v.t.*—*concatenated, concatenating.* [L. *concateno, concatenatum*, to link together—*con*, together, and *catena*, a chain. CHAIN.] To link together; to unite in a successive series or chain, as things depending on each other.—**Concatenation**, kon-kat′e-nā″shon, *n.* The state of being concatenated or linked together; a series of links united.

Concave, kon′kāv, *a.* [L. *concavus—con*, and *cavus*, hollow. CAVE.] Hollow and curved or rounded, as the inner surface of a spherical body; presenting a hollow or incurvation towards some direction expressed or understood; incurved.—*n.* A hollow; an arch or vault; a cavity.—*v.t.*†—*concaved, concaving.* To make hollow.—**Concavation**, kon-kā-vā′shon, *n.* The act of making concave.—**Concavely**, kon′kāv-li, *adv.* So as to be concave; in a concave manner.—**Concaveness**, kon′kāv-nes, *n.* The state of being concave.—**Concavity**, kon-kav′i-ti, *n.* Hollowness; a concave surface, or the space contained in it.—**Concavo-concave**, kon-kā′vō-kon-kāv, *a.* Concave or hollow on both surfaces, as a lens.—**Concavo-convex**, kon-kā′vō-kon-veks, *a.* Concave on one side and convex on the other.

Conceal, kon-sēl′, *v.t.* [From L. *concelo*, to conceal—*con*, together, and *celo*, to hide, same root as E. *hell, hole, hull*, &c.] To side; to withdraw from observation; to cover or keep from sight; to keep close or secret; to forbear to disclose; to withhold from utterance or declaration.—**Concealable**, kon-sēl′a-bl, *a.* Capable of being concealed, hid, or kept close.—**Concealedly**, kon-sēl′ed-li, *adv.* In a clandestine manner; so as not to be detected.—**Concealedness**, kon-sēl′ed-nes, *n.* A state of being concealed.—**Concealer**, kon-sēl′ėr, *n.* One who conceals.—**Concealment**, kon-sēl′ment, *n.* The act of concealing, hiding, or keeping secret; the state of being hid or concealed; privacy; shelter from observation; cover from sight.

Concede, kon-sēd′, *v.t.*—*conceded, conceding.* [L. *concedo, concessum*, to yield, grant—*con*, together, and *cedo*, to yield. CEDE.] To admit as true, just, or proper; to grant; to let pass undisputed; to grant as a privilege; to yield up; to allow; to surrender.—*v.i.* To make concession; to grant a request or petition; to yield.—**Concedence**, kon-sē′dens, *n.* The act of conceding; concession.—**Conceder**, kon-sē′dėr, *n.* One who concedes.—**Concessible**, kon-ses′i-bl, *a.* Capable of being conceded.—**Concession**, kon-sesh′on, *n.* [L. *concessio.*] The act of conceding, admitting, or granting; a yielding to demand or claim; the thing yielded; a grant; a grant empowering some scheme or work to be done.—**Concessionary, Concessionnaire**, kon-sesh′on-a-ri, kon-sesh′on-ār, *n.* [Fr. *concessionaire.*] A person to whom a concession for carrying out some scheme has been made; a member of a company to whom special powers have been granted by a government for carrying out some work.—**Concessionist**, kon-sesh′on-ist, *n.* One who favours concession or a concession.—**Concessive**, kon-ses′iv, *a.* Implying or containing concession.—**Concessively**, kon-ses′iv-li, *adv.* By way of concession.

Conceit, kon-sēt′, *n.* [O.E. *conceipt*, O.Fr. *concept*, from L. *conceptus*, a conception, from *concipio*, to conceive—*con*, and *capio*, to take; comp. *deceit, receipt.*] Opinion, estimation, view, or belief (wise in one's own *conceit*); an ill-grounded opinion; a baseless fancy; a crotchety notion; an ill-grounded opinion of one's own importance; self-conceit; vanity; a witty, happy, or ingenious thought or expression; a quaint or humorous fancy; now commonly a thought or expression intended to be striking or poetical, but rather far-fetched, insipid, or pedantic.—*Out of conceit with*, not now having a favourable opinion of; no longer pleased with.—*v.t.* To imagine wrongly; to err in believing: used *refl.*—**Conceited**, kon-sē′ted, *a.* Entertaining a flattering opinion of one's self; self-conceited; vain; egotistical.—**Conceitedly**, kon-sē′ted-li, *adv.* In a conceited manner; with vanity or egotism.—**Conceitedness**, kon-sē′ted-nes, *n.* The state of being conceited.

Conceive, kon-sēv′, *v.t.*—*conceived, conceiving.* [O.Fr. *concever, conceveir*, Fr. *concevoir*, from L. *concipere*, to conceive. CONCEIT.] To become pregnant with; to develop in the womb in an embryonic state; to form in the mind; to devise (an idea, a purpose); to realize in the mind; to form a conception of; to place distinctly before the thoughts; to comprehend: often used as a specific term in philosophy; to think; to imagine; to suppose possible.—*v.i.* To have a fetus formed in the womb; to become pregnant; to have or form a conception or idea; to think (to *conceive of* a thing).—**Conceivable**, kon-sē′va-bl, *a.* Capable of being conceived, thought, imagined, or understood.—**Conceivability, Conceivableness**, kon-sē′va-bil″i-ti, kon-sē′va-bl-nes, *n.* The quality of being conceivable.—**Conceivably**, kon-sē′va-bli, *adv.*

In a conceivable or intelligible manner.—**Conceiver**, kon-sē'vėr, *n.* One that conceives.

Concentrate, kon-sen'trāt, or kon', *v.t.*—*concentrated, concentrating.* [Fr. *concentrer*—L. *con*, together, and *centrum*, a center.] To bring to a common center or point of union; to cause to come together to one spot or point; to bring to bear on one point; to direct towards one object; in chemical manipulations, to intensify by removing non-essential matter; to reduce to a state of great strength and purity.—*v.i.* To approach or meet in a common point or center.—**Concentration**, kon-sen-trā'shon, *n.* The act of concentrating; the act of collecting into a central point or of directing to one object; the state of being concentrated; the act of increasing the strength of fluids by volatilizing part of their water.—*Concentration camp.* Barracks with stockade, patrolled by the military, used for the detention and punishment of people politically, economically, or morally adverse to the policies of the government, esp., in Europe.—**Concenter**, kon-sen'tėr, *v.t.*—*concentered, concentering.* To converge to or meet in a common center; to combine or be united in one object.—*v.t.* To draw or direct to a common center; to concentrate.—**Concentric, Concentrical**, kon-sen'trik, kon-sen'tri-kal, *a.* [L. *concentricus.*] Having a common center (circles, &c.).—**Concentrically**, kon-sen'tri-kal-li, *adv.* In a concentric manner.—**Concentricity**, kon-sen-tris'i-ti, *n.* State of being concentric.

Concept, kon'sept, *n.* [L. *conceptum*, what is conceived, from *concipio.* CONCEIVE.] *Philos.* the subject of a conception; the object conceived by the mind; a notion.—**Conceptacle**, kon-sep'ta-kl, *n.* [L. *conceptaculum.*] That in which anything is contained; a receptacle; *bot.* a hollow sac containing bodies connected with reproduction or fructification†.—**Conception**, kon-sep'shon, *n.* [L. *conceptio.*] The act of conceiving; the first formation of the embryo of an animal; the act or power of conceiving in the mind; that which is conceived in the mind; product of the imaginative or inventive faculty; *philos.* that mental act or combination of acts by which an absent object of perception is brought before the mind by the imagination; the mental operation by which such notions or conceptions are formed; a general notion; that which constitutes the meaning of a general term; thought, notion, or idea in the loose sense (you have no *conception* how clever he is).—*Immaculate conception.* IMMACULATE.—**Conceptional**, kon-sep'shon-al, *a.* Pertaining to or having the nature of a conception or notion.—**Conceptive**, kon-sep'tiv, *a.* Capable of conceiving either physically or mentally.—**Conceptual**, kon-sep'tū-al, *a.* Pertaining to conception, mental or physical.—**Conceptualism**, kon-sep'tū-al-izm, *n.* The doctrine of the conceptualists, in some sense intermediate between realizm and nominalism.—**Conceptualist, Conceptionalist**, kon-sep'tū-al-ist, kon-sep'shon-al-ist, *n.* One who holds the doctrine that the mind has the power of assigning an independent existence to general conceptions.—**Conceptualistic**, kon-sep'tū-a-lis"tik, *a.* Pertaining to conceptualism or conceptualists.

Concern, kon-sėrn', *v.t.* [Fr. *concerner*, to concern, from L. *concerno*, to mix, as in a sieve—*con*, together, and *cerno*, to sift, akin to Gr. *krinō*, to separate. Akin *decree, discreet, secret*, &c.] To relate, pertain, or belong to; to affect the interest of; to be of importance to (that does not *concern* me); *refl.* to take or have an interest in, occupy or busy one's self; to disturb, make uneasy, or cause concern to: in this sense generally in pp.—*n.* That which relates or belongs to one; business; affair; matter of importance; that which affects one's welfare or happiness; solicitude; anxiety; agitation or uneasiness of mind; disturbed state of feeling; an establishment, such as a manufacturing or commercial establishment. ∴ *Syn.* under CARE.—**Concerned**, kon-sėrnd', *p.* and *a.* Having concern; interested; engaged; anxious.—**Concernedly**, kon-sėr'ned-li, *adv.* In a concerned manner; with anxiety or solicitude.—**Concernedness**, kon-sėr'ned-nes, *n.* State of being concerned.—**Concerning**, kon-sėr'ning, *prep.* In regard to; regarding; with relation to; about.—**Concernment**, kon-sėrn'ment, *n.* A thing in which one is concerned or interested; concern; affair; business; interest; importance; participation; concern; solicitude.

Concert, kon-sėrt', *v.t.* [Fr. *concerter*, from It. *concertare*, to concert, misspelled from L. *consero, consertus*, to join together—*con*, and *sero*, to join, from root of *series.*] To contrive and settle by mutual communication of opinions or propositions; to plan; to devise.—*n.* (kon'sėrt). [From above verb, but in musical meanings L. *concentus*, a singing together, seems to have had an influence.] Agreement of two or more in a design or plan; accordance in a scheme; cooperation; concord; the music of a company of players or singers, or of both united; a public or private musical entertainment, at which a number of vocalists or instrumentalists, or both, perform singly or combined.—**Concerted**, kon-sėr'ted, *p.* and *a.* Mutually contrived or planned.—*Concerted piece*, in *music*, a composition in parts for several voices or instruments.—**Concertina**, kon-sėr-tē'na, *n.* A musical instrument held between the hands in playing, and composed of a bellows, with two faces or ends, in which are the keys or stops by pressing which with the fingers air is admitted to the free metallic reeds producing the sounds.—**Concerto**, kon-chār'tō, *n.* [It.] A musical composition, usually in a symphonic form, written for one principal instrument, with accompaniments for a full orchestra.

Concession, &c. Under CONCEDE.

Concetto, kon-chet'tō, *n.* pl. **Concetti**, kon-chet'tē. [It.=E. *conceit.*] Affected wit; an ingenious thought or turn of expression; a conceit.—**Concettism**,† kon-set'tizm, *n.* The use of affected wit or concetti.

Conch, kongk, *n.* [L. *concha*, Gr. *kongchē*, Skr. *çankha*, a shell.] A marine shell, especially a large spiral shell of a trumpet shape, which may be blown like a trumpet; the external portion of the ear, more especially the hollow part of it.—**Concha**, kong'ka, *n.* The external ear; *arch.* the plain ribless surface of a vault; the semidome of an apse; the apse.—**Conchifer**, kong'ki-fėr, *n.* [L. *concha*, and *fero*, to bear.] A mollusc of the class Conchifera, or acephalous molluscs with bivalve shells.—**Conchiferous**, kong-kif'ėr-us, *a.* Belonging to the chonchifers.—**Conchiform**, kong'ki-form, *a.* Shell-shaped.—**Conchitic**, kong-kit'ik, *a.* Composed of shells; applied to limestones and marbles in which the remains of shells are a noticeable feature.—**Conchoid**, kong'koid, *n.* The name of a special kind of curve used for finding two mean proportionals.—**Conchoidal**, kong-koi'dal, *a.* *Mineral.* having convex elevations and concave depressions like shells.—**Conchological**, kong-kō-loj'ik-al, *a.* Pertaining to conchology.—**Conchologist**, kong-kol'o-jist, *n.* One versed in conchology.—**Conchology**, kong-kol'o-ji, *n.* That department of zoology which treats of the nature, formation, and classification of the shells with which the bodies of many mollusca are protected, or of the animals themselves.—**Conchometer, Conchyliometer**, kong-kom'et-ėr, kong-kil'i-om"et-ėr, *n.* [Gr. *kongchylion*, a shell, dim. of *kongchē.*] An instrument for measuring molluscous shells and the angle of their spire.—**Concho-spiral**, *n.* A variety of spiral curve existing in certain shells.—**Conchylious, Conchyliaceous**, kong-kil'i-us, kong-kil'i-ā"shus, *a.* Pertaining to shells; resembling a shell.—**Conchyliologist, Conchyliology**, kong-kil'i-ol"o-jist, kong-kil'i-ol"o-ji. Same as *Conchologist, Conchology.*

Concierge, koṅ-syārzh, *n.* [Fr.] A door-keeper to a hotel, house, prison, &c.; a janitor, male or female; a porter.

Conciliar, Conciliary, kon-sil'i-ėr, kon-sil'i-a-ri, *a.* [From L. *concilium*, a council.] Pertaining or relating to a council.

Conciliate, kon-sil'i-āt, *v.t.*—*conciliated, conciliating.* [L. *concilio, conciliatum*, to unite in thought or feeling, from *concilium*, plan, council. COUNCIL.] To bring to entertain a friendly feeling; to make friendly from being antagonistic; to pacify; to soothe; to win, gain, or engage (to *conciliate* one's affection or regard); to show to be compatible (statements, &c.).—**Conciliable**, kon-sil'i-a-bl, *a.* Capable of being conciliated.—**Conciliating**, kon-sil'i-āt-ing, *a.* Winning; having the quality of gaining favour.—**Conciliation**, kon-sil'i-ā"shon, *n.* The act of conciliating; the act of making friendly; the act of winning or gaining favour or esteem.—**Conciliative**, kon-sil'i-ā-tiv, *a.* Tending to conciliate; conciliatory.—**Conciliator**, kon-sil'i-ā-tėr, *n.* One who conciliates or reconciles.—**Conciliatory**, kon-sil'i-a-to-ri, *a.* Tending to conciliate or bring to a friendly state of feeling; pacific.

Concise, kon-sīs', *a.* [L. *concisus*, cut off, brief, from *concido*—*con*, and *cædo*, to cut.] Comprehending much in few words; brief and comprehensive; employing as few words as possible; succinct. ∴ *Concise* refers mainly to style or manner in speaking or writing; *succinct* refers rather to the result produced by conciseness; thus we speak of a *concise* style or phrase; a *succinct* narrative or account.—**Concisely**, kon-sīs'li, *adv.* In a concise manner; briefly; in few words.—**Conciseness**, kon-sīs'nes, *n.* The quality of being concise.

Concision,‡ kon-si'zhon, *n.* Conciseness; a sect or faction; those in the apostles' time who laid too much stress on circumcision (N.T.).

Conclamation, kon-kla-mā'shon, *n.* [L. *conclamatio*, from *conclamo*—*con*, and *clamo.* CLAIM.] An outcry or shout of many together; a clamorous outcry.

Conclave, kon'klāv, *n.* [L. *conclave*, a private room, a closet—*con*, together, and *clavis*, a key.] The assembly or meeting of the cardinals shut up for the election of a pope; hence, the body of cardinals; a private meeting; a close assembly.—**Conclavist**, kon'klā-vist, *n.* An attendant whom a cardinal is allowed to take with him into the conclave for the choice of a pope.

Conclude, kon-klūd', *v.t.*—*concluded, concluding.* [L. *concludo*—*con*, and *claudo*, to shut; whence also *clause, close.*] To shut up or inclose‡; to include or comprehend (N.T.)‡; to infer or arrive at by reasoning; to deduce, as from premises; to judge; to end, finish, bring to a conclusion; to settle or arrange finally (to *conclude* an agreement, a peace).—*v.i.* To infer; to form a final judgment; to come to a decision; to resolve; to determine: generally followed by an infinitive or a clause; to end; to make a finish.—**Concluder**, kon-klū'dėr, *n.* One who concludes.—**Concluding**, kon-klū'ding, *a.* Final; ending; closing.—**Conclusion**, kon-klū'zhon, *n.* [L. *conclusio.*] The end, close, or termination; the last part: often in the phrase *in conclusion*=finally, lastly; determination; final decision; inference; *logic*, the inference of a syllogism as drawn from the premises; an experiment (obsolete except in the phrase *to try conclusions*).—**Conclusive**, kon-klū'siv, *a.* Putting an end to debate or argument; leading to a conclusion or determination; decisive; bringing out or leading to a regular logical conclusion.—**Conclusively**, kon-klū'siv-li, *adv.* In a conclusive manner.—**Conclusiveness**, kon-klū'siv-nes, *n.* The quality of being conclusive or decisive.

Concoct, kon-kokt', *v.t.* [L. *concoquo, concoctum*—*con*, and *coquo*, to cook. COOK.] To digest by the stomach‡; to ripen or mature‡; to form and prepare in the mind; to devise; to plan; to plot (a scheme); to mix by combining different ingredients.—**Concoction**, kon-kok'shon, *n.* [L. *concoctio.*] Digestion‡; The act of mixing ingredients, as for a dish in cookery—**Con-**

Coctive,† kon-kok'tiv, *a.* Maturing; ripening.

Concomitant, kon-kom'i-tant, *a.* [From L. *com*, together, and *comitor*, to accompany, from *comes*, a companion.] Accompanying; conjoined with; concurrent; attending; of things, circumstances, &c.—*n.* A thing that accompanies another; an accompaniment; an accessory.—**Concomitance, Concomitancy,** kon-kom'i-tans, kon-kom'i-tan-si, *n.* The state of being concomitant; a being together or in connection with another thing.—**Concomitantly,** kon-kom'i-tant-li, *adv.* So as to be concomitant; concurrently; unitedly.

Concord, kon'kord or kong'kord, *n.* [Fr. *concorde*, L. *con*, and *cor*, *cordis*, the heart. Accord.] Agreement or union in opinions, sentiments, views, or interests; harmony; agreement between things; suitableness; *music*, the pleasing combination of two or more sounds; the relation between two or more sounds which are agreeable to the ear; *gram.* agreement of words in construction.—**Concordance,** kon-kor'dans, *n.* The state of being concordant; agreement; harmony; a book in which the principal words used in any work, as the Scriptures, Shakespeare, &c., are arranged alphabetically, and the book, chapter, verse, act, scene, line, or other subdivision in which each word occurs are noted.—**Concordant,** kon-kor'dant, *a.* [L. *concordans*, ppr. of *concordare*, to agree.] Agreeing; agreeable; correspondent; harmonious.—**Concordantly,** kon-kor'dant-li, *adv.* In a concordant manner.—**Concordat, Concordate,** kon-kor'dat, kon-kor'dāt, *n.* [Fr.] An agreement; compact; convention; especially, a formal agreement between the see of Rome and any secular government.—**Concordist,** kon-kor'dist, *n.* The compiler of a concordance.

Concorporate, kon-kor'po-rāt, *v.t.* and *i.* —*concorporated, concorporating.* [L. *concorporo*—*con*, together, and *corpus*, a body.] To unite in one mass or body; to unite in any close union.—*a.* United in the same body.—**Concorporation,** kon-kor'po-rā"-shon, *n.* Union of things in one mass or body.

Concourse, kon'kōrs or kong'kōrs, *n.* [Fr. *concours*, from L. *concursus*, from *concurro*, to run together—*con*, and *curro*, to run.] A moving, flowing, or running together; confluence; a meeting or coming together of people; the people assembled; a throng; a crowd; an assemblage of things; agglomeration.

Concreate,† kon'krē-āt, *v.t.*—*concreated, concreating.* [Prefix *con*, and *create*.] To create with or at the same time.

Concrescible,† kon-kres'i-bl, *a.* Capable of concreting; capable of being changed from a liquid to a solid state.—**Concrescive,**† kon-kres'iv, *a.* Growing together; uniting.

Concrete, kon'krēt or kong'krēt, *a.* [L. *concretus*, from *concresco*, to grow together —*con*, and *cresco*, to grow; seen also in *decrease, increase, crescent*, &c.] Formed by union of separate particles in a mass; united in a solid form; *logic*, a term applied to an object as it exists in nature, invested with all its attributes, or to the notion or name of such an object. Abstract.—*n.* A mass formed by concretion of separate particles of matter in one body; a compound; *logic*, a concrete term; a compact mass of gravel, coarse pebbles, or stone chippings cemented together by hydraulic or other mortar, employed extensively in building, especially under water.—*v.i.* and *t.*—*concreted, concreting.* To coagulate; to congeal; to thicken.—**Concretely,** kon-krēt'li, *adv.* In a concrete manner; not abstractly.—**Concreteness,** kon-krēt'nes, *n.* A state of being concrete.—**Concretion,** kon-krē'shon, *n.* The act of concreting or growing together so as to form one mass; the mass or solid matter formed by growing together; a clot; a lump; *geol.* a lump or nodule formed by molecular aggregation as distinct from crystallization. —*Morbid concretions*, hard substances which occasionally make their appearance in different parts of the body.—**Concretional, Concretionary,** kon-krē'shon-al, kon-krē'sho-na-ri, *a.* Pertaining to concretion; formed by concretion; consisting of concretions.—**Concretive,** kon-krē'tiv, *a.* Causing to concrete or become congealed or solid.—**Concretively,** kon-krē'tiv-li, *adv.* In a concretive manner.

Concubine, kong'kū-bīn, *n.* [L. *concubina*, from *concumbo*, to lie together—*con*, and *cumbo* or *cubo*, to lie down.] A paramour, male or female†; a woman who cohabits with a man without being legally married to him; a kept-mistress; a wife of inferior condition, such as were allowed in ancient Greece and Rome; a lawful wife, but not united to the man by the usual ceremonies.—**Concubinage,** kong'kū-bi-nāj, *n.* The act or practice of having a concubine or concubines; the state of being a concubine; a living as man and wife without being married.—**Concubinary, Concubinal, Concubinarian,** kon-kū'bi-na-ri, kon-kū'bi-nal, kon-kū'bi-nā"ri-an, *a.* Relating to concubinage; living in concubinage.

Concupiscence, kon-kū'pi-sens, *n.* [L. *concupiscentia*, from *concupisco*, to lust after —*con*, and *cupio*, to desire.] Lustful feeling; lust; sinful desire.—**Concupiscent,** kon-kū'pi-sent, *a.* Desirous of unlawful pleasure; libidinous; lustful.—**Concupiscible,**† kon-kū'pis-i-bl, *a.* Concupiscent; lustful.

Concur, kon-kėr', *v.i.*—*concurred, concurring.* [L. *concurro*, to run together—*con*, and *curro*, to run; seen also in *course, current, incur, recur*, &c.] To run or meet together†; to agree, join, or unite, as in one action or opinion (to *concur with* a person *in* an opinion (to assent: with *to* (*Mil.*)†; to unite or be conjoined; to meet together; to be combined; to unite in contributing to a common object (causes that *concur* to an effect); to coincide or have points of agreement (*Shak.*).—**Concurrence, Concurrency,** kon-kur'ens, kon-kur'en-si, *n.* The act of concurring; conjunction; combination of agents, circumstances, or events; agreement in opinion; union or consent as to a design to be carried out; approbation; consent with joint aid or contribution of power or influence.—**Concurrent,** kon-kur'ent, *a.* Concurring or acting in conjunction; agreeing in the same act; contributing to the same event or effect; operating with; conjoined; associate; concomitant; joint and equal; existing together and operating on the same objects (the *concurrent* jurisdiction of law courts).—*n.* One who concurs; one agreeing to or pursuing the same course of action; that which concurs; joint or contributory cause.—**Concurrently,** kon-kur'ent-li, *adv.* So as to be concurrent; in union or combination; unitedly.—**Concurrentness,** kon-kur'ent-nes, *n.* The state of being concurrent.

Concuss, kon-kus', *v.t.* [L. *concutio, concussum*, to shake, and as a law term to extort—*con*, together, and *quatio, quassum* (in composition *cutio, cussum*), to shake. Quash.] To shake or agitate†; to force by threats to do something, especially to give up something of value; to intimidate into a desired course of action; to coerce.—**Concussive,** kon-kus'iv, *a.* Having the power or quality of shaking; agitating.—**Concussion,** kon-kush'on, *n.* [L. *concussio, concussionis*, a shock, extortion.] The act of shaking, particularly by the stroke or impulse of another body; the shock occasioned by two bodies coming suddenly into collision; a shock; *surg.* applied to injuries sustained by the brain and other organs from falls, blows, &c.; the act of extorting by threats or force; extortion.—**Concutient,**† kon-kū'shi-ent, *a.* Coming suddenly into collision; meeting together with violence.

Condemn, kon-dem', *v.t.* [L. *condemno*—*con*, intens., and *damno*, to condemn, whence *damn*.] To pronounce to be utterly wrong; to utter a sentence of disapprobation against; to pronounce to be guilty; to sentence to punishment; to utter sentence against judicially: opposed to *acquit* or *absolve*; to judge or pronounce to be unfit for use or service, or to be forfeited.—*Condemned cell* or *ward*, in *prisons*, the cell in which a prisoner sentenced to death is detained till his execution.—**Condemnable,** kon-dem'na-bl, *a.* Worthy of being condemned.—**Condemnation,** kon-dem-nā'shon, *n.* [L. *condemnatio*.] The act of condemning; the state of being condemned; the cause or reason of a sentence of condemnation (N.T.).—**Condemnatory,** kon-dem'na-to-ri, *a.* Condemning; bearing condemnation or censure.—**Condemner,** kon-dem'ėr, *n.* One who condemns.

Condense, kon-dens', *v.t.*—*condensed, condensing.* [L. *condenso*—*con*, and *denso*, to make dense. Dense.] To make more dense or compact; to reduce the volume or compass of; to bring into closer union of parts; to consolidate; to compress (to *condense* a substance, an argument, &c.); to reduce (a gas or vapour) to the condition of a liquid or solid.—*v.i.* To become close or more compact, as the particles of a body; to change from the vaporous to the liquid state.—**Condensed,** kon-denst', *a.* Made dense or close in texture or composition; compressed; compact (a *condensed* style of composition).—**Condenser,** kon-den'sėr, *n.* One who or that which condenses; a pneumatic instrument or syringe in which air may be compressed; a vessel in which aqueous or spirituous vapours are reduced to a liquid form by coldness; a lens to gather and concentrate rays collected by a mirror and direct them upon an object; an instrument employed to collect and render sensible very small quantities of electricity.—**Condensability,** kon-den'sa-bil"i-ti, *n.* Quality of being condensable. —**Condensable, Condensible,** kon-den'sa-bl, kon-den'si-bl, *a.* Capable of being condensed; capable of being compressed into a smaller compass, or made more compact.—**Condensate,**† kon-den'sāt, *v.t.* and *i.*—*condensated, condensating.* To condense.—**Condensation,** kon-den-sā'shon, *n.* [L. *condensatio*.] The act of condensing or making more dense or compact; the act of bringing into smaller compass; consolidation; the act of reducing a gas or vapour to a liquid or solid form. —**Condensative,** kon-den'sa-tiv, *a.* Having a power or tendency to condense.

Condescend, kon-dē-send', *v.t.* [Fr. *condescendre*—L. *con*, with, and *descendo*. Descend.] To descend voluntarily for a time to the level of an inferior; to stoop; to lower one's self intentionally: often followed by the infinitive or a noun preceded by *to*.—**Condescending,** kon-dē-sen'ding, *a.* Marked or characterized by condescension; stooping to the level of one's inferiors.—**Condescendingly,** kon-dē-sen'ding-li, *adv.* In a condescending manner. —**Condescension,** kon-dē-sen'shon, *n.* The act of condescending; the act of voluntarily stooping to an equality with inferiors; affability on the part of a superior.

Condign, kon-dīn', *a.* [L. *condignus*, well worthy—*con*, and *dignus*, worthy. Dignity.] Well-deserved; merited; suitable: now always applied to punishment or something equivalent.—**Condignly,** kon-dīn'li, *adv.* In a condign manner.—**Condignness,** kon-dīn'nes, *n.* The state or quality of being condign.

Condiment, kon'di-ment, *n.* [L. *condimentum*, from *condio*, to season, pickle.] Something used to give relish to food, and to gratify the taste; sauce; seasoning.

Condisciple, kon-di-sī'pl, *n.* A comrade disciple or student associate; a fellow learner; a schoolmate.

Condition, kon-di'shon, *n.* [L. *condicio, condicionis* (also *conditio*), situation, compact, &c.—*con*, and *dīco*, to declare. Diction.] A particular mode of being; situation; predicament; case; state; state with respect to the orders or grades of society or to property; rank in society; that which is requisite to be done, happen, exist, or be present in order to something else being done, taking effect, or happening; a clause in a contract embodying some stipulation, provision, or essential point.—*v.t.* To form the condition or essential accompaniment of; to regulate or determine; to stipulate; to arrange.—**Conditional**, kon-di'shon-al, *a.* Imposing conditions; containing or depending on a condition or conditions; made with limitations; not absolute; made or granted on certain terms; *gram.* and *logic*, expressing or involving a condition.—**Conditionality**, kon-di'sho-nal"i-ti, *n.* The quality of being conditional or limited; limitation by certain terms.—**Conditionally**, kon-di'shon-al-li, *adv.* In a conditional manner; with certain limitations; on particular conditions, terms, or stipulations.—**Conditionate**, kon-di'shon-āt, *v.t.* To put under conditions; to regulate.—**Conditioned**, kon-di'shond, *a.* Having a certain state or qualities, usually preceded by some qualifying term, as *well conditioned*, *ill conditioned*; *metaph.* placed or cognized under conditions or relations.

Condole, kon-dōl', *v.i.*—*condoled*, *condoling*. [L.L. *condoleo*—*con*, with, and L. *doleo*, to grieve, whence *doleful*, *dolour*.] To express pain or grief at the distress or misfortunes of another; to express sympathy to one in grief or misfortune: followed by *with*.—*v.t.*‡ To lament or grieve over.—**Condolatory**, kon-dō'la-to-ri, *a.* Expressing condolence.—**Condolence**, kon-dō'lens, *n.* The act of condoling; expression of sympathy with another's grief.—**Condoler**, kon-dō'lėr, *n.* One who condoles.

Condominium, kon-dō-min'i-um, *n.* [L. *con*, and *dominium*, rule.] Joint rule or control.

Condone, kon-dōn', *v.t.*—*condoned*, *condoning*. [L. *condonare*, to pardon—*con*, and *donare*, to present, from *donum*, a gift. DONATION.] To pardon; to forgive; to overlook an offence (never with a personal object); *law*, to forgive, or to act so as to imply forgiveness of a violation of the marriage vow.—**Condonation**, kon-dō-nā'shon, *n.* [L. *condonatio*.] The act of condoning or pardoning a wrong act; *law*, an act or course of conduct by which a husband or a wife is held to have pardoned a matrimonial offence committed by the other, the party condoning being thus barred from a remedy for that offence.

Condor, kon'dor, *n.* [Sp., from Peruv. *cuntur*.] A South American bird, one of the largest of the vulture tribe, found most commonly in the Andes at heights from 10,000 or 15,000 feet above the level of the sea.

Condottiere, kon-dot-tyā'rā, *n.* pl. **Condottieri**, kon-dot-tyā'rē. [It.] One of a class of mercenary Italian military adventurers in the fourteenth and fifteenth centuries; a free-lance.

Conduce, kon-dūs', *v.i.*—*conduced*, *conducing*. [L. *conduco*, to conduce—*con*, and *duco*, to lead; *conduct* is from the same verb.] To combine with other things in bringing about or tending to bring about a result; to lead or tend; to contribute: followed by the infinitive or a noun preceded by *to*.—**Conducible**,‡ kon-dū'si-bl, *a.* [L. *conducibilis*.] Conducive.—**Conducibleness**,‡ kon-dū'si-bl-nes, *n.* Conduciveness.—**Conducive**, kon-dū'siv, *a.* Having the quality of conducing, promoting, or furthering; tending to advance or bring about: followed by *to*.—**Conduciveness**, kon-dū'siv-nes, *n.* The quality of being conducive.

Conduct, kon'dukt, *n.* [L.L. *conductus*, L. *conductus*, pp. of *conduco*. CONDUCE. DUKE.] The act of guiding or commanding; mode of carrying on or conducting; mode of handling or wielding; administration; management; personal behaviour; deportment: applied indifferently to a good or bad course of action; the act of convoying or guarding; guidance or bringing along under protection.—*v.t.* (kon-dukt'). To accompany and show the way; to guide; to lead; to escort; to lead, as a commander; to direct; to command; to manage (affairs, &c.); *refl.* to behave; *physics*, to carry, transmit, or propagate, as heat, electricity, &c.; to lead or direct as musical conductor.—*v.i.* To carry, transmit, or propagate heat, electricity, sound, &c.; to act as musical conductor.—**Conductibility**, kon-duk'ti-bil"i-ti, *n.* Capacity of being conducted; conductivity.—**Conductible**, kon-duk'ti-bl, *a.* Capable of being conducted or conveyed.—**Conduction**, kon-duk'shon, *n.* *Physics*, the mode of transference of heat through the substance of solids and of electricity through any suitable body called a *conductor*.—**Conductive**, kon-duk'tiv, *a.* *Physics*, having the power or quality of conducting.—**Conductivity**, kon-duk-tiv'i-ti, *n.* *Physics*, the power of conducting heat, electricity, &c.; the quality of being conductive; the quantity of heat that flows in unit time through unit area of a plate of any substance of unit thickness, with one degree of difference of temperature between its faces.—**Conductor**, kon-duk'tėr, *n.* One who conducts; a leader; a guide; a commander; one who leads an army; a director or manager; the director of a chorus or orchestra; the person who attends to the passengers in a bus or a streetcar, or the like, as contradistinguished from the driver; *physics*, a body that receives and transmits or communicates heat, electricity, or force in any of its forms; hence, specifically, a lightning-rod.—**Conductory**, kon-duk'to-ri, *a.* Having the property of conducting.

Conduit, kon'dit or kun'dit, *n.* [Fr. *conduit*, pp. of *conduire*, L. *conducere*, *conductum*, to conduct.] A pipe, tube or other channel for the conveyance of fluids; a tube or pipe for protecting electric wires or cables.

Conduplicate, kon-dū'pli-kāt, *a.* Doubled or folded over or together; *bot.* applied to leaves in the bud when they are folded down the middle, so that the halves of the lamina are applied together by their faces.—**Conduplication**, kon-dū'pli-kā"shon, *n.* A doubling; a duplication.

Condyle, kon'dil, *n.* [L. *condylus*, Gr. *kondylos*, a knuckle, a joint.] *Anat.* a protuberance on the end of a bone serving to form an articulation with another bone.—**Condyloid**, kon'di-loid, *a.* *Anat.* resembling or shaped like a condyle.

Cone, kōn, *n.* [L. *conus*, Gr. *kōnos*, a cone, from root seen in E. *hone*, Skr. *ço*, to sharpen.] A solid figure rising from a circular base and regularly tapering to a point; anything shaped like, or approaching the shape of, a cone; one of the fruits of fir-trees, pines, &c.; a strobilus; the name of certain molluscous shells; the hill surrounding the crater of a volcano, formed by the gradual accumulation of ejected material; a form of storm signal.—**Cone-pulley**, *n.* A pulley shaped like the segment of a cone, that is, gradually tapering from a thick to a thin end.—**Cone-shell**, *n.* One of a family of gasteropodous molluscs, characterized by a shell of a remarkably conical form.—**Conic**, kon'ik, *a.* [L. *conicus*, Gr. *kōnikos*.] Having the form of a cone; conical; pertaining to a cone.—*Conic sections*, the figures formed by the outlines of the cut surfaces when a cone is cut by a plane, more especially the parabola, ellipse, and hyperbola, the first of which is seen when the section is made parallel to the slope of the cone.—*n.* A conic section.—**Conical**, kon'ik-al, *a.* Having the form of a cone; cone-shaped.—**Conicality**, kon-i-kal'i-ti.—**Conicalness**, kon'ik-al-nes, *n.* The state or quality of being conical.—**Conically**, kon'ik-al-li, *adv.* In the form of a cone.—**Conicity**, kō-nis'i-ti, *n.* The property of being conical.—**Conics**, kon'iks, *n.* That part of geometry which treats of the cone and the several curve lines arising from the sections of it.—**Conifer**, kō'ni-fėr, *n.* [L. *conus*, and *fero*, to bear.] *Bot.* a plant producing cones, or hard, dry, scaly seed-vessels of a conical figure, as the pine, fir, &c.—**Coniferæ**, kō-nif'ėr-ē, *n. pl.* The conifers or cone-bearing trees, including the firs, pines, yew, cypress, &c.—**Coniferous**, kō-nif'ėr-us, *a.* Bearing cones; belonging or relating to the conifers.—**Coniform**, kō'ni-form, *a.* In form of a cone; conical.—**Conoid**, kō'noid, *n.* *Geom.* a solid formed by the revolution of a conic section about its axis; *anat.* the pineal gland.—**Conoid**, **Conoidal**, kō'noid, kō-noi'dal, *a.* Approaching to a conical form; nearly conical.—**Conoidic**, **Conoidical**, kō-noi'dik, kō-noi'di-kal, *a.* Pertaining to a conoid.

Coney, *n.* CONY.

Confabulate, kon-fab'ū-lāt, *v.i.* [L. *confabulor*—*con*, and *fabulor*, to talk. FABLE.] To talk familiarly together; to chat; to prattle. This word is sometimes shortened colloquially to **Confab**, kon-fab'.—**Confabulation**, kon-fab'ū-lā"shon, *n.* [L. *confabulatio*.] A talking together; familiar talk; easy, unrestrained conversation. Often shortened to **Confab**, kon-fab'.—**Confabulator**, kon-fab'ū-lā-tėr, *n.* One engaged in familiar talk or conversation.—**Confabulatory**,† kon-fab'ū-la-to-ri, *a.* Belonging to familiar talk.

Confect,‡ kon-fekt', *v.t.* [L. *conficio*, *confectum*, to prepare—*con*, and *facio*, to make. COMFIT.] To compose, mix, put together; to make into sweetmeats.—*n.*‡ (kon'fekt). A confection; a sweetmeat.—**Confection**, kon-fek'shon, *n.* Anything prepared or preserved with sugar, as fruit; a sweetmeat; a composition or mixture‡.—**Confectionary**,‡ kon-fek'sho-na-ri *n.* A confectioner (O.T.).—*a.* Relating to confections.—**Confectioner**, kon-fek'shon-ėr, *n.* One whose occupation is to make or sell sweetmeats or confections.—**Confectionery**, kon-fek'sho-nėr-i, *n.* Sweetmeats; things prepared or sold by a confectioner; confections.

Confederacy, kon-fed'ėr-a-si, *n.* [L.L. *confœderatio*—*con*, and L. *fœdus*, a league. FEDERAL.] A contract between two or more persons, bodies of men or states, combined in support of each other, in some act or enterprise; a league; compact; alliance; the persons, states, or nations united by a league.—**Confederate**, kon-fed'ėr-āt, *a.* [L.L. *confœderatus*.] United in a league; allied by treaty; engaged in a confederacy; pertaining to a confederacy.—*Confederate States of America*, the alliance formed by eleven southern states after secession from the United States in 1860 and 1861.—**Confederation**, kon-fed'ėr-ā"shon, *n.* A confederacy; a league; alliance; the Government of the American Colonies from 1781-1789, previous to the adoption of the Constitution of the United States.—**Confederative**, kon-fed'ėr-ā-tiv, *a.* Of or belonging to a confederation.

Confer, kon-fėr', *v.t.*—*conferred*, *conferring*. [L. *confero*, to bring together, compare, bestow, consult, &c.—*con*, together, and *fero*, to bring.] To give or bestow: with *on* or *upon* before the recipient. ∴ *Confer* differs from *bestow*, inasmuch as it always implies a certain amount of condescension or superiority on the part of the giver.—*v.i.* To consult together on some special subject; to compare opinions: formerly often simply to discourse or talk, but *confer* now implies conversation on some serious or important subject.—**Conferee**, kon-fėr-ē', *n.* One on whom something is conferred.—**Conference**, kon'fėr-ens, *n.* [Fr. *conférence*.] The act of conferring or consulting together; a meeting for consultation, discussion, or instruction; a meeting of the representatives of different foreign countries in regard to some matter of importance to all; talk or conversation (*Shak.*)‡.—**Conferrable**, kon-fer'a-bl, *a.* Capable of being conferred or bestowed.—**Conferrer**, kon-fer'ėr, *n.* One who confers.

Conferva, kon-fėr'va, *n.* pl. **Confervæ**, kon-fėr'vē. [L.] A name for various aquatic plants belonging to the algæ, and chiefly composed of simple or branching filaments.—**Confervaceous**, kon-fėr-vā'shus, *a.* Of or belonging to confervæ or allied plants.—**Confervoid**, kon-fėr'void, *a.* Resembling a conferva; partaking of the character of the confervæ.

Confess, kon-fes', *v.t.* [Fr. *confesser*, from L. *confiteor*, *confessum*—*con*, and *fateor*, to own or acknowledge.] To own, acknowledge, or avow, as a crime, a fault, a charge, a debt, or something that is against one's interest or reputation; to own to; to disclose; *eccles.* to disclose or recapitulate (sins) to a priest in private with a view to absolution: in this sense sometimes *refl.*; to hear or receive the confession of: said of the priest; to acknowledge as having a certain character or certain claims; to declare belief in; to grant, concede, admit; not to dispute; to attest, reveal, let be known (poet.). ∴ Syn. under ACKNOWLEDGE.—*v.i.* To make confession or avowal; to disclose faults; to make known one's sins to a priest.—**Confessedly**, kon-fes'ed-li, *adv.* By general confession or admission; admittedly. — **Confesser**, kon-fes'ėr, *n.* One who confesses. — **Confession**, kon-fesh'on, *n.* The act of confessing; the act of making an avowal; profession (N.T.); a disclosing of sins or faults to a priest; the disburdening of the conscience privately to a confessor.—*Confession of Faith*, a formulary which comprises the articles of faith that a person, a church, &c., accepts as true. —**Confessional**, kon-fesh'on-al, *n.* [Fr. *confessional*, L.L. *confessionale.*] A compartment or cell in which a priest sits to hear confession, having a small opening or hole at each side through which the penitent, kneeling without, makes confession.—*a.* Of or pertaining to a confession.—**Confessionalist**, kon-fesh'on-al-ist, *n.* A priest who sits in the confessional; a confessor.—**Confessionary**, kon-fesh'o-na-ri, *a.* Pertaining to auricular confession.—**Confessor**, kon-fes'ėr, *n.* One who confesses; one who acknowledges a crime or fault; a priest who hears confession and assumes power to grant absolution; one who made a profession of his faith in the Christian religion, and adhered to it in the face of persecution.

Confide, kon-fīd', *v.i.*—*confided, confiding.* [L. *confido*—*con*, and *fido*, to trust. FAITH.] To rely with full assurance of mind; to rest the mind firmly without anxiety; to trust; to believe: followed by *in*.—*v.t.*—*confided, confiding.* To intrust: to commit with full reliance on the party to whom the thing is committed (to *confide* a thing *to* a person). —**Confidant**, kon'fi-dant, *n.masc.* **Confidante**, kon-fi-dant', *n.fem.* [O.Fr.] A person intrusted with the confidence of another; one to whom secrets are confided; a confidential friend.—**Confidence**, kon'fi-dens, *n.* [L. *confidentia.*] Assurance of mind; firm belief; trust; reliance; reliance on one's own abilities, resources, or circumstances; self-reliance; assurance; boldness; courage; that in which trust is placed; ground of trust; a secret; a private or confidential communication (to exchange *confidences* together). — **Confident**, kon'fi-dent, *a.* Full of confidence; having full belief; fully assured; relying on one's self; full of assurance; bold, sometimes overbold.—**Confidential**, kon-fi-den'shal, *a.* Enjoying the confidence of another; intrusted with secrets or with private affairs; intended to be treated as private, or kept in confidence; spoken or written in confidence; secret.—**Confidentially**, kon-fi-den'shal-li, *adv.* In a confidential manner.—**Confidently**, kon'fi-dent-li, *adv.* In a confident manner; with firm trust; with strong assurance; positively; dogmatically. — **Confidentness**, kon'fi-dent-nes, *n.* Confidence.—**Confider**, kon-fī'dėr, *n.* One who confides; one who trusts in or intrusts to another.—**Confiding**, kon-fī'ding, *p.* and *a.* Trusting; reposing confidence; trustful; credulous.—**Confidingly**, kon-fī'ding-li, *adv.* In a confiding manner; trustfully. — **Confidingness**, kon-fī'ding-nes, *n.* Confiding disposition; trustfulness.

Configure,† kon-fig'ūr, *v.t.* — *configured, configuring.* [L. *configuro*—*con*, and *figuro*, to form; *figura*, figure.] To form; to dispose in a certain form, figure, or shape.—**Configuration**, kon-fig'ū-rā″shon, *n.* [L. *configuratio.*] External form, figure, or shape of a thing as resulting from the disposition and shape of its parts; external aspect or appearance; shape or form.

Confine, kon'fīn, *n.* [L. *confinis*, bordering, adjoining, *confine*, a border—*con*, and *finis*, end, border, limit. FINE.] Border; boundary; frontier; the part of any territory which is at or near the end or extremity: generally in the plural and in regard to contiguous regions. — *v.t.* (kon-fīn') — *confined, confining.* [Fr. *confiner.*] To restrain within limits; to circumscribe; hence, to imprison; to immure; to shut up; to limit or restrain voluntarily in some act or practice (to *confine one's self to* a subject).—*To be confined*, to be in child-bed.—**Confinable**, kon-fī'na-bl, *a.* Capable of being confined or limited.—**Confined**, kon-fīnd', *p.* and *a.* Restrained within limits; limited; circumscribed; narrow (a *confined* scope or range).—**Confinement**, kon-fīn'ment, *n.* The state of being confined; restraint within limits; any restraint of liberty by force or other obstacle or necessity; imprisonment; the lying-in of a woman.—**Confiner**, kon-fī'nėr, *n.* One who or that which confines.

Confirm, kon-fėrm', *v.t.* [L. *confirmo*—*con*, and *firmo*, to make firm, from *firmus*, firm.] To make firm or more firm; to add strength to; to strengthen; to settle or establish; to make certain; to put past doubt; to assure; to verify; to sanction; to ratify (an agreement, promise); to strengthen in resolution, purpose, or opinion; to administer the rite of confirmation to.—**Confirmable**, kon-fėr'ma-bl, *a.* Capable of being confirmed.—**Confirmance**,† kon-fėr'mans, *n.* Confirmation.—**Confirmation**, kon-fėr-mā'shon, *n.* The act of confirming; the act of establishing; establishment; corroboration; the act of rendering valid or ratifying; the ceremony of laying on hands by a bishop in the admission of baptized persons to the full enjoyment of Christian privileges, a rite of the Roman, Greek, and English churches; that which confirms; additional evidence; proof; convincing testimony.—**Confirmative**, kon-fėr'ma-tiv, *a.* Tending to confirm or establish; confirmatory. — **Confirmatively**, kon-fėr'ma-tiv-li, *adv.* In a confirmative manner; so as to confirm.—**Confirmatory**, kon-fėr'ma-to-ri, *a.* Serving to confirm; giving additional strength, force, or stability, or additional assurance or evidence.—**Confirmed**, kon-fėrmd', *p.* and *a.* Fixed; settled; settled in certain habits, state of health, &c. (a *confirmed* drunkard or invalid); having received the rite of confirmation. — **Confirmedly**, con-fėr'med-li, *adv.* In a confirmed manner.—**Confirmer**, kon-fėr'mėr, *n.* One who or that which confirms.

Confiscate, kon-fis'kāt or kon'fis-kāt, *v.t.* —*confiscated, confiscating.* [L. *confisco, confiscatum*—*con*, together, and *fiscus*, the state treasury.] To adjudge to be forfeited to the public treasury; to appropriate to public use by way of penalty; to appropriate under legal authority as forfeited.—*a.* Confiscated. (*Shak.*) — **Confiscable**,† kon-fis'ka-bl, *a.* Capable of being confiscated; liable to forfeiture. — **Confiscation**, kon-fis-kā'shon, *n.* The act of confiscating or appropriating as forfeited.—**Confiscator**, kon'fis-kā-tėr or kon-fis', *n.* One who confiscates.—**Confiscatory**, kon-fis'ka-to-ri, *a.* Confiscating; relating to confiscation.

Conflagration, kon-fla-grā'shon, *n.* [L. *conflagratio*—*con*, with, and *flagro*, to burn, whence *flagrant.*] A great fire, or the burning of any great mass of combustibles.—**Conflagrate**, kon-flā'grāt, *v.t.* To burn up; to consume with fire. (*Carl.*)

Conflate,† kon-flāt', *v.t.*—*conflated, conflating.* [L. *conflo, conflatum*, to collect—*con*, together, and *flo*, to blow; same root as E. *blow.*] To bring together; to collect.

Conflict, kon'flikt, *n.* [L. *conflictus*, a conflict, from *confligo*—*con*, together, and *fligo*, to strike, to dash.] A fighting or struggle for mastery; a combat; a striving to oppose or overcome; active opposition; contention; strife.—kon-flikt', *v.i.* To meet in opposition or hostility; to contend; to strive or struggle; to be in opposition; to be contrary; to be incompatible or at variance.—**Conflicting**, kon-flik'ting, *a.* Being in opposition; contrary; contradictory; incompatible.—**Confliction**,† kon-flik'shon, *n.* Act of conflicting or clashing.

Confluence, kon'flū-ens, *n.* [L. *confluentia*, from *confluo*—*con*, and *fluo*, to flow.] A flowing together; the meeting or junction of two or more streams of water; also, the place of meeting; the running together of people; a crowd; a concourse. — **Confluent**, kon'flū-ent, *a.* [L. *confluens.*] Flowing together; meeting in their course, as two streams; meeting; running together; *bot.* united at some part.—*Confluent small-pox*, small-pox in which the pustules run together or unite.—*n.* A tributary stream.—**Conflux**, kon'fluks, *n.* A flowing together; a crowd; a multitude collected.

Conform, kon-form', *v.t.* [L. *conformo*—*con*, and *forma*, form.] To make of the same form or character; to make like (to *conform* anything *to* a model); to bring into harmony or correspondence; to adapt; to submit: often *refl.*—*v.i.* To act in conformity or compliance; *eccles.* to comply with the usages of the Established Church.—*a.* [L. *conformis*—*con*, and *forma*, form.] Conformable. — **Conformability**, kon-for'ma-bil″i-ti, *n.* The state or quality of being conformable. — **Conformable**, kon-for'ma-bl, *a.* Corresponding in form, character, manners, opinions, &c.; in harmony or conformity; agreeable; suitable; consistent; adapted; compliant; submissive; disposed to obey; *geol.* lying in parallel or nearly parallel planes, and having the same dip and changes of dip: said of strata or groups of strata.—**Conformableness**, kon-for'ma-bl-nes, *n.* State of being conformable. —**Conformably**, kon-for'ma-bli, *adv.* In a conformable manner; in conformity; suitably; agreeably.—**Conformation**, kon-for-mā'shon, *n.* The manner in which a body is formed; the particular disposition of the parts which compose it; configuration; form; structure.—**Conformer**, kon-for'mėr, *n.* One who conforms; one who complies with established forms or doctrines.—**Conformist**, kon-for'mist, *n.* One who conforms or complies; one who complies with the worship of the Church of England, as distinguished from a Dissenter or Nonconformist.—**Conformity**, kon-form'i-ti, *n.* Correspondence in form or manner; agreement; congruity; likeness; harmony; correspondence with decrees or dictates; submission; accordance; compliance with the usages or principles of the English Church.

Confound, kon-found', *v.t.* [Fr. *confondre*, from L. *confundo*—*con*, together, and *fundo*, *fusum*, to pour out, whence *fuse, confuse, refuse*, &c.] To mingle confusedly together; to mix in a mass or crowd so that individuals cannot be distinguished; to throw into disorder; to confuse; to mistake one for another; to make a mistake between; to throw into consternation; to perplex with terror, surprise, or astonishment; to astound; to abash; to overthrow, ruin, baffle, or bring to nought. ∴ Syn. under ABASH.—**Confounded**, kon-foun'ded, *a.* Excessive; odious; detestable. (Colloq.)—**Confoundedly**, kon-foun'ded-li, *adv.* Enormously; greatly; shamefully; odiously; detestably. (Colloq.)—**Confounder**, kon-foun'dėr, *n.* One who or that which confounds.

Confraternity, kon-fra-tėr'ni-ti, *n.* A fraternity or brotherhood.

Confront, kon-frunt', *v.t.* [Fr. *confronter* —L. *con*, together, and *frons, frontis*, the countenance or front.] To stand facing; to face; to stand in front of; to meet in hostility; to oppose; to set face to face; to bring into the presence of†: followed by *with*. — **Confrontation**†, **Confrontment**,† kon-frun-tā'shon, kon-frunt'ment, *n.* The act of confronting.—**Confronter**, kon-frun'tėr, *n.* One who confronts.

Confucian, **Confucianist**, kon-fū'shi-an, kon-fū'shi-an-ist, *n.* A follower of Confucius, the famous Chinese philosopher.—**Confucian**, kon-fū'shi-an, *a.* Relating to Confucius.—**Confucianism**, kon-fū'shi-an-izm, *n.* The doctrines or system of morality taught by Confucius, which has been long adopted in China, and inculcates the practice of virtue but not the worship of any god.

Confuse, kon-fūz', *v.t.*—*confused, confusing.* [L. *confusus*, from *confundo*. CON-

FOUND.] To mix up without order or clearness; to throw together indiscriminately; to derange, disorder, jumble; to confound; to perplex or derange the mind or ideas of; to embarrass; to disconcert. ∴ Syn. under ABASH.—**Confused**, kon-fūzd′, *p.* and *a.* Mixed up together without order or arrangement; indiscriminately mingled (a *confused* heap); disordered; perplexed; embarrassed; disconcerted.—**Confusedly**, kon-fū′zed-li, *adv.* In a confused manner; in a mixed mass; without order; indiscriminately; with agitation of mind.—**Confusedness**, kon-fū′zed-nes, *n.* A state of being confused.—**Confusion**, kon-fū′zhon, *n.* [L. *confusio.*] A state in which things are confused; an indiscriminate or disorderly mingling; disorder; tumultuous condition; perturbation of mind; embarrassment; distraction; abashment; disconcertment; overthrow; defeat; ruin.—**Confusive**, kon-fū′ziv, *a.* Having a tendency to confusion.

Confute, kon-fūt′, *v.t.*—*confuted, confuting.* [L. *confuto*, to cool down by cold water, to confute—*con*, together, and *futis*, a pitcher, from root of *fundo*, to pour. To prove (an argument, statement, &c.) to be false, defective, or invalid; to disprove; to overthrow; to prove (a person) to be wrong; to convict of error by argument or proof.—**Confutable**, kon-fū′ta-bl, *a.* Capable of being confuted.—**Confutation**, kon-fū-tā′shon, *n.* The act of confuting, disproving, or proving to be false or invalid.—**Confutative**, kon-fū′ta-tiv, *a.* Adapted or designed to confute.—**Confuter**, kon-fū′tėr, *n.* One who confutes.

Congé, kon′jē; Fr. pron. kōṅ-zhā, *n.* [Fr., leave, permission; from L. *commeatus*, leave of absence, from *commeo, commeatum* to go or come—*com*, and *meo*, to go.] Leave to depart; farewell; dismissal; a ceremonious leave-taking; an act of civility on other occasions; a bow or a courtesy.—*Congé d'élire* (leave to elect), the sovereign's license or permission to a dean and chapter to choose a bishop, the person to be chosen being recommended by the crown. The form **Congee** is also used, and sometimes as a verb; to take leave; to make a congé or bow.

Congeal, kon-jēl′, *v.t.* [L. *congelare*—*con*, together, and *gelare*, to freeze, from *gelu*, cold, whence also *gelid, jelly.*] To change from a fluid to a solid state by cold or a loss of heat; to freeze; to coagulate; to check the flow of; to make (the blood) run cold. —*v.i.* To pass from a fluid to a solid state by cold; to coagulate.—**Congealable**, kon-jēl′a-bl, *a.* Capable of being congealed. —**Congealableness**, kon-jēl′a-bl-nes, *n.* The quality of being congealable.—**Congealment**, kon-jel′ment, *n.* Congelation.—**Congelation**, kon-jē-lā′shon, *n.* [L. *congelatio.*] The act or process of congealing; the state of being congealed; what is congealed or solidified; a concretion.

Congee, CONGE.

Congener, kon′jē-nėr, *n.* [L.—*con*, together, and *genus, generis*, a kind or race.] A thing of the same kind or nearly allied; a plant or animal belonging to the same genus.—**Congeneric, Congenerical**, kon-jē-ner′ik, kon-jē-ner′ik-al, *a.* Being of the same kind or nature; belonging to the same genus.—**Congenerous**, kon-jen′ėr-us, *a.* Congeneric; *anat.* applied to muscles which concur in the same action.

Congenial, kon-jē′ni-al, *a.* [L. *con*, and *genialis*, E. *genial.*] Partaking of the same nature or natural characteristics; kindred; sympathetic; suited for each other.—**Congeniality, Congenialness**, kon-jē′ni-al′i-ti, kon-jē′ni-al-nes, *n.* The state of being congenial; natural affinity; suitableness.—**Congenialize**, kon-jē′ni-al-īz, *v.t.* To make congenial.—**Congenially**, kon-jē′ni-al-li, *adv.* In a congenial manner.

Congenital, kon-jen′i-tal, *a.* [L. *congenitus*—*con*, and *genitus*, born, *root gen*, to produce.] Belonging or pertaining to an individual from birth (a *congenital* deformity).

Conger, Conger-eel, kong′gėr, *n.* [L. *conger*, a conger-eel.] The sea-eel, a large voracious species of eel, sometimes growing to the length of 10 feet, and weighing 100 lbs.

Congeries, kon-jē′ri-ēz, *n. sing.* and *pl.* [L., from *congero*, to amass—*con*, and *gero*, to bear.] A collection of several particles or bodies in one mass or aggregate; an aggregate; a combination.

Congest, kon-jest′, *v.t.* [L. *congero, congestum*—*con*, and *gero*, to bear.] To heap together‡; *med.* to cause an unnatural accumulation of blood in.—**Congested**, kon-jes′ted, *a.* *Med.* containing an unnatural accumulation of blood; affected with congestion.—**Congestion**, kon-jest′yon, *n.* [L. *congestio.*] *Med.* an excessive accumulation of blood in an organ, the functions of which are thereby disordered.—**Congestive**, kon-jes′tiv, *a.* Pertaining to congestion; indicating an unnatural accumulation of blood in some part of the body.

Conglobate, kon′glō-bāt, *a.* [L. *conglobatus*—*con*, and *globus*, a ball. GLOBE.] Formed or gathered into a ball or small spherical body; combined into one mass. —*v.t.*†—*conglobated, conglobating.* To collect or form into a ball; to combine into one mass.—*v.i.* To assume a round or globular form.—**Conglobately**, kon′glō-bāt-li, *adv.* In a round or roundish form.—**Conglobation**, kon-glō-bā′shon, *n.* The act of forming or gathering into a ball; a round body.—**Conglobe**,† kon-glōb′, *v.t.* and *i.*—*conglobed, conglobing.* To conglobate.

Conglomerate, kon-glom′ėr-āt, *a.* [L. *conglomero, conglomeratum*—*con*, and *glomus, glomeris*, a ball, a clew.] Gathered into a ball or round body; crowded together; clustered.—*v.t.*—*conglomerated, conglomerating.* To gather into a ball or round body; to collect into a round mass.—*n.* A kind of rock made up of rounded fragments of various rocks cemented together by a matrix of siliceous, calcareous, or other cement; gravel solidified by cement into a rock; pudding-stone.—**Conglomeration**, kon-glom′ėr-ā″shon, *n.* The act of conglomerating; collection; accumulation; what is conglomerated; a mixed mass; a mixture.

Conglutinate, kon-glū′ti-nāt, *v.t.*—*conglutinated, conglutinating.* [L. *conglutino*—*con*, and *glutino*, from *gluten*, glue. GLUE.] To glue together; to unite by some glutinous or tenacious substance; to reunite; to cement.—*v.i.* To coalesce; to unite by the intervention of some glutinous substance.—*a.* Glued together; *bot.* united by some adhesive substance, but not organically united.—**Conglutinant**, kon-glū′ti-nant, *a.* Gluing; uniting.—**Conglutination**, kon-glū′ti-nā″shon, *n.* The act of gluing together; a joining by means of some tenacious substance; union; coalescence.—**Conglutinative**, kon-glū′ti-nā-tiv, *a.* Having the power of uniting by agglutination.—**Conglutinator**, kon-glū′ti-nā-tėr, *n.* That which has the power of uniting wounds.

Congou, kong′gö, *n.* [Chinese *kung-fu*, labour.] The second lowest quality of black tea, being the third picking from a plant during the season.

Congratulate, kon-grat′ū-lāt, *v.t.*—*congratulated, congratulating.*—[L. *congratulor*—*con*, and *gratulor*, from *gratus*, grateful, pleasing. GRACE.] To address with expressions of sympathetic pleasure on some piece of good fortune happening to the party addressed; to compliment upon an event deemed happy; to wish joy to; to felicitate; also *refl.* to have a lively sense of one's own good fortune; to consider one's self lucky.—**Congratulable**,† kon-grat′ū-la-bl, *a.* Capable or worthy of being congratulated.—**Congratulant**, kon-grat′ū-lant, *a.* Congratulating; expressing pleasure in another's good fortune.—**Congratulation**, kon-grat′ū-lā″shon, *n.* The act of congratulating; words used in congratulating; expression to a person of pleasure in his good fortune; felicitation.—**Congratulator**, kon-grat′ū-lā-tėr, *n.* One who congratulates.—**Congratulatory**, kon-grat′ū-la-to-ri, *a.* Containing or expressing congratulation.

Congregate, kong′grē-gāt, *v.t.*—*congregated, congregating.* [L. *congrego*—*con*, and *grex, gregis*, a herd. GREGARIOUS.] To collect into an assemblage; to assemble; to bring into one place or into a crowd or united body.—*v.i.* To come together; to assemble; to meet in a crowd.—*a.* Collected; compact; close.—**Congregation**, kong-grē-gā′shon, *n.* The act of congregating; the act of bringing together or assembling; a collection or assemblage of persons or things; an assembly, especially an assembly of persons met for the worship of God; or a number of people organized as a body for the purpose of holding religious services in common.—**Congregational**, kong-grē-gā′shon-al, *a.* Pertaining to a congregation; pertaining to the Independents or Congregationalists, or to Congregationalism. —**Congregationalism**, kong-grē-gā′shon-al-izm, *n.* A system of administering church affairs by which each congregation has the right of regulating the details of its worship, discipline, and government.—**Congregationalist**, kong-grē-gā′shon-al-ist, *n.* One who belongs to a Congregational church or society; an Independent.

Congress, kong′gres, *n.* [L. *congressus*, a meeting, from *congredior, congressum*, to come together—*con*, and *gradior*, to go; *gradus*, a step, whence *grade, degree*, &c.] A meeting together of individuals; an assembly of envoys, commissioners, deputies, &c.; a meeting of sovereign princes or of the representatives of several courts, for the purpose of arranging international affairs; the legislative assembly of the United States of America, consisting of the Senate and House of Representatives.—*v.i.*† To come together; to assemble; to meet.—**Congressional**, kon-gresh′on-al, *a.* Pertaining to a congress or to the congress of the United States.—**Congressman**, *n.* A member of the United States Congress.

Congreve, kong′grēv, *n.* A kind of lucifer match.—*Congreve rocket*, so called from the inventor, Sir William *Congreve*, an iron rocket for use in war.

Congrue,† kon-grö′, *v.i.* [L. *congruo*, to suit, to be congruous.] To be consistent; to agree. (*Shak.*)—**Congruence, Congruency**, kong′gru̧-ens, kong′gru̧-en-si, *n.* [L. *congruentia.*] Suitableness of one thing to another; agreement; consistency.—**Congruent**, kong′gru̧-ent, *a.* Suitable; agreeing; corresponding.—**Congruently**, kong′gru̧-ent-li, *adv.* In a congruent manner.—**Congruity, Congruousness**, kong-grö′i-ti, kong′gru̧-us-nes, *n.* The state or quality of being congruous; agreement between things; suitableness; pertinence; consistency; propriety.—**Congruous**, kong′gru̧-us, *a.* [L. *congruus.*] Accordant; harmonious; well adapted; appropriate; meet; fit.—**Congruously**, kong′gru̧-us-li, *adv.* In a congruous manner; suitably; pertinently; agreeably; consistently.

Conic, Conifer, &c. Under CONE.

Conidium, -ia, kon-id′i-um, *n.* [Gr. dim. of *kŏnis*, dust.] In fungi, a minute asexual spore.

Coniine, kō-nī′in, *n.* [From *conium*, the hemlock.] An alkaloid poison contained in hemlock.

Coniotheca, kon′i-ō-thē″ka, *n.* pl. **Coniothecæ**, kon′i-ō-thē″sē. [Gr. *konis, konios*, dust, and *thēkē*, a case.] *Bot.* an anther-cell.

Coniroster, kō-ni-ros′tėr, *n.* [L. *conus*, a cone, and *rostrum*, a beak.] A member of the Conirostres (kō-ni-ros′trēz), a section or sub-order of insessorial birds comprising those genera which have a strong bill, more or less conical, and without notches.—**Conirostral**, kō-ni-ros′tral, *a.* Of or pertaining to the conirosters.

Conjecture, kon-jek′tūr, *n.* [Fr. *conjecture*, L. *conjectura*, a conjecture, lit. a throwing or putting of things together, from *conjicio*, to throw together—*con*, and *jacio*, to throw.] A guess or inference based on the supposed possibility or probability of **a fact**, or on slight evidence; an opinion formed on insufficient or presumptive evidence; surmise.—*v.t.*—*conjectured, conjecturing*. To judge by guess or conjecture; to guess.—*v.i.* To form conjectures.—**Conjecturer**, kon-jek'tūr-ėr, *n.* One who conjectures; a guesser.—**Conjecturable**, kon-jek'tūr-a-bl, *a.* Capable of being guessed or conjectured.—**Conjectural**, kon-jek'tūr-al, *a.* Depending on conjecture; implying guess or conjecture.—**Conjecturalist**,† kon-jek'tūr-al-ist, *n.* One who deals in conjectures.—**Conjecturality**,† kon-jek'tū-ral"i-ti, *n.* The quality of being conjectural; guesswork.—**Conjecturally**, kon-jek'tūr-al-li, *adv.* In a conjectural manner; by conjecture; by guess.

Conjoin, kon-join', *v.t.* [*Con* and *join*; Fr. *conjoindre*.] To join together or in one; to unite; to associate or connect.—*v.i.* To unite; to join; to league.—**Conjoint**, kon-joint', *a.* United; connected; associated.—**Conjointly**, kon-joint'li, *adv.* In a conjoint manner; jointly; unitedly; in union; together.

Conjugal, kon'jū-gal, *a.* [L. *conjugalis*—*con*, together, and *jugum*, a yoke, from *jug*, root of *jungo*, to join, seen also in E. *yoke*. YOKE.] Belonging to marriage or married persons; matrimonial; connubial.—**Conjugally**, kon'jū-gal-li, *adv.* Matrimonially; connubially.

Conjugate, kon'jū-gāt, *v.t.*—*conjugated, conjugating*. [L. *conjugo, conjugatus*, to couple—*con*, and *jugo*, to yoke. CONJUGAL.] *Gram.* to inflect (a verb) through its several voices, moods, tenses, numbers, and persons, or so many of them.—*a.* United in pairs; joined together; coupled; *bot.* applied to a pinnate leaf which has only one pair of leaflets; *chem.* containing two or more radicals acting the part of a single one; *gram.* applied to words from the same root, and having the same radical signification, but modified by the affix added, or to words which have the same form but are different parts of speech; *math.* applied to two points, lines, &c., when they are considered together, with regard to any property, in such a manner that they may be interchanged without altering the way of enunciating the property.—*Conjugate foci*, in a mirror or lens, are two points such that rays proceeding from either are reflected or refracted to the other.—*n.* What is conjugate: a conjugate word.—**Conjugation**, kon-jū-gā'shon, *n.* [L. *conjugatio*.] The inflection of a verb in its different forms; a class of verbs conjugated in the same way; *biol.* the union of two sex-cells (gametes) of similar appearance.—**Conjugational**, kon-jū-gā'shon-al, *a.* Of or belonging to conjugation.

Conjunct, kon-jungkt', *a.* [L. *conjunctus*, from *conjungo*. CONJOIN.] Conjoined; united; concurrent.—**Conjunction**, kon-jungk'shon, *n.* [L. *conjunctio*.] Union; connection; association; *astron.* that position of a planet in which it is in a line with the earth or another planet and the sun; *gram.* an indeclinable particle, serving to unite words, sentences, or clauses of a sentence, and indicating their relation to one another.—**Conjunctional**, kon-jungk'shon-al, *a.* Belonging or relating to a conjunction.—**Conjunctionally**, kon-jungk'shon-al-li, *adv.* In a conjunctional manner.—**Conjunctiva**, kon-jungk-tī'va, *n.* *Anat.* the mucous membrane which lines the inner surface of the eyelids, and is continued over the fore-part of the globe of the eye.—**Conjunctive**, kon-jungk'tiv, *a.* [L. *conjunctivus*.] Uniting; serving to unite.—*Conjunctive mood*, *gram.* the mood which follows a conjunction or expresses some condition or contingency; the subjunctive.—**Conjunctively**, kon-jungk'tiv-li, *adv.* In a conjunctive manner.—**Conjunctivitis**, kon-junk-tiv-ī'tis, *n.* [From *conjunctiva*, and Gr. *-itis*, inflammation.] Inflammation of the conjunctiva.—**Conjunctly**, kon-jungkt'li, *adv.* In a conjunct manner; in union; jointly; together.—**Conjuncture**, kon-jungk'tūr, *n.* Combination of circumstances or affairs; especially, a critical time, proceeding from a union of circumstances; a crisis of affairs.

Conjure, *v.t.*—*conjured, conjuring*. [L. *conjuro*, to swear together, to conspire—*con*, with, and *juro*, to swear, whence also *jury, perjure*.] With pron. kon-jūr', to call on or summon by a sacred name or in a solemn manner; to implore with solemnity; to adjure: with pron. kun'jėr, to affect or effect by magic or enchantment; to bring about by affecting the arts of a conjurer.—*To conjure* (kun'jėr) *up*, to call up or bring into existence by conjuring or as if by conjuring.—*v.i.* (kun'jėr). To practise the arts of a conjurer; to use magic arts.—**Conjuration**, kon-jū-rā'shon, *n.* The act of conjuring or imploring with solemnity; the act of binding by an oath; adjuration; an incantation; a spell.—**Conjurement**, kon-jūr'ment, *n.* Adjuration; solemn demand or entreaty.—**Conjurer, Conjuror**, kun'jėr-ėr, *n.* An enchanter; one who practises legerdemain; a juggler.—**Conjury**, kun'jėr-i, *n.* The act or art of a conjurer; magic; legerdemain.

Connascence, Connascency, kon-nas'ens, kon-nas'en-si, *n.* [L. *con*, and *nascor*, *natus*, to be born.] The common birth of two or more at the same time; the act of growing together or at the same time.—**Connascent**, kon-nas'ent, *a.* Produced together or at the same time.—**Connate**, kon'nāt, *a.* [L. *con*, and *natus*, born.] Belonging to from birth; implanted at birth: applied chiefly in *philos.* to ideas or principles; *bot.* united in origin; growing from one base, or united at their bases (a leaf, an anther); *med.* congenital.

Connature, kon-nā'tūr, *n.* Likeness in nature; identity or similarity of character.—**Connatural**, kon-nat'ū-ral, *a.* Connected by nature; united in nature; belonging to by nature.—**Connaturality, Connaturalness**, kon-nat'ū-ral"i-ti, kon-nat'ū-ral-nes, *n.* Participation of the same nature; natural union.—**Connaturally**, kon-nat'ū-ral-li, *adv.* In a connatural manner; by the act of nature; originally.

Connect, kon-nekt', *v.t.* [L. *connecto, connexum*—*con*, and *necto*, to bind.] To fasten together; to join or unite; to conjoin; to combine; to associate.—*v.i.* To join, unite, or cohere.—**Connectedly**, kon-nek'ted-li, *adv.* By connection; in a connected manner; conjointly.—**Connection, Connexion**, kon-nek'shon, *n.* [L. *connexio*.] The act of connecting or state of being connected; also that which connects; union by something physical or by relation of any kind; relationship by blood or marriage, but more specifically by marriage; a person connected with another by this relationship; circle of persons with whom any one is brought into contact.—*In this connection*, in connection with what is now under consideration.—**Connective**, kon-nek'tiv, *a.* Having the power of connecting; tending to connect; connecting.—*n.* That which connects; *gram.* a word that connects other words and sentences; a conjunction.—**Connectively**, kon-nek'tiv-li, *adv.* In a connective manner; jointly.—**Connector**, kon-nek'tėr, *n.* One who or that which connects.

Conning-tower, *n.* An armoured structure on a warship from which the officer in charge issues his orders during the time the ship is in action.

Connive, kon-nīv', *v.i.*—*connived, conniving*. [L. *conniveo*, to wink, to connive at—*con*, together, and *niveo*, to wink.] To wink or close and open the eyelids rapidly†; *fig.* to close the eyes upon a fault or other act; to pretend ignorance or blindness; to forbear to see; to wink at or overlook a fault or other act and suffer it to pass unnoticed: followed by *at*.—**Connivance, Connivancy, Connivency**, kon-nī'vans, kon-nīv'an-si, kon-nī'ven-si, *n.* The act of conniving; voluntary blindness to an act.—**Connivent**, kon-nī'vent, *a.* Conniving; *nat. hist.* having a gradually inward direction; converging.—**Conniver**, kon-nī'vėr, *n.* One who connives.

Connoisseur, kon'is-sūr, *n.* [O.Fr. *connoisseur*, Mod.Fr. *connaisseur*, from the verb *connoitre, connaître*, from L. *cognoscere*, to know. COGNIZANCE.] A critical judge; one competent to pass a critical judgment upon anything.—**Connoisseurship**, kon'is-sūr-ship, *n.* The rôle or part of a connoisseur.

Connote, Connotate, kon-nōt', kon'ō-tāt, *v.t.*—*connoted, connoting; connotated, connotating*. [L. *con*, and *noto, notatum* to mark. NOTE.] To include in the meaning; to comprise among the attributes expressed; to imply. ∴ *Connote* and *denote* are contrasted in logic. Thus the word 'horse' *connotes* the qualities that distinguish a horse from other animals, and *denotes* the class of animals which are characterized by having these qualities. 'Thames', however, *connotes* nothing, being simply the name of the particular river which it *denotes*.—*v.i.* To have a meaning or signification in connection with another word.—**Connotation**, kon-ō-tā'shon, *n.* That which constitutes the meaning of a word; the attributes expressed by a word.—**Connotative**, kon-nō'ta-tiv, *a.* Connoting; significant.

Connubial, kon-nū'bi-al, *a.* [L. *connubialis*, from *connubium*, marriage—*con*, and *nubo*, to marry.] Pertaining to marriage; nuptial; belonging to the state of husband and wife.—**Connubiality**, kon-nū'bi-al"i-ti, *n.* The state of being connubial; anything pertaining to the state of husband and wife.—**Connubially**, kon-nū'bi-al-li, *adv.* In a connubial manner; as man and wife.

Connumerate, kon-nū'mėr-āt, *v.t.* To reckon or count in with anything else.—**Connumeration**, kon-nū'mėr-ā"shon, *n.* A reckoning together.

Conocarp, kō'nō-kärp, *n.* [Gr. *kōnos*, a cone, and *karpos*, fruit.] *Bot.* a fruit consisting of a collection of carpels arranged upon a conical centre, as the strawberry.

Conoid, Conoidal, &c. Under CONE.

Conoscente, kon-o-sen'tā, *n.* Same as *Cognoscente*.

Conquer, kong'kėr, *v.t.* [O.Fr. *conquerre, conquerrer*, Mod.Fr. *conquérir*, from L. *conquiro*, to seek for, procure—*con*, and *quæro*, to seek (whence *quest* and *query*).] To overcome and bring to subjection in war; to reduce by physical force till resistance is no longer made; to vanquish; to gain by force; to overcome or surmount (obstacles, difficulties); to gain or obtain by effort. ∴ *Conquer* is wider and more general than *vanquish*, denoting usually a succession of struggles or conflicts; while *vanquish* refers more commonly to a single conflict, and has regularly a personal object. *Subdue* implies a continued process and a complete and thorough subjection.—*v.i.* To overcome; to gain the victory.—**Conquerable**, kong'kėr-a-bl, *a.* Capable of being conquered, overcome, or subdued.—**Conquerableness**, kong'kėr-a-bl-nes, *n.*—**Conqueress**, kong'kėr-es, *n.* A female who conquers.—**Conqueror**, kong'kėr-ėr, *n.* One who conquers or gains a victory.—*The Conqueror*, an epithet applied to William I of England, as expressing his conquest of the country.—**Conquest**, kong'kwest, *n.* [O.Fr. *conquest*, Fr. *conquête*.] The act of conquering; the act of overcoming or vanquishing opposition by force, physical or moral; subjugation; that which is conquered; a possession gained by force.—*The Conquest*, by pre-eminence the conquest of England by William of Normandy.—**Conquistador**, kong-kwis'ta-dōr, *n.* [Sp.] A term applied to the early Spanish leaders who conquered Spanish America.

Consanguinity, kon-sang-gwin'i-ti, *n.* [L. *consanguinitas*—prefix *con*, and *sanguis*, *sanguinis*, blood.] The relation of persons by blood, the relation or connection of persons descended from the same stock or common ancestor, in distinction from *affinity* or relation by marriage.—**Consanguineous**, kon-sang-gwin'ē-us, *a.* [L. *consanguineus*.] Of the same blood; related by birth; descended from the same parent or ancestor.

Conscience, kon'shens, *n.* [L. *conscientia*,

from *conscio*, to know, to be privy to—*con*, with, and *scio*, to know. SCIENCE.] Private or inward thoughts or real sentiments (*Shak.*); the faculty, power, or principle within us, which decides on the rightness or wrongness of our own actions and affections; the sense of right and wrong; the moral sense; morality; what a good conscience would approve.—*A bad conscience*, a reproving conscience.—*A good conscience*, an approving conscience.—*In all conscience*, to be reasonable, to keep within the bounds of moderation: a form of asseveration.—*Conscience clause*, a clause or article in an act or law which specially relieves persons having conscientious scruples in taking judicial oaths, or having their children present at school during the time of religious instruction or service. —**Conscientious**, kon-shi-en'shus, *a.* Influenced by conscience; governed by a strict regard to the dictates of conscience, or by the known or supposed rules of right and wrong.—**Conscientiously**, kon-shi-en'shus-li, *adv.* In a conscientious manner; according to the direction of conscience.—**Conscientiousness**, kon-shi-en'shus-nes, *n.* The state or quality of being conscientious. —**Conscionable**, kon'shon-a-bl, *a.* [For *conscience-able.*] Governed by conscience; according to conscience; reasonable; just.—**Conscionableness**, kon'shon-a-bl-nes, *n.* The state or quality of being conscionable. —**Conscionably**, kon'shon-a-bli, *adv.* In a conscionable manner; reasonably; justly.

Conscious, kon'shus, *a.* [L. *conscius*—*con*, and *scio*, to know. CONSCIENCE.] Knowing what affects or what goes on in one's own mind; having direct knowledge of a thing; having such a knowledge as is conveyed by immediate sensation or perception; aware; sensible (*conscious of* something); having become the subject of consciousness; known to one's self (*conscious* guilt).—**Consciously**, kon'shus-li, *adv.* In a conscious manner; with knowledge of one's own mental operations or actions. —**Consciousness**, kon'shus-nes, *n.* The faculty of knowing what affects or what goes on in one's own mind; immediate knowledge, such as is given in sensation and perception; internal persuasion.

Conscript, kon'skript, *a.* [L. *conscriptus*, from *conscribo*, to enroll—*con*, with, and *scribo*, to write.] Enrolled.—*Conscript fathers*, a title of the senators of Rome.—*n.* One who is compulsorily enrolled for military or naval service.—kon-skript', *v.t.* to draft; to enroll by compulsion for military service.—**Conscription**, kon-skrip'shon, *n.* [L. *conscriptio.*] A compulsory enrollment of individuals of a certain age, held liable to be drafted for military or naval service.

Consecrate, kon'sē-krāt, *v.t.*—*consecrated*, *consecrating.* [L. *consecro*—*con*, with, and *sacro*, to consecrate, from *sacer*, sacred. SACRED.] To make or declare to be sacred with certain ceremonies or rites; to appropriate to sacred uses; to enrol among deities or saints; to canonize; to give episcopal rank to; to dedicate with solemnity; to render venerable; to make respected; to hallow. —**Consecrate**, kon'sē-krāt, *a.* Sacred; consecrated; devoted; dedicated. [Obs. or poet.]—**Consecration**, kon-sē-krā'shon, *n.* The act or ceremony of consecrating or separating from a common to a sacred use; dedication of a person or thing to the service and worship of God, by certain rites or solemnities; dedication; the ceremony of elevating a priest to the dignity of a bishop; the giving of the bread and wine of the eucharist their sacred character in the mass or communion service.—**Consecrator**, kon'sē-krā-tėr, *n.* One who consecrates.

Consecution, kon-sē-kū'shon, *n.* [L. *consecutio*—*con*, and *sequor*, to follow (whence *sequence*); same root as *second.*] A following; a train or series; the state of being consecutive. —**Consecutive**, kon-sek'ū-tiv, *a.* Uninterrupted in course or succession; succeeding one another in a regular order; successive; following; succeeding. —**Consecutively**, kon-sek'ū-tiv-li, *adv.* In a consecutive manner; in regular succession; successively. —**Consecutiveness**, kon-sek'ū-tiv-nes, *n.* State of being consecutive.

Consent, kon-sent', *v.i.* [L. *consentio*, to agree—*con*, with, and *sentio*, *sensum*, to feel, perceive, think; akin *sense*, *sentiment*, &c.] To agree; to accord; to yield, as to persuasion or entreaty; to comply; to acquiesce or accede.—*n.* Voluntary accordance with what is done or proposed by another; a yielding of the mind or will to that which is proposed; acquiescence; concurrence; compliance; accord of minds; agreement in opinion or sentiment; *law*, intelligent concurrence in the terms of a contract or agreement, of such a nature as to bind the party consenting.—**Consensual**, kon-sen'shū-al, *a.* *Law*, formed or existing by mere consent; *physiol.* excited or caused by sensation or sympathy and not by conscious volition.—**Consensus**, kon-sen'sus, *n.* [L.] Unanimity; agreement; concord.—**Consentaneity**,† kon-sen'ta-nē"i-ti, *n.* Mutual agreement.—**Consentaneous**, kon-sen-tā'nē-us, *a.* [L. *consentaneus.*] Accordant; agreeing; consistent; suitable.—**Consentaneously**, kon-sen-tā'nē-us-li, *adv.* Agreeably; consistently; suitably. —**Consentaneousness**, kon-sen-tā'nē-us-nes, *n.* Agreement: accordance; consistency.—**Consenter**, kon-sen'tėr, *n.* One who consents.—**Consentient**, kon-sen'shi-ent, *a.* Agreeing; accordant; unanimous.

Consequence, kon'sē-kwens, *n.* [L. *consequentia*, from *consequor.* CONSECUTION.] That which follows from any act, cause, principles, or series of actions; an event or effect produced by some preceding act or cause; inference; deduction; conclusion from premises; importance (a matter *of consequence*, a man *of* great *consequence*).—*In consequence of*, as the effect of; by reason of; through.—**Consequent**, kon'sē-kwent, *a.* [L. *consequens.*] Following as the natural effect: with *to* or *on.*—*n.* That which follows; *logic*, that member of a hypothetical proposition which contains the conclusion.—**Consequential**, kon-sē-kwen'shal, *a.* Following as the effect; produced by the connection of effects with causes; affecting airs of great self-importance, or characterized by such affectation; pompous.—*n.* An inference; a deduction; a conclusion.—**Consequentially**, kon-sē-kwen'shal-li, *adv.* In a consequential manner; with just deduction of consequences; with assumed importance; pompously. —**Consequentialness**, kon-sē-kwen'shal-nes, *n.* The quality of being consequential. —**Consequently**, kon'sē-kwent-li, *adv.* By consequence; by necessary connection of effects with their causes; in consequence of something.

Conservatoire, koṅ-sār-va-twar, *n.* [Fr., from It. *conservatorio.*] A name given to an establishment for promoting the study of any special branch, especially music.

Conserve, kon-sėrv', *v.t.*—*conserved*, *conserving.* [L. *conservo*—*con*, and *servo*, to preserve.] To keep in a safe or unimpaired state; to uphold and keep from decay, waste, or injury; to guard or defend from violation (institutions, customs, buildings, &c.); to preserve with sugar, &c., as fruits. —*n.* (kon'sėrv). That which is conserved; a sweetmeat made of the inspissated juice of fruit boiled with sugar.—**Conserver**, kon-sėr'vėr, *n.* One who conserves or preserves.—**Conservable**, kon-sėr'va-bl, *a.* That may be conserved.—**Conservation**, kon-sėr-vā'shon, *n.* [L. *conservatio.*] The act of conserving, preserving, guarding, or protecting; preservation from loss, decay, injury, or violation.—*Conservation of energy*, the principle that energy or force is indestructible, the sum of all the energy in the universe being constant. —**Conservational**, kon-sėr-vā'shon-al, *a.* Tending to preserve; preservative.—**Conservatism**, kon-sėr'va-tizm, *n.* The political principles and opinions maintained by Conservatives. —**Conservative**, kon-sėr'va-tiv, *a.* Tending to preserve; preservative; inclining to keep up old institutions, customs, and the like; having a tendency to uphold and preserve entire the institutions of a country, both civil and ecclesiastical; opposed to radical changes or innovations; pertaining to the Conservatives or their principles.—*n.* One who aims to preserve from ruin, innovation, injury, or radical change; one of the political party the professed object of which is to support and preserve all that is good in the existing institutions of a country, and to oppose undesirable changes; a Tory.—**Conservator**, kon'sėr-vā-tėr or kon-sėr'va-tėr, *n.* One who conserves; one who preserves from injury or violation; one appointed to conserve or watch over anything. —**Conservatory**, kon-sėr'va-to-ri, *a.* Having the quality of preserving from loss, decay, or injury.—*n.* A large greenhouse for preserving exotics and other tender plants. —Same as CONSERVATOIRE.

Consider, kon-sid'ėr, *v.t.* [L. *considero*, to view attentively, to consider: originally (like *contemplor*) an augurial term—*con*, together, and *sidus*, *sideris*, a constellation.] To fix the mind on, with a view to a careful examination; to think on with care; to ponder; to study; to meditate on; to observe and examine; to regard with pity or sympathy, and hence relieve (the poor); to have regard or respect to; to respect; to take into view or account, or have regard to, in examination, or in forming an estimate; to judge to be; to reckon (to *consider* a man wise).—*v.i.* To think seriously, maturely, or carefully; to reflect.—**Considerable**, kon-sid'ėr-a-bl, *a.* Worthy of consideration on account of its amount; more than a little; moderately large; somewhat important or valuable. —**Considerably**, kon-sid'ėr-a-bli, *adv.* In a degree deserving notice; in a degree not trifling or unimportant.—**Considerate**, kon-sid'ėr-āt, *a.* [L. *consideratus.*] Given to consideration or to sober reflection; circumspect; discreet; prudent; characterized by consideration or regard for another's circumstances and feelings; thoughtful or mindful of others.—**Considerately**, kon-sid'ėr-āt-li, *adv.* In a considerate manner. —**Considerateness**, kon-sid'ėr-āt-nes, *n.* The state or quality of being considerate.—**Consideration**, kon-sid'ėr-ā"shon, *n.* [L. *consideratio.*] The act of considering; mental view; regard; notice; mature thought; serious deliberation; thoughtful, sympathetic, appreciative, or due regard or respect; contemplation; meditation; some degree of importance or claim to notice or regard; motive of action; ground of conduct; ground of concluding; reason; recompense or remuneration (colloq.).—*In consideration of*, in respect or regard of; in return for.—**Considering**, kon-sid'ėr-ing, *prep.* Having regard to; taking into account; making allowance for.

Consign, kon-sīn', *v.t.* [L. *consigno*, to seal or sign—*con*, and *signum*, a sign, seal, or mark. SIGN.] To give or hand over; to transfer or deliver over into the possession of another or into a different state (to *consign* a body to the grave); to deliver or transfer in charge or trust; to intrust (as goods to a factor for sale); to commit for permanent preservation (to *consign* to writing).—**Consignatary**, kon-sig'na-ta-ri, *n.* One to whom any trust or business is consigned. —**Consignation**,† kon-sig-nā'shon, *n.* The act of consigning.—**Consignature**, kon-sig'na-tūr, *n.* Joint signing or stamping.—**Consignee**, kon-sī-nē', *n.* The person to whom goods or other things are consigned for sale or superintendence; a factor.—**Consigner**, **Consignor**, kon-sī'nėr, kon-sī'nor, *n.* The person who consigns.—**Consignment**, kon-sīn'ment, *n.* The act of consigning; the act of sending off goods to an agent for sale; goods sent or delivered to a factor for sale.

Consilience, kon-sil'i-ens, *n.* [L. *con*, *salio*, to leap.] Coincidence; concurrence.—**Consilient**, kon-sil'i-ent, *a.* Concurring.

Consist, kon-sist', *v.i.* [L. *consisto*—*con*, and *sisto*, to stand.] To hold together or remain fixed‡; to be, exist, subsist‡; to stand or be; to be comprised or contained: followed by *in*; to be composed; to be made up: followed by *of*; to be compatible, consistent, or harmonious; to accord: followed by *with*.—**Consistence, Consistency,** kon-sis'tens, kon-sis'ten-si, *n.* An indefinite degree of density or viscosity; agreement or harmony of all parts of a complex thing among themselves, or of the same thing with itself at different times; congruity, agreement, or harmony. — **Consistent,** kon-sis'tent, *a.* [L. *consistens.*] Having a certain substance or firmness; standing in agreement; compatible; congruous; not contradictory or opposed; not out of harmony with other acts or professions of the same person. — **Consistently,** kon-sis'-tent-li, *adv.* In a consistent manner; in agreement; suitably or agreeably to one's other acts or professions.

Consistory, kon'sis-tor-i, *n.* [L. *consistorium*, a place of assembly, a council. CONSIST.] A spiritual or ecclesiastical court; the court of a bishop for the trial of ecclesiastical causes arising within the diocese; an assembly of prelates; the college of cardinals at Rome; a solemn assembly or council; in some Reformed churches, an assembly or council of ministers and elders.—**Consistorial,** kon-sis-tō'ri-al, *a.* Pertaining or relating to a consistory, or ecclesiastical court.

Console, kon-sōl', *v.t.*—*consoled, consoling.* [L. *consolor*, to console—*con*, and *solor*, to comfort; akin *solace.*] To cheer the mind in distress or depression; to comfort; to soothe; to solace.—**Consolable,** kon-sōl'-a-bl, *a.* Capable of receiving consolation. —**Consolation,** kon-sōl-ā'shon, *n.* [L. *consolatio.*] The act of consoling; alleviation of misery or distress of mind; a comparative degree of happiness in distress or misfortune, springing from any circumstance that abates the evil or supports and strengthens the mind, as hope, joy, courage, and the like; comfort of the mind; that which comforts or refreshes the spirits; the cause of comfort. — **Consolatory,** kon-sol'a-tor-i, *a.* Tending to console or give comfort; refreshing to the mind; assuaging grief.—**Consoler,** kon-sōl'ėr, *n.* One that consoles. — **Consoling,** kon-sōl'ing, *a.* Adapted to console or comfort.

Console, kon'sōl, *n.* [Fr., perhaps from *consolider*, to consolidate.] A variety of bracket, either useful or ornamental; an ornamental bracket projecting from a wall, employed to support a cornice, bust, vase, or the like.—**Console-table,** *n.* A table whose leaf or slab is supported by a bracket or console at either end.

Consolidate, kon-sol'id-āt, *v.t.*—*consolidated, consolidating.* [L. *consolido, consolidatum*—*con*, and *solidus*, solid.] To make solid or compact; to harden or make dense and firm; to bring together into one close mass or body; to make firm or establish (power).—*v.i.* To grow firm and hard; to unite and become solid.—*a.* Formed into a solid mass. (*Tenn.*)—**Consolidant,** kon-sol'id-ant, *a.* Tending to consolidate or make firm.—*n.* A medicine to unite the parts of wounded flesh.—**Consolidated,** kon-sol'id-āt-ed, *p.* or *a.* Made solid, hard, or compact; united.—*Consolidated Fund.* A British public fund from which is paid the interest on the national debt.—**Consolidation,** kon-sol'id-ā"shon, *n.* The act of consolidating; a making or process of becoming solid; the act of forming into a firm compact mass, body, or system.—**Consols,** kon'solz, *n. pl.* [Contr. for *consolidated annuities.*] A term used to denote a considerable portion of the public debt of Britain, more correctly known as the three per cent consolidated annuities.

Consonance, Consonancy, kon'sō-nans, kon'sō-nan-si, *n.* [L. *consonantia*, from *consono*, to sound together—*con*, and *sono*, to sound. SOUND.] Accord or agreement of sounds; *mus.* an accord of sounds which produces an agreeable sensation in the ear, as the third, fifth, and octave; hence, agreement; accord; congruity; consistency; suitableness.—**Consonant,** kon'-sō-nant, *a.* Like in sound; agreeing generally; according; congruous; consistent: followed by *to* or *with*.—*n.* A letter that receives its proper sound only in connection with a vowel; one of the closings or junctions of the organs of speech, which precede or follow the openings of the organs with which the vowels are uttered. — **Consonantal, Consonantic,** kon-sō-nant'al, kon-sō-nant'ik, *a.* Relating to or partaking of the nature of a consonant.—**Consonantly,** kon'sō-nant-li, *adv.* In a consonant manner; consistently; in agreement.

Consort, kon'sort, *n.* [L. *consors*—*con*, and *sors*, a lot. SORT.] A partner; an intimate associate; particularly, a wife or husband; *naut.* any vessel keeping company with another.—*Queen consort*, the wife of a king, as distinguished from a *queen regnant*, who rules alone, and a *queen dowager*, the widow of a king.—*v.i.* (kon-sort'). To associate; to unite in company; to keep company: followed by *with*. — *v.t.*‡ To marry; to unite in company; to accompany.—**Consortable,**† kon-sort'a-bl, *a.* Suitable.

Conspectus, kon-spek'tus, *n.* [L.] A comprehensive view of a subject; an abstract or sketch.

Conspicuous, kon-spik'ū-us, *a.* [L. *conspicuus*, from *conspicio*, to look or see—*con*, and *specio*, to see. SPECIES.] Obvious or prominent to the eye; easy to be seen; manifest; clearly or extensively known, perceived, or understood; eminent; distinguished (*conspicuous* abilities). — **Conspicuously,** kon-spik'ū-us-li, *adv.* In a conspicuous manner; in a manner to be clearly seen; prominently; eminently; remarkably. — **Conspicuousness,** kon-spik'ū-us-nes, *n.* The state of being conspicuous.

Conspire, kon-spīr', *v.i.*—*conspired, conspiring.* [L. *conspiro*, to plot—*con*, and *spiro*, to breathe; lit. to breathe together.] To agree by oath, covenant, or otherwise to commit a crime; to plot; to form a secret plot; to hatch treason; to agree, concur, or conduce to one end (circumstances *conspired* to defeat the plan).—*v.t.* To plot; to plan; to devise; to contrive; to concur to produce.—**Conspiracy,** kon-spir'a-si, *n.* [L. *conspiratio*, from *conspiro.*] A secret combination of men for an evil purpose; an agreement or combination to commit some crime in concert; a plot; concerted treason. —**Conspirant,** kon-spī'rant, *a.* [L. *conspirans.*] Conspiring; plotting. (*Shak.*)—**Conspirator, Conspirer,** kon-spir'-at-ėr, kon-spī'rėr, *n.* One who conspires; one who engages in a plot to commit a crime, particularly treason. — **Conspiring,** kon-spī'ring, *a.* Uniting or concurring to one end.

Constable, kun'sta-bl, *n.* [O.Fr. *conestable*, from L. *comes stabuli*, count of the stable.] An officer of high rank in several of the medieval monarchies; the keeper or governor of a castle belonging to the king or to a great baron; now usually a peace officer; a police officer.—**Constablery,** kun'-sta-bl-ri, *n.* A body or jurisdiction of constables; a district in charge of a constable. —**Constableship,** kun'sta-bl-ship, *n.* The office of a constable. — **Constabulary,** kon-stab'ū-la-ri, *a.* Pertaining to constables; consisting of constables. — *n.* The body of constables of a district, city, or country.

Constant, kon'stant, *a.* [L. *constans*, pp. of *consto*—*con*, and *sto*, to stand.] Not undergoing change; continuing the same; permanent; immutable; fixed or firm in mind, purpose, or principle; not easily swayed; firm or unchanging in affection or duty; faithful; true; loyal.—*n.* That which is not subject to change; *math.* a quantity which remains the same throughout a problem. — **Constantly,** kon'stant-li, *adv.* Firmly; steadily; invariably; continually; perseveringly. — **Constancy,** kon'stan-si, *n.* [L. *constantia.*] Fixedness; a standing firm; immutability; steady, unshaken determination; fixedness or firmness of mind under sufferings; steadiness in attachments; perseverance in enterprise.

Constantia, kon-stan'shi-a, *n.* A kind of wine, both white and red, from the farms around *Constantia*, Cape of Good Hope.

Constellation, kon-stel-lā'shon, *n.* [L. *constellatio* — *con*, together, and *stella*, a star.] A group of the fixed stars to which a definite name has been given; an assemblage of splendours or excellences (a *constellation* of poetic genius).

Consternation, kon-stėr-nā'shon, *n.* [L. *consternatio*, from *consterno*—*con*, and *sterno*, to throw or strike down.] Astonishment; amazement or horror that confounds the faculties, and incapacitates a person for consultation and execution; excessive terror, wonder, or surprise.

Constipate, kon'sti-pāt, *v.i.*—*constipated, constipating.* [L. *constipo, constipatum*, to crowd together—*con*, together, and *stipo*, to crowd, to cram.] To stop up by filling a passage‡; to make costive.—**Constipation,** kon-sti-pā'shon, *n.* A state of the bowels in which the evacuations do not take place as frequently as usual, or are very hard and expelled with difficulty; costiveness.

Constituent, kon-stit'ū-ent, *a.* [L. *constituens*, ppr. of *constituo*—*con*, and *statuo*, to set. STATUE, STATUTE.] Forming or existing as an essential component or ingredient; composing, or making up as an essential part; component, elementary (the *constituent* parts of water); having the power of constituting or appointing. — *n.* One who or that which establishes or determines; that which constitutes or composes, as a part, or an essential part; an essential ingredient; one who elects or assists in electing another as his representative in a deliberative or administrative assembly; one who empowers another to transact business for him.—**Constituency,** kon-stit'ū-en-si, *n.* A body of constituents who appoint or elect persons to any office or employment, especially to municipal or parliamentary offices.

Constitute, kon'sti-tūt, *v.t.*—*constituted, constituting.* [L. *constituo, constitutum*—*con*, and *statuo*, to set. STATUE, STATUTE.] To settle, fix, or enact; to establish; to form or compose; to make up; to make a thing what it is; to appoint, depute, or elect to an office or employment; to make and empower.—**Constitution,** kon-sti-tū'shon, *n.* The act of constituting, enacting, establishing, or appointing; the peculiar structure and connection of parts which makes or characterizes a system or body; natural condition of the human body as regards general health or strength; the established form of government in a state; a system of fundamental rules, principles, and ordinances for the government of a state or nation.—*Constitution of the U. S.*, the document, ratified in 1789, creating the federal system of government, with twenty-one amendments, embodying the fundamental law.—**Constitutional,** kon-sti-tū'shon-al, *a.* Pertaining to a constitution; connected with the constitution, or natural condition of body or mind; consistent with the constitution of a state; authorized by the constitution or fundamental rules of a government.—*n.* A walk taken for health and exercise.—**Constitutionalism,** kon-sti-tū'shon-al-izm, *n.* The theory or principle of constitutional rule or authority; constitutional principles; adherence to a constitution.—**Constitutionalist, Constitutionist,** kon-sti-tū'-shon-al-ist, kon-sti-tū'shon-ist, *n.* An adherent to the constitution of government; an upholder of the constitution of his country. — **Constitutionality,** kon-sti-tū'shon-al"i-ti, *n.* The state of being constitutional.—**Constitutionalize,** kon-sti-tū'shon-al-iz, *v.i.* To take a walk for health and exercise. (*Colloq.*)—**Constitutionally,** kon-sti-tū'shon-al-li, *adv.* In a constitutional manner; in consistency with a national constitution; in accordance with the constitution of mind or body; naturally.—**Constitutive,** kon'sti-tūt-iv, *a.* Forming, composing, enacting, or establishing; constituting; instituting. *Constitutively*, kon'sti-tūt-iv-li, *adv.* In a constitutive manner.

Constrain, kon-strān', *v.t.* [O.Fr. *con-*

straindre, Fr. *contraindre*, from L. *constringo*, to bind together—*con*, and *stringo*, to strain. STRAIN.] To compel or force; to urge with a power sufficient to produce the effect; to drive; to necessitate; to confine by force; to restrain, check, repress, confine, bind.—**Constrainable**, kon-strā'na-bl, *a.* Capable of being constrained; liable to constraint or to restraint.—**Constrained**, kon-strānd', *a.* With a certain constraint or want of freedom; with a feeling of something checking (to speak in a *constrained* tone).—**Constrainedly**, kon-strā'ned-li, *adv.* In a constrained manner; with constraint; by compulsion.—**Constrainer**, kon-strā'nėr, *n.* One who constrains.—**Constraint**, kon-strānt', *n.* A constraining, compelling, or restraining; force; compulsion; restraint; confinement; feeling of reserve or being kept in check.

Constrict, kon-strikt', *v.t.* [L. *constringo, constrictum.* CONSTRAIN.] To draw together; to cramp; to contract or cause to shrink: said of canals, &c., of the body.—**Constriction**, kon-strik'shon, *n.* The state of being constricted or drawn together as by some spasm, as distinguished from compression or the pressure of extraneous bodies.—**Constrictive**, kon-strik'tiv, *a.* Tending to contract or compress.—**Constrictor**, kon-strik'tėr, *n.* That which draws together or contracts; a muscle which draws together or closes an orifice of the body; one of the larger class of serpents which envelop and crush their prey in their folds.—**Constringe**, kon-strinj', *v.t.*—*constringed, constringing.* To strain into a narrow compass; to constrict.—**Constringent**, kon-strin'jent, *a.* Having the quality of constringing.

Construct, kon-strukt', *v.t.* [L. *construo, constructum*—*con*, and *struo*, to pile up. STRUCTURE.] To put together the parts of in their proper place and order; to build up; to erect; to form; to form by the mind.—**Constructer, Constructor**, kon-struk'tėr, *n.* One who constructs or frames.—**Construction**, kon-struk'shon, *n.* [L. *constructio.*] The act of building, devising, or forming; fabrication; the form of building; the manner of putting together the parts; structure; conformation; the arrangement and connection of words in a sentence; syntactical arrangement; attributed sense or meaning to language; explanation; interpretation; the manner of describing a figure or problem in geometry for the purpose of any demonstration.—**Constructional**, kon-struk'shon-al, *a.* Pertaining to construction; deduced from construction or interpretation.—**Constructive**, kon-struk'tiv, *a.* Pertaining to construction or building; having ability to construct; created or deduced by construction or mode of interpretation.—**Constructively**, kon-struk'tiv-li, *adv.* In a constructive manner; by way of construction or interpretation; by fair inference.—**Constructiveness**, kon-struk'tiv-nes, *n.* State of being constructive; *phren.* a faculty supposed to produce constructive power.

Construe, kon'strö, *v.t.*—*construed, construing.* [L. *construo*, CONSTRUCT.] To arrange words so that their grammatical bearing and meaning are apprehended; to analyse grammatically; as applied to a foreign language, to translate; to interpret or draw a certain meaning from; to explain (to *construe* actions wrongly).

Consubstantial, Consubstantiate, kon-sub-stan'shal, kon-sub-stan'shi-āt, *a.* [L. *consubstantialis*—*con* and *substantia.* SUBSTANCE.] Having the same substance or essence; coessential.—**Consubstantialism**, kon-sub-stan'shal-izm, *n.* The doctrine of consubstantiation.—**Consubstantialist**, kon-sub-stan'shi-al-ist, *n.* One who believes in consubstantiation.—**Consubstantiality**, kon-sub-stan'shi-al"i-ti, *n.* The quality of being consubstantial; the existence of more than one in the same substance; participation of the same nature.—**Consubstantially**, kon-sub-stan'shi-al-li, *adv.* In a consubstantial manner.—**Consubstantiate**,† kon-sub-stan'shi-āt, *v.t.* and *i.*—*consubstantiated, consubstantiating.* To unite in one common substance or nature, or regard as so united.—**Consubstantiation**, kon-sub-stan'shi-ā"-shon, *n.* The union of the body of our blessed Saviour with the sacramental elements; impanation.

Consuetude,† kon'swē-tūd, *n.* [L. *consuetudo*, custom, CUSTOM.] Custom; usage.—**Consuetudinal, Consuetudinary**, kon-swē-tūd'in-al, kon-swē-tūd'in-a-ri, *a.* Customary.—*Consuetudinary law*, in contradistinction to written or statutory law, is that law which is derived by immemorial custom from antiquity.

Consul, kon'sul, *n.* [L. *consul*—*con*, together, and root seen also in *consulo, consultum*, to consult.] The title of the two chief magistrates of the ancient Roman republic, invested with legal authority for one year; the title given to the three supreme magistrates of the French republic after the dissolution of the Directory in 1799; a person commissioned by a sovereign or state to reside in a foreign country as an agent or representative, to protect the interests (especially the commercial interests) of his own country.—**Consulage**, kon'sul-āj, *n.* A duty paid by merchants for the protection of their commerce abroad.—**Consular**, kon'sū-lėr, *a.* Pertaining to a consul.—**Consulate**, kon'sū-lāt, *n.* [L. *consulatus.*] The office or jurisdiction of a consul; the official dwelling or residence of a consul; consular government.—**Consulship**, kon'sul-ship, *n.* The office of a consul, or the term of his office.—**Consul-general**, *n.* A chief consul having other consuls under him.

Consult, kon-sult', *v.i.* [L. *consulto*, intens. from *consulo*, to consult.] To seek the opinion or advice of another; to take counsel together; to deliberate in common.—*v.t.* To ask advice of; to seek the opinion of as a guide to one's own judgment; to have recourse to for information or instruction; to regard or have reference or respect to, in judging or acting (to *consult* one's safety, one's means.)—**Consultary**, kon-sult'a-ri, *a.* Relating to consultation.—**Consultation**, kon-sul-tā'shon, *n.* The act of consulting; deliberation of two or more persons with a view to some decision; a meeting of experts, as physicians or counsel, to consult about a specific case.—**Consultatory**, kon-sult'a-tō-ri, *a.* Having the privilege of consulting or deliberating; deliberative; often opposed to *executive*.—**Consultant**, kon-sul'tent, *n.* One who consults.—**Consulting**, kon-sult'ing, *a.* In the practice of giving advice; making the giving of advice one's business (a *consulting* attorney); used for consultations (*consulting* room).—**Consultive**,† kon-sult'iv, *a.* Consultatory; advisory.

Consume, kon-sūm', *v.t.*—*consumed, consuming.* [L. *consumo*, to take wholly or completely—*con*, intens., and *sumo*, to take, seen also in *assume, resume*, &c.] To destroy by separating the component parts and annihilating the form of the substance, as by fire or by eating; to destroy by dissipating or by use; to expend; to waste; to spend; to pass (time); to waste slowly; to bring to ruin.—*v.i.* To waste away slowly; to be exhausted.—**Consumable**, kon-sūm'a-bl, *a.* That may be consumed, destroyed, dissipated, or wasted.—**Consumer**, kon-sūm'-ėr, *n.* One who or that which consumes; *pol. econ.* one who uses commodities as distinguished from the producer of them.—**Consuming**, kon-sūm'ing, *p.* and *a.* Burning; wasting; destroying.—**Consumingly**, kon-sūm'ing-li, *adv.* In a consuming manner.—**Consumption**, kon-sum'shon, *n.* [L. *consumptio.*] The act of consuming, or state of being consumed; a using up or wasting away; *med.* a wasting disease affecting the lungs, and attended with a hectic fever, cough, &c.; a decline; *pol. econ.* the use or expenditure of the products of industry, or of all things having an exchangeable value.—**Consumptive**, kon-sum'tiv, *a.* Consuming, wasting, or exhausting; having the quality of consuming or dissipating; affected with or having a tendency to the disease consumption.—**Consumptively**, kon-sum'tiv-li, *adv.* In a consumptive manner.—**Consumptiveness**, kon-sum'tiv-nes, *n.* A state of being consumptive or a tendency to consumption.

Consumedly, kon-sūm'ed-li, *adv.* [*Consumed* formerly had sense of deuced, confounded.] Greatly; hugely; decedly.

Consummate, kon'sum-āt, *v.t.*—*consummated, consummating.* [L. *consummo, consummatus*—*con*, and *summa*, sum. SUM.] To finish by completing what was intended; to perfect; to bring or carry to the utmost point or degree; to make complete.—*a.* (kon-sum'āt). Complete; perfect; carried to the utmost extent or degree; thorough.—**Consummately**, kon-sum'āt-li, *adv.* Completely; perfectly.—**Consummation**, kon-sum-ā'shon, *n.* [L. *consummatio.*] Completion; end; termination; perfection of a work, process, or scheme.—**Consummative**, kon-sum'at-iv, *a.* Pertaining to consummation; consummating; final.

Contabescence, kon-ta-bes'ens, *n.* [L. *contabesco*, to waste away gradually.] Atrophy; consumption; a shrivelled up condition of the anthers of certain plants.—**Contabescent**, kon-ta-bes'ent, *a.* Wasting away.

Contact, kon'takt, *n.* [L. *contactus*, from *contingo, contactum*, to touch—*con*, and *tango* (root *tag*), to touch, whence also E. *tact, tangent*, &c.] A touching; touch; state of being so near as to touch.—**Contactual**, kon-tak'tū-al, *a.* Pertaining to contact; implying contact.

Contagion, kon-tā'jon, *n.* [L. *contagio*—*con*, and root *tag.* CONTACT.] The communication of a disease by contact, direct or indirect; that excessively subtle matter which proceeds from a diseased person or body, and communicates the disease to another person; infection; that which propagates mischief (the *contagion* of vice); pestilential influence.—**Contagioned**, kon-tā'jond, *a.* Affected by contagion.—**Contagium**, kon-tā'ji-um, *n.* That which carries the infectious element in diseases from one person to another.—**Contagious**, kon-tā'jus, *a.* Containing or generating contagion; communicated by contagion or contact; catching; containing contagion; containing mischief that may be propagated; spreading from one to another, or exciting like affections in others (*contagious* fear).—**Contagiously**, kon-tā'jus-li, *adv.* By contagion.—**Contagiousness**, kon-tā'jus-nes, *n.*

Contain, kon-tān', *v.t.* [L. *contineo*—*con*, and *teneo*, to hold, seen also in *attain, retain, tenant, tempt*, &c.] To hold within fixed limits; to comprehend; to comprise; to include; to hold or be capable of holding; to comprise, as a writing; to have for contents; to keep in check an enemy's forces; to keep occupied, to hinder progress.—*To contain one's self*, to restrain one's feelings or prevent them showing themselves.—**Containable**, kon-tā'na-bl, *a.* Capable of being contained or comprised.—**Containant, Container**, kon-tā'nant, kon-tā'nėr, *n.* One who, or that which, contains.

Contaminate, kon-tam'in-āt, *v.t.*—*contaminated, contaminating.* [L. *contamino, contaminatum*, from *contamen*, contact, contamination, contr. for *contagimen*, from root of *tango*, to touch. CONTAGION, CONTACT.] To defile; to pollute: usually in a figurative sense; to sully; to tarnish; to taint.—**Contaminable**, kon-tam'in-a-bl, *a.* Capable of being contaminated.—**Contamination**, kon-tam'in-ā"shon, *n.* The act of contaminating; what contaminates; pollution; defilement; taint.—**Contaminative**, *a.* Adapted to contaminate.

Contango, kon-tang'gō, *n.* In stock-exchange transactions, a sum of money paid to a seller for accommodating a buyer, by carrying the engagement to pay the price of shares bought over to the next account day. BACKWARDATION.

Contemn, kon-tem', *v.t.* [L. *contemno, contemptum*, to despise (whence also *contempt*)—*con*, intens., and *temno*, to despise.] To despise; to consider and treat as mean and despicable; to scorn; to reject with disdain.—**Contemner**, kon-tem'ėr, *n.* One who contemns; a despiser; a scorner.

Contemplate, kon'tem-plāt, *v.t.*—*contemplated, contemplating.* [L. *contemplor, contemplatus*, to mark out a *templum*, to view attentively, contemplate — *con*, and *templum*, the space marked out by the augur as that within which the omens should be observed. TEMPLE.] To view or consider with continued attention; to study; to meditate on; to consider or have in view in reference to a future act or event; to intend.—*v.i.* To think studiously; to study; to muse; to meditate.—**Contemplant**,† kon-tem'plant, *a.* Contemplative.—**Contemplation**, kon-tem-plā'shon, *n.* [L. *contemplatio.*] The act of contemplating; meditation; continued attention of the mind to a particular subject; a looking forward to the doing or happening of something; expectation. — **Contemplative**, kon-tem'plāt-iv, *a.* Given to contemplation, or continued application of the mind to a subject; thoughtful; meditative; having the power of thought or meditation (the *contemplative* faculty).—**Contemplatively**, kon-tem'plāt-iv-li, *adv.* With contemplation; thoughtfully. — **Contemplativeness**, kon-tem'plāt-iv-nes, *n.* State of being contemplative. — **Contemplator**, kon-tem'plāt-ėr, *n.* One who contemplates.

Contemporary, Cotemporary, kon-tem'pō-ra-ri, ko-tem'pō-ra-ri, *a.* [L. *con*, and *tempus, temporis*, time.] Living, existing, or occurring at the same time: of persons and things.—*n.* One who lives at the same time with another. [*Contemporary* is the commoner spelling and the one that is in accordance with analogy.]—**Contemporariness**, kon-tem'pō-ra-ri-nes, *n.* State of being contemporary.—**Contemporaneity**, kon-tem'pō-ra-nē″i-ti, *n.* State of being contemporaneous; contemporariness. — **Contemporaneous**, kon-tem'pō-rā″nē-us, *a.* [L. *contemporaneus.*] Contemporary: most commonly of things.—**Contemporaneously**, kon-tem'pō-rā″nē-us-li, *adv.* At the same time with some other event.—**Contemporaneousness**, kon-tem'pō-rā″nē-us-nes, *n.* Contemporaneity.

Contempt, kon-temt', *n.* [L. *contemptus*, from *contemno.* CONTEMN.] The feeling that causes us to consider and treat something as mean, vile, and worthless; disdain; scorn for what is mean; the state of being despised; *law*, disobedience to the rules or orders of a court, or a disturbance of its proceedings. — **Contemptibility**, kon-tem'ti-bil″i-ti, *n.* Quality of being contemptible.—**Contemptible**, kon-tem'ti-bl, *a.* [L. *contemptibilis.*] Worthy of contempt; deserving scorn or disdain; despicable; mean; vile; despised or neglected from insignificance (a *contemptible* plant). ∴ *Contemptible*, deserving of being scorned or looked down upon from meanness or worthlessness; *despicable*, implies a stronger feeling, scorn, and loathing, often on moral grounds; *paltry* or *pitiful*, too insignificant to waken any active feeling.—**Contemptibleness**, kon-tem'ti-bl-nes, *n.* The state of being contemptible.—**Contemptibly**, kon-tem'ti-bli, *adv.* In a contemptible manner; meanly; in a manner deserving of contempt. — **Contemptuous**, kon-tem'tū-us, *a.* Manifesting or expressing contempt or disdain; scornful; apt to despise; haughty; insolent.—**Contemptuously**, kon-tem'tū-us-li, *adv.* In a contemptuous manner; with scorn or disdain; despitefully. —**Contemptuousness**, kon-tem'tū-us-nes, *n.* Disposition to contempt; scornfulness; haughtiness.

Contend, kon-tend', *v.i.* [L. *contendo*, to strive, contend—*con*, intens., and *tendo*, stretch; whence E. *tend, tent, attend, pretend;* root also in *tender.*] To strive; to struggle in opposition; absolutely, or with *against* or *with* preceding an object; to use earnest efforts to obtain, or to defend and preserve; with *for* before the object.—**Contender**, kon-tend'ėr, *n.* One who contends; a combatant or rival.—**Contending**, kon-tend'ing, *p.* and *a.* Striving; struggling in opposition; debating; quarrelling; clashing; opposing; rival (*contending* claims).—**Contention**, kon-ten'shon, *n.* [L. *contentio.*] The act of contending; contest, struggle, or strife; strife in words; debate; angry contest; quarrel; controversy; competition; emulation; a point that a person maintains, or the argument in support of it.—**Contentious**, kon-ten'shus, *a.* [Fr. *contentieux.*] Apt to contend; given to angry debate; quarrelsome; perverse; relating to or characterized by contention or strife; involving contention.— **Contentiously**, kon-ten'shus-li, *adv.* In a contentious manner.—**Contentiousness**, kon-ten'shus-nes, *n.* The state or quality of being contentious; a disposition to contend; peevishness; quarrelsomeness.

Content, kon-tent', *a.* [L. *contentus*, from *contineo*, to contain—*con*, and *teneo*, to hold. CONTAIN.] Having a mind at peace; satisfied, so as not to repine, object, or oppose; not disturbed; contented; easy.—*Content* and *non-content*, words by which assent and dissent are expressed in the House of Lords, answering to the *aye* and *no* used in the House of Commons.—*v.t.* To make content; to quiet, so as to stop complaint or opposition; to appease; to make easy in any situation; to please or gratify. — *n.* The state of being contented; contentment.—*n.* (kon-tent' or kon'tent.) That which is contained; the thing or things held, included, or comprehended within a limit or line; *geom.* the area or quantity of matter or space included in certain lines. [Usually in the pl.]—*Table of contents*, a summary or index of all the matters treated in a book. —**Contented**, kon-tent'ed, *a.* Satisfied with what one has or with one's circumstances; easy in mind; not complaining, opposing, or demanding more. — **Contentedly**, kon-tent'ed-li, *adv.* In a contented manner; quietly; without concern. —**Contentedness**, kon-tent'ed-nes, *n.* State of being contented. — **Contentment**, kon-tent'ment, *n.* [Fr. *contentement.*] The state or feeling of being contented; content; a resting or satisfaction of mind without disquiet or craving for something else; acquiescence in one's own circumstances. ∴ *Contentment* is passive, *satisfaction* is active. The former implies the absence of fretting or craving, the latter an active feeling of pleasure.

Contention, &c. Under CONTEND.

Conterminous, kon-tėr'min-us, *a.* [L. *conterminus*—*con*, and *terminus*, a border.] Terminating at a common point; having common boundaries or limits; touching at the boundary. Also **Coterminous**, kō-tėr'mi-nus.

Contest, kon-test', *v.t.* [Fr. *contester*, from L. *contestari*, to call to witness, to call witnesses—*con*, together, and *testis*, a witness. DETEST.] To make a subject of contention or dispute; to enter into a struggle for; to struggle to defend; to controvert; to oppose; to call in question; to dispute (statements). —*v.i.*† To strive; to contend; followed by *with.*—*n.* (kon'test). A struggle for victory, superiority, or in defence; struggle in arms; dispute; debate; controversy; strife in argument. — **Contestable**, kon-tes'ta-bl, *a.* Capable of being disputed or debated; disputable; controvertible. — **Contestableness**,† kon-tes'ta-bl-nes, *n.*—**Contestant**,† kon-tes'tant, *n.* One who contests. —**Contested**, kon-test'ed, *p.* and *a.* Disputed; fought; litigated.

Context, kon'tekst, *n.* [L. *contextus*, connection, from *contexo*—*con*, and *texo*, to weave.] The parts of a book or other writing which immediately precede or follow a sentence quoted. — **Contextural**, kon-teks'tūr-al, *a.* Pertaining to contexture. —**Contexture**, kon-teks'tūr, *n.* The manner of interweaving several parts into one body; the disposition and union of the constituent parts of a thing with respect to each other; constitution. — **Contextured**,† kon-teks'tūrd, *a.* Woven; formed into texture.

Conticent,† kon'ti-sent, *a.* [L. *conticens, conticentis*, ppr. of *conticeo*—*con*, together, and *taceo*, to be silent.] Silent; hushed; quiet: said of a number of persons.

Contiguous, kon-tig'ū-us, *a.* [L. *contiguus* —*con*, and *tango*, to touch. CONTACT.] Situated so as to touch; meeting or joining at the surface or border; close together; neighbouring; bordering or adjoining.—**Contiguity**, kon-ti-gū'i-ti, *n.* The state of being contiguous; closeness of situation or place; a linking together, as of a series of objects.—**Contiguously**, kon-tig'ū-us-li, *adv.* In a contiguous manner; without intervening space. — **Contiguousness**, kon-tig'ū-us-nes, *n.* The state or quality of being contiguous; contiguity.

Continence, Continency, kon'ti-nens, kon'ti-nen-si, *n.* [L. *continentia*, from *contineo*, to hold or withhold. CONTAIN.] The restraint which a person imposes upon his desires and passions; the restraint of the passion for sexual enjoyment; forbearance of lewd pleasures; chastity.—**Continent**, kon'ti-nent, *a.* [L. *continens.*] Refraining from sexual commerce; chaste; also moderate or temperate in general.—**Continently**, kon'ti-nent-li, *adv.* In a continent manner; chastely.

Continent, kon'ti-nent, *n.* [L. *continens*, a continent or mainland, lit. land holding together.] An arbitrary term applied to a connected tract of land of great extent; one of the great divisions of the land on the globe.—**Continental**, kon-ti-nent'al, *a.* Pertaining or relating to the continent of Europe; pertaining to the confederated colonies at the time of the American Revolution; a soldier in the Continental Army; the least bit;—*not worth a Continental*—from the low value of Continental currency at the time.

Contingency, kon-tin'jen-si, *n.* [L. *contingens*, ppr. of *contingo*—to fall or happen to—*con*, and *tango*, to touch. CONTACT.] The quality of being contingent; the possibility of happening or coming to pass; fortuitousness; something that may happen; a possible occurrence; a fortuitous event, or one which may occur. Also **Contingence**, kon-tin'jens.—**Contingent**, kon-tin'jent, *a.* Possibly occurring; liable to occur; not determinable by any certain rule; accidental; casual; dependent upon what is undetermined or unknown; dependent upon the happening of something else. — **Contingent**, kon-tin'jent, *n.* A contingency†; a quota or suitable proportion, as of troops furnished for some joint enterprise.—**Contingently**, kon-tin'jent-li, *adv.* In a contingent manner.—**Contingentness**, kon-tin'jent-nes, *n.* The state of being contingent.

Continue, kon-tin'ū, *v.i.*—*continued, continuing.* [L. *continuo*, to carry on, to keep on, continue, from *continuus*, unbroken, continuous — *con*, together, and *teneo*, to hold. CONTAIN.] To remain in a state or place; to abide for any time indefinitely; to last; to endure; to be permanent; to persevere; to be steadfast or constant in any course.—*v.t.* To protract or lengthen out; not to cease from or to terminate; to extend; to make longer; to persevere in; not to cease to do or use; to suffer or cause to remain as before.—**Continuable**, kon-tin'ū-a-bl, *a.* Capable of being continued. —**Continual**, kon-tin'ū-al, *a.* [Fr. *continuel;* L. *continuus.*] Proceeding without interruption or cessation; not intermitting; unceasing; of frequent recurrence; often repeated; incessant. Syn. under CONTINUOUS.—**Continually**, kon-tin'ū-al-li, *adv.* Without pause or cessation; unceasingly; very often; in repeated succession; from time to time. Syn. under CONTINUOUSLY. —**Continuance**, kon-tin'ū-ans, *n.* The state of continuing or remaining in a particular state or course; permanence, as of habits, condition, or abode; a state of lasting; constancy; perseverance; duration; the act of continuing; continuation. Syn. under CONTINUATION. — **Continuation**, kon-tin'ū-ā″shon, *n.* [L. *continuatio.*] The act of continuing or prolonging; extension or carrying on to a further point; the portion continued or extended; a prolongation or extension. ∴ *Continuation* is the act of continuing (also the part prolonged), *continuance* the state of continuing.—**Continuative**, kon-tin'ū-āt-iv, *a.* Tending to continue, extend, prolong, or persist.—*n.*

What is continuative.—**Continuator, Continuer**, kon-tin'ū-āt-ėr, kon-tin'ū-ėr, *n.* One who or that which continues; one who carries forward anything that had been begun by another.—**Continued**, kon-tin'-ūd, *p.* and *a.* Protracted or extended; proceeding without cessation; unceasing.—*Continued fraction*, one whose denominator is an integer with a fraction, which latter fraction has for its denominator an integer with a fraction, and so on.—**Continuing**, kon-tin'ū-ing, *p.* and *a.* Abiding; lasting; enduring; permanent.—**Continuity**, kon-ti-nū'i-ti, *n.* [L. *continuitas.*] Connection uninterrupted; cohesion; close union of parts; unbroken texture.—**Continuous**, kon-tin'ū-us, *a.* [L. *continuus.*] Joined without intervening space or time; proceeding from something else without interruption or without apparent interruption; uninterrupted; unbroken. ∴ *Continuous* means unbroken, uninterrupted; *continual* does not imply unceasing continuity, but the habitual or repeated renewals of an act, state, &c. *Perpetual* is *continuous* with the idea of lastingness.—**Continuously**, kon-tin'ū-us-li, *adv.* In a continuous manner; in continuation; without interruption. ∴ *Continuously*, like its adjective, denotes unbroken continuity, *continually* close succession.—**Continuousness**, kon-tin'ū-us-nes, *n.* State or quality of being continuous.

Contort, kon-tort', *v.t.* [L. *contorqueo, contortum*, to twist—*con*, intens., and *torqueo, tortum*, to twist, whence also *torture, torment, extort*, &c.] To twist together; to bend or curve in irregular forms; to writhe.—**Contortion**, kon-tor'shon, *n.* [L. *contortio.*] The act of contorting, or state of being contorted; a twist or twisting; a wry-thing, especially spasmodic writhing; a wry motion or position; *med.* a twisting or wresting of a limb or member of the body out of its natural situation.—**Contortionist**, kon-tor'shon-ist, *n.* An acrobat who practises contortions of the body.—**Contortious**, kon-tor'shus, *a.* Affected by contortions.

Contour, kon-tör', *n.* [Fr. *contour*—*con*, and *tour*, a turn, revolution, turner's lathe, from L. *tornus*, Gr. *tornos*, a lathe; hence also Fr. *tourner*, E. *turn.*] The outline of a figure or body; the line that defines or bounds a solid body; the periphery considered as distinct from the object.—*v.t.* To delineate or draw by the contour.

Contraband, kon'tra-band, *a.* [Fr. *contrebande*—It. *contra*, against, and *bando*, a proclamation, a ban. BAN.] Prohibited or excluded by proclamation, law, or treaty.—*Contraband goods* are such as are prohibited to be imported or exported, either by the laws of a particular kingdom or state, or by the law of nations, or by special treaties.—*n.* Illegal or prohibited traffic; articles prohibited to be imported or exported.—**Contrabandism**, kon'tra-band-izm, *n.* Trafficking in contraband goods; smuggling.—**Contrabandist**, kon'tra-band-ist, *n.* One who deals in contraband goods.

Contrabasso, kon-tra-bas'sō, *n.* [It.] The largest of the violin species of instruments, of which it forms the lowest bass: usually called the double-bass.

Contract, kon-trakt', *v.t.* [Fr. *contracter*, L. *contraho, contractum*—*con*, and *traho*, to draw, whence also *tract, treat, trace, train*, &c.] To draw together or closer; to draw into a less compass, either in length or breadth; to abridge, narrow, lessen; to wrinkle; to betroth or affiance; to bring on, incur, acquire (vicious habits, debts); to shorten by omission of a letter or syllable.—*v.i.* To be drawn together; to become shorter or narrower; to shrink; to bargain; to make a mutual agreement as between two or more persons.—*n.* (kon'trakt). An agreement or mutual promise upon lawful consideration or cause which binds the parties to a performance; a bargain; a compact; the act by which a man and woman are betrothed each to the other; the writing which contains the agreement of parties.—**Contracted**, kon-trakt'ed, *a.* Narrow in scope or ideas; limited; mean (*contracted* views).—**Contractedly**, kon-trakt'ed-li, *adv.* In a contracted manner.—**Contractedness**, kon-trakt'ed-nes, *n.* The state of being contracted; narrowness; meanness.—**Contractibility**, **Contractibleness**, kon-trakt'i-bil"i-ti, kon-trakt'i-bl-nes, *n.* Quality of being contractible.—**Contractible**, kon-trakt'i-bl, *a.* Capable of contraction.—**Contractile**, kon-trakt'il, *a.* Tending to contract; having the power of shortening or of drawing into smaller dimensions.—**Contractility**, kon-trakt-il'i-ti, *n.* The inherent quality or force by which bodies shrink or contract; *physiol.* that vital property which gives to certain parts the power of contracting.—**Contraction**, kon-trak'shon, *n.* [L. *contractio.*] The act of contracting, drawing together, or shrinking; the act of shortening, narrowing, or lessening dimensions by causing the parts to approach nearer to each other; the state of being contracted; an abbreviation employed with the view of saving labour in writing, as *recd.* for *received*; the shortening of a word by the omission of one or more letters or syllables.—**Contractive**, kon-trakt'iv, *a.* Tending to contract.—**Contractor**, kon-trakt'ėr, *n.* One who contracts; one of the parties to a bargain; one who covenants to do anything for another; one who contracts to perform any work or service, or to furnish supplies, at a certain price or rate.

Contradict, kon-tra-dikt', *v.t.* [L. *contradico, contradictum*—*contra*, and *dico*, to speak, whence *diction*, &c.] To assert not to be so, or to assert to be the contrary to what has been asserted; to meet (a person, an assertion) with a statement quite different or opposite; to deny; to be directly contrary to.—**Contradictable**, kon-tra-dik'ta-bl, *a.* Capable of being contradicted; deniable; disputable.—**Contradicter**, kon-tra-dik'tėr, *n.* One who contradicts or denies.—**Contradiction**, kon-tra-dik'shon, *n.* [L. *contradictio.*] The act of contradicting; an assertion of the contrary to what has been said or affirmed; denial; contrary declaration; direct opposition or repugnancy; inconsistency with itself; incongruity or contrariety of things, words, thoughts, or propositions; the person who, or thing that, contradicts or is inconsistent with him, her, or its self.—**Contradictious**, kon-tra-dik'shus, *a.* Contradictory; given to contradict.—**Contradictive**,† kon-tra-dik'tiv, *a.* Contradictory; inconsistent.—**Contradictorily**, kon-tra-dik'tor-i-li, *adv.* In a contradictory manner; in a manner inconsistent with itself.—**Contradictoriness**, kon-tra-dik'tor-i-nes, *n.* The state or character of being contradictory; contrariety in assertion or effect.—**Contradictory**, kon-tra-dik'tor-i, *a.* Contradicting; given to contradict; affirming the contrary; implying a denial of what has been asserted; inconsistent with one another; directly opposite.—*n.* A proposition which denies or opposes another in all its terms.

Contradistinction, kon'tra-dis-tingk"-shon, *n.* Distinction by opposite qualities or characteristics; a setting or bringing (terms, notions) into contrast or opposition.—**Contradistinctive**, kon'tra-dis-tingkt"iv, *a.* Having the quality of, or characterized by, contradistinction; opposite in qualities.—*n.* A mark of contradistinction.—**Contradistinguish**, kon'-tra-dis-ting"gwish, *v.t.* To distinguish or set distinctly forward, not merely by different but by opposite qualities: used of ideas, terms, &c.

Contraindicate, kon-tra-in'di-kāt, *v.t.* or *i.*—*contraindicated, contraindicating.* To indicate, suggest, or point to something contrary or opposite.—**Contraindicant, Contraindication**, kon-tra-in'di-kant, kon-tra-in'di-kā"shon, *n.* What contraindicates.

Contrajerva, kon-tra-yėr'va, *n.* CONTRAYERVA.

Contralto, kon-tral'tō, *n.* [It.] *Mus.* the lowest voice of a woman or boy, called also the *Alto*; generally a female voice below the mezzo soprano and soprano; also the counter-tenor; the person who sings with this voice.—*a.* Pertaining to, or possessed of the quality of, contralto.

Contraposition, kon'tra-pō-zi"shon, *n.* A placing over against; opposite position.

Contrapuntal, kon-tra-punt'al, *a.* Pertaining to counterpoint.—**Contrapuntist**, kon-tra-punt'ist, *n.* One skilled in counterpoint.

Contrary, kon'tra-ri, *a.* [L. *contrarius*, from *contra*, against; Fr. *contraire.*] Opposite; adverse; moving against or in an opposite direction (*contrary* winds); contradictory; not merely different, but inconsistent or repugnant; perverse or froward (*colloq.*). [This adjective, in many phrases, is to be treated grammatically as an adverb, or as an adjective referring to a sentence or affirmation; as, this happened *contrary* to my expectations.]—*n.* A thing that is contrary or of opposite qualities; a proposition contrary to another, or a fact contrary to what is alleged.—*On the contrary*, on the other hand; quite oppositely.—*To the contrary*, to an opposite purpose or fact.—**Contrariety**, kon-tra-rī'e-ti, *n.* [L. *contrarietas.*] The state or quality of being contrary; opposition in fact, essence, quality, or principle; repugnance; inconsistency; quality or position destructive of its opposite.—**Contrarily**, kon'tra-ri-li, *adv.* In a contrary manner; in opposition; on the other hand; in opposite ways.—**Contrariness**, kon'tra-ri-nes, *n.* Contrariety; opposition.—**Contrariwise**, kon'tra-ri-wīz, *adv.* On the contrary; oppositely; on the other hand (N.T.).

Contrast, kon-trast', *v.t.* [Fr. *contraster*, from L. *contra*, opposite, and *stare*, to stand.] To set in opposition so as to show the difference between, and to exhibit the excellence of the one and the defects of the other; to compare so as to point out dissimilarity.—*v.i.* To stand in contrast or opposition to something else: followed by *with.*—*n.* (kon'trast). The viewing or comparing of things together in order to render any difference between them more vividly marked; comparison by contrariety of qualities; opposition or dissimilitude of things or qualities.

Contra-tenor, Contra-tenore, kon'-tra-ten-ėr, kon'tra-tā-nō'rā, *n.* *Mus.* a middle part between the tenor and treble; contralto; counter-tenor.

Contrate-wheel, kon'trāt-whēl, *n.* [L. *contra*, against, contrary.] A wheel having the teeth projecting perpendicularly to the plane of the wheel.

Contravallation, Countervallation, kon'tra-val-lā"shon, koun'tėr-val-lā"shon, *n.* [Fr. *contrevallation*—L. *contra*, against, and *vallum*, a rampart.] *Fort.* a chain of redoubts and breastworks raised by the besiegers about a fortress to prevent sorties of the garrison.

Contravene, kon-tra-vēn', *v.t.*—*contravened, contravening.* [L. *contravenio*—*contra*, against, and *venio*, to come, as in *convene*, &c.] To come or be in conflict with; to obstruct in operation; to act so as to violate; to transgress.—**Contravener**, kon-tra-vē'nėr, *n.* One who contravenes.—**Contravention**, kon-tra-ven'shon, *n.* The act of contravening, violating, or transgressing; violation; opposition.

Contrayerva, kon-tra-yėr'va, *n.* [Sp. *contrayerba*—*contra*, and *yerba*, an herb (L. *herba*); lit. a counter herb, an antidote.] An aromatic bitterish root which is imported from tropical America, and used as a stimulant and tonic.

Contre-temps, kōṅ-tr-täṅ, *n.* [Fr.] An unexpected and untoward accident; an embarrassing conjuncture; a hitch.

Contribute, kon-trib'ūt, *v.t.*—*contributed, contributing.* [L. *contribuo*—*con*, and *tribuo*, to grant, assign, or impart. TRIBE, TRIBUTE.] To give or grant in common with others; to give to a common stock or for a common purpose; to pay as a share.—*v.i.* To give a part; to lend a portion of power, aid, or influence; to have a share in any act or effect: with *to*.—**Contributable**, kon-trib'ūt-a-bl, *a.* Capable of being contributed.—**Contributary**, kon-trib'ūt-a-ri, *a.* Contributing to the same stock or object.—**Contribution**, kon-tri-bū'shon, *n.* The act of contributing; the payment of a share along with others; that which is given to a common stock or purpose, either by an individual or by many; the sum or thing contributed.—**Contributive**, kon-trib'ūt-iv, *a.* Tending to contribute; contributing.—**Contributor**, kon-trib'ūt-ėr, *n.* One who contributes, one who gives or pays money to a common fund; one who gives aid to a common purpose.—**Contributory**, kon-trib'ū-to-ri, *a.* Contributing to the same stock or purpose; bringing assistance to some joint design, or increase to some common stock.—*n.* A contributor.

Contrite, kon'trīt, *a.* [L. *contritus*, from *contero*, to break or bruise—*con*, and *tero*, to bruise. TRITE.] Broken-hearted for sin; deeply affected with grief and sorrow for sin; humble; penitent.—*n.* A contrite person; a penitent.—**Contritely**, kon'trīt-li, *adv.* In a contrite manner; with penitence.—**Contriteness**, **Contrition**, kon'trīt-nes, kon-trish'on, *n.* [L. *contritio.*] Grief of heart for sin; sincere penitence.

Contrive, kōn-trīv', *v.t.*—*contrived*, *contriving.* [O.Fr. *controver*, Fr. *controuver*, to invent, to fabricate—*con*, and *trouver*, to find.] To invent; to devise; to plan.—*v.i.* To form schemes or designs; to plan; to scheme.—**Contrivable**, kon-trī'va-bl, *a.* Capable of being contrived, planned, invented, or devised.—**Contrivance**, kon-trī'vans, *n.* The act of contriving, inventing, devising, or planning; the thing contrived; an artifice; scheme; invention.—**Contriver**, kon-trī'vėr, *n.* One who contrives, plans, or devises.

Control, kon-trōl', *n.* [Fr. *contrôle*, lit. counter-roll, from *contre*, against, and *rôle*, a roll, list. ROLL.] Restraining power or influence; check; restraint; power; authority; government; command.—*v.t.*—*controlled*, *controlling.* To exercise control over; to hold in restraint or check; to subject to authority; to regulate; to govern; to subjugate.—**Controllable**, kon-trōl'a-bl, *a.* Capable of being controlled, checked, or restrained; subject to command.—**Controller**, kon-trōl'ėr, *n.* One who controls; one that has the power or authority to govern or control; one who governs or regulates; an officer appointed to keep a counter register of accounts, or to oversee, control, or verify the accounts of other officers; a comptroller.—**Controllership**, kon-trōl'ėr-ship, *n.* The office of a controller; comptrollership.—**Controlment**, kon-trōl'ment, *n.* The power or act of controlling; control; restraint.

Controvert, kon'trō-vėrt, *v.t.* [L. *contra*, against, and *verto*, *versum*, to turn.] To dispute; to oppose by reasoning; to contend against in words or writings; to deny and attempt to disprove or confute.—**Controversial**, **Controversary**,† kon-trō-vėr'shal, kon-trō-vėr-sa-ri, *a.* Relating to controversy.—**Controversialist**, kon-trō-vėr'shal-ist, *n.* One who carries on a controversy; a disputant.—**Controversially**, kon-trō-vėr'shal-li, *adv.* In a controversial manner.—**Controversy**, kon'-trō-vėr-si, *n.* [L. *controversia.*] Debate; agitation of contrary opinions; a disputation or discussion between parties, particularly in writing; a litigation.—**Controverter**, **Controvertist**, kon'trō-vėr-tėr, kon'trō-vėr-tist, *n.* One who controverts; a controversial writer.—**Controvertible**, kon-trō-vėr'ti-bl, *a.* Capable of being controverted or disputed; disputable; not too evident to exclude difference of opinion.—**Controvertibly**, kon-trō-vėr'ti-bli, *adv.* In a controvertible manner.

Contumacious, kon-tū-mā'shus, *a.* [L. *contumax*, *contumacis*—*con*, and *tumeo*, to swell, seen also in *tumid*, *tumult*, *contumely.*] Resisting legitimate authority; disobedient; froward or perverse; *law*, wilfully disobedient to the orders of a court.—**Contumaciously**, kon-tū-mā'shus-li, *adv.* In a contumacious manner; obstinately; stubbornly; in disobedience of orders.—**Contumaciousness**, kon-tū-mā'shus-nes, *n.* State of being contumacious; obstinacy; perverseness; contumacy.—**Contumacy**, **Contumacity**,† kon'tū-ma-si, kon-tū-mas'i-ti, *n.* [L. *contumacia.*] Contumacious conduct; character or state of being contumacious; wilful and persistent resistance to legitimate authority; unyielding obstinacy; stubborn perverseness; *law*, wilful disregard of the orders of a court.

Contumely, kon'tū-me-li, *n.* [L. *contumelia*, from *contumeo*—*con*, and *tumeo.* CONTUMACIOUS.] Haughtiness and contempt in language or behaviour; contemptuous or insulting language; haughty insolence.—**Contumelious**, kon-tū-mē'li-us, *a.* [L. *contumeliosus.*] Indicating or expressive of contumely; contemptuous; insolent; rude and sarcastic; disposed to utter reproach or insult; insolent; proudly rude.—**Contumeliously**, kon-tū-mē'li-us-li, *adv.* In a contumelious manner; rudely; insolently.—**Contumeliousness**, kon-tū-mē'li-us-nes, *n.* State of being contumelious.

Contuse, kon-tūz', *v.t.*—*contused*, *contusing.* [L. *contundo*, *contusum*—*con*, and *tundo*, to beat, same root as Skr. *tud*, to beat.] To wound or injure by bruising; to injure without breaking the flesh.—**Contusion**, kon-tū'zhon, *n.* [L. *contusio.*] A severe bruise on the body; a hurt or injury as to the flesh or some part of the body without breaking of the skin, as by a blunt instrument or by a fall.

Conundrum, kō-nun'drum, *n.* [Origin uncertain.] A sort of riddle, in which some odd resemblance is proposed for discovery between things quite unlike, the answer involving a pun.

Convalescence, **Convalescency**, kon-va-les'ens, kon-va-les'en-si, *n.* [L. *convalesco*, to grow stronger—*con*, and *valesco*, to get strength, *valeo*, to be strong. VALID, AVAIL.] The gradual recovery of health and strength after disease; the state of a person renewing his vigour after sickness or weakness.—**Convalesce**,† kon-va-les', *v.i.*—*convalesced*, *convalescing.* To grow better after sickness; to recover health.—**Convalescent**, kon-va-les'ent, *a.* Recovering health and strength after sickness or debility.—*n.* One who is recovering his health after sickness.—**Convalescently**, kon-va-les'ent-li, *adv.* In a convalescent manner.

Convection, kon-vek'shon, *n.* [L. *convectio*, from *conveho*, to convey.] The act of carrying or conveying; a process of transmission, as of heat or electricity by means of particles of matter affected by them.—**Convective**, kon-vek'tiv, *a.* Resulting from or caused by convection.—**Convectively**, kon-vek'tiv-li, *adv.* In a convective manner; by means of convection.

Convene, kon-vēn', *v.i.*—*convened*, *convening.* [L. *convenio*—*con*, and *venio*, *ventum*, to come: seen also in *intervene*, *advent*, *event*, *revenue*, &c.] To come together; to meet; to meet in the same place; to assemble: rarely said of things.—*v.t.* To cause to assemble; to call together; to convoke; to summon judicially to meet or appear.—**Convenable**, kon-vē'na-bl, *a.* Capable of being convened or assembled.—**Convenee**, kon-vē-nē', *n.* One convened or summoned with others.—**Convener**, kon-vē'nėr, *n.* One who convenes or meets with others; one who convenes or calls a meeting.

Convenience, **Conveniency**, kon-vē'ni-ens, kon-vē'ni-en-si, *n.* [L. *convenientia*, from *convenio*, to convene; lit. a coming together.] The state or quality of being convenient; freedom from discomfort or trouble; ease; comfort; that which gives ease or comfort; that which is suited to wants; opportune conjunction of affairs; opportunity.—**Convenient**, kon-vē'ni-ent, *a.* Suitable or proper; giving certain facilities or accommodation; commodious; opportune; at hand or readily available (*colloq.*).—**Conveniently**, kon-vē'ni-ent-li, *adv.* In a convenient manner or situation; suitably; with adaptation to the end or effect; with ease; without trouble or difficulty.

Convent, kon'vent, *n.* [O.Fr. *convent*, from L. *conventus*, a meeting—*con*, together, and *venio*, *ventum*, to come. CONVENE.] A community of persons devoted to religion; a body of monks or nuns; a house for persons devoted to religion and celibacy; an abbey, monastery, or nunnery.—**Conventual**, kon-ven'tū-al, *a.* Of or belonging to a convent; monastic.—**Conventual**, kon-ven'tū-al, *n.* One who lives in a convent; a monk or nun.

Conventicle, kon-ven'ti-kl, *n.* [L. *conventiculum*, dim. of *conventus*, a meeting. CONVENT.] An assembly or gathering, especially a secret assembly; a meeting of dissenters from the established church for religious worship; a secret meeting for religious worship held by the Scottish Covenanters.—**Conventicler**, kon-ven'ti-klėr, *n.* One who supports or frequents conventicles.

Convention, kon-ven'shon, *n.* [L. *conventio.* CONVENE.] The act of coming together; a meeting; an assembly; an assembly of delegates or representatives for consultation on important concerns, civil, political, or ecclesiastical; a special agreement or contract between two countries or parties; an agreement previous to a definitive treaty; conventionality†.—**Conventional**, kon-ven'shon-al, *a.* [L. *conventionalis.*] Formed by agreement; tacitly understood; arising out of custom or tacit agreement; sanctioned by or depending on general concurrence and not on any principle; resting on mere usage.—**Conventionalism**, kon-ven'shon-al-izm, *n.* That which is conventional; something received or established by convention or agreement; a conventional phrase, form, or ceremony; anything depending on conventional rules and precepts.—**Conventionalist**, kon-ven'shon-al-ist, *n.* One who adheres to a convention or agreement.—**Conventionality**, kon-ven'shon-al"i-ti, *n.* The character of being conventional; what is conventional; a conventional mode of living, acting, or speaking, as opposed to what is natural.—**Conventionalize**, kon-ven'-tion-al-īz, *v.t.*—*conventionalized*, *conventionalizing.* To render conventional; to bring under the influence of conventional rules; to render observant of the conventional rules of society.—**Conventionally**, kon-ven'shon-al-li, *adv.* In a conventional manner.—**Conventionary**, kon-ven'-shon-a-ri, *a.* Acting under contract; settled by stipulation.—**Conventioner**, **Conventionist**, kon-ven'shon-ėr, kon-ven'-shon-ist, *n.* One who enters into a convention.

Conventual. Under CONVENT.

Converge, kon-vėrj', *v.i.*—*converged*, *converging.* [L. *con*, together, and *vergo*, to incline. VERGE.] To tend to one point; to incline and approach nearer together in position; to approach in character.—**Convergence**, **Convergency**, kon-vėr'jens, kon-vėr'jen-si, *n.* The quality of converging; tendency to one point.—**Convergent**, kon-vėr'jent, *a.* Converging; tending to one point; approaching each other.

Converse, kon-vėrs', *v.i.*—*conversed*, *conversing.* [Fr. *converser*; L. *conversor*, to associate with—*con*, and *versor*, to be engaged in anything, from *verto*, *versum*, to turn; seen also in *convert*, *reverse*, *verse*, *version*, &c. VERSE.] To associate, hold intercourse or communion; to talk familiarly; to have free intercourse in mutual communication of thoughts and opinions; to chat; to discourse.—*n.* (kon'vėrs). Acquaintance by frequent or customary intercourse; intercourse; communion; familiarity; free interchange of thoughts or opinions.—**Conversable**, kon-vėr'sa-bl, *a.* [Fr. *conversable.*] Disposed to conversation; ready or inclined to mutual communication of thoughts; sociable; free in discourse.—**Conversableness**, kon-vėr'sa-bl-nes, *n.* The quality of being conversable; disposition or readiness to converse; sociability.—

Conversably, kon-vėr'sa-bli, *adv.* In a conversable manner.—**Conversance**,† **Conversancy**,† kon'vėr-sans, kon'vėr-san-si, *n.* The state of being conversant.—**Conversant**, kon'vėr-sant, *a.* Keeping company; having frequent intercourse; intimately associating: followed by *with* or *among*; but the common meaning now is, acquainted by familiar use or study; having an intimate or thorough knowledge (of things): followed generally by *with*).—**Conversantly**, kon'vėr-sant-li, *adv.* In a conversant or familiar manner.—**Conversation**, kon-vėr-sā'shon, *n.* [Fr. *conversation*, L. *conversatio*, intercourse.] Manners, behaviour, or deportment, especially as respects morals; familiar discourse; general interchange of sentiments; chat; unrestrained talk, opposed to a formal conference (now the usual meaning); also sexual intercourse.—**Conversational**, kon-vėr-sā'shon-al, *a.* Pertaining to conversation.—**Conversationalist**, **Conversationist**, kon-vėr-sā'shon-al-ist, kon-vėr-sā'shon-ist, *n.* One who excels in conversation.—**Conversazione**, kon-vėr-sat'si-ō"nā, *n.* [It.] A meeting of a number of people for conversation or discussion, particularly on literary, scientific, antiquarian, or artistic subjects.

Converse, kon'vėrs, *a.* [L. *conversus*, turned round, *converto*, *conversum*, to turn round—*con*, and *verto*, *versum*, to turn. CONVERSE, *v.i.*] Turned so as to be transposed or inverted, put the opposite, reverse, or contrary way (*converse* statement, proposition, way).—*n.* Something forming a counterpart; what is contrary or opposite; a statement or proposition produced by inversion or interchange of terms; thus the *converse* of 'religion is true wisdom', is 'true wisdom is religion'.—**Conversely**, kon'vėrs-li, *adv.* In a converse manner; with inversion of order; put the converse way.—**Conversible**, kon-vėr'si-bl, *a.* Capable of being made converse.—**Conversion**, kon-vėr'shon, *n.* [L. *conversio*.] The act of turning or changing from one state to another; the state of being so turned or changed; transmutation; the act of changing or state of being changed in opinions or conduct; a change of heart or dispositions, succeeded by a reformation of life; a change from heathenism or from irreligion to Christianity.—**Convert** kon-vėrt', *v.t.* [L. *converto*.] To change or turn into another substance or form· to change from one state to another; to change or turn from one religion to another, or from one party or sect to another; to change from heathenism to Christianity; to turn from a bad life to a good, religious, and holy one; to turn from one use or destination to another; to interchange conversely.—*v.i.* To turn or be changed; to undergo a change.—*n.* (kon'vėrt). A person who turns from one opinion or practice to another; a person who renounces one creed, religious system, or party, and embraces another; one who is turned from sin to holiness. ∴ A *convert* is one who changes opinions, and thus goes over to another side, party, or religion; a *proselyte* is one who changes his religion; but proselytism does not, like conversion, necessarily imply conviction.—**Converter**, kon-vėr'tėr, *n.* One who converts; one who makes converts; that which converts, especially an iron retort used in the Bessemer process of steel-making.—**Convertibility**, **Convertibleness**, kon-vėr'ti-bil"i-ti, kon-vėr'ti-bl-nes, *n.* The condition or quality of being convertible; the capability of being converted.—**Convertible**, kon-vėr'ti-bl, *a.* Capable of being converted; susceptible of change; transmutable; transformable; capable of being used the one for the other, as terms of similar signification; interchangeable.—**Convertibly**, kon-vėr'ti-bli, *adv.* In a convertible manner; with interchange of terms.

Convex, kon'veks, *a.* [L. *convexus*, carried round, rounded—*con*, together, and *veho*, *vexum*, to carry; whence also *vehicle*.] Rising or swelling into a spherical or rounded form on the exterior surface: opposed to *concave*.—*n.* A convex part.—**Convexed**, kon'vekst, *a.* Made convex.—**Convexly**, **Convexedly**, kon-veks'li, kon-vek'sed-li, *adv.* In a convex form.—**Convexity**, kon-vek'si-ti, *n.* State of being convex; the exterior surface of a convex body; roundness.—**Convexness**, **Convexedness**, kon'veks-nes, kon-vek'sed-nes, *n.* Convexity.—**Convexo-concave**, *a.* Convex on one side and concave on the other: said of a lens.—**Convexo-convex**, *a.* Convex on both sides: said of a lens.

Convey, kon-vā', *v.t.* [O.Fr. *conveier*, *convoyer*, L.L. *conviare*, to convey, to convoy—L. *con*, with, and *via*, a way; whence also *voyage*, *devious*, *deviate*, *obvious*, &c.] To carry, bear, or transport; to transmit, hand over, or transfer from one person to another (rights, landed estate); to transmit or carry by any medium (air *conveys* sound, words *convey* meaning).—**Conveyable**, kon-vā'a-bl, *a.* Capable of being conveyed or transferred.—**Conveyance**, kon-vā'ans, *n.* The act of conveying; the act of bearing, carrying, or transporting; transmission; transference; the transmitting or transferring of property from one person to another; the document by which property is transferred; the means by which anything is conveyed, especially a vehicle or carriage of some kind.—**Conveyancer**, kon-vā'ans-ėr, *n.* One whose occupation is to draw conveyances of property, deeds, &c.—**Conveyancing**, kon-vā'ans-ing, *n.* The act or practice of drawing deeds, leases, or other writings for transferring the title to property from one person to another.—**Conveyer**, kon-vā'ėr, *n.* One who or that which conveys.

Convict, kon-vikt', *v.t.* [L. *convinco*, *convictum*—*con*, and *vinco*, to vanquish. CONVINCE.] To determine the truth of a charge against; to prove or find guilty of a crime charged; to determine or decide to be guilty: with *of* before the crime.—*n.* (kon'vikt). A person convicted or found guilty of a crime; a person undergoing penal servitude.—**Conviction**, kon-vik'shon, *n.* The act of convicting or the state of being convicted; the act of a legal tribunal adjudging, finding, or determining a person to be guilty of an offence charged against him; strong belief on the ground of satisfactory evidence; settled persuasion. ∴ *Conviction* is assent founded on satisfactory proofs which appeal to the reason; *persuasion* is assent founded on what appeals to the feelings and imagination.—**Convictive**,† kon-vik'tiv, *a.* Having the power to convince or convict.

Convince, kon-vins', *v.t.*—*convinced*, *convincing*. [L. *convinco*, *convictum*—*con*, and *vinco*, to vanquish, whence *victor*, *vanquish*, *evince*.] To persuade or satisfy by evidence; to bring to full belief or acquiescence by satisfactory proofs or arguments; to compel to yield assent; to convict or prove guilty (N.T.)‡; to overpower (*Shak.*)‡.—**Convincible**, kon-vin'si-bl, *a.* Capable of conviction.—**Convincingly**, kon-vin'sing-li, *adv.* In a convincing manner; in a manner to leave no room to doubt, or to compel assent.—**Convincingness**, kon-vin'sing-nes, *n.* The power of convincing.

Convivial, kon-viv'i-al, *a.* [L. *conviva*, a guest—*con*, and *vivo*, *victum*, to live, whence *victuals*, *vital*, *vivid*, &c.] Relating to a feast or entertainment; festal; social; jovial.—**Convivialist**, kon-viv'i-al-ist, *n.* A person of convivial habits.—**Conviviality**, kon-viv'i-al"i-ti, *n.* The good humour or mirth indulged at an entertainment; a convivial spirit or disposition.—**Convivially**, kon-viv'i-al-li, *adv.* In a spirit of conviviality; in a convivial manner; festively.

Convoke, kon-vōk', *v.t.*—*convoked*, *convoking*. [L. *convoco*, to convoke—*con*, and *voco*, to call. VOICE, VOCAL.] To call together; to summon to meet; to assemble by summons.—**Convocation**, kon-vō-kā'shon, *n.* The act of convoking or assembling by summons; an assembly; a convention; a congress; a council; in England, an assembly of the clergy, by their representatives, to consult on ecclesiastical affairs—a sort of ecclesiastical parliament.—**Convocational**, kon-vō-kā'shon-al, *a.* Relating to a convocation.

Convolve, kon-volv', *v.t.*—*convolved*, *convolving*. [L. *convolvo*—*con*, and *volvo*, to roll, whence *involve*, *revolve*, *volume*, *vault*. WALLOW.] To roll or wind together; to roll one part on another; to coil up.—**Convolute**, **Convoluted**, kon'vō-lūt, kon'vō-lū-ted, *a.* Rolled together, or one part on another; presenting convolutions.—**Convolution**, kon-vō-lū'shon, *n.* [L. *convolutio*, *convolutionis*.] The act of rolling or winding together, or one thing on another; a winding motion; the state of being rolled round upon itself or rolled or wound together; a turn or winding; a twisted or tortuous part of something.—**Convolutive**, kon'vō-lū-tiv, *a.* *Bot.* convolute.

Convolvulus, kon-vol'vū-lus, *n.* [L., from *convolvo*, to entwine, in reference to their twining habit.] Bindweed, a genus of plants consisting of slender twining herbs, with milky juice, and somewhat bell-shaped flowers, many of them beautiful.—**Convolvulaceous**, kon-vol'vū-lā"shus, *a.* Relating to the convolvulus or allied plants.

Convoy, kon-voi', *v.t.* [Fr. *convoyer*. *Convoy*=*convey*. CONVEY.] To accompany on the way for protection, either by sea or land; to escort, as a guard against enemies.—*n.* (kon'voi). A protecting force accompanying ships or property on their way from place to place either by sea or land; that which is conducted by such a force.

Convulse, kon-vuls', *v.t.* [L. *convello*, *convulsum*—*con*, and *vello*, to pull or pluck.] To draw together or contract spasmodically, as the muscular parts of an animal body; to affect by irregular spasms; to affect by violent irregular action; to agitate violently.—**Convulsible**,† kon-vul'si-bl, *a.* Capable of being convulsed; subject to convulsion.—**Convulsion**, kon-vul'shon, *n.* [L. *convulsio*.] A violent and involuntary contraction of the muscular parts of an animal body, with alternate relaxations; violent and irregular motion; a violent and far-reaching disturbance in nature or among peoples; turmoil; a violent commotion.—**Convulsional**,† **Convulsionary**,† kon-vul'shon-al, kon-vul'shon-a-ri, *a.* Pertaining to convulsion; of the nature of convulsion.—**Convulsive**, kon-vul'siv, *a.* Producing or tending to produce convulsion; attended with, or characterized by, convulsion or spasms.—**Convulsively**, kon-vul'siv-li, *adv.* In a convulsive manner; with convulsion.

Cony, **Coney**, kō'ni, *n.* [O.E. *coning*, *cunning*, perhaps from O.Fr. *conil*, *conin*, from L. *cuniculus*, a rabbit; comp. W. *cwning*, Gael. *coinean*, Ir. *coinin*, Manx *connee*—rabbit.] A rabbit; a rabbit-like animal found in Syria and Palestine; the daman (O.T.); a simpleton‡.—**Cony-wool**, *n.* The fur of rabbits, used in the hat manufacture.

Coo, kö, *v.i.* [Imitative of the noise of doves; comp. D. *korren*, Icel. *kurra*, Fr. *roucouler*, to coo like a dove.] To cry or make the characteristic sound uttered by pigeons or doves; to act in a loving manner.—**Cooingly**, kö'ing-li, *adv.* In a cooing manner.

Cooey, **Cooie**, kö'i, *n.* [Imitative.] The cry or call of the Australian aborigines.—*v.t.* To cry or call like the aborigines of Australia.

Cook, kuk, *v.t.* [A.Sax. *cóc*, a cock, borrowed, like Dan. *koge*, G. *kochen*, D. *kooken*, to boil, to cook, from L. *coquo*, to cook, *coquus*, a cook.] To prepare for the table by boiling, roasting, baking, broiling, &c.; to dress, as meat or vegetables, for eating; to dress up or give a colour to for some special purpose, especially, to tamper with accounts so as to give them a more favourable aspect than they ought to have; to garble; to falsify.—*n.* One whose occupation is to cook or prepare victuals for the table.—**Cookery**, kuk'ėr-i, *n.* The art or the practice of dressing and preparing victuals for the table.—**Cook-house**, *n.* An erection on a ship's deck for containing the cooking apparatus; the galley.

Cool, köl, *a.* [A.Sax. *cól* = G. *kühl*, cool; Icel. *kul*, D. *koel*, a cold blast; same root as in *chill, cold*, L. *gelu*, frost, *gelidus*.] Moderately cold; being of a temperature between hot and cold; not ardent or zealous; not excited by passion of any kind; not angry; not fond; indifferent; apathetic; chilling; frigid; deliberate; calm; quietly impudent and selfish: of persons and acts (*colloq.*).—*n.* A moderate state of cold; moderate temperature of the air between hot and cold (the *cool* of the day).—*v.t.* To make cool; to reduce the temperature of; to moderate or allay, as passion of any kind; to calm; to abate, as desire, zeal, or ardour; to render indifferent.—*v.i.* To become less hot; to lose heat; to lose the heat of excitement, passion, or emotion; to become less ardent, zealous, or affectionate.—**Cooler**, köl'ėr, *n.* That which cools; a vessel in which liquors or other things are cooled.—**Cool-headed**, *a.* Having a temper not easily excited; free from passion.—**Cooling**, köl'ing, *a.* Adapted to cool and refresh.—**Coolish**, köl'ish, *a.* Somewhat cool.—**Coolly**, köl'li, *adv.* Without heat or sharp cold; in a cool or indifferent manner; without passion or ardour; without haste; calmly; deliberately.—**Coolness**, köl'nes, *n.* The state or quality of being cool; a moderate degree of cold; a moderate degree or a want of passion; want of ardour or zeal; indifference; want of affection.

Coolie, kö'li, *n.* An East Indian porter or carrier; an emigrant labourer from India, China, and other eastern countries.

Coom, köm, *n.* [Perhaps from Fr. *écume*, foam, dross.] Soot; dirty refuse matter; the matter that works out of the naves or boxes of carriage wheels; coal-dust.

Coomb, Comb, köm, köm, *n.* [A.Sax. *cumb*, a liquid measure, a valley = Dan. and G. *kumme*, a bowl, a basin; D. *kom*, a trough, a chest.] An English dry measure of 4 bushels or half a quarter; a valley between hills (see COMB).

Coon, kön, *n.* An abbreviation of *Raccoon*; (*slang*) negro.

Coop, köp, *n.* [From L. *cupa*, a cask or vessel; akin *cup*.] A box of boards grated or barred on one side for keeping fowls in confinement; an inclosed place for small animals; a pen.—*v.t.* To put in a coop; to confine in a coop; to shut up or confine in a narrow compass: followed by *up*, *in*, or *within*.—**Cooper**, kö'pėr, *n.* One whose occupation is to make barrels, tubs, &c.—*v.t.* and *i.* To do the work of a cooper.—**Cooperage**, kö'pėr-āj, *n.* A place where coopers' work is done; the work or business of a cooper.—**Coopery**, kö'pėr-i, *n.* The trade of a cooper; a cooper's workshop.

Co-operate, kō-op'ėr-āt, *v.i.*—*co-operated, co-operating.* To act or operate jointly with another or others to the same end; to work or labour to promote a common object; to unite in producing the same effect.—**Co-operation**, kō-op'ėr-ā"shon, *n.* The act of working or operating together to one end; joint operation; concurrent effort or labour.—**Co-operant**, kō-op'ėr-ant, *a.* Operating or working together.—**Co-operative**, kō-op'ėr-ā-tiv, *a.* Operating jointly to the same end; established for the purpose of providing the members with goods at wholesale prices or at prime cost and cost of management (*co-operative* societies or stores).—**Co-operator**, kō-op'ėr-ā-tėr, *n.* One who co-operates.

Co-opt, Co-optate, kō-opt', kō-op'tāt, *v.t.* [L. *co-opto*.] To elect by co-optation into some body of which the electors are members.

Co-ordinate, kō-or'din-āt, *a.* [L. *co* for *con*, and *ordinatus*, from *ordo*, order. ORDER.] Being of equal order, or of the same rank or degree; not subordinate.—*v.t.*—*co-ordinated, co-ordinating.* To make co-ordinate; to arrange in due and relative order; to harmonize.—*n.* What is co-ordinate; *geom.* any straight line which, with another or others, serves to determine the position of certain points under consideration.—**Co-ordinately**, kō-or'di-nāt-li, *adv.* In the same order or rank; without subordination.—**Co-ordinateness**, kō-or'di-nāt-nes, *n.* The state of being co-ordinate.—**Co-ordination**, kō-or'di-nā"shon, *n.* The act of making co-ordinate or state of being co-ordinated.—**Co-ordinative**, kō-or'di-nā-tiv, *a.* Expressing or indicating co-ordination.

Coot, köt, *n.* [Same as D. *koet*, a coot; comp. W. *cwta*, short-tailed.] A British wading bird of the rail family, with a bald forehead, a black body, short tail, and lobated toes, and about 15 inches in length.

Copaiba, Copaiva, kō-pā'ba, kō-pā'va, *n.* [Sp. and Pg.] A liquid resinous juice or balsam, flowing from incisions made in the stem of certain South American trees, used in medicine, especially in affections of the mucous membranes.

Copal, kō-pal', *n.* [Mex. *copalli*, a generic name of resins.] A hard, shining, transparent, citron-coloured, and odoriferous resinous substance, the product of several different tropical trees: when dissolved and diluted with spirit of turpentine it forms a beautiful transparent varnish.

Coparcener, kō-pär'sen-ėr, *n.* [Prefix *co*, and *parcener*, ultimately from L. *pars*, a part.] A coheir; one who has an equal portion of the inheritance of his or her ancestor with others.—**Coparcenary**, kō-pär'sen-a-ri, *n.* Partnership in inheritance; joint heirship.

Copartner, kō-pärt'nėr, *n.* A partner with others; one who is jointly concerned with one or more persons in carrying on trade or other business; a sharer; a partaker.—**Copartnership, Copartnery**, kō-pärt'nėr-ship, kō-pärt'nėr-i, *n.* The state of being a copartner; joint concern in business; the persons who have a joint concern.

Cope, kōp, *n.* [A form of *cap* and *cape*, a hood.] An ecclesiastical vestment resembling a cloak, worn in processions, at vespers, at consecration, and other sacred functions; something spread or extended over the head; hence, the arch or concave of the sky, the roof or covering of a house, the arch over a door; a coping.—*v.t.*—*coped, coping.* To cover as with a cope.—**Copestone**, *n.* A head or top stone, as on a wall or roof.—**Coping**, kō'ping, *n.* The covering course of a wall, parapet, buttresses, &c.

Cope, kōp, *v.i.*—*coped, coping.* [O.Fr. *coper*, to strike (Fr. *couper*, to cut), from *colp, cop* (Fr. *coup*), a blow. COPPICE.] To strive or contend on equal terms or with equal strength; to match; to oppose with success; to encounter: followed by *with*.—*v.t.*‡ To make return for; to reward. (*Shak.*)

Copeck, kō'pek, *n.* A Russian coin, the hundredth part of a silver rouble.

Copeck, kō'pek, KOPECK.

Copernican, kō-pėr'ni-kan, *a.* Pertaining to Copernicus, who taught the solar system now received, called the *Copernican* system.

Coping. Under COPE, *n.*

Copious, kō'pi-us, *a.* [L. *copiosus*, from *copia*, plenty—*co*, and *ops, opis*, property.] Abundant; plentiful; in great quantities; furnishing abundant matter; rich in supplies.—**Copiously**, kō'pi-us-li, *adv.* In a copious manner; abundantly; plentifully; in large quantities; fully; amply; diffusely.—**Copiousness**, kō'pi-us-nes, *n.* The state or quality of being copious.

Copper, kop'ėr, *n.* [L.L. *cuprum*, from L. *cyprium* (*æs*), Cyprian brass, from *Cyprus*, whence the Romans got their best copper.] A ductile and malleable metal of a pale red colour, tinged with yellow, specific gravity 8·95, of great value both by itself and in alloys; a vessel made of copper, particularly a large boiler; a coin made of copper or partly of copper; *pl.* the cast-iron apparatus used on board ship for cooking, and erected in the cook-house or galley.—*a.* Consisting of or resembling copper.—*v.t.* To cover or sheathe with sheets of copper; as, to *copper* a ship.—**Copper-bottomed**, *a.* Having a bottom sheathed with copper: applied to ships.—**Copper-fastened**, *a.* Fastened with copper bolts, as the planking of a vessel.—**Copper-head**, *n.* [From its colour.] A poisonous American serpent.—**Coppering**, kop'ėr-ing, *n.* The act of covering with copper, or the covering itself.—**Copperish**, kop'ėr-ish, *a.* Containing copper; like copper or partaking of it.—**Copper-nose**, *n.* A red nose. (*Shak.*)—**Copper-plate**, *n.* A plate of polished copper on which some figure or design has been engraved, and from which an impression can be printed; a print or impression from such a plate.—**Copper-smith**, *n.* One whose occupation is to manufacture copper utensils.—**Coppery**, kop'ėr-i, *a.* Mixed with or containing copper; like copper in taste, smell, or colour.

Copperas, kop'ėr-as, *n.* [From L. *cuprirosa*, rose of copper, It. *copparosa*, Sp. Pg. *caparrosa*, Fr. *couperose*.] Sulphate of iron or green vitriol, a salt of a peculiar astringent taste and of various colours, but usually green.

Coppice, Copse, kop'is, kops, *n.* [O.Fr. *copeiz, coupiez*, wood newly cut, from *couper, coper*, to cut, from L.L. *colpus*, L. *colaphus*, Gr. *kolaphos*, a blow.] A wood of small growth, or consisting of underwood or brushwood; a wood cut at certain times for fuel or other purposes.—**Copse-wood**, *n.* A growth of shrubs and bushes; wood treated as coppice and cut down at certain periods.—**Copsy**, kop'si, *a.* Having copses; overgrown with copse-wood.

Copra, kop'ra, *n.* The dried kernel of the cocoa-nut, from which the oil has yet to be expressed.

Coprolite, kop'ro-līt, *n.* [Gr. *kopros*, dung, and *lithos*, a stone.] The petrified dung of extinct animals, such as lizards or sauroid fishes, found chiefly in the lias and coal-measures.—**Coprolitic**, kop-ro-lit'ik, *a.* Composed of coprolites; resembling coprolites; containing coprolites.

Coprology, kop-rol'o-ji, *n.* [Gr. *kopros*, dung, *logos*, talk]. Literary treatment of base or dunghill subject.—**Coprologist**, *n.* One who so writes.

Coprophagous, kop-rof'a-gus, *a.* [Gr. *kopros*, dung, and *phágo*, to eat.] Feeding upon dung or filth: a term particularly applied to certain insects.

Copse, kops, *n.* COPPICE.

Copt, kopt, *n.* A descendant of the ancient Egyptian race, and usually professing Christianity.—**Coptic**, kop'tik, *a.* Pertaining to the Copts.—*n.* The language of the Copts, an ancient Hamitic tongue, used in Egypt till superseded as a living language by Arabic.

Copula, kop'ū-la, *n.* [L. *copula*, a band, a link, whence E. *couple*.] *Logic*, the word which unites the subject and predicate of a proposition; as in 'man is mortal', where *is* is the copula.—**Copular**, kop'ū-lėr, *a.* Of or relating to a copula.—**Copulate**, kop'ū-lāt, *v.i.*—*copulated, copulating.* To unite in sexual embrace.—**Copulation**, kop-ū-lā'shon, *n.* [L. *copulatio*.] The act of copulating; coition.—**Copulative**, kop'ū-lā-tiv, *a.* Uniting or coupling.—*Copulative conjunction*, *gram.* a conjunction (such as *and*) which connects two or more subjects or predicates in an affirmative or negative proposition.—*n.* A copulative conjunction.—**Copulatively**, kop'ū-lā-tiv-li, *adv.* In a copulative manner.—**Copulatory**, kop'ū-la-to-ri, *a.* Relating to copulation; copulative.

Copy, kop'i, *n.* [Fr. *copie*, from L. *copia*, plenty, opportunity, permission, whence permission to reproduce. COPIOUS.] A writing like another writing; a transcript from an original; a book printed according to the original; one of many books containing the same literary matter; what is produced by imitating; a thing made in close imitation of another; that which is to be imitated; a pattern; a model; an archetype; writing engraved or penned by a master to be imitated by a pupil; written or printed matter given to a printer to be put in type.—*v.t.*—*copied, copying.* To make a copy from; to write, print, engrave, construct, draw, paint, &c., according to an original; to transcribe; to imitate; to follow as in language, style, manners, or course of life; take as one's model.—*v.i.* To make or produce a copy.—**Copybook**, *n.* A book in which copies are written or printed for learners to imitate.—**Copyhold**, kop'-i-hōld, *n.* *English law*, a tenure for which the tenant has nothing to show except the copy of the rolls made on the tenant's being admitted to the possession of the subject; land held in copyhold.—**Copyholder**, kop'i-hōl-dėr, *n.* One who is possessed of land in copyhold; a device for holding copy; a proofreader's assistant.—**Copying press**, *n.* A machine for producing duplicates of letters, invoices, and other manuscripts.—**Copyright**, kop'i-rīt, *n.* The exclusive privilege which the law allows an author (or his assignee) of printing, reprinting, publishing, and selling his own original work: an author's exclusive right of property in his work for a certain time.—*a.* Relating to, or protected by the law of copyright.—*v.t.* To secure by copyright, as a book.

Coquet, kō-ket', *v.t.*—*coquetted, coquetting.* [Fr. *coqueter*, lit. to demean one's self as a cock amongst hens, to swagger, to strut, from *coq*, a cock.] To entertain with compliments and amorous tattle.—*v.i.* To act the lover from vanity; to endeavour to gain admirers.—**Coquetry**, kok'et-ri, *n.* [Fr. *coquetterie.*] The arts of a coquette; attempts to attract admiration, notice, or love, from vanity; affectation of amorous advances.—**Coquette**, kō-ket', *n.* [Fr. *coquette.*] A vain, airy, trifling girl, who endeavours to attract admiration and advances in love, from a desire to gratify vanity; a flirt.—**Coquettish**, kō-ket'ish, *a.* Of or pertaining to coquetry; characterized by coquetry; practising coquetry.—**Coquettishly**, kō-ket'ish-li, *adv.* In a coquettish manner.

Coquilla-nut, kō-kwil'la, *n.* The seed of one of the cocoa-nut palms, a native of Brazil, extensively used in turnery.

Cor, kor, *n.* [Heb.] A Hebrew measure of capacity containing about 11 bushels.

Coracle, kor'a-kl, *n.* [W. *cwrwgl.*] An ancient form of boat made by covering a wicker frame with leather or oil-cloth, still used in Wales and Ireland.

Coracoid, kor'a-koid, *a.* [Gr. *korax, korakos*, a crow, and *eidos*, resemblance.] Shaped like a crow's beak.—*Coracoid process*, in *anat.* a small sharp process of the scapula in mammals; *coracoid bone*, a bone connecting the shoulder joint and sternum in birds.

Co-radicate, kō-rad'i-kāt, *a.* [L. prefix *co*, and *radix, radicis*, a root.] *Philol.* belonging to the same root.

Coral, kor'al, *n.* [Fr. *corail* or *coral*, L. *corallium* or *corallum*, Gr. *korallion.*] A general term for the hard calcareous substance secreted by marine cœlenterate polyps for their common support and habitation, exhibiting a great variety of forms and colours; a toy or plaything for an infant, made of coral; the unimpregnated eggs in the lobster, so called from being of a bright red colour.—*a.* Made of coral; resembling coral.—**Corallaceous**, kor-a-lā'shus, *a.* Like coral, or partaking of its qualities.—**Coralled**, kor'ald, *a.* Furnished with coral; covered with coral.—**Coralliferous**, **Coralligerous**, kor-a-lif'ėr-us, kor-a-lij'ėr-us, *a.* Containing or consisting of coral; producing coral.—**Coralliform**, kō-ral'i-form, *a.* Resembling coral.—**Coralligenous**, kor-a-lij'e-nus, *a.* Producing coral.—**Coralline**, kor'al-īn, *a.* Consisting of coral; like coral; containing coral.—*n.* One of the coral polyps or other zoophytes; a sea-weed with calcareous fronds; an orange-red colour.—**Corallite**, kor'al-īt, *n.* A mineral substance or petrifaction in the form of coral; the calcareous substance secreted by a single polyp.—**Coralloid**, **Coralloidal**, kor'al-oid, kor'al-oi-dal, *a.* Having the form of coral; branching like coral.—**Coral-rag**, *n.* *Geol.* a term for the highest member of the middle oolitic series—a variety of limestone containing an abundance of petrified corals.—**Coral-reef**, **Coral-island**, *n.* One of those reefs or islands of coral which are produced by the operation of species of polyps.—**Coral-tree**, *n.* A genus of leguminous plants, of several species, natives of Africa and America, with trifoliolate leaves and scarlet spikes of papilionaceous flowers.—**Coral-wood**, *n.* A hard cabinet wood, susceptible of a fine polish, and of a beautiful red or coral colour.

Corb, korb, *n.* [L. *corbis*, a basket.] A basket used for carrying minerals in mines; a corf; a corve; *arch.* a corbel.

Corban, kor'ban, *n.* [Heb. *corbân*, an offering, sacrifice.] *Jewish antiq.* a solemn consecration of anything to God, as of one's self, one's services, or possessions; an alms-basket; a treasury of the church.

Corbeil, kor'bel, *n.* [Fr. *corbeille*, from L. *corbicula*, dim. of *corbis*, a basket.] *Fort.* a basket, to be filled with earth and set upon a parapet to shelter men; *arch.* a carved basket with sculptured flowers and fruits.—**Corbel**, kor'bel, *n.* [L.L. *corbella*, a dim. from L. *corbis*, a basket.] *Arch.* a piece of stone, wood, or iron projecting from the vertical face of a wall to support some superincumbent object.—*v.t. corbelled, corbelling. Arch.* to support on a corbel or corbels; to provide with corbels.—**Corbel-steps**, *n.* Steps into which the sides of gables from the eaves to the apex are broken.—**Corbel-table**, *n.* An architectural arrangement which requires the support of numerous corbels.

Corcule, **Corcle**, kor'kūl, kor'kl, *n.* [L. *corculum*, a dim. of *cor*, the heart.] *Bot.* the heart of the seed or rudiment of a future plant, attached to and involved in the cotyledons.

Cord, kord, *n.* [Fr. *corde*, from L. *chorda*, Gr. *chordē*, a string or gut, the string of a lyre.] A string or small rope composed of several strands twisted together; a quantity of wood, originally measured with a cord or line, containing 128 cubic feet, or a pile 8 feet long, 4 feet high, and 4 feet broad; *fig.* what, binds, restrains, draws, or otherwise in moral effects resembles a cord: corded cloth; corduroy.—*v.t.* To bind with a cord or rope; to pile up for measurement and sale by the cord.—**Cordage**, kor'dāj, *n.* Ropes or cords collectively; the ropes in the rigging of a ship.—**Corded**, kor'ded, *p.* and *a.* Fastened with cords; made of cords (*Shak.*); striped or furrowed, as by cords (*corded* cloth).

Cordate, **Cordated**, kor'dāt, kor'dā-ted, *a.* [L. *cor*, *cordis*, the heart.] Having the form of a heart; heart-shaped.—**Cordately**, kor'dāt-li, *adv.* In a cordate form.—**Cordiform**, kor'di-form, *a.* Heart-shaped.

Cordelier, kor'de-lēr, *n.* [Fr., from *corde*, a girdle or cord worn by the order.] A Franciscan friar under the strictest rules and wearing a girdle of knotted cord.

Cordial, kor'di-al, *a.* [Fr. *cordial*, from L. *cor, cordis*, the heart; same root as E. *heart.*] Proceeding from the heart; hearty; sincere; not hypocritical; warm; affectionate; reviving the spirits; refreshing; invigorating (a *cordial* liquor).—*n.* Anything that strengthens, comforts, gladdens, or exhilarates; an exhilarating liquor; an aromatized and sweetened spirit employed as a beverage.—**Cordiality**, **Cordialness**, kor'di-al-i-ti, kor'di-al-nes, *n.* The state of being cordial; sincere affection and kindness; genial sincerity; hearty warmth of heart; heartiness.—**Cordially**, kor'di-al-li, *adv.* In a cordial manner; heartily; sincerely; without hypocrisy; with real affection.

Cordiform. Under CORDATE.

Cordillera, kor-dēl-yā'rä, *n.* [Sp., from L. *chorda*, a string. CORD.] A ridge or chain of mountains; specifically, the mountain range of the Andes in South America.

Cordite, kor'dīt, *n.* [From being made in *cord*-like forms.] A smokeless gunpowder, for use in ordnance.

Cordon, kor'don, *n.* [Fr. and Sp. *cordon*. CORD.] A line or series of military posts inclosing or guarding any particular place; a line of posts on the borders of a district infected with disease, to cut off communication; a ribbon worn across the breast by knights of the first class of an order.—**Cordon-bleu**, *n.* The blue line of defence, police force; a clever cook.

Cordovan, **Cordwain**, kor'dō-van, kord'wān, *n.* [O.Fr. *cordouan*, Sp. *cordoban*, from *Cordova* or *Cordoba*, in Spain, where it is largely manufactured.] Spanish leather; goat-skin tanned and dressed.—**Cordwainer**, kord'wān-ėr, *n.* A worker in cordwain or Cordovan leather; a shoemaker.

Corduroy, kor-dū-roi', *n.* [Fr. *corde du roy*, the king's cord.] A thick cotton stuff corded or ribbed on the surface.

Core, kōr, *n.* [O.Fr. *cor, coer*, from L. *cor*, the heart, whence *cordial.*] The heart or inner part of a thing; particularly the central part of fruit containing the kernels or seeds; a centre or central part, as the iron bar of an electro-magnet round which is wound a coil of insulated wire, the conducting wires of a submarine telegraph cable, the interior part of a column, the internal mould which forms a hollow in the casting of metals; *fig.* the heart or deepest and most essential part of anything (the *core* of a question).—*v.t.* To remove the core of.—**Coreless**, kōr'les, *a.* Wanting a core; without pith; weak.

Co-relative. CORRELATIVE.

Co-respondent, kō-rē-spon-dent, *n.* *Law*, a joint respondent, or one opposed, along with another or others, to the plaintiff; a man charged with adultery, and made a party to a suit for dissolution of marriage.

Corf, korf, *n.* CORB.

Coriaceous, kō-ri-ā'shus, *a.* [L. *coriaceus*, from *corium*, leather.] Consisting of leather or resembling leather; tough and leathery.

Coriander, kor-i-an'dėr, *n.* [L. *coriandrum*, from Gr. *koriannon*, coriander, from *koris*, a bug, from the smell of its leaves.] An annual plant of the carrot family, the seeds of which have a strong smell, and are stomachic and carminative, being used in sweetmeats, in certain liqueurs, and also in cookery.

Corinthian, ko-rin'thi-an, *a.* Pertaining to *Corinth*, a celebrated city of Greece.—*Corinthian order*, an architectural order distinguished by fluted columns and capitals adorned with acanthus leaves.—*n.* An inhabitant of Corinth; a gay, fast, or spirited fellow.—**Corinthian**, kor-in'thi-an, *n.* A gentleman who does the work on his own or a friend's yacht, opposed to a paid hand; a gentleman jockey who rides his own horse; *pl.* two epistles written by St. Paul to the church of Corinth.

Corium, kō'ri-um, *n.* [L., leather.] Leathern body-armour worn by the Roman soldiers; the innermost layer of the skin in mammals; the true skin.

Cork, kork, *n.* [G. Dan. and Sw. *kork*, Sp. *corcho*, from L. *cortex, corticis*, bark.] The outer bark of a kind of oak (the cork-oak or cork-tree) growing in Spain and elsewhere, stripped off and made into such articles as stopples for bottles and casks; a stopple for a bottle or cask cut out of cork.—*v.t.* To stop or fit with cork; to confine or make fast with a cork.—**Cork-cutter** *n.* One whose trade is to make corks.—**Corked**, korkt, *p.* and *a.* Stopped or fitted with cork or a cork; having acquired the taste of cork (*corked* wine).—**Corking-pin**, *n.* A pin of a large size formerly used.—**Cork-jacket**, *n.* A kind of jacket padded with cork, designed to buoy up a person who cannot swim.—**Cork-leg**, *n.* An artificial leg, in the formation of which cork is used. **Corkscrew**, kork'skrö, *n.* A screw to draw corks from bottles.—*v.t.* To direct or work along in a spiral; to wriggle forward.—**Corky**, kor'ki, *a.* Consisting of cork; resembling cork.

Corm, korm, *n.* [Gr. *kormos*, a stem.] *Bot.* a bulb-like part of a plant, consisting of the dilated base of the stem, as in the crocus; a solid bulb.

Cormogen, kor′mo-jen, *n.* [Gr. *kormos*, stem.] A plant with regular stem and root, as opposed to *thallogen*.

Cormorant, kor′mō-rant, *n.* [Fr. *cormoran*, from L. *corvus marinus*, sea raven.] A web-footed sea-bird of the pelican family, of several species, catching fish by swimming and diving, and extremely voracious; *fig.* a greedy fellow; a glutton.

Corn, korn, *n.* [A.Sax. *corn*, a word found throughout the Teutonic languages, of same root as L. *granum*, a seed. Akin *kernel*, *grain*.] A grain grown extensively in many parts of the United States, particularly the central west (corn belt) and southwest, and also throughout the world in most temperate zones. It is used as food for human consumption, but its principal use is for stock food. In Great Britain, corn means any of a variety of grains such as wheat, barley, &c.—*v.t.* To preserve and season with salt in grains; to sprinkle with salt (to *corn* beef.)—**Corn-beef**, **Corned beef**, *n.* Beef preserved and seasoned with salt in grains; beef cured by salting.—**Corn beetle**, *n.* A minute beetle, the larva of which is often very destructive to the stores, particularly of wheat, in granaries.—**Corn cockle**, *n.* The common name of a plant with purple flowers, a frequent weed among grain crops.—**Corn crake**, *n.* The crake or land rail, which frequents cornfields and is noted for its strange harsh cry.—**Corn exchange**, *n.* A place where grain is sold or bartered and samples shown and examined.—**Corn factor**, *n.* One who traffics in grain by wholesale, or as an agent.—**Cornfield**, *n.* A field in which corn is growing.—**Corn flag**, *n.* A popular name of the plants of the genus *Gladiolus*.—**Corn flour**, *n.* The finely-ground meal of Indian corn.—**Corn laws**, *n. pl.* In England, legislative enactments and restrictions relating to the exportation and importation of grain.—**Corn marigold**, *n.* A kind of Chrysanthemum common in cornfields.—**Corn parsley**, *n.* An umbelliferous plant found in moist places and hedge banks.—**Corn poppy**, **Corn rose**, *n.* The common red poppy, a troublesome weed in cornfields.—**Corn violet**, *n.* A species of *Campanula*, a plant found in cornfields.—**Corny**, kor′ni, *a.* Of the nature of, or furnished with, grains of corn; producing corn; containing corn; produced from corn; tasting of corn or malt.

Corn, korn, *n.* [L. *cornu*, a horn.] A hard excrescence or induration of the skin on the toes or some other part of the feet, occasioned by the pressure of the shoes.—**Corn-plaster**, *n.* A plaster to cure corns.

Corneous, kor′nē-us, *a.* [L. *corneus*, from *cornu*, a horn.] Horny; like horn; consisting of a horny substance, or a substance resembling horn; hard.—**Corniculate**, kor-nik′ū-lāt, *a.* Horned; having horns; *bot.* producing horned pods; bearing a little spur or horn.—**Cornific**, kor-nif′ik, *a.* Producing horns.—**Cornification**, kor′ni-fi-kā″shon, *n.* The growth or formation of horn.—**Corniform**, kor′ni-form, *a.* Horn-shaped.—**Cornigerous**, kor-nij′ėr-us, *a.* Horned; having horns.—**Cornute**, **Cornuted**, kor-nūt′, kor-nū′ted, *a.* Furnished with horns; horned; *bot.* horn-shaped.

Cornea, kor′nē-a, *n.* [L. *corneus*, horny, *cornu*, a horn.] The horny transparent membrane in the fore part of the eye through which the rays of light pass.—**Corneule**, kor′nē-ūl, *n.* A term applied to the minute transparent segments of which the compound eyes of insects are composed.

Cornel, **Cornel-tree**, kor′nel, *n.* [L. *cornus*, from *cornu*, a horn, from the hardness of the wood.] A species of dogwood found in Europe and Northern Asia, which produces a small, red, acid, cherry-like fruit, used in preserves and confectionery. Sometimes called *Cornelian-tree*.—**Cornelian-cherry**, *n.* The edible fruit of the cornel-tree.

Cornelian, kor-nē′li-an, *n.* Same as *Carnelian*.

Corner, kor′nėr, *n.* [Fr. *cornière*, from L. *cornu*, a horn, projection.] The point where two converging lines or surfaces meet, or the space between; an angle; a secret or retired place; a nook or out-of-the-way place; any part (every *corner* of the forest); a combination to raise the price of goods in the market.—*v.t.* In trading, to secure a monopoly or sufficient quantity of any stock or commodity, so that prospective buyers will be forced to pay the seller's price.—**Cornered**, kor′nėrd, *a.* Having corners.—**Corner-stone**, *n.* The stone which forms the corner of the foundation of an edifice; hence, that which is of the greatest importance; that on which any system is founded.

Cornet, kor′net, *n.* [Fr., dim. of *corne*, L. *cornu*, a horn.] A kind of brass wind-instrument; a cornet-a-pistons; a troop of horse: said to be so called because each company had a cornet player; formerly the title of the officer who carried the ensign or colours in a troop of horse in the British army.—**Cornet-à-pistons**, kor′net-a-pis″tonz, *n.* [Fr., cornet with pistons.] A brass or silver wind-instrument, capable of producing the notes of the chromatic scale from the valves and pistons with which it is furnished.—**Cornetcy**, kor′net-si, *n.* The commission or rank of a cornet.

Cornice, kor′nis, *n.* [O.Fr. *cornice*, It. *cornice*, from Gr. *korōnis*, a summit, from *korōnē*, a crown. CROWN.] *Arch.* any moulded projection which crowns or finishes the part to which it is affixed; specifically, the highest part of an entablature resting on the frieze.—**Corniced**, kor′nist, *a.* Having a cornice.

Corniculate, Cornific, Corniform, &c. CORNEOUS.

Cornish, korn′ish, *a.* Pertaining to Cornwall, in England.—*Cornish engine*, a single-acting steam-engine used for pumping water.—*n.* The ancient language of Cornwall, a dialect of the Celtic.—**Cornish hug**, *n.* A close grip at wrestling in the Cornish style.

Cornopean, kor-nō′pē-an, *n.* A kind of horn; the cornet-à-pistons (which see).

Cornucopia, kor-nū-kō′pi-a, *n.* [L. *cornucopiæ*, the horn of plenty.] A wreathed horn, filled to overflowing with richest fruit, flowers, and grain, used in sculpture, &c., as a symbol of plenty, peace, and concord.

Corolla, ko-rol′la, *n.* [L. *corolla*, dim. of *corona*, a crown.] *Bot.* the part of a flower inside the calyx, surrounding the parts of fructification, and composed of one or more petals, generally to be distinguished from the calyx by the fineness of its texture and the gayness of its colours.—**Corollaceous**, ko-rol-ā′shus, *a.* Pertaining to a corolla, inclosing and protecting like a wreath.—**Corollate**, **Corollated**, kor′ol-āt, kor′ol-āt-ed, *a.* *Bot.* like a corolla; having corollas.—**Corollet**, kor′ol-let, *n.* *Bot.* one of the partial flowers which make a compound one; the floret in an aggregate flower.—**Corolline**, kor′ol-lin, *a.* *Bot.* of or belonging to a corolla.

Corollary, kor′ol-la-ri, *n.* [Fr. *corollaire*, from L. *corolla*, a little crown, from as it were crowning what it refers to.] That which follows over and above what is directly demonstrated in a mathematical proposition; any consequence necessarily concurrent with or following from the main one; an inference· a conclusion; a surplus (*Shak.*)‡.

Coromandel-wood, kor-ō-man′del, *n.* A beautiful brown wood from the coast of Coromandel.

Corona, ko-rō′na, *n.* [L., a crown. CROWN.] A technical term for various things supposed to have some resemblance to a crown; *astron.* a halo or luminous circle around one of the heavenly bodies; a luminous appearance observed during total eclipses of the sun, which lies outside the chromosphere; *arch.* the lower member or drip of a classical cornice having a broad vertical face, usually of considerable projection; *bot.* the circumference or margin of a radiated composite flower; also an appendage of the corolla or petals of a flower proceeding from the base of the limb.—**Coronal**, ko-rō′nal, *a.* Pertaining to a coronat; belonging to the crown or top of the head: in this sense pron. kor′o-nal.—*n.* (kor′o-nal). A crown; wreath; garland.—**Coronamen**, kor-o-nā′men, *n.* The superior margin of an animal's hoof.—**Coronary**, kor′o-na-ri, *a.* Relating to a crown; resembling a crown; seated on the top of the head, or placed as a crown; *anat.* resembling a crown or circlet.—*n.* A small bone in the foot of a horse.—**Coronate**, kor′o-nāt, *a.* [L. *coronatus*.] Having or wearing a crown or something like one.—**Coronation**, kor-o-nā′shon, *n.* The act or solemnity of crowning a sovereign or investing him with the insignia of royalty; the pomp attending on a coronation.—**Coroner**, kor′o-nėr, *n.* [L.L. *coronator*, originally a crown officer of extensive powers, from L. *corona*, a crown. An officer appointed to hold inquests on the bodies of such as either die, or are supposed to die, a violent death.—**Coronet**, kor′o-net, *n.* [Fr., dim. of O.Fr. *corone*, L. *corona*.] An inferior crown worn by princes and noblemen, bearing crosses, fleurs-de-lis, strawberry leaves, pearls; the lower part of the pastern of a horse.—*v.t.* To adorn with a coronet or something similar.—**Coroneted**, kor′o-net-ed, *a.* Wearing or entitled to wear a coronet.—**Coroniform**, ko-rō′ni-form, *a.* Having the form of a crown.—**Coronule**, kor′o-nūl, *n.* [Dim. from L. *corona*.] *Bot.* a coronet or little crown of a seed; the downy tuft on seeds.

Coronach, kor′ō-nach, *n.* [Gael. and Ir.] A dirge; a lamentation for the dead among the Highlanders and Irish.

Coronoid, kor′o-noid, *a.* [Gr. *korōnē*, a crow, and *eidos*, form.] Resembling the beak of a crow: applied in *anat.* to one or two processes or projecting parts.

Corozo-nut, ko-rō′zō, *n.* The seed of a tropical American palm, whose hardened albumen, under the name of vegetable ivory, is used for small articles of turnery.

Corporal, kor′po-ral, *n.* [Corrupted from Fr. *caporal*, It. *caporale*, from *capo*, L. *caput*, the head.] The non-commissioned officer of a company of infantry next below a sergeant; in *ships-of-war*, a petty officer who attends to police matters.

Corporal, kor′po-ral, *a.* [L. *corporalis*, from *corpus*, body.] Belonging or relating to the body; bodily; also material or not spiritual†. ∴ Syn. under BODILY.—**Corporality**, kor-po-ral′i-ti, *n.* The state of being corporal; corporation; confraternity.—**Corporally**, kor′po-ral-li, *adv.* Bodily; in or with the body (*corporally* present).—**Corporate**, kor′po-rāt, *a.* [L. *corporatus*.] United in a body, as a number of individuals who are empowered to transact business as an individual; formed into a body; united; collectively one (*Shak.*); belonging to a corporation.—**Corporately**, kor′po-rāt-li, *adv.* In a corporate capacity.—**Corporateness**, kor′po-rāt-nes, *n.* The state of a body corporate.—**Corporation**, kor-po-rā′shon, *n.* A body corporate, formed and authorized by law to act as a single person; a society having the capacity of transacting business as an individual; the body or bodily frame of a man (*colloq.*).—**Corporeal**, kor-pō′rē-al, *a.* Of or pertaining to a body; having a body; consisting of a material body; material; opposed to *spiritual* or *immaterial*. ∴ Syn. under BODILY.—**Corporealism**, kor-pō′rē-al-izm, *n.* The principles of a corporealist; materialism.—**Corporealist**, kor-pō′rē-al-ist, *n.* One who denies the existence of spiritual substances; a materialist.—**Corporeality**, kor-pō′rē-al″i-ti, *n.* The state of being corporeal.—**Corporeally**, kor-pō′rē-al-li, *adv.* In body; in a bodily form or manner.—**Corporeity**, kor-pō-rē′i-ti, *n.* The state of having a body or of being embodied; materiality†.

Corposant, kor′pō-zant, *n.* [It. *corpo santo*, holy body.] A name given to a ball of electric light often observed on dark tem pestuous nights about the rigging; St. Elmo's light.

Corps, kōr, *n.* pl. **Corps**, kōrz. [Fr., from L. *corpus*, body.] A body of troops; any division of an army.—*Corps d'armée*, a large division of an army.—**Corpse**, korps, *n.* The dead body of a human being.—**Corpse-candle**, *n.* A candle used at ceremonious watchings of a corpse before its interment; a local name for the will-o'-the-wisp.—**Corpse-gate**, *n.* A covered gateway at the entrance to church-yards, a lich-gate.

Corpulence, **Corpulency**, kor'pū-lens, kor'pū-len-si, *n.* [L. *corpulentia*, from *corpulentus*, corpulent, *corpus*, a body.] Fleshiness or stoutness of body; excessive fatness.—**Corpulent**, kor'pū-lent, *a.* Having a great bulk of body; stout; fat; obese.

Corpus, kor'pus, *n.* A collected whole; a material substance; *anat.* a name for certain small bodies of various kinds.

Corpus Christi, kor'pus kris'ti, *n.* [L., body of Christ.] *R. Cath. Ch.* the host or eucharist; an annual festival in its honour.

Corpuscle, kor'pus-l, *n.* [L. *corpusculum*, dim. of *corpus*, body.] A minute particle, molecule, or atom; a minute animal cell generally inclosing granular matter, and sometimes a spheroidal body called a nucleus.—**Corpuscular**, **Corpusculous**, kor-pus'kū-ler, kor-pus'kū-lus, *a.* Relating to corpuscles or small particles, supposed to be the constituent materials of all large bodies.—*Corpuscular theory*, a theory which supposes light to consist of minute particles emitted by luminous bodies, and travelling through space with immense rapidity till they reach the eye.

Corral, kor-räl', *n.* [Sp., from *corro*, a circle; Pg. *curral*, a cattle-pen.] A pen or inclosure for horses or cattle, and also an inclosure formed of wagons employed by emigrants as a means of defence [Amer.]; a strong stockade or inclosure for capturing wild elephants in Ceylon.—*v.t.*—*corralled*, *corralling*. To form into a corral; to form a corral or inclosure by means of.

Corrasion, cor-rā'zhon, *n.* [L. *corrasio*, scraping.] The wear of rocks by material transported over them.

Correct, ko-rekt', *a.* [L. *correctus*, from *corrigo*—*con*, and *rego*, to set right. REGENT, RIGHT.] Set right or made straight; in accordance with a certain standard; conformable to truth, rectitude, or propriety; not faulty; free from error.—*v.t.* To make correct or right; to bring into accordance with a certain standard; to remove error or defect from; to amend or emend; to punish for faults or deviations from moral rectitude; to chastise; to discipline; to counteract or obviate, as by adding some new ingredient.—**Correctable**, **Correctible**, ko-rek'ta-bl, ko-rek'ti-bl, *a.* Capable of being corrected.—**Correction**, ko-rek'shon, *n.* [L. *correctio.*] The act of correcting; the removal of faults or errors; something written to point out an error, or substituted in the place of what is wrong; punishment; discipline; chastisement; critical notice; animadversion; the counteraction of what is inconvenient or hurtful in its effects.—*House of correction*, a house where disorderly persons are confined; a bridewell.—**Correctional**, ko-rek'shon-al, *a.* Tending to correction.—**Corrective**, ko-rek'tiv, *a.* Having the power to correct; having the quality of removing or obviating what is wrong or injurious.—*n.* That which has the power of correcting; that which has the quality of altering or obviating what is wrong or injurious.—**Correctly**, ko-rekt'li, *adv.* In a correct manner; according to a standard; in conformity with a copy or original; exactly; accurately; without fault or error.—**Correctness**, ko-rekt'nes, *n.* The state of being correct; conformity to a standard or rule; exactness; accuracy.—**Corrector**, ko-rek'tėr, *n.* One who corrects; one who amends faults; one who punishes for correction; that which corrects.—**Correctory**, ko-rek'to-ri, *a.* Containing or making correction; corrective.—*n.* A corrective.

Corregidor, ko-rej'i-dōr, *n.* [Sp., a corrector, from *corregir*, to correct.] A magistrate in Spain and Portugal.

Correl, **Corri**, kor'i, *n.* The hollow side of a hill; a corrie.

Correlate, kor'ē-lāt, *n.* [L. *cor* for *con*, and *relatus*. RELATE.] One who or that which stands in a reciprocal relation to something else, as father and son.—*v.i.*—*correlated*, *correlating*. To have a reciprocal relation; to be reciprocally related, as father and son.—*v.t.* To place in reciprocal relation; to determine the relations between, as between several objects or phenomena which bear a resemblance to one another.—**Correlatable**, kor-ē-lā'ta-bl, *a.* Capable of being correlated; assignable to correlation.—**Correlation**, kor-ē-lā'shon, *n.* Reciprocal relation; corresponding similarity or parallelism of relation or law.—**Correlative**, ko-rel'a-tiv, *a.* Having a reciprocal relation, so that the existence of one in a certain state depends on the existence of another; reciprocal.—*n.* That which is correlative; that of which the existence implies the existence of something else; one of two terms either of which calls up the notion of the other, as *husband* and *wife*; *gram.* the antecedent to a pronoun.—**Correlatively**, ko-rel'a-tiv-li, *adv.* In a correlative relation.—**Correlativeness**, ko-rel'a-tiv-nes, *n.* The state of being correlative.

Correspond, kor-ē-spond', *v.i.* [*Cor* for *con*, and *respond.*] To be adapted or suitable; to have a due relation; to be adequate or proportionate; to accord; to agree; to answer; to fit: used absolutely or followed by *with* or *to*; to communicate or hold intercourse with a person by letters sent and received.—**Correspondence**, kor-ē-spon'dens, *n.* The state of corresponding or being correspondent; mutual adaptation of one thing or part to another; intercourse between persons by means of letters sent and received; the letters collectively which pass between correspondents; friendly intercourse; reciprocal exchange of offices or civilities.—**Correspondency**, kor-ē-spon'den-si, *n.* Correspondence, in sense of relation, congruity, adaptation, friendly intercourse.—**Correspondent**, kor-ē-spon'dent, *a.* Corresponding; suitable; duly related; congruous; agreeable; answerable; adapted.—*n.* One who corresponds; one with whom an intercourse is carried on by letters or messages; a person who sends regular communications to a newspaper from a distance.—**Correspondently**, kor-ē-spon'dent-li, *adv.* In a corresponding manner.—**Corresponding**, kor-ē-spon'ding, *a.* Answering; agreeing; suiting; correspondent.—**Correspondingly**, kor-ē-spon'ding-li, *adv.* In a corresponding manner.—**Corresponsive**, kor-ē-spon'siv, *a.* Answerable; adapted. (*Shak.*)

Corridor, kor'i-dōr, *n.* [It. *corridore*, from *correre*, L. *currere*, to run. CURRENT.] *Arch.* a passage in a building leading to several chambers at a distance from each other; *fort.* the covered way round the fortifications of a place.

Corrie, kor'i, *n.* [Gael.] A steep hollow in a hill.

Corrigendum, kor-i-jen'dum, *n.* pl. **Corrigenda**, kor-i-jen'da. [L.] A thing or word to be corrected or altered.

Corrigible, kor'i-ji-bl, *a.* [Fr., from L. *corrigo*, to correct. CORRECT.] Capable of being corrected, amended, or reformed; deserving punishment or correction; punishable.—**Corrigibleness**, kor'i-ji-bl-nes, *n.* **Corrigibility**, kor'i-ji-bil"i-ti, *n.*

Corroborate, ko-rob'ō-rāt, *v.t.*—*corroborated*, *corroborating*. [L. *corroboro*, *corroboratum*—*con*, and *roboro*, to strengthen, from *robur*, strength.] To strengthen or give additional strength to; to confirm; to make more certain; to add assurance to (to *corroborate* testimony, news).—**Corroborant**, ko-rob'ō-rant, *a.* Strengthening the body; having the power or quality of giving strength.—*n.* A medicine that strengthens the body when weak; a tonic.—**Corroboration**, ko-rob'ō-rā"shon, *n.* The act of corroborating; confirmation; that which corroborates.—**Corroborative**, ko-rob'ō-rā-tiv, *a.* Having the power of corroborating or confirming.—*n.* A medicine that strengthens; corroborant.—**Corroboratory**, ko-rob'ō-ra-to-ri, *a.* Corroborative.

Corrode, ko-rōd', *v.t.*—*corroded*, *corroding*. [L. *corrodo*—*cor* for *con*, and *rodo*, to gnaw, whence also *rodent*, *erode*.] To eat away by degrees; to wear away or diminish by gradually separating small particles (nitric acid *corrodes* copper); *fig.* to gnaw or prey upon; to consume by slow degrees; to envenom or embitter; to poison, blight, canker.—**Corrodent**,† ko-rō'dent, *a.* Having the power of corroding.—*n.* Any substance or medicine that corrodes.—**Corrodibility**, ko-rō'di-bil"i-ti, *n.* The quality of being corrodible.—**Corrodible**, ko-rō'di-bl, *a.* That may be corroded.—**Corrosibility**, ko-rō'si-bil"i-ti, *n.* Corrodibility.—**Corrosible**, ko-rō'si-bl, *a.* Liable to corrosion; corrodible.—**Corrosibleness**, ko-rō'si-bl-nes, *n.*—**Corrosion**, ko-rō'zhon, *n.* The action of corroding, eating, or wearing away by slow degrees, as by the action of acids on metals; *fig.* the act of cankering, fretting, vexing, envenoming, or blighting.—**Corrosive**, ko-rō'siv, *a.* Having the power of corroding or eating into a substance; having the quality of fretting, envenoming, blighting.—*Corrosive sublimate*, a compound of chlorine and mercury, forming a white crystalline solid, an acrid poison of great virulence, and a powerful antiseptic.—*n.* That which has the quality of eating or wearing gradually; anything which irritates, preys upon one, or frets.—**Corrosively**, ko-rō'siv-li, *adv.* In a corrosive manner.—**Corrosiveness**, ko-rō'siv-nes, *n.* The quality of being corrosive.

Corrugate, kor'ụ-gāt, *v.t.*—*corrugated*, *corrugating*. [L. *corrugo*, *corrugatum*—*cor* for *con*, and *rugo*, to wrinkle.] To wrinkle; to draw or contract into folds.—*a.* Wrinkled; showing wrinkles or furrows.—**Corrugated**, kor'ụ-gā-ted, *p.* and *a.* Wrinkled; furrowed or ridged.—*Corrugated iron*, common sheet-iron or 'galvanized' iron, bent into a series of regular grooves and ridges by being passed between powerful rollers. Iron thus treated will resist a much greater strain than flat iron, each groove representing a half tube; it is used for roofing, &c.—**Corrugant**, kor'ụ-gant, *a.* Having the power of contracting into wrinkles.—**Corrugation**, kor-ụ-gā'shon, *n.* A wrinkling; contraction into wrinkles.—**Corrugator**, kor'ụ-gā-tėr, *n.* *Anat.* the small muscle situated on each side of the forehead, which knits the brows.

Corrupt, ko-rupt', *v.t.* [L. *corrumpo*, *corruptum*—*con*, and *rumpo*, *ruptum*, to break; whence also *rupture*, *abrupt*, *disrupt*, &c.] To change from a sound to a putrid or putrescent state; to cause to rot; *fig.* to deprave; to pervert; to impair; to debase; to defile, taint, pollute, or infect; to bribe; to debase or render impure by alterations or innovations (language); to falsify (a text).—*v.i.* To become putrid; to putrefy; to rot; to become vitiated; to lose purity.—*a.* Changed from a sound to a putrid state; changed from the state of being correct, pure, or true to a worse state; vitiated; perverted; debased; impure; ready to be influenced by a bribe; infected with errors or mistakes (a *corrupt* text).—**Corrupter**, ko-rup'tėr, *n.* One who or that which corrupts.—**Corruptibility**, ko-rup'ti-bil"i-ti, *n.* The possibility of being corrupted.—**Corruptible**, ko-rup'ti-bl, *a.* Capable of being made corrupt, putrid, or rotten; subject to decay and destruction, debasement, depravation, &c.—**Corruptibleness**, ko-rup'ti-bl-nes, *n.*—**Corruptibly**, ko-rup'ti-bli, *adv.* In such a manner as to be corrupted or vitiated.—**Corruption**, ko-rup'shon, *n.* [L. *corruptio.*] The act of corrupting, or state of being corrupt, putrid, or rotten; putrid matter; pus; depravity; wickedness; loss of purity or integrity; debasement; impurity; depravation; pollution; defilement; vitiating influence; more specifically, bribery; *law*, an immediate consequence of attainder by which a person was formerly disabled from holding, inheriting, or transmitting lands.—**Corruptive**, ko-rup'tiv, *a.* Having the power of corrupting, tainting, or vitiating.—**Corruptless**, ko-rupt'les, *a.* Not susceptible of corruption or decay.—**Corruptly**, ko-rupt'li, *adv.* In a corrupt manner; with corruption; impurely; by bribery.—**Corruptness**, ko-rupt'nes, *n.* Corrupt quality or state; putrid state.

Corsage, kor'sāj, *n.* [Fr.] A small bouquet for a woman; the waist of a woman's dress.

Corsair, kor'sār, *n.* [Fr. *corsaire*, It. *corsare*, from *corsa*, a course, a cruise, from L. *cursus*, a course. COURSE.] A pirate; a sea robber; a rover; a piratical vessel.

Corselet, kors'let, *n.* [Fr., a dim. of O.Fr. *cors*, L. *corpus*, the body.] A small cuirass, or armor to cover and protect the body; a type of lightly boned corset for women; that part of a winged insect to which the wings and legs are attached; the thorax.

Corset, kor'set, *n.* [Dim. of O.Fr. *cors*.] A tight, boned undergarment, reaching from the bust to below the hips, worn by women, occasionally by men, to support and mold the body.

Corsned, kor'sned, *n.* [A.Sax. *corsnaed*—*cor*, from root of *choose*, and A.Sax. *snaed*, a mouthful, a bit.] Anciently, a piece of bread consecrated by exorcism and to be swallowed by a suspected person as a trial of his innocence.

Cortège, kor-tezh', *n.* [Fr., from It. *corteggio*, from *corte*, court.] A train of attendants to a great personage on a ceremonial occasion.

Cortes, kor'täz, *n. pl.* [Sp., pl. of *corte*, court.] The present legislative assembly of Portugal and formerly, the single legislative chamber of Republican Spain.

Cortex, kor'teks, *n.* [L. *cortex*, *corticis*, bark; whence *cork*.] Bark, as of a tree; hence, an outer covering; *anat.* a membrane forming a covering or envelope for any part of the body. *Of brain*, external layer of cerebral hemispheres and cerebellum: that of cerebral hemispheres divided into *motor areas*, controlling muscles, and *sensory areas*, concerned with sensations.—**Cortical**, kor'ti-kal, *a.* Belonging to, consisting of, or resembling bark or rind; external; belonging to the external covering.—**Corticate**, **Corticated**, kor'ti-kāt, kor'ti-kā-ted, *a.* [L. *corticatus*.] Resembling the bark or rind of a tree.—**Corticiferous**, kor-ti-sif'ėr-us, *a.* Producing bark, or that which resembles it.—**Corticose**, **Corticous**, kor'ti-kōz, kor'ti-kus, *a.* Barky; full of bark.

Corundum, ko-run'dum, *n.* [Hind. *kurand*.] A mineral, next in hardness to the diamond, and consisting of nearly pure anhydrous alumina; the amethyst, ruby, sapphire, topaz, and emery are considered as varieties.

Coruscate, kor'us-kāt, *v.i.* — *coruscated*, *coruscating*. [L. *corusco*, *coruscatum*, to flash.] To flash; to lighten; to gleam; to glitter.—**Coruscation**, kor-us-kā'shon, *n.* [L. *coruscatio*.] A sudden burst of light in the clouds or atmosphere; a flash; glitter; a blaze.

Corve, korv, *n.* Same as *Corb*.

Corvee, kor'vā, *n.* [Fr.] Forced levy for labour by feudal lord on vassals.

Corvette, kor-vet', *n.* [Fr. *corvette*, from L. *corbita*, a ship of burden, from *corbis*, a basket.] A flush-decked vessel, ship-rigged, but without a quarter-deck, and having only one tier of guns.

Corvine, kor'vīn, *a.* [L. *corvus*, a crow.] Pertaining to the crow, or the crow family of birds.

Corybant, kor'i-bant, *n.* pl. **Corybants** or **Corybantes**, kor-i-ban'tēz. [L. *corybas*, *corybantis*, Gr. *korybas*.] A priest of Cybele who celebrated the mysteries with mad dances to the sound of drum and cymbal.—**Corybantic**, kor-i-ban'tik, *a.* Madly agitated like the Corybantes.

Corymb, kō'rimb, *n.* [L. *corymbus*, Gr. *korymbos*, a cluster of fruit or flowers.] *Bot.* an inflorescence in which the flowers or blossoms are so arranged as to form a mass of flowers with a convex or level top, as in the hawthorn, candytuft, &c.—**Corymbiferous**, kō-rim-bif'ėr-us, *a.* *Bot.* producing corymbs; bearing fruit in clusters.—**Corymbose**, kō-rim'bōz, *a.* *Bot.* relating to or like a corymb.—**Corymbous**, kō-rim'bus, *a.* Corymbose.

Corypheus, **Coryphæus**, kor-i-fē'us, *n.* [L. *coryphæus*, Gr. *koryphaios*, from *koryphē*, the head.] The chief of a chorus; the chief of a company.—**Coryphee**, ko-rē-fā, *n.* [Fr.] A ballet-dancer.

Coryza, ko-rī'za, *n.* [Gr.] *Med.* a cold in the head.

Co-secant, kō-sē'kant, *n.* [From *complement* and *secant*.] *Geom.* the secant of an arc or angle which is the complement of another arc or angle, that is, when added to it makes up 90°.

Cosen, **Cosenage**. COZEN, COZENAGE.

Cosey, **Cosy**, kō'zi, *a.* [Akin to Norse *koselig*, cosy, *kose sig*, to enjoy one's ease.] Well sheltered; snug; comfortable; social. Written also *Cosie*, *Cozie*, *Cozy*. (Colloq.)—*n.* A kind of padded covering or cap put over a teapot to keep in the heat after the tea has been infused.—**Cosily**, kō'zi-li, *adv.* In a cosey, snug, or comfortable manner.

Cosher, kosh'ėr, *v.i.* [Ir. *cosair*, a feast.] To levy exactions in the shape of feasts and lodgings, as formerly Irish landlords with their trains did on their tenants.—*v.t.* To treat with dainties or delicacies; to fondle; to pet. (Colloq.)—**Cosherer**, kosh'ėr-ėr, *n.* One who coshers.

Co-signatory, kō-sig'na-to-ri, *n.* One who signs a treaty or other agreement along with another or others. Also used as an adj.

Co-sine, kō'sīn, *n.* [*Complement* and *sine*.] *Geom.* the sine of an arc or angle which is the complement of another, that is, when added to it makes 90°.

Cosmetic, koz-met'ik, *a.* [Gr. *kosmētikos*, from *kosmos*, order, beauty.] Beautifying; improving beauty, particularly the beauty of the complexion.—*n.* Any preparation that renders the skin soft, pure, and white, or helps to beautify and improve the complexion.

Cosmic, **Cosmical**, koz'mik, koz'mi-kal, *a.* [Gr. *kosmikos*, from *kosmos*, the universe.] Relating to the universe and to the laws by which its order is maintained; hence, harmonious as the universe; orderly.—**Cosmically**, koz'mi-kal-li, *adv.* In a cosmic manner; with the sun at rising or setting; said of a star.—**Cosmic ray**, *n.* An electromagnetic ray of extremely high frequency and energy content that originates in outer space and bombards the earth, penetrating barriers impervious to all other radiation. Molecules of the earth's atmosphere are ionized upon impact with cosmic rays.

Cosmogony, koz-mog'o-ni, *n.* [Gr. *kosmogonia*—*kosmos*, world, and root *gen*, to bring forth.] The origin or creation of the world or universe; the doctrine of the origin or formation of the universe.

Cosmography, koz-mog'ra-fi, *n.* [Gr. *kosmographia*—*kosmos*, the world, and *graphō*, to describe.] A description of the world or universe; the science which treats of the construction of the universe.—**Cosmographer**, koz-mog'ra-fėr, *n.* One who describes the world or universe; one versed in cosmography.—**Cosmographic**, **Cosmographical**, koz-mo-graf'ik, koz-mo-graf'ik-al, *a.* Relating to cosmography.—**Cosmographically**, koz-mo-graf'ik-al-li, *adv.* In a manner relating to cosmography.

Cosmology, koz-mol'o-ji, *n.* [Gr. *kosmologia*—*kosmos*, the universe, and *logos*, discourse.] The science of the world or universe; or a theory relating to the structure of the universe and the laws which underlie it; cosmogony.—**Cosmological**, koz-mo-loj'ik-al, *a.* Pertaining to cosmology.—**Cosmologist**, koz-mol'o-jist, *n.* One who describes the universe; one versed in cosmology.

Cosmopolitan, **Cosmopolite**, koz-mo-pol'i-tan, koz-mop'o-līt, *n.* [Gr. *kosmos*, world, and *politēs*, a citizen.] A person who is nowhere a stranger, or who is at home in every place; a citizen of the world.—*a.* Free from local, provincial, or national prejudices or attachments; at home all over the world; common to all the world.—**Cosmopolitanism**, **Cosmopolitism**, koz-mo-pol'i-tan-izm, kos-mop'o-lit-izm, *n.* The state of being a cosmopolitan; disregard of local or national prejudices, attachments, or peculiarities.

Cosmorama, koz-mō-rä'ma, *n.* [Gr. *kosmos*, the world, *horama*, a view.] A view or series of views of the world; an exhibition, through a lens or lenses, of drawings or paintings of cities, buildings, landscapes, &c., with suitable arrangements for illumination.—**Cosmoramic**, koz-mo-ram'ik, *a.* Relating to a cosmorama.

Cosmos, koz'mos, *n.* [Gr. *kosmos*, order, ornament, and hence the universe as an orderly and beautiful system.] The universe as an embodiment of order and harmony; the system of order and harmony combined in the universe.—**Cosmosphere**, koz'mo-sfēr, *n.* An apparatus for showing the position of the earth at any given time, with respect to the fixed stars.

Cossack, kos'ak, *n.* [Rus. *kosak*, Turk. *kazâk*, a robber.] One of a warlike people, very expert on horseback, inhabiting the steppes in the south of Russia, about the Don, &c.

Cosset,‡ kos'et, *n.* [Comp. old *coss*, Icel *koss*, a *kiss*.] A pet; a pet-lamb; a lamb brought up by hand.

Cost, kost, *n.* [O.Fr. *cost*, from *coster*, *couster* (Mod.Fr. *coûter*), to cost, from L *constare*, to cost—*con*, and *stare*, to stand STATE.] The price, value, or equivalent of a thing purchased; amount in value expended or to be expended; charge; expense; *law.* the sum to be paid by the party losing in favour of the party prevailing, &c.; outlay, expense, or loss of any kind, as of time, labour, trouble, or the like; detriment; pain; suffering (he learned that to his *cost*).—*v.t* —pret. & pp. *cost*. To require to be given or expended in order to purchase; to be bought for; to require to be undergone, borne, or suffered: often with two objects (to *cost* a person money or labour).—**Costless**, kost'les, *a.* Without cost; costing nothing.—**Costly**, kost'li, *a.* Of a high price; costing much; expensive; dear.—**Costliness**, kost'li-nes, *n.* The state or quality of being costly, high in price, or expensive.

Costal, kos'tal, *a.* [L. *costa*, a rib.] Pertaining to the side of the body or the ribs.—**Costated**, **Costate**, kos'tā-ted, kos'tāt, *a.* Ribbed; marked with elevated lines.

Costard, kos'tärd, *n.* [Lit. a *ribbed* apple, O.Fr. *coste*, L. *costa*, a rib.] An apple; hence, humorously for the head. (*Shak.*)—**Costard-monger**, *n.* A costermonger.

Costean, kos'tē-an, *v.i.* [Corn. *cothas*, dropped, and *stean*, tin.] In *mining*, to seek for a lode by sinking small pits.

Coster, **Costermonger**, kos'tėr, kos'tėr-mung-gėr, *n.* [Originally *costard-monger*, a seller of apples.] A hawker who sells fruit or vegetables.

Costive, kos'tiv, *a.* [Contr. from It. *costipativo*, from L. *constipo*, to cram, to stuff. CONSTIPATE.] Suffering from a morbid retention of fecal matter in the bowels, in a hard and dry state; having the bowels bound; constipated.—**Costively**, kos'tiv-li, *adv.* With costiveness.—**Costiveness**, kos'tiv-nes, *n.* The state of being costive; constipation.

Costmary, kost'ma-ri, *n.* [L. *costus*, Gr. *kostos*, an aromatic plant, and *Mary* (the Virgin).] A perennial composite plant, a native of the south of Europe, cultivated for the agreeable fragrance of the leaves.

Costrel, kos'trel, *n.* [W., from *kostr*, what is consumed.] A small vessel, generally with ears so as to be suspended, used by labourers in harvest time; a vessel for holding wine.

Costume, kos'tūm, *n.* [Fr. *costume*, custom. CUSTOM.] An established mode of dress; the style of dress peculiar to a people or nation, to a particular period, or a particular class of people; a dress of a particular style.—**Costumed**, kos'tūmd, *a.* Wearing a costume; dressed.—**Costumier, Costumer**, kos-tū'mi-ėr, kos'tūm-ėr, *n.* One who prepares costumes, as for theatres, fancy-balls, &c.; one who deals in costumes.

Cosy, kō'zi, *a.* Same as *Cosey*.

Cot, kot, *n.* [A.Sax. *cot*, *cott*, a cot, chamber; Icel. and D. *kot*, a cot, G. *kot*, *kote*, a hut; *cote* is the same word. From this comes *cottage*.] A small house; a hut or cottage; a small bed or crib for a child to sleep in; *naut.* a sort of bed-frame suspended from the beams.

Co-tangent, kō-tan'jent, *n.* [*Complement* and *tangent*.] The tangent of an arc or angle which is the complement of another, that is, when added to it makes 90°.

Cote, kōt, *n.* [COT.] A shelter or habitation for animals, as a dove-*cote*; a sheep-fold (*Mil.*)‡; a cottage or hut.

Cotemporaneous, Cotemporary, kō-tem'po-rā"nē-us, kō-tem'po-ra-ri. CONTEMPORANEOUS, CONTEMPORARY.

Co-tenant, kō-ten'ant, *n.* A tenant in common.

Coterie, kō'te-rē, *n.* [Fr., from L.L. *coteria*, an association of villagers, *cota*, a cottage. COT.] A set or circle of friends who are in the habit of meeting for social or literary intercourse or other purposes; a clique.

Coterminous, kō-tėr'mi-nus, *a.* CONTERMINOUS.

Cothurnus, Cothurn, kō-thėr'nus, kō'thėrn, *n.* [L. *cothurnus*.] A buskin; a kind of high laced shoe, such as was anciently worn by tragic actors; hence, *fig.* tragedy.—**Cothurnate**, kō-thėr'nāt, *a.* Buskined; tragical; solemn and elevated.

Cotidal, kō-tī'dal, *a.* Marking an equality of tides.

Cotillion, Cotillon, ko-til'yon, *n.* [Fr. *cotillon*.] A kind of brisk dance; a tune which regulates the dance.

Cotquean,‡ kot'kwēn, *n.* A man who busies himself with the affairs which properly belong to women. (*Shak.*)

Co-trustee, kō-trus-tē', *n.* A joint trustee.

Cotswold, kots'wōld, *n.* A sheep of a breed belonging to the Cotswold Hills in Gloucestershire.

Cottage, kot'āj, *n.* [From *cot*.] A cot or small dwelling-house; a small country residence or detached suburban house, adapted to a moderate scale of living.—**Cottaged**, kot'ājd, *a.* Set or covered with cottages.—**Cottager**, kot'āj-ėr, *n.* One who lives in a hut or cottage.—**Cottage-piano**, *n.* A small upright piano.—**Cotter, Cottier**, kot'ėr, kot'i-ėr, *n.* A cottager; one who inhabits a cot or cottage, dependent upon a farm, having sometimes a piece of land. Written also *Cottar*.—**Cottierism**, kot'i-ėr-izm, *n.* The system of holding a cottage with a small portion of land directly from a proprietor, the tenancy being annual. Called also *Cottier Tenure*.

Cotton, kot'n, *n.* [Fr. *coton*, from Ar. *qoton*.] A soft downy substance resembling fine wool, growing in the pods or seed-vessels of certain plants, being the material of a large proportion of cloth for apparel and furniture; cloth made of cotton.—*a.* Pertaining to cotton; made of cotton.—*v.i.* To fraternize; to agree or get on (with). (*Colloq.*)—**Cottony**, kot'n-i, *a.* Downy or soft like cotton; pertaining to or resembling cotton.—**Cotton-gin**, *n.* A machine to separate the seeds from raw cotton.—**Cotton-grass**, *n.* A name of plants of the sedge family with white cottony spikes.—**Cotton-plant**, *n.* A malvaceous tropical perennial shrub of various species, indigenous to both the Old and the New World, with a three- or five-celled capsule, which contains numerous black seeds covered with the beautiful filamentous cotton.—**Cotton-press**, *n.* A machine for pressing cotton into bales.—**Cotton-wood**, *n.* A tree of the poplar genus, a native of North America.—**Cotton-wool**, *n.* A name sometimes given to raw cotton.

Cotyle, Cotyla, kot'i-lē, kot'i-la, *n.* [Gr. *kotylē*, a hollow.] The cavity of a bone which receives the end of another in articulation; one of the suctorial cups or disks of the arms of a cuttle-fish.

Cotyledon, kot-i-lē'don, *n.* [Gr. *kotylēdōn*, from *kotylē*, a hollow.] *Bot.* the seed-leaf; the first leaf or leaves of the embryo plant, forming, together with the radicle and plumule, the embryo, which exists in every seed capable of germination; *anat.* a tuft of vessels adhering to the chorion of some animals.—**Cotyledonal**, kot-i-lē'do-nal, *a.* Belonging to a cotyledon; resembling a cotyledon.—**Cotyledonary**, kot-i-lē'do-na-ri, *a.* *Anat.* having the tuft called cotyledon (*cotyledonary* placenta).—**Cotyledonous**, kot-i-lē'do-nus, *a.* Pertaining to cotyledons; having cotyledons.—**Cotyliform**, ko-til'i-form, *a.* Having the form of a cotyle; cup-shaped.—**Cotyloid**, kot'i-loid, *a.* Cup-shaped; cotyliform.

Couch, kouch, *v.t.* [Fr. *coucher*, O.Fr. *colcher*, Pr. *colcar*, It. *colcare*, from *collocare*, to lay, to place—*col* for *con*, and *locare*, to place.] To lie down, as on a bed or place of repose; to recline; to lie or crouch with body close to the ground, as a beast; to stoop; to bend the body or back (O.T.); to lie or be outspread (O.T.).—*v.t.* To lay down; to spread on a bed or floor (to *couch* malt); to express in obscure terms that imply what is to be understood: with *under*; to fix a spear in the rest in the posture of attack; *surg.* to cure of cataract in the eye by depressing the crystalline lens.—*n.* A bed; a seat for repose or on which one may lie down undressed; any place for repose, as the lair of a wild beast, &c.; a heap of steeped barley spread out on a floor to allow germination to take place, and so convert the grain into malt.—**Couchant**, kouch'ant, *a.* Lying down; squatting. (*Tenn.*)—**Coucher**, kouch'ėr, *n.* One who couches.

Couch-grass, kouch'gras, *n.* [A corruption of *quitch* or *quick grass*.] A species of grass which infests arable land, spreading over a field with great rapidity, being propagated both by seed and by its creeping root-stock.

Cougar, kö'gär, *n.* [Native name modified.] A quadruped of the cat kind, 7 or 8 feet in length, one of the most destructive of all the animals of America, particularly in the warmer parts. Called also *Puma* and *Red Tiger*.

Cough, kof, *n.* [Imitative of the sound; like D. *kuch*, a cough; G, *keichen*, *keuchen*, to pant, cough.] A deep inspiration of air followed by a spasmodic and sonorous expiration, excited by the sensation of the presence of some irritating cause in the air-passages.—*v.i.* To give a cough; to expel the air from the lungs suddenly with noise.—*v.t.* To expel from the lungs by a violent effort with noise; to expectorate: with *up* (to *cough up* phlegm).—*To cough down*, to put down an unpopular or too lengthy speaker by simulated coughs.—**Cougher**, kof'ėr, *n.* One that coughs.

Could, kud, *v.*, pret. of *can*. [O.E. *coude*, A.Sax. *cúthe*, pret. of *cunnan*, to be able. See CAN. *L* has been improperly introduced through the influence of *would* and *should*.] Was able, capable, or susceptible.

Coulee, kö-lā, *n.* [Fr., from *couler*, to flow.] *Geol.* a stream of lava, whether flowing or consolidated.

Coulisse, kö-lēs, *n.* [Fr.] One of the side scenes of the stage in a theatre, or the space included between the side scenes.

Coulomb, kö-lom', *n.* [From *Coulomb*, the French physicist.] In *current elect.*, the practical unit of quantity, that transferred by a current of one ampere in one sec., equal to 1/10 of the absolute electromagnetic unit of quantity.

Coulter, kōl'tėr, *n.* [L. *culter*, a knife, a coulter.] An iron blade or knife inserted into the beam of a plough for the purpose of cutting the ground and facilitating the separation of the furrow-slice by the ploughshare.

Coumarine, kö'ma-rēn, *n.* [From *coumaron*, a tree of Guiana.] A vegetable principle obtained from the Tonka-bean, used in medicine and to give flavour to the Swiss cheese called schabzieger.

Council, koun'sil, *n.* [Fr. *concile*, from L. *concilium*—*con*, together, and root *cal*, to summon; akin *conciliate*, *reconcile*. This word is often improperly confounded with *counsel*.] An assembly of men summoned or convened for consultation, deliberation, and advice (a common *council*, an ecumenical *council*, the privy-*council*); act of deliberation; consultation, as of a council.—*Council of war*, an assembly of officers of high rank called to consult with the commander-in-chief of an army or admiral of a fleet on matters of supreme importance.—**Councillor**, koun'sil-ėr, *n.* The member of a council; specifically, a member of a common council or of the privy-council.—**Council-board**, *n.* The board or table round which a council holds consultation; the council itself in deliberation or session.—**Council-man**, *n.* A member of a city common council.

Counsel, koun'sel, *n.* [Fr. *conseil*, from L. *consilium*, advice, from *consulo*, to consult, deliberate. Akin *consult*.] Opinion or advice, given upon request or otherwise, for directing the judgment or conduct of another; consultation; interchange of opinions; deliberation; the secrets intrusted in consultation; secret opinions or purposes (to keep one's *counsel*); intent or purpose; one who gives counsel in matters of law; any counsellor or advocate engaged in a cause in court, or the counsellors, barristers, or sergeants united in the management of a case collectively.—*King's* (*queen's*) *counsel*, barristers appointed counsel to the crown on the nomination of the lord-chancellor, and taking precedence over ordinary barristers.—*v.t.*—*counselled*, *counselling*. To give advice or deliberate opinion to, for the government of conduct; to advise, exhort, warn, admonish, or instruct; to recommend or give an opinion in favour of.—**Counsellor**, koun'sel-ėr, *n.* Any person who gives counsel or advice; an adviser; one whose profession is to give advice in law, and manage causes for clients; a barrister.—**Counsellorship**, koun'sel-ėr-ship, the office of a counsellor.

Count, kount, *v.t.* [Fr. *conter*, *compter*, from L. *computare*, to compute. COMPUTE.] To tell or name one by one, or by small numbers, in order to ascertain the whole number of units in a collection; to reckon; to number; to compute; to esteem, account, think, judge, or consider.—*To count out*, to bring (a meeting) to a close by numbering the members and finding a quorum not present, as in the House of Commons, where this is done by the speaker.—*v.i.* To be added or reckoned in with others; to reckon; to rely: in this sense with *on* or *upon* (to *count on* assistance).—*n.* The act of numbering; reckoning; number; *law*, a particular charge in an indictment, or narration in pleading, setting forth the cause of complaint.—**Countable**, koun'ta-bl, *a.* Capable of being counted or numbered.—**Counter**, koun'tėr, *n.* One who counts, numbers, or reckons; that which is used to keep an account or reckoning, as in games, such as a small plate of metal, ivory, wood, &c.; a counterfeit or imitation of a coin; a registering apparatus or tell-tale; a table or board on which money is counted; a table in a shop over which sales are made, and on which goods are exposed for sale.—**Countless**, kount'les, *a.* Not capable of being counted; innumerable.—**Counting-house**, *n.* A house or room appropriated by mercantile men to the business of keeping their books, accounts, &c.

Count, kount, *n.* [Fr. *comte*, from L. *comes*,

comitis, a companion, a companion of the emperor or a king—*com* for *con*, with, and stem of *eo*, *itum*, to go, seen also in *ambition*, *exit*, *transit*, *perish*, &c.] A title of foreign nobility, equivalent to the English *earl*, and whose domain is a *county*.—**Countess**, koun'tes, *n.* The wife of an earl or count, or a lady possessed of the same dignity in her own right.

Countenance, koun'te-nans, *n.* [Fr. *contenance*, demeanour, way of acting or holding one's self, from *contenir*, to contain. CONTAIN.] The whole form of the face; the features considered as a whole; the visage; the face; appearance or expression of the face; favour expressed towards a person; good-will; support.—*In countenance*, in favour or estimation; free from shame or dismay.—*Out of countenance*, confounded; abashed; not bold or assured.—*v.t.*—*countenanced*, *countenancing*. To favour; to encourage; to aid; to support; to abet.—**Countenancer**, koun'te-nan-sėr, *n.* One who countenances, favours, or supports.

Counter, koun'tėr, *adv.* [Fr. *contre*, from L. *contra*—*con*, and *tra*, denoting direction, as in *intra*, *extra*, *ultra*.] In an opposite direction; in opposition; contrariwise; in the wrong way (to run *counter* to wishes).—*a.* Adverse; opposite; opposing; antagonistic.—*n.* *Music*, formerly an under part serving for contrast to a principal part, now equivalent to *counter-tenor*; that part of a horse which lies between the shoulders and under the neck.

Counteract, koun-tėr-akt', *v.t.* To act in opposition to; to hinder, defeat, or frustrate by contrary agency; to oppose, withstand, contravene, or resist.—**Counteraction**, koun'tėr-ak-shon, *n.* Action in opposition; hindrance; resistance.—**Counteractive**, koun'tėr-ak-tiv, *a.* Tending to counteract.—*n.* One who or that which counteracts.—**Counter-agent**, *n.* Anything which counteracts or acts in opposition; an opposing agent.

Counter-approach, koun'tėr-ap-prōch, *n.* *Fort.* works thrown up by the besieged to hinder the approach of the besiegers.

Counter-attraction, koun'tėr-at-trak"-shon, *n.* Opposite attraction.—**Counter-attractive**, koun'tėr-at-trak"tiv, *a.* Attracting in an opposite way.

Counterbalance, koun-tėr-bal'ans, *v.t.* To serve as a balance to; to weigh against with an equal weight; to act against with equal power or effect.—*n.* Equal weight, power, or agency acting in opposition to anything; counterpoise.

Counterchange, koun'tėr-chānj, *n.* Exchange; reciprocation. (*Shak.*)—*v.t.* To give and receive; to cause to make alternate changes; to alternate. (*Tenn.*)

Countercharge, koun'tėr-chärj, *n.* An opposite charge.

Countercharm, koun'tėr-chärm, *n.* That which has the power of dissolving or opposing the effect of a charm.—*v.t.* To destroy the effect of a charm.

Countercheck, koun'tėr-chek, *v.t.* To oppose or stop by some obstacle; to check.—*n.* Check; stop; rebuke; a censure to check a reprover.

Countercurrent, koun'tėr-kur-ent, *n.* A current in an opposite direction.

Counterdraw, koun-tėr-dra', *v.t.* To copy, as a design or painting, by means of a fine linen cloth, an oiled paper, or other transparent substance, through which the strokes appear and are traced with a pencil.

Counter-evidence, koun'tėr-ev-i-dens, *n.* Evidence or testimony which opposes other evidence.

Counterfeit, koun'tėr-fit, *a.* [Fr. *contrefait*, made to correspond—*contre*, against, and *faire*, to make.] Made in imitation of something else, with a view to pass the false copy for genuine or original; forged; not genuine; base; assuming the appearance of something; false; spurious; hypocritical.—*n.* One who pretends to be what he is not; an impostor; a cheat; that which is made in imitation of something with a view to defraud by passing the false for the true.—*v.t.* To copy or imitate with a view to pass off as original or genuine; to make a likeness or resemblance of with a view to defraud; to forge; to imitate or copy generally; to sham or pretend.—*v.i.* To feign; to dissemble; to carry on a fiction or deception.—**Counterfeiter**, koun'tėr-fit-ėr, *n.* One who counterfeits; a forger; one who assumes a false appearance, or who makes false pretences.

Counterfoil, koun'tėr-foil, *n.* [*Counter*, and *foil*, from L. *folium*, a leaf.] A portion of a document, such as a bank cheque or draft, which is retained by the person giving the other part, and on which is noted the main particulars contained in the principal document.

Counterforce, koun'tėr-fōrs, *n.* An opposing or counteracting force.

Counter-irritant, koun'tėr-ir-i-tant, *n.* *Med.* an irritant substance employed to relieve another irritation or inflammation, as mustard, croton-oil, Spanish-flies.—**Counter-irritation**, koun'tėr-ir-i-tā"shon, *n.* *Med.* the production of an artificial irritation.

Countermand, koun-tėr-mand', *v.t.* [Fr. *contremander*—*contre*, and *mander*, L. *mando*, to command.] To revoke, as a former command; to order or direct in opposition to an order before given, thereby annulling it.—*n.* A contrary order; revocation of a former order or command by a subsequent order.

Countermarch, koun-tėr-märch', *v.i.* To march back.—*n.* A marching back; a returning; a change of measures.

Countermark, koun'tėr-märk, *n.* An additional mark made for greater security or more sure identification; the mark of the Goldsmiths' Company, to show the metal to be standard; a mark on a coin already stamped indicating a change of value, or that it had been taken from an enemy; an artificial cavity made in the teeth of horses to disguise their age.—*v.t.* To add a countermark to.

Countermine, koun'tėr-mīn, *n.* *Milit.* a mine sunk in search of the enemy's mine or till it meets it, to defeat its effect; *fig.* a stratagem or project to frustrate any contrivance; an opposing scheme or plot.—*v.t.* To mine so as to discover or destroy an enemy's mine; *fig.* to frustrate by secret and opposite measures.—*v.i.* To make a countermine; to counterplot.

Countermotion, koun'tėr-mō-shon, *n.* An opposite motion; a motion counteracting another.—**Countermove**, **Countermovement**, koun'tėr-mȯv, koun'tėr-mȯv-ment, *n.* A movement in opposition to another.

Counterpane, koun'tėr-pān, *n.* [From older *counterpoint*, O.Fr. *contrepoinct*, corruptly derived from L.L. *culcita puncta*, lit. stitched quilt. QUILT, POINT.] A bed-cover; a coverlet for a bed; a quilt.

Counterpart, koun'tėr-pärt, *n.* A part that answers to or resembles another, as the several parts or copies of an indenture corresponding to the original; a thing or person exactly resembling another; a copy; a duplicate; the thing that supplements another thing or completes it; a complement.

Counterplot, koun'tėr-plot, *v.t.* To oppose or frustrate by another plot or stratagem.—*n.* A plot or artifice set afoot in order to oppose another.

Counterpoint, koun'tėr-point, *n.* The art of writing music in several distinct parts or themes proceeding simultaneously, as distinguished from harmony, which depends more for its effects on the composition and progression of whole chords than on the melody of each separate part; so called because the points which formerly represented musical notes were written under or against each other on the lines; often used, but improperly, as equivalent to *harmony*.

Counterpoise, koun'tėr-poiz, *v.t.* To weigh against with equal weight; to equal in weight; to counterbalance; to act against with equal power or effect; to balance.—*n.* A weight equal to and acting in opposition to another weight; equal power or force acting in opposition; state of being in equilibrium by being balanced by another weight or force.

Counterpoison, koun'tėr-poi-zn, *n.* One poison that destroys the effect of another; an antidote.

Counterpressure, koun'tėr-pre-shūr, *n.* Opposing pressure; a force or pressure that acts in a contrary direction.

Counterproject, koun'tėr-proj-ekt, *n.* A project brought forward in opposition to another.

Counterproof, koun'tėr-prȯf, *n.* An impression yielded by a newly-printed proof of an engraved plate, by passing the proof again through the press with a fresh sheet of paper, on which the ink is thrown off.

Counter-revolution, koun'tėr-rev-ō-lū-shon, *n.* A revolution opposed to a former one, and restoring a former state of things.

Counterscarp, koun'tėr-skärp, *n.* *Fort.* the slope of the ditch nearest the enemy and opposite the scarp; the face of the ditch sloping down from the covered-way.

Countersign, koun'tėr-sīn, *v.t.* To sign (a document) formally or officially in proof of its genuineness; to attest or witness by signature.—*n.* A private signal, word, or phrase given to a guard with orders to let no man pass unless he first give that sign; a watchword; also, the signature of a subordinate to a writing signed by his superior, to attest its authenticity.—**Countersignature**, koun'tėr-sig-na-tūr, *n.* The name of a secretary or other subordinate officer countersigned to a writing.—**Countersignal**, koun'tėr-sig-nal, *n.* A signal to answer or correspond to another.

Countersink, koun'tėr-singk, *v.t.* To form a cavity in timber or other materials so as to receive the head of a bolt, screw, &c., and make it flush with the surface; to sink below or even with a surface, as the head of a screw, bolt, &c., by making a depression for it in the material.—*n.* A drill or brace-bit for countersinking; the cavity made by countersinking.

Counter-tenor, koun'tėr-ten-ėr, *n.* *Mus.* the highest male adult voice, having about the same compass as the alto, with which term this is sometimes confounded; a singer with this voice.

Countervail, koun'tėr-vāl, *v.t.* [Fr. *contrevaloir*. AVAIL.] To act with equivalent force or effect against anything; to balance; to compensate; to equal.—*n.* Equal weight, strength, or value; compensation; requital.

Countervallation, *n.* CONTRAVALLATION.

Counterview, koun'tėr-vū, *n.* An opposite or opposing view; a posture in which two persons front each other; opposition; contrast.

Counterweigh, koun'tėr-wā, *v.t.* To weigh against; to counterbalance.—**Counter-weight**, koun'tėr-wāt, *n.* A weight in the opposite scale; a counterpoise.

Counterwheel, koun'tėr-whēl, *v.t.* To cause to wheel in an opposite direction.

Counterwork, koun'tėr-wėrk, *v.t.* To work in opposition to; to counteract; to hinder any effect by contrary operations.—*n.* A work in opposition or in answer to another.

Country, kun'tri, *n.* [Fr. *contrée*, from L.L. *contrata*, country, from L. *contra*, against, opposite; *country* being thus literally the land opposite or before us. Akin *counter*, adv., *encounter*.] A tract of land; a region; the land occupied by a particular race of people; a state; a person's native or adopted land.—*The country*, the rural parts of a region, as opposed to cities or towns; the inhabitants of a region; the people; the public; the parliamentary electors of a state, or the constituencies of a state, collectively.—*a.* Pertaining to the country or to a district at a distance from a city;

rural; rustic.—**Countrified**, kun'tri-fīd, *a.* Having the airs or manner of a rustic. —**Countryman**, kun'tri-man, *n.* One born in the same country with another; one who dwells in the country as opposed to the town; a rustic; an inhabitant or native of a region.—**Countrywoman**, kun'tri-wụ-man, *n.* A woman belonging to the country, as opposed to the town; a woman born in the same country; a female inhabitant or native of a region.—**Country-dance**, *n.* [*Country* and *dance*; not from Fr. *contre-danse*, which is a kind of quadrille.] A dance in which the partners are arranged opposite to each other in lines.

County, koun'ti, *n.* [L.L. *comitatus*, from *comes*, *comitis*, a count. COUNT.] Originally, the district or territory of a count or earl; now, a district or particular portion of a state or kingdom, separated from the rest of the territory for certain purposes in the administration of justice; a shire (which see); a count‡; an earl or lord‡.—*a.* Pertaining to a county.—*County town*, the chief town of a county; that town where the various courts of a county are held.

Coup, kö, *n.* A French term for stroke or blow, and used in various connections, to convey the idea of promptness, force, or violence.—*Coup d'état* (kö-dā-tä), a sudden decisive blow in politics; a stroke of policy; specifically, a daring or forcible alteration of the constitution of a country without the consent or concurrence of the people. —*Coup de grâce* (köd-gräs), the finishing stroke.—*Coup de main* (köd-mañ), a sudden attack or enterprise.—*Coup d'œil* (kö-dė-yė), glance of the eye; a comprehensive or rapid view.—*Coup de soleil* (köd-so-lā-yė), sunstroke.

Coupé, kö-pā', *n.* [Fr.] A four-wheeled carriage carrying two inside, with driver's seat; a two-door automobile of one enclosed body, generally seating two but sometimes four persons.

Couple, kup'l, *n.* [Fr. *couple*, from L. *copula*, a band, bond, connection.] Two of the same class or kind, connected or considered together; a brace; a pair; a male and female connected by marriage, betrothed, or otherwise allied; *mech.* two equal and parallel forces acting in opposite directions; *elect.* one of the pairs of plates of two metals which compose a battery, called a *galvanic* or *voltaic couple*; *carp.* one of a pair of opposite rafters in a roof, united at the top where they meet.—*v.t.*—*coupled*, *coupling*. To link, chain, or otherwise connect; to fasten together; to unite, as husband and wife; to marry.—*v.i.* To copulate.—**Coupler**, kup'lėr, *n.* One who or that which couples; specifically, the mechanism by which any two of the ranks of keys, or keys and pedals, of an organ are connected together.—**Couplet**, kup'let, *n.* Two verses or lines of poetry, especially two that rhyme together; a pair of rhymes. —**Coupling**, kup'ling, *n.* The act of one who couples; that which couples or connects; a coupler; a contrivance for connecting one portion of a system of shafting with another; the chains or rods connecting the carriages, &c., of a train.—**Coupling-box**, *n.* The box or ring of metal connecting the contiguous ends of two lengths of shaft permanently coupled.

Coupon, kö'pon, *n.* [Fr., from *couper*, to cut.] An interest certificate printed at the bottom of transferable bonds, and so called because it is cut off or detached and given up when a payment is made; hence, generally one of a series of tickets which binds the issuer to make certain payments, perform some service, or give value for certain amounts at different periods, in consideration of money received.

Coupure, kö-pür', *n.* [Fr., from *couper*, to cut.] *Fort.* an intrenchment made by the besieged behind a breach, with a view to protract the defence; also a passage cut to facilitate sallies.

Courage, kur'ij, *n.* [Fr. *courage*, from L. *cor*, the heart, whence also *cordial*, &c.] That quality of mind which enables men to encounter danger and difficulties with firmness, or without fear; bravery; intrepidity; valour; boldness; resolution; disposition or frame of mind (*Shak.*)‡.—**Courageous**, ku-rā'jus, *a.* Possessing or characterized by courage; brave; bold; daring; intrepid.—**Courageously**, ku-rā'jus-li, *adv.* In a courageous manner.—**Courageousness**, ku-rā'jus-nes, *n.*

Courier, kö'rē-ėr, *n.* [Fr. *courrier*, from *courir*, L. *curro*, to run.] A messenger sent express with letters or despatches; an attendant on a party travelling abroad whose especial duty is to make all arrangements at hotels and on the journey.

Course, kōrs, *n.* [Fr. *cours*, *course*, a course, a race, direction, way, &c.; from L. *cursus*, L.L. also *cursa*, from *curro*, *cursum*, to run (whence *current*, *incur*, *recur*, &c.).] A running, race, flight, career, a moving or motion forward in any direction; a continuous progression or advance; the direction of motion; the line in which a body moves; the ground or path marked out for a race; continuous or gradual advance; progress; order of succession; stated or orderly method of proceeding; customary or established sequence; series of successive and methodical proceedings; systematized order in arts or sciences for illustration or instruction (*course* of studies, &c.); way of life or conduct; line of behaviour (to follow evil *courses*); the part of a meal served at one time; *arch.* a continued range of stones or bricks of the same height throughout the face or faces of a building; *naut.* one of the sails that hang from a ship's lowest yards; *pl.* the menstrual flux; catamenia. —*v.t. coursed*, *coursing*. To hunt; to pursue; to chase; to hunt (hares) with greyhounds; to drive with speed; to run through or over.—*v.i.* To move with speed; to run or move about.—*Of course*, by consequence; in regular or natural order; naturally; without special direction or provision. —**Courser**, kōr'sėr, *n.* One who courses; a swift horse; a war-horse: used chiefly in poetry; a swift-footed cream-coloured bird of the plover tribe; any bird of the cursorial order, or runners.

Court, kōrt, *n.* [O.Fr. *cort*, *court* (Fr. *cour*), from L. *cors*, *cortis*, contracted from *cohors*, *cohortis*, a yard, a *court*—*co* for *con*, and *hor*, a root seen in *hortus*, a garden, also in *garden*, *garth*.] An inclosed uncovered area, whether behind or in front of a house, or surrounded by buildings; a court-yard; an alley, lane, close, or narrow street; the place of residence of a king or sovereign prince; all the surroundings of a sovereign in his regal state; the collective body of persons who compose the retinue or council of a sovereign; a hall, chamber, or place where justice is administered; the persons or judges assembled for hearing and deciding causes, as distinguished from the counsel or jury; any judicial body, civil, military, or ecclesiastical; the sitting of a judicial assembly; attention directed to a person in power to gain favour; civility; flattery; address to gain favour (to pay *court* to a person).—*v.t.* To endeavour to gain the favour of or win over by attention and address; to flatter; to seek the affections or love of; to woo; to solicit for marriage; to attempt to gain by address; to solicit; to seek (to *court* applause); to hold out inducements to; to invite.—*v.i.* To pay one's addresses; to woo.—**Courteous**, kėr'tē-us, *a.* Having courtly, refined, or elegant manners; characterized by courtesy; affable; condescending, polite.—**Courteously**, kėr'tē-us-li, *adv.* In a courteous manner.—**Courteousness**, kėrt'ē-us-nes, *n.*—**Courter**, kōr'tėr, *n.* One who courts or endeavours to gain favour; one who wooes; a wooer.—**Courtesan**, **Courtezan**, kōr'te-zan, *n.* A prostitute.—**Courtesanship**, **Courtezanship**, kōr'te-zan-ship, *n.* The character or practice of a courtesan.—**Courtesy**, kėr'te-si, *n.* Politeness of manners, combined with kindness; polished manners or urbanity shown in behaviour towards others; an act of civility or respect; a movement of reverence, civility, or respect made by a woman by a slight inclination of the body and bending of the knees; a curtsey (in this sense pronounced kėrt'si); favour or indulgence, as contradistinguished from right.—*Courtesy of England*, the husband's tenure of certain kinds of property after his wife's death.—*Courtesy title*, a title assumed or popularly accorded and to which the individual has no valid claim, as the title marquis to the eldest son of a duke, viscount to the eldest son of an earl, &c.—**Courtier**, kōr'ti-ėr, *n.* One who attends or frequents the court of a sovereign; one who courts or flatters another with a view to obtain favour, &c.—**Courtly**, kōrt'li, *a.* Relating or pertaining to a prince's court; refined and dignified; elegant; polite; courteous.—**Courtliness**, kōrt'li-nes, *n.* The state or quality of being courtly.—**Courtship**, kōrt'ship, *n.* The act of courting or soliciting favour; wooing.—**Courtship coloration**. Beautiful colours possessed and displayed by animals (usually the males) as a courtship accessory.—**Courtship selection**. Preferential mating.—**Court-card**, *a.* A corruption of *coat-card* (which see).—**Court-day**, *n.* A day in which a court sits to administer justice.—**Court-dress**, *n.* A dress suitable for an appearance at court or levee.—**Court-hand**, *n.* The old manner of writing used in records and judicial proceedings.—**Court-house**, *n.* A house in which established courts are held.—**Court-martial**, *n.* pl. **Courts-martial**. A court consisting of military or naval officers, for the trial of military or naval offences.—**Court-party**, *n.* A political party attached to the court, as opposed to the nation at large.—**Court-plaster**, *n.* A fine kind of sticking-plaster. —**Courts-rolls**, *n.pl.* The records of a court.—**Court-sword**, *n.* A slight dress sword worn at levees.—**Court-yard**, *n.* A court or inclosure round a house or adjacent to it.

Cousin, kuz'n, *n.* [Fr. *cousin*, from L.L. *cosinus*, for L. *consobrinus*, a cousin—*con*, and *sobrinus*, akin to *soror*, a sister.] The son or daughter of an uncle or aunt; in a wider and now less usual sense, one collaterally related more remotely than a brother or sister; a kinsman or kinswoman; a blood-relation; a title given by a monarch to a nobleman.—**Cousinhood**, kuz'n-hụd, *n.* The state of being cousins; the individuals connected with a family regarded collectively.—**Cousinly**, kuz'n-li, *a.* Like or becoming a cousin.—**Cousinship**, kuz'n-ship, *n.* The state of being cousins; cousinhood.—**Cousin-german**, *n.* A first or full cousin.

Couvade, kö-väd', *n.* [Fr. *couver*, to hatch; L. *cubare*, to lie. COVEY.] A custom among primitive races (Basques, Corsicans, &c.) of men, by which, at the birth of a child, the father takes to bed and is attended by mother. Doubtless to prove paternity, by a survival from earlier days of promiscuity of intercourse.

Cove, kōv, *n.* [A.Sax. *cófa*, a chamber, a cave; allied to Icel. *kofi*, Sw. *kofwa*, a hut.] A small inlet, creek, or bay; a sheltered recess in the sea-shore; *arch.* any kind of concave moulding; the concavity of a vault. —*v.t. coved*, *coving*. To arch over.

Covenant, kuv'e-nant, *n.* [O.Fr. *covenant*, for *convenant*, from L. *convenire*, to agree —*con*, and *venio*, to come. CONVENE.] A mutual consent or agreement of two or more persons to do or to forbear some act or thing; a contract; a compact; a bargain, arrangement, or stipulation; a writing containing the terms of agreement or contract between parties.—*v.i.* To enter into a formal agreement; to contract; to bind one's self by contract.—*v.t.* To grant or promise by covenant. [O.T.]—**Covenantee**, kuv'e-nan-tē", *n.* The person to whom a covenant is made.—**Covenanter**, kuv'e-nan-tėr, *n.* One who makes a covenant; a term specially applied to those who joined in the Solemn League and Covenant in Scotland, and in particular those who resisted the government of Charles II., and fought and suffered for adherence to their own form of worship. —**Covenantor**, kuv'e-nan-tor", *n.* *Law*, the person who makes a covenant and subjects himself to the penalty of its breach.

Cover, kuv'ėr, *v.t.* [O.Fr. *covrir*, Fr. *couvrir*, from L. *cooperire*—*con*, intens., and *operire*, to cover.] To overspread the surface of with another substance; to lay or set over; to overspread so as to conceal; to envelop; to wrap up; to clothe; to shelter; to protect: to defend; to cloak; to screen; to invest with; to brood over; to be sufficient for; to include; to comprehend; to be equal to; to be co-extensive with.—*n.* Anything which is laid, set, or spread over another thing; anything which veils or conceals; a screen; disguise; superficial appearance; shelter; defence; protection; concealment and protection; shrubbery, woods, underbrush, &c., which shelter and conceal game; the articles laid at table for the use of one person—plate, spoon, knife and fork, &c.—**Cover-glass**. In microscopy, a very thin piece of glass for covering the object examined.—**Covered-way**, *n.* *Fort.* the level space of ground between the top of the counterscarp or outer slope of the main ditch and the glacis.—**Coverer**, kuv'ėr-ėr, *n.* One who or that which covers.—**Covering**, kuv'ėr-ing, *n.* That which covers; anything spread or laid over another, whether for security, protection, shelter, or concealment; clothing; dress; wrapper; envelope.—**Coverlet**, kuv'ėr-let, *n.* [O.Fr. *covre-lit*, *couvre-lit*, a bed-cover—*covrir*, to cover, and *lit*, L. *lectus*, a bed.] The upper covering of a bed.—**Coverlid**, kuv'ėr-lid, *n.* A coverlet. (*Tenn.*)

Covert, kuv'ėrt, *a.* [O.Fr. *covert*, part. of *covrir*, to cover.] Kept secret or concealed; not open (*covert* fraud or enmity); *law*, under cover, authority, or protection.—*n.* A place which covers and shelters; a shelter; a defence; a thicket; a shady place or a hiding-place; *pl.* feathers covering the bases of the quills of the wing or tail of birds.—**Covertly**, kuv'ėrt-li, *adv.* Secretly; in private; insidiously.—**Covertness**, kuv'ėrt-nes, *n.* Secrecy; privacy.—**Coverture**, kuv'ėr-tūr, *n.* Covering; shelter; defence; *law*, the state of a married woman, who is considered as under the cover or power of her husband.—**Covert-way**. Same as *Covered-way*: see under COVER.

Covet, kuv'et, *v.t.* [From O.Fr. *coveiter* (Fr. *convoiter*), from L. *cupidus*, desirous, *cupio*, to desire.] To desire or wish for with eagerness; to desire earnestly to obtain or possess; to desire inordinately; to desire with a greedy or envious longing; to long for; to hanker after.—*v.i.* To have or indulge inordinate desire.—**Covetable**, kuv'e-ta-bl, *a.* That may be coveted.—**Coveter**, kuv'e-tėr, *n.* One who covets.—**Covetingly**, kuv'e-ting-li, *adv.* With eager desire to possess.—**Covetous**, kuv'e-tus, *a.* Very desirous; eager to obtain; inordinately desirous; excessively eager to obtain and possess; avaricious.—**Covetously**, kuv'e-tus-li, *adv.* With a strong or inordinate desire; eagerly; avariciously.—**Covetousness**, kuv'e-tus-nes, *n.* The state or quality of being covetous; avarice; cupidity; greediness; craving.

Covey, kuv'i, *n.* [O.Fr. *covee*, Fr *couvée*, a brood, from *couver*, *cover*, to sit on or brood, L. *cubare*, to lie; seen also in *incubate*.] A brood or hatch of birds; an old fowl with her brood of young; a small flock: usually confined to partridges.

Covin, **Covine**, kuv'in, *n.* [O.Fr. *covine*, from L. *convenire*. COVENANT.] *Law*, a collusive or deceitful agreement between two or more to prejudice a third person; deceitful contrivance.—**Covinous**, kuv'i-nus, *a.* Deceitful; collusive; fraudulent.

Cow, kou, *n.* pl. **Cows**, kouz, old pl. **Kine**, kin. [A.Sax. *cú*, pl. *cý*; G. *kuh*, D. and Dan. *koe*, Icel. *kú*; the same root appears in Skr. *go*, nom. *gaus*, a cow, an ox., *Kine* is a double plural, the *en* form as in *oxen* being added to the older form.] The general term applied to the females of the bovine genus or ox, the most valuable to man of all the ruminating animals, on account of her milk, flesh, hide, &c.—**Cow-bane**, *n.* A kind of hemlock, water-hemlock, highly poisonous, being sometimes fatal to cattle who eat its leaves.—**Cow-berry**, *n.* Red whortleberry.—**Cowboy**, *n.* Boy who has charge of cows; a man who looks after cattle on a large stock farm and does this work on horseback.—**Cow-bunting**, **Cow-troopial**, *n.* An American bird belonging to the starling tribe, remarkable for dropping its eggs into the nests of other birds to be hatched.—**Cow-catcher**, *n.* A strong frame in front of locomotives for removing obstructions, such as strayed cattle, from the rails.—**Cow-chervil**, **Cow-parsley**. Popular names of several perennial herbs of the carrot family, said to be eaten by cattle.—**Cow-feeder**, **Cow-keeper**, *n.* One whose business it is to feed or keep cows; a dairyman.—**Cow-grass**, **Cow-pea**, *n.* A kind of clover having bright red flowers.—**Cow-hide**, *n.* The hide or skin of a cow, made or to be made into leather; a strong whip made of such leather.—*v.t.* To thrash or whip with a lash of cow-hide.—**Cow-parsnip**. A plant of the carrot family, sometimes used in England for fattening hogs.—**Cow-pox**, *n.* A disease which appears on the teats of the cow in the form of vesicles or blisters, the fluid or virus contained in which is capable of communicating the disease to the human subject, and of conferring, in the great majority of instances, security against small-pox.—**Cowslip**, kou'slip, *n.* [A.Sax. *cú-slyppe*, *cú-sloppe*, the latter part of the name apparently meaning dung.] A perennial herb of the primrose family, growing in moist places in Britain.—*Cowslip wine*, a beverage made by fermenting cowslips with sugar, and used as a domestic soporific.—**Cow-tree**, *n.* A name given to various species of South American trees, which on incision yield a rich milky nutritious juice in such abundance as to render it an important article of food.

Cow, kou, *v.t.* [Dan. *kue*, Icel. *kúga*, to depress, subdue, keep under.] To sink the spirits or courage of; to daunt, dishearten, intimidate, overawe.

Coward, kou'ėrd, *n.* [Fr. *couard*, It. *codardo*, from L. *cauda*, a tail, the name being originally applied to the timid hare from its short tail.] A person who wants courage to meet danger; a poltroon; a craven; a dastard; a faint-hearted, timid, or pusillanimous man.—*a.* Destitute of courage; timid; of, proceeding from, or expressive of fear or timidity.—**Cowardice**, kou'ėr-dis, *n.* [Fr. *couardise*.] Want of courage to face danger; timidity; pusillanimity; fear of exposing one's person to danger.—**Cowardly**, kou'ėrd-li, *a.* Wanting courage to face danger; timid; timorous; pusillanimous; faint-hearted; mean; base; proceeding from fear of danger; befitting a coward.—*adv.* In the manner of a coward.—**Cowardliness**, kou'ėrd-li-nes, *n.* Cowardice.

Cowdie-pine. Same as *Cowrie-pine*.

Cower, kou'ėr, *v.i.* [Same word as Sc. *curr*, to squat; Icel. *kúra*, Dan. *kure*, Sw. *kura*, to doze, to rest; G. *kauern*, to cower.] To squat; to stoop or sink downward, as from terror, discomfort, &c.

Cowhage, **Cow-itch**, kou'āj, kou'ich, *n.* [Hind. *kiwanch*, cowhage.] The short, brittle hairs of the pods of a leguminous plant, which easily penetrate the skin, and produce an intolerable itching; they are administered in honey or treacle as a vermifuge.

Cowl, koul, *n.* [A.Sax. *cufle*, Icel. *kufl*, *kofl*, a cowl; comp. also O.Fr. *coule*, from L. *cucullus*, a cowl.] A hood, especially a monk's hood; a cowl-shaped covering for the top of a chimney, which turns with the wind; a wire cap or cage on the top of an engine funnel.—**Cowled**, kould, *a.* Wearing a cowl; hooded; in shape of a cowl (*cowled* leaf).

Cowl, koul, *n.* [O.Fr. *cuvel*, dim. of *cuve*, a tub, from L. *cupa*. CUP.] A vessel to be carried on a pole betwixt two persons, for the conveyance of water.—**Cowl-staff**, *n.* Same as *Colstaff*.

Co-work, kō-wėrk', *v.i.* To work jointly; to co-operate.—**Co-worker**, kō-wėr'kėr, *n.* One that works with another; a co-operator.

Cowrie-pine, **Kauri-pine**, kou'ri, *n.* [Native name.] A coniferous tree of New Zealand, yielding gum-damar, damar-resin, or kauri-gum, and having a tall straight stem, rising to the height of 150 to 200 feet, yielding valuable timber.

Cowry, kou'ri, *n.* [Hind. *kauri*.] A small univalve shell used for coin on the coast of Guinea, and in many parts of Southern Asia.

Coxa, kok'sa, *n.* [L.] *Anat.* the hip, haunch, or hip-joint; *entom.* the joint of an insect's limb which is next the body.

Coxcomb, koks'kōm, *n.* [*Cock's comb*.] The comb resembling that of a cock which licensed fools wore formerly in their caps; hence used often for the cap itself; the top of the head, or the head itself; a vain showy fellow; a superficial pretender to knowledge or accomplishments; a fop; a dandy.—**Coxcombical**, **Coxcomical**, koks-kom'i-kal, *a.* Like or indicating a coxcomb; conceited; foppish.—**Coxcombically**, **Coxcomically**, koks-kom'i-kal-li, *adv.* After the manner of a coxcomb; foppishly.—**Coxcombry**, koks'kōm-ri, *n.* The manners of a coxcomb; foppishness.—**Coxcomicality**, koks-kom'i-kal"i-ti, *n.* Coxcombry.

Coxswain, *n.* Same as *Cockswain*.

Coy, koi, *a.* [O.Fr. *coi*, *coy*, *coit*, from L. *quietus*, quiet. QUIET.] Shrinking from familiarity; shy; modest; reserved; distant; backward; bashful.—**Coyish**, koi'ish, *a.* Somewhat coy or reserved.—**Coyly**, koi'li, *adv.* In a coy manner; with disinclination to familiarity.—**Coyness**, koi'nes, *n.* The quality of being coy; bashfulness; shyness; reserve; modesty.

Coyote, koi-ōt', koi-ō'tā, *n.* [Sp. *coyote*, Mex. *coyotl*.] The American prairie-wolf.

Coypou, **Coypu**, koi'pö, *n.* The native name of a South American rodent, beaver-like, semi-aquatic mammal, valued for its fur.

Coystrel,‡ **Coystril**,‡ kois'trel, kois'tril, *n.* A mean, cowardly, paltry fellow. (*Shak.*)

Cozen, kuz'n, *v.t.* [A form of *cousin*; Fr. *cousiner*, to sponge upon people (under pretext of relationship), from *cousin*, a cousin.] To cheat; to defraud; to deceive; to beguile.—*v.i.* To cheat; to act deceitfully.—**Cozenage**, kuz'n-āj, *n.* Trickery; fraud; deceit.—**Cozener**, kuz'n-ėr, *n.* One who cozens.

Cozy, **Cozily**. Same as *Cosey*, *Cosily*.

Crab, krab, *n.* [A.Sax. *crabba* = D. *krab*, Icel. *krabbi*, Sw. *krabba*, G. *krabbe*, a crab; all perhaps from L. *carabus*, Gr. *karabos*, a kind of crab.] A popular name for all the ten-footed, short-tailed crustaceans, having their tail folded under the body, the two fore-feet not used for locomotion, but furnished with strong claws or pincers, and several species being highly esteemed as food; Cancer, a sign in the zodiac; a name given to various machines, as a kind of portable windlass or machine for raising weights, &c.

Crab, krab, *n.* [Sw. *krabbäple*, a crab-apple, perhaps from *crab*, the animal, in allusion to its pinching or astringent juice.] A small, wild, very sour apple; the tree producing the fruit; a sour-tempered, peevish, morose person‡.—**Crab-apple**, *n.* A wild apple.—**Crabbed**, krab'ed, *a.* Rough or harsh as regards temper or disposition; sour; peevish; morose; difficult; perplexing; uninviting (a *crabbed* author).—**Crabbedly**, krab'ed-li, *adv.* In a crabbed manner; peevishly; morosely.—**Crabbedness**, krab'ed-nes, *n.* The state or quality of being crabbed.—**Crab-faced**, *a.* Having a sour, peevish face.—**Crabstick**, *n.* A walking-stick made of the wood of the crab-tree.—**Crab-tree**, *n.* The tree that bears crabs; the wild apple-tree.

Crab-oil, *n.* Carap-oil.—**Crab-wood**, *n.* The tree that yields crab-oil or carap-oil.

Crack, krak, *v.t.* [An imitative word; A.Sax. *cracian*, to crack; G. *krachen*, to crack; D. *krak*, a crack; Gael. *knac*, a crack, as of a whip, &c.] To rend, break, or burst; to break partially; to break without an entire severance of the parts; to throw out or utter with smartness (to *crack* a joke); to snap; to cause to make a sharp sudden noise (a whip).—*v.i.* To break with a sharp sound; to burst; to open in chinks; to be fractured without quite separating into different parts; to give out a loud or sharp sudden sound; to boast or brag: with *of* (*Shak.*)‡.—*n.* A chink or fissure; a partial separation of the parts of a substance, with or without an opening; a burst of sound; a sharp or loud sound uttered suddenly; a violent report; injury or impairment to the intellect or to the character; flaw; blemish; an instant; a trice.—*a.* Having qualities to be proud of; first-rate; excellent (a *crack* regiment, a *crack* horse).—**Cracked**, krakt, *p.* and *a.* Burst or split; rent; broken; impaired; crazy, as regards the mind.—**Cracker**, krak'ėr, *n.* One who or that which cracks; a noisy, boasting fellow (*Shak.*); a small kind of firework filled with powder, which explodes with a sharp crack or with a series of sharp cracks; a small hard biscuit.—**Crackle**, krak'l, *v.i.*—*crackled*, *crackling*. [Dim. of *crack*.] To make slight cracks; to make small abrupt noises, rapidly or frequently repeated; to decrepitate.—**Crackling**, krak'l-ing, *n.* A noise made up of small cracks or reports frequently repeated; the browned skin of roast pig; a kind of cake used for dogs' food, made from the refuse of tallow-melting.—**Cracknel**, krak'nel, *n.* A hard brittle cake or biscuit.—**Crack-brained**, *a.* Having a disordered intellect; insane; lunatic; mad.

Cracovienne, krä-kō'vē-en", *n.* The favourite dance of the Polish peasantry around *Cracow*; the music for the dance, written in $\frac{2}{4}$-time.

Cradle, krā'dl, *n.* [A.Sax. *cradel*, *cradol*; perhaps of Celtic origin.] A small bed, crib, or cot in which an infant is rocked; hence, the place where any person or thing is nurtured in the earlier stage of existence; something resembling a cradle in construction or use, as a case in which a broken limb is placed after being set; a rocking machine in which gold is washed from the earth, &c., containing it; a vessel or basket attached to a line or lines between a wrecked ship and the shore for bringing off the crew or passengers, &c.—*v.t.*—*cradled*, *cradling*. To lay in a cradle; to rock in a cradle; to compose or quiet by rocking; to nurse in infancy.—*v.i.* To lie or lodge as in a cradle. (*Shak.*)

Craft, kraft, *n.* [A.Sax. *cræft*, craft, cunning, a bark, a craft = G. Sw. Icel. and Dan. *kraft*, D. *kracht*, power, faculty; from root of which *cramp* is a nasalized form, akin to Skr. *grabh*, to grasp.] Cunning art, or skill, in a bad sense; artifice; guile; dexterity in a particular manual occupation; hence, the occupation or employment itself; manual art; trade; the members of a trade collectively; *naut.* a vessel: often used in a collective sense for vessels of any kind.—**Craftless**, kraft'les, *a.* Free from craft, guile, or cunning.—**Craftsman**, krafts'man, *n.* An artificer; a mechanic; one skilled in a manual occupation.—**Craftsmanship**, krafts'man-ship, *n.* The skilled work of a craftsman.—**Craftsmaster**, krafts'mas-tėr, *n.* One skilled in his craft or trade.—**Crafty**, kraf'ti, *a.* Characterized by, having, or using craft; cunning; wily; sly; deceitful; subtle; dexterous; skilful.—**Craftily**, kraf'ti-li, *adv.* In a crafty manner; cunningly; slyly; deceitfully; skilfully; dexterously.—**Craftiness**, kraf'ti-nes, *n.* The state or quality of being crafty.

Crag, krag, *n.* [Gael. *creag*, Ir. *craig*, W. *careg*, a rock, stone.] A steep, rugged rock; a rough broken rock, or point of a rock; a cliff; *geol.* shelly deposits in Norfolk and Suffolk, usually of gravel and sand, of the older pliocene period.—**Cragged**, krag'ed, *a.* Full of crags or broken rocks; craggy.—**Craggedness**, krag'ed-nes, *n.*—**Craggy**, krag'i, *a.* Full of crags; abounding with broken rocks; rugged with projecting points of rocks.—**Cragginess**, krag'i-nes, *n.* The state of being craggy.—**Cragsman**, kragz, *n.* One who is dexterous in climbing or descending rocks; one who takes sea-fowls or their eggs from crags.

Crake, krāk, *n.* [Imitative of the bird's cry, like *croak*, *creak*; comp. L. *crex*, Gr. *krex*, a landrail; Icel. *krâka*, to croak, &c.] A grallatorial bird of various species belonging to the family of the rails, the best-known species being the corncrake or landrail.

Cram, kram, *v.t.*—*crammed*, *cramming*. [A.Sax. *crammian*, to cram; Dan. *kramme*, to crush; Sw. *krama*, to press; akin *cramp*.] To press or drive, particularly in filling or thrusting one thing into another; to stuff; to crowd; to fill to superfluity; to fill with food beyond satiety; to stuff; *fig.* to endeavour to qualify for an examination, in a comparatively short time, by storing the memory with only such knowledge as is likely to serve the occasion; to coach.—*v.i.* To eat greedily or beyond satiety; to stuff; to prepare for an examination by rapidly storing the memory with crude facts.—*n.* Information got up hurriedly for an examination or other special purpose.—**Crammer**, kram'ėr, *n.* One who crams or stuffs; one who crams in study.

Crambo, kram'bō, *n.* [Origin doubtful.] A game in which one person gives a word, to which another finds a rhyme; a word rhyming with another.

Cramp, kramp, *n.* [Same as D. *kramp*, Dan. *krampe*, Sw. *kramp*, *krampa*, G. *krampf*, *krampe*, cramp, a cramp-iron; from root seen in *cram*, *crimp*, *crumple*.] The contraction of a limb or some muscle of the body, attended with pain; spasm; a feeling of restraint; a piece of iron bent at the end, serving to hold together pieces of timber, stones, &c.; a cramp-iron; a portable kind of iron screw press for closely compressing the joints of a timber framework.—*v.t.* To pain or affect with spasms or cramps; to confine, restrain, or hinder from action or expansion; to fasten, confine, or hold with a cramp or cramp-iron.—*a.* Difficult; knotty.—**Cramp-bone**, *n.* The patella of a sheep, so named because considered a charm against cramp.—**Cramp-iron**, *n.* A piece of iron, bent at each end, and let into the upper surface of two pieces of stone, when their perpendicular faces are joined together.—**Crampon**, kram'pon, *n.* [Fr. *crampon*.] *Bot.* an adventitious root which serves as a fulcrum or support in climbing, as in the ivy.—**Crampoon**, kräm'pön, *n.* An iron fastened to the shoes of a storming party, to assist them in climbing a rampart; an apparatus used in raising timber or stones for building, consisting of two hooked pieces of iron hinged together.

Cran, kran, *n.* [Gael. *crann*.] In Scotland, a measure of capacity for fresh herrings, as taken out of the net, which contains on a rough average about 750 herrings.

Cranberry, kran'be-ri, *n.* [That is *craneberry*, perhaps because the berries are eaten by cranes.] The globose, dark red berry, about the size of a currant, produced by several species of small shrubs growing in peat-bogs or swampy land in Europe and North America; the shrub producing this berry. Called also *Moss-berry* and *Moorberry*.

Cranch, kranch. CRAUNCH.

Crane, krān, *n.* [A.Sax. *cran*; cog. D. *kraan*, G. *krahn*, *kranich*, Icel. *trani*, Dan. *trane* (with *tr* for *kr*), W. *garan*, Gr. *geranos*, L. *grus*, the bird, also the lifting apparatus; from a root *gar*, seen in L. *garrio*, Gr. *geryō*, to call.] A large migratory grallatorial bird of several species, having long slender legs, a long neck, and powerful wings; a machine for raising great weights, and depositing them at some distance from their original place, the most common form consisting of a vertical shaft, with projecting arm or jib, at the outer end of which is a fixed pulley, carrying the rope or chain to receive the weight, which is raised by coiling the rope or chain round a cylinder; a movable iron arm or beam attached to the back or side of a fire-place for supporting a pot or kettle; a siphon or crooked pipe for drawing liquors out of a cask.—*v.i.*—*craned*, *craning*. To stretch out one's neck like a crane; hence, *hunting*, to look before one leaps; to pull up at a dangerous jump.—**Cranage**, krā'-nāj, *n.* The right of using a crane at a wharf, &c.; the sum paid for the use of a crane.—**Crane-fly**, *n.* A dipterous insect having very long legs, and lanceolate spreading wings; the daddy-longlegs is a well-known species.—**Crane's-bill**, *n.* The popular name given to the species of Geranium, from the long slender beak of their fruit.

Cranium, krā'ni-um, *pl.* **Crania**, krā'-ni-a, *n.* [L.L. *cranium*, from Gr. *kranion*, a skull.] The bones which inclose the brain; the skull.—**Cranial**, krā'ni-al, *a.* Relating to the cranium.—**Craniofacial**, krā'-ni-ō-fā-shal, *a.* Pertaining to the cranium and face.—**Craniology**, krā-ni-ol'o-ji, *n.* The knowledge of the cranium or skull; the art of determining the intellectual and moral peculiarities of individuals by the shape of their skulls; phrenology.—**Craniological**, krā'ni-ō-loj"ik-al, *a.* Pertaining to craniology.—**Craniologist**, krā-ni-ol'o-jist, *n.* One who treats of or is versed in craniology.—**Craniometer**, krā-ni-om'-et-ėr, *n.* An instrument for measuring skulls.—**Craniometrical**, krā'ni-ō-met"-ri-kal, *a.* Pertaining to craniometry.—**Craniometry**, krā-ni-om'et-ri, *n.* The art of measuring skulls.—**Cranioscopy**, krā-ni-os'ko-pi, *n.* An examination of the skull with the view of discovering its distinctive characters; phrenology.—**Cranioscopist**, krā-ni-os'ko-pist, *n.* One skilled in cranioscopy; a phrenologist.

Crank, krangk, *n.* [Allied to *cringe*, *crinkle*; D. *krinkel*, something bending, a curve, *krinkelen*, to bend.] An iron axis with the end bent like an elbow, serving as a handle for communicating circular motion (as in a grindstone), for changing circular motion into motion backwards and forwards or the reverse (steam-engine), or for merely changing the direction of motion (as in bell-hanging); any bend, turn, winding, or involution; a twisting or turning in speech; a man with crotchets and crabbed views.—*v.i.* To run in a winding course; to bend, wind, and turn.

Crank, krangk, *a.* [A.Sax. *cranc*, weak, sick; D. and G. *krank*, Icel. *krankr*, sick, ill.] Liable to be overset, as a ship when she has not sufficient ballast to carry full sail; in a shaky or crazy condition; loose; disjointed.—**Crankness**, krangk'nes, *n.* The condition or property of being crank.—**Cranky**, krang'ki, *a.* Liable to overset; full of crotchets or whims; not to be depended on; unsteady; crazy.

Crannog, kran'og, *n.* [Ir., from *cran*, Gael. *crann*, a tree, a pile.] The name given in Ireland and Scotland to the fortified islands in lakes, or to platforms supported by piles, which were in use as dwelling-places and places of refuge among the old Celts; a lake-dwelling.

Cranny, kran'i, *n.* [Fr. *cran*, a notch, from L. *crena*, a notch; comp. G. *krinne*, a rent.] A small narrow opening, fissure, crevice, or chink, as in a wall or other substance.—*v.i.* To become intersected with or penetrated by crannies or clefts; to enter by crannies (*Shak.*).—**Crannied**, kran'id, *p.* or *a.* Having chinks, fissures, or crannies.

Crape, krāp, *n.* [Fr. *crêpe*, O.Fr. *crespe*, from L. *crispus*, curled. CRISP.] A thin transparent stuff like gauze made of raw silk gummed and twisted on the mill, woven without crossing, and much used in mourning, light shawls, the dress of the clergy, &c.—*v.t.*†—*craped*, *craping*. To frizzle or curl; to form into ringlets.—**Crapy**, krā'pi, *a.* Like crape.

Crapulence, krap'ū-lens, *n.* [L. *crapula*, intoxication.] Drunkenness; the sickness occasioned by intemperance.—**Crapulent**, **Crapulous**, krap'ū-lent, krap'ū-lus, *a.* Drunk; sick by intemperance; connected or associated with drunkenness.

Crash, krash, *v.t.* [Imitative. Comp.

crack, clash, crush, &c.] To break to pieces violently; to dash with tumult and violence.—*v.i.* To make the loud multifarious sound of a thing or things falling and breaking; or to make any similar noise.—*n.* The loud sound of a thing or things falling and breaking; a sound made by dashing; the collapse of a commercial undertaking; bankruptcy; failure.

Crash, krash, *n.* [L. *crassus*, thick.] A coarse kind of linen cloth, mostly used for towels.

Crasis, krā'sis, *n.* [Gr. *krasis*, a mixing.] *Med.* the mixture of the constituents of a fluid, as the blood; hence, temperament; constitution; *gram.* a figure by which two different letters are contracted into one long letter or into a diphthong: called also *Synæresis.*

Crass, kras, *a.* [L. *crassus.*] Gross; thick; coarse: not thin, nor fine: applied to fluids and solids; *fig.* gross; dense; stupid; obtuse. —**Crassament**, kras'a-ment, *n.* [L. *crassamentum.*] The thick red part of the blood, as distinct from the serum or aqueous part; the clot.—**Crassitude**, kras'i-tūd, *n.* Grossness; coarseness; thickness. —**Crassness**, kras'nes, *n.* Grossness.

Crate, krāt, *n.* [L. *crates*, wicker-work.] A kind of basket or hamper of wicker-work, used for the transportation of china, glass, crockery, and similar wares.

Crater, krā'tėr, *n.* [L. *crater*, from Gr. *kratēr*, a great cup, a mixing vessel, from *kerannymi*, to mix.] The orifice or mouth of a volcano, often a circular cup-like hollow at the top of a volcanic cone.—**Crateriform**, kra-tėr'i-form, *a.* Having the form of a crater; shaped like a goblet.—**Craterous**,† krā'tėr-us, *a.* Belonging to or like a crater. (*Browning.*)

Craunch, kra̤nsh, *v.t.* [Imitative, same as *crunch, scranch.*] To crush with the teeth; to crunch.

Cravat, kra-vat', *n.* [Fr. *Cravate*, a Croat, and hence a cravat, because this piece of dress was adopted in the seventeenth century from the Croats who entered the French service.] A neckcloth; an article of muslin, silk, woollen, or other material worn by men about the neck.—**Cravatted**, kra-vat'ed, *a.* Wearing a cravat.

Crave, krāv, *v.t.—craved, craving.* [A.Sax. *crafian*, to ask = Icel. *krefja*, Sw. *krāfva*, Dan. *kræve*, to crave, to ask.] To ask for with earnestness or importunity; to ask (a thing) with submission or humility; to beg, entreat, implore, solicit; to call for, as a gratification; to long for; to require or demand, as a passion or appetite.—*v.i.* To beg, ask, beseech, or implore; to long or hanker eagerly: with *for.*—**Craver**, krā'vėr, *n.* One who craves.—**Craving**, krā'ving, *n.* Vehement or inordinate desire; a longing. — *a.* Ardently or inordinately desirous or longing. — **Cravingly**, krā'ving-li, *adv.* In an earnest or craving manner.

Craven, krā'vn, *n.* [O.Fr. *cravanter*, to overthrow, from a L.L. *crepantare*, from L. *crepare*, to break; akin *crevice, crepitate.*] Formerly one vanquished in trial by battle, and yielding to the conqueror; hence, a recreant; a coward; a weak-hearted, spiritless fellow.—*a.* Cowardly; base.

Craw, kra̤, *n.* [Of same origin as Dan. *kro*, D. *kraag*, G. *kragen*, the throat, craw.] The crop or first stomach of fowls; the stomach, in a general sense.

Crawfish, *n.* The crayfish; also the spiny lobster, a marine crustacean.

Crawl, kra̤l, *v.i.* [Of same origin as Sw. *krāla*, also *krafla*, Icel. *krafla*, Dan. *kravle*, G. *krabbeln*, to crawl.] To move slowly by thrusting or drawing the body along the ground, as a worm; to move slowly on the hands and knees, as a human being; to creep; to move or walk weakly, slowly, or timorously; to advance slowly and slyly; to insinuate one's self; to behave meanly or despicably.—*n.* The act of crawling; slow creeping motion.—**Crawler**, kra̤'lėr, *n.* One who or that which crawls; a creeper; a reptile; a mean, cringing fellow.—**Crawlingly**, kra̤'ling-li, *adv.* In a crawling manner.

Crayfish, Crawfish, krā'fish, kra̤'fish, *n.* [A curious corruption of comparatively modern origin; formerly *crevise, creveys*, from O.Fr. *crevice*, O.H.G. *krebiz*, G. *krebs* = crab. CRAB.] The river lobster, a ten-footed crustacean found in streams, and resembling the lobster, but smaller, used as food; also the spiny lobster.

Crayon, krā'on, *n.* [Fr. *crayon*, from *craie*, L. *creta*, chalk, whence *cretaceous.*] A pencil or cylinder of coloured pipe-clay, chalk, or charcoal, used in drawing upon paper; a composition pencil made of soap, resin, wax, and lamp-black, used for drawing upon lithographic stones. — *v.t.* To sketch with a crayon; hence, to sketch roughly.

Craze, krāz, *v.t.—crazed, crazing.* [Same as Sw. *krasa*, to crush, break; Dan. *krase*, to crackle; from sound of crushing. Akin *crush, crash*, &c.] To break in pieces, grind or crush‡; to put out of order; to impair the natural force or energy of; to derange the intellect of; to render insane. —*v.i.* To become crazy or insane; to become shattered; to break down.—*n.* Craziness; an inordinate desire or longing; a passion; a wild fancy or notion.—**Crazed**, krāzd, *a.* Broken down; impaired; decrepit; crazy.— **Crazy**, krā'zi, *a.* Decrepit; feeble; shattered; unsound: of the body or any structure; disordered, deranged, weakened, or shattered in mind.—**Crazily**, krā'zi-li, *adv.* In a crazy manner.—**Craziness**, krā'zi-nes, *n.* The state of being crazy; imbecility or weakness of intellect; derangement.

Creak, krēk, *v.i.* [Imitative of a more acute and prolonged sound than *crack*; comp. Fr. *criquer*, to creak; W. *crecian*, to scream.] To make a sharp harsh grating sound of some continuance, as by the friction of hard substances.—*v.t.* To cause to make a harsh protracted noise.—*n.* A sharp, harsh, grating sound.

Cream, krēm, *n.* [Fr. *crème*, from L.L. *cremum* (or *crema*), cream — a word suggested by L. *cremor*, thick juice or broth; It. Sp. and Pg. *crema*, cream.] Any part of a liquor that separates from the rest, rises, and collects on the surface; more particularly, the richer and butyraceous part of milk, which rises and forms a scum on the surface, as it is specifically lighter than the other part of the liquor; the best part of a thing; the choice part; a sweetmeat prepared from cream (as, ice *cream*). —*Cream of tartar*, the scum of a boiling solution of tartar; a salt obtained from the tartar of argol that forms on the inside of wine casks, frequently employed in medicine.—*v.t.* To skim; to take the cream off by skimming; to take off the best part of. —*v.i.* To gather cream; to gather a covering on the surface; to flower or mantle. (*Shak.*) — **Creamy**, krē'mi, *a.* Full of cream; having the nature of or resembling cream. — **Creaminess**, krē'mi-nes, *n.* The state of being creamy. — **Cream-cake**, *n.* A cake filled with custard made of eggs, cream, &c.—**Cream-cheese**, *n.* A cheese made with milk to which a certain quantity of cream is added.—**Cream-colored**, *a.* Having the color of cream. **Creamer**, krē'mėr, *n.* A pitcher for holding cream; a machine that separates cream from milk.—**Creamery**, krē'mėr-i, *n.* An establishment to which farmers send their milk to be made into butter and cheese.— **Cream-faced**, *a.* White; pale; having a coward look. (*Shak.*)—**Cream-laid**, *a.* A term applied to laid paper of a cream color.—**Cream nut**, *n.* The *Brazil nut.*

Crease, krēs, *n.* [Of Celt. origin; same as Armor. *kriz*, a wrinkle, a plait.] A line or mark made by folding or doubling anything; hence, a similar mark, however produced; specifically, the name given to certain lines marking boundaries near the wickets in the game of cricket.—*v.t. creased, creasing.* To make a crease or mark in, as by folding or doubling.—**Creasy**, krē'si, *a.* Full of creases; characterized by creases. (*Tenn.*)

Crease, krēs, *n.* [Malay.] A Malay dagger. **Creaser**, krēs'ėr, *n.* A tool, or a sewing-machine attachment for making creases on leather or cloth, as guides to see by; in *bookbinding*, a tool for making the band impression distinct on the back or for making blind lines or creases on covers.

Creasote, krē'a-sōt, *n.* CREOSOTE.

Create, krē-āt, *v.t.—created, creating.* [L. *creo, creatum*, to create; same root as Skr. *kri*, to make.] To produce from nothing; to bring into being; to cause to exist; to make or form, by investing with a new character; to constitute; to appoint (to *create* a peer); to be the occasion of; to bring about; to cause; to produce (*create* a disturbance).—**Creatable**, krē-ā'ta-bl, *a.* Capable of being created.—**Creation**, krē-ā'shon, *n.* The act of creating, producing, or causing to exist; especially, the act of bringing this world into existence; the act of investing with a new character; appointment; formation; the things created; that which is produced or caused to exist; the world; the universe.—**Creational**, krē-ā'shon-al, *a.* Pertaining to creation.—**Creative**, krē-ā'tiv, *a.* Having the power to create, or exerting the act of creating.— **Creator**, krē-ā'tėr, *n.* [L.] One who, or that which, creates, produces, causes, or constitutes; distinctively, the almighty Maker of all things.—**Creatorship**, krē-ā'tėr-ship, *n.* The state or condition of a creator. —**Creatress**, krē'āt-res, *n.* She who creates, produces, or constitutes.—**Creature**, krē'tūr, *n.* [O.Fr. *creature*, L.L. *creatura.*] Anything created‡; a thing‡; a created being: any living being; a human being, in contempt or endearment; a person who owes his rise and fortune to another; one who is entirely subject to the will or influence of another; a mere tool.—*a.* Of or belonging to the body (*creature* comforts).— **Creaturely**,† krē'tūr-li, *a.* Of or pertaing to the creature.—**Creatureship**,† krē'tūr-ship, *n.* The state of a creature.

Creatic, krē-at'ik, *a.* [Gr. *kreas, kreatos*, flesh.] Relating to flesh or animal food.— **Creatin**, krē'a-tin, *n.*—**Creatinin**, krē-at'in-in, *n.* Substances obtained from animal flesh by chemical processes.

Creche, krāsh, *n.* [Fr. *crèche*, manger.] An institution or establishment where, for a small payment, children are fed and taken care of during the day, in cases where the mothers daily go from home to work.

Credence, krē'dens, *n.* [L.L. *credentia*, belief, from L. *credens, credentis*, pp. of *credo*, to believe. CREED.] Reliance on evidence derived from other sources than personal knowledge, as from the testimony of others; belief or credit (to give a story *credence*); the small table by the side of the altar or communion table, on which the bread and wine are placed before they are consecrated: called also *Credence-table.*— **Credendum**, krē-den'dum, *n.* pl. **Credenda**, krē-den'da. [L.] A thing to be believed; an article of faith.—**Credent**,† krē'dent, *a.* Believing; giving credit; easy of belief; having credit; not to be questioned. (*Shak.*)—**Credential**, krē-den'shal, *n.* That which gives a title or claim to confidence†; *pl.* testimonials or documents given to a person as the warrant on which belief, credit, or authority is claimed for him among strangers, such as the documents given to an ambassador when sent to a foreign court.

Credible, kred'i-bl, *a.* [L. *credibilis.*] Capable of being believed; such as one may believe; worthy of credit, reliance, or confidence as to truth and correctness: applied to persons and things.—**Credibility, Credibleness**, kred-i-bil'i-ti, kred'i-bl-nes, *n.* The state or quality of being credible.—**Credibly**, kred'i-bli, *adv.* In a credible manner; so as to command belief (to be *credibly* informed).

Credit, kred'it, *n.* [Fr. *crédit*; L. *creditum.* CREED.] Reliance on testimony; belief; faith; trust; good opinion founded on a belief of a man's veracity, integrity, abilities, and virtue; reputation derived from the confidence of others; esteem; honour; what brings some honour or estimation;

reputation for commercial stability or solvency; the selling of goods or lending of money in confidence of future payment; trust; *book-keeping*, the side of an account in which payment or other item lessening the claim against a debtor is entered: opposed to *debit*; the time given for payment for goods sold on trust.—*v.t.* To believe; to confide in the truth of; to sell, or lend in confidence of future payment; to trust; to enter upon the credit side of an account; to give credit for. —*Letter of credit*, an order given by bankers or others at one place to enable a specified person to receive money from their agents at another place.—**Creditable**, kred'i-ta-bl, *a.* Accompanied with reputation or esteem; the cause of credit or honour; honourable; estimable.—**Creditability, Creditableness**, kred'-i-ta-bil"i-ti, kred'i-ta-bl-nes, *n.* The quality of being creditable.—**Creditably**, kred'i-ta-bli, *adv.* Reputably; with credit; without disgrace.—**Creditor**, kred'i-tėr, *n.* [L.] One who gives goods or money on credit; one to whom money is due; one having a just claim for money: correlative to *debtor*.

Credulous, kred'ū-lus, *a.* [L. *credulus*, from *credo*, to believe.] Apt to believe without sufficient evidence; unsuspecting; easily deceived.—**Credulously**, kred'ū-lus-li, *adv.* With credulity.—**Credulousness, Credulity**, kred'ū-lus-nes, kre-dū'-li-ti, *n.* The state or quality of being credulous; disposition or readiness to believe without sufficient evidence.

Creed, krēd, *n.* [A.Sax. *creda*, from L. *credo*, I believe, the first word of the Apostles' Creed, whence also *credence, credit, credible*, also *grant, recreant*.] A brief and authoritative summary of the articles of Christian faith; hence, a statement or profession of fundamental points of belief; a system of principles of any kind which are believed or professed.

Creek, krēk, *n.* [O.E. *creke, cryke*, a creek, a bay; D. *kreek*, Icel. *kriki*, a crack, a corner; akin to *crook*.] A small inlet, bay, or cove; a recess in the shore of the sea or of a river; a stream of water smaller than a river but larger than a brook; a narrow winding passage.

Creel, krēl, *n.* [Gael. *craidhleag*; same root as *cradle*.] An osier basket or pannier; specifically, a large deep fish-basket for carrying on the back.

Creep, krēp, *v.i.* pret. & pp. *crept.* [A.Sax. *creópan* = D. *kruipen*, Icel. *krjúpa*, Sw. *krypa*, Dan. *krybe*, to creep or crawl; akin *cripple, cramp*.] To move with the belly on the ground or any surface, as a reptile, or as many insects with feet and very short legs; to crawl; to move along a surface in growth (as a vine); to move slowly, feebly, or timorously; to move slowly and insensibly, as time; to move secretly or insidiously; to move or behave with extreme servility or humility; to cringe; to fawn; to have a sensation such as might be caused by worms or insects creeping on the skin.—**Creeper**, krē'pėr, *n.* One who or that which creeps; a creeping plant, which moves along the surface of the earth, or attaches itself to some other body, as ivy; an instrument of iron with hooks or claws for dragging the bottom of a well, river, or harbour; a popular name of birds which resemble the woodpeckers in their habits of creeping on the stems of trees in quest of insect prey.—*n.* The act of creeping, or moving slowly and insensibly.—**Creephole**, krēp'hōl, *n.* A hole for hiding in; a subterfuge; an excuse.—**Creepingly**, krē'ping-li, *adv.* By creeping; slowly; in the manner of a reptile.

Creese, krēs, *n.* A crease or Malay dagger.

Cremate, krē-māt', *v.t.—cremated, cremating.* [L. *cremo, crematum*, to burn.] To burn; to dispose of (a human body) by burning instead of interring. —**Cremation**, krē-mā'shon, *n.* The act or custom of cremating; the burning of a dead body instead of burial.—**Cremationist**, krē-mā'shon-ist, *n.* One who favours the practice of cremation.—**Crematory**, krē'ma-to-ri, *a.* Connected with or employed in cremation. —*n.* A place for cremation.

Cremona, krē-mō'na, *n.* A general name given to the unrivalled violins made at *Cremona* in North Italy in the seventeenth and eighteenth centuries.

Cremor, krē'mor, *n.* [L.] A creamy liquor, or substance resembling cream.

Crenate, Crenated, krē'nāt, krē'nā-ted, *a.* [L. *crenatus*, notched, *crena*, a notch.] Notched; indented; scalloped; *bot.* applied to a leaf having its margin cut into even and rounded notches or scallops.—**Crenature**, krē'na-tūr, *n.* A tooth of a crenate leaf, or any other part that is crenate.

Crenelle, kre-nel', *n.* [O.Fr. *crenel*, from L. *crena*, a notch.] An embrasure in an embattled parapet or breastwork to fire through; an indentation; a notch.—**Crenellate**, krē'nel-lāt, *v.t.* To furnish with crenelles or similar openings; to embattle. —**Crenellation**, krē-nel-lā'shon, *n.* The act of crenellating; a crenelle or indentation. —**Crenulate, Crenulated**, krē'nū-lāt, krē'nū-lā-ted, *a.* Having the edge cut into very small scallops, as a leaf or a shell.

Creodonta, krē'od-on"ta. [Gr. *kreas*, flesh, *ŏdons, odŏntŏs*, a tooth.] Primitive carnivorous mammals, now extinct.

Creole, krē'ōl, *n.* [Fr. *créole*, Sp. *criollo*; said to be of Negro origin.] A native of the West Indies or Spanish America, but not of indigenous blood: sometimes restricted to descendants of Europeans.—**Creolean**, krē-ō'lē-an, *a.* Pertaining to or resembling Creoles.

Creosote, krē'ō-sōt, *n.* CREASOTE.

Creosote, krē'ō-sōt, *n.* A heavy, oily colorless liquid of strong odor obtained from wood tar, used as a powerful antiseptic in surgery and for minor cuts.

Crepitate, krep'i-tāt, *v.i.—crepitated, crepitating.* [L. *crepito, crepitatum*, freq. from *crepo*, to crackle (whence *crevice*).] To burst with a small sharp abrupt sound rapidly repeated, as salt in fire or during calcination; to crackle; to snap.—**Crepitant**, krep'i-tant, *a.* Relating to the sound of the lungs in pneumonia; crackling.

Crepuscular, krē-pus'kū-lėr, *a.* [L. *crepusculum*, twilight.] Pertaining to twilight; glimmering; flying or appearing in the twilight or evening, or before sunrise, as certain insects.

Crescendo, kre-shen'dō. [It.] *Mus.* a term signifying that the notes of the passage are to be gradually swelled: usually written *Cres.*, and marked thus $<$.

Crescent, kres'ent, *a.* [L. *crescens, crescentis*, from *cresco*, to grow, seen also in *increase, decrease, accrue, concrete*, &c.] Increasing; growing; waxing. (*Mil.*)—*n.* The increasing or new moon, which, when receding from the sun, shows a curving rim of light terminating in points or horns; anything shaped like a new moon, as a range of buildings whose fronts form a concave curve; the figure or likeness of the new moon, as that borne in the Turkish flag or national standard; the standard itself, and figuratively, the Turkish power. —**Crescented**, kres'en-ted, *a.* Adorned with a crescent; shaped like a crescent.—**Crescentic**, kre-sen'tik, *a.* Crescent-shaped.

Cress, kres, *n.* [A.Sax. *cærse, cresse* = D *kers*, G. *kresse*, Sw. *karse*.] The name of various plants, mostly cruciferous, in general use as a salad, such as water-cress, common in streams, and having a pungent taste; garden cress, a dwarf cultivated species; Indian cress, a showy garden annual whose fruits are made into pickles. —**Cressy**, kres'i, *a.* Abounding in cresses. (*Tenn.*)

Cresselle, kre-sel', *n.* [Fr. *crécelle*.] A wooden rattle used in some Roman Catholic countries during Passion Week instead of bells.

Cresset, kres'et, *n.* [O.Fr. *crusset, crasset*; akin to E. *cruse*, G. *kruse*, a jar.] A term most commonly applied to a lamp or firepan suspended on pivots and carried on a pole, or to a beacon light in a kind of iron basket; also a large lamp formerly hung in churches, &c.

Crest, krest, *n.* [O.Fr. *creste*, L. *crista*, a crest.] A tuft or other excrescence upon the top of an animal's head, as the comb of a cock, &c.; anything resembling, suggestive of, or occupying the same relative position as a crest, as the plume or tuft of feathers, or the like, affixed to the top of the helmet; *her.* a figure placed upon a wreath, coronet, or cap of maintenance above both helmet and shield; the foamy, feather-like top of a wave; the highest part or summit of a hill, ridge, slope, or the like; the rising part of a horse's neck; *fig.* pride, high spirit, courage, daring (*Shak.*). —*v.t.* To furnish with a crest; to serve as a crest for; to adorn as with a plume or crest.—**Crested**, kres'ted, *a.* Furnished with a crest or crests.—**Crestless**, krest'les, *a.* Without a crest; without a family crest, and hence of low birth (*Shak.*). —**Crest-fallen**, *a.* Dejected; sunk; bowed; dispirited; spiritless.

Cretaceous, krē-tā'shus, *a.* [L. *cretaceus*, from *creta*, chalk.] Composed of or having the qualities of chalk; like chalk; abounding with chalk; chalky.—*Cretaceous group*, in *geol.* the upper strata of the secondary series, immediately below the tertiary series, and superincumbent on the oolite system, containing immense chalk beds.

Cretic, kret-ik, *n.* A metrical foot in Greek verse, consisting of — ⏑ — (i.e., long, short, long).

Cretin, krē'tin, *n.* [Fr. *crétin*.] A name given to certain deformed and helpless idiots in the valleys of the Alps.—**Cretinism**, krē'tin-izm, *n.* The state of a cretin; a peculiar endemic disease resembling rickets, but accompanied with idiocy, common in Switzerland, and found also in some other mountainous countries.

Cretonne, kre-ton', *n.* [Fr.] A cotton cloth with various textures of surface printed with pictorial and other patterns, and used for curtains, covering furniture, &c.

Creutzer, kroit'sėr, *n.* KREUTZER.

Crevasse, krē-vas', *n.* [Fr. *crevasse*. CREVICE.] A fissure or rent: generally applied to a fissure across a glacier, and in the United States to a breach in the embankment of a river.

Crevice, krev'is, *n.* [Fr. *crevasse*, from *crever*, L. *crepare*, to burst, to crack; akin *craven, crepitate, decrepit*.] A crack; a cleft; a fissure; a cranny; a rent.—*v.t.* To crack; to flaw.

Crew, krö, *n.* [From O. Icel. *krú*, a swarm; or for old *accrue*, number added, company. ACCRUE.] A company of people; an assemblage; a crowd; a band; a gang; a herd; a horde; a company; the company of seamen who man a ship, vessel, or boat; the company belonging to a vessel.

Crew, krö, pret. of *crow*.

Crewel, krö'el, *n.* [From D. *krul*, a curl.] A kind of fine worsted or thread of silk or wool, used in embroidery and fancy work.

Crib, krib, *n.* [A.Sax. *crib, cribb*, D. *kribbe*, Dan. *krybbe*, Icel. and Sw. *krubba*, G. *krippe*, a crib.] A small habitation or cottage; a hovel; the manger or rack of a stable or house for cattle; a feeding-place for cattle; a small frame or bed for a child to sleep in; a theft, or the thing stolen (*colloq.*); a literal translation of a classic author for the use of students (*colloq.*); in the game of cribbage, a set of cards made up of two thrown from the hand of each player.—*v.t. cribbed, cribbing.* To shut or confine in a narrow habitation; to cage (*Shak.*); to pilfer or purloin (*colloq.*). —**Cribbage**, krib'āj, *n.* A game at cards played with the whole pack by two, three, or four persons; so called because the dealer receives a *crib*, or additional hand partly drawn from the hands of his opponent or opponents. —*Cribbage-board*, a board used for marking in the game of cribbage.

Cribble, krib'l, *n.* [L. *cribellum*, dim. of *cribrum*, a sieve.] A corn-sieve or riddle; coarse flour or meal.—*v.t.—cribbled, cribbling.* To sift; to cause to pass through a sieve or riddle.—**Cribrate, Cribrose**, krī'brāt, krī'brōs, *a.* [L. *cribrum*, a sieve.] Perforated like a sieve.—**Cribration**, kribrā'shon, *n.* The act of sifting or riddling. —**Cribriform**, krib'ri-form, *a.* Resembling a sieve or riddle; pierced with holes.

Crick, krik, *n.* [Akin to *crook.*] A spasmodic affection of some part of the body, as of the neck or back, making motion of the part difficult.

Cricket, krik'et, *n.* [O.Fr. *criquet*, from its sharp creaking sound; comp. D. *kriek*, a cricket, *krieken*, to chirp. Akin *creak*, *crack.*] An orthopterous insect of several species, nearly allied to the grasshoppers, noted for the chirping or creaking sound produced by the friction of the bases of its wing-cases against each other.—**Cricket-bird**, *n.* The grasshopper warbler, so called from its note resembling that of a cricket.

Cricket, krik'et, *n.* [Fr. *criquet*, a kind of game.] A favorite open-air game played in England, Australia, and other British possessions, generally by two sides of eleven each, with bats, ball, and wickets. —*v.i.* To engage in the game of cricket.

Cricoid, krī'koid, *a.* [Gr. *krikos*, a ring, and *eidos*, appearance.] Ring-like: applied to a round ring-like cartilage of the larynx.

Crier, krī'ėr, *n.* Under Cry.

Crime, krīm, *n.* [Fr. *crime*, L. *crimen*, an accusation, a crime; allied to *cerno*, to sift, *cribrum*, a sieve; Gr. *krinō*, to separate, judge, condemn.] A violation of a law whether human or divine; specifically, a gross violation of law, as distinguished from a misdemeanour, trespass, or other slight offence; any great wickedness or iniquity; a foul wrong; offence. — **Crimeful**,† krīm'fụl, *a.* Criminal; wicked. (*Shak.*)—**Crimeless**, krīm'les, *a.* Free from crime; innocent. — **Criminal**, krim'i-nal, *a.* Guilty of a crime; culpable; wicked; iniquitous; atrocious; abandoned; villainous; felonious; nefarious; partaking of the nature of a crime; involving a crime; that violates public law, divine or human; relating to crime: opposed to *civil.*—*Criminal conversation*, in *law*, adultery; illicit intercourse with a married woman.—*n.* A person guilty of crime; a person indicted or charged with a public offence and found guilty; a culprit; a malefactor. — **Criminalist**, krim'i-nal-ist, *n.* An authority in criminal law; one versed in criminal law.—**Criminality, Criminalness**, krim-i-nal'i-ti, krim'i-nal-nes, *n.* The quality or state of being criminal; that which constitutes a crime; guiltiness.—**Criminally**, krim'i-nal-li, *adv.* In a criminal or wicked manner.—**Criminate**, krim'i-nāt, *v.t.*—*criminated, criminating.* [L. *criminor, criminatus.*] To accuse or charge with a crime; to involve in a crime or the consequences of a crime. — **Crimination**, krim-i-nā'shon, *n.* The act of criminating; accusation; charge.—**Criminative, Criminatory**, krim'i-nā-tiv, krim'i-na-to-ri, *a.* Relating to accusation; accusing.—**Criminology**, krim'i-nol"ō-ji, *n.* The science of crime.—**Criminous**, krim'i-nus, *a.* Criminal.

Crimp, krimp, *v.t.* A lighter form of *cramp*; D. *krimpen*, Dan. *krympe*, G. *krimpen*, to shrink; akin *crumple.*] To curl or crisp, as the hair; to flute or make regular ridges on, as on a frill; to crimple; to pinch and hold; to seize; hence, to decay for service in the army or navy (see noun); *cookery*, to gash the flesh of a live fish with a knife, to give it greater hardness and make it more crisp.—*n.* One who decoys another into the naval or military service; one who decoys sailors by treating, advancing money, boarding and lodging, giving goods on credit, &c., and when he has them in his power, induces them to engage with a shipmaster whom it is the crimp's interest to serve. —**Crimping-iron**, *n.* An iron for curling the hair.—**Crimping-machine**, *n.* A machine for forming a kind of plaiting or fluting on frills or ruffles.—**Crimple**, krim'pl, *v.t.*—*crimpled, crimpling.* [Dim. of *crimp.*] To contract or draw together; to cause to shrink; to curl; to crimp.—**Crimper**, krim'pėr, *n.* One who or that which crimps; a name of various machines.

Crimp, krimp, *a.* [Probably allied to *crumb.*] Easily crumbled; friable; brittle.

Crimson, krim'zn, *n.* [O.Fr. *cramoisin*, from L.L. *carmesinus*, from Ar. *kermez*, *qirmiz*, the kermes insect, which yields the dye; akin *carmine.*] A deep red colour; a rich red slightly tinged with blue; a red colour in general.—*a.* Of a deep red colour. —*v.t.* To dye with crimson; to make red.—*v.i.* To become of a crimson colour; to be tinged with red; to blush.

Crinal, krī'nal, *a.* [L. *crinis*, hair.] Belonging to hair.

Cringe, krinj, *v.i.* *cringed, cringing.* [A. Sax. *cringan*, *crincan*, to cringe, succumb, from root of *crank*, *crinkle*, &c.] To bend or crouch with servility; to fawn; to stoop or truckle.—*n.* A mean or fawning obeisance. — *v.t.*‡ To contract; to draw together; to distort. (*Shak.*)—**Cringeling**, krinj'ling, *n.* One who cringes meanly.—**Cringer**, krin'jėr, *n.* One who cringes or bows and flatters with servility.—**Cringingly**, krin'jing-li, *adv.* In a cringing manner.

Cringle, kring'gl, *n.* [D. *kring*, *krinkel*, a curl, bend, ring; Icel. *kringla*, an orb, from *kringr*, a circle; A.Sax. *kring*, a ring. Akin *ring, cringe.*] A withe for fastening a gate; *naut.* an iron ring, or a short rope worked into the bolt-rope of a sail so as to form a ring or eye, &c.

Crinite, krī'nīt, *a.* [L. *crinitus*, from *crinis*, hair.] Having the appearance of a tuft of hair†; *bot.* having tufts of long weak hairs on the surface.

Crinkle, kring'kl, *v.i.*—*crinkled, crinkling.* [D. *krinkelen*, to turn or wind; akin *crank.*] To turn or wind; to bend; to wrinkle; to run in and out in little or short bends or turns; to curl.—*v.t.* To form with short turns or wrinkles; to make with many flexures.—*n.* A wrinkle; a winding or turn; sinuosity.

Crinoid, krī'noid, *n.* [Gr. *krinon*, a lily, *eidos*, likeness.] A lily-star or sea-lily; one of an order of echinoderms having star-shaped bodies, supported by a long, slender, calcareous jointed stem; most of the species are fossil. —**Crinoid, Crinoidal**, krī'-noid, krī'noi-dal, *a.* Containing or consisting of the fossil remains of crinoids.

Crinoline, krin'o-lin, *n.* [Fr., from *crin*, L. *crinis*, hair, and *lin*, L. *linum*, flax] A stiff fabric of horse-hair, &c.; a skirt or petticoat stiffened by horse-hair, hoops, &c.

Crinose,† krī'nōs, *a.* Hairy.

Crio-sphinx, krī'ō-sfingks, *n.* [Gr. *krios*, a ram, and *sphinx.*] A sphinx having the head of a ram.

Cripple, krip'l, *n.* [A.Sax. *crypel* = G. *krüppel*, Icel. *kryppil*, a cripple, D. *kreupel*, lame; from stem of *creep.*] One who halts or limps; one who has lost or never enjoyed the use of his limbs; a lame person. —*a.* Lame.—*v.t.*—*crippled, crippling.* To disable by injuring the limbs, particularly the legs or feet; to lame; to deprive of the power of exertion; to disable (a *crippled* fleet).

Crisis, krī'sis, *n.* pl. **Crises**, krī'sēz. [L. *crisis*, Gr. *krisis*, from the root of *krinō*, to separate, to determine. Crime.] The change of a disease which indicates recovery or death; the decisive state of things, or the point of time when an affair has reached its height, and must soon terminate or suffer a material change; turning-point; conjuncture.

Crisp, krisp, *a.* [A.Sax. *crisp*, *crips*, from L. *crispus*, curled, crisp.] Curling in small stiff or firm curls; indented or winding†; easily broken or crumbled; brittle; friable; possessing a certain degree of firmness and freshness; fresh; brisk, effervescing or foaming; sparkling.—*v.t.* To curl; to contract or form into ringlets; to wrinkle or curl into little undulations; to ripple.—*v.i.* To form little curls or undulations; to curl. (*Tenn.*)—**Crispate**, kris'pāt, *a.* Having a crisped appearance.—**Crisper**, kris'pėr, *n.* One who or that which crisps or curls; an instrument for friezing or crisping cloth. —**Crisply**, krisp'li, *adv.* In a crisp manner.—**Crispness**, krisp'nes, *n.* State of being crisp.—**Crispy**, kris'pi, *a.* Curled; formed into ringlets; brittle; dried so as to break short.—**Crisping-iron, Crisping-pin**, *n.* A curling-iron.

Crispin, kris'pin, *n.* A colloquial name for a shoemaker, from *Crispin* or *Crispinus*, the patron saint of the craft; the anniversary of the battle of Agincourt—October 25, 1415.

Cristate, Cristated, kris'tāt, kris'tā-ted, *a.* [L. *cristatus*, from *crista*, a crest.] *Bot.* having an appendage like a crest or tuft, as some anthers and flowers; crested; tufted.

Criterion, krī-tē'ri-on, *n.* pl. **Criteria**, krī-tē'ri-a. [Gr. *kriterion*, from root of *krinō*, to judge. Crime.] A standard of judging; any established law, rule, principle, or fact by which a correct judgment may be formed.

Crith, krith. [Gr. *krithē*, a barley-corn.] The unit of mass for gases, being the mass of a litre of hydrogen gas at normal temperature and pressure (N.T.P.), equal to ·0896 gm.

Critic, krit'ik, *n.* [L. *criticus*, Gr. *kritikos*, from *kritēs*, a judge, from *krinō*, to judge. Crime.] A person skilled in judging of the merit of literary works; a judge of merit or excellence in the fine arts generally; a writer whose chief function it is to pass judgment on matters of literature and art; a reviewer; one who judges with severity; one who censures or finds fault.—**Critical**, krit'i-kal, *a.* Relating to criticism; belonging to the art of a critic; passing judgment upon literary and artistic matters; inclined to make nice distinctions; nicely judicious; exact; fastidious; inclined to find fault or to judge with severity; *med.* pertaining to the crisis or turning-point of a disease; pertaining to any crisis; decisive; important, as regards consequences (a *critical* time or juncture); momentous; attended with danger or risk; dangerous; hazardous (a *critical* undertaking.—*Critical angle. Optics*, the angle of incidence of a ray passing from one medium into a less refracting medium, when it emerges along the bounding surface. — *Critical temperature*, that temperature of a gas above which no pressure, however great, can liquefy it.—**Critically**, kri'tik-al-li, *adv.* In a critical manner; with nice discernment or scrutiny; at the crisis: at the exact time; in a critical situation, place. or condition.—**Criticalness**, kri'i-kal-nes, *n.* The state of being critical.—**Criticaster**, krit'i-kas-tėr, *n.* A small or inferior critic.—**Criticize**, krit'i-sīz, *v.t.*—*criticized, criticizing.* To judge critically, estimating beauties and defects; to pick out faults; to utter censure.—*v.t.* To examine or judge critically; to notice beauties and blemishes or faults in; to pass judgment on with respect to merit or blame; to animadvert upon. Also written **Criticise**.—**Criticizable**, krit'i-sī-za-bl, *a.* Capable of being criticized.—**Criticism**, krit'i-sizm, *n.* The art of judging with propriety of the beauties and faults of a literary performance or of any production in the fine arts; the art of judging on the merit of any performance; a critical judgment; a detailed critical examination; a critique.—**Critique**, kri-tēk', *n.* [Fr.] A written estimate of the merits of a performance, especially of a literary or artistic performance; a criticism.

Crizzle, Crizzel, kriz'l, *n.* A roughness on the surface of glass which dulls its transparency; any roughness on a surface.

Croak, krōk, *v.i.* [Purely imitative, like M.H.G. *krochzen*, G. *krächzen*, Fr. *croasser*, L. *crocire*, *crocitare*, Gr. *krōzein*, to croak.] To make a low, hoarse noise in the throat, as a frog, a raven, or crow; to produce any low harsh sound; to speak with a low, hollow voice; to forebode evil; to complain; to grumble.—*v.t.* To utter in a low hollow voice; to murmur out; to announce or herald by croaking. — *n.* The low, harsh sound uttered by a frog or a raven, or a like sound.—**Croaker**, krō'kėr, *n.* One that croaks, murmurs, or grumbles; one who complains unreasonably; one who takes a desponding view of everything; an alarmist.—**Croaking, Croaky**, krō'king, krō'ki, *a.* Having or uttering a low harsh sound; hoarse; grumbling.

Crochet, krō'shā, *n.* [Fr., dim. of *croc*, a hook.] A species of knitting performed by means of a small hook, the material being worsted, cotton, or silk.—*v.t.* To knit in this style.

Crocidolite, krō-sid'o-līt, *n.* [Gr. *krokis*, nap of cloth, *lithos*, stone.] A sort of fibrous quartz from Cape Colony, made into trinkets, &c.

Crock, krok, *n.* [A.Sax. *crocca*=D. *kruik*, Icel. *krukka*, Dan. *krukke*, G. *krug*, an earthen vessel, pitcher.] An earthen vessel; a pot or pitcher; the soot or smut from pots, kettles, &c.—**Crockery**, krok'ėr-i, *n.* Earthenware; vessels formed of clay, glazed and baked.

Crocket, krok'et, *n.* [Akin to *crochet* or to *crook.*] An architectural ornament, usually in imitation of curved and bent foliage, &c., placed on the angles of the inclined sides of pinnacles, canopies, gables, &c.; one of the terminal snags on a stag's horn.

Crocodile, krok'ō-dīl, *n.* [L. *crocodilus*, Gr. *krokodeilos.*] A large aquatic reptile of the lizard kind, sometimes reaching the length of 30 feet, and having a long and powerful tail flattened at the sides, the body covered with square bony plates, the jaws long, and the gape of enormous width; the best known species haunt the Nile.—*a.* Of or pertaining to or like a crocodile.—*Crocodile tears*, false or affected tears: in allusion to the old fiction that crocodiles shed tears over their victims.—**Crocodilean, Crocodilian**, krok-ō-dil'ē-an, krok-ō-dil'i-an, *a.* Relating to the crocodile.—**Crocodilian**, *n.* A reptile of the order (*Crocodilia*) which includes the true crocodile, the alligator, the gavial, &c.

Crocus, krō'kus, *n.* [L. *crocus*, Gr. *krokos*, saffron, also the *crocus.*] A beautiful genus of European plants, consisting of many hardy species, some of which are vernal and others autumnal, and are well known in gardens, the flowers appearing before the grass-like leaves; saffron; the long orange-reddish stigmas of an autumnal species dried; the commercial name of a red or deep yellow polishing powder made with oxide of iron.

Croft, kroft, *n.* [A.Sax. *croft*, a field; D. *kroft*, a hillock; O.D. *krocht*, a field.] A small piece of inclosed ground adjoining a dwelling-house, and used for pasture, tillage, or other purposes; a very small farm.—**Crofter**, krof'tėr, *n.* One who cultivates a croft.

Cromlech, krom'lek, *n.* [W. *cromlech*—*crom*, bent, concave, and *llech*, a flat stone.] An ancient structure (probably a sepulchral monument) consisting of two or more large unhewn stones fixed upright in the ground supporting a large flat stone in a horizontal position.

Cromorna, krō-mor'na, *n.* [From G. *krummhorn*, crooked horn.] A stop or set of pipes in an organ with a clarionet-like tone.

Crone, krōn, *n.* [Formerly *crony*, from D. *karonie*, a hussy, a slut, lit. a *carrion.* CARRION.] A contemptuous term for an old woman.—**Crony**, krō'ni, *n.* A crone‡; an intimate companion; an associate; a familiar friend.

Crook, krök, *n.* [Same as Icel. *krókr*, Sw. *krok*, Dan. *krog*, a hook or crook; D. *kruk*, a crutch; comp. W. *crwg*, Gael. *crocan*, a crook, a hook. Akin *crutch*, *crouch.*] Any bend, turn, or curve; curvature; flexure; any bent or curved instrument; especially, a shepherd's staff, curving at the end, or the staff of a bishop or abbot, fashioned in the form of a shepherd's staff, as a symbol of his sway over and care for his flock; a pastoral staff; a small curved tube applied to a trumpet, horn, &c., to change its key; an artifice; a trick.—*v.t.* To bend; to turn from a straight line; to make a curve or hook.—*v.i.* To bend or be bent; to be turned from a straight line; swindler, sharper.—**Crooked**, krö'ked, *a.* Deviating from a straight line; bent, curved, or winding; wry or deformed; deviating from the path of rectitude; perverse, deceitful, devious, or froward.—**Crookedly**, krö'ked-li, *adv.* In a crooked, curved, or perverse manner.—**Crookedness**, krö'ked-nes, *n.* The state or quality of being crooked.

Croon, krön, *v.t.* and *i.* [Imitative of sound; D. *kreunen*, to groan, to lament.] To sing in a low humming tone; to hum; to utter a low, continued, plaintive sound.

Crop, krop, *n.* [A.Sax. *crop*, top, bunch, craw of a bird; D. *krop*, G. *kropf*, a bird's crop; Icel. *kroppr*, a hump, bunch.] The first stomach of a fowl; the craw; that which is cropped, cut, or gathered from a single field; the quantity of a particular kind of grain, fruit, &c., obtained from a single field or in a single season; the corn or fruits of the earth collected; harvest; corn and other cultivated plants while growing; the act of cutting or clipping off, as hair.—*Hunting crop*, a riding-whip with loop at end, with no lash.—*Neck and crop*, bodily; altogether; bag and baggage.—*v.t.* —*cropped, cropping.* To cut off the ends of; to eat off or browse; to pull off; to pluck; to mow; to reap; to cause to bear a crop; to raise crops on.—*v.i.* To yield harvest‡. (*Shak.*)—*To crop out*, to appear on the surface; to appear incidentally and undesignedly; to come to light.—**Cropper**, krop'ėr, *n.* A breed of pigeons with a large crop; one who raises crops, generally receiving his wages in the form of shares of the crops. Known also as a *share-cropper.*—**Crop-sick**, *a.* Sick or indisposed from a surcharged stomach.

Croquet, krō'kā, *n.* [Fr. *croquer*, to crack.] An open-air game played by two or more persons with mallets, balls, pegs or posts, and a series of iron hoops or arches, the object of each party being to drive their balls through the hoops and against the posts in a certain order before their opponents.

Crore, krōr, *n.* In the East Indies, ten millions (a *crore* of rupees).

Crosier, *n.* CROZIER.

Cross, kros, *n.* [Prov. *cros*, Fr. *croix*, from L. *crux*, *crucis*, a cross used as a gibbet, from same root as that of W. *crog*, a cross, *crwg*, a hook; Ir. *crochaim*, to hang; Gael. *crocan*, a hook.] An instrument on which malefactors were anciently put to death, consisting of two pieces of timber placed across each other, either in form of +, T, or X, variously modified, such as that on which Christ suffered; hence, the symbol of the Christian religion; and hence, *fig.* the religion itself; an ornament in the form of a cross; a monument with a cross upon it to excite devotion, such as were anciently set in market-places; any figure, mark, or sign in the form of a cross, or formed by two lines crossing each other, such as the mark made instead of a signature by those who cannot write; anything that thwarts, obstructs, or perplexes; hindrance, vexation, misfortune, or opposition; a mixing of breeds; a hybrid.—*a.* Transverse; passing from side to side; falling athwart; adverse; thwarting; untoward; perverse; intractable; peevish; fretful; ill-humoured; contrary; contradictory; perplexing; made or produced by the opposite party, as a *cross* question or examination.—*v.t.* To draw or run a line or lay a body across another; to erase by marking crosses on or over; to cancel; to make the sign of the cross upon; to pass from side to side of; to pass or move over; to thwart, obstruct, hinder, embarrass; to contradict; to counteract; to clash with; to be inconsistent with; to cause to interbreed; to mix the breed of.—*v.i.* To lie or be athwart; to move or pass across.—*To cross one's path*, to thwart or oppose one's interest, purpose, designs, &c.; to stand in one's way.—*Crossed cheque*, in *banking*, a cheque crossed with two lines, between which may be written the name of a banking firm or the words 'and Co.', such marks being made as an additional security that the sum shall be paid to the proper party.—**Crossing**, kros'ing, *n.* The act of one who crosses; an intersection; a place specially set apart or adapted for passing across, as on a street or line of rails.—**Crosslet**, kros'let, *n.* A little cross.—**Crossly**, kros'li, *adv.* In a cross manner; athwart; transversely; *fig.* adversely; in opposition; unfortunately; peevishly; fretfully.—**Crossness**, kros'nes, *n.* The state or quality of being cross; peevishness; ill-humour; fretfulness; perverseness.—**Crosswise**, kros'wīz, *adv.* In the form of a cross; across.—**Cross-action**, *n. Law*, a case in which the defendant in an action brings another action against the plaintiff arising out of the same transaction.—**Cross bench**, *n.* The seats in the House of Commons for members attached to no political party.—**Cross-bill**, *n.* A bird of several species belonging to the finch family, the mandibles of whose bill curve opposite ways and cross each other at the points.—**Cross-bones**, *n. pl.* A symbol of death, consisting of two human thigh or arm bones placed crosswise, generally in conjunction with a skull.—**Cross-bow**, *n.* An ancient missive weapon formed by placing a bow athwart a stock.—**Cross-bred**, *a.* A term applied to an animal produced from a male and female of different breeds.—**Cross-breed**, *n.* A breed produced from parents of different breeds. —**Cross-breeding**, *n.* The system of breeding animals, such as horses, cattle, dogs, and sheep, from individuals of two different strains or varieties.—**Cross-cut**, *v.t.* To cut across.—*Crosscut-saw*, a saw adapted for cutting timber across the grain.—**Cross-examine**, *v.t.* To examine a witness of one party by the opposite party in the suit or his counsel.—**Cross-examination**, *n.* The examination or interrogation of a witness called by one party by the opposite party or his counsel.—**Cross-eye**, *n.* That sort of squint by which both eyes turn towards the nose.—**Cross-fertilization**, *n. Bot.* the fertilization of the ovules of one plant by the pollen of another; the fecundation of a pistilliferous plant by a staminiferous one, which is effected by the agency of insects, the action of the wind, water, &c.—**Cross-fire**, *n. Milit.* a term used to denote that the lines of fire from two or more parts of a work cross one another.—**Cross-garter**, *v.t.* To cross the garters on the leg. (*Shak.*)—**Cross-grained**, *a.* Having the grain or fibres transverse or irregular, as timber; *fig.* perverse; intractable; crabbed.—**Cross-hatching**, *n.* Engraved lines which cross each other regularly to increase or modify the depth of shadow.—**Cross-head**, *n.* A beam or rod stretching across the end of the piston of a steam-engine and moving between parallel guides.—**Cross-multiplication**, *n.* DUODECIMAL.—**Cross-pollination**, *n.* Same as *Cross-fertilisation.*—**Cross-purpose**, *n.* A contrary purpose; a misunderstanding; an inconsistency; *pl.* a sort of conversational game consisting in the mixing up of questions and answers.—*To be at cross-purposes*, to misunderstand each other, and so to act counter without intending it.—**Cross-question**, *v.t.* To cross-examine.—**Cross-reference**, *n.* A reference from one part of a book to another where additional information on the subject is to be had.—**Cross-road**, *n.* A road that crosses another, or the place where one road intersects another; a by-road.—**Cross-sea**, *n.* A swell in which the waves run in different directions, owing to a sudden change of wind, or to the opposing effect of winds and currents.—**Cross-section**, *n.* Strictly, the cutting of any body at right angles to its length, but often used to denote the area of the surface thus exposed.—**Cross-staff**, *n.* A surveying instrument consisting of a staff carrying a brass circle, divided into four equal parts or quadrants: used for taking offsets.—**Cross-stone**, *n.* A grayish-white or milk-white mineral of the zeolite family: so-called from the joint-like intersection of its rhombic crystals.—**Cross-tree**, *n. pl. Naut.* horizontal pieces of timber at the upper ends of the lower and top masts, to sustain the frame of the tops and extend the shrouds.

Crotch, kroch, *n.* [Same as CRUTCH.] A fork or forking; the parting of two branches.

Crotchet, kroch'et, *n.* [Fr. *crochet*, dim. from *croc*, a hook. CROCHET, CROOK.] A peculiar turn of the mind; a whim or fancy; a perverse conceit; *print.* a bracket; *music*, a black-faced note with a stem.—**Crotcheteer**, kroch-e-tēr', *n.* One given to some favourite theory, whim, hobby, project, or crotchet.—**Crotchety**, kroch'e-ti, *a.* Full of crotchets; whimsical; fanciful; odd.—**Crotchetiness**, kroch'e-ti-nes, *n.* The state of being crotchety.

Croton, krō'ton, *n.* [Gr. *krotōn*, a tick, from the appearance of the seeds.] A genus of East Indian shrubs from the seeds of which is extracted an oil of active and dangerous purgative properties, and which, when applied externally, acts as an irritant and suppurative.

Crouch, krouch, *v.i.* [A softened form of *crook*, with modification of meaning.] To bend down; to stoop low; to lie close to the ground, as an animal; to bend servilely; to stoop meanly; to fawn; to cringe.—*v.t.* To bend or cause to bend lowly.

Croup, kröp, *n.* [Fr. *croupe*, the rump, croup. Same origin as *crop*.] The rump or buttocks of certain animals, especially of a horse; hence, the place behind the saddle.

Croup, **Croop**, kröp, *n.* [Sc. *croup*, *roup*, hoarseness; allied to Goth. *hropjan*, to croak, to call; A.Sax. *hreópan*, to call.] A dangerous disease mostly attacking children, and consisting of inflammatory affection of the windpipe, accompanied with a short barking cough and difficult respiration, generally brought on by exposure to cold.

Croupier, krö'pē-ėr, *n.* [Fr. *croupier*, from *croupe*, the rump or hinder part.] One who superintends and collects the money at a gaming-table; one who at a public dinner party sits at the lower end of the table as assistant-chairman.

Crow, krō, *n.* [A.Sax. *cráwe*, a crow, *cráwan*, to crow or croak, from the cry; like G. *krähe*, a crow, *krähen*, to crow; Goth. *kruk*, a croaking; L. *crocio*, Gr. *krazō*, to croak. Comp. *crake*, *croak*.] The general name of such conirostral birds as the raven, rook, jackdaw, carrion crow, hooded crow, &c.; usually of a black colour, and having the voice harsh and croaking; the cry of the cock; a crowbar (which see).—*As the crow flies*, in a direction straight forward, resembling the flight of the crow.—*To have a crow to pluck with one*, to have something demanding explanation from one; to have some fault to find with one; to have a disagreeable matter to settle.—*v.i. crowed* or *crew*; pp. *crowed*. [A.Sax. *cráwan*.] To cry or make a noise as a cock in joy, gaiety, or defiance; to boast in triumph; to vaunt; to vapour; to swagger; to utter a sound expressive of pleasure, as a child.—**Crowbar**, krō'bär, *n.* A bar of iron with a bent and sometimes forked end, used as a lever for forcing open doors or raising weights.—**Crow-berry**, *n.* The jet-black berry of a small evergreen shrub common on heaths in Scotland and north of England.—**Crow-foot**, *n. Naut.* a complication of small cords spreading out from a long block, used to suspend the awnings, &c.; a popular name for the species of buttercups, from the leaf being supposed to have the shape of the foot of a crow.—**Crow-quill**, *n.* A crow's feather made into a pen and used where very fine writing is required, as in lithography, tracing, &c.—**Crow's-bill**, *n.* A kind of forceps for extracting bullets and other things from wounds.—**Crow's-feet**, *n. pl.* The wrinkles brought on by age under and around the outer corners of the eyes.—**Crow's-foot**, *n.* A caltrop (which see).—**Crow's-nest**, *n.* A barrel or box fitted up on the main-topmast cross-trees of an Arctic vessel for the shelter of the look-out man.

Crowd, kroud, *n.* [A.Sax. *crúdan*, to press; O.D. *cruden*, to press, to push; L.G. *krüden*, to oppress.] A number of persons or things collected or closely pressed together; a number of persons congregated without order; a throng; the lower orders of people; the populace; the vulgar; the mob.—*v.t.* To press into a crowd; to drive together; to fill by pressing numbers together without order; to fill to excess; to throng about; to press upon; to encumber or annoy by multitudes or excess of numbers.—*v.i.* To press in numbers; to swarm; to press or urge forward.

Crowd,‡ kroud, *n.* The crwth (which see).—**Crowder**,‡ krou'dėr, *n.* A fiddler.

Crown, kroun, *n.* [O.Fr. *corone*, Fr. *couronne*, L. *corona*—crown; Gr. *korōnē*, anything curved, a crown; akin W. *crwn*, Ir. *cruin*, round.] An ornament for the head, in the form of a wreath or garland, worn as a symbol of honour, victory, joy, &c.; a rich head-covering of gold, gems, &c., worn by monarchs on state occasions as a badge of sovereignty; hence, regal power; royalty; kingly government or executive authority; the wearer of a crown; the sovereign, as head of the state; honorary distinction; reward; honour; completion; accomplishment; highest or most perfect state; acme; the top part of anything, as of the head, or of a covering for the head, of a mountain or other elevated object; the portion of a tooth which appears above the gum; the end of the shank of an anchor, or the point from which the arms proceed; a coin anciently stamped with a crown (the English crown being a silver piece, value 5s.); paper of a particular size (15 by 20 inches), so called from formerly having the watermark of a crown.—*v.t.* To cover, decorate, or invest with, or as if with, a crown; hence, to invest with regal dignity and power; to honour; to reward; to dignify; to form the topmost or finishing part of; to terminate or finish; to complete; to consummate; to perfect.—*a.* Relating to, pertaining to, or connected with, the crown or government.—*Crown* or *demesne lands*, the lands, estate, or other real property belonging to the crown or sovereign.—**Crowning**, krou'ning, *a.* Forming the crown or summit; completing; perfecting; final.—**Crown-glass**, *n.* The finest sort of common window-glass.—**Crownless**, kroun'les, *a.* Destitute of a crown.—**Crownlet**, kroun'let, *n.* A small crown.—**Crown-prince**, *n.* The prince royal who is apparently successor to the crown.—**Crown-saw**, *n.* A species of circular saw formed by cutting the teeth round the edge of a cylinder, as the surgeon's trepan.—**Crown-wheel**, *n.* A wheel with cogs or teeth set at right angles with its plane, as in certain watches.—**Crown-work**, *n. Fort.* an outwork running into the field, consisting of two demi-bastions at the extremes, and an entire bastion in the middle, with curtains.

Crowth, krouth, *n.* CRWTH.

Crozier, **Crosier**, krō'zhi-ėr, *n.* [O.E. *croisier*, *croysier*, from Fr. *crois*, a cross. CROSS.] A staff about 5 feet long, surmounted by an ornamental cross or crucifix, borne by or before an archbishop on solemn occasions; also (and more properly) a bishop's pastoral staff terminating in a crook.—**Croziered**, **Crosiered**, krō'zhi-ėrd, *a.* Bearing a crozier.

Crucial, krö'shi-al, *a.* [Fr. *crucial*, from L. *crux*, *crucis*, a cross. CROSS.] Relating to or like a cross; having the shape of a cross; transverse; intersecting; trying or searching, as if bringing to the cross; decisive (a *crucial* experiment).—**Cruciate**,† krö'shi-āt, *v.t.* [L. *crucio*, *cruciatum*, to torture.] To torture; to torment; to afflict with extreme pain or distress.—*a.* Tormented†; *bot.* having four parts arranged like the arms of a cross; cruciform.—**Crucifer**, krö'si-fėr, *n.* [L. *crux*, and *fero*, to bear.] A plant belonging to a very extensive order, all the members of which have flowers with six stamens, two of which are short, and four sepals and petals, the spreading limbs of which form a Maltese cross, whence the name.—**Cruciferous**, krö-sif'ėr-us, *a.* Of or pertaining to the Crucifers.—**Cruciform**, krö'si-form, *a.* Cross-shaped; disposed in the form of a cross.

Crucible, krö'si-bl, *n.* [L.L. *crucibulum*, from the root seen in G. *kruse*, E. *cruse*, D. *kroes*, pitcher; akin *cresset*.] A chemical vessel or melting-pot, made of earth, black-lead, platina, &c., and so tempered and baked as to endure extreme heat without fusing; *fig.* a severe or searching test.

Crucify, krö'si-fī, *v.t.*—*crucified*, *crucifying*. [Fr. *crucifier*, L. *crux*, cross, and *figo*, to fix. CROSS, FIX.] To nail to a cross; to put to death by nailing the hands and feet to a cross or gibbet, sometimes anciently by fastening a criminal to a cross with cords; to subdue or mortify; also, to torture.—**Crucifier**, krö'si-fī-ėr, *n.* One who crucifies.—**Crucifix**, krö'si-fiks, *n.* [L. *crucifixus*, crucified.] A cross with the figure of Christ crucified upon it.—**Crucifixion**, krö-si-fik'shon, *n.* The act of nailing or fastening a person to a cross, for the purpose of putting him to death; death upon a cross, especially the death of Christ.—**Crucigerous**, krö-sij'ėr-us, *a.* Bearing the cross.

Crude, kröd, *a.* [L. *crudus*, raw, unripe; akin *crudelis*, cruel; from same root as E. *raw*. RAW.] Raw; not cooked; in its natural state; not digested in the stomach; not altered, refined, or prepared by any artificial process (*crude* salt or alum); unripe; not having reached the mature or perfect state; not brought to perfection; unfinished; immature; not matured; not well formed, arranged, or prepared in the intellect (notions, plan, theory).—**Crudely**, kröd'li, *adv.* In a crude manner; without due preparation; without form or arrangement; without maturity or digestion.—**Crudeness**, kröd'nes, *n.* The state or quality of being crude; rawness; unripeness; a state of being unformed or undigested; immatureness.—**Crudity**, krö'di-ti, *n.* [L. *cruditas*.] Crudeness; that which is crude.

Cruel, krö'el, *a.* [Fr. *cruel*, from L. *crudelis*, cruel. CRUDE.] Disposed to give pain to others in body or mind; destitute of pity, compassion, or kindness; hard-hearted; applied to persons; exhibiting or proceeding from cruelty; causing pain, grief, or distress; inhuman; tormenting, vexing, or afflicting (disposition, mood, manner, act, words, &c.).—**Cruelly**, krö'el-li, *adv.* In a cruel manner; with cruelty; inhumanly; barbarously; painfully; with severe pain or torture; extremely (*colloq.*).—**Cruelty**, krö'el-ti, *n.* [O.Fr. *cruelté*, L. *crudelitas*.] The state or character of being cruel; savage or barbarous disposition; any act which inflicts unnecessary pain; a wrong; an act of great injustice or oppression.

Cruet, krö'et, *n.* [Contr. from Fr. *cruchette*, dim. of *cruche*, a pitcher. Akin *crock*, *cruse*.] A vial or small glass bottle for holding vinegar, oil, &c.—**Cruet-stand**, *n.* A frame, often of silver, for holding cruets.

Cruise, kröz, *v.i.*—*cruised*, *cruising*. [D. *kruisen*, to cross, to cruise, from *kruis*, a cross. CROSS.] To sail hither and thither, or to rove on the ocean in search of an enemy's ships for capture, for protecting commerce, for pleasure, or any other purpose.—*n.* A voyage made in various courses; a sailing to and fro, as in search of an enemy's ships, or for pleasure.—**Cruiser**, krö'zėr, *n.* A person or a ship that cruises; an armed ship that sails to and fro for capturing an enemy's ships, for protecting commerce, or for plunder.

Cruller, krul'ėr, *n.* [O.E. *crull*, curled; D. *krullen*, to curl.] A cake shaped in the form of a curl or twist, composed of a rich batter, and fried crisp in deep fat.

Crumb, krum, *n.* [A.Sax. *cruma* = D. *kruim*, Dan. *krumme*, G. *krume*, a crumb; from root of *crimp*.] A small fragment or piece; usually, a small piece of bread or other food, broken or cut off; the soft part of bread; opposed to *crust*.—*v.t.* To break into small pieces with the fingers; to cover (meat, &c.) with bread crumbs.—**Crumb-brush**, *n.* A brush for sweeping crumbs off the table.—**Crumb-cloth**, *n.* A cloth to be laid under a table to receive falling fragments, and keep the carpet clean.—**Crumble**, krum'bl, *v.t.*—*crumbled*, *crumb-*

ling. [A dim. form from *crumb*; like D. *kruimelen*, G. *krümeln*, to crumble.] To break into crumbs or small pieces. —*v.i.* To fall into small pieces, as something friable; to moulder; to become frittered away.—**Crumbly**, krum'bli, *a.* Apt to crumble; brittle; friable. — **Crumby**, krum'i, *a.* Full of crumbs; soft like the crumb of bread.

Crumpet, krum'pet, *n.* [Allied to *crimp*, brittle.] A sort of muffin or tea-cake, very light and spongy.

Crumple, krum'pl, *v.t.*—*crumpled, crumpling.* [Closely allied to *crimp* and *cramp*.] To draw or press into wrinkles or folds; to rumple.—*v.i.* To contract; to shrink; to shrivel.

Crunch, krunsh, *v.t.* [See CRAUNCH.] To crush with the teeth; to chew with violence and noise.—*v.i.* To press with force and noise through a brittle obstacle.

Cruorin, krö'or-in, *n.* [L. *cruor*, blood.] The red colouring matter of blood corpuscles; hæmoglobin.

Crupper, krup'ėr, *n.* [Fr. *croupière*, from *croupe*, the buttocks. CROUP.] The buttocks of a horse; a strap of leather buckled to a saddle and passing under a horse's tail, to prevent the saddle from sliding forward on to the horse's neck.

Crural, krö'ral, *a.* [L. *cruralis*, from *crus*, *cruris*, the leg.] Belonging to the leg.—*Crural arch*, the ligament of the thigh.

Crusade, krų-sād', *n.* [Fr. *croisade*, from L. *crux*, a cross.] A military expedition under the banner of the cross, undertaken by Christians in the eleventh, twelfth, and thirteenth centuries, for the recovery of the Holy Land from the power of infidels or Mohammedans; any enterprise undertaken through enthusiasm.—*v.i.*—*crusaded, crusading.* To engage in a crusade; to support or oppose any cause with zeal.—**Crusader**, krų-sā'dėr, *n.* A person engaged in a crusade. — **Crusading**, krų-sā'-ding, *a.* Engaged in or relating to the Crusades.

Crusado, krų-sā'dō, *n.* A Portuguese coin of the value of 2*s.* 9*d.*, so called from having the cross stamped on it. (*Shak.*)

Cruse, krös, *n.* [Icel. *krús*, Dan. *kruus*, D. *kroes*, pot, mug; akin *cresset*, *crucible*.] A small cup; a bottle or cruet (O.T.).—**Cruset**, krö'set, *n.* [Fr. *creuzet*.] A goldsmith's crucible or melting-pot.

Crush, krush, *v.t.* [O.Fr. *cruisir*, *croissir*, to crack or crash, from the Teutonic; comp. Dan. *kryste*, Sw. *krysta*, Icel. *kreista*, to squeeze; Goth. *kriustan*, to gnash.] To press and bruise between two hard bodies; to squeeze so as to force out of the natural shape; to press with violence; to force together into a mass; to beat or force down, by an incumbent weight, with breaking or bruising; to bruise and break into fine particles by beating or grinding; to comminute; to subdue or conquer beyond resistance.—*v.i.* To press, bruise, or squeeze.—*n.* A violent pressing or squeezing; the act or effect of anything that crushes; violent pressure caused by a crowd; a crowding or being crowded together.—**Crusher**, krush'ėr, *n.* One who or that which crushes; a machine for crushing rocks, oilseeds or other materials; a worker who tends such a machine; a conclusive or overwhelming retort.—**Crushing**, krush'ing, *a.* Having the power to crush; overwhelming.—**Crush-hat**, *n.* A soft hat which may be carried under the arm without having its shape destroyed.

Crust, krust, *n.* [O.Fr. *crouste*, L. *crusta*.] A hard or comparatively hard external coat or covering; a hard coating on a surface; the hard outside portion of a loaf; an incrustation; a deposit from wine, as it ripens, collected on the interior of bottles, &c.—*Crust of the earth*, the exterior portion of our globe which is so far accessible to our inspection and observation.—*v.t.* To cover with a crust; to spread over with hard matter; to incrust. —*v.i.* To gather or form into a crust.—**Crustacea**, krus-tā'shē-a, *n. pl.* [From their crusty covering or shell.] An important division of animals, comprising crabs, lobsters, crayfish, shrimp, &c., having an external calcareous skeleton or shell in many pieces, and capable of being moulted or cast; a number of jointed limbs; head and thorax united into a single mass; abdomen often forming a kind of tail. — **Crustacean**, krus-tā'shē-an, *n.* and *a.* One of, or pertaining to the crustaceans. —**Crustaceology**, krus-tā'shē-ol"o-ji, *n.* That branch of zoology which treats of crustaceous animals. — **Crustaceous**, krus-tā'shus, *a.* Having a crust-like shell; belonging to the Crustacea; crustacean.—**Crustated**, krus'-tā-ted, *a.* Covered with a crust.—**Crustation**, krus-tā'shon, *n.* An adherent crust; incrustation.—**Crustily**, krus'ti-li, *adv.* In a crusty manner; peevishly; harshly; morosely. — **Crustiness**, krus'ti-nes, *n.* The quality of being crusty; hardness; snappishness; surliness. —**Crusty**, krus'ti, *a.* Like crust; of the nature of a crust; pertaining to a hard covering; hard: peevish; snappish; surly.

Crut, krut, *n.* [Perhaps Fr. *croûte*, crust.] The rough shaggy part of oak bark.

Crutch, kruch, *n.* [A.Sax. *cryce*, *cricc*, a staff, a crutch; D. *kruk*, G. *krücke*, Dan. *krykke*, Sw. *krycka*, a crutch; same root as in *crook*.] A staff with a curving crosspiece at the head, to be placed under the arm or shoulder to support the lame in walking; any fixture or adjustment of similar form: used in various technical meanings. — *v.t.* To support on crutches; to prop or sustain with miserable helps. — **Crutched**, krucht, *p.* and *a.* Supported with crutches; using crutches; crossed; badged with a cross.—*Crutched Friars*, an order of friars founded at Bologna in 1169, so named from their adopting the cross as their special symbol.

Crux, kruks, *n.* [L. *crux*, a cross.] Anything that puzzles greatly or torments with the difficulty of finding an explanation.

Crwth, kruth, *n.* [W.] A kind of violin with six strings, formerly much used in Wales.

Cry, krī, *v.i.* — *cried, crying.* [Fr. *crier*, from L. *quiritare*, to invoke the aid of the *Quirites*, or citizens.] To utter a loud voice; to speak, call, or exclaim with vehemence; to utter a loud voice by way of earnest request or prayer; to utter the voice of sorrow; to lament; to weep or shed tears; to utter a loud voice in giving public notice; to utter a loud inarticulate sound, as a dog or other animal.—*To cry out*, to exclaim; to vociferate; to clamour; to utter a loud voice; to utter lamentations.—*To cry out against*, to complain loudly against; to blame or censure.—*I cry you mercy*,† I beg pardon. —*v.t.* To utter loudly; to sound abroad; to proclaim; to name loudly and publicly, so as to give notice regarding; to advertise by crying. — *To cry down*, to decry; to dispraise; to condemn.—*To cry up*, to praise; to applaud; to extol.—*n.* Any loud sound articulate or inarticulate uttered by the mouth of an animal; a loud or vehement sound uttered in weeping or lamentation; a fit of weeping; clamour; outcry; an object for which a party professes great earnestness; a political catchward or the like.—**Crier, Cryer**, krī'ėr, *n.* One who cries; especially, an officer whose duty it is to proclaim the orders or commands of a court, to keep silence, &c.—**Crying**, krī'ing, *a.* Calling for vengeance and punishment; clamant; notorious; common; great (*crying* sins).

Cryolite, krī'o-līt, *n.* [Gr. *kryos*, cold, and *lithos*, stone — ice-stone.] A fluoride of sodium and aluminium found in Greenland and in the Ural Mountains, of great importance as one source of the metal aluminium.

Cryophorus, krī-of'o-rus, *n.* [Gr. *kryos*, frost, and *phoreō*, to bear.] An instrument for showing the diminution of temperature in water by evaporation.

Crypt, kript, *n.* [L. *crypta*, Gr. *kryptē*, from *kryptō*, to hide.] A subterranean cell or cave, especially one constructed for the interment of bodies; that part of a cathedral, church, &c., below the floor, set apart for monumental purposes, and sometimes used as a chapel.—**Cryptal**, krip'tal, *a.* Pertaining to or connected with a crypt.—**Cryptic**,†, **Cryptical**,† krip'tik, krip'ti-kal, *a.* Hidden; secret; occult.—**Cryptically**,† krip'ti-kal-li, *adv.* Secretly.

Cryptobranchiate, krip-tō-brang'ki-āt, *a.* [Gr. *kryptos*, concealed, and *branchia*, gills.] *Zool.* having concealed gills; destitute of distinct gills.

Cryptogam, krip'tō-gam, *n.* [Gr. *kryptos*, concealed, and *gamos*, marriage.] One of those plants forming a large division of the vegetable kingdom which do not bear true flowers consisting of stamens and pistils, and which are divided into cellular and vascular cryptogams, the former including algæ, fungi, lichens, mosses, &c., the latter the ferns, horse-tails, lycopods, &c.—**Cryptogamic, Cryptogamous**, krip-tō-gam'ik, krip-tog'a-mus, *a.* Pertaining to cryptogams.—**Cryptogamist**, krip-tog'a-mist, *n.* One who is skilled in cryptogamic botany. —**Cryptogamy**, krip-tog'a-mi, *n.* Obscure fructification, as in the cryptogams.

Cryptograph, krip'tō-graf, *n.* [Gr. *kryptos*, concealed, and *graphō*, to write.] Something written in secret characters or cipher. —**Cryptographer**, krip-tog'ra-fėr, *n.* One who writes in secret characters. — **Cryptographic, Cryptographical**, krip-tō-graf'ik, krip-tō-graf'i-kal, *a.* Written in secret characters or in cipher; pertaining to cryptography. — **Cryptography**, krip-tog'ra-fi, *n.* The act or art of writing in secret characters; also, secret characters or cipher.—**Cryptology**, krip-tol'o-ji, *n.* Secret or enigmatical language.

Cryptonym, krip'tō-nim, *n.* [Gr. *kryptos*, concealed, and *onoma*, a name.] A private, secret, or hidden name; a name which one bears in some society or brotherhood.

Crystal, kris'tal, *n.* [L. *crystallus*, Gr. *krystallos*, from *kryos*, frost.] A species of glass more perfect in its composition and manufacture than common glass; hence, collectively, all articles, as decanters, cruets, &c., made of this material; *chem.* and *mineral.* an inorganic body, which, by the operation of affinity, has assumed the form of a regular solid, terminated by a certain number of plane and smooth surfaces. —*Rock crystal*, a general name for all the transparent crystals of quartz, particularly of limpid or colourless quartz. —*a.* Consisting of crystal, or like crystal; clear; transparent; pellucid. — **Crystalline**, kris'tal-īn, *a.* Consisting of crystal; relating or pertaining to crystals or crystallography; resembling crystal; pure; clear; transparent; pellucid. — *Crystalline lens*, a lens-shaped pellucid body situated in the anterior part of the eye, and serving to produce that refraction of the rays of light which is necessary to cause them to meet in the retina, and form a perfect image there.—**Crystallizable**, kris'ta-līz-a-bl, *a.* Capable of being crystallized.—**Crystallization**, kris'tal-i-zā"shon, *n.* The act of crystallizing or forming crystals; the act or process of becoming crystallized, so that crystals are produced with a determinate and regular form, according to the nature of the substance; a body formed by the process of crystallizing.—*Water of crystallization*, the water which unites chemically with many salts during the process of crystallizing.—**Crystallize**, kris'-ta-līz, *v.t.*—*crystallized, crystallizing.* To cause to form crystals.—*v.i.* To be converted into a crystal; to become solidified, as the separate particles of a substance into a determinate and regular shape.—**Crystallogeny**, kris-ta-loj'e-ni, *n.* The origin of crystals.—**Crystallographer**, kris-ta-log'ra-fėr, *n.* One who treats of crystallography, crystals, or the manner of their formation.—**Crystallographic, Crystallographical**, kris'tal-ō-graf"ik, kris'-tal-ō-graf"i-kal, *a.* Pertaining to crystallography. — **Crystallographically**, kris'-tal-ō-graf"i-kal-li, *adv.* In the manner of crystallography. — **Crystallography**, kris-ta-log'ra-fi, *n.* The doctrine or science of crystallization, teaching the principles of the process, and the forms and structure of crystals.—**Crystalloid**, kris'tal-oid, *a.* Resembling a crystal.—*n.* The name given to a class of bodies which have the power, when in solution, of passing through membranes, as parchment-paper, easily: opposed to *colloids*, which have not this power; in *seeds*, &c., a minute crystal-shaped mass of albuminoid matter.—**Crystallomancy**, kris'tal-ō-man-si, *n.* [Gr. *manteia*, divination.] A mode of divining by means of a transparent body, as a precious stone, crystal globe, &c.—**Crystallometry**, kris-ta-lom'et-ri, *n.* The art or process of measuring the forms of crystals.

Ctenoid, ten'oid, *a.* [Gr. *kteis*, *ktenos*, a comb, and *eidos*, form.] Comb-shaped; pectinated; having the posterior edge with teeth: said of the scales of certain fishes, those of the perch and flounder being of this kind; having scales of this kind.—*n.* A fish having ctenoid scales; one of an order of fishes, mostly fossil, having scales jagged or pectinated like the teeth of a comb.—**Ctenoidian**, te-noi'di-an, *n.* and *a.* One of, or pertaining to, the ctenoids.

Cub, kub, *n.* [Etymology unknown.] The young of certain quadrupeds, as of the lion, bear, or fox; a whelp; a young boy or girl: in contempt.—*v.t.*—*cubbed, cubbing.* To bring forth a cub or cubs.

Cubation,‡ kū-bā'shon, *n.* [L. *cubatio*, from *cubo*, to lie down.] The act of lying down; a reclining.—**Cubatory**,‡ kū'ba-to-ri, *a.* Lying down; reclining; incumbent.

Cube, kūb, *n.* [Fr. *cube*, from L. *cubus*, Gr. *kybos*, a cube, a cubical die.] A solid body that is exactly square; a regular solid body with six equal sides, all squares, and containing equal angles; the product of a number multiplied into itself, and that product multiplied into the same number (4×4=16, and 16×4=64, the cube of 4).—*Cube root*, the number or quantity which, multiplied into itself, and then into the product, produces the cube (thus 4 is the cube root of 64).—*v.t.*—*cubed, cubing.* To raise to the cube or third power by multiplying into itself twice.—**Cubature**, kū'ba-tūr, *n.* The finding of the solid or cubic contents of a body.—**Cubic, Cubical**, kū'bik, kū'bi-kal, *a.* [L. *cubicus.*] Having the form or properties of a cube; pertaining to the measure of solids (a *cubic* foot, *cubic* contents).—**Cubically**, kū'bi-kal-li, *adv.* In a cubical method.—**Cubicalness**, kūb'i-kal-nes, *n.* The state or quality of being cubical.—**Cubiform**, *a.* Having the form of a cube.—**Cuboid, Cuboidal**, kū'boid, kū-boi'dal, *a.* Having the form of a cube or differing little from it.—**Cube-ore**, *n.* Arseniate of iron, a mineral of a greenish colour.—**Cube-spar**, *n.* An anhydrous sulphate of lime.

Cubeb, kū'beb, *n.* [Ar. *kabāban.*] The small spicy berry of a kind of pepper, a native of Java and other East India Isles.

Cubicular, kū-bik'ū-ler, *a.* [L. *cubiculum*, a sleeping-room.] Belonging to a bed-chamber.—**Cubiculary**,† kū-bik'ū-la-ri, *a.* Fitted for the posture of lying down.—**Cubicule**,‡ kū'bi-kūl, *n.* A bed-chamber; a chamber.

Cubit, kū'bit, *n.* [L. *cubitus*, *cubitum*, the elbow, an ell or cubit, from root of L. *cubo*, to lie or recline.] *Anat.* the fore-arm: the ulna, a bone of the arm from the elbow to the wrist; a lineal measure, being the length of a man's arm from the elbow to the extremity of the middle finger: usually taken at 18 inches.—**Cubital**, kū'bi-tal, *a.* Of the length of a cubit; pertaining to the cubit or ulna.

Cucking-stool, kuk'ing-stöl, *n.* [Icel. *kúka*, to ease one's self, *kúkr*, dung.] A chair in which an offender was placed, usually before her or his own door, to be hooted at or pelted by the mob; or it might be used for ducking its occupant.

Cuckold, kuk'old, *n.* [Lit. one who is *cuckooed*, from O.Fr. *coucoul*, L. *cuculus*, a cuckoo; from the cuckoo's habit of depositing her eggs in the nests of other birds.] A man whose wife is false to his bed; the husband of an adulteress.—*v.t.* To make a cuckold of.—**Cuckoldize**, kuk'ol-dīz, *v.t.* To cuckold.—**Cuckoldly**, kuk'old-li, *a.* Having the qualities of a cuckold. (*Shak.*)—**Cuckoldom**, kuk'ol-dum, *n.* The state of a cuckold.—**Cuckoldry**, kuk'old-ri, *n.* The debauching of other men's wives; the state of being made a cuckold.

Cuckoo, Cuckow, ku̦'kö, ku̦'kō, *n.* [Fr. *coucou*, from L. *cuculus*, like G. *kukuk*, D. *koekoek*, Gr. *kokkux*, Skr. *kokila*, names derived from its cry.] A migratory bird remarkable for its striking call-note and its habit of depositing its eggs in the nests of other birds; also the name of many allied birds in various parts of the world.—**Cuckoo-spit, Cuckoo-spittle**, *n.* A froth found on plants in summer, being a secretion formed by the larva of a small insect.

Cucullate, Cucullated, kū-kul'āt, kū-kul'ā-ted, *a.* [L. *cucullatus*, from *cucullus*, a hood or cowl.] Hooded; cowled; covered as with a hood; having the shape or resemblance of a hood.

Cucumber, kū'kum-bėr, *n.* [Fr. *concombre*, from L. *cucumis*, *cucumeris*, a cucumber.] An annual plant of the gourd family, extensively cultivated and prized as an esculent: in an unripe state used in pickles under the name of gherkins.—**Cucumber-tree**, *n.* A beautiful American tree, a species of Magnolia, abounding in the Alleghanies.—**Cucumiform**, kū-kū'mi-form, *a.* Shaped like a cucumber.

Cucurbit, Cucurbite, kū-kėr'bit, kū-kėr'bīt, *n.* [Fr. *cucurbite*, L. *cucurbita*, a gourd.] A chemical vessel originally in the shape of a gourd, but sometimes shallow, with a wide mouth, used in distillation.—**Cucurbitaceous**, kū-kėr'bi-tā"shus, *a.* Resembling a gourd.—**Cucurbital**, kū-kėr'bi-tal, *a.* Of or pertaining to the gourd or cucumber family of plants.

Cud, kud, *n.* [A.Sax. *cud*, the cud, what is chewed, from *ceówan*, to chew.] The food which going into the first stomach of ruminating animals is afterwards brought up and chewed at leisure; a portion of tobacco held in the mouth and chewed; a quid.—*To chew the cud* (*fig.*), to ponder; to reflect; to ruminate.

Cudbear, kud'bār, *n.* [After Dr. *Cuthbert* Gordon, who first brought it into notice.] A purple or violet-coloured powder, used in dyeing violet, purple, and crimson, prepared from various species of lichens.

Cuddle, kud'l, *v.i.*—*cuddled, cuddling.* [Origin doubtful; perhaps same as *coddle.*] To lie close or snug; to squat; to join in an embrace; to fondle.—*v.t.* To hug; to fondle; to press close, so as to keep warm.—*n.* A hug; an embrace.

Cuddy, kud'i, *n.* [Probably a word of East Indian origin.] *Naut.* a room or cabin abaft and under the poop-deck; also a sort of cabin or cook-room in lighters, barges, &c.

Cuddy, kud'i, *n.* [An abbrev. of *Cuthbert*, like *neddy*, also a name for the ass.] An ass; a donkey.

Cudgel, kuj'el, *n.* [W. *cogel*, a cudgel, from *cog*, a short piece of wood.] A short thick stick; a club.—*To take up the cudgels*, to stand boldly forth in defence.—*v.t.*—*cudgelled, cudgelling.* To beat with a cudgel or thick stick; to beat in general.—*To cudgel one's brains*, to reflect deeply and laboriously.—**Cudgeller**, kuj'el-ėr, *n.* One who cudgels.

Cue, kū, *n.* [Fr. *queue*, L. *cauda*, the tail; or partly from *Q*, the first letter of L. *quando*, when, which was marked on the actors' copies of the plays, to show when they were to enter and speak.] The end of a thing, as the long curl of a wig, or a long roll of hair; a queue; the last words of a speech which a player, who is to answer, catches and regards as an intimation to begin; a hint on which to act; the part which any man is to play in his turn; turn or temper of mind; the straight tapering rod used in playing billiards.

Cuff, kuf, *n.* [Akin to Sw. *kuffa*, Hamburg dialect *kuffen*, to cuff.] A blow with the fist; a stroke; a box.—*v.t.* To strike with the fist, as a man; to buffet.—*v.i.* To fight; to scuffle.

Cuff, kuf, *n.* [Perhaps from Fr. *coiffe*, It. *cuffia*, a coif, hence a covering for the hand.] The fold at the end of a sleeve; anything occupying the place of such a fold, as a loose band worn over the wristband of a shirt.

Cufic, kū'fik, *a.* [From *Cufa*, near Bagdad.] Applied to the characters of the Arabic alphabet used in the time of Mohammed, and in which the Koran was written; Kufic.

Cuirass, kwi-ras', *n.* [Fr. *cuirasse*, from *cuir*, L. *corium*, leather. The cuirass was originally made of leather.] A breastplate; a piece of defensive armour made of iron plate, well hammered, and covering the body from the neck to the girdle.—**Cuirassier**, kwi-ras-sēr', *n.* A soldier armed with a cuirass or breastplate.

Cuir-bouilly, Cuir-bouilli, kwēr'bö-il-li, kwēr-bö-ēl-lyē, *n.* [Fr.] Leather softened by boiling, then impressed with ornaments.

Cuish, Cuisse, kwis, *n.* [Fr. *cuisse*, from L. *coxa*, the hip.] Defensive armour for the thighs.

Cuisine, kwē-zēn', *n.* [Fr., from L. *coquina*, art of cooking, a kitchen, from *coquo*, to cook. COOK.] A kitchen; the cooking department; manner or style of cooking; cookery.

Culdee, kul-dē', *n.* [Gael. *ceile*, servant, and *De*, God.] One of an ancient order of monks who formerly lived in Scotland, Ireland, and Wales, and are supposed to have been originated in the sixth century by St. Columba.

Cul-de-sac, kül'de-sak, *n.* [Fr., lit. the bottom of a bag.] A place that has no thoroughfare; a blind alley; any natural cavity, bag, or tubular vessel, open only at one end.

Culilawan, kū-lil'a-wan, *a.* The name of a valuable aromatic, pungent bark, the produce of a tree of the Moluccas, useful in indigestion, diarrhœa, &c.

Culinary, kū'li-na-ri, *a.* [L. *culinarius*, from *culina*, a kitchen.] Relating to the kitchen, or to the art of cooking; used in kitchens.—**Culinarily**, kū'li-na-ri-li, *adv.* In a culinary manner.

Cull, kul, *v.t.* [Fr. *cueillir*, from L. *colligere*, to collect—*col*, and *legere*, to gather. COLLECT, COIL.] To pick out; to separate one or more things from others; to select from many; to pick up; to collect.—**Culler**, kul'ėr, *n.* One who picks or chooses from many.—**Culling**, kul'ing, *n.* Anything selected or separated from a mass.

Cullender, kul'en-dėr, *n.* A colander.

Cullet, kul'et, *n.* Broken glass for melting up with fresh materials.

Cullibility,‡ kul-i-bil'i-ti, *n.* [From *cully.*] Credulity; easiness of belief.—**Cullible**,‡ kul'i-bl, *a.* Easily cajoled or cheated.

Cullion,‡ kul'yun, *n.* [O.Fr. *couillon*, It. *coglione*, a testicle, from L. *coleus*, the scrotum.] A mean wretch; a base fellow; a poltroon or dastard (*Shak.*).

Cullis, kul'is, *n.* [Fr. *coulisse*, a groove, from *couler*, to run.] *Arch.* a gutter in a roof.

Cully, kul'i, *n.* [Said to be of Gypsy origin.] A person who is easily deceived, tricked, or imposed on.—*v.t.*—*cullied, cullying.* To deceive; to trick, cajole, or impose on; to jilt.—**Cullyism**, kul'i-izm, *n.* The state of being a cully.

Culm, kulm, *n.* [L. *culmus*, a stalk.] *Bot.* the jointed stem of grasses, which is herbaceous in most, but woody and tree-like in the bamboo.—**Culmiferous**, kul-mif'ėr-us, *a.* Bearing culms.

Culm, kulm, *n.* [Perhaps another spelling of *coom*; or akin to *coal.*] Anthracite shale, an impure shaly kind of coal.—**Culmiferous**, kul-mif'ėr-us, *a.* Abounding in culm.

Culmen, kul'men, *n.* [L.] Top; summit; highest ridge.—**Culminant**, kul'mi-nant, *a.* Being vertical, or at the highest point of altitude; hence, predominating.—**Culminate**, kul'mi-nāt, *v.i.*—*culminated, culminating.* To come or be in the meridian; to be in the highest point of altitude, as a planet; to reach the highest point, as of rank, power, size, numbers, or quality.—**Culminating**, kul'mi-nāt-ing, *p.* or *a.* Being at the meridian; being at its highest point, as of rank, power, size, &c.—**Culmination**, kul-mi-nā'shon, *n.* The transit of a heavenly body over the meridian, or highest point of altitude for the day; *fig.* the condition of any person or thing arrived at the most brilliant or important point of his or its progress.

Culpable, kul'pa-bl, *a.* [L. *culpabilis*, from *culpa*, a fault.] Deserving censure; blamable; blameworthy; immoral: said of persons or their conduct.—**Culpability, Culpableness**, kul-pa-bil'i-ti, kul'pa-bl-nes, *n.* State of being culpable; blamableness; guilt.—**Culpably**, kul'pa-bli, *adv.* In a culpable manner; blamably; in a faulty manner.—**Culpatory**, kul'pa-to-ri, *a.* Inculpatory; censuring; reprehensory.

Culprit, kul'prit, *n.* [Probably for *culpat*, from old law Latin *culpatus*, one accused, from L. *culpo*, to blame, accuse.] A person arraigned in court for a crime; a criminal; a malefactor.

Cult, cult, *n.* [Fr. *culte*, L. *cultus*, worship, from *colo*, *cultum*, to till, worship.] Homage; worship; a system of religious belief and worship; the rites and ceremonies employed in worship.

Cultch, kulch, *n.* The spawn of the oyster.

Culter, kul'tėr, *n.* [L.] A coulter.

Cultivate, kul'ti-vāt, *v.t.*—*cultivated, cultivating.* [L.L. *cultivare*, *cultivatum*, from L. *cultus*, pp. of *colo*, *cultum*, to till.] To till; to prepare for crops; to manure, plough, dress, sow, and reap; to raise or produce by tillage; to improve by labour or study; to refine and improve; to labour to promote and increase; to cherish; to foster (to *cultivate* a taste for poetry); to devote study, labour, or care to; to study (to *cultivate* literature); to study to conciliate or gain over; to labour to make better; to civilize.—**Cultivable, Cultivatable**, kul'ti-va-bl, kul'ti-vā-ta-bl, *a.* Capable of being tilled or cultivated.—**Cultivation**, kul-ti-vā'shon, *n.* The act or practice of cultivating; husbandry; study, care, and practice directed to improvement or progress; the state of being cultivated or refined; culture; refinement.—**Cultivator**, kul'ti-vā-tėr, *n.* One who cultivates; especially, a farmer or agriculturist; an agricultural implement used for the purpose of loosening the earth about the roots of growing crops.

Cultrate, Cultrated, Cultriform, kul'trāt, kul'trā-ted, kul'tri-form, *a.* [L. *cultratus*, from *culter*, a ploughshare or pruning knife.] Sharp-edged and pointed; coulter-shaped.—**Cultrirostral**, kul-tri-ros'tral, *a.* [L. *culter*, and *rostrum*, a beak.] Having a bill shaped like a coulter: said of such birds as cranes, herons, storks, &c.

Culture, kul'tūr, *n.* [L. *cultura*, from *colo*, *cultum*, to till.] Tillage; cultivation; training or discipline by which man's moral and intellectual nature is elevated; the result of such training; enlightenment; civilization; refinement.—**Culturable**, kul'tū-ra-bl, *a.* Capable of being cultured or refined.—**Cultural**, kul'tū-ral, *a.* Pertaining to culture; educational. — **Cultured**, kul'tūrd, *a.* Cultivated; tilled; having culture; refined. —**Cultureless**, kul'tūr-les, *a.* Having no culture.—**Cultus**, kul'tus, *n.* [L.] Cult or religious system.

Culver, kul'vėr, *n.* [A.Sax. *culfre.*] A pigeon; a dove.—**Culver-house**, *n.* A dove-cote.—**Culvertail**, kul'vėr-tāl, *n.* A dove-tail joint.

Culverin, kul'vėr-in, *n.* [Fr. *couleuvrine*, from L. *coluber*, a serpent.] A long, slender piece of ordinance or artillery, serving to carry a ball to a great distance.

Culvert, kul'vėrt, *n.* [O.Fr. *culvert*; Fr. *couvert*, a covered walk, from *couvrir*, to cover. COVER.] An arched drain of brick-work or masonry carried under a road, railway, canal, &c., for the passage of water.

Cumarin, kū'ma-rin, *n.* Same as *Coumarine.*

Cumas, kū'mas, *n.* Quamash (which see).

Cumber, kum'bėr, *v.t.* [O.Fr. *combrer*, from L.L. *combrus*, *cumbrus*, a mass, from L. *cumulus*, a heap (whence also *cumulate*), by insertion of *b* (comp. *number*) and change of *l* to *r.*] To overload: to overburden; to check, stop, or retard, as by a load or weight; to make motion difficult; to obstruct; to perplex or embarrass; to distract or trouble; to cause trouble or obstruction in, as by anything useless.—**Cumber**, kum'bėr, *n.* Hindrance; burdensomeness; embarrassment. — **Cumberless**, kum'bėr-les, *a.* Free from care, distress, or encumbrance.—**Cumbersome**, kum'bėr-sum, *a.* Troublesome; burdensome; embarrassing; vexatious; unwieldy; unmanageable; not easily borne or managed. — **Cumbersomely**, kum'bėr-sum-li, *adv.* — **Cumbersomeness**, kum'bėr-sum-nes, *n.*—**Cumbrance**, kum'brans, *n.* That which cumbers or encumbers; an encumbrance. — **Cumbrous**, kum'brus, *a.* Serving to cumber or encumber; burdensome; troublesome; rendering action difficult or toilsome; unwieldy.—**Cumbrously**, kum'brus-li, *adv.* In a cumbrous manner. — **Cumbrousness**, kum'brus-nes, *n.*

Cumbrian, kum'bri-an, *a.* Of or pertaining to Cumberland; *geol.* applied to the lowest slaty and partly fossiliferous beds in Cumberland and Westmorland.

Cumfrey, kum'fri, *n.* Comfrey.

Cumin, Cummin, kum'in, *n.* [L. *cuminum*, Gr. *kyminon*, Heb. *kamon*, cumin.] An annual umbelliferous plant found wild in Egypt and Syria, and cultivated for the sake of its agreeable aromatic seeds, which possess well-marked stimulating and carminative properties.

Cummer, kum'ėr, *n.* [Fr. *commère.*] Gossip, god-mother.

Cummer-bund, Kamar-band, kum'-ėr-bund, *n.* [Hind. *kamar*, the waist, and *bandhna*, to tie.] A girdle or waist-band worn in Hindustan.

Cumshaw, kum'sha, *n.* [Chinese *kom-tsie.*] In the East, a present or bonus.

Cumulate, kū'mū-lāt, *v.t.* — *cumulated, cumulating.* [L. *cumulo*, *cumulatum*, to heap up, from *cumulus*, a heap, seen also in *accumulate*; akin *cumber.*] To form a heap of; to heap together; to accumulate.—**Cumulation**, kū-mū-lā'shon, *n.* The act of heaping together; a heap.—**Cumulative**, kū'mū-lāt-iv, *a.* Forming a mass; aggregated; increasing in force. weight, or effect by successive additions (arguments, evidence).—*Cumulative system*, in elections, that system by which each voter has the same number of votes as there are persons to be elected, and can give them all to one candidate or distribute them as he pleases.—**Cumulose**, kū'mū-lōs, *a.* Full of heaps.—**Cumulo-cirro-stratus**, kū'mū-lō-sir''rō-strā-tus, *n.* A form of cloud which produces rain; a rain cloud; a nimbus.—**Cumulo-stratus**, kū'mū-lō-strā-tus, *n.* A species of cloud in which the cumulus at the top, mixed with cirri, overhangs a flattish stratum or base.—**Cumulus**, kū'mū-lus, *n.* A species of cloud which assumes the form of dense convex or conical heaps, resting on a flattish base.

Cuneal, kū'nē-al, *a.* [L. *cuneus*, a wedge, whence also *coin.*] Having the form of a wedge.—**Cuneate, Cuneated**, kū'nē-āt, kū'nē-āt-ed, *a.* Wedge-shaped; cuneiform.—**Cuneiform, Cuniform**, kū-nē'i-form, kū'ni-form, *a.* Having the shape or form of a wedge; wedge-shaped; the epithet applied to the arrow-headed inscriptions found on old Babylonian and Persian monuments, from the characters resembling a wedge.

Cunning, kun'ing, *a.* [O.E. *cunnand*, from A.Sax. *cunnan*, Icel. *kunna*, Goth. *kunnan*, to know; akin *can*, *ken*, *know.*] Having skill or dexterity; skilful; wrought with skill; ingenious; shrewd; sly; crafty; astute; designing; subtle.—*n.* Knowledge‡; skill‡; artifice; artfulness; craft; deceitfulness or deceit; fraudulent skill or dexterity.—**Cunningly**, kun'ing-li, *adv.* In a cunning manner; artfully; craftily; with subtlety; with fraudulent contrivance; skilfully: artistically.—**Cunningness**, kun'ing-nes, *n.* Cunning.

Cup, kup, *n.* [A.Sax. *cuppe*, from L. *cupa*, a tub, a cask, in later times a cup.] A vessel of small capacity, used commonly to drink from; a chalice; the contents of a cup; the liquor contained in a cup, or that it may contain; anything formed like a cup (the *cup* of an acorn, of a flower).—*In his cups*, intoxicated; tipsy.—*v.t.*—*cupped, cupping.* To perform the operation of cupping upon.—**Cup-bearer**, *n.* An attendant at a feast who conveys wine or other liquors to the guests.—**Cupboard**, kub'bėrd, *n.* Originally, a board or shelf for cups to stand on; now, a case or inclosure in a room with shelves to receive cups, plates, dishes, and the like.—**Cupful**, kup'ful, *n.* As much as a cup holds.—**Cup-moss**, *n.* A species of lichen so called from the cup-like shape of its erect frond. — **Cup-valve**, *n.* A valve, the seat of which is made to fit a cover in the form of a vase, or of the portion of a sphere.—**Cupping**, kup'ing, *n. Surg.* a species of blood-letting performed by a scarificator and a glass called a cupping-glass from which the air has been exhausted.—**Cupping-glass**, *n.* A glass vessel like a cup, to be applied to the skin in the operation of cupping.

Cupel, kū'pel, *n.* [L. *cupella*, dim. of *cupa*, a tub.] A small, shallow, porous, cup-like vessel: generally made of the residue of burned bones rammed into a mould, and used in refining metals.—**Cupellation**, kū-pel-lā'shon, *n.* The refining of gold or silver by a cupel.

Cupid, kū'pid, *n.* [L. *Cupido*, from *cupido*, desire, from *cupio*, to desire.] The god of love, and *fig.* love.

Cupidity, kū-pid'i-ti, *n.* [L. *cupiditas*, from *cupidus*, desirous, from *cupio*, to desire; akin *covet.*] An eager desire to possess something; inordinate or unlawful desire, especially of wealth or power; avarice; covetousness.

Cupola, kū'po-la, *n.* [It. *cupola*, dim. of L. *cupa*, a cup. CUP.] *Arch.* a spherical vault on the top of an edifice; a dome, or the round top of a dome; the round top of any structure, as of a furnace; the furnace itself.—**Cupola-furnace**, *n.* A furnace for melting iron, so called from the cupola or dome leading to the chimney.

Cupreous, kū'prē-us, *a.* [L. *cupreus*, from *cuprum*, copper.] Coppery; consisting of copper; resembling copper or partaking of its qualities.—**Cupric, Cuprous**, kū'-prik, kū'prus, *a.* Of or belonging to copper.—**Cupriferous**, kū-prif'ėr-us, *a.* Producing or affording copper. — **Cuprite**, kū'prīt, *n.* The red oxide of copper; red copper ore.

Cupula, Cupule, kū'pū-la, kū'pūl, *n.* [From L. *cupa.* CUP.] *Bot.* a form of involucrum, occurring in the oak, the beech, and the hazel, and consisting of bracts cohering by their bases, and forming a kind of cup.—**Cupuliferous**, kū-pū-lif'ėr-us, *a.* In *bot.* bearing cupules.

Cur, kėr, *n.* [Sw. *kurre*, D. *korre*, a dog, from root of Icel. *kurra*, to grumble or mutter.] A degenerate dog; a worthless or contemptible man; a hound.—**Currish**, kėr'ish, *a.* Like a cur; having the qualities of a cur; snappish; snarling; churlish; quarrelsome; malignant. — **Currishly**, kėr'ish-li, *adv.* In a currish manner.—**Currishness**, kėr'ish-nes, *n.* The quality of being currish; snappishness; churlishness.

Curable, kūr'a-bl, *a.* Under CURE.

Curacoa, kö-ra-sō'a, *n.* A liquor or cordial flavoured with orange-peel, cinnamon, and mace: so named from the island of *Curaçoa*, where it was first made.

Curacy, Curateship. Under CURATE.

Curari, Curara, kų'ra-rē, kų'ra-rä, *n.* A brown-black resinous substance obtained from a small tree of the Nux-vomica family; and forming a deadly poison; used by the South American Indians for poisoning arrows, especially for hunting, the animals killed by it being quite wholesome.—**Curarine**, kū-ra-rin, *n.* An alkaloid extracted from curari, and more poisonous than the curari which yields it.

Curassow, kū-ras'sō, *n.* The name given to several species of gallinaceous birds found in the warmer parts of America, about the size of turkeys, and easily domesticated and reared.

Curate, kū'rāt, *n.* [L.L. *curatus*, one intrusted with the cure of souls, from L. *cura*, care.] One who has the cure of souls; a clergyman in Episcopal churches who is employed to perform divine service in the place of the incumbent, parson, or vicar. —**Curacy**, **Curateship**, kū'ra-si, kū'rāt-ship, *n.* The office or employment of a curate.—**Curator**, kū-rā'tėr, *n.* [L., from *cura, curatum*, to take care of.] One who has the care and superintendence of anything, as a public library, museum, fine art collection, or the like; *Scots law*, a guardian.—**Curatorship**, kū-rā'tėr-ship, *n.* The office of a curator.—**Curatrix**, kū-rāt'riks, *n.* A female superintendent or guardian.—**Curé**, kū-rā, *n.* [Fr.] A curate; a parson.

Curative, kū'ra-tiv, *a.* Under CURE.

Curb, kėrb, *v.t.* [Fr. *courber*, to bend or crook, from L. *curvare*, to curve, from *curvus*, curved; same root as L. *circus*, a circle, Gr. *kurtos*, crooked.] To bend to one's will; to check, restrain, hold back; to keep in subjection; to restrain (a horse) with a curb; to guide and manage by the reins; to strengthen by a curb-stone.—*n.* What checks, restrains, or holds back; restraint; check; hindrance; a chain or strap attached to a bridle, and passing under the horse's lower jaw, against which it is made to press tightly when the rein is pulled; the edge-stone of a side walk or pavement; a curb-stone.—**Curbable**, kėr'ba-bl, *a.* Capable of being curbed or restrained.—**Curbless**, kėrb'les, *a.* Having no curb or restraint.—**Curb-roof**, *n.* A roof formed with an upper and under set of rafters on each side, the under set being less inclined to the horizon than the upper; a mansard roof.—**Curb-stone**, *n.* A stone placed against earth or stonework to hold the work together; the outer edge of a foot pavement.

Curd, kėrd, *n.* [Probably connected with W. *crwd*, a round lump, and perhaps with *crowd*.] The coagulated or thickened part of milk; the coagulated part of any liquid. —*v.t.* to cause to coagulate; to turn to curd; to curdle; to congeal.—*v.i.* To become curdled or coagulated; to become curd.—**Curdiness**, kėr'di-nes, *n.* State of being curdy.—**Curdle**, kėr'dl, *v.i.—curdled, curdling.* To coagulate or concrete: to thicken or change into curd; to run slow with terror; to freeze; to congeal.—*v.t.* To change into curd; to coagulate; to congeal or make run slow.—**Curdy**, kėr'di, *a.* Like curd; full of curd; coagulated.

Cure, kūr, *n.* [O.Fr. *cure*, L. *cura*, care.] Care†; a spiritual charge: care of the spiritual welfare of people; the employment or office of a curate curacy; remedial treatment of disease; method of medical treatment; remedy for disease; restorative; that which heals; a healing; restoration to health from disease and to soundness from a wound.—*v.t.—cured, curing.* To restore to health or to a sound state; to heal; to remove or put an end to by remedial means; to heal, as a disease; to remedy; to prepare for preservation, as by drying, salting, &c. —*v.i.* To effect a cure.—**Curability**, kūr-a-bil'i-ti, *n.* The quality of being curable.—**Curable**, kū'ra-bl, *a.* Capable of being healed or cured; admitting a remedy. —**Curableness**, kūr'a-bl-nes, *n.* Possibility of being cured.—**Curative**, kū'ra-tiv, *a.* Relating to the cure of diseases; tending to cure.—**Cureless**, kūr'les, *a.* Incurable; not admitting of a remedy.—**Curer**, kū'rėr, *n.* One who or that which cures or heals; a physician; one who preserves provisions, as beef, fish, and the like, from speedy putrefaction by means of salt, or in any other manner.

Curé, *n.* Under CURATE.

Curfew, kėr'fū, *n.* [Fr. *couvre-feu*, cover-fire, from L. *cooperire*, to cover, and *focus*, hearth, fire-place.] A bell formerly rung in the evening as a signal to the inhabitants to rake up their fires and retire to rest.

Curia, kū'ri-a, *n.* [L., the senate-house, the senate.] The Roman see in its temporal aspect, including the pope, cardinals, &c.

Curious, kū'ri-us, *a.* [L. *curiosus*, from *cura*, care, attention. CURE.] Strongly desirous to discover what is novel or unknown; solicitous to see or to know things interesting; inquisitive; addicted to research or inquiry; wrought with care and art or with nice finish; singular; exciting surprise; awakening curiosity; odd or strange. —**Curiosity**, kū-ri-os'i-ti, *n.* [L. *curiositas*.] The state or feeling of being curious; a strong desire to see something novel or to discover something unknown; a desire to see what is new or unusual, or to gratify the mind with new discoveries; inquisitiveness; a curious or singular object.—**Curio**, kū'ri-ō, *n.* A curiosity; a small interesting article or object.—**Curioso**, kū-ri-ō'sō, *n.* [It.] A curious person; a virtuoso.—**Curiously**, kū'ri-us-li, *adv.* In a curious manner; inquisitively; attentively; in a singular manner; unusually.—**Curiousness**, kū-ri-us-nes, *n.*

Curl, kėrl, *v.t.* [Akin to D. *krullen*, Dan. *krölle*, to curl.] To bend or twist circularly; to bend or form into ringlets; to crisp (the hair); to writhe; to twist; to coil; to curve; to raise in breaking waves or undulations.—*v.i.* To bend or twist in curls or ringlets; to move in or form curves or spirals; to rise in waves; to writhe; to twist: to play at the game called curling. —*n.* A ringlet of hair or anything of a like form; something curled or bent round; a waving; sinuosity; flexure.—**Curled**, kėrld, *a.* Having the hair curled; curly.—**Curler**, kėrl'ėr, *n.* One who or that which curls; one who engages in the amusement of curling.—**Curliness**, kėrl'i-nes, *n.* State of being curly.—**Curling**, kėrl'ing, *n.* A winter amusement on the ice (especially in Scotland), in which contending parties slide large smooth stones of a circular form from one mark to another, called the tee.—**Curling-irons**, **Curling-tongs**, *n.* An instrument for curling the hair.—**Curling-stone**, *n.* A stone shaped somewhat like a cheese with a handle in the upper side, used in the game of curling. —**Curly**, kėr'li, *a.* Having or forming curls: tending to curl.—**Curly-headed**, **Curly-pated**, *a.* Having curling hair.

Curlew, kėr'lū, *n.* [O.Fr. *corlieu*; imitative of the cry of the bird; Fr. *courlis*.] A bird allied to the snipe and woodcock, with a long, slender, curved bill, longish legs, and a short tail, frequenting moors and also the sea-side.

Curmudgeon, kėr-muj'on, *n.* [Said to be from *corn-mudgin*, a dealer in corn—corn-dealers being reckoned, in old times, the most flinty-hearted and avaricious of men.] An avaricious churlish fellow; a miser; a niggard; a churl.—**Curmudgeonly**, kėr-muj'on-li, *a.* Avaricious; covetous; niggardly; churlish.

Currant, kur'ant, *n.* [From *Corinth*, whence it was probably first brought.] A small kind of dried grape, brought in large quantities from Greece; the name of several species of shrubs belonging to the gooseberry family, and of their fruits, as the red currant, the white currant, and the black currant.—**Currant-jelly**, *n.* Jelly made of the juice of currants.—**Currant-wine**, *n.* Wine made from the juice of currants.

Current, kur'ent, *a.* [L. *currens, currentis*, ppr. of *curro*, to run, seen also in *concur, incur, occur, course, cursive*, &c.] Running†; passing from person to person, or from hand to hand (report, coin); circulating; common, general, or fashionable; generally received, adopted, or approved (opinions, beliefs, theories); popular; established by common estimation (the *current* value of coin); fitted for general acceptance or circulation (*Shak.*); now passing, or at present in its course (the *current* month: often in abbreviated expressions, such as, 20th *curt.*).—*Current coin*, coin in general circulation.—*n.* A flowing or passing; a stream; a body of water or air moving in a certain direction; course; progressive motion or movement; connected series; successive course (the *current* of events); general or main course (the *current* of opinion). —*Electric current*, the passage of electricity from one pole of an apparatus to the other.—**Currency**, kur'en-si, *n.* The state of being current; a passing from person to person; a passing from mouth to mouth among the public; a continual passing from hand to hand, as coin or bills of credit; circulation; that which is in circulation, or is given and taken as having value, or as representing property; circulating medium (the *currency* of a country).—*Metallic currency*, the gold, silver, and copper in circulation in any country.—*Paper currency*, bank-notes or other documents serving as a substitute for money or a representative of it.—**Currently**, kur'ent-li, *adv.* Commonly; generally; popularly; with general acceptance.—**Currentness**, kur'ent-nes, *n.* The state of being current; currency.

Curricle, kur'i-kl, *n.* [L. *curriculum*, from *curro*, to run.] A chaise or carriage with two wheels, drawn by two horses abreast.

Curriculum, ku-rik'ū-lum, *n.* [L.] A specified fixed course of study in a university, academy, school, or the like.

Currish, kėr'ish, *a.* Under CUR.

Curry, kur'i, *v.t.—curried, currying.* [Fr. *courroyer, corroyer*, originally to prepare, put right, or make ready in general, from the prefix *con*, and the Germanic stem to which belong E. *ready*, *ray* in *array*.] To dress leather after it is tanned by scraping, cleansing, beating, and colouring; to rub and clean (a horse) with a comb; to beat, drub, or thrash (*colloq.*).—*To curry favour*, to seek favour by officiousness, kindness, flattery, caresses, and the like: the phrase being corrupted from 'to *curry favel*,' from *favel*, an old name for a horse= chestnut.—**Currier**, kur'i-ėr, *n.* A man who curries leather or a horse.—**Curriery**, kur'i-ėr-i, *n.* The trade of a currier or the place where the trade is carried on.—**Curry-comb**, *n.* An iron instrument or comb with very short teeth, for combing and cleaning horses.—*v.t.* To rub down or comb with a curry-comb.

Curry, **Currie**, kur'i, *n.* [Per. *khur*, flavour, relish.] A kind of sauce much used in India, containing cayenne-pepper, garlic, turmeric, coriander seed, ginger, and other strong spices; a dish of fish, fowl, &c., cooked with curry.—*v.t.—curried, currying.* To flavour with curry.—**Curry-powder**, *n.* A condiment used for making curry.

Curse, kėrs, *v.t.—cursed, cursing.* [A.Sax. *cursian*, from *curs*, a curse—a word of doubtful connections.] To utter a wish of evil against one; to imprecate evil upon; to call for mischief or injury to fall upon; to execrate; to bring evil to or upon; to blast; to blight; to vex, harass, or torment with great calamities.—*v.i.* To utter imprecations; to use blasphemous or profane language; to swear.—*n.* A malediction; the expression of a wish of evil to another; an imprecation; evil solemnly or in passion invoked upon one; that which brings evil or severe affliction; torment; great vexation; condemnation or sentence of divine vengeance on sinners.—**Cursed**, kėr'sed, *a.* Blasted by a curse; deserving a curse; execrable; hateful; detestable; abominable; wicked; vexatious; troublesome.—**Cursedly**, kėr'sed-li, *adv.* In a cursed manner; miserably; in a manner to be cursed or detested.—**Cursedness**, kėr'sed-nes, *n.* The state of being cursed.—**Curser**, kėr'sėr, *n.* One who curses.—**Curst**, kėrst, *a.* Cursed; having a violent temper; snarling; peevish; forward.—**Curstly**, kėrst'li, *adv.* In a curst or ill-tempered manner.—**Curstness**, kėrst'nes, *n.* The character of being curst.

Cursive, kėr'siv, *a.* [L.L.*cursivus*, L. *cursus*, a running. COURSE, CURRENT.] Running; flowing: said of hand-writing.—**Cursively**, kėr'siv-li, *adv.* In a cursive manner.—**Cursor**, kėr'sėr, *n.* [L., a runner.] Any part of a mathematical instrument that slides backward and forward upon another part.—**Cursores**, kėr-sō'rēz, *n. pl.* The runners, an order of birds, such as the ostrich and some others, so named from their remarkable velocity in running.—**Cursorial**, kėr-sō'ri-al, *a.* Adapted for running: of or pertaining to the Cursores. —**Cursorily**, kėr'so-ri-li, *adv.* In a cursory or hasty manner; slightly; hastily; without attention.—**Cursoriness**, kėr'so-ri-nes, *n.* The state of being cursory.—**Cursory**, kėr'so-ri, *a.* [L. *cursorius.*] Rapid or hurried, as if running; hasty; slight; superficial; careless; not exercising close attention (a *cursory* view, a *cursory* observer).

Curst, *a.* Under CURSE.

Curt, kėrt, *a.* [L. *curtus*, short, docked.] Short; concise; brief and abrupt; short and sharp.—**Curtly**, kėrt'li, *adv.* In a curt manner; briefly.—**Curtness**, kėrt'nes, *n.* Shortness; conciseness; abruptness, as of manner.

Curtail, kėr-tāl', *v.t.* [O.Fr. *courtault*, Mod.Fr. *courteau*, from *court*, L. *curtus*, short.] To cut off the end or a part of; to make shorter; to dock; hence, to shorten in any manner; to abridge; to diminish.—**Curtailer**, kėr-tā'lėr, *n.* One who curtails.—**Curtailment**, kėr-tāl'ment, *n.* The act of curtailing.

Curtain, kėr'tin, *n.* [Fr. *curtine*, L.L. *cortina*, a little court, a curtain, from L. *cors, cortis*, an inclosure, a court. COURT.] A hanging cloth or screen before a window, around a bed, or elsewhere, that may be moved at pleasure so as to admit or exclude the light, conceal or show anything; the movable screen in a theater or like place serving to conceal the stage from the spectators; what resembles a curtain; *fort.* that part of a rampart which is between the flanks of two bastions, or between two gates.—*v.t.* To inclose or furnish with curtains.—**Curtain-lecture**, *n.* A lecture or reproof given behind the curtains or in bed by a wife to her husband.—**Curtain raiser**, *n.* In the theater, a short piece, usually of one scene with few characters, used to open a performance.

Curtal,‡ kėr'tal, *n.* [CURTAIL.] A horse or dog with a docked tail. (*Shak.*)—*a.* Short; abridged; brief.

Curtana, kėr-tā'na, *n.* [From L. *curtus*, shortened.] The pointless sword, carried before the kings of England at their coronation, and emblematically considered as the sword of mercy.

Curtate, kėr'tāt, *a.* [L. *curtatus*, from *curto*, to shorten. CURT.] Shortened; reduced.—*Curtate distance* (of a planet), the distance between the sun or earth and that point where a perpendicular let fall from the planet meets the plane of the ecliptic.

Curtsy, Curtesy, kėrt'si, kėr'te-si, *n.* [A modification of *courtesy.*] An obeisance or gesture of respect by a woman, consisting in bending the knees and slightly dropping the body. —*v.i.*—*curtsied, curtsying.* To drop or make a curtsy.

Curule, kū'röl, *a.* [L. *curulis.*] *Rom. antiq.* applied to a chair of state, something like a camp-stool, which belonged to certain of the magistrates of the republic in virtue of their office; hence, privileged to sit in such a chair.

Curve, kėrv, *a.* [L. *curvus*, crooked. CURB.] Bending circularly, or so as in no part to be straight; having a bent form; crooked. —*n.* A bending in a circular form; a bend or flexure such that no part forms a straight line; *geom.* a line which may be cut by a straight line in more points than one; a line which changes its direction at every point.—*v.t.*—*curved, curving.* To bend into the form of a curve; to crook.—*v.i.* To have a curved or bent form; to bend round.—**Curvate, Curvated**, kėr'vāt, kėr'vā-ted, *a.* Curved.—**Curvation**, kėr-vā'shon, *n.* The act of bending or curving.—**Curvative**, kėr'va-tiv, *a.* *Bot.* having leaves whose margins are slightly turned up or down.—**Curvature**, kėr'va-tūr, *n.* A bending in a regular form; the manner or degree in which a thing is curved.—**Curved**, kėrvd, *pp.* or *a.* Formed into or having the form of a curve.—**Curvity**, kėr'vi-ti, *n.* [L. *curvitas.*] A bending in a regular form; crookedness.

Curvet, kėr'vet or kėr-vet', *n.* [It. *corvetta*, from L. *curvare*, to bend or curve.] The leap of a horse when he raises both fore-legs at once, and as they are falling also his hind-legs; a gambol; a leap.—*v.i.*—*curvetted, curvetting.* To make a curvet; to bound or leap; to prance; to frisk or gambol.—*v.t.* To cause to make a curvet.

Curvicostate, kėr-vi-kos'tāt, *a.* [L. *curvus*, crooked, and *costa*, a rib.] Marked with small bent ribs.—**Curvidentate**, kėr-vi-den'tāt, *a.* [L. *dens*, a tooth.] Having curved teeth or tooth-like projections.—**Curvifoliate**, kėr-vi-fō'li-āt, *a.* [L. *folium*, a leaf.] Having reflected leaves.—**Curviform**, kėr'vi-form, *a.* Having a curved form.—**Curvilinear, Curvilineal**, kėr-vi-lin'ē-ėr, kėr-vi-lin'ē-al, *a.* [L. *linea*, a line.] Having the shape of a curve line; consisting of curve lines; bounded by curve lines.—**Curvilinead**, kėr-vi-lin'ē-ad, *n.* An instrument for describing curves.—**Curvilinearity**, kėr-vi-lin'ē-ar"i-ti, *n.* The state of being curvilinear.—**Curvilinearly**, kėr-vi-lin'ē-ėr-li, *adv.* In a curvilinear manner.—**Curvirostral**, kėr-vi-ros'tral, *a.* [L. *rostrum*, a beak.] *Ornith.* having a crooked beak.

Cusco-bark, kus'kō-bärk, *n.* A variety of Peruvian bark from *Cuzco* in Peru, applied medicinally to excite warmth in the system.

Cuscus, kus'kus, *n.* [Native name.] A name of several marsupial animals about the size of a cat, resembling opossums, with prehensile tails, living in trees, and natives of the smaller Australasian islands.

Cushat, kush'at, *n.* [A.Sax. *cusceote.*] The ring-dove or wood-pigeon.

Cushion, kush'on, *n.* [Fr. *coussin*, It. *cuscino*; from a hypothetical *culcitinum*, dim. of L. *culcita*, a cushion, a quilt.] A pillow for a seat; a soft pad to be placed on a chair or attached to some kind of seat; any stuffed or padded appliance; the padded side or edge of a billiard-table.—*v.t.* To furnish or fit with a cushion or cushions. —**Cushion-capital**, *n.* *Arch.* a capital having the shape of a cube rounded off at its lower extremities.—**Cushiony**, kush'on-i, *a.* Having the appearance of a cushion; cushion-shaped and soft.

Cusk, kŭsk, *n.* A large edible marine fish, allied to the cod; the burbot.

Cusp, kusp, *n.* [L. *cuspis*, a point, a spear.] A sharp projecting point; the point or horn of the crescent moon or other similar point; a prominence on a molar tooth; a projecting point formed by the meeting of curves, as in heads of Gothic windows and panels, &c.—**Cusped**, kuspt, *a.* Furnished with a cusp or cusps; cusp-shaped.—**Cuspidal, Cuspidate, Cuspidated**, kus'pi-dal, kus'pi-dāt, kus'pi-dā-ted, *a.* Cusp-shaped or having cusps; terminating in a cusp or spine (as leaves).

Cuspidor, kus'pi-dor, *n.* [Pg. from *cuspir*, to spit.] A spittoon.

Custard, kus'tėrd, *n.* [Probably a corruption of old *crustade*, a kind of stew served up in a raised *crust.*] A composition of milk and eggs, sweetened, and baked or boiled, forming an agreeable kind of food. —**Custard-apple**, *n.* [From the yellowish pulp.] The large, dark-brown, roundish fruit of a West Indian tree, now cultivated in all tropical countries.

Custody, kus'to-di, *n.* [L. *custodia*, from *custos, custodis*, a watchman, a keeper.] A keeping; a guarding; guardianship; care, watch, inspection, for keeping, preservation, or security; restraint of liberty; confinement; imprisonment.—**Custodial**, kus-tō'di-al, *a.* Relating to custody or guardianship.—**Custodian**, kus-tō'di-an, *n.* One who has the care or custody of anything, as of a library, some public building, &c.—**Custodianship**, kus-tō'di-an-ship, *n.* The office or duty of a custodian.—**Custodier**, kus-tō'di-ėr, *n.* A keeper; a guardian; one who has the care or custody of anything.

Custom, kus'tum, *n.* [O.Fr. *custume*, from L. *consuetudo, consuetudonis*, custom—*con*, with, and *sueo, suetum*, to be wont or accustomed. *Costume* is the same word.] Frequent or common use or practice; established manner; habitual practice; a practice or usage; an established and general mode of action, which obtains in a community; practice of frequenting a shop, manufactory, &c., and purchasing or giving orders; tribute, toll, or tax; *pl.* the duties imposed by law on merchandise imported or exported. ∴ *Custom* is the frequent repetition of the same act, *habit* being a custom continued so long as to develop a tendency or inclination to perform the customary act.—**Customable**, kus'tum-a-bl, *a.* Subject to the payment of the duties called customs.—**Customarily**, kus'tum-a-ri-li, *adv.* Habitually; commonly.—**Customariness**, kus'tum-a-ri-nes, *n.* State of being customary; frequency; commonness. —**Customary**, kus'tum-a-ri, *a.* According to custom or to established or common usage; wonted; usual; habitual; in common practice.—*n.* A book containing an account of the customs and municipal rights of a city, province, &c.—**Customer**, kus'tum-ėr, *n.* A purchaser; a buyer; a dealer; one that a person has to deal with, or one that comes across a person; a queer fellow.—**Customhouse**, *n.* An office where the customs on merchandise are paid or secured to be paid; the whole establishment by means of which the customs revenue is collected and its regulation enforced.—**Customs-duty**, *n.* The tax levied on goods and produce brought for consumption from foreign countries, or on export.

Custumal, kus'tū-mal, *a.* Of or pertaining to the customs of a city or manor; reference to customs duties.—*n.* A customary.

Cut, kut, *v.t.*—*cut* (pret. & pp.), *cutting.* [Of Celtic origin; comp. W. *cwt*, a short piece, *cwtogi*, to curtail; Ir. *cut*, a short tail; *cutach*, bob-tailed.] To separate or divide the parts of by an edged instrument, or as an edged instrument does; to make an incision in; to sever; to sever and cause to fall for the purpose of removing; to fell, as wood; to mow or reap, as corn; to sever and remove, as the nails or hair; to fashion by, or as by, cutting or carving; to hew out; to carve; to wound the sensibilities of; to affect deeply; to intersect; to cross (one line *cuts* another); to have no longer anything to do with; to quit (*colloq.*); to shun the acquaintance of (*colloq.*).—*To cut down*, to cause to fall by severing; to reduce as by cutting; to retrench; to curtail (expenditure).—*To cut off*, to sever from the other parts; to bring to an untimely end; to separate; to interrupt; to stop (communication); to intercept; to hinder from return or union.—*To cut out*, to remove by cutting or carving; to shape or form by, or as by, cutting; to fashion; to take the preference or precedence of; *naut.* to seize and carry off, as a vessel from a harbour or from under the guns of the enemy.—*To cut short*, to hinder from proceeding by sudden interruption; to shorten; to abridge.—*To cut up*, to cut in pieces; to criticise severely; to censure; to wound the feelings deeply; to affect greatly.—*To cut and run*, to cut the cable and set sail immediately; to be off; to be gone.—*To cut off with a penny*; to bequeath one's natural heir a penny; a practice adopted by a person dissatisfied with his heir, as a proof that the disinheritance was not the result of neglect—*To cut capers*, to leap or dance in a frolicsome manner.—*To cut a dash* or *figure*, to make a display.

—*To cut a joke*, to joke; to crack a jest.—*To cut a knot*, to take short measures with anything; in allusion to the well-known story of Alexander the Great and the Gordian knot.—*To cut a pack of cards*, to divide it into portions before beginning to deal or for other purposes.—*To cut one's stick*, to move off; to be off at once. (*Slang.*)—*To cut the teeth*, to have the teeth pierce the gums.—*v.i.* To do the work of an edge-tool; to serve in dividing or gashing; to admit of incision or severance; to use a knife or edge-tool; to divide a pack of cards, to determine the deal or for any other purpose; to move off rapidly (*colloq.*). — *To cut across*, to pass over or through in the most direct way (*colloq.*). —*To cut in*, to join in suddenly and unceremoniously (*colloq.*).—*p.* and *a.* Gashed; carved; intersected; pierced; deeply affected. — *Cut and dry*, or *cut and dried*, prepared for use: a metaphor from hewn timber.—*Cut glass*, glass having the surface shaped or ornamented by grinding and polishing.—*Cut nail*, a nail manufactured by being cut from a rolled plate of iron by machinery.—*n.* The opening made by an edged instrument; a gash; a notch; a wound; a stroke or blow as with an edged instrument; a smart stroke or blow, as with a whip; anything that wounds one's feelings deeply, as a sarcasm, criticism, or act of discourtesy; a part cut off from the rest; a near passage, by which an angle is cut off; the block on which a picture is carved, and by which it is impressed; the impression from such a block; the act of dividing a pack of cards; manner in which a thing is cut; form; shape; fashion; the act of passing a person without recognizing him, or of avoiding him so as not to be recognized by him.—*To draw cuts*, to draw lots, as of paper, &c., cut of unequal lengths.—**Cutter**, kut'ėr, *n.* One who or that which cuts; one who cuts out cloth for garments according to measurements; *naut.* a small boat used by ships of war; a vessel rigged nearly like a sloop, with one mast and a straight running bowsprit.—**Cutter-bar**, *n.* *Mech.* the bar of a boring machine, in which the cutters or cutting tools are fixed. —**Cutting**, kut'ing, *a.* Penetrating or dividing by the edge; serving to penetrate or divide; sharp; piercing the heart; wounding the feelings; sarcastic; satirical; severe. —*n.* The act or operation of one who cuts; a piece cut off; a portion of a plant from which a new individual is propagated; an excavation made through a hill or rising ground in constructing a road, railway, canal, &c.—**Cuttingly**, kut'ing-li, *adv.* In a cutting manner.—**Cut-purse**, *n.* One who cuts purses for the sake of stealing them or their contents; one who steals from the person; a thief; a robber.—**Cut-away**, *n.* A coat, the skirts of which are rounded or cut away: used also adjectively.—**Cut-off**, *n.* That which cuts off or shortens; that which is cut off; *steam-engines*, a contrivance for economizing steam. — **Cut-throat**, *n.* A murderer; an assassin; a ruffian.—*a.* Murderous; cruel; barbarous. —**Cutty**, *n.* Short pipe.—**Cutty-sark**, *n.* Short shirt or shift.—**Cutty-stool**, *n.* Of repentance, or of discipline, in old Scottish ecclesiastical penance.—**Cut-water**, *n.* The fore part of a ship's prow which cuts the water; the lower portion of the pier of a bridge formed with an angle or edge directed up stream.

Cutaneous. Under CUTICLE.

Cutch, kuch, *n.* The spawn of the oyster.

Cutcha, kuch'a, *n.* In Hindustan, an inferior kind of lime used in poor or temporary buildings; hence, used adjectively in the sense of temporary, makeshift, inferior. PUCKA.

Cutchery, kuch'ėr-i, *n.* In the East Indies, a court of justice or public office.

Cute, kūt, *a.* [An abbrev. of *acute*.] Acute; clever; sharp.—**Cuteness**, kūt'nes, *n.* The quality or character of being cute; attractive by reason of daintiness, usually with the idea of smallness, as a child.

Cuticle, kū'ti-kl, *n.* [L. *cuticula*, dim. of *cutis*, skin.] *Anat.* the outermost thin transparent skin which covers the surface of the body; the epidermis or scarf-skin; *bot.* the thin external covering of the bark of a plant; the outer pellicle of the epidermis. —**Cutaneous**, kū-tā'nē-us, *a.* Belonging to the skin; existing on or affecting the skin. — **Cuticular**, kū-tik'ū-lėr, *a.* Pertaining to the cuticle or external coat of the skin.—**Cuticularize**, kū-tik'ū-lėr-īz, *v.t.* To render cuticular.—**Cutin**, kū'-tin, *n.* A peculiar modification of cellulose, contained in the epidermis of leaves, petals, and fruits.—**Cutis**, kū'tis, *n.* [L.] *Anat.* the dense resisting skin which forms the general envelope of the body below the cuticle; the dermis or true skin.

Cutlass, kut'las, *n.* [Fr. *coutelas*, from O.Fr. *coutel* (Fr. *couteau*), a knife; from L. *cultellus*, dim. of *culter*, a knife.] A broad curving sword used by cavalry, seamen, &c.

Cutler, kut'lėr, *n.* [Fr. *coutelier*, from L. *culter*, a knife. CUTLASS.] One whose occupation is to make or deal in knives and other cutting instruments; one who sharpens or repairs cutlery; a knife-grinder. —**Cutlery**, kut'lėr-i, *n.* The business of a cutler; edged or cutting instruments.

Cutlet, kut'let, *n.* [Fr. *côtelette*, lit. a little side or rib, from *côte*, side. COAST.] A piece of meat, especially veal or mutton, cut for cooking; generally cut from the short ribs or shank.

Cuttle, Cuttle-fish, kut'l, *n.* [A.Sax. *cudele*, a cuttle-fish; G. *kuttel-fisch*.] A two-gilled cephalopodous mollusc, having a body enclosed in a sac, eight arms or feet covered with suckers, used in locomotion and for seizing prey, a calcareous internal shell, and a bag or sac from which the animal has the power of ejecting a black ink-like fluid (sepia) so as to darken the water and conceal it from pursuit.—**Cuttle-bone**, *n.* The internal calcareous plate of the cuttle-fish, used for polishing wood, as also for pounce and tooth-powder.

Cuzco-bark, kuz'kō-bärk, *n.* CUSCO-BARK.

Cyanic, sī-an'ik, *a.* [Gr. *kyanos*, blue.] Of or pertaining to the colour blue or azure; *chem.* containing cyanogen (*cyanic* acid, *cyanic* ether).—**Cyanide**, sī'an-id, *n.* A combination of cyanogen with a metallic base.—*Cyanide of potassium*, a poisonous substance used in photography and electrotyping.—**Cyanin**, sī'an-in, *n.* The blue colouring matter of certain flowers, as of the corn-flower and violet; a fugitive blue dye used in calico-printing.—**Cyanogen**, sī-an'ō-jen, *n.* A gas of a strong and peculiar odour, which under a pressure of between three and four atmospheres becomes liquid, and is highly poisonous and unrespirable. —**Cyanometer**, sī-a-nom'et-ėr, *n.* A meteorological instrument for estimating or measuring degrees of blueness of the sky. — **Cyanosis**, sī-a-nō'sis, *n.* A disease in which the skin has a blue tint, arising from the mingling of the venous and the arterial blood through defect in the heart.

Cyathiform, sī-ath-i-form, *a.* [L. *cyathus*, Gr. *kyathos*, a cup.] In the form of a cup or drinking-glass, a little widened at the top: used chiefly in *bot.*

Cycad, sī'kad, *n.* [Gr. *kykas*, a kind of plant.] One of a nat. order of gymnospermous plants, resembling palms in their general appearance, inhabiting India, Australia, Cape of Good Hope, and tropical America. — **Cycadaceous**, sī-ka-dā'shus, *a.* Belonging to the cycads. — **Cycadiform**, sī-kad'i-form, *a.* Resembling in form the cycads.

Cyclamen, sik'la-men, *n.* [From Gr. *kyklos*, a circle, referring to the round-shaped root-stock.] A European genus of low-growing herbaceous plants, with fleshy root-stocks and very handsome flowers, several of them being favourite spring-flowering greenhouse plants.

Cycle, sī'kl, *n.* [Gr. *kyklos*, a circle or cycle.] A circle or orbit in the heavens; a circle or round of years, or a period of time, in which a certain succession of events or phenomena is completed; a long period of years; an age; the aggregate of legendary or traditional matter accumulated round some mythical or heroic event or character (as the siege of Troy or King Arthur); a bicycle or similar conveyance.—*v.i.*—*cycled*, *cycling.* To use a cycle; *bot.* a complete turn of leaves, &c., arranged spirally.—*Cycle of the moon*, or golden number, a period of nineteen years, after the lapse of which the new and full moons return on the same days of the month.—*Cycle of the sun* is a period of twenty-eight years, which having elapsed, the dominical or Sunday letters return to their former place according to the Julian calendar.—*v.i.*—*cycled*, *cycling.* To recur in cycles.—**Cyclic**, sī'klik, *a.* Pertaining to or moving in a cycle or circle; connected with a cycle in the sense it has in literature. — *Cyclic poets*, Greek poets who wrote on matters and personages connected with the Trojan war. —**Cyclical**, sī'kli-kal, *a.* Pertaining to a cycle; cyclic. — **Cyclist**, sīk'list, *n.* One who uses a cycle. — **Cycloid**, sī'kloid, *n.* A curve generated by a point in the circumference of a circle when the circle is rolled along a straight line and kept always in the same plane, that is, such a line as a nail in the circumference of a carriage-wheel describes in the air while the wheel runs.—*a.* Having a circular form; belonging to the Cycloidians.—**Cycloidal**, sī'-kloi-dal, *a.* Of or pertaining to a cycloid. —**Cycloidian**, sī-kloi'di-an, *n.* One of an order of fishes having smooth, round or oval scales, without spines or enamel, as the salmon and herring; used also adjectively. —**Cyclo-branchiate**, sī'klō-brang'ki-āt, *a.* Having the branchia arranged circularly round the body, as in the limpets.

Cyclogen, sī'klō-jen, *n.* [Gr. *kyklos*, a circle, and root *gen*, to produce.] A dicotyledon with concentric woody circles; an exogen.

Cyclolith, sī'klō-lith, *n.* [Gr. *kyklos*, a circle, and *lithos*, a stone.] *Archæol.* a circle formed by standing stones, popularly called a *Druidical Circle*.

Cyclometry, sī-klom'et-ri, *n.* [Gr, *kyklos*, circle, and *metron*, measure.] The art of measuring circles.

Cyclone, sī'klōn, *n.* [From Gr. *kyklos*, a circle.] A circular or rotary storm of immense force, revolving at an enormous rate round a calm center, and at the same time advancing at a rate varying from 20 to 40 miles an hour. In the northern hemisphere they rotate from right to left, and in the southern from left to right.—**Cyclonic**, sī-klon'ik, *a.* Relating to a cyclone.—**Cyclonism**, sī'klon-izm, *n.* The theory of cyclones; a state of being exposed or subject to cyclones. Comp. ANTICYCLONE.

Cyclopedia, Cyclopaedia, sī-klō-pē'di-a, *n.* [Gr. *kyklos*, circle, and *paideia*, discipline.] A work containing definitions or accounts of the principal subjects in one or all branches of science, art, or learning; an encyclopedia.—**Cyclopedic, Cyclopaedic, Cyclopedical, Cyclopaedical**, sī-klō-pē'dik, sī-klō-pē'di-kal, *a.* Belonging to a cyclopedia.— **Cyclopedist, Cyclopaedist**, sī'klō-pē-dist, *n.* A writer in a cyclopedia; a compiler of a cyclopedia.

Cyclops, sī'klops, *n. sing.* and *pl.* [Gr. *kyklōps*, a Cyclops, pl. *kyklōpes*—*kyklos*, a circle, and *ōps*, an eye.] *Class. myth.* a race of giants who had but one circular eye in the middle of the forehead.—**Cyclopean**, sī-klō-pē'an, *a.* Pertaining to the Cyclops; vast; gigantic; *arch.* a term applied to a very early or primitive style of building distinguished by the immense size of the stones and the absence of any cement.—**Cyclopic**, sī-klop'ik, *a.* Pertaining to the Cyclops; gigantic; savage.

Cyclostome, sī'klō-stōm, *n.* [Gr. *kyklos*, a circle, and *stoma*, a mouth.] One of a family of cartilaginous fishes which have circular mouths, as the lamprey.—**Cyclostomous**, sī-klos'to-mus, *a.* Having a circular mouth or aperture.

Cyclostylar, sī-klō-stī'lėr, *a.* [Gr. *kyklos*, a circle, and *stylos*, a pillar.] *Arch.* composed of a circular range of columns without an interior building.

Cyclostyle, sī′klō-stīl, *n.* Apparatus for printing copies of writing from stencil-plate cut by a pen with a small toothed wheel.

Cyesiology, sī-ē′si-ol″o-ji, *n.* [Gr. *kyēsis*, pregnancy, and *logos*, a discourse.] *Physiol.* the branch of science which concerns itself with gestation.

Cygnet, sig′net, *n.* [Dim. of Fr. *cygne*, from L. *cygnus*, a swan.] A young swan.

Cylinder, sil′in-dėr, *n.* [Gr. *kylindros*, from *kylindō*, to roll.] A body shaped like a roller; an elongated, round, solid body, of uniform diameter throughout its length, and terminating in two flat circular surfaces which are equal and parallel; that chamber of a steam-engine in which the force of steam is exerted on the piston; in certain printing-machines, a roller by which the impression is made, and on which stereotype plates may be secured.—**Cylindric, Cylindrical**, si-lin′drik, si-lin′dri-kal, *a.* Having the form of a cylinder, or partaking of its properties.—**Cylindrically**, si-lin′dri-kal-li, *adv.* In the manner or shape of a cylinder.—**Cylindricity**, sil-in-dris′i-ti, *n.* The condition of possessing a cylindrical form.—**Cylindricule**, si-lin′dri-kūl, *n.* A small cylinder.—**Cylindriform**, si-lin′driform, *a.* Having the form of a cylinder.—**Cylindroid**, sil′in-droid, *n.* A solid body resembling a cylinder, but having the bases elliptical.

Cyma, sī′ma, *n.* [Gr. *kyma*, a wave, a sprout, from *kyō*, to swell.] *Arch.* a moulding of a cornice, the profile of which is a double curve, concave joined to convex; an ogee moulding; *bot.* a cyme.

Cymar, si-mar′, *n.* [Fr. *simmare.*] Woman's light garment.

Cymbal, sim′bal, *n.* [L. *cymbalum*, Gr. *kymbalon*, a cymbal, from *kymbos*, hollow.] A musical instrument, circular and hollow like a dish, made of brass or bronze, two of which are struck together, producing a sharp ringing sound.—**Cymbalist**, sim′ba-list, *n.* One who plays the cymbals.

Cymbiform, sim′bi-form, *a.* [L. *cymba*, a boat, and *forma*, form.] Shaped like a boat: applied to the seeds and leaves of plants, and also to a bone of the foot.

Cyme, sīm, *n.* [Gr. *kyma*, a wave, a sprout. CYMA.] *Bot.* an inflorescence of the definite or determinate class, in which the flowers are in racemes, corymbs, or umbels, the successive central flowers expanding first.—**Cymiferous**, sī-mif′ėr-us, *a.* *Bot.* producing cymes.—**Cymoid**, sī′moid, *a.* Having the form of a cyme.—**Cymose, Cymous**, sī′mōs, sī′mus, *a.* Containing a cyme; in the form of a cyme.

Cymophane, sī′mō-fān, *n.* [Gr. *kyma*, a wave, and *phainō*, to show.] A siliceous gem of a yellowish-green colour, the same as chrysoberyl.—**Cymophanous**, sī-mof′a-nus, *a.* Having a wavy floating light; opalescent; chatoyant.

Cymric, kim′rik, *a.* Of or pertaining to the Cymry (kim′ri), the name given to themselves by the Welsh; Welsh; pertaining to the ancient race to which the Welsh belong.—*n.* The language of the Cymry or ancient Britons; Welsh.

Cynanche, si-nang′kē, *n.* [Gr. *kynangchē*, a kind of sore throat, angina—*kyōn*, *kynos*, a dog, and *angchō*, to suffocate.] A disease of the throat or windpipe of several kinds, attended with inflammation, swelling, and difficulty of breathing and swallowing; quinsy; tonsillitis.

Cynanthropy, si-nan′thro-pi, *n.* [Gr. *kyon*, *kynos*, a dog, and *anthrōpos*, man.] A kind of madness in which a man imagines himself to be a dog, and imitates its voice and actions.

Cynegetics, sī-nē-jet′iks, *n.* [Gr. *kynēgetikē*—*kyōn*, *kynos*, a dog, and *hēgeomai*, to lead.] The art of hunting with dogs.

Cynic, sin′ik, *n.* [L. *cynicus*, Gr. *kynikos*, from Gr. *kyōn*, *kynos*, a dog.] One of an ancient sect of Greek philosophers who valued themselves on their contempt of riches, of arts, sciences, and amusements; a man of a currish temper; a surly or snarling man; a sneering fault-finder; a misanthrope.—**Cynic, Cynical**, sin′i-kal, *a.* Belonging to the sect of philosophers called Cynics; surly; sneering; captious.—**Cynically**, sin′i-kal-li, *adv.* In a cynical, sneering, captious, or morose manner.—**Cynicalness**, sin′i-kal-nes, *n.* The state or character of being cynical.—**Cynicism**, sin′i-sizm, *n.* The practice of a cynic; a morose contempt of the pleasures and arts of life.

Cynorexia, sī-nō-rek′si-a, *n.* [Gr. *kyōn*, *kynos*, a dog, and *orexis*, appetite.] A morbidly voracious appetite.

Cynosure, sī′no-zhör, *n.* [Gr. *kynosoura*, lit. dog's tail, the Little Bear—*kyōn*, *kynos*, a dog, and *oura*, tail.] An old name of the constellation Ursa Minor or the Little Bear, which contains the pole-star, and thus has long been noted by mariners and others; hence, anything that strongly attracts attention; a centre of attraction.

Cyperaceous, sī-pėr-ā′shus, *a.* [Gr. *kyperos*, an aromatic plant.] Belonging to the sedge family of plants; having the characters of the sedges.

Cypher, sī′fėr, *n.* Same as *Cipher.*

Cypress, sī′pres, *n.* [O.Fr. *cypres*, Gr. *kyparissos.*] The popular name of a genus of coniferous trees, some species of which have attained much favour in shrubberies and gardens as ornamental evergreen trees, while the wood of others is highly valued for its durability; the emblem of mourning for the dead, cypress branches having been anciently used at funerals.—**Cyprine**, sī′prīn, *a.* Of or belonging to the cypress.

Cyprian, sip′ri-an, *a.* Belonging to the island of *Cyprus*; a term applied to a lewd woman, from the worship of Venus in Cyprus and women of this island having anciently a bad character.—*n.* A native of Cyprus; a lewd woman; a courtesan; a strumpet.—**Cypriot**, sip′ri-ot, *n.* A native of Cyprus.

Cyprine, sī′prīn, *a.* [Gr. *kyprinos*, a carp.] Pertaining to the carp or allied fishes.

Cyprus,† **Cyprus-lawn**, sī′prus, *n.* A thin transparent black stuff; a kind of crape. (*Shak.*)

Cypsela, sip′se-la, *n.* [Gr. *kypselē*, any hollow vessel.] *Bot.* the one-celled, one-seeded, indehiscent, inferior fruit of composite plants.

Cyrenaic, sī-re-nā′ik, *a.* Pertaining to *Cyrene*, a Greek colony on the north coast of Africa, or to a school of Epicurean philosophers founded there by Aristippus, a disciple of Socrates. Also used as a noun.—**Cyrenian**, sī-rē′ni-an, *n.* A native or inhabitant of Cyrene.

Cyrillic, sī-ril′ik, *a.* [From St. *Cyril*, its reputed inventor.] The term applied to an alphabet adopted by all the Slavonic peoples belonging to the Eastern Church.

Cyriologic,† sī′ri-o-loj″ik, *a.* [Gr. *kyrios*, chief, *logos*, discourse.] Relating or pertaining to writing by pictures.

Cyrtostyle, sėr′tō-stīl, *n.* [Gr. *kyrtos*, curved, and *stylos*, a pillar.] *Arch.* a circular portico projecting from the front of a building.

Cyst, sist, *n.* [Gr. *kystis*, a bladder.] A close sac or bag of vegetable or animal nature; a bladder-like body; a hollow organ with thin walls (as the urinary bladder); a bladder-like bag or vesicle which includes morbid matter in animal bodies.—**Cysted**, sis′ted, *a.* Inclosed in a cyst.—**Cystic, Cystose**, sis′tik, sis′tōs, *a.* Pertaining to, or contained in, a cyst; having cysts; formed in, or shaped like, a cyst.—**Cysticercus**, sis-te-ser′kus. [Gr. *kystis*, a bladder, *kĕrkŏs*, a tail.] In tape-worms, a simple cyst with only one head.—**Cysticle**, sis′ti-kl, *n.* A small cyst.—**Cystiform**, sis′ti-form, *a.* In the form of a cyst.—**Cystirrhœa**, sis-tir-rē′a, *n.* [Gr. *rheō*, to flow.] Discharge of mucus from the bladder.—**Cystitis**, sis-tī′tis, *n.* Inflammation of the bladder.—**Cystocele**, sis′tō-sēl, *n.* [Gr. *kēlē*, a tumour.] A hernia or rupture formed by the protrusion of the urinary bladder.—**Cystolith**, sis′tō-lith. [Gr. *kystis*, a bladder, *lithos*, a stone.] *Bot.* a concretion of carbonate of lime projecting into an epidermal cell.—**Cystolithic**, sis-tō-lith′ik, *a.* *Med.* relating to stone in the bladder.—**Cystoscope**, sis′tō-skōp. [Gr. *kystis*, a bladder, *skōpeō*, I look at.] An instrument for inspecting the interior of the bladder.—**Cystotome**, sis′tō-tōm, *n.* [Gr. *tomos*, cutting.] *Surg.* an instrument for cutting into the bladder.—**Cystotomy**, sis-tot′o-mi, *n.* The act or practice of opening encysted tumours; the operation of cutting into the bladder for the extraction of a calculus.

Cytherean, sith-e-rē′an, *a.* [From *Cythera*, now Cerigo, where Venus was specially worshipped.] Pertaining to Venus.

Cytoblast, sī′tō-blast, *n.* [Gr. *kytos*, a cavity, and *blastanō*, to sprout.] *Biol.* the nucleus, cellule, or centre from which the organic cell is developed.—**Cytoblastema**, sī′tō-blas-tē″ma, *n.* The substance of which animal and vegetable cells are formed; protoplasm.—**Cytode**, sī′tōd, *n.* [Gr. *kytos*, a cavity.] *Biol.* a cell containing protoplasm but with no nucleus.

Cytogenesis, Cytogeny, sī-tō-jen′e-sis, sī-toj′e-ni, *n.* [Gr. *kytos*, a cell, and *genesis*, origin.] *Biol.* the development of cells in animal and vegetable structures.—**Cytogenetic**, sī′tō-je-net″ik, *a.* *Biol.* relating or pertaining to cell formation.—**Cytology**, sī-tol′o-ji, *n.* The biological doctrine of cells; the study of cells.—**Cytolysis**, kit-ol′is-is. [Gr. *kytŏs*, a cell, *lysis*, a loosing.] The dissolving of poisoned cells.—**Cytoplasm**, kit′ō-plasm. [Gr. *kytŏs*, a cell, *plasma*, anything formed.] Of a cell, the part of the protoplasm outside the nucleus.

Czar, zär or tsär, *n.* [Perhaps a corruption of L. *Cæsar.*] A title of the Emperor of Russia.—**Czarevna**, zä-rev′na, *n.* The wife of the czarowitz.—**Czarina**, zä-rē′na, *n.* A title of the Empress of Russia.—**Czarowitz, Czarewitch**, &c., zä′rō-vits, zä′re-vich, *n.* The title of the eldest son of the Czar of Russia.

Czech, chech, *n.* A Bohemian; one of the Slavonic inhabitants of Bohemia; the language of the Czechs or Bohemians.

D

D, in the English alphabet, is the fourth letter and the third consonant, representing a dental sound; as a numeral equivalent to 500; *mus.* the second note of the natural scale, answering to the French and Italian *re.*

Dab, dab, *v.t.*—*dabbed*, *dabbing.* [Allied to O.D. *dabben*, to dabble, probably also to *dub.*] To strike quickly but lightly with the hand or with some soft or moist substance.—*n.* A gentle blow with the hand or some soft substance; a quick but light blow; an expert (*colloq.*); a small lump or mass of anything soft or moist; a name common to many species of the flat-fishes, but especially to a kind of flounder which is found along the European and American coasts of the Atlantic Ocean.—**Dabber**, dab′ėr, *n.* One who dabs.

Dabble, dab′l, *v.t.*—*dabbled*, *dabbling.* [A dim. and freq. from *dab.*] To wet; to moisten; to spatter; to sprinkle.—*v.i.* To play in water, as with the hands; to splash in mud or water; to do or engage in anything in a slight or superficial manner; to occupy one's self with slightly; to dip into; to meddle.—**Dabbler**, dab'lėr, *n.* One who dabbles in water or mud; one who partakes casually without going thoroughly into an activity; a superficial, casual participant, as one who *dabbles* in politics.

Dabchick, dab'chik, *n.* [*Dab*, equivalent to *dip*, and *chick*, from its habit of dipping or diving below the water.] The little grebe, a small swimming bird of the diver family.

Da capo, dä kä'pō. [It.] *Mus.* a direction to repeat from the beginning of a passage or section.

Dace, dās, *n.* [O.Fr. *dars*, a dace, a dart; comp. also Fr. *vandoise*, the dace.] A small river fish resembling the roach, chiefly inhabiting the deep and clear waters of quiet streams.

Dachshund, daks'hunt, *n.* [G. *dachs*, badger, *hund*, dog.] Badger-dog; a long-bodied, short-legged dog, with pendulous ears and short hair, black with yellow extremities.

Dacoit, Dacoity. DAKOIT, DAKOITY.

Dacryoma, dak-ri-ō'ma, *n.* [Gr. *dakru*, a tear.] *Med.* the stoppage of one or both of the tear-passages to the nose, thus causing the tears to overflow on the cheek.

Dactyl, Dactyle, dak'til, *n.* [Gr. *daktylos*, a finger, a dactyl, which, like a finger, consists of one long and two short members.] A poetical foot consisting of three syllables, the first long and the others short, or the first accented, the others not, as in häppily.—**Dactylic**, dak-til'ik, *a.* Pertaining to or consisting chiefly or wholly of dactyls.—*n.* A dactylic verse.—**Dactylioglyph**, dak-til'i-ō-glif, *n.* [Gr. *daktylios*, a finger-ring, *glyphō*, to engrave.] An engraver of gems for rings, &c.; the artist's name on a finger-ring or gem.—**Dactylioglyphy**, dak-til'i-og"li-fi, *n.* The engraving of precious stones for rings, &c.—**Dactyliography**, dak-til'i-og"ra-fi, *n.* The art of gem engraving; a description of engraved finger-rings and precious stones.—**Dactyliology**, dak-til'i-ol"o-ji, *n.* Knowledge relating to the history and qualities of finger-rings.—**Dactylology**, dak-ti-lol'o-ji, *n.* The art of communicating ideas or thoughts by the fingers; the language of the deaf and dumb.

Dactylorhiza, dak'ti-lō-rī"za, *n.* [Gr. *daktylos*, a finger, and *rhiza*, a root.] A disease of the bulbs of turnips, which divide and become hard and useless, believed to be due to the nature of the soil; finger-and-toe.

Dad, Daddy, dad, dad'i, *n.* [Comp. W. *tad*, Skr. *tata*, Hind. *dada*, Gypsy *dad*, *dada*, L. *tata*, Gr. *tata*, Lapp *dadda*—father.] A childish or pet name for father.—**Daddy-long-legs**, *n.* A name given to species of the crane-fly.

Daddle,† dad'l, *v.i.* [Origin doubtful.] To walk with tottering steps, like a child or an old man.—**Dade**,† dād, *v.t.* and *i.* To hold up by leading-strings.—*v.i.* To walk slowly and hesitatingly.

Dado, dā'dō, *n.* [It., a die, a dado, same word as *die*, *n.*] That part of a pedestal which is between the base and the cornice; the finishing of the lower part of the walls in rooms, made somewhat to represent a continuous pedestal, and frequently formed by a lining of wood, by painting, or by a special wall-paper.

Dædal, Dædalian, dē'dal, dē-dā'li-an, *a.* [L. *Dædalus*, Gr. *Daidalos*, an ingenious artist.] Formed with art; showing artistic skill; ingenious; mazy; intricate.—**Dædalous**, dē'da-lus, *a.* Having a margin with various windings; of a beautiful and delicate texture: said of the leaves of plants.

Dæmon, dē'mon. Same as *Demon*.

Daff,†‡ daf, *v.t.* [A form of *doff*.] To toss aside, to put off. (*Shak.*)

Daffodil, daf'ō-dil, *n.* [O.E. *affodille*, O.Fr. *asphodile*, Gr. *asphodelos*. ASPHODEL.] Common name of a plant of the amaryllis family with bright yellow bell-shaped flowers; a variety of narcissus. Grows in woods, and meadows: called also *Daffadowndilly*, *Daffadilly*, *Daffodilly*.

Dag, dag, *n.* [Fr. *dague*; akin *dagger*.] A kind of old pistol or hand-gun.

Dag, dag, *n.* [Probably from same root as *dagger*.] A loose end, as of a lock of wool.

Dagger, dag'ėr, *n.* [W. *dagr*, Ir. *daigear*, Armor. *dager*, *dag*, a dagger or poniard; Gael. *daga*, a dagger, a pistol; Fr. *dague*, a dagger.] A weapon resembling a short sword, with usually a two-edged, sometimes a three-edged, sharp-pointed blade, used for stabbing at close quarters; *printing*, a mark of reference in the form of a dagger, thus †.—*At daggers drawn*, on hostile terms; at war.—*To look* or *speak daggers*, to look or speak fiercely, savagely.—*v.t.* To stab with a dagger.

Daggle, dag'l, *v.t.*—*daggled*, *daggling*. [A freq. form of the obsolete verb *dag*, to bedew, from Icel. *dögg*, Sw. *dagg*, dew.] To make limp by passing through water; to trail in mud or wet grass; to befoul; to draggle.—*v.i.* To run through mud and water.—**Daggle-tail**. A slattern.

Dago, dā'gō, *n.* [Sp. *Diego*, James.] A name applied to Spanish, Portuguese, or Italian immigrants, often scornfully.

Dagoba, da'gō-ba, *n.* An oriental structure, circular in form, and sometimes rising to a great height, built to contain relics of Buddha or of some Buddhist saint.

Dagon, dā'gon, *n.* [Heb. *dag*, a fish.] The national god of the Philistines, represented with the upper part of a man and the tail of a fish.

Daguerreotype, da-ger'ō-tīp, *n.* [From *Daguerre* of Paris, the inventor.] A photographic process by which the picture is fixed on a chemically coated metallic plate solely by the action of the sun's actinic or chemical rays; a picture produced by the process.

Dahabieh, da-ha-bē'ā, *n.* [Egyptian name.] A kind of boat in use on the Nile for the conveyance of travellers, and having one or two masts with a long yard supporting a triangular sail.

Dahlia, dāl'i-a, *n.* [From *Dahl*, a Swedish botanist.] A genus of American composite plants, consisting of tuberous-rooted herbs, putting forth solitary terminal flowers, well known from the varieties of one species being florists' plants.

Daily, dā'li, *a. adv.* and *n.* See under DAY.

Daimio, dī'mi-ō, *n.* [Japanese.] The title of a class of feudal lords in Japan, the greater number of whom, previous to 1871, exercised the authority of petty princes in their domains.

Dainty, dān'ti, *a.* [From O.Fr. *daintie*, *dainté*, pleasantness, an agreeable thing, same word as *dignity*, or from W. *dantaidd*, *dantaeth*, a dainty, what is toothsome, from *dant*, a tooth.] Pleasing to the palate; of exquisite taste; delicious, as food; of acute sensibility; nice in selecting what is tender and good; delicate; squeamish; luxurious, as the palate or taste; scrupulous; affectedly fine; nice; ceremonious; elegant; pretty and slight; tender; effeminately beautiful.—*n.* Something delicate to the taste; that which is delicious; a delicacy.—**Daintily**, dān'ti-li, *adv.* In a dainty manner.—**Daintiness**, dān'ti-nes, *n.* The state or quality of being dainty.

Dairy, dā'ri, *n.* [From O.E. *dey*, a dairy-maid = Sw. *deja*, a dairymaid, Icel. *deigja*, a maid servant, a dairymaid; akin *-dy* in *lady*.] The place where milk is processed and prepared for sale; a shop where milk, butter, &c., are sold; also used as an adj.—**Dairy-farm**, *n.* A farm devoted to the keeping of cows and the sale of dairy products.—**Dairying**, dā'ri-ing, *n.* The business of conducting a dairy.—**Dairymaid**, dā'ri-mād, *n.* A female whose business is to milk cows and work in the dairy.—**Dairyman**, dā'ri-man, *n.*

Dais, dā'is, *n.* [O.Fr. *dais*, *deis*, a dining-table, from L. *discus*, a dish, a quoit. *Disk*, *desk*, are the same word.] The high table at the upper end of an ancient dining-hall at which the chief persons sat; the raised floor on which the table stood; the chief seat at the high table; often with a canopy; a canopy.

Daisy, dā'zi, *n.* [A.Sax. *dæges-eáge*, day's eye, because it opens and closes its flower with the daylight.] The popular name of a composite plant, one of the most common wild flowers, being found in all pastures and meadows, and several varieties being cultivated in gardens; also the name of several other plants having a somewhat similar blossom. North Carolina's state flower.—**Daisied**, dā'zid, *a.* Full of daisies; adorned with daisies.

Dak, däk, *n.* DAWK.

Dakoit, da-koit', *n.* An East Indian name for robbers who plunder in bands, but seldom take life.—**Dakoity**, da-koi'ti, *n.* The system of robbing in bands.

Dalai-lama, da-lī'lä-ma, *n.* One of the two lama popes of Tibet and Mongolia (his fellow-pope being the Tesho-lama), each supreme in his own district.

Dale, dāl, *n.* [A.Sax. *dæl*=Icel. Sw. Goth. &c. *dal*, G. *thal*, a valley. *Dell* is akin; the root may be in *deal*.] A low place between hills; a vale or valley.—**Dalesman**, dālz'man, *n.* One living in a dale or valley.

Dally, dal'i, *v.i.*—*dallied*, *dallying*. [Probably allied to G. *dalen*, *dallen*, *tallen*, to speak or act childishly, to trifle, to toy; or perhaps E. *doll*.] To waste time in effeminate or voluptuous pleasures; to amuse one's self with idle play; to trifle; to linger; to delay; to toy and wanton; to interchange caresses; to fondle; to sport; to play; to frolic.—**Dalliance**, dal'yans, *n.* The act of dallying, caressing, fondling, trifling, deferring, or delaying.—**Dallier**, dal'i-ėr, *n.* One who dallies.

Dalmatian, dal-mā'shi-an, *a.* Of or pertaining to *Dalmatia*.—*Dalmatian dog*, a variety of dog of elegant shape, of a white colour, thickly marked with black rounded spots; usually kept as a coach-dog.—**Dalmatic**, dal-mat'ik, *n.* The vestment used by the deacon at mass, and worn also by bishops under the chasuble, so called as coming originally from Dalmatia, long, loose, and wide-sleeved.

Dal segno, dal sān'yō. [It., from the sign.] *Mus.* a direction to go back to the 𝄋 sign and repeat from thence to the close.

Daltonism, dal'ton-izm, *n.* [From *Dalton*, the chemist, who suffered from this defect, and was the first to call attention to it.] Colour-blindness.

Dalton's (or Henry's) Law. The law that while the volume of a gas dissolved in a liquid remains constant, its weight rises and falls in proportion to the pressure.

Dam, dam, *n.* [A form of *dame*.] A female parent: used now only of quadrupeds, unless in contempt.

Dam, dam, *n.* [Indian.] Name of a small Indian coin of slight value—*not worth a dam*. RAP.

Dam, dam, *n.* [Same word as Sw. and G. *damm*, Dan. and D. *dam* (as in Amster*dam*, Rotter*dam*, &c.); Lith. *tama*, a dam.] A bank, mound of earth, wall, or other structure, built across a current of water, to raise its level for the purpose of driving mill-wheels, or for other purposes.—*v.t.*—*dammed*, *damming*. To obstruct by a dam; to confine by constructing a dam.

Damage, dam'āj, *n.* O.Fr. *damage*; Fr. *dommage*, from L.L. *damnaticum*, from L. *damnum*, loss, injury. DAMN.] Any hurt, injury, or harm to person, property, character, or reputation; the value in money of what is injured, harmed, or lost; the estimated money equivalent for detriment or injury sustained: in this sense commonly in pl.—*v.t.*—*damaged*, *damaging*. To injure; to impair; to lessen the soundness, goodness, or value of.—*v.i.* To become injured or impaired in soundness or value.—**Damageable**, dam'āj-a-bl, *a.* Capable of being injured or impaired; susceptible of damage.

Daman, dā'man, *n.* A rabbit-like animal, the hyrax, or cony of Scripture.

Damar, dam'ăr, *n.* Same as *Dammar.*

Damascene, dam'as-sēn, *n.* [L. *damascenus*, from *Damascus.*] A kind of plum; a damson.—*v.t.* To damask; to damaskeen.

Damask, dam'ask, *a.* Of or belonging to *Damascus*; of the colour of the rose so called; pink or rosy.—*Damask steel*, a fine steel chiefly from Damascus, used for sword-blades. — *n.* The name given to textile fabrics of various materials, more especially silk and linen, ornamented with raised figures of flowers, &c.; a pink colour, like that of the damask-rose.—*v.t.* To form or imprint the figures of flowers upon, as upon cloth; to variegate; to diversify; to adorn with figures, as steel-work.—**Damaskeen**, dam'as-kēn, *v.t.* [Fr. *damasquiner.*] To ornament (particularly iron and steel) with designs produced by inlaying or incrusting with another metal, as gold, silver, &c., by etching, and the like; to damask.—**Damask-plum**, *n.* A small plum, the damson.—**Damask-rose**, *n.* A pink species of rose, a native of Damascus.—**Damassin**, dam'as-sin, *n.* A kind of damask, with gold and silver flowers woven in.

Dame, dām, *n.* [Fr. *dame*, from L. *domina*, a mistress, fem. of *dominus*, a lord, whence *dominate, dominion, damsel*, &c.; same root as E. *tame.*] A woman in authority; a title equivalent to *Lady, Madam, Miss*, used as a form of address; a woman in general; particularly, a woman of mature years; the mistress of an elementary school.

Dammar, dam'ăr, *n.* A gum or resin used as a colourless varnish, and produced by various species of coniferous trees (dammar or dammara-pine) belonging to the South Asiatic islands and New Zealand, kauri gum being a variety.

Damn, dam, *v.t.* [L. *damno*, to condemn, from *damnum*, damage, a fine, penalty, from root *da*, as in *dare*, to give.] To consign or send to punishment in a future state; to send to hell; to condemn, censure, reprobate severely; to condemn or destroy the success of by common consent, as by hissing in a theatre or by criticisms in the press.—*n.* A profane oath; a curse or execration.—**Damnable**, dam'na-bl, *a.* Liable to be damned or condemned; deserving damnation; odious, detestable, or pernicious.—**Damnableness**, dam'na-bl-nes, *n.* The state or quality of being damnable.—**Damnably**, dam'na-bli, *adv.* In a damnable manner; odiously; detestably; infernally. — **Damnation**, dam-nā'shon, *n.* Sentence to punishment in a future state, or the state in which such punishment is undergone; eternal punishment; penalty inflicted for sin; condemnation.—**Damnatory**, dam'na-to-ri, *a.* Containing a sentence of condemnation; condemning to damnation; condemnatory. — **Damned**, damd, *p.* and *a* Suffering punishment in hell; lost; hateful; detestable; abominable.—**Damnify**, dam'ni-fī, *v.t.*—*damnified, damnifying.* [L. *damnifico*—*damnum* and *facio.*] To cause loss or damage to.—**Damnific**, dam-nif'ik, *a.* Mischievous. — **Damning**, dam'ning, dam'ing, *a.* Exposing to damnation; calling for damnation (a *damning* sin).

Damp, damp, *a.* [Same word as D. and Dan. *damp*, G. *dampf*, steam, vapour, fog, smoke.] Being in a state between dry and wet; moderately wet; moist; humid; depressed or dejected.—*n.* Moist air; humidity; moisture; fog; dejection; depression of spirits; chill; a noxious exhalation issuing from the earth, and deleterious or fatal to animal life, such as exists in old disused wells, in mines and coal-pits.—*v.t.* To make damp; to moisten; to chill, deaden; depress, or deject; to check or restrain; to discourage; to dispirit; to abate.—**Dampen**, dam'pen, *v.t.* To make damp or moist.—*v.i.* To grow or become damp.—**Damper**, dam'pėr, *n.* One who or that which damps; an iron plate sliding across a flue of a furnace, &c., to check or regulate the draught of air; a piece of mechanism in a pianoforte which, after the finger has left the key, checks a long-continued vibration of the strings; a cake made of flour and water without fermentation (a colonial word).—**Dampish**, dam'pish, *a.* Moderately damp or moist. — **Dampishly**, dam'pish-li, *adv.* In a dampish manner. —**Dampishness**, dam'pish-nes, *n.* The state of being dampish. — **Dampness**, damp'nes, *n.* The state or condition of being damp; moistness; humidity.

Damsel, dam'zel, *n.* [Fr. *demoiselle*, O.Fr. *damoisele, damisele*, from L.L. *dominicella*, dim. of L. *domina, domna*, a mistress. DAME.] A young unmarried woman; a maiden; a virgin.

Damson, dam'zn, *n.* [Contr. from *damascene* (which see).] A small black, dark-bluish, purple, or yellow plum.

Dan, dan, *n.* [O.Fr. *dan, dans*, a master, from L. *dominus.* DAME.] An old title of honour equivalent to *master, sir, don* ('*Dan* Chaucer').

Dance, dans, *v.i.*—*danced, dancing.* [Fr. *danser*, from O.H.G. *dansôn*, to draw.] To leap or move with measured steps, regulated by music; to leap and frisk about; to move nimbly, as up and down, backwards and forwards.—*v.t.* To make to dance; to dandle. —*To dance attendance*, to be assiduous in attentions and officious civilities.—*n.* A leaping or stepping with motions of the body adjusted to the measure of a tune; the regular movements of one who dances; a tune by which dancing is regulated.—**Dancer**, dan'sėr, *n.* One who dances.—**Dancing - master**, *n.* A teacher of dancing.

Dandelion, dan'di-lī-un, *n.* [Fr. *dent de lion*, lion's tooth.] A well-known composite plant, having a naked stalk, with one large bright yellow flower, and a tapering milky perennial root of aperient and tonic properties.

Dandle, dan'dl, *v.t.* — *dandled, dandling.* [Allied to G. *tand*, prattle, frivolity, *tändeln*, to trifle, to dandle.] To shake or jolt on the knee, as an infant; to fondle, amuse, or treat as a child; to pet.—**Dandler**, dand'lėr, *n.* One who dandles.

Dandruff, dan'druf, *n.* [Probably Celtic. W. *ton*, skin, and *drwg*, bad.] A scurf which forms on the head and comes off in small scales or particles.

Dandy, dan'di, *n.* [Fr. *dandin*, a ninny, akin to E. *dandle.*] A man who pays excessive attention to dress; one who dresses with special finery; a fop; a coxcomb.—*a.* Finely or foppishly dressed; foppish; trim; gay.—**Dandify**, dan'di-fī, *v.t.* To make, form, or dress out as a dandy or fop.—**Dandyish**, dan'di-ish, *a.* Like a dandy.—**Dandyism**, dan'di-izm, *n.* The manners and dress of a dandy; foppishness.

Dane, dān, *n.* A native or inhabitant of Denmark.—**Danegelt, Danegeld**, dān'gelt, dān'geld, *n.* [*Gelt, geld*=A.Sax. *geld, gild*, a payment.] An annual tax laid on the English nation in early times for maintaining forces to oppose the Danes, or to furnish tribute to procure peace.—**Danish**, dā'nish, *a.* Belonging to the Danes or Denmark.—*n.* The language of the Danes.

Danger, dān'jėr, *n.* [Formerly control, power, Fr. *danger*, O.Fr. *dangier, dongier*, a feudal term for right to woods and waters, from L.L. *dominiarium*, from L. *dominus*, a lord; akin *dominion, dame, damsel*, &c.] Exposure to destruction, ruin, injury, loss, pain, or other evil; peril; risk; hazard; jeopardy. —**Dangerous**, dān'jėr-us, *a.* Attended with danger; perilous; hazardous; unsafe; full of risk; creating danger; causing risk of evil.—**Dangerously**, dān'jėr-us-li, *adv.* In a dangerous manner or condition.—**Dangerousness**, dān'jėr-us-nes, *n.* The state or quality of being dangerous.

Dangle, dang'gl, *v.i.*—*dangled, dangling.* [Allied to Dan. *dingle*, Sw. and Icel. *dingla*, to swing.] To hang loose, flowing, shaking, or waving; to hang and swing; to be a humble officious follower, or to hang about a person (with *about* or *after*).—*v.t.* To cause to dangle; to swing.—**Dangler**, dang'glėr, *n.* One who dangles; a man who hangs about women.

Dank, dangk, *a.* [Nasalized form allied to *daggle* and Sw. *dagg*, dew.] Damp; moist; humid. — *n.*‡ Moisture; humidity; the watery element. (*Mil.*)—**Dankish**, dangk'-ish, *a.* Somewhat damp.

Danseuse, däṅ-süz, *n.* [Fr.] A female stage-dancer.

Danubian, da-nū'bi-an, *a.* Pertaining to or bordering on the river Danube.

Dap, dap, *v.i.* [Onomatopoetic.] To drop or let fall the bait gently into the water: an angling word.

Daphnal, daf'nal, *a.* and *n.* [G. *daphnē*, laurel.] *Bot.* a term applied to the laurels and kindred plants.

Dapper, dap'ėr, *a.* [Same word as D. *dapper*, Sw. and Dan. *tapper*, G. *tapfer*, brave.] Small and active; nimble; brisk; lively; neat. — **Dapperling**, dap'ėr-ling, *n.* A dwarf; a little fellow.

Dapple, dap'l, *a.* [Icel. *depill*, a spot; perhaps akin to *dip, deep.*] Marked with spots; spotted; variegated with spots of different colors or shades of color.—*v.t.* *dappled, dappling.* To spot; to variegate with spots.—**Dapple-bay**, *a.* Of a bay color, variegated by spots of a different shade.—**Dapple-gray**, *a.* Of a gray color, variegated by spots of a different shade.

Dare, dăr, *v.i.*—pret. *dared* or *durst*; pp. *dared*; ppr. *daring.* [A.Sax. *ic dear*, I dare, *he dear*, he dare, *we durran*, we dare; *ic dorste*, I durst; Goth. *daursan*, O.H.G. *turran*; cog. Gr. *tharsein*, Skr. *dharsh*, to be courageous.] To have courage for any purpose; to make up the mind to undertake something hazardous or dangerous; to be bold enough; to venture. — *v.t.* — *dared, daring.* To challenge; to provoke; to defy. —**Dare-devil**, *n.* A desperado; one who fears nothing and will attempt anything.—**Daring**, dā'ring, *a.* Bold; audacious; courageous; intrepid; adventurous. — *n.* Courage; boldness; fearlessness; audacity. —**Daringly**, dā'ring-li, *adv.* In a daring manner. — **Daringness**, dā'ring-nes, *n.* Boldness.

Dare, dăr, *v.t.* [Perhaps akin to *daze, dazzle*, by interchange of *z* and *r*; comp. *frore, frozen.*] To stupefy by sudden terror; to daze.

Dare, dăr, *n.* The dace. DACE.

Darg, därg, *n.* [A contr. for *day-work.*] A day's work; the quantity of work turned out in a day. (Provincial.)

Dark, därk, *a.* [A.Sax. *deorc*; not found in the other Teutonic languages; comp. Gael. and Ir. *dorch*, dark, black.] Destitute of light; not radiating or reflecting light; wholly or partially black; having the quality opposite to white; gloomy; disheartening; not cheerful; concealed; secret; mysterious; not easily understood; not enlightened with knowledge; rude; ignorant (the *dark* ages); morally black; atrocious; wicked; sinister; keeping designs concealed; not fair; said of the complexion.—*n.* [Usually with *the.*] Darkness; the absence of light; a dark hue; a dark part; secrecy; obscurity; a state of ignorance. — **Darken**, där'kn, *v.t.* To make dark or black; to deprive of light; to obscure, cloud, make dim; to deprive of vision; to render gloomy; to render ignorant or stupid; to render less clear or intelligible; to make less white or clear; to tan; to sully; to taint.—*v.i.* To grow dark or darker.—**Darkish**, därk'ish, *a.* Dusky; somewhat dark.—**Darkling**, därk'ling, *adv.* [*Dark*, and term. *-ling*, as in *flatling=long* in *headlong.*] In the dark; at night.—*a.* Black-looking; lowering; gloomy. (*Thack.*)—**Darkly**, därk'li, *adv.* In a dark manner; with imperfect light, clearness, or knowledge; obscurely; dimly; blindly; uncertainly. —**Darkness**, därk'nes, *n.* The state or quality of being dark; the want of physical light; gloom; obscurity; deepness of shade or colour; physical, intellectual, or moral blindness; ignorance; sinfulness; secrecy; uncertainty; want of clearness and intelligibility.—**Darksome**, därk'sum, *a.* Dark; gloomy; obscure.—**Darky**, där'ki, *n.* A popular name for a negro.

Darling, där'ling, *a.* [A.Sax. *deórling—deóre*, dear, and dim. term. *-ling.* DEAR.] Dearly beloved; dear; favourite.—*n.* One much beloved; a favourite.

Darn, därn, *v.t.* [W. and Armor. *darn*, Ir. *darne*, a piece, a patch.] To mend a rent or hole in, by imitating the texture of the cloth or stuff with yarn or thread and a needle; to sew or repair by crossing and recrossing the stitches.—*n.* A place mended by darning.—**Darner**, där'nėr, *n.* One who darns.

Darnel, där'nel, *n.* [O.Fr. *darnelle*; same root as D. *door*, G. *thor*, a fool, Lith. *durnas*, foolish, mad; from its narcotic properties.] A troublesome weed in cornfields, with rye-like ears, which, when ground among corn, are said to be narcotic and stupefying.

Dart, därt, *n.* [O.Fr. *dart*, Mod.Fr. *dard*; of Germanic origin=Sw. *dart*, A.Sax. *daroth*, O.H.G. *tart.*] A pointed missile weapon to be thrown by the hand; a short lance; anything which pierces and wounds; a sudden or rapid rush, leap, bound, spring, or flight.—*v.t.* To throw (a dart, &c.) with a sudden thrust; to throw swiftly; to shoot.—*v.i.* To fly, as a dart; to fly rapidly; to spring and run with velocity; to start suddenly and run.—**Darter**, där'tėr, *n.* One that darts; a web-footed tropical bird of the pelican tribe, so called from darting after fish in the water.—**Dartingly**, där'ting-li, *adv.* Rapidly; like a dart.

Dartre, där'tr, *n.* [Fr.] A name for herpes, or other skin diseases.—**Dartrous**, där'trus, *a.* Pertaining to dartre.

Darwinian, där-win'i-an, *a.* Of or pertaining to Charles *Darwin*, the celebrated naturalist.—*n.* A believer in Darwinism.—**Darwinism**, där'win-izm, *n.* The doctrine as to the origin and modifications of the species of animal and plants taught by Darwin, the principal points being that there is a tendency to variation in organic beings, so that descendants may differ very widely from progenitors; that animals and plants tend naturally to multiply rapidly, so that if unchecked they would soon overstock the whole globe; that there is thus a continual struggle for existence among all organized beings; that the strongest and best fitted for particular surroundings naturally survive, and the others die out; that from a few forms (perhaps even one) sprang all existing species, genera, orders, &c., of animals and plants.

Dash, dash, *v.t.* [A Scandinavian word=Dan. *daske*, to slap, *dask*, a slap, Sw. *daska*, to beat.] To cause to strike or come against suddenly and with violence; to strike or throw violently or suddenly; to sprinkle or mix slightly; to disturb or frustrate (to *dash* courage); to confound, confuse, abash.—*To dash off*, to form or sketch out in haste carelessly; to execute hastily or with careless rapidity.—*v.i.* To rush with violence; to strike or be cast violently.—*n.* A violent striking together of two bodies; collision; something thrown into another substance; infusion; admixture; a sudden check; abashment; a rapid movement; a sudden onset; the capacity for unhesitating, prompt action; vigour in attack; a flourish or ostentatious parade; a mark or line [—] in writing or printing noting a break or pause.—**Dasher**, dash'ėr, *n.* One who or that which dashes; the float of a paddle-wheel, the plunger of a churn, and the like; also a dash-board.—**Dashing**, dash'ing, *a.* Impetuous; spirited; showy; brilliant.—**Dash-board**, *n.* A board or leathern apron on the fore part of a vehicle to intercept mud, etc.; a partition below the windshield of an automobile (instrument board).—**Dash-pot**, *a.* A cylinder partly filled with water or other fluid, and having a loosely fitted piston working in it, and thus serving to prevent shock to some piece of mechanism.—**Dash-wheel**, *n.* A wheel revolving in a tank, used to wash fabrics by dipping them in water and dashing them against the walls.

Dastard, das'tėrd, *n.* [Icel. *dæstr*, exhausted; akin to *daze*, the suffix being *-ard.*] A coward; a poltroon; one who meanly shrinks from danger.—*a.* Cowardly; meanly; shrinking from danger.—**Dastardliness**, das'tėrd-li-nes, *n.* Cowardliness.—**Dastardly**, das'tėrd-li, *a.* Cowardly; meanly timid; base; sneaking.—**Dastardness**, **Dastardy**, das'tėrd-nes, das'tėrd-i, *n.* Cowardliness; mean timorousness.

Dasyure, dā'si-ūr, *n.* [Gr. *dasys*, hairy, and *oura*, a tail.] The brush-tailed opossum, a plantigrade carnivorous marsupial found in Australia.

Data. DATUM.

Date, dāt, *n.* [Fr., from L. *datum*, given, used in a Roman letter as 'given' (at such a place and such a time).] That addition to a writing which specifies the year, month, and day when it was given or executed; the time when any event happened, when anything was transacted, or when anything is to be done; the period of time at or during which one has lived or anything has existed; an appointment (*colloq.*); a person of the opposite sex with whom one has an appointment for a social engagement. (*Slang.*)—*Out of date*, obsolete; behind the times.—*Up to date*, modern; in the latest style.—*v.t.*—*dated*, *dating.* To write down the date on; to append the date to; to note or fix the time of; to make an appointment with a person of the opposite sex for a social engagement (*Slang.*)—*Predate*, to date prior to the time of issuance.—*Postdate*, to date subsequent to the time of issuance.—*v.i.* To reckon time; to begin at a certain date (to *date* from the 10th century); to have a certain date.—**Dateless**, dāt'les, *a.* Having no date; undated; so old as to be beyond date; having no fixed limit; eternal.

Date, dāt, *n.* [O.Fr. *date*, Fr. *datte*, from L. *dactylus*, Gr. *daktylos*, a finger, a date.] The fruit of the date-palm, consisting of a soft fleshy drupe enclosing a hard seed and having a delicious flavor, used as food in North Africa and Western Asia, and imported into other countries.—**Date-palm**, **Date-tree**, *n.* A palm having a stem rising to the height of 50 or 60 feet, crowned with large feathery leaves, the female plant bearing 180 to 200 dates.

Dative, dā'tiv, *a.* [L. *dativus*, from *do*, to give.] *Gram.* a term applied to the case of nouns which usually follows verbs that express giving, or the doing of something to or for.—*n.* The dative case.

Datum, dā'tum, *n.* pl. **Data**, dā'ta. [L.] Something given or admitted; some fact, proposition, quantity, or condition granted or known, from which other facts, propositions, &c., are to be deduced.—*Datum line, engin.* the base line of a section from which all the heights and depths are measured in the plans of a railway, &c.

Daturine, dat'ū-rin, *n.* [From *Datura Stramonium*, the botanic name of the plant.] A poisonous alkaloid found in the thorn-apple.

Daub, dạb, *v.t.* [O.Fr. *dauber*, to plaster, from L. *dealbare*, to white-wash—*de*, intens., and *albus*, white.] To smear with soft adhesive matter, as with mud or slime; to plaster; to soil; to defile; to besmear; to paint coarsely; to lay or put on without taste; to load with affected finery.—*n.* A smear or smearing; a coarse painting.—**Dauber**, dạ'bėr, *n.* One who daubs; a builder of walls with clay or mud mixed with straw; a coarse painter; a low and gross flatterer.—**Dauby**, dạ'bi, *a.* Viscous; slimy; adhesive.

Daughter, dạ'tėr, *n.* [A.Sax. *dóhtor*=D. *dochter*, Dan. *dotter*, Icel. *dóttir*, G. *tochter*, Gr. *thygatēr*, Per. *doktarah*, Skr. *duhitri*, Lith. *duktė*, Ir. *dear*—daughter.] A female child of any age; a female descendant; a title of affection given to a woman by a person whose age, position, or office entitles the speaker to respect or esteem; the female offspring of an animal or plant.—**Daughter-in-law**, *n.* A son's wife.—**Daughterliness**, dạ'tėr-li-nes, *n.* The state of being daughterly.—**Daughterly**, dạ'tėr-li, *a.* Becoming a daughter; dutiful.

Dauk, dạk, *n.* Same as *Dawk.*

Daunt, dạnt, *v.t.* [O.Fr. *danter*, Fr. *dompter*, to tame, from L. *domitare*, a freq. of *domo*, to tame, from root of *dominus*, a lord. TAME.] To repress or subdue the courage of; to intimidate; to dishearten; to check by fear.—**Daunter**, dạnt'ėr, *n.* One who daunts.—**Dauntless**, dạnt'les, *a.* Bold; fearless; intrepid; not timid; not discouraged.—**Dauntlessly**, dạnt'les-li, *adv.* In a bold fearless manner.—**Dauntlessness**, dạnt'les-nes, *n.* Fearlessness; intrepidity.

Dauphin, dạ'fin, *n.* [Fr. *dauphin*, the title originally of the lords of *Dauphiny*, and afterwards attached to the French crown along with this province, from L. *delphinus*, a dolphin, the crest of the lords of Dauphiny.] The eldest son of the King of France prior to the revolution of 1830.—**Dauphiness**, dạ'fin-es, *n.* The wife of the dauphin.

Dauw, dạ, *n.* One of the South African zebras, a species only found on the plains.

Davit, da'vit, *n.* [Origin unknown.] *Naut.* either of the two projecting pieces of wood or iron on the side or stern of a vessel, used for suspending or lowering and hoisting the boats by means of pulleys.

Davy-lamp, dā'vi-lamp, *n.* A lamp whose flame is surrounded by wire, invented by Sir Humphry *Davy* to protect the miners from explosions of fire-damp.

Daw, dạ, *n.* [From cry.] A jackdaw.

Dawdle, dạ'dl, *v.i.* [Akin to *daddle*; and probably to *dowdy*, a slattern.] To waste time; to trifle; to saunter.—*v.t.* To waste by trifling.—**Dawdler**, dạ'dlėr, *n.* One who dawdles; a trifler.

Dawk, dạk, *n.* [Hind.] In the East Indies, the post; a relay of men, as for carrying letters, despatches, &c., or travellers in palanquins.

Dawn, dạn, *v.i.* [A.Sax. *dagain*, to dawn or become day, from *dæg*, day.] To begin to grow light in the morning; to grow light; to begin to show intellectual light or knowledge; to begin to become visible or appear (the truth *dawns* upon me).—*n.* The break of day; the first appearance of light in the morning; first opening or expansion; beginning; rise; first appearance (the *dawn* of civilization, &c.).—**Dawning**, dạn'ing, *n.* The growing light in the morning; dawn.

Day, dā, *n.* [A.Sax. *dæg*=D. Dan. and Sw. *dag*, Icel. *dagr*, Goth. *dags*, G. *tag*; not connected with L. *dies*, a day.] That space of time during which there continues to be light, in contradistinction to night; the time between the rising and setting of the sun; the period of one revolution of the earth on its axis, or twenty-four hours; light; sunshine (in the open *day*); any period of time distinguished from other time (the authors of that *day*); age; era; epoch; in the plural often = lifetime, earthly existence; the contest of a day or day of combat (to gain the *day*); an appointed or fixed time; time of commemorating an event; anniversary.—*Days of grace*, a certain number of days (usually three) allowed for the payment of a bill (not payable on demand) beyond the date marked on the face of it specifying when it becomes due.—*Astronomical, natural*, or *solar day*, the interval between the sun's leaving the meridian and his return to it.—*Mean solar day*, the mean of all the solar days in the year.—*Sidereal day*, the time of one apparent revolution of the fixed stars.—*Civil day*, the day beginning and ending at midnight.—*Jewish day*, the interval between sunset and sunset.—*Day's journey*, an indefinite measure of distance frequently mentioned in Scripture; the average distance one can travel on a day, say from 12 miles or more on foot, to 20 or over on horseback.—**Daily**, dā'li, *a.* Happening, being, or appearing every day; done day by day; bestowed or enjoyed every day.—*adv.* Every day; day by day.—*n.* A newspaper published daily.—**Day-bed**, *n.* A bed used for rest during the day; a couch; a sofa. (*Shak.*)—**Day-blindness**, *n.* The visual defect by which objects are seen only in the evening and at night.—**Day-book**, *n.* A book in which are recorded the debts and credits or accounts of the day.—**Daybreak**, dā'brāk, *n.* The dawn or first appearance of light in the morning.—**Daydream**, dā'drēm, *n.* A reverie; a visionary fancy indulged in when awake. — **Daydreamer**, dā'drē-mėr, *n.* One who indulges in daydreams.—**Dayfly**, dā'flī, *n.* The popular name of those neuropterous insects which, though they may exist in the larval and pupal state for several years, in their perfect form exist only from a few hours to a few days.—

Day-labor, *n.* Labor hired or performed by the day; stated or fixed labor.—**Day-laborer**, *n.* One who works by the day.—**Daylight**, dā'līt, *n.* The light of the day; the light of the sun.

—**Day-lily**, *n.* [The beauty of its flowers rarely lasts over one day.] A liliaceous plant of which the fragrant yellow species is a favourite garden flower.—**Daylong**, dā'long, *a.* Lasting all day.—**Daypeep**,† dā'pēp, *n.* The dawn. (*Mil.*)—**Day-school**, *n.* A school taught during the day, at which the scholars are not boarded: opposed to *evening-school, boarding-school.* — **Day-sight**, *n.* A defect of vision, in which the sight is clear and strong only in the daylight.—**Daysman**, dāz'man, *n.* [Lit. one who appoints a *day* for hearing a cause.] An umpire or arbiter; a mediator (O.T.).—**Dayspring**, dā'spring, *n.* The dawn; the beginning of the day (N.T.).—**Daytime**, dā'tīm, *n.* The time of daylight.

Daze, dāz, *v.t.* [The same word as Icel. *dasa*, to tire out; O.D. *daesen*, to be foolish; akin *doze, dizzy.*] To stun or stupefy, as with a blow, liquor, or excess of light; to blind by too strong a light.

Dazzle, daz'l, *v.t.*—*dazzled, dazzling.* [Freq. of *daze.*] To overpower or blind with light; to dim by excess of light; *fig.* to overpower or confound by splendour or brilliancy, or with show or display of any kind.—*v.i.* To be overpoweringly bright or brilliant; to be overpowered or dimmed by light (as the eyes). — *n.* A dazzling light; glitter. — **Dazzler**, daz'lėr, *n.* One who or that which dazzles.—**Dazzling**, daz'ling, *a.* So bright as to dazzle; excessively brilliant.—**Dazzlingly**, daz'ling-li, *adv.* In a dazzling manner.

Deacon, dē'kon, *n.* [L. *diaconus*, Gr. *diakonos*, a minister or servant.] In the Roman and Anglican churches, a member of the lowest of the three orders of priesthood (bishops, priests, and deacons); in Presbyterian churches, a functionary who attends to the secular interests of the church; among Congregationalists, Baptists and others, one who looks after the spiritual as well as temporal concerns of the congregation under the minister; in Scotland, the president of an incorporated trade.—**Deaconess**, dē'kon-es, *n.* A female deacon in the primitive church.—**Deaconhood**, dē'kon-hud, *n.* The state or office of a deacon; deacons collectively.—**Deaconry, Deaconship**, dē'kon-ri, dē'kon-ship, *n.* The office of a deacon.

Dead, ded, *a.* [A.Sax. *deád* = D. *dood*, Dan. *död*, Icel. *dauthr*, Goth. *dauths.* DEATH, DIE.] Deprived, devoid, or destitute of life; having lost the vital principle; lifeless; inanimate; hence, wanting animation, activity, spirit, vigour; numb; callous; void of perception; resembling death; deep and sound (a *dead* sleep); perfectly still or motionless (a *dead* calm); monotonous; unvarying or unbroken by apertures or projections (a *dead* level, or wall); unemployed; useless (*dead* capital or stock); unreverberating, dull, heavy (a *dead* sound); tasteless, vapid, spiritless, flat, as liquors; producing death; sure or unerring as death (a *dead* shot); in a state of spiritual death; under the power of sin; cut off from the rights of a citizen; not communicating motion or power (*dead* steam); no longer spoken, or in common use by a people (a *dead* language); having no gloss, warmth, or brightness (a *dead* colour).—*The dead* (*sing.*), the time when there is a remarkable stillness or gloom; the culminating point, as the midst of winter or of night; (*pl.*), those who are dead; the deceased; the departed.—*adv.* To a degree approaching death; to the last degree; thoroughly; completely (*dead* tired, *dead* drunk). — **Deaden**, ded'n, *v.t.*—To deprive of a portion of vigour, force, or sensibility; to abate the vigour or action of; to destroy the acuteness, pungency, spirit, or brilliancy of; to render dull, flat, heavy, or vapid.—**Deadly**, ded'li, *a.* Causing death; mortal; fatal; destructive; implacable.—*adv.* In a manner resembling death (*deadly* pale); mortally; destructively. —**Deadliness**, ded'li-nes, *n.* The quality of being deadly.—**Deadness**, ded'nes, *n.* The state of being dead; lifelessness; want of animation, spirit, vigour, activity, or force. — **Dead-beat**, *n.* In clock and watch making, a term applied to a kind of escapement in which the seconds hand is made to stand still an instant after each beat without recoil.—**Dead-center**, **Dead-point**, *n.* A position in a link motion such as that when the crank and connecting-rod of a steam-engine are in a straight line.—**Dead-coloring**, *n.* A first layer of colors, usually some shade of gray, on which are superinduced the finishing colors.—**Dead-eye**, *n.* *Naut.* a block without a pulley pierced with three holes and used to extend the shrouds and stays, &c.—**Deadhead**, ded'hed, *n.* A person who receives free tickets for theaters, or passes for conveyances.—*v.t.* To treat as a deadhead.—**Dead-heat**, *n.* The result, in a contest of speed, when two so that no one is the winner. — **Dead-house**, *n.* An apartment in a hospital or other institution where dead bodies are kept for a time.—**Dead-letter**, *n.* A letter which cannot be delivered from defect of address, and which is sent to the general post office to be opened and returned to the writer; anything, as a condition, treaty, &c., which has lost its force or authority, by lapse of time or any other cause, and has ceased to be acted on.—**Dead-light**, *n.* *Naut.* a strong wooden shutter for protecting the windows of cabins, &c., in a storm.—**Dead-load**. See LOAD.—**Dead-lock**, *n.* Such a complicated state of affairs as renders action or progress impossible; complete obstruction or standstill.—**Dead-meat**, *n.* The flesh of cattle, sheep, and pigs, slaughtered and ready for the market.—**Dead-nettle**, *n.* A perennial herb of various species so called from the resemblance of its leaves to the common nettle, though it has no stinging power. — **Dead-pay**, *n.* The continued pay of soldiers and sailors actually dead, but which dishonest officers charge and appropriate.—**Dead-reckoning**, *n.* The calculation of a ship's place at sea from the distance run by the log, and the courses steered by the compass, rectified by allowances for drift, lee-way, &c.—**Dead-set**, *n.* The fixed position of a dog in pointing game; a determined effort or attempt; a pointed attack. — **Dead-wall**, *n.* A blank wall, without windows or openings.—**Dead-weight**, *n.* A heavy or oppressive burden.

Deaf, def, *a.* [A.Sax. *deáf*=D. *doof*, Dan. *döv*, Icel. *daufr*, G. *taub*—deaf; akin Sc. *daft*, stupid, Icel. *dofi*, torpor.] Wanting the sense of hearing, either wholly or in part; disinclined to hear; inattentive; unheeding; unconcerned. — **Deafen**, def'n, *v.t.* To make deaf; to deprive of the power of hearing; to stun; to prevent the passage of sound.—**Deafening**, def'ning, *n.* Matter used to prevent the passage of sound through floors, partitions, and the like.—**Deafly**, def'li, *adv.* Without sense of sounds; obscurely heard.—**Deafness**, def'nes, *n.* The state of being deaf, or of being unable to hear sounds; want of hearing; unwillingness to hear; inattention.—**Deaf-mute**, *n.* A person who is both deaf and dumb.

Deal, dēl, *n.* [A.Sax. *dael*, a portion, a share=D. *deel*, a portion, a board or plank; Dan. *deel*, Sw. *del*, Goth. *dails*, G. *theil*, a part, a share. *Dole, dale* are akin.] A portion or part; an indefinite quantity, degree, or extent, generally implying that the amount is considerable (often qualified by *great* which hardly adds to the sense); the division or distribution of playing cards; a board or plank of fir, of some length and at least 7 inches wide; fir or pine timber.—*v.t.* —*dealt* (delt), *dealing.* [A.Sax. *daelan*, to divide.] To divide in portions; to give out; to part; to distribute; to scatter; to hurl (blows, destruction).—*v.i.* To distribute; to traffic; to trade; to negotiate; to transact; to have intercourse; to conduct one's self in relation to others; to act; to behave.—**Dealer**, dēl'ėr, *n.* One who deals; one who has to do or has concern with others; a trader, merchant, or trafficker; one who distributes cards to the players.—**Dealing**, dē'ling, *n.* Conduct; behaviour; practice (double-*dealing*, fair *dealing*); traffic; business; intercourse or business of friendship; concern: commonly in pl.—**Deal-fish**, *n.* [From *deal*, board.] A name for a fish with an extremely compressed body found in the northern seas.

Dean, dēn, *n.* [O.Fr. *dean*, *deien*, Mod.Fr. *doyen*, from L. *decanus*, one set over ten persons, from *decem*, ten.] An ecclesiastical dignitary ranking next to the bishop; an administrative officer of a college or university, under the president, supervising students in regard to their choice of courses, heading the faculty of a division or college, or adviser to men or women; a senior member of a diplomatic corps; an acknowledged leader in a profession.—**Deanery**, dē'nėr-i, *n.* The office or jurisdiction of a dean; the official residence of a dean.—**Deanship**, dēn'ship, *n.* The office or title of a dean.

Dear, dēr, *a.* [A.Sax. *deóre, dýre*, dear, beloved, high-priced; O.D. *dier*, Mod.D. *duur*, Icel. *dýrr*, Dan. and Sw. *dyr*, G. *theuer*, dear, beloved, high-priced, &c.] Bearing a high price in comparison with the usual price or the real value; high-priced: opposite to *cheap*; characterized by high prices resulting from scarcity (a *dear* year); greatly valued; beloved; precious; heartfelt‡; passionate or intense‡.—*n.* A darling; a term of affection or endearment. —*adv.* Dearly; tenderly; at a dear rate.—**Dearly**, dēr'li, *adv.* At a high price; with great fondness; fondly; tenderly.—**Dearness**, dēr'nes, *n.* The state or quality of being dear; high value in price, or estimation; preciousness; tender love.—**Dearth**, dėrth, *n.* [Comp. *warm-th, heal-th, slo(w)-th*, &c.] Scarcity, which makes food dear; want, or time of want; famine; lack or absence.—**Deary**, dē'ri, *n.* A familiar word of endearment.

Deaspirate, dē-as'pi-rāt, *v.t.*—*deaspirated, deaspirating.* To deprive of the aspirate, to pronounce without an aspirate.

Death, deth, *n.* [A.Sax. *deáth* = Goth. *dauthus*, L.G. and D. *dood*, Sw. and Dan. *död*, G. *tod*—death. DEAD, DIE.] That state of a being, animal or vegetable, in which there is a total and permanent cessation of all the vital functions; the state of being dead; the state or manner of dying; cause, agent, or instrument of death; total loss or extinction (the *death* of one's faculties); capital punishment.—*Civil death*, deprivation of the rights of citizenship, as when a man is banished or becomes a monk. —**Deathless**, deth'les, *a.* Not subject to death, destruction, or extinction; undying; immortal.—**Deathly**, deth'li, *a.* and *adv.* Resembling death; cadaverously; wanly.—**Death-agony**, *n.* The agony or struggle which immediately precedes death.—**Death-bed**, *n.* The bed on which a person dies or is confined in his last sickness. —**Death-bell**, *n.* The bell that announces death; the passing-bell.—**Death-blow**, *n.* A blow causing death; a mortal blow; any thing which extinguishes hope or blights one's prospects.—**Death-fire**, *n.* A luminous appearance or flame, as the *ignis fatuus*, supposed to presage death.—**Death-rate**, *n.* The proportion of deaths among the inhabitants of a town, country, &c.—**Death-rattle**, *n.* A peculiar rattling in the throat of a dying person.—**Death's-door**, *n.* A near approach to death; the gates of death.—**Death's-head**, *n.* The skull of a human skeleton, or a figure representing one.—*Death's-head moth*, the largest lepidopterous insect found in Britain, having markings upon the back of the thorax very closely resembling a skull or death's-head.—**Death's-man**, *n.* An executioner; a hangman.—**Death-stroke**, *n.* The stroke of death; a death-blow.—**Death-struggle**, *n.* Death agony.—**Death-token**, *n.* That which indicates approaching death. (*Shak.*) — **Death-warrant**, *n.* An order from the proper authority for the execution of a criminal.—**Death-watch**, *n.* A small beetle, the ticking noise made by which is superstitiously supposed to prognosticate death.

Debacle, dē-bak'l, *n.* [Fr., from *débâcler*, to break up—*de*, priv., and *bâcler*, to bar, from L. *baculus*, a bar.] A sudden breaking up of ice in a river; *geol.* a sudden outbreak of water; the complete collapse of an enterprise.

Debar, dē-bär', *v.t.*—*debarred*, *debarring*. To bar or cut off from entrance; to preclude; to hinder from approach, entry, or enjoyment; to shut out or exclude.—**Debarment**, dē-bär'ment, *n.* The act of debarring.

Debark, dē-bärk', *v.t.* and *i.* [Fr. *débarquer*—*de*, and *barque*, a boat or bark.] To land from a ship or boat; to disembark.—**Debarkation**, dē-bärk-ā'shon, *n.* The act of disembarking.

Debase, dē-bās', *v.t.*—*debased*, *debasing*. To impart a certain baseness to; to reduce or lower in quality, dignity, character, &c.; to degrade; to vitiate; to adulterate; to abase.—**Debasement**, dē-bās'ment, *n.* The act of debasing, or state of being debased.—**Debaser**, dē-bā'sėr, *n.* One who or that which debases.—**Debasingly**, dē-bā'sing-li, *adv.* So as to debase.

Debate, dē-bāt, *n.* [O.Fr. *debatre*, to debate—prefix *de*, and *batre*, to beat. BATTER, ABATE.] An argument or reasoning between persons of different opinions; dispute; controversy; quarrel; strife; contention.—*v.t.*—*debated*, *debating*. To discuss by arguments for and against; to dispute; to argue; to contest.—*v.i.* To discuss disputed points; to examine different arguments in the mind (to *debate* with one's self whether).—*Debating society*, a society for the purpose of debate and improvement in extemporaneous speaking.—**Debatable**, dē-bā'ta-bl, *a.* Capable of being debated; disputable; subject to controversy and contention. — **Debater**, dē-bā'tėr, *n.* One who debates; a disputant.

Debauch, dē-bạch', *v.t.* [O.Fr. *desbaucher*, Fr. *débaucher*—*de*, *des*, and *bauche*, a workshop, a task; the original meaning would therefore be to draw one away from his work or duty.] To corrupt or vitiate (as principles, &c.); to corrupt with lewdness; to bring to be guilty of unchastity: to seduce; to lead astray from duty or allegiance.—*n.* Excess or a fit of excess in eating or drinking; intemperance; drunkenness. — **Debauched**, dē-bạcht', *p.* and *a.* Vitiated in morals; given to debauchery; characterized by debauchery.—**Debauchedly**, dē-bạch'ed-li, *adv.* In a profligate manner.—**Debauchedness**, dē-bạcht'nes, *n.* The state of being debauched.—**Debauchee**, deb'o-shē, *n.* A man given to debauchery.—**Debaucher**, dē-bạ'chėr, *n.* One who debauches.—**Debauchery**, dē-bạ'chėr-i, *n.* Excessive indulgence in sensual pleasures of any kind, as gluttony, intemperance, unlawful indulgence of lust.—**Debauchment**, dē-bạch'ment, *n.* The act of debauching.

Debenture, dē-ben'tūr, *n.* [L. *debentur*, there are owing (certain things), a word used in old acknowledgments of debt. Akin *debt*, *debit*.] A deed or document charging certain property with the repayment of money lent by a person therein named, and with interest on the sum lent at a given rate; a certificate or drawback of customs duties on the exportation of certain goods.—**Debentured**, dē-ben'tūrd, *a.* Entitled to drawback or debenture; secured by debenture.

Debilitate, dē-bil'i-tāt, *v.t.*—*debilitated*, *debilitating*. [L. *debilito*, *debilitatum*, to weaken, from *debilis*, weak.] To weaken; to impair the strength of; to enfeeble; to make faint or languid.—**Debilitating**, dē-bil'i-tāt-ing, *a.* Tending or adapted to weaken.—**Debilitation**, dē-bil'i-tā"shon, *n.* The act of weakening; relaxation.—**Debility**, dē-bil'i-ti, *n.* [L. *debilitas*.] A state of general bodily weakness; feebleness; languor of body; faintness.

Debit, deb'it, *n.* [L. *debitum*, something owed, from *debeo*, to owe—*de*, from, and *habeo*, to have.] That which is entered in an account as a debt; a recorded item of debt; that part of an account in which is entered any article of goods furnished, or money paid to or on account of a person.—*v.t.* To charge with as a debt (to *debit* a person *for* or *with* goods); to enter on the debtor side of a book.

Déblai, de-blā, *n.* [Fr., from L. *de*, from, *ablatum*, taken away.] *Fort.* the earth excavated from the ditch to form the parapet.

Debonair, deb-ō-när', *a.* [Fr. *débonnaire*—*de*, from, *bon*, good, and *aire* (L. *area*), place, extraction.] Characterized by courtesy, affability, or gentleness; elegant; well-bred; winning; accomplished. — **Debonairly**, deb-ō-när'li, *adv.* In a debonair manner.—**Debonairness**, deb-ō-när'nes, *n.* The character of being debonair.

Debouch, dē-bösh', *v.i.* [Fr. *déboucher*—*de*, from, and *bouche*, mouth, L. *bucca*, the cheek.] To issue or march out of a narrow place, or from defiles, as troops.—**Débouchure**, dā-bö'shür, *n.* [An English formation, by analogy with Fr. *embouchure*.] The mouth or opening of a river or channel.

Debris, dā-brē', *n.* [Fr., from *dé*, L. *dis*, asunder, apart, and *briser*, to break.] Fragments; rubbish; ruins; *geol.* any accumulation of broken and detached matter, as that which arises from the waste of rocks, and which is piled up at their base or swept away by water.

Debt, det, *n.* [O.Fr. *debte* (now *dette*), L. *debita*, things due. DEBIT.] That which is due from one person to another; that which one person is bound to pay to or perform for another; what is incumbent on one to do or suffer; a due; an obligation; the state of owing something to another (to be in *debt*); a duty neglected or violated; a trespass; a sin (N.T.).—**Debtor**, det'ėr, *n.* [L. *debitor*.] A person who owes another either money, goods, or services: the correlative of *creditor*; one who has received from another an advantage of any kind; one indebted or in debt.

Debunk, dē-bunk', *v.t.* To show the error in false or high-flown statements. [*Colloq.*]

Debut, dā-bü, *n.* [Fr.—*de*, from, and *but*, mark, butt. The word has its meaning from the bowl being brought from the butt on one commencing to play at bowls.] Entrance upon anything; first appearance before the public, as that of an actor or actress on the stage.—**Debutant**, *fem.* **Debutante**, dā-bü-tän, dā-bü-tänt, *n.* [Fr.] One who makes a debut or first appearance before the public.

Decachord, dek'a-kord, *n.* [Gr. *deka*, ten, and *chordē*, string.] An ancient Greek musical instrument, triangular in shape, and having ten strings.

Decade, **Decad**, dek'ād, dek'ad, *n.* [L. *decas*, *decadis*, Gr. *dekas*, from *deka*, ten.] The sum or number of ten; an aggregate or group consisting of ten; specifically, an aggregate of ten years.—**Decadal**, dek'adal, *a.* Pertaining to ten; consisting of tens.

Decadence, **Decadency**, dek'a-dens, dek'a-den-si, *n.* [Fr. *décadence*, L.L. *decadentia*, from L. *de*, down, and *cado*, to fall.] Decay; a falling into a lower state.—**Decadent**, dek'a-dent, *a.* In decadence; decaying; deteriorating. — *n.* An artist or writer of a morally weak fibre and style.

Decagon, dek'a-gon, *n.* [Gr. *deka*, ten, and *gōnia*, a corner.] *Geom.* a plane figure having ten sides and ten angles.—**Decagonal**, de-kag'o-nal, *a.* Of or belonging to a decagon.

Decagram, **Decagramme**, dek'a-gram, *n.* [Fr. *décagramme*, Gr. *deka*, ten, and Fr. *gramme*.] A French weight of 10 grams, equal to 5.644 drams avoirdupois.

Decagyn, dek'a-jin, *n.* [Gr. *deka*, ten, and *gynē*, a female.] *Bot.* a plant having ten pistils.—**Decagynian**, **Decagynous**, dek-a-jin'i-an, de-kaj'i-nus, *a.* *Bot.* having ten pistils.

Decahedron, dek-a-hē'dron, *n.* [Gr. *deka*, ten, and *hedra*, a seat, a base.] *Geom.* a figure or body having ten sides.—**Decahedral**, dek-a-hē'dral, *a.* Having ten sides.

Decalcify, dē-kal'si-fī, *v.t.* [L. *de*, priv., and *calx*, *calcis*, lime, chalk.] To deprive of lime, as bones of their hardening matter, so as to reduce them to gelatine.—**Decalcification**, dē-kal'si-fi-kā"shon, *n.* The removal of calcareous matter, as from bones.

Decalcomania, dē-kal'kō-mā"nia, *n.* [Fr. *decalcomanie*.] A process in printing which permits the transfer of the ink, forming a design or picture, from the paper on which it is printed to some object such as porcelain, glassware, or automobile windshields in the case of vehicle tax certificates.

Decalogue, dek'a-log, *n.* [Gr. *deka*, ten, and *logos*, a word.] The ten commandments or precepts given by God to Moses at Mount Sinai.—**Decalogist**, de-kal'o-jist, *n.* One who explains the decalogue.

Decamp, dē-kamp', *v.i.* [Fr. *décamper*—*de*, from, and *camp*, a camp.] To remove or depart from a camp or camping ground; to march off; to depart; to take one's self off, especially in a secret or clandestine manner.—**Decampment**, dē-kamp'ment, *n.* Departure from a camp; a marching off.

Decanal, dē'kan-al, *a.* [L. *decanus*, a dean. DEAN.] Pertaining to a dean or deanery.

Decander, de-kan'dėr, *n.* [Gr. *deka*, ten, and *anēr*, *andros*, a male.] *Bot.* a plant having ten stamens.—**Decandrian**, **Decandrous**, de-kan'dri-an, de-kan'drus, *a.* *Bot.* having ten stamens.

Decangular, de-kang'gū-lėr, *a.* [Gr. *deka*, ten, and E. *angular*.] Having ten angles.

Decant, dē-kant', *v.t.* [Fr. *décanter*, to decant—*de*, and *canter*, from O.Fr. *cant*, a rim, an edge; lit. to pour out by canting or tilting. CANT.] To pour off gently, as liquor from its sediment, or from one vessel into another.—**Decantation**, dē-kan-tā'shon, *n.* The act of decanting.—**Decanter**, dē-kan'tėr, *n.* One who decants; a vessel used to decant liquors, or for receiving decanted liquors; a glass vessel or bottle used for holding wine or other liquors for filling drinking-glasses.

Decaphyllous, de-kaf'il-lus, *a.* [Gr. *deka*, ten, and *phyllon*, a leaf.] *Bot.* having ten leaves: applied to the perianth of flowers

Decapitate, dē-kap'i-tāt, *v.t.*—*decapitated*, *decapitating*. [L.L. *decapito*, *decapitatum*, to behead—L. *de*, and *caput*, head.] To behead; to cut off the head of.—**Decapitation**, dē-kap'i-tā"shon, *n.* The act of beheading.

Decapod, dek'a-pod, *n.* [Gr. *deka*, ten, and *pous*, *podos*, a foot.] One of an order of crustaceans (crabs, lobsters) having ten feet; one of that division of the cuttle-fishes which have ten prehensile arms.—*a.* Having ten feet; belonging to the decapods.—**Decapodal**, **Decapodous**, de-kap'o-dal, de-kap'o-dus, *a.* Belonging to the order of decapods; having ten feet.

Decarbonate, dē-kär'bo-nāt, *v.t.* To deprive of carbonic acid.—**Decarbonization**, **Decarburization**, dē-kär'bo-ni-zā"shon, dē-kär'bū-ri-zā"shon, *n.* The process of depriving of carbon.—**Decarbonize**, **Decarburize**, dē-kär'bo-nīz, dē-kär'bū-rīz, *v.t.*—*decarbonized*, *decarbonizing*. To deprive of carbon.

Decastich, dek'a-stik, *n.* [Gr. *deka*, ten, and *stichos*, a verse.] A poem consisting of ten lines.

Decastyle, dek′a-stīl, *n.* [Gr. *deka*, ten, and *stylos*, a column.] A portico or colonnade of ten columns.—*a.* Decorated with or having ten columns.

Decasyllabic, dek′a-sil-lab″ik, *a.* [Gr. *deka*, ten, and *syllabē*. a syllable.] Having ten syllables.

Decay, dē-kā′, *v.i.* [O.Fr. *decaer*, from L. *de*, down, and *cadere*, to fall; seen also in *cadence, chance, casual, incident*, &c.] To pass gradually from a sound, prosperous, or perfect state, to a less perfect state, or toward weakness, or dissolution; to become decomposed or corrupted; to rot; to be gradually impaired; to waste or moulder away.—*v.t.*† To impair; to bring to a worse state. (*Shak.*)—*n.* The state or process of decaying; decline to a worse or less perfect state; decomposition; putrefaction; deterioration; wasting.—**Decayedness**, dē-kād′nes, *n.* A state of being decayed.—**Decayer**, dē-kā′ėr, *n.* That which causes decay.

Decease, dē-sēs′, *n.* [Fr. *décès*, from L. *decessus*, departure—*de*, and *cedo*, *cessum*, to go. CEDE.] Departure from this life; death.—*v.i.* To depart from this life; to die.—**Deceased**, dē-sēst′, *p.* Departed from life; dead: frequently used as a noun, the word *person* being understood.—**Decedent**,† dē-sē′dent, *a.* [L. *decedens.*] Departing; removing.

Deceit, dē-sēt′, *n.* [O.Fr. *deceit*, L. *deceptus*, from *decipio*, *deceptum*, to deceive, lit. to take down—*de*, down, and *capio*, to take. CAPABLE.] The quality or act of deceiving; guilefulness; the act of misleading a person; any artifice, stratagem, or practice, which misleads another, or causes him to believe what is false; act of fraud; cheat; fallacy. ∴ Syn. under FRAUD.—**Deceitful**, dē-sēt′ful, *a.* Given to deceive; full of deceit; tending to mislead, deceive, or insnare; trickish; fraudulent; cheating.—**Deceitfully**, dē-sēt′ful-li, *adv.* In a deceitful manner.—**Deceitfulness**, dē-sēt′ful-nes, *n.* Disposition or tendency to mislead or deceive; the quality of being deceitful.—**Deceive**, dē-sēv′, *v.t.*—*deceived, deceiving.* [Fr. *décevoir*, O.Fr. *decever.*] To mislead the mind of, especially intentionally; to cause to believe what is false, or disbelieve what is true; to cause to mistake; to impose on; to delude; to frustrate or disappoint (the hopes, &c.).—**Deceivable**, dē-sē′va-bl, *a.* Capable of being or liable to be deceived.—**Deceivableness**, dē-sē′va-bl-nes, *n.* Liableness to be deceived.—**Deceivably**, dē-sē′va-bli, *adv.* In a deceivable manner.—**Deceiver**, dē-sē′vėr, *n.* One who deceives.

December, dē-sem′bėr, *n.* [L., from *decem*, ten, this being the tenth month among the early Romans, who began the year in March.] The twelfth and last month in the year, in which the sun is at his greatest distance south of the equator.—**Decemberly**, dē-sem′bėr-li, *a.* Resembling December; chilly; gloomy; cheerless.

Decemfid, dē-sem′fid, *a.* [L. *decem*, ten, and *findo*, to divide.] *Bot.* ten-cleft; divided into ten parts; having ten divisions.

Decemlocular, dē-sem-lok′ū-lėr, *a.* [L. *decem*, ten, and *loculus*, a cell.] *Bot.* having ten cells for seeds.

Decempedal, dē-sem′pē-dal, *a.* [L. *decem*, ten, and *pes*, a foot.] Having ten feet; ten feet in length.

Decemvir, dē-sem′vėr, *n.* pl. **Decemvirs**, **Decemviri**, dē-sem′vėrz, dē-sem′vi-rī. [L. *decem*, ten, and *vir*, a man.] One of ten magistrates, who had absolute authority in ancient Rome, from B.C. 449 to 447.—**Decemviral**, dē-sem′vėr-al, *a.* Pertaining to the decemvirs.—**Decemvirate**, dē-sem′vėr-āt, *n.* The office of the decemvirs; the decemvirs collectively.

Decency. Under DECENT.

Decennary, dē-sen′na-ri, *n.* [L. *decennium*, a period of ten years—*decem*, ten, and *annus*, a year.] A period of ten years.—**Decennial**, dē-sen′ni-al, *a.* Continuing for ten years; consisting of ten years; happening every ten years.

Decent, dē′sent, *a.* [L. *decens*, *decentis*, ppr. of *decet*, it becomes; akin *decorate*, *decorum.*] Becoming; having a character or show that gains general approval; suitable, as to words, behaviour, dress, and ceremony; seemly; decorous; free from immodesty; not obscene; modest; moderate, tolerable, passable, respectable (*colloq.*).—**Decency**, dē′sen-si, *n.* [L. *decentia.*] The state or quality of being decent; propriety in actions or discourse; decorum; modesty; freedom from ribaldry or obscenity; a decent or becoming ceremony or rite.—**Decentish**, dē′sent-ish, *a.* Somewhat decent; of a fairly good kind or quality; passable. (*Colloq.*)—**Decently**, dē′sent-li, *adv.* In a decent or becoming manner; tolerably, passably, or fairly (*colloq.*).—**Decentness**, dē′sent-nes, *n.* The state of being decent; decency.

Decentralize, dē-sen′tral-īz, *v.t.* To distribute what has been centralized; to remove from direct connection or dependence on a central authority.—**Decentralization**, dē-sen′tra-li-zā″shon, *n.* The act of decentralizing; *politics*, the act of distributing among a number of places throughout a country the administration of its internal affairs.

Deception, dē-sep′shon, *n.* [L. *deceptio*, *deceptionis*, a deceiving. DECEIVE.] The act of deceiving or misleading; habit of deceiving; the state of being deceived or misled; that which deceives; artifice; cheat. ∴ Syn. under FRAUD.—**Deceptibility**, dē-sep′ti-bil″i-ti, *n.* Liability to be deceived.—**Deceptible**, dē-sep′ti-bl, *a.* Liable to be deceived.—**Deceptive**, dē-sep′tiv, *a.* Tending to deceive; having power to mislead or impress false opinions; misleading.—**Deceptively**, dē-sep′tiv-li, *adv.* In a manner to deceive.—**Deceptiveness**, dē-sep′tiv-nes, *n.* The state of being deceptive; tendency or aptness to deceive.—**Deceptivity**,† dē-sep-tiv′i-ti, *n.* A thing which deceives; a sham.—**Deceptory**,† dē-sep′to-ri, *a.* Deceptive.

Decern, dē-sėrn′, *v.t.* and *i.* [L. *decerno*, *decretum*, to decree.] *Scots law*, to judge; to adjudge; to decree; to pass judgment.

Dechristianize, dē-kris′tyan-īz, *v.t.*—*dechristianized, dechristianizing.* To turn from Christianity; to banish Christian belief and principles from.

Decide, dē-sīd′, *v.t.*—*decided, deciding.* [L. *decido*—*de*, and *cædo*, to cut, seen also in *concise, precise, excision.*] To determine, as a question, controversy, or struggle, finally or authoritatively; to settle by giving the victory to one side or the other; to determine the issue or result of; to conclude; to end.—*v.t.* To determine; to form a definite opinion; to come to a conclusion; to pronounce a judgment.—**Decidable**, dē-sī′da-bl, *a.* Capable of being decided.—**Decided**, dē-sī′ded, *a.* Well marked; clear; unequivocal; that puts an end to doubt; free from ambiguity or uncertainty; unmistakable; resolute; determined; free from hesitation or wavering.—**Decidedly**, dē-sī′ded-li, *adv.* In a decided or determined manner; in a manner to preclude doubt.—**Decider**, dē-sī′dėr, *n.* One who decides.

Deciduous, dē-sid′ū-us, *a.* [L. *deciduus*, *decido*—*de*, and *cado*, to fall; akin *decay.*] Not perennial or permanent; *bot.* applied to trees whose leaves fall in autumn and to leaves or other parts of the plant that fall; *zool.* applied to parts which fall off at a certain stage of an animal's existence, as hair, horns, teeth.—**Decidua**, dē-sid′ū-a, *n.* [For *decidua membrana*, the membrane that falls off.] A membrane arising from alteration of the upper layer of the mucous membrane of the uterus, after the reception into the latter of the impregnated ovum, the name being given to it because it is discharged at parturition.—**Deciduate**, dē-sid′ū-āt, *a.* Applied to those mammals, as Man, the Quadrumana, Carnivora, &c., which throw off a decidua after parturition.—**Deciduousness**, **Deciduity**, de-sid′ū-us-nes, des-i-dū′i-ti, *n.* The quality of being deciduous.

Decigram, **Decigramme**, des′i-gram, *n.* A French weight of one-tenth of a gram.—**Deciliter**, **Decilitre**, des′i-lē-tėr, *n.* A French measure of capacity equal to one-tenth of a liter.

Decillion, dē-sil′yon, *n.* In English notation, the number denoted by a unit with 60 zeros annexed, while in the French and American notation, 33 zeros are annexed.—**Decillionth**, de-sil′yonth, *a.* Being one of a decillion equal parts.—*n.* One such part.

Decimal, des′i-mal, *a.* [L. *decimus*, tenth, from *decem*, ten.] Of or pertaining to tens; numbered or proceeding by tens; having a tenfold increase or decrease.—*Decimal fraction*, a fraction whose denominator is 10, or some number produced by the continued multiplication of 10 as a factor, such as 100, 1000, &c., but written with the denominator omitted, its value being indicated by a point placed to the left of as many figures of the numerator as there are ciphers in the denominator; thus 7/10, 3/1000, are written .7, .003.—*Decimal system*, a system of weights, measures, and moneys based on multiples of ten; the metric system; *in libraries*, a classification for books, dividing all knowledge into ten classes, indicating the specific subject of each book by a number ranging from .001 to 999.—*n.* A decimal fraction.

Decimate, des′i-māt, *v.t.*—*decimated, decimating.* [L. *decimo*, *decimatum*, to select by lot every tenth man for punishment, from *decem*, ten.] To select by lot and punish with death every tenth man of, as was done by the Romans in punishing bodies of troops, &c.; hence, to destroy a great but indefinite number of.—**Decimation**, des-i-mā′shon, *n.* A selection of every tenth by lot, as for punishment, &c.; the destruction of a great but indefinite proportion of people.—**Decimator**, des′i-mā-tėr, *n.* One who or that which decimates.

Decimeter, **Decimetre**, des′i-mē-tėr, *n.* A French measure of length equal to the tenth part of a meter, or 3.9371 inches.

Decipher, dē-sī′fėr, *v.t.* To explain what is written in ciphers, by finding what each character or mark represents; to read what is written in obscure or badly formed characters; to discover or explain the meaning of, as of something difficult to be understood.—**Decipherable**, dē-sī′fėr-a-bl, *a.* That may be deciphered or interpreted.—**Decipherer**, dē-sī′fėr-ėr, *n.* One who deciphers.—**Decipherment**, dē-sī′fėr-ment, *n.* The act of deciphering.

Decision, dē-si′zhon, *n.* [L. *decisio*, *decisionis*. DECIDE.] The act of deciding; determination, as of a question or doubt; final judgment or opinion in a case which has been under deliberation or discussion; determination, as of a contest or event; arbitrament; the quality of being decided in character; unwavering firmness.—**Decisive**, dē-sī′siv, *a.* Having the power or quality of determining; final; conclusive; putting an end to controversy; marked by decision or prompt determination.—**Decisively**, dē-sī′siv-li, *adv.* In a decisive manner.—**Decisiveness**, dē-sī′siv-nes, *n.* The quality of being decisive: conclusiveness; decision of character.—**Decisory**, dē-sī′so-ri, *a.* Able to decide or determine.

Decivilize, dē-siv′il-īz, *v.t.* To reduce from a civilized to a wild or savage state.

Deck, dek, *v.t.* [Same word as D. *dekken*, Dan. *dække*, G. *decken*, to cover, with the nouns, D. *dek*, Dan. *dæk*, a cover, a ship's deck, G. *decke*, a cover, *deck*, a deck; closely akin to E. *thatch* (Sc. *thack*), the root being that of L. *tego*, to cover. THATCH.] To clothe; to dress the person; but usually, to clothe with more than ordinary elegance; to array; to adorn; to embellish; to furnish with a deck, as a vessel.—*n.* A horizontal platform or floor extending from side to side of a ship, and formed of planking, supported by the beams; large vessels having often upper, main, and lower decks, with a quarter-deck over the upper deck towards the stern.—*To clear the decks*, to prepare a ship for action.—**Decked**, dekt, *p.* and *a.* Covered; adorned; furnished with a deck.

—**Decker**, dek′ėr, *n.* One who or that which decks or adorns; a vessel that has a deck or decks: in composition (a three-*decker*).—**Deck-cargo, Deck-load**, *n.* Cargo stowed on the deck of a vessel.—**Deck-hand**, *n.* One whose duties are confined to the deck of a vessel, he being unfit for the work of a seaman properly so called.—**Deck-passage**, *n.* A passage on the deck of a vessel.

Deck, dek, *n.* [Origin unknown.] A pack of cards.

Deckle, dek′l, *n.* [G. *deckel*, dim. of *decke*, cover.] A frame or rubber band upon a paper-making machine to limit the size of sheet.—**Deckle-edge**, *a.* Rough uncut edge.

Declaim, dē-klām, *v.i.* [L. *declamo*, to practise speaking in public—*de*, and *clamo*, to cry out. CLAIM, CLAMOUR.] To speak a set oration in public; to make a formal speech or oration; to harangue; to inveigh; to speak or write for rhetorical display.—*v.t.* To utter with rhetorical force; to deliver with inflation of tone.—**Declaimer**, dē-klā′mėr, *n.* One who declaims; one who habitually speaks for rhetorical display; one who speaks clamorously; an inveigher.—**Declaimant**, dē-klā′mant, *n.* A declaimer.—**Declamation**, dek-la-mā′shon, *n.* [L. *declamatio.*] The act or art of declaiming or making a rhetorical harangue in public; the delivery of a speech or exercise in oratory, as by the students of a college, &c.; a display of showy rhetorical oratory; pretentious rhetorical language, with more sound than sense.—**Declamatory**, dē-klam′a-to-ri, *a.* [L. *declamatorius.*] Relating to the practice of declaiming; pertaining to declamation; merely rhetorical, without solid sense or argument.

Declare, dē-klār′, *v.t.—declared, declaring.* [L. *declaro*, to declare—*de*, intens., and *claro*, to make clear, from *clarus*, clear. CLEAR.] To make known by words; to tell explicitly; to manifest or communicate plainly in any way; to exhibit; to publish; to proclaim; to assert; to affirm; to make a full statement of, as of goods on which duty falls to be paid to the custom-house.—*To declare one's self*, to throw off reserve and avow one's opinion; to show openly what one thinks, or which side he espouses.—*v.i.* To make a declaration; to make known explicitly some determination; to proclaim one's self; to pronounce adhesion in favour of a party, &c.: with *for* or *against.*—*To declare off*, to refuse to co-operate in any undertaking; to break off from one's party engagements, &c.—**Declarable**, dē-klā′ra-bl, *a.* Capable of being declared or proved.—**Declarant**,† dē-klā′rant, *n.* One who declares.—**Declaration**, dek-la-rā′shon, *n.* [L. *declaratio.*] The act of declaring, making known, or announcing; affirmation; explicit assertion; open expression; avowal; that which is declared; the document or instrument by which an announcement is authoritatively made; *law*, that part of the process or pleadings in which the plaintiff sets forth at large his cause of complaint; a simple affirmation substituted in lieu of an oath, solemn affirmation, or affidavit.—**Declarative**, dē-klar′a-tiv, *a.* Making declaration, proclamation, or publication; declaratory.—**Declaratively**, dē-klar′a-tiv-li, *adv.* In a declarative manner.—**Declarator**, dē-klar′a-tėr, *n.* *Scots law*, a form of action in the Court of Session, the object of which is to have a fact (as the existence of a marriage) declared judicially.—**Declaratorily**, dē-klar′a-to-ri-li, *adv.* By declaration or exhibition.—**Declaratory**, dē-klar′a-to-ri, *a.* Making declaration; distinctly expressive of opinions or intentions.—**Declared**, dē-klārd′, *p.* and *a.* Made known; told explicitly; avowed; manifested; proclaimed; openly professed (a *declared* enemy).—**Declaredly**, dē-klā′red-li, *adv.* Avowedly; explicitly.—**Declaredness**, dē-klā′red-nes, *n.* State of being declared.—**Declarer**, dē-klā′rėr, *n.* One who declares.

Declension. Under DECLINE.

Decline, dē-klīn′, *v.i.—declined, declining.* [L. *declino*, to bend down or aside—*de*, down, and a hypothetical *clino*=Gr. *klinō*, to bend. Root seen in L. *clivus*, sloping, and also in E. to *lean.*] To lean downward; to bend over; to hang down, as from weakness, despondency, submission, or the like; to sink to a lower level; to stoop, as to an unworthy object; to lean or deviate from rectitude (O.T.); to approach or draw toward the close (day *declines*); to avoid or shun; to refuse; not to comply; to tend to a less perfect state; to sink in character or value; to become diminished or impaired (as health, reputation); to fail; to decay.—*v.t.* To bend downward; to cause to bend; to depress; to shun or avoid; to refuse; not to accept or comply with; *gram.* to inflect, through cases and numbers; to change the termination of a word, for forming the oblique cases.—*n.* A falling off; a tendency to a worse state; diminution or decay; deterioration; a popular name for almost all chronic diseases in which the strength and plumpness of the body gradually decrease, until the patient dies; consumption.—**Decliner**, dē-klī′nėr, *n.* One who declines.—**Declinometer**, dek-li-nom′et-ėr, *n.* An instrument for measuring the declination of the magnetic needle, and for observing its variations.—**Declension**, dē-klen′shon, *n.* [L. *declinatio*, *declinationis*: in the grammatical sense it refers to the leaning away or differing of the other cases from the nominative; so *case* is lit. a falling.] The act of declining; declination; slope; a falling or declining toward a worse state; refusal; non-acceptance; *gram.* the inflection of nouns, adjectives, and pronouns by change of termination to form the oblique cases; the act of declining a word; a class of nouns declined on the same type.—**Declinable**, dē-klī′na-bl, *a.* Capable of being declined; having case inflections.—**Declinal**, dē-klī′nal, *a.* Bending downwards; declining; *geol.* applied to the slope of strata from an axis.—**Declinate, Declinous**, dek′li-nāt, dē-klī′nus, *a.* *Bot.* bending or bent downward: applied to stamens when they are thrown to one side of a flower.—**Declination**, dek-li-nā′shon, *n.* The act or state of declining; a bending down; inclination; a falling into a worse state; a falling away; deterioration; a deviation from a straight line; oblique motion; deviation from rectitude in behaviour or morals; the act of refusing; refusal; *astron.* the distance of a heavenly body from the celestial equator, measured on a great circle passing through the pole and also through the body; *physics*, the variation of the magnetic needle from the true meridian of a place—declination of the compass or magnetic declination.—**Declinator**, dek′li-nā-tėr, *n.* An instrument used in ascertaining the declination.—**Declinatory**, dē-klī′na-to-ri, *a.* Of or pertaining to declination; characterized by declining; intimating declinature or refusal.—**Declinature**, dē-klī′na-tūr, *n.* The act of declining or refusing; a refusal.

Declivity, dē-kliv′i-ti, *n.* [L. *declivitas*, a declivity, from *declivis*, sloping—*de*, and *clivus*, sloping; same root as in *decline.*] Slope or inclination downward; a slope or descent of the ground: opposed to *acclivity*, or ascent.—**Declivous, Declivitous**, dē-klī′vus, dē-kliv′i-tus, *a.* Sloping downwards.

Decoct, dē-kokt′, *v.t.* [L. *decoquo*, *decoctum*, to boil down—*de*, and *coquo*, to cook, to boil. COOK.] To prepare by boiling; to extract the strength or flavour of by boiling; to heat up or excite (*Shak.*)†.—**Decoctible**, dē-kok′ti-bl, *a.* Capable of being boiled.—**Decoction**, dē-kok′shon, *n.* The act of boiling a substance in water, for extracting its virtues; the water in which a substance has been thus boiled.

Decode, dē-kōd′, *v.t.* To decipher a telegram by code. CODE.

Decollate, dē-kol′āt, *v.t.—decollated, decollating.* [L. *decollo*, *decollatum*, to behead—*de*, from, and *collum*, the neck.] To behead.—**Decollated**, dē-kol′lā-ted, *p.* and *a.* Beheaded; *conch.* having lost the apex and become truncated.—**Decollation**, dē-kol-lā′shon, *n.* The act of beheading.

Décolleté, dā-kol-tā, *a.* [Fr.] Low-necked style of dress.

Decoloration, dē-kul′ėr-ā″shon, *n.* [L. *decoloratio*, *decolorationis*, discolouring—*de*, from, and *color*, colour.] The removal of colour; abstraction or loss of colour.—**Decolorant**, dē-kul′ėr-ant, *n.* A substance which removes colour, or bleaches.—**Decolorization, Decolourization**, dē-kul′ėr-i-zā″shon, *n.* The process of depriving of colour.—**Decolorate, Decolorize, Decolourize, Decolour**, dē-kul′ėr-āt, dē-kul′ėr-īz, dē-kul′ėr, *v.t.* To deprive of colour; to bleach.

Decomplex, dē′kom-pleks, *a.* [Prefix *de*, intens., and *complex.*] Made up of complex constituents.

Decompose, dē-kom-pōz′, *v.t.—decomposed, decomposing.* [Fr. *décomposer*—*de*, from, and *composer*, to compose. COMPOSE.] To separate the constituent parts or elementary particles of; to resolve into original elements.—*v.i.* To become resolved into constituent elements; to decay, rot, or putrefy.—**Decomposable**, dē-kom-pō′za-bl, *a.* Capable of being decomposed or resolved into constituent elements.—**Decomposition**, dē-kom′pō-zi″shon, *n.* The act of decomposing; analysis; resolution; the state of being decomposed; disintegration; decay; putrescence.

Decomposite, dē-kom′po-zit, *a.* [Prefix *de*, intens., and *composite.*] Compounded a second time; decompound.—*n.* Anything compounded with things already composite.

Decompound, dē-kom-pound′, *a.* [Prefix *de*, intens., and *compound.*] Composed of things or words already compounded; compounded a second time; *bot.* divided into a number of compound divisions, as a leaf or panicle.—*n.* A decomposite.

Deconcentrate, dē-kon-sen′trāt, *v.t.* and *i.* To spread or scatter from a point or centre, or after being concentrated.

Deconsecrate, dē-kon′sē-krāt, *v.t.* To deprive of sacred character or of the virtue conferred by consecration; to unconsecrate; to secularize.—**Deconsecration**, dē-kon′sē-krā″shon, *n.* The act of deconsecrating.

Decorate, dek′ō-rāt, *v.t.—decorated, decorating.* [L. *decoro*, *decoratum*, from *decus*, *decor*, comeliness, grace; akin *decent.*] To deck with something becoming or ornamental; to adorn; to beautify; to embellish; to make attractive the interiors of dwellings; to award a decoration of honor to.—*Decorated style*, *arch.* a style of Gothic architecture distinguished by the flowing or wavy lines of its tracery, and generally by profuse florid ornamentation.—**Decoration**, dek-ō-rā′shon, *n.* The act of adorning; ornamentation; that which decorates or adorns; ornament; any badge, as a medal, cross of honor, &c., bestowed for distinguished services.—**Decorative**, dek′ō-rā-tiv, *a.* Adorning; suited to embellish.—**Decorativeness**, dek′ō-rā-tiv-nes, *n.* Quality of being decorative.—**Decorator**, dek′ō-rā-tėr, *n.* One who decorates or embellishes.

Decorous, dē-kō′rus, *a.* [L. *decorus*, becoming.] Suitable to a character or to the time, place, and occasion; becoming; seemly; proper; befitting (speech, behaviour, dress, &c.).—**Decorously**, dē-kō′rus-li, *adv.* In a becoming manner.—**Decorousness**, dē-kō′rus-nes, *n.* Decency or propriety of behaviour.—**Decorum**, dē-kō′rum, *n.* [L., what is becoming.] Propriety of speech or behaviour; seemliness; decency; opposed to rudeness, licentiousness, or levity.

Decorticate, dē-kor′ti-kāt, *v.t.—decorticated, decorticating.* [L. *decortico*, *decorticatum*—*de*, priv., and *cortex*, bark.] To strip off the bark of; to peel; to husk.—**Decortication**, dē-kor′ti-kā″shon, *n.* The act of stripping off bark or husk.

Decoy, dē-koi′, *n.* [Properly *duck-coy*; *coy* being a provincial word from D. *kooi*, a cage, hence *vogel-kooi*, a bird-cage, an apparatus for entrapping water-fowl.] A place into which wild fowls are enticed in order to be caught, being a structure of network covering in a piece of water; a fowl, or the likeness of one, employed to entice other fowl into a net or within range of shot; a thing or person intended to lead into a snare; a stratagem employed to mislead or lead into danger; a lure.—*v.t.* To lead or lure by artifice into a snare, with a view to catch; to entrap by any means which deceive; to allure, attract, or entice.—**Decoy-bird, Decoy-duck,** *n.* A duck or other bird employed to draw others into a net or situation to be taken; a person employed to decoy persons.—**Decoy-man,** *n.* A man employed in decoying and catching fowls.

Decrease, dē-krēs′, *v.i.*—*decreased, decreasing.* [L. *decresco*—*de,* down, and *cresco,* to grow, seen also in *increase, crescent, accrue.*] To be diminished gradually in extent, bulk, quantity, or amount, or in strength, influence, or excellence; to become less.—*v.t.* To lessen; to make smaller in dimensions, amount, quality, or excellence, &c.; to diminish gradually or by small deductions.—*n.* A becoming less; gradual diminution; wane (as applied to the moon); decay.—**Decreasingly,** dē-krēs′ing-li, *adv.* By decreasing or diminishing.—**Decrement,** dek′rē-ment, *n.* [L. *decrementum.*] Decrease; waste; the quantity lost by gradual diminution or waste; *math.* the small part by which a variable quantity becomes less and less: opposed to *increment.*—**Decrescent,** dē-kres′ent, *a.* [L. *decrescens, decrescentis.*] Decreasing; becoming less by gradual diminution.

Decree, dē-krē′, *n.* [L. *decretum,* from *decerno,* to judge—*de,* and *cerno,* to judge; also seen in *concern, discern, secret,* &c.] Judicial decision or determination of a litigated cause; the judgment or award of an umpire in a case submitted to him; an edict, law, or order by a superior authority as a rule to govern inferiors.—*Decree nisi* (decree unless), *law,* the order made by an English court of divorce, after satisfactory proof is given in support of a petition for dissolution of marriage; it remains conditional for at least six months, after which, *unless* sufficient cause is shown, it is made absolute, and the dissolution takes effect.—*v.t.*—*decreed, decreeing.* To determine judicially; to resolve by sentence; to determine or resolve legislatively; to fix or appoint; to determine or decide on.—*v.i.* To determine immutably; to make an edict; to appoint by edict.—**Decreeable,** dē-krē′a-bl, *a.* Capable of being decreed.—**Decreer,** dē-krē′ėr, *n.* One who decrees.—**Decreet,** dē-krēt′, *n. Scots law,* a decree.—**Decretal,** dē-krē′tal, *a.* Appertaining to a decree; containing a decree.—*n.* An authoritative order or decree; a letter of the pope determining some point or question in ecclesiastical law; *pl.* the second part of the canon law, so called because it contains the decrees of sundry popes.—**Decretist,** dē-krē′tist, *n.* One who studies or professes a knowledge of the decretals.—**Decretive,** dē-krē′tiv, *a.* Having the force of a decree; pertaining to a decree.—**Decretory,** dek′rē-to-ri, *a.* Judicial; definitive; established by a decree.

Decrepit, dē-krep′it, *a.* [L. *decrepitus,* broken down, worn out—*de,* from, and *crepare,* to make a noise, hence originally noiseless; akin *crevice, discrepant.*] Broken down or weakened with age; wasted or worn by the infirmities of old age; being in the last stage of decay.—**Decrepitude, Decrepitness,** dē-krep′i-tūd, dē-krep′it-nes, *n.* The state of being decrepit; the broken, crazy state of the body, produced by decay and the infirmities of age.

Decrepitate, dē-krep′i-tāt, *v.t.*—*decrepitated, decrepitating.* [L. *decrepo,* to break or burst, to crackle—*de* and *crepo.* DECREPIT.] To roast or calcine in a strong heat, with a continual bursting or crackling of the substance.—*v.i.* To crackle when roasting.—**Decrepitation,** dē-krep′i-tā″shon, *n.* The act of flying asunder with a crackling noise on being heated, or the crackling noise, attended with the flying asunder of their parts, made by several salts and minerals when heated.

Decrescendo, dā-kre-shen′dō, *n.* [It.] *Mus.* a term which denotes the gradual weakening of the sound.

Decrustation, dē-krus-tā′shon, *n.* The removal of a crust.

Decry, dē-krī′, *v.t.*—*decried, decrying.* [Fr. *décrier,* O.Fr. *descrier*—*des* (=L. *dis*), and *crier,* to cry.] To cry down; to censure as faulty, mean, or worthless; to clamour against; to discredit by finding fault.—**Decrial,** dē-krī′al, *n.* The act of decrying or crying down.—**Decrier,** dē-krī′ėr, *n.* One who decries.

Decuman, Decumane, dek′ū-man, dek′ū-mān, *a.* [L. *decumanus,* from *decimus,* tenth, from *decem,* ten.] Tenth; hence, from the ancient notion that every tenth wave was the largest in a series; large; immense. Sometimes used substantively for the tenth or largest wave.

Decumbent, dē-kum′bent, *a.* [L. *decumbens,* from *decumbo,* to lie down—*de,* and *cumbo,* for *cubo,* to lie.] Lying down; reclining; prostrate; recumbent; *bot.* declined or bending down, as a stem which rests on the earth and then rises again.—**Decumbence, Decumbency,** dē-kum′bens, dē-kum′ben-si, *n.* The state of being decumbent or of lying down; the posture of lying down.—**Decumbently,** dē-kum′bent-li, *adv.* In a decumbent manner.—**Decumbiture,** dē-kum′bi-tūr, *n.* The time during which a person is confined to bed, in a disease.

Decuple, dek′ū-pl, *a.* [L.L. *decuplus,* from L. *decem,* ten.] Tenfold; containing ten times as many.—*n.* A number ten times repeated.—*v.t.*—*decupled, decupling.* To increase to a tenfold proportion.

Decurion, dē-kū′ri-on, *n.* [L. *decurio,* from *decem,* ten.] An officer in the Roman army who commanded a *decuria,* that is, a body of ten soldiers.

Decurrent, dē-kur′ent, *a.* [L. *decurrens, decurrentis*—*de,* and *curro,* to run.] *Bot.* applied to a sessile leaf having its base extended downward along the stem.—**Decurrency,** dē-kur′en-si, *n.* The prolongation of a leaf below the place of insertion on the stem.—**Decurrently,** dē-kur′ent-li, *adv.* In a decurrent manner.—**Decursive,** dē-kėr′siv, *a.* Running down; decurrent.—**Decursively,** dē-kėr′siv-li, *adv.* In a decursive manner; decurrently.

Decussate, dē-kus′āt, *v.t.*—*decussated, decussating.* [L. *decusso,* to divide crosswise in the form of a ×, from *decussis,* the number 10, which the Romans represented by X.] To intersect so as to make acute angles, thus ×; to intersect; to cross, as lines, rays of light, leaves, or nerves in the body.—**Decussate, Decussated,** dē-kus′āt, dē-kus′ā-ted, *a.* Crossed; intersected; *bot.* arranged in pairs alternately crossing each other at regular angles.—**Decussately,** dē-kus′āt-li, *adv.* In a decussate manner.—**Decussation,** dē-kus-ā′shon, *n.* The act of crossing at right or at acute angles; the crossing of two lines, rays, nerves, &c., which meet in a point and then proceed and diverge.—**Decussatively,** dē-kus′a-tiv-li. *adv.* Crosswise in the form of an ×.

Dedal, Dedalian, dē′dal, dē-dā′li-an, *a.* Same as *Dædal.*

Dedicate, ded′i-kāt, *v.t.*—*dedicated, dedicating.* [L. *dedico*—*de,* and *dico, dicare,* to devote, dedicate; akin *abdicate, diction, predict,* &c.] To set apart and consecrate to a divine Being, or to a sacred purpose; to appropriate to any person or purpose; to give wholly or earnestly up to (often *refl.*); to inscribe or address to a patron, friend, or public character (to *dedicate* a book).—*a.* Consecrated, devoted; appropriated.—**Dedicatee,**† ded′i-kā-tē″, *n.* One to whom a thing is dedicated.—**Dedication,** ded-i-kā′shon, *n.* The act of dedicating; consecration or devotion to a sacred use; solemn appropriation; an address prefixed to a book, and inscribed to a friend of the author, some public character, or other person, as a mark of esteem.—*Dedication day, dedication feast,* an annual festival commemorating the consecration of a church.—**Dedicator,** ded′i-kā-tėr, *n.* One who dedicates.—**Dedicatory, Dedicatorial,** ded′i-ka-to-ri, ded′i-ka-tō″ri-al, *a.* Serving to dedicate; serving as a dedication.

Deduce, dē-dūs′, *v.t.*—*deduced, deducing.* [L. *deduco*—*de,* and *duco,* to lead. DUKE.] To draw; to draw, bring out, or infer in reasoning; to attain or arrive at (a truth, opinion, or proposition), from premises; to infer from what precedes.—**Deducement,**† dē-dūs′ment, *n.* Deduction.—**Deducibility, Deducibleness,** dē-dū′si-bil″i-ti, dē-dū′si-bl-nes, *n.* The quality of being deducible.—**Deducible,** dē-dū′si-bl, *a.* Capable of being deduced; inferrible.—**Deducive,**† dē-dū′siv, *a.* Performing the act of deduction.—**Deduct,** dē-dukt′, *v.t.* To take away, separate, or remove, in numbering, estimating, or calculating; to subtract.—**Deduction,** dē-duk′shon, *n.* [L. *deductio, deductionis.*] The act of deducting or taking away; that which is deducted; sum or amount taken from another; abatement; the act or method of deducing from premises; that which is drawn from premises; inference; consequence drawn; conclusion.—**Deductive,** dē-duk′tiv, *a.* Deducible; pertaining to deduction; that is or may be deduced from premises.—*Deductive reasoning,* the process of deriving consequences from admitted or established premises, as distinguished from *inductive* reasoning, by which we arrive at general laws or axioms by an accumulation of facts.—**Deductively,** dē-duk′tiv-li, *adv.* By regular deduction; by deductive reasoning.

Deed, dēd, *n.* [A.Sax. *daed,* a deed, from *dón,* to do=Icel. *dád,* D. and Dan. *daad,* Goth. *deds,* G. *that,* a deed. Do.] That which is done or performed; an act; a fact; anything that is done; an exploit; achievement; *law,* a writing containing some contract or agreement, and the evidence of its execution; particularly, an instrument conveying real estate to a purchaser or donee.—*In deed,* in fact, in reality: often united to form the single word *indeed.*—**Deedful,**† dēd′fụl, *a.* Characterized or marked by deeds or exploits. (*Tenn.*)

Deem, dēm, *v.t.* [A.Sax. *déman,* to deem, to judge, from *dóm,* doom, judgment (same word as term. *-dom*); Icel. *dæma,* Dan. *dömme,* Goth. (*ga*)*domjan,* to judge; from root of *do.*] To think, judge, believe, or consider to be so or so.—*v.i.* To think or suppose.—**Deemster,** dēm′stėr, *n.* The name of two judges in the Isle of Man who act as the chief-justices of the island.

Deep, dēp, *a.* [A.Sax. *deóp*=D. *diep,* Dan. *dyb,* G. *tief,* deep; from root of *dip, dive.*] Extending or being far below the surface; descending far downward; profound: opposed to *shallow* (*deep* water, a *deep* pit); low in situation; being or descending far below the adjacent land (a *deep* valley); entering far (a *deep* wound); absorbed: engrossed; wholly occupied; not superficial or obvious; hidden; abstruse; hard to penetrate or understand; profoundly learned; having the power to enter far into a subject; penetrating; artful; concealing artifice; insidious; designing; grave in sound; great in degree; intense; profound (silence, grief, poverty); measured back from the front.—*n.* Anything remarkable for depth; the sea; the abyss of waters; any abyss.—*adv.* Deeply; to a great depth; profoundly.—**Deepen,** dē′pn, *v.t.* To make deep or deeper; to sink lower; to increase; to intensify; to make more grave (sound).—*v.i.* To become more deep, in all its senses.—**Deeply,** dēp′li, *adv.* At or to a great depth; far below the surface; profoundly; thoroughly; to a great degree; intensely; gravely; with low or deep tone; with art or intricacy (a *deeply* laid plot).—**Deepness,** dēp′nes, *n.* The state of being deep; depth.—**Deep-sea,** *a.* Relating or belonging to the deeper parts of the ocean, the parts deeper than 20 fathoms (*deep-sea* lead; *deep-sea* dredging).

Deer, dēr, *n. sing.* and *pl.* [A.Sax. *deór,*

any wild animal, a deer = Goth. *dius*, D. *dier*, Dan. *dyr*, Icel. *dyr*, Sw. *diur*, G. *thier*, any animal or beast, especially a wild beast.] A name of many ruminant quadrupeds, distinguished by having solid branching horns which they shed every year, and eight cutting teeth in the lower jaw, and none in the upper; such as the red-deer, fallow-deer, roebuck, reindeer, moose, or elk, &c.—**Deer-fold**, *n.* A fold or park for deer.—**Deer-hair**, *n.* A kind of rushy plant.—**Deer-hound**, *n.* A hound for hunting deer; a stag-hound.—**Deer-mouse**, *n.* An American rodent animal allied to the mice and the jerboas of the Old World.—**Deer-skin**, *n.* The skin of a deer; the leather made from it.—**Deer-stalker**, *n.* One who practises deer-stalking.—**Deer-stalking**, *n.* The hunting of deer (especially the red-deer) on foot by hiding and stealing within shot of them unawares.

Deface, dē-fās′, *v.t.—defaced, defacing.* To destroy or mar the face or surface of; to injure the beauty of; to disfigure; to erase or obliterate.—**Defaced**, dē-fāst′, *p.* and *a.* Injured on the surface; erased.—**Defacement**, dē-fās′ment, *n.* The act of defacing; injury to the surface or exterior; what mars or disfigures.—**Defacer**, dē-fā′sėr, *n.* One who defaces.

Defalcate,† dē-fal′kāt, *v.t.—defalcated, defalcating.* [L.L. *defalco, defalcatum*, to cut off with a sickle, hence to deduct—L. *de*, down, and *falx, falcis*, a sickle.] To take away or deduct, as money.—**Defalcation**, dē-fal-kā′shon, *n.* Deduction; abatement; that which is deducted; a deficit; a fraudulent deficiency in money matters.—**Defalcator**, def′al-kā-tėr, *n.* One who is guilty of embezzlement.

Defame, dē-fām′, *v.t.—defamed, defaming.* [L.L. *defamare*—*de*, priv., and L. *fama*, fame.] To slander; to speak evil of; to calumniate; to libel; to bring into disrepute.—**Defamation**, def-a-mā′shon, *n.* The uttering of slanderous words with a view to injure another's reputation; slander; calumny.—**Defamatorily**, dē-fam′a-to-ri-li, *adv.* In a defamatory manner.—**Defamatory**, dē-fam′a-to-ri, *n.* Containing defamation; calumnious; slanderous.—**Defamer**; dē-fā′mėr, *n.* One who defames; a slanderer; a calumniator.—**Defamingly**, dē-fā′ming-li, *adv.* In a defamatory manner.

Default, dē-fa̤lt′, *n.* [Fr. *défaut*, for *défault*, from *défaillir*, to fail—*de*, and *faillir*, to fail. FAIL, FAULT.] A failing or failure; an omission of that which ought to be done; *law*, a failure of appearance in court at a day assigned.—*In default of*, in the absence or want of; hence, in place of; in lieu of.—*v.i.* To fail in fulfilling or satisfying an engagement, claim, contract, or agreement.—*v.t. Law*, to give judgment against on account of failing to appear and answer.—**Defaulter**, dē-fa̤l′tėr, *n.* One who makes default; a delinquent; one who fails to meet his claims or to fulfil his engagements.

Defeasance, dē-fē′zans, *n.* [Fr. *défaisant*, from *défaire*, to undo—L. *dis*, and *facio*, to do.] A rendering null and void; *law*, a condition which being performed renders a deed null or void: the writing containing a defeasance.—**Defeasible**, dē-fē′zi-bl, *a.* Capable of being abrogated or annulled.—**Defeasibleness**, dē-fē′zi-bl-nes, *n.*

Defeat, dē-fēt′, *n.* [Fr. *défaite*, from *défaire*, to undo, O.Fr. *desfaire*—L. *dis*, and *facere*, to do.] An overthrow; loss of battle; check, rout, or destruction of an army by the victory of an enemy; a frustration by rendering null and void, or by prevention of success.—*v.t.* To overcome or vanquish; to overthrow; to frustrate; to prevent the success of; to disappoint; to render null and void.—**Defeatism**, de-fē′tizm, *n.* An attitude of admitting defeat, as of one's own country, or of life itself, on the ground that failure is inevitable.

Defecate, def′ē-kāt, *v.t.—defecated, defecating.* [L. *defæco*—*de*, and *fæx*, dregs.] To clear from dregs or impurities; to clarify or purify; to void excrement.—*v.i.* To become clear or pure by depositing impurities; to clarify.—*a.* Purged from lees; defecated.—**Defecation**, def-ē-kā′shon, *n.* The act of defecating or separating from lees or dregs; purification.—**Defecator**, def′ē-kā-tėr, *n.* One who or that which defecates.

Defect, dē-fekt′, *n.* [L. *defectus*, pp. of *deficio, defectum*, to fail—*de*, from, and *facio*, to make, to do.] Want or absence of something necessary or useful toward perfection; a fault; an imperfection; that which is wanting to make a perfect whole; blemish; deformity.—*v.i.*† To revolt.—**Defectible**,† dē-fek′ti-bl, *a.* Imperfect; deficient; wanting.—**Defection**, dē-fek′shon, *n.* [L. *defectio, defectionis.*] The act of abandoning a person or cause to which one is bound by allegiance or duty, or to which one has attached himself; a falling away; apostasy; backsliding.—**Defective**, dē-fek′tiv, *a.* [L. *defectivus*, imperfect.] Having some defect; wanting either in substance, quantity, or quality, or in anything necessary; imperfect; faulty; *gram.* wanting some of the usual forms of declension or conjugation (a *defective* noun or verb).—**Defectively**, dē-fek′tiv-li, *adv.* In a defective manner; imperfectly.—**Defectiveness**, dē-fek′tiv-nes, *n.* The state of being defective; faultiness.

Defense, dē-fens′, *n.* [Fr. *défense*, from L.L. *defensa*, defense, from L. *defendo, defensum*, to defend—*de*, and *fendo*, to strike, a verb used also in *offendo*, to offend.] The act of defending, upholding, or maintaining; anything that opposes attack, violence, danger, or injury; fortification; guard; protection; a speech or writing intended to repel or disprove a charge or accusation; vindication; apology; *law*, the method adopted by a person against whom legal proceedings have been taken, for defending himself against them.—*Line of defense*, a continuous fortified line or succession of fortified points.—**Defenseless**, dē-fens′les, *a.* Being without defense, or without means of repelling assault or injury.—**Defenselessness**, dē-fens′les-nes, *n.* The state of being defenseless.—**Defend**, dē-fend′, *v.t.* To protect or support against any assault or attack; to ward off an attack upon; to protect by opposition or resistance; to vindicate, uphold, or maintain uninjured by force or by argument (rights and privileges); *law*, to come forward as defendant in (to *defend* an action).—*v.i.* To make opposition; to make defense.—**Defendable**, dē-fen′da-bl, *a.* Capable of being defended.—**Defendant**, dē-fen′dant, *a.* Defensive (*Shak.*)‡; making defense.—*n.* One who defends; *law*, the party that opposes a complaint, demand, or charge; the party against whom the conclusions of a process or action are directed.—**Defender**, dē-fen′dėr, *n.* One who defends; a vindicator, either by arms or by arguments; a champion or an advocate.—*Defender of the Faith*, a title peculiar to the sovereigns of England, first conferred by Pope Leo X on Henry VIII in 1521, as a reward for writing against Luther.—**Defensibility**, dē-fen′si-bil″i-ti, *n.* Capability of being defended; defensibleness.—**Defensible**, dē-fen′si-bl, *a.* Capable of being defended, vindicated, maintained, or justified.—**Defensive**, dē-fen′siv, *a.* [Fr. *défensif.*] Serving to defend; proper for or suited to defense; carried on in resisting attack or aggression; in distinction from *offensive*.—*n.* That which defends.—*To be on the defensive*, or *to stand on the defensive*, to be or stand in a state or posture of defense or resistance, in opposition to aggression or attack.—**Defensively**, dē-fen′siv-li, *adv.* In a defensive manner; on the defensive; in defense.—**Defensory**, dē-fen′so-ri, *a.* Tending to defend; defensive.

Defer, dē-fėr′, *v.t.—deferred, deferring* [O.Fr. *differre*, L. *differo*, to delay—*dis*, from, and *fero*, to carry.] To delay; to put off; to postpone to a future time.—*v.i.* To delay; to procrastinate.—**Deferment**, dē-fėr′ment, *n.* The act of deferring; postponement or delay.—**Deferrer**, dē-fėr′ėr, *n.* One who defers or delays.

Defer, dē-fėr′, *v.i.* [L. *defero*, to carry down or away, hand over, refer—*de*, down, and *fero*, to carry.] To yield to another's opinion; to submit or give way courteously or from respect (to *defer to* a friend's judgment).—**Deference**, def′ėr-ens, *n.* A yielding in opinion; submission of judgment to the opinion or judgment of another; respect; courteous consideration; obedience.—**Deferential**, def-ėr-en′shal, *a.* Expressing deference; accustomed to defer.—**Deferentially**, def-ėr-en′shal-li, *adv.* In a deferential manner; with deference.—**Deferrer**, dē-fėr′ėr, *n.* One who defers in regard to opinion.

Defervescence, Defervescency, dē-fėr-ves′ens, dē-fėr-ves′en-si, *n.* [L. *defervesco*, to cool down—*de*, priv., and *fervesco*, to boil.] Abatement of heat; *med.* abatement or decrease of fever or feverish symptoms.

Defeudalize, dē-fū′da-līz, *v.t.* To deprive of the feudal character or form.

Defiance, Defiant, &c. Under DEFY.

Defibrinize, Defibrinate, dē-fī′bri-nīz, dē-fī′bri-nāt, *v.t.—defibrinized, defibrinizing; defibrinated, defibrinating.* To deprive of fibrin; to remove fibrin from fresh blood by whipping it with rods.—**Defibrination**, dē-fī′bri-nā″shon, *n.* Act or process of defibrinizing.

Deficient, de-fish′ent, *a.* [L. *deficiens, deficientis*, ppr. of *deficio*, to fail—*de*, and *facio*, to do.] Wanting; defective; imperfect; not sufficient or adequate; not having a full or adequate supply: with *in* (*deficient in* strength).—**Deficiency, Deficience**, de-fish′en-si, de-fish′ens, *n.* The state of being deficient; a failing or falling short; want, either total or partial; defect; absence; something less than is necessary.—**Deficiently**, de-fish′ent-li, *adv.* In a defective manner.—**Deficientness**,† de-fish′ent-nes, *n.* State of being deficient.—**Deficit**, de′fi-sit, *n.* [L., there is wanting.] A falling short of a requisite sum or amount; a deficiency (a *deficit* in revenue).

Defier dē-fī′ėr, *n.* Under DEFY.

Defilade, dē-fi-lād′, *v.t.—defiladed, defilading.* [Fr. *défilade*. DEFILE, *v.i.*] *Fort.* to surround by defensive works so as to protect the interior when in danger of being commanded by an enemy's guns.—**Defilading**, dē-fi-lā′ding, *n.* That branch of fortification which determines the most suitable construction of a fortress so that the interior of the work may not be incommoded by a fire from neighbouring eminences.

Defile, dē-fīl′, *v.t.—defiled, defiling.* [L. prefix *de*, and A.Sax. *fýlan* (O.E. and Sc. *file*, to defile), from *fúl*, foul. FOUL.] To make unclean; to render foul or dirty; to soil or sully; to tarnish, as reputation, &c.; to make ceremonially unclean; to pollute; to corrupt the chastity of; to debauch; to violate.—**Defilement**, dē-fīl′ment, *n.* The act of defiling, or state of being defiled.—**Defiler**, dē-fī′lėr, *n.* One who or that which defiles.

Defile, dē-fīl′, *v.i.—defiled, defiling.* [Fr. *défiler*—*de*, and *file*, a row or line, from L. *filum*, a thread.] To march off in a line, or file by file; to file off.—*v.t. Fort.* to defilade.—*n.* A narrow passage or way, in which troops may march only in a file, or with a narrow front; a long narrow pass; as between hills, &c.

Define, dē-fīn′, *v.t.—defined, defining.* [L. *definio*—*de*, and *finio*, to limit, from *finis*, end, whence also *final, finish, finite*, &c.] To determine or set down the limits of; to determine with precision; to mark the limit of; to circumscribe, mark, or show the outlines of clearly; to determine the extent of the meaning of; to give or describe the signification of; to enunciate or explain the distinctive properties of.—*v.i.* To give a definition.—**Defined**, dē-fīnd′, *p.* and *a.* Having the limits marked; having a determinate limit; clearly marked out as to form.—**Definable**, dē-fī′na-bl, *a.* Capable of being defined; capable of having the limits ascertained, fixed, and determined; capable of having its signification expressed with certainty or precision.—**Definably**, dē-fī'na-bli, *adv.* In a definable manner.—**Definer**, dē-fī'nėr, *n.* One who defines.—**Definite**, def'i-nit, *a.* [L. *definitus.*] Having fixed or marked limits; bounded with precision; determinate; having well-marked limits in signification; certain; precise; *gram.* defining; limiting; applied to particular things; *bot.* same as *centrifugal.*—The *definite article*, the article *the.*—**Definitely**, def'i-nit-li, *adv.* In a definite manner.—**Definiteness**, def'i-nit-nes, *n.* State or character of being definite.—**Definition**, def-i-ni'shon, *n.* [L. *definitio*, *definitionis.*] The act of defining; a brief and precise description of a thing by its properties; an explanation of the signification of a word or term; the quality or power in a telescope or other optical instrument of showing distinctly the outlines or features of any object.—**Definitive**, de-fin'i-tiv, *a.* [L. *definitivus*, definitive.] Limiting; determinate; positive; express; conclusive; final.—*n. Gram.* a word used to define or limit the extent of the signification of an appellative or common noun, as *this*, *the*, &c.—**Definitively**, dē-fin'i-tiv-li, *adv.* In a definite manner; positively; expressly; finally; conclusively; unconditionally.

Deflagrate, def'la-grāt, *v.t.*—*deflagrated*, *deflagrating.* [L. *deflagro*, *deflagratum*—*de*, intens., and *flagro*, to burn, whence *flagrant.*] To set fire to; to cause to burn rapidly; to consume.—*v.i.* To burn rapidly, or with violent combustion.—**Deflagration**, def-la-grā'shon, *n.* The act or process of deflagrating; a rapid combustion of a mixture, attended with much evolution of flame and vapor; the process of oxidizing substances by means of niter; the rapid combustion of metals by the electric spark.

Deflate, dē-flāt', *v.t.* To reduce from an inflated state by releasing of the distending gas or air.—**Deflation**, dē-flā'shon, *n.* A deflating; a reduction in the volume of currency outstanding; a reduction in the volume of purchasing power.

Deflect, dē-flekt', *v.i.* [L. *deflecto*—*de*, from, and *flecto*, to turn or bend. FLEXIBLE.] To turn away or aside; to deviate from a true course or right line; to swerve.—*v.t.* To cause to turn aside; to turn or bend from a straight line.—**Deflected**, **Deflexed**, dē-flek'ted, dē-flekst', *p.* and *a.* Turned aside; *bot.* bending downward archwise.—**Deflection**, dē-flek'shon, *n.* [L. *deflecto*, I bend down.] The strain produced by a transverse stress, such as the bending of a horizontal beam under a load; also used to denote amount of deflection.—**Deflection**, **Deflexion**, **Deflexure**, dē-flek'shon, dē-flek'sūr, *n.* Deviation; a turning from a true line or the regular course.—**Deflective**, dē-flek'tiv, *a.* Causing deflection or deviation.—**Deflector**, dē-flek'tėr, *n.* A diaphragm in a lamp, stove, &c., by means of which air and gas are mingled, and made to burn completely.

Deflower, **Deflour**, dē-flou'ėr, dē-flour', *v.t.* [Fr. *déflorer*; L.L. *defloro*—L. *de*, from, and *flos*, *floris*, a flower.] To deprive of her virginity; to violate, ravish, seduce.—**Deflowerer**, **Deflourer**, dē-flou'ėr-ėr, dē-flour'ėr, *n.* One who deflours.—**Deflorate**, dē-flō'rāt, *a. Bot.* having shed their pollen on their flowers.—**Defloration**, dē-flō-rā'shon, *n.* The act of deflowering or taking away a woman's virginity; rape.

Defluxion, dē-fluk'shon, *n.* [L. *defluxio*, *defluxionis*, from *defluo*, *defluxum*, to flow down—*de*, and *fluo*, to flow.] *Med.* a discharge or flowing of humours, as from the nose or head in catarrh.

Defoliate, **Defoliated**, dē-fō'li-āt, dē-fō'li-ā-ted, *a.* [L. *de*, priv., and *folium*, a leaf.] Deprived of leaves.—**Defoliation**, dē-fō'li-ā"shon, *n.* The fall of the leaf or shedding of leaves.

Deforce, dē-fōrs', *v.t.*—*deforced*, *deforcing.* *Law*, to keep out of lawful possession of an estate; *Scots law*, to resist (an officer of the law) in the execution of official duty.—**Deforcement**, dē-fōrs'ment, *n.* The act of deforcing.—**Deforceor**, **Deforciant**, dē-fōr'sėr, dē-fōr'si-ant, *n. Law*, one who deforces.—**Deforciation**, dē-fōr'si-ā"shon, *n. Law*, distress or seizure of goods for the satisfaction of debt.

Deform, de-form', *v.t.* [L. *deformo*—*de*, and *forma*, form.] To mar or injure the form of; to disfigure; to render ugly or unpleasing; to disfigure the moral beauty of (vices *deform* the character).—**Deformation**, dē-for-mā'shon, *n.* A disfiguring or defacing.—**Deformed**, dē-formd', *p.* and *a.* Disfigured; distorted; misshapen; ugly.—**Deformedly**, dē-for'med-li, *adv.* In a deformed manner.—**Deformedness**, dē-for'med-nes, *n.* The state or character of being deformed.—**Deformer**, dē-for'mėr, *n.* One who deforms.—**Deformity**, dē-for'mi-ti, *n.* [L. *deformitas.*] The state of being deformed; some deformed or misshapen part of the body; distortion; irregularity of shape or features; ugliness; anything that destroys beauty, grace, or propriety.

Defraud, dē-fra̤d', *v.t.* [L. *defraudo*—*de*, intens., and *fraudo*, to cheat, *fraus*, fraud.] To deprive of right, either by obtaining something by deception or artifice, or by taking something wrongfully without the knowledge or consent of the owner; to cheat; to keep out of just rights: with *of* before the thing.—**Defraudation**, **Defraudment**, dē-fra̤-dā'shon, dē-fra̤d'ment, *n.* The act of defrauding.—**Defrauder**, dē-fra̤'dėr, *n.* One who defrauds; one who takes from another his right by deception, or withholds what is his due; a cheat.

Defray, dē-frā', *v.t.* [Fr. *defrayer*—*de*, and *frais*, expense, from L.L. *fractus* or *fractum*, expense, compensation, from L. *frango*, *fractum*, to break, whence *fraction*, *fragile*, &c.] To pay for; to disburse the amount of; to discharge or bear: with *cost*, *charge*, *expense* as the object.—**Defrayal**, **Defrayment**, dē-frā'al, dē-frā'ment, *n.* The act of defraying.—**Defrayer**, dē-frā'ėr, *n.* One who defrays or pays expenses.

Deft, deft, *a.* [A.Sax. *dæft*, fit, convenient, from (*ge*)*dafan*, to become, to befit; Goth. *gadaban*, to befit.] Dexterous; clever; apt.—**Deftly**, deft'li, *adv.* In a deft manner; aptly; neatly; dexterously.—**Deftness**, deft'nes, *n.* The quality of being deft; dexterity.

Defunct, dē-fungkt', *a.* [L. *defunctus*, having finished, discharged, or performed, from *defungor*, to perform—*de*, intens., and *fungor*, to perform.] Having finished the course of life; dead; deceased; used with reference to *defunct* periodicals, commercial organizations, or other enterprises.—**Defunction**,‡ dē-fungk'shon, *n.* Death. (*Shak.*)—**Defunctive**,‡ dē-fungk'tiv, *a.* Of or pertaining to the dead; funereal. (*Shak.*)

Defy, dē-fī', *v.t.*—*defied*, *defying.* [Fr. *défier*, O.Fr. *desfier*, lit. to renounce faith or allegiance.—L. *dis*, apart, and *fides*, faith. FAITH.] To provoke to combat or strife, by appealing to the courage of another; to invite one to contest; to challenge; to dare; to brave; to set at nought; to despise or be regardless of.—*n.* A challenge.—**Defiance**, dē-fī'ans, *n.* [O.Fr.] The act of defying, daring, or challenging; a challenge to fight; invitation to combat; a challenge to meet in any contest, or to make good any assertion; contempt of opposition or danger; daring that implies contempt for an adversary, or of any opposing power.—*To bid defiance to*, or *to set at defiance*, to defy; to brave.—**Defiant**, dē-fī'ant, *a.* Characterized by defiance, boldness, or insolence.—**Defiantly**, dē-fī'ant-li, *adv.* In a defiant manner; with defiance; daringly; insolently.—**Defier**, **Defyer**, dē-fī'ėr, *n.* One who defies; one who dares to combat or encounter; one who sets at nought.

Degenerate, dē-jen'ėr-āt, *v.i.*—*degenerated*, *degenerating.* [L. *degenero*, *degeneratum*, to become unlike one's race, from *degener*, ignoble, base—*de*, from, and *genus*, *generis*, race.] To fall off from the qualities proper to the race or kind; to become of a lower type, physically or morally; to pass from a good to a worse state.—*a.* Having fallen from a perfect or good state into a less excellent or worse state; having declined in natural or moral worth; characterized by or associated with degeneracy; base or mean (*degenerate* arts or times).—**Degeneracy**, dē-jen'ėr-a-si, *n.* The state of degenerating or of being degenerate; a growing worse or inferior; a decline in good qualities; a state or condition of deterioration; lowness; meanness.—**Degenerately**, dē-jen'ėr-āt-li, *adv.* In a degenerate or base manner; unworthily.—**Degenerateness**, dē-jen'ėr-āt-nes, *n.* A degenerate state.—**Degeneration**, dē-jen'ėr-ā"shon, *n.* The state or process of becoming degenerate; degeneracy; gradual deterioration from a state physiologically superior.—**Degenerative**, dē-jen'ėr-ā-tiv, *a.* Tending to cause degeneration.

Deglutition, dē-glū-ti'shon, *n.* [L. *deglutio*, *deglutitum*, to swallow—*de*, and *glutio*. GLUTTON.] The act or power of swallowing; the process by which animals swallow.—**Deglutitious**,† dē-glū-tish'us, *a.* Pertaining to deglutition.—**Deglutitory**, dē-glū'ti-to-ri, *a.* Serving for deglutition.

Degrade, dē-grād', *v.t.*—*degraded*, *degrading.* [Fr. *dégrader*—L. *de*, down, and *gradus*, a step, a degree. GRADE.] To reduce from a higher to a lower rank or degree; to strip of honours; to reduce in estimation; to lower or sink in morals or character; to debase.—*v.i.* To degenerate; to become lower in character.—**Degradation**, degra-dā'shon, *n.* The act of degrading; a depriving of rank, dignity, or office; the state of being reduced from an elevated or more honourable station to one that is meaner or humbler; a mean or abject state to which one has sunk; debasement; degeneracy; *geol.* the lessening or wearing down of higher lands, rocks, strata, &c., by the action of water, or other causes.—**Degraded**, dē-grā'ded, *a.* Sunk to an abject or vile state; exhibiting degradation; debased; low.—**Degrading**, dē-grā'ding, *a.* Dishonouring; disgracing the character; causing degradation.—**Degradingly**, dē-grā'ding-li, *adv.* In a degrading manner.

Degree, dē-grē', *n.* [Fr. *degré*, from L. *de*, down, and *gradus*, a step. DEGRADE.] A step or single movement, upward or downward, toward any end; one of a series of progressive advances; measure, amount, or proportion (he is a *degree* worse); measure of advancement; relative position attained; rank; station (men of low *degree*); a certain distance or remove in the line of family descent, determining the proximity of blood (a relation in the third or fourth *degree*); the 360th part of the circumference of any circle, a *degree of latitude* being the 360th part of any meridian on the earth's surface, a *degree of longitude* the same part of any given parallel of latitude; an interval of musical sound, marked by a line on the scale; a division, space, or interval marked on a mathematical or other instrument, as a thermometer or barometer; in universities, a title of distinction (*bachelor*, *master*, *doctor*) conferred as a testimony of proficiency in arts and sciences, or merely as an honour.—*By degrees*, step by step; gradually; by moderate advances.—*To a degree*, to an extreme; exceedingly.

Dehisce, dē-his', *v.i.* [L. *dehisco*, to gape—*de*, intens., and *hisco*, to gape.] *Bot.* to open, as the capsules or seed-vessels of plants.—**Dehiscence**, dē-his'ens, *n. Bot.* the splitting of an organ in accordance with its structure, as the opening of the parts of a capsule or the cells of anthers, &c.—**Dehiscent**, dē-his'ent, *a. Bot.* opening; dehiscing.

Dehort, dē-hort', *v.t.* [L. *dehortor*—*de*, and *hortor*, to advise.] To dissuade; to exhort against.—**Dehortation**, dē-hor-tā'shon, *n.* Dissuasion.—**Dehortative**, dē-hor'ta-tiv, *a.* Dissuasive; dehortatory.—**Dehortatory**, dē-hor'ta-to-ri, *a.* Dissuading; belonging to dissuasion.—*n.* A dissuasive argument or reason.

Dehumanize, dē-hū'man-īz, *v.t.* To deprive of the character of humanity; to deprive of tenderness or softness of feeling.

Dehydration, dē-hī-drā'shon, *n.* *Chem.* the process of freeing a compound from the water contained in it.

Deicide,† dē'i-sīd, *n.* [Fr. *déicide*—L. *deus*, God, and *cædo*, to slay.] The act of putting to death Jesus Christ, our Saviour; one concerned in putting Christ to death.

Deictic, dīk'tik, *a.* [Gr. *deiktikos*, serving to show, from *deiknymi*, to show.] *Logic*, direct; by direct argument: applied to reasoning.—**Deictically**, dīk'ti-kal-li, *adv.* Directly.

Deify, dē'i-fī, *v.t.*—*deified, deifying.* [L. *deus*, a god, and *facio*, to make.] To make a god of; to exalt to the rank of a deity; to enroll among deities; to treat as an object of supreme regard; to praise or revere as a deity; to make godlike; to elevate spiritually.—**Deific, Deifical**, dē-if'ik, dē-if'i-kal, *a.* Making divine; god-making.—**Deification**, dē'if-i-kā"shon, *n.* The act of deifying.—**Deifier Deifyer**, dē'i-fī-ėr, *n.* One that deifies.—**Deiform**, dē'-i-form, *a.* Of a godlike form.—**Deiformity**,† dē-i-for'mi-ti, *n.* The quality of being deiform.

Deign, dān, *v.i.* [Fr. *daigner*, from L. *dignor*, to think worthy, from *dignus*, worthy, whence *dignity*, &c.] To vouchsafe; to condescend: generally followed by an infinitive.—*v.t.* To think worthy of acceptance (*Shak.*)‡; to grant or allow.

Deinornis, Deinosaur, Deinotherium. DINORNIS, DINOSAUR, &c.

Deiparous,† dē-ip'a-rus, *a.* [L. *deus*, a god, and *pario*, to bring forth.] Bearing or bringing forth a god: applied to the Virgin Mary.

Deism, dē'izm, *n.* [Fr. *déisme*, from L. *Deus*, God. DEITY.] The doctrine or creed of a deist.—**Deist**, dē'ist, *n.* [Fr. *déiste.*] One who believes in the existence of a God or supreme being but denies revealed religion, basing his belief on the light of nature and reason. ∴ The term *deist* generally implies a certain antagonism to Christianity; while the similar term *theist* is applied to Christians, Jews, Mohammedans, and all believers in one god, being opposed to *atheist* or *pantheist*.—**Deistic, Deistical**, dē-is'tik, dē-is'ti-kal, *a.* Pertaining to deism or to deists; embracing or containing deism.—**Deistically**, dē-is'ti-kal-li, *adv.* In a deistical manner.

Deity, dē'i-ti, *n.* [L.L. *deitas*, the Godhead, divine nature, from L. *Deus*, God, akin to Gr. *Zeus* (genit. *Dios*), the supreme divinity; L. *Diespiter*, *Jupiter*, and *dies*, a day; Skr. *deva*, a god; W. *Duw*, God, *dyw*, day; Gael. and Ir. *dia*, God; *Tiw*, the A.Sax. god whose name appears in *Tuesday*; all from a root implying brightness.] Godhead; divinity; the Supreme Being, or infinite self-existing Spirit; God; a fabulous god or goddess; a divinity.

Deject, dē-jekt', *v.t.* [L. *dejicio*, *dejectum*—*de*, down, and *jacio*, to throw; seen also in *abject, eject, jet, jut*, &c.] To cast down; to depress the spirits of; to dispirit; discourage, dishearten.—**Dejected**, dē-jek'-ted, *p.* and *a.* Downcast; depressed; sad; sorrowful.—**Dejectedly**, dē-jek'ted-li, *adv.* In a dejected manner; sadly; heavily.—**Dejectedness**, dē-jek'ted-nes, *n.* Dejection.—**Dejection**, dē-jek'shon, *n.* The state of being downcast; depression of mind; melancholy; lowness of spirits occasioned by grief or misfortune.—**Dejecta**, dē-jek'-ta, *n. pl.* Droppings; castings; excrement.

Déjeuner, dā-zhü-nā, *n.* [Fr., from *de*, priv., and *jeûner*, L. *jejunare*, to fast.] Breakfast; the morning meal; luncheon.

Delaine, dē-lān', *n.* [Fr. *de*, of, and *laine*, L. *lana*, wool.] A muslin made originally of wool, afterwards more commonly of a mixed fabric, generally cotton and wool, and used chiefly as a printing cloth.

Delation, dē-lā'shon, *n.* [L. *delatio*, from *de*, down, and *latus*, part. of *fero*, to bear.] *Law*, accusation; act of charging with a crime; information against.

Delay, dē-lā', *v.t.* [Fr. *délai*, It. *dilata*, delay, from L. *dilatus*, put off—*dis*, apart, and *latus*, pp. of *fero*, to carry.] To prolong the time of doing or proceeding with; to put off; to defer; to retard; to stop, detain, or hinder for a time; to restrain the motion of.—*v.i.* To linger; to move slowly; to stop for a time.—*n.* A lingering; a putting off or deferring; procrastination; protraction; hindrance.—**Delayer**, dē-lā'ėr, *n.* One who delays.—**Delayingly**, dē-lā'ing-li, *adv.* In a manner so as to delay.

Del credere, del kred'e-re, *n.* [It.] A guarantee which an agent or factor gives his principal that the persons are solvent to whom he sells goods or transfers property.

Delectable, dē-lek'ta-bl, *a.* [L. *delectabilis*, from *delectare*, to delight. DELIGHT.] Delightful; highly pleasing; affording great joy or pleasure.—**Delectableness**, dē-lek'ta-bl-nes, *n.* Delightfulness.—**Delectably**, dē-lek'ta-bli, *adv.* In a delectable manner; delightfully.—**Delectation**, dē-lek-tā'shon, *n.* A giving delight; delight.

Delegate, del'ē-gāt, *v.t.*—*delegated, delegating.* [L. *delego*, *delegatum*—*de*, and *lego*, to send as an ambassador. LEGATE.] To depute; to send on an embassy; to send with power to act as a representative; to intrust, commit, or deliver to another's care and management (power, an affair).—*n.* A person appointed and sent by another or by others, with powers to transact business as his or their representative; a deputy; a commissioner; a representative.—**Delegation**, del-ē-gā'shon, *n.* The act of delegating; appointment to act as deputy; a person or body of persons deputed to act for another or for others.

Delete, dē-lēt', *v.t.* [L. *deleo*, *deletum*, to blot out, to destroy.] To blot out; to erase; to strike or mark out, as with a pen, pencil, &c.—**Deletion**, dē-lē'shon, *n.* [L. *deletio.*] The act of deleting; an erasure; a passage deleted.

Deleterious, dē-lē-tē'ri-us, *a.* [L.L. *deleterius*, from Gr. *dēlētērios*, noxious, from *dēleomai*, to injure.] Having the quality of destroying life; noxious; poisonous; injurious; pernicious.

Delf, Delft, delf, delft, *n.* Earthenware, covered with enamel or white glazing in imitation of chinaware or porcelain, made at *Delft*, in Holland; glazed earthenware dishes.

Delian, dē'li-an, *a.* Of or pertaining to *Delos*, a small island in the Ægean Sea, the birthplace of Apollo, and the seat of one of his most famous temples.

Deliberate, dē-lib'ėr-āt, *v.i.*—*deliberated, deliberating.* [L. *delibero*, *deliberatum*—*de*, and *libro*, to weigh, from *libra*, a balance; akin *level.*] To weigh consequences or results in the mind previous to action; to pause and consider; to ponder, reflect, cogitate, or debate with one's self.—**Deliberate**, dē-lib'ėr-āt, *a.* Weighing facts and arguments with a view to a choice or decision; carefully considering probable consequences; slow in determining; formed with deliberation; well advised or considered; not sudden or rash; not hasty.—**Deliberately**, dē-lib'ėr-āt-li, *adv.* In a deliberate manner; with careful consideration; not hastily or rashly.—**Deliberateness**, dē-lib'ėr-āt-nes, *n.* The state or quality of being deliberate.—**Deliberation**, dē-lib'-ėr-ā"shon, *n.* [L. *deliberatio.*] The act of deliberating; careful consideration; mature reflection; mutual discussion and examination of the reasons for and against a measure; the act or habit of doing anything coolly or without hurry or excitement.—**Deliberative**, dē-lib'ėr-ā-tiv, *a.* Pertaining to deliberation; proceeding or acting by deliberation or discussion; having or conveying a right or power to deliberate or discuss.—**Deliberatively**, dē-lib'ėr-ā-tiv-li. *adv.* By deliberation.

Delicate, del-i-kāt, *a.* [Fr. *délicat*, L. *delicatus*, from *deliciæ*, delight, *delicio*, to allure—*de*, and *lacio*, to draw gently; akin *delight, delectable.*] Pleasing to a cultivated taste; refinedly agreeable; dainty; of a fine texture; fine; soft; smooth; tender; sensitive; easily injured; not capable of standing rough handling; nice; accurate; light or softly tinted; slender; minute; peculiarly sensitive to beauty, harmony, or their opposites; refined in manner; polite; nice.—**Delicately**, del'i-kāt-li, *adv.* In a delicate manner; with nice regard to propriety and the feelings of others; tenderly; daintily; luxuriously.—**Delicateness**, del'i-kāt-nes, *n.* The state of being delicate.—**Delicacy**, del'i-ka-si, *n.* The quality of being delicate or highly pleasing to the taste or some other sense; fineness; smoothness; softness; tenderness; slenderness; that which is pleasing to the senses; a luxury; refined taste or judgment; nicety.—**Delicious**, dē-lish'us, *a.* [Fr. *délicieux*, from L. *deliciæ*, delight.] Highly pleasing to the taste; most sweet or grateful to the senses; affording exquisite pleasure; charming; delightful; entrancing.—**Deliciously**, dē-lish'us-li, *adv.* In a delicious manner; exquisitely; delightfully.—**Deliciousness**, dē-lish'us-nes, *n.* The quality of being delicious.

Delight, dē-līt', *v.t.* [O.E. *delite*, from O.Fr. *deliter*, *deleiter*, from L. *delecto*, to delight, from *delicio*, to allure. DELICATE.] To affect with great pleasure; to please highly; to give or afford high satisfaction or joy.—*v.i.* To have or take great pleasure; to be greatly pleased or rejoiced (to *delight in* a thing).—*n.* A high degree of pleasure or satisfaction of mind; joy; rapture; that which gives great pleasure; the cause of joy; charm.—**Delighted**, dē-lī'ted, *a.* Experiencing delight; overjoyed.—**Delightedly**, dē-lī'ted-li, *adv.* In a delighted manner; with delight.—**Delightful**, dē-līt'ful, *a.* Giving delight; highly pleasing; charming; exquisite; delicious.—**Delightfully**, dē-līt'ful-li, *adv.* In a delightful manner; charmingly; exquisitely.—**Delightfulness**, dē-līt'ful-nes, *n.* The quality of being delightful.—**Delightless**, dē-līt'les, *a.* Affording no pleasure or delight; cheerless.—**Delightsome**,† dē-līt'-sum, *a.* Delightful.—**Delightsomely**,† dē-līt'sum-li, *adv.* In a delightful manner.—**Delightsomeness**, dē-līt'sum-nes, *n.* Delightfulness.

Delimit, dē-lim'it, *v.t.* To mark or settle distinctly the limits of.—**Delimitation**, dē-lim'i-tā"shon, *n.* The act of delimiting; the fixing or settling of limits or boundaries.

Delineate, dē-lin'ē-āt, *v.t.*—*delineated, delineating.* [L. *delineo*, *delineatum*—*de*, down, and *linea*, a line. LINE.] To draw the lines which exhibit the form of; to make a draught of; to sketch or design; to represent in a picture; to draw a likeness of; to portray to the mind or understanding; to depict, sketch, or describe.—**Delineation**, dē-lin'ē-ā"shon, *n.* The act or process of delineating; representation or portrayal, whether pictorially or in words; sketch; description.—**Delineator**, dē-lin'ē-ā-tėr, *n.* One who delineates.

Delinquency, dē-ling'kwen-si, *n.* [L. *delinquentia*, a fault, from *delinquo*, to abandon, fail, omit duty—*de*, out, and *linquo*, to leave.] Failure or omission of duty; a fault; a misdeed; an offence.—**Delinquent**, dē-ling'kwent, *a.* Failing in duty; offending by neglect of duty.—**Delinquent**, dē-ling'kwent, *n.* One who fails to perform his duty; one guilty of a delinquency; an offender; a culprit; a malefactor.—**Delinquently**, dē-ling'kwent-li, *adv.* So as to fail in duty.

Deliquate,† del'i-kwāt, *v.i.* and *t.* [L. *deliquo*, *deliquatum*—*de*, down, and *liquo*, to melt. LIQUID.] To melt or be dissolved; to deliquesce.—**Deliquation**,† del-i-kwā'-shon, *n.* A melting.

Deliquesce, del-i-kwes', *v.i.*—*deliquesced, deliquescing.* [L. *deliquesco*—*de*, and *liquesco*, to melt, from *liqueo*, to become liquid. LIQUID.] To melt gradually and become liquid by attracting and absorbing moisture from the air, as certain salts, acids, and alkalies.—**Deliquescence**, del-i-kwes'-ens, *n.* The process of deliquescing; a gradual melting or becoming liquid by absorption of moisture from the atmosphere.—

Deliquescent, del-i-kwes'ent, *a.* Liquefying in the air; deliquescing.—**Deliquiate**, dē-lik'wi-āt, *v.i.* To deliquesce.—**Deliquiation**, dē-lik'wi-ā"shon, *n.* Deliquescence.—**Deliquium**, dē-lik'wi-um, *n.* [L., a flowing or dropping down—*de*, and *liqueo*, to be liquid.] A melting or dissolution in the air or in a moist place; a liquid state; a swoon or faint; a melting or maudlin mood of mind†.

Delirium, dē-lir'i-um, *n.* [L., from *deliro*, to draw the furrow awry in ploughing, to deviate from the straight line, hence to be crazy, to rave—*de*, from, and *lira*, a furrow.] A temporary disordered state of the mental faculties occurring during illness, either of a febrile or of an exhausting nature; violent excitement; wild enthusiasm; mad rapture.—*Delirium tremens* (trē'menz), an affection of the brain which arises from the inordinate and protracted use of ardent spirits.—**Deliriant**, dē-lir'i-ant, *a.* Causing or tending to cause delirium.—**Delirifacient**, dē-lir'i-fa"shi-ent, *a.* Causing delirium.—**Delirious**, dē-lir'i-us, *a.* Affected with delirium; light-headed; disordered in intellect; crazy; raving; frenzied; characterized by, or proceeding from, delirium.—**Deliriously**, dē-lir'i-us-li, *adv.* In a delirious manner.—**Deliriousness**, dē-lir'i-us-nes, *n.* The state of being delirious; delirium.

Delitescence, **Delitescency**, del-i-tes'ens, del-i-tes'en-si, *n.* [L. *delitescens*, ppr. of *delitesco*, to lie hid—*de*, and *latesco*, from *lateo*, to lie hid.] The state of being concealed; latent, or not active or manifest.—**Delitescent**, del-i-tes'ent, *a.* Being latent or not active.

Deliver, dē-liv'ėr, *v.t.* [Fr. *délivrer*, from L.L. *delibero*, to set free — L. *de*, from, *libero*, to free, from *liber*, free, whence also *liberal*, *liberate*.] To release, as from restraint; to set at liberty; to free; to rescue or save; to transfer, hand over, or commit (a letter, a person to enemies); to surrender, yield, give up, resign: often followed by *up*; to disburden of a child; to utter, pronounce, speak (a sermon, address, &c.); to direct, send forth, or discharge (a blow, a broadside).—**Deliverable**, dē-liv'ėr-a-bl, *a.* Capable of being delivered.—**Deliverance**, dē-liv'ėr-ans, *n.* The act of delivering; in modern usage most commonly release or rescue, as from captivity, oppression, danger, &c., *delivery* being used in other senses.—**Deliverer**, dē-liv'ėr-ėr, *n.* One who delivers; one who releases or rescues; a preserver; a saviour.—**Delivery**, dē-liv'ėr-i, *n.* The act of delivering; release; rescue, as from slavery, restraint, oppression, or danger; the act of handing over or transferring; surrender; a giving up; a giving or passing from one to another; specifically, the distribution of letters, &c., from a post office to a district or districts; utterance; pronunciation, or manner of speaking; childbirth.

Dell, del, *n.* [DALE.] A small narrow valley between hills or rising grounds; a ravine.

Della Cruscan, del'a krus'kan, *a.* [It. of the bran, *dellà cruscà*, sifting.] Pertaining to the Florentine Academy of the name, formed for the purification of the Italian language in an authoritative dictionary.—*n.* Member of such an academy.

Delphian, **Delphic**, del'fi-an, del'fik, *a.* Relating to *Delphi*, a town in Greece, and to the celebrated oracle of that place; hence, oracular; inspired.

Delphine, del'fin, *a.* [L. *delphinus*, a dolphin.] Pertaining to the dolphin, a genus of fishes; pertaining to the Dauphin of France, a term applied to a set of Latin classics prepared for the use of the son of Louis XIV.

Delphinine, delf'in-in, *n.* [Gr. *delphinion*, larkspur.] A poisonous alkaloid used medicinally.

Delta, del'ta, *n.* The name of the Greek letter Δ, answering to the English D; the island formed by the alluvial deposits between the mouths of the Nile, from its resemblance in shape to this letter; any similar alluvial tract at the mouth of a river.—**Deltafication**,† del'ta-fi-kā"shon, *n.* The process of forming a delta at the mouth of a river.—**Deltaic**, del-tā'ik, *a.* Relating to or like a delta.—**Deltoid**, del'toid, *a.* Resembling the Greek Δ; triangular; *bot.* expressing the shape of a leaf; *anat.* applied to a muscle of the shoulder.

Delude, dē-lūd', *v.t.*—*deluded*, *deluding*. [L. *deludo*—*de*, and *ludo*, to play, *ludus*, sport, whence also *ludicrous*, *elude*, *illusion*, &c.] To cause to entertain foolish or erroneous notions; to impose on; to befool; to lead from truth or into error; to mislead; to beguile; to cheat: often *refl.* (to *delude one's self* with vain hopes).—**Deludable**, dē-lū'da-bl, *a.* Liable to be imposed on.—**Deluder**, dē-lū'dėr, *n.* One who deludes; a deceiver; an impostor; one who holds out false pretences.—**Delusion**, dē-lū'zhon, *n.* The act of deluding; a misleading of the mind; false impression or belief; illusion; error or mistake proceeding from false views; the state of being deluded or misled.—**Delusive**, dē-lū'siv, *a.* Apt to delude; tending to mislead the mind; deceptive; beguiling.—**Delusively**, dē-lū'siv-li, *adv.* In a delusive manner.—**Delusiveness**, dē-lū'siv-nes, *n.* The quality of being delusive.—**Delusory**, dē-lū'so-ri, *a.* Apt to deceive; deceptive.

Deluge, del'ūj, *n.* [Fr. *déluge*, from L. *diluvium*, a flood, a deluge—*di* for *dis*, asunder, away, and *luo* = *lavo*, to wash; akin *lave*, *ablution*, &c.] An inundation; a flood; but specifically, the great flood or overflowing of the earth by water in the days of Noah; anything resembling an inundation; anything that overwhelms, as a great calamity.—*v.t.*—*deluged*, *deluging*. To overflow, as with water; to inundate; to drown; to overwhelm.

Delve, delv, *v.t.*—*delved*, *delving*. [A.Sax. *delfan* = D. *delven*, to dig; probably connected with *dell*, a dale, Fris. *dollen*, to dig.] To turn up with a spade; to dig.—*v.i.* To dig; to labour with the spade.—**Delver**, del'vėr, *n.* One who delves.

Demagnetization, dē-mag'net-i-zā"shon, *n.* The act or process of depriving of magnetic or of mesmeric influence.—**Demagnetize**, dē-mag'ne-tīz, *v.t.* To deprive of magnetic polarity or free from mesmeric influence.

Demagogue, dem'a-gog, *n.* [Gr. *dēmagōgos*—*dēmos*, the people, and *agōgos*, a leader, from *agō*, to lead.] A leader of the people; a person who sways the people by his oratory; generally, an unprincipled factious orator; one who acquires influence with the populace by pandering to their prejudices or playing on their ignorance.—**Demagogic**, **Demagogical**, dem-a-goj'ik, dem-a-goj'i-kal, *a.* Relating to or like a demagogue; factious.—**Demagogism**, **Demagoguelsm**, dem'a-gog-izm, *n.* The practices and principles of a demagogue.

Demain, *n.* DEMESNE.

Demand, dē-mand', *v.t.* [Fr. *demander*, from L. *demando*, in its late sense of to demand, the opposite of *mando*, to commit to, lit. to put into one's hand, from *manus*, the hand, and *do*, to give; akin *mandate*, *command*.] To claim or seek as due by right (to *demand* a thing *of* a person); to ask or claim generally (a price, a reward); to ask (a thing) by authority; to question authoritatively (O.T.); to require as necessary or useful; to necessitate (a task *demands* industry).—*v.i.* To make a demand; to inquire; to ask.—*n.* An asking for or claim made by virtue of a right or supposed right to the thing sought; an asking or request with authority; the asking or requiring of a price for goods offered for sale; question; interrogation; the calling for in order to purchase (there is no *demand* for the goods).—*In demand*, in request; much sought after or courted (goods are *in demand*, his company is *in* great *demand*).—*On demand*, on being claimed; on presentation (a bill payable *on demand*).—**Demandable**, dē-man'da-bl, *a.* That may be demanded, claimed, asked for, or required.—**Demander**, dē-man'dėr, *n.* One who demands.

Demarcation, dē-mär-kā'shon, *n.* [Fr. *démarcation*—*de*, down, and *marquer*, to mark. MARK.] The act or process of marking off, or of defining the limits or boundaries of anything; separation; distinction. Also written *Demarkation*.—**Demarcate**,† dē-mär'kāt, *v.t.* To mark the limits or boundaries of.

Dematerialize, dē-ma-tē'ri-al-īz, *v.t.* To divest of material qualities or characteristics.

Deme, dēm, *n.* [Gr. *dēmos*.] A subdivision of ancient Attica and of modern Greece; a township.

Demean, dē-mēn', *v.t.* [Fr. *démener*, formerly to behave—*de*, intens., and *mener*, to lead, to manage, from L. *minare*, to drive with threats, from *mina*, a threat, whence also *menace*, *minatory*.] To behave; to carry; to conduct: used *refl.* From confusion with the adj. *mean* the word is also sometimes used in sense of to lower or degrade (one's self).—**Demeanor**, dē-mē'nėr, *n.* Behavior, especially as regards air or carriage of the person, countenance, &c.; carriage; deportment; conduct.

Demented, dē-men'ted, *a.* [L. *demens*, *dementis*, out of one's mind—*de*, out of, and *mens*, the mind.] Infatuated; mad; insane; crazy.—**Dementia**, dē-men'shi-a, *n.* [L.] A form of insanity; in psychiatry, any condition of impaired mentality.—*Dementia Praecox*, prē'koks. Occurs in late adolescence and is marked by melancholia and self-absorption.

Demerit, dē-mer'it, *n.* [Fr. *démérite*—*de*, and *mérite*, merit. MERIT.] Desert, or what one merits (*Shak.*)‡; the opposite or absence of *merit*; that which is blamable or punishable in moral conduct; vice or crime.

Demesmerize, dē-mez'mėr-īz, *v.t.* To relieve from mesmeric influence.

Demesne, **Demain**, de-mān', *n.* [O.Fr. *demaine*, *domaine*, from L. *dominus*, a lord; akin *dame*, *damsel*, *dominate*, &c.] An estate in land; the land adjacent to a manor-house or mansion kept in the proprietor's own hands, as distinguished from lands held by his tenants.

Demi, dem'i. [Fr. *demi*, from L. *dimidius*, half—*di* for *dis*, and *medius*, the middle.] A prefix signifying half. The hyphen is not always inserted in all these words.—**Demi-bastion**, dem'i-bas-ti-on, *n.* *Fort*, a bastion that has only one face and one flank.—**Demi-cadence**, dem'i-kā-dens, *n.* *Mus.* an imperfect cadence, or one that falls on any other than the key-note.—**Demi-devil**, dem'i-dev-il, *n.* Half a devil; one partaking of the diabolic nature.—**Demigod**, dem'i-god, *n.* Half a god; an inferior deity; one partaking partly of the divine, partly of the human, nature.—**Demi-monde**, dem'i-mońd, *n.* [Fr. *monde*, the world, society.] Women of questionable reputation; courtesans; the society which these women frequent.—**Demi-rep**, dem'i-rep, *n.* [A contr. for *demi-reputation*.] A woman of doubtful reputation; an adventuress.—**Demi-semiquaver**, dem'i-sem-i-kwā-vėr, *n.* *Mus.* the half of a semiquaver, or one-fourth of a quaver.—**Demi-tasse**, dem'i-täs, *n.* [Fr.] A small cup of, or for, black coffee.—**Demi-volt**, dem'i-volt, *n.* A kind of leap or curvet of a horse.—**Demi-wolf**, dem'i-wulf, *n.* A cross between a wolf and a dog. (*Shak.*)

Demijohn, dem'i-jon, *n.* [Fr. *dame-jeanne*, from Ar. *damagan*, from *Damaghan*, a town in Khorassan once famous for its glass-works.] A glass vessel or bottle with a large body and small neck, enclosed in wicker-work.

Demise, dē-mīz', *n.* [Lit. a laying off or aside, from Fr. *démettre*—*de*, L. *dis*, aside, and *mettre*, to put, L. *mitto*, to send.] The death of a person, especially of a person of distinction; decease: used with possessives; *law*, a conveyance or transfer of an estate by lease or will.—*v.t.*—*demised*, *demising*. *Law*, to transfer or convey, as an estate;

to bequeath; to grant by will.—**Demisable**, dē-mīz′a-bl, *a.* Capable of being demised.

Demit, dē-mit′, *v.t.*—*demitted, demitting.* [L. *demitto*—*de*, down, and *mitto*, to send.] To lay down formally, as an office; to resign; to relinquish; to transfer.—**Demission**, dē-mi′shon, *n.* The act of demitting; a laying down of office; resignation; transference.

Demiurge, **Demiurgus**, dem′i-ėrj, dem′i-ėr″-gus, *n.* [Gr. *dēmiourgos*, from *dēmos*, the people, and *ergon*, a work.] A maker or framer; the maker of the world; the Creator; specifically, the name given by the Gnostics to the creator or former of the world of sense.—**Demiurgic**, **Demiurgical**, dem-i-ėr′jik, dem-i-ėr′ji-kal, *a.* Pertaining to a demiurge or to creative power.

Demobilize, dē-mō′bi-līz, *v.t.*—*demobilized, demobilizing.* [L. *de*, priv., and E. *mobilize.*] To disarm and dismiss (troops) home; to disband.—**Demobilization**, dē-mō′bi-li-zā″shon, *n.* The act of demobilizing.

Democracy, dē-mok′ra-si, *n.* [Gr. *dēmokratia*—*dēmos*, people, and *kratos*, strength, power.] That form of government in which the supreme power rests with the people, ruling themselves either directly, as in the New England town meetings, or indirectly, through representatives—aptly expressed by Abraham Lincoln's phrase, "*of the people, by the people, for the people.*" The modern concept of democracy assumes the political equality of all individuals, the right to private freedom, and to petition authority for redress of grievances; a country so governed.—**Democrat**, dem′ō-krat, *n.* One who adheres to principles of democracy; a member of the Democratic party in the U. S.—**Democratically**, dem-ō-krat′i-kal-li, *adv.* In a democratical manner.—**Democratize**,† dē-mok′ra-tīz, *v.t.* To render democratic.

Demogorgon, dē-mō-gor′gon, *n.* [Gr. *daimōn*, a demon, and *gorgos*, terrible.] A mysterious divinity in classical or ancient mythology, viewed as an object of terror rather than of worship. (*Mil.*)

Demography, dē-mog′ra-fi, *n.* [Gr. *dēmos*, people, *graphō*, to write.] The description of peoples or communities in regard to their social relations and institutions, especially as compared with other communities.

Demoiselle, dé-mwą-zel′, *n.* [Fr. DAMSEL.] A young lady; a damsel; a bird, the Numidian crane, so called from its gracefulness and symmetry of form.

Demolish, dē-mol′ish, *v.t.* [Fr. *démolir, démolissant*, from L. *demolior*—*de*, priv., and *molior*, to build, from *moles*, mass, whence *molecule.*] To throw or pull down; to raze; to destroy, as a structure or artificial construction; to ruin.—**Demolisher**, dē-mol′ish-ėr, *n.* One who demolishes.—**Demolition**, dem-ō-lish′on, *n.* The act of demolishing; destruction; ruin.

Demon, dē′mon, *n.* [L. *daemon*, from Gr. *daimōn*, a spirit, evil or good, from a root meaning to know.] A spirit or immaterial being, holding a middle place between men and the celestial deities of the pagans; an evil or malignant spirit; a devil; a very wicked or cruel person.—**Demoniac**, **Demoniacal**, dē-mō′ni-ak, dē-mō-nī′a-kal, *a.* Pertaining to demons or evil spirits; influenced by demons; produced by demons or evil spirits; extremely wicked or cruel.—**Demoniac**, dē-mō′ni-ak, *n.* A human being possessed by a demon.—**Demoniacally**, dē-mō-nī′a-kal-li, *adv.* In a demoniacal manner.—**Demonian**,† dē-mō′ni-an, *a.* Having the characteristics of a demon. (*Mil.*)—**Demonism**, dē′mon-izm, *n.* The belief in demons.—**Demonist**, dē′mon-ist, *n.* A worshiper of or believer in demons.—**Demonize**, dē′mon-īz, *v.t.* To render demoniacal or diabolical; to control by a demon.—**Demonology**, dē-mon-ol′o-ji, *n.* A treatise on evil spirits and their agency, or beliefs regarding them.

Demonetize, dē-mon′e-tīz, *v.t.* To deprive of standard value, as money; to withdraw from circulation.—**Demonetization**, dē-mon′e-tī-zā″shon, *n.* The act of demonetizing.

Demonstrate, dem′on-strāt, *v.t.*—*demonstrated, demonstrating.* [L. *demonstro*—*de*, intens., and *monstro*, to show, from *monstrum*, a portent, a monster.] To point out with perfect clearness; to show clearly; to make evident; to exhibit; to exhibit the merits and operation of; to show or prove to be certain; to prove beyond the possibility of doubt.—**Demonstrable**, dē-mon′stra-bl, *a.* Capable of being demonstrated, proved, or exhibited.—**Demonstrableness**, **Demonstrability**, dē-mon′stra-bl-nes, dē-mon′stra-bil″i-ti, *n.* The state or quality of being demonstrable.—**Demonstrably**, dē-mon′stra-bli, *adv.* In a manner so as to preclude doubt.—**Demonstration**, dem-on-strā′shon, *n.* The act of demonstrating; an exhibition; a manifestation; an outward show; the act of exhibiting proof beyond the possibility of doubt; a proof by logical or mathematical reasoning; the exhibition of parts dissected for the study of anatomy; *milit.* an operation, such as the massing of men at a certain point, performed for the purpose of deceiving the enemy respecting the measures which it is intended to employ against him.—**Demonstrative**, dē-mon′stra-tiv, *a.* Serving to demonstrate; showing or proving by certain evidence; invincibly conclusive; characterized by or given to the strong exhibition of any feeling; outwardly expressive of feelings or emotions.—*Demonstrative pronoun*, one that clearly indicates the object to which it refers, as *this* man, *that* book.—**Demonstratively**, dē-mon′stra-tiv-li, *adv.* In a demonstrative manner; by demonstration; with proof which cannot be questioned; with energetic outward exhibition of feeling.—**Demonstrativeness**, dē-mon′stra-tiv-nes, *n.* Quality of being demonstrative.—**Demonstrator**, dem′on-strā-tėr, *n.* One who demonstrates or exhibits the merits or operation of something to the public, as a device or food product; an article or product used for purposes of demonstration, such as an automobile or radio.

Demoralize, dē-mor′a-līz, *v.t.*—*demoralized, demoralizing.* [Prefix *de*, priv., and *moral.*] To corrupt or undermine the morals of; to destroy or lessen the effect of moral principles on; to render corrupt in morals; *milit.* to deprive (troops) of courage and self-reliance, to render them distrustful and hopeless.—**Demoralization**, dē-mor′a-li-zā″shon, *n.* The act of demoralizing; the state of being demoralized.

Demulcent, dē-mul′sent, *a.* [L. *demulcens, demulcentis*, ppr. of *demulceo*, to stroke down—*de*, down, and *mulceo*, to stroke, to soften.] Softening; mollifying; lenient.—*n.* Any medicine which lessens the effects of irritation, as gums and other mucilaginous substances.

Demur, dē-mėr′, *v.t.*—*demurred, demurring.* [Fr. *demeurer*, to delay, to stay, from L. *demorari*—*de*, and *mora*, delay.] To pause in uncertainty; to hesitate; to have or to state scruples or difficulties; to object hesitatingly; to take exceptions; *law*—*n.* Stop; pause; hesitation as to the propriety of proceeding; suspense of proceeding or decision; exception taken; objection stated.—**Demurrable**, dē-mur′a-bl, *a.* Capable of being or liable to be demurred to.—**Demurrage**, dē-mur′āj, *n.* The time during which any common carrier, such as a vessel, railroad car, or express truck, is detained beyond that originally stipulated for loading or unloading; the payment made for such detainment; the charge made for the storage of freight or luggage beyond the collection period.—**Demurrer**, dē-mur′ėr, *n.* One who demurs; *law.* a pleading which claims that the contentions submitted by the opposing party are insufficient in law to warrant his justification in bringing action.

Demure, dē-mūr′, *a.* [From Fr. *de moeurs*, of manners, having manners, from L. *mores*, manners, whence *moral*, &c.] Affectedly modest or coy; making a show of gravity or decorousness; grave or reserved consciously and intentionally.—**Demurely**, dē-mūr′li, *adv.* In a demure manner; with a show of solemn gravity.—**Demureness**, dē-mūr′nes, *n.* The state or quality of being demure; gravity of countenance, real or affected.

Den, den, *n.* [A.Sax. *denn*, a cave or lurking-place; akin *denu*, E. *dene*, a valley.] A cave or hollow place in the earth; a cave, pit, or subterranean recess, used for concealment, shelter, protection, or security; any squalid place of resort or residence; a dell, wooded hollow, or ravine; a quiet, private retreat, as a room for reading.

Denarius, dē-nā′ri-us, *n.* [L., from *decem*, ten.] An ancient Roman silver coin originally worth 10 asses or 10 lbs. of copper.

Denationalize, dē-na′shon-al-īz, *v.t.* To divest of national character or rights.—**Denationalization**, dē-na′shon-al-i-zā″shon, *n.* The act of denationalizing.

Denaturalize, dē-nat′ū-ra-līz, *v.t.* To render unnatural; to alienate from nature; to deprive of naturalization or acquired citizenship in a foreign country.—**Denature**, dē-na′tūr, *v.t.* To change the nature of; to render unfit for human consumption, without impairing usefulness for other purposes, as alcohol.

Dendriform, den′dri-form, *a.* [Gr. *dendron*, a tree.] Having the form or appearance of a tree.—**Dendrite**, den′drīt, *n.* A stone or mineral, on or in which are figures resembling shrubs, trees, or mosses, the appearance being due to arborescent crystallization, resembling the frost-work on our windows.—**Dendritic**, **Dendritical**, den-drit′ik, den-drit′i-kal, *a.* Resembling a tree; tree-like; marked by figures resembling shrubs, moss, &c.—**Dendroid**, **Dendroidal**, den′droid, den-droi′dal, *a.* Resembling a small tree or shrub.—**Dendrolite**, den′dro-līt, *n.* A petrified or fossil shrub, plant, or part of a plant.—**Dendrology**, den-drol′o-ji, *n.* The natural history of trees.—**Dendrologist**, den-drol′o-jist, *n.* One versed in dendrology.—**Dendrometer**, den-drom′e-tėr, *n.* An instrument of various forms for measuring the height and diameter of trees.

Dene, dēn, *n* [A.Sax. *denu.* DEN.] A dell or valley; often used as an ending of place-names.

Dengue, deng′gā, *n.* [Sp.] A febrile epidemic disease of the East and West Indies, with symptoms resembling those of scarlet fever and rheumatism combined.

Denial, **Denier**. Under DENY.

Denier,‡ den′i-ėr, *n.* [Fr., from L. *denarius* (which see).] An Old French copper coin, the twelfth part of a sou. (*Shak.*)

Denigrate, den′i-grāt, *v.t.* To blacken, to soil, or to defile; to defame.

Denitrate, dē-nī′trāt, *v.t.* To set nitric acid free from.—**Denitration**, dē-nī-trā′shon, *n.* A disengaging of nitric acid.—**Denitrify**, dē-nī′tri-fī, *v.t.* To deprive of niter.

Denitrification, dē-nī′tri-fi-kā″shon. [L. *de*, from, *facio*, I make (nitrogen).] Liberation of nitrogen from organic matter by the action of bacteria. Cp. NITRIFICATION.

Denizen, den′i-zn, *n.* [O.Fr. *deinzein*, one living within a city, from *deins, dens*, Fr. *dans*, in, within, a contr. of L. *de intus*, from within, and thus opposed to *foreign.*] An alien who is admitted to the privileges of citizenship; one granted membership in a society or fellowship; hence, a stranger admitted to residence and certain rights in a foreign country; a citizen; a dweller; an inhabitant.—*v.t.* To make a denizen. —**Denization, Denizenation**, den-i-zā'-shon, den'i-zn-ā"shon, *n.* The act of making one a denizen.

Denominate, dē-nom'i-nāt, *v.t.*—*denominated, denominating.* [L. *denomino*—*de*, intens., and *nomino*, to nominate.] To give a name or epithet to; to name, call, style, or designate.—**Denomination**, dē-nom'-i-nā"shon, *n.* The act of naming; a name or appellation; a class, society, or collection of individuals called by the same name; a religious sect.—**Denominational**, dē-nom'i-nā"shon-al, *a.* Pertaining to or characterizing a denomination; pertaining to particular religious denominations or bodies. — **Denominationalism**, dē-nom'i-nā"shon-al-izm, *n.* A denominational or class spirit; adherence or devotion to a denomination; the principle or system of religious sects having each their own schools.—**Denominationally**, dē-nom'-i-nā"shon-al-li, *adv.* By denomination or sect.—**Denominative**, dē-nom'i-nā-tiv, *a.* Giving or conferring a name or distinct appellation.—*n.* That which has the character of a denomination; *gram.* a verb formed from a noun or an adjective.—**Denominatively**, dē-nom'i-nā-tiv-li, *adv.* By denomination. — **Denominator**, dē-nom'-i-nā-tėr, *n.* One who or that which denominates; the number placed below the line in vulgar fractions, showing into how many parts the integer is divided.

Denote, dē-nōt', *v.t.* — *denoted, denoting.* [L. *denoto*, to mark, to point out, to denote —*de*, intens., and *noto*, to mark, from *nota*, a mark.] To signify by a visible sign; to indicate, mark, or stand for; to be the name of or express; to be the sign or symptom of; to show; to indicate. ∴ Syn. under CONNOTE.—**Denotable**, dē-nō'ta-bl, *a.* That may be denoted or marked.—**Denotation**, dē-nō-tā'shon, *n.* [L. *denotatio.*] The act of denoting or marking off; what any word or sign denotes.—**Denotative**, dē-nō'ta-tiv, *a.* Having power to denote.

Dénouement, de-nö-moṅ, *n.* [Fr., from *dénouer*, to untie—*de*, priv., and *nouer*, to tie, from L. *nodus*, a knot.] The winding up or catastrophe of a plot, as of a novel, drama, &c.; the solution of any mystery; the issue, as of any course of conduct; the event.

Denounce, dē-nouns', *v.t.* — *denounced, denouncing.* [Fr. *dénoncer*, from L. *denuntiare*—*de*, and *nuntiare*, to declare, *nuntius*, a messenger; seen also in *announce, pronounce, renounce.*] To declare solemnly; to proclaim in a threatening manner; to announce or declare, as a threat; to threaten; to inform against; to accuse.—**Denouncement**,† dē-nouns'ment, *n.* The act of denouncing; denunciation. — **Denouncer**, dē-noun'sėr, *n.* One who denounces.—**Denunciate**,† dē-nun'shi-āt, *v.t.* To denounce.—**Denunciation**, dē-nun'shi-ā"shon, *n.* The act of denouncing; proclamation of a threat; public menace.—**Denunciative, Denunciatory**, dē-nun'shi-ā-tiv, dē-nun'shi-a-to-ri, *a.* Relating to, containing, or implying denunciation; ready or prone to denounce.—**Denunciator**, dē-nun'shi-ā-tėr, *n.* One who denounces, or solemnly and publicly threatens.

Dense, dens, *a.* [Fr. *dense*, L. *densus*, thick, whence *condense.*] Having its constituent parts closely united; close; compact; thick; crass; gross; crowded.—**Densely**, dens'li, *adv.* In a dense manner; compactly.—**Denseness**, dens'nes, *n.* Density.—**Density**, den'si-ti, *n.* [L. *densitas.*] The quality of being dense, close, or compact; closeness of constituent parts; compactness; either the mass of unit volume of a substance (*absolute density*) or the ratio of the mass of a given volume of the substance to that of an equal volume of some standard substance (*relative density*). The standard for solids and liquids is water (see SPECIFIC GRAVITY); for gases, either air or (usually in *chem.*) hydrogen.

Dent, dent, *n.* [A form of *dint.*] A mark made by a blow; especially, a hollow or depression made on the surface of a solid body.—*v.t.* To make a dent on or in.

Dental, den'tal, *a.* [L. *dentalis*, dental, from *dens, dentis*, a tooth, a word akin to E. *tooth.*] Of or pertaining to the teeth; having the characteristic sound given by the teeth and tip of the tongue (*d* and *t* are *dental* letters).—*n.* A dental letter, as *d, t*, and *th.*—*Dental formula*, a formula for showing briefly the number and kinds of teeth of an animal; thus the *dental formula* of cats is: I. $\frac{3-3}{3-3}$, C. $\frac{1-1}{1-1}$, P.M. $\frac{3-3}{2-2}$, M. $\frac{1-1}{1-1} = 30$; which signifies that they have on each side of each jaw three incisors and one canine tooth, three præmolars in the upper and two in the lower jaw on each side, and behind these one true molar.—**Dentate, Dentated**, den'tāt, den'tā-ted, *a.* [L. *dentatus*, toothed.] Toothed; having sharp teeth, with concave edges, as a leaf.—**Dentately**, den'tāt-li, *adv.* In a dentate manner.—**Denticle**, den'ti-kl, *n.* [L. *denticulus.*] A small tooth or projecting point. —**Denticulate, Denticulated**, den-tik'ū-lāt, den-tik'ū-lā-ted, *a.* Having small teeth, as a leaf, calyx, or seed.—**Denticulation**, den-tik'ū-lā"shon, *n.* The state of being denticulate.—**Denticule**, den'ti-kūl, *n.* *Arch.* the flat projecting part of a cornice, on which dentils are cut.—**Dentiform**, den'ti-form, *a.* Having the form of a tooth.—**Dentifrice**, den'ti-fris, *n.* [L. *dens*, and *frico*, to rub.] A powder, paste, or liquid to be used in cleaning the teeth.—**Dentigerous**, den-tij'ėr-us, *a.* Bearing or carrying teeth.—**Dentil**, den'til, *n.* *Arch.* the name of the little cubes or square blocks often cut for ornament on Greek cornices.—**Dentine**, den'tēn, *n.* The hard tissue lying below the enamel and constituting the body of the tooth.—**Dentiroster**, den-ti-ros'tėr, *n.* A member of the Dentirostres (den-ti-ros'trēz), a suborder or tribe of insessorial birds, characterized by having a notch and tooth-like process on each side of the upper mandible, and including the butcher-birds or shrikes, the thrushes, tits, &c.—**Dentirostrate, Dentirostral**, den-ti-ros'trāt, den-ti-ros'-tral, *a.* Having a tooth-like process on the beak.—**Dentist**, den'tist, *n.* One who makes it his business to clean and extract teeth, repair them when diseased, and replace them when necessary by artificial ones.—**Dentistic**, den-tis'tik, *a.* Relating to dentistry or a dentist.—**Dentistry**, den'tist-ri, *n.* The art or profession of a dentist.—**Dentition**, den-tish'on, *n.* [L. *dentitio.*] The breeding or cutting of teeth in infancy; the time of growing teeth; the system of teeth peculiar to an animal.—**Dentoid**, den'toid, *a.* Resembling a tooth; tooth shaped.—**Denture**, den'tūr, *n.* A dentist's term for one or more artificial teeth.

Denude, dē-nūd', *v.t.*—*denuded, denuding.* [L. *denudo*—*de*, and *nudus*, naked.] To divest of all covering; to make bare or naked; to strip; to uncover or lay bare.—**Denudation**, dē-nū-dā'shon, *n.* The act of stripping off covering; a making bare; *geol.* the carrying away, by the action of running water, of a portion of the solid materials of the land, by which the underlying rocks are laid bare.

Denunciate, Denunciation, Denunciator, &c. Under DENOUNCE.

Deny, dē-nī', *v.t.*—*denied, denying.* [Fr. *dénier*, from L. *denego*—*de*, intens., and *nego*, to say no, from *nec*, nor. NEGATION.] To declare not to be true; to affirm to be not so; to contradict; to gainsay; to refuse to grant; not to afford; to withhold (Providence *denies* us many things); to refuse or neglect to acknowledge; not to confess; to disavow; to disown; to reject.—*To deny one's self*, to decline the gratification of appetites or desires. — *To deny one's self something*, to abstain from it although desiring it.—*v.i.* To answer in the negative; to refuse; not to comply.—**Denyingly**, dē-nī'ing-li, *adv.* In a manner indicating denial. — **Denial**, dē-nī'al, *n.* The act of denying; contradiction; a contradictory statement; refusal; rejection; disownment. —**Deniable**, dē-nī'a-bl, *a.* Capable of being denied.—**Denier**, dē-nī'ėr, *n.* One who denies.

Deobstruct, dē-ob-strukt', *v.t.* To remove obstructions or impediments from; to clear from anything that hinders the passage of fluids in the proper ducts of the body.—**Deobstruent**, dē-ob'strụ-ent, *a.* *Med.* having power to clear or open the natural ducts of the fluids and secretions of the body, as the pores, lacteals, &c.—*n.* A medicine having this effect.

Deodand, dē'ō-dand, *n.* [L. *Deo dandus*, to be given to God.] *Law*, formerly a personal chattel which had been the immediate occasion of the death of a rational creature (as a horse that killed a man), and for that reason forfeited to the king to be applied to pious uses.

Deodar, dē'ō-där, *n.* [Skr. *devadāru*, that is, divine tree.] A kind of Indian cedar, closely akin to the cedar of Lebanon, yielding valuable timber, and introduced into Europe and elsewhere as an ornamental tree.

Deodorize, dē-ō'dėr-īz, *v.t.* — *deodorized, deodorizing.* To deprive of odour or smell, especially of fetid odour resulting from impurities. — **Deodorizer, Deodorant**, dē-ō'dėr-ī-zėr, dē-ō'dėr-ant, *n.* That which deodorizes; a substance which has the power of destroying fetid effluvia, as chlorine, chloride of lime, &c.—**Deodorization**, dē-ō'dėr-i-zā"shon, *n.* The act or process of deodorizing.

Deontology, dē-on-tol'o-ji, *n.* [Gr. *deon, deontos*, that which is binding or right, duty, and *logos*, discourse.] The science of duty; that doctrine of ethics which is founded on the principle of judging of actions by their tendency to promote happiness.—**Deontological**, dē-on'to-loj"i-kal, *a.* Relating to deontology.—**Deontologist**, dē-on-tol'o-jist, *n.* One versed in deontology.

Deoxidate, Deoxidize, dē-ok'si-dāt, dē-ok'si-dīz, *v.t.* [Prefix *de*, priv., and *oxide*, or the first part of *oxygen.*] To deprive of oxygen, or reduce from the state of an oxide; also called *deoxygenate* (dē-ok'si-ge-nāt). — **Deoxidation, Deoxidizement**, dē-ok'si-dā"shon, dē-ok'si-dīz-ment, *n.* The act or process of reducing from the state of an oxide; called also *deoxygenation.* —**Deoxidize**, dē-ok'si-dīz, *v.t.* — *deoxidized, deoxidizing.* To deoxidate.

Depart, dē-pärt', *v.i.* [Fr. *départir*—*de*, and *partir*, to separate. PART.] To go or move away; to go elsewhere; to leave or desist, as from a practice; to forsake, abandon, deviate, not to adhere to or follow (commonly with *from* in these senses); to leave this world; to die; to decease.—*v.t.* To leave; to retire from; with ellipsis of *from.*—**Departed**, dē-pär'ted, *p.* and *a.* Gone; vanished; dead: with the definite article used as a noun for a dead person.—**Department**, dē-pärt'ment, *n.* A separate branch of business; a distinct province, in which a class of duties are allotted to a particular person; a distinct branch, as of science, &c.; a division of territory, as in France; a district into which a country is formed for governmental or other purposes. —**Departmental**, dē-pärt-men'tal, *a.* Pertaining to a department, branch, district, &c.—**Departure**, dē-pär'tūr, *n.* The act of departing or going away; a moving from or leaving a place; death; decease; a forsaking; abandonment; deviation, as from a standard, rule, or plan.

Depasture, dē-pas'tūr, *v.t.* To put out in order to graze or feed; to pasture; to graze; to eat up by cattle.—*v.i.* To feed or pasture; to graze.

Depauperize, dē-pa̤'pėr-īz, *v.t.* To raise from a condition of poverty or pauperism; to free from paupers or pauperism; also, to reduce to a state of pauperism.

Depend, dē-pend', *v.i.* [L. *dependeo*, to

hang down—*de*, down, and *pendeo*, to hang, seen also in *pendant, pendulum, pendulous, impend*, &c.] To be sustained by being fastened or attached to something above; to hang down: followed by *from*; to be related to anything in regard to existence, operation, or effects; to be contingent or conditioned: followed by *on* or *upon* (we *depend on* air for respiration); to rest with confidence; to trust, rely, or confide; to believe fully: with *on* or *upon*. —**Dependable**, dē-pen'da-bl, *a*. Capable of being depended on; trustworthy.—**Dependability**, dē-pen'da-bil"i-ti, *n*. Reliableness.—**Dependent, Dependant**, dē-pen'dent, dē-pen'dant, *n*. One who is sustained by another, or who relies on another for support or favor; a retainer; a follower; a servant.—*a*. Hanging down; relying on something else for support; in grammar, subordinate, as a *dependent* clause.—**Dependence**, dē-pen'dens, *n*. A state of being dependent; connection and support; mutual connection; inter-relation; a state of relying on another for support or existence; a state of being subject to the operation of any other cause; reliance; confidence; trust; a resting on.—**Dependency**, dē-pen'den-si, *n*. The state of being dependent; dependence; now generally a territory remote from the kingdom or state to which it belongs, but subject to its dominion (Malta is a *dependency* of Britain).—**Dependent**, dē-pen'dent, *a*. Hanging down; subject to the power of or at the disposal of another; not able to exist or sustain itself alone; relying for support or favor (*dependent on* another's bounty.) —**Dependably**, dē-pen'da-bli, *adv*. In a dependent manner.—**Depender**, dē-pen'dėr, *n*. One who depends; a dependent.

Dephlogisticate, dē-flo-jis'ti-kāt, *v.t.* An old chemical term meaning to deprive of phlogiston, or the supposed principle of inflammability.

Depict, dē-pikt', *v.t.* [L. *depingo, depictum* —*de*, and *pingo*, to paint. PAINT, PICTURE.] To form a likeness of in colours; to paint; to portray; to represent in words; to describe.—**Depicture**,† dē-pik'tūr, *v.t.* To depict; to picture.

Depilate, dep'i-lāt, *v.t.—depilated, depilating*. [L. *depilo, depilatum*—*de*, priv., and *pilus*, hair.] To strip of hair.—**Depilation**, dep-i-lā'shon, *n*. The removal of hair.—**Depilatory**, dē-pil'a-to-ri, *a*. Having the quality or power to remove hair from the skin.—*n*. An application which is used to remove hair without injuring the texture of the skin; a cosmetic employed to remove superfluous hairs from the human skin.

Deplete, dē-plēt', *v.t.—depleted, depleting*. [L. *depleo, depletum*, to empty out—*de*, priv., and *pleo*, to fill, as in *complete*, &c.] To empty, reduce, or exhaust by draining away.—**Depletion**, dē-plē'shon, *n*. The act of depleting; *med.* the act of diminishing the quantity of blood in the vessels by blood-letting.—**Depletive**, dē-plē'tiv, *a*. Tending to deplete; producing depletion. —*n*. That which depletes; any medical agent of depletion.—**Depletory**, dē-plē'to-ri, *a*. Calculated to deplete.

Deplore, dē-plōr', *v.t.—deplored, deploring*. [L. *deploro*—*de*, intens., and *ploro*, to wail, to let tears flow (same root as *flow, flood*); seen also in *explore, implore*.] To feel or express deep and poignant grief for; to lament; to mourn; to grieve for; to bewail; to bemoan.—**Deplorable**, dē-plō'ra-bl, *a*. Lamentable; sad; calamitous; grievous; miserable; wretched; contemptible or pitiable.—**Deplorableness, Deplorability**, dē-plō'ra-bl-nes, dē-plō'ra-bil"i-ti, *n*. The state of being deplorable.—**Deplorably**, dē-plō'ra-bli, *adv*. In a manner to be deplored; lamentably.—**Deplorer**, dē-plō'rėr, *n*. One who deplores.—**Deploringly**, dē-plō'ring-li, *adv*. In a deploring manner.

Deploy, dē-ploi', *v.t.* [Fr. *déployer*—*de*, priv., and *ployer* (as in *employ*), equivalent to *plier*, to fold, from L. *plicare*, to fold. PLY.] *Milit.* to extend in a line of small depth, as a battalion which has been previously formed in one or more columns; to display; to open out.—*v.i.* To form a more extended front or line; to open out. —**Deployment**, dē-ploi'ment, *n*. The act of deploying.

Deplume, dē-plūm', *v.t.—deplumed, depluming*. [L.L. *deplumo*—L. *de*, priv., and *pluma*, a feather.] To strip of feathers; to deprive of plumage.

Depolarize, dē-pō'lėr-īz, *v.t.* To deprive of polarity.—**Depolarization**, dē-pō'lėr-i-zā"shon, *n*. The act of depriving of polarity; the restoring of a ray of polarized light to its former state.

Depone, dē-pōn', *v.i.* [L. *depono*—*de*, down, and *pono, positum*, to place. POSITION.] To give testimony; to depose: chiefly a Scots law term.—**Deponent**, dē-pō'nent, *a*. Laying down.—*Deponent verb*, in *Latin gram.* a verb which has a passive termination, with an active signification. — *n*. One who depones; a deponent verb.

Depopulate, dē-pop'ū-lāt, *v.t.—depopulated, depopulating*. [L. *de*, from, and *populus*, people.] To deprive of inhabitants, whether by death or by expulsion; to dispeople; to greatly diminish the inhabitants of.—**Depopulation**, dē-pop'ū-lā"shon, *n*. The act of depopulating.—**Depopulator**, dē-pop'ū-lā-tėr, *n*. One who or that which depopulates.

Deport, dē-pōrt', *v.t.* [Fr. *déporter*, to banish; O.Fr. *se deporter*, to amuse one's self; L. *deporto*, to banish—*de*, down, away, and *porto*, to carry.] To carry, demean, or behave: used *refl.*; also, to transport; to carry away; to eject undesirable aliens from a country, under compulsory edict. (*Mil.*)—**Deportation**, dē-pōr-tā'shon, *n*. A removal from one country to another, or to a distant place; exile; banishment.—**Deportment**, dē-pōrt'ment, *n*. Manner of acting in relation to the duties of life; behavior; demeanor; carriage; conduct.

Depose, dē-pōz', *v.t.—deposed, deposing*. [Fr. *déposer*—*de*, from, and *poser*, to place. COMPOSE.] To remove from a throne or other high station; to dethrone; to divest of office; to give testimony on oath, especially in a court of law.—**Deposable**, dē-pō'za-bl, *a*. That may be deposed.—**Deposal**, dē-pō'zal, *n*. The act of deposing or divesting of office.—**Deposer**, dē-pō'zėr, *n*. One who deposes.—**Deposition**, dē-pō-zish'on, *n*. The act of deposing or giving testimony under oath; the attested written testimony of a witness; declaration; the act of dethroning a king, or removing a person from an office or station. See also under DEPOSIT.

Deposit, dē-poz'it, *v.t.* [L. *depositum*, something deposited, a deposit, from *depono, depositum*. DEPONE. POSITION.] To lay down; to place; to put; to lay in a place for preservation; to lodge in the hands of a person for safe-keeping or other purpose; to intrust; to commit as a pledge.—*n*. That which is laid down; any matter laid or thrown down, or lodged; matter that settles down and so is separated from a fluid, as (*geol.*) an accumulation of mud, gravel, stones, &c., lodged by the agency of water; anything intrusted to the care of another; a pledge; a thing given as security or for preservation; a sum of money lodged in a bank.—**Depositary**, dē-poz'i-ta-ri, *n*. A person with whom anything is left or lodged in trust; a guardian.—**Deposition**, dē-pō-zish'on, *n*. [L. *depositio*.] The act of depositing, laying, or setting down; placing; that which is deposited, lodged, or thrown down. See also under DEPOSE.—**Depositor**, dē-poz'i-tėr, *n*. One who makes a deposit.—**Depository**, dē-poz'i-to-ri, *n*. A place where anything is lodged for safe-keeping; a person to whom a thing is intrusted for safe-keeping†.—**Deposit-receipt**, *n*. An acknowledgment for money lodged with a banker for a time and not on a current account.

Depot, dep'ō or dē'pō, *n*. [Fr. *dépôt*, O.Fr. *depost*, from L. *depono, depositum*, to deposit.] A place of deposit; a depository; a building for receiving goods for storage or sale; *milit.* the headquarters of a regiment; also a station where recruits for different regiments are received and drilled; a railway-station.

Deprave, dē-prāv', *v.t.—depraved, depraving*. [L. *depravo*, to make crooked, to deprave—*de*, intens., and *pravus*, crooked, perverse, wicked.] To make bad or worse; to impair the good qualities of; to vitiate; to corrupt.—**Depravation**, dep-ra-vā'-shon, *n*. [L. *depravatio*.] The act of depraving or corrupting; the state of being depraved; corruption; deterioration.—**Depraved**, dē-prāvd', *p.* and *a*. Vitiated; tainted; corrupted (*depraved* taste); destitute of good principles; vicious; immoral; profligate; abandoned. — **Depravedly**, dē-prā'ved-li, *adv*. In a depraved manner. —**Depraver**, dē-prā'vėr, *n*. One who depraves.—**Depravingly**, dē-prā'ving-li, *adv*. In a depraving manner.—**Depravity**, dē-prav'i-ti, *n*. The state of being depraved; a vitiated state; especially, a state of corrupted morals; destitution of good principles; sinfulness; wickedness; vice; profligacy.

Deprecate, dep'rē-kāt, *v.t.—deprecated, deprecating*. [L. *deprecor, deprecatus*, to pray against, to ward off by prayer—*de*, off, and *precor*, to pray.] To pray deliverance from, or that something may be averted; to plead or argue earnestly against; to urge reasons against; to express strong disapproval of (as of anger, a scheme, &c.).—**Deprecatingly**, dep'rē-kā-ting-li, *adv*. In a deprecating manner.—**Deprecation**, dep-rē-kā'shon, *n*. The act of deprecating; a praying against; entreaty; disapproval; condemnation.—**Deprecator**, dep'rē-kā-tėr, *n*. One who deprecates.—**Deprecatory, Deprecative**, dep'rē-ka-to-ri, dep'rē-kā-tiv, *a*. Serving to deprecate; having the character of deprecation.

Depreciate, dē-prē'shi-āt, *v.t.—depreciated, depreciating*. [L. *depretio*, to lower the price of—*de*, down, and *pretium*, price. PRICE.] To bring down the price or value of; to cause to be less valuable; to represent as of little value or merit, or of less value than is commonly supposed; to lower in estimation, undervalue, decry, disparage, or underrate.—*v.i.* To fall in value; to become of less worth.—**Depreciation**, dē-prē'shi-ā"shon, *n*. The act of depreciating; reduction in value or worth; a lowering or undervaluing in estimation; the state of being undervalued.—**Depreciative, Depreciatory**, dē-prē'shi-ā-tiv, dē-prē'shi-a-to-ri, *a*. Tending to depreciate.—**Depreciator**, dē-prē'shi-ā-tėr, *n*. One who depreciates.

Depredate, dep'rē-dāt, *v.t.—depredated, depredating*. [L. *deprædor*, to pillage—*de*, intens., and *prædor*, to plunder, from *præda*, prey. PREY.] To plunder; to pillage; to waste; to spoil.—**Depredation**, dep-rē-dā'shon, *n*. The act of depredating; a robbing; a pillaging by men or animals; a laying waste. — **Depredator**, dep'rē-dā-tėr, *n*. One who depredates; a spoiler; a waster. — **Depredatory**, dep'rē-dā-to-ri, *a*. Consisting in pillaging.

Depress, dē-pres', *v.t.* [L. *deprimo, depressum*, to depress—*de*, and *premo, pressum*, to press. PRESS.] To press down; to let fall to a lower state or position; to lower; to render dull or languid; to deject or make sad; to humble, abase, bring into adversity; to lower in value.—**Depressed**, dē-prest', *p.* and *a*. Dejected; dispirited; discouraged; sad; humbled; languid; dull; *nat. hist.* flattened in shape; flattened as regards the under and upper surfaces.—**Depressingly**, dē-pres'ing-li, *adv*. In a depressing manner.—**Depression**, dē-presh'on, *n*. The act of pressing down or depressing; a sinking or falling in of a surface; a hollow; the state or feeling of being depressed in spirits; a sinking of the spirits; dejection; a low state of strength; a prolonged period of financial and commercial stagnation characterized by unemployment, restricted credit, low prices, and general social distress.—*Angle of depression*. *Astron.* The angle by which a straight line drawn from the eye to any object dips below the horizon.—**Depressive**, dē-pres-iv, *a.* Able or tending to depress or cast down.—**Depressor**, dē-pres′ėr, *n.* One who or that which depresses; *anat.* a muscle which depresses or draws down the part to which it is attached.

Deprive, dē-prīv, *v.t.—deprived, depriving.* [L. *de*, intens., and *privo*, to take away. PRIVATE.] To take from; to dispossess; to despoil; to bereave of something possessed or enjoyed: followed by *of* (to *deprive* a person *of* a thing); to divest of an ecclesiastical preferment, dignity, or office.—**Deprivation**, dep-ri-vā′shon, *n.* The act of depriving; a taking away; a state of being deprived; loss; want; bereavement; the act of divesting a clergyman of his spiritual promotion or dignity; the taking away of a preferment; deposition.—**Depriver**, dē-prī′vėr, *n.* One who or that which deprives or bereaves.

Depth, depth, *n.* [From *deep*; comp. *width, breadth, length*, &c.] The distance or measure of a thing from the highest part, top, or surface to the lowest part or bottom, or to the extreme part downward or inward; the measure from the anterior to the posterior part; deepness: in a vertical direction opposed to *height*; a deep place; an abyss; a gulf; the inner, darker, or more concealed part of a thing; the middle, darkest, or stillest part (the *depth* of winter or of a wood); abstruseness; obscurity; immensity; infinity; intensity (the *depth* of despair or of love); extent of penetration, or of the capacity of penetrating; profoundness.

Depullulation,† dē-pul′ū-lā″shon, *n.* [L. *de*, intens., and *pullulare*, to sprout.] A sprouting with vigour or abundance of growth. (*De Quincey.*)

Depurate, dep′ū-rāt, *v.t.—depurated, depurating.* [L.L. *depuro, depuratum*, to purify—L. *de*, intens., and *puro, puratum*, to purify, from *purus*, pure.] To free from impurities, heterogeneous matter, or feculence; to purify; to clarify.—**Depuration**, dep-ū-rā′shon, *n.* The act of depurating; the cleansing of a wound.—**Depurator**, dep′ū-rā-tėr, *n.* One who or that which depurates.—**Depuratory**, dep′ū-ra-to-ri, *a.* Having the effect of purifying; purifying the blood.

Depute, dē-pūt′, *v.t.—deputed, deputing.* [Fr. *députer*, from L. *deputo*, to destine, allot—*de*, and *puto*, to prune, set in order, reckon, as in *compute, dispute*, &c.] To appoint as a substitute or agent to act for another; to appoint and send with a special commission or authority to act for the sender.—*n.* (dep′ūt). A deputy; as, a sheriff-*depute*. [Scotch.]—**Deputation**, dep-ū-tā′shon, *n.* The act of deputing or sending as a deputy; a special commission or authority to act as the substitute of another; the person or persons deputed to transact business for another.—**Deputy**, dep′ū-ti, *n.* [Fr. *député*.] A person appointed or elected to act for another; a representative, delegate, agent, or substitute.

Deracinate,† dē-ras′i-nāt, *v.t.* [Fr. *déraciner—de*, from, and *racine*, a root, from L. *radix*, a root.] To pluck up by the roots; to extirpate. (*Shak.*)

Derange, dē-rānj′, *v.t.—deranged, deranging.* [Fr. *déranger—de*, priv., and *ranger*, to set in order, to range. RANGE.] To put out of order; to throw into confusion; to disorder; to confuse; to disturb; to unsettle; to embarrass; to discompose.—**Derangement**, dē-rānj′ment, *n.* The act of deranging or state of being deranged; a putting out of order; embarrassment; confusion; disorder; delirium; insanity; mental disorder.

Derelict, der′e-likt, *a.* [L. *derelictus*, left behind, abandoned—*de*, intens., *re*, behind, and *linquo*, to leave.] Left; abandoned, especially abandoned at sea.—*n.* An article abandoned by the owner, especially a vessel abandoned at sea.—**Dereliction**, der-e-lik′shon, *n.* The act of leaving with an intention not to reclaim; desertion; relinquishment; abandonment (a *dereliction* of duty).

Deride, dē-rīd′, *v.t.—derided, deriding.* [L. *derideo—de*, intens., and *rideo*, to laugh.] To laugh at in contempt; to turn to ridicule or make sport of; to treat with scorn by laughter; to mock; to ridicule.—**Derider**, dē-rī′dėr, *n.* One who derides; a mocker; a scoffer.—**Deridingly**, dē-rī′ding-li, *adv.* By way of derision or mockery.—**Derision**, dē-rizh′on, *n.* [L. *derisio*.] The act of deriding, or the state of being derided; contempt manifested by laughter; mockery; ridicule; scorn.—**Derisive**, dē-rī′siv, *a.* Expressing or characterized by derision; mocking; ridiculing.—**Derisively**, dē-rī′siv-li, *adv.* With mockery or contempt.—**Derisiveness**, dē-rī′siv-nes, *n.* The state of being derisive.

Derive, de-rīv′, *v.t.—derived, deriving.* [L. *derivo*, to divert a stream from its channel, to derive—*de*, from, and *rivus*, a stream, whence also *rivulet, rival*.] To divert or turn aside from a natural course†; to draw from, as in a regular course or channel; to receive from a source or as from a source or origin (to *derive* power, knowledge, facts); to deduce or draw from a root or primitive word; to trace the etymology of.—*Derived units.* Units based upon and determined by the FUNDAMENTAL UNITS (which see).—*v.i.*† To come or proceed. (*Tenn.*)—**Derivable**, de-rī′va-bl, *a.* Capable of being derived.—**Derivably**, dē-rī′va-bli, *adv.* By derivation.—**Derivation**, der-i-vā′shon, *n.* The act of deriving, drawing, or receiving from a source; the drawing or tracing of a word from its root or origin; etymology.—**Derivational**, der-i-vā′shon-al, *a.* Relating to derivation.—**Derivative**, de-riv′a-tiv, *a.* Taken or having proceeded from another or something preceding; derived; secondary.—*n.* That which is derived; that which is deduced or comes by derivation from another; a word which takes its origin in another word, or is formed from it.—**Derivatively**, de-riv′a-tiv-li, *adv.* In a derivative manner; by derivation.—**Derivativeness**, de-riv′a-tiv-nes, *n.*—**Deriver**, de-rī′vėr, *n.* One who derives.

Derm, Derma, Dermis, dėrm, dėr′ma, dėr′mis, *n.* [Gr. *derma*, skin.] The true skin, or under layer of the skin, as distinguished from the cuticle, epidermis, or scarf skin.—**Dermal**, dėr′mal, *a.* Pertaining to skin; consisting of skin.—**Dermatic**, dėr-mat′ik, *a.* Pertaining to the skin.—**Dermatitis**, dėr-ma-tī′tis. [Gr. *derma*, skin, *-itis*, inflammation.] Inflammation of the skin.—**Dermatogen**, dėr′ma-tō-jen. [Gr. *derma, dermatos*, skin, *gen*, to produce.] A cellular layer at the tip of a root or stem from which the epidermis is produced.—**Dermatography**, dėr-ma-tog′ra-fi, *n.* The anatomical description of the skin.—**Dermatoid**, dėr′ma-toid, *a.* Resembling skin; skin-like.—**Dermatologist**, dėr-ma-tol′o-jist, *n.* One versed in dermatology.—**Dermatology**, dėr-ma-tol′o-ji, *n.* The branch of science which treats of the skin and its diseases.—**Dermatophyte**, dėr′ma-tō-fīt, *n.* [Gr. *phyton*, a plant.] A parasitic plant, infesting the cuticle and epidermis of men and animals, and giving rise to various forms of skin-disease, as ring-worm.—**Dermic**, dėr′mik, *a.* Relating to the skin.—**Dermoid**, dėr′moid, *a.* Resembling skin: applied to tissues which resemble skin.—**Dermo-skeleton**, *n.* The hard leathery, horny, shelly, or bony integument, such as covers many invertebrate and some vertebrate animals, taking the form of scales, plates, shells, &c. (as in crabs, crocodiles, &c.).

Derogate, der′ō-gāt, *v.t.—derogated, derogating.* [L. *derogo, derogatum*, to repeal part of a law, to restrict, to modify—*de*, priv., and *rogo*, to ask, to propose.] To repeal, annul, or revoke partially, as a law: distinguished from *abrogate*; to lessen the worth of; to disparage†.—*v.i.* To detract; to have the effect of lowering or diminishing, as in reputation; to lessen by taking away a part: with *from* (something *derogates* from a person's dignity.—**Derogation**, der-ō-gā′shon, *n.* The act of derogating; a taking away from, or limiting in extent or operation; a lessening of value or estimation; detraction; disparagement.—**Derogatory**, dē-rog′a-to-ri, *a.* Having the effect of derogating or detracting from; lessening the extent, effect, or value: with *to*.—**Derogatoriness**, dē-rog′a-to-ri-nes, *n.* The quality of being derogatory.—**Derogatorily**, dē-rog′a-to-ri-li, *adv.* In a detracting manner.

Derrick, der′ik, *n.* [The name of a London hangman of the 17th century, applied first to the gallows, and hence to a contrivance resembling it.] An apparatus for hoisting heavy weights, usually consisting of a boom supported by a central post which is steadied by stays and guys, and furnished with a purchase, either the pulley or the wheel and axle and pulley combined.—*Derrick-crane*, a kind of crane with a movable jib, combining the advantages of the derrick and of the crane.

Derringer, dėr′in-jėr, *n.* [After the inventor, an American gunsmith.] A short-barrelled pistol of large calibre, now usually breech-loading.

Dervish, dėr′vish, *n.* [Turkish *dervish*, Per. *darwesh*, poor, indigent, a dervish.] A Mohammedan friar or monk, who professes extreme poverty, and leads an austere life, partly in monasteries, partly itinerant.

Descant, des′kant, *n.* [O.Fr. *deschant*, from L.L. *discantus*—L. *dis*, and *cantus*, singing, a song.] A discourse, discussion, or disputation; *mus.* an addition of a part or parts to a subject or melody; a song or tune with various modulations.—*v.i.* (deskant′). To discourse, comment, or animadvert freely; to add a part or variation to a melody.—**Descanter**, des-kan′tėr, *n.* One who descants.

Descend, dē-send′, *v.i.* [Fr. *descendre*, L. *descendere—de*, down, *scando*, to climb. SCAN.] To move from a higher to a lower place; to move, come, or go downward; to sink; to run or flow down; to invade or fall upon hostilely; to proceed from a source or origin; to be derived; to pass from one heir to another; to pass, as from general to particular considerations; to lower or degrade one's self; to stoop.—*v.t.* To walk, move, or pass downward upon or along; to pass from the top to the bottom of.—**Descendable**, dē-sen′da-bl, *a.* Capable of descending by inheritance; descendible.—**Descendant**, dē-sen′dant, *n.* An individual proceeding from an ancestor in any degree; offspring.—**Descendent**, dē-sen′dent, *a.* Descending.—**Descender**, dē-sen′dėr, *n.* One who descends.—**Descendible**, dē-sen′di-bl, *a.* Capable of being descended or passed down; capable of descending from an ancestor to an heir.—**Descendibility**, dē-sen′di-bil″i-ti, *n.* The quality of being descendible.—**Descending**, dē-sen′ding, *p.* and *a.* Moving downward.—*Descending series, math.* a series in which each term is less than that preceding it.—**Descension**, dē-sen′shon, *n.* [L. *descensio*.] Descent; degradation.—**Descensional**, dē-sen′shon-al, *a.* Pertaining to descension.—**Descensive**, dē-sen′siv, *a.* Descending; tending downward.—**Descent**, dē-sent′, *n.* [Fr. *descente*.] The act of descending or passing from a higher to a lower place; inclination downward; slope; declivity; decline, as in station, virtue, quality, or the like; an incursion, invasion, or sudden attack on a country; transmission by succession or inheritance; a proceeding from a progenitor; extraction; lineage; pedigree; a generation; a single degree in the scale of genealogy; issue†; descendants†.

Describe, dē-skrīb′, *v.t.—described, describing.* [L. *describo*, to write down, to delineate—*de*, down, and *scribo*, to write, as in *ascribe, inscribe*, &c.; akin *scribe, scripture*.] To delineate or mark the form or figure of; to trace out; to form or trace by motion; to show or represent orally or by writing; to depict or portray in words.—*v.i.* To use the power of describing.—**Describable**, dē-skrī′ba-bl, *a.* Capable of being described.—**Describent**, dē-skrī′bent, *n.* *Geom.* the line or surface from the motion of which a surface or solid is supposed to be generated or described.—**Describer**, dē-skrī′bėr, *n.* One who describes.—**Description**, dē-skrip′shon, *n.* [L.

descriptio, descriptionis.] The act of describing; delineation; an account of the properties or appearance of a thing, so that another may form a just conception of it; the combination of qualities which constitute a class, species, or individual; hence, class, species, variety, kind (a person of this *description.*)—**Descriptive**, di-skrip'-tiv, *a.* Containing description; having the quality of representing.—**Descriptively**, di-skrip'tiv-li, *adv.* In a descriptive manner.—**Descriptiveness**, di-skrip'tiv-nes, *n.* State of being descriptive.

Descry, dē-skrī', *v.t.—descried, descrying.* [O.Fr. *descrier*, to decry, to make an outcry on discovering something. DECRY.] To espy; to discover by the sight; to see or behold from a distance; to examine by the sight (O.T.).—**Descrier**, dē-skrī'ėr, *n.* One who descries.

Desecrate, des'ē-krāt, *v.t.— desecrated, desecrating.* [From L. *de*, from, away, and *sacer*, sacred, being thus the opposite of *consecrate.*] To divert from a sacred purpose or sacred character; to render unhallowed; to profane.—**Desecration**, des-ē-krā'shon, *n.* The act of desecrating; profanation.

Desert, dez'ėrt, *a.* [L. *desertus*, pp. of *desero, desertum*, to forsake—*de*, priv., and *sero, sertum*, to unite, to join together, from root seen in *series.*] Lying waste; uncultivated and uninhabited; in the natural state and unimproved by man; pertaining to a wilderness (the *desert* air).—*n.* An uninhabited tract of land; a wilderness; a solitude; often a vast sandy, stony, or rocky expanse, almost destitute of moisture and vegetation.—*v.t.* (dē-zėrt'). To forsake; to leave utterly; to abandon; to quit, leave, or depart from in defiance of duty.—*v.i.* To quit a service or post without permission; to run away.—**Deserter**, dē-zėr'tėr, *n.* One who deserts; particularly, a soldier or seaman who quits the service without permission.—**Desertion**, dē-zėr'shon, *n.* The act of deserting; the state of being deserted or forsaken.

Desert, dē-zėrt', *n.* [O.Fr. *deserte*, merit, from *deservir*, to deserve. DESERVE.] The quality of deserving either reward or punishment; merit or demerit; what is deserved on account of good or evil done; reward or punishment merited; due return.—**Desertless**, dē-zėrt'les, *a.* Without merit or claim to favour or reward; undeserving.

Deserve, dē-zėrv', *v.t.—deserved, deserving.* [O.Fr. *deservir, desservir*, from L. *deservio*, to serve diligently—*de*, intens., and *servio*, to serve.] To merit; to be worthy of, whether of good or evil; to merit by labour, services, or qualities; to be worthy of or call for on account of evil acts or qualities (actions that *deserve* censure).—*v.i.* To merit; to be worthy of or deserving (to *deserve* well of a person).—**Deservedly**, dē-zėr'ved-li, *adv.* According to desert, whether of good or evil; justly.—**Deserver**, dē-zėr'vėr, *n.* One who deserves or merits: used generally in a good sense.—**Deserving**, dē-zėr'ving, *a.* Worthy of reward or praise; meritorious.—**Deservingly**, dē-zėr'ving-li, *adv.* Meritoriously; with just desert.

Deshabille, dez-a-bēl', *n.* [Fr.—*des*=prefix *dis*, and *habiller*, to dress; akin *habiliment.*] The state of being in undress, or of not being properly or fully dressed.

Desiccate, dē-sik'āt, *v.t.—desiccated, desiccating.* [L. *desicco*, to dry up—*de*, intens., and *sicco*, to dry, from *siccus*, dry.] To exhaust of moisture; to exhale or remove moisture from; to dry.—*v.i.* To become dry.—**Desiccant**, **Desiccative**, de-sik-ant, de-sik'a-tiv, *a.* Drying.—*n.* A medicine or application that dries a sore.—**Desiccation**, des-ik-kā'shon, *n.* The act of making dry; the state of being dried.

Desiderate, dē-sid'ėr-āt, *v.t.* [L. *desidero, desideratum*, to long for, to feel the want of, whence also *desire.*] To feel the want of; to miss; to want; to desire.—**Desiderative**, dē-sid'ėr-ā-tiv, *a.* Having or implying desire; expressing or denoting desire.—*n.* A verb formed from another verb and expressing a desire of doing the action implied in the primitive verb.—**Desideratum**, dē-sid'ėr-ā"tum, *n.* pl. **Desiderata**, dē-sid'ėr-ā"ta. [L.] That which is not possessed, but which is desirable; something much wanted.

Design, dē-zīn' or dē-sīn', *v.t.* [L. *designo*, to mark out, point out, contrive—*de*, and *signo*, to seal or stamp, from *signum*, a sign. SIGN.] To plan and delineate by drawing the outline or figure of; to sketch, as for a pattern or model; to project or plan; to contrive for a purpose; to form in idea (a scheme); to set apart in intention; to intend; to purpose.—*v.i.* To intend; to purpose.—*n.* A plan or representation of a thing by an outline; first idea represented by lines, as in painting or architecture; a sketch; a drawing; a tracing; a scheme or plan in the mind; purpose; intention; aim; the adaptation of means to a preconceived end; contrivance.—**Designable**, dē-zī'na-bl or dē-sī'na-bl, *a.* Capable of being designed or marked out; distinguishable.—**Designate**, dez'ig-nāt, *v.t.—designated, designating.* To mark out or indicate by visible lines, marks, description, &c.; to name and settle the identity of; to denominate; to select or distinguish for a particular purpose; to appoint, name, or assign.—**Designation**, dez-ig-nā'shon, *n.* The act of designating; a distinguishing from others; indication; appointment; assignment; distinctive appellation.—**Designative**, **Designatory**, dez'ig-nā-tiv, dez'-ig-na-to-ri, *a.* Serving to designate or indicate.—**Designator**, dez'ig-nā-tėr, *n.* One who designates or points out.—**Designedly**, dē-zī'ned-li or dē-sī'ned-li, *adv.* By design; purposely; intentionally.—**Designer**, dē-zī'nėr or dē-sī'nėr, *n.* One who designs.—**Designing**, dē-zī'ning or dē-sī'ning, *pp.* and *a.* Artful; insidious

Desire, dē-zīr', *v.t.—desired, desiring.* [Fr. *désirer*, from L. *desidero, desideratum*, to desire (*desiderate* being thus the same word)—prefix *de*, and *sidero*, as in *considero*. CONSIDER.] To wish for the possession or enjoyment of; to long for; to hanker after; to covet; to express a wish to obtain; to ask; to request; to petition.—*v.i.* To be in a state of desire or anxiety.—*n.* [Fr. *désir*, from the verb.] An emotion or excitement of the mind, directed to the attainment or possession of an object from which pleasure is expected; a wish, craving, or longing to obtain or enjoy; the object of desire; that which is desired.—**Desirability**, **Desirableness**, dē-zī'ra-bil"i-ti, dē-zī'ra-bl-nes, *n.* The state or quality of being desirable.—**Desirable**, dē-zī'ra-bl, *a.* Worthy of desire; calculated or fitted to excite a wish to possess.—**Desirably**, dē-zī'ra-bli, *adv.* In a desirable manner.—**Desirer**, dē-zī'rėr, *n.* One who desires.—**Desirous**, dē-zī'rus, *a.* Filled with a desire; wishing to obtain; wishful; covetous: often with *of.*—**Desirously**, dē-zī'rus-li, *adv.* With desire; with earnest wishes.

Desist, dē-zist', *v.i.* [L. *desisto*, to desist—*de*, away from, and *sisto*, to stand, as in *assist, consist, persist*, &c. STAND.] To cease to act or proceed; to forbear; to leave off; to discontinue; to cease.—**Desistance**, **Desistence**,† dē-zis'tans, dē-zis'tens, *n.* A ceasing to act or proceed; a stopping.

Desk, desk, *n.* [A.Sax. *disc*, a table, a dish; L.L. *discus*, a desk, from L. *discus*, Gr. *diskos*, a disc, a quoit; *dais, dish, disk* are the same word.] A kind of table or piece of furniture with a sloping upper surface for the use of writers and readers; a frame or case to be placed on a table for the same purpose.

Desman, des'man, *n.* The European muskrat.

Desmography, des-mog'ra-fi, *n.* [Gr. *desmos*, a ligament.] A description of the ligaments of the body.—**Desmology**, des-mol'o-ji, *n.* That branch of anatomy which treats of the ligaments and sinews.

Desolate, des'ō-lāt, *v.t.—desolated, desolating.* [L. *desolo, desolatum*, to leave alone, to forsake—*de*, intens., and *solo*, to lay waste, from *solus*, alone. SOLE, *a.*] To deprive of inhabitants; to make desert; to lay waste; to ruin; to ravage.—*a.* [L. *desolatus*, pp. of *desolo, desolatum.*] Destitute or deprived of inhabitants; desert; uninhabited; laid waste; in a ruinous condition; without a companion; solitary; forsaken; forlorn; lonely.—**Desolately**, des'ō-lāt-li, *adv.* In a desolate manner.—**Desolateness**, des'-ō-lāt-nes, *n.* A state of being desolate.—**Desolater**, **Desolator**, des'ō-lā-tėr, *n.* One who or that which desolates.—**Desolation**, des-ō-lā'shon, *n.* The act of desolating; devastation; havoc; ravage; a place depopulated, ravaged, or laid waste; the state of being desolate; gloominess; sadness; melancholy; destitution; ruin.

Despair, dė-spār', *v.i.* [O.Fr. *desperer* (now *desespérer*), from L. *despero*—*de*, priv., and *spero*, to hope, allied to Skr. root *sprih*, to desire. *Prosper* is from same root.] To give up all hope or expectation: followed by *of*; to be sunk in utter want of hope.—*n.* The state of being without hope, combined with a dread of coming evil; hopelessness; desperation; that which causes despair; *theol.* loss of hope in the mercy of God.—**Despairer**, dė-spā'rėr, *n.* One who despairs.—**Despairing**, dė-spā'ring, *a.* Indulging in despair; prone to despair; indicating despair.—**Despairingly**, dė-spā'ring-li, *adv.* In a despairing manner.

Despatch, des-pach', *v.t.* [O.Fr. *despeecher*, Fr. *dépêcher*, to despatch, to expedite, from L.L. *dispedico*—L. *dis*, apart, and *pedica*, a snare, or from a L.L. *dispactare*, from L. *dis*, and *pango, pactum*, to fasten, as in *compact, a.*] To send or send away; particularly applied to the sending of messengers, agents, and letters on special business, and often implying haste; to hasten; to expedite; to speed; to send out of the world; to put to death; to slay; to kill; to perform or execute speedily; to finish.—*n.* The act of despatching; the getting rid of or doing away with something; dismissal; riddance; speedy performance; speed; haste; expedition; a letter sent or to be sent with expedition by a special messenger; a letter on some affair of state or of public concern; a letter, message, or document, sent by some public officer on public business.—**Despatcher**, des-pach'ėr, *n.* One who despatches.—**Despatchful**, des-pach'ful, *a.* Full of despatch or haste; bent on haste; indicating haste.

Desperado, des'pėr-ā"dō, des'pėr-ā"dō, *n.* A desperate fellow; one fearless or regardless of safety; a reckless ruffian.

Desperate, des'pėr-ėt, *a.* [L. *desperatus*, pp. of *despero*, to despair. DESPAIR.] Without hope‡; regardless of safety; fearless of danger; reduced to extremity and reckless of consequences; frantic; proceeding from despair; reckless; beyond hope; irretrievable; past cure; hopeless (*desperate* disease, situation, undertaking).—**Desperately**, des'pėr-ėt-li, *adv.* In a desperate manner; recklessly; violently; furiously; madly.—**Desperateness**, des'pėr-ėt-nes, *n.* The state or quality of being desperate.—**Desperation**, des-pėr-ā'shon, *n.* The state of being desperate; a giving up of hope; disregard of safety or danger; fury; rage; violence.

Despicable, des'pi-ka-bl, *a.* [L.L. *despicabilis*, from L. *despicor, despicatus*, to despise, from *despicio*. DESPISE.] Deserving of being despised; contemptible; base; mean; vile; worthless. ∴Syn. under CONTEMPTIBLE.—**Despicableness**, des'pi-ka-bl-nes, *n.* The quality or state of being despicable.—**Despicably**, des'pi-ka-bli, *adv.* In a despicable manner; basely; vilely.

Despise, di-spīz', *v.t.—despised, despising.* [O.Fr. *despiz*, pp. of *despire*, to despise, from L. *despicere*, to despise—*de*, down, and *specio*, to look. SPECIES. Akin *despicable, despite.*] To look down upon; to have the lowest opinion of; to contemn; to disdain; to scorn.

Despite, di-spīt', *n.* [O.Fr. *despit*, Mod. Fr. *dépit*, from L. *despectus*, a looking down upon, a despising, from *despicio*, to despise.] DESPISE. Hence the shorter form *spite.*] Extreme malice; malignity; contemptuous hate; aversion; spite; defiance with contempt, or contempt of opposition; contemptuous defiance; an act of malice or contempt.—*v.t.*† To vex; to offend; to spite; to tease.—*prep.* In spite of; notwithstanding.—**Despiteful**, di-spīt′ful, *a.* Full of despite or spite; malicious; malignant.—**Despitefully**, di-spīt′ful-li, *adv.* With despite; maliciously; contemptuously.—**Despitefulness**, di-spīt′ful-nes, *n.*

Despoil, di-spoil′, *v.t.* [O. Fr. *despoiller*, L. *despolio*, to rob, plunder—*de*, intens., and *spolio*, to spoil. SPOIL.] To take from by force; to rob; to strip; to divest; to deprive (to *despoil* a person *of* a thing).—**Despoiler**, di-spoi′lėr, *n.* One who despoils; a plunderer.—**Despoliation**, di-spō′li-ā″shon, *n.* The act of despoiling; a stripping.

Despond, di-spond′, *v.i.* [L. *despondeo*, to promise in marriage, to promise away, to give up, to despond—*de*, away, and *spondeo*, *sponsum*, to promise solemnly, whence *sponsor*, *spouse*, *respond*.] To be quite cast down; to feel depressed or dejected in mind; to lose hope, heart, or resolution.—**Despondency**, di-spon′den-si, *n.* The state or quality of being despondent.—**Despondent**, di-spon′dent, *a.* Losing courage at the loss of hope; sinking into dejection.—**Despondently**, **Despondingly**, di-spon′dent-li, di-spon′ding-li, *adv.* In a despondent manner.—**Desponder**, di-spon′dėr, *n.* One who desponds.

Despot, des′pot, *n.* [Gr. *despotēs*, *potēs* being from same root as Gr. *posis*, Lith. and Skr. *patis*, lord, husband; L. *potior*, to be master of, *potis*, able, *potestas*, power; Slav. *hospodar*, *gospodar*, lord, master.] A sovereign or monarch ruling absolutely or without control; a tyrant; one who enforces his will regardless of the interests or feelings of others.—**Despotic**, **Despotical**, despot′ik, des-pot′i-kal, *a.* Absolute in power; unrestrained by constitution, laws, or men; arbitrary; tyrannical. — **Despotically**, des-pot′i-kal-li, *adv.* In a despotic manner. —**Despotism**, des′pot-izm, *n.* Absolute power; unlimited or uncontrolled authority; an arbitrary government; the rule of a despot; absolutism; autocracy; tyranny.

Despumate,† dē-spū′māt, *v.t.* and *i.* [L. *despumo*, *despumatum*—*de*, off, and *spuma*, froth, scum. SPUE.] To throw off or remove froth or scum. — **Despumation**, des-pū-mā′shon, *n.* The act of despumating.

Desquamate,† dē-skwā′māt, *v.i.* [L. *desquamo*, *desquamatum*—*de*, off, and *squama*, a scale.] To scale off; to peel off.—**Desquamation**, des-kwa-mā′shon, *n.* A scaling off. — **Desquamative**, **Desquamatory**, des-kwam′a-tiv, des-kwam′a-to-ri, *a.* Relating to desquamation.

Dessert, dē-zėrt′, *n.* [Fr. *dessert*, from *desservir*, to clear the table—*des* (=L. *dis*), and *servir*, to serve.] A service of fruits or sweetmeats at the close of a dinner or entertainment. — **Dessert-spoon**, *n.* A spoon intermediate in size between a table-spoon and tea-spoon, used for dessert.

Destine, des′tin, *v.t.*—*destined*, *destining*. [L. *destino*, to place down, to make firm or secure—*de*, and a root *stan*, a stronger form of *sta*, root of *stare*, to stand, E. *stand*, *stay*, being of the same root.] To set, ordain, or appoint to a use, purpose, state or place; to fix unalterably, as by a divine decree; to doom; to devote; to appoint inevitably. — **Destination**, des-ti-nā′shon, *n.* [L. *destinatio*.] The act of destining; the purpose for which anything is intended or appointed; predetermined object or use; the place to which a thing is appointed; the predetermined end of a journey or voyage.—**Destinist**, des′ti-nist, *n.* A believer in destiny.—**Destiny**, des′ti-ni, *n.* A person's destined fate or lot; ultimate fate; doom; fortune; invincible necessity; fate; order of things fixed or established by divine decree, or by connection of causes and effects.—*pl.* the Fates.

Destitute, des′ti-tūt, *a.* [L. *destitutus*, pp. of *destituo*, *destitutum*, to set down, to forsake—*de*, down, and *statuo*, to set. STATE, STATUE, &c.] Not having or possessing; wanting: with *of*; not possessing the necessaries of life; in abject poverty; entirely without the means of subsistence.—**Destitution**, des-ti-tū′shon, *n.* The state of being destitute; a state of utter want; poverty; indigence; deprivation†.

Destroy, dē-stroi′, *v.t.* [O.Fr. *destruire* (now *détruire*), from L. *destruo*, to destroy —*de*, priv., and *struo*, to pile, to build. STRUCTURE.] To pull down; to knock to pieces; to demolish; to ruin; to annihilate; to put an end to; to cause to cease; to kill or slay; to ravage; to spoil.—**Destroyer**, dē-stroi′ėr, *n.* One who or that which destroys; a swift class of vessel intended for the destruction of torpedo-craft, and itself armed with guns and torpedoes. — **Destructible**, dē-struk′ti-bl, *a.* Liable to destruction; capable of being destroyed. — **Destructibility**, **Destructibleness**, dē-struk′ti-bil″i-ti, dē-struk′ti-bl-nes, *n.* The state of being destructible.—**Destruction**, dē-struk′shon, *n.* [L. *destructio*.] The act of destroying; demolition; a pulling down; subversion; overthrow; ruin, by whatever means; extermination; death; murder; slaughter; the state of being destroyed; cause of destruction; a destroyer (O.T.).—**Destructive**, dē-struk′tiv, *a.* Causing destruction; having the quality of destroying; having a tendency to destroy; delighting in destruction; ruinous; mischievous; fatal; deadly: with *of* or *to*.—*Destructive distillation*, the distillation of organic products at high temperatures, by which the elements are separated or evolved in new forms, as in making gas from coal. —**Destructively**, dē-struk′tiv-li, *adv.* In a destructive manner. — **Destructiveness**, dē-struk′tiv-nes, *n.* The quality of being destructive; a propensity to destroy. —**Destructor**, dē-struk′tėr, *n.* A destroyer; a furnace for burning refuse.

Desudation, dē-sū-dā′shon, *n.* [L. *desudo*—*de*, and *sudo*, to sweat.] *Med.* a sweating; a profuse or morbid sweating.

Desuetude, des′wē-tūd, *n.* [L. *desuetudo* —*de*, priv., and *suesco*, to accustom one's self. CUSTOM.] A state of being no longer practised or customary; disuse; discontinuance of practice, custom, or fashion.

Desulphurate, **Desulphurize**, dē-sul′fū-rāt, dē-sul′fū-rīz, *v.t.* To deprive of sulphur. — **Desulphuration**, **Desulphurization**, dē-sul′fū-rā″shon, dē-sul′fū-ri-zā″shon, *n.* The act of depriving of sulphur.

Desultory, des′ul-to-ri, *a.* [L. *desultorius*, pertaining to a *desultor*, or rider in the circus, from *desilio*, *desultum*, to leap down —*de*, down, and *salio*, to leap.] Leaping or hopping about‡; passing from one thing or subject to another without order or natural connection; rambling; unconnected; immethodical; inconstant; unsettled; hasty. —**Desultorily**, des′ul-to-ri-li, *adv.* In a desultory manner; without method; loosely. —**Desultoriness**, des′ul-to-ri-nes, *n.* The character of being desultory.

Desynonymize, dē-si-non′i-mīz, *v.t.* [Prefix *de*, priv., and *synonym*.] To give a turn of meaning to so as to prevent from being absolutely synonymous; to use with kindred but not the same meanings.—**Desynonymization**, dē-si-non′i-mi-zā″shon, *n.* The act of desynonymizing.

Detach, dē-tach′, *v.t.* [Fr. *détacher*—*de*, priv., and the root from which the English noun *tack* is derived. TACK, ATTACH.] To separate or disunite; to disengage; to part from; to sever; to separate for a special purpose or service, especially some military purpose.—**Detached**, dē-tacht′, *a.* Separated; disunited; standing apart or separately; drawn and sent on a separate service. —**Detachment**, dē-tach′ment, *n.* The act of detaching; a body of troops or number of vessels selected or taken from the main army or fleet and employed on some special service or expedition.

Detail, dē-tāl′, *v.t.* [Fr. *détailler*, to cut in pieces—*de*, and *tailler*, L.L. *taleare*, *taliare*, to cut, from L. *talea*, a cutting. RETAIL, TAILOR.] To relate, report, or narrate in particulars; to recite the particulars of; to particularize; to relate minutely and distinctly; *milit.* to appoint to a particular service. — *n.* An individual fact, circumstance, or portion going along with others; an item; a particular; a minute account; a narrative or report of particulars; *milit.* an individual or small body; small detachment on special service.—*In detail*, circumstantially; item by item; individually; part by part.—**Detailed**, dē-tāld′, *p.* and *a.* Related in particulars; minutely recited; exact; minute; particular. — **Detailer**, dē-tā′lėr, *n.* One who details.

Detain, dē-tān′, *v.t.* [Fr. *détenir*, L. *detineo*, to detain—*de*, off, and *teneo*, to hold, as in *contain*, *retain*, &c., seen also in *tenant*, *tenacious*. TENANT.] To keep back or from; to withhold; to retain or keep what belongs to another; to keep or restrain from proceeding; to hinder; to stay or stop; to hold in custody.—**Detainer**, dē-tā′nėr, *n.* One who detains; *law*, a holding or keeping possession of what belongs to another. — **Detainment**, dē-tān′ment, *n.* The act of detaining; detention.—**Detent**, dē-tent′, *n.* [L. *detentus*, a keeping back.] A pin, stud, or lever forming a check in a clock, watch, tumbler-lock, or other machine; a click or pawl.—**Detention**, dē-ten′shon, *n.* The act of detaining; a wrongful keeping of what belongs to another; state of being detained; confinement; restraint; delay from necessity or from accident.

Detect, dē-tekt′, *v.t.* [L. *detego*, *detectum*, to uncover, expose—*de*, priv., and *tego*, to cover. DECK.] To discover; to find out; to bring to light (an error, crime, criminal). —**Detectable**, **Detectible**, dē-tek′ta-bl, dē-tek′ti-bl, *a.* Capable of being or liable to be detected.—**Detection**, dē-tek′shon, *n.* The act of detecting; the finding out of what is concealed, hidden, or formerly unknown; discovery.—**Detective**, dē-tek′tiv, *a.* Fitted for or skilled in detecting; employed in detecting crime.—*n.* A species of police officer, having no specific beat nor uniform, whose special duty it is to detect offences and to apprehend criminals; also a private person who engages to investigate cases, often of a delicate nature, for hire.—**Detector**, dē-tek′tėr, *n.* One who, or that which, detects or brings to light; a revealer; a discoverer.

Detent, **Detention**. Under DETAIN.

Deter, dē-tėr′, *v.t.*—*deterred*, *deterring*. [L. *deterreo*, to frighten from, to prevent—*de*, from, and *terreo*, to frighten. TERROR.] To discourage and prevent from acting or proceeding, the preventing agency being something anticipated as difficult, dangerous, or unpleasant.—**Determent**, dē-tėr′ment, *n.* The act or cause of deterring; that which deters.—**Deterrent**, dē-tėr′ent, *a.* Having the power or tendency to deter.—*n.* That which deters or tends to deter.—**Deterrer**, dē-tėr′ėr, *n.* One who or that which deters.

Deterge, dē-tėrj′, *v.t.*—*deterged*, *deterging*. [L. *detergeo*—*de*, from, and *tergeo*, *tersum*, to wipe. TERSE.] To cleanse (a sore); to clear away foul or offending matter from.—**Detergence**, **Detergency**, dē-tėr′jens, dē-tėr′jen-si, *n.* The state or quality of being detergent; cleansing or purging power.—**Detergent**, dē-tėr′jent, *a.* Cleansing; purging. — *n.* Anything that has a strong cleansing power.—**Detersion**, dē-tėr′shon, *n.* The act of cleansing.—**Detersive**, dē-tėr′siv, *a.* Having power to cleanse; cleansing.—*n.* That which has the power of cleansing; a detergent.—**Detersively**, dē-tėr′siv-li, *adv.* In a detersive manner.—**Detersiveness**, dē-tėr′siv-nes, *n.*

Deteriorate, dē-tē′ri-ō-rāt, *v.i.*—*deteriorated*, *deteriorating*. [L. *deterioro*, *deterioratum*, from *deterior*, worse, from *de*, as *exterior* from *ex*, *interior* from *in*.] To grow worse or inferior in quality; to be impaired in quality; to degenerate.—*v.t.* To make worse; to reduce in quality.—**Deterioration**, dē-tē′ri-ō-rā″shon, *n.* The process or state of growing worse.—**Deteriority**,† dē-tē′ri-or″i-ti, *n.* Deterioration.

Determine, dē-tėr′min, *v.t.*—*determined*, *determining*. [L. *determino*, to bound, to limit—*de*, intens., and *terminus*, a boundary, whence *terminate, term.*] To fix the bounds of; to set bounds or limits to; to mark off, settle, fix, establish; to end or settle conclusively, as by the decision of a doubtful or controverted point; to settle ultimately; to come to a fixed resolution and intention in respect of; to give a bent or direction to; to influence the choice of; to cause to come to a conclusion or resolution.—*v.i.* To resolve; to conclude; to decide; to settle on some line of conduct: to cease; to terminate.—**Determinability**, dē-tėr′mi-na-bil″i-ti, *n.* Quality of being determinable.—**Determinable**, dē-tėr′mi-na-bl, *a.* Capable of being determined, ascertained, decided, brought to a conclusion.—**Determinant**, dē-tėr′mi-nant, *a.* Serving to determine; determinative.—*n.* That which determines or causes determination; *math.* the sum of a series of products of several numbers, these products being formed according to certain specified laws; a group of BIOPHORES (which see).—**Determinate**, dē-tėr′mi-nāt, *a.* [L. *determinatus.*] Limited; fixed; definite; established; settled; positive; decisive; conclusive; fixed in purpose; resolute.—*Determinate inflorescence*, in *bot.* same as *centrifugal inflorescence.*—*v.t.*† To bring to an end; to terminate (*Shak.*).—**Determinately**, dē-tėr′mi-nāt-li, *adv.* In a determinate manner; precisely; with exact specification; resolutely.—**Determinateness**, dē-tėr-mi-nāt-nes, *n.* The state of being determinate.—**Determination**, dē-tėr′mi-nā″shon, *n.* The act of determining or deciding; decision in the mind; firm resolution; settled purpose; the mental habit of settling upon some line of action with a fixed purpose to adhere to it; adherence to aims or purposes; resoluteness; *chem.* the ascertainment of the exact proportion of any substance in a compound body; *med.* afflux; tendency of blood to flow to any part more copiously than is normal.—**Determinative**, dē-tėr′mi-nā-tiv, *a.* Having power to determine or direct to a certain end; directing; conclusive; limiting; bounding; having the power of ascertaining precisely; employed in determining.—**Determinator**, dē-tėr′mi-nā-tėr, *n.* One who determines.—**Determined**, dē-tėr′mind, *a.* Having a firm or fixed purpose; manifesting firmness or resolution; resolute.—**Determinedly**, dē-tėr′mind-li, *adv.* In a determined manner.—**Determiner**, dē-tėr′mi-nėr, *n.* One who decides or determines.—**Determinism** dē-tėr′mi-nizm, *n.* A system of philosophy which denies liberty of action to man, holding that the will is not free, but is invincibly determined by motives.

Deterrent. Under DETER.

Detersion, Detersive, &c. Under DETERGE.

Detest, dē-test′, *v.t.* [L. *detestor*, to invoke a deity in cursing, to detest—*de*, intens., and *testor*, to call to witness, from *testis*, a witness; so *attest, contest*, also *testify, testament.*] To abhor; to abominate; to hate extremely.—**Detestable**, dē-tes′ta-bl, *a.* Extremely hateful; abominable; very odious; deserving abhorrence.—**Detestableness, Detestability**, dē-tes′ta-bl-nes, dē-tes′ta-bil″i-ti, *n.* The state or quality of being detestable; extreme hatefulness.—**Detestably**, dē-tes′ta-bli, *adv.* In a detestable manner.—**Detestation**, dē-tes-tā′shon, *n.* Extreme hatred; abhorrence; loathing.—**Detester**, dē-tes′tėr, *n.* One who detests.

Dethrone, dē-thrōn′, *v.t.*—*dethroned, dethroning.* [Prefix *de*, from, and *throne.*] To remove or drive from a throne; to depose; to divest of royal authority and dignity; to divest of rule or power, or of supreme power.—**Dethronement**, dē-thrōn′ment, *n.* Removal from a throne; deposition.—**Dethroner**, dē-thrō′nėr, *n.* One who dethrones.

Detonate, det′ō-nāt, *v.t.* and *i.*—*detonated, detonating.* [L. *detono, detonatum*, to thunder—*de*, and *tono*, to thunder.] To explode or cause to explode; to burn with a sudden report.—**Detonating**, det′ō-nā-ting, *p.* and *a.* Exploding; explosive.—*Detonating powders*, or *fulminating powders*, certain chemical compounds, which, on being exposed to heat or suddenly struck, explode with a loud report, owing to one or more of the constituent parts suddenly assuming the gaseous state.—**Detonation**, det-ō-nā′shon, *n.* An explosion or sudden report made by the inflammation of certain combustible bodies.—**Detonator**, det′ō-nā-tėr, *n.* That which detonates; the device by which fulminate of mercury is made to explode the charge in a torpedo or submarine mine.—**Detonization**, det′ō-ni-zā″shon, *n.* The act of exploding.—**Detonize**, det′ō-nīz, *v.t.* and *i.*—*detonized, detonizing.* To cause to explode; to detonate.

Detort, dē-tort′, *v.t.* [L. *detorqueo, detortum*—*de*, intens., and *torqueo*, to twist, whence *contort, extort, torture.*] To distort; to twist, wrest, pervert; to turn from the original or plain meaning.—**Detortion, Detorsion**, dē-tor′shon, *n.* A turning or wresting; perversion.

Detour, de-tör′, *n.* [Fr. *détour*—prefix *de*, and *tour*=E. *turn.*] A roundabout or circuitous way; a going round instead of by a direct road or route.

Detract, dē-trakt′, *v.t.* [L. *detracto*—*de*, from, and *tracto*, to draw, from *traho, tractum*, to draw, whence *tract, trace*, &c.] To take away from a whole; to withdraw; to disparage†.—*v.i.* To take away a part; especially, to take away reputation; to derogate: followed by *from* (this *detracts from* his merit).—**Detracter**, dē-trak′tėr, *n.* One who detracts; a detractor.—**Detraction**, dē-trak′shon, *n.* [L. *detractio.*] The act of detracting; an attempt, by calumny, or injurious or carping statements, to take something from the reputation of another; envious or malicious depreciation of a person, or denial of his merits.—**Detractive**, dē-trak′tiv, *a.* Having the quality or power to take away; having the character of detraction.—**Detractiveness**,† dē-trak′tiv-nes, *n.* Quality of being detractive.—**Detractor**, dē-trak′tėr, *n.* One who uses detraction; one who tries to take somewhat from the reputation of another injuriously; a muscle that draws the part to which it is attached away from some other part.—**Detractory**, dē-trak′to-ri, *a.* Containing detraction; depreciatory.

Detrain, dē-trān′, *v.t.* To remove from a railway train; to cause to leave a train: said especially of bodies of men (to *detrain* troops).—*v.i.* To quit a railway train.

Detriment, det′ri-ment, *n.* [L. *detrimentum*, from *detero, detritum*, to rub off or down, to wear—*de*, down, and *tero*, to rub, whence *trite.*] A certain degree of loss, damage, or injury; injurious or prejudicial effect; harm; diminution.—**Detrimental**, det-ri-men′tal, *a.* Injurious; hurtful; causing loss or damage.

Detritus, dē-trī′tus, *n.* [L. *detritus*, worn down. DETRIMENT.] *Geol.* a mass of substances worn off or detached from solid bodies by attrition; disintegrated materials of rocks.—**Detrital**, dē-trī′tal, *a.* Of or pertaining to detritus; composed of detritus, or partaking of the nature of detritus.

Detrude, dē-tröd′, *v.t.*—*detruded, detruding.* [L. *detrudo*—*de*, down, and *trudo*, to thrust.] To thrust down; to push down.—**Detrusion**, dē-trö′zhon, *n.* The act of thrusting or driving down.

Detruncate, dē-trung′kāt, *v.t.*—*detruncated, detruncating.* [L. *detrunco*—*de*, and *trunco*, to maim, *truncus*, cut short. TRUNK.] To cut off; to lop; to shorten by cutting.—**Detruncation**, dē-trung-kā′shon, *n.* The act of detruncating.

Deuce, dūs, *n.* [Fr. *deux*, two.] A playing card or a die with two spots; the two at dice, being the lowest throw.

Deuce, dūs, *n.* [Perhaps from L. *deus*, God, used as an interjection; but comp. L.G. *duus*, G. *daus*, used similarly; Armor. *dus, teuz*, a goblin.] The devil; perdition; used only in exclamatory or interjectional phrases.—**Deuced**, dū′sed or dūst, *a.* and *adv.* Devilish; excessive; confounded. (*Slang.*)—**Deucedly**, dū′sed-li, *adv.* Confoundedly.

Deuterogamy, dū-tėr-og′a-mi, *n.* [Gr. *deuteros*, second, and *gamos*, marriage.] A second marriage after the death of the first husband or wife.—**Deuterogamist**, dū-tėr-og′a-mist, *n.* One who marries a second time.

Deuteronomy, dū-tėr-on′o-mi, *n.* [Gr. *deuteros*, second, and *nomos*, law.] Lit. the second law or second statement of the law, the fifth book of the Pentateuch: hence **Deuteronomist**, its writer.

Deuteropathy, dū-tėr-op′a-thi, *n.* [Gr. *deuteros*, second, and *pathos*, suffering.] *Med.* a secondary disease or sympathetic affection of one part with another.—**Deuteropathic**, dū′tėr-ō-path″ik, *a.* Pertaining to deuteropathy.

Deuteroscopy,† dū-tėr-os′ko-pi, *n.* [Gr. *deuteros*, second, *skopeō*, to see.] The second-sight.

Deutoplasm, dū′tō-plazm, *n.* *Biol.* that portion of the yolk of ova which furnishes nourishment for the embryo (the *protoplasm*).—**Deutoplastic**, dū-tō-plas′tik, *a.* Pertaining to or composed of deutoplasm.

Devaporation, dē-vap′ér-ā″shon, *n.* The change of vapour into water, as in the formation of rain.

Devastate, dev′as-tāt, *v.t.*—*devastated, devastating.* [L. *devasto, devastatum*, to lay waste—*de*, intens., and *vasto*, to lay waste. WASTE.] To lay waste; to ravage; to desolate.—**Devastation**, dev-as-tā′shon, *n.* [L. *devastatio.*] The act of devastating; the state of being devastated; ravage; havoc; desolation.—**Devastator**, dev-as-tā′tėr, *n.* One who or that which devastates.

Develop, dē-vel′up, *v.t.* [Fr. *développer*, O.Fr. *desveloper*—prefix *des*, L. *dis*, apart, and a Teut. verb = O.E. *wlappe*, E. *wrap*; similarly *envelop.*] To unfold gradually; to lay open part by part; to disclose or show all the ramifications of; *biol.* to make to pass through the process of natural evolution; in photography, to bring out the latent image on a sensitized surface by the action of chemical agents.—*v.t.* To be unfolded; to become manifest in all its parts; to advance from one stage to another by a process of natural or inherent evolution; to grow or expand by a natural process; to be evolved; to proceed or come forth naturally from some vivifying source.—**Developable**, dē-vel′up-a-bl, *a.* Capable of developing or of being developed.—**Developer**, de-vel′up-ėr, *n.* One who or that which develops or unfolds.—**Development**, dē-vel′up-ment, *n.* The act or process of developing; unfolding; the unraveling of a plot; a gradual growth or advancement through progressive changes; the organic changes which take place in animal and vegetable bodies, from their embryo state until they arrive at maturity; *photog.* the process following exposure, by which the image on the plate is rendered visible.—*Development theory*, *biol.* the theory that plants and animals are capable of advancing, in successive generations and through an infinite variety of stages, from a lower to a higher state of existence, and that the more highly organized forms at present existing are the descendants of lower forms.

Deviate, dē′vi-āt, *v.i.*—*deviated, deviating.* [L. *devio, deviatum*—*de*, from, and *via*, way; seen also in *convey, obvious, voyage*, &c.] To turn aside or wander from the common or right way, course, or line; to diverge; to err; to swerve; to vary from uniform state.—*v.t.* To cause to deviate.—**Deviation**, dē-vi-ā′shon, *n.* A turning aside from the right way, course, or line; variation from a common or established rule or standard.—*Deviation of the compass*, the deviation of a ship's compass from the true magnetic meridian, caused by the near presence of iron.

Device, dē-vīs′, *n.* [O.Fr. *devise*, a device; Fr. *deviser*, to imagine, devise; from L. *divido, divisum*, to divide. DIVIDE.] That which is formed by design or invented; a scheme, contrivance, stratagem, project;

invention or faculty of devising (*Shak.*); something fancifully conceived, as an ornamental design; an emblem or figure representative of a family, person, action, or quality, with or without a motto.

Devil, dev'il, *n.* [A.Sax. *deófol*, from L. *diabolus*, Gr. *diabolos*, the accuser, from *diaballō*, to accuse.] An evil spirit or being; the evil one, represented in Scripture as the traducer, father of lies, tempter, &c.; a very wicked person; a ferocious marsupial animal of Tasmania; a printer's errand-boy; a machine through which cotton or wool is first passed to prepare it for the carding machines; a teasing machine; a machine for cutting up rags and old cloth into flock and for other purposes; *cookery*, a dish, as a bone with some meat on it, grilled and seasoned with pepper.—*The devil*, is used as an expletive and also in various colloquial expressions, being equivalent to ruin or destruction, something very annoying or harassing, the deuce.—*Devil's advocate*, *R. Cath. Ch.* a person appointed to raise doubts against the claims of a candidate for canonization.—*v.t.*—*devilled, devilling.* To pepper or season excessively and broil; to tease or cut up by an instrument called a devil.—**Devilish**, dev'il-ish, *a.* Partaking of the qualities of the devil; pertaining to the devil; diabolical; very evil and mischievous.—**Devilishly**, dev'il-ish-li, *adv.* In a devilish manner.—**Devilishness**, dev'il-ish-nes, *n.* The quality of being devilish.—**Devilment**, dev'il-ment, *n.* Trickery; roguishness; devilry; prank. (*Colloq.*)—**Devilry**, dev'il-ri, *n.* Devilment; extreme wickedness; wicked mischief.—**Devil-may-care**, *a.* Rollicking; reckless. (*Slang.*)—**Devil's-bit**, *n.* A common British plant allied to the teasel, having heads of blue flowers nearly globular, and a fleshy root, which is, as it were, cut or bitten off abruptly.—**Devil's bones**, *n.* Dice.—**Devil's books**, *n.* Cards.—**Devil's-dust**, *n.* The name given to flock made by the machine called the *devil* out of old woollen materials; shoddy.

Devious, dē'vi-us, *a.* [L. *devius*—*de*, and *via*, way. DEVIATE.] Out of the common way or track; following circuitous or winding paths; rambling; erring; going astray.—**Deviously**, dē'vi-us-li, *adv.* In a devious manner.—**Deviousness**, dē'vi-us-nes, *n.* The character or state of being devious.

Devise, dē-vīz', *v.t.*—*devised, devising.* [Fr. *deviser*, to devise or invent, to dispose of. See DEVICE.] To invent, contrive, or form in the mind; to strike out by thought; to plan; to scheme; to excogitate; *law*, to give or bequeath by will.—*v.t.* To consider; to contrive; to lay a plan; to form a scheme.—*n.* The act of bequeathing by will; a will or testament; a share of estate bequeathed.—**Devisable**, dē-vī'za-bl, *a.* Capable of being devised.—**Devisee**, dev-i-zē', *n.* The person to whom a devise is made.—**Deviser**, dē-vī'zėr, *n.* One who devises; a contriver; an inventor.—**Devisor**, dē-vī'zėr, *n.* One who gives by will.

Devitalize, dē-vī'tal-īz, *v.t.* To deprive of vitality; to take away life from.

Devitrify, dē-vit'ri-fī, *v.t.*—*devitrified, devitrifying.* To deprive of the character or appearance of glass.—**Devitrification**, dē-vit'ri-fi-kā"shon, *n.* The act of devitrifying.

Devoid, dē-void', *a.* [Prefix *de*, out, from, and *void*.] Destitute; not possessing: with *of* before the thing absent.

Devoir, dev-wąr', *n.* [Fr., from L. *debere*, to owe, whence *debt*.] Service or duty; an act of civility or respect; respectful notice due to another.

Devolve, dē-volv', *v.t.*—*devolved, devolving.* [L. *devolvo*, *devolutum*—*de*, and *volvo*, to roll, seen also in *revolve, convolve, volume, voluble*, &c.] To roll down; to move from one person to another; to deliver over, or from one possessor to a successor.—*v.i.* To roll down; hence, to pass from one to another; to fall by succession from one possessor to his successor.—**Devolvement**, dē-volv'ment, *n.* The act of devolving.—**Devolution**, dev-ō-lū'shon, *n.* [L.L. *devolutio*.] The act of rolling down; the act of devolving, transferring, or handing over; a passing to or falling upon a successor.

Devonian, de-vō'ni-an, *a.* Of or pertaining to *Devonshire* in England; *geol.* a term applied to a great portion of the palæozoic strata of North and South Devon, lying between the Silurian and carboniferous rocks, and sometimes used as synonymous with 'old red sandstone'.

Devonport, dev'on-pōrt, *n.* A sort of small, generally ornamental, writing-table, fitted up with drawers and other conveniences.

Devote, dē-vōt', *v.t.*—*devoted, devoting.* [L. *devoveo*, *devotum*, to vow anything to a deity, to devote—*de*, intens., and *voveo*, to vow. VOW, VOTE.] To appropriate by vow; to set apart or dedicate by a solemn act; to consecrate; to give up wholly; to direct the attention wholly or chiefly (to *devote* one's self or one's time to science); to give up; to doom; to consign over (to *devote* one to destruction).—**Devoted**, dē-vō'ted, *a.* Strongly attached to a person or cause; ardent; zealous.—**Devotedness**, dē-vō'ted-nes, *n.* The state of being devoted.—**Devotee**, dev'ō-tē, *n.* One who is wholly devoted; a votary; particularly, one who is superstitiously given to religious duties and ceremonies.—**Devotement**, dē-vōt'ment, *n.* The act of devoting.—**Devoter**, dē-vō'tėr, *n.* One that devotes.—**Devotion**, dē-vō'shon, *n.* The state of being devoted or set apart for a particular purpose; a yielding of the heart and affections to God, with reverence, faith, and piety, in religious duties, particularly in prayer and meditation; devoutness; performance of religious duties: now generally used in the plural; ardent attachment to a person or a cause; attachment manifested by constant attention; earnestness; ardour; eagerness.—**Devotional**, dē-vō'shon-al, *a.* Pertaining to devotion; used in devotion; suited to devotion.—**Devotionalist, Devotionist**, dē-vō'shon-al-ist, dē-vō'shon-ist, *n.* A person excessively given to devotions; a religious devotee.—**Devotionally**, dē-vō'shon-al-li, *adv.* In a devotional manner; towards devotion.

Devour, dē-vour', *v.t.* [Fr. *dévorer*, L. *devorare*—*de*, intens., and *voro*, to eat greedily, whence *voracious*.] To eat up; to eat with greediness; to eat ravenously; to destroy or consume; to waste.—*v.i.*† To act as a devourer; to consume (O.T.).—**Devourable**, dē-vou'ra-bl, *a.* Capable of or fit for being devoured.—**Devourer**, dē-vou'rėr, *n.* One who devours.—**Devouring**, dē-vou'ring, *a.* Consuming; wasting; destroying.—**Devouringly**, dē-vou'ring-li, *adv.* In a devouring manner.

Devout, dē-vout', *a.* [Fr. *dévot*, devout; L. *devotus*. DEVOTE.] Yielding a solemn and reverential devotion to God in religious exercises; pious; devoted to religion; religious; expressing devotion or piety; solemn; earnest.—**Devoutly**, dē-vout'li, *adv.* In a devout manner; piously; religiously; earnestly.—**Devoutness**, de-vout'nes, *n.* The quality or state of being devout.

Dew, dū, *n.* [A.Sax. *deáw*, D. *dauw*, Dan. *dug*, G. *thau*—dew; akin *dazzle, dank*.] The aqueous vapour or moisture which is deposited in small drops, especially during the night, from the atmosphere, on the surfaces of bodies when they have become colder than the surrounding atmosphere.—*v.t.* To wet with dew; to bedew.—**Dewberry**, *n.* A species of bramble, the fruit of which is black, with a bluish bloom, and an agreeable acid taste.—**Dew-claw**, *n.* The uppermost claw in a dog's foot, smaller than the rest, and not touching the ground.—**Dewdrop**, dū'drop, *n.* A drop or spangle of dew.—**Dewfall**, dū'fąl, *n.* The falling of dew, or the time when dew begins to fall.—**Dewiness**, dū'i-nes, *n.* State of being dewy.—**Dewlap**, dū'lap, *n.* The fold of skin that hangs from the throat of oxen or cows, or a similar appendage in other animals.—**Dewlapt**, dū'lapt, *a.* Furnished with a dewlap, or similar appendage. (*Shak.*)—**Dew-point**, *n.* The temperature when dew begins to be deposited, varying with the humidity of the atmosphere.—**Dewy**, dū'i, *a.* Of or pertaining to dew; partaking of the nature or appearance of dew; like dew; moist with, or as with, dew; accompanied with dew; abounding in dew; falling gently, or refreshing, like dew (*dewy* sleep).

Dexter, deks'tėr, *a.* [L. *dexter*, right, on the right side, akin to Gr. *dexios*, Skr. *daksha*, on the right hand.] Pertaining to or situated on the right hand; right as opposed to left.—**Dexterity**, deks-ter'i-ti, *n.* [L. *dexteritas*.] Ability to use the right hand more readily than the left†; right-handedness†; expertness; skill; that readiness in performing an action which proceeds from experience or practice, united with activity or quick motion; readiness of mind or mental faculties, as in contrivance, or inventing means to accomplish a purpose; promptness in devising expedients.—**Dexterous**, deks'tėr-us, *a.* Characterized by dexterity; skilful and active with the hands; adroit; prompt in contrivance and management; expert; quick at inventing expedients; skilful; done with dexterity. Sometimes written **Dextrous**, deks'trus.—**Dexterously**, deks'tėr-us-li, *adv.* With dexterity; adroitly.—**Dexterousness**, deks'tėr-us-nes, *n.* Dexterity.—**Dextral**, deks'tral, *a.* Right as opposed to left.—**Dextrine**, deks'trin, *n.* The gummy matter into which the interior substance of starch globules is convertible,—remarkable for the extent to which it turns the plane of polarization to the right hand, whence its name.—**Dextrorse, Dextrorsal**, deks-trors', deks-tror'sal, *a.* [L. *dextrorsum*, towards the right side—*dexter*, right, and *vorsum*, for *versum*, turned.] Turned towards the right; rising from left to right, as a spiral line, helix, or climbing plant.—**Dextrose**, deks'trōs, *n.* A name for grape-sugar, from its solution rotating the plane of polarization of a ray of light to the right.

Dey, dā, *n.* [Turk. *dâi*, an uncle.] The title of the old governors or sovereigns of Algiers, Tunis, and Tripoli, under the Sultan of Turkey.

Dhole, dōl *n.* The Cingalese name for the wild dog of India.

Dhow, dou, *n.* An Arab vessel, generally with one mast, from 150 to 250 tons burden, employed in mercantile trading, and also in carrying slaves from the east coast of Africa to the Persian Gulf and the Red Sea.

Dhurra, dụr'ra, *n.* [Ar.] A kind of millet largely cultivated in Africa and elsewhere.

Diabetes, dī-a-bē'tēz, *n.* [Gr. *diabētēs*, from *diabainō*, to pass through—*dia*, and *bainō*, to go or pass.] *Med.* a disease characterized by great augmentation and often manifest alteration in the secretion of urine, one variety of it being incurable.—**Diabetic, Diabetical**, dī-a-be'tik, dī-a-bē'ti-kal, *a.* Pertaining to diabetes.

Diablerie, Diablery, di-ab'lėr-i, *n.* [Fr. *diablerie*, from *diable*, devil.] Devilry; mischief; wickedness; sorcery; witchcraft.

Diabolic, Diabolical, dī-a-bol'ik, dī-a-bol'i-kal, *a.* [L. *diabolus*, the devil. DEVIL.] Devilish; pertaining to the devil; infernal; impious; atrocious.—**Diabolically**, dī-a-bol'i-kal-li, *adv.* In a diabolical manner.—**Diabolicalness**, dī-a-bol'i-kal-nes, *n.* The state or quality of being diabolical.

Diabrosis, dī-a-brō'sis, *n.* [Gr. corrosion—*dia*, intens., and *bibrōskō*, to eat.] *Surg.* the action of corrosive substances intermediate between caustics and escharotics.

Diacaustic, dī-a-ką's'tik, *a.* [Gr. prefix *dia*, through, and E. *caustic*.] *Math.* belonging to a species of caustic curves formed by refraction.—*n.* *Math.* a diacaustic curve; *med.* cautery by a burning-glass.

Diachylon, Diachylum, dī-ak'i-lon, dī-ak'i-lum, *n.* [Gr. *dia*, through, and *chylos*, juice.] *Med.* a plaster originally composed of the juices of herbs, now made of olive-oil and finely pounded litharge.

Diaconal, dī-ak'o-nal, *a.* [L. *diaconus*, Gr. *diakonos*, a deacon.] Pertaining to a deacon.—**Diaconate**, dī-ak′o-nāt, *n.* The office or dignity of a deacon; a body of deacons.

Diacoustic, dī-a-kous′tik, *a.* [Gr. *dia*, through, and *akouō*, to hear.] Pertaining to the science or doctrine of refracted sounds.—**Diacoustics**, dī-a-kous′tiks, *n.* The science or doctrine of the properties of sound refracted by passing through different mediums; diaphonics.

Diacritical, **Diacritic**, dī-a-krit′i-kal, dī-a-krit′ik, *a.* [Gr. *diakritikos*—*dia*, and *krinō*, to separate.] Separating or distinguishing; distinctive.—*Diacritical mark*, a mark used in some languages to distinguish letters which are similar in form.

Diactinic, dī-ak-tin′ik, *a.* [Gr. *dia*, through, and *aktis*, *aktinos*, a ray.] Capable of transmitting the actinic or chemical rays of the sun.

Diadelph, dī′a-delf, *n.* [Gr. *di*, twice, and *adelphos*, a brother.] *Bot.* a plant the stamens of which are united into two bodies of bundles by their filaments.—**Diadelphous**, dī-a-del′fus, *a.* *Bot.* having the stamens united in two bundles.

Diadem, dī′a-dem, *n.* [Gr. *diadēma*—*dia*, and *deō*, to bind.] A head-band or fillet formerly worn as a badge of royalty; anything worn on the head as a mark or badge of royalty; a crown; a coronet.—*v.t.*† To adorn with or as with a diadem; to crown.

Diæresis, dī-ē′re-sis, *n.* [Gr. *diairesis*, from *diaireō*, to divide.] Separation of one syllable into two; a mark which signifies such a division, as in naïf, aërial.

Diaglyph, dī′a-glif, *n.* [Gr. *dia*, through, and *glyphō*, to carve.] A sculptured or engraved production in which the figures are sunk below the general surface; an intaglio—**Diaglyphic**, dī-a-glif′ik, *a.* Of, pertaining to, or having the character of a diaglyph.

Diagnosis, dī-ag-nō′sis, *n.* [Gr. *diagnōsis*—*dia*, through, and *gignōskō*, to know.] Scientific discrimination of any kind; *med.* the discrimination of diseases by their distinctive marks or symptoms.—**Diagnose**, dī-ag-nōs′, *v.t.*—*diagnosed*, *diagnosing*. To discriminate or ascertain from symptoms the true nature of.—**Diagnostic**, dī-ag-nos′tik, *a.* Distinguishing; characteristic; indicating the nature of a disease.—*n.* A sign or symptom by which a disease is known.—*pl.* The department of medicine which treats of the diagnosis of diseases; symptomatology.

Diagonal, dī-ag′o-nal, *a.* [Gr. *diagōnios*, from angle to angle—*dia*, and *gōnia*, an angle or corner.] Extending from one angle to the opposite of a quadrilateral figure, and dividing it into two triangles; lying in this direction.—*n.* A straight line drawn between the opposite angles of a quadrilateral figure.—**Diagonally**, dī-ag′o-nal-li, *adv.* In a diagonal direction.

Diagram, dī′a-gram, *n.* [Gr. *diagramma*—*dia*, and *graphō*, to write.] A figure or drawing for the purpose of demonstrating the properties of any geometrical figure, as a triangle, circle, &c.; any illustrative figure wherein the outlines are exclusively or chiefly delineated.—**Diagrammatic**, dī′a-gram-mat″ik, *a.* Pertaining to or partaking of the nature of a diagram.—**Diagrammatically**, dī′a-gram-mat″i-kal-li, *adv.* After the manner of a diagram.

Diaheliotropic, dī-a-hē′li-o-trop″ik, *a.* [Gr. *dia*, through, *hēlios*, the sun, and *tropē*, a turning.] *Bot.* turning transversely to the light, as the stem or other organs of a plant; pertaining to diaheliotropism.—**Diaheliotropism**, dī-a-hē′li-ot″ro-pizm, *n.* *Bot.* the disposition or tendency of a plant or of the organs of a plant to assume a more or less transverse position to the light.

Dial, dī′al, *n.* [L.L. *dialis*, daily, from L. *dies*, a day, whence also *diary*, *diurnal*, *journal*, &c.] An instrument for showing the hour of the day from the shadow thrown by means of a *stile* or *gnomon* upon a surface; the face of a watch, clock, or other timekeeper; any somewhat similar plate or face on which a pointer or index moves, as in a gas-meter or telegraphic instrument.—*v.t.* *dialled*, *dialling*. To measure with, or as with, a dial.—**Dialist**, dī′al-ist, *n.* A constructor of dials; one skilled in dialling.—**Dialling**, dī′al-ing, *n.* The art of constructing dials; the science which explains the principles of measuring time by the sun-dial.—**Dial-plate**, *n.* The plate or face of a dial of a clock or watch, &c.

Dialect, dī′a-lekt, *n.* [Fr. *dialecte*, from Gr. *dialektos*—*dia*, and *legō*, to speak.] The form or idiom of a language peculiar to a province or to a limited region or people, as distinguished from the literary language of the whole people; language; speech or manner of speaking.—**Dialectal**, dī-a-lek′tal, *a.* Pertaining to a dialect.—**Dialectic**, **Dialectical**, dī′a-lek′tik, dī-a-lek′ti-kal, *a.* Pertaining to a dialect or dialects; pertaining to dialectics.—**Dialectically**, dī-a-lek′ti-kal-li, *adv.* In a dialectic manner.—**Dialectician**, dī-a-lek-tish″an, *n.* One skilled in dialectics; a logician; a reasoner.—**Dialectics**, dī-a-lek′tiks, *n.* [Gr. *dialektikē* (*technē*), the art of discussing.] The art of reasoning or disputing; that branch of logic which teaches the rules and modes of reasoning, or of distinguishing truth from error; the art of using forms of reasoning so as to make fallacies pass for truth; word-fence. Also **Dialectic** in same sense.

Diallage, dī′a-lāj, *n.* [Gr. *diallagē*, an interchange, difference.] A silico-magnesian mineral of a lamellar or foliated structure, akin to augite and exhibiting sometimes a beautiful green colour, at other times brownish or yellowish; it includes bronzite and hypersthene.—**Diallogite**, dī-al′o-jīt, *n.* A mineral of a rose-red colour with a laminar structure and vitreous lustre.

Dialogue, dī′a-log, *n.* [Fr. *dialogue*, from Gr. *dialogos*, dialogue, from *dialegomai*, to dispute—*dia*, and *legō*, to speak.] A conversation between two or more persons; a formal conversation in theatrical performances; a composition in which two or more persons are represented as conversing on some topic.—**Dialogical**, **Dialogistic**, **Dialogistical**, dī-a-loj′i-kal, dī-al′o-jis″tik, dī-al′o-jis″ti-kal, *a.* Pertaining to, or partaking of the nature of, a dialogue; having the form of a dialogue.—**Dialogically**, **Dialogistically**, dī-a-loj′i-kal-li, dī-al′o-jis″ti-kal-li, *adv.* In the manner of a dialogue.—**Dialogism**, dī-al′o-jizm, *n.* Dialogue in the third person; oblique or indirect narrative.—**Dialogist**, dī-al′o-jist, *n.* A speaker in a dialogue; a writer of dialogues.—**Dialogize**, dī-al′o-jīz, *v.i.* To discourse in dialogue.

Dialycarpous, dī′a-li-kär″pus, *a.* [Gr. *dialyō*, to separate, and *karpos*, fruit.] *Bot.* composed of distinct carpels.—**Dialypetalous**, dī′a-li-pet″a-lus, *a.* [Gr.] In flowers, with petals distinct from one another; polypetalous.—**Dialysepalous**, dī′a-li-sep″a-lus, *a.* Polysepalous.

Dialysis, dī-al′i-sis, *n.* [Gr. *dialysis*, a separation — *dia*, and *lyō*, to dissolve.] *Chem.* the act or process of separating the crystalloid elements of a body from the colloid by diffusion through a parchment-paper septum; *med.* debility; also, a solution of continuity; in *writing* or *printing*, same as *Diæresis*.—**Dialyze**, dī′a-līz, *v.t.* To separate by a dialyzer.—**Dialyzer**, dī′a-lī-zėr, *n.* The parchment paper, or septum, stretched over a ring used in the operation of dialysis.—**Dialytic**, dī-a-lit′ik, *a.* Pertaining to dialysis.

Diamagnetic, dī′a-mag-net″ik, *a.* [Prefix *dia*, and *magnetic*.] Applied to a class of substances which, when under the influence of magnetism, and freely suspended, take a position at right angles to the magnetic meridian, that is, point east and west.—**Diamagnetism**, dī-a-mag′ne-tizm, *n.* The characteristic phenomena of diamagnetic bodies.

Diamesogamous, dī′a-me-sog″a-mus, *a.* [Fr. *dia*, through, *mesos*, middle, and *gamos*, marriage.] *Bot.* requiring an intermediate agent to produce fertilization.

Diameter, dī-am′e-tėr, *n.* [Gr. *diametros*—*dia*, and *metron*, measure.] A straight line passing through the centre of a circle or other curvilinear figure, terminated by the circumference, and dividing the figure into two equal parts; a straight line through the centre of any body; the measure transversely through a cylindrical body; thickness.—**Diametric**, **Diametrical**, **Diametral**, dī-a-met′rik, dī-a-met′ri-kal, dī-a-met′ral, *a.* Of or pertaining to a diameter; directly opposed.—**Diametrically**, **Diametrally**, dī-a-met′ri-kal-li, dī-a-met′ral-li, *adv.* In a diametrical direction or position.

Diamond, dī′a-mond, *n.* [Fr. *diamant*, corrupted from *adamant* (which see).] A most valuable gem of extreme hardness, usually clear and transparent, but sometimes yellow, blue, green, black, &c., consisting of pure carbon; a small diamond fixed to a handle and used for cutting glass; a very small variety of printing type; a four-sided figure with the sides equal or nearly so, and having two obtuse and two acute angles, called also a lozenge or rhomb; one of a set of playing-cards marked with one or more such figures in red.—*Black diamond*, a term applied colloquially to coal.—*a.* Resembling a diamond; consisting of diamonds; set with a diamond or diamonds.—**Diamond-borer**, **Diamond-drill**, *n.* A metal bar or tube, armed at the boring extremity with one or more small diamonds, by the action of which, as it rapidly revolves, rocks, gems, &c., are speedily perforated.—**Diamond type**. A kind of printing type.—**Diamond wedding**. The sixtieth anniversary, the fiftieth being the golden.

Diander, dī-an′dėr, *n.* [Gr. *di*, twice, and *anēr*, *andros*, a male.] *Bot.* a plant having two stamens.—**Diandrian**, **Diandrous**, dī-an′dri-an, dī-an′drus, *a.* *Bot.* having two stamens.

Dianoetic, dī′a-nō-et″ik, *a.* [Gr. *dianoētikos*, from *dia*, and *noeō*, to revolve in the mind.] Capable of thought; thinking; intellectual.

Diapason, dī-a-pā′zon, *n.* [Gr. *diapasōn*, lit. through all (notes).] *Mus.* an old Greek term for the octave; proportion in the constituent parts of an octave; harmony; the entire compass of a voice or an instrument; a rule or scale by which the pipes of organs, the holes of flutes, &c., are correctly adjusted; a name of certain stops in the organ, given because they extend through the scales of the instrument.

Diapedesis, dī′a-pē-dē″sis, *n.* [Gr. *diapedesis*, leaping through.] The passing of blood corpuscles through the walls of the vessels without rupture of tissue.

Diaper, dī′a-pėr, *n.* [Fr. *diapré*, pp. of *diaprer*, to variegate with colors; from L.L. *diasprus*, a kind of precious cloth, from It. *diaspro*, jasper. JASPER.] A fabric, either linen or cotton, or a mixture of the two, upon the surface of which a figured pattern is produced; an infant's breech-cloth; flowering either of sculpture in low relief, or of painting or gilding used to ornament a flat surface.—*v.t.* To variegate or diversify with figures.

Diaphane, dī′a-fān, *n.* [Gr. *dia*, through, and *phainō*, to show.] A woven silk stuff with transparent and colourless figures.—**Diaphanie**, di-af′a-ni, *n.* [Fr.] The art or process of fixing transparent pictures on glass to resemble stained glass.—**Diaphanous**, dī-af′a-nus, *a.* Having power to transmit rays of light, as glass; pellucid; transparent; clear.—**Diaphanously**, dī-af′a-nus-li, *adv.* In a diaphanous manner.

Diaphonic, dī-a-fon′ik, *a.* [Gr. *dia*, and *phōnē*, sound.] Diacoustic.—**Diaphonics**, dī-a-fon′iks, *n.* The science or doctrine of refracted sounds; diacoustics.

Diaphoresis, dī′a-fo-rē″sis, *n.* [Gr. *diaphorēsis*, perspiration—*dia*, and *phoreō*, to carry.] *Med.* a greater degree of perspiration than is natural.—**Diaphoretic**, **Diaphoretical**, dī′a-fo-ret″ik, dī′a-fo-ret″i-kal, *a.* Having the power to increase perspiration.—**Diaphoretic**, *n.* A medicine which promotes perspiration; a sudorific.

Diaphragm, dī'a-fram, *n.* [Gr. *diaphragma*, a partition—*dia*, and *phrassō*, to break off, to defend.] The midriff, a muscle separating the chest or thorax from the abdomen; a partition or dividing substance, as a circular ring used in telescopes, &c., to cut off marginal portions of a beam of light; a calcareous plate which divides the cavity of certain molluscous shells.—**Diaphragmatic**, dī'a-frag-mat"ik, *a.* Appertaining to or having the character of a diaphragm. —**Diaphragmatitis**, dī-a-frag'ma-tī"tis, *n.* *Med.* inflammation of the diaphragm.

Diarchy, dī'ăr-ki, *n.* [Gr. *di*, double, and *archē*, rule.] A form of government in which the supreme power is invested in two persons.

Diarrhœa, dī-a-rē'a, *n.* [Gr. *diarrhoia*—*dia*, through, and *rheō*, to flow.] An ailment consisting in a morbidly frequent evacuation of the intestines.—**Diarrhœtic**, dī-a-rē'tik, *a.* Producing diarrhœa.

Diarthrosis, dī-ăr-thrō'sis, *n.* [Gr., from *dia*, through, asunder, and *arthron*, a joint.] *Anat.* a joint in which the bones revolve freely in every direction, as in the shoulder joint.

Diary, dī'a-ri, *n.* [L. *diarium*, a daily allowance of food, a journal, from *dies*, a day, whence also *dial*, *diurnal*, *journal*.] A book in which daily events or transactions are noted; a journal; a blank book dated for the record of daily memoranda.—**Diarial**, **Diarian**, dī-ā'ri-al, dī-ā'ri-an, *a.* Pertaining to a diary.—**Diarist**, dī'a-rist, *n.* One who keeps a diary.

Diastase, dī'as-tās, *n.* [Gr. *diastasis*, separation—*dia*, asunder, and root *sta*, to stand.] A substance existing in barley and oats after germination: so called because in solution it possesses the property of causing starch to break up at 150° Fahr., transforming it first into dextrine and then into sugar. —**Diastema**, dī-as-tē'ma, *n.* [Gr.] The natural interval between some of the series of teeth in animals.

Diastole, dī-as'to-lē, *n.* [Gr. *diastolē*, a drawing asunder—*dia*, and *stellō*, to set.] *Physiol.* the dilatation of the heart with blood: opposed to *systole*, or contraction; *gram.* the lengthening of a syllable that is naturally short.—**Diastolic**, dī-a-stol'ik, *a.* Pertaining to or produced by the diastole.

Diastyle, dī'a-stīl, *n.* [Gr. *diastylion*—*dia*, and *stylos*, a column.] *Arch.* that mode of arranging columns in which three diameters of the columns are allowed for intercolumniations.

Diatessaron, dī-a-tes'ar-on, *n.* [Gr. *dia tessaron*, by four.] A harmony of the four gospels.

Diathermal, **Diathermic**, **Diathermous**, dī-a-thėr'mal, dī-a-thėr'mik, dī-a-thėr'mus, *a.* [Gr. *dia*, and *thermē*, heat.] Freely permeable by heat. — **Diathermanous**, dī-a-thėr'ma-nus, *a.* Having the property of transmitting or suffering radiant heat to pass through.—**Diathermancy**, dī-a-thėr'man-si, *n.* The property of transmitting radiant heat. — **Diathermanism**, dī-a-thėr'ma-nizm, *n.* The doctrine or phenomena of the transmission of radiant heat.

Diathesis, dī-ath'e-sis, *n.* [Gr.] *Med.* particular disposition or habit of body, good or bad; predisposition to certain diseases rather than to others.—**Diathetic**, dī-a-thet'ik, *a.* Pertaining to diathesis; constitutional.

Diatom, dī'a-tom, *n.* [Gr. *dia*, through, and *tomē*, a cutting, from forming often loosely connected chains.] One of a natural order of microscopic vegetable organisms with siliceous coverings, found in fresh and salt water, and in moist places—**Diatomaceous**, dī'a-to-mā"shus, *a.* Pertaining to diatoms; containing or made up of the siliceous parts of diatoms.

Diatomic, dī-a-tom'ik, *a.* [Gr. *di*, twice, and *atomos*, an atom.] *Chem.* consisting of two atoms.—**Diatomite**, dī-at'o-mīt, *n.* A name for certain earthy deposits, consisting of the minute siliceous parts of diatoms, forming when dry a fine powder, and used in making dynamite, glaze for pottery, polishing, &c.

Diatonic, dī-a-ton'ik, *a.* [Gr. *dia*, by or through, and *tonos*, sound.] *Mus.* applied to the major or minor scales, or to chords, intervals, and melodic progressions belonging to one scale.—**Diatonically**, dī-a-ton'i-kal-li, *adv.* In a diatonic manner.

Diatribe, dī'a-trīb, *n.* [Gr. *diatribē*, a discussion, amusement, passing of time—*dia*, through, and *tribō*, to rub.] A continued disputation; a lengthy invective; a harangue in which a person inveighs against something.—**Diatribist**, dī-at'ri-bist, *n.* The author of a diatribe.

Dibble, dib'l, *n.* [From *dib*, a form of *dip*.] A pointed instrument used in gardening and agriculture to make holes for planting seeds, bulbs, &c. Also called *Dibber* (dib'ėr).—*v.t.*—*dibbled*, *dibbling*. To plant with a dibble; to dig with a dibble.—**Dibbler**, dib'lėr, *n.* One who dibbles.

Dibranchiate, dī-brang'ki-āt, *a.* [Gr. *di*, double, and *branchia*, gills.] Having two gills.—*n.* A member of an order of cephalopods in which the branchiæ are two in number, one situated on each side of the body.

Dicast, dī'kast, *n.* [Gr. *dikastēs*, from *dikē* justice.] *Greek antiq.* an officer answering nearly to the modern juryman.—**Dicastery**, dī-kas'tėr-i, *n.* *Greek antiq.* a court of justice in which dicasts used to sit.

Dice, dīs, *n.* pl. of *die*, for gaming. DIE.—*v.i.*—*diced*, *dicing*. To play with dice.—**Diced**, dīst, *a.* Ornamented with square or diamond-shaped figures.—**Dice-box**, *n.* A box from which dice are thrown in gaming.—**Dicer**, dī'sėr, *n.* A player at dice.

Dicephalous, dī-sef'a-lus, *a.* [Gr. *di*, double, *kephalē*, head.] Having two heads on one body.

Dichlamydeous, dī-kla-mid'ē-us, *a.* [Gr. *di*, double, *chlamys*, a garment.] *Bot.* having both a calyx and a corolla.

Dichogamy, dī-kog'a-mi, *n.* [Gr. *dicha*, in two parts, and *gamos*, marriage.] *Bot.* a provision in hermaphrodite flowers to prevent self-fertilization, as where the stamens and pistils within the same flower are not matured at the same time. — **Dichogamous**, dī-kog'a-mus, *a.* *Bot.* exhibiting or characterized by dichogamy.

Dichotomous, dī-kot'o-mus, *a.* [Gr. *dicha*, doubly, by pairs, and *temnō*, to cut.] *Bot.* regularly dividing by pairs from top to bottom.—**Dichotomously**, dī-kot'o-mus-li, *adv.* In a dichotomous manner.—**Dichotomy**, dī-kot'o-mi, *n.*—A cutting in two‡; division‡; division or distribution of ideas by pairs; *bot.* a mode of branching by constant forking, as when the stem of a plant divides into two branches, each branch into two others, and so on.

Dichroism, dī'krō-izm, *n.* [Gr. *di*, twice, and *chroa*, colour.] *Optics*, a property possessed by several crystallized bodies of appearing under two distinct colours according to the direction in which light is transmitted through them. — **Dichroic**, dī-krō'ik, *a.* Characterized by dichroism.—**Dichroite**, dī'krō-īt, *n.* A mineral generally of a blue colour, but exhibiting different colours in different positions.—**Dichromatic**, dī-krō-mat'ik, *a.* [Gr. *di*, and *chrōma*, colour.] Having or producing two colours. — **Dichroscope**, dī'krō-skōp, *n.* [Gr. *di*, *chroa*, and *skopeō*, to see.] An instrument in which a prism of Iceland-spar is used for testing the dichroism of crystals. —**Dichroscopic**, dī-krō-skop'ik, *a.* Pertaining to the dichroscope.

Dickens, dik'enz, *interj.* [Probably a fanciful euphemism for *devil*: comp. L.G. *düker*, *duks*, the deuce.] Devil; deuce: used interjectionally. (*Shak.*)

Dicker, dik'ėr, *n.* [L.G. and Sw. *deker*, G. *decher*, ten hides, from L.L. *dacra*, *decara*, L. *decem*, ten.] The number or quantity of ten, particularly ten hides or skins.

Dickey, **Dicky**, dik'i, *n.* [Origin doubtful.] An article of dress like the front of a dress-shirt, and worn instead; the seat in a carriage on which the driver sits, whether in front or not.—**Dicky-bird**, *n.* A pet name for a little bird.

Diclinic, dī-klin'ik, *a.* [Gr. *di*, twice, and *klinō*, to incline.] Applied to crystals in which two of the axes are obliquely inclined.

Diclinous, dī'kli-nus, *a.* [Gr. *di*, double, and *klinē*, a bed.] *Bot.* having the stamens in one flower and the pistil in another.

Dicœlous, dī-sē'lus, *a.* [Gr. *di*, two, and *koilos*, hollow.] *Anat.* characterized by having two cavities; amphicœlous.

Dicondylian, dī-kon-dil'i-an, *a.* [Gr. *di*, double, *condyle*.] *Zool.* having two condyles at the base of the skull.

Dicotyledon, dī'kot-i-lē"don, *n.* [Gr. *di*, and *kotylēdōn*.] A plant whose seeds contain a pair of cotyledons or seed-leaves, which are always opposite to each other.—**Dicotyledonous**, dī'kot-i-lē"do-nus, *a.* Having two cotyledons.

Dictate, dik'tāt, *v.t.*—*dictated*, *dictating*. [L. *dicto*, *dictatum*, a freq. of *dico*, *dictum*, to say. DICTION.] To deliver or enounce with authority, as an order, command, or direction; to instruct to be said or written; to utter, so that another may write out; to direct by impulse on the mind (an action *dictated* by fear); to instigate.—*n.* An order delivered; a command; a rule, maxim, or precept, delivered with authority; rule or direction suggested to the mind (the *dictates* of reason).—**Dictation**, dik-tā'shon, *n.* The act of dictating; the act or practice of speaking or reading that another may write down what is spoken.—**Dictator**, dik'tā-tėr, *n.* [L., a supreme magistrate appointed on special occasions with unlimited power.] One invested with absolute authority; a supreme leader or guide to direct the conduct or opinion of others.—**Dictatorial**, dik-ta-tō'ri-al, *a.* Pertaining to a dictator; imperious; overbearing.—**Dictatorially**, dik-ta-tō'ri-al-li, *adv.* In an imperious manner. — **Dictatorship**, **Dictature**, dik'tā-tėr-ship, dik'ta-tūr, *n.* The office of a dictator; authority; imperiousness.—**Dictatory**, dik'ta-to-ri, *a.* Overbearing; dictatorial.—**Dictatress**, **Dictatrix**, dik-tā'tres, dik-tā'triks, *n.* A female dictator.

Diction, dik'shon, *n.* [L. *dictio*, from *dico*, *dictum*, to speak, appearing in a great many English words, as *dictate*, *addict*, *contradict*, *edict*, *condition*, *preach*, &c.] A person's choice or selection of words in speaking or writing; general mode of expressing one's self; style. ∴ *Diction* refers chiefly to the words used; *phraseology* refers more to the manner of framing the phrases, clauses, and sentences; *style* includes both, referring to the thoughts as well as the words, and especially comprehends the niceties and beauties of a composition.—**Dictionary**, dik'shon-a-ri, *n.* (L.L. *dictionarium*.) A book containing the words of a language arranged in alphabetical order, with explanations or definitions of their meanings; a lexicon; a word-book; any work which communicates information on an entire subject or branch of a subject, under entries or heads arranged alphabetically.—*a.* Pertaining to, contained in, or given by a dictionary or dictionaries. — **Dictum**, dik'tum, *n.* pl. **Dicta**, dik'ta. [L.] A positive assertion; an authoritative saying or decision.

Dictyogen, dik'ti-o-jen, *n.* [Gr. *dictyon*, network, and root *gen*, to produce.] *Bot.* the name given to a group of monocotyledonous plants, with net-veined leaves, intermediate between the monocotyledons and dicotyledons. — **Dictyogenous**, dik-ti-oj'e-nus, *a.* *Bot.* having the character of a dictyogen.

Did, did, pret. of *do*.

Didactic, **Didactical**, di-dak'tik, di-dak'ti-kal, *a.* [Gr. *didaktikos*, from *didaskō*, to teach.] Adapted to teach; containing doctrines, precepts, principles, or rules; intended to instruct. — **Didactically**, di-dak'ti-kal-li, *adv.* In a didactic manner; in a form to teach.—**Didactics**, di-dak'tiks, *n.* The art or science of teaching.

Didactyl, **Didactyle**, dī-dak'til, *a.* [Gr. prefix *di*, and *daktylos*, the finger.] Having two toes or two fingers.—*n.* An animal having two toes only.—**Didactylous**, di-dak'ti-lus, *a.* Two-toed or two-fingered.

Didapper, did'a-pėr, *n.* [For *divedapper* (*Shak.*), from *dive*, and *dap* = *dip*. DAB-CHICK.] The dab-chick or little grebe.

Diddle, did'l, *v.t.* [A.Sax. *dyderian*, to deceive or delude, originally perhaps by rapid movements or sleight of hand.] To cheat or trick, especially in money matters (slang); to dandle (provincial).

Didelphia, dī-del'fi-a, *n. pl.* [Gr. *di*, double, and *delphys*, womb.] One of the three sub-classes of Mammalia (the other two being Ornithodelphia and Monodelphia), founded on the nature of the female reproductive organs, the young being born in an immature state and carried in a pouch or second womb till perfect; they include the marsupials, as the kangaroos, opossums, &c.—**Didelphian**, **Didelphic**, dī-del'fi-an, dī-del'fik, *a.* Pertaining to the Didelphia.—**Didelphid**, dī-del'fid, *n.* A member of the Didelphia.

Diduction,† di-duk'shon, *n.* [L. *diductio* —*di* for *dis*, and *duco*, to draw.] Separation by withdrawing one part from the other.

Didunculus, dī-dung'kū-lus, *n.* [Dim. from *didus*, the generic name of the dodo.] The nearest living ally of the dodo, the tooth-billed pigeon of Samoa.

Didymium, dī-dim'i-um, *n.* [Gr. *didymos*, double, twin.] A rare metal discovered in 1841 in the oxide of cerium, and so named from being, as it were, the twin-brother of lanthanum, which was previously found in the same body.—**Didymous**, did'i-mus, *a. Bot.* twin; growing double.

Didynam, did'i-nam, *n.* [Gr. *di*, double, and *dynamis*, power, from the two larger stamens appearing to domineer over the shorter.] *Bot.* a plant of four stamens, disposed in two pairs, one being shorter than the other.—**Didynamous**, **Didynamic**, di-din'a-mus, did-i-nam'ik, *a. Bot.* having four stamens disposed in pairs, one shorter than the other.

Die, dī, *v.i.*—*died*, *dying*. [Not an A.Sax. word; closely allied to the O.Fris. *deja*, *deya*, Icel. *deya*, *deyja*, Dan. *döe*, to die; A.Sax. *dedd*, dead, a kind of participial form, *dedth*, death.] To cease to live; to expire; to decease; to perish; to become dead; to lose life: said of both animals and plants; to come to an end; to cease to have influence or effect (his fame will not *die*); to sink; to faint (his heart *died* within him); to languish with pleasure, tenderness, affection, or the like: to become gradually less distinct or perceptible to the sight or hearing: generally followed by *away* (the sound *died away*); *theol.* to suffer divine wrath and punishment in the future world.—*To die out*, to become extinct gradually.

Die, dī, *n.* [Fr. *dé*, O.Fr. *det*, from L. *datum*, something given, hence what is thrown or laid on the table.] A small cube marked on its faces with numbers from one to six, used in gaming by being thrown from a box; a square body: in the above senses the plural is *dice*; *arch.* the cubical part of a pedestal between its base and cornice; a stamp used in coining money, in foundries, &c.: in the last two senses the plural is regular, *dies*.—*The die is cast*, everything is now put to hazard; all will depend upon fortune.—**Die-sinker**, *n.* An engraver of dies for stamping or embossing.—**Die-sinking**, *n.* The process of engraving dies.

Dielectric, dī-ē-lek'trik, *n.* [Gr. *dia*, through, and E. *electric*.] *Elect.* any medium through or across which electric induction takes place between two conductors.

Dieresis, dī-ē're-sis, *n.* Same as *Diœresis*.

Diet, dī'et, *n.* [O.Fr. *diete*, L.L. *dieta*, Gr. *diaita*, a way of living, diet.] A person's regular food or victuals; manner of living as regards food and drink; course of food prescribed and limited in kind and quantity; allowance of provision.—*v.t.* To furnish diet or meals for; to prescribe a particular diet for.—*v.i.* To eat according to rules prescribed; to eat; to feed.—**Dietarian**, di-e-tā'ri-an, *n.* One who adheres to a certain or prescribed diet; a dietetist.—**Dietary**, dī'e-ta-ri, *a.* Pertaining to diet or the rules of diet.—*n.* A system or course of diet; allowance of food.—**Dieter**, dī'et-ėr, *n.* One who diets; one who prescribes rules for eating. (*Shak.*)—**Dietetic**, **Dietetical**, dī-e-tet'ik, dī-e-tet'i-kal, *a.* Pertaining to diet, or to the rules for regulating diet.—**Dietetically**, dī-e-tet'i-kal-li, *adv.* In a dietetical manner.—**Dietetics**, dī-e-tet'-iks, *n.* That department of medicine which relates to the regulation of diet.—**Dietitian**, **Dietician**, dī-e-ti'shon, *n.* One versed in dietetics; one who arranges diets.

Diet, dī'et, *n.* [Fr. *diète*, from L.L. *dieta*, the space of a day, from L. *dies*, a day, whence also *dial*, *diary*.] A meeting, as of dignitaries or delegates, held from day to day for legislative, ecclesiastical, or other purposes; session; specifically, the legislative or administrative assemblies, as the Japanese, &c.

Differ, dif'ėr, *v.i.* [L. *differo*—prefix *dif*, *dis*, and *fero*, to bear, to carry, seen also in *confer*, *offer*, *refer*, *suffer*, *infer*, &c.; root also in *fertile*.] To be unlike, dissimilar, distinct, or various, in nature, condition, form, or qualities (men and things *differ* greatly; they *differ* from each other); to disagree; not to accord; to be of another opinion (we *differ with* or *from* a person); to contend; to be at variance; to dispute; to quarrel. — **Difference**, dif'ėr-ens, *n.* The state or condition in virtue of which things differ from each other; a point or feature of disagreement; the being different; want of sameness; variation; dissimilarity; distinction; a dispute, contention, quarrel, controversy; the point in dispute; the remainder of a sum or quantity after a lesser sum or quantity is subtracted; the quantity by which one quantity differs from another.—*v.t.*—*differenced*, *differencing*. To cause a difference or distinction in; to distinguish; to discriminate.—**Different**, dif'ėr-ent, *a.* Distinct; separate; not the same; various; of various natures, forms, or qualities; unlike; dissimilar.—**Differential**, dif-ėr-en'shal, *a.* Making a difference; discriminating; distinguishing; *math.* an epithet applied to an infinitely small quantity by which two variable quantities differ; pertaining to mathematical processes in which such quantities are employed.—*Differential calculus*, an important branch of the higher mathematics which deals largely with the infinitely small differences of variable and mutually dependent quantities.—*Differential duties*, *pol. econ.* duties which are not levied equally upon the produce or manufactures of different countries, as when a heavier duty is laid on certain commodities from one country than on the same commodities from another country.—*n.* A coupling used to connect shafts, as in the driving axle of an automobile, so that a union is effected when moving straight, but allowing independent motion on a curve; *math.* an infinitesimal difference between two states of a variable quantity.—**Differentiate**, dif-ėr-en'shi-āt, *v.t.* To produce, or lead to, a difference in or between; to mark or distinguish by a difference; to set aside for a definite or specific purpose; *math.* to obtain the differential of.—*v.i.* To acquire a distinct and separate character.—**Differentiation**, dif-ėr-en'shi-ā″shon, *n.* The act of differentiating; the production or discrimination of differences or variations; the assignment of a specific agency to the discharge of a specific function; *biol.* the formation of different parts, organs, species, &c., by the production or acquisition of a diversity of new structures, through a process of evolution or development; *math.* the operation of finding the differential of any function.

Difficulty, dif'i-kul-ti, *n.* [Fr. *difficulté*; L. *difficultas*, from *difficilis*, difficult—*dis*, priv., and *facilis*, easy to be made or done.] Hardness to be done or accomplished; the state of anything which renders its performance laborious or perplexing: opposed to *easiness* or *facility*; that which is hard to be performed or surmounted; perplexity; embarrassment of affairs; trouble; objection; cavil; obstacle to belief; an embroilment; a falling out; a controversy; a quarrel. —**Difficult**, dif'i-kult, *a.* Hard to make, do, or perform; not easy; attended with labour and pains; arduous; hard to understand. — **Difficultly**, dif'i-kult-li, *adv.* Hardly; with difficulty.

Diffidence, dif'i-dens, *n.* [L. *diffidentia*, *diffidens*, ppr. of *diffido*, to distrust—*dis*, priv., and *fido*, to trust. FAITH.] Distrust; want of confidence; especially distrust of one's self; a doubt respecting some personal qualification; modest reserve.—**Diffident**, dif'i-dent, *a.* Characterized by diffidence; distrustful of one's self; not confident; backward; bashful. — **Diffidently**, dif'i-dent-li, *adv.* In a diffident manner.

Diffluent, dif'flu-ent, *a.* [L. *diffluens*, *diffluentis*, ppr. of *diffluo*—*dis*, asunder, and *fluo*, to flow.] Flowing or falling away on all sides.

Difform, dif'form, *a.* [Fr. *difforme*, from L. *dif* for *dis*, and *forma*, shape.] Irregular in form; not uniform; anomalous; dissimilar. — **Difformity**, dif-for'mi-ti, *n.* Irregularity of form; want of uniformity.

Diffract, dif-frakt', *v.t.* [L. *diffringo*, *diffractum* — prefix *dif*, *dis*, and *frango*, to break.] To break; to bend from a straight line; to deflect.—**Diffraction**, dif-frak'shon, *n.* *Optics*, the peculiar modifications which light undergoes when it passes by the edge of an opaque body; deflection.—**Diffractive**, dif-frak'tiv, *a.* Causing diffraction.

Diffuse, dif-fūz', *v.t.*—*diffused*, *diffusing*. [L. *diffundo*, *diffusum*—prefix *dif*, *dis*, and *fundo*, *fusum*, to pour, whence *fusion*.] To pour out and spread, as a fluid; to cause to flow and spread; to send out or extend in all directions (light, information, happiness).—*a.* (dif-fūs'). Widely spread; using too many words to express meaning; wanting conciseness and due condensation; verbose; prolix; *bot.* spreading widely, horizontally, and irregularly.—**Diffused**, dif-fūzd', *p.* and *a.* Spread; dispersed; loose; flowing.—**Diffusedly**, dif-fū'zed-li, *adv.* In a diffused manner.—**Diffusedness**, dif-fū'zed-nes, *n.* The state of being diffused.—**Diffusely**, dif-fūs'li, *adv.* In a diffuse manner; widely; extensively; with too many words.—**Diffuseness**, dif-fūs'nes, *n.* The quality of being diffuse; want of conciseness or due concentration in expressing one's meaning. — **Diffuser**, dif-fū'zėr, *n.* One who or that which diffuses. —**Diffusibility**, **Diffusibleness**, dif-fū'zi-bil″i-ti, dif-fū'zi-bl-nes, *n.* The quality of being diffusible.—**Diffusible**, dif-fū'zi-bl, *a.* Capable of being diffused or spread in all directions.—**Diffusion**, dif-fū'zhon, *n.* The act of diffusing or process of being diffused; a spreading abroad or scattering; dispersion; dissemination; extension; propagation; the tendency of two different gases to mix when separated by a porous partition.—**Diffusive**, dif-fū'siv, *a.* Having the quality of diffusing or becoming diffused; extending in all directions; widely reaching (*diffusive* charity); diffuse as regards expression.—**Diffusively**, dif-fū'siv-li, *adv.* In a diffusive manner; widely; extensively. — **Diffusiveness**, dif-fū'siv-nes, *n.* The character of being diffusive.—**Diffusivity**, dif-fū-siv'i-ti, *n.* The power of diffusion; in conduction of heat, the tendency to equalization of temperature; measured by the conductivity divided by the thermal capacity of unit volume.

Dig, dig, *v.t.*—*digged* or *dug*, *digging*. [Probably connected with *dike* or *dyke*, *ditch*; A.Sax. *dīc*, a dike or a ditch, *dīcian*, Dan. *dige*, to make a ditch.] To open and break, or turn up, with a spade or other sharp instrument; to excavate; to form in the ground by digging and removing the loose soil; to raise from the earth by digging (to *dig* coals, fossils, &c.).—*v.i.* To work with a spade or other similar instrument.—

Diggable, dig'a-bl, *a.* Capable of being digged.—**Digger**, dig'ėr, *n.* One who or that which digs; specifically, one who digs for gold.—**Digging**, dig'ing, *n.* The act of one who digs; *pl.* a word applied to the different localities in California, Australia, New Zealand, &c., where gold is obtained by excavations in the earth.

Digamma, dī'gam-ma, *n.* [Gr., lit. double gamma (gamma = E. *g* hard), because in form it resembled two gammas, the one set above the other, somewhat like our F.] A letter which once belonged to the alphabet of the Greeks, and appears to have had the force of *v* or *f*.

Digastric, dī-gas'trik, *a.* [Gr. *di*, double, and *gastēr*, belly.] Having a double belly. —*Digastric muscle*, a double muscle that pulls the lower jaw downwards and backwards.

Digest, di-jest', *v.t.* [L. *digero*, *digestum*, to distribute, dispose, digest food—*di* for *dis*, asunder, and *gero*, *gestum*, to bear; also in *congest*, *suggest*, *gesture*, &c.] To arrange in suitable divisions or under proper heads or titles; to dispose in due method for being conveniently studied or consulted; to arrange methodically in the mind; to think out; to separate or dissolve in the stomach, preparing the nutritious elements for entering the system; *chem.* to soften and prepare by a heated liquid; *fig.* to bear with patience or with an effort; to brook; to put up with. —*v.i.* To undergo digestion, as food.—*n.* (dī'jest). A collection of Roman laws, digested or arranged under proper titles by order of the Emperor Justinian; any orderly or systematic summary, as of laws. —**Digester**, di-jes'tėr, *n.* One who digests or disposes in order; that which assists the digestion of food; a vessel in which bones or other substances may be subjected to heat in water or other liquid.—**Digestibility**, di-jes'ti-bil"i-ti, *n.* The quality of being digestible.—**Digestible**, di-jes'ti-bl, *a.* Capable of being digested.—**Digestibleness**, di-jes'ti-bl-nes, *n.* Quality of being digestible.—**Digestion**, di-jes'tyon, *n.* [L. *digestio*.] The act of methodizing or disposing in order; the process which food undergoes in the stomach, by which it is prepared for nourishing the body; *chem.* the operation of exposing bodies to heat in a liquid to prepare them for some action on each other; or the slow action of a solvent on any substance.—**Digestive**, di-jes'tiv, *a.* Having the power to promote digestion in the stomach.—*n.* Any preparation or medicine which increases the tone of the stomach and aids digestion; a stomachic.

Digger, Digging. Under Dig.

Dight, dīt, *v.t.*—*dight*. [A.Sax. *dihtan*, from L. *dictare*, to dictate. Dictate.] To put in order; to dress; to array. (Now only poet.)

Digit, dij'it, *n.* [L. *digitus*, a finger; akin Gr. *daktylos*, a finger; root *dik*, to point out, as in Gr. *deiknymi*, to show, L. *dico*, to say.] A finger: sometimes used scientifically to signify toe, when speaking of animals; the measure of a finger's breadth or ¾ inch; *astron.* the twelfth part of the diameter of the sun or moon; *arith.* any integer under 10: so called from counting on the fingers.—**Digital**, dij'i-tal, *a.* [L. *digitalis*.] Pertaining to the fingers or to digits.—*n.* One of the keys of instruments of the organ or piano class.—**Digitalin**, dij'i-ta-lin, *n.* A strong poison obtained from digitalis.—**Digitalis**, dij-i-tā'lis, *n.* Any of a genus of Eurasian herbs of the figwort family; the dried and powdered leaf of the common foxglove, containing several important glucocides and serving as a powerful heart stimulant and a diuretic.—**Digitately**, dij'i-tāt-li, *adv.* In a digitate manner.—**Digitation**, dij-i-tā'shon, *n.* A division into finger-like processes.—**Digitiform**, dij'i-ti-form, *a.* Formed like fingers. **Digitigrade**, dij'i-ti-grād, *n.* [L. *digitus*, and *gradior*, to go.] An animal that walks on its toes, as the lion, wolf, &c.—*a.* Walking on the toes.—**Digitorium**, dij-i-tō'ri-um, *n.* A small portable instrument for giving strength and flexibility to the fingers for piano playing; a dumb piano.

Diglyph, dī'glif, *n.* [Gr. *di*, double, and *glyphō*, to carve.] *Arch.* a projecting face with two panels or channels sunk in it.

Dignify, dig'ni-fī, *v.t.*—*dignified*, *dignifying*. [Fr. *dignifier*—L. *dignus*, worthy, and *facere*, to make.] To invest with honour or dignity; to exalt in rank; to elevate to a high office; to honour; to make illustrious. —**Dignification**,† dig'ni-fi-kā"shon, *n.* The act of dignifying.—**Dignified**, dig'ni-fīd, *p.* and *a.* Invested with dignity; honoured; marked with dignity or loftiness; noble; stately in deportment.—**Dignitary**, dig'ni-ta-ri, *n.* One who holds an exalted rank or office.—**Dignity**, dig'ni-ti, *n.* [L. *dignitas*.] Nobleness or elevation of mind; loftiness; honourable place or rank; degree of elevation; elevation of aspect; grandeur of mien; height or importance; an elevated office; one who holds high rank; a dignitary.

Digraph, dī'graf, *n.* [Gr. *di*, twice, and *graphō*, to write.] A union of two vowels or of two consonants, representing a single sound of the voice (as *ea* in head).

Digress, di-gres', *v.i.* [L. *digredior*, *digressus*, to step apart—prefix *dis*, apart, and *gradior*, to step. Grade.] To depart or wander from the main subject or tenor of a discourse, argument, or narration.—**Digression**, di-gresh'on, *n.* [L. *digressio*.] The act of digressing; a departure from the main subject; the part or passage of a discourse, &c., which deviates from the main subject; transgression (*Shak.*)‡.—**Digressional, Digressive**, di-gresh'on-al, di-gres'iv, *a.* Pertaining to or consisting in digression.—**Digressively**, di-gres'iv-li, *adv.* By way of digression.

Digyn, dī'jin, *n.* [Gr. prefix *di*, twice, and *gynē*, a female.] A plant having two pistils.—**Digynian, Digynous**, dī-jin'i-an, dī'ji-nus, *a.* Having two pistils.

Dihedral, dī-hē'dral, *a.* [Gr. *di*, twice, and *hedra*, a seat or face.] Having two plane faces, as a crystal.—**Dihedron**, dī-hē'dron, *n.* A figure with two plane sides or surfaces.

Dijudicate, dī-jū'di-kāt, *v.i.*—*dijudicated*, *dijudicating*. [L. *dijudico*, *dijudicatum*, to judge between—prefix *di* for *dis*, apart, and *judico*, to judge.] To judge, determine, or decide. — **Dijudicant**, dī-jū'di-kant, *n.* One who dijudicates. — **Dijudication**, dī-jū'di-kā"shon, *n.* The act of adjudicating.

Dike, Dyke, dīk, *n.* [A.Sax. *dīc*, D. *dijk*, Dan. *dige*, a bank of earth, a ditch, the ditch being excavated and the bank formed by the same operation. *Ditch* is a softened form of this.] A ditch or channel for water; a barrier of earth, stones, or other materials, intended to prevent low lands from being inundated by the sea or a river; a low wall forming a fence; *geol.* a vein of igneous rock which has intruded in a melted state into rents or fissures of other rocks.—*v.t.*—*diked*, *diking*. To surround with a dike; to secure by a bank; to drain by one or more dikes or ditches.

Dilacerate, dī-las'ėr-āt, *v.t.* [L. *dilacero* —prefix *di* for *dis*, asunder, and *lacero*, to tear.] To tear; to rend asunder.—**Dilaceration**, dī-las'ėr-ā"shon, *n.* The act of dilacerating.

Dilapidate, di-lap'i-dāt, *v.i.*—*dilapidated*, *dilapidating*. [L. *dilapido*, *dilapidatum*—prefix *di* for *dis*, asunder, and *lapis*, *lapidis*, a stone.]—*v.t.* To suffer to go to ruin (buildings) by misuse or neglect; to waste; to squander.—*v.i.* To fall to ruin.—**Dilapidated**, di-lap'i-dā-ted, *p.* and *a.* In a ruinous condition; suffered to go to ruin.—**Dilapidation**, di-lap'i-dā"shon, *n.* The act of dilapidating; *eccles.* the ruinous neglect or actual wasting, by an incumbent, of any building or other property in his possession.—**Dilapidator**, di-lap'i-dā-tėr, *n.* One who dilapidates.

Dilate, dī-lāt', *v.t.*—*dilated*, *dilating*. [L. *dilato*, to make wider—*di* for *dis*, asunder, and *latus*, broad.] To expand or swell out, especially by filling; to distend; to enlarge in all directions: opposed to *contract*; to tell copiously or diffusely (*Shak.*)‡.—*v.i.* To expand, swell, or extend in all directions; to speak largely and copiously; to dwell in narration; to descant: with *on* or *upon*.—**Dilatability**, dī-lā'ta-bil"i-ti, *n.* The quality of being dilatable. — **Dilatable**, dī-lā'ta-bl, *a.* Capable of being dilated; possessing elasticity; elastic. — **Dilatation, Dilation**, dī-lā-tā'shon, dī-lā'shon, *n.* The act of expanding, dilating, or state of being expanded or distended.—**Dilater, Dilator**, dī-lā'tėr, *n.* One who or that which dilates. — **Dilative**, dī-lā'tiv, *a.* Tending to dilate.

Dilatory, dil'a-to-ri, *a.* [Fr. *dilatoire*, L.L. *dilatorius*, from L. *differo*, *dilatum*. Delay.] Marked with or given to procrastination or delay; making delay or resulting in delay; slow; tardy; not proceeding with diligence: of persons or things. — **Dilatorily**, dil'a-to-ri-li, *adv.* In a dilatory manner; tardily. — **Dilatoriness**, dil'a-to-ri-nes, *n.* The quality of being dilatory; delay in proceeding; tardiness.

Dilemma, di-lem'ma, *n.* [Gr. *dilēmma*—prefix *di* for *dis*, double, and *lēmma*, an assumption, from *lambanō*, to take.] *Logic*, an argument in which the adversary is caught between two difficulties, by having two alternatives presented to him, each of which is equally conclusive against him; hence, a state of things in which evils or obstacles present themselves on every side, and it is difficult to determine what course to pursue.

Dilettante, dil-e-tan'ti, *n.* pl. **Dilettanti**, dil-e-tan'tē. [It., from L. *delectare*, to delight. Delight.] An admirer or lover of the fine arts; an amateur or trifler in art; one who pursues an art desultorily and for amusement.—**Dilettantism**, dil-e-tan'-tizm, *n.* The quality characteristic of a dilettante.

Diligence, dil'i-jens, *n.* [L. *diligentia*, carefulness, diligence, from *diligo*, to love earnestly—*di* for *dis*, intens., and *lego*, to choose.] Steady application in business of any kind; constant effort to accomplish what is undertaken; due attention; industry; assiduity; care; heed; heedfulness; *Scots law*, a kind of warrant, and also a process by which persons or effects are attached.—**Diligent**, dil'i-jent, *a.* [L. *diligens*, *diligentis*.] Steady in application to business; constant in effort to accomplish what is undertaken; assiduous; attentive; industrious; not idle or negligent: of persons or things.—**Diligently**, dil'i-jent-li, *adv.* In a diligent manner.

Diligence, dē-lē-zhäṅs, *n.* [Fr.] A kind of four-wheeled stage-coach.

Dill, dil, *n.* [A. Sax. *dil*, Sw. *dill*, G. *dill*, dill; probably from its soothing qualities in *dilling* or *dulling* pain. Comp. prov. E. *dill*, Icel. *dilla*, to lull a child.] A plant of the parsley family, seeds of which are moderately pungent and aromatic, and are used as a seasoning.

Dilly-dally, dil'i-dal-i, *v.i.* [A reduplication of *dally*.] To loiter; to delay; to trifle.

Dilucidate,† dī-lū'si-dāt, *v.t.* [L. *dilucidus*—*di* for *dis*, and *lucidus*, shining.] To make clear; to elucidate.

Dilute, di-lūt', *v.t.*—*diluted*, *diluting*. [L. *diluo*, *dilutus*—prefix *di* for *dis*, and *luo*, to wash, as in *ablution*. Deluge.] To render liquid or more liquid, especially by mixing with water; to weaken (spirit, acid, &c.) by an admixture of water.—*a.* Diluted; reduced in strength by intermixture.—**Dilutedly**, di-lū'ted-li, *adv.* In a diluted form.—**Dilutedness, Diluteness**, di-lū'ted-nes, di-lūt'nes, *n.* The state or quality of being diluted.—**Diluter**, di-lū'tėr, *n.* One who or that which dilutes.—**Dilution**, di-lū'shon, *n.* The act of diluting.—**Diluent**, dil'ū-ent, *a.* [L. *diluens*, *diluentis*.] Having the effect of diluting.—*n.* That which dilutes; *med.* a substance which increases the proportion of fluid in the blood.

Diluvial, Diluvian, di-lū'vi-al, di-lū'vi-an, *a.* [L. *diluvium*, a deluge, from *diluo*. Dilute.] Pertaining to a flood or deluge, more especially to the deluge in Noah's days.—*Diluvial formation, geol.* a name of superficial deposits of gravel, clay, sand, &c., conveyed to their present sites by any unusual or extraordinary rush of water.—**Diluvialist**, di-lū'vi-al-ist, *n.* One who explains geological phenomena by the Noachian deluge.—**Diluvion, Diluvium**, di-lū'vi-on, di-lū'vi-um, *n.* [L.] A deluge or inundation; *geol.* a deposit of superficial loam, sand, gravel, pebbles, &c., caused by the extraordinary action of water.

Dim, dim, *a.* [A.Sax. *dim*, dark, obscure=O.Fris. *dim*, Icel. *dimmr*, dim; comp. Lith. *tamsa*, Skr. *tamas*, darkness.] Not seeing clearly; having the vision indistinct; not clearly seen; obscure; faint; vague; somewhat dark; not luminous; dull of apprehension; having the lustre obscured; tarnished. —*v.t.—dimmed, dimming.* To render dim or less clear or distinct; to becloud; to obscure; to tarnish or sully.—**Dimly**, dim'li, *adv.* In a dim manner. — **Dimmish, Dimmy**, dim'ish, dim'i, *a.* Somewhat dim; obscure.—**Dimness**, dim'nes, *n.* The state of being dim.

Dime, dīm, *n.* [Fr. *dîme*, a tenth, a tithe, O.Fr. *disme*, from L. *decimus*, tenth, from *decem*, ten.] A silver coin of the United States, value ten cents; the tenth of a dollar.

Dimension, di-men'shon, *n.* [L. *dimensio*, from *dimetior*, to measure—*di* for *dis*, and *metior, mensus*, to mete. METE, MEASURE.] Extension in a single direction, as length, breadth, and thickness or depth, a solid body having thus three dimensions; *pl.* measure, size, extent, capacity; *fig.* consequence; importance; *alg.* same as *degree.*—**Dimensions**, *n.* Of a derived unit, in *phys.* are the powers of the fundamental units which determine its variation with them; thus the dimensions of velocity are LT^{-1}.

Dimerous, dim'ėr-us, *a.* [Gr. *di*, twice, and *meros*, part.] Having its parts in pairs; composed of two unrelated pieces or parts; *entom.* having the tarsi two-jointed.

Dimeter, dim'e-tėr, *a.* [Gr. *dimetros—di*, twice, and *metron*, a measure.] Having two poetical measures.—*n.* A verse of two measures.—**Dimetric**, dī-met'rik, *a. Crystal*, a term applied to crystals whose vertical axis is unequal to the lateral.

Dimidiate, di-mid'i-āt, *a.* [L. *dimidiatus*, from *dimidium*, half—*dis*, asunder, and *medius*, the middle.] Divided into two equal parts; halved; *bot.* applied to an organ when half of it is so much smaller than the other as to appear to be missing; *zool.* having the organs of one side of different functions from the corresponding organs on the other.

Diminish, di-min'ish, *v.t.* [O.Fr. *demenuiser*, from L. *diminuo*, to lessen—*di* for *dis*, asunder, and *minuere*, to lessen, from root *min*, in *minor*, less.] To lessen; to make less or smaller by any means: opposed to *increase* and *augment*; to impair, degrade, or abase (O.T.).—*v.i.* To lessen; to become or appear less or smaller; decrease.—**Diminishable**, di-min'ish-a-bl, *a.* Capable of being diminished.—**Diminished**, di-min'isht, *p.* and *a.* Lessened; reduced in size or importance; degraded.—**Diminisher**, di-min'ish-ėr, *n.* One who or that which diminishes. — **Diminuendo**, di-min'ū-en"dō. [It.] *Mus.* an instruction to the performer to lessen the volume of sound from loud to soft: opposite of *crescendo.*—**Diminution**, dim-i-nū'shon, *n.* [L. *diminutio.*] The act of diminishing; a making smaller; the state of becoming or appearing less; discredit; loss of dignity; degradation. —**Diminutive**, di-min'ū-tiv, *a.* [Fr. *diminutif.*] Considerably smaller than the normal size; small; little.—*n.* Anything of very small size (*Shak.*)‡; *gram.* a word formed from another word to express a little thing of the kind (as *manikin*, a little man). — **Diminutively**, di-min'ū-tiv-li, *adv.* In a diminutive manner.—**Diminutiveness**, di-min'ū-tiv-nes, *n.* State of being diminutive; smallness; littleness.

Dimissory, di-mis'o-ri, *a.* [L.L. *dimissorius.* DISMISS.] Sending away; dismissing to another jurisdiction; granting leave to depart.

Dimity, dim'i-ti, *n.* [It. *dimito*, L.L. *dimitum*, from Gr. *dimitos*, dimity—*di*, double, and *mitos*, a thread.] A stout cotton fabric ornamented in the loom by raised stripes or fancy figures, rarely dyed, but usually employed white for beds, &c.

Dimly, Dimmish, Dimness. Under DIM.

Dimorphism, dī-mor'fizm, *n.* [Gr. *di*, double, and *morphē*, form.] The property shown by some mineral bodies of crystallizing in two distinct forms not derivable from each other; the condition when analogous organs of plants of the same species appear under two very dissimilar forms; difference of form between animals of the same species.—**Dimorphous, Dimorphic**, dī-mor'fus, dī-mor'fik, *a.* Characterized by dimorphism.

Dimple, dim'pl, *n.* [Probably a diminutive form connected with *dip* or *deep*; comp. G. *dümpel, tümpel*, a pool.] A small natural depression in the cheek or other part of the face, as the chin; a slight depression or indentation on any surface.—*v.i.—dimpled, dimpling.* To form dimples; to sink into depressions or little inequalities.—*v.t.* To mark with dimples.—**Dimpled**, dim'pld, *a.* Set with dimples; having cheeks marked by dimples.—**Dimply**, dim'pli, *a.* Full of dimples.

Dimyary, dim'i-a-ri, *n.* [Gr. *di*, double, and *mys*, a muscle.] A bivalve mollusc which closes its shell by means of two adductor muscles.

Din, din, *n.* [A.Sax. *dyn, dyne*, noise, thunder; Icel. *dynr*, din, *dynia*, to resound; from same root as Skr. *dhvan*, to sound.] Noise; a loud sound; particularly, a rattling, clattering, or rumbling sound, long continued. — *v.t. — dinned, dinning.* To strike with continued or confused sound; to stun with noise; to harass with clamour.

Dine, dīn, *v.i.—dined, dining.* [Fr. *dîner*, O.Fr. *disner*, L.L. *disnare*—L. *de*, intens. (as in *devour*), and *cœnare*, to dine, from *cœna*, dinner.) To eat the chief meal of the day; to take dinner.—*To dine out*, to take dinner elsewhere than at one's own residence.—*v.t.* To give a dinner to; to supply with dinner; to afford convenience for dining.—**Diner-out**, *n.* One who is in the habit of dining from home; one who receives and accepts many invitations to dinner.—**Dinette**, dī-net', *n.* A small dining room off the kitchen.—**Dining-room**, *n.* A room to dine in; a place for public dining.—**Dinner**, din'ėr, *n.* [Fr. *dîner.*] The principal meal of the day, taken between morning and evening, or in the afternoon or evening.—**Dinner-hour**, *n.* The hour at which dinner is taken; the hour spent in dining.—**Dinnerless**, din'ėr-les, *a.* Having no dinner.—**Dinner-table**, *n.* A table at which dinner is taken.—**Dinner-time**, *n.* The usual time of dining.

Ding, ding, *v.t.—dung* or *dinged.* [Icel. *dengja*, Dan. *dænge*, Sw. *dänga*, to knock, to beat.] To throw or dash with violence (*Mil.*)†; to dash; to drive; to break. [O.E. and Sc.]—**Ding-dong**, ding'dong, *n.* The sound of bells, or any similar sound of continuous strokes.

Dinghy, Dingey, ding'gi, *n.* An East Indian boat varying in size in different localities; a small boat used by a ship.

Dingle, ding'gl, *n.* [Apparently a form of O.E. *dimble*, a dell or dingle, and *dimple.*] A narrow dale or valley between hills; a small secluded and embowered valley.

Dingo, ding'gō, *n.* The wild Australian dog, of a wolf-like appearance, and extremely fierce.

Dingy, din'ji, *a.* [Probably connected with *dung.*] Of a dirty white or dusky colour; soiled; sullied; dusky.—**Dinginess**, din'jines, *n.* The quality of being dingy.

Dinoceras, dī-nos'e-ras, *n.* [Gr. *deinos*, terrible, *keras*, horn.] A fossil animal as large as an elephant, with three horns.

Dinornis, dī-nor'nis, *n.* [Gr. *deinos*, terrible, and *ornis*, a bird.] An extinct running bird of gigantic size (some of them being 14 feet high) which formerly inhabited New Zealand, called by the natives *moa.*—**Dinosaur, Dinosaurian**, dī'nō-sar, dī-nō-sa'ri-an, *n.* [Gr. *deinos*, and *sauros*, a lizard.] One of a group of huge, terrestrial, fossil reptiles peculiar to the upper secondary formations, some of them carnivorous.—**Dinothere, Dinotherium**, dī'nō-thēr, dī-nō-thē'ri-um, *n.* [Gr. *deinos*, and *thērion*, wild beast.] A gigantic extinct mammal allied to the elephant, occurring in the strata of the tertiary formation, with two tusks curving downwards. These words are also spelled *Dei-*.

Dint, dint, *n.* [A.Sax. *dynt*, a blow, O.E. and Sc. *dunt*, Icel. *dyntr*, a stroke; perhaps akin to *din* and *ding. Dent* is the same word.] A blow or stroke‡; the mark made by a blow; a cavity or impression made by a blow or by pressure on a substance; a dent.—*By dint of*, by the force or power of; by means of.—*v.t.* To make a dint in; to dent.

Diocese, dī'ō-sēs, *n.* [Gr. *dioikēsis*, administration, a province or jurisdiction — *dia*, and *oikēsis*, residence, from *oikeō*, to dwell, *oikos*, a house.] The circuit or extent of a bishop's jurisdiction; an ecclesiastical division of a state, subject to the authority of a bishop.—**Diocesan**, dī-os'es-an or dī'ō-sē-san, *a.* Pertaining to a diocese.—*n.* A bishop as related to his own diocese; one in possession of a diocese, and having the ecclesiastical jurisdiction over it.

Diodon, dī'o-don, *n.* [Gr. *di*, twice and *odous, odontos*, a tooth.] A name of certain fishes having each jaw appearing as a single bony piece, some of them covered with prickles, and capable of inflating themselves.

Diœcious, Diœcian, dī-ē'shus, dī-ē'shi-an, *a. Bot.* having stamens on one plant and pistils on another; *zool.* having the germ-cell or ovum produced by one individual (female), and the sperm-cell, or spermatozoid, by another (male).—**Diœciousness, Diœcism**, dī-ē'shus-nes, dī-ē'sizm, *n.* The character of being diœcious.

Diopside, dī-op'sīd, *n.* [Gr. *dia*, through, and *opsis*, a view, from being sometimes transparent.] A variety of augite, of a vitreous lustre and greenish or yellowish colour.

Dioptase, dī-op'tās, *n.* [Gr. *dia*, through, and *optazō*, from *optomai*, to see.] Emerald copper ore, a translucent mineral of a beautiful green, occurring crystallized in six-sided prisms.

Diopter, di-op'tėr, *n.* [Gr. *diopter*, a spy.] In lenses, the unit of refractive power, being that of a lens with a focal length of one metre.—**Dioptric, Dioptrical**, dī-op'trik, dī-op'tri-kal, *a.* [Gr. *dioptrikos*, from *dia*, through, and the root *op*, to see.] Pertaining to dioptrics, or to the passing of light through instruments or substances.—*Dioptric system*, the mode of illuminating lighthouses in which the illumination is produced by a central lamp, sending its rays through a combination of lenses surrounding it.—**Dioptrics**. dī-op'triks, *n.* That part of optics which treats of the refractions of light passing through different mediums, as through air, water, or glass, and especially through lenses.

Diorama, dī-ō-rä'ma, *n.* [Gr. *dia*, through, and *horama*, a view.] A scenic contrivance in which the scenes are viewed through a large aperture, partly by reflected and partly by transmitted light, the light and shade being produced by coloured screens or blinds.—**Dioramic**, dī-ō-ram'ik, *a.* Pertaining to diorama.

Diorism,† dī'ō-rizm, *n.* [Gr. *diorismos*—*dia*, through, and *horos*, a boundary.] Distinction; definition. — **Dioristic**,† **Dioristical**,† dī-ō-ris'tik, dī-ō-ris'ti-kal, *a.* Distinguishing; defining.

Diorite, dī'o-rīt, *n.* [Gr. *dia*, through, and *horos*, boundary, the stone being formed of distinct portions.] A tough crystalline trap-rock of a whitish colour, speckled with black or greenish black.

Dioxide, dī-ok′sīd, *n.* [Prefix *di*, double, and *oxide.*] An oxide consisting of one atom of a metal and two atoms of oxygen.

Dip, dip, *v.t.*—*dipped* or *dipt*, *dipping.* [A. Sax. *dippan*, *dyppan*, to dip; Fris. *dippe*, D. *doopen*, G. *taufen*, to dip, to baptize, akin *deep*, *dive.*] To plunge or immerse in water or other liquid; to put into a fluid and withdraw; to lift with a ladle or other vessel: often with *out*; to baptize by immersion.—*v.i.* To plunge into a liquid and quickly emerge; to engage in a desultory way; to concern oneself to some little extent (to *dip* into a subject); to read passages here and there (to *dip* into a volume); to sink, as below the horizon; *geol.* to incline or slope.—*n.* An immersion in any liquid; a plunge; a bath; a candle made by dipping the wick in tallow; inclination or slope.—*Dip of the needle*, the angle which the magnetic needle makes with the plane of the horizon.—*The dip of strata*, in *geol.* the inclination or angle at which strata slope or dip downwards into the earth.—**Dipper**, dip′ėr, *n.* One who or that which dips; one of a sect of American Baptists; a name given to the water-ouzel.

Dipetalous, dī-pet′a-lus, *a.* [Gr. *di*, double, and *petalon*, a petal.] Having two flower-leaves or petals; two-petaled.

Diphrelatic,† dif-rē-lat′ik, *a.* [Gr. *diphrēlatēs*, a charioteer.] Pertaining to the driving of vehicles. (*De Quincey.*)

Diphtheria, dif-thē′ri-a, *n.* [Gr. *diphthera*, a membrane.] An epidemic inflammatory disease of the air-passages, and especially of the throat, characterized by the formation of a false membrane. —**Diphtheritic**, dif-the-rit′ik, *a.* Connected with, relating to, or formed by diphtheria.

Diphthong, dif′thong or dip′thong, *n.* [Gr. *diphthongos*—*di*, twice, and *phthongos*, sound.] A union of two vowels pronounced in one syllable (as in *bound*, *oil*).—**Diphthongal**, dif-thong′gal or dip-, *a.* Belonging to a diphthong.—**Diphthongally**, dif-thong′gal-li or dip-, *adv.* In a diphthongal manner.—**Diphthongation**, **Diphthongization**, dif-thong-gā′shon or dip-, dif′thong-gi-zā″shon or dip-, *n.* The formation of a diphthong; the conversion of a simple vowel into a diphthong.—**Diphthongize**, dif′thong-gīz or dip′-, *v.t.* To form into a diphthong.

Diphycerc, **Diphycercal**, dī′fi-sėrk, dī-fi-sėr′kal, *a.* [Gr. *diphyēs*, of a double nature, and *kerkos*, a tail.] Applied to those fishes whose vertebral column extends into the upper lobe of the tail.

Diphyllous, dī-fil′us, *a.* [Gr. *di*, twice, and *phyllon*, a leaf.] *Bot.* having two leaves, as a calyx, &c.

Diphyodont, dī′fi-o-dont, *n.* [Gr. *di*, twice, *phyō*, to produce, and *odous*, *odontos*, tooth.] One of that group of the mammalia which possess two successive sets of teeth—a deciduous or milk set, and a permanent set.

Diploblastic, dip′lō-blást″ik, *a.* [Gr. *diploos*, double, *blastos*, a germ.] Of embryos, composed of two cellular layers.

Diplococcus, dip′lō-kok″us, *n.* [Gr. *diploos*, double, *kokkos*, a berry.] Of bacteria, a form consisting of a pair of cocci. See Coccus.

Diploe, dip′lō-ē, *n.* [Gr. *diploos*, double.] *Anat.* the soft medullary substance or porous part existing between the plates of the skull.

Diploma, di-plō′ma, *n.* [Gr. *diplōma*, a paper folded double, a license, from *diploō*, to fold, *diploos*, double.] A letter or writing, usually under seal and signed by competent authority, conferring some power, privilege, or honour, as that given to graduates of colleges on their receiving the usual degrees, to physicians who are licensed to practise their profession, and the like.—*v.t.* To furnish with a diploma; to fortify by a diploma.—**Diplomacy**, di-plō′ma-si, *n.* The science or art of conducting negotiations, arranging treaties, &c., between nations; the forms of international negotiations; dexterity or skill in managing negotiations of any kind; artful management or manœuvring with the view of securing advantages.—**Diplomat**, **Diplomate**, dip′lō-mat, dip′lō-māt, *n.* A diplomatist.—**Diplomatize**, di-plō′ma-tīz, *v.t.* To invest with a title or privilege by a diploma.—**Diplomatic**, **Diplomatical**, dip-lō-mat′ik, dip-lō-mat′i-kal, *a.* Pertaining to diplomacy, or to the management of any negotiations; skilful in gaining one's ends by tact and cleverness; conferred by diploma; relating to diplomatics.—**Diplomatically**, dip-lō-mat′i-kal-li, *adv.* In a diplomatic manner; artfully.—**Diplomatics**, dip-lō-mat′iks, *n.* The science of deciphering old writings, to ascertain their authenticity, date, &c.; paleography.—**Diplomatism**, di-plō′ma-tizm, *n.* Diplomacy.—**Diplomatist**, di-plō′ma-tist, *n.* A person skilled in diplomacy; a diplomat.

Diplopia, **Diplopy**, di-plō′pi-a, dip′lo-pi, *n.* [Gr. *diploos*, double, and *ōps*, the eye.] A disease of the eye, in which the patient sees an object double or even triple.

Dipolar, dī-pō′lėr, *a.* Having two poles; doubly polar, as certain crystals.

Dipper, **Dipping**. Dip.

Diprismatic, dī-priz-mat′ik, *a.* [Prefix *di*, twice, and *prismatic.*] Doubly prismatic.

Diprotodon, dī-prō′to-don, *n.* [Gr. *di*, twice, *prōtos*, first, and *odous*, *odontos*, tooth.] An extinct gigantic marsupial mammal, found in the pleistocene or recent beds of Australia.

Dipsomania, dip-sō-mā′ni-a, *n.* [Gr. *dipsa*, thirst, and *mania*, madness.] That morbid condition to which habitual drunkards of a nervous and sanguine temperament are liable to reduce themselves, and in which they manifest an uncontrollable craving for stimulants.—**Dipsomaniac**, dip-sō-mā′ni-ak, *n.* A victim of dipsomania. —**Dipsomaniacal**, dip-sō-mā′ni-a-kal, *a.* Pertaining to dipsomania.

Dipteral, dip′tėr-al, *a.* [Gr. *di*, double, and *pteron*, a wing.] *Entom.* having two wings only; dipterous; *arch.* a term applied to a temple having a double row of columns on each of its flanks.—*n.* *Arch.* a dipteral temple.—**Dipteran**, dip′tėr-an, *n.* A dipterous insect.—**Dipterous**, dip′tėr-us, *a.* *Entom.* having two wings; *bot.* a term applied to seeds which have their margins prolonged in the form of wings.

Diptych, dip′tik, *n.* [Gr. *diptychos*—*di*, double, and *ptyssō*, to fold.] Anciently, a kind of register or list as of magistrates or bishops, consisting usually of two leaves folded; a design, as a painting or carved work, on two folding compartments or tablets.

Dire, dīr, *a.* [L. *dirus*, terrible.] Dreadful; dismal; horrible; terrible; evil in a great degree.—**Direful**, dīr′ful, *a.* Same as *Dire.* —**Direfully**, dīr′ful-li, *adv.* In a direful manner.—**Direfulness**, dīr′ful-nes, *n.* The state or quality of being direful.—**Direly**, dīr′li, *adv.* In a dire manner.—**Direness**, dīr′nes, *n.* The state or quality of being dire. (*Shak.*)

Direct, di-rekt′, *a.* [L. *dirigo*, *directum*, to set in a straight line, to direct—*di* for *dis*, intens., and *rego*, *rectum*, to make straight. Right, Regent.] Straight; right: opposite to *crooked*, *circuitous*, *winding*, *oblique*; *astron.* appearing to move from west to east: opposed to *retrograde*; in the line of father and son: opposed to *collateral*; straightforward; open; ingenuous; plain; not ambiguous.—*v.t.* To point or aim in a straight line toward something; to make to act, or work, towards a certain end or object; to show the right road or course to; to prescribe a course to; to regulate, guide, lead, govern; to order or instruct; to prescribe to; to inscribe (a letter) with the address.—*v.i.* To act as a guide; to point out a course.—*n.* *Mus.* the sign ₩ placed at the end of a stave to direct the performer to the first note of the next stave.—**Direction**, di-rek′shon, *n.* The act of directing; the course or line in which anything is directed; a being directed towards a particular end; the line in which a body moves, or to which its position is referred; course; the act of governing; administration; management; guidance; superintendence; instruction in what manner to proceed; order; behest; the address on a letter, parcel, &c.; a body or board of directors; directorate.—**Directive**, di-rek′tiv, *a.* Having the power of directing.—**Directly**, di-rekt′li, *adv.* In a direct manner; in a straight line or course; straightway; immediately; instantly; soon; without delay; openly; expressly; without circumlocution or ambiguity.—**Directness**, di-rekt′nes, *n.* The state or quality of being direct.—**Director**, di-rek′tėr, *n.* One who or that which directs; one who superintends, governs, or manages; specifically, one of a body appointed to direct, control, or superintend the affairs of a company.—**Directorate**, di-rek′tėr-āt, *n.* The office of a director; a body of directors.—**Directorship**, di-rek′tėr-ship, *n.* The condition or office of a director.—**Directory**, di-rek′to-ri, *n.* A rule to direct; a book containing directions for public worship or religious services; a book containing an alphabetical list of the inhabitants of a city, town, &c., with their places of business and abode; board of directors; directorate; during the French Revolution, a body established by the Convention in 1795, and composed of five members.—**Directress**, di-rek′tres, *n.* A female who directs or manages.—**Directrix**, di-rek′triks, *n.* A directress; *geom.* a straight line of importance in the doctrine of conic sections.

Direful. Under Dire.

Dirge, dėrj, *n.* [A contraction of L. *dirige* ('direct', imperative of *dirigere*, to direct), the first word in a psalm or hymn formerly sung at funerals.] A song or tune intended to express, grief, sorrow, and mourning.

Dirigible, di′ri-ji-bl, *a.* That may be directed, turned, or guided in any direction. —*n.* A balloon or air-ship whose course can be directed by means of steering or directing apparatus.

Dirk, dėrk, *n.* [Origin doubtful.] A kind of dagger or poniard; a dagger worn as essential to complete the Highland costume. —*v.t.* To poniard; to stab.

Dirt, dėrt, *n.* [Icel. *drit*, dirt, excrement, *drita*, Sc. *drite*, A.Sax. (*ge*)*drītan*, to go to stool.] Any foul or filthy substance, as excrement, mud, mire, dust; whatever, adhering to anything, renders it foul or unclean; a gold-miner's name for the material, as earth, gravel, &c., put into his cradle to be washed.—*v.t.* To soil; to dirty.—**Dirtily**, dėr′ti-li, *adv.* In a dirty manner; nastily; filthily; meanly; sordidly.—**Dirtiness**, dėr′ti-nes, *n.* The condition of being dirty; filthiness; foulness; nastiness.—**Dirty**, dėr′ti, *a.* Foul; nasty; filthy; not clean; impure; turbid; mean; base; despicable; sleety, rainy, or sloppy (weather).—*v.t.*—*dirtied*, *dirtying.* To defile; to make dirty or filthy; to soil.—**Dirt-bed**, *n.* *Geol.* a bed or layer of mould with the remains of trees and plants, found especially in working the freestone in the oolite formation of Portland.—**Dirt-cheap**, *a.* As cheap as dirt, worthless, sold at a loss.—**Dirt-pie**, *n.* Clay moulded by children in the form of a pie.

Disable, dis-ā′bl, *v.t.*—*disabled*, *disabling.* [Prefix *dis*, priv., and *able.*] To render unable: to deprive of competent strength or power, physical or mental; to injure so as to be no longer fit for duty or service; to deprive of adequate means, instruments, or resources; to impair; to deprive of legal qualifications; to incapacitate; to render incapable.—**Disability**, dis-a-bil′i-ti, *n.* The state or quality of being disabled or unable; weakness; impotence; incapacity; inability; want of legal qualifications.—**Disablement**,† dis-ā′bl-ment, *n.* The act of disabling; disability.

Disabuse, dis-a-būz′, *v.t.*—*disabused*, *disabusing.* [Fr. *désabuser*, to disabuse.] To free from mistaken or erroneous notions or beliefs; to undeceive; to set right.

Disaccustom, dis-ak-kus'tum, *v.t.* To destroy the force of habit in by disuse; to render unaccustomed.

Disadvantage, dis-ad-van'tāj, *n.* Absence or deprivation of advantage; that which prevents success or renders it difficult; any unfavourable circumstance or state; prejudice to interest, fame, credit, profit, or other good; loss; injury; harm; damage.—**Disadvantageous**, dis-ad'van-tā"jus, *a.* Attended with disadvantage; unfavourable to success or prosperity; prejudicial.—**Disadvantageously**, dis-ad'van-tā"jus-li, *adv.* In a disadvantageous manner.—**Disadvantageousness**, dis-ad'van-tā"jus-nes, *n.*

Disaffect, dis-af-fekt', *v.t.* To alienate the affection of; to make less friendly or faithful, as to a person, party, or cause; to make discontented or unfriendly.—**Disaffected**, dis-af-fek'ted, *p.* and *a.* Having the affections alienated; indisposed to favour or support; unfriendly; hostile to the governing power.—**Disaffectedly**, dis-af-fek'ted-li, *adv.* In a disaffected manner.—**Disaffectedness**, dis-af-fek'ted-nes, *n.* The quality of being disaffected.—**Disaffection**, dis-af-fek'shon, *n.* Alienation of affection, attachment, or good-will; disloyalty.

Disaffirm, dis-af-fėrm', *v.t.* To deny; to contradict; to annul, as a judicial decision, by a contrary judgment of a superior tribunal.

Disafforest, dis-af-for'est, *v.t.* To reduce from the privileges of a forest to the state of common ground; to strip of forest laws and their oppressive privileges.

Disagree, dis-a-grē', *v.t.*—*disagreed*, *disagreeing*. To be not accordant or coincident; to be not exactly similar; to differ; to be of an opposite or different opinion; to be unsuitable to the stomach; to be in opposition; not to accord or harmonize; to become unfriendly; to quarrel.—**Disagreeable**, dis-a-grē'a-bl, *a.* The reverse of agreeable; unpleasing; offensive to the mind or to the senses; repugnant; obnoxious.—**Disagreeableness**, dis-a-grē'a-bl-nes, *n.* The state or quality of being disagreeable.—**Disagreeably**, dis-a-grē'a-bli, *adv.* In a disagreeable manner; unpleasantly.—**Disagreement**, dis-a-grē'ment, *n.* Want of agreement; difference, as of form or character; difference of opinion or sentiments; a falling out; a quarrel; discord.

Disallow, dis-al-lou', *v.t.* To refuse permission or sanction for; not to grant; not to authorize; to disapprove of; to reject, as being illegal, unnecessary, unauthorized, and the like.—**Disallowable**, dis-al-lou'a-bl, *a.* Not allowable; not to be permitted.—**Disallowance**, dis-al-lou'ans, *n.* Disapprobation; refusal; prohibition; rejection.

Disanimate, dis-an'i-māt, *v.t.* To discourage; to dishearten.

Disannul, dis-an-nul', *v.t.* To make void; to annul; to deprive of force or authority; to cancel. (*Shak.*)—**Disannulment**, dis-an-nul'ment, *n.* Annulment.

Disapparel, dis-ap-par'el, *v.t.* To disrobe; to strip of raiment.

Disappear, dis-ap-pēr', *v.i.* To cease to appear or to be perceived; to vanish from the sight; to go away or out of sight; to cease, or seem to cease, to be or exist.—**Disappearance**, dis-ap-pē'rans, *n.* Act of disappearing; removal from sight.

Disappoint, dis-ap-point', *v.t.* Fr. *désappointer*, originally to remove from an appointment or office.] To defeat of expectation, wish, hope, desire, or intention; to frustrate; to balk; to hinder from the possession or enjoyment of that which was hoped or expected (*disappointed* of the expected legacy).—**Disappointed**, dis-ap-poin'ted, *p.* and *a.* Having suffered disappointment; balked; unprepared (*Shak.*)†.—**Disappointedly**, dis-ap-poin'ted-li, *adv.* With a feeling of disappointment.—**Disappointment**, dis-ap-point'ment, *n.* The act of disappointing or feeling of being disappointed; defeat or failure of expectation, hope, wish, desire, or intention.

Disapprobation, dis-ap'rō-bā"shon, *n.* The reverse of approbation; disapproval; censure, expressed or unexpressed.—**Disapprove**, dis-a-pröv', *v.t.*—*disapproved*, *disapproving*. To censure; to regard as wrong or objectionable.—*v.i.* To express or feel disapproval: with *of* before the object.—**Disapproval**, dis-a-prö'val, *n.* Disapprobation; dislike.—**Disapprovingly**, dis-a-prö'ving-li, *adv.* In a disapproving manner.

Disarm, dis-ärm', *v.t.* To take the arms or weapons from, usually by force or authority; to reduce to a peace footing, as an army or navy; to deprive of means of attack or defence, or of annoyance, or power to terrify; to render harmless.—*v.i.* To lay down arms; to disband armed forces.—**Disarmament**, dis-är'ma-ment, *n.* Act of disarming.

Disarrange, dis-a-rānj', *v.t.* To put out of order; to unsettle or disturb the order or due arrangement of.—**Disarrangement**, dis-a-rānj'ment, *n.* The act of disarranging; disorder.

Disarray, dis-a-rā', *v.t.* To undress; to divest of clothes; to throw into disorder.—*n.* Disorder; confusion; disordered dress.

Disaster, diz-as'tėr, *n.* [Fr. *désastre*—*dis*, and L. *astrum*, a star; a word of astrological origin. Compare the adj. *disastrous* with *ill-starred*.] Any unfortunate event, especially a great and sudden misfortune; mishap; calamity; adversity; reverse.—**Disastrous**, diz-as'trus, *a.* Occasioning or accompanied by disaster; calamitous.—**Disastrously**, diz-as'trus-li, *adv.* In a disastrous manner.—**Disastrousness**, diz-as'trus-nes, *n.*

Disavow, dis-a-vou', *v.t.* To deny to be true, as a fact or charge respecting one's self; to disown; to repudiate; to reject.—**Disavowal**, dis-a-vou'al, *n.* Denial; repudiation.—**Disavower**, dis-a-vou'ėr, *n.* One who disavows.

Disband, dis-band', *v.t.* To dismiss from military service; to break up, as a band or body of men; to disperse.—*v.i.* To break up and retire from military service.—**Disbandment**, dis-band'ment, *n.* The act of disbanding.

Disbar, dis-bär', *v.t.*—*disbarred*, *disbarring*. To expel from being a member of the bar; to remove from the list of barristers.

Disbelief, dis-bē-lēf', *n.* Refusal of credit or faith; denial of belief; unbelief; infidelity; scepticism.—**Disbelieve**, dis-bē-lēv', *v.t.*—*disbelieved*, *disbelieving*. To refuse belief to; to hold not to be true or not to exist; to refuse to credit.—*v.i.* To deny the truth of any position; to refuse to believe.—**Disbeliever**, dis-bē-lē'vėr, *n.* One who disbelieves or refuses belief; an unbeliever.

Disburden, dis-bėr'den, *v.t.* To remove a burden from; to lay off or aside as oppressive; to get rid off.

Disburse, dis-bėrs', *v.t.*—*disbursed*, *disbursing*. [O.Fr. *desbourser*—prefix *dis*, and L.L. *bursa*, a purse. PURSE.] To pay out, as money; to spend or lay out; to expend.—**Disbursement**, dis-bėrs'ment, *n.* The act of disbursing; a sum paid out.—**Disburser**, dis-bėr'sėr, *n.* One who disburses.

Disburthen, dis-bėr'THen, *v.t.* and *i.* Same as *Disburden*.

Disc, Disk, disk, *n.* [L. *discus*, a quoit. DISH, DESK.] A kind of ancient quoit; any flat circular plate or surface, as of a piece of metal, the face of the sun, moon, or a planet as it appears to our sight, &c.; *bot.* the whole surface of a leaf; also, the central part of a radiate compound flower, the part surrounded by what is called the ray.—**Disciform**, dis'si-form, *a.* Having the form or shape of a disc.—**Discoid, Discous**, dis'koid, dis'kus, *a.* Shaped like a disc; resembling a disc.

Discard, dis-kärd', *v.t.* and *i.* To throw out of the hand such cards as are not played in the course of the game; to dismiss from service or employment, or from society; to cast off.

Discern, diz-zėrn', *v.t.* [L. *discerno*—*dis*, and *cerno*, to separate or distinguish, akin to Gr. *krinō*, to judge (whence *critic*); Skr. *kri*, to separate. CRIME.] To perceive or note as being different; to discriminate by the eye or the intellect; to distinguish or mark as being distinct; to discover by the eye; to see.—*v.i.* To see or understand differences; to make distinction; to have clearness of mental vision.—**Discerner**, diz-zėr'nėr, *n.* One who discerns; a clear-sighted observer; one who knows and judges; one who has the power of distinguishing.—**Discernible, Discernable**, diz-zėr'ni-bl, diz-zėr'na-bl, *a.* Capable of being discerned; discoverable by the eye or the understanding; distinguishable.—**Discernibleness**, diz-zėr'ni-bl-nes, *n.*—**Discernibly**, diz-zėr'ni-bli, *adv.* So as to be discerned.—**Discerning**, diz-zėr'ning, *p.* and *a.* Having power to discern; capable of discriminating, knowing, and judging; sharp-sighted; acute.—**Discerningly**, diz-zėr'ning-li, *adv.* In a discerning manner.—**Discernment**, diz-zėrn'ment, *n.* The act of discerning; the power or faculty of discerning by the mind; acuteness of judgment; power of perceiving differences of things or ideas, and their relations; penetration.

Discharge, dis-chärj', *v.t.*—*discharged*, *discharging*. To unload (a ship); to take out (a cargo); to free from any load or burden; to free of the missile with which anything is charged or loaded; to fire off; to let fly; to shoot; to emit or send out; to give vent to, *lit.* or *fig.*; to deliver the amount or value of to the person to whom it is owing; to pay (a debt); to free from an obligation, duty, or labour; to relieve (to *discharge* a person from a task); to clear from an accusation or crime; to acquit; to absolve; to set free; to perform or execute (a duty or office); to divest of an office or employment; to dismiss from service (a servant, a soldier, a jury); to release; to liberate from confinement.—*v.i.* To get rid of or let out a charge or contents.—*n.* The act of discharging, unloading, or freeing from a charge; a flowing or issuing out, or a throwing out; emission; that which is thrown out; matter emitted; dismissal from office or service; release from obligation, debt, or penalty; absolution from a crime or accusation; ransom; price paid for deliverance; performance; execution, as of an office, trust, or duty; liberation; release from confinement; payment of a debt; a written acknowledgment of payment; a substance used in calico-printing to remove colour, and so form a pattern.—**Discharger**, dis-chär'jėr, *n.* One who or that which discharges.

Disciform. Under DISC.

Disciple, dis-sī'pl, *n.* [L. *discipulus*, from *disco*, to learn.] One who receives instruction from another; a learner; a scholar; a pupil; a follower; an adherent.—**Discipleship**, dis-sī'pl-ship, *n.* The state of being a disciple.

Discipline, dis'si-plin, *n.* [L. *disciplina*, from *discipulus*, a disciple, from *disco*, to learn.] Training; education; instruction and the government of conduct or practice; the training to act in accordance with rules; drill; method of regulating principles and practice; punishment inflicted by way of correction and training; instruction by means of misfortune, suffering, and the like; correction; chastisement.—*v.t.*—*disciplined*, *disciplining*. To subject to discipline; to apply discipline to; to train; to teach rules and practice, and accustom to order and subordination; to drill; to correct, chastise, punish.—**Discipliner**, dis'si-plin-ėr, *n.* One who disciplines.—**Disciplinable**, dis'si-plin-a-bl, *a.* Capable of instruction and improvement in learning; capable of being made matter of discipline; subject or liable to discipline.—**Disciplinableness**, dis'si-plin-a-bl-nes, *n.*—**Disciplinarian**, dis'si-pli-nā"ri-an, *n.* One who disciplines; one who instructs in military and naval tactics and manœuvres; one who enforces rigid discipline; a martinet.—*a.* Pertaining to discipline.—**Disciplinary**, dis'si-pli-na-ri, *a.* Pertaining to discipline; intended for discipline; promoting discipline.

Disclaim, dis-klām′, *v.t.* To deny or relinquish all claim to; to reject as not belonging to one's self; to renounce; to deny responsibility for or approval of; to disavow; to disown.—**Disclaimer**, dis-klā′mėr, *n.* A person who disclaims; an act of disclaiming; abnegation of pretensions or claims; *law*, a renunciation, abandonment, or giving up of a claim.

Disclose, dis-klōz′, *v.t.*—*disclosed, disclosing.* To uncover and lay open to the view; to cause to appear; to allow to be seen; to bring to light; to make known, reveal, tell, utter.—**Discloser**, dis-klō′zėr, *n.* One who discloses. — **Disclosure**, dis-klō′zhūr, *n.* The act of disclosing; exhibition; the act of making known or revealing; utterance of what was secret; a telling; that which is disclosed or made known.

Discoid. Under Disc.

Discolor, dis-kul′ėr, *v.t.* To alter the hue or color of; to change to a different color or shade; to stain; to tinge.—**Discoloration**, dis-kul′ėr-ā″shon, *n.* The act of discoloring; alteration of color; a discolored spot or marking.

Discomfit, dis-kum′fit, *v.t.* [O.Fr. *disconfire, disconfit*—L. *dis*, priv., and *conficere*, to achieve. Comfit.] To rout, defeat, or scatter in fight; to cause to flee; to vanquish; to disconcert, foil, or frustrate the plans of.—*n.* A defeat; an overthrow. (*Mil.*) —**Discomfiture**, dis-kum′fi-tūr, *n.* Rout; defeat; overthrow; frustration; disappointment.

Discomfort, dis-kum′fėrt, *n.* Absence or opposite of comfort or pleasure; uneasiness; disturbance of peace; pain, annoyance, or inquietude.—*v.t.* To disturb the peace or happiness of; to make uneasy; to pain.—**Discomfortable**,† dis-kum′fėr-ta-bl, *a.* Wanting in comfort; uncomfortable.

Discommend,† dis-kom-mend′, *v.t.* To blame; to censure; to expose to censure or bad feeling.

Discommode, dis-kom-mōd′, *v.t.* — *discommoded, discommoding.* To put to inconvenience; to incommode.

Discommon, dis-kom′on, *v.t.* To make to cease to be common land; to deprive of the right of a common.

Discompose, dis-kom-pōz′, *v.t.*—*discomposed, discomposing.* To disorder, disturb, or disarrange; to disturb the peace and quietness of; to agitate, ruffle, fret, or vex. —**Discomposure**, dis-kom-pō′zhūr, *n.* The state of being discomposed; a certain agitation or perturbation of mind.

Disconcert, dis-kon-sėrt′, *v.t.* To throw into disorder or confusion; to undo, as a concerted scheme or plan; to defeat; to frustrate; to discompose or disturb the self-possession of; to confuse.—**Disconcertion**, dis-kon-sėr′shon, *n.* The act of disconcerting; the state of being disconcerted.

Disconformable, dis-kon-for′ma-bl, *a.* Not conformable.—**Disconformity**, dis-kon-for′mi-ti, *n.* Want of agreement or conformity; inconsistency.

Discongruity, dis-kon-grö′i-ti, *n.* Want of congruity; incongruity.

Disconnect, dis-kon-nekt′, *v.t.* To separate or sever the connection between; to disunite; to detach.—**Disconnection**, dis-kon-nek′shon, *n.* The act of disconnecting; separation; want of union.

Disconsolate, dis-kon′sō-lāt, *a.* [L. *dis*, priv., and *consolatus*, pp. of *consolor*, to console, to be consoled. Console.] Destitute of consolation; hopeless; sad; dejected; melancholy; cheerless; saddening; gloomy.—**Disconsolately**, dis-kon′sō-lāt-li, *adv.* In a disconsolate manner; without comfort.—**Disconsolateness**, dis-kon′sō-lāt-nes, *n.*

Discontent, dis-kon-tent′, *n.* Want of content; uneasiness or inquietude of mind; dissatisfaction; one who is discontented; a malcontent (*Shak.*).—*a.*‡ Uneasy; dissatisfied.—*v.t.* To make dissatisfied.—**Discontented**, dis-kon-ten′ted, *a.* Not contented; dissatisfied; not pleased with one's circumstances; given to grumble.—**Discontentedly**, dis-kon-ten′ted-li, *adv.* In a discontented manner or mood.—**Discontentedness**, dis-kon-ten′ted-nes, *n.* The state of being discontented; dissatisfaction. —**Discontentment**, dis-kon-tent′ment, *n.* The state of being discontented; discontent.

Discontinue, dis-kon-tin′ū, *v.t.*—*discontinued, discontinuing.* [Prefix *dis*, neg., and *continue.*] To continue no longer; to leave off or break off; to give up, cease from, or abandon; to stop; to put an end to.—*v.i.* To cease; to stop.—**Discontinuable**, dis-kon-tin′ū-a-bl, *a.* That may be discontinued. — **Discontinuance**, dis-kon-tin′ū-ans, *n.* Want of continuance; a breaking off; cessation; intermission; interruption.—**Discontinuation**, dis-kon-tin′ū-ā″shon, *n.* Discontinuance.—**Discontinuity**, dis-kon′ti-nū″i-ti, *n.* Want of continuity or uninterrupted connection; disunion of parts; want of cohesion.—**Discontinuous**, dis-kon-tin′ū-us, *a.* Broken off; interrupted.

Discophora, dis-kof′o-ra, *n. pl.* [Gr. *diskos*, a disc, and *pherō*, to carry.] A group of animals, comprising most of the organisms known as sea-jellies, jelly-fishes, or sea-nettles.

Discord, dis′kord, *n.* [Fr. *discorde*, L. *discordia*, disagreement, from *discors*, discordant—*dis*, and *cor, cordis*, the heart, as in *concord, accord, cordial.*] Want of concord or agreement; opposition of opinions; difference of qualities; disagreement; variance; contention; strife; *mus.* a union of sounds disagreeable or grating to the ear; dissonance; each of the *two* sounds forming a dissonance.—*v.i.* (dis-kord′). To disagree; to be out of harmony or concord; to clash.—**Discordance, Discordancy**, dis-kor′dans, dis-kor′dan-si, *n.* Disagreement; opposition; inconsistency.—**Discordant**, dis-kor′dant, *a.* Disagreeing; incongruous; being at variance; dissonant; not in unison; not harmonious; not accordant; harsh; jarring.—**Discordantly**, dis-kor′dant-li, *adv.* In a discordant manner.

Discount, dis′kount, *n.* [Prefix *dis*, neg., and *count*; O.Fr. *descompte.*] A certain sum deducted from the credit price of goods sold on account of prompt payment, or any deduction from the customary price, or from a sum due or to be due at a future time; a charge made to cover the interest of money advanced on a bill or other document not presently due; the act of discounting.—*At a discount*, below par; hence, in low esteem; in disfavour.—*v.t.* (dis-kount′). To lend or advance the amount of (a bill or similar document), deducting the interest or other rate per cent from the principal; to leave out of account or disregard; to estimate or take into account beforehand; to enjoy or suffer by anticipation.—**Discountable**, dis-koun′ta-bl, *a.* Capable of being discounted.—**Discounter**, dis′koun-tėr, *n.* One who discounts bills, &c.

Discountenance, dis-koun′te-nans, *v.t.* To put out of countenance; to put to shame; to abash; to set one's countenance against; to discourage, check, or restrain by frowns, censure, arguments, cold treatment, &c.—*n.* Cold treatment; disapprobation.—**Discountenancer**, dis-koun′te-nan-sėr, *n.* One who discountenances.

Discourage, dis-kur′āj, *v.t.*—*discouraged, discouraging.* To check the courage of; to dishearten; to deprive of self-confidence; to attempt to repress or prevent by pointing out difficulties, &c.; to dissuade.—**Discouragement**, dis-kur′āj-ment, *n.* The act of discouraging; the act of deterring or dissuading from an undertaking; that which discourages or damps ardour or hope; the state of being discouraged. — **Discourager**, dis-kur′ā-jėr, *n.* One who or that which discourages.—**Discouraging**, dis-kur′ā-jing, *a.* Tending to discourage or dishearten; disheartening.—**Discouragingly**, dis-kur′ā-jing-li, *adv.* In a discouraging manner.

Discourse, dis-kōrs′, *n.* [Fr. *discours*, from L. *discursus*, a running about, a conversation, from *discurro*, to ramble—*dis*, and *curro*, to run. Current.] A running over a subject in speech; hence, a talking together or discussing; conversation; talk; speech; a treatise; a dissertation; a homily, sermon, or other production.—*v.i.*—*discoursed, discoursing.* To communicate thoughts or ideas orally or in writing, especially in a formal manner; to hold forth; to expatiate; to converse.—*v.t.* To talk over or discuss‡; to utter or give forth.—**Discourser**, dis-kōr′sėr, *n.* One who discourses. — **Discoursive**, dis-kōr′siv, *a.* Having the character of discourse; conversable; communicative.

Discourteous, dis-kōr′tē-us, *a.* Wanting in courtesy; uncivil; rude. — **Discourteously**, dis-kōr′tē-us-li, *adv.* In a discourteous manner. — **Discourteousness**, dis-kōr′tē-us-nes, *n.*—**Discourtesy**, dis-kōr′te-si, *n.* Want of courtesy; incivility; rudeness of manner; act of disrespect.

Discous, *a.* Under Disc.

Discover, dis-kuv′ėr, *v.t.* [Prefix *dis*, priv., and *cover*; O.Fr. *descouvrir.*] To lay open to view; to disclose or reveal; to espy; to have the first sight of; to find out; to obtain the first knowledge of; to come to the knowledge of; to detect. ∴ We *discover* what before existed, though to us unknown; we *invent* what did not before exist.—**Discoverable**, dis-kuv′ėr-a-bl, *a.* Capable of being discovered, brought to light, exposed, found out, or made known.—**Discoverer**, dis-kuv′ėr-ėr, *n.* One who discovers; one who first sees or espies; one who finds out or first comes to the knowledge of something. —**Discovery**, dis-kuv′ėr-i, *n.* The act of discovering; a disclosing or bringing to light; a revealing or making known; a finding out or bringing for the first time to sight or knowledge; what is discovered or found out.

Discredit, dis-kred′it, *n.* Want of credit or good reputation; some degree of disgrace or reproach; disesteem; disrepute; want of belief, trust, or confidence; disbelief.—*v.t.* To give no credit to; not to credit or believe; to deprive of credit or good reputation; to bring into some degree of disgrace or disrepute; to deprive of credibility. — **Discreditable**, dis-kred′i-ta-bl, *n.* Injurious to reputation; disgraceful; disreputable.—**Discreditably**, dis-kred′i-ta-bli, *adv.* In a discreditable manner.

Discreet, dis-krēt′, *a.* [Fr. *discret*, from L. *discretus*, pp. of *discerno*, to discern. Discern.] Wise in avoiding errors or evil, and in selecting the best course or means; prudent in conduct; circumspect; cautious; heedful; guarded.—**Discreetly**, dis-krēt′li, *adv.* In a discreet manner; prudently.—**Discreetness**, dis-krēt′nes, *n.* The quality of being discreet.—**Discretion**, dis-kresh′on, *n.* [Fr. *discrétion*, L. *discretio.*] The quality or attribute of being discreet; discernment to judge critically of what is correct and proper, united with caution; prudence; sound judgment; circumspection; wariness; caution; liberty or power of acting without other control than one's own judgment (to leave an affair to one's *discretion*, to surrender at *discretion*, that is without stipulating for terms).—**Discretionarily**, dis-kresh′on-a-ri-li, *adv.* At discretion; according to discretion.—**Discretionary**, dis-kresh′on-a-ri, *a.* Left to a person's own discretion or judgment; to be directed according to one's own discretion (*discretionary* powers).

Discrepance, Discrepancy, dis-krep′ans, dis-krep′an-si, *n.* [L. *discrepantia*, from *discrepo*, to give a different sound, to vary —*dis*, and *crepo*, to creak. Crepitate.] A difference or inconsistency between facts, stories, theories, &c.; disagreement; divergence.—**Discrepant**, dis-krep′ant, *a.* Differing or diverging; not agreeing or according; disagreeing; dissimilar.

Discrete, dis krēt′, *a.* [L. *discretus*, separated, set apart. Discreet.] Separate; distinct; disjunct; disjunctive.—*A discrete quantity*, quantity not continued in its parts, as any number, since a number consists of units.—**Discretive**, dis-krē′tiv, *a.*

Disjunctive; denoting separation or opposition.

Discretion. Under DISCREET.

Discriminate, dis-krim′i-nāt, *v.t.*—*discriminated, discriminating.* [L. *discrimino, discriminatum*, to distinguish, from *discrimen*, difference—*dis*, asunder, and the root seen in *crimen*, accusation, *cerno*, to sift or separate. CRIME, DISCERN, DISCREET.] To distinguish from other things by observing differences; to perceive by a distinction; to discern; to separate; to select; to distinguish by some note or mark.—*v.i.* To make a difference or distinction; to observe or note a difference; to distinguish.—**Discriminately**, dis-krim′i-nāt-li, *adv.* With minute distinction; particularly.—**Discriminating**, dis-krim′i-nā-ting, *p.* and *a.* Serving to discriminate; distinguishing; distinctive; able to make nice distinctions.—**Discrimination**, dis-krim′i-nā″-shon, *n.* The act of discriminating; the faculty of distinguishing or discriminating; penetration; discernment; the state of being discriminated or set apart.—**Discriminative**, dis-krim′i-nā-tiv, *a.* Discriminating or tending to discriminate; forming the mark of distinction or difference; characteristic.—**Discriminatively**, dis-krim′-i-nā-tiv-li, *adv.* By discrimination.—**Discriminator**, dis-krim′i-nā-tėr, *n.* One who discriminates.—**Discriminatory**, dis-krim′i-na-to-ri, *a.* Discriminative.

Discrown, dis-kroun′, *v.t.* To deprive of a crown.

Discursive, dis-kėr′siv, *a.* [Fr. *discursif*, from L. *discursus.* DISCOURSE.] Passing rapidly from one subject to another; desultory; rambling; digressional; argumentative; reasoning; rational.—**Discursively**, dis-kėr′siv-li, *adv.* In a discursive manner.—**Discursiveness**, dis-kėr′siv-nes, *n.*

Discus, dis′kus, *n.* DISC.

Discuss, dis-kus′, *v.t.* [L. *discutio, discussum*, to scatter, dissipate—*dis*, asunder, and *quatio*, to shake, as in *concussion.* QUASH.] To drive away, dissolve, or resolve (a tumour, &c.: a medical use); to agitate by argument; to examine by disputation; to reason on; to debate; to argue; to make an end of, by eating or drinking; to consume (*colloq.*).—**Discussable**, dis-kus′a-bl, *a.* Capable of being discussed or debated.—**Discusser**, dis-kus′ėr, *n.* One who discusses.—**Discussion**, dis-ku′shon, *n.* The act of discussing; debate; disquisition; the agitation of a point or subject with a view to elicit truth.—**Discussive**, dis-kus′iv, *a.* Having the power to discuss.—*n.* A medicine that discusses; a discutient.—**Discutient**, dis-kū′shent, *n.* A medicine or application which disperses a tumour or morbid matter.

Disdain, dis-dān′, *v.t.* [O.Fr. *desdaigner*, Fr. *dédaigner*, from L. *dis*, priv., and *dignor*, to deem worthy, from *dignus*, worthy. DEIGN.] To deem or regard as worthless; to consider to be unworthy of notice, care, regard, esteem, or unworthy of one's character; to scorn; to contemn.—*n.* A feeling of contempt, mingled with indignation; the looking upon anything as beneath one; haughtiness; contempt; scorn.—**Disdainer**, dis-dā′nėr, *n.* One who disdains.—**Disdainful**, dis-dān′fụl, *a.* Full of or expressing disdain; contemptuous; scornful; haughty.—**Disdainfully**, dis-dān′fụl-li, *adv.* In a disdainful manner.—**Disdainfulness**, dis-dān′fụl-nes, *n.* The quality of being disdainful; haughty scorn.

Disease, di-zēz′, *n.* Want or absence of ease‡; uneasiness, distress, or discomfort‡; any morbid state of the body, or of any particular organ or part of the body; ailment; distemper; malady; disorder; any morbid or depraved condition, moral, mental, social, political, &c.—**Diseased**, di-zēzd′, *a.* Affected with disease; having the vital functions deranged; disordered; deranged; distempered; sick.—**Diseasedness**, di-zē′zed-nes, *n.* The state of being diseased; a morbid state.

Disembark, dis-em-bärk′, *v.t.* To remove from on board a ship to the land; to put on shore; to land.—*v.i.* To leave a ship and go on shore; to land.—**Disembarkation, Disembarkment**, dis-em′bär-kā″shon, dis-em-bärk′ment, *n.* The act of disembarking.

Disembarrass, dis-em-bar′as, *v.t.* To free from embarrassment or perplexity; to clear; to extricate.—**Disembarrassment**, dis-em-bar′as-ment, *n.* The act of disembarrassing.

Disembitter, dis-em-bit′ėr, *v.t.* To free from bitterness or acrimony.

Disembody, dis-em-bod′i, *v.t.* To divest of the body (a *disembodied* spirit = a ghost); to set free from the flesh; to disband (*military*).—**Disembodiment**, dis-em-bod′i-ment, *n.* The act of disembodying; the condition of being disembodied.

Disembogue, dis-em-bōg′, *v.t.* and *i.*—*disembogued, disemboguing.* To pour out or discharge at the mouth, as a stream; to discharge water into the ocean or a lake.—**Disemboguement**, dis-em-bōg′ment, *n.* Discharge of waters by a stream.

Disembowel, dis-em-bou′el, *v.t.*—*disembowelled, disembowelling.* To deprive of the bowels or of parts analogous to the bowels; to eviscerate; to gut.

Disenchant, dis-en-chant′, *v.t.* To free from enchantment; to deliver from the power of charms or spells; to free from fascination or pleasing delusion.—**Disenchanter**, dis-en-chan′tėr, *n.* One who or that which disenchants.—**Disenchantment**, dis-en-chant′ment, *n.* Act of disenchanting.

Disencumber, dis-en-kum′bėr, *v.t.* To free from encumbrance, clogs, and impediments.—**Disencumbrance**, dis-en-kum′brans, *n.* Deliverance from encumbrance.

Disendow, dis-en-dou′, *v.t.* To deprive of an endowment or endowments, as a church or other institution.—**Disendowment**, dis-en-dou′ment, *n.* The act of disendowing.

Disenfranchise, dis-en-fran′chīz, *v.t.* To disfranchise.

Disengage, dis-en-gāj′, *v.t.*—*disengaged, disengaging.* To separate or set free from union or attachment; to detach; to disunite; to free; to disentangle; to extricate; to clear, as from difficulties or perplexities; to free, as from anything that occupies the attention; to set free by dissolving an engagement.—**Disengaged**, dis-en-gājd′, *p.* and *a.* Being at leisure; not particularly occupied; not having the attention confined to a particular object.—**Disengagedness**, dis-en-gā′-jed-nes, *n.*—**Disengagement**, dis-en-gāj′ment, *n.* The act or process of disengaging; the state of being disengaged; freedom from engrossing occupation; leisure.

Disennoble, dis-en-nō′bl, *v.t.* To deprive of that which ennobles; to degrade.

Disenroll, dis-en-rōl′, *v.t.* To erase from a roll or list.

Disentail, dis-en-tāl′, *v.t.* To free from being entailed; to break the entail of.

Disentangle, dis-en-tang′gl, *v.t.* To free from entanglements; to unravel; to extricate from perplexity or complications; to disengage.—**Disentanglement**, dis-en-tang′gl-ment, *n.* Act of disentangling.

Disenthrall, dis-en-thrạl′, *v.t.* To liberate from slavery, bondage, or servitude; to free or rescue from oppression.—**Disenthralment**, dis-en-thrạl′ment, *n.* Liberation from bondage; emancipation.

Disenthrone, dis-en-thrōn′, *v.t.* To dethrone; to depose from sovereign authority. (*Mil.*)

Disentomb, dis-en-töm′, *v.t.* To take out of a tomb; to disinter.

Disestablish, dis-es-tab′lish, *v.t.* To cause to cease to be established; to withdraw (a church) from its connection with the state.—**Disestablishment**, dis-es-tab′lish-ment, *n.* The act of disestablishing; the act of withdrawing a church from its connection with the state.

Disesteem, dis-es-tēm′, *n.* Want of esteem; slight dislike; disregard.—*v.t.* To dislike in a moderate degree; to regard as unworthy of esteem.

Disfavor, dis-fā′vėr, *n.* A feeling of some dislike or slight displeasure; unfavorable regard; disesteem; a state of being unacceptable, or not favored, patronized, or befriended; a disobliging act.—*v.t.* To withdraw or withhold favor, friendship, or support from.

Disfigure, dis-fig′ūr, *v.t.*—*disfigured, disfiguring.* To mar the external figure of; to impair the shape or form of; to injure the beauty, symmetry, or excellence of; to deface; to deform.—**Disfiguration**, dis-fig′-ū-rā″shon, *n.* The act of disfiguring; disfigurement.—**Disfigurement**, dis-fig′ūr-ment, *n.* The act of disfiguring or state of being disfigured; that which disfigures.—**Disfigurer**, dis-fig′ū-rėr, *n.* One who disfigures.

Disforest, dis-for′est, *v.t.* Same as *Disafforest.*

Disfranchise, dis-fran′chīz, *v.t.*—*disfranchised, disfranchising.* To deprive of the rights and privileges of a free citizen; to deprive of any franchise, more especially of the right of voting in elections, &c.—**Disfranchisement**, dis-fran′chiz-ment, *n.* The act of disfranchising, or state of being disfranchised.

Disgorge, dis-gorj′, *v.t.*—*disgorged, disgorging.* [O.Fr. *desgorger*, to vomit—*dis*, and *gorge.* GORGE.] To eject or discharge from, or as from, the stomach, throat, or mouth; to vomit; to belch; to discharge violently (a volcano *disgorges* lava); to yield up, as what has been taken wrongfully; to give up; to surrender.—*v.i.* To give up plunder or ill-gotten gains.—**Disgorgement**, dis-gorj′ment, *n.* The act of disgorging.

Disgrace, dis-grās′, *n.* A state of being out of favour; disfavour; state of ignominy; dishonour; shame; infamy; cause of shame.—*v.t.*—*disgraced, disgracing.* To bring into disgrace; to put out of favour; to dismiss with dishonour; to treat ignominiously; to bring shame or reproach on; to humiliate or humble; to dishonour.—**Disgraceful**, dis-grās′fụl, *a.* Entailing disgrace; shameful; infamous; dishonourable.—**Disgracefully**, dis-grās′fụl-li, *adv.* In a disgraceful manner.—**Disgracefulness**, dis-grās′-fụl-nes, *n.* The state or quality of being disgraceful.—**Disgracer**, dis-grā′sėr, *n.* One who disgraces.

Disguise, dis-gīz′, *v.t.*—*disguised, disguising.* [O.Fr. *desguiser*, Fr. *déguiser*—prefix *dis*, and *guise*, way, fancy, manner. GUISE.] To conceal the ordinary guise and appearance of by an unusual habit or mask; to hide by a counterfeit appearance; to cloak by a false show, false language, or an artificial manner (anger, intentions, &c.); to change in manners or behaviour by the use of spirituous liquor; to intoxicate.—*n.* A counterfeit dress; a dress intended to conceal the identity of the person who wears it; a counterfeit show; artificial or assumed language or appearance intended to deceive.—**Disguisedly**, dis-gī′zed-li, *adv.* With disguise.—**Disguisedness**, dis-gī′zed-nes, *n.* The state of being disguised.—**Disguisement**, dis-gīz′ment, *n.* The act of disguising.—**Disguiser**, dis-gī′zėr, *n.* One who disguises.

Disgust, dis-gust′, *n.* [O.Fr. *desgoust*, Fr. *dégoût*, from L. *dis*, priv., and *gustus*, taste.] Aversion to the taste of food or drink; distaste; disrelish; nausea; aversion in the mind excited by something offensive in the manners, conduct, language, or opinions of others; loathing; repugnance; strong dislike.—*v.t.* To cause to feel disgust; to excite aversion in the stomach of; to offend the taste of; to stir up loathing or repugnance in.—**Disgustful**, dis-gust′fụl, *a.* Exciting the feeling of disgust.—**Disgusting**, dis-gus′ting, *a.* Producing or causing disgust; nauseous; loathsome; nasty.—**Disgustingly**, dis-gus′ting-li, *adv.* In a disgusting manner.—**Disgustingness**, dis-gus′ting-nes, *n.* State of being disgusting.

Dish, dish, *n.* [A.Sax. *disc*, a dish; like D.

disch, G. *tisch*, a table, from L. *discus*, Gr. *diskos*, a quoit or disc. DESK, DISC.] A broad open vessel made of various materials, used for serving up meat and various kinds of food at the table; the meat or provisions served in a dish; hence, any particular kind of food; the concavity of certain wheels, as those of vehicles.—*v.t.* To put in a dish after being cooked; to make (a wheel) concave in the centre; to damage, ruin, completely overthrow (*slang*).—**Dish-cloth, Dish-clout**, *n.* A cloth used for washing and wiping dishes. — **Dish-water**, *n.* Water in which dishes are washed.

Dishabille, dis'a-bil, *n.* Same as *Deshabille.*

Dishearten, dis-här'tn, *v.t.* To discourage; to deprive of courage; to depress the spirits of; to deject; to dispirit.

Dishevel, di-shev'el, *v.t.—dishevelled, dishevelling.* [O.Fr. *descheveler*, Fr. *décheveler*, to put the hair out of order—*des* for *dis*, priv., and O.Fr. *chevel*, Fr. *cheveu*, hair, from L. *capillus*, the hair of the head.] To spread the locks or tresses of loosely and negligently; to suffer (the hair) to hang negligently and uncombed.

Dishonest, dis-on'est, *a.* Void of honesty, probity, or integrity; not honest, fraudulent; inclined or apt to deceive, cheat, pilfer, embezzle, or defraud; proceeding from or marked by fraud; knavish; unchaste‡.—**Dishonestly**, dis-on'est-li, *adv.* In a dishonest manner; fraudulently; knavishly. —**Dishonesty**, dis-on'es-ti, *n.* The opposite of honesty; want of probity or integrity; a disposition to cheat, pilfer, embezzle, or defraud; violation of trust; fraud; treachery; deviation from probity or integrity; unchastity or incontinence‡.

Dishonor, dis-on'ėr, *n.* The opposite of honor; want of honor; disgrace; shame; anything that disgraces.—*v.t.* To disgrace; to bring shame on; to stain the character of; to lessen in reputation; to treat with indignity; to violate the chastity of; to debauch; to refuse or decline to accept or pay (a bill of exchange).—**Dishonorable**, dis-on'ėr-a-bl, *a.* Shameful; disgraceful; base; bringing shame; staining the character and lessening reputation; unhonored (*Shak.*). **Dishonorableness**, dis-on'ėr-a-bl-nes, *n.* Quality of being dishonorable. —**Dishonorably**, dis-on'ėr-a-bli, *adv.* In a dishonorable manner.—**Dishonorer**, dis-on'ėr-ėr, *n.* One who dishonors or disgraces.

Dishorse, dis-hors', *v.t.* To dismount from horseback; to unhorse. (*Tenn.*)

Disillusionize, dis-il-lū'zhon-īz, *v.t.* To free from illusion; to disenchant.

Disincline, dis-in-klīn, *v.t.* To excite slight aversion in; to make unwilling; to cause to hang back; to alienate.

Disincorporate, dis-in-kor'po-rāt, *v.t.* To deprive of corporate powers; to cause to cease from being incorporated.—**Disincorporation**, dis-in-kor'po-rā"shon, *n.* The act of so depriving.

Disinfect, dis-in-fekt', *v.t.* To cleanse from infection; to purify from contagious matter.—**Disinfectant**, dis-in-fek'tant, *n.* A substance that disinfects, or is used for destroying the power or means of propagating diseases which spread by infection or contagion. — **Disinfection**, dis-in-fek'shon, *n.* Purification from infecting matter.

Disingenuous, dis-in-jen'ū-us, *a.* Not ingenuous; not open, frank, and candid; meanly artful; insincere; sly; uncandid.—**Disingenuously**, dis-in-jen'ū-us-li, *adv.* In a disingenuous manner.—**Disingenuousness**, dis-in-jen'ū-us-nes, *n.* The state or quality of being disingenuous.

Disinherit, dis-in-her'it, *v.t.* To cut off from hereditary right; to deprive of the right to an inheritance. — **Disinheritance, Disinherison**, dis-in-her'i-tans, dis-in-her'i-son, *n.* Act of disinheriting.

Disintegrate, dis-in'tē-grāt, *v.t.* [L. *dis*, priv., and *integer*, entire, whole.] To separate the component particles of; to reduce to powder or to fragments. — **Disintegrable**, dis-in'tē-gra-bl, *a.* Capable of being disintegrated. — **Disintegration**, dis-in'tē-grā"shon, *n.* The act of separating the component particles of a substance; the gradual wearing down of rocks by atmospheric influence.

Disinter, dis-in-tėr', *v.t.—disinterred, disinterring.* To take out of a grave or out of the earth; to take out, as from a grave; to bring from obscurity into view.—**Disinterment**, dis-in-tėr'ment, *n.* The act of disinterring; exhumation.

Disinterested, dis-in'tėr-es-ted, *a.* Free from self-interest; having no personal interest or private advantage in a question or affair; not influenced or dictated by private advantage; unselfish; uninterested. —**Disinterestedly**, dis-in'tėr-es-ted-li, *adv.* In a disinterested manner.—**Disinterestedness**, dis-in'tėr-es-ted-nes, *n.* The state or quality of being disinterested.

Disinthrall, Disinthralment, dis-in-thral, dis-in-thral'ment. DISENTHRALL.

Disjoin, dis-join', *v.t.* To part asunder; to disunite; to separate; to detach; to sunder. —*v.i.* To be separated; to part. — **Disjoint**, dis-joint', *v.t.* To separate, as parts united by joints; to put out of joint; to dislocate; to break the natural order and relations of; to put out of order; to derange; to render incoherent.—*v.i.* To fall in pieces.—**Disjointed**, dis-join'ted, *a.* Unconnected; incoherent; out of joint; out of order; ill-joined together.—**Disjointedness**, dis-join'ted-nes, *n.* State of being disjointed.—**Disjointly**, dis-joint'li, *adv.* In a disjointed manner or state.

Disjunct, dis-jungkt', *a.* [L. *disjunctus*, pp. of *disjungo—dis*, and *jungo*, to join.] Disjoined; separated.—**Disjunction**, dis-jungk'shon, *n.* The act of disjoining; disunion; separation. — **Disjunctive**, dis-jungk'tiv, *a.* Tending to disjoin or separate; *gram.* marking separation or opposition, a term applied to a word or particle which unites words or sentences in construction, but disjoins the sense (as *neither, nor*); *logic*, applied to a proposition in which the parts are opposed to each other by means of disjunctives.—*n. Gram.* a word that disjoins (as *or, nor, neither*); *logic*, a disjunctive proposition. — **Disjunctively**, dis-jungk'tiv-li, *adv.* In a disjunctive manner.

Disk, *n.* DISC.

Dislike, dis-līk', *n.* A feeling the opposite of liking; disinclination; aversion; distaste; antipathy; repugnance. — *v.t.* — *disliked, disliking.* To feel dislike towards; to regard with some aversion; to have a feeling against; to disrelish. — **Dislikable**,† dis-lī'ka-bl, *a.* Worthy of, or liable to dislike; distasteful; disagreeable.

Dislimb, dis-lim', *v.t.* To tear the limbs from.

Dislink, dis-lingk', *v.t.* To unlink; to disjoin; to separate. (*Tenn.*)

Dislocate, dis'lō-kāt, *v.t.—dislocated, dislocating.* To displace; to shift from the original site; particularly, to put out of joint; to move (a bone) from its socket, cavity, or place of articulation.—**Dislocation**, dis-lō-kā'shon, *n.* The act of dislocating; particularly, the act of removing or forcing a bone from its socket; luxation; *geol.* the displacement of parts of rocks, or portions of strata, from the situations which they originally occupied.

Dislodge, dis-loj', *v.t.—dislodged, dislodging.* To drive from the fixed position or place occupied; to drive (enemies) from any place of hiding or defence, or from a position seized.—*v.i.* To go from a place of rest. — **Dislodgment**, dis-loj'ment, *n.* The act of dislodging.

Disloyal, dis-loi'al, *a.* Not loyal or true to allegiance; false to a sovereign or country; faithless; false; perfidious; treacherous; not true to the marriage-bed; false in love. —**Disloyally**, dis-loi'al-li, *adv.* In a disloyal manner.—**Disloyalty**, dis-loi'al-ti, *n.* The character of being disloyal; want of fidelity to a sovereign; violation of allegiance; want of fidelity in love.

Dismal, diz'mal, *a.* [Etym. doubtful. According to one derivation, from L. *dies malus*, an evil day; according to another, from O.Fr. *dismal*, L. *decimalis, decem*, ten, referring to the day of paying tithes.] Dark, gloomy, or cheerless to look at; depressing; sorrowful; dire; horrid; melancholy; calamitous; unfortunate; frightful; horrible.—**Dismally**, diz'mal-li, *adv.* In a dismal manner. — **Dismalness**, diz'mal-nes, *n.* The state of being dismal; gloominess; horror.—**Dismals**, *n.* Gloomy feelings; in the blues.

Dismantle, dis-man'tl, *v.t.—dismantled, dismantling.* [O.Fr. *desmanteler, desmanteller*, lit. to deprive of cloak or mantle.] To deprive of dress; to strip; to divest; more generally, to deprive or strip (a thing) of furniture, equipments, fortifications, and the like.

Dismast, dis-mast', *v.t.* To deprive of a mast or masts; to break and carry away the masts from.

Dismay, dis-mā', *v.t.* [Same word as Sp. and Pg. *desmayar*, to fall into a swoon, but no doubt directly from the French; from prefix *dis*, and O.H.G. *magan*, to be able (=E. *may*).] To deprive entirely of strength or firmness of mind; to discourage, with some feeling of dread or consternation; to confound; to daunt; to strike aghast. — *v.i.* To be daunted; to stand aghast. (*Shak.*)—*n.* A complete giving way of boldness or spirit; loss of courage together with consternation; a yielding to fear.

Disme,‡ dēm, *n.* [O.Fr. DIME.] A tenth part; the number ten. (*Shak.*)

Dismember, dis-mem'bėr, *v.t.* To divide limb from limb; to separate the members of; to mutilate; to sever and distribute the parts of; to divide into separate portions (a kingdom, &c.). — **Dismemberment**, dis-mem'bėr-ment, *n.* The act of dismembering.

Dismiss, dis-mis', *v.t.* [From L. *dimitto, dimissum*, to dismiss—*di, dis*, and *mitto*, as in *admit, commit*, &c.] To send away; to permit to depart, implying authority in a person to retain or keep; to discard; to remove from office, service, or employment; *law*, to reject as unworthy of notice, or of being granted.—**Dismissal**, dis-mis'al, *n.* The act of dismissing; dismission; discharge; liberation; manumission. — **Dismission**, dis-mish'on, *n.* The act of dismissing or sending away; leave to depart; removal from office or employment; discharge; *law*, rejection of something as unworthy of notice or of being granted.

Dismount, dis-mount', *v.i.* To alight from a horse or other animal; to come or go down.—*v.t.* To throw or remove from a horse; to unhorse; to throw or remove (cannon or other artillery) from their carriages.

Disobedience, dis-ō-bē'di-ens, *n.* Neglect or refusal to obey; violation of a command or prohibition; the omission of that which is commanded to be done, or the doing of that which is forbid.—**Disobedient**, dis-ō-bē'di-ent, *a.* Neglecting or refusing to obey; guilty of disobedience; not observant of duty or rules prescribed by authority.—**Disobediently**, dis-ō-bē'di-ent-li, *adv.* In a disobedient manner.—**Disobey**, dis-ō-bā', *v.t.* To neglect or refuse to obey; to omit or refuse obedience to; to transgress or violate an order or injunction.—*v.i.* To refuse obedience; to disregard orders.

Disoblige, dis-ō-blīj', *v.t.* To offend by acting counter to the will or desires of; to offend by failing to oblige or do a friendly service to; to be unaccommodating to.—**Disobligement**, dis-ō-blīj'ment, *n.* The act of disobliging.—**Disobliger**, dis-ō-blī'jėr, *n.* One who disobliges.—**Disobliging**, dis-ō-blī'jing, *a.* Not obliging; not disposed to gratify the wishes of another; unaccommodating.—**Disobligingly**, dis-ō-blī'jing-li, *adv.* In a disobliging manner. —**Disobligingness**, dis-ō-blī'jing-nes, *n.*

Disorder, dis-or'dėr, *n.* Want of order or regular disposition; irregularity; immethodical distribution; confusion; tumult;

disturbance of the peace of society; disturbance or interruption of the functions of the animal economy or of the mind; distemper; sickness; derangement.—*v.t.* To break the order of; to derange; to throw into confusion; to disturb or interrupt the natural functions of; to produce sickness or indisposition in; to disturb as regards the reason or judgment; to craze.—**Disordered**, dis-or′dėrd, *p.* and *a.* Disorderly; irregular; deranged; crazed.—**Disorderliness**, dis-or′dėr-li-nes, *n.* State of being disorderly.—**Disorderly**, dis-or′dėr-li, *a.* Being without proper order; marked by disorder; confused; immethodical; irregular; tumultuous; unruly; violating law and good order.—*adv.*† In a disorderly manner.

Disorganize, dis-or′ga-nīz, *v.t.* To disturb or destroy organic structure or connected system in; to throw out of regular system; to throw into confusion or disorder (a government, society, &c.).—**Disorganization**, dis-or′ga-ni-zā″shon, *n.* The act of disorganizing; the state of being disorganized.—**Disorganizer**, dis-or′ga-nī-zėr, *n.* One who disorganizes.

Disown, dis-ōn′, *v.t.* To refuse to acknowledge as belonging to one's self; to refuse to own; to deny; to repudiate (a child, a written work).

Disparage, dis-par′āj, *v.t.*—*disparaged*, *disparaging*. [O.Fr. *desparager*, to offer to a woman, or impose on her as husband, a man unfit or unworthy; to impose unworthy conditions—prefix *des* for *dis*, and *parage*, equality, from L. par, equal, whence also *peer*, *pair*.] To dishonour by a comparison with something of less value or excellence; to treat with detraction or in a depreciatory manner; to undervalue; to decry; to vilify; to lower in estimation.—**Disparagement**, dis-par′āj-ment, *n.* The act of disparaging; the act of undervaluing or depreciating; detraction; what lowers in value or esteem; disgrace; dishonour.—**Disparager**, dis-par′ā-jėr, *n.* One who disparages.—**Disparagingly**, dis-par′ā-jing-li, *adv.* In a manner to disparage.

Disparate, dis′pa-rāt, *a.* [L. *disparatus*, pp. of *disparo*, to part, separate—*dis*, asunder, and *paro*, to prepare.] Unequal; unlike; dissimilar.—*n.* One of two or more things so unequal or unlike that they cannot be compared with each other.

Disparity, dis-par′i-ti, *n.* [Fr. *disparité*, from L. *dispar*, unequal—*dis*, and *par*, equal. DISPARAGE.] Inequality; difference in degree, in age, rank, condition, or excellence; dissimilitude; unlikeness.

Dispart, dis-pärt′, *v.t.* To divide into parts; to separate, sever, burst, rend.—*v.i.* To separate; to open; to cleave.—*n.* (dis′pärt). The difference between the semi-diameter of the base ring at the breech of a gun, and that of the ring at the swell of the muzzle.

Dispassionate, dis-pash′on-āt, *a.* Free from passion; calm; composed; unmoved by feelings; not dictated by passion; not proceeding from temper or bias: impartial.—**Dispassionately**, dis-pash′on-āt-li, *adv.* Without passion; calmly; coolly.—**Dispassioned**, dis-pash′ond, *a.* Free from passion.

Dispatch, dis-pach′. DESPATCH.

Dispauper, dis-pa̤′pėr, *v.t.* To deprive of the claim of a pauper to public support.—**Dispauperize**, dis-pa̤′pėr-īz, *v.t.* To free from the state of pauperism; to free from paupers.

Dispeace, dis-pēs′, *n.* Want of peace or quiet; dissension.

Dispel, dis-pel′, *v.t.*—*dispelled*, *dispelling*. [L. *dispello*—*dis*, asunder, and *pello*, to drive, as in *compel*, *repel*, &c.] To scatter by force; to disperse; to dissipate; to drive away (clouds, doubts, fears, &c.).—*v.i.* To be dispersed; to disappear.—**Dispeller**, dis-pel′ėr, *n.* One who or that which dispels.

Dispense, dis-pens′, *v.t.*—*dispensed*, *dispensing*. [L. *dispenso*, to weigh out or pay, to manage, to act as steward—*dis*, distrib., and *penso*, freq. of *pendo*, to weigh, whence *pension*, *poise*, *expend*, *spend*.] To deal or divide out in parts or portions; to distribute; to administer; to apply, as laws to particular cases; to grant dispensation to; to relieve, excuse, or set free from an obligation.—*v.i.* To bargain for, grant, or receive a dispensation; to compound.—*To dispense with*, to permit the neglect or omission of, as a ceremony, an oath, and the like; to give up or do without, as services, attendance, articles of dress, &c.—**Dispenser**, dis-pen′sėr, *n.* One who or that which dispenses or distributes; one who administers.—**Dispensing**, dis-pen′sing, *a.* Granting dispensation; granting licence to omit what is required by law, or to do what the law forbids; dealing out or distributing.—**Dispensable**, dis-pen′sa-bl, *a.* Capable of being dispensed or administered; capable of being spared or dispensed with.—**Dispensableness**, dis-pen′sa-bl-nes, *n.* The capability of being dispensed with.—**Dispensary**, dis-pen′sa-ri, *n.* A shop in which medicines are compounded and sold; a house in which medicines are dispensed to the poor, and medical advice given gratis.—**Dispensation**, dis-pen-sā′shon, *n.* The act of dispensing or dealing out; the distribution of good and evil in the divine government; system established by God settling the relations of man towards him as regards religion and morality (the Mosaic *dispensation*); the granting of a licence, or the licence itself, to do what is forbidden by laws or canons, or to omit something which is commanded.—**Dispensative**, dis-pen′sa-tiv, *a.* Granting dispensation.—**Dispensatively, Dispensatorily**, dis-pen′sa-tiv-li, dis-pen′sa-to-ri-li, *adv.* By dispensation.—**Dispensator**, dis-pen′sā-tėr, *n.* [L.] A dispenser.—**Dispensatory**, dis-pen′sa-to-ri, *a.* Having power to grant dispensations.—*n.* A book containing the method of preparing the various kinds of medicines used in pharmacy; a pharmacopœia.

Dispeople, dis-pē′pl, *v.t.* To depopulate; to empty of inhabitants.—**Dispeopler**, dis-pē′plėr, *n.* One who or that which dispeoples.

Dispermous, dī-spėr′mus, *a.* [Gr. *di*, double, and *sperma*, seed.] *Bot.* two-seeded; containing two seeds only.

Disperse, dis-pėrs′, *v.t.*—*dispersed*, *dispersing*. [Fr. *disperser*, L. *dispersus*, from *dispergo*—*di* for *dis*, distrib., and *spargo*, to scatter, whence also *sparse*. To scatter; to cause to separate and go far apart; to dissipate; to cause to vanish. ∴ *Dissipate* is said of things that vanish or are not afterwards collected: *disperse* and *scatter* are applied to things which do not necessarily vanish, and which may again be brought together.—*v.i.* To scatter; to separate or move apart; to break up; to vanish, as fog or vapours.—**Dispersed**, dis-pėrst′, *p.* and *a.* Scattered.—**Dispersedly**, dis-pėr′sed-li, *adv.* In a dispersed manner; separately.—**Dispersedness**, dis-pėr′sed-nes, *n.* The state of being dispersed or scattered.—**Disperser**, dis-pėr′sėr, *n.* One who disperses.—**Dispersion, Dispersal**, dis-pėr′shon, dis-pėr′sal, *n.* The act of dispersing or scattering; the state of being scattered or separated into remote parts; *optics*, the separation of the different coloured rays of a beam of light by means of a prism, prisms of different materials causing greater or less dispersion.—**Dispersive**, dis-pėr′siv, *a.* Tending to scatter or dissipate.

Dispirit, dis-pir′it, *v.t.* To depress the spirits of; to deprive of courage; to discourage; to dishearten; to deject; to cast down.—**Dispirited**, dis-pir′i-ted, *p.* and *a.* Discouraged; depressed in spirits; spiritless; tame.—**Dispiritedly**, dis-pir′i-ted-li, *adv.* Dejectedly.—**Dispiritedness**, dis-pir′i-ted-nes, *n.* Want of courage; depression of spirits.—**Dispiritment**, dis-pir′it-ment, *n.* The act of dispiriting.

Displace, dis-plās′, *v.t.*—*displaced*, *displacing*. To put out of the usual or proper place; to remove from its place; to remove from any state, condition, office, or dignity.—**Displaceable**, dis-plā′sa-bl, *a.* Capable of being displaced or removed.—**Displacement**, dis-plās′ment, *n.* The act of displacing; removal; the quantity of water displaced by a body floating at rest, as a ship.

Displant, dis-plant′, *v.t.* To pluck up what is planted; to drive away or remove from residence; to strip of what is planted or settled.—**Displantation**, dis-plan-tā′shon, *n.* The act of displanting.

Display, dis-plā′, *v.t.* [O.Fr. *desployer*, Fr. *déployer*—*des*, equal to L. *dis*, priv., and *ployer*, same as *plier*, from L. *plicare*, to fold, as in *deploy*, *employ*.] To spread before the view; to set in view ostentatiously; to show; to exhibit to the eyes or to the mind; to make manifest.—*v.i.* To make a show or display.—*n.* An unfolding; an exhibition of anything to the view; ostentatious show; exhibition; parade.—**Displayer**, dis-plā′ėr, *n.* One who or that which displays.

Displease, dis-plēz′, *v.t.*—*displeased*, *displeasing*. To offend somewhat; to dissatisfy; to annoy; to make angry, usually in a slight degree; to excite aversion in; to be disagreeable to (the taste, the senses).—**Displeased**, dis-plēzd′, *p.* and *a.* Not well-pleased; offended; annoyed (to be *displeased with* a person).—**Displeasedly**, dis-plē′zed-li, *adv.* In a displeased manner.—**Displeasedness**, dis-plē′zed-nes, *n.* Displeasure; uneasiness.—**Displeaser**, dis-plē′zėr, *n.* One who displeases.—**Displeasing**, dis-plē′zing, *a.* Offensive to the mind or any of the senses; disagreeable.—**Displeasingness**, dis-plē′zing-nes, *n.*—**Displeasure**, dis-plezh′ūr, *n.* The feeling of one who is displeased; dissatisfaction; anger; vexation; annoyance; that which displeases; offence.

Displode,† dis-plōd′, *v.t.* and *i.*—*disploded*, *disploding*. [L. *displodo*—*dis*, asunder, and *plaudo*, to clap, beat.] To burst with a loud noise; to explode. (*Mil.*)

Dispondee, dī-spon′dē, *n.* [Gr. *di*, twice, and *spondee*.] *Pros.* a double spondee, consisting of four long syllables.

Dispone, dis-pōn′, *v.t.*—*disponed*, *disponing*. [L. *dispono*, to dispose—*dis*, distrib., and *pono*, to place.] *Scots law*, to make over or convey (property) to another in a legal form.—**Disponee**, dis-pō-nē′, *n.* *Scots law*, one to whom anything is disponed.—**Disponer**, dis-pō′nėr, *n.* *Scots law*, one who dispones.

Disport, dis-pōrt′, *n.* [O.Fr. *desport*, Fr. *déport*, properly diversion resorted to in order to divert the thoughts—prefix *dis*, and L. *porto*, to carry (whence *export*, &c.). *Sport* is an abbrev. of *disport*.] Play; sport; pastime.—*v.i.* To play; to sport.—**Disportment**, dis-pōrt′ment, *n.* Act of disporting; play.

Dispose, dis-pōz′, *v.t.*—*disposed*, *disposing*. [Fr. *disposer*, to dispose, arrange—prefix *dis*, and *poser*, to place (E. *pose*). COMPOSE.] To arrange, place out, or distribute; to set in a particular order; to apply to a particular end or purpose; to set the mind of in a particular frame; to incline.—*v.i.* To regulate, determine, or settle; to bargain or make terms (*Shak.*).—*To dispose of*, to part with; to alienate; to sell; to put into another's hand or power; to bestow; to do with, make use of, use, or employ (one's self, one's time, &c.); to put away or get rid of.—**Disposable**, dis-pō′za-bl, *a.* Subject to disposal; free to be used or employed as occasion may require.—**Disposal**, dis-pō′zal, *n.* The act of disposing; a setting or arranging; power of ordering, arranging, or distributing; government; management; power or right of bestowing; the act of selling or parting with; alienation.—**Disposed**, dis-pōzd′, *p.* and *a.* Inclined; minded.—**Disposer**, dis-pō′zėr, *n.* One who or that which disposes.—**Disposition**, dis-pō-zish′on, *n.* [L. *dispositio*, arrangement.] The act of disposing or state of being disposed; manner in which things or the parts of a complex body are placed or arranged; order; method; distribution; arrangement; natural fitness or tendency; temper or natural constitution of the mind; inclination; propensity; *Scots law*, disposal or settlement of property or effects.—**Dispositional**, dis-pō-zish′on-al, *a.* Pertaining to disposition.—**Disposure**,† dis-pō′zhur, *n.* Disposal; management; distribution; allotment.

Dispossess, dis-poz-zes′, *v.t.* To put out of possession; to deprive of the occupancy or ownership; to dislodge: with *of* before the thing taken away.—**Dispossession**, dis-poz-zesh′on, *n.* The act of dispossessing. —**Dispossesser**, dis-poz-zes′ėr, *n.* One who dispossesses.

Dispraise, dis-prāz′, *n.* The opposite of praise, blame; censure.—*v.t. dispraised, dispraising.* To blame; to censure.—**Dispraiser**, dis-prā′zėr, *n.* One who dispraises.

Disprejudice, dis-prej′ū-dis, *v.t.* To free from prejudice.

Disproof, dis-pröf′, *n.* Under DISPROVE.

Disproportion, dis-prō-pōr′shon, *n.* Want of proportion of one thing to another, or between the parts of a thing; want of symmetry; want of proper quantity; according to rules prescribed; want of suitableness or adequacy; disparity; inequality.—*v.t.* To violate due proportion or symmetry in. — **Disproportionable**, **Disproportional**, **Disproportionate**, dis-prō-pōr′shon-a-bl, dis-prō-pōr′shon-al, dis-prō-pōr′shon-āt, *a.* Not having due proportion to something else; not having proportion or symmetry of parts; unequal; inadequate. —**Disproportionableness**, **Disproportionalness**, **Disproportionateness**, dis-prō-pōr′shon-a-bl-nes, dis-prō-pōr′shon-al-nes, dis-prō-pōr′shon-āt-nes, *n.* Want of proportion or symmetry; unsuitableness in form, bulk, or value to something else. — **Disproportionably**, **Disproportionally**, **Disproportionately**, dis-prō-pōr′shon-ab-li, dis-prō-pōr′shon-al-li, dis-prō-pōr′shon-āt-li, *adv.* With want of proportion or symmetry; unsuitably with respect to form, quantity, or value; inadequately; unequally.—**Disproportionality**, dis-prō-pōr′shon-al″i-ti, *n.* The state of being disproportional.

Disprove, dis-pröv′, *v.t.—disproved, disproving.* To prove to be false or erroneous; to confute; to refute.—**Disprovable**, dis-prö′va-bl, *a.* Capable of being disproved or refuted.—**Disproval**, dis-prö′val, *n.* Act of disproving; disproof.—**Disprover**, dis-prö′vėr, *n.* One that disproves or confutes. —**Disproof**, dis-pröf′, *n.* Confutation; refutation; a proving to be false or erroneous.

Dispute, dis-pūt′, *v.i.—disputed, disputing.* [L. *disputo*, to compute, to weigh, examine, investigate, discuss—*dis*, asunder, apart, and *puto*, to clean, prune, clear up, reckon. COMPUTE.] To contend in argument; to reason or argue in opposition; to debate; to altercate; to wrangle; to contend in opposition to a competitor.—*v.t.* To attempt to disprove by arguments or statements; to attempt to overthrow by reasoning; to controvert (an assertion, a claim, &c.); to call in question; to strive to maintain; to contest (to *dispute* every inch of ground). —*n.* Strife or contest in words or by arguments; a difference of opinion vigorously maintained; controversy in words; a wordy war; contention; strife; contest.—**Disputer**, dis-pū′tėr, *n.* One who disputes or who is given to disputes.—**Disputable**, dis-pū′ta-bl, *a.* Capable of being disputed; liable to be called in question, controverted, or contested; controvertible; disputatious (*Shak.*).—**Disputableness**, dis-pū′ta-bl-nes, *n.* State of being disputable.—**Disputant**, dis′pū-tant, *n.* One who disputes; one who argues in opposition to another; a reasoner in opposition.—*a.* Disputing; engaged in controversy.—**Disputation**, dis-pū-tā′shon, *n.* [L. *disputatio.*] The act of disputing; controversy; verbal contest respecting the truth of some fact, opinion, proposition, or argument. — **Disputatious**, **Disputative**, dis-pū-tā′shus, dis-pū′ta-tiv, *a.* Inclined to dispute; fond of arguing; characterized by disputes.—**Disputatiously**, dis-pū-tā′shus-li, *adv.* In a disputatious manner.—**Disputatiousness**, dis-pū-tā′shus-nes, *n.*

Disqualify, dis-kwol′i-fī, *v.t.—disqualified, disqualifying.* To make unfit; to deprive of natural power, or the qualities or properties necessary for any purpose (weakness *disqualifies* a person *for* labour); to deprive of legal capacity, power, or right; to incapacitate.—**Disqualification**, dis-kwol′i-fi-kā″shon, *n.* The act of disqualifying; the state of being disqualified; disability; legal disability or incapacity; that which disqualifies or incapacitates.

Disquiet, dis-kwī′et, *n.* Want of quiet; uneasiness; anxiety.—*v.t.* To deprive of peace, rest, or tranquillity; to make uneasy or restless; to disturb, harass, fret, or vex. —*a.* Unquiet; restless. (*Shak.*) — **Disquieter**, dis-kwī′e-tėr, *n.* One who or that which disquiets.—**Disquietful**, dis-kwī′et-fụl, *a.* Producing inquietude.—**Disquieting**, **Disquietive**, dis-kwī′e-ting, dis-kwī′e-tiv, *a.* Tending to disquiet; disturbing the mind.—**Disquietly**,† dis-kwī′et-li, *adv.* Unquietly; in a disquieting manner. — **Disquietude**, **Disquietness**, dis-kwī′e-tūd, dis-kwī′et-nes, *n.* Want of peace or tranquillity; uneasiness; disquiet.

Disquisition, dis-kwi-zish′on, *n.* [L. *disquisitio*, from *disquiro, disquisitum*, to investigate—*dis*, distrib., and *quæro, quæsitum*, to ask, whence *query, question, inquire*, &c.] A formal or systematic inquiry into any subject, by discussion of the facts and circumstances bearing on it; an argumentative inquiry; a formal discussion or treatise on any matter; dissertation; essay. —**Disquisitive**, dis-kwiz′i-tiv, *a.* Relating to disquisition; fond of discussion or investigation. — **Disquisitional**, **Disquisitionary**, **Disquisitory**, dis-kwi-zish′on-al, dis-kwi-zish′on-a-ri, dis-kwiz′i-to-ri, *a.* Pertaining to disquisition; partaking of the nature of a disquisition.

Disregard, dis-rē-gärd′, *n.* Want of regard, notice, or attention; neglect; slight.—*v.t.* To omit to take notice of; to neglect to observe; to pay no heed to; to treat as unworthy of regard or notice.—**Disregarder**, dis-rē-gär′dėr, *n.* One who disregards. —**Disregardful**, dis-rē-gärd′fụl, *a.* Neglectful; heedless. — **Disregardfully**, dis-rē-gärd′fụl-li, *adv.* Negligently; heedlessly.

Disrelish, dis-rel′ish, *n.* Distaste; dislike of the palate; some degree of disgust; dislike of the mind; aversion; antipathy.—*v.t.* To dislike the taste of; to feel some disgust at.

Disrepair, dis-rē-pār′, *n.* A state of being not in repair or good condition; state of requiring to be repaired.

Disreputable, dis-rep′ū-ta-bl, *a.* Not reputable; disgracing reputation; dishonourable; discreditable; low; mean.—**Disreputability**, dis-rep′ū-ta-bil″i-ti, *n.* The state of being disreputable.—**Disreputably**, dis-rep′ū-ta-bli, *adv.* In a disreputable manner.—**Disrepute**, dis-rē-pūt′, *n.* Loss or want of reputation; disesteem; discredit; dishonour.

Disrespect, dis-rē-spekt′, *n.* Want of respect or reverence; incivility, irreverence, or rudeness; a slight or neglect.—*v.t.* To have no respect or esteem for; to show disrespect to.—**Disrespectability**, dis-rē-spek′ta-bil″i-ti, *n.* The state or quality of being disrespectable.—**Disrespectable**, dis-rē-spek′ta-bl, *a.* Not respectable; unworthy of respect.—**Disrespectful**, dis-rē-spekt′fụl, *a.* Wanting in respect; manifesting disrespect; irreverent; uncivil. — **Disrespectfully**, dis-rē-spekt′fụl-li, *adv.* In a disrespectful manner.—**Disrespectfulness**, dis-rē-spekt′fụl-nes, *n.*

Disrobe, dis-rōb′, *v.t.—disrobed, disrobing.* To divest of a robe; to divest of garments; to undress; to strip of covering; to uncover.

Disroot, dis-röt′, *v.t.* To tear up the roots of, or by the roots; to uproot.

Disrupt,† dis-rupt′, *v.t.* [L. *disruptus*, pp. of *disrumpo* (*dirumpo*), to break or burst asunder—*dis*, asunder, and *rumpo*, to burst, whence *rupture*, &c.] To tear or rive away; to rend; to sever; to break asunder.—**Disruption**, dis-rup′shon, *n.* [L. *disruptio.*] The act of rending asunder; the act of bursting and separating; breach; rent; break-up; the rupture which took place in the Established Church of Scotland in 1843, resulting in the foundation of the Free Church.—**Disruptive**, dis-rup′tiv, *a.* Causing, or tending to cause, disruption; produced by or following on disruption.—**Disrupture**, dis-rup′tūr, *n.* Disruption; a rending asunder.

Diss, dis, *n.* A grass growing wild in Algeria, now beginning to be used in the manufacture of paper.

Dissatisfaction, dis-sat′is-fak″shon, *n.* The feeling caused by want of satisfaction; discontent; uneasiness proceeding from the want of gratification, or from disappointed wishes and expectations.—**Dissatisfactoriness**, dis-sat′is-fak″to-ri-nes, *n.* The state of being dissatisfactory.—**Dissatisfactory**, dis-sat′is-fak″to-ri, *a.* Causing dissatisfaction; giving discontent; mortifying; displeasing.—**Dissatisfied**, dis-sat′is-fīd, *p.* and *a.* Not satisfied; not pleased; discontented. — **Dissatisfy**, dis-sat′is-fī, *v.t.—dissatisfied, dissatisfying.* To fail to satisfy; to render discontented; to displease; to excite displeasure in by frustrating wishes or expectations.

Dissect, dis-sekt′, *v.t.* [L. *disseco, dissectum—dis*, asunder, and *seco, sectum*, to cut, whence *section, segment, intersect*, &c.] To divide (an animal body) with a cutting instrument, by separating the joints; to cut up (an animal or vegetable) for the purpose of examining the structure and character of the several parts, or to observe morbid affections; to anatomize; *fig.* to analyse for the purpose of criticism; to describe with minute accuracy.—**Dissectible**, dis-sek′ti-bl, *a.* Capable of being dissected.—**Dissecting**, dis-sek′ting, *a.* Used in dissecting.—**Dissection**, dis-sek′shon, *n.* The act or art of dissecting or anatomizing.—**Dissector**, dis-sek′tėr, *n.* One who dissects; an anatomist.

Disseize, dis-sēz′, *v.t.—disseized, disseizing.* [Prefix *dis*, neg., and *seize*; Fr. *dessaisir*, to dispossess.] *Law*, to dispossess wrongfully; to deprive of actual seizin or possession: with *of* before the thing. — **Disseizee**, dis-sē-zē′, *n.* One who is disseized. —**Disseizin**, dis-sē′zin, *n.* The act of disseizing.—**Disseizor**, dis-sē-zor′, *n.* One who dispossesses another.

Dissemble, dis-sem′bl, *v.t.—dissembled, dissembling.* [O.Fr. *dissembler* (Fr. *dissimuler*), from L. *dissimulo—dis*, and *simulo*, to make like, to simulate, from *similis*, like. ASSEMBLE, SIMILAR. *Dissimulate* is the same word.] To hide under an assumed manner; to conceal or disguise by a false outward show; to hide by false pretences (to *dissemble* love, hate, opinions, &c.).—*v.i.* To try to appear other than reality; to put on an assumed manner or outward show; to conceal the real fact, motives, intention, or sentiments under some pretence. — **Dissembler**, dis-sem′blėr, *n.* One who dissembles; one who conceals his real thoughts or feelings.

Disseminate, dis-sem′i-nāt, *v.t.—disseminated, disseminating.* [L. *dissemino, disseminatum*, to scatter seed—*dis*, and *semen*, seed.] To spread by diffusion or dispersion; to diffuse; to spread abroad among people; to cause to reach as many persons as possible (religious doctrines, knowledge, &c.). — **Dissemination**, dis-sem′i-nā″shon, *n.* The act of disseminating.—**Disseminative**, dis-sem′i-nā-tiv, *a.* Tending to disseminate or become disseminated.—**Disseminator**, dis-sem′i-nā-tėr, *n.* One who disseminates.

Dissent, dis-sent′, *v.i.* [L. *dissentio*, to think otherwise, to dissent—*dis*, asunder, and *sentio*, to perceive, as in *consent, resent*, &c. SENSE.] To disagree in opinion; to differ; to think in a different or contrary manner: with *from*; *eccles.* to differ from an established church in regard to doctrines, rites, or government.—*n.* Difference of opinion; disagreement; declaration of disagreement in opinion; *eccles.* separation from an established church. — **Dissension**, dis-sen′shon, *n.* [L. *dissensio.*] Disagreement in opinion, usually a disagreement producing warm debates or angry words; strife; discord; quarrel; breach of friendship and union. — **Dissensious, Dissentious**, dis-sen'shus, *a.* Disposed to dissension or discord.—**Dissentaneous**, dis-sen-tā'nē-us, *a.* Disagreeing; inconsistent.—**Dissentation**,† dis-sen-tā'shon, *n.* Act of dissenting.—**Dissenter**, dis-sen'tėr, *n.* One who dissents; one who differs in opinion, or one who declares his disagreement; *eccles.* one who separates from the service and worship of any established church.—**Dissenterism**, dis-sen'tėr-izm, *n.* The spirit or the principles of dissent or dissenters.—**Dissentient**, dis-sen'shi-ent, *a.* Disagreeing; declaring dissent; voting differently. —*n.* One who disagrees and declares his dissent. —**Dissenting**, dis-sen'ting, *p.* and *a.* Disagreeing in opinion; having the character of dissent; belonging to or connected with a body of dissenters.

Dissepiment, dis-sep'i-ment, *n.* [L. *dissepimentum*—*dis*, asunder, and *sepio*, to inclose, from *sepes*, a hedge.] A kind of small partition in certain hollow parts of animals and plants; one of the partitions in the ovary of some plants formed by the sides of cohering carpels.

Dissertation, dis-sėr-tā'shon, *n.* [L. *dissertatio*, from *disserto*, a freq. of *dissero*, to argue, discuss—*dis*, asunder, and *sero*, to join, from root of *series*.] A formal discourse, intended to illustrate or elucidate a subject; a written essay, treatise, or disquisition.—**Dissertational**, dis-sėr-tā'shon-al, *a.* Relating to dissertations; disquisitional.—**Dissertationist, Dissertator**, dis-sėr-tā'shon-ist, dis'sėr-tā-tėr, *n.* One who writes dissertations.

Disserve, dis-sėrv', *v.t.* To do the reverse of a service to; to do an injury or ill turn to. —**Disservice**, *n.* An ill turn or injury; something done to one's injury.—**Disserviceable**, dis-sėr'vi-sa-bl, *a.* Injurious.

Dissever, dis-sev'ėr, *v.t.* To part in two; to divide asunder; to separate; to disunite; —**Disseverance, Disseverment**, dis-sev'ėr-ans, di-sev'ėr-ment, *n.* The act of dissevering; separation.

Dissident, dis'si-dent, *a.* [L. *dissidens, dissidentis*, ppr. of *dissideo*, to disagree—*dis*, asunder, and *sedeo*, to sit; seen also in *supersede, sedentary, session*, &c.] Dissenting; specifically, dissenting from an established church.—*n.* One who dissents from others; a dissenter; one who separates from an established religion. — **Dissidence**, dis'si-dens, *n.* Disagreement; dissent; nonconformity.

Dissilience, dis-sil'i-ens, *n.* [L. *dissilio*, to leap asunder—*dis*, and *salio*, to leap, whence *salient*.] The act of leaping or starting asunder. — **Dissilient**, dis-sil'i-ent, *a.* Starting asunder; bursting and opening with an elastic force, as the dry pod or capsule of a plant.

Dissimilar, dis-sim'i-lėr, *a.* Not similar; unlike, either in nature, properties, or external form.—**Dissimilarity**, dis-sim'i-lar"i-ti, *n.* Want of similarity; unlikeness; want of resemblance. — **Dissimilarly**, dis-sim'i-lėr-li, *adv.* In a dissimilar manner. — **Dissimilation**, dis-sim'i-lā-shon, *n.* The act or process of rendering dissimilar or different; *philol.* the change of a sound to another and a different sound when otherwise two similar sounds would come together or very close to each other.—**Dissimilitude**, dis-si-mil'i-tūd, *n.* [L. *dissimilitudo*.] Unlikeness; want of resemblance.

Dissimulation, dis-sim'ū-lā"shon, *n.* [L. *dissimulatio*, from *dissimulo, dissimulatum*, to feign that a thing is not what it is—*dis*, and *simulo*, to make like, from *similis*, like. DISSEMBLE.] The act or practice of dissembling, usually from a mean or unworthy motive; a hiding under a false appearance; false pretension; hypocrisy. — **Dissimulate**, dis-sim'ū-lāt, *v.i.* To dissemble; to make pretence; to feign.—**Dissimulator**, dis-sim'ū-lā"tėr, *n.* One who dissimulates or dissembles.

Dissipate, dis'si-pāt, *v.t.*—*dissipated, dissipating*. [L. *dissipo, dissipatum* — *dis*, asunder, and the rare *sipo, supo*, to throw, allied probably to E. verb to *sweep*.] To scatter, to disperse, to drive away (mist, care, energy, &c.); to scatter in wasteful extravagance; to waste. ∴ Syn. under DISPERSE.—*v.i.* To scatter, disperse, separate into parts and disappear; to vanish; to be wasteful or dissolute in the pursuit of pleasure. — **Dissipable**, dis'si-pa-bl, *a.* Liable to be dissipated; capable of being scattered or dispersed.—**Dissipated**, dis'si-pā-ted, *a.* Given to extravagance in the expenditure of property; devoted to pleasure and vice; dissolute.—**Dissipation**, dis-si-pā'shon, *n.* The act of dissipating; the insensible loss of the minute particles of a body, which fly off, so that the body is diminished or may altogether disappear; indulgence in dissolute and irregular courses; a reckless and vicious pursuit of pleasure; dissolute conduct.—*Dissipation of energy*, the running down of energy from higher to lower or less available forms, a process constantly going on in nature, and tending to the ultimate production of an earth uninhabitable by man as at present constituted.

Dissociate, dis-sō'shi-āt, *v.t.*—*dissociated, dissociating*. [L. *dissocio, dissociatum*—*dis*, and *socio*, to unite, from *socius*, a companion. SOCIAL.] To separate or take apart; to disunite; to part.—**Dissociability**,† dis-sō'shi-a-bil"i-ti, *n.* Want of sociability.—**Dissociable**,† dis-sō'shi-a-bl, *a.* Not well associated, united, or assorted; not sociable; incongruous; not reconcilable. — **Dissocial**, dis-sō'shal, *a.* Disinclined to or unsuitable for society; not social.—**Dissocialize**, dis-sō'sha-līz, *v.t.* To make unsocial.—**Dissociation**, dis-sō'shi-ā"shon, *n.* The act of dissociating; a state of separation; disunion; *chem.* the decomposition of a compound substance into its primary elements.—**Dissociative**, dis-sō'shi-ā-tiv, *a.* Tending to dissociate; *chem.* resolving or reducing a compound to its primary elements.

Dissoluble, dis'so-lū-bl, *a.* [L. *dissolubilis*. DISSOLVE.] Capable of being dissolved or melted; having its parts separable, as by heat or moisture; susceptible of decomposition or decay. — **Dissolubility, Dissolubleness**, dis'so-lū-bil"i-ti, dis'so-lū-bl-nes, *n.* The state or quality of being dissoluble.

Dissolute, dis'sō-lūt, *a.* [L. *dissolutus*, pp. of *dissolvo*. DISSOLVE.] Loose in behaviour and morals; given to vice or profligacy; debauched; devoted to or occupied in dissipation.—**Dissolutely**, dis'sō-lūt-li, *adv.* In a dissolute manner; profligately; in dissipation or debauchery.—**Dissoluteness**, dis'sō-lūt-nes, *n.* The state or character of being dissolute; looseness of manners and morals; vicious indulgence in pleasure, as in intemperance and debauchery; dissipation.—**Dissolution**, dis-sō-lū'shon, *n.* [L. *dissolutio*, a breaking up, a loosening, from *dissolvo*.] The act of dissolving, liquefying, or changing from a solid to a fluid state by heat; liquefaction; the reduction of a body into its smallest parts, or into very minute parts; the separation of the parts of a body by natural decomposition; decomposition; death; the separation of the soul and body; the separation of the parts which compose a connected system or body; the breaking up of an assembly, or the putting an end to its existence.

Dissolve, diz-zolv', *v.t.*—*dissolved, dissolving*. [L. *dissolvo*, to break up, to separate —*dis*, asunder, and *solvo, solutum*, to loose, to free, whence also *solve, soluble, solution, absolve*, &c.] To melt; to liquefy; to convert from a solid or fixed state to a fluid state, by means of heat or moisture; to disunite, break up, separate, or loosen; to destroy any connected system or body (parliament, a government); to break or make no longer binding (an alliance, &c.); to solve, explain, or resolve (doubts); to destroy the power of or render ineffectual (a spell or enchantment); to destroy or consume (O.T.). —*v.i.* To melt; to be converted from a solid to a fluid state; to fall asunder; to crumble; to waste away; to be decomposed; to be dismissed; to separate; to break up.—*Dissolving views*, views painted on glass slides, which, by a particular arrangement and manipulation of two magic lanterns, can be made to appear and vanish at pleasure, others replacing them.—**Dissolvability, Dissolvableness**, diz-zol'va-bil"i-ti, diz-zol'va-bl-nes, *n.* Capability of being dissolved; solubility.—**Dissolvable**, diz-zol'va-bl, *a.* Capable of being dissolved or melted; capable of being converted into a fluid.—**Dissolvent**, diz-zol'vent, *a.* Having power to melt or dissolve.—*n.* Anything that dissolves; a substance that has the power of converting a solid substance into a fluid, or of separating its parts so that they mix with a liquid.—**Dissolver**, diz-zol'vėr, *n.* One who or that which dissolves.

Dissonance, dis'sō-nans, *n.* [Fr. *dissonance*, L. *dissonantia*, discordance—*dis*, asunder, and *sono*, to sound. SOUND.] Discord; a mixture or union of harsh, inharmonious sounds; incongruity; inconsistency.—**Dissonant**, dis'sō-nant, *a.* Discordant; harsh; jarring; unharmonious; unpleasant to the ear; disagreeing; incongruous.

Disspirit, *v.t.* Same as *Dispirit*.

Dissuade, dis-swād', *v.t.*—*dissuaded, dissuading*. [L. *dissuadeo*, to advise against —*dis*, priv., and *suadeo*, to advise.] To advise or exhort against; to attempt to draw or divert from a measure by reasons or offering motives; to divert by persuasion; to turn from a purpose by argument; to render averse: the opposite of *persuade*. —**Dissuader**, dis-swā'dėr, *n.* One who dissuades.—**Dissuasion**, dis-swā'zhon, *n.* Advice or exhortation in opposition to something; dehortation: the opposite of *persuasion*.—**Dissuasive**, dis-swā'siv, *a.* Tending to dissuade. — *n.* Reason, argument, or counsel, employed to deter one from a measure or purpose; that which tends to dissuade.—**Dissuasively**, dis-swā'siv-li, *adv.* In a dissuasive manner.—**Dissuasory**, dis-swā'so-ri, *n.* A dissuasion.—*a.*† Dissuasive.

Dissyllable, dis'sil-la-bl, *n.* [Gr. *dis*, twice, and *syllabē*, a syllable.] A word consisting of two syllables only. — **Dissyllabic**, dis-sil-lab'ik, *a.* Consisting of two syllables only. — **Dissyllabification**, dis-sil-lab'i-fi-kā"shon, *n.* Act of forming into two syllables.—**Dissyllabify, Dissyllabize**, dis-sil-lab'i-fī, dis'sil-la-bīz, *v.t.* To form into or express in two syllables.

Distaff, dis'taf, *n.* [A.Sax. *distæf*, that is, *dis-* or *dise-staff*—*dis-*=O.E. *dise*, to put the flax on the distaff; allied to L.G. *diesse*, the flax on the distaff; G. *dusse*, tow, oakum.] The staff to which a bunch of flax or tow is tied, and from which the thread is drawn to be spun by the spindle.—**Distaff side**, *n.* The female side of relationship, opposed to *spear* or male side.

Distain, dis-tān', *v.t.* [O.Fr. *desteindre*, Fr. *déteindre*, to cause to lose colour—*des* for L. *dis*, priv., and *teindre*, from L. *tingere*, to stain.] To stain; to discolour; to sully, defile, tarnish.

Distal, dis'tal, *a.* [From *distant*: formed on the type of *central*.] Applied to the end of a bone, limb, or organ in plants and animals farthest removed from the point of attachment or insertion; situated away from or at the extremity most distant from the centre. — **Distally**, dis'tal-li, *adv.* Towards the distal end; towards the extremity.

Distance, dis'tans, *n.* [Fr. *distance*, L. *distantia*, from *disto*, to stand apart—*dis*, apart, and *sto*, to stand. STATE, STATUE, &c.] An interval or space between two objects; the length of the shortest line which intervenes between things that are separate; remoteness of place; space of time, past or future; ideal space or separation, as between things that differ from each other; the remoteness or ceremonious avoidance of familiarity which respect requires; the remoteness or reserve which one assumes from being offended, from dislike, &c.; *mus.* the interval between two notes; *horse-racing*, a length of 240 yards from the winning-post, marked by a post.—

v.t.—*distanced, distancing.* To place at a distance or remote; to leave at a great distance; behind; to outdo or excel greatly.—**Distance-signal**, *n.* *Rail.* the most distant of the series of signals under the control of a signal-man.—**Distant**, dis'-tant, *a.* [L. *distans*, standing apart, ppr. of *disto.*] Separate or apart, the intervening space being of any indefinite extent; remote in place; in time, past or future; in a line of succession or descent; in natural connection or consanguinity; in kind or nature, &c.; as if remote or far off; hence, slight; faint (a *distant* resemblance); characterized by haughtiness, coldness, indifference, or disrespect; reserved; shy.—**Distantly**, dis'tant-li, *adv.* Remotely; at a distance; with reserve.

Distaste, dis-tāst', *n.* Aversion of the taste; dislike of food or drink; disrelish; disinclination; a want of liking (a *distaste* for rural sports).—**Distasteful**, dis-tāst'-ful, *a.* Causing distaste; unpleasant to the taste or liking; disagreeable; slightly repulsive.—**Distastefully**, dis-tāst'ful-li, *adv.* In a distasteful manner.—**Distastefulness**, dis-tāst'ful-nes, *n.* The state or character of being distasteful.

Distemper, dis-tem'pėr, *n.* Any morbid state of an animal body or of any part of it; derangement of the animal economy; a disorder; malady; a disease of young dogs, commonly considered as a catarrhal disorder.—*v.t.* To derange the bodily functions of; to deprive of temper or moderation; to ruffle; to disturb; to make ill-humoured.—**Distempered**, dis-tem'pėrd, *p.* and *a.* Diseased in body or in mind; disordered; prejudiced or perverted; biassed.

Distemper, dis-tem'pėr, *n.* [It. *distemperare*, to dissolve or mix with liquid.] *Painting*, a preparation of opaque colour, ground with size and water; tempera; a kind of painting in which the pigments are mixed with size, and chiefly used for scene-painting and interior decoration.

Distend, dis-tend', *v.t.* [L. *distendo*—*dis*, asunder, and *tendo*, to tend, as in *extend*, *contend*. TENT.] To stretch or swell out by force acting from within; to dilate; to expand; to swell; to puff out (a bladder, the lungs).—*v.i.* To become inflated or distended; to swell.—**Distensibility**, dis-ten'si-bil"i-ti, *n.* The quality or capacity of being distensible.—**Distensible**, dis-ten'si-bl, *a.* Capable of being distended or dilated.—**Distention, Distension**, dis-ten'shon, *n.* [L. *distentio.*] The act of distending; the state of being distended; extent or space occupied by the thing distended.

Distich, dis'tik, *n.* [Gr. *distichon*—*di*, twice, and *stichos*, a row, a line, a verse.] A couplet; a couple of verses or poetic lines making complete sense.—**Distichous**, dis'ti-kus, *a.* Having two rows, or disposed in two rows, as the grains in an ear of barley.

Distill, Distil, dis-til', *v.i.*—*distilled, distilling.* [Fr. *distiller*, from L. *destillo*, to trickle down—*de*, down, and *stillo*, to drop, from *stilla*, a drop.] To drop; to fall in drops or in a small stream; to trickle; to use a still; to practise distillation.—*v.t.* To yield or give forth in drops or a small stream; to let fall in drops; to drop; to obtain or extract by distillation; to subject to the process of distillation.—**Distillable**, dis-til'a-bl, *a.* Capable of being distilled; fit for distillation.—**Distillate**, dis-til'āt, *n.* A fluid distilled, and found in the receiver of a distilling apparatus.—**Distillation**, dis-ti-lā'shon, *n.* The act of distilling or falling in drops; the volatilization and subsequent condensation of a liquid by means of an alembic, or still and refrigeratory, or of a retort and receiver; the operation of extracting spirit from a substance by evaporation and condensation.—**Distillatory**, dis-til'a-to-ri *a.* Belonging to distillation; used for distilling.—*n.* An apparatus used in distillation; a still.—**Distiller**, dis-til'ėr, *n.* One who distils; one whose occupation is to extract spirit by distillation.—**Distillery**, dis-til'ėr-i, *n.* The act or art of distilling; the building and works where distillation is carried on.

Distinct, dis-tingkt', *a.* [L. *distinctus*, pp. of *distinguo.* DISTINGUISH.] Separated or distinguished by some mark, note, or character; marked out; not the same in number or kind; different; having well-marked characteristics; standing clearly or boldly out; well-defined; obvious; plain; unmistakable.—**Distinction**, dis-tingk'shon, *n.* [L. *distinctio.*] The act of separating or distinguishing; that which distinguishes or marks as different; a note or mark of difference; distinguishing quality; eminence or superiority; elevation or honourable estimation; that which confers or marks eminence or superiority; a title or honour of some kind.—**Distinctive**, dis-tingk'-tiv, *a.* Marking or indicating distinction or difference.—**Distinctively**, dis-tingk'-tiv-li, *adv.* In a distinctive manner.—**Distinctiveness**, dis-tingk'tiv-nes, *n.* The state or quality of being distinctive; distinctive character.—**Distinctly**, dis-tingkt'li, *adv.* In a distinct manner; clearly; obviously; plainly; precisely.—**Distinctness**, dis-tingkt'nes, *n.* The quality or state of being distinct; clearness; precision.

Distinguish, dis-ting'gwish, *v.t.* [L. *distinguo*, to mark off, to distinguish—*di* for *dis*, asunder, and *stinguo*, to mark. STIGMA.] To mark or set apart as different or separate from others; to perceive or recognize the individuality of; to note as differing from something else by some mark or quality; to know or ascertain difference by the senses or the intellect; to classify or divide by any mark or quality which constitutes difference; to separate by definitions; to separate from others by some mark of honour or preference; to make eminent or known; to signalize.—*v.i.* To make a distinction; to find or show the difference.—**Distinguishable**, dis-ting'-gwish-a-bl, *a.* Capable of being distinguished or recognized; capable of being defined or classified; worthy of note or special regard.—**Distinguishableness**, dis-ting'gwish-a-bl-nes, *n.* State of being distinguishable.—**Distinguishably**, dis-ting'gwish-a-bli, *adv.* So as to be distinguished.—**Distinguished**, dis-ting'-gwisht, *p.* and *a.* Separated from others by superior or extraordinary qualities; eminent; extraordinary; transcendent; noted; famous; celebrated.—**Distinguisher**, dis-ting'gwish-ėr, *n.* One who or that which distinguishes.—**Distinguishing**, dis-ting'gwish-ing, *a.* Constituting difference or distinction from everything else; peculiar; characteristic.—**Distinguishingly**, dis-ting'gwish-ing-li, *adv.* In a distinguishing manner.—**Distinguishment**, dis-ting'-gwish-ment, *n.* Distinction; observation of difference.

Distort, dis-tort', *v.t.* [L. *distorqueo*, *distortum*—*dis*, asunder, and *torqueo*, to twist, as in *contort* (which see).] To twist out of natural or regular shape; to force or put out of the true bent or direction; to bias (the judgment); to wrest from the true meaning; to pervert.—**Distorted**, dis-tor'-ted, *p.* and *a.* Twisted out of natural or regular shape; shaped abnormally or awry.—**Distortion**, dis-tor'shon, *n.* The act of distorting; a twisting or writhing motion; an unnatural direction of parts from whatever cause, as a curved spine, a wry mouth, squinting, &c.; a perversion of the true meaning of words.—**Distortive**, dis-tor'-tiv, *a.* Causing distortion; distorted.

Distract, dis-trakt', *v.t.* [L. *distraho*, *distractum*, to pull asunder, to perplex—*dis*, asunder, and *traho*, to draw; whence *tractable*, *trace*, &c.] To draw apart or pull separate‡; to turn or draw from any object or point; to divert toward various other objects (the attention); to perplex, confound, or harass (the mind); to disorder the reason of; to render insane or frantic.—**Distracted**, dis-trak'ted, *p.* and *a.* Disordered in intellect; deranged; perplexed; crazy; frantic.—**Distractedly**, dis-trak'-ted-li, *adv.* In a distracted manner; insanely; wildly.—**Distractedness**, dis-trak'ted-nes, *n.* A state of being distracted; madness.—**Distracter**, dis-trak'tėr, *n.* One who or that which distracts.—**Distraction**, dis-trak'shon, *n.* The act of distracting; the state of being distracted; confusion from multiplicity of objects crowding on the mind and calling the attention different ways; perplexity; embarrassment; madness; frenzy; insanity; extreme folly; extreme perturbation or agony of mind, as from pain or grief; anything giving the mind a new and less onerous occupation; a diversion.—**Distractive**, dis-trak'tiv, *a.* Causing perplexity.

Distrain, dis-trān', *v.t.* [O.Fr. *destraindre*, from L. *distringere*, to draw apart, bind, molest, later to exact a pledge—*dis*, asunder, and *stringere*, to strain (as in *constrain*, *restrain*). STRAIN. Akin *distress*, *district.*] To seize or take possession of (*Shak.*)‡; specifically, *law*, to seize, as goods and chattels, for debt.—**Distrainable**, dis-trā'na-bl, *a.* Capable of being or liable to be distrained.—**Distrainer, Distrainor**, dis-trā'nėr, *n.* He who seizes goods for debt or service.—**Distraint**, dis-trānt', *n.* A distress or distraining.

Distrait, dis-trā, *a.* [Fr.] Abstracted; absent-minded; inattentive.

Distraught, dis-trąt', *a.* [Old pp. of *distract.*] Distracted; perplexed.

Distress, dis-tres', *n.* [O.F. *destresse*, *destrece*, oppression, from *destrecer*, to oppress, from a hypothetical L.L. *destrictiare*, from L. *districtus*, pp. of *distringo*, to draw apart, hinder, molest. DISTRAIN.] Extreme pain; anguish of body or mind; that which causes suffering; affliction; calamity; adversity; misery; a state of danger; *law*, the act of distraining, the seizure of any personal chattel as a pledge for the payment of rent or debt, or the satisfaction of a claim.—*v.t.* To afflict with pain or anguish; to harass; to grieve; to perplex; to make miserable.—**Distressed**, dis-trest', *p.* and *a.* Suffering distress; harassed with pain or trouble; afflicted.—**Distressful**, dis-tres'ful, *a.* Inflicting or bringing distress; calamitous; proceeding from pain or anguish; indicating distress.—**Distressfully**, dis-tres'ful-li, *adv.* In a distressful manner.—**Distressing**, dis-tres'ing, *a.* Very afflicting; affecting with severe pain.—**Distressingly**, dis-tres'ing-li, *adv.* In a distressing manner; with great pain.

Distribute, dis-trib'ūt, *v.t.*—*distributed, distributing.* [L. *distribuo*, *distributum*, to divide, distribute—*dis*, and *tribuo*, to give. TRIBUTE.] To divide among two or more; to deal out; to give or bestow in parts or portions; to dispense; to administer; to divide, as into classes, orders, genera; *printing*, to separate types and place them in their proper boxes or compartments in the cases.—**Distributable**, dis-trib'ū-ta-bl, *a.* Capable of being distributed.—**Distributer**, dis-trib'ū-tėr, *n.* One who or that which distributes or deals out; a dispenser.—**Distribution**, dis-tri-bū'shon, *n.* [L. *distributio.*] The act of distributing or dealing out; the act of dispensing or administering; the act of separating into distinct parts or classes; *printing*, the separating of the types and arranging of them in their proper places in the case; the manner of being distributed or spread over the earth (the *distribution* of animals or plants).—**Distributive**, dis-trib'ū-tiv, *a.* Serving to distribute; expressing separation or division; specifically, *gram.* an epithet applied to certain words (as *each*, *every*) which denote the persons or things that make a number taken separately and singly.—*n.* *Gram.* a distributive word, as *each* and *every*.—**Distributively**, dis-trib'ū-tiv-li, *adv.* In a distributive manner.

District, dis'trikt, *n.* [L.L. *districtum*, a district subject to one jurisdiction, from L. *districtus*, pp. of *distringo.* DISTRAIN.] A part of a country, city, &c., distinctly defined or marked out; a portion of country without very definite limits; a tract; a region, locality, quarter.

Distrust, dis-trust', *v.t.* To doubt or suspect the truth, fidelity, firmness, sincerity, reality, sufficiency, or goodness of; to have no faith, reliance, or confidence in; to be suspicious of.—*n.* Doubt or suspicion;

want of confidence, faith, or reliance.—**Distruster**, dis-trus'tėr, *n.* One who distrusts. — **Distrustful**, dis-trust'fụl, *a.* Apt to distrust; wanting confidence; suspicious; mistrustful; apprehensive; not confident; diffident; modest.—**Distrustfully**, dis-trust'fụl-li, *adv.* In a distrustful manner.—**Distrustfulness**, dis-trust'fụl-nes, *n.* The state or quality of being distrustful. —**Distrustless**, dis-trust'les, *a.* Free from distrust or suspicion.

Disturb, dis-tėrb', *v.t.* [L. *disturbo*, to throw into disorder—*dis*, asunder, and *turbo*, to confuse, from *turba*, a crowd, tumult, whence also *turbid, turbulent.*] To excite from a state of rest or tranquillity; to stir; to move; to discompose; to agitate; to throw into confusion or disorder; to excite uneasiness in the mind of; to disquiet; to render uneasy; to ruffle; to move from any regular course, operation, or purpose; to make irregular; to interfere with; to interrupt. — **Disturbance**, dis-tėr'bans, *n.* The act of disturbing; interruption of peace or quiet; interruption of a settled state of things; violent change; derangement; perturbation; agitation; disorder of thoughts; confusion; agitation in the body politic; a disorder; a tumult.—**Disturber**, dis-tėr'bėr, *n.* One who disturbs; one who causes tumults or disorders.

Disunion, dis-ūn'yon, *n.* A state of not being united; separation; disjunction; a breach of concord and its effect; contention; dissension.—**Disunite**, dis-ū-nīt', *v.t.* To separate; to disjoin; to part; to set at variance; to raise dissension between.—*v.i.* To fall asunder; to become separate.—**Disuniter**, dis-ū-nī'tėr, *n.* One who or that which disjoins.—**Disunity**, dis-ū'ni-ti, *n.* Want of unity; a state of separation; a want of concord.

Disuse, dis-ūs', *n.* Cessation of use, practice, or exercise.—*v.t.* (dis-ūz'). To cease to use; to neglect or omit to practise; to disaccustom.—**Disusage**, dis-ū'zāj, *n.* Gradual cessation of use or custom; neglect of use, exercise, or practice.

Disyoke, dis-yōk', *v.t.* To unyoke; to free from any trammel. (*Tenn.*)

Ditch, dich, *n.* [A softened form of *dike* (comp. *church* and *kirk*, &c.), both being formerly applied to the embankment as well as to the ditch. DIKE, DIG.] A trench in the earth made by digging, particularly a trench for draining wet land, or for making a fence to guard inclosures, or for preventing an enemy from approaching a town or fortress; any long artificial channel dug to contain water.—*v.i.* To dig or make a ditch or ditches.—*v.t.* To dig a ditch or ditches in; to drain by a ditch; to surround with a ditch.—**Ditcher**, dich'ėr, *n.* One who digs ditches.

Ditheism, dī'thē-izm, *n.* [Gr. *di*, double, and *theos*, a god.] The doctrine of the existence of two gods, especially that on which the old Persian religion was founded, or the opposition of the two (good and evil) principles; dualism; Manicheism. — **Ditheist**, dī'thē-ist, *n.* One who believes in ditheism. — **Ditheistic, Ditheistical**, dī-thē-is'tik, dī-thē-is'ti-kal, *a.* Pertaining to ditheism.

Dithyramb, Dithyrambic, dith'i-ramb, dith-i-ram'bik, *n.* [Gr. *dithyrambos.*] A hymn among the ancient Greeks, originally in honour of Bacchus, afterwards of other gods, composed in an elevated or wildly enthusiastic style; hence, any poem of an impetuous and irregular character. —**Dithyrambic**, *a.* Pertaining to or resembling a dithyramb; wild; enthusiastic.

Ditokous, dī'to-kus, *a.* [Gr. *di*, *tiktō*, to bring forth.] *Zool.* producing two young; laying two eggs.

Ditone, dī'tōn, *n.* [Gr. *dis*, double, and *tonos*, tone.] *Mus.* an interval comprehending two tones.

Ditrochee, dī-trō'kē, *n.* [Gr. *di*, twice, and *trochaios*, trochee.] *Pros.* a double trochee; a foot made up of two trochees.

Dittany, dit'a-ni, *n.* [L. *dictamnus*, from growing abundantly on Mount *Dicte* in Crete.] A perennial plant found in the Mediterranean region, with large white or rose-coloured flowers in terminal racemes, and having numerous glands containing a fragrant and very volatile oil.

Ditto, dit'tō. [It. *ditto*, from L. *dictum*, something said. DICTION.] A word used chiefly in lists, accounts, &c., to save writing, equivalent to same as above, or aforesaid: often contracted into *Do.*,

Ditty, dit'i, *n.* [O.Fr. *ditté*, story, poem, &c., from L. *dictatum*, pp. of *dictare*, to dictate. DICTION.] A song; a sonnet; a little poem to be sung.—*v.i.*† To sing; to warble a little tune.

Diuretic, dī-ū-ret'ik, *a* [Gr. *diourētikos*, from *dia*, through, and *ouron*, urine.] Having the power to excite the secretion of urine; tending to produce discharges of urine. —*n.* A medicine that excites the secretion of urine or increases its discharges. —**Diuresis**, dī-ū-rē'sis, *n.* *Med.* an excessive flow of urine.

Diurnal, dī-ėr'nal, *a.* [L. *diurnalis*, from *diurnus*, daily, from *dies*, a day, whence also *dial, diary*, &c. *Journal* is the same word.] Relating to a day; pertaining to the daytime; belonging to the period of daylight, as distinguished from the night; happening every day; performed every day; daily. — **Diurnally**, dī-ėr'nal-li, *adv.* Daily; every day.

Divagation,† dī-va-gā'shon, *n.* [L. *divagor, divagatus*, to wander about—*di* for *dis*, asunder, and *vagor*, to wander.] A going astray; deviation; digression. (*Thack.*)

Divan, di-van', *n.* [Per. *divân*, a collection of writings, custom-house, council, raised seat.] Among the Turks and other orientals, a court of justice; a council; council-chamber; a state or reception room; a kind of coffee-house; a cushioned seat standing against the wall of a room; a collection of poems by one author.

Divaricate, dī-var'i-kāt, *v.i.* [L. *divarico*, *divaricatum*, to spread asunder—*di* for *dis*, asunder, and *varico*, to straddle.] To fork; to part into two branches; *bot.* to diverge at an obtuse angle.—*v.t.* To divide into two branches; to cause to branch apart.—**Divarication**, dī-var'i-kā"shon, *n.* A separation into two branches; a forking.

Dive, dīv, *v.i.* — *dived, diving.* [A.Sax. *dýfan*, to dive = Icel. *dýfa*, to dip, to dive; akin *deep, dip.*] To descend or plunge into water head first; to go under water for the purpose of executing some work; to go deep into any subject; to plunge into any business or condition; to sink; to penetrate.—*n.* The act of diving; a plunge.—**Diver**, dī'vėr, *n.* One who dives; one of a family of marine swimming birds, with short wings and tail, legs far back and toes completely webbed, preying upon fish, which they pursue under water.—**Diving**, dī'ving, *n.* The act or practice of descending into water; especially, the art of descending below the surface of the water, and remaining there for some time, in order to remove objects from the bottom, &c.—**Diving-bell**, *n.* An apparatus, originally bell-shaped, in which persons descend into the water and remain for a length of time, fresh air being pumped into the bell by assistants above.—**Diving-dress**, *n.* A waterproof dress used by professional divers, variously constructed.

Diverge, di-vėrj', *v.i.*—*diverged, diverging.* [L. *di* for *dis*, asunder, and *vergo*, to incline. VERGE.] To tend or proceed from a common point in different directions; to deviate from a given course or line: opposed to *converge*; to differ or vary.—**Divergence, Divergency**, di-vėr'jens, di-vėr'jen-si, *n.* The act of diverging; a receding from each other; a going farther apart. — **Divergent**, di-vėr'jent, *a.* Diverging; separating or receding from each other, as lines which proceed from the same point.—**Divergingly**, di-vėr'jing-li, *adv.* In a manner so as to diverge.

Divers, dī'vėrz, *a.* [Fr. *divers*, from L. *diversus*, diverse, turned away, from *di* for *dis*, asunder, and *verto, versum*, to turn. VERSE.] Different; various; several; sundry; more than one, but not a great number.—**Diverse**, dī-vers' or dī'vėrs. *a.* [L. *diversus.*] Different; differing; unlike; not the same.—**Diversely**, dī-vėrs'li, *adv.* In a diverse manner; in different directions.—**Diversifiable**, di-vėr'si-fī-a-bl, *a.* Capable of being diversified or varied.—**Diversification**, di-vėr'si-fi-kā"shon, *n.* The act of diversifying; the state of being diversified.—**Diversified**, di-vėr'si-fīd, *p.* and *a.* Distinguished by various forms, or by a variety of objects.—**Diversiform**, di-vėr'si-form, *a.* Of a different form; of various forms.—**Diversify**, di-vėr'si-fī, *v.t.* —*diversified, diversifying.* [Fr. *diversifier* —L. *diversus*, and *facio*, to make.] To make diverse or various in form or qualities; to give variety or diversity to; to variegate.—**Diversion**, di-vėr'shon, *n.* The act of diverting or turning aside from any course; that which diverts or turns the mind or thoughts away; what turns or draws the mind from care, business, or study, and thus relaxes and amuses; sport; play; pastime; a feint or other movement made to mislead an enemy as to the real point of attack.—**Diversity**, di-vėr'si-ti, *n.* [L. *diversitas.*] The state of being diverse; difference; dissimilitude; unlikeness; multiplicity with difference; variety; distinctness or separateness of being, as opposed to *identity*.—**Divert**, di-vėrt', *v.t.* [L. *diverto, diversum*, to turn aside.] To turn off from any course, direction, or intended application; to turn aside (to *divert* a stream, traffic, &c.); to turn from business or study; to turn from care or serious thoughts: hence, to please; to amuse; to entertain. ∴ Syn. under AMUSE.—**Diverter**, di-vėr'tėr, *n.* One who or that which diverts.—**Diverting**, di-vėr'ting, *a.* Causing diversion; amusing; entertaining. —**Divertingly**, di-vėr'ting-li, *adv.* In a diverting manner. — **Divertissement**, dē-ver-tēs-moṅ, *n.* [Fr.] A short entertainment between the acts of longer theatrical pieces.

Dives, dī'vēz, *n.* [L. *dives*, rich.] Name in Biblical parable; type of the rich man.

Divest, di-vest', *v.t.* [O.Fr. *devestir*, from L. *devestio*, to undress—*de*, priv., and *vestio*, to clothe, from *vestis*, a garment, whence also *vest, vesture.*] To strip; to strip of dress or of anything that surrounds or attends; to deprive: with *of* before the thing removed.

Divide, di-vīd', *v.t.*—*divided, dividing.* [L. *divido*, to divide—*di* for *dis*, asunder, and *vid*, a root signifying to cut or separate, akin to Skr. *vyadh*, to penetrate.] To part or separate into pieces; to cut or otherwise separate into two or more parts; to cause to be separate; to keep apart, as by a partition or by an imaginary line or limit; to make partition of among a number; to disunite in opinion or interest; to set at variance.—*v.i.* To become separated; to part; to open; to cleave; to vote by the division of a legislative house, as in the British Parliament, into two parts, that is, the "ayes" dividing from the "noes."—*n.* The watershed of a district or region.—**Dividable**, di-vī'da-bl, *a.* Capable of being divided.—**Divided**, di-vī'ded, *p.* and *a.* Parted, separated, or disunited; showing divisions; at variance in feeling.—**Dividedly**, di-vī'ded-li, *adv.* In a divided manner; separately.—**Dividend**, div'i-dend, *n.* [L. lit. a thing to be divided.] A sum or a number to be divided; the profit or gain made by a corporation and which falls to be divided among the stockholders according to the stock of each; the sum that falls to the share of each; the share of the fund realized from the effects of a bankrupt, and apportioned according to the amount of the debt of each creditor; a share of surplus allocated by an insurance company to policy holders.—**Divider**, di-vī'dėr, *n.* One who or that which divides; *pl.* an instrument for dividing lines, &c.; compasses.

Divi-divi, div'i-div'i, *n.* The native and commercial name of a tropical American tree and its remarkably curled pods which yield tannic and gallic acid.

Divine, di-vīn', *a.* [L. *divinus*, divine, religious, divinely inspired, godlike, from *divus*, divine, a deity or divinity. DEITY.] Pertaining to God, or to a heathen deity or false god; partaking of the nature of God; godlike; heavenly; sacred; holy; excellent in the highest degree; apparently above what is human; relating to divinity or theology.—*Divine right*, the claim set up by sovereigns to the unqualified obedience of their subjects on the assumption that they themselves were appointed by God to rule, and responsible to him only for their acts.—*n.* A minister of the gospel; a priest; a clergyman; a theologian.—*v.t.*—*divined, divining.* [L. *divino.*] To foretell; to predict; to prognosticate; to conjecture; to guess.—*v.i.* To use or practise divination; to utter presages or prognostications; to bode; to guess.—**Divination**, div-i-nā'-shon, *n.* [L. *divinatio.*] The act of divining; a foretelling future events, or discovering things secret or obscure, by the aid of superior beings, or by certain rites, experiments, observations, &c.—**Divinatory**, di-vin'a-to-ri, *a.* Professing or pertaining to divination.—**Divinely**, di-vīn'li, *adv.* In a divine manner; in a manner resembling deity; by the agency or influence of God; in a supreme degree; excellently.—**Divineness**, di-vīn'nes, *n.* The state or quality of being divine, likeness to God; sacredness; superexcellence.—**Diviner**, di-vī'nėr, *n.* One who professes divination; a soothsayer; one who guesses or conjectures.—**Divineress**, di-vī'nėr-es, *n.* A female diviner.—**Divining-rod**, *n.* A rod, usually of hazel, which, if carried slowly along in suspension by an adept, dips and points downwards, it is affirmed, when brought over the spot where water or treasure is to be found.—**Divinity**, di-vin'i-ti, *n.* [L. *divinitas.*] The state of being divine; divineness; deity; godhead; divine element; divine nature; God; the Deity; a celestial being; one of the deities belonging to a polytheistic religion; supernatural power or virtue; awe-inspiring character or influence; sacredness; the science of divine things; theology.—**Divinize**,† div'-i-nīz, *v.t.* To regard as divine.

Divisible, di-viz'i-bl, *a.* [L. *divisibilis*, from *divido.* DIVIDE.] Capable of division; that may be separated or disunited; separable.—**Divisibility, Divisibleness**, di-viz'i-bil''i-ti, di-viz'i-bl-nes, *n.* The quality of being divisible; that general property of bodies by which their parts or component particles are capable of separation.—**Divisibly**, di-viz'i-bli, *adv.* In a divisible manner.—**Division**, di-vizh'on, *n.* [L. *divisio.*] The act of dividing or separating into parts; the state of being divided; separation; a dividing line; a partition; the part separated from the rest, as by a partition, line, &c., real or imaginary; a distinct segment or section; a part or distinct portion; a certain section or portion of an organized whole, as an army, a fleet; disunion; discord; dissension; variance; difference; the separation of members in a legislative house in order to ascertain the vote; *arith.* one of the four fundamental rules, the object of which is to find how often one number is contained in another.—*Division of cavalry*, 9815 men.—*Division of infantry*, three brigades of infantry, artillery, &c., 18,000 men.—**Divisional**, di-vizh'on-al, *a.* Pertaining to division; noting or making division; belonging to a division or district.—**Divisive**, di-vī'ziv, *a.* Forming division; tending to divide; creating division or discord.—**Divisor**, di-vī'zėr, *n.* *Arith.* the number by which the dividend is divided.

Divorce, di-vōrs', *n.* [Fr. *divorce*, from L. *divortium*, a separation, a divorce, from *divorto*, same as *diverto*, to turn away. DIVERT.] A legal dissolution of the bond of marriage; a legal separation between husband and wife, after which either is free to marry again; the sentence or writing by which marriage is dissolved; disunion of things closely united; separation.—*v.t.*—*divorced, divorcing.* To dissolve the marriage contract between; to separate from the condition of husband and wife; to separate or disunite from close connection; to force asunder; to put away.—**Divorceable**, di-vōr'sa-bl, *a.* Capable of being divorced.—**Divorcee**, di-vōr-sē', *n.* A person divorced.—**Divorcement**, di-vōrs'ment, *n.* Divorce. (O.T.)—**Divorcer**, di-vōr'sėr, *n.* One who or that which divorces.—**Divorcive**,† di-vōr'siv, *a.* Having power to divorce. (*Mil.*)

Divulge, di-vulj', *v.t.*—*divulged, divulging.* [L. *divulgo*, to spread among the people—*di* for *dis*, distrib., and *vulgus*, the common people, whence also *vulgar.*] To tell or make known what was before private or secret; to reveal; to disclose; to let be known.—**Divulgement**,† di-vulj'ment, *n.* The act of divulging.—**Divulger**, di-vul'jėr, *n.* One who divulges.

Divulsion, di-vul'shon, *n.* [L. *divulsio*, a tearing asunder, from *divello*, *divulsum*, to pluck or pull asunder—*di* for *dis*, asunder, and *vello*, to pull.] The act of pulling or plucking away; a rending asunder; violent separation; laceration.—**Divulsive**, di-vul'siv, *a.* Tending or having power to pull asunder or rend.

Dizen,‡ diz'n, *v.t.* [From the obsolete *dise*, *dyse*, the first part of *distaff.* Hence *bedizen.*] To dress; to attire; especially, to dress gaily or gaudily; to deck; to bedizen.

Dizzy, diz'i, *a.* [A.Sax. *dysig*, foolish; akin to L.G. *dusig*, *dōsig*, O.D. *duyzigh*, Mod.D. *duizelig*, dizzy, Dan. *dösig*, drowsy. Allied are *daze, dazzle, dose.*] Having a sensation of whirling in the head with instability or proneness to fall; giddy; vertiginous; causing giddiness (a *dizzy* height); arising from, or caused by, giddiness; thoughtless; heedless; inconstant.—*v.t.*—*dizzied, dizzying.* To make dizzy or giddy; to confuse.—**Dizzily**, diz'i-li, *adv.* In a dizzy manner.—**Dizziness**, diz'i-nes, *n.* The state or feeling of being dizzy; giddiness; vertigo.

Djereed, Djerid, je-rēd', *n.* [Ar. *jerid.*] A blunt javelin used in oriental military sports, as for hitting a distant mark, or being thrown through as many suspended rings as possible, &c.

Do, dö, *v.t.* or *auxiliary*; pret. *did*; pp. *done*; ppr. *doing.* When transitive the present tense singular is, I *do*, thou *doest* or *dost* (dö'est, dust), he *does* or *doth* (duz, duth); when auxiliary, the second person is, thou *dost.* [A.Sax. *dón*, to do, *dó*, I do = D. *doen*, G. *thun*, to do, L. *do* in *abdo*, I put away, *condo*, I put together, Skr. *dhâ*, to place. From same stem are *deed, deem, doom.*] To perform; to execute; to carry into effect; to bring about, produce, effect; to give, confer, or pay (to *do* honour, reverence, &c.); to transact; to finish or complete; to hoax, cheat, swindle (*colloq.*); to inspect the sights or objects of interest in (*colloq.*); to prepare; to cook.—*To do away*, to remove; to put away; to annul; to put an end to.—*To do into*, to translate or render (in another language).—*To do over*, to perform again; to repeat; put a coating, as of paint, upon.—*To do up*, to put up, as a parcel; to tie up; to pack.—*To do with*, to dispose of; to employ; to occupy; to deal with; to get on with (as in what shall I *do with* it? I can *do* nothing *with* him, &c.).—*v.i.* [In this usage *do* is partly the intransitive form of the preceding verb, partly from A.Sax. *dugan*, to avail, be worth, same word as Icel. *duga*, Dan. *due*, D. *deugen*, Goth. *dugan*, G. *taugen*, to be worth, but the senses are so intermingled that it would be difficult to separate them.] To act or behave in any manner, well or ill; to conduct one's self; to fare; to be in a state with regard to sickness or health (how do you *do*?); to succeed; to accomplish a purpose; to serve an end; to suffice (will this plan *do*?); to find means; to contrive; to shift (how shall we *do* for money?).—*To do for*, to suit; to be adapted for; to answer in place of; to be sufficient for; to satisfy; to ruin; to put an end to (*vulg.*); attend on or do household duties for (*colloq.*).—*To do without*, to shift without; to put up without; to dispense with.—*To have done*, to have made an end; to have finished.—*To have done with*, to have finished; to cease to have part or interest in or connection with.—*Do* is often used for a verb to save the repetition of it; as, I shall probably come, but if I *do* not, you must not wait; that is, if I *come* not.—As an auxiliary it is used most commonly in forming negative and interrogative sentences; as, *do* you intend to go? *does* he wish me to come? *Do* is also used to express emphasis; as, I *do* love her. In the imperative, it expresses an urgent request or command; as, *do* come; help me, *do*; make haste, *do.* In the past tense it is sometimes used to convey the idea that what was once true is not true now. 'My lord, you once *did* love me.' (*Shak.*)—The past participle *done*, besides being used for all the ordinary meanings of the verb, has some colloquial or familiar uses; as *done!* an exclamation expressing agreement to a proposal, that is, it is agreed or I accept; *done up*, ruined in any manner, completely exhausted, very tired or fatigued.—**Doable**, dö'a-bl, *a.* Capable of being done or executed.—**Doer**, dö'ėr, *n.* One who does, executes, performs, or acts; one who performs what is required: as opposed to a mere talker or theorizer.—**Doings**, dö'ingz, *n.pl.* Things done; transactions; feats; actions, good or bad; behaviour; conduct.

Do, dō, *n.* *Mus.* the name given to the first of the syllables used in solmization; the first or key note of the scale.

Doab, Dooab, dō'ab, dö'ab, *n.* In the East Indies, a tract of country between two rivers.

Docetes, dō-sēt'es, *n.* [Gr. *dokein*, to appear.] Early Christian sect maintaining the apparent but not real nature of the Saviour's body.

Docile, dō'sīl or dos'il, *a.* [L. *docilis*, from *doceo*, to teach, whence also *doctor*, *document.*] Teachable; easily instructed; ready to learn; tractable; easily managed.—**Docility**, dō-sil'i-ti, *n.* The state or quality of being docile.

Docimasy, dos'i-ma-si, *n.* [Gr. *dokimasia*, from *dokimazō*, to try, examine, from *dokimos*, proved, tested.] The art or practice of assaying metals; metallurgy.—**Docimastic**, dos-i-mas'tik, *a.* [Gr. *dokimastikos.*] Proving by experiments or tests; relating to the assaying of metals; metallurgic.

Dock, dok, *n.* [A.Sax. *docce*, G. *docke.*] The common name of various species of perennial herbs, most of them troublesome weeds with stout rootstalks, erect stems, and broad leaves.

Dock, dok, *n.* [Icel. *dockr*, a short tail; G. *docke*, a thick short piece; Fris. *dok*, a small bundle, bunch; comp. also W. *toc*, anything short, *tociaw*, to curtail.] The tail of a beast cut short; the stump of a tail; the solid part of the tail.—*v.t.* To cut off, as the end of a thing; to curtail; to cut short; to clip; to shorten.

Dock, dok, *n.* [D. *dok*, G. *docke*, Sw. *docka*, a dock, Flem. *docke*, a kind of cage; perhaps from L. *doga*, a kind of vessel; from Gr. *dochē*, receptacle, from *dechomai*, to receive.] The place where a criminal stands in court; a place artificially formed on the side of a harbor or the bank of a river for the reception of ships, the entrance of which is generally closed by gates; a landing pier for boats, a wharf; an elevated platform for loading freight cars.—*Dry* or *graving dock*, a dock so constructed that the water may be excluded at pleasure, allowing the bottom of a vessel to be inspected and repaired.—*Wet dock*, a dock in which there is always water.—*Floating docks* are composed of large pontoons carrying along each side pumps on suitable stiff frames. When the pontoons are filled with water, they sink to the desired depth, *e.g.*, beneath a vessel, that is raised with them when the water is pumped out of the pontoons.—**Dockage**, dok'āj, *n.* Charges for the use of docks.—**Docker**, *n.* A worker at the wharves or a longshoreman.—**Dock-master**, *n.* One who has the superintendence of docks.—**Dock-warrant**, *n.* A certificate given to the owner of goods warehoused in the docks.—**Dockyard**, dok'yärd, *n.* A yard or repository near a harbour for containing all kinds of naval stores and timber.

Docket, **Docquet**, dok'et, *n.* [A dim. of *dock*, anything curtailed or cut short.] A summary of a larger writing; a small piece of paper or parchment containing the heads of a writing: an alphabetical list of cases in a court of law; a ticket attached to goods, containing the name of the owner, the place to which they are to be sent, or specifying their measurement, &c.—*v.t.* To make an abstract of, and enter, or write it down; to mark the contents of papers on the back; to add a docket to.—**Docketed**, dok'et-ed, *p.* and *a.*

Doctor, dok'tėr, *n.* [L., from *doceo*, *doctum*, to teach. DOCILE.] A teacher‡; an instructor‡; a learned man; a person who has received the degree of this name from a university, being thus a *doctor* of divinity, laws, medicine, &c., and supposed capable of teaching the particular subject; a person duly licensed to practise medicine; a physician; one who cures diseases.—*v.t.* To treat medically; hence. to repair or patch up; to drug or adulterate (wine); to falsify; to cook (in all senses colloq.).—**Doctoral**, dok'tėr-al, *a.* Relating to the degree of a doctor.—**Doctorate**, dok'tėr-āt, *n.* The university degree of doctor.—**Doctorship**, dok'tėr-ship, *n.* The degree of a doctor; doctorate.—**Doctress**, **Doctoress**, dok'tres, dok'tėr-es, *n.* A female physician.

Doctrine, dok'trin, *n.* [L. *doctrina*, instruction, learning, from *doceo*, to teach, whence *doctor*, *docile*, &c.] In a general sense, whatever is taught; hence, a principle, view, or set of opinions maintained by any person or set of persons: whatever is laid down as true by an instructor or master; often instruction and confirmation in the truths of the gospel; one or more of the truths of the gospel.—**Doctrinaire**, dok'tri-när″, *n.* [Fr., from L. *doctrina*; the name was originally given to certain French politicians after the restoration of 1815.] One who theorizes or advocates important changes in political or social matters without a sufficient regard to practical considerations; a political theorist.—**Doctrinal**, dok'tri-nal, *a.* Pertaining to doctrine; containing a doctrine; pertaining to the act or means of teaching.—**Doctrinally**, dok'tri-nal-li, *adv.* In the form of doctrine or instruction; by way of teaching or positive direction.—**Doctrinarian**, dok-tri-nā'ri-an, *n.* A doctrinaire.—**Doctrinarianism**, dok-tri-nā'ri-an-izm, *n.* The principles or doctrines of doctrinaires.

Document, dok'ū-ment, *n.* [L. *documentum*, a lesson, a proof, from *doceo*, to teach. DOCTRINE.] Any official or authoritative paper containing instructions or proof, for information, establishment of facts, and the like; any written or printed paper.—**Documentary**, **Documental**, dok'ū-men-ta-ri, dok'ū-men-tal, *a.* Pertaining to documents or written evidence; consisting in documents.

Dodder, dod'ėr, *n.* [Dan. *dodder*, Sw. *dodra*, G. *dotter*, of unknown derivation.] The name of certain slender, twining, leafless pink or white parasitic plants, the common English species of which are found on nettles, vetches, furze, flax, &c.—**Doddered**, dod'ėrd, *a.* Overgrown with dodder.—**Doddered oak**, *a.* With the top branches blasted or withered.

Dodecagon, dō-dek'a-gon, *n.* [Gr. *dōdeka*, twelve, and *gōnia*, an angle.] A regular figure or polygon, consisting of twelve equal sides and angles.—**Dodecagyn**, dō-dek'a-jin, *n.* [Gr. *gynē*, a female.] *Bot.* a plant having twelve styles.—**Dodecagynian**, **Dodecagynous**, dō-dek'a-jin″i-an, dō-de-kaj'i-nus, *a.* *Bot.* having twelve styles. —**Dodecahedral**, dō-dek'a-hē″dral, *a.* Pertaining to a dodecahedron: consisting of twelve equal sides.—**Dodecahedron**, dō-dek'a-hē″dron, *n.* [Gr. *hedra*, a base or side.] A regular solid contained under twelve equal and regular pentagons, or having twelve equal bases.—**Dodecander**, dō-de-kan'dėr, *n.* [Gr. *anēr*, *andros*, a male.] *Bot.* a plant having twelve stamens. —**Dodecandrian**, **Dodecandrous**, dō-de-kan'dri-an, dō-de-kan'drus, *a.* Pertaining to the dodecanders.—**Dodecapetalous**, dō-dek'a-pet″a-lus, *a.* *Bot.* having twelve petals.—**Dodecasyllable**, dō-dek'a-sil-la-bl, *n.* A word of twelve syllables.

Dodge, doj, *v.i.*—*dodged*, *dodging*. [Perhaps connected with *duck*, to stoop or bend down the head, G. *ducken*, to bow, to stoop.] To start suddenly aside; to follow the footsteps of a person, but so as to escape his observation; to play tricks; to play fast and loose; to quibble.—*v.t.* To evade by a sudden shift of place; to escape by starting aside; to pursue by rapid movements in varying directions; to baffle by shifts and pretexts; to overreach by tricky knavery.—*n.* A trick; an artifice; an evasion.—**Dodger**, doj'ėr, *n.* One who dodges or evades; one who practises artful shifts or dodges.

Dodo, dō'dō, *n.* [Pg. *doudo*, silly.] An extinct bird of Mauritius, having a massive, clumsy body, covered with down, short and extremely strong legs, and wings and tail so short as to be useless for flight.

Doe, dō, *n.* [A.Sax. *dá*, Dan. *daa*.] The female of the fallow-deer, the goat, the sheep, the hare, and the rabbit: corresponding to the masculine *buck*.—**Doeskin**, *n.* The skin of a doe; a compact twilled woollen cloth.

Doff, dof, *v.t.* [Contr. for *do off*, like *don* for *do on*.] To put, take, or lay off, as dress; to lay aside.—*v.i.* To lay off some article of dress; to take off the hat.

Dog, dog, *n.* [A.Sax. *dogga* (very rare), a dog; same as D. *dog*, Dan. *dogge*, Sw. *dogg*, a large kind of dog. *Hound* (A.Sax. *hund*) was originally and long the common English word for dog.] A well-known domesticated carnivorous quadruped, closely allied to the wolf and the fox, noted for its sagacity, acute senses, and great attachment to man; a term of reproach or contempt given to a man; a mean, worthless fellow; a gay young man; a buck; a name applied to several tools, articles, &c., generally iron, as, an andiron, or kind of trestle to lay wood upon in a fireplace, an iron bar, with one or more sharp fangs or claws at one end, for fastening into a piece of wood or other heavy article, for the purpose of dragging or raising it, and the like. *Dog* is often used in composition for male; as, *dog*-fox, *dog*-otter, &c.; as also to denote meanness, degeneracy, or worthlessness; as, *dog*-Latin, *dog*-rose.—*To give* or *throw to the dogs*, to throw away as useless.—*To go to the dogs*, to go to ruin in life.—*v.t.*—*dogged*, *dogging*. To follow insidiously or indefatigably; to follow close; to hunt; to worry with importunity. —**Dogged**, dog'ed, *a.* Having the bad qualities of a dog; sullen; sour, morose; surly; severe; obstinate.—**Doggedly**, dog'ed-li, *adv.* In a dogged manner.—**Doggedness**, dog'ed-nes, *n.* The quality of being dogged.—**Doggish**, dog'ish, *a.* Snappish; surly; brutal.—**Doggishness**, dog'ish-nes, *n.*—**Dogbane**, *n.* A North American bitter plant used instead of ipecacuanha.—**Dog-berry**, *n.* The berry of the dogwood.—**Dog-brier**, *n.* A brier; the dog-rose.—**Dog-cart**, *n.* A carriage with a box for holding sportsmen's dogs, a sort of double-seated gig, the occupants before and behind sitting back to back.—**Dog-cheap**, *a.* Cheap or worthless as a dog; very cheap; in little estimation.—**Dog-days**, *n. pl.* The days when Sirius or the Dog-star (whence the term) rises and sets with the sun, extending from about the 3rd of July to about the 11th of August. —**Dog-eared**, *a.* Having the corners of the leaves turned down from careless handling (a *dog-eared* book.)—**Dogfight**, *n.* A fight, as of dogs; tenacious combat between fighter airplanes.—**Dog-fish**, *n.* A name given to several species of fishes closely allied to the sharks, but of no great size.—**Dog-grass**, *n.* [Supposed to be eaten by dogs.] A grass common in woods and waste places, having stems from 1 to 3 feet high.—**Dog-Latin**, *n.* Barbarous Latin; a jargon having a superficial resemblance to Latin.—**Dog-louse**, *n.* A parasitic insect which infests dogs.—**Dog-parsley**, *n.* A common British umbelliferous weed in cultivated grounds, having a nauseous smell, and being a virulent poison; fool's parsley.—**Dog-rose**, *n.* A common British wild rose; the wild brier, the fruit of which is known as the hip.—**Dog's-ear**, *n.* The corner of a leaf in a book turned down, especially by careless handling.—*v.t.* To turn down in dog's ears.—**Dog's-fennel**, *n.* A weed found in cultivated fields, with acrid emetic properties, and with leaves having some resemblance to those of fennel.—**Dog-sick**, *a.* Sick as a dog that has eaten till compelled to vomit.—**Dog's-tail Grass**, *n.* The popular name of several species of grasses common in Britain.—**Dog-star**, *n.* Sirius, a star of the first magnitude, whose rising and setting with the sun gives name to the dog-days.—**Dog's-tooth Violet**, *n.* A bulbous garden plant with spotted leaves and purple flowers.—**Dog-tired**, *a.* Quite tired.—**Dog-tooth**, *n.* A sharp-pointed human tooth situated between the foreteeth and grinders: a canine tooth; an eye-tooth.—**Dog-trick**, *n.* A currish trick; an ill-natured practical joke. —**Dog-trot**, *n.* A gentle trot like that of a dog.—**Dog-vane**, *n.* *Naut.* a small vane placed on the weather gunwale of a vessel to show the direction of the wind.—**Dog-watch**, *n.* *Naut.* the name of the two watches of two hours each instead of four (between 4 and 8 p.m.) arranged so as to alter the watches kept from day to day by each portion of the crew, otherwise the same men would form the watch during the same hours for the whole voyage.—**Dog-weary**, *a.* Quite tired; much fatigued.—**Dogwood**, dog'wu̇d, *n.* A name of several trees or shrubs, one of them common in copses and hedges in England, with small cream-white flowers borne in dense roundish clusters. CORNEL.

Doge, dōj, *n.* [It.] The chief magistrate of the former republics of Venice (697-1797) and Genoa (1339-1797).—**Dogal**, dō'gal, *a.* Pertaining to a doge.—**Dogate**, dō'gāt, *n.* The office or dignity of a doge.

Dogger, dog'ėr, *n.* [D. *dogger-boot*—*dogger*, a codfish, and *boot*, a boat.] A Dutch fishing vessel having two masts, employed in the North Sea especially in the cod and herring fisheries.

Doggerel, dog'ėr-el, *a.* [Possibly from *dog*.] An epithet originally applied to a kind of loose irregular measure in burlesque poetry, but now more generally to mean verses defective in rhythm and sense.—*n.* Doggerel or mean verses.

Dogma, dog'ma, *n.* [Gr. *dogma*, that which seems true, an opinion, from *dokeō*, to seem.] A settled opinion or belief; a tenet; an opinion or doctrine received on authority, as opposed to one obtained from experience or demonstration.—**Dogmatic**, **Dogmatical**, dog-mat'ik, dog-mat'i-kal, *a.* Pertaining to a dogma or dogmas; having the character of a dogma: disposed to assert opinions with overbearing or arrogance; dictatorial; arrogant; authoritative; positive.—**Dogmatically**, dog-mat'i-kal-li, *adv.* In a dogmatic manner.—**Dogmatics**, dog-mat'iks, *n.* Doctrinal theology; the essential doctrines of Christianity.—**Dogmatism**, dog'ma-tizm, *n.* The quality of being dogmatic; arrogant assertion.—**Dogmatist**, dog'ma-tist, *n.* One who is dogmatic; an upholder of dogmas; an arrogant advancer of principles or opinions.—**Dogmatize**, dog'ma-tīz, *v.i.* To teach opinions with bold and undue confidence; to assert principles arrogantly or authoritatively.—**Dogmatizer**, dog'ma-tī-zėr, *n.* One who dogmatizes.

Dohl, dōl, *n.* A kind of foreign pulse resembling dried pease.

Doily, doi'li, *n.* [Said to be named from the first maker.] A small ornamental mat used at table to put glasses on during dessert.

Doit, doit, *n.* [D. *duit*, from Fr. *d'huit*, of eight, as the eighth part of a stiver.] A small Dutch copper coin, being the eighth part of a stiver, in value half a farthing;

the ancient Scottish penny piece, of which twelve were equal to a penny sterling; any small piece of money; a trifle.

Dolabra, do-lā'bra, *n.* [L., from *dolo*, to chip, to hew.] A variety of celt or ancient hatchet.—**Dolabriform**, dō-lab'ri-form, *a.* Having the form of an axe or hatchet.

Dolce, Dolcemente, dol'chā, dol-chā-men'tā. [It.] *Mus.* an instruction that the music is to be executed softly and sweetly.

Doldrums, dōl'drumz, *n. pl. Naut.* the parts of the ocean near the equator that abound in calms, squalls, and light baffling winds; low spirits; the dumps (*colloq.*).

Dole, dōl, *n.* [DEAL.] That which is dealt out or distributed; a part, share, or portion; lot; fortune; that which is given in charity; gratuity; especially money distributed by the government during a financial depression.—*v.t.* To deal out; to distribute.

Dole, dōl, *n.* [O.Fr. *dole*, Fr. *devil*, mourning, from L. *doleo*, to grieve.] Grief; sorrow.—**Doleful**, dōl'ful, *a.* Full of dole or grief; sorrowful; expressing grief; mournful; melancholy; sad; dismal; gloomy.—**Dolefully**, dōl'ful-li, *adv.* In a doleful manner. — **Dolefulness**, dōl'ful-nes, *n.* The state or quality of being doleful.—**Dolesome**,† dōl'sum, *a.* Doleful.

Dolerite, dol'ėr-it, *n.* [Gr. *doleros*, deceptive.] A variety of trap-rock composed of augite and labradorite; so named from the difficulty of discriminating its component parts.

Dolichocephalic, Dolichocephalous, dol'i-kō-se-fal"ik, dol'i-kō-sef"a-lus, *a.* [Gr. *dolichos*, long, and *kephalē*, the head.] A term used in ethnology to denote skulls in which the diameter from side to side bears a less proportion to the diameter from front to back than 8 to 10, as seen in the West African negro tribes.—**Dolichocephalism**, dol'i-kō-sef"a-lizm, *n.* The condition of being dolichocephalic.

Doll, dol, *n.* [Of doubtful origin; perhaps for *Doll*, contr. of *Dorothy*.] A puppet or small image in the human form for the amusement of children; a girl or woman more remarkable for good looks than intelligence.

Dollar, dol'ėr, *n.* [D. Dan. and Sw. *daler*, from G. *thaler*, from *thal*, a dale, because first coined in Joachim's-*Thal*, in Bohemia, in 1518.] A silver coin of the United States, of the value of 100 cents.—*Dollar-diplomacy*, a diplomacy used to promote the financial or commercial interests of a country abroad. — **Dollar-fish**, a small smooth-scaled marine fish.

Dolman, dol'man, *n.* [Fr. *dolman*, *doliman*, from Turk. *dōlāmān*.] A long outer robe, open in front, and having narrow sleeves buttoned at the wrist, worn by Turks; a kind of garment somewhat of the nature of a wide jacket, worn by ladies.

Dolmen, dol'men, *n.* [Armor. *dolmen*; Gael. *tolmen*—*dol*, *tol*, a table, and *men*, a stone.] A rude ancient structure (probably of sepulchral origin) consisting of one large unhewn stone resting on two or more others placed erect; also applied to structures where several blocks are raised upon pillars so as to form a sort of gallery; a cromlech.

Dolomite, dol'o-mīt, *n.* [After the French geologist *Dolomieu*.] A granular, crystalline, or schistose stone or rock, being a compound of carbonate of magnesia and carbonate of lime.—**Dolomitic**, dol-o-mit'ik, *a.* Containing dolomite; of the nature of dolomite.

Dolor, Dolour, dō'lėr, *n.* [Fr. *douleur*, from L. *dolor*, *doloris*, grief, pain, from *doleo*, to grieve. Akin *dole*, *doleful*.] Grief; sorrow; lamentation. [Now only poetical.] — **Doloriferous**, dō-lo-rif'ėr-us, *a.* Producing pain. — **Dolorific**,† dō-lo-rif'ik, *a.* Causing pain or grief.—**Dolorous**, dol'ėr-us, *a.* Sorrowful; doleful; exciting sorrow or grief; painful; expressing pain or grief.—**Dolorously**, dol'ėr-us-li, *adv.* In a dolorous manner. — **Dolorousness**, dol'ėr-us-nes, *n.* The state or quality of being dolorous.

Dolphin, dol'fin, *n.* [O.Fr. *daulphin*, Mod. Fr. *dauphin*, a dolphin, the dauphin, from L. *delphinus*, a dolphin.] A name of several species of cetaceous mammals having numerous conical teeth in both jaws, as the dolphin proper, a peculiarly agile animal, the grampus, &c.; a fish about 5 feet long, celebrated for its swiftness and the brilliant and beautiful colours which it assumes in the act of dying; a spar or buoy made fast to an anchor, and usually supplied with a ring to enable vessels to ride by it; a mooring-post placed at the entrance of a dock or along a quay or wharf.—**Dolphinet**, dol'fi-net, *n.* A female dolphin.

Dolt, dōlt, *n.* [Probably connected with E. *dull*, A.Sax. *dol*, dull, stupid; *dwelan*, to err, to be stupid.] A heavy, stupid fellow; a blockhead; a thickskull.—**Doltish**, dōl'tish, *a.* Dull in intellect; stupid. — **Doltishly**, dōl'tish-li, *adv.* In a doltish manner.—**Doltishness**, dōl'tish-nes, *n.*

Dom, dom, *n.* [L. *dominus*, lord.] Roman Catholic title of dignatories of the Carthusian and Benedictine monks.

Domain, dō-mān', *n.* [Fr. *domaine*, from L.L. *domanium*, a form of L. *dominium*, ownership, property, from *dominus*, a lord.] The territory over which dominion is exercised; the territory ruled over; a dominion; an estate in land; the land about a mansion-house and in the immediate occupancy of the owner; a demesne.—**Domanial**, dō-mā'ni-al, *a.* Relating to domains or landed estates.

Dome, dōm, *n.* [Fr. *dôme*, from Eccles. L. *doma*, a house, from Gr. *dōma*, a house, from *demō*, to build.] A roof rising up in the form of an inverted cup; a large cupola; the hemispherical roof of a building; anything shaped like a dome, as the steam-chamber of a locomotive, rising above it with a rounded top, &c.—**Domed**, dōmd, *a.* Furnished with a dome.—**Domical**, dō'mi-kal, *a.* Shaped like a dome or cupola.

Domestic, dō-mes'tik, *a.* [L. *domesticus*, from *domus*, a house; from root seen in Gr. *demō*, to build, and in E. *timber*; akin *domicile*.] Belonging to the house or home; pertaining to one's place of residence and to the family; devoted to home duties or pleasures; living in or about the habitations of man; kept for the use of man; tame; not wild; pertaining to one's own country; intestine; not foreign. — *Domestic economy*, the economical management of all household affairs; the art of managing domestic affairs in the best and thriftiest manner.—*n.* One who lives in the family of another, and is paid for some service; a household servant. — **Domestically**, dō-mes'ti-kal-li, *adv.* In a domestic manner.—**Domesticate**, dō-mes'ti-kāt, *v.t.* — *domesticated*, *domesticating*. To make domestic; to accustom to remain much at home; to accustom (animals) to live near the habitations of man; to tame; to reduce from a wild to a cultivated condition (plants).—**Domestication**, dō-mes'ti-kā"shon, *n.* The act of domesticating; the state of being domesticated. — **Domesticity**, dō-mes-tis'i-ti, *n.* State of being domestic.

Domicile, dom'i-sīl, *n.* [L. *domicilium*, a mansion, from *domus*, a house, and root of *cella*, a cell. DOMESTIC.] A place of residence; a dwelling-house; the place where one lives in opposition to the place where one only remains for a time.—*v.t.*—*domiciled*, *domiciling*. To establish in a fixed residence.—**Domiciliary**, dom-i-sil'i-a-ri, *a.* Pertaining to a domicile.—*Domiciliary visit*, a visit to a private dwelling, particularly for the purpose of searching it under authority. — **Domiciliate**, dom-i-sil'i-āt, *v.t.*—*domiciliated*, *domiciliating*. To domicile.—**Domiciliation**, dom-i-sil'i-ā"shon, *n.* Permanent residence; inhabitancy.

Dominant, dom'i-nant, *a.* [L. *dominans*, ppr. of *dominor*, to rule, from *dominus*, lord, master. DAME.] Ruling; prevailing; governing; predominant.—*Dominant chord*, *mus.* that which is formed by grouping three tones, rising gradually by intervals of a third from the dominant or fifth tone of the scale.—*n. Mus.* the fifth tone of the diatonic scale; thus G is the dominant of the scale of C, and D the dominant of the scale of G.—**Dominance, Dominancy**, dom'i-nans, dom'i-nan-si, *n.* Ascendency; rule; authority. — **Dominate**, dom'i-nāt, *v.t.* — *dominated*, *dominating*. To have power, or sway over; to govern; to prevail or predominate over. — *v.i.* To predominate.—**Domination**, dom-i-nā'shon, *n.* The exercise of power in ruling; dominion; government; arbitrary authority; tyranny.—**Dominations**, *n.* The fourth rank or order in the angelic hierarchy.—**Dominative**, dom'i-nā-tiv, *a.* Presiding; governing; imperious; insolent.—**Dominator**, dom'i-nā-tėr, *n.* One that dominates; a ruler or ruling power; the presiding or predominant power.—**Domineer**, dom-i-nēr', *v.i.* To rule with insolence or arbitrary sway; to bluster; to hector.—*v.t.* To govern harshly or overbearingly; to order or command insolently.—**Domineering**, dom-i-nē'ring, *p.* and *a.* Given to domineer; overbearing. — **Dominical**, dō-min'i-kal, *a.* [L.L. *dominicalis*, connected with Sunday, from L. *dominicus* (*dies dominica*, Sunday), pertaining to a lord or master, from *dominus*, lord. DOMINANT.] Noting or marking the Lord's day or Sunday; relating to our Lord.—*Dominical letter*, one of the seven letters, A, B, C, D, E, F, G, used in almanacs, &c., to mark the Sundays throughout the year.

Dominican, dō-min'i-kan, *a.* Of or pertaining to St. Dominic or the order founded by him.—*n.* A member of a religious order instituted in 1216 at Toulouse, by Dominic de Guzman (afterwards St. *Dominic*) with the special purpose of combating the doctrines of the Albigenses: called also *Black-friar*, from the colour of the dress.

Dominie, dom'i-ni, *n.* [From L. *domine*, vocative case of *dominus*, a lord or master.] A schoolmaster; a pedagogue. [Scotch.]

Dominion, dō-min'yon, *n.* [L. *dominium*. See DOMAIN.] Sovereign or supreme authority; the power of governing and controlling; government; sway; rule; ascendency; predominance; territory under a government; country or district governed, or within the limits of the authority of a prince or state; *pl.* an order of angels (N.T.).

Domino, dom'i-nō, *n.* pl. **Dominoes**, dom'i-nōz. [Fr., a covering for the head worn by priests, from *dominus*, lord.] A masquerade dress, consisting of an ample cloak or mantle, with a cap and wide sleeves; frequently, though incorrectly, applied to a half-mask worn by ladies as a partial disguise for the features; a person wearing a domino; *pl.* a game played with twenty-eight flat, oblong pieces of ivory or bone, dotted, after the manner of dice, with a certain number of points.

Don, don. [From L. *dominus*, a lord. The feminine is *donna* or *doña*.] A title in Spain, formerly given to noblemen and gentlemen only, but now used much more widely; a fellow or one holding high office in an English college (*colloq.*).

Don, don, *v.t.*—*donned*, *donning*. [To *do on*: opposed to *doff*.] To put on; to invest one's self with.

Donation, dō-nā'shon, *n.* [L. *donatio*, an offering, from *dono*, to give; *donum*, a gift, from *do*, to give.] The act of giving or bestowing; that which is gratuitously given; a grant; a gift.—**Donative**, don'a-tiv, *n.* A gift; a largess; a gratuity; a present; a dole; *law*, a benefice given to a person by the founder or patron, without presentation, institution, or induction by the ordinary.—*a.* Vested or vesting by donation.—**Donee**, dō-nē', *n.* The recipient of a gift or grant. — **Donor**, dō'nėr, *n.* One who gives, grants, or bestows; a giver.

Done, dun, pp. of *do*.

Donga, dong'ga, *n.* A South African name for a gulley or ravine.

Donjon, don'jon, *n.* [Fr., from L.L. *domnio*, *domnionis*, for L. *dominio*, dominion.] The principal tower of a castle, which was usually situated in the innermost court, and into which the garrison could retreat in case of necessity, the lower part of it being commonly used as a prison: also called the *Keep*.

Donkey, dong'ki, *n.* [Lit. a little *dun* animal, from *dun* and diminutive term. *-key.*] An ass; a stupid or obstinate and wrong-headed fellow.—**Donkey-engine**, *n.* A small steam-engine used where no great power is required, and often to perform some subsidiary operation, as on board ships.

Donna, don'na, *n.* [It., from L. *domina*, a lady or mistress.] A lady; as, *prima donna*, the first female singer in an opera, oratorio, &c.

Donor. Under DONATION.

Dooab. DOAB.

Doob, döb, *n.* [Hind.] Indian fodder grass, acclimatized in United States.

Dooly, Doolie, dö'li, *n.* [Hind.] Light litter used in India.

Doom, döm, *n.* [A.Sax. *dóm* = O.Sax., O. Fris. *dom*, Goth. *doms*, Icel. *dómr*, the same word as the suffix *-dom* in king*dom*, &c., and derived probably from verb *to do*. Akin *deem.*] A judgment or judicial sentence; passing of sentence; the final judgment; the state to which one is doomed or destined; fate; fortune, generally evil; adverse issue; ruin; destruction.—*Crack of doom*, dissolution of nature.—*v.t.* To condemn to any punishment; to consign by a decree or sentence; to pronounce sentence or judgment on; to ordain as a penalty; to decree; to destine.—**Doomer**, dö'mėr, *n.* One who dooms.—**Doomsday**, dömz'dā, *n.* The day of doom or final judgment; a day of sentence or condemnation (*Shak.*).—*Doomsday Book*, a book compiled by order of William the Conqueror containing a survey of all the lands in England, giving the areas of estates, the amount of land under tillage, pasture, woods, &c., the number of villeins, &c.—**Doomsman**, dömz'man, *n.* A judge; an umpire.—**Doomster**, döm'stėr, *n.* Obsolete official in Scottish law courts, pronouncing the sentence of the judge.

Doom Palm. DOUM PALM.

Doonga, dön'ga, *n.* A canoe made out of a single piece of wood, employed for navigating the marshes and the branches of the mouth of the Ganges.

Door, dōr, *n.* [A.Sax. *dór*, *dúru* = O.Sax. *dur*, *dor*, Icel. *dyr*, Goth. *daur*, G. *thür*, L. *fores*, Gr. *thura*, Ir. *dorus*, Skr. *dvāra*, door.] An opening or passage into a house or apartment by which persons enter; the frame of boards or other material that shuts such an opening, and usually turns on hinges; means of approach or access.—*To lie* or *be at one's door* (*fig.*), to be imputable or chargeable to one.—*Next door to* (*fig.*), near to; bordering on (*colloq.*).—*Out of door* or *doors*, out of the house; in the open air; abroad.—*In doors*, within the house; at home.—**Door-keeper**, *n.* A porter; one who guards the entrance of a house or apartment.—**Door-nail**, *n.* The nail on which, in ancient doors, the knocker struck.—**Door-plate**, *n.* A plate upon a door bearing the name of the resident.—**Door-step, Door-stone**, *n.* The stone at the threshold.—**Doorway**, dōr'wā, *n.* The passage of a door; the entrance-way into a room or house.

Dope, dōp, *v.t.* To drug; to dose.—*n.* A narcotic; a dull or stupid person. (*Slang.*)

Doquet, dok'et, *n.* DOCKET.

Dor, Dorr, dor, *n.* [A.Sax. *dora*, drone, a humble-bee.] A common British beetle, of a stout form and black colour, often heard droning through the air towards the close of the summer twilight.—**Dor-hawk**, *n.* A name sometimes given to the common goat-sucker.

Doree, dō'rē, *n.* Same as *Dory* (the fish).

Doric, Dorian, dor'ik, dō'ri-an, *a.* Pertaining to the Dorians, a people of ancient Greece.—*Doric order*, *arch.* the oldest and simplest of the three orders of Grecian architecture, characterized by the columns having no base, and the flutings few, large, and not deep, the capital of simple character.—*Dorian* or *Doric mode*, *mus.* a composition in which the second note of the normal scale acquires something of the dignity or force of a tonic, and upon it the melody closes.—**Doric**, *n.* The language of the Dorians, a Greek dialect characterized by broadness and hardness; hence, any dialect with similar characteristics, especially to the Scottish.—**Doricism**, dor'i-sizm, *n.* A peculiarity of the Doric dialect.

Dorking, dor'king, *n.* A species of domestic fowl, distinguished by having five claws on each foot, so named because bred largely at *Dorking* in Surrey.

Dormant, dor'mant, *a.* [Fr., from *dormir*, L. *dormio*, to sleep.] Sleeping; sunk in the winter sleep or torpid state of certain animals; at rest; not in action (*dormant* energies); neglected; not claimed, asserted, or insisted on (a *dormant* title or privileges); in *heraldry*, of beast with head on paws.—*Dormant partner*, a partner who takes no active part in a commercial concern.—**Dormancy**, dor'man-si, *n.* State of being dormant.—**Dormer, Dormer-window**, dor'mėr, *n.* [Lit. the window of a sleeping apartment.] A window standing vertically on a sloping roof of a dwelling-house, and so named because such windows are found chiefly in attic bed-rooms.—**Dormitive**, dor'mi-tiv, *n.* A medicine to promote sleep; an opiate; a soporific.—*a.* Causing or tending to cause sleep.—**Dormitory**, dor'mi-to-ri, *n.* [L. *dormitorium.*] A place, building, or room to sleep in.—**Dormouse**, dor'mous, *n.* pl. **Dormice**, dor'mīs. [Prov. E. *dorm*, to sleep, and *mouse*, lit. the sleeping-mouse.] A small rodent animal which passes the winter in a lethargic or torpid state, only occasionally waking and applying to its stock of provisions hoarded up for that season.

Dornick, Dornic, dor'nik, *n.* A species of figured linen of stout fabric, so called from *Dornick*, the Flemish name for *Tournay* in Flanders, where it was first manufactured.

Dorsad, dor'sad. [L. *dorsum*, back, *ad*, toward.] Toward the dorsal aspect.

Dorsal, dor'sal, *a.* [From L. *dorsum*, the back.] Of or pertaining to the back.—**Dorsibranchiate**, dor-si-brang'ki-āt, *a.* Having the branchiæ along the back, as certain molluscs.—**Dorsi-spinal**, *a.* Of or pertaining to the back and the spine.

Dorse, dors, *n.* [G. *dorsch*, Scand. *torsk.*] A small variety of the codfish.

Dory, dō'ri, *n.* [Also called *John-Dory*, probably from Fr. *jaune dorée*, golden yellow, from its colour.] A European fish of a beautiful yellow colour, with a curious protrusible mouth, valued as food.

Dory, dō'ri, *n.* A canoe or small boat.

Dose, dōs, *n.* [Fr., from Gr. *dosis*, a giving, from *didōmi*, to give.] The quantity of medicine given or prescribed to be taken at one time; anything given to be swallowed; as much as a man can take; a quantity in general.—*v.t.*—*dosed, dosing.* To form into suitable doses; to give a dose or doses to; to physic.—**Dosage**, dō'sāj, *n.* *Med.* act of dosing; administering of medicine by doses.

Dossal, dos'al, *n.* [L.L. *dorsale*, from L. *dorsum*, back.] An ornamental cloth hung at the back of an altar or a seat.

Dossier, dos'ē-ā, *n.* [Fr. word, from *dos*, back.] A collection of documents containing information about a person or incident.

Dot, dot, *n.* [A.Sax. *dott*, a spot or speck (whence Sc. *dottle*, a small lump): comp. L.G. *dutte*, a plug, a stopper; D. *dot*, a small bundle.] A small point or spot made with a pen or other pointed instrument; a speck, used in marking a writing or other thing; a spot.—*v.t.*—*dotted, dotting.* To mark with dots; to mark or diversify with small detached objects (as clumps of trees).—*v.i.* To make dots or spots.

Dotal, dō'tal, *a.* [Fr., from L. *dotalis*, from *dos*, dower. DOWER.] Pertaining to dower or a woman's marriage portion; constituting dower, or comprised in it.—**Dotation**, dō-tā'shon, *n.* The act of bestowing a marriage portion on a woman; endowment; establishment of funds for the support of an hospital or other eleemosynary corporation.

Dote, dōt, *v.i.*—*doted, doting.* [The same word as O.D. *doten*, to dote; akin to D. *dut*, a nap, *dutten*, to take a nap; Icel. *dotta*, to nod with sleep.] To have the intellect impaired by age, so that the mind wanders or wavers; to be in a state of senile silliness; to be excessively in love; to love to excess or extravagance (to *dote on* a person).—**Doter**, dō'tėr, *n.* One who dotes.—**Dotage**, dō'tāj, *n.* Feebleness or imbecility of understanding or mind, particularly in old age; childishness of old age; senility; weak and foolish affection.—**Dotard**, dō'tėrd, *n.* A man whose intellect is impaired by age; one in his second childhood.—**Dotardly**, dō'tėrd-li, *a.* Like a dotard; weak.—**Dotingly**, dō'ting-li, *adv.* In a doting manner; foolishly; in a manner characterized by excessive fondness.—**Dotish**, dō'tish, *a.* Childishly fond; weak; stupid.—**Dotterel, Dottrel**, dot'ėr-el, dot'rel, *n.* [From the bird's supposed stupidity.] A species of plover, breeding in the highest latitudes of Asia and Europe, and migrating to the shores of the Mediterranean; a booby; a dupe; a gull.

Douane, dö-an, *n.* [Ar. *diwan.*] Foreign custom-house.

Double, dub'l, *a.* [Fr. *double*, from L. *duplus*, double—*duo*, two, and term. *-plus*, from root of *pleo*, to fill. FILL.] Forming a pair; consisting of two in a set together; coupled; composed of two corresponding parts; twofold; twice as much; multiplied by two (a *double* portion); acting two parts, one openly, the other in secret; deceitful; *bot.* having two or more rows of petals produced by cultivation from stamens and carpels.—*v.t.*—*doubled, doubling.* To make double or twofold; to fold one part upon another part of; to increase by adding an equal sum, value, or quantity; to contain twice as much as; to pass round or by; to march or sail round, so as to proceed along both sides of (to *double* a cape).—*v.i.* To increase or grow to twice as much; to turn back or wind in running.—*n.* Twice as much; a turn in running to escape pursuers; a trick; a shift; an artifice to deceive; something precisely equal or like; a counterpart; a duplicate; a copy; a person's apparition or likeness; a wraith; a fold or plait; *milit.* the quickest step in marching next to the run.—**Double-acting**, *p.* and *a.* *Mach.* acting or applying power in two directions; producing a double result.—**Double-barreled**, *a.* Having two barrels, as a gun.—**Double-bass**, *n.* The largest musical instrument of the viol kind.—**Double-breasted**, *a.* Applied to a waistcoat or coat, either side of which may be made to lap over the other and button.—**Double-dealer**, *n.* One who deceitfully acts two different parts; a deceitful, trickish person; one who says one thing and thinks or intends another; one guilty of duplicity.—**Double-dealing**, *n.* Duplicity; the profession of one thing and the practice of another.—*a.* Given to duplicity; deceitful.—**Double-dye**, *v.t.* To dye twice over.—**Double-dyed**, *p.* and *a.* Twice dyed; thorough; complete; utter (a *double-dyed* villain).—**Double-eagle**, *n.* A gold coin of the United States, worth $20; the representation of an eagle with two heads.—**Double-edged**, *a.* Having two edges; *fig.* applied to an argument which makes both for and against the person employing it.—**Double-elephant**, *n.* A large size of writing, drawing, and printing paper, 40 inches by 26½.—**Double-entendre**, or, more correctly, **Double-entente**, dö-bl-än-tän-dr, än-tänt, *n.* A phrase with a double meaning, one of which is often somewhat indelicate.—**Double-entry**, *n.* A mode of book-keeping in which two entries are made of every transaction, one on the Dr. side of one account, and the other on the Cr. side of another account, in order that the one may check the other.—**Double-faced**, *a.* Deceitful; hypocritical; showing two faces.—**Double-glo'ster**, *n.* A rich kind of English cheese, made in Gloucestershire from new milk.—**Double-lock**, *v.t.* To lock with two bolts; to fasten with double security.—**Doubleness**, dub'l-nes, *n.* The state of being double; duplicity.—**Double-quick**, *n.* *Milit.* the quickest step next to the run.—Pertaining to or in conformity with the double-quick; very quick or rapid.—**Doubler**, dub'lėr, *n.* One who or that which doubles.—**Double-security**, *n.* Two securities held by a creditor for the same debt.—**Double-shuffle**, *n.* A shuffling, noisy dance by one person.—**Double-star**, *n.* *Astron.* two stars so near each other that they are distinguishable only by the help of a telescope.—**Doublet**, dub'let, *n.* [Dim. of *double.*] A close-fitting garment covering the body from the neck to a little below the waist, now superseded by the vest or waistcoat; one of a pair; a simple form of microscope consisting of a combination of two simple lenses; one of two (or more) words really the same but different in form (as *ant* and *emmet*).—**Double-tongued**, *a.* Making contrary declarations on the same subject to different persons from deceitful motives.—**Doubling**, dub'ling, *n.* The act of making double; a fold, plait, lining, &c.; the winding course of a hare or fox; an artifice; a shift; the substitution of the main actors by less valuable talent during the taking of hazardous scenes in moving pictures.—**Doubloon**, dub-lön', *n.* [Fr. *doublon*, Sp. *doblon.*] A coin of Spain and the Spanish American States, value about $5.00 in U. S. currency.

Doubt, dout, *v.i.* [O.Fr. *doubter*, from L. *dubitare*, to doubt, from same stem as *dubius*, doubtful, from *duo*, two. Akin *dubius*, *dual*, &c.] To waver or fluctuate in opinion; to be in uncertainty respecting the truth or fact; to be undetermined.—*v.t.* To question or hold questionable; to withhold assent from; to hesitate to believe; to suspect; to be inclined to think (governing clauses: I *doubt* you are wrong) (*Scot.*); to distrust; to be diffident of (to *doubt* a person's ability).—*n.* A fluctuation of mind respecting the truth or correctness of a statement or opinion, or the propriety of an action; uncertainty of mind; want of belief; unsettled state of opinion; suspicion; apprehension.—**Doubtable**, dou'ta-bl, *a.* Liable to be doubted.—**Doubter**, dou'tėr, *n.* One who doubts.—**Doubtful**, dout'ful, *a.* Entertaining doubt; not settled in opinion; undetermined; wavering; dubious; ambiguous; not clear in its meaning; not obvious, clear, or certain; questionable; not without suspicion; not confident; not without fear; not certain or defined.—**Doubtfully**, dout'ful-li, *adv.* In a doubtful manner.—**Doubtfulness**, dout'ful-nes, *n.* The state or quality of being doubtful; uncertainty; suspense; ambiguity.—**Doubtingly**, dou'ting-li, *adv.* In a doubting manner; dubiously; without confidence.—**Doubtless**, dout'les, *adv.* Without doubt or question; unquestionably.—**Doubtlessly**, *adv.* Unquestionably.

Douceur, dö'sėr, *n.* [Fr., from *doux*, L. *dulcis*, sweet.] A present, gift, or gratuity; a bribe.

Douche, dösh, *n.* [Fr.] A kind of bath consisting in a jet or current of water or vapour directed upon some part of the body.

Dough, dō, *n.* [A.Sax. *dág*, *dáh*=D. *deeg*, Icel. and Dan. *deig*, Goth. *daigs*, G. *teig*, dough; akin Goth. *deigan*, to mould, to form.] Paste of bread; a mass composed of flour or meal moistened and kneaded but not baked.—**Doughboy**, *n.* During the World War the nickname for an infantryman in the U. S. army.—**Doughnut**, *n.* A small roundish cake, usually with a hole in the center.

Doughty, dou'ti, *a.* [A.Sax. *dohtig*, *dyhtig*, from *dugan* (Sc. *dow*), to be able; Dan. *dygtig*, G. *tuchtig*, able, fit. Do, *v.i.*] Brave; valiant; noble; illustrious: now seldom used except in irony or burlesque.—**Doughtily**, dou'ti-li, *adv.* With doughtiness.—**Doughtiness**, dou'ti-nes, *n.* The character of being doughty; valour; bravery.

Doum, Doum Palm, döm, *n.* A palm-tree, the fruit of which is about the size of an apple and tastes like gingerbread, and is eaten by the poorer inhabitants of Upper Egypt, where the tree grows.

Douse, Dowse, dous, *v.t.*—*doused*, *dousing*. [Origin doubtful; comp. Sw. *dunsa*, to plump; D. *doesen*, to strike.] To thrust or plunge into water; to immerse; to dip; *naut.* to strike or lower in haste; to slacken suddenly; to put out or extinguish (slang). —*v.i.* To fall or be plunged suddenly into water.

Dout,† dout, *v.t.* [Contr. for *do out*. Comp. *doff*, *don.*] To put out; to quench; to extinguish (*Shak.*).

Dove, duv, *n.* [A.Sax. *dúfa*, *dúfe*, from *dúfan*, to dive, to dip, probably from its habit of ducking the head, or from its manner of flight; D. *duif*, Dan. *due*, Sc. *doo*, G. *taube.*] A pigeon, some varieties being distinguished by an additional term prefixed, as *ring-dove*, *turtle-dove*, &c.; a word of endearment.—**Dove-cot, Dove-cote**, *n.* A small building or box in which domestic pigeons breed; a house for doves. —**Dove-eyed**, *a.* Having eyes like those of a dove; having eyes expressive of meekness, gentleness, or tenderness.—**Dovetail**, *n.* *Carp.* a method of fastening the ends of boards together at right angles by letting one piece, cut into projections somewhat like a dove's tail spread, into corresponding cavities in another.—*v.t.* *Carp.* to unite by the above method; *fig.* to fit or adjust exactly and firmly.

Dowager, dou'a-jėr, *n.* [From a form *dowage*, from Fr. *douer*, to endow. DOWER.] A name given to the widow of a person of title, as a prince or nobleman, to distinguish her from the wife of her husband's heir bearing the same title; thus when a duke dies leaving a widow, and his successor in the title has a wife, the widow becomes the duchess-*dowager*.

Dowdy, dou'di, *n.* [Akin to O.E. *dowde*, *dowd*, dull, sluggish; E. *dawdle*, L.G. *dödeln*, to be slow; Prov.E. *daw*, a sluggard.] An awkward, ill-dressed woman; a woman with no elegance or grace.—*a.* Awkward; ill-dressed; vulgar-looking; applied to females. —**Dowdyish**, dou'di-ish, *a.* Like a dowdy.

Dowel, dou'el, *n.* [Fr. *douille*, a groove or socket; L.L. *ductile*, a gutter, from L. *duco*, to lead.] A wooden or iron pin or tenon used in joining together two pieces of any substance edgewise (as the pieces of a barrel-end); a piece of wood driven into a wall to receive nails of skirtings, &c.—*v.t.*—*dowelled*, *dowelling*. To fasten by means of dowels, as two boards together by pins inserted in the edges.—**Dowel-joint**, *n.* A joint made by means of a dowel or dowels.—**Dowel-pin**, *n.* A pin inserted in the edges of boards to fasten them together.

Dower, dou'ėr, *n.* [Fr. *douaire*, from L.L. *dotarium*, from L. *doto*, *dotatum*, to endow, from *dos*, *dotis*, a dower, whence also *dotal*, *dowager.*] That with which one is endowed; the property which a woman brings to her husband in marriage; *law*, the right which a wife has in the third part of the real estate of which her husband died possessed.—*v.t.* To furnish with dower or a portion; to endow.—**Dowerless**, dou'ėr-les, *a.* Destitute of dower.—**Dowry**, dou'ri, *n.* The money, goods, or estate which a woman brings to her husband in marriage; dower.

Dowlas, dou'las, *n.* [Perhaps from *Doullens* in France.] A kind of coarse linen cloth.

Dowle, Dowl, doul, *n.* [O.Fr. *douille*, *doille*, soft, L. *ductilis*, from *duco*, to lead.] One of the filaments of a feather; a fibre of down; down.

Down, doun, *n.* [A.Sax. *dún*, a hill; L.G. *dünen*, Fris. *dunen*, D. *duin*, a dune; O.H.G. *dûn*, *dûna*, promontory, Sw. dial. *dun*, a hill; also W., Ir., and Gael. *dun*, a hill, hillock.] A hill or rising ground; a low, rounded, grassy hill; a tract of naked, hilly land, used chiefly for pasturing sheep; a term commonly used in the south of England; also a dune or sand-hill near the sea.

Down, doun, *prep.* [A.Sax. *adúne*, adown, for *of-dúne*, off or down the hill. DOWN, a hill.] Along in descent; from a higher to a lower part of; toward the mouth of and in the direction of the current.—*adv.* In a descending direction; from a higher to a lower position, degree, or place in a series; from the metropolis of a country to the provinces, or from the main terminus of a railway to the subordinate stations; on the ground, or at the bottom; in a low condition; in humility, dejection, calamity, &c.; below the horizon (the sun is *down*); into disrepute or disgrace (to write *down* folly, vice, an author); from a larger to a less bulk (to boil *down*); from former to more recent times; extended or prostrate on the ground or on any flat surface; paid or handed over in ready money (a thousand pounds *down*). It is often used elliptically or interjectionally for go down, kneel down, &c. (*down*! dog, *down*!); also with *with*, in energetic commands; as, *down with* the sail, that is, take it down.—*Up and down*, here and there; everywhere.—*Down in the mouth*, dispirited; dejected. (*Colloq.*)—*To be down at heel*, to have the back part of the upper, or heel, turned down, or to have on shoes with the heel turned down; to be slipshod or slovenly.—*n.* A downward fluctuation (ups and *downs*).—**Downbear**, *v.t.* To bear down; to depress.—**Downcast**, doun'kast, *a.* Cast downward; directed to the ground (*downcast* eyes); in low spirits; dejected.—*n.* *Mining*, the ventilating shaft down which the air passes in circulating through a mine.—**Downcastness**, doun'kast-nes, *n.* State of being downcast; sadness.—**Downcome**, doun'kum, *n.* A tumbling or falling down; a sudden or heavy fall; hence, ruin; destruction.—**Down-draught**, *n.* A draught or current of air down a chimney, shaft of a mine, &c.—**Downfall**, doun'fal, *n.* A falling down; a sudden descent or fall from a position of power, honour, wealth, fame, or the like; loss of rank, reputation, or fortune; loss of office; ruin; destruction.—**Downfallen**, doun'faln, *a.* Fallen; ruined.—**Downhearted**, doun'här-ted, *a.* Dejected in spirits.—**Downhill**, doun'hil, *n.* A declivity; slope.—*a.* Sloping downwards; descending; sloping.—*adv.* Down a hill or slope.—**Down-line**, *n.* The line of a railway leading from the capital, or other important centre, to the provinces.—**Down-lying**, doun'lī-ing, *n.* The time of retiring to rest; time of repose. —**Downpour**, doun'pōr, *n.* A pouring down; especially a heavy or continuous shower.—**Downright**, doun'rīt, *adv.* Right down; perpendicularly; in plain terms; completely; thoroughly.—*a.* Directed straight or right down; coming down perpendicularly; directly to the point; plain; open; mere; sheer (*downright* nonsense); straightforward; unceremonious; blunt (a *downright* man).—**Downrightly**, doun'rīt-li, *adv.* Plainly; in plain terms.—**Downrightness**, doun'rīt-nes, *n.*—**Down-rush**, *n.* A rush downward or towards a centre.—**Down-sitting**, *n.* The act of sitting down.—**Down-stairs**, *a.* Pertaining or relating to the lower flat of a house. —**Down-stroke**, *n.* A downward stroke or blow; a line drawn downward with the pen; a thick stroke of a letter.—**Downthrow**, doun'thrō, *n.* A throwing down; *geol.* a fall or sinking of strata below the level of the surrounding beds: opposed to *upheaval* or *upthrow*.—**Down-train**, *n.* A train proceeding from the capital, or other important centre, to the provinces. —**Down-trodden, Down-trod**, *a.* Trodden down; trampled upon; tyrannized over.—**Downward, Downwards**, doun'wėrd, doun'wėrdz, *adv.* From a higher place to a lower; in a descending course; in a course or direction from a spring or source; in a course of descent from an ancestor.—**Downward**, *a.* Moving or extending from a higher to a lower place (a *downward* course); descending from a head, origin, or source; tending to a lower condition or state.—**Downweigh**, doun-wā', *v.t.* To weigh or press down; to depress; to cause to sink or prevent from rising.

Down, doun, *n.* [Same word as Icel. *dún*, Dan. *duun*, G. *daune*, down.] The fine soft covering of birds under the feathers, particularly on the breasts of water-fowl, as the duck and swan; the soft hair of the human face when beginning to appear; the pubescence of plants, a fine hairy substance; any fine feathery or hairy substance of vegetable growth.—*v.t.* To cover, stuff, or line with down.—**Downiness**, dou'ni-nes, *n.* The quality of being downy; knowingness or cuteness (slang).—**Downy**, dou'ni, *a.* Covered with down or nap; covered with pubescence or soft hairs, as a plant; made of down; soft, calm, soothing (sleep); knowing, cunning, or artful (slang).

Dowry, *n.* Under DOWER.

Dowsing-rod, dou'zing-rod, *n.* A name for the divining-rod.

Doxology, dok-sol'o-ji, *n.* [Gr. *doxologia*, a praising—*doxa*, praise, glory, and *legō*, to speak.] A short hymn or form of words ascribing glory to God, and used in worship. —**Doxological**, dok-so-loj'i-kal, *a.* Pertaining to doxology.—**Doxologize**, dok-sol'o-jīz, *v.i.* To give glory to God, as in doxology.

Doxy, dok'si, *n.* [Comp. G. *docke*, Sw. *docka*, a doll, a plaything.] An old low term for a sweetheart or mistress.

Doyley, doi'li, *n.* Same as *Doily*.

Doze, dōz, *v.i.—dozed, dozing.* [Akin to Dan. *döse*, to doze; *dös*, drowsiness; G. *döseln*, *doseln*, to doze; Prov. G. *dosen*, to slumber; allied to *dizzy* and to *daze*.] To slumber; to sleep lightly; to live in a state of drowsiness; to be dull or half asleep.—*v.t.* To pass or spend in drowsiness; to make dull; to stupefy.—*n.* A light sleep; a slumber.—**Dozer**, dō'zėr, *n.* One that dozes or slumbers. — **Doziness**, dō'zi-nes, *n.* Drowsiness; heaviness; inclination to sleep. —**Dozy**, dō'zi, *a.* Drowsy; heavy; inclined to sleep; sleepy.

Dozen, duz'n, *n.* [Fr. *douzaine*, from *douze*, twelve, from L. *duodecim—duo*, two, and *decem*, ten.] A collection of twelve things of a like kind, or regarded as forming an aggregate for the time being; an indefinite or round number comprising more or less than twelve units, as the case may be.

Drab, drab, *n.* [A Celtic word; Ir. *drabhog*, a slut, dregs, from *drab*, a spot, a stain; Gael. *drabach*, dirty, slovenly; *drabag*, a drab; akin to *draff*.] A strumpet; a prostitute; a low, sluttish woman; a slattern.—*v.i.* To associate with strumpets.—**Drabber**, drab'ėr, *n.* One who keeps company with drabs. — **Drabbish**, drab'ish, *a.* Having the quality of a drab; sluttish. — **Drabble**, drab'l, *v.t.—drabbled, drabbling.* To draggle; to make dirty; to wet and befoul.

Drab, drab, *n.* [Fr. *drap*, L.L. *drappus*, cloth, from a Teut. root seen in E. *trappings*, horse furniture.] A thick woollen cloth of a dun or dull-brown colour; a dull brownish-yellow colour.—*a.* Being of a dull brown or pale brown colour, like the cloth so called.

Drachma, drak'ma, *n.* [L., from Gr. *drachmē*, a drachm, from *drassomai*, to grasp with the hand. *Dram* is the same word.] A Grecian coin, the average value of the Attic drachma being $3.00; the gold monetary unit of modern Greece, formerly equal to the Franc [$0.20], but in 1928 stabilized at $0.0193.

Draconic, **Draconian**, drā-kon'ik, drā-kō'ni-an, *a.* Relating to *Draco*, the Athenian lawgiver; hence (applied to laws), extremely severe; sanguinary.

Draff, draf, *n.* [Icel. *draf*, D. *draf*, also *drab*, Dan. *drav*, dregs, hog's-wash; allied to *drab*, a slut.] Refuse; dregs; hog's-wash; the refuse of malt which has been brewed or distilled from, given to swine and cows.—**Draffy**, draf'i, *a.* Like, or consisting of draff; waste; worthless.

Draft, draft, *n.* [A form of *draught*.] A selection of men or things for a special duty or purpose; a body of men drawn from a larger body; an order from one man to another directing the payment of money; an order authorizing a man to draw a certain sum of money; the first outlines of any writing, embodying an exposition of the purpose, as well as of the details, of the document; a drawing, delineation, or sketch in outline. — *v.t.* To make a draft of; to compose and write the first outlines of; to delineate in outline; to draw from a larger body; to select.

Drag, drag, *v.t.—dragged, dragging.* [A. Sax. *dragan*, to drag, to draw; Icel. *draga*, to drag, to carry; Goth. *dragan*, to draw, to carry; D. *dragen*, G. *tragen*, to carry, to bear. *Draw* is another form of the same word, *draggle* is a dim., and *drawl*, *dray*, *dredge*, are akin.] To pull; to haul; to draw along the ground by main force; to draw along slowly or heavily, as anything burdensome or troublesome; hence, to pass in pain or with difficulty; to search (a river, pond, &c.) with a net, hooked instrument, &c., for drowned persons, &c.—*To drag the anchor*, to draw or trail it along the bottom when it will not hold: said of a ship.—*v.i.* To be drawn along or trail on the ground, as a dress or as an anchor that does not hold; to move or proceed slowly, heavily, or laboriously; to move on lingeringly or with effort.—*n.* A net or a kind of grapnel for recovering the bodies of drowned persons; an apparatus used to recover articles lost in the water, or to dredge up oysters, &c.; a kind of heavy harrow for breaking up ground; a long coach or carriage, generally drawn by four horses, uncovered and seated round the sides; an apparatus for retarding or stopping the rotation of one wheel, or of several wheels of a vehicle, in descending hills, slopes, &c.; a person or thing forming an obstacle to one's progress or prosperity; slow and difficult motion.—**Drag-net**, *n.* A net to be drawn on the bottom of a river or pond for taking fish.

Draggle, drag'l, *v.t.—draggled, draggling.* [Dim. from *drag*, or, as some think, a form of *drabble*.] To wet and dirty by drawing on damp ground or mud, or on wet grass; to drabble. — *v.i.* To be drawn on the ground; to become wet or dirty by being drawn on the mud or wet grass.—**Draggle-tail**, *n.* A slut. — **Draggle-tailed**, *a.* Untidy; sluttish.

Dragoman, drag'ō-man, *n.* pl. **Dragomans**. [Sp. *dragoman*, from Ar. *tarjumân*, an interpreter, from *tarjama*, to interpret; Chal. *targem*, to interpret.] An interpreter and travellers' guide or agent in Eastern countries; an interpreter attached to an embassy or a consulate: a term in general use in the Levant.

Dragon, drag'on, *n.* [Fr. *dragon*, from L. *draco*, Gr. *drakōn*, from root *drak* or *derk*, as in *derkomai*, to see; Skr. *darç*, to see; so called from its fiery eyes.] A fabulous animal, conceived as a sort of winged crocodile, with fiery eyes, crested head, and enormous claws, spouting fire, and often regarded as an embodiment of watchfulness; a kind of small lizard, having an expansion of the skin on each side, which forms a kind of wing, serving to sustain the animal when it leaps from branch to branch; a fiery, shooting meteor, or imaginary serpent (*Shak.*); a fierce, violent person, male or female; more generally now, a spiteful, watchful woman; a short carbine, carried by the original dragoons, having the representation of a dragon's head at the muzzle; a variety of carrier pigeons. — **Dragonet**, drag'o-net, *n.* A little dragon; a small fish of the goby family.—**Dragon-fish**, *n.* The dragonet. —**Dragon-fly**, *n.* The popular name of a family of insects, having large strongly reticulated wings, a large head with enormous eyes, a long body, and strong horny mandibles.—**Dragonish**, drag'o-nish, *a.* Pertaining to or like a dragon.—**Dragon's-blood**, *n.* The popular name of the inspissated juice of various plants, used for colouring spirit and turpentine varnishes, for tooth-tinctures and powders, for staining marble, &c.—**Dragon-shell**, *n.* A name given to a species of limpet.—**Dragon-tree**, *n.* An evergreen tree of the Canary Islands, one of the plants that produce dragon's blood.

Dragoon, dra-gön', *n.* [From *dragon*, the carbine carried by the original dragoons raised by Marshal Brissac in 1660, on the muzzle of which, from the old fable that the dragon spouts fire, the head of the monster was worked.] Originally a soldier serving both on foot and horseback; now a cavalry soldier, there being in the British army *heavy* and *light dragoons*, now nearly alike in weight of men, horses, and appointments.—*v.t.* To harass with or abandon to the rage of soldiers; to harass; to persecute; to compel to submit by violent measures.—**Dragonade**, **Dragoonade**, drag-o-nād', dra-gö'nād, *n.* A persecution of French Protestants in the reign of Louis XIV, from dragoons generally leading the persecuting force; a military attack upon civilians.

Drain, drān, *v.t.* [Probably from A.Sax. *drehnigean*, to strain, and allied to *drag*.] To cause to pass through some porous substance; to filter; to exhaust any body of a liquid; to exhaust (land) of excessive moisture by causing it to flow off in channels; to exhaust; to deprive by drawing off gradually (to *drain* a country *of* men).—*v.i.* To flow off gradually; to be emptied or deprived of liquor by flowing or dropping.—*n.* The act of draining or drawing off, or of emptying by drawing off; gradual or continuous outflow or withdrawal; a channel through which water or other liquid flows off; a trench or ditch to convey water from wet land; a water-course; a sewer; *pl.* the grain from the mash-tub.—**Drainable**, drā'na-bl, *a.* Capable of being drained.—**Drainage**, drā'nāj, *n.* A draining; a gradual flowing off of any liquid; the system of drains and other works by which any town, surface, and the like, is freed from water; the mode in which the waters of a country pass off by its streams and rivers; the water carried away from a district by natural or other channels. — **Drainer**, drā'nėr, *n.* One who or that which drains; one who constructs channels for draining land; *cookery*, a perforated plate for letting fluids escape.—**Drain-tile**, **Draining-tile**, *n.* A hollow tile employed in the formation of drains.—**Drain-trap**, *n.* A contrivance to prevent the escape of foul air from drains, but to allow the passage of water into them.

Drake, drāk, *n.* [Contr. from a form *enedrice*, *endrake* (Icel. *andrika*, O.H.G. *antrecho*, *antricho*), a hypothetical masculine of A.Sax. *ened*, a duck, the termination *ric*, being the same as that in *bishopric*, and akin to Goth. *reiks*, ruling, G. *reich*, empire. *Ened* is cog. with L. *anas*, *anatis*, a duck.] The male of the duck kind; a species of fly used as bait in angling.

Dram, dram, *n.* [Contr. from *drachma*.] *Apothecaries' weight*, a weight of the eighth part of an ounce, or 60 grains; *avoirdupois weight*, the sixteenth part of an ounce; as much spirituous liquor as is drunk at once. —**Dram-shop**, *n.* A shop where spirits are sold in small quantities.

Drama, drä'ma, *n.* [Gr. *drama*, from *draō*, to do, to act.] A poem or composition representing a picture of human life, and accommodated to action, generally designed to be spoken in character and represented on the stage; a series of real events invested with dramatic unity and interest; dramatic composition or literature; dramatic representation and all that is connected with it. —**Dramatic**, **Dramatical**, dra-mat'ik, dra-mat'i-kal, *a.* Of or pertaining to the drama or plays represented on the stage; appropriate to or in the form of a drama; theatrical; characterized by the force and fidelity appropriate to the drama (a *dramatic* description).—**Dramatically**, dra-mat'i-kal-li, *adv.* In the manner of the drama; vividly and strikingly. — **Dramatist**, dram'a-tist, *n.* The author of a dramatic composition; a writer of plays.—**Dramatizable**, dram'a-tī-za-bl, *a.* Capable of being dramatized.—**Dramatize**, dram'a-tīz, *v.t.—dramatized, dramatizing.* To compose in the form of the drama; to adapt to the form of a play.—**Dramaturgy**, dram'a-tėr-ji, *n.* [Gr. *dramatourgia*, dramatic composition—*drama*, and *ergon*, work.] The science which treats of the rules of composing dramas and representing them on the stage.—**Dramaturgic**, dram-a-tėr′-jik, *a.* Pertaining to dramaturgy; theatrical; hence, unreal. — **Dramaturgist**, dram-a-tėr′jist, *n.* One skilled in dramaturgy.

Drank, pret. of *drink.*

Drape, drāp, *v.t.—draped, draping.* [Fr. *draper*, to drape, from *drap*, cloth. DRAB.] To cover or invest with clothing or cloth; to dispose drapery about for use or ornament.—**Draper**, drā′pėr, *n.* [Fr. *drapier.*] One who sells cloths; a dealer in cloths.—**Draperied**, drā′pėr-id, *a.* Furnished with drapery.—**Drapery**, drā′pėr-i, *n.* [Fr. *draperie.*] The occupation of a draper; cloth or textile fabrics; the clothes or hangings with which any object is draped or hung.

Drastic, dras′tik, *a.* [Gr. *drastikos*, from *draō*, to do, to act.] Acting with strength or violence; powerful; efficacious.—*n.* A strong purgative.

Draught, draft, *n.* [From *draw, drag.*] The act of drawing; the capacity of being drawn (a cart or plough of easy *draught*); the drawing of liquor into the mouth and throat; the act of drinking; the quantity of liquor drunk at once; the act of delineating, or that which is delineated; a representation by lines; a drawing or first sketch; an outline; a sweeping of the water for fish with a net; that which is taken by sweeping with a net (a *draught* of fishes); the depth of water necessary to float a ship, or the depth a ship sinks in water, especially when laden; a current of air moving through an inclosed or confined space, as through a room or up a chimney; *pl.* a game resembling chess played on a board divided into sixty-four checkered squares.—*On draught*, drawn or to be had directly from the cask, as ale, porter, &c.—*v.t.* To draw out; to sketch roughly; to draft.—*a.* Used for drawing; drawn from the barrel or other receptacle in which it is kept (*draught* ale).—**Draught-bar**, *n.* A bar to which the traces are attached in harnessing horses for draught purposes; a swing-tree or swingle-tree. — **Draught-board**, *n.* A checkered board for playing draughts.—**Draught-compasses**, *n. pl.* Compasses with movable points used for drawing the finer lines in mechanical drawings, as plans, &c. — **Draughtsman**, drafts′man, *n.* A man who draws plans or designs, or one who is skilled in such drawings.—**Draughtsmanship**, drafts′-man-ship, *n.* The office or work of a draughtsman.—**Draughty**, draf′ti, *a.* Of or pertaining to draughts of air; exposed to draughts.

Drave, drāv, old and poetical pret. of *drive.*

Dravidian, dra-vid′i-an, *a.* Of or pertaining to *Dravida*, the name of an old province of India; applied to a distinct family of tongues spoken in South India, Ceylon, &c.

Draw, dra̤, *v.t.—drew* (drö), *drawn* (dra̤n), *drawing.* [A softened form of *drag* (which see).] To pull along after one; to haul; to cause to advance by force applied in front of the thing moved or at the fore end; to pull out; to unsheathe; to bring out from some receptacle (to *draw* water); to let run out; to extract (blood, wine); to attract; to cause to move or tend toward; to allure; to lead by persuasion or moral influence; to lead, as a motive; to induce to move; to inhale; to take into the lungs; to pull more closely together, or apart (to *draw* a curtain); to lengthen; to extend in length; to form by extension (to *draw* wire); to form (a line) between two points; to represent by lines drawn on a plain surface; to form a picture or image; to describe in words or to represent in fancy; to derive, deduce, have, or receive from some source; to receive from customers or patrons; to receive or take (to *draw* money from a bank); to extort; to force out (groans, tears); to write in due form; to form in writing; to take out of a box or wheel, as tickets in a lottery; to receive or gain by such drawing; to require (so many feet of water) for floating; to bend (to *draw* the bow); to eviscerate; to finish, as a game, battle, &c., so as neither party can claim the victory.—*To draw a badger, fox*, &c., to drag or force it from its cover.—*To draw in*, to contract; to pull back; to collect or bring together; to entice, or inveigle.—*To draw off*, to draw away; to withdraw; to abstract (the mind); to draw or take from; to cause to flow from.—*To draw on*, to allure; to entice; to occasion; to cause.—*To draw over*, to persuade or induce to revolt from an opposing party, and to join one's own party.—*To draw out*, to lengthen; to extend; to compose or form in writing; to cause to issue forth; to elicit, by questioning or address; to cause to be declared; to call forth.—*To draw together*, to collect or be collected.—*To draw up*, to raise; to lift; to form in order of battle; to array; to compose in due form, as a writing; to form in writing.—*v.i.* To pull; to exert strength in drawing; to act or have influence, as a weight; to shrink; to contract; to advance; to approach; to resort or betake one's self to; to unsheathe a sword; to use or practise the art of delineating figures; to form a picture; to make a draft or written demand for payment of a sum of money upon a person.—*To draw back*, to retire; to move back; to withdraw.—*To draw near* or *nigh*, to approach; to come near.—*To draw off*, to retire; to retreat.—*To draw on*, to advance; to approach.—*To draw up*, to form themselves in regular order (as troops); to assume a certain order or arrangement; to stop a horse by pulling the reins.—*n.* The act of drawing; the lot or chance drawn; a drawn game. — **Drawable**, dra̤′a-bl, *a.* Capable of being drawn. — **Drawback**, dra̤′bak, *n.* What detracts from profit or pleasure; a discouragement or hindrance; a disadvantage; a certain amount of duties or customs dues paid back or remitted, as duty on spirits when they are sent abroad. —**Draw-bolt**, *n.* A coupling-pin. — **Drawbridge**, dra̤′brij, *n.* A bridge which may be drawn up or let down or opened or shut horizontally, to admit or hinder communication, as before the gate of a town or castle, or over a navigable river.—**Draw-cut**, *n.* A single cut with a knife in a plant, &c.—**Drawee**, dra̤-ē′, *n.* The person on whom an order or bill of exchange is drawn.—**Drawer**, dra̤′ėr, *n.* One who draws or pulls; one who takes water from a well; one who draws liquor from a cask; a waiter (*Shak.*); one who draws a bill of exchange or an order for the payment of money; a sliding box in a table, desk, &c., which is drawn out at pleasure; one of a set of such boxes in a case or bureau; *pl.* an under garment worn on the legs and lower part of the body by both sexes. CHEST. — **Draw-gate**, *n.* The valve of a sluice. — **Draw-gear**, *n.* A harness adapted for draught-horses; the apparatus or parts by which railway carriages are coupled together, &c.—**Drawing**, dra̤′ing, *n.* The act of one who draws; the representation or delineation of an object on a plain surface, by means of lines and shades, as with a pencil, crayon, pen, &c.; the amount of money taken for sales in a shop or other trading establishment.—**Drawing-board**, *n.* A board on which paper is stretched for drawing on or for painting in water-colours, &c.—**Drawing-master**, *n.* One who teaches the art of drawing.—**Drawing-paper**, *n.* A large-sized variety of stout paper, used for making drawings on.—**Drawing-pen**, *n.* A pen used in drawing lines.—**Drawing-pencil**, *n.* A black-lead pencil used in drawing. —**Drawing-room**, *n.* [For *withdrawing-room*, a room to which the company withdraws from the dining-room.] A room in a house appropriated for the reception of company; a room in which distinguished personages hold levees, or private persons receive parties; the formal reception of evening company at a royal court. — **Drawn**, dra̤n, *p.* and *a.* Pulled, hauled, allured; unsheathed; extended; delineated, &c.; not decided, from both parties having equal advantage and neither a victory (a *drawn* battle).—**Draw-net**, *n.* A net for catching birds.—**Draw-plate**, *n.* A stout plate of steel, pierced with a graduated series of conical holes, for drawing wire through in order to reduce and elongate it. — **Draw-well**, *n.* A deep well, from which water is drawn by a long cord or pole and a bucket.

Drawl, dra̤l, *v.t.* [A dim. form from *draw* or *drag.* DRAG.] To utter or pronounce in a slow lengthened tone; to while away in an indolent manner. — *v.i.* To speak with slow utterance. — *n.* A lengthened utterance of the voice. — **Drawlingly**, dra̤′ling-li, *adv.* In a drawling manner.

Dray, drā, *n.* [A.Sax. *drœge*, from *dragan.* DRAG, DRAW.] A low cart or carriage on heavy wheels, such as those used by brewers. —**Drayage**, drā′āj, *n.* The use of a dray; charge for the use of a dray. — **Dray-horse**, *n.* A horse used in a dray.—**Dray-man**, *n.* A man who attends a dray.

Dread, dred, *n.* [A.Sax. *draedan, on-draedan*, to fear.] Great fear or apprehension of evil or danger; terror; awe; fear united with respect; the cause of fear; the person or the thing dreaded (O.T.).—*a.* Exciting great fear or apprehension; terrible; frightful; awful; venerable in the highest degree. —*v.t.* To fear in a great degree.—*v.i.* To be in great fear.—**Dreader**, dred′ėr, *n.* One that dreads.—**Dreadful**, dred′fu̇l, *a.* Impressing dread or great fear; terrible; formidable; awful; venerable. — *n.* A print chiefly devoted to the narration of stories of criminal life, frightful accidents, &c. (*Colloq.*) — **Dreadfully**, dred′fu̇l-li, *adv.* In a manner to be dreaded.—**Dreadfulness**, dred′fu̇l-nes, *n.* The quality of being dreadful.—**Dreadless**, dred′les, *a.* Free from fear or dread; undaunted; intrepid.—**Dreadlessness**, dred′les-nes, *n.* Fearlessness; undauntedness. — **Dreadnought**, dred′na̤t, *n.* A person that fears nothing; a thick cloth with a long pile, used for warm clothing or to keep off rain; a garment made of such cloth; general term for battleship of the highest class.

Dream, drēm, *n.* [A.Sax. *dreám*, joy, melody; O.Fris. *drâm*, D. *droom*, G. *traum*, O.Sax. *drôm*, dream.] The thought or series of thoughts of a person in sleep; *Scrip.* impressions on the minds of sleeping persons made by divine agency; a matter which has only an imaginary reality; a visionary scheme or conceit; a vain fancy; an unfounded suspicion.—*v.i.—dreamed* or *dreamt* (dremt), *dreaming.* To have ideas or images in the mind in the state of sleep: with *of* before a noun; to think; to imagine; to think idly.—*v.t.* To see in a dream.—*To dream away*, to pass in reverie or inaction; to spend idly.—**Dreamer**, drē′mėr, *n.* One who dreams; a visionary; one who forms or entertains vain schemes.—**Dreamery**, drē′mėr-i, *n.* A habit of dreaming or musing. —**Dreamful**, drēm′fu̇l, *a.* Full of dreams. (*Tenn.*) — **Dreaminess**, drē′mi-nes, *n.* State of being dreamy. — **Dreamland**, drēm′land, *n.* The land of dreams; the region of fancy or imagination; the region of reverie.—**Dreamless**, drēm′les, *a.* Free from dreams.—**Dreamlessly**, drēm′les-li, *adv.* In a dreamless manner.—**Dreamy**, drē′mi, *a.* Full of dreams; associated with dreams; giving rise to dreams; dream-like.

Dreary, drē′ri, *a.* [A.Sax. *dreórig*, bloody, sad, sorrowful, *dreór*, blood, from *dreósan* (Goth. *driusan*), to fall, with common conversion of *s* into *r*; akin to G. *traurig*, sad, *trauern*, to mourn.] Dismal; gloomy; waste and desolate; distressing; oppressively monotonous. — **Drear**, drēr, *a.* Dismal; gloomy with solitude.—**Drearily**, drē′ri-li, *adv.* Gloomily; dismally. — **Dreariness**, drē′ri-nes, *n.* The state of being dreary.—**Drearisome**,† drē′ri-sum, *a.* Very dreary.

Dredge, drej, *n.* [From the stem of *drag*, the *g* being softened as in *bridge*, from older *brig.*] A drag-net for taking oysters, &c.; an apparatus for bringing up shells, plants, and other objects from the bottom of the sea for scientific investigation; a machine for clearing the beds of canals, rivers, harbours, &c.—*v.t.—dredged, dredging.* To take, catch, or gather with a dredge; to remove sand, silt, &c., from by the use of a dredge.—**Dredger**, drej′ėr, *n.* One who or that which dredges.—**Dredging-machine**, **Dredging-vessel**, *n.*

A machine used to take up mud or gravel from the bottoms of rivers, docks, &c.

Dredge, drej, *n.* [Fr. *dragée*, mixed provender for horses and cattle; It. *treggéa*, from Gr. *tragēmata*, dried fruits.] A mixture of oats and barley sown together.—*v.t.* To sprinkle flour on roast meat.—**Dredge-box, Dredging-box, Dredger**, drej′-ėr, *n.* A utensil for scattering flour on meats when roasting.

Dregs, dregz, *n. pl.* [Icel. *dregg*, Sw. *drägg*, dregs, lees; probably connected with *drag*, *drain*—the dregs being what remains after the liquor is drained off.] The sediment of liquors; lees; grounds; feculence; any foreign matter of liquors that subsides to the bottom of a vessel; dross; sweepings; refuse; hence, the most vile and worthless among men. *Dreg*, in the singular, is found in Spenser and Shakspere.—**Dregginess**, dreg′i-nes, *n.* State of being dreggy.—**Dreggy, Dreggish**, dreg′i, dreg′ish, *a.* Containing dregs or lees; consisting of dregs; foul; muddy; feculent.

Drench, drensh, *v.t.* [A.Sax. *drencan*, *drencean*, to give to drink, to drench, from *drincan*, to drink. DRINK.] To wet thoroughly; to soak; to saturate; to purge violently (an animal) with medicine.—*n.* [A.Sax. *drenc*, a draught.] A draught; a dose of medicine for a beast, as a horse.—**Drencher**, dren′shėr, *n.* One who drenches.

Dress, dres, *v.t.*—*dressed* or *drest*, *dressing*. [Fr. *dresser*, to make right, prepare, from a L.L. verb *directiare*, *drictiare*, to make straight, from L. *directus*, straight. DIRECT.] To make straight or in a straight line (troops); to put to rights; to put in good order; to till or cultivate; to treat (a wound or sore) with remedies or curative appliances; to prepare, in a general sense; to make suitable or fit for something (leather, a lamp, &c.); to put clothes on; to invest with garments; to adorn; to deck.—*To dress up* or *out*, to clothe elaborately, pompously, or elegantly.—*v.i. Milit.* to arrange one's self in proper position in a line; to clothe one's self; to put on garments.—*n.* Clothes, garments, or apparel; collectively, a suit of clothes; a costume; a lady's gown.—**Dress-circle**, *n.* A portion of a theatre, concert-room, or other place of entertainment set apart for spectators or an audience in evening dress.—**Dress-coat**, *n.* A coat with narrow pointed tails; a swallow-tailed coat, being the coat in which gentlemen go to full-dress parties, operas, &c.—**Dresser**, dres′-ėr, *n.* One who dresses; one employed in preparing, trimming, or adjusting anything; a hospital assistant, whose office is to dress wounds, ulcers, &c.—[Fr. *dressoir*.] A table or bench on which meat and other things are dressed or prepared for use; a kind of low cupboard for dishes and cooking utensils.—**Dressing**, dres′ing, *n.* The act of one who dresses; what is used to dress; an application to a wound or sore; manure spread over land; gum, starch, paste, and the like, used in stiffening or preparing silk, linen, and other fabrics; *cookery*, the stuffing of fowls, pigs, &c., or the unctuous ingredients to complete a salad; *arch.* mouldings round doors, windows, and other openings on an elevation.—**Dressing-case**, *n.* A box containing requisites for the toilet, such as combs, brushes, &c.—**Dressing-gown**, *n.* A light gown or wide and flowing coat worn by a person while dressing, in the study, &c.—**Dressing-room**, *n.* An apartment appropriated for dressing the person.—**Dressing-station**, *n.* Place where wounded are collected and attended to by the personnel of a field-ambulance.—**Dressing-table**, *n.* A table provided with conveniences for the toilet; a toilet-table.—**Dressmaker**, dres′māk-ėr, *n.* A maker of ladies' dresses.—**Dressy**, dres′i, *a.* Very attentive to dress; wearing rich or showy dresses. (*Colloq.*)

Drew, drö, pret. of *draw*.

Drey, drā, *n.* A squirrel's nest.

Dribble, drib′l, *v.t.*—*dribbled*, *dribbling*. [A dim. from *drip*, and properly *dripple*.] To give out or let fall in drops.—*v.i.* To fall in drops or small particles, or in a quick succession of drops.—**Dribblet, Driblet**, drib′let, *n.* One of a number of small pieces or parts; a small sum doled out as one of a series.

Drier, drī′ėr, *n.* Under DRY.

Drift, drift, *n.* [From *drive*; A.Sax. *drifan* = Icel. *drift*, a snow-drift; Dan. *drift*, impulse, drove; D. *drift*, drove, course. DRIVE, and comp. *rive*, *rift*; *shrive*, *shrift*; *thrive*, *thrift*.] A drove or flock‡; a heap of matter driven together by the wind or water (a snow-*drift*); a driving or impulse; overbearing power or influence; course of anything; tendency; aim (the *drift* of one's remarks); intention; design; purpose; a name in South Africa for a ford; *milit.* the deflection of a shell to the right of its proper course, due to the resistance of the air and the right-hand spin or rotation imparted by the rifling; the deviation of an air-craft due to the wind; *mining*, a passage cut between shaft and shaft; *naut.* the distance which a vessel drives through wind or current when lying-to or hove-to during a gale; *geol.* earth and rocks which have been conveyed by icebergs and glaciers and deposited over a country while submerged.—*Drift of a current*, the rate at which it flows.—*v.i.* To accumulate in heaps by the force of wind; to be driven into heaps; to float or be driven along by a current of water or air; to be carried at random by the force of the wind or tide; *mining*, to make a drift; to search for metals or ores.—*v.t.* To drive into heaps.—*a.* Drifted by wind or currents (*drift* sand, *drift* ice).—**Drifter**, drif′tėr, *n.* A boat that uses drift-nets.—**Driftless**, drift′les, *a.* Without drift; purposeless; aimless.—**Drift-net**, *n.* A large fishing net that hangs upright and catches herring, mackerel, &c., by the gills.—**Drift-sail**, *n.* A sail used under water to keep the ship's head right, and prevent her driving too fast.—**Drift-weed**, *n.* Same as *Gulf-weed*.—**Drift-wood**, *n.* Wood drifted or floated by water.—**Drifty**, drif′ti, *a.* Forming or characterized by drifts, especially of snow.

Drill, dril, *v.t.* [From D. *drillen*, to bore, to drill soldiers; G. *drillen*, to bore; from same root as *through*, *thrill*, *-tril* in *nostril*. (In the agricultural sense, however, perhaps of different origin.)] To pierce or perforate by turning a sharp-pointed instrument of a particular form; to bore and make a hole by turning an instrument; *agri.* to sow in rows, drills, or channels; to teach and train soldiers or others to their duty by frequent exercises; hence, to teach by repeated exercise or repetition of acts.—*v.i.* To go through the exercises prescribed to recruits, &c.—*n.* A pointed instrument used for boring holes, particularly in metals and other hard substances; the act of training soldiers, &c., to their duty, or the exercises by which they are trained; *agri.* a row of seeds deposited in the earth, or the trench or channel in which the seed is deposited; also a machine for sowing seeds in rows.—**Drill-barrow**, *n. Agri.* an implement for forming drills, sowing the seed, and covering it with earth.—**Drill-bow**, *n.* A small bow, the string of which is used for rapidly turning a drill.—**Drill-harrow**, *n.* A small harrow employed in drill-husbandry.—**Drill-plough**, *n.* A plough for sowing grain in drills.—**Drill-press, Drilling-machine**, *n.* A machine armed with one or more drills for boring holes in metal.—**Drill-sergeant**, *n.* A sergeant who drills soldiers.

Drill, Drilling, dril, dril′ing, *n.* [G. *drillich*, from *drei*, three, a fabric in which the threads are divided in a threefold way.] A kind of coarse linen or cotton cloth.

Drily. Under DRY.

Drink, dringk, *v.i.*—*drank* or *drunk* (pret.), *drunk* or *drunken* (pp.). [A.Sax. *drincan* = D. *drinken*, Icel. *drekka*, G. *trinken*, Goth. *drigkan*, to drink. Hence *drench* and *drown*.] To swallow liquor, for quenching thirst or other purpose; especially, to take intoxicating liquor; to be intemperate in the use of intoxicating liquors; to be an habitual drunkard.—*To drink to*, to salute in drinking; to drink in honour of; to wish well to, in taking the cup.—*To drink deep*, to drink a deep draught; to indulge in liquor to excess.—*v.t.* To swallow (liquids); to imbibe; to suck in; to absorb; to take in through the senses (to *drink* delight); to inhale.—*To drink down*, to take away thought or consideration of (care, &c.) by drinking.—*To drink off*, to drink the whole at a draught.—*To drink in*, to absorb; to take or receive into.—*To drink up*, to drink the whole.—*To drink the health*, or *to the health of*, to drink while expressing good wishes for; to signify good-will to by drinking; to pledge.—*n.* Liquor to be swallowed; a draught of liquor; intoxicating liquors.—*In drink*, drunk; tipsy.—**Drinkable**, dring′ka-bl, *a.* Fit or suitable for drink; potable.—*n.* A liquor that may be drunk.—**Drinkableness**, dring′ka-bl-nes, *n.*—**Drinker**, dring′kėr, *n.* One who drinks particularly one who practises drinking spirituous liquors to excess; a drunkard.—**Drinking**, dring′king, *a.* Connected with the use of intoxicating liquors.—**Drinking-bout**, *n.* A convivial revel; a set-to at drinking.—**Drinking-fountain**, *n.* A public fountain for supplying water to quench thirst.—**Drinking-horn**, *n.* A cup or goblet made of horn.—**Drinking-song**, *n.* A song in praise of drinking; a bacchanalian song.—**Drink-money**, *n.* Money given to buy liquor for drink.—**Drink-offering**, *n.* A Jewish offering of wine, &c.

Drip, drip, *v.i.*—*dripped*, *dripping*. [A.Sax. *drypan*, to drip, to drop = Dan. *dryppe*, Icel. *drjúpa*, D. *druipen*, G. *triefen*. Akin *drop*.] To fall in drops; to have any liquid falling from it in drops.—*v.t.* To let fall in drops.—*n.* A falling or letting fall in drops; a dripping; that which falls in drops; dripping, or melted fat from meat while roasting; the edge of a roof; the eaves; *arch.* a large flat member of the cornice projecting so as to throw off water; a drip-stone.—**Dripping**, drip′ing, *n.* The fat which falls from meat in roasting.—**Drip-stone**, *n. Arch.* a projecting moulding or cornice over doorways, windows, &c., to throw off the rain.

Drive, drīv, *v. t.*—*drove* (formerly *drave*); *driven*, *driving*. [A. Sax. *drīfan* = Goth. *dreiban*, D. *drijven*, Dan. *drive*, G. *treiben*, to drive, to urge or carry on. *Drift* and *drove* are derivatives.] To impel or urge forward, or away from, by force; to force or move by physical means; to propel; to compel or urge by other means than absolute physical force, or by means that compel the will; to constrain; to press or carry to a great length (an argument); to chase or hunt; to keep horses or other animals moving onward while directing their course; to guide or regulate the course of an automobile or other vehicle; to guide or regulate a machine; to convey in a vehicle; to carry on, prosecute, engage in (a trade, a bargain); *mining*, to dig horizontally; to cut a horizontal gallery or tunnel.—*v.i.* To be forced along or impelled (a ship *drives* before the wind); to rush and press with violence (a storm *drives* against the house); to go in an automobile; to travel in a vehicle drawn by horses or other animals; to aim or tend; to aim a blow; to make a stroke.—*To let drive*, to aim a blow; to strike.—*n.* A journey or airing in a vehicle; a course on which vehicles are driven; a road prepared for driving; a strong or sweeping blow or impulsion.—**Driver** drī′vėr, *n.* One who or that which drives; the person who drives a vehicle, one who conducts a team; *naut*, a large fore-and-aft quadrilateral sail, called also the *Spanker*, on the mizzen mast; *mach.* the main wheel by which motion is communicated to a train of wheels; a driving-wheel.—**Driver-ant**, *n.* A singular species of ant in West Africa, so named from its *driving* before it almost every animal that comes in its way.—**Driving**, drī′ving, *p.* and *a.* Having great force; communicating power.—

Driving-band, *n.* The copper band near the base of a shell to take the grooves of the rifling when fired, rotation being thus imparted.—**Driving-shaft**, *n.* A shaft from a driving-wheel communicating motion to a machine.—**Driving-wheel**, *n.* *Mech.* a wheel that communicates motion to another or to others; the large wheel in a locomotive engine which is fixed upon the crank-axle or main-shaft.

Drivel, driv'el, *v.i.*—*driveled, driveling.* [A modification of *dribble*, from root of *drib.*] To slaver; to let spittle drop or flow from the mouth, like a child, idiot, or dotard; to be weak or foolish; to dote.—*n.* Slaver; saliva flowing from the mouth; silly unmeaning talk; senseless twaddle.—**Driveler**, driv'el-er, *n.* One who drivels; an idiot; a fool.

Drizzle, driz'l, *v.i.* — *drizzled, drizzling.* [A dim. from A.Sax. *dreósan*, Goth. *driusan*, to fall; like Prov. G. *drieseln*, to dizzle. DREARY.] To rain in small drops; to fall from the clouds in very fine particles.—*v.t.* To shed in small drops or particles.—*n.* A small or fine rain; mizzle.—**Drizzly**, driz'-li, *a.* Shedding small rain, or small particles of snow.

Droger, Drogher, drō'gėr, *n.* A small West Indian coasting craft, for carrying goods.

Droit, droit, *n.* [Fr., from L. *directus.*] Right; law; justice; a fiscal charge or duty. —*Droits of admiralty*, perquisites attached to the office of admiral of England, or lord high-admiral.

Droll, drōl, *a.* [Same word as Fr. *drôle*, D. *drol*, G. *droll*, a thick, short person, a droll; Gael. *droll*, a slow, awkward person; perhaps from Icel. and Sw. *troll*, a kind of imp or hobgoblin.] Odd; merry; facetious; comical; ludicrous; queer; laughable; ridiculous.—*n.* One whose occupation or practice is to raise mirth by odd tricks; a jester; a buffoon; something exhibited to raise mirth or sport.—*v.i.* To jest; to play the buffoon. — **Drollery**, drō'lėr-i, *n.* The quality of being droll; something done to raise mirth; sportive tricks; buffoonery; fun; comicalness; humour. — **Drollish**, drō'lish, *a.* Somewhat droll.

Dromedary, drum'e-da-ri, *n.* [L. *dromedarius*, a dromedary, formed from Gr. *dromas, dromados*, running, from stem of *dramein*, to run.] A species of camel, called also the Arabian camel, with one hump or protuberance on the back, in distinction from the Bactrian camel, which has two humps.

Dromond, drom'ond, *n.* [Gr. *dramein*, to run.] Fast-sailing ship of war (obsolete).

Drone, drōn, *n.* [A.Sax. *drán*, the drone-bee; L.G. and Dan. *drone*, Sw. *dron, drönje*, G. *drohne*, from the sound it makes; comp. *humble-bee*, G. *hummel*, and the verb *hum.*] The male of the honey-bee; an idler; a sluggard; one who earns nothing by industry; a humming or low sound, or the instrument of humming; one of the largest tubes of the bagpipe, which emit a continued deep tone.—*v.i.*—*droned, droning.* [Dan. *dröne*, Sw. *dröna*, to drone; akin Goth. *drunjus*, a sound.] To give forth a low, heavy, dull sound; to hum; to snore; to make use of a dull monotonous tone; to live in idleness.—*v.t.* To read or speak in a dull, monotonous, droning manner.—**Dronish**, drō'nish, *a.* Like or pertaining to a drone; sluggish; lazy; inactive; slow.—**Dronishly**, drō'nish-li, *adv.* In a dronish manner.—**Dronishness**, drō'nish-nes, *n.* —**Drony**, drō'ni, *a.* Like a drone; dronish.

Droop, drōp, *v.i.* [A form of *drip, drop.*] To sink or hang down; to bend downward, as from weakness or exhaustion; to languish from grief or other cause; to fail or sink; to decline; to be dispirited; to come towards a close (*Tenn.*).—*v.t.* To let sink or hang down.—*n.* The act of drooping or of falling or hanging down; a drooping position or state.—**Drooper**, drö'pėr, *n.* One who or that which droops.—**Droopingly**, drö'ping-li, *adv.* In a drooping manner.

Drop, drop, *n.* [A.Sax. *dropa*, O.Sax. *dropo*, Icel. *dropi*, D. *drop*, G. *tropfe*, a drop; akin *dribble, drip, droop.*] A small portion of any fluid in a spherical form, falling or pendant, as if about to fall; a small portion of water falling in rain; what resembles or hangs in the form of a drop, as a hanging diamond ornament, a glass pendant of a chandelier, &c.; a very small quantity of liquor; a small quantity of anything (a *drop* of pity: *Shak.*); that part of a gallows which sustains the criminal before he is executed, and which is suddenly dropped; also the distance which he has to fall; the curtain which conceals the stage of a theatre from the audience; *pl.* a liquid medicine, the dose of which is regulated by a certain number of drops.—*v.t.*—*dropped, dropping.* [A.Sax. *dropian*, from the noun =D. *droppen*, G. *tropfen.*] To pour or let fall in drops; to let fall, lower, or let down (to *drop* the anchor); to let go, dismiss, lay aside, break off from; to quit, leave, omit; to utter (words) slightly, briefly, or casually; to send in an off-hand informal manner (*drop* me a few lines).—*v.i.* To fall in small portions, globules, or drops, as a liquid; to let drops fall; to drip; to discharge itself in drops; to fall; to descend suddenly or abruptly; to sink lower; to cease; to die suddenly; to fall, as in battle; to come to an end; to be allowed to cease; to be neglected and come to nothing; to come unexpectedly: with *in* or *into.*—*To drop astern* (*naut.*), to slacken speed so as to let another vessel get ahead. — *To drop down*, to sail, row, or move down a river.—*Dropping fire* (*milit.*), a continuous irregular discharge of small arms.—**Drop-drill**, *n.* *Agri.* an agricultural implement which drops seed and manure into the soil simultaneously. — **Droplet**, drop'let, *n.* A little drop.—**Dropper**, drop'ėr, *n.* One who or that which drops. — **Dropping**, drop'ing, *n.* The act of one who drops; a falling in drops; that which drops; *pl.* the dung of animals.—**Droppingly**, drop'ing-li, *adv.* In drops. — **Drop-hammer, Drop-press**, *n.* A machine worked by the foot, consisting of a weight raised vertically by a cord and pulley, and allowed to drop suddenly on an anvil: used for embossing, punching, &c.—**Drop-scene**, *n.* A scenic picture, suspended by pulleys, which descends or *drops* in front of the stage in theatres.—**Drop-tin**, *n.* Fine tin.

Dropsy, drop'si, *n.* [Formerly *hydropsy*, from Gr. *hydrōps*, dropsy, from *hydōr*, water.] *Med.* an unnatural collection of water in any cavity of the body, or in the cellular tissue.—**Dropsical**, drop'si-kal, *a.* Diseased with dropsy; inclined to dropsy; resembling or partaking of the nature of dropsy.—**Dropsicalness**, drop'si-kal-nes, *n.*—**Dropsied**, drop'sid, *a.* Affected with dropsy; exhibiting an unhealthy inflation.

Dropwort, drop'wėrt, *n.* A kind of Spiræa or meadow-sweet with fine-cut leaves.

Drosky, dros'ki, *n.* [Rus. *drozhki.*] A kind of light four-wheeled carriage used in Russia and Prussia.

Drosometer, dro-som'et-ėr, *n.* [Gr. *drosos*, dew, and *metron*, measure.] An instrument for ascertaining the quantity of dew that condenses on a body which has been exposed to the open air during the night.

Dross, dros, *n.* [A.Sax. *dros, drosn*, from *dreósan*, to fall; D. *droes*, Icel. *tros*, rubbish; Sc. *drush*, dregs; Dan. *drysse*, to fall. DREARY.] The refuse or impurities of metals; rust; waste matter; refuse; any worthless matter separated from the better part.—**Drossiness**, dros'i-nes, *n.* The quality or state of being drossy.—**Drossy**, dros'i, *a.* Like dross; pertaining to dross; full of or abounding with refuse matter; worthless; foul; impure.

Drought, drout, *n.* [Contr. from A.Sax. *drugath, drugoth*, from *drige, dryge*, dry; like D. *droogte*, from *droog*, dry. DRY.] Dry weather; want of rain; such a continuance of dry weather as affects the crops; aridness; thirst; want of drink; scarcity; lack.—**Droughtiness**, drou'ti-nes, *n.* The state of being droughty.—**Droughty**, drou'ti, *a.* Characterized by drought or the absence of rain or moisture; arid; thirsty.—**Drouth**, drouth, *n.* Drought; aridity; dryness of the throat and mouth; thirst; want of drink.—**Drouthiness**, drou'thi-nes, *n.*—**Drouthy**, drou'thi, *a.* Devoid of moisture; drouthy; thirsty, especially for strong drink.

Drove, drōv, pret. of *drive.*

Drove, drōv, *n.* [A.Sax. *dráf*, from *drífan*, to drive.] A number of animals, as oxen, sheep, or swine, driven in a body; a collection of animals moving forward; a crowd of people in motion; a flock.—**Drover**, drō'vėr, *n.* One who drives cattle or sheep to market, or from one locality to another.

Drown, droun, *v.t.* [From A.Sax. *druncnian*, to sink in water, to be drunk, from *druncen*, pp. of *drincan*, to drink; Dan. *drukne*, to drown. DRINK, DRENCH.] To deprive of life by immersion in water or other fluid; to overflow, overwhelm, or inundate; to put an end to, as if by drowning or overwhelming; to overpower (to *drown* care; to *drown* one's voice).—*v.i.* To be suffocated in water or other fluid; to perish in water.

Drowse, drouz, *v.i.*—*drowsed, drowsing.* [A.Sax. *drúsan, drúsian*, to be slow, to languish; allied to *dreósan*, to fall, to droop; D. *droosen*, to doze, to slumber. DREARY.] To sleep imperfectly or unsoundly; to slumber; to be heavy with sleepiness; to be heavy or dull.—*v.t.* To make heavy with sleep; to make dull or stupid.—*n.* A slight sleep; a doze; slumber. —**Drowsily**, drou'zi-li, *adv.* In a drowsy manner. — **Drowsiness**, drou'zi-nes, *n.* State of being drowsy.—**Drowsy**, drou'zi, *a.* Inclined to sleep; sleepy; heavy with sleepiness; lethargic; sluggish; stupid; disposing to sleep; lulling.

Drub, drub, *v.t.*—*drubbed, drubbing.* [Prov. E. *drab*; akin to Icel. and Sw. *drabba*, to beat; G. *treffen*, to hit.] To beat with a stick; to thrash; to cudgel.—*n.* A blow with a stick or cudgel; a thump; a knock. —**Drubber**, drub'ėr, *n.* One who drubs or beats.—**Drubbing**, drub'ing, *n.* A cudgelling; a sound beating.

Drudge, druj, *v.i.* — *drudged, drudging.* [Softened form of O.E. *drugge, drug*, to work laboriously; origin doubtful.] To work hard; to labour in mean offices; to labour with toil and fatigue.—*n.* One who labours hard in servile employments; a slave.—**Drudgery**, druj'ėr-i, *n.* Ignoble toil; hard work in servile occupations.—**Drudgingly**, druj'ing-li, *adv.* With labour and fatigue; laboriously.

Drug, drug, *n.* [Fr. *drogue*; Pr. Sp. Pg. It. *droga*; all from D. *droog*, the same word as A.Sax. *dryge*, dry—because the ancient medicines were chiefly dried herbs.] Any substance, vegetable, animal, or mineral, used in the composition or preparation of medicines; any commodity that lies on hand or is not saleable; an article of slow sale or in no demand in the market.—*v.i.*—*drugged, drugging.* To prescribe or administer drugs or medicines.—*v.t.* To mix with drugs; to introduce some narcotic into with the design of rendering the person who drinks the mixture insensible; to dose to excess with drugs or medicines; to administer narcotics to; to render insensible with a narcotic drug.—**Druggist**, drug'ist *n.* One who deals in drugs; properly, one whose occupation is merely to buy and sell drugs, without compounding or preparation.

Drugget, drug'et, *n.* [Fr. *droguet*, dim. of *drogue*, drug, trash. DRUG.] A cloth or thin stuff of wool, or of wool and thread, used for covering carpets, and also as an article of clothing.

Druid, drụ'id, *n.* [Ir. and Gael. *druidh*, W. *derwydd.*] A priest or minister of religion who superintended the affairs of religion and morality, and performed the office of judges among the ancient Celtic nations in Gaul, Britain, and Germany.—**Druidess**, drụ'i-des, *n.* A female druid. —**Druidic, Druidical**, drụ-id'ik, drụ-id'i-kal, *a.* Pertaining to the druids.—*Druidical stones*, the name popularly given to large upright stones, found in various localities and sometimes forming circles, from an uncertain assumption that they were druidical places of worship.—**Druidish**, drụ'i-dish, *a.* Pertaining to or like druids.—**Druidism**, drụ'i-dizm, *n.* The doctrines, rites, and ceremonies of the druids.

Drum, drum, *n.* [Probably, like *drone*, a word of imitative origin; Dan. *tromme*, G. *trommel*, a drum, Dan. *drum*, a booming sound; Goth. *drunjus*, a sound.] An instrument of music commonly in the form of a hollow cylinder, covered at the ends with vellum, the ends being beaten with sticks to produce the sound; a mechanical contrivance resembling a drum in shape, and used in connection with machinery of various kinds, &c.; the tympanum or barrel of the ear; a quantity packed in the form of a drum; a round box containing figs; a tea before dinner; a kettle-drum; a name formerly given to a fashionable and crowded evening party; a storm-drum.—*v.i.*—*drummed, drumming.* To beat a drum; to beat with rapid movements of the fingers; to beat with a rapid succession of strokes; to throb; to resound dully.—*v.t.* To perform on a drum; to expel with beat of drum (he was *drummed out* of the regiment); to summon by beat of drum; to din.—*To drum up*, to assemble or call together by beat of drum.—**Drum-head**, *n.* The head or top of a drum; a variety of cabbage having a large, rounded, or flattened head.—*Drumhead court-martial*, a court-martial called suddenly on the field. —*Drumhead service*, religious service on the field, at the front.—**Drum-major**, *n.* The chief or first drummer of a regiment.—**Drumlin**, drum'lin. [Celtic name.] An elongated mound of glacial material sorted by water action.—**Drummer**, drum'ėr, *n.* One who drums; one whose office is to beat the drum; commercial traveller. [American.]—**Drum-stick**, *n.* The stick with which a drum is beaten; what resembles a drum-stick, as the upper joint of the leg of a turkey.

Drunk, drungk, *a.* [From *drunken*. DRINK.] Intoxicated; inebriated; overcome, stupefied, or frenzied by alcoholic liquor.—**Drunkard**, drung'kėrd, *n.* One given to an excessive use of strong liquor; a person who habitually or frequently is drunk.—**Drunken**, drung'ken, *a.* [Part. of *drink*, but now used chiefly as an adjective.] Intoxicated; drunk; given to drunkenness; proceeding from intoxication; done in a state of drunkenness (a *drunken* quarrel).—**Drunkenly**,† drung'ken-li, *adv.* In a drunken manner. (*Shak.*)—**Drunkenness**, drung'ken-nes, *n.* The state of being drunk; the habit of indulging in intoxication; intoxication; inebriety.

Drupe, dröp, *n.* [Fr. *drupe*, L. *drupa*, Gr. *dryppa*, an over-ripe olive.] *Bot.* a stone fruit, such as the cherry or plum; a fruit in which the outer part is fleshy while the inner hardens like a nut, forming a stone with a kernel.—**Drupaceous**, drụ-pā'shus, *a.* Producing drupes; pertaining to drupes, or consisting of drupes.—**Drupel**, drö'pel, *n.* *Bot.* a little drupe.

Druse, drös, *n.* [G. *druse*, a gland.] A cavity in a rock or mineral having its interior surface studded with crystals.—**Drusy**, drö'si, *a.* Pertaining to a druse; having the surface composed of very small prominent crystals nearly equal in size.

Dry, drī, *a.* [A.Sax. *dryge, drige, drie* (D. *droog*, G. *trocken*), dry, whence *dryan, drigan*, to dry. *Drought* and *drug* are derivatives.] Destitute of moisture; free from water or wetness; free from juice, sap, or aqueous matter; not moist; arid; not giving milk; thirsty; craving drink; barren; jejune; plain; unembellished; destitute of interest; quietly sarcastic; caustic; discouraging; expressive of a degree of displeasure; cold and not friendly (a *dry* reception).—*Dry goods*, cloths, stuffs, silks, laces, ribbons, &c., in distinction from groceries.—*Dry steam*, superheated steam. —*Dry stone walls*, walls built of stone without mortar.—*Dry wines*, those in which no sweetness is perceptible.—*v.t.*—*dried, drying.* To make dry; to free from water or from moisture of any kind; to desiccate; to expose in order to evaporate moisture; to deprive of natural juice, sap, or greenness.—*To dry up*, to deprive wholly of water; to scorch or parch with thirst.—*v.i.* To grow dry; to lose moisture; to become free from moisture or juice; to evaporate wholly: sometimes with *up*.—**Drier**, drī'ėr, *n.* One who or that which dries or makes dry; a desiccative; specifically a preparation to increase the hardening and drying properties of paint.—**Dry Clean**, *v.t.* To clean textiles with solvents other than water, as benzine.—**Dry Dock**, *n.* A dock from which water may be shut or pumped out, used in constructing or repairing ships.—**Dry Ice**, *n.* A trademark for solidified carbon dioxide used as a substitute for ice.—**Drying**, drī'ing, *a.* Adapted to exhaust moisture; having the quality of rapidly becoming dry and hard. —**Dryly**, **Drily**, drī'li, *adv.* Without moisture; coldly; frigidly; without affection; severely; sarcastically; barrenly; without embellishment; without anything to enliven, enrich, or entertain.—**Dryness**, drī'nes, *n.* The state or quality of being dry. —**Drybeat**,‡ drī'bēt, *v. t.* To beat severely. (*Shak.*)—**Dryfoot**, drī'fụt, *adv.* Pursuing game by the scent.—**Dry-measure**, *n.* Measure for dry commodities by quarts, &c.; in this system two pints make one quart, eight quarts make one peck, four pecks make one bushel.—**Dry-nurse**, *n.* A nurse who attends and feeds a child by hand.—*v.t.* To act as dry-nurse to; to feed, attend, and bring up without the breast.—**Dry-pile**, *n.* A form of the ordinary voltaic pile, in which the liquid is replaced by some hygrometric substance, as paper which has been moistened with sugar and water and allowed to dry.—**Dry-point**, *n.* A sharp etching needle, used to cut fine lines in copper without the plate being covered with etching-ground or the lines bit in by acid.—**Dry-rot**, drī'rot, *n.* A well-known disease affecting timber, occasioned by various species of fungi, the mycelium of which penetrates the timber, destroying it.—**Dry-shod**, *adv.* Without wetting the feet.—**Dry-stone**, *a.* A term applied to a wall not cemented with mortar.

Dryad, drī'ad, *n.* [Gr. *dryas, dryados*, from *drys*, an oak, a tree.] *Myth.* a deity or nymph of the woods; a nymph supposed to preside over woods.—**Dryite**, drī'it, *n.* *Geol.* fragments of petrified or fossil wood in which the structure of the wood is recognized.

Dual, dū'al, *a.* [L. *dualis*, from *duo*, two; akin *duel, double, doubt, dubious*, &c.] Expressing the number two; existing as two; consisting of two; twofold; a term applied to a special form of a noun or verb used in some languages when two persons or things are spoken of.—*n.* *Gram.* that number which is used when two persons or things are spoken of.—**Dualism**, dū'a-lizm, *n.* A twofold division; a system founded on a double basis or based in belief of two fundamental existences; the belief in two antagonistic supernatural beings, the one good, the other evil; the philosophical exposition of the nature of things by the adoption of two dissimilar primitive principles not derived from each other; the doctrine of those who maintain the existence of spirit and matter as distinct substances, in opposition to idealism, which maintains we have no knowledge or assurance of the existence of anything but our own ideas or sensations.—**Dualist**, dū'a-list, *n.* One who holds the doctrine of dualism in any of its forms.—**Dualistic**, dū-a-lis'tik, *a.* Pertaining to dualism; characterized by duality.—**Duality**, dū-al'i-ti, *n.* The state of being two or of being divided into two.—**Duarchy**, dū'är-ki, *n.* [Gr. *dyō*, two, and *archē*, rule.] Government by two persons.

Dualin, dū'a-lin, *n.* Explosive compound of nitro-glycerine, saltpetre, and sawdust.

Duan, dū'an, *n.* [Gael. and Ir.] A division of a poem; a canto; a poem; a song.

Dub, dub, *v.t.*—*dubbed, dubbing.* [A.Sax. *dubban*, to strike, to dub knight; Icel. *dubba*, to dub.] To strike with a sword and make a knight; to give the accolade to; to confer any dignity or new character on; to entitle; to speak of as; to make smooth, or of an equal surface, by some operation; to smooth with an adze; to rub with grease, as leather when being curried; to raise a nap on cloth by striking it with teasles.—*n.* A blow.

Dub, dub, *n.* [Probably of same root as *dip* and *deep*.] A puddle; a small pool of foul stagnant water.

Dubious, dū'bi-us, *a.* [L. *dubius*, moving alternately in two opposite directions, from root of *duo*, two. DOUBT.] Doubtful; wavering or fluctuating in opinion; uncertain; not ascertained or known exactly; not clear or plain; occasioning or involving doubt; of uncertain event or issue.—**Dubiously**, dū'bi-us-li, *adv.* In a dubious manner.—**Dubiousness**, dū'bi-us-nes, *n.* The state of being dubious.—**Dubiety**, dū-bī'e-ti, *n.* [L. *dubietas.*] Doubtfulness; a feeling of doubt.—**Dubiosity**, dū-bi-os'i-ti, *n.* Dubiousness; doubtfulness.—**Dubitable**,† dū'bi-ta-bl, *a.* [L. *dubito*, to waver in opinion.] Liable to be doubted; doubtful; uncertain.—**Dubitancy**,† dū'bi-tan-si, *n.* Doubt; uncertainty.—**Dubitate**,† dū'bi-tāt, *v.i.* To hesitate.—**Dubitation**,† dū-bi-tā'shon, *n.* [L. *dubitatio.*] The act of doubting or hesitating; doubt.

Ducal, dū'kal, *a.* [L. *ducalis*, pertaining to a leader, from *dux, ducis*, a leader. DUKE.] Pertaining to a duke.—**Ducally**, dū'kal-li, *adv.* After the manner of a duke; in relation with a duke or a ducal family.—**Ducat**, duk'at, *n.* [Fr. *ducat*, It. *ducato*, from L.L. *ducatus*, a duchy (the particular duchy originating the name being uncertain), from L. *dux*. DUKE.] A gold coin formerly common to several European states, first coined about 1150; the average value was about $2.25.—**Ducatoon**, duk-a-tön', *n.* [Fr. *ducaton*, from *ducat.*] A silver coin once common in Europe, of different values.—**Duchess**, duch'es, *n.* [Fr. *duchesse*, from *duc*, duke.] The consort or widow of a duke; a lady who has the sovereignty of a duchy.—**Duchy**, duch'i, *n.* [Fr. *duché.*] The territory or dominions of a duke; a dukedom.

Duck, duk, *n.* [Same word as D. *doek*, Sw. *duk*, G. *tuch*, cloth.] A species of coarse cloth or canvas, used for sails, sacking of beds, &c.

Duck, duk, *n.* [Same word as Dan. *dukke*, G. *docke*, a baby or puppet; or the name of the bird used as a term of endearment.] A word of endearment or fondness.

Duck, duk, *v.t.* [Akin to D. *duiken*, to bend the head, duck, dive, Dan. *dukke*, to dive, G. *tauchen*, to dip, to dive.] To dip or plunge in water and suddenly withdraw; to bow, stoop, or nod in order to escape a blow or the like.—*v.i.* To plunge into water and immediately withdraw; to dip; to plunge the head in water or other liquid; to drop the head suddenly; to bow; to cringe.—*n.* [From the verb to *duck.*] A name of various water-fowls akin to, but distinguished from swans and geese by having broader bills, a more waddling gait from their legs being placed further back, there being also a marked difference in the plumage of the sexes; a term of endearment (*colloq.*); an inclination of the head, resembling the motion of a duck in water.—*To make ducks and drakes*, to throw a flat stone, piece of slate, &c., along the surface of water so as to cause it to strike and rebound repeatedly; hence, *to make ducks and drakes of one's money*, to squander it in a foolish manner.—**Duck-bill**, **Duck-mole**, *n.* A remarkable Australian animal with jaws which resemble the bill of a duck. ORNITHORHYNCHUS.—**Duck-billed**, *a.* Having a bill like a duck.—**Ducker**, duk'ėr, *n.* One who ducks; a plunger; a diver; a cringer; a fawner.—**Duck-hawk**, *n.* The marsh-harrier or moor-buzzard.—**Ducking-stool**, *n.* A stool or chair in which common scolds were formerly tied and plunged into water.—**Duckling**, duk'ling, *n.* A young duck.—**Duck-meat**,

Duck's-meat, Duck-weed, *n.* The popular name of several species of plants growing in ditches and shallow water, and floating on the surface, serving for food for ducks and geese.—**Duck-shot,** *n.* Large shot used for shooting wild ducks.

Duct, dukt, *n.* [L. *ductus*, a leading, conducting, from *duco, ductum*, to lead. DUKE.] Any tube or canal by which a fluid is conveyed, used especially of canals in the bodies of animals or in plants.—**Ductile,** duk'til, *a.* [L. *ductilis.*] Easy to be led or influenced (persons); tractable; yielding to persuasion or instruction; capable of being drawn out into wire or threads (used of metals).—**Ductilely,** duk'til-li, *adv.* In a ductile manner.—**Ductileness,** duk'til-nes, *n.* The quality of being ductile.—**Ductility,** duk-til'i-ti, *n.* The property of solid bodies, particularly metals, which renders them capable of being extended by drawing, while their thickness or diameter is diminished, without any actual separation of their parts; a yielding disposition of mind; ready compliance.—**Ductless glands.** Structures of various use, superficially resembling glands, but devoid of ducts for carrying off a liquid secretion, e.g. thymus, thyroid, and spleen.

Dude, dūd, *n.* A dandy; a fop. *Western slang*, an Easterner or city-bred person.

Dude Ranch, *n.* A ranch operated for, or accommodating tourists, where they may board and get a taste of ranching.

Dudgeon, duj'on, *n.* [W. *dygen*, anger, grudge; *dygn*, severe, hard, painful.] Anger; resentment; malice; ill-will; discord.

Due, dū, *a.* [O.Fr. *deu*, Fr. *dû*, pp. of *devoir*, from L. *debere*, to owe. DEBT.] Falling to be paid or done to another; owed by one to another, and by contract, justice, or propriety required to be paid; liable or meriting to be given or devoted; owing to (the attention *due* to one's studies); proper; fit; appropriate; suitable; becoming; seasonable; required by the circumstances (to behave with *due* gravity); exact; correct; owing origin or existence; to be attributed or assigned as causing (an effect *due* to the sun's attraction); that ought to have arrived or to be present; bound or stipulated to arrive (the mails are *due*).—*adv.* Directly; exactly (to sail *due* east).—*n.* What is owed or ought to be paid or done to another; that which justice, office, rank, or station, social relations or established rules of decorum, require to be given, paid, or done; a toll, tribute, fee, or other legal exaction.—**Duly,** dū'li, *adv.* In a due, fit, or proper manner; fitly; suitably; properly; at the proper time.—**Dueness,** dū'nes, *n.* State of being due; fitness; propriety; due quality.

Duel, dū'el, *n.* [Fr. *duel*, It. *duello*, from L. *duellum*, old form of *bellum*, war, from *duo*, two.] A premeditated combat between two persons with deadly weapons for the purpose of deciding some private difference or quarrel; a single combat; a fight between two fortresses, two encamped armies, and the like, carried on without the tactics of a pitched battle or an assault.—*v.i.*—*dueled, dueling.* To engage in a duel.—**Dueling,** dū'el-ing, *n.* The practice of engaging in duels.—**Duelist,** dū'el-ist, *n.* One who engages in a duel or in duels.—**Duello,** dū-el'lō, *n.* A duel; the art or practice of *dueling*, or the code of laws which regulate it (*Shak.*).

Duenna, dū-en'na, *n.* [Sp. *duenna, dueña*, a form of *doña*, fem. of *don*, from L. *domina*, a mistress.] An elderly female appointed to take charge of the younger female members of Spanish and Portuguese families; an elderly woman who is kept to guard a younger.

Duet, Duetto, dū-et', dụ-et'tō, *n.* [It. *duetto*, from *duo*, two.] A musical composition for two voices or two instruments.

Duffel, Duffle, duf'el, duf'l, *n.* [From *Duffel*, a Belgian manufacturing town.] A kind of coarse woollen cloth having a thick nap; supplies as for camping.

Duffer, duf'ėr, *n.* A peddler; a hawker of cheap, flashy articles; a hawker of sham jewelry; a person who is a sham; a useless character; a stupid person; a fogey (*colloq.*).

Dug, dug, *n.* [Akin to Sw. *dägga*, Dan. *dægge*, to suckle; from root seen in Skr. *duh*, to milk, *daughter* also being from this root.] The pap or nipple of a woman or (now generally) of an animal.

Dug, dug, pret. & pp. of *dig*.—**Dug-out,** *n.* A rudely hollowed-out canoe from trunk of tree; an underground shelter from shells and bombs in time of war.

Dugong, dụ'gong, *n.* [Malayan.] A herbivorous mammal of the Indian Seas, allied to the manatee or sea-cow, and sometimes attaining a length of 20 feet, though generally about 7 or 8.

Duke, dūk, *n.* [Fr. *duc*, from L. *dux, ducis*, a leader, from *duco*, to lead (seen also in *duct, ducat, conduct, produce, educate*, &c.); cog. A.Sax. *toga*, a leader, E. *tug* and *tow*.] A chief, prince, or leader‡; in Great Britain, one of the highest order of nobility; a title of honour or nobility next below that of a prince; in some countries on the Continent, a sovereign prince, the ruler of a state.—**Dukedom,** dūk'dum, *n.* The seigniory or possessions of a duke; the territory of a duke; the title or quality of a duke.—**Dukeship,** dūk'ship, *n.* The state or dignity of a duke.

Dukhn, dụchn, *n.* A kind of millet cultivated in Egypt, Spain, &c.

Dulcamara, dul-ka-mā'ra, *n.* [L. *dulcis*, sweet, and *amarus*, bitter. Lit. bitter-sweet.] A common British hedge-plant, the bitter-sweet or woody nightshade, the root and twigs of which have a peculiar bitter-sweet taste.

Dulcet, dul'set, *a.* [O.Fr. *dolcet*, L. *dulcis*, sweet.] Sweet to the taste; luscious; exquisite; sweet to the ear; melodious; harmonious; agreeable to the mind.—**Dulcification,** dul'si-fi-kā"shon, *n.* The act of dulcifying.—**Dulcifluous,** dul-sif'lụ-us, *a.* [L. *dulcis*, and *fluo*, to flow.] Flowing sweetly.—**Dulcify,** dul'si-fi, *v.t.*—*dulcified, dulcifying.* [Fr. *dulcifier*, from L. *dulcis*, sweet, and *facio*, to make.] To sweeten; to free from acidity, saltness, or acrimony; to render more agreeable to the taste.

Dulcimer, dul'si-mėr, *n.* [Sp. *dulcemele*, It. *dolcimello*, from L. *dulcis*, sweet.] A musical instrument consisting in its modern form of a shallow quadrilateral box without a top, across which runs a series of wires, tuned by pegs at the sides, and played on by being struck by two cork-headed hammers.

Dulcinea, dul-sin'ē-a, *n.* [Sp. name.] Lady-love; the inamorata of Don Quixote.

Dulia, dū'li-a, *n.* [Gr. *douleia*, service, from *doulos*, a slave.] An inferior kind of worship or adoration, as that paid to saints and angels in the Roman Catholic Church.

Dull, dul, *a.* [A.Sax. *dol, dwol*, erring, dull, from *dwelan*, to be torpid or dull; akin Goth. *dvals*, foolish; Icel. *dul*, foolishness; D. *dol*, L.G. *dull*, G. *toll*, mad.] Stupid; doltish; slow of understanding; heavy; sluggish; without life or spirit; slow of motion; wanting sensibility or keenness in some of the senses (sight, hearing); not quick; sad; melancholy; depressing; dismal; gross; inanimate; insensible; not pleasing; not exhilarating; cheerless; not bright or clear; tarnished; dim; obscure; blunt; obtuse; having a thick edge; cloudy; overcast.—*v.t.* To make dull; to stupefy; to blunt; to render less acute; to make less eager; to make sad or melancholy; to make insensible or slow to perceive; to render dim; to sully; to tarnish or cloud.—*v.i.* To become dull.—**Dullard,** dul'ėrd, *n.* A stupid person; a dolt; a blockhead; a dunce.—**Dullardism,**† dul'ėr-dizm, *n.* Stupidity; doltishness.—**Dull-brained,** *a.* Stupid.—**Dull-browed,** *a.* Having a gloomy brow or look.—**Dull-eyed,** *a.* With eyes dull in expression.—**Dull-head,** *n.* A person of dull understanding; a dolt; a blockhead.—**Dullish,** dul'ish, *a.* Somewhat dull; somewhat stupid; tiresome.—**Dully,** dul'i, *a.* Somewhat dull. (*Tenn.*)—*adv.* (dul'li). Stupidly; slowly; sluggishly; without life or spirit.—**Dullness, Dulness,** dul'nes, *n.* The state or character of being dull.

Dulse, duls, *n.* [Gael. *duilliasg*, Ir. *duileasg*, dulse.] A kind of edible sea-weed having a reddish-brown, or purple, frond, several inches long, found at low water.

Duma, dö'ma, *n.* The Russian parliament created in 1905, and overthrown by the Bolshevist revolution in 1917.

Dumb, dum, *a.* [A.Sax. *dumb* = Goth. *dumbs*, Dan. *dum*, G. *dumm*, dumb, stupid; allied to *dim*, and perhaps Goth. *daubs*, deaf.] Mute; silent; not speaking; destitute of the power of speech; unable to utter articulate sounds; not accompanied with speech; effected by signs (*dumb* show).—*To strike dumb*, to confound; to astonish; to render silent by astonishment.—*v.t.* To silence; to overpower with sound (*Shak.*).—**Dumbly,** dum'li, *adv.* Mutely; silently; without words or speech.—**Dumbness,** dum'nes, *n.* State of being dumb.—**Dumb-bells,** *n. pl.* Weights, usually consisting of two iron balls with a short piece for grasping between them, swung in the hands for developing the chest, the muscles of the arms, &c.—**Dumb-show,** *n.* A sort of dramatic representation performed pantomimically; gesture without words; pantomime.—**Dumb-waiter,** *n.* A framework with shelves, made to move from floor to floor in a house for conveying food, &c.; a side table or other portable piece of furniture in a dining-room, on which dessert, &c., is placed until required.—**Dumfound, Dumbfound,** dum-found', *v.t.* To strike dumb; to confuse. (*Colloq.*)—**Dumfounder,** dum-foun'dėr, *v.t.* To confuse; to stupefy; to strike dumb; to confound. (*Colloq.*)—**Dummy,** dum'i, *n.* One who is dumb; the fourth or exposed hand during the play of bridge or whist; also when there are only three playing; a sham object doing service for a real one, as sham packages, &c.; a lay figure on which merchants display clothing.—*a.* Silent; mute; sham; fictitious.—*Double dummy*, bridge or whist with only two players, each having a hand exposed.

Dumdum, dum-dum, *n.* [Indian name of station with arsenal.] A soft-nosed bullet which expands and lacerates on striking.

Dumous, Dumose, dū'mus, dū'mōs, *a.* [L. *dumosus*, from *dumus*, a bush.] Having a bushy form; abounding with bushes.

Dump, dump, *v.t.* [Akin to *bump, thump.*] To put or throw down with a bang; to deposit carelessly; to sell cheaply abroad through protection in the home market.

Dump, dump, *n.* [Allied to *damp*: Dan. *dump*, dull; G. *dampf*, steam, vapour; comp. *dumps*, melancholy, with *vapours*, in the sense of nervousness or depression.] A dull gloomy state of the mind; sadness; melancholy; low spirits; heaviness of heart: generally in the plural, and now used only when a ludicrous effect is intended; a melancholy tune (*Shak.*)‡.—**Dumpish,** dum'pish, *a.* Sad; melancholy; depressed in spirits.—**Dumpishly,** dum'pish-li, *adv.* In a moping manner.—**Dumpishness,** dum'pish-nes, *n.* State of being dumpish.

Dumpling, dump'ling, *n.* [Connected with Prov.E. *dump*, a clumsy leaden counter, a lump; also perhaps prov. *dump*, to knock.] A kind of pudding or mass of boiled paste, with or without fruit in it.—**Dumpy,** dum'pi, *a.* Short and thick.—**Dumpy-level,** *n.* A spirit-level having a short telescope with a large aperture, and a compass, used in surveying.

Dun, dun, *a.* [A.Sax. *dunn*, perhaps from W. *dwn*, Gael. *donn*, dun.] Of a grayish-brown or dull-brown colour; of a smoky colour.—**Dunnish,** dun'ish, *a.* Inclined to a dun colour; somewhat dun.

Dun, dun, *v.t.*—*dunned, dunning.* [A form of *din.*] To clamour for payment of a debt from; to demand a debt in a pressing manner from; to call on for payment repeatedly; to urge importunately.—*n.* One who duns.

Dunce, duns, *n.* [From *Duns Scotus*, the leader of the Schoolmen of the fourteenth century, opposed to the revival of classical learning; hence this name was given to his followers in contempt by their opponents.] An ignoramus; a pupil too stupid to learn; a dullard; a thick-skull.—**Duncedom**, duns′dum, *n.* The realm or domain of dunces.—**Duncery**, dun′sėr-i, *n.* Dulness; stupidity.—**Duncish**, dun′sish, *a.* Like a dunce.—**Duncishness**, dun′sish-nes, *n.* —**Dunciad**, *n.* A famous mock-heroic satire on Dunces by Pope.

Dunder, dun′dėr, *n.* [W. Indian.] The lees or dregs of the juice of the sugar-cane, used for distilling rum.

Dunderhead, **Dunderpate**, dun′dėr-hed, dun′dėr-pāt, *n.* [Comp. Dan. *dummerhoved*, a dunderhead, lit. stupid-head, from *dum*, stupid.] A dunce; a dull-head. —**Dunderheaded**, dun′dėr-hed-ed, *a.* Stupid; thick-skulled.

Dune, dūn, *n.* [A.Sax. *dún*. DOWN.] A low hill of sand accumulated on the seacoast; a name given to some ancient forts in Scotland with a hemispherical or conical roof.

Dung, dung, *n.* [A.Sax. *dung*, G. *dung*, Sw. *dynga*; connected with verb to *ding*.] The excrement of animals.—*v.t.* To manure with dung.—*v.i.* To void excrement.—**Dung-fork**, *n.* A fork with three or more prongs used to lift dung.—**Dunghill**, dung′hil, *n.* A heap of dung; the place where dung is kept collected; a mean or vile abode or situation.—*a.* Sprung from the dunghill; mean; low; vile.—**Dung-meer**, dung′mēr, *n.* A pit where dung, weeds, &c., are mixed to lie and rot.—**Dungy**, dung′i, *a.* Full of dung; filthy; vile.

Dungaree, dun-ga-rē′, *n.* [Anglo-Indian, low, common, vulgar.] A coarse unbleached Indian calico, generally blue, worn by sailors.

Dungeon, dun′jon, *n.* [Fr. *dongeon*. *donjon*. DONJON.] The innermost and strongest tower of a castle; the donjon; a close prison; a deep, dark place of confinement. —*v.t.* To confine in a dungeon.

Duniwassal, **Dunniewassal**, dų-ni-was′sal, *n.* [Gael. *duin′ uasal*, from *duine*, a man, and *uasal*, gentle.] A gentleman of secondary rank among the Scottish Highlanders; a cadet of a family of rank.

Dunker, dung′kėr, *n.* A member of a sect of Baptists originating in Philadelphia; a tunker.

Dunlin, dun′lin, *n.* [From *dune* with dim. termination *-ling*; or from *dun*, adj.] A species of sandpiper, about eight inches in length, often occurring in vast flocks along sandy shores; remarkable for the variations its plumage undergoes in summer and winter.

Dunnage, dun′āj, *n.* [For *downage*, from *down*.] Faggots, boughs, or loose wood laid on the bottom of a ship to raise heavy goods above the bottom to prevent injury from water; also loose articles of lading wedged between parts of the cargo to hold them steady.

Dunnock, dun′ok, *n.* [From *dun*, *a.*] The common hedge-sparrow.

Duodecimal, dū-ō-des′i-mal, *a.* [L. *duodecim*, twelve.] Proceeding in computation by twelves.—*n. pl.* An arithmetical method of ascertaining the number of square feet and square inches in a rectangular area or surface, whose sides are given in feet and inches.—**Duodecimo**, dū-ō-des′i-mō, *a.* Having or consisting of twelve leaves to a sheet.—*n.* A book in which a sheet is folded into twelve leaves; the size of a book consisting of sheets so folded: usually indicated thus, 12*mo*.

Duodenum, dū-ō-dē′num, *n.* [From L. *duodeni*, twelve each, so called because its length is about twelve fingers' breadth.] The first portion of the small intestines; the twelve-inch intestine.—**Duodenal**, dū-ō-dē′nal, *a.* Connected with or relating to the duodenum.—**Duodenary**, dū-ō-den′a-ri, *a.* [L. *duodenarius*.] Relating to the number twelve; twelvefold; increasing by twelves.—*Duodenary arithmetic*, that system in which the local value of the figures increases twelvefold from right to left, instead of tenfold.

Duoliteral, dū-ō-lit′ė-ral, *a.* [L. *duo*, two, and *litera*, a letter.] Consisting of two letters only; biliteral.

Duologue, dū′o-log, *n.* [L. *duo*, two, *-logue*, from *dialogue*.] A dialogue between two.

Dup,‡ dup, *v.t.* [For *do up*.] To open. (*Shak.*)

Dupe, dūp, *n.* [Fr. *dupe*, a name sometimes given to the hoopoe, and hence, from the bird being regarded as stupid, applied to a stupid person. Comp. *pigeon*.] A person who is deceived, or one easily led astray by his credulity.—*v.t.*—*duped*, *duping*. [Fr. *duper*.] To make a dupe of; to trick; to mislead by imposing on one's credulity. —**Dupability**, dū-pa-bil′i-ti, *n.* Liability to be duped; gullibility.—**Dupable**, **Dupeable**, dū′pa-bl, *a.* Liable to be or capable of being duped.—**Duper**, dū′pėr, *n.* One who dupes; a cheat; a swindler.—**Dupery**, dū′pėr-i, *n.* The art of duping.

Duple, dū′pl, *a.* [L. *duplus*, double. DOUBLE.] Double.—*Duple ratio*, that of 2 to 1, 8 to 4, &c.—*Sub-duple ratio* is the reverse, or as 1 to 2, 4 to 8, &c.—*v.t.*† To double.—**Duplet**,† dūp′let, *n.* Doublet. —**Duplex**, dū′pleks, *a.* [L.] Double; twofold; an apartment of rooms on two floors; a house with two apartments.

Duplicate, dū′pli-kāt, *a.* [L. *duplicatus*, from *duplico*, to double, from *duplex*, double, twofold—*duo*, two, and *plico*, to fold. DUAL, PLY.] Double; twofold.—*Duplicate proportion* or *ratio*, the proportion or ratio of squares.—*n.* Another corresponding to the first; a second thing of the same kind; another example or specimen of the same kind of object; a copy; a transcript; a pawnbroker's ticket.—*v.t.*—*duplicated*, *duplicating*. To double; to fold. —**Duplication**, dū-pli-kā′shon, *n.* The act of doubling; the multiplication of a number by 2; a folding; a doubling; a fold. —*Duplication of the cube*, *math.* a problem for determining the side of a cube which shall be exactly the double in solid contents of a given cube.—**Duplicative**, dū′pli-kā-tiv, *a.* Having the quality of duplicating or doubling.—**Duplicature**, dū′-pli-kā-tūr, *n.* A doubling; a fold.—**Duplicity**, dū-plis′i-ti, *n.* [Fr. *duplicité*; L. *duplicitas*, from *duplex*, *duplicis*.] The state of being double; doubleness; especially, doubleness of heart or speech; the act or practice of exhibiting a different or contrary conduct, or uttering different or contrary sentiments at different times in relation to the same thing; double-dealing; dissimulation; deceit.

Durable, dū′ra-bl, *a.* [L. *durabilis*, from *duro*, to last, *durus*, hard.] Having the quality of lasting or continuing long in being without perishing or wearing out; not perishable or changeable.—**Durability**, **Durableness**, dū-ra-bil′i-ti, dū′-ra-bl-nes, *n.* The quality of being durable. —**Durably**, dū′ra-bli, *adv.* In a durable manner.

Duralumin, dūr-al′u-min, *n.* A composite material consisting mainly of aluminium as strong as mild steel under proper heat treatment.

Dura-mater, dū′ra-mā-tėr. [L.; lit. hard mother: called *mother* as protecting the brain.] The outer membrane of the brain: so named from its hardness compared with the membrane which lies under it, called *pia-mater* (pious mother), and which also surrounds the brain.

Duramen, dū-rā′men, *n.* [L. *duramen*, hardness, *durus*, hard.] The central wood or heart-wood in the trunk of an exogenous tree.

Durance, dū′rans, *n.* [In the common sense apparently shortened from *endurance*, from the hardships of imprisonment; comp. *duress*.] Imprisonment; restraint of the person; custody; duration†.—**Duration**, dū-rā′shon, *n.* Continuance in time; length or extension of existence, indefinitely; power of continuance.

Durbar, dėr′bär, *n.* [Hind. and Per. *darbâr*—Per. *dar*, door, and *bâr*, court, assembly.] An audience room in the palaces of the native princes of India; state levee or audience held by the governor-general of India, or by a native prince; an official reception.

Dure,‡ dūr, *v.i.* [Fr. *durer*, L. *durare*, *durus*, hard.] To endure; to continue. (N.T.)

Duress, dū′res, *n.* [O.Fr. *duresse*, hardship, constraint, from L. *duritia*, harshness, hardness, from *durus*, hard.] Imprisonment; restraint of liberty; *law*, also restraint or constraint by threats of personal injury.

Durian, **Durion**, dū′ri-an, dū′ri-on, *n.* [The Malay name.] A tree of the Malayan Archipelago; also its fruit, which is extremely luscious and enticing to eat, but has an abominably offensive odour.

During, dū′ring. [From the L. phrase *vita durante*, while life lasts.] Continuing; lasting; in the time of; throughout the course of.

Durmast, dėr′mast, *n.* A highly valued species of oak, closely allied to the common oak.

Durra, dur′a, *n.* [Ar.] A species of grain much cultivated in Africa, Asia, and the south of Europe; Indian millet; Guinea corn.

Durst, dėrst, pret. of *dare*.

Dusk, dusk, *a.* [Probably akin to Sw. *dusk*, dull weather; Icel. *doska*, to dawdle; L.G. *dusken*, to slumber, perhaps also to *dose*.] Tending to darkness, or moderately dark; tending to a dark or black colour; moderately black; swarthy.—*n.* An approach to darkness; incipient or imperfect obscurity; a middle degree between light and darkness; twilight; darkness of colour.—*v.t.*† To make dusky, or somewhat dark.—*v.i.*† To begin to lose light or whiteness; to grow dark; to cause a dusky appearance.—**Dusken**, dus′kn, *v.i.* To grow dusk; to become dark.—*v.t.* To make dusk, or somewhat dark.—**Duskily**, dus′ki-li, *adv.* In a dusky manner.—**Duskiness**, dus′ki-nes, *n.* The state of being dusky.—**Duskish**, dus′kish, *a.* Moderately dusky.—**Dusky**, dus′ki, *a.* Partially dark or obscure; not luminous; tending to blackness in colour; dark-coloured; not bright; gloomy.

Dust, dust, *n.* [A.Sax. *dust*, dust; same word as Icel. and L.D. *dust*, D. *duist*, dust; akin to G. *dunst*, vapour.] Fine dry particles of earth or other matter, so attenuated that they may be raised and wafted by the wind; hence, *fig.* commotion and confusion accompanying a struggle; earth or earthy matter as symbolic of mortality; the body when it has mouldered in the grave; the grave; a low condition; money (*colloq.*).—*To throw dust in one's eyes*, to mislead; to blind as to the true character of something.—*v.t.* To free from dust; to brush, wipe, or sweep away dust; to beat; to sprinkle with dust.—**Dust-ball**, *n.* A disease in horses, in which a hard ball is formed in the intestinal canal.—**Dust-brand**, *n.* Smut, a disease of cereals.—**Dust-brush**, *n.* A brush for removing dust, as from articles of furniture.—**Dust-cart**, *n.* A cart for conveying dust and refuse from the streets.—**Duster**, dus′tėr, *n.* One who or that which clears from dust; a light overcoat worn to protect the clothing from dust.—**Dustiness**, dus′ti-nes, *n.* The state of being dusty.—**Dust-man**, *n.* One whose employment is to remove dirt and filth.—**Dust-pan**, *n.* A utensil to convey dust brushed from the floor, furniture, &c.—**Dusty**, dus′ti, *a.* Filled, covered, or sprinkled with dust; reduced to dust; like dust; of the colour of dust.

Dutch, dutsh, *n.* [G. *deutsch*, German, Germanic, pertaining to the Germanic or Teutonic race; O.H.G. *diutisc*, from *diot*, A.Sax. *theod*, Goth. *thiuda*, people. The word has latterly been narrowed from its original meaning. The term *Low Dutch* means Dutch or Low German (*Plattdeutsch*), as opposed to *High Dutch* (*Hochdeutsch*), or German proper.] *Pl.* originally, the Germanic race; the German peoples generally:

now only applied to the people of Holland; *sing.* the language spoken in Holland.—*a.* Pertaining to Holland or its inhabitants.—*Dutch auction*, an auction at which the auctioneer starts with a high price, and comes down till he meets with a bidder; a mock auction.—*Dutch courage*, false or artificial courage; boldness inspired by intoxicating spirits.—*Dutch clover*, white clover, a valuable pasture plant.—*Dutch concert*, a concert in which a company join, each singing his own song at the same time as his neighbour, or in which each member sings a verse of a song, some well-known chorus being used as the burden after each verse.—*Dutch gold, Dutch metal*, an alloy of eleven parts of copper and two of zinc.—*Dutch leaf*, false gold-leaf.—*Dutch mineral*, copper beaten out into very thin leaves.—*Dutch myrtle*, sweet gale; a fragrant shrub found in bogs and moors.—*Dutch oven*, a tin hanging screen for cooking before a kitchen range or ordinary fire-grate.—*Dutch pink*, chalk or whiting dyed yellow with a decoction of birch-leaves, French berries, and alum.—**Dutchman**, dutsh'-man, *n.* A native of Holland; a Hollander.

Dutch treat, *n.* A meal or entertaining at which each person pays his own share.

Duty, dū'ti, *n.* [From *due.*] That which a person is bound by any natural, moral, or legal obligation to do or perform; what has to be done as being due towards another; obligation to do something; obedience; submission; act of reverence or respect; any service, business, or office; particularly, military or similar service; a tax, toll, or impost; any sum of money required by government to be paid on the importation, exportation, or consumption of goods.—**Duteous**, dū'tē-us, *a.* Performing that which is due, or that which law, justice, or propriety requires; dutiful; obedient; enjoined by duty (*Shak.*)†.—**Duteously**, dū'tē-us-li, *adv.* In a duteous manner.—**Duteousness**, dū'tē-us-nes, *n.* Quality of being duteous.—**Dutiable**, dū'ti-a-bl, *a.* Subject to the imposition of duty or customs.—**Dutiful**, dū'ti-ful, *a.* Performing the duties or obligations required by law, justice, or propriety; obedient; submissive to superiors; expressive of respect or a sense of duty; respectful; reverential; required by duty.—**Dutifully**, dū'ti-ful-li, *adv.* In a dutiful manner.—**Dutifulness**, dū'ti-ful-nes, *n.* The state or character of being dutiful.—**Duty-free**, *a.* Free from tax or duty.

Duvetyn, Duvetine, dū'vė-tēn, *n.* A soft fabric with a fine velvety nap, made of wool mixed with silk or cotton, or both.

D-valve, *n.* A valve for opening and closing the induction and eduction passages of a steam-engine cylinder, so called from its plan resembling the letter D.

Dwale, dwāl, *n.* [A.Sax. *dwala, dwola*, error, from *dwelian*, to err, to be torpid or dull.] The deadly nightshade, which possesses stupefying or poisonous properties.

Dwarf, dwarf, *n.* [A.Sax. *dwerg, dweorg*, D. *dwerg*, Sw. *dwerg, dwerf*, L. G. *dwarf*, a dwarf.] A general name for an animal or plant which is much below the ordinary size of the species or kind; a very diminutive man or woman.—*v.t.* To hinder from growing to the natural size; to prevent the due development of; to stunt; to cause to look small or insignificant by comparison.—*v.i.* To become less; to become dwarfish or stunted.—**Dwarfish**, dwar'fish, *a.* Like a dwarf; below the common stature or size; very small; low; petty; despicable.—**Dwarfishly**, dwar'fish-li, *adv.* In a dwarfish manner.—**Dwarfishness**, dwar'fish-nes, *n.* The state or quality of being dwarfish.—**Dwarf-wall**, *n.* A wall of less height than a story of a building.

Dwell, dwel, *v.i.*—*dwelled*, usually contracted into *dwelt, dwelling.* [From A.Sax. *dwellan*, to deceive, prevent, hinder; Icel. *dvelja*, to hinder, to delay; Dan. *dvæle*, to loiter, delay, dwell; akin *dull.*] To abide as a permanent resident; to live in a place; to have a habitation for some time or permanently; to be in any state or condition; to continue.—*To dwell on*, or *upon*, to keep the attention fixed on; to hang upon with fondness; to occupy a long time with; to be tedious over.—**Dweller**, dwel'ėr, *n.* One who dwells; an inhabitant.—**Dwelling**, dwel'ing, *n.* Habitation; place of residence; abode; continuance; residence.—**Dwelling-house**, *n.* A house intended to be occupied as a residence, in contradistinction to a place of business, office, or other building.—**Dwelling-place**, *n.* The place of residence.

Dwindle, dwin'dl, *v.i.*—*dwindled, dwindling.* [Freq. from O.E. and Sc. *dwine*; A.Sax. *dwinan*, to pine, waste away = D. *dwijnen*, Icel. *dvína*, Dan. *tvine*, to pine.] To diminish gradually; to become small and insignificant; to shrink; to waste or consume away; to degenerate.—*v.t.* To cause to dwindle.—*n.* The process of dwindling; decline.—**Dwindled**, dwin'dld, *p.* and *a.* Shrunk; diminished in size.—**Dwindlement**, dwin'dl-ment, *n.* The act or state of dwindling.

Dyad, dī'ad, *n.* [Gr. *dyas, dyados*, from *dyo*, two.] Two units treated as one; a pair; a couple; *chem.* an elementary substance, each atom of which, in combining with other bodies, is equivalent to two atoms of hydrogen.—**Dyadic**, dī-ad'ik, *a.* Pertaining or relating to the number two, or to a dyad; consisting of two parts or elements.—**Dyas**, dī'as, *n.* [Gr.] *Geol.* a term sometimes applied to the Permian system from its being divided into two principal groups.

Dyarchy, dī'ār-ki, *n.* [Gr. *duo*, two, *archē*, rule.] The rule of two persons together.

Dye, dī, *v.t.*—*dyed, dyeing.* [A.Sax. *deâgan, deâgian*, from *deâg*, dye, color, perhaps akin to *dew.*] To give a new and permanent color to: applied particularly to cloth or the materials of cloth, as wool, cotton, silk, and linen; also to hair, skins, &c.; to stain; to color; to tinge.—*n.* A coloring liquor; color; stain; tinge.—**Dyer**, dī'ėr, *n.* One whose occupation is to dye cloth and the like.—**Dye-house**, *n.* A building in which dyeing is carried on.—**Dyer's-moss**, *n.* Same as *Archil.*—**Dyer's-weed**, *n.* Any of several dye-yielding plants, as the wood waxen.—**Dye-stuff**, *n.* Materials used in dyeing.—**Dye-wood**, *n.* A general name for any wood from which dye is extracted.—**Dye-work**, *n.* An establishment in which dyeing is carried on.

Dying, dī'ing, *a.* Mortal; destined to death; given, uttered, or manifested just before death (*dying* words); pertaining to or associated with death (*dying* hour); drawing to a close; fading away.—*n.* The act of expiring; death.—**Dyingly**, dī'ing-li, *adv.* In an expiring manner.—**Dyingness**, dī'ing-nes, *n.* The state of dying; affected languor or faintness; languishment.

Dyke, *n.* and *v.* Same as *Dike.*

Dynam, dī'nam, *n.* [Gr. *dynamis*, power.] A term proposed to express a unit of work equal to a weight of 1 lb. raised through 1 foot in a second; a foot-pound.—**Dynameter**, di-nam'e-tėr, *n.* An instrument for determining the magnifying power of telescopes.—**Dynametric, Dynametrical**, dī'na-met'rik, dī'na-met'ri-kal, *a.* Pertaining to a dynameter.—**Dynamic, Dynamical**, di-nam'ik, di-nam'i-kal, *a.* Pertaining to strength, power, or force; relating to dynamics; relating to the effects of the forces or moving agencies in nature.—*Dynamical electricity*, current electricity.—**Dynamically**, di-nam'i-kal-li, *adv.* In a dynamical manner.—**Dynamics**, di-nam'iks, *n.* The science which investigates the action of force, now usually divided into *Statics* and *Kinetics*, the former dealing with forces such as compel rest or prevent change of motion, the latter with forces that cause motion or change of motion. [Formerly the term was used as equivalent to the modern *Kinetics, Mechanics* being then equivalent to *Dynamics* as now used.]
Dynamism, dī'na-mizm, *n.* The doctrine that all substance involves force.—**Dynamite**, dī'na-mīt, *n.* An explosive substance consisting of a siliceous earth, and sometimes of charcoal, saw-dust, &c., impregnated with nitro-glycerin, and having a disruptive force estimated at about eight times that of gunpowder.—*v.t.* To shatter with dynamite.—**Dynamiter**, dīn'a-mīt-ėr, *n.* One who uses dynamite for destroying public buildings or other criminal purposes.—**Dynamo**, dī'na-mō, *n.* A machine for converting energy from a mechanical into an electric form by the use of electro-magnets.—**Dynamograph**, dī-nam'o-graf, *n.* An instrument for measuring and making a graphic record of muscular power.—**Dynamometer**, dī'na-mom"e-tėr, *n.* An instrument for measuring force or power, especially that of men, animals, machines, the strength of materials, &c.—**Dynamometric, Dynamometrical**, dī'na-mo-met"rik, dī'na-mo-met"ri-kal, *a.* Of or pertaining to a dynamometer or to the measurement of force.—**Dynamo-electric**, di-nam'ō-ē-lek"trik, *a.* With *machine*, an electric generator or motor.

Dynasty, din'as-ti, *n.* [Gr. *dynasteia*, sovereignty, from *dynastēs*, a lord or chief, from *dynamai*, to be strong, *dynamis*, power.] A race or succession of rulers of the same line or family, who govern a particular country; the period during which they rule.—**Dynastic**, di-nas'tik, *a.* Relating to a dynasty or line of kings.

Dyne, dīn, *n.* [Gr. *dynamis*, power.] *Physics*, a unit of force, being that force which, acting on a gramme for one second, generates a velocity of a centimetre per second.

Dysæsthesia, dis-ēs-thē'si-a, *n.* [Gr. *dys*, with difficulty, *aisthēsis*, perception.] *Pathol.* impaired feeling; insensibility.

Dyschroa, dis'kro-a, *n.* [Gr. *dys*, and *chroa*, colour.] *Med.* a discoloured state of the skin.

Dyscrasia, Dyscrasy, dis-krā'si-a, dis'-kra-si, *n.* [Gr. *dyskrasia*—*dys*, evil, and *krasis*, habit.] *Med.* a bad habit of body.

Dysentery, dis'en-te-ri, *n.* [Gr. *dysenteria*—*dys*, bad, and *entera*, intestines.] Inflammation of the mucous membrane of the large intestine, accompanied generally with much fever and great prostration, frequent stools, the discharges being mixed with blood and mucous or other morbid matter, griping of the bowels, and tenesmus.—**Dysenteric, Dysenterical**, dis-en-ter'ik, dis-en-ter'i-kal, *a.* Pertaining to or afflicted with dysentery.

Dyslogistic, dis-lō-jis'tik, *a.* [Formed on the model of *eulogistic*, *dys* signifying ill, and the word having therefore the opposite signification of *eulogistic.*] Conveying censure, disapproval, or opprobrium; censorious; opprobrious.—**Dyslogistically**, dis-lō-jis'ti-kal-li, *adv.* In a dyslogistic manner; so as to convey censure or disapproval.—**Dyslogy**, dis'lo-ji, *n.* Dispraise; opposite of *eulogy.*

Dysmenorrhœa, dis'men-o-rē"a, *n.* [Gr. *dys*, difficult, *men*, month, *rheō*, to flow.] Difficult or painful menstruation.

Dysodile, dis'ō-dīl, *n.* [Gr. *dys*, bad, and *ozō*, to smell, and *hylē*, matter.] A species of coal, of a greenish or yellowish-gray colour, in masses composed of thin layers, which, when burning, emits a very fetid odour.

Dysorexia, Dysorexy, dis-o-rek'si-a, dis'-o-rek-si, *n.* [Gr. *dys*, bad, and *orexis*, appetite.] *Med.* a bad or depraved appetite; a want of appetite.

Dyspepsia, Dyspepsy, dis-pep'si-a, dis-pep'si, *n.* [Gr. *dyspepsia*—*dys*, bad, and *peptō*, to concoct, to digest.] Indigestion, or difficulty of digestion; a state of the stomach in which its functions are disturbed, without the presence of other diseases, or when, if they are present, they are but of minor importance.—**Dyspeptic, Dyspeptical**, dis-pep'tik, dis-pep'ti-kal, *a.* Afflicted with dyspepsia; pertaining to or consisting in dyspepsy.—**Dyspeptic**, *n.* A person afflicted with dyspepsy.

Dysphagia, Dysphagy, dis-fā'ji-a, dis'-fa-ji, *n.* [Gr. *dys*, ill, and *phagō*, to eat.] *Med.* difficulty of swallowing.

Dysphonia, Dysphony, dis-fō'ni-a, dis'-

fo-ni, *n.* [Gr. *dys*, bad, and *phōnē*, voice.] *Med.* a difficulty of speaking occasioned by an ill disposition of the organs of speech.

Dyspnœa, disp-nē'a, *n.* [Gr. *dyspnoia*—*dys*, ill, and *pneō*, to breathe.] *Med.* difficulty of breathing.—**Dyspnoic**, disp-nō'-ik, *a.* Affected with or resulting from dyspnœa.

Dysteleology, dis'tel-ē-ol"o-ji, *n.* The doctrine of the absence of purpose or intention in the structure of animals, as seen in the existence of rudimentary organs that can be of no use in the animal economy.

Dysthymic, dis-thim'ik, *a.* [Gr. *dysthymikos*, melancholy—*dys*, bad, and *thymos*, the soul or spirit.] *Med.* affected with despondency; depressed in spirits; dejected.

Dysuria, Dysury, dis-ū'ri-a, dis-ū'ri, *n.* [Gr. *dysouria*—*dys*, ill, and *ouron*, urine.] *Med.* difficulty in discharging the urine, attended with pain and a sensation of heat.—**Dysuric**, dis-ū'rik, *a.* Pertaining to dysury.

Dziggetai, dzig'ge-tā, *n.* The wild ass of Central Asia, a fine swift animal, intermediate in appearance and character between the horse and the ass.

E

E, the second vowel and the fifth letter of the English alphabet, occurring more frequently than any other letter of the alphabet; *mus.* the third note or degree of the natural or diatonic scale.

Each, ēch, *distrib. a.* and *pron.* [O.E. *eche, ech, ych, uch, elch, elc, ilk*; A.Sax. *ælc*, from *á* = *aye*, ever, and *líc*, like; similar to D. and L.G. *elk*, G. *jeglich*. Comp. *such* and *which*.] Every one of any number separately considered or treated; every one of two or more considered individually. With *other* it is used reciprocally; as, it is our duty to assist *each other* (that is, each to assist the other).

Eager, ē'gėr, *a.* [O.E. *egre*, O.Fr. *eigre*, Mod.Fr. *aigre*, eager, sharp, biting, from L. *acer, acris*, sharp, from root which appears in *acute acid, acrid*, &c.] Sharp, sour, acid (*Shak.*)‡; excited by ardent desire in the pursuit of any object; ardent to pursue, perform, or obtain; ardently wishing or longing; vehement; fervid; earnest; impetuous; keen.—**Eagerly**, ē'gėr-li, *adv.* In an eager manner.—**Eagerness**, ē'gėr-nes, *n.* The state or character of being eager; keenness; ardour; zeal.

Eagle, ē'gl, *n.* [Fr. *aigle*, from L. *aquila*, an eagle, fem. of the rare adj. *aquilus*, dark-colored, swarthy.] A common name of many large birds of prey, characterized by a hooked beak and curved, sharp, and strong claws (talons), and by its great powers of flight and vision, often regarded as a symbol of royalty; the typical eagles constitute a genus (*Aquila*) in which the legs are feathered to the toes; a military standard having the figure of an eagle, such as that of ancient Rome and modern France; a gold coin of the United States, of the value of ten dollars, from the eagle on the reverse; a reading desk in churches in the form of an eagle with expanded wings; in golf, a score of two under par on any hole but a par-three hole.—**Eaglet**, ē'glet, *n.* A small or young eagle.—**Eagle-eyed**, *a.* Sharp-sighted as an eagle; having an acute sight.—**Eagle-owl**, *n.* A horned owl little inferior in size to the golden eagle.—**Eagle-stone**, *n.* A variety of argillaceous iron ore occurring in spherical, oval, or reniform masses varying from the size of a walnut to that of a man's head; so called from an ancient notion that they were often found in the nests of eagles.—**Eagle-wood**, *n.* A highly fragrant wood.

Eagre, ē'gėr, *n.* [A.Sax. *eágor, ēgor*, Icel. *ægir*, the sea.] A tidal wave moving up a river or estuary at spring-tide; a bore.

Eanling,‡ ēn'ling, *n.* [A.Sax. *ednian*, to bring forth, and *ling*, dim. term.] A lamb just brought forth. (*Shak.*)

Ear, ēr, *n.* [A.Sax. *eáre* = D. *oor*, Icel. *eyra*, Dan. *öre*, G. *ohr*, L. *auris*, G. *ous*.] The organ of hearing, which in man and higher animals is composed of the external ear, a cartilaginous funnel for collecting the sound waves and directing them inwards; the middle ear, tympanum or drum; and the internal ear or labyrinth; the sense of hearing; the power of distinguishing sounds; the power of nice perception of the differences of musical sounds; a favourable hearing; attention; heed; a part of any inanimate object resembling an ear; a projecting part from the side of anything; a handle of a tub, pitcher, &c.—*All ear*, all attention.—*To set by the ears*, to make strife between; to cause to quarrel.—*Up to the ears, over head and ears*, deeply absorbed or engrossed; overwhelmed.—**Eared**, ērd, *a.* Having ears: usually in compounds, as *long-eared*.—**Earless**, ēr'les, *n.* Having no ears; wanting the external ear.—**Ear-ache**, *n.* Pain in the ear.—**Ear-cockle**, *n.* A disease in wheat caused by the presence in the grain of a microscopic worm.—**Ear-drop**, *n.* An ornamental pendant for the ear.—**Ear-drum**, *n.* The tympanum (which see).—**Ear-hole**, *n.* The aperture or opening of the external ear.—**Ear-mark**, *n.* A mark on the ear for distinguishing sheep, pigs, cattle, &c.; hence any mark for distinction or identification. —*v.t.* To distinguish by putting an ear-mark on; to set apart funds for an overdue purpose or estimate.—**Ear-pick**, *n.* An instrument for cleaning the ear.—**Ear-piercing**, *a.* Piercing the ear; sharp; shrill; acute.—**Ear-ring**, *n.* An ornament ring worn hanging from the lobe of the ear, and usually carrying a jewelled pendant.—**Ear-shell**, *n.* One of a genus of gasteropodous molluscs, so called from the flatness and smallness of the spire of the shell giving it some resemblance to an ear.—**Ear-shot**, *n.* The distance the ear can perceive sound; hearing distance.—**Ear-trumpet**, *n.* An instrument, usually in the shape of a conoidal tube, used to enable persons somewhat deaf to hear more readily.—**Ear-wax**, *n.* The waxy or viscous substance secreted by the ear; cerumen.—**Earwig**, ēr'wig, *n.* [A.Sax. *wicga*, a beetle.] One of a family of insects having a long narrow body and a pair of nippers at the extremity of the abdomen: so called from a popular delusion that they have a propensity to creep into the ear.—**Ear-witness**,† *n.* One able to give evidence from his own hearing; an auditor.

Ear, ēr, *v.t.* [A.Sax. *erian*, O.Fris. *era*, Icel. *erja*, Goth. *arjan*, L. *aro*, Gr. *aroō*, to plough.] To plough or till. (O.T.)—**Earing**, ēr'ing, *n.* A ploughing of land; tilling. (O.T.)

Ear, ēr, *n.* [A.Sax. *ear*, D. *aar*, G. *ähre*, an ear.] A spike or head of corn or grain; that part of cereal plants which contains the flowers and seeds.—*v.i.* To shoot, as an ear; to form ears, as corn.

Earl, ėrl, *n.* [A.Sax. *eorl*, Icel., Dan., and Sw. *jarl*, an earl.] In Britain a nobleman, the third in rank, being next below a marquis, and next above a viscount.—**Earldom**, ėrl'dum, *n.* The jurisdiction or dignity of an earl.—**Earl-marshal**, *n.* An officer of state in Great Britain, who, as the head of the College of Arms, determines all rival claims to arms, and grants armorial bearings, through the medium of the king-of-arms.

Early, ėr'li, *a.* [A.Sax. *aerlice* (adv.), from *aer*, soon, *lic*, like. ERE.] In advance of something else as regards time; sooner than ordinary; produced or happening before the usual time (*early* fruit, *early* maturity); forward; being at the beginning; first (in *early* manhood, *early* times).—*Early English architecture*, the style of architecture into which the Norman passed, the distinctive features of which are pointed arches, long, narrow, lancet-shaped windows without mullions, and a peculiar projecting ornament in the hollows of the mouldings, called the dog-tooth ornament: called also the *First Pointed* or *Lancet Style*.—*Early Victorian*, of art, literature, or the state prevailing at the time, with a slight tinge of depreciation.—*adv.* Soon, or sooner than usual or than others; in good season; betimes.—**Earliness**, ėr'li-nes, *n.* The state of being early.

Earn, ėrn, *v.t.* [A.Sax. *earnian*, to earn, to reap the fruit of one's labours; O.D. *erne*, G. *ernte*, harvest.] To merit or deserve by labour or by any performance; to gain by labour, service, or performance; to deserve and receive as compensation.—**Earnings**, ėr'ningz, *n. pl.* That which is earned; what is gained or deserved by labour, services, or performance; wages; reward; recompense.

Earnest, ėr'nest, *a.* [A.Sax. *eornest*, earnestness, *eorneste* (adj.), earnest, serious; cog. D. and G. *ernst*, earnest, D. *ernsten*, to endeavour.] Ardent in the pursuit of an object; eager to obtain; having a longing desire; warmly engaged or incited; warm; zealous; intent; serious; grave.—*n.* Seriousness; a reality; a real event, as opposed to jesting or feigned appearance.—**Earnestly**, ėr'nest-li, *adv.* In an earnest manner. —**Earnestness**, ėr'nest-nes, *n.* The state or quality of being earnest.

Earnest, ėr'nest, *n.* [From W. *ernes*, earnest or pledge, from *ern*, a pledge.] Something given by way of token or pledge, to bind a bargain and prove a sale; a part paid or delivered beforehand, as a pledge and security for the whole, or as a token of more to come; *fig.* anything which gives assurance, promise, or indication of what is to follow; first-fruits; token.—**Earnest-money**, *n.* Money paid as earnest to bind a bargain or ratify and prove a sale.

Earth, ėrth, *n.* [A.Sax. *eorthe*; Goth. *airtha*, Icel. *jörth*, Sw. and Dan. *jord*, G. *erde*, allied to A.Sax. *eard*, soil, home, dwelling, and perhaps to Gr. *era*, Skr. *ira* —earth, and to L. *aro*, to plough.] The particles which compose the mass of the globe, but more particularly the particles which form the mould on the surface of the globe; the globe which we inhabit; the planet third in order from the sun; the world, as opposed to other scenes of existence; the inhabitants of the globe; dry land, as opposed to the sea; the ground; the hole in which a fox or other burrowing animal hides itself; *chem.* the name given to certain tasteless, inodorous, dry, and uninflammable substances, the most important of which are lime, baryta, strontia, magnesia, alumina, zirconia, glucina, yttria, and thoria.—*v.t.* To hide in the earth; to cover with earth or mould.—*v.i.* To retire under ground; to burrow.—*Earth currents*, in *elect.* strong irregular currents, which disturb telegraphic lines of considerable length, flowing from one part of the line to another, affecting the instruments and frequently interrupting telegraphic communication.—**Earthen**, ėrth'n, *a.* Made of earth; composed of clay or other like substance.—**Earthly**, ėrth'li, *a.* Pertaining to the earth or this world; worldly; temporal; gross; vile; carnal; mean; composed of earth; among the things of this earth; possible; conceivable.—**Earthliness**, ėrth'li-nes, *n.* The state or quality of being earthly.—**Earthling**, ėrth'ling, *n.* An inhabitant of the earth; a mortal; a frail creature; one much attached to worldly affairs; a worldling.—**Earthy**, ėr'thi, *a.* Of or pertaining to earth; composed of earth; partaking of the nature of earth; like earth or having some of its properties. —**Earthiness**, ėr'thi-nes, *n.* The state or quality of being earthy.—**Earth-born**, *a.*

Born of the earth; springing originally from the earth; relating to or occasioned by earthly objects; of low birth; meanly born.—**Earth-bound**, *a.* Fastened by the pressure of the earth; firmly fixed in the earth.—**Earth-closet**, *n.* A night-stool or convenience of the same kind, in which the fæces are received in a quantity of earth.—**Earthenware**, ėrth′n-wār, *n.* Every sort of household utensil made of clay hardened in the fire; crockery; pottery.—**Earth-flax**, *n.* A fine variety of asbestos, whose long flexible parallel filaments are so delicate as to resemble flax.—**Earthly-minded**, *a.* Having a mind devoted to earthly things.—**Earthly-mindedness**, *n.* The state of being earthly-minded.—**Earth-nut**, *n.* An umbelliferous plant common in woods and fields in Britain, producing a brown sweetish farinaceous tuber or nut about the size of a chestnut, formed 4 to 6 inches below the surface, and of which swine are fond; also a name given to the ground-nut.—**Earth-oil**, *n.* PETROLEUM.—**Earth-plate**, *n.* *Teleg.* a buried plate of metal connected with the battery or line wire, by means of which the earth itself is made to complete the circuit, so that a return wire is unnecessary.—**Earthquake**, ėrth′kwāk, *n.* A shaking, trembling, or concussion of the earth, sometimes a slight tremor, at other times a violent shaking or convulsion, in which vast chasms open, swallowing up sometimes whole cities; at other times a rocking or heaving of the earth: probably due to internal igneous forces.—**Earth-shine**, *n.* A name given to the faint light visible on the part of the moon not illuminated by the sun, due to the illumination of that portion by the light which the earth reflects on her.—**Earth tremor**, *n.* A slight shaking of part of the earth's surface that may be noted by special instruments—cause unknown.—**Earth-work**, *n.* A term applied to all operations where earth has to be removed or collected together, as in cuttings, embankments, &c.; a fortification constructed of earth.—**Earth-worm**, *n.* The common worm found in the soil, characterized by a long body divided by transverse furrows into a great number of rings, and destitute of legs, visible appendages, and organs of sight; a mean sordid wretch.

Ease, ēz, *n.* [Fr. *aise*, ease; O.Fr. *eise*, *ayse*, *aize*, ease; Pr. *aise*, It. *agio*, O.It. *asio*, ease: all words of very doubtful origin.] Freedom from labour or exertion, or from physical pain, disturbance, excitement, or annoyance; freedom from concern, anxiety, solicitude, or anything that frets or ruffles the mind; tranquillity; repose; freedom from difficulty or great labour; facility; freedom from constraint, formality, stiffness, harshness, forced expressions, or unnatural arrangement; unaffectedness.—*Chapel of ease*, a chapel taking off the burdens of a large parish, and having right to most part of ecclesiastical duties.—*v.t.*—*eased*, *easing.* To free from pain, suffering, anxiety, care, or any disquiet or annoyance; to relieve; to give rest to; to mitigate; to alleviate; to assuage; to allay; to abate or remove in part (to *ease* pain, grief, a burden, &c.); to render less difficult; to facilitate; to release from pressure or restraint by moving gently; to shift a little.—**Easeful**, ēz′ful, *a.* Giving ease. [Poet.]—**Easement**, ēz′ment, *n.* Convenience; accommodation; that which gives ease or relief; *law*, a privilege without profit which one proprietor has in the estate of another proprietor, distinct from the ownership of the soil, as a way, water-course, &c.; Scots law, *servitude* (q.v.).—**Easy**, ē′zi, *a.* Being at rest; having ease; free from pain, disturbance, suffering, annoyance, care, trouble, concern, anxiety, or the like; quiet; tranquil; giving no pain or disturbance; requiring no great labour or exertion; not difficult; not steep, rough, or uneven; gentle; not unwilling; ready; not constrained, stiff, or formal; not rigid or strict; smooth; flowing; not straitened or restricted as regards money or means; affluent; comfortable.—**Easily**, ē′zi-li, *adv.* In an easy manner.—**Easiness**, ē′zi-nes, *n.* The state or quality of being easy.

Easel, ē′zel, *n.* [G. *esel*, an ass, a wooden horse or stand.] The wooden frame on which painters place pictures while at work upon them.

East, ēst, *n.* [A.Sax. *eást* = D. *oost*, G. *ost*, Icel. *aust*; connected with L. *aurora* (anc. *ausosa*), Lith. *auszra*, the red of morning, Skr. *ushas*, the dawn, from a root *us*, to burn, as in L. *urere*, to burn.] One of the four cardinal points, being the point in the heavens where the sun is seen to rise at the equinox, or the corresponding point on the earth; that point of the horizon lying on the right hand when one's face is turned towards the north pole; the regions or countries which lie east of Europe; the oriental countries.—*a.* Toward or in the direction of the rising sun; opposite from west.—*v.i.* To move in the direction of the east; to veer from the north or south toward the east.—*adv.* In an easterly direction; eastwards.—**Easterling**, ēs′tėr-ling, *n.* An old name for a native of some country lying eastward of Britain, especially a trader from the shores of the Baltic.—**Easterly**, ēs′tėr-li, *a.* Coming from the east; moving or directed eastward; situated or looking toward the east.—*adv.* On the east; in the direction of east.—**Eastern**, ēs′tėrn, *a.* [A.Sax. *eástern.*] Being or dwelling in the east; oriental; situated toward the east; on the east part; going toward the east, or in the direction of east.—*Eastern Church*, the Greek Church, established in Russia, into which it was introduced from Constantinople.—*Eastern Question*, the political problem of the Balkan States and Turkey.—**Easting**, ēs′ting, *n.* The distance made good or gained by a ship to the eastward.—**Eastward**, **Eastwards**, ēst′wėrd, ēst′wėrdz, *adv.* Toward the east; in the direction of east from some point or place.—**Eastward**, *a.* Facing, pointing, or having its direction towards the east.

Easter, ēs′tėr, *n.* [A.Sax. *eástre*, Easter, from A.Sax. *Eástre*, *Eóstre*, O.H.G. *Ostarâ*, a goddess of light or spring, in honor of whom a festival was celebrated in April, whence this month was called *eastermônâth*; connected with *east.*] A movable festival of the Christian church observed in March or April in commemoration of our Savior's resurrection. Easter is the first Sunday after the first full moon that falls on or next after the vernal equinox (March 21 in the Gregorian calendar); if the full moon happens on Sunday, Easter is celebrated one week later.

Easy. Under EASE.

Eat, ēt, *v.i.* pret. *eat* or *ate* (et, āt); pp. *eat* or *eaten* (et, ē′tn). [A.Sax. *etan* = D. *eten*, Icel. *eta*, Dan. *æde*, Goth. *itan*, G. *essen*; from root seen also in L. *edo*, Gr. *edō*, Skr. *ad*, to eat.] To masticate and swallow; to partake of as food: said especially of solids; to corrode; to wear away; to gnaw into gradually.—*To eat one's heart*, to brood over one's sorrows or disappointments.—*To eat one's words*, to retract one's assertions.—*v.i.* To take food; to feed; to take a meal; to have a particular taste or character when eaten; to make way by corrosion; to gnaw; to enter by gradually wearing or separating the parts of a substance.—**Eatable**, ē′ta-bl, *a.* Capable of being eaten; esculent.—*n.* Anything that may be eaten; that which is used as food; an edible or comestible.—**Eater**, ē′tėr, *n.* One who eats; that which eats or corrodes.

Eatage, ē′tāj, *n.* Same as *Eddish.*

Eau, ō, *n.* [Fr., from L. *aqua*, water.] A word used with some other words to designate several spirituous waters, particularly perfumes.—*Eau de Cologne*, ō dė ko-lōn, *n.* A perfumed spirit, originally invented at *Cologne*, and consisting of spirits of wine flavoured by a few drops of different essential oils blended so as to yield a fine fragrant scent.—*Eau de vie*, ō dė vē, *n.* [Lit. water of life.] The French name for brandy.

Eaves, ēvz, *n.pl.* [A.Sax. *efese*, *yfese* (sing.), the eave, the edge, whence *efesian*, to shave, to trim; same word as Goth. *ubizva*, O.H.G. *obisa*, a portico, a hall; from root of *over.*] That part of the roof of a building which projects beyond the wall and casts off the water that falls on the roof.—**Eaves-drop**, *v.i.*—*eaves-dropped*, *eaves-dropping.* To stand under the eaves, or near the windows of a house to listen and learn what is said within doors; to watch for an opportunity of hearing the private conversation of others.—*n.* The water which falls in drops from the eaves of a house.—**Eaves-dropper**, *n.* One who stands near the window or door of a house to catch what is said within doors; one who tries to hear private conversation.

Ebb, eb, *n.* [A.Sax. *ebbe*, *ebba*; D. *eb*, *ebbe*, G. and Dan. *ebbe*, Sw. *ebb*; allied to E. *even*, G. *aben*, to fall off, to sink. EVENING.] The reflux of the tide; the return of tide-water toward the sea: opposed to *flood* or *flow*; a flowing backward or away; decline; decay (the *ebb* of prosperity or of life).—*v.i.* To flow back; to return, as the water of a tide toward the ocean: opposed to *flow*; to recede; to decrease; to decay; to decline.—**Ebb-tide**, *n.* The reflux of tide-water; the retiring tide.

Ebionite, ē′bi-o-nīt, *n.* [Heb. *ébionim*, the poor, the name given by the Jews to the Christians.] One of a sect of Jewish Christians who united the ceremonies of the law with the precepts of the gospel, but denied the divinity of Christ.

Ebony, eb′o-ni, *n.* [L. *ebenus*, Gr. *ebenos*, from Heb. *eben*, a stone, from its hardness and weight.] A black-coloured wood of great hardness, heavier than water, and capable of taking on a fine polish, being much used in inlaid work and turnery; the most valuable variety is the heart-wood of a large tree growing in Ceylon.—**Ebon**, eb′on, *a.* Consisting of ebony; black like ebony; dark.—**Ebonite**, eb′o-nīt, *n.* Same as *Vulcanite.*—**Ebonize**, eb′o-nīz, *v.t.* To make black or tawny; to tinge with the colour of ebony.

Ebracteate, ē-brak′tē-āt, *a.* [L. *e*, priv., and *bractea*, a thin plate.] *Bot.* without bracts.—**Ebracteolate**, ē-brak′tē-ō-lāt, *a.* Without bracteoles.

Ebriety, ē-brī′e-ti, *n.* [L. *ebrietas*, from *ebrius*, drunk.] Drunkenness; intoxication by spirituous liquors.

Ebullition, ē-bul-lish′on, *n.* [L. *ebullitio*; from *ebullio*—*e*, *ex*, out, up, and *bullio*, to boil, from *bulla*, a bubble. BOIL.] The operation or phenomenon of boiling; the bubbling up of a liquor by heat; the agitation produced in a fluid by the escape of a portion of it converted into an aeriform state by heat; effervescence; an outward display of feeling, as of anger; a sudden burst; a pouring forth; an overflowing.—**Ebullience**, **Ebulliency**, ē-bul′yens, ē-bul′yen-si, *n.* A boiling over; a bursting forth; overflow.—**Ebullient**, ē-bul′yent, *a.* Boiling over; hence, over-enthusiastic; over-demonstrative.

Eburnean, ē-bėr′nē-an, *a.* [L. *eburneus*, from *ebur*, ivory.] Relating to or made of ivory.—**Eburnine**, ē-bėr′nīn, *a.* Made of ivory.

Écarté, ā-kär-tā, *n.* [Fr., discarded.] A game of cards for two persons with thirty-two cards, the small cards from two to six being excluded: so called because the players may discard or exchange their cards for others.

Ecaudate, ē-ka′dāt, *a.* [L. *e*, priv., *cauda*, tail.] Not having a tail, tailless; used in descriptions in natural history.

Ecbatic, ek-bat′ik, *a.* [Gr. *ekbasis*, event.] *Gram.* pertaining to an event that has happened; denoting a mere consequence or result, opposed to *telic.*

Ecbolic, ek-bol′ik, *a.* and *n.* [Gr. *ekbolē*, a throwing out.] Promoting parturition; a drug that aids childbirth.

Eccaleobion, ek′kal-ē-ō″bi-on, *n.* [Gr. *ekkaleō*, to call out, and *bios*, life.] A contrivance for hatching eggs by artificial heat.

Eccentric, ek-sen′trik, *a.* [L. *eccentricus*—*ex*, from, and *centrum*, centre.] Deviating or departing from the centre; not having the same centre; not concentric though situated one within the other; having the axis out of the centre; deviating from usual practice; given to act in a way peculiar to one's self and different from other people; anomalous; singular; odd.—*n.* An eccentric person; a term applied to several mechanical contrivances for converting circular into reciprocating rectilinear motion, consisting of variously shaped discs, attached to a revolving shaft.—**Eccentrically**, ek-sen′-tri-kal-li, *adv.* With eccentricity; in an eccentric manner.—**Eccentricity**, ek-sen-tris′i-ti, *n.* The state of having a centre different from that of another related circle; the ratio, to the semi-major-axis, of the distance of the centre of a planet's orbit (an ellipse) from the centre of the sun (a focus); eccentric conduct; departure or deviation from what is regular or usual; oddity; whimsicalness.

Ecchymosis, ek-ki-mō′sis, *n.* [Gr. *ekchymōsis*, from *ek*, out, and *chymos*, juice, from *cheō*, to pour.] *Med.* a livid, black, or yellow spot produced by extravasated blood caused by a contusion, as a blow on the eye.

Ecclesiastic, Ecclesiastical, ek-klē′zi-as″tik, ek-klē′zi-as″ti-kal, *a.* [Gr. *ekklēsiastikos*, from *ekklēsia*, an assembly, the church, from *ekkaleō*, to call forth or convoke—*ek*, and *kaleō*, to call.] Pertaining or relating to the church; not civil or secular.—**Ecclesiastic**, *n.* A person in orders or consecrated to the services of the church and the ministry of religion.—**Ecclesiastically**, ek-klē′zi-as″ti-kal-li, *adv.* In an ecclesiastical manner.—**Ecclesiast**, ek-klē′zi-ast, *n.* An ecclesiastic; a preacher.—**Ecclesiastes**, ek-klē′zi-as″tēz, *n.* A canonical book of the old Testament, placed between the book of Proverbs and the Song of Solomon; translation of *Koheleth*, the Preacher.—**Ecclesiasticism**, ek-klē′zi-as″ti-sizm, *n.* Strong adherence to the principles of the Church, or to ecclesiastical observances, privileges, &c.—**Ecclesiasticus**, *n.* Book in the Apocrypha, but allowed for use in the Church.—**Ecclesiology**, ek-klē′zi-ol″o-ji, *n.* [Gr. *ekklēsia*, the church, and *logos*, discourse.] The science of antiquities as applied to churches and other ecclesiastical foundations; the science and theory of church building and decoration.—**Ecclesiologist**, ek-klē′zi-ol″o-jist, *n.* One versed in ecclesiology.

Eccoprotic, ek-ko-prot′ik, *a.* [Gr. *ek*, out, from, and *kopros*, dung.] Having the quality of promoting alvine discharges; laxative; gently cathartic.—*n.* A medicine which purges gently; a mild cathartic.

Ecderon, ek′de-ron, *n.* [Gr. *ek*, out, and *deros*, skin.] The outer layer of the integument; the epithelial layer of mucous membrane; the epidermal layer of the skin.

Ecdysis, ek′di-sis, *n.* [Gr., from *ekdyō*, to strip off—*ek*, out of, and *dyō*, to enter.] The act of shedding or casting an outer coat or integument, as in the case of serpents, certain insects, &c.

Ecgonine, ek′gō-nin, *n.* An alkaloid extracted from coca leaf.

Echelon, esh′e-lon, *n.* [Fr., from *échelle*, a ladder, from L. *scala*, a ladder.] *Milit.* the position of an army in the form of steps, or in parallel lines, each line being a little to the left or right of the preceding one.—**Echeloned**, esh′e-lond, *a.* Formed in echelon.

Echidna, ē-kid′na, *n.* [Gr., an adder, a fabulous monster.] A burrowing mammal of Australia belonging to the Monotremata and resembling the hedgehog, except that the muzzle is protracted and slender, with a small aperture at the extremity for the protrusion of a long flexible tongue, by means of which it catches its insect prey; the porcupine ant-eater.—**Echidnine**, ē-kid′nin, *n.* Serpent poison; the secretion from the poison glands of the viper and other serpents.

Echinate, Echinated, ē-kī′nāt, ē-kī′nā-ted, *a.* [L. *echinus*, Gr. *echinos*, a hedgehog, a sea-urchin.] Set with prickles; prickly, like a hedgehog; having sharp points.—**Echinite**, ē-kī′nīt, *n.* A fossil sea-urchin.—**Echinoderm**, ē-kī′nō-dėrm, *n.* [Gr. *echinos*, and *derma*, skin.] An animal of the class Echinodermata.—**Echinodermal, Echinodermatous**, ē-kī′nō-dėr-mal, ē-kī′nō-dėr″ma-tus, *a.* Relating to the Echinodermata.—**Echinodermata**, ē-kī′nō-dėr″ma-ta, *n. pl.* A class of marine invertebrate animals of the annuloid type, characterized by having a tough integument in which lime is deposited as granules (as in the star-fish and sea-cucumber), or so as to form a kind of shell like that of the sea-urchin; and by the rayed arrangement of the parts of the adult; it includes the sea-urchins, star-fishes, sand-stars, brittle-stars, feather-stars, sea-cucumbers, &c.—**Echinococcus**, ē-kī′nō-kok″us, *n.* [Gr. *echinos*, urchin, *kokkos*, berry.] The hydatid of a certain tapeworm in man and other animals.—**Echinoid**, ē-kī′noid, *a.* Resembling an echinus or sea-urchin.—**Echinozoa**, ē-kī′-nō-zō″a, *n. pl.* Same as *Annuloida*.—**Echinus**, ē-kī′nus, *n.* The generic name of the sea-urchin; *arch.* an egg-shaped moulding or ornament, alternating with an anchor-shaped or dart-shaped body.

Echo, ek′ō, *n.* pl. **Echoes**, ek′ōz. [L. *echo*, from Gr. *ēchō*, an echo, a nymph, who, for love of Narcissus, pined away till nothing remained of her but her voice; a sound: this word is also seen in *catechise*.] A sound reflected or reverberated from a distant surface; sound returned; repercussion of sound; repetition with assent; close imitation either in words or sentiments; a person who slavishly follows another in uttering sentiments.—*v.i.* To give forth an echo; to resound; to reflect sound; to be sounded back; to produce a sound that reverberates; to give out a loud sound.—*v.t.* To reverberate or send back the sound of; to repeat with assent; to adopt as one's own sentiments or opinion.

Éclaircissement, ā-klār-sēs-mäṅ, *n.* [Fr. from *éclaircir*—L. *ex*, and *clarus*, clear.] The clearing up of a plot, mystery, or the like; explanation.

Eclampsy, ek-lamp′si, *n.* [Gr. *eklampsis*—*ek*, out, and *lampō*, to shine.] A flashing of light before the eyes; convulsive motions; convulsions; epilepsy.

Éclat, ā-klä, *n.* [Fr., a splinter, noise, brightness, magnificence, from *éclater*, to split, to shiver, to glitter; from O.H.G. *skleizan*, G. *schleissen*, *schlitzen*, to split; E. *slit*, *slice*, *slate*.] A burst, as of applause; acclamation; approbation; brilliancy of success; splendour of effect; lustre; renown; glory.

Eclectic, ek-lek′tik, *a.* [Gr. *eklektikos*—*ek*, and *legō*, to choose.] Proceeding by the method of selection; choosing what seems best from others; not original nor following any one model or leader, but choosing at will from the doctrines, works, &c., of others; specifically applied to certain philosophers of antiquity who selected from the opinions and principles of various schools what they thought solid and good.—*n.* One who follows an eclectic method in philosophy, science, religion, and the like.—**Eclectically**, ek-lek′ti-kal-li, *adv.* In an eclectic manner.—**Eclecticism**, ek-lek′ti-sizm, *n.* The doctrine or practice of an eclectic.

Eclipse, ē-klips′, *n.* [L. *eclipsis*, from Gr. *ekleipsis*, defect, from *ekleipō*, to fail—*ek*, out, and *leipō*, to leave.] An interception or obscuration of the light of the sun, moon, or other luminous body, by the intervention of some other body either between it and the eye or between the luminous body and that illuminated by it; an eclipse of the moon, for instance, being caused by the earth coming between it and the sun; *fig.* a darkening or obscuring of splendour, brightness, or glory.—*v.t.*—*eclipsed*, *eclipsing*. To cause the eclipse or obscuration of; to cloud; to darken, obscure, throw into the shade; to cloud the glory of.—*v.i.* To suffer an eclipse.—**Ecliptic**, ē-klip′tik, *n.* [L. *linea ecliptica*, the ecliptic line, or line in which eclipses take place.] A great circle of the celestial sphere supposed to be drawn through the middle of the zodiac, making an angle with the equinoctial of about 23° 27′; the path which the sun, owing to the annual revolution of the earth, appears to describe among the fixed stars; a great circle on the terrestrial globe, answering to and falling within the plane of the celestial ecliptic.—*a.* Pertaining to or described by the ecliptic; pertaining to an eclipse.

Eclogue, ek′log, *n.* [L. *ecloga*, Gr. *eklogē*, selection, from *eklegō*, to select. ECLECTIC.] A poetical composition in which shepherds are introduced conversing with each other; a bucolic.

Economy, ē-kon′o-mi, *n.* [L. *œconomia*, Gr. *oikonomia*—*oikos*, house, and *nomos*, law, rule.] The management, regulation, and government of a household; especially, the management of the pecuniary concerns of a household; hence, a frugal and judicious use of money; that management which expends money to advantage and incurs no waste; a prudent management of all the means by which property is saved or accumulated; a judicious application of time, of labour, and of the instruments of labour; the disposition or arrangement of any work or the system of rules and regulations which control it; the operations of nature in the generation, nutrition, and preservation of animals and plants; the regular, harmonious system in accordance with which the functions of living animals and plants are performed; the regulation and disposition of the internal affairs of a state or nation, or of any department of government.—*Domestic economy.* DOMESTIC.—*Political economy.* POLITICAL.—**Economic, Economical**, ē-ko-nom′ik, ē-ko-nom′i-kal, *a.* Pertaining to the regulation of household concerns; managing domestic or public pecuniary concerns with frugality; frugal; thrifty; saving; not wasteful or extravagant; relating to the science of economics, or the pecuniary and other productive resources of a country; relating to the means of living.—**Economically**, ē-ko-nom′i-kal-li, *adv.* In an economical manner.—**Economics**, ē-ko-nom′iks, *n.* The science of household affairs or of domestic management; the science of the useful application of the wealth or material resources of a country; political economy.—**Economist**, ė-kon′o-mist, *n.* One who manages domestic or other concerns with frugality; one who practises economy; one versed in economics or the science of political economy.—**Economization**, ē-kon′o-mī-zā″-shon, *n.* The act or practice of economizing or managing frugally; the result of economizing; economy; saving.—**Economize**, ē-kon′o-mīz, *v.i.*—*economized*, *economizing*. To manage pecuniary concerns with frugality; to make a prudent use of money, or of the means of having or acquiring property.—*v.t.* To use with prudence; to expend with frugality.

Écorché, ā-kor-shā, *n.* [Fr.] *Paint.* and *sculp.* the subject, man or animal, flayed or deprived of its skin, so that the muscular system is exposed for the purposes of study.

Ecossaise, ā-kos-āz, *n.* [Fr.] Dance music in the Scotch style; a schottische.

Ecostate, ē-kos′tāt, *a.* [L. *e*, priv., and *costa*, a rib.] *Bot.* a term applied to leaves that have no central rib.

Ecraseur, ā-krä-zėr, *n.* [Fr., from *écraser*, to crush to pieces.] A surgical instrument for removing tumours or malignant growths.

Ecstasy, ek′sta-si, *n.* [Gr. *ekstasis*, a standing out, a displacement, distraction, astonishment—*ek*, out, and *histēmi*, to stand (from root of *stand*).] A state in which the mind is carried away as it were from the body; a state in which the functions of the senses are suspended by the contemplation of some extraordinary or supernatural object; a kind of trance; excessive joy; rapture; a degree of delight that arrests the whole mind; extreme delight; madness or distraction (*Shak.*)‡.—**Ecstatic, Ecstatical**, ek-stat′ik, ek-stat′i-kal, *a.* Pertaining to or resulting from ecstasy; suspending the senses; entrancing; rapturous; transporting; delightful beyond measure.—**Ecstatically**, ek-stat′i-kal-li, *adv.* In an ecstatic manner.

Ecthlipsis, ek-thlip′sis, *n.* [Gr. *ekthlipsis*, a squeezing out—*ek*, out, and *thlibō*, to press.] *Latin pros.* the elision of the final syllable of a word ending in *m*, when the next word begins with a vowel.

Ectoblast, ek′tō-blast, *n.* [Gr. *ektos*, outside, and *blastos*, bud, germ.] *Physiol.* the membrane composing the walls of a cell, as distinguished from *mesoblast*, the nucleus, and *entoblast*, the nucleolus.—**Ectoderm**, ek′tō-dėrm, *n.* [Gr. *derma*, skin.] *Anat.* an outer layer or membrane, as the epidermal layer of the skin. — **Ectodermal, Ectodermic**, ek-tō-dėr′mal, ek-tō-dėr′-mik, *a.* Belonging to the ectoderm.—**Ectoparasite**, ek-tō-par′a-sīt, *n.* A parasitic animal infesting the outside of animals; as opposed to *endoparasite*, which lives in the body.—**Ectosarc**, ek′tō-särk, *n.* [Gr. *sarx, sarkos*, flesh.] *Zool.* the outer transparent sarcode-layer of certain Protozoa, such as the Amœba.—**Ectozoa**, ek′-tō-zō-a, *n. pl.* [Gr. *zōon*, a living being.] Parasites (as lice, &c.) which infest the external parts of other animals: opposed to *Entozoa*.

Ectopia, ek-tō′pi-a, *n.* [Gr. *ek*, out, *topos*, place.] *Pathol.* a displacement of internal parts of the body.

Ectoplasm, ek′tō-plazm, *n.* [Gr. *ektos*, without, and *plasma*. PLASM.] *Biol.* the exterior portion of a cell; matter forming a cell-wall.

Ectropical, ek-trop′i-kal, *a.* [Gr. *ek*, out, and *tropikos*, turning. TROPIC.] Belonging to parts outside the tropics; being outside the tropics.

Ectrotic, ek-trot′ik, *a.* [Gr. *ektrotikos*, causing abortion—*ek*, out, and root of *titrōskō*, to wound.] *Med.* preventing development, especially preventing a wound from developing.

Ectype, ek′tīp, *n.* [Gr. *ektypos*, worked in high relief—*ek*, out, and *typos*, type.] A reproduction of, or very close resemblance to, an original: opposed to *prototype*; a copy in relief or embossed.—**Ectypal**, ek-tī′pal, *a.* Taken from the original; imitated.—**Ectypography**, ek-ti-pog′ra-fi, *n.* A method of etching in which the lines are in relief upon the plate instead of being sunk into it.

Ecumenic, Ecumenical, ek-ū-men′ik, ek-ū-men′i-kal, *a.* [L. *œcumenicus*, Gr. *oikoumenē*, the habitable earth, from *oikos*, a habitation.] General; universal; specifically, an epithet applied to an ecclesiastical council regarded as representing the whole Christian Church, or the whole Catholic Church.

Eczema, ek′zē-ma, *n.* [Gr., from *ekzeō*, to boil out—*ek*, out, and *zeō*, to boil.] An eruptive disease of the skin, characterized by minute vesicles which burst and discharge a thin acrid fluid, often giving rise to excoriation; one form is popularly known as grocers' itch.—**Eczematous**, ek-zem′-a-tus, *a.* Pertaining to or produced by eczema.

Edacious, ē-dā′shus, *a.* [L. *edax*, from *edo*, to eat.] Eating; given to eating; greedy; voracious.—**Edaciously**, ē-dā′-shus-li, *adv.* Greedily; voraciously.—**Edacity**, ē-das′i-ti, *n.* [L. *edacitas*.] Greediness; voracity; ravenousness; rapacity.

Edda, ed′a, *n.* [Icel., great-grandmother; a name given to indicate that it is the mother of all Scandinavian poetry.] The name of two Scandinavian books, dating from the eleventh to the thirteenth century: first, the *Elder* or *Poetic Edda*, a collection of pagan poems or chants of a mythic, prophetic, mostly all of a religious character; second, the *Younger* or *Prose Edda*, a kind of prose synopsis of Scandinavian mythology.

Eddish, ed′ish, *n.* [A.Sax. *edisc*, aftermath, probably from *ed*, a prefix signifying again, anew.] The latter pasture or grass that comes after mowing or reaping.

Eddy, ed′i, *n.* [From Icel. *itha*, an eddy, from prefix *ith*, Goth. *id*, A.Sax. *ed*, again, back.] A current of air or water turning round in a direction contrary to the main stream; a whirlpool; a current of water or air moving circularly.—*v.i.*—*eddied, eddying*. To move circularly, or as an eddy.—*v.t.* To cause to move in an eddy; to collect as into an eddy.

Edelweiss, ā′dl-vīs, *n.* [G. *edel*, noble, *weiss*, white.] A composite plant inhabiting the Alps, and having a specially woolly foliage and involucre. Now cultivated in Britain and elsewhere, but apt to lose its peculiar appearance.

Edema, Edematous. ŒDEMA.

Eden, ē′den, *n.* [Heb. and Chal. *eden*, delight, pleasure, a place of pleasure.] The garden in which Adam and Eve were placed by God; hence, a delightful region or residence.

Edentate, ē-den′tāt, *a.* [L. *edentatus*—*e*, *ex*, out of, and *dens, dentis*, a tooth.] Destitute or deprived of teeth; pertaining to the Edentata.—*n.* An animal belonging to the order Edentata.—**Edentata**, ē-den-tā′ta, *n. pl.* An order of mammals, including the sloths, armadillos, pangolins, and ant-eaters, and so called from some of the genera being absolutely toothless, while the remainder have teeth of a rudimentary structure, with no enamel or root, whilst incisors are rarely present.—**Edentulous**, ē-den′tū-lus, *a.* Without teeth; toothless.

Edge, ej, *n.* [A.Sax. *ecg*, edge, whence *ecgian, eggian*, to sharpen, to egg = D. *egge*, Icel. and Sw. *egg*, G. *ecke*, edge, corner; from an Indo-European root *ak*, seen in L. *acies*, an edge, *acus*, a needle, *acuo*, to sharpen; akin *acid, acute, eager*.] The thin cutting side of an instrument; the abrupt border or margin of anything; the brink; the border or part adjacent to a line of division; the part nearest some limit; sharpness of mind or appetite; keenness; intenseness of desire; sharpness; acrimony.—*To set the teeth on edge*, to cause a tingling or grating sensation in the teeth.—*v.t.*—*edged, edging*. To sharpen; to furnish with an edge, fringe, or border; to exasperate; to embitter; to incite; to provoke; to instigate; to move sideways; to move by little and little.—*v.i.* To move sideways or gradually; to advance or retire gradually.—**Edged**, ejd, *p.* and *a.* Furnished with an edge; having an edge of this or that kind; bordered; fringed.—**Edgeless**, ej′les, *a.* Not having a sharp edge; blunt.—**Edgewise**, ej′wīz, *adv.* With the edge turned forward or toward a particular point; in the direction of the edge; sideways; with the side foremost.—**Edging**, ej′ing, *n.* That which is added on the border or which forms the edge, as lace, fringe, trimming, added to a garment for ornament; a row of small plants set along the border of a flower-bed.—**Edge-bone**, *n.* AITCH-BONE.—**Edge-tool**, *n.* An instrument having a sharp or cutting edge; *fig.* something dangerous to deal or sport with.

Edible, ed′i-bl, *a.* [L.L. *edibilis*, from L. *edo*, to eat.] Fit to be eaten as food; eatable; esculent.—*n.* Anything that may be eaten for food; an article of food; a comestible.—**Edibility, Edibleness**, ed-i-bil′i-ti, ed′i-bl-nes, *n.* The quality of being edible.

Edict, ē′dikt, *n.* [L. *edictum*, from *edico*, utter or proclaim—*e*, out, and *dico*, to speak. DICTION.] An order issued by a prince to his subjects, as a rule or law requiring obedience; a proclamation of command or prohibition; a decree.—**Edictal**, ē-dik′tal, *a.* Pertaining to an edict.

Edify, ed′i-fī, *v.t.*—*edified, edifying*. [Fr. *édifier*, from L. *ædificare*, to build, erect, construct—*ædes*, a house, and *facio*, to make.] To build or construct†; to instruct and improve in knowledge generally, and particularly in moral and religious knowledge, or in faith and holiness.—*v.i.* To cause or tend to cause a moral or intellectual improvement.—**Edifier**, ed′i-fī-ėr, *n.* One who edifies.—**Edifying**, ed′i-fī-ing, *a.* Adapted to edify; having the effect of instructing and improving.—**Edification**, ed′i-fi-kā″shon, *n.* The act of edifying; improvement and progress of the mind in knowledge, in morals, or in faith and holiness.—**Edifice**, ed′i-fis, *n.* [L. *ædificium*, a building. EDIFY.] A building; a structure; a fabric: chiefly applied to houses and other large structures.—**Edificial**, ed-i-fish′al, *a.* Pertaining to an edifice or structure; structural.—**Edifyingly**, ed′i-fī-ing-li, *adv.* In an edifying manner.—**Edifyingness**, ed′i-fī-ing-nes, *n.*

Edile, ē′dīl, *n.* [L. *ædilis*, from *ædes*, a building.] A magistrate of ancient Rome who had the superintendence of buildings of all kinds, especially public edifices, and also the care of the highways, public places, weights and measures, &c.—**Edileship**, ē′dīl-ship, *n.* The office of an edile.

Edit, ed′it, *v.t.* [L. *edo, editum*, to give forth, to publish—*e*, forth, and *do, datum*, to give, whence *date, dative*.] To superintend the publication of; to prepare, as a book or paper, for the public eye, by writing, correcting, or selecting the matter; to conduct or manage as regards literary contents or matter; to publish.—**Edition**, ē-dish′on, *n.* A literary work as bearing a special stamp or form when first published or subsequently; a work as characterized by editorial labours; the whole number of copies of a work published at once.—**Edition de luxe**. A limited edition in luxurious style of print, binding, &c.—**Editio-princeps**, *n.* The oldest printed in date of any work, especially of a Greek or Latin classic.—**Editor**, ed′i-tėr, *n.* One who edits; a person who superintends, revises, corrects, and prepares a book, newspaper, or magazine for publication.—**Editorial**, ed-i-tō′-ri-al, *a.* Pertaining to, proceeding from, or written by an editor.—*n.* An article, as in a newspaper, written by the editor; a leading article.—**Editorially**, ed-i-tō′ri-al-li, *adv.* In the manner or character of an editor.—**Editorship**, ed′i-tėr-ship, *n.* The business of an editor; the care and superintendence of a publication.

Educate, ed′ū-kāt, *v.t.*—*educated, educating*. [L. *educo, educatum*, from *educo, eductum*, to lead forth, to bring up a child—*e*, out, and *duco*, to lead. DUKE.] To inform and enlighten the understanding of; to cultivate and train the mental powers of; to qualify for the business and duties of life; to teach; to instruct; to train; to rear.—**Education**, ed-ū-kā′shon, *n.* The act of educating, teaching, or training; the act or art of developing and cultivating the various physical, intellectual, æsthetic, and moral faculties; instruction and discipline; tuition; nurture; learning; erudition.—**Educational**, ed-ū-kā′shon-al, *a.* Pertaining to education; derived from education.—**Educationalist, Educationist**, ed-ū-kā′shon-al-ist, ed-ū-kā′shon-ist, *n.* One who is versed in or who advocates or promotes education.—**Educationally**, ed-ū-kā′shon-al-li, *adv.* By means of education; by way of instruction; with regard to education.—**Educative**, ed′ū-kā-tiv, *a.* Tending or having the power to educate.—**Educator**, ed′ū-kā-tėr, *n.* One who or that which educates.

Educe, ē-dūs′, *v.t.*—*educed, educing*. [L. *educo, eductum*—*e*, out, and *duco*, to lead. EDUCATE.] To bring or draw out; to cause to appear; to extract.—**Educible**, ē-dū′-si-bl, *a.* Capable of being educed.—**Educt**, ē′dukt, *n.* Extracted matter; a substance brought to light by separation, analysis, or decomposition; anything educed or drawn from another; an inference.—**Eduction**, ē-duk′shon, *n.* The act of educing, drawing out, or bringing into view.—**Eduction-pipe**, *n.* The pipe by which the exhaust steam is led from the cylinder of a steam-engine into the condenser or the atmosphere, according as the engine may be of the low or high pressure kind.—**Eductor**,† ē-duk′-tėr, *n.* That which brings forth, elicits, or extracts.

Edulcorate, ē-dul′kō-rāt, *v.t.*—*edulcorated, edulcorating*. [L. *e*, out, and *dulcoro, dulcoratum*, to sweeten, from *dulcor*, sweetness, *dulcis*, sweet.] To remove acidity from; to sweeten†; *chem.* to free from acids, salts, or impurities by washing.—**Edulcorant**, ē-dul′kō-rant, *a.* Edulcorative.—*n.* A substance that edulcorates.—**Edul-**

coration, ē-dul'kō-rā"shon, *n.* The act of sweetening by admixture of some saccharine substance†; *chem.* the act of freeing from acid or saline substances, or from any soluble impurities, by repeated affusions of water.—**Edulcorative**, ē-dul'kō-rā-tiv, *a.* Having the quality of sweetening or removing acidity.

Eel, ēl, *n.* [A. Sax. *ael* = Dan. D. and G. *aal*, Icel. *áll*; not connected with Gr. *echis*, Skr. *ahi*, a serpent; L. *anguilla*, an eel, *anguis*, a snake.] A fish characterized by its slimy serpent-like elongated body, by the absence of ventral fins, and the continuity of the dorsal and anal fins round the extremity of the tail; some species are marine, some fresh-water; all are remarkable for their voracity and tenacity of life, many are considered excellent food.—**Eel-basket**, **Eel-buck**, ēl'buk, *n.* A kind of basket, usually attached to a framework set in a river, for catching eels, having a sort of funnel-shaped entrance fitted into the mouth of it, and composed of flexible willow rods converging inwards to a point, so that eels can easily force their way in, but cannot escape.—**Eel-pout**, *n.* [A.Sax. *aele-puta*.] The local name of two different species of fish—the viviparous blenny and the burbot.—**Eel-spear**, *n.* A forked instrument used for catching eels.

E'en, ēn, *adv.* A contraction for *Even*.

E'er, ār, *adv.* A contraction for *Ever*.

Eerie, ē'ri, *a.* [A.Sax. *earh*, timid.] Calculated to inspire fear; dreary; lonely; weird; superstitiously affected by fear, especially when lonely.—**Eeriness**, ē'ri-nes, *n.* The state or quality of being eerie.

Efface, ef-fās', *v.t.*—*effaced*, *effacing*. [Fr. *effacer*—L. *e*, out, and *facies*, a face. Comp. *deface*.] To destroy, as a figure, on the surface of anything, so as to render it invisible or not distinguishable; to blot out; to erase, strike, or scratch out; to remove from the mind; to wear away.—**Effaceable**, ef-fā'sa-bl, *a.* Capable of being effaced.—**Effacement**, ef-fās'ment, *n.* Act of effacing; state of being effaced.

Effect, ef-fekt', *n.* [L. *effectus*, from *efficio*—*ex*, and *facio*, to make. FACT.] That which is produced by an operating agent or cause; the result or consequence of the action of a cause or agent; consequence; result; power to produce consequences or results; force, validity, or importance; purport, import, tenor, or general intent; reality and not mere appearance; fact: preceded by *in*; the impression produced on the mind, as by natural scenery, a picture, musical composition, or other work of art, by the object as a whole, before its details are examined; *pl.* goods; movables; personal estate.—*v.t.* To produce, as a cause or agent; to bring about or cause to be; to bring to pass; to achieve; to accomplish.—**Effecter**, **Effector**, ef-fek'tėr, *n.* One who effects, produces, causes, or brings about.—**Effectible**,† ef-fek'ti-bl, *a.* Capable of being effected.—**Effection**,† ef-fek'shon, *n.* Act of effecting; production.—**Effective**, ef-fek'tiv, *a.* Having the power to cause or produce effect; efficacious; operative; active; efficient; having the power of active operation; fit for duty.—**Effectively**, ef-fek'tiv-li, *adv.* In an effective manner.—**Effectiveness**, ef-fek'tiv-nes, *n.* The quality of being effective.—**Effectless**, ef-fekt'les, *a.* Without effect; without advantage; useless.—**Effectual**, ef-fek'tū-al, *a.* Producing an effect, or the effect desired or intended; having adequate power or force to produce the effect.—**Effectually**, ef-fek'tū-al-li, *adv.* In an effectual manner.—**Effectualness**, ef-fek'tū-al-nes, *n.*—**Effectuate**, ef-fek'tū-āt, *v.t.*—*effectuated*, *effectuating*. [Fr. *effectuer*.] To bring to pass; to achieve; to accomplish; to fulfil.—**Effectuation**, ef-fek'tū-ā"shon, *n.* Act of effectuating.

Effeminate, ef-fem'i-nāt, *a.* [L. *effeminatus*, from *effeminor*, to grow or make womanish, from *ex*, out, and *femina*, a woman.] Having the qualities of a woman instead of those of a man; soft or delicate to an unmanly degree; weak and unmanly; womanish; voluptuous.—*v.t.*—*effeminated*, *effeminating*. To make womanish or effeminate.—*v.i.* To grow womanish or weak.—**Effeminacy**, ef-fem'i-na-si, *n.* The state or character of being effeminate.—**Effeminately**, ef-fem'i-nāt-li, *adv.* In an effeminate manner.—**Effeminateness**, ef-fem'i-nāt-nes, *n.* Effeminacy.

Effendi, ef-fen'di, *n.* [Turk.] A title of respect frequently attached to the official title of certain Turkish officers, especially learned men and ecclesiastics.

Efferent, ef'fėr-ent, *a.* [L. *ef* for *ex*, out of, and *fero*, to carry.] *Physiol.* conveying outwards or discharging.

Effervesce, ef-fėr-ves', *v.i.*—*effervesced*, *effervescing*. [L. *effervesco*—*ef*, *ex*, out of, and *fervesco*, to begin boiling, from *ferveo*, to be hot. FERVENT.] To bubble and hiss or froth and sparkle, as fermenting liquors or any fluid when some part escapes in a gaseous form; to work, as new wine; *fig.* to exhibit signs of excitement; to exhibit feelings which cannot be suppressed.—**Effervescence**, ef-fėr-ves'ens, *n.* That commotion, bubbling, frothing, or sparkling of a fluid which takes place when some part of the mass flies off in a gaseous form, producing innumerable small bubbles; strong excitement or manifestation of feeling; flow of animal spirits.—**Effervescent**, ef-fėr-ves'ent, *a.* Effervescing.—**Effervescible**, ef-fėr-ves'i-bl, *a.* Having the quality of effervescing.

Effete, ef-fēt', *a.* [L. *effetus*, exhausted, worn out by bearing—*ex*, and *fetus*, fruitful, pregnant.] Having the energies worn out or exhausted; having the vigour lost or dissipated; barren.

Efficacious, ef-fi-kā'shus, *a.* [L. *efficax*, efficacious, from *efficio*. EFFECT.] Effectual; productive of effects; producing the effect intended; having power adequate to the purpose intended.—**Efficaciously**, ef-fi-kā'shus-li, *adv.* In an efficacious manner.—**Efficaciousness**, ef-fi-kā'shus-nes, *n.* The quality of being efficacious.—**Efficacy**, ef'fi-ka-si, *n.* [L. *efficacia*, efficacy.] Power to produce effects; production of the effect intended; effectiveness; efficiency; virtue; energy.—**Efficiency**, ef-fish'en-si, *n.* [L. *efficientia*.] The state or character of being efficient; effectual agency; power of producing the effect intended; active competent power; competence for one's duties: in any mechanical contrivance, the ratio of the useful work obtained to the energy expended.—**Efficient**, ef-fish'ent, *a.* Causing effects; causing anything to be what it is; efficacious; effectual; competent; able; operative.—*n.* One who is competent to perform the duties of a service.—**Efficiently**, ef-fish'ent-li, *adv.* In an efficient manner.

Effigy, ef'fi-ji, *n.* [L. *effigies*, from *effingo*, to fashion—*ef* for *ex*, and *fingo*, to form or devise. FEIGN.] The image, likeness, or representation of a person or thing; a likeness in sculpture, painting, or otherwise; an image: frequently applied to the figures on sepulchral monuments.—**Effigial**,† ef-fij'i-al, *a.* Exhibiting or pertaining to an effigy.—**Effigiate**, ef-fij'i-āt, *v.t.*—*effigiated*, *effigiating*. [L. *effigio*, *effigiatum*.] To make like; to form of a like figure.—**Effigiation**,† ef-fij'i-ā"shon, *n.* The act of forming in resemblance; an image or effigy.

Effloresce, ef-flo-res', *v.i.*—*effloresced*, *efflorescing*. [L. *effloresco*—*ef* for *ex*, and *floresco*, from *floreo*, to blossom, from *flos*, a flower. FLOWER.] To burst into bloom, as a flower; to break out into florid or excessive ornamentation; *chem.* to change over the surface or throughout to a whitish, mealy, or crystalline powder, from a gradual decomposition, on simple exposure to the air; to become covered with a whitish crust or light crystallization, from a slow chemical change.—**Efflorescence**, ef-flo-res'ens, *n.* The act or process of efflorescing; *bot.* the time of flowering; the production of blossoms; *med.* a redness of the skin; eruption; *chem.* the formation of a whitish substance on the surface of certain bodies, as salts; the powder or crust thus formed.—**Efflorescent**, ef-flo-res'ent, *a.* Showing efflorescence; incrusted or covered with efflorescence; liable to effloresce.

Effluence, **Effluency**, ef'flụ-ens, ef'flụ-en-si, *n.* [Fr. *effluence*, from L. *effluo*, to flow out—*e*, *ex*, and *fluo*, to flow.] The act of flowing out; that which flows out or issues; an emanation.—**Effluent**, ef'flụ-ent, *a.* Flowing out; emanating; emitted.—*n. Geog.* a stream that flows out of another stream or out of a lake.

Effluvium, ef-flū'vi-um, *n.* pl. **Effluvia**, ef-flū'vi-a. [L., from *effluo*, to flow out, FLOW.] Something flowing out in a subtle or invisible form; exhalation; emanation; especially applied to noxious or disagreeable exhalations.—**Effluviable**, ef-flū'vi-a-bl, *a.* Capable of being given off in the form of effluvium.—**Effluvial**, ef-flū'vi-al, *a.* Pertaining to or containing effluvia.—**Effluviate**,† ef-flū'vi-āt, *v.i.* To throw off effluvium.

Efflux, ef'fluks, *n.* [L. *effluo*, *effluxum*, to flow out. EFFLUENCE.] The act or state of flowing out or issuing in a stream; outflow; that which flows out; emanation.—**Effluxion**, ef-fluk'shon, *n.* The act of flowing out; that which flows out; emanation.

Effodient, ef-fō'di-ent, *a.* [L. *effodiens*, *effodientis*, ppr. of *effodio*, to dig out—*ef* for *ex*, out, and *fodio*, to dig.] Digging; accustomed to dig.

Effoliation, ef-fō'li-ā"shon, *n.* [L. *ef* for *ex*, out, and *folium*, a leaf.] *Bot.* deprivation of a plant of its leaves.

Effort, ef'fėrt, *n.* [Fr. *effort*—L. *ef* for *ex*, out, and *fortis*, strong.] An exertion of strength or power, whether physical or mental; strenuous exertion to accomplish an object; a straining to do something; endeavour.—**Effortless**, ef'fėrt-les, *a.* Making no effort.

Effranchise, ef-fran'chīz, *v.t.* [L. *ef* for *ex*, out, and E. *franchise*.] To invest with franchises or privileges.

Effrontery, ef-frun'tėr-i, *n.* [Fr. *effronterie*, from L. *effrons*, *effrontis*, barefaced, shameless—*ef* for *ex*, and *frons*, the forehead. FRONT.] Audacious impudence or boldness; assurance entirely unabashed; shamelessness; brazenness.

Effulge, ef-fulj', *v.i.*—*effulged*, *effulging*. [L. *effulgeo*—*ef* for *ex*, out, and *fulgeo*, to shine.] To send forth a flood of light; to shine with splendour.—**Effulgence**, ef-ful'jens, *n.* A flood of light; a shining forth of light or glory; great lustre or brightness; splendour.—**Effulgent**, ef-ful'jent, *a.* Shining; bright; splendid; diffusing a flood of light.—**Effulgently**, ef-ful'jent-li, *adv.* In a bright or splendid manner.

Effuse, ef-fūz', *v.t.*—*effused*, *effusing*. [L. *effundo*, *effusum*, to pour out—*ef* for *ex*, out, and *fundo*, *fusum*, to pour. FUSE.] To pour out, as a fluid; to spill; to shed.—*v.i.* To emanate; to come forth.—*a.* (ef'fūs). *Bot.* applied to a kind of panicle with a very loose one-sided arrangement; *conch.* applied to shells where the aperture is not whole behind, but the lips are separated by a gap or groove.—**Effusion**, ef-fū'zhon, *n.* The act of pouring out; that which is poured out; *pathol.* the escape of any fluid out of the vessel containing it into another part; cordiality of manner; overflowing or demonstrative kindness.—**Effusive**, ef-fū'siv, *a.* Pouring out; pouring forth largely; showing overflowing kindness or cordiality of manner.—**Effusively**, ef-fū'siv-li, *adv.* In an effusive manner.—**Effusiveness**, ef-fū'siv-nes, *n*

Efreet, ef'rēt, *n.* AFRIT.

Eft, eft, *n.* [O.E. *evete*, *ewte*, A.Sax. *efete*. *Newt* is from *ewte*, the *n* of the art. *an* having adhered to the noun.] A newt.

Eftsoons, eft'sönz, *adv.* [O.E. *eftsona*, soon after, with adverbial *s* of genitive.] Soon afterwards. [Archaic.]

Egad, ē-gad', *exclam.* [Probably a euphemistic corruption of 'by God'.] An exclamation expressing exultation or surprise.

Egence, ē'jens, *n.* [L. *egens*, ppr. of *egeo*, to suffer want.] The state of suffering from the need of something; a desire for something wanted.

Eger, ē'gėr, *n.* Same as *Eagre*.

Egest, ē-jest', *v.t.* [L. *egero*, *egestum*, to carry or bear out.—*e*, out, and *gero*, to carry.] To cast or throw out; to void excrement.—**Egestion**, ē-jest'yon, *n.* The act of voiding excrement.

Egg, eg, *n.* [A.Sax. *æg* = Icel. *egg*, Dan. *æg*, Sw. *ägg*, G. and D. *ei*; allied in origin to L. *ovum*, Gr. *ōon*, Ir. *ugh*, Gael. *ubh*, an egg.] A roundish body covered with a shell or membrane, formed in a special organ of many female animals besides birds, and in which the development of the young animal takes place; an ovum. [Animals whose young do not leave the egg till after it is laid are called *oviparous*; those in which the eggs are retained within the parent body until they are hatched are called *ovoviviparous*.]—*Egg and anchor, egg and dart, egg and tongue, arch.* same as *Echinus*.—**Egger**, eg'ėr, *n.* Any of various moths (family Lasiocampidae) whose larvae feed on the foliage of trees.—**Eggery**, eg'ėr-i, *n.* A nest of eggs; a place where eggs are deposited, as those of sea-birds.—**Egg-apple**, *n.* The fruit of the egg-plant.—**Egg-bird**, *n.* A species of tern the eggs of which are of considerable commercial importance in the West Indies.—**Egg-cup**, *n.* A cup used to hold an egg at table.—**Egg-nog**, *n.* A drink of eggs beaten up with sugar, milk, and sometimes nutmeg or wine.—**Egg-glass**, *n.* A sand-glass running about three minutes, for timing the boiling of eggs.—**Egg-plant**, *n.* A plant of the potato family (*Solanum melongena*) with egg-shaped fruits, which are boiled, stewed in sauces, &c., and served as a vegetable.—**Egg-shell**, *n.* The shell or outside covering of an egg; *fig.* anything very brittle, easily broken, or destroyed.—**Egg-slicer**, *n.* A kitchen utensil for slicing hard-boiled eggs.

Egg, eg, *v.t.* [A.Sax. *ecgian*, *eggian*, to incite, to sharpen; Icel. *eggja*, to egg. EDGE.] To incite or urge on; to stimulate; to instigate; to provoke.—**Egger**, eg'ėr, *n.* One who eggs or incites.

Egis, ē'jis, *n.* Same as *Ægis*.

Eglandulose, Eglandulous, ē-glan'dū-lōs, ē-glan'dū-lus, *a.* [L. *e*, out, and *glandulosus*, glandulous.] Destitute of glands.

Eglantine, eg'lan-tīn, *n.* [Fr. *églantine*, O.Fr. *aiglent*, from a form *aculentus*, prickly, from L. *aculeus*, a spine, a prickle, *acus*, a needle. ACID.] An old and poetical name for the sweet-brier or wild-rose.

Ego, ē'gō, *n.* [L., I.] *Philos.* the conscious thinking subject; the subject, as opposed to the *non-ego*, the not-self, the object.—**Egoism**, ē'gō-izm, *n.* [Fr. *égoïsme.*] *Philos.* the doctrine which refers the elements or all knowledge to the phenomena of personal existence; subjective idealism; a passionate love of self; egotism; selfishness.—**Egoist**, ē'gō-ist, *n.* [Fr. *égoïste*, an egotist.] An egotist; a selfish person; one holding the doctrine of egoism.—**Egoistic, Egoistical**, ē-gō-is'tik, ē-gō-is'ti-kal, *a.* Pertaining to egoism; addicted to or manifesting egoism; egotistic.—**Egoistically**, ē-gō-is'ti-kal-li, *adv.* In an egoistic manner.—**Egoity**,† ē-gō'i-ti, *n.* Personality; individuality.—**Egotheism**, ē'gō-thē-izm, *n.* [Gr. *egō*, I, and *theos*, a god.] The deification of self; self-worship.—**Egotism**, eg'o-tizm, *n.* The practice of too frequently using the word *I*; hence, a speaking or writing much of one's self; a passionate and exaggerated love of self, leading one to refer all things to one's self, and to judge of everything by its relation to one's interests or importance. ∴ *Egotism* and *self-conceit* are based on what we think of ourselves, the former being the more deep-seated and powerful; *vanity*, on what we believe others think of us.—**Egotist**, eg'o-tist, *n.* One who repeats the word *I* very often in conversation or writing; one who speaks much of himself or magnifies his own achievements.—**Egotistic, Egotistical**, eg-o-tis'tik, eg-o-tis'ti-kal, *a.* Addicted to egotism; manifesting egotism.—**Egotistically**, eg-o-tis'ti-kal-li, *adv.* In an egotistical or self-conceited manner.—**Egotize, Egoize**, eg'o-tīz, ē'gō-īz, *v.i.*—*egotized, egotizing.* To talk or write much of one's self; to exhibit egotism.

Egophony. See ÆGOPHONY.

Egregious, ē-grē'ji-us, *a.* [L. *egregius*, lit. out of the common flock or herd—*e* or *ex*, out, and *grex*, *gregis*, a flock (whence *gregarious*).] Extraordinary; remarkable; enormous: now mostly used in a bad or ironical sense (an *egregious* fool, blunder, impudence).—**Egregiously**, ē-grē'ji-us-li, *adv.* In an egregious manner. — **Egregiousness**, ē-grē'ji-us-nes, *n.*

Egress, ē'gres, *n.* [L. *egressus*, from *egredior*—*e*, and *gradior*, to step. GRADE.] The act of going or issuing out; the power of departing from any inclosed or confined place; *astron.* the passing of an inferior planet from the disc of the sun in a transit.—*v.i.* (ē-gres'). To go out; to depart; to leave.—**Egression**,† ē-gresh'on, *n.* [L. *egressio*.] Egress.—**Egressor**, ē-gres'ėr, *n.* One who goes out.

Egret, ē'gret, *n.* [Fr. *aigrette*, a dim. from an old form *aigre*, from O.H.G. *heigro*, a heron, Sw. *häger*, Icel. *hegri*, a heron. *Heron* has the same origin.] A name of those species of herons which have the feathers on the lower part of the back lengthened and the barbs loose, so that this part of the plumage is very soft and flowing; the small white heron; a plume of heron's feathers, or of feathers, diamonds, &c.; an aigret; *bot.* the flying, feathery, or hairy down of seeds, as the down of the thistle.

Egriot, ē'gri-ot, *n.* [Fr. *aigre*, sour.] A kind of sour cherry.

Egyptian, ē-jip'shan, *n.* [From *Egypt*, Gr. *Aigyptos*; akin *Gypsy*.] Pertaining to Egypt.—*Egyptian vulture*, a vulture, about the size of a raven, which frequents the streets of eastern towns, where it is protected on account of its services as a scavenger. Called also *Pharaoh's Chicken*.—*n.* A native of Egypt; an old designation for a gypsy, so called because believed to have come from Egypt.—**Egyptologer, Egyptologist**, ē-jip-tol'o-jėr, ē-jip-tol'o-jist, *n.* One well acquainted with the antiquities of Egypt, especially the hieroglyphic inscriptions and documents. — **Egyptological**, ē-jip'to-loj"i-kal, *a.* Pertaining to Egyptology; devoted to the study of Egyptology. — **Egyptology**, ē-jip-tol'o-ji, *n.* The science of Egyptian antiquities; that branch of knowledge which treats of the ancient language, history, &c., of Egypt.

Eh! ā or e, an *interj.* expressive of doubt, inquiry, slight surprise.

Eider, Eider-duck, ī'dėr, *n.* [G. *eider*, Sw. *eider*, Icel. *œdr*, Dan. *eder*.] A species of large duck, with down that is much valued, from its warmth, lightness, and elasticity.

Eidograph, ī'do-graf, *n.* [Gr. *eidos*, likeness, and *graphō*, to write.] An instrument for copying designs on a larger or smaller scale than the original.

Eidolon, ī-dō'lon, *n.* [IDOL.] An unreal or spectral form; a phantom.

Eight, āt, *a.* [A.Sax. *eahta* = G. and D. *acht*, Icel. *átta*, Dan. *aatte*, L. *octo*, Gr. *oktō*, Ir. and Gael. *achd*, Skr. *ashtan*, *ashtau*.] One of the cardinal numeral adjectives; one more than seven and less than nine.—*n.* The number composed of seven and one; the symbol representing this number.—**Eight-day**, *a.* That goes for eight days (an *eight-day* clock). — **Eighteen**, ā'tēn, *a.* and *n.* Eight and ten; the sum of ten and eight; the symbol representing this sum.—**Eighteenmo**, ā'tēn-mō, *n.* [From *eighteen* and *-mo*, in L. *decimo*, tenth.] The size of a book in which a sheet is folded into eighteen leaves: written often 18*mo*.—**Eighteenth**, ā'tēnth, *a.* and *n.* Next in order after the seventeenth; one of eighteen equal parts of a thing.—**Eightfold**, āt'fōld, *a.* Eight times the number or quantity.—**Eighth**, ātth, *a.* and *n.* Next in order after the seventh; one of eight equal parts of anything; an octave.—**Eighthly**, ātth'li, *adv.* In the eighth place.—**Eightieth**, ā'ti-eth, *a.* and *n.* Next in order to the seventy-ninth; one of eighty equal parts of anything.—**Eighty**, ā'ti, *a.* and *n.* Eight times ten; fourscore; a symbol representing this number.

Eikon-Basilike, *n.* The book purporting to be written by Charles I of England; really written by John Gauden (1605-62).

Einstein Theory, *n.* The theory of *Relativity* developed by Albert Einstein, the German-Swiss physicist and mathematician.

Eisteddfod, is-teᴛʜ'vōd, *n.* [W.] A meeting of bards and minstrels in Wales; a periodical Welsh festival for the recitation of poems and performances on the harp.

Either, ē'ᴛʜėr or ī'ᴛʜėr; the former is more in accordance with analogy, *a.* or *pron.* [A.Sax. *aegther*; contracted from *aeghwæther*, compounded of *á* = *aye*, the augment *ge*, and *hwæther*. EACH, WHETHER.] One or the other; one of two things; each of two; the one and the other; both.—*conj.* A disjunctive conjunction always used as correlative to and preceding *or* (*either* the one *or* the other).

Ejaculate, ē-jak'ū-lāt, *v.t.*—*ejaculated, ejaculating.* [L. *ejaculor*, *ejaculatus*—*e*, out, and *jaculum*, a dart, from *jacio*, to throw, seen also in *reject*, *project*, &c.] To throw out, as an exclamation; to utter suddenly and briefly.—*v.i.*† To utter ejaculations.—**Ejaculation**, ē-jak'ū-lā"shon, *n.* The uttering of a short, sudden exclamation; the exclamation uttered; a prayer consisting of a few words.—**Ejaculatory**, ē-jak'ū-la-to-ri, *a.* Of the nature of an ejaculation.

Eject, ē-jekt', *v.t.* [L. *ejicio*, *ejectum*—*e*, and *jacio*, to throw, as in *dejected*, *project*, &c.] To throw out; to cast forth; to thrust out; to drive away; to expel; to dismiss from office; to turn out.—**Ejection**, ē-jek'shon, *n.* [L. *ejectio*.] The act of ejecting; dismissal; dispossession; expulsion; rejection.—**Ejectment**, ē-jekt'ment, *n* A casting out; a dispossession; *law*, the removal of a person from the wrongful possession of land or tenements.—**Ejector**, ē-jek'tėr, *n.* One who ejects.

Eka-aluminium, ek'a-al-ū-min"i-um, *n.* [Gr. *ek*, beyond.] A hypothetical element coming between aluminium and indium, predicted by Mendeléeff, since discovered, and now called gallium.—*Eka-boron*, between calcium and titanium, and *eka-silicon*, between silicon and tin, have a similar history, and are now called scandium and germanium.

Eke, ēk, *v.t.*—*eked, eking.* [A.Sax. *écan*, to increase, to eke, Icel. *auka*, Goth. *aukan*, L. *augeo* (whence *augment*), Gr. *auxanō*, to increase.] To add to; to enlarge by addition: sometimes with *out* (he *eked out* his income by odd jobs).—*n.* Something added to another; an addition.—*adv.* [A.Sax. *eác*, D. *ook*, Sw. *och*, Dan. *og*, G. *auch*, and.] Also; likewise; in addition.—**Eking**, ē'king, *n.* That which is added.

Elaborate, ē-lab'o-rāt, *v.t.*—*elaborated, elaborating.* [L. *elaboro*, *elaboratum*—*e*, out, and *laboro*, to labour, from *labor*, labour.] To produce with labour; to work out or complete with great care; to work out fully or perfectly.—*a.* Wrought with labour; finished with great care; executed with exactness; highly finished.—**Elaborately**, ē-lab'o-rāt-li, *adv.* In an elaborate manner.—**Elaborateness**, ē-lab'o-rāt-nes, *n.* The quality of being elaborate.—**Elaboration**, ē-lab'o-rā"shon, *n.* The act of elaborating; careful or laborious finish bestowed; *physiol.* the process performed by the living organs in animals and plants by which something is produced (the *elaboration* of sap).—**Elaborative**, ē-lab'o-rā-tiv, *a.* Serving or tending to elaborate.—**Elaborator**, ē-lab'o-rā-tėr, *n.* One who or that which elaborates.

Elæoptene, el-ē-op'tēn, *n.* [Gr. *elaion*, olive-oil, and *ptēnos*, winged.] The liquid portion of volatile oils, as distinguished from the solid portion called *stearoptene*.

Elaine, e-lā'in, *n.* [Gr. *elainos*, pertaining to the olive, from *elaia*, the olive.] The liquid principle of oils and fats; oleine.—**Elaic**, e-lā'ik, *a.* Same as *Oleic*.

Elan, ā-lan', *n.* [Fr.] Ardour inspired by enthusiasm, passion, or the like; unhesitating dash resulting from an impulsive imagination.

Eland, ē'land, *n.* [D. *eland*, an elk.] An African species of antelope, the largest of all antelopes; a name sometimes given to the moose.

Elapse, ē-laps', *v.i.*—*elapsed, elapsing*. [L. *elabor, elapsus*, to slip away—*e*, out, and *labor, lapsus*, to glide. LAPSE.] To slip or glide away; to pass away silently: said of time.—**Elapsion**, ē-lap'shon, *n.* The act of elapsing; lapse.

Elasmobranchiate, ē-las'mō-brang"ki-āt, *a.* [Gr. *elasmos*, a plate, and *brangchia*, gills.] Of or belonging to an order of fishes including the sharks, dog-fishes, rays, &c.

Elastic, Elastical, ē-las'tik, ē-las'ti-kal, *a.* [Fr. *élastique*, L.L. *elasticus*, from Gr. *elastos*, beaten out, extensible, from *elaunō*, to drive, to beat out.] Having the power of returning to the form from which it is bent or extended; having the property of recovering its former figure or volume after being altered by pressure; rebounding; flying back; *fig.* possessing the power or quality of recovering from depression or exhaustion.—*Elastic limit*, for any material, is the maximum stress per unit area that can be applied without causing an appreciable permanent set. — **Elastically**, ē-las'ti-kal-li, *adv.* In an elastic manner; by elastic power.—**Elasticity**, ē-las-tis'i-ti, *n.* The quality of being elastic.

Elate, ē-lāt', *a.* [L. *elatus*, pp. of *effero*—*e*, out, and *latus*, borne or carried.] Raised or lifted up†; having the spirits lifted up; flushed, as with success; exultant; haughty.—*v.t.*—*elated, elating*. To raise; to exalt; to elevate with success; to cause to exult; to make proud. — **Elatedly**, ē-lā'ted-li, *adv.* With elation.—**Elatedness**, ē-lā'ted-nes, *n.*—**Elation**, ē-lā'shon, *n.* Elevation of mind proceeding from self-approbation; haughtiness; pride of prosperity.

Elater, el'a-tėr, *n.* [Gr. *elatēr*, a driver.] An elastic spiral filament generated in tubes in certain liverworts and scale-mosses, and supposed to assist in the dispersion of spores; a name of various small leaping beetles.

Elaterium, ē-la-tē'ri-um, *n.* [Gr. *elatērion*, from *elatērios*, driving, purgative, from *elatēr*, a driver, from *elaunō*, to drive.] A substance obtained from the fruit of the squirting cucumber, serving as a drastic purge, and administered in dropsy.

Elbow, el'bō, *n.* [A.Sax. *elboga, elnboga*—*el, eln*, forearm, an ell (akin to L. *ulna*, Gr. *ōlenē*, the forearm), and *boga*, a bow; D. *elleboog*, G. *ellbogen, ellenbogen*, Icel. *alnbogi*. ELL, BOW.] The outer angle made by the bend of the arm; the joint which unites the upper arm with the forearm; a flexure, angle, or part of a structure somewhat resembling an elbow, or which supports the arm or elbow, as the raised arm of a chair or sofa.—*Out at elbows*, having holes in the elbows of one's clothes; shabbily dressed.—*v.t.* To push or jostle with the elbow; to make or gain (a path through a crowd) by pushing with the elbows.—*v.i.* To jut into an elbow or angle; to project; to bend; to push one's way.—**Elbow-chair**, *n.* An arm-chair. — **Elbow-grease**, *n.* A colloquial or vulgar expression for energetic and continuous hand-labour, as rubbing, scouring, &c.—**Elbow-room**, *n.* Room to extend the elbows on each side; hence, ample room for motion or action.

Eld, eld, *n.* [A.Sax. *eld*, an age, *eldo*, old age. OLD.] Old age; decrepitude; old time; former ages. (*Poet.*)

Elder, el'dėr, *a.* [A.Sax. *yldra, eldra*, the compar. degree of *eald*, old. OLD.] Having lived a longer time; of greater age; born, produced, or formed before something else: opposed to *younger*; prior in origin; senior; pertaining to earlier times; earlier. — *n.* [A.Sax. *ealdor*, an ancestor, a chief, a prince.] One who is older than another or others; an ancestor; a person advanced in life, and who, on account of his age, experience, and wisdom, is selected for office; a lay official in Presbyterian churches, who acts along with the minister in the administration of discipline and government, having an equal vote with the latter in all church courts.—**Elderly**, el'dėr-li, *a.* Somewhat old; advanced beyond middle age; bordering on old age.—**Eldership**, el'dėr-ship, *n.* The office of an elder; elders collectively; order of elders.—**Eldest**, el'dest, *a.* [A.Sax. *yldest*, superl. of *eald, ald*, old.] Oldest; most advanced in age; that was born before others.

Elder, Elder-tree, el'dėr, *n.* [A.Sax. *ellern, ellen*; the *d* has been inserted in later times; D. *elloorn*, the elder; perhaps akin to *alder*.] Any tree or shrub of the honeysuckle family of rapid growth with white flowers and purple berries, and containing an unusual quantity of pith.—**Elder-berry**, *n.* The fruit of the elder.—**Elder-wine, Elder-berry Wine**, *n.* A wine made of elder-berries.—**Elderwort**, eld'ėr-wėrt, *n.* A fetid herbaceous plant found in waste places in Britain.

El Dorado, el dō-rä'dō or el dō-rā'dō, *n.* [Sp. the golden—*el*, the, and *dorado*, gilt.] A country formerly reputed to exist in South America, and possessing immense stores of gold; hence, any region rich in gold or treasure of any kind.

Eleatic, ē-lē-at'ik, *a.* Of or pertaining to *Elea*, an ancient Greek town in Southern Italy, or to a sect of philosophers that originated there.—*n.* An adherent of the Eleatic philosophy.

Elecampane, el'ē-kam-pān", *n.* [Fr. *énulecampane*, from L. *inula*, elecampane, and (probably) *campus*, a field.] A perennial plant with yellow-rayed flowers which grows in moist meadows and pastures, formerly regarded as expectorant; a coarse candy, professedly made from the root of the plant, but really composed of little else than colored sugar.

Elect, ē-lekt', *v.t.* [L. *eligo, electum*—*e*, out, and *lego, lectum*, to pick, choose, as in *collect, select*, &c.; *legend, lecture*, &c., being also akin.] To pick out or select; especially, to select or take for an office or employment; to choose from among others; to appoint to an office by vote or designation; to choose; to determine in favour of (often with an infinitive: he *elected* to go).—*a.* Chosen or elected; especially, chosen, but not inaugurated, consecrated, or invested with office (bishop-*elect*); *theol.* chosen, selected, or designated to eternal life; predestinated in the divine counsels.—*n. sing.* or *pl.* One or several chosen or set apart; *theol.* those especially favoured by God.—**Election**, ē-lek'shon, *n.* [L. *electio*.] The act of electing; the act of selecting one or more from others; the act of choosing a person to fill an office or employment, by any manifestation of preference; as by vote, uplifted hands, *viva voce*, or ballot; power of choosing or selecting; choice; voluntary preference; liberty to choose or act (it is at his *election* to accept or refuse); *theol.* predetermination of God, by which persons are distinguished as objects of mercy, become subjects of grace, are sanctified and prepared for heaven. — **Electioneer**, ē-lek'shon-ēr", *v.i.* To work or exert one's self in any way to obtain the election of a candidate. — **Electioneerer**, ē-lek'shon-ē"rėr, *n.* One who electioneers. — **Electioneering**, ē-lek'sho-nē"ring, *a.* Of or pertaining to an electioneerer.—**Elective**, ē-lek'tiv, *a.* Chosen by election; dependent on choice; bestowed or passing by election; pertaining to or consisting in choice or right of choosing; exerting the power of choice. — **Elective affinity**, *n. Chem.* the tendency to combine with some substances rather than with others. — **Electively**, ē-lek'tiv-li, *adv.* By choice; with preference of one to another.—**Elector**, ē-lek'tėr, *n.* One who elects or has the right of electing; a person who has the right of voting for any functionary; specifically, one of the persons elected, by vote of the people, to the *electoral college*, whose function is to elect the President and Vice-President of the United States.—**Electoral, Electorial**, ē-lek'tėr-al, ē-lek-tō'ri-al, *a.* Pertaining to election or electors; consisting of electors.—**Electorate**, ē-lek'tėr-āt, *n.* A body of electors; the dignity or territory of an elector.—**Electorship**, ē-lek'tėr-ship, *n.* The office of an elector.

Electric, Electrical, ē-lek'trik, ē-lek'-tri-kal, *a.* [Fr. *électrique*, from L. *electrum*, Gr. *ēlektron*, amber, from the fact that the earliest electric phenomenon observed was the attraction of amber for light substances when rubbed.] Containing electricity, or capable of exhibiting it when excited by friction; pertaining to electricity; derived from or produced by electricity; conveying electricity; communicating a shock by electricity; *fig.* full of fire, spirit, or passion, and capable of communicating it to others. —*Electric battery*, a number of primary or secondary voltaic cells, connected with each other in one circuit. — *Electric charge*, a quantity of electricity existing on the surface of a body.—*Electric clock*, a clock in which the moving power, or the controlling power, is the action of a current of electricity. — *Electric condenser*, a system of two conducting surfaces, usually plane, facing each other across a narrow layer of air or other dielectric. A small difference of potential produces large charges on conductors so placed. — *Electric current*, a current or stream of electricity traversing a closed circuit formed of conducting substances, or passing by means of conductors from one body to another.—*Electric eel*, a fish which is capable of giving electric shocks.—*Electric lamp*, a lamp of any type depending on electricity, as the incandescent lamp, or the arc lamp.—*Electric light*, a light obtained by the conversion of electric energy into light energy. The usual method is to heat some material to incandescence by passing an electric current through it. — *Electric machine*, a machine for generating static electricity, by friction or by induction; the name is also given to the electric GENERATOR.—*Electric motor*. ELECTROMOTOR.—*Electric railway*, a railway on which electricity is the motor.—*Electric spark*, one of the forms in which accumulated electricity discharges itself.—*Electric telegraph*. TELEGRAPH. — **Electrically**, ē-lek'tri-kal-li, *adv.* In the manner of electricity or by means of it. — **Electricalness**,† ē-lek'-tri-kal-nes, *n.* The state or quality of being electrical.—**Electrician**, ē-lek-trish'an, *n.* One versed in the science of electricity; one who designs, sets up, repairs, or attends to electrical instruments and machinery.—**Electricity**, ē-lek-tris'i-ti, *n.* A name for the cause or agent underlying certain phenomena, called *electric*, and usually spoken of as a fluid; the force that manifests itself in lightning, in the attraction of amber and sealing-wax when rubbed for light substances, and in many other phenomena; the science which deals with these phenomena. Besides friction there are various other sources of electricity, such as chemical action, the contact of metals, change of temperature, &c., but above all the relative motion of a conductor and a field of magnetic force, as in the GENERATOR, for producing electric current.—*Atmospheric electricity*, the electricity which is produced in the atmosphere, and which becomes visible in the form of lightning.—**Electrification**, ē-lek'tri-fi-kā"shon, *n.* The act of electrifying, or state of being electrified.—**Electrify**, ē-lek'tri-fī, *v.t.* — *electrified, electrifying*. To communicate electricity to; to charge with electricity; to affect by electricity; to give an electric shock to; *fig.* to give a sudden shock (as of surprise) to; to surprise with some sudden and brilliant effect; to thrill.—*v.i.* To become electric.—**Electro**, ē-lek'trō, *n.* A contraction for *Electrotype*.—**Electro-ballistic**, *a.* Applied to an instrument for determining by electricity the velocity of a projectile at any part of its flight.—**Electro-biologist**, *n.* One versed in electro-biology. — **Electro-biology**, *n.* That branch of science which treats of the electric currents developed in living organisms; also mesmerism or animal magnetism or a phase of this.—**Electro-chemistry**, *n.* That branch of science which treats of, or is based upon, the relations between chemical and electrical phenomena.—**Electrocute**, ē-lek'trō-kūt, *v.t.* To execute by the agency of an electric current or shock. — **Electrocution**, ē-lek'trō-kū-shon, *n.* Execution by such means. [American, on model of *execute.*]—**Electrode**, ē-lek'trōd, *n.* [*-ode* is from Gr. *hodos*, a way.] One of the terminals or poles of the voltaic circuit. — **Electro - dynamic**, **Electro - dynamical**, *a.* Pertaining to electro-dynamics. — **Electro-dynamics**, *n.* The science which treats of mechanical actions exerted on one another by electric currents. —**Electro-dynamometer**, *n.* An instrument for measuring electric currents by electro-dynamic action. — **Electro-gild**. *v.t.* To gild by means of the electric current.—**Electro-gilt**, *a.* Gilded by means of the electric current.—**Electro-kinetics**, *n.* That branch of electrical science which treats of electricity in motion. — **Electro-kinetic**, *a.* Of or pertaining to electro-kinetics or electricity in motion. —**Electrolyze**, ē-lek'tro-līz, *v.t.* To decompose by direct action of the electric current.— **Electrolyzable**, ē-lek'tro-lī-za-bl, *a.* Susceptible of being electrolyzed. **Electrolyzation**, ē-lek'tro-li-zā"shon, *n.* The act of electrolyzing.—**Electrolysis**, ē-lek-trol'i-sis, *n.* The resolution of compound bodies into their elements, or, in some cases, into groups of elements, under the action of a current of electricity.— **Electrolyte**, ē-lek'tro-līt, *n.* A compound which is decomposable, or is subjected to decomposition, by an electric current. — **Electrolytic**, **Electrolytical**, ē-lek'tro-lit"ik, ē-lek'tro-lit"i-kal, *a.* Pertaining to electrolysis. — **Electro-magnet**, *n.* A bar of soft iron rendered temporarily magnetic by a current of electricity having been caused to pass through a wire coiled round it.—**Electro-magnetic**, *a.* Having to do with the relations between electricity and magnetism. —*Electro-magnetic units*, units employed in electrical measurement based upon the force exerted between two magnetic poles. The basis of the ordinary practical units. **Electro-metallurgy**, *n.* The art of depositing metals, as gold, silver, copper, &c., from solutions of their salts by electrolysis; and of using the heating effects of the electric current. — **Electrometer**, ē-lek-trom'e-tėr, *n.* An instrument for measuring potential, or differences of electric potential between two conductors.—**Electrometric**, **Electrometrical**, ē-lek'tro-met"rik, ē-lek'tro-met"ri-kal, *a.* Pertaining to an electrometer, or the measurement of potential. — **Electrometry**, ē-lek-trom'et-ri, *n.* That branch of electric science which treats of the measurement of potential.—**Electro-motion**, *n.* The motion of electricity; mechanical motion produced by electricity. — **Electro - motive**, *a.* Causing, or tending to cause, an electric current.—*Electro-motive force*, that which determines the flow of electricity along a conductor; proportional to difference of potential, and analogous to difference of level causing a flow in water. Measured in volts.—**Electromotor**, ē-lek'tro-mō-tėr, *n.* A machine for transforming the energy of the electric current into mechanical energy, for propelling vehicles or driving machinery.—**Electron**, ē-lek'tron, *n.* One of extremely small particles of negative electricity, which form essential constituents of atoms, and by which, according to the *electron theory*, heat and electricity are conducted.—**Electro-negative**, *a.* Repelled by bodies negatively electrified, and attracted by those positively electrified. — **Electrophorus**. ē-lek-trof'o-rus, *n.* An instrument for collecting electricity, and showing the phenomena of induction. — **Electro - physiological**, *a.* Pertaining to electro-physiology.—**Electro-physiology**, *n.* That branch of science which treats of electric phenomena produced through physiological agencies.—**Electroplate**, *v.t.* To plate or give a coating of silver or other metal by means of electric currents. — *n.* Articles coated with silver or other metal by the process of electroplating.—**Electro-plater**, *n.* One who practises electro - plating. — **Electro - polar**, *a.* A term applied to conductors, one end or surface of which is positive and the other negative.—**Electro-positive**, *a.* Attracted by bodies negatively electrified or by the negative pole of the galvanic arrangement.—**Electroscope**, ē-lek'tro-skōp, *n.* An instrument for observing or detecting the existence of free electricity, and, in general, for determining its kind. **Electroscopic**, ē-lek'tro-skop"ik, *a.* Of or belonging to the electroscope.—**Electro-silver**, *v.t.* To deposit a coating of silver on by means of voltaic electricity; to electro-plate.—**Electro-statics**, *n.* The science which treats of the phenomena occasioned by electricity at rest, and of the production and discharge of stationary charges of electricity.—*Electro-static units*, units employed in electrical measurement, based upon Coulomb's law of attraction and repulsion between quantities of statical electricity. All electrical quantities may be expressed in either electro-static or electromagnetic units, but the dimensions in the two systems differ, the velocity of light entering into the difference. — **Electrotint**, *n.* An art by which drawings are traced by the action of electricity on a copper plate.—**Electrotype**, ē-lek'tro-tīp, *n.* The act of producing copies of types, woodcuts, medals, &c., by means of the electric deposition of copper upon a mould taken from the original; a copy thus produced.— *v.t.—electrotyped, electrotyping.* To stereotype or take copies of by electrotype. — **Electrotypic**, ē-lek'tro-tī"pik, *a.* Pertaining to, or effected by means of, electrotype.—**Electrotypist**, ē-lek'tro-tī-pist, *n.* One who practises electrotypy.—**Electrotypy**, ē-lek'tro-tī-pi, *n.* The process of electrotype.

Electuary, ē-lek'tū-a-ri, *n.* [L.L. *electuarium*, a word of doubtful origin.] A medicine composed of powders or other ingredients, incorporated with some conserve, honey, or syrup.

Eleemosynary, el-ē-moz'i-na-ri, *a.* [L.L. *eleemosynarius*, from Gr. *eleēmosynē*, alms, from *eleeō*, to pity, *eleos*, compassion. ALMS.] Given in charity or alms; appropriated to charity; founded by charity (an *eleemosynary* institution); relating to charitable donations; supported by charity.—*n.* One who lives by receiving alms or charity. — **Eleemosynarily**, el-ē-moz'i-na-ri-li, *adv.* In an eleemosynary manner.

Elegance, el'ē-gans, *n.* [Fr. *élégance*, from L. *elegantia*, from *elegans*, for *eligens*, from *eligo*—*e, ex*, out, and *lego*, to pick, to choose. ELECT.] The quality of being elegant; beauty resulting from perfect propriety, or from the absence of anything calculated to produce a disagreeable sensation; refinement; an elegant characteristic or feature.—**Elegancy**, el'ē-gan-si, *n.* Elegance. —**Elegant**, el'ē-gant, *a.* [Fr. *élégant*, L. *elegans.*] Having beauty or a pleasing effect resulting from grace, refinement, or polish; pleasing to good taste; graceful; refined (a lady with an *elegant* figure); having the words or style polished and appropriate (an *elegant* speech); giving expression to thought with propriety and grace; pleasing to the eye by grace of form or delicacy of colour; free from coarseness, blemish, or other defect; showing fine harmony or symmetry.— **Elegantly**, el'ē-gant-li, *adv.* In an elegant manner.

Elegy, el'ē-ji, *n.* [L. *elegia*, from Gr. *elegeia*, from *elegos*, a lament.] A mournful or plaintive poem, or a funeral song; a poem or a song expressive of sorrow and lamentation; a dirge; *class. poetry*, any poem written in elegiac verse.—**Elegiac**, el-ē-jī'ak, *a.* Belonging to elegy; plaintive; expressing sorrow or lamentation; used in elegies: said especially of a style of verse commonly used by the Greek and Latin poets, and composed of couplets consisting of alternate hexameter and pentameter lines. — **Elegiast**, **Elegist**, e-lē'ji-ast, el'ē-jist, *n.* A writer of elegies. — **Elegize**, el'ē-jīz, *v.t.* and *i.* To write or compose elegies; to celebrate or lament in an elegy; to bewail.

Element, el'ē-ment, *n.* [L. *elementum*, an element, a first principle; same root as *aliment.*] One of the simplest constituent principles, or parts, of which anything consists, or upon which its constitution is based; a fundamental or ultimate part or principle, by the combination or aggregation of which anything is composed; an ingredient; *chem.* one of the eighty-seven simple substances which hitherto have resisted resolution by chemical analysis; one of the ultimate, indecomposable constituents of any kind of matter; *pl.* the first or simplest rules or principles of an art or science; rudiments; one of the four constituents of the material world according to an old and still popular classification —fire, air, earth, water (hence such expressions as 'war of the *elements*' for a storm); the state or sphere natural to anything or suited to its existence (hence, *out of one's element*, out of one's natural sphere or position); a datum or value necessary to be taken into consideration in making a calculation or coming to a conclusion; *pl.* the bread and wine used in the eucharist. —*v.t.* To constitute; to be an element in; to make a first principle.—**Elemental**, el-ē-men'tal, *a.* Pertaining to or produced by elements or primary ingredients; pertaining to the four so-called elements of the material world or some of them (hence '*elemental* war,' applied to a tempest); arising from or pertaining to first principles; elementary†. — **Elementalism**, el-ē-men'-tal-izm, *n.* The theory which identifies the divinities of the ancients with the elemental powers. — **Elementality**,† el'ē-men'tal"i-ti, *n.* State of being elemental or elementary.—**Elementally**, el-ē-men'-tal-li, *adv.* In an elemental manner; according to elements. — **Elementarity**, **Elementariness**, el'ē-men-tar"i-ti, el-ē-men'ta-ri-nes, *n.* The state of being elementary. — **Elementary**, el-ē-men'ta-ri, *a.* Having the character of an element or primary substance; primary; simple; uncompounded; uncombined; initial; rudimentary; containing, teaching, or discussing first principles, rules, or rudiments. —*Elementary analysis, chem.* the estimation of the amounts of the elements which together form a compound body. — *Elementary substances*, the elements or substances which have hitherto resisted analysis by any known chemical means.— **Elementoid**, el-ē-men'toid, *n.* Like an element; having the appearance of a simple substance.

Elemi, el'ē-mi, *n.* The resinous exudation from various trees, used in plasters and ointments and the manufacture of varnish.

Elenchus, ē-leng'kus, *n.* [L. *elenchus*; Gr. *elenchos.*] *Logic*, a syllogism by which an opponent is made to contradict himself; a fallacious argument; a sophism.

Elephant, el'ē-fant, *n.* [L. *elephas, elephantis*, from Gr. *elephas, elephantos*, an elephant; probably from Heb. *eleph*, an ox.] The name of two species of huge quadrupeds, one inhabiting India, the other Africa, and both remarkable for having their nose prolonged into a long proboscis or trunk with the nostrils at its extremity, and for their large tusks. — **Elephantiac**, el-ē-fan'ti-ak, *a.* Affected with elephantiasis. —**Elephantiasis**, el'ē-fan-tī"a-sis, *n.* [Gr., from *elephas*, elephant.] *Med.* a skin disease in which the limbs, from their enlargement and the changed condition of the skin, have a slight resemblance to those of the elephant.—**Elephantine**, el-ē-fan'tīn, *a.* Pertaining to the elephant; resembling an elephant; hence, huge; immense. — **Elephantoid**, el-ē-fan'toid, *a.* Having the form of an elephant.—**Elephant-paper**, *n.* A writing, printing, and drawing paper, of the size of 28 inches by 23.

Eleusinian, el-ū-sin'i-an, *a.* Relating to *Eleusis* in Greece; as, *Eleusinian mysteries* or *festivals*, the mysteries and festivals of Dēmētēr (Ceres), celebrated there.

Eleutheromania, e-lū'thėr-ō-mā''ni-a, *n.* [Gr. *eleutheros*, free, and *mania*, madness.] A mania for freedom; excessive zeal for freedom.—**Eleutheromaniac**, e-lū'-thėr-ō-mā''ni-ak, *n.* A fanatic on the subject of freedom.

Elevate, el'ē-vāt, *v.t.*—*elevated, elevating.* [L. *elevo, elevatum*, to lift up—*e*, out, up, and *levo*, to raise, from *levis*, light in weight, whence *levity, lever, levy*, &c.] To raise; in a literal sense, to raise from a low or deep place to a higher; to raise to a higher state or station; to improve, refine, or dignify; to raise from a low or common state, as by training or education; to exalt; to excite, cheer, animate; to render somewhat tipsy (*colloq.*); to augment or swell; to make louder.—**Elevated**, el'ē-vā-ted, *a.* Raised; exalted; dignified; elated; excited; slightly tipsy (*colloq.*); raised above the natural pitch; somewhat loud.—**Elevatedness**, el'ē-vā-ted-nes, *n.*—**Elevating**, el'ē-vā-ting, *a.* Exalting; elating.—**Elevation**, el-ē-vā'shon, *n.* [L. *elevatio.*] The act of elevating; the act of raising or conveying from a lower place or degree to a higher; the state of being raised or elevated; exaltation; that which is raised or elevated; an elevated place; a rising ground; height; degree of height; height above the surface of the earth; altitude; *astron.* altitude; *gun.* the angle which the axis of the bore of a firearm makes with the plane of the horizon; *arch.* a geometrical representation of a building in vertical section, as opposed to *ground-plan*.—**Elevator**, el'ē-vā-tėr, *n.* One who or that which elevates, raises, lifts, or exalts; a mechanical contrivance for raising passengers or goods from a lower place to a higher; a hoist.—**Elevatory**, el'ē-va-to-ri, *a.* Tending or having power to elevate.

Eleven, ē-lev'n, *a.* [A.Sax. *endleofan, endlufon* = Icel. *ellifu*, Dan. *elleve*, D. *elf*, Goth. *ainlif*; compounded of two elements meaning one and ten, A.Sax. *-leofan*, Goth. *lif*, being allied to L. *decim*, Gr. *deka*, ten. So *twelve* = two-ten.] Ten and one added.—*n.* The sum of ten and one; a symbol representing eleven units; *football* and *cricket*, the players selected to play as a team in a football game or cricket match.—**Eleventh**, ē-lev'nth, *a.* and *n.* Next in order after the tenth; one of eleven equal parts into which anything is divided.

Elf, elf, *n.* pl. **Elves**, elvz. [A.Sax. *ælf, elf* = L.G. *elf*, Dan. *alf*, Icel. *álfr*, O.H.G. *alp*, an elf. Probably of same origin as L. *albus*, white, and the name *Alps*.] A kind of inferior spiritual being formerly believed in; a fairy; a goblin; a mischievous person; a pet name for a child.—**Elf-arrow, Elf-bolt**, *n.* Names popularly given in the British Islands to the ancient flint arrowheads still often found. Also called *Elf-dart*.—**Elfin**, el'fin, *a.* Relating or pertaining to elves.—*n.* A little elf; a little urchin.—**Elfish**, el'fish, *a.* Of or pertaining to elves; resembling an elf; suggestive of elves.—**Elf-land**, *n.* The region of the elves; fairy-land.—**Elf-lock**, *n.* A knot of hair twisted as if by elves.

Elicit, ē-lis'it, *v.t.* [L. *elicio, elicitum*—*e*, out, and *lacio*, to allure; akin *delicate, delight*.] To bring or draw out by reasoning, discussion, examination, or the like; to deduce or educe (as truth, facts, &c.).

Elide, ē-līd', *v.t.* [L. *elido*—*e*, out, and *lædo*, to strike.] *Gram.* to cut off or suppress, as a syllable.—**Elision**, ē-lizh'on, *n.* *Gram.* the act of eliding; the cutting off or suppression of a vowel or syllable.

Eligible, el'i-ji-bl, *a.* [Fr. *éligible*, from L. *eligo*—*e*, out, and *lego*, to choose. ELECT.] Fit to be chosen for some purpose or duty; worthy of choice; desirable; legally qualified to be chosen.—**Eligibility**, el'i-ji-bil''i-ti, *n.* The state or condition of being eligible; capability of being chosen.—**Eligibleness**, el'i-ji-bl-nes, *n.* Eligibility.—**Eligibly**, el'i-ji-bli, *adv.* In a manner to be worthy of choice; suitably.

Eliminate, ē-lim'i-nāt, *v.t.*—*eliminated, eliminating.* [L. *elimino, eliminatum*—*e*, out, and *limen*, threshold.] To discharge or throw off (as a secretion of the human body); to take out or separate as not being an element of value or necessary; to set aside as unimportant or not to be considered; to leave out of consideration; *alg.* to cause to disappear from an equation; to deduce or elicit† (incorrect in this sense).—**Elimination**, ē-lim'i-nā''shon, *n.* The act of eliminating.

Eliquation, ē-li-kwā'shon, *n.* [L. *eliquo*—*e*, out, and *liquo*, to melt.] An operation, now seldom employed, for the separation of silver from copper by means of lead.

Elision. Under ELIDE.

Élite, ā-lēt, *n. pl.* [Fr., lit. elected or select.] Those who are choice or select; the best; the flower.

Elixate,‡ ē-lik'sāt, *v.t.*—*elixated, elixating.* [L. *elixo*, to boil thoroughly, from *elixus*, thoroughly boiled—*e*, and *lix*, an ancient word which, according to Nonius, signified ashes, or lye mixed with ashes.] To boil; to seethe; to extract by boiling.—**Elixation**, ē-lik-sā'shon, *n.* The act of boiling or seething; extraction by boiling; also, concoction in the stomach; digestion.

Elixir, ē-lik'sėr, *n.* [Fr. *elixir*, from Sp. *elixir*, from Ar. *el-iksir*, the philosopher's stone, from Gr. *xēros*, dry.] A liquor sought for by the alchemists for transmuting metals into gold or prolonging life; quintessence; a cordial; *med.* a tincture composed of various substances held in solution by alcohol in some form.

Elizabethan, ē-liz'-a-beth''an, *a.* Pertaining to Queen Elizabeth of England or her period.—*Elizabethan architecture*, the architectural style of the times of Elizabeth and James I., when the debased Gothic and Italian were combined, characterized by large windows, tall and highly decorated chimneys, and much ornament.

Elk, elk, *n.* [Icel. *elgr*, O.H.G. *elaho*, Sw. *elg*; akin to L. *alces*, an elk.] In Europe and Asia, the largest member of the deer family, similar to the moose; in America, the wapiti, a member of the deer family, next in size to the moose.

Ell, el, *n.* [A.Sax. *eln*; D. *ell, elle*, G. *elle*, O.H.G. *elna*, Sw. *aln*, Icel. *alin*, Goth. *aleina*; akin to L. *ulna*, Gr. *ōlenē*, the forearm, and hence, a measure of length. Comp. *cubit*.] A measure of different lengths in different countries, used chiefly for measuring cloth; the English ell being 45 inches, the Flemish ell 27, the Scotch 37·2, and the French 54.

Ellagic, el-laj'ik, *a.* [From Fr. *galle*, gall, reversed.] Pertaining to or derived from gall-nuts.

Ellipse, el-lips', *n.* [Gr. *elleipsis*, an omission or defect, from *elleipō*, to leave out—*ek*, out, and *leipō*, to leave.] *Geom.* an oval figure produced when any cone is cut by a plane which passes through it, not parallel to nor cutting the base; a closed curve in which the distances of any point from two points called the *foci* have always the same sum.—**Ellipsis**, el-lip'sis, *n.* *Gram.* the omission of one or more words which the hearer or reader may supply; *printing*, the marks, — or *** or . . . , denoting the omission or suppression of letters or words; *geom.* an ellipse‡.—**Ellipsograph, Elliptograph**, el-lip'so-graf, el-lip'to-graf, *n.* An instrument for describing ellipses; a trammel.—**Ellipsoid**, el-lip'soid, *n.* *Geom.* a solid figure, all plane sections of which are ellipses or circles.—**Ellipsoidal**, el-lip-soi'dal, *a.* Pertaining to an ellipsoid; having the form of an ellipsoid.—**Elliptic, Elliptical**, el-lip'tik, el-lip'ti-kal, *a.* Pertaining to an ellipse; having the form of an ellipse; pertaining to ellipsis; having a word or words left out.—**Elliptically**, el-lip'ti-kal-li, *adv.* According to the form of an ellipse; with a word or words left out.—**Ellipticity**, el-lip-tis'i-ti, *n.* The quality of being elliptical or having the form of an ellipse.

Elm, elm, *n.* [A.Sax. *elm*, D. *olm*, Icel. *álmr*, Dan. *ælm, alm*; akin to L. *ulmus*, Bohem. *gilm* (pron. *yilm*), elm.] A valuable timber and shade tree, species of which are found in America and Europe.—**Elmen**, el'men, *a.* Made of elm.—**Elmy**, el'mi, *a.* Abounding with elms.

Elmo's-fire, el'mōz-fīr, *n.* [After Saint *Elmo*, whom sailors in the Mediterranean invoke during a storm.] A popular name for a meteoric appearance seen playing about the masts of a ship.

Elocular, ē-lok'ū-lėr, *a.* [L. *e*, without, and *loculus*, cell.] *Bot.* having but one cell; not divided by partitions.

Elocution, el-ō-kū'shon, *n.* [L. *elocutio*, from *eloquor, elocutus*, to speak out—*e*, out, and *loquor*, to speak, seen in *colloquy, eloqueni, loquacious*, &c.] The art by which, in delivering a discourse before an audience, the speaker is enabled to render it effective and impressive; mode of utterance or delivery of an address, accompanied by gestures.—**Elocutionary**, el-ō-kū'shon-a-ri, *a.* Pertaining to elocution.—**Elocutionist**, el-ō-kū'shon-ist, *n.* One who is versed in elocution; a teacher of elocution.

Eloge, ā-lōzh, *n.* [Fr., from L. *elogium.*] A funeral oration; a panegyric on the dead; a discourse pronounced in public in honour of an illustrious person recently deceased; properly of that pronounced by a member of the French Academy in honour of his predecessor.—**Elogist**, el'ō-jist, *n.* [Fr. *élogiste.*] One who delivers an éloge.—**Elogy, Elogium**, el'ō-ji, ē-lō'ji-um, *n.* A panegyric; an éloge.

Elohim, el-ō'him, *n.* One of the Hebrew names of God of frequent occurrence in the Bible, used both of the true God and of false gods, while *Jehovah* is used only of the true God.—**Elohist**, el-ō'hist, *n.* The supposed writer of the Elohistic passages of the Pentateuch, in contradistinction to the *Jehovist*.—**Elohistic**, ē-lō-his'tik, *a.* A term applied to certain passages in Scripture, especially in the Pentateuch, in which the Almighty is always spoken of as *Elohim*.

Elongate, ē-long'gāt, *v.t.*—*elongated, elongating.* [L.L. *elongo, elongatum*—L. *e*, out, and *longus*, long.] To lengthen; to extend.—*v.i.* To recede apparently from the sun: said of a planet in its orbit.—**Elongation**, ē-long-gā'shon, *n.* The act of elongating or lengthening; the state of being stretched out or lengthened; *astron.* the angular distance of a planet from the sun, as it appears to the eye of a spectator on the earth.

Elope, ē-lōp', *v.i.*—*eloped, eloping.* [From D. *loopen*, the same word as G. *laufen*, Goth. *hlaupan*, to run, to leap, E. *leap*, with prefix *e*, out, away.] To run away; to run away with a lover or paramour in defiance of duty or social restraints: said especially of a woman.—**Elopement**, ē-lōp'ment, *n.* The act of eloping; the running away of a woman, married or unmarried, with a lover.

Eloquence, el'ō-kwens, *n.* [Fr. *éloquence*, from L. *eloquentia*. ELOCUTION.] The art of expressing thoughts in such language and in such a way as to produce conviction or persuasion; oratory; that which is expressed with eloquence.—**Eloquent**, el'ō-kwent, *a.* Having the power of expressing strong emotions vividly and appropriately; adapted to express strong emotion with fluency and power; characterized by eloquence.—**Eloquently**, el'ō-kwent-li, *adv.* In an eloquent manner.

Else, els, *a.* or *adv.* [A.Sax. *elles*, else, otherwise; akin to O.H.G. *eli, ali*, Goth. *alis*; L. *alius* (see ALIEN), Gr. *allos*, another.] Other; besides; in addition; as in who *else*? nothing or nobody *else*, nowhere *else*.—*conj* Otherwise; in the other case; if the fact were different; as, he was ill, *else* he would have come.—**Elsewhere**, els'whār, *adv.* In another place; somewhere else.

Eltchi, elt'shē, *n.* An ambassador or envoy; a Persian or Turkish name.

Elucidate, ē-lū'si-dāt, *v.t.*—*elucidated, elucidating.* [L.L. *elucido, elucidatum*—L. *e*, out, and *lucidus*, bright. LUCID.] To make clear or manifest; to explain; to remove obscurity from and render intelligible; to illustrate.—**Elucidation**, ē-lū'si-dā"shon, *n.* The act of elucidating; explanation; exposition; illustration.—**Elucidative**, ē-lū'si-dā-tiv, *a.* Making or tending to elucidate; explanatory.—**Elucidator**, ē-lū'si-dā-tėr, *n.* One who elucidates or explains.—**Elucidatory**,† ē-lū'si-da-to-ri, *a.* Tending to elucidate.

Elude, ē-lūd', *v.t.*—*eluded, eluding.* [L. *eludo*—*e*, and *ludo*, to play, as in *allude, collude, delude*, &c.] To evade; to avoid by artifice, stratagem, wiles, deceit, or dexterity; to remain unseen, undiscovered, or unexplained by (to *elude* scrutiny).—**Eludible**, ē-lū'di-bl, *a.* Capable of being eluded or escaped.—**Elusion**, ē-lū'zhon, *n.* An escape by artifice or deception; an evasion.—**Elusive**, ē-lū'siv, *a.* Practising elusion; using arts to escape.—**Elusively**, ē-lū'siv-li, *adv.* With or by elusion.—**Elusoriness**, ē-lū'so-ri-nes, *n.* The state of being elusory.—**Elusory**, ē-lū'so-ri, *a.* Tending to elude; tending to deceive; evasive; fallacious.

Elul, ē'lul, *n.* [Heb.] The twelfth month of the Jewish civil year, corresponding nearly to our August.

Elutriate, ē-lū'tri-āt, *v.t.*—*elutriated, elutriating.* [L. *elutrio, elutriatum*, from *eluo, elutum*, to wash off—*e*, off, and *luo*, to wash.] To purify (ores) by washing and straining off or decanting the liquid from the substance washed, the lighter matters being then separated from the heavier.—**Elutriation**, ē-lū'tri-ā"shon, *n.* The operation of elutriating.

Elvan, el'van, *n.* A kind of rock in Cornwall, often forming dikes in other rocks; a granitic and felspar porphyritic rock.

Elves, elvz, pl. of *elf*.—**Elvish**, el'vish, *a.* Pertaining to elves or fairies; mischievous, as if done by elves; elfish.—**Elvishly**, el'vish-li, *adv.* In an elvish manner.

Élysée, ā-lē-zā, *n.* [Fr.] The official residence of the President of the French Republic.

Elysium, ē-liz'i-um, *n.* [L., from Gr. *ēlysion* (*pedion*), the Elysian fields.] *Myth.* a place assigned to happy souls after death; the seat of future happiness; hence, any place exquisitely delightful.—**Elysian**, ē-liz'i-an, *a.* Pertaining to elysium; exceedingly delightful.

Elytron, Elytrum, el'i-tron, el'i-trum, *n.* pl. **Elytra**, el'i-tra. [Gr., a cover, sheath, from *elyō*, to roll round.] The wing-sheath or coriaceous membrane which forms the superior wing in beetles, serving to cover and protect the true wing.—**Elytriform**, e-lit'ri-form, *a.* In the form of a wing-sheath.—**Elytrine**, el'i-trin, *n.* The substance of which the horny covering of crustaceous insects is composed.—**Elytroid**, el'i-troid, *a.* Like an elytron.

Elzevir, el'ze-vėr, *a.* Of or belonging to the *Elzevir* family: applied to editions of the classics, &c., published by the Elzevir family at Amsterdam and Leyden, from about 1595 to 1680, and highly prized for their accuracy and elegance; a term applied to a variety of printing type consisting of tall thin letters.

Em, em, *n.* *Print.* the unit of measurement, being a type whose breadth is equal to its depth.

Emaciate, ē-mā'shi-āt, *v.i.*—*emaciated, emaciating.* [L. *emacio, emaciatum*—*e*, intens., and *macies*, leanness.] To lose flesh gradually; to become lean from loss of appetite or other cause.—*v.t.* To cause to lose flesh gradually; to reduce to leanness.—*a.* Thin; wasted.—**Emaciation**, ē-mā'shi-ā"shon, *n.* The act of making or becoming lean or thin in flesh; the state of being reduced to leanness.

Emanate, em'a-nāt, *v.i.*—*emanated, emanating.* [L. *emano, emanatum*—*e*, out, and *mano*, to flow.] To flow forth or issue from a source: said of what is intangible, as light, heat, odour, power, &c.; to proceed from something as the source, fountain, or origin; to take origin; to arise; to spring.—**Emanant**, em'a-nant, *a.* Emanating, issuing, or flowing from something else.—**Emanation**, em-a-nā'shon, *n.* The act of emanating; that which emanates, issues, flows, or proceeds from any source, substance, or body; efflux; effluvium; any person, power, or thing emanating or proceeding from the Divine Essence.—**Emanative**,† em'a-nā-tiv, *a.* Tending to emanate.—**Emanatively**, em'a-nā-tiv-li, *adv.* After the manner of an emanation.

Emancipate, ē-man'si-pāt, *v.t.*—*emancipated, emancipating.* [L. *emancipo, emancipatum*—*e*, out, *manus*, the hand, and *capio*, to take.] To set free from servitude or slavery by the voluntary act of the proprietor; to restore from bondage to freedom; to free from bondage, restriction, or restraint of any kind; to liberate from subjection, controlling power, or influence.—**Emancipation**, ē-man'si-pā"shon, *n.* The act of emancipating; deliverance from bondage or controlling influence; liberation.—**Emancipationist**, ē-man'si-pā"shon-ist, *n.* An advocate for the emancipation of slaves.—**Emancipator**, ē-man'si-pā-tėr, *n.* One who emancipates.—**Emancipist**, ē-man'si-pist, *n.* Ex-convict who has served out his sentence.

Emanium, ē-mā'ni-um, *n.* [From *emanation.*] ACTINIUM (which see).

Emarginate, Emarginated, ē-mär'ji-nāt, ē-mär'ji-nā-ted, *a.* [L. *emarginatus*—*e*, priv., and *margo, marginis*, border, margin.] Having the margin or extremity taken away; having a blunt or obtuse notch in the margin; notched at the blunt apex: applied most commonly in *bot.* to a leaf, petal, &c.—**Emarginately**, ē-mär'ji-nāt-li, *adv.* In the form of notches.—**Emargination**, ē-mär'ji-nā"shon, *n.* The condition of being emarginate; a blunt notch in the extremity or margin.

Emasculate, ē-mas'kū-lāt, *v.t.*—*emasculated, emasculating.* [L. *e*, priv., and *masculus*, dim. of *mas*, a male. MASCULINE.] To deprive of the properties of a male; to castrate; to geld; to deprive of masculine vigour; to render effeminate; to expurgate by removing coarse passages from (a book).—**Emasculation**, ē-mas'kū-lā"shon, *n.* The act of emasculating; the state of being emasculated.—**Emasculatory**, ē-mas'kū-la-to-ri, *a.* Serving to emasculate.

Embalm, em-bäm', *v.t.* [Prefix *em*, and *balm*, balsam.] To preserve (a dead body) from decay by removing the intestines and filling their place with odoriferous and desiccative spices and drugs; to preserve from loss or decay; to cherish tenderly the memory of.—**Embalmer**, em-bä'mėr, *n.* One who embalms.

Embank, em-bangk', *v.t.* [Prefix *em*, and *bank.*] To inclose with a bank; to defend by banks, mounds, or dikes; to bank up.—**Embankment**, em-bangk'ment, *n.* The act of surrounding or defending with a bank; a mound or bank raised to protect land from being overflowed by a river or the sea, or to enable a road or railway to be carried over a valley.

Embarcation, *n.* EMBARKATION.

Embargo, em-bär'gō, *n.* [Sp. *embargo*, an embargo, embarrassment, lit. what serves as a bar—prefix *em* for *in*, and L.L. *barra*, a bar; akin *embarrass.*] A restraint or prohibition imposed by the public authorities of a country on merchant vessels, or other ships, to prevent their leaving its ports, sometimes amounting to an entire interdiction of commercial intercourse; a restraint or hindrance imposed on anything.—*v.t.* To put an embargo on; to subject to an embargo.

Embark, em-bärk', *v.t.* [Fr. *embarquer*—*en*, in, and *barque*, a bark. BARQUE.] To put or cause to enter on board a ship or boat; to engage, invest, or make to enter on in any affair.—*v.i.* To go on board of a ship, boat, or vessel; to engage or take a share in any affair; to enlist.—**Embarkation**, em-bär-kā'shon, *n.* The act of embarking; that which is embarked or put on board.

Embarrass, em-bar'as, *v.t.* [Fr. *embarrasser*, to embarrass, *embarras*, embarrassment—prefix *em*, and L.L. *barra*, a bar; akin *embargo.* BAR.] To derange, confuse, or entangle (affairs, business, &c.), so as to make a course of action difficult; to involve in pecuniary difficulties; to perplex, disconcert, or abash.—**Embarrassed**, em-bar'ast, *p.* and *a.* Entangled; involved; confused; disconcerted.—**Embarrassing**, em-bar'as-ing, *a.* Perplexing; adapted to perplex or embarrass.—**Embarrassingly**, em-bar'as-ing-li, *adv.* In an embarrassing manner.—**Embarrassment**, em-bar'as-ment, *n.* The state of being embarrassed; entanglement; perplexity arising from inability to pay one's debts; confusion of mind; abashment.

Embassador, em-bas'sa-dor, *n.* An ambassador. [This spelling is not now used, though *embassy* and not *ambassy* is the correct form.]—**Embassage**,† em'bas-sāj, *n.* An embassy; a message (*Shak.*).—**Embassy**, em'bas-si, *n.* [O.E. and Fr. *embassade.*] The mission of an ambassador; the charge or employment of an ambassador or envoy; the message of an ambassador; a message, especially a solemn or important message; the persons intrusted with ambassadorial functions; a legation; the official residence of an ambassador.

Embattle, em-bat'l, *v.t.*—*embattled, embattling.* [Prefix *em*, and *battle.*] To arrange in order of battle; to array for battle; to furnish with battlements.—*v.i.* To be ranged in order of battle.—**Embattled**, em-bat'ld, *p.* and *a.* Arrayed in order of battle; furnished with battlements; indented like a battlement.—**Embattlement**, em-bat'l-ment, *n.* An indented parapet; a battlement (which see).

Embay, em-bā', *v.t.* [Prefix *em*, and *bay.*] To inclose in a bay or inlet; to landlock.—**Embayment**, em-bā'ment, *n.* A portion of the sea closed in and sheltered by capes or promontories.

Embed, em-bed', *v.t.*—*embedded, embedding.* [Prefix *em*, and *bed.*] To lay in or as in a bed; to lay in surrounding matter.—**Embedment**, em-bed'ment, *n.* Act of embedding; state of being embedded.

Embellish, em-bel'lish, *v.t.* [Fr. *embellir*—prefix *em*, and *belle*, L. *bellus*, pretty, beautiful.] To make beautiful; to adorn; to beautify; to decorate; to deck.—**Embellisher**, em-bel'lish-ėr, *n.* One who or that which embellishes.—**Embellishment**, em-bel'lish-ment, *n.* The act of embellishing or adorning, or state of being embellished; that which embellishes or adorns; that which renders anything pleasing to the eye or agreeable to the taste; adornment; ornament; decoration.

Ember, em'bėr, *n.* [A.Sax. *æmyrian*, cinders; Dan. *emmer*, Icel. *eimyrja*, embers.] A small live coal, glowing piece of wood, &c.: used chiefly in the plural to signify live cinders or ashes; the smouldering remains of a fire.

Ember-days, *n.pl.* [A.Sax. *ymbrine, ymbren, embren*, the circle or course of the year, from *ymb* or *emb*, round, and *rinnan*, to run.] Days returning at certain seasons, being the Wednesday, Friday, and Saturday after the first Sunday in Lent, after Whitsunday, after Holyrood-day (September 14), and after St. Lucia's day (December 13), appointed in the Church of England for fasting and abstinence: called also *Embering-days*†.—**Ember-tide**, *n.* The season at which ember-days occur.—**Ember-week**, *n.* A week in which ember-days occur.

Ember-goose, *n.* [N. *ember-gaas*, G. *imber*; etym. uncertain.] A swimming bird, known also as the great northern diver.

Embezzle, em-bez'l, *v.t.*—*embezzled, embezzling.* [O.Fr. *embeasiler*, to filch, *besler*, to deceive; origin doubtful.] To appropriate fraudulently to one's own use what is intrusted to one's care; to apply to one's private use by a breach of trust, as a clerk or servant who misappropriates his employer's money or valuables.—**Embezzlement**, em-bez'l-ment, *n.* The act by which a clerk, servant, or person acting as such, fraudulently appropriates to his own use the money or goods intrusted to his care.—

Embezzler, em-bez'lėr, *n.* One who embezzles.

Embitter, em-bit'ėr, *v.t.* [Prefix *em*, and *bitter*.] To make bitter or more bitter; to make unhappy or grievous; to render distressing; to make more severe, poignant, or painful; to render more violent or malignant; to exasperate.—**Embitterer**, em-bit'ėr-ėr, *n.* One who or that which embitters. — **Embitterment**, em-bit'ėr-ment, *n.* The act of embittering.

Emblaze,‡ em-blāz', *v.t.—emblazed, emblazing.* [Prefix *em*, and *blaze*.] To kindle; to set in a blaze; to make to glitter or shine; to display or set forth conspicuously or ostentatiously; to blazon.

Emblazon, em-blā'zon, *v.t.* [Prefix *em*, and *blazon*.] To adorn with figures of heraldry or ensigns armorial; to depict or represent, as an armorial ensign on a shield; to set off with ornaments; to celebrate in laudatory terms; to sing the praises of.—**Emblazoner**, em-blā'zon-ėr, *n.* One that emblazons.—**Emblazonment**, em-blā'zon-ment, *n.* The act of emblazoning; that which is emblazoned.—**Emblazonry**, em-blā'zon-ri, *n.* The act or art of emblazoning; blazonry; heraldic decoration, as pictures or figures on shields, standards, &c.

Emblem, em'blem, *n.* [Fr. *emblême*; Gr. *emblēma*, from *emballō—em*, in, and *ballō*, to cast.] A kind of inlaid work or mosaic‡; a picture, figure, or other work of art representing one thing to the eye and another to the understanding; any object or its figure whose predominant quality symbolizes something else, as another quality or state; a symbolic figure; a type; a symbol; a device, as a balance used to symbolize justice.—**Emblematic, Emblematical**, em-ble-mat'ik, em-ble-mat'i-kal, *a.* Pertaining to or comprising an emblem; serving as an emblem or symbolic figure; symbolic.—**Emblematically**, em-ble-mat'i-kal-li, *adv.* In an emblematic manner. —**Emblematist**, em-blem'a-tist, *n.* An inventor of emblems.—**Emblematize, Emblemize**, em-blem'a-tīz, em'blem-īz, *v.t.—emblematized, emblematizing; emblemized, emblemizing.* To represent by an emblem; to serve as the emblem of.

Emblement, em'blē-ment, *n.* [From O.Fr. *embleer*, to sow with corn—prefix *em*, and *blé, bled*, L.L. *bladum*, corn.] *Law*, the produce or fruits of land sown or planted; growing crops annually produced: used chiefly in the plural.

Embody, em-bod'i, *v.t.—embodied, embodying.* [Prefix *em*, and *body*.] To lodge in a material body; to invest with a body; to incarnate; to clothe with a material form; to render obvious to the senses or mental perception (to *embody* thought in words); to form or collect into a body or united mass; to collect into a whole.—*v.i.* To unite into a body, mass, or collection; to coalesce.—**Embodier**, em-bod'i-ėr, *n.* One who embodies.—**Embodiment**, em-bod'i-ment, *n.* Act of embodying or investing with a body; the state of being embodied; bodily or material representation; the act of collecting or forming into a body or united whole.

Embogue, em-bōg', *v.i.* [Prefix *em*, and O.Fr. *bogue*, a mouth, Fr. *bouche*, from L. *bucca*, the cheek.] To discharge itself, as a river, into the sea or another river.

Embolden, em-bōl'dn, *v.t.* [Prefix *em*, and *bold*.] To give boldness or courage to; to encourage.—**Emboldener**, em-bōl'dn-ėr, *n.* One who emboldens.

Embolism, em'bol-izm, *n.* [Gr. *embolismos*, from *emballō*, to throw in, to insert.] The insertion of days, months, or years in an account of time, to produce regularity, intercalation; *surg.* the obstruction of a vessel by a clot of fibrine, a frequent cause of paralysis, and of gangrene of the part beyond the obstacle.—**Embolismal, Embolismic**, em-bo-liz'mal, em-bo-liz'mik, *a.* Pertaining to embolism or to intercalation; intercalated; inserted.

Embonpoint, äṅ-boṅ-pwaṅ, *n.* [Fr., from *em*, in, *bon*, good, and *point*, condition.] Plumpness; fleshiness; rotundity of figure; stoutness.

Emborder, em-bor'dėr, *v.t.* [Prefix *em*, and *border*.] To adorn with a border; to imborder.

Embosom, em-bö'zum, *v.t.* [Prefix *em*, and *bosom*.] To take into or hold in the bosom; to admit to the heart or affection; to cherish; to inclose in the midst; to surround.

Emboss, em-bos', *v.t.* [Prefix *em*, and *boss*.] To form bosses on; to fashion relief or raised work on; to cover with protuberances; to represent in relief or raised work; to represent in worked figures.—**Embossed**, em-bost', *a.* Flecked with bosses or flakes of foam. (*Shak.*)—**Embosser**, em-bos'ėr, *n.* One who embosses.—**Embossment**, em-bos'ment, *n.* The act of embossing; work in relief.

Embouchure, äṅ-bö-shür, *n.* [Fr., from prefix *em*, and *bouche*, mouth.] A mouth of a river; the mouth-hole of a wind-instrument of music; the shaping of the lips to the mouth-piece.

Embow, em-bō', *v.t.* [Prefix *em*, and *bow*.] To form like a bow; to vault. (*Mil.*)

Embowel, em-bou'el, *v.t.—embowelled, embowelling.* [Prefix *em*, and *bowel*.] To take out the bowels or entrails of; to eviscerate; to take out the internal parts of; to sink or inclose in; to imbed; to bury.—**Emboweller**, em-bou'el-ėr, *n.* One who embowels. —**Embowelment**, em-bou'el-ment, *n.* The act of taking out the bowels; evisceration.

Embower, em-bou'ėr, *v.i.* [Prefix *em*, and *bower*.] To lodge or rest in a bower.—*v.t.* To cover with a bower; to shelter with, or as with, trees; to form a bower for.

Embrace, em-brās', *v.t.—embraced, embracing.* [Fr. *embrasser*, to embrace—*em*, in, and *bras*, the arm. BRACE.] To take, clasp, or inclose in the arms; to press to the bosom in token of affection; to inclose, encompass, or contain; to encircle; to seize eagerly, in a figurative sense; to accept with cordiality (doctrines, religion); to comprehend, include, or take in; to comprise; to submit to (*Shak*)‡.—*v.i.* To join in an embrace.—*n.* Inclosure or clasp with the arms; pressure to the bosom with the arms; sexual intercourse; conjugal endearment. —**Embracement**, em-brās'ment, *n.* A clasp in the arms; a hug; embrace; sexual commerce (*Shak.*)‡.—**Embraceor, Embrasor**, em-brā'sėr, *n.* *Law*, one who practises embracery.—**Embracer**, em-brā'sėr, *n.* One who embraces.—**Embracery**, em-brā'sėr-i, *n.* *Law*, an attempt to influence a jury corruptly to one side, by promises, persuasions, entreaties, money, entertainments, or the like.

Embrasure, em-brā'zhür, *n.* [Fr., prefix *em*, and *braser*, to slope the edge of a stone.] *Fort.* an opening in a wall or parapet through which cannon are pointed and fired; the indent or crenelle of an embattlement; *arch.* the enlargement of the aperture of a door or window on the inside of the wall to give more room or admit more light.

Embrocate, em'brō-kāt, *v.t.—embrocated, embrocating.* [L.L. *embroco, embrocatum*, from Gr. *embrochē*, a fomentation, from *embrechō*, to foment—prefix *em* for *en*, in, and *brechō*, to wet.] *Med.* to moisten and rub, as a diseased part, with a liquid substance, as with spirit, oil, &c.—**Embrocation**, em-brō-kā'shon, *n.* The act of moistening and rubbing a diseased part with a cloth or sponge, dipped in some liquid substance, as spirit, oil, &c.; the liquid or lotion with which an affected part is rubbed or washed.

Embroglio, em-brōl'yō, *n.* IMBROGLIO.

Embroider, em-broi'dėr, *v.t.* [Prefix *em*, and *broider*. BROIDER.] To adorn with figures of needle-work, often raised above the surface.—**Embroiderer**, em-broi'dėr-ėr, *n.* One who embroiders.—**Embroidery**, em-broi'dėr-i, *n.* Work in gold, silver, silk, or other thread, formed by the needle on cloth, stuffs, and muslin into various figures; variegated needle-work; hence, variegated or diversified ornaments.

Embroil, em-broil', *v.t.* [Prefix *em*, and *broil*, a noisy quarrel.] To mix up or entangle in a quarrel or disturbance; to intermix confusedly; to involve in contention or trouble.—**Embroilment**, em-broil'ment, *n.* The act of embroiling; a state of contention, perplexity, or confusion.

Embrown, embroun', *v.t.* [Prefix *em*, and *brown*.] To make brown; to imbrown.

Embrue, em-brö'. IMBRUE.

Embryo, em'bri-ō, *n.* [Gr. *embryon—em*, in, and *bryō*, to be full of anything.] The first rudiments of an animal in the womb, before the several members are distinctly formed, after which it is called a *fœtus*; the rudimentary plant contained in the seed, produced by the action of the pollen on the ovule; the beginning or first state of anything, while yet in a rude and undeveloped condition; rudimentary state.—*Embryo buds*, spheroidal solid bodies formed in the bark of trees, and capable of developing into branches under favourable circumstances.—**Embryogeny**, em-bri-oj'e-ni, *n.* [Gr. *embryon*, and root *gen*, to produce.] The formation and development of embryos; that department of science that treats of such formation and development. —**Embryogenic**, em'bri-ō-jen"ik, *a.* Pertaining to embryogeny.—**Embryology**, em-bri-ol'o-ji, *n.* [Gr. *embryon*, and *logos*, discourse.] The doctrine of the development of embryos, whether in plants or animals.—**Embryologic, Embryological**, em'bri-ō-loj"ik, em'bri-ō-loj"i-kal, *a.* Of or belonging to embryology.—**Embryon**,‡ em'bri-on, *n.* An embryo. (*Mil.*).—**Embryonal, Embryonic**, em'-bri-on-al, em-bri-on'ik, *a.* Of or pertaining to an embryo, or the embryo stage. Also **Embryonary**, em'bri-o-na-ri, and **Embryotic**, em-bri-ot'ik.—**Embryotomy**, em-bri-ot'o-mi, *n.* [Gr. *embryon*, and *tomē*, a cutting.] The division of the fœtus in the uterus into fragments in order to effect delivery.—**Embryo-sac**, em'bri-ō, *n.* [Gr. *embryō*, an embryo.] *Bot.* a cell in the ovule within which the embryo is produced.

Emend, ē-mend', *v.t.* [L. *emendo*, to correct—*e*, priv., and *menda*, a spot or blemish. *Amend* and *mend* are virtually the same as this.] To remove faults or blemishes from; to amend; especially to amend by criticism of the text; to improve the reading of (an *emended* text of Vergil).—**Emendation**, ē-men-dā'shon, *n.* The act of emending; removal of errors or corruptions from the text of a book or writing; a textual alteration or correction.—**Emendator**, ē'men-dā-tėr, *n.* One who emends. —**Emendatory**, ē-men'da-to-ri, *a.* Contributing to emendation or correction.

Emerald, em'e-rald, *n.* [Fr. *emeraude*, Sp. *esmeralda*, It. *smeraldo*; from L. *smaragdus*, Gr. *smaragdos*, an emerald.] A precious stone whose colours are a pure lively green, varying to a pale, yellowish, bluish, or grass green, akin to the beryl, found especially in South America; a variety of printing type intermediate between minion and nonpareil.—*a.* Of a bright green, like emerald; printed with the size of type known as emerald.—*Emerald green*, a durable pigment of a vivid light-green colour, prepared from the arseniate of copper.—*Emerald Isle*, Ireland. From the green verdure of the grass, or from its being set like an emerald in the sea. First so named in song by Drennan, 1754-1820.

Emerge, ē-mėrj', *v.i—emerged, emerging.* [L. *emergo, emersum—e.* out, and *mergo*, to *plunge*, as in *immerge, submerge*. MERGE.] To rise out of a fluid or other covering or surrounding substance; to issue or proceed from something; to reappear after being eclipsed; to leave the sphere of the obscuring object; to rise out of a state of depression or obscurity; to come to notice.—**Emergence**, ē-mėr'jens, *n.* The act of emerging.—**Emergency**, ē-mėr'jen-si, *n.* The act of emerging; sudden occasion; unexpected casualty; unforeseen occurrence; any event or combination of circumstances calling for immediate action; pressing necessity. — **Emergent**, ē-mėr'jent, *a.* Emerging; rising into view or notice; coming suddenly; unexpected; calling for immediate action; urgent; pressing. — **Emergently**, ē-mėr'jent-li, *adv.* In an emergent manner.—**Emersion**, ē-mėr'shon, *n.* The act of emerging or rising out of a fluid or other substance; the act of coming forth to view; the reappearance of a heavenly body after an eclipse of occultation.

Emeritus, ē-mer'i-tus, *a.* [L. *emeritus*, having served out his time.—*e* out, and *mereor*, *meritus*, to merit, earn, serve.] Discharged from the performance of public duty with honour, on account of infirmity, age, or long service; as, a professor *emeritus*. Sometimes used as a noun.

Emerods, em'e-rodz, *n. pl.* [Corrupted from *hemorrhoids*.] Hemorrhoids; piles. [O.T.]

Emersion. Under EMERGE.

Emery, em'e-ri, *n.* [Fr. *émeri*, O.Fr. *esmeril*, from It. *smeriglio*, from Gr. *smyris*, *smiris*, *smēris*, from *smaō*, to rub.] A mineral substance, an amorphous variety of corundum and sapphire, varying in colour from deep gray to bluish or blackish gray, sometimes brownish, used for grinding and polishing metals, hard stones, and glass.—**Emery-cloth**, **Emery-paper**, *n.* Cloth or paper which has been first covered with a thin coating of glue and then dusted with emery powder, used for polishing.

Emetic, ē-met'ik, *a.* [Gr. *emetikos*, from *emeō*, to vomit.] *Med.* inducing to vomit; exciting the stomach to discharge its contents by the mouth.—*n.* A medicine that provokes vomiting.—**Emetically**, ē-met'i-kal-li, *adv.* In such a manner as to excite vomiting. — **Emetin**, em'e-tin, *n.* The active principle of ipecacuanha.

Emeu, **Emew**. ē'mū, *n.* EMU.

Emeute, e-müt', *n.* [Fr. *émeute*, from L. *ex*, intens., and *moveo*, *motum*, to move.] A seditious commotion; a riot; a tumult; an outbreak.

Emiction, ē-mik'shon, *n.* [L. *e*, and *mictio*, a making water.] The discharging of urine; urine.—**Emictory**, ē-mik'to-ri, *a.* Causing or promoting the flow of urine; diuretic. —*n.* A diuretic.

Emigrate, em'i-grāt, *v.i.*—*emigrated*, *emigrating*. [L. *emigro*, *emigratum*, to migrate, to emigrate—*e*, *out*, and *migro*, to migrate.] To quit one country, state, or region and settle in another; to remove from one country or state to another for the purpose of residence. — **Emigrant**, em'i-grant, *a.* Emigrating; pertaining to emigration or emigrants. — **Emigrant**, em'i-grant, *n.* One who emigrates.—**Emigration**, em-i-grā'shon, *n.* The act of emigrating; departure of inhabitants from one country or state to another for the purpose of residence; a body of emigrants.—**Emigrational**, em-i-grā'shon-al, *a.* Relating to emigration. — **Emigrationist**, em-i-grā'shon-ist, *n.* An advocate for or promoter of emigration.—**Émigré**, ā-mē-grā, *n.* [Fr.] One of the French nobles who became refugees during the revolution which commenced in 1789.

Eminence, em'i-nens, *n.* [Fr. *éminence*, from L. *eminentia*, from *eminens*, *eminentis*, from *emineo*—*e*, out, and *mineo*, to project, to jut.] A rising ground; a hill of moderate elevation; a part rising or projecting beyond the rest or above the surface; a projection; a prominence; an elevated situation among men; station above men in general; rank; distinction; celebrity; conspicuousness; a title of honour given to cardinals and others.—**Eminency**,† em'i-nen-si, *n.* Same as *Eminence*.—**Eminent**, em'i-nent, *a.* Standing out above other things‡; prominent‡; lofty‡; exalted in rank; high in office or public estimation; conspicuous; remarkable; distinguished.—**Eminently**, em'i-nent-li, *adv.* In an eminent manner or position.

Emir, em'ėr, *n.* [Ar. *amir*, a commander; from *amara*, Heb. *âmar*, to command.] The title given by Mohammedans to all independent chiefs, to the heads of certain departments, and to all the real or supposed descendants of Mohammed, through his daughter Fatimah.

Emissary, em'is-sa-ri, *n.* [L. *emissarius*, from *emitto*, *emissum*, to send out—*e*, out, and *mitto*, to send. EMIT.] A person sent on a mission; particularly, a secret agent, or one who carries on private negotiations or business; a spy; an outlet or channel by which water is drawn from a lake.—**Emissory**, ē-mis'o-ri, *a.* Sending or conveying out; excretory.—**Emit**, ē-mit', *v.t.* —*emitted*, *emitting*. [L. *emitto*—*e*, out, and *mitto*, *missum*, to send, whence *mission*, *missile*, *missive*, *message*, &c.] To throw or give out (light, heat, steam, &c.); to send forth; to vent; to cause or allow to issue or emanate.—**Emission**, ē-mish'on, *n.* [L. *emissio*.] The act of emitting or of sending or throwing out; that which is emitted, issued, sent, or thrown out.

Emmenagogue, em-mē'na-gog, *n.* [Gr. *emmēna*, the menses—*em*, in, *mēn*, *mēnos*, month, and *agō*, to lead.] A medicine taken to promote the menstrual discharge. —**Emmenagogic**, em-mē'na-goj"ik, *a.* Of or pertaining to an emmenagogue; promoting the menstrual discharge.

Emmensite, em'menz-īt, *n.* [From *Emmens*, the inventor.] A powerful explosive recently introduced for use in torpedoes, &c.

Emmet, em'met, *n.* [A.Sax. *æmette*, *æmete*, O.E. *emet*, *amet*, *amt*, and finally *ant*; G. *ameise*, *âmse*, an ant. Comp. *aunt*, from L. *amita*.] An ant or pismire.

Emmetropia, em-me-trō'pi-a, *n.* [Gr. *en*, in, *metron*, measure, *ōps*, eye.] The state of the eye being normal as regards the focal length: opposed to hypermetropia.

Emollescence, em-ol-les'ens, *n.* [L. *e*, and *mollesco*, to grow soft, from *mollis*, soft.] That degree of softness in a body beginning to melt which alters its shape; the first stage of fusibility.—**Emolliate**, ē-mol'li-āt, *v.t.*—*emolliated*, *emolliating*. [L. *emollio*, to soften.] To soften; to render effeminate. —**Emollient**, ē-mol'li-ent, *a.* [L. *emolliens*, *emollientis*, ppr. of *emollio*.] Softening; making supple; relaxing the solids.—*n.* A medicine which softens and relaxes living tissues that are inflamed or too tense.

Emolument, ē-mol'ū-ment, *n.* [L. *emolumentum*, a working out, from *e*, and *molior*, to exert one's self, from *moles*, a heavy mass.] The profit arising from office or employment; compensation for services; remuneration; salary; income; profit; advantage or gain in general.—**Emolumental**,† ē-mol'ū-men"tal, *a.* Producing profit; profitable; advantageous.

Emotion, ē-mō'shon, *n.* [L. *emotio*, from *emoveo*, *emotum*—*e*, out, up, and *moveo*, to move.] A moving of the mind or soul; a state of excited feeling of any kind, as pleasure, pain, grief, joy, astonishment; one of the three fundamental properties of the human mind, the other two being *volition* and *intellect*.—**Emotional**, ē-mō'shon-al, *a.* Pertaining to or characterized by emotion; attended by or producing emotion; liable to emotion.—**Emotionalism**, ē-mō'shon-al-izm, *n.* The character of being emotional; tendency to emotional excitement.—**Emotive**,† ē-mō'tiv, *a.* Emotional; indicating or exciting emotion. — **Emotively**,† ē-mō'tiv-li, *adv.* In an emotive manner. — **Emotiveness**,† ē-mō'tiv-nes, *n.* The state or quality of being emotive.

Empale, em-pāl', *v.t.*—*empaled*, *empaling*. [Fr. *empaler*, from L.L. *impalare*—L. *in*, and *palus*, a pale, a stake.] To fence or fortify with stakes or otherwise‡; to put to death by fixing on a stake set upright.—**Empalement**, em-pāl'ment, *n.* A fencing, fortifying, or inclosing with stakes; a putting to death by thrusting a stake into the body.

Empannel, **Empannelment**, em-pan'el, em-pan'el-ment. IMPANEL.

Emperor, em'pėr-ėr, *n.* [Fr. *empereur*, from L. *imperator*, from *impero*, *imperatum*, to command—prefix *im*, and *paro*, to prepare, to order.] The sovereign or supreme monarch of an empire; a title of dignity superior to that of king.—**Empress**, em'pres, *n.* The consort or spouse of an emperor; a woman who rules an empire.—**Empery**, em'pe-ri, *n.* Empire; power. (*Poet.*)

Emphasis, em'fa-sis, *n.* [Gr. *emphasis*, a setting forth, from *emphainō*, to indicate —*em*, in, and *phainō*, to show (whence *phenomenon*).] A particular stress of utterance or force of voice given to the words or parts of a discourse whose signification the speaker intends to impress specially upon his audience; a peculiar impressiveness of expression or weight of thought; impressiveness; vividness.—**Emphasize**, em'fa-sīz, *v.t.* — *emphasized*, *emphasizing*. To utter or pronounce with emphasis; to lay particular stress upon; to render emphatic.—**Emphatic**, **Emphatical**, em-fat'ik, em-fat'i-kal, *a.* Having emphasis; uttered with emphasis; forcible; expressive. —**Emphatically**, em-fat'i-kal-li, *adv.* In an emphatic manner. — **Emphaticalness**,† em-fat'i-kal-nes, *n.*

Emphractic, em-frak'tik, *a.* [Gr. *emphraktikos*, obstructing, from *emphrassō*, to block up.] *Med.* having the quality of closing the pores of the skin.

Emphysema, em-fi-sē'ma, *n.* [Gr. *emphysēma*, from *emphysaō*, to inflate.] *Med.* any white, shining, elastic, indolent tumour of the integuments, caused by the introduction of air into the cellular tissue.—**Emphysematous**, **Emphysematose**, em-fi-sē'ma-tus, em-fi-sē'ma-tōs, *a.* Pertaining to emphysema; swelled; *bot.* resembling a bladder.

Empire, em'pīr, *n.* [Fr. *empire*, from L. *imperium*. EMPEROR.] Supreme power in governing; supreme dominion; sovereignty; imperial power; the territory or countries under the dominion of an emperor or other powerful sovereign; usually a territory of greater extent than a kingdom; supreme control; rule; sway.

Empiric, em-pir'ik, *n.* [L. *empiricus*, from Gr. *empeirikos*, experienced—*en*, in, and *peira*, a trial.] One who relies only on experience and observation, as opposed to theory based on scientific conclusions; specifically, a physician who enters on practice without a regular professional education; an ignorant pretender to medical skill; a quack; a charlatan.—**Empiric**, **Empirical**, em-pir'i-kal, *a.* Pertaining to experiments or experience; depending altogether upon the observation of phenomena; depending upon experience or observation alone, without due regard to science and theory.—**Empirically**, em-pir'i-kal-li, *adv.* In an empirical manner.—**Empiricism**, em-pir'i-sizm, *n.* The quality or method of being empirical; the practice of an empiric; quackery.

Emplacement, em-plās'ment, *n.* A position specially assigned to a gun or group of guns. A solid platform with accessories prepared for the support of a gun or guns.

Employ, em-ploi', *v.t.* [Fr. *employer*, from L. *implicare*, to enfold, involve, engage—*in*, and *plicare*, to fold, seen also in *deploy*, *display*. PLY.] To occupy the time, attention, and labour of; to keep busy or at work; to make use of; to use as an instrument or means to, or as materials in forming anything; to engage in one's service; to use as an agent or substitute in transacting business; to apply or devote to an object; to occupy.—*n.* That in which one is employed; a state of being engaged by a master; occupation; employment.—**Employable**, em-ploi'a-bl, *a.* Capable of being employed. —**Employee**, em-ploi'ē, *n.* [The English form of the French *employé*, one who is employed, especially a clerk.] One who works for an employer or master; a clerk, workman, or other person working for salary or wages.—**Employer**, em-ploi'ėr, *n.* One who employs; one who uses; one who engages or keeps servants in employment.—**Employment**, em-ploi'ment, *n.* The act of employing or using; the state of being employed; occupation; business; that which engages the head or hands; vocation; trade; profession; work.

Empoison, em-poi′zn, *v.t.* [Prefix *em*, and *poison*.] To poison; to taint with poison or venom; to embitter; to destroy all pleasure in.—**Empoisoner**, em-poi′zn-ėr, *n.* One who or that which empoisons.

Emporium, em-pō′ri-um, *n.* [L., from Gr. *emporion*, an emporium or mart, from *emporos*, a merchant—*en*, in, and *poros*, a way, of same root as A.Sax. *faran*, to go, E. *fare*.] A town or city which is a center of commerce, or to which sellers and buyers resort from different countries; a commercial center; a department store.

Empoverish, em-pov′ėr-ish, *v.t.* Same as *Impoverish*.

Empower, em-pou′ėr, *v.t.* [Prefix *em*, and *power*.] To give legal or moral power or authority to; to authorize, as by law, commission, letter of attorney, verbal licence, &c.; to warrant; to license.

Empress. Under EMPEROR.

Empressement, äṅ-präs′mäṅ, *n.* [Fr.] Eagerness; cordiality.

Emprise, Emprize, em-prīz′, *n.* [O.Fr. *emprise*—prefix *em*, and *prise*, a taking, from *prendre*, to take.] An undertaking; an enterprise; adventure. (*Poet.*)

Empty, em′ti, *a.* [A.Sax. *aemti*, *aemtig*, *ėmtig*, vacant, free, idle; *aemtian*, to be at leisure, to be vacant; from *aemta*, *ėmta*, quiet, leisure.] Containing nothing, or nothing but air; void of contents or appropriate contents; destitute of solid matter; not filled; void; devoid; destitute of force or effect, or of sense or sincerity; wanting substance or solidity; wanting reality; unsatisfactory; not able to fill the mind or the desires; destitute of sense, knowledge, or judgment; vain; ignorant; unfruitful, or producing nothing (O.T.); without effect (O.T.)‡.—*n.* An empty packing-case or the like.—*v.t. emptied, emptying.* To remove the contents from; to discharge; to render void.—*v.i.* To pour out or discharge contents; to become empty.—**Emptier**, em′ti-ėr, *n.* One who or that which empties.—**Emptiness**, em′ti-nes, *n.* A state of being empty.

Empyema, em-pi-ē′ma, *n.* [Gr. *empyēma*, from *em*, in and *pyon*, pus.] *Med.* a collection of pus, blood, or other fluid matter, in some cavity of the body, especially in the cavity of the chest.

Empyreal, em-pir′ē-al, or em-pī-rē′al, *a.* [L.L. *empyrœus*, from Gr. *empyros*, prepared by fire, fiery, scorched—*en*, and *pyr*, fire.] Formed of pure fire or light; refined beyond aerial substance; pertaining to the highest and purest region of heaven.—**Empyrean**, em-pī-rē′an, *a.* Empyreal.—*n.* The highest heaven, where the pure element of fire was supposed by the ancients to exist.—**Empyreuma**, em-pī-rū′ma, *n.* [Gr. *empyreuō*, to set on fire—*em*, in, and *pyr*, fire.] *Chem.* the odour of some oily animal or vegetable substances, when burned in close vessels, or when subjected to destructive distillation. — **Empyreumatic, Empyreumatical**, em-pī′rū-mat″ik, em-pī′rū-mat″ik-al, *a.* Pertaining to or having the taste or smell of slightly burned animal or vegetable substances.

Emu, Emeu, ē-mū′, *n.* A large cursorial bird, closely allied to the ostrich and the cassowary, but differing from the former in having three toes, found in Australia.

Emulate, em′ū-lāt, *v.t.*—*emulated, emulating.* [L. *æmulor*, *æmulatus*, to make one's self a rival, from *æmulus*, a rival.] To strive to equal or excel in qualities or actions; to vie with; to come forward as a rival of. — **Emulation**, em-ū-lā′shon, *n.* The act of emulating; rivalry; desire of superiority, attended with effort to attain it; ambition to equal or excel; envy, jealousy, or malicious rivalry (*Shak.*).—**Emulative**, em′ū-lā-tiv, *a.* Inclined to emulation; striving to emulate.—**Emulatively**, em′ū-lā-tiv-li, *adv.* In an emulative manner.—**Emulator**, em′ū-lā-tėr, *n.* One who emulates; a rival; a competitor.—**Emulatory**, em′ū-la-to-ri, *a.* Arising out of emulation; indicating emulation; of or belonging to emulation.—**Emulous**, em′ū-lus, *a.* Desirous or eager to imitate, equal, or excel another; desirous of like excellence with another (*emulous* of another's prowess); rivalling; engaged in competition; factious; contentious (*Shak.*).—**Emulously**, em′ū-lus-li, *adv.* In an emulous manner. — **Emulousness**, em′ū-lus-nes, *n.*

Emulsion, ē-mul′shon, *n.* [From L. *emulgeo*, *emulsum*, to milk out — *e*, out, and *mulgeo*, to milk.] A soft liquid remedy of a colour and consistence resembling milk; any milk-like mixture prepared by uniting oil and water, by means of another substance, saccharine or mucilaginous. — **Emulsify**, ē-mul′si-fī, *v.t.* — *emulsified, emulsifying.* To make or form into an emulsion. Also **Emulsionize** in same sense.—**Emulsive**, ē-mul′siv, *a.* Softening; milk-like; yielding oil by expression (*emulsive* seeds); producing a milk-like substance.

Emunctory, ē-mungk′to-ri, *n.* [L. *emungo*, *emunctum*, to wipe.] *Anat.* any part of the body which serves to carry off excrementitious or waste matter; an excretory duct.

Enable, en-ā′bl, *v.t.* — *enabled, enabling.* [Prefix *en*, and *able*.] To make able; to supply with power, physical, moral, or legal; to furnish with sufficient power, ability, or authority; to render fit or competent; to authorize.

Enact, en-akt′, *v.t.* [Prefix *en*, and *act*.] To pass into an act or established law; to give sanction to (a bill or legislative proposal); to decree; to act or perform (*Shak.*)‡; to act the part of on the stage (*Shak.*)‡.—**Enactive**, en-ak′tiv, *a.* Having power to enact, or establish as a law.—**Enactment**, en-akt′ment, *n.* The passing of a bill or legislative proposal into a law; a law enacted; a decree; an act.—**Enactor**, en-ak′tėr, *n.* One who enacts.

Enaliosaur, Enaliosaurian, en-al′i-o-sar, en-al′i-o-sa′ri-an, *n.* [Gr. *enalios*, living in the sea, and *sauros*, lizard.] A fossil marine reptile of great size, such as the ichthyosaurus.

Enallage, en-al′la-jē, *n.* [Gr. *enallagē*, change.] *Gram.* a figure consisting in the change of one word for another, or the substitution of one gender, number, case, person, tense, &c., of the same word for another, as 'We, the king'

Enamel, en-am′el, *n.* [Prefix *en*, and old *amel*, *ammel*, *amile*, enamel, from O.Fr. *esmail*, Mod.Fr. *émail*, enamel, from G. *schmelzen*, to smelt. SMELT.] A colored substance of the nature of glass, differing from it by a greater degree of fusibility or opacity, used as an ornamental coating for various articles; a smooth, glossy surface of various colors, resembling enamel; the smooth hard substance which covers the crown of a tooth, overlying the dentine.—*v.t.*—*enameled, enameling.* To lay enamel on; to paint in enamel; to form a glossy surface like enamel upon; to variegate or adorn with different colors.—*v.i.* To practice the use of enamel or the art of enameling.—**Enameler, Enamelist**, en-am′el-ėr, en-am′el-ist, *n.* One who enamels; one whose occupation is to lay on enamels.

Enamor, en-am′ėr, *v.t.* [O.Fr. *enamourer* —*en*, and *amour*, L. *amor*, love.] To inflame with love; to charm; to captivate: commonly in the past participle, and with *of* or *with* before the person or thing that captivates.

Enantiosis, ē-nan′ti-ō″sis, *n.* [Gr., contradiction, from *enantios*, opposite.] *Rhet.* a figure of speech by which what is meant to be conveyed in the affirmative is stated in the negative, and *vice versâ*.

Enarthrosis, en-är-thrō′sis, *n.* [Gr. *enarthrōsis*—*en*, in, and *arthron*, a joint.] *Anat.* a ball-and-socket joint; an articulation which consists in the insertion of the round end of a bone in the cup-like cavity of another.

Encænia, en-sē′ni-a, *n.* [Gr. *enkainia*.] Dedication, festival of commemoration.

Encage, en-kāj′, *v.i.*—*encaged, encaging.* [Prefix *en*, and *cage*.] To shut up or confine in a cage; to coop up.

Encamp, en-kamp′, *v.i.* [Prefix *en*, and *camp*.] To take up position in a camp; to make a camp.—*v.t.* To form into or place in a camp (*Shak.*)†.—**Encampment**, en-kamp′ment, *n.* The act of encamping; the place where a body of men is encamped, together with the tents or other conveniences set in order for their accommodation; a camp.

Encaustic, en-kas′tik, *a.* [Gr. *enkaustikos*—*en*, and *kaustikos*, caustic, from *kaiō*, to burn.] Pertaining to the art of enameling and to painting in colors that are fixed by burning.—*Encaustic painting*, a kind of painting in which, by heating or burning, the colors are rendered permanent in all their original splendor—*Encaustic tiles*, decorated tiles of baked pottery, used in ornamental pavements, to cover parts of walls, &c.

Enceinte, äṅ-saṅt, *n.* [Fr., pp. of *enceindre*, from L. *incingere*, to gird in—*in*, and *cingere*, to gird.] *Fort.* the wall or rampart which surrounds a place; the area thus surrounded.

Enceinte, äṅ-saṅt, *a.* [Fr., L. *in*, not, and *cinctus*, pp. of *cingo*, to gird.] Pregnant; with child.

Encephalon, Encephalos, en-sef′a-lon, en-sef′a-los, *n.* [Gr. *enkephalos*, within the head—*en*, in, and *kephalē*, the head.] The contents of the skull, consisting of the cerebrum, cerebellum, medulla oblongata, and membranes; the brain.—**Encephalic**, en-sē-fal′ik, *a.* Situated in the head; belonging to the head or brain.—**Encephalalgia**, en′se-fa-lal″ji-a, *n.* [Gr. *en*, *kephalē*, and *algos*, pain.] *Med.* headache, cephalalgy. — **Encephalitis**, en-sef′a-lī″tis, *n.* Inflammation of the brain.—**Encephaloid**, en-sef′a-loid, *a.* Resembling the matter of the brain.—**Encephalous**, en-sef′a-lus, *a.* *Zool.* possessing a distinct head: opposed to *acephalous*.

Enchain, en-chān′, *v.t.* [Prefix *en*, and *chain*.] To fasten with a chain; to bind or hold in chains; to hold in bondage; to hold fast, restrain, confine; to link together; to connect†. — **Enchainment**, en-chān′-ment, *n.* The act of enchaining or state of being enchained; concatenation.

Enchant, en-chänt′, *v.t.* [Fr. *enchanter*—*en*, and *chanter*, to sing; L. *incanto*—*in*, and *canto*, freq. of *cano*, to sing. CHANT, CANT.] To practise sorcery or witchcraft on; to subdue by charms or spells; to hold as by a spell; to fascinate; to delight in a high degree; to charm, captivate, or enrapture.—**Enchanter**, en-chän′tėr, *n.* One who enchants; a sorcerer or magician; one who practises enchantment or pretends to perform surprising things by the agency of demons; one who charms or delights.—**Enchanting**, en-chän′ting, *a.* Charming; delighting; ravishing.—**Enchantingly**, en-chän′ting-li, *adv.* In an enchanting manner.—**Enchantment**, en-chänt′ment, *n.* The act of enchanting; the use of magic arts, spells, or charms; incantation; that which enchants; an influence or power which fascinates or delights; overpowering influence of delight.—**Enchantress**, en-chänt′res, *n.* A female enchanter.

Enchase, en-chās′, *v.t.*—*enchased, enchasing.* [Fr. *enchâsser*—*en*, and *châsse*, a frame, from L. *capsa*, a chest, a case, from *capio*, to take or receive.] To incase or inclose in a border or rim; to surround with an ornamental setting, as a gem with gold; to adorn by embossed work; to beautify by some design or figure in low relief.

Enchorial, Enchoric, en-kō′ri-al, en-kor′ik, *a.* [Gr. *enchōrios*, in or of the country—*en*, in, and *chōra*, a country.] Belonging to or used in a country; native; indigenous; demotic (which see).

Encircle, en-sėr′kl, *v.t.*—*encircled, encircling.* To form a circle about; to inclose or surround; to encompass; to environ; to embrace.

Enclasp, en-klasp′, *v.t.* To clasp; to embrace.

Enclave, äṅ-kläv, *n.* [Fr.—*en*, in, and L. *clavis*, a key.] A place or country which is entirely surrounded by the territories of another power.

Enclitic, Enclitical, en-klit′ik, en-klit′i-kal, *a.* [Gr. *enklitikos*, inclined, from *enklinō*, to incline—*en*, in, and *klinō*, to lean.] *Gram.* subjoined, and as it were leaning: said of a word or particle which always follows another word, and is so closely connected with the preceding word as to seem to be a part of it.—**Enclitic**, *n. Gram.* an enclitic word.—**Enclitically**, en-klit′i-kal-li, *adv.* In an enclitic manner.

Enclose, Enclosure, en-klōz′, en-klō′-zhūr. INCLOSE.

Encomium, en-kō′mi-um, *n.* [Gr. *enkōmion*, a laudatory ode, an encomium—*en*, in, and *kōmos*, a revel, a procession in honour.] A eulogy or commendation; a statement in praise of something or somebody; a panegyric.—**Encomiast**, en-kō′-mi-ast, *n.* [Gr. *enkōmiastēs*.] One who praises another; a panegyrist.—**Encomiastic, Encomiastical**, en-kō′mi-as″tik, en-kō′mi-as″ti-kal, *a.* Bestowing praise; laudatory.—**Encomiastically**, en-kō′-mi-as″ti-kal-li, *adv.* In an encomiastic manner.

Encompass, en-kum′pas, *v.t.* To form a circle about; to encircle; to environ, inclose, or surround; to shut in; to go or sail round.—**Encompassment**, en-kum′pas-ment, *n.* The act of encompassing or state of being encompassed.

Encore, äṅ-kōr, *adv.* [Fr., from L. (*in*) *hanc horam*, (to) this hour.] Again; once more: used by the auditors and spectators in calling for a repetition of a particular performance, song, or the like.—*v.t.*—*encored, encoring.* To call for a repetition of; to call upon to repeat.

Encounter, en-koun′tėr, *n.* [Fr. *encontre*—*en*, and *contre*, L. *contra*, against.] A meeting, particularly a sudden or accidental meeting of two or more persons; a meeting in contest; a fight; a conflict; a skirmish; a battle; an intellectual or moral conflict or contest; controversy; debate.—*v.t.* To meet face to face; to meet suddenly or unexpectedly; to meet in opposition or in a hostile manner; to engage with in battle; to come upon or light upon; to meet with; to meet and oppose; to resist.—*v.i.* To meet face to face; to meet unexpectedly; to meet in hostile fashion; to come together in combat; to conflict.—**Encounterer**, en-koun′tėr-ėr, *n.* One who encounters.

Encourage, en-kur′āj, *v.t.*—*encouraged, encouraging.* [Fr. *encourager*—*en*, and *courage*.] To give courage to; to inspire with courage; to embolden; to animate or inspirit; to help forward; to support or countenance.—**Encouragement**, en-kur′āj-ment, *n.* The act of encouraging; that which encourages; incitement; incentive.—**Encourager**, en-kur′ā-jėr, *n.* One who encourages.—**Encouraging**, en-kur′-ā-jing, *p.* and *a.* Exciting courage; furnishing ground to hope for success.—**Encouragingly**, en-kur′ā-jing-li, *adv.* In an encouraging manner.

Encrinite, en′kri-nīt, *n.* [Gr. *en*, in, and *krinon*, a lily.] A crinoid, lily-star, or stone-lily; a common name for those fossil echinodermata that have long many-jointed stalks supporting the somewhat flower-like animal.—**Encrinal, Encrinic**, en-krī′-nal, en-krin′ik, *a.* Relating to or containing encrinites. Also **Encrinital**, en-kri-nī′-tal, and **Encrinitic**, en-kri-nit′ik.

Encroach, en-krōch′, *v.i.* [Prefix *en*, and Fr. *crocher*, to hook on, from *croc*, a hook; E. *crook* (which see).] To trespass or intrude on the rights and possessions of another; to take possession of what belongs to another by gradual advances into his limits or jurisdiction (to *encroach on* one's privileges); to make inroads (the sea sometimes *encroaches on* the land); to assail gradually and stealthily.—**Encroacher**, en-krō′chėr, *n.* One who encroaches.—**Encroachingly**, en-krō′ching-li, *adv.* By way of encroachment.—**Encroachment**, en-krōch′ment, *n.* The act of encroaching; undue or unlawful trespass on the privileges, jurisdiction, &c., of another; that which is taken by encroaching.

Encrust, en-krust′, *v.t.* To incrust.

Encumber, en-kum′bėr, *v.t.* [Prefix *en*, and *cumber*; Fr. *encombrer*.] To impede the motion of with a load, burden, or anything inconvenient; to clog; to load; to embarrass; to load, as an estate, with debts.—**Encumberingly**, en-kum′bėr-ing-li, *adv.* In a manner to encumber or impede.—**Encumbrance**, en-kum′brans, *n.* Anything that impedes action or renders it difficult and laborious; clog, load, burden, impediment; liability resting on an estate; a legal claim on an estate, for the discharge of which the estate is liable, as a mortgage, &c.—**Encumbrancer**, en-kum′bran-sėr, *n.* One who holds an encumbrance on an estate.

Encyclic, Encyclical, en-sī′klik, en-sī′-kli-kal, *a.* [Gr. *enkyklikos*—*en*, in, and *kyklos*, a circle.] Sent to many persons or places; intended for many, or for a whole order of men; circular: used often as a substantive in both forms, and generally applied to a letter on some important occasion sent by the pope to the bishops.

Encyclopædia, en-sī′klō-pē″di-a, *n.* [Gr. *enkyklopaideia*—*en*, in, *kyklos*, a circle, and *paideia*, instruction.] A work in which various branches of knowledge are discussed separately, and usually in alphabetical order; a kind of dictionary of things, not words; a cyclopædia; specially of the great French Encyclopædia projected by Diderot, D'Alembert, and others.—**Encyclopædic, Encyclopædical, Encyclopædian**, en-sī′klō-pē″dik, en-sī′klō-pē″di-kal, en-sī′klō-pē″di-an, *a.* Pertaining to an encyclopædia; such as is embraced in an encyclopædia; universal as regards knowledge and information.—**Encyclopædism**, en-sī′klō-pē-dizm, *n.* The making of encyclopædias; the possession of a wide range of information; extensive learning.—**Encyclopædist**, en-sī′klō-pē-dist, *n.* The compiler of an encyclopædia, or one who assists in such compilation; a person whose knowledge is of a very wide range. These words are also spelled *Encyclopedia*, &c.

Encyst, en-sist′, *v.t.* [Gr. *en*, in, and *kystis*, a bladder, a pouch.] To inclose in a cyst, sac, or vesicle.—**Encystation, Encystment**, en-sis-tā′shon, en-sist′ment, *n.* A process undergone by certain Protozoa and Infusoria previous to fission, in which they become coated with a secretion of gelatinous matter, ultimately inclosing the body in a hard cyst.—**Encysted**, en-sis′ted, *p.* and *a.* Inclosed in a bag, bladder, or vesicle: applied to tumours which consist of a fluid or other matter inclosed in a sac or cyst.

End, end, *n.* [A.Sax. *ende* = Icel. *endi*, Dan. and G. *ende*, Goth. *andeis*, the end; Skr. *anta*, end, death.] The extreme point of a line, or of anything that has more length than breadth; the termination, conclusion, or last part of anything, as of a portion of time, of an action, of a state of things, of a quantity of materials; the close of life; death; consequence; issue; result; the ultimate point or thing at which one aims or directs his views; purpose intended; scope; aim; drift.—*On end*, resting on one end; upright; also, continuously; uninterruptedly.—*To make both ends meet*, to keep one's expenditure within one's income, or at least to keep them equal.—*v.t.* To put an end to or be the end of; to finish; to close, conclude, terminate; to destroy; to put to death.—*v.i.* To come to an end; to terminate; to close; to conclude; to cease.—**Ender**, en′dėr, *n.* One who or that which ends or finishes.—**Ending**, en′ding, *n.* The act of putting or coming to an end; conclusion; termination; the last part; the final syllable or letter of a word.—**Endless**, end′les, *a.* Without end; having no end or conclusion: applied to length and duration; perpetually recurring; interminable; incessant; continual; without object, purpose, or use; fruitless; forming a closed loop and working continuously round two wheels or pulleys in the same plane (an *endless* rope, chain, saw).—*Endless screw*, a screw on a revolving shaft, the thread of which gears into a wheel with skew teeth.—**Endlessly**, end′les-li, *adv.* In an endless manner.—**Endlessness**, end′les-nes, *n.* The state or quality of being endless.—**Endlong**, end′long, *a.* or *adv.* With the end forward; lengthwise.—**Endways, Endwise**, end′wāz, end′-wīz, *adv.* On the end; erectly; in an upright position; with the end forward.—**End-all**, *n.* What ends all; conclusion. (*Shak.*)

Endamage, en-dam′āj, *v.t.*—*endamaged, endamaging.* To bring loss or damage to; to damage; to harm; to injure.—**Endamagement**, endam′āj-ment, *n.* Act of endamaging. (*Shak.*)

Endanger, en-dān′jėr, *v.t.* To put in hazard; to bring into danger or peril; to expose to loss or injury.—**Endangerment**,† en-dān′jėr-ment, *n.* Act of endangering or state of being endangered. (*Mil.*)

Endear, en-dēr′, *v.t.* To make dear; to make more beloved; to bind by ties of affection and love.—**Endearedness**, en-dē′-red-nes, *n.* State of being endeared.—**Endearing**, en-dē′ring, *a.* Having a tendency to make dear or beloved; tender; affectionate.—**Endearment**, en-dēr′-ment, *n.* The act of endearing; the state of being beloved; tender affection; a caress (in this sense chiefly plural).

Endeavor, en-dev′ėr, *n.* [Fr. *en*, in, and *devoir*, duty, from the use of these words in such expressions as *se mettre en devoir*, to try to do, to set about; *devoir* (whence *due, duty*) is from L. *debere*, to owe, to be under obligation (whence *debt*).] An exertion of physical strength or the intellectual powers toward the attainment of an object; an effort; an essay; an attempt.—*v.i.* To labor or exert one's self for the accomplishment of an object; to strive; to try; to attempt; to essay.—*v.t.* To try to effect; to strive after: often governing an infinitive.—**Endeavorer**, en-dev′ėr-ėr, *n.* One who endeavors.

Endecagon, en-dek′a-gon, *n.* [Gr. *hendeka*, eleven, and *gōnia*, an angle.] A plane figure of eleven sides and angles.

Endeictic, en-dīk′tik, *a.* [Gr. *endeiktikos*, from *endeiknymi*, to display.] Displaying; exhibiting: in the Platonic philosophy an *endeictic* dialogue is one which exhibits a specimen of skill.

Endemic, Endemical, en-dem′ik, en-dem′i-kal, *a.* [Fr. *endémique*, from Gr. *endēmios*—*en*, in, among, and *dēmos*, people.] Peculiar to a people, locality, or region: a term applied to diseases to which the inhabitants of a particular country are peculiarly subject.—*n.* A disease of an endemic nature.—**Endemically**, en-dem′i-kal-li, *adv.* In an endemic manner.

Endermatic, Endermic, en-dėr-mat′ik, en-dėr′mik, *a.* [Gr. *en*, and *derma*, skin.] *Med.* applied or effected by rubbing into the skin, especially after the cuticle has been removed, as by a blister.

Enderon, en′de-ron, *n.* [Gr. *en*, in, and *deros*, skin.] The inner surface of the outer layer of the skin (viz. the ectoderm or epidermis).

Endirons, end-ī′ėrnz, *n.* Two movable iron cheeks in grate for expanding or contracting the fire. Not to be confused with *andirons* (q.v.).

Endive, en′div, *n.* [Fr. *endive*, from L. *intybum*; probably from Ar. *hindeb*.] A composite plant, used as a salad; garden succory.

Endocardium, en-dō-kär′di-um, *n.* [Gr. *endon*, within, and *kardia*, the heart.] *Anat.* a colourless transparent membrane which lines the interior of the heart.—**Endocardiac**, en-dō-kär′di-ak, *a.* Relating to the endocardium, or to the interior of the heart.—**Endocarditis**, en′dō-kär-dī″-tis, *n.* An inflammatory disease of the internal parts of the heart, ending in the deposit of fibrin upon the valves.

Endocarp, en′dō-kärp, *n.* [Gr. *endon*, within, *karpos*, fruit.] *Bot.* the inner layer of the pericarp of fruits, when its texture differs from the outer layer, as the stone of a plum or the flesh of an orange.

Endochrome, en′dō-krōm, *n.* [Gr. *endon*, within, *chrōma*, colour.] *Bot.* the colouring matter which fills vegetable cells, except the green.

Endocyst, en'dō-sist, *n.* [Gr. *endon*, within, *kystis*, a bag.] *Zool.* the inner membrane or layer of the body-wall of a polyzoon.

Endoderm, en'dō-dėrm, *n.* [Gr. *endon*, within, and *derma*, skin.] *Zool.* the inner skin or layer of some simple animals, as the Cœlenterata.

Endogamy, en-dog'a-mi, *n.* [Gr. *endon*, within, *gamos*, marriage.] A custom among some savage peoples of marrying only within their own tribe; opposite of *exogamy* (q.v.). —**Endogamous**, en-dog'a-mus, *a.* Pertaining to, practising, or characterized by endogamy.

Endogen, en'dō-jen, *n.* [Gr. *endon*, within, root *gen*, to produce.] Any plant, the stem of which grows by additions developed from the inside and does not increase much in thickness, and in which there is no distinction into bark, wood, and pith, the leaves also being commonly parallel-veined, as in the grasses, lilies, and palms. Endogens form a primary class of the vegetable kingdom, which contrasts with the exogens.—**Endogenous**, en-doj'e-nus, *a.* Pertaining to endogens; growing, developing, originating from within.—**Endogenously**, en-doj'e-nus-li, *adv.* In an endogenous manner; internally.

Endolymph, en'dō-limf, *n.* [Gr. *endon*, within, E. *lymph.*] *Anat.* a limpid fluid in the labyrinth of the ear.

Endomorph, en'dō-morf, *n.* [Gr. *endon*, within, *morphē*, form.] *Mineral.* a mineral inclosed in a crystal of another mineral.

Endoparasite, en-dō-par'a-sīt, *n.* [Gr. *endon*, within, and E. *parasite.*] A parasite living on the internal organs of animals, as opposed to an *ectoparasite*.

Endophlœum, en-dō-flē'um, *n.* [Gr. *endon*, within, *phloios*, bark.] *Bot.* the inner layer or liber of bark containing woody tissue lying next the wood.

Endophyllous, en-dō-fil'lus, *a.* [Gr. *endon*, within, *phyllon*, a leaf.] *Bot.* applied to the young leaves of monocotyledons, from their being formed within a sheath.

Endoplasm, en'dō-plazm, *n.* [Gr. *endon*, within, and *plasma.* PLASMA.] *Biol.* internal matter of a cell; internal protoplasm. —**Endoplast**, en'dō-plast, *n.* The nucleus of a cell.

Endopleura, en'dō-plū-ra, *n.* [Gr. *endon*, within, *pleura*, the side.] *Bot.* the innermost skin of a seed-coat.

Endorhiza, en-dō-rī'za, *n.* [Gr. *endon*, within, *rhiza*, a root.] *Bot.* the radicle of the embryo of monocotyledonous plants, which is developed inside a sheath, from which it issues in germination.—**Endorhizal**, **Endorhizous**, en-dō-rī'zal, en-dō-rī'zus, *a.* *Bot.* having the radicle protected in its early stage by a sheath.

Endorse, en-dors', *v.t.*—*endorsed*, *endorsing.* [Prefix *en*, and L. *dorsum*, a back.] To write something on the back of, as one's name as payee on the back of (a check) in order to obtain the cash or credit represented on the face of the document; hence, to assign by writing one's name on the back; to assign or transfer by endorsement; to sanction, ratify, or approve; to acknowledge the receipt of (a sum specified) by one's signature.—**Endorsable**, en-dors'a-bl, *a.* Capable of being endorsed. —**Endorsement**, en-dors'ment, *n.* The act of endorsing; a note of the contents of any paper on its back; the signature of the holder of a note or bill of exchange written on its back; ratification, sanction, or approval. *Insurance.* A provision added to an insurance contract whereby the scope of its coverage is restricted or enlarged.

Endosarc, en'dō-särk, *n.* [Gr. *endon*, within, *sarx*, flesh.] Endoplasm.

Endoskeleton, en'dō-skel-ē-ton, *n.* [Gr. *endon*, within, and *skeleton.*] The internal bony structure of man and other animals, in contradistinction to *exoskeleton*, the outer hard covering of such animals as the crab, &c.

Endosmose, **Endosmosis**, en'dos-mōs, en-dos-mō'sis, *n.* [Gr. *endon*, within, *ōsmos*, impulsion, from *ōtheō*, to push.] The transmission of fluids or gases through porous septa or partitions, from the exterior to the interior.—**Endosmometer**, en-dos-mom'e-tėr, *n.* An instrument for measuring the force of endosmotic action.—**Endosmotic**, **Endosmosmic**, en-dos-mot'ik, en-dos-mos'mik, *a.* Of or pertaining to endosmose; of the nature of or acting by endosmose.

Endosperm, en'dō-spėrm, *n.* [Gr. *endon*, within, *sperma*, seed.] *Bot.* the albuminous tissue which surrounds the embryo in many seeds, and which contains the supply of food for the germinating embryo: called also *Albumen* or *Perisperm*.—**Endospermic**, en-dō-spėr'mik, *a.* Belonging to or containing endosperm.

Endosteum, en-dos'tē-um, *n.* [Gr. *endon*, within, *osteon*, bone.] *Anat.* the lining membrane of the narrow cavity of a bone. —**Endostitis**, en-dos-tī'tis, *n.* *Med.* inflammation of endosteum.

Endostome, en'dō-stōm, *n.* [Gr. *endon*, within, *stoma*, the mouth.] *Bot.* the passage through the inner integument of a seed or ovule.

Endothecium, en-dō-thē'si-um, *n.* [Gr. *endon*, within, *thēkē*, a cell.] *Bot.* the fibrous cellular tissue lining an anther.

Endothelium, en'dō-the''li-um, *n.* [Gr. *endon*, without, *thēlē*, a nipple.] A delicate cellular membrane lining blood-vessels and cavities.

Endothermic, en-dō-ther'mik, *n.* [Gr. *endon*, within, *thermos*, heat.] Of a chemical reaction, involving absorption of heat; or of the compound so formed.

Endow, en-dou', *v.t.* [Prefix *en*, and Fr. *douer*, to endow, from L. *dos*, *dotis*, a dowry, from root seen in L. *do*, Fr. *didōmi*, to give.] To furnish with a portion of goods or estate, called *dower*; to settle a dower on; to furnish with a permanent fund or provision for support; to enrich or furnish with any gift, quality, or faculty; to indue (*endowed* with genius).—**Endowment**, en-dou'ment, *n.* The act of endowing; property, fund, or revenue permanently appropriated to any object; that which is given or bestowed on the person or mind; gift of nature; natural capacity.

Endue, en-dū', *v.t.*—*endued*, *enduing.* [L. *induo*, to put on. INDUE.] To invest; to clothe; to indue (as with virtue or other qualities).—**Enduement**, en-dū'ment, *n.* *Induement.*

Endure, en-dūr', *v.i.*—*endured*, *enduring.* [Fr. *endurer*, from *en*, and *durer*, L. *durare*, to last.] To continue in the same state without perishing; to last; to remain; to abide; to suffer without resistance or without yielding; to hold out; to bear; to suffer. —*v.t.* To bear, sustain, or support without breaking or yielding; to bear with patience; to bear without opposition or sinking under the pressure; to undergo, suffer, experience. —**Endurable**, en-dū'ra-bl, *a.* Capable of being endured.—**Endurableness**, en-dū'ra-bl-nes, *n.* State of being endurable. —**Endurably**, en-dū'ra-bli, *adv.* In an endurable manner.—**Endurance**, en-dū'rans, *n.* A state of lasting or duration; permanence; lastingness; continuance; a bearing or suffering; a continuing under pain or distress without sinking or yielding; sufferance; patience; fortitude.—**Endurer**, en-dū'rėr, *n.* One who endures.—**Enduring**, en-dū'ring, *a.* Lasting long; permanent.—**Enduringly**, en-dū'ring-li, *adv.* Lastingly; for a time.—**Enduringness**, en-dū'ring-nes, *n.*

Enema, en'ė-ma or en-ē'ma, *n.* [Gr. *enema*, from *eniēmi*, to send in—*en*, in, and *hiēmi*, to send.] A liquid or gaseous substance thrown into the rectum.

Enemy, en'e-mi, *n.* [Fr. *ennemi*, from L. *inimicus*—*in*, neg., and *amicus*, a friend.] One hostile to another; one who hates another; a foe; an adversary; an antagonist; a hostile force, army, fleet, or the like.

Energid, en-er'jid, *n.* [L.L. *energia*, energy.] *Biol.* a cell.

Energy, en'ėr-ji, *n.* [Gr. *energeia*—*en*, and *ergon*, work.] Internal or inherent power; the power of operating, whether exerted or not; power exerted; vigorous operation; force; vigour; effectual operation; efficacy; strength or force producing the effect; strength of expression; force of utterance; life; spirit; emphasis; *phys.* power to do work; it may be mechanical, electrical, thermal, chemical, &c.—*Conservation of energy*, CONSERVATION.—**Energetic**, **Energetical**, en-ėr-jet'ik, en-ėr-jet'i-kal, *a.* [Gr. *energētikos.*] Acting with or exhibiting energy; operating with force, vigour, and effect; forcible; powerful; efficacious; working; active; operative; vigorous.—**Energetically**, en-ėr-jet'i-kal-li, *adv.* In an energetic manner; with energy and effect. —**Energic**, **Energical**, e-nėr'jik, e-nėr'-ji-kal, *a.* Exhibiting energy or force; producing directly a certain physical effect.—**Energize**, en'ėr-jīz, *v.i.*—*energized*, *energizing.* To act with energy or force; to act in producing an effect.—*v.t.* To give strength or force to; to give active vigour to.

Enervate, ē-nėr'vāt, *v.t.*—*enervated*, *enervating.* [L. *enervo*, *enervatum*,—*e*, out, away, and *nervus*, a nerve.] To deprive of nerve, force, or strength; to weaken; to render feeble; to debilitate.—*a.* Without strength or force; weakened; debilitated.—**Enervation**, ē-nėr-vā'shon, *n.* The act of enervating; the state of being enervated; effeminacy.

Enfeeble, en-fē'bl, *v.t.*—*enfeebled*, *enfeebling.* To make feeble; to deprive of strength; to weaken; to debilitate or enervate.—**Enfeeblement**, en-fē'bl-ment, *n.* The act of enfeebling or state of being enfeebled.—**Enfeebler**, en-fē'blėr, *n.* One who or that which makes feeble or weakens.

Enfeoff, en-fef', *v.t.* [Prefix *en*, and L.L. *feoffo*, to confer a fief or feud. FIEF.] *Law*, to give a fief or feud to; to invest with the fee of an estate; to give any corporeal hereditament to in fee.—**Enfeoffment**, en-fef'ment, *n.* *Law*, the act of enfeoffing; the instrument or deed by which one is enfeoffed.

Enfield, en'fēld, *n.* [From *Enfield*, Government factory, as *Carronades* at Carron foundry.] A rifle.

Enfilade, en-fi-lād', *v.t.*—*enfiladed*, *enfilading.* [Fr. *en*, and *file*, a row, a rank, from *fil*, a thread, L. *filum.*] *Milit.* to rake or sweep with shot through the whole length of, as, through a work or line of troops; to fire in the flank of a line.—*n.* A firing in such a manner; the line of fire.

Enfold, en-fōld', *v.t.* To infold. (*Tenn.*)—**Enfoldment**, en-fōld'ment, *n.* The act of enfolding.

Enforce, en-fōrs', *v.t.*—*enforced*, *enforcing.* [Prefix *en*, and *force*; Fr. *enforcir.*] To give strength to; to add force, emphasis, or impressiveness to; to inculcate, urge, or press earnestly; to make or gain by force or compulsion; to force; to compel, constrain, or force; to put in execution; to cause to take effect (to *enforce* the laws).—**Enforceable**, **Enforcible**, en-fōr'sa-bl, en-fōr'-si-bl, *a.* Capable of being enforced.—**Enforcement**, en-fōrs'ment, *n.* The act of enforcing; compulsion; that which gives force, energy, or effect; sanction; that which urges or constrains; constraining power; a putting in execution (the *enforcement* of law).—**Enforcer**, en-fōr'sėr, *n.* One who enforces.—**Enforcive**, en-fōr'siv, *a.* Serving or tending to enforce; compulsive.—**Enforcively**, en-fōr'siv-li, *adv.* Of or by compulsion.

Enforest, en-for'est, *n.* To turn into or lay under forest.

Enfranchise, en-fran'chīz, *v.t.*—*enfranchised*, *enfranchising.* To set free; to liberate from slavery; to free or release, as from custody, bad habits, or any restraining power; to confer the franchise on; to endow with the right of voting for a member of parliament. — **Enfranchisement**, en-fran′chiz-ment, *n.* The act of enfranchising or the state of being enfranchised.— **Enfranchiser**, en-fran′chi-zėr, *n.* One who enfranchises.

Engage, en-gāj′, *v.t.* — *engaged, engaging.* [Fr. *engager—en*, and *gager*, from *gage*, a pledge. GAGE.] To bind or bring under an obligation, as by oath, pledge, contract, or promise: generally with reflexive pron.; to pawn, stake, or pledge; to enlist; to bring into a party; to bespeak, as for service or the like; to win and attach (to *engage* one's affections); to attract and fix (attention); to occupy (to *engage* a person in conversation); to employ the attention or efforts of (to make to embark or take concern in); to enter into contest with; to bring to conflict (to *engage* an enemy).—*v.i.* To promise or pledge one's word; to become bound; to embark in any business; to take a concern in; to undertake; to attack in conflict; to begin mutually a hostile encounter.—**Engaged**, en-gājd′, *pp.* or *a.* Pledged; affianced; enlisted; attracted; occupied; earnestly employed.—*Engaged column, arch.* a column attached to a wall so that part of it is concealed.—**Engagedly**, en-gā′jed-li, *adv.* In an engaged or occupied manner.— **Engagedness**, en-gā′jed-nes, *n.* The state of being engaged.—**Engagement**, en-gāj′ment, *n.* The act of engaging; obligation by agreement or contract; the act of betrothing or state of being betrothed; occupation; employment of the attention; affair of business; an appointment; a combat between bodies of troops or fleets; a fight; a conflict.—**Engaging**, en-gā′jing, *a.* Winning; attractive; tending to draw the attention or the affections; pleasing.— **Engagingly**, en-gā′jing-li, *adv.* In an engaging manner.—**Engagingness**, en-gā′jing-nes, *n.*

Engender, en-jen′dėr, *v.t.* [Fr. *engendrer*, from L. *ingenero—in*, and *genero*, to beget, from *genus, generis*, birth, descent. GENUS.] To beget between the different sexes; more generally, to produce; to cause to exist; to cause, excite, stir up.—*v.i.* To be caused or produced; to meet in sexual embrace.— **Engenderer**, en-jen′dėr-ėr, *n.* One who or that which engenders.

Engine, en′jin, *n.* [Fr. *engin*, a machine, a tool, ingenuity, from L. *ingenium*, disposition, ability, invention—*in*, and root *gen*, to produce, as in *genius.* INGENIOUS.] Any instrument in any degree complicated; a tool, instrument, or appliance by which any effect is produced, as a musket, a cannon, the rack, a battering-ram, &c.; a person regarded as a tool or instrument†; any mechanical instrument of complicated parts, which concur in producing an intended effect; a machine; especially, a machine for applying steam to drive machinery, to propel vessels, railway trains, &c.; a steam-engine. — *v.t.* To furnish (a steam-vessel) with an engine or engines. — **Engine-driver**, *n.* One who drives or manages an engine, especially a locomotive engine. —**Engineer**, en-ji-nēr′, *n.* [Formed on type of *charioteer, musketeer*, &c.] Originally one who managed military engines or artillery; now one who manages a steam-engine or has to do with the construction of steam-engines and steam-machinery; or a person skilled in the principles and practice of engineering, either civil or military.— *v.t.* To direct or superintend the making of in the capacity of engineer; to perform the office of an engineer in respect of (to *engineer* a canal).—**Engineering**, en-ji-nē′ring, *n.* The art of constructing and using engines or machines; the art of executing such works as are the objects of civil and military architecture, in which machinery is in general extensively employed. — *Military engineering*, that branch which relates to the construction and maintenance of fortifications, and the surveying of a country for the various operations of war.—*Civil engineering* relates to the forming of roads, bridges, and railroads, the formation of canals, aqueducts, harbours, drainage of a country, &c.—*Mechanical engineering* refers strictly to machinery. — *Electrical engineering* refers to electrical plant. — **Engineman**, en′jin-man, *n.* A man who manages a steam-engine. — **Enginery**,† en′jin-ri, *n.* Engines in general; artillery or instruments of war (*Mil.*); mechanism; machinery. — **Engine-turning**, *n.* A method of turning used for ornamental work, such as the net-work of curved lines on the backs of watches.

Engirdle, en-gėr′dl, *v.t.* To inclose; to surround.

Engiscope, en′ji-skōp, *n.* [Gr. *engys*, near, and *skopeō*, to view.] A kind of reflecting microscope.

England, ing′land, *n.* [Usually derived from A.S. *Engla land*, the land of the Angles; but may possibly come from N. *engeland*, meadow-land, so called from the rich land near the Trent and Humber.]— **English**, ing′glish, *a.* [A.Sax. *Englisc*, from the *Engle* or *Angles*, a North German tribe who settled in Britain.] Belonging to England or to its inhabitants.—*n.* One of the Low German group of languages, spoken by the people of England and the descendants of natives of that country, as the Americans, Canadian and Australian colonists, &c.; as a collective noun, the people of England; *print.* a size of type between greatprimer and pica. —*v.t.* To translate into the English language; to represent or render in English.—**Englishman**, ing′glish-man, *n.* A native or naturalized inhabitant of England.—**Englishry**, ing′glish-ri, *n.* A population of English descent; especially the persons of English descent in Ireland.

Engorge, en-gorj′, *v.t.*—*engorged, engorging.* [Fr. *engorger*—prefix *en*, and *gorge*, the throat.] To swallow; to gorge; to swallow with greediness or in large quantities.— *v.i.* To devour; to feed with eagerness or voracity.—**Engorged**, en-gorjd′, *p.* and *a.* Gulped down; *med.* filled to excess with blood; congested. — **Engorgement**, en-gorj′ment, *n.* The act of swallowing greedily; *med.* congestion.

Engraft, en-graft′, *v.t.* To ingraft.—**Engraftation, Engraftment**, en-graf-tā′shon, en-graft′ment, *n.* Ingraftment.

Engrail, en-grāl′, *v.t.* [Fr. *engrêler*, to engrail, from *grêle, gresle*, hail.] To variegate; to spot, as with hail; to indent in curved lines.—**Engrailed**, en-grāld′, *p.* and *a.* Variegated; spotted; having an indented outline; indented by curves with the points outwards.—**Engrailment**, en-grāl′ment, *n.* The ring of dots round the edge of a medal; indentation in curved lines.

Engrain, en-grān′, *v.t.* To dye with grain or kermes; hence, from the permanence and excellence of this dye, to dye in any deep, permanent, or enduring colour; to dye deep; to incorporate with the grain or texture of anything; to paint in imitation of the grain of wood; to grain. — **Engrainer**, en-grā′nėr, *n.* A person who paints articles in imitation of wood.

Engram, en′gram, *n.* [Gr. *gramma*, a picture.] *Biol.* the impression left on protoplasm by any physiological happening.

Engrave, en-grāv′, *v.t.*—*engraved*, pp. *engraved* or *engraven, engraving.* [Prefix *en*, and *grave*, to carve.] To cut figures, letters, or devices on, as on stone, metal, &c.; to delineate, copy, picture, or represent by incisions, as on stone, metal, wood, &c.; to imprint; to impress deeply; to infix.—**Engraver**, en-grā′vėr, *n.* One who engraves; a cutter of letters, figures, or devices on stone, metal, or wood.—**Engraving**, en-grā′ving, *n.* In its widest sense, the art of cutting designs, writing, &c., on any hard substance; specifically, the art of forming designs on the surface of metal plates or of blocks of wood for the purpose of taking off impressions or prints of these designs; that which is engraved; an engraved plate; an impression taken from an engraved plate; a print.

Engross, en-grōs′, *v.t.* [Fr. *en*, and *grossir*, to enlarge, from *gros*, big. GROSS.] To increase in bulk or quantity (*Shak.*)†; to seize, occupy, or take up the whole of (cares or duties *engross* one's time or attention); to purchase, with the purpose of making a profit by enhancing the price; to take or assume in undue quantity, proportion, or degree; to write a fair correct copy of in large or distinct legible characters (to *engross* a legal document).—*v.i.* To be employed in engrossing, or making fair copies of writings. — **Engrosser**, en-grō′sėr, *n.* One who or that which engrosses; one who takes or assumes in undue quantity, proportion, or degree; one who copies a writing in large fair characters.—**Engrossment**, en-grōs′ment, *n.* The act of engrossing or state of being engrossed; the copy of an instrument or writing made in large fair characters.

Engulf, en-gulf′, *v.t.* To ingulf.

Enhance, en-hans′, *v.t.* — *enhanced, enhancing.* [Pr. *enanser*, to advance, enhance, from *enant, enans*, forward, from L. *in*, in, to, *ante*, before.] To heighten; to make greater; to increase (price, pleasure, difficulty, beauty, evil, or other non-physical object).—*v.i.* To increase or grow larger.— **Enhancement**, en-hans′ment, *n.* The act of enhancing or state of being enhanced; rise; augmentation; aggravation. — **Enhancer**, en-han′sėr, *n.* One who or that which enhances.

Enharmonic, Enharmonical, en-här-mon′ik, en-här-mon′i-kal, *a.* [Fr. *enharmonique*, Gr. *enarmonikos*, in harmony— *en*, in, and *harmonia*, harmony.] *Mus.* of or pertaining to that one of the three ancient Greek scales which consisted of quarter tones; pertaining to a scale of perfect intonation which recognizes intervals less than semitones.—**Enharmonically**, en-här-mon′i-kal-li, *adv.* In the enharmonic style or system; with perfect intonation.

Enhydrite, en-hī′drīt, *n.* [Gr. *en*, and *hydōr*, water.] A mineral containing water. —**Enhydrous**, en-hī′drus, *a.* Having water within; containing water or other fluid; not *anhydrous.*

Enigma, ē-nig′ma, *n.* [L. *ænigma*, from Gr. *ainigma*, from *ainissomai*, to speak darkly, from *ainos*, a tale, a story.] A dark saying, in which something is concealed under obscure language; an obscure question; a riddle; something containing a hidden meaning which is proposed to be guessed; anything inexplicable to an observer, such as the means by which anything is effected, the motive for a course of conduct, the cause of any phenomenon, &c.; a person whose conduct or disposition is inexplicable. — **Enigmatic, Enigmatical**, ē-nig-mat′ik, ē-nig-mat′i-kal, *a.* Relating to or containing an enigma; obscure; darkly expressed; ambiguous. — **Enigmatically**, ē-nig-mat′i-kal-li, *adv.* In an enigmatic manner. — **Enigmatist**, ē-nig′ma-tist, *n.* A maker or dealer in enigmas an riddles. —**Enigmatize**, ē-nig′ma-tīz, *v.i* To utter or talk in enigmas; to deal in riddles.

Enjambement, en-jamb′ment, *n.* [Fr. *enjambement—en*, in, *jambe*, leg.] The prolongation of the words or sense beyond the second line of a couplet.

Enjoin, en-join′, *v.t.* [Fr. *enjoindre*, from L. *injungo—in*, and *jungo*, to join.] To prescribe or impose with some authority; to lay, as an order or command; to put by way of injunction; to order, direct, or urge (to *enjoin* submission or obedience *upon* a person; duties *enjoined* by law); to admonish or instruct with authority; to command.—**Enjoiner**, en-joi′nėr, *n.* One who enjoins.—**Enjoinment**, en-join′ment, *n.* The act of enjoining.

Enjoy, en-joi′, *v.t.* [O.Fr. *enjoier*, to receive with joy—prefix *en*, and *joie*=E. *joy.*] To feel or perceive with pleasure; to take pleasure or satisfaction in the possession or experience of; to have, possess, and use with satisfaction; to have, hold, or occupy, as a good or profitable thing, or as something desirable. — *To enjoy one's self*, to experience delight from the pleasures in which one partakes; to be happy.—**Enjoyable**, en-joi′a-bl, *a.* Capable of being enjoyed; capable of yielding enjoyment.— **Enjoyer**, en-joi′ėr, *n.* One who enjoys.— **Enjoyment**, en-joi′ment, *n.* The condition of enjoying; the possession or occupancy of anything with satisfaction or pleasure; that which gives pleasure or satisfaction in the possession; cause of joy or gratification; delight.

Enkindle, en-kin′dl, *v.t.*—*enkindled, enkindling.* [Prefix *en*, and *kindle*.] To kindle; to set on fire; to inflame; to excite; to rouse into action.—*v.i.* To take fire.

Enlace, en-lās′, *v.t.*—*enlaced, enlacing.* To fasten with or as with a lace; to lace; to encircle.—**Enlacement**, en-lās′ment, *n.* Act of enlacing; state of being enlaced; an encircling.

Enlarge, en-lärj′, *v.t.*—*enlarged, enlarging.* To make larger or greater in quantity or dimensions; to extend; to expand; to augment; to increase; to make more comprehensive (to *enlarge* the mind); to magnify to the eye; to set at liberty; to release from confinement or pressure.—*v.i.* To grow large or larger; to extend; to dilate; to expand; to expatiate in speaking or writing; to speak or write at length or in full detail.—**Enlarged**, en-lärjd′, *a.* Not narrow nor confined; expansive; broad; comprehensive; liberal (*enlarged* views of a question).—**Enlargement**, en-lärj′ment, *n.* The act of enlarging or state of being enlarged; augmentation; dilatation; expansion; something added on; an addition; expansion or extension, as applied to the mind or the intellectual powers; release from confinement; deliverance; a detailed discourse or argument.—**Enlarger**, en-lär′jėr, *n.* One who or that which enlarges.

Enlighten, en-lī′tn, *v.t.* [Prefix *en*, and *lighten*, to make light, to illumine.] To shed light on; to supply with light; to illuminate; to give intellectual light to; to impart knowledge or practical wisdom to; to inform; to instruct; to enable to see or comprehend.—**Enlightener**, en-lī′tn-ėr, *n.* One who or that which enlightens.—**Enlightenment**, en-lī′tn-ment, *n.* Act of enlightening; state of being enlightened.

Enlist, en-list′, *v.t.* [Prefix *en*, and *list*.] *Lit.* to enroll or enter on a list; to hire for the public service, especially military service, by entering the name in a register; to employ in advancing some interest; to engage the services of (to *enlist* a person in the cause of truth).—*v.i.* To engage in public service, especially military service, voluntarily, to enter heartily into a cause, as being devoted to its interests.—**Enlistment**, en-list′ment, *n.* The act of enlisting; the raising of soldiers by enlisting.

Enliven, en-lī′vn, *v.t.* [Prefix *en*, and adj. *live*.] To give life, action, or motion to; to make vigorous or active; to stimulate; to give spirit or vivacity to; to animate; to make sprightly, gay, or cheerful.—**Enlivener**, en-lī′vn-ėr, *n.* One who or that which enlivens or animates.

Enmity, en′mi-ti, *n.* [Fr. *inimitié*, O.Fr. *enemistie*, corresponding to a L. form *inimicitas*, from *inimicus*, unfriendly—*in*, not, and *amicus*, a friend.] The quality or state of being an enemy; hostile or unfriendly disposition; hostility; ill-will.

Ennead, en′e-ad, *n.* [Gr. *ennea*, nine, *ad*, as in *monad, triad, myriad*.] A collection of nine books, discourses, or accounts.

Enneagon, en′nē-a-gon, *n.* [Gr. *ennea*, nine, and *gōnia*, an angle.] *Geom.* a polygon or plane figure with nine sides or nine angles.—**Enneagonal**, en-nē-ag′o-nal, *a.* *Geom.* having nine angles.—**Enneagynous**, en-nē-aj′i-nus, *a.* [Gr. *gynē*, female.] *Bot.* having nine pistils or styles: said of a flower or plant.—**Enneahedral**, en′nē-a-hē″dral, *a.* [Gr. *hedra*, seat, base.] *Geom.* having nine sides.—**Enneahedria, Enneahedron**, en′nē-a-hē″dri-a, en′nē-a-hē″dron, *n.* *Geom.* a figure having nine sides; a nonagon.—**Enneander**, en-nē-an′dėr, *n.* [Gr. *anēr, andros*, a male.] *Bot.* a plant having nine stamens and hermaphrodite flowers.—**Enneandrian, Enneandrous**, en-nē-an′dri-an, en-nē-an′drus, *a.* Having nine stamens.—**Enneapetalous**, en′nē-a-pet″a-lus, *a.* Having nine petals or flower-leaves.—**Enneaspermous**, en′nē-a-spėr″mus, *a.* [Gr. *sperma*, seed.] *Bot.* having nine seeds.

Ennoble, en-nō′bl, *v.t.*—*ennobled, ennobling.* [Prefix *en*, and *noble*; Fr. *ennoblier*.] To make noble; to raise to nobility; to dignify; to exalt; to elevate in degree, qualities, or excellence.—**Ennoblement**, en-nō′bl-ment, *n.* The act of ennobling; the state of being ennobled; exaltation; elevation.

Ennui, än-nwē, *n.* [Fr., O.Fr. *anui*, annoy, like O.Venet. *inodio*, from L. *in odio*, in hate, in disgust. ODIUM, ANNOY.] Languor of mind arising from lack of occupation; want of interest in present scenes and surrounding objects; listlessness; weariness; tedium.—**Ennuyé**, än-nwē-yā, *a.* [Fr.] Affected with ennui; bored; sated with pleasure.—*n.* One affected with ennui; one indifferent to or bored by ordinary pleasures or occupations.—**Ennuyée**, än-nwē-yā, *n.* A female affected with ennui.

Enormous, ė-nor′mus, *a.* [L. *enormis*—*e*, out of, and *norma*, a rule. NORMAL.] Great beyond or exceeding the common measure; excessively large; excessively wicked; flagitious; atrocious. ∴ *Enormous*, *lit.* out of rule, hence great, far beyond common: used especially of magnitude; *immense*, that cannot be measured: used especially of quantity, extent, and number; *excessive*, beyond bounds, beyond what is fit and right: said especially of degree.—**Enormously**, ė-nor′mus-li, *adv.* Excessively; beyond measure.—**Enormousness**, ė-nor′mus-nes, *n.* The state of being enormous.—**Enormity**, ė-nor′mi-ti, *n.* [L. *enormitas*.] The state or quality of being enormous, immoderate, or excessive; excessive degree; atrociousness; a very grave offence against order, right, or decency; an atrocious crime; an atrocity.

Enough, ē-nuf′, *a.* [O.E. *inoh, enow*, A.Sax. *genóh, genóg*=D. *genoeg*, Icel. *gnógr*, O.Fris. *enoch*, Goth. *ganohs*, G. *genug*, enough, from a verb meaning to suffice.] Satisfying desire or giving content; meeting reasonable expectations; answering the purpose; adequate to want or demand. [*Enough* usually follows the noun with which it is connected.]—*n.* A sufficiency; a quantity of a thing which satisfies desire or is adequate to the wants; what is equal to the powers or abilities.—*Enough!* an exclamation denoting sufficiency.—*adv.* Sufficiently; in a quantity or degree that satisfies or is equal to the desires or wants; fully; quite; denoting a slight augmentation of the positive degree (he was ready *enough* to embrace the offer); in a tolerable or passable degree (the performance is well *enough*).—**Enow**, ē-nou′. An old form of *Enough*.

Enounce, ē-nouns′, *v.t.*—*enounced, enouncing.* [Fr. *énoncer*, L. *enuncio*—*e*, out, and *nuncio*, to declare, as in *announce, denounce, renounce*.] To declare; to enunciate; to state, as a proposition or argument.—**Enouncement**, ē-nouns′ment, *n.* Act of enouncing; enunciation; distinct statement.

Enquire, en-kwīr′, *v.t.* and *i.* **Enquirer**, en-kwī′rėr, *n.* **Enquiry**, en-kwī′ri, *n.* Same as *Inquire, Inquirer, Inquiry.*

Enrage, en-rāj′, *v.t.*—*enraged, enraging.* To excite rage in; to exasperate; to provoke to fury or madness; to make furious.—**Enraged**, en-rājd′, *p.* and *a.* Angry; furious; exhibiting anger or fury (an *enraged* countenance).

Enrapture, en-rap′tūr, *v.t.*—*enraptured, enrapturing.* To transport with rapture; to delight beyond measure.

Enravish, en-rav′ish, *v.t.* To transport with delight; to enrapture.—**Enravishment**, en-rav′ish-ment, *n.* Ecstasy of delight; rapture.

Enregister, en-rej′is-tėr, *v.t.* To register; to enroll or record.

Enrich, en-rich′, *v.t.* To make rich, wealthy, or opulent; to supply with abundant property; to fertilize; to supply with an abundance of anything desirable; to fill or store; to supply with anything splendid or ornamental; to adorn.—**Enrichment**, en-rich′ment, *n.* The act of enriching; something that enriches or adorns.

Enring, en-ring′, *v.t.* To form a circle about; to encircle; to inclose.

Enripen, en-rīp′n, *v.t.* To ripen; to bring to perfection.

Enrobe, en-rōb′, *v.t.*—*enrobed, enrobing.* To clothe with attire; to attire; to invest.

Enrockment, enrok′ment, *n.* A mass of large stones thrown in at random to form the bases of piers, quays, breakwaters, &c.

Enroll, Enrol, en-rōl′, *v.t.*—*enrolled, enrolling.* To write in a roll or register; to insert or enter the name of in a list or catalogue; to record; to insert in records; to leave in writing.—**Enroller**, en-rōl′ėr, *n.* One who enrolls or registers.—**Enrolment**, en-rōl′ment, *n.* The act of enrolling or registering; a register.

Ens, enz, *n.* [L. *ens*, being or thing, originally neuter of ppr. of verb *esse*, to be, whence *essence*.] Entity; being; existence; an actually existing being.

Ensample, en-sam′pl, *n.* [O.Fr., from L. *exemplum*, example. EXAMPLE.] An example; a pattern or model for imitation.

Ensanguine, en-sang′gwin, *v.t.*—*ensanguined, ensanguining.* [Prefix *en*, and L. *sanguis, sanguinis*, blood.] To stain or cover with blood; to smear with gore.

Ensate, en′sāt, *a.* [L. *ensis*, a sword.] *Bot.* ensiform.

Ensconce, en-skons′, *v.t.*—*ensconced, ensconcing.* To cover or shelter, as with a sconce or fort; to protect; to hide securely; to take shelter behind something; to hide: with the reflexive pronoun.

Ensemble, än-sän-bl, *n.* [Fr., from L. *insimul*, at the same time—*in*, and *simul*, together.] All the parts of anything taken together so that each part is considered only in relation to the whole; the general effect of a whole work of art, as a picture, piece of music, drama, &c.

Enshrine, en-shrīn′, *v.t.*—*enshrined, enshrining.* To enclose in or as in a shrine or chest; to preserve with care and affection; to cherish.

Enshroud, en-shroud′, *v.i.* To cover with or as with a shroud; to envelop with anything which conceals from observation.

Ensiform, en′si-form, *a.* [L. *ensiformis*, —*ensis*, sword, and *forma*, form.] Having the shape of a sword; sword-shaped: said of leaves of plants, also of a cartilage at the lower part of the human sternum or breast-bone.

Ensign, en′sīn, *n.* [Fr. *enseigne*, a sign, an ensign, from L. *insigne*, a sign, a badge—*in*, and *signum*, a mark, a sign. SIGN, SIGNAL.] A sign or token‡; a badge or mark of distinction, rank, or office; a symbol; a flag or standard; the flag or banner distinguishing a company of soldiers, an army, or vessel; the colors; *Military* (usually pronounced en′sin). The lowest commissioned officer in the United States Navy, ranking below a lieutenant, junior grade; formerly a commissioned officer of lowest rank in a British regiment of infantry, the equivalent rank now being that of second lieutenant.—**Ensign-bearer**, *n.* One who carries the flag; an ensign.—**Ensigncy, Ensignship**, en′sin-si, en′sin-ship, *n.* The rank, office, or commission of an ensign.

Ensilage, en′sil-āj, *n.* [Fr. *ensilage*, from Sp. *ensilar*, to store grain in an underground receptacle, from *en*, in, and *silo*, from L. *sirus*, a pit.] A mode of storing green fodder, vegetables, &c., by burying in pits or silos dug or built, the substance stored being pressed down with heavy weights, and undergoing a slight fermentation; the substance thus treated.—**Ensile**, en-sīl′, *v.t.* To store by this process.

Ensky, en-skī′, *v.t.* To place in heaven or among the gods. (*Shak.*)

Enslave, en-slāv′, *v.t.*—*enslaved, enslaving.* To make a slave of; to reduce to slavery or bondage; to subject to the dominant influence of; to master or overpower (*enslaved* by his passions).—**Enslavedness**, en-slā′ved-nes, *n.*—**Enslavement**, en-slāv′ment, *n.* The act of enslaving or state of being enslaved.—**Enslaver**, en-slā′vėr, *n.* One who or that which enslaves.

Ensnare, en-snar′, *v.t.—ensnared, ensnaring*. To take in a snare; to entrap; to insnare.

Ensue, en-sū′, *v.t.—ensued, ensuing*. [Prefix *en*, and *sue*; O.Fr. *ensuir*, from L. *insequor*, to follow upon.] To follow as a consequence; to follow in a train of events or course of time; to succeed; to come after. ∴Syn. under FOLLOW.

Ensure, en-shör′, *v.t.—ensured, ensuring*. To make sure or secure; to make certain to turn out, arise, or follow (to *ensure* peace, to *ensure* a good crop).

Entablature, en-tab′la-tūr, *n*. [O.Fr. *entablature—en*, and *table*; L. *tabula*, a board, plank.] The superstructure which lies horizontally upon the columns in *class. arch.*, and consists of three principal divisions, the architrave, the frieze, and the cornice.

Entail, en-tāl′, *n*. [Fr. *entaille*, a cutting, incision, from *entailler*, to cut in—*en*, and *tailler*, to cut, as in *detail, retail, tailor*.] *Law*, an estate or fee entailed or limited in descent to a particular heir or heirs, male or female; rule of descent settled for an estate.—*v.t. Law*, to settle the descent of (lands and tenements) by gift to a man and to certain heirs specified so that neither the donee nor any subsequent possessor can alienate or bequeath it; to transmit in an unalterable course; to devolve as a consequence or of necessity (crimes *entail* punishment).—**Entailer**, en-tā′lėr, *n*. One who executes an entail.—**Entailment**, en-tāl′ment, *n*. The act of entailing or state of being entailed.

Entangle, en-tang′gl, *v.t.—entangled, entangling*. [TANGLE.] To interweave in such a manner as not to be easily separated; to make confused or disordered; to involve in anything complicated, and from which it is difficult to extricate one's self; to involve in difficulties or embarrassments; to puzzle; to perplex; to involve in contradictions; to hamper.—**Entanglement**, en-tang′gl-ment, *n*. The act of entangling or state of being entangled.—**Entangler**, en-tang′glėr, *n*. One who entangles.

Entasis, en′ta-sis, *n*. [Gr., a stretching—*en*, and *teinō*, to stretch.] *Arch*. the almost imperceptible swelling of the lower part of the shaft of a column; *pathol*. constrictive or tonic spasm, as cramp, lockjaw, &c.—**Entastic**, en-tas′tik, *a*. *Med*. relating to diseases characterized by tonic spasms.

Entelechy, en-tel′e-ki, *n*. [Gr. *entelechia*.] The absoluteness, or actuality, of a thing, as opposed to simple capability or potentiality. A philosophic coinage by Aristotle, who styles the soul the *entelechy* of the body, that by which it actually is, though it had the capacity of existing before; actual, as opposed to virtual, or potential, power. In Rabelais, the kingdom of Queen Quintessence, the city of speculative science.

Entellus, en-tel′lus, *n*. [Fr. *entelle*, from Gr. *entellō*, to command.] An East Indian species of monkey, the sacred monkey of the Hindus.

Entente, äṅ-taṅt, *n*. [Fr. *entente*.] An understanding, a good feeling between two or more nations; *entente cordiale, triple entente*.

Enter, en′tėr, *v.t.* [Fr. *entrer*, from L. *intrare*, to enter, from *intro*, into the inside—*in*, in, and root seen in *trans*, across (a common prefix), and in Skr. *tri*, to pass.] To come or go into in any manner whatever; to pierce; to penetrate; to begin or commence upon, as a new period or stage in the progress of life, a new state of things, &c.; to engage or become involved in; to join; to become a member of (an army, a profession, a college); to initiate into a business, service, society, method, &c.; to set down in a book or other record; to enroll; to inscribe; to report (a ship) at the custom-house on arrival in port, by delivering a manifest; *law*, to go in or upon and take possession of (lands); to place in regular form before a court.—*v.i.* To come in; to go or pass in; sometimes with *in*; to embark or enlist in an affair; to become a member.—*To enter into*, to get into the inside or interior of; to penetrate; to engage in (to *enter into* business); to deal with or treat by way of discussion, argument, and the like; to be an ingredient in; to form a constituent part in.—*To enter on* or *upon*, to begin; to commence; to treat or deal with; to discuss or talk of; to examine.

Enteralgy, Enteralgia, en′tėr-al-ji, en-tėr-al′ji-a, *n*. [Gr. *enteron*, intestine, *algos*, pain.] Intestinal neuralgia.

Enteric, en-ter′ik, *a*. [Gr. *enterikos*, from *enteron*, intestine.] Belonging to the intestines.—*Enteric fever*, same as *Typhoid Fever*.—**Enteritis**, en-tėr-ī′tis, *n*. *Med*. inflammation of the intestines.—**Enterocele**, en-ter′ō-sēl, *n*. [Gr. *enterokēlē—enteron*, and *kēlē*, tumour.] A hernial tumour in any situation, whose contents are intestine.—**Enterography**, en-tėr-og′ra-fi, *n*. The anatomical description of the intestines.—**Enterokinase**, en′ter-o-kin-āz, *n*. [Gr. *enteron*, the intestine, *kineō*, I move.] An internal secretion of the lining of the small intestine that enables TRYPSIN (which see) to dissolve proteids.—**Enterolite, Enterolith**, en′tėr-ō-līt, en′tėr-ō-lith, *n*. [Gr. *enteron*, and *lithos*, a stone.] An intestinal concretion or calculus.—**Enterology**, en-tėr-ol′o-ji, *n*. A treatise or discourse on the viscera or internal parts of the body.—**Enteropathy**, en-tėr-op′a-thi, *n*. [Gr. *enteron*, and *pathos*, disease.] Disease of the intestines.—**Enterotomy**, en-tėr-ot′o-mi, *n*. [Gr. *enteron*, and *tomē*, a cutting.] Dissection of the bowels or intestines; incision of the bowels for the removal of strangulation, &c.

Enterprise, en′tėr-prīz, *n*. [Fr., from *entreprendre*, pp. *entrepris*, *entreprise*—*entre*, between, and *prendre*, to take, to lay hold of, from L. *prehendo, prendo*, as in *apprehend, comprehend*.] That which is undertaken or attempted to be performed; a project attempted; particularly, a bold, arduous, or hazardous undertaking; an active and enterprising spirit; readiness to engage in undertakings of difficulty, risk, or danger.—*v.t.*†—*enterprised, enterprising*. To undertake.—**Enterpriser**, en′tėr-prī′zėr, *n*. An adventurer; one who engages in an enterprise.—**Enterprising**, en′tėr-prī-zing, *a*. Having a disposition for or tendency to engage in enterprises; ready to start and carry on untried schemes.—**Enterprisingly**, en′tėr-prī-zing-li, *adv*. In an enterprising manner.

Entertain, en-tėr-tān′, *v.t.* [Fr. *entretenir*, to maintain—*entre*=L. *inter*, between, and *tenir*=L. *tenere*, to hold.] To receive into the house and treat with hospitality; to receive as a host his guests; to engage the attention of agreeably; to amuse with anything that causes the time to pass pleasantly; to take into consideration; to hold or maintain in the mind with favour; to harbour; to cherish (to *entertain* charitable sentiments). ∴ Syn. under AMUSE.—*v.i.* To give entertainments; to receive company.—**Entertainer**, en-tėr-tā′nėr, *n*. One who entertains.—**Entertaining**, en-tėr-tā′ning, *a*. Affording entertainment; pleasing; amusing; diverting.—**Entertainingly**, en-tėr-tā′ning-li, *adv*. In an amusing manner.—**Entertainingness**, en-tėr-tā′ning-nes, *n*. The quality of being entertaining.—**Entertainment**, en-tėr-tān′ment, *n*. The act of entertaining; the receiving and accommodating of guests; food, lodging, or other things required by a guest; a hospitable repast; the pleasure which the mind receives from anything interesting, and which holds or arrests the attention; that which entertains; that which serves for amusement, as a dramatic or other performance; reception; admission.

Enthrall, en-thral′, *v.t.* To reduce to the condition of a thrall; to enslave; to charm or to captivate; to hold spellbound.—**Enthralment**, en-thral′ment, *n*. The act of enthralling, or state of being enthralled.

Enthrone, en-thrōn′, *v.t.—enthroned, enthroning*. To place on a throne; to invest with sovereign authority; to exalt to an elevated place or seat; to induct or install (a bishop) into the powers and privileges of a vacant see.—**Enthronement**, en-thrōn′ment, *n*. Act of enthroning, or state of being enthroned.—**Enthronization**, en-thrō′ni-zā″shon, *n*. The act of enthroning; the placing of a bishop on his throne in his cathedral.

Enthusiasm, en-thū′zi-azm, *n*. [Gr. *enthousiasmos*, from *enthousiazō*, to infuse a divine spirit, from *enthous, entheos*, inspired, divine—*en*, and *theos*, god (whence *theist*).] An ecstasy of mind, as if from inspiration or possession by a spiritual influence; complete possession of the mind by any subject; ardent zeal in pursuit of an object; predominance of the emotional over the intellectual powers; elevation of fancy; exaltation of ideas.—**Enthusiast**, en-thū′zi-ast, *n*. [Gr. *enthousiastēs*.] One full of enthusiasm; one whose mind is completely possessed by any subject; one who is swayed to a great or undue extent by his feelings in any pursuit; a person of ardent zeal; one of elevated fancy; a highly imaginative person.—**Enthusiastic, Enthusiastical**, en-thū′zi-as″tik, en-thū′zi-as″ti-kal, *a*. Filled with or characterized by enthusiasm; prone to enthusiasm; ardent; devoted.—**Enthusiastically**, en-thū′zi-as″ti-kal-li, *adv*. With enthusiasm.

Enthymeme, en′thi-mēm, *n*. [Gr. *enthymēma—en*, and *thymos*, mind.] *Rhet*. an argument consisting of only two premises or propositions, a third proposition required to complete the syllogism being suppressed or kept in mind; as, 'we are dependent, therefore we should be humble'—the proposition omitted being 'all dependent creatures should be humble'.—**Enthymematical**, en′thi-mē-mat″i-kal, *a*. Pertaining to an enthymeme.

Entice, en-tīs′, *v.t.—enticed, enticing*. [O.Fr. *enticer, entiser*=Mod.Fr. *attiser*, from *tison*, L. *titio*, a firebrand.] To draw on by exciting hope or desire; to allure, attract, invite; to lead astray; to induce to evil.—**Enticement**, en-tīs′ment, *n*. The act or means of enticing; allurement; attraction; seduction.—**Enticer**, en-tī′sėr, *n*. One who or that which entices.—**Enticing**, en-tī′sing, *p.* and *a*. Alluring; attracting; attractive.—**Enticingly**, en-tī′sing-li, *adv*. In an enticing manner.

Entire, en-tīr′, *a*. [Fr. *entier*, from L. *integer*, whole (whence *integer, integrity*, &c.).] Whole; unbroken; complete in its parts; perfect; not mutilated; not participated with others; mere; sheer. ∴ Syn. under COMPLETE.—*Entire horse*, an uncastrated horse; a stallion.—*n*. That kind of malt liquor known also as porter or stout; so called because it combined the qualities of various sorts of beer, and did not necessitate mixing.—**Entirely**, en-tīr′li, *adv*. Wholly; completely; fully; altogether.—**Entireness**, en-tīr′nes, *n*. Completeness; unbroken form or state.—**Entirety**, en-tīr′ti, *n*. The state of being entire or whole; wholeness; completeness; the whole.

Entitle, en-tī′tl, *v.t.—entitled, entitling*. [O.Fr. *entituler*, Fr. *intituler*—L. *in*, and *titulus*, a title.] To give a name or title to; to affix a name or appellation to; to designate; to denominate; to call; to name; to furnish with a title, right, or claim (a railway ticket *entitles* a person to travel).

Entity, en′ti-ti, *n*. [L.L. *entitas*, from *ens, entis*, a thing. ENS.] Being; character of existence; essence; a being or species of being; an existing thing.—**Entitative**,† en′ti-tā-tiv, *a*. Considered as an entity or independent existence.

Entoblast, en′to-blast, *n*. [Gr. *entos*, within, and *blastos*, bud.] *Physiol*. the nucleolus of a cell.

Entomb, en-töm′, *v.t.* To deposit in a tomb; to bury; to inter.—**Entombment**, en-töm′ment, *n*. The act of entombing; burial; sepulture.

Entomology, en-to-mol′o-ji, *n*. [Gr. *entomon*, an insect, from *entomos*, cut in—*en*, in, and *temnō*, to cut; from the thorax being almost divided from the abdomen.]

That branch of zoology which treats of the structure, habits, and classification of insects. — **Entomic**, **Entomical**, en-tom′ik, en-tom′i-kal, *a.* Relating to insects. —**Entomoid**, en′to-moid, *a.* Like an insect. — **Entomoline**, en-tom′o-lin, *n.* Same as *Chitin*. — **Entomologic**, **Entomological**, en′to-mo-loj″ik, en′to-mo-loj″i-kal, *a.* Pertaining to entomology.—**Entomologically**, en′to-mo-loj″i-kal-li, *adv.* In an entomological manner.—**Entomologist**, en-to-mol′o-jist, *n.* One versed in entomology.—**Entomophagan**, en-to-mof′a-gan, *n.* [Gr. *entomon*, and *phagein*, to eat.] An insectivorous animal.—**Entomophagous**, en-to-mof′a-gus, *a.* Feeding on insects; insectivorous.—**Entomophilous**, en-to-mof′i-lus, *a.* [Gr. *entomon*, and *philos*, love.] *Bot.* applied to flowers whose pollen is conveyed from the anther to the stigma by the agency of insects.—**Entomostraca**, en-to-mos′tra-ka, *n. pl.* [Gr. *entomon*, and *ostrakon*, a shell.] A division of the crustaceous animals containing a number of the lower forms, as brine-shrimps, water-fleas, &c.

Entonic, en-ton′ik, *a.* [Gr. *entonos*, strained—*en*, and *teinō*, to stretch.] *Med.* strained; intense as regards physiological action.

Entoperipheral, en′to-pe-rif″ėr-al, *a.* [Gr. *entos*, within, and E. *peripheral*.] Within the periphery or external surface of a body.

Entophyte, en′to-fīt, *n.* [Gr. *entos*, within, and *phyton*, a plant.] A plant growing in the interior of animal or vegetable structures; a plant growing on or in living animals.—**Entophytic**, en-to-fit′ik, *a.* Pertaining to entophytes.

Entozoon, en-to-zō′on, *n.* pl. **Entozoa**, en-to-zō′a. [Gr. *entos*, within, and *zōon*, an animal.] An intestinal worm; an animal living in some part of another animal.—**Entozoal**, **Entozoic**, en-to-zō′al, en-to-zō′ik, *a.* Pertaining to the Entozoa.—**Entozoologist**, en′to-zō-ol″o-jist, *n.* A student of entozoology.—**Entozoology**, en′to-zō-ol″o-ji, *n.* That branch of zoology which treats of the Entozoa.

Entr'acte, äṅ-träkt, *n.* [Fr.] The interval between the acts of a drama; a short musical entertainment performed during such interval.

Entrails, en′trālz, *n. pl.* [Fr. *entrailles*; from L.L. *intralia*, from L. *inter*, within.] The internal parts of animal bodies; the bowels; the viscera; the guts.

Entrain, en-trān′, *v.t.* To put on board a railway train: opposed to *detrain*.—*v.i.* To take places in a railway train.

Entrammel, en-tram′el, *v.t.* — *entrammelled*, *entrammelling*. To trammel; to entangle.

Entrance, en′trans, *n.* [From *enter*.] The act of entering into a place; the power or liberty of entering; admission; the doorway or passage by which a place may be entered; initiation; beginning; the act of taking possession, as of property or an office.—**Entrant**, en′trant, *n.* One who enters; one who begins a new course of life; one becoming a member for the first time of any association or body.

Entrance, en-trans′, *v.t.* or *i.*—*entranced*, *entrancing*. To throw into a trance; to put into an ecstasy; to ravish with delight or wonder; to enrapture. — **Entrancement**, en-trans′ment, *n.* The act of entrancing or state of being entranced.

Entrap, en-trap′, *v.t.*—*entrapped*, *entrapping*. To catch as in a trap; to insnare; to catch by artifices; to entangle.

Entreat, en-trēt′, *v.t.* [Prefix *en*, and *treat*; O.Fr. *entraiter*, to treat of.] To ask earnestly (a person or a thing); to beseech; to supplicate; to solicit pressingly; to importune; to treat, handle, or deal with†.—**Entreatable**, en-trē′ta-bl, *a.* Capable of being entreated or influenced by entreaty. —**Entreater**, en-trē′tėr, *n.* One that entreats. — **Entreatingly**, en-trē′ting-li, *adv.* In an entreating manner.—**Entreaty**, en-trē′ti, *n.* Urgent prayer; earnest petition; pressing solicitation; supplication.

Entrée, äṅ-trā, *n.* [Fr.] Entry; freedom of access; a made-dish served between courses at dinner.—**Entremets**, äṅ-tr-mā, *n.* [Fr. *entre*, between, and *mets*, a dish.] A side-dish or minor dish at table, as an omelet, a jelly, &c.

Entrench, en-trensh′, *v.t.*; **Entrenchment**, en-trensh′ment, *n.* Same as *Intrench*, *Intrenchment*.

Entrepôt, äṅ-tr-pō, *n.* [Fr., from L. *inter*, between, *positum*, placed.] A warehouse for the depositing of goods; an emporium or centre for the distribution of merchandise.

Entresol, en′tėr-sol or äṅ-tr-sol, *n.* [Fr.] *Arch.* a low story between two others of greater height.

Entrochite, en′tro-kīt, *n.* [Gr. *en*, in, and *trochos*, a wheel.] A term applied to the wheel-like joints of encrinites, which frequently occur in great profusion in certain limestones. — **Entrochal**, en′tro-kal, *a.* Belonging to or consisting of entrochite.

Entropy, en′trop-i, *n.* [Gr. *en*, in, *tropē*—transformation.] A measure of the unavailability of thermal energy for conversion into mechanical work.

Entrust, en-trust′, *v.t.* [Fr. *en*, in, and E. *trust*.] To deliver in trust; to trust or confide to the care of; to commit with confidence (to *entrust* a thing *to* a person, or a person *with* a thing); consign; commit; confide.

Entry, en′tri, *n.* [Fr. *entrée*. ENTER.] The act of entering; entrance; ingress; the act of recording in a book; any single item entered or set down; the passage into a house or other building or into a room; a beginning; a first attempt; the giving an account of a ship's cargo or exhibition of her papers, and obtaining permission to land goods; *law*, the act of taking possession of lands or tenements.—**Entry-fee**, *n.* Money paid for entry; money paid when a person becomes a member of a society, or that he may be allowed to take part in a competition.

Entwine, en-twīn′, *v.t.*—*entwined*, *entwining*. To twine; to twist round.—*v.i.* To become twisted or twined. — **Entwinement**, en-twīn′ment, *n.* A twining or twisting round or together.

Enucleate,† ē-nū′klē-āt, *v.t.*—*enucleated*, *enucleating*. [L. *enucleo*, *enucleatum* — *e*, priv., and *nucleus*, a kernel.] To make manifest or plain; to disentangle; to solve. —**Enucleation**,† ē-nū′klē-ā″shon, *n.* The act of enucleating; explanation.

Enumerate, ē-nū′me-rāt, *v.t.*—*enumerated*, *enumerating*. [L. *enumero*, *enumeratum* —*e*, out, and *numerus*, number.] To count or tell, number by number; to number; to count; to mention one by one; to recount. —**Enumeration**, ē-nū′me-rā″shon, *n.* The act of enumerating; an account of a number of things each by each.—**Enumerative**,† ē-nū′me-rā-tiv, *a.* Counting; reckoning up.—**Enumerator**, ē-nū′me-rā-tėr, *n.* One who enumerates.

Enunciate, ē-nun′shi-āt, *v.t.*—*enunciated*, *enunciating*. [L. *enuncio*, *enunciatum*—*e*, out, and *nuncio*, to tell. NUNCIO.] To utter, as words or syllables; to pronounce; to declare; to proclaim; to announce; to state.—*v.i.* To utter words or syllables.—**Enunciable**, ē-nun′shi-a-bl, *a.* Capable of being enunciated or expressed.—**Enunciation**, ē-nun′shi-ā″shon, *n.* The act of enunciating; declaration; expression; utterance; announcement; statement.—**Enunciative**, ē-nun′shi-ā-tiv, *a.* Pertaining to enunciation; declarative. — **Enunciatively**, ē-nun′shi-ā-tiv-li, *adv.* Declaratively.—**Enunciator**, ē-nun′shi-ā-tėr, *n.* One who enunciates.—**Enunciatory**, ē-nun′shi-ā-to-ri, *a.* Pertaining to enunciation or utterance.

Enure, en-ūr′, *v.i.* [Same as *Inure*.] To take or have effect; to be available or of benefit.

Enuresis, en-ū-rē′sis, *n.* [Gr. *en*, in, and *ouron*, urine.] *Pathol.* incontinence or involuntary discharge of urine.

Envelop, en-vel′up, *v.t.* [Fr. *envelopper*, It. *invillupare*, to envelop—prefix *en*, in, and verb equivalent to E. *wrap*, an old form of which is *wlap*; so also *develop*.] To cover, as by wrapping or folding; to enwrap or wrap up; to surround entirely; to cover on all sides; to form a covering about; to lie around and conceal; to outflank or turn the enemy's line, so that it is partially surrounded.—**Envelope**, en′ve-lōp, *n.* What is wrapped around or envelops something; a wrapper; an enclosing cover; an integument; *bot.* one of the parts of fructification surrounding the stamens and pistils; the outer covering of a balloon or airship distended by means of enclosed gas, usually a fabric into the construction of which a rubber enters.—**Envelopment**, en-vel′up-ment, *n.* The act of enveloping; that which envelops.

Envenom, en-ven′om, *v.t.* To taint or impregnate with venom; to poison; to imbue with bitterness or malice; to enrage; to exasperate.

Enviable, **Envious**, &c. See ENVY.

Environ, en-vī′ron, *v.t.* [Fr. *environner*—*en*, and O.Fr. *vironner*, to veer, to environ, from *virer*, to veer. VEER.] To surround, encompass, or encircle; to hem in; to involve; to envelop.—**Environment**, en-vī′ron-ment, *n.* Act of surrounding; state of being environed; that which environs; surroundings.—**Environs**, en-vī′ronz, *n. pl.* The parts or places which surround another place, or lie in its neighbourhood, on different sides.

Envisage, en-viz′āj, *v.t.* [Fr. *envisager*—*en*, in, and *visage*, face.] To look in the face of; to face.—**Envisagement**, en-viz′āj-ment, *n.* The act of envisaging.

Envoy, en′voi, *n.* [Fr. *envoyer*, to send—*en*, and *voie*, L. *via*, a way, as in *convoy*, *voyage*, &c. WAY.] One despatched upon an errand or mission; a messenger; a person deputed to negotiate a treaty, or transact other business, with a foreign ruler or government; a diplomatic agent sent on a special occasion; short poem or stanzas addressed by the author to the reader, sending him 'on his way' with the book.—**Envoyship**, en′voi-ship, *n.* The office of an envoy.

Envy, en′vi, *n.* [Fr. *envie*, from L. *invidia*, envy, from *invidus*, envious—*in*, against, and root *vid*, to look. VISION.] Pain, uneasiness, mortification, or discontent excited by the sight of another's superiority or success; a feeling that makes a person begrudge another his good fortune; malice; object of envy.—*v.t.*—*envied*, *envying*. [Fr. *envier*.] To feel envy towards or on account of; to repine at; to regard with malice and longing; to desire earnestly.—*v.i.* To be affected with envy; to have envious feelings.—**Enviable**, en′vi-a-bl, *a.* Exciting or capable of exciting envy.—**Enviableness**, en′vi-a-bl-nes, *n.* The state or quality of being enviable.—**Enviably**, en′vi-a-bli, *adv.* In an enviable manner.—**Envious**, en′vi-us, *a.* [Fr. *envieux*.] Feeling or harbouring envy; tinctured with envy; excited or directed by envy.—**Enviously**, en′vi-us-li, *adv.* In an envious manner.—**Enviousness**, en′vi-us-nes, *n.*

Enwrap, en-rap′, *v.t.* To envelop; to inwrap.

Enzootic, en-zō-ot′ik, *a.* [Gr. *en*, among, and *zōon*, an animal.] Limited to the animals of a district: said of diseases. —*n.* A disease affecting the animals of a district.

Enzyme, en′zīm, *n.* [Gr. *en*, in, *zymē*, leaven.] *Physiol.* a ferment, i.e. a substance of complex nature (e.g. pepsin) of which a very small quantity can effect a large amount of chemical change without itself being appreciably used up in the process.

Eocene, ē′ō-sēn, *a.* and *n.* [Gr. *ēōs*, the dawn, and *kainos*, recent.] *Geol.* a term applied to strata at the base of the tertiary formations, having a small proportion of living species among the fossils.

Eolian, **Eolic**, ē-ō′li-an, ē-ol′ik, *a.* A name of one of the ancient Greek races.—*Eolian* *mode, mus.*, the fifth of the authentic Gregorian modes; it consists of the natural notes A B C D E F G.—*n.* The Eolian dialect; one of the Eolian race.

Eolian, ē-ō′li-an, *a.* Pertaining to *Æolus*, the god of the winds.—*Eolian lyre* or *harp*, a simple instrument that sounds by the air sweeping across its strings.

Eolipile, ē-ol′i-pīl, *n.* [L. *Æolus*, the deity of the winds, and *pila*, a ball.] A hollow ball of metal, with a pipe or slender neck, used for exhibiting the elastic power of steam.

Eolith, ē′ō-lith, *n.* [Gr. *ēōs*, dawn, *lithos*, stone.] The oldest known type of prehistoric stone implements.—**Eolithic**, ē-ō-lith′ik, *a. Archæol.* of or pertaining to the early part of the palæolithic period.

Eon, Æon, ē′on, *n.* [Gr. *aiōn*, age, duration, eternity.] A long indefinite space of time; a great cycle of years; an age; an era; *Platonic philos.* a virtue, attribute, or perfection existing throughout eternity; a sort of divine beings believed in by the Gnostics.

Eosin, ē′ō-sin, *n.* [Gr. *ēōs*, dawn.] A dye obtained from coal-tar products, giving a rose-red colour.

Eozoic, ē-ō-zō′ik, *a.* [Gr. *ēōs*, dawn, and *zōē*, life.] Of or pertaining to the oldest fossiliferous rocks, from their being supposed to contain the first or earliest traces of life in the stratified systems.—**Eozoon**, ē-ō-zō′on, *n.* The name given to a supposed fossil animal of low type, found in the Laurentian rocks of Canada and in the quartz rocks of Germany.—**Eozoonal**, ē-ō-zō′o-nal, *a.* Of or belonging to the eozoon.

Epacris, ep′a-kris, *n.* [Gr. *epi*, on, *akron*, top.] A genus of shrubby, flowering plants, type of a natural order, allied to the heaths and mostly Australian.

Epact, ē′pakt, *n.* [Gr. *epaktos*, brought in or on—*epi*, on, and *agō*, to lead.] *Chron.* the excess of the solar month above the lunar synodical month, and of the solar year above the lunar year of twelve synodical months.

Epanthous, e-pan′thus, *a.* [Gr. *epi*, upon, and *anthos*, flower.] *Bot.* growing upon flowers.

Eparch, ep′ärk, *n.* [Gr. *eparchos*—*epi*, and *archē*, dominion.] In Greece, the governor of a province or eparchy.—**Eparchy**, ep′är-ki, *n.* [Gr. *eparchia*.] The territory under the jurisdiction of an eparch.

Epaule, e-pal′, *n.* [Fr. *épaule*, the shoulder, O.Fr. *espaule*, from L. *spatula*, *spathula*, a broad, flat thing; dim. of *spatha*, a broad blade; allied to *spade*.] *Fort.* the shoulder of a bastion, or the angle made by the face and flank.—**Epaulement**, e-pal′ment, *n. Fort.* a mass of earth, &c., raised for the purpose either of protecting a body of troops at one extremity of their line, or of forming a wing or shoulder of a battery to prevent the guns from being dismounted by an enfilading fire; a kind of parapet.—**Epaulet, Epaulette**, ep′a-let, *n.* [Fr. *épaulette*.] A shoulder-piece; an ornamental badge worn on the shoulder, especially by military and naval officers.—**Epauletted**, ep′a-let-ed, *a.* Furnished with epaulets.

Epencephalon, ep-en-sef′a-lon, *n.* [Gr. *epi*, near, and *enkephalon*, the brain.] *Anat.* the hindmost of the four divisions or segments of the brain.—**Epencephalic**, ep′en-sē-fal″ik, *a. Anat.* of or belonging to the epencephalon.

Epenthesis, e-pen′the-sis, *n.* [Gr. *epi*, on, *en*, in, and *tithēmi*, to put.] *Gram.* the insertion of a letter or syllable in the middle of a word.—**Epenthetic**, ep-en-thet′ik, *a. Gram.* inserted in the middle of a word.

Epergne, e-pėrn′, *n.* [Apparently from Fr. *épargne*, thrift, economy.] An ornamental stand with a large dish and branches for the centre of a table.

Epexegesis, e-pek′se-jē″sis, *n.* [Gr. *epi*, and *exegesis*. EXEGESIS.] A full explanation or interpretation of something immediately preceding; exegesis.—**Epexegetical**, e-pek′sē-jet″i-kal, *a.* Explanatory; exegetical.

Epha, Ephah, ē′fä, *n.* [Heb.] A Hebrew measure of capacity, containing, according to one estimate, 8·6696 gallons; according to another, 4·4286.

Ephemeral, e-fem′e-ral, *a.* [Gr. *ephemeros*, lasting but a day, short-lived—*epi*, and *hēmera*, a day.] Beginning and ending in a day; continuing or existing one day only; short-lived; fleeting.—**Ephemera**, e-fem′e-ra, *n.* A small fly that lives but for a day or for a very short time; the day-fly.—**Ephemerality**, e-fem′e-ral″i-ti, *n.* The state of being ephemeral; that which is ephemeral.—**Ephemeridian**, e-fem′e-rid″i-an, *a.* Relating to an ephemeris.—**Ephemeris**, e-fem′e-ris, *n.* pl. **Ephemerides**, e-fe-mer′i-dēz. [Gr., a diary.] A journal or account of daily transactions; a diary; *astron.* a publication exhibiting the places of the heavenly bodies throughout the year, and giving other information regarding them; an astronomical almanac; a collective name for reviews, magazines, and all kinds of periodical literature.—**Ephemerist**, e-fem′e-rist, *n.* One who studies the daily motions and positions of the planets; one who keeps an ephemeris.—**Ephemeron**, e-fem′e-ron, *n.* Anything ephemeral.

Ephesian, e-fē′zhi-an, *a.* Pertaining to Ephesus in Asia Minor.—**Ephesians**, *n.* Natives of Ephesus; members of the old church, roysterers, jovial boys. (*Shak.*)

Ephod, ef′od, *n.* [Heb., from *aphad*, to put on.] A species of vestment worn by the Jewish high-priest over the second tunic, and consisting of two main pieces, one covering the back, the other the breast and upper part of the body.

Ephor, ef′or, *n.* [Gr. *ephoros*.] A name of certain magistrates among the ancient Spartans.

Epiblast, ep′i-blast, *n.* [Gr. *epi*, upon, and *blastos*, a bud.] *Bot.* a second cotyledon, consisting of a small transverse plate, found on some grasses; *anat.* the upper of the two layers of cells (the under being the *hypoblast*) forming the blastoderm.

Epic, ep′ik, *a.* [L. *epicus*, from Gr. *epikos*, from *epos*, a word, a song.] Composed in a lofty narrative style of poetry; pertaining to such a style; narrative; heroic.—*n.* A narrative poem of elevated character, describing often the exploits of heroes.

Epicalyx, ep-i-kā′liks, *n.* [Gr. *epi*, upon, and *calyx*.] *Bot.* the outer calyx in plants with two calyces, formed either of sepals or bracts.

Epicarp, ep′i-kärp, *n.* [Gr. *epi*, upon, and *karpos*, fruit.] *Bot.* the outer skin of fruits, the fleshy substance or edible portion being termed the *mesocarp*, and the inner portion the *endocarp*.

Epicene, ep′i-sēn, *a.* [Gr. *epikoinos*, common to a number—*epi*, and *koinos*, common.] *Gram.* a term applied to nouns which have but one form of gender, either the masculine or feminine, to indicate animals of both sexes.

Epicentrum, ep-i-sent′rum, *n.* [Gr. *epicentros*.] The point at which an earthquake breaks out.

Epiclinal, ep-i-klī′nal, *a.* [Gr. *epi*, upon, and *klinē*, a bed.] *Bot.* placed upon the disk or receptacle of a flower.

Epicotyl, ep′i-kot″il, *n.* [Gr. *epi*, above, *cotyl*(edon).] In seedlings, that part of the stem immediately above the seed-leaves (cotyledons).

Epicranium, ep-i-krā′ni-um, *n.* [Gr. *epi*, on, *kranion*, skull.] What is upon the cranium; the scalp; the upper surface of an insect's head.

Epicure, ep′i-kūr, *n.* [After *Epicurus*, a Greek philosopher who taught that pleasure and pain are the chief good and chief evil.] One devoted to sensual enjoyments; especially one who indulges in the luxuries of the table.—**Epicurean**, ep′i-kū-rē″an, *a.* Pertaining to Epicurus or his teaching; luxurious; given to luxury.—*n.* A follower of Epicurus; a man devoted to sensual pleasures or luxuries; an epicure.—**Epicureanism**, ep′i-kū-rē″an-izm, *n.* The principles or philosophical doctrines of Epicurus; attachment to luxurious habits.—**Epicurism**, ep′i-kū-rizm, *n.* The practices of an epicure.—**Epicurize**, ep′i-kū-rīz, *v.i.*—*epicurized*, *epicurizing*. To indulge one's self like an epicure.

Epicycle, ep′i-sī-kl, *n.* [Gr. *epi*, and *kyklos*, a circle.] In old astronomy, a little circle, whose centre moves round in the circumference of a greater circle.—**Epicyclic**, ep-i-sī′klik, *a.* Pertaining to an epicycle.—**Epicycloid**, ep-i-sī′kloid, *n. Geom.* a curve generated by the movement of a curve upon the convex or concave side of another fixed curve.—**Epicycloidal**, ep′i-sī-kloi″dal, *a.* Pertaining to the epicycloid, or having its properties.—*Epicycloidal wheel*, a fixed wheel or ring toothed on its inner side, and having in gear with it another toothed wheel of half the diameter, fitted so as to revolve about the centre of the larger.

Epideictic, Epideictical, ep-i-dīk′tik, ep-i-dīk′ti-kal, *a.* [Gr. *epideiktikos*—*epi*, and *deiknymi*, to show.] Serving to display or show off; having a rhetorical or declamatory character; demonstrative.

Epidemic, Epidemical, ep-i-dem′ik, ep-i-dem′i-kal, *a.* [Gr. *epi*, upon, and *dēmos*, people.] Common to or affecting a whole people, or a great number in a community; said of diseases; prevalent; general; generally prevailing.—**Epidemic**, *n.* A disease which, arising from a wide-spread cause, attacks many people at the same period and in the same country.—**Epidemically**, ep-i-dem′i-kal-li, *adv.* In an epidemic manner.—**Epidemiological**, ep-i-dē′mi-o-loj″i-kal, *a.* Pertaining to epidemiology.—**Epidemiologist**, ep-i-dē′mi-ol″o-jist, *n.* One skilled in epidemiology.—**Epidemiology**, ep-i-dē′mi-ol″o-ji, *n.* The doctrine of or method of investigating epidemic diseases.—**Epidemy**,† ep′i-de-mi, *n.* An epidemic.

Epidermis, Epiderm, ep-i-dėr′mis, ep′i-dėrm, *n.* [Gr. *epidermis*—*epi*, and *derma*, skin.] *Anat.* the cuticle or scarf-skin of the body; a thin membrane covering the true skin of animals; *bot.* the cellular integument, or the exterior cellular coating of the leaf or stem of a plant.—**Epidermal**, ep-i-dėr′mal, *a.* Relating to the epidermis; epidermic.—**Epidermatoid, Epidermoid**, ep-i-dėr′ma-toid, ep-i-dėr′moid, *a.* Resembling or pertaining to the epiderm.—**Epidermic, Epidermical**, ep-i-dėr′mik, ep-i-dėr′mi-kal, *a.* Pertaining to or like the epidermis.

Epidictic, Epidictical, ep-i-dik′tik, ep-i-dik′ti-kal, *a.* Same as EPIDEICTIC.

Epidote, ep′i-dōt, *n.* [Fr., from Gr. *epi*, over and above, and *didōmi*, to give, from the enlargement of the base of the primary in some of the secondary forms.] A mineral of a green or gray colour, vitreous lustre, and partial transparency, a member of the garnet family.

Epigæous, Epigeous, ep-i-jē′us, *a.* [Gr. *epi*, upon, and *ge*, *gaia*, the earth.] *Bot.* growing on or close to the earth.

Epigastric, ep-i-gas′trik, *a.* [Gr. *epi*, and *gaster*, belly.] Pertaining to the upper and anterior part of the abdomen.—**Epigastrium**, ep-i-gas′tri-um, *n.* The upper part of the abdomen.

Epigee, Epigeum, ep′i-jē, ep-i-jē′um, *n.* [EPIGÆOUS.] Same as *Perigee*.

Epigene, ep′i-jēn, *a.* [Gr. *epi*, upon, and root *gen*, to produce.] *Geol.* formed or originating on the surface of the earth: opposed to *hypogene*.

Epigenesis, ep-i-jen′e-sis, *n.* [Gr. *epi*, and *genesis*, generation.] The biological theory that organic bodies and parts are produced by superadded vital activity and not merely developed from pre-existing bodies.—**Epigenesist**, ep-i-jen′e-sist, *n.* One who supports the theory of epigenesis.—**Epigenetic**, ep′i-je-net″ik, *a.* Pertaining to or produced by epigenesis.—**Epigenous**, ep-ij′e-nus, *a. Bot.* growing upon the surface of a part.

Epiglottis, ep-i-glot′is, *n.* [Gr. *epiglōttis*—

epi, upon, and *glōttis*.] *Anat.* a cartilaginous plate behind the tongue, which covers the glottis like a lid during the act of swallowing. —**Epiglottic**, ep-i-glot'ik, *a.* Of or pertaining to the epiglottis.

Epigram, ep'i-gram, *n.* [Gr. *epigramma*, an inscription—*epi*, upon, and *gramma*, a writing, from *graphō*, to write.] A short poem usually keenly satirical, the last line of which generally contains the sting or pointed allusion; also an interesting thought represented happily in a few words, whether verse or prose; a pointed or antithetical saying. —**Epigrammatic**, **Epigrammatical**, ep'i-gram-mat"ik, ep'i-gram-mat"i-kal, *a.* Relating to, characterized by, or producing epigrams; like an epigram; antithetical; pointed. —**Epigrammatically**, ep'i-gram-mat"i-kal-li, *adv.* In an epigrammatic manner or style; tersely and pointedly.—**Epigrammatist**, ep-i-gram'-ma-tist, *n.* One who composes epigrams or deals in them.—**Epigrammatize**, ep-i-gram'ma-tīz, *v.t.* To represent or express by epigrams.

Epigraph, ep'i-graf, *n.* [Gr. *epigraphē*—*epi*, and *graphō*, to write.] An inscription on a building, tomb, monument, statue, &c., denoting its use or appropriation; a quotation or motto at the commencement of a work, or at its separate divisions.—**Epigraphic**, ep-i-graf'ik, *a.* Of or pertaining to an epigraph.—**Epigraphics**, **Epigraphy**, ep-i-graf'iks, e-pig'ra-fi, *n.* That branch of knowledge which deals with the deciphering and explaining of inscriptions.—**Epigraphist**, e-pig'ra-fist, *n.* One versed in epigraphics.

Epigynous, e-pij'i-nus, *a.* [Gr. *epi*, upon, and *gynē*, female.] *Bot.* growing or appearing to grow upon the top of the ovary.

Epilepsy, ep'i-lep-si, *n.* [Gr. *epilēpsia*—*epi*, upon, and *lambanō*, *lēpsomai*, to take, to seize.] The falling-sickness; a spasmodic disease in which the sufferer suddenly falls down without sensation or consciousness, and commonly recurring at intervals.—**Epileptic**, **Epileptical**, ep-i-lep'tik, ep-i-lep'ti-kal, *a.* Pertaining to or indicating epilepsy; affected with epilepsy; consisting of epilepsy.—**Epileptic**, *n.* One affected with epilepsy; a medicine for the cure of epilepsy. —**Epileptoid**, ep-i-lep'toid, *a.* Of or pertaining to epilepsy; resembling epilepsy.

Epilogue, ep'i-log, *n.* [L. *epilogus*, from Gr. *epilogos*, conclusion—*epi*, and *legō*, to speak.] A speech or short poem addressed to the spectators by one of the actors, after the conclusion of a drama. —**Epilogic**, **Epilogical**, ep-i-loj'ik, ep-i-loj'i-kal, *a.* Relating to or like an epilogue. Also **Epilogistic**, e-pil'o-jis"tik. —**Epiloguise**, **Epilogize**, e-pil'o-gīz, e-pil'o-jīz, *v.i.* To pronounce an epilogue. —**Epiloguiser**, **Epiloguizer**, ep'i-lo-gī"zėr, *n.* One who epiloguises.

Epimera, ep-i-mē'ra, *n. pl.* [Gr. *epi*, upon, and *mēron*, thigh.] The lateral pieces of the dorsal surface of the segment of a crustacean. —**Epimeral**, ep-i-mē'ral, *a.* A term applied to that part of the segment of a crustaceous animal which is above the joint of the limb.

Epinasty, ep'i-nas-ti, *n.* [Gr. *epi*, on, *nastos*, pressed.] *Bot.* a bending downwards of an organ owing to the more rapid growth of its upper than its under surface.

Epiperipheral, ep'i-pe-rif"e-ral, *a.* [Gr. *epi*, upon, and E. *peripheral*.] Situated or originating upon the periphery or external surface.

Epipetalous, ep-i-pet'a-lus, *a.* [Gr. *epi*, upon, and *petalon*, a leaf.] *Bot.* inserted in or growing on the petal.

Epiphany, ē-pif'a-ni, *n.* [Gr. *epiphaneia*, appearance, from *epiphainō*, to appear—*epi*, upon, and *phainō*, to show.] An appearance or a becoming manifest; specifically, a Christian festival celebrated on the sixth day of January in commemoration of the manifestation of our Saviour's birth to the wise men of the East.

Epiphlœum, ep-i-flē'um, *n.* [Gr. *epi*, upon, and *phloios*, bark.] *Bot.* the layer of bark immediately below the epiderm; the cellular integument.

Epiphragm, ep'i-fram, *n.* [Gr. *epiphragma*, a lid—*epi*, on, *phrassein*, to fence in.] A lid-like organ in animals or plants; the disc or plate with which certain snails close the aperture of their shell.

Epiphyllous, ep-i-fil'us, *a.* [Gr. *epi*, upon, and *phyllon*, a leaf.] *Bot.* inserted or growing upon a leaf.

Epiphysis, e-pif'i-sis, *n.* [Gr. *epiphysis*—*epi*, upon, and *phyō*, to grow.] *Anat.* any portion of a bone separated from the body of the bone by a cartilage which becomes converted into bone by age.—**Epiphyseal**, **Epiphysial**, ep-i-fiz'ē-al, ep-i-fiz'i-al, *a.* Pertaining to or having the nature of an epiphysis.

Epiphyte, ep'i-fīt, *n.* [Gr. *epi*, upon, and *phyton*, a plant.] A plant growing upon another plant, but not deriving its nourishment from it; an air-plant.—**Epiphytic**, **Epiphytical**, ep-i-fit'ik, ep-i-fit'i-kal, *a.* Pertaining to or having the nature of an epiphyte. Also **Epiphytal**, ep-i-fī'tal.—**Epiphytically**, ep-i-fit'i-kal-li, *adv.* In an epiphytic manner.

Epiplerosis, ep'i-plē-rō"sis, *n.* [Gr. *epi*, and *plērōsis*, repletion.] In *pathol.* excessive repletion; distension.

Epiploon, e-pip'lō-on, *n.* [Gr. *epiploon*—*epi*, upon, and *pleō*, to swim.] The caul or omentum, a membranous expansion which floats upon the intestines.—**Epiploic**, ep-i-plō'ik, *a.* Pertaining to the caul or omentum.

Epirhizous, ep-i-rī'zus, *a.* [Gr. *epi*, upon, and *rhiza*, a root.] *Bot.* growing on a root.

Epirrheology, e-pir'ē-ol"o-ji, *n.* [Gr. *epi*, upon, *rheō*, to flow, and *logos*, discourse.] That branch of botany which treats of the effects of external agents upon plants.

Episcopacy, ē-pis'kō-pa-si, *n.* [L. *episcopatus*, from Gr. *episkopos*, a bishop. BISHOP.] That form of ecclesiastical government in which bishops are established, as distinct from and superior to priests or presbyters; the collective body of bishops.—**Episcopal**, ē-pis'kō-pal, *a.* Belonging to or vested in bishops or prelates; characteristic of or pertaining to a bishop or bishops.—**Episcopalian**, ē-pis'kō-pā"li-an, *a.* Pertaining to bishops or government by bishops; episcopal.—*n.* One who belongs to an episcopal church or favours episcopacy.—**Episcopalianism**, ē-pis'kō-pā"li-an-izm, *n.* The system of episcopal religion, or government of the church by bishops.—**Episcopally**, ē-pis'kō-pal-li, *adv.* In an episcopal manner. —**Episcopate**, ē-pis'kō-pāt, *n.* A bishopric; the office and dignity of a bishop; the collective body of bishops.

Episode, ep'i-sōd, *n.* [Gr. *epeisodion*, from *epi*, and *eisodos*, an entrance—*eis*, to, in, and *hodos*, a way.] A separate incident, story, or action, introduced for the purpose of giving a greater variety to the events related in a poem, romance, tale, &c.; an incident or action more or less connected with a complete series of events; that which follows on the entrance of the chorus into the orchestra.—*Greek play*, the part of the play or dialogue between two choral odes, incident.—**Episodic**, **Episodical**, ep-i-sod'ik, ep-i-sod'i-kal, *a.* Pertaining to an episode; contained in an episode or digression. Also **Episodal**, **Episodial**, ep-i-sō'dal, ep-i-sō'di-al.—**Episodically**, ep-i-sod'i-kal-li, *adv.* In an episodic manner.

Epispastic, ep-i-spas'tik, *a.* [Gr. *epispaō*, to draw.] *Med.* drawing; blistering.—*n.* A vesicatory; a blister.

Episperm, ep'i-spėrm, *n.* [Gr. *epi*, upon, and *sperma*, a seed.] *Bot.* the testa or outer integument of a seed.—**Epispermic**, ep-i-spėr'mik, *a.* Pertaining to the episperm.

Epistaxis, ep-i-stak'sis, *n.* [Gr. *epi*, upon, and *staxis*, a dropping.] Bleeding from the nose.

Epistemology, ep-is-tē-mol'o-ji, *n.* [Gr. *epistēmē*, knowledge, *logos*, discourse.] The theory of the method or ground of knowledge. ONTOLOGY.

Episterna, ep-i-stėr'na, *n. pl.* [Gr. *epi*, upon, and *sternon*, the breast-bone.] The lateral pieces of the lower surface of the segment of a crustacean.—**Episternal**, ep-i-stėr'nal, *a.* *Anat.* a term applied to two bones forming part of the sternum, and situated upon its superior and lateral part.

Epistle, ē-pis'l, *n.* [L. *epistola*, Gr. *epistolē*, from *epistellō*, to send to—*epi*, on, and *stellō*, to send.] A writing, directed or sent, communicating intelligence to a distant person; a letter: applied particularly in dignified discourse or in speaking of the letters of the apostles or of the ancients.—**Epistler**, ē-pis'lėr, *n.* A writer of epistles; one who reads the epistle in a church service. —**Epistolary**, ē-pis'tō-la-ri, *a.* Pertaining to epistles or letters; suitable to letters; contained in or consisting of letters.—**Epistolic**, **Epistolical**, ē-pis-tol'ik, ē-pis-tol'-i-kal, *a.* Pertaining to letters or epistles. —**Epistolist**, ē-pis'to-list, *n.* A writer of letters or epistles.—**Epistolize**, ē-pis'to-līz, *v.i.*—*epistolized*, *epistolizing*. To write epistles or letters.

Epistoma, **Epistome**, e-pis'to-ma, ep'i-stōm, *n.* [Gr. *epi*, upon, and *stoma*, mouth.] A valve-like organ which arches over the mouth in many species of Polyzoa.

Epistrophe, ē-pis'tro-fi, *n.* [Gr. *epistrophē*—*epi*, upon, and *strophē*, a return.] *Rhet.* a figure in which several successive clauses or sentences end with the same word or affirmation.

Epitaph, ep'i-taf, *n.* [Gr. *epi*, upon, and *taphos* or *taphē*, a tomb.] An inscription on a tomb or monument in honour or memory of the dead; or a composition such as might be so used.—**Epitaphian**, **Epitaphic**, ep-i-taf'i-an, ep-i-taf'ik, *a.* Pertaining to an epitaph; of the nature of or serving as an epitaph.—**Epitaphist**, ep'i-taf-ist, *n.* A writer of epitaphs.

Epithalamium, ep'i-tha-lā"mi-um, *n.* [Gr. *epithalamion*—*epi*, upon, and *thalamos*, a bed-chamber.] A nuptial song or poem, in praise of a bride and bridegroom; a poem in honour of a newly-married pair. —**Epithalamic**, ep'i-tha-lam"ik, *a.* Pertaining to an epithalamium.

Epithelioma, ep'i-thē-li-ō"ma, *n.* Cancer of the skin.

Epithelium, ep-i-thē'li-um, *n.* [Gr. *epi*, upon, and *thēlē*, the nipple.] *Anat.* a thin and delicate kind of cuticle, like that which covers the nipple; the thin cellular layer which lines the internal cavities and canals of the body, as the mouth, nose, respiratory organs, blood-vessels, &c.; *bot.* an epidermis consisting of young thin-sided cells, filled with homogeneous transparent colourless sap.—**Epithelial**, ep-i-thē'li-al, *a.* Pertaining to the epithelium.

Epithem, ep'i-them, *n.* [Gr. *epithēma*—*epi*, and *tithēmi*, to place.] A kind of fomentation or poultice.

Epithet, ep'i-thet, *n.* [Gr. *epitheton*, a name added, from *epi*, upon, and *tithēmi*, to place.] An adjective expressing some real quality of the thing to which it is applied, or some quality ascribed to it; any word or name implying a quality attached to a person or thing.—**Epithetic**, **Epithetical**, ep-i-thet'ik, ep-i-thet'i-kal, *a.* Pertaining to an epithet or epithets; containing or consisting of epithets; abounding with epithets.

Epitome, e-pit'o-mi, *n.* [Gr. *epitomē*, from *epi*, upon, and *tomē*, a cutting, from *temnō*, to cut, seen also in *anatomy*, *entomology*, &c.] A brief summary or abstract of any book or writing; a compendium; an abridgement; a summary; *fig.* anything which represents another or others in a condensed form. ∴ Syn. under ABRIDGE.—**Epitomist**, **Epitomizer**, e-pit'o-mist, e-pit'o-mī-zėr, *n.* One who epitomizes; the writer of an epitome. Also **Epitomator**, ē-pit'-o-mā-tėr. —**Epitomize**, e-pit'o-mīz, *v.t.* —*epitomized*, *epitomizing*. To make an epitome of: to abstract, in a summary, the principal matters of.

Epizoon, ep-i-zō'on, *n.* pl. **Epizoa**, ep-i-zō'a. [Gr. *epi*, upon, and *zōon*, animal.] A term applied to those parasitic animals which live on or in the skin of other animals. Also **Epizoan**, ep-i-zō′an.—**Epizootic**, ep′i-zō-ot″ik, *a.* Applied to diseases prevalent among the lower animals, corresponding to *epidemic* among men.—*n.* A pestilence among animals prevailing over a district.

Epoch, ē′pok, *n.* [L. *epocha*, from Gr. *epochē*, retention, delay, from *epechō*, to hold back—*epi*, upon, and *echō*, to hold.] A fixed point of time from which succeeding years are numbered; a point from which computation of years begins; any fixed time or period; a memorable term of years; era; age; date.—**Epochal**, ē′po-kal, *a.* Belonging to an epoch; of the nature of an epoch.

Epode, ep′ōd, *n.* [Gr. *epōdē*—*epi*, upon, and *ōdē*, a song, an ode.] The third or last part of the ode, the ancient ode being divided into strophe, antistrophe, and epode; a species of lyric poem in which a longer verse is followed by a shorter one.—**Epodic**, e-pō′dik, *a.* Pertaining to or resembling an epode.

Eponym, ep′o-nim, *n.* [Gr. *epi*, upon, and *onoma*, a name.] A name of a place or people derived from that of a person; a name of a personage called into existence to account for the name of a country or people, as *Italus*, *Romulus*, for *Italy*, *Rome*. —**Eponymic**, **Eponymous**, ep-o-nim′-ik, e-pon′i-mus, *a.* Of or relating to or connected with an eponym.—*Eponymous archon.* The chief magistrate of Athens among the archons, giving his name to the year as a date or point of time.

Epopee, **Epopœia**, ep-o-pē′, ep-o-pē′ya, *n.* [Fr. *epopée*, Gr. *epopoiïa*—*epos*, a word, an epic poem, and *poieō*, to make.] An epic poem; the subject of an epic poem.—**Epos**, ep′os, *n.* [Gr.] An epic poem or its subject; an epopee; epic poetry.

Éprouvette, ā-prö-vet, *n.* [Fr., from *éprouver*, to try, assay, prove.] An instrument for ascertaining the explosive force of gunpowder.

Epsom-salt, ep′som-salt, *n.* The sulphate of magnesia, a cathartic producing watery discharges: so named from its being formerly procured by boiling down the mineral water of *Epsom*, but now prepared otherwise.

Epulotic, ep-ū-lot′ik, *a.* [Gr. *epoulōtikos*, from *epi*, upon, and *oulē*, a scar.] *Med.* healing; cicatrizing.

Epyornis. See ÆPYORNIS.

Equable, ē′kwa-bl, *a.* [L. *æquabilis*, from *æquo*, to make equal, from *æquus*, equal.] Characterized by uniformity, invariableness, or evenness; uniform in action or intensity; not varying; steady; even.—**Equability**, **Equableness**, ē-kwa-bil′-i-ti, ē′kwa-bl-nes, *n.* State or quality of being equable.—**Equably**, ē′kwa-bli, *adv.* In an equable manner.

Equal, ē′kwal, *a.* [L. *æqualis*, from *æquus*, equal (seen also in *equity*, *adequate*, *iniquity*, &c.); same root as Skr. *eka*, one, the same.] The same in size, value, qualities, or degree; neither inferior nor superior, greater nor less, better nor worse; uniform; not variable; being in just relation or proportion; of the same interest or importance; not unduly favourable to any party; just; equitable; fair; having competent power, ability, or means; adequate.—*n.* One not inferior or superior to another; a person having the same or a similar age, rank, station, office, talents, strength, &c.; a compeer.—*v.t.*—*equalled*, *equalling.* To make equal; to make of the same quantity or quality; to cause to be commensurate with or unsurpassed by; to equalize; to be equal to; to be adequate to; to be commensurate with; to rise to the same state, rank, estimation, or excellence with; to become equal to.—**Equality**, ē-kwol′i-ti, *n.* [L. *æqualitas.*] The state of being equal; likeness in size, number, quantity, value, qualities, or degree; the condition in which things or persons cannot be said to be inferior or superior, greater or less, one than another; parity; sameness in state or continued course.—**Equalize**, ē′kwa-līz, *v.t.*—*equalized*, *equalizing.* To make equal; to cause to be equal in amount or degree; to adjust so that there shall be equality between.—**Equalization**, ē′kwal-i-zā″shon, *n.* The act of equalizing, or state of being equalized.—**Equalizer**, ē′kwa-lī-zėr, *n.* One who or that which equalizes.—**Equally**, ē′kwal-li, *adv.* In an equal manner or degree; in the same degree with another; alike; in equal shares or proportions; impartially.—**Equalness**, ē′kwal-nes, *n.* A state of being equal; equality.

Equanimity, ē-kwa-nim′i-ti, *n.* [L. *æquanimitas*—*æquus*, equal, and *animus*, mind.] Evenness of mind; that calm temper or firmness of mind which is not easily elated or depressed.—**Equanimously**, ek-wan′-i-mus-li, *adv.* With equanimity. (*Thack.*)

Equate, ē-kwāt′, *v.t.*—*equated*, *equating.* [L. *æquo*, *æquatum*, to make equal, from *æquus*, equal.] To make equal; to reduce to an average; to make such correction or allowance in as will reduce to a common standard of comparison, or will bring to a true result.—**Equation**, ē-kwā′shon, *n.* The act of equating; *alg.* a statement or expression asserting the equality of two quantities, equality being denoted by the sign = (equal to) between them; *astron.* a quantity which from some imperfect method has to be taken into account in order to give a true result.—*Equation of time*, the difference between mean and apparent time, or the difference between the time given by a dial and that given by a clock. —*Personal equation*, in astronomical observations the quantity of time by which a person is in the habit of noting a phenomenon wrongly.—**Equator**, ē-kwā′tėr, *n.* [L.L. *æquator*, from L. *æquo*, *æquatum*, to make equal.] That great circle of our globe which divides it into two hemispheres (the northern and southern), and every point of which is 90° from the poles, which are also its poles, its axis being also the axis of the earth; also, the equinoctial or celestial equator.—**Equatorial**, ē-kwa-tō′ri-al, *a.* Pertaining to the equator.—*n.* An astronomical instrument, contrived for the purpose of directing a telescope upon any celestial object of which the right ascension and declination are known, and of keeping the object in view for any length of time, notwithstanding the diurnal motion.—**Equatorially**, ē-kwa-tō′ri-al-li, *adv.* In an equatorial manner; in a line with the equator.

Equerry, **Equery**, ek′we-ri, *n.* [Fr. *écurie*, a stable, so that the word means really stable (man); from L.L. *scuria*, a stable; from O.H.G. *skiura*, the Mod.G. *scheuer*, a barn or shed.] An officer of nobles or princes who has the care and management of their horses: in England, equerries are certain officers of the royal household in the department of the master of the horse.

Equestrian, ē-kwes′tri-an, *a.* [L. *equestris*, from *eques*, horseman, from *equus*, horse; akin Gr. *hippos*, Skr. *açva*, horse; Gr. *ōkys*, swift.] Pertaining to horses or horsemanship; consisting in or accompanied with performances on horseback; representing a person on horseback (an *equestrian* statue); pertaining to the class or rank of knights in ancient Rome.—*n.* A rider on horseback; one who earns his living by performing feats of agility and skill on horseback in a circus.—**Equestrianism**, ē-kwes′tri-an-izm, *n.* The performance of an equestrian; horsemanship. —**Equestrienne**, ē-kwes′tri-en, *n.* [Spurious French form.] A female rider or performer on horseback.

Equiangular, ē-kwi-ang′gū-lėr, *a.* *Geom.* consisting of or having the angles all equal.

Equidifferent, ē-kwi-dif′ėr-ent, *a.* Having equal differences; arithmetically proportional.

Equidistance, ē-kwi-dis′tans, *n.* Equal distance.—**Equidistant**, e-kwi-dis′tant, *a.* Being at an equal distance from some point or place.—**Equidistantly**, ē-kwi-dis′tant-li, *adv.* At an equal distance.

Equilateral, ē-kwi-lat′ėr-al, *a.* [L. *æquus*, equal, and *latus*, *lateris*, a side.] Having all the sides equal.

Equilibrate, ē-kwi-lī′brāt, *v.t.*—*equilibrated*, *equilibrating.* [L. *æquus*, equal, and *libro*, to poise, from *libra*, a balance.] To balance equally; to keep in equipoise.—**Equilibration**, ē′kwi-lī-brā″shon, *n.* Equipoise; the state of being equally balanced.—**Equilibrist**, ē-kwil′i-brist, *n.* One that balances equally; one who keeps his balance in unnatural positions and hazardous movements, as a rope-dancer.—**Equilibrity**,† ē-kwi-lib′ri-ti, *n.* [L. *æquilibritas.*] Equilibrium.—**Equilibrium**, ē-kwi-lib′ri-um, *n.* [L. *æquilibrium.*] Equality of weight or force; a state of rest produced by two or more weights or forces counterbalancing each other, as the state of the two ends of a balance when both are charged with equal weights, and they maintain an even or level position; a state of just poise; a position of due balance.

Equimultiple, ē-kwi-mul′ti-pl, *a.* [L. *æquus*, equal, and *multiplico*, to multiply.] Multiplied by the same number or quantity. —*n.* A number multiplied by the same number or quantity as another.

Equine, **Equinal**, ē′kwīn, ē-kwī′nal, *a.* [L. *equinus*, from *equus*, a horse. EQUESTRIAN.] Pertaining to or resembling a horse.

Equinox, ē′kwi-noks, *n.* [L. *æquinoctium*, from *æquus*, equal, and *nox*, night.] The time when the sun reaches one of the two equinoctial points, or points in which the ecliptic and celestial equator intersect each other, the *vernal equinox* being about the 21st of March, the *autumnal equinox* about the 23rd of September, the day and the night being then of equal length all over the world.—**Equinoctial**, ē-kwi-nok′shal, *a.* Pertaining to the equinoxes; occurring or manifested about that time (*equinoctial* gales); pertaining to the regions or climate under the equinoctial line or about the equator.—*Equinoctial points*, the two points of the heavens at which the equator and ecliptic intersect each other.—*n.* The celestial equator, so called because, when the sun is on it, the days and nights are of equal length in all parts of the world.

Equip, ē-kwip′, *v.t.*—*equipped*, *equipping.* [Fr. *équiper*, O.Fr. *esquiper*, to equip, to fit out a ship, from the Teut. stem *skip*, to provide, arrange, &c., as in Icel. *skipa*, to arrange; akin E. *ship*, *shape.*] To dress; to accoutre; to prepare for some particular duty or service; specifically, to furnish with arms and munitions of war; to provide with everything necessary for an expedition or voyage; to fit out for sea, as a ship.—**Equipage**, ek′wi-pāj, *n.* [Fr. *équipage.*] Materials with which a person or thing is equipped; accoutrements; equipment; the furniture and supplies of an armed ship, or the necessary preparations for a voyage; a train of dependants accompanying or following a person; a carriage with the horse or horses, harness, &c.; retinue.—**Equipment**, ē-kwip′ment, *n.* The act of equipping or fitting out; anything that is used in equipping; necessaries for an expedition, a voyage, &c.; equipage.

Equipendent, ē-kwi-pen′dent, *a.* [L. *æquus*, equal, *pendeo*, to hang.] Hanging in equipoise; evenly balanced.

Equipoise, ē′kwi-poiz, *n.* [L. *æquus*, equal, and E. *poise.*] Equality of weight or force; due balance; equilibrium; a state in which the two ends or sides of a thing are balanced.

Equipollence, **Equipollency**, ē-kwi-pol′lens, ē-kwi-pol′len-si, *n.* [Fr. *équipollence*—L. *æquus*, equal, and *polleo*, to be able.] Equality of power or force; *logic*, an equivalence between two or more propositions.—**Equipollent**, ē-kwi-pol′lent, *a.* Having equal power, force, or signification; equivalent.

Equiponderate, ē-kwi-pon′dėr-āt, *v.i.*—*equiponderated*, *equiponderating.* [L. *æquus*, equal, and *pondero*, to weigh, from *pondus*, *ponderis*, weight.] To be equal in weight; to weigh as much as another thing.—*v.t.* To weigh equally in an opposite scale; to counterbalance. — **Equiponderance, Equiponderancy**, ē-kwi-pon'dėr-ans, ē-kwi-pon'dėr-an-si, *n.* Equality of weight; equipoise. — **Equiponderant**, ē-kwi-pon'dėr-ant, *a.* Being of the same weight.

Equisetum, ek-wi-sē'tum, *n.* [L. *equus*, a horse, and *seta*, a bristle.] The generic and common name of many cryptogamous plants, popularly known as horse-tails, having hollow jointed stems, leaves in the form of whorls of teeth terminating the joints, and growing in marshy places.—**Equisetaceous**, ek-wis'e-tā"shus, *a.* Pertaining to the nat. order of equisetums or horse-tails.

Equitable, ek'wi-ta-bl, *a.* [Fr. *équitable*, from L. *æquitas*, equity, from *æquus*, equal.] Possessing or exhibiting equity; equal in regard to the rights of persons; giving each his due; just; fair; impartial; pertaining to a court of equity.—**Equitableness**, ek'-wi-ta-bl-nes, *n.* The quality of being equitable.—**Equitably**, ek'wi-ta-bli, *adv.* In an equitable manner; justly; impartially.—**Equity**, ek'wi-ti, *n.* [Fr. *équité*, L. *æquitas*.] The giving or disposition to give to each man his due; justice; impartiality; fairness; uprightness; *law*, a doing justice between parties where there is no guidance or remedy in strict law; more strictly, a system of supplemental law founded upon defined rules, recorded precedents, and established principles, the judges, however, liberally expounding and developing these to meet new exigencies.

Equitant, ek'wi-tant, *a.* [L. *equitans*, ppr. of *equito*, to ride, from *eques*, *equitis*, a horseman, from *equus*, a horse.] *Bot.* a term applied to unexpanded leaves in a leaf-bud, that overlap each other entirely without any involution, as in the iris.—**Equitation**, ek-wi-tā'shon, *n.* The act or art of riding on horseback; horsemanship.

Equivalent, ė-kwiv'a-lent, *a.* [Fr. *équivalent*—L. *æquus*, equal, and *valens*, *valentis*, ppr. of *valeo*, to be worth (seen also in *avail*, *prevail*, &c.).] Equal in value, force, power, effect, excellence, import, or meaning; interchangeable.—*n.* Something that is equivalent; that which is equal in value, weight, dignity, or force with something else; something given as a fair exchange; compensation; *chem.* the quantity by weight in which an element combines with or replaces a unit of hydrogen; *geol.* a stratum or series of strata in one district formed contemporaneously with a stratum or series of a different character in a different region, and holding a similar place.—**Equivalently**, ė-kwiv'a-lent-li, *adv.* In an equivalent manner. — **Equivalence**, ė-kwiv'a-lens, *n.* The condition of being equivalent; equality of value, signification, or force.—**Equivalency**, ė-kwiv'a-len-si, *n.* Same as *Equivalence*; *chem.* the quality in chemical elements of combining with or displacing one another in certain definite proportions.

Equivalve, **Equivalved**, ē'kwi-valv, ē'kwi-valvd, *a.* A term applied to bivalve shells in which the valves are equal in size and form. Also **Equivalvular**, ē-kwi-val'vū-lėr.

Equivocal, ė-kwiv'ō-kal, *a.* [L. *æquus*, equal, and *vox*, *vocis*, voice.] Being of doubtful signification; capable of being or liable to be understood in different senses; ambiguous; uncertain; dubious; unsatisfactory; deserving to be suspected; capable of being ascribed to different motives; doubtful; questionable. — **Equivocally**, ė-kwiv'ō-kal-li, *adv.* In an equivocal manner. — **Equivocalness**, ė-kwiv'ō-kal-nes, *n.* State of being equivocal. — **Equivocate**, ė-kwiv'ō-kāt, *v.i.*—*equivocated*, *equivocating.* To use ambiguous expressions with a view to mislead; to prevaricate; to quibble. — **Equivocation**, ė-kwiv'ō-kā"-shon, *n.* The act of equivocating; the use of words or expressions that are susceptible of a double signification, with a view to mislead; prevarication; quibbling.—**Equivocator**, ė-kwiv'ō-kā-tėr, *n.* One who equivocates; a prevaricator; a quibbler.—**Equivocatory**, ė-kwiv'ō-ka-to-ri, *a.* Indicating or characterized by equivocation.—**Equivoque**, **Equivoke**, ek'wi-vōk, ē'kwi-vōk, *n.* [Fr. *équivoque*.] An ambiguous term or expression; a quirk; pun or punning.

Era, ē'ra, *n.* [L.L. *æra*, a date, an item of an account, from L. *æra*, counters, pl. of *æs*, brass.] A fixed point of time, from which any number of years is begun to be counted; a succession of years proceeding from a fixed point, or comprehended between two fixed points; an age or period.

Eradicate, ē-rad'i-kāt, *v.t.* — *eradicated*, *eradicating.* [L. *eradico*, *eradicatum*—*e*, out, and *radix*, *radicis*, a root (whence *radical*).] To pull up by the roots; to destroy at the roots; to root out; to destroy thoroughly; to extirpate.—**Eradicable**, ē-rad'i-ka-bl, *a.* That may be eradicated. — **Eradication**, ē-rad'i-kā"shon, *n.* The act of eradicating. — **Eradicative**, ē-rad'i-kā-tiv, *a.* Serving to eradicate, uproot, extirpate, or destroy.

Erase, ē-rās', *v.t.* — *erased*, *erasing.* [L. *erado*, *erasum*—*e*, out, and *rado*, *rasum*, to scrape, to scratch. RAZE.] To rub or scrape out, as letters or characters written, engraved, or painted; to efface; to obliterate; to expunge; to remove or destroy, as by rubbing or blotting out.—**Erasable**, **Erasible**, ē-rā'sa-bl, ē-rā'si-bl, *a.* That may or can be erased.—**Erasement**, ē-rās'-ment, *n.* The act of erasing.—**Eraser**, ē-rā'sėr, *n.* One who or that which erases; a sharp instrument, prepared caoutchouc and the like, used to erase writing, &c.—**Erasion**,† ē-rā'zhon, *n.* The act of erasing; obliteration.—**Erasure**, ē-rā'zhūr, *n.* The act of erasing or scratching out; obliteration; the place where a word or letter has been erased.

Erastian, ē-ras'ti-an, *n.* One whose opinions are the same or akin to those of Thomas *Erastus*, a German divine of the sixteenth century, who maintained the complete subordination of the ecclesiastical to the secular power.—*a.* Pertaining to the doctrines of Erastus or his followers.—**Erastianism**, ē-ras'ti-an-izm, *n.* The doctrines or principles of Erastus or his followers: in a loose and inaccurate sense, the doctrine that an established church should be under the complete control of the state.

Erbium, ėr'bi-um, *n.* [From *Ytterby*, in Sweden.] A rare metal found along with yttrium, terbium, and other rare elements, in some minerals.

Ere, ār, *adv.* or *conj.* [A.Sax. *aer*=D. *eer*, Icel. *ár*, Goth. *air*, before, sooner, earlier. It is the positive form, of which *erst* is the superlative.] Before; sooner than.—*prep.* Before, in respect of time.—**Erelong**, ār-long', *adv.* Before the lapse of a long time; before long; soon.—**Erenow**, ār-nou', *adv.* Before this time. — **Erewhile**, ār'whīl', *adv.* Some time ago; a little time before.

Erebus, er'ē-bus, *n.* [L. *erebus*, Gr. *erebos*.] According to the belief of the Greeks and Romans a dark and gloomy region under the earth, through which the shades passed into Hades.

Erect, ē-rekt', *a.* [L. *erectus*, pp. of *erigo*, to erect—*e*, out, and *rego*, to straighten. REGENT.] In a perpendicular posture; upright; directed upward; raised; uplifted; firm; bold; unshaken.—*v.t.* To raise and set in an upright or perpendicular position, or nearly so; to set upright; to raise up; to construct; to set up; to build; to establish; to found; to form; to elevate; to exalt; to lift up; to encourage.—**Erectable**, ē-rek'ta-bl, *a.* Capable of being erected. — **Erecter**, ē-rek'tėr, *n.* One who or that which erects. —**Erectile**, ē-rek'tīl, *a.* Susceptible of erection.—**Erectility**, ē-rek-til'i-ti, *n.* The quality of being erectile.—**Erection**, ē-rek'-shon, *n.* The act of erecting; a raising and setting perpendicular; a setting upright; the act of constructing or building; establishment; settlement; formation; anything erected; a building of any kind.—**Erective**, ē-rek'tiv, *a.* Setting upright; raising. — **Erectly**, ē-rekt'li, *adv.* In an erect posture. — **Erectness**, ē-rekt'nes, *n.* The state of being erect.—**Erector**, ē-rek'tėr, *n.* One who or that which erects.

Eremacausis, er'e-ma-ka"sis, *n.* [Gr. *ērema*, slowly, gently, and *kausis*, burning.] A slow combustion or oxidation; the gradual combination of the combustible elements of a body with the oxygen of the air.

Eremite, er'ē-mīt, *n.* [L. *eremita*; Late Gr. *erēmitēs*, from Gr. *erēmos*, alone, desert.] One who lives in a wilderness or in retirement; a hermit.—**Eremitic**, **Eremitical**, er-ē-mit'ik, er-ē-mit'i-kal, *a.* Relating to, having the character of, or like an eremite or hermit. — **Eremitism**, er'ē-mi-tizm, *n.* A living in seclusion from social life.

Erethism, er'e-thizm, *n.* [Gr. *erethismos*, irritation, from *erethizō*, to stir.] *Med.* a morbid energy or excitement in any organ or tissue. — **Erethistic**, er-e-this'tik, *a.* Relating to erethism.

Erg, erg, *n.* [Gr. *ergon*, work.] *Physics*, a unit of work, being the work done by a force which, acting for one second upon a mass of one gramme (15·4 grains), produces a velocity of a centimetre (·3937 inch) per second.—**Ergometer**, ėr-gom'e-tėr, *n.* An instrument for measuring work.

Ergo, ėr'gō, *adv.* [L.] Therefore.

Ergot, ėr'got, *n.* [Fr. *ergot*, *argot*, a spur, ergot.] A diseased state of rye and other grasses, caused by the attack of a minute fungus on the seeds or grains; the diseased grain itself.—**Ergoted**, ėr'go-ted, *a.* Diseased with ergot.—**Ergotine**, **Ergotin**, ėr'go-tin, *n.* The narcotic and poisonous principle of the ergot of rye, obtained as a brown powder of a pungent and bitter taste.—**Ergotism**, ėr'go-tizm, *n.* An epidemic occurring in moist districts from the use of ergoted rye in food.

Ericaceous, er-i-kā'shus, *a.* [L. *erica*, heath.] Of or belonging to the nat. order of heaths.

Erin, ė'rin, *n.* [Uncertain origin.] Ireland.

Eringo, ē-ring'gō, *n.* Same as *Eryngo*.

Erinnys, e-rin'nis, *n.* pl. **Erinnyes**, e-rin'ni-ēz. *Greek myth.* one of the Furies; a goddess of discord.

Eriometer, er-i-om'e-tėr, *n.* [Gr. *erion*, wool, and *metron*, measure.] An instrument for measuring the diameters of minute particles and fibres.

Eristic, **Eristical**, ē-ris'tik, ē-ris'ti-kal, *a.* [Gr. *eristikos*, contentious, from *eris*, strife.] Pertaining to disputation or controversy; controversial; captious.

Erl-king, *n.* King of the elves, haunting the Black Forest, in poem by Goethe.

Ermine, ėr'min, *n.* [O.Fr. *ermine*, Mod. Fr. *hermine*, from the Teut.; comp. Dan. Sw. and G. *hermelin*, O.G. *harm*, *harmo*, an ermine.] A quadruped of the weasel tribe found over temperate Europe, but common only in the north, much sought after in the winter on account of its fur, which is white at that season: known also as the *stoat*; the fur of the ermine, long considered as an emblem of purity; *fig.* the office or dignity of a judge, from his state robe being ornamented or bordered with ermine.—**Ermined**, ėr'mind, *a.* Clothed or adorned with ermine.

Erne, ėrn, *n.* [A.Sax. *earn*=Dan. and Sw. *ørn*, an eagle, allied to G. *aar*, an eagle, and to Skr. *ara*, swift, from *ri*, to go.] A name sometimes given to the white-tailed sea-eagle, the bald-eagle, and other allied species.

Erode, ē-rōd', *v.t.* — *eroded*, *eroding.* [L. *erodo*—*e*, and *rodo*, to gnaw, whence *rodent*.] To eat into or away; to corrode.—**Erodent**, ē-rō'dent, *n.* A drug which eats away, as it were, extraneous growths; a caustic.—**Erose**, ē-rōs', *a.* [L. *erosus*.] *Bot.* having small irregular sinuses in the margin, as if gnawed.—**Erosion**, ē-rō'zhon, *n.* [L. *erosio*.] The act or operation of eating or wearing away; *geol.* the wearing away of soil or rock by the influence of water and ice (especially in the form of glaciers). —**Erosive**, ē-rō'siv, *a.* Having the property of eating or wearing away.

Erotic, ē-rot'ik, *a.* [Gr. *erōtikos*, from *erōs*, *erōtos*, love.] Pertaining to or prompted by love; treating of love.—*n.* An amorous composition or poem. — **Erotomania, Erotomany**, e-rō'to-mā"ni-a, er-o-tom'a-ni, *n.* [Gr. *erōs, erōtos*, and *mania*, madness.] Mental alienation or melancholy caused by love.

Erpetology, Erpetological, Erpetologist, ėr-pe-tol'o-ji, ėr'pet-o-loj"i-kal, ėr-pe-tol'o-jist. Same as HERPETOLOGY, &c.

Err, er, *v.i.* [L. *erro, erratum*, to wander, to err; allied to G. *irren*, to wander, to go astray.] To wander from the right way; to go astray; to deviate from the path of duty; to fail morally; to transgress; to mistake in judgment or opinion; to blunder; to misapprehend. — **Errant**, er'rant, *a.* [L. *errans, errantis*, ppr. of *erro*, to err.] Wandering; roving; rambling: applied particularly to the knights of yore who wandered about to seek adventures.—**Errantry**, er'-rant-ri, *n.* A wandering; a roving or rambling about; the condition or way of life of a knight-errant. — **Erratic, Erratical**, er-rat'ik, er-rat'i-kal, *a.* [L. *erraticus.*] Wandering; devious; having no certain course; irregular or peculiar in movements or actions; eccentric; peculiar; queer.—*Erratic blocks*, or *Erratics*, in *geol.* boulders or fragments of rocks which appear to have been transported from their original sites by ice in the pleistocene period, and carried often to great distances.—**Erratically**, er-rat'i-kal-li, *adv.* In an erratic manner. —**Erraticalness**, er-rat'i-kal-nes, *n.* State of being erratic.—**Erratum**, er-rā'-tum, *n.* pl. **Errata**, er-rā'ta. [L. *erratum*, a blunder.] An error or mistake in writing or printing.—**Erroneous**, er-rō'nē-us, *a.* [L. *erroneus.*] Characterized by or containing error or errors; wrong; mistaken; false; inaccurate.—**Erroneously**, er-rō'-nē-us-li, *adv.* In an erroneous manner.—**Erroneousness**, er-rō'nē-us-nes, *n.* The state of being erroneous.—**Error**, er'rėr, *n.* [L. *error.*] An unintentional wandering or deviation from truth or what is right; a going wrong; a mistake; a misapprehension; a mistake made in writing, printing, calculation, or other performance; an inaccuracy; an oversight; a transgression of law or duty; a fault; a sin.

Errand, er'rand, *n.* [A.Sax. *aerend, aerynd.* Dan. *ærrende*, Icel. *eyrendi, erendi*, O.G; *ârunti, ârunti*, an errand, a message; Goth. *airus*, a message, a messenger.] A special business intrusted to a messenger; something to be told or done by one expressly sent.

Errhine, er'rīn, *n.* [Gr. *errhinon—en*, and *rhis, rhinos*, the nose.] A medicine to be snuffed up the nose to promote discharges of mucus.

Ersatz, er-zäts', *a.* [G.] Substitute.—*n.* Any substitute product, such as a substitute food or fabric.

Ersh, Earsh, ėrsh, *n.* [Contracted and corrupted form of *eddish.*] Stubble of grain.

Erst, ėrst, *adv.* [A.Sax. *aerest*, superl. of *aer*, now *ere*, early, before.] At first; at the beginning; once; formerly; long ago.—**Erstwhile**, ėrst'whīl, *adv.* Till then or now; formerly.

Erubescence, Erubescency, er-ū-bes'-ens, er-ū-bes'en-si, *n.* [L. *erubesco*, to become red—*e*, and *ruber*, red (whence *rubric*).] A becoming red; redness of the skin or surface of anything; a blushing.—**Erubescent**, er-ū-bes'ent, *a.* Red or reddish; blushing.

Eructate, ē-ruk'tāt, *v.t.* [L. *eructo, eructatum—e*, out, and *ructo*, to belch.] To eject, as wind from the stomach; to belch. —**Eructation**, ē-ruk-tā'shon, *n.* [L. *eructatio.*] The act of belching wind from the stomach; a belch; a violent bursting forth or ejection of matter from the earth.

Erudite, er'ū-dīt, *a.* [L. *eruditus*, from *erudio*, to polish, to instruct—*e*, out, and *rudis*, rough, rude.] Fully instructed; learned; deeply read; characterized by erudition.—**Eruditely**, er'ū-dīt-li, *adv.* In an erudite manner.—**Eruditeness**, er'ū-dīt-nes, *n.* The quality of being erudite.—**Erudition**, er-ū-dish'on, *n.* Knowledge gained by study or from books and instruction; learning in literature, as distinct from the sciences; scholarship.

Eruginous, ē-rū'ji-nus, *a.* Same as *Æruginous.*

Erumpent, ē-rum'pent, *a.* [L. *erumpens, erumpentis*, ppr. of *erumpo.* ERUPT.] *Bot.* prominent, as if bursting through the epidermis.

Erupt, ē-rupt', *v.t.* [L. *erumpo, eruptum*, to break out—*e*, out, and *rumpo, ruptum*, to burst or break, as in *corrupt, disrupt*, &c.] To throw out or emit by internal and especially by volcanic action; to cast out, as lava from a volcano.—**Eruption**, ē-rup'-shon, *n.* The act of breaking or bursting forth from inclosure or confinement; a violent emission of lava, &c., from a volcano; a sudden or violent rushing forth of men or troops; the breaking out of a cutaneous disease; the rash, pustules, vesicles, &c., accompanying the disease. See EXANTHEMA. —**Eruptional**, ē-rup'shon-al, *a.* Of or pertaining to eruptions.—**Eruptive**, ē-rup'-tiv, *a.* Bursting forth; attended with eruption or rash, or producing it; *geol.* produced by eruption.

Ervalenta, ėr-va-len'ta, *n.* [From *Ervum lens*, botanical name of the lentil.] A dietetic substance consisting of the farina or meal of the common lentil.

Eryngo, ē-ring'gō, *n.* [Gr. *ēryngion*, a prickly plant.] An umbelliferous plant of many species, found on the sandy shores of Britain, and having thick and fleshy roots which were formerly candied as a sweetmeat: called also *Sea Holly.*

Erysipelas, er-i-sip'e-las, *n.* [Gr. —*erythros*, red, and *pella*, skin.] A disease characterized by diffused inflammation with fever; an eruption of a fiery acrid humour on some part of the body, but chiefly on the face and head; rose; St. Anthony's fire.—**Erysipelatous**, er'i-si-pel"a-tus, *a.* Resembling erysipelas, or partaking of its nature.

Erythema, er-i-thē'ma, *n.* [Gr., from *erythros*, red.] A superficial redness of some portion of the skin without blisters and uninfectious.—**Erythematic, Erythematous**, er'i-thē-mat"ik, er-i-them'a-tus, *a.* Of the nature of erythema.

Erythrite, e-rith'rīt, *n.* [Gr. *erythros*, red.] A mineral, a hydrous arseniate of cobalt; also a rose-red felspar.

Erythrosis, er-ith-rō'sis, *n.* [Gr. *erythros*, red.] *Pathol.* a form of plethora, in which the blood is rich in bright red pigment.

Escalade, es-ka-lād', *n.* [Fr., from L. *scala*, a ladder. SCALE.] A furious attack made by troops on a fortified place, in which ladders are used to pass a ditch or mount a rampart. — *v.t.* — *escaladed, escalading.* To mount and pass or enter by means of ladders; to scale.

Escallonia, es-ka-lō'ni-a, *n.* [From *Escallon*, the discoverer.] A South American genus of flowering plants.

Escallop, es-kal'op, *n.* [O.Fr. *escalope.* SCALLOP.] A kind of bivalve; a scallop.

Escape, es-kāp', *v.t.* — *escaped, escaping.* [O.Fr. *escaper*, Fr. *échapper*, Sp. Pg. Pr. *escapar*, to escape; from *ex*, out, and L.L. *cappa, capa*, a mantle (comp. *cape, cap*), lit. to slip out of one's mantle.] To flee from and avoid; to get out of the way of; to shun; to be unnoticed by; to obtain security from; to evade; to elude.—*v.i.* To flee, shun, and be secure from danger; to be free, or get free, from any injury; to hasten or get away; to free one's self from custody or restraint; to regain one's liberty. —*n.* Flight to shun danger or injury; the act of fleeing from danger or imprisonment; the condition of being passed by without receiving injury, when danger threatens.—**Escapable**, es-kā'pa-bl, *a.* Capable of being escaped; avoidable.—**Escapade**, es-ka-pād', *n.* [Fr.] A freak; a mad prank; a wild adventure.—**Escapement**, es-kāp'-ment, *n.* The general contrivance in a time-piece by which the rotatory motion of the wheels gives rise to or maintains the vibratory motion of the pendulum or balance-wheel.—**Escaper**, es-kā'pėr, *n.* One who or that which escapes.

Escarp, es-kärp', *v.t.* [Fr. *escarper*, to cut steep, as rocks or slopes. SCARP.] *Fort.* to slope; to form a slope to.—*n.* Same as *Scarp.*—**Escarpment**, es-kärp'ment, *n.* *Fort.* ground cut away nearly vertically about a position in order to make it inaccessible to an enemy; also, the precipitous side of any hill or rock; a steep ridge of land; a cliff.

Eschalot, esh-a-lot', *n.* Same as *Shallot.*

Eschar, es-kär', *n.* [Gr. *eschara*, a fire-place, a scab.] The crust or scab occasioned on the skin by burns or caustic applications. —**Escharotic**, es-ka-rot'ik, *a.* Caustic; having the power of searing or destroying the flesh.—*n.* An application which sears or destroys flesh.

Eschatology, es-ka-tol'o-ji, *n.* [Gr. *eschatos*, last, and *logos*, discourse.] The doctrine of the last or final things, as death, judgment, &c.

Escheat, es-chēt', *n.* [O.Fr. *eschet*, from *escheir, escheoir*, Mod.Fr. *échoir*, from L. *excadere—ex*, and *cadere*, to fall (whence *cadence, decay*, &c.). *Cheat* is shortened from this.] The resulting back or reverting of any land or tenements to the state or sovereign through failure of heirs, and formerly also by forfeiture or attainder; the property which falls to the state in this way.—*v.i.* To become an escheat.—*v.t.* To cause to be an escheat; to forfeit. —**Escheatable**, es-chē'ta-bl, *a.* Liable to escheat. — **Escheatage**, es-chē'tāj, *n.* The right of succeeding to an escheat.—**Escheator**, es-chē'tėr, *n.* An officer anciently appointed to look after the escheats of the sovereign.

Eschew, es-chö', *v.t.* [O.Fr. *eschever*, Fr. *esquiver*, to avoid, to shun, from O.G. *skiuhan*, G. *scheuen*, to avoid; akin to E. *shy.*] To flee from; to shun; to seek to avoid; to avoid.—**Eschewance**, es-chö'ans, *n.* The act of eschewing.—**Eschewer**, es-chö'ėr, *n.* One who eschews.

Escort, es'kort, *n.* [Fr. *escorte*, from It. *scorta*, a guard or guide, from *scorgere*, to guide, from L. *ex*, and *corrigere*, to correct.] A body of armed men appointed to guard an officer, or stores, money, baggage, &c., when being conveyed from place to place; a person or persons attending one as a mark of respect, honour, or attention; protection or safeguard on a journey or excursion. — *v.t.* (es-kort'). To attend and guard on a journey; to accompany as a guard or protector.

Escritoire, es-kri-twar', *n.* [O.Fr. *escriptoire*, from L. *scriptorius*, connected with writing, *scribo, scriptum*, to write. SCRIBE.] A desk or chest of drawers with an apartment for writing materials; a writing-desk.

Escuage, es'kū-āj, *n.* [O.Fr. *escuage*, from *escu*, L. *scutum*, a shield.] *Feudal law*, a species of tenure by which a military tenant was bound to follow his lord to war, afterward exchanged for a pecuniary satisfaction; scutage.

Esculapian, es-kū-lā'pi-an, *a.* Of or pertaining to *Esculapius*, the god of medicine; pertaining to the healing art.

Esculent, es'kū-lent, *a.* [L. *esculentus*, from *esca*, food, from *edo*, to eat.] Capable of or fit for being used by man for food; edible.—*n.* Something that is eatable; an edible.

Escurial, es-kū'ri-al, *n.* [L. *scoria*, Gr. *skōr*, refuse of metals in fusion.] The name of the Spanish royal palace at Madrid, erected near a slag-heap. So *Tuileries*, from tile-pit.

Escutcheon, es-kuch'on, *n.* [O.Fr. *escusson*, from L. *scutum*, a shield. ESQUIRE.] The shield on which a coat of arms is represented; the shield of a family; a plate for protecting the keyhole of a door, or to which the handle is attached; a scutcheon. —**Escutcheoned**, es-kuch'ond, *a.* Having a coat of arms.

Esker, Eskar, es'kėr, *n.* [Ir. *eiscir.*] In *geol.* a term for a long linear ridge of sand and gravel, common in regions where ice sheets have prevailed, and belonging to glacial phenomena.

Eskimo, Esquimau, es'ki-mō, *n.* pl. **Eskimos, Esquimaux**, es'ki-mōz. One of a race of men, generally short in stature, with broad oval faces and small oblique eyes, inhabiting the northern parts of North America and Greenland.

Esodic, es-od'ik, *a.* [Gr. *es*, into, and *hodos*, a way.] *Physiol.* conducting influences to the spinal marrow: said of certain nerves.

Esophagus, Esophageal, &c. Under ŒSOPHAGUS.

Esopian, Æsopian, ē-sō'pi-an, *a.* Pertaining to *Æsop*, a Greek writer of fables; composed by him or in his manner.

Esoteric, Esoterical, es-ō-ter'ik, es-ō-ter'i-kal, *a.* [Gr. *esōterikos*, from *esō*, within.] Taught only to a select number, and not intelligible to a general body of disciples; designed for, and understood only by, the initiated; private: opposed to *exoteric* or public. — **Esoterically**, es-ō-ter'i-kal-li, *adv.* In an esoteric manner.

Espalier, es-pal'yėr, *n.* [Fr., from It. *spalliera*. a support for the shoulders, from *spalla*, a shoulder, L. *spathula*, *spatula*, a broad blade, dim. of *spatha*. EPAULET.] A broad piece of trellis-work on which the branches of fruit-trees or bushes are trained; a row of trees so trained.—*v.t.* To form an espalier of, or to train as an espalier.

Esparto, es-pär'tō, *n.* [Sp., from L. *spartum*, Gr. *sparton*, *spartos*.] A name of two or three species of grass found in southern Spain and North Africa, and extensively exported to be used in the manufacture of paper, matting, baskets, &c.

Especial, es-pesh'al, *a.* [O.Fr. *especial*, Fr. *spécial*, L. *specialis*, of particular sort or kind, special, from *species*, kind. SPECIES.] Of a distinct sort or kind; special; particular; marked; peculiar. — **Especially**, es-pesh'al-li, *adv.* In an especial manner; particularly; specially; peculiarly.

Esperanto, es-per-ant'ō. A language formed for the purpose of enabling the inhabitants of all countries to converse with each other.

Espial, Espier, Espionage. Under ESPY.

Esplanade, es-pla-nād', *n.* [Fr., from the old verb *esplaner*, to make level, from L. *explanare*—*ex*, and *planus*, plain, level.] *Fort.* a wide open space between the glacis of a citadel and the first houses of the town; any open level space near a town, especially a kind of terrace along the sea-side, for public walks or drives.

Espouse, es-pouz', *v.t.*—*espoused, espousing.* [O.Fr. *espouser* (Fr. *épouser*), from L. *sponsare*, to betroth, to espouse, freq. of *spondeo, sponsum*, to pledge one's self, whence *despond, respond.*] To give or take in marriage; to promise, engage, or bestow in marriage by contract or pledge; to betroth; to marry; to wed; to become a partisan in; to embrace or to adopt (a cause, a quarrel). —**Espousal**, es-pou'zal, *n.* [O.Fr. *espousailles*, L. *sponsalia*, espousals, pl. n. of *sponsalis*, relating to betrothal.] The act of espousing or betrothing: frequently used in the plural; the adopting or taking up of a cause.—**Espousement**, es-pouz'ment, *n.* Act of espousing.—**Espouser**, es-pou'zėr, *n.* One who espouses.

Esprit, es-prē, *n.* [Fr.] Soul; spirit; intellect; mind; wit.—*Esprit de corps*, an attachment to the class or body of which one is a member; the common spirit or disposition formed by men in association.

Espy, es-pī', *v.t.*—*espied, espying.* [O.Fr. *espier*, It. *spiare*; same word as *spy*.] To see at a distance; to have the first sight of; to descry; to discover, as something concealed, or as if unexpectedly or unintentionally; to inspect; to spy.—**Espial**, es-pī'al, *n.* The act of espying; observation; discovery.—**Espier**, es-pī'ėr, *n.* One who espies.—**Espionage**, es'pi-o-nāj, *n.* The practice or employment of spies; the practice of watching the conduct and words of others as a spy.

Esquire, es-kwīr' or es', *n.* [O.Fr. *escuyer*, Fr. *écuyer*, lit. a shield-bearer, from L. *scutarius*, a soldier armed with a *scutum*, or shield, from root *sku*, to cover or protect.] Originally, a shield-bearer or armor-bearer; an attendant on a knight; hence, a title of dignity next in degree below a knight; a title properly given in Great Britain to the younger sons of noblemen, to justices of the peace, sheriffs, landed proprietors, &c.; now used as a complimentary adjunct (usually abbreviated to *Esq.*) to a name in addressing letters, &c., to almost any person of respectable standing.

Essay, es-sā', *v.t.* [Fr. *essayer*. ASSAY.] To exert one's power or faculties on; to make an effort to perform; to try; to attempt; to endeavour to do; to make experiment of.—*n.* (es'sā). An effort made for the performance of anything; a trial, attempt; or endeavour; a test or experiment; a literary composition intended to prove some particular point or illustrate a particular subject, not having the importance of a regular treatise; a short disquisition on a subject of taste, philosophy, or common life. —**Essayer**, *n.* One who essays (pronounced es-sā'ėr); one who writes essays; an essayist (pronounced es'sā-ėr).†—**Essayist**, es'sā-ist, *n.* A writer of an essay or of essays.

Essence, es'sens, *n.* [Fr., from L. *essentia*, from *esse*, to be; akin *entity*.] That which constitutes the particular nature of a thing, and which distinguishes it from all others; that which makes a thing what it is; existence; a being having existence; constituent substance; the predominant elements or principles of any plant or drug extracted, refined, or rectified from grosser matter; an extract; perfume; odour; scent; the most important or fundamental doctrines, facts, ideas, or conclusions (the *essence* of a lecture, a statement).—*v.t.* To perfume; to scent.—**Essential**, es-sen'shal, *a.* Being of or pertaining to the essence; necessary to the constitution or existence of a thing; constituting a thing what it is; important in the highest degree; indispensable; volatile; diffusible (*essential* oils).—*n.* What is essential; fundamental or constituent principle; distinguishing characteristic.—**Essentiality, Essentialness**, es-sen'shi-al"i-ti, es-sen'shal-nes, *n.* The quality of being essential.—**Essentially**, es-sen'shal-li, *adv.* In an essential manner; fundamentally.

Essene, es-sēn', *n. pl.* [Gr. *Essēnoi*, L. *Esseni*.] Among the Jews, a member of a sect remarkable for their strictness and abstinence.

Establish, es-tab'lish, *v.t.* [O.Fr. *establir* (Fr. *établir*), from L. *stabilio*, to make firm, to establish, from *sta*, root of *sto*, to stand. STAND.] To make steadfast, firm, or stable; to settle on a firm or permanent basis; to set or fix unalterably; to institute and ratify; to enact or decree authoritatively and for permanence; to ordain; to strengthen; to prove; to confirm; to originate and secure the permanent existence of; to found permanently; to set up in connection with the state and endow (a church); to set up in business.—**Establisher**, es-tab'lish-ėr, *n.* One who establishes. — **Establishment**, es-tab'lish-ment, *n.* The act of establishing; the state of being established; settlement; fixed state; confirmation; a permanent civil or military force or organization, such as a fixed garrison or a local government; that form of doctrine and church government established by the legislature in any country; the place where a person is settled either for residence or for transacting business; a person's residence and everything connected with it, such as furniture, servants, carriages, &c.; an institution, whether public or private; the quota or number of men in an army, regiment, &c.—**Establishmentarian**, es-tab'lishmen-tā"ri-an, *n.* One who supports the doctrine of establishment in religion.

Estafet, Estafette, es-ta-fet', *n.* [Fr. *estafette*, from It. *staffetta*, a courier, from *staffa*, a stirrup, from O.H.G. *stapho* = E. *step*.] A military courier; an express of any kind.

Estaminet, äs-tam-ī-nā, *n.* [Fr.] A coffee-house where smoking is allowed; a tap-room.

Estate, es-tāt', *n.* [O.Fr. *estat*, Fr. *état*, from L. *status*, a standing, state, from *sto*, *statum*, to stand. STAND.] Condition or circumstances of any person or thing; state; rank; quality; possessions; property; a piece of landed property; a definite portion of land in the ownership of some one; an order or class of men constituting a state; one of the classes of the nation invested with political rights, the *three estates of the realm*, in Britain, being the lords spiritual, the lords temporal, and the commons.—*The fourth estate*, the newspaper press; journalists.—*The Estates*, the old French and Scottish Parliament of nobles, clergy, burghers.—*The Third Estate*—*tiers état*, the commonalty.—*v.t.* To settle an estate upon (*Tenn.*)†; to bestow (*Shak.*)‡.

Esteem, es-tēm', *v.t.* [Fr. *estimer*, L. *æstimare*, *estimatum*, from same root as Skr. *esha*, a wish, G. *heischen*, to desire. Akin *aim*.] To set a value on, whether high or low; to estimate; to value; to set a high value on; to regard with reverence, respect, or friendship; to prize.—*n.* Opinion or judgment of merit or demerit; estimation; high value or estimation; great regard; favourable opinion, founded on supposed worth. — **Esteemable**, es-tē'ma-bl, *a.* Worthy of esteem; estimable.—**Esteemer**, es-tē'mėr, *n.* One who esteems. — **Estimable**, es'ti-ma-bl, *a.* Capable of being estimated or valued; worthy of esteem or respect; deserving our good opinion or regard. — **Estimableness**, es'ti-ma-bl-nes, *n.* The quality of being estimable.—**Estimably**, es'ti-ma-bli, *adv.* In an estimable manner.—**Estimate**, es'ti-māt, *v.t.*—*estimated, estimating.* [L. *æstimare, æstimatum.*] To form a judgment or opinion regarding: especially applied to value, size, weight, degree, extent, quantity, &c.; to rate by judgment, opinion, or a rough calculation; to fix the worth of; to compute; to calculate; to reckon.—*n.* A valuing or rating in the mind; an approximate judgment or opinion as to value, degree, extent, quantity, &c.—**Estimates**, *n.* The national estimate or forecast of expenditure for the year, presented to Parliament.—**Estimation**, es-ti-mā'shon, *n.* [L. *æstimatio*.] The act of estimating; calculation; computation; an estimate; esteem; regard; favourable opinion; honour. — **Estimative**, es'ti-mā-tiv, *a.* Having the power of estimating.—**Estimator**, es'ti-mā-tėr, *n.* One who estimates or values.

Ester, es'ter, *n.* Esters are compounds of the higher fatty acids, which, united with glycerine, constitute animal fats. Palmitin, stearin, and olein are the commonest forms.

Esthete, Esthetic, &c. Same as *Æsthete*.

Estival,† es-tī'val, *a.* [L. *æstivus*, from *æstas*, summer.] Pertaining to summer.—**Estivate**,† es'ti-vāt, *v.i.* [L. *æstivo, æstivatum*.] To pass the summer.—**Estivation, Æstivation**, es-ti-vā'shon, *n.* *Bot.* the manner in which the parts of a flower-bud are arranged with respect to each other before opening; the disposition of the petals within the flower-bud—*vernation* being the disposition of leaves.

Estop, es-top', *v.t.*—*estopped, estopping.* [O.Fr. *estoper*, Fr. *étouper*, to stop with tow, from L. *stupa, stuppa*, tow.] *Law*, to impede or bar by one's own act.—**Estoppel**, es-top'el, *n.* *Law*, a stop; a plea in bar, grounded on a man's own act.

Estotiland, es-tōt'i-land, *n.* A tract of land in North America in the Arctic circle. (*Mil.*, P. L., x. 685.)

Estovers, es-tō'vėrz, *n. pl.* [O.Fr. *estoveir*, *estovoir*, to be needful.] *Law*, the right of taking the necessary amount of wood from an estate for fuel, fences, repairs, and other reasonable purposes.

Estrade, es-träd, *n.* [Fr. from Sp. *estrado*, the place, strewn, L. *stratum*, with carpets. An elevated part of the floor of a room; a platform.

Estrange, es-trānj', *v.t.* — *estranged*, *estranging*. [O.Fr. *estranger*, from L.L. *extraneus*, foreign, strange. STRANGE.] To keep apart or out of friendly relations; to make to cease from being familiar; to alienate; to turn from kindness to indifference or malevolence; to apply to a purpose foreign from its original or customary one. —**Estrangedness**, es-trān'jed-nes, *n.* The state of being estranged.—**Estrangement**, es-trānj'ment, *n.* The act of estranging or state of being estranged; alienation.

Estray, es-trā', *n.* A stray, or animal that has strayed from the custody of its owner.

Estreat, es-trēt', *n.* [O.Fr. *estraite*, from L. *extraho*, *extractum*, to draw out.] *Law*, a true copy of an original writing, under which fines are to be levied.—*v.t. Law*, to levy (fines) under an estreat.

Estuary, es'tū-a-ri, *n.* [L. *æstuarium*, from *æstuo*, to boil or foam, *æstus*, heat, tide.] The wide mouth of a river where the tide meets the currents, or flows and ebbs; a firth.—**Estuarian**, **Estuarine**, es-tū-ā'ri-an, es'tū-a-rīn, *a.* Of or pertaining to an estuary; formed in an estuary.

Etærio, e-tē'ri-ō, *n.* [Gr. (*h*)*etairos*, a companion.] *Bot.* a kind of aggregate fruit, as that of the strawberry and raspberry.

Etagère, ā-tä-zhâr', *n.* [Fr. *étage*, stage.] A piece of cabinet furniture with shelves for holding ornamental articles.

État-major, ā-tä-mä-zhor, *n.* [Fr.] The staff of an army or regiment, as in England.

Et cetera, et set'ėr-a. [L. *et*, and *cætera*, other things.] And others of the like kind, an expression used after the mention of certain individuals of a class, to indicate that others might also have been mentioned by name: written also *Etcætera*, *Etcetera*, and commonly contracted *etc.*, *&c.* It is sometimes treated as a noun.

Etch, ech, *v.t.* and *i.* [From D. *etsen*, G. *ätzen*, to corrode by acids, to etch; lit. to bite into; O.H.G. *ezan*, to eat. EAT.] To produce figures or designs upon a plate of steel, copper, glass, or the like, by means of lines drawn through a thin coating or ground covering the plate and corroded or *bitten in* by some strong acid, which can only affect the plate where the coating has been removed by the etching instrument.—**Etcher**, ech'ėr, *n.* One who etches.—**Etching**, ech'ing, *n.* The art or operation of an etcher; a design or picture produced by an etcher.—**Etching-ground**, *n.* The varnish or coating with which plates to be etched are covered.—**Etching-needle**, *n.* An instrument of steel with a fine point, for tracing outlines, &c., in etching.

Eternal, ē-tėr'nal, *a.* [Fr. *éternel*; L. *æternus*, *æviternus*, from *ævum*, an age, and adj. suffix *-ternus*. AGE.] Having no beginning or end of existence; everlasting; endless; continued without intermission; ceaseless; perpetual.—*The Eternal*, an appellation of God. —**Eternalist**, ē-tėr'nal-ist, *n.* One who holds the existence of the world to be infinite. — **Eternalize**, ē-tėr'nal-īz, *v.t.* — *eternalized*, *eternalizing*. To make eternal; to give endless duration to.—**Eternally**, ē-tėr'nal-li, *adv.* In an eternal manner; without beginning or end of duration; perpetually; unceasingly; continually.—**Eternity**, ē-tėr'ni-ti, *n.* The condition or quality of being eternal; duration or continuance without beginning or end; endless past time or endless future time; the state or condition which begins at death.—**Eternize**, ē-tėr'nīz, *v.t.* — *eternized*, *eternizing*. [Fr. *éterniser*.] To make eternal or endless; to perpetuate; to make for ever famous; to immortalize.

Etesian, ē-tē'zi-an, *a.* [L. *etesius*, from Gr. *etēsios*, annual, from *etos*, a year.] Recurring every year; blowing at stated times of the year: applied to the periodical winds in the Mediterranean.

Ethane, ē'thān, *n.* A hydrocarbon (C_2H_6) allied to marsh-gas (CH_4).

Etheling, eth'el-ing, *n.* Same as *Atheling.*

Ether, ē'thėr, *n.* [L. *æther*, from Gr. *aithēr*, from *aithō*, to light up, to kindle, to burn or blaze; cog. L. *æstas*, summer heat, *Ætna*, Skr. *indh*, to set on fire, *iddhas*, bright.] The supposed subtle atmosphere in space beyond the earth's atmosphere; a hypothetical medium of extreme tenuity and elasticity supposed to be diffused throughout all space (as well as among the molecules of which solid bodies are composed), and to be the medium of the transmission of light and heat; a very light, volatile, and inflammable fluid, obtained from alcohol, an excellent solvent of fats and resins, and used as a stimulant, antispasmodic, and anæsthetic. — **Ethereal**, ē-thē'rē-al, *a.* Formed of ether or the fine atmosphere pervading all space; containing or filled with ether; belonging to the sky regions; heavenly; celestial.—**Etherealism**, **Ethereality**, ē-thē'rē-al-izm, ē-thē'rē-al''i-ti, *n.* The state or quality of being ethereal. — **Etherealize**, ē-thē'rē-al-īz, *v.t.* — *etherealized*, *etherealizing*. To convert into ether; to purify and refine; to render spirit-like or ethereal.—**Etherealization**, ē-thē'rē-al-ī-zā''shon, *n.* An ethereal or subtle spirit-like state or condition. —**Ethereally**, ē-thē'rē-al-li, *adv.* In an ethereal, celestial, or heavenly manner.—**Ethereous**, ē-thē'rē-us, *a.* Ethereal.— **Etherification**, ē-thē'ri-fi-kā''shon, *n.* The process of ether formation.—**Etheriform**, ē'thėr-i-form, *a.* Having the form of ether.—**Etherism**, ē'thėr-izm, *n. Med.* the aggregate of the phenomena produced by administering ether.—**Etherization**, ē'thėr-i-zā''shon, *n.* The act of administering ether to a patient; the state of the system when under the influence of ether. —**Etherize**, ē'thėr-īz, *v.t.*—*etherized*, *etherizing*. To convert into ether; to subject to the influence of ether.

Ethic, **Ethical**, eth'ik, eth'i-kal, *a.* [L. *ethicus*, from Gr. *ēthikos*, from *ēthos*, custom, habit.] Relating to morals; treating of morality; containing precepts of morality; moral.—**Ethically**, eth'i-kal-li, *adv.* In an ethical manner.—**Ethicist**, eth'i-sist, *n.* A writer on ethics; one versed in ethical science.—**Ethics**, eth'iks, *n.* The science which treats of the nature and grounds of moral obligation; moral philosophy, which teaches men their duty and the reasons of it; the science of duty.

Ethiop, **Ethiopian**, ē'thi-op, ē-thi-ō'pi-an, *n.* [Gr. *Aithiops*—*aithō*, to burn, and *ōps*, countenance.] A native of Ethiopia; a Negro or black man.—**Ethiopian**, *a.* Relating to Ethiopia or to its inhabitants. —**Ethiopian**, **Ethiopic**, ē-thi-op'ik, *n.* The language of Ethiopia; the literary and ecclesiastical language of Abyssinia, one of the Semitic tongues.—*a.* Relating to Ethiopia.

Ethmoid, **Ethmoidal**, eth'moid, eth-moi'dal, *a.* [Gr. *ēthmos*, a sieve, and *eidos*, form.] Resembling a sieve.—*Ethmoid bone*, a light spongy bone situated between the orbital processes at the root of the nose, its pores forming passages for the olfactory nerves.

Ethnic, **Ethnical**, eth'nik, eth'ni-kal, *a.* [L. *ethnicus*, from Gr. *ethnikos*, from *ethnos*, nation, pl. *ta ethnē*, the nations, heathens, gentiles.] Pertaining to the gentiles or nations not converted to Christianity; heathen; pagan; pertaining to race; ethnological. — **Ethnically**, eth'ni-kal-li, *adv.* In an ethnical manner.—**Ethnographer**, eth-nog'ra-fėr, *n.* One who cultivates ethnography. — **Ethnographic**, **Ethnographical**, eth-no-graf'ik, eth-no-graf'i-kal, *a.* Pertaining to ethnography.—**Ethnographically**, eth-no-graf'i-kal-li, *adv.* In an ethnographic manner.—**Ethnography**, eth-nog'ra-fi, *n.* That branch of science which has for its subject the description of the different races of men, or the manners, customs, religion, &c., peculiar to different nations.—**Ethnologic**, **Ethnological**, eth-no-loj'ik, eth-no-loj'i-kal, *a.* Relating to ethnology. — **Ethnologist**, eth-nol'o-jist, *n.* One skilled in ethnology; a student of ethnology.—**Ethnology**, eth-nol'o-ji, *n.* That branch of science which investigates the mental and physical differences of mankind and the organic laws on which they depend.

Ethology, eth-ol'o-ji, *n.* [Gr. *ethos* or *ēthos*, manners, morals, and *logos*, discourse.] The science of ethics; the science of character.—**Ethologic**, **Ethological**, eth-o-loj'ik, eth-o-loj'i-kal, *a.*

Ethyl, eth'il, *n.* [*Ether*, and Gr. *hylē*, matter.] A univalent hydro-carbon radical; the trade-mark for tetraethyl lead, or for motor fuel to which it has been added in order to raise the combustibility and reduce the formation of carbon in the motor.—**Ethylene**, eth'i-lēn, *n.* A gas to which is largely due the illuminating power of coal-gas.

Etiolate, ē'ti-ō-lāt, *v.i.*—*etiolated*, *etiolating*. [Fr. *étioler*, to blanch, from *éteule*, stubble, from L. *stipula*, a straw.] To grow white from absence of the normal amount of green colouring matter in the leaves or stalks; to be whitened by excluding the light of the sun, as plants.—*v.t.* To blanch or whiten by excluding the light or by disease. — **Etiolation**, ē'ti-ō-lā''shon, *n.* The act of etiolating or state of being etiolated or blanched.

Etiology, ē-ti-ol'o-ji, *n.* [Gr. *aitia*, cause, and *logos*, discourse.] An account of the causes of anything, particularly of diseases. —**Etiological**, ē'ti-ō-loj''i-kal, *a.* Pertaining to etiology.

Etiquette, et'i-ket, *n.* [Fr.; O.Fr. *estiquette*, a thing attached, a label, from G. *stecken*, to stick, to put. *Ticket* is same word.] Conventional forms of ceremony or decorum; the forms which are observed toward particular persons, or in particular places; social observances required by good breeding.

Etna, et'na, *n.* [From *Etna*, the Sicilian volcano.] A table cooking-utensil, heated by a spirit-lamp.

Etruscan, ē-trus'kan, *a.* Relating to Etruria, an ancient country in Central Italy.—*n.* A native of ancient Etruria.

Etude, ā-tūd, *n.* [Fr.] A musical or artistic composition designed to serve as a study.

Etui, **Etwee**, et-wē', *n.* [Fr. *étui.*] A pocket-case for small articles, such as needles, pins, &c.; a ladies' reticule.

Etymology, et-i-mol'o-ji, *n.* [Gr. *etymos*, true or real, *to etymon*, the true or literal signification of a word, its root, and *logos*, discourse.] That part of philology which explains the origin and derivation of words; derivation; that part of grammar which comprehends the various inflections and modifications of words. — **Etymologic**, **Etymological**, et'i-mo-loj''ik, et'i-mo-loj''i-kal, *a.* Pertaining to or treating of etymology or the derivation of words.— **Etymologically**, et'i-mo-loj''i-kal-li, *adv.* In an etymological manner.—**Etymologist**, et-i-mol'o-jist, *n.* One versed in etymology; one who searches into the origin of words.—**Etymologize**, et-i-mol'o-jīz, *v.i.* To search into the origin of words.—*v.t.* To trace the etymology of; to give the etymology of.—**Etymon**, et'i-mon, *n.* The root of a word.

Etypical, ē-tip'i-kal, *a.* Diverging from, not conforming to, the type.

Eucaine, ū-kā'in, *n.* A complex synthetic substance used as a local anæsthetic, which has largely superseded cocaine, being as powerful and less dangerous.

Eucalyptol, ū'ka-lip-tol, *n.* [From *eucalyptus*, and *oleum*, oil.] The oil of the blue-gum tree (*Eucalyptus globulus*), used as a remedy for asthma and other ailments.— **Eucalyptus**, ū-ka-lip'tus, *n.* [Gr. *eu*, well, and *kalyptō*, to cover—referring to the cover of the flower-bud.] The eucalyptus, a genus of very large trees of the myrtle order, natives of Australia, called gum-trees, from the gum that exudes from them, also stringy-bark, iron-bark, &c.

Eucharis, ūk'ar-is, *n.* [Gr. *eucharis*, pleasing.] South American plant of the bulbous kind, with white flowers of bell shape.

Eucharist, ū'ka-rist, *n.* [Gr. *eucharistia*, thanksgiving, the Lord's supper, *eucharis-*

tos, grateful—*eu*, well, good, and *charis*, grace, favour.] The sacrament of the Lord's supper; the Communion; the consecrated elements, and especially the bread; thanksgiving. — **Eucharistic, Eucharistical**, ū-ka-ris'tik, ū-ka-ris'ti-kal, *a.* Pertaining to the eucharist.

Euchlorine, ū-klō'rin, *n.* [Gr. *chlōros*, green.] A gaseous compound of chlorine and oxide of chlorine.

Euchology, ū-kol'o-ji, *n.* [Gr. *euchē*, prayer, *logos*, discourse.] A book of prayers; a liturgy.—**Euchologion**, ū-kol-o'ji-on.

Euchre, Eucre, ū'kėr, *n.* A game of cards, 'a modified form of the game of écarté', played by two, three, or four players with the thirty-two highest cards of the pack.

Euclase, ū'klās, *n.* [Gr. *eu*, and *klaō*, to break.] A mineral of the beryl family, of a pale-green colour and very brittle.

Eudæmonism, Eudemonism, ū-dē'-mon-izm, *n.* [Gr. *eudaimōn*, happy.] The system of philosophy which makes human happiness the highest object, declaring that the production of happiness is the foundation of virtue.—**Eudæmonist, Eudemonist**, ū-dē'mon-ist, *n.* A believer in eudæmonism.

Eudiometer, ū-di-om'e-tėr, *n.* [Gr. *eudios*, serene, and *metron*, measure.] An instrument usually in the form of a glass siphon with a graduated limb, originally designed for ascertaining the purity of the air, but now employed generally in the analysis of gases by the electric spark. — **Eudiometric, Eudiometrical**, ū'di-o-met"-rik, ū'di-o-met"ri-kal, *a.* Pertaining to a eudiometer or to eudiometry.—**Eudiometry**, ū-di-om'et-ri, *n.* The art or practice of using the eudiometer.

Eugenics, ū-jen'iks, *n.* [Gr. *eu*, well, *genos*, race.] The theory dealing with the production or treatment of a fine, healthy race.—**Eugenist**, ū-jen'ist, *n.* One who theorizes or practises *eugenics*.

Euhemerism, ū-hem'ėr-izm, *n.* [After the Greek *Euēmeros*, who explained myths in this way.] That system of interpreting myths by which the gods are regarded as representing distinguished men who formerly lived, and so the myths are considered as founded on real histories.—**Euhemerist**, ū-hem'ėr-ist, *n.* A believer in the doctrine of euhemerism. — **Euhemeristic**, ū-hem'ėr-is"tik, *a.* Of or belonging to euhemerism. — **Euhemerize**, ū-hem'ėr-īz, *v.t.* To treat or explain in the manner of Euemeros. Also written *Euemerism*, &c.

Eulogy, ū'lo-ji, *n.* [Gr. *eulogia*—*eu*, well, and *logos*, speech, from *legō*, to speak.] Praise; encomium; panegyric; a speech or writing in commendation of a person on account of his valuable qualities or services. —**Eulogic, Eulogical**, ū-loj'ik, ū-loj'i-kal, *a.* Containing or pertaining to eulogy or praise; commendatory.—**Eulogically**, ū-loj'i-kal-li, *adv.* In a eulogic manner.—**Eulogist**, ū'lo-jist, *n.* One who praises and commends another; one who pronounces a eulogy.—**Eulogistic, Eulogistical** ū-lo-jis'tik, ū-lo-jis'ti-kal, *a.* Containing or pertaining to eulogy or praise; laudatory. — **Eulogistically**, ū-lo-jis'ti-kal-li, *adv.* With commendation or eulogy. — **Eulogium**, ū-lō'ji-um, *n.* A formal eulogy.—**Eulogize**, ū'lo-jīz, *v.t.*—*eulogized, eulogizing.* To speak or write in commendation of another; to extol in speech or writing; to praise.

Eumenides, ū-men'i-dēz, *n. pl.* *Lit.* the gracious goddesses, a Greek name of the Furies, because it was considered unlawful and dangerous to name them under their true designation *Erinnyes*.

Eunuch, ū'nuk, *n.* [Gr. *eunouchos*—*eunē*, a bed, and *echō*, to keep, to have charge of.] A castrated male of the human species; hence, from the employment to which eunuchs were commonly put, a chamberlain.—**Eunuch, Eunuchate**, ū'nu-kāt, *v.t.* To make a eunuch of.—**Eunuchism**, ū'nuk-izm, *n.* The state of being a eunuch.

Eupepsia, Eupepsy, ū-pep'si-a, ū-pep'si, *n.* [Gr. *eupepsia*—*eu*, and *pepsis*, digestion, from *peptō*, to digest.] Good digestion; the opposite of dyspepsia.—**Eupeptic**, ū-pep'-tik, *a.* Having good digestion; easy of digestion.

Euphemism, ū'fem-izm, *n.* [Gr. *euphēmismos*—*eu*, well, and *phēmi*, to speak.] A figure of speech in which a delicate word or expression is substituted for one which is offensive to good manners or to delicate ears. — **Euphemistic, Euphemistical**, ū-fem-is'tik, ū-fem-is'ti-kal, *a.* Pertaining to or containing euphemism. — **Euphemize**, ū'fem-īz, *v.t.* To express by a euphemism.

Euphony, ū'fo-ni, *n.* [Gr. *euphōnia*—*eu*, well, and *phōne*, voice.] An agreeable sound; an easy, smooth enunciation of sounds; a pronunciation of letters, syllables, and words which is pleasing to the ear.—**Euphonic, Euphonical**, ū-fon'ik, ū-fon'i-kal, *a.* Of or pertaining to, or characterized by, euphony; agreeable in sound; pleasing to the ear.—**Euphonious**, ū-fō'-ni-us, *a.* Agreeable in sound; euphonic.—**Euphoniously**, ū-fō'ni-us-li, *adv.* In a euphonious manner. — **Euphonium**, ū-fō'ni-um, *n.* A brass bass instrument with three or four valves, used in military bands, and frequently in the orchestra as a substitute for the trombone.—**Euphonize**, ū'fo-nīz, *v.t.* To make agreeable in sound.

Euphorbia, ū-for'bi-a, *n.* [Gr. *euphorbia*, from the name of an ancient Greek physician.] A genus of exogenous plants, some of which are found in Britain, and are popularly called *spurges*, while the most remarkable are tropical shrubs or trees, often large, fleshy, and leafless, having the habit of a cactaceous plant. — **Euphorbium**, ū-for'bi-um, *n.* A substance obtained from several species of Euphorbia, virulently purgative and emetic.

Euphoria, ū-for'i-a, *n.* [Gr. *eu*, well, *phoreō*, I possess.] Feeling of well-being.

Euphrasy, ū'fra-si, *a.* [Gr. *euphrasia*, delight.] The herb popularly called eyebright, formerly a specific for diseases of the eye.

Euphuism, ū'fū-izm, *n.* [From the name of the hero of two works by John Lyly, written in a strange and affected style, which became fashionable at the court of Elizabeth. *Euphues* is the Gr. *euphyēs*, well-shaped — *eu*, well, and *phyē*, growth, stature.] Affectation of excessive elegance and refinement of language; high-flown artificial diction.—**Euphuist**, ū'fū-ist, *n.* One addicted to euphuism: applied particularly to certain writers, at the head of which stood John Lyly. — **Euphuistic**, ū-fū-is'tik, *a.* Belonging to the euphuists or to euphuism.

Eupnœa, ūp-nē'a, *n.* [Gr. *eu*, well, *pneō*, I breathe.] Easy, natural breathing.

Eurasian, ū-rā'shi-an, *n.* [A contraction of *European* and *Asian*.] One born in Hindustan of a Hindu mother and European father.

Eureka, ū-rē'ka. [Gr. (*h*)*eurēka*, I have found, perf. ind. act. of (*h*)*euriskō*, to find.] The exclamation of Archimedes, when, after long study, he discovered a method of detecting the amount of alloy in King Hiero's crown; hence, a discovery; especially, one made after long research; an expression of triumph at a discovery or supposed discovery.

Eurhythmy, ū-rith'mi, *n.* Artistic harmony; proportion; harmonious movement. *Med.* regularity of the pulse.

European, ū-rō-pē'an, *a.* [L. *Europa*, Gr. *Eurōpē*, Europe.] Pertaining to Europe; native to Europe.—*n.* A native of Europe.—**Europeanize**, ū-rō-pē'an-īz, *v.t.* To cause to become European; to assimilate to Europeans in manners, character, and usages.

Eustachian, ū-stā'ki-an, *a.* Named after *Eustachius* or *Eustachi*, an Italian physician, who died 1574.—*Eustachian tube*, the tube which forms a communication between the internal ear and the back part of the mouth.—*Eustachian valve*, a valve which separates the right auricle of the heart from the inferior vena cava.

Eutaxy, ū'tak-si, *n.* [Gr. *eutaxia*, good arrangement—*eu*, well, and *taxis*, order.] Good or established order.

Euthanasia, ū-tha-nā'zi-a, *n.* [Gr.—*eu*, well, and *thanatos*, death.] An easy death; a putting to death by painless means; a means of putting to a painless death.

Eutrophy, ū'tro-fi, *n.* [Gr. *eutrophia*, from *eutrophos*, healthy—*eu*, well, and *trephō*, to nourish.] *Med.* healthy nutrition; a healthy state of the nutritive organs.—**Eutrophic**, ū-trof'ik, *n.* An agent whose action is exerted on the system of nutrition.

Evacuate, ē-vak'ū-āt, *v.t.* — *evacuated, evacuating.* [L. *evacuo*, *evacuatum*—*e*, out, and *vacuus*, empty, from *vaco*, to be empty. VACANT.] To make empty; to make empty by removing one's self from (an army *evacuates* a town or a country); to void or discharge from the bowels. — **Evacuant**, ē-vak'ū-ant, *a.* Producing evacuation; purgative.—*n.* A medicine which promotes the natural secretions and excretions.—**Evacuation**, ē-vak'ū-ā"shon, *n.* The act of evacuating; that which is evacuated or discharged, especially from the bowels.—**Evacuative**, ē-vak'ū-ā-tiv, *a.* Serving or tending to evacuate; purgative.—**Evacuator**, ē-vak'ū-ā-tėr, *n.* One who or that which evacuates.

Evade, ē-vād', *v.t.*—*evaded, evading.* [L. *evado*—*e*, and *vado*, to go, as in *invade*, *pervade*; akin to E. *wade*. WADE.] To avoid, escape from, or elude in any way, as by dexterity, artifice, sophistry, address, or ingenuity; to slip away from; to elude; to escape the grasp or comprehension of; to baffle or foil.—*v.i.* To escape; to slip away; to practise artifice or sophistry for the purpose of eluding.—**Evadible**, ē-vā'di-bl, *a.* Capable of being evaded.—**Evasion**, ē-vā'-zhon, *n.* [L. *evasio*.] The act of evading, eluding, avoiding, or escaping; shift; subterfuge; equivocation; prevarication; shuffling.—**Evasive**, ē-vā'siv, *a.* Using evasion or artifice to avoid; shuffling; equivocating; containing or characterized by evasion.—**Evasively**, ē-vā'siv-li, *adv.* In an evasive manner.—**Evasiveness**, ē-vā'siv-nes, *n.*

Evaluate, ē-val'ū-āt, *v.t.* *Alg.* to find the numerical expression for a quantity.—**Evaluation**,† ē-val'ū-ā"shon, *n.* Exhaustive valuation or appraisement.

Evanesce,† ev-a-nes', *v.i.*—*evanesced, evanescing.* [L. *evanesco* — *e*, and *vanesco*, to vanish, from *vanus*, vain, empty. VAIN.] To vanish; to disappear; to be dissipated, as vapour.—**Evanescence**, ev-a-nes'ens, *n.* The state or character of being evanescent. — **Evanescent**, ev-a-nes'ent, *a.* Vanishing; subject to vanishing; fleeting; passing away; liable to disappear or come to an end.—**Evanescently**, ev-a-nes'ent-li, *adv.* In an evanescent manner.

Evangel, ē-van'jel, *n.* [L. *evangelium*, the gospel; Gr. *euangelion*, good tidings, the gospel—*eu*, well, good, and *angellō*, to announce.] The gospel; one of the gospels or four New Testament books under the names of Matthew, Mark, Luke, and John. —**Evangelical, Evangelic**, ē-van-jel'i-kal, ē-van-jel'ik, *a.* [L.L. *evangelicus*.] According to the gospel, or religious truth taught in the New Testament; sound in the doctrines of the gospel; adhering closely to the letter of the gospel; fervent and devout; *eccles.* a term applied to a section in the Protestant churches who give special prominence to the doctrines of the corruption of man's nature by the fall, of his regeneration and redemption through our Saviour, and of free and unmerited grace; applied in Germany to Protestants as distinguished from Roman Catholics, and more especially to the national Protestant church formed in Prussia in 1817 by a union of the Lutheran and Calvinistic churches.—**Evangelicalism**, ē-van-jel'i-kal-izm, *n.* Adherence to evangelical doctrines. — **Evangelically**, ē-van-jel'i-kal-i, *adv.* In an evangelical manner. — **Evangelicism**, ē-van-jel'i-sizm, *n.* Evangelical principles.—**Evangelist**, ē-van'jel-ist, *n.* One of the four writers of the gospels; a layman engaged in preaching or missionary work.—**Evangelistic**, ē-van'jel-is"tik, *a.* Evangelical;

tending or designed to evangelize.—**Evangelization**, ē-van′jel-i-zā″shon, *n.* The act of evangelizing.—**Evangelize**, ē-van′jel-īz, *v.t.*—*evangelized, evangelizing.* To instruct in the gospel; to preach the gospel to and convert.—*v.i.* To preach the gospel.

Evanish,† ē-van′ish, *v.i.* To vanish; to disappear.

Evaporate, ē-vap′ėr-āt, *v.i.*—*evaporated, evaporating.* [L. *evaporo, evaporatum*—*e*, out, and *vapor*, vapour. VAPOUR.] To pass off in vapour; to escape and be dissipated, either in visible vapour or in particles too minute to be visible; *fig.* to escape or pass off without effect; to be dissipated; to be wasted.—*v.t.* To convert or resolve into vapour; to cause to evaporate; to vaporize. — **Evaporable**, ē-vap′ėr-a-bl, *a.* Capable of being converted into vapour or of being dissipated by evaporation.—**Evaporation**, ē-vap′ėr-ā″shon, *n.* The act or process of evaporating; the conversion of a liquid by heat into vapour or steam, which becomes dissipated in the atmosphere in the manner of an elastic fluid; vaporization; the matter evaporated; vapour. — **Evaporative**, ē-vap′ėr-ā-tiv, *a.* Causing evaporation; pertaining to evaporation.—**Evaporometer**, ē-vap′ėr-om″et-ėr *n.* An instrument for ascertaining the quantity of a fluid evaporated in a given time; an atmometer.

Evasion, Evasive. Under EVADE.

Eve, ēv, *n.* [Short for *even, evening.*] The close of the day; the evening; the day or the latter part of the day before a church festival; the period just preceding some event (on the *eve* of a revolution).

Even, ē′vn, *a.* [A.Sax. *efen*, even, level, equal = D. *even*, Dan. *jevn, jævn*, Icel. *jafn*, Goth. *ibns*, G. *eben*, even, level.] Level; smooth; flat; devoid of irregularities; straight or direct; uniform; equal; not easily ruffled; on a level or on the same level; in the same or in an equally favourable position; on a level in advantage; having accounts balanced; square; adjusted; fair; equitable; capable of being divided by 2 without a remainder: opposed to *odd.*—*v.t.* To make even; to level; to lay smooth; to place in an equal state; to balance.—*adv.* Expressing a level or equality; hence, just; exactly in consonance; according (*even* as he wished); expressing equality or sameness of time (I knew it *even* then); expressing, emphatically, identity of person (*even* he did it); expressing a strong assertion; not only this or so, but more, or but also.—**Evenly**, ē′vn-li, *adv.* In an even manner; smoothly; equally; uniformly; impartially. — **Evenness**, ē′vn-nes, *n.* The state or quality of being even.—**Even-handed**, *a.* Impartial; equitable; just. — **Even-handedness**, *n.*

Even, ē′vn, *n.* [A.Sax. *aefen, ǽfen.* EVENING.] Evening. (*Poet.*)—**Evenfall**, ē′vn-fal, *n.* The fall of evening; early evening; twilight. — **Evensong**, ē′vn-song, *n.* A form of worship for the evening; vespers.—**Eventide**, ē′vn-tīd, *n.* Evening.

Evening, ēv′ning, *n.* [A.Sax. *aefnung*, verbal noun (like *morning*), from *aefen, ǽfen*, evening; cog. G. *abend*, Sw. *afton*, Icel. *aftan*, Dan. *aften*, evening. The root meaning seems to be retiring, the word being akin to A.Sax. *af, of*, off; G. *ab*, of, from L. *ab*, Skr. *apa*, from.] The close of the day, and the beginning of darkness or night; the time from sunset till darkness; the latter part of the afternoon and the earlier part of the night; the decline or latter part of life, strength, or glory; often used as an adjective.—**Evening-star**, *n.* The planet Venus when visible in the evening.

Event, ē-vent′, *n.* [L. *eventus*, from *evenio, eventum*, to come out—*e*, out, and *venio*, to come, seen also in *advent, convene, prevent, venture*, &c.] That which happens or falls out; any incident good or bad; an occurrence; the consequence of anything; that in which an action, operation, or series of operations terminates; the issue, conclusion, end. — **Eventful**, ē-vent′ful, *a.* Full of events or incidents; characterized by great changes either in public or private affairs.—**Eventual**, ē-ven′tū-al, *a.* Coming or happening as a consequence or final result; consequential; final; ultimate.—**Eventuality**, ē-ven′tū-al″i-ti, *n.* That which eventuates or happens; a contingent result. —**Eventually**, ē-ven′tū-al-li, *adv.* In the event; in the final result or issue.—**Eventuate**, ē-ven′tū-āt, *v.i.*—*eventuated, eventuating.* To issue as an event or consequence; to fall out; to happen; to come to pass.

Eventrate, ē′ven-trāt, *v.t.* To open the belly.—**Eventration**, ē-ven-trā′shon, *n.* Act of opening the belly; protrusion of an organ from the abdomen.

Ever, ev′ėr, *adv.* [A.Sax. *aefre*, always; allied to Goth. *aivs*, time, *aiv*, ever; Icel. *æfi*, an age, the space of life; L. *ævum*, Gr. *aiōn*, Skr. *âyus*, an age. Akin *aye, every.*] At any time past or future; at all times; always; eternally; constantly; incessantly; continually; in any degree.—*For ever*, eternally; to perpetuity; sometimes with a repetition for the sake of emphasis (*for ever and ever*).—*Ever and anon*, now and then; again and again; time after time.—*Ever*, in *composition*, signifies always or continually, without intermission, or to eternity; as, *ever*-active; *ever*-living. — **Evergreen**, ev′ėr-grēn, *a.* Always green; having verdant leaves throughout the year; *fig.* always fresh, vigorous, or in a good condition.—*n.* A plant that retains its verdure through all the seasons.—**Everlasting**, ev-ėr-las′ting, *a.* Lasting or enduring for ever; existing or continuing without beginning or end; eternal; perpetual; endless; continual. — *n.* Eternity; a plant whose flowers retain their form, colour, and brightness for many months after being gathered.—*The Everlasting*, the Eternal Being; God.—**Everlastingly**, ev-ėr-las′ting-li, *adv.* Eternally; perpetually; continually.—**Everlastingness**, ev-ėr-las′ting-nes, *n.*—**Evermore**, ev′ėr-mōr, *adv.* Always; eternally; for ever; at all times; continually.

Evert, ē-vėrt′, *v.t.* [L. *everto, eversum*—*e*, and *verto*, to turn, as in *convert, invert, revert, verse*, &c.] To overturn; to overthrow; to turn outward, or inside out.—**Eversion**, ē-vėr′shon, *n.* The act of everting; an overthrowing; destruction. — *Eversion of the eyelids*, a disease in which the eyelids are turned outward, so as to expose the red internal tunic.

Every, ev′ėr-i, *a.* [O.E. *everich, everilk*, from A.Sax. *aefre*, ever, and *ælc*, each. EVER, EACH.] Each individual of the whole number; each of a number singly or one by one.—**Everybody**, ev′ėr-i-bod-i, *n.* Every person.—**Everyday**, ev′ėr-i-dā, *a.* Used, occurring, or that may be seen or met with every day; common; usual; ordinary. — **Everywhere**, ev′ėr-i-whār, *adv.* In every place; in all places.

Evict, ē-vikt′, *v.t.* [L. *evinco, evictum*, to vanquish utterly—*e*, intens., and *vinco*, to overcome, as in *convince, convict, evince.* VICTOR.] To dispossess by a judicial process or course of legal proceedings; to expel from lands or tenements by law.—**Eviction**, ē-vik′shon, *n.* The act of evicting; the expulsion of a tenant from lands or tenements by law.

Evidence, ev′i-dens, *n.* [Fr. *évidence*, from L. *evidentia*—*e*, and *video, visum*, to see. VISION.] That which demonstrates or makes clear that a fact is so; that which makes evident or enables the mind to see truth; proof arising from our own perceptions by the senses, or from the testimony of others, or from inductions of reason; testimony; *law*, that which is legally submitted to a competent tribunal as a means of ascertaining the truth of any alleged matter of fact under investigation.—*State's evidence*, evidence given by an accomplice, when the ordinary evidence is defective, on the understanding that he himself shall go free for his share of the crime.—*v.t.*—*evidenced, evidencing.* To render evident; to prove; to make clear to the mind.—**Evident**, ev′i-dent, *a.* [L. *evidens.*] Open to be seen; clear to the mental or physical eye; manifest; obvious; plain.—**Evidential**, ev-i-den′shal, *a.* Affording evidence; clearly proving.—**Evidentiary**, ev-i-den′shi-a-ri, *a.* Evidential.—**Evidently**, ev′i-dent-li, *adv.* In an evident manner; clearly; manifestly.—**Evidentness**, ev′i-dent-nes, *n.*

Evil, ē′vil, *a.* [A.Sax. *efel, yfel*; D. *euvel*, O.Fris. *evel*, G. *übel*, Goth. *ubils. Ill* is a contracted form of *evil.*] Having bad qualities of a natural kind; having qualities which tend to injury, or to produce mischief; injurious; pernicious; mischievous; having bad qualities of a moral kind; wicked; corrupt; perverse; wrong; vile; vicious; unfortunate; unpropitious; calamitous.—*The evil one*, the devil.—*n.* Anything that causes injury, pain, or suffering; misfortune; calamity; mischief; injury; depravity; corruption of heart, or disposition to commit wickedness; malignity; the negation or contrary of good.—*adv.* Not well; ill. — **Evildoer**, ē′vil-dö-ėr, *n.* One who does evil; one who commits sin, crime, or any moral wrong.—**Evil-eye**, *n.* A kind of influence superstitiously ascribed in former times to certain persons, their glance being supposed to injure.—**Evil-eyed**, *a.* Having the evil-eye; looking with envy, jealousy, or bad design.—**Evil-favoured**, *a.* Having a bad countenance or external appearance.—**Evil-minded**, *a.* Having evil dispositions or intentions; disposed to mischief or sin.—**Evilness**, ē′vil-nes, *n.* Badness; viciousness; malignity of sin.—**Evil-starred**, *a.* Destined to misfortune, as if through the influence of an adverse star or planet; ill-starred.

Evince, ē-vins′, *v.t.*—*evinced, evincing.* [L. *evinco*, to vanquish, to prove or show. EVICT.] To show; to prove; to manifest; to make evident; to display as something belonging to one's own nature or character (to *evince* fear). — **Evincement**, ē-vins′-ment, *n.* Act of evincing.—**Evincible**, ē-vin′si-bl, *a.* Capable of being evinced.—**Evincibly**, ē-vin′si-bli, *adv.* In a manner to evince.

Evirate, ē′vi-rāt, *v.t.* [L. *e*, out, *vir*, man.] To castrate.

Eviscerate, ē-vis′ėr-āt, *v.t.*—*eviscerated, eviscerating.* [L. *eviscero*—*e*, and *viscera*, the bowels.] To take out the entrails of; to disembowel.—**Evisceration**, ē-vis′ėr-ā″shon, *n.* The act of eviscerating.

Evoke, ē-vōk′, *v.t.*—*evoked, evoking.* [L. *evoco*—*e*, out, and *voco*, to call.] To call or summon forth.—**Evocation**, ev-ō-kā′shon, *n.* The act of evoking; a calling forth.

Evolution, ev-ō-lū′shon, *n.* [L. *evolutio*, from *evolvo, evolutum*, to unroll, to unfold. EVOLVE.] The act of unfolding, unrolling, or expanding; a gradual development or working out; the extraction of arithmetical or algebraic roots—the reverse of involution; a regulated or systematic series of movements which a body of troops, a fleet, or a ship makes when changing a previous formation or position; that theory which sees in the history of all things, organic and inorganic, a development from simplicity to complexity, a gradual advance from a simple or rudimentary condition to one that is more complex and of a higher character.—**Evolutional, Evolutionary**, ev-ō-lū′shon-al, ev-ō-lū′shon-a-ri, *a.* Of or pertaining to evolution; produced by or due to evolution.—**Evolutionist**, ev-ō-lū′shon-ist, *n.* One skilled in evolutions, specifically in military evolutions; a believer in the doctrine of evolution.

Evolve, ē-volv′, *v.t.*—*evolved, evolving.* [L. *evolvo*—*e*, and *volvo*, to roll, which is cog. with E. to *wallow*, and is seen also in *convolve, devolve, revolve, voluble, volume*, &c.] To unfold; to open and expand; to disentangle; to unravel; to develop; to cause to pass from a simple to a complex state. —*v.i.* To open or disclose itself.—**Evolvement**,† ē-volv′ment, *n.* Act of evolving.—**Evolvent**, ē-vol′vent, *n. Geom.* the involute of a curve.—**Evolver**, ē-vol′vėr, *n.* One who or that which evolves.

Evulsion, ē-vul′shon, *n.* [L. *evulsio*—*e*, out, and *vello, vulsum*, to pluck.] The act of plucking or pulling out by force.

Ewe, ū, *n.* [A.Sax. *eowu*; allied to Fris. *ei*,

O.H.G. *avi*, *ou*, Icel. *á*, L. *ovis*, Gr. *oïs*, Skr. *avi*, a sheep.] A female sheep.

Ewer, ū'ėr, *n.* [From O.Fr. *ewe*, Mod.Fr. *eau*, water, from L. *aqua*, water (whence *aquatic*, &c.).] A large pitcher or jug with a wide spout, used to bring water for washing the hands; a sort of pitcher that accompanies a wash-hand basin for holding the water.

Exacerbate, ek-sas'ėr-bāt, *v.t.*—*exacerbated*, *exacerbating*. [L. *exacerbo*, *exacerbatum*—*ex*, intens., and *acerbus*, harsh, sharp, sour.] To irritate, exasperate, or inflame; to increase the malignant qualities of; to increase the violence of (a disease).—**Exacerbation**, ek-sas'ėr-bā"shon, *n.* The act of exacerbating; increase of malignity; a periodical increase of violence in a disease. Termed also **Exacerbescence**, ek-sas'-ėr-bes"ens, *n.*

Exact, eg-zakt', *a.* [L. *exactus*, pp. of *exigo*, to drive out, to measure—*ex*, out, and *ago*, to drive, to do, as in *agent*, *act*, *agitate*, &c.] Closely correct or regular; accurate; conformed to rule; precise; not different in the least; methodical; careful; observing strict method, rule, or order; punctual; strict. —*v.t.* [Fr. *exacter*, L.L. *exactare*.] To force or compel to be paid or yielded; to extort by means of authority or compulsion; to enforce a yielding of; to enjoin with pressing urgency.—**Exacter**, eg-zak'-tėr, *n.* One who exacts.—**Exacting**, eg-zak'ting, *p.* and *a.* Demanding or disposed to demand without pity or justice; extorting; making unreasonable claims.—**Exaction**, eg-zak'shon, *n.* The act of exacting; extortion; a wresting of contributions unjustly; that which is exacted; fees, rewards, or contributions levied with severity or injustice. —**Exactitude**, eg-zak'ti-tūd, *n.* Exactness; accuracy; nicety.—**Exactly**, eg-zakt'li, *adv.* In an exact manner.—**Exactness**, eg-zakt'nes, *n.* The state or quality of being exact; accuracy; correctness; preciseness; regularity.—**Exactor**, eg-zak'tėr, *n.* One who exacts.

Exaggerate, eg-zaj'ėr-āt, *v.t.*—*exaggerated*, *exaggerating*. [L. *exaggero*, *exaggeratum*—*ex*, intens., and *aggero*, to heap, from *agger*, a heap—*ad*, to, and *gero*, to carry.] To represent as greater than truth or justice will warrant; to heighten unduly; to magnify. —**Exaggeration**, eg-zaj'ėr-ā"-shon, *n.* The act of exaggerating; a representation of things beyond the truth or reality. —**Exaggerative**, eg-zaj'ėr-ā-tiv, *a.* Having the tendency to exaggerate.—**Exaggerator**, eg-zaj'ėr-ā-tėr, *n.* One who exaggerates. —**Exaggeratory**, eg-zaj'ėr-a-to-ri, *a.* Containing exaggeration.

Exalbuminous, eks-al-bū'mi-nus, *a. Bot.* having no albumen about the embryo, or no albumen but that of the cotyledons.

Exalt, eg-zalt', *v.t.* [Fr. *exalter*, from L. *exaltare*—*ex*, and *altus*, high (whence *altitude*, *haughty*).] To raise high; to lift up; to elevate in power, wealth, rank, or dignity, character, and the like; to elevate with joy, pride, or confidence; to elate; to praise highly; to magnify; to extol; to elevate the tone of; to elevate in diction or sentiment. —**Exaltation**, eg-zal-tā'shon, *n.* The act of exalting or state of being exalted; elevated state; state of greatness or dignity; a state of great elation; mental elevation.—**Exaltedness**, eg-zal'ted-nes, *n.* The state of being exalted.—**Exalter**, eg-zal'tėr, *n.* One who exalts.

Examine, eg-zam'in, *v.t.*—*examined*, *examining*. [L. *examino*, *examinatum*, from *examen*, *examinis*, the tongue of a balance, for *exagmen*, from *ex*, out, and *ago*, to bring, to do (whence *agent*, &c.).] To inspect or observe carefully; to look into the state of; to view and consider in all its aspects; to question, as a witness or an accused person; to put judicial inquiries to; to inquire into the qualifications, capabilities, knowledge, or progress of, by interrogatories; to try or test.—**Examinant**, eg-zam'i-nant, *n.* An examiner.—**Examinee**, eg-zam'i-nē", *n.* One who undergoes an examination.—**Examiner**, eg-zam'i-nėr, *n.* One who examines; one who inspects; a person appointed to conduct an examination, as in a university. —**Examinable**, eg-zam'i-na-bl, *a.* Capable of being examined.—**Examen**,† eg-zam'en, *n.* An examination.—**Examination**, eg-zam'i-nā"shon, *n.* The act of examining or state of being examined; a careful search or inquiry; careful and accurate inspection; a legal inquiry into facts by testimony; an attempt to ascertain truth by inquiries and interrogatories; a process for testing qualifications, knowledge, progress, of students, candidates, &c.; investigation; scrutiny; trial.—**Examinator**, eg-zam'i-nā-tėr, *n.* An examiner.

Example, eg-zam'pl, *n.* [L. *exemplum*, from *eximo*, to take out or away—*ex*, out, and *emo*, *emptum*, to take, to purchase (as in *exempt*). *Sample* is the same word.] A sample or specimen; a pattern, in morals or manners, worthy of imitation; a copy or model; one who or that which is proposed or is proper to be imitated; a former instance, to be followed or avoided; one held out as a caution or warning to others; a particular case illustrating a general rule, position, or truth.

Exanthema, ek-san-thē'ma, *n.* pl. **Exanthemata**, ek-san-them'a-ta. [Gr. *exanthēma*, from *exantheō*, to blossom—*ex*, and *anthos*, a flower.] *Med.* an eruption or breaking out, as in measles, small-pox, &c.: frequently limited to such eruptions as are accompanied with fever.—**Exanthematous**, **Exanthematic**, ek-san-them'a-tus, ek-san'the-mat"ik, *a.* Of or pertaining to exanthema; eruptive.—**Exanthesis**, ek-san-thē'sis, *n. Med.* an eruption.

Exarch, ek'särk, *n.* [Gr. *exarchos*—*ex*, and *archos*, a chief.] A viceroy or governor of an Italian or African province under the Byzantine Empire.—**Exarchate**, ek'sär-kāt, *n.* The office, dignity, or administration of an exarch.

Exarticulation, ek-sär-tik'ū-lā"shon, *n.* [L. *ex*, out, and *articulus*, a small joint.] Dislocation of a joint.

Exasperate, eg-zas'pėr-āt, *v.t.*—*exasperated*, *exasperating*. [L. *exaspero*, *exasperatum*, to irritate—*ex*, and *asper*, rough, harsh.] To irritate in a high degree; to provoke to rage; to enrage; to anger; to excite or inflame.—**Exasperation**, eg-zas'pėr-ā"shon, *n.* The act of exasperating or state of being exasperated.

Excamb, **Excambie**, eks-kamb', eks-kam'bi, *v.t.* [L.L. *excambio*, to exchange. CHANGE, EXCHANGE.] To exchange: applied specifically to the exchange of land. [Scotch.]—**Excambion**, **Excambium**, eks-kam'bi-on, eks-kam'bi-um, *n.* Exchange of pieces of land. [Scotch.]

Excandescence, eks-kan-des'ens, *n.* [L. *excandescentia*—*ex*, and *candesco*, *candeo*, to be hot.] A growing hot; glowing heat; heat of passion.

Excarnate, eks-kär'nāt, *v.t.*—*excarnated*, *excarnating*. [L. *ex*, priv., and *caro*, *carnis*, flesh.] To deprive or clear of flesh.—**Excarnation**,† eks-kär-nā'shon, *n.* The act of divesting of flesh; the opposite of *incarnation*.

Ex-cathedra, eks-ka-thed'ra, *a.* [L. *ex*, from, and *cathedra*, Gr. *kathedra*, a chair (whence *cathedral*).] *Lit.* from the chair, as of authority or instruction; hence, applied to any decision, order, &c., given in an authoritative and dogmatic manner.

Excavate, eks'ka-vāt, *v.t.*—*excavated*, *excavating*. [L. *excavo*, *excavatum*—*ex*, out, and *cavus*, hollow. CAVE.] To cut, scoop, dig, or wear out the inner part of anything and make it hollow; to hollow; to form by scooping or hollowing out.—**Excavation**, eks-ka-vā'shon, *n.* The act of excavating; a hollow or a cavity formed by removing substance.—**Excavator**, eks'ka-vā-tėr, *n.* One who or that which excavates; a machine for excavating.

Exceed, ek-sēd', *v.t.* [L. *excedo*—*ex*, out, and *cedo*, to go. CEDE.] To pass or go beyond; to proceed beyond the given or supposed limit, measure, or quantity of; to outgo; to surpass; to excel.—*v.i.* To go too far; to pass the proper bounds or limits.—**Exceeding**, ek-sē'ding, *a.* Great in extent, quantity, degree, or duration; very large. —*adv.* In a very great degree; unusually. (O.T.)—**Exceedingly**, ek-sē'ding-li, *adv.* In an exceeding manner or degree; very greatly; very much.

Excel, ek-sel', *v.t.*—*excelled*, *excelling*. [L. *excello*—*ex*, and root seen in Gr. *kellō*, to impel, L. *celsus*, raised high.] To surpass in good qualities or laudable deeds; to outdo in comparison; to surpass; to transcend; to exceed.—*v.i.* To be eminent or distinguished; to surpass others; to take a high rank.—**Excellence**, ek'sel-lens, *n.* The state of excelling in anything; the state of possessing good qualities in an eminent or unusual degree; superiority; eminence; any valuable quality; anything highly laudable, meritorious, or esteemed; a title of honour given to persons of high rank; excellency.—**Excellency**, ek'sel-len-si, *n.* Valuable quality; excellence; a title of honour given to governors, ambassadors, ministers, and the like: with *your*, *his*, &c.—**Excellent**, ek'sel-lent, *a.* Being of great virtue or worth; eminent or distinguished for what is amiable, valuable, or laudable; virtuous; good; worthy; excelling or surpassing in any quality, power, or attainment; being of great value or use; remarkable for good properties. —**Excellently**, ek'sel-lent-li, *adv.* In an excellent manner; in an eminent degree.

Excentral, eks-sen'tral, *a. Bot.* out of the centre.

Excentric, **Excentricity**. ECCENTRIC.

Except, ek-sept', *v.t.* [Fr. *excepter*, L. *excipio*, *exceptum*—*ex*, out, and *capio*, to take, seen also in *captious*, *capacious*, *capable*, *accept*, *conceive*, &c.] To take or leave out of any number specified; to exclude.—*v.i.* To object; to take exception: usually followed by *to*.—*prep.* Being excepted or left out; with exception of; excepting.—*conj.* excepting; unless.—**Excepted**, ek-sep'ted, *p.* and *a.* Left out; specially excluded.—**Excepting**, ek-sep'ting, *ppr.* used as a *prep.* and *conj.* With exception of; excluding; unless; except.—**Exception**, ek-sep'shon, *n.* The act of excepting or excluding from a number designated, or from a description; exclusion; that which is excepted or excluded; the person or thing specified as distinct or not included; an objection; that which is or may be offered in opposition to a rule, proposition, statement, or allegation; offence; slight anger or resentment (to *take exception at* a severe remark; to *take exception to* what was said). —**Exceptionable**, ek-sep'shon-a-bl, *a.* Liable to exception or objection; objectionable. —**Exceptionableness**, ek-sep'-shon-a-bl-nes, *n.*—**Exceptional**, ek-sep'-shon-al, *a.* Out of the ordinary course; relating to or forming an exception.—**Exceptionally**, ek-sep'shon-al-li, *adv.* In an exceptional manner; unprecedentedly; extraordinarily; especially.—**Exceptive**, ek-sep'tiv, *a.* Including an exception; making exception.—**Exceptor**, ek-sep'tėr, *n.* One who makes exceptions.

Excerpt, ek-sėrpt', *v.t.* [L. *excerpo*, *excerptum*—*ex*, out, and *carpo*, to pick.] To pick out or extract from a book or other literary composition; to cull; to select; to cite.—*n.* An extract from an author or from a writing of any kind.—**Excerption**, ek-sėrp'shon, *n.* [L. *excerptio*.] The act of excerpting; a gleaning; selection.

Excess, ek-ses', *n.* [L. *excessus*, from *excedo*, to exceed. EXCEED.] That which exceeds any measure or limit; that which is beyond measure, proportion, or due quantity; superfluity; superabundance; any transgression of due limits; extravagance; wastefulness; riotous living; want of restraint in gratifying the desires; intemperance; over-indulgence; the amount by which one number or quantity exceeds another.—**Excessive**, ek-ses'iv, *a.* Beyond any given degree, measure, or limit, or beyond the common measure or proportion; immoderate; extravagant; extreme. ∴ *Enormous*, *Excessive*. Syn. under ENORMOUS.—**Excessively**, ek-ses'iv-li, *adv.* In an excessive manner or degree; exceedingly;

vehemently; violently.—**Excessiveness**, ek-ses'iv-nes, *n.* The state or quality of being excessive.

Exchange, eks-chānj', *v.t.* — *exchanged, exchanging.* [O.Fr. *exchanger* — *ex*, and *changer*, to change. CHANGE.] To give or take in return for another thing; to barter; to lay aside, quit, or resign (a thing, state, or condition), and take something else; to give and receive reciprocally; to give and take; to interchange.—*v.i.* To make an exchange; to pass or to be taken as an equivalent.—*n.* The act of giving one thing or commodity for another; barter; traffic by interchange of commodities; the act of giving up or resigning one thing or state for another; the act of giving and receiving reciprocally; the thing given or the thing received in return; the place where the merchants, brokers, and bankers of a city meet to transact business: often contracted into '*Change*; the difference of value in the respective currencies of different countries. — **Exchangeable**, eks-chān'ja-bl, *a.* Capable of being exchanged; estimated by what may be procured in exchange.—**Exchangeableness, Exchangeability**, eks-chān'ja-bl-nes, eks-chān'ja-bil"i-ti, *n.* The quality or state of being exchangeable. —**Exchanger**, eks-chān'jėr, *n.* One who exchanges; one who deals in exchanging the money of one country for that of another.—**Exchange-broker**, *n.* One who negotiates foreign bills, for which he receives a small commission.

Exchequer, eks-chek'ėr, *n.* [O.Fr. *eschequier*, Fr. *échiquier*, a chess-board: the term was applied to a court of finance from its having at first held its meetings round a table covered with *checked* cloth, because accounts were taken by means of counters on the checks. CHECK, CHEQUER, CHESS.] A state treasury; hence, pecuniary property in general; a person's finances or pecuniary resources; an ancient English tribunal and court, founded chiefly for the collection and care of the royal revenues, now a division of the High Court of Justice.—*Exchequer bills*, bills for money, or bills of credit issued from the exchequer, and pledging the government to repay the sum with a certain rate of interest; a species of paper currency emitted under the authority of the government, and in Britain forming a principal part of the public unfunded debt. —*v.t.*† To institute a process against in the court of exchequer.

Excipient, ek-sip'i-ent, *n.* [L. *excipiens, excipientis*, ppr. of *excipio*, to take out. EXCEPT.] *Med.* an inert or slightly active substance employed as the medium or vehicle for the administration of the active medicine, as bread-crust, sugar, jelly, &c.

Excise, ek-sīz', *n.* [From O.D. *aksijs*, G. *accise*, excise, corruption of O.Fr. *assise*, an assize, a tax. ASSIZE.] A tax or duty imposed on certain commodities of home production and consumption, as beer, spirits, &c.; or levied on persons for licences to pursue certain callings, deal in certain commodities, as well as use certain things (armorial bearings, carriages, plate, &c.), or the like; that branch of the civil service which is connected with the collecting of such duties.—*v.t.* — *excised, excising.* To levy an excise on.—**Excisable**, ek-sī'za-bl, *a.* Liable or subject to excise.—**Exciseman**, ek-sīz'man, *n.* An inferior officer of the excise.

Excise, ek-sīz', *v.t.* — *excised, excising.* [From L. *excido, excisum*—*ex*, out, and *cædo*, to cut, as in *concise, circumcise.*] To cut out or off; to remove by cutting, as in surgery; to delete or expunge.—**Excision**, ek-sizh'on, *n.* The act of cutting out; removal by cutting; amputation; deletion.

Excite, ek-sīt', *v.t.*—*excited, exciting.* [Fr. *exciter*, from L. *excito*—*ex*, and *cito* (as in *cite, incite, recite*), intens. of *cieo* or *cio*, to excite, call; akin to Gr. *kiō*, to go, *kineō*, to move.] To call into action; to animate; to rouse, provoke, or to stir up; to cause to act, as that which is dormant, sluggish, or inactive; to give new or increased action to; to stimulate; to call forth or increase the vital activity of; to raise, create, or set afoot. — **Excitable**, ek-sī'ta-bl, *a.* Susceptible of excitement; capable of being excited; easily excited or stirred up; prone to or characterized by excitement.—**Excitability, Excitableness**, ek-sī'ta-bil"i-ti, ek-sī'ta-bl-nes, *n.* The state or quality of being excitable.—**Excitant**, ek'-si-tant, *n.* That which produces or may produce increased action in a living organizm; an agent or influence which arouses the vital activity of the body or of any of the tissues or organs; a stimulant.—**Excitation**, ek-si-tā'shon, *n.* The act of exciting; excitement.—**Excitative, Excitatory**, ek-sī'ta-tiv, ek-sī'ta-to-ri, *a.* Having power to excite; tending or serving to excite.—**Excitement**, ek-sīt'ment, *n.* The act of exciting; stimulation; the state of being excited; agitation; sensation; commotion; a state of aroused or increased vital activity in the body or any of its tissues or organs; a vitiated and abnormal state of the actions and sensations, or both, produced by stimulants, irritants, or the like; that which excites or rouses; that which moves, stirs, or induces action.—**Exciter**, ek-sī'tėr, *n.* One who or that which excites.—**Exciting**, ek-sī'ting, *p.* and *a.* Calling or rousing into action; producing excitement; deeply interesting; thrilling.—**Excitingly**, ek-sī'ting-li, *adv.* So as to excite.—**Excitive**, ek-sī'tiv, *a.* Tending to excite.

Exclaim, eks-klām', *v.i.* [L. *exclamo*—*ex*, and *clamo*, to call. CLAIM.] To utter with vehemence; to cry out; to shout; to declare with loud vociferation.—**Exclaimer**, eks-klā'mėr, *n.* One who exclaims.—**Exclamation**, eks-kla-mā'shon, *n.* The act of exclaiming or making an outcry; noisy talk; vehement vociferation; clamour; an emphatical or passionate utterance; the mark or sign in printing ! by which emphatical utterance or interjectional force is marked; *gram.* a word expressing outcry; an interjection. — **Exclamatory, Exclamative**, eks-klam'a-to-ri, eks-klam'a-tiv, *a.* Pertaining to or characterized by exclamation; expressing exclamation. — **Exclamatorily, Exclamatively**, eks-klam'a-to-ri-li, eks-klam'a-tiv-li, *adv.* In an exclamatory manner.

Exclude, eks-klūd', *v.t.*—*excluded, excluding.* [L. *excludo*, to shut out—*ex*, out, and *claudo*, to shut, whence *clause, close*, &c.] To hinder from entering or from admission; to shut out; to hinder from participation or enjoyment; to debar; to except; not to comprehend or include in a privilege, grant, argument, description, &c.; to thrust out; to eject. — **Exclusion**, eks-klū'zhon, *n.* The act of excluding, shutting out, debarring, expelling, excepting, or rejecting; the state of being excluded.—**Exclusionary**, eks-klū'zhon-a-ri, *a.* Tending to exclude or debar. — **Exclusionism**, eks-klū'zhon-izm, *n.* Exclusive principles or practice.—**Exclusionist**, eks-klū'zhon-ist, *n.* One who is in favour of exclusion.—**Exclusive**, eks-klū'siv, *a.* Having the power or effect of excluding; possessed and enjoyed to the exclusion of others (an *exclusive* privilege); not taking into account something or certain individuals; not including or comprehending certain things (an *exclusive* estimate): often with *of* (500 men *exclusive of* officers); excluding from or chary in admitting to society or fellowship; fastidious as to the social rank of associates; illiberal; narrow.—*n.* One very fastidious as to the social position or breeding of his associates. — **Exclusively**, eks-klū'siv-li, *adv.* Without admission of others; with the exclusion of all others; without comprehension in a number; not inclusively.—**Exclusiveness**, eks-klū'siv-nes, *n.* State or quality of being exclusive.—**Exclusivism**, eks-klū'siv-izm, *n.* Act or practice of being exclusive or fastidious in the choice of associates. — **Exclusory**, eks-klū'so-ri, *a.* Exclusive; excluding; able to exclude.

Excogitate, eks-koj'i-tāt, *v.t.*—*excogitated, excogitating.* [L. *excogito* — *ex*, out, and *cogito*, to think.] To strike out by thinking; to think out; to devise; to contrive.—**Excogitation**, eks-koj'i-tā"shon, *n.* The act of excogitating.

Excommunicate, eks-kom-mū'ni-kāt, *v.t.* — *excommunicated, excommunicating.* [L. *ex*, out, and *communico, communicatum*, to communicate, from *communis*, common.] To expel or eject from the communion of the church and deprive of spiritual advantages; hence, to expel from any association and deprive of the privileges of membership.—*n.* One who is excommunicated; one cut off from any privilege.—**Excommunicable**, eks-kom-mū'ni-ka-bl, *a.* Liable or deserving to be excommunicated; punishable by excommunication. — **Excommunication**, eks-kom-mū'ni-kā"shon, *n.* The act of excommunicating, or state of being excommunicated; expulsion from the communion of a church, and deprivation of its rights, privileges, and advantages.—**Excommunicator**, eks-kom-mū'ni-kā-tėr, *n.* One who excommunicates.—**Excommunicatory**, eks-kom-mū'ni-ka-to-ri, *a.* Relating to or causing excommunication.

Excoriate, eks-kō'ri-āt, *v.t.* — *excoriated, excoriating.* [L.L. *excorio* — L. *ex*, and *corium*, skin, hide.] To break or wear off the cuticle of; to abrade a part of the skin so as to reach the flesh; to gall.—**Excoriation**, eks-kō'ri-ā"shon, *n.* The act of excoriating; a galling; abrasion.

Excorticate, eks-kor'ti-kāt, *v.t.* [L. *ex*, priv., and *cortex, corticis*, the bark.] To strip of the bark or rind.—**Excortication**, eks-kor'ti-kā"shon, *n.* The act of excorticating.

Excrement, eks'krē-ment, *n.* [L. *excrementum*, from *excerno, excretum*, to sift out —*ex*, out, and *cerno*, to separate. DISCERN.] Matter discharged from the animal body after digestion; alvine discharge. — **Excremental, Excrementitial, Excrementitious**, eks-krē-men'tal, eks'-krē-men-tish"al, eks'krē-men-tish"us, *a.* Pertaining to or consisting of excrement; consisting of matter excreted from the animal body.

Excrement,† eks'krē-ment, *n.* [L. *excresco, excretum*, to grow out or forth. EXCRESCENCE.] Anything growing out of the body, as hair, nails, feathers, &c. (*Shak.*)

Excrescence, Excrescency, eks-kres'-ens, eks-kres'en-si, *n.* [Fr. *excrescence*, from L. *excrescens*, pp. of *excresco*, to grow out —*ex*, out, and *cresco*, to grow (in *crescent, concrete, increase*, &c.).] Anything which grows out of something else and is useless or disfiguring (as a wart or tumour); a useless or troublesome outgrowth; hence, a troublesome superfluity. — **Excrescent**, eks-kres'ent, *a.* Growing out of something else in an abnormal manner, as a wart or tumour.

Excrete, eks-krēt', *v.t.*—*excreted, excreting.* [L. *excerno, excretum.* EXCREMENT.] To separate and throw off from the body by vital action; to discharge.—**Excretion**, eks-krē'shon, *n.* A separation of some fluid from the blood by means of the glands; a discharge of animal fluids from the body; that which is discharged. — **Excretive, Excretory**, eks'krē-tiv, eks'krē-to-ri, *a.* Having the quality of excreting or throwing off excrementitious matter. — *n.* *Anat.* a duct or vessel destined to receive secreted fluids and to excrete them.

Excruciate, eks-krö'shi-āt, *v.t.*—*excruciated, excruciating.* [L. *excrucio, excruciatum* — *ex*, and *crucio*, to torment, from *crux*, a cross. CROSS.] To cause extreme pain or torture to; to torment; to inflict most severe pain on. — **Excruciating**, eks-krö'shi-ā-ting, *p.* and *a.* Extremely painful; distressing; torturing; tormenting. —**Excruciatingly**, eks-krö'shi-ā-ting-li, *adv.* In an excruciating manner.—**Excruciation**, eks-krö'shi-ā"shon, *n.* The act of excruciating; torture; extreme pain; vexation.

Excubitory, Excubitorium, eks-kū'-bi-to-ri, eks-kū'bi-tō"ri-um, *n.* [L. *excubitor*, a watchman — *ex*, out, and *cubo*, to lie.] *Arch.* a gallery in a church where public watch was kept at night on the eve of some festival, and from which the great shrines were observed; a watching-loft.

Exculpate, eks'kul-pāt, *v.t.*—*exculpated,*

exculpating. [L.L. *exculpo, exculpatum*—L. *ex*, and *culpo, culpatum*, to blame, from *culpa*, a fault.] To clear from a charge or imputation of fault or guilt; to vindicate from a charge of fault or crime; to relieve of or free from blame; to regard as innocent; to exonerate; to absolve; to excuse. —**Exculpation**, eks-kul-pā′shon, *n.* The act of exculpating; what exculpates; an excuse.—**Exculpatory**, eks-kul′pa-to-ri, *a.* Able to exculpate; containing excusatory evidence.

Excurrent, eks-kur′ent, *a.* [L. *excurrens, excurrentis*, ppr. of *excurro*—*ex*, out, and *curro*, to run.] *Bot.* projecting or running beyond the edge or point, as when the midrib of a leaf projects beyond the apex.

Excursion, eks-kėr′shon, *n.* [L. *excursio*, from *excurro*—*ex*, out, and *curro*, to run.] Act of running out or forth; a deviation from a fixed or usual course; a wandering from a subject or main design; digression; a journey for pleasure or health, with the view of return; a trip.—*Excursion train*, a railway train specially put on for carrying passengers on a pleasure trip for a certain distance and at a low fare.—**Excursionist**, eks-kėr′shon-ist, *n.* One who makes an excursion; specifically, one who travels by an excursion train; one who professionally provides the public with facilities for making excursions.—**Excursionize**, eks-kėr′shon-īz, *v.i.* To make an excursion; to take part in an excursion.—**Excursive**, eks-kėr′siv, *a.* Given to making excursions; rambling; wandering. — **Excursively**, eks-kėr′siv-li, *adv.* In an excursive manner. —**Excursiveness**, eks-kėr′siv-nes, *n.* The condition or character of being excursive.—**Excursus**, eks-kėr′sus, *n.* [L.] A dissertation appended to a book, discussing some important point or topic more fully than could be done in the body of the work.

Excuse, eks-kūz′, *v.t.*—*excused, excusing.* [L. *excuso*—*ex*, out, and *causa*, a cause, a suit.] To free from accusation or the imputation of fault or blame; to relieve from blame; to exculpate; to absolve; to justify; to pardon (a fault), to forgive, or to admit to be little censurable, and to overlook; to free from an obligation or duty; to release by favour.—*n.* (eks-kūs′). A plea offered in extenuation of a fault or irregular deportment; apology; that which extenuates or justifies a fault.—**Excusable**, eks-kū′za-bl, *a.* Capable of being excused; pardonable; admitting of excuse.—**Excusableness**, eks-kū′za-bl-nes, *n.* The state of being excusable.—**Excusably**, eks-kū′za-bli, *adv.* In an excusable manner; pardonably. — **Excusatory**, eks-kū′za-to-ri, *a.* Making excuse; containing excuse or apology; apologetical.—**Excuseless**, eks-kūs′les, *a.* Having no excuse; such as to exclude excuse or apology.—**Excuser**, eks-kū′zėr, *n.* One who excuses.

Exeat, ek′sē-at. [L., let him depart.] Leave of absence given to a student in the English universities; the permission granted by a bishop to a priest to go out of his diocese.

Execrate, ek′sė-krāt, *v.t.*—*execrated, execrating.* [Fr. *exécrer*, from L. *execror*—*ex*, and *sacer*, consecrated or dedicated to a deity, accursed. SACRED.] To denounce evil against, or to imprecate evil on; to curse; hence, to detest utterly; to abhor; to abominate.—**Execrable**, ek′sė-kra-bl, *a.* Deserving to be execrated or cursed; very hateful; detestable; abominable.—**Execrably**, ek′sė-kra-bli, *adv.* In a manner deserving of execration; detestably.—**Execration**, ek-sė-krā′shon, *n.* The act of execrating; a curse pronounced; imprecation of evil; utter detestation; the object execrated.—**Execrative**, **Execratory**, ek′sė-krā-tiv, ek′sė-kra-to-ri, *a.* Denouncing evil; cursing; vilifying.—**Execratory**, *n.* A formulary of execration.

Execute, ek′sė-kūt, *v.t.*—*executed, executing.* [Fr. *exécuter*, from L. *exsequor, exsecutus*, to follow to the end—*ex*, and *sequor*, to follow, as in *sequence, prosecute, persecute, pursue, ensue*, &c.] To follow out; to perform; to do; to carry into complete effect; to complete; to accomplish; to finish; to give effect to; to put in force (a law or measure); to inflict; to inflict capital punishment on; to put to death; to perform what is required to give validity to (a writing), as by signing and sealing; to perform (a piece of music) on an instrument or with the voice.—**Executable**, ek-sė-kū′ta-bl, *a.* Capable of being executed.—**Executant**, eg-zek′ū-tant, *n.* One who executes or performs; a performer. — **Executer**, ek′sė-kū-tėr, *n.* One who performs or carries into effect.—**Execution**, ek-sė-kū′shon, *n.* The act of executing; performance; the mode of producing or performing an artistic work, and the dexterity with which it is accomplished; the carrying out of the sentence of the law by putting a criminal to death; a case of the infliction of capital punishment; the carrying out of the sentence of a court by arresting the goods or body of a debtor.—*To do execution*, to cause great damage; to have a destructive effect (as a storm or a cannon-ball). — **Executioner**, ek-sė-kū′shon-ėr, *n.* One who inflicts a capital punishment in pursuance of a legal warrant.—**Executive**, eg-zek′ū-tiv, *a.* Having the quality of executing or performing; designed or fitted for execution, administering, or carrying into effect, laws; governing.—*n.* The person (or body of persons) who superintends the execution of the laws; the person or persons who administer the government.—**Executively**, eg-zek′ū-tiv-li, *adv.* In the way of executing or performing.—**Executor**, ek′sė-kū-tėr, *n.* One who executes or performs; a performer or doer; *law*, the person appointed by a testator to execute his will or to see it carried into effect: in this sense pronounced eg-zek′ū-tėr.—**Executorial**, eg-zek′ū-tō″ri-al, *a.* Pertaining to an executor. — **Executorship**, eg-zek′ū-tėr-ship, *n.* The office of an executor.—**Executory**, eg-zek′ū-to-ri, *a.* Performing official duties; carrying laws into effect; executive. — **Executrix**, **Executress**, eg-zek′ū-triks, eg-zek′ū-tres, *n.* A female executor; a woman appointed by a testator to execute his will.

Exegesis, ek-sė-jē′sis, *n.* [Gr. *exēgēsis*, from *exēgeomai*, to explain—*ex*, and *hēgeomai*, to lead, to guide.] The exposition or interpretation of any literary production, but more particularly the exposition or interpretation of Scripture; also the principles of the art of sacred interpretation; exegetics; hermeneutics.—**Exegetic**, **Exegetical**, ek-sė-jet′ik, ek-sė-jet′i-kal, *a.* Explanatory; tending to illustrate or unfold; expository.—**Exegetically**, ek-sė-jet′i-kal-li, *adv.* By way of exegesis or explanation.—**Exegetics**, ek-sė-jet′iks, *n.* The science which lays down the principles of the art of scriptural interpretation; exegesis; hermeneutics.—**Exegetist**, **Exegete**, ek-sė-jē′tist, ek′sė-jēt, *n.* One skilled in exegesis; an expounder or interpreter.

Exemplar, eg-zem′plėr, *n.* [L. EXAMPLE.] A model, original, or pattern to be copied or imitated; a person who serves as a pattern. — **Exemplary**, eg′zem-pla-ri, *a.* Serving for a pattern or model for imitation; worthy of imitation; such as may serve for a warning to others; such as may deter.—**Exemplarily**, eg′zem-pla-ri-li, *adv.* In an exemplary manner. — **Exemplariness**, eg′zem-pla-ri-nes, *n.* The state or quality of being exemplary.

Exemplify, eg-zem′pli-fī, *v.t.*—*exemplified, exemplifying.* [L.L. *exemplifico*, to exemplify—L. *exemplum*, an example, and *facio*, to make.] To show or illustrate by example; to serve as an example or instance of; to make an attested copy or transcript of. — **Exemplifiable**, eg-zem′pli-fī-a-bl, *a.* Capable of being exemplified.—**Exemplification**, eg-zem′pli-fi-kā″shon, *n.* The act of exemplifying; a showing or illustrating by example; that which exemplifies.—**Exemplifier**, eg-zem′pli-fī-ėr, *n.* One that exemplifies.

Exempt, eg-zemt′, *v.t.* [Fr. *exempter*; L. *eximo, exemptum*, to take out, to remove —*ex*, out, and *emo*, to buy, to take.] To free or permit to be free from any charge, burden, restraint, duty, &c., to which others are subject; to privilege; to grant immunity (no man is *exempted* from suffering).—*a.* Free from any service, charge, burden, tax, duty, requisition, or evil of any kind to which others are subject; not subject; not liable; not included; freed; free.—*n.* One who is exempted; one not subject.—**Exemption**, eg-zem′shon, *n.* The act of exempting; the state of being exempt; immunity; privilege.

Exequatur, ek-sė-kwā′tėr, *n.* [L., let him perform or execute.] A written recognition of a person in the character of consul or commercial agent; an official permission to perform some act.

Exequies, ek′sė-kwiz, *n. pl.* [L. *exequiæ*, from *exequor, exsequor*—*ex*, out of, and *sequor*, to follow. EXECUTE.] Funeral rites; the ceremonies of burial; obsequies.—**Exequial**,† ek-sē′kwi-al, *a.* Pertaining to funeral ceremonies.

Exercise, ek′sėr-sīz, *n.* [Fr. *exercice*, from L. *exercitium*, exercise, from *exerceo, exercitum*, to exercise—*ex*, out, and *arceo*, to inclose, to hinder.] A putting in action the powers or faculties of (the eyes, the limbs, the mind); use; employment; practice or performance; a carrying out in action, or performing the duties of anything (the *exercise* of an art, trade, occupation); exertion of the body as conducive to health; bodily exertion as a part of regimen; systematic exertion of the body for amusement or in order to acquire some art, dexterity, or grace; any such art or dexterity acquired by bodily training; training to acquire skill in the management of arms and in military evolutions; drill; moral training; discipline; a lesson or example for the practice of learners; a school task; puritan week-day service and sermon.—*v.t.*—*exercised, exercising.* To set in exercise or operation; to employ; to set or keep in a state of activity; to exert (the body, the mind) to put in practice; to carry out in action (to *exercise* authority); to train, discipline, or improve by practice; to task; to keep employed or busy; to cause to think earnestly and laboriously; to give anxiety to; to make uneasy; to task or try with something grievous; to pain or afflict.—*v.i.* To exercise one's self; to take exercise. —**Exerciser**, ek′sėr-sī-zėr, *n.* One who or that which exercises.—**Exercisible**, ek′sėr-sī-zi-bl, *a.* Capable of being exercised, enjoyed, or enforced.—**Exercitation**, ek-sėr′si-tā″shon, *n.* [L. *exercitatio*.] Exercise; practice; use.

Exergue, eg-zėrg′, *n.* [Gr. *ex*, out, and *ergon*, work.] The small space beneath the base-line of a subject engraved on a coin or medal, left for the date, engraver's name, or something of minor importance.

Exert, eg-zėrt′, *v.t.* [L. *exerto, exserto*, to stretch out, to thrust forth, freq. from *exsero, exsertum*, to thrust out or forth—*ex*, out, and *sero*, to join. SERIES.] To put forth (strength, force, ability); to put in action; to bring into active operation (the mind, the bodily powers); *refl.* to use efforts; to strive; to put forth one's powers.—**Exertion**, eg-zėr′shon, *n.* The act of exerting; a putting forth of power; an effort; a striving or struggling; endeavour; trial.

Exeunt. EXIT.

Exfoliate, eks-fō′li-āt, *v.i.*—*exfoliated, exfoliating.* [L. *exfolio, exfoliatum*, to strip of leaves—*ex*, and *folium*, a leaf.] To separate and come off in scales; to split into scales.—*v.t.* To free from scales or splinters. —**Exfoliation**, eks-fō′li-ā″shon, *n.* The process of exfoliating or separation in scales; desquamation; separation into scales or laminæ, as in a mineral.—**Exfoliative**, eks-fō′li-ā-tiv, *a.* Having the power of causing exfoliation.

Exhale, egz-hāl′, *v.t.*—*exhaled, exhaling.* [L. *exhalo*—*ex*, out, and *halo*, to breathe.] To breathe or send out (something of a vaporous or gaseous character); to emit, as vapour; also, to cause to be emitted in vapour or minute particles.—*v.i.* To rise or pass off, as vapour; to vanish.—**Exhalable**, egz-hā′la-bl, *a.* Capable of being exhaled or evaporated.—**Exhalant**, **Ex-**

halent, egz-hā'lant, egz-hā'lent, *a.* Having the quality of exhaling or evaporating. —**Exhalation**, egz-ha-lā'shon, *n.* [L. *exhalatio.*] The act or process of exhaling; evaporation; that which is exhaled; that which is emitted or which rises in the form of vapor; emanation; effluvium.

Exhaust, eg-zast', *v.t.* [L. *exhaurio, exhaustum—ex*, out, up, and *haurio*, to draw, to draw water.] To draw out or drain off the whole of; to consume or use up; to empty by drawing out the contents; to use or expend the whole of by exertion; to wear out; to tire; to treat thoroughly; to leave nothing unsaid regarding.—*n.* Gaseous or other material exhausted, as from an internal combustion engine; also the muffler through which such material is passed.—**Exhaustible**, eg-zas'ti-bl, *a.* Capable of being exhausted, drained off, consumed, or brought to an end.—**Exhaustibility**, eg-zas'ti-bil"i-ti, *n.* Capability of being exhausted; the state of being exhaustible. —**Exhausting**, eg-zas'ting, *a.* Tending to exhaust, weaken, or fatigue.—**Exhaustion**, eg-zast'shon, *n.* The act of exhausting; the state of being exhausted or emptied; the state of being deprived of strength or spirits; a state of complete fatigue and bodily weakness.—**Exhaustive**, eg-zas'tiv, *a.* Causing exhaustion; tending to exhaust; treating of a subject in such a way as to leave no part of it unexamined; thorough.—**Exhaustless**, eg-zast'les, *a.* Not to be exhausted; inexhaustible.—**Exhaust-pipe**, *n.* The pipe of an engine that conveys waste steam or other working fluid from the cylinder to the condenser, or through which it escapes to the atmosphere.—**Exhaust-steam**, *n.* The steam allowed to escape from the cylinder after it has produced motion of the piston.—**Exhaust-valve**, *n.* The valve which regulates the passage of waste steam from the cylinder.

Exhibit, eg-zib'it, *v.t.* [L. *exhibeo, exhibitum—ex*, out, and *habeo, habitum*, to hold, as in *prohibit*, &c. HABIT.] To hold out or present to view; to present for inspection; to show; to manifest publicly (to *exhibit* a noble example); *med.* to administer by way of medicine or remedy.—*v.i.* To show one's self in some particular capacity or character; to exhibit one's manufactures or productions at a public exhibition.—*n.* Anything exhibited, as at a public exhibition; a document or other thing shown to a witness when giving evidence, and referred to by him in his evidence.—**Exhibitor, Exhibiter**, eg-zib'i-tėr, *n.* One who exhibits; one who presents a petition.—**Exhibition**, eg-zi-bish'on, *n.* [L. *exhibitio.*] The act of exhibiting; a showing or presenting to view; that which is exhibited; especially a public display, as of works of art, natural products, manufactures, feats of skill, and the like; formerly an allowance, pension, or salary; hence, a benefaction settled for the maintenance of scholars in English universities; *med.* the act of administering a remedy.—**Exhibitioner**, eg-zi-bish'on-ėr, *n.* In English universities, one who has a pension or allowance granted for his maintenance.—**Exhibitionism**, eg-zi-bish'on-ism, *n.* Morbid disposition to display that which modesty conceals, physical or mental.

Exhilarate, eg-zil'a-rāt, *v.t.—exhilarated, exhilarating.* [L. *exhilaro—ex*, and *hilaro*, to make merry, from *hilaris*, merry, jovial.] To make cheerful or merry; to inspire with hilarity; to make glad or joyous; to inspirit; to gladden; to cheer.—**Exhilarant**, eg-zil'a-rant, *a.* Exhilarating.—*n.* That which exhilarates.—**Exhilarating**, eg-zil'a-rā-ting, *a.* Such as to exhilarate or make cheerful.—**Exhilaratingly**, eg-zil'a-rā-ting-li, *adv.* In an exhilarating manner.—**Exhilaration**, eg-zil'a-rā"shon, *n.* The act of exhilarating; cheerfulness; enlivenment; gladness; gaiety.

Exhort, eg-zort', *v.t.* [L. *exhortor—ex*, and *hortor*, to encourage, to advise.] To incite by words or advice; to animate or urge by arguments to laudable conduct or course of action; to advise, warn, or caution; to admonish.—*v.i.* To use words or arguments to incite to good deeds.—**Exhortation**, eg-zor-tā'shon, *n.* The act or practice of exhorting; language intended to incite and encourage; a persuasive discourse; a homily; an admonition.—**Exhortative, Exhortatory**, eg-zor'ta-tiv, eg-zor'ta-to-ri, *a.* Containing exhortation; tending to exhort; serving for exhortation.—**Exhorter**, eg-zor'tėr, *n.* One who exhorts or encourages.

Exhume, eks-hūm', *v.t.—exhumed, exhuming.* [Fr. *exhumer*, to dig out of the ground —L. *ex*, out, and *humus*, earth, ground (akin *humble*).] To dig up after having been buried; to disinter.—**Exhumation**, eks-hū-mā'shon, *n.* The act of exhuming.

Exigence, Exigency, ek'si-jens, ek'si-jen-si, *n.* [Fr. *exigence*, from L. *exigo*, to drive out or forth, to demand, to exact. EXACT.] The state of being urgent or pressing; urgent demand; urgency; a pressing necessity; emergency.—**Exigent**, ek'si-jent, *a.* Pressing; requiring immediate aid or action. — **Exigible**, ek'si-ji-bl, *a.* That may be exacted; demandable; requirable.

Exiguous, ek-sig'ū-us, *a.* [L. *exiguus*, scanty.] Small; slender; minute; diminutive.—**Exiguity**, ek-si-gū'i-ti, *n.* [L. *exiguitas.*] Smallness; slenderness.

Exile, eg'zīl, *n.* [Fr. *exil*, banishment, *exilé*, an exiled person, from L. *exsilium*, banishment, *exsul*, a banished person—*ex*, out, and root of *salio*, to leap (whence *salient, sally*); Skr. *sar*, to go.] The state of being expelled from one's native country or place of residence by authority, and forbidden to return, either for a limited time or for perpetuity; banishment; a removal to a foreign country for residence; a separation from one's country and friends by distress or necessity; the person banished or expelled from his country, or who leaves his country and resides in another.—*v.t.—exiled, exiling.* To banish; to cause to be an exile. — **Exilement**,† eg-zīl'ment, *n.* Banishment.

Exist, eg-zist', *v.i.* [Fr. *exister*, from L. *existo—ex*, and *sisto*, to stand, as in *assist, consist*, &c. STATE, STAND.] To have actual existence or being, whether in the form of matter or of spirit; to be; to live; to continue to have life or animation; to continue to be.—**Existence**, eg-zis'tens, *n.* The state of being or existing; continuance of being; that which exists; an entity. —**Existent**, eg-zis'tent, *a.* Having existence; being.—**Existential**, eg-zis-ten'-shal, *a.* Of or pertaining to, or consisting in existence.

Exit, ek'sit, *n.* [L., he goes out, from *exeo*, to go out—*ex*, out, and *eo*, to go.] The departure of a player from the stage when he has performed his part; a direction in a play to mark the time of an actor's quitting the stage; any departure; the act of quitting the stage of action or of life; death; decease; a way of departure; passage out of a place.—**Exeunt**, ek'sē-unt. They go out: a common direction in plays, referring to more of the actors than one.

Exocarp, ek'sō-kärp, *n.* [Gr. *exō*, outside, *karpos*, fruit.] *Bot.* the outer layer of a pericarp.

Exoculate,† eks-ok'ū-lāt, *v.t.* To put out the eyes of.—**Exoculation**, *n.* The act of exoculating.

Exodic, ek-sod'ik, *a.* [EXODUS.] *Physiol.* a term applied to certain nerves which conduct influences from the spinal marrow outward to the body; motor.

Exodus, ek'sō-dus, *n.* [Gr. *exodos—ex*, and *hodos*, way.] Departure from a place; especially, the emigration of large bodies of people from one country to another; the second book of the Old Testament, which gives a history of the departure of the Israelites from Egypt.

Exogamy, ek-sog'a-mi, *n.* [Gr. *exō*, without, and *gamos*, marriage.] A custom among certain savage tribes which prohibits a man from marrying a woman of his own tribe, and so leads the men to capture their wives from among other tribes. —**Exogamous**, ek-sog'a-mus, *a.* Of or belonging to exogamy; characterized by exogamy.

Exogen, ek'sō-jen, *n.* [Gr. *exō*, without, and root *gen*, to produce.] One of those plants forming a large primary class of the vegetable kingdom, so named because the growth of the stem takes place by a succession of rings of new wood externally, or from the central pith outwards to the bark or circumference.—**Exogenous**, ek-soj'e-nus, *a.* Pertaining or belonging to the class Exogens.

Exon, ek'son, *n.* [O.Fr. *exoiné*, excused, exempt.] In England the name given to four officers of the yeomen of the royal body-guard.

Exonerate, eg-zon'ėr-āt, *v.t.—exonerated, exonerating.* [L. *exonero, exoneratum—ex*, priv., and *onus, oneris*, a load (whence also *onerous*).] To relieve of a charge or of blame; to clear of something that lies upon the character as an imputation; to discharge of responsibility, obligation, duty, or liability.—**Exoneration**, eg-zon'ėr-ā"shon, *n.* The act of exonerating.—**Exonerative**, eg-zon'ėr-ā-tiv, *a.* Freeing from a burden or obligation.

Exophthalmia, eks-of-thal'mi-a, *n.* [Gr. *exō*, without, and *ophthalmos*, an eye.] *Med.* a protrusion of the eyeball through disease.

Exorable, ek'so-ra-bl, *a.* [L. *exorabilis*, from *ex*, and *oro*, to pray.] That may be moved or persuaded by entreaty.

Exorbitance, Exorbitancy, eg-zor'bi-tans, eg-zor'bi-tan-si, *n.* [L.L. *exorbitantia*, from *exorbito*, to go out of the track—L. *ex*, out, and *orbita*, a rut made by a wheel, from *orbis*, a circle. ORB.] A going beyond rule or ordinary limits; excess; extravagance (*exorbitance* of demands, of prices). — **Exorbitant**, eg-zor'bi-tant, *a.* Going beyond the established limits of right or propriety; excessive; extravagant; enormous. — **Exorbitantly**, eg-zor'bi-tant-li, *adv.* In an exorbitant manner.

Exorcise, ek'sor-sīz, *v.t.—exorcised, exorcising.* [Fr. *exorciser*, from Gr. *exorkizō—ex*, intens., and *horkizō*, to bind by oath, from *horkos*, an oath.] To expel or cast out by conjurations, prayers, and ceremonies; to purify from unclean spirits by adjurations and ceremonies; to deliver from the influence or presence of malignant spirits or demons.—**Exorciser, Exorcist**, ek'sor-sī-zėr, ek'sor-sist, *n.* One who exorcises. — **Exorcism**, ek'sor-sizm, *n.* The act of exorcising; a prayer or charm used to expel evil spirits.

Exordium, eg-zor'di-um, *n.* [L., from *exordior*, to begin a web, to lay the warp—*ex*, and *ordior*, to begin a web, to begin.] The beginning of anything; specifically, the introductory part of a discourse, which prepares the audience for the main subject. —**Exordial**, eg-zor'di-al, *a.* Pertaining to an exordium; introductory; initial.

Exorhiza, ek-sō-rī'za, *n.* [Gr. *exō*, outside, and *rhiza*, a root.] The rootlet of an exogenous plant. — **Exorhizal, Exorhizous**, ek-sō-rī'zal, ek-sō-rī'zus, *a.* *Bot.* a term applied to exogenous roots because they push out directly in a tapering manner, and do not come out in the form of numerous rootlets through sheaths, as in monocotyledons.

Exoskeleton, ek'sō-skel-ē-ton, *n.* [Gr. *exō*, without, and *skeleton.*] The external skeleton; all those structures which are produced by the hardening of the integument, as the shells of the crustacea, the scales and plates of fishes and reptiles; dermo-skeleton.

Exosmose, Exosmosis, ek'sos-mōs, ek-sos-mō'sis, *n.* [Gr. *exō*, outside, and *ōsmos*, impulsion, from *ōtheō*, to thrust, to push.] The passage of gases or liquids through membranes or porous media, from within outward, the reverse process being called *endosmose*.—**Exosmotic**, ek-sos-mot'ik, *a.* Pertaining or relating to exosmose.

Exostome, ek'sos-tōm, *n.* [Gr. *ex*, and *stoma*, a mouth.] *Bot.* the aperture through the outer integument of an ovule.

Exostosis, ek-sos-tō'sis, *n.* [Gr. *ex*, and *osteon*, a bone.] Any protuberance or enlargement of a bone which is not natural; a disease of trees, in which knots or large tumours are formed.

Exoteric, **Exoterical**, ek-sō-ter'ik, ek-sō-ter'i-kal, *a.* [Gr. *exōterikos*, external, from *exōteros*, exterior—*exō*, without.] Suitable to be imparted to the public; hence, capable of being readily or fully comprehended; public; opposed to *esoteric* or secret.—**Exoterically**, ek-sō-ter'i-kal-li, *adv.* In an exoteric manner.—**Exotericism**, ek-sō-ter'i-sizm, *n.* Exoteric doctrines or principles, or the profession or teaching of such.

Exothecium, ek-sō-thē'shi-um, *n.* [Gr. *exō*, outside, and *thēkē*, a case.] *Bot.* the coat of an anther.

Exothermic, eks-ō-ther'mik, *a.* [Gr. *exō*, outside, *thermos*, heat.] Of chemical compounds or reactions, formed with or involving evolution of heat. See ENDOTHERMIC.

Exotic, **Exotical**, eg-zot'ik, eg-zot'i-kal, *a.* [Gr. *exōtikos*, from *exō*, outward.] Introduced from a foreign country; not native; foreign; extraneous.—**Exotic**, *n.* Anything of foreign origin, as a plant, tree, word, practice, introduced from a foreign country.—**Exoticism**, eg-zot'i-sizm, *n.* The state of being exotic; anything exotic, as a foreign word or idiom.

Expand, eks-pand', *v.t.* [L. *expando*—*ex*, and *pando*, to spread out, to extend, to open (seen also in *pace*, *pass*, &c.).] To spread out so as to give greater extent to; to open out; to cause the particles or parts of to spread or stand apart, thus increasing the bulk; to dilate; to enlarge in bulk; to distend; to widen or extend.—*v.i.* To become opened, spread apart, dilated, distended, or enlarged.—**Expanse**, eks-pans', *n.* [L. *expansum*.] A widely expanded surface or space; a wide extent of space.—**Expansible**, eks-pan'si-bl, *a.* Capable of being expanded, extended, dilated, or diffused.—**Expansibility**, eks-pan'si-bil"i-ti, *n.* The capacity of being expanded.—**Expansibly**, eks-pan'si-bli, *adv.* In an expansible manner.—**Expansile**, eks-pan'sil, *a.* Capable of expanding or of being dilated.—**Expansion**, eks-pan'shon, *n.* The act of expanding or spreading out; the state of being expanded; the increase of bulk which a body undergoes by the recession of its particles from one another so that it occupies a greater space, its weight remaining still the same; enlargement; dilatation; distention; an expanse or extended surface; extension.—**Expansive**, eks-pan'siv, *a.* Having the power of expanding or dilating; having the capacity of being expanded; embracing a large number of objects; wide-extending.—**Expansively**, eks-pan'siv-li, *adv.* In an expansive manner.—**Expansiveness**, eks-pan'siv-nes, *n.*

Ex-parte, eks-pär'te, *a.* [L.] Proceeding only from one part or side of a matter in question; one-sided; partial; *law*, made or done by or on behalf of one party in a suit.

Expatiate, eks-pā'shi-āt, *v.i.*—*expatiated*, *expatiating*. [L. *exspatior*, *exspatiatus*—*ex*, and *spatior*, to walk about, from *spatium*, space. SPACE.] To move at large; to rove without prescribed limits; to enlarge in discourse or writing; to be copious in argument or discussion.—**Expatiation**, eks-pā'shi-ā"shon, *n.* Act of expatiating.—**Expatiator**, eks-pā'shi-ā-tėr, *n.* One who expatiates.—**Expatiatory**, eks-pā'shi-a-to-ri, *a.* Expatiating; amplificatory.

Expatriate, eks-pā'tri-āt, *v.t.*—*expatriated*, *expatriating*. [L. *ex*, out, and *patria*, one's fatherland, from *patrius*, fatherly, from *pater*, a father.] To banish from one's native country; to exile: often *refl.*—**Expatriation**, eks-pā'tri-ā"shon, *n.* The act of banishing or state of being banished; banishment; exile.

Expect, eks-pekt', *v.t.* [L. *exspecto*, *exspectatum*—*ex*, and *specto*, to behold, from *specio*, to look. SPECIES.] To wait for‡; to await‡; to look forward to in the future; to look for to happen; to entertain at least a slight belief in the happening of; to anticipate; to reckon or count upon.—**Expectance**, **Expectancy**, eks-pek'tans, eks-pek'tan-si, *n.* The act or state of expecting; expectation; something on which expectations or hopes are founded; the object of expectation or hope.—**Expectant**, eks-pek'tant, *a.* Expecting; looking for.—*n.* One who waits in expectation; one held in dependence by his belief or hope of receiving some good.—**Expectation**, eks-pek-tā'shon, *n.* The act of expecting or looking forward to an event as about to happen; the state of being expected or awaited; prospect of future possessions, wealth, or other good fortune; wealth in prospect: in this sense usually in the plural; the value of anything depending on the happening of some uncertain event; prospect of reaching a certain age.—**Expectative**, eks-pek'ta-tiv, *a.* Giving rise to expectation; anticipatory.—**Expectedly**, eks-pek'ted-li, *adv.* In an expected manner.—**Expectingly**, eks-pek'ting-li, *adv.* In an expecting manner.

Expectorate, eks-pek'tō-rāt, *v.t.*—*expectorated*, *expectorating*. [L. *expectoro*, *expectoratum*—*ex*, and *pectus*, *pectoris*, the breast (whence *pectoral*).] To eject from the trachea or lungs; to discharge, as phlegm or other matter, by coughing, hawking, and spitting; to spit out.—*v.i.* To eject matter by coughing and spitting; to spit.—**Expectorant**, **Expectorative**, eks-pek'tō-rant, eks-pek'tō-rā-tiv, *a.* Having the quality of promoting discharges from the mucous membrane of the lungs or trachea.—*n.* A medicine which promotes such discharges.—**Expectoration**, eks-pek'tō-rā"shon, *n.* The act of expectorating; the matter expectorated.

Expediency, **Expedience**, eks-pē'di-en-si, eks-pē'di-ens, *n.* [L. *expediens*, pp. of *expedio*, to set free. EXPEDITE.] Propriety under the particular circumstances of a case; advisability, all things being duly considered or taken into account; the seeking of immediate or selfish gain or advantage at the expense of genuine principle; time-servingness.—**Expedient**, eks-pē'di-ent, *a.* Tending to promote the object proposed; proper under the circumstances; conducive or tending to selfish ends.—*n.* That which serves to promote or advance; any means which may be employed to accomplish an end; means devised or employed in an exigency; shift; contrivance; resort; plan; device.

Expedite, eks'pē-dīt, *v.t.*—*expedited*, *expediting*. [L. *expedio*, *expeditum*, to free one caught by the feet in a snare—*ex*, out, and *pes*, *pedis*, the foot, seen also in *pedal*, *pedestal*, *pedestrian*, *despatch*, &c.] To free from impediments; to accelerate or facilitate the motion or progress of; to render quicker or easier in progress.—*a.* Clear of impediments; easy; expeditious.—**Expeditely**, eks'pē-dīt-li, *adv.* In an expedite manner.—**Expedition**, eks-pē-dish'on, *n.* Promptness in action from being free from encumbrance; speed; quickness; despatch; the march of an army or the voyage of a fleet to a distant place for hostile purposes; any important journey or voyage made by an organized body of men for some valuable end; such a body of men, together with their equipments, &c.—**Expeditionary**, eks-pē-dish'on-a-ri, *a.* Pertaining to or composing an expedition.—**Expeditious**, eks-pē-dish'us, *a.* Performed with expedition or celerity; quick; hasty; speedy; nimble; active; swift; acting with celerity.—**Expeditiously**, eks-pē-dish'us-li, *adv.* In an expeditious manner.—**Expeditiousness**, eks-pē-dish'us-nes, *n.* The quality of being expeditious.

Expel, eks-pel', *v.t.*—*expelled*, *expelling*. [L. *expello*—*ex*, out, and *pello*, to drive, as in *impel*, *repel*, *compel*, &c.] To drive or force out from any inclosed place, or from that within which anything is contained or situated; to cast or thrust out; to banish; to exclude; to drive out, as from any society or institution.—**Expellable**, eks-pel'a-bl, *a.* That may be expelled or driven out.—**Expeller**, eks-pel'ėr, *n.* One who or that which expels.

Expend, eks-pend', *v.t.* [L. *expendo*—*ex*, out, and *pendo*, to weigh out, to pay. The same word takes another form in *spend*.] To lay out in paying, purchasing, &c.; to disburse; to spend; to deliver or distribute, either in payment or in donations; to use, employ, consume (time, labour, material).—**Expenditure**, eks-pen'di-tūr, *n.* The act of expending or laying out; disbursement; that which is expended; expense.—**Expense**, eks-pens', *n.* [L. *expensum*, from *expensus*, pp. of *expendo*.] A laying out or expending; that which is expended, laid out, or consumed; especially, money expended; cost; charge; cost, with the idea of loss, damage, or discredit (he did this at the *expense* of his character).—**Expensive**, eks-pen'siv, *a.* Requiring much expense; costly; dear; extravagant; lavish.—**Expensively**, eks-pen'siv-li, *adv.* In an expensive manner.—**Expensiveness**, eks-pen'siv-nes, *n.* The quality of being expensive.

Experience, eks-pi'ri-ens, *n.* [Fr. *expérience*, L. *experientia*, from *experior*, to try, to prove—*ex*, and a root *per*, to try, to pass through, same as in E. *ferry*, &c.] Personal trial, proof, or test; frequent trial; continued and varied observation; the knowledge gained by trial, or repeated trials, or observation; practical wisdom taught by the changes and trials of life.—*v.t.*—*experienced*, *experiencing*. To make practical acquaintance with; to try, or prove, by use, by suffering, or by enjoyment; to have happen to or befall.—**Experienced**, eks-pi'ri-enst, *p.* and *a.* Taught by experience; skillful or wise by means of trials, use, or observation.—**Experiential**, eks-pi'ri-en"shal, *a.* Relating to experience; derived from or based on experience, trial, or observation; empirical.—**Experientialism**, eks-pi'ri-en"shal-izm, *n.* The doctrine that all our knowledge or ideas are derived from the experience of ourselves or others, and that none of them are intuitive.—**Experientialist**, eks-pi'ri-en"shal-ist, *n.* One who holds the doctrine of experientialism.

Experiment, eks-per'i-ment, *n.* [L. *experimentum*, from *experior*. EXPERIENCE.] An act or operation designed to discover some unknown truth, principle, or effect, or to establish it when discovered; a trial.—*v.i.* To make trial; to make an experiment.—**Experimental**, eks-per'i-men"tal, *a.* Pertaining to, derived from, founded on, or known by experiment; given to or skilled in experiment.—**Experimentalize**, **Experimentalise**, eks-per'i-men"tal-īz, *v.t.* To make experiments.—**Experimentalist**, eks-per'i-men"tal-ist, *n.* One who makes experiments.—**Experimentally**, eks-per'i-men"tal-li, *adv.* In an experimental manner; by experiment.—**Experimentation**, eks-per'i-men-tā"shon, *n.* The act or practice of making experiments.—**Experimenter**, eks-per'i-men-tėr, *n.* One who makes experiments.

Expert, eks-pėrt', *a.* [L. *expertus*, having made trial, experienced, from *experior*, to try. EXPERIENCE.] Experienced; taught by use or practice; skillful; dexterous; adroit; having a facility of operation or performance from practice.—*n.* (eks'pėrt). A skillful or practised person; a scientific or professional witness who gives evidence on matters connected with his profession.—**Expertly**, eks-pėrt'li, *adv.* In an expert manner.—**Expertness**, eks-pėrt'nes, *n.* The quality of being expert.

Expiate, eks'pi-āt, *v.t.*—*expiated*, *expiating*. [L. *expio*, *expiatum*, to make satisfaction—*ex*, out, and *pio*, to appease, to propitiate, from *pius*, pious.] To atone for; to make satisfaction or reparation for.—**Expiable**, eks'pi-a-bl, *a.* Capable of being expiated.—**Expiation**, eks-pi-ā'shon, *n.* The act of atoning for a crime; the act of making satisfaction or reparation for an offense; atonement; satisfaction; the means by which atonement, satisfaction, or reparation is made.—**Expiator**, eks'pi-ā-tėr, *n.* One who expiates.—**Expia-**

tory, eks′pi-a-to-ri, *a.* Having the power to make atonement or expiation.

Expire, eks-pīr′, *v.t.* — *expired, expiring.* [L. *exspiro*—*ex*, out, and *spiro*, to breathe. SPIRIT.] To breathe out; to expel from the mouth or nostrils in the process of respiration: opposed to *inspire*; to emit in minute particles; to exhale.—*v.i.* To emit breath; to emit one's last breath; to die; to come to an end; to close or conclude, as a given period; to terminate; to end.—**Expiration**, eks-pi-rā′shon, *n.* [L. *exspiratio.*] The act of breathing out, or forcing the air from the lungs; emission of breath; exhalation; close, end, conclusion, or termination; expiry.—**Expiratory**, eks-pī′ra-to-ri, *a.* Pertaining to the emission or expiration of breath.—**Expiring**, eks-pī′ring, *p.* and *a.* Breathing out air from the lungs; breathing the last breath; dying; pertaining to or uttered at the time of dying.—**Expiry**, eks′pi-ri, *n.* Expiration; termination.

Expiscate, eks-pis′kāt, *v.t.* [L. *expiscor*, *expiscatus* — *ex*, out, and *piscor*, to fish, from *piscis*, a fish.] To fish out; to discover by artful means or by strict examinations.—**Expiscation**, eks-pis-kā′shon, *n.* The act of expiscating; the act of getting at the truth of any matter by strict inquiry and examination.—**Expiscatory**, eks-pis′ka-to-ri, *a.* Calculated to expiscate.

Explain, eks-plān′, *v.t.* [L. *explano*—*ex*, and *plano*, to make plain, from *planus*, level, plain. PLAIN.] To make plain, manifest, or intelligible; to clear of obscurity; to make clear or evident; to expound; to give or show the meaning or reason of.—*v.i.* To give explanations.—**Explainable**, eks-plā′na-bl, *a.* Capable of being explained.—**Explainer**, eks-plā′nėr, *n.* One who explains.—**Explanation**, eks-pla-nā′shon, *n.* [L. *explanatio.*] The act of explaining; a making clear or understood; exposition; interpretation; the clearing up of matters between parties who have been at variance.—**Explanatory**, eks-plan′a-to-ri, *a.* Serving to explain; containing explanation.

Expletive, eks′ple-tiv, *a.* [Fr. *explétif*, from L. *expleo*, *expletum*, to fill full—*ex*, intens., and *pleo*, to fill (as in *complete*, &c.).] Added to fill a vacancy; superfluous: said of words.—*n.* A word or syllable inserted to fill a vacancy; an oath or a needless interjection.—**Expletively**, eks′ple-tiv-li, *adv.* In the manner of an expletive.—**Expletory**, eks′ple-to-ri, *a.* Expletive.

Explicate, eks′pli-kāt, *v.t.*—*explicated, explicating.* [L. *explico*, *explicatum*, to unfold—*ex*, priv., and *plico*, to fold, as in *complicate, implicate, apply*, &c. PLY.] To unfold the meaning or sense of; to explain; to interpret.—**Explicable**, eks′pli-ka-bl, *a.* Capable of being explicated or explained.—**Explication**, eks-pli-kā′shon, *n.* The act of explicating or explaining; explanation.—**Explicative, Explicatory**, eks′pli-kā-tiv, eks′pli-ka-to-ri, *a.* Serving to unfold or explain.—**Explicator**, eks′pli-kā-tėr, *n.* One who explains.

Explicit, eks-plis′it, *a.* [L. *explicitus*, disentangled, from *explico*, *explicitum*, to unfold, to disentangle. EXPLICATE.] Not implied only, but distinctly stated; plain in language; open to the understanding; clear; not obscure or ambiguous; open; unreserved; outspoken.—**Explicitly**, eks-plis′it-li, *adv.* In an explicit manner; expressly; plainly.—**Explicitness**, eks-plis′it-nes, *n.* The quality of being explicit.

Explode, eks-plōd′, *v.i.*—*exploded, exploding.* [L. *explodo*, to hoot off the stage, to cast out, reject—*ex*, and *plaudo*, to clap, as in *applaud, plaudit*, &c.] To burst with a loud report; to burst and expand with force and noise; to detonate; to burst into activity or into a passion.—*v.t.* To cause to explode or burst with a loud report; to drive from notice or practice and bring into disrepute; to cause to be no longer practised, held, or believed in (generally in pp.; an *exploded* custom or theory).—**Explodent**, eks-plō′dent, *n.* *Philol.* same as *explosive*.—**Exploder**, eks-plō′dėr, *n.* One who or that which explodes.—**Explosion**, eks-plō′zhon, *n.* [L. *explosio.*] The act of exploding; a bursting or sudden expansion of any elastic fluid with force and a loud report; a sudden and loud discharge caused by the application of fire, as of gunpowder or an inflammable gas; *fig.* a violent outburst of feeling, as of rage, generally accompanied by excited language or by violent actions.—**Explosive**, eks-plō′siv, *a.* Causing explosion; readily exploding; *philol.* mute, forming a complete vocal stop: said of certain consonants.—*n.* Anything liable or with a tendency to explode, as gunpowder, dynamite, &c.; *philol.* a mute or non-continuous consonant, as *k, t, b.*—**Explosively**, eks-plō′siv-li, *adv.* In an explosive manner.

Exploit, eks′ploit, eks-ploit′, *n.* [Fr. *exploit*, O.Fr. *exploict*, from L. *explico*, *explicatum*, *explicitum*, to unfold, finish. EXPLICATE.] A deed or act of note; a heroic act; a deed of renown; a notable feat; a great or noble achievement.—*v.t.* eks-ploit′. [Fr. *exploiter.*] To utilize; to make use of basely for one's own advantage.—**Exploitation**, eks-ploi-tā′shon, *n.* [Fr.] Utilization; the successful application of industry on any object, as in the cultivation of land, the working of mines, &c.; now, esp., selfish or unfair utilization.

Explore, eks-plōr′, *v.t.*—*explored, exploring.* [L. *exploro*, to cry aloud, to explore—*ex*, out, and *ploro*, to bewail, as in *deplore.*] To travel or range over with the view of making discovery, especially geographical discovery; to search by any means; to scrutinize; to inquire into with care; to examine closely with a view to discover truth.—**Explorable**, eks-plō′ra-bl, *a.* Capable of being explored.—**Exploration**, eks-plō-rā′shon, *n.* The act of exploring; close search; strict or careful examination.—**Explorative, Exploratory**, eks-plō′ra-tiv, eks-plō′ra-to-ri, *a.* Serving or tending to explore; searching; examining.—**Explorator**, eks′plō-rā-tėr, *n.* One who explores.—**Explorer**, eks-plō′rėr, *n.* One who explores.—**Exploring**, eks-plō′ring, *p.* and *a.* Employed in or designed for exploration.

Explosion. Under EXPLODE.

Exponent, eks-pō′nent, *n.* [L. *exponens*, *exponentis*, ppr. of *expono*, to expose or set forth—*ex*, out, and *pono*, to place.] One who expounds or explains anything; one who stands forth to explain the principles or doctrines of a party; *alg.* a small number placed above a quantity at the right hand to denote to what power the quantity must be understood to be raised: thus a^2 denotes a raised to the second power.—**Exponential**, eks-pō-nen′shal, *a.* Of or pertaining to an exponent or exponents.

Export, eks-pōrt′, *v.t.* (*often* eks′pōrt, *esp. in contrast with import*). [Fr. *exporter*, from L. *exporto*—*ex*, out, and *porto*, to bear, to carry, as in *import, report, support, sport.*] To send for sale or consumption in foreign countries; to send or furnish for conveyance to distant places, either by water or land.—*n.* (eks′pōrt). The act of exporting; exportation; the gross quantity of goods exported; that which is exported; a commodity that is exported.—**Exportable**, eks-pōr′ta-bl, *a.* Capable of being exported.—**Exportation**, eks-pōr-tā′shon, *n.* The act of exporting; the act of conveying or sending abroad commodities in the course of commerce.—**Exporter**, eks-pōr′tėr, *n.* (*in contrast*, eks′pōr-tėr). One who exports.

Expose, eks-pōz′, *v.t.* [Fr. *exposer*—prefix *ex*, and *poser*, to set, to place. POSE; also COMPOSE, DEPOSE, &c.] To set out or leave in a place unprotected and uncared for; to abandon; to make bare; to uncover; to disclose; to put forward or place in a position to be seen; to exhibit; to set out to view; to lay open to examination; to subject or place in the way of something to be avoided (this *exposed* him to danger); to put in danger; to hold up to censure by disclosing the faults of; to show the folly or ignorance of.—**Exposé**, eks-po-zā, *n.* [Fr.] Exposure; the exposure of something which it was desirable to keep concealed.—**Exposed**, eks-pōzd′, *p.* and *a.* Put in danger; unprotected; liable; subject; open to the wind or the cold; unsheltered.—**Exposedness**, eks-pō′zed-nes, *n.* A state of being exposed.—**Exposer**, eks-pō′zėr, *n.* One who exposes.—**Exposition**, eks-pō-zish′on, *n.* [Fr. *exposition*, L. *expositio.*] A laying open; a setting out to public view; explanation; interpretation; a laying open the sense or meaning; an exhibition or show.—**Expositor**, eks-poz′i-tėr, *n.* One who expounds or explains; an interpreter.—**Expository**, eks-poz′i-to-ri, *a.* Serving to explain; tending to illustrate.—**Exposure**, eks-pō′zhūr, *n.* The act of exposing; abandonment; the state of being exposed; openness to view; openness or liability to danger, inconvenience, &c.; position in regard to the free access of light, air, &c.

Ex-post-facto, eks-pōst-fak′tō, *a.* [L.] *Law*, done after another thing; after the deed is done; retrospective.

Expostulate, eks-pos′tū-lāt, *v.i.*—*expostulated, expostulating.* [L. *expostulo*, *expostulatum*, to demand vehemently, to find fault—*ex*, and *postulo*, to demand, from *posco*, to ask urgently, to beg. POSTULATE.] To reason earnestly with a person on some impropriety of his conduct; to remonstrate.—*v.t.*‡ To reason about; to discuss. (*Shak.*)—**Expostulation**, eks-pos′tū-lā″shon, *n.* The act of expostulating; the act of pressing on a person reasons or arguments against the impropriety of his conduct; an address containing expostulation.—**Expostulator**, eks-pos′tū-lā-tėr, *n.* One who expostulates.—**Expostulatory**, eks-pos′tū-la-to-ri, *a.* Consisting of or containing expostulation.

Exposure. Under EXPOSE.

Expound, eks-pound′, *v.t.* [O.Fr. *expondre*, from L. *exponere*, to set forth, to explain—*ex*, out, and *pono*, to place. *Compound* is similarly formed.] To explain; to lay open the meaning of; to clear of obscurity; to interpret.—**Expounder**, eks-poun′dėr, *n.* One who expounds.

Express, eks-pres′, *v.t.* [O.Fr. *expresser*, L. *exprimo*, *expressum*—*ex*, out, and *premo*, to press. PRESS.] To press or squeeze out; to force out by pressure; to give utterance to or declare by words; to represent in words; to intimate; to indicate; to make known; to tell; to represent; to exhibit; to denote; to send or convey by special fast system; *refl.* to speak what one has got to speak.—*a.* Given in direct terms; not implied or left to inference; clearly expressed; not ambiguous; plain; explicit; intended or sent for a particular purpose or on a particular errand; traveling with special speed (an *express* train).—*n.* A messenger sent with haste on a particular errand or occasion; any regular provision made for the speedy transmission of parcels, money, goods; any vehicle or other conveyance sent on a special mission; a railway train which travels at a specially high rate of speed; that sent by express.—**Expressed**, eks-prest′, *p.* and *a.* Squeezed or forced out, as juice or liquor; uttered in words; set down in writing (well *expressed* sentiments).—**Expression**, eks-presh′on, *n.* The act of expressing or forcing out by pressure, as juices and oils from plants; the act of uttering, declaring, or representing; utterance; declaration; power of expressing one's thoughts, feelings, ideas, &c.; something uttered; a phrase or mode of speech; the peculiar manner of utterance suited to the subject and sentiment; cast of countenance, as indicative of character; play of features, as expressive of feeling or any emotion; the natural and lively representation of any state or condition, as in a picture by the pose of the figure, the conformation of the features, &c.; the power or quality in a picture or other work of art of suggesting an idea; *mus.* sound suited to any particular subject; *alg.* any algebraic quantity, simple or compound, as $3a$, $\sqrt{4a+b}$, &c.—**Expressional**, eks-presh′on-al, *a.* Of or pertaining to expression.—**Expression-**

less, eks-presh'on-les, *a.* Destitute of expression. — **Expressive**, eks-pres'iv, *a.* Serving to express, utter, or represent (words *expressive of* gratitude); full of expression; vividly representing the meaning or feeling intended to be conveyed; emphatical.—**Expressively**, eks-pres'iv-li, *adv.* In an expressive manner.—**Expressiveness**, eks-pres'iv-nes, *n.* The quality of being expressive.—**Expressly**, eks-pres'li, *adv.* In an express manner; of set purpose; in direct terms; plainly.—**Expressness**, eks-pres'nes, *n.*

Expropriate, eks-prō'pri-āt, *v.t.* [L. *ex*, out of, from, and *proprius*, one's own. PROPER, PROPRIETY.] To disengage from appropriation; to give up a claim to the exclusive property of. — **Expropriation**, eks-prō'pri-ā"shon, *n.* The act of expropriating; the act of dispossessing the owner of a property wholly or to a great extent of his proprietary rights.

Expulsion, eks-pul'shon, *n.* [L. *expulsio*, a driving out, from *expello*, to expel.] The act of driving out or expelling; a driving away by violence; the state of being expelled, driven out, or away.—**Expulsive**, eks-pul'siv, *a.* Having the power of expelling.

Expunge, eks-punj', *v.t.*—*expunged*, *expunging.* [L. *expungo*, to prick out, to cross or blot out—*ex*, out, and *pungo*, to prick. POINT.] To blot out, as with a pen; to rub out; to efface; to erase; to obliterate; to wipe out or destroy; to annihilate.

Expurgate, eks'pėr-gāt, *v.t.*—*expurgated*, *expurgating.* [L. *expurgo*, *expurgatum*—*ex*, and *purgo*, to purge. PURGE, PURE.] To purify from anything noxious, offensive, or erroneous; to purge; to cleanse; to strike obscene, coarse, or offensive passages out of (a book).—**Expurgation**, eks-pėr-gā'shon, *n.* The act of expurgating, purging, or cleansing; purification. — **Expurgator**, eks-pėr'gā-tėr, *n.* One who expurgates.—**Expurgatory**, eks-pėr'ga-to-ri, *a.* Cleansing; purifying; serving to expurgate.

Exquisite, eks'kwi-zit, *a.* [L. *exquisitus*, carefully sought out, exquisite, from *exquiro*, *exquisitum*—*ex*, out, and *quæro*, to seek, whence *question*, *quest*, *query*, &c.] Of great excellence or fineness; choice; select; consummate; perfect; of keen or delicate perception; keen; nice; refined; delicate; pleasurable or painful in the highest degree; extreme.—*n.* One excessively nice in his dress; a dandy; a swell; a fop; a coxcomb.—**Exquisitely**, eks'kwi-zit-li, *adv.* In an exquisite manner.—**Exquisiteness**, eks'kwi-zit-nes, *n.*

Exsangueous, **Exsanguinous**, **Exsanguineous**, eks-sang'gwē-us, eks-sang-gwi-nus, eks-sang-gwin'ē-us, *a.* [L. *exsanguis*—*ex*, priv., and *sanguis*, blood.] Destitute of blood, or rather of red blood, as an animal.—**Exsanguinity**, eks-sang-gwin'i-ti, *n.* Destitution of blood.

Exscind, ek-sind', *v.t.* [L. *exscindo*, to cut out.] To cut out or off.

Exsect, ek-sekt', *v.t.* [L. *exseco*, to cut out.] To cut out or away.

Exsert, **Exserted**, ek-sėrt', ek-sėr'ted, *a.* [L. *exsertus*, from *exsero*, to stretch out or forth. EXERT.] Standing out; projected beyond some other part.—**Exsertile**, ek-sėr'tīl, *a.* Capable of being protruded.

Exsiccate, ek'sik-āt, *v.t.*—*exsiccated*, *exsiccating.* [L. *exsicco*, *exsiccatum*, to dry up—*ex*, intens., and *sicco*, to dry.] To exhaust of moisture; to dry up completely.—**Exsiccant**, ek-sik'kant, *a.* Having the quality of drying.—*n.* A drug having drying properties.—**Exsiccation**, ek-sik-kā'shon, *n.* The act or operation of exsiccating or drying; dryness. — **Exsiccative**, ek-sik'ka-tiv, *a.* Tending to make dry; having the power of drying. — **Exsiccator**, ek-sik'kā-tėr, *n.* An apparatus or contrivance for drying moist substances.

Exstipulate, eks-tip'ū-lāt, *a.* *Bot.* having no stipules.

Extant, eks'tant, *a.* [L. *extans*, *exstans*, *extantis*, *exstantis*, ppr. of *exsto*, to stand out—*ex*, out, and *sto*, to stand. STATE.] Still existing; in being; now subsisting; not destroyed or lost.

Extasy, **Extatic**, eks'ta-si, eks-tat'ik. ECSTASY, ECSTATIC.

Extemporaneous, **Extemporary**, eks-tem'pō-rā"nē-us, eks-tem'po-ra-ri, *a.* [L. *extemporaneus*—*ex*, priv., and *tempus*, *temporis*, time.] Performed, uttered, or made at the time without previous thought or study; unpremeditated; off-hand. — **Extemporaneously**, **Extemporarily**, eks-tem'pō-rā"nē-us-li, eks-tem'po-ra-ri-li, *adv.* In an extemporaneous manner.—**Extemporaneousness**, eks-tem'pō-rā"nē-us-nes, *n.* The quality of being extemporaneous. — **Extempore**, eks-tem'po-rē, *adv.* [L. phrase *ex tempore*, same meaning.] Without previous thought, study, or meditation; without preparation.—*a.* Extemporary; extemporaneous.—**Extemporization**, eks-tem'po-ri-zā"shon, *n.* The act of extemporizing. — **Extemporize**, eks-tem'po-rīz, *v.i.*—*extemporized*, *extemporizing.* To speak without previous thought, study, or preparation; to discourse without notes or written composition.—*v.t.* To make without forethought; to provide for the occasion; to prepare in great haste with the means within one's reach (to *extemporize* a speech or a dinner).—**Extemporizer**, eks-tem'po-rī-zėr, *n.* One who extemporizes.

Extend, eks-tend', *v.t.* [L. *extendo*, to stretch out—*ex*, out, and *tendo*, to stretch (as in *contend*, *pretend*, *tend*); same root as L. *tenuis*, thin, *tenax*, tenacious, E. *thin.*] To stretch in any direction; to carry forward or continue in length, as a line; to spread in breadth; to expand or dilate in size; to hold out or reach forth; to expand; to enlarge; to widen; to diffuse; to continue; to prolong; to communicate, bestow, or impart.—*v.i.* To stretch; to reach; to be continued in length, or breadth; to become larger or more comprehensive; to value land; to seize land for debt. — **Extendedly**, eks-ten'ded-li, *adv.* In an extended manner.—**Extender**, eks-ten'dėr, *n.* He who or that which extends or stretches.—**Extendible**, eks-ten'di-bl, *a.* Capable of being extended. — **Extensibility**, eks-ten'si-bil"i-ti, *n.* The quality of being extensible.—**Extensible**, **Extensile**, eks-ten'si-bl, eks-ten'sīl, *a.* Capable of being extended.—**Extension**, eks-ten'shon, *n.* The act of extending; the state of being extended; enlargement; expansion; prolongation; that property of any body by which it occupies a portion of space, being one of the properties of matter; *logic*, the extent of the application of a general term, that is, the objects collectively which are included under it; compass.—**Extensive**, eks-ten'siv, *a.* Having great or considerable extent; wide; large; embracing a wide area or a great number of objects; diffusive.—**Extensively**, eks-ten'siv-li, *adv.* In an extensive manner.—**Extensiveness**, eks-ten'siv-nes, *n.* The state or quality of being extensive. — **Extensor**, eks-ten'sėr, *n.* *Anat.* a muscle which serves to extend or straighten any part of the body, as an arm or a finger: opposed to *flexor*.—**Extent**, eks-tent', *n.* [L.L. *extentus*, a stretching out; L. *extentus*, extended.] Space or degree to which a thing is extended; extension; length; compass; bulk; size; valuation of land; seizure of land for debt.

Extensometer, eks-ten-som'e-tėr, *n.* [L. *extensio*, stretching, Gr. *metron*, a measure.] An instrument of precision for measuring small lengths.

Extenuate, eks-ten'ū-āt, *v.t.*—*extenuated*, *extenuating.* [L. *extenuo*, *extenuatum*, to make thin or small, to lessen—*ex*, and *tenuis*, thin, fine (whence *tenuity*); same root as E. *thin.*] To lessen or diminish; to weaken the import or force of; to palliate; to mitigate. — **Extenuation**, eks-ten'ū-ā"shon, *n.* The act of extenuating; palliation; mitigation, as opposed to *aggravation*. — **Extenuator**, eks-ten'ū-ā-tėr, *n.* One who extenuates. — **Extenuatory**, eks-ten'ū-a-to-ri, *a.* Tending to extenuate.

Exterior, eks-tē'ri-ėr, *a.* [L., compar. of *exter* or *exterus*, on the outside, outward, from *ex*, out of; akin *external*, *extreme*, *estrange*, *strange*.] External; outer; outward; bounding or limiting outwardly; situated beyond the limits of; on the outside; not arising or coming from within.—*n.* The outer surface; the outside; the external features.—**Exteriority**, eks-tē'ri-or"i-ti, *n.* The state or quality of being exterior; externality. — **Exteriorly**, eks-tē'ri-ėr-li, *adv.* In an exterior manner; outwardly; externally.

Exterminate, eks-tėr'mi-nāt, *v.t.*—*exterminated*, *exterminating.* [L. *extermino*, *exterminatum*, to remove—*ex*, and *termino*, to terminate, from *terminus*, a limit. TERM.] To destroy utterly; to extirpate; to root out; to eradicate.—**Exterminable**, eks-tėr'mi-na-bl, *a.* Capable of being exterminated. — **Extermination**, eks-tėr'mi-nā"shon, *n.* The act of exterminating; destruction; eradication; extirpation.—**Exterminator**, eks-tėr'mi-nā-tėr, *n.* One who or that which exterminates.—**Exterminatory**, eks-tėr'mi-na-to-ri, *a.* Serving or tending to exterminate.

External, eks-tėr'nal, *a.* [L. *externus*, from *exter*, on the outside. EXTERIOR.] On the outside: opposite to *internal*; on the exterior; superficial; visible; apparent; existing or situated outside; not being or arising within; outside of ourselves; relating to or connected with foreign nations; foreign.—*n.* An outward part; something pertaining to the exterior; an outward rite or ceremony.—**Externality**, eks-tėr-nal'i-ti, *n.* The state of being external; separation from the perceiving mind; exteriority. —**Externalize**, eks-tėr'nal-īz, *v.t.* To embody in an outward form; to give shape and form to.—**Externally**, eks-tėr'nal-li, *adv.* Outwardly; on the outside; apparently; exteriorly.

Exterritorial, eks-ter'i-tō"ri-al, *a.* [Prefix *ex*, and *territorial*.] Beyond the jurisdiction of the laws of the country in which one resides.—**Exterritoriality**, eks-ter'i-tō'ri-al"i-ti, *n.* Immunity from a country's laws, such as that enjoyed by an ambassador.

Extinct, eks-tingkt', *a.* [L. *extinctus*, pp. of *extinguo*, *exstinguo*. EXTINGUISH.] Extinguished; quenched; having ceased; being at an end; no longer in existence; having died out (a family or race is *extinct*).—**Extinction**, eks-tingk'shon, *n.* The act of putting out or quenching flame or fire; the state of being extinguished; a putting an end to, or a coming to an end.

Extine, eks'tīn, *n.* [L. *exter*, outside.] *Bot.* the outer coat of the pollen-grain in plants.

Extinguish, eks-ting'gwish, *v.t.* [L. *extinguo*, *exstinguo*—*ex*, and *stinguo*, to scratch out, as in *distinguish*.] To put out; to quench; to stifle; to put an end to; to suppress; to destroy; to crush; to eclipse.—**Extinguishable**, eks-ting'gwish-a-bl, *a.* Capable of being quenched, destroyed, or suppressed. — **Extinguisher**, eks-ting'gwish-ėr, *n.* One who or that which extinguishes; a hollow conical utensil to put on a candle or lamp to extinguish it.—**Extinguishment**, eks-ting'gwish-ment, *n.* The act of extinguishing; extinction.

Extirpate, eks'tėr-pāt, *v.t.*—*extirpated*, *extirpating.* [L. *extirpo*, *exstirpo*, *exstirpatum*—*ex*, out, and *stirps*, the trunk of a tree.] To pull or pluck up by the roots; to root out; to eradicate; to destroy totally; to exterminate.—**Extirpable**, eks-tėr'pa-bl, *a.* Capable of being extirpated.—**Extirpation**, eks-tėr-pā'shon, *n.* The act of rooting out; eradication; total destruction.—**Extirpator**, eks-tėr'pā-tėr, *n.* One who or that which extirpates.—**Extirpatory**, eks-tėr'pa-to-ri, *a.* Serving or tending to extirpate.

Extol, eks-tol', *v.t.*—*extolled*, *extolling.* [L. *extollo*, to raise up—*ex*, out, up, and *tollo*, to raise; from same root as in *tolero*, to endure, to tolerate.] To speak in laudatory terms of; to praise; to laud; to applaud; to eulogize; to magnify; to celebrate; to glorify.—**Extoller**, eks-tol'ėr, *n.* One who extols; a praiser or magnifier.

Extort, eks-tort', *v.t.* [L. *extorqueo*, *extortum*—*ex*, and *torqueo*, to twist, seen in *con-*

tort, distort, retort, torture, &c.] To obtain from a person by force or compulsion; to wrest or wring by physical force, by menace, torture, or authority (to *extort* contributions, a confession, a promise, &c.).—**Extorter**, eks-tor'tėr, *n.* One who extorts.—**Extorsive**, eks-tor'siv, *a.* Serving to extort.—**Extorsively**, eks-tor'siv-li, *adv.* In an extorsive manner.—**Extortion**, eks-tor'shon, *n.* The act of extorting; the act or practice of extorting or wringing money from people by any undue exercise of power; illegal compulsion to pay money; rapacity; that which is extorted.—**Extortionary**, eks-tor'shon-a-ri, *a.* Practising extortion; containing extortion.—**Extortionate**, eks-tor'shon-āt, *a.* Characterized by extortion; oppressive in exacting money.—**Extortioner, Extortionist**, eks-tor'shon-ėr, eks-tor'shon-ist, *n.* One who practises extortion.

Extra, eks'tra, *a.* [Contr. from *extraordinary*, or directly from L. *extra*, beyond.] Extraordinary; more than what is usual; beyond what is due, appointed, or expected; supplementary; additional.—*n.* Something in addition to what is due, expected, or usual; something over and above.

Extract, eks-trakt', *v.t.* [L. *extractus*, from *extraho*—*ex*, and *traho*, to draw; seen also in *contract, detract, retract, trace, tract,* &c.] To draw out; to take out; to pull out or remove from a fixed position; to draw out by distillation or other chemical process; to select as a specimen or sample; to take (a passage or passages) from a book or writing; to ascertain the root of a number.—*n.* (eks'trakt). That which is extracted or drawn from something; a passage taken from a book or writing; an excerpt; a quotation; anything drawn from a substance by heat, distillation, or a chemical process, as an essence, a tincture, and the like.—**Extractable, Extractible**, eks-trak'ta-bl, eks-trak'ti-bl, *a.* Capable of being extracted.—**Extraction**, eks-trak'shon, *n.* [L. *extractio.*] The act of extracting or drawing out; descent; lineage; derivation of persons from a stock or family; the stock or family from which one has descended; *arith.* and *alg.* the operation of finding the root of a given number or quantity.—**Extractive**, eks-trak'tiv, *a.* Capable of being extracted; tending or serving to extract; extracting.—*n.* A peculiar base or principle supposed to exist in all vegetable extracts.—**Extractor**, eks-trak'tėr, *n.* One who or that which extracts; a forceps or instrument used in lithotomy and midwifery, or in extracting teeth.

Extradition, eks-tra-dish'on, *n.* [L. *ex*, and *traditio*, a giving up, surrender, from *trado, traditum*, to give up.] Delivery of a criminal or fugitive from justice by one nation to another, on sufficient grounds shown.—An *extradition treaty* is a treaty by which either nation becomes bound to give up criminal refugees to the other.—**Extradite**, eks'tra-dīt, *v.t.* To deliver or give up (a criminal) to the authorities of the country from which he has come.

Extrados, eks-trā'dos, *n.* [Fr., from L. *extra*, without, and *dorsum*, the back.] The exterior curve of an arch; the outer curve of a voussoir.

Extraforaneous,† eks'tra-fo-rā"nē-us, *a.* [L. *extra*, beyond, and *fores*, doors.] Outdoor; out-of-door.

Extrajudicial, eks'tra-jū-dish"al, *a.* Out of the proper court, or the ordinary course of legal procedure.—**Extrajudicially**, eks'tra-jū-dish"al-li, *adv.* In an extrajudicial manner; out of court.

Extramundane, eks-tra-mun'dān, *a.* Beyond the limit of the material world or mundane affairs.

Extramural, eks-tra-mū'ral, *a.* [L. *extra*, beyond, and *murus*, a wall.] Without or beyond the walls, as of a fortified city or a university.

Extranean, eks-trā'nē-an, *n.* Outsider, not a full member of a class or body.

Extraneous, eks-trā'nē-us, *a.* [L. *extraneus*, from *extra*, without, beyond; akin *strange.*] Foreign; not belonging to a thing; existing without; not intrinsic.—**Extraneously**, eks-trā'nē-us-li, *adv.* In an extraneous manner.

Extraofficial, eks'tra-of-fish"al, *a.* Not within the limits of official duty.

Extraordinary, eks-tra-or'di-na-ri, *a.* [L. *extraordinarius*—*extra*, and *ordo, ordinis*, order.] Beyond or out of the ordinary or common order or method; not in the usual, customary, or regular course; not ordinary; exceeding the common degree or measure; remarkable; uncommon; rare; wonderful; special; particular; sent for a special purpose or on a particular occasion (an ambassador *extraordinary*).—**Extraordinarily**, eks-tra-or'di-na-ri-li, *adv.* In an extraordinary manner; in an uncommon degree; remarkably; exceedingly; eminently.—**Extraordinariness**, eks-tra-or'di-na-ri-nes, *n.* The state or quality of being extraordinary; remarkableness.

Extraparochial, eks'tra-pa-rō"ki-al, *a.* Not within or reckoned within the limits of any parish.—**Extraparochially**, eks'tra-pa-rō"ki-al-li, *adv.* Out of a parish.

Extraphysical, eks-tra-fiz'i-kal, *a.* Not subject to physical laws or methods.

Extraprofessional, eks'tra-prō-fesh"on-al, *a.* Not within the ordinary limits of professional duty or business.

Extratropical, eks-tra-trop'i-kal, *a.* Beyond the tropics; without the tropics, north or south.

Extravagance, Extravagancy, eks-trav'a-gans, eks-trav'a-gan-si, *n.* [Fr. *extravagance*—L. *extra*, beyond, and *vagans*, ppr. of *vago, vagor*, to wander. VAGABOND.] A wandering beyond proper bounds; want of restraint; wildness; irregularity; unreasonableness; prodigality; lavish spending or waste; excess; profusion; bombast.—**Extravagant**, eks-trav'a-gant, *a.* Wandering beyond bounds (*Shak.*); exceeding due bounds; unreasonable; excessive; not within ordinary limits of truth or probability or other usual bounds; unrestrained; irregular; wild; wasteful; prodigal; profuse in expenses.—**Extravagantly**, eks-trav'a-gant-li, *adv.* In an extravagant manner; unreasonably; excessively; wastefully.—**Extravaganza**, eks-trav'a-gan"za, *n.* A literary or musical composition noted for its wildness and incoherence; a burlesque.

Extravasate, eks-trav'a-sāt, *v.t.*—*extravasated, extravasating.* [L. *extra*, beyond, and *vas*, a vessel.] To force or let out of the proper vessels, as out of the blood-vessels.—**Extravasation**, eks-trav'a-sā"shon, *n.* The act of extravasating; the state of being forced or let out of the vessels or ducts of the body that contain it; effusion.—**Extravascular**, eks-tra-vas'kū-lėr, *a.* Being out of the proper vessels.

Extreme, eks-trēm', *a.* [Fr. *extrême*, from L. *extremus*, superl. of *exter* or *exterus*, on the outside, external. EXTERIOR.] Outermost; furthest; at the utmost point, edge, or border; worst or best that can exist or be supposed; greatest; most violent or urgent; utmost; last; beyond which there is none; carrying principles to the uttermost; holding the strongest possible views; ultra.—*Extreme unction*, in the *Roman ritual*, the anointing of a sick person with oil when on the point of death.—*n.* The utmost point of a thing; extremity; utmost limit or degree that can be supposed or tolerated; either of two states or feelings as different from each other as possible; height or extravagant pitch; *math.* the first or the last term of a proportion.—**Extremely**, eks-trēm'li, *adv.* In the utmost degree; to the utmost point.—**Extremist**, eks-trēm'ist, *n.* A supporter of extreme doctrines or practice.—**Extremity**, eks-trem'i-ti, *n.* [L. *extremitas.*] The utmost point or side; the verge; the point or border that terminates a thing; the highest degree; the most aggravated or intense form; extreme or utmost distress, straits, or difficulties; a limb or organ of locomotion, as opposed to the trunk of the body and the head.

Extricate, eks'tri-kāt, *v.t.*—*extricated, extricating.* [L. *extrico, extricatum*—*ex*, and *tricæ*, trifles, perplexity. See INTRICATE.] To free, as from difficulties or perplexities; to disembarrass; to disengage; to disentangle; to clear; to relieve.—**Extricable**, eks'tri-ka-bl, *a.* Capable of being extricated.—**Extrication**, eks-tri-kā'shon, *n.* The act of extricating, disentangling, or setting free.

Extrinsic, Extrinsical, eks-trin'sik, eks-trin'si-kal, *a.* [L. *extrinsecus*, from without—*exter*, outward (as in *exterior*), and *secus*, by, along with.] External; outward; coming from without; not intrinsic; not contained in or belonging to a body.—**Extrinsicality**, eks-trin'si-kal"i-ti, *n.* The state of being extrinsical; externality.—**Extrinsically**, eks-trin'si-kal-li, *adv.* In an extrinsic manner; from without.

Extrorsal, Extrorse, eks-tror'sal, eks-trors', *a.* [Fr. *extrorse*, from L. *extra*, on the outside, and *verto, versum*, to turn.] *Bot.* turned or directed outwards, or turned away from the axis: opposed to *introrse*.—**Extroversion**, eks-trō-vėr'shon, *n. Path.* a malformation consisting in an organ being turned inside out, as the bladder.

Extrude, eks-tröd', *v.t.*—*extruded, extruding.* [L. *extrudo*—*ex*, and *trudo*, to thrust, as in *intrude.*] To thrust out; to urge, force, or press out; to expel; to drive away; to displace.—**Extrusion**, eks-trö'zhon, *n.* The act of extruding; expulsion.

Exuberance, Exuberancy, eks-ū'bėr-ans, eks-ū'bėr-an-si, *n.* [Fr. *exubérance*, from L. *exuberantia*—*ex*, intens., and *ubero*, to be fruitful, from *uber*, rich, fruitful.] The state of being exuberant; superfluous abundance; an overflowing quantity; richness; excess; redundance; copiousness.—**Exuberant**, eks-ū'bėr-ant, *a.* [L. *exuberans, exuberantis*, ppr. of *exubero.*] Characterized by abundance, richness, or luxuriance; plenteous; rich; overflowing; over-abundant; superfluous.—**Exuberantly**, eks-ū'bėr-ant-li, *adv.* In an exuberant manner.

Exude, eks-ūd', *v.t.*—*exuded, exuding.* [L. *exsudo*, to discharge by sweating—*ex*, and *sudo*, to sweat, from same root as E. *sweat.*] To discharge through the pores, as moisture or other liquid matter; to give out, like sweat or juice; to let ooze out.—*v.i.* To flow from a body through the pores; to ooze out like sweat.—**Exudate**, eks'ū-dāt, *n.* [L. *exudare*, to sweat.] Material passing through the wall of a blood-vessel into surrounding parts.—**Exudation**, eks-ū-dā'shon, *n.* The act of exuding; a discharge of humours or moisture; that which is exuded.

Exulcerate, eg-zul'sėr-āt, *v.t.* [L. *exulcero, exulceratum*—*ex*, intens., and *ulcus, ulceris*, an ulcer.] To produce an ulcer or ulcers on; to ulcerate.

Exult, eg-zult', *v.i.* [L. *exulto, exsulto*, to leap or jump about—*ex*, and *salio, saltum*, to leap, seen also in *insult, result, salient*, &c.] To rejoice in triumph; to rejoice exceedingly; to be glad above measure; to triumph.—**Exultant**, eg-zul'tant, *a.* Rejoicing triumphantly.—**Exultation**, eg-zul-tā'shon, *n.* The act of exulting; great gladness; rapturous delight; triumph.—**Exultingly**, eg-zul'ting-li, *adv.* In an exulting manner.

Exuviæ, eg-zū'vi-ē, *n. pl.* [L., from *exuo*, to put off, to strip.] Cast skins, shells, or coverings of animals; any parts of animals which are shed or cast off, as the skins of serpents, &c.—**Exuvial**, eg-zū'vi-al, *a.* Relating to or containing exuviæ.—**Exuviation**, eg-zū'vi-ā"shon, *n.* The rejection or casting off of exuviæ.

Ex-voto, eks-vō'tō, *a.* [L., in consequence of a vow.] Vowed; offered in consequence of a vow: applied to votive offerings, as of a picture for a chapel, &c., presented by Roman Catholics. Used also as a noun.

Eyalet, ī'a-let, *n.* A Turkish province under the administration of a vizier or pasha of the first class.

Eyas, ī'as, *n.* [Fr. *niais*, lit. a nestling falcon, from L.L. *nidax, nidacis*, still in the nest, L. *nidus*, a nest; with loss of *n* as in *adder.*] A young hawk just taken from the nest, not able to prey for itself. (*Shak.*)—*Eyas-musket*, a young sparrow-hawk.

Eye, ī, *n.* [O.E. *ye*, *eighe*, A.Sax. *eáge*, Dan. *öie*, D. *oog*, Icel. *auga*, G. *auge*, Goth. *augo*; cog. L. *oculus*, Skr. *akshi*—eye; from a root meaning sharp. ACID.] The organ of vision, which in man and the higher animals consists of a ball or globular body set in an orbit or socket and forming an optical apparatus by means of which the figures of external objects form sensible impressions; power of seeing; delicate or accurate perception; sight; ocular perception; notice; observation; regard; respect; anything resembling or suggesting an eye in shape or general appearance, as the bud or shoot of a plant or tuber, the hole or aperture in a needle, the circular catch of a hook-and-eye, the loop or ring on a rope; *arch.* the centre of something; thus, the *eye* of a dome is the circular aperture at its apex.—*The wind's eye*, the direction right opposite to that of the wind.—*v.t.*—*eyed*, *eyeing*. To fix the eye on; to look on; to observe or watch narrowly, or with fixed attention.—**Eyed**, īd, *p.* and *a.* Furnished with eyes; having eyes of this or that character: used most frequently in composition.—**Eyeless**, ī'les, *a.* Without eyes.—**Eyeball**, ī'bal, *n.* The ball, globe, or apple of the eye.—**Eyebright**, ī'brīt, *n.* A pretty little annual European herb common in meadows, heaths, &c., which formerly enjoyed a great reputation in diseases of the eyes.—**Eyebrow**, ī'brou, *n.* The brow or hairy arch above the eye.—**Eye-glass**, *n.* A glass to assist the sight; the lens of a telescope, microscope, &c., to which the eye is applied.—**Eyelash**, ī'lash, *n.* One of the hairs that edge the eyelid.—**Eyelet**, **Eyelet-hole**, ī'let, *n.* A small hole or perforation to receive a lace or small rope or cord, or for other purposes.—**Eyelid**, ī'lid, *n.* That portion of movable skin that serves as a cover for the eyeball.—**Eye-opener**, *n.* Startling news; a drink of liquor, particularly the first of the day (*Slang*). **Eye-piece**, *n.* In an optical instrument the lens or combination of lenses to which the eye is applied.—**Eye-servant**, *n.* A servant who attends to his duty only when watched.—**Eye-service**, *n.* Service performed only under inspection or the eye of an employer.—**Eyesight**, ī'sīt, *n.* The sight of the eye; view; observation; the sense of seeing.—**Eyesore**, ī'sōr, *n.* Something offensive to the eye or sight.—**Eyetooth**, ī'töth, *n.* A tooth under the eye; a fang; a canine tooth.—**Eyewash**, *n.* A lotion to cleanse or treat the eye.—**Eye-witness**, *n.* One who sees a thing done; one who has ocular view of anything.

Eyot, ī'ot, *n.* [O.E. *ey*, Icel. *ey*, A.Sax. *íg*, an island, and dim. term *-ot*.] A little isle; a river islet with willows growing on it.

Eyre, ār, *n.* [O.Fr. *erre*, *eirre*, a journey, from L. *iter*, *itineris*, a journey.] A journey or circuit of a court; a court of itinerant justices.—*Justices in eyre*, itinerant justices who formerly traveled to hold courts in the different English counties.

Eyrie, **Eyry**, ī'ri, *n.* Same as AERIE.

F

F, the sixth letter of the English alphabet, a consonant, formed by the passage of breath between the lower lip and the upper front teeth; *mus.* the fourth note of the diatonic scale.

Fa, fä, *n.* *Mus.* the Italian name of the fourth note of the diatonic scale.

Faam-tea, fä'am-tē, *n.* The dried leaves of an orchid, used in England as a stomachic and in pulmonary complaints.

Fabaceous, fa-bā'shus, *a.* [L. *faba*, a bean.] Having the nature of the bean; like the bean.

Fabian, fā'bi-an, *a.* Like the generalship of *Fabius* Maximus, who harassed the troops of Hannibal but took care to avoid a battle (*Fabian* strategy).

Fable, fā'bl, *n.* [Fr. *fable*, L. *fabula*, from *fari*, to speak; akin *fate*.] A fictitious narration intended to enforce some useful truth or precept; a fabricated story; a fiction; the plot or connected series of events in an epic or dramatic poem; subject of talk (*Tenn.*).—*v.i.*—*fabled*, *fabling*. To tell fables or falsehoods.—*v.t.* To invent or fabricate; to speak of as true or real.—**Fabled**, fā'bld, *p.* and *a.* Celebrated in fables; fabulously imagined.—**Fabler**, fā'blėr, *n.* One who fables; a writer of fables. —**Fabliau**, fab-lē-ō, *n.* pl. **Fabliaux**, fab-lē-ō. [Fr.] A kind of metrical tale common in French literature of the twelfth and thirteenth centuries.—**Fabulist**, fab'ū-list, *n.* The inventor or writer of fables. —**Fabulize**, fab'ū-līz, *v.i.*—*fabulized*, *fabulizing*. To invent, compose, or relate fables. — **Fabulosity**,† fab-ū-los'i-ti, *n.* The quality of being fabulous; fabulousness; a fable.—**Fabulous**, fab'ū-lus, *a.* Having the nature of a fable; fictitious; invented; not real; mythical; hardly to be received as truth; incredible. — **Fabulously**, fab'ū-lus-li, *adv.* In a fabulous manner. — **Fabulousness**, fab'ū-lus-nes, *n.* The quality of being fabulous.

Fabric, fab'rik, *n.* [Fr. *fabrique*, L. *fabrica*, from *faber*, a worker: same root as *facio*, to make. *Forge* is really the same word.] A structure: a building, edifice, or construction; the frame of a building; cloth manufactured; the structure of anything; the manner in which the parts are put together; texture. — **Fabricant**, fab'ri-kant, *n.* [Fr.] A manufacturer.—**Fabricate**, fab'ri-kāt, *v.t.*—*fabricated*, *fabricating*. [L. *fabrico*, *fabricatum*.] To frame, build, make, or construct; to form into a whole by connecting the parts; to form by art and labour; to invent and form; to forge; to devise falsely.—**Fabrication**, fab-ri-kā'shon, *n.* The act of fabricating; construction; making; the act of devising falsely; forgery; that which is fabricated; a falsehood.—**Fabricator**, fab'ri-kā-tėr, *n.* One who fabricates.

Façade, fa-säd' or fa-sād', *n.* [Fr., from It. *faciata*, a façade, from *faccia*, L. *facies*, the face.] The face or front view or elevation of an edifice; exterior front or face.

Face, fās, *n.* [Fr., from L. *facies*, face, figure, form, from *facio*, to make.] The front part of an animal's head, particularly of the human head, made up of the forehead, eyes, nose, mouth, cheeks, &c.; the visage; aspect or air of the face; cast of features; look; countenance; expression of the face; the surface of a thing, or the side which presents itself to the view of the spectator; the front; the forepart; a plane surface of a solid; one of the sides bounding a solid; appearance; aspect; effrontery; boldness; assurance; the dial of a clock, watch, compass-card, or other indicator; the sole of a plane; operating edge or surface in certain implements.—*To make a face*, to distort the countenance; to make a grimace.—*To fly in the face of*, to act in direct opposition to or disregard of; to defy.—*Face to face*, both parties being present and confronting each other.—*v.t.*—*faced*, *facing*. To turn the face or front full toward; to meet in front; to stand up against in hostile encounter; to confront; to stand with the face or front toward; to finish or protect with a thin external covering over the front of; to smooth or dress the face of (a stone, &c.).—*To face down*, to oppose boldly or impudently. —*To face out*, to persist in, especially to persist in an assertion which is not true; to brave (an accusation) with effrontery.—*To face tea*, to adulterate it by mixing it with colouring matter and other substances.—*v.i.* To turn the face (to *face* to the right or left).—**Face-ache**, *n.* Tic-douloureux, a kind of neuralgia in the face.—**Faced**, fāst, *a.* Having a face; marked with a face (as a court-card). —**Facial**, fā'shi-al, *a.* Of or pertaining to the face.—*Facial angle*, an angle formed by lines drawn from nose to ear, and from nose to forehead; an angle formed by lines drawn to show to what extent the jaws are protruding and the forehead receding.—**Facially**, fā'shi-al-li, *adv.* In a facial manner; considered in regard to the features.—**Facing**, fas'ing, *n.* A covering in front for ornament, protection, defence, or other purposes; a mode of adulterating tea by mixing with colouring matter and other substances; the movement of soldiers in turning round to the left, right, &c.; *pl.* the distinctive trimmings on a regimental coat or jacket.—*Put through his facings*, to be cross-questioned; to be examined.—**Facingly**, fās'ing-li, *adv.* In a fronting position.

Facet, **Facette**, fas'et, fa-set', *n.* [Fr. *facette*, dim. of *face*.] A small flat portion of a surface; one of the small smooth surfaces on a gem or crystal.—*v.t.* To cut a facet or facets on.—**Faceted**, fas'et-ed, *a.* Having facets; formed into facets.

Facetiæ, fa-sē'shi-ē, *n. pl.* [L., from *facetus*, merry, elegant, from root of *facio*, to make.] Witty or humorous sayings; jests; witticisms. — **Facetious**, fa-sē'shus, *a.* Merry; jocular; witty; full of pleasantry; playful; exciting laughter.—**Facetiously**, fa-sē'shus-li, *adv.* In a facetious manner. —**Facetiousness**, fa-sē'shus-nes, *n.* The quality of being facetious; pleasantry.

Facial. Under FACE.

Facies, fā'shi-ēz, *n.* [L.] *Anat.* the face; *zool.* and *geol.* the general aspect presented by an assemblage of animals and plants, characteristic of a particular locality or period.

Facile, fas'il, *a.* [L. *facilis*, easy to be done or made, from *facio*, to make.] Easy to be done or performed; not difficult; easy to be dealt with; easy of access or converse; not haughty or distant; easily persuaded to good or bad; yielding; ductile to a fault; ready; dexterous (an artist's *facile* pencil).—**Facileness**,† fas'il-nes, *n.* The state of being facile.—**Facilitate**, fa-sil'i-tāt, *v.t.*—*facilitated*, *facilitating*. [Fr. *faciliter*, from L. *facilitas*, easiness.] To make easy or less difficult; to lessen the labour of.—**Facilitation**, fa-sil'i-tā"shon, *n.* The act of facilitating.—**Facility**, fa-sil'i-ti, *n.* [Fr. *facilité*, L. *facilitas*.] Easiness to be performed; freedom from difficulty; ease; ease in performance; readiness proceeding from skill or use; dexterity; pliancy or ductility in character; easiness to be persuaded, usually implying a disposition to yield to solicitations to evil; the means by which the accomplishment of anything is rendered more easy: in this sense usually in the *pl.*

Facsimile, fak-sim'i-lē, *n.* [L. *facio*, to make, and *similis*, like.] An exact copy or likeness; an imitation of an original in all its proportions, traits, and peculiarities.—**Facsimilist**, fak-sim'i-list, *n.* The producer of a facsimile or of facsimiles.

Fact, fakt, *n.* [L. *factum*, a thing done, a deed, a fact, from *facio*, to do or make, a stem which appears in many words, as *affect*, *affair*, *counterfeit*, *defeat*, *difficult*, *faculty*, *profits*, &c.] Anything done or that comes to pass; an act; a deed; an effect produced or achieved; an event; reality; truth; a true statement.

Faction, fak'shon, *n.* [L. *factio*, from *facio*, *factum*, to do. FACT.] A party combined or acting in union, in opposition to another party or a government; a party unscrupulously promoting their private ends at the expense of the public good; discord; dissension.—**Factionary**,† fak'shon-a-ri, *n.* A party man; one of a faction.—**Factionist**, fak'shon-ist, *n.* One who promotes faction. — **Factious**, fak'shus, *a.* Given to faction; prone to clamour against public measures or men; pertaining to faction; proceeding from faction. — **Fac-**

tiously, fak'shus-li, *adv.* In a factious, turbulent, or disorderly manner. —**Factiousness**, fak'shus-nes, *n.* The state or character of being factious; disposition to clamour and raise opposition; clamorousness for a party.

Factitious, fak-tish'us, *a.* [L. *factitius*, made by art, from *facio*, to make. FACT.] Made by art, in distinction from what is produced by nature; artificial; conventional. —**Factitiously**, fak-tish'us-li, *adv.* In a factitious manner. —**Factitiousness**, fak-tish'us-nes, *n.*

Factitive, fak'ti-tiv, *a.* [From L. *facio*, *factum*, to make. FACT.] Causative; tending to make or cause; *gram.* expressing the result of an action that produces a new condition in the object (in 'he struck him dead', *struck* is factitive).

Factor, fak'tėr, *n.* [L., a maker, doer, from *facio*, *factum*, to do. FACT.] An agent employed by merchants residing in other places to buy and sell or transact other business on their account; in Scotland, a person appointed by a landholder or house proprietor to manage an estate, collect rents, &c.; *arith.* the multiplier or multiplicand, from the multiplication of which proceeds the product; *alg.* any expression considered as part of a product; hence, generally, one of several elements or influences which tend to the production of a result.—*Factor of safety*, the ratio of the breaking load to the working load in any structure. —**Factorage**, fak'tėr-āj, *n.* The allowance to a factor for his services; commission.—**Factorial**, fak-tō'ri-al, *a.* Of or pertaining to a factor or factors.—**Factorship**, fak'tėr-ship, *n.* The business of a factor.—**Factory**, fak'to-ri, *n.* A name given to establishments of merchants and factors resident in foreign countries; (contr. from *manufactory*) a building or collection of buildings appropriated to the manufacture of goods; a manufactory.

Factotum, fak-tō'tum, *n.* [L. *facio*, to do, and *totum*, the whole.] A confidential agent that manages all kinds of matters for his employer.

Faculæ, fak'ū-lē, *n. pl.* [L. *facula*, a little torch, dim. of *fax*, a torch.] *Astron.* spots sometimes seen on the sun's disc, which appear brighter than the rest of his surface.—**Facular**, fak'ū-lėr, *a.* Pertaining or relating to faculæ.

Facultative, fak'ul-tā"tiv, *a.* [L. *facultas*, capability.] Of bacteria and parasites, able to adapt themselves to certain conditions of life.

Faculty, fak'ul-ti, *n.* [Fr. *faculté*, L. *facultas*, from *facio*, to do, to make. FACT.] Any mental or bodily power; capacity for any action or function; skill derived from practice, or practice aided by nature; special power or endowment; a right or power granted to a person by favor or indulgence, to do what by law he may not do; the body of individuals constituting one of the learned professions, and more specifically the medical profession; the teachers and professors of the several departments of a university, or one of the departments themselves, as *Faculty* of Arts, Law, Medicine; the teaching staff of any institution of learning.

Fad, fad, *n.* [Perhaps from A.Sax. *fadian*, to arrange.] A passing whim, hobby, style or fancy, pursued for a time with undue zeal.—**Faddist**, fad'ist, *n.* One who is enthusiastic over a fad.—**Faddish**, fad'-ish, *a.* Pertaining or given to fads, faddy.

Fade, fād, *v.i.*—*faded*, *fading*. [O.E. *vade*, to fade; comp. Fr. *fade*, insipid, from L. *vapidus*, vapid.] To wither; to lose strength, health, or vigor gradually; to decay; to lose freshness, color, or brightness; to tend from a stronger or brighter color to a more faint shade of the same color, or to lose color entirely; to grow dim or indistinct to view.—*v.t.* To cause to wither; to deprive of freshness or vigor.—**Fadedly**, fād'ed-li, *adv.* In a faded or decayed manner.—**Fadeless**, fād'les, *a.* Unfading. —**Fading**, fād'ing, *p.* and *a.* Liable to fade or lose freshness and vigor; not durable; transient. —**Fadingly**, fād'ing-li, *adv.* In a fading manner.—**Fadingness**, fād'ing-nes, *n.*

Fadge, faj, *v.i.* [A.Sax. *fœgian*, to fit, akin to *fæger*, fair; comp. G. *fügen*, D. *voegen*, Sw. *foga*, to fit.] To suit; to fit; to be found suitable or successful.

Fæces, fē'sēz, *n. pl.* [L.] Excrement; also, settlings; dregs; sediment.—**Fæcal**, fē'kal, *a.* Pertaining to fæces.

Faery, fā'ėr-i, *a.* Pertaining to fairies; fairy.

Fag, fag, *v.i.*—*fagged*, *fagging*. [Probably from verb to *flag*, by omission of *l*.] To become weary; to fail in strength; to be faint with weariness; to labor hard or assiduously; to work till wearied; to act as a fag.—*v.t.* To use or treat as a fag or drudge; to exhaust.—*n.* A laborious drudge; in certain English schools, a boy who performs menial services for another boy who is in the highest or next highest form or class; a cigarette.—**Fag-end**, *n.* [The end which *flags* or hangs loose.] The end of a web of cloth; the latter or meaner part of anything.

Fagaceous, fā-gā'shus, *a.* Pertaining to the beech family of shrubs and trees.

Fagot, **Faggot**, fag'ot, *n.* [Fr. *fagot*, It. *fagotto*, a faggot, from L. *fax*, *facis*, a faggot, a torch.] A bundle of sticks or small branches used for fuel, or for filling ditches, and other purposes in fortification; a fascine; a bundle of pieces of iron or steel in bars; a person formerly hired to take the place of another at the muster of a military company or to hide deficiency in its number; a term of contempt for a dry, shriveled old woman.—*v.t.* To bind in a fagot or bundle; to collect promiscuously. —**Fagot-vote**, *n.* A vote procured by the purchase of property under mortgage or otherwise, which is divided among a number so as to constitute a nominal qualification without a substantial basis.

Fagotto, fa-got'tō, *n.* [It. *fagotto*, the name being given, it is said, from its faggot-like appearance.] The Italian name of the instrument otherwise called the bassoon.

Faham-tea. FAAM-TEA.

Fahlerz, **Fahlore**, fäl'ėrts, fäl'ōr, *n.* [G. *fahl*, yellowish, and *erz*, ore.] Gray copper or gray copper ore.

Fahrenheit, fä'ren-hīt, *a.* [After *Fahrenheit*, who first employed quicksilver in thermometers about 1720.] The name distinguishing that kind of thermometer in which the space between the freezing and the boiling points of water is divided into 180 degrees; the freezing point being marked 32°, and the boiling 212°.

Faience, fā-i-ens' or fä-yäṅs, *n.* [Fr.] A sort of fine pottery or earthenware glazed with a fine varnish, and painted in various designs, named from *Faenza* in Italy.

Fail, fāl, *v.i.* [Fr. *faillir*, to fail, from L. *fallere*, to deceive, whence also *false*, *fallible*, *fault*, *falter*.] To become deficient; to be insufficient; to cease to be abundant for supply; to come short; not to have the due measure or degree; to decay, decline, sink, or be diminished; to become weaker; to become extinct; to be entirely wanting; to be no longer produced, furnished, or supplied; not to produce the effect; to miscarry; to be unsuccessful; to be guilty of omission or neglect; to become insolvent or bankrupt.—*v.t.* To cease or to neglect or omit to afford aid or strength to; to be wanting to; to disappoint; to desert; not to be at hand when required.—*n.* Miscarriage; failure; deficiency; want.—*Without fail*, without omission to perform something; without doubt; certainly.—**Failing**, fāl'ing, *n.* Imperfection; a weakness in character or disposition; foible; fault.—*Failing whom*. *Failing* used either as preposition or *abl. absol.* 'who failing'.—**Failingly**, fāl'ing-li, *adv.* By failing.—**Failure**, fāl'ūr, *n.* A failing; deficiency; cessation of supply or total defect; omission; non-performance; decay, or defect from decay; the act of failing or state of having failed to attain an object; want of success; a becoming insolvent or bankrupt.

Faille, fī-yė or fāl, *n.* [Fr.] A heavy silk fabric of superior quality.

Fain, fān, *a.* [A.Sax. *fægen*, joyful, *fægnian*, to rejoice; Goth. *faginon*, Icel. *fagna*, to be glad. *Fawn* (verb) is of same origin, and *fair* (adj.) is akin.] Glad or pleased under some kind of necessity; inclined; content to accept of or do something for want of better.—*adv.* Gladly; with joy or pleasure: with *would*.—**Fainness**, fān'-nes, *n.* State of being fain.

Faineant, fā-nā-aṅ, *n.* [Fr. *faire*, do, *néant*, nothing.] An idler, a do-nothing, a puppet or phantom king in the Merovingian dynasty of the Franks.

Faint, fānt, *v.i.* [O.Fr. *faint*, sluggish, negligent, pp. of *feindre*, L. *fingere*, to feign, whence also *feign*, *fiction*, &c.] To become feeble; to decline or fail in strength and vigour; to become temporarily unconscious, powerless, and motionless; to swoon; to sink into dejection; to lose courage or spirit; to become gradually weak or indistinct; to decay; to fade, disappear, or vanish.—*a.* Weak; languid; feeble; exhausted; inclined to swoon; hardly perceptible by or feebly striking the senses; indistinct; wanting in brightness or vividness, loudness, sharpness, or force; not well defined; feeble; slight; imperfect; not carried on with vigour or energy; dejected; depressed; dispirited.—*n.* A fainting fit; a swoon; *pl.* the impure spirit which comes over first and last in the distillation of whisky.—**Faint-hearted**, *a.* Cowardly; timorous; having lost courage; yielding to fear. —**Faint-heartedly**, *adv.* In a faint-hearted manner.—**Faint-heartedness**, *n.* Want of courage.—**Faintish**, fān'tish, *a.* Slightly faint.—**Faintishness**, fān'tish-nes, *n.* A slight degree of faintness.—**Faintly**, fānt'-li, *adv.* In a faint, weak, feeble, or languid manner; without vigour or activity; without vividness or distinctness. —**Faintness**, fānt'nes, *n.* The state of being faint.

Fair, fār, *a.* [A.Sax. *fæger*, fair, pleasant, beautiful; Icel. *fagr*, Dan. *feir*, Sw. *fager*, Goth. *fagrs*, bright. FAIN.] Pleasing to the eye; beautiful; handsome; white or light coloured in respect of skin or complexion; not dark or swarthy; not stormy or wet; not cloudy or overcast; clear (*fair* weather); free from obstruction, obstacle, or anything to impede (on the *fair* way to success); open, frank, or honest; not resorting to anything tricky or underhand; just; equitable; free from unfair or unfavourable circumstances or influences; civil, pleasing, or courteous (*fair* words); free from deletions, blots, and the like; perfectly or easily legible (a *fair* copy); free from stain or blemish; unspotted; untarnished (one's *fair* name); passably or moderately good; better than indifferent. —*Fair way*, the track or course that is clear of obstacles and is therefore taken by vessels in navigating a narrow bay, river, or harbour.—*adv.* Openly; frankly; civilly; complaisantly (especially in 'to speak a person *fair*'); on good terms (to keep *fair* with the world).—*To bid fair*, to promise well; to be in a fair way; to be likely.—*n.* Elliptically, a fair woman; a handsome female. (*Poet.*)—*The fair*, the female sex; specifically, the loveliest of that sex.—*v.t.* To make fair or beautiful.—**Fairish**, fār'-ish, *a.* Reasonably fair.—**Fairishly**, fār'-ish-li, *adv.* In a tolerably fair manner.—**Fairly**, fār'li, *adv.* In a fair manner; beautifully; handsomely; honestly; justly; equitably; tolerably.—**Fairness**, fār'nes, *n.* The quality or character of being fair; lightness of complexion, beauty; honesty; justice.—**Fair-play**, *n.* Equitable dealing or treatment; justice.—**Fair-spoken**, *a.* Using fair speech; bland; civil, courteous; plausible.—**Fair-weather**, *a.* In pleasant weather; showing only in fair weather or in favourable circumstances (a *fair-weather* friend).

Fair, fār, *n.* [Fr. *foire*, a fair, market; It. *feria*; L. *feriæ*, holidays, festivals.] A stated market in a particular town or city; a stated meeting of buyers and sellers for trade.—**Fairing**, fār′ing, *n.* A present given at a fair.

Fairy, fā′ri, *n.* [O.Fr. *faerie*, Fr. *féerie*, the power of a fairy, enchantment; from O.Fr. *fae*, Fr. *fée*, It. *fata*, a fairy, lit. a fate, from L. *fatum*, fate. FATE.] An imaginary being or spirit having a human form, though of a stature much below human and with sundry superhuman attributes: an elf or fay; any personage with superhuman power‡; fairy-land‡.—*a.* Pertaining to or in some manner connected with fairies; coming from fairies; resembling a fairy.—*Fairy ring* or *circle*, a ring formed by the grass in certain places growing noticeably greener than that around, long popularly supposed to be caused by fairies in their dances.—**Fairily**, fā′ri-li, *adv.* In a fairy-like manner; in a manner or fashion suggestive of the handiwork of fairies.—**Fairy-king**, *n.* The king of the fairies.—**Fairy-land**, *n.* The imaginary land or abode of fairies.—**Fairy-queen**, *n.* The queen of the fairies.—**Fairy-tale**, *n.* A tale relating to fairies.

Faith, fāth, *n.* [O.E. *feid*, *feith*, O.Fr. *feid*, from L. *fides*, faith; akin *fidelity*, *confide*, *defy*, *infidel*, &c.] The assent of the mind to the truth of what is declared by another; firm and earnest belief on probable evidence of any kind; belief; belief in what is given forth as a revelation of man's relation to God and the infinite; a settled conviction in regard to religion; a system of religious belief; that which is believed on any subject, whether in science, politics, or religion; a doctrine or system of doctrines believed; faithfulness; fidelity; word or honour pledged; promise given.—*In good faith*, in real honesty; with perfect sincerity.—**Faithful**, fāth′fu̧l, *a.* Firm in faith; firmly adhering to religious or other duty; of true fidelity; loyal; true and constant to a person to whom one is bound; true to one's word; in conformity to the letter and spirit; conformable to truth; conformable to a prototype; true or exact; worthy of belief.—*The faithful*, those who adhere to the true faith, as contrasted with the adherents of another faith.—**Faithfully**, fāth′fu̧l-li, *adv.* In a faithful manner; sincerely; with strong assurance; earnestly; conformably to truth or fact; conformably to an example or prototype.—**Faithfulness**, fāth′fu̧l-nes, *n.* The quality or character of being faithful; fidelity; truth; loyalty; constancy.—**Faithless**, fāth′les, *a.* Without faith; not adhering to allegiance, vows, or duty; disloyal; not observant of promises.—**Faithlessly**, fāth′les-li, *adv.* In a faithless manner.—**Faithlessness**, fāth′les-nes, *n.* State of being faithless.—**Faithworthiness**,† fāth′wėr-ᴛʜi-nes, *n.* Trustworthiness.—**Faithworthy**,† fāth′wėr-ᴛʜi, *a.* Worthy of faith or belief; trustworthy.

Fake, fāk, *n.* [A.Sax. *faec*, a space or interval.] One of the circles or windings of a rope as it lies in a coil; a counterfeit or imitation presented as genuine; a fraud.—*v.t.* To impart a false character to; to deceive; to feign.

Fakir, fā-kēr′, *n.* [Ar., lit. a poor man.] An oriental ascetic or begging monk.

Falcate, **Falcated**, fal′kāt, fal′kāt-ed, *a.* [L. *falcatus*, from *falx*, *falcis*, a sickle.] Hooked; in shape like a sickle or scythe.—**Falcation**, fal-kā′shon, *n.* A bending or bend in the form of a sickle.—**Falciform**, fal′si-form, *a.* In the shape of a sickle or reaping-hook.—**Falcula**, fal′kū-la, *n.* [L., a small sickle.] *Zool.* a compressed, elongated, curved, and sharp-pointed claw.—**Falculate**, fal′kū-lāt, *a.* *Zool.* having the shape of a falcula.

Falchion, fal′shon, *n.* [L. *falx*, *falcis*, a scythe.] A broad short sword with a slightly curved point.

Falcon, fa̧′kn, *n.* [O.Fr. *falcon*, Fr. *faucon*, L.L. *falco*, probably from L. *falx*, a reaping-hook, from the curved claws and beak.] The common name of various raptorial birds inferior in size to the eagles and vultures, and remarkable for their elegant form and powers of flight; especially, one trained to hunt wild fowl or other game; a hawk. [The term falcon is by sportsmen restricted to the female, the male, which is smaller and less courageous, being called *tersel* or *tiercel*.] A small cannon. MUSKET.—**Falconer**, fa̧′kn-ėr, *n.* A person who breeds and trains falcons or hawks for sport; one who follows the sport of fowling with hawks.—**Falcon-gentle**, *n.* The female of the goshawk.—**Falconine**, fa̧′kon-īn, *a.* Of or pertaining to the falcons.—**Falconry**, fa̧′kn-ri, *n.* The art of training falcons to attack wild birds or game; the sport of pursuing wild fowls or game by means of falcons or hawks.

Faldstool, fa̧ld′stöl, *n.* [*Fald* or *fold*, and *stool*.] A folding-stool similar to a camp-stool; a kind of stool at which the kings of England kneel at their coronation; a small desk at which in churches litany is said.

Falernian, fa-lėr′ni-an, *a.* Pertaining to Mount *Falernus* in Campania, in Italy.—*n.* The ancient wine made from grapes from Mount Falernus.

Fall, fa̧l, *v.i.*—*fell* (pret.), *fallen* (pp.). [A. Sax. *feallen* = D. *vallen*, Dan. *falde*, Icel. *falla*, G. *fallen*, to fall. *Fell* is the causal of this.] To sink from a higher to a lower position; to descend by the power of gravity; to drop down; to sink; to ebb; to drop from an erect posture; to empty, disembogue, or discharge itself: said of a stream; to depart from the faith or from rectitude; to sink into sin; to die, particularly by violence; to come to an end suddenly; to perish, be overthrown, or ruined; to sink into weakness; to become faint or feeble (our hopes *fall*); to sink into disrepute or disgrace; to decline in power, wealth, or glory; to pass into a new state, especially with suddenness or through inadvertence or ignorance (to *fall* asleep, to *fall* into error); to decrease; to be diminished in weight, size, value, or intensity (the price *falls*, the wind *falls*); to assume an expression of dejection, discontent, sorrow, shame, &c.: applied to the countenance; to happen; to befall; to take place; to pass or be transferred by lot, inheritance, or otherwise (something *falls* to one's share); to belong or appertain; to have to be reckoned to; to be dropped or uttered carelessly; to sink in tone or loudness.—*To fall among*, to come among or into the society of, accidentally or unexpectedly.—*To fall away*, to lose flesh; to become lean or emaciated; to renounce or desert allegiance, faith, or duty; to revolt or rebel; to apostatize; to decline gradually; to languish or become faint.—*To fall back*, to recede; to give way; to go from better to worse; to retrograde; to fail of performing a promise or purpose; not to fulfil.—*To fall back upon*, to have recourse to, generally to some support or expedient formerly tried.—*To fall down*, to prostrate one's self in worship or supplication; to sink; to come to the ground.—*To fall foul of*, to attack; to make an assault upon.—*To fall from*, to recede from; to depart; not to adhere to.—*To fall in*, to take one's place in an organized body of men, as soldiers; to terminate or lapse (an annuity *falls in* when the annuitant dies).—*To fall in with*, to meet casually; to happen to meet; to concur, agree, or comply with.—*To fall off*, to be broken or detached from something; to apostatize; to fall away; to get into disuse; to decline from former excellence; to become less valuable or interesting; to become less; to decrease: *naut.* to deviate from the course to which the head of the ship was before directed.—*To fall on* or *upon*, to begin suddenly and eagerly; to begin an attack on; to assault; to assail; to come upon, usually with some degree of suddenness and unexpectedness; to drop on; to light on; to come upon.—*To fall out*, to quarrel; to begin to contend; to happen; to befall; to chance; to turn out; to prove.—*To fall short*, to be deficient.—*To fall to*, to begin hastily and eagerly; to apply one's self to.—*To fall under*, to come under or within the limits of; to be subjected to; to become the subject of.—*n.* The act of one who or that which falls; a dropping or descending; descent; a tumble; death; destruction; overthrow; downfall; degradation; declension of greatness, power, or dominion; ruin; diminution; decrease of price or value; a sinking of tone; cadence; descent of water; a cascade or cataract; extent of descent; the distance through which anything falls or may fall; amount of slope; declivity; the season when leaves fall from trees; autumn; that which falls; a shower; a kind of ladies' veil; lapse or declension from innocence or goodness, the *fall* being specifically the lapse into sin of our first parents Adam and Eve; *naut.* the part of a tackle to which the power is applied in hoisting.—*To try a fall*, to try a bout at wrestling.—**Fallen**, fa̧l′en, *pp.* or *a.* Dropped; degraded; sunk in vice; lost to virtue; ruined; overthrown.—**Falling-in**, *n.* An indentation or hollow.—**Falling-sickness**, *n.* Epilepsy, a disease in which the patient suddenly loses his senses and falls.—**Falling-star**, *n.* A meteor appearing as a luminous point darting through the sky, and followed by a long train of light.—**Fall-trap**, *n.* A trap in which a part of the apparatus descends and imprisons or kills the victim.

Fallacious, fal-lā′shus, *a.* [Fr. *fallacieux*, from L. *fallax*, *fallacis*, deceitful, from *fallo*, to deceive. FAIL.] Pertaining to or embodying something deceptive or misleading; producing error or mistake; tending to mislead. ∴ *Fallacious* reasoning consists of arguments that deceive or mislead one, though not necessarily purposely. *Sophistical* reasoning is intendedly false reasoning, consisting of arguments so subtle as not to be easily detected and controverted, advanced purposely to mislead.—**Fallaciously**, fal-lā′shus-li, *adv.* In a fallacious manner; sophistically; with purpose or in a manner to deceive.—**Fallaciousness**, fal-lā′shus-nes, *n.* State of being fallacious.—**Fallacy**, fal′la-si, *n.* [L. *fallacia*, deceit.] A misleading or mistaken argument; an argument or proposition apparently sound but really containing some undetected error, and therefore misleading; any unsound but specious mode of arguing.

Fallible, fal′i-bl, *a.* [L.L. *fallibilis*, from L. *fallo*, to deceive. FALLACIOUS, FAIL.] Liable to fail or mistake; liable to deceive or to be deceived; liable to error or going astray.—**Fallibility**, fal-i-bil′i-ti, *n.* The state of being fallible; liableness to deceive or to be deceived.—**Fallibly**, fal′i-bli, *adv.* In a fallible manner.

Fallopian, fal-lō′pi-an, *a.* Of or pertaining to *Fallopius*, an Italian anatomist of the 16th century.—*Fallopian tubes*, the two canals or tubes which arise at each side of the uterus, and pass towards the ovarium.

Fallow, fal′ō, *a.* [A.Sax. *fealo*, *fealwe*, pale red or pale yellow; akin to G. *fahl*, *falb*; L.G. and D. *vaal*, fallow; same root as L. *pallidus*, pallid, pale. The term was applied to land from the colour of ploughed land.] Pale red or pale yellow; left to rest without a crop after tillage; untilled; uncultivated; neglected; unoccupied; unused.—*n.* Land that has lain a year or more untilled or unsown; land ploughed without being sowed; the ploughing of land, without sowing it, for a season.—*v.t.* To leave fallow or ploughed but not sown in crop.—**Fallow-deer**, *n.* [From its *fallow* or pale-yellow colour.] A European deer smaller than the stag, of a brownish-bay colour, whitish beneath.—**Fallow-chat**, **Fallow-finch**, *n.* The bird otherwise called the wheat-ear.

False, fa̧ls, *a.* [L. *falsus*, false, from *fallo*, *falsum*, to deceive. FAIL.] Not true; not conformable to fact; expressing what is contrary to that which exists, is done, said, or thought; intended to mislead; counterfeit; forged; not real or genuine; hypocritical; feigned; not agreeable to rule or propriety (*false* construction in language); not honest or just; fraudulent; not faithful or loyal; treacherous; perfidious; deceitful; unfaithful; inconstant; not well founded or based (*false* hopes); constructed for show or a subsidiary purpose (a *false* bottom, a *false* keel).—**False-faced**, *a.* Hypocritical.—**False-hearted**, *a.* Treacherous; deceitful; perfidious.

—**False-heartedness**, *n.* Perfidiousness; treachery.—**Falsehood**, fąls′hŏd, *n.* Contrariety or want of conformity to fact or truth; falseness; want of truth or veracity; untruthfulness; what is false or untrue; a lie; an untrue assertion; want of honesty; deceitfulness; perfidy; imposture. —**Falsely**, fąls′li, *adv.* In a manner contrary to truth and fact; not truly; untruly. —**Falseness**, fąls′nes, *n.* The state or quality of being false; untruthfulness; want of veracity; duplicity; deceit; unfaithfulness; perfidy.—**Falsify**, fąl′si-fī, *v.t.*—*falsified, falsifying.* [Fr. *falsifier*, from L. *falsus*, and *facio*, to make.] To represent falsely; to vitiate with false and misleading elements; to garble; to make not genuine; to disprove; to prove to be false; to cause to turn out false (to *falsify* a prediction); to violate or break by falsehood.—*v.i.* To violate the truth.—**Falsifiable**, fąl′si-fī-a-bl, *a.* Capable of being falsified.—**Falsification**, fąl′si-fi-kā″shon, *n.* The act of falsifying; a counterfeiting; the giving to a thing an appearance of something which it is not.—**Falsifier**, fąl′si-fī-ėr, *n.* One who falsifies; one who counterfeits or gives to a thing a deceptive appearance.—**Falsism, Falseism**, fąl′sizm, *n.* A statement or assertion the falsity of which is plainly apparent: opposed to *truism*.—**Falsity**, fąl′si-ti, *n.* The quality of being false; that which is false; a falsehood; a false assertion.

Falsetto, fäl-set′tō, *n.* [It., from L. *falsus*, false.] The tones above the natural compass of the voice.

Falter, fąl′tėr, *v.i.* [A freq. connected with *fault*, from a supposed Fr. verb corresponding to Sp. *faltar*, It. *faltare*, to fail, from L. *fallere*, to deceive. FAULT, FAIL.] To hesitate in the utterance of words; to speak with a broken or trembling utterance; to stammer; not to be firm and steady; to tremble.—*n.* The act of faltering; hesitation; trembling; quavering.—**Faltering**, fąl′tėr-ing, *a.* Trembling; hesitating.—**Falteringly**, fąl′tėr-ing-li, *adv.* With hesitation; with a trembling, broken voice.

Fama, fā′ma, *n.* [L. FAME.] A widely prevailing rumour affecting the character of any one; in *Rom. myth.* the deified personification of fame or rumour.

Fame, fām, *n.* [Fr. *fame*, from L. *fama*, fame, renown, from *fari*, to speak; whence also *fate*. FATE.] Public report or rumour; report or opinion widely diffused; renown; notoriety; celebrity.—**Famed**, fāmd, *p.* and *a.* Much talked of; renowned; celebrated.—**Fameless**, fām′les, *a.* Without renown.—**Famous**, fā′mus, *a.* [L. *famosus*, Fr. *fameux*.] Celebrated in fame or public report; renowned; much talked of; distinguished in story.—**Famously**, fā′mus-li, *adv.* In a famous manner.—**Famousness**,† fā′mus-nes, *n.* The state of being famous; renown; celebrity.

Familiar, fa-mil′yėr, *a.* [L. *familiaris*, from *familia*, a household, the servants of a family, from *famulus*, a servant. FAMILY.] Well acquainted; closely intimate; well versed (in a subject of study); exhibiting the manner of an intimate friend; affable; accessible; characterized by ease or absence of stiffness of pedantry; easy; well known; well understood; of everyday occurrence or use.—*Familiar spirit*, a spirit or demon supposed to be constantly at the command of some person.—*n.* An intimate; a close companion; a familiar spirit; an officer of the Inquisition employed in apprehending and imprisoning persons accused.—**Familiarity**, fa-mil′i-ar″i-ti, *n.* The state of being familiar; unconstrained intercourse; intimate acquaintance or knowledge; intimacy; *pl.* actions characterized by too much licence; liberties.—**Familiarization**, fa-mil′yėr-i-zā″shon, *n.* Act or process of making or becoming familiar.—**Familiarize**, fa-mil′yėr-īz, *v.t.*—*familiarized, familiarizing.* To make familiar or intimate; to habituate; to accustom; to make intimately acquainted; to render conversant or fully acquainted by practice or customary use, or by intercourse.—**Familiarly**, fa-mil′yėr-li, *adv.* In a familiar manner.—**Familiarness**, fa-mil′yėr-nes, *n.* Familiarity.

Family, fam′i-li, *n.* [L. *familia*, a household, the slaves or servants of a house; from *famulus*, a servant, a slave, from Oscan *famel*, a servant, from *faama*, Skr. *dhâman*, a house.] The body of persons who live in one house and under one head; the parents and children alone; the children as distinguished from the parents; those who descend from one common progenitor; a tribe or race; kindred; lineage; line of ancestors; honourable descent; noble or respectable stock (a man of *family*); in scientific classifications, a group of individuals more comprehensive than a genus, and less so than an order.—*Family Compact*, the compact formed in 1733 between the divisions of the Bourbon family, Philip V of Spain and Louis XV of France, against British supremacy.—**Family living**, *n.* A clerical gift or advowson in the patronage of a family.—**Family-man**, *n.* One who has a family or household; a married man. —**Family-way**, *n.* State of pregnancy.

Famine, fam′in, *n.* [Fr. *famine*, from L. *fames*, hunger.] Scarcity of food; dearth; a general want of provisions; destitution. —**Famish**, fam′ish, *v.t.* [O.Fr. *famis*, starving, from L. *fames*.] To kill or destroy with hunger; to starve; to cause to suffer from hunger or thirst; to distress with hunger; to force or compel by famine. —*v.i.* To die of hunger; to suffer extreme hunger or thirst; to suffer by the deprivation of any necessary.

Famous. Under FAME.

Fan, fan, *n.* [A.Sax. *fann*, *fan*, from L. *vannus*, a fan for winnowing; akin to L. *ventus*, wind, and E. *wind*, *winnow*.] The name of various instruments for exciting a current of air by the agitation of a broad surface, vanes or discs; a machine for winnowing grain; an instrument used by ladies to agitate the air and cool the face; anything resembling this; what fans or excites.—*v.t.*—*fanned, fanning.* To move or agitate as with a fan; to cool and refresh by moving the air with a fan; to winnow; to separate chaff from, and drive it away by a current of air; *fig.* to produce effects on analogous to those of a fan in exciting flame; to excite or stir up to activity; to stimulate.—**Fan-blower**, *n.* A fan for driving a current of air into a furnace by the quick revolution of a wheel with vanes. —**Fan-light**, *n.* A fan-shaped window situated over a door in a circular-headed opening; also any window over a door.—**Fanner**, fan′ėr, *n.* One who fans; a rotatory contrivance with vanes for ventilating the interior of a chamber; an arrangement of vanes for blowing fires; *pl.* a fan or machine for winnowing grain.—**Fan-tail**, *n.* A variety of the domestic pigeon; a form of gas-burner.—**Fan-tailed**, *a.* Having a tail expanding like a fan.—**Fan-window**, *n.* A window having a semicircular outline and a sash formed of radial bars.

Fanatic, Fanatical, fa-nat′ik, fa-nat′i-kal, *a.* [L. *fanaticus*, inspired, enthusiastic, from *fanum*, a place dedicated to some deity, a temple. FANE.] Wild and extravagant in opinions, particularly in religious opinions.—*n.* A person affected by excessive enthusiasm, particularly on religious subjects; one who indulges wild and extravagant notions of religion.—**Fanatically**, fa-nat′i-kal-li, *adv.* In a fanatical manner; with wild enthusiasm.—**Fanaticalness**, fa-nat′i-kal-nes, *n.* Fanaticism. —**Fanaticism**, fa-nat′i-sizm, *n.* The state or character of a fanatic; wild and extravagant notions of religion; religious frenzy; fervid zeal.—**Fanaticize**, fa-nat′i-sīz, *v.t.* To make fanatic.

Fancy, fan′si, *n.* [Contr. for *fantasy*, *phantasy*, from L. and Gr. *phantasia*, a fancy, from Gr. *phantazō*, to make visible, from *phainō*, to show; akin *phantom*, *phenomenon*.] A phase of the intellectual faculty of a lighter and less impressive cast than the imagination, or the active play of this lighter faculty; a new and pleasing thought or conception due to this faculty; the happy and poetical embodiment of such conception in words; a poetical illustration or ornament, as a simile, metaphor, and the like; an opinion or notion; an impression or supposition; a whim or conceit; inclination; liking; fondness; preference.—*The fancy*, a name for sporting characters, especially prize-fighters.—*a.* Fine; elegant; ornamental (*fancy* goods); beyond intrinsic value; extravagant (a *fancy* price).—*v.i.*—*fancied, fancying.* To imagine; to figure to one's self; to believe or suppose without proof.—*v.t.* To form a conception of; to portray in the mind; to imagine; to like; to be pleased with.—**Fancied**, fan′sid, *p.* and *a.* Portrayed or formed by the fancy; imaginary; attracting one's fancy; liked; in esteem; sought after.—**Fancier**, fan′si-ėr, *n.* One who fancies; one who is influenced by his fancies.—**Fanciful**, fan′si-fųl, *a.* Guided by fancy rather than by reason and experience; subject to the influence of fancy; whimsical: applied to persons; dictated or produced by fancy; appealing to or pleasing the fancy; full of wild images; curiously shaped: applied to things.—**Fancifully**, fan′si-fųl-li, *adv.* In a fanciful manner.—**Fancifulness**, fan′si-fųl-nes, *n.* The quality of being fanciful.—**Fanciless**, fan′si-les, *a.* Destitute of fancy.—**Fancy-ball**, *n.* A ball in which persons appear in fancy dresses, imitations of antique costumes, &c.—**Fancy-fair**, *n.* A kind of temporary market in which ladies sell various light wares, usually of their own make, for some benevolent or charitable purpose; a bazaar.—**Fancy-free**, *a.* Free from the power of love.—**Fancy-work**, *n.* Ornamental knitting, embroidery, &c., performed by ladies.

Fandango, fan-dang′gō, *n.* A lively Spanish dance borrowed from the Moors, danced by two persons, male and female, the music being in triple time.

Fane, fān, *n.* [L. *fanum*, a place dedicated to a deity, from *fari*, to speak; akin *fame*, *fate*.] A temple; a place consecrated to religion; a church. (*Poet.*)

Fanfare, fan′fār, *n.* [Fr.] A flourish of trumpets; a short tune of a cheerful cast, played with hunting horns; an ostentatious parade or boast; bravado.—**Fanfaron**, fan′fa-ron, *n.* [Fr.] A bully; a hector; a swaggerer; an empty boaster.—**Fanfaronade**, fan-far′o-nād″, *n.* [Fr.] A swaggering; ostentation; bluster.

Fang, fang, *n.* [A.Sax. *fang*, a taking, grasp, from *fón* (for *fahan*), to seize (pret. *feng*, pp. *fangen*) = G. *fangen*, Goth. *fahan*, D. *vangen*, to take.] The tusk of a boar or other animal by which the prey is seized and held; a long pointed tooth; the hollow poison tooth of a serpent; a claw or talon; the catch of a pump.—*Off the fang*, out of sorts, listless.—*v.t.* To start a pump by pouring water on it.—**Fanged**, fangd, *p.* and *a.* Furnished with fangs, tusks, or something resembling these.—**Fangless**, fang′les, *a.* Having no fangs or tusks.

Fangled, fang′gld, *a.* [From old *fangle*, a gewgaw, something to catch the eye, from old *fangen*, to catch.] Gaudy; showy; fond of finery. (Used by Shakspere, but now only in the compound *new-fangled*.)

Fanon, fan′on, *n.* [Fr. *fanon*, from Goth. *fana*, cloth, a banner.] *Eccles.* a kind of napkin or handkerchief used by the priest at mass; also an ornament attached to a priest's left arm.

Fanpalm, *n.* A name for the talipat and one or two other palms.

Fantasia, fan-tä′zē-a, *n.* [It., lit. a fantasy or fancy, from L. and Gr. *phantasia*, a fancy, whence also E. *fancy*. FANCY.] A species of musical composition having no particular theme, but ranging amidst various airs and movements.—**Fantasm**, fan′tazm, *n.* Same as *Phantasm*.—**Fantast**, fan′tast, *n.* One whose mind is full of fantastic notions.—**Fantastic, Fantastical**, fan-tas′tik, fan-tas′ti-kal, *a.* [Fr. *fantastique*, from Gr. *phantastikos*, from *phantasia*, vision, fancy.] Fanciful; existing only in imagination; imaginary; chimerical; whimsical; capricious; indulging the vagaries of imagination; having oddness of figure or appearance; whimsically shaped; grotesque.—*n.* A whimsical person; a fop. —**Fantasticality**, fan-tas'ti-kal"i-ti, *n.* Fantasticalness. — **Fantastically**, fan-tas'ti-kal-li, *adv.* In a fantastic manner; capriciously; whimsically.—**Fantasticalness, Fantasticism**, fan-tas'ti-kal-nes, fan-tas'ti-sizm, *n.* State of being fantastical.—**Fantasy**, fan'ta-si, *n.* Same as *Fancy.*

Fantoccini, fan-to-chē'nē, *n. pl.* [It.] Puppets worked by concealed wires or strings; a puppet-show; marionettes.

Fantom, fan'tom, *n.* Same as *Phantom.*

Far, fär, *a.* [A.Sax. *feor*; D. *ver*, Icel. *fjarri*, Goth. *fairra*, G. *fern*, far—allied to *fore, ferry, fare*; the root being same as that of L. *per*, through; G. *pera*, beyond; Skr. *para*, other.] Distant; separated by a wide space; hence, remote as regards wishes, feelings, affections; more distant of the two: applied to the right side of a horse.—*adv.* To a great extent or distance of space; to a remote period; in great part (the day *far* spent); in a great proportion; by many degrees; very much (*far* better or higher); to whatever point, degree, or distance (as *far* as).—*By far*, in a great degree; very much.—*From far*, from a great distance; from a remote place.—*Far other*, very different.—**Far-fetched**, *p.* and *a.* Brought from a remote place; not easily or naturally introduced; elaborately strained (a *far-fetched* explanation). — **Farmost**, fär'mōst, *a. superl.* Most distant or remote. —**Farness**, fär'nes, *n.* The state of being far off; distance; remoteness.—**Far-off**, *a.* Far-away; distant; remote in space or time. —**Far-sighted**, *a.* Seeing to a great distance; calculating carefully the distant results of present conduct or action; not capable of perceiving objects near at hand distinctly. —**Far-sightedness**, *n.* The state or quality of being far-sighted.—**Far-sought**, *a.* Sought at a distance; forced. —**Farther**, fär'THėr, *a. compar.* [Not the original compar. of *far*, which was *far-er* (*ferrer*), but assimilated to *further.*] More remote; more distant than something else; tending to a greater distance; additional.—*adv.* At or to a greater distance; more remotely; beyond; by way of progression in a subject; moreover.—**Farther**,† fär'THėr, *v.t.* To promote; to further.—**Fartherance**,† fär'THėr-ans, *n.* A helping forward; furtherance. —**Farthermore**, fär'THėr-mōr, *adv.* Besides; moreover; furthermore. —**Farthermost**, fär'THėr-mōst, *a. superl.* Being at the farthest distance; most remote.—**Farthest**, fär'THest, *a. superl.* At the greatest distance either in time or place.—*adv.* At or to the greatest distance.—**Far-west**, *n.* That portion of the United States lying beyond the Mississippi.

Farad, far'ad, *n.* [In honour of *Faraday.*] The unit of electrical capacity in the practical system of units, being the capacity of a condenser which one coulomb of electricity raises to a potential of one volt.—**Faradic**, fa-rad'ik, *a.* Applied to induction electricity. — **Faradisation, Faradism**, far'a-di-zā"shon, far'ad-izm, *n.* The medical application of the magneto-electric currents which *Faraday* discovered in 1837.

Farce, färs, *v.t.* —*farced, farcing.* [Fr. *farcir*, L. *farcio*, to stuff.] To stuff with force-meat; to fill with mingled ingredients. —*n.* [Fr. *farce*, It. *farsa*, from L. *farcio*, to stuff, from being stuffed or crammed with humour.] A dramatic composition of a broadly comic character; a comedy full of extravagant drollery; ridiculous parade; empty pageantry; mere show.—**Farceur**, fär-sėr, *n.* [Fr.] A writer or player of farces; a joker.—**Farcical**, fär'si-kal, *a.* Belonging to a farce; of the character of a farce; droll; ludicrous; ridiculous.—**Farcically**, fär'si-kal-li, *adv.* In a farcical manner. — **Farcicalness**, fär'si-kal-nes, *n.* Quality of being farcical.—**Farcing**, fär'sing, *n.* Stuffing; force-meat.

Farcy, Farcin, fär'si, fär'sin, *n.* A disease of horses intimately connected with glanders, the two diseases generally running into each other. — **Farcy-bud**, *n.* A tumour which appears early in the disease farcy.

Fardage, fär'dāj, *n.* [Fr. FARDEL.] *Naut.* same as *Dunnage.*

Fardel, fär'del, *n.* [O.Fr. *fardel*, Fr. *fardeau*, a bundle, from the Arabic. Hence *furl.*] A bundle or pack; a burden; anything cumbersome or irksome.—**Fardel-bound**, *a.* A term applied to cattle and sheep affected with a disease caused by the retention of food in the maniplies or third stomach.

Fare, fār, *v.i.* —*fared, faring.* [A.Sax. *faran*, to go = Icel. Sw. *fara*, Dan. *fare*, D. *varen*, G. *fahren*, to go, same root as L. *per*, through, *porta*, gate, Gr. *poros*, passage, *peirō*, to pierce; E. *far, ferry*, &c.] To go; to pass; to move forward; to travel; to be in any state, good or bad; to be in a certain condition as regards bodily or social comforts; to be entertained with food; to happen; to turn out or result; to be: with *it* impersonally.—*n.* The sum paid or due for conveying a person by land, air, or water; food; provisions of the table; condition; treatment by circumstances; fortune; the person or persons conveyed in a vehicle.—**Farewell**, fār'wel. [From *fare*, in the imper., and *well.*] May you fare or prosper well; a wish of happiness to those who leave or those who are left: it sometimes has the pronoun inserted between its two elements; as *fare* you *well.* Sometimes it is an expression of mere separation (like 'good-bye' or 'adieu').—*n.* Good-bye; adieu; leave; departure; final look, reference, or attention.—*a.* Leave-taking; valedictory.

Farina, fa-rī'na, *n.* [L. *farina*, flour, from *far*, a sort of grain.] Meal or flour; a soft, tasteless, and commonly white powder, obtained by trituration of the seeds of cereal and leguminous plants, and of some roots, as the potato.—**Farinaceous**, far-i-nā'shus, *a.* Consisting or made of meal or flour; containing or yielding farina or flour; mealy.—**Farinaceously**, far-i-nā'shus-li, *adv.* After the manner of farinaceous substances.—**Farinose**, far'i-nos, *a.* Yielding farina.

Farm, färm, *n.* [A.Sax. *feorm, fyrm*, food, provisions, a feast, entertainment; hence, a piece of land that has to supply a certain quantity of provisions; from L.L. *firma* (from L. *firmus*, firm, established), farm rent, sum settled or fixed.] A tract of land cultivated by either the owner of the land or a tenant, and usually divided into fields.—*v.t.* To let to a tenant on condition of paying rent; to hold and cultivate either as tenant or as owner; to lease or let, as taxes or other duties, at a certain sum or a certain rate per cent.—*v.i.* To be employed in agriculture; to cultivate the soil. —**Farmable**, färm'a-bl, *a.* Capable of being farmed.—**Farm Loan Bank**, *n.* A Federal Land Bank, loosely but incorrectly so called.—**Farmer**, färm'ėr, *n.* One who farms; one who cultivates a farm; an agriculturist; a husbandman; one who takes taxes, customs, excise, or other duties, to collect for a certain gross sum or a rate per cent.—**Farmership**, färm'ėr-ship, *n.* Skill in farming. —**Farmhouse**, färm'-hous, *n.* A house attached to a farm for the residence of a farmer.—**Farming**, färm'ing, *a.* Pertaining to agriculture.—*n.* The business of a farmer; husbandry.—**Farmstead**, färm'sted, *n.* The system of buildings connected with a farm; a homestead.—**Farmyard**, färm'yärd, *n.* The yard or inclosure surrounded by or connected with the farm buildings.

Faro, fā'rō, *n.* [Said to be from *Pharaoh* having formerly been depicted on one of the cards.] A game at cards in which a person plays against the bank. — **Faro-bank**, *n.* A bank or establishment where persons play at the game of faro.

Farrago, fa-rā'gō, *n.* [L., from *far*, meal.] A mass composed of various materials confusedly mixed; a medley.—**Farraginous**, fa-raj'i-nus, *a.* Formed of various materials mixed.

Farrier, far'i-ėr, *n.* [O.Fr. *ferrier*, from *ferrer*, to shoe a horse, from L. *ferrum*, iron.] A shoer of horses; one who combines the art of horse-shoeing with the profession of veterinary surgery.—*v.i.* To practise as a farrier.—**Farriery**, far'i-ėr-i, *n.* The art of shoeing horses; the art of curing the diseases of horses, oxen, sheep, pigs, &c.; veterinary surgery.

Farrow, far'ō, *n.* [A.Sax. *fearh*, a little pig; akin to O.H.G. *farah*, G. *ferkel*, D. *varken*, a pig; L. *porcus*, a pig, being also allied.] A litter of pigs.—*v.t.* and *i.* To bring forth pigs.

Farther. Under FAR.

Farthing, fär'THing, *n.* [A.Sax. *ferthing, feorthing*, the fourth part of a thing, from *feorth*, fourth, from *feówer*, four.] The fourth of a penny, a small copper coin of Britain, the fourth of a penny in value.

Farthingale, Fardingale, fär'THing-gāl, fär-ding-gāl, *n.* [O.Fr. *verdugalle, vertugade*, from Sp. *verdugo*, a rod or shoot of a tree, hence a hoop.] A hoop petticoat formerly worn by ladies, or the circles of hoops used to extend the petticoat.

Fasces, fas'sēz, *n. pl.* [L.] A bundle of rods, with an axe bound in along with them, anciently borne before the superior Roman magistrates as a badge of their power over life and limb; now the symbol of the Fascist party in Italy.

Fascia, fash'i-a, *n.* pl. **Fasciæ**, fash'i-ē. [L.] A band, sash, or fillet, or something resembling this in shape; a surgical bandage; *arch.* a long band of stone or brick forming a slight projection. — **Fasciate**, fash'i-āt, *a.* Banded or bound together; fasciated. — **Fasciated**, fash'i-ā-ted, *a.* Bound with a fillet, sash, or bandage; *bot.* applied to the peculiar flattened stems or branches which occur occasionally in trees. —**Fasciation**, fash-i-ā'shon, *n.* The state of being fasciated; the act or manner of binding up diseased parts; bandage.

Fascicle, fas'si-kl, *n.* [L. *fasciculus*, from *fascis*, a bundle.] A little bundle or collection; *bot.* a form of cyme in which the flowers are clustered together in a more or less compact bundle.—**Fasciculate, Fasciculated, Fascicled, Fascicular**, fas-sik'ū-lāt, fas-sik'ū-lā-ted, fas'si-kld, fas-sik'ū-lėr, *a. Bot.* growing in bundles or bunches from the same point: said of leaves, stems, roots, &c.—**Fasciculately, Fascicularly**, fas-sik'ū-lāt-li, fas-sik'ū-lėr-li, *adv.* In a fasciculate manner.—**Fascicule**, fas'si-kūl, *n.* A fascicle.—**Fasciculus**, fas-sik'ū-lus, *n.* A fascicle; one of the separate divisions or numbers in which a book is published.

Fascinate, fas'si-nāt, *v.t.*—*fascinated, fascinating.* [Fr. *fasciner*, L. *fascino, fascinatum*, to fascinate, bewitch.] To bewitch; to enchant; to operate on by some powerful or irresistible influence; to charm; to captivate; to allure irresistibly or powerfully.—*v.i.* To exercise a bewitching or captivating power.—**Fascinating**, fas'si-nā-ting, *p.* and *a.* Bewitching; enchanting; charming; captivating. — **Fascination**, fas-si-nā'shon, *n.* The act of fascinating, bewitching, or enchanting; enchantment; a charm.

Fascism, fash'izm, *n.* A totalitarian form of government in Italy administered by the Fascisti (a political organization) which advocates the building of a highly nationalistic state, recognizing private ownership except when the state determines otherwise.—**Fascist**, fash'ist, *a.* Of or pertaining to Fascism.—*n.* A member of the Fascisti.

Fashion, fash'on, *n.* [O.Fr. *fachon, facion*, from L. *factio*, a making, from *facio*, to make. FACT.] The make or form of anything; external form; shape; pattern; make according to the custom of the time; the prevailing mode of dress or ornament; manner, sort, way, or mode; custom; prevailing practice; genteel life or good breeding; genteel society.—*v.t.* To form; to give shape or figure to; to mould.—**Fashionable**, fash'on-a-bl, *a.* Conforming to the fashion or established mode; taking the public taste and being in vogue; established by custom; current; prevailing; dressing or behaving according to the prevailing fashion; genteel; well-bred.—*n.* A person of fashion. —**Fashionableness**, fash'on-a-bl-nes, *n.* The state of being fashionable.—**Fashionably**, fash'on-a-bli, *adv.* In a manner according to fashion; according to the prevailing mode.—**Fashioner**, fash'on-ėr, *n.* One who fashions.

Fassaite, Fassite, fas'sa-īt, fas'sīt, *n.* A mineral, a variety of pyroxene, found in the valley of *Fassa*, in the Tyrol.

Fast, fast, *a.* [A.Sax. *fæst, fest*, fast, firm = D. *vast*, Icel. *fastr*, Dan. *fast*, G. *fest*, firm, solid. Hence *fast*, quick, and verb to *fast*.] Firmly fixed; close; tight; closely adhering; made close; strong against attack; firm in adherence; not easily alienated (a *fast* friend); steadfast; faithful; lasting; durable (a *fast* colour).—*adv.* Firmly; immovably. — *To play fast and loose*, to act in an inconstant manner; to say one thing and do another.—**Fasten**, fas'n, *v.t.* [A.Sax. *fæstnian*, to secure.] To fix firmly; to make fast or close; to secure, as by lock, bolt, or the like; to join in close union; to unite closely; to attach; to affix. —*v.i.* To fix one's self or itself; to become attached. — **Fastener**, fas'n-ėr, *n.* One who or that which fastens.—**Fastening**, fas'n-ing, *n.* Anything that fastens, binds, attaches, &c.—**Fastly**, fast'li, *adv.* In a fast, firm, or secure manner.—**Fastness**, fast'nes, *n.* [A.Sax. *fæstnes*, firmness, a fortification.] The state of being fast, firm, or secure; strength; security; a stronghold; a fortified place; a castle; a fortress.

Fast, fast, *a.* [The same word as *fast*, fixed firm or steadfast (one who runs fast runs steadfastly) = Icel. *fast*, rapidly, quickly, from *fastr*, firm.] Swift; moving rapidly; quick in motion; rapid; dissipated; devoted to pleasure; indulging in sensual vices: said of a man; imitating the manners or habits of a man: said of a female.—*adv.* In a fast or quick manner; swiftly; rapidly; with quick steps or progression; prodigally and wastefully; with dissipation. —**Fastness**, fast'nes, *n.* The state or quality of being fast.

Fast, fast, *v.i.* [A.Sax. *fæstan*, to fast; probably from *fæst*, firm, steadfast, the meaning being to be steadfast in abstaining = D. *vasten*, Dan. *faste*, Icel. and Sw. *fasta*, G. *fasten*, Goth. *fastan*, to fast.] To abstain from food beyond the usual time; to go hungry; to abstain from food, or particular kinds of food, voluntarily, especially for religious reasons.—*n.* Abstinence from food; a withholding from the usual quantity of nourishment; voluntary abstinence from food as a religious mortification or humiliation; the time of fasting.—**Faster**, fas'tėr, *n.* One who fasts.—**Fast-day**, *n.* A day on which fasting is observed.

Fasti, fast'i, *n.* [L. *fasti*.] A calendar, a register.

Fastidious, fas-tid'i-us, *a.* [L. *fastidiosus*, from *fastidium*, loathing, fastidiousness, from *fastus*, haughtiness.] Hard or difficult to please; squeamish; delicate to a fault; overnice; difficult to suit.—**Fastidiously**, fas-tid'i-us-li, *adv.* In a fastidious manner. — **Fastidiousness**, fas-tid'i-us-nes, *n.* The condition or quality of being fastidious.

Fastigiate, Fastigiated, fas-tij'i-āt, fas-tij'i-ā-ted, *a.* [L. *fastigiatus*, pointed, from *fastigium*, a top or peak.] Peaked or pointed at top; *bot.* tapering to a narrow point like a pyramid, as a plant when the branches become gradually shorter from the base to the apex.

Fat, fat, *a.* [A.Sax. *fæt* = D. *vet*, Dan. *fed*, Icel. *feitr*, G. *fett*, fat. Hence, to *fatten*, *fatling*.] Fleshy; plump; obese; corpulent; the contrary to *lean*; oily; greasy; unctuous; coarse; heavy; dull; stupid (especially in such compounds as *fat*-brained, *fat*-witted); producing a large income; rich; fertile; nourishing.—*n.* A solid oily substance of whitish or yellow colour, a compound of carbon, hydrogen, and oxygen, found in certain parts of animal bodies, lard and tallow being varieties of it; the best or richest part of a thing.—*v.t.*—*fatted, fatting*. To make fat; to fatten.—*v.i.* To grow fat.—**Fatling**, fat'ling, *n.* Any young animal fattened for slaughter, as a lamb, kid, or the like. — **Fatly**, fat'li, *adv.* In a fat manner; grossly; greasily.—**Fatness**, fat'nes, *n.* The state or quality of being fat; corpulence; plumpness; unctuousness; oiliness; richness; fertility.—**Fatten**, fat'n, *v.t.* To make fat; to feed for slaughter; to enrich; to make fertile.—*v.i.* To grow fat; to become plump or fleshy.—**Fattener**, fat'n-ėr, *n.* One who or that which fattens; that which gives fatness, richness, or fertility.—**Fattiness**, fat'i-nes, *n.* The state or quality of being fatty; greasiness.—**Fatty**, fat'i, *a.* Having the nature or qualities of fat; oily; greasy; composed of, or containing much fat. — **Fat-lute**, *n.* A mixture of pipe-clay and linseed-oil for filling joints, holes, &c.

Fat, fat, *n.* [VAT.] A large tub or vessel; a vat. (O.T.)

Fatal, fā'tal, *a.* [L. *fatalis*, from *fatum*, fate. FATE.] Proceeding from fate or destiny‡; fraught with fate‡; fateful‡; causing death or destruction; deadly; mortal; destructive; calamitous; disastrous.—**Fatalism**, fā'tal-izm, *n.* The doctrine that all things are subject to fate, or that they take place by inevitable necessity.—**Fatalist**, fā'tal-ist, *n.* One who maintains that all things happen by inevitable necessity.—**Fatalistic**, fā-ta-lis'tik, *a.* Pertaining to fatalism; implying fatalism.—**Fatality**, fa-tal'i-ti, *n.* [L. *fatalitas*.] The state of being fatal; a fixed unalterable course of things; a fatal occurrence; a calamitous accident. — **Fatally**, fā'tal-li, *adv.* In a fatal manner.—**Fatalness**, fā'tal-nes, *n.* The state or quality of being fatal.

Fata Morgana, fä'ta mor-gä'na, *n.* [It., because supposed to be the work of a *fata* or fairy called *Morgana*.] A striking optical illusion principally remarked in the Strait of Messina, between the coasts of Sicily and Calabria—a variety of mirage.

Fate, fāt, *n.* [L. *fatum* (lit. that which has been spoken), destiny as pronounced by the gods, fate, from *fari*, to speak (whence also *fama*, fame, and *fanum*, a fane), from a root which appears also in Gr. *phanai*, to speak, and *phaos*, light; akin *fable, fairy, fay, affable*, &c.] A fixed decree or sentence, by which the order of things is prescribed; inevitable necessity settling how events are to befall; unavoidable concatenation and succession of events; destiny; predetermined lot; human destiny; the final fortune of anything; final event; death; destruction; *pl.* (*myth.*) the Destinies or Parcæ; the three goddesses supposed to preside over the birth and life of men, called Clotho, Lachesis, and Atropos.—**Fated**, fā'ted, *a.* Assigned or gifted with a certain fate; doomed; destined; regulated by fate.—**Fateful**, fāt'ful, *a.* Bringing or deciding fate or destiny; fatal.

Father, fä'ᴛʜėr, *n.* [A.Sax. *fæder* = D. *vader*, Icel. *fathir*, Dan. and Sw. *fader*, Goth. *fadar*, G. *vater*, L. *pater*, Gr. *patēr*, Per. *padar*, Skr. *pitri*—father; probably from a root *pa*. to feed.] He who begets a child; a male parent; a male ancestor more remote than a parent, especially the first ancestor; the founder of a race, family, or line; a respectful mode of address to an old man; one who exercises paternal care over another; a guardian, protector, or preserver; the first to practice any art; a distinguished example; a teacher; originator; cause; the appellation of the first person in the Trinity; the title given to dignitaries of the church, confessors, and priests; the eldest member of a profession, or other body.—*Father of the House*, in England the member in the Commons who has sat the longest period of time —*Fathers of the Church*, the name given to the early teachers and expounders of Christianity, whose writings have thrown light upon the history, doctrines, and observances of the Christian church in the early ages.—*v.t.* To beget as a father; to assume as one's own work; to profess or acknowledge one's self to be the author of; to ascribe or charge to one as his offspring or production (to *father* a book *on* a person).—**Fatherhood**, fä'ᴛʜėr-hụd, *n.* The state of being a father; the character or authority of a father.—**Father-in-law**, *n.* The father of one's husband or wife.—**Fatherland**, fä'ᴛʜėr-land, *n.* [A literal translation of the G. *Vaterland*.] One's native country; the country of one's fathers or ancestors. — **Fatherlasher**, fä'ᴛʜėr-lash-ėr, *n.* A fish; the bull-head (which see).—**Fatherless**, fä'ᴛʜėr-les, *a.* Destitute of a living father; without a known author.—**Fatherliness**, fä'ᴛʜėr-li-nes, *n.* The state or quality of being fatherly; parental kindness, care, and tenderness.—**Fatherly**, fä'ᴛʜėr-li, *a.* Like a father in affection and care; paternal; protecting; pertaining to a father.—*adv.* In the manner of a father.—**Fathership**, fä'ᴛʜėr-ship, *n.* State of being a father.

Fathom, faᴛʜ'um, *n.* [A.Sax. *fæthm*, the bosom, the space of both arms extended; Icel. *fathmr*, D. *vadem*, Sw. *famn*, G. *faden*, from a root meaning to stretch.] A measure of length containing 6 feet, being originally the space to which a man may extend his arms.—*v.t.* To try the depth of; to find the bottom or extent of; to sound; *fig.* to penetrate or comprehend. — **Fathomable**, faᴛʜ'um-a-bl, *a.* Capable of being fathomed or comprehended.—**Fathomless**, faᴛʜ'um-les, *a.* That of which no bottom can be found; bottomless; not to be penetrated or comprehended.

Fatigue, fa-tēg', *v.t.*—*fatigued, fatiguing*. [Fr. *fatiguer*, from L. *fatigo*, to weary.] To weary with labour or any bodily or mental exertion; to harass with toil; to exhaust the strength by severe or long-continued exertion; to tire or wear out.—*n.* Weariness from bodily labour or mental exertion; lassitude or exhaustion of strength; the cause of weariness; labour undergone; toil; the labours of military men distinct from the use of arms.—**Fatigue-dress**, *n.* The working dress of soldiers.—**Fatigue-duty**, *n.* The work of soldiers distinct from the use of arms.—**Fatigue-party**, *n.* Soldiers detailed for fatigue-duty. — **Fatiguing**, fa-tēg'ing, *p.* and *a.* Inducing fatigue or weariness; tiring; exhausting.

Fatling, Fatten, &c. Under FAT.

Fatuity, fa-tū'i-ti, *n.* [L. *fatuitas*, from *fatuus*, silly.] Weakness or imbecility of mind; feebleness of intellect; foolishness. —**Fatuous**, fat'ū-us, *a.* [L. *fatuus*.] Feeble in mind; weak; idiotically silly; foolish.

Faubourg, fō'börg, *n.* [Fr.] A suburb in French cities; also a district within a city which was formerly a suburb.

Fauces, fa̤'sēz, *n. pl.* [L., the throat, the gullet.] *Anat.* the gullet or windpipe; the posterior part of the mouth, terminated by the pharynx and larynx.—**Faucal**, fa̤'kal, *a.* Pertaining to the fauces.

Faucet, fa̤'set, *n.* [Fr. *fausset*, from L. *falsus*, false.] A spout fitted with a valve, for drawing liquids through a pipe; a spigot.

Faugh, fa̤. Exclamation of contempt or abhorrence.

Fault, fa̤lt, *n.* [O.Fr. *faulte*, Fr. *faute*, It. and Sp. *falta*, fault, defect, from a Romance verb (not recorded in French), from a L. freq. *fallitare*, from *fallo*, to deceive. FAIL.] A slight offence; a neglect of duty or propriety; something worthy of some blame or censure; a defect; a blemish; a flaw; among *sportsmen*, the act of losing the scent; a lost scent; *geol.* and *mining*, a break or dislocation of strata; an interruption in the continuity of strata such that the strata on either side appear elevated or depressed.—*At fault*, puzzled; in some difficulty or perplexity; also, to blame; deserving censure. —*To find fault*, to express blame; to take exception.—*To find fault with*, to take exception to; to censure.—**Faulted**, fa̤l'ted, *p.* and *a.* *Geol.* exhibiting a fault.—**Faultily**, fa̤l'ti-li, *adv.* In a faulty manner.—

Faultiness, fạl'ti-nes, *n.* The state of being faulty, defective, or erroneous.—**Faultless**, fạlt'les, *a.* Without fault; not defective or imperfect; free from blemish, vice, or offence; perfect.—**Faultlessly**, fạlt'les-li, *adv.* In a faultless manner. — **Faultlessness**, fạlt'les-nes, *n.* Freedom from faults or defects.—**Faulty**, fạl'ti, *a.* Containing faults, blemishes, or defects; defective; imperfect; guilty of a fault or of faults; blamable. — **Fault-finder**, *n.* One who censures or objects.

Faun, fạn, *n.* [L. *faunus*, a deity of the woods and fields.] *Rom. myth.* one of a kind of demigods or rural deities, differing little from satyrs.—**Fauna**, fạ'na, *n.* [A Roman goddess of fields, cattle, &c.] A collective term for the animals peculiar to a region or epoch, corresponding to the word *flora* in respect of plants.—**Faunist**, fạ'nist, *n.* One who treats of the fauna of a country or district.

Faussebraye, fōs'brā, *n.* [Fr.] *Fort.* a small mount of earth thrown up about a rampart.

Fauteuil, fō'tŭl or fō-tė-yė, *n.* [Fr., from O.H.G. *faltstuol*, lit. a folding-stool.] An arm-chair; an easy-chair.

Faux-pas, fō-pä, *n.* [Fr.] A false step; a breach of manners or moral conduct; a lapse from chastity.

Faveolate, fa-vē'o-lāt, *a.* [L. *favus*, a honey-comb.] Formed like a honey-comb; alveolate; cellular.

Favonian, fa-vō'ni-an, *a.* [L. *favonius*, the west wind.] Pertaining to the west wind.

Favor, fā'vėr, *n.* [Fr. *faveur*, from L. *favor*, *favoris*, from *faveo*, to favor, to befriend.] Kind regard; friendly disposition; a state of being looked on with good will or kindness; a kind act or office; kindness done or granted; an act of grace or good will; leave; good will; pardon; a token of love; a knot of ribbons worn at a marriage or on other festive occasions; something worn as a token of affection; convenience afforded for success (under *favor* of darkness); partiality; bias; aspect, look, or appearance (*Shak.*)‡.—*v.t.* To regard with favor or kindness; to support; to aid or have the disposition to aid; to be propitious to; to befriend; to show favor or partiality to; to afford advantages for success to; to render easier; to facilitate.—**Favorable**, fā'vėr-a-bl, *a.* Kind; propitious; friendly; affectionate; manifesting partiality; conducive; contributing; tending to promote; advantageous; affording facilities. — **Favorableness**, fā'vėr-a-bl-nes, *n.* The condition or quality of being favorable.—**Favorably**, fā'vėr-a-bli, *adv.* In a favorable manner.—**Favored**, fā'vėrd, *a.* Regarded or treated with favor; having special advantages or facilities; featured, now only in the compounds *well-favored*, *ill-favored*.—**Favoredness**, fā'vėrd-nes, *n.* State of being favored; appearance; cast of countenance (with *well* or *ill* prefixed.)—**Favorer**, fā'vėr-ėr, *n.* One who favors.—**Favorite**, fā'vėr-it, *n.* A person or thing regarded with peculiar favor, preference, and affection; one greatly beloved; often one unduly favored; one treated with undue partiality.—*The favorite*, the horse favored by betting on a horse-race.—*a.* Regarded with particular affection or preference.—**Favoritism**, fā'vėr-it-izm, *n.* The disposition to patronize favorites, or to promote the interest of a person or persons to the neglect of others having equal claims.—**Favorless**, fā'vėr-les, *a.* Not regarded with favor.

Favose, fa-vōs', *a.* [L. *favosus*, from *favus*, a honeycomb.] Resembling a honeycomb in shape or color.

Favus, fā'vus, *n.* [L., a honey-comb.] A kind of ringworm, a disease attacking the scalp, and characterized by yellowish dry incrustations somewhat resembling a honey-comb.

Fawn, fạn, *n.* [Fr. *faon*, from a form *fetonus*, from L. *fetus*, progeny.] A young deer; a buck or doe of the first year.—*v.i.* To bring forth a fawn.—*a.* Resembling a fawn in colour; light brown.

Fawn, fạn, *v.i.* [A.Sax. *faegnian*, Icel. *fagna*, to rejoice, flatter. FAIN.] To show a servile attachment; to court favour by low cringing, and the like; to flatter meanly; to cringe and bow to gain favour; to cringe and frisk about a person (as a dog).—*n.* A servile cringe or bow; mean flattery.—**Fawner**, fạ'nėr, *n.* One who fawns.—**Fawning**, fạ'ning, *p.* and *a.* Servilely courting or caressing; meanly flattering; cajoling in an abject manner. — **Fawningly**, fạ'ning-li, *adv.* In a fawning, servile way; with mean flattery.

Fay, fā, *n.* [Fr. *fée*, L.L. *fata*, a fairy. FAIRY.] A fairy; an elf.

Fay, fā, *v.t.* [A.Sax. *fœgian*, to fit.] To fit two pieces of timber together so that they lie close and fair.

Fayalite, fā'yal-īt, *n.* [*Fayal*, one of the Azores, where it is found.] A black, greenish, or brownish mineral, consisting mainly of silicate of iron.

Fayence, *n.* Same as *Faience*.

Fealty, fē'al-ti, *n.* [O.Fr. *fealté*, *feauté*, fealty, from L. *fidelitas*, faithfulness, fidelity; it is thus the same word as *fidelity*.] Fidelity to a superior; faithful adherence of a tenant or vassal to the superior of whom he holds his lands; faithfulness of any person to another; faith.

Fear, fēr, *n.* [A.Sax. *faer*, fear, peril; Icel. *fár*, harm, mischief; O.H.G. *fára*, danger, fright; Mod.G. *gefahr*, danger; from root of E. *fare*, to travel; seen also in L. *periculum*, danger (E. *peril*).] A painful emotion excited by an expectation of evil or the apprehension of impending danger; anxiety; solicitude; holy awe and reverence for God and his laws; respect; due regard, as for persons of authority or worth.—*v.t.* To feel fear or a painful apprehension of; to be afraid of; to suspect; to doubt; to reverence; to have a reverential awe of; to venerate; to affright or to terrify (*Shak.*)‡.—*v.i.* To be in fear; to be in apprehension of evil; to be afraid.—**Fearer**, fē'rėr, *n.* One who fears.—**Fearful**, fēr'fụl, *a.* Affected by fear; apprehensive with solicitude; afraid; timorous; wanting courage; impressing fear; terrible; dreadful; awful. — **Fearfully**, fēr'fụl-li, *adv.* In a fearful manner.—**Fearfulness**, fēr'fụl-nes, *n.* The quality of being fearful. —**Fearless**, fēr'les, *a.* Free from fear; bold; courageous; intrepid; undaunted.—**Fearlessly**, fēr'les-li, *adv.* In a fearless manner. — **Fearlessness**, fēr'les-nes, *n.* The state or quality of being fearless.—**Fearsome**, fēr'sum, *a.* Alarming, terrible.

Feasible, fē'zi-bl, *a.* [Fr. *faisible*, from *faire*, *faisant*, to do or make, L. *facere*, to do, to make. FACT.] Capable of being done, performed, executed, or effected; practicable. — **Feasibility**, **Feasibleness**, fē-zi-bil'i-ti, fē'zi-bl-nes, *n.* The quality of being feasible.—**Feasibly**, fē'zi-bli, *adv.* In a feasible manner.

Feast, fēst, *n.* [O.Fr. *feste* (Fr. *fête*), from L. *festum*, a holiday, a feast, from *festus*, solemn, festive.] A sumptuous repast or entertainment of which a number of guests partake; a banquet; a delicious meal; something particularly gratifying to the palate or the mind; a festival in commemoration of some great event, or in honour of some distinguished personage; a periodical or stated celebration of some event.—*v.i.* To take a meal of rich or sumptuous viands; to dine or sup on rich provisions; to be highly gratified or delighted.—*v.t.* To entertain with sumptuous food; to treat at the table magnificently; to pamper; to gratify luxuriously.—**Feaster**, fēs'tėr, *n.* One who feasts.

Feat, fēt, *n.* [Fr. *fait*, from L. *factum*, a deed, from *facio*, *factum*, to do. FACT.] An act; a deed; an exploit; in particular, any extraordinary act of strength, skill, or cunning.—*a.* [Fr. *fait*, made.] Neat; skilful; ingenious; deft. (*Shak.*) — **Featly**, fēt'li, *adv.* Neatly; dexterously.

Feather, feᴛʜ'ėr, *n.* [A.Sax. *fether* = D. *veder*, Sw. *fjäder*, Icel. *fjöthr*, G. *feder*; same root as L. *penna* (= *petna*), a feather; Skr. *pattra*, a wing, from root *pat*, to fly.] One of the growths which form the distinguishing covering of birds; a plume, consisting usually of a stem hollow at the lower part (called the quill), and having on each side of the upper part (called the shaft) the barbs, which with the shaft constitute the vane; something resembling a feather; a projection on the edge of a board which fits into a channel on the edge of another board.—*A feather in the cap*, an honour or mark of distinction.—*To be in high feather*, to appear in high spirits; to be elated.—*To show the white feather* to give indications of cowardice (a white feather in the tail of a fighting cock showed that it was not of the true game breed).—*v.t.* To dress in feathers; to fit with feathers; to cover with feathers.—*To feather one's nest*, to collect wealth, particularly from emoluments derived from agencies for others.—*To feather an oar*, to turn the blade horizontally, with the upper edge pointing aft as it leaves the water, to lessen the resistance of the air upon it.—**Feathered**, feᴛʜ'ėrd, *a.* Clothed or covered with feathers; fitted or furnished with feathers; furnished with wings; winged.—**Feather-edge**, *n.* *Carp.* the thinner edge of a board or plank. — **Feather-edged**, *a.* Having one edge thinner than the other and overlapping.—**Feathering**, feᴛʜ'ėr-ing, *n.* *Arch.* an arrangement of small arcs or curves separated by projecting points or cusps, used as ornaments in the heads of windows, &c., in Gothic architecture.—**Featherless**, feᴛʜ'ėr-les, *a.* Destitute of feathers; unfledged.—**Feathery**, feᴛʜ'ėr-i, *a.* Clothed or covered with feathers; resembling feathers in appearance, softness, or lightness. — **Feather-grass**, *n.* A wiry grass whose flowers are produced in loose panicles, which, when dried and coloured, form ornaments for rooms.—**Feather-spray**, *n.* The foamy ripple thrown from the bows of fast-sailing vessels.—**Feather-star**, *n.* A beautiful crinoid, consisting of a central body or disc, from which spring slender radiating arms furnished on both sides with processes that give a feather-like appearance.—**Feather-weight**, *n.* A weight as light as a feather; the lightest weight that is placed on a racing-horse.

Feature, fē'tūr, *n.* [O.Fr. *faiture*, *faicture* from L. *factura*, a making, from *facio* *factum*, to make. FACT.] The shape or make of the body (*Shak.*)‡; the make, form, or cast of any part of the face; any single lineament; the make or form of any part of the surface of a thing, as of a country or landscape; a prominent part, as the *feature* of a motion-picture theater program.—*v.t.* *Featuring*, starring in a motion-picture.—**Featureless**, fē'tūr-les, *a.* Having no distinct features; ugly.

Feaze, fēz, *v.t.* [A.Sax. *fœs*, a fringe; G. *fasen*, to ravel out.] To untwist the end of anything made of threads or fibres; to ravel out.

Febricula, fe-brik'ū-la, *n.* [L., dim. of *febris*, fever.] A slight fever.—**Febriculose**, fe-brik'ū-lōs, *a.* Affected with slight fever. — **Febrifacient**, feb-ri-fā'shi-ent, *a.* [L. *febris*, and *facio*, to make.] Causing fever.—**Febriferous**, fe-brif'ėr-us, *a.* [L. *febris*, and *fero*, to bring.] Producing fever. —**Febrifuge**, feb'ri-fūj, *n.* [L. *febris*, and *fugo*, to drive away.] Any medicine that mitigates or removes fever.—*a.* Having the quality of mitigating or subduing fever.—**Febrile**, fē'bril, *a.* [L. *febrilis*.] Pertaining to fever; indicating fever, or derived from it.

February, feb'rụ-a-ri, *n.* [L. *februarius*, from *februa*, purification, because a great feast of purification was held on the 15th.] The second month in the year, consisting in common years of twenty-eight days, in leap-year of twenty-nine.

Feces, Fecal. FÆCES.

Fechner's Law. fek'nėrz, *n.* *Physiol.* law that with increase of stimulus a sensation increases in proportion to the logarithm of the stimulus.

Feckless, fek'les, *a.* [Sc. for *effectless.*] Weak; impotent.

Fecula, fek'ū-la, *n.* [L. *fæcula*, lees of wine, dim. of *fæx*, *fæcis*, dregs.] Powdery matter obtained from plants by crushing, washing with water, and subsidence; starch or farina. —**Feculence, Feculency**, fek'ū-lens, fek'ū-len-si, *n.* [L. *fæculentia.*] The quality or state of being feculent; sediment; dregs.—**Feculent**, fek'ū-lent, *a.* [L. *fæculentus.*] Abounding with sediment, dregs, or impure and extraneous matter; dreggy; muddy; turbid; foul.

Fecund, fē'kund, *a.* [L. *fecundus*, fruitful, from root *fe* (as in *fetus*), meaning to produce or bring forth.] Fruitful in children; prolific.—**Fecundate**, fē'kun-dāt, *v.t.*—*fecundated, fecundating.* To make fruitful or prolific; to impregnate.—**Fecundation**, fē-kun-dā'shon, *n.* The act of fecundating.—**Fecundity**, fē-kun'di-ti, *n.* [L. *fœcunditas.*] The state or quality of being fecund or of bringing forth young abundantly; fertility; richness of invention.

Fed, fed, pret. & pp. of *feed.*

Federal, fed'ėr-al, *a.* [Fr. *fédéral*, from L. *foedus, foederis*, a league, seen also in *confederate.*] Pertaining to a league or contract, particularly between states, as the *federal* government of the United States is located in Washington, D. C.; united in a federation; founded on alliance between several states which unite for national or general purposes, each state retaining control of its home affairs, civil and criminal law, &c. (a *federal* republic); theologian, like the Cocceian School, laying emphasis on the Covenants between God and man. —*n.* A member of the Northern party in the United States who during the civil war of 1861-5 maintained the integrity of the Union, in opposition to the *Confederates*, or the Southern party, who desired to secede.—**Federalism**, fed'ėr-al-izm, *n.* The principles of federal government; the upholding and strengthening of the central government in a federal republic.—**Federalist**, fed'ėr-al-ist, *n.* One who upholds federalism; a federal.—**Federalize**, fed'ėr-al-īz, *v.t.* or *i.*—*federalized, federalizing.* To unite in a federal compact.—**Federate**, fed'ėr-āt, *a.* [L. *foederatus.*] Leagued; united by compact, as states or nations.—**Federation**, fed'ėr-a"shon, *n.* The act of uniting in a league; a federal government; a league.

Fee, fē, *n.* [A.Sax. *feoh, feó*, cattle, property, money = D. *vee*, Icel. *fé*, G. *vieh*, cattle; Goth. *faihu*, goods, money—allied to L. *pecus*, cattle (whence *pecuniary*). *Fief* is really the same word.] A reward or compensation for services; recompense: applied particularly to the reward of professional services; a fief or piece of land held of a superior on certain conditions; a feud; *law*, a freehold estate liable to alienation at the pleasure of the proprietor, who is absolute owner of the soil; hence, absolute property, possession, or ownership.—*v.t.*—pret. & pp. *feed* or *fee'd.* To give a fee to; to pay for services; to reward; to hire; to bribe.—**Fee-simple**, *n.* An estate in lands or tenements liable to alienation at the will of the owner: also called a *Fee.*—**Fee-tail**, *n.* An estate limited to a man and the heirs of his body, or to himself and particular heirs of his body.

Feeble, fē'bl, *a.* [Fr. *faible*, O.Fr. *feble, floible, foible*, It. *fievole*, from L. *flebilis*, lamentable, from *fleo*, to weep.] Destitute of physical strength; infirm; debilitated; weak; wanting force, vigour, vividness, or energy.—**Feebleness**, fē'bl-nes, *n.* The quality or condition of being feeble.—**Feebly**, fē'bli, *adv.* In a feeble manner. —**Feeble-minded**, *a.* Weak in mind; wanting firmness or constancy; irresolute. —**Feeble-mindedness**, *n.*

Feed, fēd, *v.t.*—pret. & pp. *fed.* [A.Sax. *fēdan*, to feed, from *fóda*, food. FOOD.] To give food to; to supply with nourishment; *fig.* to entertain, indulge, delight (to *feed* one's self with hopes); to furnish with anything of which there is constant consumption, waste, use, or application for some purpose (to *feed* a lake, a fire); to supply.—*v.i.* To take food; to eat; to subsist by eating; to pasture; to graze; to satisfy a longing or craving.—*n.* That which is eaten; food; fodder; an allowance of provender given to a horse, cow, &c.; the material supplied at once to a machine or other contrivance to make it act.—**Feeder**, fē'dėr, *n.* One who feeds; one who gives food or nourishment; one who eats; that which supplies something (the *feeder* of a lake).—**Feeding**, fē'ding, *n.* Food; that which furnishes food, especially for animals. —**Feeding-bottle**, *n.* A bottle for supplying milk or liquid nutriment to an infant. —**Feed-pipe**, *n.* The pipe that carries water to the boiler of a steam-engine or for some other purpose.—**Feed-pump**, *n.* The pump employed in supplying the boilers of steam-engines with water.

Feel, fēl, *v.t.*—*felt, feeling.* [A.Sax. *fēlan*, D. *voelen*, G. *fühlen*, to feel; root and connections doubtful.] To perceive by the touch; to have sensation excited by contact of with the body or limbs; to have a sense of; to be affected by; to be sensitive of (pain, pleasure, disgrace); to experience; to suffer; to examine by touching.—*v.i.* To have perception by the touch, or by the contact of any substance with the body; to have the sensibility or the passions moved or excited; to produce an impression on the nerves of sensation (iron *feels* cold); to perceive one's self to be (to *feel* sick or well); to know certainly or without misgiving.—*n.* The act of feeling; sensation or impression on being touched.—**Feeler**, fē'lėr, *n.* One who feels; an organ of touch in insects and others of the lower animals, as antennæ, palpi, &c.; any device for the purpose of ascertaining the designs, opinions, or sentiments of others.—**Feeling**, fē'ling, *a.* Expressive of great sensibility; affecting; tending to excite the passions; possessing great sensibility; easily affected or moved.—*n.* The sense of touch; the sense by which we perceive external objects which come in contact with the body, and obtain ideas of their tangible qualities; the sensation conveyed by the sense of touch; physical sensation not due to sight, hearing, taste, or smell (a *feeling* of warmth, pain, or drowsiness); mental sensation or emotion; mental state or disposition; mental perception; consciousness; conviction; tenderness of heart; nice sensibility; the quality of exciting or expressing emotion; *pl.* the emotional part of our nature; sensitiveness; susceptibility.—**Feelingly**, fē'ling-li, *adv.* In a feeling manner; tenderly; acutely; keenly.

Feet, fēt, n. pl. of *foot.* FOOT.—**Feetless**, fēt'les, *a.* Destitute of feet.

Feign, fān, *v.t.* [Fr. *feindre*, from L. *fingere*, to shape, invent, feign, from root seen also in *figment, figure, fiction, faint*, &c.] To invent or imagine; to make a show of; to pretend; to assume a false appearance of; to counterfeit.—*v.i.* To represent falsely; to pretend.—**Feigned**, fānd, *p.* and *a.* Devised; assumed; simulated; counterfeit. —**Feignedly**, fā'ned-li, *adv.* In a feigned manner.—**Feignedness**, fā'ned-nes, *n.* The state or quality of being feigned.—**Feigner**, fā'nėr, *n.* One who feigns.—**Feigningly**, fā'ning-li, *adv.* In a feigning manner; with pretence.—**Feint**, fānt, *n.* [Fr. *feinte*, from *feindre.*] A pretence; a mock attack; an appearance of aiming or thrusting at one part when another is intended to be struck.—*v.i.* To make a feint or mock attack.

Feldspar, feld'spär. FELSPAR.—**Feldspathic**, feld-spath'ik. FELSPATHIC.

Felicitate, fē-lis'i-tāt, *v.t.*—*felicitated, felicitating.* [Fr. *féliciter*; L.L. *felicito*, from L. *felix, felicis*, happy.] To congratulate; to express joy or pleasure to another at his good fortune; *refl.* to congratulate one's self.—**Felicitation**, fē-lis'i-tā"shon, *n.* The act of felicitating; expression of joy at another's good fortune.—**Felicitous**, fē-lis'i-tus, *a.* Happy; extremely appropriate, suitable, or well expressed; managed with extreme skill and success.—**Felicitously**, fē-lis'i-tus-li, *adv.* In a felicitous manner. —**Felicitousness**, fē-lis'i-tus-nes, *n.* The state of being felicitous.—**Felicity**, fē-lis'i-ti, *n.* [L. *felicitas*, from *felix*, happy.] The state of being happy or in extreme enjoyment; happiness; bliss; blissfulness; blessing; source of happiness; skilfulness; a skilful or happy turn; appropriateness.

Feline, fē'līn, *a.* [L. *felinus*, from *felis*, a cat.] Pertaining to cats or to their species; like a cat; belonging to the family Felidæ. —**Felidæ**, fē'li-dē, *n. pl.* A family of carnivorous quadrupeds, including the lion, tiger, cat, leopard, panther, &c.

Fell, fel, pret. of *fall.*

Fell, fel, *a.* [A.Sax. *fell*, D. *fel*, O.Fr. *fel, felle*, sharp, fierce, cruel, a word perhaps of Celtic origin.] Cruel; barbarous; inhuman; fierce; savage; rancorous; bloody. —**Fellness**, fel'nes, *n.* The state or quality of being fell; cruelty; ruthlessness.

Fell, fel, *n.* [A.Sax. *fell* = Icel. *fell*, G. *fell*, D. *vel*, Goth. *fill*, skin. Cog. L. *pellis*, skin.] A skin or hide of an animal; a seam or hem sewed down level with the cloth.—*v.t.* To lay a seam or hem and sew it down level with the cloth.—**Fellmonger**, fel'mung-gėr, *n.* One who deals in fells or hides.

Fell, fel, *v.t.* [A.Sax. *fellan*, from *feallan*, to fall; causative form of *fall.* Comp. *sit, set*; *lie, lay*; *rise, raise*; &c.] To cause to fall; to bring to the ground, either by cutting or by striking; to hew down; to knock down.—**Feller**, fel'ėr, *n.* One who fells or knocks or hews down.

Fell, fel, *n.* [Icel. *fell*, a hill, *fjall*, a mountain; Dan. *fjäld, fjeld*, a mountain, a rock; G. *fels*, a rock, a cliff.] A barren or stony hill; high land not fit for pasture.

Fellah, fel'lä, *n.* [Ar., a peasant; pl. *fellahin.*] An Egyptian peasant or agricultural labourer.

Felloe, fel'ō. FELLY.

Fellow, fel'ō, *n.* [Icel. *félagi*, a partner, a sharer in goods, from *félag*, a community of goods (lit. a *fee-laying*), from *fé*, money, *fee*, and *lag*, partnership, a laying.] A companion; an associate; one of the same kind; an equal in rank, endowments, character, qualifications, &c.; a peer; a compeer; one of a pair, or of two things used together and suited to each other; an appellation of contempt for a man without good breeding or worth; an ignoble man; also, familiar for person, individual; in some universities and colleges, a member of the corporation or governing body; also a graduate appointed to a fellowship; a member of any incorporated society (as of the American College of Surgeons). [Used in composition to denote community in nature, station, or employment; mutual association on equal or friendly terms: as, *fellow*-citizen, *fellow*-laborer; bed-*fellow*, school-*fellow.*]—**Fellowship**, fel'ō-ship, *n.* The condition of being a fellow or associate; mutual association on equal and friendly terms; companionship; partnership; joint interest; an association of persons having the same tastes, occupations, or interests; a brotherhood: a foundation for the maintenance, under certain requirements, of a scholar called a fellow.—**Fellow-creature**, *n.* One made by the same Creator.—**Fellow-feeling**, *n.* Sympathy; a like feeling.

Felly, fel'i, *n.* [A.Sax. *felg, felge* = Dan. *fælge*, D. *velg*, G. *felge*, a felly.] One of the curved pieces of wood which, joined together, form the circumference or circular rim of a wheel; the circular rim of a wheel. Written also *Felloe.*

Felo de se, fē'lō dē sē. [L.L., lit. a felon upon himself.] *Law*, one who commits felony by suicide, or deliberately destroys his own life.

Felon, fel'on, *n.* [Fr. *félon*, a traitor, from L.L. *felo*, a felon; origin doubtful.] A person who has committed felony; a person guilty of heinous crimes; a criminal; a malefactor; a whitlow.—*a.* Malignant; fierce; traitorous; disloyal.—**Felonious**, fe-lō'ni-us, *a.* Villainous; traitorous; perfidious; *law*, done with the deliberate purpose to commit a crime.—**Feloniously**, fe-lō'ni-us-li, *adv.* In a felonious manner.—**Feloniousness**, fe-lō'ni-us-nes, *n.* The quality of being felonious.—**Felony**, fel'o-ni, *n.* A crime which occasions the forfeiture of lands or goods, or both; a serious crime.

Felsite, fel'sīt, *n.* [From the *fels* of felspar, felstone (q.v.).] An eruptive rock, made up of quartz and orthoclase felspar, and very hard.—**Felsitic**, fel-sit'ik, *a.* Pertaining to or containing felsite.

Felspar, fel'spär, *n.* [G. *feldspath*—*feld*, field, and *spath*, spar.] A mineral widely distributed, and usually of a foliated structure, consisting of silica and alumina, with potash, soda, or lime; it is a principal constituent in granite, gneiss, porphyry, &c. Called also *Feldspar, Felspath.* — **Felspathic, Felspathose**, fel-spath'ik, fel-spath'ōs, *a.* Pertaining to felspar or containing it: written also *Feldspathic, Feldspathose.*—**Felstone**, fel'stōn, *n.* [*Fel* in *felspar*, and *stone.*] Compact felspar occurring in amorphous or vitreous rock masses.

Felt, felt, pret. & pp. of *feel.*

Felt, felt, *n.* [A.Sax. *felt* = D. *vilt*, G. *filz*, felt; allied to Gr. *pilos*, wool wrought into felt, and to L. *pileus*, a felt hat or cap. Akin *filter.*] A cloth or stuff made of wool, or wool and hair or fur, matted or wrought into a compact substance by rolling, beating, and pressure; a hat made of wool felted.—*v.t.* To make into felt; to cover with felt.—**Felter**, fel'tėr, *n.* One who makes felt, or who covers with felt.—**Felting**, fel'ting, *n.* The process by which felt is made; the materials of which felt is made, or the felt itself.

Felucca, fe-luk'a, *n.* [It. *felucca, feluca*, from Ar. *felûkah*, from *fulk*, a ship.] A long, narrow vessel, once common in the Mediterranean, with two large lateen sails, and capable of being propelled by oars.

Female, fē'māl, *n.* [Fr. *femelle*, L. *femella*, a young girl, from *femina*, a woman, from the root *fe*, as in *fetus, fecundus.*] An animal of that sex which conceives and brings forth young; that plant which produces fruit; the flower that bears the pistil and receives the pollen of the male flowers.—*a.* Belonging to the sex which produces young; feminine; delicate; weak; *bot.* pistil-bearing; producing pistillate flowers.—*Female rhymes*, double rhymes, such as *motion, notion*, the second syllable being unstressed. —*Female screw*, a concave screw, corresponding to the convex or male screw which works in it.—**Feminine**, fem'in-in, *a.* [L. *femininus*, feminine, from *femina*, a woman.] Pertaining to a woman or to women, or to the female sex; having the qualities belonging to a woman; womanly; effeminate; womanish; *gram.* denoting the gender of words which signify females, or the terminations of such words.—**Femininely**, fem'in-in-li, *adv.* In a feminine manner.—**Feminineness, Femininity**, fem'in-in-nes, fem-in-in'i-ti, *n.* The quality of being feminine.

Feme-covert, Femme-covert, fem-kuv'ėrt, *n.* [Norm. Fr.] *Law*, a married woman who is under the protection and control of her husband.—**Feme-sole**, fem-sōl', *n.* An unmarried woman, divorcee or widow; a married woman conducting business or holding property in her own right.

Femoral, fem'o-ral, *a.* [L. *femoralis*, from *femur*, the thigh.] Belonging to the thigh. —**Femur**, fē'mėr, *n.* [L.] The first bone of the leg or pelvic extremity; the thigh-bone.

Fen, fen, *n.* [A.Sax. *fen, fenn*, marsh, mud, dirt; D. *veen*, G. *fenne*, Icel. *fen*, fen, peat-bog, Goth. *fani*, mud, clay.] Low land covered wholly or partially with water, but producing sedge, coarse grasses, or other plants; boggy land; a marsh.—**Fenny**, fen'i, *a.* Having the character of a fen; marshy; boggy; inhabiting or growing in fens.

Fence, fens, *n.* [Abbrev. from *defence.*] A wall, hedge, bank, railing, or paling forming a boundary to or inclosing some area; that which defends; defence; the art of fencing; skill in fencing or swordsmanship; hence, skill in argument and repartee; a purchaser or receiver of stolen goods (*slang*). —*v.t.*—*fenced, fencing.* To inclose with a fence; to secure by an inclosure; to guard; to hedge in; to ward off or parry by argument or reasoning.—*v.i.* To use a sword or foil for the purpose of learning the art of attack and defence; to practise fencing; to fight and defend by giving and avoiding blows or thrusts; to parry arguments; to equivocate; to prevaricate. — **Fenced**, fenst, *p.* and *a.* Inclosed with a fence; guarded; fortified.—**Fenceless**, fens'les, *a.* Without a fence; uninclosed; open.—**Fencer**, fen'sėr, *n.* One who fences; one who teaches or practises the art of fencing with sword or foil.—**Fencible**, fen'si-bl, *n.* A soldier for defence of the country against invasion, and not liable to serve abroad.—**Fencing**, fen'sing, *n.* The art of using skilfully a sword or foil in attack or defence; material used in making fences; that which fences; a protection put round a dangerous piece of machinery.

Fend, fend, *v.t.* [Contr. from *defend*, from *de*, and obs. L. *fendo*, to thrust, to strike; seen also in *offendo*, to offend.] To keep off; to ward off; to shut out: usually followed by *off* (to *fend off* blows).—**Fender**, fen'dėr, *n.* One who or that which fends or wards off; a utensil employed to hinder coals of fire from rolling forward to the floor; also, a piece of timber, bundle of rope, &c., hung over the side of a vessel to prevent it from being injured by rubbing against any body.

Fenestra, fē-nes'tra, *n.* [L.] A window; an aperture; a foramen.—**Fenestral**, fē-nes'tral, *a.* [L. *fenestralis*, from *fenestra*, a window.] Pertaining to a window.—**Fenestrate**, fē-nes'trāt, *a.* Having windows or openings; *bot.* applied to leaves in which the cellular tissue does not completely fill up the interstices between the veins, thus leaving openings.—**Fenestration**, fen-es-trā'shon, *n.* The series or arrangement of windows in a building.

Fengite, fen'jīt, *n.* [Gr. *phengos*, light.] A kind of transparent alabaster or marble.

Fenian, fē'ni-an, *n.* [A name assumed from Ir. *Fionna*, a race of superhuman heroes in Irish legendary history.] A person belonging to a secret society having for its principal object the erection of Ireland into an independent republic.—*a.* Of or belonging to the Fenians.—**Fenianism**, fē'ni-an-izm, *n.* The principles or politics of the Fenians.

Fennec, fen'ek, *n.* [Moorish name.] A North African animal allied to the fox.

Fennel, fen'el, *n.* [A.Sax. *finol, finugl*, like G. *fenchel*, borrowed from the L. *fœniculum*, fennel, dim. from *fœnum*, hay.] A fragrant, umbelliferous, perennial, cultivated plant, having seeds which are carminative, and frequently employed in medicine, and leaves that are used in sauces.

Fent, fent, *n.* [Fr. *fente*, a slit.] The opening left in an article of dress, as at the top of the skirt in a gown, &c., for the convenience of putting it on; a placket.

Fenugreek, fē'nū-grēk, *n.* [L. *fœnum græcum*, Greek hay.] A leguminous annual plant resembling clover, and whose bitter and mucilaginous seeds are used in veterinary practice.

Feod, Feodal, Feodary, fūd, fū'dal, fū'da-ri. Same as *Feud*, &c.

Feoff, fef, *n.* [A form of *fief.*] A fief or fee.—**Feoffee**, fef'fē, *n.* A person who is invested with land in fee. — **Feoffer, Feoffor**, fef'ėr, *n.* One who enfeoffs or grants a fee.—**Feoffment**, fef'ment, *n.* The legal gift or transference to a person of a fee or freehold estate; the instrument or deed by which such property is conveyed.

Feracious,† fē-rā'shus, *a.* [L. *ferax, feracis*, from *fero*, to bear.] Fruitful; producing abundantly.—**Feracity**,† fē-ras'i-ti, *n.* Fruitfulness.

Feral, fē'ral, *a.* [L. *fera*, a wild beast.] Having become wild from a state of domestication, as animals, or from a state of cultivation, as plants.

Fer-de-lance, fer-de-läns, *n.* [Fr., iron of a lance, lance-head.] The lance-headed viper, a very venomous serpent of Brazil and the West Indies.

Feretory, fer'e-to-ri, *n.* [From L. *feretrum*, a bier or litter, from *fero*, to bear.] A shrine or repository for the relics of saints, variously adorned, and usually in the shape of a chest, with a roof-like top.

Ferial, fē'ri-al, *a.* [L. *ferialis*, from *feriæ*, holidays.] Pertaining to holidays or days in which business is not transacted.

Ferine, fē'rīn, *a.* [L. *ferinus*, from *fera*, a wild beast.] Relating to or resembling a wild beast; wild; untamed; savage.

Feringee, Feringhee, fe-ring'gē, *n.* [Probably a corruption of *Frank.*] The name given to Europeans by the Hindus.

Ferment, fėr'ment, *n.* [L. *fermentum*, for *fervimentum*, from *fervo* or *ferveo*, to boil, to foam. FERVENT.] Any substance, as a fungus, whose presence in another body produces the peculiar effervescence and decomposition called fermentation; commotion; heat; tumult; agitation (as of a crowd, of the feelings, &c.).—*v.t.* (fėr-ment'). To cause fermentation in; to set in brisk motion or agitation; to warm; to excite.—*v.i.* To undergo fermentation; to work; to be in agitation or excited, as by violent emotions.—**Fermentable**, fėr-men'ta-bl, *a.* Capable of fermentation.—**Fermentability**, fėr-men'ta-bil"i-ti, *n.* Capability of being fermented. — **Fermentation**, fėr-men-tā'shon, *n.* The act or process of fermenting; the decomposition or conversion of an organic substance into new compounds in presence of a ferment, generally indicated by a sensible internal motion, the development of heat, and the liberation of bubbles of gas; in common language, the process by which grape juice is converted into wine, and the wort of malt into beer; *fig.* the state of being in high activity or commotion; agitation; excitement. — **Fermentative**, fėr-men'ta-tiv, *a.* Causing fermentation; consisting in or produced by fermentation.—**Fermentativeness**, fėr-men'ta-tiv-nes, *n.* The state of being fermentative. — **Fermentescible**, fėr-men-tes'si-bl, *a.* Capable of being fermented.

Fern, fėrn, *n.* [A.Sax. *fearn* = G. *farn, farren*, D. *varen*—fern; allied to Skr. *parna*, a wing or feather.] The name of many vascular cryptogams, consisting of herbaceous, shrubby, or arborescent plants, producing leaves called fronds, which are simple or more or less divided, and bear on their under surface or edge the capsules containing the minute spores.—**Fernery**, fėr'nėr-i, *n.* A place where ferns are artificially grown.—**Fern-owl**, *n.* The common goat-sucker or night-jar. — **Fern-seed**, *n.* The seed, or more correctly the spores, of fern. Supposed to render the bearer invisible.—*We walk by fernseed*, to steal.—**Ferny**, fėr'ni, *a.* Abounding or overgrown with fern.

Ferocious, fē-rō'shus, *a.* [Fr. *féroce*; L. *ferox, ferocis*, fierce, allied to *ferus*, wild. FIERCE.] Fierce; savage; barbarous; ravenous; rapacious; indicating, or expressive of, ferocity.—**Ferociously**, fē-rō'shus-li, *adv.* Fiercely; with savage cruelty.—**Ferociousness**, fē-rō'shus-nes, *n.* State or quality of being ferocious; ferocity.—**Ferocity**, fē-ros'i-ti, *n.* [Fr. *férocité*, L. *ferocitas.*] State of being ferocious; savage wildness or fierceness; fury; cruelty.

Ferrandine, fer'an-dīn, *n.* [Fr. *ferrandine.*] A stuff made of wool and silk.

Ferrara, fer-rä'rä, *n.* A broadsword of peculiarly excellent quality, named after the famous swordsmith Andrea *Ferrara.*

Ferreous, fer'ē-us, *a.* [L. *ferrum*, iron.] Pertaining to, obtained from, or containing iron.—**Ferric**, fer'ik, *a. Chem.* pertaining to or extracted from iron (*ferric* acid and *ferric* oxide).—**Ferricalcite**, fer-i-kal'sīt, *n.* [L. *ferrum*, and *calx*, lime.] A species of calcareous earth or limestone combined with a large portion of iron.—**Ferriferous**, fe-rif'ėr-us, *a.* [L. *ferrum*, and *fero*, to produce.] Producing or yielding iron.—**Ferrocyanic**, fer'ō-sī-an"ik, *a.* Pertaining to or derived from iron and cyanogen.—**Ferrotype**, fer'ō-tīp, *n.* *Photog.* a term applied to some photographic processes in which the salts of iron are the principal agents; a photograph taken on japanned sheet-iron by a collodion process.—**Ferruginous, Ferrugineous,**† fe-rụj'i-nus, fe-rụ-jin'ē-us, *a.* [L. *ferrugineus*, rusty, from *ferrugo, ferruginis*, iron rust, from *ferrum*, iron.] Partaking of iron; irony; of the colour of the rust or oxide of iron.—**Ferruginated**, fe-rụj'i-nā-ted, *a.* Having the colour or properties of the rust of iron. —**Ferrugo**, fe-rö'gō, *n.* *Bot.* a disease of plants, commonly called *Rust*.—**Ferruminate**, fe-rụm'i-nāt, *v.t.* [L. *ferrumino*, to cement, from *ferrumen*, cement.] To unite or solder, as metals.—**Ferrumination**, fe-rụm'i-nā"shon, *n.* The soldering or uniting of metals.

Ferret, fer'et, *n.* [Fr. *furet*, It. *furetto*, a ferret, from L. *fur*, a thief.] A domesticated variety of the polecat, usually of a pale yellow colour, with red eyes—used to drive rabbits out of their holes and to kill rats. —*v.t.* To hunt with ferrets; to drive out of a lurking-place; (with *out*) to search out by perseverance and cunning.—**Ferreter**, fer'e-tėr, *n.* One who ferrets.

Ferret, fer'et, *n.* [Older *foret*, from It. *fioretti*, floss silk, from L. *flos, floris*, flower.] A kind of narrow tape, made of woollen thread, sometimes of cotton or silk.

Ferriage, fer'i-āj, *n.* Under Ferry.

Ferril, fer'il, *n.* Same as *Ferrule*.

Ferrite, fer'rīt, *n.* [L. *ferrum*, iron.] Layers of pure iron seen in sections of steel.

Ferro-, from L. *ferrum*, iron, a prefix in various words naming substances that contain iron or form compounds with this metal.—**Ferro-concrete**, fer'rō-kon"krēt, *n.* A building material consisting of concrete in which steel rods are embedded; reinforced concrete.—**Ferro-manganese**, fer'rō-man"ga-nez, *n.* An alloy of iron and manganese used in the manufacture of steel. See Ferreous.

Ferruginous, &c. Under Ferreous.

Ferrule, fer'ụl, *n.* [Formerly *verril*, from Fr. *virole*, ferrule, from *virer*, to veer, the form having been modified by the influence of L. *ferrum*, iron. Veer.] A ring of metal put round the end of a walking-stick or other thing to strengthen it or prevent its splitting.

Ferry, fer'i, *v.t.*—*ferried, ferrying.* [A.Sax. *ferian, farian*, to carry, to convey, causative of *faran*, to go. Fare.] To carry or transport over a river, strait, &c., in a boat or other conveyance.—*v.i.* To pass over a ferry.—*n.* The place or passage where boats pass over a narrow piece of water to convey passengers; the boat itself.—**Ferry-boat**, *n.* A boat that plies at a ferry.—**Ferryman**, *n.* One who keeps a ferry.—**Ferriage**, fer'i-āj, *n.* The price or fare to be paid at a ferry.

Fertile, fėr'til or fėr'tīl, *a.* [Fr. *fertile*, from L. *fertilis*, from *fero*, to bear, to produce; same root as E. *bear* (Bear); seen also in *confer, differ, refer*, &c.] Fruitful; producing fruit or crops in abundance; the opposite of barren; prolific or productive of anything, as of ideas, poetry, &c.; inventive; able to produce abundantly; *bot.* capable of producing fruit; fruit-bearing.—**Fertilely**, fėr'til-li, *adv.* In a fertile manner; fruitfully.—**Fertileness**, fėr'til-nes, *n.* Fertility.—**Fertility**, fėr-til'i-ti, *n.* [L. *fertilitas.*] The state of being fertile or fruitful; fruitfulness; fecundity; productiveness; richness; fertile invention. —**Fertilization**, fėr'til-i-zā"shon, *n.* The act or process of rendering fertile, fruitful, or productive; *bot.* the application of the pollen to the stigma of a plant, by means of which a perfect seed containing an embryo is produced; fecundation.—**Fertilize**, fėr'ti-līz, *v.t.*—*fertilized, fertilizing.* To make fertile; to make fruitful or productive; to enrich; to fecundate.—**Fertilizer**, fėr'ti-lī-zėr, *n.* One who or that which fertilizes.

Ferula, fer'ū-la, *n.* [L.] A ferula, a genus of plants, members of which yield asafetida, galbanum, &c.—**Ferulaceous**, fer-ū-lā'shus, *a.* [L. *ferula*, a reed.] Pertaining to reeds or canes, growing similar to a reed.

Ferule, fer'ụl, *n.* [L. *ferula*, a twig, a cane, a switch, from *ferio*, to strike.] A flat piece of wood used to punish children by striking them on the palm of the hand; a cane or rod for the same purpose.—*v.t.*—*feruled, feruling.* To punish with a ferule.

Fervent, fėr'vent, *a.* [L. *fervens, ferventis*, ppr. of *ferveo*, to boil, to ferment; akin *ferment*.] Hot; glowing; intensely warm; hot in temper; vehement; ardent; earnest; excited; animated; glowing with religious feeling; zealous.—**Fervently**, fėr'vent-li, *adv.* In a fervent manner or degree; earnestly; ardently; vehemently.—**Ferventness, Fervency**, fėr'vent-nes, fėr'ven-si, *n.* The state of being fervent; heat of mind; ardor; animated zeal; warmth of devotion.—**Fervescent**, fėr-ves'ent, *a.* [L. *fervescens, fervescentis*, from *ferveo*.] Growing hot.—**Fervid**, fėr'vid, *a.* [L. *fervidus*, from *ferveo*.] Very hot; burning; glowing; fervent; very warm in zeal; vehement; ardent.—**Fervidly**, fėr'vid-li, *adv.* Very hotly; with glowing warmth.—**Fervidness**, fėr'vid-nes, *n.* Glowing heat; ardor.—**Fervor**, fėr'vėr, *n.* [L. *fervor*, heat.] Heat or warmth; intensity of feeling; ardor; burning zeal; extreme earnestness in religion, particularly in prayer.

Fescennine, fes'en-īn, *a.* [From *Fescennia*, town in Etruria.] Sportive, ribald, licentious.

Fescue, fes'kū, *n.* [O.E. *festue*, from O.Fr. *festu* (Fr. *fétu*), a straw; L. *festuca*, a shoot or twig.] A straw, wire, pin, or the like, used to point out letters to children; a kind of grass, some species being excellent meadow and pasture grasses.

Fesse, fes, *n.* [O.Fr. *fesse*, Fr. *fasce*, L. *fascia*, a band.] *Her.* a band or girdle comprising the centre third part of the escutcheon, which it crosses horizontally.—**Fesse-point**, *n.* The exact centre of the escutcheon.

Festal, fes'tal, *a.* [From L. *festum*, a feast. Feast.] Pertaining to a feast; festive.—**Festally**, fes'tal-li, *adv.* Joyfully; mirthfully.—**Festival**, fes'ti-val, *a.* [L. *festivus.*] Pertaining to or befitting a feast; joyous; mirthful.—*n.* A time of feasting; an anniversary day of joy, civil or religious; a festive celebration.—**Festive**, fes'tiv, *a.* [L. *festivus.*] Pertaining to or becoming a feast; joyous; gay; mirthful.—**Festively**, fes'tiv-li, *adv.* In a festive manner.—**Festivity**, fes-tiv'i-ti, *n.* [L. *festivitas.*] The condition of being festive; social joy or exhilaration at an entertainment; something forming part of a festal celebration.

Fester, fes'tėr, *v.i.* [O.Fr. *festrir*, to fester.] To suppurate; to discharge or become full of pus or purulent matter; to rankle (passions, a sense of wrong, &c.).—*n.* Act of festering or rankling.

Festinate,‡ fes'ti-nāt, *a.* [L. *festino, festinatum*, to hasten.] Hasty; hurried. (*Shak.*)

Festoon, fes-tön', *n.* [Fr. *feston*, lit. a festal garland; It. *festone*, from L. *festum*, a feast.] A string, chain, or garland of flowers, foliage, &c., suspended so as to form one or more depending curves; *arch.* a sculptured ornament in imitation of this. —*v.t.* To adorn with festoons; to connect by festoons.—**Festoony**,† fes-tö'ni, *a.* Of or belonging to festoons.

Fetal, *a.* **Fetation**, *n.* Under Fetus.

Fetch, fech, *v.t.* [A.Sax. *feccan, gefeccan*, to fetch, to draw, to take, to seek; akin to O.Fris. *faka*, to prepare.] To go and bring; to bring; to bear toward the person speaking; to recall or bring back; to make or perform, with certain objects (to *fetch* a blow or stroke, to *fetch* a sigh); to bring or obtain as its price.—*To fetch out*, to bring or draw out.—*To fetch to*, to restore; to revive, as from a swoon; to bring up; to stop suddenly in any course; to overtake.—*v.i.* To bring things; to move or turn.—*To fetch and carry*, to perform menial services; to become a servile drudge.—*n.* A stratagem by which a thing is indirectly brought to pass; a trick; an artifice; the apparition of a living person; a wraith.—**Fetch-candle**, *n.* A light seen at night, and believed by the superstitious to portend a person's death.—**Fetcher**, fech'ėr, *n.* One who fetches.

Fête, fāt, *n.* [Fr., from L. *festum*, a feast.] A feast; a holiday; a festival-day.—*v.t.*—*fêted, fêting.* To entertain with a feast; to honour with a festive entertainment.—**Fête-champêtre**, fāt-shäṅ-pātr, *n.* [Fr.] A festival or entertainment in the open air.

Fetich, fē'tish, *n.* Same as *Fetish*.

Feticide, Fœticide, fē'ti-sīd, *n.* Under Fetus.

Fetid, fe'tid, *a.* [L. *fœtidus*, from *fœteo*, to stink.] Having an offensive smell; having a strong or rancid scent.—**Fetidness**, fe'tid-nes, *n.* The quality of smelling offensively.—**Fetor**, fē'tėr, *n.* [L. *fœtor.*] Any strong offensive smell; stench.

Fetish, fē'tish, *n.* [Fr. *fétiche*, Pg. *feitiço*, sorcery, witchcraft, from L. *factitius*, artificial, from *facio*, to make. Fact.] Any object, animate or inanimate, natural or artificial, regarded by some uncivilized races with a feeling of awe, as having mysterious powers residing in it or as being the representative or habitation of a deity; hence, any object of exclusive devotion.—**Fetishism, Feticism**, fē'tish-izm, fē'ti-sizm, *n.* The practice of worshipping fetishes practised by some African tribes. —**Fetishistic**, fē-tish-is'tik, *a.* Of or pertaining to fetishism.

Fetlock, fet'lok, *n.* [From *foot* or *feet* and *lock*.] A tuft of hair growing behind the pastern joint of horses; the joint on which the hair grows; an instrument fixed on the leg of a horse when put to pasture for the purpose of preventing him from running off.—**Fetlocked**, fet'lokt, *a.* Having a fetlock; tied by the fetlock.—**Fetlock-joint**, *n.* The joint of a horse's leg next to the hoof.

Fetlow, fet'lō, *n.* A whitlow in cattle.

Fetor. Under Fetid.

Fetter, fet'ėr, *n.* [A.Sax, *feter, fetor*, a fetter; O.G. *fezzera*, G. *fessel*, Icel. *fiötur*. Probably connected with *foot*.] A chain for the feet; a chain by which a person or animal is confined by the foot; anything that confines or restrains from motion; a restraint.—*v.t.* To put fetters on; to bind; to confine; to restrain.—**Fetterless**, fet'ėr-les, *a.* Free from fetters or restraint.—**Fetterlock**, fet'ėr-lok, *n.* An instrument for confining a horse's leg; a fetlock.

Fettle, fet'l, *v.t.* [Akin to Icel. *fitla*, to touch lightly; L.G. *fisseln*, to be occupied in cleaning.] To put in right order or trim. (*Provincial.*)

Fetus, Fœtus, fē'tus, *n.* [L., from a root *fe*, implying fruitfulness, productiveness, as in *fecund*.] The young of viviparous animals in the womb, and of oviparous animals in the egg, after it is perfectly formed; before which time it is called *Embryo*.—**Fetal, Fœtal**, fē'tal, *a.* Pertaining to a fetus.—**Fetation, Fœtation**, fē-tā'shon, *n.* The formation of a fetus.—**Feticide, Fœticide**, fē'ti-sīd, *n.* [L. *fetus*, and *cædo*, to kill.] The destruction of the fetus in the womb; the act by which criminal abortion is produced.—**Fetiferous, Fœtiferous**, fē-tif'ėr-us, *a.* [L. *fetus*, and *fero*, to bear.] Producing young.

Feu, fū, *n.* [O.Fr. *fieu, fief*, a fief.] In Scotland a piece of ground (usually small) granted by a superior in perpetuity in consideration of an annual payment called *feu-duty*, and certain other contingent burdens.—*v.t.* To give or take in feu, or by the payment of feu-duty.—**Feuar**, fū'ėr, *n.* One who holds a feu.

Feud, fūd, *n.* [L.L. *feudum*, a fief; from

O.Fr. or O.G., like *fief, feu, fee.*] A fief.—**Feudal**, fū'dal, *a.* [L.L. *feudalis*, from *feudum.*] Pertaining to feuds or fiefs; founded upon or pertaining to the system of holding lands by military services.—*Feudal system*, a system according to which grants of land were made by the sovereign to the nobles, and by them to an inferior class, on the condition that the possessor should take an oath of fealty, and do military service to him by whom the grant was made.—**Feudalism**, fū'dal-izm, *n.* The feudal system and its belongings; the system of holding lands by military services.—**Feudalist**, fū'dal-ist, *n.* A supporter of the feudal system; one versed in feudal law.—**Feudality**, fū-dal'i-ti, *n.* The state or quality of being feudal.—**Feudalization**, fū'dal-i-zā"shon, *n.* The act of feudalizing.—**Feudalize**, fū'dal-īz, *v.t.*—*feudalized, feudalizing.* To reduce to a feudal tenure; to conform to feudalism.—**Feudally**, fū'dal-li, *adv.* In a feudal manner; by feudal tenure.—**Feudary**, fū'da-ri, *a.* Held by or pertaining to feudal tenure.—*n.* A tenant who holds his lands by feudal service; a feudatory.—**Feudatory**, **Feudatary**, fū'da-to-ri, fū'da-ta-ri, *a.* Holding from another by feudal tenure.—*n.* A tenant or vassal holding his lands on condition of military service; the tenant of a feud or fief.

Feud, fūd, *n.* [O.E. *feide*, from A.Sax. *faehth*, hostility, from *fāh*, hostile (whence *foe*); D. *veede*, G. *fehde*, Dan. *fejde*, a feud; the spelling being modified through confusion with L.L. *feudum*, a feud or fief. Akin *fiend.*] A contention or quarrel; hostility; often, hostility or declared warfare between families or parties in a state.

Feu de joie, fėd-zhwą. [Fr., fire of joy.] A bonfire, or a firing of guns in token of joy.

Feuilleton, fwēl-toṅ, *n.* [Fr., from *feuille*, a leaf; lit. a small leaf.] That part of a French newspaper devoted to light literature or criticism.—**Feuilletonist**, *n.* A light journalist; a journalist on a daily sheet.

Fever, fē'vėr, *n.* [A.Sax. *fefer*, from L. *febris*, a fever; or from O.Fr. *fevre*, Mod.Fr. *fièvre*, of same origin.] A diseased state of the system, characterized by an accelerated pulse, with increase of heat, deranged functions, diminished strength, and often with excessive thirst; agitation or excitement by anything that strongly affects the passions.—*v.t.* To put in a fever.—*v.i.* To be seized with fever.—**Feverish**, fē'vėr-ish, *a.* Having fever; affected with fever, especially with a slight degree of fever; indicating or pertaining to fever.—**Feverishly**, fē'vėr-ish-li, *adv.* In a feverish manner.—**Feverishness**, fē'vėr-ish-nes, *n.* The state of being feverish; anxious, heated excitement.—**Feverous**, fē'vėr-us, *a.* Affected with fever or ague; feverish.—**Feverously**,† fē'vėr-us-li, *adv.* In a feverous manner.—**Feverfew**, fē'vėr-fū, *n.* [A.Sax. *feferfuge*, from L. *febrifugia*, from *febris*, fever, and *fugo*, to drive away.] A European composite plant with much-divided leaves, and white flowers; once supposed to be a valuable febrifuge, hence the name.

Few, fū, *a.* [A.Sax. *fedwa*, *fedwe*, Dan. *faa*, Goth. *favs*, pl. *favai*, little, few; of cognate origin with L. *paucus*, few, *paulus*, Gr. *pauroe*, little.] Not many; small in number: used frequently, by ellipsis of a noun, for not many persons or things. *A few* is often used and generally means more than *few* alone.—**Fewness**, fū'nes, *n.* The state of being few; paucity.

Fey, fe'i, *a.* [A.Sax. *fæge*, Icel. *feigr*, near to death.] On the verge of a sudden or violent death; fated soon to die, and often showing this in some peculiar way.

Fez, fez, *n.* [From *Fez*, the principal town in Morocco, where such caps are largely manufactured.] A red cap of fine cloth, fitting closely to the head, with a tassel of blue silk or wool at the crown, much worn in Turkey, on the shores of the Levant, in Egypt, and North Africa generally.

Fiacre, fē-ä-kr, *n.* [Fr., from the Hotel St. *Fiacre*, where the inventor of these carriages established in 1640 an office for the hire of them.] A small four-wheeled carriage; a hackney-coach or similar vehicle plying for hire.—*v.* To convey pilgrims and others to the shrine of the Irish saint Fiachra.

Fiancé, **Fiancée**, fē-äṅ-sā, *n. masc.* and *fem.* [Fr.] An affianced or betrothed person.

Fiasco, fē-as'kō, *n.* [It. *fiasco*, a flask or bottle, a cry in Italy when a singer fails to please, perhaps in allusion to the bursting of a bottle.] A failure in a musical performance; an ignominious and notorious failure generally; a conspicuous or chagrining frustration; a breakdown.

Fiat, fī'at, *n.* [L. let it be done, 3rd pers. sing. subj. of *fio*, to be done.] A command to do something; a decisive or effective command.—**Fiat Money**, *n.* Paper currency issued by a government as money, which does not represent coin or bullion, but is made legal tender by law.—*Fiat in Bankruptcy*, an order in chancery allowing the institution of proceedings in bankruptcy.

Fib, fib, *n.* [Probably an abbreviation and corruption from *fable.*] A lie or falsehood: a word used as a softer expression than lie.—*v.i.*—*fibbed, fibbing.* To lie; to speak falsely.—**Fibber**, **Fibster**, fib'ėr, fib'stėr, *n.* One who tells lies or fibs.

Fiber, **Fibre**, fī'bėr, *n.* [Fr. *fibre*, L. *fibra*, allied to *filum*, a thread.] A thread or filament; one of the fine slender threadlike or hair-like bodies of which the tissues of animals and plants are partly constituted; the small slender root of a plant.—**Fibered**, fī'bėrd, *a.* Having fibers.—**Fiberless**, fī'bėr-les, *a.* Having no fibers.—**Fibriform**, fī'bri-form, *a.* Like a fiber or fibers.—**Fibril**, fī'bril, *n.* [Fr. *fibrille.*] A small fiber; the branch of a fiber; a very slender thread.—**Fibrilla**, fī-bril'la, *n.* pl. **Fibrillae**, fī-bril'lē. [Dim. of L. *fibra.*] One of the elements or components of fiber; *bot.* one of the hairs produced from the epidermis which covers the young roots of plants.—**Fibrillated**, fī-bril'ā-ted, *a.* Furnished with fibrils or fibrillae; fringed.—**Fibrillation**, fī-bri-lā'shon, *n.* The state of being reduced to fibrils or fibrillae.—**Fibrillose**, fī-bril'ōs, *a. Bot.* covered with or composed of little strings or fibers.—**Fibrillous**, fī-bril'us, *a.* In the form of fibrils.—**Fibrin**, **Fibrine**, fī'brin, *n.* A peculiar organic substance found in animals and vegetables, and readily obtained from fresh blood.—**Fibrination**, fī-bri-nā'shon, *n. Med.* the acquisition of an excess of fibrine.—**Fibrinous**, fī'bri-nus, *a.* Having or partaking of the nature of fibrine.—**Fibrocartilage**, fī'brō-kär"ti-lāj, *n.* A substance intermediate between proper cartilage and ligament.—**Fibrocellular**, fī-brō-sel'lū-lėr, *a.* Partaking of the characters of fibrous and cellular tissues.—**Fibroid**, fī'broid, *a.* [From L. *fibra*, fiber.] Of a fibrous character.—*Fibroid phthisis*, consumption characterized by the growth of fibrous matter in the lungs.—**Fibrosis**, fī-brō'sis, *n. Pathol.* a morbid growth or development of fibrous matter.—**Fibroma**, fī-brō'ma, *n. Pathol.* a tumor or growth of fibrous matter.—**Fibrous**, fī'brus, *a.* Containing or consisting of fibers.—**Fibrousness**, fī'brus-nes, *n.*—**Fibrovascular**, fī-brō-vas'kū-lėr, *a. Bot.* consisting of wood fibers and vessels.

Fibula, fib'ū-la, *n.* pl. **Fibulæ**, fib'ū-lē. [L. a clasp, a brace, a pin.] An ancient clasp or buckle; *anat.* the outer and lesser bone of the lower leg; *surgery*, a needle for sewing up wounds.—**Fibular**, fib'ū-lėr, *a.* Of or pertaining to the fibula.

Fichu, fi-shö', *n.* [Fr.] A light piece of dress worn by ladies covering the neck, throat, and shoulders.

Fickle, fik'l, *a.* [A.Sax. *ficol*, inconstant; akin to G. *ficken*, to move quickly to and fro.] Wavering; inconstant; unstable; of a changeable mind; irresolute; not firm in opinion or purpose; capricious; liable to change or vicissitude.—**Fickleness**, fik'l-nes, *n.* The state or quality of being fickle; inconstancy; unsteadiness in opinion or purpose; changeableness.—**Fickly**, fik'li, *adv.* In a fickle manner.

Fico, fē'kō, *n.* [It. from *ficus*, fig.] A fig, used in expressions of contempt or scorn, originally with obscene gesture. (*Shak.*)

Fictile, fik'tīl, *a.* [L. *fictilis*, from *fingo*, *fictum*, to form. FEIGN.] Moulded into form by art; manufactured by the potter; suitable for the potter.—**Fictileness**, **Fictility**, fik'tīl-nes, fik-til'i-ti, *n.* The quality of being fictile.

Fiction, fik'shon, *n.* [L. *fictio*, a shaping, a fashioning, from *fingo*, *fictum*, to fashion. FEIGN.] The act of inventing or imagining; that which is feigned, invented, or imagined; a feigned or invented story; a tale or story composed for amusement or entertainment; fictitious literature; prose narrative in the form of romances, novels, tales, and the like.—**Fictional**, fik'shon-al, *a.* Pertaining to or characterized by fiction.—**Fictionist**, fik'shon-ist, *n.* A writer of fiction.—**Fictitious**, fik-tish'us, *a.* [L. *fictitius.*] Feigned; imaginary; not real; counterfeit; false; not genuine: invented to give literary pleasure; dealing with imaginary characters and events.—**Fictitiously**, fik-tish'us-li, *adv.* In a fictitious manner; falsely.—**Fictitiousness**, fik-tish'us-nes, *n.*—**Fictive**, fik'tiv, *a.* Feigned; imaginary; hypothetical.

Fid, fid, *n.* A bar or short piece of wood or metal, helping to support a topmast; a wooden pin for various purposes on board ship.

Fiddle, fid'l, *n.* [A.Sax. *fithele*; L.G. *fidel*, Dan. *fiddel*, Icel. *fithla*, D. *vedel*; perhaps borrowed from L.L. *vidula*, a viol. VIOL.] A stringed instrument of music; a violin.—*v.i.*—*fiddled, fiddling.* To play on a fiddle or violin; to trifle.—**Fiddle-bow**, *n.* The bow strung with horse-hair for playing the fiddle.—**Fiddle-faddle**, *a.* Trifling; making a bustle about nothing. (*Colloq.*)—*v.i.* To trifle.—**Fiddler**, fid'lėr, *n.* One who plays on a fiddle.—**Fiddle-stick**, *n.* A fiddle-bow: used often as an interjection equivalent to nonsense! pshaw! &c.—**Fiddle-string**, *n.* The string of a fiddle.—**Fiddle-wood**, *n.* A tropical American timber tree which yields a hard wood valuable for carpenter work.—**Fiddling**, fid'-ling, *a.* Trifling; trivial; fussily busy with nothing.

Fidelity, fi-del'i-ti, *n.* [L. *fidelitas*, from *fidelis*, faithful, from *fides*, trust, faith, *fido*, to trust. FAITH.] Faithfulness; careful and exact observance of duty or performance of obligations; firm adherence to a person or to a party; loyalty; honesty; veracity; adherence to truth.

Fidget, fij'et, *v.i.* [Dim. of provincial *fidge*, *fike*, *fyke*, to be restless; akin to Icel. *fika*, to hasten; G. *ficken*, O.Sw. *fika*, to move quickly to and fro.] To move uneasily one way and the other; to move irregularly or in fits and starts.—*n.* Irregular motion; restlessness.—**Fidgetiness**, fij'et-i-nes, *n.* The state or quality of being fidgety.—**Fidgety**, fij'et-i, *a.* Given to fidget; restless; uneasy.

Fiducial, fi-dū'shal, *a.* [L.L. *fiducialis*, from L. *fiducia*, trust, trustiness, from *fido*, to trust. FAITH.] Confident in trust or belief; undoubting; fiduciary.—**Fiducially**, fi-dū'shal-li, *adv.* With confidence.—**Fiduciary**, fi-dū'shi-a-ri, *a.* [L. *fiduciarius*, held in trust.] Confident in belief; trustful; undoubting; having the nature of a trust; held in trust.—*n.* One who holds a thing in trust; a trustee.

Fie, fī, *interj.* [Interjectional expression corresponding to Sc. *feigh*, Fr. *fi*, G. *pfui*, *fi*, Dan. *fy*, &c.] An exclamation denoting contempt, dislike, or impatience.

Fief, fēf, *n.* [Fr. *fief*, from O.H.G. *fihu*, property, lit. cattle. FEE, FEUD.] An estate held of a superior on condition of military or other service; an estate held on feudal tenure.

Field, fēld, *n.* [A.Sax. *feld*, a field = D. *veld*, Dan. *felt*, G. *feld*; allied to *fold*, an inclosure, *fell*, a hill; Dan. *falle*, greensward;

Sc. *fale, feal*, a turf.] A piece of land suitable for tillage or pasture; a distinct or separate division of a farm; cleared land; cultivated ground; the open country; the ground where a battle is fought or military operations carried on; hence, a battle or action (the *field* is lost); open space, or unrestricted opportunity, for action or operation; scope; compass; extent; sphere (a wide *field* for conjecture); the ground or blank space on which figures are drawn; the general surface of a heraldic shield or escutcheon; *cricket*, the fielders collectively; *sporting*, those taking part in a hunt; all the horses, dogs, or the like, taking part in a race.—*Field of vision* or *view*, in a telescope or microscope, the space or range within which objects are visible to an eye looking through the instrument.—*To keep the field*, to continue active military operations in the field.—*To take the field*, to begin military operations.—*v.i. Cricket*, to be one of the field whose duty is to watch and catch or recover the ball as it is driven by the batsman. — **Fielder**, fēl′dėr, *n*. A player who fields at cricket.—**Field-allowance**, *n*. A small extra payment to troops on active service in the field.—**Field-artillery**, *n*. Light ordnance fitted for active operations in the field.—**Field-day**, *n*. A day when troops are drawn out for instruction in field exercises and evolutions; any day of unusual display. —**Fieldfare**, fēld′fār, *n*. [*Field*, and *fare*, to go, to wander.] A small European bird of the thrush family with brown wings.—**Field-glass**, *n*. A kind of binocular telescope or opera-glass for looking at objects at a considerable distance from the spectator. — **Field-gun**, *n*. A small cannon for use in the field, acting with infantry or cavalry. A common *field-gun* is the 18-pounder quick-firing gun.—**Field-marshal**, *n*. The highest rank conferred on general officers in practically all armies. — **Field-marshalship**, *n*. The office or dignity of a field-marshal. —**Field-mouse**, *n*. One of several species of rodent animals that live in the field, burrowing in banks, &c. — **Field-officer**, *n*. A military officer above the rank of captain and below that of general, as a major or colonel.—**Field-preacher**, *n*. One who preaches in the open air.—**Field-train**, *n*. A department of artillery that has to attend to the supply of ammunition on the field.—**Field-work**, *n*. All the out-of-doors operations of a surveyor, engineer, geologist, &c.; a temporary fortification thrown up.

Fiend, fēnd, *n*. [A.Sax. *feónd, fynd*, a fiend, an enemy, from *feón*, to hate; like D. *vijand*, Icel. *fjandi*, Goth. *fijands*, G. *feind*, originally a present participle. Akin *foe*.] An infernal being; a demon; the devil; a person with devilish qualities; a wicked, cruel, or malicious person. — **Fiendish**, fēn′dish, *a*. Having the qualities of a fiend; infernal; excessively cruel; diabolic; devilish.—**Fiendishly**, fēn′dish-li, *adv*. In a fiendish manner.—**Fiendishness**, fēn′dish-nes, *n*. The quality of being fiendish.

Fierce, fērs, *a*. [O.Fr. *fers, fiers*, from L. *ferus*, wild, rude, cruel, whence *fera*, a wild beast; akin *feral* and *ferocious*.] Vehement; violent; furious; savage; ferocious; easily enraged; indicating ferocity or a ferocious disposition; very eager; vehement in anger or cruelty.—**Fiercely**, fērs′li, *adv*. In a fierce manner; furiously; with rage; with a fierce expression or aspect.—**Fierceness**, fērs′nes, *n*. The quality of being fierce, furious, or angry; violence; fury; ferocity; savageness.

Fiery, fī′ėr-i, *a*. Under Fire.

Fife, fīf, *n*. [Fr. *fifre*, a fife, from G. *pfeife*, (=E. *pipe*), a word of onomatopoetic origin. Pipe.] A small musical instrument of the flute kind, having but one key, and a compass of two octaves.—*v.i*. To play on a fife. —**Fife-major**, *n*. A non-commissioned officer who superintends the fifers of a battalion.—**Fifer**, fī′fėr, *n*. One who plays on a fife; an inhabitant of the county of Fife.

Fifteen, fif′tēn, *a*. [A.Sax. *fiftyne*, lit. five-ten.] Five and ten.—*n*. The number which consists of five and ten; a symbol representing this number, as 15 or xv.—*The Fifteen*, the old Scottish law court with its fifteen Lords of Session.—*The fifteen*, the '15, the Jacobite rebellion of 1715.—*A fifteen*, a football Rugby team of fifteen players. — **Fifteenth**, fif′tēnth, *a*. The fifth in order after the tenth; being one of fifteen equal parts into which a whole is divided.—*n*. A fifteenth part.—**Fifth**, fifth, *a*. The ordinal of five; next after the fourth; being one of five equal parts of a whole.—*n*. One of five equal parts into which anything is divided; *mus*. an interval consisting of three tones and a semitone. — *Fifth-monarchy men*, believers in the last of the great monarchies of *Daniel*, ii. 44, expecting the advent of Christ, and denying all human organizations.—**Fifth Column**, *n*. The practice of sabotage and espionage by citizens of one country for the benefit of a foreign power; traitorous political activity.

Fifty, fif′ti, *a*. [A. Sax. *fiftig*.] Five times ten.—*n*. The number which consists of five times ten; a symbol representing this number.

Fig, fig, *n*. [Fr. *figue*, like D. *vijg*, G. *feige*, from L. *ficus*, fig.] A fruit consisting of a hollow receptacle containing a great multitude of minute flowers, the ripe carpels of which, erroneously called the seed, are embedded in the pulp; the tree that bears this fruit; used also as a term of scorn or contempt (I do not care a *fig* for him; in this usage perhaps from O.Sp. *figo*, a motion denoting contempt). — **Fig-cake**, *n*. A preparation of figs and almonds pressed into round cakes.—**Fig-eater**, *n*. Same as *Beccafico*. — **Fig-leaf**, *n*. A symbol of decency for statues, &c., from *Genesis*, iii. 7.

Fig, fig, *n*. [A contr. for *figure*.] Dress: employed chiefly in the colloquial phrase *in full fig*, in full or official dress.

Fight, fīt, *v.i*. pret. & pp. *fought*. [A.Sax. *feohtan* = G. *fechten*, D. *vechten*, Dan. *fegte*, Icel. *fikta*, to fight.] To contend for victory in battle or in single combat; to contend in arms or otherwise; to carry on active opposition; to strive or struggle to resist: with *with* or *against* before an object.—*To fight shy of*, to avoid from a feeling of dislike, fear, mistrust, &c.—*v.t*. To carry on or wage (a battle); to win or gain by struggle (to *fight* one's way); to contend with; to war against; to manage or manœuvre in a fight (to *fight* one's ship).—*To fight it out*, to struggle till a decisive result is attained.—*n*. A contest; a battle; an engagement; a struggle for victory. Syn. under Battle.—**Fighter**, fī′tėr, *n*. One that fights; a combatant. — **Fighting**, fī′ting, *p*. and *a*. Qualified or trained for war; fit for battle.

Figment, fig′ment, *n*. [L. *figmentum*, from *fingo*, to feign. Feign.] An invention; a fiction; something feigned or imagined.

Figuline, fig′ū-lin, *a*. [L. *figulus*, a potter, from *fingo*, to fashion.] Made of potter's clay; made by a potter.

Figure, fig′ūr, *n*. [Fr. *figure*, from L. *figura*, figure, shape, from *fig*, root of *fingo*, to fashion, to shape; whence also *feign, fiction*, &c. Feign.] The form of anything as expressed by the outline or contour; shape; fashion; form; any form made by drawing, painting, carving, embroidering, &c.; especially the human body so represented; appearance or impression made by the conduct of a person (to cut a poor *figure*); *logic*, the form of a syllogism with respect to the relative position of the middle term; *arith*. a character denoting or standing for a number; hence, value, as expressed in numbers; price; *theol*. type or representative; *rhet*. a mode of speaking or writing in which words are deflected from their ordinary use or signification; a trope; a peculiar expression used for impressiveness as a metaphor, antithesis, &c.—*To cut a figure*, to make one's self celebrated or notorious; to appear to advantage or disadvantage.—*v.t.—figured, figuring*. To make a figure or likeness of; to represent by drawing, sculpture, carving, embroidery, &c.; to cover or adorn with figures or ornamental designs; to mark with figures; to represent by a typical or figurative resemblance; to typify; to imagine; to image in the mind. —*v.i*. To make a figure; to be a prominent figure or personage. — **Figurable**, fig′ū-ra-bl, *a*. Capable of being figured. — **Figural**, fig′ū-ral, *a*. Represented by figure or pertaining to figures; figurate.—**Figurant**, fig′ū-rant, *n. masc*.; **Figurante**, fig′ū-rant, *n. fem*. [Fr.] One who dances at the opera in groups or figures; a character on the stage who figures in its scenes, but has nothing to say.—**Figurate**, fig′ū-rāt, *a*. [L. *figuro, figuratum*, to form, to fashion.] Of a certain determinate form or shape.—*Figurate numbers*, such numbers as do or may represent some geometrical figure, being thus called triangular, square, pentagonal, &c., numbers.—**Figuration**, fig-ū-rā′shon, *n*. The act of giving figure or determinate form.—**Figurative**, fig′ū-rā-tiv, *a*. [Fr. *figuratif*.] Representing by means of a figure or type; typical; symbolical: used in a metaphorical sense; having the character of a figure or trope; metaphoric; not literal.—**Figuratively**, fig′ū-rā-tiv-li, *adv*. In a figurative manner; by a figure; in a sense different from that which words originally imply; in a metaphorical sense. — **Figurativeness**, fig′ū-rā-tiv-nes, *n*. State of being figurative.—**Figured**, fig′ūrd, *a*. Adorned with figures. — **Figure-head**, *n*. The ornamental figure on a ship immediately under the bowsprit. — **Figurine**, fig-ū-rēn′, *n*. [Fr. dim. of *figure*.] A small ornamental figure or piece of statuary; a statuette.

Filament, fil′a-ment, *n*. [L.L. *filamentum*, a slender thread, from L. *filum*, a thread, whence also *file* (a line), *fillet, profile*.] A thread; a fibre; a fine thread, of which flesh, nerves, skin, plants, roots, &c., and also some minerals, are composed.—**Filaceous**,† fi-lā′shus, *a*. Composed or consisting of threads.—**Filamentary**, fil-a-men′ta-ri, *a*. Having the character of or formed by a filament. — **Filamentose, Filamentous**, fil-a-men′tōs, fil-a-men′tus, *a*. Like a thread; consisting of fine filaments; *bot*. bearing filaments.—**Filar**, fī′lėr, *a*. Pertaining to a thread: applied to a microscope, or other optical instrument, into whose construction one or more threads or fine wires are introduced. — **Filatory**, fil′a-to-ri, *n*. A machine which forms or spins threads.—**Filature**, fil′a-tūr, *n*. A forming into threads; the reeling off silk from cocoons; a filatory.—**Filiferous**, fi-lif′ėr-us, *a*. Producing threads.—**Filiform**, fil′i-form, *a*. Having the form of a thread or filament.—**Filose**, fī′lōs, *a*. *Zool*. and *bot*. applied to a part when it ends in a threadlike process.

Filbert, fil′bėrt, *n*. [For *fill-beard*, because the nut just fills the cup made by the beards of the calyx.] The fruit of a cultivated variety of hazel; a nut of Filbert, maturing about August 22, St. Philibert's Day.

Filch, filch, *v.t*. [For *filk*, from O.E. *fele*, Icel. *fela*, to steal, like *talk* and *tell*, *stalk* (verb) and *steal*.] To steal, especially something of little value; to pilfer; to take in a thievish manner.—**Filcher**, filch′ėr, *n*. One who filches.—**Filchingly**, filch′ing-li, *adv*. In a thievish manner.

File, fīl, *n*. [Fr. *file*, from L. *filum*, a thread. Filament.] A line or wire on which papers are strung that they may be conveniently found when wanted; the papers so strung; a collection of papers arranged for ready reference; a row of soldiers ranged one behind another, from front to rear; hence, *rank and file* (*milit*.), the lines of soldiers from side to side, and from front to back; an old *file*, a sharper.—*v.t.—filed, filing*. To arrange or place in a file; to bring before a court by presenting the proper papers (to *file* a bill in chancery).—*v.i*. To march in a file or line, as soldiers, not abreast, but one by one.

File, fīl, *n*. [A.Sax. *feol*=D. *vijl*, Dan. *viil*, G. *feile*, O.H.G. *vihila*, a file.] A steel instrument, having minute teeth upon the surface for cutting, abrading, and smoothing metal, ivory, wood, &c.—*v.t.—filed, fil-*

ing. To rub smooth, or cut with a file, or as with a file; to polish.—**Filing**, fī'ling, *n.* A particle rubbed off by a file.

Filet, fē-le', fē-lā', *a.* Indicating a lace or net of square mesh.

Filet de sole, fē-le'd' sōl, *n.* [Fr.] A boneless piece of sole (fish).

Filet Mignon, fē-le' or fē-lā' mē'nyōn, *n.* [Fr.] A thick slice from the tenderloin of beef, garnished with bacon before cooking.

Filial, fil'i-al, *a.* [Fr. *filial*, from L.L. *filialis*, from L. *filius*, a son, *filia*, a daughter.] Pertaining to a son or daughter; becoming a child in relation to his parents; bearing the relation of a child.—**Filially**, fil'i-al-li, *adv.* In a filial manner.—**Filiate**, fil'i-āt, *v.t.* To adopt as a son or daughter.—**Filiation**, fil-i-ā'shon, *n.* The relation of a child to a father; adoption; the fixing of the paternity of a child.—**Filiety**, fi-lī'e-ti, *n.* The relation of a son to a parent; sonship.

Filibuster, fil'i-bus-tėr, *n.* [Fr. *flibustier*, formerly *fribustier*, a form of D. *vrijbuiter*, G. *freibeuter*, E. *freebooter*.] Originally, a buccaneer of the West Indies, now applied to any lawless adventurers who invade, with the view of occupying, a foreign country.—*v.i.* To act as a filibuster; to endeavor to defeat or to delay legislation by obstructionist tactics, as long speeches or motions.—**Filibusterism**, fil'i-bus-tėr-izm, *n.* The act or practice of filibustering.

Filical, fil'i-kal, *a.* [L. *filix*, *filicis*, a fern.] Belonging to the family of ferns.—**Filiciform**, fi-lis'i-form, *a.* Fern-shaped.—**Filicite**, fil'i-sīt, *n.* A fossil fern or filicoid plant.—**Filicoid**, fil'i-koid, *a.* Fern-like; having the form of a fern.—*n.* A plant resembling a fern.—**Filicology**, fil-i-kol'o-ji, *n.* The study of ferns.

Filigree, fil'i-grē, *n.* [Formerly *filigrane*, from Fr. *filigrane*, It. *filigrana*, from L. *filum*, a thread, and *granum*, a grain: originally it is said to have had beads in it.] Ornamental open work executed in fine gold or silver wire, formed into flowers and arabesques.—**Filigreed**, fil'i-grēd, *a.* Ornamented with filigree.

Fill, fil, *v.t.* [A.Sax. *fyllan*, to fill, from the adjective *ful*, full=Icel. and Sw. *fylla*, Goth. *fulljan*, G. *füllen*, D. *vullen*, to fill.] To make full; to cause to be occupied so that no space is left vacant; to put in so as to occupy a space; to occupy the whole space or capacity of; to occupy to a great extent; to pervade; to satisfy; to content; to glut; to press and dilate (a ship's sails); to supply with an occupant or holder; to possess and perform the duties of; to officiate in; to hold or occupy.—*To fill in*, to pour or put in for the purpose of filling something; to write in (items in a list).—*To fill out*, to distend or enlarge from within.—*To fill up*, to make quite full; to occupy or take up; to occupy the whole extent of; to engage or employ (time).—*v.i.* To grow or become full; to make something full.—*To fill out*, to become enlarged or distended.—*To fill up*, to grow or become full.—*n.* As much as fills or quite supplies; as much as gives complete satisfaction.—**Filler**, fil'ėr, *n.* One who or that which fills; a utensil for conveying a liquid into a bottle, cask, &c.—**Filling**, fil'ing, *a.* Calculated to fill, satisfy, or satiate.—*n.* Materials used for occupying some vacant space, stopping up a hole, or the like.

Fillet, fil'et, *n.* [Fr. *filet*, a thread, a band, the chine of an animal, &c., dim. of *fil*, thread, from L. *filum*, a thread. FILE.] A little band to tie about the head; a band or narrow strip; *cookery*, fi-lā', a boneless piece of lean meat, sometimes rolled and tied; fillet of beef, a slice of tenderloin; fillet of veal, a slice from the fleshy part of the calf's thigh.—*Arch.* A small molding having the appearance of a narrow band, generally used to separate ornaments and moldings; also the ridge between the flutes of a column.—*v.t.* To bind, furnish, or adorn with a fillet or little band.

Fillibeg, fil'i-beg, *n.* [Gael. *feileadh-beag*, lit. little-plaid—*feileadh*, a plaid, and *beag*, little.] The Gaelic name of the kilt worn by the Highlanders of Scotland.

Fillibuster, fil'i-bus-tėr, *n.* A filibuster.

Fillip, fil'ip, *v.t.* [Same as *flip*.] To strike with the fore or middle finger by jerking it away from the ball of the thumb; to strike with a smart stroke.—*n.* A jerk of the finger forced suddenly from the thumb; a smart blow or stroke; something which sharply rouses or stimulates.

Fillister, fil'is-tėr, *n.* A kind of plane used for grooving timber.

Filly, fil'i, *n.* [A dim. form of *foal* = Icel. *fylja*, a filly, from *foli*, a foal. FOAL.] A female or mare foal; a young mare; a young girl (*colloq.*).

Film, film, *n.* [A.Sax. *filmen*, a skin; allied to *fell*, a skin.] A thin skin or membrane; a pellicle; a lamina; a thin layer for receiving a photographic negative, especially for cinematographic purposes; a fine thread.—*v.t.* To cover with a thin skin or pellicle.—*v.i.* To be or become covered as by a film.—**Filminess**, fil'mi-nes, *n.* State of being filmy.—**Filmy**, fil'mi, *a.* Forming or like a film; showing films or fine threads.

Filoplume, fī'lo-plöm, *n.* [L. *filum*, thread, *pluma*, feather.] *Ornith.* one of the threadlike feathers of a bird.

Filose, *a.* Under FILAMENT.

Filter, fil'tėr, *n.* [Fr. *filtre*, from L.L. *filtrum*, *feltrum*, felt or fulled wool, used originally as a strainer. FELT.] A strainer; any substance or apparatus through which liquors are passed for defecation.—*v.t.* To purify by passing through a filter, or a porous substance that retains feculent matter.—*v.i.* To percolate; to pass through a filter.—**Filtrate**, fil'trāt, *v.t.*—*filtrated*, *filtrating*. [L.L. *filtro*, *filtratum*.] To filter.—*n.* The liquid which has been passed through a filter.—**Filtration**, fil-trā'shon, *n.* The act or process of filtering.

Filth, filth, *n.* [A.Sax. *fylth*, from *fúl*, foul. FOUL.] Anything that soils or defiles; dirt; foul matter; nastiness; corruption; pollution.—**Filthily**, filth'i-li, *adv.* In a filthy manner; foully.—**Filthiness**, filth'i-nes, *n.* The state of being filthy; filth; foul matter; impurity.—**Filthy**, filth'i, *a.* Dirty; foul; unclean; nasty; morally impure; licentious.

Fimbriate, fim'bri-āt, *a.* [L. *fimbriæ*, threads, a fringe.] Fringed; having a sort of fringe or border; having the edge surrounded by fibres, hairs, or bristles.—*v.t.* To hem; to fringe.—**Fimbriated**, fim'-bri-ā-ted, *a.* Fimbriate.

Fimetarious, fī-mē-tā'ri-us, *a.* [L. *fimetum*, a dunghill, from *fimus*, dung.] *Bot.* growing on or amidst dung.

Fin, fin, *n.* [A.Sax. *fin*, *finn*, L.G. and Dan. *finne*, D. *vin*, Sw. *fena*; allied to L. *pinna*, *penna*, a feather.] One of the projecting wing-like organs which enable fishes to balance themselves in an upright position, and assist in regulating their movements in the water.—**Fin-footed**, *a.* Having palmated feet, or feet with toes connected by a membrane.—**Finless**, fin'les, *a.* Destitute of fins.—**Finned**, find, *a.* Having a fin or fins or anything resembling a fin.—**Finner, Finback**, fin'ėr, fin'bak, *n.* A name given to several whales from their possessing a dorsal hump or fin.—**Finny**, fin'i, *a.* Furnished with fins; relating to or abounding with fins.—**Fin-pike**, *n.* A name of certain ganoid fishes, the long dorsal fin of which is separated into twelve or sixteen strong spines.—**Fin-spine**, *n.* A spine-shaped ray in the fin of a fish.—**Fin-spined**, *a.* Having spiny fins; acanthopterygious.

Finable. Under FINE, *a.* and *n.*

Final, fī'nal, *a.* [L. *finalis*, from *finis*, end; seen also in *fine*, adj. and noun, *confine*, *define*, *affinity*, *finance*, *finish*, &c.] Pertaining to the end or conclusion; last; ultimate; conclusive; decisive; respecting a purpose or ultimate end in view (a *final* cause).—**Finale**, fē-nä'lā, *n.* [It.] *Mus.* the last part of a concerted piece, sonata, symphony, or opera; hence, the last part, piece, or scene in any public performance or exhibition.—**Finality**, fi-nal'i-ti, *n.* The state of being final; *philos.* the doctrine that nothing exists or was made except for a determinate end.—**Finally**, fī'nal-li, *adv.* At the end or conclusion; ultimately; lastly; completely; beyond recovery.—**Finals**, fī'nals, *n.* The last deciding heat in a game; final or last, opposed to entrance, examinations.

Finance, fi-nans', *n.* [Fr., from L.L. *financia*, a money payment, from *finare*, to pay a fine, from L. *finis*, in late sense of a sum paid in final settlement of a claim. FINE, *n.*] The system or science of public revenue and expenditure; *pl.* funds in the public treasury, or accruing to it; public resources of money; also the income or pecuniary resources of individuals.—*v.i.* To conduct financial operations.—**Financial**, fi-nan'-shal, *a.* Pertaining to finance or public revenue; having to do with money matters.—**Financialist**, fi-nan'shal-ist, *n.* One skilled in financial matters; a financier.—**Financially**, fi-nan'shal-li, *adv.* In relation to finances or public funds.—**Financier**, fi-nan'sēr, *n.* One who is skilled in financial matters or in the principles or system of public revenue.

Finch, finsh, *n.* [A.Sax. *finc* = G. Dan. and Sw. *fink*, *finke*, D. *vink*; comp. W. *pinc*, a finch, Prov. E. and Sc. *pink*, *spink*.] The popular name given to a large family of small conirostral singing birds belonging to the insessorial order.

Find, fīnd, *v.t.*—pret. and pp. *found*. [A.Sax. *findan*, to find = D. *vinden*, G. *finden*, Dan. *finde*, Icel. *finna* (for *finda*), Goth. *finthan*, to find. From same root as in L. *peto*, to aim at, to seek.] To discover; to gain first sight or knowledge of (something lost); to recover; to get; to meet; to come or light upon; to gain, acquire, or procure (leisure, happiness); to supply, provide, or furnish (to *find* money for a purpose); to catch; to detect; *law*, to determine and declare by verdict.—*To find one's self*, to fare in regard to ease or pain, health or sickness; to provide one's necessaries at one's own expense.—*To find one in* (something), to supply, furnish, or provide one with (something).—*To find out*, to detect; to discover, as something before unknown, a mystery, secret, trick, &c.; to solve.—*To find fault with*, to censure.—*v.i.* *Law*, to give judgment on the merits or facts of a case.—*n.* A discovery of anything valuable; the thing found.—**Findable**, fīn'da-bl, *a.* Capable of being found.—**Finder**, fīn'dėr, *n.* One who or that which finds; *astron.* a smaller telescope attached to a larger, for the purpose of finding an object more readily.—**Finding**, fīn'ding, *n.* Discovery; that which is found; *law*, the return of a jury to a bill; a verdict.

Fin-de-siecle, fan-de-sē-ekl', *a.* [Fr. end of century.] Affected, decadent tone in art or life.

Fine, fīn, *a.* [Fr. *fin*, fine, delicate, &c.; G. *fein*, D. *fijn*, Dan. *fiin*, Sw. *fin*, Icel. *finn*, from L. *finitus*, finished, perfect, pp. of *finio*, to finish, from *finis*, an end. FINAL.] Slender; minute; very small; of very small diameter; not coarse; in very small grains or particles; thin; keen; sharp; made of fine threads or material; delicate; pure; of excellent quality; refined; elegant; perceiving or discerning minute beauties or deformities (*fine* taste); handsome; beautiful; accomplished (a *fine* gentleman); elegant; showy; splendid; free from clouds or rain; sunshiny (*fine* weather); finically or affectedly elegant; aiming too much at show or effect.—*Fine arts*, the arts which depend chiefly on the labours of the mind or imagination, generally restricted to the imitative arts which appeal to us through the eye, such as painting and sculpture.—*v.t.*—*fined*, *fining*. To refine; to purify; to free from foreign matter.—**Finable**, fī'na-bl, *a.* Capable of being refined or purified.—**Finer**, fī'nėr, *n.* One who refines or purifies. (O.T.)—**Fining**, fī'ning, *n.* The process of refining or purifying; the clarifying of wines, malt liquors, &c.; the preparation used to fine or clarify.—**Fining-pot**, *n.* A vessel in which metals are refined.—**Finedraw**, fīn'dra, *v.t.* To sew up with so much nicety that the rent is not perceived. — **Finedrawn**, fīn′dran, *a.* Drawn out to too great a degree of fineness or tenuity; drawn out with too much subtlety.—**Fine-fingered**, *a.* Nice in workmanship; dexterous at fine work.—**Finely**, fīn′li, *adv.* In a fine or finished manner; admirably; beautifully; delicately.—**Fineness**, fīn′nes, *n.* The state or quality of being fine.—**Finery**, fī′nėr-i, *n.* Fineness; ornament; showy or excessive decoration; the forge in iron-works at which the iron is hammered into what is called a bloom or square bar.—**Finespoken**, fīn′spō-kn, *a.* Using fine phrases.—**Finespun**, fīn′spun, *a.* Drawn to a fine thread; minute, hence, over-refined; over-elaborated; subtile.

Fine, fīn, *n.* [From L. *finis*, an end, and in later times and in a feudal sense, a final settlement of a claim by composition or agreement. FINANCE, FINAL.] A payment of money imposed upon a person as a punishment for an offence.—*In fine*, in conclusion; to conclude; to sum up all.—*v.t.*—*fined, fining.* To set a fine on by judgment of a court; to punish by fine.—**Finable**, fī′na-bl, *a.* Admitting of a fine; capable of being subjected to a fine or penalty.

Finesse, fi-nes′, *n.* [Fr., lit. fineness.] Artifice; stratagem; subtlety of contrivance to gain a point.—*v.i.* To use finesse.

Fingent,† fin′jent, *a.* [L. *fingo*, to make, to form. FEIGN.] Making; forming; fashioning.

Finger, fing′gėr, *n.* [A.Sax. *finger* = D. *vinger*, G. Sw. and Dan. *finger*, Goth. *figgrs*; same root as in *fang*.] One of the five extreme members of the hand or any of them but the thumb; a digit; something resembling or serving the purpose of a finger; an index.—*To have a finger in*, to be concerned in.—*To have at one's finger ends*, to be quite familiar with; to be able to make available readily.—*v.t.* To touch with the fingers; to handle; to toy or meddle with; to touch or take thievishly; to apply the fingers to in order to produce musical effects.—*v.i.* To use the fingers in playing on an instrument.—**Finger-alphabet**, *n.* Certain positions and motions of the hands and fingers answering to the common written alphabet, and used by deaf-mutes. —**Finger-and-toe**, *n.* A disease in turnips.—**Finger-board**, *n.* The board at the neck of a violin, guitar, or the like, where the fingers act on the strings; also the whole range of keys of a piano, organ, &c.; a key-board.—**Fingered**, fing′gėrd, *pp.* or *a.* Having fingers; *bot.* digitate; having leaflets like fingers; *mus.* touched or played on; produced by pressing the finger on a particular key, string, or hole. — **Fingerer**, fing′gėr-ėr, *n.* One who fingers or handles; a pilferer.—**Finger-glass**, *n.* A glass introduced at table in which to rinse the fingers after dinner. — **Fingering**, fing′gėr-ing, *n.* The act of touching lightly or handling; *mus.* the management of the fingers in playing on an instrument of music; the marking of the notes of a piece of music to guide the fingers in playing; a thick loose worsted used for knitting stockings. — **Finger-plate**, *n.* A plate fixed on the edge of a door where the handle is.—**Finger-post**, *n.* A post set up to guide travellers, generally where roads cross or divide.—**Finger-print**, *n.* An impression made by fingers, often serving to identify the person.—**Finger-stall**, *n.* A cover of leather, &c., for protection of a finger when injured.

Finial, fin′i-al, *n.* [From L. *finio*, to finish. FINAL.] The ornamental termination of a pinnacle, canopy, gable, or the like.

Finical, fin′i-kal, *a.* [From *fine*.] Affecting great nicety or elegance; overnice; unduly particular about trifles.—**Finicality**, fin-i-kal′i-ti, *n.* State of being finical; something finical.—**Finically**, fin′i-kal-li, *adv.* In a finical manner.—**Finicalness**, fin′i-kal-nes, *n.* Quality of being finical.—**Finicking**, **Finicky**, fin′i-king, fin′i-kē, *a.* [Equivalent to *finical*.] Precise in trifles; idly busy.

Finis, fī′nis, *n.* [L.] An end; conclusion: often placed at the end of a book.

Finish, fin′ish, *v.t.* [Fr. *finir*, ppr. *finissant*, from L. *finio*, *finitum*, to finish, from *finis*, end. FINAL.] To bring to an end; to make an end of; to arrive at the end of; to bestow the last required labour upon; to perfect; to polish to a high degree; to elaborate carefully.—*v.i.* To come to an end; to terminate; to expire.—*n.* The last touch to a work; polish; careful elaboration; a name for methylated spirit.—**Finished**, fin′isht, *p.* and *a.* Polished to the highest degree of excellence; complete; perfect.—**Finisher**, fin′ish-ėr, *n.* One who finishes; something that gives the finishing touch to or settles anything (*colloq.*).

Finite, fī′nīt, *a.* [L. *finitus*, from *finio*, to finish, from *finis*, limit. FINAL.] Having a limit; limited; bounded: opposed to *infinite*; *gram.* a term applied to those moods of a verb which are limited by number and person, as the indicative, subjunctive, and imperative.—**Finitely**, fī′nīt-li, *adv.* In a finite manner; limitedly; to a certain degree only. — **Finiteness**, fī′nīt-nes, *n.* State of being finite.—**Finitude**, fin′i-tūd, *n.* State of being finite; limitation.

Finn, fin, *n.* A native of Finland, or person of the same race.—**Finnish**, fin′ish, *a.* Relating to the Finns or Finland.—*n.* A language, allied to the Turkish and Hungarian, spoken by the Finns.

Finnan Haddie, fin′an had′ē, *n.* A split and cured haddock.

Finsen light, fin′sen, *n.* [From *Finsen*, a Danish physician.] A powerful arc lamp used in treatment of skin diseases.

Fiord, Fjord, fyord, *n.* [Dan. *fiord*; Icel. *fjörthr*. FIRTH.] An inlet from the sea, usually long, narrow, and very irregularly shaped, such as are common on the coast of Norway.

Florin, fī′o-rin, *n.* [Comp. Ir. *fiothran*, Gael. *feur*, grass.] A species of creeping bent grass (*Agrostis vulgaris*), not of agricultural value.

Fir, fėr, *n.* [A.Sax. *furh* = Icel. Sw. *fura*, Dan. *fyr*, *fyrre*, G. *föhre*. *Fir* represents an ancient word, which appears in L. as *quercus*, an oak, and probably meant originally tree in general.] A general name for several species of coniferous trees, sometimes used as co-extensive with the term pine (Pinus), but often restricted to trees of the section Abies, which differ from the true pines in their leaves growing singly on the stem, and the scales of the cones being smooth, round, and thin.—**Firry**, fėr′i, *a.* Of or pertaining to firs; consisting of fir; abounding in firs.

Fire, fīr, *n.* [A.Sax. *fyr* = Icel. *fyri*, Dan. and Sw. *fyr*, G. *feuer*, fire; cog. Gr. *pyr*, fire; allied to Skr. *pu*, to purify, as fire is the great purifying element.] The evolution of heat and light during combustion; fuel in combustion; the burning of a house or town; a conflagration; the discharge of a number of firearms; a spark from hot iron accidentally lodged in the eye; light; lustre; splendour; ardour of passion, whether of love, hate, anger, &c.; consuming violence of temper; liveliness of imagination; vigour of fancy; animation; vivacity; force of sentiment or expression.—*On fire*, ignited; burning; hence, *fig.* eager; ardent.—*St. Anthony's fire*, erysipelas.—*v.t.*—*fired, firing.* To set on fire; to kindle; to inflame or irritate; to animate; to give life or spirit to; to cause to explode; to discharge (a gun, a shot).—*v.i.* To take fire; to be irritated or inflamed with passion; to discharge artillery or firearms. — *To fire away*, to begin; to go on. (*Colloq.*)—*Fire-out*, to discharge or expel from office. —*To fire up*, to become irritated or angry; to fly into a passion. (*Colloq.*)—**Fiery**, fī′ėr-i, *a.* Consisting of fire; burning; flaming; blazing; highly inflammable; hot; ardent; vehement; impetuous; passionate; irritable; fierce; like fire; bright; glaring.—*Fiery cross*, a light wooden cross, the extremities of which were set fire to and then extinguished in blood; used in ancient times in Scotland as a signal to assemble under arms.—**Fierily**, fī′ėr-i-li, *adv.* In a fiery manner. — **Fieriness**, fī′ėr-i-nes, *n.* The state or quality of being fiery.—**Fireless**, fīr′les, *a.* Destitute of fire.—**Firer**, fī′rėr, *n.* One who fires or sets on fire.—**Firing**, fī′ring, *n.* The act of discharging firearms; a setting on fire; material for burning; fuel.—**Fire-alarm**, *n.* An apparatus for instantaneously communicating information of fire, as by telegraphic signal.—**Firearm**, fīr′ärm, *n.* A weapon whose charge is expelled by the combustion of powder, as cannon, pistols, muskets, &c.—**Fireball**, fīr′bal, *n.* A ball filled with combustibles to be thrown among enemies; a meteor having the appearance of a globular mass of light.—**Fire-balloon**, *n.* A balloon sent up through the buoyancy of air rarefied by means of a fire in connection with it.—**Fire-blast**, *n.* A disease in hops, in which they appear as if burned by fire.—**Fire-box**, *n.* The box (generally made of copper) in which the fire in a locomotive is placed.—**Firebrand**, fīr′brand, *n.* A piece of wood kindled; an incendiary; one who inflames factions, or causes contention and mischief. — **Fire-brick**, *n.* A brick of clay that will sustain intense heat without fusion.—**Fire-brigade**, *n.* A body of firemen organized to work in extinguishing fires in towns.—**Fire-bucket**, *n.* A bucket to convey water for extinguishing fire.—**Fire-bug**, *n.* An arsonist.—**Fire-clay**, *n.* A kind of clay capable of sustaining intense heat, and used in making fire-bricks, gas-retorts, crucibles, &c.—**Fire-cock**, *n.* A cock to let out water for extinguishing fire.—**Fire-control**, kon-trōl′, *n.* The system of controlling and directing the fire from the guns of a war-vessel, a highly scientific operation.—**Fire-cracker**, *n.* A firework consisting of a paper cylinder inclosing powder, through which a fuse is passed, and exploding with a sharp report when ignited.—**Fire-damp**, *n.* Light carburetted hydrogen gas, sometimes very abundantly evolved in coal-mines, and productive of the most dreadful results when brought into contact with a naked flame, being highly explosive.—**Fire-dog**, *n.* An andiron.—**Fire-eater**, *n.* A juggler who pretends to eat fire; a fighting character or duellist; a fireman (*Colloq.*).—**Fire-engine**, *n.* An engine, acting on the force-pump principle, for throwing jets of water to extinguish fire and save buildings.—**Fire-escape**, *n.* An apparatus for escaping from the upper part of a building when on fire; a common form consisting of an arrangement of long ladders capable of being drawn out after the manner of a telescope. —**Firefly**, fīr′flī, *n.* A name for any winged insect which possesses much luminosity.—**Fire-guard**, *n.* A framework of iron wire, to be placed in front of a fireplace to protect against fire.—**Fire-irons**, *n. pl.* Poker, tongs, and shovel.—**Fire-light, Fire-lighter**, *n.* A composition of very inflammable material, as pitch and sawdust, for lighting fires.—**Firelock**, fīr′lok, *n.* A musket or other gun with a lock furnished with a flint and steel.—**Fire-main**, *n.* A pipe for water, to be employed in case of conflagration.—**Fireman**, fīr′man, *n.* A man whose business is to extinguish fires in towns; a member of a fire-brigade; a man employed in tending fires, as of a steam-engine.—**Fire-pan**, *n.* A pan for holding or conveying fire.—**Fireplace**, fīr′plās, *n.* The lower part of a chimney which opens into an apartment. and in which fuel is burned; a hearth.—**Fire-plug**, *n.* A plug for drawing water from the pipes in the street to extinguish fire.—**Fire-pot**, *n.* A small earthen pot filled with combustibles, used in military operations.—**Fireproof**, fīr′pröf, *a.* Proof against fire; incombustible; rendered incombustible by some process.—**Fire-screen**, *n.* A kind of movable screen placed before a fire to intercept the heat. —**Fire-ship**, *n.* A vessel filled with combustibles to be set on fire for burning an enemy's ships.—**Fireside**, fīr′sīd, *n.* The side of the fireplace; the hearth; home: often used adjectively.—**Fire-stone**, fīr′stōn, *n.* Any kind of stone which resists the action of fire.—**Fire-**

unit, ū'nit, *n.* Any number of men firing at the command of one, the normal fire-unit being the section. See *Battery*.—**Fire-weed**, *n.* A plant which appears abundantly on land over which a fire has passed. —**Firewood**, fīr'wụd, *n.* Wood for fuel.—**Firework**, fīr'wėrk, *n.* A preparation of gunpowder, sulphur, and other inflammable materials to be let off for the purpose of making a show.—**Fire-worship**, *n.* The worship of fire, the highest type being the adoration of the sun, a species of worship practiced by the ancient Persians or Magians, and continued by the modern Parsees.—**Firing-tube**, fī'ring-tūb, *n.* A tube containing an explosive which when fired ignites the cordite with which a gun is loaded.

Firkin, fėr'kin, *n.* [From *four*, with dim. suffix *-kin*, being the fourth of a barrel.] An old measure of capacity equal to 7½ gallons; a small wooden vessel or cask.

Firlot, fėr'lot, *n.* [From *four*, and *lot*, part.] A former dry measure used in Scotland equal to the fourth part of a boll.

Firm, fėrm, *a.* [L. *firmus*, firm, seen also in *affirm, confirm, firmament, farm*.] Closely compressed; compact; hard; solid; fixed; steady; constant; stable; unshaken in purpose or will; resolute in mind; not easily moved; not giving way.—*n.* [Originally a signature by which a writing was *firmed* or rendered valid.] A partnership or association of two or more persons for carrying on a business; a commercial house; the name or title under which a company transact business.—*v.t.* To make firm or solid; to solidify.—*v.i.* To become firm or solid.—**Firmly**, fėrm'li, *adv.* In a firm manner. —**Firmness**, fėrm'nes, *n.* The state or quality of being firm; compactness; solidity; stability; steadfastness; resolution.—**Firmament**, fėr'ma-ment, *n.* [L. *firmamentum*, from *firmo, firmatum*, to make firm.] The region of the air; the sky or heavens.

Firman, fėr'man or fėr-män', *n.* [Per. *fermān, farmān*, a decree.] A decree, order, or grant of an Oriental sovereign, as of Turkey, &c., issued for various special purposes; a licence or grant of privileges.

First, fėrst, *a.* [A superlative, of which *fore* may be regarded as the positive. A. Sax. *fyrst*, first, most to the fore. FORE.] The ordinal of *one*; preceding all others in a series; advanced before or further than any other in progression; foremost in place; preceding all others in time, rank, dignity, or excellence.—*First floor*, the floor or story of a house next above the ground-floor.—*adv.* Before all others in place, progression, rank, order of time, &c.—*At first, at the first*, at the beginning or origin.—*First and last*, within the whole time or period; altogether.—*First or last*, at one time or another.—**Firstling**, fėrst'ling, *n.* The first produce or offspring of a beast.—**Firstly**, fėrst'li, *adv.* In the first place; first.—**First-born**, *a.* First brought forth; eldest. —**First-class**, *a.* First-rate; of the highest excellence or quality. (*Colloq.*)—**First-foot**, fėrst'fụt, *n.* In Scotland, the person who first enters a dwelling-house after the coming in of the new year.—*v.t.* To pay the first visit in the new year.—**First-fruit, First-fruits**, *n.* The fruit or produce first matured and collected in any season; the first profits of anything; the first or earliest effect of anything, in a good or bad sense.—**First-hand**, *a.* Obtained direct from the first source; obtained direct from the producer, maker, &c.—*At first-hand*, directly; without the intervention of an agent.—**First-rate**, *a.* Of the first class or rate; of the highest excellence.—*n.* A war-ship of the first or most powerful class.—**First-water**, *n.* The first or highest quality; purest lustre: applied principally to diamonds and pearls.

Firth, fėrth, *n.* [From Icel. *fjörthr*, Dan. *fiord*, N. *fjord*, a firth; same root as *fare, ferry*.] A name given to several estuaries or bays into which rivers discharge themselves in Scotland; a channel or arm of the sea (the Pentland *Firth*): written also *Frith*.

Fiscal, fis'kal, *a.* [From L. *fiscus*, the state treasury.] Pertaining to the public treasury or revenue; financial.—*Fiscal year* the twelve months for which a complete financial accounting is made.

Fish, fish, *n.* pl. **Fishes**, fish'ez, instead of which the sing. is often used collectively. [A.Sax. *fisc* = Icel. *fiskr*, Dan. and Sw. *fisk*, D. *visch*, G. *fisch*, Goth. *fisks*; cog. L. *piscis*, W. *pysg*, Gael. and Ir. *iasg*, fish.] A vertebrate animal that lives in water, breathes by gills, and has cold blood, with limbs in the form of fins; popularly applied also to whales and various other marine animals; a contemptuous or familiar term for a person (in such phrases as, a queer or strange *fish*; a loose *fish*); the flesh of fish used as food; *naut.* a purchase used to raise the flukes of an anchor up to the gunwale.—*Neither flesh nor fish*, neither one thing nor another; having no decided character or qualities; nondescript.—*v.i.* To employ one's self in catching fish; to endeavor to take fish by a rod and line or other means; to seek to obtain by artifice, or indirectly (to *fish* for compliments).—*v.t.* To catch or attempt to catch fish; to draw out or up, especially when in water, to search by dragging, raking, or sweeping; to strengthen or unite by a piece that extends on both sides of a joint or a crack.—**Fish-beam**, *n.* A beam which bellies out usually on the under side.—**Fish-cake**, *n.* A small ball of shredded fish, as codfish, mixed with potato, seasoned, and fried.—**Fish-carver**, *n.* A broad knife, generally of silver, for carving fish at table: a fish-slice.—**Fisher**, fish'ėr, *n.* One who fishes; one employed in catching fish.—**Fisherman**, fish'ėr-man, *n.* One whose occupation is to catch fish.—**Fishery**, fish'ėr-i, *n.* The business of catching fish; a place where fish are regularly caught, or other products of the sea or rivers are taken from the water.—**Fish-garth**, *n.* A garth or weir for the taking and retaining of fish.—**Fishgig, Fizgig**, fish'gig, fiz'gig, *n.* [From *fish*, and *gig*, a dart.] A kind of harpoon.—**Fish-glue**, *n.* Isinglass.—**Fish-guano**, *n.* Fish or fish-offal dried and used as manure.—**Fish-hook**, *n.* A hook for catching fish.—**Fishiness**, fish'i-nes, *n.* The state or quality of being fishy. —**Fishing**, fish'ing, *n.* The art or practice of catching fish.—*a.* Used or employed in fishery or by fishermen.—**Fishing-rod**, *n.* A long slender rod to which a line is fastened for angling.—**Fish-joint**, *n.* A railway contrivance for connecting two rails meeting end to end.—**Fish-kettle**, *n.* A kettle made long for boiling fish whole.—**Fish-knife**, *n.* A fish-carver or fish-slice.—**Fish-louse**, *n.* A name for several crustaceans parasitic on fishes.—**Fishmonger**, fish'mung-gėr, *n.* A seller of fish, a dealer in fish.—**Fish-oil**, *n.* Oil obtained from the bodies of fishes, whales, porpoises, &c.—**Fish-plate**, *n.* One of the plates composing a fish-joint in a rail. **Fish-salesman**, *n.* One who receives consignments of fish for sale, generally by auction, to retail dealers.—**Fish-sauce**, *n.* Sauce to be eaten with fish.—**Fish-slice**, *n.* Same as *Fish-carver*.—**Fish-strainer**, *n.* A utensil to drain the water from cooked fish.—**Fishtail**, fish'tāl, *a.* Shaped like a fish's tail.—*Fishtail burner*, a gas-burner whose jet takes the form of a fish's tail.—**Fish-torpedo**, *n.* A kind of torpedo or explosive apparatus for use under water, self-propelling and shaped like a fish.—**Fishy**, fish'i, *a.* Pertaining to fishes; consisting of fish; inhabited by fish; having the qualities of fish; as a slang term, worn out, as if by dissipation; seedy; applied to persons; equivocal; unsafe; unsound; applied to a project or speculation; dull; without luster (*fishy* eyes).

Fish, fish, *n.* [Fr. *fiche*, a dibble, a peg to mark distances.] A counter used in various games.

Fissile, fis'sil, *a.* [L. *fissilis*, from *findo, fissum*, to split or cleave, whence also *fissure*, the root being same as in E. *bite*.] Capable of being split in the direction of the grain (like wood), or in certain planes; readily splitting in flakes or plates.—**Fissilingual**, fis-i-ling'gwal, *a.* [L. *fissus*, cleft, *lingua*, tongue.] With the tongue cleft or forked, as in certain lizards.—**Fissility**, fis-sil'i-ti, *n.* The quality of being fissile.—**Fission**, fish'on, *n.* [L. *fissio*.] The act of cleaving, splitting, or breaking up into parts; *biol.* a species of reproduction or multiplication by means of a process of self-division seen in animals of a low type, the body becoming divided into two parts, each of which then becomes a separate and independent individual.—**Fissiparism, Fissiparity**, fis-sip'ar-izm, fis-si-par'i-ti, *n.* [L. *fissus*, split, and *pario*, to produce.] Reproduction by fission. —**Fissiparous**, fis-sip'a-rus, *a.* Reproducing by fission or spontaneous division.—**Fissiparously**, fis-sip'a-rus-li, *adv.* In a fissiparous manner.—**Fissipedes**, fis'si-pēds, *n.* [L. *fissus*, split, Gr. *pous, podos*, a foot.] Carnivorous mammals with separate digits.

Fissirostral, fis-si-ros'tral, *a.* [L. *findo, fissum*, to divide, and *rostrum*, a beak.] Belonging to the Fissirostres (fis-si-ros'trēz), a sub-order of insessorial birds characterized by a deeply-cleft bill, as swallows, goat suckers, &c., in which the gape is extended beneath the eyes.

Fissure, fish'ūr, *n.* [Fr., from L. *fissura*, from *findo*, to split. FISSILE.] A cleft; a crack; a narrow chasm made by the parting of any substance; a longitudinal opening.—*v.t.*—*fissured, fissuring*. To cleave or make a fissure in; to crack or fracture.

Fist, fist, *n.* [A.Sax. *fyst* = G. *faust*, D. *vuist*, Rus. *pjast*; same root as L. *pugnus*, Gr. *pygmē*, the fist.] The hand clenched; the hand with the fingers doubled into the palm.—*v.t.* To strike or gripe with the fist. (*Shak.*)—**Fistic**, fis'tik, *a.* Pertaining to boxing; pugilistic.—**Fisticuffs**, fis'ti-kufs, *n. pl.* Blows or a combat with the fists.—**Fisty**, fis'ti, *a.* Pertaining to the fist or fists, or to pugilism; fistic.

Fistula, fis'tū-la, *n.* [L., a pipe.] A musical pipe; *surg.* a channel excavated between an internal part (as the rectum) and the skin-surface, showing no tendency to heal, and generally arising from abscesses.—**Fistular**, fis'tū-lėr, *a.* Hollow, like a pipe or reed.—**Fistulose, Fistulous**, fis'tū-lōs, fis'tū-lus, *a.* Formed like a fistula; fistular.

Fit, fit, *n.* [Of doubtful origin; comp. A. Sax. *fit, fitt*, a song, a struggle, Icel. *fet*, a pace, a step.] A sudden effort, activity, or motion followed by an interval of relaxation; a temporary but violent mental affection or attack; a paroxysm; a temporary attack of a disease or pain; particularly a sudden and violent attack, accompanied with convulsions and loss of consciousness, as in hysteria, apoplexy, &c.—**Fitful**, fit'fụl, *n.* Full of fits; varied by paroxysms; spasmodic; varied by events; chequered.—**Fitfully**, fit'fụl-li, *adv.* In a fitful manner; by fits; at intervals.—**Fitfulness**, fit'fụl-nes, *n.* The state of being fitful; impulsiveness; waywardness.

Fit, fit, *a.* [Allied to Icel. *fitja*, to knit together, Goth. *fetjan*, to arrange, to adorn, E. *fettle*; or equivalent to *feat* (adj.), O.Fr. *feit*, L. *factum*, made.] Conformable to a standard of right, duty, taste, or propriety; of suitable kind; meet; becoming; appropriate; adapted to an end, object, or design; suitable; qualified; competent; prepared; ready.—*v.t.*—*fitted, fitting*. To make fit or suitable; to bring into some required form; to adapt; to suit; to furnish or accommodate with anything; to prepare; to put in order for; to qualify; to be properly fitted for or adjusted to; to suit; to become.—*To fit out*, to furnish; to equip; to supply with necessaries or means.—*To fit up*, to furnish (a house, &c.) with things suitable; to make proper for the reception or use of any person.—*v.i.* To be proper or becoming; to be adjusted to the shape intended; to suit or be suitable; to be adapted.—*n.* Nice adjustment; adaptation.—**Fitly**, fit'li, *adv.* In a fit manner; suitably; properly.—**Fitness**, fit'nes, *n.* The state or quality of being fit; suitableness; adaptation; preparation; qualification.—**Fittedness**, fit'ed-nes, *n.* The state of being fitted.—**Fitter**, fit'ėr, *n.* One who fits; one who puts the parts of machinery together.—**Fitting**, fit'ing, *a.* Fit or appropriate; suitable; proper.—*n.* Something fitted on or attached as subsidiary to another thing.—**Fittingly**, fit'ing-li, *adv.* In a fitting manner; suitably.

Fitch, fich, *n.* [VETCH.] A chick-pea; a vetch; a kind of cummin; also a kind of bearded wheat or spelt. (O.T.)

Fitch, fich, *n.* [O.D. *vitsche*, O.Fr. *fissau*, a pole-cat; akin *foist*.] The pole-cat; also its fur.—**Fitchet, Fitcheu**, fich'et, fich'ū, *n.* The pole-cat.

Five, fīv, *a.* [A.Sax. *fīf*=Goth. *fimf*, Icel. *fimm*, Sw. and Dan. *fem*, D. *vijf*, G. *fünf*, Lith. *penki*, W. *pump*, Gael. *coig*, L. *quinque*, Gr. *pempe, pente*, Skr. *panchan*—five.] Four and one added; the half of ten.—*n.* The number which consists of four and one; the number of the fingers and thumb of one hand; a symbol representing this number.—**Fivefold**, fīv'fōld, *a.* Consisting of five in one; five times repeated; in fives.—**Fives**, fīvz, *n.* A kind of play with a ball, originally called hand-tennis: so named probably because the ball is struck with the hand or *five* fingers.

Fix, fiks, *v.t.* [Fr. *fixer*, from L. *figo, fixum*, to fasten, seen also in *affix, prefix, suffix*.] To make stable, firm, or fast; to set or place permanently; to establish firmly or immovably; to fasten; to attach firmly; to direct steadily, as the eye, the mind, the attention, &c.; to make solid; to congeal; to deprive of volatility; to stop or keep from moving.—*v.i.* To settle or remain permanently; to cease from wandering; to become firm, so as to resist volatilization; to cease to flow or be fluid; to congeal.—*n.* A condition of difficulty; dilemma. (*Colloq.*)—**Fixable**, fik'sa-bl, *a.* That may be fixed, established, or rendered firm.—**Fixation**, fik-sā'shon, *n.* The act of fixing; that process by which a gaseous body becomes fixed or solid.—**Fixed**, fikst, *pp.* or *a.* Settled; established; firm; fast; stable; not volatile or easily volatilized.—*Fixed oils*, oils obtained by simple pressure and not readily volatilized.—*Fixed stars*, such stars as always retain the same apparent position and distance with respect to each other, and are thus distinguished from planets.—**Fixedly**, fik'sed-li, *adv.* In a fixed manner.—**Fixedness**, fik'sed-nes, *n.* A state of being fixed.—**Fixity**, fik'si-ti, *n.* State of being fixed; fixed character; fixedness; stability.—**Fixture**, fiks'tūr, *n.* Anything placed in a firm or fixed position; that which is fixed to a building; any appendage or part of the furniture of a house which is fixed to it, as by nails, screws, &c.

Fizgig, Fishgig. Under FISH.

Fizz, Fizzle, fiz, fiz'l, *v.i.* [Imitative.] To make a hissing sound.

Flabby, flab'i, *a.* [Akin to *flap*, and to G. *flabbe*, Sw. *flabb*, Dan. *flab*, hanging lips.] Soft and yielding to the touch; easily moved or shaken; hanging loose by its own weight; flaccid: said especially of flesh.—**Flabbily**, flab'i-li, *adv.* In a flabby manner.—**Flabbiness**, flab'i-nes, *n.* State of being flabby.

Flabellum, fla-bel'lum, *n.* [L.] A fan; specifically, an ecclesiastical fan anciently used to drive away flies from the chalice during the eucharist.—**Flabellate, Flabelliform**, fla-bel'lāt, fla-bel'li-form, *a.* Fan-shaped.

Flaccid, flak'sid, *a.* [L. *flaccidus*, from *flaccus*, flabby; comp. W. *llac*, slack, loose; Ir. *fluich*, flabby.] Soft and weak; limber; lax; drooping; hanging down by its own weight.—**Flaccidly**, flak'sid-li, *adv.* In a flaccid manner.—**Flaccidness, Flaccidity**, flak'sid-nes, flak-sid'i-ti, *n.* The state of being flaccid.

Flag, flag, *n.* [Not found in A.Sax.; same as D. *vlag*, Sw. *flagg, flagga*, Dan. *flag*, G. *flagge*, banner; connected with *flag*, to hang loose.] A cloth, usually bearing emblems or figures, borne on a staff, and employed to distinguish one party or nationality from another; a standard on which are certain emblems expressive of nationality, party, or opinion; a banner.—*Black flag*, a flag of a black colour displayed on a piratical vessel as a sign that no mercy will be shown to the vanquished, or on a prison to indicate that an execution has taken place.—*White flag*, a flag of truce.—*Yellow flag*, flag as sign of infection or disease on board a vessel.—*Flag of truce*, a white flag displayed as an invitation to the enemy to confer, and in the meantime as a notification that the fighting shall cease.—*To strike* or *lower the flag*, to pull it down in token of respect or submission.—*To hang the flag half mast high*, to raise a flag halfway to the top of the mast or staff, as a token or signal of mourning.—**Flag-officer**, *n.* A general distinguishing title for an admiral of any grade; the commanding officer of a squadron.—**Flag-ship**, *n.* The ship which bears the flag-officer, and on which his flag is displayed.—**Flag-staff**, *n.* The staff or pole on which a flag is displayed. **Flag-wagger**, flag-wag'ėr, *n.* A signaller.

Flag, flag, *v.i.*—*flagged, flagging*. [Formerly written *flack*, and connected with Icel. *flaka*, to hang loosely, G. *flacken*, to become languid, O.D. *flaggeren*, to be loose; akin also *flicker*.] To hang loose without stiffness; to be loose and yielding; to grow spiritless or dejected; to droop; to grow languid; to grow stale or vapid; to loose interest or relish.—**Flaggingly**, flag'ing-li, *adv.* In a drooping or listless manner.

Flag, flag, *n.* [From Icel. *flaga*, a flag, Sw. *flaga*, a flake or scale; allied to L.G. *flage*, a flat marshy place, and Gr. *plax*, a tablet.] A flat stone used for paving.—*v.t.*—*flagged, flagging*. To lay with flags or flat stones.—**Flag-stone**, *n.* Any fissile sandstone that splits up into flags; a large flat paving-stone; a flag.

Flag, flag, *n.* [Probably named from its broad leaves resembling flags or standards.] A popular name for many endogenous plants with sword-shaped leaves, mostly growing in moist situations; particularly appropriated to a species of iris.—**Flaggy**, flag'i, *n.* Abounding in or resembling flags.

Flagellate, flaj'el-lāt, *v.t.* [L. *flagello, flagellatum*, to beat or whip, from *flagellum*, a whip, scourge, dim. of *flagram*, a whip, a scourge; akin *flail*.] To whip; to scourge.—**Flagellant**, flaj'el-lant, *n.* One who whips himself in religious discipline; specifically, one of a fanatical sect founded in Italy A.D. 1260, who maintained that flagellation was of equal virtue with baptism and other sacraments.—**Flagellation**, flaj-el-lā'shon, *n.* A flogging; the discipline of the scourge.—**Flagelliform**, fla-jel'li-form, *a.* [L. *flagelliformis*.] Long, narrow, and flexible, like the thong of a whip.—**Flagellum**, fla-jel'lum, *n.* pl. **Flagella**, fla-jel'la. *Bot.* a runner or creeping branch sent out from the bottom of a stem, as in the strawberry; *zool.* the lash-like appendage exhibited by many infusoria.

Flageolet, flaj'el-et, *n.* [Fr. *flageolet*, dim. of O.Fr. *flajol*, from L.L. *flauta, flautus*, flute. FLUTE.] A small wind-instrument of music, played by a mouthpiece inserted in the bulb-shaped head of the pipe, which is holed and keyed like the flute.

Flagitious, fla-jish'us, *a.* [L. *flagitiosus*, from *flagitium*, a shameful act, from *flagito*, to demand or urge hotly or violently, from root *flag*, whence *flagro*, to burn (as in *flagrant*).] Deeply criminal; grossly wicked; vicious; abandoned; profligate; heinous; flagrant.—**Flagitiously**, fla-jish'us-li, *adv.* In a flagitious manner.—**Flagitiousness**, fla-jish'us-nes, *n.* The condition or quality of being flagitious.

Flagon, flag'on, *n.* [Fr. *flacon, flascon*, L.L. *flasca*, a flask. FLASK.] A vessel with a narrow mouth, used for holding and conveying liquors.

Flagrant, flā'grant, *a.* [L. *flagrans, flagrantis*, ppr. of *flagro*, to burn (seen in *conflagration*), the root being same as in *flamma*, flame, *flagitium*, a flagitious act.] Flaming into notice; glaring; notorious; enormous.—**Flagrantly**, flā'grant-li, *adv.* In a flagrant manner.—**Flagrancy**, flā'gran-si, *n.* The quality of being fragrant; heinousness; enormity.

Flail, flāl, *n.* [O.Fr. *flael, flaiel, flaial*, from L. *flagellum*, a whip or scourge, whence also *flagellate*.] An instrument for thrashing or beating grain from the ear, consisting of the hand-staff, which is held in the hand; the swiple, which strikes the corn; and a thong which connects the two.

Flake, flāk, *n.* [Allied to Icel. *flakna*, to flake off, *flyka*, a flake; E. *flag*, a stone for paving, and *flaw*; Sw. *flaga*, a flake.] A loose filmy or scale-like mass of anything; a scale; a small fleecy or feathery particle; a flock.—*v.i.*—*flaked, flaking*. To break or separate in layers; to peel or scale off.—**Flaky**, flā'ki, *a.* Consisting of flakes or small loose masses; lying in flakes or layers; flake-like.—**Flakiness**, flā'ki-nes, *n.* The state of being flaky.—**Flake-white**, *n.* The purest white-lead, a fine white pigment in the form of scales or flakes.

Flambeau, flam'bō, *n.* pl. **Flambeaux**, flam'bōz. [Fr., from *flambe*, a blaze, for *flamble*, from L. *flammula*, dim. of *flamma*, a flame.] A flaming torch; a light made of thick wicks covered with wax or other inflammable material.—**Flamboyant**, flam-boi'ant, *a.* [Fr., flaming.] A term applied to that style of Gothic architecture whose chief characteristic is a wavy flame-like tracery in the windows.

Flame, flām, *n.* [Fr. *flamme*, from L. *flamma*, a flame, for *flagma*, from the root *flag*, whence *flagro*, to burn, to blaze, as in *flagrant, conflagration*; root also in Gr. *phlegō*, to burn.] A blaze; burning vapour or gas rising from matter in a state of visible combustion; fire in general; heat of passion; violent contention; passionate excitement or strife; a state of ardour; warmth of affection; the passion of love; one beloved.—*v.i.*—*flamed, flaming*. To blaze; to send out a flame or blaze; to shine like burning gas or any other luminous body; to break out in violence of passion.—**Flaming**, flā'-ming, *a.* Of a bright red or yellow colour; burning; ardent; violent; vehement.—**Flamingly**, flā'ming-li, *adv.* In a flaming manner.—**Flamy**, flā'mi, *a.* Pertaining to, consisting of, or like flame.

Flamen, flā'men, *n.* [L.] The name in ancient Rome for any priest devoted to the service of one particular deity.—**Flamineous, Flaminical**, fla-min'ē-us, fla-min'i-kal, *a.* Pertaining to a flamen.

Flamingo, fla-ming'gō, *n.* [Sp. and Pg. *flamenco*, from L. *flamma*, flame, from its red colour.] A web-footed tropical bird, with long neck and long slender legs, standing from 5 to 6 feet high, and having scarlet plumage.

Flanch, flanch, *n.* Same as *Flange*.

Flaneur, flä-nėr, *n.* [Fr., from *flâner*, to saunter about.] A lounger; a gossiper.

Flange, flanj, *n.* [A form of *flank*.] A projecting edge or rim on any object, as the rims by which cast-iron pipes are connected together, or those round the wheels of railway-carriages to keep them on the rails.—*v.t.*—*flanged, flanging*. To furnish with a flange; to make a flange on.

Flank, flangk, *n.* [Fr. *flanc*, Sp. and Pg. *flanco*, It. *fianco*, the flank; of Germanic origin ultimately, same as O.H.G. *hlanca*, side, loin, flank; akin G. *gelenk*, joint.] The fleshy or muscular part of the side of an animal, between the ribs and the hip; the side of anything, particularly the extreme right or left of an army, brigade, regiment, &c., the outer ships of a fleet, or the place occupied by such forces; any part of a fortified work defending another work by a fire along its face.—*v.t.* To stand or be at the flank or side of; to place troops so as to command or attack the flank of, to pass round or turn the flank of.—**Flanker**, flangk'ėr, *n.* One who or that which flanks; one employed on the flank of an army.

Flannel, flan'el, *n.* [O.E. and Sc. *flannen*, from W. *gwlanen*, from *gwlan*, wool.] A soft nappy woollen cloth of loose texture, used for articles of underclothing, &c.—**Flanneled**, flan'eld, *a.* Covered with or wrapped in flannel.—**Flannelette**, flan-el-et', *n.* A cotton cloth with a soft nap.

Flap, flap, *n.* [Probably onomatopoetic, being imitative of a blow with a pliant flat surface; *flabby* is a kindred form.] Anything broad and flexible that hangs loose or is attached by one end or side and easily moved; a lappet, a lobe, a skirt or tail of a coat; the motion of anything broad and loose, or a stroke with it.—*v.t.*—*flapped, flapping.* To beat with or as with a flap; to move, as something broad or flap-like.—*v.i.* To move as wings, or as something broad or loose; to wave loosely or flutter. —**Flap-dragon**, *n.* A play in which the players snatch raisins out of burning brandy; snap-dragon.—**Flap-eared**, *a.* Having broad loose ears. (*Shak.*)—**Flap-jack**, *n.* A sort of broad flat pancake; a fried cake; an apple-puff.—**Flap-mouthed**, *a.* Having loose hanging lips.—**Flapper**, flap'ėr, *n.* One who or that which flaps; a young wild duck; a young girl. (*Colloq.*)

Flare, flãr, *v.i.*—*flared, flaring.* [Comp. Dan. *flagre*, G. *flackern* (freq. of *flacken*), to flicker, to flare; perhaps akin to *flash.*] To waver or flutter in burning; to burn with an unsteady light; hence, to flutter with gaudy show; to shine out with sudden and unsteady light or splendour; to give out a dazzling light.—*To flare up*, to become suddenly angry or excited.—*n.* A bright unsteady light.—**Flare-spot**, flãr'spot, *n.* A bright patch in the middle of a photographic print, caused by reflection from the lenses.—**Flaringly**, flã'ring-li, *adv.* Flutteringly; showily.

Flash, flash, *n.* [Comp. Icel. *flasa*, to rush, *flas*, a rush; also E. *flare.*] A sudden burst of light; a flood of light instantaneously appearing and disappearing; a gleam; a sudden burst of something regarded as resembling light, as wit, merriment, passion, &c.; a short and brilliant burst; momentary brightness or show; the time occupied by a flash of light; an instant.—*v.i.* To break or burst forth with a flash or flame; to give out a flash or gleam; to break forth into some new and dazzling condition; to burst out violently; to come, appear, or pass suddenly; to dart (a thought *flashes* through the mind). —*v.t.* To emit or send forth in a sudden flash or flashes; to convey or send instantaneously or startlingly.—*a.* Vulgarly showy or gaudy; forged; counterfeit (*flash* notes). —**Flashy**, flash'i, *a.* Showy or gaudy; tawdry; impulsive; fiery.—**Flashily**, flash'i-li, *adv.* In a flashy manner.—**Flashiness**, flash'i-nes, *n.* The state of being flashy.—**Flashpoint**, flash'point, *n.* Temperature at which vapour from oil or gaseous objects ignites.

Flask, flask, *n.* [A.Sax. *flasc, flasca, flaxa*, Dan. *flaske*, Sw. *flasca*; ultimate origin doubtful; comp. O.Fr. *flasche, flascon*; Sp. *flasco*, It. *fiasco*, L.L. *flasco, flasca*, a flask; L. *vasculum*, dim. of *vas*, a vessel; also W. *fflasg*, a vessel of wicker-work, a basket.] A kind of bottle; a narrow-necked globular glass bottle; a metal or other pocket dram-bottle; a vessel for containing gun-powder, carried by sportsmen.—**Flasket**, flas'ket, *n.* A vessel in which viands are served up; a long shallow basket.

Flat, flat, *a.* [Not in A.Sax.=Icel. *flatr*, Sw. *flat*, Dan. *flad*, G. *flach*, flat; akin Gr. *platys*, Skr. *prithus*, broad.] Having an even and horizontal, or nearly horizontal surface, without elevations or depressions, hills or valleys; level without inclination; level with the ground; prostrate; fallen; laid low; tasteless; stale; vapid; insipid; depressed; without interest, point, or spirit; frigid; dull; peremptory; absolute; positive; downright (a *flat* denial); *mus.* below the natural or the true pitch; not sharp or shrill; not acute; *gram.* applied to consonants, in the enunciation of which voice (in contradistinction to breath) is heard: opposed to *sharp*; as, *b, d, g, z, v.*—*n.* A flat surface; a surface without relief or prominences; a level; a plain; a low tract of land; a shoal; a shallow; a sand-bank under water; the flat part or side of anything (the *flat* of the hand, of a sword); *mus.* a mark (♭) placed on a line or in a space of the staff, which indicates that all notes on the same degree (or their octaves) are lowered a semitone; a story or floor of a building; a foolish fellow; a simpleton; one of the halves of such stage scenes or parts of scenes as are formed by two equal portions pushed from the sides of the stage and meeting in the centre.—*v.t.* and *i.*—*flatted, flatting.* To flatten.—**Flat-fish**, *n.* One of those fish which have their body of a flattened form, swim on the side, and have both eyes on one side, as the flounder, turbot, and sole.—**Flat-iron**, *n.* An iron with a flat face for smoothing cloth.—**Flatly**, flat'li, *adv.* In a flat manner; horizontally; evenly; positively; plainly.—**Flatness**, flat'nes, *n.* State or quality of being flat (in all its senses).—**Flat-race**, *n.* A race over level or clear ground, as opposed to a *hurdle-race* or *steeple-chase.*—**Flatten**, flat'n, *v.t.* To make flat or level; to lay flat; *mus.* to lower in pitch; to render less acute or sharp.—*v.i.* To grow or become flat.—**Flatting**, *n.* A mode of house-painting, in which the paint, from its mixture with turpentine, leaves the work without gloss.—**Flattish**, flat'ish, *a.* Somewhat flat; approaching to flatness.—**Flatwise**, flat'wīz, *a.* or *adv.* With the flat side downward or next to another thing: opposed to *edgewise.*

Flatter, flat'ėr, *v.t.* [Fr. *flatter*, Pr. *flatar*, to pat, stroke, caress, flatter; perhaps from Icel. *flatr*, E. *flat*; comp. also Icel. *flathra*, to fawn or flatter, *flathr*, flattery.] To gratify by praise or obsequiousness; to please by applause, favourable notice, respectful attention, or anything that confirms one's good opinion of one's self; to encourage by favourable notice or by favourable representations or indications (to *flatter* hopes); to inspire with false hopes.—**Flatterer**, flat'ėr-ėr, *n.* One who flatters; one who praises another with a view to please him, to gain his favour, or to accomplish some purpose.—**Flatteringly**, flat'ėr-ing-li, *adv.* In a flattering manner.—**Flattery**, flat'ėr-i, *n.* [Fr. *flatterie.*] The act of one who flatters; false, insincere, or venal praise; adulation; cajolery.

Flatulent, flat'ū-lent, *a.* [L.L. *flatulentus*, from L. *flatus*, a blowing, from *flo*, *flatum*, to blow (as in *inflate*).] Affected with gases generated in the alimentary canal; generating or apt to generate wind in the stomach; windy.—**Flatulence**, **Flatulency**, flat'ū-lens, flat'ū-len-si, *n.* [L.L. *flatulentia.*] The state of being flatulent, or affected with an accumulation of gases in the alimentary canal.—**Flatulently**, flat'ū-lent-li, *adv.* In a flatulent manner.

Flaunt, fląnt, *v.i.* [Connected with prov. G. *flander*, a rag or tatter, *flandern*, to flutter, G. *flattern*, to flirt, to flutter.] To make an ostentatious display; to move or act ostentatiously; to be glaring or gaudy. —*v.t.* To display ostentatiously; to display impudently or offensively.—*n.* The act of flaunting; bold or impudent parade.—**Flaunter**, fląn'tėr, *n.* One who flaunts. —**Flauntingly**, fląn'ting-li, *adv.* In a flaunting way.—**Flaunty, Flaunting**, fląn'ti, fląn'ting, *a.* Ostentatious; vulgarly or offensively showy; gaudy.

Flautist, flą'tist, *n.* [It. *flauto*, a flute.] A player on the flute; a flutist.

Flavescent, fla-ves'ent, *a.* [L. *flavesco*, to become yellow, from *flavus*, yellow.] *Bot.* yellowish or turning yellow.—**Flavicomous**, fla-vik'o-mus, *a.* Having yellow hair.—**Flavin**, flav'in, *n.* A yellow dye of vegetable origin.

Flavor, flā'vėr, *n.* [From L.L. *flavor*, yellowness, the meaning of color being changed to that of taste or smell, from L. *flavus*, yellow.] The quality of any substance which affects the taste; that quality which gratifies the palate; relish; zest; the quality of a substance which affects the smell; odor; fragrance.—*v.t.* To communicate flavor or some quality of taste or smell to.—**Flavoring**, flā'vėr-ing, *n.* Any substance used for imparting flavor; seasoning.—**Flavorless**, flā'vėr-les, *a.* Without flavor; tasteless.—**Flavorous**, flā'vėr-us, *a.* Having a rich or pleasant flavor.

Flaw, flą, *n.* [A.Sax. *flóh*, that which has flown off, a fragment; Goth. *flaga*, a fragment; Sw. *flaga*, a flaw, *flaga sig*, to scale off, akin to *flake* and *flag*; comp. also W. *fflaw*, a splinter, *ffla*, a parting from.] A crack; a defect of continuity or cohesion; a gap or fissure; any blemish or imperfection; a defect; a fault; a sudden burst of wind; a sudden gust or blast of short duration.—*v.t.* To make or produce a flaw in.—**Flawless**, flą'les, *a.* Without flaw or defect.—**Flawy**, flą'i, *a.* Full of flaws; defective; faulty; subject to sudden gusts.

Flax, flaks, *n.* [A.Sax. *fleax* = D. *vlas*, Fris. *flax*, G. *flachs*, flax; allied to Bohem. *vlas*, Rus. *volos*, Lith. *plaukas*, hair, from a root meaning to comb, weave, or twist, seen in L. *plecto*, Gr. *plekō*, to weave or plait.] A wiry, erect-stemmed annual plant, the fibre of which is used for making linen thread and cloth, lace, &c.; the fibrous part of the plant when broken and cleaned by scutching and hackling.—**Flax-dresser**, *n.* One who breaks and scutches flax, and so prepares it for the spinner.—**Flaxen**, flak'sn, *a.* Made of flax; resembling flax; of the colour of flax; fair.—**Flax-mill**, *n.* A mill where flax is spun; a mill for the manufacture of linen goods.—**Flaxy**, flak'si, *a.* Like flax; flaxen.

Flay, flā, *v.t.* [A.Sax. *fleán*, to flay; O.D. *vlaegen, vlaen*, to flay; akin *flake, flaw.*] To skin; to strip off the skin of.—**Flayer**, flā'ėr, *n.* One who flays.

Flea, flē, *n.* [A.Sax. *fleá*, from *fleón*, *fleógan*, to fly; D. *vloo*, Icel. *fló*, Sc. *flech*, G. *floh*, a flea.] An insect remarkable for its agility and its very troublesome bite.—*A flea in the ear*, an annoying, unexpected hint or reply.—*v.t.* To clean from fleas.—**Fleabane**, flē'bān, *n.* A name popularly given to several composite plants from their supposed power of destroying or driving away fleas.—**Fleabite**, flē'bīt, *n.* The bite of a flea; a trifling wound or pain; a slight inconvenience; a thing of no moment.

Fleam, flēm, *n.* [D. *vlijm*, Fr. *flamme*, O.H.G. *fliedimâ*, from L.L. *flevotomum*, *flebotomum*, from Gr. *phlebs, phlebos*, a vein, and *tomos*, a cutting. PHLEBOTOMY.] A sharp instrument used by farriers for opening veins for letting blood; a lancet.

Flèche, flāsh, *n.* [Fr.] A slight field-work, with two faces forming an angle pointing forwards. A spire at the intersection of the nave and transepts of a church.

Fleck, flek, *n.* [Icel. *flekkr*, D. *vlek*, G. *fleck*, a spot; allied to *flick.*] A spot; a streak; a dapple; a stain.—*v.t.* To spot; to streak or stripe; to variegate; to dapple.—**Flecker**, flek'ėr, *v.t.* Same as *Fleck.*—**Fleckless**, flek'les, *a.* Spotless; blameless.

Flected, flek'ted, *p.* and *a.* [L. *flecto*, to bend.] Bent.—*Flected and reflected*, bowed or bent in a serpentine form like the letter S.—**Flection**, flek'shon, *n.* [L. *flectio.*] The act of bending or state of being bent; inflection.—**Flector**, flek'tėr, *n.* A flexor.

Fled, fled, pret. & pp. of *flee.*

Fledge, flej, *v.t.*—*fledged, fledging.* [Icel. *fleygr*, able to fly, from *fljúga*, to fly; comp. G. *flück, flügge*, feathered, from *fliegen*, to fly.] To furnish with feathers; to supply with the feathers necessary for flight; chiefly in pp.—**Fledgeling**, flej'ling, *n.* A young bird just fledged.

Flee, flē, *v.i.* pret. and pp. *fled*; ppr. *fleeing.* [A.Sax. *fleón*, to flee, *ic fleó*, I flee; akin to *fleógan*, to fly, Icel. *flýja*, Dan. *flye*, Sw. *fly*, G. *fliehen*, to flee. FLY.] To hasten or run away, as from danger or evil; to resort to shelter: sometimes apparently transitive, *from* being omitted before the object.

Fleece, flēs, *n.* [A.Sax. *fleós, flýs*, a fleece, wool = D. *vlies*, G. *fliess*; root meaning doubtful.] The coat of wool that covers a sheep or that is shorn from a sheep at one time; any covering resembling wool.—*Golden Fleece*, the object of the Argonauts under Jason.—*Order of Golden Fleece*, the Flemish and Spanish order, commemorating the wool trade of Flanders, a sheep suspended by ribbon from the neck.—*v.t.*—*fleeced, fleecing.* To deprive of the fleece; to strip of money or property; to rob or cheat heartlessly.—**Fleecer**, flē'sėr, *n.* One who fleeces or strips of money.—**Fleece-wool**, *n.* Wool that is shorn from the living sheep: opposed to *skin-wool*, from the skins of dead animals.—**Fleecy**, flē'si, *a.* Covered with wool; woolly; resembling wool or a fleece.

Fleer, flēr, *v.i.* [Comp. Dan. dial. *flire*, to laugh, to sneer, N. *flira*, to titter.] To make a wry face in contempt; to grin, sneer, mock, or gibe.—*v.t.* To mock; to flout at.—*n.* The act of one who fleers.—**Fleerer**, flē'rėr, *n.* One who fleers.

Fleet, flēt, *n.* [A.Sax. *fleót*, *fliét*, a ship, from *fleótan*, to float; akin D. *vloot*, G. *flotte*, fleet. FLOAT.] A body or squadron of ships; a number of ships in company, more especially ships of war; old London prison, from the ditch or stream of the Fleet, giving its name to Fleet Street, crossing it at right angles, and entering the city by the *fleet-gate, flood-gate, Ludgate.*—**Fleet captain**, *n.* In the United States navy, an officer temporarily appointed to act as chief of staff to the admiral commanding a fleet.—**Fleet Street**, *n.* Newspaper headquarters in London.

Fleet, flēt, *a.* [Icel. *fljótr*, A.Sax. *fleótig*, quick; allied to *flit*, and *float*. FLIT, FLOAT.] Swift of pace; moving or able to move with rapidity; nimble; light and quick in motion.—*v.i.* To fly swiftly; to hasten; to flit, as a light substance.—*v.t.* To skim over the surface; to pass over rapidly.—**Fleet-footed**, *a.* Swift of foot; running or able to run with rapidity.—**Fleeting**, flē'ting, *p.* and *a.* Passing rapidly; transient; not durable (the *fleeting* moments). ∴ Syn. under TRANSIENT.—**Fleetingly**, flē'ting-li, *adv.* In a fleeting manner.—**Fleetly**, flēt'li, *adv.* In a fleet manner; rapidly; swiftly.—**Fleetness**, flēt'nes, *n.* The quality of being fleet; swiftness; rapidity; velocity; celerity; speed.

Fleming, flem'ing, *n.* A native of Flanders.—**Flemish**, flem'ish, *a.* Pertaining to Flanders.—*n.* The language of the Flemings, closely akin to Dutch; *pl.* the people of Flanders.

Flense, flens, *v.t.*—*flensed, flensing.* [Dan. *flense*; D. *vlensen.*] To cut up and obtain the blubber of a whale.

Flesh, flesh, *n.* [A.Sax. *flaesc* = D. *vleesch*, G. *fleisch*, flesh; Icel. and Dan. *flesk*, bacon or pork; further connections are doubtful.] The substance which forms a large part of an animal, consisting of the softer solids, as distinguished from the bones, the skin, and the fluids; animal food, in distinction from vegetable; beasts and birds used as food, in distinction from fish; the body, as distinguished from the soul; the bodily frame; the human race; mankind; human nature; bodily appetite; kindred; family; the soft pulpy substance of fruit; also that part of a root, fruit, &c., which is fit to be eaten.—*Flesh and blood*, the entire body; man in his physical personality.—*v.t.* To initiate to the taste of flesh (as dogs used in hunting); to accustom to flesh; to imbrue a sword in blood for the first time.—**Flesh-color**, *n.* The color of human flesh.—**Flesh-colored**, *a.* Being of the color of flesh.—**Fleshed**, flesht, *p.* and *a.* Fat; fleshy; having flesh of a particular kind.—**Flesher**, flesh'ėr, *n.* A knife used for scraping flesh from hides.—**Flesh-fly**, *n.* Same as *Blow-fly.*—**Fleshful**, flesh'ful, *a.* Plump; abounding in flesh.—**Flesh-hook**, *n.* A hook to drag flesh from a pot or caldron. (O.T.)—**Fleshiness**, flesh'i-nes, *n.* State of being fleshy; plumpness; corpulence.—**Fleshing**, flesh'ing, *n.* [Generally in plural.] A kind of drawers worn by actors, dancers, &c., resembling the natural skin.—**Fleshless**, flesh'les, *a.* Destitute of flesh; lean.—**Fleshliness**, flesh'li-nes, *n.* State of being fleshly; carnal passions and appetites.—**Fleshly**, flesh'li, *a.* Pertaining to the flesh; corporeal; carnal; worldly; lascivious; human; not celestial; not spiritual or divine.—**Flesh-meat**, *n.* Animal food; the flesh of animals prepared or used for food.—**Fleshpot**, flesh'pot, *n.* A vessel in which flesh is cooked. (O.T.)—**Flesh-pots of Egypt.** (*Ex.* xvi. 3.) Symbol of a selfish, luxurious life.—**Flesh-tint**, *n.* *Painting*, a colour which best serves to represent that of the human body.—**Flesh-wound**, *n.* A wound which does not reach beyond the flesh.—**Fleshy**, flesh'i, *a.* Characterized by or consisting of flesh; full of flesh; plump; fat; corpulent; corporeal; human; pulpy, as fruit.

Fleur-de-lis, flėr-de-lē, *n.* [Fr., flower of the lily.] A heraldic figure representing either a lily or the head of a lance or some such weapon; the distinctive bearing of the kingdom of France; *bot.* the iris.

Flew, flū, pret. of *fly.*

Flex, fleks, *v.t.* [From L. *flecto, flexum*, to bend; seen also in *deflect, inflect, reflect*, &c.] To bend.—**Flexed**, flekst, *p.* and *a.* Bent; having a bent shape.—**Flexible**, flek'si-bl, *a.* [L. *flexibilis*, from *flecto, flexum.*] Capable of being flexed or bent; pliant; yielding to pressure; not stiff; capable of yielding to entreaties, arguments, or other moral force; manageable; tractable; easy and compliant; capable of being moulded into different forms or styles; plastic; capable of being adapted or accommodated.—**Flexibility, Flexibleness**, flek-si-bil'i-ti, flek'si-bl-nes, *n.* The quality of being flexible; pliancy; easiness to be persuaded; readiness to comply; facility.—**Flexibly**, flek'si-bli, *adv.* In a flexible manner.—**Flexile**, flek'sil, *a.* [L. *flexilis.*] Pliant; pliable; flexible.—**Flexion**, flek'shon, *n.* [L. *flexio.*] The act of bending; a bending; a part bent; *gram.* an inflection.—**Flexor**, flek'sėr, *n.* *Anat.* a muscle whose office is to produce flexion.—**Flexuous**, flek'sū-us, *a.* [L. *flexuosus.*] Winding or bending; having turns or windings; *bot.* changing its direction in a curve, from joint to joint, from bud to bud, or from flower to flower: in this sense written also *Flexuose.*—**Flexure**, flek'sūr, *n.* [L. *flexura.*] A bending; the form in which a thing is bent; part bent; a bend.

Flick, flik, *n.* [Akin to *flip, flap.*] A sharp sudden stroke, as with a whip; a flip.—*v.t.* To strike with a flick; to flip.

Flicker, flik'ėr, *v.i.* [A.Sax. *flicerian*, to flutter or move the wings; G. *flackern*, to flare, to blaze, to flutter; D. *flikkeren*, to twinkle; Icel. *flaka*, to flap.] To flutter or flap the wings; to fluctuate or waver, as a flame in a current of air or about to expire.—*n.* A wavering or fluctuating gleam, as of a candle; a flutter.—**Flickeringly**, flik'ėr-ing-li. *adv.* In a flickering manner.

Flier, flī'ėr, *n.* Under FLY.

Flight, flīt, *n.* [A.Sax. *fliht*, from *fleógan*, to fly. FLY.] The act of fleeing; hasty or precipitate departure; the act or power of flying; volitation; the manner or mode of flying; a flock of birds flying in company; the birds produced in the same season; a discharge; a volley; a shower, as of arrows; a mounting or soaring; an extravagant excursion or sally, as of the imagination.—*Flight of stairs*, the series of steps or stairs from one platform or landing to another.—**Flightily**, flī'ti-li, *adv.* In a flighty, wild, capricious, or imaginative manner.—**Flightiness**, flī'ti-nes, *n.* The state of being flighty; extreme volatility.—**Flight-shot**, *n.* The distance which an arrow flies; bow-shot.—**Flighty**, flī'ti, *a.* Fleeting†; indulging in flights or sallies of imagination, humour, caprice, &c.; volatile; giddy; fickle.

Flimsy, flim'zi, *a.* [Origin doubtful.] Without strength or solid substance; of loose and unsubstantial structure; without reason or plausibility.—*n.* A thin sort of paper; a slang term for a bank-note.—**Flimsily**, flim'zi-li, *adv.* In a flimsy manner.—**Flimsiness**, flim'zi-nes, *n.* State or quality of being flimsy.

Flinch, flinsh, *v.i.* [Perhaps corrupted from *blench*, or from O.E. *flecche*, Fr. *fléchir*, L. *flectere*, to bend.] To draw back from pain or danger; to show signs of yielding or of suffering; to shrink; to wince.—**Flincher**, flinsh'ėr, *n.* One who flinches or fails.—**Flinchingly**, flinsh'ing-li, *adv.* In a flinching manner.

Flinders, *n.* Fragments; splinters. (*Archaic and dialect.*)

Fling, fling, *v.t.*—*flung, flinging.* [Akin to O.Sw. *flenga*, to strike or beat; Dan. *flenge*, to slash.] To cast, send, or throw; to hurl; to send or shed forth; to emit; to scatter; to throw to the ground; to prostrate.—*v.i.* To flounce; to throw out the legs violently; to start away with a sudden motion, as in token of displeasure; to rush away angrily.—*n.* A throw; a gibe; a sarcasm; a severe or contemptuous remark; enjoyment of pleasure to the full extent of one's opportunities (to take one's *fling*: *colloq.*); a Scotch dance, the Highland *fling.*

Flint, flint, *n.* [A.Sax. and Dan. *flint*, Sw. *flinta*; same root as Gr. *plinthos*, a brick.] A species of quartz, of a yellowish or bluish-gray or grayish-black colour, very hard and used to form an ingredient in fine pottery; a piece of flint used to strike fire with steel or in a flint-lock.—**Flinty**, flin'ti, *a.* Consisting or composed of flint; containing flints; like flint; very hard; cruel; unmerciful.—**Flintiness**, flin'ti-nes, *n.* The quality of being flinty.—**Flint-glass**, *n.* A species of glass, of which flint was formerly an ingredient, now made with quartz and fine sand, and used for table-ware, &c.—**Flint-lock**, *n.* A musket-lock in which fire is produced by a flint striking on the steel pan.

Flip, flip. *n.* [A form of *flap.*] A smart blow, as with a whip; a flick; a drink consisting of beer and spirit sweetened, and heated by a hot iron.—*v.t.* To flick.

Flippant, flip'ant, *a.* [Formed from *flip, flap*; comp. Icel. *fleipr*, tattle, *fleipinn*, pert, petulant.] Speaking fluently and confidently, without knowledge or consideration; heedlessly pert; showing undue levity.—**Flippancy, Flippantness**, flip'an-si, flip'ant-nes, *n.* The state or quality of being flippant.—**Flippantly**, flip'ant-li, *adv.* In a flippant manner; volubly.

Flipper, flip'ėr, *n.* [Equivalent to *flapper*, from *flap.*] The paddle of a sea-turtle; the broad fin of a fish; the arm of a seal.

Flirt, flėrt, *v.t.* [A.Sax. *fleard*, trifle, folly; *fleardian*, to trifle; comp. G. *flirren*, trifles, *flirren*, to make a confused noise.] To throw with a jerk or sudden effort or exertion; to fling suddenly; to move with short, quick movements; to make coquettish motions with (a fan).—*v.i.* To run and dart about; to act with levity or giddiness; to play the coquette.—*n.* A sudden jerk; a quick throw or cast; one who flirts; a woman who plays at courtship; a coquette.—**Flirtation**, flėr-tā'shon, *n.* A flirting; a playing at courtship; coquetry.—**Flirtatious**,† flėr-tā'shus, *a.* Given to flirtation.—**Flirtingly**, flėr'ting-li, *adv.* In a flirting manner.

Flit, flit, *v.i.*—*flitted, flitting.* [Dan. *flytte*, Sw. *flytta*, to remove; akin to *flee, fleet, flutter*, &c.] To fly away with a rapid motion; to dart along, as a bird; to move with celerity through the air; to move rapidly about; to flutter; to migrate.—**Flitting**, flit'ing, *n.* The act of one who flits.—**Flitty**, flit'i, *a.* Fluttering; restless; irresponsible; capricious; giddy. Same as *Flighty.*

Flitch, flich, *n.* [A.Sax. *flicce*, a flitch of bacon; Icel. *flikki*, a flitch.] The side of a hog salted and cured; *carp.* a plank fastened side by side with others to form a compound beam.

Flittern, flit'ėrn, *a.* The bark of young oak-trees used in tanning.

Float, flōt, *v.i.* [A.Sax. *flotian*, to float, *fleótan*, to fleet; *fleet, flow, flood* are closely allied. FLOW.] To rest or glide on the surface of a fluid; to swim or be buoyed up; to move as if supported by a fluid; to move gently and easily through the air.—*v.t.* To cause to float; to cause to rest or be conveyed on the surface of a fluid; to flood; to inundate; to overflow.—*To float a scheme*, to bring it prominently before public notice; to raise funds for carrying it on.—*n.* That which floats on the surface of a fluid; a collection of timber fastened together and floated down a stream; a raft; a buoy; the cork or quill on an angling line, to support it and indicate the bite of a fish; a plasterer's tool for producing a plane surface; the float-board of a water-wheel or paddle-wheel.—**Floatage, Flotage**, flō'tāj, *n.* Anything that floats on the water.—**Floatation**, flō-tā'shon, *n.* The science of floating bodies.—**Float-board**, *n.* One of the boards of an undershot water-wheel which receive the impulse of the stream; one of the boards of a paddle-wheel.—**Floater**, flō'tėr, *n.* One that floats.—**Floating**, flō'ting, *p.* and *a.* Resting on and buoyed up by a fluid; circulating; not fixed or invested: opposed to *sunk* (*floating* capital; *floating* debt); disconnected; unattached (*floating* ribs in fishes); fluctuating; unsettled (a *floating* population).—*Floating breakwater*, a series of floating frames of timber, connected by mooring chains or cables, to protect vessels from the violence of the waves.—*Floating bridge*, a bridge of timber supported wholly by the water; a large flat-bottomed steam ferry-boat, in harbours or rivers, generally running on chains laid across the bottom.—*Floating dock.* Under DOCK.—*Floating light*, a light borne on a buoy or carried by a vessel moored on sunken rocks, shoals, &c.—*Floating pier*, a pier which rises and falls with the tide.—**Floaty**, flō'ti, *a.* Buoyant; swimming on the surface; light.

Floccillation, flok-sil-lā'shon, *n.* [L. *floccus*, a lock of wool.] A delirious picking of the bed-clothes by a sick person.—**Floccose**, flok-ōs', *a.* [L. *floccosus*.] *Bot.* composed of or bearing tufts of woolly, or long and soft, hairs.—**Flocculence**, flok'ū-lens, *n.* The state of being flocculent; adhesion in small flakes.—**Flocculent**, flok'ū-lent, *a.* Coalescing and adhering in locks or flakes.

Flock, flok, *n.* [From O.Fr. *floc*, L. *floccus*, a lock of wool; comp. G. *flocke*, O.G. *floccho*, D. *vlok*, Sw. *flocka*, Dan. *flokke*.] A lock of wool or hair; the refuse of cotton and wool, or shreds of woollen goods, used for stuffing mattresses, &c.—**Flock-bed**, *n.* A bed stuffed with flocks or locks of wool, or pieces of cloth cut up fine.—**Flock-paper**, *n.* A wall-paper having raised figures resembling cloth made of powdered wool attached by size or varnish.—**Flocky**, flok'i, *a.* Abounding with flocks; floccose.

Flock, flok, *n.* [A.Sax. *floc*, *flocc*, a flock, a company of men = Dan. *flok*, Sw. *flock*, Icel. *flokkr*, flock; perhaps same as *folk*.] A company or collection of living creatures: especially applied to birds and sheep; a Christian congregation in relation to their pastor, who takes charge of them in spiritual things.—*v.i.* To gather in flocks or crowds.—**Flock-master**, *n.* An owner or overseer of a flock; a sheep-farmer.

Floe, flō, *n.* [Dan. *flage*, Sw. *flaga*, a floe; akin to *flake*.] A large mass of ice floating in the ocean.

Flog, flog, *v.t.*—*flogged*, *flogging*. [Allied to Prov. E. *flack*, to beat; *flacket*, to flap about; perhaps also to *flap* or *flag*.] To beat or whip; to chastise with repeated blows.—*To flog a dead horse*, to try to revive interest in a stale subject.—**Flogger**, flog'ėr, *n.* One who flogs.

Flood, flud, *n.* [A.Sax. *flód*, a flood = Fris. Dan. and Sw. *flod*, Icel. *flód*, D. *vloed*; from the root of *flow*.] A great flow of water; a body of water rising and overflowing the land; a river (*poet.*); the flowing in of the tide: opposed to *ebb*; a flow or stream of anything fluid; a great quantity; an overflowing; abundance; superabundance.—*The Flood*, the deluge in the days of Noah.—*v.t.* To overflow; to inundate; to cause to be covered with water.—**Flood-gate**, *n.* A gate to be opened for letting water flow, or to be shut to prevent it.—**Flooding**, flud'ing, *n.* The act of overflowing or inundating; a morbid discharge of blood from the uterus.—**Flood-mark**, *n.* The mark or line to which the tide rises; high-water mark.—**Flood-tide**, *n.* The rising tide.

Floor, flōr, *n.* [A.Sax. *flór*, a floor = D. *vloer*, a floor; G. *flur*, a field, a floor; W. *llawr*, the ground, a floor.] That part of a building or room on which we walk; a platform; a story in a building; a suite of rooms on a level.—*v.t.* To furnish with a floor; to strike or knock down level with the floor (*colloq.*).—**Floorer**, flō'rėr, *n.* One who or that which floors; a blow which floors a person (*colloq.*).—**Flooring**, flō'ring, *n.* A floor; materials for floors.—**Floor-cloth**, *n.* Oil-cloth for covering floors.

Flop, flop, *v.t.* [A form of *flap*.] To clap; to flap; to let fall or sink down suddenly.—*v.i.* To strike about with something broad and flat; to flap; to plump down suddenly.—*n.* A sudden sinking to the ground.—**Floppy**, flop'i, *a.* Having a tendency to flop.

Flora, flō'ra, *n.* [L., from *flos*, *floris*, a flower (whence also *flower*, *flour*, *flourish*, &c.).] The Roman goddess of flowers; a work describing the plants of a certain district or region; a collective term for the plants indigenous to any district, region, or period.—**Floral**, flō'ral, *a.* Containing or belonging to the flower; pertaining to flowers in general; made of flowers.—**Florally**, flō'ral-li, *adv.* In a floral manner.—**Floreated**, flō'rē-ā-ted, *a.* Decorated with floral ornament; having florid ornaments.—**Florescence**, flō-res'ens, *n.* [L. *florescens*, pp. of *floresco*.] *Bot.* a bursting into flower; the season when plants expand their flowers; inflorescence.—**Florescent**, flō-res'ent, *a.* Bursting into flower; flowering.—**Floret**, flō'ret, *n.* A single small flower in a compact inflorescence.—**Floriage**,† flō'ri-āj, *n.* Bloom; blossom.—**Floriculture**, flō'ri-kul-tūr, *n.* [L. *flos*, *floris*, and *cultura*.] The culture or cultivation of flowers or flowering plants.—**Floricultural**, flō-ri-kul'tūr-al, *a.* Relating to floriculture.—**Floriculturist**, flō-ri-kul'tūr-ist, *n.* One interested in floriculture.—

Florid, flor'id, *a.* [L. *floridus*, from *flos*, *floris*.] Flowery; bright in color; flushed with red; of a lively red color; embellished with profuse ornamentation, especially with flowers of rhetoric, or high-flown or elaborately elegant language.—**Florida**, flor'i-da, *n.* The southeasternmost state, so named because the land was discovered on Palm Sunday (*Pascua Florida*) by Juan Ponce de Leon. *Dominica* was discovered by Columbus on a Sunday (*dies dominica*), and *Natal* by Vasco da Gama on Christmas (*dies natalis*).—**Floridity, Floridness**, flo-rid'i-ti, flor'id-nes, *n.* The quality or condition of being florid.—**Floridly**, flor'id-li, *adv.* In a showy imposing way.

Floriferous, flō-rif'ėr-us, *a.* Producing flowers.—**Florification**, flō'ri-fi-kā"shon, *n.* The act, process, or time of flowering.—**Floriform**, flō'ri-form, *a.* In the form of a flower.—**Florist**, flor'ist, *n.* [Fr. *fleuriste*, a florist.] A cultivator of flowers; one who deals in flowers; one who writes a flora.—**Floroon**, flo-rön', *n.* [Fr. *fleuron*.] A border worked with flowers.

Florence, flor'ens, *n.* A kind of wine from *Florence* in Italy; a gold coin of the reign of Edward III, of Britain, value 6 shillings.—*Florence flask*, a globular bottle of thin transparent glass with a long neck.—**Florentine**, flor'en-tin, *a.* Of or pertaining to Florence.—*n.* A native of Florence; a kind of silk cloth.

Florin, flor'in, *n.* [Fr. *florin*, from It. *fiorino*, first applied to a Florentine coin, because stamped with a lily; It. *fiore*, a flower, from L. *flos*, *floris*, a flower.] A name given to different coins of gold or silver, of different values, and to moneys of account, in different countries; a British coin, value 2 shillings, about 50 cents.

Floscular, Flosculous, Flosculose, flos'kū-lėr, flos'kū-lus, flos'kū-lōs, *a.* [L. *flosculus*, dim. of *flos*, a flower.] *Bot.* applied to composite flowers, which consist of many florets.—**Floscule**, flos'kūl, *n.* A small flower; a floret.

Floss, flos, *n.* [It. *floscio*, *flosso*, soft, flaccid, from L. *fluxus*, flowing, loose.] A downy or silky substance in the husks of certain plants; untwisted filaments of the finest silk, &c.—**Floss-silk**, *n.* Floss; silk fibres broken off in unwinding the cocoons, and used for coarser fabrics.—**Flossy**, flos'i, *a.* Composed of or resembling floss.

Flotation. See FLOATATION, under FLOAT.

Flotilla, flō-til'la, *n.* [Sp. dim. of *flota*, a fleet.] A little fleet; a fleet of small vessels.

Flotsam, Flotson, flot'sam, flot'son, *n.* [From *float*.] Such a portion of the wreck of a ship and the cargo as continues floating on the surface of the water. JETSAM.

Flounce, flouns, *v.i.*—*flounced*, *flouncing*. [Akin N. and O.Sw. *flunsa*, to plunge about in water.] To throw one's self about with jerks, as if in displeasure or agitation.—*n.* A sudden jerking motion of the body.

Flounce, flouns, *n.* [Originally *frounce*, from Fr. *froncis*, a plait, from *froncer*, *fronser*, to wrinkle, from L. *frons*, *frontis*, the front or forehead. FRONT.] A strip of cloth sewed horizontally round a frock or gown, with the lower border loose and spreading.—*v.t.* To deck with a flounce or flounces.

Flounder, floun'dėr, *n.* [Gr. *flunder*, Sw. *flundra*, Dan. *flynder*, flounder.] One of the most common of the flat-fishes, found in the sea and near the mouths of rivers.

Flounder, floun'dėr, *v.i.* [Akin to D. *flodderen*, to flap like a loose garment.] To make violent motions with the limbs and body when hampered in some manner; to roll or tumble about.

Flour, flour, *n.* [Fr. *fleur*, a flower, *fleur de farine*, flour, lit. 'flour of meal', the finest part of the meal; comp. *flowers of sulphur*. *Flower* is merely another form.] The finely ground meal of wheat or of any other grain; the finer part of meal separated by bolting; the fine and soft powder of any substance.—*v.t.* To convert into flour; to sprinkle with flour.—**Flour-box, Flour-dredge, Flour-dredger**, *n.* A tin box for scattering flour.—**Flour-mill**, *n.* A mill for grinding and sifting flour.—**Floury**, flou'ri, *a.* Consisting of or resembling flour; covered with flour.

Flourish, flur'ish, *v.i.* [Fr. *fleurir*, *fleurissant*, L. *florere*, to flower, to bloom, from *flos*, *floris*, a flower. FLORA.] To grow luxuriantly; to increase and enlarge; to thrive; to be prosperous; to increase in wealth, comfort, happiness, or honour; to prosper; to live at a certain period (said of authors, painters, &c.); to use florid language; to make ornamental strokes in writing; to move or be moved in fantastic irregular figures; to play a bold prelude or fanfare.—*v.t.* To adorn with flowers or beautiful figures; to ornament with anything showy; to give a fair appearance to (*Shak.*); to make bold or irregular movements with; to hold in the hand and swing about; to brandish.—*n.* An ostentatious embellishment; parade of words and figures; show; a fanciful stroke of the pen or graver; a brandishing; the waving of a weapon or something held in the hand; the decorative notes which a singer or instrumental performer adds to a passage.—*Flourish of trumpets*, a trumpet-call, fanfare, or prelude performed on the approach of any person of distinction; hence, any ostentatious preliminary sayings or doings.—**Flourisher**, flur'ish-ėr, *n.* One who flourishes.—**Flourishing**, flur'ish-ing, *p.* and *a.* Prosperous; thriving.—**Flourishingly**, flur'ish-ing-li, *adv.* In a flourishing manner.

Flout, flout, *v.t.* [D. *fluiten*, *fluyten*, to play on the flute, to whistle, to jeer, from *fluit*, a flute. FLUTE.] To mock or insult; to treat with contempt or disrespect, to jeer at; to jibe.—*v.i.* To behave with contempt: often with *at*.—*n.* A mock; an insult.—**Flouter**, flou'tėr, *n.* One who flouts.

Flow, flō, *v.i.* [A.Sax. *flówan*, to flow = D. *vloeijen*, to flow; Icel. *flóa*, to flood; O.H.G. *flawan*, to wash; from a root seen in L. *pluvius*, rain, Gr. *pleō*, to swim; Skr. *plu*, to flow. Akin are *flood*, *float*, *fleet*, &c.]

To move along in the manner of liquids; to run like water; to melt; to proceed or issue as from a source; to abound; to have or be in abundance; to glide along smoothly, without harshness or roughness; to be smooth or pleasant to the ear; to be easily or smoothly uttered; to hang loose and waving; to rise, as the tide: opposed to *ebb*.—*v.t.* To cover with water; to overflow. —*n.* A stream of water or other fluid; a current; an outflow; the rise of the tide; abundance; copiousness; undisturbed and even movement.—**Flowage**, flō′āj, *n.* Act of flowing; state of being flowed.—**Flowing**, flō′ing, *p.* and *a.* Moving as a fluid; fluent; smooth.—**Flowingly**, flō′ing-li, *adv.* In a flowing manner.—**Flowingness**, flō′ing-nes, *n.*

Flower, flou′ėr, *n.* [O.Fr. *flour*, Mod.Fr. *fleur*, from L. *flos*, *floris*, a flower, whence also *floral*, *florid*, *florin*, &c. *Flour* is really the same word though it has taken a different signification and spelling.] The delicate and gaily-coloured leaves or petals on a plant; a circle of leaves or leaflets of some other colour than green; a bloom or blossom; more strictly, in *bot.* the organs of reproduction in a phenogamous plant, consisting of, when complete, stamens and pistils together with two sets of leaves which surround and protect them, the calyx and corolla; the early part of life or of manhood; the prime; youthful vigour; youth; the best or finest part; a figure of speech; an ornament of style; *pl.* a powdery or mealy substance (as *flowers* of sulphur); the menstrual discharge.—*v.i.* To blossom; to bloom; to flourish.—*v.t.* To embellish with figures of flowers; to adorn with imitated flowers.—**Flowerage**, flou′ėr-āj, *n.* Flowers in general.—**Flower-bud**, *n.* The bud which produces a flower.—**Flower-clock**, *n.* A means of measuring time by a collection of growing flowers that open and shut at certain hours of the day.—**Flower-de-lis**, **Flower-de-luce**, flou′ėr-de-lē, flou′ėr-de-lūs, *n.* [Fr. *fleur de lis*, flower of the lily.] Same as *Fleur-de-lis*.—**Flowered**, flou′ėrd, *p.* and *a.* Embellished with figures of flowers.—**Floweret**, flou′ėr-et, *n.* A small flower; a floret.—**Flowerful**, flou′ėr-ful, *a.* Abounding with flowers.—**Flower-garden**, *n.* A garden in which flowers chiefly are cultivated.—**Flower-head**, *n.* *Bot.* a capitulum or head of sessile flowers, as in the daisy.—**Floweriness**, flou′ėr-i-nes, *n.* The state of being flowery; floridness of speech.—**Flowering**, flou′ėr-ing, *p.* and *a.* Having or producing flowers.—**Flowering-ash**, *n.* A deciduous tree of Southern Europe which yields manna.—**Flowering-fern**, *n.* A fine fern, so called from the upper pinnae of the fronds being transformed into a handsome panicle covered with sporangia.—**Flowering-rush**, *n.* A beautiful plant, found in Europe and Asia, having leaves 2 or 3 feet long, and a large umbel of rose-colored flowers.—**Flower-leaf**, *n.* The leaf of a flower; a petal.—**Flowerless**, flou′ėr-les, *a.* Having no flowers.—**Flowerlessness**, flou′ėr-les-nes, *n.* State of being without flowers.—**Flower-piece**, *n.* A painting or picture of flowers.—**Flower-pot**, *n.* A pot in which flowering-plants or other plants are grown.—**Flower-show**, *n.* An exhibition of flowers, generally competitive.—**Flower-stalk**, *n.* *Bot.* the peduncle of a plant, or the stem that supports the flower or fructification.—**Flowery**, flou′ėr-i, *a.* Full of flowers; abounding with blossoms; richly embellished with figurative language; florid.

Flown, flōn, pp. of verb to *fly*.

Fluctuate, fluk′tū-āt, *v.i.*—*fluctuated*, *fluctuating*. [L. *fluctuo*, *fluctuatum*, from *fluctus*, a wave, from *fluo*, to flow, whence *fluent*, &c. FLUENT.] To move as a wave; to wave; to float backward and forward, as on waves; to be wavering or unsteady; to be irresolute; to rise and fall; to be in an unsettled state.—*v.t.* To put into a state of fluctuating or wave-like motion.—**Fluctuability**, fluk′tū-a-bil″i-ti, *n.* The quality of being fluctuable.—**Fluctuable**, fluk′tū-a-bl, *a.* Capable of fluctuating; liable to fluctuation.—**Fluctuant**, fluk′tū-ant, *a.* [L. *fluctuans*, *fluctuantis*.] Moving like a wave; wavering; unsteady.—**Fluctuating**, fluk′tū-ā-ting, *p.* and *a.* Wavering; moving in this and that direction; rising and falling; changeable.—**Fluctuation**, fluk-tū-ā′shon, *n.* [L. *fluctuatio*.] A motion like that of waves; a moving in this and that direction; a rising and falling; a wavering; unsteadiness.

Flue, flö, *n.* [Comp. O.Fr. *flue*, a flowing, from *fluer*, L. *fluere*, to flow.] A passage for smoke in a chimney; a pipe or tube for conveying heat, as in certain kinds of steam-boilers, &c.—**Flue-boiler**, *n.* A steam-boiler with flues running through the part that contains the water.

Flue, flö, *n.* [FLUFF.] Downy matter; fluff.—**Fluey**, flö′i, *a.* Downy; fluffy.

Fluent, flu̧′ent, *a.* [L. *fluens*, *fluentis*, ppr. of *fluo*, *fluxum*, to flow, as in *affluence*, *confluence*, *influence*, *flux*, &c.; akin Gr. *phlyō*, to bubble over.] Flowing; ready in the use of words; having words at command and uttering them with facility and smoothness; voluble; smooth.—*n.* *Math.* the variable or flowing quantity in fluxions which is continually increasing or decreasing.—**Fluently**, flu̧′ent-li, *adv.* In a fluent manner.—**Fluentness**,† flu̧′ent-nes, *n.* State of being fluent; fluency.—**Fluency**, flu̧′en-si, *n.* The quality of being fluent; readiness of utterance; volubility.

Fluff, fluf, *n.* [Also *flue*; akin to *flock*, L.G. *flog*, *flok*, flue.] Light down or nap such as rises from beds, cotton, &c.; flue.—**Fluffy**, fluf′i, *a.* Containing or resembling fluff; giving off fluff; fluey.

Flugelman. Same as *Fugelman*.

Fluid, flu̧′id, *n.* [L. *fluidus*, from *fluo*, to flow. FLUENT.] Capable of flowing or moving like water; liquid or gaseous.—*n.* A fluid body or substance; a body whose particles on the slightest pressure move and change their relative position without separation; a liquid or a gas: opposed to a *solid*.—**Fluidity**, flu̧-id′i-ti, *n.* The quality of being fluid; a liquid, aeriform, or gaseous state.—**Fluidize**, flu̧′id-īz, *v.t.* To convert into a fluid.—**Fluidness**, flu̧′id-nes, *n.* The state of being fluid; fluidity.

Fluke, flök, *n.* [Akin to G. *flunk*, a wing, the fluke of an anchor; comp. also Sw. *flik*, Dan. *flig*, a flap or lappet; Dan. *anker-flig*, anchor-fluke.] The part of an anchor which catches in the ground; one of the two triangular divisions constituting the tail of a whale; *billiards*, an accidental successful stroke; hence, any unexpected or accidental advantage.—**Fluky**, flö′ki, *a.* Formed like or having a fluke.

Fluke, flök, *a.* [A.Sax. *flóc*, a flat fish.] A flounder.—**Fluke-worm**, *n.* A species of entozoon which infests the ducts of the liver of various animals, especially those of the sheep: also called simply *fluke*.

Flume, flöm, *n.* [Connected with *flow*.] The passage or channel for the water that drives a mill-wheel; an artificial channel for gold-washing.

Flummery, flum′ėr-i, *n.* [W. *llymry*, flummery, oatmeal steeped till sour, from *llymyr*, harsh, *llym*, sharp.] A sort of jelly made of flour or meal; flour from oats steeped in water till sour and then boiled; flattery; empty compliment; nonsense.

Flung, flung, pret. & pp. of *fling*.

Flunkey, **Flunky**, flung′ki, *n.* [L.G. *flunkern*, to flaunt; D. *flonkeren*, *flinkeren*, to glitter; or from *flank*, one that keeps at his master's flank.] A male servant in livery; a term of contempt for a cringing flatterer and servile imitator of the aristocracy; a male toady.—**Flunkeydom**, **Flunkydom**, flung′ki-dum, *n.* Flunkeys collectively; the grade or condition of flunkeys.—**Flunkeyism**, **Flunkyism**, flung′ki-izm, *n.* Servility; toadyism.

Fluorite, flö′or-īt, *n.* A name of fluor-spar.

Fluor-spar, flu̧′or-spär, *n.* [L. *fluor*, a flowing (from *fluo*, to flow), and *spar*, as in *felspar*; named from its fusibility and from being used as a flux.] Calcium fluorid, a crystalline mineral sometimes colorless and transparent, but more frequently exhibiting tints of yellow, green, blue, and red. It is manufactured into various ornamental articles. Sometimes called simply *Fluor*.—**Fluorescence**, flu̧-o-res′ens, *n.* The emission of bluish or greenish light by certain substances caused by the invisible rays of the solar spectrum at the violet end.—**Fluorescent**, flu̧-o-res′ent, *a.* Possessing fluorescence.—**Fluoric**, flu̧-or′ik, *a.* Pertaining to or obtained from fluor-spar.—**Fluorin**, **Fluorine**, flu̧′o-rin, *n.* An element existing in fluor-spar, of which in a free state we know but little.—**Fluoroscope**, flu̧-or′ō-skōp, *n.* A device for observing the effects of X-rays on the human body by means of a fluorescent screen.

Flurry, flur′i, *n.* [Of doubtful origin and connections; comp. Sw. *flurig*, disordered, *flur*, disordered hair.] A sudden blast or gust of wind; a short sudden shower; agitation; commotion; bustle.—*v.t.* To put in agitation; to excite or alarm.—**Flurried**, flur′id, *p.* and *a.* Put in agitation; agitated; discomposed; excited.

Flush, flush, *v.i.* [Perhaps akin to *flash*; or from O.Fr. *flux*, a flowing, a flush at cards, from L. *fluxus*. FLUX.] To flow and spread suddenly, as the blood to the face; to become suffused; to become suddenly red; to blush.—*v.t.* To cause to blush or redden suddenly; to elate; to excite; to animate with joy; to wash out by drenching with copious supplies of water; *sporting*, to cause to start up or fly off; to spring.—*n.* A sudden flow of blood to the face; the redness so produced; any warm colouring or glow; sudden thrill or shock of feeling; bloom; vigour; a rush or flow of water; a run of cards of the same suit in cribbage.

Flush, flush, *a.* [Origin doubtful.] Fresh; full of vigour; well supplied with money (*slang*); having the surface even or level with the adjacent surface.—**Flushness**, flush′nes, *n.* State of being flush.

Fluster, flus′tėr, *v.t.* [Icel. *flauster*, fluster, *flaustra*, to be in a fluster; Norweg. *flosa*, passion.] To make hot with drinking; to heat; to agitate; to confuse.—*n.* Heat; glow; agitation; confusion of mind.—**Flustrated**,† flus′trā-ted, *a.* Flustered.

Flute, flöt, *n.* [Fr. *flûte*, O.Fr. *flaüte*, from *flaüter*, from a L.L. *flatuare* (giving *flautare* by metathesis), from L. *flatus*, a blowing, from L. *flo*, *flatum*, to blow (as in *inflate*); akin *flageolet*.] A musical wind-instrument consisting of a tapering tube with six holes for the fingers, and from one to fourteen keys which open other holes; a perpendicular furrow or channel cut along the shaft of a column or pilaster; any similar groove or channel in any material.—*v.i.*—*fluted*, *fluting*. To play on a flute.—*v.t.* To play or sing in notes resembling those of a flute; to form flutes or channels in.—**Fluted**, flö′ted, *p.* and *a.* Channelled; furrowed; *mus.* clear and mellow; flute-like.—**Fluter**, flö′tėr, *n.* A flutist; one who makes grooves or flutes.—**Flutina**, flö-tē′na, *n.* A musical instrument of the accordion kind.—**Fluting**, flö′ting, *n.* The act of forming a groove or flute, fluted work.—**Flutist**, flö′tist, *n.* A performer on the flute.—**Fluty**, flö′ti, *a.* Soft and clear in tone, like a flute.

Flutter, flut′ėr, *v.i.* [A.Sax. *floterian*, to fluctuate, from *flot*, the sea; allied to *float*, and to L.G. *fluttern*, G. *flattern*, to flutter.] To move or flap the wings rapidly, without flying, or with short flights; to move about with bustle; to move with quick vibrations or undulations; to be in agitation.—*v.t.* To agitate; to disorder; to throw into confusion.—*n.* Quick and irregular motion; vibration; agitation of the mind, confusion; disorder.—**Flutter**, *n.* A betting transaction; fluttering of bank-notes (*Colloq.*)—**Flutterer**, flut′ėr-ėr, *n.* One who flutters.—**Flutteringly**, flut′ėr-ing-li, *adv.* In a fluttering manner.

Fluvial, **Fluviatic**, **Fluviatile**, flö′vi-al, flö-vi-at′ik, flö′vi-a-til, *a.* [L. *fluvialis*, *fluviaticus*, *fluviatilis*, from *fluvius*, a river, from *fluo*, to flow.] Belonging to rivers; produced by river action; growing or living in fresh-water rivers.—**Fluviomarine**, flö'vi-ō-ma-rēn", *a.* *Geol.* formed or deposited in estuaries or on the bottom of the sea at the embouchure of a river.

Flux, fluks, *n.* [Fr., from L. *fluxus*, from *fluo*, to flow. FLUENT.] The act of flowing; a flow; the flow of the tide, in opposition to the ebb; *med.* an extraordinary evacuation from the bowels or other part; that which flows or is discharged; *metal.* any substance or mixture used to promote the fusion of metals or minerals; a liquid state from the operation of heat.—*v.t.* To melt or to fuse; *med.* to cause a flux or evacuation from; to purge.—**Fluxation**, fluk-sā'shon, *n.* A flowing or passing away, and giving place to others.—**Fluxibility**, **Fluxibleness**,† fluk'si-bil-i-ti, fluk'si-bl-nes, *n.* The quality of being fluxible or admitting fusion. — **Fluxible**, fluk'si-bl, *a.* Capable of being melted or fused, as a mineral.—**Fluxility**, fluk-sil'i-ti, *n.* The quality of admitting fusion.—**Fluxion**, fluk'shon, *n.* A flux or flowing; *med.* a flow or determination of blood or other fluid towards any organ with greater force than natural; *math.* a differential, *fluxions* being an old method of mathematical analysis superseded by the differential calculus. — **Fluxional**, **Fluxionary**, fluk'shon-al, fluk'shon-a-ri, *a.* Pertaining to fluxions; variable.—**Fluxionist**, fluk'-shon-ist, *n.* One skilled in fluxions.

Fly, flī, *v.i.*—pret. *flew*, pp. *flown*, ppr. *flying*. [A.Sax. *fleógan*, G. *fliegen*, Icel. *fljúga*, Dan. *flyue*, to fly; akin *flee*, *flight*, *fledge*, &c.] To move through air by the aid of wings; to move through the air by the force of wind or other impulse; to rise in air, as light substances; to run or pass with swiftness; to depart swiftly; to run away; to flee; to escape; to become diffused or spread rapidly; to pass quickly from mouth to mouth; to burst in pieces; to flutter, vibrate, or play, as a flag in the wind.—*To fly at*, to rush on; to fall on suddenly.—*To fly in the face of*, to set at defiance; to act in direct opposition to. — *To fly open*, to open suddenly or with violence.—*To let fly*, to discharge; to throw or drive with violence.—*v.t.* To flee from; to shun; to avoid; to cause to fly or float in the air.—*n.* [The noun is partly from A.Sax. *fleóge*, the insect, from *fleógan*, to fly, like G. *fliege*, from *fliegen*, partly from the verb directly.] A winged insect of various species, whose distinguishing characteristics are that the wings are transparent and have no cases or covers; a hook dressed so as to resemble a fly or other insect used by anglers to catch fish; an arrangement of vanes upon a revolving axis or other contrivance to regulate the motion of machinery; a flier; one of the arms that revolve round the bobbin in a spinning-frame, and twist the yarn as it is wound on the bobbin; a light carriage formed for rapid motion; a hackney-coach; a cab; a gallery in a theatre running along the side of the stage at a high level, where the ropes for drawing up parts of the scenes, &c., are worked.—**Flier**, **Flyer**, flī'ėr, *n.* One that flies or flees; a runaway; a fugitive; a part of a machine which by moving rapidly equalizes and regulates the motion of the whole; a contrivance for taking off or delivering the sheets from a printing machine.—**Flybitten**, flī'bit-n, *a.* Marked by the bite of flies.—**Flyblow**, flī'blō, *n.* The egg of a fly.—*v.t.* To deposit a fly's egg in; to taint with eggs which produce maggots. — **Flyblown**, flī'blōn, *pp.* or *a.* Tainted with maggots.—**Fly-boat**, *n.* A large flat-bottomed Dutch vessel with a high stem; a long narrow passage boat, swifter than the cargo boats, formerly much used on canals.—**Fly-catcher**, *n.* One who or that which catches flies; especially, a name of various insessorial birds which feed on flies and other winged insects; the phoebe, bee-bird, or kingbird.—**Fly-fishing**, *n.* The art or practice of angling for fish with flies, natural or artificial. —**Fly-leaf**, *n.* A blank leaf at the beginning or end of a book, pamphlet, &c. —**Fly-paper**, *n.* A kind of porous paper impregnated with poison for destroying flies.—**Fly-sickness**, *n.* Fatal tropical disease of horses, &c., caused by germs introduced by bites of a tsetse fly. — **Fly-trap**, *n.* A trap to catch or kill flies; an American sensitive plant, the leaves of which close upon and capture insects. — **Fly-wheel**, *n.* A wheel with a heavy rim placed on the revolving shaft of any machinery put in motion by an irregular or intermitting force, for the purpose of rendering the motion equable and regular by means of its momentum. — **Flying-buttress**, *n.* A buttress in the form of an arch springing from a solid mass of masonry, and abutting against and serving to support another part of the structure.— **Flying-fish**, *n.* One of those fishes which have the power of sustaining themselves for a time in the air by means of their large pectoral fins. — **Flying-fox**, *n.* A bat found in the islands of the Eastern Archipelago, so named from the resemblance of its head to that of a fox.—**Flying Dutchman**, *n.* A spectral or phantom ship seen off the Cape of Good Hope, believed to import foul weather or danger.—**Flying-jib**, *n.* *Naut.* a sail extended outside of the jib, upon a boom called the flying-jib boom.— **Flying-lemur**, *n.* An insectivorous mammal having the limbs connected by wide lateral folds of skin, which serve to bear it up when taking great leaps from tree to tree.—**Flying-man**, *n.* Aviator. —**Flying-phalanger**, *n.* A nocturnal marsupial of New Guinea and Australia, having a wing-like fold of skin similar to that of the flying-lemur.—**Flying-shot**, *n.* A shot fired at something in motion.— **Flying-squid**, *n.* A cephalopod having two large lateral fins, which enable it to leap high out of the water. — **Flying-squirrel**, *n.* One of those squirrels that have a fold of skin extending between the fore and hind legs, so as to bear them up for a moment in the air, and enable them to make very great leaps; also a name of the flying-phalanger.

Foal, fōl, *n.* [A.Sax. *fola*, a foal; Icel. *foli*, Dan. *fole*, D. *veulen*, G. *fohlen*, *füllen*; Cog. Gr. *pōlos*, a foal; L. *pullus*, a young animal. *Filly* is a dim. from *foal*.] The young of the equine genus of quadrupeds, and of either sex; a colt; a filly.—*v.t.* To bring forth her young: said of a mare or a she-ass.—*v.i.* To bring forth a foal.—**Foal-foot**, *n.* Same as *Colt's-foot*.

Foam, fōm, *n.* [A.Sax. *fám*=G. *feim*, and dial. *faum*, foam; allied to L. *spuma*, foam, from *spuo*, to spit.] Froth; spume; the aggregation of bubbles which is formed on the surface of liquids by fermentation or violent agitation. — *v.i.* To gather foam; to froth; to be in a violent rage.—*v.t.* To cause to foam; to throw out with rage or violence: with *out* (N.T.).—**Foamy**, fō'mi, *a.* Covered with foam; frothy.

Fob, fob, *n.* [Allied to Prov. G. *fuppe*, a pocket.] A little pocket made in men's breeches or trowsers, as a receptacle for a watch.

Fob, fob, *v.t.*—*fobbed*, *fobbing*. [Comp. G. *foppen*, to mock, to banter.] To cheat; to trick; to impose on. (*Shak.*)

Focus, fō'kus, *n.* pl. **Focuses**, fō'kus-ez, or **Foci**, fō'sī. [L. *focus*, a fire, the hearth, whence also *fuel*, *fusil*.] A point of concentration; a central point; a centre of special activity; *optics*, a point in which any number of rays of light meet after being reflected or refracted; *geom.* a name of two important points on the principal axis of the ellipse (which see). — *v.t.* To bring to a focus; to adjust to a focus; to focalize.—**Focal**, fō'kal, *a.* Of or pertaining to a focus. — **Focalize**, fō'kal-īz, *v.t.* To bring to a focus; to focus.—**Focimeter**, fō-sim'et-ėr, *n.* An instrument for finding the focus of a lens.

Fodder, fod'ėr, *n.* [A.Sax. *fódder*, *fóder*, from *fóda*, food=Icel. *fóthr*, L.G. *foder*, D. *voeder*, G. *futter*, fodder. FOOD.] Food for cattle, horses, and sheep, as hay, straw, and other kinds of vegetables. — *v.t.* To feed with fodder.—**Fodderer**, fod'ėr-ėr, *n.* One who fodders cattle.

Foe, fō, *n.* [A.Sax. *fá*, *fáh*, an enemy, from same stem as *fiend*. FIEND, FEUD.] An enemy; one who entertains personal enmity; an enemy in war; a hostile or opposing army; an adversary; one who opposes anything (a *foe* to virtue).—**Foeman**, fō'man, *n.* pl. **Foemen**, fō'men. An enemy in war; a personal antagonist.

Fœtal, **Fœtus**, &c. FETAL, FETUS.

Fog, fog, *n.* [Comp. Dan. *snee-fog*, a snow-storm, *fyge*, to drive with the wind, Dan. dial. *fuge*, to rain fine and blow, Icel. *fok*, snow-storm.] A dense watery vapour exhaled from the earth or from rivers and lakes, or generated in the atmosphere near the earth; a state of mental confusion or uncertainty.—*v.t.*† To envelop with or as with fog.—**Fog-bank**, *n.* At sea a bank of fog sometimes resembling land at a distance. — **Foggily**, fog'i-li, *adv.* In a foggy manner.—**Fogginess**, fog'i-nes, *n.* The state of being foggy.—**Foggy**, fog'i, *a.* Filled or abounding with fog; damp with humid vapours; misty; dull; stupid; beclouded.—**Fog-horn**, *n.* A horn to sound as a warning signal in foggy weather; a sounding instrument for warning vessels of their proximity to the coast during a fog.—**Fog-signal**, *n.* Any signal made during fog to prevent accidents; *rail.*, a detonating body placed on the rails, which explodes on the engine passing over it, and gives warning of danger ahead, &c.

Fog, fog, *n.* [W. *ffwg*, dry grass.] Aftermath; a second growth of grass; long grass that remains on land through the winter.

Fogey, **Fogy**, fō'gi, *n.* [Lit. one who is in a *fog*; or from *fog*, after-grass.] A stupid fellow; an old-fashioned or singular person. (*Colloq.*) — **Fogeyism**, **Fogyism**, fō'gi-izm, *n.* The habits or practices of a fogey.

Foh, fo, *interj.* An exclamation of abhorrence or contempt, like *poh* and *fie*.

Foible, foi'bl, *n.* [O.Fr. weak. FEEBLE.] The weak part of a sword; opposed to *forte*; a particular moral weakness; a weak point; a fault of not a very serious character.

Foil, foil, *v.t.* [Fr. *fouler*, to press, to crush, to oppress, from stem of L. *fullo*, a fuller.] To frustrate; to defeat; to render vain or nugatory, as an effort or attempt; to baffle; to balk.—*n.* Defeat; frustration; a blunt sword, or one that has a button at the end, used in fencing.—**Foilable**, foi'la-bl, *a.* Capable of being foiled.—**Foiler**, foi'lėr, *n.* One who foils or frustrates.

Foil, foil, *n.* [Fr. *feuille*, L. *folium*, a leaf (whence *foliage*).] A leaf or thin plate of metal; a thin leaf of metal placed under precious stones to improve their appearance; anything of a different character which serves to set off something else to advantage; that which, by comparison or contrast, sets off or shows more conspicuously the superiority of something else; *arch.* one of the small arcs or hollow curves in the tracery of a Gothic window, panel, &c.—**Foiled**, foild, *a.* *Arch.* having foils (a *foiled* arch).

Foin, foin, *v.i.* [From Fr. *fouine*, a fish-spear; or O.Fr. *foigner*, to feign, to make a feint.] To push in fencing. (*Shak.*)

Foison,† foi'zn, *n.* [Fr. *foison*, from L. *fusio*, *fusionis*, outpouring, from *fundo*, *fusum*, to pour. FUSE.] Plenty; abundance. (*Shak.*)

Foist, foist, *v.t.* [D. *vuist*, fist; originally, it would appear, to insert by clever movements of the *fist*; compare to *palm off*.] To insert surreptitiously, or without warrant; to pass off as genuine, true, or worthy.—*n.* A trick; an imposition.—**Foister**, fois'tėr, *n.* One who foists.

Fokker, fok'ėr, *n.* A type of aeroplane named after the designer.

Fold, fōld, *n.* [A.Sax. *fald*, *feald*, a plait, a fold, *fealdan*, to fold; cog. Fris. *fald*, G. *falte*, Goth. *falths*, a doubling, a plait; Icel. *falda*, Dan. *folde*, Goth. *falthan*, to fold; same as *fold* in *twofold*, *fivefold*.] The doubling or double of any flexible substance, as cloth; a plait; one part turned or bent and laid on another; a clasp; an embrace (*Shak.*). [Often used following a numeral in compounds, and then signifying 'times', as in two*fold*, four*fold*, ten*fold*.]—*v.t.* To lap or lay double or in plaits; to lay one part over another part of; to lay one over the other, as the hands or arms; to enfold; to embrace. — *v.i.* To become folded or doubled.—**Folder**, fōl'dėr, *n.* One who or that which folds; a flat knife-like instrument used in folding paper.—**Folding-door**, *n. pl.* A door in two upright pieces which meet in the middle. — **Folding-stool**, *n.* A camp-stool, or similar stool.—**Foldless**, fōld'les, *a.* Having no fold.

Fold, fōld, *n.* [A.Sax. *fald*=Dan. *fold*, Sw. *falla*, a fold, a pen.] A pen or inclosure for sheep or like animals; a flock of sheep; hence, *Scrip.* the church, the flock of Christ. —*v.t.* To confine in a fold.

Foliaceous, fō-li-ā'shus, *a.* [L. *foliaceus*, from *folium*, a leaf, akin to Gr. *phyllon*, a leaf.] Leafy; of the nature or form of a leaf; consisting of leaves or thin laminæ. —**Foliage**, fō'li-āj, *n.* [Fr. *feuillage*, from *feuille*, L. *folium*.] Leaves collectively; the leaves of a plant; leaves or leafy growths, represented by sculpture, &c. — **Foliar**, fō'li-ėr, *a. Bot.* inserted in or proceeding from a leaf.—**Foliate**, fō'li-āt, *v.t.* To beat into a leaf, thin plate, or lamina; to cover with tin-foil, &c.—*a. Bot.* leafy; furnished with leaves.—**Foliated**, fō'li-ā-ted, *p.* and *a.* Consisting of plates or laminæ; lamellar; *arch.* containing foils (a *foliated* arch). — **Foliation**, fō-li-ā'shon, *n.* [L. *foliatio*.] The leafing of plants; vernation; the act of beating metal into a thin plate or foil; the operation of spreading foil over a surface; the property in certain rocks of dividing into laminæ or plates; *arch.* the foils, cusps, &c., in the tracery of Gothic windows. — **Foliferous, Foliiferous**, fō-lif'ėr-us, fō-li-if'ėr-us, *a. Bot.* producing leaves.—**Foliparous**, fō-li-ip'a-rus, *a. Bot.* producing leaves only.—**Foliolate**, fō'li-o-lāt, *a. Bot.* pertaining to or consisting of leaflets.—**Foliole**, fō'li-ōl, *n. Bot.* a leaflet; a separate piece of a compound leaf.—**Foliose**, fō'li-ōs, *a. Bot.* covered closely with leaves.

Folio, fō'li-ō, *n.* [Ablative case of L. *folium*, a leaf, short for *in folio*.] A book of the largest size, formed of sheets of paper once doubled, each sheet thus containing four pages; *book-keeping*, a page, or rather both the right and left hand pages, of an account-book, expressed by the same figure; *printing*, the number appended to each page; *law*, a written page of a certain number of words.

Folk, fōk, *n.* [A.Sax. *folc*, folk, a people or nation = L.G. Fris. Dan. and Sw. *folk*; Icel. *fólk*; D. and G. *volk*; probably connected with E. *flock*; Lith. *pulkas*, multitude, crowd; but further connections doubtful.] People in general; a separate class of people: though plural in signification it is frequently used with the plural form especially with a qualifying adjective (rich *folks*, young *folks*).—**Folk-etymology**, *n.* The popular form given to words in order to explain their apparent meaning or derivation, as, for instance, *White Sheet* for *Wytscharte* and *sparrowgrass* for *asparagus*. — **Folk-land**, *n.* Public land in ancient England held by the people in common or granted for a term to individuals.—**Folk-lore**, *n.* Rural superstitions, tales, traditions, or legends.—**Folk-speech**, *n.* The dialect spoken by the common people of a country or district.

Follicle, fol'li-kl, *n.* [L. *folliculus*, dim. of *follis*, a bag or bellows.] A little bag or vesicle in animals and plants; a dry seed-vessel or pod opening on one side only; a vessel distended with air; a gland; a minute secreting cavity.—**Follicular, Folliculous**, fol-lik'ū-lėr, fol-lik'ū-lus, *a.* Pertaining to, or consisting of follicles.—**Folliculated**, fol-lik'ū-lā-ted, *a.* Having follicles; follicular.

Follow, fol'ō, *v.t.* [A.Sax. *folgian*, *fyligean* =G. *folgen*, Dan. *følge*, Icel. *fylgja*, to follow. By some regarded as connected with *folk*, *full*, &c.] To go or come after or behind; to move behind in the same direction; to pursue; to chase; to pursue as an object of desire; to go with (a leader); to be led or guided by; to accept as authority; to take as an example; to copy; to come after in order of time, rank, or office; to result from, as an effect from a cause or an inference from premises; to keep the attention fixed upon while in progress (a speech, piece of music, &c.); to understand the meaning, connection, or force of; to walk in (a road or course); to practise (a trade or calling).—*To follow suit*, in *card-playing*, to play a card of the same suit as that first played; hence, to follow the line of conduct adopted by a predecessor.—*v.i.* To go or come after another; to be posterior in time; to result, as an effect or an inference. ∴ *Follow* and *succeed* are applied to persons or things; *ensue*, in modern literature, to things only. *Succeed* implies a coming into the place previously occupied by another; *ensue*, generally that which follows is an effect or result. — **Follower**, fol'ō-ėr, *n.* One who follows; an adherent; a disciple; an imitator; a dependant.—**Following**, fol'ō-ing, *n.* A body of followers or retainers.—*p.* Being next after; succeeding; related, described, or explained next after.

Folly, fol'i, *n.* [Fr. *folie*, folly, from *fol*, a fool. FOOL.] Weakness of intellect; imbecility of mind; a weak or foolish act; foolish, weak, or light-minded conduct; criminal weakness.

Foment, fō-ment', *v.t.* [Fr. *fomenter*, L. *fomento*, from *fomentum*, for *fovimentum*, a warm application, from *foveo*, to warm, to cherish.] To apply warm lotions to; to bathe with warm medicated liquids or warm water; to encourage; to abet, used especially in a bad sense (to *foment* quarrels).—**Fomentation**, fō-men-tā'shon, *n.* The act of fomenting; encouragement; what is used to foment; a warm lotion.—**Fomenter**, fō-men'tėr, *n.* One who foments.

Fond, fond, *a.* [O.E. *fonne*, to be foolish, fond, stupid; *fon*, a fool; akin to Icel. *fána*, to play the fool; Sw. *fane*, fatuous. The word is properly a past participle, whence the final *d*.] Foolish; indiscreet; imprudent; foolishly tender and loving; doting; relishing highly; loving ardently; delighted with: followed by *of*; foolishly or extravagantly prized (*Shak.*).—**Fondle**, fon'dl, *v.t.* —*fondled*, *fondling*. To treat with tenderness; to caress.—**Fondling**, fond'ling, *n.* A person or thing fondled or caressed.—**Fondly**, fond'li, *adv.* In a fond manner; with indiscreet or excessive affection; affectionately; tenderly.—**Fondness**, fond'nes, *n.* The state of being fond; great affection or liking.

Font, font, *n.* [From L. *fons*, *fontis*, a fountain. FOUNT.] The vessel used in churches as the receptacle of the baptismal water.—**Fontal**,† fon'tal, *a.* Pertaining to a fount, source, or origin.

Font, font, *n.* [Fr. *fonte*, from *fondre*, to melt or found, from L. *fundo*, to pour out, whence also *found*, *foundry*.] A complete assortment of printing types of one size.

Fontanel, fon'ta-nel, *n.* [Fr. *fontanelle*, lit. a little fountain, from L. *fons*, a fountain.] *Anat.* a vacancy in the infant cranium between the frontal and parietal bones, and also between the parietal and occipital.

Food, föd, *n.* [A.Sax. *fóda*, food, whence *fédan*, to feed; Dan. *föde*, Sw. *foda*, food; from root meaning to feed, seen in L. *pasco*, to feed, *pastor*, a shepherd.] Whatever supplies nourishment to organic bodies; nutriment; aliment; victuals; provisions; whatever feeds, sustains, or nourishes.—**Foodless**, föd'les, *a.* Not having or not supplying food.

Fool, föl, *n.* [Fr. *fol*, *fou*, foolish, a fool, from L.L. *follus*, from L. *folles*, bellows, cheeks puffed out, the *follus* or fool being originally one who made grimaces.] One who is destitute of reason or the common powers of understanding; an idiot; a natural; a person who acts absurdly, irrationally, or unwisely; one who does not exercise his reason; a professional jester or buffoon.—*To make a fool of*, to cause to appear ridiculous.—*v.i.* To act like a fool.—*v.t.* To make a fool of; to befool; to deceive; to impose on; to cheat.—*To fool away*, to waste or spend foolishly.—**Foolery**, föl'ėr-i, *n.* Folly; the practice of folly; an act of folly; object of folly.—**Foolhardiness, Foolhardihood**, föl'här-di-nes, föl'här-di-hud, *n.* Quality of being foolhardy; mad rashness. — **Foolhardily**, föl'här-di-li, *adv.* With foolhardiness. — **Foolhardy**, föl'här-di, *a.* [O.Fr. *fol-hardi*.] Daring without judgment; madly rash and adventurous; foolishly bold. Syn. under RASH. —**Foolish**, föl'ish, *a.* Characterized by or exhibiting folly; weak in intellect; unwise; silly; vain; trifling; ridiculous.—**Foolishly**, föl'ish-li, *adv.* In a foolish manner.—**Foolishness**, föl'ish-nes, *n.* The quality or condition of being foolish; folly. —**Foolscap**, fölz'kap, *n.* Paper of the smallest regular size but one, its watermark in early times being the outline of a fool's head and cap.—**Fool's-errand**, *n.* An absurd or fruitless search or enterprise. —**Fool's-parsley**, *n.* A British plant resembling parsley, commonly believed to be poisonous, but if so only in certain localities.

Foot, fut, *n.* pl. **Feet**, fēt. [A.Sax. *fót*, pl. *fét*=Icel. *fótr*, Sw. *fot*, Goth. *fotus*, G. *fuss*; the same word also as L. *pes*, *pedis*, Gr. *pous*, *podos*, Skr. *pâda*, a foot, from a root *pad*, to go.] The lower extremity of an animal's leg; the part of the leg which treads the earth in standing or walking; that surface of the body by which progression is effected among the mollusca; step; tread; footfall; the part of a stocking, boot, &c., which receives the foot; the lower end of anything that supports a body; the part opposite to the head or top; the bottom; soldiers who march and fight on foot; infantry, as distinguished from cavalry; a measure consisting of 12 inches, taken from the length of a man's foot; *pros.* a certain number of syllables forming a distinct part of a verse.—*Square foot*, a square whose side is one foot or any equivalent area; 144 square inches.—*Cubic foot*, a cube whose side is one foot, and which therefore contains 1728 cubic inches or any equivalent solid.—*By foot*, *on foot*, by walking.—*To set on foot*, to originate; to begin; to put in motion.—*To put one's best foot foremost*, to adopt all the means at command.—*Foot-and-mouth disease*, a highly contagious affection which attacks the feet and mouths of cattle.—*v.i.* To dance; to walk, commonly followed by *it*.—*v.t.* To kick or spurn (*Shak.*)‡; to tread; to add or make a foot to (to *foot* a stocking or boot). —**Football**, fut'bal, *n.* A ball made of an inflated ox-bladder, or a hollow globe of india-rubber, cased in leather, to be driven by the foot; a game played with a football by two parties of players.—**Foot-bridge**, fut'brij, *n.* A narrow bridge for foot passengers.—**Footcloth**, fut'kloth, *n.* A sumpter cloth, or housings of a horse, covering his body and reaching to his heels. —**Footed**, fut'ed, *a.* Provided with a foot or feet: usually in composition.—**Foot-fall**, fut'fal, *n.* A footstep; tread of the foot.—**Footgear**, fut'gēr, *n.* The covering of the feet; shoes or boots.—**Foot-guards**, *n. pl.* A body of infantry so called.—**Foot-hold**, fut'hōld, *n.* That on which one may tread or rest securely; firm standing; footing; stable position; settlement.—**Footing**, fut'ing, *n.* Ground for the foot; established place; permanent settlement; foothold; basis; foundation; tread; walk (*Shak.*); relative condition; state (on a *footing* of equality). — *To pay one's footing*, to pay something by way of entrance money, as on entering a new place to prosecute one's trade.—**Foot-iron**, *n.* A carriage-step; a fetter for the feet.—**Foot-jaw**, *n.* The limb of a crustacean, modified so as to serve in mastication.—**Foot-lights**, *n. pl.* A row of lights in a theatre on the front of the stage, and serving to light it up. —**Footman**, fut'man, *n.* An infantry soldier; a male servant whose duties are to attend the door, the carriage, the table, &c.; a man in waiting.—**Footmark**, fut'märk, *n.* A track; mark of a foot.—**Foot-note**, *n.* A note of reference at the bottom of a page.—**Foot-pace**, *n.* A slow step, as in walking.—**Footpad**, fut'pad, *n.* A highwayman that robs on foot.—**Foot-pas-**

senger, *n.* One who travels on foot.—**Footpath**, fụt'path, *n.* A narrow path for foot-passengers only.—**Foot-pavement**, *n.* A paved way for passengers on foot; a footway.—**Foot-pound**, *n.* In mechanics, a unit of work or energy; the work done in raising one pound of weight through a height of one foot against the force of gravity.—**Footprint**, fụt'print, *n.* The mark of a foot.—**Foot race**, *n.* A race performed by men on foot.—**Foot rot**, *n.* A disease in the feet of sheep.—**Foot-rule**, *n.* A rule of 12 inches long; a rule for taking measurements in feet and inches.—**Foot soldier**, *n.* A soldier that serves on foot.—**Footsore**, *a.* Having the feet rendered sore or tender, as by much walking.—**Footstalk**, fụt'stąk, *n.* *Bot.* a petiole; the stalk supporting a leaf; *zool.* a process resembling the footstalk in botany; a peduncle.—**Footstep**, fụt'step, *n.* The mark or impression of the foot; footprint; tread; footfall; sound of the step.—**Footstool**, fụt'stöl, *n.* A stool for the feet when sitting.—**Foot warmer**, *n.* A contrivance for warming or keeping warm the feet.—**Footway**, fụt'wā, *n.* A path for passengers on foot.—**Footworn**, *p.* and *a.* Worn by the feet; footsore.

Fop, fop, *n.* [D. *foppen*, to banter, to make a fool of, *fopper*, a wag.] A vain man of weak understanding and much ostentation; a gay, trifling man; a coxcomb; a dandy.—**Fopling**, fop'ling, *n.* A petty fop.—**Foppery**, fop'ėr-i, *n.* The characteristics of a fop; showy folly; idle affectation; dandyism.—**Foppish**, fop'ish, *a.* Pertaining to a fop; vain of dress; dressing in the extreme of fashion; affected in manners.—**Foppishly**, fop'ish-li, *adv.* In a foppish manner.—**Foppishness**, fop'ish-nes, *n.*

For, for, *prep.* [A.Sax. *for*, for, because of, instead of; D. *voor*, G. *für*, Goth. *faur*, for—allied to E. *fore*, *far*, *fare*; L. *pro*, for or in place of; Skr. *pra*, before: before, in advance, is the root-meaning. The prefix *for-* in *forbid*, &c., is different from this.] In the place of; instead of: indicating substitution or equivalence; corresponding to; accompanying (groan *for* groan); in the character of; as being (he took it *for* truth); toward; with the intention of going to; with a tendency to (an inclination *for* drink); conducive to; tending towards; in expectation of; with a view to obtain; in order to arrive at, get, or procure (to wait *for* money, he writes *for* money); suitable or proper to; against; with a tendency to resist and destroy (a remedy *for* the headache); because of; on account of; by reason of (*for* want of time) [in this usage *but* comes very often before the *for*]; on the part of; in relation to (easy *for* you, but difficult *for* me); in proportion to (tall *for* his age); through a certain space; during a certain time; according to; as far as; so far as concerns; notwithstanding (it may be so *for* anything I know); in favour of; on the part or side of (to vote *for* a person); desirous to have; willing to receive [in this sense often in interjections: O *for* revenge!]; to take up the part or character of (nature intended him *for* a usurer); having so much laid to one's account; to the amount of (he failed *for* ten thousand). ∴ *For* was at one time common before the infinitives of verbs to denote purpose; but this usage is now vulgar.—*For all the world*, of everything else in the world; in every respect; exactly (an animal *for all the world* like a mouse).—*For ever*. Ever.—*conj.* For the cause or reason that; because: a word by which a reason is introduced of something before advanced, being really a preposition governing a clause.—*For as much as*, or *forasmuch as*, in consideration that; seeing that; since.

Forage, for'āj, *n.* [Fr. *fourrage*, O.Fr. *forrage*, from *forre*, forage; from the old German or Scandinavian word equivalent to E. *fodder*.] Food of any kind for horses and cattle; the act of searching for provisions.—*v.i.*—*foraged*, *foraging*. To collect forage; to roam in search of food or provender.—*v.t.* To collect forage from; to supply with forage.—**Forage-cap**, **Foraging-cap**, *n.* A military cap worn by soldiers sent out to forage, or when in fatigue-dress.—**Forager**, for'ā-jėr, *n.* One that forages.

Foramen, fō-rā'men, *n.* pl. **Foramina**, fō-ram'i-na. [L., from *foro*, to bore.] A small natural opening or perforation in parts of animals or plants; an opening by which nerves or blood-vessels obtain a passage through bones.—**Foraminated**, fō-ram'i-nā-ted, *a.* Having foramina or little holes.—**Foraminifer**, fō-ra-min'i-fėr, *n.* [L. *foramen*, *foraminis*, a hole, and *fero*, to bear.] An individual of the Foraminifera.—**Foraminifera**, fō-ram'i-nif″ėr-a, *n. pl.* An order of minute animals belonging to the protozoa, furnished with a shell, simple or complex, usually perforated by pores (whence the name).—**Foraminiferal**, **Foraminiferous**, fō-ram'i-nif″ėr-al, fō-ram'i-nif″ėr-us, *a.* Belonging to the Foraminifera.—**Foraminule**, fō-ram'i-nūl, *n.* A minute foramen.

Forasmuch, for-az-much', *conj.* Under For.

Foray, for'ā, *v.t.* [A form of *forage*.] To ravage; to pillage.—*n.* The act of foraging; a predatory excursion; booty.—**Forayer**, for'ā-ėr, *n.* One who takes part in a foray; a marauder.

Forbade, for-bad', pret. of *forbid*.

Forbear, for-bär', *v.i.*—*forbore* (pret.), *forborne* (pp.). [Prefix *for*, intens., and *bear*; A.Sax. *forberan*, *forbæran*.] To cease; to refrain from proceeding; to pause; to delay; to be patient; to restrain one's self from action or violence.—*v.t.* To avoid voluntarily; to abstain from; to omit; to avoid doing; to treat with indulgence†.—**Forbearance**, for-bär'ans, *n.* The act of forbearing; restraint of passions; long-suffering; indulgence towards those who injure us; lenity.—**Forbearer**, for-bär'ėr, *n.* One who forbears.—**Forbearing**, for-bär'ing, *p.* and *a.* Having forbearance; long-suffering.—**Forbearingly**, for-bär'ing-li, *adv.* In a forbearing manner.

Forbid, for-bid', *v.t.*—pret. *forbade*; pp. *forbid*, *forbidden*; *forbidding*. [Prefix *for*, implying negation, and *bid*.] To prohibit; to interdict; to command to forbear or not to do; to refuse access; to command not to enter or approach; to oppose; to hinder; to obstruct (a river *forbids* approach).—**Forbiddance**,† for-bid'ans, *n.* Prohibition; command or edict against a thing.—**Forbidden**, for-bid'n, *p.* and *a.* Prohibited; interdicted.—**Forbidden-fruit**, *n.* The fruit of the tree of knowledge prohibited to Adam and Eve in Paradise; the fruit of the shaddock when of small size.—**Forbidder**, for-bid'ėr, *n.* One who forbids.—**Forbidding**, for-bid'ing, *a.* Repelling approach; repulsive; raising abhorrence, aversion, or dislike.—**Forbiddingly**, for-bid'ing-li, *adv.* In a forbidding manner; repulsively.—**Forbiddingness**, for-bid'ing-nes, *n.*

Forçat, for-sä, *n.* [Fr., from *forcer*, to force.] A French convict condemned to forced labour; a galley-slave.

Force, fōrs, *n.* [Fr., from L.L. *forcia*, *fortia*, from L. *fortis*, strong; seen also in *fort*, *fortitude*, *fortress*, *comfort*, *effort*, &c.] Active power; vigour; might; strength; energy; that which is the source of all the active phenomena occurring in the material world; that which produces or tends to produce change; one of the modes or forms in which energy is exhibited in nature, as heat or electricity; momentum; the quantity of energy or power exerted by a moving body; violence; power exerted against will or consent; moral power to convince the mind; influence; validity; power to bind or hold (the *force* of an agreement); a military or naval armament; a body of troops; an army or navy; a body of men prepared for action in other ways (a police *force*).—*v.t.*—*forced*, *forcing*. To compel; to constrain to do or to forbear, by the exertion of a power not resistible; to impel; to press, drive, draw, or push by main strength; to compel by strength of evidence (to *force* conviction on the mind); to ravish; to violate (a female); to twist, wrest, or overstrain; to assume, or compel one's self to give utterance or expression to (to *force* a smile); to ripen or bring to maturity by heat artificially applied. In Contract Bridge, to demand a bid from one's partner, as by bidding one more of a suit than is required by the preceding bid, or by making an opening bid of two.—**Forced**, fōrst, *p.* and *a.* Unnaturally assumed; constrained; affected; overstrained; unnatural.—**Forcedly**, fōr'sed-li, *adv.* In a forced manner; constrainedly; unnaturally.—**Forcedness**, fōr'sed-nes, *n.* The state of being forced.—**Forceful**, fōrs'fụl, *a.* Possessing force; powerful; driven with force; acting with power; impetuous (*Shak.*).—**Forcefully**, fōrs'fụl-li, *adv.* Violently; impetuously.—**Forceless**, fōrs'les, *a.* Having little or no force; feeble; impotent.—**Force pump**, **Forcing pump**, *n.* A pump which delivers the water by means of pressure or force directly applied, so as to eject it forcibly to a great elevation; in contradistinction to a pump that raises water by the pressure of the air simply.—**Forcer**, fōr'sėr, *n.* One who or that which forces.—**Forcible**, fōr'si-bl, *a.* Having force; exercising force; powerful; strong; marked by force or violence; violent.—**Forcible feeding**, *n.* The administering of food to a person or animal unwilling, or unable, to eat naturally.—**Forcible entry**, *n.* *Law*, an actual entry into a house or upon lands without lawful authority.—**Forcibleness**, fōr'si-bl-nes, *n.* The condition or quality of being forcible.—**Forcing**, fōr'sing, *n.* *Hort.* the art of raising plants, flowers, and fruits at an earlier season than the natural one, as by artificial heat.

Force, fōrs, *n.* [Icel. *fors*, Dan. *fos*, a waterfall.] A waterfall. (*North of England.*)

Force, fōrs, *v.t.* [Same as *farce*; or perhaps from *force*, in old sense of to season, *forcemeat* being thus highly seasoned meat.] To stuff; to farce.—**Forcemeat**, fōrs'mēt, *n.* *Cookery*, meat chopped fine and seasoned, either served up alone or used as stuffing, *farced* meat, by corruption.

Forceps, for'seps, *n.* [L., from *for* in *formus*, warm, and *capio*, to take.] A two-bladed instrument on the principle of pincers or tongs for holding anything difficult to be held by the hand: used by surgeons, dentists, jewellers, &c.—**Forcipate**, **Forcipated**, for'si-pāt, for'si-pā-ted, *a.* Formed like a forceps.—**Forcipation**, for-si-pā'shon, *n.* Torture by pinching with forceps or pincers.

Forclose, **Forclosure**. Same as *Foreclose*, *Foreclosure*.

Ford, fōrd, *n.* [A.Sax. *ford*, connected with *faran*, to go, to fare; comp. G. *furt*, a ford, *fahren*, to go; allied to Gr. *poros*, a passage; E. *ferry*.] A place in a river or other water where it may be passed by man or beast on foot or by wading.—*v.t.* To pass or cross (a stream) by wading; to wade through.—**Fordable**, fōr'da-bl, *a.* Capable of being forded.—**Fordableness**, fōr'da-bl-nes, *n.* State of being fordable.

Fordo, for-dö', *v.t.*—*fordid* (pret.), *fordone* (pp.). [Prefix *for-*, intens., and *do*.] To destroy; to undo; to ruin; to exhaust, overpower, or overcome, as by toil.

Fore, fōr, *a.* [A.Sax. *fore*, *foran*, before; D. *voor*, Dan. *för*, G. *vor*, before; Goth. *faura*, for; L. *præ*, before, *pro*, for, *por* (as in *porrigere*, to extend), Gr. *paros*, Skr. *pra*, *puras*—before. Akin *far*, *for*, *fare*. *First* and *foremost* are its superlatives.] Advanced, or, locally, in advance of something: opposed to *hind* or *hinder*; coming first in time: opposed to *after*; anterior; prior; antecedent; in front or toward the face; situated towards the stem of a ship.—*Fore and aft* (*naut.*), in a direction from stem to stern; *fore-and-aft* sail, a sail, such as a jib or spanker, that has a position more or less in this direction.—*n.* Used in the phrase *to the fore*, that is, alive; remaining still in existence; not lost, worn out, or spent.

Foreadmonish, fōr-ad-mon′ish, *v.t.* To admonish beforehand.

Forearm, fōr-ärm′, *v.t.* To arm or prepare for attack or resistance before the time of need.

Forearm, fōr′ärm, *n.* That part of the arm which is between the elbow and the wrist.

Forebode, fōr-bōd′, *v.t.—foreboded, foreboding.* To bode beforehand; foretell; to presage; to be prescient of; to feel a secret sense of, as of a calamity about to happen.—**Forebodement**, fōr-bōd′ment, *n.* The act of foreboding.—**Foreboder**, fōr-bō′dėr, *n.* One who forebodes.

Forecast, fōr-kast′, *v.t.*—pret. & pp. *forecast.* To cast or scheme beforehand; to plan before execution; to calculate beforehand; to estimate in the future.—*v.i.* To form a scheme previously; to contrive beforehand.—*n.* (fōr′kast). Previous contrivance or determination; foresight; a guess or estimate of what will happen.—**Forecaster**, fōr-kas′tėr, *n.* One who forecasts.

Forecastle, fōr′kas-l; sailors' pronunciation, fōk′sl, *n.* A short raised deck in the forepart of a ship; the forepart of a vessel where the sailors live.

Forechosen, fōr′chō′zn, *a.* Chosen or elected beforehand.

Foreclose, fōr-klōz′, *v.t.—foreclosed, foreclosing.* [*Fore* for Fr. prefix *for* (as in *forfeit*), from L. *foris*, away, out of doors.] To preclude; to stop; to prevent.—*To foreclose a mortgage*, to compel the mortgager to pay the money due on it, or forfeit his right to the estate.—**Foreclosure**, fōr-klō′zūr, *n.* The act of foreclosing.

Foredate, fōr-dāt′, *v.t.* To date before the true time; to antedate.

Foredeck, fōr′dek, *n.* The forepart of a deck of a ship.

Foredesign, fōr-dē-sīn′ or dē-zīn′, *v.t.* To design or plan beforehand; to intend previously.

Foredetermine, fōr-dē-tėr′min, *v.t.* To determine beforehand.

Foredge, fōr′ej, *n.* The front edge of a book or folded sheet, &c.

Foredispose, fōr-dis-pōz′, *v.t.* To dispose or bestow beforehand.

Foredo, fōr-dö′, *v.t.—foredid* (pret.), *foredone* (pp.). To do beforehand.

Foredoom, fōr-döm′, *v.t.* To doom beforehand; to predestinate.

Foredoor, fōr′dōr, *n.* The door in the front of a house; in contradistinction to *backdoor.*

Fore-end, fōr′end, *n.* The end in front; the anterior part.

Forefather, fōr′fä-ᴛʜėr, *n.* An ancestor.

Forefend, fōr-fend′, *v.t.* To fend off; to avert; to prevent the approach of; to forbid or prohibit.

Forefinger, fōr′fing-gėr, *n.* The finger next to the thumb; the index.

Forefoot, fōr′fụt, *n.* One of the anterior feet of a quadruped or multiped.

Forefront, fōr′frunt, *n.* The foremost part or place.

Foregather, fōr-gaᴛʜ′ėr, *v.i.* Same as *Forgather.*

Forego, fōr-gō′, *v.t.* To forgo (which see).

Forego, fōr-gō′, *v.t.—forewent* (pret.), *foregone* (pp.). To go before; to precede.—**Foregoer**, fōr-gō′ėr, *n.* One who goes before another; an ancestor; a progenitor.—**Foregoing**, fōr-gō′ing or fōr′gō-ing, *p.* and *a.* Preceding; going before, in time or place; antecedent.—**Foregone**, fōr-gon′ or fōr′gon, *p.* and *a.* Past; preceding; predetermined; made up beforehand.

Foreground, fōr′ground, *n.* The part of a picture which is represented so as to appear nearest the eye of the observer.

Forehand, fōr′hand, *n.* The part of a horse which is before the rider; *tennis*, &c., a stroke made with palm forward (by a righthanded player on his right).—*a.* Anticipative; referring to a forehand stroke.

Forehead, fōr′hed or for′ed, *n.* The part of the face which extends from the usual line of hair on the top of the head to the eyes; the brow.

Foreign, for′in, *a.* [Fr. *forain*, from L.L. *foraneus*, from L. *foras*, out of doors (also in *forest*)—same root as E. *door.* As in *sovereign* the *g* has been improperly inserted.] Belonging or relating to another nation or country; not of the country in which one resides; alien; extraneous; not our own; remote; not belonging; not connected; irrelevant; not to the purpose: with *to* or *from.*—**Foreigner**, for′in-ėr, *n.* A person born in or belonging to a foreign country; an alien.—**Foreignism**, for′in-izm, *n.* Foreignness; a foreign idiom or custom.—**Foreignness**, for′in-nes, *n.* The quality of being foreign.

Forejudge, fōr-juj′, *v.t.* To judge beforehand or before hearing the facts and proof; to prejudge.—**Forejudgment**, fōr-juj′ment, *n.* Judgment previously formed.

Foreknow, fōr-nō′, *v.t.—foreknew* (pret.), *foreknown* (pp.). To have previous knowledge of; to know beforehand. — **Foreknowable**, fōr-nō′a-bl, *a.* Capable of being foreknown. — **Foreknowingly**, fōr-nō′ing-li, *adv.* With foreknowledge; deliberately.—**Foreknowledge**, fōr-nol′ej, *n.* Knowledge of a thing before it happens; prescience.

Foreland, fōr′land, *n.* A promontory or cape; a headland.

Foreleg, fōr′leg, *n.* One of the front or anterior legs, as of an animal, a chair, &c.

Forelock, fōr′lok, *n.* The lock or hair that grows from the forepart of the head.—*To take time by the forelock*, to make prompt use of anything; to let no opportunity escape.

Foreman, fōr′man, *n.* pl. **Foremen**, fōr′men. The first or chief man; the chief man of a jury who acts as their speaker; a chief workman who superintends others.

Foremast, fōr′mast, *n.* The mast of a ship or other vessel which is placed before the other or the others.

Forementioned, fōr′men-shond, *a.* Mentioned before; mentioned in a former part of the same writing or discourse.

Foremost, fōr′mōst or fōr′most, *a.* [Should have been *formest* (to correspond with *former*), being the A.Sax. *formest*, a double superlative, from *forma*, first, foremost (itself a superlative), and the *-est* of superlatives: the spelling has been modified by confusion with *most*; so also *hindmost, inmost, outmost.*] First in place, station, honour, or dignity; most advanced; first in time.

Forename, fōr′nām, *n.* A name that precedes the family name or surname.—**Forenamed**, fōr′nāmd, *a.* Named or mentioned before.

Forenoon, fōr′nön, *n.* The part of the day that comes before noon; the part from morning to mid-day.

Forensic, Forensical, fō-ren′sik, fō-ren′si-kal, *a.* [From L. *forensis*, from *forum*, a court, a forum; akin *forest.*] Belonging to courts of justice or to public discussion and debate; used in courts or legal proceedings, or in public discussions.—*Forensic medicine*, medical jurisprudence.

Foreordain, fōr′or-dān, *v.t.* To ordain or appoint beforehand; to preordain; to predestinate.—**Foreordination**, fōr-or′di-nā″shon, *n.* Predetermination; predestination.

Forepart, fōr′pärt, *n.* The most advanced part, or the first in time or place; the anterior part; the beginning.

Forepayment, fōr′pā-ment, *n.* Payment beforehand; prepayment.

Forepeak, fōr′pēk, *n.* *Naut.* the part of a vessel in the angle of the bow.

Forerun, fōr-run′, *v.t.* — *foreran* (pret.), *forerun* (pp.), *forerunning* (ppr.). To run before; to come before, as an earnest of something to follow.—**Forerunner**, fōr-run′ėr, *n.* A messenger sent before to give notice of the approach of others; a harbinger; a sign foreshowing something to follow.

Foresaid, fōr′sed, *a.* Spoken of or mentioned before.

Foresail, fōr′sāl, *n.* *Naut.* the principal sail set on the foremast.

Foresee, fōr-sē′, *v.t.—foresaw* (pret.), *foreseen* (pp.). To see beforehand; to see or know before it happens; to have prescience of; to foreknow.—*v.i.* To exercise foresight.—**Foreseeing**, fōr-sē′ing, *p.* and *a.* Prescient; foresighted.—**Foreseer**, fōr-sē′ėr, *n.* One who foresees.

Foreshadow, fōr-shad′ō, *v.t.* To shadow or typify beforehand.

Foreshew, fōr-shō′, *v.t.*† Same as *Foreshow.*

Foreshore, fōr′shōr, *n.* The sloping part of a shore between high and low watermark.

Foreshorten, fōr-shor′tn, *v.t.* *Persp.* to represent or depict (as an arm, a branch, directed towards the spectator) with the due impression of length, prominence, and relative position.

Foreshot, fōr′shot, *n.* The coarse spirit that first comes over in distilling.

Foreshow, fōr-shō′, *v.t.* — *foreshowed* (pret.), *foreshown* (pp.). To show, represent, or exhibit beforehand; to prognosticate; to foretell. — **Foreshower**, fōr-shō′ėr, *n.* One who foreshows.

Foreside, fōr′sīd, *n.* The front side.

Foresight, fōr′sīt, *n.* The act or power of forseeing; prescience; foreknowledge; provident care for the future; prudence in guarding against evil; wise forethought; the sight on the muzzle of a gun.—**Foresighted**, fōr′sī-ted, *a.* Having foresight; prescient; provident.

Foreskin, fōr′skin, *n.* The fold of skin that covers the anterior extremity of the male member of generation; the prepuce.

Forespend, fōr-spend′, *v.t.* [*Fore*, for prefix *for*, intens.] To weary out; to exhaust.—**Forespent**, fōr-spent′, *p.* and *a.* Tired out; exhausted.

Forest, for′est, *n.* [O.Fr. *forest*, Mod.Fr. *forêt*, from L.L. *foresta*, a forest, from L. *foris, foras*, out of doors, abroad; akin *foreign, forensic.*] An extensive wood, or a large tract of land covered with trees; a tract of mingled woodland and open uncultivated ground; *Eng. law*, a district wholly or chiefly devoted to hunting, and usually a royal domain.—*a.* Of or pertaining to a forest; sylvan; rustic.—*v.t.* To convert into a forest.—**Forestal**, for′es-tal, *a.* Pertaining to a forest.—**Forestation**, for′es-tā″shon, *n.* The act or process of planting a forest.—**Forester**, for′es-tėr, *n.* A person who possesses a knowledge of forestry, particularly one appointed to inspect and care for forests or trees; various moths; the giant kangaroo.—**Forestine**, for′es-tin, *a.* Pertaining to forests; living in forests.—**Forest-oak**, *n.* The ornamental timber of various hardwood trees of Australia; the she-oak or beefwood.—**Forest ranger**, an officer who patrols tracts of forest.—**Forestry**, for′est-ri, *n.* The art of forming or of cultivating forests, or of managing growing timber.—**Forest Service**, a division of the United States Department of Agriculture which manages and cares for national forests.—**Foresty**, for′es-ti, *a.* Abounding in forests.

Forestall, fōr-stal′, *v.t.* [A.Sax. *foresteall*, an intercepting, a placing before, from *fore*, before, and *steall*, a place, a stall.] To take too early action regarding; to realize beforehand; to anticipate; to take possession of in advance of something or somebody else; to hinder by preoccupation or prevention.—*To forestall the market*, to buy up merchandise on its way to market with the intention of selling it again at a higher price: formerly an offence at law.—**Forestaller**, fōr-stal′ėr, *n.* One who forestalls.

Foretaste, fōr′tāst, *n.* A taste beforehand;

anticipation; enjoyment in advance.—*v.t.* (fōr-tāst′). To taste before possession; to have a foretaste of.—**Foretaster**, fōr-tās′-tėr, *n.* One that foretastes.

Foretell, fōr-tel′, *v.t.*—*foretold* (pret. & pp.). To tell before happening; to predict; to prophesy; to foretoken or foreshow; to prognosticate.—*v.i.* To utter prediction or prophecy.—**Foreteller**, fōr-tel′ėr, *n.* One who foretells.

Forethought, fōr′that, *n.* A thinking beforehand; provident care; foresight.

Foretoken, fōr-tō′kn, *v.t.* To betoken beforehand; to foreshow; to presignify; to prognosticate.

Foretooth, fōr′tōth, *n.* pl. **Foreteeth**, fōr′tēth. One of the teeth in the forepart of the mouth; an incisor.

Foretop, fōr′top, *n.* Hair on the forepart of the head; *naut.* the platform erected at the head of the foremast. — **Foretop-mast**, *n.* The mast above the foremast, and below the foretop-gallant mast.

Forewarn, fōr-wạrn′, *v.t.* To warn beforehand; to give previous notice to.

Forewoman, fōr′wụ-man, *n.* A woman who superintends others in a workshop or other establishment.

Foreword, fōr′wėrd, *n.* A preface, an introduction to a book or reprint.

Forfeit, for′fit, *v.t.* [Fr. *forfait*, a crime, misdeed, from *forfaire*, to transgress, L.L. *forisfacere*, to offend—L. *foris*, out of doors, beyond (seen also in *foreclose*, *forest*), and *facere*, to do.] To lose the right to by some fault, crime, or neglect; to become by misdeed liable to be deprived of (an estate, one's life).—*n.* The act of forfeiting; that which is forfeited; a fine; a penalty; a sportive fine or penalty, whence the game of *forfeits*.—*p.* and *a.* Forfeited or subject to be forfeited; liable to deprivation or penal seizure.—**Forfeitable**, for′fit-a-bl, *a.* Liable to be forfeited; subject to forfeiture.—**Forfeiter**, for′fit-ėr, *n.* One who forfeits.—**Forfeiture**, for′fit-ūr, *n.* The act of forfeiting; the losing of some right, privilege, estate, honor, &c., by an offense, crime, breach of condition, or other act; that which is forfeited.

Forfend, for-fend′. Same as *Forefend*.

Forgat, for-gat′ Old form of the pret. of *forget*. (O.T.)

Forgather, for-gaᴛʜ′ėr, *v.i.* [*For*, intens., and *gather*; comp. O.Fris. *forgathera*, to assemble.] To meet; to convene; to come or meet together accidentally.

Forgave, for-gāv′, pret. of *forgive*.

Forge, fōrj, *n.* [Fr. *forge*, It. *forgia*, from L. *fabrica*, a workshop, from *faber*, a workman, a smith. So that *forge* = *fabric*.] A furnace in which iron or other metal is heated to be hammered into form; a workshop for this purpose; a smithy. —*v.t.*—*forged*, *forging*. To work into shape in a forge; to form or shape out in any way; to invent; to produce, as that which is counterfeit or not genuine; to counterfeit, as a signature or document.—*v.i.* To commit forgery.—**Forger**, fōr′jėr, *n.* One who forges; especially, a person guilty of forgery.—**Forgery**, fōr′jėr-i, *n.* The act of forging, fabricating, or producing falsely; the crime of counterfeiting a person's signature on a document; that which is forged, fabricated, or counterfeited.—**Forging**, fōr′jing, *n.* The act of one who forges; an article of metal forged.

Forge, fōrj, *v.i.*—*forged*, *forging*. [Perhaps from Icel. *farga*, to press.] *Naut.* to move on slowly and laboriously; to work one's way: usually with *ahead*, *off*, *past*, &c.

Forget, for-get′, *v.t.*—*forgot* (pret.), *forgot*, *forgotten* (pp.), *forgetting* (ppr.). [A.Sax. *forgitan*—*for*, priv. or neg., and *gitan*, to get. GET.] To lose the remembrance of; to let go from the memory; to cease to have in mind; not to remember or think of; to slight; to neglect; *refl.* to be guilty of something unbecoming; to commit an oversight.—**Forgetable**, **Forgettable**, for-get′a-bl, *a.* Capable of being forgotten. —**Forgetful**, for-get′fụl, *a.* Apt to forget; easily losing remembrance; careless; neglectful; inattentive.—**Forgetfully**, for-get′fụl-li, *adv.* In a forgetful manner.—**Forgetfulness**, for-get′fụl-nes, *n.* The quality of being forgetful; a ceasing to remember; oblivion; neglect; negligence; inattention.—**Forgetter**, for-get′ėr, *n.* One who forgets.—**Forget-me-not**, *n.* A well-known plant, having bright blue flowers with a yellow eye, and considered to be the emblem of friendship and fidelity in many lands.

Forgive, for-giv′, *v.t.*—*forgave* (pret.), *forgiven* (pp.), *forgiving* (ppr.). [A.Sax. *forgifan*—*for*, intens., and *gifan*, to give.] To give up resentment or claim to requital on account of; to remit, as an offence, debt, fine, or penalty; to pardon; to cease to feel resentment against; to free from a claim or the consequences of an injurious act or crime. Syn. under PARDON.—**Forgivable**, for-giv′a-bl, *a.* Capable of being forgiven; pardonable.—**Forgiveness**, for-giv′nes, *n.* The act of forgiving; disposition or willingness to forgive.—**Forgiver**, for-giv′ėr, *n.* One who forgives.—**Forgiving**, for-giv′ing, *p.* and *a.* Disposed to forgive; inclined to overlook offences; mild; merciful; compassionate. — **Forgivingness**, for-giv′ing-nes, *n.*

Forgo, for-gō′, *v.t.*—*forwent* (pret.), *forgone* (pp.). [Also spelled less correctly *forego*; from prefix *for*, intens., or with sense of away, and *go*; A.Sax. *forgán*, to forgo, pass over, neglect.] To forbear to enjoy or possess; to voluntarily avoid enjoying or possessing; to give up, renounce, resign.—**Forgoer**, for-gō′ėr, *n.* One who forgoes.

Forisfamiliate, fō′ris-fa-mil″i-āt, *v.t.* [L. *foris*, out of doors, and *familia*, family.] To emancipate or free from parental authority; to put a son in possession of property in his father's lifetime.—**Forisfamiliation**, fō′ris-fa-mil-i-ā″shon, *n.* The act of forisfamiliating.

Fork, fork, *n.* [A.Sax. *forc*, *furc*, from L. *furca*, a fork, which is also the parent of G. *furke*, D. *vork*, Fr. *fourche*.] An instrument, consisting of a handle with a shank, terminating in two or more parallel prongs, used for holding or lifting something; anything similar in shape; one of the parts into which anything is bifurcated; a prong. —*Forks of a road* or *river*, the point where a road parts into two, the point where two rivers meet and unite in one stream. —*v.i.* To divide into forks or branches. —*v.t.* To raise or pitch with a fork; to dig and break with a fork.—**Forked**, forkt, *a.* Having prongs or divisions like a fork; opening into two or more prongs, points, or shoots; furcated.—**Forkedly**, for′ked-li, *adv.* In a forked form.—**Forkedness**, for′ked-nes, *n.* The quality of being forked. —**Forkiness**, for′ki-nes, *n.* The state of being forky.—**Forky**, for′ki, *a.* Forked; furcated.

Forlorn, for-lorn′, *a.* [A.Sax. *forloren*, pp. of *forleósan*, to lose; prefix *for*, intens., *leósan*, to lose; comp. D. and G. *verloren*, forlorn, lost. LOSE.] Deserted; forsaken; abandoned; lost; helpless; wretched; solitary; bereft; destitute.—*Forlorn hope*. [D. *verloren hoop*—*hoop*, a troop.] A detachment of men appointed to lead in an assault, or perform other service attended with uncommon peril. — **Forlornly**, for-lorn′li, *adv.* In a forlorn manner. — **Forlornness**, for-lorn′nes, *n.*

Form, form, *n.* [Fr. *forme*, form, shape, manner, bench, bed of a hare, from L. *forma*, form, whence *conform*, *inform*, *reform*, &c.] The shape or external appearance of a body, as distinguished from its material; the figure, as defined by lines and angles; appearance to the eye; configuration; a shape; a phantom; manner of arranging particulars; disposition of particular things (a *form* of words); general system or arrangement (a particular *form* of government); something on or after which things are fashioned; a model, draught, pattern; proper shape or trim; high condition or fitness for any undertaking; external appearance without the essential qualities; stated method; established practice; ceremony; a long seat; a bench; a bench or class of pupils in a school; the bed of a hare; *printing*, the pages of type or stereotype plates arranged for printing a sheet, and fastened in an iron frame or chase.—*v.t.* To give form or shape to; to shape; to mould; to arrange; to combine in any particular manner; to model by instruction and discipline; to mould; to train; to devise; to contrive; to frame; to create; to be an element or constituent of; to combine to make up; to answer as; to take the shape of.—*v.i.* To take a form.—**Formal**, for′mal, *a.* Given to outward forms, observances, or ceremonies; strictly ceremonious; done or made in due form or according to regular method; acting according to rule or established mode; having the form or appearance without the substance or essence; conventional; formative. —**Formalism**, for′mal-izm, *n.* The quality of being formal or addicted to mere forms; outside and ceremonial religion.—**Formalist**, for′mal-ist, *n.* One given to formalism.—**Formality**, for-mal′i-ti, *n.* The condition or quality of being formal; form without substance; established order; rule of proceeding; mode; method; customary ceremony; ceremonial; conventionality.—**Formalize**, for′mal-īz, *v.t.*—*formalized*, *formalizing*. To reduce to a form; to give a certain form to; to render formal. —**Formally**, for′mal-li, *adv.* In a formal manner; ceremoniously; stiffly; precisely.—**Format**, for′mä, *n.* [Fr.] Size of a book as regards length and breadth.—**Formation**, for-mā′shon, *n.* The act of forming, making, creating, composing, shaping, &c.; production; the manner in which a thing is formed; *geol.* any series of rocks referred to a common origin or period; *milit.* an arrangement of troops, as in a square, column, &c. — **Formative**, for′ma-tiv, *a.* Giving form; having the power of giving form; plastic; *gram.* serving to form; inflexional.—*n.* *Gram.* that which gives form to a word and is no part of the root.—**Forme**, form, *n.* *Printing*, see FORM.—**Former**, for′mėr, *n.* One who forms.—**Formless**, form′les, *a.* Wanting form or shape; shapeless.—**Formlessness**, form′-les-nes, *n.*

Formaldehyde, form-al′de-hīd, *n.* [FORMIC and ALDEHYDE.] A colorless gas, with a strong odor, used chiefly in solution, as a preservative and disinfectant.

Former, for′mėr, *a.* *compar.* [A compar. from A.Sax. *forma*, first. FOREMOST.] Before or preceding another in time: opposed to *latter*; ancient; long past (*former* ages); preceding; earlier, as between two things mentioned together; first mentioned. — **Formerly**, for′mėr-li, *adv.* In time past, either in time immediately preceding or at an indefinite distance; of old; heretofore. ∴ *Formerly* means before the present time; *previously*, before some particular event.

Formic, for′mik, *a.* [L. *formica*, an act.] Pertaining to or produced by ants.—*Formic acid*, a pungent acid with a peculiar odour, and acting as a corrosive on the skin, originally obtained from ants.—**Formicary**, for′mi-ka-ri, *n.* A colony of ants; an ant-hill. — **Formicate**, for′mi-kāt, *a.* Pertaining to an ant. — **Formication**, for-mi-kā′shon, *n.* [L. *formicatio*.] *Med.* a sensation of the body resembling that made by the creeping of ants on the skin.

Formidable, for′mi-da-bl, *a.* [L. *formidabilis*, from *formido*, fear.] Exciting fear or apprehension; adapted to excite fear or deter from approach, encounter, or undertaking.—**Formidableness**, for′mi-da-bl-nes, *n.* The quality of being formidable.—**Formidably**, for′mi-da-bli, *adv.* In a formidable manner.

Formula, for′mū-la, *n.* pl. **Formulæ**, for′mū-lē, or **Formulas**. [L. *formula*, dim. of *forma*, a form.] A prescribed form; a prescribed form of words in which something is stated; *med.* a prescription; *eccles.* a written confession of faith; a formal enunciation of doctrines; *math.* a rule or principle expressed in algebraic symbols; *chem.* an expression by means of symbols and letters of the constituents of a compound.—**Formular**, for′mū-lėr, *a.* Of or pertaining to a formula.—**Formularization**, for′mū-lėr-i-zā″shon, *n.* The act of formularizing. — **Formularize**, for′mū-lėr-īz, *v.t.*—*formularized, formularizing.* To reduce to a formula; to formulate.—**Formulary**, for′mū-la-ri, *n.* A book containing stated and prescribed forms; a book of precedents.—*a.* Prescribed; ritual. — **Formulate**, for′mū-lāt, *v.t.*—*formulated, formulating.* To reduce to or express in a formula; to put into a precise and comprehensive statement; to state precisely.—**Formulation**, for-mū-lā′shon, *n.* The act of formulating. — **Formulization**, for′mū-li-zā″shon, *n.* The act of formulizing.—**Formulize**, for′mū-līz, *v.t.* To reduce to a formula or formulas; to formulate.

Fornicate, for′ni-kāt, *v.i.* [L. *fornicor, fornicatus*, from *fornix*, a vault, a brothel, brothels in Rome being generally in vaults or cellars.] To have unlawful sexual intercourse.—**Fornication**, for-ni-kā′shon, *n.* [L. *fornicatio.*] The incontinence or lewdness of unmarried persons, male or female. —**Fornicator**, for′ni-kā-tėr, *n.* One guilty of fornication.—**Fornicatress**, for′ni-kā-tres, *n.* An unmarried female guilty of fornication.

Forsake, for-sāk′, *v.t.*—*forsook* (pret.), *forsaken* (pp.), *forsaking* (ppr.). [A.Sax. *forsacan*, to oppose, to renounce; prefix *for*, intens., and *sacan*, to contend; Dan. *forsage*, D. *versaken*, to deny. SAKE.] To quit or leave entirely, often to leave that to which we are bound by duty or natural affection; to desert; to abandon; to depart or withdraw from; to renounce; to reject.—**Forsaker**, for-sā′kėr, *n.* One that forsakes.

Forsooth, for-söth′, *adv.* [*For* and *sooth*, that is, for or in truth. A.Sax. *forsóth.*] In truth; in fact; certainly; very well; often in ironical expressions.

Forswear, for-swār′, *v.t.*—*forswore* (pret.), *forsworn* (pp.). [Prefix *for* with negative sense.] To reject or renounce upon oath; to renounce earnestly or with protestations; *refl.* to swear falsely; to perjure one's self. —*v.i.* To swear falsely; to commit perjury. —**Forswearer**, for-swā′rėr, *n.* One who forswears; one who is perjured.

Fort, fōrt, *n.* [Fr. *fort, lit.* strong place from *fort*, L. *fortis*, strong. FORCE.] A fortified place; usually, a small fortified place, occupied only by troops.—**Fortalice**, fōr′ta-lis, *n.* [O.Fr. *fortelesse*, L.L. *fortalitium.*] A small outwork of a fortification.—**Forte**, fōr′tā, *adv.* [It.] *Mus.* direction to sing or play with force of tone. —**Forte**, fōrt, *n.* [Fr. *fort*, strong part, also a person's forte (the final *e* being an English insertion).] The strong portion of a sword-blade or rapier; peculiar talent or faculty a person has; a strong point; chief excellence.—**Fortress**, fort′res, *n.* [Fr. *forteresse*, O.Fr. *fortelesse*: same word as *fortalice.*] A fortified place, especially one of considerable extent and complication; a stronghold; a place of security.

Forth, fōrth, *adv.* [A.Sax. *forth*, from *fore*, before; G. *fort*, on, further; D. *voord*, forward. FORE.] Onward in time, place, or order (from that time *forth*); in advance from a given point; forward; out; abroad; from a state of concealment; from an interior; out into view.—**Forthcoming**, fōrth′kum-ing, *a.* Ready to appear; making appearance.—**Forthgoing**, fōrth′gō-ing, *a.* Going forth.—*n.* A going forth or utterance; a proceeding from. — **Forthright**, fōrth′rīt, *adv.* Straightforward; straightway. — *a.* Straightforward; direct; immediate.—*n.* A straight way; opposed to meanders. (*Shak.*)—**Forthwith**, fōrth′-with, *adv.* [*Forth* and *with*, forth along with that.] Immediately; without delay; directly.

Fortify, for′ti-fī, *v.t.*—*fortified, fortifying.* [Fr. *fortifier*, from L.L. *fortifico*—L. *fortis*, strong, and *facio*, to make.] To add strength to; to strengthen (an argument, resolution); to furnish with strength or means of resisting (to *fortify* one against cold); to surround with a wall, ditch, palisades, or other works, with a view to defend against the attacks of an enemy; to increase the alcoholic strength of (wine) by means of adventitious spirit.—**Fortifiable**, for′ti-fī-a-bl, *a.* Capable of being fortified.—**Fortification**, for′ti-fi-kā″shon, *n.* The act of fortifying; the art or science of strengthening military positions in such a way that they may be readily defended; the works constructed for the purpose of strengthening a position; a fortified place; a fort.—**Fortifier**, for′ti-fī-ėr, *n.* One who fortifies.

Fortissimo, for-tis′sē-mō, *adv.* *Mus.* a direction to sing with the utmost strength or loudness.

Fortitude, for′ti-tūd, *n.* [L. *fortitudo*, from *fortis*, strong. FORCE.] That strength or firmness of mind or soul which enables a person to encounter danger or to bear pain with coolness and courage; passive courage; resolute endurance.

Fortnight, fort′nīt, *n.* [Contr. from *fourteen nights*, time being formerly often reckoned by nights. SE′NNIGHT.] The space of fourteen days; two weeks.—**Fortnightly**, fort′nīt-li, *adv.* Once a fortnight; every fortnight.—*a.* Occurring or appearing once a fortnight.

Fortress. Under FORT.

Fortuitous, for-tū′i-tus, *a.* [L. *fortuitus*, from *fors, fortis*, chance. FORTUNE.] Accidental; happening by chance; occurring without any known cause.—**Fortuitously**, for-tū′i-tus-li, *adv.* In a fortuitous manner; accidentally; by chance. — **Fortuitousness**, for-tū′i-tus-nes, *n.*—**Fortuity**, for-tū′i-ti, *n.* Accident; chance; casualty.

Fortune, for′tūn, *n.* [L. *fortuna*, a lengthened form from stem of *fors, fortis*, chance, hap, luck, from *fero*, to bring (as in *fertile*).] Chance; accident; luck; fate; also, the personified or deified power regarded as determining the lots of life; the good or ill that befalls or may befall man; success, good or bad; what the future may bring; good success; prosperity; good luck; estate; possessions; especially, large estate; great wealth.—*v.i.* To befall; to fall out; to happen; to come casually to pass.—**Fortunate**, for′tū-nāt, *a.* [L. *fortunatus.*] Coming by good fortune or favourable chance; bringing some unexpected good; having good fortune; lucky; successful. ∴ *Fortunate* refers to that which is deemed beyond our own control; *successful* denotes that effective effort has been made to gain the object; *prosperous* leaves both these notions out of account, simply conveying the fact of there being a flourishing state of matters. —**Fortunately**, for′tū-nāt-li, *adv.* In a fortunate manner; luckily; happily.—**Fortunateness**, for′tū-nāt-nes, *n.* — **Fortune-hunter**, *n.* A man who seeks to marry a woman with a large fortune, with a view to enrich himself. — **Fortune-hunting**, *n.* The seeking of a fortune by marriage.—**Fortuneless**, for′tūn-les, *a.* Luckless; also, destitute of a fortune or wealth.—**Fortune-teller**, *n.* One who pretends to tell people their fortune in life. —**Fortune-telling**, *n.* The act or practice of telling fortunes.

Forty, for′ti, *a.* [A.Sax. *feówertig*—*feówer*, four, and *tig*, ten. FOUR.] Four times ten; thirty-nine and one added.—*n.* The number which consists of four times ten; or a symbol expressing it. — *The roaring forties*, the stormy area of the Atlantic between 39° and 50° N. lat.—*The forty-five*, the Jacobite rebellion of 1745, following on the '15 of 1715.—*The forty thieves*, the tale of Ali Baba in the *Arabian Nights.*—*Forty winks*, short nap.—**Fortieth**, for′ti-eth, *a.* Following the thirty-ninth; being one of forty equal parts into which anything is divided.—*n.* One of forty equal parts into which a whole is divided.

Forum, fō′rum, *n.* [L., connected with *foris*, out of doors; hence *forensic.*] A public place in Rome where causes were judicially tried and orations delivered to the people; a tribunal; a court.

Forward, for′wėrd, *adv.* [A.Sax. *foreweard*—*fore*, before, and *weard*, used to signify direction. Comp. G. *vorwärts.*] Toward a part or place before or in front; onward; progressively: opposed to *backward.*—*a.* Being at the front; anterior; fore; ready; prompt; ardent; eager; over bold; self-assertive; pert; saucy; advanced beyond the usual degree; advanced for the season.—*n.* One in advance; a front player in football.—*v.t.* To advance or help onward; to further, promote, accelerate, hasten; to send toward the place of destination; to transmit; *bookbinding*, to prepare for the finisher. — **Forwarder**, for′wėr-dėr, *n.* One who forwards. — **Forwardly**, for′-wėrd-li, *adv.* In a forward manner; eagerly; pertly; saucily.—**Forwardness**, for′wėrd-nes, *n.* The quality of being forward; promptitude; pertness.—**Forwards**, *adv.* Forward; toward the front.

Fosse, Foss, fos, *n.* [Fr. *fosse*, L. *fossa*, a ditch, a trench, from *fodio, fossum*, to dig, whence also *fossil.*] *Fort.* a ditch or moat, commonly full of water, outside the walls or rampart of a fortified place or post to be defended; *anat.* a kind of cavity in a bone with a large aperture.

Fossil, fos′sil, *a.* [Fr. *fossile*, L. *fossilis*, from *fodio, fossum*, to dig. FOSSE.] Dug out of the earth; petrified and preserved in rocks.—*n.* Originally any substance dug out of the earth; now specifically applied to the petrified remains of plants and animals which occur in the strata that compose the surface of our globe; an antiquated person, a petrified fogey.—**Fossil-cork, Fossil-flax**, *n.* Popular names for special varieties of asbestos.—**Fossiliferous**, fos-si-lif′ėr-us, *a.* Producing or containing fossils. —**Fossilification**, fos-sil′i-fi-kā″shon, *n.* Act of fossilifying, or of becoming fossil.—**Fossilify**, fos-sil′i-fī, *v.t.* To convert into a fossil; to fossilize. — *v.i.* To become a fossil.—**Fossilist**, fos′sil-ist, *n.* One who is versed in fossils; a palæontologist. — **Fossilization**, fos′sil-i-zā″shon, *n.* The act or process of fossilizing; the state of being fossilized.—**Fossilize**, fos′sil-īz, *v.t.* —*fossilized, fossilizing.* To convert into a fossil; *fig.* to render permanently antiquated; to cause to be out of harmony with present time and circumstances.—*v.i.* To become a fossil; to become antiquated, rigid, and fixed.

Fossorial, fos-sō′ri-al, *a.* [L. *fossor*, a digger, from *fodio, fossum*, to dig.] Pertaining to animals which dig dwellings and seek their food in the earth; adapted for digging.—**Fossulate**, fos′sū-lāt, *a.* [L. *fossula*, dim. of *fossa*, a ditch.] *Nat. hist.* presenting small, long, and narrow superficial depressions.

Foster, fos′tėr, *v.t.* [A.Sax. *fóstrian*, to nourish, from *fóster*, nourishment, from *fóda*, food. FOOD, FODDER.] To nourish or nurture; to bring up; to cherish; to promote the growth of; to encourage; to sustain and promote.—**Foster-brother**, *n.* One who is a brother only by being nursed at the same breast. — **Foster-child**, *n.* A child nurtured by one who is not its mother or father. — **Foster-daughter**, *n.* One who is a daughter only by nursing.—**Fosterer**, fos′tėr-ėr, *n.* One that fosters.—**Foster-father**, *n.* One who takes the place of a father in bringing up and educating a child.—**Fosterling**, fos′tėr-ling, *n.* A foster-child. — **Foster-mother**, *n.* A woman who takes the place of a mother in bringing up a child.—**Foster-parent**, *n.* A foster-father or foster-mother.—**Foster-sister**, *n.* A female, not a sister, nursed by the same person.—**Foster-son**, *n.* One brought up like a son, though not the person's son by birth.

Fother, foᴛʜ′ėr, *v.t.* [A.Sax. *fodder*, a covering or case; G. *futter*, lining.] To stop a leak by letting down a sail over it lined with oakum, spun yarn, &c.

Fother, foᴛʜ′ėr, *n.* [A.Sax. *fóther*, a cart-load; D. *voeder*, G. *fuder.*] A weight for lead = 19½ cwts.

Fougade, Fougasse, fö-gäd′, fö-gäs′, *n.* [Fr., from L. *focus*, a fire.] *Milit.* a little mine in the form of a well, 8 or 10 feet wide and 10 or 12 deep, dug under some work or post.

Fought, fat, pret. & pp. of *fight*.

Foul, foul, *a.* [A.Sax. *fūl*, foul = Icel. *fúll*, Dan. *fuul*, D. *vuil*, G. *faul*, Goth. *fuls*, putrid, corrupt; same root as L. *puteo*, Skr. *pûy*, to be putrid.] Covered with or containing extraneous matter, which is injurious, noxious, or offensive; filthy; dirty; not clean; turbid; muddy; scurrilous; obscene or profane; abusive; stormy, rainy, or tempestuous (*foul* weather); detestable; vile; shameful; odious; unfair; not lawful; *sports*, denoting, or pertaining to, an act committed contrary to the rules of the game; *naut.* entangled or in collision: opposed to *clear*.—*Foul ball, baseball*, a batted ball that falls or rolls outside the field of play bounded by two straight lines (*foul lines*) that extend from home plate past first base and third base to the boundary of the field.—*To run* or *fall foul of*, to rush upon; to attack; to run against; to stumble over or upon.—*v.t.* To make filthy; to defile; to dirty; to soil.—*v.i.* To become foul or dirty; to commit a foul; to hit a ball foul; *naut.* to come into collision; to become entangled or clogged.—*n.* The act of fouling; a colliding, or otherwise impeding due motion or progress.—**Foully**, foul'li, *adv.* In a foul manner.—**Foulness**, foul'nes, *n.* The quality or state of being foul or filthy.—**Foul-mouthed**, *a.* Using foul or vile language; uttering abuse, or profane or obscene words.

Found, found, pret. & pp. of *find*.

Found, found, *v.t.* [Fr. *fonder*, from L. *fundo*, to found, from *fundus*, the bottom of anything; hence also *fund*, *founder*.] To lay the basis of; to base; to establish on a basis literal or figurative; to take the first steps in erecting or building up; to originate.—*v.i.* To rest or rely: followed by *on* or *upon* (I *found upon* my own observation). — **Foundation**, foun-dā'shon, *n.* The act of founding, establishing, or beginning to build; the masonry or the solid ground on which the walls of a building rest; the basis or groundwork of anything; that on which anything stands and is supported; fund invested for a benevolent purpose; endowment; an endowed institution or charity. — **Foundationer**, foun-dā'shon-ėr, *n.* One who derives support from the foundation or endowment of a college or endowed school.—**Foundationless**, foun-dā'shon-les, *a.* Having no foundation. —**Foundation-stone**, *n.* A stone of a public building, laid in public with some ceremony.—**Founder**, foun'dėr, *n.* One who founds; one who fixes, originates, or establishes.—**Foundress**, foun'dres, *n.* A female founder.

Found, found, *v.t.* [Fr. *fondre*, to melt, to cast, from L. *fundo*, *fusum*, to pour out (hence *fuse*, &c.).] To form by melting a metal and pouring it into a mould; to cast. —**Founder**, foun'dėr, *n.* One who founds; one who casts metals in various forms.— **Foundry, Foundery**, foun'dri, foun'dėr-i, *n.* [Fr. *fonderie*.] The art of casting metals; the buildings and works occupied for casting metals.

Founder, foun'dėr, *v.i.* [O.Fr. *fondrer*, *afondrer*, to founder—*fond*, ground, bottom, from L. *fundus*, bottom. FOUND, to establish.] To fill or be filled and sink; to go down: said of a ship; to fail; to miscarry; to go lame: said of a horse.—*n. Farriery*, a lameness occasioned by inflammation within the hoof of a horse; an inflammatory fever or acute rheumatism.

Foundling, found'ling, *n.* [Dim. formed from *found*, as *bantling* from *band*, *darling* from *dear*.] A child found without a parent or any one to take care of it.

Fount, fount, *n.* [L. *fons*, *fontis*. FONT.] A spring of water; a fountain.—*Fount of types*. FONT, in this sense.—**Fountain**, foun'tān, *n.* [Fr. *fontaine*, L.L. *fontana*, from L. *fons*, *fontis*.] A spring or natural source of water; the head or source of a river; an artificial spout, jet, or shower of water; a basin or other structure kept constantly supplied with water for use or for ornament; the origin or source of anything. —**Fountain-head**, *n.* Primary source; origin.—**Fountainless**, foun'tān-les, *a.* Having no fountain or springs.—**Fountain-pen**, *n.* A writing pen with a reservoir for furnishing a continuous supply of ink.

Four, fōr, *a.* [A.Sax. *feówer*=Fris. *flower*, Icel. *fjórir*, Dan. *fire*, G. and D. *vier*, Goth. *fidwor*, L. *quatuor*, Gr. *tettares*, Russ. *cetvero*, W. *pedwar*, Ir. *ceathair*, Skr. *chatvâr*.] Twice two; three and one.—*n.* The number consisting of twice two; the symbol representing this number.—*On all four*, or *on all fours*. *All-fours*, under ALL.—**Four-flush**, *n.* and *v.i.* Bluff.—**Fourflusher**, *n.* One who bluffs, boasts or deceives.—**Fourfold**, fōr'fōld, *a.* Four times told; quadruple.—**Four-in-hand**, *n.* A vehicle drawn by four horses and guided by one driver holding all the reins; a necktie tied with a slip-knot at the collar and hanging down the shirt front.—**Fourpence, Fourpenny**, fōr'pens, fōr'pen-i, *n.* A British silver coin worth 8 cents.—**Four-poster**, *n.* A large bed having four posts or pillars for the curtains.—**Fourscore**, fōr'skōr, *a.* Four times twenty; eighty: often elliptically for fourscore years.—*n.* Twenty taken four times; eighty units.— **Foursome**, fōr'sum, *n.* Game of golf between two pairs; dance or reel of two pairs. —**Fourteen**, fōr'tēn, *n.* [A.Sax. *feówertýne*.] The number consisting of ten and four, or the symbol representing it.—*a.* Four and ten; twice seven.—**Fourteenth**, fōr'tēnth, *a.* The ordinal of fourteen; the fourth after the tenth.—*n.* One of fourteen equal parts in which a whole is divided.— **Fourth**, fōrth, *a.* [A.Sax. *feórtha*.] The ordinal of four; the next after the third.— *n.* One of four equal parts into which a whole is divided; *mus.* an interval composed of two tones and a semitone.—*The fourth of July*, in the U. S., the holiday celebrating the Declaration of Independence.—**Fourthly**, fōrth'li, *adv.*

Fourchette, fōr-shet', *n.* [Fr. dim. of *fourche*, fork. FORK.] A small fork-shaped piece or implement; the furculum, or wishbone, of a bird.

Fourgon, fōr-goṅ, *n.* [Fr.] An ammunition wagon; a baggage cart.

Fourierism, fō'ri-ėr-izm, *n.* A socialistic system or form of communism propounded by Charles *Fourier*, a Frenchman.—**Fourierist, Fourierite**, fō'ri-ėr-ist, fō'ri-ėr-it, *n.* An adherent of this system.

Foveate, Foveolate, fō'vē-āt, fō'vē-ō-lāt, *a.* [L. *fovea*, a pit.] *Bot.* marked by little depressions or pits; pitted.

Fovilla, fō-vil'la, *n.* [Dim. formed from L. *foveo*, to warm, to nourish.] *Bot.* the minute powder or semi-fluid matter contained in the interior of the pollen grain, and which is the immediate agent in fertilization.

Fowl, foul, *n.* [A.Sax. *fugel*, *fugol*, a fowl, a bird = D. and G. *vogel*, Icel. and Dan. *fugl*, Goth. *fugls*, a bird; can hardly be connected with *fly*.] A bird: often unchanged in the plural (the *fowl* of the air); now very commonly a cock or hen; a barndoor or domestic fowl.—*v.i.* To catch or kill wild fowls.—**Fowler**, fou'lėr, *n.* A sportsman who pursues wild fowls.—**Fowling-piece**, *n.* A light gun for shooting fowls or birds of any kind.

Fox, foks, *n.* [A.Sax. *fox*; G. *fuchs*, L.G. *voss*, *vos*, Prov.E. *faws*, Goth. *fauho*, fox. *Fixen* (E. *vixen*) was the A.Sax. for shefox.] A carnivorous animal closely allied to the dog, remarkable for his cunning, and preying on lambs, geese, hens, or other small animals; a sly, cunning fellow.—*v.t.* and *i.* To turn sour: applied to beer when it sours in fermenting.—**Fox-bat**, *n.* A name for some of the largest of the bat tribe inhabiting the Australian region.— **Fox-brush**, *n.* The tail of a fox.—**Fox-earth**, *n.* A hole in the earth to which a fox resorts to hide itself.—**Foxed**, fokst, *p.* and *a.* Marked with brownish stains or spots, as paper.—**Foxglove**, foks'gluv, *n.* [A.Sax. *foxes glofa*, lit. fox's glove.] A common plant, conspicuous by its tall spike of large showy flowers in long onesided racemes; digitalis.—**Fox-hound**, *n.* A hound for chasing foxes, of great fleetness, strength, and perseverance, and with a keen scent.—**Fox-hunt**, *n.* The chase or hunting of a fox with hounds.—**Foxish**, foks'ish, *a.* Resembling a fox in qualities; cunning.—**Fox-shark**, *n.* A kind of shark, the *Sea-fox* or *Thresher*.—**Foxtail grass**, any of certain grasses with tail-like spikelets.—**Fox terrier**, a small, smoothhaired or wire-haired dog, first bred to dig out foxes.—**Fox trot**, a form of ballroom dance in four-four time.—**Foxy**, foks'i, *a.* Pertaining to foxes; wily, as of one who is cunning or sly as a fox; suggestive of a fox or of cunning; sour: said of wine, beer, &c., which has soured in fermenting.

Foyer, fwą-yā, *n.* [Fr., L.L. *focarium*, a hearth, L. *focus*.] A lobby or anteroom in a public building, as a theater.

Fracas, fra-kä', *n.* [Fr., from *fracasser*, to crash; It. *fracassare*, to break.] An uproar; a noisy quarrel; a disturbance.

Fracid, fras'id, *a.* [L. *fracidus*, mellow, soft.] Rotten from being too ripe; overripe; *bot.* of a pasty texture, between fleshy and pulpy.

Fraction, frak'shon, *n.* [Fr. *fraction*, from L. *fractio*, a breaking, from *frango*, *fractum*, to break; akin *frail*, *fragile*, *fragment*, *fracture*, *infringe*, &c.] The act of breaking‡; a fragment; a portion; a very small part; *arith.* and *alg.* one or more of the equal parts into which a unit or whole number is divided or supposed to be divided (as $\frac{2}{5}$, two fifths, $\frac{1}{4}$, one fourth, which are called *vulgar fractions*; .56, .004, *decimal* fractions).—**Fractional**, frak'shon-al, *a.* Pertaining to fractions; constituting a fraction.—*Fractional distillation*, the distillation of a mixture of liquids that have different boiling-points, so that the most volatile comes over first, the others as more heat is applied, as in refining shale-oil or petroleum.—**Fractionary**, frak'shon-a-ri, *a.* Fractional; pertaining to a fraction or small portion of a thing.—**Fractionize, Fractionate**, frak-shon-īz', frak-shon'āt, *v.t.* To separate into fractions.

Fractious, frak'shus, *a.* [From Prov.E. *fratch*, to quarrel or chide.] Apt to quarrel; cross; snappish; peevish; fretful. — **Fractiously**, frak'shus-li, *adv.* In a fractious manner; snappishly. — **Fractiousness**, frak'shus-nes, *n.* A fractious temper.

Fracture, frak'tūr, *n.* [L. *fractura*, from *frango*, *fractum*, to break. FRACTION.] A breakage; a breach in a body, especially caused by violence; a crack; a rupture; *surg.* the breaking of a bone; *mineral.* the characteristic manner in which a mineral breaks, and by which its texture is displayed. — *v.t.* — *fractured*, *fracturing*. To cause fracture in; to break; to crack.

Fragile, fraj'il, *a.* [L. *fragilis*, from *frango*, to break. FRACTION. *Frail* is the same word.] Brittle; easily broken; easily destroyed; frail.—**Fragilely**, fraj'il-li, *adv.* In a fragile manner.—**Fragileness, Fragility**, fraj'il-nes, fra-jil'i-ti, *n.* The condition or quality of being fragile; brittleness; delicacy of substance.

Fragment, frag'ment, *n.* [L. *fragmentum*, from *frango*, to break. FRACTION.] A part broken off; a piece separated from anything by breaking; anything left uncompleted; a part separated from the rest.— **Fragmental**, frag-men'tal, *a.* Consisting of fragments; fragmentary.—**Fragmentarily**, frag'men-ta-ri-li, *adv.* In a fragmentary manner; by piecemeal. — **Fragmentariness**, frag'men-ta-ri-nes, *n.* The state or quality of being fragmentary.— **Fragmentary**, frag'men-ta-ri, *a.* Composed of fragments or broken pieces; broken up; not complete or entire; disconnected.

Fragrant, frā'grant, *a.* [L. *fragrans*, *fragrantis*, ppr. of *fragro*, to emit a scent.] Sweet of smell; affecting the olfactory nerves agreeably; having an agreeable perfume; odoriferous. — **Fragrantly**, frā'grant-li, *adv.* With sweet scent.—**Fragrance, Fragrancy**, frā'grans, frā'-

gran-si, *n.* The quality of being fragrant; sweetness of smell; pleasing scent; perfume.

Frail, frāl, *a.* [Fr. *frêle*, O.Fr. *fraile*, L. *fragilis*, fragile. FRAGILE.] Easily broken; fragile; liable to fail and decay; easily destroyed; perishable; not firm or durable; not strong against temptation to evil; liable to fall from virtue.—**Frailly**, frāl'li, *adv.* In a frail manner; weakly.—**Frailness**, frāl'nes, *n.* The condition or quality of being frail.—**Frailty**, frāl'ti, *n.* The condition or quality of being frail; weakness of resolution; infirmity; liableness to be deceived or seduced; a fault proceeding from weakness; a foible.

Frail, frāl, *n.* [O.Fr. *frael*, *frayel*.] A basket made of rushes, in which dried fruit is occasionally imported.

Fraise, frāz, *n.* [Fr., same word as *frieze* (on a building).] *Fort.* a defence consisting of pointed stakes driven into the ramparts in a horizontal or inclined position. —**Fraised**, frāzd, *a.* Fortified with a fraise.

Frambœsia, fram-bē'si-a, *n.* [Fr. *framboise*, a raspberry.] The yaws, a contagious disease prevalent in the Antilles and some parts of Africa, characterized by raspberry-like excrescences: whence the name.

Frame, frām, *v.t.*—*framed*, *framing*. [A. Sax. *fremman*, to form, make, effect, from *fram*, *from*, strong, forward = *from*, prep.; O.Sax. *fremmian*, O.Fris. *frema*, Icel. *fremja*, to accomplish.] To construct by fitting and uniting together the several parts; to make, compose, contrive, devise, invent, fabricate; to fit, as for a specific end; to adjust, shape, conform; to surround or provide with a frame, as a picture.—*n.* Anything composed of parts fitted and united; fabric; structure; specifically, bodily structure; make or build of a person; the main timbers of a structure fitted and joined together for the purpose of supporting and strengthening the whole; framework; some kind of case or structure for admitting, inclosing, or supporting things; particular state, as of the mind; temper or disposition.—**Framable**, frā'ma-bl, *a.* Capable of being framed.—**Frame-bridge**, *n.* A bridge constructed of pieces of timber framed together.—**Frame-house**, *n.* A house constructed with a wooden skeleton.—**Framer**, frā'mėr, *n.* One who frames; a maker; a contriver. —**Frame-saw**, *n.* A thin saw stretched on a frame, without which it would not have sufficient rigidity for working. —**Framework**, frām'wėrk, *n.* A structure or fabric for supporting anything; a frame; fabric; structure. —**Framing**, frā'ming, *n.* A framework or frame; a system of frames.

Frampold, fram'pōld, *a.* [Comp. W. *ffromawl*, peevish, testy; *ffromi*, to grow angry.] Unruly; peevish; quarrelsome. (*Shak.*)

Franc, frangk, *n.* [Fr., from the device *Francorum rex*, king of the French, on the coin when first struck by King John in 1360.] The French monetary unit, formerly valued at 19.3 cents, but since 1928 worth about 4 cents.

Franchise, fran'chīz, *n.* [Fr., from *franc*, free. FRANK.] A particular privilege or right granted by a government, as the right to vote, to operate a railroad, or to form, and exercise the powers of, a corporate body.

Franciscan, fran-sis'kan, *n.* A mendicant of the order founded by St. Francis of Assisi about 1210, and also called *Minorites*, *Gray Friars*, from the former color of their habit, or *Black Friars*, from the color of the habit worn by the Conventuals.

Francolin, frang'ko-lin, *n.* [Dim. of Pg. *frango*, a hen.] A bird closely allied to the partridges, found throughout the warmer parts of Europe, as well as in Asia.

Franc-tireur, frăn-tē-rėr, *n.* [Fr., lit. a free-shooter.] One of a body of irregular sharp-shooters organized in France in the war of 1870, and employed in guerrilla warfare.

Frangible, fran'ji-bl, *a.* [From L. *frango*, to break. FRACTION.] Capable of being broken; brittle. — **Frangent**, fran'jent, *a.* Causing fractures. — **Frangibility**, **Frangibleness**, fran-ji-bil'i-ti, fran'ji-bl-nes, *n.* The state or quality of being frangible.

Frangipanni, fran-ji-pan'ni, *n.* A perfume prepared from, or imitating the odour of, the flower of a West Indian tree.

Frangulin, frang'gū-lin, *n.* A yellowish colouring matter used in dyeing, obtained from the bark of the alder-buckthorn (*Rhamnus frangula*).

Frank, frangk, *a.* [Fr. *franc*, free, originally free like the *Franks*, the word being from the name of this old Germanic tribe or nation.] Free in uttering real sentiments; not reserved; open; candid; ingenuous; using no disguise; generous or liberal‡.—*n.* The privilege granted by the federal government to its bureaus, legislators, and accredited representatives of foreign governments, of sending, postage free, mail concerned with official business.—*v.t.* To send by means of a frank; to transmit free of expense.—**Frankly**, frangk'li, *adv.* In a frank manner; openly; candidly.—**Frankness**, frangk'nes, *n.* The state or quality of being frank.—**Frank-pledge**, *n.* [A pledge given by free men.] An institution in early England by which the members of a tithing, composed of ten households, were made responsible for each other, so that if one committed an offense the others were bound to make reparation.

Frank, frangk, *n.* One of the ancient German race of the Franks; a native of Franconia; a name given by the Orientals to the inhabitants of western Europe. —**Frankish**, frang'kish, *a.* Relating or pertaining to the Franks.

Frankfort-black, frangk'fort, *n.* A fine black pigment used in copperplate printing.

Frankincense, frangk'in-sens, *n.* [That is, pure, unadulterated incense.] A gum resin obtained from a tree somewhat resembling the sumach, inhabiting the mountains of India, which, when burned, exhales a strong aromatic odour.

Franklin, frangk'lin, *n.* [O.Fr. *frankeleyn*, *francheleyn*, from L.L. *franchilanus*, from *francus*, free. FRANK, *a.*] A freeholder; a yeoman; one whose estate was free of any feudal superior.

Frantic, fran'tik, *a.* [Fr. *frénétique*, from L. *phreneticus*, from Gr. *phrenitis*, mental disorder, frenzy, from *phrēn*, the mind. FRENZY.] Mad; raving; furious; outrageous; distracted (a *frantic* person); characterized by violence, fury, and disorder (a *frantic* outburst).—**Frantically**, **Franticly**, fran'ti-kal-li, fran'tik-li, *adv.* In a frantic or furious manner.—**Franticness**, fran'tik-nes, *n.*

Frap, frap, *v.t.*—*frapped*, *frapping*. [Fr. *frapper*, to strike, to frap, of Scandinavian origin.] *Naut.* to make fast or tight, as by passing ropes round a sail or a weakened vessel, or by binding tackle with yarn.

Fraternal, fra-tėr'nal, *a.* [Fr. *fraternel*; L. *fraternus*, from *frater*, brother; a word cog. with E. *brother*.] Brotherly; pertaining to brothers; becoming or proceeding from brothers. —**Fraternally**, fra-tėr'nal-li, *adv.* In a fraternal manner.—**Fraternity**, fra-tėr'ni-ti, *n.* [Fr. *fraternité*; L. *fraternitas*.] The state or relationship of a brother; a body of men associated for their common interest, business, or pleasure; a brotherhood; a society; a class or profession of men. —**Fraternization**, frat'ėr-ni-zā"shon, *n.* The act of fraternizing.—**Fraternize**, **Fraternise**, frat'ėr-nīz, *v.i.* To associate or hold fellowship; to hold sympathetic intercourse; to have congenial sympathies and intercourse.—**Fraternizer**, frat'ėr-nī-zėr, *n.* One who fraternizes. —**Fratricide**, frat'ri-sīd, *n.* [L. *fratricidium*, the crime, *fratricida*, the criminal—*frater*, and *cædo*, to kill.] The crime of murdering a brother; one who murders or kills a brother.—**Fratricidal**, frat-ri-sī'dal, *a.* Pertaining to or involving fratricide.

Fraud, fra̤d, *n.* [L. *fraus*, *fraudis*, Fr. *fraude*; hence *defraud*.] An act or course of deception deliberately practised with the view of gaining an unlawful or unfair advantage; deceit; deception; imposition. ∴ *Deceit* is used of the mental process which underlies any proceeding intended to deceive; *deception* signifies the procedure by which deceit is carried out, and also that which deceives, misleads, or imposes on; while *fraud* is an act, or a series of acts of *deceit*, by which we attempt to benefit ourselves at the expense of another.—**Fraudful**, fra̤d'fu̦l, *a.* Full of or characterized by fraud; containing fraud or deceit.—**Fraudfully**, fra̤d'fu̦l-li, *adv.* In a fraudful manner.—**Fraudless**, fra̤d'les, *a.* Free from fraud. — **Fraudlessly**, fra̤d'les-li, *adv.* In a fraudless manner.—**Fraudlessness**, fra̤d'les-nes, *n.* State or quality of being fraudless.—**Fraudulence**, **Fraudulency**, fra̤'dū-lens, fra̤'dū-len-si, *n.* [L. *fraudulentia*.] The quality of being fraudulent. — **Fraudulent**, fra̤'dū-lent, *a.* [L. *fraudulentus*.] Using fraud in making bargains, contracts, &c.; given to using fraud; founded on fraud; proceeding from fraud. — **Fraudulently**, fra̤'dū-lent-li, *adv.* In a fraudulent manner.—**Fraudulentness**, fra̤'dū-lent-nes, *n.*

Fraught, fra̤t, *a.* [A participial form from old verb *fraught*, to load, a form of *freight*. FREIGHT.] Freighted‡; *fig.* filled, stored, charged, abounding, pregnant (a scheme *fraught* with mischief).—**Fraughtage**,† fra̤'tāj, *n.* Loading; cargo. (*Shak.*)

Fray, frā, *n.* [Abbrev. of *affray*.] An affray; a broil, quarrel, or violent riot.—*v.t.* To fright; to terrify.

Fray, frā, *v.t.* [Fr. *frayer*, from L. *fricare*, to rub (whence also *friction*).] To rub; to rub away the surface of; to fret, as cloth by wearing or the skin by friction.—*n.* A frayed or rubbed place.

Freak, frēk, *n.* [A.Sax. *frec*, greedy, bold = Icel. *frekr*, greedy, exorbitant; Dan. *fræk*, bold, G. *frech*, saucy.] A sudden causeless change or turn of the mind; a whim or fancy; a capricious prank; an odd, whimsical person.—**Freakish**, frēk'ish, *a.* Addicted to freaks; whimsical; capricious; fanciful; grotesque.—**Freakishly**, frēk'ish-li, *adv.* In a freakish manner.—**Freakishness**, frēk'ish-nes, *n.* Capriciousness; whimsicalness.

Freak, frēk, *v.t.* [Connected with *freckle*, *fleck*.] To variegate; to checker.

Freckle, frek'l, *n.* [O.E. *freckens*, *frekens*, freckles (akin to *freak*, to variegate); Icel. *freknur*, Dan. *fregner*, freckles; comp. G. *fleck*, a spot.] A spot of a yellowish colour in the skin, particularly on the face, neck, and hands; any small spot or discoloration. —*v.t.* and *i.* To mark or become marked with freckles.—**Freckled**, frek'ld, *pp.* and *a.* Marked with freckles. — **Freckledness**, frek'ld-nes, *n.* The state of being freckled.—**Freckly**, frek'li, *a.* Covered with freckles.

Free, frē, *a.* [A.Sax. *frí*, *freó* = Icel. *frí*, Dan. and Sw. *fri*, D. *vrij*, G. *frei*, Goth. *freis*, free; allied to *friend*, Goth. *frijon*, to love; Skr. *pri*, to love; perhaps also to L. *privus*, one's own, *privatus*, private.] Not being under necessity or restraint, physical or moral; exempt from subjection to the will of others; being at liberty; not in confinement; not under an arbitrary or despotic government; instituted by a free people; capable of being used, enjoyed, or taken advantage of without charge; unrestricted; open; not obstructed; going beyond due limits in speaking or acting; open; candid; frank; without care; unconcerned; liberal; not parsimonious; profuse; gratuitous; given with readiness or good-will; clear; exempt; having got rid; not encumbered, affected, or oppressed: with *from*, and sometimes *of*; invested with or enjoying certain immunities; having certain privileges: with *of* (a man *free of* the city of London); *bot.* applied to parts which are not united together; *chem.* not chemically combined with any other body.—*Free agency*, the state of acting freely or without necessity or constraint of the will.—*Free Church of Scotland*, that ecclesiastical body which seceded from the Established Church at the Disruption in 1843.—*Free labour*, labour performed by free persons in contradistinction to that of slaves.—*Free love*, the right to consort with those we have conceived a passion for, regardless of the shackles of matrimony.—*To make free with*, to intermeddle with; to use liberties with; to help one's self to.—*Free and easy*, unconstrained; regardless of conventionalities.—*v.t.*—*freed, freeing*. To remove from a thing any encumbrance or obstruction; to disentangle; to disengage; to rid; to strip; to clear; to set at liberty; to rescue or release from slavery, captivity, or confinement; to manumit; to loose; to exempt, as from some oppressive condition or duty.—**Free air**, normal atmospheric air, unconfined; that portion of the atmosphere which is not greatly restricted by friction with the surface of the earth.—**Freeboard**, *n.* *Naut.* the part of a ship's side between the gunwale and the line of flotation.—**Freebooter**, frē'bö-tėr, *n.* [D. *vrijbuiter*, G. *freibeuter*. BOOTY.] One who wanders about for booty or plunder; a robber; a pillager; a plunderer.—**Freebooting**, frē'bö-ting, *a.* Living or acting as a freebooter; pertaining to or like freebooters.—*n.* Robbery; plunder; pillage.—**Freebooty**, frē'bö-ti, *n.* Pillage or plunder by freebooters.—**Freeborn**, frē'born, *a.* Born free; not in vassalage; inheriting liberty.—**Freedman**, frēd'man, *n.* A man who has been a slave and is manumitted.—**Freedom**, frē'dum, *n.* The state of being free; exemption from slavery, servitude, confinement, or constraint; liberty; independence; frankness; openness; outspokenness; unrestrictedness; permission; liberality; particular privileges (the *freedom* of a city); ease or facility of doing anything; license; improper familiarity (in this sense with a plural).—**Freedom of the seas**, doctrine that merchant ships may traverse all waters, save those territorial, in both peace and war.—**Free-for-all**, *n.* An open competition; a promiscuous fight. (*Colloq.*)—**Free grace**, *n.* Voluntary and unmerited favor.—**Free-hand**, frē'hand, *a.* Applied to drawing in which the hand is not assisted by any guiding or measuring instruments.—**Freehanded**, *a.* Open-handed; liberal.—**Freehearted**, *a.* Open; frank; unreserved; liberal; charitable; generous.—**Freehold**, frē'hōld, *n.* *Law*, an estate in real property, held either in fee-simple or fee-tail, or for life; the tenure by which such an estate is held.—**Free lance**, *n.* One of the mercenary soldiers of the middle ages, who fought for any employer able to pay; one unattached to any political party; a writer (or artist or actor) not regularly employed by any one concern (*slang*)—**Freeliver**, frē'liv-ėr, *n.* One who eats and drinks abundantly; one who gives free indulgence to his appetites.—**Freely**, frē'li, *adv.* In a free manner.—**Freeman**, frē'-man, *n.* A man who is free; one not a slave or vassal; one who enjoys or is entitled to a franchise or peculiar privilege.—**Freemartin**, frē'mär-tin, *n.* A cow-calf twin born with a bull-calf: generally barren.—**Freemason**, frē'mā-sn, *n.* A person belonging to a society or organization the members of which call themselves *free* and accepted *masons*.—**Freemasonry**, frē'-mā-sn-ri, *n.* The mysteries in which freemasons are initiated.—**Freeness**, frē'nes, *n.* The state or quality of being free.—**Free-pass**, *n.* A permission to pass free, as by railway, &c.—**Free-port**, *n.* A port where ships may be unloaded and goods deposited without payment of customs.—**Freer**, frē'ėr, *n.* One who frees.—**Free-school**, *n.* A school in which pupils are taught without paying for tuition.—**Free-spoken**, frē'spō-kn, *a.* Accustomed to speak without reserve.—**Freespokenness**, frē-spō'kn-nes, *n.* The quality of being freespoken.—**Freestone**, frē'stōn, *n.* Any species of stone composed of sand or grit, so called because it is easily cut or wrought.—**Freethinker**, frē'thingk-ėr, *n.* One who is free from the common modes of thinking in religious matters; a deist; an unbeliever; a sceptic.—**Free-thinking**, frē'thingk-ing, *n.*—*a.* Holding the principles of a freethinker.—**Free thought**, frē'that, *a.* The beliefs or ways of thinking of freethinkers.—**Free trade**, *n.* Trade or commerce free from restrictions, and in particular from customs duties levied on foreign commodities.—**Free trader**, *n.* An advocate of free-trade.—**Free will**, *n.* The power of directing our own actions without constraint by necessity or fate; voluntariness; spontaneousness.—*a.* Voluntary; spontaneous.

Freeze, frēz, *v.i.*—*froze* (pret.), *frozen* or *froze* (pp.), *freezing* (ppr.). [A.Sax. *frysan*, *freósan*=D. *vriezen*, Icel. *frjósa*, Dan. *fryse*, G. *frieren*; same root as L. *pruina*, hoar-frost. Akin *frore*, *frost*.] To be congealed by cold; to be changed from a liquid to a solid state by the abstraction of heat; to be hardened into ice; to be of that degree of cold at which water congeals: used impersonally (it *freezes* hard); to become chilled in body with cold.—*v.t.* To congeal or cause to freeze; to harden into ice; to chill; to give the sensation of cold and shivering.—*n.* The act of freezing; frost. (*Colloq.*).—**Freezable**, frē'za-bl, *n.* Capable of being frozen.—**Freezer**, frē'zėr, *n.* One who or that which freezes.—**Freezing-point**, *n.* That degree of a thermometer at which a liquid begins to freeze; the temperature at which ordinarily water freezes. By the Centigrade thermometer the freezing-point of water is 0° or zero; by Fahrenheit's thermometer 32° above zero.—**Freezing-mixture**, *n.* A mixture such as produces a degree of cold sufficient to freeze liquids.—**Frozen**, frō'zn, *p.* and *a.* Congealed by cold; frosty; subject to severe frost; void of sympathy; wanting in feeling or interest; unsympathetic.—**Frozenness**, frō'zn-nes, *n.* A state of being frozen.

Freight, frāt, *n.* [Formerly *fraht* = D. *vragt*, Dan. *fragt*, Sw. *frakt*, G. *fracht*, a freight or cargo. FRAUGHT.] A burden or load; goods laden for transportation by land, water, or air; the price charged or paid for the transportation of goods; transportation by common carrier, as opposed to express; a freight train.—*v.t.* To transport by freight; *fig. to pay the freight*, to bear the burden.—**Freightage**, frā'-tāj, *n.* The act or process of freighting; money paid for freight; freight or lading (*Mil.*).—**Freight car**, a railroad car used for the transportation of freight.—**Freighter**, frā'tėr, *n.* One who freights; a ship mainly transporting freight.—**Freight train**, a railroad train consisting of freight cars.

French, frensh, *a.* [O.Fr. *franchois*, *françois*, Mod.Fr. *français*, from *France*, which received its name from the *Franks*.] Pertaining to France or its inhabitants.—*n.* The language spoken by the people of France; collectively the French people.—**French-bean**, *n.* A species of bean; the kidney-bean.—**French-chalk**, *n.* A variety of talc resembling chalk, of a pearly white or grayish colour.—**French berries**, *n.* Yellow berries.—**French honeysuckle**, *n.* A leguminous plant grown in gardens for its scarlet flowers, and in Southern Europe as a fodder plant.—**French-horn**, *n.* A musical instrument of brass having several curves, and gradually widening from the mouth-piece to the other end.—**Frenchify**, frensh'i-fī, *v.t.* To make French; to infect with French tastes or manners.—**Frenchman**, frensh'man, *n.* A man of the French nation; a native or naturalized inhabitant of France.—**French-polish**, *n.* Gumlac dissolved in spirits of wine, used for coating wood with a fine glossy surface.—**French-white**, *n.* Finely pulverized talc.

Frenetic, Frenetical, fre-net'ik, fre-net'i-kal, *a.* [Same word as *frantic*. FRENZY.] Frenzied; frantic.—**Frenetically**, fre-net'i-kal-li, *adv.* In a frenetic or frenzied manner.

Frenzy, fren'zi, *n.* [O.Fr. *frenaisie*, Mod.Fr. *phrénésie*; from Gr. *phrenēsis*, *phrenitis*, mental derangement, from *phrēn*, the mind. FRANTIC.] Distraction; delirium; madness; any violent agitation of the mind approaching to distraction or temporary derangement of the mental faculties.—*v.t.* —*frenzied, frenzying*. To drive to madness; to render frenzied.—**Frenzical**, fren'zi-kal, *a.* Partaking of frenzy.—**Frenzied**, fren'zid, *p.* and *a.* Affected with frenzy or madness; maddened; frantic.—**Frenziedly**, fren'zid-li, *adv.* Madly; distractedly.

Frequent, frē'kwent, *a.* [Fr. *fréquent*, from L. *frequens*, *frequentis*, common, usual, full, crowded; same root as *farcio*, to cram (whence *farce*).] Often seen or done; often happening at short intervals; often repeated or occurring; doing a thing often; inclined to indulge in any practice.—*v.t.* (frē-kwent'). [L. *frequento*; Fr. *fréquenter*.] To visit often; to resort to often or habitually.—**Frequence**,† frē'kwens, *n.* [L. *frequentia*.] A crowd; a throng; a concourse; an assembly.—**Frequency**, frē'kwen-si, *n.* The state of being frequent; a frequent return or occurrence; the condition of being often repeated at short intervals.—**Frequentation**, frē-kwen-tā'shon, *n.* The act or custom of frequenting.—**Frequentative**, frē-kwen'ta-tiv, *a.* *Gram.* serving to express the frequent repetition of an action: applied to certain verbs.—*n.* A verb which denotes the frequent occurrence or repetition of an action.—**Frequenter**, frē-kwen'tėr, *n.* One who frequents.—**Frequently**, frē'kwent-li, *adv.* Often; many times, at short intervals; repeatedly; commonly.—**Frequentness**, frē'kwent-nes, *n.*

Fresco, fres'kō, *n.* pl. **Frescoes** and **Frescos**, fres'kōz. [It., fresh, from being executed on fresh plaster. FRESH.] A method of painting on walls with mineral and earthy pigments on fresh plaster, or on a wall laid with mortar not yet dry.—*v.t.* To paint in fresco, as walls.

Fresh, fresh, *a.* [A.Sax. *fersc*, whence *fresh* by a common metathesis = D. *versch*, Icel. *ferskr*, *friskr*, Dan. *fersk*, *frisk*, G. *frisch*; hence It. Sp. and Pg. *fresco*, Fr. *frais*, *fraiche*, fresh. *Frisk* is a form of the same word.] Full of health and strength; vigorous; strong; brisk; lively; bright; not faded; undecayed; unimpaired by time; in good condition; not stale; not exhausted with labour or exertion; renewed in strength; reinvigorated; refreshing; health-giving: applied to pure cool water, and also to a rather strong wind; vivid; clearly remembered; new; recently grown, made, or obtained; not salt or salted.—*n.* A freshet; a spring of fresh water; a flood; an overflowing; an inundation.—**Freshen**, fresh'n, *v.t.* To make fresh; to give a fresh appearance or character to; to make to feel fresh; to refresh; to revive.—*v.i.* To grow fresh; to grow strong (the wind *freshens*).—**Freshet**, fresh'et, *n.* A small stream of fresh water; a flood or overflowing of a river, by means of heavy rains or melted snow.—**Freshly**, fresh'li, *adv.* In a fresh manner.—**Freshman**, fresh'man, *n.* A novice; a student of the first year in a university.—**Freshness**, fresh'nes, *n.* The condition or quality of being fresh.—**Freshwater**, *a.* Pertaining to, produced by, or living in water that is fresh or not salt.

Fret, fret, *v.t.*—*fretted, fretting*. [A.Sax. *fretan*, to eat, to gnaw, devour; D. *vreten*, G. *fressen*, O.H.G. *frezzan*, Goth. *fraïtan*, to eat, all from prefix = E. *for*, intens., and verb to *eat*.] To gnaw; to eat into; to rub or wear away; to fray; to chafe; to gall; to wear away so as to diminish; to impair; to agitate; to disturb (to *fret* the surface of the sea); *fig.* to chafe the mind of; to irritate; to tease; to make angry.—*v.i.* To become frayed or chafed; to be chafed or irritated; to become vexed or angry; to utter peevish expressions; to boil or work as angry feelings; to rankle.—*n.* A state of chafing or irritation; vexation; anger.—**Fretful**, fret'ful, *a.* Disposed to fret; ill-humoured; peevish; in a state of vexation.

—**Fretfully**, fret'ful-li, *adv.* In a fretful manner; peevishly.—**Fretfulness**, fret'-ful-nes, *n.* Peevishness; ill-humour.—**Fretter**, fret'ėr, *n.* One who frets.

Fret, fret, *n.* [O.Fr. *freter*, to interlace, *frettes*, a grating; from L. *ferrum*, iron. Comp. also A.Sax. *frætwe*, ornaments.] A kind of ornament formed of bands or fillets variously combined, but most frequently arranged in rectangular forms; a piece of perforated ornamental work; one of the small cross-bars or ridges on the finger-boards of some stringed instruments, to regulate the pitch of the notes.—*v.t.* To ornament or furnish with frets; to variegate; to diversify.—**Fretted**, fret'ed, *a.* Adorned with frets or fretwork; exhibiting sunk or raised ornamentation in rectangular or other forms.—**Fretter**, fret'ėr, *n.* One who or that which frets.—**Fretty**, fret'i, *a.* Adorned with fretwork.—**Fretwork**, fret'wėrk, *n.* Ornamental work consisting of a series or combination of frets; designs cut through a thin plate of wood.—**Fret-saw**, *n.* A small saw for cutting fretwork.

Friable, frī'a-bl, *a.* [L. *friabilis*, from *frio*, *friatum*, to crumble down.] Easily crumbled or pulverized; easily reduced to powder.—**Friability**, **Friableness**, frī-a-bil'i-ti, frī'a-bl-nes, *n.* The quality of being friable.

Friar, frī'ėr, *n.* [Formerly *frere*, Fr. *frère*, O.Fr. *freire*, a brother, from L. *frater*, *fratris*, a brother. BROTHER.] A person belonging to one of the Roman Catholic mendicant religious orders or brotherhoods —Dominicans, Franciscans, Carmelites, Augustines, &c.; a monk.—**Friar's lantern**, *n.* Will o' the wisp; marsh-light.—**Friarly**, frī'ėr-li, *a.* Like or pertaining to friars.—**Friary**, frī'ėr-i, *n.* A convent of friars; a monastery.

Fribble, frib'l, *a.* [Perhaps corrupted from Fr. *frivole*, frivolous.] Frivolous; trifling; silly.—*n.* A frivolous, trifling, contemptible fellow.—*v.i.—fribbled, fribbling.* To act the fribble; to trifle.—**Fribbler**, frib'lėr, *n.* A trifler; a coxcomb.—**Fribbling**, frib'-ling, *a.* Frivolous; trifling.

Fricandeau, frik-an-dō', *n.* [Fr., etymology doubtful.] A fricassee or other preparation of veal.

Fricassee, frik-as-sē', *n.* [Fr. *fricassée*, from *fricasser*, to cook in this way: etymology doubtful.] A dish of food made by cutting chickens, rabbits, or other small animals into pieces, and dressing them with a strong sauce in a frying-pan or a like utensil.—*v.t.—fricasseed, fricasseeing.* To dress in fricassee.

Friction, frik'shon, *n.* [L. *frictio*, *frictionis*, from *frico*, *frictum*, to rub, to rub down.] The act of rubbing the surface of one body against that of another; attrition; *mech.* the effect of rubbing or the resistance which a moving body meets with from the surface on which it moves.—*Angle of friction*, the maximum angle at which one body will remain on another without sliding.—**Frication**,† fri-kā'shon, *n.* [L. *fricatio.*] The act of rubbing; friction.—**Fricative**, frik'a-tiv, *a.* A term applied to certain letters produced by the friction of the breath issuing through a narrow opening of the organs, as *f, v, s, z*, &c.—**Frictional**, frik'-shon-al, *a.* Relating to friction; moved by friction; produced by friction.—**Frictionless**, frik'shon-les, *a.* Having no friction.—**Friction-clutch**, *n.* A species of loose coupling much used for connecting pieces in machines which require to be frequently engaged and disengaged.—**Friction-powder**, *n.* A composition of chlorate of potash and antimony, which readily ignites by friction.—**Friction-rollers**, *n. pl.* Small rollers or cylinders placed under heavy bodies when they are required to be moved a short distance on the surface of the ground.—**Friction tape**, *elect.* a flat tape, both insulating and adhesive, used in repairs, &c.—**Friction-wheel**, *n.* *Mach.* one of two simple wheels or cylinders intended to assist in diminishing the friction of a horizontal axis.

Friday, frī'dā, *n.* [A.Sax. *Frige-dæg*, G. *Freytag*, the day sacred to *Frigga*, or *Freya*, the Teutonic goddess.] The sixth day of the week.—*Good Friday*, the Friday immediately preceding Easter, kept sacred as the day of Christ's crucifixion.

Friend, frend, *n.* [A.Sax. *freónd*, virtually a pres. part. of *freón*, to love; like Goth. *frijonds*, from *frijon*, to love; D. *vriend*, Icel. *frændi*, G. *freund*, a friend. *Fiend* is similarly formed. FREE.] One who is attached to another by affection; one who has esteem and regard for another and loves his society; one not hostile; one of the same nation, party, or kin; one who looks with favour upon a cause, institution, or the like; also a term of salutation or familiar address.—*Society of Friends*, the name assumed by the society of dissenters commonly called Quakers.—*To be friends with*, to feel as a friend towards; to be friendly towards: may be used when a single person is the friend of another.—*v.t.* To befriend; to support or aid.—**Friendless**, frend'les, *a.* Destitute of friends.—**Friendlessness**, frend'les-nes, *n.* The state of being friendless.—**Friendlike**, frend'līk, *a.* Like a friend; like what marks a friend.—**Friendlily**, frend'li-li, *adv.* In a friendly manner.—**Friendliness**, frend'li-nes, *n.* The condition or quality of being friendly; a disposition to favour or befriend; good-will; exercise of benevolence or kindness.—**Friendly**, frend'li, *a.* Having the temper and disposition of a friend; disposed to promote the good of another; kind; amicable; befitting friends; not hostile; favorable; propitious.—*Friendly fire*, a fire kept within a container which has been provided for it, as a fire in a heater; opposed to *hostile fire*, a fire elsewhere than within a container provided for it. (*Fire Insurance.*) ∴ Syn. under AMICABLE.—*adv.*† In the manner of friends; amicably. (*Shak.*)—**Friendship**, frend'ship, *n.* The feeling that subsists between friends or binds them to one another; attachment to a person; mutual attachment; kind regard; intimacy between friends; kindness.

Friese, frēz, *n.* The language of Friesland; Frisian.—**Friesic**, frē'zik, *a.* Frisian.

Frieze, frēz, *n.* [Fr. *frise* = It. *fregio*, Sp. *friso*, probably from Ar. *ifriz*, a ledge or a wall.] *Arch.* that part of the entablature of a column which is between the architrave and cornice, usually enriched with figures or other ornaments.

Frieze, frēz, *n.* [Fr. *frise*, probably from *Friesland*, once the principal seat of its manufacture.] A coarse woollen cloth having a shaggy nap on one side.—*Chevaux de Frieze*, 'horses of Friesland,' pointed stakes planted to keep off cavalry.—*v.t.—friezed, friezing.* To form a shaggy nap on; to frizzle; to curl.—**Friezed**, frēzd, *a.* Napped; shaggy with nap or frieze.

Frigate, frig'āt, *n.* [Fr. *frégate*, It. *fregata*; Sp. and Pg. *fragata*; origin doubtful.] Among ships of war of the older class, a vessel of a size larger than a sloop or brig, and less than a ship of the line; a ship of war with a high speed and great fighting power.—**Frigate-bird**, *n.* A tropical sea-bird allied to the cormorants, remarkable for its powers of flight.

Frigatoon, frig-a-tön', *n.*‡ [FRIGATE.] A ship-rigged sloop of war.

Fright, frīt, *n.* [A.Sax. *fyrhtu*, *fyrhto*, fear; Dan. *frygt*, G. *furcht*, D. *vrucht*, fear. *Fear* is probably akin in origin.] Sudden and violent fear; a sudden fit of fear or dread; terror; a person of a shocking, disagreeable, or ridiculous appearance in person or dress.—*v.t.* To frighten; to affright; to scare.—**Frighten**, frī'tn, *v.t.* To strike with fright; to terrify; to scare; to alarm suddenly.—**Frightenable**,† frī'-tn-a-bl, *a.* That may be frightened.—**Frightful**, frīt'ful, *a.* Causing fright; terrible; dreadful; awful; horrid; terrific.—**Frightfully**, frīt'ful-li, *adv.* In a frightful manner; dreadfully; horribly; terribly; shockingly.—**Frightfulness**, frīt'ful-nes, *n.* The quality of being frightful; the Hun or German theory of war by terrorism. (*World War.*)—**Frightless**, frīt'les, *a.* Free from fright.

Frigid, frij'id, *a.* [L. *frigidus*, from *frigeo*, to be cold, akin to *rigeo*, to be numb or stiff; Gr. *rigos*, cold. *Frill* is of same origin.] Cold; wanting heat or warmth; of a very low temperature; cold in feeling or manner; wanting warmth of affection; wanting zeal, fire, energy, spirit, or animation; stiff; haughty; forbidding; lifeless.—*Frigid zones*, in *geog.* the two zones comprehended between the poles and the polar circles, which are about 23° 28' from the poles.—**Frigidity**, fri-jid'i-ti, *n.* The state or quality of being frigid; coldness; want of warmth; coldness of feeling or manner; want of animation, ardour, or vivacity.—**Frigidly**, frij'id-li, *adv.* In a frigid manner.—**Frigidness**, frij'id-nes, *n.* The state of being frigid.—**Frigorific**, **Frigorifical**, frig-o-rif'ik, frig-o-rif'i-kal, *a.* [L. *frigorificus*—*frigus*, *frigoris*, cold, and *facio*, to make.] Causing cold.

Frill, fril, *n.* [Originally the ruffling of a hawk's feathers when shivering with cold; from Fr. *friller*, to shiver, from L. *frigidulus*, dim. from *frigidus*, cold. FRIGID.] A crimped or ornamental edging of fine linen on the bosom of a shirt; a somewhat similar trimming on something else; a ruffle.—*v.t.* To decorate with a frill.—**Frilled**, frild, *pp.* or *a.* Decked with a frill or frills, or something similar.—**Frilling**, fril'ing, *n.* Frills; ruffles.

Fringe, frinj, *n.* [Fr. *frange*, fringe, It. *frangia*, from L. *fimbria*, fringe; akin to *fibra*, a fibre.] An ornament to the borders of garments, furniture, &c., consisting of threads attached at one end, the other hanging loose; something resembling a fringe; an edging; margin; extremity; *optics*, one of the coloured bands of light in the phenomena of diffraction.—*v.t.* To adorn or border with or as with a fringe.—**Fringed**, frinjd, *pp.* and *a.* Bordered or ornamented with a fringe or fringes.—**Fringe-tree**, *n.* A small American tree having snow-white flowers, which hang down like a fringe.—**Fringy**, frin'ji, *a.* Adorned with fringes.

Fringillaceous, frin-jil-lā'shus, *a.* [L. *fringilla*, a finch.] Pertaining to the finches.

Frippery, frip'ėr-i, *n.* [Fr. *friperie*, old clothes, from *friper*, to rumple, to spoil; from O.Fr. *frepe*, rag, tatter.] Old or cast-off clothes; waste matter; useless things; trifles; traffic in old clothes; an old-clothes shop. (*Shak.*)—*a.* Trifling; contemptible.

Frisian, friz'i-an, *a.* Belonging to Friesland.—*n.* A native of Friesland; the language of Friesland.

Frisk, frisk, *v.i.* [O.Fr. *frisque*, brisk, lively, from the Germanic adjective corresponding to E. *fresh*. FRESH.] To leap, skip, dance, or gambol, as in gaiety or frolic; to frolic.—*n.* A frolic; a fit of wanton gaiety.—**Frisker**, fris'kėr, *n.* One who frisks.—**Frisket**, fris'ket, *n.* [Fr. *frisquette*, from the frequency of its motion.] *Print.* a light frame hinged to the tympan for keeping the sheet in proper position while being printed.—**Friskful**, frisk'ful, *a.* Frisky; frolicsome.—**Friskily**, fris'ki-li, *adv.* In a frisky manner.—**Friskiness**, fris'ki-nes, *n.* The state or quality of being frisky.—**Frisky**, fris'ki, *a.* Fond of frisking or capering; lively; frolicsome.

Frit, frit, *n.* [Fr. *fritte*, from *frit*, fried. pp. of *frire*, from L. *frigo*, *frictum*, to roast, FRY.] The matter of which glass is made after it has been calcined or baked in a furnace.

Frith, frith, *n.* Same as *Firth.*

Fritillary, frit'il-la-ri, *n.* [L. *fritillus*, a dice-box: from checkered markings.] The popular name of a genus of herbaceous bulbous plants.

Fritter, frit'ėr, *n.* [Fr. *friture*, lit. a frying, from L. *frigo*, *frictum*, to fry. FRY.] A fragment or shred; batter or substance contained in batter, fried in deep fat or sautéed (as apple *fritters* or corn *fritters*).—*v.t.* To cut into small pieces; to break into small pieces or fragments.—*To fritter away*, to waste or expend by little and little; to spend frivolously or in trifles.

Frivolous, friv′o-lus, *a.* [L. *frivolus*, frivolous, silly, trifling; same root as *frico*, to rub (whence *friction*).] Of little weight, worth, or importance; not worth notice; trifling; trivial; given to trifling; characterized by unbecoming levity; silly; weak.—**Frivolity, Frivolism**,† fri-vol′i-ti, friv′ol-izm, *n.* The condition or quality of being frivolous or trifling; insignificance; also, the act or habit of trifling; unbecoming levity of mind or disposition. — **Frivolously**, friv′o-lus-li, *adv.* In a frivolous manner.—**Frivolousness**, friv′o-lus-nes, *n.* The quality of being frivolous.

Friz, Frizz, friz, *v.t.—frizzed, frizzing.* [Fr. *friser*, O.Fr. *frizer*, to curl, *frise*, frieze cloth. FRIEZE.] To curl; to crisp; to form into small curls or into little burs, as the nap of cloth.—*n.* That which is frizzed or curled.—**Frizzle**, friz′l, *v.t.—frizzled, frizzling.* [Dim. from *frizz.*] To curl or crisp, as hair; to frizz.—*n.* A curl; a lock of hair crisped.—**Frizzler**, friz′lėr, *n.* One who frizzles. — **Frizzly, Frizzy**, friz′li, friz′i, *a.* Curly.

Fro, frō, *adv.* [A.Sax. or Icel. *frá*, from; short form of *from.*] From; away; back or backward; as in the phrase *to and fro.*

Frock, frok, *n.* [Fr. *froc*, a monk's habit; L.L. *frocus, flocus*, so called because *floccosa*, woolly, from L. *floccus*, a flock of wool.] Primarily, an ecclesiastical garment with large sleeves worn by monks; a kind of gown which opens behind, worn by females and children.—**Frock-coat**, *n.* A coat with full skirts having the same length before and behind; a surtout.—**Frocked**, frokt, *a.* Clothed in a frock.

Frog, frog, *n.* [A.Sax. *frocga, froga, frosc, frox*; D. *vorsch*, G. *frosch*, Dan. *frö*, Icel. *froskr.*]. The name of various amphibians, having four legs with four toes on the fore feet and five on the hind, more or less webbed, a naked body, no ribs, and no tail, and with great powers of leaping; a sort of tender horn that grows in the middle of the sole of a horse's foot.—**Frog-eater**, *n.* One who eats frogs: a term of contempt for a Frenchman.—**Froggery**,† frog′ėr-i, *n.* A place abounding in frogs. —**Frog-fish**, *n.* A fish with a wide and flattened head, larger than the body, a gaping mouth with many teeth, and spacious gill-covers.—**Frog-fly, Frog-hopper**, *n.* A small leaping insect, the larvæ of which are found on plants inclosed in a frothy liquid known as cuckoo-spit.—**Frog-spit, Frog-spittle**, *n.* The frothy liquid of the larvæ of the frog-hopper.—**Froggy**, frog′i, *a.* Having or abounding in frogs.

Frog, frog, *n.* A fastening for a frock or coat in the form of a tassel or large button passed through a loop on the breast; the loop of the scabbard of a bayonet or sword. —*v.t.—frogged, frogging.* To ornament or fasten with a frog.

Frolic, frol′ik, *a.* [From D. *vrolijk*, from *vro* = O.Fris. *fro*, Dan. *fro*, glad, and *lijk* = E. *like*; so G. *fröhlich*, from *froh*, joyful, and *lich*, like.] Gay; merry; full of mirth; dancing, playing, or frisking about.—*n.* A wild or merry prank; a flight of levity or gaiety and mirth; a scene of gaiety and mirth; a merry-making. — *v.i.* —*frolicked* (frol′ikt), *frolicking.* To play merry pranks; to play tricks of levity, mirth, and gaiety.—**Frolicsome, Frolicful**, frol′ik-sum, frol′ik-fụl, *a.* Full of gaiety and mirth; given to frolics; sportive.—**Frolicsomely**, frol′ik-sum-li, *adv.* In a frolicsome manner. —**Frolicsomeness**, frol′ik-sum-nes, *n.*

From, from, *prep.* [A.Sax. *from, fram*, O.Sax. O.H.G. and Goth. *fram*, from; Icel. *fram*, forward, *frá*, from; Dan. *frem, fra*, from; cog. with L. *peren* in *perendie*, the day after to-morrow, Gr. *peran*, Skr. *param*, beyond. Allied to *far, forth*, &c.] Out of the neighbourhood of; leaving behind; by reason of; out of; by aid of; denoting source, beginning, distance, absence, privation, or departure, sometimes literally and sometimes figuratively: the antithesis and correlative of *from* is *to.*

Frond, frond, *n.* [L. *frons, frondis*, a leaf.] *Bot.* a term used to designate the leaves of ferns and other cryptogamous plants.—**Frondent**,† fron′dent, *a.* Covered with leaves. — **Frondesce**, fron-des′, *v.i.* [L. *frondesco.*] To unfold leaves or become leafy.—**Frondescence**, fron-des′ens, *n.* *Bot.* the precise time in which each species of plants unfolds its leaves; the act of bursting into leaf.—**Frondiferous**, fron-dif′ėr-us, *a.* Producing fronds.—**Frondlet**, frond′let, *n.* A little frond.—**Frondose**, fron′dōs, *a.* *Bot.* covered with leaves; bearing a great number of leaves.—**Frondous**, fron′dus, *a.* *Bot.* producing leaves and flowers on one part.

Fronde, frond, *n.* [Fr.] The party in opposition to Mazarin, the French prime minister, 1648-53, with civil war as result.

Front, frunt, *n.* [Fr. *front*, L. *frons, frontis*, the forehead (allied to E. *brow*); seen also in *affront, confront*, &c.] The forehead, or part of the face above the eyes; the whole face; boldness of disposition; impudence; the part or side of anything which seems to look out or to be directed forward; the face or fore part; the foremost rank; position directly before the face of a person or the foremost part of anything; a set of false hair or curls for a lady; the van of war; the area of warfare in campaign; shirt front, real or false.—*To come to the front*, to take a high rank in one's profession, in society, &c.—*a.* Relating to the front or face; having a position in the front.—*v.t.* To oppose face to face; to stand in front of or over against; to face; to appear in the presence of; to confront; to supply with a front; to adorn in front.—*v.i.* To have the face or front in some direction.—**Frontage**, frun′tāj, *n.* The front part of any structure or object; extent of front. — **Frontal**, fron′tal, *n.* Something worn on the forehead; a frontlet; an ornamental band for the hair; *arch.* a little pediment over a door or window.—*a.* Belonging to the forehead.—*Frontal* attack, *a.* Attack on the front; opposed to flank or rear.—**Front-door**, *n.* The door in the front wall of a building, generally the principal entrance.—**Frontier**, fron′tēr, *n.* [Fr. *frontière*, a frontier, a border.] That part of a country which fronts or faces another country; the confines or extreme part of a country bordering on another country; the marches; the border.—**Frontispiece**, fron′tis-pēs, *n.* [L.L. *frontispicium*, from L. *frons*, and *specio*, to view.] An ornamental figure or engraving fronting the first page of a book or at the beginning. — **Frontless**, frunt′les, *a.* Wanting shame or modesty; of unblushing front.—**Frontlet**, frunt′let, *n.* A frontal or browband; a fillet or band worn on the forehead.

Frore, frōr, *a.* [A.Sax. *froren*, pp. of *freósan*, to freeze. FREEZE.] Frozen; frosty: a poetic word.

Frost, frost, *n.* [A.Sax. *frost, forst*, from *freósan*, to freeze; Icel. Dan. Sw. and G. *frost*, D. *vorst.* FREEZE.] That state or temperature of the air which occasions freezing or the congelation of water; freezing weather; frozen dew; rime; hoar-frost; coldness or severity of manner or feeling.—*v.t.* To injure by frost; to cover or ornament with anything resembling hoar-frost, as with white sugar; to furnish with frost-nails.—*Frosted glass*, glass roughened on the surface, so as to destroy its transparency.—**Frost-bite**, *n.* A state of insensibility or deadness with arrested circulation in any part of the body, such as the nose and ears, occasioned by exposure to severe frost.—*v.t.* —*frost-bit* (pret.), *frost-bitten, frost-bit* (pp.); *frost-biting* (ppr.). To affect with frost-bite.—**Frostily**, fros′ti-li, *adv.* In a frosty manner; with frost or excessive cold; without warmth of affection; coldly. —**Frostiness**, fros′ti-nes, *n.* The state or quality of being frosty.—**Frosting**, fros′ting, *n.* A coating resembling frost; the composition resembling hoar-frost used to cover cake, &c.—**Frost-nail**, *n.* A nail driven into a horse-shoe to prevent the horse from slipping on ice.—**Frostwork**, frost′wėrk, *n.* The beautiful covering of hoar-frost deposited on shrubs or other natural objects.—**Frosty**, fros′ti, *a.* Attended with frost; of a freezing temperature; affected by frost; without warmth of affection or courage; resembling hoar-frost; gray-haired.

Froth, froth, *n.* [A Scandinavian word = Icel. *frotha, frauth*, Dan. *fraade*, froth, foam.] The bubbles caused in liquors by fermentation or agitation; spume; foam; empty talk; mere words without sense; light, unsubstantial matter.—*v.t.* To cause to foam or produce froth; to vent, or give expression to what is light, unsubstantial, or worthless.—*v.i.* To foam; to throw up or out froth.—**Frothily**, froth′i-li, *adv.* In a frothy manner.—**Frothiness**, froth′i-nes, *n.* The state or quality of being frothy. —**Frothy**, froth′i, *a.* Full of or accompanied with froth; consisting of froth or light bubbles; foamy; light, empty, or unsubstantial; given to empty display.

Frounce, frouns, *v.t.—frounced, frouncing.* [Fr. *froncer*, D. *fronssen*, to wrinkle, from a hypothetical L.L. *frontiare*, to wrinkle the brows, from L. *frons*, the forehead (whence *front*). *Flounce*, (of a dress) is the same word.] To form into plaits or wrinkles; to adorn with fringes, plaits, &c.—*n.* A wrinkle, plait, or curl; a flounce.

Frow, frō, *n.* A wedge-shaped tool with a handle used for splitting wood.

Froward, frō′wėrd, *a.* [From *fro* = from, and *-ward*, denoting direction, being thus the reverse of *to-ward*, and nearly equivalent to *way-ward* (*awayward*); A.Sax. *fromweard*, turned away, about to depart.] Not willing to comply with what is right or reasonable; perverse; ungovernable; refractory; disobedient; peevish.—**Frowardly**, frō′wėrd-li, *adv.* In a froward manner.—**Frowardness**, frō′wėrd-nes, *n.* The quality of being froward.

Frown, froun, *v.i.* [Fr. *frogner*, in *se refrogner*, to knit the brow, to frown; of doubtful origin.] To express displeasure, severity, or sternness by contracting the brow; to put on a stern look; to scowl; to show displeasure or disapprobation; to be ominous of evil; to lower (the clouds *frown*). —*n.* A contraction or wrinkling of the brow, or a severe or stern look expressive of displeasure. — **Frowningly**, frou′ning-li, *adv.* In a frowning manner.—**Frowny**, frou′ni, *a.* Given to frown; scowling.

Frowzy, Frowsy, frou′zi, *a.* [Comp. Prov. E. *froust*, a musty smell, also Prov.E. *frow*, a slattern, from D. *vrouw*, G. *frau*, a woman.] Fetid; musty; rank; dingy; ill-colored; in a state of disorder; slovenly; slatternly.

Froze, frōz, **Frozen**, frō′zn. FREEZE.

Fructescence, fruk-tes′ens, *n.* [From L. *fructus*, fruit. FRUIT.] *Bot.* the time when the fruit of a plant arrives at maturity and its seeds are dispersed; the fruiting season. — **Fructiculose**, fruk-tik′ū-lōs, *a.* *Bot.* producing much fruit.—**Fructiferous**, fruk-tif′ėr-us, *a.* Bearing or producing fruit.—**Fructification**, fruk′ti-fi-kā″shon, *n.* The act of forming or producing fruit; the act of fructifying or rendering productive of fruit; fecundation; the organs concerned in the production of the fruit of a plant.—**Fructify**, fruk′ti-fi, *v.t.* [Fr. *fructifier.*] To make fruitful; to render productive; to fertilize.—*v.i.* To bear or produce fruit.—**Fructose**, fruk′tōs, *n.* A variety of sugar from fruit. — **Fructuary**, fruk′tū-a-ri, *n.* One who enjoys the produce or profits of anything.

Frugal, frö′gal, *a.* [L. *frugalis*, from *frugi*, lit. fit for food, hence, worthy, temperate, dative case of *frux, frugis*, fruit; akin to *fruit.*] Economical in regard to expenditure; thrifty; sparing; not profuse, prodigal, or lavish; saving.—**Frugality**, frö-gal′i-ti, *n.* The quality of being frugal; a prudent and sparing use of anything.—**Frugally**, frö′gal-li, *adv.* In a frugal manner. — **Frugalness**, frö′gal-nes, *n.* Frugality.

Frugiferous, frö-jif′ėr-us, *a.* [L. *frugifer* —*frux, frugis*, fruit, and *fero*, to bear.] Producing fruit or crops; fruitful; fructiferous.—**Frugivorous**, frö-jiv′ėr-us, *a.* [L.

frux, frugis, and *voro*, to eat.] Feeding on fruits, seeds, or corn, as birds and other animals.

Fruit, fröt, *n.* [Fr. *fruit*, from L. *fructus*, fruit, from *fruor, fructus*, to enjoy, from a root seen in E. verb to *brook*, originally to enjoy; akin *frugal, fruition*.] Whatever vegetable products the earth yields for the use of man and the lower animals (in this sense generally in the plural); in a more limited sense, the reproductive product of a tree or other plant; especially, the edible succulent products of certain plants, generally covering and including their seeds; such products collectively; *bot.* the seed of a plant, or the mature ovary, composed essentially of two parts, the pericarp and the seed; the produce of animals; offspring; young; something that results; effect, result, or consequence.—*v.i.* To produce or yield fruit.—**Fruitage**, frö'tāj, *n.* Fruit collectively; product or produce.—**Fruit-bearing**, *a.* Producing fruit; having the quality of bearing fruit.—**Fruitcake**, fröt'cake, *n.* A round or oblong loaf cake containing several varieties of spice and fruit; usually quite rich.—**Fruit bud**, *n.* The bud that produces fruit.—**Fruitful**, fröt'ful, *a.* Producing fruit in abundance; very productive; prolific; bearing children; not barren; producing or presenting in abundance; productive (*fruitful* in expedients).—**Fruitfully**, fröt'fu-li, *adv.* In a fruitful manner; plenteously; abundantly.—**Fruitfulness**, fröt'ful-nes, *n.* The state or quality of being fruitful; productiveness; fertility; fecundity.—**Fruit knife**, *n.* A knife, generally with a silver or plated blade, for paring and cutting fruit.—**Fruitless**, fröt'les, *a.* Not bearing fruit; destitute of fruit or offspring; productive of no advantage or good effect; vain.—**Fruitlessly**, fröt'les-li, *adv.* In a fruitless manner.—**Fruitlessness**, fröt'les-nes, *n.* The state or quality of being fruitless or unprofitable.—**Fruit pigeon**, *n.* A pigeon of very brilliant plumage, occurring in India, the warmer parts of Australia, &c.; so called because they feed entirely on fruit.—**Fruit sugar**, *n.* Fructose. — **Fruit tree**, *n.* A tree cultivated for its fruit, or whose principal value consists in its fruit.—**Fruity**, frö'ti, *a.* Resembling fruit; having the taste or flavor of fruit.

Fruition, frö-ish'on, *n.* [From L. *fruor, fructus* or *fruitus*, to use or enjoy. FRUIT.] Use or possession of anything, especially when accompanied with pleasure; the pleasure derived from use or possession; enjoyment.

Frumentaceous, frö-men-tā'shus, *a.* [L. *frumentaceus*, from *frumentum*, corn; same root as *fructus*, fruit. FRUIT.] Having the character of or resembling wheat or other cereal. — **Frumentarious**, frö-men-tā'ri-us, *a.* [L. *frumentarius*.] Pertaining to wheat or grain.—**Frumenty**, frö'men-ti, *n.* [L. *frumentum*, wheat.] A dish made of hulled wheat boiled in milk and seasoned; furmenty.

Frump, frump, *n.* [Connected with *frampold*, or with Prov.E. *frumple*, D. *frommelen*, to wrinkle or crumple.] A cross-tempered, old-fashioned female.—**Frumpish**, frump'ish, *a.* Cross-tempered; cross-grained; scornful; old-fashioned as to dress.—**Frumpishness**, frump'ish-nes, *n.* The state or quality of being frumpish.—**Frumpy**, frump'i, *a.* Cross-tempered; frumpish.

Frush,‡ frush, *v.t.* [Fr. *froisser*, to crush, to break, from L. *frustum*, a fragment.] To crush; to break in pieces. (*Shak.*)—*a.* Easily broken; brittle. (*Provincial.*)—*n.*† Noise of objects coming into collision and breaking.

Frustrate, frus'trāt, *v.t.*—*frustrated, frustrating.* [L. *frustror, frustratus*, from *frustra*, in vain, same root as *fraus*, fraud.] To make to be in vain or of no avail; to bring to nothing; to prevent from taking effect; to defeat; to balk.—**Frustrable**, frus'tra-bl, *a.* Capable of being frustrated or defeated.—**Frustration**, frus-trā'shon, *n.* The act of frustrating.—**Frustrative**, frus'tra-tiv, *a.* Tending to frustrate or defeat. — **Frustratory**, frus'tra-to-ri, *a.* Tending to frustrate; making void or of no effect; rendering null.

Frustum, frus'tum, *n.* [L., a piece, same root as *frustra*, in vain, *fraus*, fraud, &c.] *Geom.* the part of a solid (as a cone or a pyramid) left by cutting off the top portion by a plane; a truncated solid.—**Frustule**, frus'tūl, *n.* [L. *frustulum*, dim. of *frustum*.] One of the cells into which certain sea-weeds, as the diatoms, divide.—**Frustulent**,† frus'tū-lent, *a.* Abounding in fragments.—**Frustulose**, frus'tū-lōs, *a.* Consisting of small fragments or frustums.

Frutescent, frö-tes'ent, *a.* [From L. *frutex, fruticis*, a shrub.] *Bot.* having the appearance or habit of a shrub; shrubby.—**Fruticose**, frö'ti-kōs, *a.* [L. *fruticosus*.] Pertaining to shrubs; shrubby.—**Fruticulose**, frö-tik'ū-lōs, *a.* Branching like a small shrub.

Fry, frī, *v.t.*—*fried, frying.* [Fr. *frire*, to fry, from L. *frigo*, to fry, roast, or parch; Skr. *bhrij*, to parch.] To cook in a pan over a fire along with fat or butter.—*v.i.* To be cooked as above; to simmer; to be agitated or vexed.—*n.* A dish of anything fried; state of vexation or mental agitation.—**Fryer, Frier**, frī'ėr, *n.* One who or that which fries; a young chicken, suitable for frying.—**Frying pan**, *n.* A pan with a long handle, used for frying meat and vegetables; a skillet

Fry, frī, *n.* [Icel. *frœ, frjo*, spawn; Goth. *fraiv*, seed.] Young of fishes at a very early stage; a swarm of little fishes; a swarm of small animals, or of young people; small or insignificant objects collectively.

Fucate, Fucated, fū'kāt, fū'kā-ted, *a.* [L. *fucatus*, from *fuco*, to stain, *fucus*, paint for the face, deceit.] Painted; disguised with paint or with any false show.

Fuchsia, fū'shi-a, *n.* [From the discoverer Leonard *Fuchs* (= *Fox*), a German botanist.] A genus of beautiful flowering shrubs, natives of South America, Mexico, and New Zealand, having a funnel-shaped, coloured, deciduous, four-parted calyx.—**Fuchsin**, fök'sin, *n.* [From resembling the *fuchsia* in colour.] A beautiful aniline colour; magenta.

Fuciphagous, fū-sif'a-gus, *a.* [L. *fucus*, seaweed, and *voro*, to eat.] A term applied to animals that subsist on seaweed.

Fuddle, fud'l, *v.t.*—*fuddled, fuddling.* [From a form *fuzzle*, akin to L.G. *fusslig*, G. *fusselig*, drunk.] To make foolish or stupid by drink; to make tipsy or intoxicated; to confuse or muddle.—**Fuddler**, fud'lėr, *n.* A drunkard.

Fudge, fuj. *v.t.*—*fudged, fudging.* [Probably connected with *fadge* (which see). To make up or invent (a false story); to fabricate; to foist; to interpolate.—*n.* A made-up story; a creamy candy made of sugar, milk, and butter. often flavored with chocolate.

Fuel, fū'el, *n.* [Norm.Fr. *fuayl, fouoyle, foualle*, from L.L. *focale*, from L. *focus*, a hearth, a fireplace. FOCUS.] That which is used to feed fire, as wood, coal, peat, &c.; what serves to feed or increase heat, anger, or excitement.—*v.t.*—*fuelled. fuelling.* To feed with fuel; to store or furnish with fuel.

Fugacious, fū-gā'shus, *a.* [L. *fugax, fugacis*, from *fugio*, to flee.] Flying or disposed to fly; volatile; fleeting.—*Fugacious corolla, bot.* one that is soon shed.—**Fugaciousness**, fū-gā'shus-nes, *n.* The quality of being fugacious.—**Fugacity**, fū-gas'i-ti, *n.* The quality of being fugacious; fugaciousness; volatility; instability; transitoriness.—**Fugitive**, fū'ji-tiv, *a.* [Fr. *fugitif*, L. *fugitivus*, from L. *fugio*, to flee.] Apt to flee away or be dissipated; volatile; staying or lasting but a short time; fleeting; not fixed or durable (*fugitive* dyes); fleeing or running from danger or pursuit, duty or service; as a literary term, applied to compositions which are short, unimportant, and published at intervals.—*n.* One who flees; a deserter; one who flees from danger or duty; one who flees for refuge.—**Fugitively**, fū'ji-tiv-li, *adv.* In a fugitive manner.

Fugleman, Flugelman, fū'gl-man, flö'gl-man, *n.* + [G. *flügelmann*, a man at the head of a file or a wing, from *flügel*, a wing.] A soldier especially expert and well drilled, who takes his place in front of soldiers, as an example or model to the others in their exercises; a file-leader; hence, any one who sets an example for others to follow.

Fugue, fūg, *n.* [Fr., from L. *fuga*, a flight.] *Mus.* a composition in parts that do not all begin at once, but as it were follow or pursue each other successively.

Führer, Fuehrer, fū'rėr, *n.* The head of the Nazi party and chief of the German state; the leader of any local Nazi organization.

Fulcrum, ful'krum, *n.* L. pl. **Fulcra**, E. pl. **Fulcrums**. [L., the post or foot of a couch, from *fulcio*, to support.] A prop or support; *mech.* that by which a lever is sustained; the point about which a lever turns in lifting a body; *bot.* an additional or supplementary organ, as a stipule, a bract, a tendril, a gland, &c.—**Fulcrate**, ful'krāt, *a.* Having a fulcrum or fulcrums; having the character of a fulcrum.

Fulfill, Fulfil, ful-fil', *v.t.*—*fulfilled, fulfilling.* [A compound of *full* and *fill*; A. Sax. *fulfyllan*.] To accomplish or carry into effect, as a prophecy, promise, intention, design, desire, prayer, bargain, &c.; to perform; to complete by performance; to complete (a term of years)‡.—**Fulfiller**, ful-fil'ėr, *n.* One that fulfills or accomplishes.—**Fulfillment, Fulfilment**, ful-fil'ment, *n.* Execution; performance.

Fulgent, ful'jent, *a.* [L. *fulgens, fulgentis*, from *fulgeo*, to shine.] Shining; dazzling; exquisitely bright.—**Fulgency**, ful'jen-si, *n.* Brightness; splendour; glitter. — **Fulgently**, ful'jent-li, *adv.* In a fulgent manner; dazzlingly; glitteringly.—**Fulgid**, ful'jid, *a.* [L. *fulgidus*.] Shining; splendid.—**Fulgidity**, ful-jid'i-ti, *n.* Splendour.

Fulguration, ful-gū-rā'shon, *n.* [L. *fulguratio*, from *fulgur*, lightning.] The flashing of lightning; *assaying*, the sudden brightening of the melted globules of gold and silver in the cupel.—**Fulgurite**, ful'gū-rīt, *n.* Any rocky substance that has been fused or vitrified by lightning.—**Fulgurous**, ful'gū-rus, *a.* Flashing like lightning.

Fuliginous, Fuliginose, fū-lij'i-nus, fū-lij'i-nōs, *a.* [L. *fuliginosus*, from *fuligo*, soot.] Pertaining to soot; sooty; smoky; resembling smoke; dusky.—**Fuliginously**, fū-lij'i-nus-li, *adv.* In a smoky manner; duskily.—**Fuliginosity**, fū-lij'i-nos"i-ti, *n.* The condition or quality of being fuliginous.

Full, ful, *a.* [A.Sax. *ful* = Icel. *fullr*, Sw. *full*, Dan. *fuld*, Goth. *fulls*, G. *voll*; same root as L. *plenus*, full, *pleo*, to fill (as in *complete*). *Fill* is a derivative.] Having within its limits all that it can contain; replete; completely or largely supplied or furnished; abounding; supplied; occupied; not vacant; plump; filled out; inclined to be stout or corpulent; saturated; sated; abundant in quantity; plenteous; not defective or partial; entire; adequate; mature; perfect (*full* supply, accomplishment, age; a *full* stop); loud, clear, and distinct (voice); giving ample details or arguments; copious (a *full* account; the speech was *full*).—*Full brothers* or *sisters*, children of the same father and the same mother.—*Full cousin*, the son or daughter of an aunt or uncle.—*Full cry*, a term in *hunting* signifying that all the hounds have caught the scent and give tongue in chorus; hence, hot pursuit; hard chase.—*Full dress*, a dress which etiquette requires to be worn on occasions of ceremony and the like.—*Full moon*, the moon with its whole disk illuminated; also, the time when the moon is in this position.

—*n.* The state of being full; complete measure; utmost extent; highest state or degree (fed to the *full*; the *full* of the moon).—*Written in full*, written without contractions; written in words, not in figures.—*adv.* Quite; fully; equally; completely; altogether; exactly (*full* in the center); directly; straight (he looked him *full* in the face); to satiety (to sup *full* of horrors). ∴*Full* is often used, especially in poetry, to heighten or strengthen the signification of adjectives and adverbs (*full* sad), and is prefixed to other words, chiefly participles, to express utmost extent or degree (*full*-blown, *full*-grown).—**Fullback**, ful′bak, *n.* In football, a back; originally the one standing farthest behind the line of scrimmage.—**Full-blooded**, *a.* Having a full supply of blood; of pure blood or extraction; thorough-bred.—**Full-blown** *a.* Fully expanded, as a blossom; mature (*full-blown* beauty).—**Full-bound**, *a.* *Book-binding*, bound entirely in leather. —**Full-eyed**, *a.* Having large prominent eyes. —**Full-fed**, *a.* Fed to fullness; plump with fat.—**Full-grown**, *a.* Grown to full size; accompanying fullness of growth.—**Full-handed**, *a.* Bearing something valuable, especially a gift.—**Full house**, in poker, a hand containing three of a kind and a pair.—**Full-length**, *a.* Embracing the whole length or figure; extending the whole length (a *full-length* portrait).—**Fullness**, **Fulness**, ful′nes, *n.* The state or quality of being full or filled.—*In the fullness of time*, at the proper or destined time.—**Full stop**, in punctuation, a period.—**Full-swing**, *adv.* With eager haste; with violence and impetuosity. (*Colloq.*)—**Fully**, ful′li, *adv.* In a full manner; to the full extent; so as to be full; without lack or defect; completely; entirely.

Full, ful, *v.t.* [Partly from A.Sax. *fullian*, to whiten, *fullere*, a fuller, a bleacher, from L. *fullo*, a fuller; partly from Fr. *fouler*, to tread, to full or felt, from L.L. *fullare*, to full, also from L. *fullo*.] To thicken and condense the fibers of (woolen cloth) by wetting and beating; to scour, cleanse, and thicken in a mill.—*v.i.* To become fulled. —**Fuller**, ful′ėr, *n.* One who fulls; one whose occupation is to full cloth; one who bleaches or whitens (N.T.)‡.—**Fuller's earth**, *n.* A variety of clay or marl, useful in scouring and cleansing cloth.

Fulmar, ful′mär, *n.* [Icel. *fúlmár*, lit. foul mew, from its feeding on putrid substances.] A marine swimming bird which inhabits the northern seas in prodigious numbers, and is valued for its feathers, down, and the oil it yields.

Fulminate, ful′mi-nāt, *v.i.*—*fulminated*, *fulminating*. [L. *fulmino*, *fulminatum*, from *fulmen*, lightning, contr. for *fulgimen*, from *fulgeo*, to flash, whence *fulgent*.] To thunder; to explode with a loud noise; to detonate; to issue threats, denunciations, censures, and the like.—*v.t.* To cause to explode; to utter or hurl out (denunciation). —*n.* A kind of explosive compound.—**Fulminant**, ful′mi-nant, *a.* [L. *fulminans*, *fulminantis*.] Thundering; making a loud noise.—**Fulminating**, ful′mi-nā-ting, *p.* and *a.* Thundering; exploding; detonating. —*Fulminating powder*, a mixture of nitre, sulphur, and potash. — **Fulmination**, ful-mi-nā′shon, *n.* The act of fulminating; that which is fulminated or thundered forth, as a menace or censure.—**Fulminatory**, ful′mi-na-to-ri, *a.* Sending forth thunders or fulminations. — **Fulmine**, ful′min, *v.t.*—*fulmined*, *fulmining*. To fulminate or give utterance to in an authoritative or vehement manner.—*v.i.* To thunder; to fulminate or send forth denunciations, &c.—**Fulminic**, ful-min′ik, *a.* Capable of detonation: applied to an acid.

Fulness. Under FULL.

Fulsome, ful′sum, *a.* [Partly from *full*, and term. *-some*, partly from old *ful*, foul.] Cloying‡; surfeiting‡; offensive from excess of praise; gross (flattery, compliments); nauseous; disgusting.—**Fulsomely**, ful′sum-li, *adv.* In a fulsome manner.—**Fulsomeness**, ful′sum-nes, *n.*

Fulvous, ful′vus, *a.* [L. *fulvus*, yellow.] Yellow; tawny; of a tawny yellow color.

Fumarole, fū′ma-rōl, *n.* [It. *fumarola*, from L. *fumus*, smoke.] A hole from which smoke or gases issue (in a volcanic locality).

Fumble, fum′bl, *v.t.* [From D. *fommelen*, L.G. *fummelen*, to fumble, Sw. *fumla*, to handle feebly.] To feel or grope about; to grope about in perplexity; to seek or search for something awkwardly; to employ the hands or fingers in an awkward fashion; in football, baseball, and other games, to drop the ball or fail to handle it properly.—**Fumbler**, fum′blėr, *n.*

Fume, fūm, *n.* [L. *fumus*, smoke, vapour, fume; akin to Skr. *dhûma*, smoke, the root being that of E. *dust*.] Smoky or vaporous exhalation, especially if possessing narcotic or other remarkable properties; volatile matter arising from anything; exhalation: generally in the plural; mental agitation clouding or affecting the understanding; an idle conceit or vain imagination (*Shak.*). —*v.i.*—*fumed*, *fuming*. To yield fumes or exhalations; to pass off in vapours: with *away*; to be in a rage; to be hot with anger. —*v.t.* To fumigate; to perfume; to offer incense to.—**Fumeless**, fūm′les, *a.* Free from fumes.—**Fumette**, fū-met′, *n.* [Fr. *fumet*, from L. *fumus*.] The scent of meat, as venison or game when kept too long; the scent from meats cooking.—**Fumid**, fū′mid, *a.* [L. *fumidus*.] Smoky; vaporous.—**Fumidity**, **Fumidness**, fū-mid′-i-ti, fū′mid-nes, *n.* The state or quality of being fumid; smokiness.—**Fumiferous**, fū-mif′ėr-us, *a.* [L. *fumifer*.] Producing smoke.—**Fumigate**, fū′mi-gāt, *v.t.*—*fumigated*, *fumigating*. [L. *fumigo*, *fumigatum*.] To apply smoke to; to expose to fumes or vapours (as of sulphur) in cleansing infected apartments, clothing, &c.—**Fumigation**, fū-mi-gā′shon, *n.* The act of fumigating.—**Fumigatory**, fū′mi-ga-to-ri, *a.* Having the quality of fumigating.—**Fumily**, fū′-mi-li, *adv.* With fumes.—**Fumy**, fū′mi, *a.* Producing fumes; vaporous; apt to fume or fret.

Fumitory, fū′mi-to-ri, *n.* [O.E. *fumetere*, Fr. *fumeterre*, from L. *fumus*, smoke, and *terra*, the earth, because said to make the eyes water like smoke.] A common garden and field plant with much-divided leaves and purplish flowers, formerly much used in medicine.

Fun, fun, *n.* [Perhaps connected with *fond*, O.E. *fon*, foolish, *fon*, *fonne*, to be foolish; or Ir. *fonn*, delight.] Sport; mirthful drollery; frolicsome amusement.—*To make fun of*, to turn into ridicule.—*Not to see the fun*, to be unwilling to regard something in the light of a joke.—**Funnily**, fun′i-li, *adv.* In a funny, droll, or comical manner.—**Funning**, fun′ing, *n.* Jesting; joking; the playing of sportive tricks. — **Funny**, fun′i, *a.* Making fun; droll; comical; odd.—**Funny bone**, *n.* The shoulder bone at the elbow, L. *os humeri*, with play on the sound of words.

Funambulate, fū-nam′bū-lāt, *v.t.* [L. *funambulus*, a rope-walker, *funis*, rope, and *ambulo*, *ambulatum*, to walk.] To walk on a rope.—**Funambulation**, fū-nam′bū-lā″shon, *n.* Rope-dancing.—**Funambulatory**, fū-nam′bū-la-to-ri, *a.* Pertaining to a rope-dancer or rope-dancing. — **Funambulist**, fū-nam′bū-list, *n.* A rope-walker or rope-dancer.

Function, fungk′shon, *n.* [Fr. *fonction*, L. *functio*, from *fungor*, *functus*, to perform, to execute; same root as Skr. *bhuj*, to enjoy; akin *defunct*.] Office, duty, or business belonging to a person in virtue of a particular station or character; what a person or body of persons has specially to perform in some capacity (the *functions* of a bishop, of a parent); the specific office or action which any organ or system of organs performs in the animal or vegetable economy, as the body, the mind, or a faculty of the mind (the *function* of memory, of nutrition); a formal or ceremonious meeting; *math.* a quantity so connected with another that no change can be made in the latter without producing a corresponding change in the former.—**Functional**, fungk′shon-al, *a.* Pertaining to a function or functions: thus a *functional* disease is one in which some one or other of the animal functions is deranged, and is often opposed to an *organic* disease, in which an organ is directly affected.—**Functionally**, fungk′shon-al-li, *adv.* In a functional manner; by means of functions. —**Functionary**, fungk′shon-a-ri, *n.* One who holds an office or trust; one who has a special office or duties.

Fund, fund, *n.* [Fr. *fond*, land, fund, a merchant's stock, from L. *fundus*, foundation, a piece of land, estate, whence also *found*, *founder*, *profound*.] A stock or capital; a sum of money appropriated as the foundation of some commercial or other operation; money which an individual may possess or can employ for carrying on trade; in England, money lent to government and constituting part of the national debt (used in plural); money set apart for any object more or less permanent; a store laid up from which one may draw at pleasure; stock; supply (a *fund* of amusement, of anecdote).—*Sinking fund*, a fund or stock set apart, generally at certain intervals, for the reduction of a debt of a government or corporation.—*Consolidated fund*. Under CONSOLIDATE.—*v.t.* To provide and appropriate a fund or permanent revenue for the payment of the interest of; to put into the form of bonds or stocks bearing regular interest; to place in a fund.—*Funded debt*, a debt existing in the form of bonds bearing regular interest; a debt forming part of the permanent debt of a country at a fixed rate of interest.—**Fundable**, fun′da-bl, *a.* Capable of being funded or converted into a fund.—**Fundholder**, *n.* One who has property in the public funds. (*Brit.*)

Fundament, fun′da-ment, *n.* [L. *fundamentum*, a groundwork or foundation, from *fundo*, *fundatum*, to found. FUND, FOUND.] The part of the body on which one sits; the anus.—**Fundamental**, fun-da-men′tal, *a.* Pertaining to a groundwork, root, or basis; at the root or foundation of something; essential; elementary (a *fundamental* truth or principle).—*n.* A leading or primary principle, rule, law, or article; something essential.—**Fundamentality**, **Fundamentalness**, fun′da-men-tal″i-ti, fun-da-men′tal-nes, *n.* The state or quality of being fundamental.—**Fundamentally**, fun-da-men′tal-li, *adv.* In a fundamental manner.—**Fundamental units**, *a.* The three units of mass, length, time, corresponding to fundamental ideas, from which all units are or may be derived.

Fundi, fun′di, *n.* A kind of grain allied to millet, cultivated in the west of Africa.

Funeral, fū′nėr-al, *n.* [Fr. *funerailles*, from L. *funus*, *funeris*, a burial.] The ceremony of burying a dead human body; interment; burial; obsequies.—*a.* Pertaining to burial; used at the interment of the dead. — **Funereal**, fū-nē′rē-al, *a.* [L. *funereus*.] Suiting a funeral; pertaining to or calling up thoughts of death or the grave; dismal; mournful; gloomy.—**Funereally**, fū-nē′rē-al-li, *adv.* In a funereal manner.

Fungi, fun′ji, *n. pl.* [L., pl. of *fungus*, a mushroom.] A large natural order of cryptogamous plants, typical forms of which are seen in the numerous species of the mushroom tribe, and in the growths known as moulds, mildew, smut, rust, dry-rot, &c. —**Fungaceous**, fung-gā′shus, *a.* Pertaining or relating to the Fungi.—**Fungal**, fung′gal, *n.* A plant of the class of fungi and lichens.—*a.* Relating to Fungi.—**Fungic**, fun′jik, *a.* Pertaining to or obtained from fungi. — **Fungiform**, **Fungilliform**, fun′ji-form, fun-jil′i-form, *a.* Having the form of a fungus; having a termination similar to the head of a fungus.—**Fungivorous**, fun-jiv′ėr-us, *a.* [L. *fungus*, and *voro*, to devour.] Feeding on mushrooms or fungi.—**Fungoid**, fung′goid, *a.* Having the appearance or character of a fungus.—**Fungology**, fung-gol′o-ji, *n.* [L.

fungus, Gr. *logos*.] A treatise on or the science of the fungi; mycology.—**Fungosity**, fung-gos'i-ti, *n.* The quality of being fungous; fungous excrescence.—**Fungous**, fung'gus, *a.* Like a fungus; having the character of one of the fungi; hence, growing or springing up suddenly, but not substantial or durable.—**Fungus**, fung'gus, *n.* A member of the Fungi; *med.* a spongy morbid excrescence; a diseased state dependent on the growth of vegetable parasites.

Funicle, fū'ni-kl, *n.* [L. *funiculus*, dim. of *funis*, a cord.] A small cord; a small ligament; *bot.* the little stalk by which a seed is attached to the placenta.—**Funicular**, fū-nik'ū-lėr, *a.* Consisting of a funicle or small cord; dependent upon the tension of a cord.—**Funiliform**, fū-nil'i-form, *a.* *Bot.* formed of tough, flexible cordlike fibres.

Funk, funk, *n.* Fear; cowardice.—*v.i.* To be in terror. (*Colloq.*)

Funnel, fun'el, *n.* [Prov.Fr. *enfounil*, a funnel, from L. *infundibulum*, a funnel—*in*, into, and *fundo*, *fusum*, to pour, whence *fuse*, to melt. FUSE.] A utensil for conveying fluids into vessels with small openings, being a kind of hollow cone with a pipe issuing from its apex; the shaft or hollow channel of a chimney; a cylindrical iron chimney in steam-ships for the furnaces, rising above the deck.—**Funneled**, **Funnelled**, fun'-eld, *a.* Having a funnel or funnels; funnel-shaped.—**Funnel-net**, *n.* A net shaped like a funnel.

Funny, fun'i, *a.* Under FUN.

Fur, fėr, *n.* [Fr. *fourrure*, fur, O.Fr. *forre*, *fuere*, a case or cover, from an old German word corresponding to modern G. *futter*, covering, case, lining, *fur* being so called from the skins of animals being used for lining or trimming clothes.] The short, fine, soft hair of certain animals growing thick on the skin, and distinguished from the hair, which is longer and coarser; the skin of certain wild animals with the fur; peltry; a coating regarded as resembling fur, as morbid matter collected on the tongue.—*a.* Made of fur.—*v.t.*—*furred*, *furring*. To line, face, or cover with fur.—**Furrier**, fėr'i-ėr, *n.* A dealer in or dresser of furs.—**Furriery**, fėr'i-ėr-i, *n.* Furs in general; the trade of a furrier.—**Furry**, fėr'i, *a.* Covered with fur; dressed in fur; consisting of fur or skins; resembling fur; coated with a deposit of morbid matter.

Furbelow, fėr'bē-lō, *n.* [Fr. *falbala*, *farbala*, It. Sp. Pg. *falbala*, Sp. also *farfala*, flounce; origin unknown.] A kind of flounce; the plaited border of a petticoat or gown.—**Furbelowed**, fėr'bē-lōd, *a.* Having furbelows; ornamented with furbelows.

Furbish, fėr'bish, *v.t.* [Fr. *fourbir*, from O.H.G. *furban*, to clean, to furbish, G. *fürben*, to sweep.] To rub or scour to brightness; to polish up; to burnish; *fig.* to clear from taint or stain; to brighten.—**Furbishable**, fėr'bish-a-bl, *a.* Capable of being furbished.—**Furbisher**, fėr'bish-ėr, *n.* One who or that which furbishes.

Furcate, **Furcated**, fėr'kāt, fėr'kā-ted, *a.* [L. *furca*, a fork.] Forked; branching like the prongs of a fork.—**Furcation**, fėr-kā'shon, *n.* A forking or branching.—**Furcula**, fėr'kū-la, *n.* [L., dim. of *furca*.] The forked bone formed by the union of the collar-bones in many birds; the wishbone.

Furfur, fėr'fėr, *n.* [L.] Dandruff; scurf; scales like bran.—**Furfuraceous**, **Furfurous**, fėr-fėr-ā'shus, fėr'fėr-us, *a.* [L. *furfuraceus*.] Branny; scurfy; like bran.—**Furfuration**, fėr-fėr-ā'shon, *n.* The falling of scurf from the head.

Furious. Under FURY.

Furl, fėrl, *v.t.* [Contr. from *furdle*, for *fardle*, *fardel*, to make up in fardels or bundles. FARDEL.] *Naut.* to wrap or roll (a sail) close to the yard, stay, or mast, and fasten; to draw into close compass.

Furlong, fėr'long, *n.* [A.Sax. *furlang*—*furh*, a furrow, and *lang*, long.] A measure of length, being the eighth part of a mile; forty rods.

Furlough, fėr'lō, *n.* [Dan. *forlov*, D. *verlof*, G. *verlaub*, leave, furlough, lit. leave off or away—*fur* being equivalent to *for-* in *forbear*, and *lough*, akin to *leave*, *lief*.] Leave or licence given to a soldier to be absent from service for a certain time.—*v.t.* To furnish with a furlough.

Furmenty, **Furmety**, fėr'men-ti, fėr'me-ti, *n.* Same as *Frumenty*.

Furnace, fėr'nās, *n.* [Fr. *fournaise*, from L. *fornax*, an oven.] An inclosed structure in which is kept up a strong fire for melting ores or metals, heating the boiler of a steam-engine, and other such purposes; *fig.* an occasion of severe torture or trial.

Furnish, fėr'nish, *v.t.* [Fr. *fournir*, to furnish; It. *fornire*, *frunire*, Pr. *formir*, *furmir*, to finish, perfect, to furnish; from O.H.G. *frumjan*, to perfect, of kindred origin with E. *frame*.] To supply with anything necessary or useful; to equip; to offer for use; to afford; to fit up; to supply with furniture.—**Furnisher**, fėr'nish-ėr, *n.* One who furnishes.—**Furnishing**, fėr'nish-ing, *n.* Something that serves to equip or fit up; an appendage.—**Furniture**, fėr'ni-tūr, *n.* [Fr. *fourniture*, from *fournir*, to furnish.] That with which anything is furnished; equipment; specifically, the seats, tables, utensils, &c., necessary or convenient for housekeeping; the necessary appendages in various employments or arts.

Furor, fū'ror, *n.* Under FURY.

Furrier. Under FUR.

Furrow, fur'ō, *n.* [A.Sax. *furh* = O.H.G. *furich*, G. *furche*, furrow; cog. with L. *porca*, a ridge between furrows.] A trench in the earth made by a plough; a narrow trench or channel; a groove; a wrinkle in the face.—*v.t.* To make furrows in; to plough; to mark with or as with wrinkles.—**Furrow-drain**, *v.t.* To drain by a drain at each furrow.—**Furrowed**, fur'ōd, *a.* Having furrows, channels, or grooves.—**Furrowy**, fur'ō-i, *a.* Furrowed; full of furrows.

Furry, fėr'i, *a.* Under FUR.

Further, fėr'THėr, *adv.* [A.Sax. *furthor*, *furthur*, further, more, besides, compar. of *forth*, or of *fore*, before.] More in advance; still onwards; moreover; besides; farther: this word can hardly be said to differ in meaning from *farther*.—*a.* More distant; farther.—*v.t.* To help forward; to promote; to forward or assist.—**Furtherance**, fėr'THėr-ans, *n.* The act of furthering; promotion; advancement.—**Furtherer**, fėr'THėr-ėr, *n.* One who furthers; a promoter.—**Furthermore**, fėr'THėr-mōr, *adv.* Moreover; besides; in addition to what has been said.—**Furthersome**,† fėr'THėr-sum, *a.* Tending to further or promote.—**Furthest**, fėr'THest, *a.* Most distant; farthest.

Furtive, fėr'tiv, *a.* [L. *furtivus*, from *furtum*, theft, from *fur*, a thief.] Sly; accomplished by stealth; stealthy; thief-like.—**Furtively**, fėr'tiv-li, *adv.* In a furtive manner; stealthily.

Fury, fū'ri, *n.* [Fr. *furie*, L. *furia*, fury, one of the three goddesses of vengeance, from *furo*, to rage.] Rage; a storm of anger; madness; turbulence; a violent rushing; impetuous motion; inspired or supernatural excitement of the mind; a virago; an enraged woman; *class. myth.* one of the avenging deities, the daughters of Earth or of Night, three in number, and called respectively Tisiphone, Alecto, and Megæra.—**Furious**, fū'ri-us, *a.* [L. *furiosus*.] Exhibiting fury; raging; violent; transported with passion; mad; frenzied; rushing with impetuosity; violent; boisterous.—**Furiously**, fū'ri-us-li, *adv.* In a furious manner.—**Furiousness**, fū'ri-us-nes, *n.*—**Furor**, fū'ror, *n.* [L.] Fury; rage; mania.—**Furore**, fō-rō'rā, *n.* [It.] Rage; fury; great excitement; intense commotion; enthusiasm.

Furze, fėrz, *n.* [A.Sax. *fyrs*.] Whin or gorse, a spiny, almost leafless shrub, with yellow papilionaceous blossoms, growing abundantly in gravelly waste grounds in Western Europe.—**Furzy**, fėr'zi, *a.* Overgrown with furze.

Fusarole, fū'sa-rōl, *n.* [Fr. *fusarolle*, from L. *fusus*, spindle.] *Arch.* a kind of moulding used in the capitals of pillars; an astragal.

Fuscous, fus'kus, *a.* [L. *fuscus*, dark-coloured.] Brown; of a dark colour.

Fuse, fūz, *v.t.*—*fused*, *fusing*. [L. *fundo*, *fusum*, to pour out, to melt, to cast; hence *found* (to cast), also *confound*, *confuse*, *diffuse*, *refuse*, &c.; akin also *futile*.] To melt or liquefy by heat; to render fluid; to dissolve; to blend or unite as if melted together.—*v.i.* To melt by heat; to become intermingled and blended.—**Fusibility**, fū-zi-bil'i-ti, *n.* The quality of being fusible.—**Fusible**, fū'zi-bl, *a.* Capable of being fused or melted.—*Fusible metal*, an alloy, usually of lead, tin, and bismuth, compounded in such definite proportions as to melt at a given temperature.—**Fusil**, **Fusile**, fū'zil, *a.* [Fr. *fusile*, L. *fusilis*.] Capable of being melted; fusible.—**Fusion**, fū'zhon, *n.* [Fr. *fusion*, L. *fusio*.] The act or operation of fusing; the state of being melted or dissolved by heat; the act or process of uniting or blending as if melted together; complete union.

Fuse, **Fuze**, fūz, *n.* [A shortened form of *fusil*, a musket.] A tube filled with combustible matter, used in blasting, or in discharging a shell, &c.; in an electric circuit, a piece of metal which melts when the load is too great, thus breaking the circuit and preventing possible damage.

Fusee, fū-zē', *n.* [Fr. *fusée*, a spindleful, from L.L. *fusata* (same sense), L. *fusus*, a spindle.] The cone or conical piece in a watch or clock round which is wound the chain or cord.—**Fusiform**, fū'zi-form, *a.* Shaped like a spindle.

Fuselage, fū'sel-āj, *n.* [L. *fusus*, spindle.] The long, narrow, somewhat spindle-shaped body of an aeroplane, having a midway position in the structure, and having a rudder at one end for steering, and a tail.

Fusel-oil, fū'zel, *n.* [G. *fusel*, coarse spirits.] A colourless oily spirit, of a strong and nauseous odour, separated in the rectification of ordinary distilled spirits.

Fusil, fū'zil, *n.* [Fr. *fusil*, originally the part of the lock that struck fire, L.L. *focile*, from L. *focus*, a fire (whence also, *fuel*).] A light musket or firelock formerly used.—**Fusilier**, **Fusileer**, fū-zil-lēr', *n.* Properly, a soldier armed with a fusil; an infantry soldier who bore firearms, as distinguished from a pikeman and archer.—**Fusillade**, fū'zi-lād, *n.* [Fr., from *fusil*.] A simultaneous discharge of musketry.—*v.t.*—*fusilladed*, *fusillading*. To shoot down by a fusillade.

Fuss, fus, *n.* [From A.Sax. *fús*, quick, ready; Icel. *fúss*, eager.] A tumult; a bustle; unnecessary bustle in doing anything; much ado about nothing.—*v.i.* To make much ado about trifles; to make a fuss or bustle.—**Fussily**, fus'i-li, *adv.* In a fussy manner.—**Fussiness**, fus'i-nes, *n.* The state of being fussy; needless bustle.—**Fussy**, fus'i, *a.* Moving and acting with fuss; bustling; making more ado than is necessary.

Fust, fust, *n.* [O.Fr. *fusté*, tasting or smelling of the cask, *fust*, a cask, from L. *fustis*, a stick.] A strong musty smell.—*v.i.* To become mouldy or musty; to smell ill.—**Fusted**, fus'ted, *a.* Mouldy; ill smelling.—**Fustiness**, fus'ti-nes, *n.* State or quality of being fusty.—**Fusty**, fus'ti, *a.* Mouldy; musty; ill-smelling; rank; rancid.

Fustet, fus'tet, *n.* [Sp. and Pg. *fustete*, from L. *fustis*, a stick, staff.] The wood of Venice sumach, a South European shrub which yields a fine orange colour.

Fustian, fus'tyan, *a.* [O.Fr. *fustaine*, Fr. *futaine*, It. *fustagno*, from *Fostat*, the name of a suburb of Cairo, whence this fabric was first brought.] A coarse cotton stuff, or stuff of cotton and linen, with a pile like velvet, but shorter, such as corduroy, moleskin, &c.; an inflated style of writing; bombast.—*a.* Made of fustian; ridiculously tumid; bombastic.—**Fustianist**, fus'tyan-ist, *n.* One who writes bombast.

Fustic, fus'tik, *n.* [Fr. and Sp. *fustoc*, from Sp. *fuste*, wood, timber, from L. *fustis*, a stick, a staff.] The wood of a tree growing in the West Indies, extensively used as an ingredient in the dyeing of yellow.

Fustigate,† fus'ti-gāt, *v.t.* [L. *fustigo*, from *fustis*, a stick.] To beat with a cudgel.

Futile, fū'til, *a.* [Fr. *futile*, from L. *futilis*, leaky, vain, worthless, from *fundo*, *fusum*, to pour. FUSE.] Serving no useful end; of no effect; answering no valuable purpose; worthless; trivial.—**Futilely**, fū'til-li, *adv.* In a futile manner.—**Futility**, fū-til'i-ti, *n.* The quality of being futile, or producing no valuable effect; triflingness; unimportance.—**Futilitarian**, fū-til'i-tā"ri-an, *a.* [Formed on the type of *utilitarian*.] Devoted to the belief that all human aims and hopes are futile; pessimistic.

Futtock, fut'ok, *n.* [Corrupted from *foothook*.] *Naut.* one of those timbers raised over the keel which form the breadth of the ship.

Future, fū'tūr, *a.* [Fr. *futur*, from L. *futurus*, future part. of *sum*, *fui*, to be. BE.] That is to be or come hereafter; that will exist at any time after the present.—*Future tense*, that tense of a verb which expresses that something is yet to take place.—*n.* Time to come; time subsequent to the present; all that is to happen after the present time; the future tense.—**Futurist**, fū'tūr-ist, *n.* One who has regard to the future; one who holds that the prophecies of the Bible are yet to be fulfilled; member of a school of recent art and literature.—**Futuristic**, fū'tūr-is"tic, *a.* Pertaining to a twentieth-century school of art which rejects tradition and emphasizes dynamics (loosely, any recent art that is unconventional and obscure.—**Futurity**, fū-tū'ri-ti, *n.* The state of being future or yet to come; future time; time or event to come.—**Futurity race**, a race for which horses are entered a long time in advance, often even before they are born.

Fuze, fūz, *n.* FUSE.

Fuzz, fuz, *v.i.* [Comp. Prov.E. *fozy*, spongy, soft and woolly; D. *voos*, spongy.] To fly off in minute particles.—*n.* Fine, light particles; loose volatile matter.—**Fuzz-ball**, fuz'bal, *n.* A fungus which, after it becomes dry, when pressed, bursts and scatters a fine dust; a puff-ball.—**Fuzzy**, fuz'i, *a.* Light and spongy or rough and shaggy.—**Fuzzy-Wuzzy**, *n.* Soudanese warrior, with shock hair. (*Kipling.*)

Fylfot, fil'fot, *n.* A rectangular cross with arms of equal lengths and each bent at right angles at the end.

G

G, the seventh letter in the English alphabet, with two sounds, a hard (guttural), as in *good*; a soft (= j) as in *gem*, the former being the original sound; *mus.* the fifth note and dominant of the normal scale of C, called also *sol*.

G. [Initial letter of *gravity*.] The symbol always used to denote the acceleration with which any body falls freely to the earth in vacuo. It varies from place to place on the earth's surface, its value being about 32 feet per second per second.

Gab, gab, *v.i.* [Icel. *gabb*, mockery, *gabba*, to mock; akin D. *gabberen*, to joke, to chatter; Fr. *gaber*, to deceive; E. *gabble*, *gape*.] To talk much; to prate; to talk idly. (*Colloq.*)—*n.* (Dan. *gab*, Sw. *gap*, the mouth.) The mouth; idle talk; chatter. (*Colloq.*)

Gabardine, gab'ėr-dēn", gab"ėr-dēn', *n.* A wool or cotton cloth, like serge in appearance, but twilled on one side only.

Gabble, gab'l, *v.i.*—*gabbled*, *gabbling*. [Freq. from *gab*; akin to *gobble*.] To talk noisily and rapidly, or without meaning; to prate; to utter rapid inarticulate sounds.—*n.* Loud or rapid talk without meaning; inarticulate sounds rapidly uttered, as of fowls.—**Gabbler**, gab'lėr, *n.* One who gabbles.

Gabelle, ga-bel', *n.* [Fr. *gabelle*, O.It. *cabella*.] A tax or excise duty formerly imposed on salt in France.

Gaberdine, gab'ėr-dēn", gab"ėr-dēn', *n.* A coarse frock or loose upper garment, worn in medieval times.

Gaberlunzie, gab'ėr-lun-zi, *n.* Scottish beggar.

Gabion, gā'bi-on, *n.* [Fr. *gabion*, It. *gabbione*, a large cage, from *gabbia*, a cage, from L.L. *gabia* (= L. *cavea*), a cage. CAGE.] *Fort.* a large basket of wickerwork, of a cylindrical form, but without a bottom, filled with earth, and serving to shelter men from an enemy's fire.—**Gabionage**, gā'bi-on-āj, *n.* Gabions collectively.—**Gabioned**, gā'bi-ond, *a.* *Fort.* furnished with or formed of gabions.—**Gabionade**, gā'bi-on-ād, *n.* A work consisting of gabions.

Gable, gā'bl, *n.* [O.Fr. *gable*, L.L. *gabulum*, from the Teut.; comp. Dan. *gavl*, D. *gevel*, Icel. *gafl*, G. *giebel*, Goth. *gibla*, a gable.] *Arch.* the triangular end of a house from the level of the eaves to the top; also the end wall of a house.—**Gable window**, *n.* A window in the end or gable of a building.

Gaby, gā'bi, *n.* [Akin to *gape*, *gab*.] A silly, foolish person; a dunce. (*Colloq.*)

Gad, gad, *n.* [Icel. *gaddr*, Sw. *gadd*, Goth. *gazds*, a goad, a spike, a sting; akin to *goad*: comp. also Ir. *gada*, a bar or ingot of metal.] A spike, style, or other sharp thing; a wedge or ingot of steel or iron; a pointed wedge-like tool used by miners.—**Gad-steel**, *n.* Flemish steel: so called from its being wrought in gads.—**Gadfly**, gad'flī, *n.* [From *gad*, for *goad*, and *fly*.] A two-winged insect which stings cattle, and deposits its eggs in their skin: called also *Botfly* and *Breeze*; any fly that bites and annoys cattle.

Gad, gad, *v.i.*—*gadded*, *gadding*. [Probably from the restless running about of animals stung by the *gadfly*.] To rove or ramble idly or without any fixed purpose; to act or move without restraint; to wander, as in thought or speech.—**Gadabout**, gad'-a-bout, *n.* One who walks about idly. (*Colloq.*)—**Gadder**, gad'ėr, *n.* One that gads.—**Gaddish**, gad'ish, *a.* Disposed to gad.—**Gaddishness**, gad'ish-nes, *n.*

Gadget, gaj'et, *n.* A small object or device, usually of a mechanical nature; a part of a machine. (*Slang.*)

Gadid, gā'did, *n.* pl. **Gadidae**, gad'i-dē. [Gr. *gados*, a cod.] A family of sea fishes which includes the codfish, the haddock, the pollack, &c.—**Gadoid**, gā'doid, *a.* Resembling, belonging to, or relating to the gadidae family of fishes.

Gadolinite, gad'ō-lin-īt, *n.* [From *Gadolin*, a Prussian chemist.] A blackish mineral, a silicate of yttrium and cerium.

Gadwall, gad'wal, *n.* [Origin doubtful.] A duck belonging to Europe, Asia, and North America, not so large as the common wild duck.

Gaelic, gāl'ik, *a.* [Gael. *Gaidhealach*, Gaelic, from *Gaidheal*, a Gael.] Of or pertaining to the Gaels, a Celtic race inhabiting the Highlands of Scotland.—*n.* The language of the Celts inhabiting the Highlands of Scotland.—**Gael**, gāl, *n.* A Scottish Highlander.

Gaff, gaf, *n.* [Fr. *gaffe*, Sp. and Pg. *gafa*, a hook; of Celtic origin; akin L.G. D. Dan. and Sw. *gaffel*, a fork.] A harpoon; a gaff-hook; *naut.* a spar with a forked end used to extend the upper edge of some fore-and-aft sails.—*v.t.* To strike or secure (a salmon) by means of a gaff-hook.—**Gaff-hook**, *n.* An iron hook used to assist in landing large fish when they have been brought near the side by the angler.

Gaff, gaf, *n.* An ordeal; something difficult to endure, as *to stand the gaff*. (*Slang.*)

Gaffer, gaf'ėr, *n.* [Contr. from *grandfather* or *good father*.] An old rustic; a word originally of respect, now rather of familiarity or contempt; (*Brit.*) the foreman of a squad of workmen; an overseer.

Gag, gag, *v.t.*—*gagged*, *gagging*. [Perhaps from W. *cegiaw*, to choke, from *ceg*, a choking. Or it may be onomatopoetic; comp. *gaggle*.] To stop the mouth of by thrusting something into it so as to hinder speaking but permit breathing; hence, to silence by authority or violence.—*n.* Something thrust into the mouth to hinder speaking; interpolations, additions by actors to their verbal parts.

Gage, gāj, *n.* [Fr. *gage*, from L.L. *gadium*, *vadium*, from Goth. *wadi*, pledge, G. *wette*, a bet; or from L. *vas*, *vadis*, a surety, a pledge. Akin *wage*.] Something laid down or given as a security for the performance of some act by the person giving the gage; a pledge; something thrown down as a token of challenge to combat.—*v.t.*—*gaged*, *gaging*.‡ To give or deposit as a pledge or security for some act; to pledge or pawn; to bind by pledge.

Gage, gāj, *n.* and *v.t.* Same as GAUGE.

Gage, gāj, *n.* [The name of the person who first introduced them.] A name of several varieties of plum.

Gaggle, gag'l, *v.i.*—*gaggled*, *gaggling*. [Formed from the sound.] To make a noise like a goose.

Gaiety, Gaily. Under GAY.

Gain, gān, *v.t.* [Fr. *gagner*, anciently, to earn profit from pasturage, hence, to gain; from O.H.G. *weidanjan*, to pasture; partly also from Icel. and Sw. *gagn*, gain, profit.] To obtain by industry or the employment of capital; to get as profit or advantage; to acquire: opposed to *lose*; to win or obtain by superiority or success (to *gain* a battle, a prize); to obtain in general; to procure (fame, favour); to win to one's side; to conciliate; to reach, attain to, arrive at (to *gain* a mountain top).—*To gain over*, to draw to another party or interest; to win over.—*To gain ground*, to advance in any undertaking; to make progress.—*To gain time*, to obtain a longer time for a particular purpose.—*v.i.* To reap advantage or profit; to acquire gain.—*To gain on* or *upon*, to encroach on (the sea *gains on* the land); to advance nearer to, as in a race; to gain ground on.—*n.* Something obtained as an advantage; anything opposed to loss; profit; benefit derived.—**Gainable**, gā'na-bl, *a.* Capable of being gained, obtained, or reached.—**Gainer**, gā'nėr, *n.* One that gains or obtains profit or advantage.—**Gainful**, gān'ful, *a.* Producing profit or advantage; profitable; advantageous; lucrative.—**Gainfully**, gān'ful-li, *adv.* In a gainful manner.—**Gainfulness**, gān'ful-nes, *n.* The state or quality of being gainful.—**Gaining**, gā'ning, *n.* That which one gains: usually in the plural; earnings.—**Gainless**, gān'les, *a.* Not producing gain; unprofitable.—**Gainlessness**, gān'les-nes, *n.*

Gainly, gān'li, *a.* Handsome: now only in the compound *ungainly* (which see).

Gainsay, gān'sā, *v.t.*—*gainsaid*, *gainsaying*. [A.Sax. *gegn*, against (as in *again*), and E. *say*.] To contradict; to deny or declare not to be true; to controvert; to dispute.—

n. Opposition in words; contradiction.—**Gainsayer**, gān'sā-ėr, *n.* One who gainsays.

'Gainst, genst. Contr. for *Against.*

Gair-fowl, gãr'foul, *n.* [Prov.E. *gare, gair*, to stare.] The great auk, a bird now extinct.

Gairish, *a.* GARISH.

Gait, gāt, *n.* [Akin Icel. *gata*, a way.] Walk; manner of walking or stepping; carriage.—**Gaited**, gāt'ed, *a.* Having a particular gait: used in compounds (slow-*gaited*, heavy-*gaited*).

Gaiter, gā'tėr, *n.* [Fr. *guêtre*, a gaiter—origin unknown.] A covering of cloth for the leg, fitting over the shoe; a spatterdash.—*v.t.* To dress with gaiters.

Gala, gal'a or gā'la, *n.* [Fr., show, pomp; It. *gala*, finery; of Teut. origin; akin *gallant*. GALLANT.] An occasion of public festivity.—**Gala-day**, *n.* A day of festivity; a holiday with rejoicings.—**Gala-dress**, *n.* A holiday dress.

Galactic, ga-lak'tik, *a.* [Gr. *galaktikos*, milky, from *gala, galaktos*, milk.] Of or belonging to milk; obtained from milk; lactic; *astron.* pertaining to the Galaxy or Milky Way.—**Galactin**, ga-lak'tin, *n.* A substance obtained from milk.—**Galactogogue**, **Galactagogue**, ga-lak'tō-gog, ga-lak'ta-gog, *n.* [Gr. *gala*, and *agō*, to induce.] A medicine which promotes the secretion of milk.—**Galactometer**, gal-ak-tom'et-ėr, *n.* [Gr. *gala*, and *metron*, measure.] An instrument to test the quality of milk; a lactometer.—**Galactopoietic**, ga-lak'to-poi-et''ik, *a.* or *n.* [Gr. *gala*, and *poieō*, to make.] Applied to substances which increase the flow of milk. — **Galactose**, ga-lak'tōz, *n.* [Gr. *gala, galaktos*, milk.] A sweet substance derived from milk sugar.

Galago, ga-lā'gō, *n.* A name of certain animals of the lemur family.

Galanga, **Galangal**, ga-lang'ga, ga-lang'-gal, *n.* [Fr. *galanga*, O.Fr. *garingal*; of Eastern origin.] A dried rhizome brought from China and used in medicine, being an aromatic stimulant of the nature of ginger.

Galantine, gal-an-tēn', *n.* [Fr.] A dish of veal, chickens, or other white meat, freed from bones and served cold.

Galatian, ga-lā'shi-an, *n.* A native or inhabitant of Galatia, in Asia Minor.—*a.* Of or pertaining to Galatia or the Galatians.

Galaxy, gal'ak-si, *n.* [Fr. *galaxie*, from Gr. *galaxias* (*kyklos*, circle, being understood), from *gala, galaktos*, milk.] The Milky Way, that long, white, luminous tract which is seen at night stretching across the heavens, and which is formed by a multitude of stars so distant and blended as to be distinguishable only by powerful telescopes; an assemblage of splendid persons or things.

Galbanum, gal'ba-num, *n.* [L., from Heb. *chelbnah*, galbanum, from *cheleb*, fat.] A fetid gum resin brought from the Levant, Persia, and India, used in the arts, as in the manufacture of varnish, and also as a medicine.

Galbulus, gal'bū-lus, *n.* [L., the nut of the cypress.] *Bot.* a cone or strobilus, the scales of which are fleshy and combined into a uniform mass.

Gale, gāl, *n.* [Gael. and Ir. *gal*, a gale or puff of wind; or connected with Icel. *gol, gola*, a breeze.] A wind; a breeze; a wind between a breeze and a storm or tempest.

Gale, gāl, *n.* [O.E. *gawl*, A.Sax. D. and G. *gagel*, wild-myrtle.] A small shrub with a pleasant aromatic odour found in bogs and wet heaths.

Gale, gāl, *n.* [A.Sax. *gafol*, rent, tribute, probably from W. *gafael*, Gael. *gabhail*, a taking, a lease.] A periodical payment of rent.

Galea, gā'lē-a, *n.* [L., a helmet.] *Bot.* parts of a calyx or corolla when with the form of a helmet.—**Galeated**, **Galeate**, gā'lē-ā-ted, gā'lē-āt, *a.* [L. *galeatus*.] Covered as with a helmet; shaped like a helmet.

Galena, ga-lē'na, *n.* [Gr. *galēnē*, tranquillity—so named from its supposed effect upon diseases.] The principal ore of lead, of a lead-gray colour, with a metallic lustre, found massive, or sometimes granular or crystallized.—**Galenic**, **Galenical**, ga-len'ik, ga-len'i-kal, *a.* Pertaining to or containing galena.

Galenic, **Galenical**, ga-len'ik, ga-len'i-kal, *a.* Relating to *Galen*, the celebrated Greek physician of the second century.—**Galenism**, gā'len-izm, *n.* The doctrines of Galen.—**Galenist**, gā'len-ist, *n.* A follower of Galen.

Galilean, gal-i-lē'an, *a.* Of or pertaining to, or invented by *Galileo*, the Italian astronomer.

Galilee, gal'i-lē, *n.* [Named after the scriptural *Galilee*]. A portico or chapel annexed to some old churches, and used for various purposes.—**Galilean**, gal-i-lē'an, *n.* A native or inhabitant of Galilee, in Judea.—*a.* Relating to Galilee.

Galimatias, gal-i-mā'shi-as, *n.* [Fr., origin doubtful.] Confused talk; nonsense; absurd mixture.

Galingale, gal'in-gāl, *n.* [GALANGA.] A rare marsh plant which occurs in the south of England; formerly used as a synonym of *Galanga*.

Galiot, **Galliot**, gal'i-ot, *n.* [Fr. *galiote*, dim. of *galie*, a galley. GALLEY.] A small galley, or sort of brigantine, moved both by sails and oars; a two-masted Dutch cargo vessel, with very rounded ribs and flattish bottom.

Galipot, gal'i-pot, *n.* [Fr., perhaps from being sold in *gallipots*.] The French name for the resin which is obtained by incisions in the stems of the maritime pine.

Gall, gal, *n.* [A.Sax. *gealla* = Icel. *gall*, D. *gal*, G. *galle*; cog. with Gr. *cholē*, L. *fel*, bile.] A bitter fluid secreted in the liver of animals; bile; *fig.* bitterness of mind; rancor; malignity; the gall bladder; nerve, audacity, impudence, brazen assurance. (*Slang.*)—**Gall bladder**, *n. Anat.* a small membranous sac shaped like a pear, which receives the gall or bile from the liver.—**Gallstone**, *n.* A concretion formed in the gall bladder, or biliary passages.

Gall, gal, *n.* [Fr. *gale*, It. *galla*, from L. *galla*, an oak gall, a gallnut.] A vegetable excrescence produced by the deposit of the egg of an insect in the bark or leaves of a plant, especially the oak, very extensively used in dyeing and in the manufacture of ink.—**Gallfly**, **Gallinsect**, *n.* An insect that punctures plants, and occasions galls.—**Gallic**, gal'ik, *a.* Belonging to galls; derived from galls.—**Gall oak**, *n.* The oak from which the galls of commerce are obtained.

Gall, gal, *v.t.* [O.Fr. *galler*, to gall or fret, *galle*, an itching, scurf, perhaps L. *galla*, the diseased vegetable excrescence. Comp. also Armor. *gâl*, eruption.] To make a sore in the skin of by rubbing, fretting, and wearing away; to excoriate; to vex; to chagrin; to cause to have a feeling of bitterness or annoyance; to hurt the feelings of; to harass; to annoy (as by a musketry fire).—*n.* A sore place caused by rubbing.—**Galling**, gal'ing, *a.* Adapted to fret or chagrin; vexing; harassing; annoying.—**Gallingly**, gal'ing-li, *adv.* In a galling manner.

Gallant, gal'ant, *a.* [Fr. *galant*, ppr. of O.Fr. verb *galer*, to rejoice, from the Teutonic; comp. G. *geil*, wanton, Goth. *gailjan*, to rejoice, A.Sax. *gál*, merry.] Gay, showy, or splendid in attire or outward appearance; handsome; fine; brave; high-spirited; courageous; magnanimous; noble; chivalrous; (in the following senses pron. also ga-lant'), courtly; polite and attentive to ladies; courteous.—*n.* A gay sprightly man; a high-spirited brave young fellow; a daring spirit; (in the following senses pron. also ga-lant'), a man who is polite and attentive to ladies; a wooer; a suitor.—*v.t.* (ga-lant'). To act the gallant towards; to wait on or be very attentive to (a lady).—**Gallantly**, gal'ant-li, *adv.* In a gallant manner; gaily; splendidly; bravely; nobly. — **Gallantness**, gal'ant-nes, *n.* The state or quality of being gallant.—**Gallantry**, gal'ant-ri, *n.* [Fr. *galanterie*.] Show; ostentatious finery; bravery; dash; intrepidity; polite attention to ladies; court paid to females for the purpose of winning illicit favours.

Galleass, gal'ē-as, *n.* [Fr. *galeasse*, It. *galeazza*; akin to *galley*.] A large kind of galley formerly used in the Mediterranean.

Galleon, gal'ē-un, *n.* [Sp. *galeon*, It. *galeone*, augmentatives from L.L. *galea*, a galley.] A large ship formerly used by the Spaniards in their commerce with America.

Gallery, gal'ėr-i, *n.* [Fr. *galerie*, It. *galleria*, L.L. *galeria*, perhaps from L.Gr. *galē*, a gallery.] An apartment of much greater length than breadth, serving as a passage of communication between different rooms of a building; a room or building for the exhibition of paintings, statues, and other works of art; a collection of paintings, statues, &c.; a platform projecting from the walls of a building, and overlooking a ground-floor, as in a church, theatre, and the like; *fort.* any communication covered in both above and at the sides; *mining*, a narrow passage; *naut.* a frame like a balcony projecting from the stern and quarters of a ship.

Galley, gal'i, *n.* [O.Fr. *galie*, It. and L.L. *galea*—probably from Gr. *galē*, a kind of gallery, or *galeos, galē*, a sea-fish, a kind of shark, which might suggest a swift-sailing vessel. Akin are *galleon, galleass, galiot*.] A low flat-built vessel with one deck, and navigated with sails and oars, once commonly used in the Mediterranean; a ship of the ancient Greeks and Romans, propelled chiefly by oars; the boat of a warship appropriated for the captain's use; the cook-room or kitchen on board ship; *printing*, a movable frame or tray on which the types are placed when composed. — *The galleys*, certain galleys on the Mediterranean which were worked by convicts; hence, a synonym for a place of forced and severe toil.—**Galley-fire**, *n.* A ship's fireplace.—**Galley-slave**, *n.* A person condemned for a crime to work at the oar on board of a galley.

Galliard, gal'yärd, *n.* [Sp. *gallarda*.] A lively dance, originally Spanish; also the dancer of a *galliard*.

Gallic, *a.* Under GALL, a vegetable excrescence.

Gallic, **Gallican**, gal'ik, gal'i-kan, *a.* [L. *Gallicus*, from *Gallia*, Gaul, France.] Pertaining to Gaul or France (the *Gallican* church or clergy); in the days of Louis XIV and Bossuet, claiming liberty of action denied by the Papal or Ultramontane party.—**Gallicize**, gal'i-sīz, *v.t.*—*gallicized, gallicizing*. To render conformable to the French idiom or language.—**Gallicism**, gal'i-sizm, *n.* [Fr. *gallicisme*.] A mode of speech peculiar to the French nation; a custom or mode of thought peculiar to the French.

Galligaskins, gal-i-gas'kinz, *n.pl.* [From Fr. *gregues*q*ues*, O.Fr. *guarguesques, garguesques*, from It. *grechesco*, Grecian (through such forms as *gleguesques, galligasks*).] Large open breeches; wide hose; leather guards worn on the legs by sportsmen.

Gallimaufry, gal-i-ma'fri, *n.* [Fr. *galimafrée*, a ragout; of uncertain origin.] A hash; a medley; a hodge-podge.

Gallinaceous, gal-i-nā'shus, *a.* [L. *gallinaceus*, from *gallina*, a hen, *gallus*, a cock.] Pertaining to the order of birds which includes the domestic fowls, pheasants, &c.—**Gallinacean**, gal-i-nā'shē-an, *n.* One of the gallinaceous birds.—**Gallinule**, gal'i-nūl, *n.* [L. *gallinula*, dim. of *gallina*, a hen.] A grallatorial bird closely allied to the coots; the water-hen or moor-hen.

Gallipot, gal'i-pot, *n.* [Corrupted from O.D. *gleypot*, an earthen pot—*gley*, clay, and *pot*.] A small pot or vessel painted and glazed, used by druggists and apothecaries for containing medicines.

Gallium, gal'i-um, *n.* [From *Gallia*, the Latin name for France.] A rare metal, of a grayish-white colour and brilliant lustre, exceedingly fusible, discovered in 1875.

Gallivant, Gallavant, gal-i-vant′, gal-a-vant′, *v.i.* [Probably a corrupt form of *gallant*.] To gad or run about; to flirt.

Galliwasp, gal′i-wasp, *n.* A species of West Indian lizard, about 1 foot in length.

Gallomania, gal-ō-mā′ni-a, *n.* [See GAUL, MANIA.] A mania for imitating French manners, dress, literature, &c.

Gallon, gal′un, *n.* [O.Fr. *galon, jalon*; Fr. *jale*, a jar, a bowl; origin unknown.] A measure of capacity equal to 4 quarts, dry or liquid, but usually the latter; the U. S. gallon contains 231 cu. in., the English imperial gallon, 277.274 cu. in.

Galloon, ga-lön′, *n.* [Fr. and Sp. *galon*; It. *galone*, from *gala*, show. GALA.] A kind of narrow close lace made of cotton, silk, gold, or silver threads, &c.—**Gallooned**, ga-lönd′, *a.* Furnished or adorned with galloon.

Gallop, gal′up, *v.i.* [Fr. *galoper*, from O.Flem. *walop*, a galop, an extension of *wallen*, A.Sax. *weallan*, to boil.] To move or run with leaps, as a horse; to run with speed; to ride a horse that is galloping; to ride at a rapid pace; to scamper.—*n.* The movement or pace of a horse, by springs or leaps.—**Gallopade**, gal-up-äd′, *n.* [Fr. *galopade*.] A sidelong or curvetting kind of gallop; a sprightly kind of dance; a galop; the music adapted to it.—*v.i.*—*gallopaded, gallopading*. To gallop; to perform the dance called a gallopade.—**Galloper**, gal′-up-ėr, *n.* One who or that which gallops.

Galloper, *n.* An aide-de-camp.

Galloway, gal′ō-wā, *n.* A species of horses of small size but great endurance, first bred in *Galloway* in Scotland. — *Gallovidians, Galwegians*, inhabitants of Galloway.

Gallowglass, Gallowglas, gal′ō-glas, *n.* [Ir. *galloglach*—*gall*, a foreigner, an Englishman, and *oglach*, a youth; from being armed after the English model.] An ancient heavy-armed foot-soldier of Ireland and the Western Isles.

Gallows, gal′ōz, *n. sing.* or *pl.*; also **Gallowses** in pl. [A plural form: A.Sax. *galga, gealga* (sing.), a gallows = Dan. and Sw. *galge*, Icel. *gálgi*, Goth. *galga*, G. *galgen*, gallows.] An upright wooden frame with crossbar, on which criminals are executed by hanging; also a pair of suspenders or braces.

Galop, ga-lop′, *n.* [Fr. GALLOP.] A quick, lively kind of dance in 2=4 time, somewhat resembling a waltz; the music for this dance.

Galore, ga-lōr′, *n.* [Ir. and Gael. *go leòr*, enough—*go*, to, and *leòr*, enough.] Abundance; plenty.—*adv.* In abundance; bountifully. (*Colloq.*)

Galosh, Galoshe, ga-losh′, *n.* [Fr. *galoche*, from L.L. *calopedia* (through the corruptions *calop′dia, calopdja*), from Gr. *kalopodion*, a wooden shoe—*kalon*, wood, and *pous, podos*, a foot.] A shoe to be worn over another shoe to keep the foot dry; also a kind of gaiter.

Galvanic, Galvanical,† gal-van′ik, gal-van′i-kal, *a.* [From *Galvani*, an Italian physiologist, an early investigator of galvanism.] Pertaining to galvanism; containing or exhibiting galvanism.—*Galvanic electricity*, electricity arising from chemical action.—*Galvanic pair* or *cell*, a combination of two substances in an exciting liquid which acts chemically upon one more than on the other.—*Galvanic battery*, an association of galvanic pairs for the production of current electricity. — **Galvanism**, gal′-van-izm, *n.* That branch of the science of electricity which treats of the electric currents arising from chemical action. *Current electricity, voltaic* are now used instead of *galvanism, galvanic*.—**Galvanist**, gal′-van-ist, *n.* One versed in galvanism. — **Galvanization**, gal′van-i-zā″shon, *n.* The act of affecting with galvanism; the state of being affected.—**Galvanize**, gal′-van-īz, *v.t.*—*galvanized, galvanizing*. To affect with galvanizm; to electroplate by galvanism; to coat (sheets of iron) with tin or zinc in this way; to restore to consciousness by galvanic action, as from a state of suspended animation.—**Galvanizer**, gal′van-ī-zėr, *n.* One who or that which galvanizes.—**Galvanologist**, gal-van-ol′o-jist, *n.* One who describes the phenomena of galvanism. — **Galvanology**, gal-van-ol′o-ji, *n.* A description of the phenomena of galvanism.—**Galvanomagnetic**, gal′van-ō-mag-net″ik, *a.* Same as *Electro-magnetic*. — **Galvanometer**, gal-van-om′et-ėr, *n.* An instrument for detecting the existence and determining the strength and direction of an electric current.—**Galvanometry**, gal-van-om′et-ri, *n.* The art or process of determining the force of electric or galvanic currents.—**Galvanoplastic**, gal′van-ō-plas″tik, *a.* Pertaining to the art or process of electrotyping.—**Galvanoplasty**, gal′van-ō-plas-ti, *n.* Same as *Electrotypy*. — **Galvanoscope**, gal′van-ō-skōp, *n.* An instrument for detecting the existence and direction of an electric current. — **Galvanoscopic**, gal′van-ō-skop″ik, *a.* Of or pertaining to a galvanoscope.

Gama-grass, gä′ma, *n.* A tall, strong, and exceedingly productive grass cultivated in the warm parts of America and to some extent in Europe.

Gambeson, Gambison, gam′bē-zon, gam′bi-zon, *n.* [O.Fr. *gambeson*, from O.H.G. *wamba*, A.Sax. *wambe*, womb, stomach; comp. G. *wams*, doublet.] A stuffed and quilted tunic, fitting the body, and formerly worn under the habergeon.

Gambier, Gambir, gam′bēr, gam′bir, *n.* [Malayan.] An earthy-looking substance of light-brown hue, procured from the leaves of a Malayan shrub, and used medicinally as an astringent, but far more extensively employed in tanning and dyeing.

Gambit, gam′bit, *n.* [Fr., from It. *gambetto*, a tripping up of one's legs, from *gamba*, the leg.] *Chess*, the sacrifice of a pawn early in the game, for the purpose of taking up an attacking position.

Gamble, gam′bl, *v.i.*—*gambled, gambling*. [Freq. of *game*, with *b* inserted, as in *number, humble*.] To play or game for money or other stake, especially to be in the habit of doing so.—*v.t.* To lose or squander by gaming: with *away*. — **Gambler**, gam′-blėr, *n.* One who gambles.—**Gambling-house**, *n.* A gaming-house.

Gamboge, gam-bōj′, *n.* [From *Camboja, Cambodia*, a portion of the empire of Anam, in Asia.] The hardened juice or sap yielded by several species of trees, and used as a purgative in medicine, and also in the arts, chiefly in water-colour painting. — **Gambogic**, gam-bō′jik, *a.* Pertaining to gamboge.

Gambol, gam′bol, *v.i.*—*gambolled, gambolling*. [O.E. *gambolde, gambaude*, from Fr. *gambade*, gambol, *gambiller*, to wag the leg or kick, O.Fr. *gambe*, It. *gamba*, the leg, Fr. *jambe*.] To dance and skip about in sport; to frisk; to leap; to play in frolic. —*n.* A skipping or leaping about in frolic; a skip, frisk, leap, prank.

Gambrel, Gambril, gam′brel, gam′bril, *n.* [From It. *gamba*, the leg.] The hind-leg of a horse; a stick crooked like a horse's leg, used by butchers for suspending animals.—*Gambrel roof*, a hipped-roof; a mansard roof.

Game, gām, *n.* [A.Sax. *gamen*, joy, pleasure; Icel. *gaman*, Dan. *gammen*, delight, gratification; O.G. *gaman*, jest, sport. *Gamble* is a derivative, and *gammon*, humbug, is of same origin.] Sport of any kind; jest; play; some contrivance or arrangement for sport, recreation, testing skill, and the like (as baseball or football); a single contest in any such game; specifically (*pl.*), diversions or contests, as in wrestling, running, and other athletic exercises; a scheme pursued or measures planned; such animals, collectively, as are usually pursued or taken in the chase or in the sports of the field: in this sense without a plural; the animals enumerated in the game-laws.—*To make game of*, to turn into ridicule; to delude or humbug.—*v.i.*—*gamed, gaming*. [A.Sax. *gamenian*.] To gamble; to play at cards, dice, billiards, &c., for money; to be in the habit of so doing.—*a.* Having the courageous spirit of a game-cock; courageous. (*Colloq.*)—*To die game*, to maintain a bold, resolute, courageous spirit to the last. —**Game-bag**, *n.* A bag for holding the game killed by a sportsman. — **Game-cock**, *n.* A cock bred or used to fight; a cock of a good fighting breed. — **Game-fowl**, *n.* A variety of the common fowl bred for fighting.—**Gameful**, gām′ful, *a.* Full of sport or games; sportive; full of game or beasts of sport (*Pope*).—**Gamekeeper**, *n.* One who has the care of game; one who is employed to look after animals kept for sport. — **Game-laws**, *n. pl.* Laws enacted with regard to, or for the preservation of, the animals called game.—**Game leg**, *n.* [Celt. *cam*, crooked.] A crippled or bent leg.—**Game**, *n.* Cricket. *To play* the *game*, to play according to rule; to act straightforwardly.—**Gamely**, gām′-li, *adv.* In a game or courageous manner. (*Colloq.*)—**Gameness**, gām′nes, *n.* The quality of being game; pluckiness. (*Colloq.*) — **Game-preserver**, *n.* One who strictly preserves for his own sport or profit such animals as are game.—**Gamesome**, gām′sum, *a.* Sportive; playful; frolicsome. —**Gamesomely**, gām′sum-li, *adv.* Sportively; playfully. — **Gamesomeness**, gām′sum-nes, *n.* The quality of being gamesome. — **Gamester**, gām′stėr, *n.* [*Game*, and the suffix *-ster*.] One who games; a person addicted to gaming; a gambler; one skilled in games.—**Gamey, Gamy**, gā′mi, *a.* Having the flavour of game. — **Gaming-house**, *n.* A house where gaming is practised; a gambling-house. — **Gaming-table**, *n.* A table appropriated to gaming.

Gamete, ga-mēt′, *n.* [Gr. *gameō*, I marry.] A sexual cell.

Gamin, gam′in, ga-maṅ, *n.* [Fr.] A neglected street boy; an Arab of the streets.

Gammer, gam′ėr, *n.* [Contr. for *good-mother* or *grandmother*. Comp. *gaffer*.] An old wife; the correlative of *gaffer*.

Gammon, gam′un, *n.* [O.Fr. *gambon*, It *gambone*, a big leg, a gammon, from *gamba*, a leg.] The thigh of a hog, pickled and smoked or dried; a smoked ham.—*v.t.* To make into bacon; to pickle and dry in smoke.

Gammon, gam′un, *n.* [Connected with *game*; comp. Dan. *gammen*, sport.] An imposition or hoax; humbug. (*Colloq.*)—*v.t.* To delude; to hoax or humbug. (*Colloq.*)

Gamogenesis, gam-o-jen′e-sis, *n.* [Gr. *gamos*, marriage, and *genesis*.] Generation by copulation of the sexes; sexual generation.—**Gamogenetic**, gam′o-je-net″ik, *a.* Of or relating to gamogenesis.—**Gamopetalous**, gam-o-pet′a-lus, *a.* [Gr. *gamos*, and *petalon*, a flower-leaf.] *Bot.* monopetalous.—**Gamophyllous**, ga-mof′i-lus or gam-o-fil′lus, *a.* [Gr. *gamos*, and *phyllon*, a leaf.] *Bot.* having a single perianth-whorl with coherent leaves.—**Gamosepalous**, gam-o-sep′a-lus, *a.* [Gr. *gamos*, and E. *sepal*.] *Bot.* monosepalous.

Gamp, gamp, *n.* A clumsy umbrella, as carried by Mrs. Sairey Gamp, in Dickens. Fr. *Robinson*, from the umbrella of Robinson Crusoe.

Gamut, gam′ut, *n.* [Gr. *gamma*, the letter G, the last note of the scale, and L. *ut*, the syllable formerly used in singing the first note of the scale, the modern *do*.] *Mus.* a scale on which notes in music are written or printed, consisting of lines and spaces which are named after the first seven letters of the alphabet.

Gander, gan′dėr, *n.* [A.Sax. *gandra*, for *ganra*, from the root *gan* seen in G. *gans*, a goose, *gänserich*, a gander. GOOSE.] The male of the goose.

Gang, gang, *n.* [A.Sax. *gang*, a way, a passage, *genge*, a gang, a company, from *gangan*, to go. GO.] A number going in company; hence, a company or number of persons associated for a particular purpose: used especially in a depreciatory or contemptuous sense or of disreputable persons;

a number of workmen or laborers engaged on any piece of work under the supervision of one person; a squad.—**Gang boss**, *n.* One who superintends a gang of laborers. —**Gang machinery**, A combination of similar implements, acting in unison, as *gang* drills.—**Gangster**, one of a gang of toughs, or thieves. (*Colloq.*)—**Gangway**, gang'wā, *n.* A temporary means of access to some position, formed of planks or boards; a narrow framework or platform leading into or out of a ship, or from one part of a ship to another; an opening in a ship's bulwarks and the steps leading to it.

Ganglion, gang'gli-on, *n.* pl. **Ganglia** or **Ganglions**. [Gr. *ganglion*, a sort of swelling or excrescence, a tumour under the skin.] *Anat.* an enlargement occurring somewhere in the course of a nerve; a mass of nervous matter containing nerve-cells, and giving origin to nerve-fibres; *surg.* an encysted tumour situated somewhere on a tendon.—**Gangliac**, **Ganglial**, gang'gli-ak, gang'gli-al, *a.* Relating to a ganglion. —**Gangliated**, gang'gli-āt-ed, *a.* Having ganglions.—**Gangliform**, **Ganglioform**, gang'gli-form, gang'gli-o-form, *a.* Having the shape of a ganglion.—**Ganglionary**, gang'gli-on-a-ri, *a.* Composed of ganglia.—**Ganglionic**, gang-gli-on'ik, *a.* Pertaining to a ganglion.

Gangrene, gang'grēn, *n.* [L. *gangræna*, from Gr. *gangraina*, from *grainō*, to gnaw.] The first stage of mortification of living flesh; *bot.* a disease ending in putrid decay. —*v.t.*—*gangrened, gangrening.* To produce a gangrene in; to mortify.—*v.i.* To become mortified. Also **Gangrenate**, gang'grē-nāt.—**Gangrenescent**, gang-grē-nes'ent, *a.* Becoming gangrenous.—**Gangrenous**, gang'grē-nus, *a.* Attacked by gangrene; mortified; indicating mortification of living flesh.

Gangue, gang, *n.* [G. *gang*, a vein.] The stony matrix of metallic ores.

Gangway. Under GANG.

Ganister, **Gannister**, gan'is-tėr, *n.* A close-grained hard sandstone or grit found under certain coal-beds in England.

Gannet, gan'et, *n.* [A.Sax. *ganet, ganot*, a sea-fowl, a gannet; allied to *gander, goose.*] The solan-goose, an aquatic bird of the pelican family, 3 feet in length, common on insular rocks in the northern seas.

Ganoid, gan'oid, *a.* [Gr. *ganos*, splendour, and *eidos*, appearance.] Belonging to an order of fishes, the majority of them extinct, characterized by scales composed of horny or bony plates, covered with glossy enamel. —*n.* One of these fishes.

Gantlet, gant'let, *n.* A glove. Same as *Gauntlet.*

Gantlet, gant'let, *n.* [From Sw. *gatlopp*, from *gata*, a street, a line of soldiers, and *lopp*, a course, akin to E. *leap*, D. *loopen*, to run.] A punishment in which the culprit was compelled to run between two ranks of men armed with rods, &c., receiving a blow from each.—*To run the gantlet*, to undergo the punishment of the gantlet; hence, to go through much and severe criticism, controversy, or ill-treatment.

Gaol, jāl, **Gaoler**, jā'lėr. JAIL, JAILER.

Gap, gap, *n.* [Icel. and Sw. *gap*, a gap or hiatus; akin *gape, gaby.*] A break or opening, as in a fence, wall, or the like; a breach; a chasm; a hiatus.—*To stop a gap*, to fill it up; hence, to supply a temporary expedient.—*v.t.* To make a gap or gaps in; to notch or jag; to cut into teeth.—**Gap-toothed**, *a.* Having interstices between the teeth.

Gape, gāp, *v.i.*—*gaped, gaping.* [A.Sax. *geapan*, to gape or open wide, from *geap*, wide; Dan. *gabe*, Icel. *gapa*, to gaze with open mouth; D. *gapen*, G. *gaffen*, to gape; akin *gap, gaby.*] To open the mouth wide, as indicative of drowsiness, dulness, surprise, expectation, &c.; to stand open; to present a gap; to show a fissure or chasm.—*To gape for or after*, to crave; to desire or covet earnestly.—*n.* The act of gaping; *zool.* the width of the mouth when opened, as of birds, fishes, &c.; *pl.* a disease of young poultry attended with much gaping.—**Gaper**, gā'pėr, *n.* One who gapes; a bivalve mollusc with a shell permanently open at the posterior end.

Garage, gar'āj, *n.* [Fr.] A place for receiving or mending motor-cars.

Garb, gärb, *n.* [O.Fr. *garbe*, a garb, appearance, comeliness, from O.H.G. *garawi, garwi*, attire; akin to A.Sax. *gearwa*, clothing; E. *gear* and *yare.*] Clothing; vesture; costume; habit; an official or other distinguishing dress; fashion or mode.—*v.t.* To dress; to clothe. (*Tenn.*)

Garbage, gär'bāj, *n.* [O.E. *garbash*, probably from *garble*, to sift; being thus what is sifted out, refuse.] Refuse or offal; refuse animal or vegetable matter; any worthless, offensive matter.

Garble, gär'bl, *v.t.*—*garbled, garbling.* [O. Fr. *garbeller*, from Sp. *garbillar*, to sift, *garbillo*, a coarse sieve; from Ar. *gharbil*, a sieve.] To sift or bolt‡; to examine for the purpose of separating the good from the bad‡; to falsify by leaving out parts; to mutilate so as to give a false impression (to *garble* historical documents); to sophisticate; to corrupt.—**Garbler**, gär'blėr, *n.* One who garbles; formerly an official in London who looked after the purity of drugs and spices.

Garboil,‡ gär'boil, *n.* [O.Fr. *garbouil*, It. *garbuglio.*] Tumult; uproar. (*Shak.*)

Gardant, gär'dant, *a.* [Fr.] *Her.* a term applied to a lion represented as looking with full face at the observer.

Garden, gär'dn, *n.* [O.Fr. *gardin*, Mod. Fr. *jardin*, a word of Teutonic origin; comp. L.G. *garden*, G. *garten*, a garden; Goth. *gards*, A.Sax. *geard*, O.E. *garth*, an inclosed place, a yard. YARD.] A piece of ground appropriated to the cultivation of plants, fruits, flowers, or vegetables; a rich well-cultivated spot or tract of country. —*v.i.* To lay out or cultivate a garden.—**Gardener**, gär'dn-ėr, *n.* One whose occupation is to keep a garden.—**Gardening**, gär'dn-ing, *n.* The art or practice of cultivating gardens; horticulture.—*Garden city*, a town laid out with many gardens and open spaces.—*Garden party*, a party held out of doors on the lawn or in the garden of a private residence.

Gardenia, gär-dē'ni-a, *n.* [After Dr. *Garden*, an American botanist.] A name of certain plants of Asia and Africa with large white or yellowish fragrant flowers.

Garfish, gär'fish, *n.* [A.Sax. *gár*, a dart.] A fish with a remarkably elongated body and a long, narrow, beak-like snout; sea-pike or sea-needle.

Gargantua, gar-gan'tu-a, *n.* A gigantic hero of a satirical romance by Rabelais; **Gargantuan**, *a.* Gigantic; coarse.

Gargle, gär'gl, *v.t.*—*gargled, gargling.* [A word akin to *gurgle, gorge, gargoil*; Fr. *gargouiller*, to gargle; L. *gurgulio*, the gullet; Gr. *gargarizō*, to rinse the mouth; G. *gurgel*, the throat, *gurgeln*, to gargle.] To wash or rinse (the mouth or throat) with a liquid preparation.—*n.* Any liquid preparation for washing the mouth and throat.

Gargoyle, **Gargoil**, gär'goil, *n.* [Fr. *gargouille*, a gargoil or spout. GARGLE.] *Arch.* a projecting spout for throwing the water from the gutters of a building, generally carved into a grotesque figure from whose mouth the water gushes.

Garibaldi, gar-i-bald'i, *n.* A loose red blouse worn by women, named from the red-shirt troops of the Italian patriot *Garibaldi.*

Garish, **Gairish**, gā'rish, *a.* [From O.E. *gare*, to stare, probably a form of *gaze* with change from *z*-sound to *r*, as in *snore, snooze; frore, freeze*, &c.] Gaudy; showy; staring; overbright; dazzling.—**Garishly**, **Gairishly**, gā'rish-ly, *adv.* In a garish manner.—**Garishness**, **Gairishness**, gā'rish-nes, *n.* The state or quality of being garish.

Garland, gär'land, *n.* [O.E. *girlond, gerlond*, from Fr. *guirlande*, a garland, from O.H.G. *wiera*, a coronet, through a verb *wierelen*, to plait.] A wreath or chaplet made of leaves, twigs, flowers, or the like; a collection of little printed pieces; an anthology.—*v.t.* To deck with a garland or garlands.

Garlic, gär'lik, *n.* [A.Sax. *gárleác*, from *gár*, a dart or lance—from the spear-shaped leaves—and *leác*, a leek, as in hem*lock*, char*lock*, &c.] A plant allied to the onion, leek, &c., having an acrid pungent taste and very strong odour, indigenous to the south of Europe, where it forms a favourite condiment. See also RAMSON.

Garment, gär'ment, *n.* [Fr. *garnement*; O.Fr. *garniment*, from *garnir*, to garnish, to deck. GARNISH.] Any article of clothing or piece of dress, as a coat, a gown, &c.; a vestment.

Garner, gär'nėr, *n.* [Fr. *grenier*, O.Fr. *gernier*, a cornloft, from L. *granaria*, a granary, from *granum*, grain. GRANARY.] A granary; a building or place where grain is stored for preservation.—*v.t.* To store in, or as in, a granary.

Garnet, gär'net, *n.* [Fr. *grenat*, It. *granata*, from L. *granum*, grain, seed, and in later times the cochineal insect and the scarlet dye obtained from it, the stone being so called on account of its fine crimson color.] The name common to a group or family of precious stones, varying considerably in composition, the prevailing color being red of various shades, but often brown, and sometimes green, yellow, or black; *naut.* a sort of tackle fixed to a stay, and used to hoist in and out cargo.

Garnish, gär'nish, *v.t.* [Fr. *garnir*, to provide or equip; It. *guarnire, guernire*, O.Sp. *guarnir*; from the German—comp. O.H.G. *warnōn*, G. *warnen*, A.Sax. *warnian*, to take care, to warn. WARN. Akin *garment, garrison.*] To adorn; to decorate with appendages; to set off; *cookery*, to ornament (a dish) with colorful trimming; *law*, to warn, or bring into court, by garnishment.—*n.* Something added for embellishment; ornament; decoration; *cookery*, something added to food as an embellishment.—**Garnishee**, *v.t.* To obtain legal attachment on property or money owing to a debtor by his employer.—**Garnisher**, gär'nish-ėr, *n.* One who garnishes or decorates.—**Garnishing**, **Garnishment**, gär'nish-ing, gär'nish-ment, *n.* That which garnishes; ornament; *law*, a legal notice commanding one to appear in court.

Garotte, **Garotter**. GARROTE, GARROTTER.

Garret, gar'et, *n.* [O.Fr. *garite*, a place of refuge or outlook, from *garer*, to beware, from O.H.G. *werjan*, Goth. *varjan*, to defend. Akin *ward, guard, wary, warn.*] That part of a house which is on the uppermost floor, immediately under the roof; a loft.—**Garreteer**, gar-et-ēr', *n.* An inhabitant of a garret; a poor author.—**Garret-story**, *n.* The story of a house in which the garrets are situated.

Garrison, gar'i-sn, *n.* [Fr. *garnison*, from *garnir*, to garnish. GARNISH.] A body of troops stationed in a fort or fortified town; a fort, castle, or fortified town furnished with troops.—*v.t.* To place a garrison in; to secure or defend by garrisons.

Garrote, **Garrotte**, ga-rōt', ga-rot', *n.* [Fr. *garrotte*, from Sp. *garrote.*] A mode of capital punishment in Spain by strangling the prisoner by means of an iron collar attached to a post; the instrument of this punishment.—**Garrote**, **Garrotte**, ga-rōt', ga-rot', *v.t.*—*garroted, garrotted; garroting, garrotting.* To strangle by means of the garrote; to rob by suddenly seizing a person and compressing his windpipe till he become insensible, or at least helpless, usually carried out by two or three accomplices.—**Garroter**, ga-rōt'ėr, *n.* One who commits the act of garroting.

Garrulous, ga'rū-lus, *a.* [L. *garrulus*, from *garrio*, to prate, to chatter; allied to Gr. *gēryō*, *garyō*, to cry; Ir. *gairim*, to bawl.] Talkative; prating; characterized by long prosy talk, with minuteness and frequent repetition in recording details.—**Garrulity**, ga-rū'li-ti, *n.* The quality of being garrulous; talkativeness; loquacity.—**Garrulously**, ga'rū-lus-li, *adv.* In a garrulous or talkative manner.—**Garrulousness**, ga'rū-lus-nes, *n.* Talkativeness; garrulity.

Garter, gär'tėr, *n.* [From O.Fr. *gartier* = Fr. *jarretière*, from *jarret*, O.Fr. *garret*, ham, hough, from the Celtic; Armor. *gâr* or *garr*, W. *gar*, the leg, Gael. *gar*, in *gartan*, a garter.] A band or strip of elastic worn to hold up a stocking; the badge of the highest order of knighthood in Great Britain, called *the order of the Garter*; hence, also, the order itself, and the name given to the principal king-of-arms in England.—*v.t.* To bind with a garter.

Garth, gärth, *n.* [Icel. *garthr*, a yard or court = A.Sax. *geard*, a yard. GARDEN, YARD.] A yard or garden†; a small inclosed place; the greensward or grass area within the cloisters of a religious house; a dam or weir for catching fish.

Gas, gas, *n.* [A word formed by the Dutch chemist Van Helmont, who died in 1644.] An elastic, airlike fluid; a substance, such as air, the particles of which tend to fly apart from each other, thus causing it to expand indefinitely; in common usage, any gaseous substance except air, as *acetylene gas*, which in combination with oxygen is used in welding; *coal gas*, distilled from coal and used for heating, cooking, and less frequently, lighting; *laughing gas* or nitrous oxide, employed in dentistry or surgery as an anesthetic; *natural gas*, found under the earth's crust and used as a fuel and illuminant; *poison gas*, such as chlorine, employed in warfare. Fuel gases, poison gases, and firedamp are often referred to simply as *gas*. Gasoline is colloquially termed *gas*.—*v.t.* To treat with gas, as in industrial processes; to poison with gas.—**Gas burner**, a jet or series of jets where gas is burned as it issues out.—**Gaselier**, gas'e-lēr, *n.* A chandelier adapted for burning gas.—**Gas engine**, an internal-combustion engine burning gasoline.—**Gaseous**, gas'ē-us, *a.* In the form of gas; of the nature of gas.—**Gaseousness**, gas'ē-us-nes, *n.*—**Gas fitter**, a workman who fixes pipes and fits burners and other appliances for gas.—**Gas fixture**, that part of a gas pipe to which a gas burner is attached.—**Gas furnace**, a furnace of which the fuel is gas.—**Gasiform**, gas'i-form, *a.* Gaseous; aeriform.—**Gasify**, gas'i-fī, *v.t.*—*gasified*, *gasifying*. To convert into gas.—**Gasification**, gas'i-fi-kā"shon, *n.* The act of converting into gas.—**Gas lamp**, a lamp, the light of which is supplied by gas.—**Gas light**, light produced by the combustion of coal gas; a gas jet.—**Gas main**, one of the principal pipes which convey gas from the gas works to the place of consumption.—**Gas mask**, a covering for the face, worn as a protection against poison gas. It is airtight, save for a respirator in which the poison is neutralized.—**Gas meter**, an instrument through which gas is passed in order to have registered the quantity which is consumed at a particular place.—**Gasoline**, gas'ō-lēn, **Gasolene**, *n.* Refined petroleum, used as a fuel, as in automobiles; it is a volatile liquid hydrocarbon, highly inflammable; vaporized and mixed with air, it becomes explosive.—**Gasometer**, gas-om'e-tėr, *n.* An instrument or apparatus intended to measure, collect, or mix gases.—**Gas station**, a place where gasoline and oil are sold, chiefly for use in automobiles.—**Gas stove**, a stove heated by gas.—**Gassy**, gas'i, *a.* Relating to or containing gas; gaseous.—**Gas tank**, a reservoir for coal gas and other fuel gases.

Gascon, gas'kon, *n.* [Fr.; akin to *Basque*.] A native of Gascony in France; hence, a boaster, the Gascons being noted for boasting.—**Gasconade**, gas-ko-nād', *n.* [Fr.] A boast or boasting; a vaunt; a bravado; a bragging.—*v.i.*—*gasconaded*, *gasconading*. To boast; to brag, to vaunt; to bluster.—**Gasconader**, gas-ko-nā'dėr, *n.* A great boaster.

Gash, gash, *n.* [Perhaps from O.Fr. *garser*, to scarify, to pierce with a lancet; L.L. *garsa*, scarification.] A deep and long cut; an incision of considerable length, particularly in flesh.—*v.t.* To make a gash or gashes in.

Gasket, gas'ket, *n.* [Fr. *garcette*, Sp. *garceta*, a gasket.] One of the plaited cords fastened to the yard of a ship to tie the sail to it; packing for pistons, &c.

Gasp, gasp, *v.i.* [Icel. *geispa*, to yawn; Dan. *gispe*, to gasp; L.G. *japen*, *japsen*; akin to E. *gape*.] To open the mouth wide in laborious respiration; to labor for breath; to respire convulsively; to pant violently.—*v.t.* To emit or utter with gaspings or pantings; with *away*, *forth*, *out*, &c.—*n.* A labored respiration; a short painful catching of the breath.—**Gaspingly**, gasp'ing-li, *adv.* In a gasping manner.

Gastropod, Gasteropod, gas'trō-pod, gas'tėr-o-pod, *n.* [Gr. *gastēr*, the belly, and *pous*, *podos*, a foot.] One of a class of mollusks, consisting of snails, periwinkles, and other animals inhabiting a univalve shell (although some of them are destitute of a shell), the distinguishing characteristic being the *foot*, a broad muscular organ attached to the ventral surface.—**Gastropodous**, gas-trop'o-dus, *a.* Belonging to the gastropods.

Gastly, gast'li, *a.* Same as *Ghastly*.

Gastralgia, Gastralgy, gas-tral'ji-a, gas-tral'ji, *n.* [Gr. *gastēr*, *gastros*, the belly, and *algos*, pain.] Pain in the stomach or belly.

Gastric, gas'trik, *a.* [From Gr. *gastēr*, *gastros*, the belly or stomach.] Of or pertaining to the belly or stomach.—*Gastric juice*, a fluid secreted in the mucous membrane of the stomach, and the principal agent in digestion.—*Gastric fever*, a popular name for *typhoid* or *enteric fever*, from the manner in which it affects the intestines.—**Gastritis**, gas-trī'tis, *n.* Chronic inflammation of the stomach.—**Gastrocele**, gas'trō-sēl, *n.* [Gr. *kēlē*, a tumour.] *Pathol.* a hernia of the stomach.—**Gastrocnemius**, gas-trō-knē'mi-us, *n.* [Gr. *gastēr*, belly, and *knēmē*, lower half of the leg.] Muscle forming the chief part of the calf of the leg.—**Gastro-enteric**, gas'trō-en-ter"ik, *a.* [Gr. *entera*, intestines.] Pertaining to the stomach and intestines.—**Gastro-enteritis**, en-te-rī'tis, *n.* Inflammation of the stomach and intestines.—**Gastrolith**, gas'trō-lith, *n.* [Gr. *lithos*, stone.] A calculus or stony concretion in the stomach.—**Gastronomy**, gas-tron'o-mi, *n.* [Gr. *nomos*, a law.] The art or science of good living; the pleasures of the table; epicurism.—**Gastronomic, Gastronomical**, gas-tro-nom'ik, gas-tro-nom'i-kal, *a.* Pertaining to gastronomy.—**Gastronome, Gastronomer, Gastronomist**, gas'tro-nōm, gas-tron'o-mėr, gas-tron'o-mist, *n.* One versed in gastronomy; a judge of the art of cookery; a gourmet; an epicure.—**Gastrophrenic**, gas'-tro-fren'ik, *a.* [Gr. *phrēn*, diaphragm.] Pertaining to the stomach and diaphragm.—**Gastroscopy**, gas-tros'ko-pi, *n.* [Gr. *skopeō*, to view.] *Med.* an examination of the abdomen in order to detect disease.—**Gastrotomy**, gas-trot'o-mi, *n.* [Gr. *tomē*, a cutting.] *Surg.* the operation of cutting into the abdomen.—**Gastrovascular**, *a.* Belonging to digestion and circulation (the *gastrovascular* body-cavity of certain animals).

Gastrula, gas'trụ-la, *n.* [A dim. of *gaster*, Gr. *gastēr*, belly.] A germ or embryonic form developed by invagination from a morula or blastula, and having the character of a double-walled sac with an orifice leading into it.—**Gastrulation**, *n.* The process by which a gastrula is produced.

Gat, gat, old pret. of *get*.

Gate, gāt, *n.* [A.Sax. *geat*, a gate or door; Icel. *gat*, D. *gat*, a hole; from same root as *get*.] A large door such as gives entrance into a castle, a temple, palace, or other large edifice; the entrance leading into such an edifice; a frame of timber or metal which opens or closes a passage into an inclosure of some kind; the frame which shuts or stops a passage for water, as at the entrance to a dock.—**Gated**, gā'ted, *a.* Having gates.—**Gate-house**, *n.* A house at a gate, as a porter's lodge at the entrance to the grounds of a mansion.—**Gate-leg**, *a.* A style of table with folding leaves and movable legs.—**Gateman**, *n.* The person who has charge of a gate.—**Gate receipts**, *n.* Total amount of money paid for admissions at a sporting event.—**Gateway**, gāt'wā, *n.* An opening which is or may be closed with a gate.

Gather, gaᴛʜ'ėr, *v.t.* [A.Sax. *gaderian*, *gadrian*, from *gador*, *geador*, together, seen also in *together*; comp. D. *gadern*, to gather, *te gader*, L.G. *to gader*, together.] To bring together; to collect into one place or one aggregate; to assemble; to congregate; to pick; to pluck; to accumulate; to amass; to draw together; to bring together in folds or plaits, as a garment; hence, to plait; to pucker; to acquire or gain, with or without effort (to *gather* strength); to deduce by inference; to conclude.—*To gather one's self together*, to collect all one's powers for a strong effort.—*To be gathered to one's fathers*, to be interred along with one's ancestors, or simply to die.—*v.i.* To collect; to become assembled; to congregate; to take origin and grow; to come to a head (as a boil).—*n.* A plait or fold in cloth held in position by a thread drawn through it; a pucker.—**Gatherer**, gaᴛʜ'ėr-ėr, *n.* One who or that which gathers.—**Gathering**, gaᴛʜ'ėr-ing, *n.* The act of collecting or assembling; that which is gathered; a crowd; an assembly; a collection of pus; an abscess.

Gatling-gun, gat'ling-gun, *n.* A form of the mitrailleuse or repeating machine-gun, so named from the inventor.

Gaucherie, gōsh-rē, *n.* [Fr., from *gauche*, left-handed, awkward.] An awkward action; awkwardness.

Gaucho, gou'chō, *n.* A cowboy of the South American pampas, of mixed Spanish and Indian blood.

Gaud, Gawd, gąd, *n.* [L. *gaudium*, joy, gladness; in later times something showy; akin *joy*, *jewel*.] Something worn for adorning the person; a piece of showy finery (*Shak.*).—**Gaudery**,† gą'dėr-i, *n.* Finery; fine things.—**Gaudily**, gą'di-li, *adv.* In a gaudy manner.—**Gaudiness**, gą'di-nes, *n.* The quality or condition of being gaudy.—**Gaudy**, gą'di, *a.* Gay beyond the simplicity of nature or good taste; showy; tastelessly or glaringly adorned.

Gaudeamus, gą-dē-ā'mus, *n.* [L., let us rejoice.] A rejoicing; a festival. (*Scottish.*)

Gauge, Gage, gāj, *v.t.*—*gauged*, *gaged*, *gauging*, *gaging*. [O.Fr. *gauger*, perhaps of the same origin with *gallon*, and signifying to find the number of measures in a vessel.] To measure or to ascertain the contents or capacity of; to measure in respect to capability, power, character, &c.; to appraise; to estimate.—*n.* A standard of measure; an instrument to determine dimensions or capacity; a measure; means of estimating; the distance between the lines of rails of a railway, the standard distance being 4 feet 8½ inches; this is called *standard gauge*; *broad* or *wide gauge* and *narrow gauge* are respectively larger and smaller; *joinery*, a simple instrument made to strike a line parallel to the straight side of a board, &c.—**Gaugeable**, gāj'a-bl, *a.* Capable of being gauged or measured.—**Gauger**, gāj'ėr, *n.* One who gauges; an officer whose business is to ascertain the contents of casks.

Gaul, gąl, *n.* [L. *Gallus*, a Gaul, an inhabitant of *Gallia*, the country now called France.] An inhabitant of Gaul.—**Gaulish**, gą'lish, *a.* Pertaining to Gaul.

Gaultheria, gal-thē'ri-a, *n.* [After M. Gaulthier, Canadian botanist.] A shrub of a large genus of plants of the heath family that includes the American wintergreen.—*Gaultheria oil*, oil of wintergreen.

Gaunt, gant, *a.* [Comp. N. *gand*, a slender stick, a thin man.] Attenuated, as with fasting or suffering; lean; meager; haggard; slender; forbidding; desolate, as of an abandoned and dilapidated building.—**Gauntly**, gant'li, *adv.* Leanly; meagerly.—**Gauntness**, *n.*

Gauntlet, gant'let, *n.* [Fr. *gantelet*, dim. from *gant*, a glove, from the Teut.; D. *want*, Dan. *vante*, Icel. *vöttr* (for *vantr*), a glove.] A large iron glove with fingers covered with small plates, formerly worn as armour; a long glove for a lady, which envelops the hand and wrist. The gauntlet used to be thrown down in token of challenge; hence, *to throw down the gauntlet*, to challenge; *to take up the gauntlet*, to accept the challenge. — **Gauntleted**, gant'let-ed, *a.* Wearing a gauntlet.

Gaur, Gour, gour, *n.* [Indian name; Skr. *go*, a cow.] One of the largest of the ox tribe, inhabiting the mountain jungles of India.

Gauss, gows, *n.* [After the mathematician *Gauss*.] The unit of intensity of magnetic field, equal to the intensity produced by unit magnetic pole at a distance of one centimetre.

Gauze, gaz, *n.* [Fr. *gaze*, Sp. *gasa*, from the town *Gaza*, whence it was first brought.] A very thin, slight, transparent stuff, of silk, linen, or cotton; any slight open material resembling this (wire *gauze*).—**Gauzy**, ga'zi, *a.* Like gauze; thin as gauze.

Gave, gāv, pret. of *give*.

Gavelkind, gā'vel-kind, *n.* [A.Sax. *gafol*, payment, *cynd*, kind, offspring.] An old land-tenure in England, still prevailing in Kent, by which land descends to all the sons in equal shares.

Gavial, gā'vi-al, *n.* [Indian name.] A crocodile found in India, with an extremely lengthened muzzle.

Gavotte, ga-vot', *n.* [Fr., from *Gavot*, a native of the Pays de *Gap* in the Hautes Alpes, where the dance originated.] A sort of French dance; the music to which the dance was performed, or a similar instrumental movement.

Gawk, gak, *n.* [A.Sax. *gedc*, Icel. *gaukr*, Sc. *gowk*, cuckoo, simpleton.] A simpleton; a booby.—**Gawky**, ga'ki, *a.* Awkward; clumsy; clownish.—*n.* A stupid awkward fellow; a clown.

Gay, gā, *a.* [Fr. *gai*, of Teutonic origin; comp. O.H.G. *gâhi*, swift, excellent, G. *gähe*, *jähe*, quick. *Jay*, the bird, is akin.] Excited with merriment or delight; merry; sportive; frolicsome; fine; showy (a *gay* dress); given to pleasure, often to vicious pleasure; dissipated.—**Gaiety**, gā'e-ti, *n.* The state of being gay; merriment; mirth; show.—**Gaily, Gayly**, gā'li, *adv.* In a gay manner.—**Gayness**, gā'nes, *n.* The state or quality of being gay.—**Gaysome**, gā'sum, *a.* Full of gaiety.

Gayal, Gyal, gī'al, *n.* [Indian name.] A species of ox found wild in Burmah and Assam, and also domesticated.

Gaze, gāz, *v.i.*—*gazed, gazing*. [Sw. *gasa*, to gaze; allied to E. *agast*, Goth. *usgaisjan*, to terrify.] To fix the eyes and look steadily and earnestly; to look with eagerness or curiosity.—*v.t.* To view with fixed attention (*Mil.*).—*n.* A fixed look; a look of eagerness, wonder, or admiration.—*At gaze*, standing gazing; gaping in wonder. — **Gazer**, gā'zėr, *n.* One who gazes.—**Gazing-stock**, gā'zing-stok, *n.* A person gazed at; an object of curiosity or contempt.

Gazelle, ga-zel', *n.* [Fr. *gazelle*, from Sp. *gazela*, from Ar. *ghazal*.] An antelope of North Africa, Syria, Arabia, and Persia, about the size of a roebuck, of a graceful form, and with long slender limbs.

Gazette, ga-zet', *n.* [It. *gazzetta*, a gazette, from *gazzetta*, a small Venetian coin (from L. or rather Per. *gaza*, treasure), the price of the newspaper; or the name may have been equivalent to 'The Chatterer,' *gazzetta* being a dim. of *gazza*, a magpie.] A newspaper; especially an official or government newspaper containing public announcements, such as appointments to civil or military posts, the names of persons who have been declared bankrupt, &c.; hence, *to appear in the gazette* often means to be publicly announced there as a bankrupt.—*v.t.*—*gazetted, gazetting*. To insert or publish in a gazette; hence, *to be gazetted*, to have one's name announced in the gazette as appointed to some post or promoted to some rank.—**Gazetteer**, gaz-et-tēr', *n.* A manager of a gazette; more commonly a book containing geographical and topographical information alphabetically arranged; a geographical dictionary.

Gazogene. Under GAS.

Gean, gēn, *n.* [Fr. *guigne*, O.Fr. *guisne*, a word of Teutonic origin.] A kind of wild cherry-tree common in England and Scotland, with fruit of an excellent flavour.

Gear, gēr, *n.* A.Sax. *gearwe*, habiliments, equipments, from *gearu*, *gearo*, prepared, ready, whence also *yare*, ready; akin *garb*, dress.] Whatever is prepared for use or wear; hence, dress; ornaments; the harness or furniture of domestic animals; *naut.* the ropes, blocks, &c., belonging to any particular sail or spar; *mach.* the appliances or furnishings connected with the acting portions of any piece of mechanism. —*To throw machinery into* or *out of gear*, to connect or disconnect wheelwork or couplings.—*v.t.* To put gear on; to harness.—**Gearing**, gē'ring, *n.* Harness; the parts by which motion is communicated from one portion of a machine to another; a train of connected toothed wheels.—**Gearshift**, gēr'shift, *n.* A device by which transmission gears, as in an automobile, are engaged and disengaged.

Geck, gek, *n.* [Comp. D. *gek*, G. *geck*, a silly person; also E. *gawk*, a simpleton.] A dupe; a gull. (*Shak.*)

Gecko, Gekko, gek'o, *n.* A name of various nocturnal lizards of the warm parts of both hemispheres.

Geese, gēs, *n.* pl. of *goose*.

Gehenna, gē-hen'na, *n.* [L. *gehenna*, Gr. *geenna*, from the Heb. *ge-hinom*, the valley of Hinom at Jerusalem, where children were 'passed through the fire' to Moloch.] A term used in the New Testament as typical of the place of future punishment and translated hell, hell-fire.

Geisha, gā'i-shä, *n.* One of the Japanese dancing and singing girls who perform at private parties and elsewhere.

Geitonogamy, git'ōn-og"a-mē, *n.* [Gr. *geitōn*, a neighbour, *gamos*, marriage.] Cross-pollination between flowers on the same plant.

Gelatine, Gelatin, jel'a-tin, *n.* [Fr. *gélatine*, It. and Sp. *gelatina*, from L. *gelo*, to congeal. GELID.] A substance obtained from various animal tissues, and employed in the arts and as human food, being known in its coarser forms as *glue*, *size*, and *isinglass*, according to the sources whence it is obtained and the care exercised in its preparation.—**Gelatination**, je-lat'i-nā"shon, *n.* The act or process of converting into gelatine. — **Gelatinize**, je-lat'i-nīz, *v.t.* and *i.* To convert or be converted into gelatine. Also **Gelatinate**, je-lat'i-nāt.—**Gelatinous**, je-lat'i-nus, *a.* Of or pertaining to, or consisting of gelatine; resembling jelly; viscous.—**Gelose**, jē'lōs, *n.* Same as *Agar-agar*.

Geld, geld, *v.t.* [From Icel. *gelda*, Dan. *gilde*, G. *gelten*, to geld.] To castrate; to emasculate; to deprive of anything essential (*Shak.*).—**Gelder**, gel'dėr, *n.* One who castrates.—**Gelding**, gel'ding, *n.* A castrated animal; especially a castrated horse.

Gelder-rose, Guelder-rose, gel'dėr, *n.* [Brought from *Guelder*land in Holland.] A shrub of the woodbine family with handsome flowers.

Gelid, jel'id, *a.* [L. *gelidus*, from *gelo*, to freeze, seen also in *gelatine*, *congeal*, *jelly*, the root being that of *cool*.] Cold; very cold; icy or frosty.—**Gelidity**, je-lid'i-ti, *n.* The state of being gelid; extreme cold.—**Gelidly**, jel'id-li, *adv.* In a gelid manner.—**Gelidness**, jel'id nes, *n.*

Gelignite, jē-lig'nīt, *n.* A nitro-glycerine explosive.

Gelsemium, jel-sē'mi-um, *n.* [It. *gelsomino*, jasmine.] A twining shrub, the yellow jasmine of the United States; a dangerous drug derived from this plant, used in various diseases.

Gem, jem, *n.* [L. *gemma*, a bud, a precious stone.] A precious stone of any kind, as the ruby, topaz, emerald, &c., especially when cut or polished; a jewel; anything resembling a gem, or remarkable for beauty, rarity, or costliness.—*v.t.*—*gemmed, gemming*. To adorn with gems or what resembles gems; to bespangle.—**Gemmeous**, jem'ē-us, *a.* [L. *gemmeus*.] Pertaining to, of the nature of, or resembling gems.—**Gemminess**, jem'i-nes, *n.* The state of being gemmy.—**Gemmy**, jem'i, *a.* Glittering with gems; adorned with gems.

Gemara, gem-a'ra, *n.* [Aramaic, completion.] A part of the Talmud, a commentary on the Mishna.

Geminate,† jem'i-nāt, *v.t.* [L. *gemino*, *geminatum*, to double, from *geminus*, twin.] To double.—*a.* *Bot.* twin; combined in pairs; binate.—**Gemination**, jem-i-nā'shon, *n.* A doubling; duplication; repetition.—**Gemini**, jem'i-nī, *n.pl.* [L., twin brothers, Castor and Pollux.] *Astron.* the third sign of the zodiac, so named from its two brightest stars, Castor and Pollux.

Gemma, jem'a, *n.*pl. **Gemmæ**, jem'ē. [L., a bud. GEM.] *Bot.* a leaf-bud as distinguished from a flower-bud.—**Gemmaceous**, jem-ā'shus, *a.* Pertaining to leaf-buds.—**Gemmate**, jem'āt, *a.* [L. *gemmatus*.] *Bot.* having buds; reproducing by buds.—**Gemmation**, jem-ā'shon, *n.* L. *gemmatio*.] *Zool.* the process of reproduction by buds; the formation of a new individual by budding; *bot.* the act of budding; vernation.—**Gemmiferous**, jem-if'ėr-us, *a.* Producing buds; multiplying by buds.—**Gemmiparity**, jem-i-par'i-ti, *n.* The condition of being gemmiparous.—**Gemmiparous**, jem-ip'a-rus, *a.* [L. *pario*, to produce.] Producing buds; *zool.* reproducing by buds.—**Gemmule**, jem'ūl, *n.* [L. *gemmula*.] *Bot.* the growing point of the embryo in plants; one of the buds of mosses; a reproductive spore of algæ; *zool.* the ciliated embryo or reproductive body of some of the lowest animals.

Gemsbok, gemz'bok, *n.* [D. *gemsbok*, G. *gemsbock*, the male chamois, from *gemse*, chamois, and *bock*, buck.] A fine large antelope inhabiting South Africa.

Genappe, je-nap', *n.* [From *Genappe*, in Belgium.] A worsted yarn well adapted for braids, fringes, &c.

Gendarme, zhäṅ'därm, *n.* [Fr., from the pl. *gens d'armes*, men-at-arms.] A private in the armed police of France.—**Gendarmerie**, zhäṅ-därm-rē, *n.* [Fr. *gendarmerie*.] The body of gendarmes.

Gender, jen'dėr, *n.* [Fr. *genre*, from L. *genus*, *generis*, kind or sort, gender; with *d* inserted as in tender, adj. GENUS.] Kind or sort‡; a sex, male or female; *gram.* one of those classes or categories into which words are divided according to the sex, natural or metaphorical, of the beings or things they denote; a grammatical category in which words of similar termination are classed together; such a distinction in words. [In English grammar words expressing males are all said to be of the *masculine gender*; those expressing females, of the *feminine gender*; and words expressing things having no sex are of the *neuter gender*; but in other languages gender has a different basis, thus in French it has comparatively little to do with sex, all nouns being either masculine or feminine.]—*v.t.*† To beget; to engender.—*v.i.* To copulate; to breed (O.T.).

Genealogy, jē-nē-al′o-ji or jen-ē-al′o-ji, *n.* [L. and Gr. *genealogia*—Gr. *genea*, family (root *gen*, to beget), and *logos*, discourse. GENUS.] An account or synopsis tracing the descent of a person or family from an ancestor; an enumeration or table of ancestors and their children in the order of succession; pedigree; lineage; the study of pedigrees or family history.—**Genealogical**, jē′nē-a-loj″i-kal, *a.* Pertaining to genealogy; exhibiting or tracing genealogies.—*Genealogical tree*, the genealogy or lineage of a family drawn out under the form of a tree.—**Genealogically**, jē′nē-a-loj″i-kal-li, *adv.* In a genealogical manner.—**Genealogist**, jē-nē-al′o-jist, *n.* One who traces descents of persons or families.—**Genealogize**, jē-nē-al′o-jīz, *v.i.*—*genealogized, genealogizing.* To investigate or study genealogy.

Genera, jen′ėr-a, *n.* pl. of GENUS.

General, jen′ėr-al, *a.* [Fr. *général*, from L. *generalis*, belonging to a genus, generic, general, from *genus, generis*, a kind. GENUS.] Relating to a whole genus, kind, class, or order; relating to, affecting, or comprehending the whole community; public; common to many or the greatest number; extensive, though not universal; common; usual; ordinary (a *general* opinion); not restrained or limited to a particular import; not specific (a *general* term); not directed to a single object; taken as a whole; regarded in the gross. ∴This word affixed to another word is common in names expressive of rank or office, as *adjutant-general, attorney-general, &c.*—*General Assembly*, under ASSEMBLY.—*General delivery*, delivery of mail to those who call for it at the post office; the department in charge of such mail.—*General store*, a store with a mixed stock.—*General strike*, a strike by all the workmen in a region or by all the workmen in an industry.—*n.* The whole community‡; a general or comprehensive notion; a military officer of the highest rank; the commander of an army or of a division or brigade; the chief of an order of monks.—*In general*, in the main; for the most part; not always or universally; also in the aggregate, or as a whole.—**Generalissimo**, jen′ėr-a-lis″i-mō, *n.* [It.] The chief commander of an army or military force which consists of two or more grand divisions under separate commanders.—**Generality**, jen-ėr-al′i-ti, *n.* The state of being general; the quality of including species or particulars; a statement which is general or not specific, or which lacks application to any one case.—*The generality*, the main body; the bulk; the greatest part.—**Generalizable**, jen′ėr-al-ī″za-bl, *a.* Capable of being generalized.—**Generalization**, jen′ėr-al-i-zā″shon, *n.* The act or process of generalizing; a general inference.—**Generalize**, jen′ėr-al-īz, *v.t.*—*generalized; generalizing.* To reduce or bring under a general law, rule, or statement; to bring into relation with a wider circle of facts; to deduce from the consideration of many particulars.—*v.i.* To form objects into classes; to bring or classify particulars under general heads or rules.—**Generally**, jen′ėr-al-li, *adv.* In general; commonly; ordinarily; extensively, though not universally; most frequently, but not without exceptions; without detail; leaving particular facts out of account; in the whole taken together.—**Generalness**, jen′ėr-al-nes, *n.* The state of being general; frequency; commonness. **Generalship**, jen′ėr-al-ship, *n.* The office of a general; the discharge of the functions of a general; military skill exhibited in the judicious handling of troops; management or judicious tactics generally.

Generate, jen′ėr-āt, *v.t.*—*generated, generating.* [L. *genero, generatum*, to beget. GENUS.] To procreate (young); to produce; to cause to be; to bring into existence; to cause (heat, vibrations).—**Generability**, jen′ėr-a-bil″i-ti, *n.* Capability of being generated.—**Generable**, jen′ėr-a-bl, *a.* Capable of being generated.—**Generant**,† jen′ėr-ant, *n.* That which generates.—*a.* Generating; producing.—**Generation**, jen-ėr-ā′shon, *n.* The act of generating; production; formation; a single succession of the human race in natural descent, calculated at thirty years; the average period of time between one succession of children and the next following; people who are contemporary or living at the same time; a race; progeny; offspring.—*Equivocal* or *spontaneous generation*, in *biol.* the production of animals and plants without previously existing parents; abiogenesis.—*Alternate generation*, under ALTERNATE.—**Generative**, jen′ėr-ā-tiv, *a.* Having the power of generating; belonging to generation or the act of procreating.—**Generator**, jen′ėr-ā-tėr, *n.* One who or that which begets, causes, or produces; a vessel or chamber in which something is generated.

Generic, Generical, je-ner′ik, je-ner′i-kal, *a.* [Fr. *générique*, from L. *genus, generis*, kind. GENUS.] Pertaining to a genus; descriptive of, belonging to, or comprehending the genus, as distinct from the species or from another genus; referring to a large class.—**Generically**, je-ner′i-kal-li, *adv.* In a generic manner; with regard to genus.—**Genericalness**, je-ner′i-kal-nes, *n.*

Generous, jen′ėr-us, *a.* [L. *generosus*, of honourable birth, generous, from *genus, generis*, birth, extraction, family. GENUS.] Noble; honourable; magnanimous (of persons or things); liberal; bountiful; munificent; free in giving; strong; full of spirit (*generous* wine).—**Generously**, jen′ėr-us-li, *adv.* In a generous manner.—**Generosity**, jen-ėr-os′i-ti, *n.* [L. *generositas.*] The quality of being generous; nobleness of soul; liberality of sentiment; a disposition to give liberally.—**Generousness**, jen′ėr-us-nes, *n.* The quality of being generous; generosity.

Genesis, jen′e-sis, *n.* [Gr. *genesis*, from root *gen*, to beget. GENUS.] The act of producing or giving origin; a taking origin; generation; origination; the first book of the Old Testament, containing the history of the creation of the world and of the human race.—**Genesiology**, je-nē′si-ol″o-ji, *n.* [Gr. *genesis*, and *logos*, discourse.] The science or doctrines of generation.

Genet, jen′et, *n.* [Fr. *genette*, Sp. *ginete*, from the name of a Berber tribe who supplied the Moorish sultans of Grenada with cavalry.] A small-sized, well-proportioned Spanish horse: spelled also *Jennet.*

Genet, Genette, jen′et, je-net′, *n.* [Sp. *gineta*, from Ar. *jerneit.*] A carnivorous animal belonging to the civet family, a native of western Asia; the fur of the genet.

Genetic, Genetical, je-net′ik, je-net′i-kal, *a.* [From Gr. *genetēs*, a begetter, or *genesis*, generation.] Relating to generation; pertaining to the origin of a thing or its mode of production.—**Genetically**, je-net′i-kal-li, *adv.* In a genetic manner.

Geneva, je-nē′va, *n.* [From L. *juniperus*, juniper; *gin* is a contraction of this.] A spirit distilled from grain or malt, with the addition of juniper-berries; gin.

Genevan, je-nē′van, *a.* Pertaining to Geneva.—*n.* An inhabitant of Geneva; a Genevese; a Calvinist.—**Genevese**, jen-ē-vēz′, *n. sing.* and *pl.* A native or natives of Geneva.—*a.* Relating to Geneva.

Genial, jē′ni-al, *a.* [L. *genialis*, from *genius*, social disposition, genius, from root *gen.* GENUS.] Characterized by kindly warmth of disposition and manners such as promotes cheerfulness on the part of others; cordial; kindly; sympathetically cheerful; enlivening; warming; contributing to life and cheerfulness (the *genial* sun).—**Geniality, Genialness**, jē-ni-al′i-ti, jē′ni-al-nes, *n.* The state or quality of being genial; sympathetic cheerfulness or cordiality.—**Genially**, jē′ni-al-li, *adv.* In a genial manner.

Geniculated, Geniculate, je-nik′ū-lā-ted, je-nik′ū-lāt, *a.* [L. *geniculatus*, from *geniculum*, a knot or joint, from *genu*, the knee.] *Bot.* knee-jointed; having knots like knees.—**Geniculate**, je-nik′ū-lāt, *v.t.* To form joints or knots.—**Geniculation**, je-nik′ū-lā-shon, *n.* Knottiness; a knot or joint like a knee.

Genie, jē′nē, *n.* pl. **Genii**, je′nē-ī. [A form due to the influence of the word *genius.*] Same as *Jinnee.*

Genipap, jen′i-pap, *n.* [From *genipapo*, the name in Guiana.] The fruit of a South American and West Indian tree of the Madder family, about the size of an orange.

Genital, jen′i-tal, *a.* [L. *genitalis*, from *gigno, genitum*, to beget. GENUS.] Pertaining to generation or the act of begetting.—**Genitals**, jen′i-talz, *n. pl.* The parts of generation; the privates; the sexual organs.

Genitive, jen′i-tiv, *a.* [L. *genitivus*, relating to birth or origin, from *gigno, genitum*, to beget.] *Gram.* a term applied to a case in the declension of nouns, adjectives, pronouns, &c., in English called the possessive case.—*n. Gram.* the genitive case.—**Genitival**, jen′i-tī-val, *a.* Relating to the genitive.

Genius, jē′ni-us, *n.* [L., a genius or tutelary spirit, social disposition, wit or genius, from the root *gen*, to beget. GENUS.] A tutelary deity; an imaginary being ruling or protecting men, places, or things; a good or evil spirit supposed to be attached to a person and to influence his actions.—*His evil genius*, bad adviser, false friend; that disposition or bent of mind which is peculiar to every man, and which qualifies him for a particular employment; intellectual endowment of the highest kind, particularly the power of invention or of producing original combinations; a man thus intellectually endowed; peculiar character or constitution; pervading spirit or influence from associations or otherwise (the special *genius* of a language). [Plural *Genii* meaning spirits, *Geniuses* meaning men.] ∴ *Genius* implies the possession of high and peculiar natural gifts which enable their possessor to reach his ends by a sort of intuitive power. *Talent* is of a lower order, being less original and inventive.

Genoese, jen′o-ēz, *a.* Relating to Genoa.—*n.* An inhabitant or the people of Genoa in Italy.

Genre, zhähr, *n.* [Fr., from L. *genus, generis*, kind.] *Painting*, a term applied to paintings which depict scenes of ordinary life, as domestic, rural, or village scenes.

Gent, jent. A vulgar abbreviation for *Gentleman.*

Gent,† *a.* [L. *genitus.*] Well-born. 'Ladie gent' (*Spenser*).

Genteel, jen-tēl′, *a.* [Fr. *gentil*, from L. *gentilis*, belonging to the same family or nation, not foreign, latterly also gentile or pagan, from *gens, gentis*, race, stock, family. GENUS. *Gentle* and *gentile* are doublets of this.] Having the manners of well-bred people; well-bred; refined; free from anything low or vulgar; of a station above the common people; furnishing a competence (a *genteel* allowance).—**Genteelish**,† jen-tēl′ish, *a.* Somewhat genteel.—**Genteelly**, jen-tēl′li, *adv.* In a genteel manner.—**Genteelness**, jen-tēl′nes, *n.* The state or quality of being genteel.—**Gentility**, jen-til′i-ti, *n.* The state or character of being genteel; the manners or circumstances of genteel people.

Gentian, jen′shi-an, *n.* [L. *gentiana*—said to be named after *Gentius*, king of Illyria, who first experienced the virtue of gentian.] The name of certain bitter herbaceous plants with beautiful blue or yellow flowers, the roots of some species being highly valued as a tonic.

Gentile, jen′tīl, *n.* [L. *gentilis*, from *gens, gentis*, nation, race. GENTEEL.] *Scrip.* any one belonging to the non-Jewish nations; any person not a Jew or a Christian; a heathen; applied by Mormons to those outside their sect.—*a.* Belonging to the non-Jewish nations; *gram.* denoting one's race or country (a *gentile* noun).—**Gentilish**, jen′tīl-ish, *a.* Heathenish; pagan.—**Gentilism**, jen′tīl-ism, *n.* Heathenism; paganism.—**Gentilitious**,† jen-ti-lish′us, *a.* [L. *gentilitius.*] Peculiar to a people or nation; national; hereditary.

Gentility. Under GENTEEL.

Gentle, jen'tl, *a.* [Fr. *gentil.* GENTEEL.] Well-born; of a good family; soft and refined in manners; mild; meek; not rough, harsh, or severe; not wild, turbulent, or refractory; placid; bland; not rude or violent.—*n.* A person of good birth; a gentleman.—**Gentleness**, jen'tl-nes, *n.* The state or quality of being gentle.—**Gently**, jen'tli, *adv.* In a gentle manner; mildly; meekly; placidly.—**Gentlefolk**, jen'tl-fōk, *n.* Persons of good breeding and family: generally in plural, *gentlefolks.*—**Gentleman**, jen'tl-man, *n.* [*Gentle*, that is, wellborn, and *man*; Fr. *gentilhomme.* GENTEEL.] A man of good family or good social position; in a somewhat narrow and technical sense, any man above the rank of yeomen, including noblemen; in a more limited sense, a man who without a title bears a coat of arms; as commonly applied, any man whose education, occupation, or income raises him above menial service or an ordinary trade; a man of good breeding and politeness, as distinguished from the vulgar and clownish; a man of the highest honour, courtesy, and morality; often used almost as a polite equivalent for 'man': in the plural the appellation by which men are addressed in popular assemblies, whatever may be their condition or character.—**Gentlemanhood**, jen'tl-man-hŏd, *n.* The condition or attributes of a gentleman.—**Gentlemanism**, jen'tl-man-izm, *n.* The state of being a gentleman; the affectation of gentlemanliness.—**Gentlemanize**, jen'tl-man-īz, *v.t.* To bring or put into the condition of a gentleman.—**Gentlemanliness**, jen'tl-man-li-nes, *n.* The quality of being gentlemanly; gentlemanly behaviour.—**Gentlemanly, Gentlemanlike**, jen'tl-man-li, jen'tl-man-līk, *a.* Pertaining to or becoming a gentleman; like a gentleman.—**Gentleman-at-arms, Gentleman-pensioner**, *n.* One of forty gentlemen attached to the English court whose office it is to attend the sovereign to and from the chapel-royal, &c.—**Gentleman-in-waiting, Lady-in-waiting**, *n.* Persons of high social standing in personal attendance on the sovereign.—**Gentlewoman**, jen'tl-wụm-an, *n.* A woman of good family or of good breeding; a woman above the vulgar; a woman who waits about the person of one of high rank.

Gentry, jen'tri, *n.* [O.Fr. *genterise*, for *gentilise*, high birth, from *gentil*, L. *gentilis.* GENTEEL.] Rank or good birth (*Shak.*)‡; courtesy (*Shak.*)‡; *pl.* people of good position; wealthy or well-born people in general, of a rank below the nobility; also ironically applied to disreputable characters.

Genuflect, jen'ū-flekt, *v.i.* [L. *genu*, the knee, and *flecto*, to bend, as in *inflect, reflect*, &c.] To kneel, as in worship, to make a genuflection or genuflections.—**Genuflection, Genuflexion**, jen-ū-flek'shon, *n.* The act of bending the knee, particularly in worship.

Genuine, jen'ū-in, *a.* [L. *genuinus*, from root of *gigno*, to beget. GENUS.] Belonging to the original stock; hence, real; natural; true; pure; not spurious, false, or adulterated. ∴ Syn. under AUTHENTIC.—**Genuinely**, jen'ū-in-li, *adv.* In a genuine manner.—**Genuineness**, jen'ū-in-nes, *n.* The state of being genuine.

Genus, jē'nus, *n.* pl. **Genera** or **Genuses**, jen'ėr-a, jē'nus-ez. [L. *genus, generis*, a kind, class = Gr. *genos*, race, family; from root *gen*, Skr. *jan*, to beget, the same as in E. *kin, kind.* This root is seen in a great many words, as *gentle, genteel, general, genius, generous, genesis, genial, genital, genuine, indigenous, ingenious, progeny*, &c.] A kind, class, or sort; *logic*, a class of a greater extent than a species; a word which may be predicated of several things of different species; in *scientific classifications*, an assemblage of species possessing certain characters in common, by which they are distinguished from all others: subordinate to *order, tribe, family.*

Geocentric, Geocentrical, jē-ō-sen'trik, jē-ō-sen'tri-kal, *a.* [Gr. *gē*, earth, and *kentron*, centre.] *Astron.* having reference to the earth for its centre; seen from the earth: applied to the place of a planet as seen from the centre of the earth.—**Geocentrically**, jē-ō-sen'tri-kal-li, *adv.* In a geocentric manner.

Geocyclic, jē-ō-sīk'lik, *a.* [Gr. *gē*, the earth, and *kyklos*, a circle.] Of or pertaining to the revolutions of the earth; circling the earth periodically.

Geode, jē'ōd, *n.* [Gr. *geōdēs*, earthy, from *gē*, earth.] *Mineral*, a roundish hollow lump of agate or other mineral, having the cavity frequently lined with crystals.—**Geodiferous**, jē-ō-dif'ėr-us, *a.* Producing geodes.

Geodesy, Geodetics, jē-od'e-si, jē-ō-det'iks, *n.* [Gr. *geōdaisia*—*gē*, the earth, and *daiō*, to divide.] That branch of applied mathematics which determines the figures and areas of large portions of the earth's surface, the general figure of the earth, and the variations of the intensity of gravity in different regions.—**Geodesian**, jē-ō-dē'si-an, *n.* One versed in geodesy.—**Geodetic, Geodetical**, jē-ō-det'ik, jē-ō-det'i-kal, *a.* Pertaining to geodesy; obtained or determined by the operations of geodesy. Also **Geodesic, Geodesical**, jē-ō-des'ik, jē-ō-des'i-kal.—**Geodetically**, jē-ō-det'i-kal-li, *adv.* In a geodetical manner.

Geognosy, jē-og'no-si, *n.* [Gr. *gē*, the earth, and *gnōsis*, knowledge.] That part of natural science which treats of the structure of the earth—a term nearly equivalent to *geology*, but having less to do with scientific reasoning and theory.—**Geognost**,† jē'og-nost, *n.* One versed in geognosy.—**Geognostic**,† **Geognostical**,† jē-og-nos'tik, jē-og-nos'ti-kal, *a.* Pertaining to geognosy.

Geogony, jē-og'o-ni, *n.* [Gr. *gē*, the earth, and *gonē*, generation.] The doctrine of the origin or formation of the earth.—**Geogonic, Geogonical**, jē-ō-gon'ik, jē-ō-gon'i-kal, *a.* Pertaining to geogony.

Geography, jē-og'ra-fi, *n.* [Gr. *geōgraphia*—*gē*, the earth, and *graphē*, description.] The science or branch of knowledge which treats of the world and its inhabitants, describing more especially the external features of the world, and in its widest scope embracing *mathematical geography*, which deals with the figure and measurement of the earth, latitude and longitude, &c.; *physical geography*, which describes the earth's features and explains their relations to each other, treating also of climate, animals, and plants, and their distribution; the ocean and its phenomena, &c.; and *political geography*, which treats of the states and peoples of the earth and their political and social characteristics; a description of the earth or a certain portion of it; a book containing such a description.—**Geographer**, jē-og'ra-fėr, *n.* One who is versed in, or compiles a treatise on, geography.—**Geographic, Geographical**, jē-ō-graf'ik, jē-ō-graf'i-kal, *a.* Relating to geography; containing information regarding geography.—**Geographically**, jē-ō-graf'i-kal-li, *adv.* In a geographical manner.

Geology, jē-ol'o-ji, *n.* [Gr. *gē*, the earth, and *logos*, discourse.] The science which deals with the structure, especially the internal structure, of the crust of the globe, and of the substances which compose it; the science which treats of the minerals, rocks, earths, or other substances composing the globe, the relations which the several constituent masses bear to each other, their formation, structure, position, and history, together with the successive changes that have taken place in the organic and inorganic kingdoms of nature as illustrated by fossils or otherwise.—**Geologic, Geological**, jē-ō-loj'ik, jē-ō-loj'i-kal, *a.* Pertaining to geology.—**Geologically**, jē-ō-loj'i-kal-li, *adv.* In a geological manner.—**Geologist**, jē-ol'o-jist, *n.* One versed in geology. Also **Geologian**, jē-ō-lō'ji-an, *n.*—**Geologize**, jē-ol'ō-jīz, *v.i.* To study geology; to make geological investigations.

Geomancy, jē'ō-man-si, *n.* [Gr. *gē*, the earth, and *manteia*, divination.] A kind of divination by means of figures or lines formed by little dots or points, originally on the earth and afterwards on paper.—**Geomancer**, jē'ō-man-sėr, *n.* One versed in or who practises geomancy.—**Geomantic, Geomantical**, jē-ō-man'tik, jē-ō-man'ti-kal, *a.* Of or pertaining to geomancy.

Geometry, jē-om'e-tri, *n.* [Gr. *geōmetria*, *gē*, the earth, and *metron*, measure—the term being originally equivalent to land-measuring or surveying.] The science of magnitude; that science which treats of the properties of lines, angles, surfaces, and solids; that branch of mathematics which treats of the properties and relations of magnitudes.—**Geometral**,† jē-om'et-ral, *a.* [Fr. *géometral.*] Pertaining to geometry.—**Geometric, Geometrical**, jē-ō-met'rik, jē-ō-met'ri-kal, *a.* [Gr. *geōmetrikos.*] Pertaining to geometry; according to the rules or principles of geometry; done or determined by geometry.—*Geometrical elevation*, a design for the front or side of a building drawn according to the rules of geometry, as opposed to *perspective* or *natural elevation.*—*Geometrical progression*, progression in which the terms increase or decrease by a common ratio, as 2, 4, 8, 16, &c.—*Geometrical proportion*, proportion involving equal ratios in the two parts—1 : 3 :: 4 : 12.—**Geometrically**, jē-ō-met'ri-kal-li, *adv.* In a geometrical manner.—**Geometrician, Geometer**, jē-om'e-trish-an, jē-om'e-tėr, *n.* One skilled in geometry.

Geonomy, jē-on'o-mi, *n.* [Gr. *gē*, the earth, and *nomos*, law.] The science of the physical laws relating to the earth, including geology and physical geography.

Geophagism, jē-of'a-jizm, *n.* [Gr. *gē*, the earth, and *phagō*, to eat.] The act or practice of eating earth, as clay, chalk, &c.—**Geophagist**, jē-of'a-jist, *n.* One who eats earth.

Geoponic, Geoponical jē-ō-pon'ik, jē-ō-pon'i-kal, *a.* [Gr. *gē*, the earth, and *ponos*, labour.] Pertaining to tillage or agriculture.—**Geoponics**, jē-ō-pon'iks, *n.* The art or science of cultivation.

Georama, jē-ō-rä'ma, *n.* [Gr. *gē*, the earth, and *horama*, view.] A large hollow spherical globe or chamber having the geography of the earth's surface depicted on its interior.

George, jorj, *n.* [This proper name is from Gr. *geōrgos*, a husbandman—*gē*, the earth, and *ergon*, labour.] A figure of St. George on horseback encountering the dragon, worn pendent from the collar by knights of the Garter.—*St. George*, the patron saint of England, supposed to be martyred in A.D. 303 under Diocletian.—*St. George's Cross*, the English flag, a red cross on a white ground, opposed to the St. Andrew's Cross of Scotland, a silver saltire on a blue ground.—**Georgian**, jor'ji-an, *a.* Belonging or relating to the reigns of the four *Georges*, kings of Great Britain; a native of Georgia in the United States, or of Georgia in the Caucasus.—**Georgia bark**, *n.* The bark of a small tree of the southern United States belonging to the cinchona family and used in fevers.—**Georgic**, jor'jik, *n.* [Gr. *geōrgikos*, rustic.] A rural poem; a poetical composition on the subject of husbandry.—**Georgics**, *n.* Poem in four books by Virgil.—**Georgium Sidus**, jor'ji-um sī'dus, *n.* [That is 'Georgian star.'] The name given to the planet Uranus by its discoverer Sir William Herschel in honour of George III.

Geoselenic, jē'ō-sē-len''ik, *a.* [Gr. *gē*, the earth, and *selēnē*, the moon.] Relating to the earth and the moon; relating to the joint action or mutual relations of the earth and moon.

Geothermic, jē-ō-thėr'mik, *a.* [Gr. *gē*, the earth, and *thermos*, heat.] Of or pertaining to the internal heat of the earth.—**Geothermometer**, jē'ō-thėr-mom''e-tėr, *n.* An instrument for measuring the heat in mines, artesian wells, &c.

Geotropism, jē-ot'ro-pizm, *n.* [Gr. *gē*, the earth, and *tropos*, a turning.] Disposition or tendency to turn or incline towards the earth, the characteristic exhibited in a young plant when deprived of light.—**Geotropic**, jē-ō-trop′ik, *a.* Pertaining to or exhibiting geotropism.

Gerah, gē′ra, *n.* [Heb.] The smallest piece of money among the ancient Jews, equal to about three halfpennies.

Geranium, je-rā′ni-um, *n.* [L. *geranium*, Gr. *geranion*, from *geranos*, a crane—on account of the long projecting spike of the seed-capsule.] The crane's-bill genus, a genus of herbaceous plants (rarely undershrubs), natives of the temperate regions of the world, having flowers which are usually blue or red, and often handsome; the geraniums of gardens belong, however, to a different genus (pelargonium).

Gerbil, jėr′bil, *n.* [Fr. *gerbille*, from *gerbo*, the Arabic name.] A small burrowing rodent found in the sandy parts of Africa and Asia, one species, inhabiting Egypt, being about the size of a mouse.

Gerfalcon, jėr′fa-kn, *n.* The gyrfalcon.

Germ, jėrm, *n.* [Fr. *germe*, L. *germen*, an offshoot, a sprout.] *Physiol.* the earliest form under which any organism appears; the rudimentary or embryonic form of an organism; hence, that from which anything springs; origin; first principle.—**Germ-cell**, *n.* *Animal physiol.* the cell which results from the union of the spermatozoon with the germinal vesicle or its nucleus.—**Germinal**, jėr′mi-nal, *a.* Pertaining to a germ or seed-bud.—*Germinal vesicle, animal physiol.* a cell which floats in the yoke of an egg; *bot.* a cell contained in the embryo sac, from which the embryo is developed.—**Germinant**, jėr′mi-nant, *a.* [L. *germinans, germinantis.*] Sprouting; beginning to grow; growing; gradually developing.—**Germinate**, jėr′mi-nāt, *v.i.*—*germinated, germinating.* [L. *germino, germinatum*, to bud, from *germen.*] To sprout; to bud; to shoot; to begin to vegetate, as a plant or its seed.—*v.t.*† To cause to sprout or bud.—**Germination**, jėr-mi-nā′shon, *n.* The act of germinating; the first act of growth by an embryo plant.—**Germinative**, jėr′mi-nā-tiv, *a.* Of or pertaining to germination.—**Germ-theory**, *n.* The theory that living matter cannot be produced by evolution or development from not-living matter, but is produced from germs or seeds; also the theory that zymotic diseases are caused by the presence in the atmosphere of infinite multitudes of germs of cryptogamic plants ready to become developed and multiply under favourable conditions.

German, jėr′man, *a.* [L. *germanus*, a brother, for *germinanus*, from *germen*, an offshoot. GERM.] Sprung from the same father and mother or from members of the same family; germane†.—**Germane**, jėr′-mān, *a.* Closely akin; nearly related; allied; relevant; pertinent.

German, jėr′man, *n.* [L. *Germanus*, German, *Germani*, the Germans, not a native German appellation, but probably borrowed by the Romans from the Celts; of doubtful origin.] A native or inhabitant of Germany; the language of the higher and more southern districts of Germany, and the literary language of all Germany, called by the people themselves *Deutsch* (=*Dutch*), and also known as *High German*, to distinguish it from the *Low German*, or vernacular of the lowland or northern parts of Germany. See also DUTCH.—*a.* Belonging to Germany.—**Germanic**, jėr-man′ik, *a.* Pertaining to Germany; a name of certain languages otherwise called *Teutonic*.—**Germanism**, jėr′man-izm, *n.* An idiom or phrase of the German language.—**Germanium**, jėr-ma′ni-um, *n.* [*Germania*, Germany.] A metallic element discovered in 1885, of a greyish-white colour and fine lustre.—**German-millet**, *n.* A species of grass, producing a nutritious grain.—**German-paste**, *n.* A kind of paste used for feeding singing-birds.—**German-silver**, *n.* A white alloy of nickel, formed by fusing together 100 parts of copper, 60 of zinc, and 40 of nickel.—**German-tinder**, *n.* Amadou.

Germander, jėr-man′dėr, *n.* [Fr. *germandrée*, corrupted from L. *chamædrys*, Gr. *chamaidrys*, germander—*chamai*, on the ground, and *drys*, an oak.] The common name of certain labiate plants, a few species of which are common in Britain.—*Germander speedwell.* SPEEDWELL.

Germicide, jėr′mi-sīd, *n.* [E. *germ*, L. *cædo*, I kill.] A substance that destroys germs, especially disease germs.

Germinal disc, jėr′min-al disk, *n.* In large eggs full of nutritive matter (e.g. those of birds), the part which develops into the body of the embryo.—**Germinal variation**. Variation of germ-cells, female (ova) and male (sperms).

Germ-plasm, jėrm′plasm, *n.* [From *germ* and Gr. *plasma*, anything formed.] A hypothetical constituent of the nucleus in a sex-cell, by which hereditary characters are supposed to be transmitted.

Gerontocracy, jer-on-tok′ra-si, *n.* [Gr. *gerōn, gerontos*, an old man, and *kratos*, power.] Government by old men.

Geropigia, Jerupigia, jer-o-pij′i-a, *n.* [Sp. *geropigia, jeropigia.*] A mixture of grape-juice, brandy, colouring matter, &c., used to sophisticate port wine.

Gerrymander, ger′i-man″dėr, *v.t.* [From *Gerry*, governor of Massachusetts.] To divide a state into election districts in an unfair way.

Gerund, jer′und, *n.* [L. *gerundium*, from *gero*, to carry on or perform, the gerund expressing the doing or the necessity of doing something.] A part of the Latin verb, or a kind of verbal noun, used to express the meaning of the present infinitive active; a term adopted into other languages to indicate various forms or modifications of the verb, in English being applied to verbal nouns such as 'teaching' in expressions like 'fit for teaching boys'.—**Gerundial**, je-run′di-al, *a.* Pertaining to or resembling a gerund.—**Gerundive**, je-run′div, *n.* A name given originally by Latin grammarians to the future participle passive, a form similar to the gerund; sometimes used in regard to other languages.—**Gerundively**, je-run′div-li, *adv.* In the manner of a gerund or gerundive.

Gestation, jes-tā′shon, *n.* [L. *gestatio*, from *gesto, gestatum*, freq. from *gero, gestum*, to carry, seen also in *gesture, gesticulate, congest, digest, suggestion*, &c.] The act of carrying young in the womb from conception to delivery; pregnancy.—**Gestatory**, jes′ta-to-ri, *a.* Pertaining to gestation or pregnancy.—**Gestic**,† jes′tik, *a.* [From old *gest*, a deed or exploit; L. *gestum*, from *gero.*] Pertaining to deeds or exploits. (*Goldsmith.*)

Gesticulate, jes-tik′ū-lāt, *v.i.*—*gesticulated, gesticulating.* [L. *gesticulor, gesticulatus*, from *gero, gestum*, to bear or carry. GESTATION.] To make gestures or motions, as in speaking; to use postures.—*v.t.*† To represent by gesture.—**Gesticulation**, jes-tik′ū-lā″shon, *n.* [L. *gesticulatio.*] The act of gesticulating or making gestures; a gesture.—**Gesticulator**, jes-tik′ū-lā-tėr, *n.* One that gesticulates.—**Gesticulatory**, jes-tik′ū-la-to-ri, *a.* Pertaining to gesticulation.

Gesture, jes′tūr, *n.* [L.L. *gestura*, mode of acting, from L. *gestus*, posture, motion, from *gero, gestum*, to bear, to carry. GESTATION.] A motion or action intended to express an idea or feeling, or to enforce an argument or opinion; movement of the body or limbs.—*v.t. gestured, gesturing.* To express by gesture.—*v.i.* To make gestures.—**Gestural**, jes′tū-ral, *a.* Pertaining to gesture.—**Gestureless**, jes′tūr-les, *a.* Free from gestures.

Get, get, *v.t.* pret. *got* (*gat*, obs.), pp. *got, gotten*, ppr. *getting.* [A.Sax. *gitan*, to obtain; Icel. *geta*, O.H.G. *gezan*, Goth. *gitan*; probably of same root as Gr. *chandanō*, to contain, L. (*pre*)*hendo*, to catch, as in *comprehend.* Hence *beget, forget.*] To procure; to obtain; to gain possession of by any means; to beget; to procreate; to commit to memory; to learn; to prevail on; to induce; to persuade; to procure or cause to be or occur (to *get* a letter sent, to *get* things together); *refl.* to carry or betake one's self.—*To get in*, to collect and bring under cover.—*To get off*, to put or be able to put off; to take off.—*To get on*, to be able to put on; to draw or pull on.—*To get out*, to draw or be able to draw forth.—*v.i.* To make acquisition; to gain; to arrive at any place or state; to become; followed by some modifying word, and sometimes implying difficulty or labour.—*To get above*, to surmount; to surpass.—*To get along*, to proceed; to advance.—*To get at*, to reach; to make way to; to come to.—*To get away*, to depart; to leave; to disengage one's self.—*To get back*, to arrive at the place from which one departed; to return.—*To get before*, to advance to the front or so as to be before.—*To get behind*, to fall in the rear; to lag.—*To get clear*, to disengage one's self; to be released.—*To get down*, to descend; to come from an elevation.—*To get drunk*, to become intoxicated.—*To get forward*, to proceed; to advance; also, to prosper.—*To get home*, to arrive at one's dwelling.—*To get in*, to obtain admission; to insinuate one's self.—*To get loose* or *free*, to disengage one's self; to be released from confinement.—*To get off*, to escape; to depart; to get clear; to alight or come down from a thing.—*To get on*, to proceed; to advance; to succeed; to prosper; to mount.—*To get out*, to depart from an inclosed place or from confinement; to escape; to free one's self from embarrassment.—*To get over*, to pass over; to surmount; to conquer; to recover from.—*To get quit of, to get rid of*, to shift off, or to disengage one's self from.—*To get through*, to pass through and reach a point beyond; also, to finish; to accomplish.—*To get to*, to reach; to arrive at.—*To get up*, to rise from a bed or a seat; to ascend; to climb; to originate and prepare or bring forward (to *get up* a concert); to dress; to equip (the actor was well *got up*).—**Gettable, Getable**, get′a-bl, *a.* Capable of being obtained; obtainable.—**Getter**, get′-ėr, *n.* One who gets; one who begets†.—**Getting**, get′ing, *n.* The act of obtaining; acquisition.—**Get-up**, *n.* Equipment; dress and other accessories (an actor's *get-up*): initiative, spunk.

Gewgaw, gū′ga, *n.* [Formerly *gugawe, gygawe*, for old *givegove*, a reduplicated form from *give.*] A showy trifle; a pretty thing of little worth; a toy; a bauble.

Geyser, gī′zėr, *n.* [Icel. *geysir*, lit. the gusher, from *geysa*, to gush; allied to E. *gush.*] The name given to springs or fountains of hot water characterized by periodic eruptions, the water rising up in a column.

Ghastly, gast′li, *a.* [A.Sax. *gæstlic*, terrible, *gæst* being the same as *ghast* in *aghast*; akin Goth. *usgaisjan*, to terrify. AGHAST.] Terrible of countenance; deathlike; dismal; horrible; shocking; dreadful.—*adv.* In a ghastly manner; hideously.

Ghat, Ghaut, gat, gat, *n.* [Hind.] In the East Indies, a pass through a mountain; a range or chain of hills; a landing-place or stairway to the rivers of India.—**Ghat.** As at Cal*cutta*, Cali*cut*, to the shrines of the goddess *Kali*.

Ghawazee, Ghawazi, gä-wä′sē, *n.* An Egyptian dancing-girl.

Gheber, Ghebre, gā′bėr, *n.* The name given by the Mohammedans to one belonging to the Persian fire-worshippers, called in India, Parsees.

Ghee, gē, *n.* [Hind.] In India, the butter made from the milk of the buffalo converted into a kind of oil.

Gherkin, gėr′kin, *n.* [G. *gurke*, D. *agurkje*, Dan. *agurke*, from Ar. *al-khiyâr*, Per. *khiyâr*, cucumber.] A small-fruited variety of the cucumber used for pickling.

Ghetto, get′to, *n.* [It. *borghetto, borgo*, borough.] Jewish pen or quarter, a Jewry; the quarter, closed and locked at night, in Italian and Rhine-valley towns, in which Jews lived.

Ghittern, git′ėrn, *n.* Same as *Gittern*.

Ghost, gōst, *n.* [A.Sax. *gást*, a spirit, a ghost; D. *geest*, G. *geist*, a spirit: from a root seen in Icel. *geisa*, to chafe, to rage as fire; Sw. *gäsa*, to ferment; E. *yeast*.] The soul or spiritual part of man†; the visible spirit of a dead person; a disembodied spirit; an apparition; shadow (not the *ghost* of a chance).—*To give up the ghost*, to yield up the spirit; to die.—*The Holy Ghost*, the third person in the Trinity.—**Ghostlike**, gōst′līk, *a.* Like a ghost; spectral.—**Ghostliness**, gōst′li-nes, *n.* The state or quality of being ghostly.—**Ghostly**, gōst′-li, *a.* Having to do with the soul or spirit; spiritual; not carnal or secular; pertaining to apparitions (a *ghostly* visitant); suggestive of ghosts (*ghostly* gloom).—**Ghost-seer**, *n.* One who sees ghosts or apparitions.—**Ghost-story**, *n.* A story about a ghost or ghosts.

Ghoul, göl, *n.* [Per. *ghûl*, a kind of demon supposed to devour men.] An imaginary evil being among eastern nations, which is supposed to prey upon human bodies.

Ghyll, gil, *n.* Same as *Gill*, a ravine.

Giallo-antico, jäl′lō-än-tē′kō, *n.* [It. *giallo*. yellow, *antico*, ancient.] A fine yellow marble used in ancient Rome and obtained from Numidia.

Giant, jī′ant, *n.* [O.E. *geant*, Fr. *géant*, from L. *gigas*, *gigantis*, from Gr. *gigas*, *gigantos*, a giant, formed by reduplication of root *gan*, *gen*, to produce.] A man of extraordinary bulk and stature; a person of extraordinary strength or powers, bodily or intellectual.—*a.* Like a giant; extraordinary in size or strength.—**Giantess**, jī′an-tes, *n.* A female giant.—**Giantize**, jī′an-tīz, *v.i.* To play the giant.—**Giantly**, jī′ant-li, *a.* Resembling or appropriate to a giant; characteristic of a giant.—**Giantry**,† jī′ant-ri, *n.* Giants collectively.—**Giantship**, jī′ant-ship, *n.* The state or character of a giant.

Giaour, jour, *n.* [Turk., from Per. *gâwr*, an infidel.] A word used by the Turks to designate the adherents of all religions except the Mohammedan, more particularly Christians; a Frank.

Gibber, jib′ėr, *v.i.* [Akin to *jabber* and *gabble*, perhaps also to *gibe*.] To speak rapidly and inarticulately; to gabble or jabber.—**Gibberish**, gib′ėr-ish, *n.* Rapid and inarticulate talk; unintelligible language; unmeaning words.

Gibbet, jib′et, *n.* [Fr. *gibet*, O.Fr. *gibbet*; comp. O.Fr. *gibet*, a large stick.] A kind of gallows; a gallows with a cross-beam or an arm projecting from the top, on which notorious malefactors were hanged; the projecting beam or jib of a crane.—*v.t.* To hang on a gibbet or gallows; to hold up to ridicule, scorn, infamy, &c.

Gibbon, gib′on, *n.* A name of various apes of the Indian Archipelago, slender in form and with very long arms.

Gibbous, gib′us, *a.* [L. *gibbosus*, from *gibbus*, humped, a hump.] Swelling out or protuberant; exhibiting a sort of hump or convex swelling; hunched: applied to the moon when more than half and less than full; *bot.* more convex or tumid in one place than another.—**Gibbose**, gib-ōs′, *a.* Humped; having humps; gibbous.—**Gibbosity**, gib-os′i-ti, *n.* The state of being gibbous or gibbose; a protuberance or round swelling prominence; convexity.—**Gibbously**, gib′us-li, *adv.* In a gibbous or protuberant form.—**Gibbousness**, gib′-us-nes, *n.*

Gib-cat, gib′kat, *n.* [*Gib* for *Gilbert*; comp. *Tom-cat*.] A castrated cat.

Gibe, jīb, *v.i.*—*gibed*, *gibing*. [From the same root as *gab*, the mouth, *gabble*, *jabber*, &c.; comp. Sw. *gipa*, to wry the mouth.] To utter taunting sarcastic words; to flout; to fleer.—*v.t.* To assail with contemptuous words; to mock; to flout; to treat with sarcastic reflections; to taunt.—*n.* A taunt or sarcastic remark; a mocking jest; a scoff.—**Giber**, jī′bėr, *n.* One who gibes.—**Gibingly**, jī′bing-li, *adv.* In a gibing manner.

Gibeonite, gib′i-on-īt, *n.* A drudge, 'hewer of wood and drawer of water'. (*Joshua*, ix. 27).

Giblets, jib′lets, *n. pl.* [O.Fr. *gibelet*, origin unknown.] The entrails of a goose or other fowl removed before roasting; rags or tatters†.

Giddy, gid′i, *a.* [A.Sax. *gydig*, insane, from *god*, a god, a heathen deity.] Having in the head a sensation of a whirling or reeling about; affected with vertigo; dizzy; reeling; rendering giddy; inducing giddiness (a *giddy* height); suggestive of giddiness from its motion; whirling; inconstant; changeable; flighty; thoughtless; rendered wild by excitement; having the head turned.—*v.t.*—*giddied*, *giddying*. To make giddy.—*v.i.* To turn quickly; to reel.—**Giddily**, gid′i-li, *adv.* In a giddy manner.—**Giddiness**, gid′i-nes, *n.* The state of being giddy.—**Giddy-head**, *n.* A person without thought or judgment.—**Giddy-headed**, *a.* Having a giddy head; unsteady; flighty; volatile.—**Giddy-paced**, *a.* Moving irregularly; reeling; flighty.

Gier-eagle, gēr′ē-gl, *a.* [D. *gier*, G. *geier*, a vulture.] A kind of eagle. (O.T.)

Gift, gift, *n.* [A.Sax. *gift*, from *gifan*, to give. GIVE.] That which is given or bestowed; a present; a donation; the act, right, or power of giving (it is not in his *gift*); a natural quality or endowment regarded as conferred; power; faculty; talent. *v.t.* To confer as a gift; to make a gift or present to; to endow.—**Gifted**, gif′ted, *pp.* or *a.* Endowed by nature with any power or faculty; largely endowed with intellect or genius; talented.

Gig, gig, *n.* [Origin doubtful; comp. *jig*.] Any little thing that is whirled round in play; a whirligig (*Shak.*); a light one-horse carriage with two wheels; a long narrow rowing-boat; a ship's boat suited for rowing expeditiously, and generally furnished with sails; a machine for teazling woollen cloth; a kind of harpoon.—**Gigmanity**, *n.* Type of respectability, as of one that keeps a gig. (*Carlyle*).—**Gigster**, gig′stėr, *n.* A horse suitable for a gig.

Gigantic, **Gigantical**, ji-gan′tik, ji-gan′-ti-kal, *a.* [L. *giganticus*, from *gigas*, a giant. GIANT.] Of the size or proportions of a giant; colossal; huge; enormous; immense.—**Gigantesque**, jī′gan-tesk, *a.* Befitting a giant.—**Gigantically**, jī-gan′ti-kal-li, *adv.* In a gigantic manner.—**Giganticness**,† ji-gan′tik-nes, *n.* The state or quality of being gigantic.—**Gigantomachy**, jī-gan-tom′a-ki, *n.* [Gr. *gigas*, *gigantos*, giant, and *machē*, fight.] A war of giants.

Giggle, gig′l, *n.* [Imitative, like *cackle*; D. *gicken*, *gickelen*, to cackle; Swiss *gigelen*, to giggle.] A kind of laugh, with short catches of the voice or breath; a titter.—*v.i.*—*giggled*, *giggling*. To laugh with short catches of the breath or voice; to titter.—**Giggler**, gig′lėr, *n.* One that giggles.—**Giggling**, gig′ling, *a.* Characterized by giggles; tittering.—**Giglet**, **Giglot**, gig′-let, gig′lot, *n.* [From *giggle*, or from *gig* with a diminutive termination.] A light giddy girl; a wanton.—*a.* Giddy; inconstant; wanton (*Shak.*).

Gigot, jig′ot, *n.* [Fr., from O.Fr. *gigue*, the thigh, a fiddle, from O.G. *gige*, G. *geige*, a violin, from its shape.] A leg of mutton.

Gilbert, gil′bert, *n.* [After the natural philosopher *Gilbert*.] The C.G.S. unit of magneto-motive force.

Gild, gild, *v.t.*—pret. and pp. *gilded* or *gilt*. [A.Sax. *gyldan*, from *gold*.] To overlay with gold, either in leaf or powder, or in amalgam with quicksilver; to give a golden hue to; to illuminate; to brighten; to render bright; to give a fair and agreeable external appearance to.—**Gilded**, *a.* *Gilded chamber*, the House of Lords.—*Gilded youth*, wealthy young people; fashionables. [Fr. *jeunesse dorée*.] **Gilder**, gil′dėr, *n.* One who gilds.—**Gilding**, gil′ding, *n.* The art of a gilder; what is laid on by the gilder; a thin coating of gold-leaf; *fig.* fair superficial show.

Gild, gild, *n.* Same as *Guild*.

Gilder, gil′dėr, *n.* A Dutch coin; a guilder.

Gill, gil, *n.* [Not in A.Sax. or German; a Scandinavian word: Dan. *giælle*, Sw. *gäl*, *fisk-gel*, a fish-gill; comp. Gael. *gial*, a jaw, a gill.] The respiratory organ of fishes and other animals which breathe the air that is mixed in water.—*Gill arches and clefts*, in fishes, &c., those visceral arches and clefts (which see) related to gills; *pl.* the flap that hangs below the beak of a fowl; the flesh under or about a person's chin; the radiating plates on the under side of a fungus.

Gill, jil, *n.* [O.Fr. *gelle*, a wine measure; akin to *gallon*.] A measure of capacity containing the fourth part of a pint.

Gill, jil, *n.* [Abbrev. of *Gillian*, from *Juliana*; hence *jilt*.] A sweetheart; a wanton girl.—*Jack and Gill* = lad and lass.—**Gill-flirt**, *n.* A sportive or wanton girl.

Gill, gil, *n.* [Icel. *gil*, a ravine.] A ravine or chasm in a hill; a brook. (Local name, chiefly confined to the Lake district, by Norse infusion.)

Gillie, gil′i, *n.* [Gael. *gillie*, a boy, a gillie. In the Highlands an outdoor male servant, especially one who attends a person while hunting.

Gillyflower, jil′i-flou-ėr, *n.* [Formerly *gilofer*, from Fr. *girofiée*, from L. *caryophyllus*, Gr. *karophyllon*, the clove-tree—*karyon*, a nut, and *phyllon*, a leaf.] The popular name given to certain plants, as the pink or clove-pink. CLOVE.

Gilt, gilt, pp. of *gild*. Overlaid with gold.—*n.* Gold laid on the surface of a thing; gilding.—**Gilt-edged securities**. Favoured as safe by trustees, brokers, and bankers.—**Gilt-head**, *n.* The name of two fishes.

Gimbals, jim′bals, *n.pl.* [Formerly *gemmal*, *gimmal-ring*, from Fr. *gemelle*, from L. *gemellus*, twin, paired, double, from *geminus*, twin.] A contrivance consisting usually of two movable hoops or rings, supported upon horizontal pivots, the one moving within the other about two axes at right angles to each other and in the same plane; a contrivance such as supports the mariner's compass and causes it to assume a constantly vertical position, notwithstanding the rolling of the ship.

Gimcrack, jim′krak, *n.* [Probably from Prov.E. *gimp*, *gim*, neat, spruce, and old *crack*, a pert boy; originally applied to a boy.] A trivial piece of mechanism; a toy; a pretty thing.

Gimlet, **Gimblet**, gim′let, *n.* [O.Fr. *guimbelet*, same word as E. *wimble*, with dim. term.; comp. O.D. *wimpel*, a bore, D. *wemelen*, to move in an undulatory manner.] A small instrument with a pointed screw at the end, for boring holes in wood by turning.—*v.t.* To use a gimlet upon; to form by using a gimlet.

Gimmer, gim′ėr, *n.* [Icel. *gymbr*, Dan. *gimmer*, a young ewe.] A ewe that is two years old. (*Provincial*.)

Gimp, **Gymp**, gimp, *n.* [Perhaps nasalized from Fr. *guiper*, to whip about with silk, from Goth. *weipan*=E. to *whip*; comp. G. *gimf*, *gimpf*, a loop, lace, &c.] A kind of silk twist or edging.

Gin, jin, *n.* A contraction of *Geneva*, a distilled spirit.—**Gin-palace**, *n.* A shop or house where gin is retailed; a dram-shop.

Gin, jin, *n.* [A contr. of *engine*.] A trap or snare; a kind of whim or windlass worked by a horse, for raising minerals; a contrivance for raising weights, consisting of three upright poles meeting at top with block and tackle; a machine for separating the seeds from cotton; a machine for driving piles.—*v.t.*—*ginned*, *ginning*. To catch in a gin; to clear of seeds by the cotton-gin.

Gin, gin, *v.i.* [A.Sax. *ginnan*.] To begin.

Gingelly-oil, jin-jel′i, *n.* [Indian name.] The oil of Indian sesame.

Ginger, jin′jėr, *n.* [O.Fr. *gengibre*, Fr. *gingembre*, from L. *zingiber*, ultimately from Skr. *çringa-vêra*—*çringa*, horn, *vêra*, shape.] The rhizome or underground stem of a perennial herb cultivated in most tropical countries, used in medicine and largely as a condiment.—*v.t.* To put life and vigor into.—**Gingerale**, *n.* A carbonated beverage, amber colored, flavored with ginger.—**Ginger beer**, *n.* A white carbonated, non-alcoholic beverage differing from ginger ale principally in that bitters are used in the brewing of it.—**Gingerbread**, *n.* A plain cake flavored with ginger, and usually sweetened with molasses; gaudy ornamentation.—**Gingerbread tree**, *n.* A name given to the doum palm.—**Gingersnap**, *n.* A small, thin cooky flavored with ginger and molasses.

Gingerly, jin′jėr-li, *adv.* [Connected with prov. *ging*, *gang*, to go.] Cautiously; daintily (to walk, to handle a thing *gingerly*).

Gingham, ging′am, *n.* [From Malay *ginggang*, striped.] A kind of striped cotton or linen cloth; an umbrella (*colloq.*).

Gingili, jin′jil-i, *n.* [Hindi *jinjali*.] East Indian sesame, and the oil from its seeds.

Ginglymus, ging′gli-mus, *n.* [Gr. *ginglymos*.] *Anat.* a joint such as that of the elbow or knee, in which there is no rotatory movement.

Ginn, jin, *n.* Same as *Jinn*.

Ginseng, jin′seng, *n.* [Chinese name.] A name of two plants, the root of which is considered by the Chinese a panacea or remedy for all ailments.

Gipsy, jip′si, *n.* GYPSY.

Giraffe, ji-raf′, *n.* [Fr. *girafe*, *giraffe*, Sp. *girafa*, from Ar. *zurāfa*, said to mean long-necked.] The camelopard, a ruminant animal inhabiting Africa, the tallest of all animals (owing to the extraordinary length of the neck), a full-grown male reaching the height of 18 or 20 feet.

Girandole, jir′an-dōl, *n.* [Fr., from It. *girandola*, from *girare*, to turn, from L. *gyrus*, a turn.] A chandelier; a kind of revolving firework.

Girasole, jir′a-sōl, *n.* [Fr., from It. *girasole*—*girare*, to turn, L. *gyrus*, a turn, and *sole*, L. *sol*, the sun.] ARTICHOKE, *Jerusalem*. A plant, the European heliotrope or turnsole; a variety of opal showing a reddish colour when turned toward the sun or any bright light.

Gird, gėrd, *n.* [A.Sax. *gyrd*, a rod (whence also E. *yard*, a measure); D. *garde*, G. *gerte*, a twig, a switch.] A stroke with a switch or whip; hence, a twitch or pang; a sneer; a jibe.—*v.t.* To gibe; to lash.—*v.i.* To gibe; to utter severe sarcasms: with *at*.

Gird, gėrd, *v.t.* pret. & pp. *girded* or *girt*. [A.Sax. *gyrdan*=Goth. *gairdan*, Icel. *gyrtha*, Dan. *giorde*, G. *gürten*, to gird; akin *garth*, *girth*, *yard*, an inclosure.] To bind by surrounding with any flexible substance; to make fast by binding; to tie round: usually with *on*; to clothe, invest, or surround; to encircle; to encompass.—**Girder**, gėr′dėr, *n.* One who girds; a main beam, either of wood or iron, resting upon a wall or pier at each end, employed for supporting a superstructure or a superincumbent weight.—**Girder-bridge**, *n.* A bridge the roadway of which is supported by girders.—**Girdle**, gėr′dl, *n.* [A.Sax. *gyrdel*, from *gyrdan*, to gird; Sw. *gördel*, G. *gürtel*.] A band or belt for the waist; what girds or incloses. See GRIDDLE. (*Scottish.*)—*v.t.* —*girdled*, *girdling*. To bind with a girdle; to inclose or environ.

Girl, gėrl, *n.* [Formerly applied to both sexes, and probably connected with L.G. *gör*, *göre*, a child: Swiss *gurre*, *gurrli*, depreciatory term for girl.] A female child; a female not arrived at puberty; sweetheart (*colloq.*); a young woman.—**Girlhood**, gėrl′hụd, *n.* The state of being a girl; the earlier stage of maidenhood.—**Girlish**, gėr′lish, *a.* Like or pertaining to a girl; befitting a girl.—**Girlishly**, *adv.*—**Girlishness**, *n.*—**Girl Scouts**, an organization for girls 10 to 18 years old.

Girondist, ji-ron′dist, *n.* [Fr.] Member of the moderate Republican party formed in the French Legislative Assembly of 1791, and consisting of the Deputies for the Gironde district and their adherents.

Girt, gėrt, pret. & pp. of *gird*.

Girth, gėrth, *n.* [From *gird*, *v.t.*, or rather directly from Icel. *gerth*, *gjörth*, girth.] The band fastening the saddle on a horse's back; the measure round a person's body or anything cylindrical.—*v.t.* To bind with a girth.

Gist, jist, *n.* [O.Fr. *giste*, a lying-place, lodging, from *gesir*, L. *jacere*, to lie (as in *adjacent*).] The main point of a question or that on which it rests; the substance or pith of a matter.

Gittern, git′ėrn, *n.* [O.D. *ghiterne*, from L. *cithara*, Gr. *kithari*, a kind of lyre.] An instrument of the guitar kind strung with wire; a cittern.

Give, giv, *v.t.* — *gave* (pret.), *given* (pp.), *giving* (ppr.). [A.Sax. *gifan* = Dan. *give*, Icel. *gefa*, D. *geven*, G. *geben*, Goth. *giban*, to give; probably causative from same root as L. *habeo*, to have (whence *habit*, &c.) = to make to have.] To convey to another; to bestow; to communicate (an opinion, advice); to utter; to pronounce (a cry, the word of command); to grant; to cause or enable (he *gave* me to understand); to addict: often with *up*; to excite (to *give* offence); to pledge (one's word); to propose, as a toast; to ascribe; to pay; to yield, as a result or product.—*To give away*, to make over to another; to transfer.—*To give back*, to return; to restore.—*To give birth to*, to bring forth, as a child; to be the origin of. —*To give chase*, to pursue.—*To give ear*, to listen; to pay attention; to give heed.—*To give forth*, to publish; to report publicly.—*To give ground*, to retire before an enemy; to yield.—*To give in*, to yield; to declare; to make known; to tender.—*To give the lie*, to charge with falsehood.—*To give over*, to leave; to cease; to abandon; to regard as past recovery.—*To give out*, to report; to decide, give the decision that the batsman is out; to proclaim; to publish; to issue; to declare or pretend to be; to emit; to distribute.—*To give place*, to retire so as to make room. — *To give tongue*, said of dogs, to bark.—*To give up*, to resign; to yield as hopeless; to surrender; to cede; to deliver or hand over.—*To give way*, to yield; to withdraw; to yield to force; to break or break down; *naut.* to row after ceasing, or to increase exertions.—*v.i.* To make gifts; to be liberal; to yield, as to pressure; to recede; to afford entrance or view; to face or be turned (as a house).—*To give in*, to give way; to yield; to confess one's self beaten.—*To give in to*, to yield assent to. —*To give out*, to cease from exertion; to yield.—*To give over*, to cease; to act no more.—**Given**, giv′n, *p.* and *a.* Bestowed; conferred; admitted or supposed; addicted; disposed (much *given* to carping); *math.* supposed or held to be known.—**Giver**, giv′ėr, *n.* One who gives.

Gizzard, giz′ėrd, *n.* [Fr. *gésier*, O.Fr. *gezier*, from L. *gigeria*, entrails of poultry.] The third and principal stomach in birds, often very thick and muscular.

Glabrous, glā′brus, *a.* [L. *glaber*, smooth.] Smooth; having a surface devoid of hair or pubescence.

Glacial, glā′shi-al, *a.* [Fr., from L. *glacialis*, from *glacies*, ice.] Pertaining to ice or to the action of ice; pertaining to glaciers; icy; frozen; having a cold glassy look.—*Glacial period* or *epoch*, in *geol.* that interval of time in the later tertiary period during which both the arctic regions and a great part of the temperate regions were covered with a sheet of ice.—**Glacialist**, glā′shi-al-ist, *n.* One who studies or writes on glacial phenomena.—**Glaciate**, glā′shi-āt, *v.i.* To be converted into ice. — *v.t.* To convert into or cover with ice; to act upon by glaciers.—**Glaciation**, glā′shi-ā′shon, *n.* The act of freezing; the process or result of glacial action on the earth's surface; the striation and smoothing of rock-surfaces by glacial action. — **Glacier**, glā′shi-ėr, *n.* [Fr., from *glace*, ice.] An immense accumulation of ice, or ice and snow, formed in lofty valleys above the line of perpetual congelation, and slowly moving downwards into the lower valleys, reaching frequently to the borders of cultivation.—*Glacier-snow*, the coarsely granular snow from which glaciers are formed; névé.—*Glacier tables*, large stones found on glaciers supported on pedestals of ice, formed by the melting away of the ice where it is not shaded from the sun by the stone.—*Glacier theory*, a theory in regard to glaciers; the theory attributing important geological changes (as the erosion of valleys) to the action of glaciers.

Glacis, glā′sis, *n.* [Fr., from *glace*, ice—from the smoothness of its surface.] *Fort.* a sloping bank so raised as to bring the enemy advancing over it into the most direct line of fire from the fort.

Glad, glad, *a.* [A.Sax. *glæd*, glad=Dan. *glad*, glad, D. *glad*, Icel. *glathr*, smooth, polished, cheerful; G. *glatt*, smooth. Allied to *glide* and to *glow*.] Affected with pleasure or satisfaction; pleased; joyful; gratified; well contented: often followed by *of* or *at*; cheerful; bright; wearing the appearance of joy (a *glad* countenance).—*v.t.* —*gladded*, *gladding*. To make glad; to gladden. (*Poet.*)—**Gladden**, glad′n, *v.t.* To make glad; to cheer; to please; to exhilarate.—*v.i.* To become glad; to rejoice. —**Gladly**, glad′li, *adv.* With pleasure; joyfully; cheerfully.—**Gladness**, glad′nes, *n.* The state or quality of being glad.—**Gladsome**, glad′sum, *a.* Glad; cheerful; causing joy, pleasure, or cheerfulness. (*Poet.*)

Glade, glād, *n.* [Lit. a light or bright place, a glad place; Icel. *glathr*, bright, glad. GLAD.] An opening or passage through a wood; a kind of avenue in a wood or forest covered with grass.—**Glady**, glād′i, *a.* Having glades.

Gladiate, glad′i-āt, *a.* [L. *gladius*, a sword.] Sword-shaped. — **Gladiator**, glad′i-ā-tėr, *n.* [L., from *gladius*, a sword.] Among the ancient Romans one who fought with deadly weapons in the amphitheatre and other places for the entertainment of the people; hence, a combatant in general; a prize-fighter; a disputant. — **Gladiatorial**, **Gladiatorian**, glad′i-a-tō″ri-al, glad′i-a-tō″ri-an, *a.* Pertaining to gladiators; pertaining to combatants in general who fight singly, as to disputants.—**Gladiatorism**, glad-i-ā′tėr-izm, *n.* The act or practice of gladiators.—**Gladiatorship**, glad-i-ā′tėr-ship, *n.* The state or occupation of a gladiator.—**Gladiolus**, gla-dī′o-lus, glad-i-ō′lus very common, *n.* pl. **Gladioli**, gla-dī′o-li, glad-i-ō′li. [L. *gladiolus* dim. of *gladius*, a sword, from their leaves.] An extensive and very beautiful genus of bulbous-rooted plants, found most abundantly in South Africa; sword-lily.—**Gladius**, glā′di-us, *n.* The 'pen' or internal bone of some cuttle-fishes.

Glagol, glä′gol, *n.* [Slav., a word.] An ancient Slavonic alphabet, still used in liturgies, &c.—**Glagolitic**, glä-gō-lit′ik, *a.* Of or pertaining to the Glagol.

Glair, glār, *n.* [Fr. *glaire*, from L. *clarus*, clear, the glair of an egg being the clear portion. CLEAR.] The white of an egg used as varnish to preserve paintings, and as a size in gilding; any similar substance. —*v.t.* To varnish or smear with glair.—**Glairy**, **Glaireous**, **Glairous**, glā′ri, glā′rē-us, glā′rus, *a.* Like glair, or partaking of its qualities; covered with glair.

Glaive, **Glave**, glāv, *n.* [Fr. *glaive*, from L. *gladius*, a sword; allied to Gael. *claidheamh*, a sword, *claidheamhmor*, a claymore. GLADIATE.] A sword; a broadsword; a falchion; a cutting weapon formerly used by foot soldiers, fixed to the end of a pole.

Glamour, glam′ėr, *n.* [A modified form of *grammar*—*grammar*—*gramarye*, having formerly meant learning, deep learning, magic.] Magical influence causing a person to see objects differently from what they really are; fascination; witchery.

Glance, glans, *n.* [Same word as Sw. *glans*, Dan. *glands*, D. *glans*, G. *glanz*, lustre, splendour; *glint*, *glitter*, *glisten*, *gleam*, &c., are connected.] A sudden dart or flash of light or splendour; a sudden look or darting of sight; a rapid or momentary casting of the eye; a name given to some minerals which possess a metallic lustre.—*v.i.*—*glanced*, *glancing*. To shoot or dart rays of light or splendour; to emit flashes or coruscations of light; to flash; to fly off in an oblique direction; to strike or graze; to dart aside; to look with a sudden cast of the eye.—*v.t.* To shoot or dart suddenly; to cast for a moment (to *glance* the eye).—**Glance-coal**, *n.* Anthracite. — **Glancingly**, glan'sing-li, *adv.* In a glancing manner.

Gland, gland, *n.* [L. *glans*, *glandis*, an acorn.] *Anat.* a distinct soft body, formed by the convolution of a great number of vessels, generally destined to secrete some fluid from the blood; *bot.* a secreting organ occurring on the epidermis of plants; also, a kind of one-celled fruit, with a dry pericarp.—**Glanders**, glan'dėrz, *n.* A very dangerous and highly contagious disease, chiefly seen in horses, but capable of being transmitted to man, which especially affects the glands (whence the name), the mucous membrane of the nose, the lungs, &c. — **Glander**, glan'dėr, *v.t.* To affect with glanders.—**Glandered**, glan'dėrd, *p.* and *a.* Affected with glanders.—**Glandiferous**, glan-dif'ėr-us, *a.* [L. *glandis*, and *fero*, to bear.] Bearing glands; bearing acorns or other nuts. — **Glandiform**, glan'di-form, *a.* Having the shape of a gland or nut; resembling a gland.—**Glandular**, glan'dū-lėr, *a.* Consisting of a gland or glands; pertaining to glands.—**Glandularly**, glan'dū-lėr-li, *adv.* In a glandular manner.—**Glandule**, glan'dūl, *n.* [L. *glandula.*] A small gland.—**Glanduliferous**, glan-dū-lif'ėr-us, *a.* Bearing glandules.—**Glandulosity**, glan-dū-los'i-ti, *n.* The quality of being glandulous. — **Glandulous, Glandulose**, glan'dū-lus, glan'-dū-lōs, *a.* [L. *glandulosus.*] Glandular.

Glare, glār, *n.* [Akin to A.Sax. *glær*, amber; Dan. *glar*, Icel. *gler*, glass; L.G. *glaren*, to glow; E. *glass*, *glance*, *gleam*, &c.] A bright dazzling light; splendour that dazzles the eyes; a confusing and bewildering light; a fierce, piercing look.—*v.i.*—*glared*, *glaring.* To shine with a bright dazzling light; to look with fierce, piercing eyes; to have a dazzling effect; to be ostentatiously splendid.—*v.t.* To shoot out or emit, as a dazzling light.—**Glaringness**, glār'ing-nes, *n.* The state or quality of having a glaring appearance. — **Glaring**, glār'ing, *p.* and *a.* Shining with dazzling lustre; excessively bright; vulgarly splendid; forcing one's notice; notorious; open; barefaced (a *glaring* crime).—**Glaringly**, glār'ing-li, *adv.* In a glaring manner.

Glass, glas, *n.* [A.Sax. *glæs*; L.G. D. G. Sw. and Icel. *glas*: Icel. also *gler*; akin *glisten*, *glance*, *glare*, &c.] A hard, brittle, transparent artificial substance, formed by the fusion of siliceous matter (as powdered flint or fine sand) with some alkali; something made of glass; especially, a mirror or looking-glass; a glass vessel filled with running sand for measuring time; a drinking vessel made of glass; the quantity which such a vessel holds (hence, *the glass*=strong drink); an optical instrument, such as a lens or a telescope; a barometer or thermometer; *pl.* spectacles.—*a.* Made of glass. —*v.t.* To reflect; to mirror; to cover with glass.—**Glassful**, glas'ful, *n.* As much as a glass will hold.—**Glassily**, glas'i-li, *adv.* So as to resemble glass. — **Glassiness**, glas'i-nes, *n.* The quality of being glassy.—**Glassy**, glas'i, *a.* Made of glass; vitreous; resembling glass; having a lustre or surface like glass.—**Glass-blower**, *n.* One whose business it is to blow and fashion vessels of glass.—**Glass-case**, *n.* A case largely consisting of glass.—**Glass-cutter**, *n.* One who cuts glass, or grinds it into ornamental forms.—**Glass-furnace**, *n.* A furnace in which the materials of glass are melted.—**Glass-gall**, *n.* Sandiver.—**Glass-house**, *n.* A manufactory of glass; a house built largely of glass, as a conservatory or greenhouse. — **Glass-painter, Glass-stainer**, *n.* One who produces designs in colour on or in glass.—**Glass-paper**, *n.*, A polishing paper made by strewing finely-pounded glass on paper besmeared with thin glue. — **Glass-rope**, *n.* A sponge found in Japan, consisting of a cup-shaped body, supported by a rope of twisted siliceous fibres.—**Glass-shade**, *n.* A cover of glass, as for flowers, gas-jets, &c.—**Glass-snake**, *n.* A North American lizard, so called from its brittleness. — **Glass-stopper**, *n.* A stopple of glass for bottles. — **Glass-ware**, *n.* Articles made of glass.—**Glass-work**, *n.* Articles of or in glass; an establishment where glass is made. — **Glasswort**, glas'wėrt, *n.* A name of various plants common on the Mediterranean coasts yielding ashes containing much soda, and hence used in making glass.

Glauber-salt, gla̤'bėr-sa̤lt, *n.* [After *Glauber* (died 1688), a German chemist, who first prepared it.] Sulphate of soda, a well-known cathartic.

Glaucous, gla̤'kus, *a.* [L. *glaucus*, from Gr. *glaukos*, bluish-green or sea-green.] Of a sea-green colour; of a light green or bluish green; *bot.* covered with a fine bluish or greenish powder or bloom. — **Glaucescent, Glaucine**, gla̤-ses'ent, gla̤'sin, *a.* *Bot.* having a somewhat bluish-green tinge or bloom.—**Glaucescence**, gla̤-ses'ens, *n.* The state of being glaucescent. — **Glaucoma, Glaucosis**, gla̤-kō'ma, gla̤-kō'sis, *n.* [Gr. *glaukōma*, from *glaukos*, sea-green.] An almost incurable disease of the eye, being an opacity of the vitreous humour, giving the eye a bluish-green tint.—**Glaucomatous**, gla̤-kō'ma-tus, *a.* Pertaining to or resembling glaucoma.

Glave, glāv, *n.* Same as *Glaive.*

Glaze, glāz, *v.t.*—*glazed*, *glazing.* [From *glass.*] To furnish with glass or panes of glass; to incrust or overlay with glass or a vitreous coating; to give a glossy, or smooth, shining surface to.—*v.i.* To assume a dim, glassy lustre: said of the eye.—*n.* That which is used in glazing.—**Glazer**, glā'zėr, *n.* One who or that which glazes.—**Glazier**, glā'zhėr, *n.* One whose business is to fix panes of glass in windows, &c.—**Glazing**, glā'zing, *n.* The act or art of one who glazes; the substance with which anything is overlaid to give it a glassy appearance; enamel; glaze; *paint.* transparent or semi-transparent colours passed thinly over other colours, to modify the effect.

Gleam, glēm, *n.* [A.Sax. *glaem*, a glittering; comp. O.Sax. *glimo*, splendour, Sw. *glimma*, to flash; allied to *glimmer*, *glow*, *glance*, &c.] A beam or flash of light; a ray; a small stream of light; brightness.—*v.i.* To dart or throw rays of light; to glimmer; to glitter; to shine.—**Gleaming**, glēm'ing, *a.* Beaming; shining clearly and brightly; radiant. — **Gleamy**, glē'mi, *a.* Darting beams or rays of light.

Glean, glēn, *v.t.* [Fr. *glaner*, from L.L. *glenare*, to glean, from W. *glain*, *glân*, clean; comp. A.Sax. *gilm*, a handful.] To gather after a reaper, or on a reaped cornfield, the ears of grain left ungathered; hence, to collect in scattered portions; to pick up here and there; to gather slowly and assiduously. — *v.i.* To gather ears of grain left by reapers.—**Gleaner**, glē'nėr, *n.* One who gleans.

Glebe, glēb, *n.* [Fr. *glèbe*, from L. *gleba*, a clod or lump of earth.] Soil; ground; earth; the land belonging to a parish church or ecclesiastical benefice.—**Glebosity**, glē-bos'i-ti, *n.* The quality of being glebous.—**Glebous**, glē'bus, *adj.* Full of lumps or clods; like a clod of earth.

Glede, glēd, *n.* [A.Sax, *glida*, the kite, lit. glider, from its gliding flight. GLIDE.] A bird of prey, the common kite of Europe.

Glee, glē, *n.* [A.Sax. *gleó*, *gliw*, *glig*, music, sport; Icel. *gly*, laughter.] Joy; merriment; mirth; gaiety; a musical composition consisting of two or more contrasted movements, with the parts forming as it were a series of interwoven melodies.—**Glee club**, A group organized for singing songs.—**Gleeman**, glē'man, *n.* [A.Sax. *gleôman.*] A minstrel or musician of former days.—**Gleeful, Gleesome**, glē'ful, glē'-sum, *a.* Full of glee; merry; gay; joyous.

Gleed, † glēd, *n.* [A.Sax. *glēd*, a live coal, from root of *glow.*] A burning coal; a blaze.

Gleek, glēk, *n.* [G. *gleich*, equal.] A game at cards, when a set of cards is equal—three aces, three kings, &c.

Gleet, glēt, *n.* [O.Fr. *glette*, slime, phlegm; Sc. *glet*, *glit*, phlegm.] A transparent mucous discharge from the urethra, an effect of gonorrhœa; a thin ichor running from a sore.—**Gleety**, glē'ti, *a.* Of the character of gleet.

Glen, glen, *n.* [Ir. and Gael. *gleann*, W. *glyn*, a glen.] A secluded narrow valley; a dale; a depression or space between hills.

Glengarry, *n.* Highland bonnet.

Glenlivet, *n.* Whisky, from *Glenlivet* in Banffshire.

Glenoid, glē'noid, *a.* [Gr. *glēnē*, the pupil, the eyeball.] *Anat.* a term applied to any shallow, articular cavity which receives the head of a bone.

Glib, glib, *a.* [Comp. D. *glibberig*, smooth, slippery; *glibberen*, L.G. *glippen*, to slide; akin to *glide.*] Smooth; slippery; more commonly voluble; fluent; having words always ready.—**Glibly**, glib'li, *adv.* In a glib manner; smoothly; volubly.—**Glibness**, glib'nes, *n.* The quality of being glib.

Glide, glīd, *v.i.*—*glided*, *gliding.* [A.Sax. *glidan* = Dan. *glide*, D. *glijden*, G. *gleiten*, to slide; allied to *glad.*] To flow gently; to move along silently and smoothly; to pass along without apparent effort (a river, a bird, a skater *glides*)—*v.t.* To fly on a descending path, when the aircraft machine is not under engine power.—*n.* A kind of dance. (*Amer.*)—**Glider**, glī'dėr, *n.* One who glides; a form of aircraft similar to an airplane but lacking an engine. —**Glidingly**, glī'ding-li, *adv.* In a gliding manner.—**Gliding angle**, glīd'ing ang'gl, *n.* The angle, slope, or natural gradient which an aeroplane assumes of its own accord in the air when the engine-power is cut off, so that it will glide gradually to the earth, the angle varying for each machine.

Glimmer, glim'ėr, *v.i.* [A freq. of *gleam* = Dan. *glimre*, to glitter, from *glimme*, to gleam; comp. G. *glimmer*, a faint light; *glimmen*, to shine.] To emit feeble or scattered rays of light; to shine faintly; to give a feeble light; to flicker.—*n.* A faint and unsteady light; feeble scattered rays of light; glitter; twinkle; also, a name of mica. —**Glimmering**, glim'ėr-ing, *n.* A glimmer; a gleam; a faint indication; an inkling; a glimpse.

Glimpse, glimps, *n.* [Formerly *glimse*, from the stem of *gleam*, *glimmer*, &c., the *p* being inserted as in *empty*, *semptress*, &c. Comp. Swiss *glumsen*, to glow; D. *glimpen*, *glinsen*, to sparkle.] A gleam; a momentary flash; a short transitory view; a glance; a faint resemblance; a slight tinge. — *v.i.* — *glimpsed*, *glimpsing.* To appear by glimpses. — *v.t.* To see by a glimpse or glimpses.

Glint, glint, *v.i.* [Of kindred origin with *glimpse*, *glimmer*, *glance*, &c.; comp. Dan. *glimt*, a gleam, *glimte*, to flash.] To glance; to gleam; to give a flash of light.—*n.* A glance; a flash; a gleam.

Glissade, glis-äd', *n.* [Fr. *glissade*; from *glisser*, to glide or slide.] A sliding or gliding down a slope.

Glisten, glis'n, *v.i.* [A.Sax. *glisnian*, akin to G. *gleissen*, Icel. *glyssa*, O.G. *glizan*, to shine; same root as *glitter*, *gleam*, &c.] To shine; to sparkle with light; to shine with a scintillating light.—*n.*† Glitter; sparkle. —**Glister**, glis'tėr, *v.i.* To shine; to glitter.—*n.* Lustre; glitter.—**Glisteringly**, glis'tėr-ing-li, *adv.* In a glistering manner.

Glitter, glit'ėr, *v.i.* [A freq. from stem *glit*, seen in A.Sax. *glitnian*, to glitter=Sw. *glittra*, Icel. *glitra* (from *glita*, to shine), G. *glitzern*, to shine; akin to *gleam*, *glance*, &c.] To shine with a broken and scattered light; to emit rapid flashes of light; to gleam; to sparkle; to glisten; to be showy or brilliant. — *n.* Bright sparkling light; brilliancy; splendour; lustre.—**Glitteringly**, glit'ėr-ing-li, *adv.* In a glittering manner.

Gloaming, glōm′ing, *n.* [A.Sax. *glómung*, twilight, from *glóm*, E. *gloom.*] Fall of the evening; the twilight; closing period; decline. [Scotch, but adopted by English writers.]

Gloat, glōt, *v.i.* [Allied to Sw. *glutta*, *glötta*, to look at with prying eyes; G. *glotzen*, to stare.] To gaze with admiration, eagerness, or desire; to feast the eyes either actually or in thought; to contemplate with evil satisfaction.

Globe, glōb, *n.* [L. *globus*, a ball; Fr. *globe*, Sp. and It. *globo.*] A round or spherical solid body; a ball; a sphere; the earth; an artificial sphere on whose convex surface is drawn a map or representation of the earth (*a terrestrial globe*) or of the heavens (*a celestial globe*).—*v.t.* To gather into a round mass; to conglobate.—**Globate, Globated**, glō′bāt, glō′bā-ted, *a.* [L. *globatus.*] Shaped like a globe; spherical.—**Globigerina**, glō′bi-je-rī″na, *n.* [L. *globus*, a ball, *gero*, to bear.] One of the Foraminifera, a microscopic animal having a many-celled shell, both found fossil and still so abundant in our seas that its shells form calcareous deposits called 'globigerina ooze'. **Globose, Globous**, glō-bōs, glō′bus, *a.* [L. *globosus.*] Spherical; globular.—**Globosity**, glō-bos′i-ti, *n.* The quality of being globose.—**Globular**, glob′ū-lėr, *a.* Globe-shaped; having the form of a ball or sphere; round; spherical.—**Globularity**, glob-ū-lar′i-ti, *n.* State of being globular; sphericity. — **Globularly**, glob′ū-lėr-li, *adv.* In a globular or spherical form; spherically.—**Globularness**, glob′ū-lėr-nes, *n.* Sphericity.—**Globule**, glō-būl, *n.* [L. *globulus.*] A small particle of matter of a spherical form; a round body or corpuscle found in the blood.—**Globulet**, glob′ū-let, *n.* A minute globule.—**Globulin**, glob′ū-lin, *n.* The main ingredient of blood globules and resembling albumen.—**Globulose, Globulous**, glob′ū-lōs, glob′ū-lus, *a.* Having the form of a small sphere; round; globular.—**Globulousness**, glob′ū-lus-nes, *n.*—**Globy**, glō′bi, *a.* Resembling a globe.—**Globe-fish**, *n.* The name of several fishes remarkable for being able to inflate themselves into a globular form. **Globe-flower**, *n.* A European plant with a globular yellow flower.

Glochidate, glō′kī-dāt, *a.* [Gr. *glōchis*, a point.] *Bot.* barbed at the point like a fish-hook.

Glochidium, glok-id′i-um, *n.* [Gr. dim. *glōchis*, an arrow.] Larva of a fresh-water mussel.

Glomerate, glom′ėr-āt, *v.t.* [L. *glomero*, *glomeratum*, from *glomus*, *glomeris*, a ball, as in *conglomerate.*] To gather or wind into a ball; to collect into a spherical form or mass.—*a.* Congregated; gathered into a round mass or dense cluster.—**Glomeration**, glom-ėr-ā′shon, *n.* The act of glomerating; conglomeration; an aggregate.—**Glomerule**, glom′ėr-ūl, *n.* *Bot.* a cluster of flower-heads inclosed in a common involucre.

Gloom, glöm, *n.* [A.Sax. *glóm*, gloom, twilight, *glómung*, gloaming; allied to *glum*, *glow*, *gleam*, *glimmer*, &c.] Obscurity; partial darkness; thick shade; dusk; cloudiness or heaviness of mind; heaviness, dejection, anger, sullenness; a depressing state of affairs; a dismal prospect.—*v.t.* To appear dimly; to be seen in an imperfect or waning light; to look gloomy, sad, or dismal; to frown; to lower.—*v.t.* To make gloomy or dark; to fill with gloom or sadness.—**Gloomily**, glö′mi-li, *adv.* In a gloomy manner.—**Gloominess**, glö′mi-nes, *n.* The condition or quality of being gloomy.—**Gloomy**, glö′mi, *a.* Involved in gloom; imperfectly illuminated; dusky or dark; characterized by gloom; wearing the aspect of sorrow; dejected; heavy of heart; dismal; doleful.

Glory, glō′ri, *n.* [L.*gloria*, fame, glory; allied to Gr. *kleos*, fame, *kleō*, to celebrate, *klyō*, to hear.] Praise, honour, admiration, or distinction, accorded by common consent to a person or thing; honourable fame; renown; celebrity; a state of greatness or renown; pomp; magnificence; brightness; lustre; splendour; brilliancy; the happiness of heaven; celestial bliss; distinguished honour or ornament; an object of which one is or may be proud; *painting*, the radiation round the head or figure of a deity, saint, angel, &c.—*v.i.*—*gloried*, *glorying*. To exult with joy; to rejoice; to be boastful; to have pride.—**Glorification**, glō′ri-fi-kā″shon, *n.* The act of glorifying or the state of being glorified.—**Glorify**, glō′ri-fī, *v.t.*—*glorified*, *glorifying*. [Fr. *glorifier*, L. *gloria*, glory, and *facio*, to make.] To give or ascribe glory to; to praise; to magnify and honour; to honour; to extol; to make glorious; to exalt to glory.—**Gloriole**, glō′ri-ōl, *n.* [Formed on type of *aureole.*] A circle, as of rays, in ancient paintings surrounding the heads of saints.—**Glorious**, glō′ri-us, *a.* [Fr. *glorieux*, L. *gloriosus*, from *gloria.*] Characterized by attributes, qualities, or acts that are worthy of glory; of exalted excellence and splendour; noble; illustrious; renowned; celebrated; magnificent; grand; splendid; hilarious or elated (*colloq.*).—**Gloriously**, glō′ri-us-li, *adv.* In a glorious manner.—**Gloriousness**, glō′ri-us-nes, *n.* **Glory-pea**, *n.* A leguminous Australian plant with fine scarlet blossoms.

Gloss, glos, *n.* [Akin to Icel. *glossi*, flame, brightness, *glys*, finery, whence *glysligr*, showy or specious; Sw. *glossa*, to glow; G. *glotzen*, to shine, to glance; allied to *glass*, *glow*, *gloom*, *gleam*, &c.] Brightness or lustre of a body proceeding from a smooth and generally a soft surface; polish; sheen (the *gloss* of silk); a specious appearance or representation; external show that may mislead.—*v.t.* To give gloss to; to give a superficial lustre to; to make smooth and shining; hence, to give a specious appearance to; to render specious and plausible; to palliate by specious representation.—**Glosser**, glos′ėr, *n.* One who glosses; one who palliates.—**Glossily**, glos′i-li, *adv.* In a glossy manner.—**Glossiness**, glos′i-nes, *n.* The state or character of being glossy; polish or lustre of a surface.—**Glossy**, glos′i, *a.* Having a gloss; having a soft, smooth, and shining surface; lustrous with softness to the touch; specious or plausible.

Gloss, glos, *n.* [L. *glossa*, an obsolete or foreign word that requires explanation, from Gr. *glōssa*, the tongue, latterly also an obsolete or foreign word.] A marginal note or interlineation explaining the meaning of some word in a text; a remark intended to illustrate some point of difficulty in an author; comment; annotation; explanation.—*v.t.* To render clear by comments; to annotate; to illustrate.—**Glossarial**, glos-sā′ri-al, *a.* Connected with, or consisting in a glossary.—**Glossarist**, glos′a-rist, *n.* One who compiles a glossary.—**Glossary**, glos′a-ri, *n.* [L.L. *glossarium.*] A vocabulary of words used by any author, especially by an old author, or one writing in a provincial dialect, or of words occurring in a special class of works, of technical terms, &c.—**Glosser, Glossist**, glos′ėr, glos′ist, *n.* One who writes glosses.—**Glossic**, glos′ik, *n.*—A system of phonetic spelling whereby the same sound is invariably represented by the same letter or letters.—**Glossitis**, glos-ī′tis, *n.* Inflammation of the tongue.—**Glossographer**, glos-og′ra-fėr, *n.* A writer of glosses; a scholiast.—**Glossographical**, glos-o-graf′i-kal, *a.* Pertaining to glossography.—**Glossography**, glos-og′ra-fi, *n.* The writing of glosses; a knowledge of glosses.—**Glossohyal**, glos-o-hī′al, *a.* *Anat.* pertaining to the tongue and the hyoid bone.—**Glossological**, glos-o-loj′i-kal, *a.* Pertaining to glossology.—**Glossologist**, glos-ol′o-jist, *n.* One who is versed in glossology.—**Glossology**, glos-ol′o-ji, *n.* The definition and explanation of terms, as of a science; terminology; universal grammar; glottology.—**Glossopharyngeal**, glos′-o-fa-rin″jē-al, *a.* Pertaining to the tongue and pharynx (the *glossopharyngeal* nerve).—**Glossotomy**, glos-ot′o-mi, *n.* *Anat.* dissection of the tongue.

Glottis, glot′is, *n.* [Gr. *glōttis*, from *glōtta*, *glōssa*, the tongue, whence also *glossary*, &c.] The opening at the upper part of the windpipe, and between the vocal chords, which, by its dilatation and contraction, contributes to the modulation of the voice.—**Glottal**, glot′al, *a.* Relating to the glottis.—**Glottology**, glot-ol′o-ji, *n.* [Gr. *glōita*, language, and *logos*, discourse.] The science of language; comparative philology; glossology.—**Glottological, Glottic**, glot-o-loj′i-kal, glot′ik, *a.* Pertaining to glottology.—**Glottologist**, glot-ol′o-jist, *n.* One versed in glottology.

Glove, gluv, *n.* [A.Sax. *glóf*; probably from prefix *ge*, and Goth. *lofa*, Sc. *loof*, Icel. *lófi*, the palm of the hand.] A cover for the hand, or for the hand and wrist, with a separate sheath for each finger.—*To throw down the glove*. Same as *to throw down the gauntlet*, under GAUNTLET.—*v.t.*—*gloved*, *gloving*. To cover with or as with a glove.—**Glover**, gluv′ėr, *n.* One whose occupation is to make or sell gloves.

Glow, glō, *v.i.* [A.Sax. *glówan*, to glow = D. *gloeijen*, G. *glühen*, to glow; Icel. *glóa*, to glitter; Sw. *gloa*, to sparkle; allied to *gloat*, *gleam*, *gloom*, *gloaming*, *gloss*, &c.] To burn with an intense or white heat, and especially without flame; to give forth bright light and heat; to feel great heat of body; to be hot or flushed in person; to be bright or red, as with animation, blushes, or the like; to exhibit brightness of colour; to feel the heat of passion; to be ardent; to burn or be vehement; to rage.—*n.* Shining heat, or white heat; incandescence; brightness of colour; redness; vehemence of colour; ardour; animation.—**Glowing**, glō′ing, *p.* and *a.* Shining with intense heat; bright in colour; red; ardent; vehement; fervid; heated; fiery.—**Glowingly**, glō′ing-li, *adv.* In a glowing manner.—**Glowworm**, glō′wėrm, *n.* The wingless female of a kind of beetle, emitting a shining green light to attract the male.

Gloxinia, glok-sin′i-a, *n.* [*Gloksin*, a German botanist.] A genus of almost stemless plants with fine bell-shaped flowers, natives of tropical America.

Gloze, glōz, *v.i.*—*glozed*, *glozing*. [O.E. *glose*, a gloss or interpretation; the meaning being influenced by *gloss*, lustre. GLOSS.] To comment or expound†; to use specious words; to talk smoothly or flatteringly.—*v.t.* To gloss over; to extenuate.—*n.* Flattery; specious words.—**Glozer**, glō′zėr, *n.* One who glozes.

Glucinum, glö-sī′num, *n.* [From Gr. *glykys* or *glukus*, sweet, from its salts having a sweet taste.] A white metal, of specific gravity 1·9, belonging to the group of the alkaline earths, and prepared from beryl, hence its name *Beryllium*.—**Glucina**, glö-sī′na, *n.* The oxide of the metal glucinum.—**Glucose**, glö-kōs′, *n.* Grape-sugar, a variety of sugar, less sweet than cane-sugar, produced from grapes, cane-sugar, starch, &c.—**Glucoside**, glö′kō-sīd, *n.* One of those substances that yield glucose.—**Glucosuria, Glycosuria**, glö-kos-ū′ri-a, glī-kos-ū′ri-a, *n.* [Gr. *glykys* or *glukus*, sweet, *ouron*, urine.] *Pathol.* the presence of glucose in the urine.

Glue, glö, *n.* [O.Fr. *glu*, from L.L. *glutis*, L. *gluten*, *glutinis*, glue; comp. W. *glyd*, viscous matter.] Common or impure gelatine, obtained by boiling animal substances, as the skins, hoofs, &c., of animals, with water: used for uniting pieces of wood or other materials.—*v.t.*—*glued*, *gluing*. To join with glue or other viscous substance; to hold together, as if by glue; to fix; to rivet.—**Gluey**, glö′i, *a.* Having the nature of glue; viscous; glutinous.—**Glueyness**, glö′i-nes, *n.* The quality of being gluey.—**Glue-pot**, *n.* A utensil, usually consisting of two pots—the one within the other—for dissolving glue.

Glum, glum, *a.* [Akin to *gloom*, and Sc. *gloum*, a frown.] Frowning; sullen. (*Colloq.*)—**Glumly**, glum′li, *adv.* In a glum or sullen manner.—**Glumness**, glum′nes, *n.* The condition or quality of being glum; sullenness.—**Glump**, glump, *v.i.* To show sullenness. (*Colloq.*)—**Glumpy**, glum′pi, *a.* Sullen; sulky. (*Colloq.*)

Glume, glöm, *n.* [L. *gluma*, a husk, from *glubo*, to peel, akin to Gr. *glyphō*, to hollow out.] The husk or chaff of grain; the palea or pale.—**Glumaceous, Glumiferous**, glö-mā'shus, glö-mif'ér-us, *a.* Having or bearing glumes; of or pertaining to the glumales. — **Glumal**, glö'mal, *a.* *Bot.* possessing or characterized by a glume.—**Glumales**, glö-mā'lēz, *n. pl.* *Bot.* a group of monocotyledons, including the grasses and sedges. — **Glumella**, glö-mel'la, *n.* The inner husk of grasses; the innermost scale-like envelope of the ovarium.—**Glumous**, glö'mus, *a.* *Bot.* having the nature of a glume.

Glut, glut, *v.t.*—*glutted, glutting.* [L. *glutio*, *gluttio*, to swallow; whence also *englut*, *glutton*.] To swallow, or to swallow greedily (*Shak.*); to cloy, sate, or disgust; to feast or delight to satiety.—*To glut the market*, to furnish an over supply of any article, so that there is no sale for it all.—*n.* Plenty even to loathing; superabundance; an oversupply of any commodity in the market.

Gluteal, glö'tē-al, *a.* [Gr. *gloutos*, the buttock.] *Anat.* of or pertaining to certain parts connected with the buttocks.

Gluten, glö'ten, *n.* [L. See GLUE.] A tough elastic substance of a grayish colour, which becomes brown and brittle by drying, found in the flour of wheat and other grain. —**Glutinate**, glö'ti-nāt, *v.t.*—*glutinated, glutinating.* [L. *glutino*, *glutinatum*.] To unite with glue; to cement.—**Glutination**, glö-ti-nā'shon, *n.* The act of glutinating or uniting with glue.—**Glutinative**, glö'ti-nā-tiv, *a.* Having the quality of cementing; tenacious.—**Glutinous, Glutinose**, glö'ti-nus, glö'ti-nōs, *a.* [L. *glutinosus*.] Gluey; viscous; viscid; tenacious; resembling glue; *bot.* besmeared with a slippery moisture.—**Glutinosity, Glutinousness**, glö-ti-nos'i-ti, glö'ti-nus-nes, *n.* The quality of being glutinous; viscosity; viscidity.

Glutton, glut'n, *n.* [Fr. *glouton*, from L. *gluto*, *glutto*, a glutton, from *glutio*, to swallow. GLUT.] One who indulges to excess in eating, or eating and drinking; a gormandizer; a carnivorous quadruped, 2½ feet long, yielding a valuable fur, and inhabiting Northern Europe and America, known also as the *Wolverene*.—**Gluttonish**,† glut'n-ish, *a.* Gluttonous.—**Gluttonize**,† glut'n-īz, *v.i.* To eat gluttonously.—**Gluttonous**, glut'n-us, *a.* Characterized by gluttony; given to excessive eating; insatiable. —**Gluttonously**, glut'n-us-li, *adv.* In a gluttonous manner.—**Gluttony**, glut'n-i, *n.* The act or practice of a glutton; excess in eating, or eating and drinking.

Glycerine, glis'ér-in, *n.* [From Gr. *glykeros*, sweet. GLUCINUM.] A transparent colourless liquid with a very sweet taste, obtained from fats.

Glycogen, glī'ko-jen, *n.* [Gr. *glykys*, sweet, and root *gen*, to produce.] Animal starch, a substance derived from grape sugar (glucose) and stored up in the liver.—**Glycogenic**, glī-ko-jen'ik, *a.* Of or pertaining to glycogen.

Glyconian, Glyconic, glī-kō'ni-an, glī-kon'ik, *a.* [Gr. *glykōneios*, from its inventor *Glykōn*.] A kind of verse in Greek and Latin poetry, consisting of three feet—a spondee, a choriambus, and a pyrrhic.

Glyph, glif, *n.* [Gr. *glyphē*, carving, from *glyphō*, to carve.] *Sculp.* and *arch.* a channel or cavity, usually vertical, intended as an ornament.—**Glyphic**, glif'ik, *a.* Of or pertaining to carving or sculpture.—**Glyphograph**, glif'o-graf, *n.* A plate formed by glyphography.—**Glyphography**, gli-fog'ra-fi, *n.* An electrotype process by which from an etched plate a design in relief is obtained.—**Glyptic**, glip'-tik, *a.* [Gr. *glyptikos*.] Pertaining to the art of sculpture or engraving.—**Glyptodon**, glip'to-don, *n.* [Gr. *glyptos*, engraved, and *odous*, tooth—from its fluted teeth.] A gigantic fossil animal, closely allied to the armadilloes, covered with an osseous coat of mail, found in the tertiary strata of South America.—**Glyptograph**, glip'to-graf, *n.* An engraving on a gem or precious stone.—**Glyptographer**, glip-tog'ra-fér, *n.* An engraver on precious stones. —**Glyptographic**, glip-to-graf'ik, *a.* Of or pertaining to glyptography.—**Glyptography**, glip-tog'ra-fi, *n.* The art or process of engraving on precious stones.—**Glyptotheca**, glip-to-thē'ka, *n.* [Gr. *glyptos*, and *thēkē*, a repository.] A place for the preservation of works of sculpture.

Gnarl, närl, *n.* [From old *gnar*, a knot, also *knarr*, *knurr*; akin to D. *knorre*, a knot, G. *knorren*, a lump.] A protuberance on the outside of a tree; a knot.—**Gnarled**, närld, *a.* Having many knots or knotty protuberances; cross-grained; perverse. —**Gnarly**, när'li, *a.* Having knots; knotty.

Gnarr, Gnarl, när, närl, *v.i.* [O.E. *gnerr*, found in similar forms in the other Teut. languages, and probably imitative of snarling.] To growl; to murmur; to snarl.

Gnash, nash, *v.t.* [O.E. *gnaste*, *gnayste*, akin to Dan. *knaske*, D. *knarsen*, G. *knirschen*, Sw. *knastra*, *gnissta*, to gnash.] To strike together (the teeth), as in anger or pain. —*v.i.* To strike or dash the teeth together, as in rage or pain.—**Gnashingly**, nash'ing-li, *adv.* In a gnashing manner.

Gnat, nat, *n.* [A.Sax. *gnæt*, L.G. *gnid*, a gnat; perhaps akin to G. *gnatze*, the itch.] A small two-winged fly whose mouth is furnished with bristly stings which inflict irritating wounds.—**Gnatling**, nat'ling, *n.* A little gnat.

Gnathic, nath'ik, *a.* [Gr. *gnathos*, jaw.] Pertaining to the jaw or jaws.

Gnathopodite, na-thop'o-dīt, *n. pl.* [Gr. *gnathos*, a jaw, and *pous*, *podos*, a foot.] A foot-jaw of a crustacean.

Gnaw, na, *v.t.* [A.Sax. *gnagan*=D. *knagen*, G. *gnagen*, Dan. *gnave*, *nage*, Icel. and Sw. *gnaga*, *naga*, to gnaw; akin verb to *nag*.] To bite by little and little; to wear away by biting; to nibble at; to bite in agony or rage; to fret; to corrode.—*v.i.* To use the teeth in biting; to bite with repeated efforts; to cause or be affected with steady annoying pain.—**Gnawer**, na'ér, *n.* One who or that which gnaws; a rodent.

Gneiss, nīs, *n.* [G. *gneiss*, gneiss.] A kind of hard tough crystalline rock, having a structure exhibiting layers either straight or curved, and like granite composed in the main of quartz, felspar, and mica.—**Gneissoid**, nīs'oid, *a.* Resembling gneiss: having the characteristics of gneiss. Also **Gneissic, Gneissose**, nīs'ik, nīs'ōs.

Gnome, nōm, *n.* [Gr. *gnome*, formed from Gr. *gnōmē*, intelligence; see next art.] An imaginary being, fabled to inhabit the inner parts of the earth, and to be the guardian of mines, quarries, &c.; a goblin; a small misshapen person.

Gnome, nōm, *n.* [Gr. *gnōmē*, a maxim, from stem of *gnōnai*, to know. KNOW.] A brief reflection or maxim; a saw; an aphorism. — **Gnomic, Gnomical**, nō'mik, nō'mi-kal, *a.* [Gr. *gnōmikos*.] Containing or dealing in maxims (the ancient Greek *gnomic* poets).

Gnomon, nō'mon, *n.* [Gr. *gnōmōn*, an index, from stem of *gnōnai*, to know; whence also *gnome*, *Gnostic*.] The style or pin of a sun-dial, which by its shadow shows the hour of the day; a style consisting of a pillar, pyramid, &c., erected perpendicularly to the horizon, in order to find the altitudes, declinations, &c., of the sun and stars; the index of the hour-circle of a globe.—**Gnomonic, Gnomonical**, nō-mon'ik, nō-mon'i-kal, *a.* Pertaining to the art of dialling; *bot.* bent at right angles. —*Gnomonic projection*, a projection of the surface of the sphere, in which the point of sight is taken at the centre of the sphere. —**Gnomonically**, nō-mon'i-kal-li, *adv.* In a gnomonical manner.—**Gnomonics**, nō-mon'iks, *n.* The art or science of dialling. —**Gnomonist**, nō'mon-ist, *n.* One versed in gnomonics.—**Gnomonology**, nō-mon-ol'o-ji, *n.* Dialling.

Gnostic, nos'tik, *n.* [L. *gnosticus*, Gr. *gnōstikos*, from stem of *gnōnai*, to know (akin L. *gnosco*, *nosco*, to know); cog. with E. *know*.] One of a sect that arose in the first ages of Christianity, who pretended to be the only men who had a true knowledge of the Christian religion, and professed a system of doctrines based partly on Christianity, partly on Greek and Oriental philosophy. — *a.* Pertaining to the Gnostics or their doctrines. — **Gnosticism**, nos'ti-sizm, *n.* The doctrines or principles of the Gnostics.

Gnu, Gnoo, nū, nö, *n.* [Hottentot *gnu* or *nju*.] A ruminant quadruped, partaking of the form of the antelope, ox, and horse, inhabiting South Africa.

Go, gō, *v.i.*—pret. *went*, pp. *gone*. [A.Sax. *gān*, *gangan*, O. and Prov.E. and Sc. *gang*, to go; Dan. *gaae*, D. *gaan*, G. *gehen*, Goth. *gaggan* (that is *gangan*)), Icel. *ganga*, O.H.G. *gangan*. *Went* though now used as the pret., is really the past tense of *wend*, A.Sax. *wendan*, to turn, to go.] To walk; to pass, proceed, move, or be in motion; to depart or move from a place: opposed to *come*; to have currency or use; to circulate (the story *goes*); to be reckoned or esteemed; to proceed or happen in a given manner; to have course; to turn out (the case *went* against him); to have recourse (to *go* to law); to be about to (in this usage a kind of auxiliary and usually in ppr.—*going* to say, *going* to begin); to be guided or regulated (to *go* by some rule); to be with young; to be pregnant; to be alienated, sold, or disposed of (it *went* for a trifle); to extend, reach, lead (this road *goes* to London); to extend in effect, meaning, or purport; to be of force or value; to proceed or tend toward a result or consequence; to contribute, conduce, concur (frequently with *to*, *towards*, &c.); to perish; to sink or die; to become (she has *gone* mad).—*To go about*, *naut.* to tack; to turn the head of a ship.—*To go about to*, to set one's self to; to take a circuitous way to.—*To go against*, to march to attack; to be in opposition; to be disagreeable.—*To go ahead*, to make rapid progress; to be enterprising. (*Colloq.*)—*To go between*, to interpose or mediate between; to attempt to reconcile.—*To go beyond*, to overreach.—*To go by*, to pass near and beyond (*by* being a prep.); to pass away unnoticed or disregarded (*by* adv.).—*To go down*, to descend; to come to nothing; to be received as true or correct.—*To go for nothing*, to have no value, weight, or efficacy. —*To go hard with*, to bring danger of a fatal issue to; to be all but ruinous for: used impersonally.—*To go in for*, to be in favour of; to make the object of acquirement or of attainment.—*To go in to* (*Scrip.*), to have sexual commerce with.—*To go off*, to leave a place; to die; to decease; to be discharged, as firearms; to explode; to be sold. —*To go on*, to proceed: to advance forward; to be put on, as a garment.—*To go out*, to issue forth; to go on an expedition; to become extinct, as light or life.—*To go over*, to read; to peruse; to examine; to view or review (*over* being the prep.); to change sides; to pass from one party to another (*over* adv.).—*To go through*, to pass or penetrate through; to accomplish; to perform thoroughly; to undergo; to sustain to the end.—*To go through with*, to execute effectually.—*To go upon*, to proceed as on a foundation; to take as a principle supposed or settled.—*To go with*, to accompany; to side with; to be in party or design with; to agree with; to suit.—*It goes ill* or *well with* a person, he has ill or good fortune.—*To go without*, to be or remain destitute.—*To go wrong*, to become unsound, as meat, fruit; to leave the paths of virtue; to take a wrong way.—*Go to!* come; move; begin; a phrase of exhortation; also a phrase of rebuke or reproof; tush; nonsense.—[In the following usages the verb may be construed as transitive.] To undertake (to *go* a journey, to *go* equal risks).—*To go one's way*, to set forth; to depart; to move on.—*To go an errand, to go a drive, to go circuit*, to go on an errand; to go upon or for a drive; to go upon circuit.—*n.* [As a noun the word is colloq. or slang.] The fashion or mode; a glass or other measure of liquor called in when drinking; stamina, bottom, or power of endurance; spirit; animation; fire.—*Great go, little go*, university cant terms for the examination for degrees and the previous or preliminary examination.—**Goer**, gō'ėr, *n.* One who or that which goes; one that has a gait good or bad: often applied to a horse, and to a watch or clock.—**Going**, gō'ing, *n.* The act of moving in any manner; departure; procedure; behavior, or course of life: chiefly in the *pl.*—*Goings-on*, actions; conduct: used mostly in a bad sense.—**Gone**, gon, *pp.* Passed; vanished away; consumed; finished; dead; lost or destroyed; worn out, exhausted, or overpowered.—**Go-ahead**, *a.* Characterized by or disposed to progress; enterprising. (*Colloq.*)—**Go-between**, *n.* An intermediary: often an agent in disreputable negotiations.—**Go-cart**, *n.* A framework on casters, to support children while learning to walk; a baby carriage with front wheels smaller than the rear.

Goad, gōd, *n.* [A.Sax. *gád*, a point of a weapon, a goad. GAD.] A pointed instrument used to stimulate a beast to move faster; hence, anything that urges or stimulates.—*v.t.* To drive with a goad; hence, to incite; to stimulate; to instigate; to urge forward.—**Goadsman, Goadster**, gōdz'man, gōd'stėr, *n.* One who drives oxen with a goad.

Goaf, gōf, *n.* [Comp. W. *gob*, a heap.] *Mining*, that part of a mine from which the mineral has been partially or wholly removed; also the waste or rubbish left behind. Called also *Gob.*

Goal, gōl, *n.* [Fr. *gaule*, a pole, a word of Germanic origin, from Goth. *walus*, Fris. *walu*, Icel. *völr*, staff, rod.] The point set to bound a race; the space between the two upright posts in the game of football; also the act of driving the ball through between the posts; the end to which a design tends, or which a person aims to reach or accomplish.

Goat, gōt, *n.* [A.Sax. *gát* = Icel. L.G., D., and Fris. *geit*, G. *geiss*, goat; cog. with L. *haedus*, a kid. A well-known horned ruminant quadruped, nearly of the size of a sheep, but stronger, less timid, and more agile.—**Goatee**, gō-tē', *n.* A beard that hangs down from the chin without whiskers.—**Goatherd**, gōt'hėrd, *n.* One whose occupation is to tend goats.—**Goatish**, gōt'ish, *a.* Resembling a goat in any quality, especially in smell or lustfulness.—**Goatishly**, gōt'ish-li, *adv.* In a goatish manner; lustfully.—**Goatishness**, gōt'ish-nes, *n.* The quality of being goatish; lustfulness.—**Goat-moth**, *n.* A large British moth, the larvæ of which, about three inches long, damage trees by hollowing out galleries in them.—**Goat-pepper**, *n.* A species of capsicum or Cayenne pepper.—**Goat's-beard**, *n.* The name of herbaceous perennials, one species of which (*salsify*) is cultivated in gardens for its root.

Gob, gob, *n.* A mass or lump; a sailor of the U. S. navy.

Gobang, gō-bang', *n.* A Japanese game played on a checker board.

Gob, gob, *n.* Same as *Goaf.*

Gobbet, gob'et, *n.* [Fr. *gobet*, from O.Fr. *gob*, a mouthful, from the Celtic=Gael. and Ir. *gob*, the mouth.] A mouthful; a morsel; a lump.—**Gobble**, gob'l, *v.t.*—*gobbled, gobbling.* [A freq. from Fr. *gober*, to swallow.] To swallow in large pieces; to swallow hastily.—*v.i.* To make a noise in the throat, as a turkey.—*n.* A noise made in the throat, as that of a turkey-cock.—**Gobbler**, gob'ler, *n.* One who gobbles.

Gobelin, gob'e-lin, *a.* [From the *Gobelins* establishment in Paris, where tapestry, &c., is made, named from, and originally belonging to a family of dyers called *Gobelin.*] A term applied to a species of rich tapestry, also to a printed worsted cloth for covering chairs, sofas, &c., in imitation of tapestry.

Goblet, gob'let, *n.* [Fr. *gobelet*, dim. of O.Fr. *gobel*, a drinking-glass, from L.L. *gobellus*, from L. *cupa*, a tub, a cask. CUP.] A kind of cup or drinking vessel without a handle.

Goblin, gob'lin, *n.* [Fr. *gobelin*, from L. *cobalus*, Gr. *kobalos*, a kind of malignant being or goblin; whence also G. *kobold.*] An evil or mischievous sprite; a gnome; an elf; a malicious fairy.—**Goblinry**, gob'lin-ri, *n.* The acts or practices of goblins.

Goby, gō'bi, *n.* [L. *gobius*, Gr. *kōbios*, the gudgeon.] A name given to various rather small fishes.

God, god, *n.* [A.Sax. *god* = D. *god*, Icel. *goth, guth*, Dan. and Sw. *gud*, Goth. *guth*, G. *gott*, God; root unknown; not connected with *good.*] A being conceived of as possessing divine power, and therefore to be propitiated by sacrifice, worship, and the like; a divinity; a deity; the Supreme Being; Jehovah; the eternal and infinite Spirit, the Creator, and the Sovereign of the universe (in this sense written or printed with a capital letter); any person or thing exalted too much in estimation, or deified and honoured as the chief good; *pl.* the audience in the upper gallery of a theatre: so called from their elevated position (*slang*).—**Godchild**, god'child, *n.* A godson or goddaughter. — **Goddaughter**, god'da-tėr, *n.* A female for whom one becomes sponsor at baptism. — **Goddess**, god'es, *n.* A female deity; a heathen deity of the female sex; a woman of superior charms or excellence.—**Godfather**, god'fä-THėr, *n.* In the *Anglican, R. Cath.*, and several other churches, a man who at the baptism of a child makes a profession of the Christian faith in its name, and guarantees its religious education; a male sponsor.—*v.t.* To act as godfather to; to take under one's fostering care. — **God-fearing**, *a.* A term applied to one who fears or reverences God.—**Godhead**, god'hed, *n.* [*God*, and suffix *-head*, same as *-hood.*] Godship; deity; divinity; divine nature or essence.—*The Godhead*, the Deity; God; the Supreme Being.—**Godhood**, god'hud, *n.* The state or quality of being a god; divinity.—**Godless**, god'les, *a.* Having or acknowledging no God; impious; ungodly; irreligious; wicked.—**Godlessly**, god'les-li, *adv.* In a godless manner.—**Godlessness**, god'les-nes, *n.* The state or quality of being godless.—**Godlike**, god'lik, *a.* Resembling a god or God; divine; of superior excellence. —**Godlikeness**, god'lik-nes, *n.* The state of being godlike.—**Godlily**, god'li-li, *adv.* In a godly manner; piously; righteously.—**Godliness**, god'li-nes, *n.* The condition or quality of being godly.—**Godly**, god'li, *a.* Pious; reverencing God and his character and laws; devout; religious; righteous; conformed to or influenced by God's law.—*adv.* Piously; righteously.—**Godmother**, god'muTH-ėr, *n.* A woman who becomes sponsor for a child in baptism.—**Godsend**, god'send, *n.* Something sent by God; an unlooked-for acquisition or piece of good fortune.—**Godship**, god'ship, *n.* Deity; divinity; the rank or character of a god.—**Godson**, god'sun, *n.* A male for whom one has been sponsor at baptism.—**God-speed**, god'spēd, *n.* [A contraction of 'I wish that *God* may *speed* you.'] Success; prosperity; a prosperous journey: usually in phrase *to bid* a person *god-speed.*—**Godward, Godwards**, god'wėrd, god'wėrdz, *adv.* Toward God.—**God's acre**, *n.* The churchyard.

Godetia, gō-dē'shi-a, *n.* [*Godet*, Swiss botanist.] A flowering hardy annual.

Godwit, god'wit, *n.* [A.Sax. *gód*, good, and *wiht*, creature, *wight*, from the excellence of their flesh.] A name of several grallatorial birds of no great size, the flesh of which is highly esteemed.

Goffer, gof'ėr, *v.t.* [GAUFFER.] To plait or flute; to gauffer.—**Goffer, Goffering**, gof'ėr, gof'ėr-ing, *n.* An ornamental plaiting, used for the frills and borders of women's caps, &c.

Goggle, gog'l, *v.i.* [Of Celtic origin; comp. W. *gogi*, to shake; Ir. *gog*, a nod, a motion; Gael. *gog*, a nod, *gogach*, nodding.] To strain or roll the eyes.—*a.* Full or prominent and rolling or staring: said of the eyes.—*n.* A strained or affected rolling of the eye; *pl.* A kind of spectacles with fixed plain glasses surrounded by leather for protecting the eyes from wind, debris, intense light.—Colored glasses (sun or beach) to protect the eyes from the glare of the sun.

Goiter, Goitre, goi'tėr, *n.* [Fr. *goître*, from L. *guttur*, the throat.] Bronchocele neck, a morbid enlargement of the thyroid gland, forming a tumor or protuberance sometimes of extraordinary size hanging down on the front part of the neck.—**Goitered, Goitred**, goi'tėrd, *a.* Affected with goiter.—**Goitrous**, goi'trus, *a.* Pertaining to goiter; affected with goiter.

Gold, gōld, *n.* [A.Sax. *gold* = D. *goud*, Sc. *gowd*, Sw. *guld*, Icel. *gull*, Goth. *gulth*; from root of *yellow.* Hence *gild.*] A precious metal of a bright yellow color, and the most ductile and malleable of all metals, and one of the heaviest; money; riches; wealth; a symbol of what is valuable or much prized; a bright yellow color, like that of the metal; *archery*, the exact center of the target, marked with gold, or of a gold color.—*a.* Made of gold; consisting of gold.—**Gold-beater**, *n.* One whose occupation is to beat gold into thin leaves for gilding.—*Gold-beater's skin*, the prepared outside membrane of the large intestine of the ox, used by gold-beaters to lay between the leaves of the metal while they beat it.—**Gold-crest**, *n.* The smallest British bird; the golden-crested wren.—**Gold-digger**, *n.* One who digs for gold; a woman whose relations with men are for selfish mercenary advantages.—**Gold-dust**, *n.* Gold in very fine particles.—**Golden**, gōl'dn, *a.* Made of gold; of the color or luster of gold; yellow; shining; splendid; excellent; most valuable; precious; happy; marked by the happiness of mankind; pre-eminently favorable or auspicious (a *golden* opportunity).—*Golden age*, an early period in the history of the human race, fabled to have been one of primeval innocence and enjoyment; any period of great brilliancy or prosperity.—*Golden balls*, the three gilt balls placed in front of a pawnbroker's place of business; the arms of Lombardy, and the bankers settled in Lombard Street.—*Golden bull*, the edict issued in 1356, at Nuremberg, regulating the special form for election to the Holy Roman Empire.—*Golden calf* (*Exodus*, xxxii), money and its worship.—*Golden fleece*, an order of knighthood, the *toison d'or;* the order of Flanders and Spain, commemorating the wool trade of the Flemish towns; in *Greek myth.* the fleece of gold in quest of which Jason undertook the Argonautic expedition.—*Golden Horn*, the inlet of the Bosporus, separating Pera and Stamboul at Constantinople.—*Golden legend*, a collection of lives and legends of saints in high repute in the middle ages.—*Golden-mouthed*, eloquent, applied to John *Chrysostom* of Antioch, A.D. 347-407.—*Golden number*, in *chron.* a number showing the year of the moon's cycle.—*Golden wedding*, the fiftieth anniversary of a marriage, the seventy-fifth being the diamond wedding.—**Golden-eye**, *n.* A species of duck; the garrot.—**Golden-pheasant**, *n.* A beautiful species of pheasant belonging to China.—**Golden-rod**, *n.* A name of certain composite plants with rod-like stems and terminal spikes or racemes of small yellow flowers.—**Gold-fever**, *n.* A mania for digging or otherwise searching for gold.—**Gold-field**, *n.* A district or region where gold is found.—**Goldfinch**, gōld'finsh, *n.* [A.Sax. *goldfinc.*] A songbird belonging to the finches, so named from the yellow markings on its wings.—**Goldfish, Golden-carp**, *n.* A species of carp, so named from its color, now largely bred in ponds, tanks, or glass vessels.—**Gold-lace**, *n.* A lace wrought with gold or gilt thread. —**Gold-leaf**, *n.* Gold beaten into an exceedingly thin sheet or leaf.—**Gold Plate**, *n.* Dishes, spoons, &c., of gold.—**Goldsmith**, gōld'smith, *n.* An artisan who manufactures vessels and ornaments of gold.—**Gold-stick**, *n.* A title given to colonels of the British Life Guards and to captains of the gentlemen-at-arms, from the gilt rods which they bear when attending the sovereign on state occasions —**Gold-thread**, *n.* A thread formed of flattened gold laid over a thread of silk by twisting it.—**Gold-washer**, *n.* One who or that which washes away the refuse from gold ore.

Golf, golf, *n.* [D. *kolf*, a club to drive balls with; Dan. and G. *kolbe*, a club.] A game played with clubs and balls, generally over large commons, downs, or links; the object being to drive the ball, with as few strokes as possible, into holes placed at considerable distances apart.—**Golfer**, gol'fėr, *n.* One who plays golf.

Golgotha, gol'go-tha, *n.* [Heb.] A charnel-house; scene of our Lord's crucifixion; the front row of the gallery in the Cambridge University Church, occupied by heads of houses, reputed brainless and 'a place of skulls' merely.

Gollywog, gol'i-wog, *n.* A black-faced, staring-eyed doll of hideous or whimsical appearance.

Golosh, gō-losh', *n.* GALOSH.

Gomphosis, gom-fō'sis, *n.* [Gr., from *gomphos*, a nail.] *Anat.* an immovable articulation, as in the insertion of the teeth in their sockets.

Gomuti, gō-mū'ti, *n.* The Malayan name for the sago-palm, which yields a bristly useful fibre resembling black horsehair, known by the same name.

Gonangium, go-nan'ji-um, *n.* [Gr. *gonos*, offspring, and *angeion*, a vessel.] Same as *Gonotheca*.

Gondola, gon'dō-la, *n.* [It.; origin unknown.] A flat-bottomed boat, very long and narrow, and having, towards the centre, a curtained chamber for the passengers, used chiefly at Venice.—**Gondolier**, gon-dō-lēr', *n.* A man who rows a gondola.

Gone, gon, pp. of *go*.

Gonfalon, **Gonfanon**, gon'fa-lon, gon'-fa-non, *n.* [Fr. *gonfalon*, O.Fr. *gonfanon*, from O.G. *guntfano*—*gunt*, a combat (= A. Sax. *gúth*), and *fano*, a banner.] An ensign or standard, the bearer of which in many of the medieval republican cities of Italy was often the chief personage in the state. —**Gonfalonier**, gon'fal-o-nēr'', *n.* One intrusted with a gonfalon; a chief magistrate in medieval Italian cities.

Gong, gong, *n.* [Malay.] A Chinese musical instrument of percussion, made of a mixed metal and shaped like a large round flat dish, used for making loud sonorous signals, for adding to the clangour of martial instruments, &c.—**Gong-metal**, *n.* An alloy consisting of about seventy-eight parts of copper and twenty-two of tin.

Gongylus, gon'ji-lus, *n.* [Gr. *gongylos*, round.] *Bot.* a spore of certain fungi; a reproductive body in certain sea-weeds.

Gonidia, go-nid'i-a, *n. pl.* [Gr. *gonē*, generation, and *eidos*, appearance.] *Bot.* the secondary, reproductive, green, spherical cells in the thallus of lichens.

Goniometer, gō-ni-om'et-ėr, *n.* [Gr. *gōnia*, angle, and *metron*, measure.] An instrument for measuring solid angles, particularly the angles formed by the faces of mineral crystals.—**Goniometric**, **Goniometrical**, gō'ni-o-met''rik, gō'ni-o-met''ri-kal, *a.* Pertaining to or determined by a goniometer.—**Goniometry**, gō-ni-om'et-ri, *n.* The art of measuring solid angles.

Gonoblastidia, gon'o-blas-tid''i-a, *n. pl.* [Gr. *gonos*, offspring, *blastidion*, dim. of *blastos*, a bud.] The processes which carry the gonophores in many hydrozoa.—**Gonocalyx**, gon-o-kā'liks, *n.* [Gr. *gonos*, a bud, and *kalyx*, a cup.] *Zool.* the swimming bell of the medusiform gonophore.

Gonophore, gon'o-fōr, *n.* [Gr. *gonos*, seed, and *phoreō*, to bear.] *Bot.* the short stalk which bears the stamens and carpels in some plants; *zool.* one of the generative buds or receptacles of the reproductive elements in the hydrozoa.

Gonorrhea, gon-o-rē'a, *n.* [Gr. *gonorrhoia*—*gonos*, semen, and *rheō*, to flow.] An inflammatory ailment of the male urethra or the female vagina, attended with secretion of mucus intermingled with pus.

Gonosome, gon'o-sōm, *n.* [Gr. *gonos*, offspring, and *sōma*, body.] *Zool.* a collective term for the reproductive zooids of a hydrozoon.

Gonotheca, gon-o-thē'ka, *n.* [Gr. *gonos*, offspring, and *thēkē*, a case.] *Zool.* the receptacle within which the gonophores of certain hydrozoa are produced.

Good, gųd, *a.* [A.Sax. *gód*, good = D. *goed*, Dan. and Sw. *god*, Icel. *gothr*, Goth. *gods*, G. *gut*; not connected with *god*.] The opposite of bad; conducive, in general, to any useful end or purpose; serviceable; advantageous; beneficial; wholesome; suitable; useful; fit; proper; right; possessing desirable or valuable physical or moral qualities; virtuous, righteous, dutiful, pious, or religious; excellent, valuable, precious; kind, benevolent, humane, merciful, or friendly; clever, skilful, or dexterous; adequate, sufficient, or competent; valid; of unimpaired credit; able to fulfil engagements; real, actual, serious (*good* earnest); considerable; more than a little; not deficient; full or complete; not blemished; unsullied; immaculate; honourable.—*Good Friday*, a fast of the Christian Church, in memory of our Saviour's crucifixion, kept on the Friday before Easter.—*In good time*, opportunely; not too soon nor too late; in proper time.—*To make good*, to perform; to fulfil; to verify or establish (an accusation); to supply deficiency in; to make up for defect; to maintain or carry out successfully.—*To stand good*, to be firm or valid.—*To think good, to see good*, to be pleased or satisfied; to think to be expedient.—*As good as his word*, equalling in fulfilment what was promised.—*n.* What is good, especially a result that is so (no *good* can come of it); what is serviceable, fit, excellent, kind, benevolent, or the like (to do *good*); benefit; advantage: opposed to *evil*, *ill*, *harm*, &c.; welfare or prosperity (the *good* of the state); a valuable possession or piece of property: almost always in the plural in this sense, and equivalent to wares, commodities, movables, household furniture, chattels, effects.—*For good, for good and all*, to close the whole business; for the last time; finally.—**Good-breeding**, *n.* Polite manners, formed by a good education.—**Good-bye**, **Good-by**, gųd-bī'. [Corruption of *God be with you*.] A form of salutation at parting; farewell.—**Good-cheap**. Equivalent of Fr. *bon-marché*, a bargain, as in *chap*, *chapman*, *chaffer*; then, by metathesis, *dog-cheap*, very cheap, *Obsolete*.—**Good Conduct Medal**, gųd kon'dukt med'al, *n.* A medal given to a soldier as a reward for 'long service with irreproachable character and conduct.'—**Good-day**, **Good-even**, **Good-evening**, **Good-morning**, **Good-morrow**, *n.* and *interj.* A kind wish or salutation at meeting or parting.—**Good-night**, *n.* and *interj.* A kind wish between persons parting for the night.—**Good-fellow**, *n.* A man esteemed for his companionable or social qualities; a good-natured pleasant person.—**Good-fellowship**, *n.* Merry society; companionableness; friendliness.—**Good-folk**, **Good-neighbors**, *n. pl.* A euphemism for fairies or elves.—**Good-for-nothing**, *n.* An idle, worthless, person.—*a.* Worthless.—**Good-humor**, *n.* A cheerful temper or state of mind. **Good-humored**, *a.* Characterized by good-humor.—**Good-humoredly**, *adv.* In a good-humored manner; in a cheerful way.—**Goodish**, gųd'ish, *a.* Pretty good; tolerable; fair.—**Good-lack**, gųd-lak', *interj.* [*Good*, and *lack*, a contraction from *lakin* or *ladykin*, a diminutive of *lady*, that is the Virgin Mary ('Our lady').] An exclamation implying wonder, surprise, or admiration.—**Goodliness**, gųd'li-nes, *n.* The quality of being goodly. —**Goodly**, gųd'li, *a.* Being of a handsome form; fair to look on; beautiful; graceful; well-favored; pleasant; agreeable; large; considerable.—**Goodman**, gųd'man, *n.* *Archaic*. A familiar appellation of civility; a husband; the head of a family.—**Goodwife**, gųd'wīf, *n.* The mistress of a household: correlative to *goodman*.—**Good-manners**, *n. pl.* Propriety of behaviour; politeness; decorum.—**Good-nature**, *n.* Natural mildness and kindness of disposition.—**Good-natured**, *a.* Having good-nature; naturally mild in temper.—**Good-naturedly**, *adv.* In a good-natured manner.—**Good-naturedness**, *n.* The quality of being good-natured.—**Goodness**, gųd'nes, *n.* The state or quality of being good; a euphemism for God (thank *Goodness*).—**Goods-engine**, *n.* A steam-engine for drawing a goods train, or one carrying goods, not passengers.—**Good-sense**, *n.* Soundness of understanding; good judgment.—**Good-tempered**, *a.* Having a good temper; not easily irritated or annoyed.—**Good-Templar**, *n.* [Name borrowed from the knights of the Temple.] —A member of a certain society established for the promotion of teetotal principles.—**Good-will**, *n.* Benevolence; kindly feelings; heartiness; earnestness; zeal; *com.* the custom of any trade or business; the right to take up a trade or business connection, purchased of one who gives it up.—**Goody**, gųd'i, *n.* [Probably contr. from *goodwife*, as *housewife*, *hussy*.] A term of civility applied to women in humble life.—**Goody**, gųd'i, **Goody-good**, **Goody-goody**, *a.* Affected with mawkish morality; excessively squeamish in morals.

Googing, **Goodgeon**, gųj'ing, gųd'jon, *n.* One of several clamps of iron or other metal, bolted on the stern-post of a vessel, whereon to hang the rudder.

Goor, gör, *n.* The Indian name for the concentrated juice or syrup of the date-palm.

Gooroo, gö'rö, *n.* [Skr. *guru*, a teacher.] A Hindu spiritual guide.

Goosander, gös'an-dėr, *n.* [Lit. goose-duck, from *goose*, and Icel. *andar*, genit. of *önd*, A.Sax. *ened*, a duck. DRAKE.] A swimming bird allied to the ducks and divers; the merganser. MERGANSER.

Goose, gös, *n.* pl. **Geese**, gēs. [A.Sax. *gós* (pl. *gés*, *gees*), a goose=Icel. *gás*, Dan. *gaas*, D. and G. *gans*, Rus. *gus*; cog. with L. *anser*, Gr. *chēn*, Skr. *hansa*; from a root meaning to gape, seen in E. *yawn*.] The name of several well-known swimming birds larger than ducks; a silly, stupid person, from the popular notion as to the stupidity of the goose; a tailor's smoothing-iron; a game formerly common in England, played with dice on a card divided into small compartments, on certain of which a goose was figured.—*To cook one's goose*, to do for one; to finish a person (*slang*).—*v.t.* To hiss out; to condemn by hissing. (*Slang.*) —**Goose-dubs**, *n.* The dirty pool or dubs in which geese swim about.—**Goose-flesh**, **Goose-skin**, *n.* A peculiar roughness of the human skin produced by cold, fear, and other depressing causes, as dyspepsia.—**Goose-grass**, *n.* A name given to two British plants.—**Goose-neck**, *n.* A pipe shaped like the letter S.—**Goose-quill**, *n.* The large feather or quill of a goose, or a pen made with it.—**Goosery**, gös'ėr-i, *n.* A place for geese; silliness or stupidity like that of the goose.—**Goose-step**, *n.* The act of a soldier marking time by raising the feet alternately without advancing; the stiff German parade step.

Gooseberry, gös'be-ri, *n.* [A corruption of *gossberry* for *gorseberry*, from prickles on the bush giving it a resemblance to gorse; or for *grose-berry*, from Fr. *groseille*, a gooseberry, from G. *krausbeere*, *kräuselbeere*, a gooseberry—*kraus*, frizzled, curled, crisp, and *beere*, a berry.] The fruit of a prickly shrub either red, yellow, or green in colour, and hairy or smooth on the surface, well-known and much esteemed; also the shrub itself; a small ball of barbed wire.

Gopher, gō'fėr, *n.* [Fr. *gaufre*, honeycomb.] The name given in America to several burrowing animals from their honeycombing the earth; also a species of burrowing tortoise of the Southern States.

Gopher-wood, gof'ėr, *n.* [Heb. *gopher*.]

A species of wood used in the construction of Noah's ark, perhaps cypress.

Goramy, Gourami, gō-ra-mī′, gö-ra-mī′, *n.* [Javanese name.] A peculiar species of nest-building fishes, natives of China and the Eastern Archipelago, but introduced into the West India Islands and elsewhere on account of the excellence of their flesh.

Gor-belly, gor′bel-li, *n.* [A.Sax. *gor*, dirt, dung, E. *gore*, and *belly*.] A prominent belly; a person having a big belly.—**Gor-bellied**, *a.* Big-bellied.—**Gor-cock**, gor′-kok, *n.* [From its red colour; or from *gorse*, furze.] The red grouse. — **Gor-hen**, *n.* The female of the red grouse.—**Gor-crow**, *n.* The common or carrion crow.

Gordian, gor′di-an, *a.* Pertaining to *Gordius*, king of Phrygia, or the knot tied by him, and which could not be untied, but which was ultimately cut by Alexander the Great; hence, the term *Gordian knot* is applied to any inextricable difficulty; and to *cut the Gordian knot* is to remove a difficulty by bold or unusual measures.

Gore, gōr, *n.* [A.Sax. *gor*, gore, filth, Icel. and Dan. *gor*, Sw. *gorr*.] Blood that is shed; thick or clotted blood.—**Gory**, gō′ri, *a.* Covered with gore; bloody.

Gore, gōr, *n.* [A.Sax. *gára*, a point or corner of land, from *gár*, a spear; like Icel. *geiri*, a triangular piece, from *geirr*, a spear.] A triangular-shaped piece, as of cloth, let into or regarded as let into a larger piece; a gusset.—*v.t.* To cut a gore in; to piece with a gore.

Gore, gōr, *v.t.*—*gored, goring.* [Directly from A.Sax. *gár*, a spear or dart; Icel. *geirr*.] To stab; to pierce with a pointed instrument, as a spear, or with the horns (as an ox).

Gorge, gorj, *n.* [Fr. *gorge*, from It. *gorgia*, L. *gurges*, a whirlpool; akin *gargle, gurgle*, &c.] The throat or gullet; that which is swallowed; food caused to regurgitate through nausea or disgust; a narrow passage between hills or mountains; the entrance into a bastion or other outwork of a fort; *arch.* the narrowest part of the Tuscan and Doric capital; also, a cavetto. —*v.t.* — *gorged, gorging.* To swallow, especially with greediness or in large quantities; to fill the stomach of; to satiate: often *refl.*—*v.i.* To feed greedily; to stuff one's self.

Gorgeous, gor′jus, *a.* [O.Fr. *gorgias*, gaudy, flaunting, from *gorgias*, a ruff for the neck, from *gorge*, the throat (which see).] Exceedingly showy; splendid; magnificent; glittering with gay colours.—**Gorgeously**, gor′jus-li, *adv.* In a gorgeous manner.—**Gorgeousness**, gor′jus-nes, *n.*

Gorget, gor′jet, *n.* [Fr. *gorgette*, from *gorge*, the throat. GORGE.] A piece of armour for defending the throat or neck; a small crescent-shaped metallic ornament formerly worn by officers on the breast.

Gorgon, gor′gon, *n.* [Gr. *gorgō, gorgōn*, from *gorgos*, fierce, grim.] *Greek myth.* one of several monsters of terrific aspect, the sight of which turned the beholder to stone; hence, some one like a gorgon.—*a.* Very ugly or terrific.—**Gorgonean, Gorgonian**, gor-gō′nē-an, gor-gō′ni-an, *a.* Like a gorgon; pertaining to gorgons. — **Gorgonize**, gor′gon-īz, *v.t.* To turn into stone; to petrify.

Gorgonzola, gor-gon-zō′la, *n.* A kind of Italian ewe-milk cheese made at Gorgonzola, a village near Milan.

Gorilla, go-ril′la, *n.* [Originally an African name, found in use by the Phoenician navigator Hanno in the fifth century B.C.] The largest of the apes, very strong and fierce, found chiefly in the woody equatorial regions of Africa, living mostly on trees, and feeding on vegetable substances.

Gormand, gor′mand, *n.* [Fr. *gourmand*.] A gourmand.—**Gormandism**, gor′man-dizm, *n.* Gluttony.—**Gormandize, Gormandise**, gor′man-dīz, *v.i.*—*gormandized, gormandizing.* To eat greedily; to swallow voraciously.—**Gormandizer**, gor′man-dī-zėr, *n.* A voracious eater.

Gorse, gors, *n.* [A.Sax. *gorst, gost*, furze; connections doubtful.] The common furze or whin.—**Gorsy**, gor′si, *a.* Abounding in gorse; resembling gorse.

Goshawk, gos′hąk, *n.* [A.Sax. *gôshafoc*, goose-hawk—so called from being flown at geese.] A kind of large hawk, formerly much used in falconry.

Gosling, goz′ling, *n.* [A.Sax. *gôs*, goose, and the dim. term. *-ling*.] A young goose; a kind of catkin.

Gospel, gos′pel, *n.* [A.Sax. *godspell*—*gôd*, good, and *spell*, history, narration—answering to the Gr. *euangelion*, L. *evangelium*; a good or joyful message, evangel; or compounded of A.Sax. *god*, God, and *spell*—lit. God's word.] The history of Jesus Christ: any of the four records of Christ's life left by his apostles; the whole scheme of salvation as revealed by Christ and his apostles; system of gospel doctrine or of religious truth; any general doctrine (a political *gospel*); some portion of one of the four gospels appointed to be read in the service of the Anglican Church.—*a.* Accordant with the gospel; relating to the gospel; evangelical. —**Gospelize**,† gos′pel-īz, *v.t.* To instruct in the gospel; to evangelize. — **Gospeler**, gos′pel-ėr, *n.* An evangelist; the priest or minister who reads the gospel in the church service.

Gossamer, gos′a-mėr, *n.* [A name apparently applied originally to the period at which gossamer is commonly observed, and equivalent to *goose-summer*, the term having perhaps arisen from geese being then driven out to the stubble and from their well-known connection with Michaelmas; comp. the German names for gossamer, 'our lady's summer', 'flying summer', 'old wives' summer'.] A fine filmy substance, a kind of delicate cobwebs, floating in the air in calm clear weather, especially in autumn, formed by small species of spiders.—**Gossamery**, gos′a-mėr-i, *a.* Like gossamer; flimsy; unsubstantial.

Gossan, gos′an, *n.* *Mining*, an oxide of iron and quartz, a sure indication of ore at greater depth.—**Gossaniferous**, gos-an-if′ėr-us, *a.* Containing gossan.

Gossip, gos′sip, *n.* [From *God* and prov. E. *sib*, relation, related, lit. related in the service of God.] A godfather or godmother‡; a friend or neighbour; an intimate companion; an idle tattler or carrier of tales; mere tattle; groundless rumour.—*v.i.* To prate; to chat; to tell idle tales. —**Gossiper**, gos′sip-ėr, *n.* One who gossips; a gossip.—**Gossipry**, gos′sip-ri, *n.* Relationship by baptismal rites; sponsorship; idle talk or gossip.—**Gossipy**, gos′-sip-i, *a.* Full of gossip.

Gossomer, gos′o-mėr. GOSSAMER.

Got, got, pret. of *get*.—**Got, Gotten**, got′n, pp. of *get*.

Goth, goth, *n.* [L. *Gothi*, Goths.] One of an ancient Teutonic race of people. first heard of as inhabiting the shores of the Baltic, and who afterwards overran and took an important part in subverting the Roman empire; a barbarian; a rude ignorant person; one defective in taste.—**Gothic**, goth′ik, *a.* Pertaining to the Goths; rude; barbarous; the term applied to that style of architecture the characteristic feature of which is the pointed arch and the subserviency of the other parts to this feature: originally used in a depreciatory sense. — *n.* The language of the Goths; *printing*, the name of a bold-faced type, used for titling and jobbing work; the Gothic style or order of architecture. — **Gothicism**, goth′i-sizm, *n.* A Gothic idiom; conformity to the Gothic style of architecture; rudeness of manners; barbarousness. — **Gothicize**, goth′i-sīz, *v.t.* — *Gothicized, Gothicizing.* To make Gothic; to bring back to barbarism. — **Gothish**, goth′ish, *a.* Gothic.

Gothamist, Gothamite, gō′tham-ist, gō′tham-īt, *n.* A person deficient in wisdom, so called from *Gotham*, in Nottinghamshire, noted for some pleasant blunders; a term sportively applied to the inhabitants of New York.

Gouache, gwäsh, *n.* [Fr.] A method of painting in water colours so mixed as to present a dead opaque surface.

Gouda, gou′da, *a.* A kind of cheese from *Gouda*, a town in Holland.

Gouge, gouj, *n.* [Fr. *gouge*, LL. *guvia*, a gouge; origin uncertain.] A chisel with a hollow or grooved blade, used to cut holes, channels, or grooves.—*v.t.*—*gouged, gouging.* To scoop out or turn with or as with a gouge.—**Gouge-bit**, *n.* A bit, in the form of a gouge, for boring wood.

Goura, gou′ra, *n.* [Native name.] The name of pigeons with a large crest inhabiting New Guinea.

Gourd, gōrd, *n.* [Fr. *gourde*, O.Fr. *gouorde*, *gougorde*, from L. *cucurbita*, a gourd.] The popular name of the family of plants represented by the melon, cucumber, pumpkin, vegetable marrow, &c., or for their fruits. —**Gourd-tree**, *n.* A tropical American tree which produces globular or oval gourd-like fruits, the hardy woody shell of which is applied to many useful purposes. — **Gourdy**, gōr′di or gör′di, *a.* Swelled in the legs: said of a horse. — **Gourdiness**, *n.* The condition or quality of being gourdy.

Gourmand, gör′mänd, *n.* [Fr., of Celtic origin; comp. W. *gormant*, that which tends to overfill; *gormodd*, excess, from *gor*, excess.] A glutton; a greedy feeder; a dainty feeder; an epicure; a gourmet.—**Gourmandize**, gör′man-dīz, *v.i.* To gormandize.

Gourmet, gör-mā or gör′met, *n.* [Fr., a wine-taster, for *groumet*, from the O.D. word = E. *groom*.] A man of keen palate; a connoisseur in wines and meats; a nice feeder; an epicure.

Gout, gout, *n.* [Fr. *goutte*, L. *gutta*, a drop, from the old medical theory that diseases were due to the deposition of drops of morbid humour in the part.] A disease giving rise to paroxysms of acute pain with inflammation, affecting the small joints, and generally the first joint of the great toe, and often accompanied by calculi or concretions at the joints; a drop; a clot or coagulation (*Shak.*).—**Goutily**, gout′i-li, *adv.* In a gouty manner.—**Goutiness**, gout′i-nes, *n.* The state of being gouty; gouty affections.—**Goutish**, gout′ish, *a.* Having a predisposition to gout; gouty.—**Gouty**, gout′i, *a.* Diseased with or subject to the gout; pertaining to the gout.—**Goutwort, Goutweed**, gout′wėrt, gout′wēd, *n.* An umbelliferous British plant which was formerly believed to be a specific for gout; ache-weed.

Goût, gö, *n.* [Fr. *goût*, from L. *gustus*, taste.] Taste; relish.

Govern, guv′ėrn, *v.t.* [Fr. *gouverner*, from L. *gubernare*, to govern, a form of Gr. *kybernaō*, to govern.] To direct and control; to regulate by authority; to keep within the limits prescribed by law or sovereign will; to influence; to direct; to restrain; to keep in due subjection; to steer or regulate the course of; *gram.* to cause to be in a particular case, or to require a particular case. —*v.i.* To exercise authority; to administer the laws; to maintain the superiority; to have the control.—**Governable**, guv′ėr-na-bl, *a.* Capable of being governed; submissive to law or rule. — **Governableness**, guv′ėr-na-bl-nes, *n.* State or quality of being governable.—**Governance**, guv′-ėr-nans, *n.* Government; exercise of authority; control; management.—**Governess**, guv′ėr-nes, *n.* A female that governs; a lady who has the care of educating or teaching children in their homes.—**Governing**, guv′ėr-ning, *p.* and *a.* Serving to govern; directing; controlling.—**Government**, guv′ėrn-ment, *n.* The act of governing; regulation; control; restraint; the exercise of authority; direction and restraint exercised over the actions of men in communities, societies, or states; the administration of public affairs; the system of polity in a state; the mode or system according to which the sovereign powers of a nation, the legislative, executive, and judicial powers, are vested and exercised;

a body politic governed by one authority; a province or division of territory ruled by a governor; the persons or council who administer the laws of a kingdom or state; the administration; the executive power; *gram.* the influence of a word in regard to construction.—**Governmental**, guv'ėrn-men-tal, *a.* Pertaining to government; made by government.—**Governor**, guv'-ėr-nėr, *n.* One who governs; the supreme executive magistrate of a state, community, corporation, &c.; a tutor to a boy at home; a contrivance in mills and machinery for maintaining a uniform velocity with a varying resistance; a contrivance in a steam-engine which automatically regulates the admission of steam to the cylinder.—**Governor-general**, *n.* A governor who has under him subordinate or deputy-governors; a viceroy.—**Governorship**, guv'ėr-nėr-ship, *n.* The office of a governor.

Gowan, gou'an, *n.* [From *gollan*, a local name for similar yellow flowers; akin to *gold.*] The Scotch name for the daisy.

Gown, goun, *n.* [O.Fr. *goune*, L.L. *gunna*, furred robe, fur.] A woman's outer garment; a dress; a dressing gown or a night-gown; the official dress worn by members of certain professions, as divinity, medicine, law, by magistrates, university professors and students, &c.; sometimes used as the emblem of civil life, as the sword of military. 'Gowns not arms' (*Milton*, Sonnets, xvii); collectively, the students of a university or college (the town and *gown*). —*v.t. Gowned, gowning.* To put a gown on; to clothe or dress in a gown.—*v.i.* To put on a gown; to wear a gown or robe.—**Gownsman**, gounz'man, *n.* One whose professional habit is a gown, as a lawyer, professor, or student of a university.

Graafian, grä'fi-an, *a.* [From Regnier de *Graaf*, a Dutch physician.] Applied to certain vesicles developed in the ovaries of mammals for the special purpose of expelling the ovum.

Graal, grāl, *n.* Same as *Grail.*

Grab, grab, *v.t.—grabbed, grabbing.* [Sw. *grabba*, to grasp; D. *grabbelen*, to snatch; akin *grapple, gripe, graip, grope*, &c.] To seize; to snatch; to gripe suddenly. (*Colloq.*)—*n.* A sudden grasp or seizure; a catch; an advantage (*colloq.*); an implement for clutching objects.—**Grabber**, grab'ėr, *n.* One who or that which grabs.

Grace, grās, *n.* [Fr., from L. *gratia*, favour, from *gratus*, pleasant (seen also in *grateful, gratitude, agree, ingrate*, &c.); from a root seen in Gr. *chairō*, to rejoice, Gael. *gradh*, love, and E. *yearn.*] Favour, good-will, or kindness; disposition to oblige another; the love and favour of God; divine influence renewing the heart and restraining from sin; a state of reconciliation to God; virtuous or religious affection or disposition proceeding from divine influence; mercy; pardon; favour conferred; a license, dispensation, or peculiar privilege; a short prayer before or after meals acknowledging the grace or goodness of God; (with possessive pronouns) a title used in addressing or speaking of a duke or duchess; that external element in acting or speaking which renders it appropriate and agreeable; elegance with appropriate dignity; a beauty or element in what pleases the eye; an embellishment; an affectation of elegance, dignity, or refinement (a person's airs and *graces*); dispensation by university authorities to take a degree; *Greek myth.* beauty or elegance deified; one of three goddesses in whose gift were grace, loveliness, and favour; *mus.* a turn, trill, shake, &c., introduced for embellishment.—*Days of grace, com.* three days immediately following the day when a bill becomes due, which days are allowed to the debtor or payer to make payment in. — *A person's good graces*, a person's favour or friendly regard.—*With a good grace*, graciously; with at least an air of graciousness. — *With a bad grace*, ungracefully; ungraciously.—*v.t.—graced, gracing.* To lend or add grace to; to adorn; to serve to embellish or dignify; to honour. —**Grace-cup**, *n.* A final parting cup, after grace has been said.—**Graced**, grāst, *a.* Endowed with grace; beautiful; graceful; favoured; honoured. — **Graceful**, grās'fụl, *a.* Displaying grace in form or action; possessing a peculiar elegance or attraction in mien or appearance: used particularly of motion, looks, and speech.—**Gracefully**, grās'fụl-li, *adv.* In a graceful manner.—**Gracefulness**, grās'fụl-nes, *n.* The condition or quality of being graceful. — **Graceless**, grās'les, *a.* Void of grace; somewhat careless in regard to religious matters; not at all devout; unregenerate; unsanctified. — **Gracelessly**, grās'les-li, *adv.* In a graceless manner.—**Gracelessness**, grās'les-nes, *n.*—**Grace-note**, *n. Mus.* a note added by way of ornament, and printed or written in smaller characters; an appoggiatura.—**Gracious**, grā'shus, *a.* [Fr. *gracieux*, L. *gratiosus.*] Favourable; benevolent; merciful; benign; kind; friendly; proceeding from, produced by, or associated with divine grace; virtuous; good.—**Graciously**, grā'shus-li, *adv.* In a gracious manner.—**Graciousness**, grā'shus-nes, *n.*

Gracile,† gras'il, *a.* [L. *gracilis*, slender.] Slender.—**Gracility**, gra-sil'i-ti, *n.* Slenderness.

Grackle, grak'l, *n.* [L. *graculus*, a jackdaw, imitative of the cry.] Any of various birds of Asia and Africa of the starling family; any of certain blackbirds of the U. S., as the purple grackle.

Grade, grād, *n.* [Fr. *grade*, from L. *gradus*, a step, from *gradior, gressus*, to go, seen also in *congress, degrade, degree, egress, ingredient, progress, retrograde*, &c.] A degree in any series, rank, or order, relative position or standing; one of the sections of a school system, as divided into years of work; the group of pupils in one of these sections; a mark rating a pupil's work; the rate of ascent or descent; the part of a road which slopes.—*v.t.—graded, grading.* To arrange in order according to size, quality, rank, degree of advancement, and the like; to reduce (the line of a railway, &c.) to such levels or degrees of inclination as may make it suitable for being used.—**Gradation**, gra-dā'shon, *n.* [L. *gradatio.*] The act of grading; the state of being graded; arrangement by grades or ranks; a regular advance from step to step; a degree or relative position in any order or series; the gradual blending of one tint into another.—**Gradational**, gra-dā'shon-al, *a.* Of or pertaining to, or according to gradation.—**Gradatory**, grā'da-to-ri, *a.* Proceeding step by step; marking gradation. —*n. Eccles. arch.* a series of steps leading from the cloisters into the church.—**Gradient**, grā'di-ent, *a.* [L. *gradiens, gradientis*, ppr. of *gradior.*] Moving by steps†; walking†; rising or descending by regular degrees of inclination.—*n.* The degree of slope or inclination of the ground over which a railway, road, or canal passes; the rate of ascent or descent; the part of a road which slopes.—**Gradual**, grad'ū-al, *a.* [Fr *graduel.*] Proceeding by steps or degrees; advancing step by step; regular and slow; progressive.—*n.* An ancient service-book of the church: also called *Grail*; song sung between epistle and Gospel at the steps of the altar.—**Gradually**, grad'ū-al-li, *adv.* In a gradual manner; by degrees; step by step, regularly. — **Graduate**, grad'ū-āt, *v.t.—graduated, graduating.* [Fr. *graduer*, from L. *gradus.*] To mark with degrees, regular intervals, or divisions; to divide into small regular distances (to *graduate* a thermometer); to temper or modify by degrees; to characterize or mark with degrees or grades, as of intensity; to confer a university degree on; to reduce to a certain consistency by evaporation. —*v.i.* To receive a degree from a college or university; to pass by degrees; to change gradually; to shade off.—*n.* One who has been admitted to a degree in a college or university, or by some incorporated society; a vessel with graduated measurement marks.—*a.* Arranged by successive steps or degrees.—**Graduation**, grad-ū-ā'shon, *n.* The act of graduating, or state of being graduated; the marks or lines made on an instrument to indicate degrees or other divisions.—**Graduator**, grad'ū-ā-tėr, *n.* One who or that which graduates; an instrument for graduating; a contrivance for accelerating evaporation.

Graffiti, grä-fē'tē, *n. pl.* [Pl. of It. *graffito*, a scribbling, from *graffiare*, to scribble.] A class of rude scribblings or figures on the walls of Pompeii, the Catacombs, &c., dating from ancient Roman times.

Graft, graft, *n.* [O.Fr. *graffe*, Fr. *greffe*, a slip or shoot of a tree for grafting, originally a pointed instrument, from L. *graphium*, a style for writing on waxen tablets, from Gr. *graphō*, to write.] A small shoot or scion of a tree, inserted in another tree and becoming part of it, but retaining the characters of its own parent; *surg.* living tissue implanted, as in a lesion, to become an organic part; the act of grafting; corrupt gains or practices in politics.—*v.t.* To insert a graft on; to propagate by a graft; to incorporate after the manner of a graft. —*v.i.* To practice grafting or engage in corrupt but profitable pursuits.—**Grafter**, graf'tėr, *n.* One who grafts; one who gains money or material profit by graft.

Graham flour, grā'am, wheat flour made from the whole kernel.

Graham's Law, grāmz, *n.* The law that gases diffuse through porous membranes at a rate inversely proportional to the square root of their density.

Grail, Graal, grāl, *n.* [O.Fr. *graal, greal*, L.L. *gradalis, gradale*, &c.; perhaps from *cratella*, dim. of L. *crater*, Gr. *kratēr*, a cup.] The holy vessel said to have been brought to England by Joseph of Arimathea, who had caught the last drops of Christ's blood in it, and which being afterwards lost the search for it became the great work of King Arthur's Knights. For another *Grail* see under GRADE.

Grain, grān, *n.* [Fr. *grain*, from L. *granum*, a grain, seed, kernel. Of same origin are *granite, grange, garner*, &c.] A single seed of a plant, particularly of those plants whose seeds are used for food of man or beast; used collectively for edible seeds in general, or the fruits of cereal plants, as wheat, rye, oats, &c., as also for the plants themselves; *pl.* the husks or remains of grain used in brewing or distilling; any small hard particle, as of sand, sugar, salt, &c.; a minute particle; a small amount (not a *grain* of sense); the twentieth part of the scruple in apothecaries' weight, and the twenty-fourth part of a pennyweight troy; the substance of a thing regarded with respect to the size, form, or direction of the constituent particles; the fibres of wood or other fibrous substance, with regard to their arrangement or direction; texture (stone or wood of a fine *grain*); formerly the scarlet dye made from the kermes or cochineal insects, from their round, seed-like form; hence, a red-coloured dye; also, a permanent colour of any kind.—*To dye in grain*, originally, to dye with kermes; then, to dye deeply or permanently; now usually to dye in the fibre or raw material.—*Grain side of leather*, the side from which the hair has been removed. — *Against the grain*, against the fibres of wood; hence, against the natural temper; unwillingly; unpleasantly; reluctantly.—*Grains of Paradise*, the pungent, somewhat aromatic seeds of a plant of the ginger family, a native of tropical Western Africa.—*v.t.* To form into grains, as powder, sugar, and the like; to paint so as to give the appearance of grains or fibres; *tan.* to give a granular appearance to the surface; to prepare the hairy side as the outer side.—*v.i.* To form grains or to assume a granular form, as the result of crystallization.—**Grained**, grānd, *p.* and *a.* Having a certain grain or texture; having a granular surface (*grained* leather).—**Grainer**, grā'-nėr, *n.* One who or that which grains; a peculiar brush or a toothed instrument used by painters.—**Grainy**, grā'ni. *n.* Full of grains or corn; full of kernels.—**Grain-leather**, *n.* A name for leather blacked on the grain side for shoes, boots, &c.—

Grain-mill, *n.* A mill for grinding grain; a grist-mill.—**Grain-moth**, *n.* A minute moth whose larvæ devour grain in granaries.—**Granary**, gran′a-ri, *n.* [L. *granarium*, from *granum*.] A storehouse for grain after it is threshed.—**Graniferous**, gra-nif′ér-us, *a.* [L. *granum*, and *fero*, to bear.] Bearing grain or seeds like grain.—**Graniform**, gran′i-form, *a.* *Bot.* formed like grains of corn.—**Granivorous**, gra-niv′ō-rus, *a.* [L. *granum*, and *voro*, to eat.] Eating grain; feeding or subsisting on seeds.

Grain, grān, *n.* [Same word as Dan. *green*, a branch, a prong; Icel. *grein*, a branch; akin *groin*.] A tine, prong, or spike; *pl.* a kind of harpoon with four or more barbed points.

Graip, grāp, *n.* [Same as D. *greep*, Dan. *greb*, a dung-fork; akin to *gripe*, *grope*.] A dung-fork or fork for digging potatoes.

Graith, grāth, *n.* [Icel. *greithi*, preparation, equipment, *greithr*, ready; A.Sax. *geræde*, trappings; from stem of *ready*, with particle *ge-* prefixed.] Apparatus, equipments, implements, or accoutrements.

Grallatores; Grallæ, gral-a-tō′rēz, gral′ē, *n. pl.* [L. *grallæ*, stilts, *grallator* (pl. *grallatores*), one who goes on stilts, from *gradior*, to go. GRADE.] An order of birds generally characterized by very long legs, long necks, and long bills, including the cranes, plovers, snipes, rails, coots, &c., &c.; the waders.—**Grallatorial**, gral-a-tō′ri-al, *a.* Pertaining to the Grallatores.

Gram, gram, *n.* The name of a chickpea extensively cultivated in the East Indies, and used as food and fodder.

Gram, Gramme, *n.* [Fr., from Gr. *gramma*, a letter, also the weight of a scruple, from *graphō*, to write.] The unit of weight in the metric system equivalent to a cubic centimeter of water, or equal to 15.432 grains.

Gramercy, *n.* Exclamation for *grand merci*, God give you great reward; as *good-bye*, God be with you.

Gramineous, Gramineal, Graminaceous, gra-min′ē-us, gra-min′ē-al, gram-i-nā′shus, *a.* [L. *gramineus*, from *gramen*, *graminis*, grass.] Like or pertaining to grass or to the tribe of grasses.—**Graminifolious**, gram′i-ni-fō″li-us, *a.* [L. *folium*, a leaf.] *Bot* having leaves resembling those of grass.—**Graminivorous**, gram-i-niv′ō-rus, *a.* [L. *voro*, to eat.] Feeding or subsisting on grass, as oxen, &c.

Grammar, gram′mar, *n.* [Fr. *grammaire*, from a hypothetical L.L. form *grammaria*, from Gr. *gramma*, a letter, from *graphō*, to write (whence *graphic*, &c.). GRAVE, *v.t.*] The exposition of the principles which underlie the use of language; a system of general principles and of particular rules for speaking or writing a language; a book containing such principles and rules; language as regulated by rules or usage; propriety of speech (to violate *grammar*; *good* grammar, *bad* grammar, correct or incorrect language); a treatise on the elements or principles of any science; an outline of the principles of any subject.—*a.* Belonging to or contained in grammar.—**Grammarian**, gram-mā′ri-an, *n.* One versed in grammar.—**Grammatical, Grammatic**, gram-mat′i-kal, gram-mat′ik, *a.* Belonging to grammar; according to the rules of grammar.—**Grammatically**, gram-mat′i-kal-li, *adv.* In a grammatical manner; according to the rules of grammar.—**Grammaticism**, gram-mat′i-sizm, *n.* A point of grammar.—**Grammaticize**, gram-mat′i-sīz, *v.t.* To render grammatical.—**Grammar-school**, *n.* A grade school; a school including the intermediate grades between the primary grades and high school; a school in which Latin and Greek are more especially taught.—**Grammatist**, gram′a-tist, *n.* One versed in grammar; especially a pedantic grammarian.

Gramophone, gram′o-fōn, *n.* [Gr. *gramma*, letter, *phōnē*, sound.] An early form of phonograph.

Grampus, gram′pus, *n.* [Sp. *gran pez*, from L. *grandis*, great, and *piscis*, a fish; comp. *porpoise*, *porpus*.] A marine mammal of the dolphin family, which grows to the length of 25 feet, and preys on fish; in secondary sense, a person who snores.

Granadilla, gran-a-dil′la, *n.* [Sp., dim. of *granada*, a pomegranate.] The fruit of a species of passion-flower much esteemed in tropical countries; also the plant.

Granary. Under GRAIN.

Grand, grand, *a.* [Fr. *grand*, from L. *grandis*, great, grand, seen also in *aggrandize*.] Great; illustrious; high in power or dignity; noble; splendid; magnificent; principal or chief: used largely in composition (*grand*-juror, *grand*-master); conceived or expressed with great dignity; implying an additional or second generation, as in *grand*father, *grand*child, &c.—**Grandam**, gran′dam, *n.* [*Grand* and *dame*.] An old woman; a grandmother.—**Grand Army of the Republic**, an organization of soldiers and sailors of the Civil War.—**Grandaunt**, *n.* The aunt of one's father or mother.—**Grandchild**, grand′child, *n.* A son's or daughter's child or offspring.—**Granddaughter**, grand′-da-tėr, *n.* The daughter of a son or daughter.—**Grandfather**, grand′fä-THėr, *n.* A father's or mother's father.—**Grandmother**, grand′muTH-ėr, *n.* A father's or mother's mother.—**Grandnephew**, *n.* The grandson of a brother or sister.—**Grandniece**, *n.* The granddaughter of a brother or sister.—**Grandparent**, grand′-pā-rent, *n.* The parent of a parent.—**Grandsire**, grand′sīr, *n.* A grandfather; any ancestor preceding a father.—**Grandson**, grand′sun, *n.* The son of a son or daughter.—**Granduncle**, *n.* The uncle of one's father or mother.—**Grand duke**, the title of former sovereigns of certain German states; also applied to members of the former imperial family of Russia.—**Grandee**, gran-dē′, *n.* [Sp. *grande*, a nobleman.] A Spanish nobleman of the first rank; hence a nobleman or man of high rank in general.—**Grandeur**, grand′yėr, *a.* [Fr.] The state or quality of being grand.—**Grandiloquence**, gran-dil′o-kwens, *n.* The quality of being grandiloquent.—**Grandiloquent**, gran-dil′o-kwent, *a.* [L. *grandiloquens*—*grandis*, and *loquor*, to speak.] Speaking in a lofty style; expressed in high-sounding words; bombastic; pompous.—**Grandiose**, gran′di-ōs, *a.* [Fr.] Impressive from inherent grandeur; imposing; commonly, aiming at or affecting grandeur; grandiloquent; bombastic; turgid.—**Grandiosity**, gran-di-os′i-ti, *n.* The quality of being grandiose.—**Grand jury**, a jury whose duty is to examine into the grounds of accusation against offenders, and if they see just cause, to find a true bill against them.—**Grandly**, grand′li, *adv.* In a grand or lofty manner.—**Grandness**, grand′nes, *n.* Grandeur; greatness with beauty; magnificence.—**Grand opera**, opera that compares with serious drama in characterization and plot and has a completely sung text.—**Grand piano**, a large kind of piano, of great compass and strength, usually flat instead of upright.—**Grandstand**, *n.* An elevated system of seats arranged one row above another at a racecourse or athletic field, usually with a roof, whence a good view can be obtained. —**Grand vizier**, the chief minister of the former Turkish Empire.

Grange, grānj, *n.* [Fr. *grange*, a barn, from L.L. *granea*, *granica*, a barn, from L. *granum*, grain. GRAIN.] A farm, with the dwelling-house, stables, barns, &c.; one of the local lodges of the secret farmers' organization called "The Patrons of Husbandry." Nationally, the Grange dates from 1867, and includes both men and women. Its social, fraternal, and educational aims were later expanded to become an effective influence in political and legislative matters, both state and national, in the interest of the farm population.

Graniferous. Under GRAIN.

Granite, gran′it, *n.* [Fr. *granit*, from It. *granito*, lit. grained stone, from L. *granum*, a grain. GRAIN.] An unstratified rock, one of the most abundant in the earth's crust, composed generally of grains or crystals of quartz, felspar, and mica, united without regular arrangement.—**Granitic, Granitical**, gra-nit′ik, gra-nit′i-kal, *a.* Of or pertaining to granite; having the nature of granite; consisting of granite.—**Granitification**, gra-nit′i-fi-kā″shon, *n.* The process of being formed into granite.—**Granitiform**, gra-nit′i-form, *a.* Resembling granite in structure.—**Granitify**, gra-nit′i-fī, *v.t.* To form into granite.—**Granitoid**, gran′i-toid, *a.* Resembling granite.—**Graniteware**, *n.* Articles made of iron coated with vitreous enamel.

Granivorous. Under GRAIN.

Grant, grant, *v.t.* [From O.Fr. *graanter*, *graunter*, *craanter*, *creanter*, to promise, to agree, to guarantee, from (hypothetical) L.L. *credentare*, to make to believe or trust, from L. *credens*, pp. of *credo*, to believe. CREED.] To transfer the title or possession of; to convey, give, or make over; to bestow or confer, particularly in answer to prayer or request; to admit as true though not proved; to allow; to yield; to concede.—*v.i.* To make a grant; to consent (*Shak.*).—*n.* The act of granting, bestowing, or conferring; the thing granted or bestowed.—**Grantable**, gran′ta-bl, *a.* Capable of being granted or conveyed.—**Grantee**, gran-tē′, *n.* The person to whom a grant or conveyance is made.—**Granter**, gran′-tėr, *n.* One who grants.—**Grantor**, gran′-tor, *n.* *Law*, the person who makes a grant or conveyance.

Granular, Granulary, gran′ū-lėr, gran′ū-la-ri, *a.* [From L. *granum*, grain. GRAIN.] Consisting of or resembling granules or grains.—**Granularly**, gran′ū-lėr-li, *adv.* In a granular form.—**Granulate**, gran′ū-lāt, *v.t.*—*granulated*, *granulating*. [Fr. *granuler*.] To form into grains or small masses; to raise in granules or small asperities; to make rough on the surface.—*v.i.* To collect or be formed into grains; to become granular.—**Granulation**, gran-ū-lā′shon, *n.* The act of granulating; a reducing to the form of small grains; *surg.* a process by which little granular fleshy bodies form on sores when healing; the fleshy grains themselves.—**Granule**, gran′ūl, *n.* [Fr., dim. from L. *granum*, a grain.] A little grain; a small particle; a minute round body of vegetable or animal matter.—**Granuliferous**, gran-ū-lif′ėr-us, *a.* Bearing grains or granules.—**Granuliform**, gran′ū-li-form, *a.* Having the form of granules.—**Granulous**, gran′ū-lus, *a.* Abounding with granules.—**Granulite**,

Grape, grāp, *n.* [O.Fr. *grape*, grape, Mod. Fr. *grappe*, a bunch or cluster, originally a hook (a cluster of grapes being hooked or hung together), from O.G. *krapfe*, a hook; akin to *grab*, *grapple*, *gripe*, &c.] A single berry of the vine; the fruit of the vine which yields wine; *milit.* grape-shot. —*Sour grapes*, things professedly despised because they are beyond our reach: from Æsop's fable of 'The Fox and the Grapes'. —**Grapery**, grā′pėr-i, *n.* A place where grapes are grown; a vinery.—**Grapefruit**, *n.* A large, yellow citrus fruit developed from the shaddock; the tree bearing this fruit.—**Grapeshot**, *n.* Iron balls held in a frame and fired from a cannon. —**Grapestone**, *n.* The stone or seed of the grape.—**Grape sugar**, a variety of sugar from grapes; glucose.—**Grapevine**, *n.* The vine that bears grapes; also some secret means of communicating rumor.

Graph, graf, *n.* [Gr. *graphō*, I write.] A diagram representing the relation between two varying magnitudes by means of a curve referred to fixed axes.—**Graphic, Graphical**, graf′ik, graf′i-kal, *a.* Pertaining to the art of writing, engraving, or delineating; written; pictorial; describing with accuracy or vividly; vivid; portraying in vivid and expressive language.—*Graphic granite*, a variety of granite which when cut in one direction exhibits markings resembling Hebrew characters.—**Graphi-**

cally, graf'i-kal-li, *adv.* In a graphic manner. — **Graphicness**, **Graphicalness**, graf'ik-nes, graf'i-kal-nes, *n.* The quality of being graphic. — **Graphite**, graf'īt, *n.* [Gr. *graphō*, to write, being made into pencils.] One of the forms under which carbon occurs, made into pencils, and called also *Plumbago* and *Black-lead*.—**Grapholite**, graf'o-līt, *n.* [Gr. *lithos*, a stone.] A species of slate suitable for writing on.—**Graphotype**, graf'o-tīp, *n.* A process by which a drawing made on a chalky surface with special ink forms a relief for printing.

Grapnel, grap'nel, *n.* [Dim. from Fr. *grappin*, a grapnel; of same origin as *grape*.] A small anchor with four or five flukes or claws, used to hold boats or small vessels; a grappling-iron.

Grapple, grap'l, *v.t.*—*grappled, grappling.* [Directly from O.Fr. *grappil*, a grapnel; or from *grab* or *gripe*.] To lay fast hold on, either with the hands or with hooks; to seize and hold.—*v.i.* To contend in close fight, as wrestlers. — *To grapple with*, to contend with; to struggle with; to confront boldly. — *n.* A close seizure or hug; the wrestler's hold; close fight or encounter; a hook by which one ship fastens on another. —**Grappling-iron**, *n.* An instrument consisting of four or more iron claws for grappling and holding fast.

Graptolite, grap'to-līt, *n.* [Gr. *graptos*, written, inscribed, and *lithos*, stone.] A fossil of various species presenting a general resemblance to pens or quills.

Grasp, grasp, *v.t.* [From stem of *grope*, *gripe*, or *grab*; comp. G. *grapsen*, to snatch, from O.G. *grappen*, *grabben*.] To seize and hold by the fingers or arms; to lay hold of; to take possession of; to seize by the intellect; to comprehend.—*v.i.* To make a clutch or catch; to gripe.—*To grasp at*, to catch at; to try to seize.—*n.* The grip or seizure of the hand; reach of the arms; hence, the power of seizing and holding; forcible possession; power of the intellect to seize and comprehend; wide-reaching power of intellect.—**Graspable**, gras'pa-bl, *a.* Capable of being grasped.—**Grasper**, gras'pėr, *n.* One who or that which grasps.—**Grasping**, gras'ping, *a.* Covetous; rapacious; avaricious; greedy; miserly.—**Graspingly**, gras'ping-li, *adv.* In a grasping manner.

Grass, gras, *n.* [A.Sax. *græs*, *gærs*=Goth. Icel. D. and G. *gras*, Dan. *græs*, Sw. *gräs*; probably akin to *grow* and *green*.] In common usage (and without a plural), herbage; the verdurous covering of the soil; also any plant of the family to which belong the grain-yielding and pasture plants.—*China grass*, a Chinese plant of the nettle family, from the fibre of which grass-cloth is made. —*Esparto grass.* ESPARTO.—*v.t.* To cover with grass; to furnish with grass; to bleach on the grass.—**Grass-cloth**, *n.* An oriental cloth made from the fibre of China grass, &c.—**Grass-green**, *a.* Green like the colour of grass.—**Grass-grown**, *a.* Overgrown with grass. — **Grasshopper**, gras'hop-ėr, *n.* A leaping orthopterous insect allied to the locusts, commonly living among grass.—**Grassiness**, gras'i-nes, *n.* The condition of being grassy.—**Grass-land**, *n.* Land kept perpetually under grass.—**Grass-oil**, *n.* A fragrant Indian oil procured from certain scented grasses. —**Grass-tree**, *n.* An Australian plant of the lily family, having shrubby stems with tufts of long grass-like wiry foliage. — **Grass-widow**, *n.* [Originally *grace-widow*, a widow by courtesy.] Formerly, an unmarried woman who had a child: now applied to a wife temporarily separated from her husband.—**Grasswrack**, gras'-rak, *n.* A genus of grass-like marine plants widely distributed on various coasts. — **Grassy**, gras'i, *a.* Covered with grass; abounding with grass; resembling grass.

Grassum, gras'um, *n.* A fine paid by a tenant for the renewal of his lease.

Grate, grāt, *n.* [It. *grata*, a grate, lattice, hurdle, from L.L. *grata*, *crata*, L. *crates*, a hurdle. CRATE.] A series of parallel or cross bars, with interstices; a kind of lattice-work; a grating; a metallic receptacle for holding burning fuel, and formed to a greater or less extent of bars. — *v.t.* To furnish with a grate or grates; to fill in or cover with cross-bars.—**Grating**, grā'ting, *n.* A partition or frame of parallel or cross bars.

Grate, grāt, *v.t.*—*grated, grating.* [O.Fr. *grater*, Fr. *gratter*, to scratch, to rub; from the Teutonic; comp. O.H.G. *chrazôn*, G. *kratzen*, to scratch; Dan. *kratte*, *kradse*, to scratch; E. *scratch*.] To rub hard or roughly together, as a body with a rough surface against another body; to wear away in small particles by rubbing with anything rough or indented; to offend or irritate.—*v.i.* To rub roughly with the surface in contact (a body *grates* upon another); to have a galling or annoying effect (to *grate* upon the feelings); to make a harsh sound by friction; to sound disagreeably.—**Grater**, grā'tėr, *n.* One who or that which grates.—**Grating**, grā'ting, *p.* and *a.* Irritating; harsh. —*n.* The harsh sound or the feeling caused by strong attrition or rubbing.—**Gratingly**, *adv.* In a grating manner.

Grateful, grāt'fụl, *a.* [From O.Fr. *grat*. L. *gratus*, pleasing, and E. adjectival term, *ful*. GRACE.] Having a due sense of benefits; having kind feelings and thankfulness toward one from whom a favour has been received; expressing gratitude; indicative of gratitude; affording pleasure; agreeable; pleasing to the taste or the intellect; gratifying.—**Gratefully**, grāt'fụl-li, *adv.* In a grateful manner.—**Gratefulness**, grāt'-fụl-nes, *n.* The state or quality of being grateful. — **Gratitude**, grat'i-tūd, *n.* [L.L. *gratitudo*.] The feeling of one who is grateful; a warm and friendly emotion awakened by a favour received; thankfulness.

Graticulation, gra-tik'ū-lā"shon, *n.* [Fr. *graticulation*, L. *craticula*, dim. of *crates*, a hurdle, wicker-work. GRATE, *n.*] The division of a design or drawing into squares, for the purpose of producing a copy of it in larger or smaller dimensions.—**Graticule**, grat'i-kūl, *n.* [Fr.] A design or drawing so divided.

Gratify, grat'i-fī, *v.t.*—*gratified, gratifying.* [Fr. *gratifier*, L. *gratificor*—*gratus*, pleasant, agreeable, and *facio*, to make. GRATEFUL.] To please; to give pleasure to; to indulge, delight, humour, satisfy.—**Gratification**, grat'ifi-kā"shon, *n.* [L. *gratificatio*.] The act of gratifying or pleasing; that which affords pleasure; enjoyment; satisfaction; delight. — **Gratifier**, grat'i-fī-ėr, *n.* One who gratifies.

Gratis, grā'tis, *adv.* [L., from *gratia*, favour. GRACE.] For nothing; freely; without recompense (to give a thing *gratis*).—*a.* Given or done for nothing.

Gratitude. Under GRATEFUL.

Gratuitous, gra-tū'i-tus, *a.* [L. *gratuitus*, from *gratus*, pleasing, agreeable. GRATEFUL, GRACE.] Given without an equivalent or recompense; free; voluntary; not required, called for, or warranted by the circumstances; adopted or asserted without any good ground (a *gratuitous* assumption). — **Gratuitously**, gra-tū'i-tus-li, *adv.* In a gratuitous manner.—**Gratuitousness**, gra-tū'i-tus-nes, *n.*—**Gratuity**, gra-tū'i-ti, *n.* A free gift; a present; a donation.

Gratulate,† grat'ū-lāt, *v.t. gratulated, gratulating.* [L. *gratulor*, *gratulatus*, from *gratus*, pleasing, agreeable. GRACE.] To salute with declarations of joy; to congratulate.—**Gratulant**, grat'ū-lant, *a.* Congratulatory. — **Gratulation**, grat-ū-lā'-shon, *n.* [L. *gratulatio*.] Congratulation. —**Gratulatory**, grat'ū-la-to-ri, *a.* Congratulatory.—*n.* A congratulation.

Grauwacke, GRAYWACKE.

Gravamen, gra-vā'men, *n.* [L., from *gravo*, to weigh down, from *gravis*, heavy. GRAVE, *a.*] That part of an accusation which weighs most heavily against the accused; ground or burden of complaint in general.

Grave, grāv, *v.t.*—*graved* (pret.), *graven* or *graved* (pp.), *graving* (ppr.). [A.Sax. *grafan*, to dig, to grave or carve=D. *graven* Dan. *grave*, Icel. *grafa*, G. *graben*, to dig, to engrave; cog. Ir. *grafaim*, to engrave, to scrape; Gr. *graphō*, to grave, to write.] To carve or cut; to form or shape by cutting with a tool; to delineate by cutting; to engrave; hence, to impress deeply.—**Graver**, grā'vėr, *n.* One who carves or engraves; an engraving tool: a burin.

Grave, grāv, *n.* [A.Sax. *græf*, a grave, a trench, from stem of *grafan*, to dig or grave = Dan. *grav*, Icel. *gröf*, D. *graf*, G. *grab*, Rus. *grob*, a grave. GRAVE, to carve.] An excavation in the earth in which a dead human body is deposited; hence, any place of interment; a tomb; a sepulchre. — **Grave-clothes**, *n. pl.* The clothes in which the dead are interred. — **Grave-digger**, *n.* One whose occupation is to dig graves. — **Graveless**, grāv'les, *a.* Without a grave; unburied. — **Grave-stone**, *n.* A stone placed at a grave as a monument to the dead.—**Grave-yard**, *n.* A yard or inclosure for the interment of the dead.

Grave, grāv, *v.t.* [From the *graves* or dregs of melted tallow with which ships' hulls were formerly smeared.] To clean a ship's bottom of sea-weeds, &c., and pay it over with pitch or tar. — **Graves**, **Greaves**, grāvz, grēvz, *n. pl.* [L.G. *greven*, Dan. *grever*, G. *grieben*, graves; hence also *gravy*.] The insoluble parts of tallow gathered from the melting-pots. — **Graving-dock**, *n.* Under DOCK.

Grave, grāv, *a.* [Fr. *grave*, from L. *gravis*, heavy (whence also *grief*, *aggravate*, *gravid*, *gravitate*); allied to Gr. *barys*, heavy, *baros*, weight (in *barometer*); Skr. *guru*, heavy.] Solemn; serious: opposed to *light* or *jovial*; plain; not showy; important; momentous; having a serious and interesting import; *mus.* low; depressed: opposed to *sharp*, *acute*, or *high*.—**Gravely**, grāv'li, *adv.* In a grave manner.—**Graveness**, grāv'nes, *n.* The state or quality of being grave; gravity.

Gravel, grav'el, *n.* [Fr. *gravele*, from O.Fr. *grave*, sand or gravel, from the Celtic; Armor. *grouan*, sand; W. *grou*, pebbles, coarse gravel.] Small stones or very small pebbles collectively; small stones, sand, &c., combined; *pathol.* small concretions or calculi in the kidneys or bladder; the disease occasioned by such concretions.—*v.t* —*graveled, graveling*, or *gravelled, gravelling.* To cover with gravel; to cause to stick in the sand or gravel; hence, to perplex and bring to an intellectual standstill; to puzzle; to hurt the foot of (a horse) by gravel lodged under the shoe.—**Gravel-blind**, *a.* [A mistaken coinage, as in Shak., *Merchant of Venice*, ii, 2, 38, on the supposed analogy of *sand-blind*.] More blind than sand-blind and less than stone-blind.—**Gravelliness**, grav'el-i-nes, *n.* The state of being gravelly.—**Graveling**, grav'el-ing, *n.* The act of laying down gravel; the gravel itself.—**Gravelly**, grav'el-i, *a.* Abounding with gravel; consisting of gravel.—**Gravel-pit**, *n.* A pit from which gravel is dug.

Graven, grā'vn, pp. of *grave*, to carve.

Graveolent, gra-vē'ō-lent, *a.* [L. *graveolens*, *graveolentis*—*gravis*, heavy, and *oleo*, to smell.] Sending forth a strong and offensive smell.—**Graveolence**, gra-vē'ō-lens, *n.* A strong offensive smell.

Graves. Under GRAVE, to clean a ship's bottom.

Gravid, grav'id, *a.* [L. *gravidus*, from *gravis*, heavy. GRAVE, *a.*] Being with child, pregnant. — **Gravidation**, **Gravidity**, grav-i-dā'shon, gra-vid'i-ti, *n.* Pregnancy; impregnation.

Gravigrade, grav'i-grād, *n.* [L. *gravis*, heavy, and *gradus*, a step.] An animal that moves slowly, more especially a huge fossil animal, as the megatherium, mylodon, &c.

Gravimeter, gra-vim'et-ėr, *n.* [L. *gravis*, heavy, and Gr. *metron*, a measure.] An instrument for determining the specific gravities of bodies, whether liquid or solid, as a hydrometer.

Graving-dock. Under GRAVE (to clean a ship's bottom) and DOCK.

Gravitate, grav'i-tāt, *v.i.*—*gravitated, gravitating.* [Fr. *graviter*, from L. *gravitas*, from *gravis*, heavy. GRAVE, *a*]. To be affected by gravitation; to move under the influence of gravitation; *fig.* to have a tendency towards some attracting influence.—**Gravitation**, grav-i-tā'shon, *n.* The act of gravitating or tending to a centre of attraction; the force by which bodies are drawn, or by which they tend toward the centre of the earth or other centre, or the effect of that force.—**Gravitational units**, *n.* Units of force, work, &c., which depend on the value of gravity, and thus vary from place to place on the earth's surface. See ABSOLUTE UNITS.—**Gravitative**, grav'i-tā-tiv, *a.* Causing to gravitate or tend to a centre. —**Gravity**, grav'i-ti, *n.* The state or character of being grave; solemnity of deportment, character, or demeanour; seriousness; weight or weightiness; enormity (the *gravity* of an offence); the force which causes a mass of matter to tend toward a centre of attraction, especially toward the centre of the earth; the force by which the planets mutually attract each other and are attracted towards the sun; centripetal force.—*Centre of gravity.* Under CENTRE. —*Specific gravity*, the relative gravity or weight of any body or substance considered with regard to the weight of an equal bulk of pure distilled water at the temperature of 62° Fahr., which is reckoned unity.

Gravy, grā'vi, *n.* [From *graves, greaves*, the dregs of melted tallow. GRAVE, to clean a ship's bottom.] The fat and other liquid matter that drips from flesh in cooking, accompanying the meat when served up; dripping.

Gray, Grey, grā, *a.* [A.Sax. *graeg* = D. *graauw*, Icel. *grár*, Dan. *graa*, G. *grau*, gray; other connections are unknown.] Of the color of hair whitened by age; hoary; white with a mixture of black; of the color of ashes; having gray hairs; old; mature (*gray* experience).—*n.* A gray color; a dull or neutral tint; an animal of a gray color, as a horse.—**Grayback, Greyback**, a whalebone whale.—**Graybeard, Greybeard**, *n.* A man with a gray beard; an old man; a large earthen jar or bottle for holding liquor.—**Grayish**, grā'ish, *a.* Somewhat gray; gray in a moderate degree.—**Grayling**, grā'ling, *n.* [From the silvery gray of its back and sides.] A game fish of the salmon family, 16 to 18 inches long, found in cold, swift streams.—**Gray matter**, nerve tissue made up of both nerve cells and nerve fiber; hence, brains; intelligence.—**Grayness, Greyness**, grā'nes, *n.* The state or quality of being gray.—**Gray owl**, the tawny owl; a large, arctic owl.—**Gray squirrel**, a large, grayish-colored squirrel of the eastern U. S.—**Graywacke, Grauwacke**, grā-wak'e, grou-wak'e, *n.* [G. *grauwacke* —*grau*, gray, and *wacke*, a kind of rock.] A kind of sandstone in which grains or fragments of various minerals or rocks are embedded in an indurated matrix, which may be siliceous or argillaceous.—**Gray whale**, a large, fierce whale of the northern Pacific. — **Gray wolf**, the American timber wolf.

Grayhound. GREYHOUND.

Graze, grāz, *v.t.*—*grazed, grazing.* [Perhaps from the combined influence of *grate*, to rub, and *rase*; or perhaps originally meaning to skim along the grass, from *grass*, like *graze*, to pasture.] To rub or touch lightly in passing, as a missile does; to brush lightly the surface of.—*v.i.* To pass so as to touch or rub lightly.—*n.* The act of grazing; a slight rub or brush.

Graze, grāz, *v.t.*—*grazed, grazing.* [A.Sax. *grasian*, to graze or feed, from *græs*, grass; comp. D. *grazen*, to graze, and *gras*, grass, G. *grasen* and *gras.*] To feed or supply with growing grass; to furnish pasture for; to feed on; to eat from the ground.—*v.i.* To eat grass; to feed on growing herbage.—*n.* The act of grazing or feeding on grass.—**Grazer**, grā'zėr, *n.* One that grazes.—**Grazier**, grā'zhėr, *n.* One who grazes or pastures cattle for the market; a farmer who raises and deals in cattle.—**Grazing**, grā'zing, *n.* The act of feeding on grass; a pasture.

Grease, grēs, *n.* [Fr. *graisse*, O.Fr. *gresse*, from L. *crassus*, fat, gross, whence E. *crass*; akin Gael. *creis*, fat.] Animal fat in a soft state; particularly the fatty matter of land animals, as distinguished from the oily matter of marine animals; *farriery*, a swelling and inflammation in a horse's legs attended with the secretion of oily matter and cracks in the skin.—*v.t.* (grēz or grēs). — *greased, greasing.* To smear, anoint, or daub with grease or fat. — **Greasily**, grē'zi-li, *adv.* In a greasy manner.—**Greasiness**, grē'zi-nes, *n.* The quality or state of being greasy.—**Greasy**, grē'zi, *a.* Composed of or characterized by grease; fatty; unctuous; having the appearance of fat or grease; seemingly unctuous to the touch, as some minerals; gross; indecent; *farriery*, affected with the disease called grease.

Great, grāt, *a.* [A.Sax. *great* = L.G. and D. *groot*, G. *gross*, great; perhaps allied to L. *grandis.*] Large in bulk, surface, or linear dimensions; of wide extent; big; large in number; numerous; large, extensive, or unusual in degree; long continued; of long duration; important; weighty; involving important interests; holding an eminent or prominent position in respect of mental endowments or acquirements, virtue, or vice, rank, office, power, or the like; eminent; distinguished; celebrated; notorious; of elevated sentiments; generous; noble; on an extensive scale; sumptuous; magnificent; wonderful; sublime; grand; pregnant; teeming; filled; denoting a degree of consanguinity in the ascending or descending line (*great* grandfather). — *Great circle.* Under CIRCLE.—*The great*, *pl.* the powerful, the rich, the distinguished, persons of rank and position.—**Greatcoat**, grāt'kōt, *n.* An overcoat; a topcoat.—**Great Dane**, a dog of a breed noted for its great size and strength.—**Great Divide**, the Rocky Mountains, dividing continental drainage east and west.—**Great-hearted**, *a.* High-spirited; magnanimous.—**Greatly**, grāt'li, *adv.* In a great manner or degree.—**Greatness**, grāt'nes, *n.* The state or quality of being great; magnitude; dignity; eminence; distinguished rank or position.

Greave, grēv, *n.* [Fr. *grève*, armor for the leg; Sp. and Pg. *greba*, probably of Ar. origin.] Armor worn on the front of the lower part of the leg, across the back of which it was buckled.

Grebe, grēb, *n.* [Fr. *grèbe*, from Armor. *krib*, W. *crib*, a comb, a crest, one variety having a crest.] An aquatic bird of various species, having no tail, toes separate, but broadly fringed by a membrane, and legs set so far back that on land it assumes the upright position of the penguin.

Grecian, grē'shan, *a.* [GREEK.] Pertaining to Greece; Greek.—*n.* A native of Greece; or a person of the Greek race; one versed in the Greek language.—**Grecism**, grē'sizm, *n.* An idiom of the Greek language.—**Grecize**, grē'siz, *v.t.* —*grecized, grecizing.* To render Grecian: to translate into Greek.—*v.i.* To speak the Greek language.

Greedy, grē'di, *a.* [A.Sax. *grédig, graedig* =Goth. *gredags*, Icel. *gráthugr*, Dan. *graadig*, D. *gretig*, greedy. Hence *greed*, which is quite a modern word in English = Icel. *gráthr*, Goth. *gredus*, hunger.] Having a keen appetite for food or drink; ravenous; voracious; very fond of eating; gluttonous; having a keen desire for anything; covetous (*greedy* of gain).—**Greed**, grēd, *n.* An eager desire or longing; greediness.—**Greedily**, grē'di-li, *adv.* In a greedy manner; voraciously; eagerly.—**Greediness**, grē'di-nes, *n.* The quality of being greedy.

Greek, grēk, *a.* [Fr. *grec*, L. *græcus*, Greek, from the *Graikoi*, an insignificant tribe of ancient north-western Greece.] Pertaining to Greece.—*n.* A native of Greece; the language of Greece.—*Greek calends*, a supposed date, that never occurs, for payment, &c., there being calends only in the Roman calendar.—*Greek Church*, the eastern church which separated from the Roman or western church in the ninth century, and comprises the great bulk of the Christians of Russia, Greece, Rumania, Turkey, &c.—*Greek fire*, a combustible preparation, the constituents of which are supposed to have been asphalt, niter, and sulphur.—*Greek gift*, a gift presented in order to betray one.—*Greek-letter fraternity*, an organization, as in a university, designated by Greek letters.

Green, grēn, *a.* [A.Sax. *grêne* = Dan. and Sw. *grön*, Icel. *grænn*, G. *grün*; akin to *grow*; L. *holus, olus*, green vegetables; Gr. *chloē*, a young shoot, *chlōros*, pale green; Skr. *hari*, green.] Of the color of grass or herbage and plants when growing; emerald; verdant; new; fresh; recent; fresh and vigorous; flourishing; undecayed (a *green* old age); containing its natural juices; not dry; not seasoned; unripe, immature (*green* fruit); immature in age; young; raw; inexperienced; easily imposed upon.—*Green corn*, sweet Indian corn, grown for the table.—*Green tea*, tea of a greenish color from the mode in which the leaves are treated and having a peculiar flavor.—*Green turtle*, the turtle of which the soup is made.—*Green vitriol*, a name of sulphate of iron in a crystallized form.—*n.* A green color; a grassy plain or plat; a piece of ground covered with verdant herbage; a name of several pigments; *pl.* the leaves and stems of young plants used in cookery, especially certain plants of the cabbage kind.—*v.t.* To make green.—*v.i.* To grow green.—**Greenback**, grēn'bak, *n.* A note belonging to the paper money of the United States, first issued in 1862, from the back of the notes being of a green color.—**Green-crop**, *n.* A crop that is used in its growing or unripe state, as clover, grass, turnips, potatoes, &c. —**Green-earth**, *n.* A species of earth or mineral substance used by artists.—**Green-ebony**, *n.* A cabinet and dye-wood obtained from South America.—**Greenery**, grē'ner-i, *n.* A mass of green foliage, the green hue of such a mass.—**Green-eyed**, *a.* Having green eyes; seeing all things discolored or distorted; jaundiced.—**Greenfinch**, *n.* A common European finch of a greenish color: the green linnet or grosbeak.—**Green-fly**, *n.* The name given to various Aphides which infest plants.—**Greengage**, *n.* [After a person named *Gage*, who introduced it into England.] A species of plum having a juicy greenish pulp of an exquisite flavour.—**Green-grocer**, *n.* A retailer of greens and other vegetables.—**Green-heart**, *n.* BEBEERU. — **Greenhorn**, grēn'horn, *n.* A person easily imposed upon; a raw inexperienced person —**Greenhouse**, grēn'hous, *n.* A building principally consisting of glazed frames or sashes for the purpose of cultivating exotic plants which are too tender to endure the open air; often artificially heated up.—**Greening**, grēn'ing, *n.* A name given to certain varieties of apples green when ripe.—**Greenish**, grēn'ish, *a.* Somewhat green; having a tinge of green; somewhat raw and inexperienced.—**Greenishness**, grēn'ish-nes, *n.* The quality of being greenish.—**Greenjacket.** A member of a rifle regiment; applied to all ranks.—**Green-linnet**, *n.* The green-finch.—**Greenly**, grēn'-li, *adv.* In a green manner.—**Greenness**, grēn'nes, *n.* The quality of being green.—**Green-room**, *n.* A room near the stage in a theatre, to which actors retire during the intervals of their parts in the play.—**Green-sand**, *n.* A name given (from the colour of some of the beds) to two groups of strata, the one (lower green-sand) belonging to the lower cretaceous series, the other (upper green-sand) to the upper cretaceous series.—**Green-shank**, *n.* A well-known species of sandpiper with greenish legs.—**Green-sickness**, *n.* CHLOROSIS. —**Green-stone**, grēn'stōn, *n.* [From a tinge of green in the colour.] A general designation for the hard granular crystalline varieties of trap.—**Green-sward**, *n.* Turf green with grass.—**Greenth**, grēnth, *n.* The quality of being green; greenness. —**Greenwood**, grēn'wụd, *n.* A wood or forest when green, as in summer.—*a.* Pertaining to a greenwood.—**Greeny**, grēn'i, *a.* Green; greenish; having a green hue.

Greet, grēt, *v.t.* [A.Sax. *grétan*, to salute, hail, bid farewell=G. *grüssen*, D. *groeten*, to greet; comp. A.Sax. *grétan*, Prov.E. and Sc. *greet*, Goth. *gretan*, Icel. *gráta*, to weep.] To address with salutations or expressions of kind wishes; to pay respects or compliments to; to salute; to hail.—*v.i.* To meet and salute each other.—**Greeter**, grēt'ėr, *n.* One who greets.—**Greeting**, grēt'ing, *n.* Expression of kindness or joy; salutation at meeting; compliment sent by one absent.

Greet, grēt, *v.i.* [GREET, to salute.] To weep. (*Old English* and *Scotch.*)

Gregarious, grē-gā'ri-us, *a.* [L. *gregarius*, from *grex*, *gregis*, a flock or herd; seen also in *aggregate, congregate, egregious.*] Having the habit of assembling or living in a flock or herd; not habitually solitary or living alone. — **Gregariously**, grē-gā'ri-us-li, *adv.* In a gregarious manner.—**Gregariousness**, grē-gā'ri-us-nes, *n.* The state or quality of being gregarious.—**Gregarian**, grē-gā'ri-an, *a.* Gregarious; belonging to the herd or common sort; ordinary.—**Gregarine**, greg'a-rin, *n.* A name of certain minute animals of a low type, having no definite organs observable, found inhabiting the intestines of various animals.

Gregorian, gre-gō'ri-an, *a.* Belonging to Gregory.—*Gregorian calendar*, the calendar as reformed by Pope Gregory XIII in 1582. —*Gregorian year*, the ordinary year, as reckoned according to the Gregorian calendar.—*Gregorian epoch*, the time from which the Gregorian calendar dates. — *Gregorian chant*, a choral melody introduced into the service of the Christian church by Pope Gregory I about the end of the sixth century. — *Gregorian telescope*, the first and most common form of the reflecting telescope, invented by Prof. James Gregory of Edinburgh.

Grenade, gre-nād', *n.* [Fr. *grenade*, Sp. *granada*, a pomegranate, a grenade (the missile somewhat resembling the fruit), from L. *granatum*, a pomegranate. GRAIN.] A hollow ball or shell of iron or other metal, or of annealed glass, filled with powder, fired by means of a fuse, and thrown among enemies. — **Grenadier**, gren-a-dēr', *n.* Originally a soldier who threw hand-grenades; afterwards a company of tall soldiers distinguished by a particular dress; now a member of a special regiment.

Grenadine, gren'a-din, *n.* A thin gauzy silk or woolen fabric, plain, colored, or embroidered, used for ladies' dresses, shawls, &c.; also, a red sirup used in mixed drinks.

Gressorial, gres-sō'ri-al, *a.* [L. *gressus*, a going, step. GRADE.] *Ornith.* having three toes forward (two of them connected) and one behind.

Grew, grö, pret. of *grow*.

Grewsome. GRUESOME.

Grey, grā. GRAY.

Greyhound, grā'hound, *n.* [Icel. *greyhundr*, from *grey*, a greyhound, a bitch; Sc. *grew*, a greyhound; Ir. *grech*, a hound; the name has no reference to the color.] A dog kept for the chase, remarkable for its beauty of form and its great fleetness.

Grice, grīs, *n.* [Dan. *gris*, *griis*, Sw. and Icel. *gris*, a pig.] A little pig.

Griddle, grid'l, *n.* [W. *greidell*, from *greidiaw*, to heat, to scorch; Ir. *greidell*, *greidaim*, to scorch.] A broad metal disk used for frying griddle cakes.—**Griddlecake**, *n.* A batter cake browned on both sides.

Gride, grīd, *v.i.* [Partly from O.E. *girden*, to strike, pierce, cut, from *gerde*, a rod = *yard*; partly from O.E. *grede*, A.Sax. *graedan*, to cry.] To pierce; to cut through; to cut (*Mil.*); to give out a harsh creaking sound; to jar harshly (*Tenn.*)—*n.* A grating or harsh sound.

Gridelin, grid'e-lin, *n.* [Fr. *gris de lin*, flax gray.] A color mixed of white and red, or a gray violet.

Gridiron, grid'ī-ėrn, *n.* [From *grid-* of *griddle*, and *iron*.] A grated utensil for broiling flesh and fish over coals; anything likened to such a frame; a football field (*colloq.*).

Grief, grēf, *n.* [Fr. *grief*, grievance, what oppresses, from L. *gravis*, heavy. GRAVE, *a.*] Pain of mind, arising from any cause; sorrow; sadness; cause of sorrow or pain; that which afflicts; trial; grievance; bodily pain (*Shak.*)†.—*To come to grief*, to come to a bad end; to come to ruin; to meet with an accident. ∴ Syn. under AFFLICTION.—**Grievable**, grē'va-bl, *a.* Causing grief; lamentable. — **Grievance**, grē'vans, *n.* That which causes grief or uneasiness; wrong done and suffered; injury.—**Grieve**, grēv, *v.t.*—*grieved, grieving.* [O.Fr. *griever.*] To cause to feel grief; to give pain of mind to; to make sorrowful; to afflict; to sorrow over; to deplore.—*v.i.* To feel grief; to sorrow; to mourn: followed by *at*, *for*, and *over*.—**Griever**, grē'vėr, *n.* One who or that which grieves. —**Grievingly**, grē'ving-li, *adv.* In a grieving manner. — **Grievous**, grē'vus, *a.* Causing grief or sorrow; afflictive; hard to bear; heavy; severe; harmful; great; atrocious; aggravated; full of grief; indicating great grief or affliction.—**Grievously**, grē'vus-li, *adv.* In a grievous manner.—**Grievousness**, grē'vus-nes, *n.*

Grieve, Greeve, grēv, *n.* [A.Sax. *geréfa*, a bailiff or reeve. REEVE.] In Scotland, a manager of a farm; a farm-bailiff.

Griffin, Griffon, grif'in, grif'on, *n.* [Fr. *griffon*, It. *grifone*, from L. *gryps*, *gryphus*, griffin, from Gr. *gryps*, a griffon, from *grypos*, hook-beaked.] A mythical animal, in the fore part represented as an eagle, in the hinder part as a lion; a species of vulture found in the mountainous parts of Europe and in North Africa; Anglo-Indian term for a new arrival.

Grig, grig, *n.* [Connected with *cricket*; in second sense with Sw. *kräka*, to creep.] A cricket; a grasshopper; the sand-eel; a small eel of lively and incessant motion.

Grill, gril, *v.t.* [From Fr. *griller*, to broil, from *gril*, a gridiron, *grille*, a grate; O.Fr. *graille*, from L.L. *graticula*, corrupted for L. *craticula*, a small gridiron, dim. of *crates*, a hurdle. GRATE, CRATE.] To broil on a gridiron or similar instrument.—*n.* A grated utensil for broiling meat, &c., over a fire; a gridiron.—**Grillade**, gril-ād', *n.* Meat or fish broiled on a grill.—**Grillage**, gril'āj, *n.* [Fr., from *grille*, a grate, a railing.] A heavy framework of beams used to sustain foundations in soils of unequal compressibility.—**Grille**, gril, *n.* [Fr.] A lattice or grating; a piece of grated work.

Grilse, grils, *n.* [Probably a corruption of Sw. *græ-lax*, gray salmon.] The young of the salmon on its first return from the sea to fresh water.

Grim, grim, *a.* [A.Sax. *grim*, fierce, ferocious; akin to *grama*, fury; Icel. *grimmr*, savage, angry, *gramr*, wrath; Dan. *grim*, ugly; D. *gram*, angry, *grimmen*, to growl; G. *grimm*, furious, *grimmen*, to rage; comp. W. *grem*, a snarl, *gremiaw*, to snarl.] Of a forbidding or fear-inspiring aspect; fierce; stern; sullen; sour; surly.—*v.t.* To make grim; to give a forbidding or fear-inspiring aspect to (*Carl.*). — **Grimly**, grim'li, *a.* Having a grim, hideous, or stern look.—*adv.* In a grim manner. — **Grimness**, grim'nes, *n.* The state or quality of being grim.

Grimace, gri-mās', *n.* [Fr., a wry face, from the Teutonic; comp. D. *grimmen*, to snarl, to make faces. GRIM.] A distortion of the countenance expressive of affectation, scorn, disapprobation, self-satisfaction, or the like; a smirk; a wry face.—*v.i.*—*grimaced, grimacing.* To make grimaces.

Grimalkin, gri-mal'kin, *n.* [For *graymalkin*—*gray*, and *malkin*, that is *Mollkin*, dim. from *Mary*; comp. *Tom-cat*.] An old cat, especially a female cat.

Grime, grīm, *n.* [Same as Dan. *grime*, a spot or streak, *grim*, soot, lampblack.] Foul matter; dirt; dirt deeply ingrained. —*v.t.*—*grimed, griming.* To sully or soil deeply; to dirt.—**Grimily**, grī'mi-li, *adv.* In a grimy manner or condition; foully.—**Griminess**, grī'mi-nes, *n.* The state or quality of being grimy.—**Grimy**, grī'mi, *a.* Full of grime; foul; dirty.

Grin, grin, *v.i.*—*grinned, grinning.* [A.Sax. *grinnian*, *grennian*, to grin = Dan. *grine*, D. *grijnen*, G. *greinen*, to grin, to cry, to weep; perhaps allied to *groan.*] To snarl and show the teeth, as a dog; to set the teeth together and open the lips; to show the teeth as in laughter, scorn, or pain.—*v.t.* To show, set, or snap (the teeth), in grinning; to express by grinning.—*n.* The act of withdrawing the lips and showing the teeth; a forced or sneering smile.—**Grinner**, grin'ėr, *n.* One who grins.—**Grinningly**, grin'ing-li, *adv.* In a grinning manner.

Grin,‡ grin, *n.* [A.Sax. *grin*, *gyrn*, Sc. *girn*, a snare.] A snare or trap; a gin. (O.T.)

Grind, grīnd, *v.t.*—*ground* (pret. & pp.), very rarely *grinded.* [A.Sax. *grindan*, to grind; same root as Gr. *chriō*, to graze or touch lightly; Skr. *ghrish*, to grind. *Grist* and *ground* (*n.*) are from this word.] To break and reduce to fine particles or powder by friction, as in a mill; to comminute by attrition; to triturate; to wear down, smooth, or sharpen by friction; to whet; to oppress by severe exactions; to harrass; to prepare for examination in some subject of study, or to study (in these senses university slang). —*v.i.* To grind corn or other matter; to be rubbed together, as in the operation of grinding; to be ground or pulverized; to drudge or perform hard work; to study hard, especially for an examination (*slang*). —*n.* The act of one who grinds; a spell of work.—**Grinder**, grin'dėr, *n.* One who or that which grinds; a molar tooth. —**Grindstone**, grīnd'stōn, *n.* A revolving stone used for grinding or sharpening tools. —*To bring or hold a person's nose to the grindstone*, to oppress him; to punish him.

Grip, grip, *n.* [Directly from Fr. *gripper*, to grasp, which itself is from a Germanic word=E. *gripe.*] The act of grasping by the hand; grasp; the grasp peculiar to any secret fraternity as a means of recognition; a fast hold; a hilt or handle.—*v.t.*—*gripped, gripping.* To grasp by the hand; to gripe; to seize forcibly; to hold fast.—*v.i.* To take hold; to hold fast.

Grip, Gripe, grip, grīp, *n.* [A.Sax. *grœp*, a ditch; D. *grop*, *groep*, a ditch or trench.] A small ditch or furrow; a channel to carry off water or other liquid. — *v.t.* To trench; to drain.

Gripe, grīp, *v.t.*—*griped, griping.* [A.Sax. *gripan*, to gripe, to grasp = Icel. *gripa*, D. *grijpen*, Goth. *greipan*, G. *greifen*, to seize; same root as *grab*, *grope*, *grasp.*] To catch with the hand and clasp closely with the fingers; to hold tight or close; to clutch; to seize and hold fast; to clench; to tighten; to give pain in the bowels, as if by pressure or contraction; to straiten or distress. — *v.i.* To take fast hold with the hand; to clasp closely with the fingers. —*n.* Grasp; seizure; grip; oppression; affliction; pinching distress; a kind of brake to act on a wheel; *pl.* a pinching intermittent pain in the intestines, of the character of that which accompanies diarrhœa or colic. — **Griper**, grī'pėr, *n.* One who gripes.—**Griping**, grī'ping, *a.* Grasping; greedy; extortionate, causing a pinching feeling in the bowels.—**Gripingly**, grī'ping-li, *adv.* In a griping manner.

Grippe, grip, *n.* [Fr.] The influenza.

Grisaille, gre-sāl', *n.* [Fr., from *gris*, gray.] A style of painting in various gray tints employed to represent solid bodies in relief, as friezes, mouldings, bas-reliefs, &c.

Grisette, gri-zet′, *n.* [Fr. Originally, a gray woollen fabric, much used for dresses by women of the inferior classes, from *gris*, gray.] A young woman of the working-class in France; a belle of the working-class given to gaiety and gallantry.

Griskin, gris′kin, *n.* [Dim. from *grise* or *grice*. GRICE.] The spine of a hog.

Grisled, Grisly, griz′ld, griz′li, *a.* Gray; of a mixed colour; grizzled.

Grisly, griz′li, *a.* [A.Sax. *grislic*, from *grisan* or *ágrisan*, to dread, to fear greatly; allied to G. *grässlich*, horrible, *grausen*, horror; *grieseln*, to shudder; E. *grewsome*.] Frightful; horrible; terrible; grim.—**Grisliness**, griz′li-nes, *n.* Quality of being grisly.

Grist, grist, *n.* [A.Sax. *grist*, a grinding, from *grindan*, to grind. GRIND.] Corn ground in the mill or to be ground; the grain carried to the mill at one time, or the meal it produces.—*To bring grist to the mill*, to be a source of profit; to bring profitable business into one's hands.—**Grist-mill**, *n.* A mill for grinding grain.

Gristle, gris′l, *n.* [A.Sax. *gristel*, gristle; akin to *grist*, being named from the grinding or crunching it requires; comp. A.Sax. *gristlung*, a gnashing.] Cartilage.—**Gristly**, gris′li, *a.* Consisting of or like gristle; cartilaginous.

Grit, grit, *n.* [A.Sax. *greót*, sand; akin to E. *grits*, *grout*, *groats*; comp. Icel. *grjót*, stones, rubble; G. *gries*, grit.] Sand or gravel; rough hard particles; any hard sandstone in which the component grains of quartz are less rounded or sharper than in ordinary sandstones; structure of a stone in regard to fineness and closeness of texture.—**Grittiness**, grit′i-nes, *n.* Gritty state or quality.—**Gritty**, grit′i, *a.* Containing or consisting of grit; sandy.

Grits, grits, *n. pl.* [A.Sax. *grytta*, *gryttan*, grits or groats.] Coarse hominy (*U.S.*); grain hulled or coarsely ground.

Grivet, griv′et, *n.* A small green-gray Abyssinian monkey.

Grizzle, *v.i.* [Origin doubtful.] To fret; to sulk.—*n.* One who frets or sulks.

Grizzle, griz′l, *n.* [From Fr. *gris*, gray, from O.G. *gris*, gray.] A gray colour; a mixture of white and black; a mixture of white among dark hairs.—*v.i.* To grow gray or grizzly; to become gray-haired.—**Grizzled**, griz′ld, *a.* Of a grayish colour.—**Grizzly**, griz′li, *a.* Somewhat gray; grayish.—*Grizzly* or *grisly bear*, a large and ferocious bear of Western North America.

Groan, grōn, *v.i.* [A.Sax. *gránian*, to groan; perhaps imitative of the sound made in groaning; comp. A.Sax. *grunan*, to grunt; W. *grwn*, a groan.] To utter a mournful voice, as in pain or sorrow; to utter a deep, low-toned, moaning sound.—*n.* A deep, mournful sound uttered in pain, sorrow, or anguish; a deep sound uttered in disapprobation or derision.—**Groaner**, grō′nėr, *n.* One who groans.

Groat, grōt, *n.* [D. *groot*, G. *grot*, that is, *great*, a great piece or coin: so called because before this piece was coined by Edward III (1351) the English had no silver coin larger than a penny.] An old English coin and money of account, equal to fourpence; hence, colloquially, in England, fourpence, or a fourpenny piece.

Groats, grōts, *n. pl.* [A.Sax. *grátan*, groats: akin *grits*, *grout*.] Oats or wheat with the husks taken off.

Grocer, grō′sėr, *n.* [Properly a *grosser*, or one who sells things in the *gross*; O.Fr. *grossier*, one who sells by wholesale, from *gros*, great. GROSS.] A merchant who deals in tea, sugar, spices, coffee, fruits; a retail purveyor of foodstuffs.—**Grocery**, grō′sėr-i, *n.* A grocer's shop; *pl.* the commodities sold by grocers.

Grog, grog, *n.* [From 'Old *Grog*', a nickname given to Admiral Vernon, who introduced the beverage, from his wearing a *grogram* cloak in rough weather.] A mixture of spirit and water not sweetened; also used as a general term for strong drink.—**Grogginess**, grog′i-nes, *n.* The state of being groggy.—**Groggy**, grog′i, *a.* Overcome with grog; tipsy; *farriery*, moving in an uneasy, hobbling manner, owing to tenderness of the feet: said of a horse.—**Grog-shop**, *n.* A dram-shop.

Grogram, Grogran, grog′ram, grog′ran, *n.* [Fr. *grosgrain*, coarse grain, of a coarse texture. GROSS, GRAIN.] A kind of coarse stuff made of silk and mohair; also, a kind of strong, coarse silk.

Groin, groin, *n.* [Icel. *grein*, a branch, an arm of the sea, *greina*, to branch off or separate; Sw. *gren*, a branch, *grena*, to divide; Sc. *grain*, a branch, a prong of a fork.] The hollow of the human body in front at the junction of the thigh with the trunk; *arch.* the angular projecting curve made by the intersection of simple vaults crossing each other at any angle.—*v.t. Arch.* to form into groins; to ornament with groins.—**Groined**, groind, *a. Arch.* having a groin or groins; formed of groins meeting in a point.—**Groining**, groi′ning, *n. Arch.* the arrangement of groins; groins collectively.

Grommet, grum′et, *n.* [Armor. *grom*, a curb.] *Naut.* a ring of rope with or without a thimble: a loop formed at the end of a rope by splicing.

Groom, gröm, *n.* [From A.Sax. *guma*, O.E. *gome*, man, with an inserted *r*; comp. O.D. *grom*, Icel. *gromr*, a youth. *Guma* (Goth. *guma*, O.H.G. *homo*) is the Teutonic word equivalent to L. *homo*, a man. Hence *bridegroom* (A.Sax. *brydguma*).] A man or boy who has the charge of horses; one who takes care of horses or the stable; one of several officers in the English royal household; a bridegroom.—*v.t.* To curry or care for a horse.—**Groom's-man, Groomsman**, grömz′man, *n.* One who acts as attendant on a bridegroom at his marriage.

Groove, gröv, *n.* [From D. *groeve*, *groef*, a furrow, a ditch, a channel = G. *grube*, a pit, hole, grave; the stem being same as in E. *grave*, *v.t.*] A furrow or long hollow, such as is cut by a tool; a channel, usually an elongated narrow channel; the fixed routine of one's life.—*v.t.*—*grooved*, *grooving*. To cut a groove or channel in; to furrow.—**Grooved**, grövd, *p.* and *a.* Channelled; cut with grooves.—**Groover**, grö′vėr, *n.* One who or that which grooves.

Grope, grōp, *v.i.*—*groped*, *groping*. [A.Sax. *grápian*; closely allied to *gripe*, *grab*, and *grasp*.] To search or attempt to find something in the dark, or as a blind person, by feeling; to feel one's way; to attempt anything blindly.—*v.t.* To search out by feeling in or as in the dark (to *grope* our way).—**Groper**, grō′pėr, *n.* One who gropes.—**Gropingly**, grō′ping-li, *adv.* In a groping manner.

Grosbeak, *n.* GROSSBEAK.

Groschen, grō′shen, *n.* (*pl.* the same). [From L.L. *grossus*, thick—in opposition to ancient thin lead coins.] An old German coin; the ten-pfennig piece. (*Colloq.*)

Gross, grōs, *a.* [Fr. *gros*, big, thick, coarse; L.L. *grossus*, thick, crass; of doubtful origin. Hence *grocer*.] Coarse or rough; indelicate, obscene, or impure; sensual; great, palpable or enormous; shameful; flagrant (a *gross* mistake, *gross* injustice); dense; not attenuated; whole; entire; total; bulky‡; of some size‡.—*Gross weight*, the weight of merchandise or goods, with the bag, cask, chest, &c., in which they are contained.—*n.* Main body, chief part; bulk; the number of twelve dozen (being the *gross* or great hundred): has no plural form.—*A great gross*, twelve gross or 144 dozen.—*In the gross*, *in gross*, in the bulk, or the undivided whole; all parts taken together.—**Grossbeak, Grosbeak**, grōs′bēk, *n.* A name common to a group of finches distinguished by the thickness and strength of the bill.—**Grossification**, gros′i-fi-kā″shon, *n. Bot.* the swelling of the ovary of plants after fertilization.—**Grossify**, gros′i-fī, *v.t.* and *i.* To make gross or thick; to become gross or thick.—**Grossly**, grōs′li, *adv.* In a gross manner.—**Grossness**, grōs′nes, *n.* The quality of being gross; obscenity; greatness.

Grossulaceous, gros-ū-lā′shus, *a.* [L.L. *grossula*, a gooseberry.] *Bot.* pertaining to the tribe of plants comprehending the gooseberry and currant of gardens.—**Grossular**, gros′ū-lėr, *a.* Pertaining to or resembling a gooseberry.

Grot, grot, *n.* Grotto. [Poet.]

Grotesque, grō-tesk′, *a.* [Fr., from *grotte*, a grotto, from the style of the paintings found in the ancient crypts and grottos. GROTTO.] Having a wild, extraordinary, or extravagant form; of the utmost oddness; whimsical; extravagant.—*n.* A capricious variety of arabesque ornamentation; a whimsical figure or scenery.—**Grotesquely**, grō-tesk′li, *adv.* In a grotesque manner.—**Grotesqueness**, grō-tesk′nes, *n.*—**Grotesquery**, grō-tes′kėr-i, *n.* Grotesque whims or antics; grotesque conduct.

Grotto, grot′tō, *n.* pl. **Grottos** or **Grottoes**, grot′tōz. [Fr. *grotte*, It. *grotta*, from L. *crypta*, Gr. *kryptē*, a cave, a vault, from *kryptō*, to conceal. CRYPT.] A cave or natural cavity in the earth, as in a mountain or rock; an artificial cavern decorated with rock-work, shells, &c., constructed for coolness and pleasure.

Ground, ground, *n.* [A.Sax. *grund*, ground; probably from *grindan*, to grind; G. Dan. and Sw. *grund*, D. *grond*, Icel. *grunnr*, Goth. *grundus*, ground; probably the original meaning was fine dust; similarly, *mold*, earth, is connected with *meal*.] The surface of the earth; the earth we tread on and subject to tillage, &c.; the soil; the soil of a particular country or person; land; estate; that on which anything may rest, rise, or originate; basis; foundation; support; *elect.*, a general term for the connection of an electrical conductor to the earth; *painting*, the first layer of color on which the others are wrought; the primary or predominating color; a foil or background that sets off anything; *etching*, a composition spread over the surface of the plate to be etched, to prevent the acid from eating into the plate, except where an opening is made with the point of the etching-needle; *pl.* sediment at the bottom of liquors; dregs; lees.—*To break ground*, to penetrate the soil for the first time, as in cutting the first turf of a railway; hence, *fig.* to take the first step; to enter upon an undertaking.—*To fall to the ground*, to come to nought.—*To gain ground*, to advance; to obtain an advantage; to gain credit; to become more general or extensive.—*To lose ground*, to withdraw from the position taken; to lose advantage; to decline; to become less in force or extent.—*To give ground*, to recede; to yield advantage.—*To stand one's ground*, to stand firm; not to recede or yield.—*v.t.* To lay or set on or in the ground; to cause to run (a ship) aground; to settle or establish, as on a foundation or basis; to fix or settle firmly; to found; to base; to thoroughly instruct in elements or first principles; *elect.*, to connect an electrical conductor to the earth.—*v.i.* To run aground; to strike the ground and remain fixed (the ship *grounded* in two fathoms of water).—**Groundedly**, groun′ded-li, *adv.* In a grounded or firmly-established manner.—**Groundless**, ground′les, *a.* Wanting ground or foundation; wanting cause or reason; baseless; false.—**Groundlessly**, ground′les-li, *adv.* In a groundless manner.—**Groundling**, ‡ground′ling, *n.* A spectator who stood in the pit of the theater (*Shak.*)—**Ground-floor**, *n.* The floor of a house on a level, or nearly so, with the exterior ground.—**Ground ice**. Ice formed at the bottom before ice begins to appear on the surface.—**Ground-hog**, the woodchuck.—**Ground-hog day**, February 2, when the woodchuck is supposed to rouse from its sleep to see if winter is over.—**Ground ivy**, a trailing plant with purplish flowers and oval leaves; English ivy.—**Groundnut**, *n.* The peanut; also see

ARACHIS, EARTH NUT.—**Ground-plan**, *n.* A plan showing the divisions of a building on the same level as the surface of the ground.—**Ground-plane**, *n.* The horizontal plane of projection in perspective drawing.—**Ground-plate**, *n.* Same as *Groundsill.*—**Ground-rent**, *n.* Rent paid for the privilege of building on another man's land.—**Groundsill**, ground'sil, *n.* The timber of a building which lies next to the ground; the ground-plate.—**Ground-squirrel**, *n.* The name of several animals allied to the true squirrels, but having cheek-pouches, and living in holes.—**Ground-swell**, *n.* A deep swell or rolling of the sea, occasioned along the shore by a distant storm or gale.—**Ground-tackle**, *n.* *Naut.* the anchors, cables, warps, &c., used for securing a vessel at anchor.—**Groundwork**, ground'wėrk, *n.* The work which forms the foundation of anything; that to which the rest is additional; the basis.

Ground, ground, pret. & pp. of *grind.*

Groundsel, ground'sel, *n.* [O.E. *groundswell*, Sc. *groundie-swallow*, A.Sax. *grundeswelge, grundswelige*, groundsel, lit. ground-swallowing, that is entirely covering.] A common annual weed, much used as food for caged birds. Also *grunsel-edge* (Mil.)

Group, gröp, *n.* [Fr. *groupe*, a group; allied to *croupe*, the buttocks of a horse; Icel. *croppr*, a hump or bunch. CROUP (rump) and CROP (craw of a bird.)] An assemblage, either of persons or things; a number collected; a cluster; an artistic combination of figures; in scientific classifications a number of individuals having some resemblance or common characteristic.—*v.t.* To form into a group; to arrange in a group or in groups.

Grouse, grous, *n.* [Etym. doubtful; perhaps erroneously formed as a singular to the old form *grice*, a grouse, on the supposition that this was a plural like *mice*; comp. O.Fr. *poule griesche*, a moor hen—*poule*, a fowl, and *griesche*, speckled, gray.] The common name of a number of rasorial game birds with mottled plumage, more particularly applied to the red grouse and the ruffed grouse.

Grout, grout, *n.* [A.Sax. *grút*, barley or wheat meal; Icel. *grautr*, porridge; akin to *groats, grits* (which see).] Coarse meal; pollard; a thin mortar used for pouring into the joints of masonry and brickwork; a kind of thick ale; lees, grounds, dregs.

Grove, grōv, *n.* [A.Sax. *gróf*, a grove, from *grafan*, to dig, a grove being originally an alley cut out in a wood; akin *grave* (*v.* and *n.*).] A cluster of trees shading an avenue or walk; an assemblage of growing trees of no great extent; a small wood.

Grovel, grov'el, *v.i.*—*groveled, groveling*, or *grovelled, grovelling.* [Akin to O.E. *grof, groff*, flat, with the face towards the earth; Icel. *grufla*, to grovel, *gruft*, a groveling; Sw. *grufa*, prone, with the face towards the earth.] To lie prone or move with the body prostrate on the earth; to have a tendency towards or take pleasure in low or base things; to be low, abject, or mean.—**Groveler**, grov'el-ėr, *n.* One who grovels.—**Groveling**, grov'el-ing, *p.* and *a.* Indulging by preference in what is low or base.

Grow, grō, *v.i.*—*grew* (pret.), *grown* (pp.). [A.Sax. *grówan*, past *greów*, pp. *grówen* = D. *groeijen*, Icel. *gróa*, Dan. *groe*, Sw. *gro*, to grow; allied to *green.*] To become enlarged in bulk or stature, by a natural and organic process: said of animals and vegetables; to increase in any way; to become larger and stronger; to be augmented; to wax; to advance; to extend; to swell (the wind *grew* to a hurricane); to be changed from one state to another; to result, as from a cause or reason; to become (to *grow* pale).—*To grow out of*, to issue from by growth; to result from, as an effect from a cause.—*To grow up*, to advance to full stature or maturity.—*To grow together*, to become united by growth.—*v.t.* To cause to grow; to cultivate; to produce; to raise.—**Grower**, grō'ėr, *n.* One who or that which grows or increases; one who grows, raises, or produces; a cultivator.—**Grown**, grōn, pp. of *grow.* Increased in growth; having arrived at full size or stature.—*Grown over*, covered by the growth of anything; overgrown.—*Grown-up*, full-grown; having attained man's or woman's estate.—**Growth**, grōth, *n.* The process of growing; increase of bulk in animals and plants; gradual increase in any way, as in number, bulk, &c.; that which has grown; something produced by growing.

Growl, groul, *v.i.* [Comp. D. *grollen*, to growl or grumble; G. *grollen*, to roar; perhaps imitative of sound.] To murmur or snarl, as a dog; to utter an angry, grumbling sound.—*v.t.* To express by growling; to utter in an angry or grumbling tone.—*n.* The angry snarl of a dog; the inarticulate grumble of a discontented or angry person.—**Growler**, grou'lėr, *n.* One who growls; a four-wheeler, as in the 'rumble' (which see).

Groyne, groin, *n.* [GROIN.] A structure projecting into the sea or a river to check its encroachments.

Grub, grub, *v.t.* *grubbed, grubbing.* [O.E. *grubbe, grobbe*; akin to *grope*; comp. G. *gruben*, to dig.] To dig in or under the ground; to be occupied in digging.—*v.t.* To dig; to dig up by the roots; to root up by digging; generally followed by *up* or *out.*—*n.* [From grubbing in the ground, dirt, &c.] The larva of an insect, especially of beetles; food (*slang*).—**Grubber**, grub'ėr, *n.* One who grubs; an instrument for grubbing out roots, weeds, &c.—**Grub axe, Grubbing hoe**, an instrument for digging up trees, shrubs, &c., by the roots; a mattock.—**Grub-stake**, *n.* Food or equipment given to a prospector in return for a share of what he may find.

Grudge, gruj, *v.t.*—*grudged, grudging.* [Formerly *grucche, grutche, groche*, &c., from O.Fr. *groucher, grouchier, groucer*, to grumble; of doubtful origin.] To permit or grant with reluctance; to begrudge.—*v.i.* To be envious; to cherish ill-will.—*n.* Unwillingness to benefit; reluctance felt in giving; ill-will from envy or sense of injury.—**Grudger**, gruj'ėr, *n.* One that grudges.—**Grudgingly**, gruj'ing-li, *adv.* With reluctance or discontent.

Gruel, grų'el, *n.* [O.Fr. *gruel*, for *grutel*, from D. or L.G. *grut* = E. *grout* (which see).] A kind of broth made by boiling ingredients in water: usually made of the meal of oats.

Gruesome, Grewsome, grö'sum, *a.* [D. *gruwen*, Dan. *grue*, G. *grauen*, to shudder.] Causing one to shudder; frightful; horrible.

Gruff, gruf, *a.* [Same word as D. *grof*, Dan. *grov*, G. *grob*, coarse, blunt, rude.] Of a rough or stern manner, voice, or countenance; sour; surly.—**Gruffish**, gruf'ish, *a.* Somewhat gruff; rather rough and surly.—**Gruffly**, gruf'li, *adv.*—**Gruffness**, *n.*

Grum, grum, *a.* [Comp. A.Sax. *grom*, *gram*, severe.] Morose; severe of countenance; sour; surly; glum.

Grumble, grum'bl, *v.i.*—*grumbled, grumbling.* [Perhaps same as D. *grommelen*, *grommen*, Fr. *grommeler*, to grumble; akin to A.Sax. *grimman*, to murmur, to rage; E. *grim, grum.* This, like other words such as *grunt, growl*, may have been partly affected by sound-imitation.] To murmur with discontent; to utter in a low voice by way of complaint; to give vent to discontented expressions; to growl; to snarl; to rumble; to roar; to make a harsh and heavy sound.—*v.t.* To express or utter by grumbling.—**Grumbler**, grum'blėr, *n.* One who grumbles; a discontented man.—**Grumblingly**, grum'bling-li, *adv.* With grumbling or complaint.

Grume, gröm, *n.* [O.Fr. *grume*, Fr. *grumeau*, a clot; from L. *grumus*, a little heap.] A fluid of a thick, viscid consistence; a clot, as of blood.—**Grumose**, grö'mōs, *a.* *Bot.* grumous.—**Grumous**, grö'mus, *a.* Resembling or containing grume; thick; clotted; *bot.* formed of coarse grains, as some clustered tubercular roots.—**Grumousness, Grumosity**, grö'mus-nes, grö-mos'i-ti, *n.*

Grumpy, Grumpish, grum'pi, grum'-pish, *a.* [Connected with *grum, grumble.*] Surly; angry; gruff. (*Colloq.*)—**Grumpily**, grum'pi-li, *adv.* In a grumpy, surly, or gruff manner.

Grunt, grunt, *v.i.* [Probably from an imitative root seen in A.Sax. *grunan*, E. *groan*, Dan. *grynte*, G. *grunzen*, to grunt; comp. also L. *grunnio*, Fr. *grogner*, to grunt; Gr. *gru*, the cry of a pig.] To snort or make a noise like a hog; to utter a short groan or a deep guttural sound, as of a hog.—*n.* A deep guttural sound, as of a hog.—**Grunter**, grun'tėr, *n.* One that grunts; a fish that makes a grunting sound.

Gruyère, gru-yãr', *n.* A kind of cheese made from a mixture of goats' and ewes' milk, from Gruyère in Switzerland.

Grype,‡ grīp, *n.* A griffin. (*Shak.*)

Guacharo, gwa-chä'rō, *n.* [Sp.] A South American bird of the goatsucker family, valued for its fat.

Guaiacum, gwā'ya-kum, *n.* [Native name.] A South American tree and the resin obtained from it, the latter, as well as the bark and wood, being of medicinal value.

Guan, gwän, *n.* A South American gallinaceous bird, allied to the curassows.

Guanaco, gwa-nä'kō, *n.* [Sp., Peruv. *huanacu.*] A quadruped closely allied to the llama and alpaca.

Guano, gwä'nō, *n.* [Sp. *guano, huano*, from Peruv. *huanu*, dung.] A substance found on many small islands, especially in the Pacific Ocean and on the west coast of South America, chiefly composed of the excrement of sea-fowl in a decomposed state, much used as a manure.—*v.t.* To manure with guano.—**Guaniferous**, gwä-nif'ėr-us, *a.* Yielding guano.—**Guanine**, gū-ȧ'nēn, *n.* [From *guano.*] A nitrogenous waste product formed in the animal body.

Guarantee, gar-an-tē', *v.t.*—*guaranteed, guaranteeing.* [O.Fr. *guarantie*, a form of *warranty*. WARRANT, &c.] To warrant; to pledge one's self for; to become bound that an article shall be as good or useful as it is represented; to secure the performance of; to undertake to secure to another (claims, rights, possessions); to undertake to uphold or maintain.—*n.* An undertaking that the engagement or promise of another shall be performed; a pledging of one's self as surety; one who binds himself to see the stipulations of another performed; a guarantor.—**Guarantor**, gar-an-tor', *n.* A warrantor; one who gives a guarantee.—**Guaranty**. Same as *Guarantee.*

Guard, gärd, *v.t.* [The form in which the Germanic equivalent of E. *ward* passed into English through the Norman; O.Fr. *guarder*, Fr. *garder*, to guard. WARD.] To secure against injury, loss, or attack; to defend; to keep in safety; to accompany for protection; to provide or secure against objections or attacks.—*To guard one's self against*, to be on one's guard against; to take pains to avoid doing or saying.—*v.i.* To watch by way of caution or defense; to be cautious; to be in a state of caution or defense (to *guard* against mistake).—*n.* A state of caution or vigilance, or the act of observing what passes in order to prevent surprise or attack; defense; attention; watch; heed; *fencing* or *boxing*, a posture of defense; the arms or weapon in such a posture; one who guards or keeps watch; one whose business is to defend or prevent attack or surprise; a brakeman or gateman on a railway, or, *Brit.*, a conductor; *football*, one of two players in the line on either side of center; in England, the body of troops that guards the king; that which guards or protects; any appliance or attachment designed to protect or secure against injury; an ornamental border on one's dress.—*On guard*, acting as a guard or sentinel.—*To be on our* (*your, my,* &c.) *guard*), to be in a watchful state.—**Guardable**, gär'da-bl, *a.* That may be guarded or protected.—**Guarded**, gär'ded, *p.* and *a.* Protected; defended; cautious; circumspect (*guarded* in language); framed or uttered with caution.—**Guardedly**, gär'ded-li, *adv.* In a guarded or cautious manner. — **Guardedness**, gär'ded-nes, *n.*—**Guardian**, gär'di-an, *n.* [Fr. *gardien.*] One who guards; one to whom anything is committed for preservation from injury; one who has the charge or custody of any person or thing.—*a.* Protecting; performing the office of a protector. — **Guardianship**, gär'di-an-ship, *n.* The office of a guardian; protection; care; watch. — **Guard-house, Guard-room**, *n.* A house or room for the accommodation of a guard of soldiers, and where military defaulters are confined.—**Guard-ship**, *n.* A vessel of war for the protection of a harbour, river, &c. — **Guardsman**, gärdz'man, *n.* A watchman; an officer or private in a regiment of guards.

Guava, gwä'va, *n.* [The native name in Guiana.] A small tropical tree of the myrtle family, the fruit of which is made into a delicious jelly.

Gubernatorial, gū'bėr-na-tō"ri-al, *a.* [L. *gubernator*, a governor. GOVERN.] Pertaining to government or to a governor.

Gudgeon, guj'on, *n.* [Fr. *goujon*, from L. *gobio, gobius*, Gr. *kōbios*, a gudgeon.] A small fresh-water fish which is very easily caught; hence, a person easily cheated or insnared.—*v.t.* To cheat; to impose on.

Gudgeon, guj'on, *n.* [Fr. *goujon*; origin doubtful.] A metallic piece let into the end of a wooden shaft and forming a sort of axle to it; the bearing portion of a shaft.

Guebre, Gueber, gā'bėr or gē'bėr, *n.* A Per. form of Turk. *giaour*, Ar. *kafir*, an infidel.] The name given by the Mohammedans to one belonging to the Persian fire-worshippers, called in India *Parsees*.

Guelder-rose, *n.* GELDER-ROSE.

Guelphs, Ghibellines, gwelfs, gib'el-ēns, *n.* The Welfs and Waiblings, names of German-Italian political parties in the early mediæval times, favouring respectively the Pope and the Emperor; Papalists and Imperialists.

Guerdon, gėr'don, *n.* [O.Fr. *guerdon*, It. *guiderdone*, from L.L. *widerdonum*, corrupted from O.G. *widarlōn* (A.Sax. *witherlean*), a recompense, through the influence of the L. *donum*, a gift—from *widar* (G. *wider*), against, and *lōn*, reward (=E. *loan*).] A reward; requital; recompense: used both in a good and bad sense (*poet.* or *rhet.*).—*v.t.* To give a guerdon to; to reward.

Guernsey, gėrn'se, *n.* A sort of close-fitting woolen knitted shirt; a breed of dairy cattle.

Guerrilla, Guerilla, ge-ril'lä; Sp. pron. ger-rēl'yä, *n.* [Sp. *guerrilla*, dim. of *guerra*, Fr. *guerre*, war, from O.H.G. *werra*, war.] A carrying on of war by the constant attacks of independent bands; an irregular petty war; one engaged in this irregular warfare.—**Guerrillero, Guerillist**, ger-rēl-yer'ō, ge-ril'ist, *n.* One who engages in guerrilla warfare.

Guess, ges, *v.t.* [O.E. *gesse* = L.G. and D. *gissen*, Dan. *gisse*, Icel. *giska, gizka*, to guess, lit. to try to *get*. GET.] To form an opinion without good means of knowledge or sufficient evidence; to judge of at random; to suppose; to imagine: often followed by a clause. [This verb is much used colloquially in the sense of to believe, to be sure.]—*v.i.* To form a conjecture; to judge at random, or without any strong evidence: with *at.*—*n.* A conjecture.—**Guesser**, ges'ėr, *n.* One who guesses.—**Guessingly**, ges'ing-li, *adv.* By way of conjecture.—**Guesswork**, ges'wėrk, *n.* Mere conjecture; the act of working by hazard.

Guest, gest, *n.* [A.Sax. *gæst, gest* = Icel. *gestr*, Dan. *giest*, D. and G. *gast*, Goth. *gasts*, a guest, a stranger; cog. Armor. *hostiz*, Rus. *gosty*, a guest; L. *hostis*, an enemy (whence E. *host, hostile*).] A visitor or friend entertained in the house or at the table of another; a lodger at a hotel or lodging-house.—**Guestwise**, gest'wīz, *adv.* In the manner or capacity of a guest. (*Shak.*)

Guffaw, guf'fa, *n.* [Imitative.] A loud or sudden burst of laughter.—*v.i.* To burst into a loud or sudden laugh.

Guggle, gug'l, *v.i.* [Imitative, suggested by *gurgle.*] To make a sound like that of a liquid passing through a narrow aperture; to gurgle. — *n.* A sound of this kind; a gurgle.

Guide, gīd, *v.t.* — *guided, guiding.* [Fr. *guider*, It. *guidare*, Sp. *guiar*—of Teutonic origin, and akin to G. *weisen*, to show, to lead, Goth. *witan*, to watch over; A.Sax. *witan*, to know, to *wit*, with change of *w* to *gu* as in *guile, guard.* WIT.] To lead or direct in a way; to conduct in a course or path; to direct; to regulate; to influence in conduct or actions; to give direction to; to instruct and direct; to superintend. — *n.* [Fr. *guide*, It. *guida*, Sp. *guia.*] A person who guides; a leader or conductor; one who conducts travellers or tourists in particular localities; one who or that which directs another in his conduct or course of life; a director; a regulator; a guide-book; *technology*, applied to various contrivances intended to direct or keep to a fixed course or motion.—**Guidable**, gī'da-bl, *a.* Capable of being guided.—**Guidance**, gī'dans, *n.* The act of guiding; direction; government. —**Guide-book**, *n.* A book for giving travellers or tourists information about the places they visit.—**Guideless**, gīd'les, *a.* Destitute of a guide; wanting a director.—**Guidelessness**, gīd'les-nes, *n.*—**Guide-post**, *n.* A post at the parting of roads for directing travellers; a finger-post.

Guidon, gī'don, *n.* [Fr., lit. a *guiding* flag.] The flag of a troop of cavalry; a flag used to signal with at sea, &c.

Guild, gild, *n.* [A.Sax. *gild*, a payment, hence a society where payment was made for its protection and support, from *gildan*, to pay; D. *gild*, a guild. GUILT, YIELD.] An association or incorporation of men belonging to the same class or engaged in similar pursuits, formed for mutual aid and protection. — **Guild-hall**, *n.* The hall where a guild or corporation usually assembles; a town or corporation hall.—**Guildry**, gild'ri, *n.* In Scotland, a guild; the members of a guild.

Guilder, gil'der, *n.* [D. and G. *gulden*, a florin; modified as if meaning a coin of *Gelders* or *Gueldres.*] A coin of Holland worth about 40 cents in American money; same as *Gulden*.

Guile, gīl, *n.* [French form of E. *wile* (which see); O.Fr. *guile*, guile, from a Germanic form, with regular change of G. *w* into Romance *gu* (as in *guide*).] Craft; cunning; artifice; duplicity; deceit. — **Guileful**, gīl'ful, *a.* Full of guile; intended to deceive; crafty; wily; deceitful; insidious; treacherous.—**Guilefully**, gīl'-ful-li, *adv.* In a guileful manner.—**Guilefulness**, gīl'ful-nes, *n.* The state or quality of being guileful.—**Guileless**, gīl'les, *a.* Free from guile.—**Guilelessness**, gīl'les-nes, *n.*

Guillemot, gil'lē-mot, *n.* [Fr. *guillemot*, perhaps from Armor. *gwéla*, to weep, and O.Fr. *moëtte*, a gull.] A marine swimming bird allied to the auks and divers.

Guillotine, gil-o-tēn', *n.* [From Dr. *Guillotin*, who introduced in the French Convention the motion for the use of the machine, first called *Louisette*, from inventor, Dr. Louis.] An engine for beheading persons by means of a steel blade loaded with a mass of lead, and sliding between two upright posts; a machine which consists of a knife descending between grooved posts, much used for cutting paper, straw, &c.—*v.t.*—*guillotined, guillotining.* To behead by the guillotine. — **Guillotinement**, gil-ō-tēn'ment, *n.* Decapitation by the guillotine. (*Carl.*)

Guilt, gilt, *n.* [A.Sax. *gylt*, a crime, from *gildan, gyldan*, to pay, to requite; akin Icel. *gjald*, payment, retribution, *gjalda*, to pay, to yield; E. *yield, guild.*] Criminality; that state of a moral agent which results from his wilful or intentional commission of a crime or offence, knowing it to be a crime or violation of law.—**Guiltily**, gil'-ti-li, *adv.* In a guilty manner.—**Guiltiness**, gil'ti-nes, *n.* The state of being guilty; wickedness; criminality; guilt.—**Guiltless**, gilt'les, *a.* Free from guilt, crime, or offence; innocent; not having experience; ignorant (with *of*; *poet.*) — **Guiltlessly**, gilt'les-li, *adv.* In a guiltless manner.—**Guiltlessness**, gilt'les-nes, *n.* State or quality of being guiltless.—**Guilty**, gil'ti, *a.* Having incurred guilt; not innocent; criminal; morally delinquent: with *of* before the crime; pertaining to guilt; indicating guilt (a *guilty* look).

Guinea, gin'ē, *n.* [Because first coined of gold brought from *Guinea*, in Africa.] A gold coin formerly current in Great Britain of the value of 21 shillings sterling, or $5.11 (at par); a sum of money of the same amount; also abbreviated form of *guinea* fowl.—**Guinea corn**, *n.* A kind of millet cultivated in Guinea and elsewhere.—**Guinea fowl**, *n.* A fowl of the rasorial order, closely allied to the peacocks and pheasants, common in Guinea. —**Guinea pepper**, *n.* A kind of capsicum; a name of various kinds of pepper. —**Guinea pig**, *n.* [Perhaps for *Guiana-pig.*] A tailless rodent mammal, about 7 inches in length, belonging to South America, and often used for medical experimentation.—**Guinea worm**, *n.* A worm common in hot countries, which often insinuates itself under the human skin, causing intense pain.

Guipure, gē-pūr', *n.* [Fr.] An imitation of antique lace; a kind of gimp.

Guise, gīz, *n.* [Fr. *guise*, the equivalent of E. *wise*, mode, fashion, O.H.G. *wîsa*, G. *weise*, with common change from *w* to *gu* in words borrowed into French from the German; comp. *guile, wile.*] External appearance; dress; garb; manner; mien; cast or behaviour; custom; mode; practice.—**Guiser**, gī'zėr, *n.* [One who assumes a *guise* other than his own.] A masker; a mummer.

Guitar, gi-tär', *n.* [Fr. *guitare*, It. *chitarra*, from L. *cithara*, Gr. *kithara*, a kind of lyre.] A musical stringed instrument having six strings, which are played by twitching with the fingers of the right hand, while the notes are stopped by the fingers of the left.

Gular, gū'lėr, *a.* [From L. *gula*, the throat or gullet.] Pertaining to the gullet.

Gulch, gulch, *n.* [Allied to Sw. *gölka*, to swallow, D. *gulzig*, greedy.] A deep, abrupt ravine caused by the action of water; the dry bed of a torrent; a gully.

Gulden, gul'den, *n.* The unit of the Netherlands coinage, worth about 40 cents. GUILDER.

Gules, gūlz, *n.* [Fr *gueules*, from Per. *gul*, a rose.] *Her.* vertical, parallel lines in a shield indicating the color red.—**Guly**, gū'li, *a.* Of or pertaining to gules.

Gulf, gulf, *n.* [Fr. *golfe*, It. *golfo*, Mod.Gr. *kolphos*, from Gr. *kolpos*, a gulf or bay.] A large indentation on the coast-line of a country and the sea embraced in it; a bay; a bight; an abyss, chasm, or deep opening in the earth; what gulfs or swallows; a wide interval, as in station, education, and the like.—*v.t.* To swallow up; to engulf; to refuse a degree with honours, but concede a pass.—**Gulf-stream**, *n.* A current of warm water which flows from the Gulf of Mexico through the channel between Cuba and America, and sweeps north-eastwards towards Europe.—**Gulf-weed**, *n.* A sea-weed found abundantly in the Atlantic Ocean, where it covers vast areas; drift-weed.

Gull, gul, *n.* [In Old and Prov.E., a young unfledged bird, lit. a yellow bird, from the yellowness of the beak and plumage of young birds, from O.E. *gul*, yellow = Icel. *gulr*, Dan. *gul, gaul*, yellow. YELLOW.

Comp. Fr. *béjaune*, yellow-beak, novice.] A young unfledged bird (*Shak.*); one easily cheated; a simpleton; a trick (*Shak.*).—*v.t.* To make a fool of; to mislead by deception; to trick.—**Gullibility**, gul-i-bil′i-ti, *n.* The quality of being gullible.—**Gullible**, gul′i-bl, *a.* Easily gulled or cheated.—**Gullish**, gul′ish, *a.* Foolish; stupid.

Gull, gul, *n.* [From the Celtic; W. *gwylan*, Armor. *gwelan*, Corn. *gullan*, a gull.] A name for many marine swimming birds found on the shores of all latitudes, and having large wings, slender legs, webbed feet, and a small or no hind toe.

Gullet, gul′et, *n.* [Fr. *goulet*, from L. *gula*, the throat.] The passage in the neck of an animal by which food and liquor are taken into the stomach; the œsophagus; something resembling this.

Gully, gul′i, *n.* [Fr. *goulet*, a gullet, a channel for water. GULLET.] A channel or hollow worn in the earth by a current of water; a ravine; a ditch; a gutter; a large knife.—*v.t.* To wear into a gully or channel.

Gulp, gulp, *v.t.* [A form of *gulf*, to swallow; same as D. *golpen*, to swallow greedily; Dan. *gulpe*, to disgorge.] To swallow eagerly or in large draughts.—*n.* The act of taking a large swallow.

Gum, gum, *n.* [A.Sax. *góma*, Icel. *gómr*, G. *gaum*, palate, gum.] The fleshy substance on the jaws which envelops the neck of the teeth.—**Gum-boil**, *n.* A boil or small abscess on the gum.—**Gum-rash**, *n.* A mild species of papular eruption to which many children are subject soon after birth.

Gum, gum, *n.* [Fr. *gomme*, from L. *gummi*, Gr. *kommi*, gum.] A juice which exudes from trees either spontaneously or after incisions are made, and thickens on the surface, or is obtained from their seeds or roots.—*v.t.—gummed, gumming.* To smear with gum; to unite or stiffen by gum or a gum-like substance.—*v.i.* To exude or form gum.—**Gum-anime**. ANIME.—**Gum-arabic**, *n.* The juice of various species of acacia, hardened in the air.—**Gum-boots**, gum-bötz, *n.* Long waterproof boots made of india-rubber.—**Gum-elastic**, *n.* Caoutchouc; india-rubber.—**Gum-elemi**. ELEMI.—**Gum-juniper**, *n.* The resin of a coniferous tree found in Barbary.—**Gum-lac**, *n.* LAC.—**Gummiferous**, gum-if′ér-us, *a.* Producing gum.—**Gumminess**, gum′i-nes, *n.* The state or quality of being gummy; viscousness.—**Gumming**, gum′ing, *n.* A disease in trees bearing stone fruit, characterized by a morbid exudation of gum, and generally killing the tree.—**Gummous**, gum′us, *a.* Of the nature or quality of gum; gummy.—**Gummy**, gum′i, *a.* Consisting of gum; of the nature of gum; giving out gum; covered with gum or viscous matter.

Gumbo, gum′bō, *n.* A soup thickened with the mucilaginous seed pods of the okra; the plant okra or its seed pods; rich, black soil that becomes soapy or sticky when wet.

Gumption, gum′shon, *n.* [Perhaps for *goamishing*, a being *goamish*, from O.E. *gome*, O.Sax. *góma*, Icel. *gaumr*, care.] Understanding; capacity; shrewdness. (*Colloq.*)

Gun, gun, *n.* [From the name *Gunnhildr*, of fourteenth century. So Mons *Meg*, Brown *Bess*, Fat *Bertha* (Krupp), 1917.] A name applied to every species of firearm for throwing projectiles by the explosion of gunpowder or other explosive.—*Great gun*, a cannon; a person distinguished in any department (*colloq.*).—*To blow great guns*, to be a tempest.—**Gun-barrel**, *n.* The barrel or tube of a gun.—**Gun-boat**, *n.* A boat or small vessel fitted to carry one or more guns of heavy calibre, and from its light draught capable of running close inshore or up rivers.—**Gun-carriage**, *n.* The carriage on which a cannon is mounted or moved, and on which it is fired.—**Gun-cotton**, *n.* A highly explosive substance produced by soaking cotton or similar vegetable fibre in nitric and sulphuric acids, and then leaving it to dry.—**Gun-fire**, *n.* *Milit.* the hour at which the morning or evening gun is fired.—**Gun-flint**, *n.* A piece of shaped flint, fixed in the lock of a musket or pistol to fire the charge before the introduction of percussion caps.—**Gun-layer**, *n.* One who lays or gives the proper position to a gun before firing; a trained artilleryman.—**Gun-metal**, *n.* An alloy, generally of nine parts of copper and one part of tin, used for the manufacture of cannon, &c.—**Gunner**, gun′ér, *n.* One who works a gun or cannon, either on land or sea; a warrant officer in the navy connected with the charge of the ordnance.—**Gunnery**, gun′ér-i, *n.* The art of firing or managing guns; the science of artillery.—**Gun-port**, *n.* An opening in the side of a ship through which cannon are discharged.—**Gunpowder**, gun′pou-dér, *n.* An explosive mixture of saltpetre, sulphur, and charcoal, reduced to a fine powder, then granulated and dried.—*Gunpowder tea*, a fine species of green tea with a granular appearance.—**Gun-runner**, *n.* One who runs or secretly conveys guns into a district.—**Gunshot**, gun′shot, *n.* The firing of a gun; the distance to which shot can be thrown so as to be effective.—*a.* Made by the shot of a gun (*gunshot* wounds).—**Gunsmith**, gun′smith, *n.* One whose occupation is to make or repair small firearms.—**Gunsmithery**, gun′smith-ér-i, *n.* The business of a gunsmith.—**Gun-tackle**, *n.* The blocks and pulleys affixed to the sides of a gun-carriage and the side of a ship by means of which a gun is run up to or drawn back from the port-hole.—**Gun-wadding**, *n.* Circular pieces of card-board, cloth, felt, &c., used to keep down the charge in a gun.—**Gunwale**, **Gunnel**, gun′wāl, gun′el, *n.* [*Gun*, and *wale*, the upper edge of a ship's side.] *Naut.* the upper edge of a ship's or boat's side.

Gunny, gun′i, *n.* [Bengalee.] A strong coarse cloth manufactured of jute in Bengal, for making into bags, sacks, &c.

Gunter, gunt′ér, *n.* [*Gunter*, mathematician.] A flat two-foot rule, with logarithmic lines, used for surveying and navigation; a sail on topmast, sliding on rings, as in Gunter's sliding scale.

Gurge,† gerj, *n.* [L. *gurges*, a whirlpool.] A whirlpool (*Mil.*).

Gurgle, gér′gl, *v.i.—gurgled, gurgling.* [Probably imitative or connected with *gorge*; comp. G. *gurgeln*, It. *gorgogliare*, to gurgle. GARGLE.] To run or flow in an irregular, noisy current, as water from a bottle; to flow with a purling sound.—*n.* The sound made by a liquid flowing from the narrow mouth of a vessel, or generally through any narrow opening.

Gurgoyle, gér′goil, *n.* *Arch.* GARGOYLE.

Gurkha, gur-ka, *n.* A native of Nepal, in Hindostan. There are Gurkha regiments in the Indian army.

Gurnard, **Gurnet**, gér′närd, gér′net, *n.* [O.Fr. *grougnaut*, probably from *grogner*, L. *grunnire*, to grunt or grumble, from the sound these fishes make when taken from the water.] The name of certain marine fishes, having an angular head wholly covered with bony plates.

Gush, gush, *v.i.* [Icel. *gjósa*, to gush, *gusa*, a gush, to gush; a Scandinavian word, allied to A.Sax. *geótan*, Goth. *giutan*, G. *giessen*, to pour; E. *gut*, *gust* (of wind), *geyser*.] To rush forth as a fluid from confinement; to flow suddenly or copiously; to be extravagantly and effusively sentimental.—*v.t.* To emit suddenly, copiously, or with violence.—*n.* A sudden and violent issue of a fluid; an emission of liquor in a large quantity and with force; an outpour; an effusive display of sentiment.—**Gusher**, gush′ér, *n.* One who or that which gushes; a person who is demonstratively sentimental.—**Gushing**, gush′ing, *ppr.* Rushing forth with violence, as a fluid; flowing copiously; exuberantly and demonstratively affectionate; extravagantly sentimental.—**Gushingly**, gush′ing-li, *adv.* In a gushing manner.

Gusset, gus′et, *n.* [Fr. *gousset*, a gusset, from *gousse*, a husk or shell.] A triangular piece of cloth inserted in a garment for the purpose of strengthening or enlarging some part; something resembling such a piece of cloth in shape or function.

Gust, gust, *n.* [L. *gustus*, taste; *gusto*, to taste (as in *disgust*); from root seen in *choose*.] The sense or pleasure of tasting; gratification of the appetite; relish; gusto; taste.—**Gustable**, gus′ta-bl, *a.* Capable of being tasted; having a pleasant relish†.—**Gustation**,† gus-tā′shon, *n.* [L. *gustatio*.] The act of tasting.—**Gustatory**, gus′ta-to-ri, *a.* Pertaining to gust or taste.—**Gusto**, gus′tō, *n.* [It.] Nice appreciation or enjoyment; keen relish; taste; fancy.

Gust, gust, *n.* [Icel. *gustr*, a blast of wind; allied to E. *gush*.] A violent blast of wind; a sudden rushing or driving of the wind, of short duration; a sudden violent burst of passion.—**Gusty**, gus′ti, *a.* Subject to gusts or sudden blasts of wind; tempestuous; given to sudden bursts of passion.

Gut, gut, *n.* [A.Sax. *gut*, *gutt*, gut, *guttas*, entrails; comp. Prov.E. *gut*, a water channel, a drain; O.E. *gote*, a drain; from stem of A.Sax. *geótan*, Goth. *giutan*, to pour out. GUSH.] The intestinal canal of an animal from the stomach to the anus; an intestine; *pl.* the stomach and digestive apparatus generally, the viscera or entrails; a preparation of the intestines of an animal used for various purposes, as for the strings of a fiddle; a channel or passage.—*v.t.—gutted, gutting.* To take out the entrails of; to eviscerate; to plunder of contents; to destroy or take out the interior of.

Gutta, gut′ta, *n.* pl. **Guttæ**, gut′tē. [L.] A drop; specifically, *arch.* one of a series of pendent ornaments attached to the under side of the mutules and under the triglyphs of the Doric order.—**Gutta-serena**, gut′ta-sē-rē″na, *n.* An old medical name for *Amaurosis*.—**Guttate**, gut′āt, *a.* *Bot.* spotted, as if discoloured by drops.—**Guttiferous**, gut-if′ér-us, *a.* Yielding gum or resinous substances.

Gutta percha, gut′ta pér′cha, *n.* [Malay *gutta*, gum, and *percha*, the tree.] The hardened milky juice of a large tree which grows in the Malayan Peninsula and in some of the islands of the Eastern Archipelago, resembling caoutchouc in many of its properties, but stronger, more soluble, and less elastic.

Gutter, gut′ér, *n.* [Fr. *gouttière*, from *goutte*, L. *gutta*, a drop.] A channel at the side of a road, street, or the like, also at the eaves of, or on, a roof of a building for conveying away water.—*v.t.* To cut or form gutters in.—*v.i.* To become channelled.—**Guttering**, gut′ér-ing, *n.* A channel or collection of channels to carry off rainwater.

Guttle, gut′l, *v.i.* [A form of *guzzle*.] To swallow greedily; to gormandize.—**Guttler**, gut′lér, *n.* A gormandizer.

Guttural, gut′ér-al, *a.* [From L. *guttur*, the throat, whence also *goitre*.] Pertaining to the throat; uttered from the throat.—*n.* A letter or combination of letters pronounced in the throat; any guttural sound.—**Gutturalize**, gut′ér-al-īz, *v.t.* To speak or enunciate gutturally.—**Gutturally**, gut′ér-al-li, *adv.* In a guttural manner.—**Gutturalness**, **Gutturality**,†, gut′ér-al-nes, gut-ér-al′i-ti, *n.* The quality of being guttural.

Guy, gī, *n.* [Sp. *guia*, a guide, a small rope used on board ship. GUIDE.] A rope used to steady anything; a rope to steady an object which is being hoisted; a rope or rod to steady a suspension-bridge.—*v.t.* To steady or direct by means of a guy.

Guy, gī, *n.* A fright; a person of queer looks or dress: from the effigy of *Guy* Fawkes burned on the 5th November.

Guzzle, guz′l, *v.i.* and *v.t.—guzzled, guzzling.* [O.Fr. *goziller*, to gulp down; connected with Fr. *gosier*, the throat.] To swallow liquor greedily; to swill; to drink much. *n.* A debauch, especially on drink.

Guzzler, guz′lér, *n.* One who guzzles.

Gyle, gīl, *n.* A brewing; a brewer's vat.

Gymkhana, jim-kä'na, *n.* [Of Anglo-Indian origin.] A meeting for athletic or other sport contests.

Gymnasium, jim-nā'zi-um, *n.* pl. **Gymnasiums, Gymnasia.** [Gr. *gymnasion*, from *gymnos*, naked.] A place where athletic exercises are performed; in Europe, a school for the higher branches of education; a school preparatory to the universities.—**Gymnast**, jim'nast, *n.* One who teaches or practices gymnastic exercises.—**Gymnastic, Gymnastical**, jim-nas'tik, jim-nas'ti-kal, *a.* [L. *gymnasticus*; Gr. *gymnastikos*.] Pertaining to athletic exercises.—**Gymnastically**, jim-nas'ti-kal-li, *adv.* In a gymnastic manner.—**Gymnastics**, jim-nas'tiks, *n.* The art of performing athletic exercises; athletic exercises; feats of skill or address.—**Gymnic**,† jim'nik, *a.* Pertaining to gymnastics.

Gymnocarpous, jim-nō-kär'pus, *a.* [Gr. *gymnos*, naked, and *karpos*, fruit.] *Bot.* having a naked fruit.—**Gymnodont**, jim'-nō-dont, *n.* [Gr. *odous*, *odontos*, a tooth.] One of those fishes that have a projecting bony beak.—**Gymnogen**, jim'nō-jen, *n.* root *gen*, to produce.] *Bot.* a plant with a naked seed; a gymnosperm.—**Gymnogenous**, jim-noj'e-nus, *a.* *Bot.* pertaining to the gymnogens.—**Gymnogynous**, jim-noj'i-nus, *a.* [Gr. *gynē*, female.] *Bot.* having a naked ovary.—**Gymnosophist**, jim-nos'o-fist, *n.* [Gr. *sophistēs*, a philosopher.] One of a sect of ancient Hindu ascetics who lived solitarily, and wore little or no clothing.—**Gymnosperm**, jim'nō-spėrm, *n.* [Gr. *sperma*, seed.] A plant with a naked seed; a gymnogen.—**Gymnospermous**, jim-nō-spėr'mus, *a.* *Bot.* pertaining to the gymnosperms.—**Gymnospore**, jim'nō-spōr, *n.* *Bot.* a naked spore.—**Gymnosporous**, jim-nos'pō-rus, *a.* *Bot.* having naked spores.—**Gymnotus**, jim-nō'tus, *n.* [Gr. *nōtos*, the back, from having no dorsal fin.] The electric eel.

Gynander, ji-nan'dėr, *n.* [Gr. *gynē*, a female, and *anēr*, *andros*, a male.] A plant belonging to the Gynandria (ji-nan'dri-a), the character of which is to have the stamens and pistil consolidated into a single body.—**Gynandrian, Gynandrous**, ji-nan'dri-an, ji-nan'drus, *a.*

Gynarchy, jin'är-ki, *n.* [Gr. *gynē*, woman, and *archē*, rule.] Government by a female or females.

Gynecocracy, Gynaecocracy, jin-ē-kok'-ra-si, *n.* [Gr. *gynē*, *gynaikos*, a woman, and *kratos*, power.] Government by a woman; female rule.—**Gyneolatry**, jin-ē-ol'a-tri, *n.* [Gr. *latreia*, worship.] The extravagant adoration or worship of women.—**Gynecology**, jin-ē-kol'o-ji, *n.* The branch of medical science dealing with functions, diseases, and hygiene of women.—**Gynecologist**, jin-ē-kol'o-jist, *n.*

Gynobase, jin'ō-bās, *n.* [Gr. *gynē*, a female, and *basis*, a base.] *Bot.* a central axis to the base of which the carpels are attached.—**Gynobasic**, jin-ō-bā'sik, *a.* *Bot.* pertaining to or having a gynobase.—**Gynophore**, jin'ō-fōr, *n.* [Gr. *phoros*, bearing.] The stalk on which the ovary stands in certain flowers; *zool.* the generative bud of a hydrozoon containing ova.

Gyp, jip, *n.* [Said to be a sportive application of Gr. *gyps*, a vulture, from their alleged rapacity.] A college servant (English usage).—*n.*, *v.t.* and *i.* *U. S. slang*, to cheat; to swindle.

Gypsum, jip'sum, *n.* [L. *gypsum*, from Gr. *gypsos*, chalk.] A mineral which is found in a compact and crystallized state, as alabaster, or in the form of a soft chalky stone which by heat becomes a fine white powder, extensively used under the name of plaster of Paris.—**Gypseous**, jip'sē-us, *a.* Of the nature of gypsum; resembling gypsum.—**Gypsiferous**, jip-sif'ėr-us, *a.* Producing gypsum.—**Gypsoplast**, jip'so-plast, *n.* [*Gypsum*, and Gr. *plassō*, to mould.] A cast taken in plaster of Paris.

Gypsy, Gipsy, jip'si, *n.* [For *Egyptian*, from the belief that the race are descendants of the ancient people of Egypt. Called by themselves *Romany*, perhaps indicative of their first reaching Europe by *Roumania*.] One of a peculiar wandering race deriving their origin from India; a name of slight or humorous reproach to a young woman; the language of the gypsies.—*a.* Pertaining to the gypsies.—**Gypsology**, jip-sol'o-ji, *n.* That branch of knowledge which treats of the gypsies.—**Gypsy moth**, *n.* A European tussock moth, now found in the East, the caterpillars of which do much damage to trees.

Gyrate, jī'rāt, *v.i.* [L. *gyro*, *gyratum*, from *gyrus*, Gr. *gyros*, a circle.] To turn round circularly; to revolve round a central point; to move spirally.—*a.* Winding or going round, as in a circle.—**Gyral**, jī'ral, *a.* Whirling; moving in a circular form.—**Gyrant**, jī'rant, *a.* Whirling; wheeling. [Poet.]—**Gyration**, jī-rā'shon, *n.* A turning or whirling round; a circular motion.—**Gyrational**, jī-rā'shon-al, *a.* Pertaining to gyration.—**Gyratory**, jī'ra-to-ri, *a.* Moving in a circle or spirally.—**Gyre**, jīr, *n.* A circular motion, or a circle described by a moving body; a turn.—**Gyrose**, jī'rōs, *a.* *Bot.* bent round like a crook.

Gyrencephalate, jī-ren-sef'a-lāt, *a.* [Gr. *gyros*, a circle and *enkephalos*, the brain.] Belonging to a sub-class of the mammalia having the cerebrum covering the greater part of the cerebellum and the hemispheres of the brain with numerous convolutions.

Gyrfalcon, jėr-fa̤-kn, *n.* [L.L. *gyrofalco*, from *gyrus*, a circle, so called from its flight.] A species of falcon, one of the boldest and most beautiful of the tribe.

Gyroidal, jī-roi'dal, *a.* [Gr. *gyros*, a circle, and *eidos*, resemblance.] Spiral in arrangement or action.—**Gyroscope**, jī'rō-skōp, *n.* [Gr. *skopeō*, to view.] An apparatus, consisting of a pivoted disk rotating in different ways, for illustrating peculiarities of rotation; also used to increase steadiness of ships and aeroplanes.—**Gyroplane**, jī'rō-plān, *n.* An aeroplane propelled by windmill-like wings revolving about a vertical axis.—**Gyrostat**, jī'rō-stat, *n.* A kind of spinning-top.

Gyrus, jī'rus, pl. **Gyri**, jī'rī, *n.* [Gr. *gyros*, a circle.] *Anat.* a name given to the ridges or raised convolutions on the surface of the brain.

Gyve, jīv, *n.* [W. *gevyn*; Ir. *geibion*, from *geibhim*, to get, to hold; same root as L. *capio*, to take.] A shackle, usually for the legs; a fetter: commonly in the plural.—*v.t.*—*gyved*, *gyving*. To fetter; to shackle; to chain.

H

H, the eighth letter of the English alphabet, a consonant often called the *aspirate*, as being a mere aspiration or breathing.

Ha, hä. An exclamation, denoting surprise, wonder, joy, or other sudden emotion.

Haaf, haf, *n.* [N. *haf*, high sea.] Deep-sea fishing-ground.

Habeas corpus, hā'bē-as kor'pus. [L., you may have the body.] *Law*, a common-law writ designed to safeguard citizens from unjust imprisonment, directed to any person who detains another in custody and commanding him to produce the body of this person with a statement of the day and cause of his apprehension and detention that the court may deal with him.

Haberdasher, hab'ėr-dash-ėr, *n.* [Lit. a seller of *hapertas*, from O.Fr. *hapertas*, a kind of cloth.] The proprietor of a store which deals principally in men's furnishings; formerly a dealer in drapery goods, woolens, linens, silks, ribbons, &c.—**Haberdashery**, hab'ėr-dash-ėr-i, *n.*

Habergeon, ha-bėr'jon, *n.* [Fr. *haubergeon*, from *hauberc*, a hauberk. HAUBERK.] A short coat of mail or armor consisting of a jacket without sleeves.

Habiliment, ha-bil'i-ment, *n.* [Fr. *habillement*, from *habiller*, to dress, from L. *habilis*, fit, proper. HABIT.] A garment; clothing; usually plural.—**Habilimented**, ha-bil'i-ment-ed, *a.* Clothed.—**Habilitate**, ha-bil'i-tāt, *v.t.* To equip for operation, as a mine.—**Habilatory**, ha'bil-a-to-ri, *a.* Pertaining or relating to habiliments or clothing.

Habit, hab'it, *n.* [Fr. *habit*, from L. *habitus*, state, dress, manner, condition, &c., from *habeo*, *habitum*, to have, to hold: of similar origin are *habiliment*, *habitation*, *inhabit*, *exhibit*, *prohibit*, also *able*, *debt*, *duty*, &c.] The ordinary state or condition of the body, either natural or acquired; tendency or capacity resulting from frequent repetition of the same acts; practice; usage; a way of acting; a peculiar practice or custom; a characteristic item of behavior; dress; garb; the outer dress worn by ladies while on horseback. ∴ *Syn.* under CUSTOM.—*v.t.* To dress; to clothe; to array.—**Habited**, hab'it-ed, *a.* Clothed, as with a habit.—**Habit-maker**, *n.* One who makes habits; a tailor who makes ladies' riding habits or fancy costumes.—**Habitual**, ha-bit'ū-al, *a.* [Fr. *habituel*.] Formed or acquired by habit, frequent use, or custom; constantly practiced; customary; regular; as a matter of course.—**Habitually**, ha-bit'ū-al-li, *adv.* In a habitual manner.—**Habitualness**, ha-bit'ū-al-nes, *n.* **Habituate**, ha-bit'ū-āt, *v.t.*—*habituated*, *habituating*. [L. *habituo*, *habituatum*.] To accustom; to make familiar by frequent use or practice; to familiarize.—*a.* Formed by habit.—**Habituation**, ha-bit'ū-ā"shon, *n.* The act of habituating, or state of being habituated.—**Habitude**, hab'i-tūd, *n.* [Fr. *habitude*, from L. *habitudo*.] Customary manner or mode of living, feeling, or acting; long custom; habit.—**Habitué**, a-bē-tü-ā, *n.* [Fr., pp. of *habituer*, to accustom.] A habitual frequenter of any place, especially one of amusement, recreation, and the like.

Habitable, hab'i-ta-bl, *a.* [Fr., from L. *habitabilis*, from *habito*, to dwell, a freq. of *habeo*, to have.] Capable of being inhabited or dwelt in; capable of sustaining human beings.—**Habitability, Habitableness**, hab'i-ta-bil"i-ti, hab'i-ta-bl-nes, *n.* State of being habitable; capacity of being inhabited.—**Habitably**, hab'i-ta-bli, *adv.* So as to be habitable.—**Habitant**, hab'i-tant, *n.* [L. *habitans*, *habitantis*, ppr. of *habito*.] An inhabitant; a dweller; a resident.—**Habitat**, hab'i-tat, *n.* [L. *habitat*, 'it dwells'.] The natural abode or locality of a plant or animal.—**Habitation**, hab-i-tā'shon, *n.* [L. *habitatio*.] Act of inhabiting; occupancy; place of abode; a settled dwelling; a house or other place in which man or any animal dwells.

Habitude, Habitué. Under HABIT.

Habromania, hab-ro-mā'ni-a, *n.* [Gr. *habros*, gay, and *mania*, madness.] Insanity in which the delusions are of a gay character.

Hachure, hach'ūr, *n.* [Fr., from *hacher*, to hack. HACK, *v.t.*] Short lines which mark half-tints and shadows in designing and engraving.—*v.t.* To cover with hachures.

Hacienda, hä-sē-en'dä, *n.* [Sp.] In Spain, Spanish America, &c., a farmhouse; a farm.

Hack, hak, *v.t.* [A.Sax. *haccan* or *haccian*

= D. *hakken*, Dan. *hakke*, Sw. *hacka*, G. *hacken*, to hack or chop; whence Fr. *hacher*, and from the latter E. *hatch* (in engraving), *hatchet*, *hash*.] To cut irregularly and into small pieces; to notch; to mangle.—*n.* A notch; a cut.—**Hacking**, hak'ing, *p.* and *a.* Short and interrupted (a *hacking* cough).

Hack, hak, *n.* [Short for *hackney*.] A horse kept for hire; a horse much worked; a worn-out horse; a person overworked; a writer employed in the drudgery and details of book-making.—*a.* Much used or worn, like a hired horse; hired.—*v.t.* To use as a hack; to let out for hire.—**Hack-watch**, *n. Naut.* a watch with a seconds hand, used in taking observations, to obviate the necessity of constantly moving the chronometer.

Hack, hak, *n.* [A.Sax. *hœc*, a grating. HATCH, *n.*] A grated frame of various kinds; a frame for drying fish, &c.; a rack for cattle.

Hackberry, hak'be-ri, *n.* [Same as Prov.E. *hag-berry*, bird-cherry = *haw*-berry, *hedge*-berry.] A North American tree bearing sweet edible fruits as large as bird-cherries.

Hackbut, hak'but, *n.* HAGBUT.

Hackee, hak'ē, *n.* The common ground-squirrel of North America.

Hackery, hak'ér-i, *n.* A rude two-wheeled cart of India drawn by oxen.

Hackle, hak'l, *n.* [D. *hekel*, G. *hechel*, Dan. *hegle*, a hackle for flax or hemp; akin to *hook*. The secondary senses are from similarity to tufts of hackled fibres.] A hatchel, heckle, or comb for dressing flax; raw silk; any flimsy substance unspun; a long pointed feather on the neck of a fowl, or any similar feather.—*Red-hackle*, feather on Highland-regiment bonnet.—*v.t.* To comb (flax or hemp); to hatchel or heckle.—**Hackler**, hak'lér, *n.* One who hackles.

Hackmatack, hak'ma-tak, *n.* [Amer. Indian.] The American black larch.

Hackney, hak'ni. *n.* [O.Fr. *haquenee*, a pacing horse, Sp. *hacanea*, a nag; probably from O.D. *hackeneye*, *hakkenei*, a hackney; lit. perhaps a hacked or dock-tailed nag.] A horse kept for riding or driving; a pad; a nag; a horse kept for hire; a hack; a person accustomed to drudgery, often literary drudgery.—*a.* Let out for hire; much used; common; trite.—*v.t.* To use as a hackney; to devote to common or vulgar use.—**Hackney-coach**, *n.* A coach kept for hire.—**Hackneyed**, hak'nid, *p.* and *a.* Discussed or talked of without end; in everybody's mouth; trite; commonplace.

Had, had, pret. & pp. of *have*.

Haddock, had'ok, *n.* [Comp. O.Fr. *hadot*, *hadou*, Ir. *codog*, a haddock.] A well-known fish of the cod family, smaller than the cod, and having a dark spot on each side just behind the head.

Hade, hād, *n.* [A.Sax. *heald*, inclined, bent; G. *halde*, declivity.] *Mining*, a slope or inclination; inclination of a vein or bed from a vertical direction.—*v.i.* To slope or incline from the vertical.

Hades, hā'dēz, *n.* [Gr. *Hadēs*, i.e. *aidēs*, invisible, unseen, from *a* priv., and *idein*, to see.] The invisible abode of the dead; the place or state of departed souls; the world of spirits.

Hadj, haj, *n.* [Ar.] The Mohammedan pilgrimage to Mecca and Medina.—**Hadji**, **Hadjee**, haj'ē, *n.* A Mussulman who has performed his pilgrimage to Mecca.

Hadrosaurus, had-ro-sä'rus, *n.* [Gr. *hadros*, thick, large, great, and *sauros*, a lizard.] A huge extinct herbivorous reptile found fossil in North America.

Hæmal, hē'mal, *a.* [Gr. *haima*, *haimatos*, blood. Some of the words in which this forms part are spelled indifferently *he-* or *hæ-*; in others there is a preference. See also under HE-.] Pertaining to the blood; connected with the blood-vessels or the circulatory system.—*Hæmal arch*, the arch formed by the projections anteriorly of the ribs and the sternum from the vertebræ.—**Hæmapophysis**, hē-ma-pof'i-sis, *n.* [Gr. *haima*, and *apophysis*, apophysis.] *Compar. anat.* part of the typical vertebra on each side of the hæmal arch.—**Hæmastatic**, hē-ma-stat'ik, *n.* Hemastatic.—**Hæmatemesis**, hē-ma-tem'e-sis, *n.* [Gr. *emesis*, a vomiting.] A vomiting of blood from the stomach.—**Hæmatics**, hē-mat'iks, *n.* That branch of physiology which treats of the blood.—**Hæmatin**. HEMATIN.—**Hæmatite**, he'ma-tīt, *n.* HEMATITE.—**Hæmatocryal**, hē-ma-tok'ri-al, *a.* [Gr. *cryos*, cold.] *Zool.* applied to the cold-blooded vertebrates.—**Hæmatophilia**, **Hæmophilia**, hē'mat-o-fil''i-a, hē-mo-fil'-i-a, *n.* [*Phileō*, I love.] *Med.* a constitutional tendency to excessive bleeding from slight injuries, or even spontaneously, the result often being death.—**Hæmatoid**, hē'ma-toid, *a.* [Gr. *haimato-eidēs*, *eidos*, resemblance.] Having the appearance of blood.—**Hæmatosis**, hē-ma-tō'sis, *n.* [Gr., a changing into blood.] The arterialization of blood; the formation of the blood.—**Hæmatothermal**, hē'ma-to-ther''-mal, *a.* [Gr. *thermos*, warm.] Of or pertaining to the warm-blooded vertebrates.—**Hæmatoxylin**, hē-ma-tok'si-lin. HEMATOXYLIN.—**Hæmatozoa**, hē'ma-to-zō''a, *n. pl.* [Gr. *zōon*, an animal.] The entozoa which exist in the blood of mammals, birds, reptiles, &c.—**Hæmaturia**, hē-ma-tū'ri-a, *n.* [Gr. *ouron*, urine.] A discharge of bloody urine.—**Hæmaturic**, hē'ma-tū-rik, *a.* Pertaining to or showing hæmaturia or bloody urine.—*Hæmaturic fever*, a severe malarial fever common in parts of Africa.—**Hæmoglobin**, **Hæmoglobulin**, hē'mo-glō-bin, hē-mo-glō'bū-lin, *n.* [L. *globus*, a ball.] The matter of a red colour contained in the red corpuscles of the blood.—**Hæmoptysis**, hē-mop'tis-is, *n.* [Gr. *ptysis*, a spitting.] The coughing up of blood.—**Hæmorrhage**, hē'mor-āj, *n.* HEMORRHAGE.—**Hæmorrhoids**, hē'-mor-oidz, *n.* HEMORRHOIDS.—**Hæmotrophy**, hē-mot'ro-fi, *n.* [Gr. *trophē*, nourishment.] An excess of sanguineous nutriment.

Hæmony, hēm'on-i, *n.* The magical herb against danger in Milton's *Comus*.

Haft, haft, *n.* [A.Sax. *hæft*, a haft = D. and G. *heft*, a handle; Icel. *hepti* (= *hefti*), a haft, from the stem of *have* or *heave*.] A handle; that part of an instrument which is taken into the hand, and by which it is held and used.—*v.t.* To set in a haft; to furnish with a handle.

Hag, hag, *n.* [Shortened from A.Sax. *hægtesse*; akin to G. *hexe*, D. *heks*, a witch; probably from A.Sax. *haga*, a hedge, G. *hag*, a wood (the meaning being woman of the woods).] An ugly old woman; a witch; a sorceress; a she-monster; an eel-shaped fish which eats into and devours other fishes.—**Haggish**, hag'ish, *a.* Pertaining to or resembling a hag; ugly; horrid.—**Haggishly**, hag'ish-li, *adv.* In a haggish manner.—**Haggishness**, hag'ish-nes, *n.*

Hagbut, hag'but, *n.* Same as *Arquebuse*.

Haggard, hag'ärd, *a.* [Fr. *haggard*, originally a wild falcon, from G. *hag*, a wood, and affix *-ard*. In secondary sense perhaps for *hagged*, that is *hag*-like. HEDGE, HAW.] Wild; intractable (a *haggard* hawk); having the expression of one wasted by want or suffering; having the face worn and pale; lean-faced; gaunt.—*n.* An untrained or refractory hawk.—**Haggardly**, hag'ärd-li, *adv.* In a haggard manner.

Haggis, hag'is, *n.* [From *hag*, to chop, a form of *hack*; comp. Fr. *hachis*, a hash.] A Scotch dish, commonly made in a sheep's stomach, of the heart, lungs, and liver of the animal minced with suet, onions, oatmeal, salt, and pepper.

Haggle, hag'l, *v.t.* — *haggled*, *haggling*. [Freq. of *hag*, for *hack*, to hack.] To cut into small pieces; to notch or cut in an unskilful manner; to mangle.—*v.i.* To be difficult in bargaining; to hesitate and cavil; to stick at small matters; to higgle.—**Haggler**, hag'l-ér, *n.* One who haggles.

Hagiocracy, hā-ji-ok'ra-si, *n.* [Gr. *hagios*, holy, and *kratos*, rule.] The government of the priesthood; a sacred government; a hierarchy.—**Hagiographa**, hā-ji-og'ra-fa, *n. pl.* [Gr. *hagios*, holy, and *graphē*, a writing.] The last of the three Jewish divisions of the Old Testament, comprehending Psalms, Proverbs, Job, Daniel, Ezra, Nehemiah, Ruth, Esther, Chronicles, Canticles, Lamentations, and Ecclesiastes.—**Hagiography**, hā-ji-og'ra-fi, *n.* Sacred writing; the lives of the saints or holy men.—**Hagiograph**, hā'ji-o-graf, *n.* A holy writing.—**Hagiographic**, **Hagiographal**, hā'ji-o-graf''ik, hā-ji-og'ra-fal, *a.* Pertaining to hagiography.—**Hagiographer**, hā-ji-og'ra-fér, *n.* One of the writers of the hagiography; a writer of lives of the saints.—**Hagiologist**, hā-ji-ol'o-jist, *n.* One who writes or treats of the sacred writings; a writer of lives of the saints.—**Hagiology**, hā-ji-ol'o-ji, *n.* [Gr. *hagios*, and *logos*.] Sacred literature; that branch of literature which has to do with the lives and legends of the saints.

Hah, hä, *interj.* Expression of effort, surprise, &c.

Ha-ha, hä'hä, *n.* [Reduplicated form of *haw*, a hedge.] A sunk fence or ditch; a hawhaw.

Hail, hāl, *n.* [A.Sax. *hagal*, *hagol* = G., D., Dan. and Sw. *hagel*, Icel. *hagl*, hail; root doubtful.] The small masses of ice or frozen vapour falling from the clouds in showers or storms; frozen rain.—*v.i.* To pour down hail.—**Hailstone**, hāl'stōn, *n.* A single ball or pellet of hail.—**Hailstorm**, *n.* A storm of hail.—**Haily**, hā'li, *a.* Consisting of hail; full of hail. (*Pope.*)

Hail, hāl, *interj.* [Same as *hale*, adj.; Icel. *heill*, Dan. *heel*, hale. HALE, HEALTH.] A term of greeting or salutation expressive of well-wishing.—*v.t.* To call to; to greet from a distance; to call to in order to arrest attention; to designate as; to salute or address as.—*v.i.* Used only in the phrase *to hail from*, originally used of a ship, which is said *to hail from* the port whence she comes; hence, to have as one's residence or birth-place; to belong to.—*n.* Call.—*Within hail*, within call; within reach of the sound of the voice.

Hair, hār, *n.* [A.Sax. *haer*, *hér* = Icel. *hár*, O.D. *hair*, D. Dan. and G. *haar*, hair; perhaps akin to Icel. *hörr*, flax, E. *hards* (which see).] A small filament issuing from the skin of an animal, and from a bulbous root; the collection or mass of filaments growing from the skin of an animal and forming an integument or covering; such filaments in the mass; a filament resembling a hair; *bot.* a species of down or pubescence.—*To a hair*, to a nicety.—*To split hairs*, to be unduly nice in making distinctions.—**Hair-breadth**, **Hair's-breadth**, *n.* The diameter or breadth of a hair; a minute distance.—*a.* Of the breadth of a hair; very narrow (a *hair-breadth* escape).—**Hair-broom**, *n.* A broom made of hair.—**Hair-brush**, *n.* A brush for dressing and smoothing the hair.—**Hair-cloth**, *n.* A kind of cloth made of hair or in part of hair.—**Hair-dresser**, *n.* One who dresses or cuts people's hair; a barber.—**Haired**, hārd, *a.* Having hair: mostly used in composition (long-*haired*, dark-*haired*, &c.).—**Hair-grass**, *n.* The popular name of various grasses of little or no value.—**Hairiness**, hā'ri-nes, *n.* The state of being hairy.—**Hairless**, hār'les, *a.* Destitute of hair; bald.—**Hair-line**, *n.* A line made of hair; a very slender line made in writing or drawing; a hair-stroke.—**Hair-pencil**, *n.* A fine brush or pencil made of hair and used in painting.—**Hair-pin**, *n.* A pin used to keep the hair in a certain position; especially, a doubled pin or bent wire used by women.—**Hair-powder**, *n.* A fine-scented powder of flour or starch for sprinkling the hair of the head.—**Hairshirt**, *n.* Shirt or belt made of horse-hair and worn by way of self-mortification.—**Hair-sieve**, *n.* A strainer or sieve with a hair-cloth bottom.—**Hair-space**, *n.* The thinnest space used by printers.—**Hair-splitting**, *n.* The act or practice of making minute distinctions in reasoning.—**Hair-splitter**, *n.* One given to hair-splitting.—**Hair-spring**, *n.* The fine hair-like spring giving motion to the balance-wheel of a watch.—**Hair-**

stroke, *n.* The fine up-stroke in penmanship.—**Hair-trigger**, *n.* A trigger to a gun-lock, so delicately adjusted that the slightest touch will discharge the piece.—**Hair-worker**, *n.* One who works in hair; one who makes bracelets, lockets, &c., of human hair.—**Hair-worm**, *n.* A filiform animal found in fresh water or in the earth.—**Hairy**, hā'ri, *a.* Overgrown with hair; covered with hair; abounding with hair; consisting of hair; resembling hair.

Hake, **Haak**, hāk, *n.* [Prov. E. *hake*, a hook, from the hook-shaped jaw of the fish.] A fish of the cod family, one species of which is known as king of herrings, on which it preys.

Hakim, hä'kēm, *n.* [Ar.] An oriental name for a physician.

Halberd, **Halbert**, hal'bėrd, hal'bėrt, *n.* [Fr. *hallebarde*, from O.G. *helmparte*, *helmbarte*, a halberd—*helm*, a handle, a helm, and *parte*, *barte*, an axe.] An ancient military weapon, a kind of combination of a spear and battle-axe, with a shaft about 6 feet long.—**Halberdier**, hal-bėr-dēr', *n.* One who is armed with a halberd.

Halcyon, hal'si-on, *n.* [L. *halcyon*, from Gr. *halkyōn*, a kingfisher, said to be from *hals*, the sea, and *kyō*, to conceive.] An old or poetical name of the kingfisher, which was fabled to have the power of charming the winds and waves during the period of its incubation, so that the weather was then calm.—*a.* Pertaining to or connected with the halcyon; calm; quiet; peaceful.—*Halcyon days*, the seven days before and as many after the winter solstice, when the halcyon was believed to brood, and the weather was calm; hence, days of peace and tranquillity.—**Halcyonian**, hal-si-ō'ni-an, *a.* Halcyon; calm.

Hale, hāl, *a.* [Same as Icel. *heill*, Dan. *heel*, Goth. *hails*, in good health, sound, &c. (hence, *hail* in salutations); closely akin to A.Sax. *hál*, whole, sound, whence E. *whole*; cog. with Gr. *kalos*, beautiful. Akin *heal*, *health*, *hollow*, *holy*.] Sound; healthy; robust; not impaired in health.—**Haleness**, hāl'nes, *n.* The state of being hale; healthiness; soundness.

Hale, hāl, *v.t.*—*haled*, *haling*. [HAUL.] To pull or draw with force; to haul.—*n.* A violent pull; a haul.

Half, häf, *n.* pl. **Halves**, hävz. [A.Sax. *half* or *healf*=O.Fris., D., and Sw. *half*, Icel. *hálfr*, Goth. *halbs*, G. *halb*, half.] One part of a thing which is divided into two equal parts, either in fact or in contemplation; a moiety (we usually say *half* a pound, *half* a mile. &c., omitting *of*). — *To cry halves*, to claim an equal share. — *To go halves*, to agree with another for the division of anything into equal parts.—*adv.* In an equal part or degree; by half; to some extent: much used in composition and often indefinite (*half*-learned, *half*-hatched).—*a.* Consisting of a moiety or half. — **Half-and-half**, *n.* A mixture of two malt liquors, especially porter and sweet or bitter ale.—**Half-back**, *n.* Player in football, immediately behind the forwards.—**Half-binding**, *n.* A style of binding books in which the back and corners are in leather and the sides in paper or cloth.—**Half-blood**, *n.* One born of the same mother but not the same father as another, or *vice versâ*; a half-breed.—**Half-bound**, *a.* A term applied to a book in half-binding.—**Half-bred**, *a.* Imperfectly bred; mixed; mongrel; partially or imperfectly acquainted with the rules of good breeding.—**Half-breed**, *n.* One born of parents of different races: specifically applied to the offspring of American Indians and whites.—**Half-brother**, *n.* A brother by one parent, but not by both.—**Half-caste**, *n.* One born of a Hindu and a European; a half-blood or half-breed.—**Half-cock**, *n.* The position of the hammer of a gun when it is elevated only half-way and retained by the first notch.—**Half-crown**, *n.* A silver coin of Britain valued at 60 cents or 2*s.* 6*d.*—**Half-dead**, *a.* Almost dead; nearly exhausted.—**Half-dollar**, *n.* A silver coin of the United States, value fifty cents.—**Half-educated**, *a.* Imperfectly educated.—**Half-guinea**, *n.* An English gold coin, value 10*s.* 6*d.*, equivalent to $2.50 in U. S. money, no longer in circulation.—**Half-hatched**, *a.* Imperfectly hatched. — **Half-hearted**, *a.* Devoid of eagerness or enthusiasm; indifferent; lukewarm.—**Half-holiday**, *n.* A day on which work is carried on only during a portion of the usual working hours.—**Half-hourly**, *a.* Occurring at intervals of half an hour.—**Half-length**, *a.* Of half the full or ordinary length; showing only the upper half of the body, as a portrait.—*n.* A portrait showing only the upper half of the body.—**Half-measure**, *n* An imperfect plan of operation; a feeble effort.—**Half-moon**, *n.* The moon at the quarters, when half its disk appears illuminated; anything in the shape of a half-moon.—**Half-note**, *n.* *Mus.* a minim, being half a semibreve; a semitone.—**Half-past**, *adv.* Half an hour past (*half-past* six o'clock).—**Half-pay**, *n.* Half wages or salary; a reduced allowance paid to an officer in the army or navy when not in actual service.—*a.* Receiving or entitled to half-pay.—**Halfpenny**, hā'pen-i, *n.* pl. **Halfpence**, hā'pens or hā'pens. A British copper coin of the value of half a penny or one cent.—*a.* Of the price or value of a halfpenny.—**Halfpenny-worth**, *n.* The value of a halfpenny.—**Half-pike**, *n.* A weapon with a shorter shaft than the ordinary pike; a boarding-pike.—**Half-price**, *n.* Half the ordinary price; a reduced charge for admission to a place of amusement when part of the entertainment is over.—**Half-quarter**, *n.* One eighth; one eighth of a year.—**Half-read**, *a.* Superficially informed by reading.—**Half-round**, *n.* *Arch.* a molding whose profile is a semicircle.—*a.* Semicircular (*Mil.*).—**Half-royal**, *n.* A kind of millboard or pasteboard of which there are two sizes, small 20¼ by 13 inches, and large 21 by 14 inches.—**Half-seas-over**, *a.* Pretty far gone in drunkenness; half-drunk; tipsy. (*Brit.*).—**Half-sister**, *n.* A sister by the father's side only, or by the mother's side only.—**Half-sovereign**, *n.* A British gold coin, value 10*s.*, equivalent to $2.40 in U. S. money.—**Half-starved**, *a.* Almost starved; very ill fed.—**Half-tide**, *n.* The tide when half-way between the ebb and flood.—**Half-timbered**, *a.* Built half of timber, as a dwelling.—**Half-timer**, *n.* One who works or goes to school half the usual time.—**Half-tone**, *n.* A tone intermediate between the extreme lights and shades of a picture; a kind of photo-engraving.—**Half-way**, *adv.* In the middle; at half the distance.—*a.* Midway; equidistant from the extremes.—**Half-witted**, *a.* Weak in intellect; silly; foolish.—**Half-year**, *n.* Six months.—**Half-yearly**, *a.* Happening in each half of a year; semiannual.—*adv.* In each half-year; semiannually.

Halibut, **Holibut**, hal'i-but, hol'i-but, *n.* [From *hali*, that is, holy, and *but* or *butt*, a flounder = D. *heilbot*, G. *heilbutt*, *heiligbutt*.] One of the largest of the flat-fish family, allied to the turbot, but much less broad comparatively, valuable as food.

Halidom, ‡ hal'i-dom, *n.* [A.Sax. *háligdom*, holiness, from *hálig*, holy, and term. *-dom*. HOLY.] Holiness; sacred word of honor: formerly used in adjurations.

Haliography, hal-i-og'ra-fi, *n.* [Gr. *hals*, *halos*, the sea, and *graphō*, to describe.] That department of science which treats of the sea; a description of the sea.

Halitosis, hal-i-tō'sis, *n.* Condition of having foul or offensive breath.

Halitus, hal'i-tus, *n.* [L. from *halo*, to breathe out (in *exhale*).] *Physiol.* the breath or moisture of the breath; vapor exhaled from the body.

Hall, hal, *n.* [A.Sax. *heal*, *heall* = Icel. *höll*, *hall*, Sw. *hall*, D. *hal*, from root signifying to cover, seen also in E. *hell*.] A large room, especially a large public room; a room or building devoted to public business, or in which meetings of the public or corporate bodies are held; a large room at the entrance of a house; a vestibule; an entrance lobby; a manor-house; the name of certain colleges at Oxford and Cambridge; also the large room in which the students dine in common; hence, the students' dinner.—**Hall-lamp**, *n.* A lamp suspended in a lobby or hall. — **Hall-mark**, *n.* The official stamp affixed by the Goldsmiths' Company and certain assay offices to articles of gold and silver, as a mark of their legal quality.

Hallelujah, **Halleluiah**, hal-lē-lö'ya, *n.* and *interj.* ALLELUIAH.

Halliard, hal'yärd, *n.* HALYARD.

Halloo, hal-lö', *interj.* and *n.* [Comp. G. *halloh!* and Fr. *halle*, an exclamation used to cheer on dogs; *haller*, to encourage dogs.] An exclamation, used as a call to invite attention; also, a hunting cry to set a dog on the chase.—*v.i.* To call *halloo*; to shout; to cry, as after dogs.—*v.t.* To shout to.

Hallow, hal'lō, *v.t.* [A.Sax. *hálgian*, to hallow, from *hálig*, holy. HOLY.] To make holy; to consecrate; to set apart for holy or religious use; to reverence; to honour as sacred.—**Hallow-e'en**, **Hallow-even**, *n.* The eve or vigil of All-Hallows or All-Saints' Day. [Sc.]—**Hallowmas**, **Hallowtide**, hal'lō-mas, hal'lō-tīd, *n.* [A.Sax. *hálga*, a saint, and *mæsse*, mass, festival.] The feast of All-Saints or the time at which it is held.

Hallucination, hal-lū'si-nā"shon, *n.* [L. *hallucinatio*, from *hallucinor*, to wander in mind, to talk idly.] An unfounded and mistaken notion; an entire misconception; a mere dream or fancy; *med.* a morbid condition of the brain or nerves, in which objects are believed to be seen and sensations experienced; the object or sensation thus erroneously perceived.—**Hallucinatory**, hal-lū'si-na-to-ri, *a.* Partaking of hallucination.

Hallux, hal'uks, *n.* [Erroneous form, for L. *hallex*, the thumb or great toe.] The great toe or corresponding digit of an animal; the hind toe of a bird.

Halm, ham, *n.* Same as *Haulm*.

Halo, hā'lō, *n.* pl. **Halos**, **Haloes**, hā'lōz. [Gr. *halōs*, a round floor, the sun's disk, a halo.] A luminous ring, either white or colored, appearing round the sun or moon; any circle of light, as the glory round the head of saints; a colored circle round the nipple; an ideal glory investing an object (a *halo* of romance).—*v.t.* To form itself into a halo.—*v.t.* To surround with a halo.—**Haloed**, hā'lōd, *a.* Surrounded by a halo.—**Haloscope**, hā'lo-skōp, *n.* An instrument which exhibits all the phenomena connected with halos.

Halogen, hal'o-jen, *n.* [Gr. *hals*, salt, and root *gen*, to produce.] *Chem.* a name given to substances (such as chlorine or iodine) which form compounds of a saline nature by their union with metals.—**Halogenous**, ha-loj'e-nus, *a.* Having the nature of halogens.

Haloid, hal'oid, *a.* [Gr. *hals*, sea-salt, and *eidos*, resemblance.] *Chem.* resembling common salt in composition; formed by the combination of a halogen and a metal: common salt is a *haloid salt*.—*n.* A haloid salt.—**Halosel**, hal'o-sel, *n.* A haloid.

Halophyte, hal'o-fit, *n.* [Gr. *hals*, *halos*, the sea, salt, and *phyton*, a plant.] One of the plants which inhabit salt marshes, and by combustion yield barilla or Spanish soda.

Halt, halt, *v.i.* [A.Sax. *healtian*, to be lame, *healt*, lame, from Icel. *haltr*, Dan. and Sw. *halt*, Goth. *halts*, lame; Dan. and Sw. *halte*, to limp. In sense of to stop in marching, probably of German origin, from *halten*, E. to *hold*.] To limp; to be lame; to limp or be defective in regard to metre, versification, or connection of ideas; to stop in marching or walking; to cease to advance; to stand in doubt whether to proceed or what to do; to hesitate.—*v.t.* To stop; to cause to cease marching.—*a.* Lame; not able to walk without limping. — *n.* Lameness; a limp; a stopping; a stop in walking or marching.—**Halter**, hal'tėr, *n.*

One who halts or limps. — **Haltingly**, hal'ting-li, *adv.* In a halting manner.

Halter, hal'tėr, *n.* [A.Sax. *hælfter*, headstall, noose=D.L.G. and G. *halfter*; origin doubtful.] A cord or strap forming a headstall for leading or confining a horse or other animal; a rope specially intended for hanging malefactors.—*v.t.* To put a halter on.

Halteres, hal-tē'rēz, *n. pl.* [Gr. *haltēres*, weights held while leaping, from *hallomai*, to leap.] The balancers of insects; the aborted second pair of wings.

Halve, häv, *v.t.*—*halved*, *halving*. [From *half*.] To divide into two halves or equal parts; to join (timbers) by lapping or letting into each other.—**Halves**, hävz, *n. pl.* of *half*.

Halyard, hal'yärd, *n.* [*Hale* or *haul*, and *yard*.] *Naut.* a rope or tackle for hoisting and lowering sails, yards, gaffs, &c.; halliard.

Ham, ham, *n.* [A.Sax. *ham*, *hamm*, the ham = D. *ham*, Icel. *hōm*, G. *hamme*, a ham, from a root meaning to bend, seen in Gr. *kamptō*, to bend; W. Ir. and Gael. *cam*, crooked, bent.] The inner bend or hind part of the knee; the thigh of an animal, particularly of a hog, salted and cured.—*v.t.* To make into ham.—**Ham-curer**, *n.* One who makes beef, pork, &c., into ham. —**Hamstring**, ham'string, *n.* One of the tendons of the ham.—*v.t.* pret. and pp. *hamstrung* or *hamstringed*. To lame or disable by cutting the tendons of the ham.

Hamadryad, ham'a-drī-ad, *n.* [Gr. *hamadryas*, from *hama*, together, and *drys*, a tree.] In classical mythology a wood-nymph, feigned to live and die with the tree to which she was attached.

Hamal, ham'al, *n.* A porter in Constantinople.

Hamate, hā'māt, *a.* [L. *hamatus*, hooked, from *hamus*, a hook.] Hooked; set with hooks.—**Hamiform**, hā'mi-form, *a.* In the shape of a hook.

Hamburg-lake, ham'bėrg, *n.* A cochineal pigment of a purplish colour, inclining to crimson.—**Hamburg-white**, *n.* A pigment composed of barytes and white-lead.

Hame, hām, *n.* [Same as D. *haam*, a hame.] One of two curved pieces of wood or metal in the harness of a draught horse, to which the traces are fastened, and which lie upon the collar or have pads attached to them fitting the horse's neck.

Hamiltonian, ham-il-tō'ni-an, *a.* The Scottish philosophy of Sir W. Hamilton; the method of acquiring foreign languages by interlinear translations.

Hamite, ham'īt, *n.* A descendant of *Ham*; an Ethiopian.—**Hamitic**, ham-it'ik, *a.* Relating to *Ham* or his descendants; appellative of a class of African tongues, comprising Coptic, Ethiopian or Abyssinian, &c.

Hamlet, ham'let, *n.* [Dim. of A.Sax. *ham*, dwelling, inclosure; akin *home*.] A small village; a little cluster of houses in the country.—**Hammel**, ham'el, *n.* A small shed and yard used for sheltering fattening cattle.

Hammer, ham'ėr, *n.* [A.Sax. *hamor* = D. *hamer*, G. and Dan. *hammer*, Icel. *hamarr*; root doubtful.] An instrument for driving nails, beating metals, and the like, consisting usually of an iron head, fixed crosswise to a handle; a striking piece in the mechanism of a clock and a piano; that part in the lock of a gun, rifle, &c., which when the trigger is pulled falls with a smart blow, and causes the explosion of the detonating substance in connection with the powder.—*To bring to the hammer*, to sell by auction. —*v.t.* To beat, form, or forge, with a hammer; to contrive by intellectual labour; to excogitate: usually with *out*; to declare bankrupt or defaulting a member of the Stock Exchange.—*v.i.* To strike anything repeatedly, as with a hammer; to work; to labour in contrivance. — **Hammer-beam**, *n.* A short projecting beam attached to the foot of a principal rafter in a roof, in the place of the tie-beam. — **Hammer-cloth**, *n.* [Probably *hammer*, here=D. *hemel*, top of a coach, cover, canopy.] The cloth which covers the driver's seat in some kinds of carriages. —**Hammer-dressed**, *a.* Dressed or prepared with a pointed hammer or pick.— **Hammerer**, ham'ėr-ėr, *n.* One who works with a hammer.—**Hammer-fish**, *n.* A shark the head of which resembles a hammer.—**Hammer-harden**, *v.t.* To harden (metal) by hammering in the cold state. — **Hammer-head**, *n.* The iron head of a hammer; the hammer-fish. — **Hammerman**, ham'ėr-man, *n.* A smith or other worker in metal.

Hammock, ham'ok, *n.* [Sp. *hamaca*, a word of West Indian origin.] A kind of hanging bed, consisting of a piece of cloth suspended by cords and hooks.

Hamous, **Hamose**, hā'mus, hā'mōs, *a.* [L. *hamus*, a hook.] *Bot.* hooked; having the end hooked or curved.

Hamper, ham'pėr, *n.* [Contr. from *hanaper* (which see).] A kind of rude basket or wicker-work receptacle, chiefly used as a case for packing articles.—*v.t.* To put into a hamper.

Hamper, ham'pėr, *v.t.* [A nasalized form corresponding to D. *haperen*, to stammer, falter, stick fast; comp. Sc. *hamp*, to stammer; Goth. *hamfs*, *hanfs*, mutilated.] To impede in motion or progress, or to render progress difficult to; to shackle; to embarrass; to encumber.—*n.* Something that hampers or encumbers; a clog.

Hamster, ham'stėr, *n.* (G.) A burrowing animal of the rat family common in Germany, having a short tail and cheek-pouches.

Hamstring, *n.* and *v.t.* Under Ham.

Hamulus, ham'ū-lus, *n.* [L., a little book, dim. of *hamus*, a hook.] A little hook; a hook-like process in animals and plants.

Hanaper, han'a-pėr, *n.* [L.L. *hanaperium*, lit. a receptacle for cups, from L.L. *hanapus*, a cup, from O.H.G. *hnap*, A.Sax. *hnæp*, a cup; hence *hamper*, *n.*] A kind of basket used in early days by the kings of England for holding and carrying with them their money; the king's treasury.—*Clerk of the hanaper*.

Hanch, hanch, *n.* *Arch.* Haunch.

Hand, hand, *n.* [Common in similar forms, to all the Teutonic tongues; allied to Goth. *hinthan*, to capture; O.E. *hent*, to seize; perhaps also *hunt*. *Handsel*, *handle*, *handy*, *handsome* are derivatives.] The extremity of the arm, consisting of the palm and fingers, connected with the arm at the wrist; the corresponding member in certain of the lower animals; a measure of 4 inches; a palm: applied chiefly to horses; side or direction, either right or left (on the one *hand* or the other); handiwork; style of penmanship; power of performance; skill; agency; part in performing (to have a *hand* in mischief); possession; power (in the *hands* of the owner); that which performs the office of the hand or of a finger in pointing (the *hands* of a clock); a male or female in relation to an employer; a person employed on board ship or in manufactories; a person with some special faculty or ability (a good *hand* at a speech); in *card-playing*, the cards held by a single player; one of the players.—*At hand*, near in time or place; within reach or not far distant.—*At first hand*, from the producer or seller directly; *at second hand*, or simply *second hand*, from an intermediate purchaser; old or used.—*By hand*, with the hands and not by the instrumentality of tools, &c. — *For one's own hand*, on one's own account; for one's self.—*From hand to hand*, from one person to another.—*In hand*, in ready-money; in possession; in the state of preparation or execution. — *Off hand*, without hesitation or difficulty; without previous preparation. —*Off one's hands*, out of one's care or attention; ended.—*On hand*, in present possession.—*On one's hands*, under one's care or management; as a burden upon one.—*Out of hand*, at once; directly; without delay or hesitation; off one's hands.—*To one's hand*, already prepared; ready to be received.—*Under one's hand*, with the proper writing or signature of the name.—*Hand in hand*, with hands mutually clasped: hence, in union; conjointly; unitedly.—*Hand to hand*, in close union; close fight.—*Hand to mouth*, as want requires; without making previous provision or having an abundant previous supply.—*Hands off!* keep off; forbear; refrain from blows. —*Clean hands*, innocence; freedom from guilt. — *To ask the hand of*, to ask in marriage.—*To be hand and glove with*, to be intimate and familiar, as friends or associates.—*To bear a hand* (*naut.*), to give assistance quickly; to hasten.—*To change hands*, to change owners.—*To come to hand*, to be received; to come within one's reach. —*To have one's hands full*, to be fully occupied; to have a great deal to do.—*To lay hands on*, to seize; to assault.—*Laying on of hands*, a ceremony used in consecrating one to office.—*To lend a hand*, to give assistance.—*To set the hand to*, to engage in; to undertake.—*To shake hands*, to clasp the right hand mutually (with or without a shake), as a greeting or in token of friendship or reconciliation.—*To strike hands*, to make a contract or to become surety for another's debt or good behaviour (O.T.).—*To take by the hand*, to take under one's protection.—*To take in hand*, to attempt; to undertake; to seize and deal with (a person). — *To wash one's hands of*, to have nothing more to do with; to renounce all connection with or interest in. — *v.t.* To give or transmit with the hand (*hand* me a book); to lead, guide, and lift with the hand; to conduct.—*To hand down*, to transmit in succession, as from father to son, or from predecessor to successor.—*a.* Belonging to or used by the hand: much used in composition for that which is manageable or wrought by the hand.—**Hand-barrow**, *n.* A kind of litter or stretcher, with handles at each end, carried between two persons.—**Hand-basket**, *n.* A small or portable basket.—**Hand-bell**, *n.* A small bell rung when held by the hand; a table-bell.—**Hand-bill**, *n.* A printed paper or sheet to be circulated for the purpose of making some public announcement. — **Hand-book**, *n.* A small book or treatise such as may be easily held in the hand; an establishment where bets are accepted on horse races. — **Hand-breadth**, *n.* A space equal to the breadth of the hand; a palm. — **Hand-cart**, *n.* A cart drawn or pushed by hand. — **Handcuff**, hand'kuf, *n.* [Modified from A.Sax. *handcops*—*hand*, the hand, *cops*, a fetter.] A manacle or fastening for the hand.—*v.t.* To put a handcuff on; to manacle.—**Handed**, han'ded, *a.* Having a hand possessed of any peculiar property: used especially in compounds (right-*handed*, left-*handed*, empty-*handed*, full-*handed*, &c.). — **Handfasting**, *n.* An irregular marriage by agreement or mutual pledge.—**Handful**, hand'-ful, *n.* As much as the hand will grasp or contain; a small quantity or number.— **Hand-gallop**, *n.* A slow and easy gallop, in which the hand presses the bridle to hinder increase of speed.—**Hand-gear**, *n.* *Steam-engine*, the mechanism used for working the valves by hand. — **Hand-glass**, *n.* *Hort.* a glass used for placing over plants to protect them or forward growth.—**Hand-grenade**, *n.* A grenade to be thrown by the hand.—**Handline**, *n.* A small line used in fishing from boats at sea.—**Hand-loom**, *n.* A weaver's loom worked by the hand, as distinguished from a *power-loom*.—**Hand-made**, *a.* Manufactured by the hand and not by a machine. — **Handmaid**, **Handmaiden**, hand'mād, hand'mā-dn, *n.* A maid that waits at hand; a female servant or attendant.—**Hand-mill**, *n.* A small mill for grinding grain, pepper, coffee, &c., moved by hand.—**Hand-organ**, *n.* A portable or barrel organ.—**Hand-press**, *n.* A press worked by the hand, in opposition to one moved by steam-power, &c.—**Handrail**, **Handrailing**, hand'rāl, hand-rāl'ing, *n.* A rail or railing to hold by.—**Hand-saw**; *n.* A saw to be used with the hand.—

Hand-screen, *n.* A screen resembling a fan, used for keeping off the heat of the fire, too glaring light, &c.—**Hand-screw**, *n.* An appliance for raising heavy weights; a jack.—**Handspike**, hand'spik, *n.* A bar used as a lever for various purposes, as in raising weights, heaving about a windlass, &c.—**Handstaff**, hand'staf, *n.* pl. **Handstaves**, hand'stāvz. A javelin (O.T.).—**Hand-vise**, *n.* A small portable vise held in the hand while used.—**Hand-work**, *n.* Work done by the hands.—**Hand-worked**, **Hand-wrought**, *a.* Made with the hands.—**Handwrite**,† hand'rīt, *v.t.* To express in handwriting; to write out.—**Handwriting**, hand'rīt-ing, *n.* The cast of writing peculiar to each person; chirography; writing.

Handicap, han'di-kap, *n.* [For *hand i' cap*, *hand in the cap*, the allusion being to drawing a lot out of a cap, from the fairness of both principles.] *Racing*, an allowance of a certain amount of time or distance to the inferior competitors in a race to bring all as nearly as possible to an equality, or the extra weight imposed upon the superior competitors with the same object; a race so arranged.—*v.t.*—*handicapped*, *handicapping*. To put a handicap on; to equalize by a handicap.—**Handicapper**, han'di-kap-ėr, *n.* One who handicaps.

Handicraft, han'di-kraft, *n.* [Equivalent to *hand-craft*, the *i* representing old prefix *ge*, as in *handiwork*.] Manual occupation; work performed by the hand.—**Handicraftsman**, han'di-krafts-man, *n.* A man employed in manual occupation; an artisan.—**Handicuff**, **Handycuff**, han'di-kuf, *n.* [Formed in imitation of *handiwork*.] A blow or cuff with the hand.

Handiwork, **Handywork**, han'di-wėrk, *n.* [A.Sax. *handgeweorc*, from *hand*, the hand, and *geweorc* = *weorc*, work, with prefix *ge*.] Work done by the hands; hence, the work or deed of any person.

Handkerchief, hang'kėr-chēf, *n.* [*Hand* and *kerchief*. KERCHIEF.] A piece of cloth, usually silk, linen, or cotton, carried about the person for wiping the face, hands, &c.; a similar piece worn round the neck.

Handle, han'dl, *v.t.*—*handled*, *handling*. [A.Sax. *handlian*, to handle, a kind of freq. from *hand*=D. *handelen*, Dan. *handle*, Icel. *höndla*, G. *handeln*.] To bring the hand or hands in frequent contact with; to finger; to touch; to feel; to manage, ply, or wield; to treat of or deal with, as a person or a topic.—*v.i.* To use the hands; to feel with the hands.—*n.* That part of a thing which is intended to be grasped by the hand in using or moving it; the instrument or means of effecting a purpose.—*To give a handle*, to furnish an occasion.—*A handle to one's name*, a title (*colloq.*).—**Handleable**, han'di-a-bl, *a.* That may be handled.—**Handler**, han'dlėr, *n.* One who handles.—**Handling**, han'dling, *n.* A touching or using by the hand; a treating in discussion; dealing; action.

Handsel, **Hansel**, hand'sel, han'sel, *n.* [From *hand*, and stem *sell*, *sale*; Icel. *handsal* (from *hand*, and *sal*, sale), a bargain by shaking hands; Dan. *handsel*, hansel, earnest.] An earnest, or earnest penny; a sale, gift, or using, which is regarded as the first of a series; the first money received for the sale of goods.—*v.t.* To give a handsel to; to use or do for the first time.

Handsome, hand'sum, *a.* [From *hand*, and term. *-some*=D. *handzaam*, tractable, serviceable, mild; G. *handsam*, convenient, favourable.] Possessing a form agreeable to the eye or to correct taste; having a certain share of beauty along with dignity; having symmetry of parts; well formed; shapely; becoming; appropriate; ample or large (a *handsome* fortune); characterized by or expressive of liberality or generosity.—**Handsomely**, hand'sum-li, *adv.* In a handsome manner.—**Handsomeness**, hand'sum-nes, *n.*

Handy, han'di, *a.* [From *hand*; comp. the D. and L.G. *handig*, handy.] Skilled to use the hands with ease; dexterous; ready; adroit; ready to the hand; near; convenient.—**Handily**, han'di-li, *adv.* In a handy manner.—**Handiness**, han'di-nes, *n.*

Hang, hang, *v.t.* pret. & pp. *hung* or *hanged* (the latter being obsolete except in sense to put to death by the rope). [A.Sax. *hangian*, to hang or be suspended, and *hón* (contracted for *hahan*), pret. *heng*, pp. *hangen*, to suspend; O.H.G. *hahan*, G. *hangen*, *hängen*, Dan. *hænge*, Icel. *hanga*, *hengja*. Goth. *hahan*, to suspend, to hang. Akin *hank*, *hanker*, *hinge*.] To suspend; to fasten to some elevated point without support from below: often with *up*; to put to death by suspending by the neck; to fit up so as to allow of free motion (a door, a gate, &c.); to cover, furnish, or decorate by anything suspended (to *hang* an apartment with curtains); to cause or suffer to assume a drooping attitude (to *hang* the head).—*To hang fire*, to be slow in communicating fire through the vent to the charge: said of a gun; hence, to hesitate or be slow in acting; to be slow in execution.—*To hang out*, to suspend in open view; to display; to suspend in the open air.—*To hang up*, to suspend; to keep or suffer to remain undecided.—*v.i.* To be suspended; to be sustained wholly or partly by something above; to dangle; to depend; to bend forward or downward; to lean or incline; to be attached to or connected with in various ways; to hover; to impend (dangers *hang* over us); to linger, lounge, loiter; to incline; to have a steep declivity; to be put to death by suspension from the neck.—*To hang back*, to halt; to incline to retire; to go reluctantly forward.—*To hang on* or *upon*, to weigh upon; to drag; to rest; to continue (sleep *hung on* his eyelids); to be dependent on; to regard with the closest attention (he *hung* upon the speaker's words).—*To hang together*, to be closely united; to be self-consistent.—*n.* The way a thing hangs; slope or declivity; inclination, bent, or tendency.—**Hang-dog**, *n.* A base and degraded character, fit only to be the hangman of dogs.—*a.* Of or pertaining to a hang-dog; having a low, degraded, or blackguard-like appearance.—**Hanger**, hang'ėr, *n.* One who hangs; a short broad sword, incurvated at the point, which was suspended from the girdle; that from which something is hung.—**Hanger-on**, *n.* pl. **Hangers-on**. One who hangs on or sticks to a person, a place, society, &c.; a parasite; a dependant.—**Hanging**, hang'ing, *a.* Such as to incur punishment by the halter (a *hanging* matter).—*n.* Death by suspension; what is hung up to drape a room, as tapestry or the like: used chiefly in the plural.—**Hanging-buttress**, *n.* *Arch.* a merely decorative buttress supported on a corbel.—**Hanging-garden**, *n.* A garden formed in terraces rising one above the other.—**Hangman**, hang'man, *n.* One who hangs another; one employed to execute malefactors by the halter.—**Hangmanship**, hang'man-ship, *n.* The office of hangman.

Hangar, hang'ar, *n.* [Fr. *hangar*, a shed.] A shed for housing aeroplanes.

Hangnail, hang'nāl, *n.* Same as *Agnail*.

Hank, hangk, *n.* [Same as Icel. *hönk*, a hank or skein; Dan. *hank*, a hook, a clasp; Sw. *hank*, a band; akin to *hang*.] A parcel consisting of two or more skeins of yarn or thread tied together; *naut.* a ring of wood, rope, or iron, fixed to a stay to confine the stay-sails.

Hanker, hang'kėr, *v.i.* [Allied to D. *hunkeren*, to desire, to long after; probably to *hank* and *hang*.] To long for; to be uneasily desirous; to think of with longing: followed by *after*.—**Hankering**, hang'kėr-ing, *n.* The feeling of one who hankers; longing appetite.—**Hankeringly**, hang'kėr-ing-li, *adv.* In a hankering manner.

Hansard, han'särd, *n.* The published debates of the British Parliament, originally issued by the Messrs. *Hansard*.

Hanse, hans, *n.* [G. *hanse*, *hansa*, league.] A league; a confederacy.—**Hanse**, **Hanseatic**, han-sē-at'ik, *a.* Of or pertaining to a confederacy of commercial cities, associated together as early as the twelfth century; the name *Hanse towns* is still applied to Lübeck, Hamburg, and Bremen, the three free cities of Germany.—**Hansard**, han'särd, *n.* A merchant of one of the Hanse towns.

Hansom, **Hansom-cab**, han'sum, *n.* A two-wheeled cab, so named after the inventor.

Hap, hap, *n.* [Icel. *happ*, good fortune, luck; comp. A.Sax. *gehæp*, fit; D. *happen*, to snatch at; seen also in *mishap*, *perhaps*.] Chance; accident; casual event; vicissitude.—*v.i.* To happen; to befall; to come by chance.—**Haphazard**, *n.* Chance; accident.—**Hapless**, hap'les, *a.*—**Happen**, hap'n, *v.i.* [From *hap*.] To be or be brought about unexpectedly or by chance; to chance; to take place; to occur.—*To happen on*, to meet with; to fall or light upon.—**Happily**, hap'i-li, *adv.* In a happy manner, state, or circumstance.—**Happiness**, hap'i-nes, *n.* The state or quality of being happy; felicity; contentedness along with actual pleasure; good fortune.—**Happy**, hap'i, *a.* [From *hap*.] Contented in mind; highly pleased; satisfied; fortunate; successful; secure of good; bringing or attended with good fortune; prosperous; favorable; well suited for a purpose or occasion; well devised; felicitous; living in concord or friendship (a *happy* family).

Hara-kiri, ha'ra-kē'ri, *n.* [Jap. *hara*, belly, and *kiri*, cutting.] A traditional Japanese method of suicide, ceremonially performed by slashing across the abdomen with a dagger and then twisting it upward; simultaneously, the second, previously selected by the suicide, swings a sword on his friend's neck. Originally it was voluntarily practiced by nobles defeated in battle, by men as a mark of loyalty to a deceased noble, by men who had lost face or prestige; and obligatorily practiced, as an honorable way out, by men guilty of treachery or disloyalty to the mikado. It is now practiced chiefly as a mark of protest against a national policy.

Harangue, ha-rang', *n.* [Fr. *harangue*=Pr. *arengua*, It. *aringa*, a harangue, lit. a speech made to a ring, or crowd, of people.] A loud address to a multitude; a popular oration; a bombastic or pompous address; a tirade or declamation.—*v.i.* *harangued*, *haranguing*. To make a harangue; to make a bombastic or pretentious speech.—*v.t.* To address by a harangue.—**Haranguer**, ha-rang'ėr, *n.* One who harangues.

Harass, har'as, *v.t.* [Fr. *harasser*; probably connected with Fr. *harier*, to harry; vex; *harer*, to set a dog on.] To weary, fatigue, or tire with bodily labour; to weary with importunity, care, or perplexity; to perplex; to annoy by repeated attacks.—*n.*† Distress; devastation.—**Harasser**, har'as-ėr, *n.* One who harasses.—**Harassment**, har'as-ment, *n.* The act of harassing or state of being harassed.

Harbinger, här'bin-jėr, *n.* [O.E. *harbegier*, *harbergeour*, *harbesher*, &c., one who provides harborage or lodging, a harbinger; for the insertion of the *n* compare *messenger*, *passenger*. HARBOR.] One who went before to provide lodgings and other accommodations; hence, a forerunner; a precursor; that which precedes and gives notice of the expected arrival of something else.—*v.t.* To precede as harbinger; to presage or predetermine, as a harbinger.

Harbor, här'bėr, *n.* [Same as L.G. *harbarge*, D. *herberg*, Icel. *herbergi*, lit. army-shelter, the elements being the same as A.Sax. *here*, an army, and *beorgan*, *bergan*, to shelter or protect. BOROUGH.] A place of shelter, protection, or refuge; a port or haven for ships.—*v.t.* To shelter or take under protection; to protect; to entertain or cherish in the mind (to *harbor* malice).—*v.i.* To lodge or abide for a time for shelter or protection; to take shelter.—**Harborage**, här'bėr-āj, *n.* State of being harbored; shelter; lodgment.—**Harbor-dues**, *n. pl.* Charges on a ship or cargo for the use of a harbor, &c.—**Harborer**, här'bėr-ėr, *a.* One who harbors.—**Harborless**, här'bėr-les, *a.* Without a harbor; destitute of shelter.—**Harbor light**, *n.* A light or lighthouse to guide ships in entering a harbor.—**Harbor master**, *n.* An officer who attends to the berthing, &c., of ships in a harbor.

Hard, härd, *a.* [A.Sax. *heard* = Goth. *hardus*, Icel. *hardr*, Dan. *haard*, D. *hard*, G. *hart*; cog. Gr. *kratos*, *kartos*, strength (as in *aristocrat*, *democrat*, &c.). Hence *hardy*.] Not easily penetrated or separated into parts; not yielding to pressure: applied to material bodies, and opposed to *soft*; difficult to the understanding; not easy to the intellect; difficult of accomplishment; not easy to be done or executed; laborious; fatiguing; difficult to endure; oppressive; severe; cruel; distressing; painful; unfeeling; insensible; harsh; obdurate; exacting; avaricious; grasping; harsh or abusive (*hard* words); pinching with cold; rigorous (a *hard* winter); austere; rough; acid or sour (*hard* cider); forced; constrained; unnatural; coarse, unpalatable, or scanty (*hard* fare); *gram.* applied to the consonants (also called *surd*) *f*, *k*, *p*, *s*, *t*, and the sound of *th* in *thin*, and also to the sound of *c* as in *corn* and *g* as in *get*, as distinguished from the sounds in *city* and *gin*; applied to water not very suitable for washing from holding salts of lime or magnesia in solution.—*Hard cash*, gold or silver coin, as distinguished from paper-money. (*Colloq.*)—*adv.* Close; near (*hard by*); with urgency; vehemently; vigorously; energetically; violently; with great force; with difficulty or labour.—*To die hard*, to die, as it were, reluctantly, and after a struggle for life; to die unrepentant.—*Hard up*, in want of money; needy; without resources.—*Hard up for*, having difficulty in getting anything; at a loss how to find.—*Hard a-weather! hard a-port!* &c., *naut.* a direction for the helm to be turned as much as possible to the weather-side, the port-side, &c.—**Hardbake**, *n.* A species of toffee.—**Hard-billed**, *a.* Having a hard bill or beak suitable for crushing seeds, &c.: said of birds.—**Hard-earned**, *a.* Earned with difficulty.—**Harden**, här'dn, *v.t.* To make hard or more hard; to confirm in effrontery, obstinacy, wickedness, opposition, or enmity; to make insensible or unfeeling; to make firm; to inure.—*v.i.* To become hard or more hard; to acquire solidity or mere compactness; to become unfeeling; to become inured.—**Hardened**, här'dnd, *p.* and *a.* Made hard, or more hard; confirmed in error or vice (*hardened* sinner).—**Hardener**, här'dn-ėr, *n.* One who or that which hardens.—**Hard-faced, Hard-visaged, Hard-featured**, *a.* Having a hard or stern face.—**Hard-favoured**, *a.* Having coarse features; harsh of countenance.—**Hard-fisted, Hard-handed**, *a.* Having hard hands; close-fisted; covetous.—**Hard-fought**, *a.* Vigorously contested.—**Hard-headed**, *a.* Shrewd; clear-headed and firm.—**Hard-hearted**, *a.* Pitiless; unfeeling; inhuman; inexorable.—**Hardish**, här'dish, *a.* Somewhat hard; tending to hardness.—**Hardly**, härd'li, *adv.* In a hard manner; not easily; severely; harshly; scarcely; barely; not quite.—**Hard-mouthed**, *a.* Having a mouth not sensible to the bit (a *hard-mouthed* horse).—**Hardness**, härd'nes, *n.* The state or quality of being hard; *mineral*, the capacity of a substance to scratch another or be scratched by another.—**Hard-pan**, *n.* *Agri.* the name given to a hard stratum of earth below the soil proper.—**Hard-pressed, Hard-pushed**, *a.* In a strait or difficulty.—**Hardship**, härd'ship, *n.* Something hard, oppressive, toilsome, distressing, &c.; want or privation; grievance.—**Hardware**, härd'wār, *n.* Articles of iron or other metal, as pots, kettles, saws, knives, &c.—**Hardwood**, härd'wu̦d, *n.* Any wood of a close and solid texture, as beech, oak, ash, maple, ebony, &c.

Hards, härdz, *n. pl.* [Also written *hurds*; from A.Sax. *heordan* (pl.), hards, tow; Icel. *hörr*, flax; same root as L. *caro*, to card, *carduus*, thistle, *coma*, hair; perhaps E. *hair*.] The refuse or coarse part of flax or wool.

Hardy, här'di, *a.* [Fr. *hardi*, bold, daring, properly the pp. of the old verb *hardir*, to make bold, from O.H.G. *hartjan*, from *hart* (E. *hard*), hard, bold. HARD.] Bold; brave; stout; daring; resolute; intrepid; confident; full of assurance; inured to fatigue; proof against hardship; capable of bearing exposure to cold weather (a *hardy* plant).—**Hardihood**, här'di-hu̦d, *n.* Boldness; bravery; intrepidity; venturesomeness; audacity.—**Hardily**, här'di-li, *adv.* In a hardy manner.—**Hardiness**, här'di-nes, *n.* The state or quality of being hardy.

Hare, hãr, *n.* [A.Sax. *hara*=Dan. and Sw. *hare*, Icel. *héri*, D. *haas*, G. *hase*; probably allied to Skr. *çaça*, a hare, from *çaç*, to jump.] A rodent quadruped of various species, with long ears, a short tail, soft hair, a divided upper lip, and long hind legs, often hunted for sport or for its flesh, which is excellent food.—**Harebell**, hãr'-bel, *n.* A species of the campanula or bell-flower, also termed the common bell-flower and Scottish blue-bell; also applied in many districts to the wild hyacinth.—**Hare-brained**, *a.* [Comp. 'mad as a March hare'.] Giddy; volatile; heedless.—**Hare-hearted**, *a.* Timorous, like a hare; easily frightened.—**Hare-hound**, *n.* A hound for hunting hares; a greyhound.—**Hare-lip**, *n.* A malformation of the lip consisting of a fissure or vertical division of one or both lips, sometimes extending also to the palate.—**Hare-lipped**, *a.* Having a hare-lip.—**Harish**, hã'rish, *a.* Resembling a hare.

Hareld, har'eld, *n.* [Perhaps from its cry.] A marine duck inhabiting the arctic seas, the male having two very long feathers in the tail.

Harem, Hareem, hā'rem, ha-rēm', *n.* [Ar. *harām*, anything prohibited, from *harram*, to prohibit, the inmates of the harem being kept in strict seclusion.] The apartments appropriated to the female members of a Mohammedan family; the occupants.

Haricot, här'i-kō, *n.* [Fr., a ragout; O.Fr. *harigoter*, to mince, *harigote*, a morsel; *haricot*-bean = ragout-bean.] A kind of ragout of meat and roots; the kidney-bean or French bean (in this sense short for haricot-bean).

Hark, härk, *v.i.* [Contr. from *hearken*.] To listen; to hearken: now only used in the imperative.—*Hark!* a hunting cry used with various adjuncts to stimulate or direct the hounds.—**Harken**. HEARKEN.

Harl, härl, *n.* [Probably = *hardle*, from *hards*.] A filament, as of flax or hemp; a barb of one of the feathers from a peacock's tail, used in dressing fly-hooks.

Harl, härl, *v.t.* To give a rough coating of lime to the stones of a house. (Scottish.)

Harlequin, här'le-kwin, *n.* [Fr. *harlequin*, *arlequin*; O.Fr. *hellequin*, *hierlekin*, &c.; origin quite uncertain.] A performer in a pantomime, masked, dressed in tight parti-coloured clothes, covered with spangles, and armed with a magic wand or sword; a buffoon in general; a fantastic fellow.—**Harlequinade**, här'le-kwin-ād'', *n.* The portion of a pantomime in which the harlequin and clown play the principal parts.—**Harlequin-duck**, *n.* A beautiful species of duck, the male of which has the plumage fantastically marked.

Harlot, här'lot, *n.* [O.Fr. *harlot*, *herlot*, Pr. *arlot*, Sp. *arlote*, It. *arlotto*, a glutton, a lazy good-for-nothing, a word of uncertain origin; comp. W. *herlawd*, a stripling, *herlodes*, a damsel.] A woman who prostitutes her body for hire; a prostitute.—**Harlotry**, här'lot-ri, *n.* A trade or practice of prostitution.

Harm, härm, *n.* [A.Sax. *hearm*, harm, evil, grief = Dan., Sw., and G. *harm*, grief, offence; Icel. *harmr*; comp. Skr. *çram*, to weary.] Physical or material injury; hurt; damage; detriment; moral wrong; evil; mischief; wickedness.—*v.t.* To hurt; to injure; to damage.—**Harmful**, härm'fu̦l, *a.* Full of harm; hurtful; injurious; noxious.—**Harmfully**, härm'fu̦l-li, *adv.* In a harmful manner.—**Harmfulness**, härm'fu̦l-nes, *n.*—**Harmless**, härm'les, *a.* Free from harm; uninjured; free from power or disposition to harm; not injurious; innocuous; inoffensive.—**Harmlessly**, härm'les-li, *adv.* In a harmless manner.—**Harmlessness**, härm'les-nes, *n.*

Harmattan, här-mat'tan, *n.* [Arabic name.] An extremely dry and hot wind which blows periodically from the interior parts of Africa towards the Atlantic Ocean.

Harmony, här'mo-ni, *n.* [L. and Gr. *harmonia*, from Gr. *harmos*, a suiting or fitting together a joint, from *arō*, to fit, to adapt, the same root being seen in E. *arm*.] The just adaptation of parts to each other, in any system or combination of things, or in things intended to form a connected whole; concord; consonance; concord or agreement in facts, views, sentiments, manners, interests, and the like; peace and friendship; *mus.* musical concord; the accordance of two or more sounds, or that union of different sounds which pleases the ear, or a succession of such sounds called chords; the science which treats of such sounds; the agreement or consistency of the accounts of the first three (synoptic) gospels with the fourth by St. John.—**Harmonic, Harmonical**, här-mon'ik, här-mon'i-kal, *a.* Relating to harmony or music; concordant; musical; harmonious.—*Acoustics*, a secondary tone heard along with a fundamental tone, produced by secondary or partial vibrations.—*Harmonical proportion*, *math.* the relation between four quantities when the first is to the fourth as the difference between the first and second is to the difference between the third and fourth; also a similar relation between three quantities.—*Harmonical series*, a series of numbers in continued harmonical proportion.—*Harmonic triad*, *mus.* the chord of a note consisting of its third and perfect fifth, or in other words, the common chord.—*n. Mus.* a secondary and less distinct tone which accompanies any principal and apparently simple tone.—**Harmonica**, här-mon'i-ka, *n.* A collection of musical glass goblets; also an instrument, the tones of which are produced by striking rods or plates of glass or metal with hammers.—**Harmonically**, här-mon'i-kal-li, *adv.* In a harmonic manner.—**Harmonicon**, här-mon'i-kon, *n.* A large barrel-organ, containing, in addition to the common pipes, others to imitate the different wind-instruments, and an apparatus to produce the effects of drums, triangles, cymbals, &c.; also, a toy musical instrument with free reeds blown by the mouth.—**Harmonics**, här-mon'iks, *n.* The doctrine or science of musical sounds.—**Harmonious**, här-mō'ni-us, *a.* Exhibiting or characterized by harmony.—**Harmoniously**, här-mō'ni-us-li, *adv.* In a harmonious manner.—**Harmoniousness**, här-mō'ni-us-nes, *n.*—**Harmonist**, här'mon-ist, *n.* One who harmonizes; one skilled in the principles of harmony; a writer of harmony.—**Harmonium**, här-mō'ni-um, *n.* A musical instrument resembling a small organ, and much used as a substitute for it, the tones of which are produced by the forcing of air through free reeds.—**Harmoniumist**, här-mō'ni-um-ist, *n.* A player of the harmonium.—**Harmonization**, här'mon-i-zā''shon, *n.* The act of harmonizing.—**Harmonize**, här'mon-īz, *v.i.*—*harmonized*, *harmonizing*. To unite harmoniously or in harmony; to be in peace and friendship; to agree in action, effect, sense, or purport; to be musically harmonious.—*v.t.* To bring to be harmonious; to cause to agree; to show the harmony or agreement of; to reconcile the contradictions between; *mus.* to combine according to the laws of counterpoint; to set accompanying parts to, as to an air or melody.—**Harmonizer**, här'mon-ī-zėr, *n.* One who harmonizes; a harmonist.

Harmotome, här'mō-tōm, *n.* [Gr. *harmos*, a joint, and *temnō*, to cut.] CROSS-STONE.

Harness, här'nes, *n.* [W. *harnais*, *haiarnaez*, harness, from *haiarn*, iron. IRON.] The whole accoutrements or equipments of a knight; a person's armour and military furniture; the gear or tackle by which a horse or other animal is yoked and made to work; the apparatus in a loom by which the sets of warp thread are shifted alternately to form the shed.—*v.t.* To dress in armour; to equip with military accoutrements; to put harness on, as on a horse.—**Harnesser**, här′nes-ėr, *n.* One who harnesses.

Harp, härp, *n.* [A.Sax. *hearpe* = D. *harp*, Icel. *harpa*, Dan. *harpe*, Gr. *harfe*, a harp; perhaps same root as L. *carpo*, to pluck or twitch.] A stringed musical instrument of great antiquity, now usually nearly triangular in form, with wire strings stretched from the upper part to one of the sides, played with both hands while standing upright, the strings being struck or pulled by fingers and thumb.—*v.i.* To play on the harp; to dwell on a subject tiresomely and vexatiously: usually with *on* or *upon*.—*To harp on one string*, to dwell too exclusively upon one subject, so as to weary or annoy the hearers.—**Harper, Harpist**, här′pėr, här′pist, *n.* A player on the harp.—**Harp-seal**, *n.* The Greenland seal, so called from the large, black, crescent-shaped mark on each side of the back.—**Harp-shell**, *n.* A mollusc of the whelk family, the shell of which has some resemblance in shape to a harp.

Harpoon, här-pön′, *n.* [Fr. *harpon*, a harpoon, from *harper*, to clutch, from *harpe*, a claw, a hook, from Gr. *harpagē*, a hook, *harpazō*, to seize.] A spear or javelin used to strike and kill whales and large fish.—*v.t.* To strike with a harpoon.—**Harpooner**, här-pö′nėr, *n.* One who uses a harpoon.—**Harpoon-gun**, *n.* A gun for firing a harpoon.

Harpsichord, härp′si-kord, *n.* [From O.Fr. *harpechorde*, It. *arpicordo*—*harp* and *chord*; it does not appear how the *s* got inserted.] An obsolete stringed musical instrument something like a horizontal grand pianoforte.

Harpy, här′pi, *n.* [Fr. *harpie*, from L. *harpyia*, Gr. *harpuia*, from root of *harpazō*, to seize.] *Class. mythol.*, the name given to three foul monsters having the face of a woman and the body of a bird, with feet and fingers armed with sharp claws, who were sent to punish Phineus for his cruelty to his children.—**Harpy eagle**, *n.* A large and very powerful raptorial bird of Mexico and South America.

Harquebus, Harquebuse, Harquebuss, här′kwē-bus. ARQUEBUSE.

Harridan, har′i-dan, *n.* [Akin to Fr. *haridelle*, Prov. Fr. *hardele*, *harin*, a worn-out horse, a jade.] A hag; an odious old woman; a vixenish woman; a trollop.

Harrier, har′i-ėr, *n.* [From *hare*.] A small kind of dog of the hound species employed in hunting the hare.

Harrier, har′i-ėr, *n.* One who harries or pillages; a name for several species of hawks which strike their prey upon the ground and generally fly very low; also a cross-country runner; *pl.* cross-country runners who play a game of hare and hounds; a club of such athletes or the members of such a team.

Harrovian, ha-rō′vi-an, *a.* Of or pertaining to Harrow, an exclusive boys' school in England.—*n.* One who attends, or is a graduate of, Harrow.

Harrow, har′ō, *n.* [Same word as Dan. *harve*, Sw. *harf*, a harrow: akin to D. *hark*, G. *harke*, a rake.] An agricultural implement, usually formed of pieces of timber or metal crossing each other, and set with iron teeth, called tines, used for covering seed when sown, &c.—*v.t.* To draw a harrow over; *fig.* to lacerate (the feelings); to torment; to harass.—**Harrower**, har′ō-ėr, *n.* One who harrows.—**Harrowing**, har′ō-ing, *a.* Causing acute distress to the mind.—**Harrowingly**, har′ō-ing-li, *adv.* In a harrowing manner; excruciatingly.

Harry, har′i, *v.t.*—*harried*, *harrying*. [A. Sax. *hergian*, to ravage, from *here* (genit. *herges*), an army; Icel. *herja*, to lay waste, to oppress; Dan. *hærge*, *hærje*, G. (*ver*) *heeren*, to ravage. Akin *herring*, *herald*.] To pillage; to plunder; to rob; to harass.

Harsh, härsh, *a.* [O.E. and Sc. *harsk*, harsh, acid; same as Dan. and O.Sw. *harsk*, rancid; G. *harsch*, harsh, rough; root doubtful; perhaps akin to *hard*.] Grating, either to the touch, to the taste, or to the ear; austere; crabbed; morose; rough; rude; rigorous; severe.—**Harshen**, har′shn, *v.t.* To render harsh.—**Harshly**, härsh′li, *adv.* In a harsh manner.—**Harshness**, härsh′-nes, *n.* The quality or condition of being harsh.

Harslet, härs′let, *n.* HASLET.

Hart, härt, *n.* [A.Sax. *heort*=L.G. and D. *hert*, Dan. *hiort*, Sw. *hjort*, Icel. *hjörtr*, G. *hirsch*, stag; lit. horned animal; allied to Gr. *keras*, L. *cornu*, a horn. HORN.] A stag or male deer, especially when he has passed his fifth year, and the sur-royal or crown antler is formed.—**Hart's-clover, Hart's-trefoil**, *n.* The common yellow melilot.—**Hartshorn**, harts′horn, *n.* The horn of the hart or stag; an ammoniacal preparation obtained from the horn, and used medicinally; solution of ammonia.—**Hart's-tongue**, *n.* The popular name of a fern found in Britain.

Hartebeest, Hartbeest, här′te-bēst, härt′-bēst, *n.* [Dutch.] An antelope common in South Africa.

Harum-scarum, hā′rum-skā′rum, *a.* [Perhaps from O.E. *hare*, to fright, or from *hare*, the animal, and *scare*.] Hare-brained; unsettled; giddy; rash.—*n.* A giddy, hare-brained, or rash person. (*Colloq.*)

Haruspice, Haruspicy. ARUSPEX.

Harvest, här′vest, *n.* [A.Sax. *haerfest* = O.Fris. *harvest*, G. *herbst*, D. *herfst*, Icel. *haust*, Sw. and Dan. *höst*, autumn, harvest; cognate with Gr. *karpos*, fruit, L. *carpo*, to pluck.] The season of gathering a crop of any kind; the time of reaping and gathering corn and other grain; that which is reaped and gathered in; the product of any labor; gain; result; effect; consequence.—*v.t.* To reap or gather (corn and fruits).—**Harvest-bug**, *n.* A species of tick which infests the skin in the autumn.—**Harvester**, har′ves-tėr, *n.* One who or that which harvests; a mower; a reaper.—**Harvest-feast**, *n.* The feast made at the ingathering of the harvest.—**Harvest-field**, *n.* A field from which a harvest is gathered.—**Harvest home**, *n.* The bringing home of the harvest; the harvest-feast.—**Harvest-moon**, *n.* The full moon at the time of harvest, or about the autumnal equinox, when it rises nearly at the same hour for several days.

Has, haz. The 3rd pers. sing. pres. of the verb *have*.—**Has-been**, haz′bin, *n.* One who has had his day; that which has passed its usefulness. (*Colloq.*)

Hash, hash, *v.t.* [Fr. *hacher*, E. to *hack*, HACK.] To chop into small pieces; to mince and mix.—*n.* That which is hashed or chopped up; meat which has been already cooked, chopped into small pieces and served up again; any second preparation of old matter; a repetition.

Hashish, Hasheesh, hash′esh, *n.* A narcotic plant of Asia, similar to marijuana, the dried leaves of which are smoked in cigarettes.

Haslet, has′let, *n.* [For *hastelet*, from Fr. *hastille*, the pluck of an animal, lit. a little roast, from *haste*, a spit, L. *hasta*, a spear.] The cooked heart, liver, &c., of a hog.

Hasp, hasp, *n.* [A.Sax. *hæpse*, the hook of a hinge = Icel. *hespa*, G. *haspe*, *häspe*, a fastening; Dan. *haspe*, a hasp, a reel.] A clasp that passes over a staple to be fastened by a padlock; a metal hook for fastening a door; the fourth part of a spindle (of yarn).—*v.t.* To shut or fasten with a hasp.

Hassock, has′ok, *n.* [Origin doubtful; comp. W. *hesg*, sedge, also Sw. *hwass*, rushes.] A thick mat or hard cushion on which persons kneel in church; a footstool stuffed with flock or other material.

Hast, hast. The 2nd pers. sing. pres. of the verb *have*.

Hastate, has′tāt, *a.* [L. *hastatus*, from *hasta*, a spear.] Spear-shaped; resembling the head of a spear; triangular.

Haste, hāst, *n.* [Same word as G.Sw. and Dan. *hast*, haste, whence O.Fr. *haste*, Mod. Fr. *hâte*, haste; akin to *hate*.] Celerity of motion; speed; swiftness; despatch; expedition: applied only to voluntary beings, as men and animals; sudden excitement of passion; quickness; precipitance; the state of being pressed by business; hurry; urgency.—*To make haste*, to hasten; to proceed rapidly.—**Haste, Hasten**, hāst, hā′sn, *v.t.* [Sw. *hasta*, Dan. *haste*, G. *hasten*, to haste.] To drive or urge forward; to push on; to hurry; to expedite; with *me*, *him*, &c., to make haste; to be speedy or quick.—*v.i.* To move with celerity; to hurry.—**Hastener**, hā′sn-ėr, *n.* One that hastens; a metal kitchen-stand for keeping in the heat of the fire to a joint while cooking.—**Hastily**, hās′ti-li, *adv.* In a hasty manner.—**Hastiness**, hās′ti-nes, *n.* The state or quality of being hasty.—**Hasty**, hās′ti, *a.* Moving or acting with haste; quick; speedy: opposed to *slow*; precipitate; rash; inconsiderate: opposed to *deliberate*; irritable; easily excited to wrath; passionate; arising from or indicating passion (*hasty* words); early ripe (O.T.).—**Hasty-pudding**, *n.* A pudding made of milk and flour boiled quickly together; also, oatmeal and water boiled together; porridge.

Hat, hat, *n.* [A.Sax. *hæt* = Dan. *hat*, Sw. *hett*, Icel. *hattr*—hat, from a root meaning to cover.] A covering for the head; a head-dress with a crown, sides, and continuous brim, made of different materials, and worn by men and women; the dignity of a cardinal: from the broad-brimmed scarlet hat which forms part of a cardinal's dress.—*To give one a hat*, to lift the hat to one.—**Hat-band**, *n.* A band round a hat.—**Hat-block**, *n.* A block for forming or dressing hats on.—**Hat-body**, *n.* The whole body of a hat in an unfinished state.—**Hat-box, Hat-case**, *n.* A box for a hat.—**Hat-brush**, *n.* A soft brush for hats.—**Hatless**, hat′les, *a.* Having no hat.—**Hat-rack, Hat-stand, Hat-tree**, *n.* A rack or stand of various forms furnished with pegs for hanging hats on.—**Hatted**, hat′ed, *a.* Covered with a hat; wearing a hat.—**Hatter**, hat′ėr, *n.* A maker or seller of hats.—**Hatting**, hat′ing, *n.* The trade of a hatter; stuff for hats.

Hatch, hach, *v.t.* [Same word as Dan. *hække*, to hatch, or nidificate, from *hæk*, a hatching; Sw. *häcka*, to hatch; G. *hecken*, to hatch, *hecke*, the pairing of birds, a brood; connected with *hack*, from the chipping of the shell.] To produce young from eggs by incubation, or by artificial heat; to contrive or plot; to originate and produce (a scheme, mischief, &c.).—*v.i.* To perform or undergo the process of incubation.—*n.* A brood; as many young birds as are produced at once; the act of hatching.—**Hatcher**, hach′ėr, *n.* One who hatches; a contriver; a plotter.

Hatch, hach, *v.t.* [Fr. *hacher*, to hack, to shade by lines. HACK.] To shade by lines crossing each other in drawing and engraving.—**Hatching**, hach′ing, *n.* Shading made by cross lines.

Hatch, hach, *n.* [A.Sax. *hæc*, a grating; Dan. *hæk*, D. *hek*, a grating; G. *heck*, a fence of laths.] The frame of cross-bars laid over the opening in a ship's deck; the cover or a hatchway; the opening in a ship's deck; the hatchway; a similar opening in a floor; a trap-door; a half-door or a door with an opening over it; a flood-gate; a frame or weir in a river for catching fish.—*To be under hatches*, to be in the interior of a ship with the hatches down.—*Naut.* dead, gone below, opposed to *gone aloft*.—*v.t.* To close with a hatch or hatches.—**Hatchway**, hach′wā, *n.* A square or oblong opening in a ship's deck for communication with the interior.

Hatchel, hach′el, *n.* [A form of *hackle* or *heckle*.] A hackle or heckle for flax.—*v.t.* To clean by drawing through the teeth of a hatchel; to hackle or heckle.—**Hatcheler**, hach′el-ėr, *n.* One who hatchels.

Hatchet, hach'et, *n.* [Fr. *hachette*, from *hacher*, to cut, from G. *hacken*, to cut. HACK.] A small axe with a short handle, used with one hand.—*To take up the hatchet*, to make war; *to bury the hatchet*, to make peace: phrases derived from the customs of the American Indians.—**Hatchet-faced**, *a.* Having a thin face with prominent features.

Hatchment, hach'ment, *n.* [Corrupted from *achievement*.] The coat of arms of a dead person, placed on the front of a house, in a church, or elsewhere at funerals, notifying the death and the rank of the deceased. Also called *Achievement*.

Hatchway, *n.* Under HATCH, *n.*

Hate, hāt, *v.t.*—*hated, hating.* [A.Sax. *hate, hete*, hate, hatred, *hatian*, to hate; D. *haat*, Sw. *hat*, Icel. *hatr*, Goth. *hatis*, hate; Goth. *hatan*, Icel. and Sw. *hata*, D. *haten*, G. *hassen*, to hate.] To dislike greatly or intensely; to have a great aversion to; to detest.—*n.* Great dislike or aversion; hatred.—**Hatable, Hateable**, hā'ta-bl, *a.* Capable or worthy of being hated; odious.—**Hateful**, hāt'ful, *a.* Causing hate; exciting great dislike; odious; detestable; feeling hatred; malevolent.—**Hatefully**, hāt'ful-li, *adv.* In a hateful manner.—**Hatefulness**, hāt'ful-nes, *n.* The quality of being hateful.—**Hater**, hā'tėr, *n.* One that hates.—**Hatred**, hā'tred, *a.* [*Hate*, and suffix *-red*, as in *kindred* = A.Sax. *-raeden*, condition, state.] Great dislike or aversion; hate; detestation; active antipathy.

Hath, hath, 3rd pers. sing. pres. of *have*, now archaic or poetical.

Hatt, Hatti-sherif, hat, hat'ti-she-rif", *n.* [Turk.] An irrevocable order which comes immediately from the Sultan of Turkey, who subscribes it himself.

Hauberk, ha̤'bėrk, *n.* [O.Fr. *hauberc*, from O.H.G. *halsberg*—*hals*, the throat, and *bergen*, to defend; A. Sax. *healsbeorga*, Icel. *hálsbjörg*, a gorget. *Habergeon* is a diminutive. HAWSE, BOROUGH.] A coat of mail without sleeves, formed of steel rings interwoven.

Haugh, ha̤ch, *n.* [Same as A.Sax. *hath*, *heath*, a nook or corner; the original meaning would be land in the bend of a stream.] In Scotland, a piece of low-lying meadow ground on the border of a river.

Haughty, ha̤'ti, *a.* [O.Fr. *hautain*, haughty, from *haut*, *hault*, from L. *altus*, high (whence *altitude, exalt*); *gh* was inserted through influence of *high*.] Proud and disdainful; having a high opinion of one's self, with some contempt for others; lofty and arrogant; disdainful; supercilious.—**Haughtily**, ha̤'ti-li, *adv.* In a haughty manner.—**Haughtiness**, ha̤'ti-nes, *n.* The quality of being haughty.

Haul, ha̤l, *v.t.* [Same as D. *halen*, Icel. and Sw. *hala*, Dan. *hale*, to haul; G. *holen*, to fetch, to tow (whence Fr. *haler*, to haul); hence *halliard, halyard*.] To pull or draw with force; to transport by drawing; to drag; to tug.—*To haul over the coals*, to bring to a reckoning; to take to task; to reprimand.—*v.i.* *Naut.* to change the direction of sailing: with *off, up*, &c.—*n.* A pulling with force; a violent pull; a draught of fish in a net; that which is caught by one haul; hence, that which is taken, gained, or received at once.—**Haulage**, ha̤'lāj, *n.* The act of hauling or drawing; the force expended in hauling; dues or charges for hauling or towing.—**Hauler**, ha̤'lėr, *n.* One who pulls or hauls.

Haulm, Haum, ha̤lm, ha̤m, *n.* [A.Sax. *healm*=D. Dan. and Sw. *halm*, Icel. *hálmr*; cog. L. *calamus*, Gr. *kalamos*, a reed.] The stem or stalk of grain of all kinds, or of peas, beans, hops, &c.; dry stalks in general.

Haunch, ha̤nsh, *n.* [Fr. *hanche*, the haunch, from the Teutonic; Fris. *hancke, hencke*, haunch; G. *hanke*, the haunch of a horse.] The hip; the bend of the thigh; part of the body of a man and of quadrupeds between the last ribs and the thigh; *arch.* the middle part between the vertex or crown and the springing of an arch; the flank.

Haunt, ha̤nt, *v.t.* [Fr. *hanter*, to frequent, from Armor. *hent*, a way, *henti*, to frequent.] To frequent; to resort to much or often, or to be much about; to visit customarily; to appear in or about, as a spectre; to be a frequent spectral visitant of.—*v.i.* To be much about a place; to make frequent resort.—*n.* A place to which one frequently resorts; a favourite resort; a common abiding place.—**Haunted**, ha̤n'ted, *p.* and *a.* Frequently visited or resorted to, especially by apparitions or the shades of the dead.—**Haunter**, ha̤n'tėr, *n.* One who haunts.

Haustellum, ha̤s-tel'lum, *n.* [L., from *haurio, haustum*, to draw up.] The suctorial organ of certain insects, otherwise called the proboscis or antlia.—**Haustellate**, ha̤s'tel-lāt, *a.* Provided with a haustellum or sucker; suctorial.

Hautboy, Hautbois, hō'boi, *n.* [Fr. *hautbois*—*haut* (in E. *haughty*), high, and *bois* (E. *bush*), wood, from the high tone of the instrument.] An oboe; a wind instrument of wood, sounded through a double-reed.—**Hautboyist**, hō'boi-ist, *n.* A player on the hautboy.

Hautelisse, ōt'lis, *a.* [Fr. *hautelice*, high warp.] BASSELISSE.

Hauteur, ō-tėr, *n.* [Fr. HAUGHTY.] Pride; haughtiness; insolent manner or spirit.

Havana, Havannah, ha-van'a, *n.* A kind of cigar largely manufactured at *Havana*, the capital of Cuba.

Have, hav, *v.t.*—pret. & pp. *had*, ppr. *having*. Ind. pres. I *have*, thou *hast*, he *has*; we, ye, they *have*. [A.Sax. *habban*, from *hafian* (*fi* becoming regularly *bb* between vowels)=Dan. *have*, Icel. *hafa*, Goth. *haban*, G. *haben*, to have; cog. L. *capio*, to take (whence *capable*, &c.). *Behave, haft, haven* are connected.] To possess; to hold; to be in close relation to (to *have* a son, a master, a servant); to accept; to take as husband or wife; to hold or regard (to *have* in honour); to maintain or hold in opinion; to be under necessity, or impelled by duty (to *have* to do it); to procure or make to be; to cause (he *had* him murdered); to gain, procure, receive, obtain; to bring forth (a child); to experience in any way, as to enjoy, to participate in, to suffer from; to understand.—*I had as good*, it would be as well for me; *I had better*, it would be better for me; *I had best*, it would be best for me; *I had as lief* or *lieve*, I would as willingly; *I had rather*, I should prefer.—*Have after!* pursue! let us pursue!—*Have at!* go at! assail! encounter! as *have* at him!—*Have with you!* come on! agreed!—*To have away*, to remove; to take away.—*To have in*, to contain.—*To have on*, to wear; to carry, as raiment or weapons.—*To have a care*, to take care; to be on guard, or to guard.—*To have a person out*, to meet him in a duel.—*To have it out of a person*, to punish him; to retaliate on him; to take him to task. [*Have* is used as an auxiliary verb to form certain compound tenses, as the perfect and pluperfect of both transitive and intransitive verbs.] **Haver**, hav'ėr, *n.* One who has something; *Scots law*, the possessor of a document bearing on the case.—**Having**, hav'ing, *n.* The act or state of possessing; that which is had or possessed; goods; estate.

Haven, hā'vn, *n.* [A.Sax. *hæfen*=D. and L.G. *haven*, Icel. *höfn*, Dan. *havn*, G. *hafen*; connected with *have*.] A harbour; a port; a bay, recess, or inlet which affords anchorage and a station for ships; a shelter, asylum, or place of safety.—*v.i.* To shelter, as in a haven.

Haversack, hav'ėr-sak, *n.* [Fr. *havresac*, from D. *haverzak*, G. *hafersack*, a haversack, literally a sack for oats, from D. *haver*, G. *hafer*, Dan. *havre*, oats.] A bag of strong cloth worn over the shoulder by soldiers in marching order for carrying their provisions.

Haversian, ha-vėr'si-an, *a.* [After *Havers*, the discoverer.] Applied to a net-work of minute canals which traverse the solid substance of bones, conveying the nutrient vessels to all parts.

Havildar, hav'il-dar, *n.* [Hind. *hawāldār*—*hawāla*, charge, care, and *dār*, a holder.] A sepoy sergeant in Indian regiments.

Havoc, Havock, hav'ok, *n.* [From. O.Fr. *havot*, pillage, plunder.] Devastation; wide and general destruction.—*v.t.* To destroy; to lay waste (*Mil.*).

Haw, ha̤, *n.* [A.Sax. *haga*, an inclosure, a yard = Icel. *hagi*, Sw. *hage*, an inclosure, akin *hedge, haggard*.] A hedge; an inclosure; the hawthorn and its berry or seed.

Haw, ha̤, *n.* [Same as *ha*, interjection.] An intermission or hesitation of speech (hums and *haws*.)—To speak with a haw.

Haw, ha̤, *n.* [Origin unknown.] The nictitating membrane in the eye of a dog, horse, &c.

Hawhaw, ha̤'ha̤, *n.* A ha-ha or sunk fence.

Hawk, ha̤k, *n.* [A.Sax. *hafoc* = D. *havik*, G. *habicht*, Icel. *haukr*, Dan. *hög*, a hawk; from stem of *have*.] A rapacious bird of the falcon family; a falcon.—*v.i.* To hunt by means of trained hawks or falcons; to practise falconry; to fly in the manner of the hawk.—*To hawk at*, to attack on the wing.—**Hawker**, ha̤'kėr, *n.* One who hawks; a falconer.—**Hawkish**, ha̤'kish, *a.* Pertaining to or resembling a hawk; rapacious; fierce.—**Hawk-moth**, *n.* A moth, so called from its hovering motion.—**Hawk's-bill**, *n.* A turtle with a mouth like the beak of a hawk.

Hawk, ha̤k, *v.i.* [Probably imitative. Comp. D. *harke*, and W. *hochi*, to hawk.] To make an effort to force up phlegm with noise.—*v.t.* To raise by hawking.—*n.* An effort to force up phlegm by coughing.

Hawk, ha̤k, *v.t.* [From D. *heukeren*, to retail, to huckster, *heuker*, a retailer; akin to G. *höken, höcken*, to retail, *höker, höcker*, a hawker, from *hocken, hucken*, to take upon the back, to squat. Akin *huckster*.] To sell, or try to sell, by offering the goods at people's doors; to convey through town or country for sale.—**Hawker**, ha̤'kėr, *n.* [D. *heuker*, a retailer.] One who travels selling wares; a pedlar; a packman.

Hawm, ha̤m, *n.* HAULM.

Hawse, ha̤s, *n.* [O. and Prov.E. *halse*, the neck; Icel. *háls*, neck, bow of a vessel; Dan. *hals*, neck.] *Naut.* that part of a vessel's bow where the hawse-holes are cut; the hole in the vessel's bow; the distance between a ship's head and her anchors.—**Hawse-hole**, *n.* A hole in a vessel's bow through which a cable passes.—**Hawser**, ha̤'sėr, *n.* [Formerly *halser*.] *Naut.* a small cable used in warping, &c.

Hawthorn, ha̤'thorn, *n.* [A.Sax. *hagathorn, hæg-thorn*, haw-thorn, lit. hedge-thorn; like G. *hagedorn*, D. *haagedoorn*. HAW, HEDGE.] A kind of small tree, one species of which is an excellent hedge-plant, while some of its varieties are very beautiful when in full blossom.

Hay, hā, *n.* [A.Sax. *hig*=O.Fris. *hai*, Dan. *hö*, Icel. *hey*, Goth. *havi*, G. *heu*, hay; connected with verb to *hew*. HEW.] Grass cut and dried for fodder.—*To make hay when the sun shines*, to seize the favourable opportunity.—**Hay-cock**, *n.* A conical pile or heap of hay.—**Hay-fever**, *n.* A summer fever, erroneously ascribed to the effluvium of new-cut hay.—**Hay-fork**, *n.* A two-pronged fork for turning or lifting hay, &c.—**Hay-rick, Hay-stack**, *n.* A large pile of hay in the open air, laid up for preservation.—**Hay-tedder**, *n.* A machine for scattering hay so as to expose it to the sun and air.

Hazard, haz'ėrd, *n.* [Fr. *hasard*, from Sp. *azar*, an unlucky throw of the dice, from Ar. *az-zahr*, a die.] A fortuitous event; chance; danger; peril; risk; a game played with dice.—*v.t.* To expose to chance; to put in danger of loss or injury; to risk.—**Hazardable**, haz'ėr-da-bl, *a.* Liable to hazard.—**Hazarder**, haz'ėr-dėr, *n.* One who hazards.—**Hazardous**, haz'ėr-dus, *a.* Exposing to peril or danger of loss or evil; dangerous; risky.—**Hazardously**, haz'ėr-dus-li, *adv.* In a hazardous manner.—**Hazardousness**, haz'ėr-dus-nes.

Haze, hāz, *n.* [Allied to A.Sax. *haso*, dusky, dark; Icel. *höss*, gray, dusky.] Fog; a grayish or dusky vapor in the air; hence, obscurity; dimness; mental fog.—**Haze**, hāz, *v.t.* [O.Fr. *haser*, to annoy.] To harass with overwork; to bully; in some schools, colleges, &c., to annoy by practical jokes, especially freshmen by upper-classmen.—**Hazy**, hā'zi, *a.* Foggy; misty; thick with haze; mentally obscure.

Hazel, hā'zl, *n.* [A.Sax. *hæsel*, *hæsl* = Icel. *hasl*, Dan. *hassel*, G. *hasel*, hazel; cog. with L. *corylus*, for *cosylus*, a hazel.] A tree growing wild and yielding edible nuts, while the wood is employed for hoops, fishing-rods, walking-sticks, &c.—*a.* Of a light-brown color like the hazel-nut.—**Hazelly**, hā'zl-li, *a.* Of the color of the hazel-nut; of a light brown.—**Hazel-nut**, *n.* The nut of the hazel.

He, hē, *pron.* possessive *his*, objective *him* (also dative). [A.Sax. *hé*, *heó*, *hit*, he, she, it; D. *hij*, Dan. and Sw. *han*, Icel. *hann*, he; akin *hence*, *her*, *here*, *hither*. *She* is of different origin.] The masc. sing. form of the pronoun of the 3rd person. It is sometimes used as a noun, being equivalent to man or male person, and is often prefixed to the names of animals to designate the male kind (a *he*-goat).

Head, hed, *n.* [A.Sax. *heafod*=Dan. *hoved*, Icel. *höfuth*, G. *haupt*, Goth. *houbith*, head; cog. L. *caput* (whence *chief*), Gr. *kephalē*, head.] The name applied generally to the anterior part or extremity of animals; the part which forms the seat of the brain and mental faculties; hence, understanding, intellect, will or resolution, mind, an individual; a unit (a thousand *head* of sheep: used only in *sing.*); a chief; a leader; a commander; what gives a striking appearance to the head, as the hair, antlers of a deer, &c.; part of a thing resembling in position or otherwise the human head (the *head* of a spear, of a nail); the main point or part; the forepart (the *head* of a ship); the upper part (of a bed, &c.); the top; the principal source of a stream; the part most remote from the mouth or opening; a headland; promontory; the foremost place; the place of honour or command; crisis; height; pitch; division of discourse; title of a subdivision.—*Hydraulics*, the height of water or other fluid above a given level, regarded as producing pressure. — *Head and ears*, deeply; wholly; completely, — *Head and shoulders*, by force; violently (to drag in a topic *head and shoulders*); by as much as the height of the head and shoulders.—*A broken head*, a flesh wound in the head.—*To make head against*, to resist with success.—*To give, to get*, &c., *the head*, used literally of a horse that is not held in by the reins, and hence figuratively *head* means license, freedom from check, control, or restraint.—*v.t.* To be or put one's self at the head of; to lead; to direct; to behead; to decapitate; to form a head to; to fit or furnish with a head; to go in front of, so as to keep from advancing (to *head* a drove of cattle).—*a.* Belonging to the head; chief; principal: often used in composition (*head*-workman, a *head*-master, &c.).—**Headache**, hed'āk, *n.* Pain in the head. — **Headachy**, hed'āk-i, *a.* Afflicted with a headache.—**Head-band**, hed'band, *n.* A band for the head; the band at each end of a bound book. — **Head-borough**, **Head-borrow**, *n.* In England, formerly the chief of a frank-pledge, tithing, or decennary, consisting of ten families: now known by the name of *Petty Constable*. — **Head-dress**, *n.* The dress of the head; the covering or ornaments of a woman's head. — **Headed**, hed'ed, *p.* and *a.* Furnished with a head: used chiefly in composition (clear-*headed*, long-*headed*, &c.).—**Header**, hed'ėr, *n.* One who puts a head on anything; one who stands at the head of anything; a leader; a plunge or dive into water head-foremost.—**Head-foremost**, *adv.* With the head first; rashly; precipitately. — **Headily**, hed'i-li, *adv.* In a heady manner.—**Headiness**, hed'i-nes, *n.* The quality of being heady.—**Heading**, hed'ing, *n.* The act of one who heads; what stands at the head; a title of a section in a book, &c.; a drift-way or passage excavated in the line of an intended tunnel, and in which the workmen labour.—**Headland**, hed'land, *n.* A cape; a promontory. — **Headless**, hed'les, *a.* Having no head; destitute of a chief or leader.—**Headlong**, hed'long, *adv.* [*Head* and adv. term. *-long* = *ling* in *darkling*.] With the head foremost; rashly; precipitately; without deliberation. — *a.* Steep; precipitous; rash; precipitate. — **Head-mark**, *n.* The natural characteristics of each individual of a species. — **Head-master**, *n.* The principal master of a school.—**Headmost**, hed'mōst, *a.* Most advanced; first.—**Headpiece**, *n.* A helmet; a morion; the head, especially the head as the seat of the understanding. — **Head-quarters**, *n. pl.* The quarters of the commander of an army; a centre of authority or order; the place where one chiefly resides.—**Head-sea**, *n.* A sea that directly meets the head of a ship.—**Headship**, hed'ship, *n.* The state or position of being a head or chief; authority; supreme power; government.—**Headsman**, hedz'man, *n.* One that cuts off heads; an executioner.—**Head-stall**, *n.* That part of a bridle which encompasses the head. — **Head-stone**, *n.* The chief or corner stone; the keystone of an arch; the stone at the head of a grave.—**Headstrong**, hed'strong, *a.* Obstinate; ungovernable; bent on pursuing one's own course. — **Headstrongness**, hed'strong-nes, *n.*—**Head-water**, *n.* The part of a river near its source, or one of the streams that contribute to form it.—**Head-way**, hed'wā, *n.* The progress made by a ship in motion; hence, progress or success of any kind.—**Head-wind**, *n.* A wind directly opposed to a ship's course.—**Head-work**, *n.* Mental or intellectual labour.—**Heady**, hed'i, *a.* Rash; hasty; precipitate; headstrong; apt to affect the mental faculties; intoxicating; strong.

Heal, hēl, *v.t.* [A.Sax. *haelan*, to heal, from *hál*, whole, sound (=E. *whole*); comp. the related words *hale*, *hail*, *whole*, *holy*, *health*.] To make hale, sound, or whole; to cure of a disease or wound and restore to soundness; to reconcile, as a breach or difference.—*v.i.* To grow sound; to return to a sound state: sometimes with *up* or *over*.—**Healable**, hē'la-bl, *a.* Capable of being healed.—**Healer**, he'lėr, *n.* One who or that which heals.—**Healing**, hē'ling, *p.* and *a.* Curing; restoring to a sound state; conciliatory.—*Healing art*, the medical art. —**Healingly**, hē'ling-li, *adv.* In a healing manner.

Heald, hēld, *n.* A heddle.

Health, helth, *n.* [A.Sax. *haelth*, from *haelan*, to heal.] That state of a being in which all the parts and organs are sound and in proper condition; moral or intellectual soundness; salvation or divine favour or grace (O.T.). [It is often used in toasts, and hence sometimes means toast.] —**Healthful**, helth'fụl, *a.* Full of health; free from disease; promoting health; wholesome.—**Healthfully**, helth'fụl-li, *adv.* In a healthful manner. — **Healthfulness**, helth'fụl-nes, *n.* The state of being healthful or healthy. — **Healthily**, hel'thi-li, *adv.* In a healthy manner or condition.— **Healthless**, helth'les, *a.* Infirm; sickly. — **Healthlessness**, helth'les-nes, *n.* — **Health-officer**, *n.* An officer appointed to watch over the public health.—**Healthy**, hel'thi, *a.* Being in health; enjoying health; hale; sound; conducive to health; wholesome; salubrious. — **Healthiness**, hel'thi-nes, *n.* State of.

Heap, hēp, *n.* [A.Sax. *heáp*, a pile, a crowd = D. *hoop*, Dan. *hob*, Icel. *hópr*, G. *haufe*. Akin *hip*.] A pile or mass; a collection of things piled up; a large quantity; a great number.—*v.t.* To lay in a heap; to pile; to amass: often with *up* or with *on*; to round or form into a heap.—**Heaper**, hē'pėr, *n.* One who heaps.

Hear, hēr *v.t.*—pret. & pp. *heard*. [A.Sax. *hýran*, *héran*, to hear = O.Fris. *hera*, *hora*, Icel. *heyra*, D. *hooren*, G. *hören*, Goth. *hausjan*; hence *hearken*, *hark*.] To perceive by the auditory sense; to take cognizance of by the ear; to give audience or allowance to speak; to listen to; to heed; to obey; to try judicially (a cause) in a court of justice; to listen to one repeating or going over, as a task or the like.—*v.i.* To enjoy the sense or faculty of perceiving sound; to listen; to hearken; to attend; to be told; to receive by report.—**Hearer**, hē'rėr, *n.* One who hears; an auditor; one who sits under the ministry of another.— **Hearing**, hē'ring, *n.* The act of perceiving sound; the faculty or sense by which sound is perceived; audience; an opportunity to be heard; a judicial investigation before a court; reach of the ear; extent within which sound may be heard.—**Hearsay**, hēr'sā, *n.* Report; rumour; common talk. —*Hearsay evidence*, evidence repeated at second hand by one who heard the actual witness relate or admit what he knew of the transaction or fact in question.

Hearken, här'kn, *v.i.* [A.Sax. *heorcnian*, *hýrcnian*, from *hyran*, to hear. HEAR.] To listen; to lend the ear; to give heed to what is uttered; to hear with obedience or compliance.—*v.t.* To hear by listening; to hear with attention; to regard. — **Hearkener**, här'kn-ėr, *n.* One who hearkens.

Hearse, hėrs, *n.* [O.Fr. *herce*, a harrow, a kind of portcullis, a *herse*, from L. *hirpex*, *hirpicis*, a harrow; hence *rehearse* (which see).] A bier; a bier with a coffin; a carriage for conveying the dead to the grave.—*v.t.* To put on or in a hearse.—**Hearse-cloth**, *n.* A pall; a cloth to cover a hearse.

Heart, härt, *n.* [A.Sax. *heorte* = Goth. *hairto*, D. *hart*, Icel. *hjarta*, Dan. *hjerte*, G. *herz*; cog. Gael. *cridhe*, L. *cor*, *cordis*, Gr. *kardia*, Skr. *hrid*, heart; from a root meaning to leap.] A muscular organ, which is the propelling agent of the blood in the animal body, situated in the thorax of vertebrated animals; the mind, the soul, the consciousness; the thinking faculty; the seat of the affections and passions; the moral side of our nature in contradistinction to the intellectual; courage; spirit; the seat of the will or inclination; hence, disposition of mind; tendency; conscience, or sense of good and ill; the inner part of anything; the part nearest the middle or centre; the vital or most essential part; the core; the very essence; that which has the shape or form of a heart or is regarded as representing the figure of a heart; one of a suit of playing cards marked with such a figure.—*At heart*, in real character or disposition; at bottom; substantially; really (he is good *at heart*).—*To break the heart of*, to cause the deepest grief to; to kill by grief.—*To find in the heart*, to be willing or disposed.—*To get* or *learn by heart*, to commit to memory.—*To have in the heart*, to purpose; to have design or intention.— *To have the heart in the mouth*, to be terrified.—*To lay* or *take to heart*, to be much affected by; to be zealous, ardent, or solicitous about.—*To wear the heart upon the sleeve*, to expose one's feelings, wishes, or intentions to every one.—*v.i.* To form a close compact head, as a plant.—**Heartache**, härt'āk, *n.* Anguish of mind. — **Heart-break**, *n.* Overwhelming sorrow or grief.—**Heart-breaker**, *n.* One who or that which breaks hearts. — **Heart-broken**, *a.* Deeply grieved; in despair.— **Heart-burn**, *n.* An uneasy burning sensation in the stomach from indigestion and excess of acidity.—**Heart-burning**, *a.* Causing discontent.—*n.* Discontent; secret enmity.—**Hearted**, här'ted, *a.* Having a heart: frequently used in composition (hard-*hearted*, faint-*hearted*, &c.). — **Hearten**, här'tn, *v.t.* To encourage; to incite or stimulate the courage of. — **Heartener**, här'tn-ėr, *n.* One who or that which heartens.—**Heart-felt**, *a.* Deeply felt; deeply affecting.—**Heartily**, här'ti-li, *adv.* In a hearty manner.—**Heartiness**, här'ti-nes, *n.* The state of being hearty.—**Heartless**, härt'les, *a.* Without a heart; destitute of feeling or affection; cruel.—**Heartlessly**, härt'les-li, *adv.* In a heartless manner.— **Heartlessness**, härt'les-nes, *n.* The quality of being heartless.—**Heart-rending**, *a.* Breaking the heart; overpowering with anguish; very distressing.—**Heart's-blood**, *n.* The blood of the heart; hence, life; essence.—**Heart's-ease**, *n.* Ease of heart; a plant of the violet genus; the pansy.

—**Heart-sick**, *a.* Sick at heart; pained in mind; deeply depressed.—**Heart-sickening**, *a.* Tending to make the heart sick or depressed.—**Heart-sickness**, *n.* Sadness of heart; depression of spirits.—**Heartsome**, härt'sum, *a.* Inspiring with heart or courage; exhilarating; cheerful; lively.—**Heart-sore**, *a.* Sore at heart.—**Heart-sorrow**, *n.* Sincere grief.—**Heart-stirring**, *a.* Arousing, exciting, or moving the heart.—**Heart-string**, *n.* A hypothetical nerve or tendon, supposed to brace and sustain the heart.—**Heart-whole**, *a.* Not affected with love; having unbroken spirits or good courage.—**Heart-wood**, *n.* The central part of the wood of exogens; the duramen.—**Hearty**, här'ti, *a.* Having the heart engaged in anything; proceeding from the heart; sincere; warm; zealous; cordial; sound and healthy; large to satisfaction (a *hearty* meal); loud and unrestrained (a *hearty* laugh).

Hearth härth, *n.* [A.Sax. *heorth*, hearth = D. *haard*, G. *heerd*, *herd*, area, floor, hearth; root doubtful.] That portion of the floor of a room on which the fire stands, generally a pavement or floor of brick or stone below a chimney; the fireside; the domestic circle.—**Hearth-broom**, **Hearth-brush**, *n.* A broom or brush for sweeping the hearth.—**Hearth-money**, *n.* A tax on hearths, long imposed in England.—**Hearth-rug**, *n.* A small thick carpet laid before a fire.—**Hearth-stone**, *n.* The stone forming the hearth.

Heat, hēt, *n.* [A.Sax. *haetu*, *haete*, from *hát*, hot; D. and L.G. *hitte*, Icel. *hiti*, Dan. *hede*, G. *hitze*, heat; Goth. *heito*, fever; root in Gr. *kaiō*, to burn (whence *caustic*).] A phenomenon believed to consist in a certain motion or vibration of the ultimate molecules of which bodies are composed; the sensation produced by bodies that are hot; the bodily feeling when one is exposed to fire, the sun's rays, &c.; the reverse of cold; high temperature, as distinguished from low; hot weather; a hot period; a single effort, as in a race; utmost ardour or violence; rage; vehemence; agitation of mind; inflammation or excitement; exasperation; animation in thought or discourse; fervency; sexual excitement in animals; fermentation.—*v.t.* To make hot; to communicate heat to; to cause to grow warm; to make feverish; to excite; to warm with passion or desire; to animate.—*v.i.* To grow warm or hot.—**Heater**, hē'tėr, *n.* One who or that which heats.—**Heating**, hē'ting, *p.* and *a.* Promoting warmth or heat; stimulating.—**Heat-spectrum**, *n.* An invisible spectrum produced by the sun's rays, when light is decomposed by a prism.

Heath, hēth, *n.* [A.Sax. *haeth* = L.G., D., Fris., and G. *heide*, the plant, also a moor; Goth. *haithi*, a field; Icel. *heithi*, *heithr*, a waste, a fell. Hence *heathen*, *heather*.] A name of numerous shrubby plants, many of them having beautiful flowers, and three species being common in Britain; a place overgrown with heath; a waste tract of land.—**Heath-berry**, *n.* The crow-berry.—**Heath-clad**, *a.* Covered with heath.—**Heath-cock**, *n.* The black-cock (under BLACK).—**Heathy**, hē'thi, *a.* Of, pertaining to, or resembling heath; covered or abounding with heath.

Heathen, hē'THen, *n.* [A.Sax. *haethen*, lit. one inhabiting a heath, from *haeth*, a heath, so that it is similar in meaning to the L. *paganus*, a pagan, originally a countryman.] One who worships idols or does not acknowledge the true God; a pagan; an idolater; a rude, barbarous, or irreligious person.—*a.* Gentile; pagan.—**Heathendom**, hē'THen-dum, *n.* Those parts of the world in which heathenism prevails.—**Heathenish**, hē'THen-ish, *a.* Belonging to heathens or their religions; barbarous; uncivilized; irreligious.—**Heathenishly**, hē'THen-ish-li, *adv.* In a heathenish manner.—**Heathenishness**, hē'THen-ish-nes, *n.*—**Heathenism**, hē'THen-izm, *n.* The system of religion or the manners and morals of a heathen nation; paganism; barbarism.—**Heathenize**, hē'THen-īz, *v.t.* To render heathenish.—**Heathenry**, hē'THen-ri, *n.* Heathenism; heathens collectively.

Heather, heTH'ėr, *n.* [Formerly *hadder*; comp. G. *heiter*, gay.] Common heath, a low shrub with clusters of rose-coloured flowers, covering immense tracts of waste land in Britain.—**Heather-bell**, *n.* A blossom of a large-flowered British heath.—**Heathery**, heTH'ėr-i, *a.* Abounding in heather; heathy.

Heave, hēv, *v.t.*—*heaved* or *hove* (pret. and pp.), *heaving*. [A.Sax. *hebban*, pret. *hóf*, pp. *hafen* = Goth. *hafjan*, O.Fris. *heva*, D. *heffen*, *heven*, Dan. *hæve*, Icel. *hefja*, G. *heben*, to lift; akin *heavy*, *heaven*.] To lift; to raise; to elevate; to raise or force from the breast (to *heave* a sigh); to throw; to cast; *naut.* to apply power to, as by means of a windlass, in order to pull or force in any direction.—*To heave to*, to bring a ship's head to the wind and stop her motion.—*v.i.* To be thrown or raised up; to rise; to rise and fall with alternate motions; to swell up; to pant, as after severe labour or exertion; to make an effort to vomit; to retch.—*To heave in sight*, to appear; to make its first appearance, as a ship at sea. *n.* An upward motion; swell, as of the waves of the sea; an effort of the lungs, &c.; an effort to raise something; *pl.* a disease of horses, characterized by difficult and laborious respiration.—**Heaver**, hē'vėr, *n.* One who or that which heaves.—**Heaving**, hē'ving, *n.* A rising or swell; a panting.

Heaven, hev'n, *n.* [A.Sax. *heofon*, heaven; O.Sax. *hevan*, L.G. *heben*, Icel. *hifinn*; from root of *heave*.] The blue expanse which surrounds the earth, and in which the sun, moon, and stars seem to be set; the sky; the upper regions: often in the plural; the final abode of the blessed; the place where God manifests himself to the blessed: often used as equivalent to God or Providence; supreme felicity; bliss; a sublime or exalted condition.—**Heavenborn**, *a.* Born of or sent by heaven.—**Heavenliness**, hev'n-li-nes, *n.* The condition or quality of being heavenly.—**Heavenly**, hev'n-li, *a.* Pertaining to heaven; inhabiting heaven; celestial; supremely blessed; supremely excellent.—*adv.* In a heavenly manner.—**Heavenward**, hev'n-wėrd, *adv.* Toward heaven.

Heavy, hev'i, *a.* [A.Sax. *hefig*, heavy, from the stem of *hebban*, to heave = Icel. *höfigr*. HEAVE.] That can be lifted only with labour; ponderous; weighty: the opposite of *light*; large in amount or quantity (a *heavy* rain, a *heavy* crop); not easily borne; hard to endure; burdensome; oppressive; severe; hard to accomplish; weighed or bowed down; burdened with sorrow, sleep, weariness, or the like; slow; sluggish; inactive; dull; lifeless; inanimate; impeding motion or action (*heavy* roads); acting or moving with violence (a *heavy* sea, cannonade; dark; gloomy; threatening; lowering (a *heavy* sky); not easily digested (food); deep and voluminous (sound).—**Heavily**, hev'i-li, *adv.* In a heavy manner.—**Heaviness**, hev'i-nes, *n.* The state or quality of being heavy; weight; severity; sadness; dullness or lifelessness.—**Heavy-laden**, *a.* Laden with a heavy burden.—**Heavy spar**, *n.* The sulphate of baryta, occurring in veins massive, fibrous, lamellar, and in prismatic crystals.—**Heavyweight**, *n.* A boxer or wrestler, &c., of what is usually the heaviest class; one weighing not less than 175 pounds.

Hebdomadal, **Hebdomadary**, heb-dom'a-dal, heb-dom'a-da-ri, *a.* [Gr. *hebdomas*, the number seven, seven days, from *hepta*, seven.] Weekly; consisting of seven days, or occurring every seven days.—**Hebdomadally**, heb-dom'a-dal-li, *adv.* By the week; from week to week.—**Hebdomadar**, *n.* A university authority in charge for a week of discipline. [Archaic.]

Hebe, hē'bē, *n.* The goddess of youth among the Greeks; hence, a beautiful young woman.

Hebetate, heb'ē-tāt, *v.t.*—*hebetated*, *hebetating*. [L. *hebeto*, *hebetatum*, from *hebes*, dull.] To dull; to blunt; to stupefy.—**Hebetude**, heb'ē-tūd, *n.* [L. *hebetudo*.] Dulness; stupidity.

Hebrew, hē'brö, *n.* [Fr. *hébreu*, L. *hebræus*, Gr. *hebraios*, from Heb.: supposed to mean a person *from beyond* (the Euphrates).] One of the descendants of Jacob; an Israelite; a Jew; the language of the Jews, one of the Semitic tongues.—*a.* Pertaining to the Hebrews.—**Hebraic**, hē'brā'ik, *a.* Pertaining to the Hebrews or their language.—**Hebraically**, hē-brā'-i-kal-li, *adv.* After the manner of the Hebrews or their language.—**Hebraism**, hē'brā-izm, *n.* A peculiarity of Hebrew or the Hebrews.—**Hebraist**, hē'brā-ist, *n.* One versed in the Hebrew language.—**Hebraize**, hē'brā-īz, *v.t.*—*hebraized*, *hebraizing*. To convert into the Hebrew idiom; to make Hebrew.—*v.i.* To conform to the Hebrew idiom, manners, &c.

Hebridean, **Hebridian**, heb-ri-dē'an, hē-brid'i-an, *a.* Pertaining to the Hebrides, islands lying to the west of Scotland.—*n.* A native or inhabitant of the Hebrides.

Hecatomb, hek'a-tom, *n.* [Gr. *hekatombē*—*hekaton*, a hundred, and *bous*, an ox.] A sacrifice of a hundred oxen or other beasts; hence, any great sacrifice of victims; a great number of persons or animals slaughtered.

Heck, hek, *n.* A contrivance used in spinning and weaving; a rack (*Brit.*); an interjection or mild oath. (*Slang.*)

Heckle, hek'l, *n.* [Same as *hackle*.] A sort of comb for flax or hemp; a hackle or hatchel.—*v.t.* To dress with a heckle; *fig.* to tease or vex; to catechise severely.—**Heckler**, hek'lėr, *n.* One who heckles.

Hectare, hek'tār, *n.* [Fr.] A French measure containing 100 ares, or = 2·47 acres.

Hectic, hek'tik, *a.* [Gr. *hektikos*, habitual, hectic or consumptive, from *hexis*, habit of body, from *echō*, future *hexō*, to have.] A term applied to the fever which accompanies consumption; pertaining to or affected with such fever; consumptive; feverish.—*n.* A hectic fever.—**Hectically**, hek'ti-kal-li, *adv.* In a hectic manner.

Hectocotylus, hek-to-kot'i-lus, *n.* [Gr. *hekaton*, a hundred, and *kotylē*, a small cup, a sucker.] The reproductive arm of certain of the male cuttle-fishes.

Hectogram, hek'tō-gram, *n.* [Fr., from Gr. *hekaton*, a hundred, and *gramma*, a gram.] A metric measure of weight containing 100 grams, or 3 ounces 8.4383 drams avoirdupois.—**Hectoliter**, hek'tō-lē-tėr, *n.* A metric measure for liquids, containing 100 liters, or 26.418 gallons.—**Hectometer**, hec'tō-mē-tėr, *n.* A metric measure of length containing 100 meters, or 109.36 yards.

Hector, hek'tėr, *n.* [From *Hector*, the son of Priam, a brave Trojan warrior.] A bully; a blustering, turbulent, noisy fellow.—*v.t.* To treat with insolence; to bully.—*v.i.* To play the bully; to bluster; to be turbulent or insolent.

Heddle, hed'l, *n.* [By metathesis for *heald*; perhaps from A.Sax. *heald*, hold.] *Weav.* one of the parallel double threads with a centre loop or eye which raises the warp threads to form the shed and allow the shuttle to pass; a heald.

Hederaceous, hed-ėr-ā'shus, *a.* [L. *hederaceus*, from *hedera*, ivy.] Pertaining to or resembling ivy.—**Hederal**, hed'ėr-al, *a.* Pertaining to ivy.

Hedge, hej, *n.* [A.Sax. *hecg*, a hedge, closely akin to *haga*, an inclosure; Icel. *hagi*, an inclosed field; D. *hegge*, a hedge, *haag*, a hedge (whence the *Hague*); E. *hawthorn*, that is *hedge-thorn*.] A fence formed by bushes or small trees growing close together; any line of shrubbery closely planted.—*v.t. hedged*, *hedging*. To inclose or fence with a hedge; to obstruct with a barrier; to stop by any means; to surround for defence; to hem in.—*To hedge a bet*, to bet upon both sides, thus guarding one's self against great loss, whatever may be the result.—*v.i.* To hide in a hedge; to skulk (*Shak.*); to protect one's self from loss by cross-bets.—**Hedgehog**, hej'hog, *n.* An

Old World insectivorous quadruped about 9 inches long, the upper part of whose body is covered with prickles or spines; in America, the porcupine; *elec.* a kind of transformer; *milit.* a kind of barbed wire entanglement.—**Hedgehop**, hej'hop, *v.t.* & *i.* To fly an airplane at a very low altitude, just skimming the ground. (*Slang.*)—**Hedge hyssop**, any of a number of herbs, as the goldenpert.—**Hedge mustard**, a wild mustard plant.—**Hedge nettle**, plants of the genus *Stachys*, whose leaves resemble those of nettles.—**Hedge parsley**, plants with leaves similar to those of parsley.—**Hedger**, hej'ėr, *n.* One who makes or repairs hedges; one who hedges bets; one who evades.—**Hedgerow**, hej'rō, *n.* A row or series of shrubs or trees forming a hedge between fields.—**Hedge sparrow**, a red-brown European warbler.

Hedonic, hē-don'ik, *a.* [Gr. *hēdonikos*, from *hēdonē*, pleasure.] Pertaining to pleasure; pursuing, or placing the chief good in, sensual pleasure.—**Hedonics**, hedon'iks, *n.* That branch of ethics which treats of active or positive pleasure or enjoyment.—**Hedonism**, hē'don-izm, *n.* The doctrine that the chief good of man lies in the pursuit of pleasure.—**Hedonist**, hē'don-ist, *n.* One who professes hedonism.

Heed, hēd, *v.t.* [A.Sax. *hēdan*, to heed; D. *hoeden*, to care for, *hoede*, care; G. *hüten*, to look after, from *hut*, protection; akin *hood*.] To regard with care; to take notice of; to attend to; to observe.—*n.* Care; attention; notice; observation; regard: usually with *give* or *take*.—**Heedful**, hēd'ful, *a.* Full of heed; attentive; watchful; cautious; wary.—**Heedfully**, hēd'ful-li, *adv.* In a heedful manner.—**Heedfulness**, hēd'ful-nes, *n.* The quality of being heedful; attention; caution.—**Heedless**, hēd'les, *a.* Without heed; inattentive; careless.—**Heedlessly**, hēd'les-li, *adv.* In a heedless manner.—**Heedlessness**, hēd'les-nes, *n.*

Heel, hēl, *n.* [A.Sax. *hēl*=Icel. *hæll*, D. *hiel*, the heel; radically akin to L. *calx*, the heel (seen in *inculcate*).] The hinder part of the foot in man or quadrupeds; the hinder part of a covering for the foot; something shaped like the human heel, or that occupies a position corresponding to the heel: the latter or concluding part.—*To be at the heels*, to pursue closely; to follow hard; also, to attend closely.—*To be down at heel*, to be slipshod; hence, to be in decayed circumstances.—*To lay by the heels*, to fetter; to shackle; to confine.—*To show the heels*, to flee; to run away.—*To take to the heels*, to betake one's self to flight.—*v.t.* To perform by the use of the heels, as a dance (*Shak.*); to add a heel to.—**Heelball**, hēl'bal, *n.* A composition for blackening the heels of shoes; used also for taking impressions from engraved plates, monumental brasses, &c.—**Heelpiece**, *n.* A piece of leather on the heel of a shoe; armour for the heel.—**Heeltap**, *n.* A small piece of leather for the heel of a shoe; the small portion of liquor left in a glass when the main portion has been drunk.

Heel, hēl, *v.i.* [Same as A.Sax. *heldan*, D. *hellen*, Dan. *helde*, Sw. *hälla*, to tilt.] To incline or cant over from a vertical position, as a ship.—*n.* The act of so inclining; a cant.

Heft, heft, *n.* [From *heave*, to lift.] The act of heaving; violent strain or exertion; effort (*Shak.*).—**Heft, Hefty**, *a.* Vigorous, strong. (*Colloq.*)

Hegelian, he-gē'li-an, *a.* Pertaining to Hegel (hā'gl) or his system of philosophy.—*n.* A follower of Hegel.—**Hegelianism**, he-gē'li-an-izm, *n.* The system of philosophy of Hegel.

Hegemony, hej'e-mo-ni or he-jem'o-ni, *n.* [Gr. *hēgemonia*, from *hēgemōn*, guide, leader, from *hēgeomai*, to lead.] Leadership; predominance; preponderance of one state among others.—**Hegemonic**, hej-e-mon'ik, *a.* Ruling; predominant; principal.

Hegira, hej'i-ra, *n.* [Ar. *hijrah*, departure, from *hajara*, to remove.] The flight of Mohammed from Mecca, adopted by the Mohammedans in reckoning their time, their era beginning 16th July, 622, hence, any similar flight.

Heifer, hef'ėr, *n.* [A.Sax. *heahfore*; origin doubtful.] A young cow.

Heigh-ho! hī'hō. An exclamation usually expressing some degree of languor or uneasiness.

Height, hīt, *n.* [For *highth*, as in *Milton*; A.Sax. *heáhtho*, *hyhtho*, from *heáh*, high. HIGH.] The condition of being high; the distance which anything rises above its foot, basis, or foundation, or above the earth; altitude; an eminence; a summit; a hill or mountain; elevation or pre-eminence among other persons; elevation in excellence of any kind; elevation or dignity, as of sentiment, expression, or the like; extent; degree; stage in progress or advancement: *the height*, the utmost degree in extent or violence.—**Heighten**, hī'tn, *v.t.* To make high; to raise higher; to elevate; to increase; to augment; to intensify.—**Heightener**, hī'tn-ėr, *n.* One who or that which heightens.

Heinous, hā'nus, *a.* [Fr. *haineux*, from *haine*, malice, hate, from *haïr*, O.Fr. *hadir*, to hate, from Teut. verb = E. to hate.] Hateful; odious; hence, notorious; enormous; aggravated (sin or crime, sinner).—**Heinously**, hā'nus-li, *adv.* In a heinous manner.—**Heinousness**, hā'nus-nes, *n.* The condition or quality of being heinous.

Heir, ār, *n.* [O.Fr. *heir*, L. *hæres*, an heir (same root as Skr. *har*, to take or hold), whence *hereditary*, *heritage*, *inherit*.] One who succeeds or is to succeed another in the possession of property; an inheritor; one who receives any endowment from an ancestor.—*Heir apparent*, *Heir presumptive*. Under APPARENT, PRESUMPTIVE.—*v.t.* To inherit; to succeed to.—**Heirdom**, ār'dum, *n.* The state of an heir.—**Heiress**, ār'es, *n.* A female heir.—**Heirloom**, ār'lōm, *n.* [*Heir* and *loom* in old sense of tool, implement, article.] A personal chattel that descends to an heir; any piece of personal property which has belonged to a family for a long time.—**Heirship**, ār'ship, *n.* The state of an heir; right of inheriting.

Hejira, hej'i-ra, *n.* Same as *Hegira*.

Helbeh, hel'be, *n.* The seeds of a species of fenugreek used in Egypt for food.

Held, held, pret. & pp. of *hold*.

Heliac, Heliacal, hē'li-ak, hē-li'a-kal, *a.* [L. *heliacus*, from Gr. *hēlios*, the sun; akin L. *sol*, and W. *haul*, sun.] *Astron.* emerging from the light of the sun or passing into it; rising or setting at the same time, or nearly the same time, as the sun.—**Heliacally**, hē-lī'a-kal-li, *adv.* In a heliacal manner.

Helianthus, hē-li-an'thus, *n.* [Gr. *hēlios*, the sun, and *anthos*, a flower.] The sunflower; the Jerusalem artichoke genus.

Helical, Helicoid, Helicoidal, &c. Under HELIX.

Heliconian, hel-i-kō'ni-an, *a.* Pertaining to *Helicon*, the famous Grecian mountain, the residence of the muses.

Heliocentric, Heliocentrical, hē'li-o-sen"trik, hē'li-o-sen"tri-kal, *a.* [Gr. *hēlios* (akin L. *sol*, W. *haul*), the sun, and *kentron*, centre.] *Astron.* relating to the sun as a centre; appearing as if seen from the sun's centre.—**Heliochrome**, hē'li-o-krōm, *n.* [Gr. *chrōma*, colour.] A coloured photograph.—**Heliochromic**, hē'li-o-krom"ik, *a.* Pertaining to heliochromy.—**Heliochromy**, hē-li-ok'ro-mi, *n.* The art of producing coloured photographs.—**Heliograph**, hē'li-o-graf, *n.* [Gr. *graphō*, to write.] A photograph; an instrument for taking photographs of the sun; a sun telegraph; a heliostat.—*v.t.* and *i.* To convey or communicate by means of a heliostat or similar instrument.—**Heliographic**, hē'li-o-graf"ik, *a.* Of or pertaining to heliography.—**Heliography**, hē-li-og'ra-fi, *n.* Photography; also, the art or process of signalling by reflecting the sun's rays.—**Heliogravure**, hē-li-o-grāv"ūr, *n.* [Gr. *hēlios*, sun, Fr. *gravure*, engraving.] A process by which a photographic print is mechanically etched on a copper plate, from which impressions are then taken.—**Heliolater**, hē-li-ol'a-tėr, *n.* [Gr. *latreuō*, to worship.] A worshipper of the sun.—**Heliolatry**, hē-li-ol'a-tri, *n.* The worship of the sun.—**Heliometer**, hē-li-om'et-ėr, *n.* Same as *Astrometer*.—**Helioscope**, hē'li-o-skōp, *n.* [Gr. *skopeō*, to view.] A sort of telescope fitted for viewing the sun without pain or injury to the eyes.—**Helioscopic**, hē'li-o-skop"ik, *a.* Pertaining to a helioscope.—**Heliosis**, hē'li-ō-sis, *n.* [Gr. *hēlios*, sun.] Spots on leaves due to the concentration of sun's rays through glass.—**Heliostat**, hē'li-os-tat, *n.* [Gr. *statos*, fixed.] A name of various contrivances for reflecting the sun's light temporarily or continuously to an observer at a distance: used in astronomical observations in experiments on light, and for signalling in war, &c.—**Heliotrope**, hē'li-o-trōp, *n.* [Gr. *tropē*, a turning, *trepō*, to turn.] A heliostat; a variety of quartz, of a deep green colour, with bright red spots; blood-stone; a name of plants, mostly natives of warm regions, one species of which is a favourite garden plant from the fragrance of its flowers.—**Heliotropic, Heliotropical**, hē'li-o-trop"ik, hē'li-o-trop"ik-al, *a.* Pertaining to, or characterized by, heliotropism.—**Heliotropically**, hē'li-o-trop"i-kal-li, *adv.* In a heliotropic manner.—**Heliotropism**, hē-li-ot'ro-pizm, *n.* The tendency of a plant to direct its growth toward the sun or toward light.—**Heliotype**, hē'li-o-tīp, *n.* A process by which pictures can be printed with lithographic ink from a film of specially prepared gelatine exposed under a photographic negative and then wetted, the parts not acted on by the light taking the ink; a picture so produced.—**Helium**, hē'li-um, *n.* A rare gaseous element.

Helix, hē'liks, *n.* pl. **Helices**, hel'i-sēz. [Gr. a winding, a spiral.] A spiral line, as of wire in a coil; something that is spiral; a circumvolution; *geom.* such a curve as is described by every point of a screw that is turned round in a fixed nut; *arch.* a small volute or twist under the abacus of the Corinthian capital; *anat.* the whole circuit of the external body of the ear; *zool.* a genus of molluscs, comprising the land shell-snails.—**Helical**, hel'i-kal, *a.* Of or pertaining to a helix; spiral.—**Helically**, hel'i-kal-li, *adv.* In a helical manner.—**Heliciform**, he-lis'i-form, *a.* Having the form of a helix.—**Helicoid, Helicoidal**, hel'i-koid, hel'i-koi-dal, *a.* Spirally curved like the spire of a univalve shell.—**Helicoid**, hel'i-koid, *n.* *Geom.* a spirally curved surface.—**Helicometry**, hel-i-kom'et-ri, *n.* The art of measuring or drawing spiral lines on a plane.—**Helicopter**, he'li-kop-tėr, *n.* [Gr. *helix*, screw, *pteron*, feather.] A form of air-craft whose support in the air is derived from the vertical thrust of large air screws.

Hell, hel, *n.* [A.Sax. *hel*, from *helan*, to cover, conceal, lit. a place of concealment = D. and Icel. *hel*, G. *hölle*, hell; same root as L. *celo*, to conceal. Akin *helmet*, perhaps *hole*.] The place of the dead, or of souls after death; the place or state of punishment for the wicked after death; the infernal powers; a gaming-house; a haunt of the vicious or depraved.—**Hellish**, hel'ish, *a.* Pertaining to hell; infernal; malignant; wicked; detestable.—**Hellishly**, hel'ish-li, *adv.* In a hellish manner.—**Hellishness**, hel'ish-nes, *n.* The state or quality of being hellish.—**Hell-fire**, *n.* The fire of hell; the torments of hell.—**Hell-hound**, *n.* A dog of hell; an agent of hell; a miscreant.

Hellebore, hel'le-bōr, *n.* [L. *helleborus*, Gr. *helleboros*.] A name applied to plants of two very different genera, the black hellebore or Christmas rose, and the white hellebore; the powdered root of white hellebore used by gardeners for killing caterpillars.—**Helleborine**, hel'le-bō-rin, *n.* A resin obtained from the root of black hellebore.—**Helleborise**, hel'le-bōr-īz, *v.t.*

To dose with hellebore; to treat for insanity by hellebore.

Hellenes, hel-lē'nez, *n. pl.* [Gr.] The inhabitants of Greece; the Greeks.—**Hellenic**, hel-len'ik, *a.* [Gr. *hellēnikos.*] Pertaining to the Hellenes; Greek; Grecian.—**Hellenism**, hel'len-izm, *n.* A Greek idiom; the type of character usually considered peculiar to the Greeks.—**Hellenist**, hel'len-ist, *n.* One who affiliates with Greeks; one skilled in the Greek language.—**Hellenistic, Hellenistical**, hel-len-is'tik, hel-len-is'ti-kal, *a.* Pertaining to Hellenists. — **Hellenization**, hel-len-i-zā"shon, *n.* Act of hellenizing. — **Hellenize**, hel'len-īz, *v.i.* To use the Greek language or adopt Greek manners.

Helm, helm, *n.* [A.Sax. *helma*, a helm; D. *helm*, a tiller; G. *helm*, a helve, a tiller; akin to *helve.*] The instrument by which a ship is steered, consisting of a rudder, a tiller, and in large vessels a wheel; in a narrower sense, the tiller; *fig.* the place or post of direction or management.—*v.t.*† To steer; to guide.—**Helmage**, hel'māj, *n.* Guidance.—**Helmless**, helm'les, *a.* Without a helm or steering apparatus.—**Helmsman**, helmz'man, *n.* The man at the helm or wheel who steers a ship.

Helm, helm, *n.* [A.Sax. *helm*, what covers, a helmet, from *helan*, to cover; D. and G. *helm*, Goth. *hilms*, Icel. *hjálmr*, Dan. *hjelm*; *helmet* is a dim. form. HELL.] A helmet. (*Poet.*) — *v.t.* To cover with a helmet.—**Helmed, Helmeted**, helmd, hel'met-ed, *a.* Furnished with a helmet.—**Helmet**, hel'met, *n.* A defensive covering for the head; head armour composed of metal, leather, &c.; *bot.* the upper part of a ringent corolla.—**Helmet-flower**, *n.* Aconite.—**Helmet-shell**, *n.* The name of certain univalve shells, some of which furnish the material for shell cameos.

Helminthagogue, hel-min'tha-gog, *n.* [Gr. *helmins, helminthos*, a worm, and *agō*, to expel.] *Med.* a remedy against worms; an anthelmintic.—**Helminthiasis**, hel-min-thī'a-sis, *n. Med.* the disease of worms in any part of the body.—**Helminthic**, hel-min'thik, *a.* Relating to worms; expelling worms.—*n.* A medicine for expelling worms; a vermifuge.—**Helminthite**, hel-min'thīt, *n.* A fossil worm-track or worm-trail.—**Helminthoid**, hel-min'thoid, *a.* Worm-shaped; vermiform.—**Helminthologic. Helminthological**, hel-min'tho-loj"ik, hel-min'tho-loj"i-kal, *a.* Pertaining to helminthology. — **Helminthologist**, hel-min-thol'o-gist, *n.* One versed in helminthology.—**Helminthology**, hel-min-thol'o-ji, *n.* The knowledge or natural history of worms.

Heloderma, hē-lo-dėr'ma, *n.* [Gr. *helos*, a stud, a wart, and *derma*, skin.] A family of stout, sluggish lizards, including the Gila monster and its allied Mexican form, whose bite is venomous.

Helot, he'lot, *n.* [Gr. *heilōtēs.*] A slave in ancient Sparta; hence, a slave in general.—**Helotism**, hē'lot-izm, *n.* The condition of a Helot; slavery.—**Helotry**, hē'lot-ri, *n.* Helots collectively; bondsmen.

Help, help, *v.t.* [A.Sax. *helpan* = Goth. *hilpan*, D. *helpen*, Icel. *hjálpa*, Dan. *hjelpe*, G. *helfen*, to help—from same root as Skr. *kalp*, to suit, to be of service.] To give assistance or aid to; to aid; to assist; to succour, to relieve; to cure or mitigate (pain or disease); to avail against; to prevent; to remedy; to forbear; to avoid (to *help* doing something).—*To help forward*, to advance by assistance; to assist in making progress.—*To help on*, to forward; to aid.—*To help out*, to aid in delivering from difficulty, or to aid in completing a design.—*To help over*, to enable to surmount.—*To help* (a person) *to*, to supply with; to furnish with.—*v.i.* To lend aid; to be of use; to avail.—*n.* [A.Sax. *helpe*, Icel. *hjálp.*] Aid furnished; deliverance from difficulty or distress; assistance; that which gives assistance; one who or that which contributes to advance a purpose; remedy; relief; a domestic servant (U.S.). — **Helper**, hel'pėr, *n.* One that helps, aids, or assists; an assistant; an auxiliary.—**Helpful**, help'ful, *a.* Furnishing help; useful.—**Helpfulness**, help'fulnes, *n.* The quality of being helpful.—**Helpless**, help'les, *a.* Destitute of help or strength; needing help; feeble; weak; affording no help; beyond help. — **Helplessly**, help'les-li, *adv.* In a helpless manner.—**Helplessness**, help'les-nes, *n.* The state of being helpless.—**Helpmate**, help'māt, *n.* An assistant; a helper; a partner; a consort; a wife.—**Helpmeet**, help'mēt, *n.* A helpmate.

Helter-skelter, hel'tėr-skel'tėr, *adv.* [A term formed to express hustle; comp. G. *holter-polter*, D. *hulter de bulter*, Sw. *huller om buller*, &c.] An expression denoting hurry and confusion.

Helve, helv, *n.* [A.Sax. *helfe*, O.H.G. *halbe, helbe*; same root as *helm* (of a ship), *hilt.*] The handle of an axe or hatchet.—*v.t.*—*helved, helving.* To furnish with a helve, as an axe.

Helvetic, hel-vet'ik, *a.* [L. *Helveticus*, from *Helvetii*, the ancient inhabitants of Switzerland.] Of or pertaining to Switzerland.

Hem, hem, *n.* [A.Sax. *hem*, a hem; akin to Icel. *hemja*, Dan. *hemme*, O.Fris. *hemma*, D. and G. *hemmen*, to stop, check, restrain.] The border of a garment, doubled and sewed to strengthen it; edge, border, margin.—*v.t. hemmed, hemming.* To form a hem or border on; to border; to edge.—*To hem in*, to inclose and confine; to surround closely; to environ.

Hem, hem, *interj.* [Imitative and more correctly *hm.*] An exclamation consisting in a sort of half-cough, loud or subdued as the emotion may suggest: sometimes used as a noun.—*v.i.* To make the sound *hem*; hence, to hesitate or stammer in speaking.

Hemachrome, hē'ma-krōm, *n.* Same as *Hæmachrome*, some words of which Gr. *haima*, blood, forms the first part, being written *He* or *Hæ*. — **Hemadromometer**, hē'ma-dro-mom"et-ėr, *n.* [Gr. *haima*, *dromos*, course, and *metron*, measure.] An instrument for measuring the rate at which the blood moves in the arteries.—**Hemadynamometer**, hē'ma-din-a-mom"et-ėr, *n.* A contrivance for ascertaining the pressure of the blood in the arteries or veins by observing the height to which it will raise a column of mercury.—**Hemal**, hē'mal, *a.* HÆMAL. — **Hemastatic, Hemastatical**, hē-ma-stat'ik, hē-ma-stat'i-kal, *a.* [Gr. *haima*, and *statikos*, causing to stand.] *Med.* serving to arrest the escape or flow of blood.—**Hemastatics**, hē-ma-stat'iks, *n.* The doctrine as to the circulation of the blood. — **Hematherm**, hē'ma-thėrm, *n.* [Gr. *haima*, and *thermos*, hot.] A warm-blooded animal. — **Hemathermal**, hē-ma-thėr'mal, *a.* Warm-blooded.—**Hematin, Hematosin**, hē'ma-tin, hē-ma-tō'sin, *n.* [Gr. *haima, haimatos*, blood.] The red colouring matter of the blood.—**Hematite**, hē'ma-tīt, *n.* [Gr. *haimatitēs*, from *haima*, blood.] A name of two ores of iron, red hematite and brown hematite, so named from the blood-red colour of the former variety, which is one of the most important ores.—**Hematitic**, hē-ma-tit'ik, *a.* Pertaining to hematite or resembling it.—**Hematosis**, hē-ma-tō'sis, *n.* HÆMATOSIS. — **Hematoxyline**, hē-ma-tok'si-lin, *n.* [Gr. *haima, haimatos*, and *xylon*, wood.] The colouring principle of logwood.

Hemeralopia, hē'me-ra-lō"pi-a, *n.* [Gr. *hēmera*, the day, *alaos*, blind, and *ōps*, the eye.] A term sometimes used to mean night blindness, sometimes day blindness, the latter being the natural meaning: opposite of *nyctalopia*.

Hemicarp, hem'i-kärp, *n.* [Gr. *hēmi*, half, *karpos*, fruit.] *Bot.* one of the halves of a fruit which spontaneously divides into two.

Hemicrania, hem-i-krā'ni-a, *n.* [Gr. *hēmi*, half, *cranion*, the skull.] A pain that affects only one side of the head.

Hemicycle, hem'i-sī-kl, *n.* [Gr. *hēmi*, half, and *kyklos*, a circle.] A half circle; a semicircle; a semicircular area.

Hemigamous, he-mig'a-mus, *a.* [Gr. *hēmi*, half, and *gamos*, marriage.] *Bot.* having one of the two florets in the same spikelet neuter, and the other unisexual.

Hemihedral, hem-i-hē'dral, *a.* [Gr. *hēmi*, half, and *hedra*, a face.] *Mineral.* applied to a crystal having only half the normal number of faces.—**Hemihedrally**, hem-i-hē'dral-li, *adv.* In a hemihedral manner.—**Hemihedron**, hem-i-hē'dron, *n.* A solid hemihedrally divided.

Hemimetabolic, hem'i-met-a-bol"ik, *a.* [Gr. *hēmi*, half, and *metabolē*, change.] Applied to insects which undergo an incomplete metamorphosis.

Hemiopia, Hemiopsy, hem-i-ō'pi-a, hem-i-op'si, *n.* [Gr. *hēmi*, half, and *opsis*, sight.] A defect of vision in which the patient sees only a part of the object he looks at.

Hemiplegia, Hemiplegy, hem-i-plē'ji-a, hem'i-plej-i, *n.* [Gr. *hēmi*, half, and *plēgē*, a stroke.] Paralysis of one half of the body.—**Hemiplegic**, hem-i-plej'ik, *a.* Relating to hemiplegia.

Hemipter, Hemipteran, he-mip'tėr, he-mip'tėr-an, *n.* [Gr. *hēmi*, half, and *pteron*, a wing.] One of an order of four-winged insects, so named because many of them have the outer wings leathery at the base and transparent towards the tips, including the locusts, bugs, plant-lice, &c.—**Hemipterous**, he-mip'tėr-us, *a.* Pertaining to the hemipters.

Hemisphere, hem'i-sfēr, *n.* [Gr. *hēmisphairion*—*hēmi*, half, and *sphaira*, a globe.] A half sphere; one half of a sphere or globe; half the terrestrial or the celestial globe.—*Hemispheres of the brain*, the two parts, one on each side, which constitute great part of the brain.—**Hemispheric, Hemispherical**, hem-i-sfer'ik, hem-i-sfer'i-kal, *a.* Pertaining to a hemisphere.—**Hemispheroid**, hem-i-sfer'oid, *n.* The half of a spheroid.—**Hemispheroidal**, hem'i-sfe-roi"dal, *a.* Approaching to the figure of a hemisphere.

Hemistich, hem'i-stik, *n.* [Gr. *hēmistichion*—*hēmi*, half, and *stichos*, a verse.] Half a poetic verse, or a verse not completed.—**Hemistichal**, he-mis'ti-kal, *a.* Pertaining to or written in hemistichs.

Hemlock, hem'lok, *n.* [A.Sax. *hemleác.*] A poisonous plant of the carrot family, with small white flowers; various evergreen trees native to North America.—*Ground hemlock*, the American yew.

Hemoglobin, hē'mo-glō-bin, *n.* The respiratory matter of a red color contained in the red corpuscles of the blood.

Hemophilia, hē-mo-fil'i-a, *n. Med.* A constitutional tendency, usually hereditary, to excessive bleeding from slight injuries, or even spontaneously, the result often being death.

Hemorrhage, he'mor-āj, *n.* [Gr. *haimorrhagia*—*haima*, blood, and *rhēgnymi*, to break, to burst.] A discharge of blood from the blood-vessels. — **Hemorrhagic**, hē-mo-raj'ik, *a.* Pertaining to hemorrhage.

Hemorrhoids, he'mor-oidz, *n. pl.* [Gr. *haimorrhois, haimorrhoïdos*, a gushing of blood—*haima*, blood, and *rhoos*, a flowing, from *rheō*, to flow.] Piles.—**Hemorrhoidal**, he-mo-roi'dal, *a.* Pertaining to hemorrhoids.

Hemp, hemp, *n.* [A.Sax. *henep, hanep* = D. *hennep*, Dan. *hamp*, Icel. *hampr*, G. *hanf*; cog. Armor. *canib*, Ir. *cannaib*, L. *cannabis*, Gr. *kannabis*, Skr. *çana*, hemp.] An annual herbaceous plant, the prepared fibre of which, also called hemp, is made into sail-cloth, ropes, &c.; the hangman s rope. — **Hempen**, hem'pn, *a.* Made of hemp.—**Hemp-palm**, *n.* A Chinese and Japanese palm whose leaves yield a valuable fibre.

Hen, hen, *n.* [A.Sax. *hen, henn* = D. *hen*, Icel. *hæna*, G. *henne*, hen—the feminines corresponding to A.Sax. and Goth. *hana*, D. *haan*, G. *hahn*, Icel. *hani*, a cock, the root being same as in L. *cano*, to sing.] The female of any kind of bird; especially, the female of the domestic or barn-yard fowl.—**Henbane**, hen'bān, *n.* A poisonous

British plant found in waste ground, and sometimes fatal to domestic fowls, but yielding a juice that is used as a sedative and narcotic.—**Hen-coop**, *n.* A coop or cage for fowls.—**Hen-harrier**, *n.* A species of hawk, so named from its depredations in the poultry-yard.—**Hen-hearted**, *a.* Having a heart like that of a hen; timid; cowardly.—**Hen-house**, *n.* A house or shelter for fowls.—**Hennery**, hen'ėr-i, *n.* An inclosed place for hens.—**Henpeck**, hen'pek, *v.t.* To govern or rule: said of a wife who has the upper-hand of her husband.—**Henpecked**, hen'pekt, *a.* Governed by one's wife.—**Hen-roost**, *n.* A place where poultry rest at night.—**Hen-wife, Hen-woman**, *n.* A woman who takes charge of, or deals in poultry.

Hence, hens, *adv.* [O.E. *hennes*, a genit. form from older *henne*; A.Sax. *heonan*, hence; G. *hin*, Goth. *hina*, hence; from the pronominal element seen in *he*, *here*, &c.] From this place; from this time (a week *hence*); as a consequence, inference, or deduction from something just before stated; from this source or origin.—*From hence* is sometimes used tautologically for *hence*.—**Henceforth, Henceforward**, hens'fōrth, hens-for'wėrd, *adv.* From this time forward.

Henchman, hensh'man, *n.* [Probably *haunch* and *man*, a man who stands at one's haunch; compare *flunkey* (=*flank-ey*).] A servant; a male attendant; a footman; a follower.

Hendecagon, hen-dek'a-gon, *n.* [Gr. *hendeka*, eleven, and *gōnia*, an angle.] *Geom.* a plane figure of eleven sides and as many angles.

Hendecasyllable, hen-dek'a-sil-la-bl, *n.* [Gr. *hendeka*, eleven, and *syllabē*, a syllable.] A metrical line of eleven syllables.—**Hendecasyllabic**, hen-dek'a-sil-lab"ik, *a.* Having eleven syllables.

Hendiadys, hen-di'a-dis, *n.* [Gr. *hen dia dyoin*, one by two.] A figure of speech by which two nouns are used instead of one, or one and an adjective.

Henna, hen'ä, *n.* [Ar. *hinnā-a*.] A tropical plant of the Old World, the leaves of which yield a rich reddish-orange dye used for tinting hair red, having been originally employed as a stain for fingernails; the color henna, a rich, brownish red.—*v.t.* To color with henna dye or paste.

Henotheism, hen'o-thē-izm, *n.* [Gr. *heis*, *henos*, one, and *theos*, god.] The worship of one deity as supreme among others.

Henotic, he-not'ik, *a.* [Gr. *heis*, *henos*, one.] Tending to make one, to unite, or to reconcile.

Henry, *n.* The practical electrical unit of self-induction and mutual induction.

Hep, hep, *n.* A hip (the fruit).

Hepatic, Hepatical, hē-pat'ik, hē-pat'i-kal, *a.* [L. *hepaticus*, Gr. *hēpatikos*, from *hēpar*, *hēpatos*, the liver.] Pertaining to the liver.—*n.* A medicine that acts on the liver.—**Hepatica**, hē-pat'i-ka, *n.* A species of anemone with trilobed leaves; any one of the order of plants (Hepaticæ) allied to the mosses, and called liverworts.—**Hepatite**, hep'a-tīt, *n.* [L. *hepatitis*, Gr. *hēpar*, *hēpatos*, the liver.] A variety of sulphate of baryta, which when rubbed or heated exhales a fetid odour.—**Hepatitis**, hep-a-tī'tis, *n.* Inflammation of the liver.—**Hepatization**, hep'a-tī-zā"shon, *n.* The state of being hepatized; the condensation of a texture so as to resemble the liver.—**Hepatize**, hep'a-tīz, *v.t.*—*hepatized*, *hepatizing*. *Pathol.* to gorge with effused matter; to convert into a substance resembling liver. **Hepatocele**, hē-pat'ō-sel, *n.* [Gr. *kēlē*, a tumour.] Hernia of the liver.—**Hepatocystic**, hep'a-to-sis"tik, *a.* [Gr. *kystis*, bladder.] Pertaining to the liver and gall-bladder jointly.—**Hepatogastric**, *a.* [Gr. *gaster*, stomach.] Pertaining both to the liver and stomach.—**Hepatorrhœa**, hep'a-to-rē"a, *n.* [Gr. *rheō*, to flow.] A morbid flow of bile.—**Hepatotomy**, hep'a-to"to-mi, *n.* [Gr. *tomē*, cutting.] The operation of cutting into the liver.

Heptachord, hep'ta-kord, *n.* [Gr. *hepta*, seven, and *chordē*, chord.] *Anc. mus.* a diatonic octave without the upper note; an instrument with seven strings.

Heptad, hep'tad, *n.* [Gr. *heptas*, *heptados*, from *hepta*, seven.] A sum of seven.

Heptaglot, hep'ta-glot, *n.* [Gr. *hepta*, seven, and *glōtta*, language.] A book in seven languages.

Heptagon, hep'ta-gon, *n.* [Gr. *hepta*, seven, and *gōnia*, an angle.] *Geom.* a plane figure having seven sides and as many angles.—**Heptagonal**, hep-tag'on-al, *a.* Having seven angles or sides.

Heptagynous, Heptagynian, hep-taj'in-us, hep-ta-jin'i-an, *a.* [Gr. *hepta*, seven, and *gynē*, a woman.] *Bot.* having seven styles.

Heptahedron, hep-ta-hē'dron, *n.* [Gr. *hepta*, seven, and *hedra*, a base.] A solid figure with seven sides.—**Heptahedral**, hep-ta-hē'dral, *a.* Having seven sides.

Heptameron, *n.* The romance, modelled on Boccaccio's *Decameron*, by Margaret of Navarre.

Heptamerous, hep-tam'ėr-us, *a.* [Gr. *hepta*, seven, and *meros*, a part.] *Bot.* consisting of seven parts; having its parts in sevens.

Heptandrous, Heptandrian, hep-tan'drus, hep-tan'dri-an, *a.* [Gr. *hepta*, seven, and *anēr*, *andros*, a male.] *Bot.* having seven stamens.

Heptangular, hep-tang'gū-lėr, *a.* [Gr. *hepta*, seven, and E. *angular*.] Having seven angles.

Heptarchy, hep'tär-ki, *n.* [Gr. *hepta*, seven, and *archē*, rule.] A government by seven persons, or the country governed by seven persons: usually applied to the seven Anglo-Saxon kingdoms into which England was once divided.—**Heptarch, Heptarchist**, hep'tärk, hep-tär'kist, *n.* A ruler of one division of a heptarchy.—**Heptarchic**, hep-tär'kik, *a.* Pertaining to or consisting of a heptarchy.

Heptateuch, hep'ta-tūk, *n.* [Gr. *hepta*, seven, and *teuchos*, book.] The first seven books of the Old Testament.

Her, hėr, *pron.*; a form answering to several cases of *she*. [O.E. *hire*, A.Sax. *hire*, *heore*, genit. and dat. case of the pronoun, *heó*, she, the feminine of *hé*, he. HE.] The possessive case of *she* (*her* face); the dative case of *she* (give *her* that book); the objective case of *she* (I love *her*).—**Hers**, hėrz, *pron.* [From *her*, with *s* of the possessive case.] A possessive pronoun used instead of *her* and a noun, as subject, object, or predicate.—**Herself**, hėr-self', *pron.* An emphasized or reflexive form of the 3rd pers. pron. fem., used in the same way as *himsel* (which see).

Herald, her'ald, *n.* [O.Fr. *herault*, *herald*, Fr. *héraut*, from O.H.G. *hariwalt* (G. *herold*), an officer of an army—*hart*, *heri*, an army (akin E. *harry*), and *waltan*, to rule (E. *wield*).] An officer whose business was to denounce or proclaim war, to challenge to battle, to proclaim peace, to bear messages from the commander of an army, &c.; an officer who marshals processions; in Great Britain, one who records and blazons the arms of the nobility and gentry, and regulates abuses therein; a proclaimer; a fore-runner.—*v.t.* To introduce or to give tidings of, as by a herald; to proclaim.—**Heraldic**, he-ral'dik, *a.* Pertaining to heralds or heraldry.—**Heraldically**, he-ral'di-kal-li, *adv.* In a heraldic manner.—**Heraldry**, her'ald-ri, *n.* The art or office of a herald; the art of blazoning arms or ensigns armorial, or the knowledge pertaining thereto.—**Heraldship**, her'ald-ship, *n.* The office of a herald.

Herb, ėrb or hėrb, *n.* [Fr. *herbe*, L. *herba*, *herb*, from a root meaning to eat or nourish, seen in Gr. *phorbē*, pasture, fodder.] Any plant with a soft or succulent stem which dies to the root every year, as distinguished from a *tree* and a *shrub*, which have woody stems.—**Herbaceous**, hėr-bā'shus, *a.* [L. *herbaceus*.] Pertaining to herbs.—*Herbaceous plants*, plants which perish annually down to the root; soft, succulent vegetables.—**Herbage**, ėr'bāj, *n.* Herbs collectively; green food for beasts; grass; pasture.—**Herbaged**, ėr'bājd, *a.* Covered with herbage or grass.—**Herbal**, hėr'bal, *n.* A book containing the names and descriptions of plants; a collection of plants dried and preserved; a herbarium.—*a.* Pertaining to herbs.—**Herbalism**, hėr'bal-izm, *n.* The knowledge of herbs.—**Herbalist**, hėr'bal-ist, *n.* A person who makes collections of plants; a dealer in medicinal plants.—**Herbarium**, hėr-bā'ri-um, *n.* A collection of dried plants systematically arranged; a book or other contrivance for preserving dried specimens of plants.—**Herbary**, hėr'ba-ri, *n.* A garden of plants.—**Herb-bennet**, *n.* Common avens, an aromatic, tonic, and astringent plant.—**Herbescent**, hėr-bes'ent, *a.* [L. *herbescens*.] Growing into herbs.—**Herbiferous**, hėr-bif'ėr-us, *a.* Bearing herbs.—**Herbivore**, hėr'bi-vōr, *n.* A herbivorous animal.—**Herbivorous**, hėr-biv'ō-rus, *a.* [L. *herba*, and *voro*, to eat.] Eating herbs; subsisting on plants (a *herbivorous* animal).—**Herborize**, hėr'bo-rīz, *v.i.*—*herborized*, *herborizing*. [Fr. *herboriser*.] To search for plants; to seek new species of plants; to botanize.—**Herborization**, her'bo-rī-zā"shon, *n.* The act of herborizing.—**Herbose, Herbous**, hėr'bōs, hėr'bus, *a.* [L. *herbosus*.] Abounding with herbs.—**Herbulent**, hėr'bū-lent, *a.* Containing herbs.—**Herb-woman**, *n.* A woman that sells herbs.—**Herby**, ėr'bi, *a.* Having the nature of herbs; abounding in herbs.

Herculean, hėr-kū'lē-an, *a.* Pertaining to *Hercules*; resembling Hercules in strength; very difficult or dangerous (a *Herculean* task).

Herd, hėrd, *n.* [A.Sax. *heord*, *herd* = Goth. *hairda*, D. *herde*, Dan. *hjord*, Icel. *hjörth*, G. *herde*, a herd, flock, drove, &c.] A number of beasts feeding or driven together; a company of men or people, in contempt or detestation; a crowd; a rabble.—*v.i.* To form or unite in a herd; to feed or run in herds; to associate; to unite in companies. **Herd-book**, *n.* Pedigree book of cattle.—**Herdsman**, hėrdz'man, *n.* A man attending a herd.

Herd, hėrd, *n.* [A.Sax. *hirde*, a herdsman or shepherd, from *heord*, a flock or herd; Goth. *hairdeis*, Icel. *hirdi*, Dan. *hyrde*, G. *hirt*; same origin as the preceding.] A keeper of cattle or sheep: now mostly in composition, as shep*herd*, goat-*herd*, swine-*herd*.

Here, hēr, *adv.* [A.Sax. *hér* = Dan. and Goth. *her*, Icel. *hér*, G. and D. *hier*, here; based on the pronominal element seen in *he*.] In this place; in the place where the speaker is present: opposed to *there*; in the present life or state; to this place, hither (come *here*). *Here* in *Here's* for you, *Here* goes, &c., is a sort of exclamation to attract attention to something about to be done, the subject in familiar phrases having been dropped out.—*Neither here nor there*, neither in this place nor in that; hence, unconnected with the matter in hand; irrelevant; unimportant.—*Here and there*, in one place and another; thinly or irregularly dispersed.—**Hereabout, Hereabouts**, hēr'a-bout, hēr'a-bouts, *adv.* About this place; in this vicinity or neighbourhood.—**Hereafter**, hēr-af'tėr, *adv.* In time to come; in some future time or state.—*n.* A future state.—**Hereat**, hēr-at', *adv.* At or by reason of this.—**Hereby**, hēr-bī', *adv.* By this; by means of this; close by; very near.—**Herein**, hēr-in', *adv.* In this.—**Hereinafter**, hēr-in-af'tėr, *adv.* In this afterwards: applied to something afterwards to be named or described in a writing.—**Hereinto**, hēr-in'tö, *adv.* Into this.—**Hereof**, hēr-of', *adv.* Of this; concerning this; from this.—**Hereon**, hēr-on', *adv.* On this.—**Hereto**, hēr-tö', *adv.* To this.—**Heretofore**, hēr-tö-fōr', *adv.* Before or up to this time; formerly.—**Hereunto**, hēr-un-tö', *adv.* Unto this or this time; hereto.—**Hereupon**, hēr-up-on', *adv.* Upon this; hereon.—**Herewith**, hēr-with', *adv.* With this.

Hereditable, hē-red'i-ta-bl, *a.*—[L.L. *hereditabilis*, from L. *hereditas*, *hereditatis*, the act of inheriting, from *heres*, *heredis*, an heir. HEIR.] Capable of being inherited. —**Hereditability**, hē-red'i-ta-bil"i-ti, *n.* State of being hereditable.—**Hereditament**, hē-red'i-ta-ment, *n.* [L.L. *hereditamentum.*] Any species of property that may be inherited.—**Hereditarily**, hē-red'i-ta-ri-li, *adv.* By inheritance. —**Hereditary**, hē-red'i-ta-ri, *a.* [L. *hereditarius.*] Descended by inheritance; descending from an ancestor to an heir; descendible to an heir-at-law; that is or may be transmitted from a parent to a child. —**Heredity**, hē-red'i-ti, *n.* [L. *hereditas.*] Hereditary transmission of qualities of like kind with those of the parent; the doctrine that the offspring inherits the characteristics of the parent or parents.

Heresy, her'e-si, *n.* [Fr. *hérésie*, L. *hæresis*, from Gr. *hairesis*, a taking, a principle or set of principles, from *haireō*, to take.] A doctrine, principle, or set of principles at variance with established or generally received principles; especially an opinion or opinions contrary to the established religious faith, or what is regarded as the true faith; heterodoxy. —**Heresiarch**, he-rē'si-ärk, *n.* [Gr. *hairesiarchos*, *hairesis*, heresy, and *archē*, rule.] A leader in heresy; a prominent or arch heretic. —**Heresiarchy**, he-rē'si-är-ki, *n.* Chief heresy.—**Heresiographer**, he-rē'si-og"-ra-fėr, *n.* One who writes on heresies.—**Heresiography**, he-rē'si-og"ra-fi, *n.* A treatise on heresy.—**Heretic**, her'e-tik, *n.* [L. *hæreticus.*] A person who holds heretical opinions; one who maintains heresy —**Heretical**, he-ret'i-kal, *a.* Containing or pertaining to heresy. —**Heretically**, he-ret'i-kal-li, *adv.* In a heretical manner.

Heriot, her'i-ot, *n.* [A.Sax. *heregeatu*, military equipment, a heriot—*here*, an army, and *geatu*, equipment.] *Eng. law*, a chattel or payment given to the lord of a fee on the decease of the tenant or vassal.—**Heriotable**, her'i-ot-a-bl, *a.* Subject to the payment of a heriot.

Heritable, her'i-ta-bl, *a.* [O.Fr. *héritable*, abbrev. from L.L. *hereditabilis*. HEREDITABLE.] Capable of being inherited; inheritable.—*Heritable property*, the name in Scotland for *real property*.—*Heritable security*, security constituted by heritable property.—**Heritably**, her'i-ta-bli, *adv.* By way of inheritance.—**Heritage**, her'i-tāj, *n.* [Fr., from L. *hereditas*, heritage.] That which is inherited; inheritance; *Scots law*, heritable estate or realty.—**Heritor**, her'i-tėr, *n.* An inheritor; in Scotland, a proprietor or landholder in a parish.—**Heritrix**, her'i-triks, *n.* A female heritor.

Herling, Hirling, hėr'ling, *n.* The young of the sea trout. (*Scot.*)

Hermaphrodite, hėr-maf'ro-dīt, *n.* [From *Hermaphroditos* of Greek mythology, son of *Hermes* and *Aphrodite*, who became united into one body with a nymph.] An animal in which the characteristics of both sexes are either really or apparently combined; *bot.* a flower that contains both the stamen and the pistil, or the male and female organs.—*a.* Including or being of both sexes.—*Hermaphrodite brig*, a brig that is square-rigged forward and schooner-rigged aft. —**Hermaphroditic, Hermaphroditical**, hėr-maf'ro-dit"ik, hėr-maf'ro-dit"i-kal, *a.* Of or pertaining to a hermaphrodite. —**Hermaphroditically**, hėr-maf'ro-dit"i-kal-li, *adv.* After the manner of hermaphrodites.—**Hermaphrodism, Hermaphrodeity, Hermaphroditism**, hėr-maf'rod-izm, hėr-maf'ro-dē"i-ti, hėr-maf'rod-it-izm, *n.* The state of being hermaphrodite.

Hermeneutics, hėr-mē-nū'tiks, *n.* [Gr. *hermēneutikos*, from *hermēneus*, an interpreter, from *Hermēs*, Mercury.] The art or science of interpretation: especially applied to the interpretation of the Scriptures; exegesis. —**Hermeneutic, Hermeneutical**, hėr-mē-nū'tik, hėr-mē-nū'ti-kal, *a.* Interpreting; explaining; exegetical; unfolding the signification.—**Hermeneutically**, hėr-mē-nū'ti-kal-li, *adv.* According to hermeneutics. —**Hermeneutist**, hėr-mē-nū'tist, *n.* One versed in hermeneutics.

Hermetic, Hermetical, hėr-met'ik, hėr-met'i-kal, *a.* [Fr. *hermétique*, from the ancient *Hermes Trismegistus*, who was regarded as skilled in alchemy and occult science.] Appellative of or pertaining to alchemy or the doctrines of the alchemists; effected by fusing together the edges of the mouth or aperture, as of a bottle or tube, so that no air, gas, or spirit can escape (the *hermetic* method of sealing).—**Hermetically**, hėr-met'i-kal-li, *adv.* In a hermetic manner; by fusing the edges together.

Hermit, hėrmit, *n.* [Fr. *ermite*, O.Fr. *hermite*, Gr. *erēmitēs*, from *erēmos*, lonely, solitary, desert.] A person who retires from society and lives in solitude; a recluse; an anchorite. —**Hermitage**, hėr'mi-tāj, *n.* The habitation of a hermit; a kind of French wine.—**Hermitary**, hėr'mi-ta-ri, *n.* A cell for the use of a hermit annexed to some abbey. —**Hermit-crab**, *n.* A species of crab which takes possession of and occupies the cast-off shells of various molluscs, carrying this habitation about with it, and changing it for a larger one as it increases in size.—**Hermitical**, hėr-mit'i-kal, *a.* Pertaining or suited to a hermit or to retired life.

Hermodactyl, hėr-mō-dak'til, *n.* [Gr. *Hermēs*, Mercury, and *daktylos*, a finger; Mercury's finger.] A white root brought from Turkey, anciently in great repute as a cathartic.

Hern, hėrn, *n.* A heron.

Hernia, hėr'ni-a, *n.* [L.] *Surg.* a protrusion of some part from its natural cavity by an abnormal aperture; commonly the protrusion of viscera through an aperture in the wall of the abdomen; rupture.—**Hernial, Hernious**, hėr'ni-al, hėr'ni-us, *a.* Pertaining to hernia.—**Herniology**, hėr-ni-ol'o-ji, *n.* That branch of surgery which deals with ruptures.

Hernshaw, hern'sha, *n.* A heronshaw.

Hero, hē'rō, *n.* pl. **Heroes**, hē'rōz. [L. *heros*, from Gr. *hērōs*; akin to L. *vir* (seen in *virile*, *virtue*), A.Sax *wer*, a man; Skr. *vīra*, a hero.] A kind of demigod in ancient Greek mythology; hence, a man of distinguished valour or intrepidity; a prominent or central personage in any remarkable action or event; the principal personage in a poem, play, novel, &c.—**Heroic**, he-rō'ik, *a.* [L. *heroicus.*] Pertaining to a hero; becoming a hero; characteristic of a hero; brave and magnanimous; intrepid and noble; reciting the achievements of heroes; epic.—*Heroic treatment, remedies*, *med.* treatment or remedies of a violent character.—*Heroic verse*, in English poetry, the iambic verse of ten syllables, in French the iambic of twelve, and in classical poetry the hexameter.—**Heroically**, hē-rō'i-kal-li, *adv.* In a heroic manner.—**Heroine**, her'ō-in, *n.* [Fr. *héroïne.*] A female hero. —**Heroism**, hē'rō-izm, *n.* The qualities of a hero; bravery; courage; intrepidity.—**Heroize**, hē'rō-īz, *v.t.* To make a hero of; to elevate to the rank of a hero.—**Heroship**, hē'rō-ship, *n.* The character or condition of a hero. —**Hero-worship**, *n.* The worship of heroes; excessive admiration of great men.

Heron, her'un, *n.* [Fr. *héron*, O.Fr. *hairon*, from O.H.G. *heigro*, *heigero*, Icel. *hegri*, Sw. *häger*, a heron; hence also Fr. *aigre*, dim. *aigrette*, E. *egret*.] A grallatorial bird with a long bill cleft beneath the eyes, long slender legs and neck, formerly the special game pursued in falconry. —**Heronry**, her'un-ri, *n.* A place where herons breed. —**Heronshaw**, her'un-sha, *n.* [O.Fr. *heronçeau*, *heroncel*, a young heron.] A young heron; a heron.

Herpes, hėr'pez, *n.* [Gr. *herpēs*, from *herpō*, to creep.] A skin disease characterized by the eruption of inflamed vesicles, such as shingles.—**Herpetic, Herpetical**, hėr-pet'ik, hėr-pet'i-kal, *a.* Pertaining to or resembling herpes.

Herpetology, hėr-pe-tol'o-ji, *n.* [Gr. *herpeton*, a reptile, from *herpō*, to creep, and *logos*, discourse.] A description of reptiles; the natural history of reptiles.—**Herpetologic, Herpetological**, hėr-pet'o-loj"-ik, hėr-pet'o-loj"i-kal, *a.* Pertaining to herpetology. —**Herpetologist**, hėr-pe-tol'o-jist, *n.* One versed in herpetology.

Herr, her, *n.* The German equivalent of the English Mr.

Herring, her'ing, *n.* [A.Sax. *hæring* = D. *haring*, G. *häring*, Icel. *hæringr*, herring; from A.Sax. *here*, G. *heer*, an army, from the fish moving in shoals. HARRY, HERALD.] A common fish found in incredible numbers in the North Sea, the northern parts of the Atlantic, &c., of great importance as an article of food or commerce. —*Herring-bone work*, masonry in which the stones are laid angularly, giving a slight resemblance to the spine of a herring.—*Herring-bone stitch*, a kind of stitch used in woollen work.—*v.t.* and *i.* To seam with a herring-bone stitch.

Hers, hėrz, *pron.* Under HER.

Herse, hėrs, *n.* [Fr. *herse*, O.Fr. *herce*, a harrow, a portcullis; same as *hearse*.] A portcullis in the form of a harrow, set with iron spikes; a similar structure used for a cheval-de-frise; a framework whereon lighted candles were placed in some of the ceremonies of the church, and at the obsequies of distinguished persons; sometimes a hearse.

Herself. Under HER.

Hertzian waves, *n.* Long electromagnetic waves.

Hesitate, hez'i-tāt, *v.i.*—*hesitated*, *hesitating*. [L. *hæsito*, *hæsitatum*, intens. from *hæreo*, *hæsum*, to stick, as in *adhere*, *cohere*, *inherent*.] To stop or pause respecting decision or action; to be doubtful as to fact, principle, or determination; to stammer; to stop in speaking.—*v.t.*† To be undecided about; to insinuate hesitatingly (*Pope*).—**Hesitatingly**, hez'i-tā-ting-li, *adv.* In a hesitating manner.—**Hesitation**, hez-i-tā'shon, *n.* [L. *hæsitatio*, *hæsitationis*.] The act of hesitating; a stopping in speech; intermission between words; stammering. —**Hesitative**, hez'i-tā-tiv, *a.* Showing hesitation. —**Hesitancy**, hez'i-tan-si, *n.* The act of hesitating or doubting.—**Hesitant**, hez'i-tant, *a.* [L. *hæsitans*, *hæsitantis*.] Hesitating; wanting readiness.

Hesperian, hes-pē'ri-an, *a.* [L. *hesperius*, western, from Gr. *hesperos* (= L. *vesper*), the evening.] Western; situated at the west. (*Poet.*)—**Hesperides**, hes-per'i-dēz, *n. pl.* *Greek myth.* the daughters of Hesperus, possessors of the garden of golden fruit, watched over by a dragon, at the western extremities of the earth.—**Hesperidium**, hes-pe-rid'i-um, *n.* *Bot.* a fleshy fruit such as that of the orange.—**Hesperornis**, hes-pėr-or'nis, *n.* A fossil swimming bird of North America, without wings, and with strong teeth in both jaws.

Hessian, hesh'i-an, *a.* Relating to *Hesse* in Germany.—*Hessian boot*, a kind of long boot originally worn by the Hessian troops. —*n.* A native of Hesse; a Hessian boot.—**Hessian-fly**, *n.* [From the notion that it was brought into America by the Hessian troops during the revolutionary war.] A small two-winged fly nearly black, the larva of which is very destructive to young wheat.

Hest, hest, *n.* [A.Sax. *haes*, a command (the *t* being added as in *amongst*), from *hâtan*, to command; comp. G. *geheiss*, a command, *heissen*, to bid; D. *heeten*, to command. Hence *behest*.] Command; precept; injunction; order. (*Poet.*)

Hetaera, Hetaira, he-tē'rä, he-tī'rä, *n.* [Gr. *hetarē*, *hetaira*.] A courtesan of the superior class.—**Hetaerism, Hetairism**, he-tēr'izm, he-tī'rizm, *n.* Concubinage; a supposed primitive social state, in which women of a tribe were held in common.

Heterarchy, het'ėr-ăr-ki, *n.* [Gr. *hėteros*, another, and *archē*, rule.] The government of an alien.

Heterocarpous, het'e-rō-kär-pus, *a.* [Gr. *heteros*, other, and *karpos*, fruit.] *Bot.* bearing fruit of two sorts or shapes.

Heterocephalous, het'e-rō-sef"a-lus, *a.* [Gr. *heteros*, other, *kephalē*, a head.] *Bot.* having some flower-heads male and others female in the same individual.

Heterocercal, **Heterocerc**, het'e-rō-sėr-kal, het'e-rō-sėrk, *a.* [Gr. *heteros*, other, *kerkos*, a tail.] Having the vertebral column running to a point in the upper lobe of the tail, as in the sharks and sturgeons: contrasted with *homocercal*.—**Heterocercy**, het'e-rō-sėr"si, *n.* Inequality in the lobes of the tail in fishes.

Heteroclite, het'e-rō-klīt, *n.* [Gr. *heteroklitos*—*heteros*, other, and *klinō*, to incline, to lean away from the normal form.] A word which is irregular or anomalous either in declension or conjugation; something abnormal.—**Heteroclitic**, **Heteroclitical**, het'é-rō-klit"ik, het'e-rō-klit"i-kal, *a.* Irregular; anomalous.

Heterodactyle, het'e-rō-dak"til, *a.* [Gr. *heteros*, other, *daktylos*, a finger or toe.] Having the toes irregular in number or formation.

Heterodont, het'ėr-o-dont, *a.* [Gr. *heteros*, other, different, *odous*, *odontos*, a tooth.] Having teeth of different kinds, as molars, incisors, and canines: opposed to *homodont*.

Heterodox, het'e-rō-doks, *a.* [Gr. *heteros*, other, and *doxa*, opinion.] Contrary to established or generally received opinions; contrary to some recognized standard of opinion, especially in theology; not orthodox.—**Heterodoxly**, het'e-rō-doks-li, *adv.* In a heterodox manner.—**Heterodoxy**, het'e-rō-dox-si, *n.* The holding of heterodox opinions; heresy.

Heterodromous, het-e-rod'ro-mus, *a.* [Gr. *heteros*, other, *dromos*, a running.] *Bot.* running in different directions, as leaves on a stem.

Heteroecism, het'er-ēs"ism, *n.* [Gr. *heteros*, different, *oikos*, a house.] In fungi, living on more than one kind of host in the course of the life-history.

Heterogamous, het-e-rog'a-mus, *a* [Gr. *heteros*, other, *gamos*, marriage.] *Bot.* irregular in regard to the arrangement of the sexes; having florets of different sexes in the same flower-head.—**Heterogamy**, het-e-rog'a-mi, *n.* The state or quality of being heterogamous. CROSS-POLLINATION.

Heterogeneous, het'e-rō-jē"nē-us, *a.* [Gr. *heteros*, other, and *genos*, kind.] Differing in kind; composed of dissimilar or incongruous parts or elements: opposed to *homogeneous*. — **Heterogeneously**, het'e-rō-jē"nē-us-li, *adv.* In a heterogeneous manner. —Also **Heterogeneal**, het'e-rō-je"nē-al. —**Heterogeneousness**, **Heterogeneity**, het'e-rō-jē"nē-us-nes, het'e-rō-jē"nē-i-ty, *n.* The state or quality of being heterogenous.

Heterogenesis, **Heterogeny**, het'e-rō-jen"e-sis, het'e-roj'e-ni, *n.* [Gr. *heteros*, other, and *genesis*, generation.] *Biol.* spontaneous generation; also, same as *Alternate Generation*.

Heterologous, het-e-rol'o-gus, *a.* [Gr. *heteros*, other, and *logos*, analogy, proportion.] Different; not analogous or homologous.—**Heterology**, het-e-rol'o-ji, *n.* The state or quality of being heterologous; *biol.* want or absence of relation or analogy between parts; difference in structure from the type or normal form.

Heteromorphic, **Heteromorphous**, het'e-rō-mor"fik, het'e-rō-mor"fus, *a.* [Gr. *heteros*, other, *morphē*, form.] Of an irregular or unusual form; having two or more diverse shapes. — **Heteromorphism**, **Heteromorphy**, het'e-rō-mor"fizm, het'e-rō-mor-fi, *n.* The state or quality of being heteromorphic; existence under different forms at different stages of development.

Heteronomy, het-e-ron'o-mi, *n.* [Gr. *heteros*, different, *nomos*, law.] Subordination to the law of another: opposed to *autonomy*.—**Heteronomous**, het-e-ron'o-mus, *a.* Pertaining to or relating to heteronomy.

Heteronym, het'ėr-o-nim, *n.* [Gr. *heteros*, other, *onoma*, name.] A word with the same spelling as another but a different pronunciation; a different name for the same thing.

Heteropathic, het'e-rō-path"ik, *a.* [Gr. *heteros*, other, *pathos*, suffering.] ALLOPATHIC.—**Heteropathy**, het-e-rop'a-thi, *n.* ALLOPATHY.

Heterophemy, het-ėr-of'e-mi, *n.* [Gr. *heteros*, other, *phēmē*, speech.] The saying or writing one thing but intending another, resulting from mental disorder.

Heterophyllous, het-e-rof'i-lus or het-e-rō-fil'lus, *a.* [Gr. *heteros*, other, *phyllon*, leaf.] *Bot.* having two different kinds of leaves on the same stem.

Heteroplastic, het-ėr-o-plas"tik, *a.* [Gr. *heteros*, other, *plassō*, to form.] Dissimilar or abnormal in structure.

Heteropod, het'e-rō-pod, *n.* [Gr. *heteros*, other, *pous*, *podos*, a foot.] One of an order of marine molluscs, the most highly organized of the gasteropods, the foot being compressed into a kind of fin.—**Heteropodous**, het-e-rop'o-dus, *a.* Pertaining to the heteropods.

Heteropterous, het-e-rop'tėr-us, *a.* [Gr. *heteros*, other, and *pteron*, a wing.] *Entomol.* having wings partly leathery, partly membranous: said of certain hemipterous insects.

Heterosporous, het'er-ō-spōr"us, *a.* [Gr. *heteros*, different, *sporos*, seed.] With spores of different kinds.

Heterostylous, het'er-ō-stīl"us, *a.* [Gr. *heteros*, different, and E. style.] Of flowers (e.g. primrose), with styles of different length.

Heterotaxy, het'e-rō-tak"si, *n.* [Gr. *heteros*, other, and *taxis*, arrangement.] Arrangement other than normal; confused or abnormal arrangement or structure.

Heterotopy, het-ėr-ot'o-pi, *n.* [Gr. *heteros*, other, *topos*, place.] *Biol.* displacement in position; abnormal position of an organ or structure.

Heterotropal, **Heterotropous**, het-e-rot'ro-pal, het-e-rot'ro-pus, *a.* [Gr. *heteros*, other, *trepō*, to turn.] *Bot.* having the ovule oblique or transverse to the axis of the seed.

Hetman, het'man, *n.* [Pol., from G. *hauptman*, head-man, chieftain.] The title of the head (general) of the Cossacks.

Heuristic, hū-ris'tik, *a.* [Gr. *heuriskein*, to find out.] Aiding or leading on towards discovery or finding out.

Hew, hū, *v.t.*—pret. *hewed*, pp. *hewed* or *hewn*. [A.Sax. *heáwan*, D. *houwen*, G. *hauen*, Icel. *höggva*, Dan. *hugge*, to hew; akin *hoe*, *hay*.] To cut or fell with an axe or other like instrument; to shape with a sharp instrument: often with *out*.—**Hewer**, hū'ėr, *n.* One who hews.

Hexacord, hek'sa-kord, *n.* [Gr. *hex*, six, and *chordē*, a chord.] *Mus.* a series of six notes, each rising one degree over the other.

Hexagon, hek'sa-gon, *n.* [Gr. *hex*, and *gōnia*, an angle.] *Geom.* a figure of six sides and six angles.—**Hexagonal**, hek-sag'on-al, *a.* Having six sides and six angles.—**Hexagonally**, hek-sag'on-al-li, *adv.* In the form of a hexagon.

Hexagynian, **Hexagynous**, hek-sa-jin'i-an, hek-saj'i-nus, *a.* [Gr. *hex*, six, and *gynē*, a female.] *Bot.* having six styles.

Hexahedron, hek-sa-hē'dron, *n.* [Gr. *hex*, six, and *hedra*, a base or seat.] A regular solid body of six sides; a cube.—**Hexahedral**, hek-sa-hē'dral, *a.* Of the figure of a hexahedron; cubic.

Hexahemeron, hex-sa-hē'me-ron, *n.* [Gr. *hex*, six, and *hēmera*, day.] The term of six days; the six days work of creation as described in the first chapter of Genesis.

Hexameter, hex-sam'e-tėr, *n.* [Gr. *hex*, six, and *metron*, measure.] *Pros.* a verse of six feet, the first four of which may be either dactyls or spondees, the fifth normally a dactyl, though sometimes a spondee, and the sixth always a spondee.—*a.* Having six metrical feet.—**Hexametric**, **Hexametrical**, **Hexametral**, hek-sa-met'rik, hek-sa-met'ri-kal, hek-sam'et-ral, *a.* Consisting of six metrical feet; forming a hexameter.—**Hexametrist**, hek-sam'et-rist, *n.* One who writes hexameters.

Hexandrian, **Hexandrous**, hek-san'dri-an, hek-san'drus, *a.* [Gr. *hex*, six, *anēr*, *andros*, a male.] *Bot.* having six stamens, all of equal or nearly equal length.

Hexangular, hek-sang'gū-lėr, *a.* [Gr. *hex*, six, and E. *angular*.] Having six angles.

Hexapetalous, hek-sa-pet'a-lus, *a.* [Gr. *hex*, six, and *petalon*, a petal.] *Bot.* having six petals. — **Hexaphyllous**, hek-saf'i-lus or hek-sa-fil'lus, *n.* [Gr. *hex*, six, and *phyllon*, a leaf.] *Bot.* having six leaves.

Hexapla, hek'sa-pla, *n. pl.* [Gr. *hexaplous*, sixfold—*hex*, six, and term. as in *double*.] An edition of the Holy Scriptures in six languages or six versions in parallel columns.—**Hexaplar**, hek'sa-plėr, *a.* Pertaining to a hexapla.

Hexapod, hek'sa-pod, *a.* [Gr. *hex*, six, and *pous*, *podos*, a foot.] Having six feet.—*n.* An animal having six feet.

Hexastich, **Hexastichon**, hek'sa-stik, hek-sas'ti-kon, *n.* [Gr. *hex*, six, *stichos*, a verse.] A poem consisting of six lines or verses.

Hexastyle, hek'sa-stīl, *n.* [Gr. *hex*, six, and *stylos*, a column.] A portico or temple which has six columns in front.—**Hexastylar**, hek'sa-stī-lėr, *a.* *Arch.* having six columns in front.

Hey, hā. [Comp. G. and D. *hei*.] An exclamation of joy or to call attention.

Heyday, hā'dā, *exclam.* [Comp. G. *heyda*, *heidi*, *heia*, huzzah! heyday!] An exclamation of cheerfulness and sometimes of wonder.

Heyday, hā'dā, *n.* [Equivalent to *highday*.] A frolic; the wildness, or frolicsome period of youth.

Hiatus, hī-ā'tus, *n.* [L., from *hio*, to open or gape.] An opening; a gap; a space from which something is wanting; a lacuna; *pros.* the coming together of two vowels in two successive syllables or words.

Hibernal, hī-bėr'nal, *a.* [L. *hibernalis*, from *hibernus*, wintry, akin to *hiems*, winter; Gr. *chiōn*, Skr. *hima*, snow.] Belonging or relating to winter; wintry.—**Hibernate**, hī-bėr'nāt, *v.i.* — *hibernated*, *hibernating*. [L. *hiberno*, *hibernatum*.] To winter; to pass the winter in sleep or seclusion, as some animals.—**Hibernation**, hī-bėr-nā'shon, *n.* The act of hibernating.—**Hibernaculum**, hī-bėr-nak'ū-lum, *n.* The winter retreat of an animal.

Hibernian, hī-bėr'ni-an, *a.* [L. *Hibernia*, Ireland.] Pertaining to Hibernia, now Ireland; Irish.—*n.* A native or inhabitant of Ireland.—**Hibernianism**, **Hibernicism**, hī-bėr'ni-an-izm, hī-bėr'ni-sizm, *n.* An idiom or mode of speech peculiar to the Irish.—**Hibernicize**, hī-bėr'ni-sīz, *v.t.* To make Irish; to render into the Irish language or idiom. — **Hiberno-Celtic**, hī-bėr'nō-sel"tik, *n.* The Celtic language spoken in Ireland.

Hibrid, hī'brid, *n.* and *a.* HYBRID.

Hiccup, **Hiccough**, hik'up, *n.* [An imitative word; comp. Dan. *hik* or *hikken*, D. *hik*, *hikken*, Fr. *hoquet*, W. *ig*, *igian*, Armor. *hicq*—all imitative.] A spasmodic catching in the breath with a sudden sound; a convulsive catch of the respiratory muscles repeated at short intervals.—*v.i.* To have hiccup. [The second spelling is erroneous, and suggested by *cough*.]

Hickory, hik'o-ri, *n.* [North Amer. Indian.] A North American tree of the walnut family with pinnate leaves, growing from 70 to 80 feet high, the wood of which is heavy, strong, tenacious, and very valuable.

Hidalgo, hi-dal'gō, Sp. pron. ē-dăl'gō, *n.* [Sp., contr. for *hijodalgo*, *hijo de algo*, son of somewhat—*hijo*, from L. *filius*, son, and *algo*, from L. *aliquod*, something, somewhat.] In Spain, a man belonging to the lower nobility; a gentleman by birth.

Hide, hīd, *v.t.*—*hid* (pret.), *hid, hidden* (pp.), *hiding* (ppr.). [A.Sax. *hydan*, to hide; cog. W. *cuddiaw*, to cover, *cudd*, darkness, Gr. *keuthō*, to hide; akin *hide*, skin.] To withhold or withdraw from sight or knowledge; to keep secret; to conceal.—*v.i.* To conceal one's self; to lie concealed.—**Hide-and-seek**, *n.* A play among children, in which some hide themselves and one seeks them.—**Hid, Hidden**, hid, hid'n, *p.* and *a.* Concealed; placed in secrecy; secret; unseen; mysterious.—**Hiddenly**, hid'n-li, *adv.* In a hidden or secret manner.—**Hiddenness**, hid'n-nes, *n.* The state of being hidden or concealed.—**Hider**, hī'dėr, *n.* One who hides or conceals.—**Hiding-place**, *n.* A place of concealment.

Hide, hīd, *n.* [A.Sax. *hýd* = D. *huid*, Icel. *húth*, Dan. and Sw. *hud*, G. *haut*, hide; cog. L. *cutis*, Gr. *skutos*, the skin of a beast, from root meaning to cover, as in *hide*, *v.t.*] The skin of an animal; especially, the undressed skin of the larger domestic animals, as oxen, horses, &c.; the human skin, in contempt.—*v.t.* To beat; to flog. (*Colloq.*)—**Hiding**, hī'ding, *n.* A flogging or beating. (*Colloq.*)—**Hidebound**, hīd'bound, *a.* Having the skin morbidly tight on the body, as horses or cattle; having the bark so close or firm as to impede growth.

Hide, hīd, *n.* [A.Sax. *hīd*, contr. from *hígid*, a hide; same root as *hive*.] An old measure of land variously estimated at 60, 80, and 100 acres.

Hideous, hid'ē-us, *a.* [Fr. *hideux*, O.Fr. *hisdous*, rough, shaggy, hideous, from L. *hispidosus*, for *hispidus*, rough, shaggy.] Frightful to the sight; dreadful; shocking to the eye; shocking in any way; detestable; horrible.—**Hideously**, hid'ē-us-li, *adv.* In a hideous manner.—**Hideousness**, hid'ē-us-nes, *n.* The state of being hideous.—**Hideosity**, hid-ē-os'i-ti, *n.* The condition or quality of being hideous; frightfulness.

Hidrotic, hī-drot'ik, *n.* [Gr. *hidrōs, hidrōtos*, sweat.] A medicine that causes perspiration.

Hie, hī, *v.i.*—*hied, hieing.* [A.Sax. *higian*, to endeavour, to hasten; perhaps from *hyge, hige*, the mind, thought; comp. D. *hijgen*, Dan. *hige*, to covet.] To move or run with haste; to go in haste (often with *him, me*, &c., reflexively; as, he *hied him* home).

Hiemal, hī'em-al, *a.* [L. *hiemalis*, from *hiems*, winter. HIBERNAL.] Pertaining to winter; wintry.—**Hiemation**, hī-e-mā'shon, *n.* The spending or passing of the winter.

Hierapicra, hī'e-ra-pik"ra, *n.* [Gr. *hieros*, sacred, *pikros*, bitter.] A cathartic medicine, composed of aloes and canella.

Hierarch, hī'ėr-ärk, *n.* [Gr. *hieros*, sacred, and *archē*, rule.] One who rules or has authority in sacred things.—**Hierarchic, Hierarchical, Hierarchal**, hī-ėr-är'kik, hī-ėr-är'ki-kal, hī-ėr-är'kal, *a.* Pertaining to a hierarch or hierarchy.—**Hierarchically**, hī-ėr-är'ki-kal-li, *adv.* In a hierarchic manner.—**Hierarchism**, hī'ėr-ärk-izm, *n.* Hierarchical principles; hierarchal character.—**Hierarchy**, hī'ėr-är-ki, *n.* Authority in sacred things; a ranking of individuals, as of officials according to their power in government or in the church; arrangement of scientific items according to their logical relationships.

Hieratic, Hieratical, hī-ėr-at'ik, hī-ėr-at'i-kal, *a.* [Gr. *hieratikos*, from *hieros*, holy.] Consecrated to sacred uses; pertaining to priests; sacred; sacerdotal; especially applied to the characters or mode of writing used by the ancient Egyptian priests, a development from the hieroglyphics.

Hierocracy, hī-ėr-ok'ra-si, *n.* [Gr. *hieros*, holy, and *kratos*, power.] Government by ecclesiastics; hierarchy.

Hieroglyph, Hieroglyphic, hī'ėr-o-glif, hī'ėr-o-glif"ik, *n.* [Gr. *hieros*, sacred, and *glyphō*, to carve.] The figure of an animal, plant, or other object intended to convey a meaning or stand for an alphabetical character; a figure implying a word, an idea, or a sound, such as those in use among the ancient Egyptians; a figure having a hidden or enigmatical significance; a character difficult to decipher.—**Hieroglyphic, Hieroglyphical**, hī'ėr-o-glif"i-kal, *a.* Forming a hieroglyphic; consisting of hieroglyphics; expressive of meaning by hieroglyphics.—**Hieroglyphically**, hī'ėr-o-glif"i-kal-li, *adv.* In a hieroglyphic manner.—**Hieroglyphist**, hī'ėr-o-glif-ist, *n.* One versed in hieroglyphics.—**Hieroglyphize**, hī'ėr-o-glif-īz, *v.t.* To express by hieroglyphics.

Hierogram, hī'ėr-o-gram, *n.* [Gr. *hieros*, sacred, and *gramma*, letter, *graphō*, to write.] A species of sacred writing.—**Hierogrammatic**, hī'ėr-o-gram-mat"ik, *a.* Written in or pertaining to hierograms.—**Hierographer**, hī-ėr-og'ra-fėr, *n.* A writer of, or one versed in hierography.—**Hierographic, Hierographical**, hī'ėr-o-graf"ik, hī'ėr-o-graf"i-kal, *a.* Pertaining to sacred writing.—**Hierography**,† hī-ėr-og'ra-fi, *n.* Sacred writing.

Hierolatry,† hī-ėr-ol'a-tri, *n.* [Gr. *hieros*, sacred, and *latreia*, worship.] The worship of saints or sacred things.

Hierology, hī-ėr-ol'o-ji, *n.* [Gr. *hieros*, sacred, and *logos*, discourse.] Sacred lore; knowledge of hieroglyphics or sacred writing.—**Hierologic, Hierological**, hī'ėr-o-loj'ik, hī'ėr-o-loj"i-kal, *a.* Pertaining to hierology.—**Hierologist**, hī-ėr-ol'o-jist, *n.* One versed in hierology.

Hierophant, hī'ėr-o-fant, *n.* [Gr. *hierophantēs*—*hieros*, sacred, and *phainō*, to show.] A priest; one who teaches the mysteries and duties of religion.—**Hierophantic**, hī'ėr-o-fan"tik, *a.* Belonging to hierophants.

Higgle, hig'l, *v.i.*—*higgled, higgling.* [A weaker form of *haggle*, to chaffer.] To chaffer; to haggle in making a bargain; to hawk wares for sale.—**Higgledy-piggledy**, hig'l-di-pig'l-di, *adv.* In confusion, like wares in a higgler's basket; topsy-turvy. (*Colloq.*)—**Higgler**, hig'l-ėr, *n.* One who higgles.

High, hī, *a.* [A.Sax. *heáh, héh* = Goth. *hauhs*, Icel. *hár*, Dan. *hoi*, D. *hoog*, G. *hoch*, high; hence *height*.] Having a great extent from base to summit; rising much above the ground or some other object; elevated, lofty, tall; exalted, excellent, superior (mind, attainments, art); elevated in rank, condition, or office; difficult to comprehend; abstruse; arrogant, boastful, proud; loud, boisterous, threatening, or angry (*high* words); extreme, intense, strong, forcible; exceeding the common measure or degree (a *high* wind; *high* colour); full or complete (*high* time); dear; of a great price, or greater price than usual; remote from the equator north or south (a *high* latitude); *mus.* acute or elevated in tone; capital; committed against the king, sovereign, or state (*high* treason); *cook.* tending towards putrefaction; strong-scented (venison kept till it is *high*). Used substantively for people of rank or high station (*high* and low).—*On high*, aloft; in a lofty position.—*High and dry*, out of the water; out of reach of the current or waves.—*High altar*, the chief altar in a church.—*High Church*, that branch of the Church of England known as the Anglo-Catholic Church, in contradistinction to the Protestant Episcopal Church.—*High day*, a festival or gala day.—*High day, high noon*, the time when the sun is in the meridian.—*High Dutch, High German.* DUTCH, GERMAN.—*High life*, the style of living of the upper classes.—*High living*, indulgence in rich or costly food and drink.—*High mass*, principal mass, a solemn ceremony in which the priest is assisted by a deacon and sub-deacon.—*High place*, in Scrip. an eminence or mound on which sacrifices were offered, especially to heathen deities.—*High school*, the school next above a grammar or elementary school, usually public and offering a four-year course.—*To be on the high horse, to mount one's high horse*, to stand on one's dignity; to assume a lofty tone or manner; to take offense.—*adv.* In a high manner; to a great altitude; highly; richly; luxuriously.—**High-angle-fire gun**, *n.* One so mounted that a very large angle (as high as 80 degrees) of elevation may be given to it.—**Highball**, hī'bal, *n.* An iced alcoholic drink, made of spirits mixed with soda or ginger ale, &c., and served in a tall glass.—**High-born**, *a.* Being of noble birth.—**High-brow**, *n.* An intellectual. (*Slang*)—**High explosives**, *n.* Explosives of extremely powerful class, especially such as are based on nitro-glycerine.—**High-fed**, *a.* Pampered; fed luxuriously.—**High-feeding**, *n.* Luxury in diet.—**Highflier**, *n.* One who is extravagant in pretensions or manners. (*Colloq.*)—**High-flown**, *a.* Elevated; proud; turgid; extravagant (*high-flown* sentiment).—**Highflying**, *a.* Extravagant in claims, expectations, or opinions.—**Highhanded**, *a.* Oppressive; violent; arbitrary.—**Highland**, hī'land, *n.* An elevated or mountainous region: generally in plural (the *Highlands* of Scotland).—*a.* Pertaining to highlands, especially the Highlands of Scotland.—**Highlander, Highlandman**, hī'land-ėr, hī'land-man, *n.* An inhabitant of highlands, particularly the Highlands of Scotland.—**Highland fling**, *n.* A sort of dance peculiar to the Scottish Highlanders, danced by one person.—**High hat**, *n.* A snob.—*v.t.* To snub someone.—**Highly**, hī'li, *adv.* In a high manner or to a high degree; greatly; decidedly; markedly.—**High-mettled**, *a.* Having high spirit; ardent; full of fire.—**High-minded**, *a.* Proud; arrogant (N.T.); characterized by or pertaining to elevated principles and feelings; magnanimous.—**High-mindedness**, *n.*—**Highness**, hī'nes, *n.* The state or quality of being high; a title of honor given to princes or other persons of rank: used with poss. prons. *his, her*, &c.—**High-pressure**, *a.* Having a pressure much greater than that of the atmosphere (15 lbs. to the square inch); pressing, intense, urgent, as, a *high-pressure* salesman, one who, by adroit talk, presses a sale of goods upon an unwilling customer.—**High priest**, *n.* A chief priest.—**High priestship**, *n.* Office of a high priest.—**High-principled**, *a.* Of strictly honorable or noble principles; highly honorable.—**Highroad**, *n.* A highway; a much-frequented road.—**High seas**, *n. pl.* The open sea or ocean; the ocean beyond the limit of 3 miles from the shore.—**High-seasoned**, *a.* Enriched with spices or other seasoning.—**High-sounding**, *a.* Pompous; ostentatious; bombastic.—**High-spirited**, *a.* Having a high spirit; bold; manly; sensitive on the point of honor.—**High-stepper**, *n.* A horse that lifts its feet well from the ground; one who leads a fast, gay life.—**High-strung**, *a.* Strung to a high pitch; high-spirited; having some intense emotion.—**High tide**, *n.* High water.—**High-toned**, *a.* High in tone or pitch; high-principled; dignified; chic.—**High water**, *n.* The utmost flow or greatest elevation of the tide; also the time when such flow or elevation occurs.—**Highway**, hī'wā, *n.* A public road; a way open to all travelers.—**Highwayman, Highway robber**, hī'wā-man, *n.* One who robs on the public road or highway.—**High-wrought**, *a.* Wrought with exquisite art or skill; inflamed or agitated to a high degree

Hight, hīt, *v.t.* [Pp. of O.E. *hatan*, G. *heissen*.] Named, styled. (*Archaic.*)

Hilar. Under HILUM.

Hilarity, hi-lar'i-ti, *n.* [Fr. *hilarité*, from L. *hilaritas*, from *hilaris, hilarus*, Gr. *hilaros*, cheerful; hence *exhilarate*.] A pleasurable excitement of the animal spirits; mirth; merriment; gaiety.—*Hilary term*, a law term beginning near the festival of

St. *Hilary*, which is January 13.—**Hilarious**, hi-lā'ri-us, *a.* Mirthful; merry.

Hilding,‡ hil'ding, *n.* [A.Sax. *hyldan*, to bend, to crouch.] A mean cowardly person.—*a.* Cowardly; spiritless. (*Shak.*)

Hill, hil, *n.* [A.Sax. *hill*, *hyll*, a hill; O.D. *hille*, *hil*: same root as L. *collis*, a hill, *columna*, a column.] A natural elevation less than a mountain; an eminence rising above the level of the surrounding land; a heap (a mole*hill*).—**Hillbilly**, *n.* One who lives in a rough, hilly region, such as the southern Appalachians or the Ozarks. (*Colloq.*)—**Hilliness**, hil'i-nes, *n.*—**Hillside**, hil'sīd, *n.* The side or declivity of a hill.—**Hilltop**, hil'top, *n.* The top or summit of a hill.—**Hilly**, hil'i, *a.* Consisting of hills.—**Hillock**, hil'ok, *n.* [Dim. of *hill.*] A small hill.

Hilt, hilt, *n.* [A.Sax. *hilt*, hilt=Icel. *hjalt*, Dan. *hjalte*, O.H.G. *helza*; same root as *helve.*] The handle of a sword, dagger, &c. —**Hilted**, hilt'ed, *a.* Having a hilt: used in composition (a basket-*hilted* sword).

Hilum, hī'lum, *n.* [L.] The mark or scar on a seed (as the black patch on a bean) produced by its separation from the placenta.—**Hilar**, hī'lėr, *a.* Pertaining to the hilum.

Him, him, *pron.* [In A.Sax. the dative and instrumental of *he* and *hit*, he and it, afterwards used instead of *hine*, the real accusative sing. masc.; *m* is properly a dative suffix, as in *them*, *whom.*] The dative and objective case of *he*.—**Himself**, him-self', *pron.* An emphatic and reflexive form of the 3rd pers. pron. masc.; as, *himself*, he *himself*, the man *himself*, told me; it was *himself*, or he *himself*; he struck *himself*. It often implies that the person has command of himself, or is possessed of his natural frame or temper; as, he is not *himself* at all; he soon came to *himself*.—*By himself*, alone; unaccompanied.

Himalayas, him-a-lā'yas or hi-mä'la-yas, *a.* [Skr. *hima*, snow, and *ālaya*, abode.] A range of mountains in Asia between India and Tibet, usually with *The*.—**Himalayan**, *a.*

Himyaric, **Himyaritic**, him-yar'ik, him-ya-rit'ik, *a.* [From *Himyar*, an ancient king of Yemen.] Pertaining to the ancient Arabic of Southeast Arabia.—*n.* The language of Southeast Arabia.

Hin, hin, *n.* [Heb.] A Hebrew measure containing about 5 quarts.

Hind, hīnd, *n.* [A.Sax. *hind* = G. and D. *hinde*, Icel., Dan., and Sw. *hind.*] The female of the red-deer, the stag being the male.

Hind, hīnd, *n.* [A.Sax. *hine*, *hina*, with *d* affixed, as in *lend*, *sound*; akin *hive.*] In England an agricultural laborer.

Hind, hīnd, *a.* [A.Sax. *hind*, hind, *hindan*, behind; Goth. *hindana*, *hindar*, O.H.G. *hintar*, G. *hinten*, behind, *hinter*, hind: hence to *hinder.*] Backward; pertaining to the part which follows or is behind: opposite of *fore*.—**Hinder**, hīn'dėr, *a.* In the rear; following; after.—**Hindmost**, hīnd'mōst, *a.* [A.Sax. *hindema*, hindmost: the *-most* is a corruption as in *foremost* (which see).] Farthest behind; behind all others; last.—**Hindsight**, hīnd'sīt, *n.* Rear sight on a gun; judgment of an incident after it has passed: opposite of *foresight*.

Hinder, hin'dėr, *v.t.* [A.Sax. *hindrian*, to hinder, from *hinder*, compar. of *hind*, *a.* (which see).] To prevent from proceeding or from starting; to stop; to interrupt; to obstruct; to impede; to check or retard in progression or motion; to debar; to shut out; to balk: often with *from* and a verbal noun (to *hinder* him *from* going: the *from* is sometimes omitted).—*v.i.* To interpose obstacles or impediments.—**Hinderer**, hin'dėr-ėr, *n.* One who hinders.—**Hindrance**, **Hinderance**, hin'drans, hin'dėr-ans, *n.* The act of hindering; that which hinders; impediment; obstruction; obstacle.

Hindu, **Hindoo**, hin-dö' or hin'dö, *n.* A disciple of Hinduism; an Asiatic Indian.—**Hinduism**, **Hindooism**, hin'dö-izm, *n.* The doctrines and rites of the Hindus; Brahmanism.—**Hindustan**. [*Hindu*, and *stan*, place, country of Hindus, as in Kurdi*stan*, Afghani*stan*, Farsi*stan*, Kohi*stan*; *Hindu* from Sanskrit, *sindhu*, river, the Indus.]—**Hindustani**, **Hindoostanee**, hin-dö-stan'ē, *n.* A language of Hindustan, akin to Sanskrit, but having a large admixture of Persian and Arabic words, spoken more or less throughout nearly the whole Peninsula.—**Hindi**, hin'dē, *n.* A language of Northern India akin to Hindustani, but much more purely Sanskrit.

Hinge, hinj, *n.* [Probably from *hang*, O. and Prov. E. and Sc. *hing*; comp. Prov. E. *hingle*, a small hinge; D. *hengsel*, a hinge.] The hook or joint on which a door, lid, gate, or shutter, and the like turns; the joint of a bivalve shell; *fig.* that on which anything depends or turns; a governing principle, rule, or point.—*v.t.* To furnish with hinges.—*v.i.*—*hinged*, *hinging*. To stand, depend, or turn, as on a hinge.

Hinny, hin'i, *n.* [L. *hinnus*, Gr. *hinnos*, mule.] A mule, the produce of a stallion and a she-ass.—*v.i.* [L. *hinnio*, to neigh.] To neigh; to whinny.

Hint, hint, *n.* [Perhaps from O.E. *hente*, A.Sax. *hentan*, to seize; comp. also Icel. *ymtr*, a muttering.] A motive or occasion (*Shak.*); a distant allusion or slight mention; a word or two suggesting or insinuating something; a suggestion.—*v.t.* To bring to notice by a hint; to suggest indirectly. ∴ To *hint* is merely to make some reference or allusion that may or may not be apprehended; to *suggest* is to offer something definite for consideration.—*v.i.* To make or utter a hint.—*To hint at*, to allude to.—**Hinter**, hin'tėr, *n.* One who hints. —**Hintingly**, hin'ting-li, *adv.* In a hinting manner.

Hinterland, hin'tėr-land, *n.* [G.] The outlying region, remote from any towns.

Hip, hip, *n.* [A.Sax. *hype* = Icel. *huppr*, Dan. *hofte*, Goth. *hups*, D. *heup*, G. *hüfte*; akin to *heap*, perhaps to *hump.*] The fleshy projecting part of the thigh; the haunch; *arch.* the external angle at the junction of two sloping roofs or sides of a roof.—*To have a person on the hip*, to have the advantage over him; to have got some catch on him.—*To smite hip and thigh*, to overthrow completely with great slaughter (O.T.).—*v.t.*—*hipped*, *hipping*. To sprain or dislocate the hip.—**Hip-bath**, *n.* A portable bath in which the body can only be partially immersed.—**Hip-joint**, *n.* The joint of the hip, a ball-and-socket joint.—**Hip-rafter**, *n.* The rafter which forms the hip of a roof.—**Hip-roof**, **Hipped-roof**, *n.* A roof the ends of which slope inwards with the same inclination to the horizon as its two other sides.—**Hip-shot**, *a.* Having the hip dislocated; lame; awkward.

Hip, hip, *n.* [A.Sax. *heópe.*] The fruit of the dog-rose or wild-brier.

Hip, hip, *n.* [Contr. of *hypochondria.*] Hypochondria.—*v.t.* To render hypochondriac or melancholy.—**Hipped**, hipt, *p.* and *a.* Rendered melancholy; characterized by melancholy.—**Hippish**, hip'ish, *a.* Somewhat melancholy or hypochondriac.

Hip, hip, *interj.* An exclamation expressive of a call to any one or to arouse attention (*hip*, *hip*, *hip*, hurrah!).

Hipparion, hip-ā'ri-on, *n.* [Gr. *hipparion*, a little horse.] A small species of fossil horse, with three-toed feet.

Hippiatry, hip'i-at-ri, *n.* [Gr. *hippos*, a horse, and *iatros*, a physician.] Veterinary surgery.—**Hippiatric**, hip-i-at'rik, *a.* Pertaining to veterinary surgery; veterinary.

Hippocampus, hip-ō-kam'pus, *n.* [Gr. *hippos*, a horse, and *kamptō*, to bend.] A name of several small fishes of singular form, having the head and foreparts showing some similarity in shape to the head and neck of a horse, and a prehensile tail.

Hippocentaur, hip-ō-sen'tạr, *n.* [Gr. *hippokentauros*—*hippos*, a horse, and *kentauros*, centaur.] *Myth.* a fabulous monster, half man and half horse.

Hippocras, hip'ō-kras, *n.* [Fr., lit. wine of *Hippocrates.*] A medicinal drink, composed of wine with an infusion of spices and other ingredients, used as a cordial.—**Hippocratic**, hip-ō-krat'ik, *a.* Pertaining to Hippocrates, a Greek physician, born 460 B.C.—*Hippocratic oath*, pledge to a code of ethics taken by those entering upon medical practice.—**Hippocratism**, hip-pok'rat-izm, *n.* The doctrines or system of Hippocrates.

Hippocrene, hip'o-krēn, *n.* [Gr. horse-fountain.] Fountain on Mount Helicon, the seat of the Muses in Bœotia, produced by the stamp of the foot of the winged horse Pegasus; source of poetic inspiration.

Hippocrepiform, hip-ō-krep'i-form, *a.* [Gr. *hippos*, a horse, *krēpis*, a shoe.] *Bot.* horseshoe-shaped.

Hippodrome, hip'ō-drōm, *n.* [Gr. *hippodromos*—*hippos*, a horse, *dromos*, a course.] Anciently, a place in which horse-races and chariot-races were performed; a circus.

Hippogriff, **Hippogryph**, hip'ō-grif, *n.* [Gr. *hippos*, a horse, and *gryps*, a griffon.] A fabulous monster, half horse and half griffon.

Hippopathology, hip'ō-pa-thol"o-ji, *n.* [Gr. *hippos*, horse, and E. *pathology.*] The science of veterinary medicine.

Hippophagy, hip-pof'a-ji, *n.* [Gr. *hippos*, a horse, and *phagō*, to eat.] The act or practice of feeding on horse-flesh.—**Hippophagist**, hip-pof'a-jist, *n.* One who eats horse-flesh.—**Hippophagous**, hip-pof'a-gus, *a.* Feeding on horse-flesh.

Hippopotamus, hip-ō-pot'a-mus, *n.* pl. **Hippopotamuses** or **Hippopotami**, hip-ō-pot'a-musez, hip-ō-pot'a-mi. [Gr. *hippos*, a horse, and *potamos*, a river.] A hoofed quadruped of great bulk inhabiting lakes and rivers in Africa, being an excellent swimmer and diver, and feeding on herbage.

Hippotherium, hip-ō-thē'ri-um, *n.* [Gr. *hippos*, a horse, and *thērion*, a wild beast.] An extinct quadruped allied to the horse.

Hippurite, hip'ū-rīt, *n.* [Gr. *hippos*, horse, *oura*, tail.] The name of certain fossil bivalves characteristic of the cretaceous period.—**Hippuritic**, hip'ū-rit'ik, *a.* Pertaining to or abounding in hippurites.

Hircine, **Hircinous**, hėr'sīn, hėr-sī'nus, *a.* [L. *hircinus*, from *hircus*, a goat.] Pertaining to or resembling a goat; having a strong, rank smell like a goat; goatish.

Hire, hīr, *v.t.*—*hired*, *hiring*. [A.Sax. *hýrian*, from *hýr*, hire; Dan. *hyre*, to hire, *hyre*, wages, Sw. *hyra*, G. *heuer*, hire.] To procure from another person and for temporary use at a certain price or equivalent; to engage in service for a stipulated reward; to grant the temporary use or service of for compensation; to let: in this sense usually with *out*, and often reflexively.—*n.* The compensation given for the temporary use of anything; the reward or recompense paid for personal service; wages. —**Hireling**, hīr'ling, *n.* [A.Sax. *hýreling.*] One who is hired or who serves for wages; a venal or mercenary person.—*a.* Venal; mercenary.—**Hirer**, hī'rėr, *n.* One that hires.

Hirsute, hėr-sūt', *a.* [L. *hirsutus*, shaggy, from *hirtus*, hairy, connected with *horrid.*] Rough with hair; hairy; shaggy.—**Hirsuteness**, hėr-sūt'nes, *n.*

Hirundine, hi-run'dīn, *a.* and *n.* [L. *hirundo*, a swallow.] Swallow-like; a swallow.

His, hiz, *pron.* [In A.Sax. the genit. sing. of *hé*, he, and of *hit*, it.] The possessive case singular of the personal pronoun *he*; of or belonging to him; formerly also used for *its*.

Hispid, his'pid, *a.* [L. *hispidus*, rough, hairy. HIDEOUS.] Rough; shaggy; bristly; *bot.* beset with stiff bristles.—**Hispidity**, his-pid'i-ti, *n.* The state of being hispid.—

Hispidulous, his-pid'ū-lus, *a.* *Bot.* having short stiff hairs.

Hiss, his, *v.i.* [A.Sax. *hysian*, O.D. *hissen*, imitative of sound.] To make a sound like that of the letter *s*, in contempt or disapprobation; to emit a similar sound: said of serpents, of water thrown on hot metal, &c. —*v.t.* To condemn by hissing; to express disapproval of by hissing.—*n.* The sound made by propelling the breath between the tongue and upper teeth, as in pronouncing the letter *s*, especially as expressive of disapprobation; any similar sound.—**Hissingly**, his'ing-li, *adv.* With a hissing sound.

Hist, hist, *exclam.* [Comp. *hush*, *whist*, Dan. *hys*, hush, W. *hust*, a low buzzing sound.] A word commanding silence, equivalent to *hush*, be silent.

Histogeny, his-toj'e-ni, *n.* [Gr. *histos*, a tissue, and root *gen*, to produce.] The formation and development of the organic tissues.—**Histogenetic**, his'to-je-net"ik, *a.* Pertaining to histogeny.—**Histography**, his-tog'ra-fi, *n.* A description of the organic tissues.—**Histologic**, **Histological**, his-to-loj'ik, his-to-loj'i-kal, *a.* Pertaining to histology.—**Histologically**, his-to-loj'i-kal-li, *adv.*—**Histologist**, his-tol'o-jist, *n.* One versed in histology.—**Histology**, his-tol'o-ji, *n.* The doctrine of the tissues which enter into the formation of an animal or vegetable and its various organs.—**Histolysis**, his-tol'i-sis, *n.* [Gr. *lysis*, solution.] The decay and dissolution of organic tissues.—**Histonomy**, his-ton'o-mi, *n.* [Gr. *nomos*, a law.] The laws of the formation of tissues.

History, his'to-ri, *n.* [L. *historia*, a history, from Gr. *historia*, a learning by inquiry, from G. *histōr*, knowing, learned; same root as E. *wis*, *wit*, to know. *Story* is a short form of this.] That branch of knowledge which deals with events that have taken place in the world's existence; the study or investigation of the past; a narrative or account of an event or series of events in the life of a nation, or that have marked the progress or existence of any community or institution; a verbal relation of facts or events; a narrative; an account of things that exist; a description; an account of an individual person.—**Historian**, his-tō'ri-an, *n.* A writer or compiler of history; a historical writer.—**Historic**, **Historical**, his-tor'ik, his-tor'i-kal, *a.* [L. *historicus*.] Pertaining to or connected with history; containing or contained in, deduced from, suitable to, representing, &c., history.—**Historically**, his-tor'i-kal-li, *adv.* In a historic manner.—**Historify**,† **Historicise**,† his-tor'i-fi, his-tor'i-sīz, *v.t.* To record or narrate; to write as history.—**Historied**,† his'to-rid, *a.* Recorded in history.—**Historiette**, his-tō'ri-et", *n.* [Fr.] A short history or story; a tale; a novel.—**Historiographer**, his-tō'ri-og"ra-fėr, *n.* A historian; particularly, a professed or official historian.—**Historiographic**, **Historiographical**, his-tō'ri-ō-graf"ik, his-tō'ri-ō-graf"i-kal, *a.* Relating to historiography.—**Historiography**, his-tō'ri-og"ra-fi, *n.* The art or employment of a historian; the writing of history.

Histrionic, **Histrionical**, his-tri-on'ik, his-tri-on'i-kal, *a.* [L. *histrionicus*, from *histrio*, an actor; same root as Skr. *has*, to laugh at.] Pertaining to an actor or stage-player; belonging to stage-playing; theatrical; stagey; feigned for purposes of effect.—**Histrionic**,† his-tri-on'ik, *n.* A dramatic performer.—**Histrionically**, his-tri-on'i-kal-li, *adv.* In a histrionic manner.—**Histrionics**, his-tri-on'iks, *n.* The art of theatrical representation.—**Histrionism**, **Histrionicism**, his'tri-on-izm, his-tri-on'i-sizm, *n.* Stage-playing; theatrical or artificial manners or deportment.

Hit, hit, *v.t.*—*hit*, *hitting*. [Same as Icel. *hitta*, Dan. *hitte*, to hit, to meet with; Sw. *hitta*, to strike, to touch; same root as *hunt*, Goth. *hinthan*, to seize.] To strike or touch with some degree of force; to strike or touch (an object aimed at); not to miss; to give a blow to; to reach or attain to an object desired; to light upon; to get hold of or come at (to *hit* a likeness); to suit; to agree with;—*To hit off*, to represent or describe strikingly.—*v.i.* To strike; to meet; to clash: followed by *against* or *on*; to agree; suit.—*To hit on* or *upon*, to meet or find, as by chance.—*n.* The act of hitting; the blow which successfully strikes the target aimed at; a person or thing that is a noted success; *baseball*, a blow by which the ball is knocked permitting the batter to get on base; an effective phrase or remark.—**Hit-and-miss**, *a.* Sometimes effective, sometimes not; careless.—**Hitter**, hit'ėr, *n.* One who hits; *baseball*, batter.

Hitch, hich, *v.i.* [Comp. Prov. E. *hick*, to hop or spring; G. dial. *hiksen*, to limp; Sc. *hotch*, to move by jerks, to hobble; Prov.E. *huck*, to shrug.] To move by jerks or with stops; to become entangled; to be caught or hooked (the cord *hitched* on a branch); to be linked or yoked.—*v.t.* To fasten; to yoke; to make fast; to hook; to raise or pull up; to raise by jerks (to *hitch up* one's trousers).—*n.* A catch; an impediment; a break-down, especially of a casual and temporary nature; a heave or pull up; temporary help or assistance (to give one a *hitch*); *naut.* a kind of knot or noose in a rope for fastening it to an object.

Hitchhike, hich'hīk, *v.t.* To travel by getting free rides, especially in passing automobiles. (*Slang.*)

Hither, hiᴛʜ'ėr, *adv.* [A.Sax. *hider*, *hither*, Goth. *hidre*, Icel. *hethra*, hither, from stem of *he* with comparative suffix.] To this place; here: with verbs signifying motion.—*Hither and thither*, to this place and that.—*a.* On this side or in this direction; nearer.—**Hitherto**, hiᴛʜ'ėr-tö, *adv.* To this time or place; until now.—**Hitherward**, *adv.* Toward this place.

Hive, hīv, *n.* [A.Sax. *hýf*, *hýfe*, *hýfi*, a hive; probably of same root as L. *cupa*, a cup, whence E. *cup*, *cupola*, *goblet*, &c.] A box or kind of basket for the reception and habitation of a swarm of honey-bees; the bees inhabiting a hive; a place swarming with busy occupants.—*v.t.*—*hived*, *hiving*. To collect into a hive; to cause to enter a hive; to lay up in store for future use.—*v.i.* To take shelter together; to reside in a collective body.—**Hive-bee**, *n.* A bee which is housed in a hive; a domestic bee.

Hives, hīvz, *n.* [Perhaps akin to *heave*.] A disease of children, in which there is an eruption of vesicles over the body; nettle-rash or chicken-pox; also croup.

Ho, **Hoa**, hō, hō'a, *exclam.* [Fr. *ho*, Icel. *hó*.] A cry or call to arrest attention.

Hoar, hōr, *a.* [A.Sax. *hár*, hoary, gray-haired; Icel. *hárr*, hoar, *hæra*, gray hair, hoariness; comp. Sc. *haar*, a whitish mist.] White (*hoar*-frost); gray or grayish white; white with age; hoary.—*n.* Hoariness; antiquity.—*v.i.* To become mouldy or musty.—**Hoar-frost**, *n.* The white particles of frozen dew, rime.—**Hoariness**, hō'ri-nes, *n.* The state of being hoary.—**Hoary**, hō'ri, *a.* White or gray with age; hence, *fig.* remote in time past; *bot.* covered with short, dense, grayish-white hairs; canescent.—**Hoary-headed**, *a.* Having a hoary head; gray-headed.

Hoard, hōrd, *n.* [A.Sax. *hord*=O.Sax. and G. *hort*, Icel. *hodd*, Goth. *huzd*, hoard, treasure; from root of *house*, and of L. *custos*, a guardian.] A store, stock, or large quantity of anything accumulated or laid up; a hidden stock.—*v.t.* To collect and lay up in a hoard; to amass and deposit in secret: often followed by *up*.—*v.i.* To collect and form a hoard; to lay up store of money.—**Hoarder**, hōr'dėr, *n.* One who hoards.

Hoarding, hōr'ding, *n.* [O.Fr. *horde*, a barrier. HURDLE.] A timber inclosure round a building when the latter is in the course of erection or undergoing alteration or repair.

Hoarse, hōrs, *a.* [A.Sax. *hás*, hoarse, husky=Icel. *háss*, Dan. *hæs*, D. *heesch*, G. *heiser*, hoarse: the *r* is intrusive.] Having a harsh, rough, grating voice, as when affected with a cold; giving out a harsh, rough cry or sound.—**Hoarsely**, hōrs'li, *adv.* In a hoarse manner.—**Hoarsen**, hōr'sn, *v.t.* and *i.* To make or to grow hoarse.—**Hoarseness**, hōrs'nes, *n.* The state or quality of being hoarse.

Hoax, hōks, *n.* [For *hocus*.] Something done for deception or mockery; a trick played off in sport; a practical joke.—*v.t.* To play a trick upon for sport or without malice.—**Hoaxer**, hōk'sėr, *n.* One that hoaxes.

Hob, hob, *n.* [Same as *hub*; comp. Dan. *hob*, a heap; *hump* is akin, and *hobnail* is a compound.] The part of a grate or fireplace on which things are placed in order to be kept warm.

Hobble, hob'l, *v.i.*—*hobbled*, *hobbling*. From or connected with *hop*; comp. D. *hobbelen*, to hobble, to stammer.] To walk lamely, bearing chiefly on one leg; to limp; to walk awkwardly; to wabble or wobble; *fig.* to halt or move irregularly in versification.—*v.t.* To hopple.—*n.* A halting gait; a difficulty; a scrape; a clog; a fetter.—**Hobbler**, hob'lėr, *n.* One that hobbles.—**Hobblingly**, hob'ling-li, *adv.* In a hobbling manner.

Hobbledehoy, hob'l-dē-hoi, *n.* [Of uncertain origin.] A raw gawky youth approaching manhood.

Hobby, hob'i, *n.* [Comp. Fr. *hoberau*, dim. of O.Fr. *hobe*, a little bird of prey.] A small but strong-winged British falcon.

Hobby, **Hobby-horse**, hob'i, *n.* [Comp. D. *hoppe*, a mare; Prov. Sw. and Fris. *hoppa*; akin to *hop*.] A strong active horse of a middle size; a nag; a figure of a horse on which boys ride; any favourite object, plan, or pursuit.

Hobgoblin, hob-gob'lin, *n.* [From *hob*, formerly a rustic, a clown, an elf; corruption of *Robin*, *Robert*.] A goblin; an elf; an imp.

Hobnail, hob'nāl, *n.* [*Hob*, a projection, and *nail*.] A nail with a thick strong head used for shoeing horses, or for the soles of heavy boots.—**Hobnailed**, hob'nāld, *a.* Set with hobnails; rough.

Hobnob, hob'nob, *v.i.* [Lit., have or not have, drink if it please you—A.Sax. *habban*, to have, and *nabban*, for *ne habban*, not to have.] To drink familiarly; to clink glasses; to be boon or intimate companions.

Hobo, hō'bō, *n.* A migratory worker. (*Slang.*)

Hock, hok, *n.* [A.Sax. *hôh*, the heel; Icel. *há*, D. *hak*.] The joint of an animal between the knee and the fetlock; in man, the posterior part of the knee-joint.—*v.t.* To hamstring; to pawn; to pledge. (*Slang.*)

Hock, hok, *n.* [G. *Hochheimer*, from *Hochheim*, in Nassau, where it is produced.] A light sort of Rhenish wine which is either sparkling or still.

Hockey, hok'i, *n.* [From *hook*.] A game played on ice (ice hockey) or in a field (field hockey) in which opposing teams try to send a rubber disk or a ball into each other's goal.—**Hockey stick**, a club curved at the lower end, used in the game of hockey.

Hocus, hō'kus, *v.t.*—*hocussed*, *hocussing*. [The *hocus* of *hocus-pocus*.] To impose upon; to cheat; to hoax; to stupefy with drugged liquor for the purpose of cheating or robbing; to drug for this purpose.—**Hocus-pocus**, hō'kus-pō'kus, *n.* [An invented word imitative of Latin.] A juggler's trick; trickery used by conjurers.—*v.t.* To cheat; to hocus or hoax.

Hod, hod, *n.* [Northern English for *hold*.] A kind of trough for carrying mortar and bricks to masons and bricklayers, fixed to the end of a pole, and borne on the shoulder.—**Hod carrier**, **Hodman**, a worker who carries bricks or mortar in a hod.

Hodge-podge, **Hotch-potch**, hoj'poj, hoch'poch, *n.* [Corruption of *hotchpot*.] A mixed mass; a medley of ingredients; in Scotland, a thick soup of vegetables boiled with beef or mutton (in this sense always *hotch-potch*).

Hodograph, hod'o-graf, *n.* [Gr. *hodos*, a way, *graphein*, to write.] A curve whose radius vector represents in every position the magnitude and direction of the velocity of a moving particle in a corresponding position.

Hodometer, ho-dom'et-ėr, *n.* [Gr. *hodos*, a way, *metron*, a measure.] An instrument for measuring the length of way travelled by any vehicle.—**Hodometrical**, hod-o-met'ri-kal, *a.* Pertaining to a hodometer.

Hoe, hō, *n.* [O.Fr. *hoe*, Fr. *houe*, from the German; O.H.G. *houwa*, G. *haue*. HEW.] An instrument for cutting up weeds and loosening the earth in fields and gardens.—*v.t.*—*hoed, hoeing.* To cut, dig, scrape, or clean with a hoe.—*v.i.* To use a hoe.

Hog, hog, *n.* [W. *hwch*, Corn. *hoch*, Armor. *houch, hoch*, a sow, swine, hog.] A swine; a pig, or any animal of that species; a castrated boar; a sheep of a year old; a brutal fellow; one who is mean and filthy.—**Hog-backed**, *a.* Shaped like the back of a hog or sow.—**Hoggery**, hog'ėr-i, *n.* A place where hogs or swine are kept; hoggishness; brutishness.—**Hogget**, hog'et, *n.* A sheep two years old; a young boar of the second year.—**Hoggish**, hog'ish, *a.* Having the qualities of a hog; brutish; filthy.—**Hoggishly**, hog'ish-li, *adv.* In a hoggish manner.—**Hoggishness**, hog'ish-nes, *n.*—**Hogherd**, hog'hėrd, *n.* A keeper of swine.—**Hog-pen**, *n.* A hog-sty.—**Hog-plum**, *n.* A West Indian fruit used as food for hogs.—**Hog's-back**, *n.* Something shaped like the back of a hog; a ridge of a hill having this shape.—**Hog-skin**, *n.* Leather made of the skin of swine.—**Hog's-lard**, *n.* The fat of the hog.—**Hog-sty**, *n.* A pen or inclosure for hogs.—**Hog-wash**, *n.* The refuse of a kitchen or a brewery, or like matter given to swine; swill.

Hogmanay, hog'ma-nā, *n.* [Of French origin, and same as Norman *hoguinané*, O.Fr. *aguillanneuf*, a cry used in connection with New Year's gifts, and the last day of December, meaning perhaps 'to the mistletoe the New Year'.] The name given in Scotland to the last day of the year.

Hogshead, hogz'hed, *n.* [Corrupted from D. *okshoofd*, Dan. *oxehoved*, the measure called a hogshead, and lit. ox's-head; probably modified from some term of quite other meaning. A large cask, especially a cask containing from 63 to 140 gallons; a liquid measure of 63 gallons or 238.5 liters: abbreviated to *hhd.*

Hoiden, hoi'dn. HOYDEN.

Hoi polloi, hoi po-loi', [Gr.] The masses; the populace; the vulgar.

Hoist, hoist, *v.t.* [O.E. *hoise*, Sc. *heese* = D. *hijsschen, hysen*, L.G. *hissen*, Dan. *heise, hisse*, to hoist; the *t* was added as in *against, amongst*.] To heave or raise; especially to raise by means of block and tackle.—*n.* The act of hoisting; that by which anything is hoisted; a machine for elevating goods, passengers, &c., in a warehouse, hotel, and the like; an elevator.—*pp.* Hoisted.

Hoity-toity, hoi'ti-toi'ti. An exclamation denoting surprise or disapprobation, with some degree of contempt: equivalent to pshaw!—*a.* Elated; flighty; petulant.

Hokum, hō'kum, *n.* [HOCUS-POCUS.] Material, especially speech, given a deliberate simulation of significance in order to excite interest and emotion; pleasing and effective nonsense; bunk.

Holarctic, hol-ark'tik, *a.* [Gr. *holos*, all, *arktos*, the north.] Native to the colder parts of the Northern Hemisphere.

Holcus, hol'kus, *n.* [L. *holcus*, a kind of grain, Gr. *holkos*.] A genus of soft, hairy grasses of little value, but one of them is very fragrant.

Hold, hōld, *v.t.* pret. & pp. *held.* [A.Sax. *healdan* = Dan. *holde*, D. *houden*, Icel. *halda*, Goth. *haldan*, G. *halten*, to hold; hence *behold*.] To have or grasp in the hand; to grasp and retain (to *hold* a sword, a pen, a candle); to bear, put, or keep in a certain position (to *hold* the hands up); to consider; to regard (I *hold* him in honour); to account (I *hold* it true); to contain, or to have capacity to receive and contain; to retain within itself; to keep from running or flowing out; to keep possession of; to maintain, uphold, preserve; not to lose; to be in possession of; to possess, occupy, own, keep; to have or to entertain (to *hold* enmity); to derive or deduce title to (he *held* lands of the king); to stop, restrain, withhold; to keep fixed, as to a certain line of action; to bind or oblige (to *hold* one to his promise); to keep in continuance or practice (to *hold* intercourse); to prosecute or carry on, observe, pursue (a course, an argument); to celebrate, solemnize, carry out (a feast, a meeting); to occupy or keep employed; to engage the attention of.—*To hold in play*, to keep occupied so as to withdraw from something else.—*To hold water* (*fig.*), to be logically sound or capable of standing investigation.—*To hold in*, to guide with a tight rein; hence, to restrain, check, repress.—*To hold off*, to keep off; to keep from touching.—*To hold out*, to extend; to stretch forth; hence, to propose; to offer.—*To hold up*, to raise; to keep in an erect position; to sustain, support, uphold; to show, exhibit, put prominently forward.—*To hold one's own*, to keep good one's present condition; not to lose ground.—*To hold one's peace*, to keep silence.—*To hold the plough*, to guide it in ploughing.—*v.i.* To take or keep a thing in one's grasp; to maintain an attachment; to continue firm; not to give way or break; to adhere; to stand, be valid, apply (the argument *holds* good, this *holds* true); to stand one's ground: generally with *out* (the garrison *held out*); to refrain; to be dependent on for possessions, to derive right or title: with *of*, sometimes *from*; to stop, stay, or wait; to cease or give over: chiefly in the imperative.—*To hold forth*, to speak in public.—*To hold off*, to keep at a distance; to avoid connection.—*To hold on*, to continue; to keep fast hold; to cling; to proceed in a course.—*To hold to*, to cling or cleave to; to adhere.—*To hold with*, to side with; to stand up for.—*To hold together*, not to separate; to remain in union.—*Hold on! hold hard!* stop; cease.—*n.* A grasp, gripe, clutch (often in to *take hold*, to *lay hold*); *fig.* mental grasp; grasp on or influence working on the mind; something which may be seized for support; power of keeping; authority to seize or keep; claim; a place of confinement; a position of strength, a keep, stronghold; the whole interior cavity of a ship between the bottom and deck or lowest deck (in this sense seems modified from D. *hol*, a hole, a ship's hold).—**Holder**, hōl'dėr, *n.* One who or that which holds; a payee of a bill of exchange or a promissory note.—**Holdfast**, hōld'fast, *n.* Something used to secure and hold in place something else.—**Holding**, hōl'ding, *n.* A tenure; a farm held of a superior; that which holds, binds, or influences.

Hole, hōl, *n.* [A.Sax. *hol*, hollow, hole; D. *hol*, Icel. *hol, hola*, a hollow, a cavity; G. *hohl*, hollow; of same root as A.Sax. *helan*, to cover, whence *hell*; or as Gr. *koilos*, hollow.] A hollow place or cavity in any solid body; a perforation, orifice, aperture, pit, rent, fissure, crevice, &c.; the excavated habitation of certain wild beasts; a mean habitation; a wretched abode.—*v.i.*—*holed, holing.* To go into a hole.—*v.t.* To make a hole or holes in; to drive into a hole; *mining*, to undercut a coal-seam.—**Hole-and-corner**, *a.* Clandestine; underhand.

Holethnos, hol-eth'nos, *n.* [Gr. *holos*, entire, whole, and *ethnos*, nation.] A primitive stock or race of people not yet divided into separate tribes or branches.—**Holethnic**, hol-eth'nik, *a.* Pertaining to a holethnos.

Holiday, Holily, Holiness. Under HOLY

Holla, Hollo, Hollea, hol-lä', hol-lō'. [Fr. *holà*—*ho!* ho! and *là*, there.] An exclamation to some one at a distance, in order to call attention or in answer to one that hails.—*v.i.* To call, shout, or cry aloud.

Holland, hol'and, *n.* A kind of fine linen originally manufactured in *Holland*; also a coarser linen fabric used for covering furniture, carpets, &c.—**Hollander**, hol'-an-dėr, *n.* A native of Holland.—**Hollands**, hol'andz, *n.* A sort of gin imported from Holland.

Hollow, hol'ō, *a.* [A.Sax. *holg, holh*, a hollow space, from *hol*, a hole. HOLE.] Containing an empty space within; having a vacant space within; not solid; concave; sunken (eye, cheek); sounding as if reverberated from a cavity; deep or low; not sincere or faithful; false; deceitful.—*n.* A depression or excavation below the general level or in the substance of anything; a cavity.—*v.t.* To make a hollow or cavity in; to excavate.—*adv.* Utterly; completely (in certain phrases, as he beat him *hollow*).—**Hollow-eyed**, *a.* Having sunken eyes.—**Hollow-hearted**, *a.* Insincere; deceitful; not true.—**Hollowly**, hol'ō-li, *adv.* In a hollow manner.—**Hollowness**, hol'ō-nes, *n.* The state or quality of being hollow.—**Hollow-square**, *n.* A body of soldiers drawn up in the form of a square, with an empty space in the middle.—**Hollow-toned**, *a.* Having a sound as if coming from a cavity; deep-toned.—**Hollow-ware**, *n.* A trade name for such iron articles as cauldrons, kettles, saucepans, coffee-mills, &c.

Holly, Holly-tree, hol'i, *n.* [O.E. *holin*, A.Sax. *holegn, holen*, holly, allied to W. *celyn*, Gael. *cuilionn*, holly.] An evergreen tree or shrub with indented thorny leaves, and which produces clusters of beautiful red berries; also a name sometimes given to the holm-oak, an evergreen oak.—*Knee-holly*, butcher's-broom,

Hollyhock, hol'i-hok, *n.* [Lit. holy hock—*hock* being A.Sax. *hoc*, W. *hocys*, mallow: so called because brought from the Holy Land.] A tall single-stemmed biennial plant of the mallow family, a frequent ornament of gardens.

Holm, hōlm or hōm, *n.* [A.Sax., L.G., G., and Dan. *holm*, a small island in a river; Sw. *holme*, Icel. *hólmr*, an island.] A river island; a low flat tract of rich land by the side of a river.

Holm-oak, hōlm or hōm, *n.* [Lit. holly-oak, *holm* being from A.Sax. *holen*, holly, the leaves resembling those of the holly. HOLLY.] The evergreen oak.

Holoblast, hol'o-blast, *n.* [Gr. *holos*, whole, and *blastos*, a bud or germ.] *Zool.* an ovum consisting entirely of germinal matter. MEROBLAST.—**Holoblastic**, hol'o-blas-tik, *a.* Pertaining to a holoblast; of fertilized ova from which the embryo is formed by complete division or cleavage.

Holocaust, hol'o-kąst, *n.* [Gr. *holos*, whole, and *kaustos*, burned.] A burnt sacrifice or offering the whole of which was consumed by fire; a great slaughter or sacrifice of life.

Holograph, hol'o-graf, *n.* [Gr. *holos*, whole, and *graphein*, to write.] Any document, as a letter, deed, &c., wholly written by the person from whom it bears to proceed. Used also as an adj.—**Holographic, Holographical**, hol-o-graf'ik, hol-o-graf'i-kal, *a.* Being holograph; written by the grantor or testator himself.

Holometabolic, hol'o-met-a-bol"ik, *a.* [Gr. *holos*, entire, *metabolē*, change.] Applied to insects which undergo a complete metamorphosis.

Holophotal, hol-o-fō'tal, *a.* [Gr. *holos*, whole, and *phōs, phōtos*, light.] *Optics*, reflecting the rays of light in one unbroken mass without perceptible loss.

Holoptychius, hol-op-tik'i-us, *n.* [Gr. *holos*, entire, and *ptychē*, a wrinkle.] A fossil ganoid fish of the Old Red Sandstone, with wrinkled bony scales.

Holostome, hol'o-stōm, *n.* [Gr. *holos*, whole, and *stoma*, a mouth.] One of the gasteropodous molluscs in which the aperture of the shell is rounded or entire.

Holothure, Holothurian, hol'o-thūr, hol-o-thū'ri-an, *n.* [Gr. *holothourion*, a sea animal; origin doubtful.] One of the sea-cucumbers or sea-slugs, an order of echinoderms, of which the bêche-de-mer or trepang is an example.

Holp, Holpen, hōlp, hōl'pn, antiquated pret. and pp. of *help*.

Holster, hōl'stėr, *n*. [D. *holster*, a pistol-case = A.Sax. *heolster*, a cover, a recess; Icel. *hulster*, Dan. *hylster*, a case; root seen in A.Sax. *helad*, to cover, whence also *hell*.] A leather case for a pistol, usually hung on a belt or saddle.—**Holstered**, hōl'stėrd, *a*. Bearing holsters.

Holt, ‡hōlt, *n*. [A.Sax., Icel., and L.G. *holt*, grove, wood; D. *hout*, G. *holz*, wood, timber; cog. Gael. and Ir. *coil*, *coille*, pl. *coillte*, wood; W. *celt*, shelter.] A wood or woodland; a grove; a plantation.

Holt, hōlt, *n*. [Corrupted for *hold*.] A place of security; a burrow. (*Dial.*)

Holus-bolus, hō'lus-bō'lus, *adv*. [From *whole*, and *bolus*, a pill.] All at a gulp; altogether; all at once. (*Vulgar.*)

Holy, hō'li, *a*. [A.Sax. *hālig*, holy, from *hāl*, whole; similarly D. and G. *heilig*, Icel. *heilagr*, Dan. *hellig*, holy; akin *hale*, *heal*, *hallow*, *whole*, &c., same root also in Gr. *kalos*, beautiful.] Free from sin and sinful affections; pure in heart; pious; godly; hallowed; consecrated or set apart to a sacred use; having a sacred character.—**Holiday, Holyday**, hol'i-dā, *n*. A consecrated day; a religious anniversary; an occasion of joy and gaiety; a day, or a number of days, of exemption from labour.—*a*. Pertaining to or befitting a holiday; cheerful; joyous.—**Holily**, hō'li-li, *adv*. In a holy manner.—**Holiness**, hō'li-nes, *n*. The state or quality of being holy or sinless; sanctity; godliness; sacredness; *his holiness*, a title of the pope.—*Holy of holies*, the innermost apartment of the Jewish tabernacle or temple, where the ark was kept.—*Holy Ghost* or *Holy Spirit*, the Divine Spirit; the third person in the Trinity.—*Holy Office*, the Inquisition.—*Holy Thursday*, Ascension Day; also Thursday in Holy Week (so also *Holy Saturday*).—*Holy water*, in the *Roman Catholic Church*, salted water consecrated by the priest, and used in various rites and ceremonies.—*Holy week*, the week before Easter (the last week of Lent).—*Holy Writ*, the sacred Scriptures.—**Holy-grass**, *n*. An odoriferous grass strewed before the doors of churches on festival days.—**Holy-stone**, *n*. A soft sandstone used by seamen for cleaning the decks of ships.—*v.t*. To scrub with holy-stone.

Homage, hom'āj, *n*. [Fr. *hommage*, O.Fr. *homenage*, L.L. *hominaticum*, homage, from L. *homo*, *hominis*, a man, in late times a vassal. HUMAN.] Acknowledgment of vassalage made by a feudal tenant to his lord on receiving investiture of a fee; hence, obeisance; respect paid by external action; reverence directed to the Supreme Being; reverential worship; devout affection.—*v.t*. To pay homage to.—**Homageable**, hom'āj-a-bl, *a*. Bound to pay homage.—**Homager**, hom'āj-ėr, *n*. One who does or is bound to do homage.

Home, hōm, *n*. [A.Sax. *hām*, home, house, dwelling = L.G. and Fris. *ham*, D. and G. *heim*, Icel. *heimr*, Goth. *haims*, abode, village, &c.; cog. Gr. *kōmē*, a village, *keimai*, I rest; probably L. *quies*, quiet, &c.] One's own abode or dwelling; the abode of the family or household of which one forms a member; abiding place; one's own country; the seat (the *home* of war); an institute or establishment affording to the homeless, sick, or destitute the comforts of a home (a sailors' *home*, an orphans' *home*, &c.).—*At home*, in or about one's own house or abode; in one's own country.—*At home in* or *on a subject*, conversant, familiar, thoroughly acquainted with it.—*To make one's self at home*, to conduct one's self in another's house as unrestrainedly as if at home.—*a*. Connected with one's home; domestic; often opposed to *foreign*.—*Home economics*, the domestic science of making and caring for a home.—*adv*. To one's home or one's native country: often opposed to *abroad*; to one's self; to the point; to the mark aimed at; so as to produce an intended effect; effectively; thoroughly (to strike *home*).—**Homeborn**, hōm'born, *a*. Native; natural; domestic; not foreign.—**Homebred**, hōm'bred, *a*. Bred at home; originating at home; not foreign; not polished by travel.—**Home-brewed**, *a*. Brewed at home.—*n*. Beer, ale, or the like brewed at home.—**Home-circle**, *n*. The members or close intimates of a household.—**Home-grown**, *a*. Grown in one's own garden or country; not imported.—**Homeless**, hōm'les, *a*. Destitute of a home.—**Homelessness**, hōm'les-nes, *n*. The state of being homeless.—**Homelily**, hōm'li-li, *adv*. In a homely manner.—**Homeliness**, hōm'li-nes, *n*. The state or quality of being homely.—**Homely**, hōm'li, *a*. Pertaining to home; domestic‡; of plain features; not handsome; like that which is made for common domestic use; plain; coarse; not fine or elegant.—**Home-made**, *a*. Made at home; of domestic manufacture.—**Home plate**, a five-sided plate of rubber, set in the ground, beside which the batter stands (*Baseball*).—**Homer**, hō'mer, *n*. A *home run* (*Colloq.*).—**Home rule**, government of a district, colony, territory, &c., by the inhabitants themselves, particularly with regard to local matters.—**Home run**, a hit which, unaided by error, allows the batter to circle the bases and return to the home plate (*Baseball*).—**Homesick**, *a*. Ill from being absent from home; affected with home-sickness.—**Home-sickness**, *n*. Intense and uncontrolled grief at a separation from one's home or native land; nostalgia; longing for home.—**Homespun**, hōm'spun, *a*. Spun or wrought at home; hence, plain; coarse; homely.—*n*. Cloth made at home.—**Homestead**, hōm'sted, *n*. A house or mansion with the grounds and buildings immediately contiguous; a home.—**Home stretch**, the section of a race-course between the last curve and the finish.—**Homeward, Homewards**, hōm'wėrd, hōm'werdz, *adv*. Toward home; toward one's abode or native country.—*a*. Being in the direction of home.—**Homeward-bound**, *a*. Bound or destined for home; returning from a foreign country.—**Home work**, work to be done at home, especially that assigned by a teacher to students.—**Homing**, hōm'ing, *a*. Coming home: a term applied to birds, such as the carrier pigeon.

Homer, hō'mėr, *n*. [Heb.] A Hebrew measure equivalent to about 75 gallons or to 11 bushels.

Homeric, hō-mer'ik, *a*. Pertaining to *Homer*, the great poet of Greece; resembling Homer's verse or style.

Homicide, hom'i-sīd, *n*. [L. *homicidium*, the crime, *homicida*, the perpetrator—*homo*, man, and *cædo*, to strike, to kill.] The killing of one man or human being by by another; a person who kills another; a manslayer.—**Homicidal**, hom-i-sī'dal, *n*. Pertaining to homicidal; murderous.

Homily, hom'i-li, *n*. [Gr. *homilia*, intercourse or converse, instruction, a sermon, from *homilos*, a throng—*homos*, same (cog. with E. *same*), and *ilē*, a throng.] A discourse or sermon read or pronounced to an audience; a sermon; a serious discourse.—**Homiletic, Homiletical**, hom-i-let'ik, hom-i-let'i-kal, *a*. [Gr. *homilētikos*.] Relating to homilies or homiletics; hortatory.—*Homiletic theology*, homiletics.—**Homiletics**, hom-i-let'iks, *n*. The art of preaching; that branch of practical theology which treats of sermons and the best mode of composing and delivering them.—**Homilist**, hom'i-list, *n*. One that composes homilies; a preacher.

Hominy, hom'i-ni, *n*. [Amer.-Indian *auhúminea*, parched corn.] Maize hulled and coarsely ground, prepared for food by being boiled with water.

Homocarpous, hō-mō-kär'pus, *a*. [Gr. *homos*, same (cog. with E. *same*), *karpos*, fruit.] *Bot*. having all the fruits of the flower-head alike.

Homocentric, hō-mō-sen'trik, *a*. [Gr. *homos*, same, *kentron*, a center.] Having the same center; concentric.

Homocercal, hō-mō-sėr'kal, *a*. [Gr. *homos*, same, *kerkos*, tail.] *Ichthyol*. having the lobes of the tail diverging symmetrically from the backbone, as in the cod, herring, &c. HETEROCERCAL.—**Homocercy**, hō-mō-sėr'si, *n*. The state of being homocercal.

Homochromous, hō-mok'ro-mus, *a*. [Gr. *homos*, same, *chrōma*, color.] *Bot*. having all the florets of the same color.

Homodromous, Homodromal, hō-mod'ro-mus, ho-mod'ro-mal, *a*. [Gr. *homos*, same, *dromos*, a race.] *Bot*. having the spires of leaves running in the same direction.

Homeomeric, Homeomerical, hō'mē-ō-mer"ik, hō'me-ō-mer"i-kal, *a*. [Gr. *homoios*, like, from *homos*, same, and *meros*, a part.] Pertaining to or characterized by sameness of parts.—**Homeomorphous**, hō'mē-ō-mor"fus, *a*. [Gr. *morphē*, form.] ISOMORPHOUS.

Homeopathy, hō-mē-op'a-thi, *n*. [Gr. *homoios*, like, *pathos*, feeling, suffering.] The system of medicine founded upon the belief that drugs have the power of curing morbid conditions similar to those they have the power to excite in healthy persons opposed to *heteropathy* or *allopathy*.—**Homeopathic, Homeopathical**, hō'mē-ō-path"ik, hō'mē-ō-path"i-kal, *a*. Relating to homeopathy.—**Homeopathically**, hō'mē-ō-path"i-kal-li, *adv*. In a homeopathic manner.—**Homeopathist**, hō-mē-op'a-thist, *n*. One who practices or supports homeopathy.

Homeozoic, hō'mē-ō-zō"ik, *a*. [Gr. *homoios*, similar, *zōē*, life.] Inhabited by similar forms of animal or vegetable life.

Homogamous, hō-mog'a-mus, *a*. [Gr. *homos*, same, *gamos*, marriage.] *Bot*. having all the florets of a flower-head, or the florets of the spikelets in grasses, hermaphrodite.—**Homogamy**, hō-mog'a-mi, *n*. The state of being homogamous.

Homogangliate, hō-mō-gang'gli-āt, *a*. [Gr. *homos*, same, *ganglion*, a ganglion.] *Anat*. having the nervous ganglia symmetrically arranged.

Homogeneous, Homogeneal, hō-mō-jē'nē-us, hō-mō-jē'nē-al, *a*. [Gr. *homogenēs*—*homos*, like, and *genos*, kind; root *gen*, cog. with E. *kin*.] Of the same kind or nature; consisting of similar parts, or of elements of the like nature: opposite of *heterogeneous*.—**Homogeneity, Homogeneousness**, hō'mō-je-nē"i-ti, hō-mō-jē'nē-us-nes, *n*. The state or character of being homogeneous.

Homogenesis, hō-mō-jen'e-sis, *n*. [Gr. *homos*, same, *genesis*, birth.] Sameness of origin; reproduction of offspring similar to their parents.—**Homogenetic**, hō'mō-je-net"ik, *a*. Pertaining to homogenesis.

Homograph, hō'mō-graf, *n*. [Gr. *homos*, same, *graphō*, to write.] A word which has exactly the same form as another, though of a different origin and signification; a homonyn.—**Homographic**, hō-mō-graf'ik, *a*. Relating to homographs.

Homoiousian, ho-moi-ou'si-an, *n*. [Gr. *homoios*, similar, and *ousia*, being.] A person holding the belief that the nature of Christ is not the same with, but only similar to, that of the Father. HOMOOUSIAN.

Homoiozoic, hō'moi-ō-zō"ik, *a*. HOMŒOZOIC.

Homologate, hō-mol'o-gāt, *v.t*.—*homologated*, *homologating*. [L.L. *homologo*, *homologatum*, from Gr. *homos*, same, and *logos*, discourse, from *legō*, to speak.] To approve; to express approval of or assent to; to ratify.—**Homologation**, ho-mol'o-gā"shon, *n*. The act of homologating.

Homologous, hō-mol'o-gus, *a*. [Gr. *homos*, same, and *logos*, proportion.] Having the same relative position, proportion, or structure; corresponding in use or general character; of similar type.—**Homologue**, hŏ'mō-log, *n.* That which is homologous; an organ of an animal homologous with another organ.—**Homology**, hō-mol'o-ji, *n.* The quality of being homologous; correspondence in character or relation; sameness or correspondence in organs of animals as regards general structure and type, thus the human arm corresponds to the fore-leg of a quadruped and the wing of a bird.—**Homological**, hō-mō-loj'i-kal, *a.* Pertaining to homology; having a structural affinity.—**Homologically**, hō-mō-loj'i-kal-li, *adv.* In a homological manner.

Homomorphous, Homomorphic, hō-mō-mor'fus, hō-mō-mor'fik, *a.* [Gr. *homos*, same, *morphē*, shape.] Having the same external appearance or form. — **Homomorphism**, hō-mō-mor'fizm, *n.* The condition of being homomorphous.

Homonym, Homonyme, hŏ'mō-nim, *n.* [Gr. *homos*, same, *onoma*, name.] A word which agrees with another in sound, and perhaps in spelling, but differs from it in signification; a homograph; as *fair*, *a.* and *fair*, *n.* — **Homonymic, Homonymical**, hō-mō-nim'ik, hō-mō-nim'i-kal, *a.* Relating to homonymy or to homonyms.—**Homonymous**, hō-mon'i-mus, *a.* Having the same sound or spelling.—**Homonymously**, hō-mon'i-mus-ly, *adv.* In a homonymous manner.—**Homonymy**, hō-mon'i-mi, *n.* Sameness of name with a difference of meaning; ambiguity; equivocation.

Homoousian, hō-mō-ou'si-an, *n.* [Gr. *homos*, same, and *ousia*, being.] A person who maintains that the nature of the Father and the Son is the same, in opposition to the *Homoiousians*.

Homopetalous, hō-mō-pet'a-lus, *a.* [Gr. *homos*, same, *petalon*, a petal.] *Bot.* having all the petals or florets alike.

Homophone, hŏ'mō-fōn, *n.* [Gr. *homos*, same, *phōnē*, sound.] A letter or character expressing a like sound with another; a word having the same sound as another; a homonym. — **Homophonous**, hō-mof'o-nus, *a.* Of like sound; agreeing in sound but differing in sense. — **Homophony**, hō-mof'o-ni, *n.* Sameness of sound.

Homoplasmy, hŏ'mo-plas-mi, *n.* [Gr. *homos*, same, *plassō*, to form.] *Biol.* resemblance in form or structure with difference in origin.—**Homoplastic**, *a.* Similar in form or structure.

Homopter, hō-mop'tėr, *n.* [Gr. *homos*, same, *pteron*, a wing.] A hemipterous insect with wings of same consistence throughout.

Homostylous, hom'ō-stīl''us, *n.* [Gr. *homoiōs*, like, style.] Of flowers with styles of the same length.

Homotaxis, Homotaxy, hō-mō-tak'sis, hō-mō-tak'si, *n.* [Gr. *homos*, same, *taxis*, arrangement.] Agreement in arrangement; *geol.*, agreement in the arrangement of strata in different localities. — **Homotaxial**, hō-mō-tak'si-al, *a.* Pertaining to homotaxis.

Homotonous, hō-mot'o-nus, *a.* [Gr. *homos*, same, *tonos*, tone.] Of the same course or tenor; applied to diseases.

Homotropal, Homotropous, hō-mot'-ro-pal, hō-mot'ro-pus, *a.* [Gr. *homos*, same, *tropos*, turn, direction.] *Bot.* directed in the same way as the body to which it belongs.

Homotype, hŏ'mō-tīp, *n.* [Gr. *homos*, same, *typos*, type.] A part or organ of animal corresponding to or forming a repetition of another part (as on the right and left sides).—**Homotypal, Homotypic**, hŏ'mō-tī-pal, hō-mō-tip'ik, *a.* Forming a homotype. — **Homotypy**, hō-mot'i-pi, *n.* The existence of homotypes.

Homuncule, Homunculus, hō-mung'-kūl, hō-mung'kū-lus, *n.* [L., dim. of *homo*, a man.] A manikin; a dwarf.

Hone, hōn, *n.* [A.Sax. *hān*, Icel. *hein*, Sw. *hen*, a hone, a whetstone; root seen in Skr. *co*, to sharpen, and in L. *conus*, a hone.] A stone of a fine grit, used for sharpening instruments that require a fine edge.—*v.t.* To sharpen on a hone.

Honest, on'est, *a.* [O.Fr. *honeste* (Fr. *honnête*), from L. *honestus*, from *honor*, *honos*, honour. HONOUR.] Fair in dealing with others; free from trickishness, fraud, or theft; upright; just; equitable; sincere, candid, or unreserved; honourable; reputable; chaste or virtuous; pleasant-looking in features.—**Honestly**, on'est-li, *adv.* In an honest manner.—**Honesty**, on'es-ti, *n.* The state or quality of being honest; integrity; uprightness; fairness; candour.

Honey, hun'i, *n.* [A.Sax. *hunig* = D. and G. *honig*, Icel. *hunang*, honey.] A sweet, viscid juice, collected from flowers by several kinds of insects, especially bees; *fig.* sweetness or pleasantness; as a word of endearment, sweet one; darling. — *v.i.* To become sweet; to become complimentary or fawning.—*v.t.* To cover with or as with honey; to make agreeable; to sweeten. —**Honey-bee**, *n.* A bee that produces honey; the hive-bee.—**Honey-comb**, *n.* The waxy structure formed by bees for the reception of honey, and for the eggs which produce their young.—**Honey-combed**, *a.* Formed like a honey-comb; perforated with or containing many cavities.—**Honey-dew**, *n.* A sweet saccharine substance found on the leaves of trees and other plants in small drops like dew.—**Honey-dew melon**, a very sweet muskmelon with a white, smooth skin.—**Honeyed, Honied**, hun'id, *p.* and *a.* Covered with or as with honey; hence, sweet; full of compliments or tender words.—**Honeyedness**, hun'id-nes, *n.*—**Honeymoon**, hun'i-mön, *n.* The first month after marriage; the interval spent by a newly-married pair before settling down in a home of their own.—**Honey-mouthed, Honey-tongued**, *a.* Soft or smooth in speech.—**Honeysuckle**, hun'i-suk-l, *n.* [From children sucking the honey out of the nectary.] The popular name for a genus of upright or climbing shrubs with fragrant flowers of a tubular shape.

Hong, hong, *n.* [Chinese *hong*, *hang*.] The Chinese name for foreign factories or mercantile houses.—*Hong merchants*, a body of eight to twelve Chinese merchants at Canton, who once had the sole privilege of trading with Europeans.

Honor, Honour, on'ėr, *n.* [O.Fr. *honor*, *honeur*, Fr. *honneur*, from L. *honor*, *honos*, honor, whence *honestus*, honest.] Esteem paid to worth; high estimation; reverence; veneration; any mark of respect or estimation by words or actions; dignity; exalted rank or place; distinction; reputation; good name; a nice sense of what is right, just, and true; scorn of meanness; a particular virtue, as bravery or integrity in men and chastity in females; one who or that which is a source of glory or esteem; he who or that which confers dignity (an *honor* to his country); title or privilege of rank or birth; one of the highest trump cards, as the ace, king, queen, or knave, and, in bridge, ten; a title of address or respect now restricted, except among the vulgar, to the holders of certain offices (e.g. judges): with *his*, *your*, &c.; (*pl.*) civilities paid, as at an entertainment; (*pl.*) academic and university distinction or pre-eminence.—*Honors of war*, distinctions granted to a vanquished enemy, as of marching out of a camp or intrenchments armed and with colors flying.—*An affair of honor*, a dispute to be decided by a duel.—*Word of honor*, a verbal promise or engagement which cannot be violated without disgrace.—*Debt of honor*, a debt, as a bet, for which no security is required or given except that implied by honorable dealing.—*Maid of honor*, a lady whose duty it is to attend a queen in public; chief attendant, if unmarried, of a bride at a wedding; if married, *matron of honor*.—*v.t.* To regard or treat with honor; to revere; to respect; to reverence; to bestow honor upon; to elevate in rank or station; to exalt; to render illustrious; *com.* to accept and pay when due (to *honor* a bill of exchange).—**Honorarium**, on-ė-rā'ri-um, or hon', *n.* [L. *honorarium* (*donum*, gift).] A fee to a professional man for professional services.—**Honorary**, on'ėr-a-ri, *a.* [L. *honorarius*.] Done or made in honor; indicative of honor; intended merely to confer honor (an *honorary* degree); possessing a title or post without performing services, or without receiving benefit or reward (an *honorary* secretary or treasurer). — **Honorable**, on'ėr-a-bl, *a.* Worthy of being honored; estimable; illustrious or noble; actuated by principles of honor; conferring honor; consistent with honor or reputation; regarded with esteem; accompanied with marks of honor or testimonies of esteem; upright and laudable; directed to a just and proper end; not base; a title of distinction applied to certain members of noble families, persons in high position, &c., *right honorable* being a higher grade.—**Honorableness**, on'ėr-a-bl-nes, *n.* The state of being honorable.—**Honorably**, on'ėr-a-bli, *adv.* In an honorable manner.—**Honorless**, on'-ėr-les, *a.* Destitute of honor; not honored.

Hood, hụd, *n.* [A.Sax. *hōd* = D. *hoed*, G. *hut*, a hat; allied to E. *heed*; G. *hüten*, D. *hoeden*, to protect; Skr. *chad*, to cover.] A soft covering for the head worn by females and children; the part of a monk's outer garment with which he covers his head; a cowl; a similar appendage to a cloak or overcoat; an ornamental fold at the back of an academic gown; a covering for a hawk's head or eyes, used in falconry; anything that resembles a hood in form or use. —*v.t.* To dress in a hood or cowl; to put a hood on; to cover or hide.—**Hooded**, hụd'-ed, *p.* and *a.*—**Hoodwink**, hụd'wingk, *v.t.* To blind by covering the eyes; to blindfold; to deceive by external appearances.

Hoodlum, höd'lum, *n.* A rowdy; a rough. (*Colloq.*)

Hoodoo, hö'dö, *n.* VOODOO. Something which brings misfortune.—*v.t.* To bring bad luck. (*Colloq.*)

Hooey, hö'i, *n.* and *interj.* Nonsense. (*Slang.*)

Hoof, höf, *n.* pl. **Hoofs**, rarely **Hooves**, hövz. [A.Sax. *hōf*, Icel. *hófr*, D. *hoef*, Dan. *hov*, G. *huf*, a hoof.] The horny substance that covers the feet or the digits of the feet of certain animals, as horses, oxen, sheep, deer, &c. — **Hoof-bound**, *a.* *Farriery*, having a dryness and contraction of the hoof, which occasions pain and lameness.—**Hoofed**, höft *a.* Furnished with hoofs.—**Hoofless**, höf'les, *a.* Destitute of hoofs. —**Hoof-mark**, *n.* The mark or trace left by a hoof.

Hook, hụk, *n.* [A.Sax. *hóc*, a hook, a crook = D. *hoek*, Icel. *haki*, G. *haken*, O.H.G. *hako*, a hook; same root as *hang*, *hake*, *hockey*, *huckle-bone*, *hackle*.] A piece of iron or other metal bent into a curve for catching, holding, or sustaining anything; any similar appliance; a curved instrument for cutting grass or grain; a sickle; an instrument for lopping; a small metallic fastening for dresses catching in an *eye*.—*By hook or by crook*, by some means or other.—*On one's own hook*, on one's own account or responsibility. (*Colloq.*) — *v.t.* To catch or fasten with a hook or hooks; to bend into the form of a hook; to furnish with hooks; to catch by artifice; to entrap. —*v.i.* To bend; to be curving; to catch into something. — **Hook-beaked, Hook-billed**, *a.* Having a curved beak or bill; curvirostral.—**Hook-bill**, *n.* The curved beak of a bird; a bill-hook with a curved end.—**Hooked**, hụk'ed or hụkt, *p.* and *a.* Shaped or curved like a hook.—**Hookedness**, hụk'ed-nes, *n.* A state of being hooked; incurvation.—**Hooker**, hụk'ėr, *n.* One who or that which hooks. — **Hook-nose**, *n.* A curved nose.—**Hook-nosed**, *a.* Having a curvated or aquiline nose.

Hookah, hö'kä, *n.* [Ar.] A tobacco pipe with a long pliable tube and water vase so constructed that the smoke passes through the water before being inhaled.

Hooker, hụk'ėr, *n.* [D. *hoeker*, *hoekboot*.] An Irish fishing-smack.

Hooligan, hö'li-gan, *n.* [Irish personal name.] A street rough or rowdy.

Hoop, höp, *n.* [A.Sax. *hóp*, Fris. *hop*,

D. *koep*; akin *hump*.] A band of wood or metal used to confine the staves of casks, tubs, &c., or for other similar purposes; a combination of circles of thin whalebone or other elastic material used to expand the skirts of ladies' dresses; a farthingale; a crinoline.—*v.t.* To bind or fasten with hoops. — **Hooper**, hö'pėr, *n.* One who hoops; a cooper; one who makes or repairs barrels and casks.

Hoopoe, hö'pö, *n.* [Fr. *huppe*, L. *upupa*, Gr. *epops*, hoopoe: names given from its cry.] A beautiful bird with a crest, which it can erect or depress at pleasure, and a long, sharp, curved bill, found in Europe and North Africa and named for its whooping cry.

Hoosegow, Hoosgow, hös'gou, hös'gą, *n.* [Sp. *juzgado*, a court.] A place of confinement; a jail; a prison; a guardhouse. (*Slang.*)

Hoosier, hö'zhėr, *n.* A person from the State of Indiana, which is nicknamed the *Hoosier State*.

Hoot, höt, *v.i.* [From the sound; comp. Fr. *houter*, to call, to cry.] To cry out or shout in contempt; to cry as an owl.—*v.t.* To utter cries or shouts in contempt of; to utter contemptuous cries or shouts at.—*n.* A cry or shout in contempt; the cry of an owl.

Hop, hop, *v.i.*—*hopped, hopping*. [A.Sax. *hoppian* = Icel. and Sw. *hoppa*, D. *huppen*, G. *hüpfen*, to hop; akin *hobble, hobby*.] To move by successive leaps; to leap or spring on one foot; to skip, as birds; to limp; to dance.—*n.* A leap on one leg; a jump; a spring; a dance or dancing party (*colloq.*).—**Hopper**, hop'ėr, *n.* One who hops; a wooden trough through which grain passes into a mill, so named from its moving or shaking; any similar contrivance; a boat having a compartment with a movable bottom to convey matter dredged up and deposit it in deep water.—**Hop-scotch**, *n.* A children's game which consists in hopping over scores or scotches on the ground.

Hop, hop, *n.* [D. *hop, hoppe*, G. *hopfen*, hop.] A climbing plant of the hemp family, whose female flowers are used to flavour malt liquors and make them keep.—*v.t.*—*hopped, hopping*. To mix hops with. —*v.i.* To pick or gather hops.—**Hopbine**, hop'bīn, *n.* The climbing or twining stem of the hop-plant.—**Hopoast**, hop'ōst, *n.* An oven or kiln for drying hops.—**Hop-picker**, *n.* One who picks or gathers hops. —**Hop-pocket**, *n.* A coarse, heavy wrapper for containing hops, used as a measure for hops = 1½ to 2 cwt.—**Hop-pole**, *n.* A pole or stake for the stem of the hop-plant to climb.—**Hoppy**, hop'i, *a.* Abounding with hops; having the flavour of hops.

Hope, hōp, *n.* [A.Sax. *hopa*=D. *hoop*, Sw. *hopp*, Dan. *haab*, hope; G. *hoffen*, to hope; possibly akin to L. *cupio*, to desire.] A desire of some good, accompanied with at least a slight expectation of obtaining it, or a belief that it is obtainable; expectation of something desirable; confidence in a future event; trust; that which gives hope; one in whom trust or confidence is placed; the object of hope; the thing hoped for.—*Forlorn hope.* Under FORLORN.—*v.i.*—*hoped, hoping*. [A.Sax. *hopian*. D. *hopen*, to hope.] To entertain or indulge hope; to have confidence; to trust.—*v.t.* To entertain hope for; to desire with expectation.—**Hopeful**, hōp'fụl, *a.* Full of or entertaining hope; having qualities which excite hope; promising.—*n.* A boy or young man, the *hope* of his parents: often with the epithet *young*, and used sarcastically.—**Hopefully**, hōp'fụl-li, *adv.* In a hopeful manner.—**Hopefulness**, hōp'fụl-nes, *n.* The state or quality of being hopeful, or of furnishing ground for hope.—**Hopeless**, hōp'les, *a.* Destitute of hope; giving no ground of hope.—**Hopelessly**, hōp'les-li, *adv.* In a hopeless manner.—**Hopelessness**, hōp'les-nes, *n.*—**Hoper**, hō'pėr, *n.* One that hopes. — **Hopingly**, hō'ping-li, *adv.* With hope; hopefully.

Hoplite, hop'līt, *n.* [Gr. *hoplitēs*, from *hoplon*, a weapon.] A heavy-armed soldier of ancient Greece.

Hopper. Under HOP.

Hopple, hop'l, *v.t.* [From *hop*, to leap; also in form *hobble*.] To tie the feet of (a horse) near together to prevent leaping or running; to hobble.—*n.* A fetter for the legs of grazing horses or other animals.

Horary, Horal, hō'ra-ri, hō'ral, *a.* [L. *hora*, an hour.] Pertaining to the hours; occurring once an hour; hourly.—**Horæ**, hō'rē, *n.* A book of devotions for fixed hours.

Horatian, ho-rā'shan, *a.* Relating to or resembling the Latin poet *Horace* (Horatius) or his poetry.

Horde, hōrd, *n.* [Fr. *horde*, from Turk. and Per. *ordû*, court, camp, horde.] A tribe, clan, or race of Asiatic or other nomads; a wandering tribe; hence, a gang; a migratory crew; rabble.—*v.i.* To live in hordes; to huddle together.

Hordeolum, hor-dē'o-lum, *n.* [Dim. of L. *hordeum*, grain of barley.] A stye on the eyelid.

Horehound, hōr'hound, *a.* [A.Sax. *hāra-hune*—*hār*, hoar, and *hune*, the generic name of these plants.] The popular name of several European plants of the mint family, one of which, white horehound, has an aromatic smell and bitter taste, and has been much in use for coughs and asthma. Written also *Hoarhound*.

Horizon, ho-rī'zon, *n.* [Gr. *horizōn*, from *horizō*, to bound, from *horos*, a limit; lit. that which bounds.] The circle which bounds that part of the earth's surface visible to a spectator from a given point; the apparent junction of the earth and sky: called the *visible* or *apparent horizon*; an imaginary great circle, parallel to this, whose plane passes through the centre of the earth: called the *celestial horizon*.—*On the same horizon, geol.* said of fossils or strata which appear to be of the same age. —**Horizontal**, hor-i-zon'tal, *a.* Pertaining to the horizon; on the same or a parallel plane with the horizon; on a level; measured or contained in the plane of the horizon (*horizontal* distance).—**Horizontality**, hor'i-zon-tal''li-ti, *n.* The state of being horizontal.—**Horizontally**, hor-i-zon'tal-li, *adv.* In a horizontal direction or position.

Hormone, hor'mōn, *n.* [Gr. *hormaō*, I excite.] An internal secretion that stimulates the activity of a digestive gland.

Horn, horn, *n.* [A.Sax. *horn*, a horn, a trumpet = Icel., Sw., Dan., and G. *horn*, D. *horen*, Goth. *haurn*; cog. W. and Armor. *corn*, L. *cornu*, Gr. *keras*—horn. *Hornet* is a derivative, and *hart* is akin.] A hard projecting appendage growing on the heads of certain animals, and particularly on cloven-hoofed quadrupeds; the material of which such horns are composed; a wind-instrument of music, originally made of horn; a drinking-cup of horn; a utensil for holding powder for immediate use, originally made of horn; a powder-flask; something similar to a horn; the feeler of an insect, snail, &c.; an extremity of the moon when waxing or waning.—*Put to the horn*, to outlaw by three blasts on a horn at the Cross of Edinburgh for refusal to answer summons (in Scots law).—*To draw in the horns*, to repress one's ardour, or to restrain pride, in allusion to the habit of the snail withdrawing its feelers when startled.—**Hornbeam**, horn'bēm, *n.* A small bushy tree of the oak family, with a hard white wood. —**Horn-beast**, *n.* An animal with horns. (*Shak.*)—**Hornbill**, horn'bil, *n.* A name of certain birds with very large bills surmounted by an extraordinary horny protuberance.—**Hornblende**, horn'blend, *n.* [G. *horn*, horn, and *blende*, blende (from *blenden*, to dazzle), from its horny and glittering appearance.] A dark green or black lustrous mineral of several varieties, an important constituent of several rocks. —**Hornblendic**, horn-blen'dik, *a.* Containing hornblende; resembling hornblende. —**Horn-blower**, *n.* One that blows a horn.—**Hornbook**, horn'bụk, *n.* In former times a child's alphabet book or primer, with a transparent sheet of horn placed over the single page of which it usually consisted, the whole being fixed to a wooden frame.—**Horn-gate**, *n.* The gate by which true dreams come and go; opposed to the *ivory-gate*.—**Horned**, hornd, *a.* Having horns or projections resembling them (the *horned* moon); wearing horns, made a cuckold. — **Horned-horse**, *n.* The gnu. —**Hornedness**, hornd'nes, *n.* The state of being horned. — **Horned-screamer**, *n.* A South American grallatorial bird, with a long, slender, movable horn projecting from its forehead.—**Horner**, hor'nėr, *n.* One who works or deals in horn; one who blows a horn.—**Horn-fish, Horn-pike**, *n.* The garfish or sea-needle.—**Hornless**, horn'les, *a.* Having no horns. — **Horn-mad**, *a.* Outrageous; stark mad: in allusion to a mad bull. — **Horn-owl, Horned-owl**, *n.* One of those owls that have two tufts of feathers on the head.—**Hornpipe**, horn'pīp, *n.* A musical instrument formerly popular in Wales; a lively dance tune; a sprightly dance, usually performed by one person. — **Hornstone**, horn'stōn, *n.* A siliceous stone, a variety of quartz. —**Hornwork**, horn'wėrk, *n.* *Fort.* a work with one front only, thrown out beyond the glacis, which front consists of two demi-bastions connected by a curtain.—**Horny**, hor'ni, *a.* Consisting or composed of horn; resembling horn in appearance or composition; exhibiting hardened skin or callosities (a *horny* fist); having horns.

Hornet, hor'net, *n.* [A.Sax. *hyrnst*, from *horn*, a horn, from its antennæ or horns, or because its buzzing is compared to the blowing of a horn; G. *horniss*, a hornet.] A large, powerful wasp, the sting of which is very painful; hence, anyone who gives particular annoyance.

Horography, hō-rog'ra-fi, *n.* [Gr. *hōra*, hour, and *graphō*, to write.] An account of the art of constructing instruments for showing the hours; horology.—**Horologe**, hō'ro-lōj, *n.* [Fr. *horologe*, L. *horologium*, Gr. *hōrologion*—*hōra*, hour, and *legō*, to tell.] A piece of mechanism for indicating the hours of the day; a time-piece of any kind.—**Horologer, Horologist**, hō-rol'-o-jėr, hō-rol'o-jist, *n.* A maker or vender of clocks and watches; one versed in or who writes on horology. — **Horologic, Horological**, hō-ro-loj'ik, hō-ro-loj'i-kal, *a.* Pertaining to horology; *bot.* opening and closing at certain hours: said of flowers.—**Horology**, hō-rol'o-ji, *n.* The science of measuring time; the art of constructing machines for measuring time, as clocks, watches, dials. — **Horometer**, hō-rom'-et-ėr, *n.* An instrument to measure time.—**Horometrical**, hō-ro-met'ri-kal, *a.* Belonging to horometry.—**Horometry**, hō-rom'et-ri, *n.* The art of measuring time by hours and subordinate divisions.—**Horoscope**, hō'ros-kōp, *n.* [Gr. *hōroskopos*—*hōra*, hour, and *skopeō*, to view.] A scheme or figure of the heavens at a given time, used by astrologers to foretell future events and the fortunes of persons, according to the position of the stars at the time of their birth. — **Horoscopist**, hō-ros'ko-pist, *n.* One versed in horoscopy.—**Horoscopic**, hō-ros-kop'ik, *a.* Relating to horoscopy.—**Horoscopy**, hō-ros'ko-pi, *n.* The predicting of future events by the disposition of the stars and planets.

Horrible, hor'ri-bl, *a.* [L. *horribilis*, from *horreo*, to bristle or stand on end, to be terrified; akin to *hirtus*, shaggy, *hirsutus*, hirsute.] Exciting or tending to excite horror; dreadful; terrible; shocking; hideous.—**Horrent**, hor'ent, *a.* [L. *horrens*, *horrentis*.] Bristling. — **Horribleness**, hor'ri-bl-nes, *n.* The state or quality of being horrible.—**Horribly**, hor'ri-bli, *adv.* In a horrible manner; excessively; very much.—**Horrid**, hor'rid, *a.* [L. *horridus*, from *horreo*.] Fitted to excite horror; dreadful; hideous; shocking; very offensive (*colloq.*).—**Horridly**, hor'rid-li, *adv.* In a horrid manner.—**Horridness**, hor'rid-nes, *n.* The quality of being horrid. — **Horrific**, hor-rif'ik, *a.* [L. *horrificus*.] Causing horror.—**Horrify**, hor'ri-fī, *v.t.*—

horrified, horrifying. [L. *horror*, and *facio*, to make.] To strike or impress with horror.—**Horripilation**, hor'ri-pi-lā"shon, *n.* [L. *horreo*, to bristle, *pilus*, hair.] The bristling or standing on end of the hair.—**Horror**, hor'rėr, *n.* [L., from *horreo.*] A powerful feeling of fear, dread, and abhorrence; a shuddering with terror and loathing; that which excites horror.

Hors de combat, ar-dė-kon-bä'. [Fr.] Out of the fighting; disabled.

Hors d'oeuvre, ar-du'vr. [Fr.] An appetizer or relish (usually in pl.).

Horse, hors, *n.* [A.Sax. *hors* = Icel. *hross, hors*, O.H.G. *hros*, G. *ross*, D. *ros*, allied to Skr. *hreca*, neighing, or to L. *curro*, to run.] A well-known quadruped, the most important to man of all animals that are used as beasts of burden and of draught; the male animal, in distinction from the female called a *mare*; cavalry; troops serving on horseback (in this sense no plural termination); a wooden frame with legs for supporting something; *naut.* a rope attached to a yard to support the sailors while they loose, reef, or furl the sails.—[*Horse*, in compounds, often implies largeness or coarseness; as *horse*-chestnut, *horse*-play.]—*To take horse*, to mount or set out on horseback.—*v.t.*—*horsed, horsing.* To provide with a horse; to supply a horse or horses for; to sit astride; to bestride (*Shak.*).—**Horse-artillery**, *n. Milit.* field-artillery with lighter guns than ordinary field-artillery, and all the gunners mounted.—**Horseback**, hors'bak, *n.* The back of a horse; that part on which the rider sits: generally in the phrase *on horseback*, that is, mounted or riding on a horse.—**Horse-barracks**, *n. pl.* Barracks for cavalry.—**Horse-box**, *n.* A closed carriage for transporting horses by railway.—**Horse-breaker**, *n.* One whose employment is to break or train horses.—**Horse-chestnut**, *n.* A well-known tree with beautiful flowers, often planted for ornament, the nuts of which have been used as food for animals.—**Horse-cloth**, *n.* A cloth to cover a horse.—**Horse-dealer**, *n.* One who buys and sells horses.—**Horse-doctor**, *n.* One who treats the diseases of horses; a farrier.—**Horse-drench**, *n.* A dose of physic for a horse; the instrument by which it is administered.—**Horseflesh**, hors'flesh, *n.* The flesh of a horse; horses generally; a species of mahogany.—**Horsefly**, hors'flī, *n.* A large fly that sucks the blood of horses.—**Horse-guards**, *n. pl.* A body of cavalry for guards.—*The Horse-guards*, the public office appropriated to the departments under the commander-in-chief of the British army; the military authorities at the head of the British war department, in contradistinction to the civil chief, who is the secretary-at-war.—**Horse-hair**, *n. sing.* and *pl.* The hair of horses, more particularly of the mane and tail.—**Horse-hoe**, *n.* An agricultural implement consisting of hoe blades attached to a frame and drawn by a horse.—**Horse-jockey**, *n.* A jockey.—**Horse-laugh**, *n.* A loud, coarse, boisterous laugh.—**Horseleech**, *n.* A large species of leech; a horse-doctor: a farrier.—**Horse-load**, *n.* A load for a horse.—**Horse-mackerel**, *n.* A fish about the size of a mackerel, with oily rank flesh.—**Horseman**, hors'man, *n.* A man who rides on horseback; one who uses and manages a horse; a soldier who serves on horseback; a variety of pigeon.—**Horsemanship**, hors'man-ship, *n.* The art of riding and managing horses; equestrian skill.—**Horse-mill**, *n.* A mill turned by a horse or horses.—**Horse-milliner**, *n.* One who supplies ribbons and other decorations for horses.—**Horse-nail**, *n.* A nail for fastening a horse's shoe to the hoof.—**Horse-play**, *n.* Rough or rude practical jokes or the like; rude pranks.—**Horse-pond**, *n.* A pond for watering horses.—**Horse-power**, *n.* The power of a horse or its equivalent; the force with which a horse acts when drawing; the standard for estimating the power of a steam-engine, each horse-power being estimated as equivalent to 33,000 lb. raised one foot high per minute.—**Horse-race**, *n.* A race by horses; a match of horses in running.—**Horse-racing**, *n.* The practice or art of running horses.—**Horse-radish**, *n.* A perennial plant of the cabbage family, the white cylindrical root of which has a pungent taste, and is used as a condiment with roast beef.—**Horse-rug**, *n.* A woollen cover for a horse.—**Horse-shoe**, *n.* A shoe for horses, commonly a piece of iron, in shape resembling the letter U, nailed to the horse's foot; anything shaped like a horse-shoe.—*Horse-shoe magnet*, an artificial steel magnet nearly in the form of a horse-shoe.—**Horse-soldier**, *n.* A cavalry soldier.—**Horse-tail**, *n.* The tail of a horse; a standard of rank and honour among the Turks, consisting of one or more tails of horses mounted on a lance; an equisetum (which see).—**Horsewhip**, hors'whip, *n.* A whip for driving or striking horses.—*v.t.*—*horsewhipped, horsewhipping.* To lash or strike with a horsewhip.—**Horsewoman**, hors'wum-an, *n.* A woman who rides on horseback; an equestrienne.—**Horsy, Horsey**, hor'si, *a.* Connected with, fond of, or much taken up with horses.—**Horsiness**, hor'si-nes, *n.* The quality of being horsy.

Hortation, hor-tā'shon, *n.* [L. *hortatio*, from *hortor*, to exhort.] The act of exhorting; exhortation.—**Hortative**, hor'ta-tiv, *a.* Giving exhortation.—*n.* A precept given to incite or encourage; exhortation.—**Hortatory**, hor'ta-to-ri, *a.* Exhortative.

Horticulture, hor'ti-kul-tūr, *n.* [L. *hortus*, a garden (same root as *garden, yard*). and *cultura*, culture.] The cultivation of a garden; the art of cultivating or managing gardens.—**Horticultural**, hor-ti-kul'tūr-al, *a.* Pertaining to horticulture.—**Horticulturist, Horticultor**,† hor-ti-kul'tūr-ist, hor'ti-kul-tėr, *n.* One who practises horticulture.—**Hortus Siccus**, hor'tus sik'kus, *n.* [L.] *Lit.* a dry garden; a collection of specimens of plants carefully dried and preserved; a herbarium.

Hosanna, ho-zan'na, *n.* [Heb., save, I beseech you.] An exclamation of praise to God, or an invocation of blessings.

Hose, hōz, *n.* [A.Sax. *hosa* (pl. *hosan*), a leg-covering = D. *hoos*, Icel. *hosa*, G. and Dan. *hose*; comp. A.Sax. *hose*, Dan. *hase*, a husk; perhaps allied to *house.*] Stockings; socks (in these senses now used as a plural); close-fitting trousers or breeches reaching to the knee; covering for the lower part of the legs, including the feet; a flexible tube or pipe for conveying water or other fluid to any required point.—*v.t.* To apply water, &c., by means of a hose, as to *hose* a garden.—**Hose-reel**, *n.* A large revolving drum or reel for carrying hose for fire engines, &c.—**Hosiery**, hō'zhi-ėr-i, *n.* Stockings, or goods similarly knitted; also a place where knit goods are made or sold.

Hospice, hos'pis, *n.* [Fr., from L. *hospitium*, hospitality, a lodging, an inn.] A place of refuge and entertainment for travellers on some difficult road or pass, as among the Alps.

Hospitable, hos'pi-ta-bl, *a.* [Fr. *hospitable*, L. *hospitalis*, from *hospes, hospitis*, a host, a guest. HOST.] Receiving and entertaining strangers with kindness and without reward; kind to strangers and guests; pertaining to the liberal entertainment of guests.—**Hospitableness**, hos'pi-ta-bl-nes, *n.* The quality of being hospitable.—**Hospitably**, hos'pi-ta-bli, *adv.* In a hospitable manner.—**Hospital**, hos'pi-tal, *n.* [O.Fr. *hospital*, L.L. *hospitale*. *Hotel, hostel*, are doublets of this.] A building or institution for the reception and treatment of the old, sick, &c., for the education and support of orphans, or for the benefit of any class of persons who are more or less dependent upon public help.—**Hospitality**, hos-pi-tal'i-ti, *n.* [L. *hospitalitas.*] The kind and generous reception and entertainment of strangers or guests; fondness for entertaining guests at one's house; hospitable treatment or disposition.—**Hospitaler**, hos'pi-tal-ėr, *n.* A member of a religious body whose office it was to relieve the poor, the stranger, and the sick; one of an order of knights who built a hospital at Jerusalem in A.D. 1042 for pilgrims, called *Knights of St. John*, and, after their removal to Malta, *Knights of Malta.*

Hospodar, hos-pō-där', *n.* A Slavonic title formerly borne by the princes of Moldavia and Wallachia, &c.

Host, hōst, *n.* [O.Fr. *hoste*, Fr. *hôte*; from L. *hospes, hospitis*, a host, for *hostipes*, from *hostis*, an enemy, a stranger (akin E. *guest*), and root *pa*, to protect, as in L. *pater*, a father, *potens*, powerful. From *hospes* are also derived *hospital, hostler, hotel*, &c.] One who receives and entertains another at his own house; a landlord: the correlative of *guest*; an animal or organism in or on whose organs a parasite exists.—**Hostess**, hōs'tes, *n.* A female host.

Host, hōst, *n.* [O.Fr. *host*, from L. *hostis*, a stranger, an enemy, in later usage an army; *guest* is cog. with *hostis*. See also HOST, above.] An army; a number of men embodied for war; any greater number or multitude.

Host, hōst, *n.* [L. *hostia*, a sacrificial victim, from *hostire*, to strike.] The altar-bread or wafer in the eucharist, or in the Roman Catholic sacrament of the mass.

Hostage, hos'tāj, *n.* [O.Fr. *hostage*, Fr. *ôtage*. L.L. *hostagius, obstagius, obsidaticus*, from L. *obses, obsidis*, hostage—*ob*, at, near, *sedeo*, to sit.] A person handed over to an enemy as a pledge for the performance of certain conditions.

Hostel, Hostelry, hos-tel, hos'tel-ri, *n.* [HOTEL.] An inn; a lodging-house.

Hostile, hos'tīl, *a.* [L. *hostilis*, from *hostis*, an enemy. See HOST, army.] Belonging to an enemy; holding the position of an enemy or enemies; showing ill-will and malevolence.—**Hostilely**, hos'tīl-li, *adv.* In a hostile manner.—**Hostility**, hos-til'i-ti, *n.* [L. *hostilitas.*] State of being hostile; an act of an open enemy; an act of warfare (in this sense generally *pl.*).

Hostler, os'lėr, *n.* [O.Fr. *hostelier*, from *hostel*, Mod. Fr. *hôtel*, an inn, from L.L. *hospitale*, a hospital. HOTEL.] The person who has the care of horses at an inn, formerly the innkeeper; a stable-boy.

Hot, hot, *a.* [A.Sax. *hát* = Sc. *het*. D. *heet*, Sw. *het*, Dan. *hed, heed*, Icel. *heitr*, G. *heiss*, HEAT.] Having much sensible heat; exciting the feeling of warmth in a great or powerful degree; very warm; ardent in temper; easily excited or exasperated; vehement; violent; furious; animated; brisk; keen; lustful; lewd; acrid; biting; stimulating; pungent.—**Hotbed**, hot'bed, *n.* *Hort.* a bed of earth heated by fermenting substances, and covered with glass, used for growing early or exotic plants; a place which favours rapid growth or development; generally in a bad sense (a *hotbed* of sedition).—**Hot-blast**, *n.* A blast of hot air; a current of heated air injected into a smelting-furnace by a blowing-engine to further the combustion of the fuel.—**Hot-blooded**, *a.* Having hot blood; having warm passions; irritable.—**Hot-dog**, a hot frankfurter, usually served in a roll.—**Hot-headed**, *a.* Violent; rash; impetuous.—**Hothouse**, hot'hous, *n.* A greenhouse or house to shelter tender plants, artificially heated; a conservatory.—**Hotly**, hot'li, *adv.* In a hot manner.—**Hotness**, hot'nes, *n.* The condition or quality of being hot.—**Hot-press**, *v.t.* To apply heat to in conjunction with mechanical pressure in order to produce a smooth and glossy surface (to *hot-press* paper or cloth).—**Hot water**, *n.* Heated water; *fig.* strife; contention; difficulties.

Hotchpot, hoch'pot, *n.* [Fr. *hochepot*—*hocher*, to shake (from D. or Flem. *hotsen*), and *pot*, a pot or dish.] A hodge-podge or mixture; *law*, a commixture of property for equality of division.—**Hotch-potch**, *n.* HODGE-PODGE.

Hotel, hō-tel', *n.* [Fr. *hôtel*, O.Fr. *hostel*, an inn; same word as *hospital, hostel.*] A house for entertaining strangers or travellers; an inn; especially, one of some style and pretensions; a large town mansion (*French usage*).—**Hôtel-de-ville**, ō-tel-dė-vēl *n.* [Fr.] A city-hall or townhouse.—**Hôtel-dieu**, ō-tel-dyė. [Fr.] A hospital.

Hottentot, hot'n-tot, *n.* [From D. *hot en tot*, *hot* and *tot*, syllables intended to imitate sounds frequent in their language.] A member of a degraded tribe or race of South Africa; the language of this people, characterized by curious clicking or clucking sounds.

Houdah, hou'dah, *n.* HOWDAH.

Hough, hok, *n.* [Written also *hock*, which see.] The hock of a horse; the back part of the human knee-joint; the ham.—*v.t.* To hamstring; to disable by cutting the sinews of the ham. (O.T.)

Houlet, hou'let, *n.* HOWLET.

Hound, hound, *n.* [A.Sax. *hund*, a dog or hound = G. Dan. and Sw. *hund*, D. *hond*, Icel. *hundr*, Goth. *hunds*; cog. W. *cun*, Gael. *cù*, L. *canis*, Gr. *kyōn*, Skr. *çvan*, a dog.] A term restricted to particular breeds or varieties of dogs used in the chase, as in hunting the deer, the fox, the hare; sometimes used as a term of contempt for a man. —*v.t.* To set on the chase; to incite to pursuit of animals; hence, to urge, incite, or spur to action: usually with *on*.—**Houndfish**, hound'fish, *n.* A name for certain fishes of the shark family.

Hour, our, *n.* [O.Fr. *hore*, *houre*, from L. *hora*, from Gr. *hōra*, a season, an hour; seen also in *horologe*, *horoscope*.] The twenty-fourth part of a day; sixty minutes; the particular time of the day; a fixed or appointed time; a time, period, or season; *pl.* certain prayers in the Roman Catholic Church, to be repeated at stated times of the day.—*To keep good hours*, to be at home regularly in good season, or not after the usual hours of retiring to rest; *to keep bad hours*, the opposite.—*The small hours*, the early hours of the morning, as one, two, &c.—**Hour-circle**, *n.* *Astron.* any great circle of the sphere which passes through the two poles; a meridian drawn on a terrestrial globe.—**Hour-glass**, *n.* A glass in two compartments connected by a narrow neck, for measuring time by the running of a quantity of sand from one compartment to the other.—**Hour-hand**, *n.* The hand which shows the hour on a clock or watch. —**Hourly**, our'li, *a.* Happening or done every hour; frequent; often repeated; continual.—*adv.* Every hour; frequently; continually.

Houri, hou'ri or hö'ri, *n.* [Ar.] Among the Mohammedans, a nymph of paradise.

House, hous, *n.* pl. **Houses**, hou'zez. [A.Sax. *hús* = Icel. *hús*, Dan. Sw. and Goth. *hus*, D. *huis*, G. *haus*; from root meaning to cover, as in *hide*, *hose*, *sky*, &c. Akin *husband*, *hussy*.] A building serving or intended to serve as an abode; a building for the habitation of man, or for his use or accommodation; a dwelling; an abode; a household; a family; a family regarded as consisting of ancestors, descendants, and kindred; especially a noble or illustrious family; a legislative body of men (the *House* of Representatives); a legislative quorum; the audience at a place of entertainment; a firm or commercial establishment; a twelfth part of the astrological heavens.—*House of Representatives*, the lower branch of the United States Congress.—*House organ*, a publication brought out by a business concern, &c., for its members.—*House party*, a social gathering, lasting one or more nights, usually at a country house.—*To bring down the house*, to draw forth a universal burst of applause, as in a theater.—*To keep house*, to maintain an independent family establishment.—*v.t.*—*housed, housing* (houz). To put or receive into a house; to provide with a dwelling or residence; to shelter; to cause to take shelter.—*v.i.* To take shelter or lodgings; to take up abode.—**House-boat**, *n.* A boat with a wooden house, for lodgings by river in summer.—**House-breaker**, *n.* One who breaks into a house with a felonious intent; a burglar.—**House-breaking**, *n.* Burglary.—**House-carl**, *n.* [*Hus-carl.*] A member of the body-guard of king or nobleman, e.g. of Harold at Hastings.—**House-carpenter**, *n.* A carpenter chiefly employed on the wood-work of houses.—**House-dog**, *n.* A dog kept to guard a house.—**House-fly**, *n.* A well-known two-winged fly common in dwelling-houses.—**Household**, hous'hōld, *n.* Those who dwell under the same roof and compose a family; those under the same domestic government; house; family.—*a.* Pertaining to the house and family; domestic.—*Household gods*, gods presiding over the house or family among the ancient Romans; hence, objects endeared to one from being associated with home.—*Household troops*, *Household brigade*, troops whose special duty it is to attend the sovereign and guard the metropolis.—**Householder**, hous'hōl-dėr, *n.* The chief of a household; the occupier of a house.—**Housekeeper**, hous'kē-pėr, *n.* A householder; a head female servant in a household; a female who looks after a person's household.—**Housekeeping**, hous'kē-ping, *n.* The management of domestic concerns; the maintenance of a household.—**Houseleek**, *n.* A well-known plant which grows on the tops of houses and on walls, and the fleshy leaves of which are applied to bruises and other sores.—**Houseless**, hous'les, *a.* Destitute of a house or habitation; without shelter.—**Houselessness**, hous'les-nes, *n.* The condition of being houseless.—**Housemaid**, hous'mād, *n.* A female servant employed to keep a house clean, &c. —**Houseroom**, hous'röm, *n.* Room or accommodation in a house.—**House-steward**, *n.* A male domestic who has the chief management of the internal affairs of a household.—**House-warming**, *n.* A merry-making at the time a family enters a new house.—**Housewife**, hous'wīf or less formally huz'if, *n.* The mistress of a family; the wife of a householder; a female manager of domestic affairs; a little case for needles, thread, scissors, &c.; a hussif.—**Housewifely**, hous'wīf-li, *a.* Pertaining to or like a housewife; thrifty.—**Housewifery**, hous'wīf-ri or huz'if-ri, *n.* The business or management of a housewife.

Housel, hou'zel, *n.* [A.Sax. *húsel*, offering, sacrament; Goth. *hunsl.*] The eucharist; the sacrament of the Lord's supper. (*Archaic.*)

Housing, hou'zing, *n.* [HOUSE.] Act of sheltering; the providing of houses and other dwelling quarters, as by a government; a frame to support machinery, &c., or parts of a machine.

Housing, hou'zing, *n.* [From Fr. *housse*, a covering, a horse-cloth; from D. *hulse*, a husk or shell; akin *holster*, *hull*, *husk.*] A cloth laid over a saddle; a saddle-cloth; a horse-cloth.

Hove, hōv, pret. of *heave*.

Hovel, hov'el, *n.* [Dim. of A.Sax. *hof*, a house, a dwelling = Icel. *hof*, a hall, G. *hof*, a court, a farm.] A poor cottage; a small mean house.

Hover, hov'ėr, *v.i.* [Perhaps from O.E. *hove*, to abide, to linger, same origin as *hovel*.] To hang fluttering in the air or upon the wing; to be in doubt or hesitation; to be irresolute; to move to and fro threateningly or watchingly (an army *hovering* on our borders).—**Hoveringly**, hov'ėr-ing-li, *adv.* In a hovering manner.

How, hou, *adv.* [A.Sax. *hú*, *hwú*, *hwý*, instrumental case of *hwá*, *hwæt*, who, what; really the same word as *why*.] In what manner; by what means or method; to what degree or extent; by what measure or quantity (*how* long, *how* much better); in what state, condition, or plight. Besides being used as an interrogative, direct or indirect, it is sometimes used interjectionally, or even substantively (the *how* and why of it).—**Howbeit**, hou-bē'it, *adv.* [*How*, *be*, and *it*.] However it be; be it as it may; nevertheless; however.—**However**, hou-ev'ėr, *adv.* In whatever manner or degree; in whatever state.—*conj.* Nevertheless; notwithstanding; yet; still; though.—**Howsoever**, hou-sō-ev'ėr, *adj.* or *conj.* In what manner soever; however.

Howdah, hou'da, *n.* [Hind. and Ar. *haudah.*] A seat erected on the back of an elephant for two or more persons to ride in: usually covered overhead.

Howitzer, hou'it-sėr, *n.* [From G. *haubitze*, from Bohem. *haufnice*, originally a sling.] A short gun firing a heavy shell with a low velocity, fired at a high angle, reaching objects not to be reached with direct fire; it represents the old *mortar*.

Howl, houl, *v.i.* [An imitative word = D. *huilen*, G. *heulen*, Dan. *hyle*, to howl; comp. L. *ululo*, Gr. *ololyzō*, to wail, to howl; akin *owl*, L. *ulula*, an owl.] To utter a loud, protracted, mournful cry, as that of a dog or wolf; to produce any similar sound, as the wind; to wail or lament (N.T.).—*v.t.* To utter in a loud or mournful tone.—*n.* The cry of a dog or wolf or other like sound; a cry of distress.—**Howler**, hou'lėr, *n.* One who howls; a name given to a monkey of South America from its cry; an error that cries aloud for correction. (*Colloq.*)—**Howling**, hou'ling, *a.* Filled with howls or howling beasts; dreary (a *howling* wilderness).

Howlet, hou'let, *n.* [From *owlet*, with *h* prefixed through the influence of *howl.*] An owl; an owlet. (*Archaic.*)

Hoy, hoi, *n.* [D. and G. *heu* (pron. hoi); Dan. *höy.*] A heavy barge; †a small coasting vessel.

Hoyden, **Hoiden**, hoi'dn, *n.* [O.D. *heyden*, a heathen, a gypsy, a vagabond. HEATHEN.] A rude, bold girl.—*a.* Romping, roistering. —*v.i.* To romp rudely; to act like a hoyden.

Hub, hub, *n.* [HOB.] The central cylindrical part of a wheel in which the spokes are set; the nave; a block of wood for stopping a carriage wheel; a mark at which quoits, &c., are cast; the hilt of a weapon.

Hubble-bubble, hub'l-bub'l, *n.* A kind of tobacco-pipe so arranged that the smoke passes through water, making a bubbling noise—hence its name; a hookah.

Hubbub, hub'ub, *n.* [Imitative of confused noise.] A noise of many confused voices; a tumult; uproar.

Huckaback, huk'a-bak, *n.* [Originally linen *hawked* or *huckstered* by being carried on the *back*.] A kind of linen cloth with raised figures on it, used principally for towels.

Huckle, huk'l, *n.* [Connected with *hook*; lit. a thing bent or hooked; akin *huckster*.] The hip; a bunch or part projecting like the hip.—**Huckle-backed**, *a.* Having roundshoulders; hump-backed.—**Huckleberry**, huk'l-be-ri, *n.* [Corruption of *whortleberry*.] A name for North American plants allied to the whortleberry.—**Huckle-bone**, *n.* The hip-bone.

Huckster, huk'stėr, *n.* [Akin to *hawker*; the name was given from the bending of the back in carrying a pack; comp. D. *hukken*, to squat, *heuker*, a hawker; G. *hocken*, to take on the back; Dan. *hökre*, to huckster; *huckle*, *hook*, are also akin.] A retailer of small articles; a hawker; one who higgles.—*v.i.* To deal in small articles or in petty bargains; to higgle.—*v.t.* To hawk or peddle; to make a matter of bargain.—**Hucksterage**, huk'stėr-āj, *n.* The business of a huckster.—**Hucksterer**, huk'stėr-ėr, *n.* A huckster.

Huddle, hud'l, *v.i.*—*huddled, huddling*. [Same word as G. *hudeln*, Dan. *hutle*, D. *hoetelen*, to bungle; akin *hustle*.] To crowd or press together without order or regularity; to hustle.—*v.t.* To crowd together without order; to produce in a hurried manner; to hunch one's body together, often with *up*.—*n.* A crowd or confused mass; a gathering of football players behind the line of scrimmage to receive instructions, &c.

Hudibrastic, hū-di-bras'tic, *a.* Pertaining to or resembling in style the poem *Hudibras*, by Samuel Butler.

Hue, hū, *n.* [A.Sax. *hiw, heow*, appearance; Sw. *hy*, colour; Goth. *hiwi*, shape, show.] Colour, or shade of colour; dye; tint; *painting*, a compound of one or more colours forming an intervenient shade.—**Hued**, hūd, *a.* Having a hue or colour.—**Hueless**, hū'les, *a.* Destitute of hue or colour.

Hue, hū, *n.* [Fr. *huer*, to hoot, to shout; akin *hoot*.] A shouting or clamour: used only in the phrase *hue and cry*, which is the outcry raised, or public warning at once given, by a person who has been robbed, or who knows that a felony has been committed.

Huff, huf, *n.* [An imitative word meaning lit. to blow, to puff; comp. *whiff*.] A fit of peevishness or petulance; anger at some offence, real or fancied; one filled with a false opinion of his own importance.—*To take huff*, to take offence.—*v.t.* To swell or puff up‡; to treat with insolence; to bully; to make angry.—*v.i.* To swell up; to bluster; to take offence.—**Huffiness**, huf'i-nes, *n.* The state of being huffy.—**Huffish**, huf'ish, *a.* Inclined to huff; insolent.—**Huffishly**, huf'ish-li, *adv.* In a huffish manner.—**Huffishness**, huf'ish-nes, *n.*—**Huffy**, huf'i, *a.* Puffed up; swelled; arrogant or insolent; easily offended.

Hug, hug, *v.t.*—*hugged, hugging.* [Origin doubtful; comp. Icel. *hugga*, to soothe, to comfort; D. *hugen*, to coax; Dan. *huge*, to squat.] To press closely with the arms; to embrace closely; to clasp to the breast; to grasp or gripe, as in wrestling; to cherish in the mind (to *hug* delusions); to keep close to (to *hug* the land in sailing): *refl.* to congratulate one's self.—*v.i.* To lie close; to crowd together (*Shak.*).—*n.* A close embrace; a clasp or gripe.—**Hugger**, hug'ėr, *n.* One who hugs.

Huge, hūj, *a.* [O.E. *huge*, also *hogge*; comp. O.Fr. *ahuge*, huge; origin unknown.] Having an immense bulk; very large or great; enormous; very great in any respect (a *huge* difference).—**Hugely**, hūj'li, *adv.* In a huge manner.—**Hugeness**, hūj'nes, *n.* The state of being huge.

Hugger-mugger, hug'ėr-mug'ėr, *n.* [Comp. *hug*, to lie close; obsolete *hugger*, to lurk; N. *mugg*, secrecy.] †Concealment; privacy; secrecy.—*a.* Clandestine; sly; confused; slovenly.

Huguenot, hū'ge-not, *n.* [Fr.; probably corrupted from G. *eidgenoss*, a confederate, there being found various early forms, such as *higuenot, eidguenot, enguenot, anguenot*, &c.] A French Protestant of the period of the religious wars in France in the sixteenth century.—**Huguenotism**, hū'ge-not-izm, *n.* The religion of the Huguenots.

Hulin process, hö'lin. An electrical method of manufacturing alkali.

Hulk, hulk, *n.* [Same word as D. *hulk*, G. *hulk, holk*, Sw. *holk*, a kind of ship, from L.L. *hulca, olca*, from Gr. *holkas*, a ship of burden, from *helkō*, to draw.] A heavy ship‡; the body of a ship; the body of an old ship laid by as unfit for service; something bulky or unwieldy.—*The hulks*, old or dismasted ships, formerly used as prisons.—**Hulking, Hulky**, hul'king, hul'ki, *a.* Large and clumsy of body; unwieldy; loutish.

Hull, hul, *n.* [A.Sax. *hulu*, a hull or husk; akin G. *hülle*, a covering, Goth. *huljan*, to cover; same root as in *hell, holster*.] The outer covering of something, particularly of fruits, grain, &c.; the husk; the body of a ship, exclusive of her masts, yards, and rigging.—*Hull down*, said of a ship when so distant that her hull is below the horizon.—*v.t.* To deprive of the hull or hulls; to pierce the hull of, as with a cannon-ball.—'To hull on the flood', of the ark; drifting, or sinking in the flood. (*Mil.*)—**Huller**, hul'ėr, *n.* One who hulls; a machine for separating seeds from their hulls.—**Hully**, hul'i, *a.* Having husks or pods.

Hullabaloo, hul'a-ba-lö", *n.* [Imitative of confused noise; comp. *hurly-burly*.] Uproar; noisy confusion.

Hullo, hul-lō', *interj.* [Same as *Halloo*.] An exclamation to call attention.

Hum, hum, *v.i.*—*hummed, humming.* [Imitative of sound; comp. G. *hummen, summen*, D. *hommelen*, to hum. *Humble-bee, humbug, humdrum* are connected.] To make a dull, prolonged sound, like that of a bee in flight; to drone; to murmur; to buzz; to give utterance to a similar sound with the mouth; to mumble; to make a drawling, inarticulate sound in speaking.—*v.t.* To sing in a low voice; to murmur without articulation.—*n.* The noise made by bees or any similar sound; a buzz; any inarticulate, low, murmuring, or buzzing sound; a murmur of applause; a low inarticulate sound uttered by a speaker.—*interj.* A sound with a pause, implying doubt and deliberation; ahem.—**Humming**, hum'ing, *n.* The sound of that which hums; a buzzing; a low murmuring sound.—**Humming-bird**, *n.* A name given to the individuals of a family of minute and beautiful birds, from the sound of their wings in flight. — **Humming-top**, *n.* A hollow spinning top, which, when spun, emits a loud humming noise.

Human, hū'man, *a.* [Fr. *humain*, L. *humanus*, from *homo, hominis*, a man (whence also *homage*); akin to *humus*, the ground (whence *humilis*, E. *humble*); also to A. Sax. *guma*, a man (seen in *bridegroom*).] Belonging to a man or mankind; having the qualities or attributes of man.—*n.* A human being. — **Humane**, hū-mān', *a.* [Same word as *human*.] Human‡; having the feelings and dispositions proper to man; kind; benevolent; tender; merciful; tending to humanize or refine.—**Humanely**, hū-mān'li, *adv.* In a humane manner.—**Humaneness**, hū-mān'nes, *n.* The quality of being humane.—**Humanify**, hū-man'i-fī, *v.t.* To render human.—**Humanism**, hū'man-izm, *n.* Classical learning; a philosophical system. — **Humanist**, hū'man-ist, *n.* One who studies the humanities; one versed in the knowledge of human nature; one at the revival of letters devoted to the study of the ancient classics. So *Literæ Humaniores*, not rendering more humane, but as opposed to sacred studies.—**Humanistic**, hū-man-is'tik, *a.* Of or pertaining to humanity. — **Humanitarian**, hū-man'i-tā"ri-an, *n.* One who has a great regard or love for humanity; a philanthropist; one who denies the divinity of Christ, and believes him to have been a mere man; one who maintains the perfectibility of human nature without the aid of grace.—**Humanitarianism**, hū-man'i-tā"ri-an-izm, *n.* The practices or beliefs of a humanitarian.—**Humanity**, hū-man'i-ti, *n.* [Fr. *humanité*, L. *humanitas*, from *humanus*.] The quality of being human; humanness; mankind collectively; the human race; the quality of being humane; tenderness and kindness towards all created beings: opposed to *cruelty*; classical and polite literature or a branch of such literature: in this sense generally plural and with the definite article—'*the humanities*': but in the Scottish universities used in the singular and applied to Latin and Latin literature alone.—**Humanization**, hū'man-i-zā"shon, *n.* The act of humanizing.—**Humanize**, hū'man-īz, *v.t.*—*humanized, humanizing.* To render human or humane.—*v.i.* To become more humane; to become more civilized.—**Humanizer**, hū'man-ī-zėr, *n.* One who humanizes.—**Humankind**, hū'man-kīnd, *n.* The race of man; mankind; the human species.—**Humanly**, hū'man-li, *adv.* In a human manner; after the manner of men.—**Humanness**, hū'man-nes, *n.* The state or quality of being human.

Humble, hum'bl, *a.* [Fr. *humble*, from L. *humilis*, from *humus*, the earth (seen also in *exhume*). HUMILIATE, HUMAN.] Of a low, mean, or unpretending character; not grand, lofty, noble, or splendid; having a low estimate of one's self; not proud; arrogant, or assuming; lowly; modest; meek; submissive.—*v.t.*—*humbled, humbling.* To render humble; to reduce the power, independence, or state of; to bring down; to abase; to lower; to bring down the pride or vanity of: often *refl.*—*Humble-pie*. Under HUMBLES.—**Humbleness**, hum'bl-nes, *n.* The state of being humble or low.—**Humbler**, hum'blėr, *n.* One who or that which humbles.—**Humbly**, hum'bli, *adv.* In a humble manner; meekly; submissively.

Humblebee, hum'bl-bē, *n.* [From old *humble*, to hum, from *hum*; comp. G. *hummel*, Dan. *humle-bi*, Sw. *humla*, humblebee; from the humming sound it makes; whence also *bumble-bee*. HUM.] The common name of various large wild bees; the bumblebee.

Humbles, hum'blz, *n. pl.* [Fr., L. *umbilicus*, the navel.] The heart, liver, kidneys, &c., of a deer.—**Humble-pie**, *n.* A pie made of the *humbles*, or heart, liver, kidneys, &c., of the deer.—*To eat humble-pie*, to have to take a humble tone; to come down from an assumed position; to apologize, or humiliate one's self, abjectly: the phrase arose from the humbles being allotted to the huntsmen and servants, the meaning being influenced by the adj. *humble*.

Humbug, hum'bug, *n.* [From *hum* and *bug*, *hum* having its old sense of to deceive, and *bug* its old meaning of *bugbear*; hence = false alarm.] An imposition played off under fair pretences; a hoax; spirit of deception or imposition; falseness; hollowness; a cheat; a trickish fellow. — *v.t.* — *humbugged, humbugging.* To impose on; to cajole or trick; to hoax.—**Humbugger**, hum-bug'ėr, *n.* One who humbugs.—**Humbuggery**, hum'bug-ėr-i, *n.* The practice of humbugging; quackery.

Humdrum, hum'drum, *a.* [From *hum* and *drum*; originally droning, monotonous.] Commonplace; homely; dull; heavy.—*n.* A droning tone of voice; dull monotony.

Humectate, hū-mek'tāt, *v.t.* [L. *humecto, humectatum*—*humectus*, moist, *humeo*, to be moist.]† To moisten.—**Humectation**, hū-mek-tā'shon, *n.* The act of moistening or wetting†; *med.* the application of moistening remedies.—**Humective**, hū-mek'tiv, *a.* Having the power to moisten.—**Humefy**, hū'me-fī, *v.t.* To moisten; to soften with water.

Humeral, hū'mėr-al, *a.* [L. *humerus*, the shoulder.] Belonging to the shoulder.—**Humerus**, hū'mėr-us, *n.* *Anat.* the long cylindrical bone of the arm, situated between the shoulder-blade and the forearm; also the shoulder.

Humic. Under HUMUS.

Humid, hū'mid, *a.* [L. *humidus, umidus*, from *humeo, umeo*, to be moist (akin *uvidus*, moist, *uva*, a grape); whence also *humor*.] Moist; damp; wet or watery.—**Humidify**, hū-mid'i-fī, *v.t.* to moisten, to make humid, especially the atmosphere.—**Humidity, Humidness**, hū-mid'i-ti, hū'mid-nes, *n.* The state of being humid; *meteor.* the ratio of the amount of aqueous vapor in the air to the amount that would saturate it at the same temperature; expressed as a percentage.—**Humidor**, hū'mi-dōr, *n.* A box in which a suitable humidity is maintained, especially one for storing tobacco.

Humiliate, hū-mil'i-āt, *v.t.*—*humiliated, humiliating.* [L. *humilio, humiliatum*, from *humilis*, humble. HUMBLE.] To reduce to a lower position in one's own estimation or the estimation of others; to humble; to depress.—**Humiliating**, hū-mil'i-āt-ing, *p.* and *a.* Humbling; reducing self-confidence; mortifying.—**Humiliation**, hū-mil'i-ā"shon, *n.* The act of humiliating; the state of being humiliated, humbled, or mortified.—**Humility**, hū-mil'i-ti, *n.* [L. *humilitas*.] The state or quality of being humble; humbleness; lowliness of mind; a feeling of one's own insignificance.—**Humiliant**,† hū-mil'i-ant, *a.* Humiliating.

Humming, *n.* Under HUM.

Hummock, hum'ok, *n.* [Probably a dim. form of *hump*.] A rounded knoll; a mound; a hillock; a protuberance on an ice-field.—**Hummocked**, hum'okt, *a.* Characterized by hummocks.—**Hummocky**, hum'ok-i, *a.* Abounding in hummocks.

Humor, Humour, hū′mėr, ū′mėr, *n.* [Fr. *humeur*; L. *humor*, moisture, liquid, from *humeo*, to be moist. HUMID.] Moisture or moist matter; fluid matter in the human or an animal body, not blood (the vitreous *humor* of the eye); a morbid fluid collected; *old med.* a fluid, of which there were four—blood, phlegm, yellow bile, and black bile—on the conditions and proportions of which the bodily and mental health was supposed to depend; hence, turn or frame of mind; disposition, or a peculiarity of disposition, often temporary (not in the *humor* for reading); a caprice, whim, or fancy (*Shak.*); temper (as regards anger or annoyance or the opposite); that mental quality which gives to ideas a ludicrous or fantastic turn, and tends to excite laughter or mirth; a quality or faculty akin to wit, but depending for its effect rather on kindly human feeling than on point or brilliancy of expression.—*Bad humor*, feeling of irritation, annoyance, or displeasure.—*Good humor*, feeling of cheerfulness; good temper.—*Out of humor*, out of temper; displeased; annoyed.—*v.t.* To comply with the humor or inclination of; to sooth by compliance; to gratify; to indulge; to adapt one's self to.—**Humoral**, hū′mėr-al, *a.* Pertaining to or proceeding from the humors of the body (*humoral* pathology).—**Humoralism**, hū′mėr-al-izm, *n.* The doctrine that diseases have their seat in the humors.—**Humoralist**, hū′mėr-al-ist, *n.* One who favors the humoral pathology.—**Humoric**, hū′mėr-ik, *a.* Pertaining to humors.—**Humorific**, † hū-mėr-if′ik, *a.* Producing humor.—**Humorism**, hū′mėr-izm, *n.* Humoralism.—**Humorist**, hū′mėr-ist, *n.* Formerly, a person who exhibited certain strong peculiarities of disposition or manner; one who indulged in whims or eccentricities; now, one that makes use of a humorous style in speaking or writing; one whose conversation or writings are full of humor; one who has a playful fancy or genius; a wag; also, one who attributes all diseases to a depraved state of the humors.—**Humoristic**, hū-mėr-is′tik, *a.* Pertaining to or like a humorist.—**Humorize**, hū′mėr-iz, *v.t.* To fall in with the humor of anything or of any person.—**Humorous**, hū′mėr-us, *a.* Moist or humid‡; full of humor; exciting laughter; jocular; governed by humor or caprice; capricious; whimsical.—**Humorously**, hū′mėr-us-li, *adv.* In a humorous manner; pleasantly; jocosely.—**Humorousness**, hū′mėr-us-nes, *n.* The state or quality of being humorous.—**Humorsome**, hū′mėr-sum, *a.* Influenced by humors or whims; capricious; petulant.

Humous. Under HUMUS.

Hump, hump, *n.* [A nasalized form of *hub* or *hob* = L.G. *hump*, heap; D. *homp*, a lump; akin *hunch*, *heap*.] A protuberance; especially, the protuberance formed by a crooked back; a hunch.—**Humpback**, hump′bak, *n.* A back with a hump; a person who has such a back; a whale that has a hump on the back.—**Humpbacked**, hump′bakt, *a.* Having a crooked back.—**Humped**, humpt, *a.* Having a hump.—**Humpy**, hump′i, *a.* Full of humps.

Humph, humf, *interj.* An exclamation expressive of disbelief, doubt, dissatisfaction, or the like.

Humus, hū′mus, *n.* [L. *humus*, soil.] Vegetable mold; a dark-brown or blackish matter from decayed vegetable substances.—**Humic**, hū′mik, *a.* Obtained from or pertaining to humus.

Hunch, hunsh, *n.* [A form of *hump*.] A hump; a lump; a thick piece; a push or jerk with the fist or elbow.—*v.t.* To make a hunch on; to push with the elbow.—**Hunchback**, hunsh′bak, *n.* A humpback; a humpbacked person.—**Hunchbacked**, hunsh′bakt, *a.* Humpbacked.—**Hunched**, hunsht, *a.* Having a hunch or hump.

Hundred, hun′dred, *a.* [A.Sax. *hundred* = Icel. *hundrath*, Dan. *hundrede*, D. *honderd*, G. *hundert*; from *hund*, cog. with L. *centum*, Skr. *catam*, a hundred, and a termination akin to E. *read*, and to Goth. *garathjan*, to reckon.] Ten times ten; ninety and ten added.—*n.* The product of ten multiplied by ten; a collection of ten times ten individuals or units; a division of a county in England, supposed to have originally contained a *hundred* families or freemen.—**Hundred-fold**, *n.* A hundred times as much.—**Hundredth**, hun′dredth, *a.* The ordinal of a hundred; one portion of a hundred equal parts into which anything is divided.—*n.* The one after the ninety-ninth; one of a hundred equal parts of a thing.—**Hundred-weight**, hun′dred-wāt, *n.* A weight, usually denoted by *cwt.*, containing 100 pounds in the United States; in England, 112 pounds.

Hung, hung, pret. & pp. of *hang*.

Hungarian, hung-gā′ri-an, *n.* A native of Hungary; a Magyar; the language of the Hungarians; Magyar. — *a.* Pertaining to Hungary. — **Hungary-balsam**, *n.* A kind of turpentine.—**Hungary-water**, *n.* A perfume and stimulant from water and alcohol flavoured with rosemary, &c., and then distilled: first made for a queen of Hungary.

Hunger, hung′gėr, *n.* [A.Sax. *hunger*, *hungor* = G. Dan. and Sw. *hunger*, Icel. *hungr*, Goth. *huhrus*, hunger.] An uneasy sensation occasioned by the want of food; a craving for food; craving appetite; strong or eager desire.—*v.i.* To feel hunger; to crave food; to desire eagerly; to long.—**Hunger-bit, Hunger-bitten**, *a.* Pained, pinched, or weakened by hunger.—**Hungerer**, hung′gėr-ėr, *n.* One who hungers. — **Hungerly**,† hung′gėr-li, *a.* Hungry (*Shak.*).—*adv.* With keen appetite (*Shak.*). — **Hungrily**, hung′gri-li, *adv.* In a hungry manner. — **Hungry**, hung′gri, *a.* [A.Sax. *hungrig*.] Feeling hunger; having a keen appetite; eagerly desirous; proceeding from hunger.

Hunk, hungk, *n.* [A form of *hunch*.] A large lump; a hunch.

Hunks, hungks, *n.* [Perhaps from *hunk*, a piece, a lump.] A covetous sordid man; a miser; a niggard.

Hunky, Hunky-dory, *a.* All right; satisfactory; comfortable. (*Slang.*)

Huns, hunz, *n.* The barbarous race of Tartar origin, invading Italy under Attila, the Scourge of God, A.D. 451-3; derogatory name applied to German soldiers during the World War.

Hunt, hunt, *v.t.* [A.Sax. *huntian*, to hunt, akin to *hentan*, to seize; O.G. *hundjan*, Goth. (*fra*)*hinthan*, to catch: allied to E. *hand*, and to *hind* (female deer).] To chase, search for, or follow after (wild animals, particularly quadrupeds), for the purpose of catching or killing; to search after, pursue, follow closely; to pursue game or wild animals over (to *hunt* a district).—*To hunt up* or *out*, to seek for; to search for. — *To hunt down*, to pursue and kill or capture; to exterminate in a locality.—*v.i.* To follow the chase; to go in pursuit of game or other wild animals; to seek by close pursuit; to search: with *after* or *for*. —*n.* The chasing of wild animals; a pursuit; a chase; a pack of hounds; an association of huntsmen in a district.—**Hunter**, hun′tėr, *n.* One who hunts; a huntsman; a horse used in the chase; a watch whose glass is protected by a metal cover.—**Hunting-horn**, *n.* A bugle; a horn used in hunting. — **Hunting-box, Hunting-lodge, Hunting-seat**, *n.* A residence occupied for the purpose of hunting.—**Hunting-watch**, *n.* Under HUNTER. —**Huntress**, hunt′res, *n.* A female that hunts or follows the chase.—**Huntsman**, hunts′man, *n.* One who hunts or who practises hunting; a person whose office it is to manage the chase. — **Huntsmanship**, hunts′man-ship, *n.* The qualifications of a huntsman. — **Hunt's-up**, *n.* The tune formerly played on the horn under the windows of sportsmen to awaken them, to show that the game was roused by the hounds, and the hunt was to begin.

Hurdle, hėr′dl, *n.* [A.Sax. *hyrdel*, a dim. corresponding to G. *horde*, *hürde*, a hurdle; Icel. *hurth*, Goth. *haurds*, a door; akin E. *hoarding*.] A movable frame made of interlaced twigs or sticks, or of bars or rods crossing each other varying in form according to its use.—*v.t.*—*hurdled*, *hurdling*. To fence or provide with hurdles.—**Hurdle-race**, *n.* A race of men or horses over hurdles or fences.

Hurds, hėrdz, *n. pl.* [HARDS.] The coarse part of flax or hemp; hards.

Hurdy-gurdy, hėr′di-gėr′di, *n.* [Intended to suggest its sound.] A stringed instrument, whose tones are produced by the friction of a wheel acting the part of a bow against four strings; various instruments, usually playing street music, operated by turning a handle.

Hurl, hėrl, *v.t.* [A contracted form of *hurtle*, influenced by *whirl*.] To send whirling or flying through the air; to throw or dash with violence; to emit or utter with vehemence. — *v.i.*† To move rapidly; to whirl.—*n.* The act of throwing with violence. — **Hurler**, hėr′lėr, *n.* One who hurls. — **Hurling**, hėrl′ing, *n.* An old game of ball.

Hurly, Hurly-burly, hėr′li, hėr′li-bėr′li, *n.* [Intended to express by its sound noise or confusion, suggested by *hurl* or *hurry*; comp. Dan. *hurlumhei*, hurry-scurry; Fr. *hurluberlu*, a hare-brained person.] Tumult; bustle; confusion.

Hurrah, Hurray, hu̥-rä′, hu̥-rā, *interj.* [Comp. E. *huzza*, G. *hurrah*, Dan. and Sw. *hurra*, Pol. *hura*.] An exclamation expressive of joy, applause, or encouragement; also used as a noun.—*v.i.* To utter a hurrah.—*v.t.* To receive with hurrahs; to encourage by cheering.

Hurricane, hur′i-kān, *n.* [Sp. *huracan*, Fr. *ouragan*, D. *orkaan*, G. *orkan*, all from a native American word.] An extremely violent tempest or storm of wind; anything resembling a violent tempest.—*Hurricane-deck*, an elevated deck in steamboats, especially the deck above a saloon.

Hurry, hur′i, *v.t.*—*hurried*, *hurrying*. [Akin to G. *hurren*, to move hastily; Icel. *hurr*, a confused noise; Dan. *hurre*, to buzz; Sw. *hurra*, to whirl; imitative like *whirr*, *hurly-burly*, &c.] To impel to greater speed or haste; to urge to act or proceed with precipitance; to cause to be performed with great or undue rapidity; to impel to violent or thoughtless action.—*v.i.* To move or act with haste; to proceed with precipitation; to make great haste in going.—*n.* The act of hurrying; urgency; bustle; confusion.—**Hurried**, hur′id, *p.* and *a.* Done in a hurry; evidencing hurry. — **Hurriedly**, hur′id-li, *adv.* In a hurried manner.—**Hurriedness**, hur′id-nes, *n.* State of being hurried.—**Hurrier**, hur′i-ėr, *n.* One who hurries.—**Hurryingly**, hur′i-ing-li, *adv.* In a hurrying manner. — **Hurry-skurry**, hur′i-skur′i, *adv.* [*Hurry* and *scurry*.] Confusedly; in a bustle.—*n.* Fluttering haste; great confusion.

Hurst, hėrst, *n.* [A.Sax. *hyrst*, O.D. *horst*, O.H.G. *hurst*, *horst*, Sw. *hurst*, a grove, a wood.] A wood or grove.

Hurt, hėrt, *v.t.* pret. & pp. *hurt*. [O.Fr. *hurter*, Mod.Fr. *heurter*, to knock against; perhaps of Celtic origin; comp. W. *hwyrdd*, a push, a thrust, a blow. Hence *hurtle*, *hurl*.] To cause physical pain to; to wound or bruise painfully; to cause mental pain; to wound the feelings of; to cause injury, loss, or diminution to; to impair; to damage; to harm.—*n.* A wound, a bruise, or the like; injury; loss; damage; detriment. —**Hurtful**, hėrt′fu̥l, *a.* Causing hurt; harmful; injurious; mischievous; detrimental.—**Hurtfully**, hėrt′fu̥l-li, *adv.* In a hurtful manner. — **Hurtfulness**, hėrt′fu̥l-nes, *n.* The quality of being hurtful.—**Hurtless**, hėrt′les, *a.* Inflicting no injury; harmless; receiving no injury. — **Hurtlessly**, hėrt′les-li, *adv.* Without harm.—**Hurtlessness**, hėrt′les-nes, *n.*

Hurtle, hėr′tl, *v.i.* — *hurtled*, *hurtling*. [From *hurt*.] To clash or meet in shock; to make a sound suggestive of hostile clash; to clash; to sound threateningly; to resound.

Hurtleberry, hėr'tl-be-ri, *n.* WHORTLEBERRY.

Husband, huz'band, *n.* [A.Sax. *húsbonda*, the master of the house, from Icel. *hús-bóndi* (*hús*, house, and *búandi*, dwelling in), Dan. *huusbond*, Sw. *husbonde*, the master of the house; A.Sax. *búan*, Icel. *búa*, G. *bauen*, to inhabit, to cultivate. HOUSE, BOOR.] A man joined to a woman by marriage: the correlative of *wife*.—*Ship's husband*, an agent of the owners who sees that a ship is supplied with stores and properly repaired before she proceeds to sea.—*v.t.* To spend, apply, or use with economy; to keep from spending in view of an effort required.—**Husbandless**, huz'-band-les, *a.* Destitute of a husband.—**Husbandly**, huz'band-li, *a.* Frugal; thrifty.—**Husbandman**, huz'band-man, *n.* A farmer; a cultivator; one engaged in agriculture. — **Husbandry**, huz'band-ri, *n.* Domestic economy; good management; frugality; thrift; the business of a husbandman; agriculture.

Hush, hush, *a.* [Akin to *hist*, *whist*, *hiss*; G. *husch*, Dan. *hys*, *hyst*, a sound made to enjoin silence.] Silent; still; quiet.—*v.t.* To still; to silence; to make quiet; to repress the noise or clamour of.—*To hush up*, to suppress; to procure silence concerning; to keep concealed.—*v.i.* To be still; to be silent: used chiefly in the imperative; be still; make no noise.—*n.* Stillness; quiet.—**Hush-money**, *n.* A bribe to secure silence; money paid to prevent disclosure of facts.

Husk, husk, *n.* [Akin to D. *hulze*, G. *hülse*, a husk; equivalent to E. *hull*, a husk, with *sk* as a termination. HULL.] The external covering of certain fruits or seeds of plants; glume; hull; rind; chaff.—*v.t.* To deprive of the husk.—**Husked**, huskt, *a.* Covered with a husk.—**Husker**, hus'kėr, *n.* One who or that which husks.—**Husky**, hus'ki, *a.* Abounding with husks; consisting of husks; resembling husks.

Husky, hus'ki, *a.* [Allied to *hoarse*; A. Sax. *hwōsta*, Sc. *hoast*, a cough.] Rough in tone, as the voice; powerful; burly.—**Huskily**, hus'ki-li, *adv.* In a husky manner.—**Huskiness**, hus'ki-nes, *n.* The state of being husky; hoarseness; burliness.

Hussar, hu̧-zär', *n.* [Hung. *huszar*, from *husz*, twenty, because in the wars against the Turks every twenty families were bound to furnish one cavalry soldier.] Originally one of the national cavalry of Hungary; now a light cavalry soldier of European armies.

Hussif, huz'if, *n.* [Contr. for *housewife*.] A case for holding such implements as needles, thimble, thread, &c.

Hussite, hus'īt, *n.* A follower of John *Huss*, the Bohemian religious reformer, burned in 1415.

Hussy, huz'i, *n.* [Contr. from *huswife*, *housewife*.] A bad or worthless woman or girl; a jade; a jilt; a forward girl; a pert, frolicsome wench; also a hussif.

Hustings, hus'tingz, *n. pl.* [A.Sax. *hústing*, from Icel. *hús-thing*, an assembly, a council —*hús*, house, and *thing*, cause, council. THING.] *Eng.* the platform on which parliamentary candidates stood when addressing the electors; now, any such place; election campaign proceedings. *Hustings court*, a local court in Virginia.

Hustle, hus'l, *v.t.* [From D. *hutselen*, *hutsen*, to jumble or shake together; Sw. *hutla*, to shuffle; akin *hotch*-pot.] To crowd upon so as to shove about roughly; to push or elbow out or about rudely; to jostle.—*v.i. hustled*, *hustling*. To push or crowd; to move in a confused crowd; to shamble hurriedly.

Huswife, huz'if, *n.* A housewife.

Hut, hut, *n.* [Same word as D. *hut*, G. *hütte*, Dan. *hytte*, Sw. *hydda*, a hut; comp. W. *cwt*, a hovel.] A small house, hovel, or cabin; a mean dwelling; a wooden house for troops in camp or for settlers in a wild country.—*v.t.*—*hutted*, *hutting*. To place in huts, as troops encamped in winter-quarters.—*v.i.* To take lodgings in huts.

Hutch, huch, *n.* [Fr. *huche*, a chest, from L.L. *hutica*, a chest; probably of Teutonic origin and akin to *hut*.] A chest, box, coffer, bin, or other receptacle in which things may be stored or animals confined; a low wagon in which coal is drawn up out of the pit; a measure of two bushels.—*v.t.* To place in a hutch.

Huzza, hu̧-zä', *interj.* A form of *Hurrah*.

Hyacinth, hī'a-sinth, *n.* [Gr. *Hyakinthos*, the name of a youth said to have been slain by Apollo, and changed into the flower.] A liliaceous bulbous plant, of which there are many varieties cultivated; a mineral; a variety of zircon, transparent or translucent, of a red colour tinged with yellow or brown: the name is also given to varieties of the garnet, the sapphire, and the topaz.—**Hyacinthine**, **Hyacinthian**, hī-a-sin'-thīn, hī-a-sin'thi-an, *a.* Made of hyacinth; resembling hyacinth.

Hyades, **Hyads**, hī'a-dēz, hī'adz, *n. pl.* [Gr. *hyades*, from *hyō*, to rain.] A cluster of seven stars supposed by the ancients to indicate the approach of rainy weather when they rose with the sun.

Hyæna, hī-ē'na, *n.* HYENA.

Hyalescence, hī-a-les'ens, *n.* [Gr. *hyalos*, glass.] The act or process of becoming transparent as glass.—**Hyaline**, hī'al-īn, *a.* Glassy; crystalline; transparent.—**Hyalite**, hī'al-īt, *n.* A pellucid variety of opal, resembling colourless gum or resin.—**Hyalography**, hī-al-og'ra-fi, *n.* The art of writing or engraving on glass.—**Hyaloid**, hī'al-oid, *a.* Resembling glass; vitriform; transparent.—**Hyalotype**, hī-al'o-tīp, *n.* A positive photographic picture taken on glass.

Hybernate, **Hybernation**, hī'bėr-nāt, hī-bėr-nā'shon. HIBERNATE, HIBERNATION.

Hyblæan, hī-blē'an, *a.* Pertaining to *Hybla*, in Sicily, noted for its honey.

Hybrid, hī'brid or hib'rid, *n.* [From L. *hybrida*, *hibrida*, a hybrid; origin doubtful.] A mongrel; an animal or plant, the produce of a female animal or plant which has been impregnated by a male of a different variety, species, or genus.—*a.* Mongrel; produced from the mixture of two species.—**Hybridism**, **Hybridity**, hī'brid-izm, hib-rid'i-ti, *n.* The state of being hybrid; mongrel state. — **Hybridizable**, hī'-brid-īz'a-bl, *a.* Capable of being hibridized.—**Hybridization**, hī'brid-i-zā"shon, *n.* The act of hybridizing.—**Hybridize**, hī'-brid-īz, *v.t.* To bring into the condition of producing a hybrid; to render hybrid.—**Hybridizer**, hī'brid-īz-ėr, *n.* One who hybridizes.

Hydatid, hid'a-tid, *n.* [Gr. *hydatis*, a vesicle, from *hydōr*, water.] A term applied to larval forms of tape-worms, found in the bodies of men and certain animals, or to similar vesicular or cyst-like bodies.—**Hydatiform**, hid'at-i-form, *a.* Resembling a hydatid.—**Hydatoid**, hid'a-toid, *a.* *Anat.* applied to the membrane inclosing the aqueous humour of the eye.

Hyde, hīd, *n.* A portion of land; a hide.

Hydra, hī'dra, *n.* [L. *hydra*; Gr. *hydra*, from *hydōr*, water.] A monster of Greek mythology destroyed by Hercules, and represented as having many heads, one of which, being cut off, was immediately succeeded by another, unless the wound was cauterized; hence, evil or misfortune arising from many sources and not easily to be surmounted; a genus of fresh-water polyps of a very low type of structure.—**Hydroid**, hī'droid, *a.* Resembling the hydra polyp in character.—**Hydroida**, hī-droi'da, *n.pl.* A division of Hydrozoa, including the hydra and animals which generally grow attached to objects.

Hydragogue, hī'dra-gog, *n.* [Gr. *hydragōgos*—*hydōr*, water, and *agō*, to lead.] A medicine causing a watery discharge; a diuretic.

Hydrangea, hī-dran'jē-a, *n.* [Gr. *hydōr*, water, and *angeion*, a vessel, from the shape of its capsules.] An Asiatic shrub cultivated in gardens for the beauty of its flowers.

Hydrant, hī'drant, *n.* [Gr. *hydrainō*, to irrigate, from *hydōr*, water.] A pipe with suitable valves and a spout by which water is raised and discharged from a main pipe.

Hydrargyrum, hī-drär'ji-rum, *n.* [L., from Gr. *hydōr*, water, and *argyros*, silver.] Quicksilver or mercury.

Hydrate, hī'drāt, *n.* [Gr. *hydōr*, water.] A chemical compound in which water is a characteristic ingredient.—**Hydrated**, hī'drā-ted, *a.* Formed into a hydrate.

Hydraulic, hī-dra̧'lik, *a.* [Fr. *hydraulique*, L. *hydraulicus*, Gr. *hydraulikos*, from *hydraulis*, an instrument played by water—*hydōr*, water, and *aulos*, a pipe.] Pertaining to fluids in motion, or the action of water utilized for mechanical purposes.—*Hydraulic cement*, a cement having the property of becoming hard under water.—*Hydraulic press*, a machine for the application of great power by means of water.—*Hydraulic ram*, a machine by which descending water can be made to raise a portion of itself to a considerable height.—**Hydraulics**, hī-dra̧'liks, *n.* That branch of science which treats of the motion of liquids, and deals with the application of water in machinery.

Hydric, hī'drik, *a.* [Gr. *hydōr*, water.] Of or pertaining to hydrogen.—**Hydride**, hī'-drīd, *n.* A chemical compound of hydrogen and a metal, or some base.

Hydrobarometer, hī'drō-ba-rom"et-ėr, *n.* [Gr. *hydōr*, water, and E. *barometer*.] An instrument for determining the depth of the sea by the pressure of the superincumbent water.

Hydrocarbon, hī-drō-kär'bon, *n.* A chemical compound of hydrogen and carbon.—*Hydrocarbon furnace*, *hydrocarbon stove*, one in which liquid fuel is used.

Hydrocele, hī'drō-sēl, *n.* [Gr. *hydōr*, water, and *kēlē*, a tumour.] *Med.* a morbid collection of serous fluid in the scrotum or testicle.

Hydrocephalus, hi-drō-sef'a-lus, *n.* [Gr. *hydōr*, water, and *kephalē*, the head.] *Med.* an accumulation of fluid within the cavity of the cranium; water in the head.—**Hydrocephalic**, hī'drō-sē-fal"ik, *a.* Pertaining to hydrocephalus.

Hydrochloric, hī-drō-klō'rik, *a.* *Chem.* pertaining to, or compounded of, chlorine and hydrogen, as *hydrochloric* acid, a concentrated aqueous solution of which is commonly known as spirit of salt and muriatic acid.

Hydrocyanic, hī'drō-sī-an"ik, *a.* [*Hydrogen* and *cyanogen*.] Derived from the combination of hydrogen and cyanogen: *hydrocyanic* acid, or *prussic acid*, found in laurel leaves, the kernels of fruits, &c., is one of the most deadly poisons known, though valuable as a medicine.

Hydrodynamic, hī'drō-di-nam"ik, *a.* [Gr. *hydōr*, water, and *dynamis*, power.] Pertaining to the force or pressure of water.—**Hydrodynamics**, hī'drō-di-nam"iks, *n.* That branch of science which treats of the application of forces to fluids, especially when producing motion in fluids.

Hydro-electric, hī'drō-ē-lek"trik, *a.* Pertaining to the production of electric current by water-power; of a frictional electric machine worked by steam.

Hydro-extractor, hī'dro-eks-trak"tėr, *n.* A machine for expelling water from textile fabrics by the action of centrifugal force.

Hydrofluoric, hī'drō-flū-or"ik, *a.* Consisting of fluorin and hydrogen (*hydrofluoric* acid, a most powerful corrosive).

Hydro-galvanic, hī'drō-gal-van"ik, *a.* Pertaining to electricity evolved by liquids.

Hydrogen, hī'drō-jen, *n.* [Gr. *hydōr*, water, and root *gen*, to generate.] One of the elements of water (the other being oxygen) and a component of all vegetable and animal products; an important elementary substance, long known only in the gaseous form, but now shown to be the vapour of a metal, and itself capable of solidification.—**Hydrogenize**, hī'drō-jen-īz, *v.t.—hydrogenized, hydrogenizing.* To combine with hydrogen.—**Hydrogenous**, hī-droj'e-nus, *a.* Pertaining to or containing hydrogen; formed or produced by the action of water: said of rocks.

Hydrography, hī-drog'ra-fi, *n.* [Gr. *hydōr*, water, and *graphō*, to describe.] That branch of science which has for its object the measurement and description of the sea, lakes, rivers, and other waters, and includes marine surveying, the drawing of charts, &c.—**Hydrographer**, hī-drog'ra-fėr, *n.* One who is proficient in hydrography.—**Hydrographic**, **Hydrographical**, hī-drō-graf'ik, hī-drō-graf'i-kal, *a.* Relating to or treating of hydrography.

Hydroid. Under HYDRA.

Hydrokinetics, hī'drō-ki-net"iks, *n.* Same as *Hydrodynamics.*

Hydrology, hī-drol'o-ji, *n.* [Gr. *hydōr*, water, and *logos*, discourse.] The science that treats of water, its properties, laws, distribution, &c.—**Hydrological**, hī-drō-loj'i-kal, *a.* Pertaining to hydrology.—**Hydrologist**, hi-drol'o-jist, *n.* One skilled in hydrology.

Hydromancy, hī'drō-man-si, *n.* [Gr. *hydōr*, water, and *manteia*, divination.] A method of divination by water.—**Hydromantic**, hī-drō-man'tik, *a.* Pertaining to divination by water.

Hydromania, hī-drō-mā'ni-a, *n.* [Gr. *hydōr*, water, and *mania*, madness.] A species of mental disease under the influence of which the sufferers are led to commit suicide by drowning.

Hydromel, hī'drō-mel, *n.* [Fr., from Gr. *hydōr*, water, and *meli*, honey.] A liquor consisting of honey diluted in water; when fermented it forms mead.

Hydrometallurgy, hī-drō-met'al-ėr-ji, *n.* The process of assaying or reducing ores by liquid reagents.

Hydrometeorology, hī-drō-mē'tē-ėr-ol"-o-ji, *n.* The branch of meteorology which concerns itself with water in the atmosphere in the form of rain, clouds, snow, &c.—**Hydrometeorological**, hī-drō-mē'tē-ėr-ō-loj"i-kal, *a.* Pertaining to this.

Hydrometer, hī-drom'et-ėr, *n.* [Gr. *hydōr*, water, *metron*, a measure.] An instrument to measure the specific gravity or density of water and other fluids, and hence the strength of spirituous liquors and of various solutions.—**Hydrometric**, **Hydrometrical**, hī-drō-met'rik, hī-drō-met'ri-kal, *a.* Pertaining to a hydrometer or hydrometry.—**Hydrometry**, hī-drom'et-ri, *n.* The art or operation of determining the specific gravity, density, force, &c., of fluids.

Hydropathy, hī-drop'a-thi, *n.* [Gr. *hydōr*, water, and *pathos*, affection.] The treatment of disease by the use of cold water externally or internally; the water-cure.—**Hydropathic**, hī-drō-path'ik, *a.* Relating to hydropathy.—*n.* An establishment in which persons are boarded and receive the hydropathic treatment if they wish.—**Hydropathist**, hī-drop'a-thist, *n.* One who practises or advocates hydropathy.

Hydrophane, hī'drō-fān, *n.* [Gr. *hydōr*, water, and *phainō*, to show.] A variety of opal made transparent by immersion in water.

Hydrophid, hī'drō-fid, *n.* [Gr. *hydōr*, water, and *ophis*, a snake.] A water-snake.

Hydrophobia, **Hydrophoby**, hī-drō-fō'bi-a, hī'drō-fō-bi, *n.* [Gr. *hydōr*, water, *phobos*, fear.] A morbid unnatural dread of water; a disease produced by the bite of a mad animal, especially of a mad or rabid dog, one of the characteristics of which is an aversion to or inability to swallow liquids.—**Hydrophobic**, hī-drō-fob'ik, *a.* Of or pertaining to hydrophobia.

Hydrophone, hī'drō-fōn, *n.* [Gr. *hydōr*, water, and *phōnē*, sound.] An instrument used on ships for the detection of submarines.

Hydrophora, hī-drof'o-ra, *n. pl.* Same as *Hydroida*, under HYDRA.

Hydrophyte, hī'drō-fīt, *n.* [Gr. *hydōr*, water, and *phyton*, a plant.] A plant which lives and grows in water.—**Hydrophytology**, hī'drō-fī-tol"o-ji, *n.* The botany of water-plants.

Hydropic, **Hydropical**, hī-drop'ik, hī-drop'i-kal, *a.* [L. *hydropicus*, Gr. *hydrōpikos*, from *hydrōps*, dropsy—*hydōr*, water, and *ōps*, the face.] Dropsical; pertaining to dropsy.—**Hydropically**, hī-drop'i-kal-li, *adv.* In a hydropical manner.—**Hydropsy**, hī'drop-si, *n.* Dropsy.

Hydroplane, hī'drō-plān, *n.* [Gr. *hydōr*, water, and *plane.*] An aeroplane fitted with floats instead of wheels, to enable it to rise or alight on the surface of the water, in the former case having to 'taxi' or glide for some distance, so as to gain the necessary flying speed.

Hydropult, hī'drō-pult, *n.* [Gr. *hydōr*, water, and the term *-pult* of *catapult.*] A machine for throwing water by hand-power.

Hydrorhiza, hī-drō-rī'za, *n.* [*Hydra*, and Gr. *rhiza*, a root.] *Zool.* the adherent base of any hydrozoon.

Hydroscope, hī'drō-skōp, *n.* [Gr. *hydōr*, water, and *skopeō*, to view.] An instrument to mark the presence of water in the air; a kind of ancient water-clock.

Hydroselenic, hī-drō-se-len'ik, *a.* Pertaining to a combination of hydrogen and selenium (*hydroselenic* acid).

Hydrosoma, **Hydrosome**, hī-drō-sō'-ma, hī'drō-sōm, *n.* [*Hydra*, and Gr. *sōma*, body.] The entire organism of any hydrozoon.

Hydrostatic, hī-drō-stat'ik, *a.* [Gr. *hydōr*, water, and *statikos.* STATICS.] Relating to hydrostatics; pertaining to the principles of the equilibrium of fluids.—*Hydrostatic balance*, a balance used for determining very accurately the specific gravity of bodies by weighing them in water.—*Hydrostatic bed.* Same as *Water-bed.*—*Hydrostatic press.* Same as *Hydraulic press.*—*Hydrostatic paradox*, the principle that any quantity of water however small may be made to balance any weight however great.—**Hydrostatically**, hī-drō-stat'i-kal-li, *adv.* According to hydrostatic principles.—**Hydrostatics**, hī-drō-stat'iks, *n.* The science which treats of the weight and equilibrium of fluids, particularly of water; that branch of science which treats of the properties of fluids at rest.

Hydrosulphuric, hī'drō-sul-fū"rik, *a.* Derived from or containing hydrogen and sulphur (*hydrosulphuric* acid).

Hydrotheca, hī'drō-thē-ka, *n.* [*Hydra*, and Gr. *thēkē*, a case.] *Zool.* a little chitinous cup, in which each polypite of the hydrozoa is protected.

Hydrothermal, hī-drō-thėr'mal, *a.* [Gr. *hydōr*, water, and *thermos*, hot.] Of or relating to heated water.

Hydrothorax, hī-drō-thō'raks, *n. Med.* dropsy in the thorax or chest.

Hydrotic, hī-drot'ik, *a.* [Fr. *hydrotique*, from Gr. *hydōr*, water.] *Med.* causing a discharge of water or phlegm.

Hydrotropism, hīd'rō-trōp"ism, *n.* [Gr. *hydōr*, water, *trepō*, I turn.] *Bot.* curving towards or away from moisture.

Hydrous, hī'drus, *a.* Containing water; watery.

Hydroxide, hīd-roks'īd, *n.* [Gr. *hydōr*, water, *oxys*, acid.] A compound formed by the union of a metallic or basic radical with one or more hydroxyl groups.

Hydroxyl, hīd-roks'il, *n.* [Gr. *hydōr*, water, *oxys*, acid.] The univalent radical OH.

Hydrozoon, hī-drō-zō'on, *n.* pl. **Hydrozoa**, hī-drō-zō'a. [Gr *hydra*, a hydra, and *zōon*, a living creature.] *Zool.* one of a class of animals forming, with the Actinozoa, the sub-kingdom Cœlenterata, consisting mostly of marine animals and including the jelly-fishes or sea-nettles, the sea-firs, the hydra or fresh-water polyp, &c., many of them being permanently attached to objects, and somewhat resembling plants.—**Hydrozoal**, hī-drō-zō'al, *a.* Pertaining to the hydrozoa.

Hyemal, hī'e-mal, *a.* Same as *Hiemal.*

Hyena, hī-ē'na, *n.* [L. *hyæna*, from Gr. *hyaina*, a hyena, from *hys*, a hog, from its hog-like back.] A digitigrade carnivorous animal of several species, belonging to Asia and Africa, strong and fierce, feeding chiefly on carrion, and of nocturnal habits.—**Hyena-dog**, *n.* A large wild dog of Cape Colony.

Hyetal, hī'e-tal, *a.* [Gr. *hyetos*, rain, from *hyō*, to rain.] Relating to rain, or its distribution with reference to different regions.—**Hyetograph**, hī'e-to-graf, *n.* A chart showing the rainfall in different regions.—**Hyetographic**, **Hyetographical**, hī'-e-to-graf"ik, hī'e-to-graf"i-kal, *a.* Pertaining to hyetography.—**Hyetography**, hī-e-tog'ra-fi, *n.* The science of the distribution of rain.—**Hyetology**, hī-e-tol'o-ji, *n.* That branch of meteorology which treats of the phenomena connected with rain.—**Hyetometer**, hī-e-tom'et-ėr, *n.* A rain-gauge.

Hygeian, hī-jē'yan, *a.* [From Gr. *hygieia*, *hygeia*, health, from *hygiēs*, healthy.] Pertaining to health or its preservation.—**Hygeist**, **Hygienist**, hī'jē-ist, hī'ji-en-ist, *n.* One versed in hygiene.—**Hygienal**, hī'ji-en-al, *a.* Relating to hygiene.—**Hygiene**, **Hygeine**, hī'ji-ēn, hī'jē-īn, *n.* [Fr. *hygiène*, from Gr. *hygieinos*, healthy, wholesome.] A system of principles or rules designed for the promotion of health, especially the health of households or communities; sanitary science.—**Hygienic**, hī-ji-en'ik, *a.* Relating to hygienic or sanitary matters.—**Hygienically**, hī-ji-en'i-kal-li, *adv.* In a hygienic manner.—**Hygienics**, **Hygienism**, hī-ji-en'iks, hī'ji-en-izm, *n.* The science of health; hygiene; sanitary science.

Hygrograph, hī'grō-graf, *n.* [Gr. *hygros*, moist, and *graphō*, I write.] An instrument which registers automatically the variations of the atmosphere as regards moistness.—**Hygrometer**, hī-grom'et-ėr, *n.* An instrument for measuring the degree of moisture of the atmosphere.—**Hygrometric**, **Hygrometrical**, hī-grō-met'-rik, hī-grō-met'ri-kal, *a.* Pertaining to hygrometry; readily absorbing and retaining moisture.—**Hygrometry**, hī-grom'et-ri, *n.* The determination of humidity, or of the moisture of the atmosphere.—**Hygrophyte**, hī'grō-fīt, *n.* [Gr. *hygros*, moisture, *phyton*, a plant.] A land-plant adapted to moist surroundings.—**Hygroscope**, hī'-grō-skōp, *n.* An instrument for indicating the presence of moisture in the atmosphere.—**Hygroscopic**, hī-grō-skop'ik, *a.* Pertaining to the hygroscope; imbibing moisture from the atmosphere.

Hyksos, hik'sos, *n.* The Shepherd Dynasty invading Egypt, with their capital named Avaris in the Delta, and ruling for 511 years, during the 13th to 17th Dynasty. From Egyptian *Heq*, ruler, and *Shashu*, name of pastoral races of eastern deserts.

Hylæosaurus, hī'lē-ō-sā"rus, *n.* [Gr. *hylaios*, belonging to woods (*hylē*, wood), and *sauros*, a lizard.] A gigantic fossil lizard discovered in the Wealden formation.

Hylism, hī'lizm, *n.* [Gr. *hylē*, a wood, timber, matter.] A theory which regarded matter as the original principle of evil, in opposition to the good spirit.—**Hylogenesis**, **Hylogeny**, hī-lō-jen'e-sis, hī loj'e-ni, *n.* [Gr. *genesis*, birth.] The origin of matter.—**Hylopathism**, hī-lop'ath-izm, *n.* [Gr. *pathos*, feeling.] The doctrine that matter is sentient.—**Hylopathist**, hī-lop'ath-ist, *n.* A believer in hylopathism.—**Hylophagous**, hī-lof'a-gus, *a.* [Gr. *phagō*, to eat.] Feeding upon the young shoots of trees, roots, &c.—**Hylotheism**, hī-lō-thē'izm, *n.* [Gr. *Theos*, God.] The doctrine or belief that matter is God, or that there is no God except matter and the universe.—**Hylotheist**, hī-lō-thē'ist, *n.* One who believes that matter is God.—**Hylozoism**, hī-lō-zō'izm, *n.* [Gr. *zōē*, life.] The doctrine that matter possesses a species of life, or that life and matter are inseparably connected.—**Hylozoist**, hī-lō-zō'ist, *n.* A believer in hylozoism.—**Hylozoic, Hylozoical**, hī-lō-zō'ik, hī-lō-zō'i-kal, *a.* Pertaining to hylozoism.

Hymen, hī'men, *n.* [Gr. *hymēn*, a skin, a membrane; *Hymēn*, the God of marriage.] *Anat.* the virginal membrane, situated at the entrance of the vagina; *bot.* the fine pellicle which incloses a flower in the bud. **Hymeneal, Hymenean**, hī-men-ē'al, hī-men-ē'an, *a.* Pertaining to marriage.—*n.* A marriage song.

Hymenium, hī-mē'ni-um, *n.* [Gr. *hymēn*, a membrane.] *Bot.* the fructifying surface in fungi.—**Hymenogeny**, hī-men-oj'e-ni, *n.* *Physiol.* the production of membranes. —**Hymenology**, hī-men-ol'o-ji, *n.* A treatise on the membranes of the animal system.

Hymenopter, Hymenopteran, hī-men-op'tėr, hī-men-op'tėr-an, *n.* [Gr. *hymēn*, a membrane, and *pteron*, a wing.] A member of an order of insects, having four membranous wings, and including the bees, wasps, ants, &c.—**Hymenopterous**, hī-men-op'tėr-us, *a.* Belonging or pertaining to the hymenopters.

Hymenotomy, hī-men-ot'o-mi, *n.* [Gr. *hymēn*, membrane, and *tomos*, a cutting.] The cutting or dissection of membranes.

Hymn, him, *n.* [L. *hymnus*, from Gr. *hymnos*, a song, a song of praise.] A song or ode in honour of God, or in honour of some deity; a sacred lyric; a song of praise, adoration, or thanksgiving.—*v.t.* To praise or celebrate in hymn or song; to sing.—*v.i.* To sing in praise or adoration. — **Hymnal, Hymn-book**, him'nal, *n.* A collection of hymns, generally for use in public worship. — **Hymnic**, him'nik, *a.* Relating to hymns. — **Hymnography**, him-nog'ra-fi, *n.* The art of writing hymns. — **Hymnologist, Hymnographer**, him-nol'o-jist, him-nog'ra-fėr, *n.* A composer of hymns.—**Hymnology, Hymnody**, him-nol'o-ji, him'no-di, *n.* A body of sacred lyrics composed by several authors of a particular period or country; hymns collectively.

Hyoid, Hyoidean, hī'oid, hī-oi'dē-an, *a.* [Gr. *hyoeidēs*, shaped like the letter *u* or *y*.] Applied to a movable bone having somewhat the shape of the letter U, between the root of the tongue and the larynx.—**Hyoideal**, hī-oi'dē-al, *a.* Connected with the hyoid bone.

Hyoscine and **Hyoscyamine**, hī'os-in, hī-ō-sī'am-in, *n.* [From *hyoscyamus*.] Alkaloid poisons occurring in henbane (*Hyoscyamus*).

Hyp, hip, *v.t.*—*hypped*, *hypping*. To make melancholy; to hip.

Hypæthral, Hypethral, hī-pē'thral, *a.* [Gr. *hypaithros*, under the sky—*hypo* under, and *aithēr*, ether.] *Arch.* applied to a building not covered by a roof.

Hypallage, hī-pal'la-jē, *n.* [Gr. *hypallagē*, change—*hypo*, under, and *allagē*, change, from *allasso*, to change.] A figure of speech consisting of a transference of attributes from their proper subjects to others.

Hypanthium, hī-pan'thi-um, *n.* [Gr. *hypo*, under, *anthos*, flower.] *Bot.* the fleshy enlarged hollow of the end of a flower-stalk, as in the rose.

Hypapophysis, hī-pa-pof'i-sis, *n.* [Gr. *hypo*, under, and *apophysis*, a process.] *Anat.* a process on the lower side of a vertebra.

Hyperæmia, hī-per-ē'mi-a, *n.* [Gr. *hyper*, over or above, and *haima*, blood.] An excessive accumulation of blood in a part of the body.—**Hyperæmic**, hī-pėr-ē'mik, *a.* Pertaining to or affected with hyperæmia.

Hyperæsthesis, Hyperæsthesia, hī'-pėr-es-thē"sis, hī'pėr-es-thē"zi-a, *n.* [Gr. *over*, and *aisthēsis*, sensation.] Morbid excess of sensibility.

Hyperbaton, hī-pėr'ba-ton, *n.* [Gr., from *hyper*, beyond, *bainō*, to go.] *Gram.* a figurative construction inverting the natural order of words and sentences.—**Hyperbatic**, hī-pėr-bat'ik, *a.* Pertaining to hyperbaton.

Hyperbola, hī-pėr'bō-la, *n.* [Gr. *hyperbolē*. HYPERBOLE.] *Geom.* a curve formed by a plane that cuts a cone in a direction parallel to its axis, or so that the plane makes a greater angle with the base than the side of the cone makes.—**Hyperboliform**, hī-pėr-bol'i-form, *a.* Having the form of a hyperbola. — **Hyperboloid, Hyperbolic**, hī-pėr-bol-oid, hī-pėr-bol'ik, *a.* Having the properties of the hyperbola.—**Hyperboloid**, *n.* A hyperbolic conoid.

Hyperbole, hī-pėr'bō-lē, *n.* [Gr. *hyperbolē*, excess—*hyper*, beyond, *ballō*, to throw.] A figure of speech which expresses much more or less than the truth; an exaggerated statement; exaggeration.—**Hyperbolic, Hyperbolical**, hī-pėr-bol'ik, hī-pėr-bol'i-kal, *a.* Belonging to or containing hyperbole; exaggerated in terms.—**Hyperbolically**, hī-pėr-bol'i-kal-li, *adv.* In a hyperbolic manner.—**Hyperbolism**, hī-pėr'bol-izm, *n.* The use of hyperbole.—**Hyperbolist**, hī-pėr'bol-ist, *n.* One who uses hyperboles. **Hyperbolize**, hī-pėr'bol-īz, *v.i.* and *t.* To speak or write with exaggeration; to exaggerate.

Hyperborean, hī-pėr-bō'rē-an, *a.* [Gr. *hyper*, beyond, *boreas*, the north.] Belonging to a region very far north; northern; arctic; frigid. — *n.* An inhabitant of the most northern region of the earth.

Hypercatalectic, hī-pėr-kat'a-lek"tik, *a.* [Gr *hyper*, beyond, and *katalēxis*, termination.] *Pros.* having a syllable or two beyond the regular measure.

Hypercritic, hī-pėr-krit'ik, *n.* [Gr. *hyper*, beyond, and *kritikos*, critical. CRITIC.] One who is critical beyond measure or reason; an over-rigid critic; a captious censor.—**Hypercritical**, hī-pėr-krit'i-kal, *a.* Over-critical; critical beyond use or reason; excessively nice or exact.—**Hypercritically**, hī-pėr-krit'i-kal-li, *adv.* In a hypercritical manner.—**Hypercriticise**, hī-pėr-krit'i-sīz, *v.t.* To criticise with excessive severity.—**Hypercriticism**, hī-pėr-krit'i-sizm, *n.* Excessive rigour of criticism; captious criticism.

Hyperdulia, Hyperduly, hī-pėr-dū'-li-a, hī-pėr-dū'li, *n.* [Gr. *hyper*, beyond, and *douleia*, service.] The worship offered by Roman Catholics to the Virgin Mary, so called because higher than that given to saints (which is known as *dulia*).

Hyperinosis, hī-pėr-i-nō"sis, *n.* [Gr. *hyper*, above, and *is*, *inos*, fibre.] An excess of fibrin in the blood.

Hyperkinesis, hī'pėr-kī-nē"sis, *n.* [Gr. *hyper*, beyond, and *kinēsis*, motion.] Abnormal increase of muscular movement; spasmodic action. — **Hyperkinetic**, hī-pėr-kī-net"ik, *a.* Relating to or characterized by hyperkinesis.

Hypermeter, hī-pėr'me-tėr, *n.* [Gr. *hyper*, beyond, and *metron*, measure.] A hypercatalectic verse; something beyond ordinary measure.—**Hypermetrical**, hī-pėr-met'ri-kal, *a.* Exceeding the common measure; redundant.

Hypermetropia, Hypermetropy, hī'-pėr-me-trō"pi-a, hī-pėr-met'ro-pi, *n.* [Gr. *hyper*, over, *metron*, measure, *ops*, the eye.] A defect of the eyesight in which the focus for all objects falls behind the retina, and which is corrected by convex glasses; long-sightedness.

Hyperphysical, hī-pėr-fiz'i-kal, *a.* Beyond what is merely physical, immaterial, supernatural.

Hyperplasia, hī-pėr-plā'sia, *n.* [Gr. *hyper*, beyond, *plassō*, to form.] *Pathol.* excessive growth of a part by multiplication of cells.

Hyperpyrexia, hī'pėr-pi-rek"si-a, *n.* [Prefix *hyper* and *pyrexia*.] An excessive degree of fever.

Hypersarcoma, Hypersarcosis, hī'-pėr-sär-kō"ma, hī-pėr-sär-kō"sis, *n.* [Gr. *hyper*, beyond, *sarx*, *sarkos*, flesh.] Proud or fungous flesh.

Hypersthene, hī'pėr-sthēn, *n.* [Gr. *hyper*, beyond, *sthenos*, strength; from its difficult frangibility as compared with hornblende.] A mineral of the hornblende group, a constituent of some rocks; also called *Labrador hornblende*.

Hypertrophy, hī-pėr'tro-fi, *n.* [Gr. *hyper*, above, and *trophē*, nutrition.] A morbid enlargement of a part of the body from excessive nutrition. — **Hypertrophic, Hypertrophical**, hī-pėr-trof'ik, hī-pėr-trof'i-kal, *a.* Producing or tending to produce hypertrophy.—**Hypertrophied**, hī-pėr'-tro-fid, *a.* Affected with hypertrophy; excessively developed.

Hypethral, *a.* HYPÆTHRAL.

Hypha, hī'fa *n.*; pl. **Hyphæ**, hī'fē. [Gr. *hyphē*, a web.] The thready or filamentous matter forming the mycelium of a fungus. —**Hyphal**, hī'fal, *a.* Pertaining to.

Hyphen, hī'fen, *n.* [Gr. *hyphen*, strictly *hyph'hen*, into or in one, together—*hypo*, under, and *hen*, one.] A mark or short line made between two words to show that they form a compound word, or used to connect the syllables of a divided word.—*v.t.* To join by a hyphen.

Hyphomycetes, hī'fō-mī-sē"tēz, *n. pl.* [Gr. *hyphaō*, *hyphaino*, to weave, and *mykēs*, *mykētos*, a fungus.] One of the great divisions of fungi, containing those species of microscopic vegetable moulds which have naked spores borne on free or only fasciculate threads.—**Hyphomycetous**, hī'fō-mī-sē"tus, *a.* Pertaining to the Hyphomycetes.

Hypnosis, hip-nō'sis, *n.* The hypnotic state; a sort of sleep artificially induced, often by the person fixing his attention upon some bright object, being accompanied by more or less unconsciousness.—**Hypnotist**, hip'no-tist, *n.* One who hypnotizes.

Hypnotic, hip-not'ik, *a.* [Gr. *hypnos*, sleep; akin L. *sopor*, sleep, A.Sax. *swefen*, a dream.] Having the quality of producing sleep; tending to produce sleep; soporific.—*n.* A medicine that produces sleep; a soporific.—**Hypnotism**, hip'no-tizm, *n.* A sleep-like condition brought on by artificial means.—**Hypnotize**, hip'no-tīz, *v.t.* To affect with hypnotism.—**Hypnologist**, hip-nol'o-jist, *n.* One versed in hypnology.—**Hypnology**, hip-nol'o-ji, *n.* Facts relating to the phenomena of sleep.

Hypoblast, hī'pō-blast, *n.* [Gr. *hypo*, under, and *blastos*, a bud.] *Bot.* the flat dorsal cotyledon of a grass; *anat.* the lower of the two layers of cells forming the blastoderm, the upper being the epiblast.

Hypocaust, hī'pō-kąst, *n.* [Gr. *pypokauston*—*hypo*, under, and *kaiō*, to burn.] *Anc. arch.* an arched chamber in which a fire was kindled for the purpose of giving heat to the rooms above it; also a compartment of some modern stoves.

Hypochondria, hī-pō-kon'dri-a, *n.* [From the *hypochondrium* being regarded as the seat of the disease. See below.] *Med.* a disease characterized by exaggerated uneasiness and anxiety, mainly as to what concerns the health, &c.; spleen; vapours; low spirits.—**Hypochondriac, Hypochondriacal**, hī-pō-kon'dri-ak, hī'po-kon-drī"a-kal, *a.* Pertaining to hypochondria or to the hypochondrium: affected with hypochondria.—**Hypochondriac**, *n.* A person affected with hypochondria.—**Hypochondriacally**, hī'pō-kon-drī"a-kal-li, *adv.* In a hypochondriac manner.—**Hypochondriasis, Hypochondriasm**, hī'pō-kon-drī"a-sis, hī-pō-kon'dri-azm, *n.* Hypochondria. — **Hypochondrium**, hī-pō-kon'dri-um, *n.* pl. **Hypochondria**. [Gr. *hypochondrion*, from *hypo*, under, and *chondros*, cartilage — from its situation.] *Anat.* the name of the two regions of the abdomen under the cartilages of the false ribs on the right and left side.

Hypocotyl, hī'pō-kot"il, *n.* [Gr. *hypo*, under, *cotyl*(edon).] In seedlings, that part of the stem below the seed-leaves (cotyledons).

Hypocrateriform, hī'pō-krā-tē"ri-form, *a.* [Gr. *hypo*, under, *kratēr*, a goblet.] *Bot.* salver-shaped; applied to a corolla having a straight tube surmounted by flat spreading limbs, as in the cowslip.

Hypocrisy, hi-pok'ri-si, *n.* [Fr. *hypocrisie*, L. *hypocrisis*, Gr. *hypokrisis*, a playing a part on the stage, simulation, from *hypokrinomai*, to play a part, to feign—*hypo*, and *krinō*, to separate, discern. CRITIC.] The act or practice of simulating or feigning to be what one is not; especially, the assuming of a false appearance of piety and virtue; dissimulation; insincerity.—**Hypocrite**, hip'ō-krit, *n.* [Fr. *hypocrite*, Gr. *hypokritēs*.] One who practises hypocrisy.—**Hypocritical**, hip-ō-krit'i-kal, *a.* Pertaining to, or proceeding from, hypocrisy; characterized by hypocrisy; pretending goodness or religion; insincere.—**Hypocritically**, hip-ō-krit'i-kal-li, *adv.* In a hypocritical manner; insincerely.

Hypocycloid, hī-pō-sī'kloid, *n.* [Gr. *hypo*, under, and E. *cycloid*.] A curve generated by the movement of a curve upon the concave side of a fixed curve.

Hypodermal, **Hypodermic**, hī-pō-dėr'mal, hī-pō-dėr'mik, *a.* [Gr. *hypo*, under, *derma*, the skin.] Pertaining to or relating to parts under the skin or to the introduction of medicines under the skin.

Hypogæan, **Hypogæal**, **Hypogæous**, hī-pō-jē'an, hī-pō-jē'al, hī-pō-jē'us, *a.* [Gr. *hypo*, beneath, *gē*, the earth.] *Lit.* subterranean; *bot.* a term applied to parts of plants which grow beneath the surface of the earth.

Hypogastrium, hī-pō-gas'tri-um, *n.* [Gr. *hypo*, under, and *gastēr*, the belly.] *Anat.* the lower anterior region of the abdomen.—**Hypogastric**, hī-pō-gas'trik, *a.* Relating to the hypogastrium.—**Hypogastrocele**, hī-pō-gas'trō-sēl, *n.* [Gr. *kēlē*, a tumour.] A hernia through the walls of the lower belly.

Hypogene, hī'pō-jēn, *a.* [Gr. *hypo*, under, and root *gen*, to produce.] *Geol.* formed or originating under the surface of the earth (as crystalline rocks).

Hypoglossal, hī-pō-glos'al, *a.* [Gr. *hypo*, under, *glōssa*, the tongue.] *Anat.* pertaining to the under side of the tongue.

Hypogynous, hī-poj'i-nus, *a.* [Gr. *hypo*, under, *gynē*, a female.] *Bot.* placed below the ovary or seed-vessel; having the corolla and stamens inserted below the ovary.

Hypomenous, hī-pom'en-us, *a.* [Gr. *hypo*, under, *menō*, to remain.] *Bot.* arising below an organ without adhering to it.

Hyponasty, hī'pō-nas-ti, *n.* [Gr. *hypo*, under, *nastos*, pressed.] *Bot.* excessive growth of the under surface of an organ, causing it to bend upwards: as opposed to *epinasty*.

Hypophosphite, hī-pō-fos'fit, *n.* The name of certain bodies containing phosphorus, some of which are used medicinally.

Hypophyllous, hī-pof'i-lus or hī-pō-fil'-lus, *a.* [Gr. *hypo*, under, and *phyllon*, a leaf.] *Bot.* placed under a leaf.

Hypostasis, hī-pos'ta-sis, *n.* pl. **Hypostases**, hī-pos'ta-sēz. [Gr. *hypostasis*—*hypo*, under, *stasis*, a standing.] That which underlies something else; the reality underlying or assumed to underlie a phenomenon; *theol.* the distinct substance or subsistence of the Father, Son, and Holy Spirit in the Godhead.—**Hypostatic**, **Hypostatical**, hī-pō-stat'ik, hī-pō-stat'i-kal, *a.* Relating to hypostasis.—*Hypostatic union*, the union of the three persons in the Godhead, or the union of the divine and human nature in the person of Christ.—**Hypostatically**, hī-pō-stat'i-kal-li, *adv.* In a hypostatic manner.—**Hypostatize**, **Hypostasize**, hī-pos'ta-tīz, hī-pos'ta-sīz, *v.t.* To regard as a distinct substance.

Hypostyle, hī'pō-stīl, *n.* [Gr. *hypo*, under, *stylos*, a pillar.] *Arch.* a covered colonnade; a pillared hall.—*a.* Having the roof supported by pillars.

Hyposulphite, hī-pō-sul'fit, *n.* The name of certain substances containing sulphur, of which the hyposulphite of sodium is used in medicine and the arts.

Hypotenuse, **Hypothenuse**, hī-pot'e-nūs, *n.* [Gr. *hypoteinousa*—*hypo*, under, and *teinō*, to stretch.] *Geom.* the longest side of a right-angled triangle; the line that subtends the right angle.

Hypothec, hī-poth'ek, *n.* [L. *hypotheca*, Gr. *hypothēkē*, a pledge, from *hypotithēmi*, to put under, to pledge.] *Scots law*, a lien such as that which a landlord has over the furniture or crops of his tenant in respect of the current rent.—**Hypothecary**, hī-poth'e-ka-ri, *a.* Of or pertaining to hypothecation.—**Hypothecate**, hī-poth'e-kāt, *v.t.*—*hypothecated*, *hypothecating*. To pledge in security for a debt, but without transfer; to mortgage.—**Hypothecation**, hī-poth'e-kā"shon, *n.* The act of hypothecating.—**Hypothecator**, hī-poth'e-kā-tėr, *n.* One who hypothecates.

Hypothesis, hī-poth'e-sis, *n.* pl. **Hypotheses**, hī-poth'e-sēz. [Gr. *hypothesis*, a supposition, from *hypo*, under, and *tithēmi*, to place.] A supposition; something not proved, but assumed for the purpose of argument; a theory imagined or assumed to account for what is not understood.—**Hypothesize**,† hī-poth'e-sīz, *v.i.* To form hypotheses.—**Hypothetic**, **Hypothetical**, hī-pō-thet'ik, hī-pō-thet'i-kal, *a.* Including or characterized by a supposition or hypothesis; conjectural; conditional.—**Hypothetically**, hī-pō-thet'i-kal-li, *adv.* In a hypothetical manner or relation.—**Hypothetist**, hī-poth'e-tist, *n.* One who defends a hypothesis.

Hypozoic, hī-pō-zō'ik, *a.* [Gr. *hypo*, under, and *zōon*, an animal.] *Geol.* applied to such rocks as occur below the undoubtedly fossiliferous strata, and which have hitherto yielded no organic remains.

Hypsometer, hip-som'et-ėr, *n.* [Gr. *hypsos*, height, *metron*, measure.] A special kind of barometer for measuring altitudes; an apparatus used for measuring heights by noting the boiling point of water.—**Hypsometric**, **Hypsometrical**, hip-sō-met'rik, hip-sō-met'ri-kal, *a.* Pertaining to hypsometry.—**Hypsometrically**, hip-sō-met'ri-kal-li, *adv.* According to hypsometry.—**Hypsometry**, hip-som'et-ri, *n.* The art of measuring the heights of places upon the surface of the earth.

Hyrax, hī'raks, *n.* [Gr., a shrew-mouse.] A small rabbit-like animal of Syria, believed to be the 'coney' of Scripture; a kindred species of South Africa.

Hyson, hī'son, *n.* [Chinese *hi-tshun*, lit. first crop.] A species of green tea from China.

Hyssop, his'op, *n.* [Gr. *hyssōpos*, hyssop.] The name of small bushy herbs of the mint family, the medicinal properties of which were formerly held in estimation, the plants being aromatic and stimulating.

Hysteranthous, his-tėr-an'thus, *a.* [Gr. *hysteron*, afterwards, *anthos*, a flower.] *Bot.* having the leaves appearing after the flowers, as the willows, &c.

Hysteresis, hist'ėr-ē-sis, *n.* [Gr. *hysteros*, later.] The lagging of magnetic effects behind their causes.

Hysteria, **Hysterics**, his-tē'ri-a, his-ter'iks, *n.* [L.L. *hysteria*, from Gr. *hystera*, the womb.] A nervous affection characterized by alternate fits of laughing and crying, convulsive struggling, rumbling in the bowels, sense of suffocation, &c.—**Hysteric**, **Hysterical**, his-ter'ik, his-ter'i-kal, *a.* Pertaining to hysterics or hysteria; affected by or subject to hysterics.—**Hysterically**, his-ter'i-kal-li, *adv.* In a hysterical manner.—**Hysterioid**, his-tē'ri-oid, *a.* Resembling hysteria.

Hysteron-proteron, his'tėr-on-prot"ėr-on, *n.* [Gr. *hysteron*, last, and *proteron*, first.] An inversion of the natural order in words; a putting first what should be last.

Hysterotomy, his-tėr-ot'o-mi, *n.* [Gr. *hystera*, the uterus, *tomē*, a cutting.] The operation of cutting into the uterus to take out a fetus which cannot be excluded by the usual means.

I

I, the ninth letter, and the third vowel of the English alphabet, in which it represents not only several vowel sounds but also the consonantal sound of *y*.

I, ī, *pron.* pos. *my* or *mine*, dat. and obj. *me*; pl. nom. *we*, pos. *our* or *ours*, dat. and obj. *us*. [A.Sax. *ic*, D. *ik*, Goth. *ik*, G. *ich*, Icel. *ek*, Dan. *jeg*, L. *ego*, Gr. *egō*, Skr. *aham*, W. *ym*, Armor. *em*—I.] The nominative case of the pronoun of the first person; the word by which a speaker or writer denotes himself: sometimes used as a noun; the ego.

Iambus, ī-am'bus, *n.* pl. **Iambuses** or **Iambi**, ī-am'bus-ez, ī-am-bī. [Gr. *iambos*, from *iaptō*, to assail, the iambus being much used in satiric poetry.] *Pros.* a foot consisting of two syllables, the first short and the last long, or the first unaccented and the last accented, as in *delight*.—**Iambic**, ī-am'bik, *a.* [Gr. *iambikos*.] Pertaining to the iambus; composed of iambics.—*n.* An iambic foot; a verse consisting of iambi.—**Iambically**, ī-am'bi-kal-li, *adv.* In iambics.—**Iambize**,† ī-am'bīz, *v.t.* To satirize in iambic verse.—**Iambographer**, ī-am-bog'ra-fėr, *n.* A writer of iambic poetry.

Iatric, **Iatrical**, ī-at'rik, ī-at'ri-kal, *a.* [Gr. *iatrikos*, from *iatros*, a physician.] Relating to medicine or physicians.

Iatrochemical, ī-ā'trō-kem"ik-al, *a.* [Gr. *iatros*, physician.] Pertaining to an old medical theory in which chemistry was relied on as explaining physiological or pathological phenomena.—**Iatrophysical**, ī-ā'trō-fiz"ik-al, *a.* *Med.* explaining phenomena by physics or natural philosophy.

Iberian, ī-bē'ri-an, *n.* One of the primitive inhabitants of Spain; the language of the ancient Iberians, of which Basque is supposed to be the representative.

Ibex, ī'beks, *n.* [L., a kind of goat.] An animal of the goat family found in the Alps and Pyrenees, with large horns directed backwards and marked with prominent transverse ridges in front.

Ibidem, ib-ī'dem. [L.] In the same place.

Ibis, ī'bis, *n.* [Gr. and L.] A name of certain grallatorial birds allied to the storks, the most remarkable species of which, the sacred ibis, was revered by the ancient Egyptians.

Icarian, ī-kā'ri-an, *a.* [From *Icarus*, in Greek mythol., who, flying with a pair of artificial wings, soared so high that the sun melted the wax that cemented his wings, and caused him to fall into the sea.] Adventurous in flight; soaring too high for safety, like Icarus.

Ice, īs, *n.* [A.Sax. *īs*=D. *ijs*, Dan. and Sw. *is*, Icel. *iss*, G. *eis*, referred along with *iron*, G. *eisen*, to a root meaning to shine or glance.] Water or other fluid congealed or in a solid state in consequence of the abstraction of the heat necessary to preserve its fluidity; cream and milk sweetened, variously flavoured, and frozen; ice cream.—*To break the ice*, to make the first opening to any attempt; to open the way.—*v.t.*—*iced*, *icing*. To cover with ice; to convert into ice; to cool with ice; to freeze; to cover with concreted sugar.—**Ice-anchor**, *n.* An anchor used for securing vessels to ice.—**Iceberg**, īs'bėrg, *n.* [D. *ijsberg*—*ijs*, ice, and *berg*, a mountain.] A vast and lofty body of ice floating on the ocean.—**Ice-blink**, *n.* A bright yellowish-white tint near the horizon, reflected from ice in arctic regions.—**Ice-boat**, *n.* A strong boat that can break a passage through ice; a boat for sailing with runners on the surface of ice.—**Icebound**, Is'bound, *a.* Surrounded with ice so as to be immovable, or inaccessible.—**Ice-breaker**, *n.* A massive and powerful steamer that smashes and forces a way through ice.—**Ice-cream**, *n.* Cream variously flavoured, and congealed by means of a freezing-mixture.—**Iced**, 1st, *p.* Covered with ice; cooled with ice; frosted.—**Ice-field**, *n.* A large sheet of sea ice whose limits cannot be seen.—**Ice-floe**, *n.* A sheet of ice, smaller than an ice-field, but still of considerable size.—**Icefoot**, Is'fut, *n.* A belt or fringe of ice that forms round the shores in arctic regions.—**Icehouse**, Is'hous, *n.* A repository for the preservation of ice during warm weather.—**Ice-plane**, *n.* An instrument for smoothing the surface of ice before cutting for storage.—**Ice-plant**, *n.* A plant belonging to Greece, the Canaries, and the Cape, so called from being studded with pellucid watery vesicles which shine like pieces of ice.—**Ice-plough**, *n.* A plough for cutting grooves on ice previously to its removal, or to open a passage for boats.—**Ice-saw**, *n.* A large saw used for cutting through ice, to relieve ships when frozen up, or to remove ice for storage.—**Ice-sheet**, *n.* A thick sheet of ice covering a land area and not limited to valleys.—**Ice-water**, *n.* Water from melted ice; iced water.—**Icicle**, I'si-kl, *n.* [A.Sax. *is-gicel*, from *is*, and *gicel*, an icicle; akin to Icel. *jökull*, icicle, *jaki*, a piece of ice.] A pendent conical mass of ice formed by the freezing of water or other fluid as it drops from something.—**Icily**, I'si-li, *adv.* In an icy manner.—**Iciness**, I'si-nes, *n.* The state of being icy or very cold.—**Icy**, I'si, *a.* Pertaining to, composed of, produced by, resembling or abounding with ice; *fig.* characterized by coldness or coolness, as of manner, &c.; frigid; chilling; indifferent.

Icelander, Is'lan-dėr, *n.* A native of Iceland.—**Icelandic**, Is-lan'dik, *a.* Pertaining to Iceland.—*n.* The language of the Icelanders or of their literature, the oldest of the Scandinavian group of tongues.—**Iceland-moss**, *n.* A species of lichen found in the arctic regions and on lofty mountains, used in medicine and as a nutritious article of diet.—**Iceland-spar**, *n.* A transparent variety of calcareous spar, or carbonate of lime, valuable for experiments on the double refraction and polarization of light.

Ichneumon, ik-nū'mon, *n.* [Gr., from *ichneuō*, to track out, from *ichnos*, a footstep—the animal searches out crocodiles' eggs.] A digitigrade carnivorous animal of Egypt, resembling a weasel, and feeding on crocodiles' eggs, snakes, rats, lizards, mice, &c.; a hymenopterous insect whose larvæ are parasitic on other insects (called also *ichneumon fly*).—**Ichneumonidan**, ik-nū-mon'i-dan, *a.* One of the ichneumon flies.

Ichnite, ik'nīt, *n.* [Gr. *ichnos*, a footprint.] *Geol.* a fossil footprint; the footprint of an extinct animal marked on rocks.—**Ichnolite**, ik'no-līt, *n.* [Gr. *ichnos*, a footmark, and *lithos*, a stone.] An ichnite or stone marked with an animal's footprint.—**Ichnology**, **Ichnolithology**, ik-nol'o-ji, ik'nō-li-thol"o-ji, *n.* The fossil footmarks of animals.

Ichnography, ik-nog'ra-fi, *n.* [Gr. *ichnos*, a footstep, and *graphō*, to describe.] The horizontal section of a building or other object, showing its true dimensions according to a geometric scale; a ground-plan.—**Ichnographic**, **Ichnographical**, ik-nō-graf'ik, ik-nō-graf'i-kal, *a.* Pertaining to ichnography.

Ichor, I'kor, *n.* [Gr.] An ethereal fluid that supplied the place of blood in the veins of the gods of the Greeks and Romans; *med.* a thin watery humour, like serum or whey; a thin watery acrid discharge from an ulcer, wound, &c.—**Ichorous**, I'ko-rus, *a.* Like ichor; thin; watery; serous.

Ichthin, ik'thin, *n.* [Gr. *ichthys*, a fish.] A constituent of the eggs of cartilaginous fishes.—**Ichthyic**, ik'thi-ik, *a.* Pertaining to fishes; fishlike.—**Ichthyocol**, **Ichthyocolla**, ik'thi-ō-kol, ik'thi-ō-kol-la, *n.* [Gr. *kolla*, glue.] Fish-glue; isinglass.—**Ichthyodorulite**, ik'thi-ō-dor"ū-līt, *n.* [Gr. *dory*, spear, *lithos*, a stone.] A spine of certain fossil fishes.—**Ichthyography**, ik-thi-og'ra-fi, *n.* The description of fishes.—**Ichthyoid**, **Ichthyoidal**, ik'thi-oid, ik-thi-oi'dal, *a.* More or less fishlike.—**Ichthyol**, ik'thi-ol, *n.* An ointment obtained from fossil fishes.—**Ichthyolatry**, ik-thi-ol'a-tri, *n.* [Gr. *latreia*, worship.] Worship of fish or a fishlike god.—**Ichthyolite**, ik'thi-ō-līt, *n.* A fossil fish or part, or its mark.—**Ichthyologic**, **Ichthyological**, ik'thi-ō-loj"ik, ik'thi-ō-loj"i-kal, *a.* Pertaining to ichthyology.—**Ichthyologist**, ik-thi-ol'o-jist, *n.* One versed in ichthyology.—**Ichthyology**, ik-thi-ol'o-ji, *n.* The science of fishes; that branch of zoology which treats of fishes.—**Ichthyomorphous**, **Ichthyomorphic**, ik'thi-ō-mor"fus, ik'thi-ō-mor"fik, *a.* Fish-shaped.—**Ichthyophagist**, ik-thi-of'a-jist, *n.* [Gr. *phagō*, to eat.] One who eats or subsists on fish.—**Ichthyophagous**, ik-thi-of'a-gus, *a.* Eating or subsisting on fish.—**Ichthyophagy**, ik-thi-of'a-ji, *n.* The practice of eating fish.—**Ichthyopsida**, ik-thi-op'si-da, *n. pl.* [Gr. *opsis*, appearance.] The primary division of the Vertebrata that comprises the fishes and amphibia.—**Ichthyornis**, ik-thi-or'nis, *n.* [Gr. *ornis*, a bird.] A fossil bird with vertebræ like those of fishes, and with teeth set in sockets.—**Ichthyosaurus**, **Ichthyosaur**, ik'-thi-ō-sa"rus, ik'thi-ō-sar", *n.* [Gr. *sauros*, a lizard.] A fishlike lizard; an immense fossil marine reptile, combining many of the characters of lizards and fishes.—**Ichthyosis**, ik-thi-ō'sis, *n.* A disease of the skin, portions of which become hard and scaly, with a tendency to excrescences.—**Ichthyotomist**, ik-thi-ot'om-ist, *n.* A dissector of fishes.—**Ichthyotomy**, ik-thi-ot'o-mi, *n.* [Gr. *tomē*, a cutting.] Dissection of fishes.

Icicle, **Icily**, **Iciness**. Under ICE.

Icon, I'kon, *n.* [Gr. *eikōn*, an image, from *eikō*, to resemble.] An image or representation; a portrait; the holy picture or emblem regarded as sacred in the Greek and Russian Church.—**Iconoclasm**, I-kon'o-klazm, *n.* The act, principles, or proceedings of an iconoclast.—**Iconoclast**, I-kon'o-klast, *n.* [Gr. *eikōn*, and *klastēs*, a breaker, from *klaō*, to break.] A breaker of images; any destroyer or exposer of shams or superstitions; one who makes attacks upon cherished beliefs.—**Iconoclastic**, I-kon'o-klas"tik, *a.* Pertaining to an iconoclast.—**Iconography**, I-ko-nog'ra-fi, *n.* [Gr. *eikōn*, and *graphō*, to describe.] That branch of knowledge which treats of ancient statues, busts, paintings in fresco, mosaic works, engraving on gems or metals, and the like.—**Iconographic**, I-kon'o-graf"ik, *a.* Relating to iconography; representing by diagrams or pictures.—**Iconolater**, I-ko-nol'at-ėr, *n.* [Gr. *eikōn*, and *latreia*, service.] One that worships images.—**Iconolatry**, I-ko-nol'at-ri, *n.* The worship or adoration of images.—**Iconology**, I-ko-nol'o-ji, *n.* The doctrine of images or emblematical representations; iconography.—**Iconomachy**, I-ko-nom'a-ki, *n.* [Gr. *eikōn*, and *machē*, a fight.] A war against images; hostility to images or pictures as objects of worship or reverence.

Icosahedral, I'kos-a-hē"dral, *a.* [Gr. *eikosi*, twenty, and *hedra*, seat, side.] Having twenty equal sides.—**Icosahedron**, I'kos-a-hē"dron, *n.* A solid of twenty equal sides.

Icosander, I-ko-san'dėr, *n.* [Gr. *eikosi*, twenty, and *anēr*, a male.] *Bot.* a plant having twenty or more stamens inserted in the calyx.—**Icosandrian**, **Icosandrous**, I-ko-san'dri-an, I-ko-san'drus, *a.* Pertaining to such plants.

Icteric, **Icterical**, ik-ter'ik, ik-ter'i-kal, *a.* [L. *icterus*, jaundice.] Affected with jaundice; curative of jaundice.—**Icteritious**, **Icteroid**, ik-ter-ish'us, ik'tėr-oid, *a.* Pertaining to jaundice; yellow, as if jaundiced.

Ictus, ik'tus, *n.* [L., from *ico*, to strike.] A stroke; the stress laid on an accented syllable.

Icy. Under ICE.

Id, id, *n.* [Gr. *idios*, distinct.] A group of DETERMINANTS (which see).

Idalian, I-dā'li-an, *a.* Pertaining to *Idalium* or to Aphroditē (Venus), that ancient town being sacred to her.

Idant, id'ant, *n.* [Gr. *idios*, distinct.] A group of IDS (which see).

Idea, I-dē'a, *n.* [L. *idea*, from Gr. *idea*, the form or appearance of a thing, kind or species, from *idein*, to see; same root as E. *wit*.] The form, image, or model of anything in the mind; that which is held or comprehended by the understanding or intellectual faculties; as a philosophical term, now generally used to designate subjective notions and representations, with or without objective validity; popularly it signifies notion, conception, thought, opinion, belief.—**Ideal**, I-dē'al, *a.* Existing in idea; existing in fancy or imagination only; visionary.—*n.* An imaginary model of perfection; a standard of perfection or beauty.—*Beau Ideal*. Under BEAU.—**Idealess**, I-dē'a-les, *a.* Destitute of ideas.—**Idealism**, I-dē'al-izm, *n.* That system of philosophy according to which nothing exists but the mind itself and ideas perceived by the mind, or which maintains that we have no rational grounds for believing in the reality of anything but percipient minds and ideas.—**Idealist**, I-dē'-al-ist, *n.* One who holds the doctrine of idealism; one who idealizes; one who indulges in flights of fancy or imagination; a visionary.—**Idealistic**, I-dē'al-is"tik, *a.* Pertaining to idealism or idealists.—**Ideality**, I-dē-al'i-ti, *n.* The condition or quality of being ideal; capacity to form ideals of beauty and perfection.—**Idealization**, I-dē'al-i-zā"shon, *n.* The act of idealizing.—**Idealize**, I-dē'al-īz, *v.t.*—*idealized*, *idealizing*. To make ideal; to give form to in accordance with any preconceived ideal; to embody in an ideal form.—*v.i.* To form ideals.—**Idealizer**, I-dē'al-ī-zėr, *n.* One who idealizes; an idealist.—**Ideally**, I-dē'al-li, *adv.* In an ideal manner.—**Idealogic**, I-dē'a-loj"ik, *a.* Pertaining to an idealogue, or to his theories or ideas.—**Idealogue**, I-dē'a-log, *n.* One given to form ideals; a theorist; a dreamer.—**Ideation**, I-dē-ā'shon, *n.* The faculty of the mind for forming ideas; the establishment of a distinct mental representation or idea of an object.—**Ideational**, I-dē-ā'-shon-al, *a.* Pertaining to ideation.—**Ideograph**, **Ideogram**, id'ē-ō-graf, id'ē-ō-gram, *n.* In some systems of writing, a character, symbol, or figure which suggests the idea of an object without expressing its name; a hieroglyphic.—**Ideographic**, **Ideographical**, id'ē-ō-graf"ik, id'ē-ō-graf"i-kal, *a.* Representing ideas independently of sounds; pertaining to that mode of writing which, by means of symbols, figures, or hieroglyphics, suggests the ideas of objects.—**Ideographically**, id'ē-ō-graf"i-kal-li, *adv.* In an ideographic manner.—**Ideography**, id-ē-og'ra-fi, *n.* Writing in ideographic characters or symbols.—**Ideology**, id-ē-ol'o-ji, *n.* The science of ideas or of the understanding; that system of mental philosophy which exclusively derives our knowledge from sensation. Also written **Idealogy**, id-ē-al'o-ji.—**Ideological**, id'ē-ō-loj"i-kal, *a.* Pertaining to ideology.—**Ideologist**, id-ē-ol'o-jist, *n.* One who treats of ideas; one who indulges in ideas or theories; a supporter of ideology.

Identical, **Identic**, I-den'ti-kal, I-den'tik, *a.* [L.L. *identicus*, from L. *idem*, the same.] The same; not another or different.—*Identical proposition*, a proposition in which the terms of the subject and the predicate comprise the same idea, as that the whole is equal to its parts.—**Identically**, I-den'-

ti-kal-li, *adv.* In an identical manner.—**Identicalness**, ī-den'ti-kal-nes, *n.* Sameness.—**Identifiable**, ī-den'ti-fī-a-bl, *a.* That may be identified.—**Identification**, ī-den'ti-fi-kā"shon, *n.* The act of identifying.—*Identification tag*, A disk worn around the neck by both officers and men in active military service, showing name, number, unit, &c.—**Identify**, ī-den'ti-fī, *v.t.*—*identified, identifying.* [From *identi-* in *identity*, and L. *facio*, to make.] To make to be the same: to unite or combine in such a manner as to make one; to determine or establish the identity of; to ascertain or prove to be the same with something described or claimed.—*v.i.* To become the same.—**Identity**, ī-den'ti-ti, *n.* [L.L. *identitas*, from L. *idem*, same.] The state or fact of being identical; sameness, as distinguished from similitude and diversity.—*Personal identity*, our being the same persons from the commencement to the end of life while the matter of the body, the dispositions, habits, thoughts, &c., are continually changing.—*Principle of identity, philos.* the principle that a thing is what it is and not another.

Ideograph, Ideology, &c. Under IDEA.

Ides, īdz, *n. pl.* [L. *idus*, the ides, from *iduo*, to divide.] In the ancient Roman calendar the 13th of January, February, April, June, August, September, November, and December, and the 15th of March, May, July, and October.

Idiocrasy, id-i-ok'ra-si, *n.* [Gr. *idios*, peculiar, and *krasis*, mixture, temperament.] Peculiarity of constitution; temperament or constitution peculiar to a person; idiosyncrasy.—**Idiocratic, Idiocratical**, id'i-ō-krat"ik, id'i-ō-krat"i-kal, *a.* Peculiar in constitution; idiosyncratic.

Idiocy. Under IDIOT.

Idioelectric, id'i-ō-ē-lek"trik, *a.* [Gr. *idios*, one's own, and E. *electric.*] Electric by virtue of its own peculiar properties.

Idiograph, id'i-ō-graf, *n.* [Gr. *idios*, peculiar, private, and *graphō*, to write.] A mark, signature, or the like, peculiar to an individual; a private or trade mark.—**Idiographic**, id'i-ō-graf"ik, *a.* Pertaining to or consisting of an idiograph or idiographs.

Idiolatry, id-i-ol'a-tri, *n.* [Gr. *idios*, belonging to one's self, and *latreia*, worship.] Self-worship; excessive self-esteem.

Idiom, id'i-om, *n.* [Fr. *idiome*, L. *idioma*, from Gr. *idiōma*, from *idios*, proper, or peculiar to one's self.] A mode of expression peculiar to a language or to a person; a phrase or expression having a special meaning from usage, or a special grammatical character; the genius or peculiar cast of a language; a peculiar form or variety of language; a dialect.—**Idiomatic, Idiomatical**, id'i-ō-mat"ik, id'i-ō-mat"i-kal, *a.* Having the character of an idiom; pertaining to the particular modes of expression which belong to a language.—**Idiomatically**, id'i-ō-mat"i-kal-li, *adv.* In an idiomatic manner.

Idiomorphic, id'i-ō-mor"fik, *a.* [Gr. *idios*, one's own, *morphē*, form.] Having a peculiar or distinctive form.

Idiopathy, id-i-op'a-thi, *n.* [Gr. *idios*, proper, peculiar, and *pathos*, suffering.] A morbid state or condition not preceded and occasioned by any other disease.—**Idiopathic, Idiopathetic, Idiopathical**, id'i-ō-path"ik, id'i-ō-pa-thet"ik, id'i-ō-path"i-kal, *a.* Pertaining to idiopathy; not symptomatic.—**Idiopathically, Idiopathetically**, id'i-ō-path"i-kal-li, id'i-ō-pa-thet"i-kal-li, *adv.* In the manner of an idiopathic disease.

Idiosyncrasy, id'i-ō sin"kra-si, *n.* [Gr. *idios*, proper, *syn*, with, and *krasis*, temperament.] A personal peculiarity of constitution or temperament; a mental or moral characteristic belonging to and distinguishing an individual; peculiar way of thinking or feeling.—**Idiosyncratic, Idiosyncratical**, id'i-ō-sin-krat"ik, id'i-ō-sin-krat"i-kal, *a.* Relating to idiosyncrasy.

Idiot, id'i-ot, *n.* [L. *idiota*, from Gr. *idiōtēs*, a private, vulgar, unskilled person, from *idios*, private, peculiar to one's self.] A private person†; a human being destitute of reason or the ordinary intellectual powers of man; one hopelessly insane.—*a.* Pertaining to an idiot; afflicted with idiocy.—**Idiocy, Idiotcy**, id'i-o-si, id'i-ot-si, *n.* State of being an idiot; hopeless insanity.—**Idiotic, Idiotical**, id-i-ot'ik, id-i-ot'i-kal, *a.* Like or relating to an idiot; foolish; utterly absurd.—**Idiotically**, id-i-ot'i-kal-li, *adv.* In an idiotic manner.—**Idiotish**, id'i-ot-ish, *a.* Like an idiot; idiotic.

Idioticon, id-i-ot'i-kon, *n.* [Gr. *idiōtikon*, from *idios*, proper to one's self.] A dictionary of idioms; a dictionary or dialectal words. — **Idiotism**, id'i-ot-izm, *n.* [Gr. *idiōtismos*, a vulgar idiom.] An idiom; a peculiar or abnormal idiom.

Idle, ī'dl, *a.* [A.Sax. *idel*, vain, empty, idle = D. *ijdel*, G. *eitel*, idle; Dan. *idel*, mere; from root meaning to shine (Skr. *idh*, Gr. *aithō*, to burn).] Not engaged in any occupation; unoccupied; doing nothing; slothful; averse to labour or employment; lazy; vacant, or not spent in work (*idle* hours); remaining unused; producing no effect; useless, vain, ineffectual, or fruitless (*idle* rage); trifling or irrelevant (an *idle* story).—*v.i.*—*idled, idling.* To lose or spend time in inaction or without being employed. — *v.t.* To spend in idleness: generally followed by *away*.—**Idleness**, ī'dl-nes, *n.* The condition or quality of being idle.—**Idler**, īd'lėr, *n.* One who idles.—**Idle-wheel**, *n.* In machinery, a wheel placed between two others for the purpose simply of transferring the motion from one axis to the other without change of direction.—**Idly**, īd'li, *adv.* In an idle manner.

Idocrase, ī'dō-krās, *n.* [Gr. *eidos*, form, and *krasis*, mixture, from the mixture of forms its crystals display.] A mineral differing from garnet chiefly in form, occurring, variously coloured, in the lavas of Vesuvius and elsewhere; pyramidal garnet or Vesuvian.

Idol, ī'dol, *n.* [Fr. *idole*, L. *idolum*, from Gr. *eidōlon*, an image, form, phantom, idol, from *eidos*, form; same root as in *idea.*] An image, representation, or symbol of a deity made or consecrated as an object of worship; any person or thing on which we strongly set our affections; that to which we are excessively, often improperly, attached.—**Idolater**, ī-dol'a-tėr, *n.* [Fr. *idolâtre*, L. *idololatre*, Gr. *eidōlolatrēs*, an idol-worshipper. IDOLATRY.] A worshipper of idols; one who worships as a deity that which is not God; a pagan; an adorer; a great admirer.—**Idolatress**, ī-dol'at-res, *n.* A female worshipper of idols.—**Idolatrize**, ī-dol'at-rīz, *v.i.* To worship idols.—*v.t.* To adore; to worship.—**Idolatrous**, ī-dol'at-rus, *a.* Pertaining to idolatry; partaking of the nature of idolatry; worshipping false gods; consisting in or partaking of an excessive attachment or reverence.—**Idolatrously**, ī-dol'at-rus-li, *adv.* In an idolatrous manner.—**Idolatry**, ī-dol'at-ri, *n.* [Fr. *idolatrie*, L. *idololatria*, from Gr. *eidōlolatreia*—*eidōlon*, idol, and *latreuō*, to worship.] The worship of idols, images, or anything made by hands, or which is not God; excessive attachment to or veneration for any person or thing.—**Idolism**,† ī'dol-izm, *n.* The worship of idols.—**Idolize**, ī'dol-īz, *v.t.*—*idolized, idolizing.* To worship as an idol; to make an idol of; to love to excess; to love or reverence to adoration.—**Idolizer**, ī'dol-ī-zėr, *n.* One who idolizes.—**Idoloclast**, ī-dol'o-klast, *n.* [Gr. *eidōlon*, and *klaō*, to break.] An idol or image breaker; an iconoclast.

Idyl, Idyll, ī'dil, *n.* [L. *idyllium*, Gr. *eidyllion*, from *eidos*, form.] A short highly wrought descriptive poem, consisting generally of scenes or events of pastoral life.—**Idyllic**, ī-dil'ik, *a.* Of or belonging to idyls or pastoral poetry; pastoral.

If, if, *conj.* [A.Sax. *gif*, if; Icel. *ef*, *if*, if; akin O.G. *ibu*, G. *ob*, if, whether; Goth. *iba*, whether, *jabai*, if.] A particle used to introduce a conditional sentence, equal to—in case that, granting that, supposing that, allowing that; also, whether: in dependent clauses (I know not *if* he will).

Igneous, ig'nē-us, *a.* [L. *igneus*, from *ignis*, fire, allied to Skr. *agni*, fire.] Pertaining to, consisting of, or resembling fire; produced by or resulting from the action of fire.—**Ignescent**, ig-nes'ent, *a.* [L. *ignescens.*] Emitting sparks of fire when struck, especially with steel.— *n.* A mineral that gives out sparks when struck.—**Ignicolist**, ig-nik'ol-ist, *n.* [L. *ignis*, and *colo*, to worship.] A worshiper of fire.—**Igniferous**, ig-nif'ėr-us, *a.* [L. *ignifer.*] Producing fire.—**Ignigenous**, ig-nij'e-nus, *a.* [L. *ignis*, and root *gen*, to produce.] Produced by fire.—**Ignipotent**, ig-nip'o-tent, *a.* [L. *ignipotens*—*ignis*, and *potens*, powerful.] Presiding over fire.—**Ignis-fatuus**, ig'nis-fat'ū-us, *n.* pl. **Ignes-fatui**, ig'nēz-fat'ū-ī. [L., foolish-fire.] A phosphorescent light appearing in the air over marshlands, visible at night; popularly known by such names as *Will-o'-the-wisp*, *Jack-o'-lantern;* something that is misleading.—**Ignite**, ig-nīt', *v.t.*—*ignited, igniting.* To kindle or set on fire; to communicate fire to.—*v.i.* To take fire; to become red with heat.—**Ignition**, ig-nish'on, *n.* The act of igniting, or state of being ignited; the act or means of exploding the charge of gases in the cylinder of an internal-combustion engine.

Ignoble, ig-nō'bl, *a.* [L. *ignobilis*—*in*, not, and *gnobilis*, or *nobilis*, noble. NOBLE.] Of low birth or family; not noble; not illustrious; mean; worthless; not honourable; base.—**Ignobleness**, ig-nō'bl-nes, *n.* The condition or quality of being ignoble.—**Ignobly**, ig-nō'bli, *adv.* In an ignoble manner.

Ignominy, ig'no-mi-ni, *n.* [L. *ignominia*—*in*, not, and *gnomen*, *nomen*, name, from root seen in E. *know.*] Public disgrace; shame; dishonour; infamy.—**Ignominious**, ig-nō-min'i-us, *a.* [L. *ignominiosus.*] Marked with ignominy; shameful; dishonourable; infamous; despicable.—**Ignominiously**, ig-nō-min'i-us-ly, *adv.* In an ignominious manner.

Ignoramus, ig-nō-rā mus, *n.* pl. **Ignoramuses**, ig-nō-rā'mus-ez. [1st pers. pl. pres. ind. of L. *ignoro*—lit. we are ignorant. IGNORE.] An ignorant person; a vain pretender to knowledge.

Ignorant, ig'nō-rant, *a.* [L. *ignorans*, *ignorantis*, ppr. of *ignoro*, to be ignorant. IGNORE.] Destitute of knowledge in general, or with regard to some particular: with *of* before an object; uninstructed or uninformed; untaught; unenlightened; unacquainted; unconscious. — **Ignorantly**, ig'nō-rant-li, *adv.* In an ignorant manner.—**Ignorance**, ig'nō-rans, *n.* [L. *ignorantia.*] The state of being ignorant; want of knowledge; the condition of not being cognizant or aware; inacquaintance.

Ignore, ig-nōr', *v.t.*—*ignored, ignoring.* [L. *ignoro*, to be ignorant of, from *ignarus*, not knowing—*in*, not, and *gnarus*, knowing, from root of *gnosco*, to know, and E. *know.*] To pass over or by without notice; to act as if one were unacquainted with; to shut the eyes to; to leave out of account; to disregard; to reject.—**Ignorement**,† ig-nōr'ment, *n.* The act of ignoring.

Iguana, ig-wä'na, *n.* [Sp., from the Haytian language.] A reptile of the lizard family, with pendulous dewlaps, native of tropical America, some species of which are much esteemed as food.

Iguanodon, ig-wä'no-don, *n.* [*Iguana* and Gr. *odous*, *odontos*, a tooth, from the character of its teeth.] A colossal fossil lizard found in the Wealden strata.

Ileum, il'ē-um, *n.* [From Gr. *eilō*, to roll, from its convolutions; or from L. *ilia*, intestines. ILIAC.] *Anat.* the lower three-fifths of the small intestine in man.

Ileus, ī'lē-us, *n.* [Gr. *ileos*, *eileos*, a severe pain in the intestines.] *Med.* colic; iliac passion.

Iliac, il'i-ak, *a.* [L. *iliacus*, from *ilia*, the flank, the groin, the intestines.] Pertaining to the bowels, especially the lower bowels, or to the part of the abdomen containing them.—*Iliac region*, the side of the abdomen between the ribs and the hips. —*Iliac arteries*, the arteries formed by the bifurcation of the aorta near the last lumbar vertebra.—*Iliac passion*, a dangerous ailment, consisting in obstruction of the bowels, accompanied with severe griping pain, and often vomiting of fecal matter.—**Ilium**, il'i-um, *n.* [Properly *os ilium*, bone of the ilia or flank.] *Anat.* a bone that forms the outer portion of the pelvis on either side; the hip-bone.

Ilk, ilk, *a.* [A.Sax. *ilc*, *ylc*, same.] Same. [Old E.]—*Of that ilk*, in Scot., a phrase sometimes used after the name of a landed gentleman to denote that his surname and the title of his estate are the same.

Ill, il, *a.* [From the Scandinavian; Icel. *illr*, adj. ill; Icel. and Sw. *illa*, adv. ill; a contracted form of *evil*. Its comparative and superlative, *worse* and *worst*, are from a different root.] Bad or evil; the opposite of good; wicked; wrong: used of things rather than persons; producing evil or misfortune; calamitous or unfortunate (an *ill* end); cross, crabbed, surly, or peevish (*ill* nature, *ill* temper); suffering from disease or sickness; sick or indisposed; unwell (*ill* of a fever); not proper; rude or unpolished (*ill* manners, *ill* breeding).—*Ill turn*, an unkind or injurious act.—*n.* Wickedness; evil; misfortune; calamity; whatever annoys or impairs happiness or prevents success. —*adv.* Not well; not rightly or perfectly (*ill* at ease); not easily; with pain or difficulty (he is *ill* able to sustain the burden). [*Ill*, prefixed to participles, or adjectives having the form of participles, forms a great number of compound words the meaning of which is generally obvious.]—**Illness**, il'nes, *n.* The state or condition of being ill; an ailment or sickness.—**Ill-advised**, *a.* Badly advised; resulting from bad advice or the want of good; injudicious.—**Ill-affected**, *a.* Not well inclined or disposed. —**Ill-blood**, *n.* Resentment; enmity —**Ill-bred**, *a.* Not well bred; badly educated or brought up; impolite. —**Ill-conditioned**, *a.* Having bad qualities; having a rude, surly temper.—**Ill-considered**, *a.* Not well considered; done without due deliberation.—**Ill-disposed**, *a.* Not well disposed; wickedly or maliciously inclined. —**Ill-fated**, *a.* Having an ill or evil fate; ill-starred: unfortunate —**Ill-favored**, *a.* Having ill features; ugly.—**Ill-got**, **Ill-gotten**, *a.* Gained by unfair or improper means; dishonestly come by.—**Ill-humor**, *n.* Ill temper, fretfulness.—**Ill-judged**, *a.* Not well judged; injudicious; unwise.—**Ill-luck**, *n.* Misfortune; bad luck.—**Ill-mannered**, *a.* Uncivil; rude; impolite.—**Ill-matched**, *a.* Badly assorted; not well suited.—**Ill-meaning**, *a.* Having malicious intentions; ill-intentioned.—**Ill-nature**, *n.* Evil nature or disposition; bad temper; crossness; crabbedness.—**Ill-natured**, *a.* Having ill-nature; of habitual bad temper; bad-tempered.—**Ill-naturedly**, *adv.* In an ill-natured manner; crossly.—**Ill-omened**, *a.* Having unlucky omens; unfortunate.—**Ill-starred**, *a.* Having an evil star presiding over one's destiny; hence, fated to be unfortunate; ill-fated.—**Ill-tempered**, *a.* Of bad temper.—**Ill-timed**, *a.* Attempted, done, or said at an unsuitable time.—**Ill-will**, *n.* A desire that evil will befall a person; enmity.

Illapse, il-laps', *v.i.* [L. *illabor*, *illapsus*, to slip or slide into—*il* for *in*, into, and *labor*, to slip.]† To fall, pass, or glide; to lapse.—*n.* A sliding in; an immission or entrance of one thing into another; a falling on; an attack.

Illaqueate, il-lak'wē-āt, *v.t.* [L. *illaqueo*, *illaqueatum*—*il* for *in*, in, and *laqueus*, a snare.]† To ensnare; to entangle.

Illation, il-lā'shon, *n.* [L. *illatio*—*il* for *in*, in, on, and *latio*, a bearing, from *fero*, *latum*, to bear.] The act of inferring from premises or reasons; inference; an inference, deduction, or conclusion.—**Illative**, il'la-tiv, *a.* Relating to illation; capable of being inferred or of inferring; denoting an inference (*then* or *therefore* is an *illative* word).—*n.* An illative word.—**Illatively**, il'la-tiv-li, *adv.* By illation or inference.

Illaudable, il-la̦'da-bl, *a.* [Prefix *il* for *in*, not, and *laudable*.] Not laudable.—**Illaudably**, il-la̦'da-bli, *adv.* In an illaudable manner.

Illegal, il-lē'gal, *a.* [Prefix *il* for *in*, not, and *legal*.] Not legal; contrary to law; unlawful; illicit. —**Illegality**, **Illegalness**, il-lē-gal'i-ti, il-lē'gal-nes, *n.* The condition or quality of being illegal.—**Illegalize**, il-lē'gal-īz, *v.t.* —*illegalized*, *illegalizing*. To render illegal or unlawful. —**Illegally**, il-lē'gal-li, *adv.* In an illegal manner.

Illegible, il-lej'i-bl, *a.* [Prefix *il* for *in*, not, and *legible*.] Incapable of being read; obscure or defaced so that the words cannot be known. —**Illegibility**, **Illegibleness**, il-lej'i-bil"i-ti, il-lej'i-bl-nes, *n.* The state or quality of being illegible. —**Illegibly**, il-lej'i-bli, *adv.* In an illegible manner.

Illegitimate, il-lē-jit'i-māt, *a.* [Prefix *il* for *in*, not, and *legitimate*.] Not legitimate; born out of wedlock; not in conformity with law; not authorized; not legitimately inferred or deduced; not warranted (an *illegitimate* inference).—*v.t.*—*illegitimated*, *illegitimating*. To render illegitimate; to bastardize.—**Illegitimacy**, il-lē-jit'i-ma-si, *n.* The state of being illegitimate, bastardy.—**Illegitimately**, il-lē-jit'i-māt-li, *adv.* In an illegitimate manner.—**Illegitimation**, il-lē-jit'i-mā"shon, *n.* The act of illegitimating.

Illeviable, il-lev'i-a-bl, *a.* [Prefix *il* for *in*, not, and *leviable*.] Incapable of being levied or collected.

Illiberal, il-lib'ėr-al, *a.* [Prefix *il* for *in*, not, and *liberal*.] Not liberal; not free or generous; of narrow or contracted mind or opinions. —**Illiberality**, **Illiberalism**, **Illiberalness**, il-lib'ėr-al"i-ti, il-lib'ėr-al-izm, il-lib'ėr-al-nes, *n.* The quality of being illiberal.—**Illiberalize**, il-lib'ėr-al-īz, *v.t.* To make illiberal. —**Illiberally**, il-lib'ėr-al-li, *adv.* In an illiberal manner.

Illicit, il-lis'it, *n.* [L. *illicitus*—*il*, not, and *licitus*, lawful, from *liceo* to be allowed.] Not permitted, sanctioned, or allowed by law, rule or tradition; prohibited; unlawful.—**Illicitly**, il-lis'it-li, *adv.* In an illicit manner.—**Illicitness**, il-lis'it-nes, *n.* The state or quality of being illicit.

Illimitable, il-lim'it-a-bl, *a.* [Prefix *il* for *in*, not, and *limitable*.] Incapable of being limited or bounded; boundless; immeasurable.—**Illimitably**, il-lim'it-a-bli, *adv.* Without possibility of being bounded; without limits.—**Illimitableness**, il-lim'it-a-bl-nes, *n.*—**Illimited**, il-lim'it-ed, *a.* Unbounded; interminable. **Illimitedness**, il-lim'it-ed-nes, *n.*

Illinition, il-li-nish'on, *n.* [L. *illinio*, *illinitum*, to spread or lay on—*il* for *in*, on, and *lino*, to smear.] A smearing or rubbing in or on, as of an ointment.

Illiterate, il-lit'ėr-āt, *a.* [L. *illiteratus*—*il* for *in*, not, and *literatus*, lettered, learned, from *litera*, a letter. LETTER.] Ignorant of letters or books; untaught; unlearned; ignorant.—**Illiteracy**, il-lit'ėr-a-si, *n.* The state of being illiterate; a literary error†. —**Illiterately**, il-lit'ėr-āt-li, *adv.* In an illiterate manner.

Illness. Under ILL.

Illogical, il-loj'i-kal, *a.* [Prefix *il* for *in*, not, and *logical*.] Ignorant or negligent of the rules of logic or correct reasoning; contrary to logic or sound reasoning. —**Illogically**, il-loj'i-kal-li, *adv.* In an illogical manner. —**Illogicalness**, il-loj'i-kal-nes, *n.* The quality of being illogical.

Illude, il-lūd', *v.t.*—*illuded*, *illuding*. [L. *illudo*, *illusum*—prefix *il* for *in*, on, and *ludo*, to play. DELUDE.]† To deceive; to mock; to make sport of.

Illuminate, il-lū'mi-nāt, *v.t.* —*illuminated*, *illuminating*. [L. *illumino*, *illuminatum*—prefix *il* for *in*, in, and *lumen*, *luminis*, light. LUMINARY, LUCID.] To enlighten; to throw light on; to supply with light; to light up with festal lamps, bonfires, or the like; to adorn (a manuscript) with gilded and coloured decorations or illustrations.—**Illume**, il-lūm', *v.t.*—*illumed*, *illuming*. To illumine or illuminate. (*Poet.*)—**Illuminable**, il-lū'mi-na-bl, *a.* Capable of being illuminated.—**Illuminant**, il-lū'mi-nant, *n.* That which illuminates or affords light.—**Illuminary**, il-lū'mi-na-ri, *a.* Pertaining to illumination. —**Illuminati**, il-lū'mi-nā"tī, *n. pl.* A term formerly applied to certain sects and secret societies, now applied to persons who affect to possess extraordinary knowledge whether justly or otherwise.—**Illumination**, il-lū'mi-nā"shon, *n.* [L. *illuminatio*, *illuminationis*.] The act of illuminating, or state of being illuminated; a festive display of lights, &c.; an ornament or illustration in colours and gilding, such as those with which ancient manuscripts or books were embellished. —**Illuminative**, il-lū'mi-nā-tiv, *a.* Having the power of illuminating; tending to throw light; illustrative. —**Illuminator**, il-lū'mi-nā-tėr, *n.* One who or that which illuminates.—**Illumine**, il-lū'min, *v.t.* To illuminate. (*Poet.*)

Illusion, il-lū'zhon, *n.* [L. *illusio*, *illusionis*, from *illudo*. ILLUDE.] The act of deceiving or imposing upon; deception; mockery; a deceptive appearance; an unreal vision presented to the bodily or mental eye; hallucination.—**Illusionable**, il-lū'zhon-a-bl, *a.* Subject to illusions.—**Illusionist**, il-lū'zhon-ist, *n.* One given to illusion.—**Illusive**, il-lū'siv, *a.* Deceiving by false show; illusory.—**Illusively**, il-lū'siv-li, *adv.* In an illusive manner. —**Illusiveness**, il-lū'siv-nes, *n.*—**Illusory**, il-lū'so-ri, *a.* [Fr. *illusoire*, from L. *illudo*, *illusum*.] Causing illusion; deceiving or tending to deceive by false appearances; false and deceptive; fallacious.

Illustrate, il'us-trāt, *v.t.* —*illustrated*, *illustrating*. [L. *illustro*, *illustratum*, to light up, to illuminate—*il* for *in*, and *lustro*, to make light. LUSTRE.] To illuminate†; to glorify†; to make bright or conspicuous†; to make clear, intelligible, or obvious; to throw light on by examples, by comparisons, and the like; to ornament and elucidate by means of pictures, drawings, &c.—**Illustrable**,† il-lus'tra-bl, *a.* Capable of being illustrated; admitting of illustration —**Illustration**, il-lus-trā'shon, *n.* The act of illustrating; that which illustrates; a particular case or example intended to throw light on one's meaning; a picture accompanying and illustrating the text of a book.—**Illustrative**, il-lus'tra-tiv, *a.* Tending to illustrate.—**Illustratively**, il-lus'tra-tiv-li, *adv.* By way of illustration or elucidation.—**Illustrator**, il-lus'trā-tėr, *n.* One who illustrates.

Illustrious, il-lus'tri-us, *a.* [From L. *illustris*, lighted up, clear, distinguished; probably contr. for *illucestris*—*il* for *in*, into, and *lux*, *lucis*, light. LUCID.] Distinguished by greatness, nobleness, or eminence among men; conspicuous for praiseworthy qualities, renowned; eminent; glorious; brilliant (an *illustrious* man, an *illustrious* action).—**Illustriously**, il-lus'tri-us-li, *adv.* In an illustrious manner.—**Illustriousness**, il-lus'tri-us-nes. *n.*

Ilmenite, il'men-īt, *n.* A black ore of iron found in the *Ilmen* Mountains in Russia.

Image, im'āj, *n.* [Fr., from L. *imago*, an image, likeness, apparition, &c., from stem of *imitor*, to imitate.] A representation of any person or thing, sculptured, painted, or otherwise made visible; a statue, picture, or stamped representation; an effigy; an idol; what forms a counterpart or likeness of something else; likeness; embodiment; a picture drawn by fancy; semblance; show; appearance; *optics*, the figure or appearance of an object made by reflection or refraction.—*v.t.*—*imaged*, *imaging*. To represent by an image; to reflect the image or likeness of; to mirror; to represent to the mental vision; to form a likeness of in the mind.—**Imageable**, im'āj-a-bl, *a.* Capable of being imaged.—**Imageless**, im'āj-les, *a.* Having no image.—**Imagery**, im'a-jėr-i, *n.* Images in general or collectively; forms of the fancy; imaginary phantasms; rhetorical figures collectively; comparisons, similes, &c., in discourse.—**Image-worship**, *n.* The worship of images; idolatry.

Imagine, im-aj'in, *v.t.—imagined, imagining.* [Fr. *imaginer*, L. *imaginor*, *imaginatum*, to imagine, from *imago*, image. IMAGE.] To form a notion or idea of in the mind; to bring before the mind's eye; to produce by the imagination; to conceive in thought; to think, scheme, or devise (O.T.).—*v.i.* To conceive; to suppose; to fancy; to think.—**Imaginable**, im-aj'i-na-bl, *a.* Capable of being imagined or conceived.—**Imaginableness**, im-aj'i-na-bl-nes, *n.*—**Imaginably**, im-aj'i-na-bli, *adv.* In an imaginable manner.—**Imaginal**,† im-aj'i-nal, *a.* Characterized by imagination; imaginative.—**Imaginarily**, im-aj'i-na-ri-li, *adv.* In an imaginary manner.—**Imaginariness**, im-aj'i-na-ri-nes, *n.* The condition or quality of being imaginary.—**Imaginary**, im-aj'i-na-ri, *a.* [L. *imaginarius*.] Existing only in imagination or fancy; conceived by the imagination; not real; fancied.—**Imagination**, im-aj'i-nā"shon, *n.* [L. *imaginatio*, *imaginationis*.] The power or faculty of the mind by which it conceives and forms ideas of things from knowledge communicated to it by the organs of sense; the faculty by which we can bring absent objects and perceptions forcibly before the mind; the power or faculty which enables a person to produce a new, impressive, and artistic whole by selecting and working up ideas derived through observation and memory, and which thus includes a certain share of invention; an image or conception in the mind; idea; an unsolid or fanciful opinion; a scheme or plot (O.T.).—**Imaginative**, im-aj'i-nā-tiv, *a.* Forming imaginations; endowed with imagination; owing existence to, or characterized by, imagination.—**Imaginativeness**, im-aj'i-nā-tiv-nes, *n.* Quality of being imaginative.—**Imaginer**, im-aj'i-nėr, *n.* One who imagines.

Imago, im-ā'gō, *n.* [L., an image.] The last or perfect state of an insect, usually that in which it has wings; *Psychoanalysis*, the childhood conception of the parent retained in the unconscious.

Imam, Imaum, Iman, i-mäm', i-mam', i-män', *n.* [Ar. *imâm*, from *amma*, to walk before, to preside.] A minister or priest who performs the regular service of the mosque among the Mohammedans; a title given to the successors of Mohammed; one who has followers in law or theology.

Imamate, i-mam'āt, *n.* The region that is ruled by an imam.

Imbecile, im'be-sil, *a.* [L. *imbecillis*, *imbecillus*, feeble in body or mind—origin doubtful.] Destitute of strength; weak; feeble; mentally feeble; fatuous; with mental faculties greatly impaired.—*n.* One that is imbecile or impotent either in body or mind.—**Imbecilitate**, im-be-sil'i-tāt, *v.t.* To render imbecile or feeble.—**Imbecility**, im-be-sil'i-ti, *n.* [L. *imbecillitas*.] The condition or quality of being imbecile; fatuity.

Imbed, im-bed', *v.t.* To embed.

Imber, Immer, im'bėr, im'ėr, *n.* The ember-goose.

Imbibe, im-bīb', *v.t.—imbibed, imbibing.* [L. *imbibo—im* for *in*, in, into, and *bibo*, to drink, whence also *beverage*.] To drink in; to absorb; to receive or admit into the mind and retain.—**Imbiber**, im-bī'bėr, *n.* One who or that which imbibes.—**Imbibition**, im-bi-bish'on, *n.* The act of imbibing.

Imbitter, Imblazon, Imbody, Imbolden, Imborder, Imbosom, Imbowel, Imbower. EMBITTER, &c.

Imbricate, Imbricated, im'bri-kāt, im'bri-kā-ted, *a.* [L. *imbricatus*, from *imbrex*, *imbricis*, a hollow tile for a roof, from *imber*, a shower=Gr. *ombros*, rain.] Formed like a bent or hollow tile; lapping over each other, like tiles on a roof, or the scales of fishes and reptiles.—**Imbrication**, im-bri-kā'shon, *n.* State of being imbricate; a hollow like that of a roof tile.

Imbroglio, im-brō'lyō, *n.* [It., from prefix *im* for *in*, and *brogliare*, to confound or mix together; akin *broil*.] An intricate and perplexing state of affairs; a misunderstanding between persons or nations of a complicated nature.

Imbrown, im-broun', *v.t.* To make brown, to embrown.

Imbrue, im-brö', *v.t.—imbrued, imbruing.* [O.Fr. *embruer*, *s'embruer*, to dabble one's self, from prefix *im* for *in*, in, and L. *bibere*, to drink; comp. Fr. *breuvage*, beverage, also from *bibere*.] To soak or drench in a fluid, as in blood.—**Imbruement**, im-brö'ment, *n.* The act of imbruing.

Imbrute, im-bröt', *v.t.—imbruted, imbruting.* To degrade to the state of a brute.—*v.i.* To sink to the state of a brute. (*Mil.*)

Imbue, im-bū', *v.t.—imbued, imbuing.* [L. *imbuo*, allied to *imber*, a shower; Skr. *ambu*, water. IMBRICATE.] To soak, steep, or tinge deeply; *fig.* to inspire, impress, or impregnate (the mind); to cause to become impressed or penetrated.—**Imbuement, Imbution**, im-bū'ment, im-bū'shon, *n.* The act of imbuing.

Imitate, im'i-tāt, *v.t.—imitated, imitating.* [L. *imitor*, *imitatus*, from a root which gives also *imago*, image.] To follow as a model, pattern, or example; to copy or endeavour to copy in acts, manners, or otherwise, to produce a likeness of in form, colour, qualities, conduct, manners, and the like, to counterfeit.—**Imitability, Imitableness**, im'i-ta-bil"i-ti, im'i-ta-bl-nes, *n.* The condition or quality of being imitable.—**Imitable** im'i-ta-bl, *a.* Capable of being imitated or copied.—**Imitation**, im-i-tā'shon, *n.* [L. *imitatio*, *imitationis*.] The act of imitating; that which is made or produced as a copy, a likeness; a copy; a counterfeit; *mus.* the repetition of the same melodic idea by different parts or voices in a composition.—**Imitational**, im-i-tā'shon-al, *a.* Relating to imitation.—**Imitationist**, im-i-tā'shon-ist, *n.* A mere imitator; one who wants originality.—**Imitative**, im'i-tā-tiv, *a.* Inclined to imitate or copy; aiming at imitation; exhibiting an imitation of a pattern or model, formed after a model or original; intended to represent an actual sound by the sound of the letters (an *imitative* word).—**Imitatively**, im'i-tā-tiv-li, *adv.* In an imitative manner.—**Imitativeness**, im'i-tā-tiv-nes, *n.* Quality of being imitative.—**Imitator**, im'i-tā-tėr, *n.* One who imitates.

Immaculate, im-mak'ū-lāt, *a.* [L. *immaculatus—im* for *in*, not, and *maculatus*, from *macula*, a spot.] Spotless; pure; unstained; undefiled; without blemish.—*Immaculate conception*, the dogma of the Roman Catholic Church (settled in 1854), that the Virgin Mary was conceived and born without original sin.—**Immaculately**, im-mak'ū-lāt-li, *adv.* In an immaculate manner.—**Immaculateness**, im-mak'ū-lāt-nes, *n.* The condition or quality of being immaculate.

Immalleable, im-mal'lē-a-bl, *a.* [Prefix *im* for *in*, not, and *malleable*.] Not malleable.

Immanate, im'ma-nāt, *v.i.* [L. *im* for *in*, in, and *mano*, to flow.] To flow or issue in: said of something intangible.—**Immanation**, im-ma-nā'shon, *n.* A flowing in.

Immanent, im'ma-nent, *a.* [L. *immanens*, *immanentis*, ppr. of *immaneo—im* for *in*, in, and *maneo*, to remain (as in *remain*, *mansion*).] Remaining in or within; hence, not passing out of the subject; inherent and indwelling; internal or subjective: opposed to *transitive*.—**Immanence, Immanency**, im'ma-nens, im'ma-nen-si, *n.* The condition of being immanent.

Immantle, im-man'tl, *v.t.* To envelop, as with a mantle.

Immanuel, im-man'ū-el, *n.* [Heb.—*im*, with, *anu*, us, and *El*, God.] God with us: an appellation of our Saviour.

Immarginate, im-mär'ji-nāt, *a.* [Prefix *im* for *in*, not, and *marginate*.] Without a margin.

Immaterial, im-ma-tē'ri-al, *a.* [Prefix *im* for *in*, not, and *material*.] Not consisting of matter; incorporeal; spiritual; of no essential consequence; unimportant.—**Immaterialism**, im-ma-tē'ri-al-izm, *n.* The doctrine that immaterial substances or spiritual beings exist or are possible; the doctrine that there is no material world, but that all exists only in the mind.—**Immaterialist**, im-ma-tē'ri-al-ist, *n.* One who professes immaterialism.—**Immateriality, Immaterialness**, im-ma-tē'ri-al"i-ti, im-ma-tē'ri-al-nes, *n.* The quality of being immaterial or not consisting of matter; absence of matter.—**Immaterialize**, im-ma-tē'ri-al-īz, *v.t.* To make immaterial or incorporeal.—**Immaterially**, im-ma-tē'ri-al-li, *adv.* In an immaterial manner.

Immature, im-ma-tūr', *a.* [L. *immaturus*, unripe—*im* for *in*, not, and *maturus*, ripe.] Not mature or ripe; unripe; not brought to a complete state; too early; premature.—**Immaturely**, im-ma-tūr'li, *adv.* In an immature manner.—**Immatureness, Immaturity**, im-ma-tūr'nes, im-ma-tū'ri-ti, *n.* The state or quality of being immature; unripeness.

Immeasurable, im-mezh'ū-ra-bl, *a.* [Prefix *im* for *in*, not, and *measurable*.] Incapable of being measured.—**Immeasurableness, Immeasurability**, im-mezh'ū-ra-bl-nes, im-mezh'ū-ra-bil"i-ti, *n.* The state of being immeasurable.—**Immeasurably**, im-mezh'ū-ra-bli, *adv.* In an immeasurable manner; immensely; beyond all measure.

Immediate, im-mē'di-āt, *a.* [Prefix *im* for *in*, not, and *mediate*.] Not separated by anything intervening; placed in the closest relation; not separated by an interval of time; instant; acting without a medium, or without the intervention of another object as a cause, means, or condition; produced, acquired, or obtained without the intervention of a medium; direct.—**Immediacy**, im-mē'di-a-si, *n.* The relation of being immediate; immediateness; proximity.—**Immediately**, im-mē'di-āt-li, *adv.* In an immediate manner; without the intervention of anything; directly; without delay; instantly; forthwith.—**Immediateness**, im-mē'di-āt-nes, *n.*

Immelodious, im-me-lō'di-us, *a.* [Prefix *im* for *in*, not, and *melodious*.] Not melodious.

Immemorial, im-me-mō'ri-al, *a.* [L. *im* for *in*, not, and *memoria*, memory.] Beyond memory; extending beyond the reach of record or tradition.—**Immemorially**, im-me-mō'ri-al-li, *adv.* Beyond memory; from time out of mind.

Immense, im-mens', *a.* [L. *immensus—im* for *in*, not, and *mensus*, measured, pp. of *metior*, *mensus*, to measure. MEASURE.] Vast in extent or bulk; very great; very large; boundless; huge; enormous. ∴ Syn. under ENORMOUS.—**Immensely**, im-mens'li, *adv.* In an immense manner; vastly.—**Immenseness**, im-mens'nes, *n.* The condition or quality of being immense.—**Immensity**, im-men'si-ti, *n.* [L. *immensitas*.] The condition or quality of being immense; that which is immense; extent not to be measured; infinity.

Immensurable, im-men'sū-ra-bl, *a.* [L. *im* for *in*, not, and *mensurabilis*, from *mensura*, measure. MEASURE.] Not to be measured; immeasurable.—**Immensurability**, im-men'sū-ra-bil"i-ti, *n.* The quality of being immensurable.

Immerge, im-mėrj', *v.t.—immerged, immerging.* [L. *immergo—im* for *in*, into, and *mergo*, to plunge.] To plunge into or under anything, especially into or under a fluid.—*v.i.* To disappear by entering into any medium.

Immerse, im-mėrs', *v.t.—immersed, immersing.* [L. *immergo*, *immersum—im* for *in*, into, and *mergo*, to plunge. MERGE.] To plunge into anything that covers or surrounds, as into a fluid; to dip; *fig.* to engage deeply; to involve (to be *immersed* in business).—**Immersible**, im-mėr'si-bl, *a.* Capable of being immersed.—**Immersion**, im-mėr'shon, *n.* [L. *immersio, immersionis.*] The act of immersing, or state of being immersed; a sinking or dipping into anything; *astron.* the disappearance of a celestial body by passing either behind another or into its shadow: opposed to *emersion.*—**Immersionist**, im-mėr'shon-ist, *n.* One who holds that immersion is essential to Christian baptism.

Immesh, im-mesh', *v.t.* [Prefix *im* for *in*, and *mesh.*] To entangle in the meshes of a net or anything similar.

Immethodical, im-me-thod'i-kal, *a.* [Prefix *im* for *in*, not, and *methodical.*] Not methodical; without system, order, or regularity. — **Immethodically**, im-me-thod'i-kal-li, *adv.*—**Immethodicalness**, im-me-thod'i-kal-nes, *n.*

Immigrate, im'mi-grāt, *v.i.* [L. *immigro* —*im* for *in*, into, and *migro*, to migrate.] To remove into a country of which one is not a native for the purpose of permanent residence.—**Immigrant**, the correlative of *emigrant.*—**Immigration**, im-mi-grā'-shon, *n.* The act of immigrating; the number of immigrants arriving in a certain country in a specific time.

Imminent, im'mi-nent, *a.* [L. *imminens, imminentis*, ppr. of *immineo*, to hang over —*im* for *in*, on, and *mineo*, as in *eminent.*] Hanging over; threatening to fall or occur (*imminent* danger, war); impending; near at hand; threatening evil.—**Imminence**, im'mi-nens, *n.* The quality or condition of being imminent.—**Imminently**, im'mi-nent-li, *adv.* In an imminent manner; threateningly.

Immit, im-mit', *v.t.* [L. *immitto*—*im* for *in*, in, into, and *mitto*, to send.] To send in; to inject: the correlative of *emit.*—**Immission**, im-mish'on, *n.* [L. *immissio.*] The act of immitting: the correlative of *emmission.*

Immix, im-miks', *v.t.* [Prefix *im* for *in*, and *mix.*] To mix; to mingle.

Immobile, im-mob'il, *a.* [Prefix *im* for *in*, not, and *mobile*; L. *immobilis.*] Not mobile; immovable; fixed; stable.—**Immobility**, im-mō-bil'i-ti, *n.* The condition or quality of being immobile.

Immoderate, im-mod'e-rāt, *a.* [Prefix *im*, not, and *moderate*; L. *immoderatus.*] Not moderate; exceeding just or usual bounds; excessive; extravagant; unreasonable. — **Immoderately**, im-mod'e-rāt-li, *adv.* In an immoderate manner.—**Immoderateness, Immoderacy, Immoderation**, im-mod'e-rāt-nes, im-mod'e-ra-si, im-mod'e-rā"shon, *n.* The condition or quality of being immoderate.

Immodest, im-mod'est, *a.* [Prefix *im* for *in*, not, and *modest.*] Not modest; wanting in the reserve or restraint which decency requires; indelicate; unchaste.—**Immodestly**, im-mod'est-li, *adv.* In an immodest manner.—**Immodesty**, im-mod'es-ti, *n.* The quality of being immodest.

Immolate, im'mō-lāt, *v.t.*—*immolated, immolating.* [L. *immolo, immolatum*, to sacrifice—*im* for *in*, on, and *mola*, meal, which was thrown on the head of the victim.] To sacrifice; to kill, as a victim offered in sacrifice; to offer in sacrifice.—**Immolation**, im-mō-lā'shon, *n.* The act of immolating; a sacrifice offered.—**Immolator**, im'mō-lā-tėr, *n.* One who immolates.

Immomentous, im-mō-men'tus, *a.* [Prefix *im* for *in*, not, and *momentous.*] Not momentous; unimportant.

Immoral, im-mor'al, *a.* [Prefix *im* for *in*, not, and *moral.*] Not moral; inconsistent with morality or rectitude; contrary to morals; wicked; unjust.—**Immorality**, im-mō-ral'i-ti, *n.* The quality of being immoral; an immoral act or practice.—**Immorally**, im-mor'al-li, *adv.* In an immoral manner.

Immortal, im-mor'tal, *a.* [L. *immortalis* —*im* for *in*, not, and *mortalis*, mortal.] Not mortal; having life that shall never end; undying; connected with immortality (*immortal* hopes); imperishable (*immortal* fame).—*n.* One who is immortal: often applied to the gods of classical mythology. —**Immortality**, im-mor-tal'i-ti, *n.* [L. *immortalitas.*] The condition or quality of being immortal; exemption from death and annihilation; unending existence. —**Immortalization**, im-mor'tal-ī-zā"shon, *n.* The act of immortalizing.—**Immortalize**, im-mor'tal-īz, *v.t.*—*immortalized, immortalizing.* To render immortal; to make famous for ever.—**Immortally**, im-mor'tal-li, *adv.* In an immortal manner.—**Immortelle**, im-mor-tel', *n.* A flower of the sort called *Everlasting*, or a wreath made of such flowers.

Immovable, im-mö'va-bl, *a.* [Prefix *im* for *in*, not, and *movable.*] Not movable; incapable of being moved in place; firmly fixed; fast; not to be moved from a purpose; steadfast; unalterable; unchangeable; not impressible; unfeeling. —**Immovability, Immovableness**, im-mö'va-bil"i-ti, im-mö'va-bl-nes, *n.* The condition or quality of being immovable.—**Immovably**, im-mö'va-bli, *adv.*

Immunity, im-mū'ni-ti, *n.* [L. *immunitas*, from *immunis*, exempt—*im* for *in*, not, and *munus*, office, duty.] Exemption from obligation, duty, office, tax, &c.; a particular privilege; freedom or exemption in general. In medicine, the ability of the body to resist the growth and products of microörganisms.—**Immune**, im-mūn'. *a.* Proof against disease or poison.

Immunize, im'ū-nīz, *v.t.* To produce immunity.

Immure, im-mūr', *v.t.*—*immured, immuring.* [O.Fr. *emmurer*—L. *in*, and *murus*, a wall. MURAL.] To inclose or imprison within walls; to shut up; to confine.—**Immurement**, im-mūr'ment, *n.* The act of immuring or state of being immured.

Immutable, im-mū'ta-bl, *a.* [Prefix *im* for *in*, not, and *mutable.*] Not mutable; not subject to mutation; unchangeable; invariable; unalterable.

Imp, imp, *n.* [Originally a shoot or scion; from L.L. *impotus*, a graft or scion, from Gr. *emphytos*, engrafted—*en*, in, and *phyō*, to grow, to produce; similarly Sw. *ymp*, Dan. *ympe*, twig, shoot, scion.] A scion or graft‡; a son, offspring, or progeny (*Shak.*)‡; a young or little devil; a little malignant spirit; hence, a mischievous child; also something added or united to another to repair or lengthen it out.—*v.t.* To graft; to strengthen or enlarge by something inserted or added; to mend a deficient wing by the insertion of a feather; to strengthen.—**Impish**, imp'ish, *a.* Having the qualities of an imp; fiendish.—**Impishly**, imp'ish-li, *adv.* After the manner of an imp.

Impact, im'pakt, *n.* [From L. *impingo*, *impactum*, to drive or strike. IMPINGE.] A forcible touch; a collision; a stroke; communicated force; *mech.* the shock or collision occasioned by the meeting of two bodies.

Impair, im-pār', *v.t.* [Fr. *empirer*, from prefix, *em*, intens., *pire*, worse, from L. *pejor*, worse.] To make worse; to lessen in some good quality, as in quantity, value, excellence, strength; to deteriorate.—*v.i.* To become worse; to deteriorate. — **Impairer**, im-pā'rėr, *n.* One who or that which impairs.—**Impairment**, im-pār'ment, *n.* The act of impairing.

Impale, im-pāl', *v.t.*—*impaled, impaling.* [L. *im* for *in*, on, and *palus*, a pole, stake, pale.] To put to death by fixing on an upright sharp stake; to empale; *her.* to join, as two coats of arms, by an upright line. — **Impalement**, im-pāl'ment, *n.* The act of impaling.

Impalpable, im-pal'pa-bl, *a.* [Prefix *im* for *in*, not, and *palpable.*] Not to be felt; incapable of having its individual particles distinguished by the touch (an *impalpable* powder); not easily or readily apprehended or grasped by the mind.—**Impalpably**, im-pal'pa-bli, *adv.* In an impalpable manner.—**Impalpability**, im-pal'pa-bil"i-ti, *n.* The quality or state of being impalpable.

Impanate, impā'nāt, *a.* [L. *in*, in, into, and *panis*, bread.] Embodied in the bread used in the eucharist.—**Impanation**, im-pa-nā'shon, *n.* The supposed real presence in, and union of the body and blood of Christ with the bread and wine, after consecration, in the eucharist; consubstantiation: distinct from *transubstantiation*, which holds that there is a change of the elements into the real body and blood of Christ.

Impanel, im-pan'el, *v.t.*—*impanelled, impanelling.* [Prefix *im* for *in*, and *panel.*] To form, complete, or enrol the list of jurors in a court of justice.—**Impanelment**, im-pan'el-ment, *n.* The act of impanelling.

Imparidigitate, im-par'i-dij"i-tāt, *a.* [L. *impar*, unequal (*im*, not, *par*, equal), and *digitus*, a finger.] *Zool.* having an uneven number of fingers or toes.—**Imparipinnate**, im-par'i-pin"āt, *a.* *Bot.* applied to a pinnate leaf when there is a terminal or odd leaflet at the end. —**Imparisyllabic**, im-par'i-sil-lab"ik, *a.* *Gram.* not consisting of an equal number of syllables: applied to a noun which has not the same number of syllables in all the cases.

Imparity, im-par'i-ti, *n.* [From L. *impar*, unequal—*im*, not, and *par*, equal. PAIR, PEER.] Inequality; disproportion; want of equality; disparity.

Impart, im-pärt', *v.t.* [O.Fr. *impartir*, from L. *impartio, impertio*—*im* for *in*, and *partio*, to divide, from *pars, partis*, a part.] To bestow a part, share, or portion of; to give, grant, confer, or communicate; to communicate the knowledge of; to make known; to show by words or tokens.—*v.i.* To give a part or share.—**Impartation**, im-pär-tā'shon, *n.* The act of imparting. —**Imparter**, im-pär'tėr, *n.* One who imparts.—**Impartibility**, im-pär'ti-bil"i-ti, *n.* The quality of being impartible.—**Impartible**, im-pär'ti-bl, *a.* Capable of being imparted.—**Impartment**, im-pärt'-ment, *n.* The act of imparting.

Impartial, im-pär'shal, *a.* [Prefix *im* for *in*, not, and *partial.*] Not partial; not favouring one party more than another; unprejudiced; equitable; just.—**Impartiality, Impartialness**, im-pär'shi-al"i-ti, im-pär'shal-nes, *n.* The quality of being impartial.—**Impartially**, im-pär'shal-li, *adv.* In an impartial manner; without bias; fairly.

Impartible, im-pär'ti-bl, *a.* [Prefix *im* for *in*, not, and *partible.*] Not partible or subject to partition. — **Impartibility**, im-pär'ti-bil"i-ti, *n.* The quality of being impartible.

Impassable, im-pas'a-bl, *a.* [Prefix *im* for *in*, not, and *passable.*] Not passable; incapable of being passed.—**Impassableness**, im-pas'a-bl-nes, *n.*

Impasse, im-pas', *n.* A blind alley; a cul-de-sac; a road having no way out; *fig.* a position from which there is no escape; a deadlock.

Impassible, im-pas'i-bl, *a.* [L. *impassibilis*—*im* for *in*, not, and *passibilis*, capable of feeling, from *patior, passus*, to suffer. PATIENT.] Incapable of pain, passion, or suffering; not to be moved to passion or sympathy; without or not exhibiting feeling. — **Impassibility, Impassibleness**, im-pas'i-bil"i-ti, im-pas'i-bl-nes, *n.* The quality or condition of being impassible.

Impassion, im-pash'on, *v.t.* [Prefix *im* for *in*, intens., and *passion.*] To move or affect strongly with passion.—**Impassionable**, im-pash'on-a-bl, *a.* Easily excited; susceptible of strong emotion.—**Impassionate**, im-pash'on-āt, *a.* Strongly affected.—**Impassioned**, im-pash'ond, *a.* Actuated or animated by passion, ardour, or warmth of feeling; animated; excited (an *impassioned* orator or discourse).

Impassive, im-pas'iv, *a.* [Prefix *im* for *in*,

intens., and *passive.*] Not susceptible of pain or suffering; impassible; not exhibiting feeling or sensibility.—**Impassively**, im-pas'iv-li, *adv.* In an impassive manner. —**Impassiveness, Impassivity**, im-pas'iv-nes, im-pa-siv'i-ti, *n.* The state or quality of being impassive.

Impaste, im-pāst', *v.t.* [Prefix *im* for *in*, and *paste.*] To knead or make into paste; *painting*, to lay on (colours) thickly and boldly; *engrav.* to intermix lines and points on (a plate) so as to represent thickness of colouring. — **Impastation**, im-pas-tā'shon, *n.* The act of impasting; a combination of materials of different colours and consistencies united by a cement and hardened. — **Impasto**, im-pas'to, *n.* [It.] *Painting*, the thickness of the layer of pigment applied by the painter.

Impatient, im-pā'shent, *a.* [Prefix *im* for *in*, not, and *patient.*] Not patient; uneasy under given conditions and eager for change: followed by *of*, *at*, *for*, *under*; prompted by impatience; exhibiting or expressing impatience (an *impatient* gesture). —**Impatiently**, im-pā'shent-li, *adv.* In an impatient manner.—**Impatience**, im-pā'shens, *n.* The condition or quality of being impatient.

Impeach, im-pēch', *v.t.* [Fr. *empêcher*, O.Fr. *empeechier*, Pr. *empedigar*; from L. *impedicare*, to entangle—*in*, and *pedica*, a snare, from *pes*, *pedis*, the foot. IMPEDE.] To charge with a crime or misdemeanour; to accuse: specifically, to exhibit charges of maladministration against, as against a minister of state or other high official, before a competent tribunal; to call in question (motives, sincerity); to disparage or detract from.—**Impeachable**, im-pēch'a-bl, *a.* Liable to impeachment.—**Impeacher**, im-pēch'ėr, *n.* One who impeaches. —**Impeachment**, im-pēch'ment, *n.* Impediment or obstruction†; the act of impeaching, or state of being impeached.

Impeccable, Impeccant, im-pek'a-bl, im-pek'ant, *a.* [L. *impeccabilis*—prefix *im* for *in*, not, and *pecco*, to sin.] Not liable or subject to sin; exempt from the possibility of doing wrong.—*n.* A person exempt from the possibility of sinning.—**Impeccability, Impeccance, Impeccancy**, im-pek'a-bil"i-ti, im-pek'ans, im-pek'an-si, *n.* The condition or quality of being impeccant or impeccable.

Impecunious, im-pē-kū'ni-us, *a.* [Prefix *im* for *in*, not, and *pecunia*, money.] Not having money; hard-up; without funds.—**Impecuniosity**, im-pē-kū'ni-os"i-ti, *n.* State of being impecunious.

Impedance, im-ped'ans, *n.* *Elect.* virtual resistance due to self-induction: opposed to true or ohmic resistance.

Impede, im-pēd', *v.t.*—*impeded, impeding.* [L. *impedio*, to entangle the feet of—*im* for *in*, and *pes*, *pedis*, the foot; seen also in *pedestrian, expedite, biped, pedestal, impeach*, &c.] To hinder; to stop or delay the progress of; to obstruct.—**Impedible**, im-pē'di-bl, *a.* That may be impeded.—**Impediment**, im-ped'i-ment, *n.* [L. *impedimentum.*] That which impedes; obstruction; a voice defect. — **Impedimenta**. [L.] Baggage.—**Impedimental**, im-ped'i-men"tal, *a.* Of the nature of an impediment. —**Impeditive**, im-ped'i-tiv, *a.* Impeding.

Impel, im-pel', *v.t.*—*impelled, impelling.* [L. *impello*—*im* for *in*, on, and *pello*, to drive (as in *compel, dispel, repel, pulse*).] To drive or urge forward; to press on; to excite to motion or action in any way.—**Impellent**, im-pel'ent, *a.* Having the quality of impelling.—*n.* A power or force that impels.—**Impeller**, im-pel'ėr, *n.* One who or that which impels.

Impend, im-pend', *v.i.* [L. *impendeo*—*im* for *in*, in, on, over, and *pendeo*, to hang (as in *depend, pendant*, &c.).] To hang over; to threaten from near at hand; to be imminent. — **Impendence, Impendency**, im-pen'dens, im-pen'den-si, *n.* The state of being impendent.—**Impendent**, im-pen'dent, *a.* Impending; imminent.

Impenetrable, im-pen'ē-tra-bl, *a.* [Prefix *im* for *in*, not, and *penetrable.*] Not penetrable; incapable of being penetrated or pierced; hence, incapable of intellectual or emotional impression; obtuse or unsympathetic; *physics*, preventing any other substance from occupying the same place at the same time.—**Impenetrably**, im-pen'ē-tra-bli, *adv.* In an impenetrable manner. —**Impenetrability, Impenetrableness**, im-pen'ē-tra-bil"i-ti, im-pen'ē-tra-bl-nes, *n.* The quality of being impenetrable.

Impenitent, im-pen'i-tent, *a.* [Prefix *im* for *in*, not, and *penitent.*] Not penitent; not repenting of sin; obdurate; of a hard heart. —*n.* One who does not repent; a hardened sinner.—**Impenitence, Impenitency**, im-pen'i-tens, im-pen'i-ten-si, *n.* The condition of being impenitent.—**Impenitently**, im-pen'i-tent-li, *adv.*

Impennate, im-pen'āt, *a.* [L. *im* for *in*, not, and *penna*, a feather.] *Ornithol.* having short wings covered with feathers resembling scales, as the penguins.

Imperative, im-per'a-tiv, *a.* [L. *imperativus*, from *impero*, to command. EMPEROR.] Expressive of command; containing positive command; authoritative; not to be avoided or evaded; obligatory (*imperative* duty); *gram.* applied to the mood or form of a verb which expresses command, entreaty, advice, or exhortation (*go, write, attend*): in this sense often used *substantively*.—**Imperatival**, im-per'a-tī-val, *a.* Belonging to the imperative mood.—**Imperatively**, im-per'a-tiv-li, *adv.* In an imperative manner; also, by way of, or as, the imperative mood. — **Imperatorial**, im-per-a-tō'ri-al, *a.* [From L. *imperator*, a commander.] Pertaining to a commander or emperor; commanding; imperial.

Imperceptible, im-pėr-sep'ti-bl, *a.* [Prefix *im* for *in*, not, and *perceptible.*] Not perceptible; not to be perceived; not discernible; not easily apprehended.—**Imperceptibility, Imperceptibleness**, im-pėr-sep'ti-bil"i-ti, im-pėr-sep'ti-bl-nes, *n.* The state or quality of being imperceptible. —**Imperceptibly**, im-pėr-sep'ti-bli, *adv.* In an imperceptible manner.—**Imperception**, im-pėr-sep'shon, *n.* Want of perception.—**Imperceptive, Impercipient**, im-pėr-sep'tiv, im-pėr-sip'i-ent, *a.* Not perceiving.

Imperfect, im-pėr'fekt, *a.* [Prefix *im* for *in*, not, and *perfect*; L. *imperfectus.*] Not perfect; not complete in all parts; wanting something necessary to completeness; defective; not reaching a certain standard or ideal; morally deficient or defective; not completely good.—*Imperfect tense*, *gram.* a tense expressing an uncompleted action or state, especially in time past.—*n.* An imperfect tense.—**Imperfectible**, im-pėr-fek'ti-bl, *a.* Incapable of being made perfect. —**Imperfection**, im-pėr-fek'shon, *n.* The condition or quality of being imperfect; defect; flaw; blemish.—**Imperfectly**, im-pėr'fekt-li, *adv.* In an imperfect manner or degree; defectively; faultily.—**Imperfectness**, im-pėr'fekt-nes, *n.* The state or quality of being imperfect.

Imperforate, im-pėr'fo-rāt, *a.* [Prefix *im* for *in*, not, and *perforate.*] Not perforated or pierced; having no opening or pores.

Imperial, im-pē'ri-al, *a.* [L. *imperialis*, from *imperium*, empire, supreme command, from *impero*, to command. EMPEROR.] Pertaining to an empire or to an emperor; pertaining to supreme authority or to one who wields it; sovereign; supreme; suitable for an emperor; of superior excellence.—*n.* A tuft of hair on a man's lower lip (the style of beard made fashionable by Napoleon III); a trade term for an article of unusual size or excellence, as a large decanter, &c.; a size of paper measuring 23 by 31 inches.—**Imperialism**, im-pē'ri-al-izm, *n.* Imperial state or authority: the spirit of empire. —**Imperialist**, im-pē'ri-al-ist, *n.* A subject or soldier of an emperor; one favorable to empire or imperial government.—**Imperiality, Imperialty**, im-pē'ri-al"i-ti, im-pē'ri-al-ti, *n.* Imperial power; an imperial right or privilege.—**Imperialize**, im-pē'ri-al-īz, *v.t.* To invest with the state, authority, or character of an emperor; to bring to the form of an empire.—**Imperially**, im-pē'ri-al-li, *adv.* In an imperial manner.

Imperil, im-per'il, *v.t.*—*imperilled, imperilling.* [Prefix *im* for *in*, into, and *peril.*] To bring into peril; to endanger.—**Imperilment**, im-per'il-ment, *n.* Act of putting in peril.

Imperious, im-pē'ri-us, *a.* [L. *imperiosus*, from *imperium*, empire. IMPERIAL.] Giving orders or commands in an arbitrary or absolute manner; dictatorial; haughty; arrogant; domineering; urgent, pressing, or overmastering (*imperious* necessity).—**Imperiously**, im-pē'ri-us-li, *adv.* In an imperious manner. — **Imperiousness**, im-pē'ri-us-nes, *n.*

Imperishable, im-per'ish-a-bl, *a.* [Prefix *im* for *in*, not, and *perishable.*] Not perishable; not subject to decay; indestructible; enduring permanently.—**Imperishableness, Imperishability**, im-per'ish-a-bl-nes, im-per'ish-a-bil"i-ti, *n.* The quality of being imperishable.—**Imperishably**, im-per'ish-a-bli, *adv.*

Impermeable, im-pėr'mē-a-bl, *a.* [Prefix *im* for *in*, not, and *permeable.*] Not permeable; impervious.—**Impermeability, Impermeableness**, im-pėr'mē-a-bil"i-ti, im-pėr'mē-a-bl-nes, *n.* — **Impermeably**, im-pėr'mē-a-bli, *adv.*

Impersonal, im-pėr'son-al, *a.* [Prefix *im* for *in*, not, and *personal.*] Not having personal existence; not endued with personality. — *Impersonal verb*, *gram.* a verb (such as *it rains, it becomes* us to be modest) which is used only with an impersonal nominative or subject.—*n.* That which wants personality; an impersonal verb.—**Impersonality**, im-pėr'so-nal"i-ti, *n.* The condition of being impersonal. — **Impersonally**, im-pėr'son-al-li, *adv.* In an impersonal manner.

Impersonate, im-pėr'son-āt, *v.t.*—*impersonated, impersonating.* [Prefix *im* for *in*, in (or *in* intens.), and *personate.*] To invest with personality; to assume the person or character of; to represent in character (as on the stage).—**Impersonation**, im-pėr'so-nā"shon, *n.* The act of impersonating.—**Impersonator**, im-pėr'son-ā-tėr, *n.* One who impersonates.

Impertinent, im-pėr'ti-nent, *a.* [Prefix *im* for *in*, not, and *pertinent.*] Not pertinent or pertaining to the matter in hand; having no bearing on the subject; not to the point; irrelevant; unbecoming in speech or action; meddling with matters in which one has no concern; petulant and rude; uncivil.—*n.* One who acts impertinently.—**Impertinently**, im-pėr'ti-nent-li, *adv.* In an impertinent manner; irrelevantly; in a rude, saucy manner. — **Impertinence, Impertinency**, im-pėr'ti-nens, im-pėr'ti-nen-si, *n.* The quality of being impertinent; that which is impertinent; impertinent conduct or language.

Imperturbable, im-pėr-tėr'ba-bl, *a.* [Prefix *im* for *in*, not, and *perturb.*] Incapable of being perturbed or agitated; unmoved; calm; cool.—**Imperturbability**, im-pėr-tėr'ba-bil"i-ti, *n.* Quality of being imperturbable.—**Imperturbation**, im-pėr'tėr-bā"shon, *n.* Freedom from agitation of mind.

Impervious, im-pėr'vi-us, *a.* [Prefix *im* for *in*, not, and *pervious.*] Not pervious; not admitting entrance or passage; incapable of being passed through.—**Imperviously**, im-pėr'vi-us-li, *adv.* In an impervious manner. — **Imperviousness**, im-pėr'vi-us-nes, *n.*

Impetigo, im-pe-tī'gō, *n.* [L., from *impeto*, to assail. IMPETUOUS.] *Med.* an eruption of itching pustules in clusters on the skin.—**Impetiginous**, im-pe-tij'i-nus, *a.* Pertaining to impetigo.

Impetrate, im'pe-trāt, *v.t.*—*impetrated, impetrating.* [L. *impetro*, *impetratum*, to obtain—prefix *im* for *in*, intens., and *patro*, to bring to pass.] To obtain by prayer or petition.—**Impetrable**, im'pe-tra-bl, *a.* Capable of being impetrated.—**Impetration**, im-pe-trā'shon, *n.* The act of impetrating; formerly specifically applied to the obtaining from the Roman see of benefices belonging to lay patrons.—**Impetrative, Impetratory**, im'pe-trā-tiv, im'pet-ra-to-ri, *a.* Containing or expressing entreaty.

Impetuous, im-pet'ū-us, *a.* [L. *impetuosus*, from *impetus*, an attack—*im*, in, and *peto*, to assail (whence *petition, compete*).] Rushing with force and violence; furious in motion; forcible; fierce; raging; vehement in feeling; passionate; violent.—**Impetuously**, im-pet'ū-us-li, *adv.* In an impetuous manner.—**Impetuosity, Impetuousness**, im-pet'ū-os"i-ti, im-pet'ū-us-nes, *n.* The quality of being impetuous; fury; vehemence.—**Impetus**, im'pe-tus, *n.* [L.] Force of motion; the force with which any body is driven or impelled; momentum.

Impeyan, Impeyan Pheasant, im'-pi-an. [After Lady *Impey*, who attempted to introduce it into Britain.] A large bird of the pheasant tribe, belonging to the high cold regions of the Himalaya.

Impi, im'pi, *n.* A brigade or large body of Kafir soldiers.

Impignorate,† im-pig'nō-rāt, *v.t.* [L. *in*, in, and *pignus, pignoris*, a pledge.] To pledge or pawn, to transfer as security.

Impinge, im-pinj', *v.i.* [L. *impingo, impactum*—*im* for *in*, on, and *pango*, to strike. PACT.] To strike, knock, or dash against; to clash upon; to strike; to hit.—**Impingement**, im-pinj'ment, *n.* Act of impinging. —**Impingent**, im-pin'jent, *a.* Striking against or upon.

Impious, im'pi-us, *a.* [L. *impius*—*im* for *in*, not, and *pius*, pious.] The reverse of pious; irreverent towards the Supreme Being; wanting in veneration for God and His authority; irreligious; irreverent; profane (*impious* men, deeds, words).—**Impiously**, im'pi-us-li, *adv.* In an impious manner.—**Impiousness**, im'pi-us-nes, *n.* Impiety.—**Impiety**, im-pī'e-ti, *n.* [L. *impietas.*] The condition or quality of being impious; an act of wickedness or irreligion: in this latter sense with a plural.

Impish, Impishly. Under IMP.

Implacable, im-plā'ka-bl, *a.* [Prefix *im* for *in*, not, and *placable.*] Not placable; not to be appeased or pacified; inexorable; stubborn or constant in enmity.—**Implacability, Implacableness**, im-plā'ka-bil"i-ti, im-plā'ka-bl-nes, *n.* The quality of being implacable.—**Implacably**, im-plā'-ka-bli, *adv.* In an implacable manner.

Implacental, im'pla-sen-tal, *a.* [Prefix *im* for *in*, not, and *placental.*] Destitute of a placenta, as marsupials and monotremes. —*n.* A mammal destitute of a placenta.

Implant, im-plant', *v.t.* [Prefix *im* for *in*, in, into, and *plant.*] To plant; to set in soil (lit. or fig.); to insert; to sow (to *implant* truths, principles, virtue, &c.).—**Implantation**, im-plan-tā'shon, *n.* The act of implanting.

Implead, im-plēd', *v.t.* [Prefix *im* for *in*, and *plead.*] To institute and prosecute a suit against in court; to sue at law.—**Impleader**, im-plē-dėr, *n.* One who impleads; an accuser.

Implement, im'plē-ment, *n.* [L.L. *implementum*, lit. what accomplishes, from L. *impleo*, to fill up—*im* for *in*, and *pleo*, to fill, as in *complete, replete*, &c., the root being in E. *full.*] An instrument, tool, or utensil; an article assisting in carrying on manual labours. ∴ Syn. under TOOL.—*v.t.* To fulfil or satisfy the conditions of; to fulfil or perform; to carry into effect (to *implement* a bargain).—**Implemental**, im-plē-men'tal, *a.* Pertaining to implements; characterized by the use of implements (*implemental* stage in civilization).

Implex, im'pleks, *a.* [L. *implexus*, pp. of *implecto*, entangle—*im* for *in*, in, and *plecto*, to plait.] Infolded; intricate; entangled.—**Implexous**, im-plek'sus, *a.* *Bot.* entangled; interlaced.

Implicate, im'pli-kāt, *v.t.*—*implicated, implicating.* [L. *implico, implicatum*—*im* for *in*, in, into, and *plico*, to fold. PLY.] To entangle to a certain extent in some affair; to show or prove to be connected or concerned; to involve (*implicated* in a conspiracy. ∴ *Implicate* is a less strong word than *involve*, a person who is *implicated* being connected only to a small extent, while one who is *involved* is deeply concerned or entangled.—**Implication**, im-pli-kā'shon, *n.* The act of implicating or state of being implicated; an implying, or that which is implied but not expressed; an inference, or something which may fairly be understood though not expressed in words.—**Implicative**, im'pli-kā-tiv, *a.* Tending to implicate.—**Implicatively**, im'pli-kā-tiv-li, *adv.* By implication.

Implicit, im-plis'it, *a.* [L. *implicitus*, from *implico, implicitum*, and *implicatum*, to infold. IMPLICATE.] Fairly to be understood, though not expressed in words, implied (an *implicit* promise); entirely depending or resting on something or some one else; hence, free from doubt or questioning; settled; deep rooted (*implicit* faith in one's word).—**Implicitly**, im-plis'it-li, *adv.* In an implicit manner.—**Implicitness**, im-plis'it-nes, *n.*

Impliedly. Under IMPLY.

Implore, im-plōr', *v.t.*—*implored, imploring.* [L. *imploro*—*im* for *in*, on, upon, and *ploro*, to cry out (as in *deplore, explore*).] To call upon or for, in supplication, to beseech; to pray earnestly; to entreat; to beg (to *implore* forgiveness, to *implore* a person to forgive).—*v.i.* To entreat; to beg.—**Imploration**, im-plō-rā'shon, *n.* The act of imploring; earnest supplication.—**Imploratory**, im-plō'ra-to-ri, *a.* Earnestly supplicating; imploring; entreating.—**Implorer**, im-plō'rer, *n.* One who implores. —**Imploringly**, im-plō'ring-li, *adv.* In an imploring manner.

Imply, im-plī', *v.t.*—*implied, implying.* [From L. *implico*—*in*, and *plico*, to fold, whence also *implicate* (which see); comp. *apply, reply, ply.*] To involve or contain by fair inference; to contain by implication or as a consequence; to include virtually (words *imply* a promise; an effect *implies* a cause).—**Impliedly**, im-plīd'li, *adv.* In an implied manner; by implication.

Impolite, im-pō-līt', *a.* [Prefix *im* for *in*, not, and *polite.*] Not polite; unpolite; uncivil; rude.—**Impolitely**, im-pō-līt'li, *adv.* In an impolite manner.—**Impoliteness**, im-pō-līt'nes, *n.*

Impolitic, Impolitical, im-pol'i-tik, im-pō-lit'i-kal, *a.* [Prefix *im* for *in*, not, and *politic.*] Not politic; wanting policy or prudent management; unwise; imprudent; indiscreet; injudicious.—**Impolicy**, im-pol'i-si, *n.* The quality of being impolitic. —**Impoliticly, Impolitically**, im-pol'i-tik-li, im-pō-lit'i-kal-li, *adv.*—**Impoliticness**, im-pol'i-tik-nes, *n.*

Imponderable, im-pon'dėr-a-bl, *a.* Not ponderable; without sensible weight.—*n.* A thing which has no appreciable weight. —**Imponderability, Imponderableness**, im-pon'dėr-a-bil"i-ti, im-pon'-dėr-a-bl-nes, *n.* The quality of being imponderable.

Import, im-pōrt', *v.t.* [Fr. *importer*, to bring from abroad, to matter or be of consequence, L. *importo*, to bring in, to cause—*im* for *in*, and *porto*, to bring or carry, whence *port*, a person's bearing, *porter.* PORT.] To bring into a place from abroad; to bring into one's own country: opposed to *export*; to bear or carry as a signification; to mean; to signify; to imply; to be of importance, moment, or consequence to; to matter to.—*n.* (im'pōrt). That which is imported or brought into a country from abroad; that which a word bears as its signification; purport; meaning; the application or interpretation of an action, of events, &c.; bearing; importance, weight, or consequence.—**Importable**, im-pōr'-ta-bl, *a.* Capable of being imported.—**Importation**, im-pōr-tā'shon, *n.* The act or practice of importing; a quantity imported.—**Importer**, im-pōr'tėr, *n.* One who imports.

Important, im-por'tant, *a.* [Fr. *important*, lit. being of great import or moment. IMPORT.] Full of or bearing import, weight, or consequence; momentous, weighty, material; influential; grave.—**Importantly**, im-por'tant-li, *adv.* In an important manner.—**Importance**, im-por'tans, *n.* The quality of being important; weight; consequence; moment.

Importune, im-por-tūn', sometimes im-por'tūn, *v.t.*—*importuned, importuning.* [Fr. *importuner*, to importune, pester, from L. *importunus*, distressing, rude—*im* for *in*, not, and *portus*, a port or harbour, access.] To press with solicitation; to solicit or urge with frequent or unceasing application; to annoy with unremitting demands.—*v.i.* To solicit earnestly and repeatedly.—**Importunate**, im-por'tū-nāt, *a.* Troublesome by frequent demands; incessant in solicitation; urgent; unreasonable.—**Importunately**, im-por'tū-nāt-li, *adv.* In an importunate manner.—**Importuner**, im-por-tū'nėr, *n.* One who importunes.—**Importunity, Importunacy, Importunateness**, im-por-tū'-ni-ti, im-por'tū-na-si, im-por'tū-nāt-nes, *n.* The quality of being importunate; application urged with troublesome pertinacity.

Impose, im-pōz', *v.t.*—*imposed, imposing.* [Fr. *imposer*—*im* for *in*, on, upon, and *poser*, to place. COMPOSE, POSE.] To lay, set, or place on (to *impose* the hands), to lay or enjoin as a burden, tax, penalty, command, law, &c.; to palm or pass off; *printing*, to arrange and adjust (pages) and fasten into a chase.—*v.i.* Used in phrase *to impose on* or *upon*, to pass or put a trick or deceit on, to deceive, to victimize.—**Imposable**, im-pō'za-bl, *a.* Capable of being imposed.—**Imposableness**, im-pō'za-bl-nes, *n.*—**Imposer**, im-pō'zėr, *n.* One who imposes; one who enjoins.—**Imposing**, im-pō'zing, *a.* Impressive in appearance; commanding; stately; majestic.—**Imposingly**, im-pō'zing-li, *adv.* In an imposing manner.—**Imposingness**, im-pō'zing-nes, *n.*—**Imposing-stone, Imposing-table**, *n.* *Printing*, a table of stone or metal on which the pages or columns of type are imposed or made into forms.—**Imposition**, im-pō-zish'on, *n.* The act of imposing or laying on; that which is imposed, levied, inflicted, enjoined, and the like, the act of tricking or deceiving; a trick or deception; a fraud; an imposture; an exercise enjoined on students as a punishment.

Impossible, im-pos'i-bl, *a.* [L. *impossibilis*—*im* for *in*, not, and *possibilis*, possible. POSSIBLE.] Not possible; not capable of being or being done; incapable of being accomplished, thought, endured, &c.—**Impossibly**, im-pos'i-bli, *adv.* Not possibly.—**Impossibility**, im-pos'i-bil"i-ti, *n.* The state or quality of being impossible; that which is impossible.

Impost, im'pōst, *n.* [O.Fr. *impost*, Fr. *impôt*, L. *impositum*, from *impono, impositum*, to lay upon—*in*, on, and *pono*, to place.] That which is imposed or levied; a tax, tribute, or duty; *arch.* the point where an arch rests on a wall or column.

Imposthume, im-pos'tūm, *n.* [A corruption of *aposteme, apostume.*] Same as *Aposteme.*

Impostor, im-pos'tėr, *n.* [L. *impostor*, from *impono*—*in*, on, and *pono*, to place.] One who imposes on others; a person who assumes a character for the purpose of deception; a deceiver under a false character. —**Impostrous**,† im-pos'trus, *a.* Characterized by imposition.—**Imposture**, im-pos'tūr, *n.* [L. *impostura*, from *impono, impositum.*] The act or conduct of an impostor; fraud or imposition.

Impotent, im'pō-tent, *a.* [L. *impotens, impotentis*—*im* for *in*, not, and *potens*, able, *potent.*] Entirely wanting power, strength, or vigour of body or mind; deficient in capacity; weak; feeble; destitute of the power of sexual intercourse or of begetting children.—**Impotently**, im'pō-tent-li, *adv.* In an impotent manner.—**Impotence, Impotency**, im'pō-tens, im'pō-ten-si, *n.* The condition or quality of being impotent.

Impound, im-pound′, *v.t.* [Prefix *im* for *in*, and *pound.*] To put in a pound (as a straying animal); to confine; to take possession of, as of a document, for use when necessary.—**Impoundage**, im-poun′dāj, *n.* The act of impounding.—**Impounder**, im-poun′dėr, *n.* One who impounds.

Impoverish, im-pov′ėr-ish, *v.t.* [Prefix *im*, intens., and Fr. *pauvre*, poor. POOR.] To make poor; to reduce to poverty or indigence; to exhaust the strength, richness, or fertility of (to *impoverish* land).—**Impoverisher**, im-pov′ėr-ish-ėr, *n.* One who or that which impoverishes. — **Impoverishment**, im-pov′ėr-ish-ment, *n.* The act of impoverishing.

Impower, im-pou′ėr, *v.t.* To empower.

Impracticable, im-prak′ti-ka-bl, *a.* Not practicable; not to be performed or effected by human means or by the means at command; not to be dealt with or managed; unmanageable; incapable of being passed or travelled (an *impracticable* road).—**Impracticably**, im-prak′ti-ka-bli, *adv.* In an impracticable manner. — **Impracticability, Impracticableness**, im-prak′ti-ka-bil″i-ti, im-prak′ti-ka-bl-nes, *n.* The state or quality of being impracticable. —**Impractical**, im-prak′ti-kal, *a.* Not practical; not taking a common-sense view of things; full of theories.

Imprecate, im′prē-kāt, *v.t.*—*imprecated, imprecating.* [L. *imprecor, imprecatus*—*im* for *in*, on, and *precor*, to pray. PRAY.] To call down, as a curse, calamity, or punishment, by prayer; to invoke (a curse or some evil). — **Imprecation**, im-prē-kā′shon, *n.* [L. *imprecatio.*] The act of imprecating; a prayer that a curse or calamity may fall on any one; a curse.—**Imprecatory**, im′prē-ka-to-ri, *a.* Of the nature of or containing an imprecation.

Impregnable, im-preg′na-bl, *a.* [O.Fr. *imprenable* (the *g* being inserted as in *pregnable*)—*im* for *in*, not, and *prendre*, to take.] Not to be taken; incapable of being reduced by force (an *impregnable* fortress); not to be moved, impressed, or shaken.—**Impregnability, Impregnableness**, im-preg′na-bil″i-ti, im-preg′na-bl-nes, *n.* State of being impregnable.—**Impregnably**, im-preg′na-bli, *adv.*

Impregnate, im-preg′nāt, *v.t.*—*impregnated, impregnating.* [L.L. *imprægno, imprægnatum* — L. *im* for *in*, in, and *prægnans*, pregnant PREGNANT.] To make pregnant or with young; to cause to conceive; to transmit or infuse an active principle into; to imbue; to communicate qualities to by mixture. — **Impregnation**, im-preg-nā′shon, *n.* The act of impregnating.

Impresario, im-pres-ä′ri-o, *n.* [It.] One who organizes, manages, or conducts a company of concert or opera performers.

Imprescriptible, im-prē-skrip′ti-bl, *a.* [Prefix *im* for *in*, not, and *prescriptible.*] Incapable of being lost by neglect to use, or by the claims of another founded on prescription. — **Imprescriptibility**, im-prē-skrip′ti-bil″i-ti, *n.* State of being imprescriptible.

Impress, im-pres′, *v.t.* [L. *imprimo, impressum*—*im* for *in*, on, upon. and *premo*, to press. PRESS.] To press or stamp in or upon; to mark by pressure; to make a mark or figure upon; to stamp (to *impress* a design on; to *impress* with a design); to stamp on the mind; to inculcate (truth, facts, &c.); to affect deeply the feelings or sentiments. — *n.* (im′pres). A mark or figure made by pressure, or as by pressure; stamp; impression. — **Impressibility, Impressibleness**, im-pres′i-bil″i-ti, im-pres′i-bl-nes, *n.* The quality of being impressible.—**Impressible**, im-pres′i-bl, *a.* Capable of being impressed; susceptible of impression; easily affected; susceptive.—**Impressibly**, im-pres′i-bli, *adv.* In an impressible manner.—**Impression**, im-presh′on, *n.* [L. *impressio, impressionis.*] The act of impressing; that which is impressed, printed, or stamped; a copy taken by pressure from type, from an engraved plate, and the like; the aggregate of copies taken at one time; edition; effect or influence on the senses, on the mind, feelings, or sentiments; an indistinct notion, remembrance or belief.—**Impressionability, Impressionableness**, im-presh′on-a-bil″i-ti, im-presh′on-a-bl-nes, *n.* The quality of being impressionable. — **Impressionable**, im-presh′on-a-bl, *a.* Susceptible of impression; having the mind or feelings easily affected. — **Impressionist**, im-presh′on-ist, *n.* One who lays much stress on impressions; an artist who tries to depict scenes by their general and most striking characteristics as they first impress the spectator. — **Impressionism**, *n.* The views or practice of an impressionist.—**Impressionistic**, *a.* Of or pertaining to impressionism.—**Impressive**, im-pres′iv, *a.* Making or tending to make an impression; having the power of affecting or of exciting attention and feeling. — **Impressively**, im-pres′iv-li, *adv.* In an impressive manner.—**Impressiveness**, im-pres′iv-nes, *a.*

Impress, im-pres′, *v.t.* [Influenced by *press*, but originally meaning to hire by ready money, from O.E. *prest*, ready money; O.Fr. *prester*, to give, to lend; L. *præsto*, in readiness (*præ*, before, and *sto*, to stand).] To compel to enter into public service, as a seaman; to seize and take into service by compulsion; to take for public use.—*n.* The act of impressing; compulsion to serve.—**Impress-gang**,‡ *n.* A press-gang.—**Impressment**, im-pres′ment, *n.* The act of impressing.

Imprimatur, im-pri-mā′tėr, *n.* [L., let it be printed.] A license to print a book, &c.; hence, a mark of approval in general.

Imprimis, im-prī′mis, *adv.* [L.] In the first place; first in order.

Imprint, im-print′, *v.t.* [O.E. *empreut*, Fr. *empreint*, pp. of *empreindre*, to imprint, L. *imprimere*, to impress. PRINT.] To mark by pressure; to stamp; to print; to fix indelibly or permanently, as on the mind or memory; to impress. — *n.* (im′print). Whatever is impressed or printed; especially, the name of the printer or publisher on a book, with the place and often the time of publication.

Imprison, im-priz′on, *v.t.* [Prefix *im* for *in*, in, and *prison.*] To put into a prison; to incarcerate; to confine.—**Imprisoner**, im-priz′on-ėr, *n.* One who imprisons.—**Imprisonment**, im-priz′on-ment, *n* The act of imprisoning or state of being imprisoned.

Improbable, im-prob′a-bl, *a.* [Prefix *im* for *in*, not, and *probable.*] Not probable; not likely to be true; unlikely.—**Improbability, Improbableness**, im-prob′a-bil″i-ti, im-prob′a-bl-nes, *n.* The quality of being improbable.—**Improbably**, im-prob′a-bli, *adv.* In an improbable manner.

Improbity, im-prob′i-ti, *n.* [L. *improbitas*—*im* for *in*, not, and *probitas*, probity.] Want of probity; want of integrity or rectitude of principle; dishonesty.

Impromptu, im-promp′tū, *adv.* [L. *in promptu*, in readiness, from *promptus*, readiness. PROMPT.] Off-hand; without previous study.—*n.* A saying, poem, epigram, or the like made off-hand, or without previous study; an extemporaneous effusion. —*a.* Off-hand; extempore.

Improper, im-prop′ėr, *a.* [Prefix *im* for *in*, not, and *proper.*] Not proper; not suitable, adapted, or suited; unbecoming; indecent.—*Improper fraction*, a fraction whose numerator is equal to or greater than its denominator.—**Improperly**, im-prop′ėr-li, *adv.* In an improper manner.—**Impropriety**, im-prō-prī′e-ti, *n.* [Fr. *impropriété*, from L. *improprius*, improper.] The quality of being improper; that which is improper; an unsuitable act, expression, and the like.

Impropriate, im-prō′pri-āt, *v.t.*—*impropriated, impropriating.* [L. *im* for *in*, and *proprio, propriatum*, to appropriate, from *proprius*, one's own. PROPER.] To appropriate; *eccles.* to place the profits or revenue of in the hands of a layman; to put in the possession of a layman or lay corporation.—*a.* Devolved into the hands of a layman.—**Impropriation**, im-prō′pri-ā″shon, *n.* The act of impropriating; that which is impropriated.—**Impropriator**, im-prō′pri-ā-tėr, *n.* One who impropriates.

Impropriety. Under IMPROPER.

Improve, im-pröv′, *v.t.*—*improved, improving.* [Prefix *im* for *in*, intens., and O.Fr. *prover*, to test, to show to be sufficient. PROVE.] To make better; to increase the value, worth, or good qualities of; to use or employ to good purpose; to turn to profitable account (to *improve* the time).—*v.i.* To grow or become better; to advance in goodness, knowledge, wisdom, or anything else desirable.—*To improve on* or *upon*, to make additions or amendments to; to make an advance in; to bring nearer to perfection. ∴ Syn. under AMEND.—**Improvability, Improvableness**, im-prö′va-bil″i-ti, im-prö′va-bl-nes, *n.* The state or quality of being improvable. — **Improvable**, im-prö′va-bl, *a.* Capable of being improved.—**Improvement**, im-pröv′ment, *n.* The act of improving, or state of being improved; that which improves; that by which the value of anything is increased, its excellence enhanced, and the like; a beneficial or valuable addition or alteration.—**Improver**, im-prö′vėr, *n.* One who improves. —**Improving**, im-prö′ving, *a.* Tending to advance in good qualities. — **Improvingly**, im-prö′ving-li, *adv.* In an improving manner.

Improvident, im-prov′i-dent, *a.* [Prefix *im* for *in*, not, and *provident.*] Not provident; wanting forecast; wanting care to make provision for future exigencies; thriftless; thoughtless.—**Improvidence**, im-prov′i-dens, *n.* The quality of being improvident.—**Improvidently**, im-prov′i-dent-li, *adv.* In an improvident manner; thriftlessly.

Improvise, Improvisate, im-pro-vīz′, im-prō′vi-sāt, *v.t.*—*improvised, improvising; improvisated, improvisating.* [Fr. *improviser*, It. *improvvisare*, to sing in extempore rhymes, from L. *in*, not, *pro*, before, and *visus*, seen.] To compose and recite or sing without premeditation; to speak extempore, especially in verse; to do or form on the spur of the moment for a special occasion; to bring about in an off-hand way.—*v.i.* To recite or sing compositions without previous preparation.—**Improvisation**, im-prō′vi-sā″shon, *n.* The act or faculty of improvising; a song or other poem which is improvised.—**Improviser, Improvisator**, im-pro-vī′zėr, im-prō′vi-sā-tėr, *n.* One who improvisates or improvises. — **Improvisatory**, im-prō-vis′a-tō-ri, *a.* Relating to improvisation or improvisers.—**Improvvisatore**, im-prov-vis′a-tō-rā, *n.* pl. **Improvvisatori**, im-prov-vis′a-tō″rē. [It.] An extempore versifier, who can, without preparation, recite or sing a quantity of verses upon a given subject. — **Improvvisatrice**, im-prov-vis′a-trē″chā, *n.* [It.] A female improvvisatore; an extempore poetess. [These Italian words are spelled less correctly with one *v.*]

Imprudent, im-prö′dent, *a.* [L. *imprudens*—*im* for *in*, not, and *prudent.*] Not prudent; wanting prudence or discretion; indiscreet; injudicious; rash; heedless.—**Imprudence**, im-prö′dens, *n.* The quality of being imprudent; an imprudent act or course of conduct.—**Imprudently**, im-prö′dent-li, *adv.* In an imprudent manner.

Impudent, im′pū-dent, *a.* [L. *impudens, impudentis*, without shame—*in*, not, and *pudens*, from *pudeo*, to be ashamed.] Offensively forward in behaviour; intentionally treating others without due respect; wanting modesty; shameless; impertinent. —**Impudently**, im′pū-dent-li, *adv.* In an impudent manner.—**Impudence**, im′pū-dens, *n.* The quality of being impudent; impudent language or behaviour; offensive forwardness.

Impugn, im-pūn′, *v.t.* [Fr. *impugner*; L. *impugno*—*im* for *in*, against, and *pugno*, to fight or resist (akin *pugnacious, repugnant, pugilism.*] To attack (a statement, truthfulness, &c.) by words or arguments; to contradict; to call in question; to gainsay.—**Impugnable**, im-pū'na-bl, *a.* Capable of being impugned.—**Impugner**, im-pū'nėr, *n.* One who impugns.—**Impugnment**, im-pūn'ment, *n.* The act of impugning.

Impulse, im'puls, *n.* [L. *impulsus*, from *impello*, *impulsum*, to drive on. IMPEL.] Force communicated suddenly; motion produced by suddenly communicated force; thrust; push; influence acting on the mind suddenly or unexpectedly; sudden thought or determination; a force of infinitely large magnitude acting for an infinitely short time so as to produce a finite change of momentum.—**Impulsion**, im-pul'shon, *n.* [L. *impulsio*, *impulsionis.*] The act of impelling or state of being impelled; instigation; impulse.—**Impulsive**, im-pul'siv, *a.* [Fr. *impulsif.*] Having the power of impelling; impellant; actuated or liable to be actuated by impulses; under the sway of one's emotions.—**Impulsively**, im-pul'siv-li, *adv.* In an impulsive manner.—**Impulsiveness**, im-pul'siv-nes, *n.*

Impunity, im-pū'ni-ti, *n.* [Fr. *impunité*, from L. *impunitas*, from *impunis*, unpunished—*im* for *in*, not, and *punio*, to punish. PUNISH.] Exemption from punishment or penalty; freedom or exemption from injury, suffering, or loss.

Impure, im-pūr', *a.* [Fr. *impur*, from L. *impurus*—*im* for *in*, not, and *purus*, pure.] Not pure; mixed or impregnated with foul or extraneous substance; foul; obscene; unchaste; lewd; unclean; defiled by sin or guilt; unhallowed or unholy.—**Impurely**, im-pūr'li, *adv.* In an impure manner.—**Impureness**, im-pūr'nes, *n.* The quality or condition of being impure.—**Impurity**, im-pū'ri-ti, *n.* [L. *impuritas.*] The condition or quality of being impure; foulness; that which is impure; foul matter.

Impute, im-pūt', *v.t.* [L. *imputo*—*in*, into, and *puto*, think, consider, reckon (as in *compute*, *repute*, *putative*).] To charge, attribute, or ascribe; to set to the account of; *theol.* to reckon or set down to the account of one what does not belong to him.—**Imputability**, **Imputableness**, im-pū'ta-bil''i-ti, im-pū'ta-bl-nes, *n.* The quality of being imputable.—**Imputable**, im-pū'ta-bl, *a.* Capable of being imputed.—**Imputation**, im-pū-tā'shon, *n.* [L. *imputatio*, *imputationis.*] The act of imputing; that which is imputed or charged; charge, as of evil; censure; reproach; *theol.* the charging or reckoning to the account of one something which properly attaches to another.—**Imputative**, im-pū'ta-tiv, *a.* Coming by imputation; imputed.—**Imputatively**, im-pū'ta-tiv-li, *adv.* By imputation.—**Imputer**, im-pū'tėr, *n.* One that imputes.

In, in, *prep.* [A.Sax. *in* = D. and Goth. *in*, Icel. *inn*, *i*, Dan. *ind*, *i*, G. *in*, *ein*, forms corresponding to L. *in*, Gr. *en*, W. *yn*, Armor. *enn*; akin to *on*.] Within; inside of; surrounded by; indicating presence or situation within limits, whether of place, time, or circumstances (*in* the house, *in* the year, *in* sickness); or existence as a part, constituent, or quality of (evil *in* a man's disposition); or a certain state (a vehicle *in* motion, to put *in* operation).—*In as much as*, or *inasmuch as*, seeing that; considering that; since.—*In that*, because; for the reason that.—*In name of*, by way of; as (a sum paid *in name of* damages).—*In the name of*, in behalf of; on the part of; by the authority of.—*adv.* In or within some place; in some state, affair, or circumstances; not out (he is *in*, that is, in the house; the Tories are *in*, that is, in office; the ship is *in*, that is, in port); into some place or state, implying motion or change (come *in*, that is, into the house).—*To breed in and in*, to breed among members of the same family.—*To keep one's hand in*, to keep up one's acquirements; to maintain one's skill by practice.—Sometimes used substantively, as in the phrase '*ins* and outs', nooks and corners; all the details and intricacies of a matter.

Inability, in-a-bil'i-ti, *n.* [Prefix *in*, not, and *ability.*] The state of being unable; want of the necessary power or ability.

Inaccessible, in-ak-ses'i-bl, *a.* [Prefix *in*, not, and *accessible.*] Not accessible; not to be reached, obtained, or approached.—**Inaccessibly**, in-ak-ses'i-bli, *adv.* In an inaccessible manner.—**Inaccessibility**, **Inaccessibleness**, in-ak-ses'i-bil''i-ti, in-ak-ses'i-bl-nes, *n.* The quality or state of being inaccessible.

Inaccurate, in-ak'kū-rāt, *a.* [Prefix *in*, not, and *accurate.*] Not accurate, exact, or correct; making or containing incorrect statements; not according to truth; erroneous.—**Inaccurately**, in-ak'kū-rāt-li, *adv.* In an inaccurate manner.—**Inaccuracy**, in-ak'kū-ra-si, *n.* The state of being inaccurate; an inaccurate statement; a mistake in a statement; an error.

Inaction, in-ak'shon, *n.* [Prefix *in*, not, and *action.*] Want of action; state of being inactive; idleness; rest.—**Inactive**, in-ak'tiv, *a.* [Prefix *in*, not, and *active.*] Not active; inert; having no power to move; not engaged in action or effort; idle; indolent; sluggish; *chem.* and *med.* inoperative.—Syn. under INERT.] **Inactively**, in-ak'tiv-li, *adv.* In an inactive manner.—**Inactivity**, in-ak-tiv'i-ti, *n.* The quality or condition of being inactive.

Inadequate, in-ad'ē-kwāt, *a.* [Prefix *in*, not, and *adequate.*] Not adequate; not equal to the purpose; insufficient; defective.—**Inadequacy**, **Inadequateness**, in-ad'ē-kwa-si, in-ad'ē-kwāt-nes, *n.* The state or quality of being inadequate.—**Inadequately**, in-ad'ē-kwāt-li, *adv.*

Inadmissible, in-ad-mis'i-bl, *a.* [Prefix *in*, not, and *admissible.*] Not admissible; not proper to be admitted, allowed, or received.—**Inadmissibly**, in-ad-mis'i-bli, *adv.* In a manner not admissible.—**Inadmissibility**, in-ad-mis'i-bil''i-ti, *n.* The quality of being inadmissible.

Inadvertent, in-ad-vėr'tent, *a.* [L. prefix *in*, not, and *advertens*, *advertentis*, ppr. of *adverto*, to attend to. ADVERT.] Not paying strict attention; failing to notice or observe; heedless; unwary.—**Inadvertently**, in-ad-vėr'tent-li, *adv.* In an inadvertent manner.—**Inadvertence**, **Inadvertency**, in-ad-vėr'tens, in-ad-vėr'ten-si, *n.* The quality of being inadvertent; an oversight, mistake, or fault which proceeds from some degree of heedlessness.

Inalienable, in-āl'yen-a-bl, *a.* [Prefix *in*, not, and *alienable.*] Incapable of being alienated or transferred to another.—**Inalienability**, **Inalienableness**, in-āl'yen-a-bil''i-ti, in-āl'yen-a-bl-nes, *n.* The state or quality of being inalienable.—**Inalienably**, in-āl'yen-a-bli, *adv.* In a manner that forbids alienation.

Inalterable, in-al'tėr-a-bl, *n.* [Prefix *in*, not, and *alterable.*] Not alterable; unalterable.

Inamorato, in-ä'mō-rä''tō, *n.* [It. *innamorato*, fem. *innamorata*, from L. *in*, in, *amor*, love.] A male lover.—**Inamorata**, in-ä'mō-rä''ta, *n.* A female in love; a mistress.

Inane, in-ān', *a.* [L. *inanis*, empty.] Empty; void; frivolous; worthless; void of sense or intelligence.—*n.* That which is void or empty; infinite void space. (*Tenn.*)—**Inanition**, in-a-nish'on, *n.* The condition of being inane; exhaustion from want of food.—**Inanity**, in-an'i-ti, *n.* The state of being inane; mental vacuity; silliness.

Inanimate, in-an'i-māt, *a.* [Prefix *in*, not, and *animate.*] Not animate; destitute of life or animation; without vivacity or briskness; dull; inactive; sluggish.—**Inanimateness**, **Inanimation**, in-an'i-māt-nes, in'an-i-mā''shon, *n.*

Inappetence, **Inappetency**, in-ap'pē-tens, in-ap'pē-ten-si, *n.* [Prefix *in*, not, and *appetence*, *appetency.*] Want of appetence, desire, or inclination.

Inapplicable, in-ap'pli-ka-bl, *a.* [Prefix *in*, not, and *applicable.*] Not applicable; incapable of being applied; not suited or suitable to the purpose.—**Inapplicability**, **Inapplicableness**, in-ap'pli-ka-bil''i-ti, in-ap'pli-ka-bl-nes, *n.*—**Inapplicably**, in-ap'pli-ka-bli, *adv.*—**Inapplication**, in-ap'pli-kā''shon, *n.* Want of application, attention, or assiduity; neglect of industry.

Inapposite, in-ap'pō-zit, *a.* [Prefix *in*, not, and *apposite.*] Not apposite, fit, or suitable; not pertinent.

Inappreciable, in-ap-prē'shi-a-bl, *a.* [Prefix *in*, not, and *appreciable.*] Not appreciable; so small as hardly to be noticed or estimated.

Inapproachable, in-ap-prōch'a-bl, *a.* [Prefix *in*, not, and *approachable.*] Not approachable; inaccessible; that cannot be equalled; unrivalled.

Inappropriate, in-ap-prō'pri-āt, *a.* [Prefix *in*, not, and *appropriate.*] Not appropriate; unsuited; unsuitable; not proper.—**Inappropriately**, in-ap-prō'pri-āt-li, *adv.* In an appropriate manner.—**Inappropriateness**, in-ap-prō'pri-āt-nes, *n.*

Inapt, in-apt', *a.* [Prefix, *in*, not, and *apt.*] Unapt; not apt; unsuitable; unfit.—**Inaptitude**, **Inaptness**, in-ap'ti-tūd, in-apt'nes, *n.* Unfitness; unsuitableness.—**Inaptly**, in-apt'li, *adv.* Unfitly; unsuitably.

Inarch, in-ärch', *v.t.* [Prefix *in*, into, and *arch.*] To graft by uniting to the stock without separating (for a time) the scion from its parent tree.

Inarticulate, in-är-tik'ū-lāt, *a.* [Prefix *in*, not, and *articulate.*] Not articulate; not uttered with distinctness of sounds or syllables; *zool.* not jointed or articulated.—**Inarticulated**, in-är-tik'ū-lā-ted, *a.* Not articulated; not jointed.—**Inarticulately**, in-är-tik'ū-lāt-li, *adv.* In an inarticulate manner.—**Inarticulateness**, in-är-tik'ū-lāt-nes, *n.* The state or quality of being inarticulate.—**Inarticulation**, in-är-tik'ū-lā''shon, *n.* Want of articulation; indistinctness of sounds in speaking.

Inartificial, in-är'ti-fish''al, *a.* [Prefix *in*, not, and *artificial.*] Not artificial; formed without art; simple; artless.—**Inartificially**, in-är'ti-fish''al-li, *adv.* In an inartificial manner.

Inasmuch, in-az-much', *adv.* Under IN.

Inattention, in-at-ten'shon, *n.* [Prefix *in*, not, and *attention.*] Want of attention; heedlessness.—**Inattentive**, in-at-ten'tiv, *a.* Not attentive; not fixing the mind on an object; heedless.—**Inattentively**, in-at-ten'tiv-li, *adv.* Carelessly; heedlessly.—**Inattentiveness**, in-at-ten'tiv-nes, *n.*

Inaudible, in-a'di-bl, *a.* [Prefix *in*, not, and *audible.*] Not audible; incapable of being heard.—**Inaudibly**, in-a'di-bli, *adv.* In an inaudible manner.—**Inaudibility**, **Inaudibleness**, in-a'di-bil''i-ti, in-a'di-bl-nes, *n.* The quality of being inaudible.

Inaugurate, in-a'gū-rāt, *v.t.*—*inaugurated*, *inaugurating.* [L. *inauguro*, *inauguratum*, to inaugurate, to install—*in*, into, and *augur*, an augur.] To introduce or induct into an office with solemnity or suitable ceremonies; to invest in a formal manner; to begin or set in progress with formality or some degree of solemnity, pomp, or ceremony; to initiate; to perform in public initiatory ceremonies in connection with; to celebrate the completion of.—**Inaugural**, in-a'gū-ral, *a.* Pertaining to an inauguration.—**Inauguration**, in-a'gū-rā''shon, *n.* The act of inaugurating, or the ceremonies connected with such an act.—**Inaugurator**, in-a'gū-rā-tėr, *n.* One who inaugurates.—**Inauguratory**, in-a'gū-ra-to-ri, *a.* Suited or pertaining to inauguration.

Inaurate, in-a'rāt, *v.t.* [L. *inauro*, *inauratum*, from prefix *in*, and *aurum*, gold.] To cover with gold; to gild.

Inauspicious, in-a-spish'us, *a.* [Prefix *in*, not, and *auspicious.*] Not auspicious; ill-omened; unlucky; unfavourable.—**Inauspiciously**, in-a-spish'us-li, *adv.* In an inauspicious manner.—**Inauspiciousness**, in-a-spish'us-nes, *n.*

Inauthoritative, in-a-thor'i-tā-tiv, *a.* [Prefix *in*, not, and *authoritative.*] Having no authority.

Inboard, in'bōrd, *a.* Within a ship or other vessel (an *inboard* cargo). — *adv.* Within the hold of a vessel; on board of a vessel.

Inborn, in'born, *a.* Innate; implanted by nature.

Inbreak, in'brāk, *n.* A sudden, violent inroad or incursion; an irruption; opposed to *outbreak*. — **Inbreaking**, in'brā-king, *n.* The act of breaking in; incursion; invasion; inroad.

Inbreathe, in-brēTH', *v.t.* To breathe in, or infuse by breathing.

Inbred, in'bred, *a.* Bred within; innate; natural.—**Inbreed**, in-brēd', *v.t.* To produce or generate within; to cross or mate closely-related individuals.

Inca, in'ka, *n.* A king or prince of Peru before the conquest of that country by the Spaniards.

Incage, in-kāj', *v.t.* To encage.

Incalculable, in-kal'kū-la-bl, *a.* [Prefix *in*, not, and *calculable*.] Not calculable; beyond calculation; very great.—**Incalculableness**, in-kal'kū-la-bl-nes, *n.*—**Incalculably**, in-kal'kū-la-bli, *adv.* In an incalculable manner; immeasurably; infinitely.

Incalescent, in-ka-les'ent, *a.* [L. *incalesco*, to grow warm—*in*, and *calesco*, to grow warm, *caleo*, to be warm. CALID.] Growing warm; increasing in heat.—**Incalescence, Incalescency**, in-ka-les'ens, in-ka-les'en-si, *n.* The state of being incalescent.

Incandescent, in-kan-des'ent, *a.* L. *incandesco*, to become warm—*in*, intens., and *candesco*, to begin to glow, from *candeo*, to shine. CANDID.] White or glowing with heat.—**Incandescence**, in-kan-des'ens, *n.* The condition of being incandescent.

Incanescent, in-ka-nes'ent, *a.* [*In*, intens., and *canescent*.] *Bot.* having a hoary or gray aspect, from hairs upon the surface.

Incantation, in-kan-tā'shon, *n.* [L. *incantatio*, *incantationis*, from *incanto*, to chant a magic formula over one—*in*, on, and *canto*, to sing. CHANT.] The act of using certain words and ceremonies for the purpose of raising spirits or performing magical actions; the form of words so used; a magical spell, charm, or ceremony.—**Incantatory**, in-kan'ta-to-ri, *a.* Dealing by enchantment; magical.

Incapable, in-kā'pa-bl, *a.* [Prefix *in*, not, and *capable*.] Not capable; possessing inadequate power; not admitting; not susceptible; not equal to anything; unable; unqualified or disqualified: generally followed by *of*. ∴ *Incapable* properly denotes a want of passive power, and is applicable particularly to the mind, or said of something inanimate; *unable* denotes the want of active power or power of performing, and is applicable to the body or mind.—*n.* One physically or mentally unable to act with effect; an inefficient or silly person.—**Incapability, Incapableness**, in-kā'pa-bil"i-ti, in-kā'pa-bl-nes, *n.* The quality of being incapable.—**Incapably**, in-kā'pa-bli, *adv.* In an incapable manner.

Incapacitate, in-ka-pas'i-tāt, *v.t.*—*incapacitated*, *incapacitating*. [Prefix *in*, not, and *capacitate*.] To deprive of capacity or natural power; to render or make unable or unfit; to disqualify or render incompetent. — **Incapacitation**, in-ka-pas'i-tā"shon, *n.* The act of incapacitating.—**Incapacity**, in-ka-pas'i-ti, *n.* Want of capacity, power, or ability; inability; incompetency.

Incarcerate, in-kär'sėr-āt, *v.t.*—*incarcerated*, *incarcerating*. [L. *in*, in, into, and *carcer*, a prison.] To imprison; to confine in a jail; to shut up or inclose.—**Incarceration**, in-kär'sėr-ā"shon, *n.* The act of incarcerating; imprisonment.—**Incarcerator**, in-kär'sėr-ā-tėr, *n.* One who incarcerates.

Incarnadine, in-kär'na-din, *v.t.* [Fr. *incarnadin*, flesh-coloured — L. *in*, in, and *caro*, *carnis*, flesh.] To tinge with the colour of flesh; to dye red.

Incarnate, in-kär'nat, *v.t.*—*incarnated*, *incarnating*. [L.L. *incarno*, *incarnatum*—L. *in*, into, and *caro*, *carnis*, flesh (whence also *carnage*, *carnal*, *carnation*).] To clothe with flesh; to embody in flesh.—*a.* Invested with flesh; embodied in flesh or a human body.—**Incarnation**, in-kär-nā'shon, *n.* The act of assuming flesh or taking a human body and the nature of man; the state of being incarnated; a visible embodiment; a vivid exemplification in person or act (he is the *incarnation* of wickedness).

Incase, in-kās', *v.t.*—*incased*, *incasing*. To inclose in, or as in, a case.

Incautious, in-ka'shus, *a.* [Prefix *in*, not, and *cautious*.] Not cautious; unwary; heedless. — **Incautiously**, in-ka'shus-li, *adv.* In an incautious manner.—**Incautiousness**, in-ka'shus-nes, *n.*

Incendiary, in-sen'di-a-ri, *n.* [L. *incendiarius*, from *incendo*, to burn—*in*, and *candeo*, to shine or be on fire. CANDID.] A person who wilfully and maliciously sets fire to a building, &c.; one who sets fire to another's property; one who is guilty of arson; one who excites or inflames factions and promotes quarrels.—*a.* Pertaining to wilful and malicious fire-raising; tending to excite or inflame factions, sedition, or quarrel. — **Incendiarism**, in-sen'di-ar-izm, *n.* The act or practice of an incendiary.

Incense, in'sens, *n.* [Fr. *encens*, from L. *incensum*, what is set on fire, from *incensus*, pp. of *incendo*, to burn. INCENDIARY.] The odours of spices and gums, burned in religious rites, or as an offering to some deity; the materials burned for making perfumes. —*v.t.* — *incensed*, *incensing*. To perfume with incense.

Incense, in-sens', *v.t.*—*incensed*, *incensing*. [L. *incensus*, provoked, inflamed; same word as *Incense*, above.] To enkindle or inflame to violent anger; to excite to angry passions; to provoke, irritate, exasperate. —**Incensed**, in-senst', *p.* and *a.* Inflamed with anger; exasperated; exhibiting violent anger.—**Incensive**, in-sen'siv, *a.* Tending to incense; inflammatory.

Incentive, in-sen'tiv, *a.* [L. *incentivus*, striking up or leading a melody—*in*, on, and *cano*, to sing. CHANT.] Inciting; encouraging or stirring up.—*n.* That which incites or has a tendency to incite to determination or action; what prompts to good or ill; motive; spur.—**Incentively**, in-sen'tiv-li, *adv.* In an incentive manner.

Inception, in-sep'shon, *n.* [L. *inceptio*, *inceptionis*, from *incipio*, to begin—prefix *in*, and *capio*, to take. CAPABLE.] The act of beginning; a beginning; commencement; first stage.—**Inceptive**, in-sep'tiv, *a.* [L. *inceptivus*.] Pertaining to inception; beginning; applied to a verb which expresses the beginning of an action.—*n.* An inceptive verb.—**Inceptively**, in-sep'tiv-li, *adv.* In an inceptive manner.—**Inceptor**, in-sep'tėr, *n.* A beginner; one who is on the point of taking the degree of Master of Arts at an English university.

Incertitude, in-sėr'ti-tūd, *n.* [Prefix *in*, not, and *certitude*.] Uncertainty; doubtfulness; doubt.

Incessant, in-ses'ant, *a.* [L. prefix *in*, not, and *cessans*, *cessantis*, ppr. of *cesso*, to cease. CEASE.] Continuing without interruption; unceasing; unintermitted; uninterrupted; continual; ceaseless.—**Incessantly**, in-ses'ant-li, *adv.* In an incessant manner; continually.—**Incessantness**, in-ses'ant-nes, *n.*

Incest, in'sest, *n.* [Fr. *inceste*, L. *incestum*, unchastity, incest, from *incestus*, unchaste—*in*, not, and *castus*, chaste (whence *chaste*).] The offence of sexual commerce between persons related within the degrees wherein marriage is prohibited by law.—**Incestuous**, in-ses'tū-us, *a.* Guilty of incest; involving the crime of incest.—**Incestuously**, in-ses'tū-us-li, *adv.* In an incestuous manner.—**Incestuousness**, in-ses'tū-us-nes, *n.*

Inch, insh, *n.* [A.Sax. *ince*, *ynce*, an inch, the twelfth part of a foot; from L. *uncia*, a twelfth part. *Ounce* is the same word.] A lineal measure, being the twelfth part of a foot; proverbially, a small quantity or degree.—*By inches*, by slow degrees; gradually.—*a.* Measuring an inch: used in composition (two-*inch*, four-*inch*).—**Inchmeal**, insh'mēl, *adv.* [The term -*meal*= A.Sax. -*maelum*, by parts, from *mael*, a part.] By inches; little by little.—*By inchmeal*, by parts or slow degrees.

Inch, insh, *n.* [Gael. *innis*, an island, probably allied to L. *insula*.] An island: common in place-names belonging to Scotland.

Inchoate,† in'kō-āt, *v.t.* [L. *inchoo*, *inchoatum*, to begin.] To begin.—*a.* Recently or just begun; incipient; rudimentary; incomplete.—**Inchoately**, in'kō-āt-li, *adv.* In an inchoate state.—**Inchoation**, in-kō-ā'shon, *n.* The act of beginning; inception.—**Inchoative**, in'kō-ā-tiv, *a.* Expressing or indicating beginning; inceptive. —*n.* That which serves to begin; *gram.* an inceptive verb.

Incidence, in'si-dens, *n.* [L.L. *incidentia*, from E. *incido*, to fall upon—*in*, into, upon, and *cado*, to fall (whence *cadence*, *chance*, *case*, &c.).] A falling or occurring; the manner of falling (the *incidence* of taxation in a state); *physics*, the direction in which a body, or a ray of light, heat, &c., falls upon any surface, this direction, as regards the surface on which the body or ray falls, being called the *line of incidence*.—*Angle of incidence*, the angle formed by the line of incidence, and a line drawn from the point of contact, perpendicular to the surface.—*Point of incidence*, the point where an incident ray meets a surface.—**Incident**, in'si-dent, *a.* [L. *incidens*, *incidentis*, ppr. of *incido*.] Falling or striking, as a ray of light upon a surface; liable to happen; apt to occur; hence, naturally happening or appertaining (ills *incident to* human life).—*n.* What falls out, happens, or takes place; an event; an appertaining fact; *law*, a thing appertaining to, or passing with another or principal thing.—**Incidental**, in-si-den'tal, *a.* Happening as an occasional event forming an incident; casual; not necessary to the chief purpose; appertaining and subsidiary.—**Incidentally**, in-si-den'tal-li, *adv.* In an incidental manner.—**Incidentalness**,† in-si-den'tal-nes, *n.*

Incinerate, in-sin'ėr-āt, *v.t.* [L. *in*, into, and *cinis*, *cineris*, ashes.] To burn to ashes. —**Incinerable**, in-sin'ėr-a-bl, *a.* Capable of being reduced to ashes.—**Incineration**, in-sin'ėr-ā"shon, *n.* The act of incinerating.

Incipient, in-sip'i-ent, *a.* [L. *incipiens*, *incipientis*, ppr. of *incipio*, to begin—*in*, and *capio*, to take. CAPABLE.] Beginning; commencing; beginning to show itself.—**Incipience, Incipiency**, in-sip'i-ens, in-sip'i-en-si, *n.* The condition of being incipient.—**Incipiently**, in-sip'i-ent-li, *adv.* In an incipient manner.

Incircle, in-sėr'kl, *v.t.* To encircle.

Incise, in-sīz', *v.t.*—*incised*, *incising*. [Fr. *inciser*, from L. *incido*, *incisum*—*in*, into, and *cædo*, to cut, as in *concise*, *decide*, *excision*, &c.] To cut into; to make a deep cut in; to carve.—**Incised**, in-sīzd', *p.* and *a.* Cut; made by cutting.—**Incision**, in-sizh'on, *n.* The act of cutting into a substance; that which is produced by incising; a cut; a gash; *fig.* sharpness; trenchancy.—**Incisive**, in-sī'siv, *a.* [Fr. *incisif*, incisive.] Cutting in; sharply and clearly expressive; trenchant (*incisive* language or style).—**Incisor**, in-sī'zėr, *n.* *Zool.* a fore-tooth; one of those teeth the special task of which is to cut or separate.—**Incisory**, in-sī'zo-ri, *a.* Having the quality of cutting. —**Incisure**, in-sī'zhūr, *n.* A cut; an incision.

Incite, in-sīt', *v.t.*—*incited*, *inciting*. [L. *incito*—*in*, on, and *cito*, to urge, to rouse. CITE.] To move to action; to stir up; to stimulate, urge, provoke, spur on.—**Incitative**, in-sī'ta-tiv, *a.* Tending to incite; inciting; provocative.—*n.* That which excites; a stimulant; a provocative.—**Incitement, Incitation**, in-sīt'ment, in-si-tā'shon, *n.* The act of inciting; that which incites or moves to action; incentive; impulse; spur; stimulus.—**Inciter**, in-sī'tėr, *n.* One who incites.—**Incitingly**, in-sī'ting-li, *adv.* So as to incite.

Incivil, in-siv'il, *a.* [Prefix *in*, not, and *civil.*] Not civil; rude; unpolite.—**Incivility**, in-si-vil'i-ti, *n.* Want of courtesy; rudeness; impoliteness.

Incivism, in-siv'izm, *n.* In French Revolution the charge of lack of patriotism, of bad performance of civic duties; disaffection.

Incle, ing'kl, *n.* Same as *Inkle.*

Inclement, in-klem'ent, *a.* [Prefix *in*, not, and *clement.*] Not clement; unmerciful, severe, or harsh; tempestuous, rough, stormy, boisterous, or otherwise hard to bear (weather).—**Inclemency**, in-klem'en-si, *n.* The condition or quality of being inclement.

Incline, in-klīn', *v.i.*—*inclined, inclining.* [L. *inclino*, to incline—*in*, in, on, and *clino*, Gr. *klinō*, to bend. DECLINE.] To deviate from a direction which is regarded as normal; to bend, lean, tend; to tend, as towards an opinion, course of action, &c.—*v.t.* To cause to deviate from a line, position, or direction; to give a leaning to; to give a tendency or propensity to; to dispose; to bend, stoop, or bow (the body, the head).—*n.*, in'klīn, an ascent or descent, as in a road; a slope.—**Inclinable**, in-klī'na-bl, *a.* [L. *inclinabilis*, from *inclino.*] Tending; inclined; somewhat disposed.—**Inclinableness**, in-klī'na-bl-nes, *n.* The state of being inclinable.—**Inclination**, in-kli-nā'shon, *n.* [L. *inclinatio, inclinationis.*] The act of inclining, leaning, or bending; deviation from a direction regarded as the normal one; *geom.* the approach or leaning of two lines or planes towards each other, so as to make an angle at the point where they meet, or where their lines of direction meet; a disposition more favourable to one thing or person than to another; leaning; feeling in favour; propensity.—*Inclination of an orbit, astron.* the angle which the plane of an orbit makes with the ecliptic. DIP.—**Inclinatory**, in-klī'na-to-ri, *a.* Having the quality of inclining.—**Inclined**, in-klīnd', *p.* and *a.* Having a leaning or tendency; disposed.—*Inclined plane*, a plane inclined to the horizon, or forming with a horizontal plane any angle whatever excepting a right angle: it is one of the mechanical powers.

Inclose, in-klōz', *v.t.*—*inclosed, inclosing.* [Prefix *in*, in, and *close.*] To surround, shut in, or confine on all sides; to shut up; to environ or encompass; to separate from common grounds by a fence (to *inclose* lands); to cover with a case, wrapper, or envelope.—**Incloser**, in-klō'zėr, *n.* One who incloses.—**Inclosure**, in-klō'zhūr, *n.* The act of inclosing; what is inclosed; a space inclosed or fenced; something inclosed along with a letter or the like.

Include, in-klūd', *v.t.*—*included, including.* [L. *includo*—*in*, in, and *claudo*, to shut up, as in *conclude, exclude*, &c. CLOSE.] To confine, hold, or contain; to comprise; to comprehend; to embrace or involve.—*Included style, included stamens, bot.* a style or stamens which do not project beyond the mouth of the corolla.—**Includible**, in-klū'di-bl, *a.* Capable of being included.—**Inclusion**, in-klū'zhon, *n.* [L. *inclusio.*] The act of including.—**Inclusive**, in-klū'siv, *a.* [Fr. *inclusif*, from L. *includo.*] Inclosing; encircling; comprehended in the number or sum; comprehending the stated limit or extremes.—**Inclusively**, in-klū'siv-li, *adv.* In an inclusive manner

Incogitable, in-koj'i-ta-bl, *a.* [Prefix *in*, not, and *cogitable.* COGITATE.] Not cogitable; incapable of being made the object of thought.—**Incogitability**, in-koj'i-ta-bil"i-ti, *n.* The quality of being incogitable.—**Incogitance, Incogitancy**, in-koj'i-tans, in-koj'i-tan-si, *n.* [L. *incogitantia.*] Want of thought or the power of thinking.—**Incogitant**, in-koj'i-tant, *a.* Not thinking; thoughtless.—**Incogitantly**, in-koj'i-tant-li, *adv.* In an incogitant manner.—**Incogitative**, in-koj'i-tā-tiv, *a.* Not cogitative; wanting the power of thought.

Incognito, in-kog'ni-tō, *a.* or *adv.* [It., Sp., and Fr., from L. *incognitus*, unknown—*in*, not, and *cognitus*, known. COGNITION.] In disguise; in an assumed character and under an assumed name.—*n.*, the fem. being **Incognita**, in-kog'ni-ta. One unknown, or in disguise, or passing under an assumed name; assumption of a disguised or feigned character.—**Incog**, in-kog', *a.*, *adv.* & *n.* Incognito. (*Colloq.*)

Incognizable, in-kog'ni-za-bl or in-kon'i-za-bl, *a.* [Prefix *in*, not, and *cognizable.*] Not cognizable; incapable of being recognized, known, or distinguished.—**Incognizance**, in-kog'ni-zans or in-kon'i-zans, *n.* Failure to recognize, know, or apprehend.—**Incognizant**, in-kog'ni-zant or in-kon'i-zant, *a.* Not cognizant; unacquainted with.—**Incognoscible**, in-kog-nos'i-bl, *a.* [Prefix *in*, not, and *cognoscible.*] Not cognoscible; incapable of being comprehended, known, or distinguished.—**Incognoscibility**, in-kog-nos'i-bil"i-ti, *n.* The state of being incognoscible.

Incoherent, in-kō-hē'rent, *a.* [Prefix *in*, not, and *coherent.*] Not coherent; not cohering or attached together; unconnected (*incoherent* particles); wanting coherence or rational connection (ideas, language, &c.); rambling and unintelligible.—**Incoherence, Incoherency**, in-kō-hē'rens, in-kō-hē'ren-si, *n.* The quality of being incoherent.—**Incoherently**, in-kō-hē'rent-li, *adv.* In an incoherent manner.

Incombustible, in-kom-bus'ti-bl, *a.* [Prefix *in*, not, and *combustible.*] Not combustible; incapable of being burned or consumed by fire.—**Incombustibility, Incombustibleness**, in-com-bus'ti-bil"i-ti, in-kom-bus'ti-bl-nes, *n.* The quality of being incombustible.—**Incombustibly**, in kom-bus'ti-bli, *adv.* So as to resist combustion.

Income, in'kum, *n.* [From *in* and *come*, lit. that which comes in; comp. *outcome.*] Receipts or benefits (usually in the form of money) regularly accruing from labor, business, or property (as, his annual *income* is $2,000); revenue.—**Income-tax**, *n.* A tax levied on incomes according to their amount.—**Incomer**, in'kum-ėr, *n.* One who comes in; a stranger, not a native.—**Incoming**, in'kum-ing, *a.* Coming in, as an occupant (an *incoming* tenant).—*n.* The act of coming in.

Incommensurable, in-kom-men'sū-ra-bl, *a.* [Prefix *in*, not, and *commensurable.*] Not commensurable; having no common measure.—*n.* One of two or more quantities which have no common measure.—**Incommensurability, Incommensurableness**, in-kom-men'sū-ra-bil"i-ti, in-kom-men'sū-ra-bl-nes, *n.*—**Incommensurably**, in-kom-men'sū-ra-bli, *adv.*—**Incommensurate**, in-kom-men'sū-rāt, *a.* [Prefix *in*, not, and *commensurate.*] Not commensurate; incommensurable; not adequate or of sufficient amount.—**Incommensurately**, in-kom-men'sū-rāt-li, *adv.* Not in due measure or proportion; inadequately.

Incommode, in-kom-mōd', *v.t.*—*incommoded, incommoding.* [Fr. *incommoder*, from L. *incommodo*, to be troublesome to—*in*, not, *commodus*, convenient.—COMMODIOUS.] To give inconvenience to; to inconvenience; to put about; to trouble.—**Incommodious**, in-kom-mō'di-us, *a.* [Prefix *in*, not, and *commodious.*] Not commodious; inconvenient; tending to incommode.—**Incommodiously**, in-kom-mō'di-us-li, *adv.* In an incommodious manner.—**Incommodiousness**, in-kom-mō'di-us-nes, *n.*

Incommunicable, in-kom-mū'ni-ka-bl, *a.* [Prefix *in*, not, and *communicable.*] Not communicable; incapable of being communicated, told, or imparted to others.—**Incommunicability, Incommunicableness**, in-kom-mū'ni-ka-bil"i-ti, in-kom-mū'ni-ka-bl-nes, *n.*—**Incommunicably**, in-kom-mū'ni-ka-bli, *adv.*—**Incommunicative**, in-kom-mū'ni-kā-tiv, *a.* [Prefix *in*, not, and *communicative.*] Not communicative; not inclined to impart information to others; not disposed to hold communion or intercourse.—**Incommunicatively**, in-kom-mū'ni-kā-tiv-li, *adv.*—**Incommunicativeness**, in-kom-mū'ni-kā-tiv-nes, *n.*

Incommutable, in-kom-mū'ta-bl, *a.* [Prefix *in*, not, and *commutable.*] Not commutable; incapable of being exchanged.—**Incommutability, Incommutableness**, in-kom-mū'ta-bil"i-ti, in-kom-mū'ta-bl-nes, *n.* The quality of being incommutable.

Incomparable, in-kom'pa-ra-bl, *a.* [Prefix *in*, not, and *comparable.*] Not comparable; admitting of no comparison with others; without a match, rival, or peer; unequalled; transcendent.—**Incomparableness**, in-kom'pa-ra-bl-nes, *n.* The quality of being incomparable.—**Incomparably**, in-kom'pa-ra-bli, *adv.* In an incomparable manner; beyond comparison or compare; in the highest degree.

Incompatible, in-kom-pat'i-bl, *a.* [Prefix *in*, not, and *compatible.*] Not compatible; incapable of subsisting, being possessed, or being made to accord with something else; incapable of harmonizing (feelings or tempers *incompatible with* each other).—*n.* A thing that is incompatible.—**Incompatibility, Incompatibleness**, in-kom-pat'i-bil"i-ti, in-kom-pat'i-bl-nes, *n.* The quality or condition of being incompatible.—**Incompatibly**, in-kom-pat'i-bli, *adv.*

Incompetent, in-kom'pe-tent, *a.* [Prefix *in*, not, and *competent.*] Not competent; wanting adequate strength, power, capacity, means, qualifications, &c.; unable; incapable; inadequate; wanting necessary legal or constitutional qualifications (an *incompetent* witness in a court); not permissible or admissible (an *incompetent* defence).—**Incompetence, Incompetency**, in-kom'pē-tens, in-kom'pē-ten-si, *n.* The condition or quality of being incompetent.—**Incompetently**, in-kom'pē-tent-li, *adv.* In an incompetent manner.

Incomplete, in-kom-plēt', *a.* [Prefix *in*, not, and *complete.*] Not complete; not finished; imperfect; defective.—**Incompletely**, in-kom-plēt'li, *adv.* In an incomplete manner.—**Incompleteness, Incompletion**, in-kom-plēt'nes, in-kom-plē'shon, *n.* The state of being incomplete.

Incompliant, in-kom-plī'ant, *a.* [Prefix *in*, not, and *compliant.*] Not compliant; not disposed to comply.—**Incompliance**, in-com-plī'ans, *n.* The quality of being incompliant.—**Incompliantly**, in-kom-plī-ant-li, *adv.* In an incompliant manner.

Incomposite, in-kom'po-zit, *a.* [Prefix *in*, not, and *composite.*] Not composite; uncompounded; simple.

Incomprehensible, in-kom'prē-hen"si-bl, *a.* [Prefix *in*, not, and *comprehensible.*] Not comprehensible; incapable of being comprehended or understood; beyond the reach of human intellect; inconceivable; *theol.* as in Athanasian Creed; illimitable; infinite; not comprehended in or bounded by space.—**Incomprehensibility, Incomprehensibleness**, in-kom'prē-hen'si-bil"i-ti, in-kom'prē-hen"si-bl-nes, *n.* The quality of being incomprehensible.—**Incomprehensibly**, in-kom'prē-hen"si-bli, *adv.* In an incomprehensible manner.—**Incomprehension**, in-kom'prē-hen"shon, *n.* Want of comprehension or understanding.—**Incomprehensive**, in-kom'prē-hen"siv, *a.* Not comprehensive; not extensive; limited.—**Incomprehensively**, in-kom'prē-hen"siv-li, *adv.*—**Incomprehensiveness**, in-kom'prē-hen"siv-nes, *n.*

Incompressible, in-kom-pres'i-bl, *a.* [Prefix *in*, not, and *compressible.*] Not compressible; resisting compression.—**Incompressibility, Incompressibleness**, in-kom-pres'i-bil"i-ti, in-kom-pres'i-bl-nes, *n.* The quality of being incompressible.

Incomputable, in-kom-pū'ta-bl, *a.* [Prefix *in*, not, and *computable.*] Not computable; incapable of being computed or reckoned.

Inconcealable, in-kon-sēl'a-bl, *a.* [Prefix *in*, not, and *concealable.*] Not concealable; not to be hid or kept secret.

Inconceivable, in-kon-sē'va-bl, *a.* [Prefix *in*, not, and *conceivable.*] Not conceivable; incapable of being conceived or thought of; incomprehensible.—**Inconceivability, Inconceivableness**, in-kon-sē'va-bil"i-ti, in-kon-sē'va-bl-nes, *n.* The quality of being inconceivable.—**Inconceivably**, in-kon-sē'va-bli, *adv.* In an inconceivable manner; beyond conception.

Inconclusive, in-kon-klū'siv, *a.* [Prefix *in*, not, and *conclusive.*] Not conclusive; not producing a conclusion; not settling a point in debate or a doubtful question.—**Inconclusively**, in-kon-klū'siv-li, *adv.* In an inconclusive manner.—**Inconclusiveness**, in-kon-klū'siv-nes, *n.* The quality of being inconclusive.

Incondensable, Incondensible, in-kon-den'sa-bl, in-kon-den'si-bl, *a.* [Prefix *in*, not, and *condensable.*] Not condensable; incapable of being condensed.—**Incondensability, Incondensibility**, in-kon-den'sa-bil"i-ti, in-kon-den'si-bil"i-ti, *n.*

Incondite, in-kon'dit, *a.* [L. *inconditus*, confused, rude—*in*, not, and *conditus*, pp. of *condo*, to put together, to join.] Rude; unpolished: said of literary compositions.

Inconformity, in-kon-for'mi-ti, *n.* [Prefix *in*, not, and *conformity.*] Nonconformity: lack of conformity.

Incongealable, in-kon-jēl'a-bl, *a.* [Prefix *in*, not, and *congealable.*] Not congealable; incapable of being frozen.—**Incongealableness**, in-kon-jēl'a-bl-nes, *n.*

Incongenial, in-kon-jē'ni-al, *a.* [Prefix *in*, not, and *congenial.*] Not congenial; not of a like nature; unsuitable; uncongenial.

Incongruous, Incongruent, in-kong'-grų-us, in-kong'grų-ent, *a.* [L. *incongruus*—*in*, not, and *congruus*, congruous.] Not congruous; not of a kind or character to mingle well together; not such as to make a harmonious whole; not suiting each other; inharmonious; inconsistent (*incongruous* parts, elements, mixtures).—**Incongruity, Incongruence**, in-kon-grų'i-ti, in-kong'grų-ens, *n.* The quality of being incongruous; that which is incongruent; something exhibiting a want of congruity.—**Incongruously**, in-kong'grų-us-li, *adv.* In an incongruous manner.—**Incongruousness**, in-kong'grų-us-nes, *n.* The state or quality of being incongruous.

Inconsequent, in-kon'sē-kwent, *a.* [Prefix *in*, not, and *consequent*; L. *inconsequens.*] Not following from the premises; not in accordance with logical method; inconclusive.—**Inconsequence**, in-kon'sē-kwens, *n.* [L. *inconsequentia.*] The condition or quality of being inconsequent; want of logical sequence.—**Inconsequential**, in-kon'sē-kwen"shal, *a.* [Prefix *in*, not, and *consequential.*] Not consequential; inconsequent; not of consequence or importance; of little moment.—**Inconsequentiality**, in-kon'sē-kwen'shi-al"i-ti, *n.* State of being inconsequential.—**Inconsequentially**, in-kon'sē-kwen"shal-li, *adv.* In an inconsequential manner.—**Inconsequentness**, in-kon'sē-kwent-nes, *n.*

Inconsiderable, in-kon-sid'ér-a-bl, *a.* [Prefix *in*, not, and *considerable.*] Not worthy of consideration or notice; unimportant; small; trivial; insignificant.—**Inconsiderableness**, in-kon-sid'ér-a-bl-nes, *n.*—**Inconsiderably**, in-kon-sid'-ér-a-bli, *adv.* In an inconsiderable manner or degree.

Inconsiderate, in-kon-sid'ér-āt, *a.* [Prefix *in*, not, and *considerate*; L. *inconsideratus.*] Not considerate; not acting with due consideration; hasty; imprudent; thoughtless; heedless.—**Inconsiderately**, in-kon-sid'ér-āt-li, *adv.* In an inconsiderate manner.—**Inconsiderateness**, in-kon-sid'ér-āt-nes, *n.* The condition or quality of being inconsiderate.—**Inconsideration**, in-kon-sid'ér-ā"shon, *n.* Want of due consideration.

Inconsistent, in-kon-sis'tent, *a.* [Prefix *in*, not, and *consistent.*] Not consistent; irreconcilable in conception or in fact; contrary; contradictory; incompatible; incongruous; not exhibiting uniformity of sentiment or conduct, steadiness to principle or the like.—**Inconsistently**, in-kon-sis'-tent-li, *adv.* In an inconsistent manner.—**Inconsistency, Inconsistence**, in-kon-sis'ten-si, in-kon-sis'tens, *n.* The condition or quality of being inconsistent; opposition or disagreement of particulars; self-contradiction; incongruity in action or conduct.

Inconsolable, in-kon-sōl'a-bl, *a.* [Prefix *in*, not, and *consolable.*] Incapable of being consoled; grieved beyond consolation.—**Inconsolableness**, in-kon-sōl'a-bl-nes, *n.* State of being inconsolable.—**Inconsolably**, in-kon-sōl'a-bli, *adv.* So as to be inconsolable.

Inconsonant, in-kon'sō-nant, *a.* [Prefix *in*, not, and *consonant.*] Not consonant or agreeing; inconsistent; discordant.—**Inconsonantly**, in-kon'sō-nant-li, *adv.* In an inconsonant manner.—**Inconsonance, Inconsonancy**, in-kon'sō-nans, in-kon'sō-nan-si, *n.* Want of harmony; discordance.

Inconspicuous, in-kon-spik'ū-us, *a.* [Prefix *in*, not, and *conspicuous.*] Not conspicuous or readily noticed; not to be easily perceived.—**Inconspicuously**, in-kon-spik'ū-us-li, *adv.* In an inconspicuous manner.—**Inconspicuousness**, in-kon-spik'-ū-us-nes, *n.* Want of conspicuousness.

Inconstant, in-kon'stant, *a.* [Prefix *in*, not, and *constant*; L. *inconstans*, Fr. *inconstant.*] Not constant; subject to change of opinion, inclination, or purpose; not firm in resolution; unsteady; fickle; capricious: said of persons; mutable, changeable, or variable: said of things.—*n.* A thing which is not constant; a variable.—**Inconstantly**, in-kon'stant-li, *adv.* In an inconstant manner.—**Inconstancy**, in-kon'stan-si, *n.* [L. *inconstantia.*] The quality of being inconstant.

Inconsumable, in-kon-sū'ma-bl, *a.* [Prefix *in*, not, and *consumable.*] Not consumable; incapable of being consumed.

Inconsummate, in-kon-sum'āt, *a.* [Prefix *in*, not, and *consummate.*] Not consummate; not finished; not complete.—**Inconsummateness**, in-kon-sum'āt-nes, *n.*

Incontestable, in-kon-tes'ta-bl, *a.* [Prefix *in*, not and *contestable.*] Not contestable; not to be disputed; too clear to be controverted; incontrovertible.—**Incontestability, Incontestableness**, in-kon-tes'ta-bil"i-ti, in-kon-tes'ta-bl-nes, *n.* The state or quality of being incontestable.—**Incontestably**, in-con-tes'ta-bli, *adv.* In an incontestable manner; incontrovertibly; indubitably.

Incontinent, in-kon'ti-nent, *a.* [Prefix *in*, not, and *continent*; L. *incontinens*; Fr. *incontinent*, incontinent, and (as adv.) forthwith, immediately.] Not continent; not restraining the passions or appetites, particularly the sexual appetite; unchaste; lewd; *med.* unable to restrain natural discharges or evacuations.—**Incontinence, Incontinency**, in-kon'ti-nens, in-kon'ti-nen-si, *n.* [L. *incontinentia*, Fr. *incontinence.*] The condition or quality of being incontinent.—**Incontinently**, in-kon'ti-nent-li, *adv.* In an incontinent manner; immediately; instantly; forthwith; at once.

Incontrovertible, in-kon'trō-vér"ti-bl, *a.* [Prefix *in*, not, and *controvertible.*] Not controvertible; too clear or certain to admit of dispute or controversy.—**Incontrovertibility, Incontrovertibleness**, in-kon'trō-vér'ti-bil"i-ti, in-kon'trō-vér"ti-bl-nes, *n.* State of being incontrovertible.—**Incontrovertibly**, in-kon'trō-vér"ti-bli, *adv.* In an incontrovertible manner; incontestably.

Inconvenient, in-kon-vē'ni-ent, *a.* [Prefix *in*, not, and *convenient.*] Not convenient; incommodious; giving some trouble; wanting due facilities; causing embarrassment; inopportune.—**Inconveniently**, in-kon-vē'ni-ent-li, *adv.* In an inconvenient manner.—**Inconvenience, Inconveniency**, in-kon-vē'ni-ens, in-kon-vē'ni-en-si, *n.* The quality of being inconvenient; something that incommodes or gives trouble or uneasiness.—**Inconvenience**, in-kon-vē'ni-ens, *v.t.*—*inconvenienced, inconveniencing.* To put to inconvenience; to incommode.

Inconversant, in-kon'ver-sant, *a.* [Prefix *in*, not, and *conversant.*] Not conversant; not familiar; not versed.

Inconvertible, in-kon-vėr'ti-bl, *a.* [Prefix *in*, not, and *convertible.*] Not convertible; incapable of being converted into or exchanged for something else.—**Inconvertibility, Inconvertibleness**, in-kon-vėr'ti-bil"i-ti, in-kon-vėr'ti-bl-nes, *n.* The quality of being inconvertible.—**Inconvertibly**, in-kon-vėr'ti-bli, *adv.* So as not to be convertible.

Inconvincible, in-kon-vin'si-bl, *a.* [Prefix *in*, not, and *convincible.*] Incapable of being convinced.

Incorporate, in-kor'po-rāt, *v.t.*—*incorporated, incorporating.* [L. *incorporo, incorporatum*—*in*, into, and *corpus, corporis*, a body.] To form into one body; to combine or mix into one mass; to unite with another body or substance; to combine or unite intimately (to *incorporate* things together or one thing *with* another); to embody or give material form to; to form into a corporation or body of individuals that can act as one.—*v.i.* To unite so as to form a part of another body; to be mixed or blended; to grow into: usually followed by *with.*—*a.* Incorporated; united in one body.—**Incorporated**, in-kor'po-rā-ted, *p.* and *a.* Mixed or united in one body; associated so as to form a corporation; united in a legal body.—**Incorporation**, in-kor'po-rā"shon, *n.* The act of incorporating or state of being incorporated; that which is incorporated; a society or body formed by the union of individuals and authorized by law to act as a single person.—**Incorporative**, in-kor'po-rā-tiv, *a.* Tending to incorporate; incorporating; *philol.* tending to combine many elements into one long word.

Incorporeal, in-kor-pō'rē-al, *a.* [Prefix *in*, not, and *corporeal.*] Not corporeal; not consisting of matter; not having a material body; immaterial; intangible.—**Incorporealism**, in-kor-pō'rē-al-izm, *n.* The condition of being incorporeal.—**Incorporeally**, in-kor-pō'rē-al-li, *adv.* In an incorporeal manner; immaterially.—**Incorporeality, Incorporeity**, in-kor-pō'rē-al"i-ti, in-kor'pō-rē"i-ti, *n.* The quality of being incorporeal.

Incorrect, in-ko-rekt', *a.* [Prefix *in*, not, and *correct.*] Not correct; not exact; inexact; erroneous; faulty; not according to fact.—**Incorrectly**, in-ko-rekt'li, *adv.* In an incorrect manner.—**Incorrectness**, in-ko-rekt'nes, *n.*

Incorrigible, in-kor'i-ji-bl, *a.* [Prefix *in*, not, and *corrigible.*] Incapable of being corrected or amended; bad beyond correction or reform.—*n.* One who is bad beyond correction or reform.—**Incorrigibility, Incorrigibleness**, in-kor'i-ji-bil"i-ti, in-kor'i-ji-bl-nes, *n.* The condition or quality of being incorrigible.—**Incorrigibly**, in-kor'i-ji-bli, *adv.* In an incorrigible manner.

Incorrodible, in-ko-rō'di-bl, *a.* [Prefix *in*, not, and *corrodible.*] Incapable of being corroded.

Incorrupt, Incorrupted, in-ko-rupt', in-ko-rup'ted, *a.* [Prefix *in*, not, and *corrupt*; L. *incorruptus.*] Not corrupt or corrupted; not suffering from corruption or decay; not depraved; pure; untainted; above the influence of corruption or bribery.—**Incorruptibility, Incorruptibleness**, in-ko-rup'ti-bil"i-ti, in-ko-rup'ti-bl-nes, *n.* The condition of being incorruptible.—**Incorruptible**, in-ko-rup'ti-bl, *a.* Incapable of corruption, decay, or dissolution;

incapable of being corrupted or bribed; inflexibly upright.—**Incorruptibly**, in-ko-rup'ti-bli, *adv.* In an incorruptible manner.—**Incorruption**, in-ko-rup'shon, *n.* Absence of or exemption from corruption or decay.—**Incorruptly**, in-ko-rupt'li, *adv.* In an incorrupt manner; without corruption.—**Incorruptness**, in-ko-rupt'-nes, *n.* The condition or quality of being incorrupt; probity; integrity.

Incrassate, in-kras'āt, *v.t.*—*incrassated, incrassating.* [L. *incrasso, incrassatum*—*in*, intens., and *crassus*, thick, crass.] To make thick or thicker; to make less fluid; to inspissate; to thicken.—**Incrassation**, in-kras-ā'shon, *n.* The act of thickening; inspissation.—**Incrassative**, in-kras'a-tiv, *a.* Having the quality of thickening.—*n.* That which has the power to thicken.

Increase, in-krēs', *v.i.*—*increased, increasing.* [Prefix *in* or *en*, and O.Fr. *creser*, L. *crescere*, to grow, allied to *creare*, to create—similarly *decrease.*] To become greater; to grow; to augment; to advance; to multiply by the production of young; *astron.* to show a gradually enlarging luminous surface; to wax (the moon *increases*).—*v.t.* To make greater or larger; to augment in bulk, quantity, amount, or degree; to add to.—*n.* (in'krēs). Augmentation; a growing greater or larger; enlargement; extension; the amount by which anything is augmented; increment: interest of money; produce; issue or offspring (O.T.): *astron.* the period of waxing, as of the moon.—**Increasable**, in-krēs'a-bl, *a.* Capable of being increased.—**Increasableness**, in-krēs'a-bl-nes, *n.* The quality of being increasable.—**Increaser**, in-krēs'ėr, *n.* One who or that which increases.—**Increasingly**, in-krēs'ing-li, *adv.* In the way of increase; by continual increase.

Incredible, in-kred'i-bl, *a.* [Prefix *in*, not, and *credible.*] Not credible; impossible to be believed; too extraordinary and improbable to admit of belief.—**Incredibility**, in-kred'i-bil"i-ti, *n.* The quality of being incredible; that which is incredible.—**Incredibleness**, in-kred'i-bl-nes, *n.* The quality of being incredible.—**Incredibly**, in-kred'i-bli, *adv.* In an incredible manner.

Incredulous, in-kred'ū-lus, *a.* [Prefix *in*, not, and *credulous.*] Not credulous; not given to believe readily; refusing or withholding belief; sceptical.—**Incredulity**, **Incredulousness**, in-krē-dū'li-ti, in-kred'ū-lus-nes, *n.* The quality of being incredulous.—**Incredulously**, in-kred'ū-lus-li, *adv.* In an incredulous manner.

Incremate, in'krē-māt, *v.t.* To cremate.—**Incremation**, in-krē-mā'shon, *n.* The act of incremating; cremation.

Increment, in'krē-ment, *n.* [L. *incrementum*, from *incresco*, to increase. INCREASE.] Act or process of increasing; augmentation or growth; something added; increase; *math.* the increase of a quantity from its present value to its next ascending value; *rhet.* an amplification without necessarily involving a true climax.

Increscent, in-kres'ent, *a.* [L. *increscens, increscentis*, ppr. of *incresco*, to increase.] Increasing; growing; augmenting; swelling.

Incriminate, in-krim'i-nāt, *v.t.*—*incriminated, incriminating.* [L.L. *incrimino, incriminatum*—L. *in*, and *crimino*, to accuse one of a crime, from *crimen, criminis*, a charge.] To charge with a crime or fault; to accuse; to criminate.—**Incriminatory**, in-krim'i-nā-to-ri, *a.* Accusatory; tending to criminate.

Incrust, in-krust', *v.t.* [L. *incrusto*—*in*, in, on, and *crusta*, crust.] To cover with a crust or with a hard coat; to form a crust on the surface of.—**Incrustation**, in-krus-tā'shon, *n.* The act of incrusting; a crust or hard coating on the surface of a body; a covering or inlaying.

Incubate, in'kū-bāt, *v.t.* [L. *incubo, incubatum*, to lie in or upon—prefix *in*, in, on, and *cubo*, to lie, seen also in *incubus, incumbent, covey.*] To care for in such a way as to induce hatching (of eggs) or promote development (of embryos, &c.)—*v.i.* To be incubated: to brood.—**Incubation**, in-kū-bā'shon, *n.* Act of incubating; *pathol.* the period of maturation, without visible symptoms, of a contagious disease.—**Incubative**, in-kū-bā'tiv, *a.*—**Incubator**, in-kū-bā'tėr, *n.* An apparatus for hatching eggs by artificial heat; an apparatus for maintaining proper body temperature in babies born prematurely or otherwise physically subnormal; an apparatus for incubating bacteriological cultures, &c.

Incubus, in'kū-bus, *n.* pl. **Incubuses**, **Incubi**, in'kū-bus-ez, in'kū-bi. [L., from *incubo*, to lie on. INCUBATE.] Nightmare; an imaginary being or demon, formerly supposed to be the cause of nightmare; hence something that weighs heavily on the mind or feelings; an incumbrance of any kind; a dead weight.

Inculcate, in-kul'kāt, *v.t.*—*inculcated, inculcating.* [L. *inculco, inculcatum*—*in*, in, and *calco*, to tread; akin *calx*, the heel.] To impress by frequent admonitions; to teach and enforce by frequent repetitions; to urge on the mind.—**Inculcation**, in-kul-kā'shon, *n.* The act of inculcating.—**Inculcator**, in-kul'kā-tėr, *n.* One who inculcates.

Inculpable, in-kul'pa-bl, *a.* [Prefix *in*, not, and *culpable.*] Not culpable; not to be accused; blameless.—**Inculpableness**, in-kul'pa-bl-nes, *n.* Blamelessness.

Inculpate, in-kul'pāt, *v.t.*—*inculpated, inculpating.* [L.L. *inculpo, inculpatum*—L. *in*, into, and *culpa*, a fault; akin *culpable, culprit.*] To show to be in fault; to accuse of crime; to impute guilt to; to incriminate: opposed to *exculpate.*—**Inculpation**, in-kul-pā'shon, *n.* The act of inculpating.—**Inculpatory**, in-kul'pa-to-ri, *a.* Tending to inculpate or criminate.

Incult, in-kult', *a.* [L. *incultus*—prefix *in*, not, and *cultus*, pp. of *colo*, to cultivate.] Uncultivated; rude; not polished or refined.

Incumbent, in-kum'bent, *a.* [L. *incumbens, incumbentis*, ppr. of *incumbo*, to lie—*in*, on, and *cumbo*, to lie down. INCUBATE.] Lying or resting upon; resting upon a person as a duty or obligation to be performed; imposed and calling for performance.—*n.* A person in possession of an ecclesiastical benefice or other office.—**Incumbently**, in-kum'bent-li, *adv.* In an incumbent manner.—**Incumbency**, in-kum'ben-si, *n.* The state of being incumbent; what is incumbent; *eccles.* the state of holding or being in possession of a benefice.

Incumber, in-kum'bėr, *v.t.* Same as *Encumber.*

Incunabulum, in-kū-nab'ū-lum, *n.* pl. **Incunabula**, in-kū-nab'ū-la. [L. *incunabula*, swaddling-clothes, birthplace, origin—prefix *in*, and *cunabula*, from *cunæ*, a cradle.] A book printed in the early times of printing; generally, a book printed before the year 1500.

Incur, in-kėr', *v.t.*—*incurred, incurring.* L. *incurro*, to run against—*in*, and *curro*, to run. CURRENT.] To run in danger of or liability to; to expose one's self to; to become liable to; to become subject to (to *incur* danger, inconvenience, &c.); to contract (to *incur* a debt).—**Incurrence**, in-kėr'ens, *n.* The act of incurring.

Incurable, in-kū'ra-bl, *a.* [Prefix *in*, not, and *curable.*] Not curable; beyond the power of skill and medicine; not admitting remedy.—*n.* A person diseased beyond the reach of cure.—**Incurability**, **Incurableness**, in-kū'ra-bil"i-ti, in-kū'ra-bl-nes, *n.* The state of being incurable.—**Incurably**, in-kū'ra-bli, *adv.* In an incurable manner.

Incurious, in-kū'ri-us, *a.* [Prefix *in*, not, and *curious.*] Not curious or inquisitive; destitute of curiosity.—**Incuriously**, in-kū'ri-us-li, *adv.* In an incurious manner.—**Incuriosity**, **Incuriousness**, in-kū'ri-os"i-ti, in-kū'ri-us-nes, *n.* The quality of being incurious.

Incursion, in-kėr'shon, *n.* [L. *incursio, incursionis*, from *incurro.* [INCUR.] An entering into a territory with hostile intention; an invasion not followed by continued occupation; an inroad.—**Incursive**, in-kėr'siv, *a.* Making an attack or incursion; aggressive.

Incurvate, **Incurve**, in-kėr'vāt, in-kėrv', *v.t.*—*incurvated, incurvating; incurved, incurving.* [L. *incurvo, incurvation*—*in*, in, and *curvo*, to bend. CURVE.] To curve inwards; to make curved; to bend; to crook.—**Incurvate**, *a.* Curved inward or upward.—**Incurvation**, in-kėr-vā'shon, *n.* The act of incurvating; a bending or bend.—**Incurvity**, in-kėr'vi-ti, *n.* A state of being bent inwards.

Incus, ing'kus, *n.* [L., an anvil.] A bone of the internal ear, so called from its shape.

Incuse†, in-kūz', *v.t.* [L. *incudo, incusum*, to forge.] To impress by striking or stamping.

Indagate,† in'da-gāt, *v.t.* [L. *indago, indagatum.*] To search or seek out.

Indear, in-dēr', *v.t.* **Indearment**, in-dēr'ment, *n.* Same as *Endear, Endearment.*

Indebted, in-det'ed, *a.* [Prefix *in*, in, and *debt.*] Being under a debt; having incurred a debt; held to payment or requital; obliged by something received, for which restitution or gratitude is due.—**Indebtedness**, in-det'ed-nes, *n.* The state of being indebted; the amount of debt owed.

Indecent, in-dē'sent, *a.* [Prefix *in*, not, and *decent*; L. *indecens*, unseemly.] Offending against decency; unfit to be seen or heard; offensive to modesty and delicacy; immodest; unseemly.—**Indecently**, in-dē'sent-li, *adv.* In an indecent manner.—**Indecency**, in-dē'sen-si, *n.* The quality of being indecent; what is indecent in language, actions, or manners; grossness in speech or behaviour; immodesty.

Indeciduate, in-dē-sid'ū-āt, *a.* [Prefix *in*, not, and *deciduate.*] Not deciduate; not having a decidua.

Indeciduous, in-dē-sid'ū-us, *a.* [Prefix *in*, not, and *deciduous.*] Not deciduous; evergreen.

Indecipherable, in-dē-sī'fėr-a-bl, *a.* [Prefix *in*, not, and *decipherable.*] Not decipherable; incapable of being deciphered.

Indecision, in-dē-sizh'on, *n.* [Prefix *in*, not, and *decision.*] Want of decision or settled purpose; a wavering of mind; irresolution.—**Indecisive**, in-dē-sī'siv, *a.* [Prefix *in*, not, and *decisive.*] Not decisive; not bringing to a final close or ultimate issue; not having come to a decision; irresolute; vacillating; hesitating.—**Indecisively**, in-dē-sī'siv-li, *adv.* In an indecisive manner.—**Indecisiveness**, in-dē-sī'siv-nes, *n.*

Indeclinable, in-dē-klī'na-bl, *a.* [Prefix *in*, not, and *declinable.*] *Gram.* not declinable; not varied by terminations.—*n. Gram.* a word that is not declined.

Indecomposable, in-dē'kom-pō"za-bl, *a.* [Prefix *in*, not, and *decomposable.*] Not decomposable; incapable of decomposition.—**Indecomposableness**, in-dē'kom-pō"za-bl-nes, *n.*

Indecorous, in-dek'o-rus, *a.* [Prefix *in*, not, and *decorous.*] Not decorous; violating decorum or propriety; unseemly; unbecoming.—**Indecorously**, in-dek'ō-rus-li, *adv.* In an indecorous manner.—**Indecorousness**, in-dek'ō-rus-nes, *n.* The quality of being indecorous.—**Indecorum**, in-dē-kō'rum, *n.* Want of decorum; impropriety of behavior.

Indeed, in-dēd', *adv.* [Prep. *in*, and *deed.*] In reality; in truth; in fact: sometimes used as intimating a concession or admission; sometimes interjectionally, as an expression of surprise, or for the purpose of obtaining confirmation.

Indefatigable, in-dē-fat'i-ga-bl, *a.* [L. *indefatigabilis*, from *in*, not, and *defatigo*, to tire completely—*de*, intens., and *fatigo*, to fatigue.] Incapable of being fatigued; not yielding to fatigue; unremitting in labour or effort; unwearied; untiring.—**Indefatigably**, in-dē-fat'i-ga-bli, *adv.* In an indefatigable manner; unremittingly; sedulously.—**Indefatigability**, **Indefatigableness**, in-dē-fat'i-ga-bil"i-ti, in-dē-fat'i-ga-bl-nes, *n.* The quality of being indefatigable.

Indefeasible, in-dē-fē'zi-bl, *a.* [Prefix *in*, not, and *defeasible.*] Not defeasible; not to be defeated or made void (right, claim, or title).—**Indefeasibly**, in-dē-fē'zi-bli, *adv.* In an indefeasible manner.—**Indefeasibility**, in-dē-fē'zi-bil"i-ti, *n.* The quality of being indefeasible.

Indefensible, in-dē-fen'si-bl, *a.* [Prefix *in*, not, and *defensible.*] Not defensible; incapable of being defended, vindicated, or justified.—**Indefensibility**, in-dē-fen'-si-bil"i-ti, *n.* The quality or state of being indefensible.—**Indefensibly**, in-dē-fen'-si-bli, *adv.* In an indefensible manner.

Indefinable, in-dē-fī'na-bl, *a.* [Prefix *in*, not, and *definable.*] Incapable of being defined; unsusceptible of definition; not to be clearly explained by words.—**Indefinably**, in-dē-fī'na-bli, *adv.* In an indefinable manner.

Indefinite, in-def'i-nit, *a.* [Prefix *in*, not, and *definite.*] Not definite; not limited or defined; not precise or certain; having no determinate or certain limits; *bot.* too numerous or various to make a particular enumeration important: said of the parts of a flower.—*Indefinite inflorescence, bot.* one in which the flowers all arise from axillary buds, the stem growing indefinitely.—**Indefinite article**, *Gram.*, *a* or *an.*—**Indefinitely**, in-def'i-nit-li, *adv.*—**Indefiniteness**, in-def'i-nit-nes, *n.*

Indehiscent, in-dē-his'ent, *a.* [Prefix *in*, not, and *dehiscent.*] *Bot.* not dehiscent; not opening spontaneously when ripe, as a capsule.—**Indehiscence**, in-dē-his'ens, *n. Bot.* the property of being indehiscent.

Indelible, in-del'i-bl, *a.* [L. *indelebilis*—*in*, not, and *deleo*, to delete.] Not to be blotted out; incapable of being effaced, cancelled, or obliterated.—**Indelibility**, **Indelibleness**, in-del'i-bil"i-ti, in-del'i-bl-nes. *n.* Quality of being indelible.—**Indelibly**, in-del'i-bli, *adv.* In an indelible manner; ineffaceably.

Indelicate, in-del'i-kāt, *a.* [Prefix *in*, not, and *delicate.*] Wanting delicacy; offensive to modesty or purity of mind; tending towards indecency or grossness; somewhat immodest.—**Indelicately**, in-del'i-kāt-li, *adv.* In an indelicate manner.—**Indelicacy**, in-del'i-ka-si, *n.* The condition or quality of being indelicate; a certain want of modesty or purity of mind.

Indemnify, in-dem'ni-fī, *v.t.*—*indemnified, indemnifying.* [L. *indemnis*, free from loss or injury, and *facio*, to make. INDEMNITY.] To save harmless; to secure against loss, damage, or penalty; to reimburse for expenditure made.—**Indemnification**, indem'ni-fi-kā"shon, *n.* The act of indemnifying; that which indemnifies.

Indemnity, in-dem'ni-ti, *n.* [Fr. *indemnité*, from L. *indemnitas*, from *indemnis*, uninjured—prefix *in*, not, and *damnum*, loss, damage. DAMN.] Security or exemption from damage, loss, injury, or punishment; compensation or equivalent for loss, damage, or injury sustained.

Indent, in-dent', *v.t.* [L.L. *indenture*, O.Fr. *endenter*, from L. *in*, in, and *dens, dentis*, a tooth. DENTAL.] To notch, jag, or cut into points or inequalities, like a row of teeth; to indenture; *printing*, to begin (a line) farther in from the margin than the rest of the paragraph.—*n.* A notch in a margin; an indentation; *printing*, the blank space at the beginning of a paragraph; *com.*, an order for goods.—**Indentation**, in-den-tā'shon, *n.* The act of indenting; a cut or notch in a margin; an angular recess or depression like a notch in any border.—**Indented**, in-den'ted, *p.* and *a.* Having notches or points like teeth on the margin; toothed; bound by indenture.—**Indentedly**, in-den'ted-li, *adv.* With indentations.—**Indenture**, in-den'tūr, *n.* The act of indenting; an indentation; *law*, a deed under seal, entered into between two or more parties, each party having a duplicate: so called from the duplicates having originally been written on one skin, which was divided by a jagged cut, so that the correspondence of the two halves was at once manifest.—*v.t.*—*indentured, indenturing.* To indent; to bind by indentures, as in apprenticeship.

Independent, in-dē-pen'dent, *a.* [Prefix *in*, not, and *dependent.*] Not dependent; not subject to the control of others; not relying on others; with *of* before an object; not subordinate; moderately wealthy, as an *independent* fortune; acting and thinking for one's self; not swayed by bias or influence; self-directing; proceeding from or expressive of a spirit of independence in air or manner; in England, pertaining to the Independents or Congregationalists.—*adv.* Irrespective; without taking note or regard; not to make mention: with *of.*—*n.* In politics, one not bound by party; *eccles.* one who maintains that every congregation forms a church or independent religious society in itself.—*Independent clause, gram.*, a clause not dependent on other words of a sentence.—**Independence, Independency**,† in-dē-pen'dens, in-dē-pen'den-si, *n.* The state of being independent; that which renders one independent; property or income sufficient to make one independent of others or of his own exertions.—**Independence Day**, the 4th of July, an annual holiday, in the United States, commemorative of the adoption of the Declaration of Independence in 1776.—**Independently**, in-dē-pen'dent-li, *adv.* In an independent manner; leaving out of consideration (he is richer *independently of* that).

Indescribable, in-dē-skrī'ba-bl, *a.* [Prefix *in*, not, and *describable.*] Not describable; incapable of being described.

Indestructible, in-dē-struk'ti-bl, *a.* Prefix *in*, not, and *destructible.*] Not destructible; incapable of being destroyed.—**Indestructibility, Indestructibleness**, in-dē-struk'ti-bil"i-ti, in-dē-struk'ti-bl-nes, *n.* The quality of being indestructible.—**Indestructibly**, in-dē-struk'ti-bli, *adv.* In an indestructible manner.

Indeterminate, in-dē-tėr'mi-nāt, *a.* [Prefix *in*, not, and *determinate.*] Not determinate; not settled or fixed; not definite; uncertain; not precise; *math.* applied to problems which have an indefinite number of solutions, not arbitrary but correlated; of a sentence, one making the imprisonment or release of the prisoner dependent on his conduct and amendment. —*Indeterminate inflorescence.* Same as *indefinite inflorescence.*—**Indeterminable**, in-dē-tėr'mi-na-bl, *a.* [Prefix *in*, not, and *determinable.*] Incapable of being determined, ascertained, or fixed; not to be determined or ended; interminable.—**Indeterminably**, in-dē-tėr'mi-na-bli, *adv.* In an indeterminable manner.—**Indeterminately**, in-dē-tėr'mi-nāt-li, *adv.* In an indeterminate manner. —**Indeterminateness**, in-dē-tėr'mi-nāt-nes, *n.* The state or quality of being indeterminate.—**Indetermination**, in-dē-tėr'mi-nā"-shon, *n.* Want of determination; an unsettled or wavering state, as of the mind.—**Indetermined**, in-dē-tėr'mind, *a.* Undetermined; unsettled. —**Indeterminism**, *n.* The philosophic theory maintaining that not all our actions are determined or conditioned by motives; the opposite of rigid determinism.

Indevout, in-dē-vout', *a.* [Prefix *in*, not, and *devout.*] Not devout; not having devout affections. —**Indevoutly**, in-dē-vout'li, *adv.* Without devotion.

Index, in'deks, *n.* pl. **Indexes**, in'dek-sez, or **Indices**, in'di-sez. [L., one who or that which points out, a table of contents—*in*, in, and stem of *dico*, to say (DICTION); seen in Skr. *diç*, Gr. *deiknymi*, to show.] Something that points out, shows, indicates, or manifests; a pointer or hand that points or directs to anything; the hand ☞ used by printers, &c., to call attention; a table of the contents of a book in alphabetical order; *anat.* the forefinger; *math.* the figure or letter which shows to what power any quantity is evolved; the exponent.—*Index of refraction, optics*, the ratio of the sine of the angle of incidence to the sine of the angle of refraction when a ray passes from one medium into another (*relative index*), or from a vacuum into a medium (*absolute index*).—*Index Expurgatorius* (Index Expurgatory), *Index Prohibitorius* (Index Prohibitory), or more fully *Index Librorum Prohibitorum* (Index of Prohibited Books), a catalogue of books which are forbidden by the Roman Catholic Church to be read by the faithful.—*v.t.* To provide with an index; to place in an index.—**Indexer**, in'dek-sėr, *n.* One who makes an index.—**Index-finger**, *n.* The forefinger.—**Indexical**, in-dek'si-kal, *a.* Having the form of an index; pertaining to an index.—**Indexically**, in-dek'si-kal-li, *adv.* In the manner of an index.

Indexterity, in-deks-ter'i-ti, *n.* [Prefix *in*, not, and *dexterity.*] Want of dexterity.

India, in'di-a, *n.* [From *Indus*, the name of a river in Asia; akin Skr. *sindhu*, a river, *syand*, to flow.] A country in Asia, forming part of the British Empire; a color darker than cream and lighter than tan. —*India ink*, a black writing fluid used chiefly by draftsmen.—*Indiaman*, a large ship formerly employed in the India trade. —*India paper*, a thin opaque paper used in printing.—*India rubber*, caoutchouc; a soft variety of rubber.—**Indian**, *a.* Of or pertaining to either of the Indies, East or West, or to the aborigines of America, so called by Columbus who mistook his discovery of America for the finding of a new route to India; made of maize or Indian corn.—*Department of Indian Affairs*, a division of the Department of the Interior with jurisdiction over affairs between the Indians and the Federal government.—*Indian club*, a wooden club used in calisthenics.—*Indian corn*, a native American plant, otherwise called *Maize*, and its ripened ears.—*Indian file*, single file.—*Indian red*, a species of ochre; a very fine purple earth used in both oil and water-color painting.—*Indian summer*, summer-like weather, with calm and absence of rain, occurring in autumn.—*Indian turnip*, Jack-in-the-pulpit.—*Indian yellow*, a bright yellow pigment.—*n.* An East Indian, West Indian or Anglo-Indian; one of the aborigines of America; a Red Indian.—**Indic**, in'dik, *a.* Applied to that branch of the Indo-European languages of India which includes Hindustani, Prakrit, Pali, and Sanskrit.

Indican, in'di-kan, *n.* [From *indigo.*] A substance which is present in the indigo plant, and is the source of indigo blue.

Indicate, in'di-kāt, *v.t.*—*indicated, indicating.* [L. *indico, indicatum*, from *index, indicis.* INDEX.] To point out; to direct the mind to a knowledge of; to show; to intimate.—**Indicant**, in'di-kant, *a.* [L. *indicans, indicantis.*] Serving to point out; indicating. —**Indication**, in-di-kā'shon, *n.* The act of indicating or pointing out; what serves to indicate or point out; intimation; mark; token; sign; symptom.—**Indicative**, in-dik'a-tiv, *a.* [L. *indicativus.*] Pointing out or indicating; serving as an indication; giving intimation or knowledge of (movements *indicative of* uneasiness); *gram.* applied to that mood of the verb that declares directly or that asks questions.—*n. Gram.* the indicative mood. —**Indicatively**, in-dik'a-tiv-li, *adv.* In an indicative manner.—**Indicator**, in'di-kā-tėr, *n.* One who or that which indicates, an instrument for ascertaining and recording the pressure of steam in the cylinder of a steam-engine; a recording instrument of various kinds; a South African cuckoo that by its movements indicates the presence of the nests of wild bees.—*Indicator diagram*, the diagram traced by the indicator in a steam-engine. It represents the pressures at all stages of the piston stroke, and its area gives the work done by the piston during the stroke.—**Indicatory**, in'di-ka-to-ri, *a.* Serving to indicate.

Indict, in-dīt', *v.t.* [O.Fr. *inditer, indicter*, from L. *indico, indictum*, to declare publicly—*in*, and *dico*, to say, to speak. INDEX.] To accuse or charge with a crime or misdemeanour in due form of law.—**Indictable**, in-dī'ta-bl, *a*. Capable of being or liable to be indicted; that may bring an indictment on one (an *indictable* offence).—**Indictment**, in-dīt'ment, *n*. The act of indicting; a formal accusation or charge against a person; a written accusation.—**Indicter, Indictor**, in-dī'tėr, *n*. One who indicts.—**Indiction**, in-dik'shon, *n*. *Chron.* a cycle of fifteen years.

Indies, West Indies, Caribbean islands; East Indies, south Asia and Malay islands.

Indifferent, in-dif'ėr-ent, *a*. [L. *indifferens, indifferentis*—*in*, not, and *differens*, ppr. of *differo*, to differ. DIFFER.] Impartial; unbiased; uninterested; unconcerned; careless; having no preference; of no account or moment; neither very good nor very bad, but rather bad than good; middling; tolerable.—Formerly used adverbially (*indifferent* honest).—**Indifference**, in-dif'ėr-ens, *n*. The state or quality of being indifferent; absence of feeling or interest; unconcern; apathy; mediocrity or some degree of badness.—**Indifferentism**, in-dif'er-ent-izm, *n*. Systematic indifference; reasoned disregard; want of zeal.—**Indifferently**, in-dif'ėr-ent-li, *adv*. In an indifferent manner; impartially; no more than passably.

Indigene, in'di-jēn, *n*. [L. *indigena*—*indu*, old form of *in*, and *gen*, root of *gigno*, to beget. GENUS.] One born in a country; a native animal or plant.—**Indigenous**, in-dij'en-us, *a*. Originating or produced naturally in a country or climate; native; not foreign or exotic.

Indigent, in'di-jent, *a*. [L. *indigens, indigentis*, from *indigeo*, to want—*ind*, a form of *in*, and *egeo*, to be in want.] Destitute of the means of comfortable subsistence; needy; poor.—**Indigently**, in'di-jent-li, *adv*. In an indigent, destitute manner.—**Indigence, Indigency**, in'di-jens, in'-di-jen-si, *n*. The condition of being indigent; penury; poverty.

Indigested, in-di-jes'ted, *a*. [Prefix *in*, not, and *digested*.] Not digested; undigested; not reduced to due form; not methodized; crude; not prepared or softened by heat, as chemical substances.—**Indigestibility, Indigestibleness**, in-di-jes'ti-bil"i-ti, in-di-jes'ti-bl-nes, *n*. The quality of being indigestible.—**Indigestible**, in-di-jes'ti-bl, *a*. [Prefix *in*, not, and *digestible*.] Not digestible; digested with difficulty.—**Indigestibly**, in-di-jes'ti-bli, *adv*. So as not to be digestible.—**Indigestion**, in-di-jest'yon, *n*. [Prefix *in*, not, and *digestion*.] Incapability of or difficulty in digesting food; dyspepsia.

Indignant, in-dig'nant, *a*. [L. *indignans, indignantis*, ppr. of *indignor*, to consider as unworthy, to disdain—*in*, not, and *dignor*, to deem worthy, from *dignus*, worthy (whence *dignity, deign*).] Displeased at what is unworthy or base; affected with indignation.—**Indignantly**, in-dig'nant-li, *adv*. In an indignant manner.—**Indignation**, in-dig-nā'shon, *n*. [L. *indignatio, indignationis*.] A feeling of displeasure at what is unworthy or base; anger, mingled with contempt, disgust, or abhorrence; violent displeasure.—**Indignity**, in-dig'ni-ti, *n*. [L. *indignitas*.] Any action toward another which manifests contempt for him or design to lower his dignity; an insult; an affront; an outrage.

Indigo, in'di-gō, *n*. [Sp. and It. *indigo*, from L *indicum*, indigo, from *Indicus*, Indian, from *India*.] A deep, slightly reddish blue, one of the seven chief colors of the spectrum, as named by Newton; a blue dye, extensively employed, now usually synthesized from amino compounds, but originally obtained from various plants native to the East and West Indies.—**Indigo blue**, the color indigo; the substance indigotin.—**Indigo bunting**, a small bird of the eastern United States.—**Indigo bush**, a shrub with handsome blue flowers, found in the southwestern U. S.—**Indigoid**, in'di-goid, *a*. Referring to a class of dyes, similar in structure to indigo.—**Indigo plant**, a plant yielding indigo.—**Indigotin**, in-dig'o-tin, *n*. A powder, the coloring principle of indigo.

Indirect, in-di-rekt', *a*. [Prefix, *in*, not, and *direct*.] Not direct; deviating from a direct line or course; circuitous; not tending directly to an aim or end; round-about; not open and straightforward; not resulting directly; having something mediate or interposed.—**Indirection**, *n*. Roundabout methods; deceit. (*Shak.*)—**Indirectly**, in-di-rekt'li, *adv*. In an indirect manner.—**Indirectness**, in-di-rekt'nes, *n*.

Indiscernible, in-diz-zėr'ni-bl, *a*. [Prefix *in*, not, and *discernible*.] Incapable of being discerned; undiscernible.—**Indiscernibleness**, in-diz-zėr'ni-bl-nes, *n*.—**Indiscernibly**, in-diz-zer'ni-bli, *adv*. So as not to be perceived.

Indisciplinable, in-dis'si-plin-a-bl, *a*. [Prefix *in*, not, and *disciplinable*.] Incapable of being disciplined or subjected to discipline.

Indiscoverable, in-dis-kuv'ėr-a-bl, *a*. [Prefix *in*, not, and *discoverable*.] Incapable of being discovered; undiscoverable.

Indiscreet, in-dis-krēt', *a*. [Prefix *in*, not, and *discreet*.] Not discreet; wanting in discretion or sound judgment; injudicious; inconsiderate.—**Indiscreetly**, in-dis-krēt'li, *adv*. In an indiscreet manner.—**Indiscreetness**, in-dis-krēt'nes, *n*. The quality of being indiscreet.—**Indiscretion**, *n*. The condition or quality of being indiscreet; want of discretion; an indiscreet act; an ill-judged act.

Indiscriminate, in-dis-krim'i-nāt, *a*. [Prefix *in*, not, and *discriminate*.] Without discrimination or distinction; not making any distinction; confused; promiscuous.—**Indiscriminately**, in-dis-krim'i-nāt-li, *adv*. In an indiscriminate manner.—**Indiscriminating**, in-dis-krim'i-nat-ing, *p.* and *a*. Not discriminating; not making any distinction.—**Indiscrimination**, in-dis-krim'i-nā"shon, *n*. Want of discrimination.—**Indiscriminative**, in-dis-krim'i-nā-tiv, *a*. Not discriminative; making no distinction.

Indispensable, in-dis-pen'sa-bl, *a*. [Prefix *in*, not, and *dispensable*.] Incapable of being dispensed with; absolutely necessary or requisite.—**Indispensability, Indispensableness**, in-dis-pen'sa-bil"i-ti, in-dis-pen'sa-bl-nes, *n*. The quality of being indispensable.—**Indispensably**, in-dis-pen'sa-bli, *adv*. In an indispensable manner; absolutely.

Indispose, in-dis-pōz', *v.t.*—*indisposed, indisposing*. [Fr. *indisposer*—prefix *in*, not, and *disposer*, to dispose. DISPOSE.] To disincline; to render averse or unfavourable; to render unfit or unsuited; to disqualify; to affect with indisposition.—**Indisposed**, in-dis-pōzd', *p.* and *a*. Not disposed; disinclined; averse; slightly disordered in health; somewhat ill.—**Indisposedness**, in-dis-pō'zed-nes, *n*.—**Indisposition**, in-dis'pō-zish"on, *n*. The state of being indisposed; disinclination; want of tendency; slight ailment or disorder of the health.

Indisputable, in-dis'pū-ta-bl, *a*. [Prefix *in*, not, and *disputable*.] Incapable of being disputed; incontrovertible; incontestable.—**Indisputability, Indisputableness**, in-dis'pū-ta-bil"i-ti, in-dis'pū-ta-bl-nes, *n*. The state or quality of being indisputable.—**Indisputably**, in-dis'pū-ta-bli, *adv*. In an indisputable manner; incontrovertibly.—**Indisputed**, in-dis-pū'ted, *a*. Not disputed or controverted; undisputed.

Indissociable, in-dis-sō'shi-a-bl, *a*. [Prefix *in*, not, and *dissociable*.] Incapable of being dissociated; inseparable.

Indissoluble, in-dis'so-lū-bl, *a*. [Prefix *in*, not, and *dissoluble*; L. *indissolubilis*.] Not capable of being dissolved; not capable of being broken or rightfully violated; perpetually binding or obligatory (agreement, ties, &c.); firm; stable.—**Indissolubility, Indissolubleness**, in-dis'so-lū-bil"i-ti, in-dis'so-lū-bl-nes, *n*. The quality of being indissoluble.—**Indissolubly**, in-di'so-lū-bli, *adv*. In an indissoluble manner.

Indissolvable, in-diz-zol'va-bl, *a*. [Prefix *in*, not, and *dissolvable*.] Not capable of being dissolved or melted; indissoluble.—**Indissolvableness**, in-diz-zol'va-bl-nes, *n*.

Indistinct, in-dis-tingkt', *a*. [Prefix *in*, not, and *distinct*; L. *indistinctus*.] Not distinct; not readily distinguishable; faint to the sight; obscure to the mind; not clear; confused; imperfect or dim (*indistinct* vision).—**Indistinctly**, in-dis-tingkt'li, *adv*. In an indistinct manner; not clearly; dimly or obscurely.—**Indistinctness**, in-dis-tingkt'nes, *n*. The quality or condition of being indistinct.

Indistinguishable, in-dis-ting'gwish-a-bl, *a*. [Prefix *in*, not, and *distinguishable*.] Incapable of being distinguished; undistinguishable.—**Indistinguishably**, in-dis-ting'gwish-a-bli, *adv*. So as not to be distinguishable.

Indite, in-dīt', *v.t.*—*indited, inditing*. [O. Fr. *inditer*. INDICT.] To compose or write; to direct, prompt, or dictate.—*v.i.* To compose; to write; to pen.—**Inditement**, in-dīt'ment, *n*. The act of inditing.—**Inditer**, in-dī'tėr, *n*. One who indites.

Indium, in'di-um, *n*. [From the *indigo* lines in its spectrum.] A soft lead-coloured metallic element, discovered by two indigo lines which it shows under spectrum analysis.

Individual, in-di-vid'ū-al, *a*. [Fr. *individuel*, from L. *individuus*, indivisible—*in*, not, and *dividuus*, divisible. DIVIDE.] Subsisting as one indivisible entity or distinct being; single; one; pertaining to one only; peculiar to or characteristic of a single person or thing.—*n*. A being or thing forming one of its kind; a single person, animal, or thing; especially, a human being; a person.—**Individualism**, in-di-vid'ū-al-izm, *n*. The quality of being individual; individuality; self-interest; a system or condition in which each individual works for his own ends, in either social, political, or religious matters.—**Individualistic**, in-di-vid'ū-al-is"tik, *a*. Pertaining to or characterized by individualism.—**Individuality**, in-di-vid'ū-al"i-ti, *n*. The condition of being individual; existence as an individual; oneness; the sum of the characteristics or traits peculiar to an individual.—**Individualization**, in-di-vid'-ū-al-ī-zā"shon, *n*. The act of individualizing.—**Individualize**, in-di-vid'ū-al-iz, *v.t.*—*individualized, individualizing*. To mark as an individual; to distinguish by peculiar or distinctive characters.—**Individualizer**, in-di-vid'ū-al-ī-zėr, *n*. One who individualizes.—**Individually**, in-di-vid'ū-al-li, *adv*. In an individual manner; separately; each by itself.—**Individuate**, in-di-vid'ū-āt, *v.t*—*individuated, individuating*. To give the character of individuality to; to individualize.—*v.i.* To become individual.—**Individuation**, in-di-vid-ū-ā"-shon, *a*. The act of individuating, or state of being.

Indivisible, in-di-viz'i-bl, *a*. [Prefix *in*, not, and *divisible*.] Not divisible; not separable into parts.—*n*. That which is indivisible.—**Indivisibility, Indivisibleness**, in-di-viz'i-bil"i-ti, in-di-viz'i-bl-nes, *n*. The state or property of being indivisible.—**Indivisibly**, in-di-viz'i-bli, *adv*. In an indivisible manner.

Indocile, in-dos'il or in-dō'sil, *a*. [Prefix *in*, not, and *docile*; L. *indocilis*, unteachable.] Not docile or teachable; intractable.—**Indocility**, in-dō-sil'i-ti, *n*. The quality of being indocile.

Indoctrinate, in-dok'tri-nāt, *v.t.*—*indoctrinated, indoctrinating*. L. *in*, in, and *doctrina*, learning. DOCTRINE.] To instruct in any doctrine; to imbue or cause to imbibe certain principles; to instruct.—**Indoctrination**, in-dok'tri-nā"shon, *n*. The act of indoctrinating; instruction.

Indo-European, *a*. A term applied to that family of languages which includes the Sanskrit and the kindred tongues of India and Persia, Greek, Latin, and the Romance tongues, the Teutonic, Celtic, and Slavonic tongues.—*n*. An Aryan.

Indo-Germanic, *a.* A term sometimes used as equivalent to *Indo-European* or *Aryan.*

Indolent, in'dō-lent, *a.* [Fr. *indolent*—L. *in*, not, and *dolens, dolentis*, ppr. of *doleo*, to feel pain (whence *dolour, dole*).] Habitually idle or indisposed to labour; lazy; slothful; sluggish; idle (person, life); *med.* causing little or no pain (an *indolent* tumour). —**Indolently**, in'dō-lent-li, *adv.* In an indolent manner.—**Indolence**, in-dō'lens, *n.* The condition or quality of being indolent; laziness; sloth.

Indomitable, in-dom'i-ta-bl, *a.* [L. prefix *in*, not, and *domito*, freq. of *domo, domitum*, to tame. DAUNT, DAME.] Not to be tamed or subdued; unconquerable; untamable.—**Indomitableness**, in-dom'i-ta-bl-nes, *n.* The character of being indomitable.—**Indomitably**, in-dom'i-ta-bli, *adv.* In an indomitable manner.

Indoor, in'dōr, *a.* Being within doors; domestic (an *indoor* servant).—**Indoors**, in'dōrz, *adv.* Within doors; inside a house.

Indorse, in-dors', *v.t.* Same as *Endorse.*

Indow, in-dou', *v.t.*† Same as *Endow.*

Indri, in'dri, *n.* [Native name, signifying 'man of the woods'.] A tailless quadrumanous animal of the lemur family, a native of Madagascar, about the size of a cat.

Indubitable, in-dū'bi-ta-bl, *a.* [Prefix *in*, not, and *dubitable*; L. *indubitabilis.*] Not dubitable; too plain to admit of doubt; incontestable; unquestionable.—**Indubitableness**, in-dū'bi-ta-bl-nes, *n.* State of being indubitable.—**Indubitably**, in-dū'bi-ta-bli, *adv.* In an indubitable manner; undoubtedly; unquestionably.

Induce, in-dūs', *v.t.*—*induced, inducing.* [L. *induco, inductum*—*in*, in, and *duco*, to lead. DUKE.] To lead by persuasion or argument; to prevail on; to draw by motives; to impel; to bring on, produce, cause (an ailment *induced* by over-study).—*Induced current*, an electric current excited by the presence of a primary current.—*Induced magnetism*, magnetism produced in soft iron when a magnet is held near, or a wire through which an electric current is passing is coiled round it.—**Inducement**, in-dūs'ment, *n.* The act of inducing; that which induces or leads one to act; a motive; a consideration that leads to action.—**Inducer**, in-dū'sėr, *n.* One who or that which induces.—**Inducible**, in-dū'si-bl, *a.* Capable of being induced; capable of being inferred by induction.—**Induct**, in-dukt', *v.t.* [L. *induco, inductum.*] To bring in or introduce; to introduce, as to a benefice or office; to put in possession of an ecclesiastical living or any other office.—**Induction**, in-duk'shon, *n.* The act of inducting; introduction; the introduction of a clergyman into a benefice, or of a person into an office, with the customary forms and ceremonies; *logic.* the method of reasoning from particulars to generals; the deriving of a general principle or conclusion from particular facts, as that heat expands bodies, from observing its effect in particular cases; the conclusion or inference thus drawn or arrived at; *physics*, the property by which one body, having electrical, galvanic, or magnetic polarity, causes or induces it in another body without direct contact.—*Induction coil*, an apparatus for producing electric currents by induction and for utilizing them.—**Inductional**, in-duk'shon-al, *a.* Pertaining to or proceeding by induction; inductive.—**Inductive**, in-duk'tiv, *a.* Proceeding by induction; employed in drawing conclusions by induction; *elect.* able to produce electricity by induction; operating by induction; facilitating induction.—*Inductive sciences*, those sciences which are based upon induction, as astronomy, zoology, &c.—**Inductively**, in-duk'tiv-li, *adv.* In an inductive manner.—**Inductor**, in-duk'tėr, *n.* One who inducts.

Inductile, in-duk'til, *a.* [Prefix *in*, not and *ductile.*] Not ductile.—**Inductility**, in-duk-til'i-ti, *n.* The quality of being inductile.

Indue, in-dū', *v.t.*—*indued, induing.* [L. *induo*, from *indu*, old form of *in*, in, and verbal stem seen also in *exuo*, to put off (whence *exuviæ*).] To put on, as clothes; to clothe or invest; hence, to furnish; to supply; to endow.—**Induement**, in-dū'ment, *n.* The act of induing.

Indulge, in-dulj', *v.t.*—*indulged, indulging.* [L. *indulgeo*, to indulge or give one's self up to; origin doubtful.] To give one's self up to; not to restrain or oppose; to give free course to (to *indulge* the passions); to gratify by compliance; to humour to excess (to *indulge* children).—*v.i.* To indulge one's self; to practise indulgence; to be self-indulgent (to *indulge* in pleasure).—**Indulgence**, in-dul'jens, *n.* [L. *indulgentia.*] The act or practice of indulging; an indulgent act; favour granted; intemperance in eating and drinking; readiness to forgive faults; tolerance; *R. Cath. Ch.* remission, by church authority, to a repentant sinner, of the penance attached to certain sins.—*The Declaration of Indulgence*, illegal declarations or proclamations by Charles II in 1672, and by James II in 1687, dispensing with penal laws against Roman Catholics and Dissenters.—**Indulgent**, in-dul'jent, *a.* [L. *indulgens, indulgentis*, ppr. of *indulgeo.*] Prone to indulge or humour; over-compliant; not strict.—**Indulgently**, in-dul'jent-li, *adv.* In an indulgent manner.—**Indulger**, in-dul'jėr, *n.* One who indulges.

Induplicate, in-dū'pli-kāt, *a.* [L. *in*, in, and *duplicatus*, doubled.] *Bot.* having the edges bent or rolled inward, as petals or leaves in the bud.

Indurate, in'dū-rāt, *v.i.* [L. *induro, induratum*—prefix *in*, intens., and *duro*, to harden, from *durus*, hard, whence also *durable, durance*, &c.] To grow hard; to harden or become hard.—*v.t.*—*indurated, indurating.* To make hard; to harden; to make unfeeling; to render obdurate.—**Induration**, in-dū-rā'shon, *n.* The act of hardening or process of growing hard; the state of being indurated.

Indusium, in-dū'si-um, *n.* pl. **Indusia**, in-dū'si-a. [L., a woman's under-garment, from *induo*, to put on. INDUE.] *Bot.* United hairs forming a sort of cup inclosing the stigma of a flower; the covering of the capsules or spore-cases in ferns; *zool.* the case or covering of a larva; *anat.* the amnion.—**Indusial**, in-dū'si-al, *a.* Pertaining to an indusium; composed of or containing indusia or the cases of larvæ (*indusial* limestone).

Industrious, in-dus'tri-us, *a.* [L. *industrius*, from *indu*, old form of *in*, and *struo*, to fabricate. STRUCTURE.] Given to or characterized by industry; diligent in business or study; always working at something.—**Industriously**, in-dus'tri-us-li, *adv.* In an industrious manner.—**Industrial**, in-dus'tri-al, *a.* Pertaining to, involving, or characterized by industry (arts, establishment, capacity).—*Industrial exhibition, industrial museum*, an exhibition, museum of industrial products.—*Industrial school*, a school for training youth in the industrial arts and in habits of industry.—**Industrialism**, in-dus'tri-al-izm, *n.* Devotion to or employment in industrial pursuits.—**Industrialist**, in-dus'tri-al-ist, *n.* One engaged in industry, usually as promoter or director.—**Industrialize**, in-dus'tri-al-ize, *v.t.* To make industrial.—**Industrially**, in-dus'tri-al-li, *adv.* In an industrial manner.—**Industry**, in'dus-tri, *n.* [L. *industria*, from *industrius.*] Diligence in employment; steady attention to work or business; assiduity; the industrial arts generally, or any one of them; any productive occupation, especially one in which numbers of people are employed.

Induviæ, in-dū'vi-ē, *n. pl.* [L., clothes, from *induo*, to put on. INDUE.] *Bot.* the withered leaves which remain on the stems of some plants, not being joined to them by articulations, which allow of their falling off.—**Induviate**, in-dū'vi-āt, *a. Bot.* covered with induviæ.

Indwell, in'dwel, *v.t.* To abide within; to occupy.—*v.i.* To dwell or exist in or within some place.—**Indweller**, in'dwel-ėr, *n.* One who dwells in a place; an inhabitant.

Inebriate, in-ē'bri-āt, *v.t.*—*inebriated, inebriating.* [L. *inebrio, inebriatum*—*in*, intens., and *ebrio*, to intoxicate, from *ebrius*, drunk, whence also *ebriety*: akin *sober.*] To make drunk; to intoxicate; to disorder the senses of; to turn the head of.—*n.* An habitual drunkard.—**Inebriation**, in'ē-bri-ā"shon, *n.* The act of inebriating or state of being inebriated.—**Inebriety**, in-ē-brī'e-ti, *n.* Drunkenness; intoxication.—**Inebriant**, in-ē'bri-ant, *a.* [L. *inebrians, inebriantis*, ppr. of *inebrio.*] Intoxicating.—*n.* Anything that intoxicates.

Inedible, in-ed'i-bl, *a.* Not edible.

Inedited, in-ed'it-ed, *a.* [Prefix *in*, not, and *edited.*] Not edited; unpublished.

Ineffable, in-ef'a-bl, *a.* [L. *ineffabilis*—prefix *in*, not, and *effabilis*, speakable, from *effor*, to speak—*ef* for *ex*, out, and *for, fari*, to speak. FATE.] Incapable of being expressed in words.—**Ineffability, Ineffableness**, in-ef'a-bil"i-ti, in-ef'a-bl-nes, *n.* The quality of being ineffable or unutterable.—**Ineffably**, in-ef'a-bli, *adv.* In an ineffable manner; unutterably.

Ineffaceable, in-ef-fā'sa-bl, *a.* [Prefix *in*, not, and *effaceable.*] Incapable of being effaced.—**Ineffaceably**, in-ef-fā'sa-bli, *adv.* So as not to be effaceable; indelibly.

Ineffective, in-ef-fek'tiv, *a.* [Prefix *in*, not, and *effective.*] Incapable of producing any effect, or the effect intended; inefficient; useless; impotent; wanting energy.—**Ineffectively**, in-ef-fek'tiv-li, *adv.* In an ineffective manner.—**Ineffectiveness**, in-ef-fek'tiv-nes, *n.* Quality of being ineffective.—**Ineffectual**, in-ef-fek'tū-al, *a.* [Prefix *in*, not, and *effectual.*] Not effectual; inefficient; weak.—**Ineffectually**, in-ef-fek'tū-al-li, *adv.* In an ineffectual manner.—**Ineffectualness**, in-ef-fek'tū-al-nes, *n.*

Inefervescent, in-ef'fėr-ves"ent, *a.* [Prefix *in*, not, and *effervescent.*] Not effervescent or effervescing; not susceptible of effervescence.—**Inefervescence**, in-ef'fėr-ves"ens, *n.* A state of not effervescing.—**Inefervescible**, in-ef'fėr-ves"i-bl, *a.* Not capable of effervescence.

Inefficacious, in-ef'fi-kā"shus, *a.* [Prefix *in*, not, and *efficacious.*] Not efficacious; not producing the effect desired; of inadequate power.—**Inefficaciously**, in-ef'fi-kā"shus-li, *adv.* In an inefficacious manner.—**Inefficaciousness, Inefficacy**, in-ef'fi-kā"shus-nes, in-ef'fi-ka-si, *n.* Want of efficacy; ineffectualness; failure of effect.

Inefficient, in-ef-fish'ent, *a.* [Prefix *in*, not, and *efficient.*] Not efficient; not producing the required effect; incapable of effective action; incompetent.—*n.* One who is incompetent to perform the duties of a service.—**Inefficiency**, in-ef-fish'en-si, *n.* The condition or quality of being inefficient.—**Inefficiently**, in-ef-fish'ent-li, *adv.* In an inefficient manner.

Inelaborate, in-ē-lab'o-rāt, *a.* [Prefix *in*, not, and *elaborate.*] Not elaborate; not wrought with care.

Inelastic, in-ē-las'tik, *a.* [Prefix *in*, not, and *elastic.*] Not elastic; wanting elasticity; unelastic.—**Inelasticity**, in-ē'las-tis"i-ti, *n.* Want of elasticity.

Inelegant, in-el'e-gant, *a.* [Prefix *in*, not, and *elegant*; L. *inelegans, inelegantis*, inelegant.] Not elegant; wanting in elegance; wanting in anything which correct taste requires.—**Inelegance, Inelegancy**, in-el'ē-gans, in-el'ē-gan-si, *n.* [L. *inelegantia*; Fr. *inélégance.*] The condition or quality of being inelegant; an inelegant point or feature.—**Inelegantly**, in-el'ē-gant-li, *adv.* In an inelegant manner.

Ineligible, in-el'i-ji-bl, *a.* [Prefix *in*, not, and *eligible.*] Not eligible; not capable of or fit for being elected or adopted; not worthy to be chosen or preferred.—**Ineligibility**, in-el'i-ji-bil"i-ti, *n.* Condition of being ineligible.—**Ineligibly**, in-el'i-ji-bli, *adv.* In an ineligible manner.

Ineloquent, in-el'ō-kwent, *a.* [Prefix *in*, not, and *eloquent.*] Not eloquent; wanting in eloquence; not eloquently written or delivered.—**Ineloquently**, in-el'ō-kwent-li, *adv.* In an ineloquent manner.—**Ineloquence**, in-el'ō-kwens, *n.* The quality of being ineloquent.

Inept, in-ept', *a.* [L. *ineptus*—prefix *in*, not, and *aptus*, fit, apt. APT.] Unsuitable; improper; foolish; silly; nonsensical.—**Ineptitude**, **Ineptness**, in-ep'ti-tūd, in-ept'nes, *n.* [L. *ineptitudo.*] The condition or quality of being inept; unfitness; inaptitude; foolishness.—**Ineptly**, in-ept'li, *adv.* In an inept manner.

Inequable, in-ē'kwa-bl, *a.* [Prefix *in*, not, and *equable*; L. *inæquabilis.*] Not equable; unequable.

Inequal, in-ē'kwal, *a.* [Prefix *in*, not, and *equal*; L. *inæqualis.*] Not equal; unequal; uneven; varying.—**Inequality**, in-ē-kwol'-i-ti, *n.* [L. *inæqualitas.*] The condition or quality of being inequal or unequal; disparity; unevenness; want of levelness; an elevation or a depression of a surface.

Inequitable, in-ek'wi-ta-bl, *a.* [Prefix *in*, not, and *equitable.*] Not equitable; not just or fair.—**Inequity**, in-ek'wi-ti, *n.* Unfairness; injustice.

Ineradicable, in-ē-rad'i-ka-bl, *a.* [Prefix *in*, not, and *eradicable.*] Incapable of being eradicated. — **Ineradicably**, in-ē-rad'i-ka-bli, *adv.* So as not to be eradicated.

Inermous, in-ėr'mus, *a.* [L. *inermis*, *inermus* — prefix *in*, not, and *arma*, arms.] *Bot.* unarmed; destitute of prickles or thorns, as a leaf.

Inert, in-ėrt', *a.* [L. *iners*, *inertis*, unskilled, inactive—*in*, not, and *ars*, acquired skill, art. ART.] Destitute of the power of moving itself, or of active resistance to motion impressed; not moving or acting; indisposed to move or act; sluggish; inactive. ∴ *Inert* refers rather to the external manifestation of a habit which may be either natural or induced; *inactive*, not exhibiting activity, often refers to a temporary, perhaps voluntary, state.—**Inertia**, in-ėr'shi-a, *n.* [L.] Passiveness; inactivity; inertness; sluggishness; *physics*, the property of matter by which it retains its state of rest or of uniform rectilinear motion so long as no foreign cause occurs to change that state: called also *vis inertiæ*.—**Inertly**, in-ėrt'li, *adv.* In an inert manner.—**Inertness**, **Inertion**, **Inertitude**, in-ėrt'nes, in-ėr'shon, in-ėr'ti-tūd, *n.* The state or quality of being inert.

Inerudite, in-er'ū-dīt, *a.* [Prefix *in*, not, and *erudite.*] Not erudite; unlearned.

Inessential, in-es-sen'shal, *a.* [Prefix *in*, not, and *essential.*] Not essential; unessential.

Inestimable, in-es'ti-ma-bl, *a.* [Prefix *in*, not, and *estimable*; L. *inæstimabilis.*] Incapable of being estimated or computed; too valuable or excellent to be rated or fully appreciated; incalculable.—**Inestimably**, in-es'ti-ma-bli, *adv.* In a manner not to be estimated.

Inevitable, in-ev'i-ta-bl, *a.* [L. *inevitabilis*, from *in*, not, and *evito*, to avoid—*e*, out, and *vito*, to shun.] Incapable of being avoided; unavoidable; admitting of no escape or evasion; certain to befall.—**Inevitability**, **Inevitableness**, in-ev'i-ta-bil"i-ti, in-ev'i-ta-bl-nes, *n.* Unavoidableness; certainty.—**Inevitably**, in-ev'i-ta-bli, *adv.* Unavoidably; certainly.

Inexact, in-eg-zakt', *a.* [Prefix *in*, not, and *exact.*] Not exact; not precisely correct or true.—**Inexactness**, in-eg-zakt'nes, *n.* The state of being inexact; incorrectness.

Inexcitable, in-ek-sī'ta-bl, *a.* [Prefix *in*, not, and *excitable.*] Not excitable; not susceptible of excitement. — **Inexcitability**, in-ek-sī'ta-bil"i-ti, *n.* The state or quality of being inexcitable.

Inexcusable, in-eks-kū'za-bl, *a.* [Prefix *in*, not, and *excusable.*] Incapable of being excused or justified; unpardonable; indefensible.—**Inexcusableness**, in-eks-kū'-za-bl-nes, *n.* The condition or quality of being inexcusable. — **Inexcusably**, in-eks-kū'za-bli, *adv.* In an inexcusable manner; without excuse.

Inexecutable, in-ek'sē-kū"ta-bl, *a.* [Prefix *in*, not, and *executable.*] Not executable; incapable of being executed or performed.

Inexhaustible, in-egz-ạs'ti-bl, *a.* [Prefix *in*, not, and *exhaustible.*] Not exhaustible; incapable of being exhausted or spent; unfailing. — **Inexhausted**, in-egz-ạs'ted, *a.* Not exhausted; unexhausted.—**Inexhaustedly**, in-egz-ạs'ted-li, *adv.* Without exhaustion.—**Inexhaustibility**, **Inexhaustibleness**, in-egz-ạs'ti-bil"i-ti, in-egz-ạs'ti-bl-nes, *n.* The state of being inexhaustible. — **Inexhaustibly**, in-egz-ạs'ti-bli, *adv.* In an inexhaustible manner or degree.

Inexorable, in-ek'so-ra-bl, *a.* [Prefix *in*, not, and *exorable.*] Incapable of being moved by entreaty or prayer; too firm and determined to yield to supplication; unyielding; unbending; implacable.—**Inexorability**, **Inexorableness**, in-ek'so-ra-bil"i-ti, in-ek'so-ra-bl-nes, *n.* The state or quality of being inexorable.—**Inexorably**, in-ek'so-ra-bli, *adv.* In an inexorable manner.

Inexpansible, in-eks-pan'si-bl, *a.* [Prefix *in*, not, and *expansible.*] Incapable of being expanded, dilated, or diffused.

Inexpedient, in-eks-pē'di-ent, *a.* [Prefix *in*, not, and *expedient.*] Not expedient; inappropriate; unsuitable to time and place; not advisable.—**Inexpedience**, **Inexpediency**, in-eks-pē'di-ens, in-eks-pē'di-en-si, *n.* The condition or quality of being inexpedient. — **Inexpediently**, in-eks-pē'di-ent-li, *adv.* In an inexpedient manner.

Inexpensive, in-eks-pen'siv, *a.* [Prefix *in*, not, and *expensive.*] Not expensive.

Inexperience, in-eks-pē'ri-ens, *n.* [Prefix *in*, not, and *experience.*] Want of experience.—**Inexperienced**, in-eks-pē'ri-enst, *a.* Not having experience.

Inexpert, in-eks-pėrt', *a.* [Prefix *in*, not, and *expert.*] Not expert; not skilled.—**Inexpertness**, in-eks-pėrt'nes, *n.*

Inexpiable, in-eks'pi-a-bl, *a.* [Prefix *in*, not, and *expiable*; L. *inexpiabilis.*] Incapable of being expiated; not to be atoned for; unpardonable. — **Inexpiableness**, in-eks'pi-a-bl-nes, *n.* — **Inexpiably**, in-eks'pi-a-bli, *adv.*

Inexplicable, in-eks'pli-ka-bl, *a.* [Prefix *in*, not, and *explicable*; L. *inexplicabilis.*] Incapable of being explained or interpreted; unaccountable; mysterious.—**Inexplicability**, **Inexplicableness**, in-eks'pli-ka-bil"i-ti, in-eks'pli-ka-bl-nes, *n.* The quality of being inexplicable.—**Inexplicably**, in-eks'pli-ka-bli, *adv.* In an inexplicable manner; unaccountably.

Inexplicit, in-eks-plis'it, *a.* [Prefix *in*, not, and *explicit.*] Not explicit; not clear in statement; not clearly stated.

Inexplosive, in-eks-plō'siv, *a.* [Prefix *in*, not, and *explosive.*] Not liable to explode or burst with a loud report.—*n.* A substance which is not liable to explode.

Inexpressible, in-eks-pres'i-bl, *a.* [Prefix *in*, not, and *expressible.*] Not expressible; not to be uttered; unspeakable; unutterable.—**Inexpressibles**, in-eks-pres'i-blz, *n. pl.* A colloquial euphemism for trousers.—**Inexpressibly**, in-eks-pres'i-bli, *adv.* In an inexpressible manner.—**Inexpressive**, in-eks-pres'iv, *a.* Not expressive; wanting in expression; inexpressible; ineffable. — **Inexpressiveness**, in-eks-pres'-iv-nes, *n.*

Inextinct, in-eks-tingkt', *a.* [Prefix *in*, not, and *extinct.*] Not extinct.

Inextinguishable, in-eks-ting'gwish-a-bl, *a.* [Prefix *in*, not, and *extinguishable.*] Incapable of being extinguished; unquenchable (flame, thirst, desire). — **Inextinguishably**, in-eks-ting'gwish-a-bli, *adv.* In an inextinguishable manner.

Inextricable, in-eks'tri-ka-bl, *a.* [Prefix *in*, not, and *extricable*; L. *inextricabilis.*] Incapable of being extricated or disentangled; not permitting extrication.—**Inextricableness**, in-eks'tri-ka-bl-nes, *n.*—**Inextricably**, in-eks'tri-ka-bli, *adv.*

Infallible, in-fal'i-bl, *a.* [Prefix *in*, not, and *fallible.*] Not fallible; not capable of erring or falling into error; not leading into error; perfectly reliable; certain (*infallible* testimony).—**Infallibly**, in-fal'i-bli, *adv.* In an infallible manner.—**Infallibilism**, in-fal'i-bil-izm, *n.* Adherence to the dogma of the infallibility of the pope.—**Infallibilist**, in-fal'i-bil-ist, *n.* One who maintains the infallibility of the pope.—**Infallibility**, **Infallibleness**, in-fal'i-bil"i-ti, in-fal'i-bl-nes, *n.* The quality of being infallible. — *Infallibility of the pope*, the dogma established as an article of faith in 1870, that the pope, when speaking as pope upon matters of faith or morals, is infallible.

Infamy, in'fa-mi, *n.* [L. *infamia*, ill fame, ill report, from *infamis*, infamous—*in*, not, and *fama*, fame.] Total loss of reputation; public disgrace; bad or disgraceful repute; shamefulness; disgracefulness; scandalousness; extreme baseness or vileness.—**Infamous**, in'fa-mus, *a.* Having a reputation of the worst kind; scandalous; notoriously vile; shameful; branded with infamy. — **Infamously**, in'fa-mus-li, *adv.* Scandalously; disgracefully; shamefully.

Infant, in'fant, *n.* [L. *infans*, *infantis*, that cannot speak, an infant—prefix *in*, not, and *fari*, to speak. FAME.] A child in the first two or three years of life; *law*, a person not of legal age.—*a.* Pertaining to infancy.—**Infancy**, in'fan-si, *n.* [L. *infantia.*] The state of being an infant; earliest period of life; *law*, the period from birth to twenty-one; nonage; minority; the first age of anything.—**Infanta**, in-fan'tä, *n.*, *fem.*; **Infante**, in-fan'tā, *n.*, *m.* Formerly in Spain and Portugal, children of the king except the eldest son.—**Infanticide**, in-fan'ti-sīd, *n.* [L. *infanticidium*, the crime, *infanticida*, the perpetrator—*infans*, and *cædo*, to kill.] The murder and murderer of an infant; child-murder.—

Infantile, **Infantine**, in'fan-tīl, in'fan-tīn, *a.* Pertaining to or characteristic of infancy or an infant.—*Infantile paralysis*, *n.* A specific, infectious, and contagious disease believed to be caused by a filterable virus. It attacks the motor nerves of the spinal cord, and often causes paralysis.

Infantry, in'fant-ri, *n.* [Fr. *infanterie*, It. *infanteria*, infantry (lit. a band of youths), from *infante*, a young person, originally an infant.] The soldiers or troops that serve on foot, as distinguished from *cavalry*.

Infatuate, in-fat'ū-āt, *v.t.*—*infatuated*, *infatuating*. [L. *infatuo*, *infatuatum*, to make foolish—prefix *in*, intens., and *fatuus*, foolish (whence *fatuous*).] To make foolish; to inspire with folly; to inspire with an extravagant passion that cannot be controlled. — **Infatuated**, in-fat'ū-ā-ted, *p.* and *a.* Affected with folly; besotted; inspired with foolish passion. — **Infatuation**, in-fat'ū-ā"shon, *n.* The act of infatuating or state of being infatuated; extreme folly; foolish passion.

Infeasible, in-fē'zi-bl, *a.* [Prefix *in*, not, and *feasible.*] Not feasible; impracticable.

Infect, in-fekt', *v.t.* [Fr. *infecter*, from L. *inficio*, *infectum*, to put in, to stain—*in*, into, and *facio*, to do. FACT.] To taint with disease; to contaminate with morbid or noxious matter; to communicate bad qualities to; to corrupt.—**Infecter**, in-fek'tėr, *n.* One who or that which infects.—**Infection**, in-fek'shon, *n.* The act or process of infecting; that which infects: as distinguished from *contagion* it does not imply actual contact, as the latter properly does.—**Infectious**, **Infective**, in-fek'-shus, in-fek'tiv, *a.* Capable of infecting; likely to communicate disease; contagious; corrupting or contaminating; easily diffused or spread from person to person.—**Infectiously**, in-fek'shus-li, *adv.* In an infectious manner; by infection.—**Infectiousness**, in-fek'shus-nes, *n.* The quality of being infectious.

Infecund, in-fē'kund, *a.* [Prefix *in*, not, and *fecund*; L. *infecundus.*] Not fecund;

unfruitful; barren.—**Infecundity**, in-fē-kun'di-ti, *n.* State of being infecund.

Infeftment, in-feft'ment, *n.* The Scotch equivalent of *Enfeoffment.*

Infelicity, in-fē-lis'i-ti, *n.* [Prefix *in*, not, and *felicity*; L. *infelicitas.*] The state of being unhappy; unhappiness; misery; unfavourableness.—**Infelicitous**, in-fē-lis'i-tus, *a.* Not felicitous; unhappy; unfortunate.

Infelt, in'felt, *a.* [Prefix *in*, within, and *felt.*] Felt within or deeply; heart-felt.

Infeoff, in-fēf'. To enfeoff.

Infer, in-fėr', *v.t.*—*inferred, inferring.* [L. *infero*, to bring in or on, to conclude—*in*, upon, and *fero*, to bear. FERTILE.] To gather or derive either by induction or deduction; to deduce, as a fact or consequence; to conclude or arrive at by reasoning.—**Inferable**, in-fėr'a-bl, *a.* Capable of being inferred; inferrible.—**Inference**, in'fėr-ens, *n.* The act of inferring; conclusion drawn or inferred; deduction; consequence.—**Inferential**, in-fėr-en'shal, *a.* Of or pertaining to an inference.—**Inferentially**, in-fėr-en'shal-li, *adv.* In an inferential manner; by way of inference.—**Inferrible**, in-fėr'i-bl, *a.* Such as may be inferred; to be gathered or concluded by reasoning.

Inferior, in-fē'ri-ėr, *a.* [L. compar. from *inferus*, low; akin *infernal.*] Lower in place, station, rank, value, importance; subordinate; *bot.* growing below some other organ; *astron.* situated between earth and sun (the *inferior* planets).—*n.* One lower in station, rank, intellect, than others.—**Inferiority**, in-fē'ri-or"i-ti, *n.* The state of being inferior.—*Inferiority complex*, a feeling of personal inferiority (real or imaginary).—**Inferiorly**, in-fē'ri-ėr-li, *adv.* In an inferior manner.

Infernal, in-fėr'nal, *a.* [L. *infernalis*, from *infernus*, infernal; akin *inferior.*] Pertaining to the lower regions, or regions of the dead; pertaining to hell; inhabiting hell; characteristic or worthy of hell or the inhabitants of hell; hellish; diabolical; wicked and detestable.—*Infernal machine*, a machine or apparatus of an explosive nature, contrived for the purposes of assassination or other mischief.—**Infernally**, in-fėr'nal-li, *adv.* In an infernal manner.—**Inferno**, *n.* A hell upon earth, with general reference to the poem of Dante, the first part of his *Divine Comedy.*

Infertile, in-fėr'til or in-fėr'tīl, *a.* [Prefix *in*, not, and *fertile.*] Not fertile; not fruitful or productive; barren.—**Infertilely**, in-fėr'til-li, *adv.* In an infertile manner.—**Infertility**, in-fėr-til'i-ti, *n.* Unproductiveness; barrenness.

Infest, in-fest', *v.t.* [Fr. *infester*; L. *infestare*, to attack, to molest, from *infestus*, hostile—*in*, in, and same root as *fendo* in *offendo, defendo*, to offend, defend.] To make hostile attacks or depredations on; to harass, torment, disturb, annoy.—**Infestation**, in-fes-tā'shon, *n.* [L. *infestatio.*] The act of infesting.—**Infester**, in-fes'tėr, *n.* One who infests.

Infeudation, in-fū-dā'shon, *n.* [L. *in*, into, and *feudum*, a fief.] *Law*, the act of putting in possession of an estate in fee; the granting of tithes to laymen.

Infidel, in'fi-del, *n.* [L. *infidelis*, faithless, unbelieving—prefix *in*, not, and *fidelis*, faithful. FIDELITY.] A disbeliever; one who has no religious faith; an atheist; not holding the true faith.—*a.* Unbelieving.—**Infidelity**, in-fi-del'i-ti, *n.* [Fr. *infidélité*; L. *infidelitas.*] Want of faith or belief; atheism or disbelief in God or religion; skepticism; unfaithfulness in married persons; adultery; unfaithfulness to a charge or moral obligation; treachery; deceit.

Infield, in'fēld, *n.* *Baseball*, the square or diamond portion of a playing field marked off by four bases; collectively, the shortstop and three basemen.

Infiltrate, in-fil'trāt, *v.i.* [Prefix *in*, and *filtrate.*] To enter by penetrating the pores or interstices of a substance.—**Infiltration**, in-fil-trā'shon, *n.* The process of infiltrating; that which infiltrates.

Infinite, in'fi-nit, *a.* [Prefix *in*, not, and *finite*; L. *infinitus.*] Not finite; without limits; not limited or circumscribed: applied to time, space, and the Supreme Being and his attributes; exceedingly great in excellence, degree, capacity, and the like; boundless; limitless; immeasurable.—*n.* That which is infinite; an infinite space or extent; the infinite being; the Almighty.—**Infinitely**, in'fi-nit-li, *adv.* In an infinite manner.—**Infiniteness**, in'fi-nit-nes, *n.* The state of being infinite.—**Infinitesimal**, in'fin-i-tes"i-mal, *a.* [Fr. *infinitésimal.*] Infinitely or indefinitely small; less than any assignable quantity.—*n. Math.* an infinitely small quantity, or one less than any assignable quantity.—**Infinitesimally**, in'fin-i-tes"i-mal-li, *adv.* To an infinitesimal extent or in an infinitesimal degree.—**Infinitive**, in-fin'i-tiv, *a.* [L. *infinitivus*, unlimited, indefinite.] Not limiting or restricting: a grammatical term applied to that mood of a verb which expresses the action of the verb, without limitation of person or number.—*n.* The infinitive mood.—**Infinitival**, in-fin'i-ti-val, *a. Gram.* of or belonging to the infinitive mood.—**Infinitively**, in-fin'i-tiv-li, *adv. Gram.* in the manner of an infinitive mood.—**Infinitude**, in-fin'i-tūd, *n.* The quality or state of being infinite; infinite extent; infinity; immensity; boundless number.—**Infinity**, in-fin'i-ti, *n.* [L. *infinitas.*] Unlimited extent of time, space, quantity, excellence, energy, &c.; boundlessness; endless or indefinite number.

Infirm, in-fėrm', *a.* [Prefix *in*, not, and *firm*; L. *infirmus*, not strong, weak, feeble.] Not firm or sound; weak as regards the body; feeble; not steadfast; irresolute; not solid or stable.—**Infirmary**, in-fėr'ma-ri, *n.* A place where the infirm or sick, or those suffering from accidents, are lodged and nursed, or have their ailments attended to.—**Infirmity**, in-fėr'mi-ti, *n.* [L. *infirmitas.*] The state of being infirm; an unsound or unhealthy state of the body; a disease; a malady; an ailment, weakness, failing, defect, foible.—**Infirmly**, in-fėrm'li, *adv.* In an infirm manner.—**Infirmness**, in-fėrm'nes, *n.* The state of being infirm.

Infix, in-fiks', *v.t.* [L. *infigo, infixum*—*in*, in, into, and *figo*, to fix.] To fix or fasten in; to cause to remain or adhere, as in the mind; to implant or fix, as principles, thoughts, &c.—*n.* A part of a word similar to a prefix or suffix, but inserted in the body of a word.

Inflame, in-flām', *v.t.*—*inflamed, inflaming.* [L. *inflammo*—*in*, and *flammo*, to inflame, from *flamma*, flame. FLAME.] To set on fire; to kindle; to redden or make fiery (the eyes, the face); to excite or increase, as passion or appetite; to enkindle into violent action; to enrage or exasperate; *med.* to make morbidly red and swollen.—*v.i.* To take fire; to grow angry; to grow hot and painful.—**Inflamer**, in-flā'mėr, *n.* One who or that which inflames.—**Inflammability, Inflammableness**, in-flam'a-bil"i-ti, in-flam'a-bl-nes, *n.* The state or quality of being inflammable.—**Inflammable**, in-flam'a-bl, *a.* Capable of being set on fire; easily kindled; combustible.—**Inflammably**, in-flam'a-bli, *adv.* In an inflammable manner.—**Inflammation**, in-fla-mā'shon, *n.* [L. *inflammatio.*] The act of inflaming; *med.* a redness and swelling of any part of an animal body, attended with heat, pain, and febrile symptoms.—**Inflammative**,† in-flam'a-tiv, *a.* Inflammatory.—**Inflammatory**, in-flam'a-to-ri, *a.* Tending to inflame; tending to excite inflammation; accompanied with great heat and excitement of arterial action; tending to excite anger, animosity, or the like.

Inflate, in-flāt', *v.t.*—*inflated, inflating.* [L. *inflo, inflatum*—*in*, into, and *flo*, to blow. FLATULENT.] To swell or distend by injecting air; to puff up; to elate, as with pride; to raise above the real value or value according to sound commercial principles (*inflated prices*).—**Inflatable**, in-flā'ta-bl, *a.* Capable of being inflated.—**Inflated**, in-flā'ted, *p.* and *a.* Distended with air; puffed up; turgid; tumid; bombastic (an *inflated* style of writing.)—**Inflation**, in-flā'shon, *n.* [L. *inflatio, inflationis.*] The act of inflating; the state of being inflated; sharp increase in amount of money and credit causing advances in the price level.—**Inflationist**, in-flā'shon-ist, *n.* One who causes or believes in manipulated expansion of prices.

Inflect, in-flekt', *v.t.* [L. *inflecto*—*in*, intens., and *flecto*, to bend. FLEX.] To bend; to turn from a direct line or course; to modulate (the voice); *gram.*, to go over the inflections of; to decline or conjugate.—**Inflected**, in-flek'ted, *p.* and *a.* Bent or turned from a direct line or course (an *inflected* ray of light); *bot.* bent or curved inwards; *gram.* having inflections.—**Inflection, Inflexion**, in-flek'shon, *n.* [L. *inflexio, inflexionis.*] The act of inflecting, or the state of being inflected; modulation or rise and fall of the voice; *optics*, deflection or diffraction; *gram.* the variation of nouns, &c., by declension, and of verbs by conjugation.—**Inflectional**, in-flek'shonal, *a.* Pertaining to or having inflection.—**Inflective**, in-flek'tiv, *a.* Having the power of inflecting.—**Inflexed**, in-flekst', *a.* [L. *inflexus*, pp. of *inflecto.*] Curved; bent.—*Inflexed leaf, bot.* a leaf curved or bent upwards and inwards at the apex.—**Inflexibility**, in-flek'si-bil"i-ti, *n.* The quality of being inflexible.—**Inflexible**, in-flex'si-bl, *a.* [L. *inflexibilis*, that cannot be bent.] Incapable of being bent; firm in purpose; not to be prevailed on; incapable of being turned from a purpose; inexorable; unalterable.—**Inflexibleness**, in-flek'si-bl-nes, *n.* Inflexibility.—**Inflexibly**, in-flek'si-bli, *adv.* In an inflexible manner; firmly; inexorably.

Inflict, in-flikt', *v.t.* [L. *infligo, inflictum*—*in*, upon, and *fligo*, to strike, as in *afflict, conflict.*] To cause to bear or suffer from; to cause to feel or experience; to impose (pain, disgrace, punishment).—**Inflicter**, in-flik'tėr, *n.* One who inflicts.—**Infliction**, in-flik'shon, *n.* [L. *inflictio, inflictionis.*] The act of inflicting or imposing; that which is inflicted.—**Inflictive**, in-flik'tiv, *a.* Tending to inflict.

Inflorescence, in-flō-res'ens, *n.* [From L. *inflorescens*, ppr. of *infloresco*, to begin to blossom—*in*, intens., and *floresco*, to begin to blossom. FLOURISH.] A flowering; the unfolding of blossoms; *bot.* a mode of flowering or the manner in which blossoms are arranged and supported on their footstalks or peduncles.

Influence, in'flu̇-ens, *n.* [Fr. *influence*, from L. *influens, influentis*, ppr. of *influo*, to flow in—*in*, in, *fluo*, to flow. FLUENT.] Agency or power serving to affect, modify, or sway in some way; ability or power sufficient to produce some effect; sway; effect; power or authority arising from elevated station, wealth, and the like; acknowledged ascendancy with people in power.—*v.t.*—*influenced, influencing.* To exercise influence on; to modify or affect in some way; to act on; to bias; to sway.—**Influent**, in'flu̇-ent, *a.* [L. *influens, influentis.*] Flowing in.—**Influential**, in-flu̇-en'shal, *a.* Exerting influence, physical or other; possessing power or influence.

Influenza, in-flū-en'za, *n.* [It. *influenza*, lit. influence. INFLUENCE.] An acute, infectious, and highly contagious disease affecting the respiratory tract, and producing symptoms not unlike a severe cold; pneumonia is a frequent complication, particularly when the disease is epidemic; intestinal, or abdominal, influenza attacks the digestive system; the etiology of the disease has not been definitely established.

Influx, in'fluks, *n.* [L. *influxus*, a flowing in, from *influo.* INFLUENCE.] The act of flowing in; infusion; inflow; a coming in; introduction; importation in abundance (an *influx* of money); the point at which one stream runs into another or into the sea.—**Influxion**, in-fluk'shon, *n.* [L. *influxio, influxionis.*] Infusion; intromission.—**Influxive**, in-fluk'siv, *a.* Having a tendency to flow in.

Infold, in-fold', *v.t.* To fold in; to wrap up or inwrap; to clasp with the arms; to embrace.

Inform, in-form', *v.t.* [Fr. *informer*, to apprise, L. *informo*, to shape, to describe—*in*, intens., and *formo*, to form, from *forma*, form.] To give form or shape to; to inspire and give life to; to actuate with vitality; to animate; to communicate knowledge to; to instruct, to tell, acquaint, apprise (to *inform* a person *of* something).—*v.i.* To give information.—*To inform against*, to communicate facts by way of accusation against.—**Informant**, in-for'mant, *n.* One who informs; an informer.—**Information**, in-for-mā'shon, *n.* [L. *informatio.*] The act of informing; news or intelligence communicated by word or writing; intelligence; knowledge derived from reading or instruction, or gathered in any way; a statement of facts laid before a court of justice.—**Informatory, Informative**, in-for'ma-to-ri, in-for'ma-tiv, *a.* Affording knowledge or information; instructive.—**Informer**, in-for'mėr, *n.* One who informs; an accomplice who in order to escape punishment gives evidence against another or others; one who makes a business of informing against others.

Informal, in-for'mal, *a.* [Prefix *in*, not, and *formal.*] Not in the regular or usual form; not in accordance with official, conventional, or customary forms; without ceremony.—**Informality**, in-for-mal'i-ti, *n.* The state of being informal; want of formality.—**Informally**, in-for'mal-li, *adv.* In an informal manner.

Infra-axillary, in-fra-ak'sil-la-ri, *a.* [L. *infra*, beneath, and *axilla*, axil.] *Bot.* situated beneath the axil.—**Infracostal**, in-fra-kos'tal, *a.* [L. *infra*, and *costa*, rib.] *Anat.* situated beneath the ribs.

Infraction, in-frak'shon, *n.* [L. *infractio, infractionis*, a breaking in pieces, from *infringo, infractum.* INFRINGE.] The act of infringing; breach; violation; infringement.

Infralapsarian, in'fra-lap-sā"ri-an, *a.* and *n.* The doctrine of the sect holding that God's election or predestination of some was consequent on his prescience of the fall, and contemplated man as already fallen. Modifications are *sublapsarian, supralapsarian.*

Infra-maxillary, in-fra-mak'sil-la-ri, *a.* [L. *infra*, beneath, and *maxilla*, a jaw.] *Anat.* situated under the jaw; belonging to the lower jaw.—**Infra-mundane**, in-fra-mun'dān, *a.* [L. *infra*, and *mundus*, the world.] Lying or being beneath the world.

Infranchise, in-fran'chīz, *v.t.* Same as *Enfranchise.*

Infrangible, in-fran'ji-bl, *a.* [Prefix *in*, not, and *frangible.*] Not capable of being broken; not to be violated or infringed.—**Infrangibility, Infrangibleness**, in-fran'ji-bil"i-ti, in-fran'ji-bl-nes, *n.* State or quality of being infrangible.

Infra-orbital, Infra-orbitary, in-fra-or'bi-tal, in-fra-or'bi-ta-ri, *a.* [Prefix *infra*, and *orbit.*] *Anat.* situated below the orbit.—**Infrared**, *a.* Pertaining to rays beyond the visible red of the spectrum.—**Infra-scapular**, in-fra-skap'ū-lėr, *a.* [Prefix *infra*, and *scapula.*] *Anat.* below the scapula or shoulder-blade.

Infrequent, in-frē'kwent, *a.* [L. *infrequens*—*in*, not, and *frequens*, frequent.] Not frequent; seldom; rare.—**Infrequence, Infrequency**, in-frē'kwens, in-frē'kwen-si, *n.*—**Infrequently**, in-frē'kwent-li, *adv.* Not frequently; seldom.

Infringe, in-frinj', *v.t.*—*infringed, infringing.* [L. *infringo*—*in*, intens., and *frango*, to break. FRACTION.] To break, as laws or contracts; to violate; to contravene; to impair or encroach on.—*v.i.* To encroach: followed by *on* or *upon.*—**Infringement**, in-frinj'ment, *n.* Act of infringing or violating.—**Infringer**, in-frin'jėr, *n.* One who infringes; a violator.

Infula, in'fū-la, *n.* [L.] A sort of head-dress worn by ancient Roman priests, &c.; a pendant to a bishop's mitre.

Infume, Infumate, in-fūm', in'fū-māt, *v.t.* [L. *infumo, infumatum*—*in*, in, and *fumus*, smoke. FUME.] To dry in smoke.

Infundibular, Infundibulate, Infundibuliform, in-fun-dib'ū-lėr, in-fun-dib'ū-lāt, in-fun-dib'ū-li-form, *a.* [From *infundibulum*, a funnel—*in*, in, and *fundo*, to pour. FUSE.] Having the form of a funnel.

Infuriate, in-fū'ri-āt, *v.t.*—*infuriated, infuriating.* [L.L. *infurio, infuriatum*—L. *in*, intens., and *furia*, rage, madness.] To render furious or mad; to enrage.—*a.* Enraged; mad; raging.

Infuse, in-fūz', *v.t.*—*infused, infusing.* [Fr. *infuser*, from L. *infundo, infusum*, to pour into—*in*, into, and *fundo*, to pour. FUSE.] To pour in, as a liquid; to pour; to shed; to instil, as principles or qualities; to introduce; to diffuse; to steep in liquor without boiling, in order to extract medicinal or other qualities.—**Infuser**, in-fū'zėr, *n.* One who infuses.—**Infusibility**, in-fū'zi-bil"i-ti, *n.* The capability of being infused.—**Infusible**, in-fū'zi-bl, *a.* Capable of being infused.—**Infusion**, in-fū'zhon, *n.* The act or process of infusing; that which is infused or instilled; liquor obtained by infusing or steeping.—**Infusive**, in-fū'siv, *a.* Having the power of infusion.—**Infusoria**, in-fū-sō'ri-a, *n. pl.* [L.] A class of minute, mostly microscopic, animals, so named from being frequently developed in organic infusions.—**Infusorial, Infusory**, in-fū-sō'ri-al, in-fū'so-ri, *a.* Pertaining to the Infusoria; composed of or containing Infusoria.—**Infusorian**, in-fū-sō'ri-an, *n.* One of the Infusoria.

Infusible, in-fū'zi-bl, *a.* [Prefix *in*, not, and *fusible.*] Not fusible; incapable of fusion.—**Infusibility**, in-fū'zi-bil"i-ti, *n.* Absence of fusibility.

Ingathering, in'gaTH-ėr-ing, *n.* The act of gathering in; the collecting and securing of the fruits of the earth; harvest.

Ingeminate, in-jem'i-nāt, *v.t.* [L. *ingemino, ingeminatum*—*in*, intens., and *gemino*, to double. GEMINATE.] To double or repeat.—*a.* Redoubled; repeated.—**Ingemination**, in-jem'i-nā"shon, *n.* Repetition; reduplication.

Ingender, in-jen'dėr, *v.t.* Same as *Engender.*

Ingenerate, in-jen'ėr-āt, *v.t.* [L. *ingenero, ingeneratum*—*in*, and *genero*, to generate.] To generate or produce within.—*a.* Generated within; inborn; innate; inbred.—**Ingeneration**, in-jen'ėr-ā"shon, *n.* The act of ingenerating or producing within.

Ingenious, in-jē'ni-us, *a.* [L. *ingeniosus*, able, ingenious, from *ingenium*, ability, cleverness—*in*, in, and root *gen*, to beget. GENUS. Possessed of cleverness or ability†; having the faculty of invention; skilful or prompt to invent; apt in contriving or forming new combinations of ideas; contrived with ingenuity; of curious design, structure, or mechanism; witty or well conceived (an *ingenious* compliment).—**Ingeniously**, in-jē'ni-us-li, *adv.* In an ingenious manner.—**Ingeniousness**, in-jē'ni-us-nes, *n.* Ingenuity.—**Ingenuity**, in-jen-ū'i-ti, *n.* [Fr. *ingénuité*, L. *ingenuitas*, from *ingenuus.* INGENUOUS.] Ingenuousness‡; the quality or power of being ingenious; ready invention; skill in contrivance. [In form, though not in meaning, this word belongs to the next entry.]

Ingenuous, in-jen'ū-us, *a.* [L. *ingenuus*, inborn, freeborn, ingenuous—*in*, and root *gen*, to produce. GENUS.] Honourable, noble, or generous‡; open, frank, or candid; free from reserve, disguise, equivocation, or dissimulation; of persons or things.—**Ingenuously**, in-jen'ū-us-li, *adv.* In an ingenuous manner; openly; candidly.—**Ingenuousness**, in-jen'ū-us-nes, *n.* The condition or quality of being ingenuous; openness of heart; frankness.—**Ingénue**, an-zhā-nū, *n.* An ingenuous, artless, naïve girl or young woman; used often of female parts in plays; also, an actress who plays such parts.

Ingest, in-jest', *v.t.* [L. *ingero, ingestum*—*in*, into, and *gero*, to bear. GESTURE.] To take into the stomach.—**Ingestion**, in-jest'shon, *n.* The act of taking into the stomach.—**Ingesta**, in-jes'ta, *n. pl.* [Lit. things carried in. INGEST.] Substances absorbed by an organism, or entering the alimentary canal; things taken into the mind.

Inglorious, in-glō-ri-us, *a.* [Prefix *in*, not, and *glorious*; L. *inglorius.*] Not glorious; without renown; obscure; bringing disgrace rather than glory; disgraceful; ignominious.—**Ingloriously**, in-glō'ri-us-li, *adv.* In an inglorious manner.—**Ingloriousness**, in-glō'ri-us-nes, *n.*

Ingluvies, in-glū'vi-ēz, *n.* [L.] *Zool.* the crop, craw, or gorge of birds; the stomach or paunch of ruminant animals.—**Ingluvial**, in-glū'vi-al, *a.* Of or pertaining to the ingluvies.

Ingoing, in'gō-ing, *n.* The act of entering; entrance.—*a.* Going in; entering, as on an office.

Ingorge, in-gorj', *v.t.* To engorge.

Ingot, in'got, *n.* [From *in*, and A.Sax. *geótan*, D. *gieten*, to pour; originally meaning a mass of molten metal. GUSH.] A mass or wedge of gold or silver cast in a mould; a mass of unwrought metal.

Ingraft, in-graft', *v.t.* [*In* and *graft.*] To graft; to attach by grafting; hence, to insert; to introduce; to set or fix deeply and firmly.—**Ingrafter**, in-graf'tėr, *n.* One who ingrafts.—**Ingraftment**, in-graft'ment, *n.* The act of ingrafting.

Ingrail, in-grāl', *v.t.* To engrail.

Ingrain, in-grān', *v.t.* To engrain.

Ingrate, in'grāt, *n.* [Fr. *ingrat*, from L. *ingratus*, ungrateful—*in*, not, and *gratus*, grateful.] An ungrateful person.

Ingratiate, in-grā'shi-āt, *v.t.*—*ingratiated, ingratiating.* [L. *in*, into, and *gratia*, favour. GRACE.] To introduce or commend to another's good-will, confidence, or kindness: always *refl.*

Ingratitude, in-grat'i-tūd, *n.* [Prefix *in*, not, and *gratitude.*] Want of gratitude; insensibility to favours, and want of a disposition to repay them; unthankfulness.

Ingrave,† in-grāv', *v.t.* To engrave.

Ingredient, in-grē'di-ent, *n.* [L. *ingrediens, ingredientis*, ppr. of *ingredior*, to go in—*in*, into, and *gradior*, to go. GRADE.] That which enters into a compound or is a component part of any compound or mixture; an element, component, or constituent.

Ingress, in'gres, *n.* [L. *ingressus*, a going into, from *ingredior.* INGREDIENT.] Entrance; *astron.* the entrance of the moon into the shadow of the earth in eclipses, the sun's entrance into a sign, &c.; power or liberty of entrance; means of entering.—*v.i.* (in-gres'). To go in or enter.—**Ingression**, in-gresh'on, *n.* [L. *ingressio.*] The act of entering; entrance.

Ingross, in-gros', *v.t.* Same as *Engross.*

Inguinal, in'gwi-nal, *a.* [L. *inguinalis*, from *inguen, inguinis*, the groin.] Pertaining to the groin.

Ingulf, in-gulf', *v.t.* To swallow up in or as in a gulf or whirlpool; to overwhelm by swallowing.—**Ingulfment**, in-gulf'ment, *n.* The act of ingulfing.

Ingurgitate, in-gėr'ji-tāt, *v.t.*—*ingurgitated, ingurgitating.* [L. *ingurgito, ingurgitatum*, to gorge—*in*, into, and *gurges*, a gulf. GORGE.] To swallow eagerly or in great quantity.—*v.i.* To drink largely; to swill.—**Ingurgitation**, in-gėr'ji-tā"shon, *n.* The act of ingurgitating.

Inhabit, in-hab'it, *v.t.* [L. *inhabito*—*in*, and *habito*, to dwell. HABIT.] To live or dwell in; to occupy as a place of settled residence.—*v.i.* To dwell; to live; to abide.—**Inhabitable**, in-hab'i-ta-bl, *a.* Capable of being inhabited; habitable.—**Inhabi-**

tance, **Inhabitancy**, in-hab'i-tans, in-hab'i-tan-si, *n.* The condition of an inhabitant; habitancy.—**Inhabitant**, in-hab'i-tant, *n.* [L. *inhabitans, inhabitantis,* ppr. of *inhabita.*] One who inhabits; one who dwells or resides permanently in a place, as distinguished from an occasional visitor.—**Inhabitation**, in-hab'i-tā"shon, *n.* The act of inhabiting; an abode.—**Inhabiter**, in-hab'i-tėr, *n.* One who inhabits; an inhabitant (N.T.).

Inhale, in-hāl', *v.t.*—*inhaled, inhaling.* [L. *inhalo*—*in*, in, into, and *halo*, to breathe, as in *exhale.*] To draw into the lungs; to inspire; to suck in.—**Inhaler**, in-hā'lėr, *n.* One who inhales; *med.* an apparatus for inhaling vapours and volatile substances, as steam of hot water, vapour of chloroform, iodine, &c.; a respirator.—**Inhalant**, **Inhalent**, in-hā'lant, in-hā'lent, *a.* Inhaling.—**Inhalation**, in-ha-lā'shon, *n.* The act of inhaling.

Inhance, in-hans', *v.t.* Same as *Enhance.*

Inharmonic, **Inharmonical**, in-här-mon'ik, in-här-mon'i-kal, *a.* Not harmonic; inharmonious; discordant.—**Inharmonious**, in-här-mō'ni-us, *a.* Not harmonious; discordant.—**Inharmoniously**, in-här-mō'ni-us-li, *adv.* In an inharmonious manner.—**Inharmoniousness**, **Inharmony**, in-här-mō'ni-us-nes, in-här'mo-ni, *n.* Want of harmony; discord.

Inhere, in-hēr', *v.i.*—*inhered, inhering.* [L. *inhæreo, inhæsum*—*in.* and *hæreo*, to stick, as in *adhere, cohere, hesitate.*] To exist or be fixed in; to belong, as attributes or qualities, to a subject; to be innate.—**Inherence**, **Inherency**, in-hē'rens, in-hē'ren-si, *n.* The state of inhering; existence in something.—**Inherent**, in-hē'rent, *a.* [L. *inhærens, inhærentis*, ppr. of *inhæreo.*] Inhering; inseparable; naturally pertaining; inborn; innate.—**Inherently**, in-hē'rent-li, *adv.* In an inherent manner.—**Inhesion**, in-hē'zhon, *n.* [L. *inhæsio.*] Inherence.

Inherit, in-her'it, *v.t.* [O.Fr. *enheriter*, L. *inhæredito*, to inherit, from *hæres, hæredis*, an heir. HEIR.] To receive or obtain by descent from an ancestor; to take by being the heir; to receive from a progenitor as part of one's nature; to come into possession of; to hold as belonging to one's lot.—*v.i.* To take an inheritance; to take the position of heir or heirs.—**Inheritability**, in-her'i-ta-bil"i-ti, *n.* The quality of being inheritable.—**Inheritable**, in-her'i-ta-bl, *a.* Capable of being inherited; capable of being transmitted from parent to child.—**Inheritably**, in-her'i-ta-bli, *adv.* By inheritance.—**Inheritance**, in-her'i-tans, *n.* That which is or may be inherited; an estate derived or to be derived from an ancestor to his heir; a possession received by gift or without purchase.—**Inheritor**, in-her'i-tėr, *n.* One who inherits or may inherit; an heir.—**Inheritress**, **Inheritrix**, in-her'it-res, in-her'it-riks, *n.* An heiress.

Inhesion, in-hē'zhon, *n.* Under INHERE.

Inhibit, in-hib'it, *v.t.* [L. *inhibeo, inhibitum*, to restrain—*in*, in, and *habeo*, to have. HABIT.] To restrain by command or interdict; to hinder; to forbid, prohibit, or interdict.—**Inhibiter**, in-hib'i-tėr, *n.* One who inhibits.—**Inhibition**, in-hi-bish'on, *n.* [L. *inhibitio.*] The act of inhibiting; prohibition; a legal writ inhibiting a judge from further proceeding in a cause.—**Inhibitory**, in-hib'i-to-ri, *a.* Conveying an inhibition; prohibitory.

Inhospitable, in-hos'pi-ta-bl, *a.* [Prefix *in*, not, and *hospitable.*] Not hospitable; wanting in hospitality; hence, affording no subsistence or shelter to strangers (*inhospitable* shores).—**Inhospitality**, **Inhospitableness**, in-hos'pi-tal"i-ti, in-hos'pi-ta-bl-nes, *n.* The quality of being inhospitable.—**Inhospitably**, in-hos'pi-ta-bli, *adv.* In an inhospitable manner.

Inhuman, in-hū'man, *a.* [Prefix *in*, not, and *human*; L. *inhumanus.*] Destitute of the kindness and tenderness that belong to human beings; cruel; barbarous; savage; unfeeling.—**Inhumanity**, in-hū-man'i-ti, *n.* [L. *inhumanitas.*] The state of being inhuman.—**Inhumanly**, in-hū'man-li, *adv.* In an inhuman manner.

Inhume, in-hūm', *v.t.*—*inhumed, inhuming.* [Fr. *inhumer*, L. *inhumo, inhumatum*—*in*, in, and *humus*, the ground. HUMBLE.] To deposit in the earth; to bury; to inter (a dead body).—**Inhumation**, in-hū-mā'shon, *n.* The act of burying; interment.

Inia, in'i-a, *n.* A cetaceous animal belonging to the dolphin family, frequenting the tributaries of the river Amazon.

Inial. Under INION.

Inimical, in-im'i-kal, *a.* [L. *inimicus*—*in*, not, and *amicus*, friendly. AMICABLE.] Unfriendly; hostile; adverse; hurtful (*inimical* to commerce).—**Inimicality**, in-im'i-kal"i-ti, *n.* The state of being inimical.—**Inimically**, in-im'i-kal-li, *adv.* In an inimical manner.

Inimitable, in-im'i-ta-bl, *a.* [Prefix *in*, not, and *imitable.*] Incapable of being imitated or copied; surpassing imitation.—**Inimitability**, **Inimitableness**, in-im'i-ta-bil"i-ti, in-im'i-ta-bl-nes, *n.* The quality of being inimitable.—**Inimitably**, in-im'i-ta-bli, *adv.* In an inimitable manner.

Inion, in'i-on, *n.* [Gr. *inion*, the nape.] *Anat.* the ridge of the occiput; the nape.—**Inial**, in'i-al, *a.* Pertaining to the inion.

Iniquity, in-ik'wi-ti, *n.* [L. *iniquitas*, from *iniquus*, unequal, from *in*, not, and *æquus*, equal. EQUAL.] Want of equity; a deviation from rectitude; unrighteousness; a sin or crime; wickedness; an act of injustice.—**Iniquitous**, in-ik'wi-tus, *a.* Characterized by iniquity; unjust; wicked; unrighteous.—**Iniquitously**, in-ik'wi-tus-li, *adv.* In an iniquitous manner.

Initial, in-ish'al, *a.* [L. *initialis*, from *initium*, beginning, from *ineo, initum*, to go in—*in*, in, and *eo, itum*, to go, present also in *ambition, exit, circuit, issue, transient*, &c. AMBITION.] Placed at the beginning (an *initial* letter); of or pertaining to the beginning; beginning; incipient.—*n.* The first letter of a word: a person's *initials* are the first letters in proper order of the words composing his name.—*v.t.*—*initialled, initialling.* To put one's initials on or to; to sign or mark by initials.—**Initially**, in-ish'al-li, *adv.* In an initial manner; by way of beginning.—**Initiate**, in-ish'i-āt, *v.t.*—*initiated, initiating.* [L. *initio, initiatum*, from *initium.*] To begin or enter upon; to set afoot; to be the first to practise or bring in; to guide or direct by instruction in rudiments or principles; to let into secrets; to indoctrinate; to introduce into a society or organization; to admit.—*a.* Initiated; introduced to the knowledge of something.—**Initiation**, in-ish'i-ā"shon, *n.* The act or process of initiating.—**Initiative**, in-ish'i-ā-tiv, *a.* Serving to initiate; initiatory.—*n.* An introductory act or step; the first active procedure in any enterprise; power of taking the lead or of originating.—**Initiatory**, in-ish'i-a-to-ri, *a.* Pertaining to initiation or introduction; introductory; initiating or serving to initiate.

Inject, in-jekt', *v.t.* [L. *injicio, injectum*—*in*, into, and *jacio*, to throw, as in *abject, eject, reject*, &c. DEJECT, JET.] To throw in; to cast in or into.—**Injection**, in-jek'shon, *n.* The act of injecting; the throwing of a liquid medicine into a cavity of the body by a syringe or pipe; that which is injected.—*Injection pipe*, a pipe through which water is injected into the condenser of a steam-engine, to condense the steam.—**Injector**, in-jek'tėr, *n.* One who or that which injects; an apparatus for supplying the boilers of steam-engines with water.

Injudicial, in-jū-dish'al, *a.* [Prefix *in*, not, and *judicial.*] Not judicial; not according to the forms of law.

Injudicious, in-jū-dish'us, *a.* [Prefix *in*, not, and *judicious.*] Not judicious; acting without judgment; not according to sound judgment or discretion; unwise; indiscreet; inconsiderate.—**Injudiciously**, in-jū-dish'us-li, *adv.* In an injudicious manner.—**Injudiciousness**, in-jū-dish'us-nes, *n.*

Injunction, in-jungk'shon, *n.* [L. *injunctio, injunctionis*, from *injungo*, to enjoin—*in*, and *jungo*, to join. JOIN.] The act of enjoining or directing; that which is enjoined; a command, order, precept; *law*, a writ requiring a person to do or refrain from doing certain acts.

Injure, in'jur, *v.t.*—*injured, injuring.* [Fr. *injurier*, L. *injurior, injuriari*, from *injuria*, injury, *injurius*, injurious, from *in*, not, and *jus, juris*, right, justice. JURY.] To do harm or injury to; to impair the excellence, value, strength, &c., of; to hurt; to damage.—**Injurer**, in'jur-ėr, *n.* One who or that which injures.—**Injurious**, in-jū'ri-us, *a.* [L. *injurius.*] Tending to injure; hurtful; harmful; prejudicial.—**Injuriously**, in-jū'ri-us-li, *adv.* In an injurious or hurtful manner.—**Injuriousness**, in-jū'ri-us-nes, *n.* The quality of being injurious.—**Injury**, in'ju-ri, *n.* [L. *injuria*, from *injurius.*] The doing of harm; harm or damage occasioned; a wrong or loss received; mischief; detriment.

Injustice, in-jus'tis, *n.* [L. *injustitia*—*in*, not, and *justitia*, justice.] Want of justice or equity; any violation of another's rights; iniquity; wrong.

Ink, ingk, *n.* [O.E. *enke, inke*, O.Fr. *enque* (Fr. *encre*), Pr. *encaut*, from L. *encaustum*, purple ink used by the Roman emperors, from Gr. *enkaustos*, burned in—*en*, in, and *kaiō*, to burn (whence *caustic, encaustic, calm*).] A coloured liquid, usually black, used for writing, printing, and the like; a pigment, as China or Indian *ink* (under INDIAN).—*v.t.* To blacken, colour, or daub with ink.—**Ink-bag**, **Ink-sac**, *n.* A sac found in some cuttle-fishes, containing a black viscid fluid resembling ink, by ejecting which they discolour the water and escape from enemies.—**Ink-fish**, *n.* The cuttle-fish.—**Inkhorn**, ingk'horn, *n.* [From horns being formerly used for holding ink.] A small vessel used to hold ink on a writing table or desk, or for carrying it about the person.—**Inkiness**, ingk'i-nes, *n.* The state or quality of being inky.—**Inking-roller**, *n.* A soft tough roller made of glue and treacle, used by printers to supply the types with ink.—**Inking-table**, *n.* A table on which to spread the ink and supply the inking-roller.—**Ink-stand**, ingk'stand, *n.* A vessel for holding ink and other writing utensils.—**Ink-well**, *n.* An ink-bottle fitted into a hole in the top of a writing-desk.—**Inky**, ingk'i, *a.* Consisting of ink; containing ink; smeared with ink; resembling ink; black.

Inkle, ingk'l, *n.* [Formerly *lingle*, then, by loss of *l*, *ingle, inkle*, from Fr. *ligneul, lignol*, strong thread used by shoemakers, L. *linum*, flax (whence *linen*).] Formerly, a kind of crewel or worsted; afterwards a sort of broad linen tape.

Inkling, ingk'ling, *n.* [Prefix *in* or *en*, and Fr. *clin*, a wink, *cligner*, to wink, L. *clinare*, to bend, as in *inclinare*, to incline.] A hint or whisper; an intimation; inclination; desire.—**Inkle**, ingk'l, *v.t.* To guess; to conjecture. (*Colloq.*)

Inlaid, in-lād', pp. of *inlay.*

Inland, in'land, *a.* [That is, *in the land* or interior as opposed to the coast.] Interior; remote from the sea; carried on within a country; domestic, not foreign; confined to a country; drawn and payable in the same country (an *inland* bill of exchange).—*adv.* In or towards the interior of a country.—*n.* The interior part of a country.—**Inlander**, in'lan-dėr, *n.* One who lives in the interior of a country.—*Inland Revenue*, the revenue raised by taxes or duties on commodities or products made in the country, as opposed to customs-duties on imported goods.

Inlay, in-lā', *v.t.*—pret. & pp. *inlaid.* [*In* and *lay.*] To lay or insert in; to ornament or diversify by inserting precious stones, metals, fine woods, ivory, &c., in a groundwork of some other material.—*n.* Pieces inlaid and forming a pattern.—**Inlayer**, in-lā'ėr, *n.* One who inlays.

Inlet, in'let, *n.* [Something *let in.*] A passage or opening by which an inclosed place may be entered; place of ingress; entrance; a creek or narrow recess in a shore.

Inlier, in-lī'ėr, *n.* *Geol.* a portion of one formation lying in and completely surrounded by another formation: opposed to *outlier*.

Inlock, in-lok', *v.t.* To lock or inclose one thing within another.

Inly, in'li, *adv.* [Adv. *in*, and suffix *-ly*.] Internally; in the heart; secretly.

Inmate, in'māt, *n.* [*In* or *inn*, and *mate*.] A person who lodges or dwells in the same house with another; one of the occupants of hospitals, asylums, prisons, &c.

Inmesh, in-mesh', *v.t.* Same as Enmesh. To involve in meshes, as of a net; to entangle or ensnare.

Inmost, in'mōst, *a.* [A.Sax. *innemest*, a double superlative of the prep. or adv. *in*, altered erroneously like *foremost*. FOREMOST.] Farthest within; remotest from the surface or external part.

Inn, in, *n.* [A.Sax. *inn*, a chamber, a house, an inn; Icel. *inni*, a house; from the prep. *in*.] A house for the lodging and entertainment of travellers; a college of law professors and students.—*Inns of Court*, certain colleges or corporate societies in London, to one of which all barristers and serjeants-at-law and all aspirants to these dignities must belong; they are now four, the Inner Temple, the Middle Temple, Lincoln's Inn, and Gray's Inn.—**Innkeeper**, in'kē-pėr, *n.* The keeper of an inn; a taverner.

Innate, in-nāt', *a.* [L. *innatus*—*in*, in, and *natus*, born. NATAL.] Inborn; belonging to the body or mind by nature; natural; derived from the constitution of the mind, as opposed to being derived from experience (*innate* ideas).—**Innately**, in-nāt'li, *adv.* In an innate manner.—**Innateness**, in-nāt'nes, *n.* The quality of being innate.

Inner, in'ėr, *a.* [A.Sax. *innera*, compar. of *in*.] Interior; farther inward than something else; internal; not outward (the *inner* man); not obvious; esoteric.—*n.* The centre, or that part of a rifle target next the bull's-eye; a shot that strikes the centre.—**Innermost**, in'ėr-mōst, *a.* Farthest inward.

Innerve, in-nėrv', *v.t.* [Prefix *in*, in, and *nerve*.] To give nerve to; to invigorate; to strengthen.—**Innervation**, in-nėr-vā'shon, *n.* Act of innerving or strengthening; *physiol.* the properties or functions of the nervous system; a special activity in any part of the nervous system.

Inning, in'ing, *n.* [Lit. the state of being *in*; a sort of verbal noun.] *Baseball, Cricket*, &c. A team's turn at bat and to score; opposing teams having innings each in a game of baseball; a turn or opportunity in other ways.

Innocent, in'nō-sent, *a.* [L. *innocens*, *innocentis*, harmless—*in*, not, and *nocens*, ppr. of *noceo*, to hurt. NOXIOUS.] Not noxious or hurtful; innoxious; free from guilt; not having done wrong or violated any law; guiltless; sinless; pure; upright; free from the guilt of a particular crime or evil action.—*n.* One free from guilt or harm; an innocent person; a natural or simpleton.—**Innocently**, in'nō-sent-li, *adv.* In an innocent manner.—**Innocence**, **Innocency**, in'nō-sens, in'nō-sen-si, *n.* [L. *innocentia*.] The quality of being innocent; harmlessness; freedom from crime, guilt, or sin; freedom from the guilt of a particular crime.

Innocuous, in-nok'ū-us, *a.* [L. *innocuus*—*in*, not, and *nocuus*, hurtful, from *noceo*, to hurt. INNOCENT.] Harmless; producing no ill effect.—**Innocuously**, in-nok'ū-us-li, *adv.* In an innocuous manner.—**Innocuity**, **Innocuousness**, in-no-kū'i-ti, in-nok'ū-us-nes, *n.*

Innominable, in-nom'i-na-bl, *a.* [L. *innominabilis*—*in*, not, and *nomen*, a name.] Not to be named.—**Innominate**, in-nom'i-nāt, *a.* [L. *innominatus*.] Having no name.—*Innominate bone*, the bony mass forming either side of the pelvis and consisting of three bones that have grown together.

Innovate, in'nō-vāt, *v.t.*‡—*innovated*, *innovating*. [L. *innovo*, *innovatum*, to renew—*in*, intens., and *novus*, new (whence *novel*). NEW.] To change or alter by introducing something new.—*v.i.* To introduce novelties; to make changes in anything established: with *on* or *in* (to *innovate on* established customs).—**Innovation**, in-nō-vā'shon, *n.* The act of innovating; change made in established laws, customs, rites, and practices by the introduction of something new.—**Innovator**, in'nō-vā-tėr, *n.* One who innovates.—**Innovationist**, in-nō-vā'shon-ist, *n.* One who favours or introduces innovations.—**Innovative**, in'nō-vā-tiv, *a.* Introducing or tending to introduce innovations.

Innoxious, in-nok'shus, *a.* [L. *innoxius*—*in*, not, and *noxius*, hurtful. NOXIOUS.] Free from mischievous qualities; innocent; harmless.—**Innoxiously**, in-nok'shus-li, *adv.*—**Innoxiousness**, in-nok'shus-nes, *n.*

Innuendo, in-nū-en'dō, *n.* [L. *innuendo* (ablative of gerund), by giving a nod, *innuo*, to give a nod—*in*, and *nuo*, Gr. *neuō*, to nod.] An oblique hint; a remote intimation; an insinuation.—**Innuent**, in'nū-ent, *a.* [L. *innuens*, *innuentis*, ppr. of *innuo*.] Conveying a hint; insinuating; significant.

Innumerable, in-nū'mėr-a-bl, *a.* [L. *innumerabilis*—*in*, not, and *numerabilis*, from *numero*, to number.] Incapable of being enumerated or numbered for multitude; hence, extremely numerous; countless.—**Innumerably**, in-nū'mėr-a-bli, *adv.* Without number.—**Innumerous**,† in-nū'mėr-us, *a.* [L. *innumerus*.] Innumerable. [*Mil.*]—**Innumerability**, **Innumerableness**, in-nū'mėr-a-bil"i-ti, in-nū'mer-a-bl-nes, *n.*

Innutrition, in-nu-trish'on, *n.* [Prefix *in*, not, and *nutrition*.] Want of nutrition or nourishment.—**Innutritious**, **Innutritive**, in-nū-trish'us, in-nū'tri-tiv, *a.* Not nutritious; not nourishing.

Inobservable, in-ob-zėr'va-bl, *a.* [Prefix *in*, not, and *observable*.] Incapable of being seen, perceived, or observed.—**Inobservance**, in-ob-zėr'vans, *n.* Want of observance; disobedience.—**Inobservant**, in-ob-zėr'vant, *a.* [Prefix *in*, not, and *observant*.] Not taking notice; not quick or keen in observation; heedless; disobedient.—**Inobservantly**, in-ob-zėr'vant-li, *adv.* In an inobservant manner.

Inobtrusive, in-ob-trö'siv, *a.* [Prefix *in*, not, and *obtrusive*.] Unobtrusive.—**Inobtrusively**, in-ob-trö'siv-li, *adv.* Unobtrusively.

Inoculate, in-ok'ū-lāt, *v.t.*—*inoculated*, *inoculating*. [L. *inoculo*, *inoculatum*, to ingraft an eye or bud of one tree into another—*in*, into, and *oculus*, an eye (whence *ocular*).] To graft by inserting a bud; to bud; *med.* to communicate a disease to by morbid matter introduced into the blood, especially that of small-pox; hence, generally, to infect, to contaminate.—*v.i.* To practise inoculation.—**Inoculable**, in-ok'ū-la-bl, *a.* Capable of being inoculated, or of being communicated by inoculation.—**Inoculation**, in-ok'ū-lā"shon, *n.* The act or practice of inoculating; communication of a disease by contagious matter introduced into the blood; especially artificial communication of small-pox formerly employed instead of vaccination.—**Inoculator**, in-ok'ū-lā-tėr, *n.* One who inoculates.

Inodorous, in-ō'dėr-us, *a.* [Prefix *in*, not, and *odorous*.] Wanting scent; having no smell.—**Inodorousness**, in-ō'dėr-us-nes, *n.*

Inoffensive, in-of-fen'siv, *a.* [Prefix *in*, and *offensive*.] Giving no offence or provocation; harmless; doing no injury or mischief.—**Inoffensively**, in-of-fen'siv-li, *adv.* In an inoffensive manner.—**Inoffensive**, in-of-fen'siv-nes, *n.*

Inofficial, in-of-fish'al, *a.* [Prefix *in*, not, and *official*.] Not official; not proceeding from the proper officer; not done in an official character.—**Inofficially**, in-of-fish'al-li, *adv.* In an inofficial manner.

Inoperative, in-op'e-rā-tiv, *a.* [Prefix *in*, not, and *operative*.] Not operative; producing no effect.

Inopercular, in-ō-pėr'kū-lėr, *n.* [L. *in*, not, and *operculum*, a lid.] Having no operculum.

Inopportune, in-op'por-tūn, *a.* [Prefix *in*, not, and *opportune*; L. *inopportunus*.] Not opportune; inconvenient; unseasonable.—**Inopportunely**, in-op'por-tūn-li, *adv.* In an inopportune manner.

Inordinate, in-or'di-nāt, *a.* [L. *inordinatus*—*in*, not, and *ordinatus*, well-ordered. ORDER.] Excessive; immoderate; not limited by rules prescribed or to usual bounds.—**Inordinacy**, **Inordinateness**, in-or'di-na-si, in-or'di-nāt-nes, *n.* The state or quality of being inordinate.—**Inordinately**, in-or'di-nāt-li, *adv.* In an inordinate manner; excessively.

Inorganic, in-or-gan'ik, *a.* [Prefix *in*, not, and *organic*.] Having no organs; devoid of an organized structure, or the structure of a living being; pertaining to or embracing the department of unorganized substances (*inorganic* chemistry).—**Inorganical**, in-or-gan'i-kal, *a.* Inorganic.—**Inorganically**, in-or-gan'i-kal-li, *adv.* In an inorganic manner; without organs or organization.—**Inorganization**, in-or'gan-i-zā"shon, *n.* The state of being inorganized.—**Inorganized**, in-or'gan-īzd, *a.* Void of organs; unorganized.

Inosculate, in-os'kū-lāt, *v.i.*—*inosculated*, *inosculating*. [L. *in*, and *osculor*, *osculatus*, to kiss. OSCULATION.] To unite by apposition or contact, as arteries, nerves, geometrical curves, &c.; to anastomose; to run into one another.—*v.t.*—*inosculated*, *inosculating*. To cause to unite in this way.—**Inosculation**, in-os'kū-lā"shon, *n.* The act of inosculating; a point where vessels are inosculated; anastomosis.

Inosite, ī'no-sit, *n.* Gr. *is*, *inos*, strength, nerve.] A saccharine substance found in the human body and also in plants.

In-patient, *n.* A patient who is lodged, fed, and treated in hospital or infirmary.

Inphase, in'fāz, *a.* *Elec.* In the same phase.

Input, in'put, *n.* Amount put in, as power into a machine or electric apparatus.

Inquest, in'kwest, *n.* [O.Fr. *enquests*, from L. *inquiro*, to seek after. INQUIRE.] Act of inquiring; inquiry; search; *law*, a judicial inquiry, especially one before a jury; the jury itself.—*Coroner's inquest*, an inquest held by a coroner on bodies of such as die a violent death.

Inquietude, in-kwī'e-tūd, *n.* [L. *inquietudo*—*in*, not, and *quietudo*, quietude.] Want of quiet; restlessness; uneasiness, either of body or mind.

Inquire, in-kwīr', *v.i.*—*inquired*, *inquiring*. [L. *inquiro*, to seek after—*in*, into, and *quæro*, to seek. QUERY, QUEST.] To ask a question or questions; to seek for information by asking questions; to seek for truth by argument or the discussion of questions, or by investigation (to *inquire* of a person, *after*, *concerning*, *into*, &c., a thing).—*v.t.* To ask about; to seek by asking (to *inquire* the way of a person).—**Inquirer**, in-kwī'rėr, *n.* One who inquires; an investigator.—**Inquiringly**, in-kwī'ring-li, *adv.* In an inquiring manner; by way of inquiry.—**Inquiry**, in-kwī'ri, *n.* [From *inquire*, like *expiry* from *expire*.] The act of inquiring; a question or interrogation; search for information or knowledge; research; investigation.

Inquisition, in-kwi-zish'on, *n.* [L. *inquisitio*, *inquisitionis*, from *inquiro*, *inquisitum*, to seek after. INQUIRE.] The act of inquiring; inquiry; investigation; a judicial inquiry; an inquest; in *R. Cath. Ch.* a court or tribunal established for the examination and punishment of heretics, and which formerly in some countries was the means of great cruelties being perpetrated.—**Inquisitional, Inquisitionary**, in-kwi-zish'on-al, in-kwi-zish'on-a-ri, *a.* Pertaining or relating to inquisition or inquiry; relating to the Inquisition.—**Inquisitive**, in-kwiz'i-tiv, *a.* Addicted to inquiry; inclined to seek information; given to pry into anything; troublesomely curious; prying.—**Inquisitively**, in-kwiz''i-tiv-li, *adv.* In an inquisitive manner.—**Inquisitiveness**, in-kwiz'i-tiv-nes, *n.* The quality of being inquisitive.—**Inquisitor**, in-kwiz'i-tėr, *n.* One whose official duty it is to inquire and examine; a member of the Inquisition.—**Inquisitorial**, in-kwiz'i-tō''ri-al, *a.* Pertaining to inquisition, especially to the Court of Inquisition; making strict or searching inquiry.—**Inquisitorially**, in-kwiz'i-tō''ri-al-li, *adv.* In an inquisitorial manner.

Inroad, in'rōd, *n.* [A *road* or rather a *raid* or riding into a country.] The hostile entrance of an enemy into a country; a sudden incursion or invasion; an encroachment; loss or impairment (to make *inroads* on one's health).

Inroll, in-rōl', *v.t.*—**Inrolment**, in-rōl'-ment, *n.* **Enrol, Enrolment**.

Insalivation, in-sal'i-vā''shon, *n.* The blending of the saliva with the food in eating.

Insalubrious, in-sa-lū'bri-us, *a.* [Prefix *in*, not, and *salubrious*.] Not salubrious; unfavourable to health; unhealthy.—**Insalubrity**, in-sa-lū'bri-ti, *n.* The state or quality of being insalubrious; unhealthiness.

Insalutary, in-sal'ū-ta-ri, *a.* [Prefix *in*, not, and *salutary*.] Not salutary; unhealthy; productive of evil.

Ins and outs, *n.* The parties out of or in office, as 'the haves and have-nots', those with and without property or possessions.

Insane, in-sān', *a.* [Prefix *in*, not, and *sane*; L. *insanus*.] Not sane; unsound or deranged in mind or intellect; mad; crazy; delirious; distracted; intended for insane persons.—**Insanely**, in-sān'li, *adv.* In an insane manner.—**Insanity, Insaneness**, in-san'i-ti, in-sān'nes, *n.* The state of being insane or of unsound mind; madness; lunacy.

Insanitary, in-san'i-ta-ri, *n.* [Prefix *in*, not, and *sanitary*.] Not sanitary; injurious to health.

Insatiable, in-sā'shi-a-bl, *a.* [Prefix *in*, not, and *satiable*; L. *insatiabilis*.] Incapable of being satiated, satisfied, or appeased.—**Insatiability, Insatiableness**, in-sā'shi-a-bil''i-ti, in-sā'shi-a-bl-nes, *n.* The quality of being insatiable.—**Insatiably**, in-sā'shi-a-bli, *adv.* In an insatiable manner.—**Insatiate**, in-sā'shi-āt, *a.* [L. *insatiatus*.] Not satisfied; insatiable.—**Insatiately**, in-sā'shi-āt-li, *adv.* In an insatiate manner.—**Insatiateness, Insatiety**, in-sā'shi-āt-nes, in-sa-tī'e-ti, *n.* State of not being satiated.

Inscient, in'si-ent, *a.* [L. *in*, not, and *sciens, scientis*, ppr. of *scio*, to know. SCIENCE.] Not knowing; ignorant.—**Inscience**, in'si-ens, *n.* [L. *inscientia*.] Ignorance; want of knowledge.

Insconce, in-skons', *v.t.* To ensconce.

Inscribe, in-skrīb', *v.t.*—*inscribed, inscribing.* [L. *inscribo, inscriptum*—*in*, and *scribo*, to write. DESCRIBE.] To write down or engrave; to mark down (to *inscribe* a motto); to mark with characters or words (to *inscribe* a monument); to assign, address, or dedicate (to *inscribe* a poem to a person); to imprint deeply; to impress; *geom.* to draw or delineate within another figure so that the boundaries of the two are in contact at certain points.—**Inscribable**, in-skrī'ba-bl, *a.* Capable of being inscribed.—**Inscribableness**, in-skrī'ba-bl-nes, *n.*—**Inscriber**, in-skrī'bėr, *n.* One who inscribes.—**Inscriptible**, in-skrip'ti-bl, *a.* *Geom.* capable of being inscribed.—**Inscription**, in-skrip'shon, *n.* [L. *inscriptio, inscriptionis*.] The act of inscribing; any words or writing engraved on stone, metal, or other hard substance for public inspection; an address of a book, poem, &c., to a person as a mark of respect, less formal than a dedication; *numis.* the words placed in the middle of the reverse side of some coins and medals.—**Inscriptive**, in-skrip'tiv, *a.* Of the character of an inscription.

Inscrutable, in-skrö'ta-bl, *a.* [Fr. *inscrutable*, L. *inscrutabilis*—*in*, not, and *scrutor*, to search. SCRUTINY.] Incapable of being searched into and understood; incapable of being penetrated or understood by human reason; not to be satisfactorily accounted for or explained.—**Inscrutably**, in-skrö'ta-bli, *adv.* In an inscrutable manner.—**Inscrutability, Inscrutableness**, in-skrö'ta-bil''i-ti, in-skrö'ta-bl-nes, *n.*

Insculp,† in-skulp', *v.t.* [L. *insculpo*—*in*, and *sculpo*, to engrave.] To engrave; to carve.

Inseam, in-sēm', *v.t.* To impress or mark with a seam or cicatrix.

Insect, in'sekt, *n.* [L. *insectum*, something cut in (from their shape), from *inseco, insectum*, to cut into—*in*, into, and *seco*, to cut. DISSECT.] One of a class of small animals that in their mature state have the three divisions of the body—the head, thorax, and abdomen—always distinct from one another, and usually have three pairs of legs and two pairs of wings, as the numerous creatures known as flies, beetles, bees, &c.; a puny contemptible person.—*a.* Pertaining to insects; resembling an insect; mean; contemptible.—**Insecticide**, in-sek'ti-sīd, *n.* [*Insect*, and L. *cædo*, to kill.] One who or that which kills insects; the killing of insects.—**Insectivore**, in-sek'ti-vōr, *n.* [*Insect*, and L. *voro*, to devour.] An animal that eats insects.—**Insectivorous**, in-sek-tiv'ō-rus, *a.* Feeding or subsisting on insects; belonging to an order of animals (shrew, hedge-hog, mole) which live to a great extent on insects.

Insecure, in-sē-kūr', *a.* [Prefix *in*, not, and *secure*.] Not secure; not confident of safety; apprehensive of danger or loss; not sufficiently strong or guarded; not furnishing security or safety; unsafe.—**Insecurely**, in-sē-kūr'li, *adv.* In an insecure manner.—**Insecurity, Insecureness**, in-sē-kū'ri-ti, in-sē-kūr'nes, *n.* The state of being insecure; want of security.

Insensate, in-sen'sāt, *a.* [L.L. *insensatus*,—L. *in*, not, and *sensus*, sensation, sense. SENSE.] Destitute of sense or sensation; wanting sensibility; stupid.—**Insensateness**, in-sen'sāt-nes, *n.* The state of being insensate.

Insensible, in-sen'si-bl, *a.* [L. *insensibilis* —prefix *in*, not, and *sensibilis*, sensible.] Not apprehended by the senses; imperceptible; incapable of being felt or perceived; so slow or gradual that the stages are not noted; destitute of the power of feeling or perceiving; numb or dead to pain; not susceptible of emotion or passion; void of feeling; unfeeling; callous; apathetic; indifferent.—**Insensibly**, in-sen'si-bli, *adv.* In an insensible manner; imperceptibly; by slow degrees.—**Insensibility, Insensibleness**, in-sen'si-bil''i-ti, in-sen'si-bl-nes, *n.* The condition or quality of being insensible; dulness; apathy; numbness; torpor.—**Insensitive**, in-sen'si-tiv, *a.* Not sensitive; having little sensibility.—**Insensuous**, in-sen'sū-us, *a.* Not sensuous.—**Insentient**, in-sen'shi-ent, *a.* Not sentient.

Inseparable, in-sep'a-ra-bl, *a.* [Prefix *in*, not, and *separable*; L. *inseparabilis*.] Incapable of being separated or disjoined; not to be parted; always together.—**Inseparably**, in-sep'a-ra-bli, *adv.* In an inseparable manner.—**Inseparability, Inseparableness**, in-sep'a-ra-bil''i-ti, in-sep'a-ra-bl-nes, *n.*

Insert, in-sėrt', *v.t.* [L. *insero, insertum*—*in*, and *sero*, to put (as in *assert, exert, concert*). SERIES.] To set in or among; to put or thrust in; to introduce.—**Inserted**, in-sėr'ted, *p.* *Bot.* attached to or growing out of some part.—*Inserted column*, same as *Engaged Column*.—**Insertion**, in-sėr'shon, *n.* [L. *insertio*.] The act of inserting; something inserted; *bot.* the place or mode of attachment of an organ to its support; of a muscle, the end attached to a relatively movable part.

Insessores, in-ses-sō'rēz, *n. pl.* [Pl. of L. *insessor*, one that sits—*in*, and *sedeo*, to sit.] The order of perchers or passerine birds, comprehending all those which live habitually among trees, with the exception of the birds of prey and climbing birds.—**Insessorial**, in-ses-sō'ri-al, *a.* Belonging to the Insessores or perching birds.

Inset, in-set', *v.t.* To set in; to infix or implant.—*n.* (in'set). That which is set in; insertion.

Insheathe, in-shēᴛʜ', *v.t.* To hide or cover in a sheath.

Inshore, in'shōr, *a.* or *adv.* Near the shore.

Inshrine, in-shrīn', *v.t.* To enshrine.

Inside, in'sīd, *a.* [Lit., within the sides.] Being within; interior; internal.—*n.* That which is within; specifically, the entrails or bowels; an inside passenger in a vehicle.—*prep.* In the interior of; within.

Insidious, in-sid'i-us, *a.* [L. *insidiosus*, from *insidiæ*, an ambush, from *insideo*, to sit upon—*in*, in, upon, and *sedeo*, to sit. SIT.] Characterized by treachery or stealthy and guileful acts; treacherous; guileful; working evil secretly (an *insidious* person, plot, disease).—**Insidiously**, in-sid'i-us-li, *adv.* In an insidious manner.—**Insidiousness**, in-sid'i-us-nes, *n.*

Insight, in'sīt, *n.* [Prefix *in*, and *sight*.] Deep inspection or view; thorough knowledge; power of observation; discernment; penetration.

Insignia, in-sig'ni-a, *n. pl.* [L., pl. of *insigne*, a mark, neut. of *insignis*, remarkable—*in*, intens., and *signum*, a mark. SIGN.] Badges or distinguishing marks of office or honour; any characteristic marks or signs.

Insignificant, in-sig-nif'i-kant, *a.* [Prefix *in*, not, and *significant*.] Void of signification; having no weight or effect; unimportant; trivial or trifling; without weight of character; mean; contemptible.—**Insignificantly**, in-sig-nif'i-kant-li, *adv.* In an insignificant manner.—**Insignificance, Insignificancy**, in-sig-nif'i-kans, in-sig-nif'i-kan-si, *n.* The condition or quality of being insignificant.

Insincere, in-sin-sēr', *a.* [Prefix *in*, not, and *sincere*; L. *insincerus*.] Not sincere; dissembling; hypocritical; false; deceitful: of persons, statements, &c.—**Insincerely**, in-sin-sēr'li, *adv.* In an insincere manner.—**Insincerity**, in-sin-ser'i-ti, *n.* The quality of being insincere.

Insinuate, in-sin'ū-āt, *v.t.*—*insinuated, insinuating.* [L. *insinuo, insinuatum*—*in*, and *sinuo*, to wind, from *sinus*, a bending, curve, bosom.] To introduce gently, or as by a winding or narrow passage; hence, *refl.* to push or work gradually into favour; to introduce one's self by slow or artful means; to infuse gently or artfully; to instil (to *insinuate* a doubt); to hint or suggest.—*v.i.* To creep or wind; to act by insinuation; to make an insinuation; to wheedle.—**Insinuating**, in-sin'ū-āt-ing, *p.* and *a.* Given to or characterized by insinuation; wheedling; insensibly winning favour and confidence.—**Insinuatingly**, in-sin'ū-āt-ing-li, *adv.* In an insinuating manner.—**Insinuation**, in-sin'ū-ā''shon, *n.* [L. *insinuatio, insinuationis*. The act of insinuating; a wheedling manner; a suggestion, hint, or innuendo.—**Insinuative, Insinuatory**, in-sin'ū-ā-tiv, in-sin'ū-a-to-ri, *a.* Insinuating; stealing on the affections.—**Insinuator**, in-sin'ū-ā-tėr, *n.* One who insinuates.

Insipid, in-sip'id, *a.* [L. *insipidus*—*in*, not, and *sapidus*, savoury, from *sapio*, to taste. SAVOUR.] Tasteless; destitute of taste; vapid; wanting interest, spirit, life, or animation; dull, heavy, or uninteresting.—**Insipidity, Insipidness**, in-si-pid'i-ti, in-sip'id-nes, *n.* The quality of being insipid.—**Insipidly**, in-sip'id-li, *adv.* In an insipid manner.

Insist, in-sist', *v.i.* [L. *insisto*—*in*, and *sisto*, to stand, as in *consist, desist, persist, resist*, &c. STATE.] To rest, dwell, or dilate upon as a matter of special moment; to be persistent, urgent, peremptory, or pressing; usually with *on* or *upon*.—**Insistence** in-sis'tens, *n.* Act of insisting; persistency; urgency.

Insnare, in-snār', *v.t.*—*insnared, insnaring.* To catch in a snare; to entrap; to involve in difficulties or perplexities; to inveigle; to entangle.—**Insnarer**, in-snār'ėr, *n.* One that insnares.—**Insnaringly**, in-snār'ing-li, *adv.* So as to insnare.

Insobriety, in-sō-brī'e-ti, *n.* [Prefix *in*, not, and *sobriety*.] Want of sobriety; intemperance; drunkenness.

Insociable, in-sō'shi-a-bl, *a.* [Prefix *in*, not, and *sociable*.] Not sociable; unsociable; taciturn.—**Insociably**, in-sō'shi-a-bli, *adv.* In an unsociable manner; unsociably.—**Insociability**, in-sō'shi-a-bil''i-ti, *a.* The quality of being insociable.

Insolate, in'so-lāt, *v.t.*—*insolated, insolating.* [L. *insolo, insolatum*—*in*, and *sol*, the sun (whence *solar*).] To dry or prepare in the sun's rays; to expose to the heat of the sun.—**Insolation**, in-so-lā'shon, *n.* [L. *insolatio, insolationis*.] The act of exposing, or condition of being exposed, to the rays of the sun; sunstroke.

Insolent, in'sō-lent, *a.* [L. *insolens, insolentis*, contrary to custom, immoderate, haughty, insolent—*in*, not, and *solens*, ppr. of *soleo*, to be wont.] Showing haughty disregard of others; using rude and haughty or defiant language; overbearing; saucy; proceeding from insolence.—**Insolently**, in'sō-lent-li, *adv.* In an insolent manner.—**Insolence**, in'sō-lens, *n.* [L. *insolentia*, from *insolens*.] Haughtiness manifested in contemptuous and overbearing treatment of others; insolent language.

Insolidity, in-so-lid'i-ti, *n.* [Prefix *in*, not, and *solidity*.] Want of solidity.

Insoluble, in-sol'ū-bl, *a.* [Prefix *in*, not, and *soluble*.] Incapable of being dissolved, particularly by a liquid; not to be solved or explained.—**Insolubility, Insolubleness**, in-sol'ū-bil''i-ti, in-sol'ū-bl-nes, *n.* The quality of being insoluble.

Insolvable, in-sol'va-bl, *a.* [Prefix *in*, not, and *solvable*.] Not solvable; not to be solved or explained; not admitting solution.

Insolvent, in-sol'vent, *a.* [Prefix *in*, not, and *solvent*.] Not solvent; not having money, goods, or estate sufficient to pay all debts.—*n.* A debtor unable to pay his debts.—**Insolvency**, in-sol'ven-si, *n.* The condition of being insolvent; inability of a person to pay all his debts.

Insomnious, in-som'ni-us, *a.* [L. *insomniosus*, from *insomnia*, sleeplessness—*in*, not, and *somnus*, sleep.] Restless in sleep, or being without sleep.—**Insomnia**, in-som'ni-a, *n.* [L.] Want of sleep; morbid or unnatural sleeplessness.

Insomuch, in-sō-much', *adv.* [*In, so*, and *much*.] To such a degree; in such wise; so: followed by *that*, sometimes *as*.

Insouciant, aṅ-sö-syaṅ, *a.* [Fr.—*in*, not, and *soucier*, to care, *souci*, care, from L. *sollicitus*, uneasy, solicitous.] Careless; heedless; regardless; unconcerned.—**Insouciance**, aṅ-sö-syäṅs, *n.* The quality of being insouciant.

Inspan, in-span', *v.t.* [D. *inspannen*—*in*, in, and *spannen*, to yoke.] To yoke, as draught oxen: correlative of *outspan*. [South African]

Inspect, in-spekt', *v.t.* [L. *inspicio, inspectum*—*in*, and *specio*, to view. SPECIES.] To view or examine for the purpose of ascertaining the quality or condition, discovering errors, &c.; to examine officially.—**Inspection**, in-spek'shon, *n.* [L. *inspectio*.] The act of inspecting; official view or examination.—**Inspector**, in-spek'tėr, *n.* One who inspects or oversees. **Inspectorate**, in-spek'tėr-at, *n.* A body of inspectors or overseers; inspectorship.—**Inspectorship**, in-spek'tėr-ship, *n.* The office or district of an inspector.

Inspire, in-spīr', *v.i.*—*inspired, inspiring.* [L. *inspiro*—*in*, and *spiro*, to breathe, whence *spirit, expire, respire*.] To draw in breath; to inhale air into the lungs.—*v.t.* To breathe in; to draw into the lungs; to infuse by or as if by breathing; to instil; to communicate divine instructions to the mind of; to animate by supernatural infusion; to rouse or animate in general.—**Inspired**, in-spīrd, *p.* and *a.* Breathed in; inhaled; directed by the Holy Spirit; instructed or affected by a superior influence; produced under the direction or influence or inspiration (*inspired* writings).—**Inspirer**, in-spī'rėr, *n.* One who inspires.—**Inspiring**, in-spī'ring, *p.* and *a.* Infusing spirit or courage; animating.—**Inspirable**, in-spī'ra-bl, *a.* Capable of being inspired; inhalable.—**Inspiration**, in-spi-rā'shon, *n.* [L. *inspiratio*.] The act of inspiring; the divine influence by which the sacred writers were instructed; influence emanating from any object, giving rise to new and elevated thoughts or emotions; the state of being inspired; something conveyed to the mind when under extraordinary influence.—*Verbal, plenary inspiration*, the doctrine maintaining that the very words were inspired, as opposed to general inspiration by the Spirit; textual inerrancy.—**Inspirational**, in-spi-rā'shon-al, *a.* Pertaining to inspiration.—**Inspiratory**, in-spī'ra-to-ri, *a.* Pertaining to or assisting in inspiration (the *inspiratory* muscles).

Inspirit, in-spir'it, *v.i.* [Prefix *in*, and *spirit*.] To infuse or excite spirit in; to enliven, animate, encourage, invigorate.

Inspissate, in-spis'āt, *v.t.*—*inspissated, inspissating.* [L. *inspisso, inspissatum*—*in*, intens., and *spissus*, thick.] To thicken by boiling so as to evaporate the water; to bring to greater thickness by evaporation.—*a.* Thick; inspissated.—**Inspissation**, in-spis-ā'shon, *n.* The act or operation of inspissating.

Instable, in-stā'bl, *a.* [L. *instabilis*—*in*, not, and *stabilis*, stable.] Not stable; unstable.—**Instability**, in-sta-bil'i-ti, *n.* Want of stability; inconstancy; want of firmness in construction.

Install, in-stąl', *v.t.* [Fr. *installer*—*in*, in, and O.H.G. *stal*, a place, E. *stall*. STALL.] To place in an office or post; to invest formally with a charge, office, or rank; to set up or establish for use (as a heating system).—**Installation**, in-stą-lā'shon, *n.* Act of installing; something installed.—**Installment**, in-stąl'ment, *n.* Installation; a part of a whole (especially a novel) produced at stated periods; one part of a sum to be paid at stated intervals.

Instance, in'stans, [L. *instantia*, a standing near, importunity, urgency—*in*, on, and *sto*, to stand. STATE.] The act or state of being instant or urgent; urgency; a case occurring; a case offered as an exemplication or precedent; an example; an occurrence.—*v.t.*—*instanced, instancing.* To mention as an instance, example, or case in point.—**Instant**, in'stant, *a.* [E. *instans, instantis*.] Pressing, urgent, importunate, or earnest (N.T.); immediate; without intervening time (send him to *instant* execution); quick; making no delay; present or current: usually abbreviated to *inst.*, as 10th *inst.*, that is, 10th day of the present month.—*n.* A point in duration; a moment; a part of duration that occupies the time of a single thought.—**Instantaneity, Instantaneousness**, in'stanta-nē''i-ti, in-stan-tā'nē-us-nes, *n.* The quality of being instantaneous.—**Instantaneous**, in-stan-tā'nē-us, *a.* [Made on the model of *contemporaneous*.] Done in an instant; occurring without any perceptible lapse of time.—**Instantaneously**, in-stan-tā'nē-us-li, *adv.* In an instant; in a moment.—**Instanter**, in-stan'tėr, *adv.* [L., from *instans*.] Immediately; forthwith; on the moment.—**Instantly**, in'stant-li, *adv.* With urgency; earnestly; immediately; forthwith; at once.

Instate, in-stāt', *v.t.*—*instated, instating.* [Prefix *in*, and *state*.] To establish, as in a rank or condition; to install.

Instead, in-sted', *adv.* [From *in*, and *stead*, place; *stead* retaining its character o. a noun, and being followed by *of*.] In the place or room. [When *instead* is used without *of* following, there is an ellipsis of a word or words that would otherwise follow the *of*.]

Instep, in'step, *n.* [Formerly *instop, instup*, perhaps from *in* and *stoop*, lit. the bend in.] The forepart of the upper side of the human foot, near its junction with the leg; part of the hind leg of a horse from the ham to the pastern-joint.

Instigate, in'sti-gāt, *v.t.*—*instigated, instigating.* [L. *instigo, instigatum*—*in*, on, and root *stig*, to prick. INSTINCT, STIGMA.] To incite; to set on; to provoke; to urge: used chiefly or wholly in a bad sense.—**Instigation**, in-sti-gā'shon, *n.* [L. *instigatio*.] act of instigating; incitement, as to evil or wickedness.—**Instigator**, in'sti-gā-tėr, *n.* One who instigates.

Instill, Instil, in-stil', *v.t.*—*instilled, instilling.* [L. *instillo*—*in*, and *stillo*, to drop. DISTIL.] To pour in by drops; hence, to infuse slowly or by degrees into the mind; to cause to be imbibed; to insinuate imperceptibly.—**Instillation**, in-stil-ā'shon, *n.* The act of instilling.—**Instillatory**, in-stil'a-to-ri, *a.* Relating to instillation.—**Instiller**, in-stil'ėr, *n.* One who instills.—**Instillment**, in-stil'ment, *n.* The act of instilling.

Instinct, in'stingkt, *n.* [L. *instinctus*, instigation, impulse, from *instinguo, instinctum*, to impel—*in*, on, and root meaning to prick, as in *stimulus, sting*.] An impulse to a particular kind of action which the being needs to perform as an individual, but which it could not possibly learn to perform before it needs to act; as a general term it includes all original impulses and that apparent knowledge and skill which animals have without experience; hence, natural feeling or sense of what is correct or effective in artistic matters or the like.—*a.* (in-stingkt'). Animated or stimulated from within; inspired; fully suffused and breathing out (a portrait *instinct* with life).—**Instinctive**, in-stingk'tiv, *a.* Prompted by or proceeding from instinct; determined by natural impulse or propensity; spontaneous.—**Instinctively**, in-stingk'tiv-li, *adv.* In an instinctive manner.—**Instinctivity**, in-stingk-tiv'i-ti, *n.* The quality of being instinctive.

Institute, in'sti-tūt, *v.t.*—*instituted, instituting*, [L. *instituo, institutum*—*in*, and *statuo*, to set, place, from *sto, statum*, to stand. STATE.] To set up or establish; to ordain; to originate; to found; to set in operation; to begin (an investigation, &c.).—*n.* That which is instituted or formally established; an established law, precept, or principle; a society established according to certain laws or regulations for the furtherance of some particular object (a philosophic *institute*, a literary *institute*, a mechanics *institute*); *pl.* a book of elements or principles, particularly a work containing the principles of a system of jurisprudence.—**Institution**, in-sti-tū'shon, *n.* [L. *institutio*.] The act of instituting; *eccles.* the ceremony of investing a clerk with the spiritual part of a benefice; something instituted or established; a permanent rule of conduct or of government; something forming a prominent or established feature in social or national life; a society established or body organized for promoting any object, public or social.—**Institutional**, in-sti-tū'shon-al, *a.* Relating to institutions; instituted by authority; relating to elementary knowledge.—**Institutionary**, in-sti-tū'shon-a-ri, *a.* Relating to an institution or to institutions.—**Institutive**, in'sti-tū-tiv, *a.* Tending or intended to institute or establish.—**Institutor**, in'sti-tū-tėr, *n.* [L.] One who institutes.

Instruct, in-strukt', *v.t.* [L. *instruo, instructum*—*in*, and *struo*, to join together, to pile up.—STRUCTURE.] To teach; to educate; to impart knowledge or information to; to enlighten; to direct or command; to furnish with orders; to order or enjoin.—**Instructible**, in-struk'ti-bl, *a.* Capable of being instructed; teachable; docile. —**Instruction**, in-struk′shon, *n.* [L. *instructio.*] The act of instructing; that which is communicated for instructing; that with which one is instructed; information; order, mandate, or direction.—**Instructional**, in-struk′shon-al, *a.* Relating to instruction; educational. —**Instructive**, in-struk′tiv, *a.* Conveying knowledge; serving to instruct or inform.—**Instructively**, in-struk′tiv-li, *adv.* In an instructive manner.—**Instructiveness**, in-struk′tiv-nes. *n.*—**Instructor**, in-struk′tėr, *n.* [L.] One who instructs; a teacher.

Instrument, in′strụ-ment, *n.* [L. *instrumentum*, from *instruo*, to prepare. INSTRUCT.] That by which work is performed or anything is effected; a tool; a utensil; an implement; one who or that which is subservient to the execution of a plan or purpose; means used or contributing to an effect; any contrivance from which music is produced, as an organ, harp, violin, flute, &c.; *law*, a writing instructing one in regard to something that has been agreed upon.—**Instrumental**, in-strụ-men′tal, *a.* Conducive as an instrument or means to some end; pertaining to instruments, especially musical instruments.—**Instrumentalist**, in-strụ-men′tal-ist, *n.* One who plays upon a musical instrument.—**Instrumentality**, **Instrumentalness**, in′strụ-men-tal″i-ti, in-strụ-men′tal-nes, *n.* The condition of being instrumental; subordinate or auxiliary agency; agency as means to an end.—**Instrumentally**, in-strụ-men′tal-li, *adv.* By way of an instrument; as means to an end; with instruments of music.—**Instrumentation**, in′strụ-men-tā″shon, *n.* The art of arranging music for a number of instruments; the music for a number of instruments; execution of music on an instrument.

Insubjection, in-sub-jek′shon, *n.* [Prefix *in*, not, and *subjection.*] Want of subjection; state of disobedience to government.

Insubmission, in-sub-mish′on, *n.* [Prefix *in*, not, and *submission.*] Want of submission; disobedience.

Insubordinate, in-sub-or′di-nāt, *a.* [Prefix *in*, not, and *subordinate.*] Not submitting to authority; mutinous; riotous.—*n.* One who is unruly.—**Insubordination**, in-sub-or′di-nā″shon, *n.* The quality of being insubordinate.

Insubstantial, in-sub-stan′shal, *a.* [Prefix *in*, not, and *substantial.*] Unsubstantial.

Insuetude, in′swē-tūd, *n.* [L. *insuetudo*, from *insuetus*, unaccustomed—*in*, not, and *suetus*, accustomed.] The state of being unaccustomed; absence of use or custom.

Insufferable, in-suf′fėr-a-bl, *a.* [Prefix *in*, not, and *sufferable.*] Not to be suffered, borne, or endured; intolerable; unendurable.—**Insufferably**, in-suf′fėr-a-bli, *adv.*

Insufficient, in-suf-fish′ent, *a.* [Prefix *in*, not, and *sufficient.*] Not sufficient; inadequate to any need, use, or purpose.—**Insufficiency**, in-suf-fish′en-si, *n.* The condition or quality of being insufficient.—**Insufficiently**, in-suf-fish′ent-li, *adv.* In an insufficient manner.

Insular, in′sū-lėr, *a.* [L. *insularis*, from *insula*, an island.] Of or pertaining to an island or the opinions or views of islanders; hence, narrow-minded (*insular* prejudices); contracted.—**Insularity**, in-sū-lar′i-ti, *n.* The state of being insular.—**Insularly**, in′sū-lėr-li, *adv.* In an insular manner.—**Insulate**, in′sū-lāt, *v.t.*—*insulated, insulating.* To make an island of; to isolate; to separate, as an electrified or heated body, from other bodies by inserting non-conductors; to free from combination with other substances, as a chemical substance. —**Insulation**, in-sū-lā′shon, *n.* The act of insulating, or state of being insulated; materials for insulating.—**Insulator**, in′sū-lā-tėr, *n.* One who or that which insulates; *elec.* a non-conducting piece, as of glass, used to insulate wires, &c.

Insulin, in′sū-lin, *n.* [L. *insula*, island, and *in.*] *Med.* Product of islands of Langerhans of the pancreas; a drug gotten from the organs of animals for diabetics.

Insult, in′sult, *n.* [Fr. *insulte*; L. *insultus*, from *insilio*, *insultum*, to leap on—*in*, and *salio*, to leap; seen also in *assail, assault, desultory, result, sally, salient.*] Any gross affront or indignity offered to another, either by words or actions; act or speech of insolence or contempt.—*v.t.* (in-sult′). To treat with insult, gross abuse, insolence, or contempt.—*v.i.* To behave with insolent triumph.—**Insulter**, in-sult′ėr, *n.* One who insults.—**Insulting**, in-sult′ing, *a.* Containing or conveying insult.—**Insultingly**, in-sult′ing-li, *adv.* In an insulting manner; so as to insult.

Insuperable, in-sū′pėr-a-bl, *a.* [L. *insuperabilis*—*in*, not, and *supero*, to overcome. SUPERIOR.] Incapable of being overcome or surmounted; insurmountable (difficulties, objections, obstacles, &c.).—**Insuperability**, **Insuperableness**, in-sū′pėr-a-bil″i-ti, in-sū′pėr-a-bl-nes, *n.* The quality of being insuperable.—**Insuperably**, in-sū′pėr-a-bli, *adv.* In an insuperable manner.

Insupportable, in-sup-pōr′ta-bl, *a.* [Prefix *in*, not, and *supportable.*] Not to be supported or borne; insufferable; intolerable.—**Insupportableness**, in-sup-pōr′ta-bl-nes, *n.*—**Insupportably**, in-sup-pōr′ta-bli, *adv.*

Insuppressible, in-sup-pres′i-bl, *a.* [Prefix *in*, not, and *suppressible.*] Incapable of being suppressed or concealed.—**Insuppressibly**, in-sup-pres′i-bli, *adv.* So as not to be suppressed.—**Insuppressive**,† in-sup-pres′iv, *a.* Not tending to suppress; insuppressible (*Shak.*).

Insure, in-shör′, *v.t.*—*insured, insuring.* [Prefix *in*, intens., and *sure.*] To make sure; to ensure (which is the word now commonly used in this general sense); to contract for the payment of a certain sum in the event of loss or damage happening to, or at the death or termination of (to *insure* a house against fire, a ship against damage, to *insure* one's life); to make a subject of insurance; to assure (one's life). —**Insurer**, in-shö′rėr, *n.* One who insures. —**Insurable**, in-shö′ra-bl, *a.* Capable of being insured.—**Insurance**, in-shö′rans, *n.* The act of insuring; a contract by which a person or company, in consideration of a sum of money or percentage (technically called a *premium*), becomes bound to indemnify the insured or his representatives against loss by certain risks; the premium paid for insuring property or life.—*Marine insurance* is the term used for the insurance on ships, goods, &c., at sea.—*Fire insurance* is for the insuring of property on shore from fire.—*Life insurance* is for securing the payment of a certain sum at the death of the individual insured, or when he reaches a given age, or of an annuity.—*Social Insurance*, a type of insurance which provides benefits for unemployment, sickness, old age, &c., obtained from funds into which usually the worker, employer, and government contribute.—*Insurance policy*, the document by which the insurance is ratified.

Insurgent, in-sėr′jent, *a.* [L. *insurgens*, *insurgentis*, ppr. of *insurgo*, to rise against —*in*, on, and *surgo*, to rise, whence *surge, source*, &c.] Rising in opposition to lawful civil or political authority; rebellious.—*n.* A person who rises in opposition to civil or political authority. ∴ An *insurgent* differs from a *rebel* in holding a less pronounced position of antagonism, and may or may not develop into a rebel. INSURRECTION.—**Insurgency**, in-sėr′jen-si, *n.* The condition of being insurgent.

Insurmountable, in-sėr-moun′ta-bl, *a.* [Prefix *in*, not, and *surmountable.*] Incapable of being surmounted, passed over, or overcome.—**Insurmountability**, **Insurmountableness**, in-sėr-moun′ta-bil″i-ti, in-sėr-moun′ta-bl-nes, *n.*—**Insurmountably**, in-sėr-moun′ta-bli, *adv.*

Insurrection, in-sėr-rek′shon, *n.* [L. *insurrectio, insurrectionis*, from *insurgo*, *insurrectum*. INSURGENT.] The open and active opposition of a number of persons to the civil or political authorities of a city or country, in defiance of law and order; a revolt by a number of persons against constituted authorities. ∴ An *insurrection* is less serious than a *rebellion*, for the latter attempts to overthrow the government, to establish a different one, or to place the country under another jurisdiction; a *mutiny* is a movement of revolt against minor institutions, or against the authorities in the army or navy; a *revolt* is a less strong form of a rebellion.—**Insurrectional**, **Insurrectionary**, in-sėr-rek′shon-al, in-sėr-rek′shon-a-ri, *a.* Pertaining to insurrection.—**Insurrectionist**, in-sėr-rek′shon-ist, *n.* One who favours insurrection.

Insusceptible, in-sus-sep′ti-bl, *a.* [Prefix *in*, not, and *susceptible.*] Not susceptible; not capable of being affected or impressed (a heart *insusceptible of* pity).—**Insusceptibility**, in-sus-sep′ti-bil″i-ti, *n.* The quality of being insusceptible.—**Insusceptive**, in-sus-sep′tiv, *a.* Not susceptive; not susceptible or receptive.

Intact, in-takt′, *a.* [L. *intactus*—prefix *in*, not, and *tactus*, touched, pp. of *tango*, to touch; whence also *tangent, tact*, &c.] Untouched by anything that harms or defiles; uninjured; unimpaired; left complete, whole, or unharmed.

Intaglio, in-tal′yō, *n.* [It., from *intagliare*, to carve—*in*, and *tagliare*, to cut, Fr. *tailler* (whence *tailor*). Any figure engraved or cut into a substance so as to form a hollow; a gem with a figure or device sunk below the background; the reverse of *cameo*, which has the figure in relief.—**Intagliated**, in-tal′yā-ted, *a.* Cut in intaglio.—*Intaglio relievato* (rel-i-ā-vä′-to). Same as *Cavo-relievo.*

Intake, in′tāk, *n.* A point where a water supply is diverted from a main stream; amount taken in (hourly *intake*).

Intangible, in-tan′ji-bl, *a.* [Prefix *in*, not, and *tangible.*] Not tangible; incapable of being touched; not perceptible to the touch.—**Intangibleness**, **Intangibility**, in-tan′ji-bl-nes, in-tan′ji-bil″i-ti, *n.*—*n. pl.* Certain properties, as good will.—**Intangibly**, in-tan′ji-bli, *adv.*

Integer, in′tē-jėr, *n.* [L. *integer*, whole, entire—*in*, not, and *tag*, root of *tango*, to touch. ENTIRE, TANGENT.] *Arith.* a whole number, in contradistinction to a fraction. —**Integral**, in′tē-gral, *a.* Whole; entire; complete; belonging to or forming a necessary part of a whole; *math.* pertaining to a whole number or undivided quantity; not fractional; pertaining to integration. —*Integral calculus*, a branch of mathematical analysis which is the inverse of the *differential calculus*, its object being the deriving of the primitive function from its differential, or its differential coefficient.—*n.* A whole; an entire thing.—**Integrally**, in′tē-gral-li, *adv.* In an integral manner. —**Integrant**, in′tē-grant, *a.* Making part of a whole; integral.—**Integrate**, in′tē-grāt, *v.t.*—*integrated, integrating.* [L. *integro, integratum.*] To make entire; to form into one whole; to perfect; to give the sum or total of.—**Integration**, in-tē-grā′shon, *n.* The act of integrating; *math.* the determination of a function from its differential or its differential coefficient.—**Integrity**, in-teg′ri-ti, *n.* [L. *integritas*, from *integer.*] The state of being entire or complete; entireness; a genuine or unimpaired state; honesty; uprightness in mutual dealings; probity.

Integument, in-teg′ū-ment, *n.* [L. *integumentum*, *intego*, to cover—*in*, intens., and *tego*, to cover (same root as E. *thatch*).] *Anat.* the skin, membrane, or shell which covers any part; *bot.* the cellular skin of seed, leaf, or stem.—**Integumentary**, in-teg′ū-men″ta-ri, *a.* Belonging to or composed of integument.—**Integumentation**, in-teg′ū-men-tā″shon, *n.* A covering with integument.

Intellect, in′tel-lekt, *n.* [L. *intellectus*, from *intelligo*, to understand—*inter*, between, and *lego*, to choose or pick, to read; seen also in *collect, elect, select, legend, lesson, lecture*, &c.] That faculty of the human mind which receives or comprehends ideas, as distinguished from the power to feel and to will; the understanding faculty; also, the capacity for higher forms of knowledge.—**Intellection**, in-tel-lek'shon, *n.* The act of understanding; simple apprehension.—**Intellective**, in-tel-lek'tiv, *a.* Pertaining to the intellect; perceivable by the understanding only, not by the senses.—**Intellectively**, in-tel-lek'tiv-li, *adv.* In an intellective manner.—**Intellectual**, in-tel-lek'tū-al, *a.* Relating to the intellect or understanding; appealing to or perceived by the intellect; existing in the understanding; ideal; having or characterized by intellect.—**Intellectualism**, in-tel-lek'tū-al-izm, *n.* Intellectuality; the doctrine that knowledge is derived from pure reason.—**Intellectualist**, in-tel-lek'tū-al-ist, *n.* One who overrates intellectualism.—**Intellectuality**, in-tel-lek'tū-al"li-ti, *n.* The state of being intellectual; intellectual power.—**Intellectualize**, in-tel-lek'tū-al-iz, *v.t.* To endow with intellect; to give an intellectual or ideal character to.—**Intellectually**, in-tel-lek'tū-al-li, *adv.* In an intellectual manner.—**Intelligence**, in-tel'i-jens, *n.* [L. *intelligentia.*] Intellectual power; knowledge imparted or acquired; general information; information communicated; news or notice; an intelligent or spiritual being.—*Intelligence quotient, Abbr. I.Q.*, mental rating found by test. (Divide age into mental age shown.) *Intelligence test*, a psychological test used to show comparative mental capacity.—**Intelligencer**, in-tel'i-jen-sėr, *n.* One who conveys intelligence; a messenger or spy.—**Intelligent**, in-tel'i-jent, *a.* [L. *intelligens, intelligentis*, ppr. of *intelligo.*] Endowed with the faculty of understanding or reason; endowed with a good intellect; having superior intellectual capacities; well informed.—**Intelligently**, in-tel'i-jent-li, *adv.* In an intelligent manner.—**Intelligibility**, **Intelligibleness**, in-tel'i-ji-bil"i-ti, in-tel'i-ji-bl-nes, *n.* The quality or state of being intelligible.—**Intelligible**, in-tel'i-ji-bl, *a.* [L. *intelligibilis.*] Capable of being understood or comprehended; comprehensible; clear.—**Intelligibly**, in-tel'i-gi-bli, *adv.*

Intelligentsia, in-tel-li-jen'si-a, *n. pl.* Intellectuals; the broadly educated.

Intemperance, in-tem'pėr-ans, *n.* [Prefix *in*, not, and *temperance*; L. *intemperantia*, want of moderation. TEMPER.] Want of moderation or due restraint; excess of any kind; specifically, habitual indulgence in the use of alcoholic liquors, especially with intoxication.—**Intemperant**, in-tem'pėr-ant, *n.* One who intemperantly indulges in alcoholic liquors.—**Intemperate**, in-tem'pėr-āt, *a.* [L. *intemperatus*, immoderate.] Not exercising due moderation or restraint; addicted to an excessive or habitual use of alcoholic liquors; excessive, immoderate, or inordinate (*intemperate* language).—*n.* One who is not temperate; an intemperant.—**Intemperately**, in-tem'pėr-āt-li, *adv.* In an intemperate manner.—**Intemperateness**, in-tem'pėr-āt-nes, *n.* State of being intemperate.

Intenable, in-ten'a-bl, *a.* [Prefix *in*, not, and *tenable.*] Not tenable; untenable.

Intend, in-tend', *v.t.* [L. *intendo*, to stretch forth, to intend—*in*, and *tendo*, to stretch (as in *attend, contend*, &c.). TEND.] To fix the mind upon, as the object to be effected or attained; to mean; to design; to purpose.—**Intendancy**, in-ten'dan-si, *n.* The office, employment, or district committed to the charge of an intendant.—**Intendant**, in-ten'dant, *n.* [Fr., from L. *intendo.*] One who has the charge or management of some public business; a superintendent.—**Intended**, in-ten'ded, *p.* and *a.* Betrothed; engaged.—*n.* A person engaged to be married to another; an affianced lover.—**Intendedly**, in-ten'ded-li, *adv.* With purpose or intention; by design.—**Intender**, *n.* One who intends.

Intense, in-tens', *a.* [L. *intensus*, stretched, tight, pp. of *intendo*, to stretch. INTEND.] Closely strained; kept on the stretch (study, thought, &c.); extreme in degree; vehement; violent; severe (pain, cold, &c.).—**Intensely**, in-tens'li, *adv.* In an intense manner.—**Intensative**, in-ten'sa-tiv, *a.* Adding intensity; intensifying.—**Intenseness**, in-tens'nes, *n.* The state of being intense. **Intensation**,† **Intensification**,† in-ten-sā'shon, in-ten'si-fi-kā"shon, *n.* The act of intensifying or making more intense.—**Intensifier**, in-ten'si-fī-ėr, *n.* One who or that which intensifies.—**Intensify**, in-ten'si-fī, *v.t.*—*intensified, intensifying.* To render intense or more intense.—*v.i.* To become intense or more intense.—**Intension**, in-ten'shon, *n.* [L. *intensio, intensionis.*] Act of straining or intensifying; the state of being strained: opposed to *remission* or *relaxation.*—**Intensity**, in-ten'si-ti, *n.* The state of being intense; relative degree, vigour, or activity; keenness (of feeling, &c.); *physics*, the amount of energy with which a force operates or a cause acts.—*Intensity of field*, the force experienced by a unit pole when placed in a field of magnetic force.—*Intensity of magnetization*, in a uniformly magnetized mass, is the quotient of the moment (q.v.) of the magnet by its volume.—*Intensity of pressure*, where the pressure is uniform over an area, is the total pressure divided by the area; measured in dynes or grammes per square centimetre or pounds per square inch.—**Intensive**, in-ten'siv, *a.* Serving to give force or emphasis (an *intensive* particle or prefix.—*Intensive cultivation*, thorough cultivation of the soil by free use of stimulating manures, &c.—*Intensive drill*, a method of drill especially adopted for particular purposes of attack by shock or storm troops in war. (*Recent.*)—**Intensively**, in-ten'siv-li, *adv.* In an intensive manner.—**Intensiveness**, in-ten'siv-nes, *n.* The quality of being intensive.—**Intent**, in-tent', *a.* [L. *intentus*, pp. of *intendo.*] Having the mind strained or bent on an object; sedulously applied; eager in pursuit of an object; anxiously diligent: with *on* before a noun.—*n.* Design, purpose, or intention; meaning; drift; aim.—*To all intents and purposes*, in all applications or senses; practically; really.—**Intention**, in-ten'shon, *n.* [L. *intentio*, attention, design.] Determination to act in a particular manner; purpose; design; end; aim; the state of being strained or intensified; intension; *logic*, any mental apprehension of an object.—**Intentional**, in-ten'shon-al, *a.* Done with intention, design, or purpose; intended; designed.—**Intentionally**, in-ten'shon-al-li, *adv.* With intention; by design; of purpose.—**Intentioned**, in-ten'shond, *a.* Having intentions or designs; usually in composition.—**Intently**, in-tent'li, *adv.* In an intent manner.—**Intentness**, in-tent'nes, *n.* The state of being intent.

Inter, in-tėr', *v.t.*—*interred, interring.* [Fr. *enterrer*—*en*, and *terre*, L. *terra*, the earth (whence *terrace, terrestrial*, &c.).] To bury; to inhume.—**Interment**, in-tėr'ment, *n.* The act of interring; burial.

Interact, in'tėr-akt, *n.* [Prefix *inter*, and *act.*] The interval between two acts of a drama; an interlude; any intermediate employment of time.—*v.i.* To act reciprocally; to act on each other.—**Interaction**, in-tėr-ak'shon, *n.* Intermediate action; mutual or reciprocal action.

Interblend, in-tėr-blend', *v.t.* and *i.* [Prefix *inter*, and *blend.*] To blend or mingle together.

Interbreed, in-tėr-brēd', *v.t.* and *i.* [Prefix *inter*, and *breed.*] To breed by crossing one kind of animals or plants with another.

Intercalary, in-tėr'ka-la-ri, *a.* [L. *intercalarius*—*inter*, between, and *calo*, to call or proclaim, seen also in *calendar, council.*] Inserted or introduced among others, as the odd day (February 29th) inserted in leap-year.—**Intercalate**, in-tėr'ka-lāt, *v.t.*—*intercalated, intercalating.* [L. *intercalo.*] To insert between others; *chron.* to insert between other days or other portions of time; *geol.* to insert, as a layer or series of layers, between the regular series of the strata.—**Intercalation**, in-tėr'ka-lā"shon, *n.* [L. *intercalatio.*] The act of intercalating.—**Intercalative**, in-tėr'ka-lā-tiv, *a.* Tending to intercalate; intercalating.

Intercede, in-tėr-sēd', *v.i.*—*interceded, interceding.* [L. *intercedo*—*inter*, between, and *cedo*, to go; lit. to pass between. CEDE.] To act between parties with a view to reconcile those who differ or contend; to plead in favour of another; to interpose; to mediate or make intercession.—**Interceder**, in-tėr-sē'dėr, *n.* One who intercedes.—**Intercession**, in-tėr-sesh'on, *n.* [L. *intercessio.*] The act of interceding; mediation.—**Intercessional**, in-tėr-sesh'on-al, *a.* Pertaining to or containing intercession.—**Intercessor**, in'tėr-ses-sėr, *n.* One who intercedes.—**Intercessory**, **Intercessorial**,† in-tėr-ses'so-ri, in'tėr-ses-sō"ri-al, *a.* Containing intercession; interceding.

Intercellular, in-tėr-sel'lū-lėr, *a.* [Prefix *inter*, between, and *cellular.*] *Bot.* and *zool.* lying between cells or cellules.

Intercept, in-tėr-sept', *v.t.* [Fr. *intercepter*; L. *intercipio, interceptum*, to intercept—*inter*, between, and *capio*, to take. CAPABLE.] To take or stop by the way; to interrupt the journey or passage of (a messenger, a letter); to stop on its passage; to obstruct the progress of (rays of light, &c.).—**Intercepter**, in-tėr-sep'tėr, *n.* One who or that which intercepts.—**Interception**, in-tėr-sep'shon, *n.* The act of intercepting; obstruction of a course or proceeding.—**Interceptive**, in-tėr-sep'tiv, *n.* Serving to intercept.

Intercession, &c. Under INTERCEDE.

Interchain, in-tėr-chān', *v.t.* [Prefix *inter*, and *chain.*] To chain or link together, to unite closely or firmly.

Interchange, in-tėr-chānj', *v.t.*—*interchanged, interchanging.* [Prefix *inter*, and *change.*] To change reciprocally; to put each in the place of the other; to cause to succeed alternately.—*v.i.* To change reciprocally; to succeed alternately.—*n.* (in'tėr-chānj). The act or process of mutually giving and receiving; exchange between two or more; alternate succession.—**Interchangeable**, in-tėr-chān'ja-bl, *a.* Capable of being interchanged.—**Interchangeability**, **Interchangeableness**, in-tėr-chān'ja-bil"i-ti, in-tėr-chān'ja-bl-nes, *n.*—**Interchangeably**, in-tėr-chān'ja-bli, *adv.*

Interclavicle, in-tėr-klav'i-kl, *n.* [Prefix *inter*, and *clavicle.*] A bone between the clavicles or in front of the breast-bone in many vertebrates.—**Interclavicular**, in'tėr-kla-vik"ū-lėr, *a.* Pertaining to the spaces between the clavicles.

Interclude, in-tėr-klūd', *v.t.*—*intercluded, intercluding.* [L. *intercludo*—*inter*, between, and *claudo*, to shut.] To shut from a place or course by something intervening; to intercept.

Intercolline, in-tėr-kol'lin, *a.* [L. *inter*, between, and *collis*, a hill.] Lying between hills or hillocks.

Intercolonial, in-tėr-ko-lō"ni-al, *a.* [Prefix *inter*, between, among, and *colonial.*] Subsisting between different colonies.—**Intercolonially**, in'tėr-ko-lō"ni-al-li, *adv.* As between colonies.

Intercolumniation, in'tėr-ko-lum'ni-ā"shon, *n.* [Prefix *inter*, between, and *column.*] *Arch.* the space between two columns measured at the lowest part of their shafts.

Intercommunicate, in'tėr-kom-mū"ni-kāt, *v.i.* and *t.* [Prefix *inter*, and *communicate.*] To communicate mutually; to hold mutual communication.—**Intercommunicable**, in'tėr-kom-mū"ni-ka-bl, *a.* Capable of being mutually communicated.—**Intercommunication**, in'tėr-kom-mū'ni-kā"shon, *n.* Reciprocal communication.

Intercommunion, in'tėr-kom-mūn"yon, *n.* [Prefix *inter*, and *communion.*] Mutual communion; mutual intercourse.—**Intercommunity**, in'tėr-kom-mū"ni-ti, *n.* A mutual communication or community.

Intercomparison, in'tėr-kom-par"i-son, *n.* [Prefix *inter*, and *comparison.*] Comparison between the various features of one thing and the corresponding features of another.

Interconnect, in'tėr-kon-nekt", *v.t.* [Prefix *inter*, and *connect*.] To connect or unite closely or by various bonds.—**Interconnection**, in'tėr-kon-nek"shon, *n.* The state of being interconnected; what serves to interconnect.

Intercontinental, in'tėr-kon-ti-nen"tal, *a.* [Prefix *inter*, and *continent*.] Subsisting between different continents.

Intercostal, in-tėr-kos'tal, *a.* [L. *inter*, between, and *costa*, a rib.] *Anat.* placed or lying between the ribs.

Intercourse, in'tėr-kōrs, *n.* [Prefix *inter*, between, and *course*; L. *intercursus*.] Reciprocal dealings between persons or nations; interchange of thought and feeling; communication; commerce; communion; sexual connection.

Intercross, in-tėr-kros', *v.t.* and *i.* [Prefix *inter*, and *cross*.] To cross mutually; to cross one another, as lines; to interbreed.

Intercurrent, in-tėr-kur'ent, *a.* [Prefix *inter*, between, and *current*; L. *intercurrens, intercurrentis*.] Running between or among; intervening; *med.* applied to diseases which occur sporadically during the prevalence of other diseases.

Intercutaneous, in'tėr-kū-tā"nē-us, *a.* [Prefix *inter*, between, and *cutaneous*.] Being within or under the skin.

Interdependence, Interdependency, in'tėr-dē-pen"dens, in'tėr-dē-pen"den-si, *n.* [Prefix *inter*, and *depend*.] Reciprocal dependence; dependence each upon the others reciprocally.—**Interdependent**, in'tėr-dē-pen"dent, *a.* Reciprocally dependent.

Interdict, in tėr-dikt', *v.t.* [L. *interdico, interdictum—inter*, between, and *dico*, to speak. DICTION.] To debar, forbid, or prohibit; to restrain by an interdict.—*n.* (in'tėr-dikt). [L. *interdictum*.] A prohibition; a prohibiting order or decree; a papal prohibition of the performance of divine service and the administration of religious rites.—**Interdiction**, in-tėr-dik'shon, *n.* The act of interdicting; prohibition.—**Interdictive, Interdictory**, in-tėr-dik'tiv, in-tėr-dik'to-ri, *a.* Having power to interdict or prohibit.

Interdigital, in-tėr-dij'i-tal, *a.* [Prefix *inter*, and *digit*.] *Anat.* being between the digits; between toes or fingers, as the web which forms the wing of a bat.—**Interdigitate**, in-tėr-dij'i-tāt, *v.i.* To run into each other, like the fingers of one hand inserted between those of the other.—**Interdigitation**, in-tėr-dij'i-tā"shon, *n.* The act or state of interdigitating; *anat.* the space between two fingers.

Interest, in'tėr-est, *n.* [O.Fr. *interest*, Fr. *intérêt*, from L. *interest*, it concerns, it is of importance, from L. *interesse — inter*, between, and *esse*, to be (whence also *essence, entity*).] Concern; sympathy, or regard (to excite one's *interest*); advantage; good; profit (it is for your *interest* to do so); share, part, or participation in value; the profit per cent derived from money lent or invested (which in reference to the interest is called the *principal*); hence, something in addition to a mere equivalent (to repay injury with *interest*); influence with a person, especially with persons in power (to get a post by *interest*); a collective name for those interested in any particular business (the landed *interest*, the shipping *interest*).—*Simple interest* is that which arises from the principal sum only.—*Compound interest* is that which arises from the principal with the interest of one year added together to form a new principal for the next year, and so on successively.—*v.t.* To engage the attention of; to awaken interest or concern in.—**Interested**, in'tėr-es-ted, *p.* and *a.* Having an interest or share; affected; moved; having attention roused; concerned in a cause or in consequences; liable to be biassed by personal considerations; chiefly concerned for one's own private advantage.—**Interestedness**, in'tėr-es-ted-nes, *n.*—**Interesting**, in'tėr-es-ting, *a.* Engaging the attention or curiosity; exciting or adapted to excite attention and sympathy.—**Interestingly**, in'tėr-es-ting-li, *adv.* In an interesting manner.—**Interestingness**, in'tėr-es-ting-nes, *n.*

Interface, in'tėr-fās, *n.* [Prefix *inter*, and *face*.] The meeting or union of two surfaces.—**Interfacial**, in-tėr-fā'shi-al, *a.* Pertaining to an interface; included between two faces or plane surfaces.

Interfemoral, in-tėr-fem'o-ral, *a.* [L. *inter*, between, *femora*, thighs.] Between the thighs (the *interfemoral* membrane of bats).

Interfere, in-tėr-fēr', *v.i.*—*interfered, interfering*. [O.Fr. *entreferir*, to exchange blows —L. *inter*, between, and *ferio*, to strike (whence *ferule*).] To interpose; to intermeddle; to enter into or take a part in the concerns of others; to clash, come in collision, or be in opposition; *physics*, to act reciprocally upon each other so as to modify the effect of each.—**Interference**, in-tėr-fē'rens, *n.* The act of interfering or intermeddling; *physics*, the mutual action of waves of any kind (water, sound, heat, or light) upon each other, by which the vibrations and their effects are increased, diminished, or neutralized.—**Interferer**, in-tėr-fē'rėr, *n.* One who interferes.—**Interfering**, in-tėr-fē'ring, *a.* Prone or given to interfere or intermeddle.—**Interferingly**, in-tėr-fē'ring-li, *adv.* In an interfering manner.

Interfluent, Interfluous, in-tėr'flu-ent, in-tėr'flu-us, *a.* [L. *interfluens, interfluus—inter*, between, and *fluo*, to flow.] Flowing between.

Interfoliaceous, in-tėr-fō'li-ā"shus, *a.* [L. *inter*, between, and *folium*, a leaf.] *Bot.* being between opposite leaves, but placed alternately with them.—**Interfoliate**, in-tėr-fō'li-āt, *v.t.* To interleave.

Interfuse, in-tėr-fūz', *v.t.*—*interfused, interfusing*. [L. *interfusus*, pp. of *interfundo —inter*, between, and *fundo*, to pour. FUSE.] To pour or spread between or among; to mix up together; to make interdependent. —**Interfusion**, in-tėr-fū'zhon, *n.* Act of interfusing or that which is interfused.

Interganglionic, in-tėr-gang'gli-on"ik, *a.* [Prefix *inter*, between, and *ganglion*.] *Anat.* lying or passing between ganglia.

Interglacial, in-tėr-glā'shi-al, *a.* [Prefix *inter*, and *glacial*.] *Geol.* formed or occurring between two periods of glacial action.

Interhemal, Interhaemal, in-tėr-hē'mal, *a.* [Prefix *inter*, and *hæmal*.] *Anat.* situated between the arches

Interim, in'tėr-im, *n.* [L., in the meantime.] The meantime; time intervening.—*a.* Belonging to an intervening time; belonging to the meantime; temporary.

Interior, in-tē'ri-ėr, *a.* [L., inner, interior, compar. of *interus*, internal, itself a compar. from *in*. Akin *entrails, internal, intestine*.] Internal; being within any limits, inclosure, or substance: opposed to *exterior* or *superficial*; inland; remote from the frontiers or shore.—*Interior angles*, *geom.* the angles made within any figure by the sides of it.—*Interior planets*, *astron.* the planets between the earth's orbit and the sun; inferior planets.—*Interior screw*, a screw cut on the interior surface of anything hollow. —*n.* The internal part of a thing; the inside; the inland part of a country; the department of a government having charge of home affairs.—**Interiority**, in-tē'ri-or"i-ti, *n.* The quality of being interior.—**Interiorly**, in-tē'ri-or-li, *adv.* Internally; inwardly.

Interjacent, in-tėr-jā'sent, *a.* [L. *interjacens*, ppr. of *interjaceo—inter*, between, and *jaceo*, to lie, as in *adjacent, subjacent*, &c.] Lying or being between; intervening.—**Interjacence, Interjacency**, in-tėr-jā'sens, in-tėr-jā'sen-si, *n.* The condition of being interjacent.

Interject, in-tėr-jekt', *v.t.* [L. *interjicio, interjectum—inter*, between, and *jacio*, to throw. JET.] To throw between; to throw in between other words.—**Interjection**, in-tėr-jek'shon, *n.* [L. *interjectio*.] The act of throwing between; a word thrown in between words connected in construction, to express some emotion or passion, as exclamations of joy, grief, astonishment, &c. —**Interjectional, Interjectionary**, in-tėr-jek'shon-al, in-tėr-jek'shon-a-ri, *a.* Thrown in between other words; partaking of the character of an interjection.—**Interjectionally**, in-tėr-jek'shon-al-li, *adv.* In an interjectional manner.

Interknit, in-tėr-nit', *v.t.* [Prefix *inter*, and *knit*.] To knit together closely.

Interlace, in-tėr-lās', *v.t.*—*interlaced, interlacing*. [Prefix *inter*, and *lace*; Fr. *entrelacer*.] To weave or twine together; to entangle or interweave one thing with another.—*v.i.* To be intertwined or interwoven; to have parts crossing or intersecting.—**Interlacement**, in-tėr-lās'ment, *n.* The act or state of interlacing.

Interlard, in-tėr-lärd', *v.t.* [Prefix *inter*, and *lard*.] Primarily, to mix fat with lean; hence, to mix by something frequently occurring; to diversify by mixture (talk *interlarded* with oaths).

Interleave, in-tėr-lēv', *v.t.*—*interleaved, interleaving*. [Prefix *inter*, and *leaf*.] To insert a blank leaf or blank leaves in; to insert between the other leaves of (a book).

Interline, in-tėr-līn', *v.t.*—*interlined, interlining*. [Prefix *inter*, and *line*.] To write or print in alternate lines; to write or print between the lines of.—**Interlineal, Interlinear, Interlineary**, in-tėr-lin'ē-al, in-tėr-lin'ē-ėr, in-tėr-lin'ē-a-ri, *a.* Written or printed between lines before written or printed.—**Interlinearly**, in-tėr-lin'ē-ėr-li, *adv.* In an interlinear manner.—**Interlineation**, in-tėr-lin'ē-ā"shon, *n.* The act of interlining; that which is interlined.

Interlock, in-tėr-lok', *v.i.* [Prefix *inter*, and *lock*.] To unite or be locked together by a series of connections.—*v.t.* To lock one in another firmly.

Interlocution, in'tėr-lō-kū"shon, *n.* [L. *interlocutio*, from *interloquor — inter*, between, and *loquor*, to speak (in *loquacious, elocution*, &c.).] Dialogue; interchange of speech; *law*, an intermediate act or decree before final decision.—**Interlocutor**, in-tėr-lok'ū-tėr, *n.* One who speaks in a dialogue or conversation; *Scots law*, the term, judgment, or order of any court of record.—**Interlocutory**, in-tėr-lok'ū-to-ri, *a.* Consisting of dialogue or conversation.

Interlope, in-tėr-lōp', *v.i.*—*interloped, interloping*. [From the noun, which is from D. *enterlooper*, a smuggler or smuggling vessel—Fr. *entre*, between, and D. *loopen*, to leap, to run=E. to *leap*. LEAP.] To traffic without a proper license; to run into a matter in which one has no right.—**Interloper**, in-tėr-lō'pėr, *n.* One who unwarrantably intrudes or thrusts himself into a business, position, or matter.

Interlude, in'tėr-lūd, *n.* [L.L. *interludium*, an interlude—L. *inter*, between, and *ludus*, a play. DELUDE.] A short lively entertainment performed between the acts of a play, or between the play and the afterpiece; a piece of music played between the verses of a canticle or hymn, or between certain portions of a church service.

Interlunar, Interlunary, in-tėr-lū'nėr, in-tėr-lū'na-ri, *a.* [L. *inter*, between, *luna*, the moon.] Belonging to the time when the moon is invisible.

Intermarry, in-tėr-mar'i, *v.i.*—*intermarried, intermarrying*. [Prefix *inter*, and *marry*.] To marry together; to become connected by marriage, as two families, ranks, tribes, or the like.—**Intermarriage**, in-tėr-mar'ij, *n.* Marriage between two families, tribes, or nations.

Intermaxillary, in-tėr-mak'sil-la-ri, *a.* [Prefix *inter*, and *maxillary*.] *Anat.* being between the maxillary bones.—*n.* The bone in mammalia which supports the upper incisors.

Intermeddle, in-tėr-med'l, *v.i.*—*inter-*

meddled, intermeddling. [Prefix *inter*, and *meddle.*] To meddle in affairs in which one has no concern; to meddle officiously; to interfere. — **Intermeddler**, in-tėr-med′lėr, *n.* One who intermeddles.—**Intermeddlesome**, in-tėr-med′l-sum, *a.* Prone to intermeddle.—**Intermeddlesomeness**, in-tėr-med′l-sum-nes, *n.*

Intermediate, in-tėr-mē′di-āt, *a.* [Fr. *intermédiat*, L. *intermedius*—*inter*, between, and *medius*, middle (whence *medium*, *mediate*, &c.).] Lying or being between; in the middle place or degree between two extremes; intervening; interposed. Also **Intermedial, Intermediary**, in-tėr-mē′di-al, in-tėr-mē′di-a-ri, in same sense.—**Intermediately**, in-tėr-mē′di-āt-li, *adv.* In an intermediate position.—**Intermediation**, in-tėr-mē′di-ā″shon, *n.* Intervention; interposition.—**Intermediary**, in-tėr-mē′di-a-ri, *n.* One who or that which interposes or is intermediate; an intervening agent.—**Intermediator**, in-tėr-mē′di-ā-tėr, *n.* A mediator between parties.—**Intermedium**, in-tėr-mē′di-um, *n.* Intermediate space; an intervening agent or instrument.

Interment. Under INTER.

Intermezzo, in-tėr-met′zō, *n.* [It.] *Mus.* a short composition, generally of a light sparkling character, played between more important pieces; an interlude.

Intermigration, in′tėr-mī-grā″shon, *n.* [Prefix *inter*, and *migration.*] Reciprocal migration.

Interminable, in-tėr′mi-na-bl, *a.* [L. *interminabilis* — *in*, not, and *terminus*, a bound or limit. TERM.] Boundless; endless; admitting no limit; wearisomely spun out or protracted.—**Interminableness**, in-tėr′mi-na-bl-nes, *n.*—**Interminably**, in-tėr′mi-na-bli, *adv.* In an interminable manner; endlessly.—**Interminate**, in-tėr′mi-nāt, *a.* Endless.—*Interminate decimal*, one that may be continued to infinity, as that given by ⅓.

Intermingle, in-tėr-ming′gl, *v.t.*—*intermingled, intermingling.* [Prefix *inter*, and *mingle.*] To mingle or mix together; to mix up; to intermix.—*v.i.* To be mixed or incorporated.

Intermission. Under INTERMIT.

Intermit, in-tėr-mit′, *v.t.*—*intermitted, intermitting.* [L. *intermitto*, to let go between, to interrupt—*inter*, and *mitto*, to send. MISSION.] To cause to cease for a time; to interrupt; to suspend or delay.—*v.i.* To cease for a time; to cease or relax at intervals, as a fever.—**Intermittence**, in-tėr-mit′ens, *n.* The act or state of intermitting; intermission. — **Intermittent**, in-tėr-mit′ent, *a.* Ceasing at intervals.—*Intermittent* or *intermitting spring*, a spring which flows for some time and then ceases, again flows and again ceases, and so on, usually having a siphon-shaped channel of outflow.—*n.* A fever which entirely subsides or ceases at certain intervals. —**Intermitting**, in-tėr-mit′ing, *ppr.* and *a.* Ceasing for a time; pausing.—**Intermittingly**, in-tėr-mit′ing-li, *adv.* In an intermittent manner. — **Intermission**, in-tėr-mish′on, *n.* [L. *intermissio.*] The act or state of intermitting; cessation for a time; pause; the temporary subsidence of a fever.—**Intermissive**, in-tėr-mis′iv, *a.* Intermittent.

Intermix, in-tėr-miks′, *v.t.* [Prefix *inter*, and *mix.*] To mix together; to intermingle.—*v.i.* To be mixed or intermingled. —**Intermixture**, in-tėr-miks′tūr, *n.* A mass formed by mixture; a mass of ingredients mixed; admixture.

Intermundane, in-tėr-mun′dān, *a.* [L. *inter*, between, *mundus*, a world.] Being between worlds or between orb and orb (*intermundane* spaces).

Intermural, in-tėr-mū′ral, *a.* [L. *inter*, between, *murus*, a wall.] Between walls.

Intern, Interne, in′tėrn, *n.* [Fr. *interne.*] A graduated physician serving in a hospital for experience; also, any resident doctor or surgeon.

Intern, in-tėrn′, *v.t.* [Fr. *interner*, from L. *internus*, internal.] To send to or cause to remain in the interior of a country without permission to leave it; to disarm and quarter in some place, as a defeated body of troops.—**Internment**, in-tėrn′ment, *n.* The act of interning; the state of being interned.

Internal, in-tėr′nal, *a.* [L. *internus*, internal. INTERIOR.] Inward; interior; being within any limit or surface; not external; pertaining to the mind or thoughts, or to one's inner being; pertaining to itself, its own affairs, or home interests: said of a country; domestic; not foreign. — *Internal combustion*, the principle employed in the engines or motors of air-craft, motor-cars, &c., by which a mixture of fuel (usually gasoline) and air is exploded in the cylinder, the force acting on the piston.—*Internal revenue*, taxes derived from levies on certain domestic transactions.—*Internal secretion*, a complex substance secreted by some part of the body, and absorbed into the blood to play some part in body economy.—**Internality**, in-tėr-nal′i-ti, *n.* The state or quality of being internal.—**Internally**, *adv.*

International, in-tėr-nash′on-al, *a.* [Prefix *inter*, and *national.*] Pertaining to or reciprocally affecting nations; regulating the mutual intercourse between different nations. — *International law*, the law of nations; those maxims or rules that regulate states in their conduct towards one another.—**International**, *n.* The International Congress of Socialistic Workers, regulating and propounding the course of joint action between workers at home and abroad.—**Internationally**, in-tėr-nash′on-al-li, *adv.*

Internecine, in-tėr-nē′sin, *a.* [L. *internecinus*, deadly, murderous—*inter*, between, among, and *neco*, to kill.] Marked by destructive hostilities or much slaughter; causing great slaughter, as between fellow-citizens (*internecine* war).

Interneural, in-tėr-nū′ral, *a.* [Prefix *inter*, and *neural.*] Situated between the neural processes or spines: said of those bones which support the fin-rays on a fish's back.

Internode, in′tėr-nōd, *n.* [L. *inter*, between, and *nodus*, knot.] *Bot.* the space which intervenes between two nodes or leaf-buds.—**Internodal**, in-tėr-nō′dal, *a. Bot.* of or pertaining to an internode.

Internuncio, in-tėr-nun′shi-ō, *n.* [L. *internuncius*—*inter*, between, and *nuncius*, a messenger.] A messenger between two parties; an envoy of the pope, sent to small states and republics while a nuncio is sent to emperors and kings.—**Internuncial**, in-tėr-nun′shi-al, *a.* Belonging to an internuncio.

Interoceanic, in-tėr-ō′shē-an″ik, *a.* Prefix *inter*, and *ocean.*] Between oceans (*interoceanic* railway, canal, &c.).

Interocular, in-tėr-ok′ū-lėr, *a.* [L. *inter*, and *oculus*, the eye.] Situated between the eyes.

Interorbital, in-tėr-or′bi-tal, *a.* [Prefix *inter*, and *orbit.*] Situated between the orbits, as of the eyes.

Interosculate, in-tėr-os′kū-lat, *v.i.* [Prefix *inter*, and *osculate.*] To touch or run into one another at various points; to form a connecting link between objects or groups by having characters in common.

Interosseal, Interosseous, in-tėr-os′sē-al, in-tėr-os′sē-us, *a.* [L. *inter*, between, and *os*, a bone.] *Anat.* situated between bones.

Interpellate, in-tėr′pel-lāt, *v.t.*—*interpellated, interpellating.* [L. *interpello*, *interpellatum*, to interrupt in speaking—*inter*, between, and *pello*, to drive (seen in *appeal*, *compel*, *pulse*, &c.).] To question, especially to question imperatively; to interrupt by a question. — **Interpellation**, in′tėr-pel-lā″shon, *n.* [L. *interpellatio.*] The act of interrupting; an interruption by speaking; a question put by a member of a legislative assembly to a minister or member of the government.

Interpenetrate, in-tėr-pen′e-trāt, *v.t.* and *i.*—*interpenetrated, interpenetrating.* [Prefix, *inter*, and *penetrate.*] To penetrate between or within; to penetrate mutually. —**Interpenetration**, in-tėr-pen′e-trā″shon, *n.* The act of interpenetrating.—**Interpenetrative**, in-tėr-pen′e-trā-tiv, *a.* Mutually penetrative.

Interpetiolar, in-tėr-pet′i-ō-lėr, *a.* [Prefix *inter*, and *petiole.*] *Bot.* situated between the petioles.

Interplanetary, in-tėr-plan′e-ta-ri, *a.* [Prefix *inter*, and *planetary.*] Situated or existing between the planets.

Interplead, in-tėr-plēd′, *v.i.* [Prefix *inter*, and *plead.*] *Law*, to proceed by interpleader. — **Interpleader**, in-tėr-plē′dėr, *n. Law*, one who interpleads; a legal process by which a person threatened with a suit in which he has no real interest gets the proper parties to plead in the matter.

Interpolate, in-tėr′pō-lāt, *v.t.* — *interpolated, interpolating.* [L. *interpolo*, *interpolatum*, to interpolate or falsify, from *interpolus*, vamped up, falsified—*inter*, between, and *polio*, to polish.] To foist in; to insert, as a spurious word or passage in a manuscript or book; to corrupt or vitiate by the insertion of new matter; *math.* and *physics*, to fill up intermediate terms of, as of a series, according to the law of the series.—**Interpolable**, in-tėr′pō-la-bl, *a.* Capable of being interpolated or inserted.—**Interpolation**, in-tėr′pō-lā″shon, *n.* [L. *interpolatio.*] The act of interpolating; that which is interpolated or inserted; a spurious word or passage inserted.—**Interpolator**, in-tėr′pō-lā-tėr, *n.* One who interpolates.

Interpose, in-tėr-pōz′, *v.t.*—*interposed, interposing.* [Fr. *interposer*—*inter*, between, and *poser*, to place. POSE, COMPOSE.] To place between; *fig.* or *lit.* to present or bring forward by way of interruption or for some service (to *interpose* one's hand, one's self, one's aid or services).—*v.i.* To step in between parties at variance; to mediate; to interfere; to put in or make a remark by way of interruption.—**Interposer**, in-tėr-pō′zėr, *n.* One who interposes.—**Interposition**, in-tėr′pō-zish″on or in′tėr-pō-zish″on, *n.* The act of interposing; a coming between; mediation; intervention.

Interpret, in-tėr′pret, *v.t.* [L. *interpretor*, from *interpres*, *interpretis*, an interpreter —*inter*, between, and root seen in (*pre*)*paro*, to prepare.] To explain the meaning of; to expound; to translate from an unknown to a known language, or into intelligible or familiar words; to free from mystery or obscurity; to make clear; to unravel; to represent artistically (as by an actor on the stage). — **Interpretable**, in-tėr′pre-ta-bl, *a.* Capable of being interpreted.—**Interpretation**, in-tėr′pre-tā″shon, *n.* [L. *interpretatio.*] The act of interpreting; translation; explanation; the sense given by an interpreter; conception and representation of a character on the stage.—**Interpretative**, in-tėr′pre-tā-tiv, *a.* Designed or fitted to explain; explanatory. — **Interpretatively**, in-tėr′pre-tā-tiv-li, *adv.* In an interpretative manner.— **Interpreter**, in-tėr′pre-tėr, *n.* One who or that which interprets.

Interregnum, in-tėr-reg′num, *n.* [L., from *inter*, between, and *regnum*, reign.] The time between the death or abdication of a king and the accession of his successor; the interval between the cessation of one government and the establishment of another.

Interrelation, in′tėr-rē-lā″shon, *n.* [Prefix *inter*, and *relation.*] Mutual; reciprocal, or corresponding relation; correlation.

Interrogate, in-tėr′ō-gāt, *v.t.* [L. *interrogo*, *interrogatum* — *inter*, between, and *rogo*, to ask (as in *abrogate*, *arrogant*, *derogate*, *prorogue*, &c.).] To question; to examine by asking questions.—**Interrogation**, in-ter′ō-gā″shon, *n.* [L. *interrogatio.*] The act of questioning; a question put; the sign ?, indicating that the sentence immediately preceding it is a question, or used to express doubt or to mark a query.—

Interrogative, in-ter-rog'a-tiv, *a.* [L. *interrogativus.*] Denoting a question; expressed in the form of a question.—*n. gram.* a word used in asking questions; as *who? what? which?*—**Interrogatively**, in-ter-rog'a-tiv-li, *adv.* In an interrogative manner. — **Interrogator**, in-ter'ō-gā-tėr, *n.* One who interrogates or asks questions.—**Interrogatory**, in-ter-rog'a-to-ri, *n.* [L. *interrogatorius.*] A question; an interrogation.—*a.* Containing a question; expressing a question.

Interrupt, in-tėr-rupt', *v.t.* [L. *interrumpo, interruptum—inter*, between, and *rumpo*, to break. RUPTURE.] To stop or hinder by breaking in upon the course or progress of; to break the current or motion of; to cause to stop in speaking; to cause to be delayed or given over; to break the uniformity of. — **Interrupted**, in-tėr-rup'ted, *a.* Having interruptions; broken; intermitted. — **Interruptedly**, in-tėr-rup'ted-li, *adv.* With breaks or interruptions. — **Interrupter**, in-tėr-rup'tėr, *n.* One that interrupts.—**Interruption**, in-tėr-rup'shon, *n.* [L. *interruptio.*] The act of interrupting or breaking in upon; a break or breach; intervention; interposition; obstruction or hindrance; cause of stoppage. — **Interruptive**, in-tėr-rup'tiv, *a.* Tending to interrupt; interrupting.—**Interruptively**, in-tėr-rup'tiv-li, *adv.* In an interruptive manner.

Intersect, in-tėr-sekt', *v.t.* [L. *interseco, intersectum — inter*, between, and *seco*, to cut. SECTION.] To cut into or between; to cut or cross mutually; to divide into parts by crossing or cutting.—*v.i.* To cut into one another; to meet and cross each other.—**Intersection**, in-tėr-sek'shon, *n.* [L. *intersectio.*] The act or state of intersecting; the point or line in which two lines or two surfaces cut each other.—**Intersectional**, in-tėr-sek'shon-al, *a.* Relating to or formed by an intersection.

Intersidereal, in'tėr-sī-dē"rē-al, *a.* [L. *inter*, between, and *sidus, sideris*, a star.] Situated between or among the stars.

Intersperse, in-tėr-spėrs', *v.t.* — *interspersed, interspersing.* [L. *interspergo, interspersum—inter*, between, and *spargo*, to scatter.] To scatter or set here and there among other things; to diversify by scattering objects.—**Interspersion**, in-tėr-spėr'shon, *n.* The act of interspersing.

Interspinal, Interspinous, in-tėr-spī'nal, in-tėr-spī'nus, *a.* [Prefix *inter*, and *spine.*] *Anat.* lying between the processes of the spine, as muscles, nerves, &c.

Interstate, in-tėr-stāt', *a.* Relations of or between states, as *interstate* commerce. *Interstate Commerce Commission* (*I. C. C.*), established by the U. S. in 1887 to regulate commerce between the states, especially railroads and express companies, or rail and water transport when combined. It passes on rates, financing, building and abandonment of railroads.

Interstellar, Interstellary, in-tėr-stel'ėr, in-tėr-stel'la-ri, *a.* [Prefix *inter*, and *stellar.*] Situated among the stars.

Interstice, in-tėr'stis, *n.* [Fr., from L. *interstitium—inter*, between, and *sto*, to stand. STATE.] A narrow or small space between things close together, or between the component parts of a body; a chink, crevice, or cranny.—**Interstitial**, in-tėr-stish'al, *a.* Of or containing interstices.

Interstratify, in-tėr-strat'i-fī, *v.t.* [Prefix *inter*, and *stratify.*] *Geol.* to cause to occupy a position between other strata; to intermix as to strata.—*v.i.* To assume a position between other strata.—**Interstratification**, in-tėr-strat'i-fi-kā"shon, *n.* The condition of being interstratified.

Intertexture, in-tėr-teks'tūr, *n.* [Prefix *inter*, and *texture.*] The act of interweaving; state of things interwoven; what is interwoven.

Intertraffic, in'tėr-traf-ik, *n.* [Prefix *inter*, and *traffic.*] Reciprocal traffic between two or more places.

Intertropical, in-tėr-trop'i-kal, *a.* [Prefix *inter*, and *tropic.*] Situated between or within the tropics.

Intertwine, in-tėr-twīn', *v.t.*—*intertwined, intertwining.* [Prefix *inter*, and *twine.*] To unite by twining or twisting one with another; to interlace.—*v.i.* To be mutually interwoven.

Intertwist, in-tėr-twist', *v.t.* [Prefix *inter*, and *twist.*] To twist one with another; to interweave or interlace.

Interval, in'tėr-val, *n.* [L. *intervallum*, the space between the rampart of a camp and the soldiers' tents—*inter*, between, and *vallum*, an earthen rampart set with palisades, from *vallus*, a stake. WALL.] A space or distance between things; an unoccupied space intervening; space of time between two definite points or events; intervening time or space; the lateral space between units having the same alignment or frontage; *music*, the difference in point of gravity or acuteness between two given sounds.

Intervene, in-tėr-vēn', *v.i.*— *intervened, intervening.* [L. *intervenio—inter*, between, and *vento*, to come, as in *advene, convene*, &c. VENTURE.] To come or be between persons or things; to be situated between; to occur, fall, or come between points of time or events; to come in the way.—**Intervener, Interventionist**, in-tėr-vē'nėr, in-tėr-ven'shon-ist, *n.* One who intervenes or advocates intervention.—**Intervention**, in-tėr-ven'shon, *n.* [L. *interventio.*] Act of intervening; a coming between; interference affecting interests.

Intervertebral, in-tėr-vėr'tē-bral, *a.* [Prefix *inter*, and *vertebra.*] *Anat.* situated between the vertebræ.

Interview, in'tėr-vū, *n.* [Prefix *inter*, and *view*; Fr. *entrevue.*] A meeting between two or more persons face to face; a conference or mutual communication of thoughts.—*v.t.* (in-tėr-vū'). To wait or call on for the purpose of having an interview and getting information for publication.—**Interviewer**, in-tėr-vū'ėr, *n.* One who interviews; a newspaper reporter who visits and interrogates a person of position or notoriety.

Interweave, in-tėr-wēv', *v.t.*—*interwove* (pret.); *interwoven* (pp.); *interweaving* (ppr.). To weave together; to intermingle as if by weaving; to unite intimately; to interlace.

Intestate, in-tes'tāt, *a.* [L. *intestatus—in*, not, and *testatus*, having made a will, pp. of *testor*, to make a will. TESTAMENT.] Dying without having made a will; not disposed of by will; not devised or bequeathed.—*n.* A person who dies without making a will, or a valid will.—**Intestable**, in-tes'ta-bl, *a.* [L. *intestabilis.*] Legally unqualified to make a will.—**Intestacy**, in-tes'ta-si, *n.* The state of being intestate.

Intestine, in-tes'tin, *a.* [L. *intestinus*, inward, *intestinum*, an intestine, from *intus*, within, from *in*, in; akin *interior.*] Internal with regard to a state or country; domestic; not foreign. — *n.* The canal or tube that extends with convolutions from the stomach to the anus; *pl.* entrails or viscera in general. — **Intestinal**, in-tes'ti-nal, *a.* Pertaining to the intestines of an animal body. — *Intestinal canal*, the intestine or tube through which food passes in being digested.

Intextine, in-teks'tin, *n.* [L. *intus*, within, and E. *extine.*] *Bot.* that membrane of the pollen-grain which is situated next to the *extine* or outermost membrane.

Inthral, Inthrall, in-thral', *v.t.* To enthral.

Inthrone, in-thrōn', *v.t.* To enthrone.

Intimate, in'ti-māt, *a.* [Fr. *intime*, L. *intimus*, inmost, superl. of obs. *interus*, internal. INTERIOR.] Inward or internal‡; close in friendship; on very familiar terms (also refers to illicit sex relationship); very close as regards connection or relation (an *intimate* union).—*n.* An intimate friend; a close associate.—**Intimacy**, in'ti-ma-si, *n.* The state of being intimate.—**Intimately**, in'ti-māt-li, *adv.* In an intimate manner.

Intimate, in'ti-māt, *v.t.*—*intimated, intimating.* [L. *intimo, intimatum*, to publish or make known, from *intimus*, inmost. INTIMATE, *a.*] To hint, indicate, or suggest‡; to announce; to make known. — **Intimation**, in-ti-mā'shon, *n.* [L. *intimatio.*] The act of intimating; a hint; an explicit announcement or notification.

Intimidate, in-tim'i-dāt, *v.t.* — *intimidated, intimidating.* [L.L. *intimido, intimidatum* — L. *in*, intens., and *timidus*, timid.] To inspire with fear; to dishearten; to cow; to deter by threats.—**Intimidation**, in-tim'i-dā"shon, *n.* The act of intimidating; the deterring of a person by threats or otherwise. — **Intimidatory**, in-tim'i-da-to-ri, *a.* Causing intimidation.

Intine, in'tīn, *n.* [L. *intus*, within.] *Bot.* the inner coat of the shell of the pollen-grain in plants.

Intitle, in-tī'tl. ENTITLE.—**Intituled**, in-ti'tūld, *pp.* Entitled; distinguished by a title: a term used in acts of parliament.

Into, in'tö, *prep.* [A.Sax. *in tó, in* being the adv. and *tó* the prep.] A compound preposition expressing motion or direction towards the inside of, whether literally or figuratively; or expressing a change of condition (to go *into* a house, to fall *into* a fever).

Intolerable, in-tol'ėr-a-bl, *a.* [L. *intolerabilis—in*, not, and *tolerabilis*, bearable, from *tolero*, to bear. TOLERATE.] Not to be borne or endured; unendurable; insufferable.—**Intolerableness, Intolerability**, in-tol'ėr-a-bl-nes, in-tol'ėr-a-bil"i-ti, *n.* The state or quality of being intolerable.—**Intolerably**, in-tol'ėr-a-bli, *adv.* In an intolerable manner; unendurably.—**Intolerant**, in-tol'ėr-ant, *a.* [L. *intolerans, intolerantis — in*, not, and *tolero*, to bear.] Not enduring; not able to endure (an animal *intolerant* of cold); refusing to tolerate others in the enjoyment of their opinions, rights, or worship; unduly impatient of difference of opinion on the part of others.—**Intolerantly**, in-tol'ėr-ant-li, *adv.* In an intolerant manner.—**Intolerance, Intolerancy, Intoleration**, in-tol'ėr-ans, in-tol'ėr-an-si, in-tol'ėr-ā"shon, *n.* The quality of being intolerant; want of toleration; want of capacity to endure.

Intomb, in-töm', *v.t.* To entomb.

Intonate, in'tō-nāt, *v.i.* [L. *in*, in, and *tonus*, tone.] To modulate the voice; to sound the notes of the musical scale.—*v.t.* to pronounce with a certain tone or modulation. — **Intonation**, in-tō-nā'shon, *n.* The act or manner of intonating; modulation of the voice musically as in reading; the act of intoning; utterance with a special tone. — **Intone**, in-tōn', *v.i.* To use a musical monotone in pronouncing or repeating; to chant.—*v.t.* To pronounce with a musical tone; to chant.

Intort, in-tort', *v.t.* [L. *intorqueo, intortum—in*, and *torqueo*, to twist. TORTURE.] To twist inwards; to wreathe. — **Intorsion**, in-tor'shon, *n.* A winding or twisting inwards.

Intoxicate, in-tok'si-kāt, *v.t.*—*intoxicated, intoxicating.* [L.L. *intoxico, intoxicatum*—L. *in*, and *toxicum*, poison = Gr. *toxikon*, a poison in which arrows were dipped, from *toxon*, a bow.] To inebriate; to make drunk, as with spirituous liquor; *fig.* to excite the spirits of to a very high pitch; to elate to enthusiasm, frenzy, or madness. *v.i.* To have the power of intoxicating, or making drunk.—**Intoxicable**, in-tok'si-ka-bl, *a.* Capable of being intoxicated.—**Intoxicant**, in-tok'si-kant, *n.* That which intoxicates; an intoxicating liquor or substance. — **Intoxicatedness**, in-tok'si-kā-ted-nes, *n.*—**Intoxicating**, in-tok'si-kā-ting, *p.* and *a.* Inebriating; causing intoxication or high mental excitement.—**Intoxication**, in-tok'si-kā"shon, *n.* The act of intoxicating; the state of being intoxicated; inebriation; drunkenness.

Intra-cellular, in-trā-sel'ū-lar. [L. *intra*, within, *cellula*, a little cell.] Within a cell.

Intractable, in-trak'ta-bl, *a.* [Prefix *in*, not, and *tractable*; L. *intractabilis*.] Not tractable; not to be governed or managed, perverse; refractory; indocile.—**Intractableness**, **Intractability**, in-trak'ta-bl-nes, in-trak'ta-bil"i-ti, *n.* The quality of being intractable. — **Intractably**, in-trak'ta-bli, *adv.* In an intractable manner

Intrados, in-trā'dos, *n.* [Fr., from L. *intra*, within, and *dorsum*, back.] *Arch.* the interior and lower line or curve of an arch. EXTRADOS.

Intrafoliaceous, in'tra-fō-li-a"shus, *a.* [Prefix *intra*, and *foliaceous*.] *Bot.* growing on the inside of a leaf.

Intramundane, in-tra-mun'dān, *a.* [Prefix *intra*, and *mundane*.] Being within the world; belonging to the material world.

Intramural, in-tra-mū'ral, *a.* [Prefix *intra*, and *mural*.] Being within the walls or boundaries, as of a university, city, or town.

Intrance, in-trans', *v.t.* ENTRANCE

Intransigent, in-tran'si-jent, *a.* [Fr. *intransigeant*, from L. *in*, not, and *transigo*, to transact, to come to a settlement.] Refusing to agree or come to a settlement; irreconcilable: used especially of some extreme political party. — *n.* An irreconcilable person.—**Intransigentes**, in-tran-si-hen'tāz, *n. pl.* [Sp., the irreconcilables.] The name given to the extreme left in the Spanish Cortes, and afterwards to a very advanced republican party.

Intransitive, in-tran'si-tiv, *a.* [Prefix *in*, not, and *transitive*.] *Gram.* expressing an action or state that is limited to the subject; not having an object (an *intransitive* verb).—**Intransitively**, in-tran'si-tiv-li, *adv.* In an intransitive manner.

Intransmissible, intrans-mis'i-bl, *a.* [Prefix *in*, not, and *transmissible*.] That cannot be transmitted.

Intransmutable, in-trans-mū'ta-bl, *a.* [Prefix *in*, not, and *transmutable*.] That cannot be transmuted or changed into another substance —**Intransmutability**, in-trans-mū'ta-bil"i-ti, *n.*

Intrant, in'trant, *a.* [L. *intrans*, *intrantis*, ppr. of *intro*, to go into, to enter.] Entering—*n.* One who makes an entrance; one who enters upon public duty or office.

Intraparietal, in'tra-pa-ri"et-al, *a.* [L. *intra*, and *paries*, *parietis*, a wall.] Situated or happening within walls; shut from public view; private.

Intrastate, in'tra-state, *a.* Within a state, as intrastate shipping of goods.

Intratropical, in-tra-trop'i-kal, *a.* [Prefix *intra*, and *tropical*.] Situated within the tropics; pertaining to regions within the tropics.

Intravenous, in'tra-vē-nus, *a.* [Prefix *intra*, and *venous*.] Introduced within the veins.

Intrench, in-trensh', *v.t.* [Prefix *in*, and *trench*.] To dig or cut a trench or trenches round, as in fortification; to fortify with a ditch and parapet; to lodge within or as within an intrenchment; to place in a strong position. — *v.i.* To invade; to encroach: with *on* or *upon*. — **Intrenchment**, in-trensh'ment, *n.* The act of intrenching; *fort.* a work consisting of a trench or ditch and a parapet (the latter formed of the earth dug out of the ditch), constructed for a defence against an enemy; an inroad or encroachment on the rights of others.

Intrepid, in-trep'id, *a.* [L. *intrepidus*—*in*, not, and *trepidus*, alarmed. TREPIDATION.] Fearless; bold; brave; undaunted. —**Intrepidity**, in-tre-pid'i-ti, *n.* Fearlessness; fearless bravery in danger; undaunted courage.—**Intrepidly**, in-trep'id-li, *adv.* In an intrepid manner.

Intricacy. Under INTRICATE.

Intricate, in'tri-kāt, *a.* [L. *intricatus*, pp. of *intrico*, to entangle—*in*, into, and *tricæ*, trifles, hindrances, as in *extricate*; akin *intrigue*.] Entangled; involved; difficult to unravel or follow out in all the windings; complicated,—**Intricately**, in'tri-kāt-li, *adv.* In an intricate manner. — **Intricateness**, in'tri-kāt-nes, *n.* The state of being intricate; intricacy. — **Intricacy**, in'tri-ka-si, *n.* The state of being intricate or entangled; a winding or complicated arrangement; entanglement; complication.

Intrigue, in-trēg' or in'trēg, *n.* [Fr. *intriguer*, from L. *intrico*, to entangle. INTRICATE.] A plot or scheme of a complicated nature, and especially political in character; the plot of a play, poem, or romance; an illicit intimacy between two persons of different sexes; a liaison.—*v.i.* —*intrigued*, *intriguing*. To form an intrigue; to engage in an intrigue; to carry on a liaison. — **Intriguer**, in-trē'gėr, *n.* One who intrigues. — **Intriguery**, in-trē'gėr-i, *n.* Arts or practice of intrigue. **Intriguing**, in-trēg'ing, *p.* and *a.* Addicted to intrigue. — **Intriguingly**, in-trēg'ing-li, *adv.* In an intriguing manner.

Intrinsic, **Intrinsical**, in-trin'sik, in-trin'si-kal, *a.* [L. *intrinsecus* — *intra*, inwards, *in*, in, and *secus*, beside, from root of *sequor*, to follow (whence *sequence*).] Inherent; essential; belonging to the thing in itself; not extrinsic or accidental (the *intrinsic* value of gold or silver, *intrinsic* merit). — **Intrinsically**, in-trin'si-kal-li, *adv.* By intrinsic character; in its nature; essentially; inherently.—**Intrinsicality**, **Intrinsicalness**, in-trin'si-kal"i-ti, in-trin'si-kal-nes, *n.*

Introduce, in-trō-dūs', *v.t.*—*introduced*, *introducing*. [L. *introduco*—*intro*, within, and *duco*, to lead. DUKE.] To lead or bring in; to conduct or usher in; to pass in; to put in; to insert; to make known by stating one's name: often used of the action of a third party with regard to two others; to bring to be acquainted; to present (to *introduce* one person, one's self, to another); to bring into use or practice a fashion, custom, &c.); to bring before the public; to bring into a country; to bring forward (a topic) with preliminary or preparatory matter.—**Introducer**, in-trō-dū'sėr, *n.* One who introduces.—**Introduction**, in-trō-duk'shon, *n.* [L. *introductio*.] The act of introducing, bringing in, making persons acquainted, &c.; the part of a book or discourse which precedes the main work, and which gives some general account of its design and subject; a preface or preliminary discourse; a treatise introductory to more elaborate works on the same subject.—**Introductive**, in-trō-duk'tiv, *a.* Serving to introduce.—**Introductory**, in-trō-duk'to-ri, *a.* Serving to introduce something else; serving as or given by way of an introduction; prefatory preliminary.

Introflexed, in-trō-flekst', *a.* [Prefix *intro*, within, to the inside, and *flexed*.] Flexed or bent inward.

Introit, in-trō'it, *n.* [L. *introitus*, an entrance, from *intro*, within, and *eo*, to go. INITIAL.] *R. Cath. Ch.* the beginning of the mass; a piece sung or chanted while the priest proceeds to the altar to celebrate mass; a musical composition designed for opening the church service.

Intromit, in-trō-mit', *v.t.* — *intromitted*, *intromitting*. [L. *intromitto*—*intro*, within, and *mitto*, *missum*, to send.] To send in, put in, or let in.—*v.i.* *Scots law*, to intermeddle with the effects, of another.—**Intromittent**, in-trō-mit'ent, *a.* Letting or conveying into or within.—**Intromitter**, in-trō-mit'ėr, *n.* One who intromits.—**Intromission**, in-trō-mish'on, *n.* The act of sending or letting in; admission; *Scots law*, the transactions of an agent or subordinate with the money of his superior.

Introrse, in-trors', *a.* [L. *introrsum*, inwards — *intro*, within, and *versus*, pp. of *verto*, to turn.] Turned or facing inwards; turned towards the axis to which they appertain, as the anthers in plants.

Introspect, in-trō-spekt', *v.t.* [L. *introspicio*, *introspectum* — *intro*, within, and *specio*, to look.] To look into or within; to view the inside of.—**Introspection**, in-trō-spek'shon, *n.* The act of looking inwardly; examination of one's own thoughts or feelings. — **Introspectionist**, in-trō-spek'shon-ist, *n.* One given to introspection.—**Introspective**, in-trō-spek'tiv, *a.* Viewing inwardly; examining one's own thoughts.

Introsusception, in'trō-sus-sep"shon, *n.* [L. *intro*, within, and *susceptio*, *susceptionis*, a taking up or in.] The act of receiving within; *anat.* intussusception

Introvert, in-trō-vėrt', *v.t.* [L. *intro*, within, and *verto*, to turn.] To turn inward: to turn thought on self. — In'tro-vėrt, *n* That which can be introverted; *psych* one inclined to introversion.—**Introversion**, in-trō-vėr'shon, *n.* A turning inward; *psych.* the tendency to give interests and motives an inward reference and to seek satisfaction (not necessarily egotistical) in an inner life.

Intrude, in-trōd', *v.t.*—*intruded*, *intruding*. [L. *intrudo*—*in*, in, into, and *trudo*, to thrust, as in *detrude*, *obtrude*, *protrude*, *abstruse*.] To thrust one's self forwardly or unwarrantably into any place or position; to force one's self upon others; to encroach; to enter unwelcome or uninvited into company; *geol.* to penetrate, as into fissures or between the layers of rocks.—*v.t.* To thrust in, or cause to enter without right or welcome: often with the reflexive pronoun.—**Intruder**, in-trō'dėr, *n.* One who intrudes.—**Intrusion**, in-trō'zhon, *n.* The act of intruding; unwarrantable entrance; *law*, an unlawful entry into lands and tenements void of a possessor by a person who has no right to the same; *geol.* the penetrating of one rock, while in a melted state, into fissures, &c., of other rocks.—**Intrusional**, in-trō'zhon-al, *a.* Belonging to intrusion.—**Intrusionist**, in-trō'zhon-ist, *n.* One who intrudes or who favors intrusion.—**Intrusive**, in-trō'siv, *a.* Characterized by intrusion; apt to intrude; of the nature of an intrusion.—**Intrusively**, in-trō'siv-li, *adv.* In an intrusive manner.—**Intrusiveness**, *n*

Intrust, in-trust', *n.* ENTRUST

Intubation, in-tūb-ā'shon, *n.* [L. *in*, in, *tuba*, tube.] The process of inserting a tube into a body organ to keep it open.

Intuition, in-tū-ish'on, *n* [From L. *intueor*, *intuitus*, to look upon, to contemplate —*in*, in, upon, and *tueor*, to look (whence *tutor*, *tuition*).] *Philos.* the act by which the mind perceives the agreement or disagreement of two ideas, or the truth of things immediately, and without reasoning and deduction; a truth discerned by the mind directly and necessarily as so; a truth that cannot be acquired by, but is assumed in experience.—**Intuitional**, in-tū-ish'on-al, *a.* Pertaining to, derived from, or characterized by intuition; intuitive.—**Intuitionalism**, in-tū-ish'on-al-izm, *n.* The doctrine that the perception of truth is from intuition.—**Intuitive**, in-tū'i-tiv, *a* Perceived by the mind immediately without the intervention of reasoning; based on intuition; received or obtained by intuition; having the power of discovering truth without reasoning.—**Intuitively**, in-tū'i-tiv-li, *adv.* In an intuitive manner; by intuition.

Intumesce, in-tū-mes', *v.i.* — *intumesced*, *intumescing*. [L. *intumesco* — *in*, and *tumesco*, to begin to swell, incept. of *tumeo*, to swell. TUMID.] To enlarge or expand with heat; to swell out in bulk.—**Intumescence**, **Intumescency**, in-tū-mes'ens, in-tū-mes'en-si, *n.* The state or process of intumescing.

Intussuscept, in'tus-sus-cept, *v.t.* [L. *intus*, within, and *suscipio*, to take or receive. SUSCEPTIBLE.] To take into the interior; to receive by intussusception.—**Intussusception**, in'tus-sus-cep"shon, *n.* The reception of one part within another; the descent or doubling in of a higher portion of intestine into a lower one; the act of taking foreign matter into the substance of a living body; the process by which nutriment is absorbed into and goes to form part of the system.

Intwine, in-twīn′, *v.t.*—*intwined, intwining.* To twine or twist in or together; to wreathe; to entwine.—**Intwinement**, in-twīn′ment, *n.* The act of intwining.

Inunction, in-ungk′shon, *n.* [L. *inunctio, inunctionis*, from *inungo, inunctum*, to anoint.] The action of anointing; unction.

Inundate, in′un-dāt or in-un′dāt, *v.t.*—*inundated, inundating.* [L. *inundo, inundatum*—*in*, and *undo*, to overflow (also in *abound*), from *unda*, a wave. UNDULATE.] To spread or flow over; to overflow; to deluge; to flood; to submerge; to fill with an overflowing abundance or superfluity.—**Inundation**, in-un-dā′shon, *n.* [L. *inundatio.*] The act of inundating or state of being inundated; a flood; a rising and spreading of waters over low grounds.—**Inundant**, in-un′dant, *a.* Overflowing; inundating.

Inure, in-ūr′, *v.t.*—*inured, inuring.* [Prefix *in*, in, and obsol. *ure*, operation, work, from O.Fr. *eure*, Mod.Fr. *œuvre*, from L. *opera*, work. The *-ure* of this word therefore = *ure* of *manure.* OPERATE.] To apply or expose in use or practice till use gives little or no pain or inconvenience, or makes little impression; to habituate; to accustom (to toil or hardships).—**Inurement**, in-ūr′ment, *n.* The act or process of inuring.

Inurn, in-ėrn′, *v.t.* [Prefix *in*, and *urn.*] To put in an urn, especially a funeral urn; hence, to bury; to intomb. (*Poet.*)

Inutility, in-ū-til′i-ti, *n.* [Prefix *in*, not, and *utility*; L. *inutilitas.*] The quality of being useless or unprofitable; uselessness; unprofitableness.

Inutterable, in-ut′ėr-a-bl, *a.* [Prefix *in*, not, and *utterable.*] Unutterable. (*Mil.*)

Invade, in-vād′, *v.t.*—*invaded, invading.* [L. *invado*—*in*, into, and *vado*, to go, seen also in *evade, pervade*; akin *wade.*] To enter with hostile intentions; to enter as an enemy, with a view to conquest or plunder; to enter by force; to make an inroad or incursion on; to intrude upon; to infringe, encroach on, or violate (rights or privileges).—*v.i.* To make an invasion.—**Invader**, in-vā′dėr, *n.* One who invades.—**Invasion**, in-vā′shon, *n.* [L. *invasio*, from *invado.*] The act of invading; a hostile entrance into the country or possessions of another; an attack on the rights of another.—**Invasive**, in-vā′siv, *a.* Tending to invade; aggressive.

Invaginate, in-vaj′i-nāt, *v.i.* [L. *in*, in, into, and *vagina*, a sheath.] To enter as into a sheath; to enter by intussusception into another part.—**Invagination**, in-vaj′i-nā″shon, *n.* *Anat.* the reception of one part within another by being doubled backwards; intussusception.

Invalid, in-val′id, *a.* [Prefix *in*, not, and *valid*; L. *invalidus.*] Not valid; of no force, weight, or cogency; weak (an *invalid* argument); *law*, having no force, effect, or efficacy; void; null.—*n.* (in′va-lid). [Directly from Fr. *invalide.*] A person who is weak and infirm; a sufferer from ill health; one who is disabled for active service, especially a soldier or seaman worn out in service.—*a.* In ill health; infirm; disabled for active service.—*v.t.* To render an invalid; to enrol on the list of invalids in the military or naval service.—**Invalidate**, in-val′i-dāt, *v.t.*—*invalidated, invalidating.* To render invalid or not valid; to render of no legal force or effect.—**Invalidation**, in-val′i-dā″shon, *n.* Act of invalidating.—**Invalidism**, in′va-lid-izm, *n.* The condition of being an invalid.—**Invalidity, Invalidness**, in-va-lid′i-ti, in-val′id-nes, *n.* Want of validity; want of cogency; want of legal force or efficacy.

Invaluable, in-val′ū-a-bl, *a.* [Prefix *in*, not, and *valuable.*] Precious above estimation; so valuable that its worth cannot be estimated; inestimable.—**Invaluably**, in-val′ū-a-bli, *adv.* Inestimably.

Invar, in′var, *n.* [From *invar*iable.] An alloy of nickel and steel which is practically unaffected by extremes of temperature.

Invariable, in-vā′ri-a-bl, *a.* [Prefix *in*, not, and *variable.*] Not variable; constant in the same state; always uniform; never varying.—*n.* *Math.* an invariable quantity; a constant.—**Invariableness, Invariability**, in-vā′ri-a-bl-nes, in-vā′ri-a-bil″i-ti, *n.* State of not varying.—**Invariably**, in-vā′ri-a-bli, *adv.* Constantly; uniformly; always.

Invasion, Invasive. Under INVADE.

Invective, in-vek′tiv, *n.* [Fr., from L. *invectivus*, abusive, from *inveho*, to inveigh. INVEIGH.] A severe or violent utterance of censure or reproach; something uttered or written intended to cast opprobrium, censure, or reproach on another; railing language; vituperation.—*a.* Containing invectives; abusive; vituperative.—**Invectively**, in-vek′tiv-li, *adv.* In an invective manner; abusively.—**Invectiveness**, in-vek′tiv-nes, *n.* The quality of being invective or vituperative.

Inveigh, in-vā′, *v.i.* [L. *invehor*, to attack with words, to inveigh against—*in*, into, against, and *veho*, to carry. VEHICLE.] To utter invectives; to exclaim or rail against a person or thing; to utter censorious or opprobrious words: with *against.*—**Inveigher**, in-vā′ėr, *n.* One who inveighs or rails; a railer.

Inveigle, in-vē′gl, *v.t.* [Norm. *enveogler*, to inveigle, to blind, for Fr. *aveugler*, to blind, from *aveugle*, blind—L. *ab*, priv., and *oculus*, the eye. OCULAR.] To persuade to something evil by deceptive arts or flattery; to cajole into wrong-doing; to entice; to seduce.—**Inveiglement**, in-vē′gl-ment, *n.* The act of inveigling.—**Inveigler**, in-vē′gl-ėr, *n.* One who inveigles.

Invenom, in-ven′om, *v.t.* To *Envenom.*

Invent, in-vent′, *v.t.* [Fr. *inventer*, from L. *invenio, inventum*, to come upon, to find—*in*, upon, and *venio*, to come, as in *advent, convent, convene, prevent*, &c. VENTURE.] To contrive and produce; to devise, make, or construct as the originator of something that did not before exist; to frame by the imagination; to excogitate; to concoct; to fabricate. ∴ Syn. under DISCOVER.—**Inventible**, in-ven′ti-bl, *a.* Capable of being invented.—**Inventibleness**, in-ven′ti-bl-nes, *n.*—**Invention**, in-ven′shon, *n.* [L. *inventio, inventionis.*] The act of inventing; the contrivance of that which did not before exist; origination; something invented or contrived; a contrivance; the power of inventing; that skill or ingenuity which is or may be employed in contriving anything new; that faculty by which a poet or novelist produces plots, incidents, and characters, &c.—**Inventive**, in-ven′tiv, *a.* Able to invent; quick at invention or contrivance; ready at expedients.—**Inventively**, in-ven′tiv-li, *adv.* By the power of invention.—**Inventiveness**, in-ven′tiv-nes, *n.* The faculty of inventing.—**Inventer, Inventor**, in-vent′ėr, in-ven′tŏr, *n.* One who invents or creates some new contrivance or device.

Inventory, in′ven-to-ri, *n.* [L. *inventarium*, an inventory, lit. a list of goods *found* in a place, from *invenio.* INVENT.] A list containing a description, with the values, of goods and chattels, made on various occasions, as on the sale of goods, or at decease of a person; any catalogue of goods or wares; a catalogue or account of particular things.—*v.t.*—*inventoried, inventorying.* To make an inventory, list, catalogue, or schedule of; to insert or register in an account of goods.—**Inventorial**, in-ven-tō′ri-al, *a.* Of or pertaining to an inventory.—**Inventorially**, in-ven-tō′ri-al-li, *adv.* In the manner of an inventory.

Inverse, in-vėrs′, *a.* [L. *inversus*, pp. of *inverto*—*in*, on, to, and *verto*, to turn, as in *advert, convert, revert, subvert*, &c. VERSE.] Opposite in order or relation; inverted; having what usually is or should be after placed before; proceeding the backward or reverse way; *math.* opposite in nature and effect; thus, subtraction is *inverse* to addition, division to multiplication.—*Inverse proportion*, proportion such that one thing is greater or less as another is less or greater.—**Inversely**, in-vėrs′li, *adv.* In an inverse order or manner; in inverse proportion.—**Inversion**, in-vėr′shon, *n.* [L. *inversio, inversionis*, from *inverto, inversum.*] The act of inverting or the state of being inverted; a change of order or position so that what was after is now before, and *vice versâ*; a making inverse in order; *gram.* and *rhet.* transposition of words so that they are out of their natural order ('wise was Solomon for 'Solomon was wise'); *mus.* change of position, as of an interval or a chord; *math.* a change in the order of the terms of a proportion, so that the second takes the place of the first, and the fourth of the third.—**Invert**, in-vėrt′, *v.t.* [L. *inverto.*] To turn upside down; to place in a contrary order or position; to put in inverse order or position.—**Inverted**, in-vėr′ted, *p.* and *a.* Turned to a contrary direction; turned upside down; changed in order; *bot.* having the apex in an opposite direction to that which is normal.—*Inverted arch*, an arch with its curve turned downwards, as in a sewer, in foundations, &c.—*Inverted commas*, commas turned upside down to mark the beginning of a quotation, the end being indicated by apostrophes.—**Invertedly**, in-vėr′ted-li, *adv.* In an inverted position; in reversed order.—**Invertible**, in-vėr′ti-bl, *a.* Capable of being inverted.

Invertebrate, Invertebrated, Invertebral, in-vėr′tē-brāt, in-vėr′tē-brā-ted, in-vėr′tē-bral, *a.* [Prefix *in*, not, and *vertebrate.* VERTEBRA.] Destitute of a backbone or vertebral column; morally or mentally without stamina or backbone.—**Invertebrate**, in-vėr′tē-brāt, *n.* An animal belonging to one of the two great divisions of the animal kingdom, the **Invertebrata** (in-vėr′tē-brā″ta), including all animals that have no vertebral column or spine, and in many cases no hard parts at all.

Invest, in-vest′, *v.t.* [L. *investio*—*in*, and *vestio*, to clothe, from *vestis*, a garment. VEST.] To put garments on; to clothe, to dress, to array: usually followed by *with*, sometimes by *in*, before the thing put on; to clothe, as with office or authority; to place in possession of an office, rank, or dignity; *milit.* to inclose or surround for the purpose of besieging; to lay siege to; to lay out (money or capital) on some species of property, usually of a permanent nature, and with the purpose of getting a return (to *invest* money *in* bank shares).—*v.i.* To make an investment.—**Investiture**, in-ves′ti-tūr, *n.* The act of investing; the act or right of giving possession of an office, dignity, &c.; that which invests or clothes; clothing; covering (*poet.* in this sense); the long mediæval contest between Kings and the Papacy for the right of investing bishops and others with ecclesiastical or feudal dignities and rights.—**Investment**, in-vest′ment, *n.* The act of investing; the act of besieging by an armed force; the laying out of money in the purchase of some species of property; money laid out for profit; that in which money is invested.—**Investor**, in-ves′tėr, *n.* One who invests.

Investigate, in-ves′ti-gāt, *v.t.*—*investigated, investigating.* [L. *investigo, investigatum*—*in*, and *vestigo*, to follow a track, to search, from *vestigium*, a track. VESTIGE.] To search into; to inquire and examine into with care and accuracy; to make careful research or examination into.—**Investigable**, in-ves′ti-ga-bl, *a.* Capable of being investigated.—**Investigation**, in-ves′ti-gā″shon, *n.* [L. *investigatio, investigationis.*] The act of investigating; the process of inquiring into a subject; research; inquiry.—**Investigative**, in-ves′ti-gā-tiv, *a.* Given to or concerned with investigation.—**Investigator**, in-ves′ti-gā-tėr, *n.* One who investigates.

Inveterate, in-vet′ėr-āt, *a.* [L. *inveteratus*, pp. of *invetero*, to render old—*in*, in, and *vetus, veteris*, old. VETERAN.] Firmly established by long continuance; deep-rooted or ingrained in a person's nature or constitution; firmly fixed by time or habit (*inveterate* disease, custom); confirmed in any habit by practice (an *inveterate* liar).—**Inveterately**, in-vet′ėr-āt-li, *adv.* In an inveterate manner. — **Inveteracy, Inveterateness**, in-vet′ėr-a-si, in-vet′ėr-āt-nes, *n.* The state or quality of being inveterate; obstinacy confirmed by time.

Invidious, in-vid′i-us, *a.* [L. *invidiosus*, from *invidia*, envy, *invidus*, envious. ENVY.] Envious†; likely to bring on envy, ill-will, or hatred; likely to provoke envy; entailing odium (*invidious* distinctions, preference, position).—**Invidiously**, in-vid′i-us-li, *adv.* In an invidious manner.—**Invidiousness**, in-vid′i-us-nes, *n.* The quality of being invidious.

Invigorate, in-vig′or-āt, *v.t.*—*invigorated, invigorating.* [L. *in*, intens., and *vigor*, strength. VIGOUR.] To give vigour to; to cause to feel fresh and vigorous; to strengthen; to give life and energy to.—**Invigoration**, in-vig′o-rā″shon, *n.* Act of invigorating; state of being invigorated.

Invincible, in-vin′si-bl, *a.* [L. *invincibilis*—*in*, not, and *vincibilis*, conquerable, from *vinco*, to conquer. VICTOR.] Incapable of being conquered or subdued; incapable of being overcome; unconquerable; insuperable.—*n.* One who is invincible.—**Invincibility, Invincibleness**, in-vin′si-bil″i-ti, in-vin′si-bl-nes, *n.* The quality of being invincible.—**Invincibly**, in-vin′si-bli, *adv.* In an invincible manner; unconquerably; insuperably.

Inviolable, in-vī′ō-la-bl, *a.* [L. *inviolabilis*—*in*, not, and *violabilis*, that may be violated, from *violo*, to violate. VIOLATE.] Not to be violated or profaned; not to be polluted or treated with irreverence; not to be broken or infringed (agreement, secrecy); not to be injured or tarnished (chastity, honour); not susceptible of hurt or wound (*Mil.*).—**Inviolably**, in-vī′ō-la-bli, *adv.* In an inviolable manner; without violation or profanation.—**Inviolability, Inviolableness**, in-vī′ō-la-bil″i-ti, in-vī′ō-la-bl-nes, *n.* The state or quality of being inviolable.—**Inviolate, Inviolated**, in-vī′ō-lāt, in-vī′o-lā-ted, *a.* [L. *inviolatus.*] Not violated; unprofaned; unpolluted; unbroken; inviolable.—**Inviolately**, in-vī′ō-lāt-li, *adv.* In an inviolate manner.—**Inviolateness**, in-vī′ō-lāt-nes, *n.*

Invisible, in-viz′i-bl, *a.* [Prefix *in*, not, and *visible*; L. *invisibilis.*] Incapable of being seen; imperceptible by the sight.—*Invisible green*, a shade of green so dark as scarcely to be distinguishable from black.—**Invisibleness, Invisibility**, in-viz′i-bl-nes, in-viz′i-bil″i-ti, *n.* The state of being invisible; imperceptibleness to the sight.—**Invisibly**, in-viz′i-bli, *adv.* In an invisible manner; imperceptibly to the eye.

Invite, in-vīt′, *v.t.*—*invited, inviting.* [L. *invito*, to invite, perhaps for *invicto, invecto*—*in*, and root of *vox*, voice.] To ask, request, bid, or call upon to do something; to summon; to ask to an entertainment or to pay a visit; to allure or attract; to tempt to come.—*v.i.* To give invitation; to allure or entice.—*n.* An invitation. (*Genteel slang.*)—**Invitation**, in-vi-tā′shon, *n.* [L. *invitatio, invitationis.*] The act of inviting; solicitation; the requesting of a person's company as to an entertainment, on a visit, or the like.—**Invitatory**, in-vī′ta-to-ri, *a.* Using or containing invitations.—**Inviter**, in-vī′tėr, *n.* One who invites.—**Inviting**, in-vī′ting, *p.* and *a.* Alluring; tempting; attractive (an *inviting* prospect).—**Invitingly**, in-vī′ting-li, *adv.* In an inviting manner; attractively.—**Invitingness**, in-vī′ting-nes, *n.* Attractiveness.

Invitrifiable, in-vit′ri-fī-a-bl, *a.* [Prefix *in*, not, and *vitrifiable.*] Incapable of being vitrified.

Invocate, in′vō-kāt, *v.i.*—*invocated, invocating.* [L. *invoco, invocatum*—*in*, and *voco*, to call, *vox*, voice. VOICE, VOCAL.] To invoke; to call on in supplication; to implore; to address in prayer.—**Invocation**, in-vō-kā′shon, *n.* [L. *invocatio, invocationis.*] The act of invoking or addressing in prayer; the form or act of calling for the assistance or presence of any being, particularly of some divinity.—**Invocatory**, in-vō′ka-to-ri, *a.* Making invocation; invoking.

Invoice, in′vois, *n.* [Fr. *envois*, things sent, goods forwarded, pl. of *envoi*, a sending, a thing sent, from *envoyer*, to send—L. *in*, and *via*, a way. ENVOY.] A written account of the particulars of merchandise sent to a purchaser, consignee, factor, &c., with the value or prices and charges annexed.—*v.t.*—*invoiced, invoicing.* To write or enter in an invoice.

Invoke, in-vōk′, *v.t.*—*invoked, invoking.* [Fr. *invoquer*, L. *invocare.* INVOCATE.] To address in prayer; to call on for assistance and protection; to call for solemnly or with earnestness.

Involucre, Involucrum, in-vō-lū′kėr, in-vō-lū′krum, *n.* [L. *involucrum*, a wrapper or envelope, from *involvo*, to involve or wrap round—*in*, and *volvo*, to roll. INVOLVE.] *Bot.* any collection of bracts round a cluster of flowers; *anat.* a membrane which surrounds or incloses a part, as the pericardium.—**Involucral**, in-vō-lū′kral, *a.* Pertaining to or having an involucre.—**Involucred, Involucrate, Involucrated**, in-vō-lū′kėrd, in-vō-lū′krāt, in-vō-lū′krā-ted, *a.* *Bot.* having an involucre, as umbels, &c.—**Involucel, Involucellum**, in-vol′ū-sel, in-vol′ū-sel″lum, *n.* [Dim. of *involucre, involucrum.*] *Bot.* the secondary involucrum or small bracts surrounding an umbellule of an umbelliferous flower.—**Involucellate**, in-vō-lū′sel-lāt, *a.* Surrounded with involucels.

Involuntary, in-vol′un-ta-ri, *n.* [Prefix *in*, not, and *voluntary.*] Not voluntary; not able to act or not acting according to will or choice (an *involuntary* agent); independent of will or choice (an *involuntary* movement); not proceeding from choice; not done willingly; unwilling. — **Involuntarily**, in-vol′un-ta-ri-li, *adv.* In an involuntary manner.—**Involuntariness**, in-vol′un-ta-ri-nes, *n.*

Involute, Involuted, in′vō-lūt, in′vō-lū-ted, *a.* [L. *involutus*, pp. of *involvo.* INVOLVE.] Involved; twisted; confusedly mingled; *bot.* rolled inward from the edges; said of leaves and petals in vernation and estivation; *zool.* turned inwards at the margin: said of the shells of molluscs.—**Involute**, *n.* A curve traced by any point of a tense string when it is unwrapped from a given curve. — **Involution**, in-vō-lū′shon, *n.* [L. *involutio, involutionis*, from *involvo.*] The action of involving or infolding; the state of being entangled or involved, or of being folded in; complication; *arith.* and *alg.* the raising of a quantity from its root to any power assigned; the multiplication of a quantity into itself a given number of times: opposite of *evolution.*

Involve, in-volv′, *v.t.*—*involved, involving.* [L. *involvo*—*in*, into, and *volvo*, to roll, as in *convolve, devolve, evolve, revolve, voluble*, &c. WALLOW.] To roll or wrap up; to envelop in folds; to entwine; to envelop; to cover with surrounding matter (*involved* in darkness); to imply or comprise, as a logical consequence (a statement that *involves* a contradiction); to connect by way of natural result or consequence; to entangle; to implicate; to complicate; to blend; to mingle confusedly; *arith.* and *alg.* to raise to any assigned power. ∴ Syn. under IMPLICATE.—**Involved**, in-volvd′, *p.* and *a.* Complicated; entangled; intricate.—**Involvedness**, in-vol′ved-nes, *n.* State of being involved.—**Involvement**, in-volv′ment, *n.* Act of involving.

Invulnerable, in-vul′nėr-a-bl, *a.* [Prefix *in*, not, and *vulnerable*; L. *invulnerabilis.*] Not vulnerable; incapable of being wounded or of receiving injury; unassailable, as an argument; able to reply to all arguments.—**Invulnerability, Invulnerableness**, in-vul′nėr-a-bil″i-ti, in-vul′nėr-a-bl-nes, *n.* The quality or state of being invulnerable. — **Invulnerably**, in-vul′nėr-a-bli, *adv.* In an invulnerable manner.—**Invulnerate**, in-vul′nėr-āt, *a.* [L. *invulneratus.*] Unwounded; unhurt.

Inward, in′wėrd, *a.* [A.Sax. *inneweard*—prep. *in*, and suffix *-ward*, as in *backward, toward*, &c.] Internal; interior; placed or being within; in or connected with the mind, thoughts, soul, or feelings.—*adv.* also **Inwards** (in′wėrdz). Toward the inside; toward the centre or interior; into the mind or thoughts.—*n. pl.* the inner parts of an animal; the viscera.—**Inwardly**, in′wėrd-li, *adv.* In an inward manner; internally; mentally; privately.—**Inwardness**, in′wėrd-nes, *n.* The state of being inward or internal.

Inweave, in-wēv′, *v.t.*—*inwove* (pret.), *inwoven* (pp.), *inweaving* (ppr.). To weave together; to intermix or intertwine by weaving.

Inwrap, in-rap′, *v.t.*—*inwrapped, inwrapping.* [Prefix *in*, and *wrap.*] To cover by wrapping; to involve; to infold.

Inwreathe, in-rēTH′, *v.t.* — *inwreathed, inwreathing.* [Prefix *in*, and *wreathe.*] To surround or twine, as with a wreath; to infold or involve.

Inwrought, in′rąt, *p.* and *a.* [Prefix *in*, and *wrought.*] Wrought or worked in or among other things; adorned with figures worked in.

Iodine, ī′ō-dīn, *n.* [Gr. *iōdēs*, resembling a violet (from its colour)—*ion*, a violet, and *eidos*, resemblance.] One of the non-metallic elements, a solid substance, of a bluish-black or grayish-black colour, existing in sea-water, in marine molluscous animals, and in sea-weeds, from the ashes of which it is chiefly procured; much used in medicine.—**Iodic**, ī-od′ik, *a.* Pertaining to or containing iodine (*iodic* silver).—*Iodic acid*, an acid formed by the action of oxidizing agents on iodine in presence of water or alkalies.—**Iodide**, ī′o-dīd, *n.* A compound of iodine and a metal.—**Iodism**, ī′o-dizm, *n.* *Pathol.* a peculiar morbid state produced by the use of iodine.—**Iodize**, ī′o-dīz, *v.t.*—*iodized, iodizing.* To treat with iodine; to impregnate or affect with iodine.—**Iodizer**, ī′o-dī-zėr, *n.* One who or that which iodizes.—**Iodoform**, ī-od′ō-form, *n.* A compound of carbon, hydrogen, and iodine, analogous to chloroform.

Iodol, ī′od-ōl. [From *iodine.*] An antiseptic derived from coal-tar.

Iolite, ī′o-līt, *n.* [Gr. *ion*, a violet, and *lithos*, stone.] A mineral of a violet blue colour; dichroite.

Ion, ī′on, *n.* One of the elements of an electrolyte, or compound body undergoing electrolysation. See Supplement.

Ionian, Ionic, ī-ō′ni-an, ī-on′ik, *a.* Relating to *Ionia*, or to the Ionian Greeks.—*Ionic order*, one of the five orders of architecture, the distinguishing characteristic of which consists in the volutes of its capital.—*Ionic dialect*, a dialect of the ancient Greek language.

Ionization, ī′on-iz-ā″shon. [Gr. *iōn*, going.] Of substances in solution, breaking up into IONS (which see).

Iota, ī-ō′ta, *n.* [Gr. *iōta*: hence *jot.*] Primarily the name of the Greek letter *ι*, which in certain cases is indicated by a sort of dot under another letter (as ῳ); hence, a very small quantity; a tittle; a jot.

I O U, ī′ ō ū, *n.* [A phonetic equivalent of *I owe you.*] A paper addressed to a person having on it these letters, followed by a sum, and duly signed; serving as an acknowledgment of a debt.

Ipecac, Ipecacuanha, ip′é-kak, ip′é-kak′ū-an″a, *n.* [The Brazilian name.] An emetic or tonic substance, of a nauseous odor and bitterish taste, obtained from the root of the Brazilian cinchona plant.

Iracund,† ī′ra-kund, *a.* [L. *iracundus*, angry, from *ira*, anger; whence *ire, irate*, &c.] Angry; passionate. (*Carl.*)

Irade, i-rā′dē, *n.* [Turk.] A decree or proclamation of the Sultan of Turkey.

Iranian, ī-rā′ni-an, *a.* Pertaining to *Iran*, the native name of Persia; applied to certain languages, including Persian, Zend, and cognate tongues.

Irascible, i-ras′i-bl, *a.* [L. *irascibilis*, from *irascor*, to be angry, from *ira*, anger, whence also *ire*, *irate*.] Readily made angry; easily provoked; apt to get into a passion; irritable. — **Irascibility, Irascibleness**, i-ras′i-bil″i-ti, i-ras′i-bl-nes, *n.* The quality of being irascible.—**Irascibly**, i-ras′i-bli, *adv.* In an irascible manner.

Irate, i-rāt′, *a.* [L. *iratus*, angry, from *irascor*, to be angry. IRASCIBLE.] Angry; enraged; incensed.

Ire, īr, *n.* [O.Fr., from L. *ira*, wrath.] Anger; wrath; keen resentment.—**Ireful**, īr′ful, *a.* Full of ire; angry; wroth.—**Irefully**, īr′ful-li, *adv.* In an ireful or angry manner.—**Irefulness**, īr′ful-nes, *n.* The condition of being ireful; wrath; anger.

Iricism, ī′ri-sizm, *n.* An Irish mode of expression; a characteristically Irish blunder; a bull; any Irish peculiarity.

Iridal, Iridian, ī′rid-al, ī-rid′i-an, *a.* [Gr. *iris*, *iridos*, the rainbow. IRIS. Pertaining to the iris; belonging to or resembling the rainbow. — **Iridescence**, ir-i-des′ens, *n.* The condition of being iridescent. — **Iridescent**, ir-i-des′ent, *a.* Giving out colors like those of the rainbow; gleaming or shimmering with rainbow colors. — **Iridium**, ī-rid′i-um, *n.* [From the iridescent colors it exhibits when dissolving in hydrochloric acid.] A rare metal of a whitish color, not malleable, very infusible, and not readily affected by acids, found in the ore of platinum and in a native alloy with osmium.—**Iridosmine, Iridosmium**, ir-i-dos′min, ir-i-dos′mi-um, *n.* A native compound of iridium and osmium used for pointing gold pens.

Iris, ī′ris, *n.* pl. **Irises**, ī′ris-ez, **Irides**, ī′ri-dēz (especially of the eye). [L. *iris*, *iridis*, Gr. *iris*, *iridos*, the rainbow, the plant iris, the iris of the eye.] The rainbow; an appearance resembling the rainbow; the hues of the rainbow as seen in sunlit spray, the spectrum of sunlight, &c.; a kind of muscular curtain stretched vertically in the anterior part of the eye, in the midst of the aqueous humour, separating the anterior from the posterior chamber, and perforated by the pupil for the transmission of light; the flower-de-lis or flag-flower, a plant of various species. — **Irisated, Irised**, ī′ri-sā-ted, ī′rist, *a.* Exhibiting the prismatic colours; resembling the rainbow.—**Iriscope**, ī′ri-skōp, *n.* A philosophical toy for exhibiting the prismatic or rainbow colours.—**Iritis, Iriditis**, ī-rī′tis, ī-ri-dī′tis, *n.* Inflammation of the iris.

Irish, ī′rish, *a.* Pertaining to Ireland or its inhabitants; Erse. —*n.* The Irish language; with plural signification, the people of Ireland.—**Irishism**, ī′rish-izm, *n.* An Iricism.—*Irish moss*, *n.* CARRAGEEN.—*Irish stew*, meat and potatoes stewed together.

Irk, ėrk, *v.t.* [The same word as Sw. *yrka*, to urge, enforce, press, from root of *work*, *wreak*, and *urge*.] To weary; to give annoyance or uneasiness to; to be distressingly tiresome to; to annoy: used chiefly or only impersonally (it *irks* me). — **Irksome**, ėrk′sum, *a.* Wearisome; burdensome; vexatious; giving uneasiness (*irksome* labour, delay, &c.). — **Irksomely**, ėrk′sum-li, *adv.* In an irksome manner.—**Irksomeness**, ėrk′sum-nes, *n.* The quality or state of being irksome; vexatiousness.

Iron, ī′ėrn, *n.* [A.Sax. *iren*, *isen*, Goth. *eisarn*, Icel. *járn* (from older *isarn*), Dan. *jern*, O.H.G. *isarn*, Mod. G. *eisen*; D. *ijzer*; comp. Skr. *ayas*, W. *haiarn*, Armor. *houarn*. The word appears to be in form an adj., and the name may be akin to *ice*—from its glancing.] The commonest and most useful of all the metals, of a livid whitish colour inclined to gray, seldom found native; an instrument or utensil made of iron; an instrument that when heated is used for smoothing cloth; *pl.* fetters; chains; manacles; handcuffs.—*To have many irons in the fire*, to be engaged in many undertakings. [*Cast iron* is iron direct from the smelting furnace (blast-furnace), also called *pig-iron*; *wrought* or *malleable iron* has to undergo the further process of puddling; *steel* is a variety of iron containing more carbon than malleable iron and less than cast iron.]—*a.* Made of iron; consisting of iron; resembling iron, either really or metaphorically; hence, harsh, rude, severe; capable of great endurance; firm; robust; inflexible.—*v.t.* To smooth with an iron; to fetter or handcuff; to furnish or arm with iron.—**Iron Age**, that cultural epoch chiefly distinguished by the use of iron; roughly, the last thousand years B. C. — **Ironbark**, ī′ėrn-bärk, *n.* Certain Australian eucalypti with hard bark. — **Iron-bound**, *a.* Bound with iron; faced or surrounded with rocks; rugged (an *iron-bound* coast). — **Ironclad**, *a.* Covered or clothed with iron plates; armor-plated.—*n.* A vessel prepared for naval warfare by being cased or covered, wholly or partially, with thick iron plates. — **Ironer**, ī′ėrn-ėr, *n.* One who irons.—**Iron Gates**. The passage of the Danube at Orsova. — **Iron-gray**, *n.* The color of freshly fractured iron. Used also adjectively. — **Iron-hearted**, *a.* Hard-hearted; unfeeling. — **Iron horse**, a locomotive. (*Colloq.*) —**Ironing board**, a flat board, covered with fabric, on which clothes are ironed. — **Iron-liquor**, *n.* Acetate of iron, used as a mordant by dyers, &c. — **Iron-master**, *n.* One who employs a number of people in the manufacture of iron. — **Iron-mold**, *n.* A spot on cloth occasioned by iron rust. — **Iron-pyrites**. PYRITES. — **Ironsides**, ī′ėrn-sīds, *n. pl.* The cavalry of Oliver Cromwell in the English revolution; an ironclad vessel (as, *Old Ironsides*). — **Iron-smith**, ī′ėrn-smith, *n.* A worker in iron, as a blacksmith, locksmith, &c. — **Iron-stone**, *n.* A general name applied to the ores of iron containing oxygen and silica. — **Ironware**, ī′ėrn-wār, *n.* Utensils, tools, and various light articles of iron. — **Iron-weed**, ī-ėrn-wēd, *n.* A plant of the genus Vernonia found in the eastern U.S.—**Iron-wood**, *n.* The popular name given to several very hard and very heavy woods in different countries. — **Iron-work**, ī′-ėrn-wėrk, *n.* A general name of the parts of a building, vessel, bridge, &c., which consist of iron; a work or establishment where iron is manufactured. — **Irony**, ī′ėrn-i, *a.* Pertaining to or resembling iron in any qualities.

Irony, ī′ron-i, *n.* [Fr. *ironie*, L. *ironia*, from Gr. *eirōneia*, from *eirōn*, a dissembler in speech, from *eirō*, to speak.] A mode of speech by which words express a sense contrary to that really intended; sarcasm, in which apparent praise really conveys disapprobation.—**Ironical, Ironic**, ī-ron′i-kal, ī-ron′ik, *a.* Relating to or containing irony; addicted to irony; using irony. —**Ironically**, ī-ron′i-kal-li, *adv.* In an ironical manner. — **Ironicalness**, *n.*

Iroquois, ir′o-kwoi, *n.* sing., pl. An early Indian confederation of New York state, composed of Cayugas, Mohawks, Oneidas, Onondagas, Senecas and later the Tuscaroras, referred to as the Five Nations; a member of one of these tribes.

Irradiate, ir-rā′di-āt, *v.t.* — *irradiated*, *irradiating*. [L. *irradio*, *irradiatum*—*in*, in or on, and *radius*, a ray.] To illuminate or shed a light upon; to cast splendor or brilliancy upon; to illuminate; to penetrate by radiation; to treat for healing by radiation, as by that of X rays or ultraviolet rays.—*v.i.* To emit rays; to shine. —**Irradiance, Irradiancy**, ir-rā′di-ans, ir-rā′di-an-si, *n.* Emission of rays of light on an object; luster; splendor.—**Irradiant**, ir-rā′di-ant, *a.* Emitting rays of light. — **Irradiation**, ir-rā′di-ā″shon, *n.* The act of irradiating; illumination; brightness emitted; *physics* and *astron.* Apparent enlargement of an object strongly illuminated, because of the vivid impression of light on the retina.

Irrational, ir-rash′on-al, *a.* [Prefix *ir* for *in*, not, and *rational*.] Not rational; void of reason or understanding; contrary to reason; absurd; *math.* not capable of being exactly expressed by an integral number or by a vulgar fraction; surd. — **Irrationality, Irrationalness**, ir-rash′on-al″i-ti, ir-rash′on-al-nes, *n.* The condition or quality of being irrational. — **Irrationally**, ir-rash′on-al-li, *adv.* In an irrational manner.

Irrealizable, ir-rē′al-īz″a-bl, *a.* [Prefix *ir* for *in*, not, and *realizable*.] Incapable of being realized or defined.

Irreclaimable, ir-rē-klā′ma-bl, *a.* [Prefix *ir* for *in*, not, and *reclaimable*.] Incapable of being reclaimed or recalled from error or vice; incapable of being reformed; incorrigible.—**Irreclaimably**, ir-rē-klā′-ma-bli, *adv.* So as not to be reclaimed.

Irrecognizable, ir-rek′og-nī″za-bl, *a.* [Prefix *ir*, not, and *recognizable*.] Incapable of being recognized; not recognizable.

Irreconcilable, ir-rek′on-sī″la-bl, *a.* [Prefix *ir* for *in*, not, and *reconcilable*.] Not reconcilable; not to be reconciled; implacable (an enemy, enmity); incapable of being made to agree or be consistent; inconsistent.—*n.* One who is not to be reconciled; especially, a member of a political body who will not work in harmony with his comembers. — **Irreconcilability, Irreconcilableness**, ir-rek′on-sī′la-bil″i-ti, ir-rek′on-sī″la-bl-nes, *n.* The quality of being irreconcilable. — **Irreconcilably**, ir-rek′on-sī″la-bli, *adv.* So as to preclude reconciliation.

Irrecoverable, ir-rē-kuv′ėr-a-bl, *a.* [Prefix *ir* for *in*, not, and *recoverable*.] Incapable of being recovered or regained; not capable of being restored, remedied, or made good.—**Irrecoverableness**, ir-rē-kuv′ėr-a-bl-nes, *n.* The state of being irrecoverable.—**Irrecoverably**, ir-rē-kuv′ėr-a-bli, *adv.* In an irrecoverable manner; beyond recovery.

Irredeemable, ir-rē-dē′ma-bl, *a.* [Prefix *ir* for *in*, not, and *redeemable*.] Not redeemable; not subject to be paid at its nominal value: specifically applied to a depreciated paper currency.—**Irredeemability, Irredeemableness**, ir-rē-dē′ma-bil″i-ti, ir-rē-dē′ma-bl-nes, *n.* The quality of being not redeemable.—**Irredeemably**, ir-rē-dē′ma-bli, *adv.* So as not to be redeemed.

Irreducible, ir-rē-dū′si-bl, *a.* [Prefix *ir* for *in*, not, and *reducible*.] Not reducible; incapable of being reduced.—**Irreducibleness, Irreductibility**, ir-rē-dū′si-bl-nes, ir′re-duk-ti-bil″i-ti, *n.* — **Irreducibly**, ir-rē-dū′si-bli, *adv.*

Irreflection, ir-rē-flek′shon, *n.* [Prefix *ir* for *in*, not, and *reflection*.] Want or absence of reflection.

Irrefragable, ir-ref′ra-ga-bl, *a.* [Prefix *ir* for *in*, not, and L. *refragor*, to withstand or gainsay—*re*, back, and root of *frango*, to break. FRACTION.] Incapable of being refuted or overthrown; incontestable; undeniable; incontrovertible. — **Irrefragability, Irrefragableness**, ir-ref′ra-ga-bil″i-ti, ir-ref′ra-ga-bl-nes, *n.* The quality of being irrefragable.—**Irrefragably**, ir-ref′ra-ga-bli, *adv.* In an irrefragable manner; incontestably.

Irrefutable, ir-ref′ū-ta-bl or ir-rē-fū′ta-bl, *a.* [Prefix *ir* for *in*, not, and *refutable*.] Not refutable; incapable of being refuted or disproved. — **Irrefutably**, ir-rē-fū′ta-bli or ir-ref′ū-ta-bli, *adv.* In an irrefutable manner.

Irregular, ir-reg′ū-lėr, *a.* [Prefix *ir* for *in*, and *regular*.] Not regular; not according to rules, established principles, or customs; not conformable to the usual operation of natural laws; deviating from the rules of moral rectitude; vicious; not straight or uniform; *gram.* deviating from the common form in respect to the inflectional terminations; *geom.* applied to a figure whose sides as well as angles are not all equal and similar among themselves; *bot.* not having the parts of the same size or form, or arranged with symmetry.—*n.* One not conforming to settled rule; especially, a soldier not in regular service.—**Irregu-**

larity, ir-reg'ū-lar"i-ti, *n.* State or character of being irregular; want of regularity; that which is irregular; a part exhibiting or causing something to be irregular or impairing uniformity; an action or behaviour constituting a breach of morality; vicious conduct.—**Irregularly**, ir-reg'ū-lėr-li, *adv.* In an irregular manner.

Irrelative, ir-rel'a-tiv, *a.* [Prefix *ir* for *in*, not, and *relative.*] Not relative; without mutual relations.—**Irrelatively**, ir-rel'a-tiv-li, *adv.*

Irrelevant, ir-rel'ē-vant, *a.* [Prefix *ir* for *in*, not, and *relevant.*] Not relevant; not applicable or pertinent; not bearing on the case in point or matter in hand.—**Irrelevantly**, ir-rel'ē-vant-li, *adv.* In an irrelevant manner.—**Irrelevance, Irrelevancy**, ir-rel'ē-vans, ir-rel'ē-van-si, *n.* The quality of being irrelevant.

Irreligion, ir-rē-lij'on, *n.* [Prefix *ir* for *in*, not, and *religion.*] Want of religion or contempt of it; impiety.—**Irreligious**, ir-rē-lij'us, *a.* Characterized by irreligion; disregarding or contemning religion; contrary to religion; profane; impious; ungodly.—**Irreligiously**, ir-rē-lij'us-li, *adv.* In an irreligious manner.—**Irreligiousness**, ir-rē-lij'us-nes, *n.*

Irremeable,† ir-rē-mē'a-bl, *a.* [L. *irremeabilis*—*ir* for *in*, not, *re*, back, and *meo*, to go.] Not permitting of a person's return.

Irremediable, ir-rē-mē'di-a-bl, *a.* [Prefix *ir* for *in*, not, and *remediable.*] Incapable of being remedied or cured; not to be corrected or redressed; incurable; irreparable.—**Irremediableness**, ir-rē-mē'di-a-bl-nes, *n.*—**Irremediably**, ir-rē-mē'di-a-bli, *adv.*

Irremissible, ir-rē-mis'i-bl, *a.* [Prefix *ir*, for *in*, not, and *remissible.*] Not remissible; unpardonable; not capable of being remitted.—**Irremissibleness**, ir-rē-mis'i-bl-nes, *n.*—**Irremissibly**, ir-rē-mis'i-bli, *adv.*—**Irremission**, ir-rē-mish'on, *n.* The act of withholding remission.—**Irremissive**, ir-rē-mis'iv, *a.* Not remissive or remitting.—**Irremittable**, ir-rē-mit'a-bl, *a.* Irremissible; unpardonable.

Irremovable, ir-rē-mö'va-bl, *a.* [Prefix *ir* for *in*, not, and *removable.*] Not removable; immovable; inflexible.—**Irremovably**, ir-rē-mö'va-bli, *adv.* In an irremovable manner.—**Irremovability**, ir-rē-mö'va-bil"i-ti, *n.* The quality or state of being irremovable.

Irreparable, ir-rep'a-ra-bl, *a.* [Prefix *ir* for *in*, not, and *reparable.*] Not reparable; incapable of being repaired; irremediable.—**Irreparability, Irreparableness**, ir-rep'a-ra-bil"i-ti, ir-rep'a-ra-bl-nes, *n.* State of being irreparable.—**Irreparably**, ir-rep'a-ra-bli, *adv.* In an irreparable manner; irrecoverably.

Irrepealable, ir-rē-pēl'a-bl, *a.* [Prefix *ir* for *in*, not, and *repealable.*] Not repealable; incapable of being legally repealed or annulled.—**Irrepealability, Irrepealableness**, ir-rē-pēl'a-bil"i-ti, ir-rē-pēl'a-bl-nes, *n.* The quality of being irrepealable.—**Irrepealably**, ir-rē-pēl'a-bli, *adv.*

Irreprehensible, ir-rep'rē-hen"si-bl, *a.* [Prefix *ir* for *in*, not, and *reprehensible.*] Not reprehensible; not to be blamed or censured; blameless.—**Irreprehensibleness**, ir-rep'rē-hen"si-bl-nes, *n.*—**Irreprehensibly**, ir-rep'rē-hen"si-bli, *adv.* In an irreprehensible manner; blamelessly.

Irrepressible, ir-rē-pres'i-bl, *a.* [Prefix *ir* for *in*, not, and *repressible.*] Not repressible; incapable of being repressed, restrained, or kept under control.—**Irrepressibly**, ir-rē-pres'i-bli, *adv.* In a manner or degree precluding repression.

Irreproachable, ir-rē-prōch'a-bl, *a.* [Prefix *ir* for *in*, not, and *reproachable.*] Incapable of being reproached; not occasioning reproach; upright; innocent; faultless; unblemished.—**Irreproachableness**, ir-rē-prōch'a-bl-nes, *n.* The quality or state of being irreproachable.—**Irreproachably**, ir-rē-prōch'a-bli, *adv.* In an irreproachable manner; faultlessly; blamelessly.

Irreprovable, ir-rē-prö'va-bl, *a.* [Prefix *ir* for *in*, not, and *reprovable.*] Not reprovable; blameless; upright; unblamable.—**Irreprovableness**, ir-rē-prö'va-bl-nes, *n.*—**Irreprovably**, ir-rē-prö'va-bli, *adv.* So as not to be liable to reproof or blame.

Irresistance, ir-rē-zis'tans, *n.* [Prefix *ir* for *in*, not, and *resist.*] Forbearance to resist; non-resistance.—**Irresistible**, ir-rē-zis'ti-bl, *a.* Not resistible; incapable of being successfully resisted or opposed; resistless; invincible.—**Irresistibility**, ir-rē-zis'ti-bil"i-ti, *n.* The quality of being irresistible.—**Irresistibly**, ir-rē-zis'ti-bli, *adv.* In an irresistible manner; resistlessly.

Irresoluble,† ir-rez'o-lū-bl, *a.* [Prefix *ir* for *in*, not, and *resoluble.*] Incapable of resolution into parts; indissoluble.—**Irresolubleness**, ir-rez'o-lū-bl-nes, *n.*

Irresolute, ir-rez'o-lūt, *a.* [Prefix *ir* for *in*, not, and *resolute.*] Not resolute; not firm or constant in purpose; undecided; wavering; given to doubt or hesitation; vacillating.—**Irresolutely**, ir-rez'o-lūt-li, *adv.* In an irresolute manner.—**Irresoluteness**, ir-rez'o-lūt-nes, *n.* The quality of being irresolute.—**Irresolution**, ir-rez'o-lū"shon, *n.* Want of resolution or decision; a fluctuation of mind; vacillation.

Irresolvable, ir-rē-zol'va-bl, *a.* [Prefix *ir* for *in*, not, and *resolvable.*] Incapable of being resolved.—**Irresolvability, Irresolvableness**, ir-rē-zol'va-bil"i-ti, ir-rē-zol'va-bl-nes, *n.*

Irrespective, ir-rē-spek'tiv, *a.* [Prefix *ir* for *in*, not, and *respective.*] Having no respect to particular circumstances: generally used in the prepositional phrase *irrespective of*, that is, leaving out of account.—**Irrespectively**, ir-rē-spek'tiv-li, *adv.* Without regard to certain circumstances (*irrespectively of* these matters).

Irrespirable, ir-rē-spī'ra-bl, *a.* [Prefix *ir* for *in*, not, and *respirable.*] Not respirable; unfit for respiration.

Irresponsible, ir-rē-spon'si-bl, *a.* [Prefix *ir* for *in*, not, and *responsible.*] Not responsible; not liable to answer for consequences.—**Irresponsibly**, ir-rē-spon'si-bli, *adv.* In an irresponsible manner.—**Irresponsibility**, ir-rē-spon'si-bil"i-ti, *n.* Want of responsibility.

Irresponsive, ir-rē-spon'siv, *a.* [Prefix *ir* for *in*, not, and *responsive.*] Not responsive.

Irrestrainable, ir-rē-strā'na-bl, *a.* [Prefix *ir* for *in*, not, and *restrainable.*] That cannot be restrained; not to be kept back or held in check.

Irretraceable, ir-rē-trā'sa-bl, *a.* [Prefix *ir* for *in*, not, and *retraceable.*] Not retraceable.

Irretrievable, ir-rē-trē'va-bl, *a.* [Prefix *ir* for *in*, not, and *retrievable.*] Not retrievable; irrecoverable; irreparable.—**Irretrievableness**, ir-rē-trē'va-bl-nes, *n.*—**Irretrievably**, ir-rē-trē'va-bli, *adv.* In an irretrievable manner; irrecoverably.

Irreverence, ir-rev'ėr-ens, *n.* [Prefix *ir* for *in*, not, and *reverence*; L. *irreverentia.*] Want of reverence or veneration; want of a due regard to the authority and character of a superior; irreverent conduct or an irreverent action.—**Irreverent**, ir-rev'ėr-ent, *a.* [L. *irreverens.*] Exhibiting or marked by irreverence (person, conduct, words); wanting in respect to superiors.—**Irreverently**, ir-rev'ėr-ent-li, *adv.* In an irreverent manner; with want of reverence; disrespectfully.

Irreversible, ir-rē-vėr'si-bl, *a.* [Prefix *ir* for *in*, not, and *reversible.*] Not reversible; incapable of being reversed.—**Irreversibleness**, ir-rē-vėr'si-bl-nes, *n.* State of being irreversible.—**Irreversibly**, ir-rē-vėr'si-bli, *adv.* In an irreversible manner; so as not to be reversed; immutably.

Irrevocable, ir-rev'ō-ka-bl, *a.* [Prefix *ir* for *in*, not, and *revocable.*] Not to be recalled or revoked; incapable of being reversed, repealed, or annulled; irreversible (fate, decree, &c.).—**Irrevocability, Irrevocableness**, ir-rev'ō-ka-bil"i-ti, ir-rev'ō-ka-bl-nes, *n.* State of being irrevocable.—**Irrevocably**, ir-rev'ō-ka-bli, *adv.* In an irrevocable manner; irreversibly; immutably.

Irrigate, ir'ri-gāt, *v.t.*—*irrigated*, *irrigating.* [L. *irrigo*, *irrigatum*—*ir* for *in*, and *rigo*, to water. RAIN.] To bedew or sprinkle; to water (land) by causing a stream to flow upon it and spread over it; to water by various artificial channels for water.—**Irrigation**, ir-ri-gā'shon, *n.* [L. *irrigatio.*] The act or operation of irrigating.—**Irriguous**, ir-rig'ū-us, *a.* [L. *irriguus.*] Having many streams; well watered. (*Mil.*)

Irritant, ir'ri-tant, *a.* [L. *irrito*, to make void, from *in*, not, and *ratus*, ratified.] *Scots law*, rendering null and void.—**Irritancy**, ir'ri-tan-si, *n.* The state of being irritant or null and void.

Irritate, ir'ri-tāt, *v.t.* [L. *irrito*, *irritatum*, to incite, stir up, provoke; perhaps from *hirrire*, to snarl.] To excite anger in; to provoke; to tease; to exasperate; to excite heat and redness in, as in the skin or flesh; to inflame; to fret; *physiol.* to excite by certain stimuli; to cause to exhibit irritation.—**Irritation**, ir-ri-tā'shon, *n.* [L. *irritatio*, *irritationis.*] The act of irritating or state of being irritated; provocation; exasperation; angry feeling; feeling of heat and pain in a part of the body; *physiol.* the change or action which takes place in muscles or organs when a nerve or nerves are affected by the application of external bodies.—**Irritative**, ir'ri-tā-tiv, *a.* Serving to excite or irritate.—**Irritable**, ir'ri-ta-bl, *a.* [L. *irritabilis.*] Capable or susceptible of being irritated; readily provoked or exasperated; of a fiery temper; *physiol.* susceptible of responding to or being acted upon by stimuli.—**Irritability, Irritableness**, ir'ri-ta-bil"i ti, ir'ri-ta-bl-nes, *n.* The state or quality of being irritable.—**Irritably**, ir'ri-ta-bli, *adv.* In an irritable manner.—**Irritant**, ir'ri-tant, *a.* [L. *irritans*, *irritantis*, ppr. of *irrito.*] Irritating; producing pain, heat, or tension; producing inflammation (an *irritant* poison).—*n.* That which excites or irritates; a medical application that causes pain or heat (as a fly blister); an irritant poison.

Irruption, ir-rup'shon, *n.* [L. *irruptio*, *irruptionis*, from *irrumpo*, *irruptum*—*in*, in, and *rumpo*, to break. RUPTURE.] A bursting in; a breaking, or sudden, violent rushing into a place; a sudden invasion or incursion.—**Irruptive**, ir-rup'tiv, *a.* Rushing in or upon.

Irvingite. [As Pusey*ite*, Sybar*ite*, Darwin*ite*.] A follower of Edward Irving, 1792–1834, founder of the sect known as the Catholic Apostolic Church, with the revival of healing and tongues. Deposed by the Church of Scotland.

Is, iz. [A.Sax. is = Goth. *ist*, L. *est*, Gr. *esti*, Skr. *asti*, is. AM.] The 3rd. pers. sing. of the verb *to be*. BE.

Isabel, Isabelline, iz'a-bel, iz'a-bel-in, *n.* [Fr. *isabelle*, from a queen or princess of this name.] A pale brownish yellow colour.

Isagogic, Isagogical, ī-sa-goj'ik, ī-sa-goj'i-kal, *a.* [Gr. *eisagōgikos*, from *eisagō*, to introduce—*eis*, in, into, and *agō*, to lead.] Introductory; especially, introductory to the study of theology.—**Isagogics**, ī-sa-goj'iks, *n.* The department of theological study introductory to exegesis.

Isagon, ī'sa-gon, *n.* [Gr. *isos*, equal, and *gōnia*, an angle.] *Math.* a figure whose angles are equal.

Isapostolic, ī'sa-pos-tol"ik, *a.* [Gr. *isos*, equal, and *apostolos*, an apostle.] Almost apostolic in character or standing; the name of Constantine the Great in the Russian Church, from his part in the Nicæan Council and its influence on the Creed.

Ischiadic, is-ki-ad'ik, *a.* [L. *ischiadicus*, from *ischias*, sciatica, from *ischium*, Gr. *ischion*, the hip.] Pertaining to sciatica.—*Ischiadic passion* or *disease*, sciatica.—**Ischial**, is'ki-al, *a.* Belonging to the ischium or hip-bone.—**Ischialgia**, is-ki-al'-

ji-a, *n.* [Gr. *algos*, pain.] Pain in the hip; sciatica.—**Ischiatic**, is-ki-at'ik, *a.* Pertaining to the ischium of the hip.—**Ischium**, is'ki-um, *n.* [Gr. *ischion.*] *Anat.* the posterior and inferior part of the pelvic arch at the hip-joint.

Ischnophonia, isk-no-fō'ni-a, *n.* [Gr. *ischnos*, slender, and *phōnē*, voice.] Shrillness or thinness of the voice.

Ischuria, Ischury, is-kū'ri-a, is'ku-ri, *n.* [Gr. *ischouria*, from *ischō*, to stop, and *ouron*, urine.] A stoppage, retention, or suppression of urine.—**Ischuretic**, is-kū-ret'ik, *a.* Having the quality of relieving ischury.—*n.* A medicine of this kind.

Iserine, ī'sėr-in, *n.* [From the river *Iser* in Silesia.] A mineral of an iron-black color, and of a splendent metallic luster, an ore of the metal titanium.

Ishmaelite, ish'mā-el-īt, *n.* [From *Ishmael*: Gen. xvi. 12.] A descendant of Ishmael; one resembling Ishmael, whose hand was against every man and every man's hand against him; one at war with society. **Ishmaelitish**, ish'mā-el-īt-ish, *a.* Like Ishmael or an Ishmaelite.

Isiac, ī'si-ak, *a.* Under Isis.

Isinglass, ī'zing-glas, *n.* [Corrupted from D. *huizenblas*—*huizen*, a sturgeon, and *blas*, a vesicle, a bladder (akin to *blow*, *bladder*).] A gelatinous substance from air-bladders of certain fishes, particularly species of sturgeon found in the rivers of Russia, used in clarifying liquors, as a cement, &c.; also thin sheets of mica.

Isis, ī'sis, *n.* One of the chief deities in the Egyptian mythology, regarded as the sister or sister-wife of Osiris.—**Isiac**, ī'si-ak, *a.* Relating to Isis.

Islam, iz'lam, *n.* [Ar., from *salama*, to be free, safe, or devoted to God.] The religion of Mohammed, and also the whole body of those who profess it throughout the world.—**Islamism**, iz'lam-izm, *n.* The faith of Islam; Mohammedism.—**Islamite**, iz'lam-īt, *n.* A Mohammedan.—**Islamitic**, iz-la-mit'ik, *a.* Pertaining to Islam; Mohammedan.—**Islamize**, iz'lam-īz, *v.t.* or *i.* To conform to Islamism; to Mohammedanize.

Island, ī'land, *n.* [From A.Sax. *igland*, lit. island-land, from *ig* (= Icel. *ey*, Dan. and Sw. *ö*), an island, and *land*, land; the *s* is due to erroneous connection with L. *insula*, O.Fr. *isle*. Isle. A.Sax. *ig* = *-ea*, or *-ey* in Anglesea, Anglesey, *ey-* in *eyot*; akin to G. *aue*, a meadow, Goth. *ahwa*, L. *aqua*, water.] A tract of land surrounded by water, whether of the sea, a river, or a lake; anything resembling an island.—*v.t.* To cause to become or appear like an island; to isolate; to dot, as with islands.—**Islander**, ī'lan-dėr, *n.* An inhabitant of an island.

Isle, īl, *n.* [O.Fr. *isle*, Fr. *île*, Prov. *isla*, from L. *insula*, an island. Insulate.] An island. [Chiefly poet.]—*v.t.*—*isled*, *isling*. To cause to become or appear like an isle; to isolate; to island.—**Islet**, īl'et, *n.* [Dim. of *isle*.] A little isle or something similar.

Isobar, ī'sō-bär, *n.* [Gr. *isos*, equal, and *baros*, weight.] A line drawn on a map connecting places at which the mean height of the barometer at sea-level is the same. —**Isobaric**, ī-sō-bar'ik, *a.* Isobarometric. —**Isobarometric**, ī-sō-bar'ō-met"rik, *a.* Indicating equal barometric pressure.—*Isobarometric line.* Same as *Isobar*.

Isobrious, ī-sob'ri-us, *a.* [Gr. *isos*, equal, and *briaō*, to be strong.] *Bot.* applied to the dicotyledonous embryo, because both lobes seem to grow with equal vigour.

Isocheim, ī'sō-kīm, *n.* [Gr. *isos*, equal, and *cheima*, *cheimōn*, winter.] A line drawn on a map through places which have the same mean winter temperature.—**Isocheimal, Isochimal**, ī-sō-kī'mal, *a.* Of the same mean winter temperature; marking places with the same mean winter temperature.—*Isocheimal line.* Same as *Isocheim*. Also **Isocheimonal, Isochimonal**, ī-sō-kī'mon-al.

Isochromatic, ī'sō-krō-mat"ik, *a.* [Gr. *isos*, equal, and *chrōma*, colour.] Having the same color; marking correspondence in tint as colored light passes through biaxial crystals.

Isochronal, Isochronous, ī-sok'ron-al, ī-sok'ron-us, *a.* [Gr. *isos*, equal, and *chronos*, time.] Uniform in time; of equal time; performed in equal times (as oscillations of pendulums).—**Isochronally**, ī-sok'ron-al-li, *adv.* So as to be isochronal.—**Isochronism**, ī-sok'ron-izm, *n.* State or quality of being isochronous.

Isochrous, ī'sok-rus, *a.* [Gr. *isochroos*, like-colored—*isos*, equal, and *chroa*, color.] Being of equal color throughout.

Isoclinal, Isoclinic, ī-sō-klī'nal, ī-sō-klin'ik, *a.* [Gr. *isos*, equal, and *klinō*, to incline.] Of equal inclination or dip.—*Isoclinal* or *isoclinic lines*, curves connecting places at which the dip of the magnetic needle is equal.

Isocryme, ī'sō-krim, *n.* [Gr. *isos*, equal, *krymos*, cold.] A line drawn on maps connecting places corresponding in regard to the extreme degree of cold.—**Isocrymal**, ī-sō-krī'mal, *a.* Pertaining to or having the nature of an isocryme.

Isodynamic, ī'sō-di-nam"ik, *a.* [Gr. *isos*, equal, and *dynamis*, power.] Having equal power or force.—*Isodynamic lines*, lines connecting those places where the intensity of the terrestrial magnetism is equal.—**Isodynamous**, ī-sō-din'a-mus, *a.* Having equal force; of equal size; *bot.* isobrious.

Isogeotherm, ī-sō-jē'ō-thėrm, *n.* [Gr. *isos*, equal, *gē*, the earth, and *thermē*, heat.] An imaginary line or plane under the earth's surface passing through points having the same mean temperature.—**Isogeothermal**, ī-sō-jē'ō-thėr"mal, *a.* Pertaining to isogeotherms.

Isogonic, ī-sō-gon'ik, *a.* [Gr. *isos*, equal, and *gōnia*, an angle.] Having equal angles. —*Isogonic lines*, lines connecting those places where the deviation of the magnetic needle from the true north is the same.

Isohel, ī'sō-hel, *n.* [Gr. *helios*, sun.] A line drawn on a map through places having the same amount of bright sunshine.

Isohyetose, ī-sō-hī'e-tōs, *a.* [Gr. *isos*, equal, and *hyetos*, rain.] Applied to lines connecting those places on the surface of the globe where the quantity of rain which falls annually is the same.

Isolate, ī'sō-lāt or is'ō-lāt, *v.t.*—*isolated*, *isolating*. [Fr. *isoler*, It. *isolare*, from *isola* = L. *insula*, an island. Insulate.] To place or leave in a detached situation; to place apart; *elect.* to insulate; *chem.* to obtain (a substance) free from all its combinations.—**Isolated**, ī'sō-lā-ted, *p.* and *a.* Standing detached from others of a like kind; placed by itself or alone.—**Isolatedly**, ī'sō-lā-ted-li, *adv.* In an isolated manner.—**Isolating**, ī'sō-lā-ting, *a. Philol.* applied to that class of languages in which each word is a simple, uninflected root; monosyllabic.—**Isolation**, ī-sō-lā'shon, *n.* State of being isolated or alone.—**Isolable**, ī'sō-la-bl, *a.* Capable of being isolated.

Isomerism, ī-som'ėr-izm, *n.* [Gr. *isos*, equal, and *meros*, a part.] *Chem.* identity or close similarity of composition with difference of physical or both chemical and physical properties.—**Isomeric, Isomerical**, ī-sō-mer'ik, ī-sō-mer'i-kal, *a.* Pertaining to or characterized by isomerism.—**Isomeride**, ī-som'ėr-īd, *n.* A compound that exhibits isomerism.—**Isomeride**, ī-som'ėr-īd, *n.* A compound that exhibits isomerism.—**Isomerous**, ī-som'ėr-us, *a. Bot.* having organs composed each of an equal number of parts.

Isometric, Isometrical, ī-sō-met'rik, ī-sō-met'ri-kal, *a.* [Gr. *isos*, equal, *metron*, measure.] Pertaining to, or characterized by equality of measure.—*Isometrical perspective* or *projection*, a method of drawing plans whereby the elevation and ground-plan are represented in one view.

Isomorphism, ī-sō-mor'fizm, *n.* [Gr. *isos*, like, and *morphē*, form.] A similarity of crystalline form in minerals.—**Isomorphous**, ī-sō-mor'fus, *a.* Exhibiting the property of isomorphism.

Isoneph, ī'sō-nef, *n.* [Gr. *nephos*, cloud.] A line drawn on a map through places having the same amount of cloudiness.

Isonomy, ī-son'o-mi, *n.* [Gr. *isos*, equal, and *nomos*, law.] Equal law; equal distribution of rights and privileges.—**Isonomic**, ī-sō-nom'ik, *a.* Pertaining to isonomy.

Isoperimetric, Isoperimetrical, ī-sō-per'i-met"rik, ī-sō-per'i-met"ri-kal, *a.* [Gr. *isos*, equal, and *perimetron*, perimeter.] Having equal boundaries or perimeters.

Isopod, ī'sō-pod, *n.* [Gr. *isos*, equal, and *pous*, *podos*, the foot.] One of an order of crustaceans, comprehending those whose feet are of equal size and move in the same direction; the wood-lice, and slaters are examples.—**Isopodous**, ī-sop'o-dus, *a.* Belonging to the isopods.

Isopolity, ī-sō-pol'i-ti, *n.* [Gr. *isos*, equal, and *politeia*, polity.] Equal rights of citizenship.

Isopycnic, ī-sō-pik'nik, *a.* [Gr. *isos*, equal, *pyknos*, dense.] Showing an equal degree of thickness.

Isopyre, ī'sō-pīr, *n.* [Gr. *isos*, like, and *pyr*, fire.] A mineral of a grayish or black colour which occurs massive.

Isosceles, ī-sos'se-lēz, *a.* [Gr. *isoskelēs*—*isos*, equal, and *skelos*, leg.] Having two legs or sides only that are equal (an *isosceles* triangle).

Isoseismal, Isoseismic, ī-sō-sīs'mal, ī-sō-sīs'mik, *a.* [Gr. *isos*, equal, and *seismos*, an earthquake, from *seiō*, to shake.] Marking equal earthquake disturbance on the earth's surface.

Isostemonous, ī-sō-stem'on-us, *a.* [Gr. *isos*, equal, and *stēmōn*, a stamen.] *Bot.* having the stamens equal in number to the petals.

Isothere, ī'sō-thēr, *n.* [Gr. *isos*, equal, and *theros*, summer.] An imaginary line on the earth's surface passing through points having the same mean summer temperature.—**Isotheral**, ī-soth'ėr-al, *a.* Pertaining to or marked by isotheres.

Isotherm, ī'sō-thėrm, *n.* [Gr. *isos*, equal, proper, and *therme*, heat.] An imaginary line on the earth's surface passing through places having a corresponding temperature either throughout the year or at any particular period.—**Isothermal**, ī-sō-thėr'mal, *a.* Pertaining to an isotherm or isotherms; marking correspondence in temperature.—*Isothermal line*, an isotherm.

Isotherombrose, ī'sō-the-rom"brōs, *a.* [Gr. *isos*, equal, *theros*, summer, and *ombros*, rain.] Said of lines marking places where the same quantity of rain falls during the summer.

Isotonic, ī-sō-ton'ik, *a.* [Gr. *isos*, equal, and *tonos*, tone.] Having or indicating equal tones.

Isotropic, ī-sō-trop'ik, *a.* [Gr. *isos*, equal, and *tropē*, a turning, from *trepō*, to turn. A term applied to bodies whose elastic forces are alike in all directions. Æolotropic.

Israelite, iz'ra-el-īt, *n.* A descendant of *Israel*, or Jacob; a Jew.—**Israelitic, Israelitish**, iz'ra-el-it"ik, iz'ra-el-īt"ish, *a.* Pertaining to Israel; Jewish; Hebrew.

Issue, ish'ū, *n.* [Fr. *issue*, issue, outlet, event, from O.Fr. *issir*, to go out, to flow forth, and that from L. *exeo*, *exire*, to go out—*ex*, out, and *eo*, to go (in *circuit*, *exit*, *initial*, &c.). Itinerant.] The act of passing or flowing out; a moving out of any inclosed place; the act of sending out; delivery (of commands, money, &c.); the whole quantity sent forth or issued at one time (an *issue* of bank-notes; yesterday's *issue* of the *Times*); what happens or turns out; event; consequence; progeny; a child or children; offspring; all persons descended from a common ancestor; a flux of blood (*N.T.*); *surg.* an artificial ulcer made in some part of the body to promote a secretion of pus; *law*, the close or result of pleadings; the point or matter depending in a suit on which two parties join and put their cause to trial; hence, a material point turning up in any argument or debate, when one party takes the negative, the other the positive side on an important point.—*At issue*, in controversy; disputed; opposing or contesting.—*To join issue, to take issue*, said of two parties who take up a positive and negative position respectively on a point in debate.—*v.i.*—*issued, issuing.* To pass, flow, or run out, as from any inclosed place; to proceed, as from a source; to rush out; to proceed, as progeny; to be produced, as an effect or result; to close, end, terminate.—*v.t.* To send out; to deliver for use; to deliver authoritatively (orders, &c.); to put (notes, coin, newspapers) into circulation.—**Issuable**, ish'ū-bl, *a.* Capable of being issued; admitting of issue being taken upon it.—**Issuably**, ish'ū-a-bli, *adv.* In an issuable manner; by way of issue.—**Issuance**, ish'ū-ans, *n.* The act of issuing or giving out.—**Issueless**, ish'ū-les, *a.* Having no issue or progeny.—**Issuer**, ish'ū-er, *n.* One who issues or emits.

Isthmus, ist'mus, *n.* [L., from Gr. *isthmos*, a neck of land or narrow passage.] A neck or narrow slip of land by which two continents are connected, or by which a peninsula is united to the mainland.—**Isthmian**, ist'mi-an, *a.* Of or pertaining to an isthmus.—*Isthmian games*, ancient Greek games celebrated at the Isthmus of Corinth, in the first and third year of each olympiad, in honour of Poseidōn.

It, it, *pron.* [A.Sax. nom. *hit*, neut. corresponding to *hē*, he, genit. or pos. *his*, dat. and instrumental *him*; Goth. *ita*, D. *het*, O.H.G. *iz*, G. *es*. HE.] A pronoun of the neuter gender corresponding with the masculine *he* and the feminine *she*, having the same plural *they*. Besides standing in place of neuter nouns *it* is used (1) as the nominative to impersonal verbs (*it* rains; *it* snows); (2) to introduce a sentence, preceding a verb as a nominative, but referring to a clause or distinct member of the sentence following (*it* is well ascertained that the figure of the earth is an oblate spheroid); (3) for a preceding clause of a sentence (we have been defeated for the present, *it* is true); (4) to begin a sentence when a personal pronoun, or the name of a person, or a masculine or feminine noun follows, where it may represent any one of the three persons or of the three genders (as, *it* is I; *it* was they); (5) for state of matters, condition of affairs, or the like (has *it* come to this?); (6) after intransitive verbs very indefinitely (to walk *it*, to run *it*). ∴ The possessive case *its* does not appear till a year or two before 1600, *his* being used both for the masculine and the neuter possessive.

Italian, i-tal'yan, *a.* Pertaining to *Italy*.—*n.* A native of Italy; the language used in Italy or by the Italians.—*Italian iron*, a smoothing iron, consisting essentially of a metal tube with a closed rounded end heated by a metal bolt: used for fluting or gauffering.—*Italian warehouse*, a name assumed by shops where groceries, including some Italian products, are sold.—*Italian handwriting*, the method of penmanship, practically the copper-plate hand of clear lettering, adopted from Italy, opposed to the old Gothic script.—**Italianism, Italicism**, i-tal'yan-izm, i-tal'i-sism, *n.* An Italian expression, manner, or custom.—**Italianize**, i-tal'yan-īz, *v.t.* To give an Italian colour or character to.—**Italic**, i-tal'ik, *a.* Pertaining to Italy; the name of a printing type sloping towards the right, invented about A.D. 1500 by Aldus Manutius, a Venetian printer.—*n.* An italic letter or type.—**Italicize**, i-tal'i-sīz, *v.t.*—*italicized, italicizing.* To write or print in italic characters; to distinguish by italics.—**Italiote**, i-tal'i-ōt, *n.* A native or colonist of Magna Græcia, in the south of Italy.

Itch, ich, *n.* [O.E. *ichyn*, *gykin*, A.Sax. *giccan*, to itch; G. *jucken*, to itch; D. *jeuking, jeukte*, Sc. *yuik*, itch.] A sensation in the skin causing a great desire to scratch or rub; a cutaneous disease due to a minute species of mite; a constant teasing desire (an *itch* for praise).—*v.i.* To feel an itch; to have an uneasy or teasing sensation impelling to something.—**Itching**, ich'ing, *n.* The sensation of itch; an uneasy desire or hankering.—*p.* and *a.* Having a sensation that leads to scratching; having a teasing uneasy sensation.—**Itch-mite**, *n.* The microscopic animal which produces itch.—**Itchy**, ich'i, *a.* Infected with or having the sensation as if suffering from itch.—**Itchiness**, ich'i-nes, *n.* The state of being itchy.

Item, ī'tem, *adv.* [L. *item*, also.] Also: used in accounts or lists of articles.—*n.* One thing in a list; a scrap of news.—**Itemize**, ī'tem-īz, *v.t.* To list or state the items, to particularize.

Iterate, it'ėr-āt, *v.t.*—*iterated, iterating.* [L. *itero, iteratum*, to do again, to repeat, from *iterum*, again, from *id*, it, with the comparative suffix; akin Skr. *itara*, another.] To utter or do a second time; to repeat.—**Iteration**, it-ėr-ā'shon, *n.* [L. *iteratio, iterationis.*] Repetition; recital or performance a second time.—**Iterative**, it'ėr-ā-tiv, *a.* Repeating.

Itinerant, ī-tin'ėr-ant, *a.* [L.L. *itinerans, itinerantis*, travelling, from L. *iter, itineris*, a way or journey; from root *i*, to go, seen also in *circuit, exit, transit, ambition, initial, issue, perish*, &c.] Passing or travelling about a country or district; wandering; not settled; strolling.—*n.* One who travels from place to place.—**Itineracy**, ī-tin'ėr-a-si, *n.* Practice of itinerating.—**Itinerancy**, ī-tin'ėr-an-si, *n.* A passing from place to place; the passing from place to place in the discharge of official duty.—**Itinerantly**, ī-tin'ėr-ant-li, *adv.* In an itinerant, unsettled, or wandering manner.—**Itinerary**, ī-tin'ėr-a-ri, *n.* [L.L. *itinerarium.*] A work containing notices of the places and stations to be met with in pursuing a particular line of road.—*a.* Travelling; pertaining to a journey.—**Itinerate**, ī-tin'ėr-āt, *v.i.*—*itinerated, itinerating.* To travel from place to place, particularly for the purpose of preaching; to wander without a settled habitation.

Its, its. Possessive case of the pronoun it.—**Itself**, it-self', *pron.* The neuter pronoun corresponding to *himself, herself.*

Ittrium, it'ri-um, *n*, Yttrium.

Ivory, ī'vō-ri, *n.* [O.Fr. *ivurie*, Fr. *ivoire*, from L. *eboreus*, made of ivory, from *ebur*, ivory; akin Skr. *ibha*, an elephant.] The substance of elephant tusks; a similar substance obtained from the tusks of the walrus, the hippopotamus, the narwhal, &c., a color, like ivory. *pl.* Articles made of ivory, such as piano keys or dice.—*a.* Consisting or made of ivory.—**Ivory-black**, *n.* A fine black pigment, prepared from ivory-dust by calcination.—**Ivory-gate**, *n.* The gates by which false dreams come and go: opposed to the *horn-gate*, by which true dreams come.—**Ivory-nut**, *n.* The seed of a South American palm, about as large as a hen's egg, and resembling ivory in texture and color; vegetable ivory.—**Ivory-palm**, *n.* The tree which bears the ivory-nut.

Ivy, ī'vi, *n.* [A.Sax. *ifig*; akin to G. *epheu*, O.G. *ebeheu, ebah*, ivy.] An evergreen climbing plant, growing in hedges, woods, on old buildings, rocks, and trunks of trees.—**Ivied**, ī'vid, *a.* Covered or overgrown with ivy.

Ixolyte, ik'sō-līt, *n.* [Gr. *ixos*, bird-lime, and *lyō*, to dissolve.] A mineral of a greasy lustre found in bituminous coal, and becoming soft and tenacious when heated.

Ixtle, iks'tle, *n.* A name for a kind of fibre obtained in Mexico from a species of agave.

Izard, Izzard, iz'ärd, *n.* The wild goat of the Pyrenees; the ibex.

J

J. Tenth letter in the English alphabet, the seventh consonant, sounding like *g* in *genius*. [Not originally English.]

Jab, jab, *v.t., v.i.* To stab, as with a sharp stick.

Jabber, jab'ėr, *v.i.* [A form equivalent to *gabble*, Sc. *gabber*, freq. of *gab*, to talk much or pertly, GAB.] To talk rapidly, indistinctly, or nonsensically; to chatter.—*v.t.* To utter rapidly (to *jabber* French).—*n.* Rapid, indistinct utterance.—**Jabberer**, jab'ėr-ėr, *n.* One who jabbers.

Jabiru, jab'i-rö, *n.* [Brazilian name.] A tall wading bird resembling the stork, a native of Africa and America.

Jaborandi, jab-ō-ran'di, *n.* [Brazilian.] A drug obtained from a Brazilian plant of the rue family, causing increase of saliva and profuse perspiration.

Jaborine, jab'o-rin, *n.* An alkaloid extracted from jaborandi.

Jacamar, jak'a-mär, *n.* [Brazilian *jacamarica.*] The name of certain climbing birds of tropical America, nearly allied to the kingfishers.

Jacana, jak'a-na, *n.* The name of sundry tropical grallatorial birds, having very long toes, so that they can easily walk on the leaves of aquatic plants.

Jacaranda, jak-a-ran'da, *n.* The name of several Brazilian trees yielding fancy woods.

Jacare, jak'a-rā, *n.* [Brazilian.] A species of Brazilian alligator.

Jacinth, jā'sinth, *n.* The gem also called *Hyacinth.*

Jack, jak, *n.* [From Fr. *Jacques*, L. *Jacobus*, James. Being the commonest christian name in France, it became synonymous with rustic or clown, a meaning which it also had in England, where, however, it came to be used as a familiar substitute for the common name *John*, instead of for *James.*] A familiar substitute for the name John; a popular name for a sailor; a name of various contrivances or implements; an implement to assist a person in pulling off his boots; a boot-jack; a contrivance for raising great weights by the action of screws; a contrivance for turning a spit; a coat quilted and covered with leather, formerly worn over a coat of mail; a pitcher of waxed leather; a black-jack; a small bowl thrown out for a mark to the players in the game of bowls; a flag displayed from a staff on the end of a bowsprit; the union flag of Britain (made by uniting the crosses of St. George, St. Andrew, and St. Patrick); the male of certain animals, as the ass; the fish more commonly called the pike; a young pike; any of the knaves in a pack of cards.—**Jack-in-a-box**, *n.* A kind of toy consisting of a box, out of which, when the lid is opened, a figure springs.—**Jack-in-office**, *n.* One who is vain of his petty office.—**Jack-of-all-trades**, *n.* A person who can turn his hand to any kind of business.—**Jack-with-a-Lantern, Jack-a-Lantern**, *n.* Will-o'-the-wisp, a meteor that appears in low moist lands.—**Jackanape, Jackanapes**, jak'a-nāp, jak'a-nāps, *n.* [*Jack the ape*, or *Jack of Apes.*] A monkey; a coxcomb; an impertinent fellow.—**Jackass**, jak'ass, *n.* The male of the ass; an ignorant or stupid person.—*Laughing jackass*, a species of Australian kingfisher.—**Jack-boot**, *n.* A kind of large boot reaching up over the knee.—**Jackdaw**, jak'da, *n.* [A name of like kind with *Magpie*, *Robin redbreast*, &c.] A small species of crow.—**Jack-of-all-trades**, *n.* A man handy with tools; a man possessing a superficial skill in several trades, hence, *Jack-of-all-trades, and master of none.*—**Jackknife**, *n.* A large strong clasp-knife for the pocket.—**Jack-plane**, *n.* A plane about 18 inches long used by joiners for coarse work.—**Jack pot**, *n. Poker.* The pool which is opened when one player has a pair of jacks or something higher.—**Jack rabbit**, *n.* One of the large hares, several species of which have long ears and long hind legs, destructive to crops in the middle west and west.—**Jackscrew**, *n.* A jack for lifting heavy objects.—**Jacksnipe**, *n.* A small species of snipe.—**Jack staff**, *n.* A staff on the bowsprit of a vessel on which the jack is flown.—**Jackstones**, *n.* A children's game, played with small stones or metal pieces.—**Jackstraw**, *n.* A figure of a man made of straw; pl. a game played with straws or strips of wood, &c.—**Jack towel**, *n.* A coarse towel for general use, hanging from a roller.

Jackal, jak'al, *n.* [Fr. *chacal*, Turk. *chakal*, Per. *shaghâl*, *shagâl*, a jackal.] A carnivorous animal closely allied to the dog and the wolf: from an erroneous notion that the jackal hunted up prey for the king of beasts, he was often called the lion's provider; hence, a person who performs a similar office for another.

Jacket, jak'et, *n.* [Fr. *jaquette*, dim. of *jaque*, a coat of mail, a jacket. JACK.] A short outer garment extending downward to the hips; an outer casing of cloth, felt, wood, &c.; a casing to prevent the radiation of heat from a steam-boiler.—*v.t.* To cover or furnish with a jacket.—**Jacketed** jak'et-ed, *p.* and *a.* Wearing or furnished with a jacket.

Jacks, jaks, *n.* The ivory or wooden keys in harpsichords or other musical instruments. (*Shak.*)

Jacobean, **Jacobian**, ja-kō'bē-an, ja-kō'bi-an, *a.* [L. *Jacobus*, James, from Heb. *Jacob.*] *Arch.* the term sometimes applied to the later style of Elizabethan architecture prevailing in the age of James I.—**Jacobin**, jak'ō-bin, *n.* [Fr., from L. *Jacobus*, James.] A Gray or Dominican Friar, from these friars having first established themselves in Paris in the Rue St. Jacques (Saint James Street); a member of a club of violent republicans in France during the revolution of 1789; a politician of similar character; a variety of pigeon whose neck-feathers form a hood.—**Jacobinic**, **Jacobinical**, jak-ō-bin'ik, jak-ō-bin'i-kal, *a.* Pertaining to or resembling the Jacobins of France.—**Jacobinically**, jak-ō-bin'i-kal-li, *adv.* In a manner resembling the Jacobins.—**Jacobinism**, jak'ō-bin-izm, *n.* The principles of Jacobins.—**Jacobinize**, jak'ō-bin-iz, *v.t.*—*jacobinized*, *jacobinizing.* To taint with Jacobinism.—**Jacobite**, jak'ō-bīt, *n.* [From L. *Jacobus*, James.] A partisan or adherent of James II of England after he abdicated the throne, and of his descendants.—*a.* Pertaining to the Jacobites.—**Jacobites**, *n.* The sect of Monophysites, following James, bishop of Edessa, in the sixth century.—**Jacobitic**, **Jacobitical**, jak-ō-bit'ik, jak-ō-bit'i-kal, *a.* Pertaining to the Jacobites.—**Jacobitically**, jak-ō-bit'i-kal-li, *adv.* In a manner resembling the Jacobites.—**Jacobitism**, jak'ō-bit-ism, *n.* The principles of the Jacobites.—**Jacob's-ladder**, *n.* A favourite cottage-garden plant with handsome blue (sometimes white) flowers; *naut.* a rope-ladder with wooden steps or spokes.—**Jacob's-staff**, *n.* CROSS-STAFF.—**Jacobus**, ja-kō'bus, *n.* A gold coin, value about $6.00, struck in the reign of James I.

Jaconet, jak'ō-net, *n.* [Fr. *jaconas*; origin doubtful.] A light soft muslin of an open texture, used for dresses, neckcloths, &c.

Jacquard-loom, jak-kärd', *n.* [From *Jacquard* of Lyons, who died in 1834.] An ingenious loom for weaving figured goods.

Jacquerie, zhäk-rē, *n.* [Fr., from *Jacques*, James, used to typify a peasant. JACK.] An insurrection of peasants; originally a revolt of the peasants against the nobles of Picardy, France, in 1358.

Jactitation, jak-ti-tā'shon, *n.* [L. *jactito*, freq. from *jacto*, freq. of *jacio*, to throw. JET.] A frequent tossing of the body; restlessness; also, vain boasting; bragging.

Jaculate, jak'ū-lāt, *v.t.* [L. *jaculor*, *jaculatus*, to throw the javelin, from *jaculum*, javelin, *jacio*, to throw.] To dart; to throw out. — **Jaculatory**, jak'ū-la-to-ri, *a.* Throwing out suddenly, or suddenly thrown out; uttered in short sentences.

Jade, jād, *n.* [Sc. *yaud*, *jaud*, an old mare; Icel. *jalda*, Prov. Sw. *jälda*, a mare.] A mean or poor horse; a worthless nag; a mean or vile woman; a hussy: used opprobriously; a young woman: used in humour or slight contempt.—*v.t.*—*jaded*, *jading.* To ride or drive severely; to overdrive; to weary or fatigue.—*v.i.* To become weary; to lose spirit. — **Jaded**, jā'ded, *p.* and *a.* Wearied out; fatigued; harassed.—**Jadery**, jā'dėr-i, *n.* The tricks of a jade.—**Jadish**, jā'dish, *a.* Like or pertaining to a jade.

Jade, jād, *n.* [Fr. and Sp. *jade*; origin unknown.] A kind of hard, tenacious gem or stone of a color more or less green, of a resinous or oily aspect when polished, capable of being carved, and used, especially by the Chinese, for ornaments.

Jag, jag, *v.t.*—*jagged*, *jagging.* [Origin doubtful; comp. W. and Gael. *gag*, a cleft or chink; Gael. *gag*, to notch.] To notch; to cut into notches or teeth like those of a saw.—*n.* A notch or denticulation; a sharp protuberance or indentation; state of inebriation (*slang*).—**Jagged**, jag'ed, *p.* and *a.* Having notches or teeth; cleft; divided; laciniate.—**Jaggedness**, jag'ed-nes, *n.*—**Jagger**, jag'ėr, *n.* One who or that which jags.

Jaggery, **Jagghery**, jag'ėr-i, *n.* [Hind. *jāgri.*] In the East Indies sugar in its coarse state; imperfectly granulated sugar; also, the inspissated juice of the palmyra-tree.

Jaghire, jag-hēr', *n.* In the East Indies, an assignment of the government share of the produce of land to an individual, either personal or for the support of a public establishment.—**Jaghirdar**, jag-hēr-där', *n.* A person holding a jaghire.

Jaguar, ja-gwär', *n.* [Brazilian *jaguara.*] The American tiger; a powerful, spotted member of the cat family found mostly in South America.

Jahve, yä've, *n.* [Heb.] Jehovah.

Jail, jāl, *n.* [Fr. *geôle*, O.Fr. *gaiole*, a prison; L.L. *gabiola*, from L. *cavea*, a cage, coop, den, from *cavus*, hollow. CAVE.] A prison; a building or place for the confinement of persons arrested for crime; a lockup.—*v.t.* To put in prison; to imprison.—**Jailbird**, jāl'bėrd, *n.* One who has been confined in jail.—**Jail-fever**, *n.* A fever generated in jails and other places when overcrowded.

Jain, **Jaina**, jān, jā'na, *n.* One of a Hindu religious sect believing doctrines similar to those of Buddhism.—**Jainism**, jān'izm, *n.* The doctrines of the Jains.

Jalap, jal'ap, *n.* [Fr. *jalap*; Sp. *jalapa*, from *Jalapa* in Mexico.] A purgative medicine, principally obtained from the tuberous roots of a climbing plant of the convolvulus family, a native of Mexico.—**Jalapic**, ja-lap'ik, *a.* Relating to jalap.

Jalousie, zhäl-ō-zē', *n.* [Fr., from *jaloux*, jealous. JEALOUS.] A wooden frame or blind for shading from the sunshine, much used in hot countries; a venetian blind.

Jam, jam, *n.* [Ar. *jamd*, congelation, concretion; *jamid*, concrete, congealed.] A conserve of fruits boiled with sugar and water.

Jam, jam, *v.t.*—*jammed*, *jamming.* [Perhaps from *jamb*, pressing between two uprights or jambs.] To wedge in; to squeeze tight; to press in.—*n.* A crush of people; a squeeze.—**Jamming**, jam'ing, *n. Wireless tel.* interference between two wireless stations caused by a third.

Jamb, jam, *n.* [Fr. *jambe*, a leg, a jamb.] The side or vertical piece of any opening in a wall, such as a door or window.

Jamboree, jam-bo-rē', *n.* A boy scout assembly; a noisy gathering.

Jangle, jang'gl, *v.i.*—*jangled*, *jangling.* [O.Fr. *jangler*, *gangler*, from L.G. and D. *jangelen*, to brawl; imitative of sound.] To sound discordantly or harshly; to quarrel in words; to altercate; to bicker; to wrangle.—*v.t.* To cause to sound harshly or inharmoniously; to utter in a discordant manner.—*n.* Discordant sound; prate; babble.—**Jangler**, jang'glėr, *n.* A prater; a babbler.

Janitor, jan'i-tėr, *n.* [L., from *janua*, a door.] A doorkeeper; a porter; a caretaker of a building.

Janizary, jan'i-za-ri, *n.* [Turk. *yeni*, new, and *tcheri*, militia, soldiers.] A soldier of the Turkish footguards, a body originally composed of Christian slaves, but suppressed after a terrible struggle in 1826.

Jansenist, jan'sen-ist, *n.* A follower of *Jansen*, R. Catholic bishop of Ypres in Flanders, who leaned to the doctrine of irresistible grace as maintained by Calvin.—**Jansenism**, jan'sen-izm, *n.* The doctrine of the Jansenists.

Jantu, **Janta**, jän'tö, jän'ta, *n.* A machine for raising water to irrigate land, used in Hindustan.

Janty, &c. See JAUNTY.

January, jan'ū-a-ri, *n.* [L. *januarius*, the month consecrated to the god *Janus*, a deity represented with two faces looking opposite ways.] The first month of the year according to the present computation. — **Janus-faced**, *a.* Having two faces; double-dealing; deceitful.—**Janus-headed**, *a.* Double-headed.

Japan, ja-pan', *n.* [From the country so called.] Work varnished and figured in the manner practised by the natives of Japan; the varnish employed in japanning articles; japan-lacquer. — *v.t.* — *japanned*, *japanning.* To varnish or cover with japan-lacquer. — *Japanned leather*, a species of enamelled or varnished leather.—**Japan-earth**, *n.* A name of catechu or cutch, an astringent matter procured from a species of acacia.—**Japanese**, jap'a-nēz, *a.* Pertaining to Japan or its inhabitants. — *n.* A native or natives of Japan; the language of the inhabitants of Japan. — **Japan-lacquer**, *n.* A valuable black hard varnish used in japanning.—**Japanner**, ja-pan'ėr, *n.* One who japans.

Jape, jāp, *n.* A merry jest, or joke.

Japhetic, ja-fet'ik, *a.* Pertaining to *Japheth*, one of the sons of Noah (the *Japhetic* nations).

Japonica, ja-po'ni-ka, *n.* Japanese species of pear or quince.

Jar, jär, *v.i.*—*jarred*, *jarring.* [Also found in forms *chur*, *jur*, and imitative of sound; comp. night-*jar*, night-*churr*, names of the goat-sucker from its cry; also *jargon*, L. *garrio*, to chatter.] To strike together with a short rattle or tremulous sound; to give out a harsh sound; to sound discordantly; to be inconsistent; to clash or interfere; to quarrel; to dispute.—*v.t.* To cause a short tremulous motion to; to cause to shake or tremble.—*n.* A rattling vibration of sound; a harsh sound; clash of interest or opinions; collision; discord.—**Jarringly**, jär'ing-li, *adv.* In a jarring manner.

Jar, jär, *n.* [Fr. *jarre*, Sp. *jarra*, a jar, from Ar. *jarra*, a water-pot.] A vessel of earthenware or glass, of various shapes and dimensions; the contents of a jar.

Jardinière, zhär-dēn-yār, *n.* [Fr., a female gardener, a gardener's wife.] An ornamental stand for plants and flowers, used as a decoration of an apartment.

Jargon, jär'gon, *n.* [Fr.; origin doubtful. JAR, *v.i.*] Confused; unintelligible talk or language; gabble; gibberish; phraseology peculiar to a sect, profession, or the like; professional slang.—*v.i.* To utter unintelligible sounds.—**Jargonize**, jär′gon-īz, *v.i.* To utter jargon.

Jargon, Jargoon, jär′gon, jär′gön, *n.* [Fr. *jargon*, from It. *giargone*, properly a yellow stone, from Pers. *zargūn*, gold-coloured.] A variety of zircon, colourless or coloured, the colourless forms resembling the diamond.—**Jargonelle**, jär-go-nel′, *n.* [Fr., from *jargon*, the mineral.] A variety of early pear.

Jarl, yarl, *n.* Norse and Danish variety of *earl*.

Jarool, jä-röl′, *n.* A magnificent timber-tree of India and Burmah, the wood of which being very durable in water is much valued for boat and ship building.

Jarrah, jar′ra, *n.* A valuable timber-tree of West Australia, a species of eucalyptus.

Jarvey, Jarvy, jär′vi, *n.* A hackney-coach; the driver of a coach, cab, or similar conveyance. (*Slang.*)

Jasey, jā′zi, *n.* [Possibly a corruption of *Jersey*, as being made of Jersey yarn.] A worsted wig.

Jasmine, Jasmin, jas′min, *n.* [Fr. *jasmin*; Ar. and ultimately Pers. *yāsemin*, jasmine.] The name of several elegant erect or climbing shrubs, with white or yellow flowers, from some of which delicious perfumes are extracted.

Jasper, jas′pėr, *n.* [O.Fr. *jaspre*, Fr. *jaspe*, L., Gr. *iaspis*, Ar. *yashb*, Heb. *yashpheh*; hence *diaper*.] An impure opaque coloured quartz, which admits of an elegant polish, and is used for vases, seals, &c.—**Jasperated**, jas′pėr-ā-ted, *a.* Mixed with jasper; containing particles of jasper.—**Jaspery**, jas′pėr-i, *a.* Having the qualities of jasper; mixed with jasper.—**Jaspidean, Jaspideous**, jas-pid′ē-an, jas-pid′ē-us, *a.* Like jasper; consisting of jasper, or partaking of jasper.—**Jaspoid**, jas′poid, *a.* Resembling jasper.—**Jasponyx**, jas′pō-niks, *n.* [L., Gr. *iasponyx*—*iaspis*, jasper, and *onyx*.] The purest horn-coloured onyx, with beautiful green zones.

Jaumange, zhō-manzh, *n.* [Fr. *jaune*, yellow, and *manger*, meat.] A variety of blanc-mange; Dutch flummery. Also called *Jaune-mange*.

Jaundice, jạn′dis, *n.* [O.E. *jaunes*, *jaunis*, Fr. *jaunisse*, from *jaune*, O.Fr. *jalne*, L. *galbanus*, *galbinus*, yellowish, *galbus*, yellow; same root as *yellow*.] A disease characterized by suppression and alteration of the liver functions, yellowness of the eyes and skin, with loss of appetite and general languor and lassitude; any feeling or emotion disordering the judgment.—*v.t.*—*jaundiced*, *jaundicing*. To affect with jaundice; to affect with prejudice.

Jaunt, jänt, *v.i.* [Formerly *jaunce*, from O.Fr. *jancer*; of doubtful origin.] To wander here and there; to make an excursion or trip; to ramble.—*n.* An excursion; a ramble; a short journey.—**Jaunting-car**, *n.* A light car used in Ireland in which the passengers ride back to back on folding-down seats placed at right angles to the axle.

Jaunty, jän′ti, *a.* [O.E. *gent*, Sc. *genty*, elegant, pretty; from *gentle*, genteel, but modified by *jaunt*.] Gay and easy in manner or actions; airy; sprightly; affecting elegance; showy.—**Jauntily**, jän′ti-li, *adv.* Briskly; airily; gaily.—**Jauntiness**, jän′ti-nes, *n.* The quality of being jaunty.

Java, jä′va, *n.* A Malay island; a variety of coffee; slang for coffee.—**Javanese**, jav′a-nēz, *a.* Relating to Java.—*n.* A native of, or the language of Java.

Javelin, jav′lin, *n.* [Fr. *javeline*, It. *giavelina*, Sp. *jabalina*.] A light spear used in ancient warfare by horse and foot.—*v.t.* To strike or wound with a javelin.

Jaw, ja, *n.* [O.E. *chaw*, that which *chaws* or *chews*. CHEW.] The bones of the mouth in which the teeth are fixed; the upper or lower bony portion of the mouth; anything resembling a jaw in form or use (the *jaws* of a vice); loquacity or talk (a vulgar usage).—*v.i.* To talk or gossip; also, to scold (vulgar).—*v.t.* To use impudent language towards (vulgar).—**Jaw-bone**, *n.* The bone of the jaw in which the teeth are fixed.—**Jawed**, jad, *a.* Having jaws: mostly in composition.—**Jaw-foot**, *n.* The foot of a crustacean near its mouth.—**Jaw-tooth**, *n.* A molar tooth; a grinder.

Jay, jā, *n.* [Fr. *geai*, O.Fr. *gai*, Pr. *gai*, *jai*, Sp. *gayo*; same origin as adjective *gay*; lit. the gay or lively bird.] A bird allied to the crows, and one species of which, a beautiful bird with a crest of erectile feathers, is a native of Britain, another (the blue jay) is a native of North America.

Jaywalk, jā′wak, *v.i.* To cross a street carelessly amid traffic and away from a regular crossing place.

Jealous, jel′us, *a.* [O.Fr. *jalous*, Fr. *jaloux*, It. *geloso*, from L.L. *zelosus*—L. *zelus*, Gr. *zēlos*, zeal. Another form of *zealous*.] Uneasy through fear of, or on account of, preference given to another; suspicious in love; apprehensive of rivalry; zealous.—**Jealously**, jel′us-li, *adv.* In a jealous manner.—**Jealousness**, jel′us-nes, *n.* The state of being jealous.—**Jealousy**, jel′us-i, *n.* [Fr. *jalousie*.] The quality of being jealous; uneasiness from fear of being, or on account of being, supplanted by a rival; earnest solicitude.

Jean, jēn, *n.* [Probably from *Genoa*.] A twilled cotton cloth.—*Satin jean*, a species of jean with a smooth and satiny surface.

Jedding-axe, jed′ing-aks, *n.* A cavil.

Jedwood, Jeddart, Jedburgh, jed′-wöd, jed′art, jed′buru, *a.* Of justice, rough and ready in the Scottish Borders, by which the criminal was hanged first and tried afterwards.

Jeer, jēr, *v.i.* [Perhaps from O.Fr. *girer*, It. *girare*, L. *gyrare*, to turn in a circle.] To utter severe sarcastic reflections; to scoff; to make a mock of some person or thing (to *jeer at* a person).—*v.t.* To treat with scoffs or derision; to make a mock of; to deride; to flout.—*n.* A scoff; a taunt; a flout; a gibe; derision.—**Jeerer**, jē′rėr, *n.*—**Jeeringly**, jē′ring-li, *adv.*

Jeffersonian, jef-fer-sō′ni-an, *a.* Of Thomas Jefferson (third U. S. president, 1801-9) or his political teachings, advocating broad rights of the states.

Jehovah, jē-hō′va, *n.* A Scripture name of the Supreme Being, the proper form of which, according to most scholars, should be *Yahveh* or *Yahweh*.—**Jehovist**, jē-hō′vist, *n.* The supposed author or authors of the *Jehovistic* portions of the Old Testament. ELOHIST.—**Jehovistic**, jē-hō-vis′tik, *a.* Pertaining to those passages in the Old Testament, especially of the Pentateuch, in which the Supreme Being is spoken of under the name *Jehovah*. ELOHISTIC.

Jehu, jē′hū, *n.* [From *Jehu*, the son of Nimshi, 2 Ki. ix. 20.] A slang name for a coachman or one fond of driving.

Jejune, jē-jūn′, *a.* [L. *jejunus*, hungry, dry, barren.] Devoid of interesting matter, or attractiveness of any kind: said especially of literary productions; bare; meagre; barren; unprofitable.—**Jejunely**, jē-jūn′li, *adv.* In a jejune manner.—**Jejuneness, Jejunity**, je-jūn′nes, jē-jū′ni-ti, *n.* The quality or condition of being jejune.

Jejunum, jē-jū′num, *n.* [L., from *jejunus*, hungry or empty.] *Anat.* the second portion of the small intestine comprised between the duodenum and ileum.

Jelly, jel′i, *n.* [Fr. *gelée*, from *geler*, L. *gelo*, to freeze; so *gelatine*, *congeal*. GELID.] Matter in a viscous or glutinous state; the inspissated juice of fruit boiled with sugar; a transparent gluey matter obtained from animal substances by decoction.—**Jellied**, jel′id, *a.* Brought to the consistence of jelly.—**Jelly-bag**, *n.* A bag through which jelly is strained.—**Jelly-fish**, *n.* The popular name of various marine animals which have a jelly-like appearance; a medusa; a sea-nettle.

Jemidar, Jemadar, jem-i-där′, jem-a-där′, *n.* [Hind. *jamadâr*, from *jama*, a number or body, and *dâr*, a holder.] A native officer in the Anglo-Indian army having the rank of lieutenant.

Jemmy, jem′i, *a.* [Possibly for *gemmy*, or connected with *gim* of *gimcrack*.] Spruce; neat; smart. (*Colloq.*)—**Jemminess**, jem′i-nes, *n.* Spruceness; neatness. (*Colloq.*)

Jemmy, jem′i, *n.* [Slang—from *James*.] A short stout crowbar used by house-breakers for opening doors.

Jennet, jen′et, *n.* GENET.

Jenneting, jen′et-ing, *n.* [Perhaps for *jeanneton*, from Fr. *Jean*, John; St. John's apple.] A species of early apple.

Jenny, jen′i, *n.* [For *ginny*, from *gin*, short for *engine*, influenced by its resemblance to a common female name.] A machine for spinning, moved by water or steam.

Jeopardy, jep′ėr-di, *n.* [O.E. *jupartie*, from Fr. *jeu parti*, lit. a divided game; L.L. *jocus partitus*, an even chance. JOKE, PART.] Exposure to death, loss, or injury; hazard; danger; peril.—*v.t.*†—*jeopardied*, *jeopardying*. To jeopardize.—**Jeopard**, jep′ėrd, *v.t.* To put in danger; to hazard.—**Jeoparder**, jep′ėr-dėr, *n.* One who jeopards.—**Jeopardize**, jep′ėr-dīz, *v.t.* To expose to loss or injury; to jeopard.—**Jeopardous**, jep′ėr-dus, *a.* Perilous; hazardous.—**Jeopardously**, jep′ėr-dus-li, *adv.* With risk or danger; hazardously.

Jerboa, jėr-bō′a, *n.* [Ar. *yerbôa*, *yerbûa*.] A name of certain small rodents mainly characterized by the disproportionate length of the hind-limbs.

Jereed, Jerid, je-rēd′, *n.* A wooden javelin used in Persia and Turkey, especially in mock fights.

Jeremiad, Jeremiade, jer-ē-mī′ad, *n.* [From *Jeremiah*, the prophet.] A lamentation; a tale of grief, sorrow, or complaint: used with a spice of ridicule or mockery.

Jerfalcon, jėr′fa-kn, *n.* The gyrfalcon.

Jergue. JERQUE.

Jerk, jėrk, *v.t.* [Comp. O.E. and Sc. *yerk*, a quick, smart lash or blow; prov. *girk*, a rod; perhaps same as *gird* (*n.*).] To thrust with a sudden effort; to give a sudden pull, twitch, thrust, or push to; to throw with a quick smart motion.—*v.i.* To make a sudden motion; to give a start.—*n.* A short sudden thrust, push, or twitch; a jolt; a sudden spring; a start; a leap or bound.—**Jerker**, jėr′kėr, *n.* One who jerks; also same as *Jerquer*.—**Jerkingly**, jėr′king-li, *adv.* In a jerking manner.—**Jerky**, jėr′ki, *a.* Moving by or exhibiting jerks.

Jerk, jėrk, *v.t.* [Chilian, *charqui*.] To cut (beef) into long thin pieces, and dry in the sun, as is done in S. America. CHARQUI.

Jerkin, jėr′kin, *n.* [Dim. of D. *jurk*, a frock.] A jacket; a short coat; a close waistcoat.

Jeroboam, jer-o-bō′am, *n.* A fanciful name for a large old-fashioned bottle or jar for liquor.

Jerque, Jergue, jėrk, jėrg, *v.t.* [Probably from It. *cercare* (pron. *cher-*), Fr. *chercher*, to search.] To search a ship (by a custom-house officer) for smuggled goods.—**Jerquer, Jerguer**, jėr′kėr, jėr′gėr, *n.* An officer who searches vessels.

Jerry-builder, je′ri-bil″dėr, *n.* [Origin dubious.] A builder of hastily-worked materials, unstable and cheap.

Jersey, jėr′zi, *n.* [From the island so called.] Fine yarn of wool; a kind of close-fitting knitted woolen upper shirt or similar article of dress; a species of dairy cow developed on the island and noted for its rich milk.

Jerusalem-artichoke, jėr-ū′sa-lem, *n.* [*Jerusalem* is here a corruption of the Italian *girasole*. GIRASOLE.] A well-known plant, the tubers of which are of a sweetish farinaceous nature, somewhat akin to the potato.

Jerusalem Chamber. The Chapter House of Westminster Abbey.

Jess, jes, *n.* [O.Fr. *ges, gest, get,* &c., from L.L. *jactus*, a jess, from L. *jacio, jactum*, to throw. JET.] A short strap of leather fastened round each of the legs of a hawk, to which the leash tied round the falconer's hand was attached.—**Jessed**, jest, *a.* Having jesses.

Jessamine, jes'a-min, *n.* Jasmine.

Jesse, jes'sē, *n.* [From its resemblance to the genealogical tree of *Jesse*, the father of David, of which a picture used to be hung up in churches.] A large brass candlestick branched into many sconces, used in churches.—*Jesse tree*, alluding to Isaiah, xi. 1: 'A rod out of the stem of Jesse'.

Jest, jest, *n.* [O.E. *geste*, a jest, a tale, from L. *gestum*, something done, a deed, a feat, from *gero*, to do, whence *gesture*, &c.] A joke; something ludicrous uttered and meant only to excite laughter; the object of laughter; a laughing-stock.—*In jest*, for mere sport or diversion; not in truth and reality; not in earnest.—*v.i.* To make merriment by words or actions; to utter jests; to talk jokingly; to joke.—**Jest-book**, *n.* A book containing jests, jokes, or funny anecdotes.—**Jester**, jes'tėr, *n.* One who jests; a person given to jesting; a buffoon; a merry-andrew; a person formerly retained by persons of rank to make sport for them.—**Jestingly**, jes'ting-li, *adv.* In a jesting manner; not in earnest.

Jesuit, jez'ū-it, *n.* [One of the order or Society of *Jesus*.] One of a religious order belonging to the Roman Catholic Church, founded by Ignatius Loyola in 1534, and approved by Pope Paul III in 1540.—**Jesuitic, Jesuitical**, jez-ū-it'ik, jez-ū-it'ikal, *a.* Of, or pertaining to, or resembling, the principles, practices, and methods of the Jesuits.—**Jesuitically**, jez-ū-it'i-kal-li, *adv.* In a jesuitical manner.—**Jesuitish**, jez'ū-it-ish, *a.* Somewhat jesuitic.—**Jesuitism**, jez'ū-it-izm, *n.* The methods, principles, and practices of the Jesuits.—**Jesuitry**, jes'ū-it-ri, *n.* The methods, principles, and practices of the Jesuits.—**Jesuit bark**, *n.* Peruvian bark; the marsh elder (U.S.).

Jesus, jē'zus, *n.* [Gr. *Iēsous*, from Heb. *Jeshuah, Jehosuah*, 'help of Jehovah'.] The Son of God; the Saviour of men: frequently conjoined with Christ (which see).

Jet, jet, *n.* [Old forms *jeat, jayet*, O.Fr. *jayet, gayet*, from Gr. *gagatēs*, from *Gagæ*, a town and river in Lycia, where it was obtained.] A highly compact species of coal susceptible of a good polish, deep black and glossy, wrought into buttons and ornaments of various kinds.—**Jet-black**, *a.* Of the deepest black, the colour of jet.—**Jettiness**, jet'i-nes, *n.* Quality of being jetty; blackness.—**Jetty**, jet'i, *a.* Made of jet, or black as jet.

Jet, jet, *n.* [Fr. *jet*, a throw, a jet, a fountain, from L. *jactus*, a throwing, from *jacio*, to throw, which, with the connected *jaceo*, to lie (to be thrown), enters into a number of E. words, as *abject, adjective, adjacent, conjecture, gist, interjection, jetty, reject*, &c.] A shooting forth or spouting; what issues or streams forth from an orifice, as water or other fluid, gas or flame.—*v.i.*—*jetted, jetting*. [Fr. *jeter*, to throw, from L. *jactare*, freq. of *jacio*, to throw. *Jut* is the same word.] To issue in a jet; to shoot out; to project; to jut.—*v.t.* To emit; to spout forth.

Jettee, jet-ē', *n.* A strong silky fibre produced by an Indian plant (genus Marsdenia, order Asclepiadaceæ).

Jettison, Jetsam, Jetson, jet'i-sun, jet'sam, jet'sun, *n.* [O.Fr. *gettaison*, L. *jactatio*, a throwing, from *jacio*, to throw.] The throwing of goods overboard in order to lighten a ship in danger; the goods thus thrown away.—*v.t* To throw overboard.

Jetty, jet'i, *n.* [O.Fr. *jettée*, Fr. *jetée*, from O.Fr. *jetter*, to throw. JET.] A projecting portion of a building; a projecting structure (generally of piles), affording a convenient landing place for vessels or boats; a kind of small pier.—**Jettyhead**, jet'i-hed, *n.* A projecting part at the outer end of a wharf.

Jew, jū, *n.* [O.Fr. *Juis*; L. *Judæus*, from *Judæa*, so named from *Judah*, the tribe which had the first and largest portion west of the Jordan.] A Hebrew or Israelite.—**Jewess**, jū'es, *n.* A Hebrew woman.—**Jewish**, jū'ish, *a.* Pertaining to the Jews or Hebrews.—**Jewishly**, jū'ish-li, *adv.* In a Jewish manner.—**Jewishness**, jū'ish-nes, *n.* The condition of being Jewish.—**Jewry**, jū'ri, *n.* Judæa; also, a city quarter inhabited by Jews.—**Jews'-harp, Jews'-trump**, *n.* An instrument of music which is held between the teeth and by means of a thin bent metal tongue struck by the finger, gives out a sound.

Jewel, jū'el, *n.* [O.Fr. *jouel, joiel, joel* (Fr. *joyau*), either from L.L. *jocale*, a jewel, from L. *jocare*, to jest, *jocus*, a jest (whence *joke*), or from L.L. *gaudiale*, from L. *gaudium*, joy (whence *joy*).] A personal ornament in which precious stones form a principal part; a precious stone; anything of exceeding value or excellence.—*v.t.*—*jewelled, jewelling*. To dress or adorn with jewels; to fit or provide with a jewel (as a watch); to deck or adorn as with jewels.—**Jewel-case**, *n.* A case for holding ornaments and jewels.—**Jeweller**, jū'el-ėr, *n.* One who makes or deals in jewels and other ornaments.—**Jewellery, Jewelry**, jū'el-ėr-i, jū'el-ri, *n.* The trade or occupation of a jeweller; jewels in general.

Jezebel, jez'e-bel, *n.* [From *Jezebel*, the infamous wife of Ahab, king of Israel.] An unscrupulous, daring, vicious woman.

Jib, jib, *n.* [From Dan. *gibbe*, D. *gijpen*, to turn suddenly, said of sails.] The foremost sail of a ship, triangular in shape and extended from the outer end of a jib-boom toward the foretopmast-head; in sloops, a sail on the bowsprit, and extending towards the lower masthead; the projecting beam or arm of a crane.—**Jib, Jibe**, jib, jīb, *v.t.*—*jibbed, jibbing, jibed, jibing*. *Naut.* to shift (a fore-and-aft sail) from one side to the other.—**Jib-boom**, *n.* A spar run out from the extremity of the bowsprit, and which serves as a continuation of it.

Jib, Jibe, jib, jīb, *v.i.*—*jibbed, jibbing; jibed, jibing*. [O.Fr. *giber*, to struggle; *regibber*, to kick.] To pull against the bit, as a horse; to move restively sideways or backwards.—**Jibber**, jib'ėr, *n.* One who jibs; a horse that jibs.

Jibe, jīb, *v.t.* To jeer. GIBE.

Jiffy, jif'i, *n.* [Prov.E. *jiffle*, to be restless; comp. *jib*, to turn suddenly.] A moment; an instant. (*Colloq.*)

Jig, jig, *n.* [O.Fr. *gigue, gige*, a stringed instrument; the same word as *gig*.] A quick light dance: a light quick tune or air, generally in triple time.—*v.i.*—*jigged, jigging*. To dance a jig; to move with a light jolting motion.—*v.t.* To sing in the style of a jig, or in jig time. (*Shak.*)—**Jiggish**, jig'ish, *a.* Pertaining to or suitable to a jig.

Jigger, jig'ėr, *n.* *Mining*, a man who cleans ores by means of a wire-bottom sieve; the sieve itself; a kind of light tackle used in ships; a potter's wheel by which earthenware vessels are shaped.—**Jigger-mast**, *n.* The mast furthest aft in a four-masted vessel, bearing the *jigger*, a sail extended by a gaff and boom. Similarly **Jigger-topmast, Jigger-stay**, &c.

Jigger, jig'ėr, *n.* [CHIGOE.] The chigoe.

Jigjog, jig'jog, *n.* [Reduplication of *jog*.] A jolting motion; a jog; a push.—*a.* Jolting.

Jig-saw, *n.* A saw with a vertical motion, moved by a vibrating lever or crank rod.

Jilt, jilt, *n.* [Contr. from *jillet*, a dim. of *jill, gill*, a young woman, a giddy girl. GILL.] A woman who gives her lover hopes and capriciously disappoints him; sometimes used of a man; a name of contempt for a woman.—*v.t.* To treat as a jilt does her lover; to play the jilt to; to trick in love.—*v.i.* To play the jilt.

Jimcrack, jim'krak, *n.* GIMCRACK.

Jimmy, jim'i, *n.* JEMMY.

Jingle, jing'gl, *v.i.*—*jingled, jingling*. [Probably imitative, like *jangle, chink, tinkle*, G. *klingeln*.] To sound with a tinkling metallic sound; to clink, as money, chains, or bells.—*v.t.* To cause to give a tinkling metallic sound.—*n.* A rattling or clinking sound, as of metal; something that jingles; a little bell or rattle; correspondence of sound in rhymes.

Jingo, jing'gō, *n.* An expletive used as a mild oath (*By jingo!*); a person exaggeratedly patriotic and clamorous for war.—**Jingoism**, jing'gō-izm, *n.* Exaggerated and bellicose patriotism.—**Jingoist**, jing'gō-ist, *n.* & *a.*—**Jingoistic**, jing'gō-is"tic, *a.*

Jinks, jingks, *n.* (Chiefly in *high jinks*.) Frolics; pranks.

Jinni, Jinnee, ji-nē', *n.* pl. **Jinn**, jin. *Mohammedan myth.* one of a race of Genii, angels, or demons.

Jinrikisha, jin-rik'shä, *n.* [Japanese.] A small, two-wheeled vehicle, drawn by one or more men.

Jinx, jingks, *n.* & *v.* Something which brings bad luck; a hoodoo. (*Slang.*)

Jitney, jit'ni, *n.* A nickel; five cents; a bus or taxicab having a low fare. (*Slang.*)

Jitter, jit'ėr, *v.t.* To behave nervously.—**Jitterbug**, jit'ėr-bug, *n.* A frenzied devotee of swing music and jazz.—**Jitters**, jit'ėrz, *n. pl.* Excessive nervousness. (*Slang.*)

Job, job, *n.* [A form of Prov.E. *gob*, a lump, a portion; akin *gobbet*.] A piece of work undertaken; employment; position; a public transaction made for private profit; an undertaking set agoing professedly in the public interest, but really to benefit the promoters.—*v.t.*—*jobbed, jobbing*. To let out to be done in several portions or jobs; to buy in large quantity and sell in smaller lots.—*v.i.* To work at chance jobs; to deal in the public stocks; to buy and sell as a broker; to pervert some public undertaking to private advantage.—*a.* Applied to goods bought and sold under special circumstances, and generally under the ordinary trade-price.—**Jobber**, job'ėr, *n.* One who jobs; one who works at jobs; one who deals in goods as middle man; one who deals or dabbles in stocks; a stock-jobber.—**Jobbery**, job'ėr-i, *n.* Act or practice of jobbing; unfair and underhand means used to procure some private end at public expense.—**Jobbing**, job'ing, *a.* Applied to a person who works by the job (a *jobbing* gardener, &c.).—**Job lot**, *n.* A miscellaneous collection sold.—**Job printer**, *n.* A printer who does miscellaneous work, as bills, circulars, &c.

Job's-comforter, jōb, *n.* [From *Job* of Scripture.] One who pretends to sympathize with you, but attributes your misfortunes to your own misconduct.

Jockey, jok'i, *n.* [For *Jackey*, dim. of *Jack*, for *John*; *Jockey* and *Jock* being Northern English forms. JACK.] A man whose profession it is to ride horses in horse races.—*v.t.*—*jockeyed* or *jockied, jockeying*. To ride in a race; to maneuver (to *jockey* for position); to jostle by riding against; to cheat; to trick; to deceive in trade.—**Jockeyism**, jok'i-izm, *n.* Practice of jockeys.—**Jockeyship**, jok'i-ship, *n.* The art or practice of riding horses.

Jocose, jō-kōs', *a.* [L. *jocosus*, from *jocus*, a joke. JOKE.] Given to jokes and jesting; merry; waggish; containing a joke; sportive; merry.—**Jocosely**, jō-kōs'li, *adv.* In a jocose manner.—**Jocoseness**, jō-kōs'nes, *n.* The quality of being jocose.—**Jocoserious**, jō-kō-sē'ri-us, *a.* Partaking of mirth and seriousness.—**Jocosity**, jō-kos'i-ti, *n.* Jocularity; merriment; waggery; a jocose act or saying.—**Jocular**, jok'ū-lėr, *a.* [L. *jocularis*, from *jocus*.] Given to jesting; jocose; merry; waggish; containing jokes; facetious.—**Jocularity**, jok-ū-lar'i-ti, *n.* The quality of being jocular.—**Jocularly**, jok'ū-lėr-li, *adv.* In a jocular manner.

Jocund, jok'und, *a.* [L. *jocundus, jucundus*; connected with *juvenis*, a young man, *juvare*, to assist (as in *adjutant*, *coadjutor*); E. *young*.] Merry; cheerful; blithe; gleeful; gay; sprightly; sportive; light-hearted. —**Jocundity**, **Jocundness**, jo-kun′di-ti, jok′und-nes, *n*. State of being jocund.—**Jocundly**, jok′und-li, *adv*.

Jodhpurs, jŏd′pŏrs, *n. pl.* [From Jodhpur, India.] Riding breeches that fit tightly from the knees to the ankles.

Jog, jog, *v.t.*—*jogged*, *jogging*. [Perhaps a form of *jag*, or allied to W. *gogi*, to shake.] To push or shake with the elbow or hand; to give notice or excite attention by a slight push.—*v.i.* To move at a slow trot; to walk or travel idly or slowly; to move along with but little progress: generally followed by *on*—*n*. A push; a slight shake; a shake or push intended to give notice or awaken attention; *carp.* and *masonry*, a square notch.—**Jogger**, jog′ėr, *n*. One who jogs. —**Joggle**, jog′l, *v.t.*—*joggled*, *joggling*. [Freq. of *jog*.] To shake slightly; to give a sudden but slight push; *carp.* to join or match by jogs or notches so as to prevent sliding apart.—*v.i.* To push; to shake; to totter.—*n*. A joint made by means of jogs or notches; a joint held in place by means of pieces of stone or metal introduced into it; the piece of metal or stone used in such a joint.—**Jog-trot**, *n*. A slow, easy trot; hence, a slow routine of daily duty to which one pertinaciously adheres.—*a*. Monotonous; easy-going; humdrum.

Johannine, jō-han′in, *a*. Of or pertaining to the author of the Fourth Gospel.

Johannisberg, jo-han′is-bėrg, *n*. [From the castle of the name near Wiesbaden, where the wine is made.] The finest and most expensive of the Rhenish wines.

John, jon, *n*. [L. *Johannes*, *Joannes*, Gr. *Iōannēs*, from Heb.] A proper name of men.—*John Bull*, a humorous designation of the English people, first used in Arbuthnot's satire *The History of John Bull*.—**John Chinaman**. A John, a native of China.—**John Doe**, *n*. *Law*. Name used for an unknown person.—**John Dory**, *n*. DORY.—**John Hancock**, han′kok, *n*. One's signature, from the exceptionally legible writing of John Hancock.—**Johnnycake**, jon′i, *n*. Bread or cake made of corn meal, salt, water, and shortening.—**Johnny-jump-up**, *n*. The wild pansy.—**Johnny-raw**, *n*. A raw beginner.

Johnsonese, jon-son-ēz′, *n*. The style or language of Dr. Johnson, or an imitation of it; a pompous inflated style.

Join, join, *v.t.* [Fr. *joindre*, from L. *jungere*, *junctum*, to join, seen in many E. words, as *junction*, *juncture*, *adjoin*, *conjoin*, *enjoin*, *rejoin*, *conjugal*, *conjugate*, &c.; same root as Skr. *yuj*, to join; E. *yoke*.] To connect or bring together, physically or otherwise; to place in contiguity; to couple; to combine; to associate; to engage in (to *join* the fray); to make one's self a party in; to become connected with; to unite with; to enter or become a member of; to merge in (to *join* the army, one river joins another).—*To join battle*, to engage in battle. —*To join issue*. Under ISSUE.—*v.i.* To be contiguous or in contact; to form a physical union; to coalesce; to unite or become associated, as in marriage, league, partnership, society; to confederate; to associate; to league.—**Joiner**, joi′nėr, *n*. One who joins; a mechanic who does the wood-work of houses; a carpenter.—**Joinery**, joi′nėr-i, *n*. The art of a joiner; carpentry.—**Joining**, joi′ning, *n*. A joint.

Joint, joint, *n*. [Fr. *joint*, from *joindre*, pp. *joint*, to join. JOIN.] The place or part at which two separate things are joined or united; the mode of connection of two things; junction; articulation; one of the large pieces into which a carcass is cut up by the butcher; *anat.* the joining of two or more bones, as in the elbow, the knee, or the knuckle; *bot.* a node or knot; also, the part between two nodes; an internode; *geol.* a fissure or line of parting in rocks at any angle to the plane of stratification; *building*, the surface of contact between two bodies that are held firmly together by means of cement, mortar, &c., or by a superincumbent weight; the place where or the mode in which one piece of timber is connected with another. DOVETAIL, SCARF, MITRE, MORTISE, TENON. —*Universal joint*, a mechanical arrangement by which one part may be made to move freely in all directions in relation to another connected part.—*Out of joint*, dislocated, as when the head of a bone is displaced from its socket; hence, figuratively, confused; disordered.—*a*. Shared by two or more (*joint* property); having an interest in the same thing (*joint* owner); united; combined; acting in concert (a *joint* force, *joint* efforts).—*v.t.* To form with a joint or joints; to articulate; to unite by a joint or joints; to fit together; to cut or divide into joints or pieces.—*v.i.* To coalesce by joints. —**Jointed**, join′ted, *p.* and *a*. Provided with joints; formed with knots or nodes.—**Jointedly**, join′ted-li, *adv*. In a jointed manner.—**Jointer**, join′tėr, *n*. One who or that which joints.—**Joint-heir**, *n*. An heir having a joint interest with another.—**Jointly**, joint′li, *adv*. In a joint manner; together; unitedly; in concert.—**Joint-stock**, *n*. Stock held in company.—*Joint-stock company*, an association of a number of individuals who jointly contribute funds for the purpose of carrying on a specified business or undertaking, of which the shares are transferable by each owner without the consent of the other partners.—**Joint-tenant**, *n*. *Law*, one who holds an estate along with another, and if the other dies takes the whole.—**Jointure**, join′tūr, *n*. Property settled on a woman in consideration of marriage, and which she is to enjoy after her husband's decease.—*v.t.*—*jointured*, *jointuring*. To settle a jointure upon.

Joist, joist, *n*. [O.Fr. *giste*, Fr. *gîte*, a bed, a place to lie on, L.L. *gista*, from L. *jacitum*, pp. of *jacere*, to lie. JET, GIST.] One of the stout pieces of timber to which the boards of a floor or the laths of a ceiling are nailed, and which are supported by the walls or on girders.—*v.t.* To fit or furnish with joists.

Joke, jōk, *n*. [L. *jocus*, Fr. *jeu*, It. *giuoco*, *gioca*, a jest; same root as *jacio*, to throw (JET). Akin *jocose*, *jocular*, *juggler*, *jeopardy*.] Something said for the sake of exciting a laugh; something witty or sportive; a jest; what is not in earnest or actually meant.—*A practical joke*, a trick played on one, usually to the injury or annoyance of his person.—*In joke*, in jest; with no serious intention.—*v.i.*—*joked*, *joking*. To jest; to utter jokes; to jest in words or actions.—*v.t.* To cast jokes at; to make merry with; to rally.—**Joker**, jō′kėr, *n*. A jester; a merry fellow; in a legal document, a seemingly harmless clause which greatly alters the apparent meaning; an extra playing card which, when used, as in poker or euchre, has special privileges.—**Jokingly**, *adv*.

Jole, **Joll**, jōl, *n*.† [JOWL. Hence *jolt*.] The jowl; the head.

Jolly, jol′i, *a*. [O.Fr. *joli*, *jolif*, Fr. *joli*, gay, merry, from the Scand., and originally referring to the festivities of Christmas; from Icel. *jól*, Sw. and Dan. *jul*, E. *yule*, Christmas. YULE.] Merry; gay; lively; full of life and mirth; jovial; expressing mirth; exciting mirth or gaiety; plump; in excellent condition of body.—**Jollification**, jol′i-fi-kā″shon, *n*. A scene of merriment, mirth, or festivity; a carouse; merry-making.—**Jollily**, jol′i-li, *adv*. In a jolly manner.—**Jolliness**, jol′i-nes, *n*. The quality or condition of being jolly.—**Jollity**, jol′i-ti, *n*. The quality of being jolly; mirth; gaiety; festivity; joviality.

Jolly-boat, *n*. [*Jolly* here is same as Dan. *jolle*, D. *jol*, a yawl, a jolly-boat.] One of a ship's boats, about 12 feet in length, with a bluff bow; a yawl.

Jolt, jōlt, *v.i.* [From *jole*, *joll*.] To shake with short abrupt risings and fallings, as a carriage moving on rough ground.—*v.t.* To shake with sudden jerks, as in a carriage or on a high-trotting horse.—*n*. A shock or shake by a sudden jerk, as in a carriage.—**Jolter**, jōl′tėr, *n*. One who or that which jolts.—**Joltingly**, jōl′ting-li, *adv*. In a jolting manner.

Jonathan, jo′na-than, *n*. Brother Jonathan, the typical American; perhaps from *Jonathan* Trumbull, governor of Connecticut.

Jongleur, jon′glūr, *n*. [Fr.] A juggler; a mediæval wandering minstrel; akin to *juggler*, *jingler*.

Jonquil, **Jonquille**, jon′kwil, *a*. [Fr. *jonquille*; It. *giunchiglia*, dim. from L. *juncus*, a rush.] A species of narcissus or daffodil, with rush-like leaves and flowers that yield a fine perfume.

Jorum, jō′rum, *n*. [Perhaps a corruption of *jordan*, a vessel in which pilgrims brought home water from the *Jordan*.] A colloquial term for a bowl or drinking vessel with liquor in it.

Joseph, jō′zef, *n*. [Probably in allusion to *Joseph's* coat of many colours.] A riding coat or habit for women, formerly much in use.

Joss, jos, *n*. [Chin. *joss*, a deity, from Pg. *deos*, from L. *deus*, a god.] A Chinese idol. —**Joss-house**, *n*. A Chinese temple.—**Joss-stick**, *n*. In China, a small reed covered with the dust of odoriferous woods, and burned before an idol.

Jostle, jos′l, *v.t.*—*jostled*, *jostling*. [A dim. from *joust*.] To push against; to crowd against; to elbow; to hustle.—*v.i.* To hustle; to shove about as in a crowd.

Jot, jot, *n*. [From *iōta*, the smallest letter in the Greek alphabet. IOTA.] An iota; a point; a tittle; the least quantity assignable.—*v.t.*—*jotted*, *jotting*. To write down in a diary or memorandum-book; to make a memorandum of.—**Jotter**, jot′ėr, *n*. One who jots; a book for memoranda.—**Jotting**, jot′ing, *n*. A memorandum.

Jougs, jögz, *n. pl.* [Fr. *joug*, L. *jugum*, yoke.] An instrument of punishment formerly used in Scotland, consisting of an iron collar with a short chain attached, which again was fastened to a wall or post.

Joule, jöl, *n*. [*Joule*, scientist.] The unit of electric energy, equal to the work done in maintaining for one second a current of 1 ampere against a resistance of 1 ohm; equal to 10^7 ergs.

Journal, jėr′nal, *n*. [Fr., from L. *diurnalis*, diurnal, from *dies*, a day. DIURNAL, DIAL, DIARY.] A diary; an account of daily transactions and events, or the book containing such account; a newspaper or other periodical published daily; a periodical; *book-keeping*, a book in which every particular article or charge is entered under each day's date, or in groups at longer periods; *naut.* a daily register of the ship's course and distance, the winds, weather, and other occurrences; a log-book; *mach.* that part of an axle or shaft which rests and moves in the bearings.—**Journalism**, jėr′nal-izm, *n*. The trade or occupation of publishing, writing in, or conducting a journal.—**Journalist**, jėr′nal-ist, *n*. The conductor of or writer in a public journal; a newspaper editor or regular contributor.—**Journalistic**, jėr-nal-is′tik, *a*. Pertaining to journalism.—**Journalize**, jėr′nal-īz, *v.t.*—*journalized*, *journalizing*. To enter in a journal; to give the form of a journal to.

Journey, jėr′ni, *n*. [Fr. *journée*, a day, a day's work, a day's journey, from L. *diurnus*, daily, from *dies*, a day. JOURNAL.] Travel from one place to another; a passage made between places; a distance travelled at a time.—*v.i.* To travel from place to place; to pass from home to a distance.—**Journeyer**, jėr′ni-ėr, *n*. One who journeys.—**Journeyman**, jėr′ni-man, *n*. Strictly, a man hired to work by the day; but in fact, any mechanic or workman who has served his apprenticeship, and is thus supposed to have learned his special occupation.

Joust, just, *n*. [O.Fr. *juste*, *jouste*, *joste*, jousting, from O.Fr. *juster*, *jouster*, *joster*, to tilt; from L. *juxta*, near to, nigh.] An encounter with spears on horseback for trial of skill; a combat between two knights at a tournament for sport or for exercise.—*v.i.* To engage in a mock fight on horseback; to tilt.—**Jouster**, jus'tėr, *n.* One who jousts.

Jove, jōv, *n.* [L. *Jovis, Diovis*, the old name of *Jupiter* (that is Jove-father), latterly appearing only in the oblique cases; same root as *deus*, a god. See DEITY.] The chief divinity of the Romans; Jupiter; the planet Jupiter.—**Jovial**, jō'vi-al, *a.* [L.L. *Jovialis*, because the planet Jupiter was believed to make those born under it of a jovial temperament.] Gay; merry; joyous; jolly.—**Jovialist**, jō'vi-al-ist, *n.* One who lives a jovial life.—**Joviality**, **Jovialty**, **Jovialness**, jō-vi-al'i-ti, jō'vi-al-ti, jō'vi-al-nes, *n.* The state or quality of being jovial.—**Jovially**, jō'vi-al-li, *adv.* In a jovial manner.—**Jovian**, jō'vi-an, *a.* Pertaining to the planet Jupiter.

Jowl, **Joul**, jōl, *n.* [Also in forms *jole, joll, chowl*, from A.Sax. *ceafl*, jaw, snout. Akin *jolt*.] The cheek.—*Cheek by jowl*, with heads close together; side by side.

Joy, joi, *n.* [O.Fr. *joye, joie, goie*, Fr. *joie*, It. *gioja*, from L. *gaudium*, joy, *gaudere*, to rejoice; seen also in *gaudy, rejoice, jewel*.] Excitement of pleasurable feeling caused by the acquisition or expectation of good; gladness; pleasure; delight; exultation; exhilaration of spirits; the cause of joy or happiness.—*v.i.* To rejoice; to be glad; to exult.—*v.t.* To give joy to; to gladden. (*Shak.*)—**Joyance**, joi'ans, *n.* [O.Fr. *joiant*, joyful.] Enjoyment; happiness; delight. (*Poet.*)—**Joyful**, joi'ful, *a.* Full of joy; very glad; exulting; joyous; gleeful.—**Joyfully**, joi'ful-li, *adv.* In a joyful manner.—**Joyfulness**, joi'ful-nes, *n.* The state of being joyful.—**Joyless**, joi'les, *a.* Destitute of joy; wanting joy; giving no joy or pleasure.—**Joylessly**, joi'les-li, *adv.* In a joyless manner.—**Joylessness**, joi'les-nes, *n.* State of being joyless.—**Joyous**, joi'us, *a.* [O.Fr. *joyous*; Fr. *joyeux*; from L. *gaudiosus*, from *gaudium*.] Glad; gay; merry; joyful; giving joy.—**Joyously**, joi'us-li, *adv.* In a joyous manner.—**Joyousness**, joi'us-nes, *n.* The state of being joyous.—**Joy-stick**, *n.* The control lever of an aeroplane.

Jubate, jö'bāt, *a.* [L. *juba*, a mane.] Having a mane, or hair similar to a mane.

Jube, jö'bē, *n.* [Fr. *jubé*.] *Arch.* a name given to a rood-loft or a rood-screen.

Jubilant, jū'bi-lant, *a.* [L. *jubilans*, ppr. of *jubilo*, to shout for joy, from *jubilum*, a shout of joy; not connected with *jubilee*.] Uttering songs of triumph; rejoicing; shouting or singing with joy.—**Jubilate**, jū'bi-lāt, *v.i.* To rejoice; to exult; to triumph.—**Jubilation**, jū-bi-lā'shon, *n.* [L. *jubilatio*.] A rejoicing; a triumph; exultation.

Jubilee, jū'bi-lē, *n.* [Fr. *jubilé*, L. *jubilæus*, jubilee, from Heb. *yôbēl*, the blast of a trumpet, and hence the sabbatical year announced by the sound of the trumpet.] Among the Jews every fiftieth year, being the year following the revolution of seven weeks of years, at which time there was a general release of all debtors and slaves; hence a season of great public joy and festivity; any occasion of rejoicing or joy; a celebration of a marriage, pastorate, or the like, after it has lasted fifty years.

Judaic, **Judaical**, jū-dā'ik, jū-dā'i-kal, *a.* [L. *Judaicus*, from *Judæa*. JEW.] Pertaining to the Jews.—**Judaically**, jū-dā'i-kal-li, *adv.* After the Jewish manner.—**Judaism**, jū'dā-izm, *n.* The religious doctrines and rites of the Jews, as enjoined in the laws of Moses; conformity to the Jewish rites and ceremonies.—**Judaist**, jū'dā-ist, *n.* An adherent to Judaism.—**Judaistic**, jū-dā-is'tik, *a.* Relating or pertaining to Judaism.—**Judaization**, jū'dā-i-zā"shon, *n.* The act of judaizing.—**Judaize**, jū'dā-iz, *v.i.*—*judaized, judaizing*. To conform to the religious doctrines and rites of the Jews; to assume the manners or customs of the Jews.—*v.t.* To bring into conformity with what is Jewish.—**Judaizer**, jū'dā-i-zėr, *n.* One who judaizes.—**Judean**, jū-dē'an, *n.* A native or inhabitant of Judæa.—*a.* Relating to Judæa.

Judas, jö'das, *n.* [After the false apostle.] A treacherous person; one who betrays under the semblance of friendship; a judas-hole.—**Judas-colored**, *a.* Red; applied to hair; from the notion that Judas had red hair.—**Judas-hole**, *n.* A small hole for peeping into a chamber without the knowledge of those within it.

Judge, juj, *n.* [Fr. *juge*, from L. *judex, judicis*, a judge, from *jus, juris*, law or right, and *dico*, to pronounce (JURY, DICTION). This word appears in *adjudge, judicature, judicial, judicious*, &c.] A civil officer invested with power to hear and determine causes, civil and criminal, and to administer justice between parties in courts held for the purpose; one who has skill to decide on the merits of a question or on the value of anything; a critic; a connoisseur; *Jewish hist.* a chief magistrate with civil and military powers; hence, *pl.* the name of the seventh book of the Old Testament.—*v.i.*—*judged, judging*. [Fr. *juger*, L. *judicare*, to judge.] To hear and determine, as in causes on trial; to pass judgment upon any matter; to sit in judgment; to compare facts, ideas, or propositions, and perceive their agreement or disagreement; to form an opinion; to express censorious opinions; to determine; to estimate; to discern.—*v.t.* To hear and determine authoritatively, as a cause or controversy; to examine into and decide; to examine and pass sentence on; to try; to be censorious towards; to esteem, think, reckon.—**Judgeship**, juj'ship, *n.* The office of a judge.—**Judgment**, juj'ment, *n.* [Fr. *jugement*.] The act of judging; the act of deciding or passing decision on something; the act or faculty of judging truly, wisely, or skilfully; good sense; discernment; understanding; opinion or notion formed by judging or considering; the act or mental faculty by which man compares ideas and ascertains the relations of terms and propositions; a determination of the mind so formed, producing when expressed in words a proposition; *law*, the sentence pronounced in a cause by the judge or court by which it is tried; hence, a calamity regarded as inflicted by God for the punishment of sinners; the final trial of the human race.—*Judgment of God*, a term formerly applied to trials of crimes by single combat, by ordeal, &c.—**Judgment-day**, *n.* The last day, when final judgment will be pronounced on men.—**Judgment-debt**, *n.* *Law*, a debt secured to the creditor by a judge's order.—**Judgment-hall**, *n.* The hall where courts are held.—**Judgment-seat**, *n.* The seat on which judges sit in court; a court; a tribunal.

Judicable, jū'di-ka-bl, *a.* [L. *judicabilis*, from *judico*, to judge, from *judex*, a judge. JUDGE.] Capable of being tried or decided.—**Judicative**, jū'di-kā-tiv, *a.* Having power to judge.—**Judicatory**, jū'di-ka-to-ri, *a.* [L. *judicatorius*.] Pertaining to the passing of judgment; belonging to the administration of justice; dispensing justice.—*n.* A court of justice; a tribunal; administration of justice.—**Judicature**, jū'di-kā-tūr, *n.* The power of distributing justice; a court of justice; a judicatory; extent of jurisdiction of a judge or court.

Judicial, jū-dish'al, *a.* [L. *judicialis*, from *judicium*, a trial, a judicial inquiry, judgment, discernment, from *judex, judicis*, a judge. JUDGE.] Pertaining or appropriate to courts of justice or to a judge thereof; proceeding from, issued or ordered by, a court of justice; inflicted as a penalty or in judgment; enacted by law or statute.—**Judicially**, jū-dish'al-li, *adv.* In a judicial manner.—**Judiciary**, jū-dish'i-a-ri, *a.* [L. *judiciarius*.] Pertaining to the courts of judicature or legal tribunals; judicial.—*n.* The system of courts of justice in a government; the judges taken collectively.—**Judicious**, jū-dish'us, *a.* [Fr. *judicieux*, from L. *judicium*, judgment.] According to sound judgment; adapted to obtain a good end by the best means; well considered: said of things; acting according to sound judgment; possessing sound judgment; directed by reason and wisdom: said of persons.—**Judiciously**, jū-dish'us-li, *adv.* In a judicious manner.—**Judiciousness**, jū-dish'us-nes, *n.* The quality of being judicious.

Jug, jug, *n.* [From *Jug* or *Judge*, an old familiar form of *Joan* or *Jenny*, the name being jocularly given to the vessel, like *jack, black-jack*.] A vessel, usually of earthenware, metal, or glass, of various sizes and shapes, and generally with a handle or ear, used for holding and conveying liquors; a drinking vessel; a mug; a pitcher.—*v.t. jugged, jugging*. To put in a jug; to cook by putting into a jug, and this into boiling water (*jugged* hare).

Jug, jug, *n.* The sound fancied to resemble the note uttered by the nightingale.

Jugate, **Jugated**, jū'gāt, jū'gā-ted, *a.* [L. *jugum*, a yoke, a ridge or summit.] *Bot.* coupled together, as the pairs of leaflets in compound leaves.

Juggernaut, jug'ėr-nat, *n.* [Properly *Jagannâtha*, 'lord of the world', the famous idol to which people in India used to sacrifice themselves at festivals.] Any idea, custom, fashion, or the like, to which one either devotes himself or is blindly or ruthlessly sacrificed.

Juggle, jug'l, *v.t.*—*juggled, juggling*. [O.Fr. *jogler*, Fr. *jongler*, It. *giocolare*, from L. *joculor*, to jest or joke, from L. *jocus*, a jest. JOKE.] To play tricks by sleight of hand; to practice artifice or imposture; to toss and catch articles, keeping several continuously in the air.—**Juggler**, jug'lėr, *n.* [O.Fr. *jugleor, jogleor*, from L. *joculator*, one who jokes.] One who juggles.—**Jugglery**, jug'lėr-i, *n.* The art or performances of a juggler; legerdemain; trickery; imposture.—**Jugglingly**, jug'ling-li, *adv.*

Jugular, jū'gū-lėr, *a.* [L. *jugulum*, the collar-bone, the neck, from root of *jungo*, to join. JOIN.] *Anat.* pertaining to the neck or throat.—*Jugular vein*, one of the large trunks (two on each side) by which the greater part of the blood that has circulated in the head, face, and neck is returned to the heart.

Juice, jūs, *n.* [O.E. *jows*, Fr. *jus*, from L. *jus*, broth, soup; cog. Skr. *yûsha*, broth.] The sap or watery part of vegetables, especially of fruits; also, the fluid part of animal substances; electricity. (*Slang.*)—**Juiceless**, jūs'les, *a.*—**Juiciness**, jū'si-nes, *n.* The state of being juicy.—**Juicy**, jū'si, *a.* Abounding with juice; succulent; also, interesting, amusing.

Jujitsu, jö-jit'sö, *n.* [Japan.] A style of Japanese wrestling resting on a knowledge of muscular action.

Jujube, **Jujub**, jö'jöb, *n.* [Fr. *jujube*, a jujube, from L. *zizyphum*, Gr. *zizyphon*, Ar. *zizuf*, the jujube-tree.] The fruit of a spiny shrub or small tree of lands about the Mediterranean sea; the tree itself; a confection made of gelatin, sweetened and flavored to resemble the jujube fruit.

Julep, jū'lep, *n.* [Fr. *julep*, Ar. *julâb*, from Per. *gulâb*, rose-water—*gul*, rose, and *âb*, water.] A sweet drink; a sweetened mixture serving as a vehicle to some form of medicine; a drink composed of spirituous liquor, as bourbon whisky, sugar, crushed ice, and mint leaves.

Julian, jū'li-an, *a.* Pertaining to or derived from *Julius* Caesar.—*Julian calendar*, the calendar as adjusted by Julius Caesar. *Julian year*, the year of 365 days 6 hours, adopted in the Julian calendar.

Julienne, jö'li-en, *n.* [Fr.] A kind of soup made with various herbs or vegetables cut in very small pieces.

July, jū-lī', *n.* The seventh month of the year, during which the sun enters the sign Leo: so called from *Julius* Cæsar, who was born in this month, and by whom the calendar was reformed.

Jumart, jū'märt, *n.* [Fr.] The supposed offspring of a bull and a mare.

Jumble, jum'bl, *v.t.*—*jumbled, jumbling.*

[O.E. *jombre, jumbre, jumpre*, to agitate, to shake together; akin to *jump*, and to Dan. *gumpe*, to jolt.] To mix in a confused mass; to put or throw together without order: often followed by *together* or *up*.—*v.i.* To meet, mix, or unite in a confused manner.—*n.* Confused mixture, mass, or collection without order; disorder; confusion.—**Jumble sale.** Sale at a bazaar of mingled or confused goods.—**Jumblement**, jum'bl-ment, *n.* The act of jumbling together; confused mixture.—**Jumbler**, jum'blér, *n.* One who jumbles.—**Jumblingly**, jum'bling-li, *adv.* In a confused or jumbled manner.

Jump, jump, *v.i.* [Akin Dan. *gumpe*, Prov. G. *gumpen*, to jolt or jump; Icel. *goppa*, to jump or skip; also *jumble*.] To throw one's self in any direction by lifting the feet wholly from the ground and again alighting upon them; to leap; to spring; to bound; to agree, tally, or coincide (this *jumps* with my ideas).—*To jump at*, to embrace or accept (an offer) with eagerness (*Colloq.*).—*v.t.* To pass by a leap; to pass over eagerly or hastily; to skip over; to leap.—*n.* The act of jumping; a leap; a spring; a bound.—**Jumper**, jump'ér, *n.* One who or that which jumps; a long iron chisel pointed with steel used to prepare a hole for blasting or the like; a kind of jacket; *Elec.* a piece of wire across a broken circuit.—**Jumpy**, *a.* Nervous, restless.

Junco, jun'kō, *n.* A snowbird; a genus of American finches.

Juncaceous, jung-kā'shus, *a.* [L. *juncus*, a rush.] *Bot.* pertaining to or resembling the order of plants of which the rush is the type.

Junction, jungk'shon, *n.* [From L. *junctio*, from *jungo*, to join. JOIN.] The act or operation of joining; the state of being joined; the place or point of union; joint; juncture; the place where two or more railways meet.—**Juncture**, jungk'tūr, *n.* [L. *junctura*.] The line or point at which two bodies are joined; a point of time; particularly, a point rendered critical or important by a concurrence of circumstances.

June, jūn, *n.* [L. *Junius*, perhaps after L. *Junius* Brutus, who abolished regal power at Rome; same root as *junior*, L. *juvenis*, a youth; E. *young*.] The sixth month of the year.

Jungle, jung'gl, *n.* [Hind. *jangal*, forest, jungle.] Land covered with forest-trees, thick, impenetrable brushwood, or any coarse, rank vegetation.—**Jungle-fever**, *n.* A disease prevalent in the East Indies and other tropical regions, a severe variety of remittent fever.—**Jungle-fowl**, *n.* A name given to two birds, the one a native of Australia, the other of India.—**Jungly**, jung'gli, *a.* Of the nature of a jungle; consisting of jungles; abounding with jungles.

Junior, jū'ni-ér, *a.* [L., contracted from *juvenior*, comp. of *juvenis*, young. JUVENILE, YOUNG.] Younger; not as old as another: applied to distinguish the younger of two persons bearing the same name; opposed to *senior*; lower or younger in standing, as in a profession.—*n.* A person younger than another; one of inferior standing in his profession to another.—**Juniority, Juniorship**, jū-ni-or'i-ti, jū'ni-ér-ship, *n.* The state of being junior.

Juniper, jū'ni-pėr, *n.* [L. *juniperus*—*juvenis*, young, and *pario*, to produce (from its being evergreen); *gin* (the liquor) is from this. JUNE, PARENT.] A coniferous shrub, the berries of which are used in the preparation of gin, varnish, &c., and in medicine as a powerful diuretic.—**Juniper-resin**, *n.* Sandarac.

Junk, jungk, *n.* [Fr. *jonc*, L. *juncus*, a bulrush, of which ropes were made in early ages. JUNKET.] Pieces of old cable or old cordage; waste material; salt beef supplied to vessels for long voyages.

Junk, jungk, *n.* [Fr. *jonque*, Sp. and Pg. *junco*, said to be from Chinese *chouen*, a vessel.] A flat-bottomed ship used in China and Japan, often of large dimensions.

Junk, jungk, *n.* [A form of *chunk, chump*, a thick piece.] A thick piece; a chunk.

Junker, yung'kėr, *n.* [G. *jung herr*, young master.] A young German nobleman, especially one who cherishes aristocratic and feudal prejudices; one of the militant or jingo party in Germany.

Junket, jung'ket, *n.* [Formerly written *juncate*, from It. *giuncata*, cream-cheese brought to market in rushes, from L. *juncus*, a rush. JUNK (rope).] Curds mixed with cream, sweetened and flavoured; a sweetmeat; delicate food; a feast; a gay entertainment of any kind.—*v.i.* To feast; to banquet; to take part in a gay entertainment.—*v.t.* To entertain; to feast.—**Junketing**, jung'ket-ing, *n.* A private feast or entertainment; a junket.

Juno, jū'nō, *n.* [L.; the root is the same as that of *Jove*.] The highest divinity of the Latin races in Italy, next to Jupiter, of whom she was the sister and wife, the equivalent of the Greek Hera.

Junta, jun'ta, *n.* [Sp. *junta*, a meeting or council, *junto*, united, from L. *junctus*, joined. JOIN.] A meeting; a council; specifically, a grand council of state in Spain.—**Junto**, jun'tō, *n.* A select council or assembly which deliberates in secret on any affair of government; a faction; a cabal.

Jupati-palm, ju-pa-tē', *n.* The South American palm, yielding the raphia fibre.

Jupiter, jū'pi-tėr, *n.* [L., equivalent to *Jovis pater*, lit. Jove-father. JOVE.] The supreme deity among the Latin races in Italy, the equivalent of the Greek Zeus; one of the superior planets, remarkable for its size and brightness.

Jupon, Juppon, ju-pon', *n.* [Fr. from Sp. *jupon*, from Ar. *jubbah*, an outer garment.] A tight-fitting military garment without sleeves, formerly worn over the armour; a petticoat.

Jurassic, jū-ras'ik, *a.* *Geol.* of or belonging to the formation of the *Jura* mountains between France and Switzerland.—*Jura limestone*, the limestone rocks of the Jura corresponding to the oolite formation.—*Jurassic system*, the system of rocks of the Mesozoic era between the Triassic and the Cretaceous.

Jurat, Jurate, jū'rat, *n.* [Fr., from L. *juratus*, sworn, from *juro*, to swear. JURY.] A person under oath; specifically, a magistrate in some corporations; an alderman, or an assistant to a bailiff.—**Juratory**, jū'ra-to-ri, *a.* Of or pertaining to, or comprising an oath.

Juridical, Juridic, jū-rid'i-kal, jū-rid'ik, *a.* [L. *juridicus*—*jus, juris*, law, and *dico*, to pronounce. JURISDICTION.] Acting in the distribution of justice; pertaining to a judge, or the administration of justice; used in courts of law or tribunals of justice.—**Juridically**, jū-rid'i-kal-li, *adv.* In a juridical manner.

Jurisconsult, jū'ris-kon-sult, *n.* [L. *juris consultus*—*jus, juris*, law, and *consultus*, from *consulo*, to consult.] One who gives his opinion in cases of law; anyone learned in jurisprudence; a jurist.

Jurisdiction, jū-ris-dik'shon, *n.* [L. *jurisdictio*—*jus, juris*, law, and *dictio*, from *dico*, to pronounce. JURY, DICTION.] The extent of the authority which a court has to decide matters tried before it; the right of exercising authority; the extent of the authority of a government, an officer, &c., to execute justice; the district or limit within which power may be exercised.—**Jurisdictional**, jū-ris-dik'shon-al, *a.* Pertaining to jurisdiction.—**Jurisdictive**, jū-ris-dik'tiv, *a.* Having jurisdiction.

Jurisprudence, jū-ris-prö'dens, *n.* [L. *jurisprudentia*—*jus, juris*, law, and *prudentia*, skill. JURY, PRUDENT.] The science of law; the knowledge of the laws, customs, and rights of men in a state or community, necessary for the due administration of justice.—*Medical jurisprudence*, the application of the principles of medical science in aid of the administration of justice; forensic medicine.—**Jurisprudent**, jū-ris-prö'dent, *a.* Understanding law.—*n.* One learned in the law; a jurist.—**Jurisprudential**, jū'ris-prö-den"shal, *a.* Pertaining to jurisprudence.

Jurist, jū'rist, *n.* [Fr. *juriste*; from L. *jus, juris*, law. JURY.] A man who professes the science of law; one versed in the law, or more particularly in the civil law.—**Juristic, Juristical**, jū-ris'tik, jū-ris'ti-kal, *a.* Relating to a jurist or to jurisprudence.

Juror, jū'rėr, *n.* [O.Fr. *jureur*, a sworn witness, from *jurer*, to swear. JURY.] One that serves on a jury; a member of a jury; a juryman.

Jury, jū'ri, *n.* [O.Fr. *jurie*, an assize, from Fr. *jurer*, L. *jurare*, to swear; same origin as *jus, juris*, right, law (whence *jurist*, &c.), *justus*, just, from root meaning to bind, seen in *jungo*, to join (see JOIN), and in E. *yoke*.] A certain number of men selected according to law and sworn to inquire into or to determine facts, and to declare the truth according to the evidence legally adduced; a body of men selected to adjudge prizes, &c., at a public exhibition.—**Jury-box**, *n.* The place in a court where the jury sit.—**Juryman**, jū'ri-man, *n.* One who is impanelled on a jury, or who serves as a juror.—**Jury-process**, *n.* The writ for the summoning of a jury.

Jury, jū'ri, *a.* [The origin of this term is quite uncertain; perhaps from Pg. *ajuda*, help.] *Naut.* a term applied to a thing employed to serve temporarily in room of something lost, as a *jury*-mast, a *jury*-rudder.

Jussieuan, jus-sū'an, *a.* Applied to the natural system of classifying plants which superseded the Linnæan, promulgated by *Jussieu*, a French botanist.

Jussive, jus'iv, *a.* [From L. *jussum*, an order, from *jubeo, jussi*, to command.] Conveying or containing a command or order.

Just, just, *a.* [Fr. *juste*, L. *justus*, what is according to *jus*, the rights of man. JURY.] Acting or disposed to act conformably to what is right; rendering or disposed to render to each one his due; equitable in the distribution of justice; upright; impartial; fair; blameless; righteous; conformed to rules or principles of justice; equitable; due; merited (*just* reward or punishment); rightful; proper; conformed to fact; exact.—*adv.* Exactly or nearly in time (*just* at that moment, *just* now); closely in place (*just* by, *just* behind him); exactly; nicely; accurately (*just* as they were); narrowly; barely; only.—**Justly**, just'li, *adv.* In a just manner.—**Justness**, just'nes, *n.* The quality of being just.—**Justice**, jus'tis, *n.* [L. *justitia*, from *justus*, just.] The quality of being just; justness; propriety; correctness; rightfulness; just treatment; vindication of right; requital of desert; merited reward or punishment; a judge holding a special office; used as an element in various titles, as Chief-*Justice* and the eight associate *justices* of the U. S. Supreme Court.—*Justices of the peace*, local judges or magistrates appointed to keep the peace, to inquire into felonies and misdemeanors, and to discharge numerous other functions.—**Justiceship**, jus'tis-ship, *n.* The office or dignity of a justice.—**Justiciable**,† justish'i-a-bl, *a.* Proper to be brought before a court of justice.—**Justiciary, Justiciar**, jus-tish'i-a-ri, jus-tish'i-ėr, *n.* [L. *justiciarius*.] An administrator of justice; in England, a lord chief-justice.—*High Court of Justiciary*, the supreme criminal tribunal of Scotland.

Justify, jus'ti-fī, *v.t.*—*justified, justifying*. [Fr. *justifier*; L. *justus*, just, and *facio*, to make.] To prove or show to be just or conformable to law, right, justice, propriety, or duty; to defend or maintain; to vindicate as right; to absolve or clear from guilt or blame; to prove by evidence; to verify; to make exact; to cause to fit, as the parts of a complex object; to adjust, as lines and words in printing; *theol.* to pardon and clear from guilt; to treat as just, though guilty and deserving punishment.—*v.i.* To form an even surface or true line with something else.—**Justifiable**, jus'ti-fī-a-bl, *a.* Capable of being justified; defensible; vindicable; warrantable; excusable.—**Justifiableness**, jus'ti-fī-a-bl-nes, *n.* The quality of being justifiable. — **Justifiably**, jus'ti-fī-a-bli, *adv.* In a manner that admits of justification; defensibly; excusably. — **Justification**, jus'ti-fi-kā"shon, *n.* The act of justifying or state of being justified; *theol.* acceptance of a sinner as righteous through the merits of Christ.—**Justificative**, jus'ti-fi-kā-tiv, *a.* Justifying; justificatory. — **Justificatory**, jus-tif'i-ka-to-ri, *a.* Vindicatory; defensory.—**Justifier**, jus'ti-fī-ėr, *n.* One who justifies.

Justle, jus'l, *v.i.* — *justled, justling.* [JOSTLE.] To clash; to jostle. [O.T.]—*v.t.* To push; to drive or force by rushing against; to jostle. — *n.* An encounter or shock.

Jut, jut, *v.i.*—*jutted, jutting.* [A different spelling of *jet.*] To shoot out or to protect beyond the main body.—*n.* That which juts; a projection.—**Juttingly**, jut'ing-li, *adv.* In a jutting manner; projectingly.—**Jutty**, jut'i, *n.* A jetty.

Jute, jūt, *n.* [Hind. *jût.*] A fibrous substance resembling hemp, obtained from an Indian plant of the linden family, and used in the manufacture of carpets, bagging, &c.; the plant itself.

Juvenile, jū've-nīl, *a.* [L. *juvenilis*, from *juvenis*, young; cog. Skr. *yuvan*, young, E. *young*. *Junior* is comparative of *juvenis*.] Young; youthful; pertaining or suited to youth. — *n.* A young person or youth. — **Juvenileness**, jū-ve-nīl'nes, *n.* Juvenility.—**Juvenility**, jū-ve-nil'i-ti, *n.* The state of being juvenile; youthfulness; youthful age.—**Juvenescent**, jū-ve-nes'ent, *a.* [L. *juvenescens*, ppr. of *juvenesco*, to grow young.] Becoming young. — **Juvenescence**, jū-ve-nes'ens, *n.* The state of being juvenescent.

Juxtapose, juks-ta-pōz', *v.t.* [L. *juxta*, near, and E. *pose.*] To place near or next; place side by side.—**Juxtaposit**, juks-ta-poz'it, *v.t.* To place contiguous or in close connection. — **Juxtaposition**, juks'ta-pō-zish"on, *n.* The act of juxtaposing, or state of being juxtaposed; proximity.

K

K, the eleventh letter and the eighth consonant of the English alphabet; in Anglo-Saxon represented by c.

Kaaba, kä'a-ba, *n.* CAABA.

Kaama, kä'ma, *n.* A South African antelope; the hartbeest.

Kab, kab, *n.* A Hebrew measure. CAB.

Kabala, kab'a-la, *n.* Cabala.

Kabyle, ka-bēl', *n.* [Ar. *k'bila*, a league.] One belonging to a race of Berbers inhabiting Algeria and Tunis.

Kadi, kad'i or kä'di, *n.* CADI.

Kaffir, Kafir, Kaffer, kaf'ėr, *n.* [Ar. *Kâfir*, an unbeliever, an infidel.] One of a race spread over a considerable region in South-eastern Africa, and living partly in British territory; the language of the Kafirs.—*a.* Of or belonging to the Kafirs. **Kaffir-bread**, *n.* A kind of sago produced by one or two cycads of South Africa. —**Kaffir-corn**, *n.* A kind of millet (sorghum) cultivated in parts of Africa. — **Kaffir-ox**, *n.* The Cape buffalo.

Kaftan, kaf'tan, *n.* [Per.] A garment worn in Turkey, Egypt, &c., consisting of a kind of long vest tied round at the waist with a girdle and having sleeves longer than the arms.

Kail, Kale, kāl, *n.* [Icel. *kál*, Dan. *kaal*. COLE.] Cabbage having curled or wrinkled leaves, but not a close head; colewort.—**Kail-yard**, *n.* A kitchen garden. [Scotch.] —**Kailyarder**, *n.* A member of the Scottish-dialect school in fiction, overdoing the tone of rural life.

Kail, kāl, *n.* [D. and G. *kegel*, Dan. *kegle*, a nine-pin, a cone.] A nine-pin.

Kaim, Kame, kām, *n.* [A form of *comb*; comp. Icel. *kambr*, a comb, a crest or ridge.] A low ridge; the crest of a hill; *geol.* a narrow, elongated, generally flat-topped ridge of gravel of the post-glacial period in a valley. [Scotch.] ESKAR.

Kainite, kā'nīt, *n.* [Gr. *kainos*, recent.] A mineral obtained at Stassfurt and elsewhere in Prussia, since recent times used as a manure, more especially on account of the potash it contains.

Kainozoic, kā-no-zō'ik, *n.* CAINOZOIC.

Kairin, kī'rin, *n.* [Gr. *kairos*, nick of time.] An alkaloid drug used with marked effect in reducing fever.

Kaiser, kī'zer, *n.* [G.] An emperor. CÆSAR.

Kaka, kä'kä, *n.* [From its cry.] A New Zealand parrot of the same genus as the kea, which latter attacks sheep and tears out portions of flesh from their backs.

Kakapo, kak'a-po, *n.* [Native name.] The owl parrot, a New Zealand parrot resembling an owl.

Kakemono, kak-e-mō'nō, *n.* A Japanese name for a painting on paper or silk, hung on a wall like a map.

Kakodyle, kak'ō-dīl, *n.* [Gr. *kakos*, bad, *odōdē*, smell, *hylē*, matter.] A compound of hydrocarbon and arsenic; a clear liquid with an insupportably offensive smell and poisonous vapour.

Kale, kāl, *n.* KAIL.

Kaleidoscope, ka-lī'dō-skōp, *n.* [Gr. *kalos*, beautiful, *eidos*, form, and *skopeō*, to view.] An optical instrument which exhibits, by reflection, a variety of beautiful colours and symmetrical forms, consisting in its simplest form of a tube containing two reflecting surfaces inclined to each other at a suitable angle, with loose pieces of coloured glass, &c., inside.—**Kaleidoscopic, Kaleidoscopical**, ka-lī'dō-skop"ik, ka-lī'dō-skop"i-kal, *a.* Relating to the kaleidoscope.

Kalendar, kal'en-dėr. CALENDAR.

Kali, kā'li, *n.* [Ar. *qali*. ALKALI.] Glasswort, a plant the ashes of which are used in making glass.—**Kaligenous**, ka-lij'e-nus, *a.* Producing alkalies: applied to certain metals which form alkalies with oxygen. —**Kalium**, kā'li-um, *n.* Another name for potassium.

Kalif, kā'lif. CALIF.

Kalmia, kal'mi-a, *n.* [From Peter *Kalm*, a botanist.] A genus of American evergreen shrubs of the heath family, with showy flowers in corymbs.

Kalmuk, Kalmuck, kal'muk, *n.* Calmuck.

Kalong, kā'long, *n.* [Native name.] A name given to several species of fox-bats.

Kamala, kam'a-la, *n.* [Of Asiatic origin.] A drug obtained from an Asiatic tree, used as a vermifuge and a dye-stuff.

Kamar-band, *n.* CUMMER-BUND.

Kamptulicon, kamp-tū'li-kon, *n.* [Gr. *kamptos*, flexible, and *oulos*, thick, close-pressed.] A kind of floor-cloth composed of ground cork, wool, &c., with melted india-rubber spread on canvas.

Kamsin, kam'sin, *n.* [Ar. *khamsin*, fifty, because it blows about fifty days.] A hot southerly wind in Egypt; the simoom.

Kamtchadale, kamt'cha-dāl, *n.* A native of Kamtchatka.

Kanacka, Kanaka, ka-nak'a, *n.* A native of the Sandwich Islands.

Kangaroo, kang'ga-rö, *n.* The native name of certain marsupials of Australia, with long and powerful hind-legs for leaping, and small and short fore-legs.—**Kangaroo-grass**, *n.* A valuable Australian fodder grass.—**Kangaroo-rat**, *n.* The bettong.

Kantianism, kant'i-ä-nizm, *n.* The philosophic system of Immanuel Kant.

Kaolin, kā'ō-lin, *n.* [Chinese *kau-ling*, high ridge, the name of a hill where it is found.] A fine variety of clay, resulting from the decomposition of the felspar of a granitic rock under the influence of the weather; porcelain or China clay.

Karma, kär'ma, *n.* [Skr., act, fate.] In the Buddhist religion, the quality belonging to actions in virtue of which they entail on the actor a certain fate or condition in a future state of existence; a term also used in theosophy.

Karob, kā'rob, *n.* A tree whose seeds were formerly used as standards of weight.

Karpholite, kär'fo-līt, *n.* [Gr. *karphos*, straw, and *lithos*, a stone.] A mineral with a fibrous structure and a yellow color.—**Karphosiderite**, kär-fō-sid'ėr-īt, *n.* [Gr. *sidēros*, iron.] A straw-colored mineral, hydrated sulphate of iron.

Karroo, Karoo, ka-rö', *n.* [Hottentot *karusa*, hard, from the hardness of their soil under drought.] The name given to the immense arid tracts of clayey table-lands of South Africa, which are covered with verdure only in the wet season.

Karyokinesis, kar'ē-ō-ki-nē"sis, *n.* [Gr. *karyon*, a nut, *kinēsis*, movement.] Indirect cell-division.

Katabolism, ka-tab'ol-ism, *n.* [Gr. *katabolē*, a casting down.] Down-breaking chemical changes in living bodies.

Katalysis. CATALYSIS.

Kathode, kath'ōd, *n.* CATHODE.

Kation, kat'i-on, *n.* CATION.

Katydid, kā'ti-did, *n.* A species of grasshopper found in the United States; it gives out a loud sound which its name is intended to imitate.

Kauri-pine, kou'ri, *n.* [Native name.] A coniferous tree of New Zealand, yielding gum-damar, damar-resin, or kauri-gum, and having a tall straight stem, rising to a height of 150 to 200 ft., yielding valuable timber.

Kava, kā'vä, *n.* A Polynesian shrub of the pepper family, and beverage made from it.

Kavass, Kawass, ka-vas', ka-was', *n.* Turk. *kawwās.*] In Turkey, an armed constable; also, a government servant or courier.

Kaw, ka, *v.i.* and *n.* Caw.

Kay, kā, *n.* Cay.

Kayak, Kayack, kā-ak', *n.* [Probably a corruption of the eastern *caique*, applied to it by early voyagers.] A light fishing-boat in Greenland, made of seal-skins stretched round a wooden frame.—**Kayaker, Kayacker**, kā'ak-ėr, *n.* One who fishes in a kayak.

Kayle, kāl, *n.* A nine-pin. KAIL.

Kea, kē'a, *n.* See KAKA.

Keblah, keb'la, *n.* [Ar. *kiblah*, from *kabala*, to lie opposite.] The direction of the temple at Mecca, being the point toward which Mohammedans turn their faces in prayer.

Keck, kek, *v.i.* To vomit.

Kecksy, kek'si, *n.* [Also *kex*; from W. *cecys*, reeds, canes.] A strong hollow stalk or stem of a plant. (*Shak.*)

Kedge, kej, *n.* [Softened form of *keg*; Icel. *kaggi*, a keg, a cask fastened as a float to an anchor, hence, the anchor itself.] A small anchor used to keep a ship steady when riding in a harbour or river, or to assist in warping her.—*v.t. kedged, kedging.* To warp (a ship) by means of a rope attached to a kedge.

Keel, kēl, *n.* [From Icel. *kjölr*, Dan. *kjöl*, Sw. *köl*, a keel of a vessel; D. *kiel*, a keel; in sense of barge, from Icel. *kjóll*, a barge = A.Sax. *ceól*, barge, O.H.G. *kiol*, a ship.] The principal timber in a ship, extending from stem to stern at the bottom, and supporting the whole frame; the corresponding part in iron vessels; *fig.* the whole ship; a projecting ridge on a surface; a low, flat-bottomed vessel used in the river Tyne for loading the colliers; a coal-barge; *bot.* the lower petal of a papilionaceous corolla, inclosing the stamens and pistil.—*v.i.* To turn up the keel; to capsize.—**Keelage**, kēl′āj, *n.* A duty for a ship entering a harbour.—**Keeled**, kēld, *a.* Having a keel or ridge; carinate.—**Keelhaul**, kēl′hal, *v.t.* To punish by dropping into the sea on one side of a ship and hauling up on the other.—**Keelson**, kēl′sun or kel′sun, *n.* [Dan. *kjölsviin*, Sw. *kölsvin*, G. *kielschwein*, lit. *keelswine*; comp. *pig* of lead.] An internal keel laid on the middle of the floor-timbers over the keel.

Keen, kēn, *a.* [A.Sax. *céne*, *cén* = Icel. *kœnn*, wise, clever; D. *koen*, G. *kühn*, keen, bold; same root as *ken*.] Acute of mind; penetrating; quick-witted; eager; vehement; full of relish or zest; sharp (a *keen* appetite); having a very fine edge (a *keen* razor); piercing; penetrating; severe (cold or wind); bitter, acrimonious (*keen* satire).—**Keenly**, kēn′li, *adv.* In a keen manner.—**Keenness**, kēn′nes, *n.* The state or quality of being keen; acuteness; eagerness.

Keen, kēn, *v.i.* [Ir. *caoinim*.] To lament in a wailing tone.

Keep, kēp, *v.t.* pret. & pp. *kept*. [A.Sax. *cépan*, to keep, observe, regard; Fris. *kijpen*, to look.] To hold; to retain in one's power or possession; not to lose or part with; to have in custody for security or preservation; to preserve; to protect; to guard; to restrain; to detain or delay; to tend or have the care of; to maintain, as an establishment, institution, &c.; to manage; to hold in any state; to continue or maintain, as a state, course, or action (to *keep* silence; to *keep* the same pace; to *keep* step); to remain confined to; not to quit (the house, one's bed); to observe in practice; not to neglect or violate; to fulfil; to observe or solemnize; to board, maintain, supply with necessaries of life; to have in the house; to entertain (to *keep* lodgers, company); to be in the habit of selling; to have a supply of for sale.—*To keep back*, to reserve; to withhold; not to disclose or communicate; to restrain; to prevent from advancing; not to deliver.—*To keep down*, to prevent from rising; to hold in subjection; to restrain.—*To keep house*, to maintain a separate residence for one's self, or for one's self and family; to remain in the house; to be confined to the house.—*To keep in*, to prevent from escape; to hold in confinement; not to tell or disclose; to restrain; to curb, as a horse.—*To keep off*, to hinder from approach or attack.—*To keep on foot*, to maintain, as a standing army.—*To keep one's self to one's self*, to shun society; to keep one's own counsel; to keep aloof from others.—*To keep out*, to hinder from entering or taking possession.—*To keep under*, to hold in subjection.—*To keep up*, to maintain; to prevent from falling or diminution; to continue; to hinder from ceasing.—*v.i.* To remain in any position or state; to continue; to abide; to stay; not to be impaired; to continue fresh or wholesome; not to become spoiled.—*To keep at it*, to continue hard at work. (*Colloq.*)—*To keep from*, to abstain from; to refrain from.—*To keep on*, to proceed; to continue to advance.—*To keep to*, to adhere strictly to; not to neglect or deviate from.—*To keep up*, to retain one's spirits; to be yet active or not to be confined to one's bed.—*n.* Guard, care, or heed; the state of being kept; the means by which one is kept; subsistence; provisions; the stronghold of an ancient castle; a donjon.—**Keeper**, kēp′ėr, *n.* One who or that which keeps; one who has the care of a prison and the custody of prisoners; one who has the charge of patients in a lunatic asylum; one who has the care, custody, or superintendence of anything; something that keeps or holds safe; a ring which keeps another on the finger.—**Keeperless**, kēp′ėr-les, *a.* Not having a keeper.—**Keepership**, kēp′ėr-ship, *n.* The office of a keeper.—**Keeping**, kēp′ing, *n.* A holding; custody; guard; maintenance; support; food; just proportion; conformity; consistency; harmony.—*To be in keeping with*, to accord or harmonize with; to be consistent with.—**Keepsake**, kēp′sāk, *n.* Anything kept or given to be kept for the sake of the giver; a token of friendship.

Keeve, kēv, *n.* [A.Sax. *cyf*, a tub, from L. *cupa*, a tub, a cask. CUP.] A large vessel to ferment liquors in; a mashing-tub.

Keg, keg, *n.* [Formerly *kag*; Icel. *kaggi*, Sw. *kagge*, a keg. KEDGE.] A small cask or barrel.

Kehul, kē-hul′, *n.* [Ar. *kuhaul*, antimony.] A mixture of antimony and frankincense, used by the Arab women to darken their eyebrows and eyelashes.

Keitloa, kīt-lō′a, *n.* [Native name.] A species of rhinoceros found in South Africa.

Kelp, kelp, *n.* [Origin unknown.] The alkaline substance yielded by sea-weeds when burned, containing soda and iodine.

Kelpie, Kelpy, kel′pi, *n.* [Perhaps connected with *yelp*, from his bellowing.] In Scotland, a malignant spirit of the waters, generally seen in the form of a horse.

Kelson, kel′son, *n.* Same as *Keelson*.

Kelt, Keltic, kelt, kel′tik. CELT, CELTIC.

Kelt, kelt, *n.* [Comp. Gael. *caillte*, lost, ruined.] The name in Scotland for a salmon in its spent state after spawning; a foul fish.

Kelter, Kilter, kel′tėr, kil′tėr, *n.* [Comp. *kilt*, to tuck up the clothes.] Regular or proper state. (*Colloq.*)

Ken, ken, *v.t.* — *kenned, kenning.* [Icel. *kenna*, D. and G. *kennen*, A.Sax. *cunnan*, to ken, to know; allied are *can*, *cunning*, *know*. KNOW.] To know; to take cognizance of; to see at a distance; to descry; to recognize. (Now only provincial and poetical.) — *n.* Cognizance; reach of sight or knowledge.

Kennel, ken′el, *n.* [Norm. Fr., from *ken*, Fr. *chien*, a dog, from L. *canis*, a dog.] A shelter for dogs; a doghouse; a place where dogs are bred; a pack of dogs.—*v.i.*—*kenneled, kenneling*, or *kennelled, kennelling.* To live in, as a dog.—*v.t.* To keep or confine in a kennel.

Kennel, ken′el, *n.* [A form of *channel*, *canal*.] The water-course of a street; a gutter.

Kenosis, ken′ō-sis, *n.* [Gr. *kenōsis*, emptying.] The renunciation for a time of the divine nature by Christ during the incarnation.

Kentish, ken′tish, *a.* Of or pertaining to the county of Kent.

Kentledge, kent′lej, *n.* Pig iron for ballast laid on the floor of a ship.

Kentucky bluegrass, ken-tuk′i *n.* [From its jointed, bluish-green stem.] A perennial, rough-stalked pasture grass of the U. S., Europe, and Asia, grown in its finest state in the limestone regions of Kentucky and Tennessee. Kentucky is called the *Bluegrass State*.

Kepi, kep′i, *n.* A military cap.

Keplerian, kep-lē′ri-an, *a.* [Johann *Kepler*, 1571-1630.] Pertaining to Kepler; propounded by Kepler.—*Keplerian* or *Kepler's laws*, the laws of the courses of the planets established by Kepler.

Kept, kept, pret. & pp. of *keep*.

Keramic, ke-ram′ik, *a.* Ceramic.

Kerargyrite, Kerate, ke-rär′ji-rīt, ker′āt, *n.* [Gr. *keras*, horn, and *argyros*, silver.] Chloride of silver; horn silver, so named from its cutting like horn.—**Keratode, Keratose**, ker′a-tōd, ker′a-tōs, *n.* [Gr. *keras*, *keratos*.] The horny substance of which the skeleton of many sponges is composed.

Keratin, ker′a-tin, *n.* [Gr. *keras*, *keratos*, horn.] The complex compound of which horny substances (*e.g.* hair and nails) are mainly composed.

Keratitis, ker-a-tī′tis, *n.* *Pathol.* inflammation of the cornea of the eye, alluding to the horny cornea.

Kerb-roof, Kerb-stone. Curb-roof; curb-stone. Under CURB.

Kerchief, kėr′chēf, *n.* [O.E. *coverchief*, O.Fr. *couvrechief*, *couvrechef*—Fr. *couvrir*, to cover, and *chef*, the head. COVER, CHIEF.] A cloth to dress or cover the head; hence, any loose cloth used in dress.—**Kerchiefed, Kerchieft**, kėr′chēft, *a.* Dressed or covered with a kerchief.

Kerf, kėrf, *n.* [A.Sax. *cyrf*, a cutting off, from *ceorfan*, *cearfan*, to cut, to carve. CARVE.] The cut or way made through wood by a saw or other cutting instrument.

Kermes, kėr′mēz, *n.* [Ar. and Per. *kermes*, *kirmis*, from Skr. *krimi*, a worm; *crimson*, *carmine*, are derivatives.] A scarlet dye-stuff consisting of the dried bodies of the females of certain insects found on various species of oak round the Mediterranean.—**Kermes-mineral**, *n.* A substance containing antimony, used in medicine.

Kern, Kerne, kėrn, *n.* [O.Gael. and Ir. *cearn*, a man.] A light-armed foot-soldier of ancient Ireland and the Highlands of Scotland: opposed to *gallowglass*.

Kern, kėrn, *n.* [Probably from L. *crena*, notch.] *Printing*, that part of a type which hangs over the body or shank.

Kernel, kėr′nel, *n.* [A.Sax. *cyrnel*, a little corn, a kernel, dim. of *corn*, a grain. CORN, GRAIN.] The edible substance contained in the shell of a nut or the stone of a fruit; anything inclosed in a shell, husk, or integument; a grain of corn; the seed of pulpy fruit; a small mass around which other matter is concreted; a nucleus; *fig.* the main or essential point, as opposed to matters of less import; the core; the gist.—*v.i.* To harden or ripen into kernels, as the seeds of plants.—**Kernelled**, kėr′neld, *a.* Having a kernel.—**Kernelly**, kėr′nel-i, *a.* Full of kernels; resembling kernels.

Kerolite, ker′o-līt, *n.* [Gr. *kēros*, wax, and *lithos*, a stone.] A mineral of a white or green colour, greasy feel, and vitreous or resinous lustre, found in Silesia.

Kerosene, ker′o-sen, *n.* [Gr. *kēros*, wax.] A liquid hydrocarbon distilled from coals, bitumen, petroleum, &c., extensively used in lamps, stoves, &c.

Kersey, kėr′zi, *n.* [Said to be from *Kersey*, in Suffolk.] A species of coarse woollen cloth, usually ribbed, made from long wool.—*a.* Consisting of kersey; hence, home-spun; homely.

Kerseymere, kėr′zi-mēr, *n.* [CASSIMERE.] A thin twilled stuff woven from the finest wools, used for men's garments; cassimere.

Keslop, kes′lop, *n.* [A.Sax. *cése-lib*, *cyse-lib*, rennet—*cése*, *cyse*, cheese, and *lib*, a drug; Goth. *lubi*, a drug.] The stomach of a calf prepared for rennet.

Kestrel, kes′trel, *n.* [Fr. *quercerelle*, *cresserelle*, kestrel; L. *querquedula*, a teal.] A common British species of falcon, 13 to 15 inches in length, regarded as a mean or base kind of hawk, and hence the word was often used as a contemptuous epithet.

Ketch, kech, *n.* [Comp. D. and G. *kits*, G. *kitz*; origin unknown.] A strongly-built vessel, usually two-masted, and from 100 to 250 tons burden, formerly much used as bomb-vessels.

Ketchup, kech′up, *n.* [From *kitjap*, a kind of East Indian pickles.] A sauce for meat and fish, made from mushrooms, unripe walnuts, tomatoes, &c.; usually, a thick, seasoned, tomato sauce.

Kettle, ket′l, *n.* [A.Sax. *cetel* = D. *ketel*,

Icel. *ketill*, Sw. *kettel*, Goth. *katils*, G. *kessel*, kettle; from L. *catillus*, dim. of *catinus*, a deep bowl, a vessel for cooking food.] A vessel of iron or other metal, of various shapes and dimensions, used for heating and boiling water or other liquor.—**Kettle-drum**, *n.* A drum consisting of a copper vessel, usually hemispherical, covered with parchment.—**Kettle-drummer**, *n.* One who beats the kettle-drum.—**Kettle-holder**, *n.* A mat or cloth to use in handling a hot kettle.—**Kettle hole**, *n. Geol.* A deep depression in glacial drift.

Keuper, koi'pėr, *n.* *Geol.* the German name for the highest member of the trias or upper new red sandstone formation.

Kevel, kev'el, *n.* [Dan. *kievle*, a peg, a rolling-pin.] *Naut.* a piece of timber serving to belay great ropes to.—**Kevel-head**, *n.* *Naut.* the end of one of the top timbers used as a kevel.

Kex, keks, *n.* Same as *Kecksy.*

Key, kē, *n.* [A.Sax. *caeg*, *caege*, Fris. *kai*, *kei*, a key; affinities doubtful.] An instrument for shutting or opening a lock; that whereby any mystery is disclosed or anything difficult explained; a guide; a solution; an explanation; an instrument by which something is screwed or turned; something that fastens, keeps tight, prevents movement, or the like; a binding or connecting piece; a movable piece in a musical instrument, struck or pressed by the fingers in playing to produce the notes; the key-note.—*v.t.* To furnish or fasten with a key; to fasten or secure firmly.—**Key-board**, *n.* The series of levers in a keyed musical instrument, as a pianoforte, organ, or in a typewriter or typesetting machine, on which the fingers press.—**Keyed**, kēd, *a.* Having a key; marked with symbols, as a map and its caption.—**Key-hole**, *n.* A hole in a door or lock for receiving a key.—**Keynote**, *n.* The main idea; *mus.*, the first note, or "do" tone, of a scale.—**Keynote address**, a speech, as at a political convention, to arouse enthusiasm and present the basic issues.—**Keystone**, kē'stōn, *n.* The stone at the apex of an arch which, when put in, keys or locks the whole.

Key, kē, *n.* A quay.

Key, kē, *n.* CAY.

Khaki, kä-kē, *n.* [Hind., from *khâk*, dust.] A light-brown thin material used for uniforms.

Khaliff, kā'lif *n.* Calif.

Khamsin, kam'sin, *n.* Kamsin.

Khan, kan, *n.* [Tartar and Turk. *khân.*] In Asia, a governor; a king; a prince; a chief.—**Khanate**, kan'āt, *n.* The dominion or jurisdiction of a khan.

Khan, kän, *n.* [Per. *khân*, a house, a tent.] An eastern inn; a caravansary.

Khedive, ke-dēv', *n.* A Turkish title formerly applied to the Pasha or governor of Egypt, implying a rank or authority superior to a prince or viceroy, but inferior to an independent sovereign.

Khitmutgar, kit-mut'gär, *n.* [Hind. *khidmat-gâr*—*khidmat*, service, duty, and *gâr*, a doer.] In India, a waiter at table; an under butler.

Kiabooca-wood, ki-a-bö'ka, *n.* Amboyna-wood.

Kibble, kib'l, *n.* [Armor. *kibel.*] *Mining*, a large bucket, generally of iron, in which the ore, &c., are brought to the surface.

Kibe, kib, *n.* [W. *cibwst*—*cib*, cup, and *gwst*, moist, fluid.] A chilblain.

Kibitzer, kib'it-ser, *n.* [Yiddish, from G. *kiebitzen*, to look on, from *kiebitz*, a bothersome spectator.] One who gives unwanted advice; especially, such a one looking on at a card game.

Kibosh, ki-bosh', kī'bosh, *n.* Nonsense.—*Put the kibosh on*, squelch; stop. (*Slang.*)

Kick, kik, *v.t.* [W *ciciaw*, to kick, *cic*, the foot.] To strike with the foot; to strike in recoiling, as a gun.—*To kick the beam*, to fly up and strike the beam, as the lighter scale of a balance outweighed by the heavier.—*To kick up a row or a dust*, to create a disturbance. (*Colloq.*)—*v.i.* To strike with the foot or feet; to be in the habit of so striking; to manifest repugnance to restraint; to be recalcitrant; to recoil, as a musket or other firearm.—*n.* A blow with the foot or feet; a striking or thrust of the foot; the recoil of a firearm.—**Kicker**, kik'ėr, *n.* One that kicks.—**Kickup**, kik'up, *n.* A disturbance; a row.

Kickshaw, kik'shą, *n.* [Originally *kickshaws*, as a singular noun, from Fr. *quelque chose*, something.] Something fantastical or uncommon; a light, unsubstantial dish.

Kid, kid, *n.* [Dan. and Sw. *kid*, Icel. *kith*, G. *kitz*, *kitze*, a kid; akin *chit*, *child.*] A young goat; leather made from the skin of a kid, or in imitation of it.—*v.t.* or *i.* *kidded*, *kidding.* To bring forth a young goat.

Kid, kid, *n.* [A form of *kit.*] A small wooden tub or vessel.

Kidderminster, kid'ėr-min-stėr, *n.* A carpeting, so named from the town where formerly it was principally manufactured.

Kiddle, kid'l, *n.* [Armor. *kidel*, a net at the mouth of a stream.] A kind of weir formed of basket-work for catching fish in a stream.

Kidnap, kid'nap, *v.t.*—*kidnapped*, *kidnapping.* [Slang E. *kid*, a child, and *nap* for *nab*, to steal.] To forcibly abduct or steal a human being; to seize and forcibly carry away.—**Kidnapper**, kid'nap-ėr, *n.* One who kidnaps.

Kidney, kid'ni, *n.* [O.E. *kidnere*=Sc. *kite*, A.Sax. *cwith*, Icel. *kvithr*, Sw. *qued*, the belly; and Sc. *neer*, Icel. *nyra*, G. *niere*, a kidney.] Either of the two oblong, flattened, bean-shaped glands which secrete the urine, situated in the belly on either side of the backbone; sometimes colloquially used for constitution, sort, kind, character, or temper (a man of that *kidney*).—**Kidney-bean**, *n.* A well-known culinary vegetable, of which there are two principal varieties in our gardens; the French or haricot bean.—**Kidney-pota-**

Kilderkin, kil'der-kin, *n.* [O.D. *kindeken*, *kinneken.*] A small barrel; an old liquid measure containing the eighth part of a hogshead or 18 gallons.

Kill, kil, *v.t.* [O.E. *kylle*, *kulle*, *culle*, to strike, Sc. *cole*, to cut short or lop; N. *kylla*, to lop; comp. Icel. *kolla*, to harm, *kollr*, the head.] To deprive of life, animal or vegetable, in any manner or by any means; to render inanimate; to put to death; to slay; to deprive of active qualities; to deaden (pain); to overpower.—**Killer**, kil'ėr, *n.* One who kills; a murderer; that which kills, as a beast of prey.—**Killing**, kil'ing, *p.* and *a.* Depriving of life; irresistible; irresistibly fascinating; dangerous; too fast to last (a *killing* pace).—**Killingly**, kil'ing-li, *adv.*

Killdeer, Killdee, kil'dēr, kil'dē, *n.* [From its clear, plaintive cry.] An American plover, a shore bird with a grayish-brown back and a white breast.

Kiln, kil, *n.* [A.Sax. *cylene*, *cyln*, perhaps from L. *culina*, a kitchen (whence *culinary*).] A fabric of brick or stone which may be heated for the purpose of hardening, burning, or drying anything placed in it; a kind of large stove in which something is dried or baked.—**Kiln-dry**, *v.t.* To dry in a kiln.

Kilocycle, kil'ō-sī-kl, *n.* A thousand cycles; *radio*, a thousand cycles per second.

Kilodyne, kil'ō-dīn, *n.* [Gr *chilioi*, a thousand, and E. *dyne.*] A thousand dynes.

Kilogram, Kilogramme, kil'ō-gram, *n.* [Fr. *kilogramme*, from Gr. *chilioi*, a thousand, and Fr. *gramme.*] A French measure of weight, being 1000 grams, or 2.2 lbs. avoirdupois.—**Kilogram-meter**, *n.* A unit of work, or the amount taken to raise one kilogram one meter (almost 7¼ foot-pounds).—**Kiloliter, Kilolitre**, kil'ō-lē-tėr, *n.* 1000 liters, or 220.09 gallons.—

Kilometer, Kilometre, kil'ō-mē-tėr, *n.* 1000 meters, equivalent to five-eighths of a mile, or 1093.633 yards. The *square kilometer* is equal to 247.11 acres.—**Kilowatt**, kil'ō-wot, *n.* An electric unit of power, equivalent to 1000 watts, or to 1.34 horsepower.

Kilt, kilt, *n.* [A Scandinavian word; comp. Icel. *kilting*, a skirt, *kjalta*, a person's lap; Dan. *kilte*, to tuck up or kilt.] A kind of short petticoat worn by men as an article of dress in lieu of trousers: regarded as peculiarly the national dress of the Highlanders of Scotland; the fillibeg.—*v.t.* To tuck up like a kilt, for greater freedom of movement.

Kimono, ki-mō'na, properly, ki-mō'nō, *n.* [Jap.] A loose, robe-like garment usually made of silk worn by both Japanese men and women; a similar garment worn indoors by occidental women; a dressing gown.

Kin, kin, *n.* [A.Sax. *cynn*, *cyn*, Icel. *kyn*, Goth. *kuni*, O.H.G. *chunni*, kin, kind, family, race; akin are *kind*, *n.* and *a.*, *king*; D. and G. *kind*, a child; L. *genus*, Gr. *genos*, race, offspring. GENUS.] Relationship; consanguinity or affinity; connection by blood; relatives collectively; kindred: used in this sense with a verb in the plural.—*a.* Of the same nature or kind; kindred; congenial.—**Kinless**, kin'les, *a.* Destitute of kin or kindred.—**Kinsfolk**, kinz'fōk, *n. pl.* Relations; kindred.—**Kinship**, kin'ship, *n.* Relationship; consanguinity.—**Kinsman**, kinz'man, *n.* A man of the same race or family; one related by blood.—**Kinswoman**, kinz'wum-an, *n.* A female relation.

Kincob, kin'kob, *n.* [Indian word.] A silken fabric made in India, enriched with gold or silver thread.

Kind, kīnd, *n.* [A.Sax. *cynd*, (*ge*)*cynd*, nature, kind, race, generation, from same root as *cyn*, offspring. KIN.] Race; genus; generic class; sort; variety; nature; style; manner; character.—*In kind*, with produce or commodities, as opposed to *in money* (to pay one *in kind*).

Kind, kīnd, *a.* [A.Sax. *cynde*, *gecynde*, natural, harmonious; closely akin to *kind*, *n.* KIN.] Disposed to do good to others, and to make them happy; having tenderness or goodness of nature; benevolent; benignant; friendly; proceeding from or dictated by tenderness or goodness of heart.—**Kind-hearted**, *a.* Having much kindness of nature; characterized by kindness of heart.—**Kind-heartedness**, *n.* Kindness of heart.—**Kindliness**, kīnd'li-nes, *n.* The quality of being kindly.—**Kindly**, kīnd'li, *adv.* In a kind manner.—*a.* Of a kind disposition or character; sympathetic; congenial; benevolent; favourable; refreshing (*kindly* showers).—**Kindness**, kīnd'nes, *n.* The state or quality of being kind; good-will; benevolence; a kind act; an act of good-will.—**Kind-spoken**, *a.* Spoken in a kind way; characterized by speaking kindly.

Kindergarten, kin'dėr-gär-tn, *n.* [G.; lit. children's garden. CHILD. GARDEN.] A kind of infants' school, intermediate between the nursery and the primary school, in which systematically arranged amusements are combined with a certain amount of instruction.

Kinderkin, kin'dėr-kin, *n.* KILDERKIN.

Kindle, kin'dl, *v.t.*—*kindled*, *kindling.* [Allied to or derived from Icel. *kynda*, to kindle, *kyndill*, a torch or candle; perhaps from L. *candela*, E. *candle.*] To set on fire; to cause to burn with flame; to light; to inflame, as the passions; to rouse; to provoke; to excite to action.—*v.i.* To take fire; to grow warm or animated; to be roused or exasperated.—**Kindler**, kind'lėr, *n.* One who or that which kindles.—**Kindling**, kind'ling, *n.* The act of one who kindles; materials for lighting a fire.—**Kindling-coal**, *n.* An ignited piece of coal used to light a fire.

Kindred, kind'red, *n.* [O.E. *kinrede*, kindred, from *kin*, and term. *-red*, as in hat*red* (which see): the *d* is inserted, as in gen*d*er, thun*d*er. KIN.] Relationship by birth or marriage; consanguinity; kin; in plural sense, relatives by blood or marriage, more properly the former; relations or relatives.—*a.* Related; congenial; allied.

Kine, kīn, old pl. of *cow*.

Kinematics, ki-nē-mat'iks, *n.* [Gr. *kinēma*, movement, from *kineō*, to move.] That branch of the science of mechanics which treats of motion, without reference to the forces producing it.—**Kinematic, Kinematical**, ki-nē-mat'ik, ki-nē-mat'i-kal, *a.* Of or belonging to kinematics.—*Kinematic viscosity*, the relation of absolute viscosity to density; air being fourteen times as kinematically viscous as water.—**Kinetic**, ki-net'ik, *a.* Causing motion; motory: applied to force actually exerted.—*Kinetic energy*, energy of motion, equal (in absolute measure) to $\frac{1}{2}mv^2$, where *m* represents the mass and *v* the velocity of the moving body; in gravitational measure it is $mv^2/2g$.—**Kinetics**, ki-net'iks, *n.* That branch of the science of dynamics which treats of forces causing or changing motion in bodies. DYNAMICS. — **Kinematograph**, ki-nē-mat'o-graf (popularly, sin-e-mat'o-graf), *n.* A method of casting upon a screen a series of instantaneous photographs, producing the effect of motion.

Kinesodic, ki-nē-sod'ik, *a.* [Gr. *kinēsis*, motion, *hodos*, way.] Transmitting motor impulses: said of nerves.

King, king, *n.* [A.Sax. *cyning*, from *cyn*, kin, race, and term. *-ing*, one of, descendant (as in *atheling*); D. *koning*, Icel. *konungr*, Dan. *konge*, G. *könig*, king. KIN.] The sovereign of a nation; a man invested with supreme authority over a nation, tribe, or country; a monarch; a prince; a ruler; a playing-card having the picture of a king; the chief piece in the game of chess; a crowned man in the game of draughts; *pl.* the title of two books in the Old Testament, relating particularly to the Jewish kings.—*v.t.* To rule over as king.—*v.i.* To act like a king.—*a.* Most important; main: often in combination (*king*-post).—**Kingbird**, *n.* Certain of the various birds of the flycatcher family.—**King-crab**, *n.* A kind of crustacean with a carapace of horse-shoe shape, and a long tail-spine.—**Kingcraft**, king'kraft, *n.* The art of governing; royal polity or policy.—**Kingdom**, king'dum, *n.* The power or authority of a king (*Shak.*); the territory or country subject to a king; the dominion of a king or monarch; domain or realm in a general sense; *nat. hist.* one of the most extensive divisions into which natural objects are classified (the animal, vegetable, and mineral *kingdoms*).—**Kingfisher**, king'fish-ėr, *n.* A crested and bright-colored bird with a short tail and long sharp-pointed bill. It frequents the banks of rivers and dives for fish.—**Kinghood**, king'hųd, *n.* State of being a king.—**Kingless**, king'les, *a.* Having no king.—**Kinglet**, king'let, *n.* A little king; a tiny bird, similar to the warbler, the golden-crowned or ruby-crowned kinglet.—**Kinglike**, king'līk, *a.* Like a king.—**Kingliness**, king'li-nes, *n.* State of being kingly.—**Kingly**, king'li, *a.* Belonging or pertaining to a king or to kings; royal; monarchical; becoming a king; august; splendid. ∴ Syn. under ROYAL.—*adv.* With an air of royalty; as becoming a king.—**Kingpin**, *n. Bowling*, the number-one pin; the leader; the chief person.—**King-post, King-piece**, *n.* The middle post standing at the apex of a pair of rafters, and having its lower end fastened to the middle of the tie-beam.—**King's-evil**, *n.* A disease of the scrofulous kind, formerly believed curable by the touch of a king.—**Kingship**, king'ship, *n.* Royalty; the state, office, or dignity of a king; royal government.—**King's-yellow**, *n.* A pigment formed by mixing orpiment and arsenious acid.—**King-truss**, *n.* A truss for a roof framed with a king-post.—**King-vulture**, *n.* An American species of vulture, so called because other vultures are said to stand quietly by until it has finished its repast.—**King-wood**, *n.* A Brazilian wood beautifully streaked with violet tints, and used in cabinet-work.—**King-worship**, *n.* Excessive or extravagant loyalty to the monarch.

Kink, kingk, *n.* [D., G., and Sw. *kink*, a twist or coil in a cable.] A twist in a rope or thread such as prevents it running freely; an unreasonable and obstinate notion; a crotchet.—*v.i.* To get into a kink; to twist or run into knots.

Kinkajou, king'ka-jö, *n.* A plantigrade carnivorous mammal of South America, resembling the lemurs in structure and aspect, but allied to the bear.

Kino, kī'nō, *n.* [An East Indian word.] An astringent extract resembling catechu, obtained from various tropical trees.

Kinsfolk, Kinship, Kinsman, Kinswoman. Under KIN.

Kiosk, ki-osk', *n.* A Turkish word signifying a kind of open pavilion or summer house.

Kip, kip, *n.* A tanner's name for the hide of a young beast.—**Kip-leather, Kip-skin**, *n.* Leather prepared from the skin of young cattle, intermediate between calf-skin and cowhide.

Kipper, kip'ėr, *n.* [D. *kippen*, to hatch, to exclude ova.] A salmon at or directly after the spawning season, when it is unfit to be eaten fresh; a fish, as a salmon or herring, split open, salted, and dried or smoked: so called because at the spawning season salmon were cured in this way to make them eatable.—*v.t.* To cure (salmon) by splitting open, salting, and drying.

Kirk, kirk, *n.* [The old form of *church*; A.Sax. *cyrc*. CHURCH.] A church: still in common use in Scotland.—**Kirk-session**, *n.* The lowest court of the Established Church of Scotland.

Kirsch-wasser, kērsh'väs-sėr, *n.* [G., from *kirsche*, cherry, and *wasser*, water.] An alcoholic liquor distilled from the fermented juice of the small black cherry.

Kirtle, kėr'tl, *n.* [A.Sax. *cyrtel*, Icel. *kyrtill*, Dan. *kjortel*; akin to *short*.] A kind of short gown; a petticoat.—*v.t.* To tuck up so as to give the appearance of a kirtle to.—**Kirtled**, kėr'tld, *a.* Wearing a kirtle.

Kish, kish, *n.* [Gr. *kies*, *kiss*, gravel, pyrites.] A substance resembling plumbago found in some iron-smelting furnaces.

Kismet, kis'met, *n.* [Per. *kusmut*.] A Mohammedan expression for fate or destiny.

Kiss, kis, *v.t.* [A.Sax. *cyssan*, from *coss*, a kiss; Icel. and Sw. *kyssa*, Dan. *kysse*, G. *küssen*, to kiss; the corresponding nouns being Icel. *koss*, Dan. *kys*, G. *kuss*; from same root as L. *gusto*, to taste, also as *choose*.] To touch with the lips in salutation or as a mark of affection; to caress by joining lips; to touch gently, as if with fondness.—*v.i.* To join lips in love or respect; to meet or come in contact (as curved lines, &c.).—*n.* A salute given with the lips; a kind of confection.—**Kisser**, kis'ėr, *n.* One that kisses.—**Kissing-comfit**, *n.* A perfumed sugar-plum to sweeten the breath. (*Shak.*)—**Kissing-crust**, *n.* A portion of the crust of a loaf that touches another.

Kist, kist, *n.* A place of interment of a prehistoric period; a cist.

Kit, kit, *n.* [D. *kit*, a large bottle; O.D. *kitte*, a beaker, decanter.] A large bottle; a kind of wooden tub for holding fish, butter, &c.; that which contains necessaries or tools, and hence the necessaries and tools themselves; a sailor's chest and contents; an outfit.

Kit, kit, *n.* [Probably an abbreviated form of *guitar*, *gittern*, *cittern*.] A diminutive fiddle, used generally by dancing-masters.

Kit-cat, kit'kat *a.* and *n.* [From the portraits of the members of the *Kit-cat* Club in London, to which Addison and Steele belonged, painted in this size by Sir G. Kneller; the club itself being so called from *Christopher Cat*, a pastry-cook, in whose house it met.] A term applied to a three-quarter length portrait on a canvas 36 inches in length by 28 or 29 inches in width; or to any portrait about half-length in which the hands are shown.

Kitchen, kich'en, *n.* [A.Sax. *cycene*, from L. *coquina*, kitchen, from *coquo*, to cook. COOK.] The room of a house appropriated to cookery; style of cooking or of food prepared.—**Kitchener**, kich'en-ėr, *n.* A servant in the kitchen; a cookstove.—**Kitchenette, Kitchenet**, *n.* A small room or recess compactly furnished as a kitchen.—**Kitchen cabinet**, a kind of cupboard with various conveniences practically arranged.—**Kitchen garden**, a garden in which vegetables are grown for the table.—**Kitchen-maid**, *n.* A female servant who works in the kitchen.—**Kitchen-midden**, *n.* [Dan. *kjøkken-modding*.] A refuse heap of a prehistoric people.—**Kitchen-stuff**, *n.* Fat drippings from pans.—**Kitchenware**, *n.* Utensils used in a kitchen.

Kite, kīt, *n.* [A.Sax. *cyta*, a kite.] A bird of the falcon family having a somewhat long forked tail, long wings, and comparatively weak bill and talons; a light frame of wood and paper constructed for flying in the air for amusement; an accommodation bill or other paper representing fictitious value (*commercial slang*).—**Kite-flier**, *n.* One who starts schemes of various kinds to test or gauge public opinion.

Kith, kith, *n.* [A.Sax. *cytth*, knowledge, relationship, native country, from *cúth*, known, pp. of *cunnan*, to know. CAN.] Acquaintances or friends collectively.—*Kith and kin*, friends and relatives.

Kithara, kith'a-ra, *n.* Same as *Cithara*.

Kitmutgar, kit-mut'gär, *n.* Same as *Khitmutgar*.

Kitten, kit'n, *n.* [Dim. of *cat*.] A young cat, or the young of the cat.—*v.i.* To bring forth young, as a cat.—**Kittenhood**, kit'n-hųd, *n.* The state of being a kitten.—**Kittenish**, kit'n-ish, *a.* Like a kitten or what pertains to a kitten; fond of playing.

Kittiwake, kit'i-wāk, *n.* [From its cry.] A species of gull found in great abundance in the northern parts of the world.

Kitty, kit'i, *n.* A kitten; a pool or common fund into which participants contribute for a particular purpose.

Kleptomania, klep-tō-mā'ni-a, *n.* [Gr. *kleptō*, to steal, and *mania*, madness.] A form of neurosis marked by an irresistible impulse to steal, usually for no economic reason.—**Kleptomaniac**, klep-tō-mā'ni-ak, *n.* One affected with kleptomania.

Klinometer. CLINOMETER.

Kloof, klöf, *n.* [D., a gap, a chasm.] In South Africa, a common name for a ravine or gully.

Knack, nak, *n.* [Imitative of sound, like D. *knak*, Dan. *knæk*, G. *knack*, a crack, a snap; originally a snap of the fingers, then a trick or way of doing a thing as if with a snap.] Readiness; habitual facility of performance; dexterity; adroitness; a knick-knack or toy (*Shak.*).

Knacker, nak'ėr, *n.* [From Icel. *hnakkr*, a saddle: originally it meant a saddler and harness-maker.] One whose occupation is to slaughter diseased or useless horses.

Knag, nag, *n.* [Comp. Dan. *knag*, a wooden peg; Prov.G. *knagge*, Sw. *knagg*, a knot in wood; Ir. *cnag*, a peg, a knob.] A knot in wood; a protuberant knot; a wart; the shoot of a deer's horns.—**Knagged**, nag'ed, *a.* Knotty.—**Knagginess**, nag'i-nes, *n.* The state of being knaggy.—**Knaggy**, nag'i, *a.* Knotty; full of knots.

Knap, nap, *v.t.*—*knapped*, *knapping*. [Same as D. *knappen*, to crack, to munch, to lay hold of; G. *knappen*, to crack, to snap.] To bite; to bite off; to break short; to snap; to make a short sharp sound.—*n.* A short sharp noise; a snap.

Knapsack, nap'sak, *n.* [L.G. *knappsack*, D. *knapzak*, G. and D. *knappen*, to snap, to eat, and *sack*—lit. a provision-sack.] A bag of leather or strong cloth for carrying a soldier's necessaries, strapped to the back between the shoulders; any similar bag, such as those used by tourists and others for carrying light personal luggage.

Knar, Knarl, när, närl, *n.* [GNARL.] A knot in wood.—**Knarled, Knarred,** närld, närd, *a.* Gnarled; knotty.—**Knarry**, när'i, *a.* Knotty; stubby.

Knave, nāv, *n.* [A.Sax. *cnapa* or *cnafa*, a boy, a youth, a son; D. *knaap*, G. *knabe*, a boy or young man, Icel. *knapi*, a servant boy; root doubtful; comp. *knight*.] A boy‡; a male servant‡; a false deceitful fellow; a dishonest man or boy; a rascal; in a pack of playing cards, a card with a soldier or servant painted on it: a jack.—**Knavery**, nā'vėr-i, *n.* The conduct of a knave; dishonesty; deception in traffic; trickery; petty villainy; fraud.—**Knavish**, nā'vish, *a.* Acting like or belonging to a knave; dishonest; fraudulent; mischievous‡.—**Knavishly**, nā'vish-li, *adv.* In a knavish manner.—**Knavishness**, nā'vish-nes, *n.* The quality or habit of being knavish.

Knead, nēd, *v.t.* [A.Sax. *cnedan*, *cnædan*; D. *kneedan*, G. *kneten*, Icel. *knotha*, to knead; akin Slav. *gneta*, *gnesti*, to press, to knead.] To work and press into a mass; particularly, to work into a well-mixed mass, as the materials of bread, cake, or paste; to beat or pommel.—**Kneader**, nē'dėr, *n.* One who kneads.

Knee, nē, *n.* [A.Sax. *cneó*, *cneów* = Icel. *kné*, Dan. *knæ*, D. and G. *knie*, Goth. *kniu*; cognate with L. *genu*, Gr. *gonu*, Skr. *jânu*, knee.] The joint connecting the two principal parts of the leg; the articulation of the thigh and bones of the lower leg; something resembling or suggestive of this; a piece of bent timber or iron used to connect the beams of a ship with her sides or timbers.—**Knee action**, *n.* In an automobile, independent front wheel suspension.—**Knee breeches**, *n. pl.* Breeches that do not reach farther down than the knee.—**Kneecap**, *n.* The movable bone covering the knee joint in front; the knee-pan; the patella; a leather cap or covering for the knee of a horse.—**Kneed**, nēd, *a.* Having knees: chiefly in composition (in-*kneed*, out-*kneed*); *bot.* geniculated.—**Knee-deep**, *a.* as deep as would come to the knee.—*adv.* so as to be up to the knees in something.—**Knee joint**, *n.* The joint which connects the thigh and leg bones.—**Knee-jointed**, *a.* Having joints or knots like knees; *bot.* geniculate.—**Knee-pan**, *n.* The bone covering the knee joint; the kneecap.—**Knee-piece, Knee-rafter**, *n.* A bent rafter, the lower end or foot being crooked downwards.—**Knee-stop**, *n.* A stop or lever in an organ or harmonium acted on by the knee.—**Knee-swell**, *n.* A contrivance in a harmonium for producing a diminuendo and crescendo effect, worked by the knee.

Kneel, nēl, *v.i.*—pret. & pp. *kneeled*, *knelt*. [O.E. *kneole*, *kneoli*, from *knee*; corresponding to D. *knielen*, Dan. *knæle*, to kneel. Comp. *handle*, from *hand*.] To bend the knee; to fall on the knees.—**Kneeler**, nēl'ėr, *n.* One who kneels or worships by kneeling.

Knell, nel, *n.* [A.Sax. *cnyll*, a sound of a bell; *cnyallan*, to sound a bell; comp. G. *knellen*, *knallen*, to make a loud noise; G. and D. *knal*, Sw. *knall*, a loud sound; Icel. *knylla*, to beat, *gnella*, to scream; imitative of sound; *knoll* is akin.] The sound of a bell rung at a funeral; a passing bell; a death signal in general.—*v.i.* To sound as a funeral knell; to sound as an omen or warning of coming evil.—*v.t.* To summon by, or as by, a knell.

Knelt, nelt, pret. & pp. of *kneel*.

Knew, nū, pret. of *know*.

Knickerbockers, nik'ėr-bok-ėrz, *n. pl.* [Properly Dutch breeches, after Washington Irving's character Diedrich *Knickerbocker*, as representative of a Dutchman.] A kind of loose breeches reaching just below the knee, where they are gathered in so as to clasp the leg.—**Knickers**, *n. pl.* A short form for *Knickerbockers*.

Knick-knack, nik'nak, *n.* [A reduplication of *knack*; comp. *click-clack*, *tip-top*, *ding-dong*, &c.] A trifle or toy; any small article more for ornament than use.

Knife, nīf, *n.* pl. **Knives**, nivz. [A.Sax. *cnif* = D. *knijf*, Icel. *knifr*, Dan. *kniv*, Sw. *knif*; akin to *nip*. NIP.] A cutting instrument consisting of a sharp-edged blade of small or moderate size attached to a handle.—*War to the knife*, a war carried on to the utmost extremity; mortal combat.—**Knife-blade**, *n.* The cutting part of a knife.—**Knife-board**, *n.* A board on which knives are cleaned and polished; the narrow seat on the top of an omnibus. (*Colloq.*).—**Knife-edge**, *n.* A piece of steel with a fine edge, serving to support with the least friction an oscillating body, as the beam of a pair of scales.—**Knife-grinder**, *n.* One whose business it is to grind or sharpen knives.—**Knife-rest**, *n.* An article used to rest the blades of carving-knives at table.

Knight, nīt, *n.* [A.Sax. *cniht*, a boy, a servant, a military follower; D. and G. *knecht*, a male servant, Dan. *knegt*, a fellow, the knave at cards: perhaps from root of *kin* or of *knave*.] In feudal times, a man admitted to a certain military rank, with special ceremonies; in the British Empire, one holding a dignity conferred by the sovereign and entitling the possessor to have the title of *Sir* prefixed to his Christian name, but not hereditary like the dignity of baronet; a member of an order of chivalry; a champion; one of the pieces in the game of chess, usually the figure of a horse's head.—*Knight of the shire*, a county member of the British Parliament.—*v.t.* To dub or create a knight; to confer the honor of knighthood upon, the accolade or blow of a sword being commonly a part of the ceremony.—**Knightage**, nīt'āj, *n.* In England, aggregate of those persons who have been created knights.—**Knight-errant**, *n.* A knight who traveled in search of adventures and to exhibit his prowess.—**Knight-errantry**, *n.* The role, character, or practice of a knight-errant.—**Knighthood**, nīt'hụd, *n.* The character or dignity of a knight; the rank or honor accompanying the title of knight; knights collectively.—*Order of Knighthood*, in England, an organized and duly constituted body of knights, as those of the Garter or the Bath.—**Knightlike**, nīt'lik, *a.* Resembling a knight.—**Knightliness**, nīt'li-nes, *n.* The character or quality of being knightly.—**Knightly**, nīt'li, *a.* Pertaining to a knight; becoming a knight; chivalrous.—*adv.* In a manner becoming a knight.—**Knights of Columbus**, a Roman Catholic society.—**Knight Templar**, member of a branch of Freemasonry.

Knit, nit, *v.t.*—*knit* or *knitted*, *knitting*. [A.Sax. *cnyattan*, to knit, to tie, from *cnotta*, a knot; Icel. *knyta*, from *knútr*, a knot; Dan. *knytte*, to knit, to knot. KNOT.] To tie together; to tie with a knot; to fasten by tying; to weave or form by looping or knotting a continuous thread by means of wires or needles; to cause to grow together; to join closely; to contract into folds or wrinkles (to *knit* the brows).—*v.i.* To make a fabric by interlooping yarn or thread by means of needles, &c.; to unite closely; to grow together.—**Knitster**, nit'stėr, *n.* A female who knits.—**Knittable**, nit'a-bl, *a.* Capable of being knitted.—**Knitter**, nit'ėr, *n.* One that knits; a knitting-machine.—**Knitting-needle**, *n.* A needle used for knitting, usually a straight piece of wire with rounded ends.

Knives, nīvz, *n.* pl. of *knife*.

Knob, nob, *n.* [Older form *knop*; comp. A.Sax. *cnæp*, a top, a knob, D. *knop*, *knoop*, G. *knopf*, Icel. *knappr*, Dan. *knop*, *knap*, a knob, button, bud, &c.; also W., Ir., and Gael. *cnap*, a knob.] A hard protuberance; a hard swelling or rising; a round ball at the end of anything; the more or less ball-shaped handle for a door, drawer, or the like; a boss; a knot; a bunch of foliage carved or cast for ornament.—*v.i.*—*knobbed*, *knobbing*. To grow into knobs; to bunch.—**Knobbed**, nobd, *a.* Containing knobs; full of knobs.—**Knobbiness**, nob'i-nes, *n.* The quality of having knobs.—**Knobby**, nob'i, *a.* Full of knobs or hard protuberances.—**Knobstick**, nob'stik, *n.* A stick or club having a knob at the end; a knobkerrie, a hurling weapon used by Kaffirs.

Knock, nok, *v.t.* [A.Sax. *cnocian*, *cnucian*, to knock; to beat; Icel. *knoka*, Sw. *knacka*, to knock; also seen in Gael. and Ir *cnag*, a knock; W. *cnociaw*, to knock; akin *knack*, *knag*, *knuckle*, &c.] To strike or beat with something thick, hard, or heavy; to drive or be driven so as to come in collision with something; to strike against; to clash; to criticize, belittle, or disparage. (*Colloq.*)—*To knock about*, to wander here and there; to move about in the world. (*Colloq.*)—*To knock off*, to cease from labor; to stop work. (*Colloq.*)—*To knock under*, to yield; to submit; to acknowledge one's self conquered. (*Colloq.*)—*To knock up*, to be worn out; to fall from fatigue.—*v.t.* To dash; to drive; to cause to collide; to drive or force by a succession of blows.—*To knock down*, to strike down; to fell; to prostrate by a blow; at *auctions*, to assign to a bidder, generally by a blow with a hammer.—*To knock on the head*, to stun or kill by a blow or blows on the head; hence, to frustrate, as a project or scheme; to render abortive. (*Colloq.*)—*n.* A blow; a stroke with something thick, hard, or heavy; a stroke on a door, intended as a request for admittance; a rap.—**Knocker**, nok'ėr, *n.* One that knocks; a contrivance fastened to a door to knock for admittance.—**Knock-kneed**, *a.* Having the legs so much curved inwards that they touch or knock together in walking; hence, feeble (a *knock-kneed* argument).—**Knock-out**, *n.* A person or thing strikingly attractive (*slang*); *boxing*, a blow which fells an opponent for a minimum period of ten seconds.

Knoll, nol, *n.* [A.Sax. *cnoll*, a knoll, a summit; N. *knoll*, Dan. *knold*, a knoll; G. *knolle*, *knollen*, a lump; comp. W. *cnol*, the top, a round hillock.] The top or crown of a hill; a small or low round hill; a small elevation of earth.

Knop, nop, *n.* [KNOB.] A knob; a boss; a bunch. (O.T.)

Knot, not, *n.* [A.Sax. *cnotta*, a knot = D. *knot*, Icel. *knútr*, Sw. *knut*, G. *knoten*, a knot; cog. L. *nodus*, that is, *gnodus* (whence *node*). KNIT.] A complication of a thread, cord, or rope, or of two or more, by tying, knitting, or entangling; a fastening made by looping a cord or thread on itself; a tie; a figure with interlaced lines; a bond of association; a union (the nuptial *knot*); a cluster, collection, group; a difficulty or perplexity; something not easily solved; a hard part in timber caused by the shooting out of a branch; a protuberance; a nodule; a bunch; a knob; *naut.* a division of the logline, forming the same fraction of a mile as half a minute is of an hour, that is, the hundred and twentieth part of a nautical mile; so that the number of knots run off the reel in half a minute shows the vessel's speed per hour in miles; hence, a nautical mile or 6080 feet.—*v.t.*—*knotted*, *knotting*. To tie in a knot or knots; to form a knot on; to entangle; to unite closely.—*v.i.* To become knotted; to form knots or joints, as in plants.—**Knot-grass**, *n.* A common, low weed, with branched trailing stems and knotted joints.—**Knotless**, not'les, *a.* Free from knots; without knots.—**Knotted**, not'ed, *a.* Full of knots; having knots; *bot.* having knobs or enlargements as on a stem.—**Knottiness**, not'i-nes, *n.* The quality of being knotty.—**Knotty**, not'i, *a.* Full of knots; having many knots; difficult; intricate; involved; hard to unravel (a *knotty* question or point).

Knotweed, Knotwort, *n.* Knot-grass.

Knot, not, *n.* [Said to be named after King *Canute* (*Cnut*), who was very fond of it.] A small grallatorial bird, closely allied to the snipe.

Knout, nout, *n.* [Russ. *knute.*] An instrument of punishment used in Russia consisting of a handle 2 feet long, a leather thong 4 feet, with a metal ring at the end to which the striking part, a flat tongue of hardened hide 2 feet long is attached; the punishment inflicted with the knout.—*v.t.* To punish with the knout.

Know, nō, *v.t.*—*knew* (pret.), *known* (pp.). [A.Sax. *cnáwan*, pret. *cneów*, pp. *cnáwen*, to know; Icel. *kná*, to be able; comp. the allied words E. *can*, to be able, *ken*, to know, Icel. *kunna*, used in both senses; G. *können*, to be able (*ich kann*, I can), *kennen*, to know; from a root *gna*, *gan*, to know, seen also in *name*, *noble*, *narrate* (these words have lost *g* before the *n*, as in *ignoble*, *ignorant*), *uncouth*; L. *gnosco*, *nosco*, Gr. *gignōskō*, to know.] To perceive with certainty; to understand clearly; to be convinced or satisfied regarding the truth or reality of; to be assured of; to be aware of; to distinguish (to *know* a star from a planet); to be familiar or acquainted with (a person, a topic, &c.); to have experience of.—*v.i.* To have clear and certain perception; not to be doubtful; to be informed.—**Knowable**, nō'a-bl, *a.* Capable of being known. —**Knowableness**, nō'a-bl-nes, *n.* The quality of being knowable. — **Knower**, nō'ėr, *n.* One who knows.—**Knowing**, nō'ing, *a.* Well-informed; well-instructed; intelligent; sagacious; conscious; expressive of knowledge or cunning (a *knowing* look). — **Knowingly**, nō'ing-li, *adv.* In a knowing manner.—**Knowingness**, nō'ing-nes, *n.*—**Knowledge**, nol'ej, *n.* [O.E. *knowleche*, from *know*, and term. seen in Icel. *kunnleikr*, knowledge, and in E. *wedlock*, and which is derived from A.Sax. *lác*, Icel. *leikr*, Goth. *laiks*, sport, play, gift.] The clear and certain perception of that which exists, or of truth and fact; indubitable apprehension; cognizance; learning; erudition; information; skill in anything; familiarity gained by actual experience; acquaintance with any fact or person.—**Known**, nōn, *p.* and *a.* Perceived; understood; recognized; familiar.

Knubs, nubz, *n. pl.* Waste silk formed in winding off the threads from cocoons.

Knuckle, nuk'l, *n.* [A.Sax. *cnucel*, D. *knokkel*, *kneukel*, Dan. *knokkel*, G. *knöchel*, a knuckle, *knochen*, a bone; comp. W. *cnwc*, a knob or knot; allied are probably *knock*, *knag*, *knack.*] The joint of a finger, particularly when protuberant by the closing of the fingers; the knee-joint of a calf or pig (a *knuckle* of veal).—*v.t.*—*knuckled*, *knuckling*. To strike with the knuckles; to pommel.—*v.i.* Only used in the colloquial phrases *to knuckle down*, *to knuckle under*, to yield; to submit; to acknowledge one's self beaten; phrases of doubtful origin.—**Knuckled**, nuk'ld, *a.* Jointed. — **Knuckle-duster**, *n.* An iron instrument with knobs or points projecting, contrived to cover the knuckles, and which renders a blow struck more powerful. — **Knuckle-joint**, *n.* *Mach.* any flexible joint formed by two abutting links.

Knur, Knurl, nėr, nėrl, *n.* Same as GNARL.

Koala, kō-a'la, *n.* [Native name.] A marsupial animal of Australia, arboreal in habit.

Kobold, kō'bold, *n.* [GOBLIN.] A domestic spirit or elf in German mythology; a kind of goblin.

Kodak, kō'dak, *n.* Trade name of a photographic camera.—*v.t.* To photograph by *kodak*.

Kohinoor, kō'i-nör, *n.* [Per. *kohi nur*, mountain of light.] The great Indian diamond of the Deccan, owned first by the Mogul kings, and finally, in 1849, the property of the British Crown.

Kohl, kōl, *n.* A black pigment used by Eastern women as a cosmetic.

Kohlrabi, kōl-rä'bē, *n.* [G., from *kohl*, kale, and L. *rapa*, a turnip; kale or cabbage turnip.] A variety of cabbage distinguished by a globular swelling immediately above the ground, which is the part used.

Kola-nut, COLA-NUT.

Koodoo, kö'dö, *n.* KUDU.

Koord, **Koordish**, körd, kör'dish. KURD.

Kop, **Kopje**, kop, kop'i or kop'ye, *n.* [D.] In South Africa, a hill; a small hill.

Kopeck, **Kopek**, kō'pek, *n.* A small Russian coin, one hundredth part of a ruble, worth about half a cent.

Koran, kō'ran or ko-rän', *n.* ALKORAN.

Kos, kos, *n.* A Jewish measure of capacity equal to about 4 cubic inches.

Kosher, kosh'ėr, *a.* [Heb. *kasher*, right.] Designating food prepared in the way prescribed by Jewish ceremonial rites.

Kosmos. COSMOS.

Koumiss, kö'mis, *n.* KUMISS.

Kousso, kus'so, *n.* The dried flowers of a plant of Abyssinia, employed as an anthelmintic.

Kow-tow, **Ko-tow**, kou-tou', ko-tou', *n.* [Chinese.] Formerly the mode of saluting the Emperor of China by prostrating one's self and touching the ground with the forehead nine times.—*v.i.* To perform the kowtow.

Kraal, kral, *n.* [D.; probably from a native word.] A native village or collection of huts in South Africa.

Kraken, krä'ken, *n.* A supposed enormous sea monster, said to have been seen at different times off the coast of Norway.

Krang, **Kreng**, krang, kreng, *n.* [D. *kreng*, a carcass.] The carcass of a whale after the blubber has been removed.

Kreasote, krē'a-sōt. CREASOTE.

Kreatic, krē-at'ik, *a.* CREATIC.—**Kreatine**, krē'a-tin, *n.* CREATIN.

Kremlin, krem'lin. [Rus. *kreml.*] The religious citadel, palace, and buildings at Moscow.

Kreosote, krē'ō-sōt, *n.* CREASOTE.

Kreutzer, **Kreuzer**, kroit'sėr, *n.* [G. *kreuzer*, from *kreuz*, a cross, because formerly stamped with a cross.] An old South German copper coin, the sixtieth part of the gulden or florin; an Austrian coin equal to the hundredth part of a florin; both coins are valued at about half a cent.

Kriegspiel, krēg'spēl, *n.* [G., game of war—*krieg*, war, and *spiel*, game.] A game of German origin, played by means of pieces representing troops on a map exhibiting all the features of a country.

Kris, krēs, *n.* A Malay dagger; a creese.

Krone, krō'ne, *n.* [Dan., a crown.] A Scandinavian monetary unit equal to \$0.268 in U. S. money at par.

Kruller, krul'ėr, *n.* [O.E. *crull*, curled; D. *krullen*, to curl.] CRULLER.

Krummhorn, krum'horn, *n.* [G., crooked horn.] An old crooked wind-instrument of wood; an eight-foot reed-stop in an organ.

Kshatriya, kshat'ri-a, *n.* A member of the second or military caste in the social system of the Brahmanical Hindus.

Kudos, kū'dos, *n.* [Gr.] Glory; fame; renown.

Kudu, kö'dö, *n.* [Native name.] A striped antelope of South Africa, the male having long and twisted horns.

Kufic, *a.* CUFIC.

Kuhhorn, kö'horn, *n.* [G. *kuh*, a cow, and *horn.*] An alpen-horn (under ALP).

Kultur, kul-tur', *n.* German education: of which the chief doctrines were that the State should be supreme in Germany and Germany supreme in the world.

Kumiss, kö'mis, *n.* [Of Tartar origin.] A liquor made from mare's milk fermented and distilled; milk-spirit, used by the Tartars.

Kümmel, küm'l or kim'l, *n.* [G. *kümmel*, caraway.] A liqueur made in Germany, Russia, &c., flavoured with caraway seeds.

Kumquat, kum'kwat, *n.* [A Chinese word.] A delicious variety of orange about the size of a large gooseberry.

Kunkur, ken'kėr, *n.* [Hind., limestone.] A calcareous deposit spread over the surface of India, and apparently corresponding to the boulder drift of England.

Kupfernickel, kup'fėr-nik-l, *n.* [G.—*kupfer*, copper, and *nickel.*] An ore of nickel, an alloy of nickel and arsenic, of a copper colour.—**Kupferschiefer**, kup'fėr-shē-fėr, *n.* [G., copper-slate.] A term applied by German geologists to certain dark shales of the permian series of Thuringia.

Kurd, kurd, *n.* An inhabitant of Kurdistan.—**Kurdish**, kur'dish, *a.* Of or relating to Kurdistan or the Kurds.

Kursaal, kör'säl, *n.* [G., lit. cure-hall—*kur*, cure, and *saal*, a hall.] A public hall or room for the use of visitors in connection with many German watering-places or health resorts.

Kutch, kuch, *n.* CUTCH.

Kyabooca-wood, ki-a-bö'ka, *n.* KIABOOCA-WOOD.

Kyanite, kī'an-īt, *n.* [Gr. *kyanos*, blue.] A gem of the garnet family of a blue colour, somewhat resembling sapphire.

Kyanize, kī'an-īz, *v.t.*—*kyanized*, *kyanizing*. [From *Kyan*, the inventor.] To preserve (timber) from dry-rot by steeping in a solution of corrosive sublimate.

Kyle, kīl, *n.* [Gael. *caol*, *caoil*, a firth, a channel.] A sound; a strait: used in some Scotch place-names.

Kyloe, kī'lō, *n.* [Gael. *caol*, slender, small.] One of a breed of small-sized cattle of the Hebrides and Western Highlands.

Kymograph, kī'mō-grâf, *n.* [Gr. *kyma*, a wave, *graphō*, I write.] An instrument for graphically recording variations in blood pressure.

Kyrie-eleison, kī'ri-ē-ē-lī'son, *n.* [Gr. *kyrie*, Lord, *eleēson*, have mercy.] A form of invocation in ancient Greek liturgies and still used in the Roman Catholic service.

L

L, the twelfth letter and ninth consonant of the English alphabet.

La, la, *exclam.* [A.Sax. *lá*, lo! behold!] Look; see; behold.

La, lä. *Mus.* the sixth of the seven syllables that represent the seven sounds in the diatonic scale.

Laager, lä'gėr, *n.* [D., a camp.] In South Africa, an encampment; a temporary defensive inclosure, formed of wagons.—*v.i.* To encamp; to form a temporary defence by means of wagons.

Labarum, lab'a-rum, *n.* [L. *labarum*, *laborum*, Gr. *labaron*, *labōron*; etym. doubtful.] The standard adopted by Constantine the Great after his conversion to Christianity; a banner bearing the Greek letters X P (that is, *Chr*), conjoined so as to form a monogram of the name of Christ.

Labdanum, lab'da-num. LADANUM.

Labefaction, lab-e-fak'shon, *n.* [L. *labefactio*, from *labefacio*—*labo*, to totter, and *facio*, to make.] A weakening: decay; downfall.

Label, lā'bl, *n.* [O.Fr. *label, lambel*, a rag, a tatter, a shred; of Germanic or Celtic origin.] A slip of paper, parchment, or other material, containing a name, title, address, statement of contents, nature, or the like, affixed to anything; a narrow slip affixed to diplomas, deeds, or writings to hold the appended seal; *arch.* a projecting tablet or molding over doors, windows, &c.—*v.t.*—*labeled, labeling*, or *labelled, labelling*. To affix a label to; to classify and name.—**Labeler, Labeller**, lā'bl-ėr, *n.* One who labels.

Labellum, la-bel'lum, *n.* [L., a little lip, dim. of *labrum*, a lip.] *Bot.* one of the three pieces forming the corolla in orchidaceous plants, usually turned downwards.

Labial, lā'bi-al, *a.* [From L. *labium*, a lip. LIP.] Pertaining to the lips; uttered by the lips; owing its special character to the lips (a *labial* consonant).—*n.* A vowel or consonant formed chiefly by the lips, as *b, m, p, o*.—**Labialize**, lā'bi-al-īz, *v.t.* To give a labial sound or character to; to utter labially.—**Labially**, lā'bi-al-li, *adv.* In a labial manner; by means of the lips.—**Labiate, Labiated**, lā'bi-āt, lā'bi-ā-ted, *a.* [L.L. *labiatus*, from L. *labium*, lip.] *Bot.* applied to an irregular gamopetalous corolla, the limb or expanded portion cleft so as to present an upper and lower lip.—**Labiodental**, lā'bi-ō-den-tal, *a.* and *n.* [L. *labium*, a lip, and *dens*, a tooth.] Formed or pronounced by the co-operation of the lips and teeth; a sound thus formed (*f* and *v*).—**Labium**, lā'bi-um, *n.* [L.] One of the lip-like folds of the vulva, *Labia major*, the two outer folds, and *Labia minor*, the two inner folds; the lower lip of insects.

Laboratory, lab'o-ra-to-ri, *n.* [L.L. *laboratorium*, from L. *labor*, labor. LABOR.] A building or room designed for investigation and experiment in chemistry, physics, or other subject; a chemist's workroom; the shop of a druggist.

Labor, Labour, lā'bėr, *n.* [O.Fr. *labour*, Fr. *labeur*, L. *labor, laboris*, labor.] Exertion, physical or mental, or both, undergone in the performance of some task or work; particularly, the exertion of the body in occupations by which subsistence is obtained; the performance of work; toil; work done or to be done; laborers or producers in the aggregate (the claims or rights of *labor*); travail; the pangs and efforts of childbirth. — *v.i.* To engage in labor; to work; to toil; to exert the body or mind, or both, in the prosecution of any design; to proceed or act with difficulty; to be burdened; to suffer (to *labor* under a disease); *naut.* to pitch and roll heavily, as a ship in a turbulent sea.—*v.t.* To till; to cultivate; to prosecute with effort.—*Labor Day*, in the U. S., the first Monday in September, observed as a legal holiday in honor of the working classes.—*Labor Party*, a party claiming to represent the interests of the working classes. *Labor union*, a trade union; an organization of wage earners designed to advance the economic interests and general working conditions of its members.—**Labored**, lā'bėrd, *p.* and *a.* Produced with labor; bearing the marks of constraint and effort: opposed to *easy* or *natural* (a *labored* speech).—**Laborer**, lā'bėr-ėr, *n.* One who labors; a man who does work that requires little skill or special training, as distinguished from an artisan.—**Labor-saving**, *a.* Saving labor; adapted to supersede or diminish the labor of men.—**Laborious**, la-bō'ri-us, *a.* [L. *laboriosus*.] Requiring labor; toilsome; not easy; diligent in work or service; industrious; assiduous.—**Laboriously**, la-bō'ri-us-li, *adv.* In a laborious manner.—**Laboriousness**, la-bō'ri-us-nes, *n.*

Laborite, lā'bėr-īte, *n.* One who upholds the theories and practices of labor organizations.

Labradorite, lab'ra-dor-īt, *n.* A mineral, a kind of felspar, found on the coast of Labrador, distinguished by its splendent changeability of colour: called also *Labrador felspar*.

Labret, lab'ret, *n.* [L. *labrum*, lip.] A lip-ornament worn by certain savage peoples, consisting of a piece of bone, wood, or the like, inserted in an artificial opening.

Labrum, lā'brum, *n.* [L.] An upper or outer lip. LABIUM.—**Labrose**, lā'brōs, *a.* Having thick lips.

Laburnum, la-bėr'num, *n.* [L.] A leguminose tree, well known for the beauty of its pendulous racemes of yellow pea-shaped flowers, and having wood which is much valued for turnery work.

Labyrinth, lab'i-rinth, *n.* [L. *labyrinthus*; Gr. *labyrinthos*.] A structure having numerous intricate winding passages; a place full of inextricable windings; an ornamental maze or wilderness in gardens; an intricate arrangement of bands or lines used for ornamentation; any intricate matter or business; *anat.* that part of the internal ear which lies behind the tympanum; *metal.* a series of troughs attached to a stamping mill, through which a current of water passes so as to carry off and deposit in certain places the ground ore.—**Labyrinthian, Labyrinthal**, lab-i-rinth'i-an, lab'i-rinth-al, *a.* Labyrinthine. — Also **Labyrinthic**, lab-i-rinth'ik, **Labyrinthical**, lab-i-rinth'i-kal. — **Labyrinthine**, lab-i-rinth'īn, *a.* Pertaining to or like a labyrinth; full of windings; intricate; mazy.—**Labyrinthodon**, lab-i-rinth'ō-don, *n.* [Gr. *labyrinthos*, and *odous, odontos*, a tooth.] A fossil amphibian allied to the crocodile and to the frog, 10 or 12 feet long.

Lac, lak, *n.* [Per. *lak*, Skr. *lākshā* and *rākshā*, the lac insect, from *ranj*, to dye; hence *lacquer, lake* (colour).] A resinous substance produced mainly upon the banyan-tree, by the puncture of a small insect, and used in preparing lacquers, varnishes, &c.—*Stick lac* is the substance in its natural state, incrusting small twigs; when broken off and washed with water it is called *seed lac*; when melted and reduced to a thin crust it is called *shell-lac, shellac*.—*Lac dye* and *lac lake*, scarlet colouring matters obtained from stick lac.—**Laccic**, lak'sik, *a.* Pertaining to lac or produced from it.

Lac, Lakh, lak, *n.* [Hind. *lakh*, Skr. *laksha*.] In the East Indies a word used to denote 100,000 (a *lac* of rupees).

Lace, lās, *n.* [O.Fr. *las*, from L. *laqueus*, a noose, a snare; akin *lasso, latchet*.] A string or cord used for fastening boots or some other part of the dress, or plaited and otherwise ornamented and used for decoration; a delicate kind of net-work, used for the ornamenting of female dresses, &c.—*v.t.*—*laced, lacing*. To fasten with a lace or string through eyelet-holes; to adorn with lace, or as with a lace; to strengthen *beer, tea*, with some alcoholic flavouring.—*v.i.* To be fastened or tied by a lace; to have a lace.—**Lace-boot**, *n.* A boot which is fastened by a lace.—**Laced**, lāst, *p.* and *a.* Fastened with lace; tricked out with lace.—**Lace-frame**, *n.* A machine for making lace.—**Lace-leaf**, *n.* Lattice-leaf.—**Lace-pillow**, *n.* A pillow or cushion for making lace on.—**Lacing**, lās'ing, *n.* The act of fastening with a lace; a cord used in drawing tight or fastening.

Lacerate, las'ėr-āt, *v.t.*—*lacerated, lacerating*. [L. *lacero, laceratum*, to tear, from *lacer*, mangled, torn.] To tear; to rend; to make a ragged wound or gash in by violence or tearing; *fig.* to torture; to harrow.—**Lacerable**, las'ėr-a-bl, *a.* Capable of being lacerated or torn.—**Lacerate, Lacerated**, las'ėr-āt, las'ėr-ā-ted, *p.* and *a.* Rent; torn; *bot.* having the appearance of being torn.—**Laceration**, las-ėr-ā'shon, *n.* The act of lacerating; the breach made by rending. — **Lacerative**, las'ėr-ā-tiv, *a.* Tending to lacerate.

Lacertian, Lacertilian, la-sėr'shi-an, las-ėr-til'i-an, *a.* [L. *lacerta*, a lizard.] Belonging to the family of lizards.—**Lacertine**, la-sėr'tīn, *a.* Like a lizard.

Laches, lach'es or lash'ez, *n.* [Norm.Fr. *lachesse*, remissness, lit. looseness, from O.Fr. *lasche*, from L. *laxus*, lax, slow.] *Law*, neglect; negligence; remissness; inexcusable delay.

Lachrymæ Christi, lak'ri-mē kris'ti, *n.* [L., lit. Christ's tears.] A sweet but piquant muscatel wine of most agreeable flavour produced from the grapes of Mount Somma, near Vesuvius.

Lachrymal, lak'ri-mal, *a.* [L. *lachryma, lacryma, lacrima*, a tear; cog. with Gr. *dakry*, a tear, and E. *tear*.] Pertaining to tears; generating or secreting tears (the *lachrymal* gland); conveying tears (*lachrymal* canal).—**Lachrymary**, lak'ri-ma-ri, *a.* Containing tears.—**Lachrymation**,† lak-ri-mā'shon, *n.* The act of shedding tears. — **Lachrymatory**, lak'ri-ma-to-ri, *n.* A vessel found in sepulchres of the ancients, in which it has been supposed the tears of a deceased person's friends were collected and preserved with the ashes and urn. Also called *Lachrymal*.—**Lachrymose**, lak'ri-mōs, *a.* Generating or shedding tears; appearing as if shedding or given to shed tears; tears; tearful.—**Lachrymosely**, lak'ri-mōs-li, *adv.* In a lachrymose manner.

Lacing. Under LACE.

Laciniate, Laciniated, la-sin'i-āt, la-sin'i-ā-ted, *a.* [L. *lacinia*, a lappet, fringe, or border.] Adorned with fringes; *bot.* jagged: applied to leaves or petals which are divided by deep tapering incisions.

Lack, lak, *v.t.* [Same as D. *laken*, to blame, O.D. *laecken*, to fail, to decrease; Dan. *lak*, fault, want; Icel. *lakr*, defective; perhaps connected with *leak*.] To be destitute of; not to have or possess; to want; to need; to require.—*v.i.* To be in want; to be wanting; to be lacking.—*n.* Want; destitution; need; failure.—**Lack-all**, lak'al, *n.* A person thoroughly destitute; a needy fellow. (*Carl.*)—**Lacker**, lak'ėr, *n.* One who lacks.—**Lack-luster**, *a.* Wanting luster or brightness.

Lack, *n.* LAC.

Lack-a-day, lak-a-dā'. [Contr. for *alack, the-day*.] Exclamation of sorrow or regret; alas! — alas! the day. — **Lackadaisical, Lackadaisy**, lak-a-dā'zi-kal, lak-a-dā'zi, *a.* Affectedly pensive; listless; maudlinly sentimental. — **Lackadaisy**, lak'a-dā-zi, *exclam.* Used ludicrously for *Lack-a-day*.

Lacker, lak'ėr, *n.* Lacquer.

Lackey, lak'i, *n.* [Fr. *laquais*, from Sp and Pg. *lacayo, alacay*, probably from Ar. *lakiyy*, attached to some one.] An attending male servant; a footboy or footman; any servile follower.—*v.t.* To wait on as a lackey; to attend servilely.—*v.i.* To act as a lackey; to pay servile attendance on some person.

Lacmus, lak'mus. LITMUS.

Laconic, Laconical, la-kon'ik, la-kon'i-kal, *a.* [Fr. *laconique*, L. *laconicus*, from *Lacones*, the Spartans.] Short; brief; pithy; sententious; expressing much in few words, after the manner of the Spartans, who were Laconians.—**Laconically**, la-kon'i-kal-li, *adv.* In a laconic manner; concisely; in few words.—**Laconism, Laconicism**, lak'on-izm, la-kon'i-sizm, *n.* [L. *laconismus*.] A concise style; a brief sententious phrase or expression.

Lacquer, Lacker, lak'ėr, *n.* [Pg. *lacre*, from *laca*, lac. LAC.] A solution of shell-lac (sometimes sandarach, mastic, &c.) in alcohol, coloured by arnotto, gamboge, saffron, and other colouring matters, forming a yellow varnish for brass and other metals. —*v.t.* To varnish with lacquer. — **Lacquered, Lackered**, lak'ėrd, *p.* and *a.* Covered with lacquer; varnished.

Lacrosse, la-kros', *n.* [Fr.] A game which originated with the North American Indians, played with two opposing teams of twelve men each, the object of the game being to score by throwing a hard-rubber ball about the size of a baseball into the opponents' goal with a crosse or lacrosse stick.

Lacrymal, &c. Under LACHRYMAL.

Lactarene, Lactarine, lak'ta-rēn, lak'ta-rin, *n.* [L. *lac, lactis*, milk; cog. with Gr. *gala, galaktos*, Ir. *laith*, milk.] A preparation of the casein of milk, extensively used by calico-printers.—**Lactary**,† lak'ta-ri, *a.* [L. *lactarius*, milky.] Milky; full of white juice like milk.—*n.*† A dairy-house.—**Lactate**, lak'tāt, *n.* *Chem.* a salt of lactic acid, or acid of sour milk.—**Lactation**, lak-tā'shon, *n.* [L. *lacto*, to give suck.] The act of giving suck, or the time of suckling; the function of secreting and excreting milk.—**Lacteal**, lak'tē-al, *a.* Pertaining to or resembling milk; milky; conveying chyle (a *lacteal* vessel).—*n.* *Anat.* one of numerous minute tubes which absorb or take up the chyle or milk-like fluid from the alimentary canal and convey it to the thoracic duct.—**Lacteally**, lak'tē-al-li, *adv.* Milkily; in the manner of milk.—**Lactean**, lak'tē-an, *a.* Milky; lacteal.—**Lacteous**, lak'tē-us, *a.* [L. *lacteus.*] Milky; lacteal.—**Lactescence**, lak-tes'ens, *n.* The state of being lactescent; milkiness or milky colour; the milky liquor which flows from a plant when wounded.—**Lactescent**, lak-tes'ent, *a.* [L. *lactescens*, ppr. of *lactesco*, to become milky.] Becoming milky; having a milky appearance or consistence.—**Lactic**, lak'tik, *a.* [Fr. *lactique.*] Pertaining to milk or procured from sour milk or whey (*lactic acid*).—**Lactiferous**, lak-tif'ėr-us, *a.* [L. *lactifer.*] Producing or conveying milk or milky juice.—**Lactific**, **Lactifical**, lak-tif'ik, lak-tif'i-kal, *a.* [L. *lac*, and *facio*, to make.] Causing, producing, or yielding milk.—**Lactifuge**, lak'ti-fūj, *n.* [L. *lac*, and *fugo*, to expel.] A medicine which checks or diminishes the secretions of milk.—**Lactine**, **Lactose**, lak'tin, lak'tōs, *n.* Sugar of milk, a substance obtained by evaporating whey, filtering through animal charcoal, and crystallizing.—**Lactometer**, lak-tom'et-ėr, *n.* [L. *lac*, and Gr. *metron*, measure.] An instrument for ascertaining the different qualities of milk.

Lactucarium, lak-tū-kā'ri-um, *n.* [From L. *lactuca*, lettuce, from *lac*, *lactis*, milk.] The inspissated milky juice of lettuce, possessing slight anodyne properties, and sometimes used for opium.

Lacuna, la-kū'na, *n.* pl. **Lacunæ**, la-kū'nē. [L., a hollow.] A pit or depression on a surface; a small blank space; a gap; a hiatus; one of the spaces left among the tissues of the lower animals, serving in place of vessels for the circulation of the fluids.—**Lacune**,† la-kūn', *n.* A lacuna.—**Lacunal**, la-cū'nal, *a.* Pertaining to or having lacunæ.—**Lacunar**, la-kū'nėr, *n.* pl. **Lacunars**, **Lacunaria**, la-kū'nėrz, lak-u-nā'ri-a. [L.] *Arch.* one of the sunk compartments or panels in ceilings, &c.—*a.* Pertaining to or having lacunæ or lacunars.—**Lacunous**, **Lacunose**, la-kū'nus, la-kū'nōs, *a.* [L. *lacunosus.*] Having lacunæ; furrowed or pitted.

Lacustrine, **Lacustral**, la-kus'trin, la-kus'tral, *a.* [From L. *lacus*, a lake.] Pertaining to a lake.—*Lacustrine* or *lake dwellings*, the name given to ancient habitations built on small islands in lakes, or on platforms supported by piles near the shores of lakes.

Lad, lad, *n.* [Of doubtful origin; comp. W. *llawd*, Ir. *lath*, a lad, a youth; *lass* is the feminine corresponding.] A young man or boy; a stripling; a familiar term applied to grown men; fellow; comrade.

Ladanum, lad'a-num, *n.* [Gr. *ladanon*, from Per. *lâdan*, the shrub.] The resinous juice which exudes from several species of cistus growing in Spain and Portugal, Crete, Syria, &c., formerly used in plasters, &c.

Ladder, lad'ėr, *n.* [A.Sax. *hlædder* = O.Fris. *hladder*, D. *ladder*, O.H.G. *hleitra*, *hleitara*, Mod.G. *leiter*, a ladder; cog. L. *clathri*, a trellis or grate.] An article of wood, metal, or rope, consisting of two long side-pieces connected by cross-pieces at suitable distances, forming steps by which persons may ascend a building, &c.; *fig.* a means of rising to eminence.

Lade, lād, *v.t.*—pret. *laded*, pp. *laded laden* (the former always in second sense), ppr. *lading.* [A.Sax. *hladan*, to load, to lade water; O.Sax. and O.H.G. *hladan*, Icel. *hlatha*, Goth. *hlathan*, D. *laden*, G. (*be*)*laden*, to load. *Load* is almost the same word, and *ladle* is a derivative.] To load; to put a load or cargo on or in; to lift or throw in or out (a fluid) with some utensil; to lave.—**Laden**, lā'dn, *p.* and *a.* [Pp. of *lade* in first sense.] Loaded; charged with a burden or freight; *fig.* oppressed; burdened.—**Lading**, lā'ding, *n.* That which constitutes a load or cargo; freight; burden.—*Bill of lading.* Under BILL.

Lade, lād, *n.* [A.Sax. *lád*, a canal, way, course, from *lithan*, to go.] A water-course; a channel for water; in Scotland, a mill-race.

Ladle, lā'dl, *n.* [A.Sax. *hlædel*, from *hladan*, to draw water. LADE, *v.*] A sort of dish with a long handle, used for lifting or serving out liquids from a vessel; the receptacle of a mill-wheel which receives the water that moves it; *founding*, an iron vessel in which liquid metal is carried from the furnace to the mould.—*v.t.*—*ladled*, *ladling.* To lift or deal out with a ladle; to lade.—**Ladleful**, lā'dl-fụl, *n.* The quantity contained in a ladle.

Lady, lā'di, *n.* [A.Sax. *hlaefdige*, *hlaefdie*, lit. bread-maid, from *hlâf*, bread, loaf, and *-dige*. O.E. *dey*, servant-maid (seen in *dairy*). LORD.] A woman of rank or distinction; correlative to *lord*; in the British Empire, the proper title of any woman whose husband is above the rank of a baronet or knight, or who is the daughter of a nobleman not lower than an earl, though often the wife of a baronet or a knight is called by this title; a term applied by courtesy to any woman; one of the fair sex: specifically, a woman of good breeding, education, and refinement of mind: the correlative to *gentleman*; the wife of a gentleman or man in good position: the mistress or possessor of an estate; an apparatus in the stomach of a lobster for grinding its food.—*Our Lady*, the Virgin Mary.—**Ladies'-man**, **Lady's-man**, *n.* One who much affects the society of ladies; a beau.—**Ladify**, lā'di-fī, *v.t.* To render ladylike; to make a lady of.—**Lady-bird**, **Lady-bug**, **Lady-beetle**, *n.* A small beetle, the larva of which feeds on aphides or plant-lice.—**Lady-chapel**, *n.* A chapel dedicated to the Virgin Mary, frequently attached to large churches.—**Lady-day**, *n.* The day of the annunciation of the Virgin Mary, March 25th.—**Lady-fern**, *n.* A common species of fern, of a remarkably elegant, plumy structure.—**Lady-finger**, *n.* A kind of finger-shaped spongecake.—**Lady-help**, *n.* A lady engaged to help in a household, and to be treated as one of the family.—**Ladyhood**, lā'di-hụd, *n.* The condition or rank of a lady.—**Ladyism**, lā'di-izm, *n.* Airs or conceits adopted by a lady.—**Lady-killer**, *n.* A man whose fascinations are irresistible among the ladies; a general lover.—**Lady-killing**, *n.* Act or practice of a lady-killer; gallantry.—**Ladylike**, lā'di-līk, *a.* Like a lady in any respect.—**Lady-love**, *n.* A female sweetheart; a lady who is loved.—**Lady's-bower**, *n.* A woody climbing-plant, a species of clematis; virgin's bower.—**Ladyship**, lā'di-ship, *n.* The condition or rank of a lady, employed as a title (with *her*, *your*, &c.)—**Lady's-maid**, *n.* A female attendant upon a lady.—**Lady's-slipper**, *n.* An orchid having flowers resembling a slipper; in the U. S., the garden balsam.—**Lady's-mantle**, *n.* An herbaceous plant of temperate regions having numerous small flowers and large, many-lobed, serrated leaves.

Lafitte, la-fēt', *n.* A Bordeaux wine, a kind of claret, so called from the vineyard of Château *Lafitte.*

Lag, lag, *a.* [Of Celtic origin: W. *llag*, weak, languid; Gael. *lag*, feeble; akin L. *laxus*, loose, lax, *languidus*, languid.] Coming after or behind; slow; sluggish; tardy.—*n.* The quantity of retardation of some movement (the *lag* of the valve of a steam-engine; the *lag* of the tide).—*v.i.*—*lagged*, *lagging.* To walk or move slowly; to loiter; to stay behind.—**Lag-end**, *n.* The last or extreme end of anything.—**Laggard**, lag'ărd, *a.* [*Lag*, and suffix *-ard.*] Slow; sluggish; backward.—*n.* One who lags; a loiterer; a lazy, slack fellow.—**Lagger**, lag'ėr, *n.* One who lags or loiters.—**Laggingly**, lag'ing-li, *adv.* Loiteringly.

Lagan, lag'an, *n.* Same as *Ligan.*

Lager beer, lä'gėr-bēr, *n.* [G. *lagerbier*—*lager*, a storehouse, and *bier*, beer.] A beer, so called from its being stored for some months before use.

Lagniappe, **Lagnappe**, lan-yap', *n.* [Creole, *la*, the, Sp. *ñapa*, *llapa*, lagniappe.] In Louisiana, a small present given by a storekeeper to a customer.

Lagomorphous, lag-ō-mor'fus, *a.* [Gr. *lagōs*, a hare, *morphē*, shape.] Having the structure or appearance of a hare.

Lagoon, **Lagune**, la-gön', la-gūn', *n.* [It. and Sp. *laguna*, from L. *lacuna*, from *lacus*, a lake. LAKE.] A shallow lake or sheet of water connected with the sea or a river.

Lagophthalmia, lag-of-thal'mi-a, *n.* [Gr. *lagos*, a hare, and *ophthalmos*, the eye.] The abnormal retraction of the upper eyelid which prevents it covering the eyeball during sleep.

Lagostoma, la-gos'to-ma, *n.* [Gr. *lagōs*, a hare, and *stoma*, the mouth.] Hare-lip.

Laic, **Laical**, lā'ik, lā'i-kal, *a.* [L. *laicus*, from Gr. *laikos*, from *laos*, people. LAY, *a.*] Belonging to the laity or people, in distinction from the clergy.—*n.* A layman.—**Laicality**, lā-i-kal'i-ti, *n.* The condition or quality of being laical; the state of a layman.—**Laically**, lā'i-kal-li, *adv.* In a laic manner.

Laid, lād, pret. & pp. of *lay*: so written for *Layed.*—*Laid paper*, writing paper with a slightly ribbed surface, called *cream-laid*, *blue-laid*, &c., according to colour.

Lain, lān, pp. of *lie.*

Lair, lār, *n.* [A.Sax. *leger*, a bed, a couch, a grave, from the root of *lay*, *lie* = D. *leger*, G. *lager.* LAY.] A place to lie or rest; especially the resting-place of a wild beast, &c.; in Scotland, a portion of a burying-ground sufficient for one grave.

Laird, lārd, *n.* [A form of *lord.*] In Scotland, a land-owner or house-proprietor.—**Lairdship**, lārd'ship, *n.* An estate; landed property. [Scotch.]

Laissez-faire, **Laisser-faire**, lā-sā-fār, *n.* [Fr. *laisser*, leave, let, *faire*, to do.] A letting alone, non-interference; a term especially used in regard to the interference of a government with social, commercial or other matters.

Laity. Under LAY, *a.*

Lake, lāk, *n.* [Fr. *lac*, from L. *lacus*, a lake; cog. *loch.*] A sheet or body of water wholly surrounded by land, and having no direct communication with the sea, or having so only by means of rivers.—**Lake-basin**, *n.* The basin in which the waters of a lake rest; the whole area drained by a lake.—**Lake-dwelling**, *n.* Under LACUSTRINE.—**Lakelet**, lāk'let, *n.* A little lake.—**Laky**, lā'ki, *a.* Pertaining to a lake or lakes.

Lake, lāk, *n.* [Fr. *laque.* LAC.] A pigment consisting of an earthy substance impregnated with red colouring matter of certain animal and vegetable substances, there being thus cochineal and lac lakes, madder lake, &c.

Lakh, lak, *n.* LAC.

Lakist, lā'kist, *a.* The name of the poetical school of Coleridge, Southey, Wordsworth, the *lake poets*, from their English Cumberland Lake residence.

Lallation, lal-lā'shon, *n.* [Fr. *lallation*, from the letter *l.*] The imperfect pronunciation of the letter *r*, which is made to sound like *l.*

Lama, lä'mä, *n.* [Tibetan.] A priest or ecclesiastic belonging to that variety of Buddhism which is known as Lamaism, and prevails in Tibet and Mongolia.—**Lamaism**, lä'mä-izm, *n.* A variety of Buddhism chiefly prevailing in Tibet and

Mongolia.—**Lamaist, Lamaite**, lä′mä-ist, lä′mä-īt, *n.* One belonging to the religion of Lamaism.—**Lamaistic**, lä-mä-is′tik, *a.* Pertaining to lamaism.—**Lamasery**, lä′-mä-sėr-i, *n.* A Buddhist religious society presided over by a lama.

Lama, lä′mä, *n.* An animal, same as *Llama*.

Lamantin, Lamentin, la-man′tin, la-men′tin, *n.* [Fr.; from Sp. *manate, manatin*, from the native W. Indian term.] The American manatee or sea-cow.

Lamarckian, la-mark′i-an, *a.* [*Lamarck*, French zoologist.] The theory of organic evolution by inherited modifications of the individual through habit or other causes.

Lamb, lam, *n.* [A.Sax., O.Sax., Goth., Icel., and O.H.G. *lamb*; D. and Dan. *lam*, G. *lamm*, lamb.] The young of the sheep kind; a person as gentle or innocent as a lamb.—*The Lamb, The Lamb of God*, the Saviour Jesus Christ, who was typified by the paschal lamb.—*v.i.* To bring forth a lamb or lambs.—**Lambkin**, lam′kin, *n.* A small lamb; one fondly cherished.—**Lamblike**, lam′līk, *a.* Like a lamb; gentle; humble; meek.—**Lambling**, lam′-ling, *n.* A young or small lamb.—**Lambskin**, lam′skin, *n.* The skin of a lamb dressed with the fleece on, or made into leather.—**Lambs′-wool**, *n.* Wool obtained from lambs; spiced wine or beer with roasted apples.

Lambdacism, lam′da-sizm, *n.* [Gr. *lambdakismos*, from *lambda*, the Greek letter L.] A faulty pronunciation of *ll*, as when the tongue is pressed against the palate and produces a sound similar to *lli* in *million*; an imperfect pronunciation of the letter *r*; lallation.

Lambdoidal, lam′doi-dal, *a.* [Gr. *lambdoeidēs*—*lambda* (Λ), and *eidos*, resemblance.] In the form of the Greek letter lambda (Λ).

Lambent, lam′bent, *a.* [L. *lambens, lambentis*, ppr. of *lambo*, to lick, a nasalized form akin to *lap*.] Licking; playing about; touching lightly; gliding over (a *lambent* flame); gleaming; twinkling; flickering.

Lame, lām, *a.* [A.Sax. *lama*=D. Dan. and Sw. *lam*, G. *lahm*, lame; Icel. *lama*, a lame person; akin prov. E. *lam*, to beat.] Crippled or disabled in one or more of the limbs; crippled; disabled (a *lame* arm); imperfect, defective, not sound or unassailable (a *lame* excuse).—*v.t.*—*lamed, laming.* To make lame; to cripple or disable; to render imperfect.—**Lame-duck**, *n.* A slang term for a defaulter on the stock-exchange.—**Lamely**, lām′li, *adv.* In a lame or imperfect manner.—**Lameness**, lām′nes, *n.* The condition of being lame.

Lamella, la-mel′la, *n.* pl. **Lamellæ**, la-mel′lē. [Dim. of *lamina*.] A thin plate or scale; one of an aggregate of thin plates; one of the thin plates which compose the gills of certain molluscs; one of the gills forming the hymenium of an agaric.—**Lamellar**, la-mel′lėr, *a.* Composed of thin plates or lamellæ; disposed in thin plates or scales.—**Lamellarly**, la-mel′-lėr-li, *adv.* In thin plates or scales.—**Lamellate, Lamellated**, lam′el-lāt, lam′el-lā-ted, *a.* Formed in thin plates or lamellæ, or covered with them; furnished with lamellæ.—**Lamellibranchiate**, la-mel′li-brang″ki-āt, *a.* [L. *lamella*, a thin plate, and *branchiæ*, gills.] Having lamellar gills, especially having lamellar gills and bivalve shells as the molluscs of the class or order (Lamellibranchiata) of which mussels, cockles, and oysters are familiar examples. Also used as a noun.—**Lamellicorn**, la-mel′li-korn, *a.* [L. *lamella*, a plate, and *cornu*, a horn.] Having lamellar antennæ; having antennæ the three last joints of which are plate-like and disposed somewhat like the teeth of a comb: said of beetles, such as the cockchafers, &c. Used also as *n.*—**Lamelliferous**, la-mel-lif′ėr-us, *a.* Producing or composed of plates or layers; having a foliated structure.—**Lamelliform**, la-mel′li-form, *a.* Having a lamellar form.—**Lamellirostral**, la-mel′li-ros″tral, *a.* [L. *rostrum*, a beak.] Having a beak furnished along its margins with numerous lamellæ or dental plates as the ducks, geese, swans, &c.—**Lamellose**, la-mel′lōs, *a.* Covered with or in the form of lamellæ.

Lament, la-ment′, *v.i.* [L. *lamentor*, to wail, from *lamentum*, a wail; same root as *latrare*, to bark, an onomatopoetic word.] To mourn; to weep or wail; to express sorrow; to regret deeply; to grieve.—*v.t.* To bewail; to mourn for; to bemoan; to deplore.—*n.* Lamentation; an elegy or mournful ballad or air.—**Lamentable**, lam′en-ta-bl, *a.* [L. *lamentabilis*.] To be lamented; exciting or calling for sorrow; grievous; mournful; miserable; pitiful; wretched.—**Lamentableness**, lam′en-ta-bl-nes, *n.* The state of being lamentable.—**Lamentably**, lam′en-ta-bli, *adv.* In a lamentable manner.—**Lamentation**, lam-en-tā′-shon, *n.* [L. *lamentatio*.] The act of lamenting; a wailing; expression of sorrow; cries or words expressive of grief; *pl.* a book of Scripture containing the Lamentations of Jeremiah.—**Lamenter**, la-ment′-ėr, *n.* One who laments.—**Lamentingly**, la-ment′ing-li, *adv.* In a lamenting manner.

Lamia, lā′mi-a, *n.* [Gr.] A female monster sucking the blood of infants.

Lamina, lam′i-na, *n.* pl. **Laminæ**, lam′i-nē. [L., a thin plate or lamina; perhaps from same root as Gr. *e-launō*, to drive.] A thin plate or scale; a layer or coat lying over another: applied to the plates of minerals, bones, &c.; *bot.* the upper broad part of the petal in a polypetalous corolla; the blade of a leaf.—**Laminable**, lam′i-na-bl, *a.* Capable of being formed into thin plates.—**Laminar**, lam′i-nėr, *a.* Formed of laminæ or plates; consisting of thin plates or layers.—**Laminaria**, lam-i-nā′ri-a, *n.* The generic name of various sea-weeds having no definite leaves but a plain ribless expansion, which is either simple or cloven, one of these plants being the common tangle.—**Laminarian**, lam-i-nā′ri-an, *a.* Pertaining to Laminaria; a term applied to that belt or zone of marine life which extends from low-water mark to a depth of from 40 to 90 feet.—**Laminary**, lam′i-na-ri, *a.* Composed of laminæ or plates.—**Laminate, Laminated**, lam′i-nāt, lam′i-nā-ted, *a.* Consisting of laminæ, scales, or thin layers, one over another.—**Laminate**, lam′i-nāt, *v.i.*—*laminated, laminating.* To separate or split up into thin plates or layers.—**Lamination**, lam-i-nā′shon, *n.* State of being laminated; arrangement in laminæ or thin plates.—**Laminiferous**, lam-i-nif′ėr-us, *a.* Having a structure consisting of laminæ or layers.

Lammas, lam′as, *n.* [A.Sax. *hlāf-mæsse*, that is *loaf-mass*, bread-feast, so called because on this day offerings were formerly made of the first-fruits of harvest.] The first day of August.—**Lammas-tide**, *n.* The time of Lammas.

Lammergeier, Læmmergeyer, lam′-mėr-gī-ėr, lem′mėr-gī-ėr, *n.* [G. *lämmergeier*—*lämmer*, pl. of *lamm*, a lamb, and *geier*, a vulture.] The bearded vulture, the largest European bird of prey, inhabiting the Alps, as well as Asia and Africa.

Lamp, lamp, *n.* [Fr. *lampe*, L. and Gr. *lampas*, from Gr. *lampō*, to shine; akin *lantern*.] A vessel for containing oil or other liquid inflammable substance, to be burned by means of a wick; any contrivance adapted to contain an artificial light; something metaphorically communicating light.—**Lampblack**, lamp′blak, *n.* A fine soot formed by the condensation of the smoke of burning oil, pitch, or resinous substances in a chimney terminating in a cone of cloth.—**Lamp-glass**, *n.* The glass tube used for lamps burning particular oils; the glass shade for a lamp or glass-burner.—**Lampion**, lam′pi-on, *n.* [Fr.; dim. of *lampe*.] A small lamp suitable for illuminations.—**Lamp-light**, *n.* The light shed by a lamp.—**Lamp-lighter**, *n.* A man employed to light street or other public lamps.—**Lamp-post**, *n.* A post or pillar for supporting a street or other outdoor lamp.—**Lamp-shade**, *n.* A shade placed over the flame of a lamp to mellow or intercept it.—**Lamp-shell**, *n.* One of the molluscs of the class Brachiopoda.

Lampas, Lampass, lam′pas, *n.* [Fr. *lampas*.] A swelling in the roof of a horse's mouth immediately behind the fore-teeth.

Lampern, lam′pėrn, *n.* [Corruption of *lamprey*.] The name given to two species of fresh-water lampreys.

Lampoon, lam-pön′, *n.* [Fr. *lampon*, a drinking or scurrilous song, from *lamper*, to drink, to guzzle; akin *lap*, to lick.] A personal satire in writing; a satiric or abusive attack in prose or verse.—*v.t.* To write a lampoon against; to assail in a lampoon.—**Lampooner**, lam-pön′ėr, *n.* The writer of a lampoon.—**Lampoonry**, lam-pön′ri, *n.* The act of lampooning; the matter in a lampoon.

Lamprey, lam′pri, *n.* [Fr. *lamproie*, It. *lampreda*, from L.L. *lampetra*—L. *lambo*, to lick, and *petra*, a stone, from their habit of attaching themselves to stones by their mouths.] The name of several marsipobranchiate, eel-like, scaleless fishes, with suctorial mouths, inhabiting both fresh and salt water.

Lanary, lā′na-ri, *n.* [L. *lanaria*, a wool-store, from *lana*, wool.] A store-place for wool.—**Lanate, Lanated**, lā′nāt, lā′nā-ted, *a.* [L. *lanatus*.] Woolly; covered with a growth or substance resembling wool.

Lance, lans, *n.* [Fr. *lance*, from L. *lancea*, a lance, supposed to be of same root as *lacero*, to lacerate.] An offensive weapon consisting of a long wooden shaft with a sharp-pointed head of steel or other metal, used in war by both ancient and modern nations; a spear.—*v.t.*—*lanced, lancing.* To pierce with a lance or other pointed instrument; to open with a lancet or other sharp instrument.—**Lance-corporal**, *n.* A private soldier performing the duties of a corporal with a temporary rank as such.—**Lance-head**, *n.* The head or sharp end of a lance.—**Lance-jack**, lans-jak, *n.* A lance-corporal.—**Lancelet**, lans′let, *n.* A small worm-like transparent fish of very anomalous structure, the lowest of the class fishes.—**Lanceolar**, lan′sē-o-lėr, *a.* [L. *lanceola*, dim. of *lancea*.] *Bot.* tapering toward each end.—**Lanceolate, Lanceolated**, lan′sē-o-lāt, lan′sē-o-lā-ted, *a.* [L. *lanceola*, dim. of *lancea*, a lance.] Shaped like a lance-head.—**Lancer**, lan′sėr, *n.* One who lances; one who carries a lance; a cavalry soldier armed with a lance.—**Lancers**, *n.* A kind of dance.—**Lancet**, lan′set, *n.* [Fr. *lancette*, dim. of *lance*.] A small surgical instrument, sharp-pointed and generally two-edged, used in opening veins, tumours, abscesses, &c.—**Lancet-window**, *n.* A high and narrow window pointed like a lancet.—**Lancet-arch**, *n.* An arch whose head is shaped like the point of a lancet: generally used in lancet-windows.—**Lancet-fish**, *n.* A fish distinguished by its compressed shape and lancet-like spines placed on each side of the tail.—**Lance-wood**, *n.* [So named from its being suitable for making the shafts of lances.] The wood of several trees of the custard-apple family, natives of Guiana and the West Indies, which possesses great toughness and elasticity, and is much used for carriage-shafts, whip-handles, tops of fishing-rods, &c.—**Lanciform**, lan′si-form, *a.* Lance-shaped; lanceolate.

Lancinate, lan′si-nāt, *v.t.* [L. *lancino, lancinatum*; akin to *lance, lacerate*.] To tear; to lacerate.—**Lancinating**, lan′si-nā-ting, *a.* Piercing: applied to a sudden sharp shooting pain, as in cancer.—**Lancination**, lan-si-nā′shon, *n.* A sudden, sharp, shooting pain; laceration; wounding.

Land, land, *n.* [A.Sax. D. Dan. Icel. Sw. Goth. and G. *land*; connections very doubtful.] The solid or fixed part of the surface of the globe, in distinction from the sea or other waters, which constitute the fluid or movable part; a definite portion of the solid surface of the globe as set apart or belonging to an individual or a people, as a country, estate, or farm (to travel in all *lands*, his *land* adjoins mine); the people of a country or region; ground or soil (good *land*, poor *land*); in Scotland, a building including houses occupied by different families.—*To make the land*, or *to make land* (*naut.*), to discover land from the sea as the ship approaches it.—*v.t.* To set on shore; to disembark; to bring to or put in a certain place or condition (to *land* a person at the theater, in difficulties).—*v.i.* To go on shore from a ship or boat; to disembark; to arrive; to reach.—**Land-agent**, *n.* A person employed by the proprietor of an estate to collect rents, to let farms, and the like.—**Land-breeze**, *n.* A current of air setting from the land toward the sea.—**Land-crab**, *n.* A crustacean whose habits are terrestrial, as distinguished from one whose habits are aquatic.—**Landed**, lan'ded, *a.* Having an estate in land; consisting in real estate or land (*landed* property).—**Lander**, lan'dėr, *n.* One who lands.—**Landfall**, land'fąl, *n.* The first land discovered after a voyage; a landslip.—**Land-force**, *n.* A military force or body of troops serving on land.—**Land-fowl**, *n.* Birds that frequent land: as opposed to *water-fowl*.—**Land-grant school**, in the U. S., a college or university which received federal aid by the Morrill Act of 1862 for teaching vocational subjects, as agriculture, &c.—**Land-holder**, *n.* A holder, owner, or proprietor of land.—**Land-ice**, *n.* A field or floe of ice stretching along the land between two headlands.—**Landing**, land'ing, *a.* Connected with the process of bringing to land, or of unloading anything from a vessel; a bringing to earth of an airplane.—*Landing gear*, the under-structure of an aircraft, consisting of rubber-tired wheels, or of floats, and their supporting frame.—*Landing net*, a small bag-shaped net used to take the fish from the water after being hooked.—*Landing stage*, a stage or platform, frequently so constructed as to rise and fall with the tide, for the convenience of landing or shipping passengers and goods.—*n.* The act of going or setting on land; a place where persons land or where goods are set on shore; the first part of a floor at the end of a flight of steps; also, a resting-place in a series or flight of steps.—**Land-jobber**, *n.* One who speculates in buying and selling land.—**Landlady**, land'lā'di, *n.* A woman who has tenants under her; the mistress of an inn or of a lodging-house: correlative to *landlord*.—**Landless**, land'les, *a.* Destitute of land; having no property in land.—**Landlocked**, land'lokt, *pp.* Inclosed or encompassed by land. — **Landloper**, land'lō-pėr (Scottish land *louper*), *n.* [*Land*, and *loper*, as in *interloper*.] A vagabond or vagrant; one who has no settled habitation.—**Landlord**, land'lord, *n.* The owner of land or of houses who has tenants under him; the master of an inn, tavern, lodging-house; a host.—**Landlubber**, land'lub-ėr, *n.* A contemptuous term among seamen for a landsman.—**Landmark**, land'märk, *n.* A mark to designate the boundary of land; any mark or fixed object by which the limits of a portion of territory may be known and preserved, any prominent and distinguishing feature of a locality; some elevated object on land that serves as a guide to seamen; what marks a stage in any course of development; any striking historical event to which others may be referred.—**Land-measure**, *n.* The system of quantities used in computing the area of pieces of land.—**Land-office**, *n.* A government office in which the sales of public lands are recorded.—*Land-office business*, a rushing, profitable business (*colloq.*).—**Land-owner**, *n.* A proprietor of land.—**Land-poor**, *a.* Financially embarrassed by having too much money invested in land, or by too much expense for upkeep of land.—**Landscape**, land'skāp, *n.* [D. *landschap*, Dan. *landskab*, equivalent to *land-shape*.] A picture representing a tract of country with the various objects it contains; such pictures in general, or the painting of such pictures; a natural scene that might form the subject of such a picture.—**Landscape-gardener**, *n.* One who is employed in landscape gardening.—**Landscape-gardening**, *n.* The art of laying out grounds, arranging trees, shrubbery, &c., so as to produce the effect of natural landscape.—**Landscape-painter**, *n.* A painter of landscapes.—**Land-shark**, *n.* A sailor's term for a sharper.—**Landslip, Landslide**, land'slip, land'slīd, *n.* The slipping or sliding down of a considerable portion of land or earth from a higher to a lower level; the earth which so slides or slips.—**Landsman**, landz'man, *n.* One who lives on the land: opposed to *seaman*. — **Land-spring**, land'spring, *n.* A spring of water which comes only into action after heavy rains. — **Land-steward**, *n.* A person who has the care of many matters connected with a landed estate.—**Landsturm**, lant'-stųrm, *n.* [G., lit. land-storm.] A local militia of Germany, which is never called from its own district but in case of actual invasion. — **Land-surveying**, *n.* The act of determining the boundaries and superficial extent of portions of land, and of laying down an accurate map of the whole.—**Land-surveyor**, *n.* One whose employment is land-surveying. — **Land-tax**, *n.* A tax assessed upon land and houses. — **Land-tortoise, Land-turtle**, *n.* A tortoise or turtle inhabiting the land.—**Land-urchin**, *n.* A hedgehog.—**Landward**, land'wėrd, *adv.* Toward the land.—*a.* Lying toward the land, or toward the interior, or away from the sea-coast; situated in or forming part of the country, as opposed to the town; rural. — **Landwehr**, lant'vär, *n.* [G. — *land*, country, and *wehr*, defence (E. *ware*, *beware*).] That portion of the military forces of some European nations who in time of peace follow their occupations, excepting when called out for training.—**Land-wind**, *n.* A wind blowing from the land.

Landau, lan-dą', *n.* [From *Landau*, a town in Germany, where first made.] A kind of automobile carriage whose top may be opened and thrown back.

Lande, land, *n.* [Fr. *lande*, It. and Sp. *landa*, a heath.] A heath; a heathy or sandy plain incapable of bearing cereals; specifically, *pl.* extensive areas in France stretching from the mouth of the Garonne along the Bay of Biscay and inward towards Bordeaux.

Landgrave, Landgraf, land'grāv, land'-graf, *n.* [G. *landgraf*, D. *landgraaf*—*land*, land, and *graf*, *graaf*, an earl or count.] In Germany, originally, the title of district or provincial governors; later, the title of three princes of the empire, whose territories were called landgraviates.—**Landgraviate**, land-grā'vi-āt, *n.* The territory or office of a landgrave.—**Landgravine**, land'gra-vēn, *n.* The wife of a landgrave.

Lane, lān, *n.* [A.Sax. *lane*, a lane; D. *laan*, alley, avenue; Icel. *lōn*, row of houses; Fris. *lona*, *lana*, a lane.] A narrow way or passage, as between hedges or buildings; a narrow street; an alley; a narrow pass.

Langrage, Langrel, lang'grāj, lang'grel, *n.* Old bolts, nails, and pieces of iron bound together and fired from a ship's guns.

Langsyne, lang-sīn', *n.* [Sc. *lang*, long, and *syne*, since.] The time long ago. (*Scotch.*)

Language, lang'gwāj, *n.* [Fr. *langage*, from *langue*, L. *lingua*, the tongue; which is cog. with E. *tongue* (*l* corresponding to *t*, as in L. *lacrima*, E. *tear*).] Human speech; the expression of thoughts by words or articulate sounds; the aggregate of the words employed by any community for intercommunication; the speech peculiar to a nation; words appropriate to or especially employed in any branch of knowledge (the *language* of chemistry); general style or manner of expression; the expression of thought in any way articulate or inarticulate (the *language* of the eyes, of flowers, &c.). — **Languaged**, lang'gwājd, *a.* Having a language of this or that kind; skilled in language. — **Languageless**, lang'gwāj-les, *a.* Wanting speech or language. (*Shak.*)

Languid, lang'gwid, *a.* [L. *languidus*, from *langueo*, to droop or flag. LANGUISH.] Flagging; drooping; weak; heavy; dull; indisposed to exertion; slow; tardy; without animation. — **Languidly**, lang'gwid-li, *adv.* In a languid manner.—**Languidness**, lang'gwid-nes, *n.* The state or quality of being languid.

Languish, lang'gwish, *v.i.* [Fr. *languir*, ppr. *languissant*, from L. *langueo*, to languish; akin to *lax*, *lag*, *slack*.] To lose strength or animation; to be or become dull, feeble, or spiritless; to pine; to be or to grow heavy; to droop; to wither; to fade; to be no longer active and vigorous. —*n.* Act of pining; also, a soft and tender look or appearance.—**Languisher**, lang'-gwish-ėr, *n.* One who languishes.—**Languishing**, lang'gwish-ing, *p.* and *a.* Losing strength; becoming feeble; pining; having a soft and tender expression (a *languishing* eye). — **Languishingly**, lang'-gwish-ing-li, *adv.* In a languishing manner.—**Languishment**, lang'gwish-ment, *n.* The state of languishing or pining; softness of look or mien.—**Languor**, lang'-gwėr, *n.* [L. *languor*.] The state of body induced by exhaustion of strength; feebleness; faintness; lassitude of body; dulness of intellect; listlessness; an agreeable listless or dreamy state. — **Languorous**, lang'gwėr-us, *a.* Characterized by languor.

Laniard, lan'yärd, *n.* LANYARD.

Laniary, lan'i-a-ri, *n.* [L. *laniarius*, pertaining to a butcher, from *lanius*, a butcher.] Shambles‡; a place of slaughter‡; one of the canine teeth of the carnivorous animals. —*a.* Used for lacerating or tearing flesh (*laniary* teeth).—**Laniariform**, lan-i-ar'-i-form, *a.* Shaped like the laniaries or canine teeth of the Carnivora.—**Laniate**,† lā'ni-āt, *v.t.* [L. *lanio*, *laniatum*.] To tear in pieces.—**Laniation**,† lā-ni-ā'shon, *n.* A tearing in pieces.

Laniferous, la-nif'ėr-us, *a.* [L. *lanifer*—*lana*, wool, *fero*, to produce.] Bearing or producing wool.—**Lanifical**, la-nif'i-kal, *a.* [L. *lana* and *facio*.] Working in wool. —**Lanigerous**, la-nij'ėr-us, *a.* [L. *lana*, and *gero*, to bear.] Bearing or producing wool.

Lank, langk, *a.* [A.Sax. *hlanc*; connections doubtful.] Loose or lax and easily yielding to pressure‡; languid or drooping‡; not distended; not plump; of a thin or slender habit of body.—**Lankly**, langk'li, *adv.* In a lank manner; loosely; laxly.—**Lankness**, langk'nes, *n.* The state or quality of being lank.—**Lanky**, lang'ki, *a.* Lank.

Lanner, lan'ėr, *n.* [Fr. *lanier*, L. *laniarius*, *lanius*, a butcher.] A species of hawk, especially the female of the species, found in the south and east of Europe.—**Lanneret**, lan'ėr-et, *n.* The male of the lanner.

Lanolin, lan'ō-lin, *n.* [L. *lana*, wool, *oleum*, oil.] An oily or greasy substance obtained from unwashed wool, said to have valuable therapeutic properties in ointments, &c.

Lansch, lan'se, *n.* [Indian name.] The fruit of a Malayan tree which is highly esteemed.

Lansquenet, lans'ke-net, *n.* [Originally a foot soldier, from G. *landsknecht*, a foot-soldier—*land*, country, *knecht*, a servant, a *knight*.] An old game at cards.

Lantern, lan'tėrn, *n.* [Fr. *lanterne*, L. *lanterna*, from Gr. *lamptēr*, a light, a beacon, from *lampō*, to shine, whence also *lamp*.] A case inclosing a light and protecting it from wind and rain, sometimes portable and sometimes fixed; *arch.* an erection on the top of a dome, the roof of an apartment, &c., to give light, for ventilation, or for ornament; a tower which has the whole or a considerable portion of the interior open to view; a light open erection on the top of a tower; the upper part of a lighthouse where the light is shown.—*Chinese lantern.* Under CHINESE.—*Dark lantern*, one with a single opening, which may be closed so as to conceal the light.—*Magic lantern.* Under MAGIC.—**Lantern-fly**, *n.* A hemipterous insect of South America which emits a strong light in the dark.—**Lantern-jawed**, *n.* Having lantern-jaws; having a long thin visage. (*Colloq.*)—**Lantern-jaws**, *n. pl.* Long thin jaws; a lean visage. (*Colloq.*)

Lanthanum, Lanthanium, lan′tha-num, lan-thā′ni-um, *n.* [Gr. *lanthanō*, I lie hid, because its existence long remained unknown.] A rare metal obtained from cerite, of little interest or importance.

Lanthorn, lan′tėrn, *n.* An old and erroneus spelling of *Lantern*, due to the fact that lanterns used to have *horn* sides.

Lanuginous, Lanuginose, la-nū′ji-nus, la-nū′ji-nōs, *a.* [L. *lanuginosus*, from *lanugo*, down, from *lana*, wool.] Downy; covered with down or fine soft hair.

Lanyard, lan′yärd, *n.* [Also written *lanier*, *laniard*, from Fr. *lanière*, a thong, strap, originally a woollen band, from L. *lana*, wool.] *Naut.* a short piece of rope or line used for fastening something in ships; *milit.* a piece of strong twine with an iron hook at one end, used in firing cannon with a friction-tube.

Laodicean, la-od′i-sē″an, *a.* Like the Christians of Laodicea; lukewarm in religion.—**Laodiceanism**, la-od′i-sē″an-izm, *n.* Lukewarmness in religion.

Lap, lap, *n.* [A.Sax. *læppa*; D. and Dan. *lap*, Sw. *lapp*, G. *lappen*, a lap, a loose flap, *lappen*, to hang loose; akin to *label*, *lobe*, *limp* (*a.*), *lapse*; *lapel*, *lappet*, are derivatives.] The lower part of a garment that hangs loosely; the part of clothes that lies on the knees when a person sits down; hence, the upper part of the legs in this position; the part of one body which lies on and covers a part of another (as a slate in roofing); the last part or round in a race.—**Lap-board**, *n.* A board resting on the lap, employed by tailors for cutting out or ironing work upon.—**Lapdog**, lap′dog, *n.* A small dog fondled in the lap; a pet dog.—**Lapful**, lap′ful, *n.* As much as the lap can contain.—**Lap-stone**, *n.* A stone on which shoemakers beat leather on the knees.

Lap, lap, *v.t.*—*lapped*, *lapping*. [From O.E. *wlap*, to wrap, a form of *wrap* (which see).] To wrap or twist round; to infold; to fold; to double over; to lay partly above.—*v.i.* To be spread or laid; to be turned over; to lie over something in part (as slates on a roof).—**Lapper**, lap′ėr, *n.* One who laps or folds; one who folds cloth.

Lap, lap, *v.i.*—*lapped*, *lapping*. [A.Sax. *lapian*, *lappian*, Icel. *lepja*, O.D. *lappen*, *lapen*, L.G. *lappen*, to lap or lick up; allied to L. *lambo*, Gr. *laptō*—to lap or lick.] To take up liquor or food with the tongue; to feed or drink by licking up; to make a sound like that produced by taking up water by the tongue.—*v.t.* To take into the mouth with the tongue; to lick up.—*n.* A lick, as with the tongue; a sound made in this way; a sound as of water rippling against the beach.—**Lapper**, lap′ėr, *n.* One who laps or takes up with the tongue.

Lap, lap, *n.* [Short for *lapidary* wheel.] A wheel or revolving disk of soft metal, which by means of a polishing powder is used in cutting glass, gems, &c.

Laparectomy, lap′ar-ek″to-mi, *n.* [Gr. *lapara*, flanks, *ektomē*, cutting out.] The excision of intestines at the side.

Laparotomy, lap′ar-ot″o-mi, *n.* Cutting of the abdominal walls.

Lapel, Lapelle, la-pel′, *n.* [Dim. from *lap*, part of a garment.] That part of a garment which is made to lap or fold over; the part in the front of a coat or waistcoat that is folded back.—**Lapelled**, la-peld′, *a.* Furnished with lapels.

Lapidary, lap′i-da-ri, *n.* [L. *lapidarius*, from *lapis*, *lapidis*, a stone; akin Gr. *lepas*, a rock.] An artificer who cuts, polishes, and engraves gems or precious stones; a dealer in precious stones.—*a.* Of or pertaining to the art of polishing and engraving precious stones.—*Lapidary style*, pompous style of language adopted on monuments; sonorous Latinity.—**Lapidarian**, lap-idā′ri-an, *a.* Pertaining to a lapidary; inscribed on stone.—**Lapideous**,† la-pid′ē-us, *a.* [L. *lapideus.*] Of the nature of stone; stony.—**Lapidescent**, lap-i-des′ent, *a.* [L. *lapidesco*, to become stone.] Growing or turning to stone; having the quality of petrifying bodies.—*n.* A substance which has the quality of petrifying bodies.—*n.* **Lapidescence**, lap-i-des′ens, *n.* The state or quality of being lapidescent.—**Lapidific, Lapidifical**, lap-i-dif′ik, lap-i-dif′i-kal, *a.* [L. *lapis*, and *facio*, to make.] Forming or converting into stone.—**Lapidification**, la-pid′i-fi-kā″shon, *n.* The act of lapidifying or converting into stone; the state of being lapidified.—**Lapidify**, la-pid′i-fī, *v.t.*—*lapidified*, *lapidifying*. To form into stone.—*v.i.* To turn into stone; to become stone.—**Lapidist**, lap′i-dist, *n.* A lapidary.—**Lapidose**, lap′i-dōs, *a.* *Bot.* growing in stony places.

Lapilli, la-pil′lī, *n. pl.* [L. *lapillus*, a little stone, contr. of *lapidulus*, dim. of *lapis*, a stone. LAPIDARY.] Volcanic ashes which consist of small angular fragments or particles.

Lapis-lazuli, lā-pis-laz′ū-li, *n.* [L. *lapis*, a stone, and L.L. *lazulum*, this mineral; same origin as *azure.*] An aluminous mineral of a rich blue colour, used in mosaic work and other kinds of ornament, and when powdered yielding ultramarine.

Lappet, lap′et, *n.* [Dim. of *lap*, a loose part, &c.] A little lap or flap, as on a dress, especially on a head-dress; a cotton fabric with imitation of embroidery on surface.

Lapps, *n.* The natives of Lapland, in northern Scandinavia.—**Laponian**, *a.* Of or pertaining to Lapland.

Lapse, laps, *n.* [L. *lapsus*, from *labor*, *lapsus*, to slide, to fall (as in *collapse*, *elapse*, *relapse*, &c.); akin *lap* (*n*)., *lobe*, &c. LAP.] A gliding, slipping, or gradually falling; an unobserved or very gradual advance; an unnoticed passing away (of time); a slip or error; a failing in duty; a deviation from truth or rectitude; *eccles law*, the omission of a patron to present a clerk to a benefice within six months after it becomes void.—*v.i.*—*lapsed*, *lapsing*. To pass slowly, silently, or by degrees; to glide away; to fall gradually; to slip in moral conduct; to fail in duty; to commit a fault; to fall or pass from one person to another, through some omission or negligence; *law*, to become ineffectual or void.—**Lapsable**, lap′sa-bl, *a.* Capable of lapsing.—**Lapsed**, lapst, *p.* and *a.* Exhibiting or having undergone a lapse; having fallen away from connection with any church (the *lapsed* masses).

Lap-sided, *a.* LOP-SIDED.

Lapwing, lap′wing, *n.* [O.E. *lapwinke*, A.Sax. *hlēdpewince*, equivalent to *leap-wink*; from its leaping or jerking mode of flight.] A well-known and handsome bird belonging to the plover family, about the size of a pigeon, often called the *pee-wit* from its cry.

Lar, lär, *n.* pl. **Lares**, lā′rēz. [L., lit. the shining one, allied to Skr. *las*, to shine.] A household deity among the ancient Romans, regarded as the spirit of a deceased ancestor.

Larboard, lär′bōrd, *n.* [D. *laar*, empty—as not occupied by the steersman.] *Naut.* the left-hand or port side of a ship, a term now given up in favour of *port*, the latter being shorter and more distinctive in sound: opposite of *starboard*.

Larceny, lär′se-ni, *n.* [Contr. for *latrociny*, from L. *latrocinium*, from *latro*, a robber.] The unlawful taking and carrying away of any article or piece of goods with intent to deprive the right owner of the same; theft.—**Larcener, Larcenist**, lär′sen-ėr, lär′-sen-ist, *n.* One who commits larceny; a thief.—**Larcenous**, lär′sen-us, *a.* Pertaining to or having the character of larceny; guilty of or inclined to larceny.

Larch, lärch, *n.* [L. and G. *larix*, the larch.] A well-known coniferous tree remarkable for the elegance of its form and the durability and value of its wood.—**Larchen**, lär′chen, *a.* Of or pertaining to larch.

Lard, lärd, *n.* [Fr. *lard*, L. *lardum*, *laridum*, allied to Gr. *larinos*, fat, from *laros*, dainty.] The fat of swine after being melted and separated from the flesh.—*v.t.* To mix with lard or bacon; to stuff with pieces of bacon (as in cooking a fowl); to fatten; to enrich; to mix with something by way of improvement; to interlard.—*v.i.* To grow fat.—**Lardaceous**, lär-dā′shus, *a.* Of the nature of lard; consisting of lard.—**Larder**, lär′dėr, *n.* [O.Fr. *lardier.*] A room, house, box, or the like, where meat is kept before eating.—**Lard-oil**, *n.* A valuable oil made from lard, used for burning and for lubricating machinery.—**Lardon**, lär′don, *n.* [Fr.] A strip of lard; a bit of bacon.—**Lardy**, lär′di, *a.* Containing lard; full of lard.

Lares, *n. pl.* LAR.

Large, lärj, *a.* [Fr. *large*, L. *largus*, abundant, large.] Being of great size; having great dimensions; big; bulky; great; containing or consisting of a great quantity or number; abundant; plentiful; numerous; liberal, many-sided, comprehensive (a *large* mind); generous, noble, sympathetic (a *large* heart.—*At large*, without restraint or confinement; diffusely; fully; with all details; elected at large (by the whole state), as congressman-*at-large*.—**Large-hearted**, *a.* Having a large heart; generous; magnanimous; sympathetic.—**Large-heartedness**, *n.* Largeness of heart.—**Largely**, lärj′li, *adv.* In a large manner; to a large or great degree or extent; widely; extensively.

Largess, lär′jes, *n.* [Fr. *largesse*, from L. *largitio*, a bounty, from *largiri*, to bestow, from *largus*, large.] A present; a gift or donation; a bounty bestowed.

Larghetto, lär-get′to. [It.] *Mus.* somewhat slowly, but not so slowly as *largo*.—**Largo**, lär′gō. [It.] *Mus.* slowly; slowly, with breadth and dignity.

Lariat, lä′ri-at, *n.* [Sp. *lariata.*] The lasso; a long cord or thong of leather with a noose used in catching wild horses, &c.

Lark, lärk, *n.* [A.Sax. *lāwerce*, *lāferce*, O. and Prov.E. *lavrock*. *laverock* = D. *leeuwerik*, *leeuwrik*, Dan. *lærke*, Icel. *lævirki*, G. *lerche*—a lark; the Icel. *lævirki* seems to literally mean *craft-worker.*] One of a genus of perching birds characterized by having a long straight hind claw, and of which there are various species, as the sky-lark, wood-lark, shore-lark, &c., the sky-lark being celebrated for its song.—**Lark-bunting**, *n.* The snow-bunting.—**Lark-spur**, lärk′spėr, *n.* [From the long spur of one of the sepals.] The common name of a genus of plants, several species of which are common in gardens.

Lark, lärk, *n.* [From A.Sax. *lāc*, Icel. *leikr*, Goth. *laiks*, sport, play.] Sport; frolic; a piece of merriment. (*Slang* or *colloq.*) To sport; to make sport. (*Slang* or *colloq.*)

Larmier, lär′mi-ėr, *n.* [Fr., from *larme*, a tear or drop.] *Arch.* another name for the *Corona*; *zool.* a pouch which secretes a blackish humour, situated at the inner corner of the eye in the deer and antelope.

Larrikin, lar′i-kin, *n.* Australian hooligan; street-corner rough.

Larrup, lär′up, *v.t.* To whip or flog.

Larum, lar′um, *n.* An old form of *Alarm*.

Larva, lär′va, *n.* pl. **Larvæ**, lär′vē. [L. *larva*, a mask, a spectre.] The early form of any animal which during its development is unlike its parent; an insect in the caterpillar or grub state, that is, the first stage after the egg, preceding the chrysalis and the perfect insect.—**Larval**, lär′val, *a.* Pertaining to a larva.—**Larvarium**, lär-vā′ri-um, *n.* A case or covering made by a caterpillar; a place in which insects are hatched.—**Larvate, Larvated**, lär′vāt, lär′vā-ted, *a.* Masked; clothed as with a mask.—**Larve**, lärv, *n.* A larva.—**Larviform**, lär′vi-form, *a.* Like or having the form of a larva.—**Larviparous**, lär-vip′-a-rus, *a.* [L. *larva*, and *pario*, to bring forth.] Producing young in the state of larvæ.

Larynx, lar′ingks, *n.* [Gr.] *Anat.* the upper part of the windpipe or trachea, a cartilaginous cavity which plays an important part in the utterance of articulate sounds.—**Laryngeal**, **Laryngean**, lar-in-jē′al, lar-in-jē′an, *a.* Pertaining to the larynx. — **Laryngitis**, la-rin-jī′tis, *n.* [Term. *-itis* denotes inflammation.] An inflammation of the larynx of any sort.—**Laryngoscope**, la-ring′go-skōp, *n.* A reflecting contrivance for examining the larynx and commencement of the trachea. —**Laryngoscopic**, la-ring′go-skop″ik, *a.* Pertaining to the inspection of the larynx. —**Laryngotomy**, lar-in-got′o-mi, *n.* [Gr. *tomē*, a cutting.] The making of an incision into the larynx for assisting respiration when obstructed, for removing foreign bodies, or for other reasons.

Lascar, las′kär, *n.* In the East Indies, properly, a camp-follower; but by Europeans applied to a native sailor.

Lascivious, las-siv′i-us, *a.* [L. *lascivia*, lewdness, *lascivus*, wanton, allied to Skr. *las*, to embrace, *lash*, to desire, Gr. *lilaiomai*, to desire.] Wanton; lewd; lustful; exciting voluptuous emotions. — **Lasciviously**, las-siv′i-us-li, *adv.* In a lascivious manner. — **Lasciviousness**, las-siv′i-us-nes, *n.* The state or quality of being lascivious.

Lash, lash, *n.* [Akin to G. *lasche*, a flap, a thong, a latchet, also a scarf joint; D. *lasch*, a piece joined on, a joining; Dan. *laske*, Sw. *laska*, to scarf.] The thong or cord at the point of a whip; any thong, cord, or the like for flogging; a whip; a scourge; a stroke with a whip or anything pliant and tough; a stroke of satire; a sarcasm or cutting remark.—*v.t.* To strike with a lash or anything pliant; to whip or scourge; to beat, as with something loose; to dash against (as waves); to satirize; to censure with severity; to tie, bind, secure, or fasten with a rope or cord.—*v.i.* To ply the whip; to aim sarcasms; to hit.—*To lash out*, to strike out with the hind legs; to kick.—**Lasher**, lash′ėr, *n.* One who or that which lashes; water rushing or lashing over a weir; a weir.—**Lashing**, lash′ing, *n.* A piece of rope binding or making fast one thing to another.—**Lashings**, *n.* Abundance of grog, drink, rations. (*Colloq.*)

Lass, las, *n.* [A contr. for *ladess*, fem. of *lad*, or a contr. of W. *llodes*, a lass. LAD.] A young woman; a girl: in familiar language often applied to a woman of any age. —**Lassie**, las′i, *n.* [Dim. of *lass*.] A young girl; a term of endearment for a young woman. (*Colloq.*)

Lassitude, las′i-tūd, *n.* [L. *lassitudo*, from *lassus*, weary; same root as *late*.] The state of having the energies weakened; weakness; weariness; languor of body or mind; enervation.

Lasso, las′sō, *n.* [Sp. *lazo*, Pg. *laço*, from *laqueus*, a noose. LACE.] A lariat, rope or cord, with a noose, used for catching wild horses and other animals.—*v.t.* To catch with a lasso.

Last, last, *a.* [A.Sax. *last*, a contr. for *latost*, latest; comp. *best* for *betst*. LATE.] Coming after all the others; latest; hindmost; closing; final; next before the present; most recent; utmost; extreme; lowest; meanest; farthest of all from possessing a given quality, character, use, or the like; most unlikely (you are the *last* man I should consult).—*At last*, formerly *at the last*, at the end; in the conclusion.—*To the last*, to the end; till the conclusion.—*adv.* On the last occasion; the time before the present; after all others; lastly; finally.

Last, last, *v.i.* [A.Sax. *laestan*, to follow, to observe or perform, to last, to endure; Goth. *laistjan*, to trace footsteps, to follow, from A.Sax. *last*, Goth. *laists*, a footstep. See LAST, for shoes.] To continue in time; to endure; to remain in existence; to hold out and be sufficient in quantity (provisions to *last* a week); to continue unimpaired; not to decay or perish.—**Lasting**, las′ting, *p.* and *a.* Such as will or can continue or endure; durable; of long continuance (*lasting* good, evil, impression).—*n.* A species of stiff and very durable woollen stuff, used for making shoes and other purposes.—**Lastingly**, las′ting-li, *adv.* In a lasting manner. — **Lastingness**, las′ting-nes, *n.* The state or quality of being lasting.—**Lastly**, last′li, *adv.* In the last place; at last; finally.

Last, last, *n.* [A.Sax. *hlæst*, from *hladan*, to lade; D., Dan., and G. *last*, Icel. *lest*, a load. LADE.] A load; hence, a certain weight or measure, which varies in different articles, but is generally estimated at 4000 lb.; the burden of a ship.

Last, last, *n.* [A.Sax. *lást*, *laest*, D. *leest*, Dan. *læst*, a last; Goth. *laists*, footstep; Icel. *leistr*, the foot below the ankle, a short sock. LAST, *v.i.*] A mould or form of the human foot, made of wood, on which boots and shoes are formed.—*v.t.* To form on or by a last.

Latakia, lat-a-kē′a, *n.* A fine variety of Turkish tobacco, so named from *Latakia* (anciently *Laodicea*), near which it is produced.

Latch, lach, *n.* [From O.E. *lacche*, *latche*, A.Sax. *læccan*, to seize, to take hold of; comp. Icel. *láss*, a latch, a lock.] A simple contrivance or catch for fastening a door.—*v.t.* To fasten with a latch.—**Latch-key**, *n.* A key used to raise the latch of a door.

Latchet, lach′et, *n.* [Fr. *lacet*, a lace or string. LACE.] The string or thong that fastens a shoe or sandal.

Late, lāt, *a.* [A.Sax. *læt*, D. *laat*, Icel. *latr*, Dan. *lad*, Sw. *lat*, late, slow, tardy; Goth. *lats*, sluggish; G. *lass*, wearied; akin L. *lassus* (for *ladtus*); the root is that of *let*. This adjective is compared by *later*, *latter*, *latest* or *last*.] Coming after the usual time; slow; tardy; long delayed; far advanced toward the end or close (a *late* hour of the day); existing not long ago, but not now; deceased; departed; last or recently in any place, office, or character. — *adv.* After the usual time, or the time appointed; after delay; not long ago; lately; far in the night, day, week, or other particular period. —*Of late*, lately, in time not long past, or near the present.—**Lately**, lāt′li, *adv.* Not long ago; recently.—**Lateness**, lāt′nes, *n.* The state of being late; tardiness; far advanced period.—**Latish**, lāt′ish, *a.* Somewhat late.

Lateen, la-tēn, *a.* [Fr. *voile lateen*, lit. Latin sail.] A term applied to a triangular sail having its foremost edge fastened to a yard which hoists obliquely to the mast: used in xebecs, feluccas, &c., in the Mediterranean.

Latent, lā′tent, *a.* [L. *latens*, *latentis*, from *lateo*, to lurk; allied to Gr. *lanthanō*, *lathein*, to escape notice.] Not visible or apparent; not seen; not manifested; under the surface or what outwardly appears.—*Latent heat*, that portion of heat which exists in any body without producing any effect upon another, or upon the thermometer.—**Latently**, lā′tent-li, *adv.* In a latent manner.—**Latency**, lā′ten-si, *n.* The state of being latent.

Lateral, lat′ėr-al, *a.* [L. *lateralis*, from *latus*, *lateris*, a side, as in *collateral*, *equilateral*.] Pertaining to the side; directed to the side; proceeding from the side; situated on the side (as opposed to the front or back).—**Laterality**, lat-ėr-al′i-ti, *n.* The quality of being lateral.—**Laterally**, lat′-ėr-al-li, *adv.* In a lateral manner, direction, or position; sideways.—**Laterifolious**, lā′tėr-i-fō″li-us, *a.* [L. *latus*, and *folium*, leaf.] *Bot.* growing on the side of a leaf.

Laterite, lat′ėr-īt, *n.* [L. *later*, a brick or tile.] An argillaceous sandstone of a reddish colour, found in South India and Ceylon.—**Lateritic**, lat-ėr-it′ik, *a.* Pertaining to or characterized by laterite.—**Lateritious**, lā-tėr-ish′us, *a.* [L. *lateritius*.] Like brick; of the colour of bricks.

Latescent,† la-tes′ent, *a.* [L. *latesco*, to hide one's self. LATENT.] Lying hid; latent.—**Latescence**,† la-tes′ens, *n.* The quality or condition of being latescent.

Latex, lā′teks, *n.* [L., a fluid juice.] *Bot.* the elaborated sap of plants, often a white milky fluid.

Lath, lath, *n.* [A.Sax. *lætta*, D. and G. *latte*, whence Fr. *latte*, It. *latta*, a lath, a pole, &c. Akin *lattice*, *latten*.] A thin narrow board or slip of wood that is nailed to the rafters of a building to support the tiles or covering; a thin narrow slip of wood, perforated metal, or wire mesh that is nailed to a wall to support the plastering; such materials collectively; any similar piece of wood.—*v.t.* To cover or line with laths.—**Lath-brick**, *n.* A long slender brick, used in kilns to dry malt on.—**Lather**, *n.* One who applies laths.—**Lathing**, *n.* Lath materials; lath work on a wall; work of putting on lath materials.—**Lathy**, läth′i, *a.* Thin as a lath.

Lathe, lāTH, *n.* [A.Sax. *laeth*.] A division of a county, now confined to the county of Kent, in which there are five. (*Brit.*)

Lathe, lāTH, *n.* [Icel. *löth*, Dan. *lad*, a lathe, *dreielad*, a turning-lathe; in second sense it corresponds with Sw. and G. *lade*, a lay or lathe in a loom.] An apparatus for turning and polishing wood, ivory, metals, &c., by supporting and causing the article to revolve while being operated on; the part of a loom to which the reed is fixed, and by the movements of which the weft-threads are driven home in weaving: called also *lay*.

Lather, laTH′ėr, *n.* [A.Sax. *ledthor*; akin to Icel. *lauthr*, *lōthr*, froth of sea water, also a kind of soap; Sw. *lodder*, soap; from root meaning to wash, seen also in *lave*.] Foam or froth made by soap and water; foam or froth from profuse sweat, as of a horse.—*v.i.* To form a foam with soap and water; to become frothy.—*v.t.* To spread over with lather.

Laticiferous, lat-i-sif′ėr-us, *a.* [L. *latex*, sap, and *fero*, to bear.] *Bot.* bearing or containing latex or elaborated sap.

Latifoliate, **Latifolious**, lā-ti-fō′li-āt, lā-ti-fō′li-us, *a.* [L. *latus*, broad, and *folium*, a leaf.] Broad-leaved, as a plant.

Latin, lat′in, *a.* [L. *Latinus*, from *Latium*, the district of Italy in which Rome was built.] Pertaining to the Latins, a people of Latium in Italy; Roman; pertaining to or composed in the language spoken by the Latins or Romans.—*Latin Church*, the Western Church; the Church of Rome, as distinct from the Greek or Eastern Church. —*Latin races*, the Italian, French, Spanish, &c., whose language is based on the Latin, and among whose ancestors were Roman colonists.—*n.* The language of the ancient Romans.—*v.t.* To turn into Latin.—**Latinism**, lat′in-izm, *n.* A Latin idiom; a mode of speech peculiar to the Latins.—**Latinist**, lat′in-ist, *n.* One skilled in Latin.—**Latinitaster**, la-tin′i-tas-tėr, *n.* One who has a smattering of Latin.—**Latinity**, la-tin′i-ti, *n.* Latin style or idiom; purity of Latin style.—**Latinization**, lat′in-i-zā″-shon, *n.* The act of rendering into Latin. —**Latinize**, lat′in-īz, *v.t.*—*latinized*, *latinizing*. To translate into Latin; to give Latin terminations or forms to, as to foreign words. — *v.i.* To use words or phrases borrowed from the Latin.

Latirostrous, lat-i-ros′trus, *a.* [L. *latus*, broad, *rostrum*, beak.] Having a broad beak, as a bird.

Latitude, lat′i-tūd, *n.* [L. *latitudo*, lit. breadth, from *latus*, broad, wide; as applied in geography this term was adopted because ancient geographers thought the breadth (latitude) of the earth from north to south was much less than its length (longitude) from east to west.] Extent from side to side; breadth; width; room or scope; comprehensiveness or looseness of application; extent of deviation from a standard; freedom from rules or limits; laxity; extent; amplitude; distance north or south of the equator, measured on a meridian and expressed in degrees, minutes, and seconds, the greatest possible latitude being 90° north or south, and any latitude approaching this being a *high* latitude, the opposite being a *low* latitude; *astron.* the distance of a star north or south of the ecliptic, measured on a circle at right angles to the ecliptic and passing through the body.—*Parallels of latitude*, circles parallel to the equator, used in measuring latitude.—**Latitudinal**, lat-i-tū'di-nal, *a*. Pertaining to latitude; in the direction of latitude.—**Latitudinarian**, lat'i-tū-di-nā"ri-an, *a*. Embracing a wide circle or range; having a wide scope; characterized by freedom, independence, or want of respect for the usual standards of belief or opinion; lax in religious principles or views; free-thinking; liberal.—*n*. One who is liberal or loose in his notions; one who has no respect for commonly accepted doctrines or opinions; one who indulges a latitude of thinking and is careless of orthodoxy.—**Latitudinarianism**, lat'i-tū-di-nā"ri-an-izm, *n*. The principles of latitudinarians; freedom of opinion, particularly in theology.

Latria, la-trī'a, *n*. [L., from Gr. *latreia*, service.] The highest kind of worship, or that paid to God, distinguished by Roman Catholics from *dulia*, or the inferior worship paid to saints.

Latrine, la-trēn', *n*. [L. *latrina*, a bath, a water-closet, from *lavo*, to wash.] A privy; a water-closet.

Latten, lat'en, *n*. [O.Fr. *laton*, Fr. *laiton*, brass; It. *latta*, tin-plate; akin to *lath*: so called from the material being used in flat pieces or plates. LATH.] A fine kind of brass or bronze anciently used for crosses, candlesticks, brasses of sepulchral monuments, &c.; as a modern commercial term, metal in sheets or strips, especially sheet or plate brass or thin plates of mixed metal.—**Latten-brass**, *n*. Milled brass in sheets of different thicknesses.

Latter, lat'ėr, *a*. [An irregular comparative of *late*. LATE.] More late or recent; the second of two: opposed to *former*; mentioned the last of two; modern; lately past (in these *latter* ages).—**Latter-day Saint**, *n*. MORMON.—**Latterly**, lat'ėr-li, *adv*. Of late; in time not long past; lately; ultimately; at last.—**Latter-math**, *n*. The latter mowing; after-math.

Lattice, lat'is, *n*. [Fr. *lattis*, from *latte*, lath. LATH.] A structure of wood or iron made by crossing laths, rods, or bars, and forming open chequered or reticulated work; a window made of laths or strips of iron which cross one another like network, so as to leave open interstices.—*v.t.*—*latticed, latticing*. To give the form or appearance of a lattice to; to furnish with a lattice.—**Lattice-bridge**, *n*. A bridge having its sides constructed with cross-framing so as to resemble lattice-work.—**Lattice-girder**, *n*. A girder of which the side consists of diagonal pieces arranged like lattice-work.—**Lattice-leaf, Lattice-plant**, *n*. An aquatic plant of Madagascar, the leaf of which resembles lattice-work, consisting of reticulated nerves with open interstices.—**Lattice-window**, *n*. A window made of strips crossing one another, with open interstices.

Laud, lạd, *v.t.* [L. *laudo*, to praise, from *laus, laudis*, praise; *allow* is a derivative.] To praise in words alone, or with words and singing; to extol; to celebrate.—*n*. Praise; a song or hymn of praise; *pl*. a service of the church comprising psalms of praise, and generally included in matins.—**Laudability**,† **Laudableness**, lạ-da-bil'i-ti, lạ'da-bl-nes, *n*. The quality of being laudable.—**Laudable**, lạ'da-bl, *a*. [L. *laudabilis*.] Praiseworthy; commendable.—**Laudably**, lạ'da-bli, *adv*. In a laudable or commendable manner.—**Laudation**, lạ-dā'shon, *n*. Praise; commendation.—**Laudatory**, lạ'da-to-ri, *a*. Containing or expressing praise; tending to praise.—*n*. That which contains or expresses praise.—**Lauder**, lạ'dėr, *n*. One who lauds or praises.

Laudanum, lạ'da-num, *n*. [From L. *ladanum*, a resinous juice. LADANUM.] Opium prepared in spirit of wine by maceration, straining, and filtering; tincture of opium.

Laugh, läf, *v.i.* [A.Sax. *hlehhan, hlihhan*, to laugh; comp. Goth. *hlahjan*, O.H.G. *hlahhan*, Icel. *hlæja*, D. *lagchen*, G. *lachen*, to laugh; imitative of sound made in laughing.] To make that convulsive or chuckling noise which sudden merriment excites; when said of things, to appear gay, bright, or brilliant.—*To laugh at*, to ridicule; to treat with some degree of contempt.—*To laugh in the sleeve*, to laugh to one's self or so as not to be observed, especially when apparently maintaining a demure countenance.—*To laugh on the wrong side of the mouth*, to weep or cry; to be made to feel vexation or disappointment after exhibiting a boastful or exultant spirit.—*n*. The inarticulate expression of sudden mirth peculiar to man.—*v.t.* To express by laughing; to ridicule or deride: with *out* or *down*.—*To laugh to scorn*, to deride; to treat with mockery, contempt, and scorn.—**Laughable**, läf'a-bl, *a*. That may justly excite laughter; comical; ludicrous.—**Laughableness**, läf'a-bl-nes, *n*. The quality of being laughable.—**Laughably**, läf'a-bli, *adv*. In a manner to excite laughter.—**Laugher**, läf'ėr, *n*. One who laughs or is fond of merriment.—**Laughing-gas**, *n*. Nitrous oxide, or protoxide of nitrogen: so called because, when inhaled, it usually produces exhilaration.—**Laughingly**, läf'ing-li, *adv*. In a laughing or merry way; with laughter.—**Laughing-stock**, *n*. A person or thing that is an object of ridicule; a butt for laughter or jokes.—**Laughter**, läf'tėr, *n*. [A.Sax. *hleahtor*, Icel. *hlátr*, O.H.G. *hlahtar*.] The act or sound of laughing; an expression of mirth, manifested chiefly in certain convulsive and partly involuntary actions of the muscles of respiration, which produce a succession of short abrupt sounds, with certain movements of the muscles of the face, and often of other parts of the body; any expression of merriment perceivable in the countenance, as in the eyes.—**Laughterless**, läf'tėr-les, *a*. Without laughter; not laughing.—**Laughy**,† läf'i, *a*. Inclined or disposed to laughter. (*Thack.*)

Launce, läns, *n*. A name of two species of sand-eels, from their lancelike form.

Launch, länsh, *v.t.* [Also written *lanch*, a form of *lance*; Fr. *lancer*, O.Fr. *lanchier*, to throw or dart.] To throw, as a lance; to dart; to let fly; to move or cause to slide from the land into the water; to set afloat for the first time after being built (to *launch* a ship); *fig*. to put out into another sphere of duty, another field of activity, or the like.—*v.i.* To glide forward, as a ship into the water; to enter upon a new field of activity; to enter upon a new topic (to *launch* into a discussion).—*n*. The setting afloat of a ship or boat; a kind of boat, longer, lower, and more flat-bottomed than a long-boat; the largest boat carried by a man-of-war.

Launder, län'dėr, *n*. [Contr. from O.E. *lavander*, from Fr. *lavandier, lavandière*, from *laver*, L. *lavo*, to wash. LAVE.] A washerwoman; a long trough used by miners for washing ore.—*v.t.*‡ To wash; to wet.—**Launderer**, län'dėr-ėr, *n*. A man who follows the business of washing clothes.—**Laundress**, län'dres, *n*. A female whose employment is to wash, and especially to dress, underclothing, table-linen, &c.—**Laundry**, län'dri, *n*. [Contr. for *lavendery*.] The place or room where clothes are washed.

Laureate, lạ'rē-āt, *a*. [L. *laureatus*, from *laurea*, a laurel, from *laurus*, a laurel. LAUREL.] Decked or invested with laurel.—*Poet laureate*, in Great Britain, an officer belonging in virtue of his office to the royal household, who was formerly required to compose an ode annually for the sovereign's birthday, for a great national victory, and the like—a requirement discontinued since the reign of George III, the post being now a sinecure.—*n*. One crowned with laurel; a poet laureate.—*v.t.*—*laureated, laureating*. To honour with a wreath of laurel; to invest with the office of poet laureate.—**Laureateship**, lạ'rē-āt-ship, *n*. Office of a laureate; the post of a poet laureate.

Laurel, lạ'rel, *n*. [O.E. *laurer, lorer*, Fr. *laurier*, Sp. Pr. *laurel*, from L. *laurus*, a laurel, for *daurus*, being akin to Gr. *drys*, W. *derw*, an oak, E. *tree*.] The sweet-bay, a native of the North of Africa and south of Europe, cultivated in gardens from its elegant appearance and the aromatic fragrance of its evergreen leaves; a name also given to several other shrubs botanically very different, but somewhat similar in their evergreen foliage, as the cherry-laurel and Portugal laurel, both of the cherry genus; *pl*. a crown of laurel, formerly bestowed as a distinction on poets, heroes, &c.; hence, honour, fame, distinction.—**Laurelled**, lạ'reld, *a*. Crowned or decorated with laurel, or with a laurel wreath; laureate.—**Laurel-water**, *n*. A poisonous water distilled from the leaves of the cherry-laurel, containing prussic acid.—**Lauriferous**, lạ-rif'ėr-us, *a*. Producing or bringing laurel.

Laurentian, lạ-ren'shi-an, *a*. [From the river St. *Lawrence*.] *Geol*. a term applied to a vast series of stratified and crystalline rocks of gneiss, mica-schist, quartzite, serpentines and limestones, occurring northward of the St. Lawrence in Canada.

Laurustine, Laurustinus, Laurestine, lạ'rus-tīn, lạ-rus-tī'nus, lạ'res'tīn, *n*. [L. *laurus*, laurel, and *tinus*, this plant.] A popular garden evergreen shrub or tree, native of the south of Europe, with pinkish or white flowers.

Lava, lä'vä, *n*. [It., from L. *lavo*, to wash. LAVE.] The general term for all rock-matter that flows in a molten state from volcanoes.—*Lava ware*, a kind of coarse ware resembling lava made from iron slag, cast into urns, tiles, table-tops, &c.—**Lavatic, Lavic**, lä-vat'ik, lä'vik, *a*. Consisting of or resembling lava.

Lave, lāv, *v.t.*—*laved, laving*. [Fr. *laver*, L. *lavo*, to wash, to bathe; akin to *luo*, Gr. *louō*, to wash; connected are *laundress, lavender, lava, ablution, alluvial, deluge, lotion*.] To wash; to bathe.—*v.i.* To wash one's self; to bathe; to wash, as the sea on the beach.—**Lavation**, la-vā'shon, *n*. [L. *lavatio*.] A washing or cleansing.—**Lavatory**, lav'a-to-ri, *a*. Washing or cleansing by washing.—*n*. A room or place for washing or personal ablutions; a wash or lotion.—**Laver**, lā'vėr, *n*. A vessel for washing; a large basin; in *Scrip. hist*. a basin placed in the court of the Jewish tabernacle, where the officiating priests washed their hands and feet.

Lave, lāv, *v.t.* [A.Sax. *laflan, gelafian*, to refresh, D. *laven*, to refresh, G. *laben*, O.H.G. *labon*, to wash, to refresh. LAVISH.] To throw up or out, as water from any receptacle; to lade out; to bale.

Lavender, lav'en-dėr, *n*. [L.L. *lavendula, lavandula*, It. *lavandola, lavanda*, Fr. *lavande*, G. *lavandel*, lavender, from L. *lavo*, to wash, from its distilled water being used in ablution.] An aromatic plant of the mint family, the flower spikes of which are used to perfume clothes, and afford by distillation a valuable essential oil; a pale blue colour with a slight mixture of gray, like the flower of lavender.—*To lay in lavender*, to lay by (clothes) with sprigs of lavender.—**Lavender-water**, *n*. A perfume composed of spirits of wine, essential oil of lavender, and ambergris.

Laver, Laverwort, lā'vėr, lā'vėr-wėrt, *n*. [Comp. Ir. *leabhar*, broad, trailing.] A name given to two species of sea-weed employed as food, and said to be useful in scrofulous affections.

Laverock, lā'vėr-ok, *n*. The sky-lark.

Lavic, lä'vik, *a*. Under LAVA.

Lavish, lav'ish, *v.t.* [Irregularly formed from E. *lave*, to pour out.] To expend or bestow with profusion; to expend without necessity or use; to waste; to squander.—*a*. Expending or bestowing with profusion; profuse; liberal to a fault; wasteful; being overflowing or in profusion; superabundant; superfluous.—**Lavisher**, lav'ish-ėr, *n*. One who lavishes.—**Lavishly**, lav'ish-li, *adv*. In a lavish manner.—**Lavishment**, lav'ish-ment, *n*. The act of lavishing.—**Lavishness**, lav'ish-nes, *n*.

Lavolt, Lavolta, la-vōlt', la-vōl'ta, *n.* [It. *la volta*, the turn.] An old dance in which was much turning and capering. (*Shak.*)

Law, la̦, *n.* [A.Sax. *lagu*, from same root as *lie*, *lay*, *low*; cog. Sw. *lag*, Icel. *lag*, *lög*, Dan. *lov*, a law; the root is also in L. *lex*, a law (whence *legal*). LIE.] A rule of action or conduct laid down or prescribed by authority; an edict or decree of a ruler or a government; a general command or order expressly laid down; such rules, edicts, or decrees collectively; the whole body of rules regulating and controlling the individuals of a state or community (to break the *law*, a violation of *law*, a father-in-*law*); legal procedure; litigation; the science dealing with legal enactments and procedure; jurisprudence; rights established by law; justice; one of the rules or principles by which any matter or proceeding is regulated (the *laws* of versification, of horse-racing); an allowance in distance or time granted to a a weaker competitor in a race or the like; a theoretical principle deduced from practice or observation; a formal statement of facts invariably observed in natural phenomena (the *law* of gravitation).—*The law*, *theol.* the code of Moses, or the books containing it; the preceptive part of revelation in contradistinction to the doctrinal, that is, to *the gospel*.—*Law French*, the Norman dialect or old French, still employed in certain formal state proceedings.—*Law language*, the language used in legal writings and forms.—*Law Latin*, corrupt Latin used in law and legal documents.—*Law merchant*, mercantile or commercial law; international law regulating commerce. See also under CIVIL, COMMERCIAL, COMMON, CRIMINAL, ECCLESIASTICAL, &c.—**Law-abiding**, *a.* Observant of the law: obeying the law.—**Law-breaker**, *n.* One who violates the law.—**Lawful**, la̦'fu̦l, *a.* Agreeable or conformable to law; allowed by law; legitimate; permissible (*lawful* but not expedient); competent; free from objection; rightful (*lawful* owner).—**Lawfully**, la̦'fu̦l-li, *adv.* In a lawful manner; legitimately; legally.—**Lawfulness**, la̦'fu̦l-nes, *n.* The quality of being lawful.—**Lawless**, la̦'les, *a.* Not obedient or conforming to law; unrestrained by the law of morality or of society; contrary to or unauthorized by law; illegal; apparently uncontrolled by any law; capricious.—**Lawlessly**, la̦'les-li, *adv.* In a lawless manner.—**Lawlessness**, la̦'les-nes, *n.* Illegality; disregard of law; arbitrariness; violence.—**Law-maker**, *n.* A legislator; a law-giver.—**Law of diminishing return**, the fact that an increase in the capital or labor of any industry causes a proportionate increase in production up to a certain point, and thereafter a less proportional and eventually unprofitable increase.—**Law of gravitation**, the principle that any two bodies, such as the earth and the moon or the earth and a ball thrown up, attract one another with a force directly proportionate to the product of their masses and inversely proportionate to the square of the distance between them.—**Law of nations**, international law.—**Law of nature**, an instinct or natural tendency observed in man or animals; *pl.* the more important generalizations of science.—**Lawsuit**, la̦'sūt, *n.* A suit in law for the recovery of a supposed right; an action before a court instituted by a party to compel another to do him justice.—**Lawyer**, la̦'yėr, *n.* [From *law*; comp. *bowyer*, *sawyer*.] One versed in the laws; or a practitioner of law; one whose profession is to institute suits in courts of law, or to prosecute or defend the cause of clients.

Lawn, la̦n, *n.* [O.E. *laund*, *lawnde*, a clear space in a forest, a wild shrubby or woody tract, from W. *llan*, an inclosed space, or from Fr. *lande*, a heath or wild tract.] A glade in a forest; a vista through trees; a space of ground covered with grass, and kept smoothly mown, generally in front of or around a mansion.—**Lawn-mower**, *n.* machine for mowing lawns.—**Lawn-tennis**, *n.* An outdoor game played with balls and rackets on a lawn and resembling tennis.—**Lawny**, la̦'ni, *a.* Resembling a lawn.

Lawn, la̦n, *n.* [Perhaps same as preceding word, and so called from its transparency, being seen through as we see through a lawn or vista, but more probably derived from the earlier term *laune lynen*, i. e., lawn linen, from *Laon*, a town in France.] A fabric of linen or cotton, sheer, fine, and plain-woven, thinner than cambric, employed in handkerchiefs, dresses, &c.—**Lawny**, la̦n'i, *a.*

Lax, laks, *a.* [L. *laxus*, loose, from same root as *langueo*, to languish, and probably E. *slack*; hence *relax*, *lease*, *leash*, *release*.] Loose; flabby; soft; not tense, firm, or rigid; not tightly stretched or drawn; not rigidly exact or precise; vague; equivocal; not sufficiently strict or rigorous; remiss; having too frequent discharges from the bowels.—**Laxation**, lak-sā'shon, *n.* [L. *laxatio*.] The act of loosening or slackening.—**Laxative**, lak'sa-tiv, *a.* [Fr. *laxatif*.] Having the power or quality of loosening or opening the intestines and relieving from constipation.—*n.* A medicine that acts as a gentle purgative.—**Laxativeness**, lak'sa-tive-nes, *n.*—**Laxity, Laxness**, lak'si-ti, laks'nes, *n.* [L. *laxitas*.] The state or quality of being lax; looseness; want of strictness; remissness.—**Laxly**, laks'li, *adv.* In a lax manner; loosely; without exactness.

Lay, lā, pret. of *lie*.

Lay, lā, *v.t.*—pret. & pp. *laid*; ppr. *laying*. [A.Sax. *lecgan* (pret. *legde*, *léde*, pp. *gelegd*, *geléd*), a causal corresponding to *lie*, A.Sax. *licgan*; similarly Goth. *lagjan*, Icel. *leggja*, Dan. *lægge*, D. *leggen*, G. *legen*. to lay, from corresponding intrans. verbs. [LIE.] To place in a lying position; to cause to lie; to prostrate; to put, set, or place in general; to impose (taxes, commands, blame, &c.); to bring into a certain state: with various adjectives (to *lay* bare; to *lay* open, &c.); to settle (dust); to still (the wind); to allay (pain); to dispose with regularity in building or in other technical operations; to place at hazard; to wager; to stake; to contrive, scheme, plan (a plot); to place before a court of justice (an indictment, damages).—*To lay aside*, to put off or away; not to retain; to abandon.—*To lay away*, to reposit in store; to put aside for preservation.—*To lay before*, to exhibit or show to; to present to the view of.—*To lay by*, to reserve for future use; to put off.—*To lay by the heels*, to put in the stocks; to confine; to put in prison.—*To lay claim*, to claim; to advance or bring forward a claim.—*To lay down*, to give up or resign; to declare (to *lay down* a proposition or principle); to delineate on paper; to stake, or deposit as a pledge, equivalent, or satisfaction.—*To lay down the law*, to assert dictatorially what the speaker holds to be right.—*To lay eggs*, to produce them naturally from the body, as a bird or reptile.—*To lay hold of*, *to lay hold on*, to seize; to catch; to apprehend.—*To lay in*, to collect and store; to provide previously.—*To lay it on*, to do something to excess, as to charge an exorbitant price.—*To lay on*, to apply with force; to supply, as water, gas, &c., to houses by means of pipes leading from a main reservoir.—*To lay one's self open to*, to expose one's self to.—*To lay one's self out for*, to be ready to take part in; to put one's self in the way of.—*To lay one's hand on a thing*, to find it when wanted.—*To lay open*, to open; to make bare; to uncover; also, to show; to expose; to reveal.—*To lay out*, to expend; to plan or dispose in order the several parts of (to *lay out* a garden); to dress in grave-clothes and place in a decent posture (to *lay out* a corpse).—*To lay to heart*, to consider seriously and intently; to feel deeply or keenly.—*To lay to one's charge*, to accuse him of.—*To lay up*, to store; to treasure; to reposit for future use; to confine to the bed or chamber; *naut.* to dismantle (a ship) and put in a dock or other place of security.—*To lay siege to*, to besiege; to importune; to annoy with constant solicitations.—*To lay wait*, to lie in ambush.—*To lay waste*, to devastate; to desolate.—*v.i.* To bring forth or produce eggs; *betting*, to wager; to bet; to stake money.—*To lay about one*, to strike on all sides; to act with vigour.—*To lay at*, to endeavour to strike.—*To lay on*, to deal blows with vehemence. [*To lay* is sometimes erroneously used, even by good writers, for *to lie*, but this should be carefully avoided. See under LIE.]—*n.* A stratum; a layer; a fold; the direction or lie in which the different strands of a rope are twisted.—**Laying**, lā'ing, *v.t.* The aiming of a gun.—**Layoff**, lā'of, *n.* Discharge, as of workmen; a period of closing down; the act of laying off.—**Layout**, *n.* Plan, arrangement, as of a newspaper; the equipment, as of an office or shop; also the plan outlining the arrangement.

Lay, lā, *a.* [Fr. *lai*, from L. *laicus*, Gr. *laikos*, from *laos*, people.] Pertaining to the people, as distinct from the clergy; not clerical; not professional; not appertaining to one who has professional knowledge.—*Lay brother*, a person received into a convent of monks, under vows, but not in holy orders.—*Lay clerk*, in the *English Ch.* a person not in orders who leads the people in their responses.—*Lay sister*, one received into a convent of nuns, under vows, but who does not perform any sacred office.—**Laity**, lā'i-ti, *n.* Collectively all people who do not belong to the clergy; people outside of any profession as distinguished from those in it.—**Layman**, lā'man, *n.* Any man not a clergyman; one of the laity; a man not professionally or specially devoted to a pursuit.—**Lay-sermon**, *n.* A sermon by a layman; a sermon on secular subjects.

Lay, lā, *n.* [O.Fr. *lai*, from the Celtic; Ir. and Gael. *laoi*, a verse, hymn, poem; same root as in G. *lied*, a song.] A song; a ballad; a narrative poem.

Lay, lā, *n.* [LATHE.] A part of a loom; a lathe.

Lay, lā, *n.* Same as *Lea*.

Layer, lā'ėr, *n.* [Partly from *lay*, the verb; partly same as *lair*.] One who or that which lays; a stratum; a coat, as of paint; a row or course of masonry, brickwork, or the like; a shoot or twig of a plant, not detached from the stock, partly laid under ground for growth or propagation.—*v.t.* *Gardening*, to propagate by bending the shoot of a living stem into the soil, the shoot striking root while being fed by the parent plant.

Layette, lā-et', *n.* [Fr.] Clothing, blankets, &c., for a new-born child.

Lay-figure, Layman, lā'fig-ūr, lā'man, *n.* [D. *leeman*, lit. joint-man, *lee* being for *lede*, from *leden*, pl. of *lid* (A.Sax. *lith*, Dan. *lid*, Goth. *lithus*), a joint.] A jointed figure used by painters in imitation of the human body, and which can be placed in any attitude so as to serve when clothed as a model for draperies, &c.

Lazar, lā'zär, *n.* [O.Fr. *lazare*, from *Lazarus* of the New Testament (Luke, xvi. 20).] A leper; any person infected with a nauseous and pestilential disease.—**Lazaretto, Lazaret**, laz-a-ret'tō, laz'a-ret, *n.* [Sp. *lazareto*, It. *lazzeretto*, Fr *lazaret*.] A hospital for the reception of diseased persons, particularly those affected with contagious distempers; at seaports often a vessel used for this purpose; a hospital for quarantine.—**Lazar-house**, *n.* A lazaretto.—**Lazarlike, Lazarly**, lā'zär-līk, lā'zär-li, *a.* Like a lazar; full of sores; leprous.

Lazuli, laz'ū-lī, *n.* Lapis-lazuli.—**Lazulite**, laz'ū-līt, *n.* Blue-spar, a phosphate of aluminium, magnesium, and iron.

Lazy, lā'zi, *a.* [Origin doubtful; perhaps for *late-sy* (from *late*), with term. as in *tricksy*, *tipsy*; or O.Fr. *lasche*, lax, slow, remiss, from L. *laxus*.] Disinclined to action or exertion; sluggish; indolent; averse to labour; heavy in motion; moving slowly or apparently with labour.—**Laze**, lāz, *v.i.* To live in idleness.—*v.t.* To spend in sloth or idleness.—**Lazily**, lā'zi-li, *adv.* In a lazy manner.—**Laziness**, lā'zi-nes, *n.* The state or quality of being lazy; indolence; sloth.—**Lazybones**, lā′zi-bōnz, *n.* A lazy fellow; an idler.

Lazzaroni, lät-sä-rō′nē, *n.pl.* sing. **Lazzarone**, lät-sä-rō′nā. [It., from *Lazarus* in the parable.] The poor class of people at Naples who have no fixed habitation.

Lea, lē, *n.* [Also written *lay*, from A.Sax. *leáh*, untilled land, pasture; Dan. dialect *lei*, fallow; D. *leeg*, empty, fallow.] A meadow or grassy plain; land under grass or pasturage.

Leach, lēch, *n.* *Naut.* the side edge of a sail. LEECH.

Leach, lēch, *v.t.* and *i.* LETCH.

Lead, led, *n.* [A.Sax. *ledd*; akin D. *lood*, Sw. and Dan. *lod*, G. *loth*, a plummet, the lead for taking soundings.] A metal of a bluish-gray colour, characterized chiefly by its softness and fusibility; a plummet or mass of lead used in sounding at sea; *printing*, a thin plate of metal used to give space between lines; a small piece of black lead or plumbago used in pencils; *pl.* the leaden covering of a roof.—*Black lead*, a name of graphite or plumbago. Under GRAPHIC.—*White lead*, carbonate of lead, forming a white substance much used in painting.—*a.* Made or composed of lead; consisting more or less of lead; produced by lead.—*v.t.* To cover with lead; to fit with lead; *printing*, to widen the space between (lines) by inserting a lead or thin plate of type-metal. — **Leaded**, led′ed, *p.* and *a.* Covered with lead; fitted with lead; set in lead; *printing*, separated by thin plates of lead, as lines in printing. —**Leaden**, led′n, *a.* Made of lead; resembling lead (a *leaden* sky); sluggish; slow; inert; heavy; dull; gloomy.—**Lead-glance**, *n.* Lead-ore; galena. — **Lead-gray, Leaden-gray**, *a.* Coloured like lead.—**Leaden-paced**, *a.* Slow in movement.—**Leadless**, led′les, *a.* Having no lead; not charged with a bullet.—**Lead-mine**, *n.* A mine containing lead or lead-ore.—**Lead-pencil**, *n.* An instrument for drawing or writing, usually made by inclosing a slip of plumbago or graphite (black lead) in a casing of wood.—**Leadsman**, ledz′man, *n.* *Naut.* the man who heaves the lead.—**Lead-spar**, *n.* A mineral, the carbonate of lead or cerusite. — **Leady**, led′i, *a.* Pertaining to or resembling lead in any of its properties.

Lead, lēd, *v.t.* pret. & pp. *led*. [A.Sax. *laeden*, to lead, from *lād*, a course, from *līthan*, to go or travel; D. *leiden*, Icel. *leitha*, Dan. *lede*, to lead; akin *lode*, *lodestone*.] To guide by the hand; to guide or conduct by showing the way; to direct; to conduct, as a chief or commander; to head; to direct and govern; to precede; to hold the first place in rank or dignity among; to show the method of attaining an object; to direct, as in an investigation; to draw, entice, allure; to induce; to prevail on; to influence; to pass or spend (to *lead* a life of gaiety); to cause to spend or endure (he *led* his wife a sad life); *card-playing*, to commence a round or trick with.—*To lead captive*, to carry into captivity.—*To lead one a dance* or *a fine dance*, to cause one more exertion or trouble than necessary or expected.—*To lead the way*, to go before and show the way.—*v.i.* To go before and show the way; to have precedence or pre-eminence; to take the first place; to have a position of authority; to be chief, commander, or director; to conduct, bring, draw, induce (gambling *leads* to other evils); *card-playing*, to play the first card of a round or trick.—*To lead off* or *out*, to begin.—*n.* A going before; guidance; act of leading; precedence; the right of playing the first card in a round or trick.—**Leader**, lē′dėr, *n.* One that leads or conducts; a guide; a conductor; a chief; a commander; the chief of a party, faction, or any body of people; a musical performer who leads a band or choir; a leading article in a newspaper, *i.e.* an editor's own political or other disquisition; one of the front horses in a team.—**Leaderette**, lē-dėr-et′, *n.* A short leading article in a newspaper. —**Leadership**, lē′dėr-ship, *n.* The office of a leader; guidance.—**Leading**, lē′ding, *p.* and *a.* Guiding; conducting; chief; principal; most influential.—*Leading question*, a question which suggests the answer.—**Leadingly**, lē′ding-li, *adv.* In a leading manner. — **Leading-strings**, *n. pl.* Strings by which children are supported when beginning to walk; hence, *to be in leading-strings*, to be a mere puppet in the hands of others.

Leaf, lēf, *n.* pl. **Leaves**, lēvz. [A.Sax. *leáf* =O.Sax. *lōf*, Goth. *laufs*, Icel. *lauf*, Dan. *lōv*, D. *loof*, G. *laub*, a leaf; allied to Lith. *lapas*, a leaf; Gr. *lepis*, a scale.] One of the external parts of a plant, usually shooting from the sides of the stem and branches, and ordinarily green in colour; something resembling a leaf; the part of a book or folded sheet containing two pages; a side, division, or part of a flat body, the parts of which move on hinges, as folding-doors, window-shutters, a firescreen, &c.; the part of a table which can be raised or lowered at pleasure; a very thin plate of metal (gold-*leaf*); the brim of a soft hat.—*To turn over a new leaf*, to adopt a different and better line of conduct.—*v.i.* To shoot out leaves; to produce leaves.—**Leafage**, lēf′āj, *n.* Leaves collectively; abundance of leaves; foliage. — **Leaf-bud**, *n.* A bud from which leaves only are produced. — **Leafed**, lēft, *a.* Having leaves: used frequently in composition (broad-*leafed*, thin-*leafed*, &c.).—**Leafiness**, lē′fi-nes, *n.* State of being leafy or full of leaves. — **Leaf-insect**, *n.* The popular name of insects whose wings resemble or mimic leaves; a walking-leaf.—**Leafless**, lēf′les, *a.* Destitute of leaves.—**Leaflessness**, lēf′les-nes, *n.*—**Leaflet**, lēf′let, *n.* A little leaf; a small printed folder; *bot.* one of the divisions of a compound leaf; a foliole.—**Leaf-louse**, *n.* An aphis or plant-louse.—**Leaf-mold**, *n.* Leaves decayed and reduced to the state of mold, used as manure for plants.—**Leaf-stalk**, *n.* The petiole or stalk which supports a leaf.—**Leafy**, lē′fi, *a.* Full of leaves; abounding with leaves.—**Leave**, lēv, *v.t.* To produce leaves; to leaf.—**Leaved**, lēvd, *a.* With leaves; and compounded, as two-*leaved*.

League, lēg, *n.* [Fr. *ligue*, It. *lega*, L.L. *liga*, from L. *ligo*, to bind (in *ligament*, *ligature*, *ally*, &c.).] A combination of parties for promotion of their mutual interests, or for executing any design in concert, as of states for military aid or defense.—*League of Nations*, a group of nations formed after the World War (1920) to cooperate in world affairs. It assigned mandates of surrendered territories and planned arbitration in disputes between nations.—*Baseball*, *National League* (organized 1876), *American League* (1900), of eight teams each in major cities.

League, lēg, *n.* [O.Fr. *legue*, Fr. *lieue*, from L.L. *leuca*, *leuga*, &c., and that from the Celtic.] A measure of length varying in different countries, the English land league being 3 statute miles, the nautical league nearly 3½.

Leaguer, lē′gėr, *n.* [D. *leger*, G. *lager*, a bed, a couch, a camp; allied to *lair*, *lie*, *lay*.] A camp; the camp of a besieging army; a siege.

Leak, lēk, *n.* [Icel. *leki*, a leak; *lekr*, leaky; D. *lek*, Dan. *læk*, G. *leck*, a leak, leaky. See the verb.] A crack, fissure, or hole in a vessel that admits water, or permits a fluid to escape; the passing of liquid through such a crack or aperture.—*To spring a leak*, to open or crack so as to let in water; to begin to let in water.—*v.i.* [Icel. *leka*, Dan. *lække*, D. *lekken*, to leak; allied to A.Sax. *leccan*, to wet, to moisten, and to E. *lack*.] To let water or other liquor in or out through a hole or crevice (the vessel *leaks*); to ooze or pass, as water or other fluid, through a crack, fissure, or aperture in a vessel. —*To leak out*, to find vent; to find publicity in a clandestine or irregular way.—**Leakage**, lēk′āj, *n.* A leaking; the quantity of a liquor that enters or issues by leaking; *com.* a certain allowance for the leaking of casks, or the waste of liquors by leaking. —**Leakiness**, lēk′i-nes, *n.* State of being leaky.—**Leaky**, lēk′i, *a.* Letting water or other liquid pass in or out by leaks; *fig.* apt to disclose secrets; tattling; not close.

Leal, lēl, *a.* [O.Fr. *leal*; the same word as *legal* and *loyal*.] Loyal; true; faithful; honest; upright.—**Lealness**, lēl′nes, *n.* The state or quality of being leal.

Leam,† lēm, *n.* [O.Fr. *liem*; same as *lien*.] A cord or string to lead a dog.

Lean, lēn, *v.i.*—pret. & pp. *leaned* or *leant* (lent). [A.Sax. *hlaenan*, to make to lean, *hlinian*, to lean; O.Sax. *hlinon*, O.H.G. *hlinen*, G. *lehnen*, D. *leunen*, to lean; cog. with Gr. *klinō*, to make to bend, and L. *clino*, *inclino*, to bend, to *incline*.] To slope or incline from a straight or perpendicular position or line; to slant; to incline in feeling or opinion; to tend toward; to rest as for support; hence, to depend for consolation, comfort, and the like: usually with *against*, *on*, or *upon*.—*v.t.* To cause to lean; to incline; to support or rest.—**Lean-to**, lēn′tö, *a.* Having rafters pitched against or leaning on another building or a wall.

Lean, lēn, *a.* [A.Sax. *hlaene*, L.G. *leen*, lean; allied to *lean*, *v.*] Wanting flesh or fat on the body; meagre; not fat; not rich, fertile, or productive; barren of thought; jejune.—*n.* That part of flesh which consists of muscle without fat.—**Leanly**, lēn′li, *adv.* In a lean manner or condition; meagrely. — **Leanness**, lēn′nes, *n.* The condition or quality of being lean; meagreness; thinness.

Leap, lēp, *v.i.*—*leaped*, pret. & pp., rarely *leapt* (lept). [A.Sax. *hleápan*, to leap, to run, pret. *hleóp*; Sc. *loup*, D. *loopen*, to run (seen in *elope*, *interlope*); Icel. *hlaupa*, Dan. *löbe*, Goth. *hlaupan*, G. *laufen*; allied to Gr. *kraipnos*, *karpalimos*, swift.] To spring or rise from the ground with feet in the air; to move with springs or bounds; to jump, vault, bound, skip; to make a sudden transition.—*v.t.* To pass over by leaping; to spring or bound from one side to the other of; to cause (one's horse) to take a leap; to make to pass by leaping.—*n.* The act of leaping; the space passed over or cleared in leaping; a jump; a spring; a bound; a sudden transition. — **Leaper**, lēp′ėr, *n.* One who or that which leaps.—**Leap-frog**, *n.* A game in which one player, by placing his hands on the back or shoulders of another in a stooping posture, leaps over his head.—**Leapingly**, lēp′ing-li, *adv.* By leaps.—**Leap-year**, *n.* Bissextile; every fourth year, in which February has an additional day, and there are thus 366 days in all; so called because after February the days of the week *leap* an extra day as compared with other years.

Learn, lėrn, *v.t.*—*learned*, *learnt* (lėrnd, lėrnt), pret. & pp. [A.Sax. *leornian*, to learn, to teach; akin to *laeran*, to teach, *lār*, learning, lore; comp. G. *lernen*, to learn, *lehren*, to teach; D. *leeren*, Icel. *læra*, to teach, to learn; Goth. *laisjan*, to teach; allied to A.Sax. *lesan*, Icel. *lesa*, to gather.] To gain or acquire knowledge of or skill in; to acquire by study; to teach (*Shak.*). —*v.i.* To gain or receive knowledge, information, or intelligence; to receive instruction; to be taught.—**Learnable**, lėr′na-bl, *a.* Capable of being learned.—**Learned**, lėr′ned, *a.* Possessing knowledge; having a great store of information obtained by study; erudite; well acquainted; having much experience; skilful: often with *in* (*learned in* martial arts); containing or indicative of learning (a *learned* book).—**Learnedly**, lėr′ned-li, *adv.* In a learned manner.—**Learnedness**, lėr′ned-nes, *n.* The state of being learned; erudition.—**Learner**, lėr′nėr, *n.* A person who learns; one who is taught; a scholar; a pupil.—**Learning**, lėr′ning, *n.* Acquired knowledge in any branch of science or literature; knowledge acquired by the study of literary productions; erudition.

Lease, lēs, *n.* [Norm. *lees*, *leez*, a lease, L.L. *lessa*; from L. *laxare*, to loosen, relax, from *laxus*, lax. LAX.] A letting of lands, tenements, &c., to a person for a specified rent or compensation; the written contract for such letting; any tenure by grant or permission; the time for which such a tenure holds good.—*v.t.*—*leased, leasing.* To grant by lease; to let for a specified rent; to let; to occupy in terms of a lease.—**Leasable**, lēs'a-bl, *a.* Capable of being leased.—**Leasehold**, lēs'hōld, *a.* Held by lease.—*n.* A tenure by lease.—**Leaseholder**, lēs'hōl-dėr, *n.* A tenant under a lease.

Leash, lēsh, *n.* [Fr. *laisse*, O.Fr. *lesse*, a leash, from L.L. *laxa*, a loose cord, from L. *laxus*, loose. LAX.] A thong or line by which a dog (or two or three dogs) is held in in hunting; a line holding in a hawk; three creatures of any kind, especially greyhounds, foxes, bucks, and hares; hence, three things in general.—*v.t.* To hold or fasten by a leash.

Leasing, lē'zing, *n.* [A.Sax. *leásung*, from *leásian*, to lie, from *leás*, false; allied to *lose, loose, loss.*] Falsehood; lies.

Least, lēst, *a.* [A.Sax. *lǽst, lǽsast*, superl. of *lǽssa*, less.] Smallest; little beyond others, either in size, degree, value, worth, importance, or the like.—*adv.* In the smallest or lowest degree.—*At least, at the least*, to say no more; at the lowest degree; on the lowest estimate.—**Leastways**, **Leastwise**, lēst'wāz, lēst'wīz, *adv.* At least; however. (*Vulgar.*)

Leather, leᴛʜ'ėr, *n.* [A.Sax. *lether* = L.G. *ledder, lier*, Icel. *lethr*, Dan. *læder, lær*, G. and D. *leder*; root unknown.] The skin of animals dressed and prepared for use by tanning, tawing, or other processes; tanned hide.—*a.* Consisting of leather.—*v.t.* To furnish with leather; to beat as with a thong of leather. (*Vulgar*)—**Leatherneck**, *n.* A marine, from the stock once worn around the neck.—**Leatherette**, leᴛʜ-ėr-et', *n.* A kind of imitation leather.—**Leathery**, leᴛʜ'ėr-i, *a.* Pertaining to or resembling leather; tough.

Leave, lēv, *n.* [A.Sax. *leáf, geleáf*, leave, permission; same as the *-lieve* in *believe*; akin D. *-lof* in *oorlof*, permission; Icel. *leyfi*, permission, *lof*, praise, permission; G. (*er*)*lauben*, to permit; allied also to E. *love, lief*; L. *libet*, it is pleasing.] Liberty granted to act; permission; allowance; a formal parting of friends or acquaintances; farewell: used chiefly in the phrase to *take leave*. ∴ *Leave* is usually employed on familiar or unimportant occasions; *liberty* in relation to more important matters.—*Ticket of leave*, permitting absence.—**Leave-taking**, *n.* The act of taking leave; a bidding good-bye.

Leave, lēv, *v.t.*—*left* (pret. & pp.), *leaving.* [A.Sax. *laefan*, to leave, to cause to remain, from *lifian*, to remain; Icel. *leifa*, O.Fris. *leva*, O.H.G. *bi-lîban*, Mod.G. *b-leiben*, to remain; same stem as *live.*] To suffer to remain; not to take or remove; to have remaining at death; to commit or trust to, as a deposit; to bequeath; to give by will; to withdraw or depart from; to forsake, desert, abandon; to relinquish, resign, renounce; to refer; to commit for decision; to let remain without further discussion.—*To be left to one's self*, to be left alone; to be permitted to follow one's own opinions or desires.—*To leave off*, to desist from; to forbear; to cease wearing or practising.—*To leave out*, to omit.—*v.i.* To set out; to take one's departure; to desist.—*To leave off*, to cease; to desist; to stop.

Leaven, lev'n, *n.* [Fr. *levain*, from *lever*, L. *levare*, to raise; akin *levity, lever, relieve*, &c.] A substance that produces fermentation, as in dough, yeast, barm; what resembles leaven in its effects; tincture, mixture.—*The old leaven*, unregenerate man.—*v.t.* To mix with leaven; to impregnate or imbue.

Lebensraum, lā'bens-roum, *n.* [G. *leben*, life, living, and *raum*, space.] A term used by Germans to indicate area in Europe which they consider vital to their national existence.

Lecher, lech'ėr, *n.* [O.Fr. *lechcor*, gourmand, parasite, libertine; Fr. *lécher*, to lick; from G. *lecken*, O.H.G. *leccôn*, to lick. LICK, LICKERISH.] A man given to lewdness.—*v.i.* To practise lewdness.—**Lecherous**, lech'ėr-us, *a.* Addicted to lewdness; prone to indulge lust; lustful; lewd.—**Lecherously**, lech'ėr-us-li, *adv.* In a lecherous manner.—**Lecherousness**, lech'ėr-us-nes, *n.*—**Lechery**, lech'ėr-i, *n.* [O.Fr. *lecherie.*] Lewdness; free indulgence or practice of lust.

Lecithin, les'ith-in, *n.* [Gr. *lekithos*, egg-yolk.] A complex fatty compound containing nitrogen and phosphates, and widely distributed through the animal body.

Lectern, lek'tėrn, *n.* [O.Fr. *lectrin*; L.L. *lectrinum*, from *lectrum*, pulpit, Gr. *lektron*, a couch.] A desk or stand on which the larger books used in the services of the Roman Catholic and other churches are placed; in Scotland, the precentor's desk in front of the pulpit.

Lection, lek'shon, *n.* [L. *lectio*, from *lego*, to read. LECTURE.] The act of reading; a difference or variety in copies of a manuscript or book; a reading; a lesson or portion of Scripture read in divine service.—**Lectionary**, lek'shon-a-ri, *n.* A book containing portions of Scripture to be read for particular days.—**Lector**, lek'tėr, *n.* [L.] A person in the Church of Rome whose office it is to read the lessons in church.

Lecture, lek'tūr, *n.* [Fr. *lecture*, from L. *lectura*, a reading, from *lego*, to read, whence also *legend, lesson, legible*, &c. LEGEND.] A discourse on some subject read or delivered before an audience; a formal or methodical discourse intended for instruction; a reprimand, as from a superior; a formal reproof.—*v.t.*—*lectured, lecturing.* To give a lecture to; to speak to dogmatically or authoritatively; to reprimand; to reprove.—*v.i.* To read or deliver a formal discourse; to deliver lectures for instruction.—**Lecturer**, lek'tū-rėr, *n.* One who lectures; a professor or instructor who delivers formal discourses to students.—**Lectureship**, lek'tūr-ship, *n.* The office of a lecturer.

Led, led, pret. & pp. of *lead.*—**Led-horse**, *n.* A horse that is led; a spare horse led by a groom or servant, to be used in a case of emergency.

Ledge, lej, *n.* [From stem of *lie*; comp. Sc. *leggin*, Icel. *lögg*, the ledge or rim at the bottom of a cask.] A shelf on which articles may be placed; anything which resembles such a shelf; a part rising or projecting beyond the rest; a ridge or shelf of rocks; *arch.* a small moulding; also, a string course; *joinery*, a piece against which something rests.—**Ledgy**, lej'i, *a.* Abounding in ledges.

Ledger, lej'ėr, *n.* [Perhaps lit. a book that rests on a *ledge* or shelf; in any case from the same stem; comp. old *leger, ledger*, resting in a place; D. *legger*, one that lies; akin *lie* (to rest).] The principal book of accounts among merchants and others, so arranged as to exhibit on one side all the sum at the debit of the accounts and on the other all those at the credit; *arch.* a flat slab of stone, such as is laid horizontally over a grave; the covering-slab of an altar-tomb.—**Ledger-line**, *n.* *Mus.* a short line added above or below the staff for the reception of a note too high or too low to be placed on the staff.

Lee, lē, *n.* [Icel. *hlé*, Dan. *læ*; D. *lij*, G. *lee*, lee; akin A.Sax. *hleó*, a shade, a shelter, Goth. *hlija*, a tent.] The quarter toward which the wind blows, as opposed to that from which it proceeds; the shelter caused by an object interposed, and keeping off the wind: almost exclusively a nautical term.—*Under the lee of*, on that side of which is sheltered from the wind; protected from the wind by; opposed to on the *weather* side of.—*a.* *Naut.* of or pertaining to the part or side towards which the wind blows; opposite to *weather.*—*Lee-shore*, the shore under the lee of a ship, or that toward which the wind blows.—*Lee-tide*, a tide running in the same direction as the wind is blowing.—**Lee-board**, *n.* A long flat piece of wood attached to each side of a flat-bottomed vessel (as a Dutch galiot), intended to prevent her from drifting fast to leeward.—**Lee-gage**, *n.* *Naut.* a greater distance from the point whence the wind blows than another vessel has.—**Leeward**, lē'wėrd or lū'wėrd, *a.* Pertaining to the part towards which the wind blows.—*n.* The quarter or direction towards the lee.—**Leeway**, lē'wā, *n.* The drifting of a ship to the leeward of her course; the deviation from her true course which a vessel makes by drifting to leeward.—*To make up leeway*, to make up for lost time; to overtake work which has fallen behind.

Lee, lē, *n.* Dregs or sediment. LEES.

Leech, lēch, *n.* [A.Sax. *laece*, a physician; Goth. *leikeis*, Icel. *læknari*, Sw. *läkare*, a physician; Sw. *läka*, Dan. *læge*, Icel. *lækna*, A.Sax. *lǽcnian*, to heal: the animal is so called from its use in healing.] A physician; a doctor; the common name of several blood-sucking wormlike animals, some of which are used in medicine.—*v.t.* To treat with medicaments; to heal; to bleed by the use of leeches.—**Leech-craft**, *n.* The art of healing.

Leech, lēch, *n.* [L.G. *leik*, Icel. *lík*, Sw. *lik*, Dan. *lig*, leech-line, bolt-rope.] *Naut.* the border or edge of a sail which is sloping or perpendicular.

Leech, lēch, *v.t.* LETCH.

Leek, lēk, *n.* [A.Sax. *leác*, an herb, a leek = L.G. and D. *look*, Icel. *laukr*, Sw. *lök*, Dan. *løg*, G. *lauch*, Rus. *luk*; this gives the term. in *garlic, hemlock.*] A well-known culinary vegetable with a bulbous root; the national badge of the Welsh.—*To eat the leek*, to be compelled to withdraw one's statements; to have to retract one's words. See Shakespeare's *Henry V*, act v.)

Leer, lēr, *n.* [A.Sax. *hleór*, O.E. *lere, lire*, O.Sax. *hlear*, Icel. *hlýr*, face, cheek.] A side glance expressive of malignity, amorousness, or some unworthy feeling; an arch or affected glance or cast of countenance.—*v.i.* To cast a look expressive of contempt, malignity, or amorousness; to cast a sly or amorous look.—*v.t.* To allure with a leer.—**Leeringly**, lē'ring-li, *adv.* In a leering manner.

Lees, lēz, *n. pl.* [Fr. *lie*, Walloon *lizi*, L.L. *liæ*; origin unknown.] The grosser parts of any liquor which have settled on the bottom of a vessel; dregs; sediment.

Leet, lēt, *n.* [Icel. *leiti*, a share or part.] In Scotland, a list of candidates for any office.

Leeward, Leeway. Under LEE.

Left, left, pret. & pp. of *leave.*—**Left-off**, *a.* Laid aside; no longer worn (*left-off* clothes).

Left, left, *a.* [A.Sax. *left*, worthless; O.E. *lift, luft*, O.D. *lucht, luft*, left; probably allied to A.Sax. *lef*, O.Sax. *lef*, weak, infirm.] Denoting the part opposed to the *right* of the body; belonging to the side next which the heart is situated (the *left* hand, arm, or side); in a political sense, a party or individuals opposed to conservatism; espousing progressive and advanced liberal policies and legislation.—*The left bank of a river*, that which would be on the left hand of a person whose face is turned down stream.—*n.* The side opposite to the right; that part which is on the left side.—**Left-handed**, *a.* Having the left hand more capable of being used than the right; using the left hand with more facility than the right; turned towards the left hand.—*Left-handed marriage.* MORGANATIC.—**Left-handedness**, *n.* The state or quality of being left-handed.—**Leftward**, left'wėrd, *adv.* Towards the left; on the left hand or side.

Leg, leg, *n.* [A Scandinavian word: Icel. *leggr*, a leg, hollow bone, stem or trunk; Dan. *læg*, Sw. *lägg*, the calf or shin.] The limb of an animal, used in supporting the body and in walking and running; in a narrower sense, that part of the limb from the knee to the foot; a long slender support, as the *leg* of a chair or table; one of the sides of a triangle as opposed to the base; the part of a stocking or other article of dress that covers the leg; *cricket*, the part of the field that lies to the left and behind the batsman as he faces the bowler; the fielder who acts in that part of the field; a blackleg (*slang*).—*To put one's best leg foremost*, to do one's utmost endeavour.—*To have not a leg to stand on*, to have exhausted all one's strength or resources.—*On one's legs*, standing, especially to speak. —**Legged**, legd, *a.* Having legs: used in composition (bandy-*legged*, two-*legged*). —**Legging**, leg'ing, *n.* A covering for the leg, usually worn over the trousers and reaching to the knees; a long gaiter.—**Leggy**, leg'i, *a.* Long-legged; having legs of a length disproportionate to the rest of the body.—**Legless**, leg'les, *a.* Having no legs.

Legacy, leg'a-si, *n.* [From L. *legatum*, a legacy, from *lego*, to bequeath, to appoint. LEGATE.] A bequest; a particular thing or certain sum of money given by last will or testament; anything handed down by an ancestor or predecessor. — **Legacy-hunter**, *n.* One who flatters and courts for legacies.

Legal, lē'gal, *a.* [Fr. *légal*, from L. *legalis*, from *lex*, *legis*, law (also in *alloy*, *legitimate*, *legislator*, &c.); akin to *legare*, to delegate (as in *legate*); root same as in E. *lay*, *lie*. *Loyal* is the same word.] According to law; in conformity with law; permitted by law; pertaining to law; created by law.—**Legalism**, lē'gal-izm, *n.* Strict adherence to law; a legal doctrine; inclination to the doctrine of works as opposed to grace.—**Legalist**, lē'gal-ist, *n.* A stickler for adherence to law.—**Legality, Legalness**, le-gal'i-ti, lē'gal-nes, *n.* The state or quality of being legal.—**Legalization**, lē'gal-iz-ā"shon, *n.* The act of legalizing. —**Legalize**, lē'gal-īz, *v.t.*—*legalized*, *legalizing*. To make legal or lawful; to render conformable to law.—**Legally**, lē'gal-li, *adv.* In a legal manner; by permission of or in conformity with law.

Legate, leg'āt, *n.* [L. *legatus*, from *lego*, to send, to delegate. LEGAL.] An ambassador; especially, the pope's ambassador to a foreign prince or state. — **Legateship**, leg'āt-ship, *n.* The office of a legate.—**Legatine**, leg'a-tin, *a.* Pertaining to a legate; made by or proceeding from a legate. — **Legation**, lē-gā'shon, *n.* [L. *legatio*.] A person or persons sent as envoys or ambassadors to a foreign court; an embassy; a diplomatic minister and his suite; a district ruled by a papal legate.

Legatee, leg-ā-tē', *n.* [From L. *legatum*, a legacy. LEGACY.] One to whom a legacy is bequeathed.

Legato, le-gä'tō. [It., tied, from L. *ligare*, to tie.] *Mus.* played or sung in an even, smooth, gliding manner.

Legend, lē'jend or lej'end, *n.* [Fr. *légende*, from L. *legenda*, lit. things to be read, from *lego*, to read; originally applied to lives of the saints that had to be read as a religious duty. *Lego*, to read, originally to gather, appears in a great many English words, as in *lecture*, *lesson*, *coil*, *cull*, *collect*, *intellect*, *neglect*, *diligent*, *elegant*, &c.] A story generally of a marvellous character told respecting a saint; hence, any marvellous story handed down from early times; a tradition; a non-historical narrative; an inscription; *numismatics*, the words arranged circularly on a medal or coin, as distinguished from the inscription, which is across it.—**Legendary**, lej'en-da-ri, *a.* Consisting of legends; like a legend; fabulous.

Legerdemain, lej'ėr-dē-mān", *n.* [Fr. *léger de main*, light of hand—*léger*, L.L. *leviarius*, from L. *levis*, light (whence *levity*), and *main*, L. *manus*, hand.] Sleight of hand; a deceptive performance which depends on dexterity of hand; trickery or deception generally.—**Legerdemainist**, lej'ėr-dē-mān"ist, *n.* One who practises legerdemain; a juggler.

Leger-line, lej'ėr-līn. Same as *Ledger-line*.

Leghorn, leg'horn, *n.* A kind of straw plait for bonnets and hats imported from Leghorn; a hat made of that material. A Mediterranean breed of domesticated fowl.

Legible, lej'i-bl, *a.* [L. *legibilis*, from *lego*, to read. LEGEND.] Capable of being read; consisting of letters or figures that may be distinguished by the eye. — **Legibility, Legibleness**, lej-i-bil'i-ti, lej'i-bl-nes, *n.* The quality of being legible.—**Legibly**, lej'i-bli, *adv.* In a legible manner.

Legion, lē'jon, *n.* [L. *legio*, from *lego*, to collect. LEGEND.] A body of ancient Roman infantry consisting at different periods of from 3000 to above 6000, often with a complement of cavalry; hence, a body of troops in general; a great number. —*Legion of honor*, an order instituted in France by Napoleon I, as a reward for merit, both civil and military, now greatly altered in character.—*American Legion*, veterans of the World War, organized Nov. 8, 1919, in the interests of fellowship, world peace, justice, freedom, democracy. Has state and national bodies.—*v.t.* To enroll or form into a legion.—**Legionary**, lē'jon-a-ri, *a.* Belonging to a legion or legions.—*n.* One of a legion; a Roman soldier belonging to a legion.

Legislate, lej'is-lāt, *v.i.*—*legislated*, *legislating*. [L. *lex*, *legis*, law, and *fero*, *latum*, to give, pass, or enact. LEGAL.] To make or enact a law or laws.—**Legislation**, lej-is-lā'shon, *n.* The act of legislating or enacting laws; laws when enacted.—**Legislative**, lej'is-lā-tiv, *a.* Enacting laws; having power or authority to enact laws; pertaining to the enacting of laws.—*n.* The branch of government which makes and repeals laws.—**Legislatively**, lej'is-lā-tiv-li, *adv.* In a legislative manner.—**Legislator**, lej'is-lā-tėr, *n.* A law-giver; one who frames or establishes the laws and polity of a state or kingdom; a member of a national or supreme legislative assembly. —**Legislature**, lej'is-lā-tūr, *n.* The body of men in a state or kingdom invested with power to make and repeal laws; the supreme legislating power of a state.—**Legist**, lē'jist, *n.* One skilled in the laws.

Legitimate, lē-jit'i-māt, *a.* [L.L. *legitimatus*, from *legitimare*, to legitimate, from L. *legitimus*, lawful, from *lex*, law. LEGAL.] Lawfully begotten or born; born in wedlock; genuine; not false or spurious; following by logical or natural sequence; allowable (a *legitimate* argument or influence); rightful; *politics*, according to law or established usage; in a narrower sense, according to the doctrine of divine right.—*Legitimate drama*, drama or plays performed on the stage, as opposed to motion picture, vaudeville, or radio performances.—*v.t.*—*legitimated*, *legitimating*. To make lawful (*Mil.*); to render legitimate. — **Legitimately**, lē-jit'i-māt-li, *adv.* In a legitimate manner.—**Legitimacy, Legitimateness**, lē-jit'i-ma-si, lē-jit'i-māt-nes, *n.* The state or quality of being legitimate. —**Legitimation**, lē-jit'i-mā"shon, *n.* The act of making or rendering legitimate.—**Legitimatize**, lē-jit'i-ma-tīz, *v.t.* To make legitimate. — **Legitimism**, lē-jit'im-izm, *n.* The principles of the legitimists. — **Legitimist, Legitimatist**, lē-jit'i-mist, lē-jit'i-ma-tist, *n.* One who supports legitimate authority; one who believes in the sacredness of hereditary monarchies or the doctrine of divine right.—**Legitimize**, lē-jit'i-mīz, *v.t.*—*legitimized*, *legitimizing*. To legitimate.

Legume, leg'ūm, *n.* [L. *legumen*, pulse—said to be from *lego*, to gather, because gathered and not cut. LEGEND.] *Bot.* a seed-vessel of two valves, like the pod of a pea, in which the seeds are fixed to the ventral suture only; *pl.* the fruit of leguminous plants of the pea kind; pulse.—**Legumin**, leg'ū-min, *n.* A nitrogenous substance obtained from peas; vegetable casein.—**Leguminous**, le-gū'mi-nus, *a.* *bot.*, bearing legumes.

Lei, lā'ē, *n.*, pl. **leis**, lā'ēz [Hawaiian]. A garland headdress of leaves and flowers.

Leiotrichous, lī-ot'ri-kus, *a.* [Gr. *leios*, smooth, and *thrix*, *trichos*, hair.] Of or belonging to the smooth-haired races, one of the two great divisions into which Huxley has classified man. ULOTRICHOUS.

Leipoa, lī-pō'a, *n.* [Native word.] One of the megapodes or mound birds of Australia.

Leister, lēs'tėr, *n.* [Icel. *ljóstr*, Sw. *ljustra*, a leister.] A pronged and barbed instrument for striking and taking fish; a salmon-spear. (Scotch.)

Leisure, lē'zhūr or lezh'ūr, *n.* [O.E. *leisere*, *leiser*, &c., Fr. *loisir*, from O.Fr. *leisir*, *loisir* (infin.), from L. *licere*, to be allowed, to be lawful; comp. *pleasure*, which is similarly formed. Akin *license*.] Freedom from occupation or business; vacant time; time free from employment; time which may be appropriated to any specific object. —*At leisure*, free from occupation; not engaged.—*At one's leisure*, at one's ease or convenience. — *a.* Not used or spent in labour or business; vacant: said of time.—**Leisured**, lē'zhūrd or lezh'ūrd, *a.* Having leisure or much unoccupied time. —**Leisurely**, lē'zhūr-li or lezh'ūr-li, *adv.* Not in haste or hurry; slowly; at leisure.—*a.* Done at leisure; not hasty; deliberate.

Leman, lē'man, *n.* [From *lief*, A.Sax. *leóf*, dear, and *man*. LIEF.] An old term for a sweetheart of either sex; a gallant or a mistress: often in a bad sense.

Lemma, lem'ma, *n.* [Gr. *lēmma*, from *lambanō*, to receive.] *Math.* a preliminary or preparatory proposition laid down and demonstrated for the purpose of facilitating something more important that follows.

Lemming, lem'ing, *n.* [Dan.] A rodent mammal found in Norway, Lapland, Siberia, &c., vast hordes of which periodically migrate towards the sea, destroying all vegetation in their path.

Lemnian, lem'ni-an, *a.* Pertaining to *Lemnos*, an island in the Egean Sea.—*Lemnian earth*, a kind of astringent medicinal earth, of a fatty consistence and reddish colour, used in the same cases as bole.

Lemon, lem'on, *n.* [Sp. *limon*, It. *limone*, Ar. *laymun*, Hind. *limu*, *limbu*.] A fruit resembling the orange, but having a much more acid pulp, and furnishing a cooling acid juice, which forms an ingredient in certain beverages; the tree that produces lemons.—*a.* Belonging to or impregnated with lemon.—**Lemonade**, lem-on-ād', *n.* [Fr. *limonade*; Sp. *limonada*.] A liquor consisting of lemon juice mixed with water and sweetened; an aerated drink flavoured with the juice or essence of lemons.—**Lemon-grass**, *a.* A name of several grasses yielding a fragrant oil. — **Lemon-kali**, *n.* Effervescent drink of tartaric acid, bicarbonate of soda, with water.—**Lemon-peel**, *n.* The rind of a lemon; the rind dried, preserved, and candied by cooks and confectioners. — **Lemon-squash**, *n.* Lemon juice and soda water.—**Lemon-yellow**, *n.* A beautiful, vivid, light yellow colour.

Lemur, lē'mėr, *n.* [L., a spectre; so called from its nocturnal habits and stealthy step.] A name of certain quadrumanous mammals inhabiting Madagascar, the East Indian Islands, &c., allied to the monkeys, insectivores, and rodents. — **Lemures**, lem'ū-rez, *n.* [L.] The ghosts or spirits of the dead, regarded as mischievous.—**Lemurine**, lem'ū-rin, *a.* Pertaining to or resembling the lemurs.—**Lemuroid**, lem'ū-roid, *a.* Resembling the lemurs; belonging to the family or group of the lemurs.

Lend, lend, *v.t.*—pret. & pp. *lent*. [A.Sax. *laenan*, to lend, from *laen*, a loan (from *lîhan* = G. *leihen*, to lend); the *d* has erroneously attached itself to the word; comp. D. *leenen*, Dan. *laane*, Icel. *lána*, to lend. LOAN.] To grant to another for temporary use; to furnish on condition of the thing or its equivalent in kind being returned; to afford, grant, or furnish in general (assistance, an ear to a discourse, &c.); *refl.* to accommodate; to give up so as to be of assistance (he *lent himself* to the scheme).—*To lend a hand*, to assist. — **Lendable**, len'da-ble, *a.* Capable of being lent.—**Lender**, len'dėr, *n.* One who lends.

Length, length, *n.* [A.Sax. *length*, from *lang*, long; comp. *strength*, from *strong*. LONG.] The longest measure of any object, in distinction from *depth*, *thickness*, *breadth*, or *width;* extent from end to end; one of the three dimensions of space; distance to a place; a portion of space considered as measured longwise; some definite long measure (to cut a rope into *lengths*); long continuance; duration of any extent in time; detail or amplification in language; extent, degree, height, as in conduct or action (to go to great *lengths*); extent of progress; one of the three fundamental conceptions (corresponding to space) represented by a fundamental unit. United States and British scientific unit, the foot; French, the centimeter.—*At length,* at or in the fullest extent; with amplitude of detail; at last; after a long period; at the end or conclusion.—**Lengthen**, leng'thn, *v.t.* To make long or longer; to extend in length (often followed by *out*).—*v.i.* To grow longer.—**Lengthily**, leng'thi-li, *adv.* In a lengthy manner.—**Lengthiness**, leng'thi-nes, *n.* The state of being lengthy.—**Lengthwise**, length-wīz, *adv.* In the direction of the length; in a longitudinal direction.—**Lengthy**, leng'thi, *a.* Long or moderately long; protracted, as a *lengthy* discourse.

Lenient, lē'ni-ent, *a.* [L. *leniens*, from *lenio*, to soften, from *lenis*, soft, mild; akin *lentus*, slow (in *relent*).] Softening‡; mitigating‡; acting without rigour or severity; gentle; merciful; clement.—**Leniently**, lē'ni-ent-li, *adv.* In a lenient manner.—**Lenience, Leniency**, lē'ni-ens, lē'ni-en-si, *n.* The quality of being lenient; clemency.—**Lenitive**, len'i-tiv, *a.* Having the quality of softening or mitigating, as pain; assuasive; emollient.—*n.* A medicine or application of this kind.—**Lenity**, len'i-ti, *n.* [L. *lenitas.*] Gentleness; clemency; tenderness; mercy.

Leno, lē'nō, *n.* A kind of cotton gauze used for window curtains, &c.

Lens, lenz, *n.* pl. **Lenses**, len'zez. [L. *lens*, a lentil—a convex lens somewhat resembles a lentil seed.] A transparent substance, usually glass, so formed that rays of light passing through it are made to change their direction, and thus cause objects to appear magnified or diminished in size; one of the glasses of a telescope, microscope, &c. Lenses are double-convex, or convex on both sides; double-concave, or concave on both sides; plano-convex, that is, with one side plane and the other convex, &c.—*Crystalline lens.* Under CRYSTAL.

Lent, lent, pret. and pp. of *lend.*

Lent, lent, *n.* [A.Sax. *lencten*, spring, *lencten-fæsten*, spring fast, Lent; D. *lente*, G. *lenz*, spring; perhaps connected with *long*, the days becoming longer in spring.] A fast of forty days, beginning at Ash-Wednesday and continuing till Easter, observed in the Christian Church in commemoration of the forty days' fast of Christ.—**Lenten**, len'ten, *a.* Pertaining to Lent; as meagre as the fasting diet of Lent; hence, spare; plain (*lenten* fare).

Lenticel, Lenticelle, len'ti-sel, *n.* [Fr. *lenticelle*, L. *lenticula*, dim. of *lens, lentis*, a lentil. LENS.] *Bot.* one of the small oval spots found on the surface of young stems; a small lens-shaped gland on the under side of some leaves.—**Lenticellate**, len'-ti-sel-āt, *a.* Pertaining to or having lenticels.—**Lenticular**, len-tik'ū-lėr, *a.* [L. *lenticularis.*] Resembling a lentil in size or form; having the form of a double-convex lens.—**Lenticularly**, len-tik'ū-lėr-li, *adv.* In a lenticular form; like a lens.—**Lentiform, Lentoid**, len'ti-form, len'toid, *a.* Of the form of a lens; lenticular.

Lentigo, len-tī'gō, *n.* [L. *lentigo*, a freckle, from L. *lens, lentis*, a lentil.] *Med.* a freckly eruption on the skin.—**Lentiginose**, len-tij'i-nōs, *a.* *Bot.* covered with minute dots as if dusted.—**Lentiginous**, len-tij'i-nus, *a.* Pertaining to lentigo; freckly; scurfy.

Lentil, len'til, *n.* [Fr. *lentille*, from L. *lens, lentil*, a lentil. LENS.] An annual pea-like leguminous plant cultivated in Egypt and Palestine from remote antiquity, having seeds used in soups, &c., and forming a very nutritious diet.

Lento, len'tō. [It., from L. *lentus*, slow.] *Mus.* a direction that the music is to be performed slowly.

Lentor, len'tor, *n.* [L.] Slowness; sluggishness.

L'envoi, L'envoy, len'voi, *n.* [Fr. ENVOY.] A sort of postscript appended to literary compositions.

Leo, lē'ō, *n.* [L., a lion.] The Lion, the fifth sign of the zodiac.—**Leonides**, lē-on'i-dēz, *n. pl.* A name for the group of meteors observed annually in November, which seem to radiate from the constellation *Leo.*—**Leonine**, lē'o-nīn, *a.* [L. *leoninus.*] Belonging to a lion; resembling a lion or partaking of his qualities.—**Leoninely**, lē'o-nīn-li, *adv.* In a leonine manner; like a lion.

Leonine, lē'o-nīn, *a.* [From *Leon* or *Leoninus*, an ecclesiastic of the twelfth century, who wrote largely in this measure.] A term applied to a certain Latin measure popular in the middle ages, consisting of hexameter and pentameter verses, rhyming at the middle and end.

Leopard, lep'ärd, *n.* [L. *leo*, lion, and *pardus*, a panther.] A carnivorous animal of the cat genus, inhabiting Africa, Persia, China, and India, of a yellowish-fawn colour variegated with dark spots.

Leper, lep'ėr, *n.* [Originally meant the disease, being from Fr. *lepre*, L. *lepra*, from Gr. *lepra*, leprosy, from *lepros*, scaly, connected with *lepos*, a husk.] A person affected with *leprosy.*—**Leperous**, lep'ėr-us, *a.* Leprous. (*Shak.*)—**Leprosy**, lep'ro-si, *n.* A disease which prevailed during the middle ages, and is still met with in various parts of the world, characterized by dusky red or livid tubercles on the face, ears, and extremities, thickened or rugose state of the skin, &c.—**Leprosity, Leprousness**, lē-pros'i-ti, lep'rus-nes, *n.* The state of being leprous.—**Leprous**, lep'rus, *a.* Infected with leprosy.—**Leprously**, lep'rus-li, *adv.* In a leprous manner.

Lepidodendron, lep'i-dō-den"dron, *n.* [Gr. *lepis, lepidos*, a scale, *dendron*, a tree.] A genus of fossil plants common in the coal formation, many of which are large trees having characters resembling those of the conifers and club-mosses.

Lepidoganoid, lep'i-dō-gan"oid, *n.* and *a.* [Gr. *lepis, lepidos*, a scale, *ganos*, splendour, *eidos*, resemblance.] A term applied to a sub-order of ganoid fishes, covered with ganoid scales, and not plates.

Lepidoid, lep'i-doid, *n.* and *a.* [Gr. *lepis*, a scale, and *eidos*, shape.] A term applied to fossil fishes covered with large rhomboidal bony ganoid scales.

Lepidolite, lep'i-do-līt, *n.* [Gr. *lepis, lepidos*, a scale, and *lithos*, a stone.] A mineral found in scaly masses, ordinarily of a violet or lilac colour, allied to mica.

Lepidopterous, Lepidopteral, lep-i-dop'tėr-us, lep-i-dop'tėr-al, *a.* [Gr. *lepis*, a scale, and *pteron*, a wing.] Of or belonging to the order of insects called Lepidoptera (lep-i-dop'tėr-a), comprising the butterflies and moths.

Lepidosiren, lep'i-do-sī"ren, *n.* [Gr. *lepis, lepidos*, a scale, and *seirēn*, a siren.] A fish found in Western Africa and South America, having both gills and lungs, and being thus enabled to lie packed in the mud of their native rivers during the dry season. Called also *Mud-fish.*

Lepidosis, lep-i-dō'sis, *n.* [Gr. *lepis, lepidos*, a scale.] *Med.* a growth of scales over different parts of the body.

Lepidote, lep'i-dōt, *a.* [Gr. *lepidōtos*, scaly, from *lepis*, a scale.] *Bot.* covered with scurfy scaly spots.

Lepisma, le-pis'ma, *n.* [Gr. *lepis*, a scale.] The name of certain small wingless insects covered with silvery scales and living about houses.

Leporine, lep'o-rīn, *a.* [L. *leporinus*, from *lepus, leporis*, a hare.] Pertaining to a hare; having the qualities of the hare.

Lepra, lep'ra, *n.* [L., leprosy.] *Med.* a non-contagious skin-disease, in which scales occur, generally on the limbs.—**Leprose**, lep'rōs, *a.* *Bot.* having a scurfy appearance.

Leprosy, Leprous, &c. Under LEPER.

Leptodactylous, lep-tō-dak'ti-lus, *a.* [Gr. *leptos*, slender, *daktylos*, a digit.] Having slender toes.

Leptorhine, lep'to-rīn, *a.* [Gr. *leptos*, thin, *rhis, rhinos*, nose.] Having the nasal bones thin or slender.

Lesbian, les'bi-an, *a.* [Gr. Island of Lesbos.] Addicted to the unnatural vice attributed to Sappho.

Lese-majesty, lēz'maj-es-ti, *n.* LEZE-MAJESTY.

Lesion, lē'zhon, *n.* [L. *læsio*, from *lædo*, to hurt; seen also in *collide, elide.*] *Med.* derangement; injury; a morbid change in the texture or substance of organs.

Less, les, *a.* serving as the comparative of *little.* [A.Sax. *læs, læssa*; O.Fris. *lessa*; allied to Goth. *lasiws*, weak, Icel. *lasinn*, feeble; the superl. *least.* *Little* is from a different root. Hence *lest.*] Smaller; not so large or great.—*adv.* In a smaller or lower degree.—*n.* Not so much; a quantity not so great as another quantity; what is below a certain standard.—*No less*, nothing of inferior consequence or moment; nothing else.—**Lessen**, les'n, *v.t.* To make less or smaller; to diminish; to reduce; to reduce in dignity; to depreciate; to disparage.—*v.i.* To become less or smaller; to decrease or diminish.—**Lesser**, les'ėr, *a.* [A double compar. from *less.*] Less; smaller; especially common with the definite article, and where there is opposition to *greater*: not used in comparisons with *than.*—*adv.* Less. (*Shak.*)

Lessee, les-sē', *n.* [LEASE.] The person to whom a lease is given.—**Lessor**, les-sor', *n.* One who leases or lets to a tenant for a term of years.

Lesson, les'n, *n.* [Fr. *leçon*, from L. *lectio, lectionis*, from L. *lego, lectum*, to read. LEGEND.] Anything read or recited to a teacher by a pupil or learner; what is assigned by a preceptor to a pupil to be learned at one time; something to be learned; piece of instruction conveyed; what is learned or may be learned from experience; a portion of Scripture read in divine service; a doctrine or notion inculcated; a precept; a reproof or rebuke.

Lessor. Under LESSEE.

Lest, lest, *conj.* [O.E. *leste*, for *les the*, shortened from A.Sax. *thý, læs the*, the less that, lest—*thý*, by that (= *the* in *the* more, &c.), *læs* = *less*, *the*, indeclinable relative.] For fear that; in case; that . . . not.

Let, let, *v.t.*—*let* (pret. & pp.), *letting.* [A. Sax. *laetan, lētan* = D. *laten*, Icel. *láta*, Goth. *letan*, G. *lassen*; allied to E. *late*, and L. *lassus*, weary.] To permit; to allow; to suffer; to give leave; not to prevent; to lease; to grant possession and use of for a compensation.—In such phrases as *let us* go, *let* often expresses merely a suggestion for mutual action, in *let him* go, &c., it often has the force of a command. (When *let* governs an infinitive the latter never takes *to.*)—*To let alone*, to leave untouched; to suffer to remain without intermeddling.—*To let be*, to suffer to be as at present; to let alone.—*To let blood*, to open a vein and suffer the blood to flow.—*To let down*, to permit to sink or fall; to lower.—*To let drive* or *let fly*, to send forth or discharge with violence, as an arrow, stone, &c.—*To let go*, to allow or suffer to go; to relax hold of anything.—*To let in* or *into*, to permit or suffer to enter; to admit; to place in as an insertion.—*To let loose*, to free from restraint; to permit to wander at large.—*To let off*, to allow to escape; to release, as from a penalty or an engagement; to discharge, as an arrow; to fire, as a gun.—*To let out*, to allow to issue; to suffer to escape; to extend; to lease or let on hire.—*To let slip*, to let go from one's hold; to let loose; to lose (an opportunity) by negligence.—*To let well alone*, to forbear trying to improve what is already satisfactory.—*v.i.* To yield a certain rent by being hired out; to be taken on hire.—*To let in*, to leak; to admit water.

Let, let, *v.t.*—*letted, letting.* [A.Sax. *lettan*, from *læt*, late=D. *letten*, Icel. *letja*; comp. *hinder*, from *hind.* LATE.] To hinder; to impede; to interpose obstructions to.—*n.* A hindrance; obstacle; impediment.

Letch, lech, *v.t.* [A.Sax. *leccan*, to wet, to moisten; akin *leak.*] To wash, as wood ashes, by causing water to pass through them, and thus to separate from them the alkali.—*v.i.* To pass through by percolation.—**Letch-tub**, *n.* A wooden vessel or tub in which ashes are letched.—**Letchy**, lech'i, *a.* Allowing water to percolate.

Lethal, lē'thal, *a.* [L. *lethalis, letalis*, mortal, from *letum*, death.] Deadly; mortal; fatal.—**Lethality**, lē-thal'i-ti, *n.* Mortality.

Lethargy, leth'är-ji, *n.* [L. *lethargia*, from Gr. *lēthargia*, oblivion, *lēthargos*, forgetful, from *lēthē*, oblivion.] Unnatural sleepiness; morbid drowsiness; profound sleep, from which a person can scarcely be awaked; dulness; inaction; inattention.—**Lethargic, Lethargical**, le-thär'jik, le-thär'ji-kal, *a.* Affected with lethargy; morbidly inclined to sleep; dull; heavy; pertaining to lethargy.—**Lethargically**, le-thär'ji-kal-li, *adv.* In a lethargic manner.—**Lethargize**, leth'är-jīz, *v.t.* To render lethargic.

Lethe, lē'thē, *n.* [Gr. *lēthē*, forgetfulness; akin L. *lateo*, to lie hid.] *Greek myth.* the river of oblivion; one of the streams of the infernal regions; hence, oblivion; a draught of oblivion.—**Lethean**, lē-thē'an, *a.* Pertaining to the river Lethe; inducing forgetfulness or oblivion.

Lett, let, *n.* A member of a race inhabiting the Baltic provinces of Russia.—**Lettish, Lettic**, let'ish, let'ik, *a.* Pertaining to the Letts.—*n.* The language spoken by the Letts, one of the Aryan tongues.

Letter, let'ėr, *n.* [Fr. *lettre*, from L. *litera*, a letter, from *lino, litum*, to besmear; same root as *liquid.*] A mark or character used as the representative of a sound; a character standing for a vowel or a consonant; a written or printed message; an epistle; *printing*, a single type or character; also types collectively; *pl.* learning; erudition (a man of *letters*).—*The letter*, neither more nor less than what words literally express; the literal or verbal meaning.—*Letter of credit.* Under CREDIT.—*Letter of Marque.* Under MARQUE.—*Letters patent*, in Britain, a writing proceeding from the crown, by which power and authority are granted to a person to do some act or enjoy some right.—*Letter-perfect*, of actors or others perfect in their parts.—*v.t.* To impress or form letters on (to *letter* a book).—**Letter-box**, *n.* A box for receiving letters; a post-office box.—**Letter-carrier**, *n.* A man who carries about and delivers letters; a postman.—**Lettered**, let'ėrd, *a.* Versed in literature or science; belonging to learning; marked or designated with letters.—**Letter file**, *n.* A file in which letters or copies of letters sent, are filed.—**Lettering**, let'ėr-ing, *n.* The act of impressing letters; the letters impressed.—**Letter-paper**, *n.* Paper for writing letters on.—**Letter-press**, *n.* Words impressed by types; print; a copying-press.—*a.* Consisting of, relating to, or employed in, type-printing.—**Letter-writer**, *n.* One who writes letters; a book giving instruction in writing letters.

Lettish, Lettic, *a.* and *n.* Under LETT.

Lettre-de-cachet, let-r-de-ka-shā. Under CACHET.

Lettuce, let'is, *n.* [From L. *lactuca*, a lettuce; from *lac, lactis*, milk (as in *lacteal*).] The popular name of several species of annual composite plants, the leaves of some of which are used as salads.

Leucine, Leucin, lū'sin, *n.* [Gr. *leukos*, white.] A white pulverulent substance obtained by treating muscular fiber with sulphuric acid, and afterwards with alcohol.—**Leucite**, lū'sīt, *n.* A mineral, so called from its whiteness, found among volcanic products at Vesuvius.—**Leucitic**, lū-sit'ik, *a.* Pertaining to leucite.

Leucocyte, lūk'ō-sīt, *n.* [Gr. *leukos*, white, *kytos*, a cell.] A white or colorless blood corpuscle.—**Leucocytosis**, lūk'ō-sīt-ō"-sis, *n.* [Gr. *leukos, kytos.*] An increase in the number of leucocytes in the blood, esp. as in certain pathologic conditions: fevers, anemia, &c.—**Leukemia**, lū-kē'mia, *n.* [Gr. *leukos*, white, *kytos*, a cell, and *haima*, blood.] *Med.* A fatal disease in which there is a pronounced increase in the number of leucocytes, attended by progressive anemia and complications.

Leucoma, lū-kō'ma, *n.* [Gr. *leukōma*, from *leukos*, white.] A white opacity of the cornea of the eye, the result of acute inflammation.

Leucopathy, lū-kop'a-thi, *n.* [Gr. *leukos*, white, and *pathos*, affection.] The condition of an albino; albinism.

Leucophlegmacy, lū-kō-fleg'ma-si, *n.* [Gr. *leukophlegmatia*—*leukos*, white, and *phlegma*, phlegm.] A tendency to a dropsical state, with paleness and flabbiness.—**Leucophlegmatic**, lū'kō-fleg-mat"ik, *a.* Pertaining to leucophlegmacy.

Leucorrhœa, lū-ko-rē'a, *n.* [Gr. *leukos*, and *rheō*, to flow.] *Med.* a morbid discharge of a white or yellowish mucus from the female genital organs; the whites.

Leucosis, lū-kō'sis, *n.* [Gr. *leukōsis*, from *leukos*, white.] Same as *Leucopathy.*

Levant, lē-vant', *n.* [It. *levante*, the east, the direction of sunrise, from L. *levare*, to raise, *se levare*, to rise. LEVITY.] The eastern portion of the Mediterranean and its seaboard or the contiguous countries, as Syria, Asia Minor, Egypt, &c.—**Levanter**, lē-van'tėr, *n.* A wind in the Mediterranean from the direction of the Levant.—**Levantine**, lē-van'tīn or lev'an-tīn, *a.* Pertaining to the Levant; designating a particular kind of silk cloth.—*n.* A native of the Levant; a vessel of the Levant; a particular kind of silk cloth.

Levant, lē-vant', *v.i.* [Sp. *levantar*, to raise, to remove; *levantar la casa*, to break up house—from L. *levare*, to raise. See above.] To run away; to decamp; to run away without paying debts.—**Levanter**, lē-van'tėr, *n.* One who levants.

Levator, lē-vā'tėr, *n.* [L., what raises, from *levo*, to raise.] *Anat.* a name applied to many muscles, such as raise the lips, eyelids, &c.; a surgical instrument used to raise a depressed part of the skull.

Levee, lev'ē, *n.* [Fr. *lever*, a rising, a levee or reception; *levée*, a levy, an embankment, from *lever*, L. *levare*, to raise, from *levis*, light. LEVITY.] A morning reception of visitors held by a prince or great personage; any similar assemblage; in America, an embankment on the margin of a river, to confine it within its natural channel.

Level, lev'el, *n.* [O.Fr. *level, livel* (now *niveau*), from L. *libella*, dim. of *libra*, a level, a balance; akin *deliberate, equilibrium.*] An instrument by which to find or draw a straight line parallel to the plane of the horizon; a line or surface which coincides with the plane of the horizon; a surface without inequalities; usual elevation; customary height; equal elevation with something else; a state of equality; natural position; position to which anything is entitled; *mining*, a horizontal gallery in a mine.—*a.* Horizontal; coinciding with the plane of the horizon, or parallel to it; not having one part higher than another; even; flat; on the same line or plane; equal in rank or degree; having no degree of superiority.—*v.t.*—*levelled, levelling.* To make level; to remove inequalities of surface in; to lay flat on the ground; to reduce to equality of condition, state, or degree; to point, in taking aim; to aim; to direct or point at.—*To level up*, to raise to the level of anything higher; to raise to a higher status.—*To level down*, to lower to the same level or status.—*v.i.* To accord, agree, or suit†; to point a gun or the like to the mark; to aim.—**Leveler**, lev'el-ėr, *n.* One who levels; one who would destroy social distinctions and reduce all men to equality.—**Leveling**, lev'el-ing, *n.* The act of one who levels; the art or operation of ascertaining the different elevations of objects on the surface of the earth, as in surveying.—**Leveling-pole, Leveling-rod, Leveling-staff**, *n.* An instrument used in leveling in conjunction with a spirit-level and telescope.—**Levelly**, lev'el-li, *adv.* In a level manner; evenly—**Levelness**, lev'el-nes, *n.* The condition of being level; evenness.

Lever, lē'vėr, *n.* [Fr. *levier*, from *lever*, L. *levare*, to raise. LEVITY.] A bar of metal, wood, or other substance turning on a support called the fulcrum or prop, and used to overcome a certain resistance (called the weight), encountered at one part of the bar, by means of a force (called the power) applied at another part; a watch having a vibrating lever to connect the action of the escape-wheel with that of the balance.—**Leverage**, lē'vėr-āj, *n.* The action of a lever; lever power; the mechanical advantage or power gained by using a lever.—**Lever-valve**, *n.* A safety-valve kept down by the pressure of a spring or an adjustable weight.

Leveret, lev'ėr-et, *n.* [Fr. *levrette*, dim. of O.Fr. *levre* (now *lièvre*), a hare, from L. *lepus, leporis*, a hare.] A hare in the first year of its age.

Leverock, lev'ėr-ok, *n.* A lark.

Leviable. Under LEVY.

Leviathan, lē-vī'a-than, *n.* [Heb. *livyāthān*, a term which etymologically seems to mean a long jointed monster.] An aquatic animal described in the book of Job, ch. xli; a fabulous sea-monster of immense size.

Levigate, lev'i-gāt, *v.t.*—*levigated, levigating.* [L. *lævigo*, from *lævis*, smooth.] To make smooth; to polish; to rub or grind to a fine impalpable powder, especially with the use of a liquid.—**Levigable**, lev'i-ga-bl, *a.* Capable of being levigated.—**Levigation**, lev-i-gā'shon, *n.* The operation of grinding or rubbing a solid substance to a fine impalpable powder.

Levin, lev'in, *n.* [O.E. *levene, levening*, connected with *light*, and Prov.E. *lowe*, Icel. *log*, flame.] Lightning. (*Poet.*)

Levirate, Leviratical, lev'i-rāt, lev-i-rat'i-kal, *a.* [L. *levir*, a husband's brother; akin Gr. *daēr.*] Pertaining to marriage with a husband's brother; applied to the Jewish law according to which a woman whose husband died without issue was to be married to the husband's brother.—**Leviration**, lev-i-rā'shon, *n.* Marriage according to the levirate law.

Levitate, lev'i-tāt, *v.t.* [L. *levitas*, lightness, from *levis*, light.] To cause to become buoyant in the atmosphere; to cause to float in the air.—**Levitation**, lev-i-tā'shon, *n.* The act of making light or buoyant; lightness; buoyancy.

Levite, lē'vīt, *n.* [From *Levi*, one of the sons of Jacob.] In *Jewish history*, one of the tribe or family of Levi; a descendant of Levi; more particularly, an inferior or subordinate priest.—**Levitic, Levitical**, lē-vit'ik, lē-vit'i-kal, *a.* Belonging to or connected with the Levites; priestly.—*Levitical degrees*, degrees of kindred within which persons are prohibited (in the book of Leviticus) to marry.—**Levitically**, lē-vit'i-kal-li, *adv.* After the manner of the Levites.—**Leviticus**, lē-vit'i-kus, *n.* A book of the Old Testament containing the ceremonial law or the laws and regulations relating to the priests and Levites and to offerings.

Levity, lev'i-ti, *n.* [L. *levitas*, from *levis*, light; akin to E. *light*, G. *leicht*, easy, slight, Gr. *elachys*, small. L. *levis* gives *lever, levy, elevate, alleviate, relieve*, &c.] Lightness; especially lightness of temper or conduct; want of seriousness; disposition to trifle; fickleness; capriciousness; volatility.

Levogyrate, lē-vō-jī'rāt, *a.* [L. *lævus*, left, *gyro*, to turn. GYRE.] Turning rays to the left in the polarization of light: said of crystals; opposite of *dextrogyrate*.

Levy, lev′i, *n.* [Fr. *levée*, from *lever*, L. *levare*, to raise. LEVITY, LEVEE.] The act of raising, collecting, or enlisting troops; the raising of taxes; that which is levied; a body of troops raised.—*v.t.*—*levied*, *levying*. To raise or enlist (troops); to collect (taxes).—*To levy war*, to raise or begin war; to raise troops for attack.—**Leviable**, lev′i-a-bl, *a.* Capable of being levied.—**Levier**, lev′i-ėr, *a.* One who levies.

Lewd, lūd, *a.* [O.E. *lewed*, A.Sax. *laewed*, lay, ignorant, pp. of *laewan*, to weaken, to betray; akin Icel. *lœ*, Goth. *lew*, craft.] Vile, despicable, profligate, or wicked (*N.T.*); given or pertaining to the unlawful indulgence of lust; lustful; libidinous; lascivious.—**Lewdly**, lūd′li, *adv.* In a lewd manner.—**Lewdness**, lūd′nes, *n.* The state or quality of being lewd; lechery; lasciviousness.

Lewis, Lewisson, lū′is, lū′is-son, *n.* An instrument of iron used in raising large stones, operating by the dove-tailing of one of its ends into the stone.

Lewis gun, lū′is gun, *n.* An automatic rifle, gas-operated and air-cooled, capable of firing forty-seven rounds without reloading.

Lexicon, lek′si-kon, *n.* [Gr. *lexicon*, from *lexis*, a speaking, speech, a word, from *legō*, to speak. LEGEND.] A dictionary; a book containing an alphabetical arrangement of the words in a language, with the definition or an explanation of the meaning of each: usually applied to dictionaries of the Greek or Hebrew tongues.—**Lexiconist**, lek′si-kon-ist, *n.* A writer of a lexicon.—**Lexical**, lek′si-kal, *a.* Pertaining to a lexicon.—**Lexically**, lek′si-kal-li, *adv.* According to lexicography or a lexicon.—**Lexicographer**, lek-si-kog′ra-fėr, *n.* The author or compiler of a lexicon or dictionary.—**Lexicographic, Lexicographical**, lek′si-kō-graf″ik, lek′si-kō-graf″i-kal, *a.* Pertaining to lexicons or lexicography.—**Lexicography**, lek-si-kog′ra-fi, *n.* The act or art of compiling a lexicon or dictionary; the occupation of composing dictionaries.—**Lexicologist**, lek-si-kol′o-jist, *n.* One skilled in lexicology.—**Lexicology**, lek-si-kol′o-ji, *n.* The science of words, their derivation and signification; that branch of learning which treats of the proper signification and just application of words.—**Lexigraphic, Lexigraphical**, lek-si-graf′ik, lek-si-graf′i-kal, *a.* Pertaining to lexigraphy.—**Lexigraphy**, lek-sig′ra-fi, *n.* The art or practice of defining words; lexicography.

Lexiphanic,† lek-si-fan′ik, *a.* [Gr. *lexis*, a word, and *phainō*, to show.] Grandiloquent; bombastic; turgid; inflated.—**Lexiphanicism**,† lek-si-fan′i-sizm, *n.* Grandiloquence; an inflated style.

Ley, lē, *n.* Same as *Lea*.

Ley, lē, *n.* Same as *Lye*.

Leyden-phial, Leyden-jar, lā′dn, *n.* [So named from having been invented at *Leyden*, Holland.] A glass phial or jar coated inside and outside, usually with tin-foil, to within a third of the top, that it may be readily charged with electricity.

Leze-majesty, lēz′maj-es-ti, *n.* [Fr. *lèse-majesté*, high treason, from L. *læsa majestas*—*lædo*, *læsum*, to injure (whence *lesion*), and *majestas*, majesty.] Any crime committed against the sovereign power in a state; treason.

Liable, lī′a-bl, *a.* [Either from the verb to *lie*, with the sense of lying open or subject to, or from Fr. *lier*, to bind, and hence akin to *ally*, *lien*. Comp. *rely* and *reliable*.] Answerable for consequences; bound to make good a loss; responsible; apt or not unlikely to incur something undesirable; subject; exposed: with *to*. ∴ *Liable* is used chiefly with regard to what may befall; *subject* to what is likely to do so, and does so customarily.—**Liability**, lī-a-bil′i-ti, *n.* The state of being liable; that for which one is liable; *pl.* sums or amount which one is under obligation to pay; debts.—*Limited Liability*.—Under LIMITED.—**Liableness**, lī′a-bl-nes, *n.* The state of being liable; liability.

Liaison, lē-ā-zoṅ, *n.* [Fr., from L. *ligatio*, a binding, from L. *ligare*, to bind. LIGAMENT.] A bond of union; an entanglement; commonly, an illicit intimacy between a man and a woman.—*Liaison officer*, an officer employed in linking up troops under different commands.

Liana, lē-ä′nä, *n.* [Fr. *liane*, from *lier*, L. *ligare*, to bind; akin *lien*. LIAISON.] A term applied to the larger climbing and twining plants in tropical forests.

Liar, lī′ėr, *n.* One who tells lies. Under LIE.

Lias, lī′as, *n.* [Fr. *liais*, O.Fr. *liois*, Arm. *liach*, Gael. *leac*, a stone.] *Geol.* that series of strata, consisting principally of thin layers of limestone embedded in thick masses of blue argillaceous clay, lying at the basis of the oolitic series, and above the triassic or new red sandstone.—**Liassic**, li-as′ik, *a.* Pertaining to or of the age of the lias formation.

Libant,† lī′bant, *a.* [L. *libans*, ppr. of *libo*, to taste. LIBATION.] Sipping; touching lightly.

Libation, lī-bā′shon, *n.* [L. *libatio*, *libationis*, from *libo*, to taste, to make libation; Gr. *leibō*; same root as *liquid*.] The act of pouring a liquid, usually wine, either on the ground or on a victim in sacrifice, in honour of some deity; a portion of wine or other liquor poured out in honour of a deity by the person who is to drink.—**Libatory**, lī′ba-to-ri, *a.* Pertaining to libation.

Libel, lī′bel, *n.* [Fr. *libelle*, L. *libellus*, a libel or lampoon, lit. a little book, dim. of *liber*, the inner bark or rind of a tree used for paper, and hence a book; akin *library*.] A defamatory writing; a malicious publication containing representations tending to bring a person into contempt, or expose him to public hatred or derision; *law*, the writ commencing a suit and containing the plaintiff's allegations.—*v.t.*—*libeled*, *libeling*. To publish a libel against; to defame by libel; to lampoon.—**Libelant**, lī′bel-ant, *n.* One who brings a libel in a court.—**Libeler**, lī′bel-ėr, *n.* One who libels; a lampooner.—**Libelous**, lī′bel-us, *a.* Containing matter of the nature of a libel; defamatory.—**Libelously**, lī′bel-us-li, *adv.* In a libelous manner.

Liber, lī′bėr, *n.* [L. LIBEL.] *Bot.* the inner lining of the bark of exogenous trees; endophlœum; bast.

Liberal, lib′ėr-al, *a.* [L. *liberalis*, from *liber*, free; akin to *libet*, *lubet*, it pleases, it is agreeable, Skr. *lubh*, to desire. L. *liber* gives also *liberate*, *liberty*, *libertine*, *livery*, *deliver*.] Befitting a freeman or one well-born (the *liberal* arts, a *liberal* education); of a free heart; bountiful; generous; giving largely; ample, large, abundant, profuse (donation, supply, &c.); not characterized by selfish, narrow, or contracted ideas or feelings; favourable to civil, political, and religious liberty; favourable to reform or progress, and in politics often opposed to *conservative*; not too literal or strict; free. It is used in various self-explanatory compounds; as, *liberal*-hearted; *liberal*-minded; *liberal*-souled.—*n.* An advocate of freedom from restraint, especially in politics and religion; a member of that party which advocates progressive reform.—*Liberal Arts*, the modern curriculum of an undergraduate academic or collegiate education, as distinguished from professional training; the languages, science, history and philosophy which are the requisites for a baccalaureate degree.—**Liberalism**, lib′ėr-al-izm, *n.* Liberal principles; the principles or practice of Liberals.—**Liberality**, lib-ėr-al′i-ti, *n.* [L. *liberalitas*; Fr. *libéralité*.] The quality of being liberal; largeness of mind or view; disposition to give largely; munificence; generosity; a particular act of generosity (in this sense with a plural).—**Liberalize**, lib′ėr-al-īz, *v.t.*—*liberalized*, *liberalizing*. To render liberal; to free from narrow views or prejudices.—**Liberally**, lib′ėr-al-li, *adv.* In a liberal manner.

Liberate, lib′ėr-āt, *v.t.*—*liberated*, *liberating*. [L. *libero*, *liberatum*, from *liber*, free. LIBERAL.] To release from restraint or bondage; to set at liberty; to free; to deliver; to disengage.—**Liberation**, lib-ėr-ā-shon, *n.* [L. *liberatio*.] The act of liberating.—**Liberationist**, *n.* One of the party advocating the disestablishment of State Churches.—**Liberator**, lib′ėr-ā-tėr, *n.* One who liberates.—**Liberatory**, lib′ėr-a-to-ri, *a.* Tending to liberate or set free.—**Liberomotor**, lib′ėr-ō-mō″tor, *a.* Letting out or liberating nerve-force.

Libertarian. Under LIBERTY.

Liberticide, lib′ėr-ti-sīd, *n.* [*Liberty*, and L. *cædo*, to kill.] Destruction of liberty; a destroyer of liberty.

Libertine, lib′ėr-tīn, *n.* [L. *libertinus*, a freedman, from *liber*, free. LIBERAL.] A freedman or manumitted slave (N.T.); one unconfined; one free from restraint (*Shak.*); one who indulges his lust without restraint; one who leads a dissolute, licentious life; a rake.—*a.* Licentious; dissolute.—**Libertinism**, lib′ėr-tin-izm, *n.* The conduct of a libertine or rake.

Liberty, lib′ėr-ti, *n.* [Fr. *liberté*, L. *libertas*, from *liber*, free. LIBERAL.] The state or condition of one who is free; exemption from restraint; power of acting as one pleases; freedom; permission granted to do something; leave; immunity enjoyed; a special privilege or exemption; a place or district within which certain exclusive privileges may be exercised; freedom of action or speech beyond the ordinary bounds of civility or decorum; freedom from occupation or engagements; state of being disengaged.—*Liberty of the press*, the free power of publishing what one pleases, subject only to punishment for publishing what is mischievous to the public or injurious to individuals.—*Cap of liberty*, a cap or hat used as a symbol of liberty; a red cap worn by French revolutionaries. ∴ Syn. under LEAVE.—**Libertarian**, lib-ėr-tā′ri-an, *a.* Pertaining to the doctrine of free-will, as opposed to the doctrine of necessity.—*n.* One who holds the doctrine of the freedom of the will.—**Libertarianism**, lib-ėr-tā′ri-an-izm, *n.* The principles or doctrines of libertarians.

Libidinous, li-bid′i-nus, *a.* [L. *libidinosus*, from *libido*, *lubido*, lust, from *libet*, *lubet*, it pleases. LIBERAL.] Characterized by lust or lewdness; having an eager appetite for sexual indulgence; fitted to excite lustful desire; lustful; lewd.—**Libidinously**, li-bid′i-nus-li, *adv.* In a libidinous manner.—**Libidinosity, Libidinousness**, li-bid′i-nos″i-ti, li-bid′i-nus-nes, *n.* The quality of being libidinous; lustfulness.—**Libidinist**, li-bid′i-nist, *n.* One who indulges in lust.

Libra, lī′bra, *n.* [L., a balance.] The Balance, the seventh sign in the zodiac, which the sun enters at the autumnal equinox in September.

Library, lī′bra-ri, *n.* [L. *librarium*, a bookcase, *libraria*, a bookseller's shop, from *liber*, a book. LIBEL.] A collection of books belonging to a private person or to a public institution, &c.; an apartment, suite of apartments, or a whole building appropriated to the keeping of a collection of books.—**Librarian**, li-brā′ri-an, *n.* The keeper of a library.—**Librarianship**, li-brā′ri-an-ship, *n.* The office of a librarian.

Librate, lī′brāt, *v.t.*—*librated*, *librating*. [L. *libro*, *libratum*, from *libra*, a balance, a level. LEVEL.] To hold in equipoise; to poise; to balance.—*v.i.* To balance; to be poised.—**Libration**, lī-brā′shon, *n.* The act of balancing; a state of equipoise; *astron.* a real or apparent motion like that of a balance before coming to rest; an apparent irregularity of the moon's motion, whereby those parts very near the border of the lunar disc alternately become visible and invisible.—**Libratory**, lī′bra-to-ri, *a.* Moving like a balance; oscillating.

Libretto, lē-bret′tō, *n.* [It., a little book. LIBEL, LIBRARY.] A book containing the words of an extended musical composition, as an opera.

Libyan, lib'yan, *a.* Of or pertaining to *Libya*, the ancient name of a large portion of North Africa, and sometimes applied to all Africa.—*n.* A group of tongues, otherwise called *Berber*.

Lice, līs, *n.* pl. of *louse*.

License, Licence, lī'sens, *n.* [Fr. *licence*, from L. *licentia*, from *licet*, it is permitted (seen also in *illicit*, *leisure*); akin to *linquo*, to leave.] Authority given to act in a particular way; power conferred upon a person by proper authority, to do particular acts, practise in professions, conduct certain trades, &c.; the document containing such authority; excess of liberty; undue freedom; freedom abused, or used in contempt of law or decorum; deviation from an artistic standard.—**License**, *v.t.*—*licensed*, *licensing*. To permit or empower by license; to grant a license to.—**Licensed**, lī'senst, *p.* and *a.* Having a license; permitted by authority.—**Licensable**, lī'sen-sa-bl, *a.* Capable of being licensed.—**Licensee**, lī-sen-sē', *n.* One to whom a license is granted.—**Licenser**, lī'sen-sėr, *n.* One who licenses.—**Licentiate**, lī'sen'shi-āt, *n.* One who has a license to practise some profession; a person licensed in medicine or theology; in Scottish church, one licensed but not ordained to a charge; a probationer; corresponding largely to the French *abbé*.—**Licentious**, lī-sen'shus, *a.* [L. *licentiosus*.] Characterized by license; overpassing due bounds; loose in behaviour; profligate; dissolute; libidinous.—**Licentiously**, lī-sen'shus-li, *adv.* In a licentious manner.—**Licentiousness**, lī-sen'shus-nes, *n.* The state of being licentious.

Lichen, lī'ken or lich'en, *n.* [Gr. *leichēn*, the plant, the disease, from *leichō*, to lick.] *Bot.* one of an order of cryptogamic plants without stem and leaves, growing on the bark of trees, on rocks, &c., and including rock-moss, tree-moss, &c.; *med.* an eruption of small pimples, of a red or white colour, clustered together or spread over the surface of the skin.—**Lichened**, lī'kend or lich'end, *a.* Covered with lichens.—**Lichenic**, lī-ken'ik, *a.* Relating to or derived from lichens.—**Licheniform**, lī-ken'i-form, *a.* Resembling a lichen.—**Lichenographic, Lichenographical**, lī'ken-ō-graf''ik, lī'ken-ō-graf''i-kal, *a.* Pertaining to lichenography.—**Lichenographist, Lichenographer**, lī-ken-og'ra-fist, lī-ken-og'ra-fėr, *n.* One versed in lichenography.—**Lichenography**, lī-ken-og'ra-fi, *n.* A botanical description of the lichens.—**Lichenology**, lī-ken-ol'o-ji, *n.* That department of botany which treats of the lichens.—**Lichenologist**, lī-ken-ol'o-jist, *n.* One versed in lichenology.—**Lichenous**, lī'ken-us or lich'en-us, *a.* Relating to or covered with lichens; pertaining to the disease called lichen.

Lich-gate, lich'gāt, *n.* [Lit. corpse-gate, from A.Sax. *lic*, Icel. *lík*, Goth. *leik*, form, body; G. *leiche*, a corpse. Akin *like*.] A church-yard gate, with a porch under which a bier might stand while the introductory part of the service was read.—**Lich-way**, *n.* The path by which the dead are carried to the grave.

Licit,† lis'it, *a.* [L. *licitus*, lawful, from *liceo*, to be permitted. LICENSE.] Lawful.—**Licitly**,† lis'it-li, *adv.* Lawfully.

Lick, lik, *v.t.* [A.Sax. *liccian*=D. *likken*, Dan. *likke*, G. *lecken*, Goth. *laigon* (in *bi-laigon*); cog. Ir. *lighim*, L. *lingo*, Gr. *leichō*, Skr. *lih*, to lick. Akin *lecher*, *lickerish*.] To pass or draw the tongue over the surface of; to lap; to take in by the tongue; to flog, beat, or conquer (*colloq.*).—*To lick up*, to devour; to consume entirely (O.T.).—*To lick the dust*, to be slain; to perish in battle; to act abjectly and servilely.—*To lick into shape*, to give form or method to, from the old notion that the young bear is born shapeless and its mother licks it into shape.—*n.* A rubbing or drawing of the tongue over anything; a slight smear or coat, as of paint; a blow or stroke (*colloq.*).—**Lick-platter, Lick-trencher**, *n.* A sneaking parasite; a lickspittle.—**Lickspittle**, lik'spit-l, *n.* A flatterer or parasite of the most abject character.

Lickerish, lik'ėr-ish, *a.* [From the stem *lick*, and akin to *lecher*, *lecherous*; comp. G. *lecker*, lickerish, dainty, delicate.] Nice in the choice of food; dainty; eager to taste or enjoy; appetizing.—**Lickerishly**, lik'ėr-ish-li, *adv.* In a lickerish manner.—**Lickerishness**, lik'ėr-ish-nes, *n.* The quality of being lickerish.

Licorice, Liquorice, lik'or-is, *n.* [Fr. *liquerice*, L.L. *liquiritia*, from Gr. *glykyrrhiza*—*glykys*, sweet, and *rhiza*, root.] A perennial plant of the bean family, the roots of which supply a sweet juice.

Lictor, lik'tor, *n.* [L., from *ligare*, to bind.] A Roman officer whose ensigns of office were an ax and fasces, and who attended the chief magistrates in public.

Lid, lid, *n.* [A.Sax. *hlid*, lid, cover, protection; D. *lid*, O.Fris. *hlid*, *lid*, G. *lied*, as in *augen-lied*, an eyelid; Icel. *hlith*, a gate, gateway, interval; allied to L. *claudo*, to shut.] A movable cover for the opening of a vessel, box, &c.; the cover of the eye; the eyelid.—**Lidless**, lid'les, *a.* Having no lid.

Lie, lī, *v.i.*—*lied*, *lying*. [A.Sax. *leógan*=D. *liegen*, Goth. *liugan*, Icel. *ljúga*, G. *lügen*, to lie; comp. Gael. *leog*, idle talk.] To utter falsehood with an intention to deceive; to knowingly utter untruth.—*n.* [A.Sax. *lige*, *lyge*, a lie, from *leógan*, to lie; Icel. *lygi*, D. *logen*, G. *lüge*, a lie.] A falsehood uttered for the purpose of deception; an intentional violation of truth.—*To give the lie to*, to charge with falsehood; to prove to be false; to belie.—**Liar**, lī'ėr, *n.* One who lies or tells lies; a person who knowingly utters falsehood; one who declares to be a fact what he knows is not.

Lie, lī, *v.i.*—pret. *lay*; pp. *lain* (*lien*, obsolete); ppr. *lying*. [A.Sax. *licgan*, to lie (of which *lecgan*, to lay, is a causative)=Goth. *ligan*, D. *liggen*, Dan. *ligge*, Icel. *liggja*, G. *liegen*, to lie; same root as L. *lectus*, Gr. *lechos*, a bed, also seen in L. *lex*, E. *law*; *ledge*, *layer*, *lair*, &c., being also akin.] To occupy a horizontal or nearly horizontal position; to rest lengthwise, or be flat upon the surface of anything; to be placed and remain without motion; to lay or place one's self in a horizontal or nearly horizontal position: often with *down*; to be in bed; to sleep or pass the night; to lean or recline; to be situated; to have place or position (Ireland *lies* west of England); to be posted or encamped, as an army; to remain or be in some condition: with words denoting the particular condition (to *lie* waste, to *lie* fallow, to *lie* open, to *lie* hid, &c.); to be present or contained; to be found; to exist; to depend (it does not *lie in* my power; success *lies* in vigilance); to weigh or press; to be sustainable in law; to be capable of being maintained (an action will not *lie*).—*To lie at one's heart*, to be an object of affection, desire, or anxiety.—*To lie by*, to rest untouched or unnoticed.—*To lie hard* or *heavy*, to press; to oppress; to burden.—*To lie in*, to be in childbed.—*To lie in the way*, to be an obstacle or impediment.—*To lie in wait*, to wait in ambush or concealment.—*To lie on* or *upon*, to be incumbent on; to be a matter of obligation or duty; to depend on.—*To lie on hand, to lie on one's hands*, to be or remain unsold or undisposed of.—*To lie over*, to remain for future attention; to be deferred to some future occasion, as a motion or resolution in a deliberative assembly.—*To lie to*, *naut.* to stop in her course and remain stationary, as a ship.—*To lie under*, to be subject to; to suffer; to be oppressed by.—*To lie with*, to lodge or sleep with; to have carnal knowledge of; to belong to (it *lies with* you to make amends. [The trans. verb *to lay* is often erroneously used for *to lie*. This is a gross blunder which should be carefully avoided, and may easily be so by attending to the meaning and conjugation of the two verbs. *To lay* is always transitive, and has for its preterit *laid*; as, he told me to *lay* it down, and I *laid* it down. Hence it is utterly wrong to say, we must know how the land *lays*; I went and *laid* down for a little.]—*n.* The relative position of one object with regard to another or to a point of the compass; general bearing or direction; position or state of an affair; *geol.* the manner in which strata are disposed.—**Lie detector**, a polygraph that simultaneously records respiration, blood pressure, pulse, and the psychogalvanic response, used in criminology to reveal attempted deception.

Lief, lēf, *adv.* [A.Sax. *leóf*, loved, beloved; D. *lief*, Icel. *ljúfr*, G. *lieb*, Goth. *liubs*, loved; akin *love*, *leave* (permission), *believe*.] Gladly; willingly; readily (used in such phrases as, I had as *lief* go as not).

Liege, lēj, *a.* [Fr. *lige*, Pr. *litje*, It. *ligio*, L.L. *ligius*, *legius*; origin uncertain; perhaps O.G. *lidic* (G. *ledig*), free.] Connected by loyalty or duty; bound by or resting on feudal ties (a *liege* lord, *liege* vassalage).—*n.* A vassal or person owing duties to his feudal lord; a lord or superior; a sovereign; a law-abiding citizen or citizen in general (in this sense usually in the *pl.*).—**Liegeman**, lēj'man, *n.* A vassal; a liege.

Lien, lī'en, obs. pp. of *lie*, now *lain*.

Lien, lī'en, *n.* [Fr. *lien*, from L. *ligamen*, from *ligo*, to bind. LIGAMENT.] *Law*, a legal claim; a right in one man to retain the property of another until some claim of the former is paid or satisfied.

Lientery, lī'en-tėr-i, *n.* [Gr. *leienteria*—*leios*, smooth, and *enteron*, an intestine.] *Med.* a species of diarrhœa, in which the food is discharged undigested.—**Lienteric**, lī-en-tėr'ik, *a.* Pertaining to a lientery.

Lier, lī'ėr, *n.* Under LIE.

Lieu, lū, *n.* [Fr., from L. *locus*, place.] Place; room; stead: preceded by *in* (to give goods *in lieu* of wages).

Lieutenant, lū-ten'ant, *n.* [Fr., composed of *lieu*, L. *locus*, place, and *tenant*, L. *tenens*, holding.] An officer, civil or military, who supplies the place of a superior in his absence; a commissioned officer in the army, ranking next below a captain; in the navy the ranking is: ensign, lieutenant junior grade, lieutenant, lieutenant commander, commander.—**Lieutenancy**, lū-ten'an-si, *n.* The office or commission of a lieutenant.—**Lieutenant-colonel**, *n.* An army officer next in rank below a colonel.—**Lieutenant-general**, *n.* An army officer next in rank below a general.—**Lieutenant-governor**, *n.* An officer ranking next below a governor.

Lieve, lēv, *a.* Same as *Lief*.

Life, līf, *n.* pl. **Lives**, līvz. [A.Sax. *līf*, Icel. *líf*, Dan. *liv*, D. *lijf*, Goth. *libains*, life. LIVE.] That state of an animal or a plant in which its organs are capable of performing their functions, or in which the performance of functions has not permanently ceased; animate existence; vitality; the time during which such a state continues; the mundane existence of a human being; the period from birth to death; period during which anything continues to exist; outward manifestation of life; a person's condition or circumstances; mode, manner, or course of living, as morally good or bad; social surroundings and characteristics (high or low *life*); that which makes alive; animating or inspiring principle; animation; vivacity; energy; the living form, or nature itself, in opposition to a copy or imitation; a living person (many *lives* were sacrificed); collectively, human beings in any number (a great loss of *life*); animated beings in the aggregate (the abundance of *life* on the globe); narrative of a person's life; a biography or memoir; human affairs; course of things in the world; happiness in the favour of God; eternal felicity.—*For life*, for the whole term of one's existence; so as to save or to strive to save one's own life (to run *for life*, to swim *for life*).—*To the life*, so as to closely resemble the living person or original; hence, exactly; perfectly (drawn *to the life*).—**Life-annuity**, *n.* A sum of money paid to a person yearly during the person's life.—**Life-assurance**, *n.* See

INSURANCE.—**Life-belt**, *n.* A belt made of pieces of cork fastened together, or of india-rubber hollow and inflated, used to support the body in the water. — **Life-blood**, *n.* The blood necessary to life; vital blood; that which is essential to existence or strength.—**Life-boat**, *n.* A boat for saving persons from drowning, constructed with great strength, and at the same time possessing sufficient buoyancy to enable it to float though loaded with men and filled with water.—**Life-buoy**, *n.* BUOY.—**Life cycle**, *n.* A series of activities including development, changes of environment, dormancy and return to original status, experienced by various organisms.—**Life-guard**, *n.* A skilled swimmer employed at a beach to save bathers from drowning.—**Life history**, An account of the activity and environment of an individual from birth to death —**Life-insurance**, *n.* INSURANCE.—**Lifeless**, lif'les, *a.* Deprived of life; dead; inanimate; inorganic; destitute of life or spirit; spiritless; dull; heavy; inactive.—**Lifelessly**, lif'les-li, *adv.* In a lifeless manner.—**Lifelessness**, lif'lesnes, *n.* The state of being lifeless.—**Lifelike**, lif'lik, *a.* Like a living person; true to the life.—**Life line**, *n* A rope projected to a foundering ship, or to a drowning person; a line by which a diver is kept in touch with the surface; a line marking the limits of shallow water on a beach. —**Lifelong**, lif'long, *a* Lasting or continuing through life —**Life-preserver**, *n.* One who or that which preserves life; a life-belt.—**Life-rate**, *n* The rate or amount for which a life is insured.—**Life-rent**, *n* A right which entitles a person to use and enjoy property during life — **Life-spring**, *n.* The spring or source of life —**Life-table**, *n.* A statistical table exhibiting the probability of life at different ages.—**Lifetime**, lif'tīm, *n* the time that life continues, duration of life.

Lift, lift, *v.t* [From O F. *lift*, A.Sax *lyft*, air, sky, comp. Icel *lypta* (pron. *lifta*), from *lopt* (pron. *loft*), air: Sw. *lyfta*, Dan *löfte*, G. *lüften*, to lift, from Sw. Dan and G. *luft*, air, atmosphere. LURE.] To bring from a lower to a higher position or place; to raise, elevate, upheave; to elevate, exalt, or improve, as in fortune, estimation, dignity, or rank, to elate: often with *up*, to take and carry away to remove by stealing (to *lift* cattle) —*To lift up the eyes*, to look, to raise the eyes in order to look —*To lift the hand*, to raise the hand for the purpose of striking to strike or threaten to strike —*To lift the hand against* to strike, to assail, to injure; to oppress —*To lift up the voice*, to cry aloud; to call out either in grief or joy —*v.i.* To raise or try to raise, to rise, or to be raised or elevated (the fog *lifts*) — *n.* The act or manner of raising or lifting; elevation; *naut* a rope from the cap and masthead to the extremity of a yard for supporting or raising it.—**Liftable**, lif'ta-bl, *a* Capable of being lifted —**Lifter**, lif'tėr, *n* One who or that which lifts, a thief (in the compound shop-*lifter*) —**Lift-bridge**, *n.* A sort of drawbridge.—**Lift-pump**, *n.* A pump in which the piston raises the water by lifting it without atmospheric pressure.

Ligament, lig'a-ment, *n.* [L. *ligamentum*, from *ligo*, to bind (whence also *ligation*, *ligature*, *lien*, *league*, *-ly* in *ally*, &c.).] What ties or unites one thing or part to another; a band; a bond; a strong flexible fastening; *anat.* a strong, compact, tendinous substance, serving to bind one bone to another — **Ligamental, Ligamentous**, lig-a-men'tal, lig-a-men'tus, *a.* Of the nature of a ligament.

Ligan, lī'gan, *n.* [Contr. for *ligamen*, a band, from *ligo*, to bind.] Goods sunk in the sea, but having something buoyant attached to mark their position.

Ligation, lī-gā'shon, *n.* [L. *ligatio*, *ligationis*. LIGAMENT.] The act of binding; a bond; a ligature —**Ligature**, lig'a-tūr, *n.* [L. *ligatura*.] Something that binds; a cord, thong, band, or bandage; a ligament; the act of binding; *mus.* a line connecting notes; *printing*, a type consisting of two or more letters or characters cast on the same body, as *fi*, *fl*; *surg.* a cord or string for tying blood-vessels to prevent hemorrhage; a thread or wire to remove tumours, &c., by strangulation.—**Ligatured**, lig'a-tūrd, *a.* Bound by a ligature.

Light, līt, *n.* [A.Sax. *leóht*, bright, shining, *leóht*, *liht*, a light; D. and G. *licht*, Icel. *ljos*, Dan. *lys*, Goth. *liuhath*; allied to L. *lux*, *lumen*, light, *luceo*, to shine, *luna*, the moon; Gr. *leukos*, white, *leussō*, to see; W. *llug*, Gael. *leus*, light. LUCID.] That agent or force by the action of which upon the organs of sight objects from which it proceeds are rendered visible; that from which this agent or force emanates, or is supposed to emanate; a radiant body, as the sun, the moon, a candle, &c.; mental or spiritual illumination; knowledge; information; a person who is conspicuous or eminent in any study; a model or example; the phenomena constituting day; hence, open view, public observation, publicity; a compartment of a window; the illuminated part of an object or picture; the point of view or position in which or from which anything is looked at or considered; aspect.—*Northern lights*, the aurora borealis. See under AURORA.—*To stand in one's own light*, to be the means of preventing one's own good, or frustrating one's own purposes.—*To bring to light*, to bring to knowledge, detection, or discovery.—*To come to light*, to be detected; to be discovered or found. —*a.* Bright; clear; not dark or obscure; white or whitish; not intense or deep, as a colour; not dark in hue.—*v.t.*—pret. & pp. *lighted*, sometimes *lit.* To set fire to; to kindle; to ignite; to set burning; to give light to; to fill or spread over with light; to show the way to by means of a light; to illuminate.—**Lightable**, lī'ta-bl, *a.* Capable of being lighted.—**Light-due**, *n.* A duty or toll levied on ships for the maintenance of lighthouses, &c.—**Lighten**, lī'tn, *v.i.* To exhibit the phenomenon of lightning; to give out flashes; to flash; to become lighter; to become less dark or gloomy; to clear.—*v.t.* To make light or clear; to dissipate darkness from; to illuminate; to enlighten; to flash forth.†—**Lighter**, lī'tėr, *n.* One who or that which lights.—**Lighthouse**, līt'hous, *n.* A tower or other lofty structure with a powerful light at top, erected as a guide or warning of danger to navigators at night; a pharos.—**Lightkeeper**, *n.* One who has charge of the lights in a lighthouse, light-ship, or the like.—**Lightless**, līt'les, *a.* Destitute of light; dark; not giving out light.—**Lightness**, līt'nes, *n.* Want of darkness or intensity; clearness. — **Lightning**, līt'ning, *n.* [From verb to *lighten*.] A flash of light the result of a discharge of atmospheric electricity.—**Lightning-conductor, Lightning-rod**, *n.* A metallic rod attached to buildings or vessels to protect them from lightning by conducting it into the earth or water.—**Light-ship**, *n.* A ship anchored and hoisting a strong light to serve as a lighthouse. — **Lightsome**, līt'sum, *a.* Bright; light; gay; cheering. — **Lightsomely**, līt'sum-li, *adv.* In a lightsome manner.—**Lightsomeness**, līt'sum-nes, *n.*

Light, līt, *a.* [A.Sax. *leóht*, D. *ligt*, G. *leicht*, Icel. *léttr*, Dan. *let*, light; allied to L. *levis* (whence *levity*), Gr. *elachys*, Skr. *laghu*, light. Hence *alight*, *lighter* (boat), *lights*.] Not heavy; having little weight; not burdensome; easy to be lifted, borne, or carried; not oppressive; easy to be suffered or endured; easy to be performed; not difficult; easy to be digested; not oppressive to the stomach; not heavily armed, or armed with light weapons; swift; nimble; not dense or gross; not strong; not copious or vehement (a *light* rain); inconsiderable; easily influenced by trifling considerations; unsteady; volatile; trifling; gay; airy; wanton; unchaste; not of legal weight (*light* coin); loose; sandy; easily pulverized (a *light* soil); having a sensation of giddiness; employed in light work (a *light* porter).—*To set light by*, to slight; to treat as of no importance.—*To make light of*, to treat as of little consequence; to slight; to disregard.—**Lighten**, lī'tn, *v.t.* To make lighter or less heavy; to relieve of a certain amount of weight; to make less burdensome or oppressive; to alleviate.—**Lighter**, lī'tėr, *n.* A large open flat-bottomed barge, often used in lightening or unloading and loading ships. — **Light-fingered**, *a.* Thievish; addicted to petty thefts: often applied to pickpockets.—**Light-footed**, *a.* Nimble in running or dancing; active. — **Light-headed**, *a.* Having dizziness or giddiness in the head; dizzy; delirious; thoughtless; heedless; weak; volatile; unsteady.—**Light-headedness**, *n.* State of being light-headed; dizziness; giddiness. — **Light-hearted**, *a.* Free from grief or anxiety; gay; cheerful; merry.—**Light-heartedness**, *n.*—**Light-horse**, *n.* Light-armed cavalry.—**Light-horseman**, *n.* A light-armed cavalry soldier.—**Light-infantry**, *n.* Infantry selected and trained for rapid evolutions. — **Lightly**, līt'li, *adv.* In a light manner; with little weight; nimbly; airily; easily; slightly; cheerfully; gaily.—**Lightness**, līt'nes, *n.* The condition or quality of being light; the opposite of heaviness; agility; briskness; levity.—**Lights**, līts, *n. pl.* The lungs. (*Colloq.*) —**Lightweight**, *n.* *Sporting*, a man weighing not more than 135 pounds.

Light, līt, *v.i.*—pret. & pp. *lighted*, sometimes *lit.* [A.Sax. *lihtan*, to descend, alight, from *leóht*, light, not heavy: to *alight* from horseback or a vehicle is to make it lighter by relieving it of weight.] To descend, as from a horse or carriage (with *down*, *off*, *from*); to fly or fall and settle; to come to rest; to fall or come by chance; to happen to find: with *on* or *upon*.

Lign-aloes, līn-al'ōz, *n.* [*Lign-* is from L. *lignum*, wood.] Aloes-wood or agallochum.

Ligneous, lig'nē-us, *a.* [L. *ligneus*, from *lignum*, wood.] Made of wood; consisting of wood; resembling wood; woody; wooden. —**Ligniferous**, lig-nif'ėr-us, *a.* Producing wood; yielding wood. — **Lignification**, lig'ni-fi-kā"shon, *n.* The act of lignifying, or the state of being lignified. — **Ligniform**, lig'ni-form, *a.* Like wood; resembling wood.—**Lignify**, lig'ni-fī, *v.t.*—*lignified*, *lignifying.* [L. *lignum*, and *facio*, to make.] To convert into wood. — *v.i.* To become wood. — **Lignin, Lignine**, lig'nin, *n.* A modification of cellulose; vegetable fibre.—**Ligniperdous**, lig-ni-pėr'dus, *a.* [L. *lignum*, and *perdo*, to destroy.] Wood-destroying: said of certain insects.—**Lignite**, lig'nīt, *n.* Fossil-wood, wood-coal, or brown coal, a combustible substance mineralized to a certain degree, but retaining distinctly its woody texture. — **Lignitic**, lig'nit-ik, *a.* Containing lignite; resembling lignite.—**Lignitiferous**, lig-ni-tif'ėr-us, *a.* *Geol.* applied to strata containing beds of lignite.—**Lignous, Lignose**, lig'nus, lig'nōs, *a.* Ligneous.—**Lignum-vitæ**, lig-num-vī'tē, *n.* [L., wood of life, from its hardness and durability.] The popular name of a small West Indian and South American tree, the wood of which is valued for its extreme hardness.

Ligroine, lig'rō-in, *n.* An oil of medium density distilled from crude petroleum.

Ligula, Ligule, lig'ū-la, lig'ūl, *n.* [L. *ligula*, a strap, from *ligo*, to bind. LIGAMENT.] *Bot.* a strap-shaped petal of composite flowers; the membrane at the base of a grass leaf.—**Ligulate, Ligulated**, lig'ū-lāt, lig'ū-lā-ted, *a.* Like a bandage or strap; *bot.* having the form of a ligula: applied especially to the ray florets of composite flowers.

Ligure, lī'gūr, *n.* [Gr. *linggourion*, *ligurion*.] A kind of precious stone (O.T.)

Ligurite, lig'ū-rīt, *n.* [From *Liguria*.] A kind of gem of an apple-green colour, occasionally speckled.

Like, līk, *a.* [A.Sax. *lic*, *gelic* = D. *lijk*, *gelijk*, Icel. *likr*, *glikr*, G. *gleich*, Goth. *leiks*, *galeiks*, like. From A.Sax. *lic*, form, body (see LICHGATE). Hence the termination in *each*, *such*, *which*, and the *-ly* of adjectives and adverbs, as also the verb *to like*.] Equal; exactly corresponding; of the same kind; similar; resembling (*like* passions); probable; likely (it is *like* he will); feeling equal or disposed to.—*Had like*, was like; had nearly; came little short of. *Like* is frequently suffixed to nouns to form adjectives denoting resemblance, as child*like*, &c.—*n.* Some person or thing resembling another; an exact counterpart.—*adv.* In the same or a similar manner; similarly; likely; probably. — **Likelihood**, līk'li-hụd, *n.* Likeliness; probability.—**Likeliness**, līk'li-nes, *n.* The condition or quality of being likely.—**Likely**, līk'li, *a.* Like the truth; credible; probable (a *likely* story); giving a probability of something (I am *likely* to be from home to-morrow); suitable, well adapted, or convenient for some purpose.—*adv.* Probably; as may be expected or reasonably thought. — **Like-minded**, *a.* Having a like disposition or purpose.—**Liken**, lī'kn, *v.t.* To make like; to cause to resemble; to compare; to represent as resembling.—**Likeness**, līk'nes, *n.* The condition or quality of being like; similarity; what exactly resembles something else; especially, a portrait.—**Likewise**, līk'wīz, *conj.* and *adv.* In like manner; also; moreover; too.

Like, līk, *v.t.*—*liked, liking.* [A.Sax. *lícian, gelícian*, to please, to suit, lit. to be *like* one's tastes: originally impersonal; D. *lijken*, to suit; Icel. *líka*, to please, to like; from the adjective (which see).] To please or suit: used impersonally‡; to be pleased with in a moderate degree; to approve; to take satisfaction in; to enjoy.—*v.i.* To be pleased; to choose. — *n.* A liking; a fancy: used chiefly in the phrase *likes and dislikes*.—**Likeable**, līk'a-bl, *a.* Such as to attract liking; lovable.—**Likeableness**, līk'a-bl-nes, *n.* Quality of being likeable.—**Liking**, līk'ing, *n.* Inclination; desire; satisfaction: often with *for* or *to* (an amusement to your *liking*).

Lilac, lī'lak, *n.* [Sp. *lilac*, Ar. *līlak*, lilac; Per. *līlaj*; from a word meaning blue.] A beautiful flowering shrub with flowers generally bluish or lavender, originally a native of Persia.

Lilliputian, lil-i-pū'shan, *n.* A member of the diminutive race of beings described in Swift's imaginary kingdom of *Lilliput* in *Gulliver's Travels*; a person of very small size.—*a.* Very small; pigmean.

Lillypilly, *n.* [Native Australian.] An Australian tree of the myrtle family, with white flowers.

Lilt, lilt, *v.t.* and *i.* [Akin to *lull.*] To sing, especially in a cheerful manner; to give musical or harmonious utterance. (*Tenn.*)—*n.* A song; a tune.

Lily, lil'i, *n.* [A.Sax. *lilie*, from L. *lilium*, Gr. *leirion.*] The popular name of many bulbous plants with showy and fragrant flowers, as the white lily, orange-lily, tiger-lily, scarlet lily, &c.—*Lily of the valley*, a perennial plant with small white bell-shaped flowers.—**Liliaceous**, lil-i-ā'shus, *a.* Pertaining to the order of lilies; lily-like.—**Lily-encrinite**, *n.* Same as *Encrinite.* — **Lily-faced**, *a.* Pale-faced. — **Lily-handed**, *a.* Having white delicate hands.—**Lily-hyacinth**, *n.* A bulbous plant with blue flowers, a kind of squill.—**Lily-livered**, *a.* White-livered; cowardly. (*Shak.*)—**Lily-white**, *a.* White as a lily.

Limaceous, lī-mā'shus, *a.* [L. *limax, limacis*, a slug, a snail.] Of or pertaining to the slugs or garden snails without shells.

Limb, lim, *n.* [A.Sax. *lim*, Icel. *limr*, Dan. and Sw. *lem*, a limb. The *b* is added as in crum*b*, thum*b*, &c.] One of the jointed members of the human body or of any animal; an arm or leg, more especially the latter; a pretty large or main branch of a tree.—*v.t.* To supply with limbs; to dismember; to tear the limbs from.—**Limbed**, limd, *a.* Having limbs: mostly in composition (large-*limbed*, short-*limbed*).

Limb, lim, *n.* [L. *limbus*, a border, edging, or fringe.] *Astron.* the border or outermost edge of the sun or moon; the graduated edge of a circle or other astronomical or surveying instrument, &c.; *bot.* the border or upper spreading part of a monopetalous corolla, or of a petal or sepal.—**Limbate**, lim'bāt, *a.* *Bot.* bordered, as when one colour is surrounded by an edging of another.

Limber, lim'bėr, *a.* [Closely allied to *limp*, pliant, flaccid.] Easily bent; flexible; pliant.—*v.t.* To render limber or pliant.—**Limberness**, lim'bėr-nes, *n.* The quality of being limber.

Limber, lim'bėr, *n.* [Really a plural form from Icel. *limar*, limbs, branches of a tree; akin to *limb.*] *Artill.* a carriage on two wheels with the ammunition boxes and shafts for the horses, attached to the gun-carriage, properly so called, of a field gun or cannon; *pl.* thills; shafts of a carriage (*local*).—*v.t.* To attach the limber to.

Limbo, lim'bō, *n.* [It., from L. *limbus*, a hem or edge.] A supposed region where souls of the innocent are detained till the final judgment; any similar region apart from this world; a prison or other place of confinement (*colloq.*).

Limburger, lim'bėrg-ėr, *n.* A soft cheese with a characteristic odor.

Lime, līm, *n.* [A.Sax. *lím*, glue, cement = D. *lijm*, Icel. *lím*, G. *leim*, glue; allied to *loam*, L. *limus*, slime, Skr. *li*, to be viscous.] A viscous substance for catching birds; bird-lime; calcium oxide, prepared by heating limestone or shells; quicklime, as used in mortar, in industry, and to counteract acidity in soil.—*v.t.*—*limed, liming.* To smear with bird-lime; to entangle; to ensnare; to manure with lime; to cement or glue (*Shak.*).—**Limekiln**, līm'kil, *n.* A kiln in which limestone is exposed to a strong heat and reduced to lime.—**Limelight**, *n.* A powerful light produced by an oxyhydrogen flame on a piece of lime; on the stage, a spotlight; *fig.* center of public interest.—**Limestone**, līm'stōn, *n.* A kind of stone consisting of varieties of carbonate of lime.—**Limewash**, *n.* A coating given with limewater; whitewash.—**Limewater**, *n.* A water solution of calcium hydroxide, used in medicine as an antacid, and in the chemical industry; natural water containing calcium carbonate or calcium sulphate.—**Limy**, lī'mi, *a.*

Lime, līm, *n.* [Formerly *line*, from A.Sax. *lind*, D. and G. *linde*, Dan. Sw. Icel. *lind*, the tree.] The linden tree.

Lime, līm, *n.* [Fr. *lime*, from Per. *limû, limûn*, whence also *lemon.*] A species of tree cultivated in southern Europe, the U. S., &c., and producing a small, yellow fruit used for flavoring punch, sherbet, &c.—**Lime juice**, *n.* The juice of the lime, used as a specific against scurvy, and in the mixing of drinks.

Limerick, lim'rik, *n.* A jingling verse form of five lines, with lines 1, 2, and 5 rhyming, as do lines 3 and 4, popularized by Edward Lear (1812-88) in his *Book of Nonsense*, 1846.

Liminal, lim'in-al, *a.* [L. *limen*, threshold.] Belonging to the lowest limit (or threshold) of perception.

Limit, lim'it, *n.* [Fr. *limite*, from L. *limes, limitis*, a bound or limit; allied to *limen*, a threshold; akin *lintel, eliminate.*] That which terminates, circumscribes, or confines; bound, border, utmost extent; *math.* a determinate quantity to which a variable one continually approaches, but can never exceed.—*v.t.* To set limits or bounds to; to bound; to confine within certain bounds; to circumscribe; to restrain; to narrow or confine the signification of; to apply exclusively (words or conceptions).—**Limitable**, lim'i-ta-bl, *a.* Capable of being limited.—**Limitarian**, lim-i-tā'ri-an, *n.* One that holds that a part of the human race only are to be saved.—**Limitary**, lim'i-ta-ri, *a.* Circumscribed or bounded in power or authority.—**Limitation**, lim-i-tā'shon, *n.* The act of limiting, bounding, or circumscribing; the condition of being so limited; that which limits; limiting circumstance; restriction; qualification.—**Limitations**, *n.* The period of limit, fixed by statute, beyond which no action at law can be brought against a person or estate.—**Limited**, lim'i-ted, *p.* and *a.* Confined within limits; narrow; circumscribed.—*Limited liability*, such liability as that of a company whose partners or shareholders are liable only for the amount of the shares subscribed.—*Limited monarchy*, a monarchy in which the monarch shares the supreme power with a class of nobles, with a popular body, or with both.—**Limitedly**, lim'i-ted-li, *adv.* In a limited manner or degree.—**Limitedness**, lim'i-ted-nes, *n.*—**Limiter**, lim'i-tėr, *n.* One who limits.—**Limitless**, lim'it-les, *a.* Having no limits; unbounded; boundless; infinite.

Limn, lim, *v.t.* [Fr. *enluminer*, from L. *illumino*, to illuminate.] To draw or paint; to make a portrait or likeness of.—**Limner**, lim'nėr, *n.* One who limns; a painter of portraits or miniatures.

Limnophilous, lim-nof'i-lus, *a.* [Gr. *limnē*, like, *phileō*, to love.] Loving, or living in, pools and marshes.

Limonene, li'mō-nēn, *n.* [Fr. *limon*, a lemon.] A hydrocarbon in oil of lemon.

Limonite, lī'mon-īt, *n.* [Gr. *leimōn*, meadow.] An important ore of iron, a variety of which is brown hematite.

Limousine, lim'o-zēn", *n.* [From *Limousin*, an old French province.] A closed automobile with the driver partitioned off from the passengers.

Limp, limp, *v.i.* [A.Sax. *limp-halt, lemphealt*, limping-halt, lame; comp. L.G. *lumpen*, to limp; Icel. *limpa*, weakness; allied to *limp, limber*, and probably to *lame.*] To halt or walk lamely.—*n.* The act of limping; a halt in one's gait; the Jacobite toast, with a limping motion, from the initial letters of Louis XIV, James, Mary (of Modena, wife of James II), Prince (the old Pretender).—**Limpingly**, lim'ping-li, *adv.* In a limping or halting manner.

Limp, limp, *a.* [Akin to *limp*, the verb, and to *limber*; comp. Skr. *lamb*, to hang.] Easily bent; flexible; pliant; lacking stiffness; flaccid.

Limpet, lim'pet, *n.* [O.Fr. *limpine*, a limpet; comp. Gr. *lepas, lepados*, a limpet.] A univalve mollusc with a conical shell, found adhering to rocks.

Limpid, lim'pid, *a.* [L. *limpidus*; allied to Gr. *lampō*, to shine, hence akin to *lamp.*] Characterized by clearness or transparency; clear and bright; translucent; transparent: said of water.—**Limpidity, Limpidness**, lim-pid'i-ti, lim'pid-nes, *n.* The state of being limpid.

Limy, *a.* Under Lime.

Linage, līn'ij, *n.* The number of printed lines on a page; measure of space sold for advertising; alignment.

Linch-pin, linsh, *n.* [Lit. axle-pin, from A.Sax. *lynis*, an axle-tree; D. *luns, lens*, G. *lünse*, a linch-pin.] A pin used to prevent the wheel of a carriage or other vehicle from sliding off the axle-tree; an axle-pin.

Lincture, lingk'tūr, *n.* [L. *lingo, linctum*, to lick.] A medicine to be taken by licking.

Linden, lin'den, *n.* [An adj. form from A.Sax. Icel. Sw. and Dan. *lind*, D. and G. *linde*, the linden. Lime, the tree.] The lime tree; the basswood tree.

Line, līn, *n.* [A.Sax. *line*, a cord or line, from L. *linea*, a linen thread, a string, a line or stroke, from *lineus*, flaxen, *linum*, flax; Fr. *ligne*, a line. Linen.] A small rope or cord; a thread-like marking, as with a pen, pencil, &c.; a stroke or score; a marking or furrow upon the hands or face; a mark traced or imagined to show latitude, longitude, temperature, or the like on a map or the globe: *the line* being specifically the equator; a row of things; a straight row of soldiers drawn up with an extended front; a similar disposition of ships in preparation for an engagement; a straight row of words or figures between two margins (a page of thirty *lines*); the words which form a certain number of poetical feet; a verse; an outline, contour, lineament (a statue of fine *lines*); a short epistle; course of thought, conduct, occupation, policy, or the like; a continuous or connected series, as of descendants from a common progenitor; a series of public conveyances, as buses, steamships, airplanes, &c., passing between places with regularity; a railroad *line*, a rail transportation system between points; a *line* of track; *fort.* (*pl.*) works made to cover extended positions; as a measure, the twelfth part of an inch.—*Line engraving, photoengraving*, an engraving, usually on zinc, without a screen (*line cut*). —*Line of defense, mil.* fortifications or trenches used as protective barriers; the standing army.—*Line drive*, in baseball, a low-hit ball which approximately parallels the ground the greater part of its course.—*Equinoctial line*, the equator; the equinoctial.—*Isoclinal, isodynamic, isogonic lines*. See the adjectives.—*Meridian line*, a line drawn at any station to show the directions of true north and south.—*Fraunhofer's lines*, the dark lines observed crossing a spectrum at right angles to its length.—**Streamline**, *n.* The design of form which permits passage through the air or water with a minimum of resistance, as in the shape of an airplane or boat.—*v.t.*—*lined, lining*. To draw lines upon; to mark with lines or thread-like strokes.—**Liner**, lī'nėr, *n.* One of a line of ocean-going ships.—**Lineman**, *n.* A repair man who works on electric light, power, telephone or telegraph lines; in football, one who plays forward; in surveying, one who handles the line.—**Linesman**, *n.* A referee in football or tennis.—**Line-up**, *n.* Arrangement of players in football or baseball; schedule of the positions of players.

Line, lin, *v.t.*—*lined, lining*. [O.E. *line*, to double a garment with *linen*.] To cover on the inside; to protect by a layer on the inside (to *line* a garment).—**Lining**, līn'-ing, *n.* The covering of the inner surface of anything, as a coat *lining*; a substance forming an inside and strengthening layer.

Lineage, lin'ē-āj, *n.* [Fr. *lignage*, from *ligne*, L. *linea*, a line. LINE.] Descendants in a line from a common progenitor; line of descent from an ancestor; race; progeny. —**Lineal**, lin'ē-al, *a.* [L. *linealis*.] Composed of lines; in a direct line from an ancestor; hereditary; pertaining to or ascertained by a line or lines (*lineal* measure).—**Lineally**, lin'ē-al-li, *adv.* In a lineal manner; in a direct line of descent.—**Lineament**, lin'ē-a-ment, *n.* [L. *lineamentum*.] The outline or contour of a body or figure, particularly of the face; a line of form or feature.—**Linear**, lin'ē-ėr, *a.* [L. *linearis*.] Pertaining to a line; consisting of lines; lineal; in *bot.* like a line in form; long and slender.—*Linear perspective*, that which regards only the positions, magnitudes, and forms of the objects delineated.—**Linearly**, lin'ē-ėr-li, *adv.* In a linear manner.—**Lineate, Lineated, Lineolate**, lin'ē-āt, lin'ē-ā-ted, lin'ē-ō-lāt, *a. Bot.* marked longitudinally with depressed parallel lines.

Linen, lin'en, *n.* [Properly an adj. signifying made of flax, from A.Sax. *lin*, flax, L. *linum*, Gr. *linon*, flax; comp. Armor. *lin*, W. *llin*, flax.] Cloth made of flax; a flaxen fabric or material; underclothing in general, because chiefly made of linen or similar materials.—*a.* Made of flax, or yarn from flax.—**Linen-draper**, *n.* A person who sells linen goods by retail.

Ling, ling, *n.* [D. *ling*; Dan. and N. *lange*; G. *leng, langfisch*, so named from being *long*.] A fish of the cod family, rather long in proportion to its thickness, found in the North Atlantic Ocean, and when salted and dried, is used as food.

Ling, ling, *n.* [Icel. and Dan. *lyng*, heather.] Common heather.

Lingam, ling'gam, *n.* [Skr.] A conventional symbol of the male organ of generation, held sacred among the Hindus.

Linger, ling'gėr, *v.i.* [From. A.Sax. *lengra*, compar. of *lang*, long; comp. the verb *lower*, from compar. of *low*.] To delay; to loiter; to lag or hang behind; to be slow to move or act; to hesitate; to remain long (the disease *lingers*).—*v.t.* To spend in a wearisome manner: with *out* or *away*.—**Lingerer**, ling'gėr-ėr, *n.* One who lingers.—**Lingering**, *p.* and *a.* Remaining or continuing long; protracted (a *lingering* disease).

Lingerie, län'zhe-rē, *n.* [Fr.] Linen articles, especially women's underwear. Now used for feminine intimate apparel.

Lingo, ling'gō, *n.* [L. *lingua*, the tongue.] Language; speech; a contemptuous term for language one does not understand. (*Vulgar.*)

Lingua Franca. A compound or mongrel language in the Levant, made up of words from French, Italian, Spanish, and modern Greek, serving as a common medium of communication.

Lingual, ling'gwal, *a.* [L. *lingua*, the tongue, originally *dingua*; cog. with E. *tongue* (comp. L. *lacrima*, E. *tear*).] Pertaining to the tongue; pronounced chiefly by means of the tongue.—*n.* A letter pronounced chiefly by means of the tongue, as *l, r*.—**Linguadental**, ling-gwa-den'tal, *a.* [L. *lingua*, tongue, and *dens*, a tooth.] Uttered by the joint use of the tongue and teeth, as the letters *d* and *t*.—*n.* A sound so uttered.—**Linguiform**, ling'gwi-form, *n.* Having the form or shape of a tongue.—**Linguist**, ling'gwist, *n.* A person skilled in languages; one who knows several languages.—**Linguister**,† ling'gwis-tėr, *n.* A dabbler in linguistics.—**Linguistic**, ling-gwis'tik, *a.* Relating to language or to the affinities of language; philological. — **Linguistics**, ling'gwis'tiks, *n.* The science of language, or of the origin, significations, affinities, and application of words; comparative philology.—**Lingula**, ling'gū-la, *n.* [Lit. little tongue, from the shape of the valves.] A remarkable genus of brachiopodous molluscs found fossil in the early Silurian period and still living.—**Lingulate**, ling'gū-lāt, *a.* Shaped like the tongue or a strap; ligulate.

Linhay, lin'hā, *n.* [Possibly from *lin*, to lean, and A.S. *haga*, enclosure.] A kind of open shed, forming part of farm buildings.

Liniment, lin'i-ment, *n.* [L. *linimentum*, from *lino*, to anoint (*letter, literature*, being from same stem).] *Med.* a species of soft ointment, of a stimulating or soothing character, to be rubbed into the skin.

Lining, *n.* Under LINE.

Link, lingk, *n.* [A.Sax. *hlence*, Sw. *länk*, Dan. *lœnke*, Icel. *hlekkr*, a link; G. *gelenk*, a joint, a link (from *lenken*, to bend).] A single ring or division of a chain; anything doubled and closed like a link; something that serves to connect one thing or part with another; any constituent part of a connected series; *land-measuring*, a division of Gunter's chain, having a length of 7.92 inches; *mach.* any straight rod connecting two rotating pieces by flexible joints.—*v.t.* To connect by, or as if by, a link or links; to unite or join.—*v.i.* To be joined or connected: with *together* or *in*. — **Link-motion**, *n.* Motion communicated by links, applied especially to a system of gearing for working the valves of a locomotive-engine.

Link, lingk, *n.* [Origin uncertain; perhaps equivalent to *lint*, the first part of *linstock*.] A torch made of tow or other materials, with tar or pitch. — **Link-boy, Linkman**, *n.* A boy or man that carries a link to light passengers.

Links, lingks, *n. pl.* [A.Sax. *hlinc*, rising ground; same root as L. *clivus*, sloping. DECLINE.] A stretch of flat or slightly undulating ground on the sea-shore lying uncultivated. (*Scotch.*) A golf course.

Linnaean, Linnean, lin-nē'an, *a.* Pertaining to Linnæus, the celebrated botanist.

Linnet, lin'et, *n.* [A.Sax. *linet*; Fr. *linot, linotte*, from L. *linum*, flax.] One of the commonest of Old World singing birds, frequenting open places.

Linoleum, li-nō'lē-um, *n.* [L. *linum*, flax, and *oleum*, oil.] A preparation of linseed-oil with chloride of sulphur, which when mixed with ground cork and pressed upon canvas forms floor-cloth; the floor-cloth thus produced.

Linotype, *n.* [A 'line o' type'.] In printing, a machine for setting and casting lines of type by the operation of a keyboard.

Linseed, lin'sēd, *n.* [O.E. *lin*, flax. LINE.] The seed of flax.—**Linseed-cake**, *n.* The solid mass which remains when oil is expressed from flax-seed, used as food for cattle and sheep. — **Linseed-meal**, *n.* Meal made from flax-seed.—**Linseed-oil**, *n.* An oil procured by pressure from the seed of flax. — **Linsey-woolsey**, lin'si-wul-si, *n.* A fabric made of linen and wool; an incongruous mixture (*Shak.*)—*a.* Made of linen and wool mixed; of different and unsuitable ingredients.

Linstock, lin'stok, *n.* [For *lintstock, luntstock*, from D. *lont*, Dan. *lunte*, a match, and *stock*, a stick.] A staff with a crotch or fork at one end to hold a lighted match, used in firing cannon.

Lint, lint, *n.* [A.Sax. *linet*, L. *linteum, linteus*, from *linum*, flax. LINE.] Flax; linen scraped into a soft substance, and used for dressing wounds and sores.

Lintel, lin'tel, *n.* [O.Fr. *lintel*, Fr. *linteau*, from L.L. *limitellus*, dim. from L. *limes, limitis*, a limit. LIMIT.] The horizontal piece of timber or stone over a door, window, or similar opening.

Lion, lī'on, *n.* [Fr. *lion*, from L. *leo, leonis*, a lion; Gr. *leōn*.] A well-known carnivorous animal, of a tawny colour, having a full-flowing mane in the male, and a tufted tail; a sign of the zodiac; Leo; an object of interest and curiosity (the *lion* of the day; to visit the *lions* of the place): a usage derived from the time when the lions kept in the Tower of London were one of the chief sights to which strangers were taken. —*Lion's provider*, a popular name for the jackal.—*Lion's share*, the whole or a very disproportionate share in advantages.—**Lionel, Lionet**, lī'on-el, lī'on-et, *n.* A lion's whelp; a young lion.—**Lioness**, lī'-on-es, *n.* The female of the lion.—**Lion-hearted**, *a.* Having a lion's courage; brave and magnanimous.—**Lionism**, lī'-on-izm, *n.* The attracting of notice as a lion; the treating of a person as an object of curiosity.—**Lionize**, lī'on-īz, *v.t.* To visit, as the objects of curiosity in a place; to treat as a lion or object of curiosity and interest.—*v.i.* To visit the objects of interest of a place.

Lip, lip, *n.* [A.Sax. *lippe* = D. *lip*, Dan. and G. *lippe*; allied to verb to *lap*; Lith. *lupa*, Per. *lab*, Hind. *lub*, L. *labium*, lip; *lambo*, to lap.] The name of the two fleshy or muscular parts (upper and lower) covering the front teeth in man and many other animals; something similar; the edge or border of something hollow (as a vessel, a wound); brink or margin.—*v.t.* To touch, as with the lip; to kiss.—**Lip-devotion**, *n.* Prayers uttered by the lips without the desires of the heart.—**Lip-language**, *n.* Oral or articulate language, in contradistinction to the language of signs.—**Lipped**, lipt, *a.* Having lips.—**Lip-reading**, *n.* Understanding what one says from the movement of his lips: used in regard to the deaf and dumb. — **Lip-service**, *n.* A mere verbal profession of service.—**Lip-wisdom**, *n.* Wisdom in talk without practice.

Lipogram, lī'pō-gram, *n.* [Gr. *leipō*, to leave, and *gramma*, a letter.] A writing in which a particular letter is wholly omitted. —**Lipogrammatic**, lī-pō-gram-mat''ik, *a.* Pertaining to lipograms.—**Lipogrammatism**, lī-pō-gram'mat-izm, *n.* The art of writing lipograms. — **Lipogrammatist**, lī-pō-gram'mat-ist, *n.* One who writes lipograms.

Lipoma, lip-ō'ma, *n.* [Gr. *lipos*, fat, *oma*, a tumour.] A fatty tumour.

Lippitude, lip'i-tūd, *n.* [L. *lippitudo*, from *lippus*, blear-eyed.] Soreness of eyes; bleareness.

Liquate, lī'kwāt, *v.i.* and *t.* — *liquated, liquating.* [L. *liquo, liquatum.* LIQUID.] To melt; to liquefy; *metal.* to separate from a less fusible metal, by applying just sufficient heat to melt the more easily liquefiable. —**Liquation**, lī'kwā'shon, *n.* The act or operation of liquating. —**Liquefacient**, lik-wē-fā'shi-ent, *n.* That which causes to melt.—**Liquefaction**, lik-wē-fak'shon, *n.* [L. *liqueo*, to be fluid, and *facio*, to make.] The act or operation of melting or dissolving; a becoming liquid; the state of being melted. —**Liquefiable**, lik'wē-fī-a-bl, *a.* Capable of being liquefied.—**Liquefy**, lik'-wē-fī, *v.t.*—*liquefied, liquefying.* To convert from a solid form to that of a liquid; to melt by heat.—*v.i.* To be melted; to become liquid. — **Liquescency**, li-kwes'en-si, *n.* The condition of being liquescent. — **Liquescent**, li-kwes'ent, *a.* [L. *liquesco*, to melt.] Melting; becoming fluid.

Liqueur, li-kėr' or li-kūr', *n.* [Fr. lit. liquor.] A sweet, alcoholic beverage with some infusion or extract from fruits, spices, or various aromatic substances, usually served after dinner.

Liquid, lik'wid, *a.* [L. *liquidus*, from *liqueo*, to melt, from root seen also in *lino*, to smear (whence *liniment*), *litera*, a letter (whence *letter, literature, obliterate*); Skr. *li*, to melt.] Composed of particles that move freely among each other on the slightest pressure; fluid; not solid; flowing smoothly or easily to the ear; devoid of harshness; pronounced with a slight contact of the organs of articulation; smooth in sound (a *liquid* letter).—*n.* A liquid; matter in the form of water, wine, milk, &c.; a non-elastic fluid; a letter or sound pronounced with a smooth flowing sound, as *l* and *r*.—**Liquidambar**, lik'wid-am-bar, *n.* [That is *liquid amber.*] A kind of fragrant gum or resin from several trees.—**Liquidate**, lik'wi-dāt, *v.t.*—*liquidated, liquidating.* [Fr. *liquider*, L. *liquido.*] To make liquid; to ascertain or reduce to precision in amount; to adjust; to dissolve or clear off (debts or liabilities); to pay; *com.* to wind up, as the affairs of a firm or company, by settling with its debtors and creditors, apportioning the amount of profit and loss of each partner or shareholder, &c.—**Liquidation**, lik-wi-dā'shon, *n.* The act of liquidating. — **Liquidator**, lik-wi-dā'tėr, *n.* One who liquidates; a person appointed to conduct the winding up of the affairs of a firm or company.—**Liquidity**, lik-wid'-i-ti, *n.* The state or quality of being liquid. —**Liquidize**, lik'wid-īz, *v.t.* To make liquid.—**Liquidly**, lik'wid-li, *adv.* In a liquid manner.—**Liquidness**, lik'wid-nes, *n.* The quality of being liquid.—**Liquor**, lik'ėr, *n.* [L. *liquor*, from *liqueo*, to melt.] A liquid or fluid substance; often specifically, an intoxicating beverage; drink.—*In liquor*, intoxicated. —*v.t.* To moisten; to drench. — *v.i.* To drink, especially intoxicating liquor. (*Colloq.*)

Liquorice, lik'ėr-is, *n.* LICORICE.

Lira, lē'ra, *n.* pl. **Lire**, lē'rā. [From L. *libra*, a pound, whence also Fr. *livre.*] An Italian silver coin equivalent to a franc, or 10*d.* nearly (nominally).

Lisk, lisk, *n.* [Dan. *lyske*, the groin.] The flank or groin. (*Old and Provincial.*)

Lisle, līl, *n.* A kind of thread made of linen, or linen and cotton; material made of lisle.

Lisp, lisp, *v.i.* [A.Sax. *wlisp, wlips*, lisping; D. *lispen*, Dan. *læspe*, Sw. *läspa*, to lisp; G. *lispeln*, to whisper, to lisp.] To pronounce the sibilant letters *s* and *z* imperfectly, as by giving the sound of *th* or *dh*; to speak imperfectly, as a child.—*v.t.* To pronounce with a lisp or imperfectly.—*n.* The habit or act of lisping; the habitual utterance of *th* for *s*.—**Lisper**, lis'pėr, *n.* One who lisps.—**Lispingly**, lis'ping-li, *adv.* In a lisping manner.

Lissencephalous, Lissencephalate, lis-en-sef'a-lus, lis-en-sef'a-lāt, *a.* [Gr. *lissos*, smooth, and *enkephalos*, brain.] Having the hemispheres of the brain smooth or with few surface convolutions: said of animals (bats, rodents, &c.).

Lissom, Lissome, lis'um, *a.* [Fr. *lithesome.* LITHE.] Supple; flexible; lithe; nimble; active. — **Lissomeness**, lis'umnes, *n.* State of being lissome.

List, list, *n.* [A.Sax. *list*, selvedge = Icel. *listi*, Sw. *list*, Dan. *liste*, a fillet, a selvedge; G. *leiste*, a strip, a border; D. *lijst*, border, margin, catalogue.] The edge or selvedge woven on cloth; a strip of cloth; a fillet; a limit or boundary; a line inclosing a field of combat or tournament ground; hence, *pl.* the ground or field inclosed for a combat or competition; a roll or catalogue (a *list* of names).—*Civil list.* Under CIVIL.—*v.t.* To enrol; to enlist; to fit or cover with list. —*v.i.* To enlist, as in the army.

List, list, *v.i.* [A.Sax. *lystan*, to wish (used impers.), from *lust*, pleasure; so Icel. *lysta*, Dan. *lyste*, D. *lusten*, from the noun. LUST.] To desire or choose; to be disposed; to please. [Sometimes impers. with dative of a pronoun.]—*n. Naut.* an inclination to one side (the ship has a *list* to port).

List, list, *v.i.* [Original form of *listen*, which is a lengthened form from A.Sax. *hlystan*, to listen, from *hlyst*, hearing, like Icel. *hlusta*, to listen, from *hlust*, an ear, allied to A.Sax. *hlosnian*, to hear; W. *clust*, an ear; L. *cluo*, Gr. *kluō*, to hear; and to E. *loud.*] To hearken; to attend; to listen. —*v.t.* To listen to.—**Listen**, lis'n, *v.i.* To attend closely with a view to hear; to give ear; to hearken. — **Listener**, lis'n-ėr, *n.* One who listens; a hearkener.—**Listening-post**, *n.* A position or post in front of an army's lines, occupied by a sentry or sentries charged with the duty of detecting enemy movements by hearing.

Listerism, lis'tėr-izm, *n.* [From Sir Joseph *Lister.*] The antiseptic system in surgery, the object of which is to exclude living germs from wounds.—**Listerian**, lis-tē'-ri-an, *a.* Pertaining to this system.

Listless, list'les, *a.* [O.E. *list*, A.Sax. *lyst*, desire, pleasure. See LIST, to desire.] Indifferent to or taking no pleasure in what is passing; languid and indifferent; uninterested; vacant.—**Listlessly**, list'les-li, *adv.* In a listless manner.—**Listlessness**, list'les-nes, *n.* The state of being listless.

Lit, lit, pret. & pp. of *light*, to kindle; also sometimes of *light*, to alight, to chance.

Litany, lit'a-ni, *n.* [Fr. *litanie*; Gr. *litaneia*, from *litaneuō*, to pray, *litē*, a prayer.] A solemn supplication used in public worship; a collection of short supplications in the *Book of Common Prayer*, uttered by the priest and people alternately.

Litchi, lich'i, *n.* A delicious fruit yielded by a tree belonging to China and the Malayan Archipelago.

Liter, lē'tr, *n.* [From Gr. *litra*, a pound.] Metric measure of capacity, a cubic decimeter, or 61.025 cu. in., or 1.0567 U. S. liquid quarts.

Literal, lit'ėr-al, *a.* [L. *literalis*, from *litera*, a letter. LETTER.] According to the letter or verbal expression; not figurative or metaphorical; following the letter or exact words; not free (a *literal* translation); consisting of or expressed by letters. —**Literalism**, lit'ėr-al-izm, *n.* The act of adhering to the letter; a mode of interpreting literally.—**Literalist**, lit'ėr-al-ist, *n.* One who practices literalism; an interpreter according to the letter.—**Literally**, lit'ėr-al-li, *adv.* In a literal manner or sense; according to the primary and natural import of words; not figuratively. —**Literalness**, lit'ėr-al-nes, *n.* The state or quality of being literal.—**Literary**, lit'ėr-a-ri, *a.* [L. *literarius.*] Pertaining to letters or literature; treating of or dealing with learning or learned men; engaged in literature; consisting in written or printed compositions (*literary* property).—**Literate**, lit'ėr-āt, *a.* [L. *literatus.*] Instructed; learned; lettered.—*n.* One who has received a certain university education, but has not graduated; a literary man.—**Literatim**, lit-ėr-ā'tim, *adv.* [L.] Letter for letter.—**Literato**, lit-ėr-ā'tō, *n.* pl. **Literati**, lit-ėr-ā'ti. [It. *litterato.*] A literary man; a litterateur. [Rare in singular.]—**Literator**,† lit'ėr-ā-tėr, *n.* [L.] A literary man; a litterateur.—**Literature**, lit'ėr-a-tūr, *n.* [L. *litteratura.*] Learning; literary knowledge; literary productions collectively; the literary productions upon a given subject, or a particular branch of knowledge; the collective writings of a country or period; the class of writings in which beauty of style is a characteristic feature; the calling of authors of books, &c.

Lith, lith, *n.* [A.Sax. *lith*=D. *lid*, Dan. *led*, Icel. *lithr*, Goth. *lithus*, limb, joint.] A limb; a joint; a symmetrical part or division; a member.

Litharge, lith'ärj, *n.* [Gr. *lithargyros*—*lithos*, stone, *argyros*, silver.] An oxide of lead, much used in assaying as a flux, and entering into the composition of the glaze of common earthenware.

Lithe, LITH, *a.* [A.Sax. *lithe*, gentle; G. *linde, gelind*, Dan. *lind*, Icel. *linr*, soft, mild; allied to L. *lentus*, pliant, *lenis*, mild (whence *lenity*). Hence *lissome.*] That may be easily bent; pliant; flexible; limber. —**Litheness**, LITH'nes, *n.* Pliancy; flexibility; limberness. — **Lithesome**, LITH'-sum, *a.* Pliant; lissome.

Lithia, lith'i-a, *n.* [From Gr. *lithos*, a stone.] The oxide of the metal lithium, of a white color, acrid and caustic; *med.* the formation of stone or concretions in the human body.—**Lithic**, lith'ik, *a.* Pertaining to or consisting of stone; pertaining to stone in the bladder.—**Lithium**, lith'i-um, *n.* The lightest of known metals.—**Lithia water**, *n.* A mineral water containing lithium salts.

Lithocarp, lith'o-kärp, *n.* [Gr. *lithos*, a stone, and *karpos*, fruit.] A fossil fruit.

Lithodome, lith'o-dōm, *n.* [Gr. *lithos*, stone, and *domos*, a dwelling.] One of those molluscous animals which make holes in rocks, shells, &c., in which they lodge.—**Lithodomous**, li-thod'o-mus, *a.* Relating to molluscs which perforate stones, &c.

Lithofracteur, lith-ō-frak'tėr, *n.* [Fr., from Gr. *lithos*, and Fr. *fracturer*, to fracture.] A powerful explosive compound, composed of nitro-glycerine, siliceous earth, nitrate of soda, sulphur, &c.

Lithogenous, li-thoj'e-nus, *a.* [Gr. *lithos*, a stone, and root *gen*, to produce.] Stone-producing; pertaining to animals which form coral.

Lithoglyphics, Lithoglyptics, lith'o-glif-iks, lith-o-glip'tiks, *n.* [Gr. *lithos*, a stone, and *glyphō*, to engrave.] The art of engraving on precious stones, &c.—**Lithoglyphic**, lith-o-glif'ik, *a.* Relating to this art.

Lithograph, lith'o-graf, *v.t.* [Gr. *lithos*, a stone, and *graphō*, to write.] To engrave or trace on stone and transfer to paper, &c., by printing.—*n.* A print from a drawing on stone.—**Lithographer**, li-thog'ra-fėr, *n.* One who practises lithography.—**Lithographic, Lithographical**, lith-o-graf'ik, lith-o-graf'i-kal, *a.* Pertaining to lithography; engraved upon or printed from stone. — *Lithographic stone, lithographic slate*, a slaty compact limestone, of a yellowish colour and fine grain, used for receiving the designs in lithography.—**Lithographically**, lith-o-graf'i-kal-li, *adv.* By the lithographic art.—**Lithography**, li-thog'ra-fi, *n.* The art of writing or drawing with special pigments on a peculiar kind of stone, and of producing impressions from it on paper.

Lithoid, Lithoidal, lith'oid, li-thoi'dal, *a.* [Gr. *lithos*, a stone.] Resembling a stone; of a stony structure.

Lithologic, Lithological, lith-o-loj'ik, lith-o-loj'i-kal, *a.* [Gr. *lithos*, a stone, and *logos*, discourse.] Of or pertaining to lithology or the science of stones.—**Lithologically**, lith-o-loj'i-kal-li, *adv.* In a lithological manner; from a lithological point of view.—**Lithologist**, li-thol'o-jist, *n.* A person skilled in the science of stones.—**Lithology**, li-thol'o-ji, *n.* The science or natural history of stones; the study of the mineral structure of rocks.

Lithomarge, lith'o-märj, *n.* [Gr. *lithos*, stone, L. *marga*, marl.] A term applied to varieties of clay of great fineness and capable of being fused into a soft slag.

Lithontriptor, lith'on-trip-tėr, *n.* [Gr. *lithos*, stone, and *tribō*, to grind down.] Same as *Lithotritor*.

Lithophagous, li-thof'a-gus, *a.* [Gr. *lithos*, stone, and *phagō*, to eat.] Eating or swallowing stones or gravel; also, perforating stones, as certain mollusca.

Lithophane, lith'o-fān, *n.* [Gr. *lithos*, a stone, and *phainō*, to show.] A style of ornamentation produced by impressing thin sheets of porcelain in a soft state with figures, which become visible by transmitted light, as in lamps, windows, &c.

Lithophotography, lith'o-fō-tog"ra-fi, *n.* The art of producing prints from lithographic stones by means of photographic pictures developed on their surface.

Lithophyl, lith'o-fil, *n.* [Gr. *lithos*, stone, *phyllon*, a leaf.] A fossil leaf or impression of a leaf, or a stone containing such.

Lithophyte, lith'o-fīt, *n.* [Gr. *lithos*, stone, *phyton*, a plant.] A polyp whose substance is stony or horny, as the corals.—**Lithophytic, Lithophytous**, lith-o-fit'ik, li-thof'i-tus, *a.* Pertaining to lithophytes.

Lithotint, lith'o-tint, *n.* A tinted picture produced by lithography.

Lithotome, lith'o-tōm, *n.* [Gr. *lithos*, stone, and *temnō*, to cut.] A surgical instrument for cutting into the bladder in operations for the stone.—**Lithotomic, Lithotomical**, lith-o-tom'ik, lith-o-tom'i-kal, *a.* Pertaining to or performed by lithotomy.—**Lithotomist**, li-thot'o-mist, *n.* One who performs the operation of lithotomy.—**Lithotomy**, li-thot'o-mi, *n.* The operation, art, or practice of cutting for the stone in the bladder.

Lithotripsy, lith'o-trip-si, *n.* Same as *Lithotrity*.—**Lithotriptist**, lith'o-trip-tist, *n.* Same as *Lithotrist*.—**Lithotriptor**, lith'o-trip-tėr, *n.* Same as *Lithotritor*.

Lithotrity, li-thot'ri-ti, *n.* [Gr. *lithos*, a stone, and L. *tero*, *tritum*, to grind.] The operation of crushing to pieces a stone in the bladder by means of an instrument called a lithotritor.—**Lithotritic**, lith-o-trit'ik, *a.* Pertaining to lithotrity.—**Lithotritist**, lith'o-trit-ist, *n.* One who performs lithotrity.—**Lithotritor**, lith'o-trī-tėr, *n.* An instrument for breaking to pieces a stone in the bladder.

Lithotypy, lī-thot'i-pi, *n.* A peculiar process of stereotyping by pressing into a mould taken from a form of type a composition which hardens into a stony substance.—**Lithotype**, lith'o-tīp, *n.* A kind of stereotype plate produced by lithotypy.

Litigate, lit'i-gāt, *v.t.*—*litigated, litigating*. [L. *litigo, litigatum*—*lis, litis*, strife, dispute, and *ago*, to carry on.] To make the subject of a lawsuit; to bring before a court of law for decision.—*v.i.* To carry on a suit by judicial process.—**Litigable**, lit'i-ga-bl, *a.* Capable of being litigated or defended at law.—**Litigant**, lit'i-gant, *a.* Disposed to litigate; contending in law; engaged in a lawsuit.—*n.* A person engaged in a lawsuit.—**Litigation**, lit-i-gā'shon, *n.* The act or process of litigating; the proceedings in a suit at law; a lawsuit.—**Litigator**, lit'i-gā-tėr, *n.* One who litigates.—**Litigiosity**, li-tij'i-os"i-ti, *n.* The character of being litigious.—**Litigious**, li-tij'us, *a.* [L. *litigiosus*, from *litigium*, a dispute.] Inclined to go to law; fond of litigation; given to bringing lawsuits; contentious.—**Litigiously**, li-tij'us-li, *adv.* In a litigious manner.—**Litigiousness**, li-tij'us-nes, *n.*

Litmus, lit'mus, *n.* [From G. *lackmus*, D. *lakmoes*—*lack*, lacker, and *mus, moes*, pulp, pap.] A colouring matter procured from certain lichens, used as a test for acids, paper tinged blue with it turning red with acids, and blue again with alkalies.

Litotes, lī'to-tēz, *n.* [Gr. *litotēs*, plainness, simplicity.] *Rhet.* a figure which expresses less than what is intended to be conveyed. Thus, 'a citizen of no mean city,' means 'of an illustrious or important city.'

Litre, lē'tr, *n.* [Fr., from Gr. *litra*, a pound.] The French standard measure of capacity, equal to 61.025 cubic inches. *See* LITER.

Litter, lit'ėr, *n.* [Fr. *litière*, from L.L. *lectaria*, from L. *lectus*, a bed; same root as *lie, lay*.] A kind of frame for supporting a bed, in which a person may be borne by men or by a horse; straw, hay, or other soft substance, used as a bed for horses and other animals; articles scattered in a slovenly manner; scattered rubbish; a condition of disorder.—*v.t.* To furnish (animals) with litter or bedding; to spread straw, &c., for; to scatter in a careless or slovenly manner.—*v.i.* To lie or sleep in litter.

Litter, lit'ėr, *n.* [Comp. Icel. *látr*, the place where animals lay their young, from *lag*, a laying; Sc. *lachter*, the quantity of eggs a hen lays.] The young produced at a birth by a quadruped which brings forth several at a birth; a birth or bringing forth, as of pigs, kittens, rabbits, puppies, &c.—*v.t.* To bring forth or give birth to: said of such quadrupeds as the sow, cat, rabbit.—*v.i.* To bring forth a litter.

Litterateur, lit'ėr-a-tėr, *n.* [Fr. *littérateur*. LITERAL.] A literary man; one who adopts literature as a profession.

Little, lit'l, *a.*—comparative *less*, superlative *least* (both from a different root); superlative very rarely *littlest*. [A.Sax. *lytel*, D. *luttel*, Icel. *lítill*, Sw. *liten*, Dan. *liden, lille*, Goth. *leitils*, little; same root as *lout*.] Small in size or extent; not great or large; short in duration; small in quantity or amount; of small dignity, power, or importance; of small force or weight; slight; inconsiderable; small in mind; petty; mean; narrow.—*n.* That which is little; a small quantity, space, &c.; small degree or scale; miniature.—*A little*, somewhat; to or in a small degree; to a limited extent.—*Little by little*, by slow degrees; gradually.—*adv.* In a small quantity or degree.—**Littleness**, lit'l-nes, *n.* The state or quality of being little.

Littoral, lit'ō-ral, *a.* [L. *littoralis*, from *littus, littoris*, the shore.] Pertaining to a shore; inhabiting the sea-shore.—*Littoral zone*, the interval or zone on a sea-coast between high and low water mark; a coast strip or district (the Red Sea *littoral*).

Lituate, Lituiform, lit'ū-āt, lit'ū-i-form, *a.* [L. *lituus*, a staff used by the augurs in taking omens, with a curled end.] Curled or bent at one end somewhat similar to a bishop's pastoral staff.—**Lituite**, lit'ū-īt, *n.* A fossil cephalopod shell of a spiral form at its smaller extremity.

Liturgy, lit'ėr-ji, *n.* [Gr. *leitourgia*—*leitos*, public, from *laos, leōs*, the people, and *ergon*, work.] The ritual or established formulas for public worship in those churches which use prescribed forms.—**Liturgic, Liturgical**, li-tėr'jik, li-tėr'ji-kal, *a.* Pertaining to a liturgy or to public prayer and worship.—**Liturgics**, li-tėr'jiks, *n.* The doctrine or theory of liturgies.—**Liturgiology**, lit'ėr-ji-ol"o-ji, *n.* The science or system of public ecclesiastical ceremonies.—**Liturgist**, lit'ėr-jist, *n.* One who favours or adheres to a liturgy.

Live, liv, *v.i.*—*lived, living*. [A.Sax. *lifian*, to live or dwell; L.G. and D. *leven*, Icel. *lifa*, Dan. *leve*, G. *leben*, Goth. *liban*, to live; akin *life*; same root as *leave*, the original meaning being to be left, to survive.] To have life; to be capable of performing the vital functions; to continue; to remain still effective; not to perish; to pass or spend life in a particular manner; to conduct one's self in life; to regulate one's life; to abide, dwell, reside; to feed; subsist, be nourished and supported (to *live* on grass or insects); to acquire a livelihood; *Scrip.* to be exempt from spiritual death.—*v.t.* To pass or spend (to *live* a life of ease).—*To live down*, to live so as to subdue or give the lie to; to prove false by the course of one's life (to *live down* a calumny).—**Liver**, liv'ėr, *n.* One who lives; one who resides; a resident; one who lives in a certain manner (the manner being expressed by an adjective).—**Living**, liv'ing, *p.* and *a.* Having life; not dead; producing action, animation, and vigour; quickening.—*Living force*, in *physics*, the force of a body in motion.—*Living rock*, rock in its natural place and condition.—*The living*, those who are alive.—*Living wage*, sufficient to live by, enough for bare life.—*n.* Means of subsistence; livelihood; power of continuing life; manner of life; the benefice of a clergyman.—**Livingly**, liv'ing-li, *adv.* In a living state or manner.—**Livingness**, liv'ing-nes, *n.* State of being alive.

Live, līv, *a.* [Short for *alive*, that is, in life'.] Having life; alive; not dead (a *live* ox; a *live* plant); ignited; not extinct (a *live* coal); vivid, as colour.—*Live salesman*, a person whose business it is to sell live stock.—*Live stock*, the quadrupeds and other animals employed or reared on a farm.—**Lived**, līvd, *a.* Having a life; existing; used in composition (long-*lived*, short-*lived*).—**Livelihood**, līv'li-hųd, *n.* [Corrupted from O.E. *liflode, livelode*, A. Sax. *líf-láde*, lit. life-leading, lead or course of life; from *lif*, life, and *lád*, a leading, as in *lode, lode*stone.] Means of maintaining life; support of life; maintenance.—**Livelily**, līv'li-li, *adv.* In a lively manner.—**Liveliness**, līv'li-nes, *n.* The quality or state of being lively or animated.—**Livelong**, liv'long, *a.* That endures long; lasting; durable.—*Livelong day*, day throughout its whole length; entire day; with undercurrent of joy or lassitude; originally *lefe* (LIEF) *long*.—**Lively**, līv'li, *a.* Brisk; vivacious; active; animated; spirited; living; lifelike; strong, energetic, keen (a *lively* faith or hope); fresh; bright: said of colours.—*adv.* In a lively manner.—**Live-oak**, *n.* A species of oak of the United States yielding very valuable timber.

Liver, liv'ėr, *n.* [A.Sax. *lifer*, D. and Dan. *lever*, Icel. *lifr*, G. *leber*; root doubtful.] The glandular organ which in animals secretes the bile; in man placed in the right upper side and towards the front of the abdominal cavity.—**Liver-colour, Liver-coloured**, *a.* Of the colour of the liver; reddish-brown.—**Livered**, liv'ėrd, *a.* Having a liver: used in composition (white-*livered*).—**Liver-fluke**, *n.* A fluke-worm.—**Liverwort**, liv'ėr-wėrt, *n.* [From the appearance of the plants.] One of an order of cryptogamic plants, closely allied to the mosses.

Livery, liv'ėr-i, *n.* [Fr. *livrée*, a giving out, something given out or delivered over, from *livré*, pp. of *livrer*, to deliver, from L. *libero*, to liberate. LIBERAL.] Release†; deliverance (*Mil.*)‡; an allowance of food statedly given out, as to a family, to servants, to horses, &c.‡; hence, the state of a horse that is kept and fed at a certain rate (to keep horses at *livery*); a distinctive dress in which the male servants of some person of position are clad; a distinctive garb worn by any body or association of persons; the body or association of persons wearing such a garb; characteristic covering or outward appearance (the *livery* of May, of grief).—*v.t.* To clothe in, or as in, livery.—**Livery-company**, *n.* A company of London liverymen.—**Liveryman**, liv'ėr-i-man, *n.* One who wears a livery; one who keeps horses for hire; keeper of a livery-stable.—**Livery-servant**, *n.* A servant who wears a livery.—**Livery-stable**, *n.* A stable where horses are kept for hire.

Livid, liv'id, *a.* [L. *lividus*, from *liveo*, to be black and blue.] Black and blue; of a lead colour; discoloured, as flesh by contusion.—**Lividity, Lividness**, li-vid'i-ti, liv'id-nes, *n.* The state of being livid.

Livraison, lē-vrā-zoṅ, *n.* [Fr., from *livrer*, to deliver. LIVERY.] One of the parts or numbers of a book issued in parts.

Livre, lē-vr, *n.* [Fr., from L. *libra*, a pound.] An old French money of account, superseded by the franc.

Lixivial, Lixivious, lik-siv'i-al, lik-siv'i-us, *a.* [L. *lixivius*, made into lye, *lixivium*, lye, from *lix*, ashes.] Pertaining to lye or the water impregnated with alkaline salt extracted from wood-ashes; of the nature of lye; obtained by lixiviation.—**Lixiviate**, lik-siv'i-āt, *v.t.* To subject to the process of lixiviation.—**Lixiviation**, lik-siv'i-ā"shon, *n.* The process of extracting alkaline salts from ashes by pouring water on them, the water passing through them taking up the salts and thus forming lye.—**Lixivium**, lik-siv'i-um, *n.* Lye, that is, water impregnated with alkaline salts taken up from wood-ashes.

Lizard, liz'ėrd, *n.* [Fr. *lézard*, from L. *lacerta*, a lizard.] The popular name of many four-footed, tailed reptiles; *naut.* a piece of rope with one or more iron thimbles in it for ropes to lead through.

Llama, lä'mä or lyä'mä, *n.* [A Peruvian word.] A hoofed ruminating quadruped of South America, allied to the camel, but smaller and not having a hump.

Llanos, lan'ōz or lyä'nōz, *n. pl.* [Sp., from L. *planus*, level.] Vast and almost entirely level grassy plains in the northern part of South America.—**Llanero**, lya-ner'ō, *n.* [Sp., from *llano.*] An inhabitant of the llanos of South America.

Lloyd's, loidz, *n.* [Because the headquarters of the underwriters were originally (from 1716) *Lloyd's* coffee-house.] A society of underwriters and others in London, Eng., for the collection and diffusion of maritime intelligence, the insurance, classification, and certification of vessels, and the transaction of business of various kinds connected with shipping.—*Lloyd's numbers*, numbers selected to designate the size of various parts of ships.—*Lloyd's Register*, an annual register of ships, their size, classification, etc.

Lo, lō, *exclam.* [A.Sax. *lā.*] Look; see; behold; observe.

Loach, Loche, lōch, *n.* [Fr. *loche*, a loach, origin unknown.] A small, fresh-water fish of the Old World, related to the carp family.

Load, lōd, *n.* [O.E. *lode*, a load, from A. Sax. *hladan*, to load, pret. *hlód.* LADE.] What is laid on or put in anything for conveyance; a burden; as much as can be carried at one time by any conveyance; a grievous weight; an encumbrance; something that burdens or oppresses the mind or spirits; in building construction, the external forces acting upon a structure and the weight of the structure itself.—*Dead-load*, one gradually applied and remaining steady.—*Live-load*, one suddenly applied and accompanied by shock or vibration.—*Load line*, a line drawn on the side of a vessel to show the depth to which she may safely sink in the water—*v.t.* To charge with a load; to lay a burden on; to weigh down, oppress, encumber; to bestow or confer in great abundance; to fill; to stuff; to make heavier for some purpose by adding special weight; to charge, as a gun with powder, or with powder and ball or shot.—*To load a cane* or *a whip*, to make it serve as a weapon by weighting it with lead or iron.—*To load dice*, to make one side heavier than the other, so as to cause the opposite to come regularly up.—*To load wine*, to drug or hocus wine.—**Loader**, lō'dėr, *n.* One who loads.

Loadstar, Lodestar, lōd'star, *n.* [*Lode, load*, is from A.Sax. *lád*, course, way (the termination of *livelihood*), from *líthan*, to go (akin to *lead*).] A star that leads or serves to guide; especially the pole-star.—**Loadstone, Lodestone**, lōd'stōn, *n.* An ore of iron; the magnetic oxide of iron, which possesses the property of attracting iron, and the power of communicating this property to iron and steel, thus forming artificial magnets; hence, a magnet.

Loaf, lōf, *n.* pl. **Loaves**, lōvz. [A.Sax. *hláf*; Icel. *hleifr*, Goth. *hlaibs, hlaifs*, O.H.G. *hlaib*, G. *laib, leib*, allied to Rus. *chljeb*, Pol. *chleb*, bread, loaf. This word forms part of *lord, lady*, and *lammas.*] A regularly shaped or moulded mass of bread of some size; a conical lump of sugar.—**Loaf-sugar**, *n.* Sugar refined and formed into a conical mass.

Loaf, lōf *v.i.* [The verb is from the noun *loafer*, G. *läufer*, D. *looper*, one that runs or gads about. Akin *leap.*] To lounge; to idle away one's time.—*v.t.* To pass or spend in idleness, as time; to spend lazily.—**Loafer**, lō'fėr, *n.* A lazy or disreputable lounger; a lazy fellow who picks up a living anyhow.

Loam, lōm, *n.* [A.Sax. *lám*; D. *leem*, G. *lehm*, loam, clay, allied to E. *lime*, and probably L. *limus*, slime, mud.] A rich soil compounded of sand, clay, vegetable mould, &c.; a mixture of sand, clay, &c., used for moulding in iron-founding.—*v.t.* To cover with loam; to clay.—**Loamy**, lō'mi, *a.* Consisting of loam; partaking of the nature of loam.

Loan, lōn, *n.* [A.Sax. *lán* (?), *laen*, a loan, from *líhan*, to lend; Icel. *lán*, Dan. *laan*, D. *leen*, a loan; same root as L. *linquo*, to leave (whence *relinquish*). LEND.] The act of lending or condition of being lent; a lending; that which is lent; especially, a sum of money lent at interest.—*v.t.* and *i.* To lend.—**Loanable**, lō'na-bl, *a.* That may be lent.—**Loan-office**, *n.* An office where money is lent, usually to be repaid by instalments; a pawnbroker's place of business.—**Loan-society**, *n.* A society established for advancing money to the industrious classes, and receiving back the same by instalments with interest.

Loath, lōth, *a.* [A.Sax. *láth*, hateful, odious; Icel. *leithr*, Dan. and Sw. *led*, O.H.G. *leit*, odious. Often written *loth.*] Filled with disgust or aversion; unwilling; reluctant; averse.—**Loathe**, lōᴛʜ, *v.t.*—*loathed, loathing.* [A.Sax. *láthian*, to hate.] To feel disgust at; to have an extreme aversion of the appetite towards; to dislike greatly; to abhor.—*v.i.* To feel nausea, disgust, or abhorrence.—**Loather**, lōᴛʜ'ėr, *n.* One who loathes or abhors.—**Loathful**, lōᴛʜ'ful, *a.* Full of loathing.—**Loathing**, lōᴛʜ'ing, *n.* Extreme disgust, nausea, or aversion; abhorrence; detestation.—**Loathingly**, lōᴛʜ'ing-li, *adv.* With loathing.—**Loathliness**, lōᴛʜ'li-nes, *n.* Loathsomeness.—**Loathly**, lōᴛʜ'li, *a.* Loathsome.—**Loathness**, lōᴛʜ'nes, *n.* The state of being loath.—**Loathsome**, lōᴛʜ'sum, *a.* Causing to loathe; exciting disgust; disgusting; odious; detestable.—**Loathsomely**, lōᴛʜ'sum-li, *adv.* In a loathsome manner.—**Loathsomeness**, lōᴛʜ'sum-nes, *n.*

Loaves, *n.* pl. of *loaf.*

Lob, lob, *n.* [W. *llob*, a dolt; allied to *lubber.*] A dolt; a lout.

Lobar, lō'bär, *a.* Pertaining to a lobe, as of the liver or brain.—*Lobar pneumonia*, inflammation of a whole lobe of the lungs, as distinguished from *lobular pneumonia*, which attacks the lungs in patches.

Lobate, Lobated. Under LOBE.

Lobby, lob'i, *n.* [L.L. *lovia, lobium*, &c., a portico, from O.H.G. *laubja*, G. *laube*, an arbor, from *laub*, a leaf, foliage. LEAF. *Lodge* is another form of this word.] An entrance hall, especially one used as a waiting room; a large public room in a hotel, where guests register and check out, etc.; a foyer; an open room or hallway at a theater entrance; in politics, a group of people who endeavor by personal persuasion to influence legislators.—*v.i.* To persuade by lobbying.—*v.t.* To accomplish by lobbying.

Lobe, lōb, *n.* [Fr. *lobe*, L.L. *lobus*, from Gr. *lobos*, a lobe.] A round projecting part of an organ, as of the liver, lungs, brain, &c.; the lower soft part of the ear; *bot.* a rounded projection or division of a leaf.—**Lobate, Lobated**, lō'bāt, lō'bā-ted, *a.* Consisting of or having lobes; applied to the foot of a bird furnished at the side with a broad-lobed membrane.—**Lobed**, lōbd, *a.* Lobate.—**Lobe-foot**, *n.* A lobe-footed bird; a lobiped.—**Lobe-footed**, *a.* Having the toes lobate or bordered with membranes, as the grebes.—**Lobiped**, lō'bi-ped, *n.* A lobe-footed bird, such as the coot.—**Lobular**, lob'ū-lėr, *a.* Having the character of a lobule.—**Lobulated**, lob'ū-lā-ted, *a.* Consisting of lobules; having small lobed divisions.—**Lobule**, lob'ūl, *n.* [Dim. of *lobe.*] A small lobe.

Lobelia, lō-bē'li-a, *n.* [From Matthew *Lobel*, physician and botanist to James I.] A genus of beautiful plants belonging to the bell-flower family, a blue species being common in gardens.

Lobscouse, lob'skous, *n.* [For *lobs-course*, from *lob* and *course*, that is, course or dish for lubbers.] *Naut.* a hash of meat, biscuit, &c., baked.

Lobsided, lob'sī-ded, *a.* Same as *Lopsided.*

Lobster, lob'stėr, *n.* [A.Sax. *loppestere, lopystre*, corrupted from L. *locusta*, a lobster, a locust.] The name of certain long-tailed (macrurous), ten-footed crustaceans with large claws, allied to the crabs, and used for food.

Lobular, Lobule. Under LOBE.

Lobworm, lob'wėrm, *n.* The lugworm.

Local, lō'kal, *a.* [L. *localis*, from *locus*, a place, seen also in *lieu, lieutenant, allocate, collocate, couch, allow*, &c.] Pertaining to a particular place; limited or confined to a spot, place, or definite district; *med.* confined to a particular part or organ.—*Local option*, the principle by which the inhabitants of a locality vote directly on the sale there of intoxicants.—*n.* A local item of news; a local railway train. (*Colloq.*)—**Locale**, lō-käl', *n.* [Fr. *local*, a locality, the *e* being erroneous, as in *morale.*] A locality.—**Localism**, lō'kal-izm, *n.* The state of being local; a local idiom or peculiarity of speech.—**Locality**, lō-kal'i-ti, *n.* Position; situation; place; district; geographical place or situation.—**Localization**, lo'kal-i-zā"shon, *n.* The act of localizing.—**Localize**, lō'kal-īz, *v.t.*—*localized, localizing.* To fix in or assign to a particular place; to discover or detect the place of.—**Locally**, lō'kal-li, *adv.* With respect to place; in place.—**Locate**, lō'kāt, *v.t.*—*located, locating.* [L. *loco, locatum.*] To set in a particular spot or position; to place; to settle.—*v.i.* To reside; to adopt a fixed residence.—**Location**, lō-kā'shon, *n.* The act of locating; situation with respect to place; place.—**Locative**, lō'ka-tiv, *a. Gram.* indicating place (a *locative* adjective; a *locative* case).—*n.* The locative case; a case expressing position.

Loch, loch, *n.* [Gael.; allied to *lake.*] A lake; an arm of the sea running into the land, especially if narrow or to some extent landlocked.

Lochaber-axe, loch-ab'ėr, *n.* [From *Lochaber*, in Inverness-shire.] A weapon consisting of a pole with an axe at its upper end, formerly used by the Highlanders of Scotland.

Lochia, lo-kī'a, *n.* [Gr. *locheia.*] The evacuations from the womb and vagina which follow childbirth.—**Lochial**, lo-kī'al, *a.* Pertaining to the lochia.

Lock, lok, *n.* [A.Sax. *loca, loc*, a lock; Icel. *lok*, a cover, shutter; *lúka*, to shut; Dan. *lukke*, a lock, *lukke*, to lock; D. *luiken*, to shut.] An appliance used for fastening doors, chests, drawers, &c., its main feature being a bolt moved with a key; the mechanism by which a firearm is discharged; a fastening together; a state of being closely entangled; a grapple in wrestling; an inclosure in a canal, with gates at each end, used in raising or lowering boats as they pass from one level to another.—*v.t.* To fasten with a lock and key; to fasten so as to impede motion (to *lock* a wheel); to shut up or confine with, or as with, a lock, or in an inclosed place; to close fast; to seal; to join or unite firmly, as by intertwining or infolding; to embrace closely.—*To lock out*, to close the doors of an industrial establishment against the operatives; to throw out of employment, so as to bring workmen to the master's terms.—*To lock up*, to close or fasten with a lock; to confine; to restrain.—*v.i.* To become fast; to unite closely by mutual insertion of parts.—**Lockage**, lok'āj, *n.* Works which form the locks on a canal; toll paid for passing the locks.—**Locker**, lok'ėr, *n.* A closed receptacle, as a drawer or small cupboard in a ship, that may be closed with a lock.—**Locket**, lok'et, *n.* [Dim. from *lock*.] A little case worn as an ornament, often pendent to a necklace.—**Lock-nut**, *n.* A nut, usually of metal, so constructed that it cannot work itself loose when properly applied.—**Lock-jaw**, *n.* *Med.* a form of tetanus consisting in spasmodic rigidity of the under jaw, so that the mouth cannot be opened.—**Lock-keeper**, *n.* One who attends the locks of a canal.—**Lock-out**, *n.* The closing of a place of work against the workmen on the part of the employers, in order to bring the men to their terms as to hours, wages, &c.—**Locksmith**, lok'smith, *n.* A mechanic whose occupation is to make or repair locks.—**Lock step**, step used by a file of men keeping as close as possible to one another.—**Lock stitch**, stitch formed by the locking of two threads.—**Lock-up**, *n.* A room or place in which persons under arrest are temporarily confined.

Lock, lok, *n.* [A.Sax. *locc* = D. and Dan. *lok*, Icel. *lokkr*, G. *locke*, a curl or ringlet.] A tuft of hair or wool; a tress; a ringlet; a tuft of hay or other like substance.

Locomotion, lō-kō-mō'shon, *n.* [L. *locus*, place, and *motio*, motion. LOCAL.] The act or power of moving from place to place.—**Locomotive**, lō-kō-mō'tiv, *a.* Pertaining to locomotion; moving from place to place.—*n.* A railroad engine (usually steam) used for hauling passenger or freight cars; a steam-engine that runs on rails. Also called *Locomotive-engine*.

Loculament, lok'ū-la-ment, *n.* [L. *loculamentum*, from *loculus*, a cell, dim. of *locus*, a place. LOCAL.] *Bot.* the cell of a pericarp in which the seed is lodged.—**Locular**, lok'ū-lėr, *a.* *Bot.* having one or more cells or loculi.—**Loculose, Loculous**, lok'ū-lōs, lok'ū-lus, *a.* *Bot.* divided by internal partitions into cells.—**Loculi**, lok'ū-lī, *n.pl.* A series of little cells or compartments.

Locum-tenens, lō'kum-tē'nenz, *n.* [L.] One who temporarily acts for another; a deputy or substitute.

Locus, lō'kus, *n.* pl. **Loci**, lō'sī. [L. LOCAL.] A place; specifically, *geom.* the line traversed by a point which is constrained to move in accordance with certain determinate conditions.—*Locus classicus*, the classical or all-important passage in an author or book dealing with a specific point.—*Locus standi*, recognized place or position; the right of a party to appear and be heard on the question before any tribunal.

Locust, lō'kust, *n.* [L. *locusta* (whence *lobster*).] The name of several large insects allied to the grasshoppers and crickets, and some of which appear in immense multitudes and eat up every green thing; the locust-tree.—**Locust-bean**, *n.* The sweet pod of the carob-tree.—**Locust-tree**, *n.* The carob-tree; also a name given to certain beautiful American trees, some of them now cultivated in Europe.

Locution, lō-kū'shon, *n.* [L. *locutio*, *locutionis*, from *loquor*, to speak. LOQUACIOUS.] A mode of speech; a phrase.

Lode, lōd, *n.* [A.Sax. *lād*, a way, a course, same as *load* in *loadstar*, *loadstone*.] An open ditch; a straight water channel; *mining*, a metallic vein, or any regular mineral vein.

Lodestar, *n.* Same as *Loadstar*.

Lodestone, *n.* Same as *Loadstone*.

Lodge, loj, *n.* [Fr. *loge*, It. *loggia*, from L.L. *lobia*. LOBBY.] A small house in a park, forest, or domain; a small country residence; a temporary habitation; a hut; a small house connected with a larger (a porter's *lodge*); a place where a society or branch of a society, as freemasons, holds its meetings; the body of members who meet at such a place.—*v.t.*—*lodged*, *lodging*. To furnish with temporary house accommodation; to provide with a temporary place of abode; to set, lay, or deposit for keeping (to *lodge* money in a bank); to plant, fix, or settle (to *lodge* an arrow in one's breast); to beat down or lay flat (growing crops).—*v.i.* To have a temporary abode; to dwell at some one else's house; to be deposited or fixed; to settle; to reside; to dwell or have a fixed position.—**Lodger**, loj'ėr, *n.* One who lodges; especially, one who lives in a hired room or rooms in the house of another.—**Lodging**, loj'ing, *n.* A place of temporary rest or residence; a room or rooms hired for residence by a person in the house of another: often in this sense spoken of as plural.—**Lodging-house**, *n.* A house in which lodgers are accommodated.—**Lodgment**, loj'ment, *n.* The act of lodging; accumulation of something deposited; deposition; *milit.* the occupation of a position, as in a siege, by the besieging party.

Lodicule, lō'di-kūl, *n.* [L. *lodicula*, a coverlet.] *Bot.* one of the scales which occur at the base of the fruit of grasses.

Loess, lės, *n.* A German geological term, applied to an alluvial deposit in the Rhine valley, the Danube valley, China, &c.

Loft, loft, *n.* [Dan. *loft*, a ceiling, loft; Icel. *lopt* (pron. loft), air, sky, a loft: same root as the verb to *lift*; A.Sax. *lyft*, Sc. *lift*, air, sky; hence, *a-loft*, Icel. *a-lopt*.] The room or space between a ceiling or flooring and the roof immediately above it; the space below and between the rafters; also a gallery raised within a larger apartment, as in a church, hall, &c.—**Loftily**, lof'ti-li, *adv.* In a lofty manner or position.—**Loftiness**, lof'ti-nes, *n.* The state or quality of being lofty or high.—**Lofty**, lof'ti, *a.* [From *loft*, *aloft*.] Much elevated in place; high; tall; elevated in condition or character; dignified; indicative of pride or haughtiness; proud; haughty; elevated in language or style; sublime; stately.

Log, log, *n.* [Icel. *lāg*, a felled tree; D. Dan. and G. *log*, the nautical log; akin *lie*, *lay*.] A bulky piece of timber unhewed; a large lump or piece of wood not shaped for any purpose; *naut.* a contrivance for measuring the rate of a ship's velocity through the water, consisting essentially in a piece of board in form of a quadrant of a circle, loaded so as to float upright, which, being thrown from a ship, drags on the line to which it is attached and causes it to unwind at a rate corresponding to the ship's velocity; the record of a ship's progress; a log-book.—**Log-book**, *n.* *Naut.* a book in which are entered all particulars relating to the weather, winds, courses, &c., with any other matters relating to the vessel's voyage that are considered worthy of being registered; a book for memoranda kept by a public teacher.—**Log-cabin, Log-house, Log-hut**, *n.* A house or hut whose walls are composed of logs laid on each other.—**Log-chip, Log-ship**, *n.* The log or board attached to the log-line.—**Log-glass**, *n.* *Naut.* the sand-glass used along with the log to obtain the rate of sailing.—**Log-line**, *n.* *Naut.* the line fastened to the log, and wound on a reel, by means of which the rate of sailing is ascertained, from the *knots* into which it is divided (see KNOT).—**Log-roller**, *n.* A lumberman who, in rolling a log down a declivity, and finding it stick, rolls another on to it to give both the necessary impulse; the union of politicians or authors to praise or puff each other's work (*Colloq.*).

Log, log, *n.* A Hebrew measure of liquids, containing three-quarters or five-sixths of a pint.

Logan, Loggan, log'an, *n.* A rocking-stone; a large stone or rock so balanced as to be easily moved.

Logan-berry, *n.* A cross between a blackberry and a raspberry.

Logarithm, log'a-rithm, *n.* [Gr. *logos*, ratio, and *arithmos*, number.] *Math.* the exponent of the power to which a given invariable number (or base) must be raised in order to produce another given number. Thus, in the common system of logarithms, in which the base is 10, the logarithm of 1000 is 3, because 10 raised to the third power is 1000. Many calculations are greatly facilitated by the use of logarithms, but for this special tables are required.—**Logarithmic, Logarithmical**, log-a-rith'mik, log-a-rith'mi-kal, *a.* Pertaining to logarithms; consisting of logarithms.—**Logarithmically**, log-a-rith'mi-kal-li, *adv.* By the use or aid of logarithms.

Loggerhead, log'ėr-hed, *n.* [From *log* and *head*; comp. *blockhead*.] A blockhead; a dunce; a dolt; a species of turtle found in the south seas.—*To be at loggerheads*, to be engaged in a fight; to be involved in a dispute.—*To come to loggerheads*, to come to a quarrel.

Loggia, loj'ä, *n.* pl. **Loggie**, loj'e [It. LODGE.] *Italian arch.* a term applied to a gallery or arcade in a building running along the front or part of the front and open on one side to the air, on which side are a series of pillars or slender piers.

Logic, loj'ik, *n.* [Fr. *logique*; L. *logica*; Gr. *logikē* (*technē*, art, understood), from *logos*, reason.] The science of reasoning; the science of the operations of the understanding subservient to the estimation of evidence; the science whose chief end is to ascertain the principles on which all valid reasoning depends, and which may be applied to test the legitimacy of every conclusion that is drawn from premises; the art or practice of reasoning.—**Logical**, loj'i-kal, *a.* Pertaining to logic; used in logic; according to the rules or principles of logic; skilled in logic; discriminating.—**Logicality, Logicalness**, loj-i-kal'i-ti, loj'i-kal-nes, *n.* The state or quality of being logical.—**Logically**, loj'i-kal-li, *adv.* In a logical manner.—**Logician**, lō-jish'an, *n.* A person skilled in logic.—**Logicise**, loj'i-sīz, *v.i.* To exercise one's logical powers.—**Logistic, Logistical**, lō'jis-tik, lō-jis'ti-kal, *a.* [Gr. *logistikos*, from *logizomai*, to calculate or reckon.] Pertaining to judging, estimating, or calculating.

Logogram, lō'gō-gram, *n.* [Gr. *logos*, a word, and *gramma*, a letter.] A single printing type that forms a word; a phonographic symbol that, for the sake of brevity, represents a word.—**Logographer**, lō-gog'ra-fėr, *n.* A general name for the school of historians, writers of narratives or tales, before the rise of the Herodotean and Thucydidean method of critical investigation; a writer of speeches for the Athenian law courts.—**Logographic, Logographical**, lō-gō-graf'ik, lō-gō-graf'i-kal, *a.* Pertaining to logography.—**Logography**, lō-gog'ra-fi, *n.* A method of printing, in which a type forms a word, instead of forming a letter.

Logomachy, lō-gom'a-ki, *n.* [Gr. *logos*, word, and *machē*, contest.] A contention about words; a war of words.—**Logomachist**, lō-gom'a-kist, *n.* One who contends about words.

Logomania, lō-gō-mā'ni-a, *n.* [Gr. *logos*, a word, and *mania*, madness.] A disease through which, while ideas remain clear, the power of associating these with the proper words is lost.

Logos, log'os, *n.* [Gr., word, speech, reason, from *legō*, to speak.] The Word; the Divine Word; Christ.

Logotype, log'ō-tīp, *n.* A word or group of words cast together, as the name of a magazine, or the mast-head of a paper, as opposed to a *ligature*, two or three letters united and cast together, as æ, ﬂ.

Logwood, log'wụd, *n.* [From being imported in *logs*.] A dark-red dyewood, imported from Central America and the West Indies, much employed in dyeing and in calico-printing to give a black or brown colour.

Loin, loin, *n.* [O.Fr. *logne* (Fr. *longe*), from L. *lumbus*, the loin.] The part of an animal on either side between the false ribs and the haunch-bone; the part on either side of the trunk from the ribs to the lower limbs.

Loiter, loi'tėr, *v.i.* [Allied to D. *leuteren*, to waggle or waver; perhaps to *late*, like Icel. *lōtra*, to linger, from *latr*, late; comp. E. *linger*, from *long*.] To be slow in moving; to delay; to spend time idly; to hang about.—*v.t.* To consume in trifles; to waste carelessly: used with *away*.—**Loiterer**, loi'tėr-ėr, *n.* One who loiters.—**Loiteringly**, loi'tėr-ing-li, *adv.* In a loitering manner.

Lok, Loki, lok, lō'ki, *n.* [Icel. *loki.*] *Scandinavian myth.* the evil deity, the author of all calamities.

Loll, lol, *v.t.* [Akin to Icel. *lulla*, to loll, *lalla*, to toddle as a child.] To lie at ease; to lie in a careless attitude; to recline; to hang extended from the mouth, as the tongue of a dog when heated from exertion; to move in a lax, lazy manner.—*v.t.* To suffer to hang out, as the tongue.

Lollard, lol'ärd, *n.* [L.G. and D. *lollen*, *lullen*, to sing, from the practice of the original Lollards of singing dirges at funerals.] A member of a society for the care of the sick and the burial of the dead, originating at Antwerp about 1300, and blamed for holding heretical opinions; one of the followers of Wickliffe in England.—**Lollardism, Lollardy**, lol'ärd-izm, lol'är-di, *n.* The principles of the Lollards.

Lollipop, lol'i-pop, *n.* [From *loll*, to protrude the tongue, and *pop*, probably same as *pap*, infants' food.] Candy; usually a hard candy that is sucked rather than chewed, and so each piece is on a short stick, for easy handling; a sucker. (*Colloq.*)

Lombard, lom'bärd, *n.* [L.L. *Longobardi*, lit. 'long beards', being a latinized form of the German words for *long* and *beard*.] A native of Lombardy in Italy; an old name for a banker or money-lender. Hence —*Lombard Street*, in London, where a large number of the principal bankers, money-brokers, and bullion-dealers have their offices.—*a.* Of or pertaining to Lombardy or the Lombards.—**Lombardic**, *a.*

Lombardy poplar, lom'bär-di, *n.* A variety of *Populus nigra italicus*, or black poplar, whose branches lie close to the upright, tapering tree trunk, used for beauty in landscaping rather than for shade.

Loment, Lomentum, lō'ment, lō-men'tum, *n. Bot.* an indehiscent legume which separates spontaneously by a transverse division between every two seeds.—**Lomentaceous**, lō-men-tā'shus, *a.* Bearing loments; pertaining to a loment.

Londoner, lun'dun-ėr, *n.* A native or citizen of London.—**London-clay**, *n. Geol.* the most considerable of the eocene tertiary formations of Britain; so called from being found under and around the metropolis.—**London-pride**, *n.* A pretty British plant, common in cottage gardens.

Lone, lōn, *a.* [A contr. from *alone*.] Solitary; retired; unfrequented; without any companion or fellow; not having others near; single; unmarried, or in widowhood. —**Loneliness**, lōn'li-nes, *n.* The condition of being lonely.—**Lonely**, lōn'li, *a.* Unfrequented by man; retired; sequestered; not having others near; apart from fellows or companions; sad from want of companionship or sympathy.—**Loneness**, lōn'nes, *n.* The state of being lone; solitude; seclusion.—**Lonesome**, lōn'sum, *a.* Dreary from want of company or animation; lonely

Long, long, *a.* [A.Sax. *lang*, *long*=D., Dan., and G. *lang*, Icel. *langr*, Goth. *laggs* (*langs*); same as (but not borrowed from) L. *longus*, long. Hence verb to *long*, *along*, *belong*, *length*, *ling*, *linger*, &c.] Drawn out in a line or in the direction of length: opposed to *short*, and contradistinguished from *broad* or *wide*; drawn out or extended in time; lasting during a considerable time; continued or protracted; extended to any specified measure; having certain linear extent (a yard *long*; a mile *long*); occurring after a protracted interval; late; containing much verbal matter (a *long* speech or book). *Long home*, the grave or death. (O.T.)—*In the long run*, in the ultimate result.—*Long cloth*, a kind of fine cotton or calico fabric.—*Long clothes*, a baby's dress, which stretches much below the feet.—*Long firm*, a fictitious or pretended firm, consisting of swindlers who order goods without any intention of paying.—*Long ton*, the weight of 2240 pounds avoirdupois.—*n.* Something that is long.—*The long and the short*, or *the short and the long*, the sum of a matter in a few words; the whole.—*adv.* To a great extent in time; at a time far distant, either prior or posterior (not *long* before or after); throughout; without intermission (in such phrases as all my life *long*, forty years *long*).—**Long-ago**, *n.* A time long or far past. (*Poet.*)—**Long-boat**, *n.* The largest and strongest boat carried by a ship.—**Long-bow**, *n.* The old English archer's weapon, measuring about 6 feet long, the arrow being usually half the length of the bow.—*To draw the long-bow*, to exaggerate; to tell improbable stories.—**Long-dozen**, *n.* Thirteen.—**Longhand**, long'hand, *n.* Ordinary written characters, as contradistinguished from *shorthand*, *phonography*, or *stenography*.—**Long-headed**, *a.* Having a long head; dolichocephalic; shrewd; far-seeing; discerning.—**Longhorn**, *n.* A type of cattle so called because of their very long horns. In the U. S., found mostly in Texas.—**Long-lived**, long'livd, *a.* Having a long life or existence; lasting long.—**Long-measure**, *n.* Measure of length; lineal measure.—**Long-sighted**, *a.* Able to see at a great distance; far-seeing; sagacious; of acute intellect.—**Longsome**, long'sum, *a.* Tiresome on account of length; tedious. —**Longshoreman**, *n.* A stevedore; a dock laborer employed at loading cargo, &c.—**Longspun**, long'spun, *a.* Spun or extended to a great length; tedious.—**Long-suffering**, *a.* Bearing injuries or provocation for a long time; patient; not easily provoked.—*n.* Long endurance; patience of offense.—**Long-tongued**, *a.* Loquacious; prating; talkative.—**Longways, Longwise**, long'wāz, long'wīz, *adv.* In the direction of length; lengthwise.—**Long-winded**, *a.* Tedious in speaking, argument, or narration.

Long, long, *v.i.* [A. Sax. *langian*, to lengthen, to long, from *lang*, long; similarly Icel. *langa*, G. *verlangen*, to wish for.] To desire earnestly or eagerly: usually followed by the infinitive, or *for* or *after*; to have an eager appetite; to have a morbid craving: usually followed by *for*.—**Longer**, long'ėr, *n.* One who longs.—**Longing**, long'ing, *n.* An eager desire; a craving or morbid appetite.—**Longingly**, long'ing-li, *adv.* With eager wishes or appetite.

Longan, long'gan, *n.* A delicious Asiatic fruit akin to the litchi.

Longeval, Longevous, lon-jē'val, lon-jē'vus, *a.* [L. *longus*, long, and *ævum*, age.] Long-lived.—**Longevity**, lon-jev'i-ti, *n.* [L. *longævitas.*] Length or duration of life; more generally, great length of life.

Longicorn, lon'ji-korn, *a.* [L. *longus*, long, and *cornu*, a horn.] Long-horned: applied to certain insects of the beetle family, from the length of their antennæ.

Longimetry, lon-jim'et-ri, *n.* [L. *longus*, long, and Gr. *metron*, measure.] The measurement of distances or lengths.

Longing, Longingly. Under LONG, *v.i.*

Longipennate, lon-ji-pen'āt, *a.* [L. *longus*, long, *penna*, a wing.] Having long wings: said especially of a family of aquatic birds, including the albatross, gulls, terns, &c.

Longirostral, lon-ji-ros'tral, *a.* [L. *longus*, long, *rostrum*, a beak.] Having a long bill: applied to wading birds with long, slender, soft bills, such as the snipes, sandpipers, &c.

Longitude, lon'ji-tūd, *n.* [L. *longitudo*, from *longus*, long. LONG.] Length; measure along the longest line; *geog.* distance (in degrees, minutes, and seconds, or in miles) on the surface of the globe measured on an arc of the equator or a parallel of latitude, the meridian of Greenwich being selected as a starting-point, and called the first meridian, and longitude being called *east* or *west* accordingly; *astron.* distance measured on the ecliptic from the first point of Aries.—**Longitudinal**, lon-ji-tū'di-nal, *a.* Pertaining to longitude; running lengthwise, as distinguished from *transverse* or across.—*Longitudinal vibrations*, vibrations executed in the same line as that in which the undulation advances, as in the transmission of sound-waves through air.—**Longitudinally**, lon-ji-tū'di-nal-li, *adv.* In a longitudinal manner; lengthwise.

Loo, lö, *n.* [Originally called *lanterloo*, Fr. *lanturlu*, the meaningless refrain of a famous song.] A game at cards, formerly played with five cards, now commonly with three.—**Loo-table**, *n.* A round table for a sitting-room, often used for playing at loo.

Looby, lö'bi, *n.* [Allied to *lob*, *lubber*; W. *llabi*, a looby; *llab*, a blockhead.] An awkward, clumsy fellow; a lubber.

Loofa, lö'fa, *n.* [Ar. name.] The dried fibrous interior of a kind of gourd grown in Egypt and elsewhere, used as a flesh-brush in washing or bathing. Also written *Lufa*, *Loofar*.

Look, luk, *v.i.* [A.Sax. *lócian*, to look; akin Prov.G. *lugen*, O.H.G. *luogen*, *luoken*, to look, G. *loch*, a hole.] To direct the eye toward an object; to gaze; to apply the mind or understanding; to consider; to have expectation or anticipation; to expect; to take heed or care; to mind; to have a particular direction or situation; to face; to front; to appear; to have a particular aspect; to give certain indications; to have or assume any air or manner.—*To look about*, to look on all sides or in different directions.—*To look after*, to tend; to take care of; to seek; to search for.—*To look down on* or *upon*, to regard as an inferior; to regard with contempt; to despise.—*To look for*, to expect (*to look for* news); to seek or search for.—*To look into*, to inspect closely; to examine.—*To look on*, to regard; to consider; to think or judge.—*To look over*, to examine one by one.—*To look out*, to be on the watch.—*To look to*, to watch; to take care of; to depend on for fulfilling some expectation.—*To look through*, to see through; to penetrate with the eye or with the understanding; to take a view of the contents of.—*v.t.* To express or manifest by a look.—*To look out*, to search for and discover.—*To look up*, to search for till found; to pay a visit to. (*Colloq.*)—*n.* Cast of countenance; air of the face; aspect; the act of looking or seeing.—**Looker**, luk'ėr, *n.* One who looks.—*A looker on*, a mere spectator.—**Looking-for**, *n.* Anticipation; expectation.—**Looking-glass**, *n.* A glass silvered on the back and intended to show by reflection the person looking on it; a mirror.—**Look-out**, *n.* A careful looking or watching for any object or event; a place from which such observation is made; the person or party watching.

Loom, löm, *n.* [O.E. *lome*, A.Sax. *lóma*, tool, utensil, vessel; connections unknown. Hence *heir-loom*.] A frame or machine by means of which thread is worked into cloth, being either driven by the person weaving (a *hand-loom*) or driven and worked by steam or other motive-power (a *power-loom*); that part of an oar which is within the boat when used in rowing.

Loom, löm, *v.i.* [Icel. *ljóma*, to shine, *ljómi*, a ray; A.Sax. *leóman*, *leóma*, a ray or beam.] To appear larger than the real dimensions and indistinctly; to show large in darkness or fog: said of distant objects; to appear to the mind faintly or as at a distance.—**Looming**, löm'ing, *n.* The indistinct and magnified appearance of objects in particular states of the atmosphere.

Loon, lön, *n.* [Same word as O.D. *loen*, a stupid man.] A sorry fellow; a rogue; a rascal; a worthless fellow. (*Shak.*)

Loon, lön, *n.* [O.E. *loom*, Dan. *loom*, Icel. *lómr*, G. *lohme*, *lomme*, a loon.] A bird, the great northern diver.

Loop, löp, *n.* [Ir. *lup*, Gael. *lub*, *luib*, loop, noose, thong, &c.] The doubled part of a string, rope, chain, &c.; a noose; a bight; anything resembling a loop, as the bend of a river.—*v.t.* To form into a loop or loops; to furnish or fasten with a loop or loops.—*Aviation*, to make a complete circle vertically in the air, the machine being temporarily upside down, with the topside of the aeroplane remaining inside the circle; in an *outside loop*, the aeroplane remains outside the circle.

Loop, lōp, *n.* [G. *luppe*, a loop, akin *lupp*, rennet; same root as E. *leap*, D. *loopen*, to run; comp. *run*, in sense of melting.] A mass of half-melted iron taken from the furnace in a pasty state for the forge or hammer.

Loophole, lōp'hōl, *n.* [D. *luipen*, to peep.] A small aperture in the wall of a fortification through which small arms are fired at an enemy; a hole that gives a passage or the means of escape; *fig.* an underhand or unfair opportunity of escape or evasion.—**Loopholed**, lōp'hōld, *a.* Full of holes or openings for escape.—**Loop-light**, *n.* A small narrow light or window; a loophole for the admission of light.

Loose, lös, *a.* [A.Sax. *leás*, D. and G. *los*, Dan. Sw. *lös*, Icel. *laus*, loose; Goth. *laus*, empty; same as term. *-less*. *Lose*, *loss*, are closely allied.] Not attached together or to something fixed; untied; not fastened or confined; *fig.* free from ties; not tight or close (a *loose* garment); not dense, close, or compact (*loose* texture); not precise or exact; vague; indeterminate; lax; careless; unconnected; rambling; having lax bowels; dissolute; unchaste.—*To break loose*, to escape from confinement; to gain liberty by violence; *fig.* to cast off moral restraint.—*To let* or *set loose*, to free from restraint or confinement. Used substantively in the phrases.—*On the loose*, escaped from restraint; leading a loose life.—*To give a loose*, to give free vent. (*Thack.*)—*v.t.*—*loosed*, *loosing*. [Partly from the adj., partly from the allied A.Sax. *losian*, to set free.] To untie or unbind; to free from any fastening; to set free; to liberate; to relax; to loosen; to free from obligation, burden, or the like.—**Loose-box**, *n.* A roomy stall in a stable for a horse that is not tied.—**Loosely**, lös'li, *adv.* In a loose manner; laxly; slackly; carelessly; negligently; dissolutely.—**Loosen**, lös'n, *v.t.* To make loose; to untie; to unfix or unsettle; to free from restraint, tightness, tension, firmness, or fixedness.—*v.i.* To become loose.—**Loosener**, lös'n-ėr, *n.* One who or that which loosens.—**Looseness**, lös'nes, *n.* The state of being loose or relaxed; slackness; laxity; dissoluteness.

Loot, löt, *n.* [Hind. *lūt*, plunder.] Booty; plunder: especially such as is taken in a sacked city.—*v.t.* To plunder, as a sacked city; to ransack in search of plunder.—**Looter**, lö'tėr, *n.* One who loots.

Loover, lö'vėr, *n.* LOUVER.

Lop, lop, *v.t.*—*lopped*, *lopping*. [Akin O.D. *luppen*, to maim.] To cut off, as the top or extreme part of anything or superfluous parts; to trim by cutting.—*n.* The act of lopping; that which is lopped off.—**Lopper**, lop'ėr, *n.* One that lops.

Lop, lop, *v.i.* [Allied to *lap*.] To be pendulous, as the ears of some varieties of rabbits.—**Lop-eared**, *a.* Having pendulous ears.—**Loppy**, lop'i, *a.* Hanging loose; pendulous.—**Lop-sided**, *a.* Heavier at one side than the other; lying or inclining to one side.

Lophobranchiate, lō-fō-brang'ki-āt, *a.* [Gr. *lophos*, a crest or tuft, and *branchia*, gills.] Having the gills disposed in tufts along the branchial arches, as in the pipe-fish and hippocampus.

Lophophore, lō'fō-fōr, *n.* [Gr. *lophos*, a crest, and *pherō*, to carry.] *Zool.* the disc or stage upon which the tentacles of the Polyzoa are borne.

Loquacious, lo-kwā'shus, *a.* [L. *loquax*, *loquacis*, from *loquor*, to speak; Skr. *lap*, to speak, to talk; seen also in *locution*, *colloquy*, *eloquent*, *obloquy*, &c.] Talkative; given to continual talking; prating.—**Loquaciously**, lo-kwā'shus-li, *adv.* In a loquacious manner.—**Loquaciousness**, **Loquacity**, lo-kwā'shus-nes, lo-kwas'i-ti, *n.* The quality of being loquacious; talkativeness.

Loquat, lō'kwat, *n.* A Chinese and Japanese evergreen tree of the apple family, yielding a fruit the size of a large gooseberry, with the flavour of an apple.

Lorate, lō'rāt, *a.* [L. *lorum*, a thong, a strap.] *Bot.* shaped like a thong or strap.

Lorcha, lor'cha, *n.* A light Chinese sailing vessel, carrying guns, and built after the European model, but rigged like a junk.

Lord, lord, *n.* [O.E. *laverd*, *loverd*, &c., A.Sax. *hlaford*, a lord, from *hlāf*, bread, a loaf, and *weard*, E. *ward*, that is bread-ward. *Lady* also has *loaf* as first element.] A master; a person possessing supreme power and authority; a lady's husband; a ruler, governor, monarch; the proprietor of a manor; a nobleman; a title in Britain given to those who are noble by birth or creation, being thus applied to peers of the realm (dukes, marquises, earls, viscounts, and barons), and by courtesy to the sons of dukes and marquises, and to the eldest sons of earls; an honorary title of certain official personages, generally as part of a designation (*Lord* chancellor, *Lord*-mayor, *Lord*-provost). Also, and in this usage always with a capital letter, a designation of the Supreme Being; Jehovah; or applied to Christ, especially in the expression *our Lord*.—*The Lord's Supper*, the sacrament of the eucharist.—*Lords of Session*, the judges of the Court of Session in Scotland.—*Lords temporal*, those lay peers who have seats in the House of Lords.—*Lords spiritual*, the archbishops and bishops who have seats in the House of Lords.—*House of Lords*, that branch of the British legislature which consists of the lords spiritual and temporal assembled in one house.—*v.i.* To domineer; to rule with arbitrary or despotic sway: often followed by *over* and an indefinite *it* (to *lord it over* us).—**Lord-lieutenant**, *n.* In Britain, an official representing the sovereign, the principal official in a county.—**Lordlike**, lord'lik, *a.* Becoming a lord; haughty; proud.—**Lordliness**, lord'li-nes, *n.* The state or quality of being lordly.—**Lordly**, lord'li, *a.* Pertaining to, befitting, or suitable for a lord; large; liberal; haughty; imperious.—*adv.* Proudly; imperiously; despotically.—**Lord's-day**, *n.* The first day of the week; Sunday.—**Lordship**, lord'ship, *n.* The state or quality of being a lord; (with *his*, *your*, *their*) a title given to a lord; a title used in addressing judges and certain other persons in authority and office; dominion; sovereignty; the territory over which a lord holds jurisdiction.

Lore, lōr, *n.* [A.Sax. *lár*, from stem of *laeran*, to teach; D. *leer*, Dan. *laere*, G. *lehre*, lore. LEARN.] The store of knowledge which exists regarding anything; learning; erudition.—*Folk-lore*, the study of customs and legendary institutions.

Lore, lōr, *n.* [L. *lorum*, a strap.] *Ornith.* the space between the bill and the eye of a bird; *entom.* a horny process observed in the mouth of some insects.

Lorgnette, lor-nyet, *n.* [Fr., from *lorgner*, to spy or peep.] An opera-glass with folding handle; eyeglasses with hollow handle, into which they fold.

Lorica, lo-rī'ka, *n.* [L., originally a corselet of leather thongs, from *lorum*, a thong.] An ancient Roman cuirass or corselet; a kind of lute or clay with which vessels are coated before they are exposed to the fire, as in chemical processes; *zool.* the protective case with which certain infusoria are provided.—**Loricate**, lor'i-kāt, *v.t.*—*loricated*, *loricating*. To cover with some protective coating or crust.—**Loricate**, **Loricated**, lor'i-kā-ted, *pp.* Covered or plated over; covered as with plates of mail.—**Lorication**, lor-i-kā'shon, *n.* The act of loricating; a protective crust or covering.

Lorikeet, lor'i-kēt, *n.* [A dim. of *lory*, formed on the type of *parrakeet*.] The name of certain small Australian birds belonging to the parrot tribe.

Loriot, lor'i-ot, *n.* [Fr. *loriot*, for *loriol*, *l'oriol*, from L. *aureolus*, golden, from *aurum*, gold.] The golden oriole of Europe.

Loris, lō'ris, *n.* [Native name.] A quadrumanous mammal allied to the lemurs.

Lorn, lorn, *a.* [An old or poetic pp. of *loss*. FORLORN.] Undone; forsaken; forlorn.

Lorry, **Lorrie**, lor'i, *n.* [Comp. Prov. E. *lurry*, to pull or drag.] A four-wheeled truck or railroad car for heavy or bulky loads, with or without sides; a low, flat motor-driven or horse-drawn truck.

Lory, lō'ri, *n.* [Malay *luri*.] A name of certain Oriental birds of the parrot family with brilliant plumage.

Lose, löz, *v.t.*—*lost* (pret. & pp.), *losing*. [A. Sax. *losian*, to become loose, to lose, from *los*, loss, also *leósan*, to lose, usually in the compound form *forleósan*, like Goth. *fraliusan*, Dan. *forlise*, D. *verliezen*, G. *verlieren*. The old pp. was *loren*, hence E. *lorn*.] To cease to have in possession, as through accident; to become dispossessed or rid of unintentionally; to cease to possess; to forfeit, as by unsuccessful contest; not to gain or win; to wander from and not be able to find; to miss; to cease to perceive, as from distance or darkness; to cease or fail to see or hear.—*To lose one's self*, to lose one's way; to be bewildered.—*To lose one's temper*, to become angry.—*To lose sight of*, to cease to see; to overlook; to omit to take into calculation.—*v.i.* To forfeit anything in contest; to fail in a competition; not to win; to suffer by comparison.—**Loser**, lö'zėr, *n.* One who loses, or is deprived of anything by defeat, forfeiture, or the like.—**Losing**, lö'zing, *a.* Causing or incurring loss.—**Losingly**, lö'zing-li, *adv.* In a losing manner.—**Loss**, los, *n.* [A.Sax. *los*, damage.] The act of losing something; privation from something being lost; deprivation; forfeiture; failure to win or gain; that which is lost; quantity or amount lost; defeat; overthrow; ruin; misuse; failure to utilize (*loss* of time).—*To bear a loss*, to make it good; also, to sustain it without sinking under it.—*To be at a loss*, to be puzzled; to be unable to determine; to be in a state of uncertainty.—**Lost**, lost, *p.* and *a.* Parted with; not to be found; no longer held or possessed; missing (a *lost* book or sheep); forfeited, as in an unsuccessful contest; not gained (a *lost* prize, a *lost* battle); not employed or enjoyed; misspent; squandered; wasted; having wandered from the way, bewildered; perplexed; ruined; quite undone; wrecked or drowned at sea; hardened beyond sensibility or recovery (*lost* to shame); no longer perceptible to the senses; not visible (a person *lost* in a crowd).—*The lost*, those who are doomed to misery in a future state.

Losel,† lōz'l, *n.* A wastrel, worthless fellow.

Lot, lot, *n.* [A.Sax. *hlot*, from *hleótan*, to get by lot; D. *lot*, Dan. *lod*, Icel. *hlutr*, G. *loos*, Goth. *hlauts*, lot. Hence *allot*; akin *lottery*.] Something selected by or falling to a person by chance, and adopted to determine his fate, portion, or conduct; the part, fate, or fortune which falls to one by chance; part in life allotted to a person; a distinct portion or parcel (a *lot* of goods); a large or considerable quantity or number (a *lot* of people): often in plural in same sense (he has *lots* of money).—*To cast in one's lot with*, to connect one's fortunes with.—*To cast lots*, to throw dice or use similarly some other contrivance to settle a matter as by previous agreement determined.—*To draw lots*, to determine an event by drawing so many lots from a number whose marks are concealed from the drawers.—*v.t.*—*lotted*, *lotting*. To allot; to assign; to distribute; to sort; to catalogue; to portion.

Loth, lōth, *a.* [See LOATH.] Unwilling; not inclined; reluctant; loath.

Lothario, lō-thā'ri-ō, *n.* [From *Lothario*, one of the characters in Rowe's *Fair Penitent*.] A gay libertine; a seducer of female virtue; a gay deceiver: as *Lovelace*, the character in Richardson's *Clarissa*.

Lotion, lō'shon, *n.* [L. *lotio*, from *lavo*, to wash. LAVE.] A wash or fluid preparation for improving the complexion, &c.;

a fluid applied externally in cutaneous diseases to relieve pain, and the like.

Lottery, lot'ėr-i, *n.* [Fr. *loterie*. LOT.] Allotment or distribution by lots or chance; a procedure or scheme for the distribution of prizes by lot; the drawing of lots.

Lotto, lot'ō, *n.* [It. *lotto*, lottery.] A game of chance, played with a series of balls or knobs, numbering from one to ninety, with a set of cards or counters having corresponding numbers.

Lotus, Lotos, lō'tus, lō'tōs, *n.* [Gr. *lōtos*.] A name vaguely applied to a number of different plants famous in mythology and tradition; especially, a tree, the fruit of which was fabled among the ancient Greeks to have the property of making people forget their country and friends and to remain idle in the lotus-land; a name also applied to the Egyptian water-lily and other plants. — **Lotophagi**, lō-tof'a-ji, *n. pl.* [Lit. lotus-eaters.] The name of a mythological people who lived on the fruit of the lotus-tree.—**Lotus-eater, Lotos-eater**, *n.* One of the Lotophagi.—**Lotus-land, Lotos-land**, *n.* The country of the lotus-eaters.

Loud, loud, *a.* [A.Sax. *hlúd*, loud; O.Sax. O.Fris. *hlúd*, D. *luid*, G. *laut*, loud; Icel. *hljóth*, G. *laut*, sound; akin *listen*; cog. Gr. *klyō*, to hear, *klytos*, famous; L. *(in)clytus*, famous; *laus*, praise, whence E. *laud*.] Strong or powerful in sound; high-sounding; making use of high words; clamorous; vehement; flashy; showy: colloquially applied to dress or manner.—*adv.* Loudly.—**Loudly**, loud'li, *adv.* In a loud manner; with great sound or noise; noisily; clamorously; vehemently.—**Loudness**, loud'nes, *n.* The quality of being loud; noise; clamour.

Lough, lok, *n.* The Irish form of *Loch*.

Louis-d'or, lö-ē-dor, *n.* [Fr., a Louis of gold, as *Napoleon*, *Daric* (Darius), *Philip*, *Jacobus*.] A gold coin of France, first struck in 1640, in the reign of *Louis* XIII, and ranging in value from about 16*s.* 7*d.* to 18*s.* 9½*d.* sterling.

Lounge, lounj, *v.i.*—*lounged*, *lounging*. [O.E. *lungis*, an awkward, slow-moving fellow, from O.Fr. *longis*, *longin*, a lout, from *long*, L. *longus*, long.] To dawdle or loiter; to spend the time in idly moving about; to recline in a lazy manner; to loll.—*n.* A sauntering or strolling; the act of reclining at ease or lolling; a place which idlers frequent; a kind of couch or sofa.—**Lounger**, loun'jėr, *n.* One who lounges.—**Lounging**, loun'jing, *a.* Pertaining to a lounger; lolling.

Louse, lous, *n.* pl. **Lice**, līs. [A.Sax. *lús*, pl. *lys* = D. *luis*, Dan. *lus*, Icel. *lús*, G. *laus*, perhaps from root of *lose*.] The common name of various wingless insects, parasitic on man and other animals.—*v.t.* (louz)—*loused*, *lousing*. To clean from lice.—**Lousily**, lou'zi-li, *adv.* In a lousy manner.—**Lousiness**, lou'zi-nes, *n.* The state of being lousy.—**Lousy**, lou'zi, *a.* Swarming with lice; infested with lice.

Lout, lout, *v.i.* [A.Sax. *lútan*, to bow or stoop; Icel. *lúta*, Dan. *lude*, to stoop; same root as *little*.] To bend, bow, or stoop down.—*n.* A mean awkward fellow; a bumpkin; a clown.—**Loutish**, lout'ish, *a.* Clownish; rude; awkward.—**Loutishly**, lout'ish-li, *adv.* In a loutish manner.—**Loutishness**, lout'ish-nes, *n.*

Louver, Loover, lö'vėr, *n.* [Fr. *lover*, *lovier*, a louver; a word of which the origin is unknown.] A dome or turret rising out of the roof of a hall or other apartment, formerly open at the sides, and intended to allow the smoke to escape.—*Louver window*, a window partially closed by sloping boards or bars called *louver boards* (corrupted into *luffer* or *lever boards*), placed across so as to admit air, but exclude rain.

Lovage, lov'āj, *n.* [By corruption from L. *ligusticum*, lovage, from *Ligusticus*, Ligurian.] A name of certain stout, umbelliferous plants of Europe, one of them specially known as Scottish lovage.

Love, luv, *v.t.*—*loved*, *loving*. [A.Sax. *lufian*, from *lufu*, love; D. *lieven*, G. *lieben*, to love, *liebe*, love; allied to *lief*, dear, *leave*, permission, *believe*; L. *libido*, desire, *liber*, free (whence *liberal*); *libeo*, *lubeo*, to please; Skr. *lubh*, to desire.] To regard with a strong feeling of affection; to have a devoted attachment to; to regard with the characteristic feelings of one sex towards the other; to like; to be pleased with; to delight in.—*v.i.* To be in love; to love each other; to be tenderly attached.—*n.* A strong feeling of affection; devoted attachment to a person; especially, devoted attachment to a person of the opposite sex; courtship (as in the phrase to *make love to*, that is, to court, to woo); fondness; strong liking (*love* of home, of art, &c.); the object beloved; a sweetheart; a representation or personification of love; a Cupid.—*Love* is the first element in a great number of compound words of obvious signification.—**Lovable, Loveable**, luv'a-bl, *a.* Worthy of love; amiable.—**Love-apple**, *n.* The tomato.—**Love-bird**, *n.* A name of a diminutive bird belonging to the parrot family, so called from the great attachment shown to each other by the male and female.—**Love-charm**, *n.* A charm by which love was supposed to be excited; a philtre.—**Love-child**, *n.* An illegitimate child.—**Love-feast**, *n.* AGAPE.—**Love-in-idleness**, *n.* A plant, the heart's-ease.—**Love-knot**, *n.* A complicated knot, or a figure representing such; so called from being symbolic of love.—**Loveless**, luv'les, *a.* Void of love.—**Love-letter**, *n.* A letter professing love; a letter of courtship.—**Lovelily**,† luv'li-li, *adv.* In a lovely manner.—**Loveliness**, luv'li-nes, *n.* The state or quality of being lovely; great beauty.—**Love-lock**, *n.* A particular curl or lock of hair hanging by itself or so as to appear prominently.—**Love-lorn**, *a.* Forsaken by one's love; pining or suffering from love.—**Lovely**, luv'li, *a.* Fitted to attract or excite love; exciting admiration through beauty; extremely beautiful.—**Love-making**, *n.* Courtship; paying one's addresses to a lady.—**Love-match**, *n.* A marriage entered into for love alone.—**Lover**, luv'ėr, *n.* One who loves or is attached to another; a person in love; a man who loves a woman; one who likes or has a fondness for anything (a *lover* of books).—**Love-sick**, *a.* Sick or languishing with love; expressive of languishing love.—**Loving**, luv'ing, *p.* and *a.* Fond; affectionate; expressing love or kindness.—**Loving-cup**, *n.* A large cup containing liquor passed from guest to guest at banquets, especially those of a ceremonious character.—**Lovingkindness**, luv'ing-kind-nes, *n.* Tender regard; mercy; favour: a scriptural word.—**Lovingly**, luv'ing-li, *adv.* In a loving manner; affectionately.—**Lovingness**, luv'ing-nes, *n.*

Lover. LOUVRE.

Low, lō, *a.* [O.E. *law*, *lagh*, &c.; not in A. Sax. = Icel. *lágr*, Dan. *lav*, D. *laag*; akin to *lie*, and to *law*.] Not rising to any great elevation; of little height; the opposite of *high*; not of the usual height; much below the adjacent ground; not much above sea-level; below the usual rate or amount (*low* wages; a *low* estimate); not loud; grave; depressed in the scale of sounds; indicative of a numerical smallness (a *low* number); near or not very distant from the equator (a *low* latitude, as opposed to a *high* latitude); dejected; depressed; humble in rank; in a mean condition; mean; vulgar; grovelling; base; dishonourable; feeble; having little vital energy (a *low* pulse; a *low* state of health); not excessive or intense; not violent (a *low* temperature); plain; not rich, high-seasoned, or nourishing (a *low* diet).—*Low Church*, the party in the *Ch.* of *Eng.* which is opposed to the High Church Party.—*Low Dutch*, *Low German*. DUTCH, GERMAN.—*Low Sunday*, the Sunday next after Easter.—*Low water*, *low tide*, the lowest point of the ebb or receding tide.—*Low wine*, a liquor produced by the first distillation of alcohol; the first run of the still.—*adv.* Not aloft or on high; near the ground; under the usual price; in a mean condition;—**Low-born**, *a.* Of mean or lowly birth.—**Low-brow**, *a.* (*Slang.*) A term applied to a person having a low forehead, and, supposedly, limited culture.—*n.* One who is supposed not to appreciate intellectual influences.—**Lower-case**, *n.* *Printing*, the case of boxes that contains the small letters of printing-type; hence, small letters of printing-type.—**Lower-class**, *a.* Pertaining to persons of the humbler ranks.—**Lower Empire**. The later Greek Empire, succeeding Constantine, with depreciatory sense.—**Low-down**, *a.* Mean; sneaking; treacherous.—*n.* The facts in the case; the truth of the matter.—**Lowland**, lō'land, *n.* Land which is low with respect to the neighboring country; a low or level country.—*The Lowlands*, applies to the southern parts of Scotland.—**Low-life**, *n.* Low condition or social position; mean social position.—**Lowliness**, lō'li-nes, *n.* The state of being lowly.—**Lowly**, lō'li, *a.* Low or humble in position of life; not lofty or exalted; meek; free from pride.—*adv.* In a low manner or condition.—**Lowness**, lō'nes, *n.* The state of being low; want of elevation; depression; dejection; meanness.—**Low-pressure**, *a.* Having a low degree of expansive force, and consequently exerting a low degree of pressure; applied to steam or steam-engines.—**Low-spirited**, *a.* Cast down in spirit; dejected; depressed.

Low, lō, *v.i.* [A.Sax. *hlówan* = D. *loeijen*, Icel. *hlóa*, O.H.G. *hlojan*, to low.] To bellow, as an ox or cow.—*n.* The sound uttered by a bovine animal, as a bull, ox, cow; a moo.—**Lowing**, lō'ing, *n.* The bellowing or cry of cattle.

Lower, lō'ėr, *v.t.* [From *lower*, compar. of *low*; comp. *linger*, from *long*, adj.] To make lower in position; to let down; to take or bring down; to reduce or humble; to make less high or haughty; to reduce, as value or amount.

Lower, lou'ėr, *v.i.* [Same word as D. *loeren*, to frown; L.G. *luren*, to look sullen; akin to *leer*.] To frown; to look sullen; to appear dark or gloomy; to be clouded; to threaten a storm.—**Lowering**, lou'ėr-ing, *p.* and *a.* Threatening a storm; cloudy; overcast.—**Loweringly**, lou'ėr-ing-li, *adv.* In a lowering manner.—**Lowery**, lou'ėr-i, *a.* Cloudy; gloomy.

Lown, loun, *n.* A low fellow; a loon. (*Shak.*)

Loxodromic, lok-so-drom'ik, *a.* [Gr. *loxos*, oblique, and *dromos*, a course.] Pertaining to oblique sailing, or sailing by the rhumb.—*Loxodromic curve*, or *line*, or *spiral*, the path of a ship when her course is directed constantly towards the same point of the compass, in a direction oblique to the equator, so as to cut all the meridians at equal angles.—**Loxodromics, Loxodromy**, lok-so-drom'iks, lok-sod'ro-mi, *n.* The art of oblique sailing by the loxodromic curve.

Loyal, loi'al, *a.* [Fr. *loyal*, O.Fr. *loial*, *leial*, *leal*, from L. *legalis*, legal, from *lex*, *legis*, a law. *Leal* is another form. LEGAL.] True or faithful in allegiance; faithful to the lawful government, to a prince or superior; true to plighted faith, duty, or love; not treacherous; constant.—**Loyalist**, loi'al-ist, *n.* A person who adheres to his sovereign or to constituted authority.—**Loyally**, loi'al-li, *adv.* In a loyal manner; faithfully.—**Loyalness, Loyalism**, loi'al-nes, loi'al-izm, *n.* Loyalty.—**Loyalty**, loi'al-ti, *n.* The state or quality of being loyal; fidelity; constancy.

Lozenge, loz'enj, *n.* [Fr. *losange*, probably from Sp. *losa*, a slate or flat stone for paving.] A rectilineal figure with four equal sides, having two acute and two obtuse angles: called also a *diamond*; a small cake of sugar, &c., originally in the form of a lozenge, but now variously shaped; a small diamond-shaped pane of glass in a window.

Lubber, lub'ėr, *n.* [Allied to *looby*, *lob*, W. *llob*, *llabi*, a lubber.] A clumsy or awkward fellow; a term applied by sailors to one who does not know seamanship.—

Lubber's point, a black vertical mark drawn on the inside of the case of the mariner's compass in a line with the ship's head, as a guide to show the vessel's course.—*Lubber's hole*, the hole in the top or platform at the head of a lower mast through which sailors may mount without going over the rim by the futtock-shrouds.—**Lubberly**, lub'ėr-li, *a.* Like a lubber; clumsy; clownish.

Lubra, lö'bra, *n.* Australian name for a female of aboriginal race.

Lubricate, lū'bri-kāt, *v.t.*—*lubricated, lubricating.* [L. *lubrico*, from *lubricus*, slippery.] To soften with an emollient or mucilaginous substance; to rub or supply with an oily or greasy substance, for diminishing friction.—**Lubricant**, lū'bri-kant, *a.* Lubricating.—*n.* That which lubricates.—**Lubrication**, lū-bri-kā'shon, *n.* The act of lubricating.—**Lubricator**, lū'bri-kā-tėr, *n.* One who or that which lubricates; an oil-cup attached to a machine. —**Lubricity**, lū-bris'i-ti, *n.* Smoothness or slipperiness; instability; shiftiness; lasciviousness.

Lucarne, lū'kärn, *n.* [Fr. *lucarne*, L. *lucerna*, a lamp, from *luceo*, to shine.] A dormer or garret window.

Luce, lūs, *n.* [L. *lucius.*] The fish called the pike.

Lucent, lū'sent, *a.* [L. *lucens, lucentis*, ppr. of *luceo*, to shine. LUCID.] Shining; bright; resplendent.—**Lucency**, lū'sen-si, *n.* The state or quality of being lucent.

Lucernal, lū-sėr'nal, *a.* [L. *lucerna*, a lamp.] Pertaining to a lamp or other artificial light.—*Lucernal microscope*, a microscope in which the object is illuminated by artificial light.

Lucerne, Lucern, lū'sėrn, *n.* [Fr. *luzerne, luserne*; origin unknown.] A leguminous plant cultivated for fodder in the U. S. and Europe; also called alfalfa.

Lucid, lū'sid, *a.* [L. *lucidus*, from *luceo*, to shine.] Clear; bright; shining; transparent; of normal intellectual faculties; sane.—**Lucida**, lū'si-da, *n.* A term in astronomy, applied to the brightest star in a constellation.—**Lucidity**, lū-sid'i-ti, *n.* The state or quality of having a clear mind.—**Lucidly**, lū'sid-li, *adv.* In a lucid manner; clearly; brightly; sanely.—**Lucidness**, lū'sid-nes, *n.* The state or quality of being lucid. —**Lucifugal**, lū-sif'ū-gal, *a.* Avoiding bright light.

Lucifer, lö'si-fėr, *n.* [L. *lux, lucis*, light, and *fero*, to bring.] The morning-star; Satan (from an erroneous interpretation of the term as applied by Isaiah); a person of Satanic attributes; a match ignitible by friction: called also *Lucifer-match.*—**Luciferian**, lö-si-fē'ri-an, *a.* Pertaining to Lucifer; devilish.—**Luciferous**, lö-cif'ėr-us, *a.* Light-giving.

Luciferin, lö-cif'ėr-in, *n.* A substance generated by luminescent fishes and insects which causes their luminosity.

Lucifugal, Lucifugous, lū-sif'ū-gal, lū-sif'ū-gus, *a.* [L. *lux, lucis*, light, and *fugio*, to flee.] Shunning or avoiding the light of day, as bats and cockroaches.

Luck, luk, *n.* [O.Fris. *luk*, D. *luk, geluk*, G. *glück*, fortune, prosperity; allied to D. *lokken*, Dan. *lokke*, G. *locken*, to entice.] What is regarded as happening by chance; what chance or fortune sends; fortune; chance; accident; hap; good fortune; success.—**Luckily**, luk'i-li, *adv.* In a lucky manner.—**Luckiness**, luk'i-nes, *n.* The state or quality of being lucky.—**Luckless**, luk'les, *a.* Without luck; ill-fated; unfortunate.—**Lucklessly**, luk'les-li, *adv.* In a luckless manner.—**Lucklessness**, luk'les-nes, *n.*—**Lucky**, luk'i, *a.* Favoured by luck; fortunate; meeting with good success; sent by good luck; favourable; auspicious.

Lucrative, lū'kra-tiv, *a.* [Fr. *lucratif*, from L. *lucrativus*, from *lucror*, to profit, from *lucrum*, gain; same root as G. *lohn*, reward.] Yielding lucre or gain; gainful; profitable.—**Lucratively**, lū'kra-tiv-li, *adv.* In a lucrative manner.—**Lucre**, lū'kėr, *n.* [Fr. *lucre*, L. *lucrum.*] Gain in money; profit; pelf: often in sense of base or unworthy gain.—**Lucrous**, lū'krus, *a.* Pertaining to lucre or gain.

Lucubrate, lū'kū-brāt, *v.i.* [L. *lucubro, lucubratum*, to study by candle-light, from obs. adj. *lucuber*, bringing light, from *lux*, light.] To study by candle-light or a lamp; to study by night.—*v.t.* To elaborate, as by laborious night-study.—**Lucubration**, lū-kū-brā'shon, *n.* Nocturnal study; what is composed, or supposed to be composed, by night; a literary composition of any kind.—**Lucubrator**, lū'kū-brā-tėr, *n.* One who makes lucubrations.

Luculent, lū'kū-lent, *a.* [L. *luculentus*, from *luceo*, to shine.] Lucid; bright; evident; unmistakable.

Lucullan, lū-kul'lan, *a.* [From the Roman consul *Lucullus*, who was famous for luxurious living.] Bountiful, voluptuous.—**Lucullite**, lū-kul'līt, *n.* A variety of limestone used for ornamental purposes.

Luddite, lud'īt, *n.* In 18th Century England, one of the rioters against the displacement of factory workers by machinery. (From a leader, Ned Lud.)

Ludicrous, lū'dik-rus, *a.* [L. *ludicrus*, from *ludus*, sport or game; seen also in *allude, delude, elude, illusion, prelude.*] Adapted to raise good-humoured laughter; very ridiculous; comical; droll.—**Ludicrously**, lū'dik-rus-li, *adv.* In a ludicrous manner.—**Ludicrousness**, lū'dik-rus-nes, *n.*

Lues, lū'ēz, *n.* [L.] A poison or pestilence; a plague.—*Lues venerea*, the venereal disease.

Luff, luf, *n.* [Formerly *loof*, from D. *loef*, Dan. *luv*, G. *luf*, weather-gauge; akin to A.Sax. *lyft*, the air, to the verb to *lift*, and to *loft*. Hence *aloof.*] *Naut.* the weather-gauge; the weather part of a fore-and-aft sail, or the side next the mast or stay to which it is attached.—*v.i.* To turn the head of a ship toward the wind; to sail near the wind.—**Luff-tackle**, *n.* *Naut.* a purchase composed of a double and single block, each fitted with a hook.

Lug, lug, *v.t.*—*lugged, lugging.* [A.Sax. *geluggian*, to lug; Sw. *lugga*, to draw, to haul, *lugg*, N. *lug*, the forelock or hair of the head; comp. A.Sax. *lyccan*, Dan. *luge*, to pluck.] To haul; to drag; to pull along or carry, as something heavy and moved with difficulty.—*n.* The ear; a projecting part of an object resembling the human ear, as the handle of a vessel.—**Luggage**, lug'āj, *n.* Anything cumbersome and heavy to be carried; a traveller's packages or baggage.—**Luggage-van**, *n.* A wagon or carriage for holding luggage.—**Lugger**, lug'ėr, *n.* [A vessel having *lug*-sails; Dan. *lugger*, D. *logger.*] A vessel carrying either two or three masts with lug-sails and a running bowsprit.—**Lug-sail**, *n.* [Perhaps from the upper corner of the sail forming a kind of *lug.*] A square sail bent upon a yard that hangs obliquely to the mast at one-third of its length.

Lugubrious, lū-gū'bri-us, *a.* [L. *lugubris*, mournful, from *lugeo*, to weep; akin Gr. *lygros*, sad.] Mournful; indicating or expressive of sorrow; doleful.—**Lugubriously**, lū-gū'bri-us-li, *adv.* In a lugubrious manner.—**Lugubriousness, Lugubriosity**, lū-gū'bri-us-nes, lū-gū'bri-os''i-ti, *n.* The quality of being lugubrious.

Lugworm, lug'wėrm, *n.* [Sw. *lugg*, tuft of hair, the forelock; it has tufts and bristles along its sides.] An annelid or worm which burrows in the muddy sand of the shore, and is much esteemed for bait. Also called *Lob-worm.*

Lukewarm, lūk'wạrm, *a.* [O.E. *luke*, lukewarm, D. *leuk*, A.Sax. *wlæc*, lukewarm; O.E. *lewe*, G. *lau*, lukewarm.] Moderately warm; tepid; not ardent; not zealous; cool; indifferent.—**Lukewarmly**, lūk'wạrm-li, *adv.* In a lukewarm degree or manner.—**Lukewarmness**, lūk'wạrm-nes, *n.* The state or quality of being lukewarm.

Lull, lul, *v.t.* [Dan. *lulle*, Sw. *lulla*, G. *lullen*, to sing to sleep, D. *lollen*, to sing badly; probably an imitation of the sound; comp. L. *lallo*, to sing lullaby.] To sing to in order to induce to sleep; to cause to rest by gentle, soothing means; to quiet; to compose.—*v.i.* To subside; to cease; to become calm (the wind *lulls*).—*n.* A season of temporary quiet after storm, tumult, or confusion.—**Lullaby**, lul'a-bī, *n.* A song to lull or quiet babes; that which quiets.

Lumachel, Lumachella, lū'ma-kel, lū'ma-kel-la, *n.* [It. *lumachella*, properly a little snail or shell, from L. *limax*, a snail.] A calcareous stone composed of shells and coral agglomerated, and so hard as to admit of polish.

Lumbago, lum-bā'gō, *n.* [L., from *lumbus*, loin.] Rheumatism or rheumatic pains affecting the lumbar region.—**Lumbaginous**, lum-baj'i-nus, *a.* Pertaining to lumbago.—**Lumbar, Lumbal**, lum'bär, lum'bal, *a.* [L. *lumbus*, a loin. LOIN.] Pertaining to the loins.—*Lumbar region*, the portion of the body between the false ribs and the upper part of the hip bone: the small of the back.

Lumber, lum'bėr, *n.* [Originally a pawnbroking establishment, from the *Lombards*, who were famed as pawnbrokers or money-lenders.] Things bulky and thrown aside as of no use: old furniture, discarded utensils, or the like; timber sawed or split for use as beams, boards, planks, &c.—*v.t.* To heap together in disorder; to fill with lumber.—*v.i.* To move heavily, as a vehicle; to cut timber in the forest and prepare it for the market.—**Lumbering**, *n.* Logging; cutting and removing timber for commercial purposes.—*a.* Clumsy; awkward.—**Lumberjack**, *n.* A timber-cutter. (*Colloq.*)

Lumbrical, lum'bri-kal, *a.* [L. *lumbricus*, a worm.] Pertaining to or resembling a worm.—*n.* A worm-like muscle of the fingers and toes.

Lumbricus, *n.* An earthworm; familiarly known as angleworm or fishworm.

Lumen, lö'men, *n.* [L. for *light.*] The cavity of a blood-vessel or other tube.

Luminary, lū'mi-na-ri, *n.* [Fr. *luminaire*, L. *luminare*, from *lumen, luminis*, light, for *lucmen*, from *luceo*, to shine. LUCID.] Any body that gives light, but chiefly one of the heavenly bodies; a person who enlightens mankind.—**Luminant**, lū'mi-nant, *a.* Emitting light; shining; luminous. —**Luminescence**, *n.* The emission of light by certain bodies that have been exposed to light or radiant energy, or self-generated light, as in fireflies and certain deep-sea fishes.—**Luminiferous**, lū-mi-nif'ėr-us, *a.* Producing light; yielding light; serving as the medium for conveying light (the *luminiferous* ether).—**Luminosity, Luminousness, Luminance**,† lū-mi-nos'i-ti, lū-mi-nus-nes, lū'mi-nans, *n.* The quality of being luminous; brightness; clearness.—**Luminous**, lū'mi-nus, *a.* [L. *luminosus.*] Shining; emitting light; bright; brilliant; giving mental light; clear (a *luminous* essay or argument).

Lummox, lum'uks, *n.* A dull-witted, awkward person.

Lump, lump, *n.* [O.D. *lompe*, Sw. *lump*, N. *lump*, piece, mass; allied to *lubber, lunch.*] A small mass of matter, of no definite shape; a mass of things blended or thrown together without order or distinction.—*In the lump*, the whole together; in gross.—*v.t.* To throw into a mass; to take in the gross. —**Lumpfish, Lumpsucker**, lump'fish, lump'suk-ėr, *n.* A fish of the northern seas, having the ventral fins modified into a sucker, by means of which it adheres to bodies.—**Lump-sugar**, *n.* Loaf-sugar in small lumps or pieces.—**Lumpy**, lump'i, *a.* Full of lumps or small compact masses.

Lunacy, lū'na-si, *n.* [From L. *lunaticus*, lunatic, moon-struck, from *luna*, the moon (lunatics being at one time supposed to be affected by the moon), for *lucna*, from root of *luceo*, to shine. LUCID.] The state or quality of being lunatic; insanity; properly the kind of insanity which is broken by intervals of reason; the height of folly.—**Lunatic**, lū'na-tik, *a.* Affected by lunacy;

mad; insane.—*n.* A person affected by lunacy; an insane person.—*Lunatic asylum*, a house or hospital established for the reception of lunatics.

Lunar, lū'nėr, *a.* [L. *lunaris*, from *luna*, the moon. LUNACY.] Pertaining to the moon; measured by the revolutions of the moon (*lunar* days or years).—*Lunar caustic*, nitrate of silver (silver being called *Luna* by the alchemists).—*Lunar cycle*, the period required for the new moons to return on the same days of the year.—*Lunar distance*, the distance of the moon from the sun or a star, by means of which the longitude of a ship at sea is found.—*Lunar month*, the period of a complete revolution of the moon, 29½ days.—*Lunar theory*, the theory that analyses and explains the perturbations to which the moon is subject in her revolution.—*Lunar year*, a period of twelve lunar months.—**Lunate, Lunated**, lū'nāt, lū'nā-ted, *a.* Having a form like that of the half-moon; crescent-shaped.—**Lunation**, lū-nā'shon, *n.* The time from one new moon to the following.

Lunatic. Under LUNACY.

Lunch, lunsh, *n.* [A form of *lump*, as *hunch* of *hump*, *bunch* of *bump*.] A luncheon.—*v.t.* To eat a lunch.—**Luncheon**, lunsh'-on, *n.* [A longer form of *lunch*, perhaps for *lunching*.] A slight repast or meal between breakfast and dinner.—**Lunch-room**, *n.* A room where lunch may be eaten; a restaurant where quick meals are served.

Lune, lūn, *n.* [L. *luna*, the moon. LUNACY.] Anything in the shape of a crescent or half-moon; a geometrical figure in shape of a crescent.—**Lunette**, lū-net', *n.* [Fr. *lunette*, dim. from L. *luna*.] *Fort.* a work in the form of a redan with flanks, used as an advanced work; *arch.* an aperture for the admission of light in a concave ceiling; *archæol.* a crescent-shaped ornament for the neck.—**Luniform**, lū'ni-form, *a.* Resembling the moon.

Lung, lung, *n.* [A.Sax. *lunge*, pl. *lungan*, Icel. *lunga*, D. *long*, D. and G. *lunge*, a lung; same root as *light*, from their lightness (comp. the name *lights*).] One of the two organs of respiration in air-breathing animals, light and spongy and full of air-cells.—**Lunged**, lungd, *a.* Having lungs: chiefly in composition.—**Lungwort**, lung'-wėrt, *n.* A common garden flower, having leaves speckled like lungs; also a kind of lichen used in diseases of the lungs.

Lunge, lunj, *n.* [Formerly *longe*, *allonge*, from Fr. *allonger*, to lengthen, to thrust—L. *ad*, to, *longus*, long.] A sudden thrust or pass, as with a sword. — *v.i. lunged*, *lunging.* To make a thrust or pass, as with a sword or rapier.—*v.t.* To exercise (a horse) by making him run round in a ring while held by a *long* rein.

Lunisolar, lū-ni-sō'lėr, *a.* [L. *luna*, moon, and *sol*, sun.] Compounded of the revolutions of the sun and moon; resulting from the united action of the sun and moon.—**Lunula, Lunule**, lū'nū-la, lū'nūl, *n.* [Dim. of L. *luna*, the moon.] Something in the shape of a little moon or crescent. Also **Lunulet**, lū'nū-let. — **Lunular**, lū'nū-lėr, *a.* Having the form of a small crescent.—**Lunulate, Lunulated**, lū'-nū-lāt, lū'nū-lā-ted, *a.* Resembling a small crescent.

Lupercal, lū-pėr'kal or lū'pėr-kal, *a.* Pertaining to the Lupercalia, or feasts of the Romans in honour of Lupercus or Pan.—*n.* pl. **Lupercalia**, lū-pėr-kā'li-a. An ancient Roman feast in honour of Pan.

Lupine, lū'pīn, *a.* [L. *lupus*, a wolf; cog. with E. *wolf*.] Like a wolf; wolfish; ravenous.—**Lupine**, lū'pin, *n.* [Fr. *lupin*; L. *lupinus*, in allusion to its destroying or exhausting land.] The name of various leguminous plants, some of which are commonly cultivated in gardens for the sake of their gaily-coloured flowers.

Lupulin, Lupuline, lū'pū-lin, *n.* [L. *lupulus*, hops.] The peculiar bitter aromatic principle of the hop; the fine yellow powder of hops, which contains the bitter principle, largely used in medicine.

Lupus, lū'pus, *n.* [L., a wolf.] A disease which eats away the flesh, producing ragged ulcerations of the nose, cheeks, forehead, eyelids, and lips.

Lurch, lėrch, *n.* [O.Fr. *lourche*, It. *lurcio*, G. *lurz*, *lurtsch*, a lurch at cribbage.] A term in the game of cribbage, denoting the position of a player who has not made his thirty-first hole when his opponent has pegged his sixty-first. Hence, *to leave in the lurch*, to leave in a difficult situation or in embarrassment; to leave in a forlorn state or without help.

Lurch, lėrch, *v.i.* [A form of *lurk*, as *church* of *kirk*, *birch* of *birk*, &c. LURK.] To lie in ambush or in secret; to lie close; to lurk; to shift or to play tricks (*Shak.*); to roll suddenly to one side, as a ship in a heavy sea; to stagger to one side, as a tipsy man.—*n.* A sudden roll of a ship; a roll or stagger of a person.—**Lurcher**, lėrch'ėr, *n.* One that lies in wait or lurks; a dog that lies in wait for game.

Lurdan, Lurdane, lėr'dan, lėr'dān, *a.* [O.Fr. *lourdin*, *lourdein*, from *lourd*, heavy, dull.] Blockish; stupid; clownish; lazy and useless. (*Tenn.*)

Lure, lūr, *n.* [Fr. *leurre*, from M.H.G. *luodar*, a lure, G. *luder*, carrion, a bait for wild beasts.] Any artificial bait, usually imitating the appearance of insects or small fish, used in angling; any enticement; that which invites by the prospect of advantage or pleasure.—*v.t.*—*lured*, *luring.* To attract by a lure or to a lure; to entice; to attract; to invite.

Lurid, lū'rid, *a.* [L. *luridus*.] Pale yellow, as flame; ghastly pale. Also vivid; violent; harshly terrible; as a *lurid* crime or *lurid* story

Lurk, lėrk, *v.i.* [Akin to N. *luska*, Dan. *luske*, to lurk, to skulk; Dan. *lur*, G. *lauer*, an ambush or watching.] To lie hid; to lie in wait; to lie concealed or unperceived.—**Lurker**, lėr'kėr, *n.* One that lurks.—**Lurking-place**, *n.* A place in which one lurks; a hiding-place; a den.

Luscious, lush'us, *a.* [Perhaps for *lustious*, from *lusty*.] Very sweet; delicious; delightful; sweet to excess, hence, unctuous; fulsome. — **Lusciously**, lush'us-li, *adv.* In a luscious manner.—**Lusciousness**, lush'us-nes, *n.* The state or quality of being luscious.

Lush, lush, *a.* [Shortened from *luscious*.] Fresh, luxuriant, and juicy; succulent.

Lust, lust, *n.* [A.Sax., D., G., and Sw. *lust*, Icel. and Dan. *lyst*, Goth. *lustus*, desire. Hence the verbs to *lust*, to *list*, and adj. *lusty*. LIST.] Longing desire; eagerness to possess or enjoy; depraved affection or desire; more especially, sexual appetite; unlawful desire of sexual pleasure; concupiscence.—*v.i.* To desire eagerly; to long; to have carnal desire: with *after*.—**Lustful**, lust'ful, *a.* Inspired by lust or the sexual appetite; provoking to sensuality.—**Lustfully**, lust'ful-li, *adv.* In a lustful manner. — **Lustfulness**, lust'ful-nes, *n.* The state of being lustful.

Luster, Lustre, lus'tėr, *n.* [Fr. *lustre*, from L. *lustrum*, purificatory sacrifice (see LUSTRAL), or from stem of *luceo*, to shine (see LUCID).] Brightness; splendor; brilliance; sheen; *mineral.* a variation in the nature of the reflecting surface of minerals; the splendor of birth, of deeds, or of fame; renown; distinction; a branched chandelier ornamented with drops or pendants of cut glass; a fabric for ladies' dresses, consisting of cotton warp and woolen weft.—**Lusterless**, lus'tėr-les, *a.* Destitute of luster.—**Lustring**, lus'tring, *n.* A species of glossy silk cloth.—**Lustrous**, lus'trus, *a.* Characterized by luster; bright; shining; luminous.—**Lustrously**, lus'trus-li, *adv.* Brilliantly; luminously.

Lustily, Lustiness. Under LUSTY.

Lustral, lus'tral, *a.* [L. *lustralis*, from *lustro*, to purify, from *lustrum*, a purificatory sacrifice, from stem of *luo*, *lavo*, to wash. LAVE.] Used in purification; pertaining to purification.—**Lustrate**, lus'trāt, *v.t.* [L. *lustro*, *lustratum*, to cleanse.] To purify as by water.—**Lustration**, lus-trā'shon, *n.* A cleansing or purifying.—**Lustrum**, lus'trum, *n.* pl. **Lustrums** or **Lustra**, lus'trumz, lus'tra. [L.] In ancient Rome, the purification of the whole people performed at the end of every five years; hence a period of five years.

Lusty, lus'ti, *a.* [From *lust* = D. and G. *lustig*, D. *lystig*, merry, jovial.] Characterized by life, spirit, vigour, health, or the like; stout; vigorous; robust; healthful; bulky; large; lustful; hot-blooded.—**Lustihood**, lus'ti-hud, *n.* The quality of being lusty; vigour of body. (*Tenn.*)—**Lustily**, lus'ti-li, *adv.* In a lusty manner; vigorously; stoutly. —**Lustiness**, lus'ti-nes, *n.* The state of being lusty.

Lutarious, lū-tā'ri-us, *a.* [L. *lutarius*, from *lutum*, mud.] Pertaining to, living in, or of the colour of mud.

Lute, lūt, *n.* [Fr. *luth*, *lut*, Sp. *laud*, from Ar. *al ûd*, the wood (*al* being the definite article).] A stringed musical instrument of the guitar kind, formerly very popular in Europe.—*v.t.* To play on a lute.—**Lutanist, Lutenist, Lutist**, lū'tan-ist, lū'tenist, lūt'ist, *n.* A performer on the lute.

Lute, Luting, lūt, lūt'ing, *n.* [L. *lutum*, mud, clay, from *luo*, to wash.] *Chem.* a composition of clay or other substance used for stopping the juncture of vessels so closely as to prevent the escape or entrance of air, or applied as a coating to glass retorts in order that they may support a high temperature. — **Lute**, *v.t.* — *luted*, *luting.* To close or coat with lute.—**Lutation**, lū-tā'shon, *n.* The act of luting.

Lutestring, lūt'string, *n.* [A corruption of *lustring*. LUSTER.] A stout glossy kind of silk used for ladies' dresses.

Lutheran, lū'ther-an, *a.* Pertaining to Martin *Luther*, the reformer.—*n.* A disciple or follower of Luther; one who adheres to the doctrines of Luther.—**Lutheranism, Lutherism**, lū'thėr-an-izm, lū'thėr-izm, *n.* The doctrines of religion as taught by Luther.

Lutose, lū'tōs, *a.* [L. *lutosus*, from *lutum*, clay.] Miry; covered with clay.

Luxate, luk'sāt, *v.t.*—*luxated*, *luxating.* [L. *luxo*, *luxatum*, from *luxus*, dislocated, Gr. *loxos*, slanting.] To put out of joint, as a limb; to dislocate.—**Luxation**, luk-sā'shon, *n.* The act of luxating; a dislocation.

Luxuriant, lug-zū'ri-ant, *a.* [L. *luxurians*, from *luxurio*, to luxuriate, from *luxuria*, luxury, *luxus*, excess.] Exuberant in growth; rank; abundant; growing to excess; excessive or superfluous.—**Luxuriantly**, lug-zū'ri-ant-li, *adv.* In a luxuriant manner or degree.—**Luxuriance, Luxuriancy**, lug-zū'ri-ans, lug-zū'ri-an-si, *n.* The state of being luxuriant.—**Luxuriate**, lug-zū'ri-āt, *v.i.*—*luxuriated*, *luxuriating.* [L. *luxurio*, to be rank or luxurious, to be wanton.] To grow rankly or exuberantly; to feed or live luxuriously; *fig.* to indulge or revel without restraint.—**Luxuriation**, lug-zū'ri-ā"shon, *n.* The act of luxuriating.—**Luxurious**, lug-zū'ri-us, *a.* [L. *luxuriosus*.] Characterized by indulgence in luxury; given to luxury; voluptuous; administering to luxury; furnished with luxuries.—**Luxuriously**, lug-zū'ri-us-li, *adv.* In a luxurious manner.—**Luxuriousness**, lug-zū'ri-us-nes, *n.* The state or quality of being luxurious.—**Luxurist**, lug'zū-rist, *n.* One given to luxury. — **Luxury**, lug'zū-ri, *n.* [L. *luxuria*.] A free or extravagant indulgence in the pleasures of the table, or in costly dress and equipage; that which is delightful to the senses, the feelings, &c.; that which gratifies a nice and fastidious appetite; anything not necessary, but used for personal gratification.

Lycanthrope, lī'kan-thrōp, *n.* [Gr. *lykos*, a wolf, and *anthrōpos*, a man.] Formerly a man believed to be transformed into a wolf; a werwolf; now, a person affected with lycanthropy. — **Lycanthropy**, lī-kan'thro-pi, *n.* A kind of insanity in which the patient supposes himself to be a wolf.

Lycée, lē-sā, *n.* [Fr.] Higher or secondary school in France.

Lyceum, lī-sē'um, *n.* [L. *Lyceum*, Gr. *Lykeion*, from a temple dedicated to Apollo *lykeios*, Apollo the wolf-slayer, from *lykos*, a wolf.] A building at ancient Athens where Aristotle taught; hence a building appropriated to instruction by lectures; a literary institute; a cultural association which provides lectures, concerts, &c.

Lycopod, lī'kō-pod, *n.* [Gr. *lykos*, a wolf, and *pous, podos*, a foot.] A plant belonging to an order intermediate between mosses and ferns, and in some respects allied to the conifers.—**Lycopode**, lī'kō-pōd, *n.* Vegetable brimstone, the highly inflammable powder contained in the spore-cases of some lycopods.—**Lycopodium**, lī-kō-pō'di-um, *n.* A genus of lycopods.

Lyddite, lid'īt, *n.* [From *Lydd*, in Kent.] An explosive prepared from picric acid.

Lydian, lid'i-an, *a.* Pertaining to ancient *Lydia* in Asia Minor; a term applied to one of the ancient Greek modes of music of a soft pleasing character.—*Lydian stone*, a jasper-like siliceous rock used by the ancients as a touchstone.

Lye, lī, *n.* [A.Sax. *leáh*, G. *lauge*, D. *loog*, lye; allied to Icel. *laug*, a bath, and probably L. *lavo*, to wash.] Water impregnated with alkaline salt imbibed from the ashes of wood; a solution of an alkali used for cleaning purposes.

Lye, lī, *n.* [Probably from *lie*, to rest.] A siding on a railway in which a train may stand for a time, wagons remain for loading, &c.

Lyencephalous, li-en-sef'a-lus, *a.* [Gr. *lyō*, to loose, and *enkephalos*, the brain.] Having the cerebral hemispheres without folds: applied to a primary division of mammals, including the monotremes and marsupials.

Lying, lī'ing, ppr. of *lie*, to recline. Being prostrate.—**Lying-in**, *n.* The act of bearing a child; inlying.—*ppr.* or *a.* Being in childbirth; pertaining to childbirth (a *lying-in* hospital).

Lying, lī'ing, ppr. of *lie*, to utter falsehood. —**Lyingly**, lī'ing-li, *adv.* In a lying manner; falsely; by telling lies.

Lymph, limf, *n.* [Fr. *lymphe*, L. *lympha*, allied to *limpidus*, clear, limpid.] Water, or a clear transparent fluid like water; a fluid in animal bodies contained in certain vessels called *lymphatics*, which differs from the blood in its corpuscles being all of the colourless kind.—*Vaccine lymph*, the fluid used in vaccination.—**Lymphadenoma**, limf'ad-e-nō"ma, *n.* [*Lymph* and *adenoma*.] A disease affecting the lymphatic glands.—**Lymphatic**, lim-fat'ik, *a.* Pertaining to lymph; phlegmatic; sluggish.—*n.* A vessel or duct in an animal body containing lymph. —**Lymphy**, limf'i, *a.* Containing or like lymph.

Lynch, linsh, *v.t.* [Said to be from a Virginian farmer of the name of *Lynch*, noted for taking the law into his own hand.] To inflict punishment upon, without the forms of law, as by a mob or by unauthorized persons.—**Lynch-law**, *n.* The practice of punishing men by unauthorized persons without a legal trial.

Lynx, lingks, *n.* [L. and G. *lynx*; same root as in L. *lux*, light, from its bright eyes.] A name given to several carnivorous mammals of the cat family, long famed for their sharp sight.—**Lynx-eyed**, *a.* Having extremely acute sight.

Lyonnaise, li-o-nāz', *a.* [From French *Lyonnais*, Lyon.] Of Lyon; a term used in cookery, signifying prepared with onions, as *lyonnaise* potatoes.

Lyre, līr, *n.* [Fr. *lyre*, L. and Gr. *lyra*; etymology uncertain.] One of the most ancient stringed instruments of music, used by the Egyptians, Assyrians, and Greeks. —**Lyrate**, **Lyrated**, lī'rāt, lī'rā-ted, *a.* Shaped like a lyre; *bot.* pinnatifid with large terminal lobe and smaller ones towards the petiole.—**Lyre-bird**, *n.* An Australian bird somewhat smaller than a pheasant, having erect tail-feathers in form resembling an ancient lyre.—**Lyric**, **Lyrical**, lir'ik, lir'i-kal, *a.* [L. *lyricus*.] Pertaining to a lyre or harp.—*Lyric poetry*, poetry for the lyre; in modern usage, songs and short poems having reference to the poet's own thoughts and feelings.—**Lyric**, *n.* A lyric poem; a writer of such poems. —**Lyricism**, lir'i-sizm, *n.* Lyric composition; a lyrical form of language.—**Lyrist**, līr'ist, *n.* A musician who plays on the lyre.

Lysis, lī'sis, *n.* [Gr., a solution, from *lyō*, to dissolve.] *Med.* the gradual ending of a disease, without critical symptoms.

Lysol, lī'sol, *n.* A disinfectant made of soap dissolved in coal-tar oil.

Lyssa, lis'a, *n.* [Gr. *lyssa*, madness.] A name for hydrophobia.

M

M is the thirteenth letter and tenth consonant of the English alphabet, representing a labial and nasal articulation.

Ma, mä, *n.* A childish or shorter form of *Mama*.

Ma'am, mäm, *n.* A colloquial contraction for *Madam*.

Mac, mak. A Gaelic word signifying son, and prefixed to many surnames, as *Mac* Donald, *Mac* Grigor, &c.

Macabre, **Macaber**, ma-kä'bėr, *a.* [Fr. *macabre*, death.] Ghastly; hideous; gruesome. Probably from a character in an old French morality play, which represented death.—*Danse macabre*, dance of death; a dance which depicts skeletons leaving their graves to dance until cockcrow.

Macadamize, mak-ad'am-īz, *v.t.*—*macadamized*, *macadamizing*. [From *Macadam*, the inventor.] To cover, as a road, with small broken stones, which, when consolidated, form a firm surface.—**Macadamization**, mak-ad'am-i-zā"shon, *n.* The act or art of macadamizing.

Macaque, ma-käk', *n.* [Fr.] An Old World monkey with short tail and prominent eyebrows.

Macaroni, mak-a-rō'ni, *n.* pl. **Macaronis** or **Macaronies**, mak-a-rō'niz. [Fr. and Prov. It. *macaroni*, It. *maccheroni*, originally a mixture of flour, cheese, and butter.] A dough of fine wheaten flour made into a tubular or pipe form, a favorite food among the Italians; a medley; a sort of droll or fool; a name formerly given to fops or dandies; a confused mixture of things; a macaronic verse or poem.

Macaroon, mak-a-rön', *n.* A small sweet cake, with egg white and sugar basis, containing almond meal or shredded cocoanut.

Macassar-oil, ma-kas'ar, *n.* An oil used for promoting the growth of the hair, named from *Macassar*, in Celebes, from which it was originally procured; also a perfumed mixture of castor-oil and olive-oil.

Macaw, ma-ka', *n.* [Native name in the Antilles.] One of a genus of beautiful birds of the parrot family, having cheeks destitute of feathers, and long tail-feathers. —**Macaw-tree**, *n.* A name for several species of palm tree of tropical America.

Maccabean, mak-ka-bē'an, *a.* Pertaining to the Jewish princes called *Maccabees*.—**Maccabees**, mak'ka-bēz, *n. pl.* Two books treating of Jewish history under the Maccabean princes, included in the Apocrypha.

Mace, mās, *n.* [O.Fr. *mace*, Fr. *masse*, It. *mazza*, a club; from L. *matea* (only found in the dim. *mateola*), a kind of mallet.] A weapon of war consisting of a staff with a heavy metal head frequently in the form of a spiked ball, used for breaking armor; an ornamental staff of metal borne before a dignitary as a symbol of his authority.—**Mace-bearer**, *n.* A person who carries a mace before public functionaries.—**Macer**, mās'ėr, *n.* A mace-bearer: an officer attending several Scottish courts.

Mace, mās, *n.* [Fr. *macis*, It. *mace*, L. *macis*, *macir*, Gr. *maker*, an Indian spice.] A spice, the dried aril or covering of the seed of the nutmeg, chiefly used in cooking or in pickles.

Macédoine, mas-e-dwän', *n.* [Fr., early meaning, Macedonian parsley.] A combination or mixture; used to designate a sauce or jellied salad containing mixed small or diced vegetables.

Macerate, mas'ėr-āt, *v.t.*—*macerated*, *macerating*. [L. *macero*, *maceratum*, to make soft: same root as *mass*, a lump.] To steep almost to solution; to soften and separate the parts of by steeping in a fluid, or by the digestive process; to mortify‡; to harass‡.—**Maceration**, mas-ėr-ā'shon, *n.* The act of macerating; state of being macerated.

Machete, **Machette**, mä-chā'tā, *n.* [Sp.] A kind of large knife or cutlass used in South America and the West Indies as a tool or a weapon.

Machiavelian, mak'i-a-vē"li-an, *a.* Pertaining to *Machiavel* (Nicolo *Machiavelli*), an Italian writer, secretary and historiographer to the Republic of Florence (died 1527); in conformity with Machiavel's principles; cunning in political management; crafty.—*n.* One who adopts the principles of Machiavel.—**Machiavelianism**, **Machiavelism**, mak'i-a-vē"li-an-izm, mak'i-a-vel-izm, *n.* The principles or system of statesmanship of Machiavel, who inculcated the systematic subordination of right to expediency; political cunning and artifice.

Machicolation, ma-chik'o-lā"shon, *n.* [Fr. *mâchicoulis*, *mâchecoulis*; origin doubtful.] *Milit. arch.* a vertical opening in the floor of a projecting gallery, parapet, &c., for hurling missiles or pouring boiling lead, pitch, &c., upon the enemy; a part thus projecting, as at the top of a tower, without any such opening.—**Machicolate**, ma-chik'o-lāt, *v.t.* To form with machicolations.—**Machicolated**, ma-chik'o-lā-ted, *a.* Having machicolations.

Machinate, mak'i-nāt, *v.t.* and *i.*—*machinated*, *machinating*. [L. *machinor*, *machinatus*, from *machina*. MACHINE.] To plan; to contrive; to form, as a plot or scheme.—**Machination**, mak-i-nā"shon, *n.* The act of machinating; a plot; an artful design or scheme formed with deliberation.—**Machinator**, mak'i-nā-tėr, *n.* One who machinates or plots with evil designs.

Machine, ma-shēn', *n.* [Fr. *machine*, L. *machina*, from Gr. *mēchanē*, machine, device, contrivance, from *mechos*, means, expedient; same root as *make*.] Any contrivance or appliance which serves to increase or regulate the effect of a given force or to produce motion (*simple machines* or mechanical powers being such as the lever, pulley, &c.); a complex structure, consisting of a combination or peculiar modification of the mechanical powers; a term of contempt applied to a person whose actions do not appear to be under his own control, but to be directed by some external agency; a mere tool or creature; a term formerly applied to a coach or cart, now particularly to an automobile, aeroplane, &c.—*v.t.* To apply machinery to; to produce by machinery.—**Machine gun**, *n.* A piece of ordnance that is loaded and fired mechanically, and can discharge a number of projectiles in rapid succession, having usually two or more barrels, as in the case of the Gatling gun, the mitrailleuse, &c.—**Machiner**, ma-shēn'ėr, *n.* A machinist.—**Machinery**, ma-shēn'ėr-i, *n.* A complicated apparatus, or combination of mechanical powers, designed to increase, regulate, or apply motion and force; machines in general; any complex system of means and appliances designed to carry on any particular work or effect a specific purpose.—**Machine-shop**, *n.* A workshop in which machines are made.—**Machine-tool**, *n.* An adjustable machine for cutting metals into any required shape. — **Machine-work**, *n.* Work done by a machine, as distinguished from that done by manual labour.—**Machinist**, ma-shēn'ist, *n.* A constructor of machines; one who tends or works a machine.

Mackerel, mak'ėr-el, *n.* [O.Fr. *maquerel*, Fr. *maquereau*, D. *makreel*, G. *makrele*, Dan. *makrel*, from L.L. *macarellus*, from L. *macula*, a spot—in allusion to the blue blotches on it.] An excellent table fish, well known by its elegant shape and brilliant colours.—*Mackerel gale*, a gale that ripples the surface of the sea, rendering it favourable for catching mackerel.—*Mackerel sky*, a sky in which the clouds have the form called *cirro-cumulus*, somewhat resembling the blotches on a mackerel.

Mackintosh, mak'in-tosh, *n.* A term applied, from the name of the inventor, to a garment, particularly an overcoat, rendered waterproof by a solution of india-rubber.

Macle, mak'l, *n.* [Fr.; L. *macula*, a spot, the mesh of a net.] A double crystal, particularly a flat, double crystal of diamond.

Macramé, mak-rä-mā', *n.* [Ar. *miqramah*, embroidered veil, Turk. *maqramah*, kerchief.] Fringe or heavy lace of knotted thread, usually in geometrical patterns.

Macrobiotic, mak'ro-bī-ot"ik, *a.* [Gr. *makros*, long, and *bios*, life.] Long-lived.—**Macrocephalous**, mak-ro-sef'a-lus, *a.* [Gr. *kephalē*, the head.] Having a long or large head.—**Macrocosm**, mak'ro-kozm, *n.* [Gr. *kosmos*, world.] The great world; the universe, regarded as analogous to the *microcosm*, or little world constituted by man.—**Macrodactyl**, mak-ro-dak'til, *n.* [Gr. *daktylos*, a finger.] One of a family of grallatorial birds, having very long toes, comprising the coot, rail, water-hen, &c.—**Macrodiagonal**, mak'ro-dī-ag"on-al, *n.* The longer of the diagonals of a rhombic prism.—**Macrognathic**, mak-rog-nath'ik, *a.* [Gr. *makros*, long, *gnathos*, a jaw.] Having long or prominent jaws.—**Macrology**, mak-rol'o-ji, *n.* [Gr. *logos*, discourse.] Long and tedious talk; superfluity of words.—**Macrometer**, mak-rom'et-ėr, *n.* [Gr. *metron*, measure.] An instrument for measuring inaccessible heights. — **Macron**, mak'rōn, *n.* [Gr. *makros*, long.] A mark placed over a vowel to show that it is long, as fāte, mē, nōte, tūbe.—**Macronucleus**, mak'rō-nū"klē-us, *n.* [Gr. *makros*, large.] In animalcules, the large nucleus.—**Macropetalous**, mak-ro-pet'a-lus, *a.* *Bot.* having large petals.—**Macrophyllous**, mak-ro-fil'us, *a.* [Gr. *phyllon*, a leaf.] *Bot.* having large leaves.—**Macropod**, mak'ro-pod, *n.* [Gr. *pous*, *podos*, foot.] An individual belonging to the kangaroo family.—**Macropterous**, mak-rop'tėr-us, *a.* [Gr. *pteron*, a wing.] *Zool.* having long wings or fins.—**Macroscopic**, mak-rō-skop'ik, *a.* [Gr. *makros*, long, *skopeō*, I see.] Visible to the naked eye; opposed to *microscopic*.—**Macrospore**, mak'rō-spōr, *n.* [Gr. *makros*, long, *sporos*, seed.] *Bot.* a large (female) spore.—**Macrotous**, mak-rō'tus, *a.* [Gr. *ous*, *ōtos*, the ear.] *Zool.* long-eared.

Macrura, **Macroura**, mak-rų'ra, mak-rou'ra, *n. pl.* [Gr. *makros*, long, and *oura*, a tail.] A family of stalk-eyed decapod crustaceans, including the lobster, prawn, shrimp, so called in contrast to the Brachyura (crabs), because their flexible abdomen extends straight backward, and is used in swimming. — **Macrural**, **Macrurous**, mak-rų'ral, mak-rų'rus, *a.* Belonging to the Macrura. — **Macruran**, **Macrouran**, mak-rų'ran, mak-rou'ran, *n.* One of the Macrura.

Macula, mak'ū-la, *n.* pl. **Maculæ**, mak'ū-lē.] [L. *macula*, a spot; hence, *mackerel*, *mail* (armour).] A spot, as on the skin.—**Maculate**, mak'ū-lāt, *v.t.* [L. *maculo*.] To spot; to stain; to blur.—*a.* Marked with spots; blotted; hence, defiled; impure.—**Maculation**, mak-ū-lā'shon, *n.* The act of spotting; a spot; a stain.—**Maculature**, mak'ū-la-tūr, *n.* A sheet blotted in printing.—**Macule**, mak'ūl, *n.* A spot; *printing*, a blur causing the impression of a page to appear double.—**Maculose**, mak'ū-lōs, *a.* Spotted; maculated.

Mad, mad, *a.* [O.E. *maad*, A.Sax. *mād*, *gemaed*, mad; allied to Goth. *gamaids*, injured; O.H.G. *gameit*, blunt, dull; Icel. *meitha*, to hurt.] Disordered in intellect; deprived of reason; distracted; crazy; insane; beside one's self; frantic; furious; wildly frolicsome; infatuated; furious from disease or otherwise: said of animals.—*Like mad*, madly; furiously. (*Colloq.*)—*v.t.* — *madded*, *madding*. To make mad; to madden. — *Madding crowd*, distracting (*v.t.*) or raving madly (*v.i.*) (?) Gray's 'madding crowd's ignoble strife', taken by him from Drummond of Hawthornden's 'madding worldling's hoarse discords', apparently *v.i.* — **Mad-apple**, *n.* The fruit of the egg-plant.—**Madcap**, mad'kap, *n.* A person of wild or eccentric behaviour; a flighty or hare-brained person; one who indulges in frolics. — *a.* Pertaining to a madcap.—**Madden**, mad'n, *v.t.* To make mad; to craze; to excite with violent passion; to enrage.—*v.i.* To become mad; to act as if mad.—**Madding**, mad'ing, *a.* Raging; furious; wild.—**Mad-house**, mad'hous, *n.* A house where insane persons are confined; a lunatic asylum.—**Madly**, mad'li, *adv.* In a mad or frenzied manner; frantically; furiously. — **Madman**, mad'man, *n.* A lunatic; a crazy person; one inflamed with extravagant passion, and acting contrary to reason. — **Madness**, mad'nes, *n.* The state or quality of being mad; lunacy; insanity; frenzy; extreme folly.

Madam, mad'am, *n.* [Fr. *ma*, my, and *dame*, lady, from L. *mea domina*, in same sense.] *Lit.* my lady: a term of compliment used in address to ladies, chiefly to married and elderly ladies: sometimes used with a slight shade of disrespect (a proud *madam*). Pl. **Mesdames**, mā'damz.

Madder, mad'ėr, *n.* A.Sax. *mæddere*, madder.] A climbing perennial plant, largely cultivated in Southern Europe, the root of which furnishes several valuable dyes and pigments, such as *madder-red*, *madder-lake*, *madder-yellow*.—*v.t.* and *i.* To dye with madder.

Made, mād, *pret. and pp.* of *make*. The pp. besides being used in the senses of the verb is often equivalent to destined, fitted, suitable ('a place *made* for murders', *Shak.*).—**Made-dish**, *n.* A dish of meat, poultry, &c., recooked; an entrée.

Madefaction, mad-ē-fak'shon, *n.* [L. *madefactio*—*madeo*, to be wet, and *facio*, to make.] The act of making wet.—**Madefy**, mad'ē-fī, *v.t.* [Fr. *madéfier*.] To make wet or moist; to moisten.

Madeira, ma-dē'ra, *n.* A rich wine made in the island of Madeira.

Mademoiselle, mad-mwä-zel, *n.* [Fr. *ma*, my, and *demoiselle*, damsel. DAMSEL.] The title given to a young unmarried lady in France; miss.

Madia, mā'di-a, *n.* [From *madi*, the Chilian name.] A composite plant allied to the sunflower, cultivated for the oil obtained from its seeds.

Madonna, ma-don'a, *n.* [It. *madonna*, from L. *mea domina*, my lady. MADAM.] An Italian form of address equivalent to *Madam*; the Virgin Mary, pictures of whom are called *madonnas*.

Madras, ma-dras', *n.* A cotton cloth of fine thread and close weave much used for men's shirts; a large cotton kerchief.

Madrepore, mad'rē-pōr, *n.* [Fr. *madrépore*, from It. *madrepora*, from *madre*, mother, and Gr. *pōros*, a kind of stone.] A common variety of reef-coral, of a stony hardness and of a spreading or branching form; the coral-building polyp itself. — **Madreporal**, mad-rē-pō'ral, *a.* Pertaining to or consisting of madrepore.—**Madreporiform**, mad-rē-pō'ri-form, *a.* Perforated with small holes like a madrepore coral.—**Madreporite**, mad'rē-pō-rīt, *n.* A variety of limestone; fossil madrepore.

Madrier, mad'ri-ėr, *n.* [Fr.] *Milit. engin.* a plank used for supporting the earth in a mine or for other purposes.

Madrigal, mad'ri-gal, *n.* [Fr. *madrigal*; It. *madrigale*, older It. *mandriale*, from L. and Gr. *mandra*, a sheepfold; originally a shepherd's song.] A little amorous poem, consisting of not less than three or four stanzas, and containing some tender and delicate, though simple thought, suitably expressed; a vocal composition, now commonly of two or more movements, and in five or six parts.

Madrilenian, mad-ri-lē'ni-an, *a.* and *n.* [Sp. *Madrileno*.] Of or belonging to or a native of Madrid.

Mæcenas, me-sē'nas, *n.* A munificent patron of art or literature, after Horace's friend.

Maelstrom, māl'strom, *n.* [Dutch *malen*, to grind, *stroom*, a stream.] A great whirlpool off the coast of Norway. Hence, *fig.* a vortex or gulf; some dangerous movement or current in social life.

Maenad, mē'nad, *n.* [Gr. *mainas*, *mainados*, from *mainomai*, to rave.] A votaress of Bacchus; hence, a raving, frenzied woman.

Maestoso, mä-es-tō'zō. [It., majestic.] A direction in music to play with grandeur and strength.

Maestro, mä-es'trō, *n.* [It., from L. *magister*, a master.] A master of any art; specifically, a master in music; a musical composer.

Maffia, **Mafia**, maf'fē-ä, *n.* A secret organization in Sicily which disregards or flouts laws and legal restrictions; branch organizations in other countries, where the members are lawless and defiant toward all government.

Magazine, mag-a-zēn', *n.* [Fr. *magasin*, a storehouse, Sp. *magacen*, *almagacen*, from Ar. *al-makhzen*, a warehouse, from *khazana*, to store.] A receptacle in which anything is stored; a warehouse; a storehouse; a building or chamber constructed for storing in security large quantities of gunpowder or other explosive substances; a publication issued in a series of numbers or parts and containing papers of an entertaining or instructive character.—*v.t.* To store up in a magazine; to accumulate for future use.—*Magazine-rifle*, a rifle with an attached magazine or chamber, containing a number of cartridges that can be fired off in rapid succession by special mechanism.—**Magaziner**, **Magazinist**, mag-a-zēn'ėr, mag-a-zēn'ist, *n.* One who writes in a magazine.

Magdalen, mag'da-len, *n.* [From Mary *Magdalene*, erroneously supposed to be the woman mentioned in St. Luke vii. 36-50.] A reformed prostitute.—*Magdalen hospital* or *asylum*, a house into which prostitutes are received with a view to their reformation.

Magellanic, mag-el-lan'ik, *a.* Pertaining to *Magellan*, the celebrated navigator.—*Magellanic clouds*, two conspicuous whitish nebulæ, of a cloud-like appearance, near the south pole.

Magenta, ma-jen'ta, *n.* [Discovered in 1859, the year of the battle of *Magenta*.] A brilliant blue-red colour derived from coal-tar.

Maggot, mag'ot, *n.* [W. *magiad*, a maggot or grub, from *magu*, to breed.] The larva of a fly or other insect; a grub; a whim; an odd fancy; a crotchet.—**Maggotiness**, mag'ot-i-nes, *n.* The state of being maggoty.—**Maggoty**, mag'ot-i, *a.* Full of or invested with maggots; capricious; whimsical.

Magi, mā'jī, *n. pl.* [L. *magus*, from Gr. *magos*, a Magian, from Per. *mag*, a priest, same root as L. *magnus*, great.] The caste of priests among the ancient Medes and Persians; hence holy men or sages of the

East.—**Magian**, mā'ji-an, *a*. Pertaining to the Magi.—*n*. One of the Magi; a priest of the Zoroastrian religion.—**Magianism**, mā'ji-an-izm, *n*. The philosophy or doctrines of the Magi.

Magic, maj'ik, *n*. [L. *magicus*, pertaining to sorcery, from *magia*, Gr. *mageia*, the theology of the Magians, magic. MAGI.] The art of producing effects by superhuman means, as by spiritual beings or the occult powers of nature; sorcery; enchantment; necromancy; power or influence similar to that of enchantment.—*Natural magic*, the art of applying natural causes, whose operation is secret, to produce surprising effects.—*a*. Pertaining to magic; used in magic; working or worked by or as if by magic. — *Magic square*, a square figure formed by a series of numbers disposed in parallel and equal ranks, and such that the sums of each row or line taken perpendicularly, horizontally, or diagonally are equal. *Magic lantern*, a kind of lantern by means of which small pictures are represented on the wall of a dark room, or on a white sheet, magnified to any size at pleasure.—**Magical**, maj'i-kal, *a*. Pertaining to magic; proceeding from magic; having supernatural qualities; acting or produced as if by magic. ∴ *Magical* differs from *magic*, chiefly in the fact that the latter is not used predicatively; thus we do not say 'the effect was *magic*'.—**Magically**, maj'i-kal-li, *adv*. In a magical manner.—**Magician**, ma-jish'-an, *n*. One skilled in magic; an enchanter; a necromancer.

Magilp, Magilph, ma-gilp', ma-gilf', *n*. A mixture of linseed-oil and mastic varnish used by artists as a vehicle for colours.

Magisterial, maj-is-tē'ri-al, *a*. [L. *magisterius*, from *magister*, a master. MASTER.] Belonging to a master or ruler; pertaining to a magistrate or his office; authoritative; arrogant; imperious; domineering.—**Magisterially**, maj-is-tē'ri-al-li, *adv*. In a magisterial manner.—**Magisterialness**, *n*. **Magistral**, maj'is-tral, *a*. Imperious; authoritative; *phar*. specially prepared.—**Magistrand**, maj-is-trand', *n*. A student in Arts in the Scottish universities in the fourth year, preparing for graduation.

Magistrate, maj'is-trāt, *n*. [L. *magistratus*, a magistrate, from *magister*, a master.] A public civil officer invested with the executive government or some branch of it; a justice of the peace; a person who dispenses justice in police courts, &c.—**Magistratic**, maj-is-trat'ik, *a*. Pertaining to a magistrate.—**Magistracy**, maj'is-tra-si, *n*. The office or dignity of a magistrate; the body of magistrates.

Magma, mag'ma, *n*. [Gr., a mass, dregs, from *massō*, to knead. MASS.] A mixture of mineral or other matters in a pasty state; a thick residuum separated from a fluid.

Magnalium, mag-nā'li-um, *n*. [From names of components.] An alloy of magnesium and aluminium, light, strong, and easily worked.

Magnanimous, mag-nan'i-mus, *a*. [L. *magnanimus*—*magnus*, great (MAGNITUDE), and *animus*, mind (ANIMAL).] Great of mind; elevated in soul or in sentiment; raised above what is low, mean, or ungenerous, said of persons; exhibiting nobleness of soul: said of actions, &c.—**Magnanimously**, mag-nan'i-mus-li, *adv*. In a magnanimous manner.—**Magnanimity**, mag-na-nim'i-ti, *n*. The quality of being magnanimous; greatness of mind; elevation, nobility, or dignity of soul; lofty generosity.

Magnate, mag'nāt, *n*. [L. *magnates* (pl.), powerful persons, the great, from *magnus*, great. MAGNITUDE.] A person of rank; a noble or grandee; a person of note or distinction in any sphere.

Magnesia, mag-nē'shi-a, *n*. [From *Magnesia* in Asia Minor, whence also *magnet*.] Oxide of magnesium, a white tasteless earthy substance, possessing alkaline properties.—*Sulphate of magnesia*, Epsom salts.—**Magnesian**, mag-nē'shi-an, *a*. Pertaining to magnesia; containing or resembling magnesia. — *Magnesian limestone*, a rock composed of carbonates of lime and magnesia, more or less useful for building or ornamental purposes; dolomite. — **Magnesium**, mag-nē'shi-um, *n*. The metallic base of magnesia, a white malleable metal, obtained by decomposing chloride of magnesium by means of potassium.—*Magnesium light*, a dazzlingly bright light produced by burning magnesium.

Magnet, mag'net, *n*. [L. *magnes*, *magnetis*, from Gr. *magnēs*, from *Magnesia* in Asia Minor, whence the stone was first brought.] The loadstone; also a bar or mass of iron or steel to which the peculiar properties of the loadstone have been imparted, either by contact or by other means. ELECTRO-MAGNET, HORSE-SHOE MAGNET.—**Magnetic**, mag-net'ik, *a*. Pertaining to the magnet or magnetism; possessing the properties of the magnet, or corresponding properties; pertaining to the earth's magnetism; attractive, as if magnetic.—*Magnetic amplitude, azimuth*, &c., *navig*. the amplitude, azimuth, &c., indicated by the compass.—*Magnetic battery*, a kind of battery formed of several magnets (usually horse-shoe magnets) combined together with all their poles similarly disposed.—*Magnetic compensator*, a contrivance connected with a ship's compass for compensating or neutralizing the effects upon the needle of the iron of the ship. — *Magnetic dip*. Under DIP.—*Magnetic elements*, for any place, are the intensity of the earth's attraction, the DIP (which see), and the DECLINATION (which see).—*Magnetic equator*, a line passing round the globe near its equator, in every part of which the dip of the needle is nothing.—*Magnetic intensity*, the force of attraction which magnets exert on surrounding bodies capable of being influenced by them.—*Magnetic iron-ore*. Same as *Magnetite*.—*Magnetic meridian*, a great circle, the plane of which at any place corresponds with the direction of the magnetic needle at that place. — *Magnetic moment*. See MOMENT.—*Magnetic needle*, any small magnetized iron or steel rod turning on a pivot, such as the needle of the mariner's compass.—*Magnetic north*, that point of the horizon which is indicated by the direction of the magnetic needle.—*Magnetic oxide of iron*, magnetite. —*Magnetic poles*, nearly opposite points on the earth's surface where the dip of the needle is 90°, at some distance from the earth's poles. — *Magnetic reluctance*. See RELUCTANCE. — *Magnetic susceptibility*. See SUSCEPTIBILITY.—*Magnetic storm*, a violent disturbance in the earth's magnetism; a sudden alteration in the magnetic elements of a place.—**Magnetical**, mag-net'i-kal, *a*. Magnetic.—**Magnetically**, mag-net'i-kal-li, *adv*. In a magnetic manner; by magnetism.—**Magnetics**, mag-net'iks, *n*. The science of principles of magnetism. — **Magnetism**, mag'net-izm, *n*. A peculiar property possessed by certain bodies, whereby, under certain circumstances, they naturally attract or repel one another according to determinate laws; that branch of science which treats of the properties of the magnet, and magnetic phenomena in general; power of attraction. —*Animal magnetism*. MESMERISM.—*Terrestrial magnetism*, the magnetic force exerted by the earth.—**Magnetician, Magnetist**, mag-net-ish'an, mag'net-ist, *n*. One versed in the science of magnetism.—**Magnetite**, mag'net-īt, *n*. A black oxide of iron, which sometimes possesses polarity, and is highly magnetic; magnetic iron ore. —**Magnetizable**, mag-net-ī'za-bl, *a*. Capable of being magnetized.—**Magnetization**, mag'net-i-zā"shon, *n*. The act of magnetizing, or state of being magnetized. —**Magnetize**, mag'net-īz, *v.t.*—*magnetized, magnetizing*. To communicate magnetic properties to; to attract as if by a magnet; to put under the influence of animal magnetism.—*v.i.* To acquire magnetic properties; to become magnetic. — **Magnetizer**, mag'net-ī-zėr, *n*. One who or that which communicates magnetism.—**Magneto-electric, Magneto-electrical**, *a*. Pertaining to magneto-electricity. — *Magneto-electric induction*, the communication of magnetic properties to iron by means of electric currents.—**Magneto-electricity**, *n*. Electricity evolved by the action of magnets; the science which treats of phenomena connected with both magnetism and electricity.—**Magnetometer**, mag-net-om'et-ėr, *n*. An instrument for measuring any of the terrestrial magnetic elements, as the dip, inclination, and intensity, especially the latter.—**Magnetometric**, mag'net-ō-met"rik, *a*. Pertaining to the magnetometer. — *Magnetomotive force*, the magnetizing influence to which a magnetic substance is subjected in a magnetic field: its unit is the GILBERT (which see).

Magnificat, mag-nif'i-kat, *n*. Canticle of the Virgin Mary in Luke, i. 46-55: 'My soul doth magnify (L. *magnificat*) the Lord'.

Magnificent, mag-nif'i-sent, *a*. [L. *magnificens*—*magnus*, great, *facio*, to make. MAGNITUDE.] Grand in appearance; splendid; fond of splendour; showy; stately.—**Magnificently**, mag-nif'i-sent-li, *adv*. In a magnificent manner. — **Magnifiable**, mag'ni-fī a-bl, *a*. Capable or worthy of being magnified.—**Magnific, Magnifical**, mag-nif'ik, mag-nif'i-kal, *a*. [L. *magnificus*, noble, splendid.] Grand; splendid; illustrious.—**Magnifically**, mag-nif'i-kal-li, *adv*, In a magnificent manner.—**Magnificence**, mag-nif'i-sens, *n*. [L. *magnificentia*.] The condition or quality of being magnificent.—**Magnifico**, mag-nif'i-kō, *n*. pl. **Magnificoes**. A grandee; a magnate. —**Magnifier**, mag'ni-fī-ėr, *n*. One who or that which magnifies.—**Magnify**, mag'-ni-fī, *v.t.*—*magnified, magnifying*. [Fr. *magnifier*, L. *magnificare*.] To make great or greater; to increase the apparent dimensions of; to enlarge; to augment; to increase the power or glory of; to sound the praises of; to extol; to exalt; to represent as greater than reality; to exaggerate.—*v.i.* To possess the quality of causing objects to appear larger than reality; to increase the apparent dimensions of objects.—*Magnifying glass*, a plano-convex or double-convex lens: so called because objects seen through it have their apparent dimensions increased.

Magniloquence, mag-nil'o-kwens, *n*. [L. *magniloquentia*—*magnus*, great (MAGNITUDE), and *loquens*, speaking (LOCUTION).] A lofty manner of speaking or writing; tumid, pompous words or style; grandiloquence; bombast.—**Magniloquent**, mag-nil'o-kwent, *a*. Big in words; speaking loftily or pompously; tumid; grandiloquent. —**Magniloquently**, mag-nil'o-kwent-li, *adv*. In a magniloquent manner.

Magnitude, mag'ni-tūd, *n*. [L. *magnitudo*, from *magnus*, great; same root as Gr. *megas*, great, E. *may, might, much, more*, &c. More or less akin are *magnate, majesty, master*, &c.] Greatness; the comparative extent, bulk, size, quantity, or amount of anything that can be measured; any quantity that can be expressed in terms of a quantity of the same kind taken as a unit; *geom*. that which has one or more of the three dimensions, length, breadth, and thickness; importance; consequence (an affair of *magnitude*).

Magnolia, mag-nō'li-a, *n*. [After Pierre *Magnol*, professor of botany at Montpellier.] A genus of trees and shrubs, chiefly natives of North America, India, China, Japan, &c., much admired for their flowers and foliage.

Magnum, mag'num, *n*. [L., a large thing. MAGNITUDE.] A bottle holding two quarts. — **Magnum bonum**, *n*. [L.] Something large and good. — **Magnum opus**, *n*. [L.] Literally, a great work; the major production of an author or artist.

Magpie, mag'pī, *n*. [*Mag*, for *Margaret*, and *pie*, a magpie, from L. *pica*, a pie or magpie; comp. *Jenny*-wren, *Robin*-redbreast, &c.] A well-known bird of the crow family, about 18 inches in length, plumage black and white, tail very long; a shot on the target, near the outer rim.

Magyar, mag'yär; Hung. pron. mod-yor', *n*. A Hungarian of Asiatic race, allied to the Turks and Finns; the language of the Hungarians, belonging to the Turanian class of tongues.

Mahaleb, ma-hä'leb, *n.* [Ar. *mahleb.*] A species of cherry of the middle and south of Europe.

Maharajah, ma-hä-rä'ja, *n.* [Skr. *mahā*, great, and *rājā*, a prince or king.] The title assumed by some Indian princes ruling over a considerable extent of territory.—**Maharani**, **Maharanee**, ma-hä'ra-nē, *n.* [Skr., great queen or princess.] A female Indian ruler.

Mahatma, ma-hät'ma, *n.* [Skr. *maha*, great, *âtmâ*, mind, soul.] A name among theosophists for certain Asiatic chiefs of their faith, said to be able to communicate by occult or non-material means with other persons at any distance.

Mahdi, mä'dē, *n.* [Ar., the director.] A name assumed by some of the successors of Mohammed; a descendant of Mohammed who is to arise and at the head of the faithful spread Mohammedanism over the world.

Mahee, ma-hē', *n.* [Hind.] The gall-nut of the tamarisk-tree, imported from India for dyeing and photographic purposes.

Mahl-stick, mal'stik, *n.* MAUL-STICK.

Mahogany, ma-hog'an-i, *n.* [*Mahagoni*, native American name.] A valuable timber-tree, the wood of which is of a reddish colour, very hard, and susceptible of a fine polish; a dinner-table or table in general (over the *mahogany*).

Mahomedan, **Mahometan**, &c., ma-hom'e-dan, ma-hom'e-tan. MOHAMMEDAN, &c.

Mahound, ma-hound', *n.* An old corruption of Mohammed; also applied to the devil or other evil spirit.

Mahout, ma-hout', *n.* [Hind.] In the East Indies, an elephant driver or keeper.

Mahratta, ma-rat'ta, *n.* One of a race of Hindus inhabiting Central India.

Maid, mād, *n.* [Short for *maiden*, A.Sax. *mægden*, dim of *mægeth*, a maiden, Goth. *magaths*, G. *magd*, maid; akin A.Sax. *magu*, Goth. *magus*, Icel. *mōgr*, a boy, a son; allied to Gael. *mac*, a son.] A young unmarried woman; a virgin; an unmarried woman who has preserved her chastity; a female servant; a female slave.—*Maid of all work*, a female servant who does housework of every kind.—**Maid of honor**, an unmarried woman who accompanies a bride to the altar.—**Maiden**, mā'dn, *n.* A young unmarried woman; a virgin or maid; an instrument of capital punishment; a race horse that has not yet won a race.—*a.* Pertaining to a maiden or virgin; consisting of virgins; like a maiden; fresh; unpolluted; unused.—*Maiden fortress*, one hitherto impregnable to assaults from the enemy; uncaptured.—*Maiden over* (*cricket*), one during whose delivery no runs are made.—*Maiden speech*, a person's first public speech.—*Maiden sword*, a sword hitherto unused and unstained with blood.—**Maidenhair**, mā'dn-hār, *n.* An elegant fern found growing on rocks and walls.—**Maidenhead**, mā'dn-hed, *n.* [*Maiden*, and term. *-head.*] Virgin purity; virginity.—**Maidenhood**, mā'dn-hụd, *n.* The state of being a maid or maiden; the state of an unmarried female; virginity.—**Maiden-like**, mā'dn-līk, *a.* Like a maid.—**Maidenliness**, mā'dn-li-nes. *n.* Behaviour that becomes a maid; modesty.—**Maidenly**, mā'dn-li, *a.* and *adv.* Like a maid; modest.—**Maidhood**, mād'hụd, *n.* Virginity.—**Maid-servant**, *n.* A female servant; a female domestic.

Maieutic, mā-ū'tik, *a.* [Gr. *maieutikos*, pertaining to midwifery, from *maia*, a midwife.] Serving to assist or accelerate childbirth; pertaining to the obstetric art; aiding in bringing forth, in a metaphorical sense.

Maigre, mā'gr, *a.* [Fr., lean, spare, meagre.] *Cookery*, a term applied to a preparation cooked merely with butter.—*Maigre dishes, maigre food*, dishes used by Roman Catholics on the days when their church forbids flesh-meats.

Mail, māl, *n.* [Fr. *maille*, the mesh of a net, a link of mail; from L. *macula*, a spot, a mesh. MACULA.] Armour; a defensive covering for warriors, and sometimes their steeds; any defensive covering, as the shell of a lobster.—*v.t.* To put on mail or armour; to arm defensively.—**Mail-clad**, *a.* Clad with a coat of mail.—**Mailed**, māld, *p.* and *a.* Covered with mail or armour; *zool.* protected by an external covering of scales or hard substance.

Mail, māl, *n.* [Fr. *malle*, O.Fr. *male*, a bag, a mail; either from Armor. *mal*, Ir. and Gael. *mala*, a bag, or from O.H.G. *malaha*, a wallet; Icel. *malr*, a knapsack.] Originally a bag; hence, a bag for the conveyance of letters and papers; the letters, papers, &c., conveyed in such a bag; the person or conveyance by which the mail is conveyed.—*v.t.* To put in the mail; to post.—**Mailable**, māl'a-bl, *a.* Capable of being carried in the mail.—**Mail-bag**, *n.* A bag in which the public mail is carried.—**Mail-boat**, *n.* A boat which carries mail.—**Mailer**, *n.* A machine for addressing mail.—**Mailman**, *n.* A postman.—**Mail order**, *n.* An order sent by mail for goods to be shipped to the buyer.—**Mail-steamer**, *n.* A steamer for conveying the mails.—**Mail-car**, *n.* A car usually in the fore part of a train, for carrying mail.

Mail, māl, *n.* [Icel. *māl*, stipulation, agreement; *mæla*, to stipulate.] A term in Scots law for a rent or sum payable regularly.

Maim, mām, *v.t.* [O.E. *main*, to hurt or maim; from O.Fr. *mehaigner*, Pr. *maganhar*, It. *magagnare*, to maim; origin doubtful.] To deprive of the use of a limb; to mutilate; to cripple; to disable.—*n.* An injury by which a person is maimed or mutilated.—**Maimedness**, mām'ed-nes, *n.* A state of being maimed.

Main, mān, *a.* [Icel. *megn*, *meginn*, main, strong, mighty; *megin*, might, main, main part; A.Sax. *mægn*, *mægen*, power, strength; same root as *may*, *might*.] Principal, chief, or most important among other things; most to be regarded or considered; first in size, rank, importance, &c. (the *main* branch of a river, the *main* timbers of an edifice, the *main* consideration); mighty; vast (the *main* ocean); directly applied; used with all one's might (*main* strength).—*Main body*, the corps of an army which marches between the advance and rear guard.—*The main chance*, the chance of making gain; one's own interests generally.—*n.* All one's strength; violent effort (in the phrase 'with might and *main*'); the chief or main portion; the gross, bulk, greater part; the ocean, the great sea, the high sea; a principal gas or water pipe in a street, as distinguished from the smaller ones supplied by it.—*In the main*, for the most part; speaking generally.—**Main-couple**, *n.* *Carpentry*, the principal truss in a roof.—**Main-hatch**, *n.* *Naut.* the hatch which gives entrance to the *main-hold*, the central portion of the hold.—**Main-keel**, *n.* The principal keel, as distinguished from the false keel.—**Mainland**, mān'land, *n.* The continent; territory of great extent as compared with an island near it.—**Mainly**, mān'li, *adv.* In the main; chiefly; principally.—**Main-mast**, *n.* *Naut.* the principal mast in a ship or other vessel; the middle lower mast of a ship.—**Main-rigging**, *n.* The rigging of the main-mast.—**Main-sail**, *n.* *Naut.* the principal sail in a ship; the chief sail on the main-mast bent on the main-yard.—**Main-sheet**, *n.* *Naut.* a rope at one or both of the lower corners of a main-sail to keep it properly extended.—**Mainspring**, mān'spring, *n.* The principal spring of any piece of mechanism, as in a watch; *fig.* the main cause of any action.—**Main-stay**, *n.* *Naut.* the stay extending from the top of the main-mast to the deck; hence, *fig.* chief support.—**Main-top**, *n.* *Naut.* a platform placed at the head of the main-mast.—**Main-yard**, *n.* *Naut.* the yard on which the main-sail is extended.

Main, mān, *n.* [Fr. *main*, L. *manus*, hand.] A hand at dice; a match at cock-fighting.

Mainpernor, mān'pėr-nėr, *n.* [Fr. *main*, the hand, and *pernor* for *preneur*, a taker, from *prendre*, to take.] *Law*, formerly a surety for a prisoner's appearance in court on a fixed day.—**Mainprise**, **Mainprize**, mān'prīz, *n.* [Fr. *main*, hand, *prise*, taken.] *Law*, a writ formerly directed to the sheriff, commanding him to take sureties for a prisoner's appearance.

Maintain, mān-tān', *v.t.* [Fr. *maintenir*—*main*, L. *manus*, the hand, and Fr. *tenir*, L. *teneo*, to hold.] To preserve or keep in any particular state or condition; to keep up or in action or operation; to support; to keep possession of; not to lose or surrender; to continue (a conversation); to support with food, clothing, &c.; to uphold; to vindicate or justify (one's right or cause); to assert, as a tenet or opinion; to allege.—**Maintainable**, mān-tā'na-bl, *a.* Capable of being maintained.—**Maintainer**, mān-tā'nėr, *n.* One who maintains.—**Maintenance**, mān'ten-ans, *n.* The act of maintaining, upholding, or keeping up; support; vindication; that which maintains or supports; means of support; *law*, intermeddling in a suit in which the person has no interest, by assisting either party with money or means to prosecute or defend it.—*Cap of maintenance*, a cap of dignity carried before the sovereigns of England at their coronation.

Maize, māz, *n.* [Sp. *maiz*, from Haytian *mahiz*, the native name.] Indian corn, a cereal plant, a native of America, now commonly cultivated in the warmer parts of the world.—**Maizena**, mā-zē'na, *n.* The starch prepared from maize; corn-flour.

Majesty, maj'es-ti, *n.* [L. *majestas*, from *majus*, compar. form of *magnus*, great. MAGNITUDE.] Grandeur or dignity of rank, character, or manner; imposing loftiness of person or mien; stateliness; dignity or elevation of literary style; sublimity; a title of emperors, kings, and queens; generally with a possessive pronoun (may it please *your majesty*).—**Majestic**, ma-jes'tik, *a.* Possessing majesty; having dignity of appearance; august; splendid; grand; sublime; stately.—**Majestical**, ma-jes'ti-kal, *a.* Majestic.—**Majestically**, ma-jes'ti-kal-li, *adv.* In a majestic manner.

Majolica, ma-jol'i-ka, *n.* [It. *Maiolica* or *Maiorica*, for *Majorca*, whence the first specimens came.] A kind of earth used for making dishes, vases, &c.; afterwards applied to the ware itself, which resembles porcelain.

Major, mā'jėr, *a.* [L., compar. of *magnus*, great. MAGNITUDE.] The greater in number, quantity, extent, or dignity; the more important; *music*, applied to the modes in which the third is four semitones above the tonic or key-note, and to intervals consisting of four semitones.—*Major tone* or *interval*, an interval represented by the ratio of 8 to 9, while a minor tone is represented by the ratio of 9 to 10.—*Major term* of a syllogism, in *logic*, the predicate of the conclusion; the *major premise* is that which contains the major term.—*n.* An officer in the army next in rank above a captain and below a lieutenant-colonel; the lowest field-officer; *law*, a person of full age to manage his own concerns, which both in male and female is twenty-one years complete; *logic*, the first proposition of a regular syllogism, containing the major term.—**Majorate**, mā'jėr-at, *n.* The office or rank of major.—**Major-domo**, mā-jėr-dō'mō, *n.* [It. *maggiordomo*—L. *major*, greater, and *domus*, a house.] A man who takes charge of the management of a large household; a steward; a chief minister or great officer of a palace.—**Major-general**, *n.* A military officer the next in rank below a lieutenant-general.—**Major-generalship**, *n.* The office of a major-general.—**Majority**, ma-jor'i-ti, *n.* [Fr. *majorité.*] The state of being major or greater; the greater number; more than half; the number by which one quantity which can be counted exceeds another; full age; the age at which the law permits a young person to manage his own affairs; the office, rank, or commission of a major.—*To join the majority*, to pass over to the dead.—**Majorship**, mā'jėr-ship, *n.* Office or rank of major; majority.

Majuscule, ma-jus'kūl, *n.* [L. *majuscula* (*litera*, letter, understood), from *majusculus*, somewhat great, dim. from *major*, *majus*, greater.] A capital letter: opposed to *minuscule*.—*Majuscule writing*, writing composed entirely of capital letters, as in ancient manuscripts.

Make, māk, *v.t.* pret. & pp. *made*; ppr. *making*. [A.Sax. *macian*, L.G. and D. *maken*, G. *machen*, to make: same root as *may*, and L. *magnus*, great.] To cause to exist as a distinct thing; to create, frame, fashion, fabricate; to produce or effect, as agent or cause (money *makes* friends): to cause to be or to become: with words expressive of the result or condition of the object (to *make* a matter public; to *make* a man king); to constrain, compel, cause, occasion, with infinitives after the object (to *make* a person laugh: *to* the sign of the infinitive, being omitted); to gain, acquire (money, profit, &c.); to get or ascertain, as the result of computation or calculation; to pass over in sailing or travelling; to put in a desired or desirable position or condition; to prepare for use (a bed, a fire); to compose, as parts united in a whole; to constitute; to serve or answer for (she *makes* a good wife); to complete, as by being added to a sum; *naut.* to arrive at; to have within sight (to *make* a port, land). —*Make* is often used periphrastically with substantives, the two together being thus equal to a single verb; thus to *make complaint*=to complain; to *make answer* = to answer; to *make haste* = to hasten, &c.—*To make believe*, to pretend; to make pretence —*To make good*, to maintain; to establish (to *make good* one's footing); to accomplish (to *make good* one's word); to supply an equivalent for (to *make good* a loss).—*To make little of*, to treat as insignificant; to be able to get little or no meaning or satisfaction from.—*To make love to*, to court.—*To make much of*, to treat with fondness; to consider as of great value.—*To make nothing for*, to have no effect in assisting or supporting.—*To make nothing of*, to regard or think as nothing; to treat as of no value; to be unable to understand; to get no satisfaction from (I can *make nothing of* him).—*To make out*, to discover; to decipher; to prove or establish by evidence or argument; to find to the full; as, he was not able to *make out* the whole sum.—*To make over*, to transfer the title of; to convey; as, he *made over* his estate in trust.—*To make sail* (*naut.*), to increase the quantity of sail already set.—*To make shift*, to contrive or manage with such means or appliances as are available.—*To make up*, to make full or complete; to collect into a sum or mass; to compose, as ingredients or parts; to constitute; to compensate for or make good (to *make up* a loss); to reconcile, settle, adjust (quarrels, &c.); to bring to a definite conclusion (to *make up* one's mind).—*To make water*, to leak, as a ship; to void the urine.—*To make way*, to make progress; to open a passage; to clear the way.—*v.i.* To act or do: often with adjectives to express the manner of acting (to *make bold*, &c.); to interfere; to proceed, move, direct one's course (he *made* toward home; he *made* after the boy); to rise or flow toward land: said of the tide.—*To make against*, to tend to injure; to be adverse to; to form an argument against; to tend to disprove.—*To make as if*, to act as if; to pretend that.—*To make at*, to make a hostile movement against.—*To make away with*, to take away and put out of reach; to remove by killing; to murder secretly.—*To make bold*, to venture; to take leave or liberty (to *make bold* to say).—*To make for*, to contribute towards; to be of service to; to favour (this *makes for* the argument).—*To make free with*, to treat with freedom or without ceremony; to make free use of.—*To make light of*, to regard as trifling or of no consequence; to belittle.—*To make out*, to succeed and no more.—*To make sure*, to ascertain with certainty.—*To make sure of*, to consider as certain; to secure to one's self.—*To make up*, to dress, &c., as an actor.—*To make up to*, to approach; to court.—*To make up for*, to serve as compensation for.—*n.* Structure; construction; shape; form (a man of slender *make*).—**Makable**, mā'ka-bl, *a.* Capable of being made.—**Make-believe**, *n.* Making believe or pretending; pretence; pretext; sham. —*a.* Unreal; sham.—**Maker**, mā'kėr, *n.* One who makes; the Creator; one who composes verses; a poet.—**Make-shift**, *n.* Something to serve a present purpose; a temporary substitute.—**Make up**, *v.* To arrange, compose, prepare, adjust, assume a guise, compensate or reconcile; in printing, to arrange the type in columns or pages; in the theater and motion pictures, to apply cosmetics, dress, or accessories for a part; in education, to remove a deficiency.—**Make-up**, *n.*

Malacca, ma-lak'ka, *a.* Pertaining to Malacca, in the Malay Peninsula.—*Malacca cane*, a cane made of the brown mottled or clouded stem of a kind of palm.

Malachite, mal'a-kīt, *n.* [Fr. *malachite*, from Gr. *malachē*, a mallow, from its colour resembling that of the leaves of mallow.] A mineral; a carbonate of copper found in solid masses of a beautiful green colour, the *Green Carbonate of Copper*, used for many ornamental purposes.

Malacology, mal-a-kol'o-ji, *n.* [Gr. *malakos*, soft, and *logos*, discourse.] The branch of zoology that treats of the mollusca or soft-bodied animals.—**Malacologist**, mal-a-kol'o-jist, *n.* One versed in malacology.

Malacopterygian, **Malacopterygious**, mal-a-kop'tėr-ij"i-an, mal-a-kop'tėr-ij"i-us, *a.* [Gr. *malakos*, soft, and *pterygion*, a fin, a little wing, from *pteryx*, a wing.] A term applied to those osseous fishes that have all the rays of the fins soft.—**Malacopteri**, **Malacopterygii**, mal-a-kop'-tėr-i, mal-a-kop'tėr-ij"i-ī, *n.pl.* The malacopterygious fishes.—**Malacopterygian**, *n.* An individual of the Malacopterygii.—**Malacosteon**, mal-a-kos'tē-on, *n.* [Gr. *osteon*, a bone.] *Med.* a softening or atrophy of the bones.—**Malacostomous**, mal-a-kos'to-mus, *a.* [Gr. *stoma*, mouth.] Having soft jaws without teeth, as certain fishes.—**Malacostracan**, mal-a-kos'tra-kan, *n.* [Gr. *astrakon*, a shell.] A division of crustaceans, including the shrimps, lobsters, &c.—**Malacostracan**, **Malacostracous**, mal-a-kos'tra-kus, *a.*

Maladjustment, mal-ad-just'ment, *n.* [Prefix *mal*, bad.] A bad or wrong adjustment; *psychology*, a lack of harmony between an individual's desires or capacities and his mode of living.

Maladministration, mal-ad-min'is-trā"shon, *n.* [Prefix *mal*, bad.] Faulty administration; bad management of public affairs.

Maladroit, mal-a-droit', *a.* [Prefix *mal*, bad.] Not adroit or dexterous; awkward.—**Maladroitly**, mal-a-droit'li, *adv.* Clumsily; awkwardly.—**Maladroitness**, mal-a-droit'nes, *n.* Clumsiness; awkwardness.

Malady, mal'a-di, *n.* [Fr. *maladie*, from *malade*, O.Fr. *malabde*, ill, from L. *male*, *habitus*, in bad condition. HABIT.] Any disease of the human body; an ailment; an indisposition; moral or mental disorder.

Mala fides, mā'la fī'dēz, *n.* [L.] Bad faith.—*Mala fide*, with bad faith; deceitfully: opposed to *bona fide*.

Malaga, mal'a-ga, *n.* A wine imported from Malaga in Spain; the white grape from which the wine is made, grown also in California.

Malagasy, mal'a-gas-i, *a.* and *n.* The language of Madagascar.

Malaise, mal-āz, *n.* [Fr., from *mal*, bad, and *aise*, ease.] State of being ill at ease; morbid and indefinite feeling of uneasiness.

Malambo-bark, ma-lam'bō, *n.* [South American.] The name of a tropical American shrub, used as a remedy for diarrhœa and as a vermifuge, also in adulterating spices.

Malanders, mal'an-dėrz, *n.* [Fr. *malandres*, L. *malandria*.] A dry scab or scurfy eruption on the hock of a horse or at the bend of the knee.

Malapert, mal'a-pėrt *a.* [O.Fr. *malappert*, over-ready—prefix *mal*, badly, and O.Fr. *appert*, ready, prompt, from L. *apertus*, open. PERT.] Pert; saucy; impudent; forward.—*n.* A pert, saucy person.—**Malapertly**, mal'a-pėrt-li, *adv.* Saucily; with impudence.—**Malapertness**, mal'a-pėrt-nes, *n.* Sauciness; impudent pertness.

Malapropos, mal-ap'rō-pō", *a.* and *adv.* [Prefix *mal*, badly, and *apropos*.] The opposite of apropos; ill to the purpose.—**Malapropism**, mal'a-prop-izm, *n.* The blundering use of words characteristic of Mrs. *Malaprop* in Sheridan's *Rivals*, e.g. 'an allegory on the banks of the Nile'.

Malar, mā'lėr, *a.* [From L. *mala*, the cheek-bone, the jaw.] Pertaining to the cheek or cheek-bone.—*n.* *Anat.* the cheek-bone.

Malaria, ma-lā'ri-a, *n.* [It. *mala arta*, bad air, from L. *malus*, bad, and *aer*, air.] An infectious febrile disease formerly believed contracted from air tainted by deleterious emanations from animal or vegetable matter, but now known to be caused by a blood parasite transmitted by the bite of certain mosquitoes.—**Malarial**, **Malarian**, **Malarious**, *a.*

Malassimilation, mal'as-sim-i-lā"shon, *n.* [Prefix *mal*, bad.] Imperfect or morbid assimilation or nutrition; faulty digestion.

Malay, **Malayan**, ma-lā', ma-lā'yan, *n.* A native of the Malay Peninsula; the language of the Malays.—*a.* Belonging to the Malays or to their country.

Malconformation, mal'kon-for-mā"-shon, *n.* [Prefix *mal*, bad.] Imperfect conformation; disproportion of parts.

Malcontent, mal'kon-tent, *n.* [Prefix *mal*, ill.] A discontented person; a discontented subject of a government.—**Malcontent**, **Malcontented**, mal'kon-ten-ted, *a.* Discontented with the government.—**Malcontentedly**, mal'kon-ten-ted-li, *adv.* In a malcontented manner.—**Malcontentedness**, mal'kon-ten-ted-nes, *n.*

Male, māl, *a.* [Fr. *mâle*, O.Fr. *masle*, from L. *masculus*, male, from *mas*, *maris*, a male. MASCULINE.] Pertaining to the sex that begets young, as distinguished from the *female*; masculine; *bot.* having fecundating organs, but not fruit-bearing. —*Male rhymes*, rhymes in which only the final syllables correspond.—*Male screw*, the screw whose threads enter the grooves of the female screw.—*n.* One of the sex which begets young; *bot.* a plant which bears stamens.

Malediction, mal-e-dik'shon, *n.* [L. *maledictio*, *maledictionis*—*male*, evil, and *dico*, to speak. DICTION.] Evil speaking; a curse or execration; an imprecation.

Malefactor, mal-e-fak'tėr, *n.* [L., evildoer—*male*, ill, and *facio*, to do.] One who commits a crime; a criminal.

Malefic, ma-lef'ik, *a.* [L. *maleficus*, that does ill—*male*, ill, and *facio*, to do.] Doing mischief.—**Maleficence**, ma-lef'i-sens, *n.* [L. *maleficentia*.] The quality of being maleficent.—**Maleficent**, ma-lef'i-sent, *a.* Doing evil; harmful.

Malevolent, ma-lev'ō-lent, *a.* [L. *malevolens*, *malevolentis*—*male*, ill, and *volens*, willing or disposed. VOLITION.] Having an evil disposition towards another or others; malicious; spiteful.—**Malevolently**, ma-lev'ō-lent-li, *adv.* In a malevolent manner; with ill-will.—**Malevolence**, ma-lev'ō-lens, *n.* [L. *malevolentia*.] The quality of being malevolent; ill-will; personal hatred. ∴ Syn. under MALICE.

Malexecution, mal'ek-sē-kū"shon, *n.* [Prefix *mal*, bad.] Evil execution; bad administration.

Malfeasance, mal-fē'zans, *n.* [Fr. *malfaisance*—*mal*, ill, and *faire*, L. *facere*, to do.] *Law*, doing what a person ought not to do; illegal deed.

Malformation, mal-for-mā'shon, *n.* [Prefix *mal*, bad.] Ill or wrong formation; a deviation from the normal structure of an organ.

Malic, mā′lik, *a.* [L. *malum*, an apple.] Pertaining to apples; obtained from the juice of apples.—*Malic acid*, an acid found in many fruits, particularly in the apple.

Malice, mal′is, *n.* [Fr. *malice*, L. *malitia*, from *malus*, evil; cog. Gr. *melas*, black; Skr. *malam*, filth; Ir. *maile*, evil. *Malus* is seen also in *malady*, *malign*, *malignant*, &c.] Enmity of heart; a disposition to injure others for mere personal gratification, or from a spirit of revenge; spite; ill-will; *law*, a formed design of doing mischief to another; called also *malice prepense* or *aforethought*. ∴ *Malice* is a deeper and more abiding feeling than *malevolence*, *malevolence* being of a more casual and temporary character. *Malignity* is malice intensified, proceeding from an innate love of doing harm to others.—**Malicious**, ma-lish′us, *a.* [L. *malitiosus*.] Indulging malice; harbouring ill-will without provocation; proceeding from ill-will; dictated by malice.—*Malicious mischief*, an injury to property from sheer malice, in some instances a felony, in others a misdemeanour.—*Malicious prosecution*, a prosecution preferred without reasonable cause.—**Maliciously**, ma-lish′us-li, *adv.* In a malicious manner.—**Maliciousness**, ma-lish′us-nes, *n.* The quality of being malicious.

Malign, ma-līn′, *a.* [L. *malignus* for *maligenus*, of an evil nature—*malus*, bad, and *genus*, kind (Malice, Genus). Comp. *benign*, with exactly the opposite sense.] Of an evil nature, disposition, or character; malicious; pernicious; tending to injure or produce evil effects.—*v.t.* To speak evil of; to traduce, defame, vilify.—**Malignance**, **Malignancy**, ma-lig′nans, ma-lig′nan-si, *n.* The quality of being malignant; extreme malevolence; bitter enmity; *med.* virulence.—**Malignant**, ma-lig′nant, *a.* [L. *malignans*, from *maligno*, to act maliciously.] Having extreme malevolence or enmity; virulently inimical; malicious; exerting pernicious influence; *med.* threatening a fatal issue; virulent (a *malignant* ulcer); extremely heinous. ∴ Syn. under Malice.—*n.* *English history*, one of the adherents of Charles I and his son: so called by the Roundheads.—**Malignantly**, ma-lig′nant-li, *adv.* In a malignant manner.—**Maligner**, ma-līn′ėr, *n.* One who maligns.—**Malignity**, ma-lig′ni-ti, *n.* [L. *malignitas*.] The state or quality of being malignant; evil disposition of heart toward another; malice without provocation; rancour; virulence.—**Malignly**, ma-līn′li, *adv.* In a malign manner.

Malinger, ma-ling′gėr, *v.i.* [Fr. *malingre*, sickly, weakly; from mal, ill, and O.Fr. *hingre*, *heingre*, feeble, nasalized form of L. *æger*, sick.] *Milit.* to feign illness in order to avoid duty.—**Malingerer**, ma-ling′gėr-ėr, *n.* A soldier who feigns himself ill.—**Malingery**, ma-ling′gėr-i, *n.* A feigning illness to avoid military duty.

Malison, mal′i-zn, *n.* [O.Fr. *malison*, *maleiçon*, contr. from *malediction*. Comp. *benison*, for *benediction*.] A malediction; curse; execration.

Malkin, ma̤′kin, *n.* [Dim. of *Mal*, Mary; comp. the name *jack*, an implement for various homely purposes.] A wench employed in a kitchen (*Shak.*); a mop made of clouts; a stuffed figure; a scarecrow.

Mall, mal, *n.* [Fr. *mail*, It. *maglio*, *malleo*, L. *malleus*, a hammer. Malleable.] A heavy wooden beetle or hammer; (originally an alley where the game of *pall-mall* was played with *malls* and balls) a public walk; a level shaded walk.

Mallard, mal′ärd, *n.* [O.Fr. *malard*, Prov. Fr. *maillard*, from *maille* (L. *macula*), a spot on a bird's feather, from the iridescent spot on the wing.] The common wild duck.

Malleable, mal′lē-a-bl, *a.* [Fr. *malléable*, from L.L. *malleo*, to beat with a hammer, from L. *malleus*, a hammer (akin *mallet*, *maul*).] Capable of being shaped or extended by beating with the hammer: said of metals.—**Malleability**, **Malleableness**, mal′lē-a-bil″i-ti, mal′lē-a-bl-nes, *n.* The quality of being malleable.—**Malleate**,† mal′lē-āt, *v.t.* To hammer; to beat out.—**Malleation**, mal-lē-ā′shon, *n.* The act of hammering; extension by beating.

Mallee, mal′lē, *n.* Kind of dwarf Eucalyptus.

Mallein, mal′lē-in, *n.* [L. *malleus*, a hammer, in allusion to the shape of the bacteria concerned.] A preparation made from a culture of the bacilli of glanders, used in diagnosing that disease.

Malleolus, mal′lē-ō-lus, *n.* [L., dim. of *malleus*, a hammer.] One of the two projections of the leg-bones at the ankle.—**Malleolar**, mal′lē-ō-lėr, *a.* *Anat.* pertaining to the ankle.

Mallet, mal′et, *n.* [Dim. of *mall*.] A wooden hammer, used chiefly by stone-cutters, joiners, &c.

Malleus, mal′ē-us, *n.* [L., a mallet.] *Anat.* one of the chain of small bones in the ear; *zool.* a hammer-shaped body forming part of the masticatory apparatus in some microscopic animals.

Mallow, mal′ō, *n.* [A.Sax. *malwe*, G. *malve*, from L. *malva*, mallow, allied to Gr. *malachē*, mallow. *malakos*, soft—from its emollient properties.] The common name of a number of plants, chiefly herbaceous or annual, some of them valuable for medicinal properties. Also called *Mallows*, as a singular.

Malm, mäm, *n.* [A.Sax. *mealm*, Goth. *malma*, sand; akin to *meal*, from root meaning to grind.] A soft, grayish limestone, easily crumbled; *Eng.* marl; a soil containing clay and chalk.

Malmsey, mäm′zi, *n.* [O.E. *malvesie*, Fr. *malvoisie*; from Napoli di *Malvasia*, in the Morea, the white and red wines produced at which first received the name.] A kind of grape; a strong sweet white wine made in Madeira.

Malnutrition, mal′nū-trish″un, *n.* Insufficient or otherwise faulty nutrition.

Malodor, **Malodour**, mal-ō′dėr, *n.* [Prefix *mal*, bad.] An offensive odor.—**Malodorous**, mal-ō′dėr-us, *a.* Having a bad or offensive odor.

Malpighian, mal-pig′i-an, *a.* [After *Malpighi*, an eminent Italian anatomist and botanist.] *Anat.* applied to certain small round bodies in the cortical substance of the kidney, and to corpuscles in the spleen.—**Malpighiaceous**, mal-pig′i-ā″shus, *a.* *Bot.* applied to hairs which are attached by the middle.

Malposition, mal-pō-zish′on, *n.* [Prefix *mal*, bad.] A wrong position.

Malpractice, mal-prak′tis, *n.* [Prefix *mal*, bad.] Professional malfeasance or improper and careless performance of duty, as of a physician or lawyer.

Malt, ma̤lt, *n.* [A.Sax. *mealt* (Icel., Sw., and Dan. *malt*, D. *mout*, G. *malz*), from *meltan*, to melt. Melt.] Grain, usually barley, steeped in water and made to germinate, the starch of the grain being thus converted into saccharine matter, after which it is dried in a kiln, and then used in brewing and distilling; liquor produced from malt; beer.—*v.t.* To make into malt.—*v.i.* To be converted into malt.—**Malt-barn**, *n.* A barn in which malt is made or kept.—**Malt-drink**, **Malt-liquor**, *n.* A beverage prepared from malt.—**Malt-dust**, *n.* The grains or remains of malt.—**Malt-floor**, *n.* A floor on which malt is dried in a malt-kiln.—**Malt-house**, *n.* A house in which malt is made.—**Malt-kiln**, *n.* A heated chamber in which malt is dried.—**Maltman**, **Maltster**, ma̤lt′man, ma̤lt′stėr, *n.* A man whose occupation is to make malt.—**Malt-mill**, *n.* A mill for grinding malt.—**Malt-vinegar**, *n.* Vinegar made from an infusion of malt.—**Maltworm**, ma̤lt′wėrm, *n.* A person fond of beer or other liquor; a tippler.

Maltese, ma̤l′tēz, *n. sing.* and *pl.* A native or natives of Malta.—*a.* Belonging to Malta.

Maltha, mal′tha, *n.* [Gr., a mixture for caulking ships.] A variety of bitumen like pitch, intermediate between liquid petroleum and solid asphalt.

Malthusian, mal-thū′zi-an, *a.* Relating to the theory of the Rev. T. R. *Malthus*, that population, when unchecked, goes on increasing in a higher ratio than the means of subsistence can be made to increase; and hence, that early marriages and unrestricted child-bearing should be discouraged.—*n.* One who holds the doctrines of Malthus.—**Malthusianism**, mal-thū′zi-an-izm, *n.* The doctrines inculcated by Malthus.

Maltose, ma̤lt′ōz, *n.* [From *malt*.] Malt sugar.

Maltreat, mal-trēt′, *v.t.* [Prefix *mal*, badly.] To treat ill.—**Maltreatment**, mal-trēt′ment, *n.* The act of maltreating; ill-usage.

Malvaceous, mal-vā′shus, *a.* [L. *malva*, mallow.] Pertaining to the plants of the mallow family.

Malversation, mal-vėr-sā′shon, *n.* [Fr. *malversation*—L. *male*, badly, and *versor*, to occupy one's self, from *verto*, *versum*, to turn. Verse.] Evil conduct; fraudulent tricks; misbehaviour in an office or employment, as fraud, breach of trust, &c.

Mamma, **Mama**, mä′mä, *n.* [A repetition of the infantile utterance *ma*, *ma*.] Mother; a word of tenderness and familiarity, used chiefly by young persons in addressing, or reference to, mother.

Mameluke, **Mamaluke**, mam′e-lūk, mam′a-lūk, *n.* [Ar. *mamlūk*, that which is possessed, a slave, from *malak*, to possess.] One of the former mounted soldiery of Egypt, a powerful body broken up and massacred in 1811.

Mamelon, mam′e-lon, *n.* [Fr., a nipple, from L. *mamma*, a breast.] A small hill or mound with a rounded top.

Mamma, mam′ma, *n.* pl. **Mammæ**, mam′mē. [L., the female breast, from root meaning to swell, to swell with juice.] The breast; the organ in females that secretes the milk.—**Mammal**, mam′mal, *n.* An animal of the class Mammalia.—**Mammalia**, mam-mā′li-a, *n. pl.* [Lit. breast-animals.] The highest class in the animal kingdom, whose distinctive characteristic is that the female suckles the young.—**Mammalian**, mam-mā′li-an, *a.* Pertaining to the mammals.—**Mammaliferous**, mam-ma-lif′ėr-us, *a.* *Geol.* containing mammalian remains.—**Mammalogist**, mam-mal′o-jist, *n.* A naturalist who treats of the mammalia.—**Mammalogy**, mam-mal′o-ji, *n.* The science of mammals.—**Mammary**, mam′ma-ri, *a.* Pertaining to the female breasts or paps.—**Mammifer**, mam′mi-fėr, *n.* A mammal.—**Mammiferous**, mam-mif′ėr-us, *a.* Having the distinguishing characteristics of a mammifer.—**Mammiform**, mam′mi-form, *a.* Having the shape or form of paps.—**Mammilla**, mam-mil′la, *n.* [L. *mamilla*, a little breast.] A little breast; something of this form.—**Mammillary**, mam′mil-a-ri, *a.* Pertaining to or resembling a nipple or pap; *anat.* applied to two small protuberances like nipples in the brain; *mineral.* studded with mammiform protuberances.—**Mammillate**, **Mammillated**, mam′mil-āt, mam′mil-ā-ted, *a.* In the form of a pap or nipple; having small protuberances like nipples.—**Mammillation**, mam-mi-lā′shon, *n.* A small mammillate prominence.—**Mammilloid**, mam′mil-oid, *a.* Shaped like a pap or nipple.

Mammee, mam-mē′, *n.* An American tree yielding a large and nourishing fruit.—**Mammee-Sapota**, mam-mē′sa-pō′ta̤, *n.* A large tree of the West Indies and tropical America, yielding a fruit which is called natural marmalade.

Mammelière, mam-mel-yãr, *n.* [Fr. *mamellière*, from *mamelle*, L. *mamilla*, dim. of *mamma*, a breast.] In *anc. armour*, one of two circular plates fastened to the surcoat right above the breasts of a knight.

Mammon, mam′mon, *n.* [L. *mammona*, Gr. *mammōnas*, mammon, riches, from Chal.

mammōn, māmōn.] The Syrian god of riches, mentioned in the New Testament as a personification of worldliness; hence, riches; wealth.—**Mammonism**, mam′-mon-izm, *n.* Devotion to the service of Mammon or the pursuit of wealth.—**Mammonist, Mammonite**, mam′mon-ist, mam′mon-īt, *n.* A person entirely devoted to the acquisition of wealth.

Mammoth, mam′moth, *n.* [Rus. *mamant, mamont*, from Tart. *mamma*, the earth, because their remains being found in the earth the natives believed that they burrowed like moles.] An extinct species of elephant of enormous size and covered with dense, shaggy hair, the remains of which are found in Siberia and elsewhere. —*a.* Resembling the mammoth in size; very large; gigantic.—**Mammoth tree**, *n.* The giant sequoia tree of California, specimens having reached more than 325 feet with a diameter of 25 feet.

Man, man, *n.* pl. **Men**, men. [A.Sax. *man, mann*, man, person = D., O.H.G., and Sw. *man*, G. *mann*, Icel. *mathr, mannr*, Dan. *mand*, Goth. *manna*; from root *man*, to think, seen in Skr. *man*, to think, *manas*, mind, *manushya*, man, and also in E. *mean*, to intend, *mind*, L. *mens*, the mind (whence *mental*).] A human being; a person; particularly, a male adult of the human race; the human race; mankind: in this sense without article or plural (*man* is born to trouble); a male servant; an adult male in some person's employment or under his direction; a piece with which a game, as chess or draughts, is played.—*Man of straw*, a man of no substantial character, influence, or means; in commercial language, a person destitute of capital put forward by way of decoy.—*v.t. manned, manning.* To supply with men; to furnish with a sufficient force or complement of men; to infuse courage into.—**Man-at-arms**, *n.* A term applied to a fully equipped or heavily armed soldier of the middle ages.—**Man-eater**, *n.* A cannibal; one of those tigers which have acquired a special preference for human flesh.—**Man-engine**, *n.* A sort of elevator for the workmen in a mine; a vertical rod with platforms working up and down in a shaft.—**Manful**, man′ful, *a.* Manly; bold; brave.—**Manfully**, man′ful-li, *adv.* In a manful manner. — **Manfulness**, man′ful-nes, *n.* The quality of being manful. — **Manhole**, man′hōl, *n.* A hole through which a man may creep into a drain, cess-pool, steam-boiler, &c., for cleaning or repairing.—**Manhood**, man′hud, *n.* The state of being a man; the qualities of or becoming a man.—**Manikin**, man′i-kin, *n.* A little man; a dwarf; an anatomic model of the human body.—**Mankind**, man-kīnd′ or man′kīnd, *n.* The human race; man taken collectively; the males of the human race. — **Manlike**, man′līk, *a.* Resembling a man; having the qualities proper to a man.—**Manliness**, man′li-nes, *n.* The quality of being manly. —**Manly**, man′li, *a.* Pertaining to or becoming a man; having the nobler attributes of a man; self-reliant; brave.—**Man-mercer**, *n.* One who deals by retail in cloths, &c., for male attire.—**Man-midwife**, *n.* A man who practises obstetrics; an accoucheur. — **Mannish**, man′ish, *a.* Characteristic of or resembling a man; as applied to a woman, masculine; unwomanly. **Mannishly**, man′ish-li, *adv.* In a mannish manner.—**Mannishness**, man′ish-nes, *n.* The state or quality of being mannish.—**Man-of-war**, *n.* A government vessel employed for the purposes of war.— **Man-of-war's-man**, *n.* A seaman belonging to a ship of war.—**Man-rope**, *n.* *Naut.* one of the ropes suspended on each side of a gangway, hatchway, &c.—**Man-servant**, *n.* A male servant. — **Manslaughter**, *n.* The slaughter or killing of a man or men; especially, the unlawful killing of a man without malice.—**Manstealer**, *n.* One who steals human beings, generally for the purpose of selling them as slaves.—**Man-trap**, *n.* A mechanism for catching trespassers.

Manacle, man′a-kl, *n.* [Fr. *manicle*, L. *manicula*, dim. of *manica*, a manacle, from *manus*, the hand. MANAGE.] An instrument of iron for fastening the hands; handcuff; shackle: generally in plural. — *v.t.*— *manacled, manacling.* To put handcuffs or other fastening upon; to shackle.

Manage, man′āj, *v.t.*—*managed, managing.* [Fr. *manége*, the management of a horse, management or guidance in general; It. *maneggiare*, to handle, to manage; from L. *manus*, the hand, whence also *manacle, manual*, &c. MANUAL.] To have under control and direction; to conduct, carry on, guide, administer; to make tractable, or get under due control; to wield; to move or use in the manner desired (tools or the like); to treat (a person) with caution or judgment; to govern with address. —*v.i.* To direct or conduct affairs; to carry on concerns or business.—**Manageability**, man′āj-a-bil″i-ti, *n.* State of being manageable. — **Manageable**, man′āj-a-bl, *a.* Capable of being managed; easily made subservient to one's views or designs.—**Manageableness**, man′āj-a-bl-nes, *n.* The quality of being manageable.—**Manageably**, man′āj-a-bli, *adv.* In a manageable manner. — **Management**, man′āj-ment, *n.* The act of managing; the manner of treating, directing, carrying on, or using for a purpose; conduct; administration; cautious handling or treatment; the body of directors or managers of any undertaking, concern, or interest collectively. — **Manager**, man′āj-ėr, *n.* One who manages; one who has the guidance or direction of anything; one who is directly at the head of an undertaking.—**Managerial**, man-a-jē′ri-al, *a.* Of or belonging to a manager. —**Managership**, man′āj-ėr-ship, *n.* The office of a manager.

Manakin, man′a-kin, *n.* [Dim. of *man*, as applied to birds, originally the name of a species with a beard-like tuft of feathers on the chin.] A manikin; a name for certain small tropical American birds.

Manatee, Manatin, man-a-tē′, man′a-tin, *n.* [Haytian.] The sea-cow, an aquatic herbivorous mammal allied to the cetaceans, and found on the coasts of South America, Africa, and Australia.

Manchet, man′shet, *n.* [Comp. Fr. *miche, michette*, a manchet or small loaf.] A small loaf of fine bread; fine white bread.—*a.* Fine and white: said of bread or flour.

Manchineel, man-chi-nēl′, *n.* [It. *mancinelto*, Fr. *manzanille*, Sp. *manzanillo*, from *manzana*, an apple, from L. *malum Matianum*, a kind of apple, from *Matius*, a Roman name.] A tree of the West Indies and Central America, abounding in acrid and highly poisonous juice; the wood being valuable for cabinet work.

Manchu, Manchoo, man-chö′, *n.* A native of Manchuria, or one of the same race; one of the reigning dynasty in China; the language of the Manchus; the court language of China.

Manciple, man′si-pl, *n.* [O.Fr. *mancipe*, L. *manceps*, one who purchases anything at a public sale—*manus*, the hand, and *capio*, to take.] A steward; a purveyor, particularly of a college or inn of court.

Mandamus, man-dā′mus, *n.* [L., lit. we command.] *Law*, a command or writ issuing from a superior court, directed to any person, corporation, or inferior court, requiring them to do some specified act.

Mandarin, man-da-rēn′, *n.* [Pg. *mandarim*, from Skr. *mantrin*, a counsellor, a minister, from *mantra*, counsel, from *man*, to think, to know. MAN.] The general name given by Europeans to Chinese magistrates or public officials, whether civil or military.—*Mandarin duck*, a beautiful kind of duck, a native of China. — **Mandarinic**, man-da-rēn′ik, *a.* Pertaining or appropriate to a mandarin.

Mandate, man′dāt, *n.* [L. *mandatum*, an order, from *mando*, to command (from *manus*, the hand, and *do*, to give), seen also in *command, commend, demand, remand, recommend*, &c.] A command; an order, precept, or injunction; written authority by one person to another to act for him.— **Mandatory, Mandatary**, man′dā-to-ri, man′dā-ta-ri, *n.* [Fr. *mandataire.*] One to whom a mandate or charge is given; one who receives special written authority to act for another.—**Mandatory**, *a.* Containing a command; directory.

Mandible, man′di-bl, *n.* [L. *mandibulum*, the jaw, from *mando*, to chew.] An animal's jaw, particularly, the under jaw of a mammal; the upper or lower jaw of a bird; one of the upper or anterior pair of jaws of an insect or other articulate animal. —**Mandibular**, man-dib′ū-lėr, *a.* Belonging to a mandible.—**Mandibulate, Mandibulated**, man-dib′ū-lāt, man-dib′ū-la-ted, *a.* Provided with mandibles, as many insects.

Mandolin, man′dō-lin, *n.* [Fr. *mandoline*, from It. *mandola, mandora, pandora*, a species of lute. BANDORE.] A musical instrument of the guitar kind.

Mandragora, man-drag′o-ra, *n.* [L. and Gr. *mandragoras*, the mandrake.] The genus of plants popularly called mandrakes; a medicinal preparation obtained from the mandrake (*Shak.*). — **Mandrake**, man′-drāk, *n.* [From *mandragora.*] A plant of the Mediterranean region, with large thick roots, and possessing strong purgative and narcotic properties, formerly the subject of various superstitions.

Mandrel, Mandril, man′drel, man′dril, *n.* [Fr. *mandrin*. from Gr. *mandra*, an inclosed space, the bed in which the stone of a ring is set.] A bar of iron on which an article is fitted to be turned on a lathe; any straight bar upon which a tube or ring is welded.

Mandrill, man′dril, *n.* [Fr. *mandrille*, from the West African name.] The great blue-faced or rib-nosed baboon, the largest and most hideous of the baboons.

Manducate, man′dū-kāt, *v.t.* — *manducated, manducating.* [L. *manduco, manducatum*, from *mando*, to chew; akin *mandible, manger.*] To masticate; to chew.—**Manducable**, man′dū-ka-bl, *a.* Capable of being chewed.—**Manducation**, man-dū-kā′shon, *n.* The act of chewing.—**Manducatory**, man′dū-ka-to-ri, *a.* Pertaining to or employed in chewing.

Mane, mān, *n.* [O.D. *mane*, D. *manen*, Dan. *man*, Icel. *mōn*, O.H.G. *mana*, G. *mähne*; allied to W. *mwng*, a mane, *mwn*, the neck.] The long hair on the upper side of the neck of some animals, as the horse, lion, &c., usually hanging down on one side.— **Maned**, mānd, *a.* Having a mane. — **Maneless**, mān′les, *a*, Not having a mane.

Manège, ma-nāzh′, *n.* [Fr. *manège*, from It. *maneggio*, management. MANAGE.] A school for training horses and teaching horsemanship; the art of breaking, training, and riding horses; the art of horsemanship.

Maneh, mā′nē, *n.* [Heb.] A Hebrew weight for gold and silver.

Mannequin, man′ē-kin, *n.* [A corruption of *manikin.*] An artist's model fashioned of wood or wax; a woman who serves as a model by wearing clothes for display.

Manes, mā′nēz, *n.pl.* [L., from O.L. *manus*, good, benevolent.] Among the Romans the ghosts, shades, or souls of deceased persons; the deified shades of the dead.

Maneuver, man-nö′vėr, *n.* MANŒUVRE.

Manful, &c. Under MAN.

Manganese, man′ga-nēz, *n.* [By metathesis from *magnesium*, the name first given to it.] A metal of a dusky white or whitish-gray colour, very hard and difficult to fuse, not known native, on account of its powerful affinity for oxygen, but having ores of considerable value in the industrial arts.— **Manganese-bronze**. A variety of bronze containing a certain quantity of manganese and iron, alleged to possess valuable qualities for various purposes.— **Manganesian**, man-ga-nē′zi-an, *a.* Pertaining to manganese; consisting of it or partaking of its qualities. — **Manganic, Manganesic**, man-gan′ik, man-ga-nē′zik, *a.* Obtained from manganese.—**Manganite**, man′gan-īt, *n.* One of the ores of manganese, used in the manufacture of glass.

Mange, mānj, *n.* [O.Fr. *mangeson*, Fr. *démangeaison*, an itching, from *manger*, L. *manduco*, to eat. MANDUCATE.] A cutaneous disease very similar to itch, and to which horses, cattle, dogs, and other beasts are subject.—**Mangily**, mān'ji-li, *adv.* In a mangy manner.—**Manginess**, mān'ji-nes, *n.* The quality or condition of being mangy.—**Mangy**, mān'ji, *a.* Infected with the mange; scabby; mean.

Mangel-wurzel, mang'gl-wėr'zl, *n.* [G., lit. want-root, but the proper form is *mangold-wurzel*—G. *mangold*, beet, and *wurzel*, root=beet-root.] A variety of beet, extensively cultivated as food for cattle.

Manger, mān'jėr, *n.* [Fr. *mangeoire*, from *manger*, from L. *manducare*, to eat. MANDUCATE.] A trough or box in which fodder is laid for horses or cattle; the receptacle from which horses or cattle eat in a stable or cow-house.

Mangle, mang'gl, *v.t.*—*mangled*, *mangling*. [Perhaps from L. *mancus*, maimed, through L.L. *mangulare*, to mangle; comp. A.Sax. *bemancian*, to maim; L.G. *mank*, mutilated; D. *mank*, lame; G. *mangel*, a defect; *mangeln*, to be wanting.] To cut by repeated blows, making a ragged or torn wound, or covering with wounds; to cut in a bungling manner; to hack; to lacerate: applied chiefly to the cutting of flesh; *fig.* to destroy the symmetry or completeness of; to mutilate.—**Mangler**, mang'glėr, *n.* One who mangles; one who mutilates.

Mangle, mang'gl, *n.* [D. and G. *mangel*, from O.Fr. *mangonel*, Gr. *manganon*, a war engine, the axis of a pulley.] A well-known machine for smoothing table-cloths, sheets, and other articles of linen or cotton.—*v.t.* To smooth cloth with a mangle.—**Mangler**, mang'glėr, *n.* One who uses a mangle.

Mango, mang'gō, *n.* [Malay.] The fruit of the mango-tree, a native of tropical Asia, but widely cultivated throughout the tropics; a fruit highly valued for dessert.—**Mango-fish**, *n.* [From its beautiful yellow colour resembling that of a ripe *mango*.] A fish of the Ganges, about 15 inches long, and highly esteemed for food.

Mangold-wurzel, mang'gōld-wėr'zl, *n.* MANGEL-WURZEL.

Mangonel, man'go-nel, *n.* [O.Fr. *mangonel*, It. *manganello*, *mangano*, from Gr. *manganon*. MANGLE, *n.*] An engine formerly used for throwing stones and battering walls.

Mangosteen, mang'gō-stēn, *n.* [Malay *mangusta*.] A tree of the East Indies, the fruit of which is about the size of an orange, and most delicious.

Mangrove, man'grōv, *n.* [Malay *manggi-manggi*.] A tropical tree growing on the banks of rivers and on the sea-coast, remarkable for giving off adventitious roots from the stem and branches.

Mangy. Under MANGE.

Manhaden, man-hā'den, *n.* MENHADEN.

Manhood. Under MAN.

Mania, mā'ni-a, *n.* [L., from Gr.; allied to Gr. *menos*, the mind; E. *mind* and *man*.] Madness; also rage or eager desire for anything; insane or morbid craving.—**Maniac**, mā'ni-ak, *a.* [L. *maniacus*.] Raving with madness; proceeding from disordered intellect; mad.—*n.* One raving with madness; a madman.—**Maniacal**, ma-nī'a-kal, *a.* Pertaining to or connected with madness.

Manicate, man'i-kāt, *a.* [L. *manicatus*, sleeved, from *manicæ*, sleeves; from *manus*, the hand.] *Bot.* covered with hairs interwoven into a mass that can be easily separated from the surface.

Manichaean, **Manichean**, man-i-kē'an, *n.* [From the founder *Manes* or *Manichæus*, who lived in the third century.] One of a sect in Persia who maintained that there are two supreme principles, the one good, the other evil, which produce all the happiness and calamities of the world. —**Manichaean**, *a.* Pertaining to the Manichaeans or their doctrines. —**Manichaeanism**, *n.*

Manichord, **Manicordon**, man'i-kord, man'i-kor-don, *n.* [O.Fr. *manicordon*, It. *monocordo*; from Gr. *monochordon*. MONOCHORD.] A musical instrument in the form of a spinet.

Manicure, man'i-kūr, *n.* [L. *manus*, hand, *cura*, care.] The care of the nails and the hands; a person whose occupation is to trim the nails and improve the condition of the hands.—*v.t.* & *i.* To trim or care for the nails. —**Manicurist**, *n.*

Manifest, man'i-fest, *a.* [L. *manifestus*, lit. that may be laid hold of by the hand —*manus*, the hand, and root seen in obs. *fendo*, to dash against (as in *offend*).] Clearly visible to the eye or obvious to the understanding; not obscure or difficult to be seen or understood; evident; plain.—*n.* A document signed by the master of a vessel at the place of lading; to be exhibited at the custom-house, containing a description of the ship and her cargo, the destination of the ship and the goods, &c.—*v.t.* To disclose to the eye or to the understanding; to show plainly; to display; to exhibit.—**Manifestable**, **Manifestible**, man'i-fes-ta-bl, man'i-fes-ti-bl, *a.* Capable of being manifested.—**Manifestation**, man'i-fes-tā"shon, *n.* The act of manifesting; a making evident to the eye or to the understanding; the exhibition of anything by clear evidence; display; what is the means of displaying.—**Manifestly**, man'i-fest-li, *adv.* In a manifest manner; clearly; evidently; plainly.—**Manifestness**, man'i-fest-nes, *n.* The condition or quality of being manifest.—**Manifesto**, man-i-fes'to, *n.* [It.] A public declaration, usually of a sovereign or government.

Manifold, man'i-fōld, *a.* [*Many* and *fold*.] Numerous and various in kind or quality; many in number; multiplied (*manifold* mercies); exhibiting or embracing many points, features, or characteristics (the *manifold* wisdom of God). —*adv.* Many times, or by many times.—*v.t.* To multiply impressions of, as of a letter, by means of a manifold-writer.—*n.* A copy made by a manifold-writer. — **Manifoldly**, man'i-fōld-li, *adv.* In a manifold manner. — **Manifoldness**, man'i-fōld-nes, *n.* — **Manifold-writer**, *n.* A writing apparatus for taking several copies of a letter or document at once.

Maniform, man'i-form, *a.* [L. *manus*, the hand.] Shaped like the hand.

Manihot, man'i-hot. Same as *Manioc*.

Manikin. Under MAN.

Manila, mä-nil'ä. *n.* A kind of cheroot manufactured in *Manila*, the capital of the Philippine Islands. — **Manila hemp**, *n.* A fibrous material from a plant which grows in the Philippine Islands, &c. — **Manila paper**, *n.* A paper of strong fiber made from manila hemp.

Manioc, man'i-ok, *n.* [Pg. and Brazil *mandioca*.] A plant cultivated in tropical America and the West Indies, from the large fleshy root of which tapioca and cassava are prepared.

Maniple, man'i-pl, *n.* [L. *manipulus*, *maniplus*, a handful, a company of soldiers —*manus*, the hand, and root of *plenus*, full (as in *plenary*, &c.).] *Rom. antiq.* a company of soldiers consisting of sixty common soldiers, two centurions, and a standard-bearer; in the Latin Ch., originally a handkerchief, now only a symbolical ornament attached to the left arm of the celebrant at mass.—**Manipular**, manip'ū-lėr, *a.* Pertaining to a maniple.—**Manipulate**, ma-nip'ū-lāt, *v.t.* — *manipulated*, *manipulating*. [L.L. *manipulo*, *manipulatum*.] To handle or operate on with the hands, as in artistic or mechanical operations; to subject to certain processes; to operate upon for the purpose of giving a false appearance to (to *manipulate* accounts). —*v.i.* To use the hands, as in artistic processes, mechanical operations, or the like. —**Manipulation**, ma-nip'ū-lā"shon, *n.* The art or mode of manipulating or working by hand; the act of operating upon skilfully, for the purpose of giving a false appearance to. — **Manipulative**, **Manipulatory**, ma-nip'ū-lā-tiv, ma-nip'ū-la-to-ri, *a.* Pertaining to or performed by manipulation. — **Manipulator**, ma-nip'ū-lā-tėr, *n.* One who manipulates.

Manis, mā'nis, *n.* [The assumed singular of L. *manes*, ghosts, from their seeking their food by night.] A genus of edentate mammals covered with large, hard scales; the pangolin or scaly ant-eater.

Manito, **Manitou**, man'i-tō, man'i-tö, *n.* Among North American Indians, a good or evil spirit or a fetish.

Manitrunk, man'i-trungk, *n.* [L. *manus*, hand, *truncus*, trunk.] *Entom.* the segment of the trunk near the head.

Manjak, man'jak, *n.* [W. Indian.] A kind of asphalt or mineral pitch.

Mankind, **Manly**, &c. Under MAN.

Manna, man'na, *n.* [Generally derived from the Heb. *man hu*, what is it?] A substance miraculously furnished as food for the Israelites in their journey through the wilderness of Arabia; the sweet solidified juice which is obtained by incisions made in the stem of a species of ash.—**Mannite**, man'īt, *n.* A peculiar variety of sugar obtained from manna.—**Manna-croup**, man'na-kröp, *n.* A granular preparation of wheat-flour deprived of bran, used for soups, puddings, &c.

Manner, man'ėr, *n.* [From Fr. *manière*, manner, O.Fr. *manier*, belonging to the hand, from L. *manus* the hand—properly, the method of handling a thing. MANAGE, MANUAL.] The mode in which anything is done; the way of performing or effecting anything; a person's peculiar or habitual way of carriage; bearing or conduct; deportment; *pl.* carriage or behaviour, considered as decorous or indecorous, polite or unpolite, pleasing or displeasing; ceremonious behaviour; polite or becoming deportment (he has no *manners*); sort; kind: in this use having often the sense of a plural = sorts, kinds (all *manner* of things).—*In a manner*, in a certain degree or measure: to a certain extent (it is *in a manner* done already).—**Mannered**, man'ėrd, *a.* Having manners of this or that kind; exhibiting the peculiar style of an author or artist, more particularly in its objectionable form.—**Mannerism**, man'ėr-izm, *n.* Excessive adherence to a characteristic mode or manner of action or treatment; a personal and prominent peculiarity of style, as in a writer or an artist.—**Mannerist**, man'ėr-ist, *n.* One addicted to mannerism.—**Mannerliness**, man'ėr-li-nes, *n.* The quality of being mannerly.—**Mannerly**, man'ėr-li, *a.* Showing good manners; correct in deportment; polite; not rude or vulgar.—*adv.* With good manners; without rudeness.

Mannheim Gold, man'hīm, *n.* [From *Mannheim*, in Baden, where it was originally made.] A brass containing 80 parts copper and 20 parts zinc, used by jewellers to imitate gold.

Mannish, &c. Under MAN.

Mannite. Under MANNA.

Mannose, man'ōz, *n.* [From *manna*.] A kind of sugar related to glucose.

Manœuvre, ma-nö'vėr, or ma-nū'vėr, *n.* [Fr. *manœuvre*—*main*, L. *manus*, the hand, and *œuvre*, L. *opera*, work. *Manure* is the same word.] A regulated dexterous movement, particularly in an army or navy; any movement of troops, ships, &c., for attack on or defence against an enemy; management with address or artful design; an adroit procedure; intrigue; stratagem.—*v.i.* — *manœuvred*, *manœuvring*. To perform manœuvres, especially military or naval manœuvres; to employ intrigue or stratagem to effect a purpose.—*v.t.* To make to perform manœuvres or evolutions.—**Manœuvrer**, ma-nö'vėr-ėr, or ma-nū'vėr-ėr, *n.* One who manœuvres.

Man-of-war. Under MAN.

Manometer, **Manoscope**, ma-nom'et-ėr, man'ō-skōp, *n.* [Gr. *manos*, rare, not dense.] An instrument to measure the elastic force of gases or vapours.—**Manometric**, **Manometrical**, man-ō-met'-

rik, man-ō-met′ri-kal, *a.* Pertaining to the manometer.

Manor, man′or, *n.* [O.Fr. *manoir, maneir, maner*, L.L. *manerium*, a dwelling-place, a mansion, from L. *maneo*, to stay, to dwell. MANSION.] The land belonging to a lord or nobleman, or so much land as a lord formerly kept in his own hands for the use and subsistence of his family; a residence with a certain portion of land annexed to it.—**Manor-house**, *n.* The mansion belonging to a manor.—**Manorial**, ma-nō′ri-al, *a.* Pertaining to a manor.

Manoscope, *n.* MANOMETER.

Mansard-roof, *n.* [From Francois *Mansard*, a French architect, the inventor, who died in 1666.] A curb-roof.

Manse, mans, *n.* [L.L. *mansus, mansum*, a residence, from L. *maneo, mansum*, to stay, to dwell. MANSION.] In Scotland, properly the dwelling-house of a parochial clergyman; also the dwelling-house reserved for the minister of any Presbyterian church.

Man-servant. Under MAN.

Mansion, man′shon, *n.* [L. *mansio, mansionis*, from *maneo, mansum*, to dwell (seen also in *manor, menial, remain, remnant*, &c.).] A dwelling or residence, especially one of considerable size and pretension; a habitation; an abode.—**Mansion-house**, *n.* A mansion; a manor-house.—*The Mansion-house*, the official residence of the Lord-mayor of London.

Man-slaughter, **Man-stealer**. Under MAN.

Mansuete, man′swēt, *a.* [L. *mansuetus*, tame—*manus*, the hand, and *suesco, suetum*, to become accustomed.] Tame; gentle.

Mantel, **Mantel-piece**, man′tel, *n.* [O. Fr. *mantel*, Fr. *manteau*—same as *mantle.*] The ornamental work above a fireplace; a narrow shelf or slab there.—**Mantel-shelf**, *n.* The shelf above the lintel of a fireplace.

Mantelet, **Mantlet**, man′tel-et, mant′let, *n.* [Dim. of *mantle.*] A small cloak worn by women; *fort.* a kind of movable parapet or penthouse set on wheels for protecting sappers from musketry fire.

Mantic,† man′tik, *a.* [Gr. *mantikos*, from *mantis*, a prophet.] Relating to prophecy or divination; prophetic.

Mantilla, man-til′la, *n.* [Sp.; same origin as *mantle.*] A hood; a Spanish head covering for women, which falls down upon the shoulders and may be used as a veil; a light cloak thrown over the dress of a lady.

Mantis, man′tis, *n.* [Gr., a prophet, the mantis.] A genus of orthopterous insects, frequently resembling twigs and leaves, the praying-mantis being so called from the position of the anterior legs resembling that of a person's hands at prayer.

Mantissa, man-tis′a, *n.* [L., addition, increase.] The decimal part of a logarithm following the integral part.

Mantle, man′tl, *n.* [O.Fr. *mantel*, Fr. *manteau*, It. *mantello*, from L. *mantellum, mantelum*, a mantle, a napkin.] Hence *mantel.*] A kind of cloak or loose garment to be worn over other garments; a covering; something that covers and conceals; *zool.* the external fold of the skin in most molluscs. Sometimes used in same sense as *mantel.*—*v.t.*—*mantled, mantling.* To cloak or cover.—*v.i.* To be expanded or spread out like a mantle; to become covered with a coating, as a liquid; to send up froth or scum; to cream; to display superficial changes of hue.—**Mantling**, mant′ling, *n.* The cloak or mantle often represented behind a heraldic escutcheon.

Mantlet, *n.* MANTELET.

Mantua, man′tū-a, *n.* [Either a corruption of Fr. *manteau*, a mantle, or from *Mantua* in Italy (comp. *milliner*, from *Milan*).] A lady's gown. — **Mantua-maker**, *n.* One who makes dresses for females; a dressmaker.

Manual, man′ū-al, *a.* [L. *manualis*, pertaining to the hand, from *manus*, the hand (root *ma*, to measure), seen also in *manacle, manage, manifest, manner, manure, maintain*, &c.] Performed or done by the hand; such as to require bodily exertion (*manual* labor); used or made by the hand. — *Manual alphabet*, the letters made by the fingers and hand, used by the deaf and dumb. — *Manual training*, training in handicraft, as the work of carpenters, plumbers, or machinists.—*n.* A small book, such as may be carried in the hand or conveniently handled; any book of instructions or orders; the key-board of an organ or the like.—**Manually**, *adv.*

Manubrium, ma-nū′bri-um, *n.* [L., a handle, from *manus*, the hand.] *Anat.* the upper bone of the sternum.

Manufactory, man-ū-fak′to-ri, *n.* [L. *manus*, the hand, and *factura*, a making, from *facio*, to make.] A building in which goods are manufactured; a factory.—**Manufactural**, man-ū-fak′tū-ral, *a.* Pertaining to manufactures. — **Manufacture**, man-ū-fak′tūr, *n.* The operation of making wares of any kind; the operation of reducing raw materials into a form suitable for use, by more or less complicated operations; something made from raw materials. — *v.t.* — *manufactured, manufacturing.* To make or fabricate from raw materials, and work into forms convenient for use, especially by more or less complicated processes.—*v.i.*—To be occupied in manufactures.—**Manufacturer**, man-ū-fak′tū-rer, *n.* One who manufactures; one who employs workmen for manufacturing; the owner of a manufactory.—**Manufacturing**, man-ū-fak′tū-ring, *pp.* and *a.* Employed in making goods; pertaining to manufactures.

Manumit, man-ū-mit′, *v.t.*—*manumitted, manumitting.* [L. *manumitto* — *manus*, hand, and *mitto*, to send.] To release from slavery; to free, as a slave; to emancipate. —**Manumission**, man-ū-mish′on, *n.* [L. *manumissio.*] The act of manumitting; emancipation.

Manure, ma-nūr′, *v.t.*—*manured, manuring.* [Originally to work by manual labour or by the hand, the same word as *manœuvre.*] To cultivate by manual labour‡; to enrich (soils) with fertilizing substances; to treat with manure.—*n.* Any matter or substance added to the soil with the view of fertilizing it, or of accelerating vegetation and increasing the production of the crops, such as guano, dung, bone-dust, the drainage from a dung-heap (liquid *manure*), &c.—**Manurer**, ma-nū′rėr, *n.* One that manures lands.—**Manurial**, ma-nū′ri-al, *a.* Pertaining to manures.

Manus, mā′nus, *n.* [L., the hand.] The hand; the part of an animal's fore-limb corresponding to the hand in man.

Manuscript, man′ū-skript, *n.* [L. *manuscriptum*, written with the hand—*manus*, the hand, and *scribo, scriptum*, to write.] A book or paper written with the hand or pen; a writing of any kind, in contradistinction to what is printed: often contracted to *MS.*, pl. *MSS.*—*a.* Written with the hand; not printed.

Manx, mangks, *n.* The native language of the inhabitants of the Isle of Man; *pl.* the natives of Man.—*a.* Belonging to the Isle of Man or its language.

Many, men′i, *a.* [A.Sax. *manig, mænig, monig*; D. *menig*, Dan. *mange*, Goth. *manags*, O.H.G. *manac*, G. *manch*, many.] Numerous; forming or comprising a great number (*many* men): always followed by *an* or *a* before a noun in the singular number (*many* a man), and then with more of a distributive force.—*The many*, the great majority of people; the crowd; the common herd.—*So many*, the same number of; a certain number indefinitely. — *Too many*, too strong; too powerful; too able (*colloq.*). [*Many* is prefixed to a great number of adjectives forming compounds which explain themselves (*many*-coloured, *many*-cornered, *many*-eyed, &c.).]—**Many-sided**, *a.* Having many sides; showing mental or moral activity in many different directions; exhibiting many phases.—**Many-sidedness**, *n.*

Maori, mä′o-ri, *n.* [A New Zealand word signifying native or indigenous.] One of the native inhabitants of New Zealand.—*a.* Of or belonging to the native inhabitants of New Zealand.

Map, map, *n.* [L. *mappa*, a napkin—*mappa mundi* (Fr. *mappemonde*, It. *mappamondo*), a map of the world; akin are *apron, napery.*] A representation of the surface of the earth or of any part of it, or of the whole or any part of the celestial sphere, usually on paper or other material.—*v.t.*—*mapped, mapping.* To delineate in a map, as the figure of any portion of land.

Maple, mā′pl, *n.* [A.Sax. *mæpel.*] The name given to a genus of trees of the sycamore kind, the wood of which is valuable. —*Sugar maple*, a maple of North America, the juice of which, obtained in early spring by tapping, is converted into sugar.

Mar, mär, *v.t.*—*marred, marring.* [A.Sax. *myrran, merran, ámyrran, ámerran*, to hinder, to spoil; D. *marren*, to retard; Icel. *merja*, to crush; O.H.G. *marrjan*, to hinder. Akin *moor* (verb).] To injure in any way; to spoil, impair, deface, deform. —**Marplot**, mär′plot, *n.* One who, by his officious interference, mars or defeats a design or plot.

Marabou, mar′a-bö, *n.* The name of two large storks, the delicate white feathers beneath the wing and tail of which form the marabou-feathers imported.

Marabout, **Maraboot**, mä-rä-böt′, *n.* In Northern Africa one of a kind of saints who are held in high estimation.

Maranatha, mar-a-nä′tha, *n.* [Syr., the Lord comes or has come.] An ejaculation used by the apostle Paul to emphasize a curse. (It has been mistaken for part of a compound '*anathema-maranatha*' in 1 *Corinthians*, xvi. 22-3; really 'Let him be anathema. Maran atha', the Lord cometh.)

Maraschino, mar-as-kē′nō, *n.* [It., from *marasca, amarasca*, a kind of sour cherry, from L. *amarus*, bitter.] A kind of liqueur made in Dalmatia from cherries.

Marasmus, ma-ras′mus, *n.* [Gr. *marasmos*, from *marainō*, to cause to pine or waste away.] A wasting of flesh without fever or apparent disease; atrophy.

Maraud, ma-ra̤d′, *v.i.* [Fr. *marauder*, to beg, play the rogue, from *maraud*, a rogue; perhaps from stem of *mar.*] To rove in quest of plunder; to make an excursion for booty.—*n.* Spoliation by marauders.—**Marauder**, ma-ra̤′dėr, *n.* One who marauds; a rover in quest of booty or plunder; a plunderer.

Maravedi, mar-a-vā′dē, *n.* [Sp., from *Marâbitin*, an Arabian dynasty which reigned in Spain.] A very small copper coin formerly used in Spain.

Marble, mär′bl, *n.* [Fr. *marbre*, from L. *marmor*, marble, Gr. *marmaros*, any stone or rock which sparkles in the light, from *marmairō*, to flash, to gleam.] The popular name of any species of calcareous stone, of a compact texture and of a beautiful appearance, susceptible of a good polish; a column, tablet, or the like, of marble, remarkable for some inscription or sculpture; a little ball of marble, of other stone, or of baked clay, used by children in play.—*a.* Composed of marble; stained or veined like marble; *fig.* hard or insensible like marble (*marble*-hearted, *marble*-breasted). — *v.t.* — *marbled, marbling*). To give an appearance of marble to; to stain or vein like marble.—**Marble-edged**, *a.* Having the edges marbled, as a book.—**Marble-paper**, *n.* Paper marked in imitation of variegated marble.—**Marbling**, mär′bling, *n.* Imitation of marble; any marking resembling that of veined marble.—**Marbly**, mär′bli, *a.* Resembling marble in structure or appearance.

Marc, märk, *n.* [Fr.] The refuse matter which remains after the pressure of fruit, as of grapes, olives, &c.

Marcasite, mär′ka-sīt, *n.* [Fr. *marcassite*, a word of Arabic origin.] Iron pyrites or bisulphide of iron, nearly of the colour of tin, used for industrial or ornamental purposes.—**Marcasitic, Marcasitical,** mär-ka-sit'ik, mär-ka-sit'i-kal, *a.* Pertaining to marcasite.

Marcescent, mär-ses'ent, *a.* [L. *marcescens, marcescentis,* ppr. of *marcesco,* to fade.] Withering; fading; decaying; specifically, *bot.* withering, but not falling off till the part bearing it is perfected. — **Marcescible,** *a.* Liable to decay.

March, märch, *n.* [A.Sax. *mearc,* a mark, sign, boundary; Icel. *mark,* O.H.G. *marcha* (whence Fr. *marche,* boundary). MARK.] A frontier or boundary of a territory: most common in pl., and especially applied to the boundaries or confines of political divisions; in Scotland the boundary line of conterminous estates or lands, whether large or small.—*v.i.* To be contiguous; to be situated next, with a boundary line between.—**March-man,** *n.* A borderer.

March, märch, *v.i.* [Fr. *marcher;* It. *marciare;* either from Fr. *marche,* a boundary (MARCH, a frontier), through such usages as in 'aller de *marche* en *marche*', to wander from boundary to boundary; or from L. *marcus,* a hammer, through L.L. *marcare,* to beat the ground with the feet, to march.] To move by steps and in order, as soldiers; to move in a military manner; to walk with a steady regular tread.—*Marching regiment,* a colloquial term for an infantry regiment of the line.—*v.t.* To cause to march.—*n.* The measured and uniform walk of a body of men, as soldiers, moving simultaneously and in order; stately and deliberate walk; steady or laboured progression; an advance of soldiers from one halting-place to another; the distance passed over; progressive advancement; progress (the *march* of intellect); a musical composition designed to accompany and regulate the movement of troops or other bodies of men.—*March past,* a march past the reviewing officer or some high dignitary on parade.

March, märch, *n.* [O.Fr. *march,* from L. *Martius,* pertaining to Mars, the god of war; *Martius mensis,* Mars' month.] The third month of the year.—*Mad as a March hare,* quite mad or crazy, from March being the rutting month of hares, during which they are in an excited state.

Marchioness, mär'shun-es, *n.* [A fem. from L.L. *marchio,* a marquis. MARQUIS.] The wife or widow of a marquis; a female having the rank of a marquis.

Marchpane, märch'pān, *n.* [O.Fr. *marcepain,* It. *marzapane,* L. Gr. *maza,* a barley-cake, and L. *panis,* bread.] A kind of sweet bread or biscuit containing almonds.

Marcid, mär'sid, *a.* [L. *marcidus,* from *marceo,* to pine.] Withered; feeble; drooping.

Marconigram, mär-kō'ni-gram, *n.* A message sent by Marconi's system of wireless telegraphy.

Mare, mär, *n.* [A.Sax. *mere, miere,* a mare, fem. of *mear, mearh,* a horse; Icel. *mar,* a horse, *merr,* a mare, G. *mähre,* a mare, O.H.G. *marah, march,* a horse; allied to Ir. *marc,* W. *march,* a horse.] The female of the horse.—*Mare's nest,* a discovery that is no discovery, and that a person merely fancies he has made.—**Mare's-tail,** *n.* A common marsh plant somewhat resembling in appearance the equisetum or horse-tail, but quite distinct.

Maremma, ma-rem'ma, *n.* pl. **Maremme,** ma-rem'me. [It.] Marshy and malarious tracts of country in middle Italy.

Margaric, mär-gar'ik, *a.* [L. *margarita,* Gr. *margaritēs,* pearl, from Per. *mervarid,* a pearl.] Pertaining to pearl; having a pearly appearance.—*Margaric acid,* a so-called acid, a mixture of palmitic and stearic acid obtained from oils and fats, and often in the form of pearly scales.—

Margarine, Margarin, mär'ga-rēn, *n.* A mixture of artificially prepared edible fats, extracted from animal fats and vegetable oils, sold as a substitute for butter after treatment with lactic acid bacilli to give it a butter odor.—**Margaritaceous,** mär'ga-ri-tā"shus, *a.* Pearly, or resembling pearl.—**Margaritic,** mar-ga-rit'ik, *a.* Pertaining to or resembling pearl or margarite.—**Margaritiferous,** mär'ga-ri-tif"-ėr-us, *a.* Producing pearls.

Margay, mär'gā, *n.* A Brazilian carnivorous animal about the size of a cat.

Margin, mär'jin, *n.*; poetically **Marge,** märj. [Formerly *margine,* or *margent,* Fr. *marge,* It. *margine,* from L. *margo, marginis,* a brink, a margin.] A border; edge; brink; verge (of a river, &c.); the edge of the leaf or page of a book, left blank or partly occupied by notes; a sum or quantity reserved to meet contingencies in addition to what is known to be necessary; the difference between the cost of an article and its selling price; *bot.* the edge or border of a leaf or other organ of a plant; *fig.* a certain latitude to go and come upon.—**Marginal,** mär'ji-nal, *a.* Pertaining to a margin; written or printed in the margin of a page.—**Marginalia,** mär-ji-nā'li-a, *n. pl.* Notes written on the margins of books.—**Marginally,** mär'ji-nal-li, *adv.* In the margin of a book.—**Marginated, Marginate,** mär'ji-nā-ted, mär'ji-nāt, *a.* Having a margin.

Margrave, mär'grāv, *n.* [Fr. *margrave,* from D. *markgraaf,* G. *markgraf—mark,* a march or border, and *graf,* an earl or count.] Originally, like marquis, a lord or keeper of the marches or borders; a title of nobility in Germany, &c.—**Margravate, Margraviate,** mär'gra-vāt, mär-grā'vi-āt, *n.* The territory or jurisdiction of a margrave.—**Margravine,** mär'gra-vīn, *n.* [Fr. *margravine,* G. *markgräfin.*] The wife of a margrave.

Marigenous, ma-rij'e-nus, *a.* [L. *mare,* the sea, and root *gen,* to produce.] Produced in or by the sea.

Marigold, mar'i-gōld, *n.* [*Mary,* that is, the Virgin Mary, and *gold.*] The popular name applied to several composite plants bearing bright yellow flowers.—*Marigold window, arch.* a rose-window.

Marinade, mär-i-nad, *n.* [Fr., from *marin,* marine, L. *mare,* the sea.] A compound liquor, generally of wine and vinegar, with herbs and spices, in which fish or meats are steeped before dressing to improve their flavour.—*v.t.* To salt or pickle (fish) and then preserve in oil or vinegar.

Marine, ma-rēn', *a.* [L. *marinus,* from *mare,* the sea; allied to W. *môr,* the sea, A.Sax. *mere,* a lake, and E. *marsh*; the root being same as in L. *mors,* death (dead or stagnant water).] Pertaining to or in some way connected with the sea; found or formed in the sea; inhabiting the sea (*marine* forms of life); used at sea; suited for use at sea (a *marine* engine); naval; maritime (a *marine* officer; *marine* forces).—*n.* The whole navy of a kingdom or state; the collective shipping of a country.—*Marine engine,* a form of engine used in sea-going vessels.—*Marines,* troops serving on a war vessel or at shore-stations, as a separate unit of the Navy to supplement naval activities. They are used primarily as landing forces in wartime, and to guard American lives and property abroad.—**Marine-glue,** *n.* A cement made by dissolving shellac, caoutchouc, and naphtha.—**Mariner,** mar'i-nėr, *n.* [Fr. *marinier.*] A seaman or sailor; one whose occupation is to assist in navigating ships.—*Mariner's Compass.* COMPASS.—**Marine-store,** *n.* A place where old ships' materials are bought and sold, as canvas, junk, iron, &c.—**Marinorama,** ma-rēn'ō-rä"ma, *n.* A representation of a sea-view.

Mariolatry, mā-ri-ol'a-tri, *n.* [L. *Maria,* Mary, the Virgin Mary, and Gr. *latreia,* service, worship.] The adoration of the Virgin Mary.—**Mariolater,** mā-ri-ol'a-tėr, *n.* One who practises Mariolatry.

Marionette, mar'i-o-net", *n.* [Fr., for *Mariolette,* a dim. of *Mariole,* a little figure of the Virgin *Mary.*] A puppet moved by strings.

Mariotte's Law. [From *Mariotte,* French mathematician.] The law in physics that the volume of a gas is inverse to its pressure.

Marischal, mär'shal. MARSHAL.

Marish,† mär'ish, *n.* A fen; a marsh. (*Poet.*)

Marist, mā'rist, *a.* Pertaining or relating to the Virgin Mary; devoted to the service of the Virgin.—*n.* Member of R. Cath. society.

Marital, mar'i-tal, *a.* [L. *maritalis,* from *maritus,* a husband, from *mas, maris,* a male. MASCULINE.] Pertaining to a husband.

Maritime, mar'i-tīm, *a.* [L. *maritimus,* from *mare,* the sea. MARINE.] Relating or pertaining to navigation or commerce by sea; connected or belonging to shipping; naval; having a navy and commerce by sea (*maritime* powers); bordering on the sea: situated near the sea (a *maritime* town).—*Maritime law,* the law relating to harbours, ships, and seamen. ∴ *Maritime* refers more especially to the sea as a field of human action, to some use of the sea by man, or some human interest connected with the sea, or to position on or near the sea; *marine* refers rather to the sea in its merely physical aspect.

Marjoram, mär'jo-ram, *n.* [G. *marjoran,* It. *marjorana,* L.L. *marjoraca,* from L. *amaracus,* Gr. *amarakos,* marjoram.] A perennial plant of the mint family, of several species; the sweet marjoram is aromatic and fragrant, and used in cookery.

Mark, märk, *n.* [A.Sax. *mearc,* mark, sign, limit, boundary = Goth. *marka,* a boundary; Icel. *mark,* mark, landmark, *merki,* a boundary; Dan. *mærke,* mark, token, *mark,* a field; D, *merk,* a mark; G. *mark,* a boundary, a district. *March* (a boundary) is another form, and hence also *remark, marquis, marchioness,* &c.] A visible sign or impression on something, as a dot, line, streak, stamp, figure, or the like; any sign by which a thing can be distinguished; a certain sign which a merchant puts upon his goods in order to distinguish them from others; a trade-mark; an indication, visible token, or evidence; pre-eminence, distinction, importance, eminent position (a man of *mark*); respectful attention or regard; heed; anything to which a missile may be directed; the point to be reached; the proper standard; the extreme estimate or allowance (below or within the *mark*); a character, generally in the form of a cross, made by a person who cannot write his name, and intended as a substitute for it; a mark in paper (a water *mark*), a translucent stamp of the maker's trade mark; a former German coin worth nearly 25c; the district of land held by a Teutonic village community.—*To make one's mark,* often to make one's influence felt; to gain a position of influence and distinction.—*v.t.* To make a mark on; to single out, point out, stamp, or characterize; to denote: often with *out;* to take particular observation of; to take note of; to regard, observe, heed.—*To mark time, milit.* to lift and bring down the feet alternately at the same rate as in marching.—*v.i.* To note; to observe critically; to take particular notice; to remark.—**Marker,** mär'kėr, *n.* One who marks; one who marks the score at games, as at billiards; a counter used in card-playing.—**Marking,** mär'king, *n.* The act of impressing a mark; a mark or series of marks upon something; characteristic arrangement of natural colouring (the *markings* on a bird's egg).—**Marking-ink,** *n.* An indelible ink used for marking linen, &c.—**Marking-nut,** *n.* A tree of the cashew family, the black juice of the unripe fruits of which is used as marking-ink.—**Marksman,** märks'man, *n.* One that is skilful to hit a mark; one who shoots well.—**Marksmanship,** märks'man-ship, *n.* The state of being a marksman; ability to shoot well.

Markee, mär-kē'. MARQUEE.

Market, mär'ket, *n.* [O.Fr. *markiet,* It. *mercato,* L. *mercatus,* from *mercor,* to buy, from *merx, mercis,* merchandise. MER-

CANTILE.] An occasion on which goods are publicly exposed for sale and buyers assemble to purchase; a fair; a public place in a city or town where goods are exposed for sale, whether a building or an open space; country or place of sale (the U. S. *market*, the foreign *market*); purchase or sale, or rate of purchase and sale; demand for commodities.—*v.i.* To deal in a market; to make bargains for provisions or goods.—*v.t.* To offer for sale in a market; to vend; to sell.—**Marketable**, mär′ket-a-bl, *a.* Capable of being sold; salable; fit for the market; current in the market.—**Market-cross**, *n.* A cross or small architectural structure set up where a market is held, sometimes of a very elaborate construction. **Market-day**, *n.* The fixed day on which a market is held in towns.—**Market-garden**, *n.* A garden in which vegetables and fruits are raised for the market.—**Market-gardener**, *n.* One who raises vegetables and fruits for sale.—**Market-price**, **Market-rate**, *n.* The price at which anything is currently sold; current value.—**Market-town**, *n.* A town in which markets are held, by privilege, at stated times.

Marking, **Marksman**, &c. Under MARK.

Marl, märl, *n.* [O.Fr. *marle*, D., Dan., Sw., and G. *mergel*, L.L. *margila*, from L. *marga*, marl—a word of Celtic origin.] A mixture of calcareous and argillaceous earth found at various depths under the soil, and extensively used for the improvement of land, there being several varieties of it, as clay-marl, shell-marl, &c.—*v.t.* To overspread or manure with marl.—**Marlaceous**, mär-lā′shus, *a.* Partaking of the qualities of marl.—**Marlite**, mär′līt, *n.* A variety of marl.—**Marlitic**, mär-lit′ik, *a.* Partaking of the qualities of marlite.—**Marl-stone**, *n.* *Geol.* the name of certain sandy, calcareous, and ferruginous strata.—**Marly**, mär′li, *a.* Resembling marl; abounding with marl.

Marline, mär′lin, *n.* [D. *marling*, *marlijn* —*marren*, to tie, to moor, and *lijn*, a line, a cord. MOOR, LINE.] *Naut.* a small line composed of two strands little twisted, used for winding round ropes to prevent their being chafed.—*v.t.* *Naut.* to wind marline round, as a rope. Also **Marl**, in this sense.—**Marlinespike**, **Marlinspike**, mär′lin-spīk, *n.* A sort of iron spike with an eye or hole on one end, used to separate the strands of a rope in splicing.

Marmalade, mär′ma-lād, *n.* [Fr. *marmelade*; Pg. *marmelada*, from *marmelo*, a quince; from L. *melimelum*, Gr. *melimēlon*, lit. a sweet apple—*meli*, honey, and *mēlon*, an apple, peach, orange.] A name applied to preserves made from various fruits, especially bitter and acid fruits, such as the orange, lemon, &c.—**Marmalade-tree**, *n.* The *Mammee-Sapota*.

Marmolite, mär′mō-līt, *n.* [Gr. *marmairō*, to shine, and *lithos*, a stone.] A mineral of a pearly or metallic lustre, a variety of serpentine.

Marmorate, **Marmorated**, mär′mo-rāt, mär′mo-rā-ted, *a.* [L. *marmoratus*, from *marmor*, marble. MARBLE.] Covered with marble; variegated like marble.—**Marmoration**, mär-mo-rā′shon, *n.* A covering or incrusting with marble; variegating so as to resemble marble.—**Marmoraceous**, mär-mo-rā′shus, *a.* Pertaining to or like marble.—**Marmoratum**, mär-mo-rā′tum, *n.* [L.] An ancient cement formed of pounded marble and lime mortar well beaten together.—**Marmoreal**, **Marmorean**, mär-mō′rē-al, mär-mō′rē-an, *a.* Pertaining to marble; made of marble.

Marmose, mär′mōs, *n.* A small species of opossum inhabiting South America.

Marmoset, mär′mō-zet, *n.* [O.Fr. *marmoset*, Fr. *marmouset*, originally a small grotesque figure, from L.L. *marmoretum*, a small marble figure, from L. *marmor*, marble.] A beautiful American monkey with long tail, long fur, and tufted ears.

Marmot, mär′mot, *n.* [Fr. *marmotte*; It. *marmotta*, *marmontana*, from L. *mus* (*muris*) *montanus*, mountain mouse.] A rodent quadruped, an inhabitant of northern latitudes, living in colonies, in extensive burrows, and hibernating in winter.

Marone, ma-rōn′, *n.* [MAROON, a colour.] Any colour or pigment produced from black and red pigments mixed.

Maronite, mā′ron-īt, *n.* [From *Maron*, the founder.] One of a Christian sect in Syria in connection with the Roman Church.

Maroon, ma-rön′, *n.* [Fr. *marron*, runaway, from Sp. *cimarron*, wild, unruly, from *cima*, the top of a hill; *negro cimarron*, and simply *cimarron*, in Cuba, a fugitive negro.] A name given to fugitive slaves living on the mountains in the West Indian Islands and Guiana.—*v.t.* To put ashore and leave on a desolate island, by way of punishment, as was done by the buccaneers, &c.

Maroon, ma-rön′, *a.* [Fr. *marron*, It. *marrone*, a chestnut.] Brownish-crimson; of a colour resembling claret.—*n.* A brownish-crimson or claret colour.

Maroon, ma-rön′, *n.* A rocket having the case bound round with tarred twine, so that it explodes with a great noise.

Marque, märk, *n.* [Fr. *marque*, a boundary; letters of marque originally empowered the receivers to cross the boundaries or marches of an enemy. MARK, MARCH (a frontier).] A license granted to a private vessel to make attacks on the ships or belongings of a public enemy, usually in the phrase *letters of marque* or *letters of marque and reprisal*, which constitute a vessel a *privateer*.

Marquee, mär-kē′, *n.* [Fr. *marquise*, a marchioness, a marquee.] An officer's field tent; a large tent erected for a temporary purpose.

Marquess, *n.* MARQUIS.

Marquetry, mär′ket-ri, *n.* [Fr. *marqueterie*, from *marqueter*, to spot, to inlay, from *marque*, a mark. MARK.] Inlaid work, often consisting of thin pieces of fine woods of different colours, arranged on a ground so as to form various patterns.

Marquis, **Marquess**, mär′kwis, mär′kwes, *n.* [Fr. *marquis*, It. *marchese*, L.L. *marchisus*, *marchensis*, a prefect of the *marches* or border territories. MARK, and MARCH, a boundary.] A title of dignity in Britain next in rank to that of duke, and hence the second of the five orders of English nobility.—**Marquisate**, mär′kwis-āt, *n.* The seigniory, dignity, or lordship of a marquis.—**Marquise**, mär-kēz, *n.* [Fr.] The wife of a marquis; a marchioness.

Marriage, mar′ij, *n.* [Fr. *mariage*, L.L. *maritaticum*, marriage, from L. *maritus*, a husband, from *mas*, *maris*, a male. MASCULINE.] The act of marrying; the legal union of a man and woman for life; the ceremony by which they are so united; a wedding.—*Marriage portion*, dower given by a father to his daughter at her marriage. *Marriage settlement*, an arrangement made before marriage whereby a jointure is secured to the wife, and portions to children, in the event of the husband's death. ∴ *Marriage*, the union, or the act of forming or entering into the union; *wedding*, the ceremonies celebrating the union; *nuptials*, a more dignified word for wedding; *matrimony*, the married state; *wedlock*, the vernacular English word for matrimony.—

Marriageable, mar′ij-a-bl, *a.* Of an age suitable for marriage.—**Marriageableness**, mar′ij-a-bl-nes, *n.* State of being marriageable.—**Marriage-license**, *n.* A written permit issued by a qualified government official to a couple intending to marry.—**Married**, mar′id, *p.* and *a.* Formed or constituted by marriage; conjugal; connubial (the *married* state).—

—**Marry**, mar′i, *v.t.*—*married*, *marrying*. [Fr. *marier*, L. *maritare*, to marry, from *maritus*, a husband.] To unite in wedlock or matrimony; to constitute man and wife (the clergyman *marries* a couple); to dispose of in wedlock (as a father his daughter); to take for husband or wife; to wed; *fig.* to unite by some close bond of connection.—*v.i.* To enter into a conjugal state; to take a husband or a wife.—**Marrying**, mar′i-ing, *a.* Disposed to marry (a *marrying* man).

Marrow, mar′ō, *n.* [A.Sax. *mearh*, *mearg* = D. *marg*, *merg*, Dan. *marv*, Icel. *mergr*, G. *mark*, marrow; comp. A.Sax. *mearu*, D. *murw*, tender, soft.] The fat contained in the osseous tubes and cells of the bones; *fig.* the essence; the best part; a kind of gourd yielding an oblong fruit used as a vegetable, also called *vegetable marrow*.—*Spinal marrow*, the spinal cord or cord of nervous matter extending through the spine.—**Marrow-bone**, *n.* A bone containing marrow.—*To go down on one's marrow-bones*, to assume a kneeling position. [Humorous.]—**Marrow-fat**, *n.* A kind of rich pea.—**Marrowless**, mar′ō-les, *a.* Destitute of marrow.—**Marrow-squash**, *n.* An American name for the vegetable marrow.—**Marrowy**, mar′ō-i, *a.* Full of marrow; resembling marrow.

Marry, mar′i. Indeed; forsooth: a term of asseveration derived from the practice of swearing by the Virgin *Mary*.

Mars, märz, *n.* A Latin deity, the god of war, identified at an early period by the Latins themselves with the Greek Arēs; the fourth planet from the sun or the first outside of the earth's orbit.

Marsala, mär-sä′la, *n.* A wine resembling sherry, from *Marsala* in Sicily.

Marseillais, mär-sā-yā, *n. mas.*, **Marseillaise**, mär-sā-yāz, *n. fem.* A native or inhabitant of Marseilles.—*a.* Belonging or pertaining to Marseilles.—*The Marseillaise*, the national song of the French Republic, dating from the first revolution, being written in 1792, and first sung in Paris by revolutionaries from Marseilles.

Marsh, märsh, *n.* [A.Sax. *mersc*, for *merisc* (= *mere-ish*), a marsh or bog, an adj. form from *mere*, a mere; L.G. *marsch*, O.D. *maersche*, *meersch*; allied to L. *mare*, the sea. MARINE.] A tract of low and very wet land; a fen, swamp, morass.—*a.* Pertaining to marshes or swampy places; applied to various plants (*marsh*-mallow, *marsh*-marigold).—**Marsh-gas**. Same as *Fire-damp*.—**Marsh-harrier**, *n.* A British bird of prey frequenting marshes, and living on water-birds, mice, frogs, fish, &c.—**Marshiness**, märsh′i-nes, *n.* State of being marshy.—**Marsh-marigold**, *n.* A marsh plant of the ranunculus family with a bright yellow flower.—**Marshy**, märsh′i, *a.* Partaking of the nature of a marsh or swamp; swampy; fenny; produced in marshes.

Marshal, mär′shal, *n.* [O.F. *mareschal*, Fr. *maréchal*, L.L. *mariscalcus*, from O.H.G. *marahscalc*—O.G. *marah*, a horse, and *scalc* (Mod.G. *schalk*), a servant. MARE.] Formerly an officer whose duty was to regulate tournaments or combats in the lists; one who regulates rank and order at a feast or any other assembly, directs the order of procession, and the like; in France, the highest rank of military officer; in other countries of Europe, a military officer of high rank, called in full *field-marshal*; in U. S., a civil officer in each judicial district, to execute court orders, and with other duties paralleling those of sheriff.—*v.t.*—*marshaled*, *marshaling*. To dispose in due order (an army, troops); to arrange in a suitable or most effective order (arguments, evidence, &c.).—**Marshalship**, mär′shal-ship, *n.* The office or dignity of a marshal.

Marshmallow, *n.* A plant of the hollyhock genus, growing naturally in marshes, and possessed of valuable demulcent properties; a soothing confection obtained from marshmallow, a medicinal root; a corn sirup and gelatin confection, sometimes with beaten egg whites, used in melted form in frostings and icings, and in candy dipped in powdered sugar, or mixed with other ingredients.

Marsipobranch, **Marsipobranchiate**, mär-sip′ō-brangk, mär-sip′ō-brang″ki-āt, *a.* and *n.* [Gr. *marsipos*, a pouch, and *branchia*, gills.] Applied to certain fishes, as the hag-fishes and sea-lampreys, with pouch-like gills.

Marsupial, Marsupiate, mär-sū'pi-al, mär-sū'pi-āt, *a.* [L. *marsupium*, Gr. *marsupion*, a pouch.] Having an external abdominal pouch; belonging to the order of marsupials. — **Marsupial, Marsupialian**, mär-sū'pi-ā"li-an, *n.* One of an extensive group of mammalia characterized by the absence of a placenta, and the consequent premature production of the fetus, which immediately on its birth is placed by the mother in an external abdominal pouch, in which are the teats, and there nurtured until fully developed.—**Marsupium**, mär-sū'pi-um, *n.* The pouch of the marsupials.

Mart, märt, *n.* [Contr. from *market.*] A place of sale or traffic, where buying and selling are active; an emporium, a center; as Furniture Mart or Merchandise Mart.

Martello-tower, mär-tel'lō-tou-ėr, *n.* [From *Mortella* in Corsica, where a tower of this kind made a strong resistance to an English naval force in 1794.] A small circular fort, with very thick walls, built chiefly to defend the seaboard.

Marten, mär'ten, *n.* [Older *martern*, Fr. *martre*, from D. *marter*, G. *marder*, a marten.] A carnivorous quadruped of the weasel family, very destructive to game, poultry, and eggs; the pelt of a marten, frequently called *sable* by fur traders.

Martial, mär'shal, *a.* [L. *martialis*, from *Mars, Martis*, the god of war.] Pertaining to war; suited to war; military; given to war; warlike.—*Martial law*, an arbitrary kind of law, proceeding directly from the military power, and proclaimed in times of war, insurrection, rebellion, or other great emergency.—**Martially**, mär'shal-li, *adv.* In a martial manner.

Martian, mär'shan, *a.* Pertaining to Mars, god of war, or to the planet Mars or its supposed inhabitants.

Martin, mär'tin, *n.* [From the proper name *Martin*; comp. *robin*-redbreast, &c.] A general name applied to various species of swallows, the best-known being the *sand martin* or bank swallow and the *purple martin*.

Martinet, mär'ti-net, *n.* [From General *Martinet*, a very strict French officer in the reign of Louis XIV.] A military or naval officer who is an excessively strict disciplinarian; one who lays stress on a rigid adherence to the details of discipline, dress, &c.

Martingale, mär'tin-gāl, *n.* [Fr. *martingale*, Sp. *martingala*, a martingale, old kind of breeches; from *Martigal*, an inhabitant of *Martigues*, in Provence.] A strap from a horse's head to the girth under his belly and passing between the fore-legs, to prevent him from rearing; *naut.* a short perpendicular spar under the bowsprit.

Martinmas, mär'tin-mas, *n.* [*Martin* and *mass.*] The feast of St. Martin, the 11th of November, a Scotch term-day, on which rents are paid, servants hired, &c.

Martlet, märt'let, *n.* [Dim. of *martin.*] The martin, a kind of swallow. (*Shak.*)

Martyr, mär'tėr, *n.* [Gr. *martyr*, a martyr, a form of *martys*, a witness.] One who by his death bears witness to the truth; one who suffers death rather than renounce his religious opinions; one who suffers death or persecution in defence of any cause.—*v.t.* To persecute as a martyr; to torment or torture.—**Martyrdom**, mär'tėr-dom, *n.* The state of being a martyr; the death of a martyr.—**Martyrize**, mär'tėr-īz, *v.t.* To devote to martyrdom.—**Martyrologic, Martyrological**, mär'tėr-o-loj"ik, mär-tėr-o-loj"i-kal, *a.* Pertaining to martyrology.—**Martyrologist**, mär-tėr-ol'o-jist, *n.* A writer of a martyrology.—**Martyrology**, mär-tėr-ol'o-ji, *n.* A history or account of martyrs with their sufferings; a register of martyrs.

Marvel, mär'vel, *n.* [Fr. *merveille*; It. *maraviglia*; from L. *mirabilia*, wonderful things, from *mirabilis*, wonderful, from *miror*, to wonder. MIRACLE.] A wonder; an object of great astonishment.—*v.i.*—*marveled, marveling.* To be struck with surprise or astonishment; to wonder.—**Marvelous**, mär'vel-us, *a.* Exciting wonder; wonderful; strange; astonishing; surpassing credit; partaking of the miraculous or supernatural.—*The marvelous* things almost beyond belief; incredible, tales or narratives; also first rate. (*Colloq.*).—**Marvelously**, mär'vel-us-li, *adv.* In a marvelous manner.—**Marvelousness**, mär'vel-us-nes, *n.*

Marzipan, mär'zi-pan, *n.* [G.] Same as *Marchpane* (which see).

Mascle, mas'kl, *n.* [O.Fr. *mascle*, Fr. *macle*, from L. *macula*, a spot, the mesh of a net.] *Armour*, a lozenge-shaped plate or scale.—**Mascled**, mas'kld, *a.* Exhibiting mascles; covered with mascles for defence.

Mascot, mas'kot, *n.* [Fr. *mascotte.*] A thing or person supposed to bring good luck.

Masculine, mas'kū-lin, *a.* [L. *masculinus*, from *masculus*, male, from *mas, maris*, a male; of same origin are *marry, marital, male.*] Of the male sex; not female; strong; robust; powerful; manly; not soft or effeminate; (said of a woman) coarse, bold, forward, or unwomanly (her manners are rough and *masculine*); *gram.* denoting or pertaining to the gender of words which are especially applied to male beings or things regarded grammatically as male.—*Masculine rhymes.* Of rhymes those are feminine that are double, such as *motion, notion*, the second syllable being short; those are masculine where the vowel sound alone is stressed, or rhymes.—*n. Gram.* the masculine gender; a word of this gender.—**Masculinely**, mas'kū-lin-li, *adv.* In a masculine manner. — **Masculineness, Masculinity**, mas'kū-lin-nes, mas-kū-lin'i-ti, *n.* The quality or state of being masculine.

Mash, mash, *n.* [Akin to Dan. *mask*, a mash, Sw. *mäska*, to mash; Sc. *mask*, to infuse, as tea, G. *meisch*, mash (of malt), *meischen*, to mash, mix; E. *mess*, a mixture.] A mixture of ingredients beaten or blended together in a promiscuous manner; especially, a mixture for feeding horses; *brewing*, a mixture of ground malt and warm water yielding wort. —*v.t.* To beat into a confused mass; to crush by beating or pressure; to mix (malt) and steep in warm water for brewing.—**Masher**, mash'ėr, *n.* [From being supposed to *mash* the hearts of the fair sex.] An affected fop who dresses in the extremest fashion, and lounges about fashionable resorts; a weak, would-be gallant. (*Slang.*)—**Mash-tub, Mash-tun**, *n.* A tub or vat for containing the mash in breweries.

Mask, mask, *n.* [Fr. *masque*, from Sp. and Pg. *mascara*, a mask, from Ar. *maskharat*, a buffoon, jeer, laugh, from *sakhira*, to ridicule.] A cover for the face, often intended to conceal identity; a disguise, pretence, or subterfuge; a masquerade; a piece of mummery; a sort of play or histrionic spectacle, much patronized during the sixteenth and seventeenth centuries. — *v.t.* To cover the face with a mask; to disguise for concealment.—*To mask a fortress*, to render it ineffective or powerless by leaving sufficient troops to command it while the main body proceeds to other operations.—**Masked**, maskt, *p.* and *a.* Having the face covered; wearing a mask; concealed; disguised. — *Masked battery*, a battery so situated and constructed as not to be perceived by the enemy till it opens fire upon them.—*Masked ball*, a ball at which the company wear masks, or appear in masquerade.—**Masker**, mas'kėr, *n.* One that wears a mask; one that plays in a mask or masquerade.

Maslin, maz'lin. MESLIN.

Mason, mā'sn, *n.* [Fr. *maçon*; L.L. *macio, machio, machionis*, from root seen in L. *maceria*, a wall.] A builder in stone or brick; one who constructs the walls of buildings, &c.; a member of the fraternity of freemasons.—**Masonic**, mā-son'ik, *a.* Pertaining to the craft or mysteries of freemasons.—*Masonic lodge*, a place where freemasons hold their meetings; a local branch of the fraternity of freemasons.—**Masonry**, mā'sn-ri, *n.* [Fr. *maçonnerie.*] The art or occupation of a mason; the work produced by a mason; the mysteries, principles, and practices of freemasons.

Mason jar, mā'sn jär, *n.* A preserve glass with porcelain-insert metal top.

Masoretic, mas-o-ret'ik, *a.* Jewish interpretation of the Masorah, the great traditional body of Biblical information.

Masque, mask, *n.* A kind of theatrical spectacle. MASK.—**Masquerade**, mas'-kėr-ād, *n.* [Fr. *masquerade.*] An assembly of persons wearing masks, and amusing themselves with various diversions, as dancing, walking in procession, &c.; a disguise. —*v.i.* — *masqueraded, masquerading.* To wear a mask; to take part in a masquerade; to go in disguise.—**Masquerader**, mas-kėr-ā'dėr, *n.* A person taking part in a masquerade; one disguised.

Mass, mas, *n.* [Fr. *masse*, L. *massa*, a lump, from Gr. *maza*, a barley-cake, from *massō*, to knead; akin *macerate.*] A body of matter collected into a lump; a lump; a collective body of fluid matter; a great quantity collected; an assemblage (a *mass* of foliage); bulk; magnitude; the main body of things collectively; the generality; the bulk (the *mass* of the people); *physics*, the quantity of matter in any body, or the sum of all the material particles of a body, always proportional to the weight, whatever the bulk or figure.—*The masses*, the great body of the people, more especially of the working-class and lower orders; the populace.—*v.t.* To form into a mass; to collect into masses; to assemble in crowds. —**Massiness**, mas'i-nes, *n.* The state of being massy.—**Massive**, mas'iv, *a.* [Fr. *massif.*] Forming or consisting of a large mass; having great size and weight; ponderous; *mineral.* having a crystalline structure, but not a regular form as a whole.—**Massively**, mas'iv-li, *adv.* With massiveness; ponderously.—**Massiveness**, mas'-iv-nes, *n.* The state or quality of being massive. — **Mass-meeting**, *n.* A large or general meeting called for some specific purpose. — **Massy**, mas'i, *a.* Possessing great mass or bulk; massive.

Mass, mas, *n.* [A.Sax. *mæsse*, Fr. *messe*, Dan. and G. *messe*, L.L. *missa*, mass, from the proclamation—Ite; *missa* est: 'Go; the assembly is dismissed' (L. *missus*, pp. of *mitto*, to send)—made in the ancient churches when the catechumens were dismissed after a portion of the service, whereupon followed the communion. MISSION.] The service of the Eucharist in the Roman Catholic and Greek Churches, the Roman Catholic communion service; the elaborate musical setting of certain portions of the service of the mass.—*High mass*, a mass performed on solemn occasions, by a priest or prelate, attended by a deacon and subdeacon, with choral music.—*Low mass*, the ordinary mass performed by the priest, assisted by one altar-servant only.

Massacre, mas'a-kėr, *n.* [Fr. *massacre*, probably from such a German word as L.G. *matsken, matschkern*, to cut in pieces, or G. *metzger*, a butcher, *metzeln*, to cut to pieces; O.G. *meizan*, to cut down.] The indiscriminate killing of human beings, especially without authority or necessity, and without forms civil or military; a great slaughter. — *v.t.* — *massacred, massacring.* To kill with indiscriminate violence; to butcher; to slaughter; usually of killing human beings.—**Massacrer**, mas'a-krėr, *n.* One who massacres.

Massage, ma-säzh' or mas'aj, *n.* [Fr., from Gr. *massō*, to knead.] The process of kneading, rubbing, pressing, slapping, &c., parts of a person's body suffering from neuralgic or certain other ailments, in order to bring relief or effect a cure. Also used as *v.t.*—**Massagist**, ma-säzh'ist, mas'a-jist, *n.* A person who practises the operation of massage; also called a *masseur* (mas-ėr).—**Masseuse**, ma-sūz'. *n.* A woman who practices massage.

Masseter, mas-se-tėr, mas-sē'ter, *n.* [Gr. *masētēr*, *massētēr*, lit. a chewer, from *massaomai*, to chew.] Either of the pair of muscles which raise the under jaw.

Massicot, **Masticot**, mas'i-kot, mas'ti-kot, *n.* [Fr. *massicot.*] Protoxide of lead or yellow oxide of lead of a deep yellow colour and used as a pigment.

Massymore, mas'i-mōr, *n.* [Moorish *mazmorra.*] A dungeon in feudal prisons or castles. (*Scott.*)

Mast, mast, *n.* [A.Sax. *mæst*=D., G., Sw., and Dan. *mast*, a mast.] A long, round piece of timber or a hollow pillar of iron or steel standing upright in a vessel, and supporting the yards, sails, and rigging in general.—*v.t.* To fix a mast or masts in; to erect the masts of.—**Masted**, mas'ted, *a.* Having a mast or masts: chiefly in composition.—**Master**, mas'tėr, *n.* Having a mast or masts: in composition (a *three-master*).—**Mast-head**, *v.t.* To send to the top of a mast and cause to remain there for a time by way of punishment.—**Mastless**, mast'les, *a.* Having no mast.

Mast, mast, *n.* (no pl.). [A.Sax. *mæst*, G. *mast*, mast; akin to *meat.*] The fruit of the oak and beech or other forest trees; nuts; acorns. — **Mastful**, mast'ful, *a.* Abounding with mast.—**Mastless**, mast'les, *a.* Bearing no mast.—**Mast-tree**, *n.* A tree that produces mast.—**Masty**, mas'ti *a.* Abounding with mast.

Master, mas'ter, *n.* [O.E. *maister*, *maistre*, O.Fr. *maïstre*, from L. *magister*, master, from root *mag*, seen in L. *magnus*, great (MAGNITUDE): same root as *may*, *might*, *much.*] One who rules, governs, or directs; one who has others under his immediate control; an employer; correlative to *slave*, *servant*, &c. (often in compounds, as, *master*-printer, *master*-builder, &c.); one who has possession and the power of controlling or using at pleasure; the owner; proprietor; a chief, principal, head, leader; the person intrusted with the care and navigation of a merchant ship: otherwise the *captain*: an artist, a sculptor, an architect, whose accomplishments rank far above those of their contemporaries, a Raphael, a Michelangelo, a Brunelleschi; a man so well trained in his profession as to be able to follow it alone; in the *navy*, formerly an officer who navigated the ship under the direction of the captain; the head of or a teacher in a school; a man eminently skilled in any pursuit, accomplishment, art, or science: a proficient or adept (a *master* of the violin; a *master* of sarcasm); a civil or respectful title of address used before a person's name, and when the person is grown up always pronounced mis'tėr and written *Mr.* (*Mr.* John Smith); when applied to a boy or young gentleman, however, written in full and pronounced mas'tėr; a title of dignity; a degree in colleges and universities (*Master* of Arts); the title of the head of some societies or corporations; the title of certain high legal or other functionaries (*Master* in chancery).—*The old masters*, ancient painters of eminence.—*To be master of one's self*, to have the command or control of one's own passions.—*v.t.* To become the master of; to overpower; to subdue; to make one's self master of. —*a.* Belonging to a master; chief; principal: often used as the first element in a compound word; as *master*-piece, *master*-mind, &c.—**Master-builder**, *n.* A chief builder; one who employs workmen in building.—**Master-chord**, *n.* The chief chord; the chord of the dominant.—**Masterful**, mas'tėr-ful, *a.* Inclined to exercise mastery; imperious; arbitrary; headstrong. — **Masterfully**, mas'tėr-ful-li, *adv.* In a masterful manner.—**Masterfulness**, mas'tėr-ful-nes, *n.* The quality of being masterful.—**Master-hand**, *n.* The hand of a person extremely skilful; a person eminently skilful.—**Master-joint**, *n.* *Geol.* one of the larger planes of partition which traverse rock-masses, running parallel to each other for considerable distances.—**Master-key**, *n.* The key that opens many locks; *fig.* a general clue to lead out of many difficulties.—**Masterless**, mas'tėr-les, *a.* Destitute of a master or owner; ungovernable; beyond control.—**Masterliness**, mas'tėr-li-nes, *n.* The quality of being masterly; masterly skill.—**Masterly**, mas'tėr-li, *a.* Formed or executed with superior skill; suitable to a master; most able or skilful (a *masterly* design or performance). — *adv.* With the skill of a master.—**Master-mariner**, *n.* The captain of a merchant-vessel.—**Master-mind**, *n.* A chief or superior mind; a predominant intellect. — **Master-passion**, *n.* A predominant or ruling passion. —**Master-piece**, *n.* Something superior to any other performance of the same person; anything done or made with superior skill.—**Mastership**, mas'tėr-ship, *n.* The state or office of a master; pre-eminence; mastery.—**Master-singer**, *n.* One of a society of German poets of the fifteenth and sixteenth centuries.—**Master-spirit**, *n.* A predominant mind; a master-mind. — **Master-stroke**, *n.* A masterly achievement.—**Master-work**, *n.* Principal performance; chef-d'œuvre.—**Mastery**, mas'tėr-i, *n.* The act of mastering; dominion or command over something; superiority in competition; pre-eminence; victory in war; eminent skill.

Mastic, **Mastich**, mas'tik, *n.* [Fr. *mastic*, L. *mastiche*, *mastichum*, Gr. *mastichē*, from *mastax*, the jaws: so named because chewed in the East.] A resin exuding from a tree of Southern Europe, &c., yielding a varnish; the tree itself; a kind of mortar or cement for plastering walls.

Masticate, mas'ti-kāt, *v.t.* — *masticated*, *masticating.* [L. *mastico*, *masticatum*, from G. *mastichaō*, to gnash the teeth. MASTIC.] To grind with the teeth and prepare for swallowing and digestion; to chew.—**Masticable**, mas'ti-ka-bl, *a.* Capable of being masticated.—**Mastication**, mas-ti-kā'shon, *n.* The act of masticating. — **Masticator**, mas'ti-kā-tėr, *n.* One who or that which masticates; a machine for cutting up meat for persons unable to chew properly, also for kneading up raw india-rubber or gutta-percha.—**Masticatory**, mas'ti-kā-to-ri, *a.* Adapted to perform the office of chewing.—*n.* *Med.* a substance to be chewed to increase the saliva.

Masticot, mas'ti-kot. MASSICOT.

Mastiff, mas'tif, *n.* [From a hypothetical Fr. *mastif*, from G. *masten*, to fatten, O.H.G. *mastjan*, to feed, from *mast*, food, mast (acorns, &c.).] A variety of dog of old English breed, large and very stoutly built, and with deep and pendulous lips.

Mastitis, mas-tī'tis, *n.* [Gr. *mastos*, the breast, and term. *-itis*, denoting inflammation.] Inflammation of the breast of women. — **Mastodon**, mas'tō-don, *n.* [Gr. *mastos*, breast, mammilla, and *odous*, a tooth.] A genus of extinct fossil quadrupeds resembling the elephant, but larger, named from the mammillary processes on its teeth.—**Mastodontic**, mas-tō-don'tik, *a.* Pertaining to or resembling a mastodon.—**Mastodynia**, mas-tō-din'i-a, *n.* [Gr. *mastos*, and *odynē*, pain.] Pain in the breast; a kind of neuralgia.—**Mastoid**, mas'toid, *a.* Resembling a nipple or breast; a term applied to a process or projection of certain bones and to parts connected therewith.—**Mastology**,† mas-tol'o-ji, *n.* The natural history of mammals.

Masula-boat, ma-sö'la, *n.* MASOOLA-BOAT.

Mat, mat, *n.* [A.Sax. *meatta*, G. *matte*, D. *mat*, Dan. *matte*, Ir. *mata*, all from L. *matta*, a mat made of rushes.] An article of interwoven rushes, straw, cocoa-nut fibre, twine, or other material to be laid down for cleaning the boots and shoes of those who enter a house, or to keep the feet from the bare floor; some kind of coarse fabric used for packing, or for covering floors, &c.; an article of various materials, flat and of little thickness, put below dishes on the table; anything growing thickly or closely interwoven so as to resemble a mat in form or texture (a *mat* of hair).—*v.t.*—*matted*, *matting.* To cover or lay with mats; to interweave like a mat; to entangle.—*v.i.* To grow thick together.—**Matting**, mat'ing, *n.* Materials for mats; mat-work; *naut.* a texture made of strands of old rope, &c., used to prevent chafing.—**Mat-work**, *n.* Matting; mats.

Mat, **Matt**, mat, *a.* [G. *matt*, dull.] Without lustre; dull in surface; lustreless.

Matador, mat'a-dōr, *n.* [Sp., lit. a killer, from *matar*, L. *mactare*, to kill, to sacrifice.] The man appointed to kill the bull in bull-fights.

Match, mach, *n.* [Fr. *mèche*, Pr. *mecha*, from L. *myxus*, a wick, Gr. *myxa*, the nozzle of a lamp.] A small body that catches fire readily, and is used for conveying and communicating fire; a small slip of wood with a composition on one end that ignites with friction; a lucifer.—*Quick match*, *slow match*, matches in a rope-like form made to burn at a certain rate and used for military and other purposes.—**Matchlock**, mach'lok, *n.* Originally, the lock of a musket containing a match for firing; hence, a musket fired by means of a match.

Match, mach, *n.* [O.E. *make*, a mate, A.S. *mæcca*, *maca*, a mate, a wife. MATE.] A person equal to another; one who is able to mate or cope with another; an equal; a mate; the coming together of two parties suited to one another, as for a trial of strength or skill, or the like; a contest; union by marriage; one to be married or gained in marriage.—*v.t.* To be a match or mate for; to be able to compete with; to equal; to show an equal to; to place in competition or comparison with; to oppose as equal; to suit; to make to correspond; to marry; to give in marriage; to join in any way, combine, couple. — *v.i.* To be united in marriage; to be of equal size or quality; to tally, suit, correspond.—**Matchable**, mach'a-bl, *a.* That may be matched; fit to be joined; comparable.—**Matchless**, mach'les, *a.* Having no match or equal; unequalled; unrivalled. — **Matchlessly**, mach'les-li, *adv.* In a matchless manner.—**Matchlessness**, mach'les-nes, *n.* The state or quality of being matchless. — **Match-maker**, *n.* One who contrives or effects a union by marriage. — **Match-making**, *a.* and *n.* Working to bring about marriages.

Mate māt, *n.* [A form of old *make*, a mate, and also of *match* (an equal); O.D. *maet*, D. *maat*, companion, mate; same root as *mete*, to measure.] One who customarily associates with another; a companion; an equal; a match; an officer in a ship whose duty is to assist the master or commander; a husband or wife; one of a pair of animals which associate for propagation and the care of their young.—*v.t.*—*mated*, *mating.* To match; to marry; to match one's self against; to cope with; to equal.—**Mateless**, māt'les, *a.* Having no mate.

Mate, māt, *v.t.* [Fr. *mater*, to enfeeble, from *mat*, worn out or exhausted, from the chess term, Per. *shāh māt*=E. *checkmate.*] To confound; to subdue; to crush; *chess*, to checkmate.—*n.* Same as *Checkmate.*

Maté, mä'tā, *n.* [Sp.] Paraguay tea, a shrub whose leaves are used in South America as a substitute for tea.

Mater, mā'tėr, *n.* [L. MOTHER.] A mother; *anat.* either of the two membranes that cover the brain, distinguished from each other by the epithets *dura* and *pia*. DURA-MATER, PIA-MATER.—**Materfamilias**, mā'tėr-fa-mil''i-as, *n.* [L.] The mother of a family: correlative of *paterfamilias.*

Material, ma-tē'ri-al, *a.* [L. *materialis*, material, from *materia*, matter. MATTER.] Pertaining to matter; consisting of matter; not spiritual; not mental; pertaining to the physical nature of man, or to the bodily wants, interests, and comforts; important; weighty; momentous; more or less necessary; *logic*, pertaining to the matter of a thing and not to the form.—*n.* What is composed of matter; the substance or matter of which anything is made.—*Raw mate-*

rial, unmanufactured material; material in its natural state.—**Materialism**, ma-tē′ri-al-izm, *n.* The doctrine which denies the existence of spirit or anything but matter; due care of our material nature.—**Materialist**, ma-tē′ri-al-ist, *n.* One who holds the doctrine of materialism.—**Materialistic**, ma-tē′ri-al-is″tik, *a.* Relating to or partaking of materialism.—**Materiality**, ma-tē′ri-al″i-ti, *n.* The quality of being material; material, as opposed to spiritual existence; importance.—**Materialization**, ma-tē′ri-al-i-zā″shon, *n.* The act of materializing; among spiritualists, the alleged assumption by a spirit of a material or bodily form.—**Materialize**, ma-tē′ri-al-īz, *v.t.*—*materialized, materializing.* To invest with matter; to make material; to regard as matter; to explain by the laws appropriate to matter.—**Materializing**, ma-tē′ri-al-īz-ing, *a.* Directed towards materialism. — **Materially**, ma-tē′ri-al-li, *adv.* In a material manner; in the state of matter; substantially; in an important manner or degree; essentially.—**Materialness**, ma-tē′ri-al-nes, *n.* — **Materia Medica**, ma-tē′ri-a med′i-ka, *n.* [L.] That branch of medical science which treats of the drugs, &c., employed in medicine; collectively, all the curative substances, employed in medicine. — **Matériel**, ma-tā-rē-el, *n.* [Fr.] Material or instruments employed, as the baggage, &c., of an army, in distinction from the *personnel*, or the men; or the buildings, &c., of a college, in distinction from its officers.

Maternal, ma-tėr′nal, *a.* [L. *maternus*, from *mater*, mother (which is cog. with E. *mother*); akin *matrimony, matriculate, matron*, &c.] Pertaining to a mother; becoming a mother; motherly.—**Maternally**, ma-tėr′nal-li, *adv.* In a maternal manner. —**Maternity**, ma-tėr′ni-ti, *n.* The state, character, or relation of a mother.

Math, math, *n.* [A.Sax. *mæth*, from *mâwan*, to mow. Mow.] A mowing, or what is gathered from mowing: chiefly in composition (after-*math*).

Mathematics, math-e-mat′iks, *n.* [L. *mathematica*, Gr. *mathematikē* (*technē*, art, understood), from stem of *manthanō, mathēsomai*, to learn.] The science that treats of the properties and relations of quantities, comprising *pure mathematics*, which considers quantity abstractly, as arithmetic, geometry, algebra, trigonometry; and *mixed*, which treats of magnitude as subsisting in material bodies, and is consequently interwoven with physical considerations (astronomy, optics, &c.). — **Mathematical, Mathematic**, math-e-mat′i-kal, math-e-mat′ik, *a.* [L. *mathematicus.*] Pertaining to mathematics, according to the principles of mathematics.—**Mathematically**, math-e-mat′i-kal-li, *adv.* In a mathematical manner.—**Mathematician**, math′e-ma-tish″an, *n.* One versed in mathematics.—**Mathesis**, ma-thē′sis, *n.* [Gr. *mathēsis.*] Mental discipline; learning or science in general, especially mathematics.

Matico, ma-tē′kō, *n.* [Peruvian.] A drug from a South American plant of the pepper family, having styptic properties.

Matin, mat′in, *a.* [Fr. *matin*, from L. *matutinus*, pertaining to the morning; same root as *mature.*] Pertaining to the morning; used in the morning.—*n.pl.* Morning worship or service; morning prayers or songs; time of morning service; the first canonical hour in the Roman Church.—**Matinal**, mat′in-al, *a.* Relating to the morning or to matins.—**Matinée**, mat-i-nā′ *n.* [Fr.] An entertainment or reception held early in the day.

Matrass, mat′ras, *n.* [Fr. *matras*, a mattrass.] A chemical vessel with a tapering neck used for digestion, evaporation, &c.

Matriarchy, mā′tri-är-ki, *n.* [Gr. *matēr*, mother, *archē*, rule.] The rule or predominance of the mother in a family; the principle of determining descent and inheritance on the mother's side and not on the father's, as is done by certain primitive tribes. — **Matriarchal**, mā-tri-är′kal, *a.* Pertaining to matriarchy. — **Matriarchalism**, mā-tri-är′kal-izm, *n.* The practices belonging to matriarchy.

Matricide, māt′ri-sīd, *n.* [L. *matricidium*, the crime, *matricida*, the perpetrator—*mater, matris*, mother, and *cædo*, to slay.] The killing or murder of one's mother; the killer or murderer of one's mother.—**Matricidal**, māt′ri-sī-dal, *a.* Pertaining to matricide.

Matriculate, ma-trik′ū-lāt, *v.t.*—*matriculated, matriculating.* [L. *matricula*, a public register, dim. of *matrix*, a womb, a parent stem, a register, from *mater*, a mother. Maternal.] To enter in a register; to enrol; especially, to admit to membership in a college or university, by enrolling the name in a register.—*v.i.* To be entered as a member of a society.—*a.* Matriculated; enrolled. — *n.* One who is matriculated.—**Matriculation**, ma-trik′ū-lā″shon, *n.* The act of matriculating.

Matrimony, mat′ri-mō-ni. *n.* [L. *matrimonium*, from *mater, matris*, a mother. Maternal.] Marriage; the nuptial state. ∴ Syn. under marriage.—**Matrimonial**, mat-ri-mō′ni-al, *a.* [L. *matrimonialis.*] Pertaining to matrimony or marriage; connubial.—**Matrimonially**, mat-ri-mō′ni-al-li, *adv.* In a matrimonial manner.

Matrix, mā′triks, *n.* pl. **Matrices**, mā′tri-sēz. [L. *matrix*, from *mater*, mother.] The womb; that which incloses anything or gives origin to anything, like a womb; the form or mold in which something is shaped; the rock or main substance in which a crystal, mineral, or fossil is embedded; in *Type founding*, a metal plate engraved to serve as a mold for the type; *linotype*, a brass mold with an incised letter that is brought out in relief by casting; *stereotype*, a papier mâché impression of type serving as a mold for casting an entire page.

Matron, mā′tron, *n.* [Fr. *matrone*, L. *matrona*, from *mater*, mother. Maternal.] A married woman, expecially an elderly married woman; the mother of a family; a head nurse in a hospital.—**Matronage**, mā′tron-ij. *n.* The state of a matron; matrons collectively.—**Matronal**, mā′tron-al, *a.* [L. *matronalis.*] Pertaining to a matron.—**Matronhood**, mā′tron-hud, *n.* State of a matron.—**Matronize**, mā′tron-iz, *v.t.* To render matronlike; to act as a mother to; to chaperon.—**Matronly**, mā′tron-li, *a.* Becoming a wife or matron; sedate.

Matter, mat′ėr, *n.* [O.Fr. *matere*, Fr. *matière*, from L. *materia*, matter, from root of *mother.*] That which occupies space and which becomes known to us by our senses; that of which the whole sensible universe is composed; body; substance; not mind; the substance of any speech or writing; the ideas or facts as distinct from the words; the meaning; *logic* and *metaph.* that which forms the subject of any mental operation, as distinguished from the *form*; good sense; substance, as opposed to empty verbosity or frivolous jesting; thing treated; that about which we think, write, or speak; affair or business (thus the *matter* ended); cause or occasion of trouble, disturbance, &c. (as in the phrase, what is the *matter*?); import; consequence; moment (as in 'no *matter* which'); indefinite amount or quantity (a *matter* of 7 miles); substance excreted from living animal bodies; that which is discharged in a tumour, boil, or abscess; pus.—*Matter of fact*, a reality, as distinguished from what is fanciful.—*v.i.* To be of importance; to signify (in such phrases as, it does not *matter*; what does it *matter*?). —**Matterless**, mat′ėr-les, *a.* Void of matter, substance, or good sense.—**Matter-of-fact**, *a.* Treating of facts or realities; not fanciful, imaginative, or ideal; adhering to facts; not given to wander beyond realities; prosaic.—**Mattery**, mat′ėr-i, *a.* Purulent; generating pus.

Matting. Under Mat.

Mattock, mat′ok, *n.* [A.Sax. *mattoc*, a mattock.] A pick-axe with one or both of its ends broad instead of pointed.

Mattoid, mat′oid, *n.* [G. *matt*, dull.] A kind of stupid monomaniac.

Mattress, mat′tres, *n.* [O.Fr. *materas*, Fr. *matelas*, It. *materasso*, from Ar. *ma'-tra'h*, a quilted cushion.] A quilted bed; a bed stuffed with hair, wool, or other soft material, and quilted.

Matty, mat′i, *n.* The trade name for a small herring.

Maturate, mat′ū-rāt, *v.t.*—*maturated, maturating.* [L. *maturo, maturatum*, to make ripe, from *maturus*, ripe, same root as *mater*, mother.] To bring to ripeness or maturity; to mature; *med.* to promote perfect suppuration in.—*v.i.* To ripen; to come to or towards maturity.—**Maturation**, mat-ū-rā′shon, *n.* [L. *maturatio.*] The process of maturing or ripening; *med.* a beginning to suppurate.—**Maturative**, ma-tū′ra-tiv, *a.* Ripening; conducing to suppuration.—*n.* *Med.* anything that promotes suppuration. Also **Maturant**, ma-tū′rant, *n.* in this sense.—**Mature**, ma-tūr′, *a.* [L. *maturus*, ripe.] Ripe; perfected by time or natural growth; brought by natural process to a complete state of development; ripe or ready to be put in action; *med.* in a state of perfect suppuration; *com.* become payable; having reached the time fixed for payment. — *v.t.* — *matured, maturing.* [L. *maturo.*] To make mature; to ripen; to make ripe or ready for any special use; *med.* to maturate.—*v.i.* To advance towards ripeness, to become mature or ripe; *com.* to reach the time fixed for payment; *med.* to maturate.—**Maturely**, ma-tūr′li, *adv.* In a mature manner; with ripeness; with full deliberation. — **Matureness**, ma-tūr′nes, *n.* The state of being mature; maturity.— **Maturescent**, mat-ū-res′ent, *a.* [L. *maturesco*, to become ripe.] Approaching to maturity. — **Maturity**, ma-tū′ri-ti, *n.* The state or quality of being mature; ripeness; a state of perfection or completeness; *com.* the time when a note or bill of exchange becomes due.

Matutinal, mat-ū′ti-nal, *a.* [L. *matutinus* pertaining to the morning. Matin.] Pertaining to the morning; early in the day.

Maud, mạd, *n.* A plaid of undyed brown wool; a gray woollen plaid worn by shepherds in Scotland.

Maudlin, mạd′lin, *a.* [From *Maudlin*, Mary *Magdalen*, who is drawn by painters with eyes swelled and red with weeping.] Tearful‡; approaching to intoxication; overemotional; sickly sentimental.

Mauger, Maugre, mạ′gėr, *prep.*‡ [O.Fr. *maugrē*, Fr. *malgrē*, in spite of, from L. *male*, badly, and *gratus*, agreeable.] In spite of; in opposition to.

Maul, mạl, *n.* [Same as *Mall.*] A kind of large hammer or mallet.—*v.t.* To beat with a maul, or as with a maul; to maltreat severely.

Maul-stick, mạl′stik, *n.* [G. and D. *malen*, to paint, and E. *stick.*] A stick used by painters to steady and support the hand in working.

Maum, mạm, *n.* A kind of soft rock. Malm.

Maund, mạnd, *n.* In the East Indies, a measure of weight, differing according to locality from a quarter of a cwt. to about thrice this.

Maund, mạnd, *n.* [A.Sax. *mand, mond*, D. *mand*, a basket.] A handbasket. (*Shak.*) —**Maunder**, mạn′dėr, *v.i.* [From old *maunder*, a beggar, one who carries a *maund.*] To speak with a beggar's whine; to grumble; to wander in talking like a drunk or silly old person; to drivel. — **Maunderer**, mạn′dėr-ėr, *n.* One who maunders.

Maundril, mạn′dril, *n.* [Comp. *mandrel.*] A collier's pick with two points or prongs.

Maundy-Thursday, mạn′di, *n.* [O.E. *maundee*, a command, Fr. *mandé*, from L. *mandatum*—the first word used in the Vulgate to render the words of our Saviour, when, after supper, he washed his apostles' feet: '*Mandatum* novum do vobis', a new commandment I give unto you.] The Thursday before Good Friday, on which the sovereign of England distributes alms to a certain number of poor persons at Whitehall. —*Maundy money*, small silver coins (including twopenny and penny pieces) struck for this distribution.

Mauresque, mą-resk′, *n.* MORESQUE.

Mauser, mou′zėr, *n.* [Inventor's name.] A kind of rifle.

Mausoleum, mą-sō-lē′um, *n.* [Gr. *mausōleion*, from *Mausolus*, king of Caria, to whom Artemisia his widow erected a stately monument so called.] A magnificent tomb or stately sepulchral monument.—**Mausolean**, mą-sō-lē′an, *a.* Pertaining to a mausoleum; monumental.

Mauve, mōv, *n.* [Fr., mallow, L. *malva*, a mallow—its petals having purple markings.] One of the coal-tar colors, a purple dye obtained from aniline.

Mavis, mā′vis, *n.* [Fr. *mauvis*, Sp. *malvis*, from the Celtic; comp. Armor *milvid*, a mavis.] The throstle or song-thrush.

Maw, mą, *n.* [A.Sax. *maga* = D. *maag*, Icel. *magi*, O.H.G. *mago*, G. *magen*, the stomach.] The stomach of brutes: applied to the stomach of human beings in contempt or humour; the crop of fowls. —**Maw-seed**, *n.* A name given to poppy-seed from its being used as food for cage-birds, especially when moulting.—**Maw-worm**, mą′wėrm, *n.* A worm which infests the maw or stomach and bowels.

Mawkish, mąk′ish, *a.* [From old *mawk*, *mauk*, a maggot; Icel. *mathkr*, N. *makk*.] Apt to cause satiety or loathing; sickly; nauseous.—**Mawkishly**, mąk′ish-li, *adv.* In a mawkish way. — **Mawkishness**, mąk′ish-nes, *n.* Quality of being mawkish.

Maxilla, mak-sil′la, *n.* pl. **Maxillæ**, mak-sil′lē. [L., a jaw, dim. of *mala*, a jaw, from root of *macerate*.] A term applied to each of the bones supporting the teeth of either jaw: often restricted to the upper jaw of the inferior vertebrates. — **Maxillar, Maxillary**, mak′sil-lar, mak′sil-la-ri, *a.* Pertaining to the jaw or the maxilla (the *maxillary* bones or glands).—**Maxilliped**, mak-sil′li-ped, *n.* [L. *maxilla*. and *pes*, foot.] A jaw-foot; one of the short foot-like appendages that cover the mouth in a crab, lobster, &c.

Maxim, mak′sim, *n.* [Fr. *maxime*, from L. *maxima* (*sententia*, opinion, understood), the greatest or chief opinion, *maximus*, superlative of *magnus*, great. MAGNITUDE.] An established principle; a principle or formula embodying a rule of conduct. ∴ Syn. under APHORISM. — **Maximist**, mak′sim-ist, *n.* One who deals in maxims. —**Maximize**, mak′sim-īz, *v.t.* To make as great as possible; to raise to the maximum. —**Maximum**, mak′si-mum, *n.* [L., from *maximus*, the greatest.] The greatest quantity or degree attainable or attained in any given case, as opposed to *minimum*, the smallest.—*a.* Greatest [the *maximum* velocity).

Maxim gun, mak′sim, *n.* A quick-firing machine-gun, single-barrelled, with water-casing to keep the parts cool, so called from Sir Hiram *Maxim*, the inventor.

May, mā, *n.* [Fr. *mai*, Pr. *mai*, May, from L. *Maius*, from the goddess *Maia*, a goddess of growth or increase, from root of L. *magnus*, great, and E. *may*, the auxiliary.] The fifth month of the year; *fig.* the early part of life; hawthorn blossom, so named because the hawthorn blooms in this month. —*v.i.* To celebrate the festivities of May-day: used only as a participial noun in such phrases as *to go a maying*, &c. — **May beetle**, *n.* The cockchafer.—**May Day**, *n.* The first day of May, on which various festivities were, and in some places still are, observed.—**May dew**, *n.* The dew gathered on the first day of May, and supposed to have virtue in preserving youthful beauty.—**May Duke**, *n.* [Corruption of *Médoc*, in France, from which these cherries were introduced.] A variety of the common cherry —**Mayflower**, *n.* The trailing arbutus; the name of the ship that brought the Pilgrims to America in 1620.—**May fly**, *n.* A neuropterous insect that appears first in May.—**May game**, *n.* Sport or diversion, such as is used on the first of May.—**May lady**, *n.* The queen or lady of May, in old May games. —**May meetings**, *n.* The meetings of religious or charitable associations held in London during the month of May.—**May morn**, *n.* Morning of May Day.—**Maypole**, *n.* A pole wreathed with flowers and set up to be danced round on May Day.— **May queen**, *n.* A young woman honored as queen at the games or pageants held on May Day.

May, mā, *verb auxiliary*; pret. *might*. Used similarly to *can*, *could*. [A.Sax. *mugan*, *magan* = L.G. and D. *mogen*, Goth. and O.H.G. *magan*, G. *mögen*, Icel. *mega*, Dan. *maa*, to be able; from same root are *much*, *maid*, L. *magnus*, Gr. *megas*, Skr. *mahâ*, great.] Formerly often used in sense of *can*, implying personal power or ability; now to imply possibility with contingency (it *may* be so, the king *may* be killed); opportunity; moral power; permission granted (you *may* now go); desire, as in prayer, aspiration, imprecation, benediction, &c. (*may* he perish miserably!); frequently used to form the compound tenses of the potential mood (you *might* have gone had you pleased).—**Maybe**, mā′bē, *adv.* [That is, 'it *may* be'.] Perhaps; possibly; probably. (*Colloq.*)—*n.* A possibility; a probability,— **Mayhap**, mā-hap′, *adv.* Peradventure; it may happen; perhaps.

Maya, mä′yä, *n.* An Indian belonging to an extinct tribe of Central America that was far advanced in civilization when discovered about 1500; also the language spoken by those people.

Mayhem, mā′hem, *n.* *Law*, the act of maiming a man. MAIM.

Mayonnaise, Mayonaise, mā-on-āz, *n.* [Fr.] A dish composed of yolks of eggs and salad-oil beaten together, used as a sauce to lobster, salmon, &c.

Mayor, mā′ėr, *n.* [Fr. *maire*, Sp. *mayor*, from L. *major*, greater, compar. of *magnus*, great. MAGNITUDE.] The chief magistrate of a city or borough; the chief officer of a municipal corporation.—*Mayor of the Palace*, the chief official in the palaces of the Merovingian kings, wielding and controlling all power, rendering the kings *fainéants* or idle puppets in his hands.—**Mayoralty**, mā′ėr-al-ti, *n.* The office of a mayor, and the time of his service.—**Mayoress**, mā′ėr-es, *n.* The wife of a mayor. —**Mayorship**, mā′ėr-ship, *n.* The office or dignity of a mayor.

Mazarine, maz-a-rēn′, *n.* [After Cardinal *Mazarin*.] A deep blue color.—**Mazarine-gown**, *n.* In England a common councilman's gown.

Mazdean, maz′dē-an, *a.* [From *Ahura-Mazdao*, the chief deity of the ancient Persians, the Ormuzd of English writers.] Pertaining or relating to Mazdeism. — **Mazdeism**, maz′dē-izm, *n.* The religion of the ancient Persians; the worship of Ormuzd.

Maze, māz, *n.* [Akin to Prov.E. *mazle*, to wander as if stupefied; Icel. *masa*, to chatter or prattle; Dan. *mase*, to have trouble; comp. also W. *masu*, to swoon. *Amaze* is from this.] A confusing net-work of paths or passages; a winding and turning; an intricacy; a labyrinth; confusion of thought; perplexity.—*v.t.*—*mazed*, *mazing*. To confound; to stupefy; to bewilder.—**Mazily**, mā′zi-li, *adv.* In a mazy manner.—**Maziness**, mā′zi-nes, *n.* The state of being mazy.—**Mazy**, mā′zi, *a.* Having the character of a maze; intricate; perplexed.

Mazer,† mā′zėr, *n.* [Originally a cup made of maple or spotted wood, from O.Fr. *mazre*, spotted wood, or A.Sax. *maser*, a maple (from being spotted); O.H.G. *masar*, G. *maser*, a knur, a spot in wood, G. *mase*, a spot; akin *measles*.] A cup or large goblet, generally of valuable material.

Mazi, mā′zi, *n.* The Turkish name for galls.

Mazurka, Mazourka, ma-zųr′ka, *n.* A lively Polish round dance in 3-8 or 3-4 time; the music written for this dance.

Mazzard, *n.* MAZARD.

Me, mē, *pron. pers.* [A.Sax. *mē*, *mec* (accusative), *mē* (dat.), G. *mich* (acc.), *mir* (dat.); Icel. *mik*, *mér*, Goth. *mik*, *mis*, L. *me*, *mihi*, Gr. *eme*, *emoi*, Skr. *mâm*, *mahyam*, me, to me.] The objective or accusative, as also the dative, of *I*, the pronoun of the first person. It stands as a dative in *me*thinks; woe is *me*; give *me* a drink, and the like.

Mead, mēd, *n.* [A.Sax. *medu* = D. *mede*, Icel. *mjöthr*, Dan. *miöd*, Sw. *mjöd*, W. *medd*, Ir. *meadh*, mead; Gr. *methy*, wine; Lith. *medus*, Rus. *med*, Skr. *madhu*, honey.] A fermented liquor made from honey and water flavoured with spices.

Meadow, med′ō, *n.*; poetical, **Mead**, mēd. [A.Sax. *maedu*, a meadow, shorter form *maed*, a mead, allied to *math* (after-*math*) and *mow*.] A low, level tract of land under grass, and generally mown annually or oftener for hay; a piece of grassland in general.—*a.* Belonging to or growing in a meadow.—**Meadow foxtail**, *n.* A high grade of pasture grass resembling timothy. —**Meadow-grass**, *n.* Variety known as June grass or Kentucky blue in U. S.— **Meadow lark**, *n.* The American genus *Sturnella* with clear, but melancholy note. It is as large as a robin; its plumage is brown, with yellow breast.—**Meadow-sweet**, *n.* The plant genus *Spiraea*, containing many beautiful herbs and low deciduous shrubs.—**Meadowy**, med′ō-i, *a.* Pertaining to or resembling a meadow.

Meager, Meagre, mē′gėr, *a.* [Fr. *maigre*, from L. *macer*, lean; same root as Gr. *mikros*, *smikros*, little; G. *schmähen*, to despise.] Having little flesh; thin; lean; wanting richness, fertility, strength, &c.; small; scanty; *mineral*, dry and harsh to the touch, as chalk.—**Meagerly, Meagrely**, mē′gėr-li, *adv.* Poorly; thinly; sparely; feebly.—**Meagerness, Meagreness**, mē′gėr-nes, *n.* The condition of being meager.

Meal, mēl, *n.* [A.Sax. *mael*, time, portion, repast; D. and Dan. *maal*, G. *mahl*, *mal*, Icel. *mál*, part, repast, time; from root seen in *measure*, *mete*, *moon*. It is the termination seen in piece*meal*, &c.] A portion of food taken at one of the regular times for eating; occasion of taking food; a repast.—**Meal-time**, *n.* The usual time of eating meals.

Meal, mēl, *n.* [A.Sax. *melu*, *melo* = Icel. Sw. *mjöl*, D. Dan. *meel*, G. *mehl*, meal; from the verbal stem seen in Icel. *mala*, Goth. *malan*, G. *mahlen*, L. *molo*, to grind. MILL, MOLAR, MELLOW, MOLLIFY.] The edible part of wheat, oats, rye, barley, &c., ground into flour or a powdery state.— **Mealies**, mē′lēz, *n. pl.* A name given in South Africa to maize or Indian corn.— **Mealiness**, mēl′i-nes, *n.* The quality of being mealy.—**Mealman**, *n.* One who deals in meal.—**Meal tub**, *n.* A large tub or barrel for holding meal.—**Mealy**, mēl′i, *a.* Having the qualities of meal, or resembling meal; powdery like meal; overspread with something that resembles meal.—**Mealymouthed**, *a.* Unwilling or hesitating to tell the truth in plain language; inclined to speak of anything in softer terms than the truth will warrant.

Mean, mēn, *a.* [A.Sax. *maene*, mean, false, bad, from *mân*, evil, wickedness; Icel. *meinn*, mean; comp. D. and Dan. *gemeen*, Goth. *gamains*, G. *gemein*, common.] Low in rank or birth; ignoble; humble; low-minded; base; spiritless; of little value; contemptible; despicable.—**Meanly**, mēn′li, *adv.* In a mean manner; in a low condition; poorly; sordidly.—**Meanness**, mēn′nes, *n.* The state or quality of being mean; want of dignity or rank; want of spirit or honour; mean or base conduct or action.— **Mean-spirited**, *a.* Having a mean spirit.

Mean, mēn, *a.* [O.Fr. *meien*, *moien*, Fr. *moyen*, Pr. *meian*, from L. *medianus*, middle, from *medius*, middle. MEDIUM, MID.] Occupying a middle position; middle; midway between extremes; intermediate; *math.* having an intermediate value between two extremes (*mean* distance, *mean* motion).—*Mean proportional*, the second of any three quantities in continued proportion.—*Mean time*, the time according to an ordinary clock, which makes every day of exactly the same length, though if days are measured by the sun they are not so.—*n.* What is midway or intermediate between two extremes; the middle or average rate or degree; medium; *math.* a quantity having an intermediate value between several others, the simple average formed by adding the quantities together and dividing by their number being called an *arithmetical mean*, while a *geometrical mean* is the square root of the product of the quantities; *pl.* the medium or what is used to effect an object; measure or measures adopted; agency; instrumentality (though pl. in form generally used as sing.; by *this means*, *a means* to an end); income, revenue, resources, estate (his *means* were large).—*By all means*, certainly; on every consideration.—*By no means*, not at all; certainly not.—**Meantime**, mēn′tīm, *adv.* During the interval; in the interval between one specified period and another.—*n.* The interval between one specified period and another.—**Meanwhile**, mēn′whīl, *adv.* and *n.* Meantime.

Mean, mēn, *v.t.*—pret. & pp. *meant* (ment). [A.Sax. *maenan*, to mean, to intend; D. *meenen*, Dan. *mene*, G. *meinen*, to think, to mean; same root as *man*, *mind*, *mental*, Skr. *man*, to think.] To have in the mind, view, or contemplation; to intend; to purpose; to design; to signify or be intended to signify (what does the word *mean*?); to import; to denote.—*v.i.* To be minded or disposed; to have such and such intentions (he *means* well).—**Meaning**, mēn′ing, *p.* and *a.* Significant; intended to convey some idea (a *meaning* look).—*n.* That which a person means; aim or purpose; intent; what is to be understood, whether by act or language; the sense of words; signification; import; force.—**Meaningless**, mēn′ing-les, *a.* Having no meaning.—**Meaningly**, mēn′ing-li, *adv.* In a meaning manner; so as to hint at something indirectly; significantly.

Meander, mē-an′dėr, *n.* [L. *Mæander*, Gr. *Maiandros*, a river in Phrygia proverbial for its windings.] The winding of a river; a winding course; a maze; a labyrinth; a kind of ornamental or decorative design having a labyrinthine character.—*v.t.* To wind or flow over.—*v.i.* To wind or turn; to have an intricate or winding course.—**Meandrian**, mē-an′dri-an, *a.* Winding; having many turns.

Meanly, Meanness, &c. Under MEAN (low).

Meantime, Meanwhile. Under MEAN (intermediate).

Mease, mēz, *n.* [From *measure*.] The quantity of 500 (a *mease* of herrings).

Measles, mē′zlz, *n.* [Lit. the spots or spotted sickness; D. *mazelen*, G. *masern*, pl. of *maser* (also *mase*, *masel*), O.G. *mâsa*, *masar*, a spot. MAZER.] A contagious disease of the human body, usually characterized by a crimson rash upon the skin; rubeola; a disease of swine, characterized by reddish watery pustules on the skin.—**Measly, Measled**, mēz′li, mē′zld, *a.* Infected with measles or eruptions like measles.—**Measliness, Measledness**, mēz′li-nes, mē′zld-nes, *n.* State of being measly.

Measure, mezh′ūr, *n.* [Fr. *mesure*, from L. *mensura*, from *metior*, *mensus*, to measure (seen also in *immense*, *dimension*, *commensurate*); from root *ma*, to measure, whence also *moon*, *mete*, &c.] The extent of a thing in length, breadth, and thickness, in circumference, capacity, or in any other respect; a standard of measurement; a fixed unit of capacity or extent; the instrument by which extent or capacity is ascertained; a measuring rod or line; a certain definite quantity (a *measure* of wine); that which is allotted or dealt out to one; moderation; just degree: in such phrases as, *beyond measure*, within *measure*; indefinite quantity or degree (in some *measure* erroneous); action or proceeding directed to an end; something done with a view to the accomplishment of purpose; *music*, that division by which the time of dwelling on each note is regulated; musical time; *poetry*, the metrical arrangement of the syllables in each line with respect to quantity or accent; a grave solemn dance with slow and measured steps, like the minuet; *geol.* beds; strata: used in the term *coal-measures*.—*Measure of a number or quantity*, *math.* a number or quantity contained in the other a certain number of times exactly.—*Greatest common measure of numbers*, the greatest number which divides them all without a remainder.—*v.t.*—*measured*, *measuring*. To ascertain the extent, dimensions, or capacity of; to judge of the greatness of; to appreciate; to value; to pass through or over; to proportion; to allot or distribute by measure (often with *out*).—*To measure one's* (own) *length*, to fall or be thrown down.—*To measure strength*, to ascertain by trial which of two parties is the stronger.—*To measure swords*, to fight with swords.—*v.i.* To take a measurement or measurements; to result or turn out on being measured; to be in extent.—**Measurable**, mezh′ūr-a-bl, *a.* That may be measured; not beyond measure; moderate.—**Measurableness**, mezh′ūr-a-bl-nes, *n.* The quality of being measurable.—**Measurably**, mezh′ūr-a-bli, *adv.* In a measurable manner or degree; moderately.—**Measured**, mezh′ūrd, *p.* and *a.* Deliberate and uniform; slow and steady; stately; formal; restricted; within bounds; moderate.—**Measureless**, mezh′ūr-les, *a.* Without measure; immeasurable.—**Measurement**, mezh′ūr-ment, *n.* The act of measuring; the amount ascertained by measuring.—**Measurer**, mezh′ūr-ėr, *n.* One who measures; one whose occupation or duty is to measure work or commodities.—**Measuring**, mezh′ūr-ing, *p.* and *a.* Used in measuring; serving to measure.

Meat, mēt, *n.* [A.Sax. *mete* = D. *met*, Icel. *matr*, D. *mad*, Sw. *mat*, Goth. *mats*, food; farther connections doubtful.] Food in general; anything eaten as nourishment; the flesh of animals used as food; the edible portion of something (the *meat* of an egg).—*The meat of* a discourse, book or article, its underlying thoughts or argument.—**Meat biscuit**, *n.* A concentrated preparation of the most nutritious parts of meat, made with meal into a biscuit.—**Meatiness**, mēt′i-nes, *n.* The quality of being meaty.—**Meat offering**, *n.* An offering or sacrifice consisting of meat or food.—**Meat pie**, *n.* A pie made of meat or flesh.—**Meat salesman**, *n.* One who sells meat for resale.—**Meaty**, mēt′i, *n.* Abounding in meat; resembling meat.

Meatus, mē-ā′tus, *n.* [L., from *meo*, to go.] A passage: applied to various ducts and passages of the body; as, *meatus auditorius*, the passage of the ear.

Mechanic, mė-kan′ik, *n.* [L. *mechanicus*, Gr. *mēchanikos*, from *mēchanē*, a machine. MACHINE.] An artisan; an artificer; one who follows a handicraft for his living: sometimes restricted to those employed in making and repairing machinery.—*Mechanics' institute*, an institution for the instruction and recreation of persons of the artisan classes, by means of lectures, a library, museum, courses of lessons, &c.—*a.*, Same as *Mechanical*, but not so common.

Mechanical, mė-kan′i-kal, *a.* Pertaining to or in accordance with the laws of mechanics; resembling a machine; hence, acting without thought or independence of judgment; done as if by a machine, that is, by the mere force of habit (a *mechanical* motion of the hand); pertaining to artisans or mechanics or their employments; acting by or resulting from weight or momentum (*mechanical* pressure); physical; opposed to *chemical* (a *mechanical* mixture, that is, one in which the ingredients do not lose their identity).—*Mechanical equivalent of heat*, the number of units of mechanical work equivalent to one unit of heat: 778 foot-pounds per pound-degree F., or 1400 foot-pounds per pound-degree C., or 41·9 million ergs per gramme-degree C.—*Mechanical philosophy*, that which explains the phenomena of nature on the principles of mechanics.—*Mechanical powers*, the simple elements of which every machine, however, complicated, must be constructed; they are the lever, the wheel and axle, the pulley, the inclined plane, the wedge, and the screw.—*Mechanical solution of a problem*, a solution by any art or contrivance not strictly geometrical, as by means of the ruler and compasses or other instruments.—**Mechanically**, mė-kan′i-kal-li, *adv.* In a mechanical manner; without thought or intelligence; by the mere force of habit.—**Mechanicalness**, mė-kan′i-kal-nes, *n.* The state of being mechanical.—**Mechanician**, mek-an-ish′an, *n.* One skilled in mechanics.—**Mechanics**, mė-kan′iks, *n.* The science which treats of motion and force; often divided into—*statics*, embracing the principles which apply to bodies at rest; and *dynamics*, the principles of equilibrium and action of bodies in a state of motion. See also DYNAMICS, KINEMATICS.—*Practical mechanics*, the application of mechanics to practical purposes, as in the construction of machines, &c.—**Mechanism**, mek′an-izm, *n.* The parts collectively, or the arrangement and relation of the parts of a machine, contrivance, or instrument; mechanical construction; machinery.—**Mechanist**, mek′an-ist, *n.* A maker of machines, or one skilled in machinery.—**Mechanize**, mek′an-īz, *v.t.*—*mechanized*, *mechanizing*. To subject to contrivance; to form mechanically.—**Mechanography**, mek-an-og′ra-fi, *n.* Writing or copying by the use of a machine.—**Mechanographist**, mek-an-og′ra-fist, *n.* One who uses mechanography.

Mechlin, mek′lin, *n.* A species of fine lace made at *Mechlin* or Malines in Belgium.

Mechoacan, mė-chō′a-kan, *n.* From *Mechoacan*, in Mexico.] The large thick tuber of a Mexican plant which yields a kind of jalap.

Mecometer. See MEKOMETER.

Meconic, mė-kon′ik, *a.* [Gr. *mēkōn*, a poppy.] A term applied to the peculiar acid with which morphia is combined in opium.—**Meconate**, mē′kon-āt, *n.* A salt of meconic acid.—**Meconin, Meconine**, mē′kon-in, *n.* A white neutral substance existing in opium.—**Meconium**, mē-kō′ni-um, *n.* The inspissated juice of the poppy; the first fæces of infants.

Medal, med′al, *n.* [Fr. *médaille*, It. *medaglia*, from L. *metallum*, Gr. *metallon*, metal. METAL.] A coin, or a piece of metal in the form of a coin, stamped with some figure or device, often issued to commemorate a noteworthy event or as a reward of merit.—**Medalist, Medallist**, med′al-ist, *n.* An engraver, stamper, or molder of metals; a person skilled in medals; one who has gained a medal as a reward of merit; in golf tournament the one who qualifies with the lowest score.—**Medallion**, mē-dal′yun, *n.* [Fr. *médaillon*.] A large antique medal, usually of gold or silver; anything resembling such a piece of metal, as a circular or oval tablet, bearing on it objects represented in relief.—**Medallurgy**, med′al-ėr-ji, *n.* [*Medal*, and Gr. *ergon*, work.] The ancient art of making and striking medals and coins.

Meddle, med′l, *v.i.*—*meddled*, *meddling*. [O.E. *medlen*, to mix, from O.Fr. *medler*, *mesler* (Fr. *mêler*), to mix, *se mesler de*, to mix one's self up with; from L.L. *misculare*, from L. *misceo*, to mix. MEDLEY, MIX.] To mix one's self; to deal, treat, tamper (followed by *with*); to interfere; to take part in another person's affairs in an officious, impertinent, or offensive manner (often followed by *with* or *in*).—**Meddler**, med′lėr, *n.* One that meddles; a busybody.—**Meddlesome**, med′l-sum, *a.* Given to meddling; officiously intrusive.—**Meddlesomeness**, med′l-sum-nes, *n.*—**Meddling**, med′ling, *p.* and *a.* Given to meddle, officious; officiously interposing or interfering in other men's affairs.—**Meddlingly**, *adv.*

Mede, mēd, *n.* A native or inhabitant of *Media*, an ancient kingdom of Asia.

Media, *n. pl.* MEDIUM.

Mediad, mē'di-ad, *n.* [From *median* + L. *ad*, towards.] Towards the median plane or line.

Mediæval, Medieval, med-i-ē'val, *a.* [L. *medius*, middle, and *ævum*, age.] Relating to the middle ages or the period between the eighth and the middle of the fifteenth century, A.D.—**Mediævalism, Medievalism**, med-i-ē'val-izm, *n.* The spirit or principles of the middle ages.—**Mediævalist, Medievalist**, med-i-ē'val-ist, *n.* One versed in the history of the middle ages.

Medial, mē'di-al, *a.* [L. *medialis*, from *medius*, middle (akin to *mid*), seen also in *mediate, medium, mediæval, mediocre, meridian, moiety*, &c.] Mean; pertaining to a mean or average.—**Median**, mē'di-an, *a.* [L. *medianus*.] Situated in the middle; passing through or along the middle.—*Median line, anat.* a vertical line, supposed to divide the body longitudinally into two equal parts.—**Mediant**, mē'di-ant, *n.* [It. *mediante*.] *Mus.* an appellation given to the third above the key-note.

Mediastinum, mē'di-as-tī"num, *n.* [L. *mediastinus*, in the middle, from *medius*, middle.] The division of the chest from the sternum backwards between the lungs, dividing the cavity into two parts.—**Mediastinal**, mē-di-as'ti-nal, *a.* Relating to the mediastinum.

Mediate, mē'di-it, *a.* [L. *medio, mediatum*, to be in the middle, from *medius*, middle. MEDIAL.] Being between two extremes; middle; acting as a means or medium; not direct or immediately; effected by the intervention of a medium.—*v.t.* mē'di-āt, *mediated, mediating.* To interpose between parties as the equal friend of each; to negotiate between persons at variance with a view to reconciliation.—*v.t.* To effect by mediation or interposition between parties (to *mediate* a peace).—**Mediately**, mē'di-āt-li, *adv.* In a mediate manner; indirectly.—**Mediateness**, mē'-di-āt-nes, *n.* The state or quality of being mediate or intervening.—**Mediation**, mē-di-ā'shon, *n.* The act of mediating; entreaty for another; intercession; interposition; intervention.—**Mediative**, mē'-di-ā-tiv, *a.* Of or belonging to a mediator; mediatorial.—**Mediatize**, mē'di-at-īz, *v.t.* —*mediatized, mediatizing.* To render mediately dependent.—**Mediatization**, mē'di-at-i-zā"shon, *n.* The act of mediating; the term applied to the annexation of the smaller German sovereignties to larger contiguous states, when they were made mediately, instead of immediately, dependent on the empire.—**Mediator**, mē'-di-ā-tėr, *n.* One that mediates or interposes between parties at variance for the purpose of reconciling them; by way of eminence, Christ is called THE MEDIATOR, being our intercessor with God.—**Mediatorial**, mē'di-a-tō"ri-al, *a.* Belonging to a mediator.—**Mediatorially**, mē'di-a-tō"-ri-al-li, *adv.*—**Mediatress, Mediatrix**, mē'di-āt-res, mē'di-āt-riks, *n.* A female mediator.

Medic, Medick, me'dik, *n.* [Gr. *mēdikē*, lit. a plant of *Media*.] A name of certain leguminous plants yielding fodder and allied to clover; alfalfa.

Medical, med'i-kal, *a.* [L.L. *medicalis*, from L. *medicus*, medical, *medeor*, to heal, to cure; allied to *meditor*, to meditate; Gr. *mēdos*, care.] Pertaining to or connected with medicine or the art of healing diseases; medicinal; tending to cure; intended or instituted to teach medical science.—*Medical jurisprudence.* Under JURISPRUDENCE.—**Medically**, med'i-kal-li, *adv.* In a medical manner; according to the rules of the healing art. — **Medicament**, me-dik'a-ment, *n.* [L. *medicamentum*.] Anything used for healing diseases or wounds; a healing application. — **Medicamental**, med'i-ka-men"tal, *a.* Relating to healing applications.—**Medicamentally**, med'i-ka-men"tal-li, *adv.* After the manner of healing applications.—**Medicate**, med'i-kāt, *v.t.*—*medicated, medicating.* [L. *medico, medicatum*.] To imbue with healing substances.—**Medication**, med-i-kā'shon, *n.* The act or process of medicating.—**Medicative**, med'i-kā-tiv, *a.* Tending to cure or heal.—**Medicinal**, me-dis'i-nal, *a.* [L. *medicinalis*.] Having the property of healing or of mitigating disease; containing healing ingredients (*medicinal* springs); pertaining to medicine.—**Medicinally**, me-dis'i-nal-li, *adv.* In a medicinal manner.—**Medicine**, med'i-sin, *n.* [Fr. *médecine*. L. *medecina*, from *medicus*, healing.] Any substance used as a remedy for disease; a drug; physic; the science and art of preventing, curing, or alleviating disease.—**Medicine case**, *n.* A portable bag for holding medicines and medical appliances.—**Medicine man**, *n.* Among the American Indians and other savage tribes any man whom they suppose to possess mysterious or supernatural powers.

Medieval, &c. MEDIÆVAL, &c.

Mediocre, mē'di-ō-kėr, *a.* [Fr. *médiocre*, from L. *mediocris*, middling. MEDIAL.] Of moderate degree or quality; of middle rate; middling.—**Mediocrity**, mē-di-ok'-ri-ti, *n.* [L. *mediocritas*.] The quality or state of being mediocre; a middle state or degree; a person of mediocre talents or abilities of any kind.

Meditate, med'i-tāt, *v.i.*—*meditated, meditating.* [L. *meditor, meditatus*, to meditate. MEDICAL.] To dwell on anything in thought; to cogitate; to turn or revolve any subject in the mind.—*v.t.* To plan by revolving in the mind; to intend; to think on.—**Meditation**, med-i-tā'shon, *n.* [L. *meditatio*.] The act of meditating; close or continued thought; the revolving of a subject in the mind.—**Meditative**, med'i-tā-tiv, *a.* Addicted to meditation; pertaining to meditation.—**Meditatively**, med'i-tā-tiv-li, *adv.* In a meditative manner.—**Meditativeness**, med'i-ta-tiv-nes, *n.*

Mediterranean, med'i-te-rā"nē-an, *a.* [L. *mediterraneus*—*medius*, middle, and *terra*, land.] Surrounded by or in the midst of land; inland: now applied exclusively to the *Mediterranean* Sea between Europe and Africa; pertaining to, situated on or near the Mediterranean Sea.

Meditullium, med-i-tul'li-um, *n.* [L. *medius*, middle.] DIPLOE.

Medium, mē'di-um, *n* pl. **Media** or **Mediums**, mē'di-a, mē'di-umz. [L. *medium*, the middle, midst, a means. MEDIAL.] Something placed or ranked between other things; a mean between two extremes; a state of moderation; something serving as a means of transmission or communication; necessary means of motion or action; agency of transmission; that by or through which anything is accomplished, conveyed, or carried on; agency; instrumentality; a person through whom spiritual manifestations are claimed to be made by believers in spiritualism, or who is said to be capable of holding intercourse with the spirits of the deceased; the liquid vehicle with which dry colours are ground and prepared for painting. — *Circulating medium*, coin and bank-notes, or paper convertible into money on demand.—*a.* Middle; middling.

Medlar, med'lėr, *n.* [O.Fr. *meslier, mesler, medler*, from L. *mespilus*, Gr. *mespilon*, medlar.] A tree found wild in Central Europe, and cultivated in gardens for its fruit, which resembles a pear.

Medley, med'li, *n.* [O.Fr. *medlée, meslée* (Fr. *mêlée*), from *medler, mesler*, to mix. MEDDLE.] A mingled and confused mass of ingredients; a jumble; a hodge-podge; a kind of song made up of scraps of different songs.

Medoc, mā-dok', mā'dok, *n.* An excellent red French wine, from *Médoc*, in the department of Gironde.

Medulla, mė-dul'a, *n.* [L., marrow, from *medius*, middle.] *Anat.* the fat substance or marrow which fills the cavity of the bones; *bot.* pith.—*Medulla oblongata*, the upper enlarged portion of the spinal cord and the base of the brain.—*Medulla spinalis*, the spinal marrow or cord.—**Medullary, Medullar**, med"u-ler'i, me-dul'ėr, *a.* [L. *medullaris*.] Consisting of or resembling marrow; relating to the pith of plants.—*Medullary sheath, bot.* a thin layer of spiral vessels formed immediately over the pith.—*Medullary rays*, the vertical plates of cellular tissue which connect the pith of exogenous plants with the bark.—*Medullary substance*, the white substance composing the greater part of the brain, spinal marrow, and nerve fibers.

Medusa, me-dū'sa, *n.* [Gr. *Medousa*, originally the fem. of *medōn*, a ruler.] *Myth.* one of the three Gorgons who had her hair changed into serpents by Athene; *zool.* (pl. **Medusæ**), in zoophytes, a free-swimming sexual stage (jellyfish).—**Medusidæ**, me-dū'si-dē, *n. pl.* [From their tentacles being compared to Medusa's snaky locks.] The jelly-fishes or sea-nettles, the latter name derived from the property which some of them have of stinging.—**Medusidan**, me-dū'si-dan, *n.* A member of the Medusidæ.—**Medusiform**, me-dū'si-form, *a.* Resembling a medusa in shape.—**Medusoid**, me-dū'soid, *a.* Pertaining to a medusa.

Meed, mēd, *n.* [A.Sax. *méd, meord* = L.G. *mede*, D. *miede*, G. *miethe*, Goth. *mizdo*, reward, recompense; allied to Gr. *misthos*, pay, hire.] That which is bestowed in consideration of merit; reward; recompense; a gift.

Meek, mēk, *a.* [Same as Sw. *miuk*, Icel. *mjúkr*, soft, meek, Dan. *myg*, pliant, supple; Goth. *muks*, soft, meek.] Mild of temper; gentle; submissive; not easily provoked or irritated; marked by meekness.—**Meekly**, mēk'li, *adv.* In a meek manner; gently; submissively. — **Meekness**, mēk'nes, *n.* The quality of being meek; mildness; gentleness; forbearance under injuries and provocations.—**Meek-eyed**, *a.* Having eyes indicating meekness.

Meerschaum, mēr'shum, *n.* [G., lit. sea-foam—*meer*, the sea, and *schaum*, foam: from having been found on the sea-shore in lumps resembling petrified sea-foam. MERE (*n.*), SCUM.] A silicate of magnesium occurring as a fine white clay, and largely made into tobacco-pipes; a tobacco-pipe made of meerschaum.

Meet, mēt, *a.* [A.Sax. *gemet*, fit, proper, from *metan*, to measure; Icel. *mætr*, meet, worthy. METE.] Fit; suitable; proper; appropriate.—**Meetly**, mēt'li, *adv.* In a meet manner; fitly.—**Meetness**, mēt'nes, *n.* Fitness; suitableness.

Meet, mēt, *v.t.*—pret. & pp. *met.* [A.Sax. *métan*, to meet, from *mót*, a meeting; Dan. *mōde*, Sw. *mōta*, Icel. *mæta*, Goth. *motjan*, *gamotjan*, to meet; akin *moot*.] To come face to face with; to come in contact with; to come to be in company with; to come in hostile contact with; to encounter; to join battle with; to find; to light on; to get, gain, or receive; to satisfy, gratify, answer (to *meet* a demand, one's views or wishes).—*To meet the ear*, to strike the ear; to be heard.—*To meet the eye*, to come into notice; to become visible.—*v.i.* To come together by mutual approach; to come together in hostility; to encounter; to assemble; to come together by being extended; to join.—*To meet with*, to light on; to find; to suffer; to suffer unexpectedly (to *meet with* a loss, an accident).—*n.* A meeting as of huntsmen.—**Meeting**, mēt'ing, *n.* A coming together; an interview; an assembly; a hostile encounter; a duel.

Megacephalous, meg-a-sef'a-lus, *a.* [Gr. *megas*, great, and *kephalē*, the head.] Large-headed; having a large head.

Megacycle, meg"a-sī'kl, *n.* [Gr. *megas*, great, and *kyklos*, circle.] In radio, a thousand kilocycles; a million cycles.

Megadyne, meg'a-dīn, *n.* [Gr. *megas*, great, and *dyne*.] A force of a million dynes.

Megafarad, meg'a-far-ad, *n.* [Gr. *megas*,

great, and E. *farad.*] *Electrometry*, a million farads.

Megalesian, meg-a-lē'si-an, *a.* [L. *megalesius*, from Gr. *Megalē*, the great, an epithet applied to Cybele.] Of or belonging to Cybele, the mother of the gods.

Megalichthys, meg-a-lik'this, *n.* [Gr. *megas*, *megalē*, great, and *ichthys*, a fish.] A fossil ganoid fish, with large scales, and with immense laniary teeth.

Megalith, meg'a-lith, *n.* [Gr. *megas*, great, *lithos*, stone.] A huge stone, such as those in cromlechs, dolmens, the Cyclopean architecture of the Greeks, &c.—**Megalithic**, meg-a-lith'ik, *a.* Pertaining to such stones or structures.

Megalomania, meg'a-lō-mā"ni-a, *n.* [Gr. *megalē*, great.] A mania or craze for big things, whether in talk or in fact.

Megalosaur, Megalosaurus, meg'a-lō-sạr, meg'a-lō-sạ"rus, *n.* [Gr. *megas*, *megalē*, great, and *sauros*, a lizard.] A fossil carnivorous reptile found in the oolite and Wealden strata, 40 to 50 feet long.

Megapode, Megapodius, meg'a-pod, meg-a-pō'di-us, *n.* [Gr. *megas*, great, and *pous*, *podos*, a foot.] The Australian jungle-fowl, remarkable for erecting large mounds of vegetable matter in which its eggs are laid and left to be hatched by the heat of the fermenting mass.

Megass, Megasse, me-gas', *n.* Same as *Bagasse*.

Megatherium, meg-a-thē'ri-um, *n.* [Gr. *megas*, great, and *thērion*, a wild beast.] A fossil genus of very large mammals, allied to the sloths, but having feet adapted for walking on the ground.

Megaweber, meg'a-vā-bėr, *n.* [Gr. *megas*, great, and E. *weber*.] *Electrometry*, a million webers.

Megilp, Megilph, mē-gilp', mē-gilf', *n.* A mixture of linseed oil and mastic varnish which artists employ as a vehicle for colors.

Megohm, meg'ōm, *n.* *Electrometry*, a million ohms.

Megrim, mē'grim, *n.* [Fr. *migraine*, corrupted from Gr. *hemicrania*, half the head —*hēmi*, half, and *kranion*, the head.] A neuralgic pain in the side of the head, also called *migraine*; *pl.* low spirits; whims or fancies.

Meibomian, mī-bō'mi-an, *a.* [From *Meibom*, a German physician.] *Anat.* a name for the small sebaceous glands of the eyelids.

Meiocene, mī'ō-sēn, *a.* Miocene.

Meiosis, mī-ō'sis, *n.* [Gr., a lessening, from *meiōn*, less.] A rhetorical figure by which a thing is represented as less than it is.

Meiostemonous, Miostemonous, mī-ō-stem'on-us, *a.* [Gr. *meiōn*, less, and *stēmōn*, a thread.] *Bot.* having stamens fewer in number than the petals.

Meizoseismic, mī-zō-sīs'mik, *a.* [Gr. *meizōn*, greater, and *seismos*, an earthquake.] A term applied to the line or curve of maximum disturbance by an earthquake.

Mekometer, *n.* [Gr. *mēkos*, length, + *metron*, measure.] A sort of range-finder or device employed for similar purposes, consisting of a pair of sextants used simultaneously at the ends of a cord, an observer being required for each sextant.

Melaconite, Melaconise, me-lak'on-īt, me-lak'on-iz, *n.* [Gr. *melas*, black, and *konis*, powder.] A black or grayish-black, impure, earthy oxide of copper.

Melada, me-lä'da, *n.* [Sp., pp. of *melar*, to candy, from L. *mel*, honey.] Crude or impure sugar as it comes from the pans.

Melanemia, mel-a-nē'mi-a, *n.* [Gr. *melas*, black, *haima*, blood.] A condition of the blood in which it contains blackish particles.

Melancholy, mel'an-kol-i, *n.* [Gr. *melancholia*, excess of black bile, melancholy madness—*melas*, *melaina*, black, and *cholē*, bile.] A variety of mental alienation characterized by excessive gloom, mistrust, and depression; hypochondria; depression of spirits induced by grief; dejection; sadness. —*a.* Gloomy; depressed in spirits; dejected; calamitous; afflictive; sombre.—**Melancholia**, mel-an-kō'li-a, *n.* Morbid melancholy.—**Melancholic**, mel'an-kol-ik, *a.* Disordered by melancholy; hypochondriac; pertaining to melancholy; gloomy; mournful.—**Melancholily**, mel'an-kol-i-li, *adv.* In a melancholy manner.—**Melancholiness**, mel'an-kol-i-nes, *n.* The condition of being melancholy.

Melanesia, mel-a-nē'si-a, *n.* [Gr. *melas*, black, *nēsos*, island.] The group of South Sea Islands north-west of the New Hebrides.

Mélange, mā-länzh, *n.* [Fr., from *mêler*, to mix. Meddle.] A mixture; a medley.

Melanic, me-lan'ik, *a.* [Gr. *melas*, *melan*, black.] Of or pertaining to melanism.—**Melanism**, mel'an-izm, *n.* An undue development of colouring material in the skin and its appendages; the opposite of *albinism*.—**Melanite**, mel'an-īt, *n.* A mineral, a variety of garnet, of a velvet-black or grayish-black colour.—**Melanochroic**, mel'an-ō-krō"ik, *a.* [Gr. *melas*, and *chroia*, colour.] A term applied to the dark-skinned white races of men.—**Melanosis**, mel-a-nō'sis, *n.* *Pathol.* a disease in which the tissue is converted into a black, hard substance, near which ulcers or cavities may form.—**Melanotic**, mel-a-not'ik, *a.* Relating to melanosis.

Melaphyre, mel'a-fīr, *n.* A compact black or blackish-gray trap-rock, consisting of a matrix of labradorite and augite, with embedded crystals of the same minerals.

Melasma, me-las'ma, *n.* [Gr., from *melas*, black.] A disease of aged persons, in which black spots appear upon the skin, sometimes ulcerous.

Melchite, mel'kīt, *n.* One of an eastern sect of Christians, who, while adhering to the liturgy of the Greek Church, acknowledge the authority of the pope.

Mêlée, mā-lā, *n.* [Fr., a participial substantive, from *mêler*, to mix. Meddle.] A fight in which the combatants are mingled in confused mass; an affray.

Melibean, Melibœan, mel-i-bē'an, *a.* [After *Melibœus*, one of the speakers in the first eclogue of Virgil.] Proceeding by alternate utterances: alternately responsive.

Melic, mel'ik, *a.* [Gr. *melikos*, from *melos*, a song.] Relating to song; lyric.

Melica, Melic-grass, mel'i-ka, mel'ik, *n.* [It. *melica*, the great millet, from L. *mel*, honey.] A perennial woodland grass, two species of which, valuable in agriculture, are found in the western United States.

Meliceris, mel-i-sē'ris, *n.* [Gr. *melikēris*—*meli*, honey, and *kēros*, wax.] *Pathol.* an encysted tumour, the contents of which resemble wax or honey in consistence.

Melilot, mel'i-lot, *n.* [Gr. *melilōton*, *melilōtos*—*meli*, honey, and *lōtos*, lotus.] A leguminous annual or biennial plant allied to the clovers, and cultivated for fodder; hart's-clover.

Melinite, mel'in-īt, *n.* A French explosive, the basis or chief ingredient of which is picric acid.

Meliorate, mēl'yor-āt, *v.t.*—*meliorated*, *meliorating*. [L. *melioro*, *melioratum*, from *melior*, better, compar. of *bonus*, good.] To make better; to improve; to ameliorate. —*v.i.* To grow better.—**Meliorater, Meliorator**, mēl'yor-ā-tėr, *n.* One who meliorates.—**Melioration**, mēl-yor-ā'-shon, *n.* Improvement; amelioration.—**Meliorism**, mēl'yor-izm, *n.* The doctrine or opinion that everything in nature is so ordered as to produce a progressive improvement.

Meliphagous, me-lif'a-gus, *a.* [Gr. *meli*, honey, *phagein*, to eat.] Feeding upon honey.

Mellay, Melley, mel'lā, *n.* A mêlée; a conflict.

Melliferous, mel-lif'ėr-us, *a.* [L. *mellifer*—*mel*, *mellis*, honey, and *fero*, to produce.] Producing honey.—**Mellification**, mel-lif'i-kā"shon, *n.* [L. *mellifico*—*mel*, and *facio*, to make.] The making or production of honey.—**Mellifluence**, mel-lif'lū-ens, *n.* [L. *mel*, and *fluo*, to flow.] The quality of being mellifluent; a flow of sweetness, or a sweet smooth flow.—**Mellifluent, Mellifluous**, mel-lif'lū-ent, mel-lif'lū-us, *a.* Flowing as with honey; sweetly flowing.—**Mellifluently, Mellifluously**, mel-lif'lū-ent-li, mel-lif'lū-us-li, *adv.* In a mellifluent manner.—**Melligenous**, mel-lij'-en-us, *a.* [L. *melligenus*—*mel*, and *genus*, kind.] Having the qualities of honey.—**Melliloquent**,† mel-lil'ō-kwent, *a.* [L. *mel*, *mellis*, honey, and *loquor*, to speak.] Speaking sweetly.—**Melliphagous**, mel-lif'a-gus, *a.* Meliphagous.—**Mellite, Mellilite**, mel'īt, mel'i-līt, *n.* [L. *mel*, *mellis*, Gr. *meli*, honey, and *lithos*, a stone.] Honey-stone, a very rare mineral of a honey-yellow colour, resinous lustre, and more or less transparent.—**Mellitic**, mel-lit'ik, *a.* Pertaining to mellite.—**Mellivorous**, mel-liv'ō-rus, *a.* [L. *mel*, and *voro*, to devour.] Honey-eating; fond of honey.

Mellow, mel'ō, *a.* [Allied to Prov.G. *möll*, soft, ripe, *mölich*, mellow, *mollig*, soft, L. *mollis*, Gr. *malakos*, Skr. *mridu*, tender, soft, and to E. *meal*, from root *mar*, to grind or crush.] Soft with ripeness; soft to the senses; rich or delicate to the eye, ear, palate, &c., as colour, sound, flavour, and the like; toned down by the lapse of time; softened or matured by length of years; rendered good-humoured by liquor; half-tipsy.—*v.t.* To render mellow; to soften by ripeness or age; to give richness, flavour, or delicacy; to tone or smooth down; to soften in character; to mature.—*v.i.* To become mellow; to soften in character; to become toned down.—**Mellowly**, mel'ō-li, *adv.* In a mellow manner.—**Mellowness**, mel'ō-nes, *n.* The state or quality of being mellow.

Melodeon, me-lō'dē-on, *n.* [From *melody*, Gr. *melōdia*.] A wind-instrument furnished with metallic free reeds and a key-board; a variety of the harmonium.

Melodrama, mel-ō-drä'ma, *n.* [Gr. *melos*, a song, and *drama*, drama.] A romantic play, generally of a serious character, in which effect is sought by startling incidents, striking situations, and exaggerated sentiment, aided by splendid decoration and music.—**Melodramatic, Melodramatical**, mel'ō-dra-mat"ik, mel'ō-dra-mat"i-kal, *a.* Pertaining to, suitable for, or having the character of a melodrama.—**Melodramatically**, mel'ō-dra-mat"i-kal-li, *adv.* In a melodramatic manner; in an affected and exaggerated manner.—**Melodramatist**, mel-ō-dram'a-tist, *n.* One who acts in melodramas or who writes them.

Melody, mel'ō-di, *n.* [Gr. *melōdia*, a tune, a choral song—*melos*, a limb, a part, and *ōdē*, a song, an ode.] An agreeable succession of sounds; sweetness of sound; sound highly pleasing to the ear; *mus.* a succession of tones produced by a single voice or instrument, and so arranged as to please the ear or to express some kind of sentiment; the particular air or tune of a musical piece.—**Melodic**, me-lod'ik, *a.* Of the nature of melody; relating to melody.—**Melodics**, me-lod'iks, *n.* That branch of music which investigates the laws of melody. —**Melodious**, me-lō'di-us, *a.* Containing or characterized by melody; musical; agreeable to the ear by a sweet succession of sounds.—**Melodiously**, me-lō'di-us-li, *adv.* In a melodious manner.—**Melodiousness**, me-lō'di-us-nes, *n.* The quality of being melodious.—**Melodist**, mel'ō-dist, *n.* A composer or singer of melodies. —**Melodize**, mel'ō-dīz, *v.t.*—*melodized*, *melodizing*. To make melodious.

Melon, mel'on, *n.* [Fr. *melon*, L. *melo*, an apple-shaped melon, from Gr. *mēlon*, an apple or apple-shaped fruit.] A climbing or trailing annual plant and its fruit, which is large and fleshy; especially the musk-melon or cantaloupe, and the watermelon.

Melopiano, mel'ō-pi-ä-nō, *n.* [Gr. *melos*, a song, and E. *piano*.] An invention by which sustained sounds can be produced on a pianoforte by a series of small hammers set into rapid vibration by winding up a spring.

Melpomene, mel-pom'e-nē, *n.* [Gr. *Melpomenē*, from *melpomai*, to sing.] The muse of tragedy; also a small asteroid.

Melt, melt, *v.t.* [A.Sax. *meltan*, allied to *malt*, *mellow*, &c.; Gr. *meldō*, to liquefy; probably also in *smelt*.] To reduce from a solid to a liquid or flowing state by heat; to liquefy; to dissolve; to fuse; *fig.* to soften, as by a warming and kindly influence; to render gentle or susceptible to mild influences, as to love, pity, or tenderness.—*v.i.* To become liquid; to dissolve; to pass by imperceptible degrees; to blend; to shade; to become tender, mild, or gentle; to be subdued, as by fear.—**Meltable**, mel'ta-bl, *a.* Capable of being melted; fusible.—**Melter**, mel'tėr, *n.* One who melts.—**Melting**, mel'ting, *p.* and *a.* Fusing; dissolving; affecting; moving (a *melting* speech); feeling or showing tenderness (*melting* charity).—**Meltingly**, mel'ting-li, *adv.* In a melting manner.—**Meltingness**, mel'ting-nes, *n.*—**Melting-pot**, *n.* A crucible.

Member, mem'bėr, *n.* [L. *membrum*, a limb, a member of the body; comp. Skr. *marman*, a joint.] A part of an animal body capable of performing a distinct office; an organ; a limb; part of an aggregate or a whole; one of the persons composing a society, community, or the like; a representative in a legislative body.—*Member of Congress*, a representative elected by the voters of a congressional district to that branch of Congress called the House of Representatives.—**Membered**, mem'bėrd, *a.* Having limbs or members: used chiefly in composition.—**Membership**, mem'bėr-ship, *n.* The state of being a member; the members of a body regarded collectively.

Membrane, mem'brān, *n.* [L. *membrana*, a thin skin, parchment, from *membrum*, a limb.] A thin tissue of the animal body which covers organs, lines the interior of cavities, takes part in the formation of the walls of canals, &c.; a similar texture in vegetables.—**Membranaceous**, mem-bra-nā'shus, *a.* Membranous; *bot.* thin, like membrane, and translucent.—**Membraniferous**, mem-bra-nif'ėr-us, *a.* Having or producing membranes.—**Membraniform**, mem-bran'i-form, *a.* Having the form of a membrane.—**Membranology**,† mem-bra-nol'o-ji, *n.* The science which relates to membranes.—**Membranous**, mem'bra-nus, *a.* Belonging to a membrane; consisting of membranes; resembling a membrane.

Memento, mē-men'tō, *n.* [L., remember, be mindful, from *memini*, to remember.] A suggestion, notice, or memorial to awaken memory; something that reminds.

Memoir, mem'oir, mem'wạr, *n.* [Fr. *mémoire*, from L. *memoria*, memory, from *memor*, mindful; same root as Skr. *smar*, to remember.] A notice of something remembered or deemed noteworthy; an account of transactions or events written familiarly; a biographical notice; recollections of one's life (in this sense usually in the pl.); a biography or autobiography; a communication to a scientific society on some subject of scientific interest.—**Memoirist**, mem'oir-ist, *n.* A writer of memoirs.—**Memorabilia**, mem'or-a-bil''i-a, *n. pl.* [L.] Things remarkable and worthy of remembrance or record.—**Memorable**, mem'or-a-bl, *a.* [L. *memorabilis.*] Worthy to be remembered; illustrious; remarkable; distinguished.—**Memorability**, **Memorableness**, mem'or-a-bil''i-ti, mem'or-a-bl-nes, *n.* The quality of being memorable.—**Memorably**, mem'or-a-bli, *adv.* In a manner worthy to be remembered.—**Memorandum**, mem-or-an'dum, *n.* pl. **Memoranda**, mem-or-an'da, less commonly now **Memorandums**. [L., something to be remembered.] A note to help the memory; a brief entry in a diary; *diplomacy*, a summary of the state of a question, or a justification of a decision adopted.—**Memorial**, me-mō'ri-al, *a.* [L. *memorialis.*] Preservative of memory; serving as a memorial; contained in the memory.—*n.* That which serves to perpetuate the memory of something; a monument; a written representation of facts made to a legislative or other body or to some person; a species of informal state paper much used in diplomatic negotiations.—**Memorialist**, me-mō'ri-al-ist, *n.* One who writes or presents a memorial or memorials.—**Memorialize**, me-mō'ri-al-īz, *v.t.*—*memorialized*, *memorializing*. To present a memorial to; to petition by memorial.—**Memoriter**, me-mor'it-ėr, *adv.* [L.] From memory; by heart.—**Memorize**, mem'or-īz, *v.t.*—*memorized*, *memorizing*. To cause to be remembered; to record; to hand down to memory by writing.—**Memory**, mem'o-ri, *n.* [L. *memoria*, memory, from *memor*, mindful.] The power, capacity, or faculty of the mind by which it retains the knowledge of past events or ideas; that faculty which enables us to treasure up and preserve for future use the knowledge which we acquire; remembrance; the state of being remembered; that which is remembered about a person or event; the time within which a person may remember what is past. ∴ *Memory* is the faculty or capacity of retaining in the mind and recalling what is past; *recollection* and *remembrance* are exercises of the faculty, the former being a calling to mind, the latter a holding in mind; while *reminiscence* always, and *recollection* often, are used of the thing remembered.

Memphian, mem'fi-an, *a.* [From *Memphis*, the ancient metropolis of Egypt.] Pertaining to Memphis; Egyptian (*Memphian* darkness).

Men, men, pl. of *man*.

Menace, men'ās, *v.t.*—*menaced*, *menacing*. [Fr. *menacer*, from L. *minax*, threatening, *mina*, a threat, from root *min*, seen in *mineo*, to project (in *prominent*, *eminent*); akin *mien*, *demean*, *amenable*, &c.] To threaten; to show a disposition to inflict punishment or other evil on: followed by *with* before the evil threatened (*threatened* him *with* death); to hold out threats of (to *threaten* revenge).—*n.* A threat or threatening; the indication of a probable evil or catastrophe to come.—**Menacer**, men'ās-ėr, *n.* One who menaces.—**Menacing**, men'ās-ing, *p.* and *a.* Threatening; indicating a threat.—**Menacingly**, men'ās-ing-li, *adv.* In a menacing manner.

Menage, men-äzh', *n.* [Fr. *ménage*, a household; O.Fr. *mesnage*, L.L. *mansionaticum*, from L. *mansio*, a dwelling. MANSION.] A household; housekeeping; household management.—**Menagerie**, me-naj'ėr-i, *n.* [Fr. *ménagerie.*] A collection of wild animals, especially of wild or foreign animals kept for exhibition.

Mend, mend, *v.t.* [Shorter form of *amend.*] To repair, as something broken, rent, decayed, or the like; to restore to a sound state; to patch up; to alter for the better; to improve (to *mend* one's manners); to better; to improve upon (to *mend* one's pace).—*v.i.* To advance to a better state; to improve; to act or behave better.—**Mendable**, men'da-bl, *a.* Capable of being mended.—**Mender**, men'dėr, *n.* One who mends.

Mendacious, men-dā'shus, *a.* [L. *mendax*, *mendacis*, lying, from stem of *mentior*, to lie: same root as *mens*, mind (whence *mental*).] Lying; false; given to telling untruths.—**Mendacity**, men-das'i-ti, *n.* The quality of being mendacious; lying; falsehood; a lie.

Mendelism, men'del-ism, *n.* [From *Mendel*, an Austrian abbot.] A theory of breeding which has led to the production of improved strains of wheat and other plants.

Mendicant, men'di-kant, *a.* [L. *mendicans*, *mendicantis*, ppr. of *mendico*, to beg, from *mendicus*, a beggar (akin to *menda*, a fault).] Practising beggary; poor to a state of beggary; begging as part of religious discipline (a *mendicant* friar).—*n.* A beggar; a member of a begging order or fraternity; a begging friar.—**Mendicancy**, men'di-kan-si, *n.* Beggary; a state of begging.—**Mendication**, men-di-kā'shon, *n.* The act of begging.—**Mendicity**, men-dis'i-ti, *n.* [L. *mendicitas.*] The state or practice of begging; the life of a beggar.

Menhaden, men-hā'den, *n.* [American Indian.] A salt-water fish of the herring family, abounding on the shores of New England.

Menhir, men'hir, *n.* [W. *maen*, a stone, and *hir*, long.] A name for tall, rude, or sculptured stones of unknown antiquity, standing singly or in groups.

Menial, mē'ni-al, *a.* [O.E. *meyneal*, &c., O.Fr. *meignial*, from *meignee*, *maisgnee*, a household, L.L. *masnata*: same origin as *mansion.*] Pertaining to household or domestic servants; servile.—*n.* A domestic servant; especially one of a train of servants: mostly as a term of disparagement.

Meninges, me-nin'jēz, *n. pl.* [Gr. *mēningx*, *mēningos*, a membrane.] *Anat.* the three membranes that envelop the brain, the *dura mater*, *pia mater*, and *arachnoid membrane*.—**Meningeal**, me-nin'jē-al, *a.* Relating to the meninges.—**Meningitis**, men-in-jī'tis, *n.* Inflammation of the membranes of the brain or spinal cord.

Meniscus, me-nis'kus, *n.* pl. **Menisci**, me-nis'si, or **Meniscuses**. [Gr. *mēniskos*, a little moon, from *mēn*, *mēnos*, the moon.] A lens, convex on one side and concave on the other, and in which the two surfaces meet, or would meet if continued, so that it resembles a crescent.—**Meniscal**, me-nis'kal, *a.* Pertaining to a meniscus.—**Meniscoid**, me-nis'koid, *a.* Like a meniscus; crescent-shaped.

Meniver, men'i-vėr, *n.* MINIVER.

Mennonite, **Mennonist**, men'non-īt, men'non-ist, *n.* [From Simon *Menno*, the founder, 1496-1561.] One of a sect of Anabaptists who do not believe in original sin, and object to taking oaths, making war, or going to law.

Menology, mē-nol'o-ji, *n.* [Gr. *mēn*, a month, *logos*, account.] A register or calendar of events according to the days of the months; a calendar of saints and martyrs with their feasts throughout the year.

Menopause, men'o-pạz, *n.* [Gr. *mēn*, month, *pausis*, a stopping.] The cessation of menstruation at the change of life in woman.

Menopome, **Menopoma**, men'ō-pōm, men-ō-pō'ma, *n.* [Gr. *menō*, to remain, and *pōma*, a drinking-cup, because its gill-openings are permanent, though it loses its gills when adult.] A tailed amphibian of the fresh waters of North America.

Menorrhagia, men-or-rā'ji-a, *n.* [Gr. *mēn*, *mēnos*, a month, and *rheō*, to flow.] *Med.* an immoderate menstrual discharge: hæmorrhage from the uterus.

Mensal, men'sal, *a.* [L. *mensis*, a month; same root as Gr. *mēn*, a month. MONTH.] Occurring once a month; monthly.—**Menses**, men'sēz, *n. pl.* The catamenial or monthly discharge of a woman.—**Menstrual**, men'strö-al, *a.* [L. *menstrualis*, monthly.] Monthly; pertaining to the menses of females; menstruous.—**Menstruant**, men'strö-ant, *a.* Subject to menstruation.—**Menstruate**, men'strö-āt, *v.i.*—*menstruated*, *menstruating*. To discharge the menses.—**Menstruation**, men-strö-ā'shon, *n.* The act of menstruating; the period of menstruating.—**Menstruous**, men'strö-us, *a.* [L. *menstruus.*] Pertaining to the monthly flow of females.

Menstruum, men'strö-um, *n.* pl. **Menstrua**, **Menstruums**. [From L. *menstruus*, monthly, from *mensis*, a month; from some old belief of the alchemists about the influence of the moon.] Any fluid which dissolves a solid; a solvent.

Mensurable, men'shụ-ra-bl, *a.* [L. *mensurabilis*, from *mensuro*, to measure, from *mensura*, measure. MEASURE.] Capable of being measured; measurable.—**Mensurability**, **Mensurableness**, men'shụ-ra-bil''i-ti, men'shụ-ra-bl-nes, *n.* Quality of being mensurable.—**Mensural**, men'-

shụ-ral, *a.* Pertaining to measure.—**Mensurate,**† men'shụ-rat, *v.t.* To measure.—**Mensuration,** men-shụ-rā'shon, *n.* The act or art of measuring or taking the dimensions of anything; the process of finding any dimension of a figure, or its area or solid content, by means of the most simple measurements possible.

Mentagra, men-tag'ra, *n.* [L., from *mentum,* the chin, and Gr. *agra,* a seizing.] An eruption about the chin, forming a crust.

Mental, men'tal, *a.* [Fr. *mental,* from L. *mens, mentis,* mind. MENTION.] Pertaining to the mind or intellect; wholly depending on the mind; intellectual.—**Mentality,** men-tal'i-ti, *n.* The state of being mental; mental cast or habit.—**Mentally,** men'tal-li, *adv.* By or in the mind of intellect: intellectually; in thought.

Mentation, men-tā'shon, *n.* [L. *mens,* mind.] The act or operation of the mind.

Menthol, men'thol, *n.* L. *mentha,* mint, *oleum,* oil.] A white crystalline substance obtained from oil of peppermint, used externally in cases of nervous headache.

Mention, men'shon, *n.* [L. *mentio, mentionis,* from same root as *mens,* mind, Skr. *man,* to think. MAN.] A brief notice or remark in regard to something; a cursory speaking of anything: often in the phrase *to make mention of,* to name or say something in regard to.—*v.t.* To make mention of. — **Mentionable,** men'shon-a-bl, *a.* That can or may be mentioned.

Mentor, men'tor, *n.* [From *Mentor,* the counsellor of Telemachus, according to Homer.] A wise or faithful adviser or monitor. — **Mentorial,** men-tō'ri-al, *a.* Containing advice or admonition.

Menu, mė-nü, *n.* [Fr., lit. minute or detailed list, from L. *minutus,* minute.] A list of the dishes, &c., to be served at a dinner, supper, or the like; a bill of fare.

Mephistophelean, Mephistophelian, mef'i-stof-i-lē"an, me-fis'to-fē"li-an, *a.* Resembling the character of Mephistopheles, the diabolic spirit of Gœthe's Faust and the Faust legend generally; diabolical; sardonic.

Mephitis, Mephitism, me-fī'tis, mef'it-izm, *n.* [L. *mephitis,* a pestilential exhalation.] Noxious exhalations from decomposing substances, filth, or other source.—**Mephitic, Mephitical,** me-fit'ik, me-fit'i-kal, *a.* Pertaining to mephitis; offensive to the smell; noxious; pestilential.—**Mephitically,** me-fit'i-kal-li, *adv.* With mephitis.

Mercantile, mėr'kan-til, *a.* [Fr. *mercantile,* from L. *mercans, mercantis.* MERCHANT.] Pertaining to merchants, or their traffic; pertaining to trade or commerce; commercial.—*Mercantile System,* the economic program which superseded that of medieval feudalism and advocated that each nation seek to establish a favorable balance of trade and so accumulate bullion.

Mercator's Chart, Mercator's Projection, mėr-kā'tėr. [From Gerard *Mercator,* a Flemish geographer.] A projection or map of the earth's surface, with the meridians and parallels of latitude all straight lines.

Mercenary, mėr'se-na-ri, *a.* [Fr *mercenaire,* L. *mercenarius,* from *merces,* reward, wages. MERCHANT.] Hired; obtained by hire (services, troops); that may be hired; moved by the love of money; greedy of gain; venal; sordid; entered into from motives of gain (a *mercenary* marriage).—*n.* One who is hired; a soldier that is hired into foreign service.—**Mercenarily,** mėr'se-na-ri-li, *adv.* In a mercenary manner.—**Mercenariness,** mėr'se-na-ri-nes, *n.* The quality or character of being mercenary.

Mercerize, mėr'sėr-īz, *v.t.* [From John *Mercer,* the originator.] To subject to treatment with certain chemical agents, as caustic soda, sulphuric acid, zinc chloride, &c., in order to produce desired results on textile fabrics, especially cotton goods.

Merchant, mėr'chant, *n.* [O.Fr. *marchant,* from L. *mercans, mercantis,* ppr. of *mercor, mercatus,* to barter, to deal, from *merx,* merchandise; akin *mercer, mercenary, mercantile, mercy,* &c.; same root as *merit.*] One who carries on trade on a large scale; especially, a man who exports and imports goods and sells them by wholesale.—*a.* Relating to trade or commerce; commercial.—**Merchantable,** mėr'chant-a-bl, *a.* Fit for market; such as is usually sold in market.—**Merchantman, Merchant-ship,** mėr'chant-man, *n.* A ship engaged in commerce, as distinguished from a ship of war; a trading vessel.—**Merchant Marine,** the commercial vessels belonging to a nation.—**Merchant-prince,** *n.* A great merchant; a merchant of great wealth.—**Merchantry,** mėr'chant-ri, *n.* The business of a merchant; merchants collectively.—**Merchant-seaman,** *n.* A seaman employed in a merchant-ship.—**Merchant-service,** *n.* The mercantile marine or trading ships of a country.—**Merchant-tailor,** *n.* A tailor who furnishes the materials for the garments which he makes.—**Merchandise,** mėr'chan-diz, *n.* [Fr. *marchandise,* from *marchand,* a merchant.] The objects of commerce; wares; goods; commodities.

Merciful, &c. Under MERCY.

Mercury, mėr'kū-ri, *n.* [L. *Mercurius,* from root of *merces,* wares. MERCHANT.] The name of a Roman divinity, identified in later times with the Greek Hermes; quicksilver, one of the heavier metals and the only metal that is liquid at common temperatures; *astron.* the planet that revolves round the sun within the orbit of the planet Venus and next to it; a newspaper; a messenger; an intelligencer.—*Mercury-vapor* lamp, a lamp in which an electric discharge, passing through mercury vapor, produces ultraviolet and actinic radiation.—**Mercurial,** mėr-kū'ri-al, *a.* [L. *mercurialis.*] Like the god Mercury or what belongs to him; light-hearted; gay; sprightly; flighty; fickle; pertaining to quicksilver; containing or consisting of quicksilver or mercury.—*n.* A preparation of mercury used as a drug.—**Mercurially,** mėr-kū'ri-al-li, *adv.* In a mercurial manner.—**Mercuric, Mercurous,** mėr-kū'rik, mėr'kū-rus, *a.* Containing mercury; terms used as part of the name of certain chemical compounds, the former indicating that they contain a smaller proportion of mercury than the latter.—**Mercurification,** mėr-kū'ri-fi-kā"shon, *n.* The act or process of mercurifying.—**Mercurify,** mėr-kū'ri-fī, *v.t.* To obtain mercury from metallic minerals; to combine or mingle with mercury; to mercurialize.

Mercy, mėr'si, *n.* [Fr. *merci,* from L. *merces, mercedis,* pay, recompense, in L.L. mercy, from stem of *mereo,* to deserve (whence *merit*); akin *mercantile, merchant, market, amerce,* &c.] That benevolence, mildness, or tenderness of heart which disposes a person to overlook injuries; the disposition that tempers justice and leads to the infliction of a lighter punishment than law or justice will warrant; clemency; an act or exercise of mercy or favour; a blessing; compassion; pity; unrestrained exercise of will or authority: often in the phrase *at one's mercy,* that is, completely in one's power.—*To cry mercy,* to beg pardon.—*Sisters of Mercy,* members of female religious communities founded for the purpose of nursing the sick and the performance of similar works of charity and mercy. — **Mercy-seat,** *n.* The place of mercy or forgiveness; the covering of the ark of the covenant among the Jews.—**Merciful,** mėr'si-fụl, *a.* Full of mercy; unwilling to punish for injuries; compassionate; tender; not cruel.—**Mercifully,** mėr'si-fụl-li, *adv.* In a merciful manner.—**Mercifulness,** mėr'si-fụl-nes, *n.*—**Merciless,** mėr'si-les, *a.* Destitute of mercy; pitiless; hard-hearted. — **Mercilessly,** mėr'si-les-li, *adv.* In a merciless manner.—**Mercilessness,** mėr'si-les-nes, *n.*

Mere, mēr, *a.* [O.Fr. *mier,* L. *merus,* pure, unmixed.] This or that and nothing else; simple; absolute, entire, utter (*mere* folly).—**Merely,** mēr'li, *adv.* Solely; simply; only; for this and no other purpose.

Mere, mēr, *n.* [A.Sax. *mere,* a mere or lake; D. *meer,* Icel. *marr,* Goth. *marei,* G. *meer,* the sea, a lake; allied to *moor, marsh, morass,* and L. *mare,* the sea. Hence the *mer* in *mer*maid.] A pool. (*Obs.*)

Mere, mēr, *n.* [A.Sax. *maere, gemaere,* O.D. *meer,* a boundary; Icel. *moerr,* borderland.] A boundary; a boundary-stone.

Merenchyma, mē-ren'ki-ma, *n.* [Gr. *meros,* part, and *enchyma,* an infusion.] *Bot.* spherical cellular tissue.

Meretricious, mer-ē-trish'us, *a.* [L. *meretricius,* from *meretrix, meretricis,* a prostitute, from *mereo,* to earn. MERIT, MERCY.] Pertaining to prostitutes; alluring by false show; having a gaudy but deceitful appearance; showy, but in bad taste.—**Meretriciously,** mer-ē-trish'us-li, *adv.* In a meretricious manner.—**Meretriciousness,** mer-ē-trish'us-nes, *n.*

Merganser, mėr-gan'sėr, *n.* [L. *mergo,* to dive, and *anser,* a goose.] A diving duck having a narrow bill and subsisting on fish.

Merge, mėrj, *v.t.*—*merged, merging.* [L. *mergo,* to dip, to dive; seen also in *emerge, immerge, immersion, submerge.*] To cause to be swallowed up, absorbed, or incorporated; to sink; to bury; chiefly figurative (the smaller grief was *merged* in the greater).—*v.i.* To be sunk, swallowed, incorporated, or absorbed.—**Merger,** mėrj'ėr, *n.* The absorption of one estate, contract, or interest, in another.

Mericarp, mer'i-kärp, *n.* [Gr. *meros,* a part, and *karpos,* fruit.] *Bot.* one of the halves of the double fruits or seeds of umbelliferous plants.

Meridian, me-rid'i-an, *a.* [L. *meridianus,* from *meridies,* for *medidies,* mid-day—*medius,* middle, and *dies,* day.] Pertaining to mid-day or noon, when the sun is on the meridian.—*Meridian altitude of the sun* or *stars,* their altitude when on the meridian of the place where they are observed.—*n.* Mid-day; noon; *fig.* the culmination; the point of greatest splendour; one of the innumerable imaginary circles or lines on the surface of the earth passing through both poles, and through any other given place, and used in denoting the longitudes of places; a similar imaginary line in the heavens passing through the poles of the heavens and the zenith of any place (often called a *celestial meridian*), noon therefore occurring at all places directly under this line when the sun is on it.—*First meridian,* that from which all the others are counted eastward and westward, and from which longitudes are reckoned, usually the meridian of Greenwich.—*Meridian of a globe,* the brazen circle in which it turns, and by which it is supported.—*Magnetic meridian,* one of the great circles which pass through the magnetic poles.—**Meridional,** me-rid'i-on-al, *a.* Pertaining to the meridian; hence, southern; having a southern aspect.—*Meridional distance, navig.* the distance or departure from the meridian; the easting or westing.—**Meridionality,** me-rid'i-on-al"i-ti, *n.* The state of being meridional.—**Meridionally,** me-rid'i-on-al-li, *adv.* In the direction of the meridian.

Meringue, mė-rang', *n.* A light delicacy made of powdered sugar and the beaten whites of eggs.

Merino, me-rē'nō, *n.* [Sp. *merino,* moving from pasture to pasture, from *merino,* an inspector of sheep-walks, from L.L. *majorinus,* from L. *major,* greater.] A breed of sheep with long, fine wool; a soft twilled fabric.

Merismatic, mer-is-mat'ik, *a.* [Gr. *merismos,* division, from *merizō,* to divide, *meros,* a part. *Zool.* and *bot.* dividing by the formation of internal partitions; taking place by internal partition into cells or segments.

Meristem, me-ris'tem, *n.* [Gr. *merizō,* I divide.] *Bot.* embryonic tissue.

Merit, mer'it, *n.* [Fr. *mérite*, L. *meritum*, what is deserved, from *mereo*, to earn or deserve. MERCY.] Desert of good or evil; excellence entitling to honour or reward; worth; reward deserved or merited; *pl.* the rights of a case or question; the essential points or circumstances.—*v.t.* To deserve, in a good sense; to have a right to claim, as a reward, regard, honour; to deserve, in a bad sense; to incur.—**Merited**, mer'i-ted, *a.* Deserved. — **Meritedly**, mer'i-ted-li, *adv.* Deservedly. — **Meritorious**, mer-i-tō'ri-us, *a.* [L. *meritorius*.] Possessing merit; deserving reward or praise; praiseworthy. — **Meritoriously**, mer-i-tō'ri-us-li, *adv.* In a meritorious manner.—**Meritoriousness**, mer-i-tō'ri-us-nes, *n.*—**Merit system**, *n.* The system whereby government employees receive appointment and promotion on the basis of ability rather than by political pressure.

Merle, mėrl, *n.* [Fr. *merle*, a blackbird.] The European blackbird.—**Merlin**, mėr'lin, *n.* [Fr. *émerillon*, from L. *merula*, a blackbird, meaning blackbird hawk.] A courageous species of hawk about the size of a blackbird.

Merlon, mėr'lon, *n.* [Fr. *merlon*; comp. L. *mœrus*, for *murus*, a wall.] *Fort.* the part of an embattled parapet which lies between two embrasures.

Mermaid, Mermaiden, mėr'mād, mėr'mā-dn, *n.* [*Mer* is same as *mere*, a lake.] A fabled marine creature, having the upper part like a woman and the lower like a fish. —**Merman**, mėr'man, *n.* The male corresponding to *mermaid*; a man of the sea, with the tail of a fish instead of legs.

Meroblast, mer'ō-blast, *n.* [Gr. *meros*, a part, and *blastos*, a sprout.] *Biol.* an ovum consisting both of a protoplasmic or germinal portion and an albuminous or nutritive one, as contradistinguished from *holoblast*, an ovum entirely germinal. — **Meroblastic**, mer-ō-blas'tik, *a.* Pertaining to a meroblast.

Merohedral, mer-o-hed'ral, *n.* [Gr. *meros*, part, *hedra*, seat, base.] Of crystals with less than the admissible number of faces.

Merosome, mer'ō-sōm, *n.* [Gr. *meros*, a part, and *sōma*, a body.] *Zool.* one of the sections or parts of which an animal is formed.

Merovingian, mer-o-ving'i-an, *a.* Of or relating to the Merovingian line of Franks founded by Clovis, and lasting from A.D. 500 to 750.

Merry, mer'i, *a.* [O.E. *myrie*, *murie*, A. Sax. *merg*, *mirig*, perhaps from root of *mearo*, tender, soft, delicate; or from the Celtic; comp Ir. and Gael, *maer*, Gael. *mir*, merry.] Pleasant; causing cheerfulness; gay and noisy; in overflowing good spirits; hilarious; mirthful; sportive. — *To make merry*, to be jovial; to indulge in hilarity; to feast with mirth.—**Merrily**, mer'i-li, *adv.* In a merry manner; with mirth.—**Merriment**, mer'i-ment, *n.* Gaiety with laughter or noise; mirth; hilarity.—**Merriness**, mer'i-nes, *n.* The state or quality of being merry.—**Merry-andrew**, *n.* [From Andrew Borde, a physician to Henry VIII, who attracted attention by his facetious speeches.] One whose business is to make sport for others; a buffoon.—**Merry Dancers**, *n.* The Aurora Borealis. — **Merry-go-round**, *n.* A circular frame, made to revolve, and on which children are treated to a ride.—**Merry-making**, *n.* A convivial entertainment; a festival. — **Merry-man**, *n.* A merry-andrew; a buffoon; a clown.—**Merry-thought**, *n.* The furcula or forked bone of a fowl's breast.

Mesa, mā'sa, *n.* [Sp., from L. *mensa*, a table.] A table-land of small extent rising abruptly from a surrounding plain.

Mesalliance, mā'zal-yäns, *n.* [Fr.] A misalliance; an unequal marriage.

Mesaraic, mes-a-rā'ik, *a.* [Gr. *mesaraion* —*mesos*, middle, and *araia*, intestines.] *Anat.* pertaining to the mesentery; mesenteric.

Mesaticephalic, mes'a-ti-se-fal"ik, *a.* [Gr. *mesatos*, midmost, *kephalē*, head.] Having a medium cephalic index, between brachycephalic and dolichocephalic.

Meseems, mē-sēmz', *v. impersonal*—pret. *meseemed.* [Not properly a simple verb, being really an impersonal verb preceded by a pronoun in the dative = it seems to me. Comp. *methinks*.] It seems to me.

Mesencephalon, mes-en-sef'a-lon, *n.* [Gr. *mesos*, middle, and *enkephalos*, the brain.] The middle or central portion of the brain.

Mesentery, mes'en-tėr-i, *n.* [Gr. *mesenterion*—*mesos*, middle, and *enteron*, intestine.] A membrane in the cavity of the abdomen, the use of which is to retain the intestines and their appendages in a proper position.—**Mesenteric**, mes-en-tėr'ik, *a.* Pertaining to the mesentery. — **Mesenteritis**, mes'en-tėr-ī"tis, *n.* Inflammation of the mesentery.

Mesh, mesh, *n.* [A.Sax. *masc*, *max*, a noose, *mæscre*, a mesh, a net; D. *maas*, Dan. *maske*, Icel. *möskvi*, G. *masche*, a mesh; W. *masg*, a mesh, Lith. *megsti*, to knit, are allied.] The opening or space between the threads of a net; geared wheels.—*v.t.* To catch in a net; to ensnare.—**Meshwork**, *n.* Network.—**Meshy**, mesh'i, *a.* Formed like network.

Mesial, mē'zi-al, *a.* [Gr. *mesos*, middle.] Middle; median.—*Mesial line*, *mesial plane*, an imaginary line and plane dividing the body longitudinally into symmetrical halves, one towards the right and the other towards the left.

Meslin, Maslin, mez'lin, maz'lin, *n.* [From O.Fr. *mestillon*, from L.L. *mestillio*, mixed grain (Fr. *méteil*), from L. *mistum*, mixed. MIXTURE.] A mixed crop of different sorts of grain, as of wheat and rye.

Mesmerism, mez'mėr-izm, *n.* [After *Mesmer*, a German physician, who propounded the doctrine in 1778.] The doctrine that one person can exercise influence over the will and nervous system of another by virtue of a supposed emanation proceeding from him, or simply by the domination of his will over that of the person operated on; the influence itself; animal magnetism.—**Mesmeric, Mesmerical**, mez-mer'ik, mez-mer'i-kal, *a.* Pertaining to mesmerism. —**Mesmerist**, mez'mėr-ist, *n.* One who practises or believes in mesmerism.—**Mesmerization**, mez'mėr-i-zā"shon, *n.* The act of mesmerizing.—**Mesmerize**, mez'mėr-īz, *v.t.*—*mesmerized*, *mesmerizing.* To bring into a state of mesmeric sleep.—**Mesmerizer**, mez'mėr-īz-ėr, *n.* One who mesmerizes.

Mesne, mēn, *a.* [Norm. *mesne*, middle, from L. *medianus*, middle. MEAN, *a.*, middle.] *Law*, middle, intervening; as, a *mesne* lord, *i.e.* a lord who holds land of a superior but grants a part of it to another person.

Mesoblast, mes'o-blast, *n.* [Gr. *mesos*, middle, and *blastos*, a bud.] *Physiol.* the layer between the epiblast and hypoblast, the two primary layers of the embryo.

Mesocæcum, mes'o-sē-kum, *n.* [Gr. *mesos*, middle, and L. *cæcum*.] That part of the peritoneum which embraces the cæcum and its appendages.

Mesocarp, mes'o-kärp, *n.* [Gr. *mesos*, middle, and *karpos*, fruit.] *Bot.* the middle part or layer of the pericarp, immediately under the epicarp.

Mesocephalic, Mesocephalous, mes'-o-se-fal"ik, mes-o-sef'a-lus, *a.* [Gr. *mesos*, middle, and *kephalē*, the head.] A term applied to the human skull when it is of medium breadth.

Mesochilium, mes-o-kī'li-um, *n.* [Gr. *mesos*, middle, and *cheilos*, a lip.] *Bot.* the middle portion of the labellum of an orchid.

Mesocolon, mes'o-kō-lon, *n.* [Gr. *mesos*, middle, and E. *colon*.] *Anat.* that part of the mesentery to which the colon is attached.

Mesoderm, mes'o-dėrm, *n.* [Gr. *mesos*, middle, and *derma*, skin.] *Zool.* the middle layer of tissue between the ectoderm and the endoderm.

Mesogastric, mes-o-gas'trik, *a.* [Gr. *mesos*, middle, *gastēr*, the belly.] *Anat.* applied to the membrane which sustains the stomach, and by which it is attached to the abdomen.—**Mesogastrium**, mes-o-gas'tri-um, *n.* *Anat.* the umbilical region of the abdomen.

Mesogloea, me-sō-glē'a, *n.* [Gr. *mesos*, middle, *gloios*, a jelly.] In zoophytes, a middle layer of the body, often jelly-like.

Mesognathous, me-sog'na-thus, *a.* [Gr. *mesos*, middle, *gnathos*, jaw.] *Anthropol.* intermediate between prognathous and orthognathous.

Mesonephros, mes'ō-nef"ros, *n.* [Gr. *mesos*, middle, *nephros*, a kidney.] In vertebrates, the second of three successive renal organs.

Mesophlœum, mes-o-flē'um, *n.* [Gr. *mesos*, middle, *phloios*, bark.] *Bot.* the middle cellular layer of the bark.

Mesophyllum, mes-o-fil'lum or me-sof'il-lum, *n.* [Gr. *mesos*, middle, and *phyllon*, a leaf.] *Bot.* the tissue forming the fleshy part of a leaf between the upper and lower integuments.

Mesosperm, mes'o-spėrm, *n.* [Gr. *mesos*, middle, and *sperma*, seed.] *Bot.* a membrane of a seed, the second from the surface.

Mesothorax, mes-o-thō'raks, *n.* [Gr. *mesos*, middle, and *thōrax*, the chest.] *Entom.* the middle ring of the thorax.

Mesozoic, mes-o-zō'ik, *a.* [Gr. *mesos*, middle, and *zōē*, life.] *Geol.* pertaining to the secondary age, between the palæozoic and cainozoic.

Mesquite, mes'kēt, *n.* [Sp. *mezquite*, probably of American origin.] A leguminous shrub of southwestern U. S. and Mexico.

Mess, mes, *n.* [O.Fr. *mes*, a dish, a course of dishes at table; It. *messo*; properly that which is sent, from L. *missus*, pp. of *mitto*, to send. MISSION.] A dish or quantity of food set on a table at one time; food for a person at one meal; a number of persons who eat together at the same table, especially in the army or navy.—*v.i.* To take meals in common with others, as one of a mess; to associate at the same table.—**Mess-mate**, *n.* A regular associate in taking meals; a fellow-sailor.

Mess, mes, *n.* [Formerly *mesh*, which is same as *mash*, lit. a mixture.] A disorderly mixture; a state of dirt and disorder; *fig.* a situation of confusion or embarrassment; a muddle.

Message, mes'āj, *n.* [Fr. *message*, It. *messaggio*, L.L. *missaticum*, message, from L. *mitto*, *missum*, to send. MISSION.] Any communication, written or verbal, sent from one person to another; an official communication delivered by a messenger. —**Messenger**, mes'en-jėr, *n.* [O.E. *messager*, Fr. *messager*. The *n* has intruded as in *passenger*.] One who delivers a message or performs an errand; one who conveys dispatches from one government to another; an envoy; an emissary; a harbinger; a herald.—**Messenger boy**, *n.* A youth employed to deliver messages and run errands.

Messiah, mes-sī'a, *n.* [Heb. *māshiach*, anointed, from *māshach*, to anoint.] The deliverer and savior promised to the Hebrews; Christ, the Anointed; the Savior of the world.—**Messiahship**, mes-sī'a-ship, *n.* The office of the Savior.—**Messianic**, mes-sī-an'ik, *a.* Relating to the Messiah.

Messidor, mes'i-dor, *n.* [L. *messis*, harvest, *dōron*, gift.] The harvest month, or tenth month, in the French Revolution calendar.

Messieurs, mes'ėrz, *n.* [Fr. pl. of *Monsieur* (which see).] Sirs; gentlemen; the plural of *Mr.*, employed in addressing firms or companies of several persons, and generally contracted into *Messrs.*

Messuage, mes'wij, *n.* [O.Fr. *messuage*, *mesnage*, L.L. *messuagium*, *mansionaticum*, from L. *mansio*, a dwelling. MANSION.] *Law*, a dwelling-house, with the adjacent buildings, &c., appropriated to the use of the household; a manor house.

Mestizo, mes-tē′zō, *n.* [Sp. *mestizo*, from L. *mixtus*, pp. of *misceo*, to mix.] The offspring of a Caucasian and an East Indian, Malay, or Negro, or a Chinese and a Filipino; an individual of mixed breed. (*Latin America and the Philippines.*)

Met, met, pret. & pp. of *meet.*

Metabasis, me-tab′a-sis, *n.* [Gr., from *meta*, beyond, and *bainō*, to go.] *Rhet.* a passing from one thing to another; transition.

Metabolic, met-a-bol′ik, *a.* [Gr. *metabolē*, change.] Pertaining to change of food into living tissues or to excretion of waste.—**Metabolism**, me-tab′o-lizm, *n.* [Gr. *metabolē*, change.] *Physiol.* the final process by which nutritive matter is absorbed into the substance of cells or is prepared for excretion.—**Metabolize**, me-tab′o-līz, *v.t.* To subject to metabolism.

Metacarpus, met-a-kär′pus, *n.* [Gr. *meta*, beyond, *karpos*, the wrist.] *Anat.* the part of the hand between the wrist and the fingers.—**Metacarpal**, met-a-kär′pal, *a.* Pertaining to the metacarpus.

Metacenter, met-a-sen′tėr, *n.* [Gr. *meta*, beyond, and *kentron*, center.] *Physics*, that point in a floating body on the position of which its stability depends, and which must be above the center of gravity to prevent the body from turning over.

Metachronism, me-tak′ron-izm, *n.* [Gr. *meta*, beyond, and *chronos*, time.] An error committed in chronology by placing an event after its real time.

Metacism, met′a-sizm, *n.* [L. *metacismus*, Gr. *metakismos.*] A defect in pronouncing the letter *m.*

Metage, mēt′āj, *n.* [From *mete.*] Measurement of coal; charge for measuring.

Metagenesis, met-a-jen′e-sis, *n.* [Gr. *meta*, after, change, and *genesis.*] *Zool.* the changes of form which the representative of a species undergoes in passing, by a series of successively generated individuals, from the ovum or egg to the perfect state; alternation of generation.—**Metagenetic**, **Metagenic**, met′a-je-net″ik, met-a-jen′ik, *a.* Pertaining to metagenesis.

Metagrammatism, met-a-gram′mat-izm, *n.* [Gr. *meta*, beyond, and *gramma*, a letter.] The transposition of the letters of a name into such a connection as to express some perfect sense applicable to the person named; anagrammatism.

Metal, met′al, *n.* [L. *metallum*, from Gr. *metallon*, a mine, a metal—*meta*, after, and root meaning to go or search.] A name given to certain substances of which gold, silver, iron, lead, are examples, having a luster and generally fusible by heat; the name given by workers in glass, pottery, &c., to the material on which they operate when in a state of fusion; gunpower of a war vessel.—*Road metal*, stones broken small, used in macadamized roads.—*v.t.—metalled., metalling.* To put metal on; to cover, as roads, with broken stones or metal.—**Metal-broker**, *n.* One who trades or deals in metals.—**Metallic**, me-tal′ik, *a.* [L. *metallicus.*] Pertaining to metals; consisting of metal; like a metal.—*Metallic oxide*, a compound of metal and oxygen.—*Metallic paper*, paper the surface of which is washed over with a solution of whiting, lime, and size, and which is written on with a pewter pencil.—**Metalliferous**, met-al-if′ėr-us, *a.* Producing metal; yielding metal.—**Metalliform**, me-tal′i-form, *a.* Having the form of metal; like metal.—**Metalline**, met′al-īn, *a.* Consisting of or containing metal.—**Metalling**, met′al-ing, *n.* Metal for roads.—**Metallist**, met′al-ist, *n.* A worker in metals, or one skilled in metals.—**Metallize**, met′al-īz, *v.t.—metallized, metallizing.* To form into metal; to give its proper metallic properties to (an ore).—**Metallography**, met-al-og′ra-fi, *n.* The science or description of metals: the study of metals by the microscope.—**Metallographist**, met-al-og′ra-fist, *n.* A writer on metallography.—**Metalloid**, met′al-oid, *n.* A metallic base of a fixed alkali or alkaline earth; any non-metallic elementary substance.—*a.* Like metal; having the form or appearance of a metal.—**Metalloidal**, met-al-oi′dal, *a.* Metalloid.—**Metallurgy**, met′al-ėr-ji, *n.* [Gr. *ergon*, work.] The art of working metals; the process of separating them from other matters in the ore, smelting, refining, &c.—**Metallurgic**, **Metallurgical**, met-al-ėr′jik, met-al-ėr′ji-kal, *a.* Pertaining to metallurgy.—**Metallurgist**, met′al-ėr-jist, *n.* One engaged in metallurgy.

Metalepsis, met-a-lep′sis, *n.* [Gr. *metalēpsis*, participation—*meta*, with, and *lambanō*, to take.] *Rhet.* the continuation of a trope or figure in one word through a succession of significations, or the union of two or more tropes of a different kind in one word.—**Metaleptic**, **Metaleptical**, met-a-lep′tik, met-a-lep′ti-kal, *a.* Pertaining to metalepsis.—**Metaleptically**, met-a-lep′ti-kal-li, *adv.* In a metaleptical manner; by transposition.

Metalloid, **Metallurgy**, &c. Under METAL.

Metalogical, met-a-loj′i-kal, *a.* [Gr. prefix *meta*, beyond, and E. *logical.*] Beyond the province of logic; transcending the sphere of logic.

Metamere, met′a-mēr, *n.* [Gr. *meta*, with or among, and *meros*, a part.] *Compar. anat.* one of a series of similar parts; in segmented animals, one of the segments.—**Metamerism**, me-tam′ėr-izm, *n.* *Chem.* the character in certain compound bodies, differing in chemical properties, of having the same elements combined in the same proportion and with the same molecular weight.

Metamorphosis, met-a-mor′fō-sis, *n.* [Gr. *metamorphōsis—meta*, denoting change, and *morphē*, form, shape.] Change of form, shape, or structure; transformation; *zool.* the alterations which an animal undergoes after its exclusion from the egg, and which alter extensively the general form and life of the individual; such changes as those from the caterpillar to the perfect butterfly.—**Metamorphic**, met-a-mor′fik, *a.* Pertaining to or producing metamorphosis.—*Metamorphic rocks, geol.* stratified rocks of any age whose texture has been rendered less or more crystalline by subterranean heat, pressure, or chemical agency; the lowest and non-fossiliferous stratified rocks, originally deposited from water and crystallized by subsequent agencies.—**Metamorphism**, met-a-mor′fizm, *n.* The process of metamorphosing; the change undergone by stratified rocks under the influence of heat and chemical or mechanical agents.—**Metamorphose**, met-a-mor′fōs, *v.t.—metamorphosed, metamorphosing.* To change into a different form; to change the shape or character of; to transform.—**Metamorphoses**, *n. pl.* The poem by Ovid dealing with the various changes of human beings and others into different characters.—**Metamorphoser**, met-a-mor′fōs-ėr, *n.* One that transforms.

Metanephros, met′a-nef″ros, *n.* [Gr. *meta*, after, *nephros*, a kidney.] In vertebrates, the third of three successive renal organs. The definitive kidney of mammals, birds, and reptiles.

Metaphor, met′a-fėr, *n.* [Gr. *metaphora*, from *metapherō*, to transfer—*meta*, over, and *pherō*, to carry.] A figure of speech founded on resemblance, by which a word is transferred from an object to which it properly belongs to another in such a manner that a comparison is implied, though not formally expressed. Thus, 'that man is a fox', is a metaphor; but 'that man is like a fox', is a simile or comparison.—**Metaphoric**, **Metaphorical**, met-a-for′ik, met-a-for′i-kal, *a.* Pertaining to metaphor; comprising a metaphor; not literal; figurative.—**Metaphorically**, met-a-for′i-kal-li, *adv.* In a metaphorical manner; not literally.—**Metaphoricalness**, met-a-for′i-kal-nes, *n.*

Metaphrase, **Metaphrasis**, met′a-frāz, me-taf′ra-zis, *n.* [Gr. *metaphrasis—meta*, according to or with, and *phrasis*, phrase.] A verbal translation of one language into another, word for word: opposed to *paraphrase.*—**Metaphrast**, met′a-frast, *n.* A literal translator.—**Metaphrastic**, **Metaphrastical**, met-a-fras′tik, met-a-fras′ti-kal, *a.* Close or literal in translation.

Metaphysics, met-a-fiz′iks, *n.* [L. *metaphysica*, pl. neut. from Gr. *meta*, after, and *physica*, physics, from *physis*, nature, the science of natural bodies or *physics* being regarded as properly first in the order of studies, and the science of mind or intelligence to be the second.] That science which seeks to trace the branches of human knowledge to their first principles in the constitution of our nature, or to find what is the nature of the human mind and its relations to the external world; the science that seeks to know the ultimate grounds of being or what it is that really exists, embracing both psychology and ontology.—**Metaphysic**, met-a-fiz′ik, *n.* Metaphysics.—**Metaphysic**, **Metaphysical**, met-a-fiz′i-kal, *a.* Pertaining to metaphysics; according to rules or principles of metaphysics.—**Metaphysically**, met-a-fiz′i-kal-li, *adv.* In a metaphysical manner.—**Metaphysician**, met-a-fi-zish′an, *n.* One who is versed in metaphysics.

Metaphyta, met′a-fīt″a, *n.* [Gr. *meta*, after, *phyton*, a plant.] The higher or many-celled plants. Cp. PROTOPHYTA.

Metaplasm, met′a-plazm, *n.* [Gr. *metaplasmos*, transformation—*meta*, over, and *plassō*, to form.] *Gram.* a change in a word by adding, transposing, or retrenching a syllable or letter.

Metasome, met′a-sōm, *n.* [Gr. *meta*, after, and *sōma*, the body.] The posterior portion of the body of a cephalopod.

Metastasis, me-tas′ta-sis, *n.* [Gr. *metastasis—meta*, over, and *stasis*, position.] *Med.* a translation or removal of a disease from one part to another.—**Metastatic**, met-a-stat′ik, *a.* Relating to metastasis.

Metatarsus, met-a-tär′sus, *n.* [Gr. *meta*, beyond, and *tarsos*, tarsus.] The middle of the foot, or part between the ankle and the toes.—**Metatarsal**, met-a-tär′sal, *a.* Belonging to the metatarsus.—*n.* A bone of the metatarsus.

Metathesis, me-tath′ē-sis, *n.* [Gr. *metathesis—meta*, over, and *tithēmi*, to set.] *Gram.* transposition of the letters, sounds, or syllables of a word.—**Metathetic**, **Metathetical**, met-a-thet′ik, met-a-thet′i-kal, *a.* Relating to metathesis.

Metathorax, met-a-thō′raks, *n.* [Gr. *meta*, after, and *thōrax*, the chest.] *Entom.* the third and last segment of the thorax.

Métayer, me-tā′yėr, *n.* [Fr. *mētayer*, L.L. *medietarius*, from L. *medietas*, middle state, from *medius*, middle.] A cultivator who tills the soil on condition of receiving a share of its produce, the owner furnishing the whole or part of the stock, tools, &c. (*Brit. and Europ. Hist.*)

Metazoa, met-a-zō′a, *n. pl.* [Gr. *meta*, after, *zōon*, animal.] All animals that are higher in the scale of life than the protozoa.—**Metazoan**, met-a-zō′an, *a.* and *n.* Belonging to one of the metazoa.

Mete, mēt, *v.t.—meted, meting.* [A.Sax. *metan* = D. *meten*, Goth. *mitan*, G. *messen*, to measure; Icel. *meta*, to value; from root of L. *modus*, a measure (whence *mode*); Gr. *metron*, a measure; Skr. *mā*, to measure.] To measure; to ascertain the quantity, dimensions, or capacity of by any rule or standard.—**Mete-wand**, **Mete-yard**, *n.* A measuring rod.

Metempirical, met-em-pir′i-kal, *a.* [Gr. *meta*, beyond, and *empeiria*, experience, from *en*, in, and *peira*, trial, experiment.] *Metaph.* beyond or outside of experience; not based on experience; transcendental; a priori: opposed to *empirical* or *experiential.*—**Metempiric**, **Metempiricist**, met-em-pir′ik, met-em-pir′i-sist, *n.* One who believes in the transcendental philosophy.—**Metempiricism**, met-em-pir′i-sizm, *n.* *Metaph.* the system of philosophy based on a priori reasoning; transcendentalism.

Metempsychosis, me-tem'si-kō"sis, *n.* [Gr. *meta*, denoting change, *en*, in, and *psychē*, soul.] Transmigration; the passing of the soul of a man after death into some other animal body.

Metensomatosis, me-ten'sō-ma-tō"sis, *n.* [Gr. *meta*, implying change, *en*, in, and *sōma*, *sōmatos*, the body.] The transference of the elements of one body into another body and their conversion into its substance, as by decomposition and assimilation.

Meteor, mē'tē-ėr, *n.* [From Gr. *meteōros*, raised on high—*meta*, beyond, and *aeirō*, to raise.] A transient celestial body that enters the earth's atmosphere with terrific velocity, white with heat generated by the resistance of the air.—**Meteoric**, mē-tē-or'ik, *a.* Pertaining to a meteor or meteors; *fig.* transiently or irregularly brilliant.—*Meteoric iron*, iron as found in meteoric stones.—*Meteoric stones*, those aerolites which fall from the heavens on the surface of the earth, and usually consist of metallic iron and certain silicates.—*Meteoric showers*, showers of shooting-stars occurring periodically.—**Meteorite**, mē'tē-ėr-it, *n.* A meteoric stone; an aerolite; especially a meteor which has reached the earth's crust without being completely consumed.—**Meteorograph**, mē'tē-ėr-ō-graf, *n.* An instrument or apparatus for registering meteorological phenomena.—**Meteorology**, mē'tē-ėr-ol"o-ji, *n.* [Gr. *meteōrologia*.] The science which treats of atmospheric phenomena, more especially as connected with or in relation to weather and climate.—**Meteorologic**, **Meteorological**, mē'tē-ėr-ō-loj"ik, mē'tē-ėr-ō-loj"-i-kal, *a.* Pertaining to meteorology or to the atmosphere and its phenomena.—**Meteorologist**, mē'tē-ėr-ol"o-jist, *n.* A person skilled in meteorology.—**Meteoromancy**, mē'tē-ėr-ō-man-si, *n.* [Gr. *manteia*, divination.] Divination by meteoric phenomena.

Meter, mē'tėr, *n.* [Fr. *mètre*, L. *metrum*, meter, Gr. *metron*, meter, a measure; same root as in *measure*, *mete*.] Rhythmical arrangement of syllables into verses, stanzas, strophes, &c.; rhythm; measure; verse.—**Metric**, **Metrical**, met'rik, met'ri-kal, *a.* Pertaining to rhythm or meter; consisting of verse.—**Metrically**, met'ri-kal-li, *adv.* In a metrical manner; according to poetic measure.—**Metrist**, mē'trist, *n.* A composer of verses.

Meter, mē'tėr; Fr. pron. mā-tr, *n.* [Fr. *mètre*, from Gr. *metron*, a measure. See above.] A French measure of length, equal to 39.37 inches, the standard of linear measure.—**Metric**, met'rik, *a.* Pertaining to a system of weights, measures, and moneys, first adopted in France—the decimal system. Under DECIMAL.—**Metrical**, met'ri-kal, *a.* Pertaining to or employed in measuring.—**Metrochrome**, met'rō-krōm, *n.* [Gr. *chrōma*, color.] An instrument for measuring colors.—**Metrograph**, met'rō-graf, *n.* An apparatus on a railway engine which measures and records the rate of speed at any moment, and the time of arrival and departure at each station.—**Metrology**, mē-trol'o-ji, *n.* An account of weights and measures; the art and science of mensuration.—**Metronome**, met'rō-nōm, *n.* [Gr. *nomos*, a law.] An instrument, consisting of a pendulum set in motion by clock-work, that determines the quickness or slowness of musical compositions.—**Metronomy**, mē-tron'o-mi, *n.* The measuring of musical time by the metronome.

Meter, mē'tėr, *n.* [From *mete*.] One who or that which measures; an instrument that measures and records automatically, as a gas-meter, water-meter, &c.

Methane, me'thān, *n.* Marsh gas (CH_4), the simplest hydrocarbon

Metheglin, mē-theg'lin, *n* [W *meddyglyn*—*medd*, mead, and *llyn*, liquor.] A Welsh variety of the liquor mead

Method, meth'od, *n.* [Fr. *méthode*, L. *methodus*, from Gr. *methodos*—*meta*, after, and *hodos*, a way.] A way or mode by which we proceed to the attainment of some aim; mode or manner of procedure; logical or scientific arrangement or mode of acting; systematic or orderly procedure; system; *nat. hist.* principle of classification (the Linnæan *method*).—**Methodic**, **Methodical**, meth-od'ik, meth-od'i-kal, *a.* Characterized by method; systematic; orderly.—**Methodically**, meth-od'i-kal-li, *adv.* In a methodical manner.—**Methodics**, meth-od'iks, *n.* The science of method.—**Methodism**, meth'od-izm, *n.* The doctrines and worship of the *Methodists*.—**Methodist**, meth'od-ist, *n.* One characterized by strict adherence to method; one of a sect of Christians founded by John Wesley, so called from the regularity of their lives and the strictness of their observance of religious duties.—**Methodistic**, **Methodistical**, meth-o-dis'tik, meth-od-is'ti-kal, *a.* Relating to method or the Methodists.—**Methodistically**, meth-o-dis'ti-kal-li, *adv.* In a methodistical manner.—**Methodize**, meth'od-iz, *v.t.*—*methodized*, *methodizing*. To reduce to method; to dispose in due order.—**Methodizer**, meth'od-iz-ėr, *n.* One who methodizes.—**Methodology**, meth-od-ol'o-ji, *n.* The science of method or of classification.

Methyl, mēth'il, *n.* [Gr. *meta*, after, with, and *hylē*, wood.] A univalent hydrocarbon radical (CH_3).—**Methylamine**, me-thil'-a-min, *n.* A colorless gas having a strong ammoniacal odor, and resembling ammonia in many of its reactions.—**Methylated**, meth'i-lā-ted, *a.* Impregnated or mixed with methyl.—*Methylated spirit*, ordinary, or ethyl, alcohol denatured with wood alcohol, which renders it unfit for drinking.—**Methylic**, me-thil'ik, *a.* Pertaining to methyl.

Methystic, me-this'tik, *a.* [Gr. *methystikos*, from *methy*, wine.] Intoxicating.—*n.* An intoxicant.

Meticulous, me-tik'ū-lus, *a.* [Fr. *méticuleux*, L. *metus*, fear.] Timidly scrupulous; too careful or fastidious.

Metier, mā-tē-ā, *n.* [Fr.] Profession; specialty; rôle.

Metis, mē'tis, *n.* [Fr. on analogy of *mestizo* (q.v.).] A child of white and American Indian parents (*Canada*): an octoroon (*U.S.*).

Metonic, mē-ton'ik, *a.* Pertaining to *Meton*, an ancient astronomer.—*Metonic cycle*, the cycle or period of nineteen years, in which the phases of the moon return to the same days of the month.

Metonymy, me-ton'i-mi, *n.* [Gr. *metōnymia*—*meta*, denoting change, and *onoma*, a name.] *Rhet.* a figure by which one word is put for another on account of some actual relation between the things signified, as when we say, 'We read *Virgil*', that is, his *poems* or *writings*.—**Metonymic**, **Metonymical**, met-ō-nim'ik, met-ō-nim'i-kal, *a.* Pertaining to metonymy.

Metope, met'o-pē, *n.* [Gr. *metopē*—*meta*, between, and *opē*, an aperture.] *Arch.* the space between the triglyphs of the Doric frieze.

Metoposcopy, met-ō-pos'ko-pi, *n.* [Gr. *metōpon*, forehead, and *skopeō*, to view.] The study of physiognomy

Metre, mē'tėr, *n* METER.

Metronymic, met-rō-nim'ik, *n.* and *a.* [Gr. *mētrōnymikos*—*mētēr*, *mētros*, a mother, and *onoma*, a name] A term applied to a name derived from a mother, as opposed to *patronymic*.

Metropolis, mē-trop'o-lis, *n.* [Gr. *mētropolis*—*mētēr*, *mētros*, a mother, and *polis*, a city, properly a mother-city in relation to its colonies.] The chief city or capital of a kingdom, state, or country; the see or seat of a metropolitan bishop.—**Metropolitan**, met-rō-pol'i-tan, *a.* Belonging to a metropolis; *eccles.* having the authority of a metropolitan; proceeding from a metropolitan.—*n.* *Eccles.* a bishop having authority over the other bishops of a province; an archbishop; *Greek Ch.* a dignitary intermediate between patriarchs and archbishops.—**Metropolitanate**, met-rō-pol'i-tan-āt, *n.* The office or see of a metropolitan bishop.—**Metropolitic**, **Metropolitical**, met-rō-pol'i-tik, met-rō-pō-lit"i-kal, *a.* Pertaining to a metropolis; metropolitan.

Metrotomy, mē-trot'o-mi, *n.* [Gr. *mētra*, womb, *tomē*, cutting.] The operation of cutting into the womb; hysterotomy.

Mettle, met'l, *n.* [Merely an altered spelling of *metal*, which was formerly used in the same sense.] Moral or physical constitution; stuff or material (to try what *mettle* he is made of); temper; spirit; constitutional ardor; courage; fire.—*To put a man on* or *to his mettle*, to stimulate a man to do his uttermost; to put him where he must do his utmost.—**Mettled**, met'ld, *a.* Full of mettle; high-spirited; ardent; full of fire.—**Mettlesome**, met'l-sum, *a.* Full of mettle or spirit; brisk; fiery.—**Mettlesomely**, met'l-sum-li, *adv.* In a mettlesome manner.—**Mettlesomeness**, met'l-sum-nes, *n.* The state of being mettlesome.

Mew, mū, *n.* [A.Sax. *maew*, a gull or mew = Sc. *maw*, D. *meeuw*, G. *mōve*, Icel. *már*, a mew.] A sea-mew; a gull.

Mew, mū, *n.* [Fr. *mue*, a molting, a mew or cage, from L.L. *muta*, a mew, from L. *mutare*, to change. MUTABLE.] The molting of a hawk; a cage for hawks or other birds while molting; a coop for fowls; a place of confinement in general.—*v.t.* To shed or cast; to molt; to shut up, inclose, confine, as in a cage or other inclosure.—*v.i.* To cast the feathers; to molt.—**Mews**, mūz, *n. pl.* The royal stables in London, England, so called because built where the king's hawks were once *mewed* or confined; hence (with verbs, &c., in *sing.*), a place where carriage-horses are kept in large towns; a lane or alley in which stables or mews are situated.

Mew, mū, *v.i.* [Imitative, and also written *meaw*, *miaw*, &c.; comp. W. *mewian*, G. *miauen*, to mew.] To cry as a cat.—*n.* The cry of a cat.—**Mewl**, mūl, *v.i.* [Imitative; comp. *miaul*, Fr. *miauler*.] To cry or squall, as a child. (*Shak.*)—*n.* The cry of a child.

Mezereon, me-zē'rē-on, *n.* [Fr. *mézereon*, Sp. *mezereon*, from Ar. and Per. *māzariyūn*, the camellia.] A common garden shrub whose fragrant pink flowers appear in spring before the leaves expand.

Mezzanine, mez'za-nēn, *n.* [It. *mezzanino*, from *mezzo*, middle. MEZZO.] *Arch.* an entresol or low story between two higher ones.

Mezzo, med'zō or met'zō, *a.* [It., from L. *medius*, middle.]—*Mus.* middle; mean.—*Mezzo soprano*, a treble voice of medium range, lower than soprano and higher than contralto.—**Mezzorilievo**, med'zō-rē-lē'-vō, *n.* Middle relief.—**Mezzotint**, **Mezzotinto**, med'zō-tint, med-zō-tin'tō, *n.* [It. *mezzo*, middle, *tinto*, tint.] A manner of engraving on copper or steel in imitation of drawing in India ink, the lights being scraped and burnished out of a prepared dark ground.

Mi, mē, *n.* The third note in the musical scale, between *re* and *fa*.

Miasma, mi-az'ma, *n.* pl. **Miasmata**, mi-az'ma-ta. [Gr. *miasma*, *miasmatos*, from *miainō*, to stain, sully.] Evil-smelling vapor, formerly supposed to be the effluvia or fine particles of any putrefying bodies, rising and floating in the atmosphere, and considered to be noxious to health; noxious emanation.—**Miasmal**, mi-az'mal, *a* Containing miasma; miasmatic.—**Miasmatic**, **Miasmatical**, mi-az-mat'ik, mi-az-mat'i-kal, *a.* Pertaining to miasma

Miaul, myal, *v.i.* [MEW.] To cry as a cat or kitten; to mew

Mica, mī'ka, *n.* [L. *mico*, to glitter.] A mineral of a foliated structure, consisting of thin flexible laminæ or scales, having a shining and almost metallic lustre.—*Mica schist, mica slate*, a metamorphic rock composed of mica and quartz, highly fissile and passing by insensible gradations into clay-slate.—**Micaceous**, mī-kā'shus, *a.* Pertaining to or containing mica; resembling mica or partaking of its properties.—*Micaceous rocks*, rocks of which mica is the chief ingredient, as mica slate.—*Micaceous schist*, mica schist.

Mice, mīs, *n.* pl. of *mouse*.

Michaelmas, mik'el-mas, *n.* [*Michael*, and *mass*, a feast.] The feast of St. *Michael*, the archangel, which falls on the 29th of September.

Miche, mich, *v.i.* [O.Fr. *muchier*, *mucher*, to hide, to skulk.] To skulk; to retire or shrink from view. (*Dial.*)—**Micher**, mich'ėr, *n.* One who skulks.—**Miching**, mich'ing, *p.* and *a.* Skulking; mean.

Mickle, mik'l, *a.* [A.Sax. *micel*, *mycel* = Icel. *mikill*. MUCH.] Much; great. (*Obs.*)

Microbe, mī'krōb, *n.* [Gr. *mikros*, small, *bios*, life.] A microscopic organism such as a bacillus or bacterium.

Microcephalous, mī-krō-sef'a-lus, *a.* [Gr. *mikros*, small, and *kephalē*, the head.] Having a very small skull.

Microchronometer, mī'krō-kro-nom"-et-ėr, *n.* [Gr. *mikros*, small, and E. *chronometer*.] An instrument for registering very small periods of time; a kind of chronograph.

Micrococcus, mī-krō-kok'us, *n.* [Gr. *mikros*, small, and *kokkos*, a berry.] *Zool.* a microscopic organism of a round form.

Microcosm, mī'krō-kozm, *n.* [Gr. *mikros*, small, and *kosmos*, world.] *Lit.* a little world or cosmos, applied to man, as supposed to be an epitome of the universe or great world (the *macrocosm*).—**Microcosmic**, **Microcosmical**, mī-krō-koz'mik, mī-krō-koz'mi-kal, *a.* Pertaining to the microcosm or man.

Microcoustic, mī-krō-kous'tik, *a.* [Gr. *mikros*, small, and *akouō*, to hear.] Serving to augment weak sounds.—*n.* An instrument to augment small sounds, and assist in hearing.

Microfarad, mī'krō-far-ad, *n.* [Gr. *mikros*, small, and E. *farad*.] The millionth part of a farad.

Microgeology, mī'krō-jē-ol"o-ji, *n.* [From *microscope* and *geology*.] That department of the science of geology whose facts are ascertained by the use of the microscope.—**Microgeological**, mī'krō-jē-ō-loj"i-kal, *a.* Pertaining to microgeology.

Micrography, mī-krog'ra-fi, *n.* [Gr. *mikros*, small, and *graphō*, to describe.] The description of objects too small to be discerned without the aid of a microscope.—**Micrographer**, mī-krog'ra-fėr, *n.* One versed in micrography.—**Micrographic**, mī-krō-graf'ik, *a.* Connected with or relating to micrography.

Microhm, mī'krōm, *n.* [Gr. *mikros*, small, and E. *ohm*.] The millionth part of an ohm.

Microlestes, mī'krō-les-tēz, *n.* [Gr. *mikros*, small, and *lestēs*, a robber.] An extinct marsupial, the earliest known mammalian inhabitant of our planet.

Microlithic, mī'krō-lith-ik, *n.* [Gr. *mikros*, small, and *lithos*, a stone.] Of or pertaining to, or consisting of, small stones: opposed to *megalithic*.

Micrology, mī-krol'o-ji, *n.* [Gr. *mikros*, small, and *logos*, description.] That part of science dependent on microscopic investigations; micrography.

Micrometer, mī-krom'et-ėr, *n.* [Gr. *mikros*, small, and *metron*, a measure.] An instrument or appliance fitted to a telescope or microscope, for measuring very small distances, or the apparent diameters of objects which subtend very small angles.—**Micrometric**, **Micrometrical**, mī-krō-met'rik, mī-krō-met'ri-kal, *a.* Belonging to the micrometer.—**Micrometrically**, mī-krō-met'ri-kal-li, *adv.* By means of a micrometer.—**Micrometry**, mī-krom'et-ri, *n.* The art of measuring with a micrometer.

Micromillimeter or **Micron** (μ), mī'-krō-mil"li-mē-tėr, mī'kron, *n.* [Gr. *mikros*, small, and *millimetre*.] 1/1000000 millimeter; the unit of microscopical measurement.

Micronucleus, mik-rō-nū'klē-us, *n.* [Gr. *mikros*, small.] In animalcules, the small nucleus.

Micro-organism, mi-krō-or'gan-izm, *n.* [Gr. *mikros*, small, and E. *organism*.] A microscopic organism, as a bacterium or bacillus.

Micropantograph, mī-krō-pan'tō-graf, *n.* [Gr. *mikros*, small, and E. *pantograph*.] An instrument for executing extremely minute writing and engraving.

Microphone, mī'krō-fōn, *n.* [Gr. *mikros* small, and *phōnē*, sound.] An instrument for transmitting or intensifying sounds by means of electricity; an instrument for converting sound waves into electrical waves, used especially in radiobroadcasting; often referred to as a *mike*.—**Microphonics**, mī-krō-fon'iks, *n.* The science of augmenting small sounds.

Microphotography, mī'krō-fō-tog"ra-fi, *n.* [Gr. *mikros*, small, and E. *photography*.] A photographic representation of microscopic size; the photography of microscopic objects.

Microphyllous, mī-krof'il-us, *a.* [Gr. *mikros*, small, and *phyllon*, a leaf.] *Bot.* having small leaves.

Microphyte, mī'krō-fīt, *n.* [Gr. *mikros*, small, and *phyton*, a plant.] A microscopic plant, especially one parasitic in its habits.

Micropyle, mī'krō-pīl, *n.* [Gr. *mikros*, small, *pylē*, gate.] *Bot.* the opening by which a pollen-tube enters the ovule; *zool.* an opening by which the spermatozoa fertilize an ovum.

Microscope, mī'krō-skōp, *n.* [Gr. *mikros*, small, and *skopeō*, to view.] An optical instrument consisting of a lens or combination of lenses for rendering minute objects distinctly visible.—**Microscopic**, **Microscopical**, mī-krō-skop'ik, mī-krō-skop'i-kal, *a.* Pertaining to the microscope; made by the aid of a microscope (*microscopic* observations); resembling a microscope; capable of seeing small objects; visible only by the aid of a microscope.—**Microscopically**, mī-krō-skop'i-kal-li, *adv.* In a microscopic manner; by the microscope.—**Microscopist**, mī'krō-skō-pist or mī-kros'-ko-pist, *n.* One skilled or versed in microscopy.—**Microscopy**, mī-kros'ko-pi, *n.* The use of the microscope; investigation with the microscope.

Microspectroscope, mī-krō-spek'trō-skōp, *n.* [Gr. *mikros*, small, and E. *spectroscope*.] A spectroscope placed in connection with a microscope, for more accurate examination of the spectrum.

Microspore, mik'rō-spōr, *n.* [Gr. *mikros*, small, *sporos*, seed.] *Bot.* a small (male) spore.

Microstylar, mī-krō-stī'lėr, *a.* [Gr. *mikros*, small, and *stylos*, a column.] *Arch.* having a small style or column.

Microtome, mī'krō-tōm, *n.* [Gr. *mikros*, small, and *tomos*, a cutting.] An instrument for making very fine sections or slices of objects for the microscope.

Microzoa, **Microzoaria**, mī-krō-zō'a, mī'krō-zō-ā"ri-a, *n. pl.* [Gr. *mikros*, small, and *zōa*, animals.] A name given to very minute animals, such as the infusoria.

Microzyme, mī'krō-zīm, *n.* [Gr. *mikros*, small, and *zymē*, yeast.] One of a class of extremely small organic particles, existing in the atmosphere, and furnishing the germs from which many epidemic diseases arise; a disease germ.

Micturition, mik-tū-rish'on, *n.* [L. *micturio*, to desire to make water.] The desire of making water; a morbid frequency in the passage of urine.

Mid, mid, *a.*; no compar.; superl. *midmost*. [A.Sax. *mid*, mid, in the middle; Goth. *midjis*, Icel. *midr* (*mithr*); cog. L. *medius* (see MEDIAL); Gr. *mesos*, Skr. *madhyas*, middle.] Middle; at equal distance from extremes; intervening.—**Mid-air**, *n.* The middle of the air; a lofty position in the air.—**Mid-channel**, *n.* The middle of a channel.—**Mid-day** *n.* The middle of the day; noon.—*a.* Pertaining to noon; meridional.—**Mid-heaven**, *n.* The middle of the sky or heaven; *astron.* the point of the ecliptic which is on the meridian at any given moment.—**Midland**, mid'land, *a.* Being in the interior country; distant from the coast or sea-shore; inland.—*n.* The interior of a country.—**Midleg**, mid'leg, *n.* The middle of the leg.—**Midlent**, mid'-lent, *n.* The middle of Lent.—**Midmost**, mid'mōst, *a.* In the very middle; middlemost.—**Midnight**, mid'nīt, *n.* The middle of the night; twelve o'clock at night.—*a.* Being or occurring in the middle of the night; dark as midnight; very dark.—**Mid-noon**, *n.* The middle of the day; noon. (*Tenn.*)—**Midrib**, mid'rib, *n.* *Bot.* a continuation of the petiole extending from the base to the apex of the lamina of a leaf.—**Midship**, mid'ship, *a.* Being or belonging to the middle of a ship.—**Midshipman**, mid'ship-man, *n.* [From his rank being between that of a superior officer and a common seaman.] A petty officer in the navy, occupying the highest rank among the petty officers, and eligible for promotion to higher rank.—**Midstream**, mid'strēm, *n.* The middle of the stream.—**Midsummer**, mid'sum-ėr, *n.* The middle of summer; the summer solstice, about the 21st of June.—**Midway**, mid'wā, *n.* A middle way or the middle of the way.—*a.* Being in the middle of the way or distance.—*adv.* In the middle of the way or distance; halfway.—**Mid-winter**, *n.* The middle of winter, or the winter solstice, December 21.

Midden, mid'n, *n.* [A.Sax. *midding*, same word as Dan. *mödding*, *mögdynge*, from *mög*, dung, and *dynge*, a heap.] A dunghill. [Prov.E. and Scot.]—*Kitchen-midden*. Under KITCHEN.

Middle, mid'l, *a.*; no compar; superl. *middlemost*. [From *mid*; A.Sax. D. and Dan. *middel*, G. *mittel*, middle. MID.] Equally distant from the extremes; forming a mean; intermediate; intervening.—*Middle Ages*, the period extending from the decline of the Roman Empire till the revival of letters in Europe, or from the eighth to the middle of the fifteenth century of the Christian era.—*Middle term, logic*, that term of a categorical syllogism with which the two extremes of the conclusion are separately compared.—*Middle voice, gram.* that voice which has as its proper function to express that the subject does something to or for himself.—*n.* The point or part equally distant from the extremities; an intervening point or part in space, time, or order; something intermediate; a mean.—**Middle-aged**, *a.* Being about the middle of the ordinary human life span.—**Middle class**. Originally, people having a social position between wage-earners and the leisure class; now many wage-earners, such as clerks and office-workers, are included; the term is variously used to refer to financial status, standard of living, and cultural background.—**Middle ground**, *n.* The part of a picture between the foreground and the background.—**Middleman**, *n.* An intermediary between two parties; a jobber.—**Middlemost**, mid'l-mōst, *a.* Being in the middle, or nearest the middle of a number of things that are near the middle.—**Middle-sized**, *a.* Being of middle or average size.—**Middle tint**, *n.* *Painting*, a tint in which bright colors do not predominate.—**Middling**, mid'-ling, *a.* Of middle state, size, or quality; moderate; mediocre.—**Middlingly**, mid'-ling-li, *adv.* Passably; indifferently.—**Middlings**, mid'lingz, *n. pl.* The coarser part of flour.

Midge, mij, *n.* [A.Sax. *micge*, a midge = D. *mug*, Dan. *myg*, G. *mücke*; allied to Gr.

myia, a fly.] The common name of numerous minute species of gnats or flies.—**Midget**, mij'et, *n.* [Dim. of *midge*.] A very small creature.

Midriff, mid'rif, *n.* [A.Sax. *midhrif—mid*, and *hrif*, the belly.] The diaphragm; the respiratory muscle dividing the cavity of the thorax from that of the abdomen.

Midst, midst, *n.* [From old *middes* (with *t* appended, as in *against, amongst*), the genit. of *mid*, middle, afterwards converted into a noun.] The middle.—*In the midst*, among; involved in; in the thickest part, or in the depths of (*in the midst* of afflictions). —*In our, your, their midst*, in the midst of us, &c.; in the country, community, or society, in which we, you, they, live.—*prep.* Poetically used for *Amidst*.

Midwife, mid'wīf, *n.* [From O.E. and A. Sax. *mid*, with, together with (G. *mit*), and *wife*: comp. Sp. and Pg. *comadre*, a midwife, *co* = L. *cum*, with, and *madre*, a mother.] A practical nurse, as distinguished from a registered nurse, who assists a mother in childbirth.—**Midwifery**, mid'wif-ri, *n.* The art or practice of a midwife: obstetrics.—**Midwifish**, mid'wīf-ish, *a.* Pertaining to a midwife.

Mien, mēn, *n.* [Fr. *mine*, air, mien; It. *mina*, course, behaviour, L.L. *minare*, to lead, conduct, properly to drive with threats, from L. *mina*, a threat. MENACE. Or from Arm. *min*, face.] External air or manner of a person; look; bearing; appearance; carriage.

Miff, mif, *n.* [Comp. Prov.G. *muff*, sullenness.] A slight quarrel. (*Colloq.*)

Might, mīt, *n.* [A.Sax. *miht*, also *meaht*, might, from stem of *may*, to be able; D. Sw. and Dan. *magt*, G. *macht*, might. MAY.] Strength; force; power; often bodily strength or physical power; but also mental power; power of will; political power.—*With might and main*, with the utmost strength or bodily exertion.—**Mightful**, mīt'ful, *a.* Mighty; powerful. (*Poet.*)—**Mightily**, mīt'i-li, *adv.* Powerfully; vehemently; greatly; highly.—**Mightiness**, mīt'i-nes, *n.* State or attribute of being mighty: also, with possessives, a title of dignity.—**Mighty**, mīt'i, *a.* [A.Sax. *mihtig*.] Having great power or dominion; strong; powerful: often an epithet of honour (most *mighty* prince); very great; vast; eminent in intellect or acquirements; displaying great power; performed with great power (*mighty* works).—*adv.* In a great degree; very (*mighty* wise; *mighty* thoughtful). (*Colloq.*)

Might, mīt, past tense of *may*.

Mignonette, min'yon-et, *n.* [Fr. *mignonnette*, a dim. of *mignon*, darling. MINION.] An annual plant, a native of Egypt, but universally cultivated in gardens on account of the sweet scent of its flowers.

Migrate, mī'grāt, *v.i.*—*migrated, migrating.* [L. *migro, migratum*, to migrate; seen also in *emigrate, immigrate, transmigration*.] To remove from one place of residence to another at a distance, especially from one country to another.—**Migrant**, mī'grant, *a.* Migratory.—*n.* One who migrates; a migratory bird or other animal.—**Migration**, mī-grā'shon, *n.* [L. *migratio*.] The act of migrating; *zool.* transit of a species of animals from one locality or latitude to another.—**Migratory**, mī'gra-to-ri, *a.* Given to migration; migrating at certain seasons (as birds); roving or wandering in one's mode of life; unsettled.

Mikado, mi-kä'dō, *n.* [Japanese, lit. the Venerable.] The emperor of Japan, the spiritual as well as temporal head of the empire.

Milanese, mil-an-ēz', *n. sing.* and *pl.* A citizen or citizens of *Milan*.—*a.* Of or belonging to Milan or the people of Milan.

Milch, milsh, *a.* [A.Sax. *melc*, milch, giving milk; comp. L.G. *melke*, Icel. *milkr*, G. *melk*, milch, but L.G. *melk*, *mjölk*, G. *milch*, milk. MILK.] Giving milk; applied only to beasts (a *milch* cow).

Mild mīld, *a.* [A.Sax. *milde* = D. Dan. Sw. and G. *mild*, Icel. *mildr*, Goth. *milds*; from a root meaning to grind or crush, and hence allied to *mellow, meal, mould*, L. *mollis*, soft (whence *mollify*).] Tender and gentle in temper or disposition; not severe or cruel; not fierce, rough, or angry; placid; not stern; not frowning; gently and pleasantly affecting the senses; not violent; soft; bland; gentle (a *mild* temperature); not acrid, pungent, corrosive, or drastic; moderately sweet or pleasant to the taste (*mild* fruit).—**Milden**, mīl'den, *v.t.* To render mild; to soften; to make less severe, stringent, or intense.—*v.i.* To become mild; to soften.—**Mildly**, mīld'li, *adv.* In a mild manner.—**Mildness**, mīld'nes, *n.* The state or quality of being mild; gentleness; softness; clemency; blandness.

Mildew, mil'dū, *n.* [A.Sax. *mildedw, melededw*; O.H.G. *militou*, G. *mehlthau*; probably='honey-dew'; comp. L. *mel*, honey.] Decay produced in living and dead vegetable matter, and in some manufactured products of vegetable matter, by very minute parasitical fungi; a sort of blight; the minute fungi causing this condition.—*v.t.* To affect with mildew.—*v.i.* To become affected with mildew.—**Mildewy**, mil'dū-i, *a.* Abounding in mildew; mouldy; resembling mildew.

Mile, mīl, *n.* [A.Sax. *mīl*, like D. *mijl*, Dan. *miil*, G. *meile*, a mile, from L. *mille*, a thousand, used shortly for *mille passus* (or *passuum*), a thousand paces, a Roman mile. Akin *million, milliard*, &c.] A land measure of distance used in the United States and Great Britain, and equal to 1,760 yards, or 5,280 feet; the nautical or sea mile, in the United States, is equal to 6,080.20 feet.—*Last mile*, the last walk of a condemned man to the execution chamber. (*Slang.*)—**Mileage**, mīl'āj, *n.* A fee or allowance paid for travel by the mile; the aggregate of miles in a railway, canal, &c.; aggregate of miles gone over by vehicles such as automobiles, railroad trains, &c.—**Milestone**, mīl'stōn, *n.* A stone or post set up on the side of a road or highway to mark the miles.

Milesian, mi-lē'zhi-an, *n.* A native of Ireland, whose inhabitants, according to Irish legend, are descended from *Milesius*, a king of Spain.—*a.* Pertaining to the ancient Irish race.

Milesian, mi-lē'zhi-an, *n.* A native or inhabitant of the ancient city of *Miletus*, in Asia Minor.—*a.* Pertaining to Miletus or the inhabitants of Miletus.

Milfoil, mil'foil, *n.* [Fr. *mille-feuille*, from L. *millefolium*, lit. thousand-leaf.] The yarrow.

Miliary, mil'i-a-ri, *a.* [L. *miliarius*, from *milium*, millet.] Resembling millet-seeds; accompanied with an eruption like millet-seeds (a *miliary* fever).

Milieu, mē-lyu', *n.* [Fr., from Old Fr. *mi*, middle, and *lieu*, place.] Environmental setting.

Miliolite, mil'i-ō-līt, *n.* [From L. *milium*, millet, from resembling a millet-seed.] The fossil shell of a minute foraminifer whose remains form almost the sole constituent of the limestone of the Paris basin.—**Miliolitic**, mil'i-ō-lit"ik, *a.* Composed of or relating to miliolites.

Militant, mil'i-tant, *a.* [L. *militans, militantis*, ppr. of *milito*, to fight, from *miles, militis*, a soldier; perhaps connected with *mille*, a thousand.] Fighting; serving as a soldier.—*Church militant*, the Christian church on earth, which is supposed to be engaged in constant warfare and struggle: as distinguished from the *church triumphant*, or in heaven.—**Militantly**, mil'i-tant-li, *adv.* In a militant or warlike manner.—**Militancy**, mil'i-tan-si, *n.* Warfare; militarism.—**Militarily**, mil'i-ta-ri-li, *adv.* In a military or soldierly manner.—**Militarism**, mil'i-ta-rizm, *n.* [Fr. *militarisme*.] The system that leads a nation to pay excessive attention to military affairs; the keeping up of great armies.—**Militarist**, mil'i-ta-rist, *n.* A military man; one proficient in the art of war (*Shak.*); one in favour of militarism; one who favours a warlike policy.—**Military**, mil'i-ta-ri, *a.* [L. *militaris*.] Pertaining to soldiers or the profession of a soldier; becoming the profession of a soldier; pertaining to war; warlike; martial.—*Military attaché*, an army officer, resident abroad with his nation's diplomatic representative, whose duty it is to observe and report on the military developments of a foreign power. —*Military brush*, a hair brush without a handle.—*Military hospital*, a hospital for the treatment of sick and wounded soldiers.—*Military police*, that part of the army which performs police duty among soldiers.—**Militate**, mil'i-tāt, *v.i.* [L. *milito, militatum*, to fight.] To stand opposed; to have weight or influence on the opposite side: said of arguments, considerations, &c., and followed by *against* (another fact *militated against* that theory).—**Militia**, mi-lish'a, *n.* [L., military service, soldiery.] A body of men enrolled and trained as military reserves for the defense of a nation in time of war; the organized militia of the individual states is called the National Guard.—**Militiaman**, *n.* One who belongs to the militia.

Milk, milk, *n.* [A.Sax. *meolc, milc*, milk = D. Dan. and L.G. *melk*, Icel. *mjölk*, Sw. *mjölk*, Goth. *miluks*, G. *milch*, milk; also Rus. *moloko*, Pol. and Bohem. *mleko*, milk; root also in L. *mulgeo*, Gr. *amelgō*, to milk.] A whitish fluid secreted by the mammary glands of females of the class Mammalia, including the human species, and drawn from the breasts for the nourishment of their young; the white juice of certain plants; an emulsion of which juice expressed from seeds is one of the constituents (the *milk* of almonds).—*v.t.* To draw milk from the breasts or udder of by the hand (to *milk* a cow).—**Milk-and-water**, *a.* Tasteless; insipid; characterless; wishy-washy (*Colloq.*).—**Milker**, milk'ėr, *n.* One who or that which milks; a cow or other animal giving milk.—**Milk-fever**, *n.* A fever which sometimes accompanies the first secretion of milk in females after childbirth.—**Milkily**, milk'i-li, *adv.* In a milky manner.—**Milkiness**, milk'i-nes, *n.* State of being milky; qualities like those of milk.—**Milk-livered**, *a.* Cowardly; timorous (*Shak.*).—**Milkmaid**, milk'mād, *n.* A woman that milks or is employed in the dairy.—**Milkman**, milk'man, *n.* A man that sells milk or carries milk to market.—**Milk-punch**, *n.* A drink made by mixing milk with spirits and sweetening it.—**Milk-quartz**, *n.* A variety of quartz of a milk-white color.—**Milk sickness**, *n.* A disease contracted from the consumption of milk or meat of a cow that has grazed on certain poisonous plants.—**Milksop**, *n.* An effeminate man or boy; one devoid of manliness.—**Milk sugar**, *n.* LACTINE.—**Milk thrush**, *n.* APHTHAE.—**Milk tooth**, *n.* One of the first, or temporary, set of teeth in young animals and children; a child's full set consists of twenty such teeth, and is later replaced by thirty-two permanent ones.—**Milk-white**, milk'whīt, *a.* White as milk.—**Milky**, milk'i, *a.* Pertaining to, resembling, or containing milk; yielding milk; soft; timorous (*Shak.*).—**Milky-way**, *n.* GALAXY.

Mill, mil, *n.* [L. *mille*, a thousand.] A money of account of the United States, value the thousandth of a dollar, or one-tenth of a cent.

Mill, mil, *n.* [O.E. *miln*, A.Sax. *mylen myln*, from L. *molina*, a mill, from *mola*, a mill or millstone, from *molo*, to grind—root same as in *meal, mould*, &c.] A machine for grinding and reducing to fine particles grain, fruit, or other substance; applied also to many machines for grinding or polishing by circular motion, or to complicated machinery for working up raw material, &c.; the building where grinding or some process of manufacturing is carried on; *calico-printing*, a copper printing cylinder; a pugilistic contest; a fight with the fists (*slang*).—*v.t.* To grind in a mill; to pass through a mill; to stamp in a coining-press; especially to stamp so as to make a transversely grooved edge round; to throw, as silk; to full, as cloth.—**Millboard**, *n.* A stout kind of pasteboard made in a paper-mill.—**Milldam**, *n.* A dam crossing a watercourse and raising the water to a height sufficient to turn a mill-wheel; in Scotland, a millpond.—**Milled**, mild, *p.* and *a.* Having undergone the operation of a mill; having the edge transversely grooved, as a dime or the head of a screw that is to be turned by the fingers; fulled, as cloth.—**Milling**, mil'ing, *n.* The process of passing through a mill; the grooves on the edge of a coin.—**Miller**, mil'ėr, *n.* One who keeps or attends a mill, especially a flour-mill.—**Miller's-thumb**, *n.* A small fish found in streams; the bull-head.—**Mill-hand**, *n.* A workman employed in a mill.—**Mill-pond, Mill-pool**, *n.* A pond or reservoir of water for driving a mill-wheel.—**Mill-race**, *n.* The stream of water that drives a mill-wheel, or the channel in which it runs.—**Mill-spindle**, *n.* The vertical shaft by which the revolving millstone is supported.—**Millstone**, mil'stōn, *n.* One of the stones for grinding the grain in a mill; stone or rock from which such stones are made.—*Millstone grit*, a siliceous conglomerate rock used for millstones, building, &c., forming one of the members of the carboniferous group of strata underlying the true coal-measures.—*To see into or through a millstone*, to see with acuteness or to penetrate into abstruse subjects.—**Mill-tail**, *n.* The current of water leaving a mill-wheel after turning it.—**Mill-wheel**, *n.* A wheel used to drive a mill; a water-wheel.—**Mill-work**, *n.* The machinery of mills.—**Mill-wright**, *n.* A mechanic or wright whose occupation it is to construct the machinery of mills.

Millenarian, mil-le-nā'ri-an, *a.* [L. *millenarius*, containing a thousand, from *mille*, a thousand. MILE.] Consisting of a thousand; especially consisting of a thousand years; pertaining to the millennium.—**Millenarian, Millennarian**, mil-le-nā'ri-an, *n.* One who believes in the millennium.—**Millenarianism, Millennialism, Millenniarism**, mil-le-nā'ri-an-izm, mil-len'i-al-izm, mil-len'i-är-izm, *n.* The doctrine of millenarians.—**Millenary**, mil'le-na-ri, *a.* Consisting of a thousand.—*Millenary Petition*, the petition presented by the Puritan and Conformist parties to James I in 1603, signed by a thousand ministers, complaining that they were overburdened with the human rites and ceremonies' in the Prayer Book.—*n.* The space of a thousand years; a thousandth anniversary.—**Millennial**, mil-len'i-al, *a.* Pertaining to the millennium, or to a thousand years.—**Millennialist**, mil-len'i-al-ist, *n.* A millenarian.—**Millennium**, mil-len'i-um, *n.* [L. *mille*, a thousand, and *annus*, year.] An aggregate of a thousand years; the thousand years mentioned in Rev. xx. 1-5, during which millenarians believe Christ will reign on earth with his saints.

Millepede, Millipede, mil'e-pēd, mil'i-pēd, *n.* [L. *mille*, a thousand, and *pes*, a foot.] A name common to worm-like articulated animals, from the number of their feet; a myriapod.

Millepore, mil'le-pōr, *n.* [L. *mille*, a thousand, and *porus*, a pore.] One of the reef-building corals, so named from their numerous minute cells or pores.

Miller, *n.* See under MILL; also a dusty-winged type of moth.

Millesimal, mil-les'i-mal, *a.* [L. *millesimus*, from *mille*, a thousand.] Thousandth.

Millet, mil'et, *n.* [Fr. *millet*, dim. of *mil*, from L. *milium*, millet; from root meaning to grind as in *mill*.] A common name for various species of small grain cultivated largely in many parts of Europe, Asia, and Africa as food for men; various forage grasses; the seed of any of these grains and grasses.

Milliard, mil-yärd', *n.* [Fr.] A thousand millions, usually called a *billion* in America.—**Millier**, mē-lyā', *n.* [Fr.] A metric ton; a weight equal to a thousand kilograms, or 2205 lbs.—**Milligram**, mil'i-gram, *n.* The thousandth part of a gram; equal to a cubic millimeter of water or .0154 of a grain.—**Millimeter**, mil"i-mē'tėr, *n.* The thousandth part of a meter, 0.03937 of an inch.—**Millimicron**, mil"i-mī'kron, *n.* The millionth part of a millimeter, or thousandth part of a micron.

Milliary, mil'i-a-ri, *a.* [L. *milliarius*, from *mille*, a thousand.] Pertaining to the ancient Roman mile of a thousand paces or five thousand feet; denoting a mile.

Milliner, mil'i-nėr, *n.* [Supposed to be for *Milaner*, from *Milan*, in Italy, famous for its silks and ribbons.] A person, now usually a woman, who makes and sells head-dresses, hats, or bonnets, &c., for females.—**Millinery**, mil'i-nėr-i, *n.* The business or occupation of a milliner; the articles made or sold by milliners.

Million, mil'yon, *n.* [Fr. *million*, from L. *mille*, a thousand. MILE.] The number of ten hundred thousand, or a thousand thousand; with the definite article, the great body of the people; the multitude; the public; the masses.—**Millionaire, Millionnaire**, mil'yon-är, *n.* [Fr. *millionnaire*.] A man worth a million of money; a man of great wealth.—**Millionary**, mil'yon-a-ri, *a.* Pertaining to millions; consisting of millions.—**Millionth**, mil'yonth, *a.* Ten hundred thousandth; constituting one of a million.—*n.* One of a million parts; a ten hundred thousandth part.

Milreis, mil'rēs, *n.* [Pg. *mil*, a thousand, and *reis*, pl. of *real*, a small denomination of money.] A Brazilian money of account, written 1$000; an old Portuguese coin.

Milt, milt, *n.* [A.Sax. *milte*, Dan. *milt*, Icel. *milti*, G. *milz*, the spleen; D. *milt*, the spleen, the milt of fishes; same root as *melt*; applied to the milt of fishes from the resemblance of the word to *milk*, and from the milky appearance of the milt.] The spleen of an animal; the soft roe of fishes, or the spermatic organ of the males.—**Milter**, milt'ėr, *n.* [D. *milter*.] A male fish, or one having a milt.

Miltonic, mil-ton'ik, *a.* Relating to *Milton* or his poetry.

Milvine, mil'vīn, *a.* [L. *milvus*, a kite.] Belonging to or resembling birds of the kite family.

Mime, mīm, *n.* [L. *mimus*, from Gr. *mimos*, an actor, a mime.] A species of ancient dramatic entertainment in which gestures and mimicry predominated; an actor in such performances.—**Mimesis**, mī-mē'sis, *n.* [Gr.] *Rhet.* imitation of the voice or gestures of another; *nat. hist.* same as *Mimicry*.—**Mimetic**, mī-met'ik, *a.* Apt to imitate; given to aping or mimicry; *nat. hist.* characterized by mimicry.—**Mimetism**, mī'met-izm, *n.* Mimicry, as among certain insects.—**Mimic, Mimical**, mim'ik, mim'i-kal, *a.* [L. *mimicus*, Gr. *mimikos*.] Imitative; inclined to imitate or ape; imitating; consisting of or made in imitation (*mimic* gestures).—**Mimic**, *n.* One who imitates or mimics; one who attempts to excite laughter or derision by acting or speaking in the manner of another.—*v.t.*—*mimicked, mimicking.* To imitate or ape, especially for sport; to ridicule by imitation; to act or speak like intentionally.—**Mimically**, mim'i-kal-li, *adv.* In a mimic or imitative manner.—**Mimicalness**, mim'i-kal-nes, *n.*—**Mimicker**, mim'ik-ėr, *n.* One who mimics.—**Mimicry**, mim'ik-ri, *n.* Imitation, often ludicrous imitation for sport or ridicule; *nat. hist.* the close resemblance presented by certain plants and animals to certain other plants or animals, or to the natural objects among which they live, this resemblance serving for protection.

Mimeograph, mim"ē-ō-graf', *n.* Trade name of a device for copying (typewritten material, usually), using a stencil.

Mimographer, mīm-og'ra-fėr, *n.* [Gr. *mimos*, a mime, and *graphō*, to write.] A writer of mimes or farces.

Mimosa, mi-mō'sa, *n.* [From Gr. *mimos*, a mimic, from their sensitive leaves.] A genus of plants, some of which are remarkable for the irritability of their leaves, hence their name *sensitive-plants*.

Mimulus, mim'ū-lus, *n.* [Dim. of L. *mimus*, an actor, from corolla resembling a mask.] A genus of plants with showy flowers, many grown for ornament.

Mina, mī'na, *n.* Among the Greeks, a weight of 100 drachmæ; also, a piece of money valued at 100 drachmæ.

Mina, mī'na, *n.* [Ind. name.] An Indian bird of the starling family that can be taught to speak, and is often kept in cages in Europe and America.

Minacious, mi-nā'shus, *a.* [L. *minax*, *minacis*, threatening, MENACE.] Threatening; menacing.—**Minacity**,† mi-nas'i-ti, *n.* Disposition to threaten.

Minaret, min'a-ret, *n.* [Fr. *minaret*, Sp. *minarete*, from Ar. *menāra*, a lighthouse, a minaret, from *nār*, to shine.] A slender lofty turret rising by different stages or stories, surrounded by one or more projecting balconies, common in mosques in Mohammedan countries, and used for summoning the people to prayers.

Minatory, min'a-to-ri, *a.* [L. *minatorius*, from *minator*, a threatener, *mina*, a threat. MENACE.] Threatening; menacing.—**Minatorily**, min'a-to-ri-li, *adv.* In a minatory manner.

Mince, mins, *v.t.*—*minced, mincing.* [A.Sax. *minsian*, from *min*, small; also O.Fr. *mincer*, from *mince*, fine, small; root same as that of *minor, minister*.] To cut or chop into very small pieces (to *mince* meat); to diminish in speaking; to extenuate; to palliate (to *mince* the matter, to *mince* matters); to pronounce with affected elegance.—*v.i.* To walk with short steps; to affect delicacy in manner; to speak with affected elegance.—**Mincemeat, Minced meat**, *n.* Meat chopped fine; chopped mixture of raisins, apples, other fruit, spices, suet, &c.—**Mince pie**, *n.* A pie made of mincemeat.—**Mincer**, mins'ėr, *n.* One who minces; a detractor.—**Mincing**, mins'ing, *p.* and *a.* Speaking or walking affectedly.—**Mincingly**, mins'ing-li, *adv.* With a mincing manner.

Mind, mīnd, *n.* [A.Sax. *mynd, gemynd*, mind, thought, intention; Dan. *minde*, Icel. *minni*, memory; from root *man*, to think, seen also in *mean*, to intend; L. *mens, mentis*, mind (whence *mental*); Gr. *menos*, mind. MAN, MEAN.] The intellectual power in man; the understanding (not in one's right *mind*); cast of thought and feeling; opinion (of the same *mind*); intention; purpose; memory; remembrance (to call to *mind*, to keep in *mind*).—*To be in two minds* about a thing, to be in doubt.—*v.t.* To attend to; to fix the thoughts on; to heed; to notice; to pay attention to; to attend with submission; to obey.—**Minded**, mīn'ded, *a.* Disposed; inclined; having a mind, as in high-*minded*, low-*minded*.—**Mindedness**, mīn'ded-nes, *n.* Disposition; inclination; in composition (heavenly-*mindedness*).—**Minder**, mīn'dėr, *n.* One who minds.—**Mindful**, mīnd'ful, *a.* Attentive; bearing in mind; heedful.—**Mindfully**, mīnd'ful-li, *adv.* Attentively; heedfully.—**Mindfulness**, mīnd'ful-nes, *n.* Attention.—**Mindless**, mīnd'les, *a.* Destitute of mind; stupid; unthinking; inattentive; heedless; careless: with *of*.

Mine, mīn, *pronominal adjective.* [A.Sax. *min*, genit. or adj. corresponding to *me* = Dan. and Sw. *min*, Icel. *minn*, Goth. *meina*, D. *mijn*, G. *mein*. *My* is a shortened form. Comp. *thy, thine*.] My; belonging to me: once regularly used before nouns beginning with a vowel, now generally used similarly to *thine, hers, ours, yours, theirs*, as equivalent to *my* followed by a noun, and serving either for a nominative or an objective.

Mine, mīn, *n.* [Fr. *mine*, a mine, *miner*, to form a mine, from L. *minare*, to drive, to conduct, originally to drive (animals) with threats, from *mina*, a threat. MENACE.] A pit or excavation in the earth, from which coal, metallic ores, or other mineral substances are taken by digging; a contrivance floating on, or near, the surface of the sea to destroy ships by explosion; *milit.* an underground gallery or passage dug under a fortification, in which a quantity of powder or other explosive may be lodged for blowing up the works; *fig.* a rich source or store of wealth or anything highly valued. —*v.i.—mined, mining.* To dig a mine; to burrow.—*v.t.* To dig away the foundation from; to undermine; to sap.—**Minelaying,** *n.* The laying or dropping into the sea of mines intended to act against an enemy's vessels, such mines having a weight attached by way of anchor. — **Minesweeping,** *n.* The 'sweeping' of the sea to clear an area of hostile mines.—**Mining,** mīn'ing, *p.* and *a.* Of burrowing habits; insidious.—**Miner,** mīn'ėr, *n.* One who mines; one who digs or works in a mine for metals or other minerals.

Mineral, min'ėr-al, *n.* [Fr. *minéral,* from *miner,* to mine. MINE.] Any ingredient in the earth's crust; an inorganic body with a definite chemical composition, and which naturally exists within the earth or at its surface.—*a.* Pertaining to minerals; consisting of minerals; impregnated with minerals or mineral matter (*mineral* waters).—*Mineral acids,* a name given to sulphuric, nitric, and hydrochloric acids. —*Mineral caoutchouc,* a variety of bitumen, much resembling india-rubber in its softness and elasticity.—*Mineral charcoal,* a fibrous variety of non-bituminous mineral coal. — *Mineral green,* carbonate of copper. — *Mineral kingdom,* that grand division of natural objects which includes all minerals, and of which mineralogy is the science.—*Mineral oil.* PETROLEUM.— *Mineral pitch,* a solid softish bitumen.— *Mineral tar,* bitumen of a tarry consistence. —*Mineral waters,* a term applied to certain waters, either naturally or artificially impregnated with gases, carbonates, sulphates, iron, &c.—*Mineral wax,* ozocerite.—**Mineralist,** min'ėr-al-ist, *n.* One skilled in or concerned about minerals.—**Mineralization,** min'ėr-al-i-zā"shon, *n.* The act or process of mineralizing; the process of being converted into a mineral.—**Mineralize,** min'ėr-al-īz, *v.t.—mineralized, mineralizing.* To convert into a mineral; to impregnate with mineral substance.—**Mineralizer,** min'ėr-al-īz-ėr, *n.* A substance or agent that mineralizes.—**Mineralogy,** min-ėr-al'o-ji, *n.* The science which treats of the properties of mineral substances, and teaches us to characterize, distinguish, and classify them according to their properties. — **Mineralogic, Mineralogical,** min'ėr-a-loj"ik, min'ėr-a-loj"i-kal, *a.* Pertaining to mineralogy.—**Mineralogically,** min'ėr-a-loj"i-kal-li, *adv.* According to the principles of mineralogy.—**Mineralogist,** min-ėr-al'o-jist, *n.* One versed in the science of minerals.—**Mineralogize,** min'ėr-al-o-jīz, *v.i.* To collect mineralogical specimens; to study mineralogy.

Minerva, mi-nėr'va, *n.* [L., from root of *mens,* mind. MIND, MENTAL.] One of the chief divinities of the Romans, a daughter of Jupiter; in later times identified with the Greek goddess Athēnē, the goddess of wisdom, of war, and of the liberal arts.—

Minestrone, mē'nā-strō"nā, *n.* A thick Italian soup, consisting of a rich broth, in which float vegetables, barley, fine spaghetti, etc.

Minever, min'e-vėr, *n.* MINIVER.

Mingle, ming'gl, *v.t.—mingled, mingling.* [From A.Sax. *mengan,* to mix, with freq. term. *-le;* D. *mengen, mengelen,* G. *mengen, mengeln,* Icel. *menga,* to mingle; G. *menge,* multitude; akin *among, mongrel.*] To mix up together so as to form one whole; to blend; to join in mutual intercourse or in society; to debase by mixture.—*v.i.* To become mixed; to become united in the same whole; to join (to *mingle with* or *in* a crowd). — **Mingledly,** ming'gld-li, *adv.* Confusedly.—**Mingler,** ming'glėr, *n.* One that mingles.—**Mingle-mangle,** *n.* [A reduplication of *mingle.*] A medley; a hotchpotch.

Miniate, min'i-āt, *v.t.* [L. *mineo, miniatum,* from *minium,* red-lead or vermilion.] To paint with red-lead or vermilion.—*a.* Of the colour of minium or vermilion.—**Miniature,** min'i-tūr, *n.* [It. *miniatura,* originally a design such as drawn on the margins of old manuscripts, from *miniare,* to write with *minium* or red-lead, this pigment being much used in the ornamenting of old manuscripts.] A painting of very small dimensions, usually executed in water-colours, on ivory, vellum, &c.; anything represented on a greatly reduced scale; a small scale (shown in *miniature*).—*a.* On a small scale.—**Miniaturist,** min'i-tūr-ist, *n.* One who paints miniatures.

Minify, min'i-fī, *v.t.* [L. *minus,* less, and *facio,* to make.] To make little or less: opposite of magnify; to lessen; to diminish; to slight; to depreciate.

Minikin,† min'i-kin, *n.* [O.D. *minneken,* darling, from *minne,* love; akin *minion.*] A darling; a favourite.—*a.* Small; diminutive.

Minim, min'im, *n.* [Fr. *minime,* L. *minimus,* least, superlative corresponding to *minor,* small. MINOR.] A note in music, equal in time to half a semibreve or two crotchets; the smallest liquid measure, generally regarded as about equal to one drop, the fluid drachm being divided into sixty minims.—**Minimum,** min'i-mum, *n.* [L.] The smallest amount or degree; least quantity assignable in a given case: opposed to *maximum.*—**Minimize,** min'i-mīz, *v.t.* To reduce to a minimum, or the smallest possible proportion or part.

Minion, min'yon, *n.* [Fr. *mignon,* a darling, from O.G. *minne,* love, originally remembrance; akin *mind.*] A darling‡; an unworthy favourite; a servile dependant; one who is the creature of another; a small kind of printing type.—**Minionette,** min-yon-et', *n.* A small fancy type.

Minish, min'ish, *v.t.* [O.Fr. *menuster, menuisier,* to diminish, from L.L. *minutiare,* from L. *minutus,* minute. Hence *diminish.* MINUTE.] To lessen; to diminish.

Minister, min'is-tėr, *n.* [L. *minister,* from stem of *minor, minus,* less.] One who acts under the authority of another; a servant; an attendant; one authorized to conduct Christian worship, as a priest or clergyman; one to whom the executive head of a government entrusts the direction of affairs of state; one engaged in the administration of government.—*v.t.* To give; to supply.—*v.i.* To act as a minister or attendant; to perform service; to afford supplies; to give things needful; to supply the means of relief; to furnish (to *minister to* one's necessities).—**Ministerial,** min-is-tē'ri-al, *a.* Pertaining to ministry or the performance of service; pertaining to a ministry or to ministers of state; pertaining to ministers of the gospel.—**Ministerialist,** min-is-tē'ri-al-ist, *n. Politics,* a supporter of the ministry in office.—**Ministerially,** min-is-tē'ri-al-li, *adv.* In a ministerial manner or character.—**Ministering,** min'is-tėr-ing, *p.* and *a.* Attending and serving as a subordinate agent.—**Ministrant,** min'is-trant, *a.* [L. *ministrans, ministrantis.*] Performing service; acting as minister or attendant; attendant on service.—**Ministration,** min-is-trā'-shon, *n.* [L. *ministratio.*] The act of ministering or performing service; service or attendance given; ecclesiastical function.—**Ministrative,** min'is-trā-tiv, *a.* Affording service; assisting.—**Ministry,** min'is-tri, *n.* [L. *ministerium.*] The act of ministering; service; aid; instrumentality; the office or functions of a minister of the gospel; the body of ministers of state or the chief officials of the executive government; duration of the office of a minister, civil or ecclesiastical.

Minium, min'i-um, *n.* [L. Hence *miniature.*] Red oxidė of lead; red-lead.

Miniver, min'i-vėr, *n.* [O.Fr. *menuveir, menuvair,* a grayish fur—*menu* (L. *minutus*), small, and *vair,* fur.] The fur of the Siberian squirrel; a fine white fur.

Mink, mingk, *n.* An American and European quadruped, allied to the polecat and weasel, yielding a fur of some value.

Minnesinger, min'ne-sing-ėr, *n.* [O.G. *minne,* love (MINION), and *singer,* a singer.] One of a class of German lyric poets of the twelfth and thirteenth centuries, so called from love being their chief theme.

Minnow, min'ō, *n.* [A.Sax. *myne,* a minnow, from root *min,* small. MINOR.] Any of various small fishes of the carp family; loosely, any of several other small fishes.

Minoan, mi-nō'an, *a.* Referring to the prehistoric Cretan culture.

Minor, mī'nor, *a.* [L. *minor,* smaller (without a positive), from a root *min,* small, seen also in A.Sax. *min,* small; Dan., Sw., *mindre,* Icel. *minni,* G. *minder,* less; Ir. and Gael. *min,* small, fine. Akin *minute, minister, minish,* &c.] Lesser; smaller: used relatively, and opposed to *major;* absolutely small; petty; *music,* less by a lesser semitone, as applied to an interval; having a tone and semitone between the key-note and its third: applied to a scale. —*Minor term, logic,* the subject of the conclusion of a categorical syllogism.—*Minor premiss,* that which contains the minor term.—*n.* A person of either sex under full age (not yet twenty-one years); one under the authority of his parents or guardians; *logic,* the minor term or premiss; *music,* the minor key.—**Minorite,** mī'nor-īt, *n.* A Franciscan friar.—**Minority,** mi-nor'i-ti, *n.* [Fr. *minorité.*] The state of being a minor or not come of age; the period or interval before one is of full age, generally the period from birth until twenty-one years of age; the smaller number out of a whole divided into two: opposed to *majority.*

Minotaur, min'o-taur, *n.* [Gr.] Mythical monster, reputed half man, half bull, offspring of Pasiphaë, wife of Minos, the ancient King of Crete, and connected with the legend of Theseus.

Minster, min'stėr, *n.* [A.Sax. *mynster,* (like G. *münster,* D. *monster*), from L. *monasterium,* a monastery. MONASTERY.] Originally, a monastery; afterwards, the church of a monastery; latterly, a cathedral church.

Minstrel, min'strel, *n.* [O.Fr. *menestrel,* from L.L. *ministrellus,* a harper, one who ministered to the amusement of the rich by music or jesting; a dim. from L. *minister,* a servant.] A singer or musical performer; in the middle ages, one of a class of men who subsisted by the arts of poetry and music.—**Minstrel show,** a performance of jokes, melodies, &c., given by comedians usually made up as Negroes.—

Minstrelsy, min'strel-si, *n.* The art or occupation of minstrels; music; a body of songs or ballads.

Mint, mint, *n.* [A.Sax. *mynet,* from L. *moneta,* the mint, money, from *Moneta,* a surname of *Juno,* in whose temple at Rome money was coined, from *moneo,* to remind (whence *monition, monitor*).] The place where money is coined by public authority; a great supply or store that may be drawn on (a *mint* of reasons).—*v.t.* To coin; to make and stamp into money; to invent; to fabricate.—**Mintage,** mint'āj, *n.* That which is coined or stamped; the duty paid for coining.—**Minter,** mint'ėr, *n.* A coiner.—**Mint-mark,** *n.* A private mark put upon coins by those that coin them, for the purpose of identification.

Mint, mint, *n.* [A.Sax. *minte,* from L. *mentha,* Gr. *mintha, minthē,* mint.] The name of several herbaceous aromatic plants which partake largely of the tonic properties found in all labiate plants. *Spearmint* and *peppermint* are the popular names of two well-known species.—**Mint-julep,** *n.* A drink made of whisky, usually Bourbon, with sugar, cracked ice, and mint leaves.—**Mint-sauce,** *n.* Mint chopped up with vinegar and sugar, used as a sauce for lamb.

Minuend, min'ū-end, *n.* [L. *minuendus,* to be lessened, *minuo,* to lessen. MINOR.] *Arith.* the number from which another number is to be subtracted.

Minuet, min'ū-et, *n.* [Fr. *menuet,* from *menu,* small, from L. *minutus,* minute—on account of the small steps of the dance.]

A slow graceful dance and the tune or air for it.

Minus, mī'nus, *a.* [Neut. of L. *minor*, less. MINOR.] Less; *alg.* applied to the negative or subtractive sign −, which, when placed between two quantities, signifies that the latter is to be taken from the former.—**Minuscule**, mi-nus'kūl, *n.* [L. *minusculus*, small, minute.] A small sort of letter used in MSS. in the middle ages.

Minute, mi-nūt', *a.* [L. *minutus*, pp. of *minuo*, to lessen, from root *min*, small. MINOR.] Very small; characterized by attention to small things or details; precise; attentive to the smallest particulars.—**Minutely**, mi-nūt'li, *adv.* With minuteness; exactly; nicely.—**Minuteness**, mi-nūt'nes, *n.* Extreme smallness; critical exactness.

Minute, min'it, *n.* [Fr. *minute*, from L. *minuta*, a minute portion. MINUTE, *a.*] A small portion of time, strictly the sixtieth part of an hour; sixty seconds; *geom.* the sixtieth part of a degree of a circle; *arch.* the sixtieth part of the diameter of a column at the base; a short sketch of any agreement or other subject, taken in writing; a note to preserve the memory of anything. — *v.t.* — *minuted*, *minuting*. To set down in a short sketch or note.—**Minutely**, min'it-li, *adv.* Every minute; with very little time intervening. — **Minute-book**, *n.* A book in which minutes are recorded.—**Minute-glass**, *n.* A glass, the sand of which measures a minute.—**Minute-gun**, *n.* A gun discharged at intervals of a minute as a signal from a vessel in distress.—**Minute-hand**, *n.* The hand that points to the minutes on a clock or watch.

Minutia, mi-nū'shi-a, *n.*; generally in pl. —**Minutiæ**, mi-nū'shi-ē. [L. from *minutus*, small. MINUTE, *a.*] Small, minor, or unimportant particulars or details.—**Minutiose**, mi-nū'shi-ōs, *a.* Dealing with minutiæ.

Minx, mingks, *n.* [Perhaps a sort of abbrev. form of *minikin*.] A pert, wanton girl; a hussy; a she-puppy.

Miocene, mī'o-sēn, *a.* [Gr. *meiōn*, less, and *kainos*, recent.] *Geol.* the name given to the middle subdivision of the tertiary strata, being applied to those strata which overlie the eocene and are below the pliocene. Spelled also *Meiocene*.—*n. Geol.* the miocene strata.

Miostemonous, mī-ō-stem'on-us, *a. Bot. Meiostemonous.*

Miracle, mir'a-kl, *n.* [Fr. *miracle*, from L. *miraculum*, something wonderful, from *miror*, to wonder; akin *marvel*, *mirror*, *mirage*, *admire*, &c.] A wonder or wonderful thing; something that excites astonishment; a sensible deviation from the known laws of nature, held to be wrought by a supernatural being; a supernatural event.—*To a miracle*, wonderfully; astonishingly.—**Miracle-play**, *n.* Formerly a dramatic representation exhibiting the lives of the saints, or other sacred subjects.—**Miraculous**, mi-rak'ū-lus, *a.* Of the nature of a miracle; effected by the direct agency of almighty power; exceedingly surprising or wonderful. — **Miraculously**, mi-rak'ū-lus-li, *adv.* In a miraculous manner; by miracle; supernaturally; wonderfully. — **Miraculousness**, mi-rak'ū-lus-nes, *n.*

Mirage, mi-räzh', *n.* [Fr., from *mirer*, to look; *se mirer*, to be reflected. MIRACLE, MIRROR.] The name given to a natural optical illusion, consisting in an apparent elevation or approximation of coasts, mountains, ships, &c., accompanied by inverted images; in deserts often causing a plain to assume the appearance of a lake.

Mire, mīr, *n.* [Same as Icel. *mýrr*, *mýri*, Sw. *myra*, N. *myre*, a swamp, fen; same root as *moor*, *marsh*.] Wet, clayey soil; mud.—*v.t.*—*mired*, *miring*. To fix or sink in mire (as a carriage); to soil or daub with mud.—*v.i.* To sink in mud, so as to be unable to advance.—**Miriness**, mī'ri-nes, *n.* The state of being miry.—**Miry**, mī'ri, *a.* Full of or covered with mire or mud.

Mirific, Mirifical, mi-rif'ik, mi-rif'i-kal, *a.* [L. *mirificus*—*mirus*, wonderful, and *facio*, to do. MIRACLE.] Wonder-working; wonderful.

Mirror, mir'ėr, *n.* [Fr. *miroir*, a mirror, from *mirer*, to look at, from L. *miror*, to admire. MIRACLE.] A looking-glass; any polished substance that forms images by the reflection of rays of light; a pattern; an exemplar.—*v.t.* To furnish with mirrors; to reflect as in a mirror.

Mirth, mėrth, *n.* [A.Sax. *myrgth*, *mirhth*, &c., from *mirig*, *merg*, merry. MERRY.] The feeling of being merry; merriment; noisy gaiety; glee; hilarity.—**Mirthful**, mėrth'fụl, *a.* Merry; jovial; causing or provoking mirth. — **Mirthfully**, mėrth'fụl-li, *adv.* In a mirthful manner. — **Mirthfulness**, mėrth'fụl-nes, *n.* Mirth; merriment. — **Mirthless**, mėrth'les, *a.* Without mirth; joyless.

Mirza, mėr'za, *n.* [Persian, for *emirzadeh*, son of the prince—*emir*, prince, and *zadeh*, son.] A common title of honour in Persia.

Misacceptation, mis-ak'sep-tā"shon, *n.* Act of understanding in a wrong sense.

Misadventure, mis-ad-ven'tūr, *n.* A mischance; ill luck; an unlucky accident.

Misadvertence, mis-ad-vėr'tens, *n.* Want of proper care, heed, or attention; inadvertence.

Misadvise, mis-ad-vīz', *v.t.* To give bad advice to.—**Misadvised**, mis-ad-vīzd', *a.* Ill-advised; ill-directed.

Misalliance, mis-al-lī'ans, *n.* Any improper alliance or association; specifically, an improper connection by marriage. MESALLIANCE. — **Misallied**, mis-al-līd', *a.* Improperly allied or connected.

Misanthrope, Misanthropist, mis'-an-thrōp, mis-an'thrōp-ist, *n.* [Gr. *misanthrōpos* — *miseō*, to hate, and *anthrōpos*, man.] A hater of mankind. — **Misanthropic, Misanthropical**, mis-an-throp'ik, mis-an-throp'i-kal, *a.* Pertaining to a misanthrope; hating mankind.—**Misanthropy**, mis-an'thro-pi, *n.* Hatred or dislike to mankind.

Misapply, mis-ap-plī', *v.t.* To apply to a wrong purpose.—**Misapplication**, mis-ap'pli-kā"shon, *n.* The act of misapplying.

Misappreciate, mis-ap-prē'shi-āt, *v.t.* Not properly or fully to appreciate.—**Misappreciation**, mis-ap-prē'shi-ā"shon, *n.* Defective appreciation.

Misapprehend, mis-ap'prē-hend, *v.t.* To misunderstand; to take in a wrong sense. —**Misapprehension**, mis-ap'prē-hen"-shon, *n.* A mistaking; wrong apprehension of one's meaning or of a fact.

Misappropriate, mis-ap-prō'pri-āt, *v.t.* To appropriate wrongly; to put to a wrong purpose. — **Misappropriation**, mis-ap-prō'pri-ā"shon, *n.* Wrong appropriation.

Misarrange, mis-a-rānj', *v.t.* To arrange in a wrong order.—**Misarrangement**, mis-a-rānj'ment; *n.* Disorderly arrangement.

Misbecome, mis-bē-kum', *v.t.*—pret. *misbecame*, ppr. *misbecoming*, pp. *misbecome* or *misbecomed*. Not to become; to suit ill; not to befit. — **Misbecoming**, mis-bē-kum'-ing, *p.* and *a.* Unbecoming; unseemly.—**Misbecomingly**, mis-bē-kum'ing-li, *adv.* In an unbecoming manner.

Misbegot, Misbegotten, mis-bē-got', mis-bē-got'n, *p.* and *a.* Unlawfully or irregularly begotten: used also as a general epithet of opprobrium.

Misbehave, mis-bē-hāv', *v.t.* To behave ill; to conduct one's self improperly: often used with the reflexive pronouns.—**Misbehaved**, mis-bē-hāvd', *a.* Guilty of ill behavior; ill bred; rude.—**Misbehavior, Misbehaviour**, mis-bē-hāv'yėr, *n.* Improper, rude, or uncivil behavior.

Misbelief, mis-bē-lēf', *n.* Erroneous belief; false religion; unbelief. — **Misbeliever**, mis-bē-lē'vėr, *n.* One who holds a false religion. — **Misbelieving**, mis-bē-lē'ving, *a.* Believing erroneously; irreligious.

Miscalculate, mis-kal'kū-lāt, *v.t.* To calculate erroneously; to make a wrong guess or estimate of.—**Miscalculation**, mis-kal'kū-lā"shon, *n.* Erroneous calculation or estimate.

Miscall, mis-kạl', *v.t.* To call by a wrong name; to name improperly; to give a bad name or character to†.

Miscarriage, mis-kar'ij, *n.* Unfortunate issue or result of an undertaking; failure; non-success; *med.* abortion.—**Miscarry**, mis-kar'i, *v.i.* To fail to reach its destination, as a letter; to fail of the intended effect; not to succeed (the project, scheme, design, &c., *miscarried*); to bring forth young before the proper time.

Miscegenation, mis'sē-je-nā"shon, *n.* [L. *misceo*, to mix, and *genus*, a race.] Mixture or amalgamation of races.

Miscellaneous, mis-sel-lā'nē-us, *a.* [L. *miscellaneus*, from *misceo*, to mix. MEDDLE.] Consisting of several kinds or things mingled; diversified; promiscuous; producing written compositions of various sorts (a *miscellaneous* writer). — **Miscellaneously**, mis-sel-lā'nē-us-li, *adv.* In a miscellaneous manner. — **Miscellaneousness**, mis-sel-lā'nē-us-nes, *n.* — **Miscellanist, Miscellanarian**, mis-sel'la-nist, mis-sel'a-nā"ri-an, *n.* A writer of miscellanies. — **Miscellany**, mis'sel-a-ni, *n.* [Fr. *miscellanée*.] A mixture of various kinds; a collection of written compositions on various subjects; a collection of various kinds of compositions, treatises, or extracts.

Mischance, mis-chans', *n.* Ill luck; misfortune; mishap; misadventure.

Mischief, mis'chif, *n.* [O.Fr. *mescheif*, *meschef*, mischief; from Fr. *mes*, Sp. and Pg. *menos*=L. *minus*, less, and *chef*=L. *caput*, the head. MINOR, CHIEF.] Harm; hurt; injury; damage; evil, whether intended or not; source of vexation, trouble, or annoyance; troublesome or annoying conduct; conduct causing injury; wrong-doing. — **Mischief-maker**, *n.* One who makes mischief; one who excites or instigates quarrels or enmity.—**Mischief-making**, *a.* Causing harm; exciting enmity or quarrels.—**Mischievous**, mis'chi-vus, *a.* Harmful; injurious; fond of mischief; annoying or troublesome in conduct.—**Mischievously**, mis'chi-vus-li, *adv.* In a mischievous manner. — **Mischievousness**, mis'chi-vus-nes, *n.* The quality of being mischievous.

Miscible, mis'i-bl, *a.* [Fr. *miscible*, from L. *misceo*, to mix. MEDDLE.] Capable of being mixed.—**Miscibility**, mis-i-bil'i-ti, *n.* State of being miscible.

Misconceive, mis-kon-sēv', *v.t.* or *i.* To receive a false notion or opinion of anything; to misjudge; to have an erroneous understanding of anything. — **Misconceiver**, mis-kon-sē'vėr, *n.* One who misconceives. — **Misconception**, mis-kon-sep'shon, *n.* Erroneous conception; false opinion; wrong notion or understanding of a thing.

Misconduct, mis-kon'dukt, *n.* Wrong or bad conduct; misbehaviour.—*v.t.* (mis-kon-dukt'). To conduct amiss; *refl.* to misbehave.

Misconstrue, mis-kon'strö, *v.t.* To construe or interpret erroneously; to take in a wrong sense; to misjudge; to misunderstand.—**Misconstruer**, mis-kon'strö-ėr, *n.* One who misconstrues. — **Misconstruction**, mis-kon-struk'shon, *n.* The act of misconstruing.

Miscount, mis-kount', *v.t.* To count erroneously; to misjudge. — *v.i.* To make a wrong reckoning.—*n.* An erroneous counting or numbering.

Miscreant, mis'krē-ant, *n.* [O.Fr. *mescreant*—*mes*, prefix, from L. *minus*, less, and *creant*, believing, from L. *credo*, to believe. MINOR, CREED.] An infidel, or one who embraces a false faith‡; a vile wretch; a scoundrel; a detestable villain.

Miscredit, mis-kred'it, *v.t.* To give no credit or belief to; to disbelieve. (*Carl.*)

Misdate, mis-dāt', *v.t.* To date erroneously.

Misdeal, mis-dēl′, *n. Card-playing*, a wrong deal; a deal in which each player does not receive his proper cards. — *v.t.* or *i.* To divide cards wrongly or unfairly.

Misdeed, mis-dēd′, *n.* An evil deed; a wicked action.

Misdeem, mis-dēm′, *v.t.* To judge erroneously; to misjudge; to mistake in judging.

Misdemean, mis-dē-mēn′, *v.t.* To behave ill: used *refl.*—**Misdemeanant**, mis-dē-mē′nant, *n.* One who commits a misdemeanor.—**Misdemeanor**, mis-dē-mē′nėr, *n.* Ill behavior; evil conduct; a fault or transgression; *law*, an offense of a less atrocious nature than a crime.

Misdirect, mis-di-rekt′, *v.t.* To give a wrong direction to; to direct into a wrong course; to direct to a wrong person or place. —**Misdirection**, mis-di-rek′shon, *n.* A wrong direction.

Misdo, mis-dö′, *v.t.* or *i.* To do wrong; to do amiss; to commit a crime or fault.—**Misdoer**, mis-dö′ėr, *n.* One who does wrong; one who commits a fault or crime. —**Misdoing**, mis-dö′ing, *n.* A wrong done; a fault or crime; an offence.

Misdoubt, mis-dout′, *n.* Suspicion of crime or danger.—*v.t.* To suspect of deceit or danger.

Misemploy, mis-em-ploi′, *v.t.* To employ to no purpose, or to a bad purpose.—**Misemployment**, mis-em-ploi′ment, *n.* The act of misemploying.

Miser, mī′zėr, *n.* [L. *miser*, wretched, akin to *mæstus*, sorrowful, and Gr. *misos*, hatred.] One wretched or afflicted (*Shak.*)‡; a sordid wretch; a niggard; one who in wealth makes himself miserable by the fear of poverty.—**Miserly**, mī′zėr-li, *a.* Like a miser in habits; pertaining to a miser; penurious; sordid; niggardly.

Miserable, miz′ėr-a-bl, *a.* [Fr. *misérable*, L. *miserabilis*, from *miser*, wretched. MISER.] Very unhappy; suffering misery; wretched; filled with misery; abounding in misery; causing misery; very poor or mean; worthless; despicable.—**Miserableness**, miz′ėr-a-bl-nes, *n.* The state or quality of being miserable. — **Miserably**, miz′ėr-a-bli, *adv.* In a miserable manner.—**Miserere**, miz-e-rē′rē, *n.* The name given to the 50th Psalm in the Vulgate, corresponding to the 51st Psalm in the English version, beginning '*Miserere* mei, Domine' ('Pity me, O Lord'); a piece of music composed to this psalm.—**Misery**, miz′ėr-i, *n.* [L. *miseria*, from *miser*, wretched.] Great unhappiness; extreme distress; wretchedness; calamity; misfortune; cause of misery.

Misfeasance, mis-fē′zans, *n.* [Fr. *mes*, wrong (L. *minus*), and *faisance*, from *faire*, to do.] *Law*, a trespass; a wrong done.

Misfit, mis-fit′, *n.* A wrong or bad fit; a bad match.—*v.t.* To make (a garment, &c.) of a wrong size; to supply with something that does not fit, or is not suitable.

Misform, mis-form′, *v.t.* To make of an ill form. — **Misformation**, mis-for-mā′shon, *n.* An irregularity of formation.

Misfortune, mis-for′tūn, *n.* Ill fortune; ill luck; calamity; some accident that prejudicially affects one's condition in life.

Misgive, mis-giv′, *v.t.* To fill with doubt; to deprive of confidence; to fail: usually with 'heart' or 'mind', &c., as subject, and a pronoun as object. — **Misgiving**, mis-giv′ing, *n.* A failing of confidence; doubt; distrust.

Misgovern, mis-guv′ėrn, *v.t.* To govern ill; to administer unfaithfully.—**Misgovernment**, mis-guv′ėrn-ment, *n.* The act of misgoverning; bad administration or management of public or private affairs; irregularity in conduct.

Misguide, mis-gīd′, *v.t.* To lead or guide into error; to direct ill; to direct to a wrong purpose or end.—**Misguidance**, mis-gī′dans, *n.* Wrong direction; guidance into error. — **Misguided**, mis-gī′ded, *p.* and *a.* Led astray by evil counsel or wrong direction.—**Misguidingly**, mis-gī′ding-li, *adv.* In such a way as to mislead.

Mishap, mis-hap′, *n.* Mischance; evil accident; ill luck; misfortune.

Mishna, mish′na, *n.* [Heb. *shanah*, to repeat.] The collection of precepts that constitute the basis of the Talmud.

Misincline, mis-in-klīn′, *v.t.* To cause to incline wrongly; to give a bad direction or inclination to.

Misinform, mis-in-form′, *v.t.* To give erroneous information to; to communicate an incorrect statement of facts to.—**Misinformation**, mis′in-for-mā″shon, *n.* Wrong information.

Misinterpret, mis-in-tėr′pret, *v.t.* To interpret erroneously; to understand or explain in a wrong sense.—**Misinterpretation**, mis-in-tėr′pre-tā″shon, *n.* The act of interpreting erroneously. — **Misinterpreter**, mis-in-tėr′pre-tėr, *n.* One who interprets erroneously.

Misjudge, mis-juj′, *v.t.* To mistake in judging of; to judge erroneously.—*v.i.* To err in judgment; to form false opinions or notions. — **Misjudgment**, mis-juj′ment, *n.* A wrong or unjust determination.

Mislay, mis-lā′, *v.t.* To lay in a wrong place; to lay wrongly; to lay in a place not recollected.

Misle, miz′l, *v.i.* [MIZZLE.] To rain in very fine drops; to mizzle.—*n.* A drizzle.

Mislead, mis-lēd′, *v.t.* To lead astray; to guide into error; to deceive.—**Misleader**, mis-lē′dėr, *n.* One who misleads.—**Misleading**, mis-lēd′ing, *p.* and *a.* Leading astray; leading into error; causing mistake.

Misletoe, miz′l-tō, *n.* MISTLETOE.

Mislike, mis-līk′, *v.t.* To dislike; to disapprove; to have aversion to.

Mismanage, mis-man′āj, *v.t.* To manage ill; to administer improperly.—**Mismanagement**, mis-man′āj-ment, *n.* Ill or improper management.

Mismate, mis-māt′, *v.t.* To mate or match amiss or unsuitably. [*Tenn.*]

Mismeasure, mis-mezh′ūr, *v.t.* To measure incorrectly: to form a wrong estimate of. — **Mismeasurement**, mis-mezh′ūr-ment, *n.* Wrong measurement.

Misname, mis-nām′, *v.t.* To call by the wrong name.

Misnomer, mis-nō′mėr, *n.* [Prefix *mis*, from Fr. prefix *mes*, wrong (L. *minus*, less), and *nommer*, to name, *nom*, L. *nomen*, a name.] A mistaken or inapplicable name or designation; a misapplied term.

Misocapnic, mi-sō-kap′nik, *a.* [Gr. *miseō*, to hate, *kapnos*, smoke.] Hating smoke, particularly tobacco smoke.

Misogamist, mi-sog′am-ist, *n.* [Gr. *miseō*, to hate, and *gamos*, marriage.] A hater of marriage. — **Misogamy**, mi-sog′a-mi, *n.* Hatred of marriage.

Misogynist, mi-soj′i-nist, *n.* [Gr. *miseō*, to hate, and *gynē*, woman.] A woman-hater.—**Misogyny**, mi-soj′i-ni, *n.* Hatred of the female sex.

Misotheism,† mi-soth′ē-izm, *n.* [Gr. *misos*, hatred, and *theos*, god.] Hatred of God.

Mispersuade, mis-pėr-swād′, *v.t.* To persuade amiss, or to lead to a wrong notion.

Mispickel, mis′pik-el, *n.* [G.] Arsenical pyrites; an ore of arsenic, containing this metal in combination with iron.

Misplace, mis-plās′, *v.t.* To put in a wrong place; to set on an improper object. —**Misplacement**, mis-plās′ment, *n.* The act of misplacing or putting in the wrong place.

Misprint, mis-print′, *v.t.* To mistake in printing; to print wrong.—*n.* A mistake in printing; a deviation from the copy.

Misprision, mis-prizh′on, *n.* [From Fr. prefix *mes* (=L. *minus*, less), and L. *prehensio*, a taking, from *prehendo*, to take.] Mistake; misconception; *law*, any high offence under the degree of capital, but nearly bordering thereon. — *Misprision of treason*, a bare knowledge and concealment of treason, without assenting to it.

Misprize, Misprise, mis-prīz′, *v.t.* [O.Fr. *mespriser* (Fr. *mépriser*), to despise—prefix *mes*, *mis* = L. *minus*, less, and *priser* = L. *pretiare*, to prize, from *pretium*, price. PRICE.] To slight or undervalue.

Mispronounce, mis-prō-nouns′, *v.t.* or *i.* To pronounce erroneously.—**Mispronunciation**, mis-prō-nun′si-ā″shon, *n.* A wrong or improper pronunciation.

Misproportion, mis-prō-pōr′shon, *v.t.* To err in proportioning one thing to another: to join without due proportion.

Misquote, mis-kwōt′, *v.t.* or *i.* To quote erroneously; to cite incorrectly.—**Misquotation**, mis-kwō-tā′shon, *n.* An erroneous quotation; the act of quoting wrong.

Misrate, mis-rāt′, *v.t.* To rate erroneously; to estimate falsely.

Misread, mis-rēd′, *v.t.* To read amiss; to mistake the sense of.

Misreckon, mis-rek′n, *v.t.* To reckon or compute wrong.

Misreport, mis-rē-pōrt′, *v.t.* To report erroneously; to give an incorrect account of. —*n.* An erroneous report; a false or incorrect account given.

Misrepresent, mis-rep′rē-zent″, *v.t.* To represent falsely or incorrectly; to give a false or erroneous representation of.—**Misrepresentation**, mis-rep′rē-zen-tā″shon, *n.* The act of misrepresenting; a false or incorrect representation.—**Misrepresentative**, mis-rep′rē-zen-ta-tiv, *a.* Tending to misrepresent.—**Misrepresenter**, mis-rep′rē-zen-tėr, *n.* One who misrepresents.

Misrule, mis-röl′, *n.* Bad rule; disorder; confusion.—*v.t.* To rule amiss; to govern badly or oppressively.

Miss, mis, *n.* [Contr. from *mistress.*] An unmarried female; a young unmarried lady; a girl; a title or address prefixed to the name of an unmarried female; a kept mistress; a concubine.—**Missish**, mis′ish, *a.* Like a miss; prim; affected.—**Missishness**, mis′ish-nes, *n.*

Miss, mis, *v.t.* [A.Sax. *missan*, to miss = D. and G. *missen*, Icel. *missa*, Dan. *miste*, to miss; closely akin to Teut. prefix *mis*; same root as A.Sax. *mīthan*, to conceal, avoid; G. *meiden*, to avoid.] To fail in hitting, reaching, obtaining, finding, seeing, and the like; to discover the absence of; to feel or perceive the want of; to mourn the loss of; to omit; to let slip; to pass over.—*To miss fire*, to fail to go off or explode from dampness or other cause (said of a gun).—*To miss stays* (*naut.*). Under STAY.—*v.i.* To fail to hit or strike what is aimed at.—*n.* A failure to hit, reach, obtain, &c.; loss, want.—**Missing**, mis′ing, *a.* Absent from the place where it was expected to be found; not to be found; wanting; lost.

Missal, mis′al, *n.* [L.L. *missale*, *liber missalis*, from *missa*, the mass. MASS.] The Roman Catholic mass-book or book containing the office of the mass.

Missel, Missel-thrush, mis′el, *n.* [From its feeding on the *mistletoe*; comp. G. *mistel-drossel*, mistletoe-thrush.] A common British thrush rather larger than the common thrush.

Misseltoe, mis′el-tō, *n.* MISTLETOE.

Missend, mis-send′, *v.t.* To send amiss or incorrectly.

Misshape, mis-shāp′, *v.t.* To shape ill; to give an ill form to; to deform. — **Misshapen**, mis-shā′pn, *a.* Ill formed; deformed; malformed; distorted.—**Misshapenness**, mis-shā′pn-nes, *n.* The state of being misshapen; deformity.

Missile, mis′il, *a.* [L. *missilis*, from *mitto*, *missum*, to send, to throw. MISSION.] Capable of being thrown or projected from the hand or from any instrument or engine. —*n.* A weapon or projectile thrown or to be thrown with a hostile intention, as a lance, an arrow, a bullet.

Mission, mish′on, *n.* [L. *missio*, a sending, from *mitto*, *missum*, to send, which enters into a great many English words; as *admit*, *commit*, *permit*, *remit*, *dismiss*, *remiss*, *promise*, *message*, *mess*, &c.] A sending or delegating; duty on which one is sent; a commission; an errand; persons sent by authority to perform any service; particularly, persons sent on some political business or to propagate religion; a station of missionaries; the persons connected with such a station.—**Missionary**, mish'on-a-ri, *n.* One who is sent upon a religious mission; one who is sent to propagate religion.—*a.* Pertaining to missions.

Missish, Missishness. Under Miss (lady).

Missive, mis'iv, *n.* [Fr. *missive*, a letter, from L. *missus*, sent. MISSION.] That which is sent; a message; a letter sent.—*a.* Sent or proceeding from some authoritative or official source; intended to be thrown, hurled, or ejected; missile.

Misspell, mis-spel', *v.t.* To spell wrong.—**Misspelling**, mis-spel'ing, *n.* A wrong spelling; false orthography.

Misspend, mis-spend', *v.t.* To spend amiss, to no purpose, or to a bad one; to waste.—**Misspender**, mis-spen'dėr, *n.* One who misspends.—**Misspent**, mis-spent', *p.* Ill-spent; wasted.

Misstate, mis-stāt', *v.t.* To state wrongly; to make an erroneous statement of.—**Misstatement**, mis-stāt'ment, *n.* The act of misstating; a wrong statement.

Mist, mist, *n.* [A.Sax. *mist*, gloom, cloud = L.G., D., and Sw. *mist*, Icel. *mistr*, mist; akin G. *mist*, dung; from root seen in Skr. *mih*, to sprinkle.] Visible watery vapour suspended in the atmosphere at or near the surface of the earth; aqueous vapour falling in numerous but separately almost imperceptible drops; cloudy matter; something which dims or darkens, and obscures or intercepts vision.—*v.t.* To cover with mist; to cloud. (*Shak.*)—*v.i.* To be misty or drizzling.—**Mistily**, mis'ti-li, *adv.* In a misty manner; vaguely; obscurely.—**Mistiness**, mis'ti-nes, *n.* The state of being misty.—**Misty**, mis'ti, *a.* Accompanied or characterized by mist; overspread with mist; dim; *fig.* obscure; not perspicuous.

Mistake, mis-tāk', *v.t.*—pret. *mistook*, pp. *mistaken*, ppr. *mistaking*. To take in error; to select wrongly; to conceive or understand erroneously; to regard otherwise than as the facts warrant; to misjudge; to take for a certain other person or thing; to regard as one when really another.—*v.i.* To be under a misapprehension or misconception; to be in error.—*To be mistaken*, to be misunderstood or misapprehended; to make or have made a mistake; to be in error.—*n.* An error in opinion or judgment; misapprehension; misunderstanding; a slip; a fault; a wrong act done unintentionally.—**Mistakable**, mis-tāk'a-bl, *a.* Capable of being mistaken or misconceived.—**Mistaken**, mis-tā'kn, *p.* and *a.* Erroneous; incorrect; having made, or labouring under, a mistake; wrong.—**Mistakenly**, mis-tā'kn-li, *adv.* By mistake.—**Mistaker**, mis-tāk'ėr, *n.* One who mistakes.

Misteach, mis-tēch', *v.t.* To teach wrongly; to instruct erroneously.—**Mistaught**, mis-tạt', *pp.* Wrongly taught or instructed.

Mister, mis'tėr, *n.* MASTER.

Mistime, mis-tīm', *v.t.* To time wrongly; not to adapt to the time.

Mistitle, mis-tī'tl, *v.t.* To call by a wrong title or name.

Mistletoe, miz'l-tō, *n.* [A.Sax. *misteltān*, Icel. *mistel-teinn*; *tān*, *teinn* (D. and Dan. *teen*, Goth. *tains*), meaning a twig or sprout; meaning of *mistel*, doubtful.] A European evergreen plant growing parasitically on various trees, with oblong, entire leaves, small yellowish-green flowers, and in winter small white berries.

Mistral, mis'tral, *n.* [Pr. from L. *magistralis*, lit. the master-wind.] A violent cold north-west wind experienced in Southern France, especially in winter, and forming a great scourge.

Mistranslate, mis-trans-lāt', *v.t.* To translate erroneously.—**Mistranslation**, mis-trans-lā'shon, *n.* An erroneous translation or version.

Mistreat, mis-trēt', *v.t.* To treat amiss; to maltreat.—**Mistreatment**, mis-trēt'ment, *n.* Wrong treatment; abuse.

Mistress, mis'tres, *n.* [O.Fr. *maistresse* (Fr. *maîtresse*), fem. corresponding to *maistre*, L. *magister*, a master. MASTER.] The female appellation corresponding to *master*; a woman who is chief or head in a certain sphere; a woman who has authority, command, ownership, &c.; the female head of some establishment, as a family, school, &c.; a female who is well skilled in anything, or has mastered it; a female sweetheart; a woman filling the place but without the rights of a wife; a concubine; a title of address or term of courtesy pretty nearly equivalent to *madam*: now applied only to married or matronly women, and written in the abbreviated form *Mrs.*, which is pronounced mis'is, and used before personal names.

Mistrust, mis-trust', *n.* Want of confidence or trust; suspicion.—*v.t.* To suspect; to doubt; to regard with jealousy or suspicion.—**Mistrustful**, mis-trust'fụl, *a.* Suspicious; doubting; wanting confidence.—**Mistrustfully**, mis-trust'fụl-li, *adv.* In a mistrustful manner.—**Mistrustfulness**, mis-trust'fụl-nes, *n.* The state or quality of being mistrustful.—**Mistrustingly**, mis-trust'ing-li, *adv.* With distrust or suspicion.

Misty. Under MIST.

Misunderstand, mis-un'dėr-stand", *v.t.* To misconceive; to mistake; to take in a wrong sense.—**Misunderstanding**, mis-un'dėr-stand"ing, *n.* Misconception; mistake of meaning; error; disagreement; dissension.

Misuse, mis-ūz', *v.t.* To treat or use improperly; to use to a bad purpose; to abuse; to maltreat.—*n.* (mis-ūs'). Improper use; employment in a wrong way or to a bad purpose; abuse; ill-treatment.—**Misusage**, mis-ū'zāj, *n.* Ill usage; abuse.—**Misuser**, mis-ū'zėr, *n.* One who misuses.

Mite, mīt, *n.* [A.Sax. *mite*=D. *mijt*, L.G. *mite*, Dan. *mide*, G. *miete*—mite; from root seen in Icel. *meita*, Goth. *maita*, to cut.] A name common to numerous small, in some cases microscopic, animals, of the class Arachnida (cheese-*mite*, sugar-*mite*, itch-*mite*, &c.).—**Mity**, mī'ti, *a.* Abounding with mites.

Mite, mīt, *n.* [D. *mijt*, a small coin; perhaps lit. something cut small, the origin being same as *mite*, a small insect.] A small coin formerly current, equal to about one-third of a farthing; anything proverbially very small; a very little particle or quantity.

Miter, Mitre, mī'tėr, *n.* [Fr. *mitre*, L. *mitra*, from Gr. *mitra*, headband, turban.] The headdress anciently worn by the inhabitants of Asia Minor; a sort of cap pointed and cleft at the top worn on the head by bishops and archbishops (including the pope), cardinals, and in some instances by abbots, upon solemn occasions, as also by a Jewish high-priest.—*v.t.*—*mitered*, *mitred; mitering*, *mitring*. To adorn with a miter; to raise to a rank which entitles to a miter; to unite or join by a miter-joint.—**Mitral**, mī'tral, *a.* Pertaining to a miter; resembling a miter.—**Mitered**, mī'tėrd, *p.* and *a.* Wearing a miter; entitled to wear a miter; *carp.* and *masonry*, cut or jointed at an angle of 45°.—**Miter-joint**, *n.* *Carp.* and *masonry*, a joint connecting two pieces of wood, stone, &c., at right angles, the line of the joint making an acute angle, or an angle of 45° with both pieces.—**Miter-shell**, *n.* A mollusc abounding in the seas of hot climates.—**Miter-sill**, *n.* A clap-sill.—**Miter-wheel**, *n.* One of a pair of bevel-wheels of equal diameter, working into each other with axes at right angles.—**Mitriform**, mī'triform, *a.* Resembling a miter.

Mithridate, mith'ri-dāt, *n.* [From *Mithridates*, king of Pontus, who was celebrated for his knowledge of poisons and antidotes.] An antidote against poisons.

Mitigate, mit'i-gāt, *v.t.*—*mitigated*, *mitigating*. [L. *mitigo*, *mitigatum*, to mitigate, from *mitis*, mild.] To alleviate or render less painful, rigorous, intense, or severe; to assuage, lessen, abate, moderate.—**Mitigable**, mit'i-ga-bl, *a.* Capable of being mitigated.—**Mitigant**, mit'i-gant, *a.* Mitigating; softening; lenitive; soothing; alleviating.—**Mitigation**, mit-i-gā'shon, *n.* The act of mitigating; alleviation; abatement; diminution.—**Mitigative**, mit'i-gā-tiv, *a.* Lenitive; tending to alleviate.—**Mitigator**, mit'i-ga-tėr, *n.* One who or that which mitigates.—**Mitigatory**, mit'i-gā-to-ri, *a.* Tending to mitigate; softening.

Mitosis, mi-tō'sis, *n.* [Gr. *mitos*, thread.] *Biol.* a somewhat complicated process of cell division.

Mitrailleuse, me-trā-yėz, *n.* [Fr. *mitraille*, small missiles, case shot, as in *mite*.] A breech-loading machine-gun discharging small missiles at one time or in quick succession.

Mitten, mit'n, *n.* [Fr. *mitaine*, from G. *mitte*, the middle, O.H.G. *mittamo*, half, the mitten being a kind of half or half-divided glove (akin *mid*).] A covering for the hand, differing from a glove in not having a separate cover for each finger, the thumb only being separate.—*To handle without mittens*, to treat roughly.—**Mitt**, mit, *n.* [Abbrev. of *mitten*.] A mitten; also a covering for the hand and wrist only, and not for the fingers. In baseball, a glove, heavily padded on the palm side.

Mittimus, mit'i-mus, *n.* [L., we send.] *Law*, a warrant of commitment to prison; a writ for removing records from one court to another.

Mix, miks, *v.t.* [A.Sax. *miscan*, which by common metathesis would become *mixan* (=*micsan*); O.H.G. *miscan*. *misgan*, G. *mischen*, to mix; cog. L. *misceo*, *mixtum* (MEDLEY, MEDDLE), Gr. *mignymi*, *misgō*, to mix.] To unite or blend promiscuously, as various ingredients, into one mass or compound; to mingle; to blend; to join; to associate; to unite with in company; to produce by blending different ingredients.—*v.i.* To become united or blended promiscuously in a mass or compound; to be joined or associated: to mingle.—**Mixable**, mik'sa-bl, *a.* Capable of being mixed.—**Mixed, Mixt**, mikst, *p.* and *a.* United in a promiscuous mass or compound; blended; mingled; consisting of various kinds or different things.—**Mixedly**, mik'sed-li, *adv.* In a mixed manner.—**Mixer**, mik'sėr, *n.* One who or that which mixes or mingles.

Mixen, mik'sn, *n.* [A.Sax. *mixen*, from *mix*, *meox*, dung.] A dunghill. (*Tenn.*).

Mixtilineal, Mixtilinear, miks-ti-lin'ē-al, miks-ti-lin'ē-ėr, *a.* [L. *mixtus*, mixed, and *linea*, a line.] Containing a mixture of lines, right, curved, &c.

Mixture, miks'tūr, *n.* [L. *mixtura*, from *misceo*, to mix. MIX.] The act of mixing, or state of being mixed; a mass or compound, consisting of different ingredients blended without order; a liquid medicine formed by mixing several ingredients together.

Mizzen, Mizen, miz'n, *n.* [Fr. *misaine*, from It. *mezzana*, mizzen, from *mezzano*, middle, from *mezzo*, middle: originally a large lateen sail on a middle mast. MEZZO, MEDIAL.] *Naut.* a fore-and-aft sail on the mast of a ship or barque next the stern: called also *Spanker*.—*a.* *Naut.* belonging to the mizzen; applied to the mast supporting the mizzen, and the rigging and shrouds connected with it.

Mizzle, miz'l, *v.i.* [For *mistle*, *misle*, a dim. and freq. from *mist*.] To rain in very fine drops; to drizzle.—*n.* Small rain.

Mnemonics, nē-mon'iks, *n.* [Gr. *mnēmonikos*, pertaining to memory, from *mnēmōn*, mindful, *mnaomai*, to remember; same root as in E. *mind*.] The art of memorizing; the precepts and rules intended to teach some method of assisting the memory; an organized system of memory training.—**Mnemonic, Mnemonical**, nē-mon'ik, nē-mon'i-kal, *a.* Pertaining to mnemonics; assisting or training the memory.

Mnemonician, nē-mon-ish'an, *n.* One skilled in mnemonics; a teacher of mnemonics.

Moa, mō'a, *n.* The native New Zealand name for the *Dinornis.*

Moan, mōn, *v.i.* [O.E. *mone, moone,* &c., A.Sax. *maenan,* to moan; perhaps an imitative word.] To utter a low dull sound under the influence of grief or pain; to make lamentations; to utter a prolonged groan; to give out a low dull noise.—*n.* A low dull sound due to grief or pain; a sound resembling that made by a person moaning.—**Moanful**, mōn'ful, *a.* Sorrowful.—**Moanfully**, mōn'ful-li, *adv.* With lamentation.

Moat, mōt, *n.* [Fr. *mote,* L.L. *mota,* the mound of earth dug from a trench, a hill or mound on which a castle was built; origin unknown.] A ditch or deep trench round the rampart of a castle or other fortified place to serve as a defence, often filled with water.—*v.t.* To surround with a ditch for defence.—**Moated**, mō'ted, *a.* Furnished with a moat.

Mob, mob, *n.* [Abbreviated from L. *mobile vulgus,* the fickle crowd, from *mobilis,* movable, fickle, from *moveo,* to move. MOVE, VULGAR.] A crowd; a promiscuous multitude of people, rude and disorderly; a rabble; a riotous assembly.—*v.t.*—*mobbed, mobbing.* To crowd round and annoy.—**Mobbish**, mob'ish, *a.* Pertaining to a mob; tumultuous.—**Mob-law**, *n.* The rule of the mob; the rough administration of justice by a mob; lynch-law.—**Mobocracy**, mob-ok'ra-si, *n.* [*Mob,* and Gr. *kratos,* power.] The rule or ascendancy of the mob.

Mob, mob, *n.* [Comp. D. *mop,* a pug-dog, *mopmuts,* a mob-cap.] A mob-cap.—**Mob-cap**, *n.* A plain cap for females.

Mobile, mō'bil, *a.* [Fr. *mobile,* L. *mobilis,* fickle, mobile, movable, from *moveo,* to move. MOVE.] Capable of being easily moved; readily liable to change (*mobile* features); changeable; fickle.—**Mobilize**, mob'il-īz, *v.t.*—*mobilized, mobilizing.* [Fr. *mobiliser.*] *Milit.* to put in a state of readiness for active service.—**Mobilization**, mob'il-ī-zā"shon, *n.* *Milit.* the act of mobilizing, calling, or putting into active service or readiness for active service; the act of placing upon a war footing.—**Mobility**, mō-bil'i-ti, *n.* [Fr. *mobilité,* L. *mobilitas.*] The state of being mobile; susceptibility of motion; readiness to move or change; fickleness; inconstancy.

Mobocracy. Under MOB.

Moccasin, mok'a-sin, *n.* [Spelled *mawcahsuns* in old glossary of North American Indian words.] A kind of shoe made of deer-skin or other soft leather, without a stiff sole, worn by the North American Indians; a venomous snake, genus *Agkistrodon,* found in North America.

Mocha-stone, mok'a, *n.* [From *Mocha,* where it is plentiful.] A variety of agate, containing the appearance of vegetable filaments in it; moss-agate.

Mock, mok, *v.t.* [Fr. *moquer,* in *se moquer,* to mock. flout; origin doubtful; comp. It. *mocca,* a grimace; also Gr. *mōkos,* mockery.] To imitate or mimic, especially in contempt or derision; to deride or flout; to ridicule; to fool, tantalize, disappoint, deceive; to set at naught; to defy.—*v.i.* To use ridicule; to gibe or jeer.—*n.* Ridicule; derision; gibe; flout; sneer.—*a.* False; counterfeit; assumed: often in compounds.—**Mocker**, mok'ėr, *n.* One that mocks; a scoffer; a derider; one that deceives or disappoints.—**Mockery**, mok'ėr-i, *n.* The act of mocking; derision; ridicule; sportive insult; sport; subject of laughter; imitation; counterfeit; appearance; false show; vain effort. —**Mock-heroic**, *a.* Burlesquing the heroic in poetry, action, character, &c.—**Mockingly**, mok'ing-li, *adv.* By way of derision; in contempt.—**Mocking-bird**, *n.* An American bird of the thrush family; much sought for on account of its wonderful faculty of imitating sounds.—**Mock-lead**, *n.* An ore of zinc. BLENDE.—**Mock-orange**, *n.* A common shrub with creamy white flowers having an odour which at a distance resembles that of orange-flowers; the syringa.—**Mock-sun**, *n.* A parhelion. PARHELION.—**Mock-turtle**, *n.* A soup prepared from calf's head, in imitation of real turtle-soup.

Mode, mōd, *n.* [Fr. *mode,* from L. *modus,* mode, manner, measure, &c.: same root as *mete.* Akin are *modify, modest, moderate; mood* (in gram.) is same word.] Manner; method; way (of speaking, acting, &c.); fashion; custom; *the mode,* the prevailing fashion or style; *gram.* and *logic,* same as *Mood; mus.* a species of scale of which modern musicians recognize only two, the *major* and the *minor modes.* MAJOR, MINOR.—**Modal**, mō'dal, *a.* Relating to a mode or mood; pertaining to the mode, manner, or form, not to the essence.—*Modal proposition,* in *logic,* one which affirms or denies with a qualification or limitation.—**Modality**, mō-dal'i-ti, *n.* The quality of being modal; *philos.* that quality of propositions in respect of which they express possibility or impossibility, existence or non-existence, necessity or contingency.—**Modally**, mō'dal-li, *adv.* In a manner or relation expressing or indicating a mode.

Model, mod'el, *n.* [Fr. *modèle,* O.Fr. *modelle,* from. It. *modello,* a model, lit. 'a little measure', dim. from L. *modus,* measure. MODE.] A pattern of something to be made; a form in miniature of something to be made on a larger scale; a copy, in miniature, of something already made or existing; an image, copy, facsimile; standard; that by which a thing is to be measured; anything serving or worthy of serving as a pattern; an example; a person, male or female, from whom a painter or sculptor studies his proportions, details, postures, &c. —*v.t.*—*modeled, modelled, modeling, modelling.* To plan or form after some model; to form in order to serve as a model; to mold; to shape.—*v.i.* To make a model; *sculp.* to form a work of some plastic material, as clay.—**Modeler**, **Modeller**, mod'el-ėr, *n.* One who models in clay, wax, etc.

Moderate, mod'ėr-āt, *v.t.*—*moderated, moderating.* [L. *modero* and *moderor, moderatus,* to limit, moderate, from *modus,* a measure. MODE.] To restrain from excess of any kind; to reduce in intensity (rage, passion, desire, joy, &c.); to qualify; to temper; to lessen; to allay.—*v.i.* To become less violent or intense; to preside as a moderator.—*To moderate in a call,* in Presbyterian churches, to preside at a meeting at which a call is addressed to a minister.—*a.* [L. *moderatus.*] Applied to persons, not going to extremes; temperate in opinions or views; applied to things, not extreme or excessive; not very great; mediocre.—*n.* A member of a party in the Church of Scotland which claimed the character of moderation in doctrine, discipline, and church government.—**Moderately**, mod'ėr-āt-li, *adv.* In a moderate manner or degree; not excessively.—**Moderateness**, mod'ėr-āt-nes, *n.* State of being moderate.—**Moderation**, mod'ėr-ā'shon, *n.* [L. *moderatio.*] The act of moderating, tempering, or repressing; the state or quality of being moderate; the keeping of a due mean between extremes; freedom from excess; due restraint; the act of presiding as a moderator.—*Moderations,* at Oxford University, the first public examination for degrees.—**Moderatism**, mod'ėr-āt-izm, *n.* Adherence to moderate views or doctrines.—**Moderator**, mod'ėr-ā-tėr, *n.* One who or that which moderates or restrains; the person who presides at a meeting or discussion: now chiefly applied to the chairman of meetings or courts in Presbyterian churches.—**Moderator-lamp**, *n.* A lamp for burning oil, in which the passage of the oil up towards the wick is regulated, or *moderated,* by an ingenious arrangement.—**Moderatorship**, mod'ėr-ā-tėr-ship, *n.* The office of a moderator.

Modern, mod'ėrn, *a.* [Fr. *moderne,* from L.L. *modernus,* modern, belonging to the present mode, from L. *modus,* mode, manner. MODE.] Pertaining to the present time, or time not long past; recent; not ancient.—*n.* A person of modern times: opposed to *ancient.*—**Modernism**, mod'ėrn-izm, *n.* The state of being modern; deviation from ancient manner, practice, or mode of expression, notably in literature and the arts; a tendency in churches towards rationalistic interpretation of doctrine.—**Modernist**, mod'ėrn-ist, *n.* One who admires what is modern.—**Modernistic**, mod-ėrn-is'tic, *a.* Having modern appearance or characteristics.—**Modernize**, mod'ėrn-īz, *v.t.*—*modernized, modernizing.* To give a modern character to; to adapt to modern times; to cause to conform to modern ideas or style.—**Modernizer**, mod'ėrn-ī-zėr, *n.* One who renders modern or modernizes.—**Modernization**, mod'ėrn-i-zā"shon, *n.* The act of modernizing; what is produced by modernizing.

Modest, mod'est, *a.* [Fr. *modeste,* L. *modestus,* from *modus,* a limit. MODE.] Restrained by a sense of propriety; not forward or bold; unpretending; bashful; diffident; free from anything suggestive of sexual impurity; pure; moderate; not excessive, extreme, or extravagant.—**Modestly**, mod'est-li, *adv.* In a modest manner; with modesty; diffidently; bashfully; not wantonly; not excessively.—**Modesty**, mod'es-ti, *n.* [L. *modestia.*] The state or quality of being modest; absence of tendency to forwardness, pretence, or presumption; bashful reserve; absence of anything suggestive of sexual impurity; chastity; moderation; freedom from excess.

Modicum, mod'i-kum, *n.* [L., a small or moderate quantity, from *modicus,* moderate, from *modus,* measure. MODE.] A little; a small quantity; a scanty allowance or allotment.

Modify, mod'i-fī, *v.t.*—*modified, modifying.* [Fr. *modifier,* from L. *modifico*—*modus,* limit, manner, and *facio,* to make. MODE, FACT.] To change the external qualities of; to give a new form or external character to; to vary; to alter in some respect.—**Modifier**, mod'i-fī-ėr, *n.* One who or that which modifies.—**Modifiable**, mod'i-fī-a-bl, *a.* Capable of being modified.—**Modifiability**, mod'i-fī-a-bil"i-ti, *n.* The capability of being modified.—**Modification**, mod'i-fi-kā"shon, *n.* The act of modifying; the state of being modified; some alteration in form, appearance, or character; a particular form or manner of being; a mode.—**Modificatory**, mod'i-fi-kā-to-ri, *a.* Tending to modify or produce change.

Modillion, mō-dil'yon, *n.* [Fr. *modillon,* from L. *modulus,* a model, dim. of *modus,* a measure. MODE.] *Arch.* a block carved into the form of an enriched bracket used in cornices of buildings.

Modish, mōd'ish, *a.* [From *mode.*] According to the mode or fashion; affectedly fashionable.—**Modishly**, mōd'ish-li, *adv.* In a modish manner.—**Modishness**, mod'ish-nes, *n.* The quality of being modish; affectation of the fashion.—**Modist**, mōd'ist, *n.* A follower of the fashion.—**Modiste**, mō-dēst', *n.* [Fr. *modiste,* a milliner, from *mode,* fashion.] A female who deals in articles of ladies' dress; particularly, a milliner or dressmaker.

Modulate, mod'ū-lāt, *v.t.*—*modulated, modulating.* [L. *modulor, modulatus,* from *modus,* limit, measure, mode. MODE.] To proportion; to adjust; to vary or inflect the sound of in such a manner as to give expressiveness to what is uttered; to vary (the voice) in tone; *music,* to change the key or mode of in the course of composition; to transfer from one key to another. —*v.i.* *Music,* to pass from one key into another.—**Modulation**, mod-ū-lā'shon, *n.* The act of modulating; adjustment; the act of inflecting the voice or any instrument musically; melodious sound; *music,* the change from one scale or mode to another in the course of a composition.—**Modulator**, mod'ū-lā-tėr, *n.* One who or that which modulates; in the tonic sol-fa system of music, a sort of map of musical sounds representing the relative intervals of the notes of a scale, its chromatics, and its more closely related scales.

Module, mod'ūl, *n.* [Fr., from L. *modulus*, dim. of *modus*, a measure. MODE.] *Arch.* a measure taken to regulate the proportions of an order or the disposition of the whole building.—**Modulus**, mod'ū-lus, *n.* pl. **Moduli**. *Math.* and *physics.* a term for some constant multiplier or quantity required to be used in certain calculations.—*Modulus of elasticity*, the quotient of a stress (in units of force per unit area) by the resulting strain.—**Modular**, mod'ū-lėr, *a.* Pertaining to a module or modulus.—**Modus**, mō'dus, *n.* Mode, manner, or method; *law*, a fixed payment by way of tithe.—*Modus operandi*, method of working.—*Modus vivendi*, lit. way of living; a temporary arrangement between parties pending the final settlement of matters in dispute.

Mœso-Gothic, mē-sō-goth'ik, *n.* and *a.* The language of the Mœso-Goths (or Goths of Mœsia), in which we have the earliest written example of a Teutonic dialect, namely, parts of the Scriptures translated by Ulfilas in the fourth century.

Mogul, mō-gul', *n.* [Per., a Mongolian.] *Lit.* a Mongolian or Mongol.—*The Great Mogul*, the sovereign of the empire founded in Hindustan by the Mongols under Babir in the sixteenth century, which terminated in 1806.

Mohair, mō'hār, *n.* [From Ar. *mokhayyar*, a kind of camlet or haircloth = Fr. *moire*.] The hair of the Angora goat; cloth made of this hair; camlet; a wool-and-cotton cloth made in imitation of real mohair.

Mohammedan, mō-ham'med-an, *a.* Pertaining to Mohammed, or the religion founded by him.—*n.* A follower of Mohammed; one who professes Mohammedanism.—**Mohammedanism, Mohammedism**, mō-ham'med-an-izm, mō-ham'med-izm, *n.* The religion of Mohammed, contained in the Koran.

Mohawk, mō'hąk, *n.* A tribe of North American Indians in what is now New York State, one of the Five Nations confederacy; a member of the tribe; the language of the tribe.

Moiety, moi'e-ti, *n.* [Fr. *moitié*, from L. *medietas*, from *medius*, middle. MEDIAL.] The half; one of two equal parts; a portion or share in general.

Moil, moil, *v.i.* [From O.Fr. *moiller*, Fr. *mouiller*, to wet, to soften, from L. *mollis*, soft. MOLLIFY.] To labor; to toil; to work with painful efforts.

Moire, mwąr, *n.* [MOHAIR.] A clouded or watered appearance on metals or textile fabrics; watered silk.—**Moire-antique**, *n.* Silk watered so as to resemble materials worn in olden times.—**Moiré-métallique**, mwą-rā-mā-tä-lēk, *n.* [Fr.] Tinplate the surface of which gives crystalline reflections from the action of acids.

Moist, moist, *a.* [O.Fr. *moiste*, from L. *musteus*, fresh, hence juicy, from *mustus*, fresh (whence *mustum*, must or new wine).] Moderately wet; damp; not dry; humid.—**Moisten**, mois'n, *v.t.* To make moist or damp.—*v.i.* To become moist.—**Moisture**, mois'tūr, *n.* Diffused wetness; damp.

Molar, mō'lėr, *a.* [L. *molaris*, from *mola*, a mill; same root as *meal*. MILL.] Serving to bruise or grind the food in eating; grinding.—*n.* A grinding tooth; a tooth having a flattened, triturating surface.

Molar, mō'lėr, *a.* [L. *moles*, a mass.] Pertaining to a mass or body as a whole.

Molasses, mō-las'ez, *n.* [Also *melasses*, a better spelling, being from Fr. *mélasse*, Sp. *melaza*, L. *mellaceus*, resembling honey, from *mel*, *mellis*, honey.] The uncrystallized syrup produced from sugar in the process of making.

Mold, mōld, *n.* [A.Sax. *molde*, mold, earth, dust; Icel. *mold*, Dan. *muld*, D. *molde*, *moude*, mold, earth; also Dan. *mul*, D. *mol*, *mul*, mold, moldiness, from root seen in Goth. *malan*, L. *molo*, to grind; the root of *meal* (comp. *grind* and *ground*).] Fine soft earth; mustiness or mildew; a minute fungoid or other vegetable growth, especially such as appears on bodies which lie in warm, damp air, animal and vegetable tissues, &c.; dust from incipient decay.—*v.t.* To cause to contract mold; to cover with mold or soil.—*v.i.* To become moldy.—**Moldiness**, mōl'di-nes, *n.* The state of being moldy.—**Moldy**, mōl'di, *a.* Overgrown with mold; musty; decaying.

Mold, mōld, *n.* [Fr *moule*, *molle* (with *d* added), also *modle*, from L. *modulus*, dim. of *modus*, a measure. MODE.] The matrix in which anything is cast and receives its form; a hollow tool for producing a form by percussion or compression; cast; form; shape; character.—*v.t.* To form into a particular shape; to shape; to model; to fashion.—**Mold-board**, *n.* The curved board or metal plate in a plough, which serves to turn over the furrow.—**Molder**, mōl'dėr, *n.* One who molds; one who is employed in making castings in a foundry.—**Molding**, mōl'ding, *n.* Something cast in a mold; *arch.* a general term applied to the varieties of outline or contour given to cornices, bases, door or window jambs, lintels, &c.—**Molding-sand**, *n.* A mixture of sand and loam for molds in a foundry.

Molder, mōl'dėr, *v.i.* [From *mold*, earth, mustiness; lit. to turn to *mold*.] To turn to dust by natural decay; to waste away by a gradual separation of the component particles; to crumble; to perish.

Moldwarp, mōld'wärp, *n.* The mole.

Mole, mōl, *n.* [Same word as *mold*, earth, being abbreviated from the fuller name *moldwarp*, *mouldwarp*, lit. earth-caster, from *mold*, and *warp*, to cast.] An insectivorous animal which forms burrows just under the surface of the ground, throwing up the excavated soil into little hills; a kind of plough for making drains.—**Mole-cast**, *n.* A mole-hill.—**Mole-cricket**, *n.* A name given to certain cricket-like burrowing insects.—**Mole-hill**, *n.* A heap of earth thrown up by a mole; something insignificant as contrasted with something important.—**Moleskin**, mōl'skin, *n.* A strong twilled fustian or cotton cloth, so called from its being soft like the skin of a mole.

Mole, mōl, *n.* [A.Sax. *mâl*, a blot, a spot = O.D. *mael*, Dan. *maal*, G. *mal*, a spot; cog. L. *macula*, a spot.] A spot, or small discolored protuberance on the human body.

Mole, mōl, *n.* [Fr., from L. *moles*, a mass, a dam, a mole; same root as *magnus*, great.] A mound or breakwater formed so as to partially inclose a harbor or anchorage, and protect it from the waves.

Molecule, mol'e-kūl, *n.* [Fr. *molécule*, dim. of L. *moles*, a mass. MOLE (a mound).] A small quantity of matter; a chemical entity that consists of one or more atoms existing as a specific chemical substance.—**Molecular**, mō-lek'ū-lėr, *a.* Pertaining to or consisting of molecules.—*Molecular attraction*, that force which acts between the molecules or particles of a body, keeping them together in one mass. It is distinct from gravitational attraction and is of much greater magnitude.—**Molecularity**, mō-lek'u-lar"i-ti, *n.* The state of being molecular.

Molendinary, mo-len'di-na-ri, *a.* [L. *molendinum*, a mill.] Pertaining to a mill or milling.—Also **Molinary**, mol'i-na-ri, *a.* [L. *molina*, a mill.]

Molest, mō-lest', *v.t.* [Fr. *molester*, from L. *molestus*, troublesome, from *moles*, trouble, a great mass. MOLECULE.] To annoy; to disturb; to vex.—**Molestation**, mol-es-tā'shon, *n.* The act of molesting; disturbance; annoyance.

Molinist, mō'lin-ist, *n.* A follower of the opinions of *Molina*, a Spanish Jesuit of the sixteenth century, in respect to grace, free-will, and predestination.

Mollify, mol'i-fī, *v.t.*—*mollified*, *mollifying*. [O.Fr. *mollifier*, L. *mollificare*—*mollis*, soft, and *facio*, to make. MEAL, MELLOW.] To assuage, as pain or irritation; to pacify; to reduce in harshness; to tone down.—**Mollification**, mol'i-fi-kā"shon, *n.* The act of mollifying; mitigation; pacification.—**Mollities**, mol-lish'i-ēz, *n.* [L., softness.] *Med.* diseased softening of an organ.

Mollusca, mo-lus'ka, *n. pl.* [L. *molluscus*, soft, from *mollis*, soft. MOLLIFY.] An animal sub-kingdom, comprising those soft-bodied animals which are usually provided with a shell, as mussels, oysters, land and sea snails, and all such animals, as well as the cuttle-fishes.—**Molluscan**, mol-lus'kan, *n.* A mollusk.—**Molluscous**, mol-lus'kus, *a.* Pertaining to the mollusca.—**Molluscoid**, mol-lus'koid, *n.* A member of the molluscoida.—**Molluscoida**, mol-lus-koi'da, *n. pl.* A group of animals (Polyzoa, Tunicata, and Brachiopoda) regarded as a class in the sub-kingdom mollusca.—**Mollusk**, one of the mollusca.

Molluskite, mol-lus'kīt, *n.* A dark coal-like substance found in shell-marbles, and originating in the petrifaction of the bodies of mollusks.

Mollycoddle, mol'i-kod-l, *n.* [From *Molly*, as general name for a female, and *coddle*.] An effeminate person. (*Slang.*)

Moloch, mō'lok, *n.* [Heb. *molech*, king.] The chief god of the Phoenicians and of the Ammonites, whose worship consisted chiefly of human sacrifices, ordeals by fire, mutilation, &c.; a genus of lizards found in Australia of repulsive appearance.

Molt, mōlt, *v.i.* [O.E. *moute*, *mowte* (the *l* having intruded as in *could*), like D. *muiten*, O.L.G. *muton*, from L. *muto*, *mutare*, to change. MEW.] To shed or cast the feathers, hair, skin, horns, &c., as birds and other animals do; most commonly used of birds, but also of crabs, serpents, &c.—*v.t.* To shed or cast, as feathers, hair, skin, &c.—The act of molting; the shedding or changing of feathers.

Molten, mōl'tn, *p.* and *a.* Melted.

Molto, mol'tō, *adv.* [It.] *Mus.* very, as *molto allegro*, very gay and lively.

Moly, mō'li, *n.* [Gr. *mōly*.] A fabulous herb of magic power spoken of by Homer.

Molybdena, mol-ib-dē'na, *n.* [L. *molybdæna*, from Gr. *molybdaina*, galena, from *molybdos*, lead.] A mineral, a sulphide of molybdenum, used for preparing a blue pigment for pottery ware.—**Molybdenous, Molybdous**, mo-lib'den-us, mo-lib'dus, *a.* Obtained from molybdenum; containing a larger proportion of that metal than the compounds called molybdic.—**Molybdenum**, mol-ib-dē'num, *n.* A brittle and rare metal of a white color obtained from the native sulphide of molybdena.—**Molybdic**, mo-lib'dik, *a.* Pertaining to or containing molybdenum.

Moment, mō'ment, *n.* [L. *momentum*, movement, impulse, brief space of time, importance, contr. for *movimentum*, from *moveo*, to move. MOVE.] A minute portion of time; an instant; importance; consequence. In *phys.* the moment (or importance) of a force round a point is the product of the magnitude of the force into the perpendicular distance of the point from its line of action.—*The moment of a couple* is the product of either force into the arm.—*The moment of a magnet* is the strength of either pole multiplied by the distance between the poles.—*Moment of inertia*, of a body or system of bodies round an axis, is the sum of the products of each small element of mass by the square of its distance from the axis; similarly with reference to a point and a plane.—*Momentum*, the product of a moving mass into its velocity.—**Momentarily**, mō'men-ta-ri-li, *adv.* Every moment; from moment to moment.—**Momentary**, mō'men-ta-ri, *a.* Lasting but a moment or a very short time; fleeting.—**Momently**, mō'ment-li, *adv.* From moment to moment; every moment.—**Momentous**, mō-men'tus, *a.* Of moment or importance; weighty; of great consequence.—**Momentously**, mō-men'tus-li, *adv.* Weightily; importantly.—**Momentum**, mō-men'tum, *n.* The force possessed by a body in motion; the product of the mass and velocity of a body; impetus.

Momier, mō'mi-ėr, *n.* [Fr. *momier*, from O.Fr. *momer*, to mumm, to mask.] A term given by the Calvinists in Switzerland to dissenters from their body.

Momus, mō'mus, *n.* [Gr. *mōmos*, derision.] *Greek myth.* the god of raillery and ridicule.

Monachal, mon'a-kal, *a.* [L. *monachus*, Gr. *monachos*, a monk, from *monos*, alone. MONK.] Pertaining to monks or a monastic life; monastic.—**Monachism**, mon'ak-izm, *n.* [Fr. *monachisme.*] The monastic life or system; monkery; monkishness.

Monad, mon'ad, *n.* [Gr. *monas*, *monados*, unity, from *monos*, alone.] An ultimate atom or simple substance without parts; *zool.* a microscopical organism of an extremely simple character developed in organic infusions; *chem.* a univalent element, such as hydrogen, chlorine, &c.; an imaginary entity in the philosophy of Leibnitz.—**Monadic**, **Monadical**, mo-nad'ik, mo-nad'i-kal, *a.* Having the nature or character of a monad.

Monadelph, mon'a-delf, *n.* [Gr. *monos*, sole, and *adelphos*, brother.] *Bot.* a plant whose stamens are united in one body by the filaments; *zool.* a mammal in which the uterus is single. — **Monadelphia**, mon-a-del'fi-a, *n. pl.* *Bot.* and *zool.* the monadelphs.—**Monadelphian**, **Monadelphous**, mon-a-del'fi-an, mon-a-del'fus, *a.* Belonging to the monadelphs.

Monander, mon-an'dėr, *n.* [Gr. *monos*, single, and *anēr*, *andros*, a male.] *Bot.* a monoclinous plant having one stamen only. —**Monandria**, mon-an'dri-a, *n. pl.* A class of plants having only one stamen or male organ.—**Monandrian**, **Monandrous**, mon-an'dri-an, mon-an'drus, *a.* *Bot.* monoclinous, and having one stamen only; belonging to the class monandria.—**Monandry**, mon-and'ri, *n.* Marriage to one husband only: as opposed to *polyandry.*

Monanthous, mon-an'thus, *a.* [Gr. *monos*, single, *anthos*, flower.] *Bot.* producing but one flower.

Monarch, mon'ėrk, *n.* [L. *monarcha*, from Gr. *monarchēs*, a monarch, *monarchos*, ruling alone—*monos*, alone, and *archē*, rule.] A sole ruler; the hereditary ruler of a state; a sovereign, as an emperor, king, queen, prince, &c.; one who is superior to others of the same kind (an oak is called the *monarch* of the forest).—**Monarchal**, mon-är'kal, *a.* Pertaining to a monarch; sovereign.—**Monarchic**, **Monarchical**, mon-är'kik, mon-är'ki-kal, *a.* Vested in a monarch or single ruler; pertaining to a monarchy.—**Monarchically**, mon-är'ki-kal-li, *adv.* In a monarchical manner.—**Monarchism**, mon'ėrk-izm, *n.* The principles of monarchy; love or preference of monarchy.—**Monarchist**, mon'ärk-ist, *n.* An advocate of monarchy.—**Monarchize**, mon'ärk-iz,*v.i.* To play the king; to act the monarch.—**Monarchy**, mon'ėr-ky, *n.* [Gr *monarchia.*] A state or country in which the supreme power is either actually or nominally lodged in the hands of a single person; the system of government in which the supreme power is vested in a single person; the territory ruled by a monarch; a kingdom; an empire.

Monastery, mon'as-tėr-i, *n.* [L.L. *monasterium*, from Gr. *monastērion*, from *monastēs*, a solitary, *monazō*, to be alone, from *monos*, alone, sole.] A house of religious retirement, or of seclusion from ordinary temporal concerns, whether an abbey, a priory, a nunnery, or convent: usually applied to the houses for monks.—**Monasterial**, mon-as-tē'ri-al, *a.* Pertaining to a monastery.—**Monastic**, **Monastical**, mon-as'tik, mon-as'ti-kal, *a.* [Gr. *monastikos.*] Pertaining to monasteries; pertaining to religious or other seclusion.—**Monastic**, *n.* A member of a monastery; a monk.—**Monastically**, mon-as'ti-kal-li, *adv.* In a monastic manner; reclusely.—**Monasticism**, mon-as'ti-sizm, *n.* Monastic life; the monastic system or condition —**Monasticon**, mon-as'ti-kon, *n.* A book giving an account of monasteries, convents, &c.

Monatomic, mon-a-tom'ik, *a.* *Chem* said of an element the molecule of which contains only one atom; in older use = univalent.

Monday, mun'dā, *n.* [A.Sax. *mónandæg*—*mónan*, genit. of *móna*, the moon, and *dæg*, day.] The second day of the week.

Monde, mond, *n.* [Fr., the world, from L. *mundus*, the world.] A French word used in certain phrases, as '*beau monde*', the world of fashion.

Monembryary, mon-em'bri-a-ri, *a.* [Gr. *monos*, single, and *embryon*, an embryo.] Having a single embryo.

Monetary, mon'e-ta-ri, *a.* [L. *moneta*, money. MONEY.] Pertaining to money or consisting in money.—*Monetary unit*, the standard of currency. — **Monetize**, mon'e-tiz, *v.t.* To form into coin or money. —**Monetization**, mon'et-i-zā"shon, *n.* The act of monetizing.

Money, mun'i, *n.* pl. **Moneys** or **Monies**, mun'iz. [O.Fr. *moneie*, *monnoie*, Fr. *monnaie*, from L. *moneta*, the mint, money, originally a surname of Juno (lit. the warner or admonisher, from *moneo*, to admonish), in whose temple at Rome money was coined; whence also *mint*. MONITION.] Coin; gold, silver, or other metal, stamped by public authority and used as the medium of exchange; in a wider sense, any equivalent for commodities, and for which individuals readily exchange their goods or services; a circulating medium; wealth; affluence (a man of *money*). The plural is used in the sense of sums of money or denominations of money.—*A money of account*, a denomination used merely for convenience in keeping accounts, and not represented by any coin.—*To make money*, to gain money; to be in the way of becoming rich.—*Paper money*, bank-notes, bills, &c., representing value and passing current as so.—**Money bill**, *n.* A bill imposing taxes or providing other means for raising government funds. —**Moneyed**, mun'id, *a.* Rich.—**Money-making**, *n* The process of accumulating money.—*a.* Lucrative; profitable.—**Money market**, *n.* The market or field for the investment or employment of money.—**Money-matter**, *n.* A matter or affair in which money is concerned.—**Money order**, *n.* An order granted upon payment of a sum and a small commission, by one post-office or express or telegraph company, and payable at another.—**Money's worth**, *n.* Something as good as or that will bring money; full value.

Monger, mung'gėr, *n.* [A.Sax. *mangere*, a dealer, from *mangian*, to traffic; Icel. *mangari*, *mang*, traffic, O.D *mangher*, O.H.G. *mangari*, a merchant; perhaps from L. *mango*, dealer.] A trader; a dealer; now only or chiefly in composition.

Mongol, **Mongolian**, mon'gol, mon-gō'li-an, *n* A native of Mongolia.—*a.* Belonging to Mongolia; an epithet sometimes applied to the whole Turanian tongues.—*Mongolian race*, one of the great divisions of the human family, named from the Mongols.

Mongolism, mon'gol-ism, *n.* In an occidental, an abnormal formation of head, with Mongolian appearance of eyes; usually accompanied by imbecility.

Mongoose, mon'gös, *n* [East Indian name.] A quadruped somewhat larger than a rat, one of the ichneumons, kept in houses in India to rid them of snakes and vermin.

Mongrel, mung'grel, *a* [From A.Sax *mang*, mixture, with dim. suffix as in *cockerel*; akin *mingle*, *among*.] Of a mixed breed; of mingled origins; hybrid.—*n.* A cross between two plants or animal varieties (breeds, races). Usually fertile, e.g. crosses between varieties of apple or breeds of sheep. Cp. HYBRID.—**Mongrelize**, mung'grel-iz, *v t* To make a mongrel of.

Monied, mun'id, *a.* MONEYED.

Moniliform, mō-nil'i-form, *a.* [L. *monile*, a necklace.] Like a necklace; like a series or string of beads: used especially in natural history.

Moning, mō'ning, *n.* A fine black tea.

Monism, mon'izm, *n.* [Gr. *monos*, alone, single.] The doctrine which holds that in the universe there is only a single element or principle from which everything is developed, this single principle being either mind (*idealistic monism*) or matter (*materialistic monism*).—**Monistic**, mon-is'tik, *a* Pertaining to monism; pertaining to or derived from a single source.

Monition, mō-nish'on, *n.* [L. *monitio*, *monitionis*, from *moneo*, to admonish (hence *moneta*, E. *money*): root in *monstrum*, a monster, *monstrare*, to show (*demonstrate*); *mens*, mind (whence *mental*), E. *mind*.] Admonition; warning; advice by way of caution; indication; intimation.—**Monitive**, mon'i-tiv, *a.* Admonitory; conveying admonition.—**Monitor**, mon'i-tėr, *n.* [L.] One who admonishes or warns of faults and informs of duty; an admonisher; a senior pupil in a school appointed to instruct and look after juniors; a genus of large lizards, popularly believed to give warning of the presence of crocodiles; a name for a class of shallow heavily-armed iron-clad steam-vessels sunk deeply in the water: so called from the name of the first vessel of the kind.—**Monitorial**, mon-i-tō'ri-al, *a.* Pertaining to a monitor or monitors in a school; conducted or carried on by monitors; monitory; admonitory.—**Monitorially**, mon-i-tō'ri-al-li, *adv.* By monitors.—**Monitory**, mon'i-to-ri, *a.* Giving admonition; admonitory. — **Monitress**, **Monitrix**, mon'i-tres, mon'i-triks, *n.* A female monitor.

Monk, mungk, *n.* [A.Sax *monec*, *munec*, from L.L. *monachus*, Gr. *monachos*, one who lives alone, from *monos*, alone.] One of a community of males inhabiting a monastery, and bound by vows to celibacy and religious exercises.—**Monk-fish**, *n.* The angel-fish.—**Monkhood**, mungk'hụd, *n.* Character or condition of a monk.—**Monkish**, mungk'ish, *a.* Like a monk, or pertaining to monks; monastic.—**Monkishness**, mungk'ish-nes, *n.* The quality of being monkish.—**Monk-seal**, *n.* A species of seal found in the Mediterranean.

Monkey, mung'ki, *n.* [O.Fr. *monne*, a monkey, It. *monna*, a female ape, properly dame, mistress, a contr. of *madonna*, the term *-key* being diminutive, as in *donkey*.] A name used in its wider sense to include all the quadrumana except the lemurs and their allies; but in a more restricted sense designating the long-tailed members of the order as distinguished from the apes and baboons; a term applied to a boy or girl either in real or pretended disapproval; a pile-driving apparatus; a sort of power-hammer; a comical person.—**Monkey block**, *n.* *Naut* a small single block strapped with a swivel.—**Monkey bread**, *n.* BAOBAB.—**Monkeyism**, mung'ki-izm, *n.* An act or conduct like that of a monkey. **Monkey jacket**, *n.* A close-fitting jacket, generally of some stout material.—**Monkey pot**, *n.* The fruit of a gigantic Brazilian tree consisting of a capsule furnished with a lid, containing nuts of which monkeys are fond.—**Monkey puzzle**, *n.* A name for the araucaria.—**Monkey wrench**, *n.* A screw-key with a movable jaw, which can be adjusted by a screw.

Monobasic, mon-ō-bās'ik, *a.* [Gr. *monos*, single, and *basis*, a base.] *Chem.* applied to acids which enter into combination with one equivalent of a base.

Monocarp, **Monocarpon**, mon'ō-kärp, mon-ō-kär'pon, *n.* [Gr. *monos*, single, and *karpos*, fruit.] *Bot.* a plant that perishes after having once borne fruit; an annual plant.—**Monocarpous**, **Monocarpic**, mon-ō-kär'pus, mon-ō-kär'pik, *a.* *Bot.* a term applied to annual plants.

Monocephalous, mon-ō-sef'a-lus, *a.* [Gr. *monos*, single, *kephalē*, head.] Having only one head; *bot.* applied to fruits that have but one organic head or summit, also to flowers disposed in umbels.

Monoceros, mon-os'e-ros, *n.* [Gr. *monos*, sole, *keras*, a horn.] A one-horned creature; a unicorn.

Monochlamydeous, mon'ō-kla-mid"ē-us,

a. [Gr. *monos*, single, and *chlamys*, *chlamydos*, a cloak.] *Bot.* having a single perianth; having no corolla.

Monochord, mon′ō-kord, *n.* [Gr. *monos*, sole, and *chordē*, a chord.] *Mus.* a single string stretched across a sound-board, and having under it a movable bridge, used to show the lengths of string required to produce the notes of the scale, &c.

Monochromatic, mon′ō-krō-mat″ik, *a* [Gr. *monos*, sole, and *chrōma*, colour.] Consisting of one colour, or presenting rays of light of one colour only.—**Monochrome**, mon′ō-krōm, *n.* A painting in one colour, but relieved by light and shade.—**Monochromy**, mon-ok′rō-mi, *n.* The art of painting in a single colour.

Monochronic, mon-ō-kron′ik, *a.* [Gr. *monos*, single, and *chronos*, time.] Existing or happening at the same time; belonging to one period; contemporaneous.

Monocle, mon′o-kl, *n.* [MONOCULAR.] A single eye-glass.

Monoclinal, mon-ō-klī′nal, *a.* [Gr. *monos*, single, and *klinō*, to bend.] *Geol.* applied to strata that dip for an indefinite length in one direction.—**Monoclinic, Monoclinohedric**, mon-ō-klin′ik, mon′ō-klī-nō-hed″rik, *a.* *Mineral.* having three unequal axes, two intersecting at an oblique angle, and cut by the third at right angles. —**Monoclinous**, mon-ok′li-nus, *a.* *Bot.* having both stamens and pistils in the same flower; *geol.* monoclinal.

Monocondylous, mon-ō-kon′di-lus, *a.* [Gr. *monos*, single, *kondylos*, joint.] Having a single occipital condyle, as birds and reptiles.

Monocotyledon, mon′ō-kot-i-lē″don, *n.* A plant with one cotyledon only; a monocotyledonous plant. — **Monocotyledonous**, mon′ō-kot-i-lē″do-nus, *a.* *Bot.* Having only one seed-lobe or cotyledon, as endogenous plants have.

Monocracy, mon-ok′ra-si, *n.* [Gr. *monos*, sole, and *kratos*, rule.] Government or rule by a single person; autocracy.—**Monocrat**, mon′ō-krat, *n.* One who governs alone.

Monocular, Monoculous, mon-ok′ū-lėr, mon-ok′ū-lus, *a.* [Gr. *monos*, sole, and L. *oculus*, an eye.] Having one eye only; adapted to be used with one eye only (a *monocular* microscope.

Monodactylous, mon-ō-dak′til-us, *a.* [Gr. *monos*, single, and *daktylos*, finger.] Having one finger or toe only.

Monodelphia, mon-ō-del′fi-a, *n. pl.* [Gr. *monos*, single, and *delphys*, womb.] The highest sub-class of the class Mammalia, including all animals having a single uterus. DIDELPHIA, ORNITHODELPHIA.—**Monodelph, Monodelphian**, mon′ō-delf, mon-ō-del′fi-an, *n.* A mammal of the Monodelphia.—**Monodelphic**, mon-ō-del′fik, *a.* Belonging to the Monodelphia.

Monodrama, Monodrame, mon′ō-drä-ma, mon′ō-drām, *n.* [Gr. *monos*, single, and *drama*, a drama.] A dramatic performance by a single person. — **Monodramatic**, mon′ō-dra-mat″ik, *a.* Pertaining to a monodrama.

Monody, mon′ō-di, *n.* [Gr. *monōdia*—*monos*, single. and *ōdē*, a song.] A mournful kind of song, in which a single mourner is supposed to give vent to his grief.—**Monodical**, mon-od′i-kal, *a.* Pertaining to a monody.—**Monodist**, mon′od-ist, *n.* One who writes or sings a monody.

Monodynamic, mon′ō-di-nam″ik, *a.* [Gr. *monos*, single, and *dynamis*, power.] Having but one power, capacity, or talent.

Monœcious, Monœcian, mo-nē′shus, mo-nē′shi-an, *a.* [Gr. *monos*, one, and *oikos*, a house.] *Bot.* having male and female flowers on the same plant; *zool.* having male and female organs of reproduction in the same individual. — **Monœcism**, mo-nē′sizm, *n.* The state of being monœcious.

Monogamic, mon-ō-gam′ik, *a.* [Gr. *monos*, sole, and *gamos*, marriage.] *Bot.* having flowers distinct from each other, and not collected in a head; monogamous.—**Monogamist**, mo-nog′a-mist, *n.* One who practises or upholds monogamy, as opposed to a *bigamist* or *polygamist*.—**Monogamous**, mo-nog′a-mus, *a.* Upholding or practising monogamy; *zool.* having only one mate; *bot.* monogamic.—**Monogamy**, mo-nog′a-mi, *n.* The practice or principle of marrying only once; the marrying of only one at a time; *zool.* the having only one mate.

Monogenesis, mon-ō-jen′e-sis, *n.* [Gr. *monos*, single, and *genesis*, origin.] *Biol.* direct development of an embryo from a parent similar to itself; descent of an individual from one parent form; development of all the beings in the universe from a single cell. — **Monogenetic**, mon′ō-je-net″ik, *a.* Of or relating to monogenesis.—**Monogenist**, mo-noj′e-nist, *n.* One who maintains the doctrine of monogeny.—**Monogeny**, mo-noj′e-ni, *n.* Origin from a single species; the unity of the human species.

Monogram, mon′ō-gram, *n.* [Gr. *monos*, sole, and *gramma*, letter.] A character or cipher composed of one, two, or more letters interwoven, being an abbreviation of a name, used for instance on seals, letter-paper and envelopes, &c.—**Monogrammic, Monogrammatic**, mon-ō-gram′ik, mon′ō-gram-mat″ik, *a.* In the style or manner of a monogram; pertaining to monograms.

Monograph, mon′ō-graf, *n.* [Gr. *monos*, single, and *graphē*, description.] An account or description of a single thing or class of things; the only book written by some distinguished writer on a topic.—**Monographer, Monographist**, mon-og′ra-fėr, mon-og′ra-fist, *n.* A writer of monographs. — **Monographic, Monographical**, mon-ō-graf′ik, mon-ō-graf′i-kal, *a.* Pertaining to a monograph. — **Monographically**, mon-ō-graf′i-kal-li, *adv.* In the manner or form of a monograph.—**Monography**, mon-og′ra-fi, *n.* The writing of monographs; delineation in lines without colour being used.

Monogyn, mon′ō-jin, *n.* [Gr. *monos*, sole, and *gynē*, a female.] *Bot.* a plant having only one style or stigma.—**Monogynian, Monogynous**, mon-ō-jin′i-an, mo-noj′-i-nus, *a.* Pertaining to a Linnæan order of plants having only one style or stigma.—**Monogyny**, mo-noj′-i-ni, *n.* Marriage to one woman only; the state of having but one wife at a time.

Monolith, mon′ō-lith, *n.* [Gr. *monos*, single, and *lithos*, a stone.] A pillar, column, and the like formed of a single stone, generally applied to such only as are noted for their magnitude.—**Monolithic**, mon-ō-lith′ik, *a.* Formed of a single stone; consisting of monoliths.

Monologue, mon′ō-log, *n.* [Fr. *monologue*, from Gr. *monos*, sole, and *logos*, speech.] That which is spoken by one person alone; a dramatic soliloquy; a long speech or dissertation, uttered by one person in company. —**Monologist**, mo-nol′o-jist, *n.* One who soliloquizes; one who monopolizes conversation.—**Monology**, mo-nol′o-ji, *n.* The act or habit of indulging in monologues.

Monomania, mon-ō-mā′ni-a, *n.* [Gr. *monos*, single, and *mania*, madness.] That form of mania in which the mind of the patient is absorbed by one idea, or is irrational on one subject only. — **Monomaniac, Monomane**, mon-ō-mā′ni-ak, mon′ō-mān, *n.* A person affected by monomania.—**Monomaniac, Monomaniacal**, mon-ō-mā′ni-ak, mon′ō-mā-nī″a-kal, *a.* Affected with, pertaining to, or resulting from monomania.

Monometallism, mon-ō-met′al-izm, *n.* [Gr. *monos*, single, E. *metal*.] The fact of having only one metal as a standard in the coinage of a country; the theory of a single metallic standard. **Monometallic**, mon-ō-me-tal″ik, *a.* Pertaining to monometallism.—**Monometallist**, mon-ō-met′al-ist, *n.* A supporter of monometallism.

Monometer, mo-nom′et-ėr, *n* [Gr. *monos*, single, and *metron*, measure.] *Pros.* a rhythmical series consisting of a single meter.—**Monometrical**, mon-ō-met′ri-kal, *a.* Pertaining to or consisting of monometres. —**Monometric**, mon-ō-met′rik, *a.* *Mineral.* a term applied to crystals with the axes equal or of one kind.

Monomial, mo-nō′mi-al, *n.* [Gr. *monos*, sole, and *onoma*, a name.] *Alg.* an expression or quantity consisting of a single term. —*a.* *Alg.* consisting of only one term or letter.

Monomorphic, Monomorphous, mon-ō-mor′fik, mon-ō-mor′fus, *a.* [Gr. *monos*, single, and *morphē*, form.] *Biol.* retaining the same form throughout the various stages of development.

Monomyaria, mon′ō-mī-ā″ri-a, *n. pl.* [Gr. *monos*, single, and *mys*, *myos*, a muscle.] Those bivalve molluscs whose shell is closed by a single adductor muscle, as the oyster. —**Monomyarian**, mon′ō-mī-ā″ri-an, *n.* and *a.* One of or pertaining to the Monomyaria.

Monopathy, mo-nop′a-thi, *n.* [Gr. *monos*, sole, and *pathos*, suffering.] A disease or affection in which only one organ or function is disordered.—**Monopathic**, mon-ō-path′ik, *a.* Pertaining to monopathy.

Monopersonal, mon-ō-pėr′son-al, *a.* [Gr. *monos*, single, and E. *person*.] Having but one person: used in theology.

Monopetalous, mon-ō-pet′al-us, *a.* [Gr. *monos*, single, and *petalon*.] *Bot.* having the petals united together into one piece by their edges; gamopetalous.

Monophthong, mon′of-thong, *n.* [Gr. *monos*, sole, and *phthongos*, sound.] A simple vowel-sound; two or more written vowels pronounced as one.—**Monophthongal**, mon-of-thong′gal, *a.* Consisting of a simple vowel-sound.

Monophyletic, mon′ō-fi-let″ik, *a.* [Gr. *monos*, single, *phylē*, a tribe.] Pertaining to a single family or tribe.

Monophyllous, mo-nof′il-us, *a.* [Gr. *monos*, sole, and *phyllon*, leaf.] *Bot.* having one leaf only, or formed of one leaf.

Monophyodont, mon-ō-fī′o-dont, *n.* and *a.* [Gr. *monos*, single, *phyō*, to generate, and *odous*, a tooth.] A term applied to those mammals in which only a single set of teeth is ever developed.

Monophysite, mo-nof′i-sīt, *n.* [Gr. *monos*, single, and *physis*, nature.] One who maintains that Jesus Christ had but one nature. Used also as adj.

Monoplane, mon′ō-plān, *n.* A flying apparatus with its wings or carrying surfaces arranged in the same plane. AEROPLANE.

Monopoly, mo-nop′o-li, *n.* [Fr. *monopole*, L. *monopolium*, Gr. *monopōlion* — *monos*, single, and *pōleō*, to sell.] An exclusive trading privilege; the sole right or power of selling something, or full command over the sale of it; that which is the subject of a monopoly; the possession or assumption of anything to the exclusion of others.—**Monopolist, Monopolizer**, mo-nop′-o-list, mo-nop′o-lī-zėr, *n.* One that monopolizes or possesses a monopoly.—**Monopolize**, mo-nop′o-līz, *v.t.*—*monopolized*, *monopolizing*. [Fr. *monopoliser*.] To obtain a monopoly of; to have full command of for trade purposes; to obtain or engross the whole of; to assume exclusive possession of.

Monopteron, Monopteros, mo-nop′-tėr-on, mo-nop′tėr-os, *n.* [Gr. *monos*, single, and *pteron*, a wing.] *Arch.* a temple without walls, composed of columns arranged in a circle and supporting a cupola or a conical roof. — **Monopteral**, mo-nop′tėr-al, *a.* *Arch.* formed as a monopteron.

Monoptote, mo-nop′tōt, *n.* [Gr. *monos*, only, and *ptōsis*, case.] *Gram.* a noun having only one oblique case-ending.

Monopyrenous, mon-ō-pī-rē′nus, *a.* [Gr. *monos*, single, *pyrēn*, kernel.] *Bot.* having but one kernel or stone.

Monorail, mon′ō-rāl, *n.* [Gr. *monos*, one, and *rail*.] A system of vehicular propulsion requiring only one rail. Balance is secured by a GYROSTAT (which see).

Monorganic, mon-or-gan'ik, *a.* [Gr. *monos*, single, and *organon.*] Belonging to or affecting one organ, or set of organs.

Monorhyme, mon'ō-rīm, *n.* [Gr. *monos*, single, and E. *rhyme.*] A composition in verse, in which all the lines end with the same rhyme.

Monosepalous, mon-ō-sep'al-us, *a.* [Gr. *monos*, one, and E. *sepal.*] *Bot.* composed of sepals which are united by their edges; gamosepalous.

Monoses, mon-ō'sēz, *n.* [Gr. *monos*, one.] The simplest CARBOHYDRATES (which see).

Monosperm, mon'ō-spėrm, *n.* [Gr. *monos*, single, and *sperma*, seed.] A plant of one seed only. — **Monospermous**, mon-ō-spėr'mus, *a.* *Bot.* having one seed only.

Monostachous, mo-nos'ta-kus, *a.* [Gr. *monos*, single, and *stachys*, ear of corn.] *Bot.* having one spike.

Monostich, mon'ō-stik, *n.* [Gr. *monos*, single, and *stichos*, a verse.] A poem consisting of one verse only.

Monostrophe, mo-nos'trō-fē, *n.* [Gr. *monos*, single, and *strophē*, strophe.] A metrical composition having only one strophe.—**Monostrophic**, mon-ō-strof'ik, *a.* Having one strophe only; written in unvaried measure.

Monostyle, mon'ō-stīl, *a.* [Gr. *monos*, alone, single, and *stylos*, a pillar.] *Arch.* applied to pillars when they consist of a single shaft.

Monosyllabic, mon'ō-sil-ab''ik, *a.* [Gr. *monos*, single, and *syllabē*, a syllable.] Consisting of one syllable; consisting of words of one syllable.—*Monosyllabic languages*, a class of languages in which each word is a simple uninflected root.—**Monosyllable**, mon'ō-sil-a-bl, *n.* A word of one syllable.

Monotessaron, mon-ō-tes'sa-ron, *n.* [Gr. *monos*, single, and *tessares*, four.] A harmony of the four Gospels.

Monothalamous, mon-ō-thal'a-mus, *a.* [Gr. *monos*, single, and *thalamos*, a chamber.] *Zool.* consisting of a cavity or chamber undivided by partitions; unilocular.

Monothecal, mon-ō-thē'kal, *a.* [Gr. *monos*, single, and *thēkē*, case.] *Bot.* having only one loculament.

Monotheism, mon'o-thē-izm, *n.* [Gr. *monos*, single, and *Theos*, God.] The doctrine or belief of the existence of one God only. — **Monotheist**, mon'ō-thē-ist, *n.* One who believes in one God only.—**Monotheistic**, mon'ō-thē-is''tik, *a.* Pertaining to monotheism.

Monothelite, mon'ō-thel-īt, *n.* [Gr. *monos*, single, *thelō*, to wish.] An early sect maintaining that there was only one will, the divine, in the Saviour.

Monotomous, mo-not'o-mus, *a.* [Gr. *monos*, single, and *tomē*, a cutting.] *Mineral.* having its cleavage distinct only in a single direction.

Monotone, mon'ō-tōn, *n.* [Gr. *monos*, single, and *tonos*, tone, sound.] A sameness of sound, or the utterance of successive syllables on one unvaried key, without inflection or cadence; sameness of style in writing or speaking.—**Monotonous**, mo-not'o-nus, *a.* Characterized by monotony or monotone.—**Monotonously**, mo-not'o-nus-li, *adv.* In a monotonous manner.—**Monotonousness**, mo-not'o-nus-nes, *n.* The state or quality of being monotonous.—**Monotony**, mo-not'o-ni, *n.* [Gr. *monotonia.*] Uniformity of tone or sound; want of inflections of voice in speaking or reading; want of cadence or modulation; tiresome sameness; want of variety.

Monotremata, mon-ō-trem'a-ta, *n. pl.* [Gr. *monos*, single, *trēma*, aperture.] The lowest sub-class of mammals, oviparous, and with a single outlet for the fæces and the products of the urinary and generative organs, comprising only the Ornithorhynchus and Echidna.—**Monotrematous**, mon-ō-trem'a-tus, *a.* Belonging to or characteristic of the Monotremata.—**Monotreme**, mon'ō-trēm, *n.* One of the Monotremata.

Monotype, Monotypic, mon'ō-tīp, mon-ō-tip'ik, *a.* [Gr. *monos*, single; and *typos*, a type.] Having but one type; consisting of a single representative.—**Monotype**, *n.* In printing, a mechanical method of setting and casting types in single letters.

Monovalent, mo-nov'a-lent, *n.* [Gr. *monos*, single, and L. *valens, valentis*, ppr. of *valeo*, to be worth.] *Chem.* applied to an elementary substance one atom of which enters into combination with a single atom of another elementary substance.

Monoxylon, mo-nok'si-lon, *n.* [Gr. *monos*, one, and *xylon*, wood.] A canoe or boat made from one piece of timber.—**Monoxylous**, mo-nok'si-lus, *a.* Formed of a single piece of wood.

Monroe Doctrine. The doctrine formulated by President Monroe of the United States that any attempt at colonizing by a European power within the American area constitutes an unfriendly act, leading to war.

Monseigneur, mon-sen-yėr, *n.* pl. **Messeigneurs**, mā-sen-yėr. [Fr. *mon*, my, and *seigneur*, lord. SENIOR.] A French title of honour given to princes, bishops, and other high dignitaries.—**Monsieur**, mos'yē, *n.* pl. **Messieurs**, mes'yė. [Fr., contr. of *monseigneur.*] The common title of courtesy and respect in France, answering to the English *Sir* and *Mr.*; abbreviated *Mons.*, *M.*; plural *Messrs.*, *MM.*

Monsoon, mon-sön', *n.* [Fr. *monson, mousson*, Sp. *monzon*, Pg. *mousão*, from Ar. *mausim*, a time, a season, the favourable season for sailing to India.] The trade-wind of the Arabian and Indian seas, for six months (November to March) blowing from about N.E.; and for the next six months (April to October) from about S.W.; an alternating wind in any region.

Monster, mon'stėr, *n.* [Fr. *monstre*, from L. *monstrum*, a marvel, a monster, from *moneo*, to admonish. MONITION.] A plant or animal of abnormal structure or greatly different from the usual type; an animal exhibiting malformation in important parts; a person looked upon with horror on account of extraordinary crimes, deformity, or power to do harm; an imaginary creature, such as the sphinx, mermaid, &c.—*a.* Of inordinate size or numbers (a *monster* meeting).—**Monstrosity**, mon-stros'i-ti, *n.* The state of being monstrous; that which is monstrous; an unnatural production.—**Monstrous**, mon'strus, *a.* [L. *monstrosus.*] Unnatural in form; out of the common course of nature; enormous; huge; extraordinary; shocking; frightful; horrible.—*adv.* Exceedingly; very much (now vulgar or colloquial).—**Monstrously**, mon'strus-li, *adv.* In a monstrous manner.—**Monstrousness**, mon'strus-nes, *n.*

Monstrance, mon'strans, *n.* [L.L. *monstrantia*, from L. *monstro*, to show.] *R. Cath. Ch.* the transparent or glass-faced shrine in which the consecrated host is presented for the adoration of the people.

Montanic, mon-tan'ik, *a.* [L. *montanus*, from *mons*, mountain.] Pertaining to mountains; consisting in mountains.

Montanist, mon'tan-ist, *n.* A follower of the heresiarch *Montanus*, who, in the second century, pretended he was inspired by the Holy Spirit and instructed in several points not revealed to the apostles.—**Montanism**, mon'tan-izm, *n.* The tenets of Montanus or his followers.—**Montanistic**, mon-tan-is'tik, *a.* Pertaining to the heresy of Montanus.

Montant, mon'tant, *n.* [Fr., from *monter*, to mount.] An upright blow or thrust in fencing (*Shak.*); an upright piece in carpentry.

Mont-de-piété, mon-de-pē-ā-tā, *n.* [Fr., lit. mountain of piety, from It. *monte di pietà.*] On the Continent a class of establishments for advancing money to the poor at a reasonable rate of interest; a public pawn-shop.

Monte, mon'tā, *n.* [Sp., the stock of cards which remain after each player has received his share, from L. *mons*, a mountain.] A Spanish gambling game played with dice or cards.

Montepulciano, mon'tā-pōl-chä''nō, *n.* A wine made from grapes growing near *Montepulciano* in Tuscany.

Montero, Montero-cap, mon-tē'ro, *n.* [Sp. *montero*, a huntsman, from *monte*, a mountain.] A kind of cap with a flap round it.

Month, munth, *n.* [A.Sax. *mónath, mónth*, from *móna*, the moon=Icel. *mánathr*, Dan. *maaned*, D. *maand*, G. *monath*; allied to L. *mensis*, Gr. *mēn*, a month. MOON.] One of the twelve parts of the calendar year, consisting unequally of 30 or 31 days, except February, which has 28, and in leap-year 29 days: called distinctively a *calendar month*; the period between change and change of the moon, reckoned as twenty-eight days.—**Monthly**, munth'li, *a.* Continued a month or performed in a month; happening once a month, or every month.—*adv.* Once a month; in every month.—*n.* A magazine or other literary periodical published once a month.—**Month's-mind**, *n.* A celebration in remembrance of a deceased person held a month after the death.

Monticle, Monticule, mon'ti-kl, mon'ti-kūl, *n.* [L. *monticulus*, dim. of *mons, montis*, a mountain.] A little mount; a hillock.

Monument, mon'ū-ment, *n.* [L. *monumentum*, from *moneo*, to remind, to warn. MONITION.] Anything by which the memory of a person, period, or event is perpetuated; a memorial; especially something built or erected in memory of events, actions, or persons; any enduring evidence or example; a singular or notable instance.—**Monumental**, mon-ū-men'tal, *a.* Pertaining to a monument; serving as a monument; memorial; preserving memory.—**Monumentally**, mon-ū-men'tal-li, *adv.* By way of monument or memorial; by means of monuments.

Moo, mö, *v.i.* To low, as a cow: imitated from the sound.—*n.* The low of a cow.

Mood, möd, *n.* [Fr. *mode*, L. *modus*; merely a different spelling of *mode.*] *Gram.* a special form of verbs expressive of certainty, contingency, possibility, or the like; *logic*, the determination of propositions according to their quantity and quality, that is, whether universal, affirmative, &c.

Mood, möd, *n.* [A.Sax. *mód*, mind, passion, disposition = D. *moed*, Icel. *módr* (*móthr*), Dan. and Sw. *mod*, Goth. *mods*, G. *muth*, mood, spirit, passion, courage, &c.; root doubtful.] Temper of mind; state of the mind in regard to passion or feeling; temporary disposition; humour; a fit of temper or sullenness.—**Moodily**, möd'i-li, *adv.* In a moody manner.—**Moodiness**, möd'i-nes, *n.* The state or quality of being moody.—**Moody**, möd'i, *a.* [A.Sax. *módig*, angry.] Subject to or indulging in moods or humours; fretful; out of humour; gloomy; sullen; melancholy.

Moon, mön, *n.* [A.Sax. *móna* (masc.) = Icel. *máni*, Dan. *maane*, D. *maan*, G. *mond*, Goth. *mena*, Lith. *menu*, Gr. *mēnē*, Skr. *mâs*; from root *ma*, to measure: the moon being early adopted as a measurer of time. *Month* is a derivative.] The heavenly orb which revolves round the earth; a secondary planet or satellite of the earth; a satellite of any planet (the *moons* of Jupiter); the period of a revolution of the moon; a month (poetical); something in the shape of a moon or crescent.—*v.i.* To wander or gaze idly or moodily, as if moon-struck (*colloq.*)—**Moon-beam**, *n.* A ray of light from the moon.—**Moon-blink**, *n.* A temporary evening blindness from sleeping in the moonshine in tropical climates.—**Moon-calf**, *n.* A monster; a deformed creature; a dolt; a stupid fellow.—**Moon-culminating**, *a.* An epithet for those stars which pass the meridian soon before or after the moon.—**Mooner**, mön'ėr, *n.* One who moons.—**Moonish**, mön'ish, *a.* Variable, as the moon; fickle.—**Moonless**, mōn'les, *a.* Destitute of a moon; without moonlight.—**Moonlight**, mōn'līt, *n.* The light afforded by the moon.—*a.* Illuminated by the moon; occurring during or by moonlight.—**Moon-lit**, *a.* Lit or illuminated by the moon.—**Moon-raker**, **Moon-sail**, *n.* A sail rigged above a sky-sail.—**Moonshine**, mōn'shīn, *n.* The light of the moon; fig. show without substance or reality; pretence; empty show.—**Moon-shiny**, mōn'shīn-i, *a.* Illuminated by the moon.—**Moonstone**, mōn'stōn, *n.* ADULARIA. — **Moonstruck**, mōn'struk, *a.* Affected by the influence of the moon; lunatic. — **Moony**, **Mooney**, mōn'i, *a.* Pertaining to the moon; like a moon; moon-shaped; bewildered or silly, as if moon-struck.

Moonshee, mōn'shē, *n.* [Arab. *munshi.*] In Hindustan, an interpreter; a teacher of languages.

Moor, mör, *n.* [A.Sax. *môr* = Icel. *môr*, a heath; D. *moer*, a morass; Dan. *mor*, a moor, a marsh; G. *moor*, a marsh, a moor; same root as *mire*; *morass* is a derivative.] A tract of waste land, especially when covered with heath; a tract of ground on which game is preserved for sport. (*Brit.*) —**Moor buzzard**, *n.* The marsh harrier. (*Brit.*)—**Moor cock**, **Moorfowl**, *n.* The red grouse. GROUSE.—**Moor hen**, *n.* The gallinule or water hen; also the female of the red grouse.—**Moorland**, mör'land, *n.* A waste, barren district; a moor.—Used also adjectively.—**Moorish**, **Moory**, mö'-rish, mö'ri, *a.*

Moor, mör, *n.* [Fr. *Maure*, from L. *Maurus*, Gr. *Mauros*, a Moor; comp. Gr. *mauros*, black or dark-coloured.] A native of the northern coast of Africa.—**Moorish**, mö'-rish, *a.* Pertaining to the Moors or Saracens.

Moor, mör, *v.t.* [D. *marren*, *maren*, to tie, to moor; same word as E. *mar*, A.Sax. *merran*, to hinder, to mar, O.H.G. *marrjan*, to stop.] To confine or secure (a ship) in a particular station, as by cables and anchors, or by chains; to fix firmly.—**Mooring**, mör'ing, *n.* *Naut.* the act of one who moors; that by which a ship is moored; *pl.* the place where a ship is moored.

Moose, mös, *n.* [American Indian name.] A large animal of the deer family, with broadly palmated antlers, found in Canada and northern U. S.

Moot, möt, *v.t.* [A.Sax. *môtian*, to meet for deliberation, to discuss, from *môt*, a meeting, whence *mêtan*, to meet. MEET.] To debate; to bring forward and discuss; to argue; to discuss. (*Obs.*)—*n.* Dispute; discussion; a debate on a hypothetical legal case by way of practice.—*a.* Debatable; subject to discussion; discussed or debated (a *moot* subject).—**Mootable**, möt'a-bl, *a.* Capable of being mooted.—**Moot hall**, *n.* A hall of meeting; a hall of judgment.—**Moot point**, *n.* A point debated or liable to be debated.

Mop, mop, *n.* [A Celtic word: W. *mop*, a mop; Gael. *mob*, a tuft, tassel, mop.] A piece of cloth, or a collection of thrums or coarse yarn fastened to a long handle and used for cleaning floors, carriages, &c.—*v.t.*—*mopped*, *mopping*. To rub or wipe with a mop.—**Moppet**, **Mopsey**, mop'et, mop'si, *n.* [Dim. of *mop.*] A rag baby; a pet name of a little girl or a woman; a woolly variety of dog.

Mop, mop, *n.* [Comp. D. *moppen*, to pout, to make a sulky face. MOPE.] A wry mouth; a grimace.

Mope, mōp, *v.i.*—*moped*, *moping*. [Connected with *mop*, a wry mouth; D. *moppen*, to pout.] To show a dull, downcast, or listless air; to be spiritless or gloomy.—*n.* One who mopes; a low-spirited person.—**Mopingly**, mōp'ing-li, *adv.* In a moping manner. — **Mopish**, mōp'ish, *a.* Dull; spiritless; dejected.—**Mopishly**, mōp'ish-li, *adv.* In a mopish manner.—**Mopishness**, mōp'ish-nes, *n.* Dejection; dulness.

Moppet. Under MOP.

Moraine, mō-rān', *n.* [Fr., akin to It. *mora*, a heap of stones.] An accumulation of stones or other debris on the surface of glaciers or in the valleys at their foot, a regular feature in glacier phenomena.

Moral, mor'al, *a.* [Fr. *moral*, from L. *moralis*, from *mos*, *moris*, manner, *mores*, manners, morals (seen also in *demoralize*, *demure*, *morose*).] Relating to right and wrong as determined by duty; relating to morality or morals; ethical; capable of distinguishing between right and wrong; governed by the laws of right and wrong; appealing to man as engaged in the practical concerns of life; sufficient for practical purposes (*moral* evidence, certainty); the condition of troops, &c., with respect to discipline, spirit, &c.—*Moral law*, the law prescribing moral duties and teaching right and wrong.—*Moral philosophy*, the science which treats of the nature and grounds of moral obligation; ethics.—*Moral sense*, the capacity to perceive what is right and wrong, and to approve or disapprove; conscience.—*n.* The practical lesson inculcated by any story; *pl.* general conduct or behaviour as right or wrong; principles and mode of life; also moral philosophy or ethics.—**Morale**, mō-räl', *n.* [An erroneous spelling of Fr. *moral*, used in same sense.] Mental condition of soldiers, &c., as regards courage, zeal, hope, confidence, and the like.—**Moralist**, mor'al-ist, *n.* One who teaches morals; a writer or lecturer on ethics; one who inculcates or practises moral duties.—**Morality**, mō-ral'i-ti, *n.* [Fr. *moralité.*] The doctrine of moral duties; morals; ethics; the practice of the moral duties; virtue; moral character or quality; the quality of an action, as estimated by a standard of right and wrong; a kind of drama among our forefathers in which the personages were abstractions or allegorical representations of virtues, vices, &c.—**Moralize**, mor'al-īz, *v.t.* *moralized*, *moralizing*. To apply to a moral purpose; to draw a moral from.—*v.i.* To make moral reflections; to draw practical lessons from the facts of life.—**Moralizer**, mor'al-ī-zėr, *n.* One who moralizes.—**Morally**, mor'-al-li, *adv.* In a moral manner; from a moral point of view; virtuously; uprightly; virtually; to all intents and purposes.

Morass, mō-ras', *n.* [Same as D. *moeras*, from *moer*, a moor; Sw. *moras*, G. *morast*. MOOR.] A tract of low, soft, wet ground; a marsh; a swamp; a fen.—*Morass ore*, bog-iron-ore.—**Morassy**, mō-ras'i, *a.* Marshy; fenny.

Moratorium, mō-ra-tō'ri-um, *n.* [L. *moratorius*, from *mora*, delay.] A special period of delay granted by law to debtors.

Moravian, mō-rā'vi-an, *a.* Pertaining to Moravia or the Moravians.—*n.* A native of Moravia; one of a religious sect, also called United Brethren, tracing its origin to John Huss, and holding evangelical principles.—**Moravianism**, mō-rā'vi-an-izm, *n.* The principles of the Moravians.

Morbid, mor'bid, *a.* [L. *morbidus*, from *morbus*, a disease; akin to *mori*, Skr. *mri*, to die. MORTAL.] Diseased; sickly; not sound and healthful; relating to disease.—**Morbidity**, **Morbidness**, mor-bid'i-ti, mor'bid-nes, *n.* The state of being morbid; diseased state. — **Morbidly**, mor'bid-li, *adv.* In a morbid manner.—**Morbific**, mor-bif'ik, *a.* Causing disease; generating a sickly state.

Morbillous, mor-bil'us, *a.* [Fr. *morbilleux*, from L.L. *morbilli*, measles, from L. *morbus*, disease. MORBID.] Pertaining to the measles; measly.

Morceau, mor-sō, *n.* [Fr., from O.Fr. *morsel*. MORSEL.] A morsel; a small piece; a short piece or passage of literary or musical composition.

Mordacious, mor-dā'shus, *a.* [L. *mordax*, *mordacis*, from *mordeo*, to bite. MORSEL.] Biting; sarcastic.—**Mordaciously**, mor-dā'shus-li, *adv.* In a biting manner; sarcastically.—**Mordacity**, mor-das'i-ti, *n.* [L. *mordacitas.*] The quality of biting; readiness to bite.—**Mordant**, mor'dant, *n.* [Fr. *mordant*, from L. *mordeo*, to bite.] A substance employed in the process of dyeing which serves to fix the colours; sticky matter by which gold-leaf is made to adhere.—*a.* Biting; caustic; severe.—**Mordantly**, mor'dant-li, *adv.* In a mordant manner.

More, mōr, *a.* Serving as the comparative of *much* and *many*, the superlative being *most.* [A.Sax. *māra*; D. *meer*, Dan. *meer*, *meere*, G. *mehr*, Icel. *meiri*, *meirr*, Goth. *mais*, *maiza*, more; from same root as L. *magnus*, great, E. *may.*] With singular nouns (as comparative of *much*): greater in amount, extent, degree, &c. (*more* land, *more* light); with plural nouns (as comparative of *many*): greater in number; in greater numbers (*more* men); added to some former number; additional (one day *more*, or one *more* day).—*adv.* In a greater degree, extent, or quantity; in addition; besides; again (once *more*, no *more*).—*To be no more*, to be destroyed or dead; to have perished. ∴ *More* is used to modify an adjective (or adverb) and form the comparative degree, having the same force and effect as the termination *er* in comparatives; as *more* wise (= *wiser*); *more* wisely; *more* illustrious; *more* illustriously.—*n.* What is more or greater; something farther or in addition.

Moreen, mō-rēn', *n.* [Connected with *mohair*, Fr. *moire.*] A watered woollen, or woollen and cotton fabric used for curtains, heavy dresses, &c.

Morel, mor'el, *n.* [Fr. *morelle*, nightshade, from L.L. *morellus*, dark-coloured, L. *morulus*, dark. So also the morel cherry is a dark-coloured cherry.] Garden nightshade; a kind of cherry. MORELLO.—**Morelle**, mo-rel', *n.* Garden nightshade.

Morel, mor'el, *n.* [Fr. *morille*, from O.H.G. *morilha*, G. *morchel*, Sw. *murkla.*] A kind of edible fungus.

Morello, mo-rel'lō, *n.* [It. *morello*, dark-coloured. MOREL.] A kind of cherry with a dark-red skin.

Moreover, mōr-ō'vėr, *adv.* [*More* and *over.*] Beyond what has been said; further; besides.

Morepork, *n.* [Properly *mopoke*, from its cry.] An Indian species of owl.

Moresque, mō-resk', *a.* [Fr., from It. *moresco*, from *Moro*, L. *Maurus*, a Moor.] Moorish; after the manner of the Moors.—*n.* A style of ornamentation for flat surfaces; same as *Arabesque.*

Morganatic, **Morganatical**, mor-ga-nat'ik, mor-ga-nat'i-kal, *a.* [L.L. *morganatica*, a kind of dowry paid on the morning before or after marriage, a dowry accepted in lieu of other claims; corrupted from G. *morgen-gabe*, lit. morning gift (A.Sax. *morgen-gifu*).] Said of a kind of marriage between a monarch, or one of the highest nobility, and a lady of inferior rank; called also a *left-handed marriage*, the offspring of which do not inherit the father's rank or possessions, but are considered legitimate in most other respects. — **Morganatically**, mor-ga-nat'i-kal-li, *adv.* In the manner of a morganatic marriage.

Morgay, mor'gā, *n.* [W. *morgi*, dog-fish—*mor*, the sea, and *ci*, dog.] The small spotted dog-fish. (*Brit.*)

Morgue, morg, *n.* [Fr. Origin unknown.] A place where the bodies of persons found dead are exposed, that they may be claimed by their friends; reference files in a newspaper office.

Moribund, mor'i-bund, *a.* [L. *moribundus*, from *morior*, to die. MORTAL.] In a dying state.

Moril, mor'il, *n.* A kind of mushroom. MOREL.

Moringa, mō-ring'ga, *n.* [From *muringo*, the name in Malabar.] The tree which yields the ben-nut and ben-oil.

Morion, mor'i-on, *n.* [Fr. *morion*, from Sp. *morrion*, a morion: origin doubtful.] A kind of helmet of iron, steel, or brass, somewhat like a hat in shape, and without beaver or visor.

Morisco, mo-ris'ko, *n.* [Sp. *morisco*, Moorish, from *Moro*, a Moor.] A name applied to the ancient Moorish population of Spain and to their language; a morris dance.

Morling, Mortling, mor'ling, mort'ling, *n.* [Fr. *mort*, dead, with dim. term. *-ling*.] Wool taken off a dead sheep. (*Obs.*).

Mormon, mor'mon, *n.* [From the Book of *Mormon*, accepted by them as of divine origin, and said to have been made known to Joseph Smith by an angel.] A term generally applied to a member of that religious body properly known as the Church of Jesus Christ of Latter-day Saints.—**Mormonism**, mor'mon-izm, *n.* The religion or doctrines of the Mormons.—**Mormonite**, mor'mon-it, *n.* A Mormon; a Latter-day Saint.

Morn, morn, *n.* [Contr. from O.E. *morwen*, A.Sax. *morgen*, morning, whence also *morrow*.] The first part of the day; the morning: used chiefly in poetry.—**Morning**, morn'ing, *n.* [O.E. *morwening*, from A.Sax. *morgen* (D., Dan., and G. *morgen*, Icel. *morginn*, Goth. *maurgins*) by common change of *g* to *w*, with the *-ing* of verbal nouns. (Comp. *even, evening, dawn, dawning*.) The root is seen in Lith. *mirgu*, to glimmer, to gleam.] The first part of the day, beginning at twelve o'clock at night and extending to twelve at noon; in a more limited sense, the time beginning at break of day and extending to the hour of breakfast and of beginning the labors of the day or considerably later; *fig.* the first or early part (as of life). It is often used adjectively.—**Morning glory**, *n.* A name given to several climbing plants of the convolvulus family, with handsome flowers.—**Morning-star**, *n.* Any of the planets, Venus, Jupiter, Mars, Mercury, Saturn, when it rises before the sun.—**Morning-tide**, *n.* Morning time; morning.

Morocco, mo-rok'ō, *n.* A fine leather made from the skins of goats, first imported from Morocco, and extensively used in the binding of books, upholstering furniture, making ladies' shoes, &c.

Moron, mō'ron, *n.* [Gr. *mōros*, sluggish.] A person whose mental capacity is a slight degree below normal, by psychological standards.

Morose, mō-rōs', *a.* [L. *morosus*, wayward, peevish, morose, from *mos, moris*, a custom, habit. MORAL.] Of a sour temper; severe; sullen and austere.—**Morosely**, mō-rōs'li, *adv.* In a morose manner; sourly; with sullen austerity.—**Moroseness**, mō-rōs'nes, *n.* The quality of being morose; sourness of temper; sullenness.

Morosis, mō-rō'sis, *n.* [Gr. *mōros*, foolish.] *Med.* stupidity; fatuity; idiocy.

Morpheus, mor'fūs, *n.* [Gr. from *morphē*, form, from the forms he causes to appear to people in their dreams.] *Greek myth.* the god of sleep and dreams.—**Morphean**, mor'fē-an, *n.* Of or belonging to *Morpheus*.

Morphia, Morphine, mor'fi-a, mor'fin, *n.* [Gr. *Morpheus*, the god of sleep.] The narcotic principle of opium, a vegetable alkaloid of a bitter taste, of medicinal value as an anodyne.

Morphinomania, Morphiomania, mor'fin-ō-mān"i-a, mor'fi-ō-mān"i-a, *n.* [From *morphine, morphia, mania*.] A morbid and uncontrollable craving for morphia; the habitual practice of taking morphia, especially by subcutaneous injection. —**Morphinomaniac**, mor'fin-ō-mān"i-ak, *n.* One given to this practice.

Morphology, mor-fol'o-ji, *n.* [Gr. *morphē*, form, and *logos*, description.] That department of science which treats of the form and arrangement of the structures of plants and animals; the science of form in the organic world. — **Morphologic, Morphological**, mor-fo-loj'ik, mor-fo-loj'i-kal, *a.* Pertaining to morphology.—**Morphologically**, mor-fo-loj'i-kal-li, *adv.* In a morphological manner. — **Morphologist**, mor-fol'o-jist, *n.* One versed in morphology.—**Morphonomy**, mor-fon'o-mi, *n.* [Gr. *morphē*, form, and *nomos*, law.] *Biol.* the laws of organic formation or configuration.

Morris, mor'is, *n.* **Morris Dance**, [Fr. *moresque*, from Sp. *morisco*, from *Moro*, a Moor.] A dance borrowed from the Moors, or in imitation of their dances; a fantastic dance formerly practiced in England, as in the May games.

Morris chair, a comfortable armchair having an adjustable back.

Morris plan, a method for making small loans employed by an industrial bank in the United States.

Morrow, mor'ō, *n.* [MORNING.] The day next after the present or after any day specified.—*Good morrow*, good morning, a term of salutation.—*To-morrow*, on the morrow: next day.

Morse alphabet or **code**. [After its inventor, Professor *Morse*, of Massachusetts.] A system of symbols, consisting of dashes and dots, to be used in telegraphic messages; any system on the same principle, as carried out by long and short blasts of a steam-whistle, &c.

Morsel, mor'sel, *n.* [O.Fr. *morcel* (Fr. *morceau*), from L.L. *morcellum*, a dim. from L. *morsus*, a bite, from *mordeo, morsum*, to bite; allied to G. *schmerz*, pain.] A bite; a mouthful; a small piece of food, a fragment; a little piece in general.

Mort, mort, *n.* [Fr. *mort*, death. MORTAL.] A flourish sounded at the death of game.

Mortal, mor'tal, *a.* [L. *mortalis*, from *mors, mortis*, death: same root as Skr. *mri*, to die, *mrita*, dead; this root meaning to crush or grind, and being also that of *meal, mild, murder*, &c.] Subject to death; destined to die; deadly; destructive to life; causing death; fatal; incurring the penalty of death or divine condemnation; not venial (*mortal* sin); human; belonging to man who is mortal. Colloquially applied to periods of time felt to be long or tedious (ten *mortal* hours).—*n.* A being subject to death; a man; a human being.—**Mortally**, mor'tal-li, *adv.* In the manner of a mortal; in a deadly manner or manner that must cause death.—**Mortality**, mor-tal'i-ti, *n.* [L. *mortalitas*.] The state of being mortal; death; frequency of death; death of numbers in proportion to a population; humanity; human nature; the human race.—*Bills of mortality*, abstracts showing the numbers that have died during certain periods of time.—*Tables of mortality*, tables showing how many out of a certain number of persons of a given age will probably die successively in each year till the whole are dead.

Mortar, mor'tėr, *n.* [From L. *mortarium*, a mortar in which things are pounded.] A vessel, usually in form of an inverted bell, in which substances are pulverized or pounded with a pestle; a short piece of ordnance, thick and wide, used for throwing shells, &c., and named from its resemblance to the above utensil; a mixture of lime and sand with water, used as a cement for stones and bricks in walls.—**Mortarboard**, mor'tėr-bōrd, *n.* A board for holding mortar; a square-topped academic cap.

Mortgage, mor'gāj, *n.* [Fr. *mort*, dead, and *gage*, pledge—the estate pledged becomes *dead* or entirely lost by failure to pay.] An assignment or conveyance of land or house property to a person as security for the payment of a debt due to him, and on the condition that if the money shall be paid according to contract the grant shall be void; the deed by which this conveyance is effected. — *v.t.* — *mortgaged, mortgaging.* To grant or assign on mortgage; to pledge; to make liable to the payment of any debt.—**Mortgagee**, mor-ga-jē', *n.* The person to whom an estate is mortgaged. — **Mortgager**, mor'gāj-ėr, *n.* The person who mortgages.

Mortice, mor'tis, *n.* MORTISE.

Mortify, mor'ti-fī, *v.t.*—*mortified, mortifying.* [Fr. *mortifier*—L. *mors, mortis*, death, and *facio*, to make. MORTAL.] To affect with gangrene or mortification; to subdue or bring into subjection by abstinence or rigorous severities; to humiliate; to chagrin; to affect with vexation; *Scots law*, to dispose of by mortification.—*v.i.* To lose vitality and organic structure while yet a portion of a living body; to become gangrenous. — **Mortifying**, mor'ti-fī-ing, *p.* and *a.* Humiliating; causing chagrin.—**Mortifyingly**, mor'ti-fī-ing-li, *adv.* In a mortifying manner.—**Mortification**, mor'ti-fi-kā"shon, *n.* The act of mortifying or the condition of being mortified; *med.* the death of a part of an animal body while the rest is alive; gangrene; the subduing of the passions and appetites by penance, abstinence, &c.; humiliation or slight vexation; chagrin; *Scots law*, the disposal of lands for religious or charitable purposes.

Mortise, mor'tis, *n.* [Fr. *mortaise*, a mortise; origin unknown.] A hole cut in one piece of material to receive a corresponding projecting piece called a *tenon*, on another piece, in order to fix the two together.—*v.t.* —*mortised, mortising.* To cut a mortise in; to join by tenon and mortise.

Mortling, *n.* MORLING.

Mortmain, mort'mān, *n.* [Fr. *mort*, dead, and *main*, hand.] *Law*, possession of lands or tenements in dead hands, or hands that cannot alienate, as those of a corporation; the holding of property more particularly by religious houses, which has been restricted by various statutes.

Mortuary, mor'tū-a-ri, *n.* [L.L. *mortuarium*, from L. *mortuus*, dead, from *mori*, to die. MORTAL.] A place for the temporary reception of the dead; a dead-house. *a.* Pertaining to the burial of the dead.

Morula, mor'ū-la, *n.* [Dim. of L. *morum*, mulberry, from the appearance of the mass of cells.] *Physiol.* a roundish mass of cells (called blastomeres) resulting from the division or segmentation of an ovum or its yolk in the process of development.

Mosaic, Mosaical, mō-zā'ik, mō-zā'i-kal, *a.* Relating to *Moses*, the Hebrew lawgiver, or his writings and institutions.—**Mosaism**, mō-zā'izm, *n.* The system propounded by Moses.

Mosaic, mō-zā'ik, *a.* [Fr. *mosaïque*, from It. *mosaico, musaico*, from L. Gr. *mousaikos*, belonging to the Muses, from *Mousa*, a Muse.] A term applied to inlaid work formed by little pieces of enamel, glass, marble, precious stones, &c., of various colours, cut, and disposed on a ground of cement in such a manner as to form designs, and to imitate the colours and gradations of painting.—*n.* Mosaic or inlaid work. —*Mosaic gold*, an alloy of copper and zinc, called also *ormolu*.—**Mosaical**, mō-zā'i-kal, *a.* Same as *Mosaic*.—**Mosaically**, mō-zā'i-kal-li, *adv.* In the manner of mosaic work.—**Mosaicist**, mō-zā'i-sist, *n.* One who makes mosaics.

Mosasaurus, Mososaurus, mos-a-sa'rus, mos-ō-sa'rus, *n.* [L. *Mosa*, the river Meuse or Maas, and Gr. *sauros*, a lizard.] A gigantic fossil reptile of the cretaceous formation, and first found in the Maestricht beds.

Moschatel, mos'ka-tel, *n.* [Fr. *moscatelle*, from L.L. *muscatus*, having the odour of musk. MUSK.] A plant of the temperate regions, with pale green flowers which smell like musk.

Moselle, mo-zel', *n.* A species of white French and German wine, so named from the river *Moselle*.

Moslem, moz'lem, *n.* [Ar. *moslem, muslim*, a true believer, from *salama*, to resign one's self to God.] A mussulman or Mohammedan. — *a.* Mohammedan. — **Moslim**, moz'lim, *n.* and *a.* Same as *Moslem*.

Mososaurus. MOSASAURUS.

Mosque, mosk, *n.* [Fr. *mosquée*, It. *moschea*, Sp. *mezquita*, from Ar. *mesjid*, the place of adoration, from *sajad*, to adore.] A Mohammedan temple or place of religious worship.

Mosquito, mos-kē'tō, *n.* [Sp. and Pg. *mosquito*, dim. from *mosca*, L. *musca*, a fly.] A name applied to several species of gnat-like flies, common in many regions, and which are very annoying from their severe bites.—*Mosquito nets* or *curtains*, of gauze, are often used to ward off attacks by mosquitoes upon persons reposing or asleep.

Moss, mos, *n.* [D., O.G., and Dan. *mos*, Sw. *mossa*, Icel. *mosi*, A. Sax. *meós*, G. *moos*, moss, a bog. Cog. L. *muscus*. moss; Gr. *moschos*, a sprout or tender shoot.] A name common to many cryptogamic plants of small size with simple branching stems and numerous, generally narrow leaves; also a name of various lichens; a bog; a place where peat is found.—*v.t.* To cover with moss.—**Mossy**, mos'i, *a.* Overgrown with moss; abounding with moss; like moss. —**Mossiness**, mos'i-nes, *n.* The state of being mossy, or overgrown with moss.—**Moss-agate**, *n.* A kind of agate having internally a moss-like appearance.—**Moss-capped**, *a.* Capped or covered with moss. **Moss-clad**, *a.* Clad or covered with moss. —**Moss-grown**, *a.* Overgrown with moss. —**Moss-land**, *n.* Land abounding in peat-moss.—**Moss-rose**, *n.* A beautiful variety of rose, so named from the calyx being covered with a moss-like growth.—**Moss-trooper**, *n.* One of the marauders upon the borders of England and Scotland previous to the union of the crowns, from the mosses so common on the borders.

Most, mōst, *a.* superl. of *more.* [A.Sax. *maest*, for *má-est*, superl. of old positive *má*, more; Goth. *maists*, Icel. *mestr*, D. and Dan. *meest*, G. *meist*. MORE.] Greatest in any way: with singular nouns (*most* wisdom, need, &c.); greatest in number; amounting to a considerable majority: with plurals (*most* men: *most* sorts of learning).—*adv.* In the greatest or highest, or in a very great or high degree, quantity, or extent; mostly; chiefly: often used before adjectives and adverbs to form the superlative degree, as *more* is to form the comparative.—*The Most High*, the Almighty.—*n.* The greatest or greater number; the majority: in this case plural; greatest amount or advantage; utmost extent, degree, effect, &c.: often with *the*, and in this sense singular.—*At most* or *at the most*, at furthest; at the utmost extent.—**Mostly**, mōst'li, *adv.* For the most part; chiefly; mainly.

Mot, mō, *n.* [Fr. *mot*, a word, a motto, L.L. *muttum*, from L. *muttio*, to mutter.] A pithy or witty saying; a bon-mot.

Mote, mōt, *n.* [A.Sax. *mot*, a mote; comp. D. *mot*, dust, sweepings.] A small particle; a mere atom; anything proverbially small.

Motet, Motett, mo-tet', *n.* [Fr. *motet*, from It. *mottetto*, a dim. of *motto*. MOTTO.] *Mus.* a sacred cantata; a choral composition, usually of a sacred character.

Moth, moth, *n.* [A.Sax. *moththe*; D. *mot*, Icel. *motti*, G. *motte*, Sw. *mott*, a moth.] The name of numerous lepidopterous insects allied to the butterflies, but seldom seen on the wing except in the evening or at night; the clothes-moth, the caterpillar of which is notoriously destructive to woollen materials, furs, skins, &c.—**Mothy**, moth'i, *a.* Full of moths; eaten by moths. —**Moth-eat**, *v.t.* To eat or prey upon, as a moth eats a garment.—**Moth-eaten**, *a.* Eaten by moths or rather their larvæ.

Mother, muᴛʜ'ėr, *n.* [A.Sax. *módor*, D. *moeder*, Dan. and Sw. *moder*, Icel. *móthir*, G. *mutter*, Ir. *matair*, Gael. *mathair*, L. *mater*, Gr. *mētēr*, Skr. *mātā*, *mātar*, Per. *māder*; from root *ma* to bring forth, the term., as in *father*, denoting an agent.] A female parent, especially one of the human race; a woman who has borne a child; that which has produced anything; source of anything; generatrix; a familiar term of address to elderly females; an abbess or other female holding an important position in religious or semi-religious institutions.—*Mother Carey's chicken*, a name given by sailors to the storm-petrel.—*a.* Native; natural (*mother* wit); giving birth or origin; originating (*mother* country).—**Mother-church**, *n.* An original or oldest church; the metropolitan church of a diocese.—**Mother-country**, *n.* A country which has sent out colonies, in relation to the colonies; a country as the mother or producer of anything.—**Motherhood**, muᴛʜ'ėr-hụd, *n.* The state of being a mother.—**Mother-in-law**, *n.* The mother of one's husband or wife.—**Motherless**, muᴛʜ'ėr-les, *a.* Destitute of a mother; having lost a mother.—**Motherliness**, muᴛʜ'ėr-li-nes, *n.* Quality of being motherly.—**Motherly**, muᴛʜ'ėr-li, *a.* Pertaining to a mother; becoming a mother; tender and affectionate.—**Mother-naked**, *a.* [Comp. G. *mutter-nackt.*] Stark naked; naked as at birth.—**Mother-of-pearl**, *n.* The hard silvery brilliant internal layer of several kinds of shells extensively used in the arts. Called also *Nacre.*—**Mother-tongue**, *n.* One's native language; a language to which other languages owe their origin.—**Mother-water**, *n.* A saline solution from which crystals have been obtained by evaporation. Termed also *Mother-liquor*, *Mother-lye.*—**Mother-wit**, *n.* Native wit; common sense.

Mother, muᴛʜ'ėr, *n.* [L.G. *moder*, D. *modder*, Dan. *mudder*, G. *mutter*—dregs, mud, slime, &c.; allied to *mud.*] A thick slimy substance that gathers in liquors, particularly vinegar.—*v.i.* To become mothery.—**Mothery**, muᴛʜ'ėr-i, *a.* Containing mother; resembling or partaking of the nature of mother.

Motif, mō-tēf', *n.* [Fr.] A passage or theme that reappears in varying form throughout a musical composition; the prevailing idea an artist or writer has endeavored to express.

Motific, mō-tif'ik, *a.* [L. *motus*, motion, and *facio*, to make.] Producing motion.—**Motile**, mō'til, *a.* Having inherent power of motion, as certain organs of plants.—**Motility**, mō-til'i-ti, *n.* Capability of motion.

Motion, mō'shon, *n.* [L. *motio*, *motionis*, from *moveo*, *motum*, to move. MOVE.] The act or process of changing place; the passing of a body from one place to another; opposed to *rest*; the power of moving; a single act of motion; a movement; movement of the mind or soul; internal impulse; proposal made; a proposition made in a deliberative assembly; the proposing of any matter for the consideration of an assembly or meeting; *med.* evacuation of the intestine; alvine discharge.—*v.t.* and *i.* To make a significant motion or gesture for guidance, as with the hand or head.—**Motionless**, mō'shon-les, *a.* Wanting motion; being at rest.—**Motion picture**. A form of drama produced by means of a series of photographs projected upon a screen to give an illusion of continuous, lifelike motion; any series of pictures photographed and presented in this way.

Motivate, mō'ti-vāt, *v.t. Motivated, motivating.* To furnish with a motive; to be the motive of; to impel; to induce.

Motive, mō'tiv, *n.* [Fr. *motif*, a motive, L.L. *motivus*, moving, from L. *moveo*, *motum*, to move. MOVE.] That which incites to action; that which determines the choice or moves the will; cause; object; inducement; prevailing design; the theme or leading subject in a piece of music; the prevailing idea in the mind of an artist, to which he endeavors to give expression in his work.—*a.* Causing motion.—*Motive power* or *force*, the power or force acting upon any body or quantity of matter to move it. —*v.t.* To supply a motive to or for; to prompt.—**Motiveless**, mō'tiv-les, *a.* Having no motive or aim.—**Motivity**, mō-tiv'i-ti, *n.* The power of producing motion.

Motley, mot'li, *a.* [W. *mudliw*, a changing color, a motley color—*mud*, change, and *lliw*, a stain, a hue; or akin to *mottle.*] Consisting of different colors; parti-colored (a *motley* coat); exhibiting a combination of discordant elements; heterogeneous (a *motley* style); of a dress of various colors, or the usual dress of a domestic fool.

Motor, mō'tėr, *n.* [L., A mover, from *moveo*, to move.] That which imparts motion; a prime mover; especially, a machine which develops power through rotary action, as an electric motor or an internal-combustion engine; an automobile.—*a.* Imparting motion; equipped with a motor; designating or pertaining to a nerve which stimulates the movement of a muscle or the secretory activity of glands.—*v.i.* To travel in, or drive, an automobile or other automotive vehicle.—**Motorboat**, *n.* A boat propelled by an internal-combustion engine or by electricity.—**Motorbus**, **Motorcoach**, *n.* A public vehicle propelled by an internal-combustion engine.—**Motorcar**, *n.* An automobile.—**Motorcycle**, *n.* A two-wheeled vehicle propelled by an internal-combustion engine.—**Motordrome**, *n.* An enclosed, circular track where motorcycles or automobiles are raced or tested. —**Motoring**, *n.* The recreation or act of driving, or traveling in, an automobile.—**Motorist**, *n.* A person who drives, or travels in, an automobile.—**Motorize** —*motorized, motorizing, v.t.* To provide with a motor or with motor-powered equipment.—**Motorman**, *n.* A man who operates a motor-powered vehicle, as a streetcar or electric locomotive.—**Motorship**, *n.* A ship propelled by internal-combustion (usually Diesel-electric) engines.

Motte, Mott, mot, *n.* In the United States, a clump of trees.

Mottle, mot'l, *n.* [O.Fr. *mattelé*, clotted, curdled; probably from the German; comp. Prov. G. *matte*, curds.] A blotched or spotted sort of surface as seen in woods employed in cabinet work when polished. —*v.t.* To mark with spots or blotches as if mottled.—**Mottled**, mot'ld, *p.* and *a.* Spotted; marked with blotches of color, as some kinds of cabinet wood.

Motto, mot'tō, *n.* [It. *motto*, Fr. *mot*, a word, from L.L. *muttum*, a word, from L. *muttio*, to mutter.] A short pithy sentence or phrase, or even a single word, adopted as expressive of one's guiding idea or principle, appended to a coat of arms, or otherwise put prominently forward.

Mouffion, Mouflon, mōf'lon, *n.* [Fr. *mouflon.*] An animal of the sheep kind inhabiting Corsica, Sardinia, and Greece.

Mouillé, mū-yā', *a.* [Fr., wet.] Given a softened, liquid sound, usually caused by a succeeding *y*-sound, as *l* in *William*.

Mould, **Mouldiness**, **Mouldy**. Under MOLD.

Mould, **Mouldable**, **Moulding**, &c. Under MOLD.

Moult. Under MOLT.

Moulin, mō-lan, *n.* [Fr. *moulin*, L.L. *molinus*, from L. *mola*, a mill.] A deep cylindrical hole in a glacier, formed by a rill on its surface draining into it.—**Moulinage**, mō'lin-āj, *n.* [Fr. *moulinage.*] The twisting and doubling of raw silk.

Mound, mound, *n.* [A.Sax. and G. *mund*, a defense; same root as *mount.*] An elevation of earth, generally artificial; a rampart; a hillock or knoll.—*v.t.* To fortify or enclose with a mound.—**Mound builder**, *n.* An Indian of any of the various groups that once lived in the Mississippi River and Great Lakes regions and built earthworks used in religious rites or for burial places or fortifications.

Mound, mound, *n.* [Fr. *monde*, from L. *mundus*, the world.] The ball or globe which forms part of the regalia of an emperor or king.

Mount, mount, *n.* [A.Sax. *munt*, Fr. *mont*, from L. *mons*, *montis*, a hill, from root seen in *eminent*, *prominent.*] A hill; a mountain: now chiefly poetical, or used in proper names, as *Mount* Vesuvius, *Mount* Sinai; a bulwark for offence or defence (O.T.); the cardboard or other material on which a picture or drawing is mounted or fixed; the setting of a gem or something similar; the opportunity or means of riding on horseback.—*v.i.* [Fr. *monter*, from *mont*, a hill.] To rise on high; to go up; to ascend; to be built to a great altitude; to get on or upon anything, specifically, to get on horseback; to amount; to reach in value.—*v.t.* To raise aloft; to ascend; to climb up to or upon; to place one's self upon (a throne or the like); to furnish with a horse or horses; to put on or cover with something necessary, useful, or ornamental (to *mount* a map on cloth); to prepare for use; to carry or be furnished with (a fort *mounts* a hundred cannon). — *To mount guard*, to take the station and do the duty of a sentinel.—**Mountable**, moun'ta-bl, *a.* Capable of being mounted.—**Mounter**, moun'tėr, *n.* One that mounts. **Mounting**, moun'ting, *n.* The act of ascending; that with which an article is mounted or set off, or finished for use, as the setting of a gem, the furnishings of a sword, of harness, cardboard on which a picture is pasted, &c.

Mountain, moun'tin, *n.* [O.Fr. *muntaine, montaigne*, Fr. *montagne*, from L.L. *montaneus*, mountainous, from L. *mons, montis*, a mountain. MOUNT.] A huge mass of earth and rock rising above the common level of the earth or adjacent land; an elevated mass higher than a hill; something very large or great.—*Chain of mountains*, a group of mountains linked together, thus forming a series, a system, or a chain, as the Allegheny Mountains which range over four states.—*The Mountain*, the extremists of the revolutionary party during the first French Revolution who occupied the highest benches in the National Convention.—*a.* Of, or pertaining to, a mountain.—**Mountain ash**, *n.* A genus of trees found in the United States and Europe, having ash-colored leaves, white corymbose flowers and scarlet fruit; in Europe, called the rowan tree.—**Mountaineer**, moun'tin-ēr", *n.* An inhabitant of a mountainous district; a climber of mountains.—*v.i.* To climb mountains.—**Mountain fastness**, *n.* A stronghold in a mountain, easily defended against attack.—**Mountain fortress**, *n.* A fortified section of a mountain; a mountain fastness.—**Mountain goat**, *n.* A goat native to the mountainous regions of the northwestern United States and Canada.—**Mountain lion**, *n.* A puma, also called cougar, panther or catamount, largest American species of the cat kind.—**Mountainous**, moun'tin-us, *a.* Full of mountains; large as a mountain; huge.—**Mountain pass**, *n.* A gap, or defile, in the mountains making passage possible.—**Mountain range**, *n.* A chain of mountains, forming a system, as the Rocky Mountain range, which stretches throughout the western portion of the entire North American continent and continues on throughout the western portion of South America, where it is identified as the Andes.

Mountebank, moun'ti-bangk, *n.* [It. *montimbanco, montambanco*—*montare*, to mount, and *banco*, bench.] One who mounts a bench or stage in the market or other public place, and vends medicines which he pretends are infallible remedies; a quack doctor; any boastful and false pretender; a charlatan.—*v.t.* To gull (*Shak.*).—**Mountebankery, Mountebankism**, moun'ti-bangk-ėr-i, moun'ti-bangk-izm, *n.* The practices of a mountebank; quackery.

Mourn, mōrn, *v.i.* [A.Sax. *murnan*=Icel. *morna*, O.H.G. *mornan*, Goth. *maurnan*, to grieve; root same as *murmur*.] To express grief or sorrow; to grieve; to be sorrowful; to lament; to wear the dress or appearance of grief.—*v.t.* To grieve for; to lament; to deplore; to bewail.—**Mourner**, mōr'nėr, *n.* One that mourns; one that follows a funeral in the habit of mourning.—**Mournful**, mōrn'fụl, *a.* Expressing sorrow; exhibiting the appearance of grief; doleful; causing sorrow; sad; calamitous; sorrowful; feeling grief.—**Mournfully**, mōrn'fụl-li, *adv.* In a mournful manner; dolefully; sorrowfully; sadly.—**Mournfulness**, mōrn'fụl-nes, *n.* The state or character of being mournful.—**Mourning**, mōr'ning, *n.* The act of expressing grief; lamentation; the dress or customary habit worn by mourners.—*a.* Employed to express grief (a *mourning* ring).—**Mourning clock**, *n.* A handsome purplish brown butterfly with wings bordered with yellow, brown and blue. It is found from the arctic south, in both Europe and America.—**Mourning dove**, a small wild dove found in the United States, having a lamenting cry.

Mouse, mous, *n.* pl. **Mice**, mīs. [A.Sax. *mūs*, pl. *mȳs* (like *lūs, lȳs*, louse, lice); Icel. *mūs*, Dan. *muus*, D. *muis*, G. *maus*; cog. L. *mus*, Gr. *mys*, Per. *mūsh*, Skr. *mūsha*, mouse.] A well-known small rodent quadruped that infests dwelling-houses, granaries, fields, &c.; a name of various allied animals; a term of endearment.—*v.i.* (mouz)—*moused, mousing*. To hunt for or catch mice.—**Mouse-ear**, *n.* Any of various plants, so named from their soft, hairy leaves which seem to resemble in shape the ear of a mouse; the blue or white flowered forget-me-not, symbolic of fidelity.—**Mousehole**, *n.* The hole of a mouse; a hole used by a mouse; a very small hole or entrance.—**Mouser**, mou'zer, *n.* A cat good at catching mice; one who snoops about; a detective (*slang*).—**Mousetrap**, *n.* A trap for catching mice.—**Mousing**, mou'zing, *a.* Given to or engaged in catching mice.

Mousseline, mös-lēn, *n.* [Fr.] Muslin.—*Mousseline-de-laine, Muslin-de-laine*, under MUSLIN.

Moustache, mus-tash', *n.* MUSTACHE.

Mouth, mouth, *n*; pl. **Mouths**, mouᴛʜz. [A.Sax. *mūth* = Icel. *muthr, munnr*, Sw. *mun*; Dan. and G. *mund*, D. *mond*, Goth. *munths*—mouth. Like *tooth, sooth*, &c., this word has lost an *n* before the *th*.] The aperture in the head of an animal through which food is received and voice uttered; the aperture between the lips or the portion of the face formed by the lips; the cavity within the lips; the opening of anything hollow, as of a pitcher or other vessel; the entrance to a cave, pit, or den, the opening of a well, &c.; the part of a river, creek, &c., by which it joins with the ocean or any large body of water.—*To make a mouth* or *to make mouths*, to distort the mouth; to make a wry face, as in derision.—*Down in the mouth*, chapfallen; dejected; mortified.—*To give mouth to*, to utter, to express.—*v.t.* (mouᴛʜ). To utter with a voice affectedly big or swelling; to seize or shake with the mouth.—*v.i.* To speak with a full, round, or loud, affected voice; to vociferate; to rant; to make wry faces, to grimace (*Tenn.*).—**Mouthed**, mouᴛʜd, *a.* Having a mouth of this or that kind: used in composition (foul-*mouthed*).—**Mouther**, mou'ᴛʜėr, *n.* One who mouths; an affected declaimer.—**Mouthful**, mouth'fụl, *n.* As much as the mouth contains at once; a small quantity.—**Mouthpiece**, mouth'pēs, *n.* The part of a musical instrument that is applied to the mouth; a tube by which a cigar is held in the mouth while being smoked; one who speaks on behalf of others.

Move, möv, *v.t.*—*moved, moving*. [O.Fr. *mover, mouver*, Mod. Fr. *mouvoir*, from L. *movere, motum*, to move; seen also in *remove, motion, emotion, motive, moment, remote, promote, mobile*, &c.] To carry, convey, or draw from one place to another; to cause to change place or posture; to set in motion; to stir; to excite into action; to influence; to prevail on; to rouse or excite the feelings of; to make an impression on; to affect, usually with tender feelings; to touch; to stir up; to awaken (laughter, terror); to offer formally, as a motion for consideration by a deliberative assembly; *chess, draughts*, &c., to change the position of (a piece) in the regular course of play. *v.i.* To change place or posture; to stir; to pass or go; to walk; to carry or bear one's self; to change residence; to take action; to begin to act; *chess, draughts*, &c., to change the position of one of the pieces in the course of play.—*n.* Proceeding; action taken; the moving of a piece in playing chess, &c.—*To be on the move*, to be stirring about.—**Movable, Moveable**, mö'va-bl, *a.* [O.Fr. *movable, mouvable*.] Capable of being moved; changing from one time to another (a *movable* feast, that is a feast or festival like Easter, the time for holding which varies within certain limits).—*n.* Any part of a man's goods capable of being moved; *pl.* goods, wares, commodities, furniture.—**Movableness, Moveableness, Movability**, mö'va-bl-nes, mö-va-bil'i-ti, *n.* The state or quality of being movable.—**Movably, Moveably**, mö'va-bli, *adv.* In a movable manner or state.—**Moveless**, möv'les, *a.* Incapable of being moved; fixed.—**Movement**, möv'ment, *n.* Act of moving; course or process of change; motion; an individual act of motion; a gesture; an agitation set on foot by one or more persons for the purpose of bringing about some result desired; *music*, motion or progression in time, also a detached and independent portion of a composition; the train of wheelwork in a watch or clock.—**Mover**, mö'vėr, *n.* One who or that which gives motion; one who or that which is in motion; one that offers a motion in an assembly.—**Moving**, mö'ving, *p.* and *a.* Causing to move or act; impelling; exciting the feelings; touching; pathetic; affecting.—*Moving force*, in *mech.* force considered with reference to the effect or momentum it produces.—**Movingly**, mö'ving-li, *adv.* In a moving manner; in a manner to excite the feelings; pathetically.—**Moving picture**, *n.* MOTION PICTURE.

Mow, mō, *v.t.*—*mowed* (*pret.*) *mowed* or *mown* (*pp.*) [A.Sax. *māwan*; akin. Icel. *mūgr, mūgi*, a swathe; Dan. *meie*, D. *maaijen*, G. *mähen*, to mow; allied to L. *meto*, Gr. *amaō*, to mow. *Meadow* is from this root.] To cut down with a scythe or mowing-machine (to *mow* grass); to cut the grass from (to *mow* a meadow); to cut down (men, &c.) indiscriminately, or in great numbers or quantity.—*v.i.* To cut grass; to use the scythe or mowing-machine.—**Mower**, mō'ėr, *n.* One who mows; a mowing-machine.—**Mowing-machine**, *n.* An agricultural machine employed to cut down grass, clover, grain, &c.

Mow, mō, *n.* [A.Sax. *muga*, a heap, a mow, N. *muga, mua*, a heap of hay.] A pile of hay or sheaves of grain deposited in a barn; the part of a barn where they are packed.—*v.t.* To put or pile in a mow.—**Mowburn**, mō'bėrn, *v.i.* To heat and ferment when in the mow, and thus receive injury: said of hay or grain.

Mow, mou, *n.* [From Fr. *moue*, a wry face; comp. D. *mouwe*, a mow.] A wry face.—*v.i.* To make mouths.

Moxa, mok'sa, *n.* [Chinese.] A soft downy substance prepared in China and Japan from the young leaves of certain plants, used for the gout, &c., by burning it on the skin; any substance used in this way as a counter-irritant.—**Moxibustion**, mok-si-bust'yon, *n.* *Med.* cauterization by means of a moxa.

Mucedine, mū'se-dīn, *n.* [L. *mucedo*, mould.] A sort of fungus forming moulds and mildews.—**Mucedinous**, mū-sed'i-nus, *a.* *Bot.* having the character of mould or mildew.

Much, much, *a.*; *more* and *most* serve as its comparative and superlative. [Shortened form of old *mochel, muchel*, much, from A.Sax. *mycel, micel*, much, great, many; akin Icel. *mjög, mjök*, much, *mikill*, great; Goth. *mikils*, O.H.G. *mihil*; same root as L. *magnus*, great, E. *may*. MAGNITUDE, MAY.] Great in quantity or amount; abundant: used with singular nouns (*much* food, seed, water, money, &c.).—*adv.* In a great degree; to a great amount or extent; greatly: used especially with comparatives and past participles (*much* better, larger, sooner, surprised, &c.); nearly (*much* as it was).—*Much about the same*, nearly equal.—*n.* A great quantity; a great deal; equivalent to an adjective with a noun omitted, and often qualified by *too, as*, and *so*.—**Muchness**, much'nes, *n.* State of being much; quantity.

Mucific, mū-sif'ik, *a.* [L. *mucus*, mucus, and *facio*, to make.] Generating mucus.—

Muciform, mū'si-form, *n.* *Med.* having the character of or resembling mucus.

Mucilage, mū'si-laj, *n.* [L. *mucilago*, from *mucus*, slime, mucus.] A gummy vegetable matter contained in gum tragacanth, many seeds, roots, &c.; a solution in water of gummy matter of any kind.—**Mucilaginous**, mū-si-laj'i-nus, *a.* Pertaining to or secreting mucilage; slimy; ropy; soft, and slightly viscid. — **Mucilaginousness**, mū-si-laj'i-nus-nes, *n.* The state of being mucilaginous.

Muciparous, mū-sip'a-rus, *a.* [L. *mucus*, slime, and *pario*, to produce.] Secreting or producing mucus.

Muck, muk, *n.* [From Icel. *mykr*, Dan. *mög*, dung (whence *mödding*, midden).] Dung in a moist state, or a mass of dung and rotten vegetable matter; something mean, vile, or filthy.—*v.t.* To manure with muck; to remove muck from.—**Mucker**, muk'ėr, *n.* A dishonorable and impolite person; an impudent boor. (*Slang*).—**Muckrake**, muk'rāk, *n.* A rake for removing muck.—*v.i.* To accuse of bad faith or broadcast accusation of corruption, especially if unjustly.

Mucous, Mucose, Mucosity. Under Mucus.

Mucronate, mū'kro-nāt, *a.* [L. *mucronatus*, from *mucro*, a sharp point.] *Bot.* and *zool.* narrowed to a point; terminating in a sharp point.—**Mucronately**, mū'kro-nāt-li, *adv.* In a mucronate manner.

Mucus, mū'kus, *n.* [L., mucus from the nose; akin *mungo*, to wipe the nose; *mucilage*.] A viscid fluid secreted by the mucous membrane of animals, which it serves to moisten and defend; *bot.* gummy matter soluble in water.—**Mucopurulent**, mū-kō-pū'ru-lent, *a.* [From *mucus* and *purulent*.] Consisting of mucus and pus, a *mucopurulent* discharge from a sore.—**Mucous, Mucose**, mū'kus, mū'kōs, *a.* [L. *mucosus*.] Pertaining to or resembling mucus; slimy; ropy; secreting a slimy substance.—*Mucous membrane*, a membrane that lines all the cavities of the body which open externally (such as the mouth, nose, intestines), and secretes mucus.—**Mucousness, Mucosity**, mū'kus-nes, mū-kos'i-ti, *n.* The state of being mucous; sliminess.

Mud, mud, *n.* [Allied to L.G. *mod, mudde*, D. *modder*, Dan. *mudder*, Sw. *modd*, mud, mire; Icel. *moð*, dust; E. *mother*, slimy sediment. *Muddle* is a derivative.] Wet and soft earth or earthy matter as in a puddle; sediment from turbid waters; mire.—*Mud wall*, a wall built of mud or clay, rendered firm by drying.—*v.t.*—*mudded, mudding.* To soil with mud; to muddy.—**Muddily**, mud'i-li, *adv.* In a muddy manner; turbidly; obscurely; confusedly.—**Muddiness**, mud'i-nes, *n.* The quality or condition of being muddy.—**Muddy**, mud'i, *a.* Abounding in mud; foul with mud; turbid; miry; cloudy in mind; confused; stupid; obscure; wanting in perspicuity. — *v.t.* — *muddied, muddying.* To soil with mud; to dirty; to make turbid; to cloud or make dull.—**Muddy-brained, Muddy-headed**, *a.* Of a dull understanding; stupid.—**Mudguard**, *n.* A cover over the wheel of a conveyance to stop flying mud.—**Mud hen**, *n.* One of several species of waterfowl.—**Mud puppy**, *n.* A kind of salamander.—**Mudsill**, *n.* The base or lowest sill of a structure, as of a bridge, at the bottom of a river, &c.—**Mud turtle**, *n.* A name of the soft tortoises and terrapins.

Muddle, mud'l, *v.t.*—*muddled, muddling.* [Freq. from *mud*.] To make foul, turbid, or muddy; to intoxicate partially; to cloud or stupefy, particularly with liquor; to bring into a state of confusion; to make a mess of.—*v.i.* To become muddy; to be in a confused state.—*n.* A mess; dirty confusion; intellectual confusion; bewilderment.—**Muddled**, mud'ld, *p.* and *a.* Made turbid or muddy; stupefied; confused.—**Muddle-headed**, *a.* Having the brains muddled; stupidly confused or dull; doltish.

Muezzin, Mueddin, mu̧-ed'zin, mu̧-ed'in, *n.* [A. *muezzin*, from *azzana*, to inform, from *azana*, to hear.] A Mohammedan crier attached to a mosque, whose duty it is to proclaim from the balcony of a minaret the summons to prayers five times a day.

Muff, muf, *n.* [Dan. *muffe*, D. *mof*, L.G. *muffe, muff*, G. *muff*, a muff, akin to O.H. G. *mouwa*, D. *mouw*, a long sleeve; comp. also D. *mof*, a clown, *muf*, musty, silly, doting. Hence *muffle*.] A cylindrical cover, usually made of fur, into which both hands may be thrust in order to keep them warm; a soft, useless fellow; a mean, poor-spirited person (*colloq.*); in various games, an unsuccessful attempt to hold a caught ball.—*v.t.* To bungle; to miss a chance; in games, to fail to hold a caught ball.

Muffin, muf'in, *n.* A quick bread baked in individual cup-shaped molds; a drop biscuit.

Muffle, muf'l, *v.t.*—*muffled, muffling.* [O.E. also *muffle*, akin to *muff*; comp. D. *muffel*, a muff; Fr. *moufle*, a mitten.] To enfold or wrap up so as to conceal from view or protect from the weather; to wrap up or cover close, particularly the neck and face; to deaden the sound of (to *muffle* an oar or a drum); to restrain from speaking by wrapping up the head; to put to silence; *fig.* to wrap up or envelop; to involve.—*n.* [Fr. *moufle*, a kind of glove, a chemical vessel.] An arched vessel, resisting the strongest fire, and made to be placed over cupels in the operation of assaying, to preserve them from coming in contact with fuel, smoke, or ashes; a pulley-block containing several sheaves. — **Muffled**, muf'ld, *p.* and *a.* Wrapped up closely, especially about the face; treated so as to deaden the sound (as when an oar is wrapped with a mat at the rowlock); dulled or deadened: applied to sound.—**Muffler**, muf'lėr, *n.* A wrapper for muffling or enveloping the neck, and often also the face; a stuffed glove for lunatics.

Muffle, muf'l, *n.* [Fr. *mufle*, from G. *muffel*, an animal with large hanging lips.] The tumid and naked portion of the upper lip and nose of ruminants and rodents.

Mufti, Muftee, muf'ti, muf'tē, *n.* [Ar. *mufti*, from *áftā*, to judge, to give a decision.] The chief of the ecclesiastical order among the Mohammedans; a doctor of Mohammedan law; an Anglo-Indian term for plain dress worn by officers off duty; civilian dress.

Mug, mug, *n.* [N. *mugge*, a ewer, a mug; Sw. *mugg*, an earthen cup; Ir. *mugan*, a mug.] A familiar name for an earthen or metal vessel for drinking from; a jug.

Mug, mug, *n.* [Perhaps a Gypsy word = Skr. *mukha*, the face.] The face or mouth; a grimace. (*Slang*.)

Muggletonian, mug'el-tōn'i-an, *n.* A follower of Ludovic *Muggleton* (1610-97) and John Reeve, who claimed to be the 'two witnesses' of Revelation and to have the gift of prophecy. This English act is no longer treated as extant.

Muggy, Muggish, mug'i, mug'ish, *a.* [Prov.E. *mug*, mist; Icel. *mugga*, mugginess, drizzle; comp. Gael. *mugach*, cloudy; W. *mwg*, smoke.] Damp and close: said of the atmosphere or weather; warm and humid; moist; moldy.

Mugwort, mug'wėrt, *n.* [A.Sax. *mucgwyrt*, lit. midge-wort.] A kind of wormwood, or several herbs resembling it.

Mugwump, mug'wump, *n.* [Algonkin, a great man, a chief.] A person who takes an independent position in politics; a highly superior person in his own eyes.

Mulatto, mū-lat'tō, *n.* [Sp. *mulato*, from *mulo*, a mule. Mule.] A person that is the offspring of parents of whom one is a Caucasian and the other a Negro; loosely, any individual of mixed Caucasian and Negro blood.

Mulberry, mul'be-ri, *n.* [For *murberry*; A.Sax. *múrberie*, a mulberry, also *múr, mór*, from L. *morus*, a mulberry-tree.] The berry or fruit of a well-known tree, and also the tree itself cultivated from a remote period for silk-worm rearing. — **Mulberry-faced**, *a.* Having the face spotted as if with mulberry stains.

Mulch, mulsh, *n.* [Akin to *mols* in A.Sax. *molsnian*, to rot, G. *mulsch, molsch*, rotten; D. *molsemen*, to moulder.] Strawy dung in a somewhat moist state, but not rotten, used for protecting the roots of newly planted shrubs or trees, &c.—*v.t.* To cover with mulch.

Mulct, mulkt, *n.* [L. *mulcta, multa*, a fine.] A fine or penalty imposed on a person guilty of some offense or misdemeanor, usually a pecuniary fine.—*v.t.* To punish by fine or forfeiture; to punish by depriving; to deprive (to *mulct* a person *of* or *in* $300).—**Mulctuary**, mulk'tū-a-ri, *a.* Consisting of a pecuniary penalty.

Mule, mūl, *n.* [A.Sax. *mūl*, Fr. *mule*, from L. *mulus*, a mule.] A quadruped of a mongrel breed, the offspring of an ass and a mare, or a horse and a she-ass; also any animal produced by a mixture of different species; a hybrid; a hybrid plant; a spinning machine invented by Crompton in 1775, so called from being a combination of the drawing rollers of Arkwright and the jenny of Hargreaves.—**Mule-skinner**, *n.* A driver of mules. (*Colloq.*)—**Muleteer**, mū-le-tēr', *n.* [Fr. *muletier*.] A mule-driver.—**Mulish**, mūl'ish, *a.* Like a mule; sullen; stubborn.—**Mulishly**, mūl'ish-li, *adv.* In a mulish manner.—**Mulishness**, mūl'ish-nes, *n.* Obstinacy or stubbornness.

Mule, mūl, *n.* A backless slipper.

Muliebrity, mū-li-eb'ri-ti, *n.* [L. *muliebritas*, from *muliebris*, womanly, womanish, from *mulier*, a woman.] Womanhood; puberty in a female; womanishness; effeminacy; softness.

Mull, mul, *v.t.* [From the spurious participle *mulled* in *mulled ale*, equivalent to *mold-ale*, that is funeral ale, from *mold*, earth, the earth of the grave.] To heat, sweeten, and flavor with spices (to *mull* wine).—**Muller**, mul'ėr, *n.* One who mulls; a vessel for mulling wine.

Mull, mul, *v.i.* & *t.* To cogitate; to contemplate thoughtfully. (*Colloq.*)

Mull, mul, *n.* [Icel. *múli*, a promontory; comp. also Gael. *maol*, a promontory, *maol*, bare or bald.] A term for a cape or promontory applied to various projecting parts of Scotland.

Mull, mul, *n.* [Hind. *mul-mul*, muslin.] A thin, soft kind of muslin.

Mullein, Mullen, mul'en, *n.* [A.Sax. *molegn*; comp. Dan. *môl*, a moth: one species is used to drive away moths.] The common name of a genus of wild plants used in domestic medicine.

Muller, mul'ėr, *n.* [O.Fr. *moulleur*, from *moulre, mouldre* (Fr. *moudre*), L. *molere*, to grind, from *mola*, a millstone.] A sort of flat-bottomed pestle used for grinding pigments, &c.

Mullet, mul'et, *n.* [Fr. *mulet*, from L. *mullus*, the surmullet.] A name common to spiny-rayed fishes of two somewhat widely separate families, the gray mullets and the red mullets, or surmullets.

Mulligan, mul'i-gan, *n.* A stew of meat and vegetables. (*Slang*.)

Mulligatawny, mul'i-gā-ta″ni, *n.* [Tamil *milagutunni*, lit. pepper-water.] An East Indian curry soup.

Mullion, mul'yon, *n.* [For *munnion*, a word equivalent to Fr. *moignon*, Sp. *muñon*, a stump, the mullion of a window being the stump below the tracery.] *Arch.* a vertical division between the lights of windows, screens, &c., in Gothic architecture; also a division between the panels in wainscoting.—**Mullioned**, mul'yond, *a.* Having mullions.

Mulse, muls, *n.* [L. *mulsum* (*vinum*, wine, understood), sweetened wine.] Wine boiled and mingled with honey.

Multangular, mul-tang'gū-lėr, *a.* [L. *multus*, many, and *angulus*, angle.] Having many angles; polygonal.—**Multangular-**

ly, mul-tang'gū-lėr-li, *adv.* With many angles.—**Multangularness**, mul-tang'-gū-lėr-nes, *n.*

Multanimous, mul-tan'i-mus, *a.* [L. *multus*, many, and *animus*, mind.] Exhibiting many phases of mental or moral character; many-sided.

Multarticulate, **Multiarticulate**, mult-är-tik'ū-lāt, mul'ti-är-tik"ū-lāt, *a.* [L. *multus*, many, and *articulus*, a joint.] Having many joints or articulations, as the legs of crustaceans.

Multicapsular, mul-ti-kap'sū-lėr, *a.* [L. *multus*, many, E. *capsule*.] Having many capsules: used especially in botany.

Multicarinate, mul-ti-kar'i-nāt, *a.* [L. *multus*, many, *carina*, a keel.] Having many keel-like ridges.

Multicavous, mul-ti-kā'vus, *a.* [L. *multus*, many, *cavus*, hollow.] Having many holes or cavities.

Multicipital, mul-ti-sip'i-tal, *a.* [L. *multus*, many, *caput*, *capitis*, the head.] Having many heads.

Multicostate, mul-ti-kos'tāt, *a.* [L. *multus*, many, *costa*, a rib.] Having many ribs; *bot.* having two or more diverging ribs: said of leaves.

Multicuspidate, mul-ti-kus'pi-dāt, *a.* [L. *multus*, many, and *cuspis*, a point.] Having many cusps or points.

Multidentate, mul-ti-den'tāt, *a.* [L. *multus*, many, and *dens*, a tooth.] Having many teeth or teeth-like processes.

Multidigitate, mul-ti-dij'i-tāt, *a.* [Many-fingered; having many finger-like processes.

Multifarious, mul-ti-fā'ri-us, *a.* [L. *multifarius*, manifold—*multus*, many.] Having great multiplicity; having great diversity or variety; made up of many differing parts.—**Multifariously**, mul-ti-fā'ri-us-li, *adv.* In a multifarious way.—**Multifariousness**, mul-ti-fā'ri-us-nes, *n.*

Multifid, **Multifidous**, mul'ti-fid, mul-tif'i-dus, *a.* [L. *multifidus*—*multus*, many, and *findo*, to divide.] Cleft or cut by many divisions; *bot.* divided into several parts by clefts extending to about the middle (a *multifid* leaf).

Multiflorous, mul-ti-flō'rus, *a.* [L. *multus*, many, *flos*, *floris*, a flower.] Many-flowered; having many flowers.

Multifoil, mul'ti-foil, *a.* [L. *multus*, many, and E. *foil*.] *Arch.* having more than five foils or divisions (a *multifoil* arch).

Multiform, mul'ti-form, *a.* [L. *multiformis*—*multus*, many, and *forma*, form.] Having many forms, shapes, or appearances.—**Multiformity**, mul-ti-for'mi-ti, *n.* The state of being multiform.

Multijugous, **Multijugate**, mul-ti-jū'gus, mul-ti-jū'gāt, *a.* [L. *multus*, many, and *jugum*, a yoke, a pair.] Consisting of many pairs.

Multilateral, mul-ti-lat'ėr-al, *a.* [L. *multus*, many, and *latus*, side.] Having many sides; polygonal.

Multilineal, **Multilinear**, mul-ti-lin'ē-al, mul-ti-lin'ē-ėr, *a.* [L. *multus*, many, and *linea*, a line.] Having many lines.

Multilocular, mul-ti-lok'ū-lėr, *a.* [L. *multus*, many, *loculus*, a cell.] Having many cells, loculi, or compartments.

Multiloquence, mul-til'ō-kwens, *n.* [L. *multus*, many, *loquor*, to speak.] Use of many words; talkativeness.—**Multiloquent**, **Multiloquous**, mul-til'ō-kwent, mul-til'ō-kwus, *a.* Speaking much; talkative.

Multimillionaire, mul-ti-mil'yun-ar", *n.* A very wealthy individual; one whose wealth is measured in millions of dollars, pounds sterling, francs, &c.

Multiparous, mul-tip'a-rus, *a.* [L. *multus*, many, *pario*, to bear.] Producing many at a birth.

Multipartite, mul'ti-pär-tīt, *a.* [L. *multus*, many, and *partitus*, divided—*pars*, a part.] Divided into several or many parts; *bot.* more deeply cleft than *multifid*.

Multipede, **Multiped**, mul'ti-pēd, *n.* [L. *multus*, many, *pes*, *pedis*, a foot.] An animal that has many feet, as a centipede.

Multiphase, mul'ti-fās, *a.* [L. *multus*, many, *phasis*, phase.] Showing many phases.

Multiple, mul'ti-pl, *a.* [Fr. *multiple*, from L.L. *multiplus*—*multus*, many, and term. as in *triple*.] Manifold; having many parts or divisions.—*n.* A number which contains another an exact number of times without a remainder: a *common multiple* of two or more numbers containing each of them a certain number of times exactly (thus 24 is a common multiple of 3 and 4); the *least common multiple* being the smallest number that will do this (thus 12 is the least common multiple of 3 and 4).

Multiplex, mul'ti-pleks, *a.* [L. *multiplex*—*multus*, many, and stem of *plico*, to fold. PLY.] Manifold; complex; *bot.* having petals lying over each other in folds.—**Multipliable**, mul'ti-plī-a-bl, *a.* Capable of being multiplied.—**Multiplicable**, mul'ti-pli-ka-bl, *a.* Multipliable.—**Multiplicand**, mul'ti-pli-kand, *n.* [L. *multiplicandus*.] *Arith.* the number to be multiplied by another, which is called the multiplier.—**Multiplicate**, mul'ti-pli-kāt, *a.* [L. *multiplicatus*.] Multiplex.—**Multiplication**, mul'ti-pli-kā"shon, *n.* [L. *multiplicatio*, *multiplicationis*.] The act or process of multiplying; the state of being multiplied; *arith.* and *alg.* the operation by which any given number or quantity may be added to itself any number of times proposed.—*Multiplication table*, a table containing the product of all the simple digits multiplied into each other, and onwards, to some assumed limit, as to 12 times 12.—**Multiplicative**, mul'ti-pli-kā-tiv, *a.* Tending to multiply; having the power to multiply.—**Multiplicator**, mul'ti-pli-kā-tėr, *n.* A multiplier.—**Multiplicity**, mul-ti-plis'i-ti, *n.* [L. *multiplicitas*, from *multiplex*.] The state of being multiplex, numerous, or various; an extensive aggregate of individuals of the same kind; a great number.—**Multiplier**, mul'ti-plī-ėr, *n.* One, who or that which multiplies; the number in arithmetic by which another is multiplied; *teleg.* an instrument for increasing by repetition the strength of an electric current.—**Multiply**, mul'ti-plī, *v.t.*—*multiplied*, *multiplying*. [Fr. *multiplier*, from L. *multiplicare*, from *multiplex*.] To increase in number; to make more by natural reproduction or by addition; to make more numerous; *arith.* to add to itself any given number of times.—*v.i.* To grow or increase in number, or to become more numerous by reproduction; to extend; to spread.—**Multiplying-glass**, **Multiplying-lens**, *n.* A sort of lens or glass with a number of facets, causing one object to appear multiplied many times.

Multipotent, mul-tip'ō-tent, *a.* [L. *multipotens*, *multipotentis*—*multus*, much, and *potens*, powerful.] Having manifold power, or power to do many things.

Multipresence, mul'ti-prez-ens, *n.* [L. *multus*, many, and E. *presence*.] The power or act of being present in more places than one at the same time.—**Multipresent**, mul'ti-prez-ent, *a.* Having power of multipresence.

Multiradiate, mul-ti-rā'di-āt, *a.* [L. *multus*, many, *radius*, a ray.] Having many rays.

Multiramose, mul'ti-rā-mōs, *a.* [L. *multus*, many, *ramus*, a branch.] Having many branches.

Multisect, mul'ti-sekt, *a.* [L. *multus*, many, and *seco*, *sectum*, to cut.] Divided into many segments.

Multiserial, mul'ti-sē-ri-al, *a.* [L. *multus*, many, and *series*, a row.] Having or arranged in many rows.

Multisiliquous, mul-ti-sil'i-kwus, *a.* [L. *multus*, many, and *siliqua*, a pod.] Having many pods or seed-vessels.

Multisonous, mul-tis'ō-nus, *a.* [L. *multus*, many, *sonus*, sound.] Having many sounds, or sounding much.

Multispiral, mul-ti-spī'ral, *a.* [L. *multus*, many, *spira*, a coil.] Having many spiral coils or convolutions.

Multistriate, mul-ti-strī'āt, *a.* [L. *multus*, many, *stria*, a streak.] Marked with many streaks or striæ.

Multisulcate, mul-ti-sul'kāt, *a.* [L. *multus*, many, *sulcus*, a furrow.] Having many furrows.

Multisyllable, mul-ti-sil'la-bl, *n.* [L. *multus*, many, and E. *syllable*.] A word of many syllables; a polysyllable.

Multitubular, mul-ti-tū'bū-lėr, *a.* [L. *multus*, many, and E. *tubular*.] Having many tubes (a *multitubular* boiler).

Multitude, mul'ti-tūd, *n.* [L. *multitudo*, from *multus*, much, many.] The state of being many; a great number, collectively; a great many, indefinitely; a crowd or throng; a gathering of people.—*The multitude*, the populace, or the mass of men without reference to an assemblage.—**Multitudinous**, mul-ti-tū'di-nus, *a.* Pertaining or belonging to a multitude; consisting of a multitude.—**Multitudinously**, mul-ti-tū'di-nus-li, *adv.* In a multitudinous manner.—**Multitudinousness**, mul-ti-tū'di-nus-nes, *n.*

Multivalve, **Multivalvular**, mul'ti-valv, mul-ti-val'vū-lėr, *a.* [L. *multus*, many, and E. *valve*.] Having many valves (a *multivalve* shell).—**Multivalve**, *n.* An animal which has a shell of many valves or pieces.

Multocular, mul-tok'ū-lėr, *a.* [L. *multus*, many, *oculus*, eye.] Having many eyes, or more eyes than two.

Multum, mul'tum, *n.* [L. *multum in parvo*, much in little.] An extract of quassia and liquorice, used in brewing for the purpose of economizing malt and hops.

Multungulate, mul-tung'gū-lāt, *a.* [L. *multus*, many, and *ungula*, a hoof.] Having the hoof divided into more than two parts, as the elephant, rhinoceros, &c.

Multure, mul'tūr, *n.* [O.Fr. *multure*, from L. *molitura*, a grinding, from *molo*, to grind.] The grinding of grain; grist; in Scotland, the fee given to the proprietor of a mill in return for the grinding of corn.

Mum, mum, *a.* [Imitative of a low sound made with the lips closed, like L. and Gr. *mu*; akin *mumble*.] Silent; not speaking. Often used as an exclamation = be silent; hush.

Mum, mum, *n.* [G. *mumme*, from Christian *Mumme*, who first brewed it at Brunswick in 1492.] A species of malt liquor used in Germany, made of wheat malt.

Mum, **Mumm**, mum, *v.i.* [Of Dutch or German origin; comp. G. *mummen*, to mask, *mumme*, a mask, *mummel*, a bugbear; D. *mommen*, to mask, *mom*, a mask, whence O.Fr. *momer*, to mask, *momerie*, mummery; originally perhaps to cover the face and cry *mum*, or similar sound.] To sport or make diversion in a mask or disguise.—**Mummer**, mum'ėr, *n.* A masker; a masked buffoon.—**Mummery**, mum'-ėr-i, *n.* A masking or masquerade; buffoonery; farcical show; hypocritical disguise and parade.—**Mumming**, mum'ing, *n.* A masking or masquerade.

Mumble, mum'bl, *v.i.*—*mumbled*, *mumbling*. [Freq. from *mum*; like D. *mommelen*, Dan. *mumle*, G. *mummeln*, to mumble.] To mutter; to speak so as to render the sounds inarticulate and imperfect; to chew or bite softly; to eat with the lips closed.—*v.t.* To utter with a low inarticulate voice; to chew gently, or to eat with a muttering sound.—**Mumbler**, mum'blėr, *n.* One who mumbles.—**Mumblingly**, mum'bling-li, *adv.* In a mumbling manner.

Mumbo-Jumbo, mum'bō-jum-bō, *n.* A god of certain Negro tribes; any senseless object of popular idolatry.

Mummy, mum'i, *n.* [Fr. *mumie*, *momie*, Sp. *momia*, It. *mummia*, from Ar. *mūmia*, from *mūm*, wax.] A dead human body embalmed and dried after the manner of those taken from Egyptian tombs; a human body dried up and preserved, either artificially or by accident; a sort of wax used in grafting and planting trees; a sort of brown bituminous pigment. — *To beat to a mummy*, to beat soundly, or till senseless.—*v.t.* To embalm.—**Mummy-cloth**, *n.* The cloth in which mummies are swathed. — **Mummify**, mum′i-fī, *v.t.* To make into a mummy; to embalm and dry, as a mummy. — **Mummification**, mum′i-fi-kā″shon, *n.* The act of mummifying; the process of becoming a mummy.—**Mummiform**, mum′i-form, *a.* Resembling a mummy.

Mump, mump, *v.i.* [An imitative word, allied to *mumble* and *munch*.] To mumble or mutter, as in sulkiness; to move the lips with the mouth closed; to nibble; to chew; to munch; to grin or make mouths; to implore alms; to play the beggar.—*v.t.* To munch or chew; to utter unintelligibly. —**Mumper**, mump′ėr, *n.* A beggar.—**Mumping**, mump′ing, *n.* Begging tricks; mockery.—**Mumpish**, mump′ish, *a.* Sullen; sour. — **Mumpishly**, mump′ish-li, *adv.* In a mumpish manner; sullenly.—**Mumpishness**, mump′ish-nes, *n.* — **Mumps**, mumps, *n. pl.* [From *mump*.] Sullenness; a disease consisting in an inflammation of the salivary glands, with swelling along the neck; parotitis.

Munch, munsh, *v.t.* and *i.* [Imitative of sound; akin *mumble*, *mump*.] To chew audibly; to mump; to nibble.—**Muncher**, munsh′ėr, *n.* One who munches.

Mundane, mun′dān, *a.* [L. *mundanus*, from *mundus*, the world.] Belonging to this world; worldly; terrestrial; earthly.—**Mundanely**, mun′dān-li, *adv.* In a mundane manner; with reference to worldly things.

Mundic, mun′dik, *n.* A Cornish name for iron pyrites or arsenical pyrites; marcasite.

Mundungus, mun-dung′gus, *n.* [Comp. Sp. *mondongo*, paunch, tripes, black-pudding.] An old name for tobacco of an ill smell.

Munerary, mū′ne-ra-ri, *a.* [L. *munus*, *muneris*, a gift.] Having the nature of a gift.

Mungo, mung′gō, *n.* [Perhaps from some person of this name.] Artificial short-staple wool formed by tearing to pieces and disintegrating old woollen fabrics; akin to shoddy.

Mungoose, mun′gōs, *n.* MONGOOSE.

Municipal, mū-nis′i-pal, *a.* [L. *municipalis*, from *municipium*, a town governed by its own laws—*munia*, official duties, and *capio*, to take.] Pertaining to local self-government; pertaining to the corporation of a town or city, or to the citizens of a state.—*Municipal bond*, a bond issued by a municipal government to provide funds for a public undertaking.—*Municipal law*, the law which pertains to the citizens of a state in their private capacity.—**Municipalism**, mū-nis′i-pal-izm, *n.* Municipal state or condition.—**Municipality**, mū-nis′i-pal″i-ti, *n.* A town or city possessed of local self-government; a community under municipal jurisdiction. —**Municipally**, mū-nis′i-pal-li, *adv.*

Munificence, mū-nif′i-sens, *n.* [L. *munificentia*—*munus*, a gift or favour, and *facio*, to make.] The quality of being munificent; a giving with great liberality; bounty; liberality.—**Munificent**, mū-nif′i-sent, *a.* Liberal in giving or bestowing; bounteous; generous.—**Munificently**, mū-nif′i-sent-li, *adv.* In a munificent manner; liberally.

Muniment, mū′ni-ment, *n.* [L. *munimentum*, a defence, from *munio*, to fortify, from *mœnia*, walls.] A fortification; a stronghold; support; defence; a writing by which claims and rights are defended or maintained; a title-deed, charter, record, &c.—*Muniment house*, *Muniment room*, a house or room for keeping deeds, charters, &c.

Munition, mū-nish′on, *n.* [L. *munitio*, *munitionis*, from *munio*, to fortify; hence *ammunition*.] A fortification (O.T.)‡; materials used in war; military stores; ammunition; material for any enterprise.—**Munitionette**, mū-nish′on-et, *n.* [By analogy with *Suffragette*.] A female munition war-worker. (*Recent.*)

Muntz's Metal, munts′ez, *n.* [From Mr. *Muntz* of Birmingham, the inventor.] An alloy of 60 parts copper and 40 parts zinc, used for sheathing ships.

Muræna, mū-rē′na, *n.* [L.] A kind of eel found in the Mediterranean.

Murage, mū′rāj, *n.* [Fr. *murage*, from L. *murus*, a wall.] Money paid for keeping the walls of a town in repair.

Mural, mū′ral, *a.* [L. *muralis*, from *murus*, a wall; same root as *munio*, to fortify. MUNITION.] Pertaining to a wall; resembling a wall; perpendicular or steep.—*Mural circle*, an astronomical instrument for measuring angular distances in the meridian, permanently fixed exactly perpendicular in the plane of the meridian.—*Mural crown*, a golden crown bestowed among the ancient Romans on him who first mounted the wall of a besieged place and lodged a standard. —*Mural literature*, placards or posters on walls by political parties during elections. —*Mural painting*, a painting in distemper colours upon a wall.

Murder, mėr′dėr, *n.* [A.Sax. *morthor*, *morther*, from *morth*, death; Goth. *maurthr*, D. *moord*, Dan., Sw., and G. *mord*, Icel. *morth*; from root *mar*, to crush, whence also L. *mors*, death (E. *mortal*); Skr. *mri*, to die.] The act of unlawfully killing a human being with premeditated malice, the person committing the act being of sound mind.—*The murder is out*, something is disclosed which was wished to be kept concealed. [The spelling *Murther* is nearly given up.]—*v.t.* To kill (a human being) with premeditated malice; to slay feloniously; *fig.* to abuse or violate grossly (to *murder* the king's English).—**Murderer**, mėr′dėr-ėr, *n.* A person who commits murder.—**Murderess**, mėr′dėr-es, *n.* A female who commits murder. — **Murderous**, mėr′dėr-us, *a.* Pertaining to murder; guilty of murder; accompanied or marked by murder; bloody. —**Murderously**, mėr′dėr-us-li, *adv.* In a murderous manner.

Murenger, mū′ren-jėr, *n.* [Fr. *murager*, from *murage*. MURAGE.] An officer appointed to see town walls kept in proper repair.

Murex, mū′reks, *n.* pl. **Murices**, mū′ri-sēz. [L.] A mollusc resembling the whelk, in esteem from the earliest ages on account of the purple dye that some of them yielded; the dye itself.—**Murexide**, mū-rek′sīd, *n.* A substance yielding a beautiful purple colour.

Muriate, mū′ri-āt, *n.* [L. *muria*, brine.] The old name for *Chloride*.—**Muriatic**, mū-ri-at′ik, *a.* Pertaining to or obtained from brine or sea-salt.—*Muriatic acid*, the older name of *Hydrochloric acid*.—**Muriatiferous**, mū′ri-a-tif″ėr-us, *a.* Producing muriatic substances or salt.

Muricate, Muricated, mū′ri-kāt, mū′ri-kā-ted, *a.* [L. *muricatus*, from *murex*, the point of a rock.] Full of sharp points or prickles; armed with prickles.

Muriform, mū′ri-form, *a.* [L. *murus*, a wall, and *forma*, form.] *Bot.* resembling brickwork: applied to the cellular tissue of the medullary rays.

Murine, mū′rīn, *a.* [L. *murinus*, from *mus*, *muris*, a mouse.] Pertaining to a mouse or to mice.

Murk, mėrk, *n.* [A.Sax. *murc*, *mirce*, dark, Icel. *myrkr*, Dan. and Sw. *mörk*, dark.] Darkness or gloom. (*Shak.*) — **Murky**, mėr′ki, *a.* Dark; obscure; gloomy. — **Murkily**, mėr′ki-li, *adv.* In a murky manner; darkly. — **Murkiness**, mėr′ki-nes, *n.* State of being murky; darkness; gloom.

Murmur, mėr′mėr, *n.* [Fr. *murmure*, from L. *murmur*, a reduplication of an imitative syllable *mur*, seen in G. *murren*, D. *morren*, Icel. *murra*, Dan. *murre*, to murmur.] A low sound continued or continually repeated, as that of a stream; a low indistinct sound; a hum; a complaint uttered in a low, muttering voice; a grumble or mutter. —*v.i.* To utter or give out a murmur or hum; to grumble; to utter complaints; to mutter. — *v.t.* To utter indistinctly; to mutter. — **Murmurer**, mėr′mėr-ėr, *n.* One who murmurs.—**Murmuring**, mėr′mėr-ing, *p.* and *a.* Making or consisting in a low continued noise; uttering complaints in a low voice or sullen manner.—*n.* A continued murmur; a low confused noise. — **Murmuringly**, mėr′mėr-ing-li, *adv.* With murmurs; with complaints.—**Murmurous**, mėr′mėr-us, *a.* Attended by murmurs; murmuring. — **Murmurously**, mėr′mėr-us-li, *adv.*

Murrain, mur′ān, *n.* [O.Fr. *morine*, from L. *morior*, to die. MORTAL.] A disease that rages among cattle; a cattle plague or epizootic disease of any kind; foot-and-mouth disease.—*Murrain take you*, *murrain on you*, &c., plague take you, plague upon you.

Murre, mur, *n.* [Etymology doubtful.] A name for the common Guillemot.

Murrey, mur′i, *n.* [O.Fr. *morée*, a dark-red colour, from L. *morum*, a mulberry.] A dark-red or mulberry colour.

Murrhine, mur′in, *a.* [L. *murrhinus*, from *murrha*, a material, supposed to be fluorspar.] A name given to a delicate kind of ware anciently brought from the East, and much prized among the Romans. Called also *Myrrhine*.

Murrion, mur′i-on, *n.* A morion.

Murry, mur′i, *n.* The muræna.

Musaceous, mū-sā′shus, *a.* [From *Musa*, the typical genus.] Pertaining to the order of plants to which belong the banana and plantain.

Musang, mū-sang′, *n.* [Malay.] An animal of South-east Africa allied to the civet.

Muscadel, Muscatel, Muscadine, mus′ka-del, mus′ka-tel, mus′ka-din, *n.* [Fr. *moscatelle*, from L.L. *muscatus*, smelling like musk, L. *muscus*, musk. MUSK.] The name of several sweet and strong Italian and French wines, whether white or red; the grapes which produce these wines; a fragrant and delicious pear.

Muscæ, mus′sē, *n. pl.* [L. *musca*, a fly.] *Pathol.* specks like motes floating before the eyes.

Muscardine, mus-kär′din, *n.* [Fr.] A fungus, the cause of a very destructive disease in silk-worms; the disease itself.

Muscatel, *n.* MUSCADEL.

Muschelkalk, mush′el-kalk, *n.* [G. *muchel*, shell, and *kalk*, lime or chalk.] A limestone of the new red sandstone of Germany, abounding in organic remains.

Musciform, mus′si-form, *a.* [L. *musca*, a fly, and *forma*, form.] Having the character of the common fly.

Muscite, mus′īt, *n.* [L. *muscus*, moss.] A fossil plant of the moss family.

Muscle, mus′l, *n.* [Fr. *muscle*, from L *musculus*, a little mouse, a mussel, a muscle, dim. of *mus*, a mouse—probably from the appearance under the skin. *Mussel* is the same word.] A band or mass of contractile tissue in an animal organism by means of which bodily movement is effected. The two main kinds of muscles are the *voluntary*, which can be controlled at will, and the *involuntary*, which function without regard to will, such as the muscles of the digestive tract, the heart, the blood vessels, &c.—**Muscled**, mus′ld, *a.* Furnished with strong muscles; muscular.—**Muscular**, mus′kū-lėr, *a.* Pertaining to or consisting of muscles (*muscular fiber* or *tissue*, that which forms the substance of muscles); performed by or dependent on muscles (*muscular* exertion); having well-developed muscles; strong; brawny.—**Muscle-bound**, *a.* Having the muscles enlarged, overstrained, and rendered inelastic by overexercise.—**Muscularity**, mus-kū-lar′i-ti, *n.* The state of being muscular or brawny.—**Muscularly**, mus′kū-lėr-li, *adv.* In a muscular manner.

Muscoid, mus′koid, *a.* [L. *muscus*, moss.]

Bot. moss-like; resembling moss.—*n.* A moss-like plant.—**Muscology**, mus-kol′o-ji, *n.* That part of botany which investigates mosses.

Muscovado, mus-kō-vä′dō, *n.* or *a.* [Sp. *mascabado*, from *mas*, more, and *acabado*, finished (further advanced than when in syrup).] A term applied to unrefined sugar, the raw material from which loaf and lump sugar are procured by refining.

Muscovite, mus′ko-vīt, *n.* A native of Muscovy, or Russia; Muscovy-glass. — **Muscovy-duck**, mus′ko-vi, *n.* The musk-duck. — **Muscovy-glass**, *n.* A variety of mica from Russia.

Muscular. Under MUSCLE.

Musculocutaneous, mus′kū-lo-kū-tā″-nē-us, *a.* [L. *musculus*, muscle, *cutis*, skin.] Pertaining to the muscles and skin: said of nerves that give off motor branches to muscles, but terminate in the skin as nerves of sensation.

Muse, mūz, *n.* [Fr. *muse*, L. *musa*, from Gr. *mousa*, a muse. *Music*, *museum*, *mosaic* are derivatives.] *Greek myth.* one of the daughters of Zeus and Mnemosynē, who presided over the different kinds of poetry, and the sciences and arts, nine in number, as *Clio*, the muse of history; *Thalia*, the muse of comedy; *Melpomenē*, the muse of tragedy; *Calliopē*, the muse of epic poetry, &c.; hence, poetic inspiration; the inspiring goddess of song.—**Museless**, mūz′les, *a.* Without a muse; disregarding the power of poetry.

Muse, mūz, *v.i.* — *mused*, *musing*. [Fr. *muser*, to muse, dawdle, loiter, from O.H.G. *muoza*, idleness, *muozon*, to be idle, G. *musze*, inactivity, leisure. From this comes *amuse* with prefix *a*.] To ponder; to think or meditate in silence; to be absent in mind.—*v.t.* To think or meditate on.—*n.* A fit of abstraction.—**Museful**, mūz′ful, *a.* Musing; thoughtful.—**Musefully**, mūz′-ful-li, *adv.* Thoughtfully.—**Muser**, mū′-zėr, *n.* One who muses.—**Musing**, mū′-zing, *a.* Meditative; absent-minded.—*n.* Meditation; absent-mindedness. — **Musingly**, mū′zing-li, *adv.* In a musing way.

Museum, mū-zē′um, *n.* [L., from Gr. *mouseion*, originally a temple of the Muses. MUSE.] A building or apartment appropriated as a repository of interesting objects connected with literature, art, or science; a cabinet of curiosities; a collection of objects in natural history.

Mush, mush, *n.* [G. *mus*, pap.] The meal of maize boiled in water.

Mush, mush, *v.t.* [Fr. *marchons*, a starting order.] (*Colloq.*, North America.) To journey on foot, particularly over snow, by dog-team and sled.—*n.* Such a trip; the call of a musher to start his dogs.

Mushroom, mush′röm, *n.* [Fr. *mousseron*, from *mousse*, L. *muscus*, moss. MOSS.] The common name of numerous fungi, especially such as are edible, a common species being well known as an ingredient in sauces; *fig.* an upstart; one that rises suddenly from a low condition of life: from the rapidity with which mushrooms grow.—*a.* Pertaining to mushrooms; resembling mushrooms in rapidity of growth.—**Mushroom-ketchup**, *n.* Ketchup made from mushrooms. — **Mushroom-spawn**, *n.* The reproductive matter or mycelium of mushrooms.

Music, mū′zik, *n.* [Fr. *musique*, L. *musica*, from Gr. *mousikē* (*technē*, art, understood), music, art, culture. MUSE, *n.*] A succession of sounds so modulated as to please the ear; melody or harmony; the art of producing melody or harmony; the written or printed score of a composition. — *Chamber music*, compositions suitable for performance in a private room.—**Music-box**, *n.* A small instrument, having a toothed barrel operating on vibrating tongues, which plays one or more tunes on being wound up. — **Musical**, mū′zi-kal, *a.* Belonging to music; producing music or agreeable sounds; melodious; harmonious.—*Musical glasses*, glass vessels on which music may be played by striking them. — **Musical-clock**, *n.* A clock which plays tunes at certain fixed times. — **Musical-comedy**, a theatrical production with little plot, but with much music and some dancing, good-looking performers and beautiful costumes and settings. — **Musician**, mū-zish′an, *n.* A person skilled in music; one that sings or performs on instruments of music. — **Music-master**, *n.* One who teaches music. — **Music-stand**, *n.* A light frame to hold music while it is being played.— **Music-stool**, *n.* A seat for one who performs on a piano or similar instrument.

Musimon, mus′i-mon, *n.* Same as *Mouflon*.

Musing. Under MUSE (verb).

Musk, musk, *n.* [Fr. *musc*, It. and Sp. *musco*, from L. *muscus*, musk, from Per. *mosk*, musk; allied to Skr. *mushka*, a testicle.] A substance obtained from a cyst or bag near the navel of the musk-deer, having a strong, peculiar, and highly diffusible odour, used as a perfume; a musky smell; a popular name for one or two plants.—**Musky**, mus′ki, *a.* Having the odour of musk.—**Muskiness**, mus′ki-nes, *n.* The quality of being musky; the scent of musk.—**Musk-ball**, *n.* A ball for the toilet, containing musk.—**Musk-beaver**, *n.* The musk-rat.—**Musk-deer**, *n.* A deer of Central Asia, the male of which has long tusks and yields the well-known perfume musk.—**Musk-duck**, *n.* A duck with a musky smell, often erroneously called the Muscovy-duck, a native of America.— **Musk-mallow**, *n.* A British plant, with a peculiar musky odour.—**Musk-melon**, *n.* A delicious and fragrant variety of melon.—**Musk-ox**, *n.* A kind of small hardy ox which inhabits the extreme north of North America, and smells strongly of musk.—**Musk-pear**, *n.* A fragrant kind of pear.—**Musk-plum**, *n.* A fragrant kind of plum.—**Musk-rat**, *n.* An American rodent allied to the beaver, which smells of musk in summer: called also *musquash*; the name is also given to two insectivorous animals smelling of musk.— **Musk-rose**, *n.* A species of rose, so called from its fragrance.—**Musk-wood**, *n.* The musky-smelling timbers of certain trees.

Muskallonge, *n.* MUSKELLUNGE.

Muskat, mus′kat, *n.* MUSCAT.

Muskellunge, mus′kel-lunj, *n.* [American Indian.] A large variety of pike found in the lakes and rivers of Northern U. S. and Canada.

Musket, mus′ket, *n.* [Fr. *mousquet*, O.Fr. *mousket*, *moschet*, originally a sparrow-hawk, lit. fly-hawk, from L. *musca*, a fly (comp. *falcon*, *falconet*, *saker*, &c., as names of fire-arms).] A general term used for any hand-gun employed for military purposes. Formerly spelled *Musquet*.—**Musketeer**, mus-ket-ēr′, *n.* A soldier armed with a musket. — **Musketoon**, mus-ket-ön′, *n.* [Fr. *mousqueton*.] A short musket with a wide bore.—**Musket-proof**, *a.* Capable of resisting the force of a musket-ball.— **Musket-rest**, *n.* A staff or rod with a forked top, formerly used to rest the musket in firing.—**Musketry**, mus′ket-ri, *n.* The fire of muskets; troops armed with muskets; the art or science of firing small-arms.

Muslim, muz′lim, *n.* Same as *Moslem*.

Muslin, muz′lin, *n.* [Fr. *mousseline*, said to be derived from *Mosul* or *Moussul*, a town in Mesopotamia where first made.] A fine thin cotton fabric, of which there are many different kinds. — *a.* Made of muslin (a *muslin* gown). — **Muslin-de-laine**, muz′lin-dē-lān, *n.* [Fr. *mousseline-de-laine*, muslin of wool.] A woollen, or cotton and woollen fabric of light texture, used for ladies' dresses, &c.—**Muslinet**, muz′lin-et, *n.* A sort of coarse muslin.

Musmon, mus′mon, *n.* The moufflon.

Musquash, mus′kwosh, *n.* A musk-rat.

Musquet, mus′ket, *n.* MUSKET.

Musquito, mus-kē′tō. MOSQUITO.

Musrole, muz′rōl, *n.* [Fr. *muserolle*, from *museau*, muzzle.] The nose-band of a horse's bridle.

Mussel, mus′el, *n.* [Same as *muscle*, with different spelling and meaning.] The common name of a genus of bivalve shell-fish, one species of which is largely used for food and bait.

Mussulman, mus′ul-man, *n.* pl. **Mussulmans**, mus′ul-manz. [Corrupted from *moslemin*, pl. of *moslem*.] A Mohammedan or believer in Mohammed; a Moslem. — **Mussulmanism**, mus′ul-man-izm, *n.* Mohammedanism.

Must, must, *v.i.*; without inflection and used as a present or a past tense. [A.Sax. *ic mōste*, *wē mōston*, I must, we must, a past tense; pres. *ic mōt*, I may or must; similar forms in Goth., D., Sw., and G.] A defective or auxiliary verb expressing obligation or necessity, physical or moral; or often merely expressing the conviction of the speaker (you *must* be wrong).

Must, must, *n.* [L. *mustum*, new wine, from *mustus*, new, fresh.] Wine or juice pressed from the grape but not fermented.

Must, must, *n.* [MUSTY.] Mold or moldiness; fustiness.

Mustache, Mustachio, mus-täsh′, mus-täsh′i-ō, *n.* [Fr. *moustache*, It. *mostaccio*, from Gr. *mystax*, the upper lip, the beard upon it.] The hair on the upper lip of men; the unshaven hair of the upper lip; often spoken of as plural.—**Mustached**, mus-tasht′, *p.* and *a.* Provided with or wearing a mustache.

Mustang, mus′tang, *n.* [Sp. *mesteno*, belonging to the *mesta*, or body of graziers.] The wild horse of America, a descendant of horses imported.

Mustard, mus′tėrd, *n.* [O.Fr. *moustarde*, It. *mostarda*, mustard, from L. *mustum*, must, because it is made with a little must mixed in it. MUST, MOIST.] An annual cruciferous plant extensively cultivated for its pungent seeds, which when ground and properly prepared form the well-known condiment of same name.—**Mustard-gas**, mus′tėrd, *n.* A poisonous gas with a pungent smell resembling that of mustard.

Musteline, mus′te-līn, *a.* [L. *mustelinus*, from *mustela*, a weasel.] Pertaining to the weasel and kindred animals.

Muster, mus′tėr, *v.t.* [O.Fr. *moustrer*, *mostrer*, *monstrer*, to exhibit, from L. *monstrare*, to show, from *monstrum*, a monster. MONSTER.] To collect, as troops for service, review, parade, or exercise; to assemble or bring together generally; to collect for use or exhibition.—*To muster up*, to gather, collect, or summon up: generally *fig.* (to *muster up* courage).—*v.i.* To assemble or meet in one place, as soldiers. —*n.* An assembling of troops for review or for service; the act of assembling; an assemblage.—*To pass muster*, to pass without censure, as one among a number on inspection; to be allowed to pass.—**Muster-roll**, *n.* A roll or register of the men in each company, troop, or regiment; a roll or register of a ship's crew.

Musty, mus′ti, *a.* [Probably connected with *moist*, or with L. *mucidus*, mouldy; comp. Sp. *mustio*, musty.] Mouldy; turned sour; fusty; stale; spoiled by age; having an ill flavour; vapid.—**Mustily**, mus′ti-li, *adv.* In a musty manner.—**Mustiness**, mus′ti-nes, *n.* The state or quality of being musty; staleness.

Mutable, mū′ta-bl, *a.* [L. *mutabilis*, from *muto*, to change; akin to *moveo*, to move; *mew*, *moult*, *mutual*, &c., are akin.] Capable of being altered; subject to change; changeable; inconstant in mind or feelings; unsettled; unstable; variable.—**Mutably**, mū′ta-bli, *adv.* In a mutable manner.—**Mutability, Mutableness**, mū-ta-bil′i-ti, mū′ta-bl-nes, *n.* The state of being mutable; changeableness; inconstancy; instability; fickleness. — **Mutation**, mū-tā′shon, *n.* [L. *mutatio*.] The act or process of changing; change; alteration; modification; *philol.* umlaut.—**Mutatory**, mū′ta-to-ri, *a.* Changing; mutable.

Mutacism, mū'ta-sizm, *n.* Inability to enunciate correctly or freely the labial consonants (*p, b, m*).

Mutchkin, much'kin, *n.* [Comp. D. *mutsje*, a little cap, a quartern; Sc. *mutch*, a kind of cap.] A liquid measure in Scotland containing four gills.

Mute, mūt, *a.* [L. *mutus*, silent, dumb; akin to *mutio*, to mumble; Gr. *mu*, a sound with closed lips. MUM, MUTTER.] Silent; not speaking; incapable of utterance; not having the power of speech; dumb; *gram.* and *philol.* silent, not pronounced, or having its sound suddenly and completely checked by a contact of the vocal organs: applied to certain consonants (as *t, p*).—*n.* A dumb person; one unable to use articulate speech; a hired attendant at a funeral; *gram.* and *philol.* a mute letter; *mus.* a utensil applied to a musical instrument to deaden or soften the sounds.—**Mutely**, mūt'li, *adv.* In a mute manner; silently; dumbly.—**Muteness, Mutism**, mūt'nes, mūt'izm, *n.* The state of being mute.

Mute, mūt, *v.i.* [Fr. *mutir, émeutir*.] To eject the contents of the bowels: said of birds.

Muticous, mū'ti-kus, *a.* [L. *muticus*, docked, curtailed.] *Bot.* without any pointed process or awn.

Mutilate, mū'ti-lāt, *v.t.*—*mutilated, mutilating.* [L. *mutilo, mutilatum*, to lop, from *mutilus*, maimed; akin Gr. *mitylos*, docked.] To cut off a limb or essential part of; to maim; to remove any material part from so as to render the thing imperfect.—**Mutilated**, mū'ti-lā-ted, *p.* and *a.* Deprived of some part; *bot.* not producing a corolla, though not regularly apetalous.—**Mutilation**, mū-ti-lā'shon, *n.* The act of mutilating or state of being mutilated.—**Mutilator**, mū'ti-lā-tėr, *n.* One who mutilates.

Mutiny, mū'ti-ni, *n.* [From Fr. *mutin*, O.Fr. *meutin*, mutinous, riotous, *meute*, a revolt, an *emeute*, from L.L. *mota*, a body of men raised for an expedition, from L. *moveo, motus*, to move. MOVE.] A resistance to or revolt against constituted authority; specifically an insurrection of soldiers or seamen against the authority of their commanders; open resistance to officers or opposition to their authority.—*v.i.*—*mutinied, mutinying.* To engage in mutiny; to rise against military or naval officers; to be guilty of mutinous conduct.—**Mutineer**, mū-ti-nēr', *n.* One guilty of mutiny.—**Mutinous**, mū'ti-nus, *a.* Engaged in or disposed to mutiny.—**Mutinously**, mū'ti-nus-li, *adv.* In a mutinous manner.—**Mutinousness**, mū'ti-nus-nes, *n.* The state or quality of being rebellious or of inciting mutiny.

Mutoscope, mū'to-skōp, *n.* [*Mut-* of *mutation*, and *-scope*.] A kind of small cinematograph, showing moving figures.

Mutter, mut'ėr, *v.i.* [An imitative word; comp. G. *muttern*, L. *muttire*, to mutter, *mu*, the sound produced by closing the lips. MUMBLE.] To utter words with a low voice and compressed lips; to grumble; to murmur; to sound with a low rumbling noise.—*v.t.* To utter with a low murmuring voice.—*n.* Murmur; obscure utterance (*Mil.*).—**Mutterer**, mut'ėr-ėr, *n.* One that mutters.—**Muttering**, mut'ėr-ing, *n.* The sound made by one who mutters.—**Mutteringly**, mut'ėr-ing-li, *adv.*

Mutton, mut'n, *n.* [Fr. *mouton*, It. *moltone*, a sheep; supposed to be from L. *mutilus*, mutilated, through L.L. *multo, mutilo*, a wether, a castrated ram.] The flesh of sheep, raw, or dressed for food.—**Mutton-chop**, *n.* A rib-piece of mutton for broiling, having the bone cut, or *chopped* off at the small end.

Mutual, mū'tū-al, *a.* [Fr. *mutuel*, from a L.L. *mutualis*, from L. *mutuus*, mutual, from *muto*, to change. MUTABLE.] Reciprocally given and received; pertaining alike or reciprocally to both sides; interchanged; equally relating to, affecting, proceeding from two or more together; common to two or more combined; shared alike.—**Mutuality**, mū-tū-al'i-ti, *n.* The state or quality of being mutual.—**Mutually**, mū'tū-al-li, *adv.* In a mutual manner; reciprocally; conjointly; in common.

Mutule, mū'tūl, *n.* [L. *mutulus*.] *Arch.* a projecting block under the corona of the Doric cornice.—**Mutuled**, mū'tūld, *a.* Having mutules.

Muzarabic, mu-za-rab'ik, *a.* Belonging to the Muzarabs, or Christians formerly living among the Moors in Spain.

Muzzle, muz'l, *n.* [O.Fr. *musel* (Mod.Fr. *museau*), dim. of O.Fr. *muse*, L.L. *musus*, a mouth, from L. *morsus*, a bite, from *mordeo, morsum*, to bite. MORSEL.] The projecting mouth and nose of an animal, as of a horse, dog, &c.; the open end of a gun or pistol, &c.; a fastening for the mouth which hinders an animal from biting.—*v.t.*—*muzzled, muzzling.* To put a muzzle on; to bind the mouth of, to prevent biting or eating; to put to silence.—**Muzzle-energy**, *n.* The force or weight of the blow which a projectile can deliver when leaving the muzzle of the gun.—**Muzzle-loader**, *n.* A gun loaded by the muzzle: opposed to *breech-loader*.—**Muzzle-velocity**, *n.* The velocity in feet per second with which a projectile leaves the muzzle.

Muzzy, muz'i, *a.* [Akin to *muse*, to be absent-minded.] Absent in mind; bewildered; tipsy.—**Muzziness**, muz'i-nes, *n.* The state of being muzzy.

My, mī, *pronom. adj.* [Contr. from *mine*, A.Sax. *min*. MINE.] Belonging to me (this is *my* book): always used before a noun or attributively, *mine* being used predicatively (this book is *mine*). [Formerly *mine* was used before a vowel, and *my* before a consonant, but *my* is now used before both.] MINE.

Myalgia, mī-al'ji-a, *n.* [Gr. *mys*, muscle, and *algos*, pain.] Cramp.

Myall, mī'al, *n.* [Austral.] An Australian species of acacia with hard violet-scented wood used for making tobacco-pipes, &c.

Mycelium, mī-sē'li-um, *n.* pl. **Mycelia**, mī-sē'li-a. [Gr. *mykēs*, a fungus.] The cellular filamentous spawn of fungi, consisting of whitish filaments spreading like a network.—**Mycelioid**, mī-sē'li-oid, *a.* *Bot.* resembling a mycelium.

Mycoderm, Mycoderma, mī'kō-dėrm, mī-kō-dėr'ma, *n.* [Gr. *mykēs*, a mushroom or fungus, and *derma*, skin.] The vegetable flocculent substance which forms in various infusions when they become mothery.—**Mycology**, mī-kol'o-ji, *n.* [Gr. *mykēs*, and *logos*.] That department of botany which investigates fungi.—**Mycologic, Mycological**, mī-kō-loj'ik, mī-kō-loj'i-kal, *a.* Relating to mycology.—**Mycologist**, mī-kol'o-jist, *n.* One versed in mycology.

Mycorhiza, mī'kō-rī''za, *n.* [Gr. *mykēs*, a fungus, *rhiza*, a root.] A sheath of fungal threads surrounding a root. Probably a case of SYMBIOSIS (which see).

Mydriatic, mid'rē-at''ik, *n.* [Gr. *mydriasis*, undue dilation of the pupil.] Causing dilation of the pupil; a drug for effecting this.

Myelencephalous, mī'el-en-sef''al-us, *a.* [Gr. *myelos*, marrow, and *enkephalon*, the brain.] Exhibiting a nervous system concentrated in a brain and spinal cord, as the higher animals.—**Myelitis**, mī-e-lī'tis, *n.* [Gr. *myelos*, and *-itis*, denoting inflammation.] *Med.* inflammation of the substance of the brain or spinal marrow.—**Myeloid**, mī'el-oid, *a.* Resembling marrow.

Mylodon, mī'lō-don, *n.* [Gr. *mylos*, a grinder, or molar, and *odous*, a tooth.] A large and heavy extinct animal, allied to the sloths; a sort of ground sloth.

Myodynamics, mī'ō-di-nam''iks, *n.* [Gr. *mys, myos*, a muscle, and *dynamis*, force.] That department of science which investigates the principles of muscular force.

Myography, mī-og'ra-fi, *n.* [Gr. *mys, myos*, a muscle, and *graphō*, to describe. A description of the muscles of the body; myology.—**Myographic, Myographical**, mī-ō-graf'ik, mī-ō-graf'i-kal, *a.* Pertaining to a description of the muscles.—**Myographist**, mī-og'ra-fist, *n.* One who describes the muscles.

Myology, mī-ol'o-ji, *n.* [Gr. *mys, myos*, muscle, and *logos*, discourse.] The scientific knowledge or description of the muscles of the human body.—**Myologic, Myological**, mī-ō-loj'ik, mī-ō-loj'i-kal, *a.* Pertaining to myology.—**Myologist**, mī-ol'o-jist, *n.* One who is versed in myology.

Myonicity, mī-ō-nis'i-ti, *n.* [Gr. *myōn*, a muscle.] The characteristic vital property of the muscular tissue.

Myop, Myops, mī'op, mī'ops, *n.* [Gr. *myōps*—*myō*, to shut, and *ōps*, the eye.] A short-sighted person.—**Myopia, Myopy**, mī-ō'pi-a, mī'o-pi. *n.* Short-sightedness; near-sightedness.—**Myopic**, mī-op'ik, *a.* Pertaining to or affected with myopia.

Myosin, mī'ō-sin, *n.* [Gr. *mys, myos*, a muscle.] A peculiar constituent of muscle.

Myosis, mī-ō'sis, *n.* [Gr. *myō*, to close the eye.] *Pathol.* an abnormal contraction of the pupil of the eye.—**Myotic**, mī-ot'ik, *a.* and *n.* Causing such contraction, or a drug that causes it.

Myositis, mī-ō-sī'tis, *n.* [Gr. *mys*, a muscle, and term. *-itis*.] Inflammation of a muscle.

Myosotis, mī-ō-sō'tis, *n.* [Gr. *mys, myos*, a mouse, and *ous, ōtos*, an ear.] The plant forget-me-not.

Myotomy, mī-ot'o-mi, *n.* [From *mys*, a muscle, and *tomē*, a cutting.] The anatomy of the muscles; the operation of cutting through muscles to remove deformity.

Myriad, mir'i-ad, *n.* [Gr. *myrias, myriados*, from *myria*, ten thousand, innumerable.] The number of ten thousand collectively; an immense number indefinitely.—*a.* Innumerable; multitudinous but indefinite.

Myriagram, Myriagramme, mir'i-a-gram, *n.* [Gr. *myria*, ten thousand, and Fr. *gramme*, a gram.] A French weight of 10,000 grams, or 22 lbs. avoirdupois.—**Myrialiter, Myrialitre**, mir'i-a-lē-tėr, *n.* A French measure of capacity containing 10,000 liters, or 610,280 cubic inches.—**Myriameter, Myriametre**, mir'i-a-mē-tėr, *n.* A French measure of length equal to 10 kilometers or 6.21 miles.

Myriapod, mir'i-a-pod, *n.* [Gr. *myria*, ten thousand, and *pous, podos*, a foot.] An individual belonging to the class of animals that includes the centipeds and millipeds, having bodies of a lengthened form and in numerous segments, each segment being provided with one pair of feet.

Myriologue, mir'i-ō-log, *n.* [Fr. *myriologue*, Mod.Gr. *myriologi*.] In modern Greece, an extemporary funeral song, composed and sung by females on the death of some person.—**Myriological**, mir'i-ō-loj''i-kal, *a.* Relating to a myriologue.—**Myriologist**, mir-i-ol'o-jist, *n.* One who composes or sings a myriologue.

Myriophyllous, mir-i-of'il-us, *a.* [Gr. *myria*, ten thousand, *phyllon*, a leaf.] Having ten thousand or numerous leaves.

Myriorama, mir'i-ō-rä''ma, *n.* [Gr. *myrios*, innumerable, and *horama*, view.] A sort of landscape kaleidoscope, forming an almost endless variety of scenes by means of several portions of landscapes on cards.

Myrmecobius, mėr-mē-kō'bi-us, *n.* [Gr. *myrmēx, myrmēkos*, an ant, and *bios*, life.] The ant-eater of Australia, a marsupial resembling a squirrel.

Myrmecophilous, mer-mē-kof'il-us, *n.* [Gr. *myrmex, -ēkos*, an ant, *phileō*, I love.] In plants, species protected by ants, to which they afford food and shelter.

Myrmidon, mėr'mi-don, *n.* One of an ancient Greek race in Thessaly, whom Achilles ruled, and who accompanied him to Troy; hence, a soldier of a rough character; one of a ruffianly band under a daring or unscrupulous leader; an unscrupulous follower.—*Myrmidons of the law*, bailiffs, sheriffs' officers, policemen, and other law menials. — **Myrmidonian**, mėr-mi-dō'-ni-an, *a.* Pertaining to myrmidons.

Myrobalan, mī-rob'a-lan, *n.* [L. *myrobalanum*, Gr. *myrobalanos—myron*, unguent, and *balanus*, a nut.] A dried fruit of different species of the plum kind, brought from the East Indies, and used by dyers and tanners.

Myrrh, mėr, *n.* [L. *myrrha*, Gr. *myrrha*, Ar. *murr*, bitter.] The gummy resinous exudation of a spiny shrub of Arabia and Abyssinia, long in use as an aromatic and medicament; a British plant, with fern-like foliage and large umbels of white flowers; sweet-cicely.—**Myrrhic**, mėr'rik, *a.* Pertaining to or obtained from myrrh.—**Myrrhine**, mėr'rīn, *n.* MURRHINE.

Myrtle, mėr'tl, *n.* [L. *myrtus*, Gr. *myrtos*, from *myron*, perfume.] An evergreen shrub of the south of Europe having buds and berries that yield a volatile oil, while the distilled flowers yield a perfume.—**Myrtle-wax**, *n.* Wax from the candleberry tree.—**Myrtaceous**, mėr-tā'shus, *a.* Of or pertaining to the myrtles.—**Myrtiform**, mėr'ti-form, *a.* Resembling myrtle or myrtle berries.

Myself, mī-self', *pron.* pl. **Ourselves**, our-selvz'. As a nominative it is used, generally after I, to express emphasis and mark distinction; I, and not another: in the objective often used reflexively and without any emphasis.

Mystagogue, Mystagogus, mis'ta-gog, mis-ta-gō'gus, *n.* [Gr. *mystagōgos—mystēs*, one initiated in mysteries, and *agōgos*, a leader.] One who instructs in or interprets mysteries. — **Mystagogy**, mis'ta-gō-ji, *n.* The practice or doctrines of a mystagogue; the interpretation of mysteries.—**Mystagogic, Mystagogical**, mis-ta-goj'ik, mis-ta-goj'i-kal, *a.* Pertaining to a mystagogue or mystagogy.

Mystery, mis'tėr-i, *n.* [L. *mysterium*, from Gr. *mystērion*, from *mystēs*, one initiated, from *myō*, to close, to shut.] Something hidden from human knowledge and fitted to inspire a sense of awe; something incomprehensible through being above human intelligence; something intentionally kept hidden; a secret; a species of dramatic performance in the middle ages, the characters and events of which were drawn from sacred history; a trade, craft, or calling (properly *mistery*, being from L. *ministerium*, service, ministry); *pl.* rites and ceremonies in ancient, chiefly Greek and Roman, religions, only known to and practised by those who had been initiated. —**Mysterious**, mis-tē'ri-us, *a.* Partaking of or containing mystery; not revealed or explained; unintelligible; beyond human comprehension; occult; enigmatical. — **Mysteriously**, mis-tē'ri-us-li, *adv.* In a mysterious manner. — **Mysteriousness**, mis-tē'ri-us-nes, *n.*

Mystic, Mystical, mis'tik, mis'ti-kal, *a.* [L. *mysticus*, Gr. *mystikos*, from *mystēs*, one initiated. MYSTERY.] Hidden from or obscure to human knowledge or comprehension; involving some secret meaning or import; mysterious; occult; pertaining to the ancient mysteries; pertaining to mystics or mysticism.—**Mystic**, *n.* One who is addicted to mysticism. — **Mystically**, mis'ti-kal-li, *adv.* In a mystic manner.—**Mysticalness**, mis'ti-kal-nes, *n.*—**Mysticism**, mis'ti-sizm, *n.* Views or tendencies in religion which aspire towards a communication between man and his Maker through the inward perception of the mind, more direct than that which is afforded us through revelation; a seeking to solve the mysteries of existence by internal illumination or special revelation; a dreamy contemplation on ideas that have no foundation in human experience.

Mystify, mis'ti-fī, *v.t.—mystified, mystifying.* [Coined from *mystic*, and *-fy*, Fr. *-fier*, L. *facere*, to make.] To perplex purposely; to play on the credulity of; to bewilder; to befog.—**Mystification**, mis'ti-fi-kā''-shon, *n.* The act of mystifying or state of being mystified.—**Mystificator**, mis'ti-fi-kā-tėr, *n.* One who mystifies.

Myth, mith, *n.* [Gr. *mythos*, a word, a fable, a legend.] A fable or legend of natural upgrowth, embodying the convictions of a people as to their gods or other divine personages, their own origin and early history and the heroes connected with it, the origin of the world, &c.; in a looser sense, an invented story; something purely fabulous or having no existence in fact.—**Mythic, Mythical**, mith'ik, mith'-i-kal, *a.* Relating to myths; described in a myth; fabulous; fabled.—**Mythically**, mith'i-kal-li, *adv.* In a mythical manner. —**Mythographer**, mi-thog'ra-fėr, *n.* A framer or writer of myths.—**Mythological, Mythologic**, mith-o-loj'i-kal, mith-o-loj'ik, *a.* Relating to mythology; proceeding from mythology; of the nature of a myth; fabulous. — **Mythologically**, mith-o-loj'i-kal-li, *adv.* In a mythological manner.—**Mythologist, Mythologer, Mythologian**, mi-thol'o-jist, mi-thol'o-jėr, mith-o-lō'ji-an, *n.* One versed in mythology.—**Mythologize**, mith-ol'o-jīz, *v.i.*—*mythologized, mythologizing.* To relate or explain myths.—**Mythology**, mith-ol'o-ji, *n.* The science or doctrine of myths; the myths of a people or nation collectively.—*Comparative mythology*, the science which investigates myths with a view to their interpretation, and to discover the degree of relationship existing between the myths of different peoples. — **Mythopœic, Mythopoetic**, mith-ō-pē'ik, mith'ō-pō-et''ik, *a.* [Gr. *mythos*, and *poieō*, to make.] Myth-making; producing or tending to produce myths; suggesting or giving rise to myths.

Mytiloid, mī'til-oid, *a.* [Gr. *mytilos*, a mussel.] Resembling the mussel.

Myxine, mik-sī'nē, *n.* [Gr. *myxinos*, slimy, *myxa*, slime.] The fish called the hag.

Myxœdema, miks-ē-dē'ma. [Gr. *myxa*, mucus, *oidēma*, a swelling.] A disease due to deficient secretion of the THYROID GLAND (which see).

N

N, the fourteenth letter and the eleventh consonant of the English alphabet.

Nab, nab, *v.t.* [Same as Dan. *knappe*, Sw. *knappa*, to snatch; comp. D. and G. *knappen*, to snap.] To catch or seize suddenly or unexpectedly. (*Colloq.*)

Nabob, nā'bob, *n.* [Corruption of Hind. *nawwāb*, from Ar. *nuwwāb*, pl. of *nāyib*, a deputy, from Ar. *nāba*, to take one's turn.] A governor of a province or commander of an army in India under the Mogul empire: a person who has acquired great wealth in the East and uses it ostentatiously.

Nacre, nā'kėr, *n.* [Fr. *nacre*, Sp. *nacar*, from Per. *nakar*, an ornament of different colours.] Mother-of-pearl. — **Nacreous**, nā'krē-us, *a.* Consisting of or resembling nacre or mother-of-pearl.—**Nacrite**, nā'-krīt, *n.* A mineral of a greenish-white colour and pearly lustre.

Nadir, nā'dėr, *n.* [Fr. *nadir*, Ar. and Per. *nadir*, *nazir*, the nadir, from *nazara*, to correspond, to be opposite.] That point of the heavens or lower hemisphere directly opposite to the zenith; the point directly under the place where we stand; *fig.* the lowest point; the point or time of extreme depression.

Nævus, nē'vus, *n.* [L.] A natural mark, spot, or blemish on the skin of a person; a birth-mark.

Nag, nag, *n.* [Same as Sc. *naig*, D. *negge*, a pony; perhaps akin to *neigh*.] A small horse, or in familiar language any horse.

Nag, nag, *v.t.* and *i.* [N. and Sw *nagga*, to gnaw, irritate, scold=G. *nagen*, E. to *gnaw*. NAIL, GNAW.] To scold pertinaciously: to find fault constantly.—**Naggy**, nag'i, *a.* Given to nagging or scolding

Nagana, nā-ga'na. [Native word.] 'Fly disease' of horses in tropical Africa. Due to a microscopic parasite introduced by the bite of the tsetse fly.

Nagelfluh, nā'gel-flö, *n.* [G. *nagel*, a nail, and O.G. and Swiss *fluh*, a rock.] A conglomerate rock of Switzerland and Italy, the pebbles in it resembling nail-heads.

Naiad, nā'yad, *n.* [Gr. *naias*, *naiados*, a naiad, from *naō*, to flow.] A water nymph; a female deity that presides over rivers and springs.—**Naiant**, nā'yant. NATANT.

Naick. NAIK.

Naïf, nä-ēf, *a.* [Fr. See NAIVE.] Ingenuous; artless; having a natural lustre without being cut: said of jewels.

Naik, Naick, nā'ik, *n.* In India, a sepoy corporal.

Nail, nāl, *n.* [A.Sax. *nægel*, D. and G. *nagel*, the human or a metallic nail; Icel. *nagl*, Dan. *negl*, a human nail, *nagli* and *nagle*, a metallic nail; cog. Lith. *nagas*, L. *unguis*, Skr. *nakha*, a human nail; allied to *nag* (verb).] The horny scale growing at the end of the human fingers and toes; a similar appendage in the lower animals; a claw; a small pointed piece of metal, with some sort of a head, used for driving through or into timber or other material for the purpose of holding separate pieces together, or left projecting that things may be hung on it; a stud or boss; a measure of length, being 2¼ inches, or 1-16th of a yard. —*To hit the nail on the head*, to hit or touch the exact point, in a figurative sense.—*v.t.* To fasten with nails; to drive nails into; to stud with nails.—**Nail-brush**, *n.* A small brush for cleaning the nails.—**Nailer**, nāl'ėr, *n.* One that nails; one whose occupation is to make nails. —**Naileress**, nāl'ėr-es, *n.* A female maker of nails.—**Nailery**, nāl'ėr-i, *n.* A manufactory where nails are made. — **Nail-head**, *n.* *Arch.* a Norman Gothic ornament. See below. — **Nail-headed**, *a.* Shaped so as to resemble the head of a nail. —*Nail-headed character*, ARROW-HEADED. —*Nail-headed moulding*, a moulding in Norman architecture formed by a series of projections resembling heads of nails.

Nainsook, nān'suk, *n.* [Hind.] A kind of muslin, plain and striped, originally made in India.

Naïve, nä-ēv', *a.* [Fr. *naïf*, fem. *naïve*, from L. *nativus*, native, latterly also rustic, simple.] Ingenuous; artless; showing candour or simplicity; unsophisticated. — **Naïvely**, nä-ēv'li, *adv.* In a naïve manner. —**Naïveté**, nä-ēv'te, *n.* [Fr.] Native simplicity of soul; unaffected ingenuousness.

Naked, nā'ked, *a.* [A.Sax. *nacod*, naked, a participial form; D. *naakt*, Icel. *naktr*, *nakinn*, Dan. *nögen*, Goth. *naqviths*, G. *nackt*; same root as L. *nudus*, nude; Skr. *nagna*, naked.] Not having clothes on; bare; nude; not having a covering, especially a customary covering (a *naked* sword); *bot.* not having a calyx; not inclosed in a pod, or the like; *zool.* not having a calcareous shell; *fig.* open to view; not concealed; manifest; mere, bare, simple; unarmed; defenceless; unprovided; destitute. —*The naked eye*, the eye unassisted by any instrument, as spectacles, telescope, or microscope.—**Nakedly**, nā'ked-li, *adv.* In a naked manner; without covering.—**Nakedness**, nā'ked-nes, *n.* The state of being naked; nudity; bareness; plainness.

Namable. NAMEABLE.

Namaycush, na-mā'kush, *n.* A large North American species of salmon.

Namby-pamby, nam'bi-pam'bi, *a.* [Contemptuously formed from the name of *Ambrose* Phillips, a rather weak poet of Addison's time.] Affectedly pretty; weakly sentimental; insipid; vapid (*namby-pamby* sentiment, rhymes).

Name, nām, *n.* [A.Sax. *nama*, a name; D. *naam*, G *name*, Goth. *namo*, Icel. *nafn*, Dan. *navn* (for *namn*), Sw. *namn*, all cog. with L. *nomen*, for *gnomen* (whence E. *noun*), Skr. *nâman*, for *jnâman* or *gnâman*, a name; from same root as *know*.] That by which a person or thing is called or designated, in distinction from other persons or things; appellation; reputation; character (one's good or bad *name*); renown; fame; eminence; the mere word by which anything is called; sound only; not reality; authority; behalf; persons having a certain name; a family; *gram.* a noun†.—*To call names*, to apply opprobrious names.—*Christian name*, a personal name preceding the family name, and usually bestowed at baptism: as distinguished from a *surname*.—*v.t.*—*named*, *naming*. To give a name or distinctive appellation to; to denominate; to mention by name; to nominate; to designate for any purpose by name; to pronounce to be; to speak of or mention as.—*To name a day*, to fix a day for anything; *to name the day*, said of a lady's fixing her marriage-day.—**Namable**, **Nameable**, nām'a-bl, *a.* Capable or worthy of being named.—**Nameless**, nām'les, *a.* Without a name or appellation; not known to fame; obscure; without family or pedigree; that cannot or ought not to be named; inexpressible.—**Namelessly**, nām'les-li, *adv.* In a nameless manner.—**Namelessness**, nām'les-nes, *n.* The state of being nameless.—**Namely**, nām'li, *adv.* To mention by name; to particularize; that is to say.—**Name-plate**, *n.* A plate bearing a person's name, such as is placed on the door of a dwelling.—**Namer**, nām'ėr, *n.* One that names or calls by name.—**Namesake**, nām'sāk, *n.* One that has the same name as another; one named after another for that other's sake.

Nandu, nan'dū, *n.* [Braz. *nhandu*.] The rhea or South American ostrich.

Nankeen, **Nankin**, nan-kēn', *n.* A sort of cotton cloth, usually of a yellow colour, originally manufactured and imported from *Nankin* in China; *pl.* trousers or breeches made of this material.

Naos, nā'os, *n.* [Gr. *naos*, a temple.] *Arch.* the body of an ancient temple.

Nap, nap, *v.i.*—*napped*, *napping*. [A.Sax. *hnappian*, *hnæppian*, to take a nap, to doze.] To have a short sleep; to drowse; to be in a careless, secure state.—*n.* A short sleep or slumber; a game at cards. (Contraction of *Napoleon*.)

Nap, nap, *n.* [A.Sax. *hnoppa*, the nap of cloth = D. *nop*, *noppe*, Dan. *noppe*, L.G. *nobbe*, nap; allied to *knob* or *knop*, from the little tufts on coarse cloth.] The woolly substance on the surface of cloth, &c.; the pile, as of a hat; what resembles this, as the downy substance on some plants.—*v.t.*—*napped*, *napping*. To raise or put a nap on.—**Napless**, nap'les, *a.* Without nap; threadbare.—**Nappy**, nap'i, *a.* Having much nap.—**Nappiness**, nap'i-nes, *n.*

Nape, nāp, *n.* [Same as A.Sax. *cnæp*, a top; akin *nap*, *knob*, *knop*.] The back part of the neck; the prominent part of the neck behind.

Napery, nā'pėr-i, *n.* [Fr. *napperie*, from *nappe*, a towel, from L. *mappa*, a towel, whence also *map*; akin *napkin*, *apron*.] A collective term for linen cloths used for domestic purposes, especially for the table.

Napha-water, nā'fa, *n.* A fragrant perfume distilled from orange flowers.

Naphtha, nap'tha or naf'tha, *n.* [Gr. Chal., Syr., and Ar. *naphtha*, Per. *naft*, naphtha.] A variety of bitumen, fluid, inflammable, emitting a strong odour, and generally of a yellow colour, used as a source of light, as a solvent for caoutchouc, &c.—*Native naphtha*, petroleum or rock-oil.—**Naphthalene**, nap'tha-lēn, *n.* A white crystallizable solid formed during the distillation of coal for gas, or obtained by re-distilling coal-tar.—**Naphthalic**, nap-thal'ik, *a.* Pertaining to or obtained from naphtha.—**Naphthalize**, nap'thal-īz, *v.t.* To impregnate or saturate with naphtha.

Napiform, nā'pi-form, *a.* [L. *napus*, a turnip, and *forma*, form.] Having the general shape of a turnip (a *napiform* root).

Napkin, nap'kin, *n.* [Dim. of Fr. *nappe*, a cloth, a table-cloth, from L. *mappa*, a napkin. NAPERY.] A cloth used for wiping the hands; a towel; a handkerchief†.—**Napkin-ring**, *n.* A ring of ivory, metal, &c., to inclose a table-napkin.

Napoleon, na-pō'lē-on, *n.* [After *Napoleon* I.] Formerly, a French gold coin, worth 20 francs, or $3.86; a card game.

Nappy, nap'i, *n.* Strong ale; a small, round, shallow, flat-bottomed dish; a sauce dish.

Naprapathy, nā-prap'ā-thi, *n.* [From Czech *naprava*, correction.] A system of treatment of disease or illness by manipulation and adjustment of joints and muscles.

Narceine, när'sē-in, *n.* [Gr. *narkē*, torpor.] An alkaloid contained in opium.

Narcissism, när-cis'sizm, *n.* (*Psychoanalysis.*) A morbid love and admiration of self.—**Narcissist**, *n.*—**Narcissistic**, *a.*

Narcissus, när-sis'us, *n.* [L., from Gr. *narkissos*, from *narkē*, torpor: from the narcotic properties of the plants.] An extensive genus of bulbous plants, including the daffodil, the jonquil, &c.; in Gr. mythology a handsome youth who died from hopeless love of his own reflection in water, and was transformed into a narcissus.

Narcosis, när-kō'sis, *n.* [Gr. See below.] The effect of a narcotic; the state produced by narcotics.

Narcotic, när-kot'ik, *n.* [Gr. *narkōtikos*, from *narkoō*, to render torpid, from *narkē*, torpor.] A substance which relieves pain, produces sleep, and in large doses brings on stupor, coma, and even death, as opium, hemlock, alcohol, &c.—**Narcotic**, **Narcotical**, när-kot'i-kal, *a.* Having the properties of a narcotic.—**Narcotism**, när'-kot-izm, *n.* Narcosis.—**Narcotize**, när'-kot-īz, *v.t.* To bring under the influence of a narcotic; to affect with stupor.

Nard, närd, *n.* [L. *nardus*, from Gr. *nardos*, Heb. and Per. *nard*, nard.] A plant, same as *Spikenard*; an unguent prepared from the plant.—**Nardine**, när'dīn, *a.* Pertaining to nard or spikenard.

Narghile, **Nargileh**, när'gi-le, *n.* [Persian and Turkish name.] A kind of tobacco-pipe or smoking apparatus used by the Orientals in which the smoke is passed through water. Spelled also *Nargile*.

Narial, nā'ri-al, *a.* [L. *naris*, a nostril.] Pertaining to the nostril; nasal.—**Nariform**, nar'i-form, *a.* Formed like the nose; nose-shaped.—**Narine**, nar'īn, *a.* Belonging to the nostrils.—**Narisonant**, nar'i-sō-nant, *a.* Having a nasal sound.

Narrate, nar-rāt', *v.t.*—*narrated*, *narrating*. [L. *narro*, *narratum*, to relate, for *gnarro*, from root *gna*, seen also in E. *know*; comp. *gnarus*, knowing. KNOW.] To tell or recite, as a story; to relate the particulars of in speech or writing.—**Narration**, nar-rā'shon, *n.* The act of narrating; that which is related; a narrative; *rhet.* that part of a discourse which recites the time, manner or consequences of an action.—**Narrative**, nar'a-tiv, *a.* Pertaining to narration.—*n.* That which is narrated or related; a relation or narration; a relation in words or writing of the particulars of any transaction or event.—**Narratively**, nar'a-tiv-li, *adv.* By way of narration.—**Narrator**, nar-rā'tėr, *n.* One who narrates or produces a narrative.

Narrow, nar'ō, *a.* [A.Sax. *nearu*, *nearo*, narrow, troublesome or painful; cog. O.Sax. *naru*, Fris. *naar*; supposed to be connected with *snare* (by loss of initial *s*).] Of little breadth; having little distance from side to side; of little extent; limited or contracted; limited as to means; straitened; contracted in mind; of confined views; bigoted; not liberal or bountiful; niggardly; near; within but a little; hence, barely sufficient to avoid evil, &c. (a *narrow* escape, majority); close; scrutinizing.—*Narrow gauge*, in railways, a gauge or distance between the rails of less than 4 feet 8½ inches, which is considered the standard gauge and is the most common.—*n.* A narrow channel of water between one sea or lake and another; a strait or sound: usually in the plural.—*v.t.* To make narrow or contracted, literally or figuratively.—*v.i.* To become narrow or narrower.—**Narrower**, nar'ō-ėr, *n.* One who or that which narrows.—**Narrowly**, nar'ō-li, *adv.* In a narrow manner; contractedly; sparingly; closely; rigorously; nearly; within a little.—**Narrow-minded**, *a.* Of confined views or sentiments; illiberal.—**Narrowness**, nar'ō-nes, *n.* The quality or condition of being narrow; illiberality; want of enlarged views.—**Narrow-souled**, *a.* Illiberal; void of generosity.

Narthex, när'theks, *n.* [Gr.] A kind of vestibule in the after-part of a church.

Narwhal, **Narwal**, när'whal, när'wal, *n.* [Dan. *narhval*, Icel. *ná-hvalr*, 'corpse-whale', Icel. *ná*, *nár*, a corpse, from the animal's pale colour.] A cetaceous mammal of northern seas, with no teeth except two canines in the upper jaw, of which one is frequently developed into a long projecting tusk; the sea-unicorn.

Nasal, nā'zal, *a.* [Fr. *nasal*, from L. *nasus*, the nose. NOSE.] Pertaining to the nose; uttered through the nose or through both the nose and mouth simultaneously (as *m* in English, *en* in French).—*Nasal fossæ*, *anat.* the two cavities which constitute the internal part of the nose.—*n.* An elementary sound uttered through or partly through the nose; a medicine that operates through the nose; an errhine; the nose-guard of an ancient helmet.—**Nasality**, nā-zal'i-ti, *n.* The state or quality of being nasal.—**Nasalization**, nā'zal-i-zā"shon, *n.* The act of nasalizing or uttering with a nasal sound.—**Nasalize**, nā'zal-īz, *v.t.*—*nasalized*, *nasalizing*. To render nasal, as the sound of a letter; to insert a nasal letter in, especially *n* or *m* (L. *tundo*, is a *nasalized* form from the root *tud*, to strike).—**Nasally**, nā'zal-li, *adv.* In a nasal manner; by or through the nose.

Nascent, nas'ent, *a.* [L. *nascens*, *nascentis*, ppr. of *nascor*, to be born. NATAL.] Beginning to exist or to grow; coming into being; arising.—**Nascency**, nas'en-si, *n.* The state of being nascent.

Nase, nāz, *n.* A ness, cape, headland. NOSE.

Naseberry, nāz'ber-i, *n.* [Sp. *nispero*, medlar, from L. *mespilus*, medlar; modified so as to have an English form, like *barberry*.] The fruit of the sapodilla.

Nasicorn, nā'zi-korn, *a.* [L. *nasus*, nose, *cornu*, horn.] Having a horn on the nose.—**Nasiform**, nā'zi-form, *a.* Shaped like a nose.—**Nasolabial**, nā-zō-lā'bi-al, *a.* [L. *labium*, the lip.] Pertaining to the nose and lips.—**Nasopalatal**, nā-zō-pal'a-tal, *a.* Pertaining to the nose and palate.

Nasturtium, nas-tėr'shi-um, *n.* [L., from *nasus*, the nose, and *torqueo*, *tortum*, to twist, from the acridity of its smell.] A genus of herbs, including the common water-cress; also a name given to the Indian cress, an American annual with pungent fruit.

Nasty, nas'ti, *a.* [O.E. *nasky*, connected with L.G. *nask*, Sw. *naskug*, *nasket*, unclean, dirty.] Filthy; dirty; indecent; obscene; disgusting to taste or smell; disagreeable; troublesome.—**Nastily**, nas'ti-li, *adv.* In a nasty manner; filthily; obscenely.—**Nastiness**, nas'ti-nes, *n.* The quality of being nasty, or what is nasty; filthiness; filthy matter; obscenity.

Nasute, nā'sūt, *a.* [L. *nasutus*, large-nosed, keen-smelling, from *nasus*, the nose. NASAL.] Having a quick or delicate perception of smell; keen-scented; critical; censorious. — **Nasuteness**, nā'sūt-nes, *n.* Acuteness of smell; nice discernment.

Natal, nā'tal, *a.* [L. *natalis*, from *nascor*, *natus*, to be born (whence also *nature*, *native*, *nation*); from same root as *genus*, *kind*. NATURE, GENUS.] Pertaining to one's birth; dating from one's birth.—**Natalitial**, nā-tal-ish'al, *a.* [L. *natalitius*.] Pertaining to one's birth or birth-day.

Natal, nā'tal, *a.* [L.L. *nates*, the buttocks.] Pertaining to the buttocks (the *natal* callosities of monkeys).

Natant, nā'tant, *a.* [L. *natans*, *natantis*, ppr. of *nato*, to swim, freq. of *no*, *natum*, to swim; same root as *navis*, a ship. NAVAL.] Floating on the surface of water; swimming, as the leaf of an aquatic plant. —**Natantly**, nā'tant-li, *adv.* In a natant manner; by swimming.—**Natation**, na-tā'shon, *n.* [L. *natatio*.] The art or act of swimming.—**Natatores**, nā-ta-tō'rēz, *n. pl.* [Lit. swimmers.] The order of swimming birds, characterized by their toes being webbed, and including ducks, geese, swans, penguins, grebes, &c.—**Natatorial**, nā-ta-tō'ri-al, *a.* Swimming or adapted to swimming; belonging to the Natatores.—**Natatorium**, nā-ta-tō'ri-um, *n.* A swimming pool, particularly, one indoors.

Natch, nach, *n.* [AITCHBONE.] The rump of an ox.—*Natch-bone*, the aitchbone.

Nathless, Natheless, nāᴛʜ'les, nā'thē-les, *adv.* [A.Sax. *nā thȳ laes*, not the less, lit. not by that less.] Nevertheless; notwithstanding. (*Archaic*.)

Nation, nā'shon, *n.* [L. *natio*, from *natus*, born, *nascor*, to be born. NATAL.] A people inhabiting a certain extent of territory, and united by common political institutions; an aggregation of persons speaking the same or a cognate language; a division of students in some universities, according to their place of birth; a great number; a great deal, by way of emphasis. —*Law of nations*. Same as *International Law*.—**National**, nash'on-al, *a.* Pertaining to a nation; common to a whole people or race; public; general.—*National air*, a popular tune peculiar to a particular nation; a tune by national consent sung or played on certain public occasions.—*National Church*, the established church of a country or nation.—*National debt*, the sum which is owing by a government to individuals who have advanced money to it for public purposes.—*National Guard*, in the U. S., organizations of militia in the several states, subject to both state and federal government.—**Nationalism**, nash'on-al-izm, *n.* Nationality; a national idiom or trait; advocacy of making one's own nation distinct and separate from others in social, cultural, and political matters; a socialist program for national control or ownership of industries and resources.—**Nationality**, nash-on-al'i-ti, *n.* The qualities that distinguish a nation; national character; strong attachment to one's own nation or countrymen; the people constituting a nation; a nation; a race of people; separate existence as a nation; national unity and integrity.—**Nationalize**, nash'on-al-īz, *v.t.*—*nationalized*, *nationalizing*. To make national; to make the common property of the nation as a whole; to give the character of a distinct nation.—**Nationally**, nash'on-al-li, *adv.* In a national manner; as a whole nation.

Native, nā'tiv, *a.* [L. *nativus*, born, innate, natural, native, from *nascor*, *natus*, to be born. NATAL.] Pertaining to the place or circumstances of one's birth; being the scene of one's origin (our *native* land); conferred by birth; belonging to one's nature or constitution; not artificial or acquired; occurring in nature pure or unmixed with other substances: said of mineral bodies (as iron or silver when found almost pure). —*n.* One born in a place or country, and not a foreigner or immigrant; an oyster raised in an artificial bed.—**Natively**, nā'tiv-li, *adv.* By birth; naturally; originally. — **Nativeness**, nā'tiv-nes, *n.* State of being native. — **Nativity**, na-tiv'i-ti, *n.* [L. *nativitas*.] A coming into life or the world; birth; the circumstances attending birth; a picture representing the birth of Christ; *astrol.* same as *Horoscope*.—*To cast a nativity*, to draw out one's horoscope, and calculate the future influence of the predominant stars.—*The nativity*, the birth of Our Saviour.

Natron, nā'tron, *n.* [Fr. and Sp. *natron*, from Ar. *natrun*, native carbonate of soda: same word as *nitre*.] Native carbonate of soda, or mineral alkali, found in the ashes of several marine plants, in some lakes, and mineral springs.—**Natrolite**, nā'tro-līt, *n.* [Gr. *lithos*, a stone.] A mineral substance occurring in trap-rocks, and containing a great quantity of soda.

Natterjack, nat'ėr-jak, *n.* [For *atter*-jack, from A.Sax. *ātor*, poison, from its disgusting smell.] A species of English toad which does not leap or crawl but walks or runs, and has a deep hollow voice.

Natty, nat'i, *a.* [Akin to *neat*.] Neat; tidy; spruce.—**Nattily**, nat'i-li, *adv.* In a natty manner; sprucely; tidily. — **Nattiness**, nat'i-nes, *n.* State of being natty.

Nature, nā'tūr, *n.* [Fr. *nature*, from L. *natura*, from *natus* (for *gnatus*), born, produced, from root *gna* or *gan*, seen in E. *know*, *kind*, *kin*; Skr. *jan*, to produce. GENUS.] The universe; the system of things of which ourselves are a part; the world of matter or of matter and mind; the creation, especially that part of it by which man is more immediately surrounded; often also the agent, author, or producer of things, or the powers that carry on the processes of the creation; the total of all agencies and forces in the creation; the inherent qualities of anything; the essential qualities which constitute it what it is; disposition of mind; personal character; individual constitution; quality; sort; natural affection; life or reality as distinguished from that which is artificial.—*To go the way of nature*, *to pay the debt of nature*, and similar phrases, to die.—*Laws of nature*, those generalizations which express the order observed in the phenomena of nature. —*In a state of nature*, naked as when born; in a state of sin; unregenerated.—**Nature-printing**, *n.* A process by which plants &c., are impressed on a metal plate so as to engrave themselves, copies or casts being then taken for printing.—**Natural**, nat'ū-ral, *a.* [L. *naturalis*.] Pertaining to nature; produced by nature; not artificial, acquired, or assumed (*natural* colour, strength, heat), in conformity with the laws of nature; regulated by the laws which govern events, actions, sentiments, &c. (a *natural* enemy, supposition); happening in the ordinary course of things (the *natural* consequence); connected with the existing physical system of things, or creation at large (*natural* philosophy, laws, &c.); according to life and reality; without affectation or artificiality (he was always *natural*); born out of wedlock; bastard; in a state of nature; unregenerated; *mus.* a term applied to the diatonic or normal scale of C.—*Natural history*, originally the study or description of nature in its widest sense, now commonly applied collectively to the sciences of zoology and botany, or sometimes to zoology alone.—*Natural numbers*, the numbers 1, 2, 3 and upwards.—*Natural order*, an order of plants belonging to the natural system or classification, in contradistinction to the artificial system of Linnæus. — *Natural philosophy*, physics. PHYSICS. — *Natural religion*, religion such as may be attained by the light of nature or reason alone, without revelation.—*Natural science*, much the same as *natural history* in its wide sense. — *Natural selection*. SELECTION.— *n.* One born without the usual powers of reason or understanding; an idiot; a fool; *mus.* a character marked thus ♮, the use of which is to make a sharpened note a semitone lower, and a flattened one a semitone higher.—**Natural-born**, *a.* Native; not alien.—**Naturalesque**, nat'ū-ral-esk, *a.* Preserving pretty closely the characteristics of natural objects: said of ornamental designs, &c.—**Naturalism**, nat'ū-ral-izm, *n.* Natural religion; the doctrine that there is no interference of any supernatural power in the universe.—**Naturalist**, nat'ū-ral-ist, *n.* One versed in natural science or natural history; one who holds the doctrine of naturalism.—**Naturalistic**, nat'ū-ral-is"tik, *a.* Pertaining to naturalism; in accordance with nature; based on natural objects. — **Naturalization**, nat'ū-ral-i-zā"shon, *n.* The act of naturalizing; the act of investing an alien with the rights and privileges of a natural subject.—**Naturalize**, nat'ū-ral-īz, *v.t.*—*naturalized*, *naturalizing*. To make natural; to confer the rights and privileges of a native subject upon; to accustom to a climate; to acclimatize; to adopt as native or vernacular (to *naturalize* foreign words).—**Naturally**, nat'ū-ral-li, *adv.* In a natural manner; according to nature; not by art or habit; without affectation; according to the usual course of things; spontaneously; without cultivation.—**Naturalness**, nat'ū-ral-nes, *n.* The state of being natural; conformity to nature; absence of affectation.

Naught, nąt, *n.* [A.Sax. *nāht*, *nōht*, *nāwiht*, lit. *no whit*, not a whit (see AUGHT). *Naught* is the same and *not* is an abbreviated form.] Nought; nothing.—*To set at naught*, to slight, disregard, or despise.— *a.* Worthless; of no value or account; bad; vile.—**Naughty**, ną'ti, *a.* [From *naught*.] Bad: mischievous; ill-behaved; very wrong (a *naughty* child).—**Naughtily**, ną'ti-li, *adv.* In a naughty manner; mischievously. —**Naughtiness**, ną'ti-nes, *n.* The state of being naughty; misbehaviour, as of children.

Naumachia, Naumachy, ną-mā'ki-a, ną'-ma-ki, *n.* [Gr. *naumachia*—*naus*, a ship, and *machē*, fight.] *Rom. antiq.* a show or spectacle representing a sea-fight; the place where these shows were exhibited.

Nauplius, nąʹplē-us, *n.* [Gr. *Nauplios*, a son of Neptune.] In lower crustacea, an ovoid unsegmented larva, possessing only the three first pairs of head-limbs, which are used as swimming organs.

Nausea, ną'shē-a, *n.* [L., from Gr. *nausia*, from *naus*, a ship. NAVAL.] Sea-sickness; any similar sickness of the stomach, accompanied with a propensity to vomit; loathing. —**Nauseant**, ną'shē-ant, *n.* A substance which produces nausea.—**Nauseate**, ną'-shē-āt, *v.i.* — *nauseated*, *nauseating*. [L. *nauseo*.] To feel nausea; to be inclined to vomit.—*v.t.* To loathe; to reject with disgust; to affect with disgust.—**Nauseous**, ną'shus, *a.* Exciting or fitted to excite nausea; loathsome; disgusting. — **Nauseously**, ną'shus-li, *adv.* In a nauseous manner.—**Nauseousness**, ną'shus-nes, *n.* The quality of being nauseous; loathsomeness.

Nautch-girl, nąch. *n.* In the East Indies, a native professional dancing-girl.

Nautical, ną'ti-kal, *a.* [L. *nauticus*, from *nauta*, a seaman, for *navita*, from *navis*, a ship. NAVAL.] Pertaining to seamanship or navigation. — *Nautical mile*. MILE.— **Nautically**, ną'ti-kal-li, *adv.* In a nautical manner.

Nautilus, ną'ti-lus, *n.* [Gr. *nautilos*, a sailor, a nautilus, from *naus*, a ship. NAVAL.] A genus of cephalopods with many-chambered shells in the form of a flat spiral, the animal residing in the external chamber, and the others being separated by partitions; also a name for the argonaut or paper nautilus; a form of diving-bell which requires no suspension, sinking and rising by means of condensed air.—*Nautilus propeller*, a hydraulic device for propelling ships.—**Nautilite**, ną'ti-līt, *n.* Any fossil shell allied to the existing nautilus.—**Nautiloid**, ną'ti-loid, *a.* Resembling the nautilus or its shell.

Naval, nā'val, *a.* [L. *navalis*, from *navis*, a ship (whence also *nautical*, *navigate*, *navy*); cog. Gr. *naus*, Skr. *naus*; from a root *nu* for *snu*, meaning to float or flow.] Consisting of ships, or of forces fighting in ships; pertaining to a navy or to ships of war; maritime.—*Naval officer*, one belonging to the navy of a country.—*Naval crown*, among the ancient Romans, a crown conferred for bravery at sea.—*Naval decorations*, specifically, three awards presented by the naval authorities to men in the service who perform acts of bravery beyond the call of duty: Medal of Honor, Distinguished Service Medal, and Navy Cross.—*Navy List*, an official publication containing the names of all the officers in the navy, the names of the vessels composing the fleet, with particulars of the power, armament, &c., of the vessels, and other naval information.

Nave, nāv, *n.* [A.Sax. *nafu*, *nafa* = D. *nave*, *naaf*, Dan. *nav*, Icel. *nöf*, G. *nabe*, a nave; cog. Skr. *nâbhi*, a nave, a navel. *Navel* is a dim. from this, and *auger* is partly derived from it.] The thick piece in the center of a wheel in which the spokes are inserted; the hub.

Nave, nāv, *n.* [Lit. ship, from O.Fr. *nave* (Mod.Fr. *nef*), It. *nave*, from L. *navis*, a ship. NAVAL.] The middle part, lengthwise, of a church; the part between the aisles and extending from the entrance.

Navel, nā'vl, *n.* [A.Sax. *nafel*, *nafol* = D. *navel*, Dan. *navle*, Icel. *nafle*, G. *nabel*—navel; dim. forms from words signifying nave of a wheel. NAVE.] A depression in the center of the abdomen, the point where the umbilical cord passes out of the fetus.

Navew, nā'vū, *n.* [From O.Fr. *naveau*, from L.L. *napellus*, a dim. of L. *napus*, turnip.] The wild turnip.

Navicular, na-vik'ū-lėr, *a.* [L. *navicula*, a little ship, from *navis*, a ship. NAVAL.] Shaped like a boat (the *navicular* bone of the wrist or ankle).

Navigate, nav'i-gāt, *v.i.*—*navigated*, *navigating*. [L. *navigo*, *navigatum*, from *navis*, a ship, *ago*, to do. NAVAL.] To pass on water in ships; to manage a ship; to sail.—*v.t.* To pass over in ships; to sail on; to steer or manage in sailing.—**Navigation**, nav-i-gā'shon, *n.* [L. *navigatio*.] The act of navigating; the science or art of managing ships.—*Aerial navigation*, the art and science of operation through the air of lighter- and heavier-than-air machines; the setting of a course along a known route; the application of directional knowledge gained by the use of landmark maps, previous flying experience, and the extensive use of various instruments for dead reckoning and position finding, such as radio compass, direction finders, altimeters, artificial horizon gauges, drift indicators, barometers, and the radio telephone.—**Navigator**, nav'i-gā-tėr, *n.* One that navigates; one who directs the course of a ship.—**Navigable**, nav'i-ga-bl, *a.* Capable of being navigated; affording passage to ships.—**Navigableness**, **Navigability**, nav'i-ga-bl-nes, nav'i-ga-bil"i-ti, *n.* The quality or state of being navigable.

Navvy, nav'i, *n.* [Abbrev. from *navigator*—the name being first given to men engaged on works connected with inland navigation.] In England, a common laborer, engaged in such works as the making of canals or railways.

Navy, nā'vi, *n.* [O.Fr. *navie*, from L. *navis*, a ship. NAVAL.] The collective name for such vessels as are built and maintained for war or for other purposes pertaining to national defense; the institutions and equipment, such as navy yards, stores, fueling stations, naval academies, &c., for the maintenance of sea defenses and vessels of war.

Nawab, na-wąb', *n.* [See NABOB.] A viceroy; a deputy.

Nay, nā, *adv.* [Equivalent to *ne aye* (A.Sax. *ne*, not), that is, not ever; from Icel. and Dan. *nei*, Sw. *nej*, no, nay; comp. *nor* for *ne or*, not or; *neither*, for *ne either*, not either, &c. No.] No; a word that expresses negation or refusal; also used to intimate that something is to be added to an expression; not only so; not this alone.—*To say nay*, to deny; to refuse.—*n.* Denial; refusal.

Nazarene, **Nazarean**, naz-a-rēn', *n.* An inhabitant of *Nazareth*; a name given to Christ and the early converts to Christianity, in contempt.

Nazarite, naz'a-rīt, *n.* [Heb. *nazir*, separated.] A Jew who by certain vows and acts devoted himself to the peculiar service of Jehovah for a certain time or for life. Num. vi. 2-21.

Nazi, nä'tsē, *a.* Of or pertaining to, or embodying the principles of, Naziism.—*n.* A member of the German National Socialist Workers' Party.—**Naziism**, nä'-tsē-izm, *n.* A totalitarian form of government administered by the Nazi Party (the German National Socialist Workers' Party) which advocates the building of a highly nationalistic Aryan state, with the revival and substitution of Germanic Hero Worship for Christianity, and recognizes private ownership except when the state determines otherwise.

Neanderthal, nā-an'der-tąl, *a.* A valley in the Rhine province, Prussia, where the skeletal remains of a prehistoric man were discovered in 1856; *n.* the species of man in Europe in paleolithic times.

Neap, nēp, *a.* [A.Sax. *nêp*, neap; akin to Dan. *knap*, Icel. *hneppr*, narrow, scanty, and probably to *nip*.] Low, or not rising high: applied to the lowest tides, being those that happen in the middle of the second and fourth quarters of the moon, taking place about four or five days before the new and full moons.—**Neap**, **Neap-tide**, *n.* One of the lowest tides or the time of one: opposite to *spring*-tide.

Neapolitan, nē-a-pol'i-tan, *a.* [L. *Neapolis*, Naples.] Of Naples or its inhabitants. *n.* An inhabitant or native of Naples.

Near, nēr, *a.* [A.Sax. *neár*, compar. of *neáh*, nigh (*nearer* being thus a double compar.) = Icel. *nær*, *nærri*, Dan. *nær*, near; nearer. NEXT, NIGH.] Nigh; not far distant in place, time, or degree; closely connected by blood (*near* relations); intimate; familiar (a *near* friend); close or literal; narrow (a *near* escape); on the left of a horse: opposed to *off*, in riding or driving (the *near* fore-leg); short, or not circuitous (a *near* way home); close, narrow, niggardly.—*prep.* At no great distance from; close to; nigh.—*adv.* Almost; within a little; closely; *naut* close to the wind: opposed to *off*.—*v.t.* and *i.* To approach; to come near.—**Nearly**, nēr'li, *adv.* Almost; within a little; not remotely; closely; intimately; in a parsimonious or niggardly manner.—**Nearness**, nēr'nes, *n.* The state or attribute of being near in any sense; closeness in time or place; proximity; parsimony.—**Near-sighted**, *a.* Short-sighted; seeing at a small distance only.

Neat, nēt, *n.* [A.Sax. *neát* (sing. and pl.); Sc. *nowt*, Icel. *naut*, Sw. *nöt*, Dan. *nöd*, cattle, an ox; from verbal stem Iceb *njóta*, A.Sax. *neótan*, to use, to enjoy; Goth. *niutan*, to take.] Cattle of the bovine genus, as oxen or cows: used either collectively or of one individual.—*Neat's-foot oil*, an oil obtained from the feet of *neat* cattle.

Neat, nēt, *a.* [Fr. *net*, *nette*, from L. *nitidus*, shining, from *niteo*, to shine.] Having everything in perfect order; tidy; trim; expressed in few and well-chosen words; chaste: said of style; pure or unmixed with water (a glass of brandy *neat*); with all deductions made (usually written *Net* or *Nett*).—**Neat-handed**, *a.* Using the hands with neatness; deft.—**Neatly**, nēt'li, *adv.* In a neat manner; tidily; with good taste.—**Neatness**, nēt'nes, *n.* The state or quality of being neat; tidiness; simple elegance.

Nebris, neb'ris, *n.* [Gr.] A fawn's skin; in works of art, the covering of Bacchus, bacchanals, fauns, &c.

Nebula, neb'ū-la, *n.* pl. **Nebulae**, **Nebulas**, neb'ū-lē, neb'ū-läs. [L. *nebula*, a cloud; allied to Gr. *nephĕlē*, a cloud; G. *nebel*, mist.] The name for celestial objects resembling white clouds, in many cases resolved by the telescope into clusters of stars, though many nebulæ consist of masses of incandescent gas; a white spot or a slight opacity of the cornea of the eye.—**Nebular**, neb'ū-lėr, *a.* Pertaining to nebulæ.—*Nebular hypothesis*, a hypothesis that the bodies composing the solar system once existed in the form of a nebula, from which, when condensed by refrigeration, the planets were constituted, the main body forming the sun.—**Nebulist**, neb'ū-list, *n.* One who upholds the nebular hypothesis.—**Nebulosity**, neb-ū-los'i-ti, *n.* The state of being nebulous; the faint misty appearances surrounding certain stars.—**Nebulous**, neb'ū-lus, *a.* [L. *nebulosus*.] Cloudy; hazy; literally or figuratively; *astron.* pertaining to or having the appearance of a nebula; nebular.—**Nebulousness**, neb'ū-lus-nes, *n.*

Necessary, nes'es-sa-ri, *a.* [L. *necessarius*, from *necesse*, necessary, unavoidable; origin doubtful.] Such as must be; inevitable; unavoidable; indispensable; essential; that cannot be absent; acting from necessity: opposed to *free* (as regards the will).—*Necessary truths*, those truths which cannot from their very nature but be true.—*n.* Anything necessary or indispensably requisite.—**Necessarian**, nes-es-sā'ri-an, *n.* A necessitarian.—**Necessarily**, nes'es-sa-ri-li, *adv.* In a necessary manner; by necessity; indispensably.—**Necessariness**, nes'es-sa-ri-nes, *n.* The state of being necessary.—**Necessitarian**, **Necessarian**, nē-ses'i-tä"ri-an, *n.* One who maintains the doctrine of philosophical necessity in opposition to the freedom of the will.—**Necessitarianism**, **Necessarianism**, nē-ses'i-tä"ri-an-izm, nes-es-sā'ri-an-izm, *n.* The doctrine of philosophical necessity.—**Necessitate**, nē-ses'i-tāt, *v.t.*—*necessitated*, *necessitating*. To make necessary or indispensable; to render necessary; to compel; to force.—**Necessitous**, nē-ses'i-tus, *a.* Exhibiting indigence; pressed with poverty; indigent; destitute.—**Necessitously**, nē-ses'i-tus-li, *adv.* In a necessitous manner.—**Necessitousness**, nē-ses'i-tus-nes, *n.* Extreme poverty; pressing want.—**Necessity**, nē-ses'i-ti, *n.* [L. *necessitas*.] The state of being necessary; condition demanding that something must be; unavoidableness; indispensableness; need; irresistible compulsion; compulsion of circumstances; the absolute determination of the will by motives; that which is requisite; a necessary; extreme indigence; pinching poverty.

Neck, nek, *n.* [A.Sax. *hnecca*, the neck = D. *nek*, Dan. *nakke*, Icel. *hnakki*, the nape; G. *nacken*, the neck; connections doubtful.] The part of an animal's body between the head and the trunk and connecting them; part of a thing corresponding to the neck of animals; a narrow tract of land connecting two larger tracts; an isthmus; the slender part of a vessel, as a bottle; that part of a violin or similar instrument which connects the scroll or head and body.—*Neck and crop*. Under CROP.—*Neck or nothing*, at every risk.—*A stiff neck*, in *Scrip.* obstinacy in sin.—*To break the neck of an affair*, to destroy the main force of it; to get over the worst part of it.—*To tread on the neck of* (*fig.*), to subdue utterly.—*Neck and neck*, close, as in a race.—*To get it in the neck*, to get the worst of it.—*On the neck of*, adhering to, or immediately following.—**Neckband**, *n.* The band of a shirt round the neck, to which the collar is attached.—**Neckcloth**, nek'kloth, *n.* A piece of linen or cotton cloth worn round the neck as part of a gentleman's dress.—**Neckerchief**, nek'ėr-chif, *n.* A kerchief for the neck.—**Necklace**, nek'lis, *n.* A string of beads, precious stones, or other ornamental objects worn on the neck.—**Necklet**, nek'let, *n.* A small chain worn round the neck for suspending a locket.—**Neck-or-nothing**, *a.* Involving great risk; desperate.—**Necktie**, *n.* A band of cloth worn round the neck under the collar and knotted in front; a cravat; a scarf or tie.

Necrobiosis, nek'rō-bī-ō"sis, *n.* [Gr. *nekros*, dead, and *bios*, life.] *Med.* the degeneration or wearing away of living tissue.—**Necrobiotic**, nek'rō-bi-ot"ik, *a.* Pertaining to necrobiosis. — **Necrographer**,† nek-rog'ra-fėr, *n.* [*Graphō*, to write.] One who writes an obituary notice. (*Thack.*) — **Necrolatry**, nek-rol'a-tri, *n.* [Gr. *latreia*, worship.] Excessive veneration for or worship of the dead.—**Necrolite**, nek'rol-īt, *n.* [Gr. *lithos*, a stone.] A kind of felspar, which, when struck or pounded, exhales an odour like that of putrid flesh. —**Necrology**, nek-rol'o-ji, *n.* A register of deaths; a collection of obituary notices.— **Necrologic, Necrological**, nek-rō-loj'-ik, nek-rō-loj'i-kal, *a.* Pertaining to a necrology.—**Necrologist**, nek-rol'o-jist, *n.* One who writes obituary notices.—**Necromancy**, nek'rō-man-si, *n.* [Gr. *manteia*, divination.] Divination by means of a pretended communication with the dead; the black art; the art of magic or sorcery.— **Necromancer**, nek'rō-man-sėr, *n.* One who practices necromancy; a sorcerer; a wizard. — **Necromancing**, nek'rō-man-sing, *n.* The art or practice of a necromancer. — **Necromantic, Necromantical**, nek-rō-man'tik, nek-rō-man'ti-kal, *a.* Pertaining to necromancy. — **Necromantically**, nek-rō-man'ti-kal-li, *adv.* By necromancy.—**Necrophagous**, nek-rof'a-gus, *a.* [Gr. *phagein*, to eat.] Feeding on the dead, or putrescent substances.— **Necrophilism**, nek-rof'il-izm, *n.* [Gr. *phileō*, to love.] An unnatural attachment to dead bodies.—**Necrophobia, Necrophoby**, nek-rō-fō'bi-a, nek'rō-fō-bi, *n.* [Gr. *phobos*, fear.] A horror of dead bodies; exaggerated fear of death.—**Necropolis**, nek-rop'o-lis, *n.* [G. *polis*, a city; the city of the dead.] A cemetery, especially one that is extensive and ornamentally laid out. —**Necroscopy**, nek-ros'ko-pi, *n.* Examination of the dead; a post-mortem examination — **Necroscopic, Necroscopical**, nek-rō-skop'ik, nek-rō-skop'i-kal, *a.* Relating to post-mortem examinations.— **Necrosis**, nē-krō'sis, *n.* [Gr. *nekrōsis*, deadness.] *Pathol.* death of the bone substance, a condition corresponding to what gangrene is to the flesh; *bot.* a disease of plants chiefly found upon the leaves and soft parts.—**Necrosed**, nē-krōst', *a.* Affected by necrosis.

Nectar, nek'tėr, *n.* [Gr.] *Greek myth.* the drink of the gods, ambrosia being their solid food; hence, any delicious drink; *bot.* the honey of a flower.—**Nectareal**, nek-tā'rē-al, *a.* Pertaining to nectar or a nectary. — **Nectarean**, nek-tā'rē-an, *a.* Resembling nectar; very delicious. — **Nectared**, nek'tėrd, *a.* Imbued or abounding with nectar. — **Nectareous**, nek-tā'rē-us, *a.* Nectarean. — **Nectareousness**, nek-tā'rē-us-nes, *n.*—**Nectariferous**, nek-ta-rif'ėr-us, *a.* Producing nectar.—**Nectarine**, nek'tėr-īn, *a.* Sweet as nectar. — *n.* A variety of the common peach, having a smoother rind and firmer pulp.—**Nectarous**, nek'tėr-us, *a.* Sweet as nectar.— **Nectary**, nek'ta-ri, *n.* The part of a flower that contains or secretes the nectar.

Nectocalyx, nek'tō-kā-liks, *n.* pl. **Nectocalyces**, nek'tō-kā'li-sēz. [Gr. *nēktos*, swimming, and *kalyx*, a cup.] The swimming-bell or disc of a medusa or jelly-fish, by the contractions of which it is propelled.

Née, nā, *pp.* [Fr., from L. *natus*, born. NATAL.] Born: a term placed before a married woman's maiden name to indicate her parentage: as, Madame de Staël, *née* Necker, that is, whose family name was Necker.

Need, nēd, *n.* [A.Sax. *nēd*=D. *nood*, Icel. *nauth*, Dan. *nōd*, G. *noth*, Goth. *nauths*, need, necessity.] A state that requires supply or relief; pressing occasion for something; urgent want; necessity; want of the means of subsistence; poverty; indigence. — *v.t.* To have necessity or need for; to want, lack, require. *Need* is often used as a sort of auxiliary, especially in negative and interrogative sentences without the personal termination of the 3rd person singular, and without the infinitive sign *to* before the following verb (he or they *need* not go; *need* he do it?).—*v.i.* To be wanted; to be necessary: not used with a personal nominative (there needs nothing more). — **Needfire**, nēd'fīr, *n.* [Lit. fire of *need* or necessity.] Fire produced by friction, of old the subject of superstitions. **Needful**, nēd'fųl, *a.* Needy; necessitous; necessary; requisite.—*The needful*, anything necessary; specifically, ready-money (*colloq.*). —**Needfully**, nēd'fųl-li, *adv.* In a needful manner. — **Needfulness**, nēd'fųl-nes, *n.* The state of being needful.—**Needily**, nē'di-li, *adv.* In a needy manner.—**Neediness**, nē'di-nes, *n.* Want; poverty; indigence.—**Needless**, nēd'les, *a.* Not wanted; unnecessary; not requisite.—**Needlessly**, nēd'les-li, *adv.* In a needless manner.— **Needlessness**, nēd'les-nes, *n.* — **Needs**, nēdz, *adv.* [An adverbial genitive of *need.*] Of necessity; necessarily; indispensably; generally with *must.* — **Needy**, nē'di, *a.* Necessitous; indigent; very poor; distressed by want of the means of living.

Needle, nē'dl, *n.* [A.Sax. *naedl*, a needle = O.Fris. *nedle*, Goth. *nethla*, G. *nadel*, D. *naald*, Icel. *nál*, a needle, from root seen in D. *naad*, a seam, G. *nähen*, to sew, L. *neo*, Gr. *neō*, to spin.] A small instrument of steel pointed at one end, and having an eye or hole through which is passed a thread, used for sewing; an instrument of iron or steel, bone, wood, &c., used for interweaving or interlacing a thread or twine in knitting, netting, embroidery, &c.; a name of sundry long and sharp-pointed surgical instruments; a magnetized bar of steel in a mariner's or other compass, in the needle-telegraph, &c.; a sharp pinnacle of rock; a needle-shaped crystal. — **Needle-book**, *n.* Pieces of cloth in the form of the leaves of a book, used for sticking needles into.—**Needle-fish**, *n.* The pipe-fish, also the sea-urchin.—**Needle-gun**, *n.* A breech-loading rifle fired by the striking of a *needle* or small spike on detonating powder in the cartridge.—**Needle-ore**, *n.* Acicular bismuth glance; native sulphide of bismuth, lead and copper, occurring in long, thin, steel-gray crystals.—**Needle-telegraph**, *n.* A telegraph in which the indications are given by the deflections of a magnetic needle.—**Needle-woman**, *n.* A seamstress.—**Needle-work**, *n.* Work executed with a needle; sewed work; embroidery; the business of a seamstress.— **Needle-zeolite**, *n.* Natrolite.—**Needly**, nēd'li, *a.* Relating to or resembling a needle.

Needless, Needs, Needy, &c. Under NEED.

Ne'er, nār. A contraction of *Never.*

Neese, nēz, *v.i.* [A.Sax. *niesan*, D. *niezen*, G. *neisen*; a form of *sneeze.*] To sneeze.

Nefarious, nē-fā'ri-us, *a.* [L. *nefarius*, from *nefas*, impious, unlawful, from *ne*, not, and *fas*, law, from *for*, *fari*, to utter. FATE.] Wicked in the extreme; atrociously sinful or villainous; detestably vile. — **Nefariously**, nē-fā'ri-us-li, *adv.* In a nefarious manner. — **Nefariousness**, nē-fā'ri-us-nes, *n.*

Negation, nē-gā'shon, *n.* [L. *negatio*, a denying, from *nego*, to deny—*ne*, not, and verbal affix, *-go*, *-igo*. Akin *deny*, *renegade.*] Denial; a declaration that something is not, has not been, or will not be: opposed to *affirmation*; contradiction or contradictory condition.—**Negative**, neg'-a-tiv, *a.* [Fr. *négatif*, L. *negativus.*] Implying or containing denial or negation: opposed to *affirmative*; tending in the direction of denial without directly denying or controverting: opposed to *positive* (a *negative* result); *photog.* applied to a picture in which the lights and shades are the opposites of those in nature. — *Negative electricity*, the opposite of positive electricity. See POSITIVE.—*Negative pole*, the metal, or equivalent, placed in opposition to the *positive*, in the voltaic battery.—*Negative quantities*, *alg.* quantities which have the sign − (minus) prefixed to them.—*n.* A proposition by which something is denied; an opposite or contradictory term or conception; a negative proposition; a word that denies (*not*, *no*); that side of a question which denies or refuses; a decision or answer expressive of negation; *photog.* a photographic picture on glass or sensitized film, in which the lights and shades are the opposite of those in nature, used as a plate from which to print positive impressions.—*v.t. negatived*, *negativing*. To disprove; to prove the contrary; to say *no* to; to reject; to refuse to enact or sanction.—**Negatively**, neg'a-tiv-li, *adv.* In a negative manner.— **Negativeness, Negativity**, neg'a-tiv-nes, neg-a-tiv'i-ti, *n.* The state or quality of being negative.—**Negatory**,† neg'a-to-ri, *a.* Expressing denial; of negation.

Neglect, neg-lekt', *v.t.* [L. *negligo*, *neglectum*, lit. not to pick up—*nec*, not, nor, and *lego*, to pick up. LEGEND.] To treat with no regard or attention or with too little; to slight; to set at naught; to omit to do; to leave undone; to forbear: often with an infinitive as object (to *neglect* to pay a visit). —*n.* Omission; forbearance to do anything that should be done; carelessness; omission of due attention or civilities; negligence; habitual want of regard; state of being disregarded.—**Neglectedness**, neg-lek'ted-nes, *n.* State of being neglected.— **Neglecter**, neg-lek'tėr, *n.* One that neglects.—**Neglectful**, neg-lekt'fųl, *a.* Apt to neglect; treating with neglect; negligent; careless; inattentive.—**Neglectfully**, neg-lekt'fųl-li, *adv.* In a neglectful manner.— **Neglectfulness**, neg-lekt'fųl-nes, *n.*— **Neglectingly**, neg-lek'ting-li, *adv.* With neglect; carelessly; heedlessly (*Shak.*).

Negligee, neg'lē-zhā", *n.* [Fr. *negligé*, from *negliger*, to neglect.] An informal dressing gown or wrapper worn by women.

Negligent, neg'li-jent, *a.* [L. *negligens*, *negligentis*, ppr. of *negligo*, to neglect. [NEGLECT. Characterized by neglect; apt to neglect; careless; heedless; neglectful.— **Negligently**, neg'li-jent-li, *adv.* In a negligent manner.—**Negligence, Negligency**, neg'li-jens, neg'li-jen-si, *n.* [L. *negligentia.*] The quality of being negligent; neglect; remissness; an act of negligence. —**Negligible**, neg'li-ji-bl, *a.* That may be neglected.

Negociate, &c. See NEGOTIATE.

Negotiate, nē-gō'shi-āt, *v.i.* [L. *negotior*, *negotiatus*, from *negotium*, want of leisure, business—*nec*, not, and *otium*, leisure.] To treat with another respecting purchase and sale; to hold intercourse in bargaining or trade; to hold diplomatic intercourse with another, as respecting a treaty, league, or other matter; to treat; to conduct communications in general. — *v.t.*—*negotiated*, *negotiating*, To procure or bring about by negotiation (a treaty, a loan); to pass in the way of business; to put into circulation (to *negotiate* a bill of exchange); to *negotiate* a corner, said of a motor car or other vehicle, taking an obstacle carefully in order to overcome it.—**Negotiable**, nē-gō'shi-a-bl, *a.* Capable of being negotiated; transferable by assignment from one person to another, as a bill or promissory note.— **Negotiability**, nē-gō'shi-a-bil"i-ti, *n.* The quality of being negotiable.—**Negotiation**, nē-gō'shi-ā"shon, *n.* The act of negotiating; the treating with another respecting sale or purchase; the intercourse of governments by their agents, in making treaties and the like.—**Negotiator, Negotiant**,† nē-gō'shi-ā-tėr, nē-gō'shi-ant, *n.* One that negotiates.—**Negotiatory**, nē-gō'shi-a-to-ri, *a.* Relating to negotiation.

Negro, nē'grō, *n.* pl. **Negroes**, nē'grōz. [It. and Sp. *negro*, black, from L. *niger*, black.] A member of the African branch of the black race, formerly called the Ethiopian, which is characterized by the black or very dark color of the skin and the possession of hair of a woolly or crisp nature.—*a.* Relating to Negroes; black.— **Negroid**, nē'groid, *a.* Resembling Negroes; having Negro characteristics.—**Negress**, nē'gres, *n.* A female Negro.—**Negrito, Negrillo**, ne-grē'tō, ne-gril'lō, *n.* and *a.* [Dim. of *Negro.*] A name given to the diminutive Negro-like tribes inhabiting the Philippines and the Eastern Archipelago.

Negus, nē'gus, *n.* [From the inventor Col. *Negus* of Queen Anne's time.] A beverage made of wine, hot water, sugar, nutmeg, and lemon-juice, or only of wine, water, and sugar: the former ruler of Ethiopia.

Neigh, nā, *v.i.* [A.Sax. *hnaegan*, Icel. *hneggja*, *gneggja*, Sw. *gnägga*, probably an imitative word; comp. L. *hinnio*.] To utter the cry of a horse; to whinny.—*n.* The cry of a horse; a whinnying.—**Neighing**, nā'ing, *n.* A whinnying.

Neighbor, nā'bėr, *n.* [A.Sax. *neáh-búr*, *nēh-būr*, lit. a near-dweller, from *nēah*, near (NIGH), and *būr*, *gebūr*, a dweller, a boor (BOOR).] One who lives near another; one who lives in a neighborhood; one in close proximity; one who lives on friendly terms with another; often used as a familiar term of address.—*a.* Being in the vicinity; adjoining; next—*v.t.* To adjoin; to border on or be near to.—**Neighborhood**, nā'bėr-hụd, *n.* A place or district the inhabitants of which may be called neighbors; vicinity; the adjoining district or locality; neighbors collectively; a district or locality in general (a low *neighborhood*) —**Neighboring**, nā'bėr-ing, *a.* Living as neighbors; being situated near.—**Neighborliness**, nā'bėr-li-nes, *n.* State or quality of being neighborly.—**Neighborly**, nā'bėr-li, *a.* Becoming a neighbor; acting as a good neighbor; social.

Neither, nē'THėr or nī'THėr, *pron.* and *pronominal adjective.* [Used as negative of either; earlier forms *nather*, *naither*, *nouther*, A.Sax. *nāuther*, *nāhwæther* = *nowhether*.] Not one of two; not either; not the one or the other: used either alone or with a noun following.—*conj.* Not either: generally prefixed to the first of two or more co-ordinate negative propositions or clauses, the others being introduced by *nor*; sometimes used instead of *nor* in the second of two clauses, the former containing *not*.

Nelumbo, nē-lum'bō, *n.* The Hindu and Chinese lotus, a beautiful water-plant with rose-coloured flowers.

Nemæan, ne-mē'an, *a.* NEMEAN.

Nematocyst, nem'a-to-sist, *n.* [Gr. *nēma*, *nēmatos*, a thread, and *kystis*, a bag.] *Physiol.* a thread-cell or stinging apparatus of cœlenterate animals.

Nematoid, nem'a-toid, *n.* [Gr. *nēma*, *nēmatos*, a thread, from *neō*, to spin.] One of an order of entozoa having a long cylindrical, and often filiform body; a round-worm.—**Nematode**, **Nematoid**, nem'a-tōd, *a.* Pertaining to or resembling the nematoids.

Nemean, nē'mē-an or ne-mē'an, *a.* Of or belonging to *Nemea* in Argolis, Greece.—*Nemean games*, ancient games or festivals celebrated at Nemea every second year.

Nemertid, nē-mėr'tid, *n.* A name of marine annelids remarkable for the length which they attain, namely 30 or 40 feet, which they can suddenly contract to 3 or 4.—**Nemertine**, **Nemertean**, nē-mėr'tīn, nē-mėr-tēan, *a.* Pertaining to the nemertids.—**Nemertines**, nē-mer-tīns, *n.* [Gr. *nēma*, a thread.] Unsegmented worms, mostly marine, which possess a thread-like proboscis that protrudes from a pore near the mouth and secures prey.

Nemesis, nem'e-sis, *n.* [Gr., from *nemesis*, distribution of what is due.] A Greek goddess personifying retributive justice; one who takes vengeance; act of retribution.

Nemoral,† nem'or-al, *a.* [L. *nemoralis*, from *nemus*, *nemoris*, a wood.] Pertaining to a wood or grove.—**Nemorose**, nem'or-ōs, *a.* [L. *nemorosus*.] *Bot.* growing in groves or among wood.—**Nemorous**, nem'or-us, *a.* Woody; pertaining to a wood.

Neocomian, nē-ō-kō'mi-an, *a.* [L. *Neocomum*, *Neufchâtel*, in Switzerland, where the strata are largely developed.] *Geol.* a term applied to the lowest of the cretaceous deposits, being the lower green-sand and wealden.

Neocosmic, nē-ō-koz'mik, *a.* [Gr. *neos*, new, and *kosmos*, the world.] New concepts of the universe and the forces which operate within it.

Neocracy, nē-ok'ra-si, *n.* [Gr. *neos*, new, and *kratos*, power.] Government by new or inexperienced officials; upstart rule or supremacy.

Neogene, nē'ō-jen, *a.* [Gr. *neos*, new, and root *gen*, to produce.] *Geol.* a name for the pliocene and miocene tertiaries to distinguish them from the eocene strata.

Neo-Lamarckism, nē'ō-la-mark″ism, *n.* [Gr. *neos*, new, and *Lamarck*, an eminent French naturalist.] A theory of evolution postulating the existence of definite laws of growth.

Neo-Latin, nē'ō-lat-in, *a.* and *n.* [Gr. *neos*, new.] Applied to the Romance languages, as having grown immediately out of the Latin; Latin as written by authors of modern times.

Neolithic, nē-ō-lith'ik, *a.* [Gr. *neos*, new, *lithos*, a stone.] *Archæol.* applied to the more recent of the two periods into which the stone age has been subdivided, as opposed to *palæolithic*. During the neolithic age, stone implements were polished, domesticated animals became common, cereals and fruit trees were grown, pottery made, linen woven, and boats used.

Neology, nē-ol'o-ji, *n.* [Gr. *neos*, new, and *logos*, a word.] The introduction of a new word or of new words into a language; novel doctrines; rationalistic views in theology.—**Neologic**, **Neological**, nē-ō-loj'ik, nē-ō-loj'i-kal, *a.* Pertaining to neology.—**Neologically**, nē-ō-loj'i-kal-li, *adv.* In a neological manner.—**Neologism**, **Neologianism**, nē-ol'o-jizm, nē-ō-lō'ji-an-izm, *n.* A new word or phrase, or new use of a word; the use of new words or of old words in a new sense; new doctrines.—**Neologist**, **Neologian**, nē-ol'o-jist, nē-ō-lō'ji-an, *n.* One who introduces new words or phrases; an innovator in doctrines or beliefs.

Neon, nē'on, *n.* [Gr. *neon*, new.] An inert, gaseous element found in the atmosphere, without color, odor, or taste.—**Neon lamp**, neon contained in a vacuum tube, through which an electric current passes, producing a reddish-orange glow, valuable in electric advertising signs (*neon signs*), and in aeronautics for beacons.

Neophyte, nē'ō-fīt, *n.* [Gr. *neos*, new, and *phyton*, a plant, from *phyō*, I grow.] A new convert or proselyte; a novice; one newly admitted to the order of priest; a tyro; a beginner in learning.

Neoplasm, nē'o-plasm, *n.* Any new and abnormal body tissue, such as a cancer, tumors, or false membranes.

Neo-Platonism, nē-ō-plā'ton-izm, *n.* [Gr. *neos*, new, and E. *Platonism*.] A philosophical system growing up in Alexandria, and prevailing chiefly from the 3rd to the 5th century after Christ, deriving elements from the philosophy of Plato, and from Christianity, Gnosticism, and Oriental beliefs.

Neoteric, **Neoterical**, nē-ō-ter'ik, nē-ō-ter'i-kal, *a.* [Gr. *neōterikos*, young, from *neos*, new.] New; recent in origin; modern.—**Neoterism**, nē-ot'ėr-izm, *n.* The introduction of new words or phrases; a new word or phrase introduced; a neologism.—**Neoterize**, nē-ot'ėr-īz, *v.i.*—*neoterized*, *neoterizing*. To coin new words or phrases; to neologize.

Neotropical, nē-ō-trop'i-kal, *a.* [Gr. *neos*, new, and E. *tropical*.] Applied to a region of the earth in reference to its characteristic fauna, including all America south of the isthmus of Tehuantepec.

Neozoic, nē-ō-zō'ik, *a.* [Gr. *neos*, new, recent, and *zōē*, life.] *Geol.* a name given to strata from the beginning of the trias up to the most recent deposits, including the mesozoic and cainozoic divisions.

Nepenthe, **Nepenthes**, nē-pen'thē, nē-pen'thēz, *n.* [Gr. *nēpenthēs*—*nē*, not, and *penthos*, grief.] A kind of magic potion, supposed to make persons forget their sorrows and misfortunes; any draught or drug capable of removing pain or care.

Nephalism, nef'al-izm, *n.* [Gr. *nēphalios*, sober, from *nēphō*, to abstain from wine.] Teetotalism.—**Nephalist**, nef'al-ist, *n.* A teetotaller.

Nepheloid, nef'el-oid, *a.* [Gr. *nephelē*, a cloud.] Cloudy, as liquors.

Nephew, nev'ū, *n.* [Fr. *neveu*, from L. *nepos*, *nepotis*, a nephew; cog. A.Sax. *nefa*, Icel. *nefi*, G. *neffe*, Skr. *napat*, a nephew. Akin *niece*.] The son of a brother or sister.

Nephralgia, **Nephralgy**, ne-fral'ji-a, ne-fral'ji, *n.* [Gr. *nephros*, a kidney, and *algos*, pain.] Pain in the kidneys.—**Nephrite**, nef'rīt, *n.* [Gr. *nephritēs*.] The mineral otherwise called jade.—**Nephritic**, **Nephritical**, ne-frit'ik, ne-frit'i-kal, *a.* Pertaining to the kidneys; relieving disorders of the kidneys.—**Nephritis**, nē-frī'tis, *n.* [Gr. term. *-itis*, signifying inflammation.] Inflammation of the kidneys.—**Nephroid**, nef'roid, *a.* Kidney-shaped.—**Nephrolithic**, nef-rō-lith'ik, *a.* [Gr. *nephros*, and *lithos*, a stone.] *Med.* relating to the stone, or calculi in the kidneys.—**Nephrology**, ne-frol'o-ji, *n.* A description of the kidneys.—**Nephrotomy**, ne-frot'o-mi, *n.* [Gr. *tomē*, a cutting.] *Surg.* the operation of cutting for stone in the kidney.

Nephridium, pl. **-ia**, nef-rid'i-um, *n.* [Gr. dim. of *nephros*, a kidney.] In animals, an excretory tube placing the CŒLOM (which see) in communication with the interior.

Nepotism, nep'o-tism, *n.* [Fr. *népotisme*, from L. *nepos*, nephew. NEPHEW.] Favoritism shown to nephews and other relations; patronage bestowed in consideration of family relationship and not of merit.—**Nepotic**, **Nepotious**, nē-pot'ik, nē-pō'shus, *a.* Belonging to nepotism; practicing nepotism.—**Nepotist**, nep'o-tist, *n.* One who practices nepotism.

Neptune, nep'tūn, *n.* [L. *Neptunus*.] The chief marine divinity of the Romans, identified by them with the Greek Poseidon; a planet beyond the orbit of Uranus, the third largest and second remotest from the sun.—**Neptunian**, nep-tū'ni-an, *a.* Pertaining to the ocean or sea; formed by water or aqueous solution (as rocks).—*Neptunian theory*, in *geol.* the theory of Werner, which refers the formation of all rocks and strata to the agency of water: opposed to the *Plutonic* theory.

Nereid, nē'rē-id, *n.* [Gr. *nērēis*, *nērēidos*, from *Nēreus*, a marine deity.] *Myth.* one of the daughters of Nereus, the constant attendants of Neptune; a sea nymph; a marine annelid; a sea-centiped.

Neritic zone, ne-rit'ik, *n.* [Gr. *nēritēs*, a sea-snail.] The shallow waters of the sea.

Neroli, ner'ō-li, *n.* [The name of an Italian princess, its discoverer.] The fragrant essential oil from the flowers of the bitter orange.

Nerve, nėrv, *n.* [L. *nervus*, a sinew, strength, vigour, from root *snar* (with initial *s*), seen in E. *snare*.] A sinew or tendon‡; strength; muscular power; self-command or steadiness, especially under trying circumstances; firmness of mind; courage; one of the whitish fibres which proceed from the brain and spinal cord, or from the central ganglia, of animals, and ramify through all parts of the body, and whose function is to convey sensation and originate motion; *pl.* the general tone of one's system; *bot.* one of the ribs or principal veins in a leaf.—*v.t.*—*nerved*, *nerving*. To give nerve, strength, or vigour to; to arm with force.—**Nervation**, nėr-vā'shon, *n.* The arrangement or distribution of nerves; *bot.* the distribution of the veins of leaves; venation.—**Nerve-cell**, **Nerve-corpuscle**, *n.* One of the nucleated cells numerous in the gray portion of the brain and spinal cord, &c.—**Nerved**, nėrvd, *a.* Having nerves; having nerves of this or that character.—**Nerve-fiber**, *n.* One of the primary fibers of the nerves and of the white substance of the brain and spinal cord.—**Nerveless**, nėrv'les, *a.* Without nerve; destitute of strength; weak.—**Nervine**, nėr'vīn, *a.* Capable of acting upon the nerves.—*n.* A medicine for nervous affections (as for toothache).—**Nervous**, nėr'vus, *a.* Pertaining to the nerves; affecting the nerves; having the nerves affected; having weak or diseased nerves; easily agitated; strong; vigorous; sinewy; characterized by force or strength in sentiment or style.—*Nerve centers*, the organs whence the nerves originate, as the brain and spinal marrow.—*Nervous system*, the nerves and nervous centers collectively.—*Nervous temperament*, that in which the predominating characteristic is a great excitability of the nervous system, and an undue predominance of the emotional impulses.—**Nervously**, nėrv'us-li, *adv.* — **Nervousness**, nėr'vus-nes, *n.* The state or quality of being nervous.—**Nervure**, nėr'vūr, *n. Bot.* the vein or nerve of a leaf; *entom.* one of the corneous tubes which help to expand the wing and keep it tense.—**Nervy**, nėr'vi, *a.* Sinewy; vigorous; cocky, bold, nervous.

Nescience, nē'shi-ens, *n.* [L. *nescientia*, from *nescio*, not to know—*ne*, not, and *scio*, to know. SCIENCE.] The state of not knowing; want of knowledge; ignorance.—**Nescious**, nē'shi-us, *a.* Ignorant.

Ness, nes, *n.* [A.Sax. *næs*, Icel. *nes*, Dan. *næs*, a ness; probably a form of *nose*.] A promontory; a cape; a headland.

Nest, nest, *n.* [A.Sax., L.G., D., and G. *nest*; allied to L. *nidus*, a nest, for *nisdus*, from root *nas*, to dwell, seen in Greek *nostos*, return.] The place or bed formed or used by a bird for incubation and rearing the young; a place where the eggs of insects, turtles, &c., are produced; a place in which the young of various small animals (as mice) are reared; a number of persons frequenting the same haunt: generally in a bad sense; a set of articles of diminishing sizes, each enveloping the one next smaller (a *nest* of boxes); a set of small drawers.—*v.i.* To build a nest; to nestle.—**Nest-egg**, *n.* An egg left in the nest to prevent the hen from forsaking it; something laid up as a beginning or nucleus.—**Nestle**, nes'l, *v.i.*—*nestled*, *nestling*. [Freq. from *nest*.] To make or occupy a nest; to take shelter; to lie close and snug.—*v.t.* To house or shelter, as in a nest; to cherish and fondle closely.—**Nestling**, nest'ling, *n.* [A dim. from *nest*.] A young bird in the nest, or just taken from the nest.

Nestor, nest'or, *n.* The type of an old and faithful counsellor, from Nestor in Homer, King of Pylus in Messenia.

Nestorian, nes-tō'ri-an, *n.* An adherent of Nestorius, patriarch of Constantinople in the fifth century, who maintained that the two natures in Christ were separate; one of those modern Christians of Persia and India who are the remains of the Nestorian sect.

Net, net, *n.* [A.Sax. *net*, *nett*, a net=Icel., Dan., and D. *net*, Sw. *nät*, Goth. *nati*, G. *netz*, a net; cog. L. *nassa*, a basket for catching fish; from root seen in Skr. *nada*, a stream.] An instrument formed of thread, twine, or other fibrous materials, wrought or woven into meshes, used for catching fish, birds, &c., and also for securing or containing articles of various kinds; a fabric of fine open texture.—*v.t.*—*netted*, *netting*. To make into a net or net-work; to take in a net; hence, to capture by wile or stratagem; to inclose in a net or net-work.—*v.i.* To form net-work.—**Netted**, net'ed, *p.* and *a.* Made into a net or net-work; reticulated. — **Netting**, net'ing, *n.* The process of making nets; a piece of net-work; a net of small ropes, to be stretched along the upper part of a ship's quarter to contain hammocks.—**Netting-needle**, *n.* A kind of shuttle used in netting.—**Netty**, net'i, *a.* Like a net; netted.—**Net-work**, *n.* Work formed in the same manner as a net; any net-like fabric; an interlacement.

Net, Nett, net, *a.* [Fr. *net*, It. *netto*, neat, net. NEAT.] Free from all deductions (*net* profits, *net* produce, *net* rent, *net* weight).—*v.t.*—*netted*, *netting*. To gain as clear profit.

Nether, neᴛʜ'ėr, *a.* [A.Sax. *nither*, *nithor*, *neothra*, compar. of *nithe*, under, downward (whence *neothan*, *beneothan*, *beneath*); cog. L.G., D., and Dan. *neder*, Icel. *netharr*, G. *nieder*; root seen in Skr. *ni*, downwards.] Lower; lying or being beneath or in the lower part: opposed to *upper*.—**Netherlands**. [D. *Nederland*.] The lands lying at the foot of the Rhine, Holland.—**Nethermost**, neᴛʜ'ėr-mōst, *a.* [A double superlative, like *hindmost*.] Lowest.—**Netherwards**, neᴛʜ'ėr-wėrdz, *adv.*

Nettle, net'l, *n.* [A.Sax. *netele* = D. *netel*, Dan. *nælde*, *nelde*, G. *nessel*, a nettle; root doubtful.] A sort of plants consisting chiefly of neglected weeds with stinging hairs.—*v.t.*—*nettled*, *nettling*. To irritate or vex; to cause to feel displeasure or vexation not amounting to anger.—**Nettle-cloth**, *n.* A thick cotton stuff, japanned and used for the peaks of caps, waist-belts, &c., in place of leather.—**Nettle-rash**, *n.* An eruption upon the skin much resembling the effects of the sting of a nettle; urticaria.

Network, net'wŭrk, *n.* An interlacement of threads, wires, or strings into a fabric or web; a complicated intermingling of lines as of a railroad system; a political undercover group, whose members are separated, but in indirect communication; in radio, a series of stations or broadcasting units called a hookup.

Neural, nū'ral, *a.* [Gr. *neuron*, a nerve; akin to L. *nervus*. NERVE.] Pertaining to the nerve or nervous system.—*Neural arch*, the arch or projection posteriorly inclosing and protecting the spinal cord of the vertebra.—*Neural axis*, the central trunk of the nervous system, also called the *cerebro-spinal axis*. — **Neuralgia**, nū-ral'ji-a, *n.* [Gr. *algos*, pain.] Pain in a nerve; an ailment the chief sympton of which is acute pain, apparently seated in a nerve or nerves.—**Neuralgic**, nū-ral'jik, *a.* Pertaining to neuralgia.—**Neurasthenia**, nū'ras-thē"ni-a, *n.* [Gr. *neuron*, nerve, *astheneia*, weakness. ASTHENIA.] *Med.* nervous debility or exhaustion; *psychol.* a form of mental disturbance characterized by excessive irritability, fatigue, and worry.—**Neuration**, nū-ra'shon, *n.* The arrangement of the veins or nervures in the wings of insects; nervation.—**Neurin**, **Neurine**, nū'rin, *n.* The nitrogenized substance of nerve-fiber and cells.—**Neuritis**, nū-rī'tis, *n. Med.* inflammation of a nerve.—**Neurapophysis**, nū-ra-pof'i-sis, *n.* [Gr. *apophysis*, a projecting part.] *Compar. anat.* a posterior process or projection of the vertebral column.—**Neuro-hypnology**, **Neuro-hypnotism**, *n.* [Gr. *hypnos*, sleep.] The doctrine of nervous sleep or animal magnetism; mesmerism.—**Neurological**, nū-rō-loj'i-kal, *a.* Pertaining to neurology.—**Neurologist**, nū-rol'o-jist, *n.* One versed in neurology.—**Neurology**, nū-rol'o-ji, *n.* That branch of science which treats of the nerves.—**Neuromuscular**, nū-rō-mus'kū-lėr, *a.* Pertaining to or having the character of both nerves and muscles.—**Neuron**, nū'ron, *n.* [Gr. for *nerve*.] A nerve-cell with its prolongations.—**Neuropathic**, nū-rō-path'ik, *a.* Pertaining to affections of the nerves.—**Neuropathology**, **Neuropathy**, nū'rō-pa-thol"o-gi, nū-rop'a-thi, *n.* An affection of the nervous system.—**Neuropter**, **Neuropteran**, nū-rop'tėr, nū-rop'tėr-an, *n.* [Gr. *pteron*, a wing.] An individual belonging to an order of insects (*Neuroptera*) having four membranous, transparent, naked wings, reticulated with veins or nervures, as the dragon-flies. **Neuropteral**, **Neuropterous**, nū-rop'tėr-al, nū-rop'tėr-us, *a.* Belonging to the Neuropters.—**Neurosis**, nū-rō'sis, *n.* A functional disorder of the nervous system without any apparent physical counterpart.—**Neuroskeletal**, nū-rō-skel'ē-tal, *a.* Pertaining to the neuroskeleton.—**Neuroskeleton**, nū-rō-skel'ē-ton, *n.* The bones of vertebrate animals connected with the nervous axis and locomotion.—**Neurotic**, nū-rot'ik, *a.* Of the nerves; relating to or acting on the nerves; affected by neurosis.—*n.* A disease of the nerves; a medicine for nervous affections; a neurotic person. — **Neurotomical**, nū-rō-tom'i-kal, *a.* [Gr. *tomē*, a cutting.] Pertaining to the dissection of nerves.—**Neurotomist**, nū-rot'om-ist, *n.* One engaged in neurotomy; one who dissects the nerves.—**Neurotomy**, nū-rot'o-mi, *n.* The act or practice of dissecting nerves.—**Neurotonic**, nū-rō-ton'ik, *n.* [Gr. *tonikos*, bracing.] A medicine employed to strengthen the nervous system.

Neuter, nū'tėr, *a.* [L., not either, not one nor the other—compounded of *ne* and *uter*, either of two.] Neutral‡; *gram.* of neither gender; neither masculine nor feminine (in *Eng. gram.* applied to all names of things without life); neither active nor passive; intransitive (a *neuter* verb); *bot.* having neither stamens nor pistils; *zool.* having no fully developed sex (*neuter* bees).—*n.* An animal of neither sex, or incapable of propagation; one of the imperfectly developed females of certain social insects, as ants and bees; *bot.* a plant which has neither stamens nor pistils; *gram.* a noun of the neuter gender.—**Neutral**, nū'tral, *a.* [L. *neutralis*.] Not taking an active part with one of certain contending parties; not interested one way or another; indifferent.—*Neutral colours*, those in which the hue is broken by partaking of the reflected colours of the objects which surround them.—*Neutral salts*, *chem.* salts which do not exhibit any acid or alkaline properties. — *Neutral tint*, a dull, grayish hue, partaking of the character of none of the brilliant colours.—*n.* A person or nation that takes no part in a contest between others. — **Neutrality**, nū-tral'i-ti, *n.* The state of being neutral; the state of taking no part on either side. — **Neutralization**, nū'-tral-i-zā"shon, *n.* The act of neutralizing; *chem.* the process by which an acid and an alkali are so combined as to disguise each other's properties or render them inert.—**Neutralize**, nū'tral-īz, *v.t.*—*neutralized*, *neutralizing*. To render neutral; to destroy the peculiar properties or opposite dispositions of; to render inoperative; to counteract; *chem.* to destroy or render inert or imperceptible the peculiar properties of by combination with a different substance.—**Neutralizer**, nū'tral-ī-zėr, *n.* One who or that which neutralizes.—**Neutrally**, nū'tral-li, *adv.* In a neutral manner.

Névé, nā'vā *n.* [Fr., from L. *nix*, *nivis*, snow.] The French name for the coarsely granular snow from which glaciers are formed.

Never, nev'ėr, *adv.* [The neg. of *ever*; A. Sax. *naefre*, from *ne*, not, and *aefre*, ever; comp. *neither*, *either*, &c.] Not ever; at no time, whether past, present, or future; in no degree (*never* fear); not at all; none (*never* the better); not, emphatically (he answered *never* a word).—*Never so*, to any or to whatever extent or degree (*never so* much, little, well, &c.; now less common than *ever so*).—*Never* is much used in composition, as in *never*-ending, *never*-failing, *never*-dying, &c.; but in all such compounds it has its usual meaning.—**Nevermore**, nev'ėr-mōr, *adv.* Never again; at no future time. — **Nevertheless**, nev'ėr-ᴛʜē-les", *conj.* [The *the* is the old instrumental case of the demonstrative used before comparatives; A.Sax. *thý læs*, the or by that less.] Not the less; notwithstanding; in spite of, or without regarding that.

New, nū, *a.* [A.Sax. *niwe*, *neówe*, new=D. *nieuw*, Goth. *niujis*, G. *neu*; cog. W. *newydd*, Ir. *nuadh*, L. *novus*, Gr. *neos*, Skr. *navas*, —new; connected with *now*.] Lately made, invented, produced, or come into being; recent in origin; novel; opposed to *old*, and used of things; not before known; recently discovered; recently produced by change; different from a former (to lead a *new* life); not habituated; not familiar; unaccustomed; fresh after any event; never used before, or recently brought into use; not second-hand (a *new* copy of a book); recently commenced; starting afresh (the *new* year, a *new* week).—*New Red Sandstone*. Under SANDSTONE.—*New Testament*. TES-

TAMENT.—*New World*, a name frequently given to North and South America; the western hemisphere.—*New* is much used adverbially in composition for *newly*; as in *new*-born, *new*-made, *new*-grown, *new*-formed, *new*-found.—**Newcomer**, *n.* One who has lately come.—**New Deal**, *n.* A term attached to the policies advocated by the Franklin Delano Roosevelt Administrations and its adherents; and legislation enacted by Congress.—**New-fangled**, *a.* [FANGLED, FANG.] New-fashioned.—**New-fashioned**, *a.* Made in a new fashion; lately come into fashion.—**Newish**, nū'ish, *a.* Somewhat new; nearly new.—**Newly**, nū'li, *adv.* Lately; freshly; recently; with a new form, different from the former; anew; afresh; as before; in a new and different manner.—**New-made**, *a.* Newly made or formed.—**Newness**, nū'nes, *n.* The state or quality of being new; novelty.—The state or quality of being new.—**News**, nūz, *n.* [From *new*; probably the old genit. of *new*, from such phrases as A.Sax. *hwæt niwes?* what of new, what news? It is almost always used as a singular.] Recent intelligence regarding any event; fresh information of something that has lately taken place, or of something before unknown; tidings; a newspaper.—**News agency**, *n.* An organization that gathers news and photographs rapidly, syndicating their services to newspapers, usually by teletype and wire-photo machines; an establishment which sells periodical publications.—**News agent**, *n.* A person who deals in newspapers; a news vender.—**Newsboy**, *n.* A boy who sells or delivers newspapers.—**News editor**, *n.* The editor of a newspaper in charge of local and telegraphic news; one who supervises the editing or writing of newspaper copy.—**Newsletter**, *n.* A letter-like report or analysis of a specialized nature, printed for periodic distribution to subscribers.—**Newsmonger**, nūz'mung-gėr, *n.* One who deals in news; a gossip; a teller of tales.—**Newspaper**, nūz'pā-pėr, *n.* A periodic publication issued daily or weekly, disseminating news, opinions, and reports of immediate significance; the organization that composes, publishes, and distributes newspapers.—**Newspaperman**, *n.* One who writes for, edits, or owns a newspaper; a gatherer of news.—**Newsprint**, *n.* An inexpensive paper manufactured from woodpulp, machine-finished, used mostly for newspapers.—**Newsreel**, nūz'rēl, *n.* A motion picture film depicting current news events.—**Newsstand**, *n.* A booth or stand where newspapers and periodicals are sold.—**Newsy**, nūz'i, *n.* A newsboy. (*Colloq.*); *a.* Full of news.

Newfoundland, Newfoundland Dog, nū-found'land or nū'found-land, *n.* A well-known and fine variety of the dog, supposed to be derived from Newfoundland, remarkable for its sagacity, good-nature, and swimming powers.

Newt, nūt, *n.* [A corruption of *an ewt*, *ewt*, *evet* being old forms. EFT.] One of a genus of small-tailed batrachians of lizard-like appearance, living in ponds, ditches, and moist places; an eft.

Newtonian, nū-tō'ni-an, *a.* Pertaining to Sir Isaac *Newton*, or formed or discovered by him.—*Newtonian telescope*, a form of reflecting telescope.

Newton pippin, nū'tn pip'n, *n.* A kind of apple; a kind of rifle-grenade.

Next, nekst, *a.* superl. of *nigh.* [A.Sax. *nēhst*, *nēhsta*, superl. of *nēh*, *neáh*, nigh.] Nearest in place, time, rank, or degree. [When *next* stands before an object without *to* after it it may be regarded as a preposition.]—*Next door to*, close to; allied to; not far removed from.—*adv.* At the time or turn nearest or immediately succeeding (who follows *next?*).

Nexus, nek'sus, *n.* [L.] Tie; connection; interdependence existing.

Niagara, nī-ag'a-ra, *n.* The great falls of the Niagara River; metaphorically, of an overpowering flow or torrent of language.—*Shooting Niagara*, taking grave social risks leading to a political crisis. (*Carlyle.*)

Nib, nib, *n.* [Same as *neb.*] The bill or beak of a fowl; the point of anything, particularly of a pen; a small pen adapted to be fitted into a holder.—*v.t.*—*nibbed*, *nibbing.* To furnish with a nib; to mend the nib of, as a pen.

Nibble, nib'l, *v.t.*—*nibbled*, *nibbling.* [A freq. from *nib*, or from *nip.*] To bite by little at a time; to eat in small bits; to bite, as a fish does the bait; just to catch by biting.—*v.i.* To bite gently; *fig.* to carp; to make a petty attack: with *at.*—*n.* A little bite, or the act of seizing with the mouth as if to bite.—**Nibbler**, nib'lėr, *n.* One that nibbles.—**Nibblingly**, nib'ling-li, *adv.* In a nibbling manner.

Niblick, nib'lik, *n.* An iron-headed golf club with a wide face at an angle of 45 degrees or more from the vertical, used to lift the ball into the air from sandtraps and to approach the green.

Nice, nīs, *a.* [O.Fr. *nice*, *nisce*, simple, from L. *nescius*, from *ne*, not, *scio*, to know. NESCIENCE.] Foolish or silly‡; unimportant‡; over-scrupulous; fastidious; punctilious; distinguishing minutely; made with scrupulous exactness; precise; pleasant to the senses; delicious; dainty; pleasing or agreeable in general: a modern sense.—**Nicely**, nīs'li, *adv.* In a nice manner; fastidiously; critically; with delicate perception; accurately; exactly; becomingly; pleasantly.—**Niceness**, nīs'nes, *n.* State or quality of being nice; fastidiousness; minute exactness; agreeableness; pleasantness.—**Nicety**, nīs'e-ti, *n.* [O.Fr. *niceté.*] State or quality of being nice; excess of delicacy; fastidiousness; delicacy of perception; precision; delicate management; a minute difference or distinction.

Nicene, nī-sēn', *a.* Pertaining to *Nicæa* or *Nice*, a town of Asia Minor.—*Nicene creed*, a summary of Christian faith composed by the Council of Nice against Arianism, A.D. 325, altered and confirmed by the Council of Constantinople, A.D. 381.

Niche, nich, *n.* [Fr. *niche*, from It. *nicchia*, originally a shell-shaped recess, from *nicchio*, a shell-fish, from L. *mytilus*, a mussel.] A recess in a wall for the reception of a statue, a vase, or some other ornament.—**Niched**, nicht, *a.* Having a niche or niches; placed in a niche.

Nick, nik, *n.* [A name among the Teutonic nations for a water-goblin; A.Sax. *nicor*, Dan. *nök*, Icel. *nykr*, N. *nykk*, *nök*, G. *nix*, *nixe.*] Originally, a goblin or spirit of the waters, but now applied only to the Evil One, generally with the addition of *Old.*

Nick, nik, *n.* [Same as D. *knik*, Sw. *nick*, a nod, a wink; G. *nicken*, to nod; or connected with *nick*, a notch.] The exact point of time required by necessity or convenience; the critical time.—*v.t.* To strike at the lucky time; to hit; to make a hit at by some trick (*Shak.*).

Nick, nik, *n.* [Comp. G. *knick*, a flaw; also E. *notch*, O.D. *nocke*, a notch.] A notch; a notch in the shank of a type to guide the hand of the compositor in setting.—*v.t.* To make a nick or notch in; to cut in nicks or notches.

Nickel, nik'el, *n.* [Sw. *nickel*, nickel; a name connected with *nick*, the evil spirit, and given to this metal because its copper-coloured ore deceived the miners by giving no copper.] A metal of a white color, of great hardness, always magnetic, and when perfectly pure malleable and ductile; the five-cent coin composed of copper and nickel. (*U. S.*)—**Nickel-bloom**, *n.* Same as *Nickel-ocher.*—**Nickel-glance**, *n.* A grayish-white ore of nickel.—**Nickel-green**, *n.* Same as *Nickel-ocher.*—**Nickelic**, ni-kel'ik, *a.* Pertaining to or containing nickel.—**Nickeliferous**, nik-el-if'ėr-us, *a.* Containing nickel.—**Nickeline**, nik'el-in, *n.* One of the chief ores of nickel, consisting principally of nickel and arsenic.—**Nickel-ocher**, *n.* A mineral containing nickel, or an apple-green color.—**Nickel-plating**, *n.* The plating of metals with nickel.—**Nickel-silver**, *n.* An alloy composed of copper, zinc, and nickel.

Nick-nack, nik'nak, *n.* [KNICK-KNACK.] A trinket; a gimcrack; a trifle. Spelled also *Nick-knack*, *Knick-knack.*—**Nick-nackery**, nik'nak-ėr-i, *n.* A collection of nick-nacks; a nick-nack; a trifle.

Nickname, nik'nām, *n.* [Probably for *ekename* (Icel. *auk-nefni*), the initial *n* being that of *an*, the indef. art., like *newt* for *ewt.*] A name given to a person in contempt or derision; a familiar or contemptuous name or appellation; a familiar form of a proper name, such as "Bill," for William.

Nicolaitan, nik-ō-lā'i-tan, *n.* [From the founder *Nicolas.*] One of a sect in the early Christian Church who inclined to licentious and pagan practices.

Nicotian, ni-kō'shi-an, *a.* [Fr. *nicotiane*, the earliest name of tobacco, from M. *Nicot*, who introduced the plant into France in 1560.] Pertaining to or derived from tobacco.—**Nicotianine**, ni-kō'shi-a-nin, *n.* An oil extracted from tobacco.—**Nicotine**, nik'ō-tin, *n.* A volatile alkaloid from tobacco, highly poisonous.

Nictitate, Nictate, nik'ti-tāt, nik'tāt, *v.t.*—*nictitated*, *nictated*; *nictitating*, *nictating.* [From L. *nicto*, *nictatum*, to wink.] To wink with the eyes.—*Nictitating membrane*, a thin movable membrane, most largely developed in birds, which covers and protects the eyes from dust or too much light.—**Nictitation, Nictation**, nik-ti-tā'shon, nik-tā'shon, *n.* The act of winking.

Nidamental, nid-a-men'tal, *a.* [L. *nidamentum*, a nest, from *nidus*, a nest. NEST.] Pertaining to the nests of birds or other animals.

Nidge, nij, *v.t.* [Perhaps akin to *nag* (verb), *gnaw.*] *Masonry*, to dress with a sharp-pointed hammer.

Nidicolæ, nid-ik'ō-lē, *n.* [L. *nidus*, a nest, *colo*, I inhabit.] In birds, species with helpless young.

Nidificate, nid'i-fi-kāt, *v.i.* [L. *nidifico*, from *nidus*, a nest, *facio*, to make. NIDULANT.] To make a nest.—**Nidification**, nid'i-fi-kā"shon, *n.* The act of building a nest.

Nidifugæ, nīd-i-fūg'ē, *n.* [L. *nidus*, a nest, *fugio*, I run away.] In birds, species with young that are active as soon as hatched.

Nid-nod, nid'nod, *v.i.* [A reduplication of *nod.*] To nod frequently.

Nidor, nī'dor, *n.* [L.] Scent; savour; smell of cooked food.

Nidulant, nid'ū-lant, *a.* [L. *nidulans*, ppr. of *nidulor*, to nestle, from *nidus*, a nest. NEST.] Nestling; *bot.* lying loose in the form of pulp or cottony matter within a berry or pericarp.—**Nidulate**, nid'ū-lāt, *a.* *Bot.* same as *Nidulant.*—*v.i.* To build a nest; to nidificate.—**Nidulation**, nid-ū-lā'shon, *n.* The act of nidulating.—**Nidus**, nī'dus, *n.* [L., a nest.] Any part of a living organism where a parasite finds nourishment; *med.* the bodily seat of a zymotic disease; the part of the organism where such a disease is developed.

Niece, nēs, *n.* [Fr. *nièce*, O.Fr. *niepce*, from L. *neptis*, a granddaughter; allied to *nepos*, *nepotis*, a nephew. NEPHEW.] The daughter of a brother or sister; also, the daughter of a brother or sister in law.

Niello, ni-el'lō, *n.* [It., from L.L. *nigellum*, from L. *nigellus*, dim. of *niger*, black.] A method of ornamenting metal plates by cutting lines in the metal and filling them up with a black or coloured composition.

Nig, nig, *v.t.* *Masonry*, same as *Nidge.*

Niggard, nig'ėrd, *n.* [From Icel. *hnöggr*, Sw. *njugg*, niggardly, with term. *-ard.*] A miser; a person meanly covetous; a sordid, parsimonious wretch.—**Niggard, Niggardly**, nig'ėrd-li, *a.* Miserly; meanly covetous; sordidly parsimonious.—**Niggardly**, *adv.* In a niggard manner.—**Niggardliness**, nig'ėrd-li-nes, *n.* The quality of being niggardly; sordid parsimony.

Nigger, nig'ėr, *n.* A familiar or contemptuous name for a negro or other person of coloured race.

Nigh, nī, *a.* compar. *nigher*, superl. *next.* [A.Sax. *nedh, nêh*, nigh, near; D. *na*, Icel. *ná-*, G. *nah, nahe*, near, prep. *nach*, to, Goth. *nehwa*—nigh. NEAR, NEIGHBOUR.] Near; not distant or remote in place or time; closely at hand; ready to aid.—*adv.* Near; close; almost; nearly.—*prep.* Near to; at no great distance from.—**Nighness**, nī'nes, *n.* Nearness; proximity.

Night, nīt, *n.* [A.Sax. *niht, neaht* = Icel. *nátt*, Sw. *natt*, Dan. *nat*, Goth. *nahts*, D. and G. *nacht*; cog. Ir. *nochd*, W. *nos*, Armor. *noz*, Lith. *naktis*, L. *nox, noctis*, Gr. *nyx, nyktos*, Skr. *nakti, nakta*—night; from root *nak*, to vanish, to perish.] That part of the natural day when the sun is beneath the horizon, or the time from sunset to sunrise; *fig.* a state or time of darkness, depression, misfortune, and the like; a state of ignorance or intellectual darkness; obscurity; the darkness of death or the grave; a time of sadness or sorrow.—**Nightless**, nīt'les, *a.* Having no night.—**Nightly**, nīt'li, *a.* Done by night; happening in the night; done every night.—*adv.* By night; every night.—**Nightward**, nīt'-wėrd, *a.* Approaching toward night. *Night* is much used as a first element in compounds, many of them self-explanatory.—**Night-bell**, *n.* A door-bell, as at the house of a physician, to be rung at night.—**Night-bird**, *n.* A bird that flies in the night.—**Night-blindness**, *n.* A disease in which the eyes can see by daylight but not by artificial light.—**Night-cap**, *n.* A cap worn in bed; toddy or other potation taken before going to bed.—**Night clothes**, *n. pl.* Clothes worn in bed.—**Night club**, *n.* A short, hardwood stick carried by police for use in hand-to-hand fighting; a café or restaurant, serving liquors and presenting entertainment for the enjoyment of night pleasure-seekers.—**Nightfall**, nīt'fąl, *n.* The fall of night; the close of the day; evening.—**Night-glass**, *n.* A telescope so constructed as to concentrate as much light as possible, so as to enable objects to be seen at night.—**Nightgown**, *n.* A loose gown worn in bed; a night-dress.—**Night-hag**, *n.* A witch supposed to wander or fly abroad in the night.—**Nighthawk**, *n.* A species of goat-sucker; a person up and about during the night.—**Night-jar**, *n.* [*Jar* or *churr* is from the sound of its voice.] A name of the common or British goat-sucker.—**Night lamp**, *n.* A lamp to be kept burning during the night.—**Night letter**, *n.* A telegram sent at night for delivery the following morning at a per-word rate lower than a straight telegram.—**Night light**, *n.* A candle or taper for burning at night, often placed in a dish of water.—**Nightlong**, *a.* Lasting a night—**Nightmare**, nīt'mãr, *a.* [*Night*, and A.Sax. and Icel. *mara*, G. *mahr*, incubus, nightmare; Pol. *mara*, nightmare, phantom.] A state of oppression or feeling of suffocation felt during sleep, and accompanied by a feeling of intense anxiety, fear, or horror; hence, some overpowering, oppressive, or stupefying influence.—**Night piece**, *n.* A picture representing a night scene; a written piece descriptive of a scene by night.—**Night porter**, *n.* A servant who attends during the night in hotels, infirmaries, &c.—**Nightshade**, nīt'shād, *n.* [A.Sax. *nihtscada*, lit. the shade or shadow of night; so D. *nachtschade*, G. *nachtschatten*, the nightshade.] The popular name of various plants of the potato genus which possess narcotic or poisonous properties; also applied to plants of different genera.—*Deadly nightshade*, belladonna.—**Nightshirt**, *n.* A pull-over sleeping garment for men and boys.—**Nightwalker**, *n.* One that walks in his sleep; a somnambulist; one that roams in the night for evil purposes.—**Night watch**, *n.* A watch or period of the night; a watch or guard in the night.—**Night watchman**, *n.* One who acts as a watchman during the night.

Nightingale, nīt'in-gāl, *n.* [A.Sax. *nihtegale*, lit. the night-singer, from *niht*, night, *galan*, to sing; so D. *nachtegaal*, Dan. *nattergal*, G. *nachtigall*. The *n* medial is intrusive, as in *passenger*, *messenger*.] A well-known migratory bird that sings at night, often called in poetry Philomela or Philomel.

Nigrescent, nī-gres'ĕnt, *a.* [L. *nigresco*, to grow black, from *niger*, black.] Growing black; approaching to blackness.—**Nigrification**, nig'ri-fi-kā"shon, *n.* [L. *niger*, and *facio*, to make.] The act of making black.—**Nigritude**, nig'ri-tūd, *n.* [L. *nigritudo*.] Blackness.

Nihil, nī'hil, *n.* [L., from *ne*, not, and *hilum*, a little thing, a trifle.] Nothing, a word used in sundry law phrases, &c.—**Nihilism**, nī'hil-izm, *n.* Nothingness; *metaph.* the denial of all existence or of the knowledge of all existence; the doctrines or principles of the Nihilists.—**Nihilist**, nī'-hil-ist, *n.* One who holds the doctrine or principles of nihilism; a member of a Russian secret society, the adherents of which maintain the need for an entire reconstruction of society and hold revolutionary ideas generally.—**Nihilistic**, nī-hil-is'tik, *a.* Relating to nihilism; characterized by nihilism.—**Nihility**, nī-hil'i-ti, *n.* A state of being nothing; nothingness.

Nil, nil, *n.* [L. NIHIL.] Nothing; as, his liabilities were over $5000 and his assets *nil*.

Nilghau, nil'gą, *n.* NYLGHAU.

Nill,‡ nil, *v.t.* and *i.* pret. *nilled* or *nould.* [A.Sax. *nillan*, that is, *ne*, not, and *willan*, to will.] Not to will; to refuse or reject; to be unwilling.

Nilometer, nī-lom'et-ėr, *n.* [Gr. *Neilos*, Nile, and *mĕtron*, measure.] An instrument for measuring the rise of water in the Nile during its periodical floods.—**Nilotic**, nī-lot'ik, *a.* Pertaining to the Nile.

Nimbiferous, nim-bif'ėr-us, *a.* [L. *nimbus*, a rain-cloud, and *fero*, to bring.] Bringing black clouds, rain, or storms.

Nimble, nim'bl, *a.* [O.E. *nemel*, capable, A.Sax. *numol*, capable, catching, from *niman*, to take = Icel. *nema*, D. *nemen*, G. *nehmen*, Goth. *niman*, to take; akin *numb*, *benumb*.] Light and quick in motion; moving with ease and celerity; agile; prompt; swift.—**Nimble-fingered**, *a.* Dexterous: generally in a bad sense; given to pilfer.—**Nimbleness**, nim'bl-nes, *n.* Agility; quickness; celerity.—**Nimbly**, nim'bli, *adv.* In a nimble manner; with agility.

Nimbus, nim'bus, *n.* [L., a cloud.] A cloud; a rain-cloud; a kind of halo or disc surrounding the head in representations of divine or sacred personages.

Nincompoop, nin'kom-pŏp, *n.* [A corruption of L. *non compos*, not of sound mind.] A fool; a blockhead; a simpleton.

Nine, nīn, *a.* [A.Sax. *nigon* = L.G. and D. *negen*, G. *neun*, Goth. *niun*, Icel. *níu*, Sw. *niu*, Dan. *ni*; cog W. *naw*, Ir. *naov*, L. *novem*, Gr. *ennea*, Skr. *navam*—nine. NOON.] One more than eight, or one less than ten.—*Nine days' wonder*, a subject of astonishment and gossip for a short time.—*The nine worthies*, certain famous personages, often alluded to by old writers, like the seven wonders of the world, &c.—*n.* The number composed of eight and one.—*The Nine*, among English poets, the nine Muses.—**Ninefold**, nīn'fōld, *a.* Nine times repeated.—**Nine-pins**, *n. pl.* A game with nine pins of wood set on end, at which a ball is rolled.—**Nineteen**, nīn'tēn, *a.* and *n.* [A.Sax. *nigontyne*, i.e. *nine, ten.*] Nine and ten.—**Nineteenth**, nīn'tēnth, *a.* The ordinal of nineteen.—*n.* A nineteenth part.—**Ninety**, nīn'ti, *a.* and *n.* [A.Sax. (*hund*) *nigontig*—*nigon*, nine, and *tig*, ten.] Nine times ten.—**Ninetieth**, nīn'ti-eth, *a.* The ordinal of ninety.—*n.* A ninetieth part.—**Ninth**, nīnth, *a.* The ordinal of nine; the next preceding ten.—*n.* A ninth part; *mus.* an interval containing an octave and a tone.—**Ninthly**, nīnth'li, *adv.* In the ninth place.

Ninny, nin'i, *n.* [A contr. for *nincompoop*, or from It. *ninno*, Sp. *niño*, a child.] A fool; a simpleton.—**Ninnyhammer**, nin'-i-ham-ėr, *n.* A simpleton.

Niobium, nī-ō'bi-um, *n.* [From *Niobe.*] A rare metal discovered in the mineral columbite and called also *Columbium*.

Nip, nip, *v.t.*—*nipped* or *nipt*, *nipping*. [Not found in A.Sax.; akin to Dan. *nippe*, to twitch, *knibe*, to nip, to pinch; D. *knippen*, to nip, *nijpen*, to pinch; Icel. *kneif*, pincers; G. *kneipen*, *kneifen*, to pinch, *knippen*, to fillip; akin *knife*, *neap*.] To catch and compress sharply between two surfaces or points, as of the fingers; to pinch; to cut, bite, or pinch off the end of; to blast, as by frost; to benumb; to chill.—*To nip in the bud*, to destroy in the first stage of growth.—*n.* A pinch, as with the points of the fingers, nails, &c.; a blast by frost.—**Nip and tuck.** Uncertainty as to the probable success of alternate element.—**Nipper**, nip'ėr, *n.* One who or that which nips; a foretooth of a horse.—**Nippers**, nip'ėrz, *n. pl.* Small pincers.—**Nippingly**, nip'ing-li, *adv.* In a nipping manner; sarcastically.—**Nippy**, *a.* Brisk or tangy, as of the air or of a cheese.

Nip, nip, *n.* [Dan. *nip*, a sip, *nippe*, D. and G. *nippen*, to nip; akin *nipple.*] A sip or small draught, especially of some strong spirituous beverage.

Nipper, nip'ėr, *n.* In the plural, pincers; a tool.

Nipple, nip'l, *n.* [A.Sax. *nipele*; probably connected with *nip*, a sip, L.G. *nippen*, Dan. *nippe*, to sip.] The spongy protuberance by which milk is drawn from the breasts of females; a pap; a teat; something like a nipple, as that part of a gun over which the cap is placed; a connecting piece of pipe.

Nirvana, nir-vä'na, *n.* [Skr. *nir*, out, and *vâna*, blown; lit. blown out.] The Buddhist belief in the emancipation of the soul; hence, ecstacy; the oblivion of passion, suffering, hatred, and delusion.

Nisan, nī'zan, *n.* A month of the Jewish calendar, originally called Abib.

Nisi, nī'sī. [L.] Unless.—*Decree nisi*, in *law*, under DECREE.—*Nisi prius*. [L.] A law phrase meaning 'unless before', prominent words occurring in a certain writ; a civil action trial in a court of record before a judge and jury.

Nissen hut, nis'n hut, *n.* A fairly portable wooden hut with iron roof. It was said to be warm in winter and cool in summer; actually it was the reverse.

Nit, nit, *n.* [A.Sax. *hnitu*; D. *neet*, Icel. *nitr*, Dan. *gnid*, Sw. *gnet*, G. *niss*, a nit; cog. Gr. *konis*, a nit.] The egg of a louse or other small insect.—**Nitter**, nit'ėr, *n.* An insect that deposits nits on horses.—**Nitty**, nit'i, *a.* Full of nits.

Nitency, nī'ten-si, *n.* [L. *niteo*, to shine.] Brightness; luster.—**Nitid**, nī'tid, *a.* [L. *nitidus*.] Bright; shining; gay; spruce; *bot.* having a smooth polished surface.

Niter, nī'tėr, *n.* [Fr. *nitre*, L. *nitrum*, Gr. *nitron*, from some oriental source.] A substance called also saltpeter, and in the nomenclature of chemistry nitrate of potassium or potassic nitrate, used for making gunpowder, in dyeing, metallurgy, medicine, &c.—**Nitrate**, nī'trāt, *n.* A salt of nitric acid.—*Nitrate of potash*, niter.—*Nitrate of silver*, a caustic substance obtained in crystals from silver oxidized and dissolved by nitric acid diluted with two or three times its weight of water; lunar caustic.—*Nitrate of soda*, a salt analogous to nitrate of potash or niter imported from South America and used as a manure.—**Nitriary**, nī'tri-a-ri, *n.* An artificial bed of animal matter for the formation of niter; a place where niter is refined.—**Nitric**, nī'trik, *a.* A term in the nomenclature of the oxygen compounds of nitrogen, indicating more oxygen than *nitrous*.—*Nitric acid*, an important acid prepared from sulphuric acid and niter, employed in etching, in metallurgy and assaying, also in medicine, and popularly called *Aqua fortis*.—**Nitriferous**, nī-trif'ėr-us, *a.* Producing or containing nitre (*nitriferous* strata).—**Nitrification**, nit'rif-i-kā''shon, *n.* [L. *facio*, I make (nitrogen).] Formation of nitrates as plant-food by the action of certain bacteria on organic substances. See DENITRIFICATION.—**Nitrify**, nī'tri-fī, *v.t.* To convert into nitre.—**Nitrite**, nī'trīt, *n.* A salt of nitrous acid.—**Nitrobenzole**, *n.* A liquid prepared by adding benzole drop by drop to fuming nitric acid, important as a source of aniline.—**Nitrocalcite**, *n.* Native nitrate of lime, seen often as an efflorescence on old walls.—**Nitrogen**, nī'trō-jen, *n.* [From Gr. *nitron*, nitre, and root *gen*, to produce.] That element which is the principal ingredient of atmospheric air, of which it constitutes about four-fifths, the rest being principally oxygen, possessing neither taste nor smell.—**Nitrogenize**, nī'trō-jen-īz, *v.t.* To impregnate or imbue with nitrogen.—**Nitrogenized**, nī'trō-jen-īzd, *a.* Containing nitrogen.—**Nitrogenous**, nī-troj'e-nus, *a.* Pertaining to or containing nitrogen.—**Nitro-glycerine**, *n.* A compound produced by the action of a mixture of strong nitric and sulphuric acids on glycerine at low temperatures, a most powerful explosive.—**Nitrometer**, nī-trom'et-ėr, *n.* An instrument for ascertaining the quality or value of nitre.—**Nitrous**, nī'trus, *a. Chem.* applied to compounds containing less oxygen than those called *nitric*.—*Nitrous oxide gas*, a combination of nitrogen and oxygen which, when inhaled, causes insensibility, and hence is used as an anæsthetic during short surgical operations: diluted with air it produces an exhilarating effect; hence the name of *laughing-gas*.

Nitwit, *n.* A dull-witted or stupid person; doltish. (*Slang.*)

Nival, nī'val, *a.* [L. *nivalis*, from *nix*, *nivis*, snow.] Abounding with snow; snowy; growing among snow or flowering during winter.—**Niveous**, nī'vē-us, *a.* [L. *niveus.*] Snowy; resembling snow.

Nizam, ni-zäm', *n.* [Hind. and Ar., from Ar. *nazama*, to govern.] The title of the ruler of Hyderabad in southern Hindustan.

No, nō, *adv.* [A.Sax. *ná*, *nó*, no, from the negative particle, *ne*, *n-*, and *á*, ever; this negative particle = Icel. *ne*, Goth. *ni*, Bohem. and Russ. *ne*, Armor. and Gael. *na*, L. *ne*, Zend. *na*, Skr. *na*; akin *nor*, *not*, *nay*, *non*.] A word of denial or refusal, expressing a negative, and opposed to *yes*. When repeated or when used with another negative it is specially emphatic. It may be used as the correlative of *whether* (*whether* or *no*), though now less common than *not*.—*n.* A negative vote, or a person who votes in the negative (the *noes* have it).—**Noway**, **Noways**, **Nowise**, nō'wā, nō'wāz, nō'wīz, *adv.* In no way, manner, or degree.—**Nowhere**, nō'whār, *adv.* Not in or to any place.—**Nowhither**, nō'whiтн-ėr, *adv.* Not in any direction or to any place.

No, nō, *a.* [From A.Sax. *nán*, none, by loss of *n*; it is related to *none* as *my* and *thy* to *mine* and *thine*.] Not any; not one; none.—*No end*, an indefinitely great number or quantity (*no end* of things). (*Colloq.*)—*adv.* Not in any degree; not at all; not: with comparatives (*no* sooner).

Noachian, nō-ā'ki-an, *a.* Relating to *Noah*, the patriarch, or his time.

Nob, nob, *n.* [From *knob.*] The head: in humour or contempt.

Nob, nob, *n.* [An abbreviation of *nobleman.*] A member of the aristocracy; a swell. (*Slang.*)—**Nobby**, nob'i, *a.* Showy; stylish; smart. (*Slang.*)

Nobble, nob'l, *v.t.* [Akin to *nab.*] To get possession of dishonestly. (*Slang.*)

Noble, nō'bl, *a.* [Fr. *noble*, from L. *nobilis*, high-born, noble; for *gnobilis*, from stem of *gnosco*, *nosco*, to know, seen also in E. *note.*] High in excellence or worth; lofty in character; magnanimous (a *noble* mind); proceeding from or characteristic of greatness of mind (*noble* sentiments); of the best kind; choice; pertaining to the nobility or peerage; magnificent; stately (a *noble* edifice).—*Noble metals*, those which can be separated from oxygen by heat alone: gold, silver, platinum, rhodium, iridium, osmium, and mercury.—*n.* A nobleman; an English gold coin in the reign of Edward III, equivalent to $1.62.—**Nobility**, nō-bil'i-ti, *n.* [L. *nobilitas.*] The quality of being noble; nobleness; the state of being of noble birth or rank; the persons collectively who are of rank above commoners; the peerage.—**Nobly**, nō'bli, *adv.* In a noble manner; heroically; with magnanimity; splendidly; magnificently.—**Nobleman**, nō'bl-man, *n.* One of the nobility; a noble; a peer.—**Noble-woman**, nō'bl-wu̇-man, *n.* A female of noble rank.—**Nobleness**, nō'bl-nes, *n.* The state or quality of being noble; nobility; noble rank; stateliness; magnificence.—**Noblesse**, nō-bles', *n.* [Fr. *noblesse*, L.L. *nobilitia*, from L. *nobilis.*] The nobility; persons of noble rank collectively.—**Noble-minded**, *a.* Possessed of a noble mind; magnanimous.

Nobody, nō'bod-i, *n.* [*No* and *body.*] No person; no one; an insignificant or contemptible person; a person of no standing or position.

Nobstick, nob'stik, *n.* KNOBSTICK.

Noctambulation, **Noctambulism**, nok-tam'bū-lā''shon, nok-tam'bū-lizm, *n.* [L. *nox*, *noctis*, night, and *ambulo*, to walk.] Somnambulism; sleep-walking.—**Noctambulist**, nok-tam'bū-list, *n.* A somnambulist.—**Noctiflorous**, nok-ti-flō'rus, *a.* [L. *nox*, *noctis*, night, and *flos*, *floris*, a flower.] *Bot.* flowering in the night.—**Noctilucous**, nok-ti-lū'kus, *a.* [L. *luceo*, to shine.] Shining in the night.—**Noctivagant**, nok-tiv'a-gant, *a.* [L. *vagor*, to wander.] Wandering in the night.—**Noctivagation**, nok'ti-vā-gā''shon, *n.* A wandering in the night.—**Noctivagous**, nok-tiv'a-gus, *a.* Noctivagant.—**Noctograph**, nok'tō-graf, *n.* [L. *nox*, and Gr. *graphō*, to write.] A writing frame for the blind; an instrument which records the presence of watchmen on their beats.—**Noctuary**,† nok'tū-a-ri, *n.* An account of what passes in the night; the converse of a diary.—**Nocturne**, nok'tėrn, *n.* [F.] In music, a serenade concerning the night; a light, dreamy composition, variable in form; the musical piece of that name made famous by Chopin.—**Nocturnal**, nok-tėr'nal, *a.* Pertaining or belonging to the night; done or occurring at night; *zool* active by night; *bot.* closing during the day and expanding during the night: said of flowers.—**Nocturnally**, nok-tėr'nal-li, *adv.* By night; nightly.—**Nocturnal-sight**, *n.* DAY-BLINDNESS.—**Nocturne**, nok'tėrn, *n.* [Fr.] A painting exhibiting some of the characteristic effects of night light; a night-piece; *mus.* NOTTURNO.

Nod, nod, *v.i.*—*nodded*, *nodding*. [Allied to O.H.G. *nuoton*, *knoton*, to shake; Dan. *noder*, gestures; or perhaps to W. and Ir. *nod*, a mark, a notice; Gael. *nodadh*, a wink or nod.] To incline the head with a quick motion, either forward or sidewise; to let the head sink from sleep; to make an inclination of the head, as in assent or in beckoning; to bend or incline the top with a quick motion (*nodding* plumes).—*v.t.* To incline, as the head or top; to signify by a nod; to beckon by a nod.—*n.* A quick downward motion of the head as a sign of assent, salutation, from drowsiness, &c.—**Nodder**, nod'ėr, *n.* One who nods.—**Nodding**, nod'ing, *p.* and *a.* Bending with a quick motion.

Noddle, nod'l, *n.* [A dim. corresponding to D. *knod*, *knodde*, a knob, a knot; Dan. *knude*, a knot; akin to *knot.*] The head: used humorously.

Noddy, nod'i, *n.* [Probably from *nod*, and equivalent to sleepy-head; comp. *noodle.*] A simpleton; a fool; a sea-fowl: so called from its being easily taken.

Node, nōd, *n.* [L. *nodus* (for *gnodus*), a knot; cog. *knot*, *noddle.*] A knot; a knob; a protuberance; *bot.* a sort of knot on a stem where leaves arise; *mus.* a nodal point; *astron.* one of the two points in which two great circles of the celestial sphere (as the ecliptic and equator) intersect each other; one of the points in which the orbit of a satellite intersects the plane of the orbit of its primary.—*Lunar nodes*, the points at which the orbit of the moon cuts the ecliptic.—**Nodal**, nō'dal, *a.* Pertaining to a node or to nodes; nodated.—*Nodal points* and *nodal lines*, the points or lines of a vibrating body which remain at rest during the vibration.—**Nodated**, nō'dā-ted, *a.* [L. *nodatus.*] Knotted.—**Nodical**, nod'i-kal, *a. Astron.* relating to nodes.—**Nodose**, nō-dōs', *a.* [L. *nodosus.*] Knotted; jointed.—**Nodosity**, nō-dos'i-ti, *n.* The state or quality of being nodose; knottiness; a knotty protuberance.—**Nodular**, nod'ū-lėr, *a.* Pertaining to or in the form of a nodule.—**Nodule**, nod'ūl, *n.* [L. *nodulus*, dim. from *nodus*, a knot.] A little knot or lump; *bot.* a small woody body found in bark; *geol.* a rounded irregular-shaped mineral mass.—**Nodulose**, **Nodulous**, nod'ū-lōs, nod'ū-lus, *a.* Having little knots; knotty.

Noel, no'el, *n.* [Fr. from L. *dies natalis*, birthday of Christ.] Christmas carols with cry of *Noel*.

Noetic, **Noetical**, nō-et'ik, nō-et'i-kal, *a.* [Gr. *noētikos*, from *nous*, the mind.] Relating to the mind or intellect.

Nog, nog, *n.* [Same as Dan. *knag*, *knage*, a wooden peg; D. *knog*, a yard-arm; akin *knag.*] A wooden pin; a tree-nail or pin used in ship-building; a brick-shaped piece of wood inserted in a wall; a timber-brick; a square piece of wood used to prop up the roof of a mine.—*Eggnog*, a drink containing an egg beaten with sugar, milk, flavoring, and usually liquors, served hot or cold.—**Nogging pieces**, horizontal pieces of timber in brick work.

Noggin, nog'in, *n.* [Ir. *noigin*, Gael. *noigean*, a noggin.] A small mug or wooden cup; a measure equivalent to a gill.

Noils, noilz, *n.* [Origin doubtful.] The knots and short wool separated out from the long wool in combing.

Noise, noiz, *n.* [Fr. *noise*, strife, quarrel, noise, probably through a form *noxia*, for L. *noxa*, injury, hurt. NOXIOUS.] A sound of any kind or proceeding from any cause; more especially a din, a confused mixture of sounds; outcry; clamour; frequent talk; much public conversation or discussion.—*v.i. noised*, *noising*. To sound loud.—*v.t.*—*noised*, *noising*. To spread by rumour or report; to report.—**Noiseless**, noiz'les, *a.* Making no noise; silent.—**Noiselessly**, noiz'les-li, *adv.* In a noiseless manner; silently.—**Noiselessness**, noiz'les-nes, *n.* The state of being noiseless; silence.—**Noisy**, noi'zi, *a.* Making a loud noise; clamorous; full of noise.—**Noisily**, noi'zi-li, *adv.* In a noisy manner; with noise.—**Noisiness**, noi'zi-nes, *n.* The state of being noisy.

Noisome, noi'sum, *a.* [From obsol. *noye*, annoyance, to annoy, shortened from *annoy*, with term. *-some.*] Noxious to health; morally noxious or injurious; offensive to the smell or other senses; fetid.—**Noisomely**, noi'sum-li, *adv.* In a noisome manner.—**Noisomeness**, noi'sum-nes, *n.*

Noli-me-tangere, nō'li-me-tan''jėr-e, *n.* [L. touch me not.] The plant called 'Touch-me-not', or Balsam; also the wild cucumber; an ulcerous disease; lupus.

Nolle prosequi, nol'ē pros'e-kwī, *n.* [L., to be unwilling to prosecute.] *Law*, the refusal of a plaintiff in an action to proceed any further.

Nomad, nō'mad, *n.* [Gr. *nomas*, *nomados*, living on pasturage, from *nemō*, to feed, to pasture.] One of those people whose chief occupation consists in feeding their flocks, and who shift their residence according to the state of the pasture.—*a.* Nomadic.—**Nomadic**, nō-mad'ik, *a.* [Gr. *nomadikos.*] Pertaining to nomads; subsisting by the tending of cattle, and wandering for the sake of pasturage; pastoral.—**Nomadically**, nō-mad'i-kal-li, *adv.* In a nomadic manner.—**Nomadism**, nō'mad-izm, *n.*

The state of being a nomad.—**Nomadize**, nō'mad-iz, *v.i.* To live a nomadic life.

No man's land. The ground between hostile trenches, as belonging to neither side; unclaimed or uninhabited land.

Nome, nōm, *n.* [Gr. *nomos*, a district.] A province or other political division of a country, especially of modern Greece.—**Nomarch**, nom'ärk, *n.* [Gr. *archō*, to rule.] The governor or chief magistrate of a nome.—**Nomarchy**, nom'är-ki, *n.* The jurisdiction of a nomarch.

Nom de plume, nom' de plöm, *n.* Pen name.

Nomenclator, nō'men-klā-tėr, *n.* [L., from *nomen*, name, and *calo*, to call (seen in *calendar*).] A person who gives names to things; one who settles and adjusts the names of things in any art or science.—**Nomenclatory**, nō-men'kla-to-ri, *a.* Pertaining to naming.—**Nomenclatural**, nō'men-klā-tū-ral, *a.* Pertaining to a nomenclature.—**Nomenclature**, nō'men-klā-tūr, *n.* A system of names; the systematic naming of things; the vocabulary of names or technical terms which are appropriated to any branch of science. ∴ As distinguished from *terminology* it is applied to the names for individual things, while the latter is generally applied to the technical terms describing the characteristics of things.—**Nomenclaturist**, nō'-men-klā-tūr-ist, *n.* One versed in nomenclatures.

Nominal, nom'i-nal, *a.* [L. *nominalis*, from *nomen*, *nominis*, a name. NAME.] Pertaining to a name or term; nounal; existing in name only; not real; merely so called.—**Nominalism**, nom'i-nal-izm, *n.* The principles of the nominalists.—**Nominalist**, nom'i-nal-ist, *n.* One of a sect of scholastic philosophers who maintained that general notions (such as the notion of a tree) have no realities corresponding to them, and have no existence but as names (*nomina*) or words: opposed to *realist*.—**Nominalistic**, nom'i-nal-is"tik, *a.* Relating to nominalism.—**Nominally**, nom'-i-nal-li, *adv.* In a nominal manner; in name only, not really (*nominally* king).—**Nominate**, nom'i-nāt, *v.t.*—*nominated*, *nominating*. [L. *nomino*, *nominatum*.] To name; to mention by name; to designate by name for an office or place; to propose by name, or offer the name of, as a candidate for an office or place; to set down in express terms (*Shak.*).—**Nominately**, nom'i-nāt-li, *adv.* By name; particularly.—**Nomination**, nom-i-nā'shon, *n.* The act of nominating; the act of proposing by name for an office; the state of being nominated; the power of nominating or appointing to office.—**Nominatival**, nom'i-na-tī"val, *a.* Pertaining to the nominative case.—**Nominative**, nom'i-na-tiv, *a.* [L. *nominativus*, naming.] A term applied to that form of a noun or pronoun which is used when the noun or pronoun is the subject of a sentence.—*n.* The nominative case; a nominative word.—**Nominatively**, nom'i-na-tiv-li, *adv.* In the manner of a nominative.—**Nominator**, nom'i-nā-tėr, *n.* One that nominates.—**Nominee**, nom-i-nē', *n.* A person nominated; one proposed to fill a place or office.

Nomography, nō-mog'ra-fi, *n.* [Gr. *nomos*, a law, and *graphō*, to write.] Exposition of the proper manner of drawing up laws.—**Nomographer**, nō-mog'ra-fėr, *n.* A writer on nomography.—**Nomology**, nō-mol'o-ji, *n.* [Gr. *nomos*, and *logos*.] The science or knowledge of law, legislation, and government.

Non-acceptance, *n.* A refusal to accept.

Nonage, non'āj, *n.* [L. *non*, not, and E. *age*.] The time of life before a person becomes legally of age; minority; period of immaturity in general.

Nonagenarian, non'a-je-nā"ri-an, *n.* [L. *nonagenarius*, from *nonageni*, ninety each, *nonaginta*, ninety, *novem*, nine.] A person ninety or between ninety and a hundred years old.—**Nonagesimal**, non-a-jes'i-mal, *a.* [L. *nonagesimus*.] Belonging to the number 90.

Nonagon, non'a-gon, *n.* [L. *nōnus*, ninth, and Gr. *gonia*, an angle.] A figure having nine sides and nine angles.

Non-appearance, *n.* A failure to appear; default of appearance.—**Non-arrival**, *n.* Failure to arrive.—**Non-attendance**, *n.* A failure to attend; personal absence.—**Non-attention**, *n.* Inattention.—**Non-bituminous**, *a.* Containing no bitumen.

Nonce, nons, *n.* Same as *once*, with an initial *n* belonging to the old dative of the article, seen in the phrases *for then anes*, *for then ones*, for the nonce, *anes*, *ones*, being an adverbial genitive from A.Sax. *ān*, one, used substantively; comp. *the tother*, for *that other*.] Present occasion or purpose: used only in the phrase *for the nonce*.

Nonchalant, non'sha-lant or noṅ-sha-laṅ, *a.* [Fr., from *non*, not, *chaloir*, to care for, from L. *calere*, to be warm or ardent; akin *chafe*, *caldron*.] Indifferent; careless; cool.—**Nonchalantly**, non-sha-lant'li, *adv.* In a nonchalant manner.—**Nonchalance**, non'sha-lans or noṅ-sha-laṅs, *n.* Want of earnestness or feeling of interest; indifference; coolness.

Non-combatant, *n.* Any one connected with a military or naval force whose duty it is not to fight; civilians in a place occupied by troops.—**Non-commissioned**, *n.* Not having a commission.—*Non-commissioned officers*, subordinate officers below the rank of lieutenant, as sergeants and corporals in the army, and quarter-masters and gunners' mates in the navy.—**Non-committal**, *a.* Indicating a refusal to commit oneself; revealing no preference.—**Non-compliance**, *n.* Neglect or failure of compliance.—**Non-concurrence**, *n.* A refusal to concur.—**Non-conducting**, *a.* Not conducting; not transmitting.—**Non-conductor**, *n.* A substance which resists or conducts with difficulty such a force as heat or electricity.—**Nonconforming**, non-kon-for'ming, *a.* Dissenting from the established religion of a country.—**Nonconformist**, non-kon-for'mist, *n.* One who does not conform; especially, one who refuses to conform to an established church.—**Nonconformity**, non-kon-for'mi-ti, *n.* Neglect or failure of conformity; the neglect or refusal to unite with an established church in its rites and mode of worship.—**Non-contagious**, *a.* Not contagious.

Nondescript, non'dē-skript, *a.* [L. *non*, not, and *descriptus*, described.] Not hitherto described or classed; not easily described; abnormal or amorphous; odd; indescribable.—*n.* Anything that has not been described; a person or thing not easily classed.

None, nun, *n.* or *pron.* [A.Sax. *nān*—*ne*, not, and *ān*, one; the loss of the final *n* produced the adjective *no*, to which it now stands in the same relation as *mine* and *thine* to *my* and *thy*. NO, ONE.] Not one: used of persons or things; not any; not a part; not the least portion.—*None the more*, *none the less*, not the more, not the less on that account.—**None-so-pretty**, *n.* LONDON-PRIDE.—**Nonesuch**, nun'such, *n.* A person or thing such as to have no parallel; a certain kind of apple.

Non-effective, *a.* Having no power to produce an effect; causing no effect.—**Non-efficient**, *a.* Not efficient; specifically, *milit.* a term applied to a volunteer who has not attended a prescribed number of drills and passed a certain standard in shooting.—*n.* One who is not efficient.—**Non-ego**, *n.* [L., not I.] *Metaph.* all beyond or outside of the *ego* or conscious thinking subject; the object as opposed to the subject.—**Non-elastic**, *a.* Not elastic; destitute of the property of elasticity.—**Non-elect**, *n. sing.* and *pl.* One who is or those who are not elect; those who are not chosen to salvation.—**Non-election**, *n.* Failure of election.—**Non-electric**, **Non-electrical**, *a.* Not electric; conducting electricity.—*n.* A non-electric substance.

Nonentity, non-en'ti-ti, *n.* [L.L. *nonentitas*. ENTITY.] Non-existence; a thing not existing; a person utterly without consequence or importance.

Nones, nōnz, *n. pl.* [L. *nonæ*, from *nonus*, for *novenus*, ninth, from *novem*, nine. NINE.] In the *Rom. calendar*, the fifth day of the months January, February, April, June, August, September, November, and December, and the seventh day of March, May, July, and October: so called as falling on the *ninth* day before the ides, both days included; the office for the ninth hour, one of the breviary offices of the Catholic Church.

Non-essential, *a.* Not essential or necessary; not absolutely necessary.—*n.* A thing that is not absolutely necessary.—**Non-existence**, *n.* Absence of existence; the negation of being.—**Non-existent**, *a.* Not having existence.—**Non-extensile**, *a.* Not extensile; incapable of being stretched.

Nonfeasance, *n.* *Law.* Omission of performance of legal duty.—**Non-fulfillment**, *n.* Absence of fulfillment; neglect or failure to fulfill.

Nonillion, nō-nil'li-on, *n.* [L. *nonus*, nine, and E. *million*.] The number produced by involving a million to the ninth power; a unit with fifty-four ciphers annexed.

Non-intervention, *n.* Abstention from intervening; a policy of not interfering in foreign politics excepting where a country's own interests are distinctly involved.

Nonius, nō'ni-us, *n.* [From a Portuguese of the sixteenth century, once credited with the invention.] Same as *Vernier*.

Nonjuring, non-jūr'ing, *a.* [L. *non*, not, and *juro*, to swear.] Not swearing allegiance: an epithet applied to those who would not swear allegiance to the government after the Revolution of 1688.—**Nonjuror**, non-jū'rėr, *n.* One who refused to take the oath of allegiance to the government of England at the Revolution of 1688.

Non-luminous, *a.* Not luminous; not giving out light.—**Non-metallic**, *a.* Not consisting of metal.—**Non-obedience**, *n.* Neglect of obedience.—**Non-observance**, *n.* Neglect or failure to observe or fulfil.

Nonpareil, non-pa-rel', *n.* [Fr. *non*, not or no, and *pareil*, equal, from L. *par*, equal (whence *pair*).] A person or thing of peerless excellence; a small printing type, a size larger than that used here.

Nonpartisan, *n.* One not bound by party ties or obligations.—**Non-payment**, *n.* Neglect of payment; failure of payment.—**Non-performance**, *n.* A failure or neglect to perform.

Nonplus, non'plus, *n.* [L. *non*, not, and *plus*, more, further (whence *plural*).] A state in which one is unable to proceed or decide; inability to say or do more; puzzle: usually in the phrase *at a nonplus*.—*v.t.*—*nonplussed*, *nonplussing*. To puzzle; to confound; to stop by embarrassment.

Non-preparation, *n.* The state of being unprepared; want of preparation.—**Non-production**, *n.* A failure to produce or exhibit.—**Non-professional**, *a.* Not belonging to a profession; not done by or proceeding from professional men.—**Non-proficiency**, *n.* Failure of proficiency.—**Non-proficient**, *n.* One who has failed to improve or make progress in any study or pursuit.—**Non-residence**, *n.* Failure or neglect of residing where official duties require one to reside, or on one's own lands; residence by clergymen away from their cures.—**Non-resident**, *a.* Not residing in a particular place, on one's own estate, or in one's proper place.—*n.* One who is non-resident.—**Non-resistance**, *n.* The omission of resistance; submission to authority, power, or usurpation without opposition.—**Non-resistant**, *a.* Making no resistance to power or oppression.—*n.* One who is non-resistant.—**Non-resisting**, *a.* Making no resistance.—**Non-ruminant**, *a.* Not ruminating or chewing the cud.

Nonsense, non'sens, *n.* [*Non*, not, and *sense*, the two elements being closely welded together.] No sense; that which is not sense; words or language conveying no just ideas; absurdity; things of no importance.—**Nonsensical**, non-sen'si-kal, *a.* Having no sense; unmeaning; absurd.—**Nonsensically**, non-sen'si-kal-li, *adv.* In a nonsensical manner.—**Nonsensicalness**, nonsen'si-kal-nes, *n.*

Non-sensitive, *a.* Not sensitive; not keenly alive to impression.—**Non-sequitur**, non-sek'wi-tėr, *n.* [L., it does not follow.] An inference or conclusion which does not follow from the premises.—**Nonsexual**, *a.* Destitute of sex; sexless; neuter; asexual.—**Nonskid**, *a.* Corrugated or with special tread to resist skidding. —**Non-solvency**, *n.* Inability to pay debts.—**Non-solvent**, *a.* Not able to pay debts; insolvent.—**Non-striated**, *a.* Not striated.—*Non-striated fiber*, the fiber constituting the involuntary muscles. —**Nonsuit**, non'sūt, *n.* A stoppage of a suit at law ordered by a judge when the plaintiff fails to make out a legal cause of action.—*v.t.* To subject to a nonsuit.

Noodle, nö'dl, *n.* [A form akin to *noddy*.] A ribbon-like flour-and-egg paste.

Nook, nök, *n.* [Comp. Sc. *neuk*, Ir. *niuc*, a nook.] A corner; a recess; a secluded retreat.

Noology, nō-ol'o-ji, *n.* [Gr. *noos*, the mind, and *logos*, discourse.] The science of intellectual facts or phenomena.—**Noölogical**, nō-ō-loj'i-kal, *a.* Pertaining to noölogy.—**Noologist**, nō-ol'o-jist, *n.* One versed in noölogy.

Noon, nön, *n.* [A.Sax. *nón*, L. *nona* (*hora*), the ninth hour; originally 3 p.m., the time of eating the chief meal, but afterwards the term became applied to the mid-day hour, the chief meal being no doubt also shifted correspondingly.] The middle of the day; the time when the sun is in the meridian; twelve o'clock; the time of greatest brilliancy or power; the prime.—**Noonday**, nön'dā, *n.* Mid-day; twelve o'clock in the day.—*a.* Pertaining to midday; meridional.—**Noontide**, nön'tīd, *n.* The time of noon; mid-day.

Noose, nös or nöz, *n.* [Probably from O. or Prov. Fr. *nous*, a knot, from L. *nodus*, a knot. NODE.] A running knot, which binds the closer the more it is drawn.—*v.t.* (nöz)—*noosed*, *noosing*. To catch in a noose; to entrap; to ensnare.

Nopal, nō'pal, *n.* [Mexican *nopalli*.] A name of several cactaceous plants cultivated for the cochineal insect.

Nor, nor, *conj.* [*Or* with the neg. particle *ne*, *n-* prefixed: old forms were *nother*, *nouther*. OR, NO.] A word used to render negative the second or a subsequent member of a clause or sentence: correlative to *neither* or other negative; also equivalent to *and not*, and in this case not always corresponding to a foregoing negative.

Nordic, nor'dik, *a.* One of the three divisions of the Caucasian race; the blond peoples from northern Europe.—*n.* An individual with Nordic characteristics.

Noria, nō'ri-a, *n.* [Sp.] A hydraulic machine used in Spain, Syria, Palestine, &c., for raising water; a Persian wheel.

Norm, norm, *n.* [L. *norma*, a carpenter's square, a rule, for *gnorima*, from root *gno*, to know (see NOBLE); hence *enormous*.] A rule; a pattern; a model; an authoritative standard; a type.—**Normal**, nor'mal, *a.* [L. *normalis*.] According to a rule, principle, or norm; conforming with a certain type or standard; not abnormal; regular; *geom.* perpendicular.—*Normal pressure*, perpendicular: a *pressure* is said to be *normal* to a surface when it acts at right angles to it or perpendicularly thereon.—*Normal school* (from Fr. *école normale*, lit. a school that serves as a model), a school in which teachers are instructed in the principles of their profession and trained in the practice of it; a training-college.—*n. Geom.* a straight line at right angles to the tangent or tangent plane at any point of a curve or curved surface. — **Normalization**, nor'mal-i-zā"shon, *n.* Reduction to a standard or type.—**Normalize**, nor'mal-īz, *v.t.*—*normalized, normalizing*. To make normal; to reduce to a standard or type.—**Normally**, nor'mal-li, *adv.* In a normal manner or state.

Norman, nor'man, *n.* A native or inhabitant of Normandy.—*a.* Pertaining to Normandy, or the Normans.—*Norman architecture*, the round-arched style of architecture, a variety of the Romanesque.—*Norman-French*, the language of the Normans at the English Conquest, and still to a small extent made use of in several formal proceedings of state in England.

Norroy, nor'oi, *n.* [*North*, and *roy*, king, north king.] The third of the three English kings-at-arms, whose jurisdiction lies to the north of the Trent.

Norse, nors, *n.* The language of Norway. —*Old Norse*, the ancient language of Scandinavia, represented by the classical Icelandic and still with wonderful purity by modern Icelandic. — *a.* Belonging to ancient Scandinavia or its language.—**Norseman**, nors'man, *n.* A native of ancient Scandinavia.

North, north, *n.* [A.Sax. *north* = Icel. *northr*, G., Sw., and Dan. *nord*, north; origin unknown.] One of the cardinal points, being that point of the horizon which is directly opposite to the sun in the meridian; the opposite of *south*; a region, tract, or country lying opposite to the south.—*a.* Northern; being in the north.—**North-east**, *n.* The point midway between the north and east.—*a.* Pertaining to, proceeding from, or directed towards that point; north-eastern.—**North-easter**, *n.* A wind from the north-east.—**North-easterly**, *a.* Towards or from the north-east.—**North-eastern**, *a.* Pertaining to or being in the north-east, or in a direction to the north-east.—**North-eastward**, *adv.* Towards the north-east. —**Northerliness**, nor'THėr-li-nes, *n.* The state of being northerly.—**Northerly**, nor'THėr-li, *a.* Pertaining to or being in or towards the north; northern; proceeding from the north.—**Northern**, nor'THėrn, *a.* Pertaining to or being in the north; in a direction toward the north; proceeding from the north (the *northern* wind). —*Northern diver*, a marine swimming bird. DIVER.—*Northern hemisphere*, that half of the earth north of the equator.—*Northern lights*, the popular name of the aurora borealis. — **Northern, Northerner**, nor'THėr-nėr, *n.* A native or inhabitant of the north, of a northern country or part. — **Northern-drift**, *n. Geol.* a name formerly given to boulder-clay of the pleistocene period, when its materials were supposed to have been brought by polar currents from the north.—**Northernmost, Northmost**, nor'THėrn-mōst, north'mōst, *a.* Situated at the point farthest north.—**Northing**, north'ing, *n.* The distance of a planet from the equator northward; north declination; *navig.* and *surv.* the difference of latitude northward from the last point of reckoning: opposed to *southing*. — **Northman**, north'man, *n.* pl. **Northmen**. A name given to the inhabitants of the north of Europe, especially the ancient Scandinavians.—**North-polar**, *a.* Pertaining to the north pole or regions near the north pole.—**North Pole**, *n.* That point of the heavens towards the north which is 90° distant from the equinoctial; the northern extremity of the earth's axis.—**North-star**, *n.* The north polar star; a star of the constellation Ursa Minor (Little Bear), about 1° 20′ from the North Pole. — **Northward**, north'wėrd, *adv.* and *a.* [A.Sax. *northweard*.] Toward the north.—*n.* The northern part.—**Northwards**, north'wėrdz, *adv.* Towards the north; northward.—**North-west**, *n.* The point midway between the north and west. —*a.* Pertaining to or being between the north and west; north-westerly; proceeding from the north-west (a *north-west* wind).—**North-wester**, *n.* A wind from the north-west. — **North-westerly**, *a.* Towards the north-west; from the north-west. —**North-western**, *a.* Pertaining to or being in the north-west; from the north-west.—**North-westward**, *adv.* Towards the north-west. — **North-wind**, *n.* The wind that blows from the north.

Norwegian, nor-wē'ji-an, *a.* Belonging to Norway. — *Norwegian haddock*. BERGYLT.—*n.* A native of Norway.

Nose, nōz, *n.* [A.Sax. *nosu*, *nasu* = Icel. *nös*, Dan. *näse*, Sw. *näsa*, G. *nase*; cog. Pol. *nos*, Rus. *nas*, L. *nasus*, Skr. *nâsâ*, *nasâ*—nose. *Ness* is akin.] The part of the face where the nostrils are located; the organ of smell and scent; the olfactory organ; the organ for smelling; hence, scent; sagacity; a nozzle.—*To lead by the nose*, to lead blindly.—*To thrust one's nose into the affairs of others*, to meddle officiously in other people's matters; to be a busybody.—*To turn up the nose*, to show contempt.— *Under one's nose*, under his immediate range of observation.—*v.t.*—*nosed*, *nosing*. To smell; to twang through the nose; to touch with the nose. — *v.i.* To smell; to pry officiously.—**Nose-bag**, *n.* A bag which may be fastened to a horse's head while he eats the provender in it.—**Nosed**, nōzd, *a.* Having a nose of a certain kind: used in compounds (long-*nosed*). —**Nose dive**, *n.* Of an aeroplane diving headlong, with the 'nose' of the machine pointing downwards.—**Nosegay**, nōz'gā, *n.* A bunch of flowers to carry for smelling; a bouquet; a posy.—**Noseless**, nōz'les, *a.* Destitute of a nose.—**Nose-piece**, *n.* A nozzle; a piece on a helmet coming down in front of the nose.—**Nose-ring**, *n.* A ring worn in the nose as an ornament; a ring for the nose of an animal, as a bull, a pig, &c.—**Nosing**, nōz'ing, *n. Arch.* the projecting edge of a moulding; a projecting moulding.

Nosography, nō-sog'ra-fi, *n.* [Gr. *nosos*, disease, and *graphō*, to write.] The science of the description of diseases.—**Nosology**, nō-sol'o-ji, *n.* [Gr. *nosos* and *logos*.] A systematic arrangement or classification of diseases; that branch of medical science which treats of the classification of diseases. — **Nosological**, nos-o-loj'i-kal, *a.* Pertaining to nosology.—**Nosologist**, nō-sol'o-jist, *n.* One versed in nosology. — **Nosonomy**, nō-son'o-mi, *n.* [Gr. *onoma*, name.] The nomenclature of diseases.—**Nosotaxy**, nos'o-tak-si, *n.* [Gr. *taxis*, arrangement.] The classification of diseases.

Nostalgia, nos-tal'ji-a, *n.* [Gr. *nostos*, return, and *algos*, pain.] A longing desire to revisit one's native country; home-sickness.—**Nostalgic**, nos-tal'jik, *a.* Relating to nostalgia; home-sick.

Nostoc, nos'tok, *n.* [G. *nostok*, *nostoch*.] A sort of gelatinous algæ often found after wet weather, especially on sandy soils.

Nostril, nos'tril, *n.* [O.E. *nosethril*, *nosethirl*, A.Sax. *nósthyrl*, lit. nose-hole, *thyrl* or *thyrel* meaning a hole, whence *thyrlian*, to bore (same word as *thrill*).] One of the two apertures of the nose which give passage to air.

Nostrum, nos'trum, *n.* [L. *nostrum*, ours, that is, a medicine belonging to us alone.] A medicine, the ingredients of which are kept secret; a quack medicine; any scheme or device proposed by a quack or charlatan in any department.

Not, not, *adv.* [Older *nat*, contr. from *naught*, nought, and equivalent to *ne aught*. NAUGHT.] A word that expresses negation, denial, refusal, or prohibition.

Notable, nō'ta-bl, *a.* [Fr. *notable*, L. *notabilis*, from *noto*, to mark or note, from *nota*, a mark, for *gnota*, from *notus*, *gnotus*, known. NOTE, NOBLE.] Worthy of notice; remarkable; memorable; noted or distinguished; conspicuous; manifest; observable.—*n.* A person or thing of note or distinction; *French hist.* one of the nobles or notable men selected by the king to form a parliament, before the revolution.—**Notableness**, nō'ta-bl-nes, *n.* The quality of being notable.—**Notably**, nō'ta-bli, *adv.* In a notable manner; remarkably; eminently; especially.—**Notabilia**, nō-ta-bil'i-a, *n. pl.* Notable things; things worthy of notice.—**Notability**, nō-ta-bil'i-ti, *n.* The quality of being notable; a notable person or thing; a person of note.

Notalgia, nō-tal'ji-a, *n.* [Gr. *nōton*, the

back, *algos*, pain.] *Med.* pain in the back; irritation of the spine.

Notary, nō'ta-ri, *n.* [L. *notarius*, from *nota*, a note. NOTE.] An officer authorized to attest written documents, to authenticate deeds, contracts, &c., and to administer oaths: called also *Notary Public.*—**Notarial**, nō-tā'ri-al, *a.* Pertaining to a notary; done or taken by a notary.—**Notarially**, nō'tā'ri-al-li, *adv.*

Notation, nō-tā'shon, *n.* [L. *notatio*, from *noto*, to mark. NOTE.] The act or practice of noting; the art of recording by marks or characters; a system of signs or characters used for expressing briefly facts connected with an art or science, as in arithmetic, algebra, music, &c.

Notch, noch, *n.* [Softened form of old *nock*, a notch = O.D. *nock*, O.Sw. *nocka*, a notch; akin *nick.*] A hollow cut in anything; a nick; what resembles such a cutting; a gap in a mountain or hill.—*v.t.* To cut a notch or notches in; to nick; to indent; to fit to a string by the notch, as an arrow.—**Notching**, noch'ing, *n.* A series of notches.

Note, nōt, *n.* [Fr. *note*, from L. *nota*, a mark, sign, character, from *notus*, known, for *gnotus*, from *gnosco*, *nosco*, to know. NOBLE, KNOW.] A mark on the margin of a book‡; a mark, character, or symbol‡; a statement subsidiary to the text of a book elucidating or adding something; an explanatory or critical comment; an annotation; a memorandum or short writing intended to assist the memory or for after use or reference; a list of items; a reckoning, bill, account; a written or printed paper acknowledging a debt and promising payment (a promissory *note*; a bank-*note*); a diplomatic or official communication in writing; a short letter; a billet; notice; heed; observation; reputation; consequence; distinction; *pl.* a newspaper reporter's or shorthand writer's report; *mus.* a character which represents a sound; a musical sound; voice; harmonious or melodious sound.—*v.t.—noted, noting.* To observe carefully; to heed; to attend to; to set down in writing; to make a memorandum of; to mark (a bill) as being dishonoured—a proceeding done by a notary.—**Note-book**, *n.* A book in which notes or memoranda are written.—**Noted**, nō'ted, *a.* Being of note; much known by reputation or report; celebrated.—**Notedness**, nō'ted-nes, *n.* The state or quality of being noted.—**Noteless**, nōt'les, *a.* Not attracting notice; not conspicuous.—**Note-paper**, *n.* Paper of a small size for writing notes or letters on.—**Noteworthy**, nōt'wėr-thi, *a.* Worthy of note; worthy of observation or notice.

Nothing, nu'thing, *n.* [*No thing.*] Not anything: opposed to *anything* and *something*; non-existence; nothingness; a trifle; a thing of no consideration or importance; *arith.* a cipher.—*adv.* In no degree; not at all.—**Nothingness**, nu'thing-nes, *n.* Nihility; non-existence; insignificance.

Notice, nō'tis, *n.* [Fr. *notice*, from L. *notitia*, notice, from *nosco*, *notum*, to know. NOTE.] The act of noting, observing, or remarking; heed; regard; cognizance; note; information; intelligence; direction; order; premonition; warning; intimation beforehand; a paper that communicates information; attention; respectful treatment; civility; a short statement; a brief critical review.—*v.t.—noticed, noticing.* To take cognizance or notice of; to perceive; to become aware of; to observe; to mention or make observations on; to treat with attention and civilities.—**Noticeable**, nō'tis-a-bl, *a.* Worthy of being noticed or observed; observable; likely to attract attention.—**Noticeably**, nō'tis-a-bli, *adv.* In a noticeable manner; evidently; distinctly.—**Noticer**, nō'tis-ėr, *n.* One who notices.

Notify, nō'ti-fī, *v.t.—notified, notifying.* [Fr. *notifier*, L. *notificare*, from *notus*, known, and *facio*, to make. NOTE.] To make known; to declare; to publish; to give notice to; to inform by words or writing.—**Notification**, nō'ti-fi-kā"shon, *n.* The act of notifying or giving notice; notice given in words or writing, or by signs; intimation; the writing which communicates information; an advertisement, citation, &c.

Notion, nō'shon, *n.* [L. *notio*, from *notus*, known. NOTE.] A mental conception; mental apprehension of whatever may be known or imagined; idea; an opinion; a belief or view entertained; a fancy article; an article of smallware; chiefly in the plural, needles, thread, pins, &c.; a gadget.—**Notional**, nō'shon-al, *a.* Pertaining to a notion or conception; imaginary; ideal; existing in idea only; visionary; whimsical; fanciful.—*Notional words*, those words which express *notions* or objects of the understanding, as verbs and nouns, in distinction from *relational* words or words expressing relation, as prepositions.—**Notionality**, nō-shon-al'i-ti, *n.* The state of being notional or fanciful.—**Notionist**, nō'shon-ist, *n.* One who holds ungrounded opinions.

Notochord, nō'tō-kord, *n.* [Gr. *nōtos*, the back, and *chordē*, a string.] A fibro-cellular rod in the embryo of vertebrates, usually replaced in the adult by the vertebral column.

Notorhizal, nō'tō-rī-zal, *a.* [Gr. *nōtos*, the back, and *rhiza*, a root.] *Bot.* having the radical in the embryonic plant at the back of the cotyledons.

Notorious, nō-tō'ri-us, *a.* [L.L. *notorius*, from L. *notoria*, *notorium*, an indictment, *notor*, a voucher, *notare*, to mark. NOTE.] Publicly or generally known and spoken of; manifest to the world; known to disadvantage; publicly known from something discreditable.—**Notoriety**, nō-tō-rī'e-ti, *n.* The state or attribute of being notorious; the state of being publicly known to disadvantage; discreditable publicity.—**Notoriously**, nō-tō'ri-us-li, *adv.* In a notorious manner.—**Notoriousness**, nō-tō'ri-us-nes, *n.* The state of being notorious; notoriety.

Notornis, nō-tor'nis, *n.* [Gr. *notos*, the south wind, the south, and *ornis*, a bird.] A genus of rare or extinct grallatorial birds of New Zealand, allied to the coots, but of larger size and with rudimentary wings.

Notoryctes, no-to-rik'tēz, *n.* [Gr. *notos*, south, *oryctēs*, a digger.] A mole-like eyeless marsupial living in Australia.

No-trump, *n. Bridge*, and some other card games, play declared in which no suit is designated as trumps.

Notwithstanding, not-with-stan'ding, a participial compound passing into a *prep.* and a *conj.* [*Not with*, in the old sense of against, and *standing.*] In spite of; without hindrance or obstruction from; despite; nevertheless; however.

Nougat, nö'gä, nö'gat, *n.* [Fr.] Candy made of egg white, sugar, corn sirup, or honey, with chopped nuts or fruits.

Nought, nąt, *n.* [A.Sax. *nâwihe*, i.e. no whit. NAUGHT.] Not anything; nothing; a cipher.

Noumenon, nou'men-on, *n.* pl. **Noumena**, nou'men-a. [Gr., the thing perceived, from *noeō*, to perceive, from *nous*, the mind.] *Metaph.* an object conceived by the understanding or thought of by the reason, as opposed to a *phenomenon.*

Noun, noun, *n.* [O.Fr. *noun*, *non*, *nom*, Mod. Fr. *nom*, from L. *nomen*, name. NAME.] *Gram.* a word that denotes any object of which we speak, whether that object be animate or inanimate, material or immaterial.—**Nounal**, noun'al, *a.* Pertaining to a noun; having the character of a noun.

Nourish, nur'ish, *v.t.* [O.Fr. *nurrir*, *norrir*, Mod.Fr. *nourrir*, from L. *nutrire*, to nourish; akin *nurse*, *nutritious*, *nurture.*] To feed and cause to grow; to supply with nutriment; *fig.* to supply the means of support and increase to; to encourage; to foster; to cherish; to comfort.—**Nourishable**, nur'ish-a-bl, *a.* Capable of being nourished.—**Nourisher**, nur'ish-ėr, *n.* One who or that which nourishes.—**Nourishing**, nur'ish-ing, *a.* Promoting growth; nutritious.—**Nourishingly**, nur'ish-ing-li, *adv.* In a nourishing manner.—**Nourishment**, nur'ish-ment, *n.* The act of nourishing; nutrition; food; sustenance; nutriment; *fig.* that which promotes any kind of growth or development.

Nouveau riche, nö'vō rĕsh, [Fr.] One who is newly rich; an upstart.

Novargent, nov-är'jent, *n.* [L. *novus*, new, and *argentum*, silver.] A preparation from silver for resilvering plated articles.

Novel, nov'el, *a.* [O.Fr. *novel*, Fr. *nouvelle*, novel, a novel, from L. *novellus*, a dim. from *novus*, new. NEW.] Of recent origin or introduction; new and striking; of a kind not known before; unusual; strange.—*n.* In *Roman Law*, a new decree issued as additional to the Codex. A lengthy fictitious prose narrative having an almost unlimited range of subject matter and varied techniques. It may contain one or more plots, and its treatment may range from photographic realism to highly imaginative themes.—**Novelette**, *n.* A small novel; recently, an intensive method of narration for condensation purposes.—**Novella**, *n.* A story vehicle, shorter than a novel, yet greater than the novelette.—**Novelist**, nov'el-ist, *n.* A writer of a novel or of novels.—**Novelize**, nov'el-īz, *v.t.* To put into the form of a novel.—**Novelty**, nov'el-ti, *n.* The quality of being novel; a noticeable newness; recentness of origin; freshness; something new or strange.

November, nō-vem'bėr, *n.* [L., from *novem*, nine; the ninth month, according to the ancient Roman year, which began in March.] The eleventh month of the year, containing 30 days.

Novena, nō-vē'na, *n.* [L. *novem*, nine.] *R. Cath. Ch.* A special nine days' devotion.—**Novenary**, nō'vē-na-ri, *a.* Pertaining to the number nine.—*n.* An aggregate of nine; nine collectively.—**Novennial**, nō-ven'i-al, *a.* [From L. *novennis*, novennial, and *annus*, a year.] Done or recurring every ninth year.

Novice, nov'is, *n.* [Fr., from L. *novitius*, new fresh, from *novus*, new. NOVEL.] One who is new to the circumstances in which he or she is placed; one newly converted to the Christian faith; one that has entered a religious house, but has not taken the vow; a probationer; one who is new in any business; a beginner.—**Novitiate**, **Noviciate**, nō-vish'i-āt, *n.* The state or time of being a novice; apprenticeship; a year or other time of probation.

Novocain, nō'vō-kān", *n.* [L. *novus*, new, and *cocaine.*] A local anesthetic.

Now, nou, *adv.* [A.Sax. *nú*, a word common to all the Teutonic tongues; cog. L. *nunc*; Gr. *nun*, now; perhaps allied to *new.*] At the present time; at a particular past time (he was *now* king); at that time; after this had happened. It often implies a connection between a subsequent and a preceding proposition, or it introduces an inference or an explanation of what precedes ('*now* Barabbas was a robber').—*But now*, only a little while ago; very lately.—*Now and then*, at one time and another; indefinitely; occasionally; at intervals.—*Now..now*, at one time—at another time; alternately. Similarly *now..then.*—*n.* Present time or moment.—**Nowadays**, nou'a-dāz, *adv.* At the present time; in these days.

Noway, Noways. Under No.

Nowel, nou'el, *n.* [Same as *newel.*] In *founding*, the inner portion of the mould for castings of large hollow articles, answering to the *core* of smaller castings.

Nowhere, Nowhither, Nowise, *adv.* Under No.

Noxal, nok'sal, *a.* [L. *noxa*, injury. NOXIOUS.] A legal word; pertaining to damage or injury.

Noxious, nok'shus, *a.* [L. *noxius*, from *noxa*, injury, from root of *noceo*, to hurt (as in *innocent*, *innocuous*), same as that of *night*; akin *noise*, *nuisance.*] Hurtful; harmful; pernicious; unwholesome; injurious, in a moral sense.—**Noxiously**, nok'shus-li, *adv.* In a noxious manner; hurtfully.—**Noxiousness**, nok'shus-nes, *n.*

Noyade, nwa-yäd, *n.* [Fr., from *noyer*, to drown.] A putting to death by drowning: a mode of executing victims during the reign of terror in France, practised by Carrier at Nantes in 1789.

Noyau, nwa-yō, *n.* [Fr. *noyau*, a stone of a fruit, from L. *nucalis*, like a nut, from *nux, nucis*, a nut.] A cordial generally prepared from spirits, bitter almonds, sugar-candy, grated nutmeg, and mace.

Nozzle, noz'l, *n.* [For *nosle*, a dim. of *nose*.] The projecting spout of something; a terminal pipe or terminal part of a pipe (the *nozzle* of a bellows).

N.T.P. Normal temperature and pressure, a phrase used to denote a temperature of 0° C., and an atmospheric pressure represented by the barometer at 760 mm.; the temperature taken as the standard in measurements of the volumes of gases.

Nuance, nū-äṅs, *n.* [Fr., from *nue*, L. *nubes*, a cloud.] A gradation by which a color passes from its lightest to its darkest shade; shade of color; delicate degree of meaning, as of words and phrases.

Nub, nub, *n.* The heart of; the point of a story.

Nubecula, nū-bek'ū-la, *n.* [L., a little cloud, dim. of *nubes*, a cloud.] Cloudy matter; a cloudy speck; one of the Magellanic clouds.—**Nubiferous**, nū-bif'ėr-us, *a.* [L. *nubifer*—*nubes*, and *fero*, to bring.] Bringing or producing clouds.

Nubile, nū'bīl, *a.* [L. *nubilis*, from *nubo*, to marry. NUPTIAL.] Of an age suitable for marriage; marriageable.

Nubilous, nū'bil-us, *a.* [L. *nubilus*, from *nubes*, a cloud.] Cloudy.

Nucament, nū'ka-ment, *n.* [L. *nucamentum*, a fir cone.] *Bot.* a catkin; the blossom of the hazel, pine, willow, &c.—**Nucamentaceous**, nū'ka-men-tā"shus, *a. Bot.* pertaining to a nucament or catkin.

Nucellus, nū-sel'lus. [Dim. of L. for a *kernel*.] The central part of an ovule, containing the EMBRYO-SAC (which see).

Nuchal, nū'kal, *a.* [L.L. *nucha*, from Ar.] Pertaining to the nape of the neck.

Nuciferous, nū-sif'ėr-us, *a.* [L. *nux, nucis*, a nut, and *fero*, to bear.] Bearing or producing nuts.—**Nuciform**, nū'si-form, *a. Bot.* resembling a nut; nut-shaped.

Nucleo-protein, nūk'lē-ō-prō"tē-in. [From *nucleus* and *protein*.] A nucleus rich in phosphorus occurring in the nucleus of a cell.

Nucleus, nū'klē-us, *n.* pl. **Nuclei**, nū'klē-ī. [L., a kernel, from *nux, nucis*, a nut.] A kernel or something similar; a central mass about which matter is collected; *bot.* the central succulent part of an ovule in which the embryo plant is generated; *physiol.* the solid or vesicular body found in many cells; the germ of a cell; *astron.* the body of a comet, called also its *head*.—**Nucleal, Nuclear**, nū'klē-al, nū'klē-ar, *a.* Pertaining to or having the character of a nucleus; constituted by a nucleus.—**Nucleate, Nucleated**, nū'klē-āt, nū'klē-ā-ted, *a.* Having a nucleus; applied to cells.—**Nucleiform, Nucleoid**, nū-klē'i-form, nū'klē-oid, *a.* Formed like a nucleus.—**Nucleolus**, nū-klē'ō-lus, *n.* pl. **Nucleoli**, nū-klē'ō-lī. [Dim. of *nucleus*.] The minute solid particle in the interior of the nucleus of some cells. Also called *Nucleole*, nū'klē-ōl.

Nucula, Nucule, nū'kū-la, nū'kūl, *n.* [Dim. from L. *nux, nucis*, a nut.] *Bot.* a hard pericarp of a horny or bony texture.

Nude, nūd, *a.* [L. *nudus*, naked (seen also in *denude*); same root as *naked*.] Naked; not covered with clothes or drapery.—*n.* A nude or naked figure or statue; generally the *nude*, that is, the undraped human figure.—**Nudely**, nūd'li, *adv.* In a nude or naked manner; nakedly.—**Nudeness**, nūd'nes, *n.* The state or quality of being nude or naked.—**Nudity**, nū'di-ti, *n.* The state of being naked; nakedness.

Nudge, nuj, *n.* [Allied to Prov.G. *knütschen*, Dan. *knuge*, to squeeze; E. to *knock*.] A jog with the elbow, or a poke in the ribs.—*v.t.*—*nudged, nudging.* To give a hint or signal by a private touch with the hand, elbow, or foot.

Nudibranchiate, nū-di-brang'ki-āt, *a.* [L. *nudus*, naked, and Gr. *branchia*, gills.] Having naked gills; having no shell, and the branchiæ or gills exposed: said of certain molluscs.—*n.* A nudibranchiate mollusc.

Nudity. Under NUDE.

Nugatory, nū'ga-to-ri, *a.* [L. *nugatorius*, from *nugor, nugatus*, to trifle, from *nugæ*, trifles.] Trifling; futile; worthless; of no force; inoperative.

Nugget, nug'et, *n.* [Formerly *nigot, niggot*, an ingot; perhaps a corruption of *ingot* (*an ingot*, a *ningot*, a *nigot*).] A lump; especially, one of the larger lumps of native gold found in the diggings.

Nuisance, nū'sans, *n.* [O.Fr. *nuisance, noisance*, from *nuisir, noisir* (Mod.Fr. *nuire*), L. *nocere*, to annoy. NOXIOUS.] Something that annoys or gives trouble; that which is offensive or irritating; an annoyance; a plague or pest; a bore.

Null, nul, *a.* [L. *nullus*, not any, none—*ne*, not, and *ullus*, any.] Of no legal or binding force or validity; void; invalid (as in *null and void*); having no character or expression (as the features).—**Nullify**, nul'i-fī, *v.t.*—*nullified, nullifying.* [L. *nullus*, and *facio*, to make.] To annul; to render invalid; to deprive of legal force or efficacy.—**Nullification**, nul'i-fi-kā"shon, *n.* The act of nullifying; a rendering void and of no effect.—**Nullity**, nul'i-ti, *n.* The state or quality of being null; want of validity.

Nullah, nul'lä, *n.* In British India, a bed of a rivulet; a rivulet.

Numb, num, *a.* [Lit. taken, being from A.Sax. *numen*, pp. of *niman*, O.E. *nim*, Goth. *niman*, to seize; hence also *benumb* (with prefix *be*); *nimble.* The final *b* is excrescent.] Torpid, benumbed, or deadened; having lost the power of sensation and motion.—*v.t.* To make numb or torpid.—**Numbness**, num'nes, *n.* The state of being numb; torpidity; torpor.

Number, num'bėr, *n.* [O.Fr. *numbre*, Fr. *nombre*, from L. *numerus*, number (whence also *numeral, numerous, enumerate*), same root as *nomad*, Gr. *nemō*, to distribute. (As to inserted *b* comp. *humble, nimble*.)] That which may be counted; an aggregate of units, or a single unit considered as part of a series; an aggregate of several individuals; not a few; many; one of a numbered series of things, as a division of a book published in parts; a part of a periodical; metrical arrangement of syllables; poetical rhythm or measure; *gram.* that distinction in the form which a word assumes according as it is spoken of or expresses one individual or several individuals; the form that denotes one individual being the *singular number*, that set apart for two the *dual number*, that which refers to two or more the *plural number*.—*Number one*, self.—*v.t.* To count; to reckon; to enumerate; to reckon, rank, or consider; to put a number or numbers on; to amount to; to reach the number of.—**Numberer**, num'bėr-ėr, *n.* One that numbers.—**Numberless**, num'bėr-les, *a.* That cannot be counted; innumerable.—**Numbers**, num'bėrz, *n.* The fourth book of the Pentateuch.

Numen, nū'men, *n.*, pl. **Numina**, nū'mi-na. A divine or leading spirit, as in the Roman Catholic Church.

Numerable, nū'mėr-a-bl, *a.* [L. *numerabilis*, from *numerus*, number. NUMBER.] Capable of being numbered or counted.—**Numeral**, nū'mėr-al, *a.* [L. *numeralis*.] Pertaining to number; consisting of number; expressing number; representing number.—*n.* A figure or character used to express a number; *gram.* a word expressing a number (one, two, three, &c.).—**Numerally**, nū'mėr-al-li, *adv.* According to number; in number.—**Numerary**, nū'mėr-a-ri, *a.* Belonging to a certain number.—**Numerate**, nū'mėr-āt, *v.t.* and *i.* [L. *numero, numeratum*.] To count.—**Numeration**, nū-mėr-ā'shon, *n.* [L. *numeratio*.] The act or art of numbering; *arith.* the art of expressing in figures any number proposed in words, or of expressing in words any number proposed in figures.—**Numerator**, nū'mėr-ā-tėr, *n.* One that numbers; *arith.* the number in fractions which shows how many parts of a unit are taken—the number above the line.—**Numerical**, nū-mer'i-kal, *a.* Belonging to number; denoting number; consisting in numbers.—**Numerically**, nū-mer'i-kal-li, *adv.* In numbers; with respect to numerical quantity.—**Numerology**, nū'-mėr-ol"ō-ji, *n.* Belief in the occult influence of numbers upon the life of an individual.—**Numerous**, nū'mėr-us, *a.* [L. *numerosus*.] Consisting of many individuals.

Numismatic, Numismatical, nū-mis-mat'ik, nū-mis-mat'i-kal, *a.* [L. *numisma*, coin, from Gr. *nomisma*, coin, lit. what is sanctioned by law, from *nomizō*, to sanction, from *nomos*, law.] Pertaining to coins or medals.—**Numismatics**, nū-mis-mat'iks, *n.* The science of coins and medals.—**Numismatist**, nū-mis'mat-ist, *n.* One versed in numismatics.—**Numismatography**, nū-mis'ma-tog"ra-fi, *n.* The science which treats of coins and medals in their relation to history.—**Numismatology**, nū-mis'ma-tol"o-ji, *n.* Same as *Numismatography*.

Nummary, num'a-ri, *a.* [L. *nummus*, a coin.] Relating to money.—**Nummular, Nummulary**, num'ū-lėr, num'ū-la-ri, *a.* Pertaining to coin or money; having the form of a coin.—**Nummuline**, num'ū-lin, *a.* Resembling a nummulite.—**Nummulite**, num'ū-līt, *n.* [Gr. *lithos*, a stone.] The name of fossil organisms having externally somewhat the appearance of a piece of money.—**Nummulitic**, num-ū-lit'ik, *a.* Containing nummulites; composed of nummulites.

Numnah, num'nah, *n.* [Hind. *namda*, Per. *namad*, carpet.] A piece of thick cloth or felt put under a saddle for the comfort of the horse. (*Anglo-Indian*.)

Numskull, num'skul, *n.* [*Numb* and *skull*.] A dunce; a stupid fellow.

Nun, nun, *n.* [A.Sax. *nunne*, from Eccles. L. *nonna*, a nun, *nonnus*, a monk, L.Gr. *nonna, nonnos*, from Coptic or Egypt. *nane, nanu*, good, beautiful, monasteries and convents having first arisen in Egypt.] A woman devoted to a religious life who lives in a convent or nunnery, under a vow of perpetual chastity; the blue titmouse; a kind of pigeon having its head almost covered with a veil of feathers.—**Nunnery**, nun'ėr-i, *n.* A convent in which nuns reside.—**Nunnish**, nun'ish, *a.* Like a nun; pertaining to a nun.

Nunc dimittis, nungk dī-mit'tis, *n.* [L., now thou lettest depart.] The canticle of Simeon (Luke, ii. 29-32).

Nunc dimittis, nungk dī-mit'tis, *n.* [L., now thou lettest depart.] The canticle of Simeon (Luke, ii. 29-32).

Nuncio, nun'shi-ō, *n.* [Sp. *nuncio*, It. *nunzio*, from L. *nuncius*, a messenger, for *noventius*, from *novus*, new; akin *announce, renounce, pronounce, enunciate*, &c.] An ambassador of the first rank (not a cardinal) representing the pope at the seat of a foreign government (an ambassador of the first rank who is a cardinal being styled a *legate*).—**Nunciature**, nun'shi-āt-ūr, *n.*

the verbal declaration of the testator.—**Nuncupatory**, nun-kū'pa-to-ri, *a.* Nuncupative; oral.

Nundinal, nun'di-nal, *a.* [L. *nundinalis*, from *nundinæ*, a fair or market.] Pertaining to a fair or to a market-day.

Nunnery. Under NUN.

Nuptial, nup'shal, *a.* [L. *nuptialis*, from *nuptiæ*, marriage, from *nubo, nuptum*, to marry; akin *nubes*, *nimbus*, a cloud (from the veiling of the bride).] Pertaining to marriage; used or done at a wedding.—

Nuptials, nup'shalz, *n. pl.* [L. *nuptiæ* (pl.), a wedding.] A wedding or marriage. ∴ Syn. under MARRIAGE.

Nurl, nėrl, *v.t.* [Same as *knurl*, *knarl*, *gnarl*.] To mill or indent on the edge.—**Nurling**, nėr'ling, *n.* The milling on the edge of a coin or the head of a screw.

Nurse, nėrs, *n.* [Fr. *nourrice*, from L. *nutrix*, *nutricis*, a nurse, from *nutrio*, to nourish. NOURISH.] One who tends or takes care of the young, sick, or infirm; a female who has the care of a child or children; a female attendant in a hospital; one who or that which nurtures, cherishes, or protects; *hort.* a shrub or tree which protects a young plant.—*v.t.*—*nursed*, *nursing*. To feed and tend generally in infancy; to suckle; to rear; to nurture; to tend in sickness or infirmity; to promote growth or vigour in; to foment; to foster; to manage with care and economy, with a view to increase.—**Nurse-maid**, *n.* A maid-servant employed in nursing children.—**Nursery**, nėr'sėr-i, *n.* A place or apartment in a house set apart for children; a place where trees, shrubs, flowering plants, &c., are raised from seed or otherwise in order to be transplanted, or where they are propagated in order to be sold; a place where anything is fostered and the growth promoted.—*Nursery rhyme*, a tale for children, usually written in rhyming verse.—**Nursery-man**, *n.* One who has a nursery of plants, or is employed in one.—**Nursling**, nėrs'ling, *n.* [*Nurse*, and dim. term. *-ling*.] One who or that which is nursed; a child; a fondling.

Nurture, nėr'tūr, *n.* [Fr. *nourriture*, from *nourrir*, to nourish. NOURISH, NURSE.] The act of nursing or nourishing; education; that which nourishes; food; diet.—*v.t.*—*nurtured*, *nurturing*. To nourish; to educate; to bring or train up.

Nut, nut, *n.* [A.Sax. *hnutu* = Icel. *hnot*, O.H.G. *hnuz*, Dan. *nöd*, G. *nuss*, Gael. *cnudh*.] The fruit of certain trees and shrubs which have the seed inclosed in a bony, woody, or leathery covering, not opening when ripe; *bot.* a bony pericarp containing a single seed, to which it is not closely attached; a small block of metal or wood, with an internal or female screw put upon the end of a screw-bolt to keep it firmly in its place.—*A nut to crack*, a difficult problem to solve; a puzzle to be explained.—*v.i.*—*nutted*, *nutting*. To gather nuts.—**Nutty**, nut'i, *a.* Abounding in nuts; having the flavor of nuts; enthusiastic; mentally unbalanced; crazy. (*Slang*)—**Nutcracker**, *n.* An instrument for cracking hard-shelled nuts; a brown spotted bird of Europe and a related greyish-white bird of North America.—**Nuthatch**, *n.* [*Hatch* is a softened form of *hack*.] Various small creeping birds of Europe and America, related to the titmice.—**Nut-oil**, *n.* An oil obtained from walnuts.—**Nutpecker**, *n.* The nuthatch.—**Nutshell**, *n.* The hard shell of a nut.—*To be* or *lie in a nutshell*, to be in small compass; to admit of a very simple explanation or statement.—**Nut tree**, *n.* The hazel.

Nutant, nū'tant, *a.* [L. *nutans*, *nutantis*, ppr. of *nuto*, to nod, freq. of *nuo*, to nod. INNUENDO.] *Bot.* drooping or nodding.—**Nutation**, nū-tā'shon, *n.* [L. *nutatio*.] A nodding; *astron.* a slight gyratory movement of the earth's axis tending to make the pole describe a minute ellipse, due to the attraction of the sun and moon and connected with *precession*.

Nutmeg, nut'meg, *n.* [From *nut*, and O.Fr. *muguette*, nutmeg, from L. *muscus*, musk; lit. the scented nut.] The kernel of the fruit of a tree of the Malayan Archipelago agreeably aromatic, and much used in cookery.—*Nutmeg butter*, a solid oil extracted from the nutmeg.—**Nutmegged**, nut'megd, *a.* Seasoned with nutmeg.

Nutria, nū'tri-a, *n.* [Sp. *nutria*, *lutria*, from L. *lutra*, an otter.] The commercial name for the skins or fur of the coypou.

Nutrient, nū'tri-ent, *a.* [L. *nutrio*, to nourish. NURSE.] Nourishing; nutritious.—*n.* Any substance which nourishes.—**Nutriment**, nū'tri-ment, *n.* [L. *nutrimentum*.] That which nourishes; nourishment; food; aliment.—**Nutrimental**, nū-tri-men'tal, *a.* Nutritious; nourishing.—**Nutrition**, nū-trish'on, *n.* [L. *nutritio*, from *nutrio*.] The act or process by which organisms whether vegetable or animal, absorb into their system their proper food; the process of assimilating food; that which nourishes; nutriment.—**Nutritious**, nū-trish'us, *a.* Containing or serving as nutriment; promoting the growth or repairing the waste of organic bodies; nourishing.—**Nutritiously**, nū-trish'us-li, *adv.* In a nutritious manner.—**Nutritiousness**, nū-trish'us-nes, *n.* The quality of being nutritious.—**Nutritive**, nū'tri-tiv, *a.* Having the quality of nourishing; nutritious; pertaining to nutrition.—**Nutritively**, nū'tri-tiv-li, *adv.* In a nutritive manner.—**Nutritiveness**, nū'tri-tiv-nes, *n.*

Nux-vomica, nuks-vom'i-ka, *n.* [From L. *nux*, a nut, and *vomeo*, to vomit.] The fruit of an East Indian tree, containing the virulent poison strychnine; a drug containing strychnine.

Nuzzle, nuz'l, *v.t.*—*nuzzled*, *nuzzling*. [A form of *nozzle*.] To put a ring into the nose of; to root up with the nose.—*v.i.* To work with the nose, as a pig; to hide the head, as a child in its mother's bosom.

Nyctalopia, nik-ta-lō'pi-a, *n.* [Gr. *nyktalōpia*, from *nyktalōps*, seeing by night only —*nyx*, *nyktos*, night, and *ōps*, the eye.] The faculty or defect of seeing in darkness or in a faint light, with privation of sight in daylight; also applied to night-blindness, the exactly opposite defect of vision.—**Nyctalops**, nik'ta-lops, *n.* One afflicted with nyctalopia.

Nyctitropic, nik-ti-trop'ik, *a.* [Gr. *nyx*, *nyktos*, night, *tropos*, a turn.] *Bot.* said of certain plants, the leaves of which assume certain positions at night.

Nylon, nī'lon, *n.* A trade-marked name for a thread used as a substitute for silk in the manufacture of ladies' garments.

Nymph, nimf, *n.* [L. *nympha*, Gr. *nymphē*, a nymph.] One of a numerous class of inferior divinities, imagined among the Greeks and Romans as beautiful maidens, not immortal, but always young; those who presided over rivers, brooks, and springs being called *Naiads*; over mountains *Oreads*; over woods and trees, *Dryads* and *Hamadryads*; over the sea, *Nereids*; hence, a young and attractive woman; a maiden; a damsel. Also same as *Nympha*.—**Nympha**, nim'fa, *n.* The pupa or chrysalis of an insect.—**Nymphal**, **Nymphean**, **Nymphic**, nim'fal, nim-fē'an, nim'fik, *a.* Pertaining to nymphs.—**Nympholepsy**, nim'fō-lep-si, *n.* [Gr. *nymphē*, and *lēpsis*, a taking.] A species of ecstasy, or fascination, seizing any one who looked on a nymph.

Nymphomania, nim-fō-mā'ni-a, *n.* [Gr. *nymphē*, a bride, and *mania*, madness.] Morbid and incontrollable sexual desire in females.

Nystagmus, nis-tag'mus, *n.* [Gr. *nystagmos*, a nodding.] *Med.* an involuntary rolling motion of the eyes.

O

O is the fifteenth letter and the fourth vowel in the English alphabet.

O, *interj.* An exclamation used in earnest or solemn address, appeal, or invocation, and prefixed to the noun of address; the sign of the vocative: often confounded with *Oh*, which is strictly a particle expressive of emotion prefixed to a sentence or clause. When O is the word, the mark of exclamation, if used, should follow the noun of address ('Hear, O Israel!'); when *oh* is the word, the mark should follow it, or the exclamatory clause of which it is a part, thus: *Oh! Oh, dear! Oh, dear me!* exclamations of surprise, uneasiness, fear, pain, &c., regarded as corruptions of Fr. *O Dieu!* It. *O Dio!* O God! It. *O Dio mio!* O my God.

Oaf, ōf, *n.* [From Icel. *álfr*, an elf. ELF.] A fairy changeling; a dolt; a blockhead.—**Oafish**, ōf'ish, *a.* Stupid; dolt; doltish.—**Oafishness**, ōf'ish-nes, *n.* Stupidity; dulness.

Oak, ōk, *n.* [A.Sax. *ác*=Sc. *aik*, Icel. *eik*, D. *eik*, L.G. *eeke*, Dan. *eeg*, Sw. *ek*, G. *eiche*; root unknown.] A well-known and valuable timber tree, or its wood, which is hard, tough, and strong, and was long extensively used in ship-building, the bark being used for tanning.—**Oak-apple**, *n.* An oak-gall.—**Oaken**, ō'kn, *a.* Made of oak or consisting of oak.—**Oak-gall**, *n.* A gall of the oak.—**Oakleather**, *n.* A fungous growth of leathery appearance in the fissures of old oaks.—**Oakling**, ōk'ling, *n.* A young oak.—**Oak-paper**, *n.* Paper-hangings stained like oak.

Oaks. A race for fillies run at Epsom Downs, Eng., established by Edward Smith Stanley, Earl of Derby, May 14, 1779.

Oakum, ō'kum, *n.* [A.Sax. *ácumba*, tow, oakum, lit. matter combed out, from prefix *á*, away, out, and *camb*, a comb. COMB.] The substance of old ropes untwisted and pulled into loose fibres: used for caulking the seams of ships, stopping leaks, &c.

Oar, ōr, *n.* [A.Sax. *ár*; Icel. *ár*, Dan. *aare*, Sw. *åra*; perhaps from root *ar*, seen in A. Sax. *erian*, Goth. *arjan*, L. *aro*, to plough; or allied to *rudder*, *row*.] A long piece of timber, flat at one end and round at the other, used to propel a boat, barge, or galley through the water.—*To feather the oars*. FEATHER, *v.t.*—*To lie on the oars*, to suspend rowing; hence, *fig.* to cease from work; to rest.—*To muffle the oars*, to wrap some soft substance round the part that lies in the rowlock.—*To put one's oar in*, to interfere in the business or concerns of others.—*v.i.* To row.—*v.t.* To impel by rowing.—**Oared**, ōrd, *a.* Furnished with oars (a four-*oared* boat).—**Oar-lock**, *n.* A row-lock.—**Oarsman**, ōrz'man, *n.* One who rows with an oar; a boatman.

Oasis, ō-ā'sis, *n.* pl. **Oases**, ō-ā'sēz. [L. and Gr., from Coptic *oueh*, to dwell, and *saa*, to drink.] A fertile tract where there is water, in the midst of a desert or waste; a green spot in the midst of barrenness; often used figuratively.

Oast, ōst, *n.* [D. *ast*, *eest*, *eijst*, a kiln.] A kiln to dry hops or malt.—**Oasthouse**, ōst'hous, *n.* A building for oasts or hop-kilns.

Oat, ōt, *n.* [O.E. *ote*, *ate*, *cote*, A.Sax. *áta*, the oat; Icel. *æti*, an eatable, oats; from the root of *eat*.] A cereal plant valuable for the grain it produces; an oaten pipe, typical of pastoral poetry (*Mil.*); *pl.* a quantity of the plant in cultivation or of the grain (field of *oats*).—*Wild oats*, youthful excesses: generally in the phrase *to sow one's wild oats*, to indulge in youthful excesses, dissipations, or follies; *to have sown one's wild oats*, to have given up youthful follies.—**Oat-cake**, *n.* A cake made of the meal of oats.—**Oaten**, ō'tn, *a.* Pertaining to or made of oats or oatmeal.—**Oatmeal**, ōt'mēl, *n.* Meal made from oats.

Oath, ōth, *n.* pl. **Oaths**, ōTHz. [A.Sax. *áth* = Sc. *aith*, Icel. *eithr*, Dan. and Sw. *ed*, Goth. *aiths*, D. *eed*, G. *eid*, oath.] A solemn affirmation or declaration, made with an appeal to God for the truth of what is affirmed: a solemn swearing; a blasphemous use of the name of the Divine Being; an imprecation.

Obbligato, ob'li-gä-tō, *n.* [It. OBLIGATE.] An instrumental part or accompaniment of such importance that it cannot be dispensed with.

Obcompressed, ob-kom-prest', *a.* Prefix *ob*, implying inversion, and *compressed*.] *Bot.* compressed or flattened back and front. —**Obconic**, **Obconical**, ob-kon'ik, ob-kon'i-kal, *a.* [Prefix *ob*, and *conic*.] *Bot.* conical, but having the apex downward.—**Obcordate**, ob-kor'dāt, *a.* [Prefix *ob*, and *cordate*.] *Bot.* shaped like a heart, with the apex downward.

Obdurate, ob'dū-rāt, *a.* [L. *obduratus*, from *obduro*, to harden—*ob*, intensive, *duro*, to harden, from *durus*, hard (seen in *indurate*, *endure*, *duration*.] Hardened in heart; persisting obstinately in sin; stubborn; inflexible; inexorable; harsh or rough†.—**Obduracy**, ob'dū-ra-si, *n.* The state or quality of being obdurate; invincible hardness of heart; obstinacy in wickedness.—**Obdurately**, ob'dū-rāt-li, *adv.* In an obdurate manner; inflexibly.—**Obdurateness**, *n.* Obduracy; stubbornness.

Obeah, o-bē'a, *n.* A species of sorcery or witchcraft among the African negroes.

Obedience, ō-bē'di-ens, *n.* [Fr. *obédience*, from L. *obedientia*, obedience. OBEY.] The act or habit of obeying; compliance with a command, prohibition, or known law and rule prescribed; submission to authority.—*Passive obedience*, unqualified obedience to authority, whether the commands be reasonable or unreasonable, lawful or unlawful. —**Obedient**, ō-bē'di-ent, *a.* [L. *obediens*, ppr. of *obedio*.] Submission to authority; complying with all commands; yielding compliance; dutiful.—**Obediential**, ō-bē'di-en"shal, *a.* According to the rule of obedience; in compliance with commands. —**Obediently**, ō-bē'di-ent-li, *adv.* In an obedient manner; dutifully; submissively.

Obeisance, ō-bā'sans, *n.* [Fr. *obéissance*, from L. *obedientia*. OBEDIENCE.] A bow or courtesy; an act of reverence, deference, or respect.

Obelisk, ob'e-lisk, *n.* [Gr. *obeliskos*, dim. of *obelos*, a spit.] A column or monumental structure of rectangular form, diminishing towards the top, and generally finishing with a low pyramid; a mark (thus †) referring the reader to a note in the margin or at the foot of the page: called also a *dagger*.

Obelus, ob'e-lus, *n.* [Gr. *obelos*, a spit.] A mark in ancient MSS. or old editions of the classics, indicating a suspected passage or reading.—**Obelize**, ob'e-līz, *v.t.* To mark as spurious or suspicious.

Oberon, ōb'ėr-on, *n.* [Fr. *Auberon*, *Alberon*, G. *Alberich*.] King of the Fairies, married to Titania.

Obese, ō-bēs', *a.* [L. *obesus*, fat—*ob*, intens., and *edo*, *esum*, to eat. EAT.] Excessively corpulent; fat; fleshy.—**Obeseness**, **Obesity**, ō-bēs'nes, ō-bes'i-ti, *n.* [L. *obesitas*.] The state or quality of being obese; excessive corpulency.

Obey, ō-bā', *v.t.* [Fr. *obéir*, from L. *obedio*, *obedire*, to obey, O.L. *obœdire*—prefix *ob*, and *audio*, to hear. AUDIBLE.] To give ear to; to comply with the commands of; to be under the government of; to be ruled by; to submit to the direction or control of. —*v.i.* To submit to commands or authority; to do as one is bid.—**Obeyer**, ō-bā'ėr, *n.* One who yields obedience.—**Obeyingly**, ō-bā'ing-li, *adv.* Obediently.

Obfuscate, ob-fus'kāt, *v.t.*—*obfuscated*, *obfuscating*. [L. *obfusco*, *obfuscatum*—prefix *ob*, and *fusco*, to obscure, from *fuscus*, dark.] To darken; to obscure; to bewilder; to confuse; to muddle.—**Obfuscation**, ob-fus-kā'shon, *n.* The act of obfuscating; confusion or bewilderment of mind.

Obi, ō'bi, *n.* Same as *Obeah*.

Obit, ob'it, *n.* [L. *obitus*, death, from *obeo*, *obitum*, to die—*ob*, against, and *eo*, to go. ITINERANT.] A person's decease; an anniversary of one's death.—**Obitual**, o-bit'ū-al, *a.* Pertaining to obits.—**Obituary**, o-bit'ū-a-ri, *n.* [Fr. *obituaire*.] A list of the dead, or a register of obitual anniversary days; an account of a person or persons deceased.—*a.* Relating to the decease of a person; written about a person at his death (an *obituary* notice).

Obiter Dictum. [L.] A remark by the way; an off-hand aphorism or statement.

Object, ob'jekt, *n.* [L. *objectum*, lit. something thrown before or against—*ob*, against, and *jacio*, to throw (as in *deject*, *eject*, *reject*, &c.). JET (of water).] That towards which the mind is directed in any of its states or activities; what is thought about, believed, or seen; some visible and tangible thing; a concrete reality (*objects* of interest in a museum); that to which efforts are directed; aim; end; ultimate purpose; a deformed person; *gram.* the word, clause, or member of a sentence expressing that on which the action expressed by a transitive verb is exercised, or the word or member governed by a preposition.—*v.t.* (ob-jekt'). [Fr. *objecter*, L. *objicio*, *objectum*.] To place before or in the way‡; to bring forward as a matter of reproach, or as an adverse ground or reason; to state or urge in opposition; to state as an objection (I have nothing to *object against* him).—*v.i.* To make opposition in words or arguments; to offer adverse reasons.—**Object-glass**, *n.* In a telescope or microscope, the lens or combination of lenses directed upon the object and producing an image of it, which is viewed through the eye-piece.—**Objectify**, **Objectivate**, ob-jek'ti-fī, ob-jek'ti-vāt, *v.t.* To form into an object; to give the character of an object to.—**Objection**, ob-jek'shon, *n.* The act of objecting; that which is or may be objected; adverse reason, argument, or charge; fault found.—**Objectionable**, ob-jek'shon-a-bl, *a.* Such as might reasonably be objected to; justly liable to objection; calling for disapproval; reprehensible (as actions, language, &c.).—**Objectionably**, ob-jek'shon-a-bli, *adv.* In an objectionable manner; reprehensibly.—**Objectivation**, ob-jek'ti-vā"shon, *n.* The act of forming into or causing to assume the character of an object.—**Objective**, ob-jek'tiv, *a.* [Fr. *objectif*.] Belonging to what is external to the mind; hence, when used of *literature* or *art*, containing no trace of the writer's or artist's own feelings or individuality: opposed to *subjective*; *gram.* belonging to the object of a transitive verb or a preposition (the *objective* case, an *objective* clause).—*n.* The objective case; an object-glass; the aim of a military manœuvre or operation.—**Objective genitive**. Opposed to subjective, e.g. E. 'Love of God', and L. *amor dei*; the love of which God is the subject, or which He feels towards us (subjective); the love of which He is the object, or which we feel towards Him (objective).—**Objectively**, ob-jek'tiv-li, *adv.* In an objective manner.—**Objectiveness**, ob-jek'tiv-nes, *n.* The state or relation of being objective.—**Objectivity**, ob-jek-tiv'i-ti, *n.* The quality or state of being objective.—**Objectize**, ob'jek-tīz, *v.t.* To put in the position of an object.—**Objectless**, ob'jekt-les, *a.* Having no object; purposeless; aimless.—**Object-lesson**, *n.* A lesson to the young by means of articles themselves or pictures of them. —**Objector**, ob-jek'tėr, *n.* One that objects.

Objuration, ob-jū-rā'shon, *n.* [From L. *objuro*, to bind by oath—prefix *ob*, and *juro*, to swear. JURY.] The act of binding by oath.—**Objure**,† ob-jūr', *v.i.* To swear.

Objurgate, ob-jėr'gāt, *v.t.* and *i.*—*objurgated*, *objurgating*. [L. *objurgo*, *objurgatum* —prefix *ob*, and *jurgo*, to chide.] To chide, reprove, or reprehend.—**Objurgation**, ob-jėr-gā'shon, *n.* The act of objurgating; a reproof.—**Objurgatory**, ob-jėr'ga-to-ri, *a.* Containing objurgation or reproof.

Oblate, ob'lāt, *a.* [L. *oblatus*, thrust forward (i.e. at the equator), also offered, devoted—*ob*, against, before, and *latus*, carried, borne.] *Geom.* flattened or depressed at the poles.—*Oblate spheroid*, a spherical body flattened at the poles, that is, having the shape of the earth.—*n. Eccles.* a secular person who offered or devoted himself and his property to some monastery, into which he was admitted as a kind of lay brother; a member of a congregation of secular priests who live in community.—**Oblateness**, ob'lāt-nes, *n.* The quality or state of being oblate.—**Oblation**, ob-lā'shon, *n.* [L. *oblatio*, an offering.] Anything offered or presented in worship or sacred service.

Obligate, ob'li-gāt, *v.t.*—*obligated*, *obligating*. [L. *obligo*, *obligatum*, to bind, to bring under an obligation—prefix *ob*, and *ligo*, to bind. LIGAMENT.] To bring or place under some obligation; to hold to some duty: a word not much used by good writers.—**Obligate**, *a.* Of bacteria and parasites, bound to particular conditions of life.—**Obligant**, ob'li-gant, *n.* One who binds himself to pay or perform something. —**Obligation**, ob-li-gā'shon, *n.* [L. *obligatio*, from *obligo*, to bind, oblige.] That which binds or obliges to do something; binding or constraining power or effect; an external act or duty imposed by the relations of society; a claim upon one; the position in which one is bound or indebted to another for a favour received; a favour bestowed and binding to gratitude.—**Obligatorily**, ob li'ga-to-ri-li, *adv.* In an obligatory manner.—**Obligatoriness**, ob li'ga-to-ri-nes; *n.* State of being obligatory.—**Obligatory**, ob li'ga-to-ri, *a.* Imposing obligation or duty; binding in law or conscience; requiring performance or forbearance of some act (*obligatory on* a person).

Obligato, ob-le-gä'tō. OBBLIGATO.

Oblige, ō-blīj', *v.t.*—*obliged*, *obliging*. [Fr. *obliger*, from L. *obligo*, to bind, to oblige —*ob*, and *ligo*, to bind. OBLIGATION.] To constrain by any force, physical, moral, or legal; to compel; to bind by any restraint; to bind by some favour done; to lay under obligation of gratitude.—**Obliged**, ō-blījd', *p.* and *a.* Having received some obligement or favour; laid under obligation; indebted.—**Obligee**, ō-bli-jē', *n. Law*, the person to whom another is bound.—**Obligement**, ō-blīj'ment, *n.* A favour conferred; obligation.—**Obliger**, ō-blī'jėr, *n.* One that obliges.—**Obliging**, ō-blī'jing, *a.* Having the disposition to do favours; conferring favours or kindnesses; complaisant; kind.—**Obligingly**, ō-blī'jing-li, *adv.* In an obliging manner.—**Obligingness**, ō-blī'jing-nes, *n.* The state or quality of being obliging.—**Obligor**, ob-li-gor', *n. Law*, the person who binds himself to another.

Oblique, ob-lēk' or ob-līk', *a.* [Fr. *oblique*, L. *obliquus*—prefix *ob*, and *liquis*, awry.] Having a direction neither perpendicular nor parallel to some line or surface which is made the standard of reference; not direct; aslant; slanting; *fig.* indirect or by allusion; not direct in descent; collateral. —*Oblique angle*, any angle except a right angle.—*Oblique arch*, a skew-arch.—*Oblique bridge*, a skew-bridge.—*Oblique case*, *gram.* any case except the nominative.—*Oblique cone* or *cylinder*, one whose axis is oblique to the plane of its base.—*Oblique speech*, *oblique narration*, *rhet.* that which is quoted indirectly, or in a different person from that employed by the original speaker.—**Obliquely**, ob-lēk'li or ob-līk'li, *adv.* In an oblique manner or direction; indirectly; by a side glance; by an allusion; not in the direct or plain meaning.—**Obliqueness**, **Obliquity**, ob-lēk'nes or ob-līk'nes, ob-lik'wi-ti, *n.* [L. *obliquitas*.] The state of being oblique; deviation from parallelism or a perpendicular; deviation from moral rectitude; a mental or moral twist.—*Obliquity of the ecliptic*, the angle which the plane of the ecliptic makes with that of the equator.

Obliterate, ob-lit'ėr-āt, *v.t.* [L. *oblitero*, to blot out, to cause to be forgotten—prefix *ob*, and *litera*, a letter. LETTER.] To efface; to erase or blot out; to make undecipherable; to cause to be forgotten.—**Ob-**

literation, ob-lit′ér-ā″shon, *n.* The act of obliterating or effacing.—**Obliterative**, ob-lit′ér-ā-tiv, *a.* Tending to obliterate.

Oblivion, ob-liv′i-on, *n.* [L. *oblivio, oblivionis*, from *obliviscor*, to forget—prefix *ob*, and *liveo*, to become black. LIVID.] The state of being blotted out from the memory; a being forgotten; forgetfulness; the act of forgetting; a forgetting of offences, or remission of punishment.—**Oblivious**, ob-liv′i-us, *a.* [L. *obliviosus.*] Causing forgetfulness (*Shak.*); forgetful; mentally absent.—**Obliviously**, ob-liv′i-us-li, *adv.* In an oblivious manner.—**Obliviousness**, ob-liv′i-us-nes, *n.* State of being oblivious.

Oblong, ob′long, *a.* [L. *oblongus*, oblong—*ob*, against, inversely, and *longus*, long.] Rectangular, and having the length greater than the breadth; longer than broad.—*n.* An oblong figure.—**Oblongish**, ob′long-ish, *a.* Somewhat oblong.—**Oblongly**, ob′long-li, *adv.* In an oblong form.—**Oblongness**, ob′long-nes, *n.*—**Oblong-ovate**, *a.* *Bot.* between oblong and ovate.

Obloquy, ob′lo-kwi, *n.* [L. *obloquium*, from *obloquor*—*ob*, against, and *loquor*, to speak. LOQUACIOUS.] Censorious speech; reproachful language; language that causes reproach and odium to rest on men or their actions; odium.—**Obloquious**,† ob-lō′kwi-us, *a.* Containing obloquy.

Obnoxious, ob-nok′shus, *a.* [L. *obnoxius*—*ob*, and *noxa*, harm, hurt. NOXIOUS.] Liable or exposed to harm, injury, or punishment‡; liable or exposed in general‡; reprehensible; censurable; odious; hateful; offensive; unpopular.—**Obnoxiously**, ob-nok′shus-li, *adv.* In an obnoxious manner.—**Obnoxiousness**, ob-nok′shus-nes, *n.*

Oboe, ō′boi, *n.* [It. *oboe*, from Fr. *hautbois*, an oboe.] A hautboy. HAUTBOY.—**Oboist**, ō′bō-ist, *n.* A player on the oboe.

Obolus, ob′o-lus, *n.* [Gr. *obolos.*] A small coin of ancient Greece equal to 1½*d.*

Oboval, **Obovate**, ob-ō′val, ob-ō′vāt, *a.* [Prefix *ob*, implying inversion.] *Bot.* inversely ovate; having the narrow end downward.—**Obovoid**, ob-ō′void, *a.* *Bot.* approaching the obovate form.

Obscene, ob-sēn′, *a.* [L. *obscenus, obscœnus*, filthy, repulsive, obscene: etymol. doubtful.] Impure in language or action; indecent; offensive to chastity and delicacy; inauspicious; ill-omened.—**Obscenely**, ob-sēn′li, *adv.* In an obscene manner.—**Obsceneness**, **Obscenity**, ob-sēn′nes, ob-sen′i-ti, *n.* The state or quality of being obscene; impurity; ribaldry; lewdness

Obscure, ob-skūr′, *a.* [Fr. *obscur*, from L. *obscurus*—prefix *ob*, and root seen in *scutum*, a shield, Skr. *sku*, to cover.] Imperfectly illuminated; gloomy; not clear or distinct to view; dim; not easily understood; not obviously intelligible; abstruse; indistinct; not much known or observed; unknown to fame; unnoticed.—*v.t.*—*obscured, obscuring.* To darken; to make dark or dim; to make less intelligible, legible, or visible; to hide; to prevent from being seen or known.—**Obscurely**, ob-skūr′li, *adv.* In an obscure manner; darkly; dimly; not clearly; in retirement; not conspicuously.—**Obscureness**, ob-skūr′nes, *n.* State of being obscure; obscurity.—**Obscurer**, ob-skū′rér, *n.* One who or that which obscures.—**Obscurity**, ob-skū′ri-ti, *n.* [L. *obscuritas.*] The quality or state of being obscure; darkness; dimness; darkness of meaning; a state of being unknown to fame.—**Obscurant**, **Obscurantist**, ob-skū′rant, ob-skū′rant-ist, *n.* One who obscures; one who opposes the progress of knowledge, or labours to prevent enlightenment, inquiry, or reform.—**Obscurantism**, ob-skū′rant-izm, *n.* The system or principles of an obscurant.—**Obscuration**, **Obscurement**, ob-skū-rā′shon, ob-skūr′ment, *n.* The act of obscuring or darkening; the state of being darkened or obscured.

Obsecrate, ob′sē-krāt, *v.t.* [L. *obsecro*, to entreat—prefix *ob*, and *sacer*, sacred. SACRED.] To beseech; to entreat; to supplicate.—**Obsecration**, ob-sē-krā′shon, *n.* The act of obsecrating; entreaty; supplication.—**Obsecratory**,† ob-sek′ra-to-ri, *a.* Supplicatory; expressing entreaty.

Obsequious, ob-sē′kwi-us, *a.* [From L. *obsequiosus*, obsequious, from *obsequium*, compliance, from *obsequor*, to follow—prefix *ob*, and *sequor*, to follow. SEQUENCE.] Promptly obedient or submissive to the will of another; compliant; officious; devoted; servilely condescending; compliant to excess; cringing; fawning.—**Obsequiously**, ob-sē′kwi-us-li, *adv.* In an obsequious manner; servilely; cringingly.—**Obsequiousness**, **Obsequience**, ob-sē′kwi-us-nes, ob-sē′kwi-ens, *n.* The quality of being obsequious.—**Obsequies**, ob′sē-kwiz, *n.* [L. *obsequiæ*, obsequies.] Funeral rites, ceremonies, or solemnities.

Observe, ob-zérv′, *v.t.*—*observed, observing.* [L. *observo*—*ob*, before, in front, and *servo*, to keep or hold. SERVE.] To look on with attention; to regard attentively; to watch; to notice; to perceive; to detect; to discover; to remark in words; to mention; to keep with due ceremonies; to celebrate; to keep or adhere to in practice; to comply with; to obey. ∴ Syn. under SEE.—*v.i.* To be attentive; to remark; to comment.—**Observer**, ob-zér′vér, *n.* One who observes.—**Observing**, ob-zér′ving, *a.* Observant; attentive.—**Observingly**, ob-zér′vingli, *adv.* In an observing manner.—**Observable**, ob-zér′va-bl, *a.* Capable of being observed; worthy of observation.—**Observableness**, ob-zér′va-bl-nes, *n.*—**Observably**, ob-zér′va-bli, *adv.*—**Observance**, ob-zér′vans, *n.* The act of observing; performance; a rite or ceremony; an act of respect, worship, and the like; obedient regard or attention; respectful or servile attention; homage.—**Observant**, ob-zér′vant, *a.* Characterized by observation; taking notice; attentively noticing; attentive to duties or commands; obedient; adhering to in practice (*observant of* duties).—**Observantly**, ob-zér′vant-li, *adv.* In an observant manner.—**Observation**, ob-zér-vā′shon, *n.* [L. *observatio.*] The act, power, or habit of observing; a taking notice or paying attention; *science*, the act of taking notice of particular phenomena as they occur in the course of nature; the observing of some phenomenon, often by the assistance of an instrument; information gained by such an act; a remark based or professing to be based on what has been observed; notice; observance†.—*Observation officer*, an artillery officer placed so as to command a view of enemy positions, and in communication by telephone with those in charge of the guns to which he is attached. He directs the laying of the guns so as to bring selected objects under fire, the objects being commonly invisible to the gunners.—*Observation post*, the position occupied by an observation officer. Often called an 'O. Pip'.—**Observational**, ob-zér-vā′shon-al, *a.* Relating to or based on observations.—**Observative**, ob-zér′va-tiv, *a.* Observant.—**Observatory**, ob-zér′va-to-ri, *n.* A place used for making observations of natural phenomena; a building constructed for astronomical observations; a place of outlook.

Obsess, ob-ses′, *v.t.* [L. *obsideo*, to besiege—*ob*, before, *sedeo*, to sit.] To beset or besiege; to vex or harass, as an evil spirit.—**Obsession**, ob-se′shon, *n.* Act of obsessing.

Obsidian, ob-sid′i-an, *n.* [L. *Obsidianus*, from *Obsidius* or *Obsius*, its alleged discoverer.] Vitreous lava, or volcanic glass, a glassy mineral of several varieties.

Obsidional, ob-sid′i-on-al, *a.* [L. *obsidionalis*, from *obsidio*, a siege—*ob*, before, and *sedeo*, to sit.] Pertaining to a siege.—*Obsidional coins*, coins of base metal, struck to be used in besieged places.—*Obsidional crown*, a crown anciently given by the Romans for services in a siege.

Obsolete, ob′sō-lēt, *a.* [L. *obsoletus*, pp. of *obsolesco*, to go out of use—prefix *ob*, and *soleo*, to use, to be wont.] Gone into disuse; disused; neglected; out of fashion; *biol.* imperfectly developed or abortive.—**Obsoletism**, ob′sō-lēt-izm, *n.* A custom, fashion, word, or the like which has become obsolete.—**Obsoleteness**, ob′sō-lēt-nes, *n.* The state of being obsolete.—**Obsolesce**,† ob-sō-les′, *v.i.* To become obsolescent.—**Obsolescence**, ob-sō-les′ens, *n.* The state or process of becoming obsolete.—**Obsolescent**, ob-sō-les′ent, *a.* [L. *obsolescens.*] Becoming obsolete; going out of use, passing into desuetude.

Obstacle, ob′sta-kl, *n.* [Fr. *obstacle*, from L. *obstaculum*, from *obsto*, to withstand—*ob*, against, and *sto*, to stand. STATE, STAND.] Anything that stands in the way and hinders progress; a hindrance; an obstruction or impediment, either physical or moral.

Obstetric, **Obstetrical**, ob-stet′rik, ob-stet′ri-kal, *a.* [L. *obstetrix*, a midwife—*ob*, before, and *sto*, to stand. OBSTACLE.] Pertaining to midwifery, or care of a woman in pregnancy and labor.—**Obstetrician**, ob-ste-trish′an, *n.* One skilled in obstetrics.—**Obstetrics**, ob-stet′riks, *n.* That branch of medical science which includes prenatal care, as well as childbirth and any complications arising therefrom.

Obstinate, ob′sti-nāt, *a.* [L. *obstinatus*, pp. of *obstino, obstinatum*, to resolve, from *obsto*, to stand against—*ob*, against, and *sto*, to stand. OBSTACLE.] Pertinaciously adhering to an opinion or purpose; fixed firmly in resolution; not yielding to reason, arguments, or other means; stubborn: said of persons; not yielding or not easily subdued or removed (an *obstinate* fever; an *obstinate* cough). ∴ To be *obstinate* implies the doing what we ourselves choose; to be *stubborn* denotes, rather, determination not to do what others advise or desire.—**Obstinacy**, **Obstinateness**, ob′sti-na-si, ob′sti-nāt-nes, *n.* The state or quality of being obstinate.—**Obstinately**, ob′sti-nāt-li, *adv.* In an obstinate manner.

Obstipation, ob-sti-pā′shon, *n.* [L. *ob*, against, and *stipo*, to cram.] *Med.* extreme constipation, where there is no alvine discharge.

Obstreperous, ob-strep′ér-us, *a.* [L. *obstreperus*, from *obstrepo*, to roar—*ob*, intens., and *strepo*, to make a noise.] Making a tumultuous noise; clamorous; vociferous; noisy; loud.—**Obstreperously**, ob-strep′ér-us-li, *adv.* In an obstreperous manner.—**Obstreperousness**, ob-strep′ér-us-nes, *n.* Clamour; noisy turbulence.

Obstriction,† ob-strik′shon, *n.* [L. *ob*, and *stringo*, to strain. STRAIN.] The condition of being bound or constrained.

Obstruct, ob-strukt′, *v.t.* [L. *obstruo, obstructum*—*ob*, against, and *struo*, to pile up. STRUCTURE.] To block up, stop up, or close, as a passage; to fill with obstacles or impediments that prevent passing; to hinder from passing; to impede; to stand in the way of; to retard, interrupt, render slow.—**Obstructer**, ob-struk′tér, *n.* One that obstructs or hinders.—**Obstruction**, ob-struk′shon, *n.* The act of obstructing; anything that stops or closes a way, passage, or channel; obstacle; impediment; that which impedes progress; check; hindrance; the state of having the vital functions obstructed†.—**Obstructionist**, ob-struk′shon-ist, *n.* One who practises obstruction; an obstructive.—**Obstructive**, ob-struk′tiv, *a.* Obstructing or tending to obstruct.—*n.* One who obstructs; one who hinders the transaction of business.—**Obstructively**, ob-struk′tiv-li, *adv.* In an obstructive manner.—**Obstruent**, ob′stru-ent, *a.* [L. *obstruens*, ppr. of *obstruo.*] Blocking up; obstructing; hindering.—*n.* Anything that obstructs; something that blocks up the natural passages of the body.

Obtain, ob-tān′, *v.t.* [L. *obtineo*—prefix *ob*, and *teneo*, to hold. TENANT.] To gain possession of; to gain, procure, receive, get, acquire.—*v.i.* To be received in customary or common use; to be established in practice; to hold good; to subsist (the custom still *obtains*).—**Obtainable**, ob-tā′na-bl, *a.* Capable of being obtained.—**Obtainer**, ob-tā′nér, *n.* One who obtains.—**Obtainment**, ob-tān′ment, *n.* The act of obtaining; attainment.

Obtected, ob-tek′ted, *a.* [L. *obtectus*—prefix *ob*, and *tego, tectus*, to cover.] Covered; *zool.* covered with a hard shelly case.

Obtest, ob-test′, *v.t.* [L. *obtestor*—prefix *ob*, and *testor*, to witness. TESTAMENT.] To call upon earnestly; to entreat, implore, conjure; to supplicate.—**Obtestation**, ob-tes-tā′shon, *n.* The act of obtesting.

Obtrude, ob-tröd′, *v.t.*—*obtruded, obtruding.* [L. *obtrudo*—prefix *ob*, and *trudo*, to thrust. INTRUDE.] To thrust prominently forward; to force into any place or state unduly or without solicitation: often *refl.* (to *obtrude* one's self upon a person's notice); to offer with unreasonable importunity.—*v.i.* To obtrude one's self; to enter when not invited.—**Obtruder**, ob-trö′dėr, *n.* One who obtrudes.—**Obtrusion**, ob-trö′zhon, *n.* The act of obtruding.—**Obtrusive**, ob-trö′siv, *a.* Disposed to obtrude; forward; intrusive.—**Obtrusively**, ob-trö′siv-li, *adv.* In an obtrusive manner.—**Obtrusiveness**, ob-tro′siv-nes, *n.*

Obtuse, ob-tūs′, *a.* [L. *obtusus*—prefix *ob*, and *tundo, tudi* (Skr. *tud*), to beat. CONTUSE.] Not pointed or acute; blunt; not having acute sensibility; stupid; dull.—*Obtuse angle*, one larger than a right angle of 90°.—**Obtuse-angled, Obtuse-angular**, *a.* Having an obtuse angle or angles.—**Obtusely**, ob-tūs′li, *adv.* In an obtuse manner.—**Obtuseness, Obtusity**, ob-tūs′nes, ob-tū′si-ti, *n.* The state of being obtuse.

Obverse, ob′vėrs, *a.* [L. prefix *ob*, and *versus*, turned.] Pertaining to the one of two possible sides or theories; *numis.* bearing the face or head.—*n.* The one of two possible ways of looking at a thing; *numis.* that side of a coin or medal which has the face or head on it, the other being the *reverse*.—**Obversely**, ob′vėrs-li, *adv.* In an obverse form or manner.—**Obversion**, ob-vėr′shon, *n.* The act of obverting.—**Obvert**, ob-vėrt′, *v.t.* To turn towards.—*In logic*, to infer another proposition with a contradictory predicate by changing the quality of the proposition.

Obviate, ob′vi-āt, *v.t.*—*obviated, obviating.* [L. *obvio, obviatum*, to meet—*ob*, against, and *via*, a way. VOYAGE, WAY.] To meet, as difficulties or objections; to overcome; to clear out of the way.—**Obviation**,† ob-vi-ā′shon, *n.* The act of obviating.—**Obvious**, ob′vi-us, *a.* [L. *obvius*, in the way.] Easily discovered, seen, or understood; perfectly plain, manifest, or evident.—**Obviously**, ob′vi-us-li, *adv.* In an obvious manner.—**Obviousness**, ob′vi-us-nes, *n.* State of being obvious.

Obvolute, Obvoluted, ob′vo-lūt, ob′vo-lū-ted, *a.* [L. *ob*, against, and *volutus*, rolled.] Rolled or turned in; *bot.* having the margins of opposite leaves alternately overlapping.

Ocarina, ō-ka-rē′na, *n.* [It.] A small musical instrument of terra cotta pierced with holes, there being seven instruments in a set.

Occasion, ok-kā′zhon, *n.* [L. *occasio, occasionis*, from *occido, occasum*, to fall—*ob*, and *cado*, to fall. ACCIDENT.] Time of an occurrence, incident, or event; opportunity; favourable time, season, or circumstances; incidental cause; a cause acting on the will; a motive or reason; incidental need; casual exigency; requirement (*to have occasion* or *no occasion* for a thing); peculiar position of affairs; juncture; exigency.—*v.t.* To cause incidentally; to produce; to induce.—**Occasional**, ok-kā′zhon-al, *a.* Incidental; occurring at times, but not regular or systematic; made or happening as opportunity requires or admits.—**Occasionally**, ok-kā′zhon-al-li, *adv.* In an occasional manner; at times; sometimes but not often.

Occident, ok′si-dent, *n.* [Fr. *occident*, L. *occidens, occidentis*, ppr. of *occido*, to fall, to set, as the sun. OCCASION.] The western quarter of the hemisphere; the west: the opposite of *orient*.—**Occidental**, ok-si-den′tal, *a.* Pertaining to the occident or west; western: opposed to *oriental*; having an inferior degree of beauty and excellence: applied to gems in opposition to *oriental*.—**Occidentally**, ok-si-den′tal-li, *adv.* In the occident or west; after the sun.

Occipital, ok-sip′i-tal, *a.* [From L. *occiput*, the back part of the head—prefix *ob*, and *caput*, the head.] Pertaining to the back part of the head.—**Occiput**, ok′si-put, *n.* [L.] The hinder part of the head.

Occlude, ok-klūd′, *v.t.*—*occluded, occluding.* [L. *occludo*—*ob*, and *claudo*, to shut.] To shut up†; *chem.* to absorb or take up without chemical combination.—**Occlusion**, ok-klū′zhon, *n.* The act of occluding; *chem.* absorption without combination.

Occult, ok-kult′, *a.* [L. *occultus*, pp. of *occulo*, to cover over—prefix *ob*, and root of *celo*, to conceal, and E. *hell*.] Hidden from the eye or understanding; invisible and mysterious; unknown.—*Occult sciences*, certain so-called sciences of the middle ages, as alchemy, necromancy or magic, astrology.—**Occultation**, ok-kul-tā′shon, *n.* *Astron.* the hiding of a star or planet from our sight by passing behind some other of the heavenly bodies; the time of a planet or star being so hidden; hence, *fig.* disappearance from view; withdrawal from public notice.—**Occulted**, ok-kul′ted, *a.* *Astron.* concealed by occultation.—**Occultism**, ok′ult-izm, *n.* A system of occult or mysterious doctrines; the beliefs of the theosophists, typified in such works as Bulwer-Lytton's *Zanoni, A Strange Story; The Coming Race. The Occult Review* (1905): 'A magazine devoted to the investigation of super-normal phenomena and the study of the truths underlying all religious beliefs.'—**Occultly**, ok-kult′li, *adv.* In an occult manner.—**Occultness**, ok-kult′nes, *n.*

Occupy, ok′kū-pī, *v.t.*—*occupied, occupying.* [L. *occupo*, to take possession of, possess—prefix *ob*, and *capio*, to take. CAPABLE.] To take possession of; to possess; to hold and use; to take up, as room or space; to cover or fill; to employ or use (one's time); to engage; to busy: often *refl.*—*v.i.* To be an occupant; to hold possession.—**Occupancy**, ok′kū-pan-si, *n.* The act of occupying; a holding in possession; term during which one is occupant.—**Occupant**, ok′kū-pant, *n.* [L. *occupans, occupantis*, ppr. of *occupo*, to occupy.] An occupier.—**Occupation**, ok-kū-pā′shon, *n.* [L. *occupatio*.] The act of occupying or taking possession; possession; tenure; state of being employed or occupied in any way; that which engages one's time and attention; the principal business of one's life; a vocation; calling; trade.—*Army of Occupation*, army provisionally occupying territory that has been overrun, until a form of government is established.—**Occupier**, ok′kū-pi-ėr, *n.* One that occupies; an occupant.

Occur, ok-kėr′, *v.i.*—*occurred, occurring.* [L. *occurro*—*ob*, against, and *curro*, to run. CURRENT.] To meet or come to the mind, imagination, or memory; to befall; to happen; to take place; to exist so as to be capable of being found or seen; to be found; to be met with.—**Occurrence**, ok-kur′ens, *n.* The act of occurring or taking place; any incident or accidental event; an observed instance.

Ocean, ō′shan, *n.* [L. *oceanus*, from Gr. *ōkeanos*, the ocean, the deity of the ocean.] The vast body of water which covers more than three-fifths of the surface of the globe; the sea; also, one of the great basins or areas into which it has been divided; any immense expanse (the boundless *ocean* of eternity).—*a.* Pertaining to the main or great sea (the *ocean* wave).—**Oceana**, ō-se′an-a, *n.* The political romance, issued in 1656, by James Harrington, in which Oceana represents England, Marpesia Scotland, Panopaea Ireland; propounding the theory that the natural element of power in states is property, of which land is the most important. Also the name of a work by Froude in 1886, discussing Australia and Imperial Federation.—**Oceanic**, ō-shē-an′ik, *a.* Pertaining to the ocean; occurring in or produced by the ocean, as distinguished from smaller seas; pertaining to Oceania (the islands lying between Asia and America) or its inhabitants.—*Oceanic island*, an island that has never formed part of a continent, e.g. Azores.—**Oceanography**, ō-shan-og′ra-fi, *n.* The department of knowledge that deals with oceanic phenomena.—**Oceanology**, ō-shan-ol′o-ji, *n.* The knowledge of the ocean.

Ocellus, ō-sel′lus, *n.* pl. **Ocelli**, ō-sel′lī. [L. *ocellus*, dim. of *oculus*, an eye. OCULAR.] One of the minute simple eyes of insects, many spiders, crustaceans, molluscs, &c.—**Ocellate, Ocellated**, ō-sel′lāt, ō-sel′lā-ted, *a.* [L. *ocellatus*.] Resembling an eye; studded with the figures of little eyes.

Ocelot, ō′sē-lot, *n.* [Mex. *ocelotl*.] A carnivorous animal of the cat kind, an inhabitant of Mexico.

Ochlocracy, ok-lok′ra-si, *n.* [Gr. *ochlos*, the multitude, and *kratos*, power.] The rule or ascendency of the multitude or common people; a mobocracy.—**Ochlocratic, Ochlocratical**, ok-lō-krat′ik, ok-lō-krat′i-kal, *a.* Relating to ochlocracy.—**Ochlocratically**, ok-lō-krat′i-kal-li, *adv.*

Ocher, Ochre, ō′kėr, *n.* [L. *ochra*, Gr. *ochra*, from *ochros*, pale, pale yellow.] A name applied to clays colored with the oxides of iron in various proportions, and varying in color from pale yellow to brownish red, much used in painting.—**Ocherous, Ochreous, Ochery**, ō′kėr-us, ō′kėr-i, *a.* Pertaining to ocher; consisting of ocher; resembling ocher.

Ocrea, ok′rē-a, *n. pl.* **Ocreae**. [L. *ocrea*, a greave or legging.] *Bot.* the union of two stipules around the stem in a kind of sheath.—**Ocreate**, ok′rē-āt, *a.* *Bot.* furnished with ochreae

Octachord, ok′ta-kord, *n.* [Gr. *oktō*, eight, and *chordē*, a string.] A musical instrument having eight strings.

Octagon, ok′ta-gon, *n.* [Gr. *oktō*, eight, and *gōnia*, angle.] *Geom.* a figure of eight sides and eight angles.—**Octagonal**, ok-tag′on-al, *a.* Having eight sides and eight angles.

Octahedron, ok-ta-hē′dron, *n.* [Gr. *oktō*, eight, *hedra*, a base.] *Geom.* a solid contained by eight faces, which take the form of equal and equilateral triangles.—**Octahedral**, ok-ta-hē′dral, *a.* Having eight equal surfaces.

Octameter, ok-tam′et-ėr, *n.* [Gr. *oktō*, eight, *metron*, a measure.] A verse of eight feet.

Octandrian, Octandrous, ok-tan′dri-an, ok-tan′drus, *a.* [Gr. *oktō*, eight, and *anēr, andros*, a male.] Applied to plants having eight distinct stamens.

Octangular, ok-tang′gū-lėr, *a.* [L. *octo*, eight, and E. *angular*.] Having eight angles.

Octant, ok′tant, *n.* [L. *octans*, an eighth part, from *octo*, eight.] The eighth part of a circle; an instrument resembling a sextant or quadrant in principle, but having an arc the eighth of a circle, or 45°.

Octapla, ok′ta-pla, *n.* [Gr. *oktaploos*, eightfold, from *oktō*, eight.] A polyglot Bible in eight languages.

Octastyle, ok′ta-stīl, *n.* [Gr. *oktō*, eight, and *stylos*, a column.] *Arch.* a temple or other building having eight columns in front.

Octateuch, ok′ta-tūk, *n.* [Gr. *oktō*, eight, and *teuchos*, a book.] The first eight books of the Old Testament.

Octave, ok′tāv, *n.* [L. *octavus*, eighth, from *octo*, eight.] The eighth day after a church festival, the festival itself being counted; the week immediately following a church festival; the first two stanzas in the sonnet of four verses each; a stanza of eight lines; *music*, an eighth, or an interval of seven degrees or twelve semitones; one sound eight tones higher than another.—*Octave flute.* PICCOLO.—*a.* Consisting of eight.—**Octavo**, ok-tā′vō, *n.* The size of one leaf of a sheet of paper folded so as to make eight leaves: usually written *8vo*; a book having eight leaves to each sheet: often used as an adjective.

Octennial, ok-ten′i-al, *a.* [L. *octo*, eight, and *annus*, a year.] Happening every eighth year; lasting eight years.—**Octennially**, ok-ten'i-al-li, *adv.* Once in eight years.

Octet, ok'tet, *n.* [L. *octo*, eight.] *Music*, a musical composition for eight parts.

Octillion, ok-til'yon, *n.* [L. *octo*, eight, and term of *million*.] The figure 1 followed by 27 zeros (*American and French*). or 1 followed by 48 zeros (*English*).

October, ok-tō'bėr, *n.* [L., from *octo*, eight: the eighth month of the primitive Roman year, which began in March.] The tenth month of the year; ale or cider brewed in October.—*October club*, a political club of squires in Queen Anne's day, devoted to the consumption of October ale and to the policy of enforcing strong anti-Whig measures on the Government.

Octodecimo, ok-tō-des'i-mō, *n.* [L. *octodecim*, eighteen — *octo*, eight, and *decem*, ten.] The size of one leaf of a sheet of paper folded so as to make eighteen leaves; a book in which each sheet is folded into eighteen leaves: usually written *18mo*. Also used as an adjective.

Octodentate, ok-tō-den'tāt, *a.* [L. *octo*, eight, *dens*, a tooth.] Having eight teeth.

Octofid, ok'tō-fid, *a.* [L. *octo*, eight, and *findo*, *fido*, to cleave.] *Bot.* cleft or separated into eight segments, as a calyx.

Octogenarian, ok'tō-je-nā"ri-an, *n.* [L. *octogenarius*, from *octogeni*, eighty, *octo*, eight.] A person eighty years of age; any one whose age is between eighty and ninety.—*a.* Of eighty years of age; between eighty and ninety years of age.

Octogynous, ok-toj'i-nus, *a.* [Gr. *oktō*, eight, and *gynē*, a female.] *Bot.* having eight pistils or styles.

Octohedron, ok-tō-hē'dron, *n.* OCTAHEDRON.

Octolocular, ok-tō-lok'ū-lėr, *a.* [L. *octo*, eight, and *loculus*, dim. of *locus*, a place.] *Bot.* having eight cells for seeds.

Octopede, ok'tō-pēd, *n.* [L. *octo*, eight, and *pes*, *pedis*, a foot.] An eight-footed animal.

Octopetalous, ok-tō-pet'a-lus, *a.* [Gr. *oktō*, eight, and *petalon*, a petal.] *Bot.* having eight petals.

Octopod, ok'tō-pod, *n.* [Gr. *oktō*, eight, and *pous*, *podos*, a foot.] An animal having eight feet; a cuttle-fish, having eight arms or tentacles.—**Octopus**, ok'tō-pus, *n.* A genus of two-gilled cuttle-fishes, having eight arms furnished with suckers; they have attained a notoriety from tales concerning their ferocity and the gigantic size of some.

Octoroon, ok-tō-rön', *n.* [L. *octo*, eight.] The offspring of a quadroon and a white person.

Octostyle, ok'tō-stīl. OCTASTYLE.

Octosyllabic, ok'tō-sil-lab"ik, *a.* [Gr. *oktō*, eight, and *syllabē*, a syllable.] Consisting of eight syllables.—*n.* A word of eight syllables.

Octroi, ok-trwą, *n.* [Fr., from L. *auctor*, an author.] A duty levied at the gates of French cities on articles brought in.

Octuple, ok'tū-pl, *a.* [L. *octuplus*—*oktō*, eight.] Eightfold.

Ocuba wax, ō-kū'ba, *n.* A vegetable wax, obtained from trees of the nutmeg genus.

Ocular, ok'ū-lėr, *a.* [L. *ocularis*, from *oculus*, the eye, a word cognate with E. *eye*. EYE.] Pertaining to the eye; depending on the eye; received by actual sight.—*n.* The eyepiece of an optical instrument.—**Ocularly**, ok'ū-lėr-li, *adv.* In an ocular manner; by the eye, sight, or actual view.—**Oculate**; **Oculated**, ok'ū-lāt, ok'ū-lā-ted, *a.* [L. *oculatus*.] Furnished with eyes; having spots resembling eyes.—**Oculiform**, ok'ū-li-form, *a.* In the form of an eye.—**Oculist**, ok'ū-list, *n.* One skilled in diseases of the eyes.

Od, od, *n.* The name invented by Reichenbach for a peculiar force which he fancied he had discovered associated with magnetism, and which was said to explain the phenomena of mesmerism or animal magnetism. Called also *Odic force*.—**Odic**, od'ik, *a.* Pertaining to od.

Odal, ō'dal, *a.* Same as *Udal*.—**Odaller**, ō'dal-ėr, *n.* Same as *Udaller*.

Odalisk, **Odalisque**, ō'da-lisk, *n.* [Fr. *odalisque*, from Turk. *odalik*, from *oda*, a chamber.] A female slave or concubine in the sultan's seraglio or a harem.

Odd, od, *a.* [From Icel. *oddi*, a triangle, an odd number, *odda-mathr*, an odd man, *odda-tala*, an odd number; Dan. *od*, a point, *odde*, a tongue of land; akin to A. Sax. *ord*, a point, G. *ort*, place, spot, originally a point.] Not even; not exactly divisible by 2; left over after the pairs have been reckoned; additional to a whole mentioned in round numbers; not included with others; hence, unheeded; of little value or account (*odd* times, *odd* trifles); incidental; casual; forming one of a pair of which the other is wanting; belonging to a broken set; singular; strange; peculiar; eccentric; queer.—**Oddfellow**, od'fel-ō, *n.* A member of an extensively ramified friendly society, originally modelled on freemasonry.—**Oddity**, od'i-ti, *n.* The state or quality of being odd; singularity; something odd or singular; a singular person.—**Oddly**, od'li, *adv.* In an odd manner; not evenly; strangely; whimsically; singularly.—**Oddment**, od'ment, *n.* An odd article or one left over.—**Oddness**, od'nes, *n.* The state of being odd; state of not being even; singularity; strangeness.—**Odds**, odz, *n. sing.* or *pl.* Excess of one amount or quantity compared with another; difference in favour of one and against another; amount by which the bet of one party exceeds that of the other.—*At odds*, at variance; in controversy or quarrel.—*Odds and ends*, small miscellaneous articles.

Ode, ōd, *n.* [L. *ode*, Gr. *ōdē*, song or poem, from *aeidō*, to sing; seen in *parody*, *prosody*.] A short poem or song; a poem to be set to music or sung; a lyric poem of a lofty cast.

Odeon, **Odeum**, ō-dē'on, ō-dē'um, *n.* [Gr. *ōdeion*, from *ōdē*, a song.] A theatre for musical or dramatic performances.

Odic. Under OD.

Odin, **Woden**, ō'din, wō'den, *n.* [Former from Scandinavian, latter Anglo-Saxon and German.] The chief god of Northern mythology, after whom is named Wednesday.—**Odinic**, ō-din'ik, *a.* Belonging to Odin.

Odious, ō'di-us, *a.* [L. *odiosus*, from *odium*, hatred, *odi*, I hate; same root as A.Sax. *atol*, hateful, horrible. ANNOY, NOISOME.] Of such a character as to be hated or greatly disliked; hateful; causing disgust or repugnance; offensive.—**Odiously**, ō'di-us-li, *adv.* In an odious manner; hatefully.—**Odiousness**, ō'di-us-nes, *n.* The quality of being odious.—**Odium**, ō'di-um, *n.* [L.] Hatred; dislike; the quality that provokes hatred.—*Odium theologicum*, theological hatred; the hatred of contending divines towards each other.

Odometer, ō-dom'et-ėr, *n.* A hodometer.

Odontalgia, **Odontalgy**, ō-don-tal'ji-a, ō'don-tal-ji, *n.* [Gr. *odous*, *odontos*, tooth, *algos*, pain.] Pain in the teeth; toothache.—**Odontalgic**, ō-don-tal'jik, *a.* Pertaining to the toothache.—*n.* A remedy for the toothache.—**Odonto**, ō-don'tō, *n.* [Gr. *odous*, *odontos*.] A dentifrice; a toothwash.—**Odontoglossum**, ō-don-tō-glos'um, *n.* [Gr. *odous*, *odontos*, a tooth, and *glōssa*, a tongue.] A genus of tropical American orchids, with magnificent flowers.—**Odontography**, ō-don-tog'ra-fi, *n.* A description of the teeth.—**Odontoid**, ō-don'toid, *a.* Tooth-like.—*Odontoid process*, the part of the first vertebra of the neck, forming a pivot for the head.—**Odontolite**, ō-don'tō-līt, *n.* [Gr. *lithos*, a stone.] A fossil tooth.—**Odontological**, ō-don'tō-loj"i-kal, *a.* Belonging to odontology.—**Odontology**, ō-don-tol'o-ji, *n.* That branch of anatomical science which treats of the teeth.—**Odontophore**, ō-don'tō-fōr, *n.* [Gr. *phoros*, bearing.] The so-called tongue or lingual ribbon of certain molluscs, covered with minute teeth.

Odor, ō'dėr, *n.* [L. *odor*, a smell; allied to Gr. *ozō*, to smell; akin *olfactory*.] Any scent or smell, whether pleasant or offensive; when used alone most commonly a sweet smell; fragrance.—*In bad odor*, in bad repute; in disfavor.—*Odor of sanctity*, the reputation of being a saint.—**Odoriferous**, ō-dėr-if'ėr-us, *a.* [L. *odoriferus*.] Giving odor or scent; diffusing fragrance; fragrant.—**Odoriferously**, ō-dėr-if'ėr-us-li, *adv.* In an odoriferous manner.—**Odoriferousness**, ō-dėr-if'ėr-us-nes, *n.*—**Odorous**, ō'dėr-us, *a.* Having or emitting an odor; sweet of scent; fragrant.—**Odorously**, ō'dėr-us-li, *adv.* In an odorous manner; fragrantly.—**Odorousness**, ō'dėr-us-nes, *n.* The quality of being odorous. **Odorless**, ō'dėr-les, *a.* Having no odor.

Odyssey, od'is-i, *n.* The poem in twenty-four books in which Homer sets forth the wanderings and return of Odysseus, or Ulysses, from Troy to his home in Ithaca.

Œcology, ēk'ol-o-jē, *n.* [Gr. *oikos*, a dwelling, *logos*, a discourse.] The relations of plants to their surroundings.

Œcumenical. ECUMENIC.

Œdema, ē-dē'ma, *n.* [Gr. *oidēma*, a swelling, from *oideō*, to swell.] *Med.* a puffiness or swelling of parts arising from water collecting.—**Œdematous**, **Œdematose**, ē-dē'ma-tus, ē-dē'ma-tōs, *a.* Relating to œdema.

Œil-de-bœuf, e-il-de-bėf, *n.* [Fr., ox-eye.] *Arch.* a round or oval opening in a frieze or roof to admit light.

Œnanthic, ē-nan'thik, *a.* [Gr. *oinos*, wine, and *anthos*, a flower.] Having or imparting the characteristic odour of wine.—*Œnanthic acid*, an acid obtained from œnanthic ether.—*Œnanthic ether*, an oily liquid which gives to wine its characteristic odour.—**Œnolin**, ē'nol-in, *n.* A colouring matter obtained from red wine.—**Œnology**, ē-nol'o-ji, *n.* That branch of knowledge which deals with wine.—**Œnometer**, ē-nom'et-ėr, *n.* A hydrometer for determining the alcoholic strength of wines.—**Œnophilist**, ē-nof'il-ist, *n.* [Gr. *phileō*, to love.] A lover of wine.

O'er, ōr. A contraction (generally poetical) of *over*.

Œrsted, er'sted, *n.* [After *Œrsted*, the physicist.] The C.G.S. unit of magnetic reluctance, equal to the reluctance of a magnetic circuit of unit length, unit area, and unit permeability.

Œsophagus, ē-sof'a-gus, *n.* [Gr. *oisophagos*—*oisō*, I will bear, and *phagō*, to eat.] The gullet; the canal through which food and drink pass to the stomach.—**Œsophageal**, ē-sō-faj'ē-al, *a.* Pertaining to the œsophagus.

Oestrus, ēs'trūs, *n.* [Gr. *oistros*, gadfly.] Irresistible impulse; passion; sexual impulse of animals.

Of, ov, *prep.* [A.Sax. *of* = Icel., Sw., Dan., and D. *af*, Goth. *af*, G. *ab*; cog. L. *ab*, Gr. *apo*, Skr. *apa*, from, away from. *Off* is the same word.] A word used in regard to source, cause, origin, motive, &c.; possession or ownership; attribute, quality, or condition (his state *of* mind); an aggregate or whole with a partitive reference (all, some, *of* us); the relation of object to a verbal notion (a desire *of* fame); to express concerning, relating to, about; distance or time (within a mile *of*); identity, equivalence, or apposition—appositive use of *of* (the city *of* London); on or in: with indefinite expressions of time, as a quarter *of* (an hour); so *of* late, in recent times.

Off, of, *adv.* [OF.] Away; distant (a mile *off*); from or away by removal or separation (to cut *off*); not on; from, in the way of departure, abatement, remission (the fever goes *off*); away; not toward.—*Off and on*, *on and off*, with interruptions and resumptions; at intervals.—*To come off*, to escape; to take place (the marriage did not *come off*).—*To get off*, to alight; to make escape.—*To go off*, to depart; to explode (a gun); to take place —*To pass off*, to pass away; to take place.—*To take off*, to take away; to mimic.—*Well off, ill off*, as an adjective phrase, in good or bad circumstances.—*a.* Distant; as applied to horses, right hand: opposed to *near*; in cricket, applied to that part of the field which is on the left of the bowler.—*prep.* Not on; away from; from or out of (a lane leading *off* a street); to seaward from: a nautical use (hence *offing*).—*interj.* A command to depart; away! begone!—**Offcast**, of'kast, *n.* That which is rejected as useless.—**Offing**, of'ing, *n.* The position of a vessel, or of a portion of the sea within sight of land, relatively to the coast.—**Off-colour**, *n.* A defective colour in gems, &c.—**Off-day**, *n.* A day on which any usual occupation is discontinued.—**Off-hand**, *adv.* Readily; with ease.—*a.* Done without study or hesitation; unpremeditated.—**Offlet**, of'let, *n.* A pipe or other appliance to let off water.—**Offprint**, *n.* A copy thrown off by the printer of a magazine article, or short piece of writing, for distribution among friends of the writer.—**Offscouring**, of'skou-ring, *n.* Refuse; what is vile or despised: often of persons.—**Offset**, of'set, *n.* A sum or amount set off against another as an equivalent; *surveying*, a perpendicular distance measured from a main line in order to get the area of an irregular portion; *hort.* a young bulb or a scion used to propagate a plant; also, an offshoot.—**Offshoot**, of'shöt, *n.* A branch from a main stem, stream, mountain range, &c.—**Offspring**, of'spring, *n. sing.* or *pl.* What is sprung from a stock or parent, a child or children; what arises or is produced from something.—**Off-street**, *n.* A small street leading from a larger one.—**Off-time**, *n.* Time when a person is off duty.

Offal, of'al, *n.* [Lit. *off-fall*; so D. *afval*, Icel. *affall*, G. *abfall*, with similar meanings.] Waste meat; a trade term for kidneys, heart, tongue, liver, and other parts of a carcass; carrion; refuse; rubbish.

Offence, of-fens', *n.* [Fr. *offense*, from L. *offensa*, an offence, from *offendo, offensum*, to strike against—*ob*, against, and old *fendo*, to strike, seen in *defend*, also in *manifest*.] A striking against or assailing (arms of *offence*); hurt; injury; an affront, insult, or wrong; the state of being offended; displeasure; any transgression of law, divine or human; a crime or sin; a misdemeanour.—*To take offence*, to become angry or displeased at something said or done.—**Offend**, of-fend', *v.t.* [L. *offendo*.] To displease; to make angry; to affront; to mortify; to shock, annoy, or pain (the taste or smell); to sin against; to disobey (*Shak.*).—*v.i.* To transgress the moral or divine law; to sin; to cause dislike or anger; to take offence (N.T.).—**Offender**, of-fen'dėr, *n.* One who offends; a criminal; a transgressor.—**Offending**, of-fen'ding, *n.* A transgression; crime.—**Offense**. American spelling of *offence*.—**Offensive**, of-fen'siv, *a.* [Fr. *offensif*.] Causing offence; giving provocation; irritating; disgusting; disagreeable (as to the senses); pertaining to offence; used in attack: opposed to *defensive*; consisting in attack; proceeding by attack.—*Alliance offensive and defensive*, one that requires the parties to make war together, and each party to defend the other in case of being attacked.—*n.* With the definite article: the act of attacking (to act on the *offensive*).—**Offensively**, of-fen'siv-li, *adv.* In an offensive manner.—**Offensiveness**, of-fen'siv-nes, *n.* The quality of being offensive; unpleasantness.

Offer, of'ėr, *v.t.* [A.Sax. *offrian*, and Fr. *offrir* (*j'offre*, I offer), from L. *offerre*, to offer—*ob*, towards, and *fero*, to bring. FERTILE.] To present for acceptance or rejection; to tender; to present to notice; to proffer; to present, as an act of worship; to sacrifice (often with *up*); to attempt or do with evil intent (to *offer* violence, an insult); to bid, as a price or wages.—*v.i.* To present itself (an opportunity *offers*); to declare a willingness; to make an attempt.—*n.* The act of offering; a proposal to be accepted or rejected; the act of bidding a price, or the sum bid.—**Offerable**, of'ėr-a-bl, *a.* Capable of being offered.—**Offerer**, of'ėr-ėr, *n.* One who offers.—**Offering**, of'ėr-ing, *n.* The act of an offerer; that which is offered; a gift offered or consecrated to a deity; a sacrifice; an oblation.—**Offertory**, of'ėr-to-ri, *n.* [L.L. *offertorium*, from *offertor*, an offerer.] The sentences in the communion service of the Church of England read while the alms are being collected; the alms collected.

Office, of'is, *n.* [Fr. *office*, from L. *officium*, duty, office, from prefix *ob*, and *facio*, to do, or from *opem*, aid (OPULENCE), and *facio* (FACT).] Employment or business; duty or duties falling on or intrusted to a person; that which is performed or assigned to be done by a particular thing; function; act of good or ill voluntarily tendered: usually in a good sense; service; *eccles.* a formulary of devotion, or a service appointed for a particular occasion; a house or apartment in which persons transact business; a place where official acts are done; a body of persons intrusted with certain duties; persons who transact business in an office (often applied to an insurance company); *pl.* kitchens, outhouses, &c., of a mansion, dwelling-house, or farm.—*Holy Office*, the Inquisition, or the authorities at Rome who direct it.—*Office hours*, the hours during which offices are open for the transaction of business.—**Office-bearer**, *n.* One who holds office.—**Officer**, of'is-ėr, *n.* A person who holds an office; a person commissioned or authorized to fill a public situation or to perform any public duty; one who holds a commission in the army or navy.—*v.t.* To furnish with officers; to appoint officers over.—**Officered**, of'is-ėrd, *a.* Supplied with officers (as troops).—**Official**, of-fish'al, *a.* [L. *officialis*.] Pertaining to an office or public duty; derived from the proper office or officer, or from the proper authority (an *official* permission); communicated by virtue of authority.—*n.* One invested with an office of a public nature; *eccles.* a deputy appointed by a bishop, chapter, archdeacon, &c.—**Officialism**, of-fish'al-izm, *n.* A system of official government; a system of excessive official routine; red-tapism.—**Officially**, of-fish'al-li, *adv.* In an official manner; by virtue of the proper authority.—**Officiate**, of-fish'i-āt, *v.i.*—*officiated*, *officiating*. To perform official duties.—**Officiator**, of-fish'i-ā-tėr, *n.* One who officiates.

Officinal, of-fis'i-nal, *a.* [From L. *officina*, a shop; same origin as *office*.] Used in a shop, or belonging to it; *phar.* used in the preparation of recognized medical recipes (an *officinal* plant).—*n.* A drug sold in an apothecary's shop.

Officious, of-fish'us, *a.* [L. *officiosus*, dutiful, obliging, from *officium*, an office. OFFICE.] Obliging‡; doing kind offices‡; excessively forward in kindness; interposing services not wanted; annoyingly eager to oblige or assist; meddling.—**Officiously**, of-fish'-us-li, *adv.* In an officious manner; with forward zeal; meddlesomely.—**Officiousness**, of-fish'us-nes, *n.* Improper forwardness; meddlesomeness.

Offing, Offlet, Offscouring, Offset, Offshoot, Offspring, &c. Under OFF.

Oft, oft, *adv.* [A.Sax., Icel., and G. *oft*, Dan. *ofte*, Sw. *ofta*, Goth. *ufta*, oft, often; *often* is a later form; akin to *over*.] Often; frequently. (*Poet.*)—**Often**, of'n, *adv.* Frequently; many times; not seldom.—*a.* Frequent.—**Oftenness**, of'n-nes, *n.* Frequency.—**Oftentimes**, of'n-tīmz, *adv.* Frequently; often; many times.—**Ofttimes**, oft'tīmz, *adv.* Frequently; often.

Ogam, og'am, *n.* OGHAM.

Ogee, ō-jē', *n.* [Fr. *ogive*, *augive*; etymology doubtful.] *Arch.* a moulding consisting of two members, the one concave, the other convex, the outline thus resembling the letter S (sometimes expressed by O G).

Ogham, og'ham, *n.* A kind of writing practised by the ancient Irish, the characters of which also were called *oghams*.

Ogive, ō'jīv, *n.* [Fr. OGEE.] *Arch.* a French term for the Gothic or pointed arch.—**Ogival**, ō-jī'val, *a.* *Arch.* of or pertaining to an ogive or ogee.

Ogle, ō'gl, *v.t.*—*ogled*, *ogling*. [Same as L.G. *oogeln*, to eye, G. *äugeln*, to ogle, from *auge*, D. *oog*, the eye. EYE.] To view with side glances, as in fondness or with a design to attract notice.—*v.i.* To cast side glances.—*n.* A side glance or look.—**Ogler**, ō'glėr, *n.* One that ogles.

Ogre, ō'gėr, *n.* [Fr. *ogre*, from L. *Orcus*, the god of the infernal regions, hell.] A monster of popular legends who lived on human flesh; a person likened to an ogre.—**Ogress**, ō'gres, *n.* [Fr. *ogresse*.] A female ogre.—**Ogreish**, ō'gėr-ish, *a.* Resembling or suggestive of an ogre.—**Ogreism, Ogrism**, ō'gėr-izm, *n.* The character or practices of ogres.

Ogygian, ō-gij'i-an, *a.* Pertaining to *Ogyges*, a legendary monarch in Greece; hence, of great and dark antiquity.

Oh, ō, *exclam.* O.

Ohm, Ohmad, ōm, ōm'ad, *n.* [From *Ohm*, the propounder of the law known by his name.] The practical unit of electrical resistance, equal to 10^9 absolute electromagnetic units of resistance. The international ohm adopted in 1893 is the resistance of a column of mercury at 0° C., of 14·4521 gm. mass, of uniform cross-section, and of 106·3 cm. height.—*Ohm's Law*, an important law referring to the causes that tend to impede the action of a voltaic battery.

Oidium, ō-id'i-um, *n.* [A dim. form of Gr. *ōon*, egg.] A microscopic fungus growing upon and very destructive to vines; the disease thus caused.

Oil, oil, *n.* [O.Fr. *oile*, *oille*, from L. *oleum*, oil; akin *olive*.] A substance of animal and vegetable origin, liquid at ordinary temperatures, insoluble in water, and burning with a more or less luminous flame; a substance of somewhat similar character of mineral origin (as petroleum). Oils are divided into *fixed* and *volatile* or *essential oils*, the latter being diffusible in vapour by heat.—*v.t.* To smear or rub over with oil.—*Oiled silk*, silk prepared with oil, &c., so as to be impervious to moisture and air.—*Oiled paper*, paper besmeared with oil so as to render it transparent, used for tracing designs.—**Oily**, oi'li, *a.* Consisting of or containing oil; resembling oil; fat; greasy; *fig.* unctuous; sanctimonious; hypocritically pious.—**Oiliness**, oi'li-ness, *n.* The quality of being oily; unctuousness.—**Oil-bag**, *n.* A bag, cyst, or gland in animals containing oil.—**Oil-cake**, *n.* A cake or mass of compressed linseed, rape, or other seed from which oil has been extracted, linseed-cake being much used as food for cattle.—**Oil-cloth**, *n.* Painted canvas for floor-covering, &c.; floor-cloth.—**Oil-colour**, *n.* A pigment made by grinding a colouring substance in oil.—**Oiler**, oil'ėr, *n.* One who oils.—**Oilery**, oil'ėr-i, *n.* The commodities of an oilman.—**Oil-gas**, *n.* An inflammable gas obtained from oils.—**Oil-mill**, *n.* A mill for expressing vegetable oils.—**Oil-nut**, *n.* A name given to various nuts and seeds yielding oil, and to plants producing them, such as the butter-nut.—**Oil-painting**, *n.* The art of painting with oil-colours, the highest branch of the painter's art; a picture painted in oil-colours.—**Oil-palm**, *n.* A West African palm whose fruit yields palm-oil.—**Oil-press**, *n.* A mill or machine for squeezing out oil from seeds or pulp.—**Oil-skin**, *n.* Waterproof cloth; prepared linen for making garments to keep out the rain.—**Oil-spring**, *n.* A spring which yields mineral oils, as petroleum.—**Oil-stone**, *n.* A fine-grained stone on which tools receive a fine edge by the aid of oil.—**Oil-well**, *n.* A well sunk into an oil-bearing mineral bed.

Ointment, oint'ment, *n.* [From Fr. *oindre*, pp. *oint*, to anoint, from L. *ungere*. UNCTION.] Any soft unctuous substance used for smearing, particularly the body or a diseased part; an unguent.

Okapi, ō-kä'pi, *n.* An African animal akin to the giraffe, but smaller and striped.

Oke, ōk, *n.* An Egyptian and Turkish weight equal to about 2¾ lb.

Okra, ō'kra, *n.* A plant of the mallow family (genus *Abelmoschus*) cultivated as a vegetable in tropical countries.

Old, ōld, *a.* [A.Sax. *ald*, *eald*; D. *oud*, G. *alt*, Goth. *altheis*, old; Icel. *aldinn*, old, *aldr*, age; cog. with L. *alo*, to nourish, *altus*, lofty (whence *altitude*), ad-*ultus*, adult.] Advanced far in years or life (an *old* man or tree); not new or fresh; long made or produced (*old* clothes, wine); not modern; ancient; of any duration whatever (a year *old*); former (*old* habits); long practised; experienced (*old* offender); having the feelings of an old person; crafty or cunning (*colloq.*); a familiar term of affection or cordiality.—*Of old*, long ago; from ancient time.—*Old age*, the portion of a person's life during which he can be called old; advanced years.—*Old bachelor*, an unmarried man somewhat advanced in years.—*Old Catholics*, the party in the Church of Rome who refuse to accept the decree of the Vatican Council of 1870, settling the infallibility of the pope.—*The old country*, a name given by foreign-born residents in the Americas to the country of their origin.—*Old Glory*, the United States flag (*colloq.*).—*Old gold*, a brownish-yellow color.—*Old Guard*, Napoleon's original bodyguard (1804).—*Old maid*, an unmarried woman no longer young.—*Old Nick*, the devil. NICK.—*Old rose*, *n.* A slightly grayed tint of red-purple.—*Old school*, persons having the character, manner, or opinions of a bygone age.—*Old style*. STYLE.—*Old Testament*. TESTAMENT.—*Old One*, *Old Harry*, the Devil.—*Old World*, the eastern hemisphere, or Europe, Asia, and Africa. ∴Syn. under ANCIENT.—**Oldclothesman**, *n.* A man who purchases cast-off garments.—**Olden**, ōl'dn, *a.* Old; ancient.—*v.i.* To grow old; to age; to become affected by age.—*v.t.* To age; to cause to appear old.—**Old-fashioned**, *a.* Formed according to obsolete fashion or custom; characterized by antiquated fashions or customs; aping old people.—**Oldness**, ōld'nes, *n.* The state of being old; old age; antiquity.—**Old-world**, *a.* Belonging to a far bygone age or to the eastern hemisphere; antiquated.

Oleaginous, ō-lē-aj'i-nus, *a.* [L. *oleaginus*, from *oleum*, oil. OIL.] Having the qualities of oil; unctuous; *fig.* (applied to persons, manners, &c.) smoothly sanctimonious; unwholesomely fawning.—**Oleaginousness**, ō-lē-aj'i-nus-nes, *n.* Oiliness.

Oleander, ō-lē-an'dėr, *n.* [Fr. *oléandre*, from L.L. *arodandrum*, by corruption for *rhododendron*.] A beautiful evergreen flowering shrub.

Oleaster, ō-lē-as'tėr, *n.* [L., from *olea*, the olive tree.] The so-called wild olive, a plant resembling the olive.

Olecranon, ō-lek'ra-non, *n.* [Gr. *ōlekranon*.] A process of the ulna, one of the bones of the forearm, forming part of the elbow-joint.

Olefiant, ō-lē'fi-ant, *a.* [L. *oleum*, oil, and *facio*, to make.] Forming or producing oil.—*Olefiant gas*, a gas obtained from a mixture of sulphuric acid and alcohol forming with chlorine an oily compound.—**Olefines**, ō'le-fins, *n.* Hydrocarbons of the ethylene (olefiant gas) series.—**Oleic**, ō-lē'ik, *a.* Pertaining to or derived from oil.—**Oleiferous**, ō-lē-if'ėr-us, *a.* Producing oil.—**Oleine**, *n.* ELAINE.—**Olein**, ōl'ē-in, *n.* [L. *oleum*, oil.] One of the chief constituents of animal fat.—**Oleograph**, ō'lē-ō-graf, *n.* A picture produced in oils by a process analogous to that of lithographic printing.

Oleomargarine, ō'lē-ō-mar"ja-rēn, *n.* [L. *oleum*, and E. *margarin*.] Margarine; a substitute for butter made from animal fat boiled and churned with fresh milk.—**Oleometer**, ō-lē-om'et-ėr, *n.* An instrument to find the weight and purity of oil.

Oleraceous, ol-ėr-ā'shus, *a.* [L. *oleraceus*, from *olus*, *oleris*, pot-herbs.] Applied to vegetables fit for kitchen use; having the nature of a pot-herb.

Olfactory, ol-fak'to-ri, *a.* [L. *olfacio*, *olfactum*, to smell, *oleo*, to smell, and *facio*, to make. ODOUR.] Pertaining to smelling; connected with the sense of smelling.—*n.* An organ of smelling.

Olibanum, o-lib'a-num, *n.* [L.L. *olibanum*, from L. *oleum*, oil, and *libanus*, frankincense.] A kind of incense; frankincense.

Oligæmia, ol-i-gē'mi-a, *n.* [Gr. *oligos*, little, *haima*, blood.] Deficiency of blood in the human system.

Oligarchy, ol'i-gär-ki, *n.* [Gr. *oligarchia*—*oligos*, few, and *archē*, rule.] A form of government in which the supreme power is placed in the hands of a small exclusive class; those who form such a class or body.—**Oligarch**, ol'i-gärk, *n.* A member of an oligarchy.—**Oligarchic**, **Oligarchical**, ol-i-gär'kik, ol-i-gär'ki-kal, *a.* Pertaining to oligarchy.

Oligist, ol'i-jist, *n.* [Fr. *oligiste*, from Gr. *oligistos*, least, from being poor in metal.] A variety of iron ore.

Oligocene, o-li'gō-sēn, *a.* [Gr. *oligos*, little, and *kainos*, recent.] *Geol.* slightly recent; somewhat more recent than *eocene*.

Oligoclase, o-li'gō-klās, *n.* [Gr. *oligos*, small, and *klasis*, a fracture.] A kind of felspar, occurring in granite, porphyry, and other metamorphic and volcanic rocks.

Olio, ō'li-o, *n.* [From Sp. *olla* (pron. *olya*), a dish of meat, from L. *olla*, a pot.] A dish of stewed meat; a mixture; a medley; a miscellany or collection of various compositions.

Olitory, ol'i-to-ri, *a.* [L. *olitorius*, from *olus*, pot-herbs.] Belonging to a kitchen-garden.

Olive, ol'iv, *n.* [Fr. *olive*, L. *oliva*, an olive, akin to Gr. *elaia*, an olive; same root as *oleum*, oil.] An evergreen tree much cultivated in Southern Europe, &c., for the valuable oil contained in its berries, formerly sacred to Minerva, furnishing wreaths used by the Greeks and Romans to crown the brows of victors, and still universally regarded as an emblem of peace; the berry or drupe of the olive; the colour of the olive, a brownish-green colour or one composed of violet and green mixed in nearly equal proportions.—*a.* Relating to the olive; of the colour of the olive; brown, tending to a yellowish-green.—**Olivaceous**, ol-i-vā'shus, *a.* Of the colour of the olive; having the qualities of olives.—**Olivary**, ol'i-va-ri, *a.* Resembling an olive.—**Olive-branch**, *n.* A branch of the olive tree: the emblem of peace; *fig.* a child.—**Olive-green**, *n.* A colour resembling that of the olive.—**Olivenite**, ol'iven-īt, *n.* A mineral of an olive-green colour, containing copper and arsenic. Called also *Olive-ore*.—**Olive-oil**, *n.* An oil obtained from the fruit of the olive, and much used in cookery and for medicinal and manufacturing purposes.—**Olive-yard**, *n.* A piece of ground in which olives are cultivated.—**Olivine**, ol'iv-in, *n.* An olive-green variety of chrysolite.

Olla, ol'la, *n.* [Sp. *olla*, a jar or pot, L. *olla*.] A jar or urn.—*Olla podrida*, po-drē'da. [Sp., lit. rotten or putrid pot], a favourite dish in Spain, consisting of a mixture of various kinds of meat stewed with vegetables; hence, a mixture or miscellaneous collection.—**Ollite**, ol'līt, *n.* *Mineral*, potstone.

Olympiad, ō-lim'pi-ad, *n.* [Gr. *olympias*, *olympiados*, from *Olympia*, where the Olympic games were held.] A period of four years reckoned from one celebration of the Olympic games to another, by which the ancient Greeks computed time, from 776 B.C.—**Olympian**, **Olympic**, ō-lim'pi-an, ō-lim'pik, *a.* Pertaining to Olympus or to Olympia in Greece.—*Olympic games*, a great national festival of the ancient Greeks, celebrated at intervals of four years on the plain of Olympia in Peloponnesus; a modern revival (Athens, Greece, 1896) in which athletes of the world meet quadrennially in various countries.

Omasum, o-mā'sum, *n.* [L.] The third stomach of ruminating animals; the many-plies.

Omber, **Ombre**, om'bėr, *n.* [Fr., from Sp. *hombre*, man, L. *homo*.] An old game at cards, usually played by three persons.

Omega, o-mē'ga, o-mā'ga, ō'me-ga, *n.* [Gr. *o*, and *mega*, great, lit. the great or long *o*.] The name of the last letter of the Greek alphabet, hence in Scripture *Omega* denotes the last, the ending.

Omelet, **Omelette**, om'e-let, *n.* [Fr. *aumelette*, *omelette*.] Beaten eggs fried, at times with cheese, chopped meat, fruit, &c.

Omen, ō'men, *n.* [L. *omen*, older *osmen*, from *os*, *oris*, the mouth, or connected with *auris*, the ear; hence *abominate*.] A casual event or occurrence thought to portend good or evil; a prognostic; an augury.—*v.i.* To prognosticate as an omen; to augur; to betoken.—*v.t.* To divine; to predict.—**Omened**, ō'mend, *a.* Containing an omen or prognostic.—**Omening**, ō'men-ing, *n.* An augury; a prognostication.—**Ominous**, om'i-nus, *a.* [L. *ominosus*.] Containing an ill omen; foreboding or betokening evil; inauspicious.—**Ominously**, om'i-nus-li, *adv.* In an ominous manner; with ill omen.—**Ominousness**, om'i-nus-nes, *n.*

Omentum, ō-men'tum, *n.* [L.] *Anat.* the caul or epiploon.—**Omental**, ō-men'tal, *a.* Relating to the omentum.

Omer, ō'mėr, *n.* [Heb.] HOMER.

Omit, ō-mit', *v.t.*—*omitted*, *omitting*. [L. *omitto*, to neglect, disregard, say nothing of—prefix *ob*, and *mitto*, to send. MISSION.] To pass over or neglect; to let slip; to fail to do or to use; to leave out; not to insert.—**Omission**, ō-mish'on, *n.* [L. *omissio*.] The act of omitting; a neglect or failure to do something that should have been done; the act of leaving out; something omitted or left out.—**Omissible**, ō-mis'i-bl, *a.* Capable of being omitted.—**Omissive**, ō-mis'iv, *a.* Leaving out; neglectful.—**Omissively**, ō-mis'iv-li, *adv.* In an omissive manner.—**Omitter**, ō-mit'ėr, *n.* One who omits.

Omnibus, om'ni-bus, *n.* [L., for all, pl. dat. from *omnis*, all.] Originally applied to a horse-drawn carriage driven on tracks, but with the advent of the automobile, the name has been shortened to 'bus'; a motor-driven, four-wheeled vehicle containing many seats for the convenience of passengers.

Omniferous, om-nif'ėr-us, *a.* [L. *omnifer*—*omnis*, all, and *fero*, to bear.] All-bearing; producing all kinds.

Omnific, om-nif'ik, *a.* [L. *omnis*, all, and *facio*, to make.] All-creating.

Omniform, om'ni-form, *a.* [L. *omnis*, all, and *forma*, form.] Having every form or shape.

Omnigenous, om-nij'en-us, *a.* [L. *omnigenus*—*omnis*, all, every, and *genus*, kind.] Consisting of all kinds.

Omniparity, om-ni-par'i-ti, *n.* [L. *omnis*, all, and *par*, equal.] General equality.

Omniparous, om-nip'a-rus, *a.* [L. *omnis*, all, and *pario*, to produce.] All-bearing, bringing forth all things.

Omnipercipient, om'ni-pėr-sip"i-ent, *a.* [L. *omnis*, all, and *percipiens*, perceiving.] Perceiving everything; all-seeing.—**Omnipercipience**, om'ni-pėr-sip"i-ens, *n.* Perception of everything.

Omnipotence, om-nip'o-tens, *n.* [L. *omnipotens*, omnipotent—*omnis*, all, and *potens*, powerful. POTENT.] Unlimited or infinite power; almighty power: an attribute of God; hence sometimes used for God (being then written with a capital).—**Omnipotency**, om-nip'o-ten-si, *n.* Omnipotence.—**Omnipotent**, om-nip'o-tent, *a.* Almighty; all-powerful.—*The Omnipotent*, the Almighty.—**Omnipotently**, om-nip'o-tent-li, *adv.* In an omnipotent manner.

Omnipresence, om-ni-prez'ens, *n.* [L. *omnis*, all, and *præsens*, present.] The faculty or power of being present in every place at the same time, an attribute peculiar to God.—**Omnipresent**, om-ni-prez'ent, *a.* Present in all places at the same time; ubiquitous.

Omniscience, **Omnisciency**, om-nish'i-ens, om-nish'i-en-si, *n.* [L. *omnis*, all, and *scientia*, knowledge. SCIENCE.] The faculty of knowing everything; knowledge unbounded or infinite: an attribute of God. —**Omniscient**, om-nish'i-ent, *a.* Having knowledge of all things; infinitely knowing. —**Omnisciently**, om-nish'i-ent-li, *adv.* In an omniscient manner.

Omnium, om'ni-um, *n.* [L., of all (things).] A term used on the Stock Exchange to express the aggregate value of the different stocks in which a loan is funded.—**Omnium-gatherum**, om'ni-um-gaTH"ėr-um, *n.* A miscellaneous collection of things or persons. (*Colloq.*)

Omnivorous, om-niv'o-rus, *a.* [L. *omnivorus*—*omnis*, all, and *voro*, to eat.] All-devouring; eating food of every kind indiscriminately (*omnivorous* animals).

Omohyoid, ō-mō-hī'oid, *a.* and *n.* [Gr. *ōmos*, the shoulder, and E. *hyoid*.] *Anat.* applied to a muscle situated at the sides and front of the neck, and attached to the hyoid bone and the shoulder.

Omoplate, ō'mō-plāt, *n.* [Gr. *omoplatē*—*ōmos*, shoulder, and *platē*, flat surface.] The shoulder-blade or scapula.

Omphalic, om-fal'ik, *a.* [Gr. *omphalos*, the navel.] Pertaining to the navel.—**Omphalocele**, om'fa-lō-sēl, *n.* [Gr. *kēlē*, tumour.] A rupture at the navel.—**Omphalode**, **Omphalodium**, om'fa-lōd, om-fa-lō'di-um, *n.* *Bot.* the central part of the hilum, through which the nutrient vessels pass. —**Omphalotomy**, om-fa-lot'o-mi, *n.* The operation of dividing the navel-string.

On, on, *prep.* [A.Sax. *on*, *an*, on, in; D. *aan*, G. *an*, Goth. *ana*, Skr. *anu*, in; akin to *in* and *under*.] Above and so as to touch; not off; performing by means of (to play *on* a harp, a violin); in addition to (loss *on* loss); at or near (*on* the coast); expressing reliance, dependence, basis, &c. (a statement founded *on* error); at or in the time of (we say *on* the day, *at* the hour, *in* the week, month, year); at the time of or during (*on* public occasions); immediately after and as a result (he retired *on* the ratification of the treaty); in reference or relation to (*on* our part); toward or so as to affect (mercy *on* him); denoting a pledge, engagement, or affirmation (*on* my word, *on* his honour); *betting*, in support of the chances of; among the staff of or contributors to: with names of periodicals; pointing to a state, condition, occupation, &c. (*on* fire, *on* duty).—*On a sudden*, suddenly.—*On fire*, in a state of burning; in a passion or eager state.—*On hand*, in present possession (goods *on hand*). —*On high*, in an elevated place.—*On the way*, *on the road*, proceeding, journeying, or making progress.—*On the wing*, in flight; flying; *fig.* departing.—*adv.* Forward, in progression (move *on*); forward, in succession (and so *on*); without interruption or ceasing (sleep *on*, say *on*); attached to the body (his clothes are not *on*). Also used elliptically as an imperative = go on, advance.—**Oncoming**, *a.* Approaching; nearing.—*n.* A coming or drawing near; approach.—**On-going**, *n.* A going on; conduct; behaviour: generally in *pl.*—**Onlooker**, on'-luk-ėr, *n.* A looker on; a spectator. —**Onrush**, on'rush, *n.* A rush or dash onwards; a rapid or violent onset.—**Onset**, on'set, *n.* A violent attack; an assault; an assault by an army or body of troops.—**Onslaught**, on'slat, *n.* [From *on*, and A. Sax. *sleaht*, a blow, from *slagan*, *sleán*, to strike (to *slay*).] An attack or onset; an assault.

Onager, on'a-jėr, *n.* [L., from Gr. *onagros* —*onos*, ass, and *agrios*, wild.] The wild ass of Central Asia.

Once, wuns, *adv.* [O.E. *ones*, *onis*, an adverbial genit. of *one*; comp. *twice* and *thrice*. NONCE.] One time; on one occasion only; at one former time; formerly; immediately after; as soon as. Used as a noun preceded by *this* or *that* (*this once*, *that once*).—*At once*, at the same time; all together; suddenly; precipitately; not gradually; immediately; forthwith; without delay.—*Once and again*, repeatedly.—*Once in a way*, corrupted from *once and away*, on one particular occasion; on rare occasions.

Oncotomy, ong-kot'o-mi, *n.* [Gr. *ongkos*, a tumour, and *tomē*, a cutting.] *Surg.* the opening of an abscess, or the excision of a tumour.

One, wun, *a.* [O.E. *oon*, A.Sax. *án* = D., L.G., and Dan. *een*, Sw. *en*, Icel. *einn*, G. *ein*, Goth. *ains*; cog. L. *unus*, W. *un*, Gael. *aon*, *an*, Armor. *unan*—one. The indefinite article *an*, *a* is the same word; *once* and *only* are derivatives, and *atone* = *at one*.] Being but a single thing or a unit; not two or more; indicating a contrast or opposition to some other thing; closely united; forming a whole; undivided; single in kind. *One* occurs in many compound words of obvious meaning, as *one*-armed, *one*-handed, *one*-masted, &c.—*One day*, on a certain or particular day; at an indefinite time, either past or future.—*All one*, just the same; of no consequence; no matter.—*n.* The first of the simple units; the symbol representing this (= 1); a particular individual, whether thing or person (in this sense with a plural). —*At one*, in union; in concord or agreement. —*pron.* Any single person; any man, any person (*one* may speak *one's* mind).—*One another*, one or each the other. —**One-horse**, *n.* Drawn by a single horse.—**Oneness**, wun'nes, *n.* The state of being one; singleness; unity. —**Oneself**, wun-self', *pron.* One's self; himself or herself.—**One-sided**, *a.* Related to, or having but one side; partial; unjust; unfair. —**One-sidedly**, *adv.* In a one-sided manner.—**One-sidedness**, *n.* State of being one-sided; partiality.

Oneirocritic, o-nī'rō-krit"ik, *n.* [Gr. *oneiron*, a dream, *kritikos*, discerning.] An interpreter of dreams. —**Oneirocritic**, **Oneirocritical**, o-nī'rō-krit"i-kal, *a.* Having the power of interpreting dreams. —**Oneirologist**, o-nī-rol'o-jist, *n.* One versed in oneirology.—**Oneirology**, o-nī-rol'o-ji, *n.* The doctrine or theory of dreams.—**Oneiromancy**, o-nī'rō-man-si, *n.* [Gr. *manteia*, divination.] Divination by dreams.—**Oneiroscopist**, o-nī-ros'ko-pist, *n.* An interpreter of dreams.—**Oneiroscopy**, o-nī-ros'ko-pi, *n.* The art of interpreting dreams.

Onerary, on'ėr-a-ri, *a.* [L. *onerarius*, from *onus*, *oneris*, a load (seen also in *exonerate*).] Fitted or intended for the carriage of burdens; comprising a burden.—**Onerate**,† on'ėr-āt, *v.t.* To load; to burden.—**Oneration**,† on-ėr-ā'shon, *n.* The act of loading. —**Onerous**, on'ėr-us, *a.* [L. *onerosus*.] Burdensome; troublesome in the performance; oppressive.

Onicolo, ō-nik'o-lō, *n.* [It. dim. of *onice*. ONYX.] A variety of onyx used for cameos.

Onion, un'yun, *n.* [Fr. *oignon*, *ognon*, from L. *unio*, *unionis*, unity, an onion with one bulb, from *unus*, one. UNITY.] A biennial cultivated plant of the lily family, and particularly its bulbous root, much used as an article of food.

Onirocritic, &c. ONEIROCRITIC, &c.

Oniscus, o-nis'kus, *n.* [Gr. *oniskos*, lit. a little ass.] The wood-louse or slater.

Onlooker. Under ON.

Only, ōn'li, *a.* [*One*, with its old pronunciation, and term. *-ly*; A.Sax. *ánlic*.] Single; alone in its class; solitary.—*adv.* For one purpose alone; simply; merely; barely; solely; singly. —*Only not*, all but; very nearly; almost.—*conj.* But; excepting that.

Onomancy, on'o-man-si, *n.* [Gr. *onoma*, a name, *manteia*, divination.] Divination by the letters of a name.—**Onomantic**, **Onomantical**, on-o-man'tik, on-o-man'ti-kal, *a.* Pertaining to onomancy.

Onomasticon, on-o-mas'ti-kon, *n.* Gr. *onomastikon*, from *onoma*, a name.] A work containing words or names with their explanation; a sort of dictionary or vocabulary.

Onomatology, on'o-ma-tol"o-ji, *n.* [Gr. *onoma*, *onomatos*, a name, *logos*, a discourse.] The doctrine of names; the rules to be observed in forming names or terms.—**Onomatologist**, on'o-ma-tol"o-jist, *n.* One versed in onomatology.

Onomatopœia, **Onomatopeia**, on'o-ma-tō-pē"a, *n.* [Gr. *onomatopoiia*—*onoma*, *onomatos*, a name, and *poieō*, to make.] The formation of words by imitation of sounds; the expressing by sound of the thing signified; thus *buzz*, *hum*, *pewit*, *whip-poor-will*, &c., are produced by *onomatopœia*.—**Onomatope**, o-nom'a-tōp, *n.* A word formed to resemble the sound made by the thing signified.—**Onomatopoetic**, **Onomatopœous**, on'o-ma-tō-pō-et"ik, on'-o-mat-ō-pē"us, *a.* Pertaining to or formed by onomatopœia.

Onset, **Onslaught**. Under ON.

Ontogenesis, **Ontogeny**, on-to-jen'e-sis, on-toj'e-ni, *n.* [Gr. *on*, *ontos*, being, and *genesis*—root *gen*, to produce.] *Biol.* the history of the individual development of an organized being.—**Ontogenetic**, on'to-je-net"ik, *a.* Pertaining to ontogenesis. —**Ontogenetically**, on'to-je-net"i-kal-li, *adv.* By way of ontogenesis.

Ontology, on-tol'o-ji, *n.* [Gr. *on*, *ontos*, being, and *logos*, discourse.] The doctrine of being; that part of metaphysics which investigates and explains the nature of all things or existences, treating of whatever does or can exist: sometimes equivalent to *metaphysics*.—**Ontologic**, **Ontological**, on-to-loj'ik, on-to-loj'i-kal, *a.* Pertaining to ontology, or the science of being.—**Ontologically**, on-to-loj'i-kal-li, *adv.* In the manner of ontology. —**Ontologist**, on-tol'o-jist, *n.* One versed in ontology.

Onus, ō'nus, *n.* [L.] A burden: often used for *onus probandi*, the burden of proof; the burden of proving what has been alleged.

Onward, on'wėrd, *adv.* [*On* and *ward*, denoting direction, similar to *toward*; A.Sax. *onweard*.] Toward the point before or in front; forward; on; in advance.—*a.* Advanced or advancing (an *onward* course); carried so far towards an end; forward; advanced.—**Onwards**, on'wėrdz, *adv.* Same as *Onward*.

Onycha, on'i-ka, *n.* [From Gr. *onyx*, the nail, onyx.] The shell of a species of Oriental mussel used in the composition of perfume. [O.T.]

Onyx, on'iks, *n.* [Gr. *onyx*, the nail: the colour of the gem resembles that of the nail.] A semi-pellucid gem with variously-coloured zones or veins; an agate with layers of chalcedony, one of which is flesh-coloured: used for cameos.

Oocyst, ō'o-sist, *n.* [Gr. *ōon*, an egg, and *kystis*, a bladder.] The chamber in certain of the polyzoa which holds the eggs; an ovicell.

Oocyte, ō'o-sīt, *n.* [Gr. *ōon*, an egg, *kytos*, a cell.] Ovarian egg, the grandmother-cell of an egg-cell or ovum.

Oof, ōf, *n.* Money. Yiddish (which see) term, from the German 'ready money', *auf dem tische*, on the table.—*Oof-bird*, a rich man.

Oogonium, ō'o-gōn"i-um, *n.* [Gr. *ōon*, an egg, *gonos*, offspring.] In lower plants, the female organ, producing one or more egg-cells.

Ooid, **Ooidal**, ō-oid', ō-oi'dal, *n.* [Gr. *ōon*, an egg, and *eidos*, a form, shape, appearance.] Egg-shaped; having albumen.

Oolite, ō'ol-īt, *n.* [Gr. *ōon*, an egg, and *lithos*, stone, from its resemblance to the roes of fish.] *Geol.* a species of limestone composed of globules clustered together, commonly without any visible cement or base; the oolitic formation or system.—**Oolitic**, ō-o-lit'ik, *a.* Pertaining to oolite; composed of oolite; resembling oolite.—*Oolitic system*, a series of strata comprehending limestones, calcareous sandstones, marls, shales, and clays which underlie the chalk formation and rest on the trias; the Jurassic system. —**Oolitiferous**, ō'o-li-tif"ėr-us, *a.* Producing oolite.

Oology, ō-ol'o-ji, *n.* [Gr. *ōon*, an egg, and *logos*, a treatise.] The branch of knowledge that deals with birds' eggs. —**Oologist**, ō-ol'o-jist, *n.* One versed in oology.

Oophyte, ō'o-fīt, *n.* [Gr. *ōon*, an egg, *phyton*, a plant.] *Bot.* the GAMETOPHYTE (which see).

Oosperm, ō'o-sperm, *n.* [Gr. *ōon*, an egg, *sperma*, seed.] A fertilized ovum.

Oospore, ō'o-spōr, *n.* [Gr. *ōon*, an egg, and E. *spore.*] *Bot.* a spore that receives impregnation before germination.

Ootheca, ō-o-thē'ka, *n.* [Gr. *ōon*, an egg, and *thēca*, a case.] An egg-case, as that for the eggs of some insects.

Ootrum, ō'trum, *n.* [Indian name.] A strong, white, silky fibre, obtained from the stem of an Indian plant.

Ooze, öz, *v.i.—oozed, oozing.* [A.Sax. *wós*, juice, liquor, *wáse*, mire, mud; Icel. *vás*, wetness; same root as *water.*] To percolate, as a liquid, through the pores of a substance, or through small openings; to flow in small quantities from the pores of a body: often used figuratively (the secret *oozed* out).—*v.t.* To emit in the shape of moisture.—*n.* Soft mud or slime, as at the bottom of any sheet of water; *tanning*, a solution of tannin; the liquor of a tan-vat.—**Oozy**, ö'zi, *a.* Containing or resembling ooze; miry.

Opacity. Under OPAQUE.

Opah, ō'pa, *n.* A large and beautiful sea-fish of the Eastern Seas.

Opal, ō'pal, *n.* [L. *opalus*, Gr. *opallios*, an opal; comp. Skr. *upala*, a precious stone.] A precious stone of various colours and varieties, the finest characterized by its iridescent reflection of light, and formerly believed to possess magical virtues. —**Opalesce**, ō-pal-es', *v.i.—opalesced, opalescing.* To give forth a play of colours like the opal.—**Opalescence**, ō-pal-es'ens, *n.* A play of colours like that of the opal; the reflection of a milky and iridescent light.—**Opalescent**, ō-pal-es'ent, *a.* Resembling opal; having the iridescent tints of opal.—**Opaline**, ō'pal-īn, *a.* Pertaining to or like opal. — *n.* A semi-translucent glass, whitened by the addition of special ingredients.—**Opalize**, ō'pal-īz, *v.t.—opalized, opalizing.* To make or resemble opal. —**Opal-jasper**, *n.* A kind of opal containing a large amount of iron-oxide.

Opaque, o-pāk', *a.* [Fr. *opaque*, from L. *opacus*, shady, dark, obscure.] Impervious to the rays of light; not transparent.—*n.* Opacity (*Young*). — **Opaquely**, o-pāk'li, *adv.* In an opaque manner.—**Opaqueness**, o-pāk'nes, *n.* The quality of being opaque.—**Opacity**, o-pas'i-ti, *n.* [L. *opacitas.*] State or quality of being opaque; want of transparency.—**Opacous**, o-pā'kus, *a.* Opaque.

Ope, ōp, *v.t.* and *i.—oped, oping.* To open: used only in poetry.

Opeidoscope, o-pī'do-skōp, *n.* [Gr. *ops*, voice, *eidos*, form, *skopeō*, to see.] An instrument for rendering visible vibratory movements caused by sound. It consists of a small mirror attached to a membrane and reflecting rays of light on a screen.

Open, ō'pn, *a.* [A.Sax. *open*, open=D. *open*, Icel. *opinn*, Dan. *daben*, G. *offen*, open; akin to *up.*] Not shut; not closed; not covered; not stopped (as a bottle); unsealed (as a letter); free to be used or enjoyed; not restricted; affording free ingress; accessible; public; spread; expanded; not drawn together or contracted (an *open* hand; *open* arms); hence, free, liberal, bounteous; free from dissimulation; candid; not secret or concealed; clear; unobstructed (an *open view*; an *open* country); not frosty; free from frost and snow (an *open* winter); exposed to view; laid bare; exposed or liable to be assailed; fully prepared; attentive; not yet decided (an *open* question); not settled, balanced, or closed (an *open* account); enunciated without closing the mouth, or with a full utterance (an *open* vowel); *mus.* produced without stopping by the finger or without using a slide, key, piston, &c.—*Open verdict*, a verdict upon an inquest finding that a crime has been committed, but without specifying the criminal; or which finds that a sudden or violent death has occurred, but does not decide on the cause.—*n.* An open or clear space.—*The open*, the open country; a place or space clear of obstructions. — *v.t.* [A.Sax. *openian.*] To make open; to unclose; to remove any fastening or obstruction from, so as to afford an entrance, passage, or view of the inner parts; to spread; to expand (the fingers, the arms); to enter upon; to commence (to *open* a negotiation or correspondence); to declare open; to set in operation with some ceremony; to reveal; to disclose (to *open* one's mind).—*To open fire*, to begin to fire or discharge firearms.—*v.i.* To unclose itself; to be unclosed; to be parted; to begin to be seen from a distance; to commence; to begin; to begin to fire (as a battery).—**Open Door Policy**, *n.* A general agreement between certain nations made in 1899 which guaranteed to them free access and commercial advantages in China.—**Open-eyed**, *a.* Having the eyes open; hence, watchful; vigilant. — **Open-handed**, *a.* Generous; liberal; munificent. — **Open-hearted**, *a.* Candid; frank; sincere; not sly.—**Open-heartedly**, *adv.* In an open-hearted manner.—**Opening**, ōp'ning, *a.* First in order; commencing (an *opening* speech).—*n.* The act of one who or that which opens; an open place; a break or breach in something; a hole or perforation; an aperture; beginning; commencement; a vacancy; an opportunity of commencing a business or profession; a thinly wooded space without underwood, as in a forest.—**Openly**, ō'pn-li, *adv.* In an open manner; publicly; candidly; frankly.—**Open-mouthed**, *a.* Having the mouth open; gaping, as with astonishment.—**Open Shop**, *n.* An establishment where union and non-union workers are employed without discrimination.—**Open-work**, *n.* Ornamental work, with openings through its substance.

Opera, op'e-ra, *n.* [It. *opera*, work, composition as opposed to improvisation, from L. *opera*, work; akin to *opus.* OPERATE.] A musical drama; a dramatic composition set to music and sung and acted on the stage, accompanied with musical instruments; the score or words of a musical drama. — **Opera-bouffe**, op'e-ra-bụf, *n.* pl. **Operas-bouffes** (same pron.). An exaggerated or farcical form of comic opera. —**Opera-cloak**, *n.* A cloak, generally of showy colours, worn by ladies at the opera, or other evening meeting.—**Opera-glass**, *n.* A small binocular telescope of low magnifying power, used in theatres, &c.; a lorgnette.—**Opera-house**, *n.* A theatre for the performance of operas.—**Opera-singer**, *n.* A professional who sings in operas.—**Operatic**, **Operatical**, op-e-rat'ik, op-e-rat'i-kal, *a.* Pertaining to the opera.

Operameter, op-e-ram'et-ėr, *n.* [L. *opera*, work, and Gr. *metron*, measure.] An apparatus attached to a machine to indicate the revolutions of a shaft, the strokes of a piston, &c.

Operate, op'e-rāt, *v.i.—operated, operating.* [L. *operor*, *operatum*, to work, from *opus*, *operis*, a work.] To exert power or strength, physical or mechanical; to work; to act; to have agency; to produce an effect; to issue in a designed result; *med.* to take appropriate effect on the human system; *surg.* to perform some manual act in a methodical manner upon a human body. —*v.t.* To effect; to accomplish; to put into operation; to work; to drive (a machine).—**Operant**, op'e-rant, *a.* Having power to produce an effect: operative.—*n.* One who operates; an operator.—**Operation**, op-e-rā'shon, *n.* [L. *operatio*,] The act or process of operating; a working or proceeding; process; manipulation; the carrying out of preconcerted measures by regular movements (military or naval *operations*); a surgical proceeding to which the human body is subjected for curative ends.—**Operative**, op'e-rā-tiv, *a.* Operating; exerting force; active in the production of effects; efficacious; producing the effect; having to do with manual or other operations.—*n.* A skilled workman; an artisan. — **Operatively**, op'e-rā-tiv-li, *adv.* In an operative manner.—**Operator**, op'e-rā-tėr, *n.* One who operates; *surg.* the person who performs an operation upon the human body.

Operculum, ō-pėr'kū-lum, *n.* [L., from *operio*, to close or shut.] A little lid or cover; the cover or lid of the spore-cases of mosses; the lid of a pitcher-form leaf; a horny or shelly plate serving to close the aperture of the shell of many molluscs when the animal is retracted within it; the bony apparatus which protects the gills of fishes.—**Opercular**, **Operculated**, **Operculate**, ō-pėr'kū-lėr, ō-pėr'kū-lā-ted, ō-pėr'kū-lāt, *a.* Pertaining to or having an operculum.—**Operculiform**, ō-pėr'kū-li-form, *a.* Having the form of a lid or cover.

Operetta, op-e-ret'ta, *n.* [It. dim. of *opera.*] A short musical drama of a light character.

Operose, op'e-rōs, *a.* [L. *operosus*, from *opera*, work. OPERA.] Laborious; attended with labour; tedious.—**Operosely**, op'e-rōs-li, *adv.* In an operose manner.—**Operoseness**, **Operosity**, op'e-rōs-nes, op-e-ros'i-ti, *n.* Labouriousness.

Ophicleide, of'i-klīd, *n.* [From Gr. *ophis*, a serpent, and *kleis*, a key; lit. key-serpent, being made to supersede the old serpent.] *Music*, a large and powerful brass wind-instrument having a compass of three octaves.

Ophidian, o-fid'i-an, *a.* [Gr. *ophis*, a serpent.] Pertaining to serpents; having the characters of the serpents; serpentine. —*n.* One of an order of reptiles which comprises all the snakes or serpents.—**Ophidious**, o-fid'i-us, *a.* Snake-like.

Ophiolatry, of-i-ol'a-tri, *n.* [Gr. *ophis*, *ophios*, a serpent, and *latreia*, worship.] Serpent-worship.—**Ophiolite**, of'i-o-līt, *n.* A variety of serpentine; ophite.—**Ophiologic**, **Ophiological**, of'i-o-loj"ik, of'i-o-loj"i-kal, *a.* Pertaining to ophiology. —**Ophiologist**, of-i-ol'o-jist, *n.* One versed in ophiology.—**Ophiology**, of-i-ol'o-ji, *n.* That branch of zoology which treats of serpents; the natural history of serpents.—**Ophiomorphous**, of'i-o-mor"fus, *a.* [Gr. *morphē*, form.] Having the form of a serpent. — **Ophiophagous**, of-i-of'a-gus, *a.* [Gr. *phagō*, to eat.] Eating or feeding on serpents.

Ophite, of'īt, *n.* [Gr. *ophis*, a serpent.] Green porphyry or serpentine, a metamorphic rock; also a name for certain Gnostics of the second century, who held that the serpent by which Eve was tempted was Christ, and hence regarded the serpent as sacred.

Ophiuchus, of-i-ū'kus, *n.* [Gr. *ophiouchos* —*ophis*, a serpent, and *echō*, to have.] The serpent-bearer; one of the northern constellations.

Ophiure, **Ophiuran**, of'i-ūr, of-i-ū'ran, *n.* [Gr. *ophis*, serpent, *oura*, a tail.] A name for star-fishes with a central disc very distinct from the surrounding arms.

Ophthalmia, of-thal'mi-a, *n.* [Gr., from *ophthalmos*, the eye, from root *op*, to see, as in *optic.*] Inflammation of the eye or its appendages.—**Ophthalmic**, of-thal'mik, *a.* Pertaining to the eye.—**Ophthalmitis**, of-thal-mī'tis, *n.* Inflammation of the eye.—**Ophthalmodynia**, of-thal'mō-din"i-a, *n.* [Gr. *odynē*, pain.] Pain, especially rheumatic pain, of the eye.—**Ophthalmology**, of-thal-mol'o-ji, *n.* That branch of science which deals with the eye.—**Ophthalmologist**, of-thal-mol'o-jist, *n.* A person versed in ophthalmology. — **Ophthalmoplegia**, of-thal'mō-plē"-ji-a, *n.* [Gr. *plēgē*, a stroke.] Paralysis of one or more of the muscles of the eye.—**Ophthalmoscope**, of-thal'mō-skōp, *n.* An instrument for viewing the interior of the eye by means of a mirror.—**Ophthalmoscopy**, of-thal-mos'ko-pi, *n.* The art of using the ophthalmoscope.—**Ophthalmotomy**, of-thal-mot'o-mi, *n.* [Gr. *tomē*, a cutting.] The art or practice of cutting into the eye, as in surgical operations.

Opiate, ō'pi-āt, *n.* [From *opium.*] Any medicine that contains opium and has the quality of inducing sleep or repose; a narcotic; anything that dulls sensation, mental or physical.—*a.* Inducing sleep; soporific; narcotic.—**Opiated**, ō'pi-ā-ted, *a.* Mixed with opium; affected by opium.

Opine, ō-pīn', *v.i.* and *t.—opined, opining.* [Fr. *opiner*, from L. *opinor*, to think. OPINION.] To think; to suppose; to be of opinion.—**Opinable**, o-pī'na-bl, *a.*

Capable of being opined or thought.—**Opiner**, ō-pī′nėr, *n.* One who opines.

Opiniative, o-pin′ya-tiv, *a.* OPINIONATIVE.

Opinion, o-pin′yun, *n.* [L. *opinio, opinionis*, from *opinor*, to think; same root as *opto*, to wish, *optimus*, best. OPTATIVE.] A judgment or belief formed without certain evidence; belief stronger than impression, less strong than positive knowledge; judgment or sentiments on persons or things as regards their character or qualities; settled judgment or persuasion; belief (religious *opinions*).—**Opinionable**, o-pin′yun-a-bl, *a.* Capable of being made matter of opinion; not to be settled dogmatically.—**Opinionate, Opinionated**, o-pin′yun-āt, o-pin′yun-ā-ted, *a.* Obstinate in opinion; opinionative; conceited.—**Opinionately**, o-pin′yun-āt-li, *adv.*—**Opinionative**, o-pin′yun-ā-tiv, *a.* Unduly attached to one's own opinions; dogmatic; obstinate in beliefs.—**Opinionatively**, o-pin′yun-ā-tiv-li, *adv.* In an opinionative manner.—**Opinionativeness**, o-pin′yun-ā-tiv-nes, *n.*—**Opinioned**, o-pin′yund, *a.* Attached to particular opinions; conceited.—**Opinionist**, o-pin′yun-ist, *n.* One unduly attached to his own opinions.

Opisthobranchiate, o-pis′thō-brang″ki-āt, *a.* [Gr. *opisthen*, behind, and *branchia*, gills.] Of or pertaining to those gasteropodous molluscs in which the gills are placed posterior to the heart.

Opisthocœlous, Opisthocœlian, o-pis′tho-sē″lus, o-pis′tho-sē″li-an, *a.* [Gr. *opisthen*, behind, and *koilos*, hollow.] A term applied to vertebræ the bodies of which are hollow or concave behind, as in some extinct crocodiles.

Opisthographic, ō-pis′thō-graf″ik, *a.* [Gr. *opisthen*, and *graphō*, to write.] Having writing on the back as well as on the front.

Opium, ō′pium, *n.* [L. *opium*, Gr. *opion*, from *opos*, vegetable juice.] A drug derived from dried juice of the unripe seed pod of the poppy; a narcotic or medicinal sedative.—**Opiate**, ō′pi-āt, *n.* Any drug derived from or containing opium; anything soothing or calming.—**Opium den**, *n.* A resort for opium smokers.

Opodeldoc, op-ō-del′dok, *n.* [Probably an arbitrary name coined by Paracelsus.] A saponaceous camphorated liniment; a solution of soap in alcohol, with the addition of camphor and essential oils.

Opopanax, o-pop′a-naks, *n.* [Gr., from *opos*, juice, and *panax*, a plant (lit. all-heal).] The inspissated juice of an umbelliferous plant, a native of Mediterranean Europe, used as an antispasmodic; also the name of a perfume.

Opossum, ō-pos′um, *n.* [From *opassom*, its native American name.] The name of several marsupial mammals of America.

Oppidan, op′i-dan, *n.* [L. *oppidanus*, from *oppidum*, a city or town.] An inhabitant of a town‡; at Eton College a student not on the foundation, and who lives in a boarding-house.

Opponent, op-pō′nent, *a.* [L. *opponens, opponentis*, ppr. of *oppono*, to oppose—*ob*, against, and *pono*, to place. POSITION.] Opposing; antagonistic; opposite.—*n.* One that opposes; an adversary; an antagonist; one that supports the opposite side in controversy, disputation, or argument.

Opportune, op-or-tūn′, *a.* [Fr. *opportun*, from L. *opportunus*, lit. offering a port or harbour—prefix *op*, for *ob*, and *portus*, a port, harbour, haven. PORT.] Seasonable; timely; well timed; convenient.—**Opportunely**, op-or-tūn′li, *adv.* In an opportune manner.—**Opportuneness**, op-or-tūn′nes, *n.* Quality of being opportune or seasonable.—**Opportunism**, op-or-tūn′izm, *n.* The practice of seizing or turning opportunities to advantage; a political attitude dispensing with a fixed and moral programme, but merely waiting for something to turn up to be utilized for immediate service.—**Opportunity**, op-or-tū′ni-ti, *n.* [L. *opportunitas.*] Fit or convenient time or occasion; a time favourable for the purpose; a suitable time, combined with other favourable circumstances.

Oppose, op-pōz′, *v.t.*—*opposed, opposing.* [Fr. *opposer*—prefix *op*, and *poser*, to place. POSE, COMPOSE.] To place in front; to set opposite; to place as an obstacle; to put with a view to hinder, defeat, destroy, or prevent effect; to act against; to resist, either by physical or other means; to act as an opponent to; to confront; to check; to withstand; to resist effectually.—*v.i.* To make objections; to act obstructively.—**Opposability**, op-pō′za-bil″i-ti, *n.* The capability of being placed so as to act in opposition.—**Opposable**, op-pō′za-bl, *a.* Capable of being opposed or resisted; capable of being opposed to something else.—**Opposed**, op-pōzd′, *p.* and *a.* Placed over against; opposite; antagonistic; hostile; being against or adverse.—**Opposer**, op-pō′zėr, *n.* One that opposes.

Opposite, op′pō-zit, *a.* [L. *oppositus*—*ob*, before, and *positus*, placed. POSITION, COMPOSE.] Standing or situated in front; facing; adverse; opposed; hostile; different in nature or quality; mutually antagonistic; contrary; inconsistent; repugnant; *bot.* growing in pairs; each pair crosswise to that above or below it.—*n.* One who or that which opposes; one who or that which is opposite or adverse.—**Oppositely**, op′pō-zit-li, *adv.* In an opposite or adverse manner.—**Oppositeness**, op′pō-zit-nes, *n.* The state of being opposite or adverse.—**Opposition**, op-pō-zish′on, *n.* [Partly from *oppose*, partly from *opposite*.] Situation so as to front something; a standing over against; the state of being opposed or contrasted; the state of being adverse; the act of opposing; attempt to check, restrain, or defeat resistance; that which opposes; the collective body of opposers; the party in either house of Congress or a state legislature opposed to the administration or the party in power; *astron.* the situation of two heavenly bodies when diametrically opposite to each other, or when their longitudes differ by 180°. Also used adjectively (an *opposition* scheme).—**Oppositive**, op-poz′i-tiv, *a.* Capable of being put in opposition; serving or tending to oppose.

Oppress, op-pres′, *v.t.* [Fr. *oppresser*, from L. *oppressus*, from *opprimo*—*ob*, and *premo*, *pressum*, to press. PRESS.] To load or burden with cruel, unjust, or unreasonable impositions; to treat with unjust severity, rigour, or hardship; to overburden; to overwhelm; to subdue; to sit or lie heavy on (as food in the stomach).—**Oppression**, op-presh′on, *n.* The act of oppressing; excessively rigorous government; severity; hardship; calamity; depression; a sense of heaviness or weight in the mind or body.—**Oppressive**, op-pres′iv, *a.* Unreasonably burdensome; unjustly severe; given to oppression; tyrannical; overpowering; overwhelming.—**Oppressively**, op-pres′iv-li, *adv.* In an oppressive manner.—**Oppressiveness**, op-pres′iv-nes, *n.* The quality of being oppressive.—**Oppressor**, op-pres′ėr, *n.* One that oppresses or harasses.

Opprobrium, op-prō′bri-um, *n.* [L., from *ob*, against, and *probrum*, a shameful or disgraceful act.] Scurrilous or abusive language; contemptuous reproaches; scurrility; disgrace; infamy.—**Opprobrious**, op-prō′bri-us, *a.* Containing or expressive of opprobrium; scurrilous; abusive; infamous.—**Opprobriously**, op-prō′bri-us-li, *adv.* Scurrilously.—**Opprobriousness**, op-prō′bri-us-nes, *n.*

Oppugn, op-pūn′, *v.t.* [L. *oppugno*—*ob*, against, and *pugno*, to fight, from *pugnus*, the fist. PUGNACIOUS.] To attack by arguments or the like, not by weapons; to oppose; to resist; to exercise hostile reasoning against.—**Oppugnancy**, op-pug′nan-si, *n.* Opposition; resistance; contention.—**Oppugnant**, op-pug′nant, *a.* Resisting; opposing; hostile.—**Oppugner**, op-pūn′ėr, *n.* One who oppugns.

Opsiometer, op-si-om′et-ėr, *n.* [Gr. *opsis*, sight, and *metron*, measure.] An optometer.

Opsonic, op-son′ik, *a.* [Gr. *opson*, cooked meat.] Having the effect on bacteria of making them easier of consumption by phagocytes.—**Opsonin**, op′so-nin, *n.* The substance in a patient's blood produced by the injection of dead cultures of the bacteria of his disease.

Optative, op′tā-tiv, *a.* [L. *optativus*, from *opto*, to desire or wish (as in *adopt, option*); root same as in *opinion, opulence, optimism*.] Expressing desire or wish; *gram.* applied to that mood of the verb in which wish or desire is expressed.—*n. Gram.* the optative mood of a verb.—**Optatively**, op′tā-tiv-li, *adv.* By desire; by means of the optative mood; in the optative mood.

Optic, op′tik, *a.* [Fr. *optique*, from Gr. *optikos*, from root *op*, to see—L. *oculus*, E. *eye*, being from same root.] Relating or pertaining to vision or sight; pertaining to the organ of vision; subservient to vision; relating to the science of optics.—*Optic axis*, the axis of the eye, or a line going through the middle of the pupil and the center of the eye.—*n.* An organ of sight; an eye.—**Optic nerve**, the nerve of sight which connects the eye with the optic centers of the brain.—**Optical**, op′ti-kal, *a.* Relating to or connected with the science of optics.—**Optically**, op′ti-kal-li, *adv.*—**Optician**, op-tish′an, *n.* A person skilled in the science of optics; one who makes or sells optic glasses and instruments.—**Optics**, op′tiks, *n.* That branch of physical science which treats of the nature and properties of light and vision, optical instruments, &c.—**Optigraph**, op′ti-graf, *n.* A telescope used in drawing landscapes.

Optimates, op-ti-mā′tēz, *n. pl.* [L., aristocrats, from *optimus*, best. OPTIMISM.] The Roman aristocracy; hence, an aristocracy or nobility in general.—**Optime**, op′ti-mē, *n.* In the University of Cambridge, a student in the second rank of honours, next to the wranglers.

Optimeter, op-tim′et-ėr, *n.* OPTOMETER.

Optimism, op′ti-mizm, *n.* [From L. *optimus*, best. OPTATIVE.] The doctrine that everything in nature is ordered for the best; the tendency to always take the most hopeful view of matters social or political; belief in the world's improvement.—**Optimist**, op′ti-mist, *n.* One who believes in optimism.—**Optimistic**, op-ti-mis′tik, *a.* Relating to or characterized by optimism.—**Optimize**, op′ti-mīz, *v.i.* To hold the doctrines of an optimist.

Optimum, op′ti-mum, *n.* The greatest number or degree; the most favorable of conditions, as for plant growth.

Option, op′shon, *n.* [L. *optio*, option, from *opto*, to wish or desire. OPTATIVE.] The power or liberty of choosing; right of choice; the power of deciding on any course of action; choice; election; preference; *stock exchange*, a right to effect a certain transaction or not at a certain date, at the desire of the person bargaining, who pays for the right.—*Local option*, the principle by which the people of a certain locality may decide as to the sale of intoxicating liquors there.—**Optional**, op′shon-al, *a.* Left to one's option or choice; depending on choice or preference.—**Optionally**, op′shon-al-li, *adv.* In an optional manner; at pleasure.

Optometer, op-tom′et-ėr, *n.* [From *opt-* of *optic*, and Gr. *metron*, a measure. OPTIC.] An instrument for testing and measuring the visual adjustment of the eye, used to determine the focal lengths of lenses needed to correct defects of vision.—**Optometrist**, *n.* One skilled in optometry.—**Optometry**, *n.* Scientific measurement of the range of vision and the fitting of lenses to effect needed adjustments.

Opulence, Opulency, op′ū-lens, op′ū-len-si, *n.* [L. *opulentia*, from *opes*, wealth. OPTATIVE.] Wealth; riches; affluence.—**Opulent**, op′ū-lent, *a.* [L. *opulentus*.] Wealthy; rich; affluent; having large means.—**Opulently**, op′ū-lent-li, *adv.*

Opuntia, ō-pun′shi-a, *n.* A kind of cactus largely cultivated in Mexico for rearing the cochineal insect.

Opus, ō′pus, *n.* [L. *pl.* OPERA.] A work; especially a musical composition.

Opuscule, Opuscle, ō-pus′kūl, ō-pus′l, *n.* [L. *opusculum*, dim. from *opus*, work. OPERATE.] A small work; a little book.

Or, or, *conj.* [Contr. from the older *other*, formerly used both for 'either' and 'or', the same word as *either*.] A particle that marks, or seems to mark, an alternative, frequently corresponding to a preceding *either*, and also to *whether*, with which words it is sometimes interchangeable in poetry; it often connects a series of words or propositions, presenting a choice between any two of them (he may study law *or* medicine *or* divinity, *or* he may enter into trade); beginning a sentence it expresses an alternative with the foregoing sentence.

Or, or, *adv.* [A form of *ere*.] Ere; before.

Or, or, *n.* [Fr. *or*, L. *aurum*, gold.] *Her.* gold, expressed in engraving by numerous small points or dots.

Orach, Orache, or′ach, *n.* [Formerly *arrach*, from Fr. *arroche*, orache; origin unknown.] A name of several plants of which a garden species is used like spinach.

Oracle, or′a-kl, *n.* [L. *oraculum*, from *oro*, to speak, to pray, from *os*, *oris*, the mouth; akin *oral*, *orifice*, *orator*, *adore*, &c.] The answer of a god or the inspired priest or priestess of a god, to an inquiry made respecting some affair; the deity who gave or was supposed to give answers to inquiries; the place where the answers were given; the sanctuary (O.T.); a divine communication, revelation, or message; any person reputed uncommonly wise, and whose opinions have great weight.—**Oracular**, o-rak′ū-lėr, *a.* Pertaining to an oracle or oracles; uttering oracles; resembling the utterance of an oracle; authoritative; sententious; ambiguous, like the ancient oracles.—**Oracularly**, o-rak′ū-lėr-li, *adv.* In the manner of an oracle.—**Oracularness**, o-rak′ū-lėr-nes, *n.*

Oragious, ō-rā′jus, *a.* [Fr. *orageux*, stormy.] Stormy; tempestuous.

Oral, ō′ral, *a.* [Fr., from L. *or*, *oris*, the mouth. ORACLE.] Uttered by the mouth or in words; spoken, not written; *zool.* pertaining to the mouth of animals.—**Orally**, ō′ral-li, *adv.* In an oral manner; by word of mouth; verbally.

Orang, ō-rang′, *n.* ORANGUTAN.

Orange, or′anj, *n.* [Fr. *orange*, It. *arancia*, *arancio*, Sp. *naranja*, from Ar. *nâranj*, an orange, the form of the word being influenced by Fr. *or*, gold.] A tree cultivated abundantly in the south of Europe, the Azores, America, &c., and also its fruit, which is imported into other countries in great quantities.—*a.* Belonging to an orange; coloured as an orange.—**Orangeade**, or-anj-ād′, *n.* Drink made from orange juice or flavoured with orange-peel.—**Orange-blossom, Orange-flower**, *n.* The blossom of the orange-tree, a wreath of which is commonly worn by a bride at her marriage.—**Orange-lily**, *n.* A garden plant with large orange-coloured flowers.—**Orange-peel**, *n.* The rind of an orange separated from the fruit; the peel of the bitter orange dried and candied, and used in flavouring puddings, &c.—**Orangery**, or′an-jėr-i, *n.* [Fr. *orangerie*.] A place where oranges are cultivated; a house for orange-trees.—**Orange-tawny**, *n.* A colour between yellow and brown.

Orangeman, or′anj-man, *n.* [From William III of England, Prince of *Orange*, a place now in France.] A member of a secret society instituted in Ireland in 1795, to uphold Protestant ascendency, and to oppose the Catholic religion and influence.—**Orangeism**, or′anj-izm, *n.* The tenets or principles of the Orangemen.

Orangutan, Orangoutang, o-rang′ō-tan, o-rang′ō-tang, *n.* [Malay *orang-utan*, lit. man of the woods.] One of the largest of the anthropoid apes, a native of Sumatra and Borneo.

Oration, o-rā′shon, *n.* [L. *oratio*, from *oro*, *oratum*, to pray. ORACLE.] A speech or discourse composed according to the rules of oratory, and spoken in public; a set speech; a formal discourse pronounced on a special occasion.—**Orate**, or-āt′, *v.i.* To deliver an oration, with under-current idea of pomposity.—**Orator**, or′a-tėr, *n.* [L.] A public speaker; one who delivers an oration; one who is skilled as a speaker; an eloquent man.—**Oratorian**, or-a-tō′ri-an, *n.* *Eccles.* a priest of the oratory.—**Oratorical**, or-a-tor′i-kal, *a.* Pertaining to an orator or to oratory; rhetorical.—**Oratorically**, or-a-tor′i-kal-li, *adv.* In an oratorical manner.—**Oratorio**, or-a-tō′ri-ō, *n.* [It.] A sacred musical composition, consisting of airs, recitatives, duets, trios, choruses, &c., the subject of which is generally taken from Scripture.—**Oratory**, or′a-to-ri, *n.* [Partly from *orator*, partly from L. *oratorium*, a place of prayer.] The art of public speaking; the art of an orator; exercise of eloquence; eloquence; a place for prayer; a small apartment for private devotions.—*Priests of the Oratory*, a religious order, the members of which are not bound by any special vow.

Orb, orb, *n.* [Fr. *orbe*, from L. *orbis*, a circle, a ring, a disc; seen also in *orbit*, *exorbitant*.] A spherical body; a sphere or globe; also a circular body or disc; *anc. astron.* a hollow globe or sphere forming part of the solar or sidereal system; *arch.* a plain circular boss. BOSS.—*v.i.*† To exhibit or assume the appearance of an orb.—*v.t.* To encircle; to inclose.—**Orbed**, orbd, *a.* Having the form of an orb; round; circular.—**Orbicular**, or-bik′ū-lėr, *a.* [L. *orbicularis*.] In the form of an orb; spherical; circular.—*Orbicular leaf*, a circular leaf with the stalk attached to the centre of it.—*Orbicular muscles*, muscles with circular fibres surrounding some natural opening of the body.—**Orbicularly**, or-bik′ū-lėr-li, *adv.* Spherically; circularly.—**Orbicularness**, or-bik′ū-lėr-nes, *n.*—**Orbiculate, Orbiculated**, or-bik′ū-lāt, or-bik′ū-lā-ted, *a.* [L. *orbiculatus*.] In the form of an orb; orbicular.—**Orbiculation**, or-bik′ū-lā″shon, *n.* The state of being orbiculate.—**Orby**, or′bi, *a.* Resembling an orb; spherical.

Orbit, or′bit, *n.* [L. *orbita*, a wheel-track, a circuit, from *orbis*, an orb. ORB.] The path of a planet or comet through space; the curve-line which a planet describes in its periodical revolution round its central body (the *orbit* of Jupiter or Mercury); *anat.* the bony cavity in which the eye is situated; *ornith.* the skin which surrounds the eye of a bird.—**Orbital**, or′bi-tal, *a.* Pertaining to an orbit.—**Orbitary**, or′bi-ta-ri, *a.* Connected with or surrounding the orbit (*orbitary* feathers).

Orcadian, or-kā′di-an, *a.* Relating to the *Orcades*, or Orkney Islands.—*n.* A native or inhabitant of Orkney.

Orcein, or′sē-in, *n.* The chief ingredient of archil, a purple dyestuff obtained from orcinol (which see).

Orchard, or′chėrd, *n.* [A.Sax. *ortgeard*, *wyrtgeard*, lit. a wort-yard; so Dan. *urtgaard*, Goth. *aurti-gards*, a garden. WORT, YARD.] A garden‡; an inclosure devoted to the culture of fruit-growing or nut-bearing trees.—**Orchard house**, *n.* A glass-roofed shed for cultivating fruits without the aid of artificial heat.—**Orchardist**, or′chėrd-ist, *n.* One that cultivates orchards; a fruit grower.

Orchella, Orchella-weed, or-kel′la, *n.* A lichen yielding archil.

Orchestra, or′kes-tra, *n.* [Gr. *orchēstra*, from *orcheomai*, to dance.] The part of a theatre appropriated to the musicians; in the Grecian theatres a part of the stage allotted to the chorus; the whole instrumental band performing together in public places of amusement.—**Orchestral**, or-kes′tral, *a.* Pertaining to an orchestra.—**Orchestration**, or-kes-trā′shon, *n.* The arrangement of music for an orchestra; instrumentation.

Orchid, Orchis, or′kid, or′kis, *n.* [Gr. *orchis*, a testicle, hence an orchid, from the form of the root.] The name of an order of perennial plants, with tuberous fleshy roots, and beautiful flowers of remarkable form, found almost everywhere and prized by florists; a light reddish-blue color.—**Orchidaceous, Orchideous**, or-ki-dā′shus, or-kid′ē-us, *a.* Pertaining to the orchids.—**Orchidologist**, or-ki-dol′o-jist, *n.* One versed in orchids.—**Orchidology**, or-ki-dol′o-ji, *n.*

Orcinol, Orcin, or′si-nōl, or′sin, *n.* [Fr. *orcine*, from *orchella*.] A colorless phenol obtained from lichens celebrated as dyeweeds (orchella-weed).

Ordain, or-dān′, *v.t.* [O.E. *ordeyne*, *ordeine*, O.Fr. *ordener* (Fr. *ordonner*), from L. *ordino*, to order, from *ordo*, *ordinis*, order. ORDER.] To set in order or arrange‡; to decree, appoint, establish, institute; to set apart for an office; to invest with ministerial or sacerdotal functions.—**Ordainable**, or-dā′na-bl, *a.* Capable of being ordained.—**Ordainer**, or-dā′nėr, *n.* One who ordains.—*Ordainers*, the Committee of Regency, composed of twenty-one members, named by Parliament in 1310, to draw up a scheme for the better management of the realm, in opposition to Edward II and Piers Gaveston.—**Ordainment**, or-dān′ment, *n.* The act of ordaining; appointment.

Ordeal, or-de-al, *n.* [A.Sax. *ordēl*, *ordāl*, decision, ordeal, lit. *out-deal* (like D. *oordeel*, G. *urtheil*, a decision), from A.Sax. prefix *or*, Goth. *us*, out, and verb meaning to *deal*. DEAL.] An ancient form of trial to determine guilt or innocence, as by causing the accused to handle red-hot iron or put the hand into boiling water, escape from injury being considered a proof of innocence; hence, any severe trial or strict test.

Order, or′dėr, *n.* [Fr. *ordre*, from L. *ordo*, *ordinis*, a row, a regular series, from root *or*, seen in *orient*, *origin*; connected are *ordain*, *ordinary*, *ordinance*, *extraordinary*, *subordinate*, &c.] Regular disposition or methodical arrangement; established succession; a proper state or condition; the established usage or settled method; regularity; public tranquillity; absence of confusion or disturbance; a mandate, precept, or authoritative direction; a rule or regulation, oral or written; a direction, demand, or commission to supply goods; a written direction to pay money; a free pass for admission to a theatre or other place of entertainment; a rank or class of men; a body of men of the same rank or profession constituting a separate class in the community; a religious fraternity; a body of men having had a common honorary distinction conferred on them; the distinction, rank, or dignity itself (the *order* of the Garter); a large division in the classification of natural objects, as plants or animals; *arch.* a column entire, with a superincumbent entablature, viewed as forming an architectural whole, there being five architectural orders, viz. Doric, Ionic, Tuscan, Corinthian, and Composite.—*Close order*, said of the ranks of soldiers when drawn up at the distance of a pace between each other.—*General orders*, the commands or notices which military headquarters issue on routine matters of general importance.—*Holy orders*, the clerical or ecclesiastical character conferred on a person by ordination or consecration to the ministry in the church; often used without the word 'holy' (*to be in orders*, *to take orders*).—*In order*, for the purpose; with a view; to the end; as means to an end.—*Religious orders*, religious brotherhoods or communities, as monastic, military, and mendicant *orders*.—*Standing orders*, certain general rules and instructions in force until specifically changed, as in a military post or legislative body.—*Order in council*, an order issued by the British sovereign, by and with the advice of the privy-council.—*Order of battle*, the arrangement and disposition of the different parts of an army for the purpose of engaging an enemy.—*Order of the day*, a parliamentary phrase denoting the business regularly set down for consideration on the minutes or votes; *milit.* specific directions issued by a superior officer to the troops under his command.—*v.t.* To put in order; to dispose or arrange; to manage or conduct; to command; to give an order to; to give an order or commission for.—*v.i.* To give command or direction.—**Order book**, *n.* A book for orders; a book in which a salesman or sales clerk keeps a record of orders of customers.—**Orderer**, or'dėr-ėr, *n.* One that gives orders; one that regulates.—**Orderless**, or'dėr-les, *a.* Disorderly; out of rule.—**Orderliness**, or'dėr-li-nes, *n.* The state or quality of being orderly; regularity.—**Orderly**, or'dėr-li, *a.* In accordance with good order; well ordered; methodical; regular; *milit.* being on duty (an *orderly* officer).—*n.* A private soldier or non-commissioned officer who attends on a superior officer to carry orders or messages.—*adv.* According to due order.

Ordinal, or'di-nal, *a.* [L. *ordinalis*, from *ordo*, *ordinis*, a row. ORDER.] Applied to a number which expresses order or succession (the *ordinal* numbers, *first*, *second*, *third*, &c.); *nat. hist.* pertaining to an order.—*n.* A number denoting order (as *first*); a book containing the ordination service.

Ordinance, or'di-nans, *n.* [O.Fr. *ordenance*, (Fr. *ordonnance*), from *ordener*, to ordain. ORDAIN.] A rule established by authority; a law, edict, decree, or the like; an established rite or ceremony; a law or provision enacted by a municipal government for local application.

Ordinand, or'di-nand, *n.* One about to be ordained or receive orders.—**Ordinant**, or'di-nant, *n.* One who ordains; a prelate conferring orders.

Ordinary, or'di-na-ri, *a.* [L. *ordinarius*, from *ordo*, *ordinis*, order. ORDER.] Established; regular; customary; common; usual; frequent; habitual; met with at any time; hence, somewhat inferior; of little merit.—*Ordinary seaman*, a seaman capable of the commoner duties, but not considered fit to be rated as an able seaman.—*n.* A person who has ordinary or immediate jurisdiction in matters ecclesiastical; an ecclesiastical judge (usually a bishop); a meal prepared for all comers, as distinguished from one specially ordered; an eating-house where there is a fixed price for the meal; one of the common heraldic figures formed with straight lines (as the bend, cross, saltire).—*In ordinary*, in actual and constant service; statedly attending and serving (a physician or chaplain *in ordinary*). An ambassador *in ordinary* is one constantly resident at a foreign court.—*Lord Ordinary*, one of the five judges of the Scottish Court of Session constituting the Outer House.—A ship *in ordinary* is one not in actual service, but laid up under the direction of a competent person.—**Ordinarily**, or'di-na-ri-li, *adv.* In an ordinary manner; usually; generally; in most cases.

Ordinate, or'di-nāt, *a.* [L. *ordinatus*, well-ordered. ORDINARY.] Regular; methodical.—*n.* *Geom.* one of those lines of reference which determine the position of a point; a straight line drawn from a point in the abscissa. The abscissa and ordinate, when spoken of together, are called *co-ordinates*. CO-ORDINATE.]—**Ordinately**, or'di-nāt-li, *adv.* *Geom.* in the manner of an ordinate.

Ordination, or-di-nā'shon, *n.* [L. *ordinatio*, regulation, from *ordino*, to ordain.] The act of ordaining; the act of settling or establishing; appointment; settled order of things; the act of conferring holy orders.

Ordnance, ord'nans, *n.* [Same as *ordinance*, Fr, *ordonnance*, arrangement, equipment; originally it had reference to guns of a particular size or equipment.] Cannon, mortars and howitzers collectively; artillery and small arms, ammunition and supplies, equipment for manufacture and repair of ordnance; equipment and supplies for naval warfare.—*Ordnance Department*, U. S., the department in charge of arsenals and depots and the purchase, manufacture and distribution of ordnance to the army and militia.

Ordovician, or'dō-vis"i-an, *n.* [L. *Ordovices*, a North Welsh tribe. A series of strata succeeding the CAMBRIAN (which see).

Ordure, or'dūr, *n.* [Fr. *ordure*, from O.Fr. *ord*, It. *ordo*, filthy, from L. *horridus*, horrid.] Dung; excrement; fæces.—**Ordurous**, or'dū-rus, *a.* Pertaining to or consisting of ordure.

Ore, ōr, *n.* [A.Sax. *ár*, brass, copper=Icel. *eir*, brass, O.G. *ēr*, Goth. *aiz*, ore; cog. L. *æs*, *æris*, ore, brass; Skr. *ayas*, iron.] A mineral consisting of a metal and some other substance, as oxygen, sulphur, or carbon, in combination, being the source from which metals are usually obtained by smelting (metals found free from such combination being called *native metals*); metal, sometimes gold (*poetical*).

Oread, ō'rē-ad, *n.* [Gr. *oreias*, *oreiados*, from *oros*, mountain.] A mountain nymph.

Orectic, ō-rek'tik, *a.* [Gr. *oregō*, I desire.] Appetitive.

Oreography, or-ē-og'ra-fi, *n.* [Gr. *oros*, *oreōs*, a mountain, and *graphō*, to describe.] The science of mountains; orography.

Orfray, or'frā, *n.* [O.F. *orfreis*, L. *auriphrygium*, Phrygian gold.] The embroidered border of ecclesiastical vestments.

Organ, or'gan, *n.* [L. *organum*, from Gr. *organon*, an instrument, implement, from *ergō*, to work; same root as E. *work*.] An instrument or means; that which performs some office, duty, or function; more commonly, a part of an animal or vegetable by which some function is carried on (as the heart, the eye); a means of communication between one person or body of persons and another; a medium of conveying certain opinions; specifically, a newspaper; the largest and most harmonious of wind-instruments of music, consisting of a great number of pipes and with keys similar to those of the piano.—**Organ-blower**, *n.* One who blows the bellows of an organ; a mechanical appliance for this purpose.—**Organ-builder**, *n.* One whose occupation is to construct musical organs.—**Organ-loft**, *n.* The loft where an organ stands in a church, &c.—**Organ-screen**, *n.* An ornamental screen of stone or timber on which a church organ is placed.—**Organic**, or-gan'ik, *a.* [L. *organicus*.] Pertaining to an organ or to organs of animals and plants; pertaining to objects that have organs, hence to the animal and vegetable worlds; exhibiting animal or vegetable life and functions (*organic* bodies, tissues, &c.); forming a whole with a systematic arrangement of parts; organized; systematized.—*Organic chemistry*. CHEMISTRY.—*Organic disease*, a disease in which the structure of an organ is morbidly altered; opposed to *functional disease*.—*Organic laws*, laws directly concerning the fundamental parts of the constitution of a state.—*Organic remains*, these organized bodies whether animals or vegetables, found in a fossil state.—*Organic selection*, the co-operation of ACCOMMODATION and ADAPTATION (which see) in the production of new species.—**Organical**, or-gan'i-kal, *a.* Organic.—**Organically**, or-gan'i-kal-li, *adv.* In an organic manner; by or with organs.—**Organicalness**, or-gan'i-kal-nes, *n.*—**Organism**, or'gan-izm, *n.* Organic structure; a body exhibiting organization and organic life; a member of the animal or vegetable kingdoms.—**Organist**, or'gan-ist, *n.* One who plays on the organ.—**Organizability**, or'gan-iz-a-bil"i-ti, *n.* The property of being organizable.—**Organizable**, or-gan-iz'a-bl, *a.* Capable of being organized.—**Organization**, or-gan-i-zā"shon, *n.* The act or process of organizing; the act of systematizing or arranging; a whole or aggregate that is organized; organic structure; arrangement of parts or organs for the performance of vital functions.—**Organize**, or'gan-iz, *v.t.*—*organized*, *organizing*. To give an organic structure to; to arrange the several parts of for action or work; to establish and systematize.—**Organizer**, or'gan-iz-ėr, *n.* One who organizes, establishes, or systematizes.—**Organogenesis, Organogeny**, or'gan-ō-jen-e-sis, or-ga-noj'e-ni, *n.* [Gr. *organon*, an organ, and *genesis*, birth.] The development of an organ or of organs in plants or animals.—**Organogenic**, or'gan-ō-jen"ik, *a.* Pertaining to organogeny.—**Organographic, Organographical**, or'gan-ō-graf"ik, or'gan-ō-graf"i-kal, *a.* Pertaining to organography.—**Organographist**, or-gan-og'ra-fist, *n.* One who describes the organs of animal or vegetable bodies.—**Organography**, or-gan-og'ra-fi, *n.* A description of the organs of plants or animals.—**Organological**, or'gan-ō-loj"i-kal, *a.* Pertaining to organology.—**Organology**, or-gan-ol'o-ji, *n.* The physiology of the different organs of animals or plants.—**Organon, Organum**, or'ga-non, or'ga-num, *n.* A body of rules and canons for the direction of the scientific faculty. The *Novum Organum* of Bacon is the new, in relation to the old or Aristotelian method or instrument of logical thought.—**Organo-therapy**, or-gan'ō-ther"a-pē, *n.* [Gr. *organon*, and *therapeuō*, I heal.] *Med.* the use of animal extracts for curative and other purposes. Cp. THYROID GLAND and ADRENALIN.

Organdy, Organdie, or'gan-di, *n.* [Fr. *organdi*.] A fine muslin, plain or figured.

Organzine, or'gan-zin, *n.* [Fr. *organsin*, It. *organzino*.] A silk thread of several threads twisted together; a fabric made of such thread.

Orgasm, or'gazm, *n.* [Gr. *orgasmos*, from *orgaō*, to swell.] Extreme excitement or action, especially in coition.

Orgeat, or'zhat, *n.* [Fr., from *orge*, barley.] A preparation extracted from barley and almonds, used to mix in certain drinks, or medicinally as a mild demulcent.

Orgiastic, or-ji-as'tik, *a.* Pertaining to the Greek orgies, or mystic festivals. ORGY.

Orgues, orgz, *n. pl.* [Fr.] *Milit.* long thick pieces of timber, pointed and shod with iron and hung over a gateway, to be let down in case of attack.

Orgy, or'ji, *n.* [Gr. *orgia*, secret rites, from *orgē*, violent passion, anger.] Secret rites or ceremonies connected with the worship of some of the pagan deities; particularly revels of the Greeks in honour of Dionysus or Bacchus: properly only plural in this sense; hence, a wild or frantic revel; drunken revelry.

Orichalc, or'i-kalk, *n.* [L. *orichalcum*, from Gr. *oros*, a mountain, and *chalkos*, copper.] A metallic substance resembling gold in colour; the brass of the ancients.

Oriel, ō'ri-el, *n.* [O.Fr. *oriol*, L.L. *oriolum*, a porch, a hall; origin doubtful.] A large window projecting from a wall, and forming a bay or recess inside; a bay-window.

Orient, ō'ri-ent, *a.* [L. *oriens*, rising, ppr. of *orior*, *ortus*, to arise; whence also *origin*, (*ab*)*ortion*; root also in *order*.] Rising, as the sun or moon; eastern; oriental; bright; shining.—*The orient*, the east; oriental countries.—*v.t.* [Fr. *orienter*.] *Surv.* to define the position of, in respect to the east or other points of the compass.—**Oriental**, ō-ri-en'tal, *a.* Eastern; situated in the east; proceeding from the east; applied to gems as a mark of excellence; precious: opposed to *occidental*.—*Oriental region*, Southern Asia, together with the western part of the East Indies, the Philippines, and Formosa.—*n.* A native of some eastern part of the world; an Asiatic.—**Orientalism**, ō-ri-en'tal-izm, *n.* An eastern mode of thought or expression; erudition in oriental languages or literature.—**Orientalist**, ō-ri-en'tal-ist, *n.* An oriental; one versed in the eastern languages and literature.—**Orientality**, ō'ri-en-tal"i-ti, *n.* The state of being oriental.—**Orientalize**, ō-ri-en'tal-iz, *v.t.* To render oriental or conformed to oriental manners.—**Orientate**, ō'ri-en-tāt, *v.t.* To cause to assume an easterly direction.—**Orientation**, ō'ri-en-tā"shon, *n.* A turning towards the east; position east and west; as applied to churches, such a position as that the chancel shall point to the east; *surv.* the determining of the points of the compass in taking bearings.—**Orientator**, ō'ri-en-tā-tėr, *n.* An instrument used in orientation.

Orifice, or'i-fis, *n.* [Fr. *orifice*, from L. *orificium—os, oris*, the mouth, and *facio*, to make. ORAL.] The mouth or aperture of a tube, pipe, or other similar object; a perforation; an opening; a vent.

Oriflamme, or'i-flam, *n.* [Fr., from L. *aurum*, gold, *flamma*, flame.] The ancient royal standard of France; a piece of red silk fixed on a gilt spear with the anterior edge cut into points.

Origanum, o-rig'an-um, *n.* [Gr. *origanon.*] Wild marjoram.

Origin, or'i-jin, *n.* [Fr. *origine*, from L. *origo, originis*, from *orior*, to rise. ORIENT.] The first existence or beginning of anything; the commencement; fountain; source; that from which anything primarily proceeds; of a muscle, the end attached to a relatively fixed part.—**Original**, o-rij'i-nal, *a.* [L. *originalis.*] Pertaining or belonging to the origin or early state of something; primitive; pristine; having the power to originate new thoughts or combinations of thought; produced by an author; not copied.—*Original sin, theol.* the first sin of Adam, namely the eating of the forbidden fruit; hence, either the imputation of Adam's sin to his posterity, or that corruption of nature and tendency to sin inherited from him.—*n.* Origin; source; first copy; archetype; that from which anything is copied; a work not copied from another, but the work of an artist himself; the language in which any work is composed as distinguished from a translation; a person of marked individuality of character; a primary stock or type from which varieties have been developed.—**Originality**, o-rij'i-nal"i-ti, *n.* The quality or state of being original; the power of originating new thoughts, or uncommon combinations of thought.—**Originally**, o-rij'i-nal-li, *adv.* In an original manner; at the very beginning; from the first.—**Originate**, o-rij'i-nāt, *v.t.*—*originated, originating.* To give origin or beginning to; to cause to be; to produce.—*v.i.* To take first existence; to have origin.—**Origination**, o-rij'i-nā"shon, *n.* The act or mode of originating; production.—**Originative**, o-rij'i-nā-tiv, *a.* Having power to originate.—**Originatively**, o-rij'i-nā-tiv-li, *adv.* In an originative manner.—**Originator**, o-rij'i-nā-tėr, *n.* A person who originates.

Orillon, o-ril'on, *n.* [Fr. *orillon*, from *oreille*, an ear, L. *auricula*, dim. of *auris*, the ear.] *Fort.* a rounded work of earth on the shoulder of a bastion.

Oriole, ō'ri-ōl, *n.* [O.Fr. *oriol*, from L. *aureolus*, dim. of *aureus*, golden, from *aurum*, gold.] The name of certain birds of the crow family with plumage generally of a golden colour.

Orion, ō-rī'on, *n.* [A celebrated hunter of Greek mythology.] A constellation of the southern hemisphere represented by the figure of a man with a sword by his side, three stars on a line forming his *belt*.

Orison, or'i-zon, *n.* [O.Fr. *orison, oreison*, from L. *oratio*, a prayer, from *oro*, to pray. *Oration* is a doublet of this.] A prayer or supplication. (*Poet.*)

Orle, orl, *n.* [Fr. *orle*, dim. from L. *ora*, a border.] *Her.* a figure on an escutcheon resembling a smaller escutcheon with the interior cut out; *arch.* a fillet under the ovolo of a capital (also called *orlet*).

Orleans, or'le-anz, *n.* A kind of cloth made of worsted and cotton, used for dresses, &c.

Orlop, or'lop, *n.* [D. *overloop—over*, over, and *loopen*, to run. OVER, LEAP.] *Naut.* the lowest deck in a ship of war or merchant vessel that has three decks; sometimes a temporary deck.

Ormer, or'mėr, *n.* [Fr. *ormier*, L. *auris, maris*, ear of the sea.] An edible univalve shell-fish.

Ormolu, or'mo-lū, *n.* [Fr. *or-moulu—or*, gold, and *moulu*, pp. of *moudre*, L. *molere*, to grind.] A variety of brass containing 25 per cent zinc and 75 per cent copper, made to imitate gold.

Ornament, or'na-ment, *n.* [Fr. *ornement*, L. *ornamentum*, from *orno, ornatum*, to adorn.] That which embellishes or adorns; something which, added to another thing, renders it more beautiful to the eye; decoration; fair outward show; that which adds beauty to the mind or character.—*v.t.* To adorn; to embellish.—**Ornamental**, or-na-men'tal, *a.* Serving to ornament; pertaining to ornament.—**Ornamentally**, or-na-men'tal-li, *adv.* In an ornamental manner.—**Ornamentation**, or'na-men-tā"shon, *n.* The act of ornamenting; the ornaments or decorations produced.—**Ornamenter**, or'na-men-tėr, *n.* One who ornaments.—**Ornamentist**, or'na-men-tist, *n.* One employed in ornamentation; a decorator.

Ornate, or'nāt, *a.* [L. *ornatus*, pp. of *orno*, to adorn. ORNAMENT.] Adorned; decorated; ornamental; richly and artistically finished; much embellished.—**Ornately**, or'nāt-li, *adv.* In an ornate manner.—**Ornateness**, or'nāt-nes, *n.*

Ornis, or'nis, *n.* [Gr. *ornis*, a bird.] The birds of a region, or its avifauna.—**Ornithotomy**, or-ni-thot'o-mi, *n.* [Gr. *tomē*, cutting.] The anatomy of birds.

Ornithic, or-nith'ik, *a.* [Gr. *ornis, ornithos*, a bird.] Of or pertaining to birds.—**Ornithichnite**, or-nith'ik-nīt, *n.* [Gr. *ichnos*, a footstep.] A fossil footprint of a bird, or resembling that of a bird.—**Ornithodelphia**, or'ni-thō-del"fi-a, *n. pl.* [Gr. *delphys*, a womb.] The lowest sub-class of mammals, consisting of the Echidna and the Ornithorhynchus, in which the structure of the reproductive organs recalls that in birds.—**Ornithodelphic**, or'ni-thō-del"fik, *a.* Pertaining to the Ornithodelphia.—**Ornithoidichnite**, or'ni-thoid-ik"nīt, *n.* An ornithichnite.—**Ornitholite**, or-nith'ō-līt, *n.* [Gr. *lithos*, a stone.] The fossil remains of birds.—**Ornithological**, or'ni-thō-loj"i-kal, *a.* Pertaining to ornithology.—**Ornithologist**, or-ni-thol'o-jist, *n.* A person skilled in ornithology.—**Ornithology**, or-ni-thol'o-ji, *n.* That branch of zoology which treats of the form, structure, classification, and habits of birds.—**Ornithomancy**, or-nith'ō-man-si, *n.* [Gr. *manteia*, divination.] Augury, a species of divination by means of birds, their flight, &c.—**Ornithopter**, or-ni-thop'tėr, *n.* [Gr. *pteron*, wing.] A form of aircraft deriving its support and propelling force from flapping surfaces.—**Ornithorhynchus**, or'ni-thō-ring"kus, *n.* [Gr. *rhynchos*, a beak.] An oviparous mammal of Australia and Tasmania, one of the monotremata, with a body like that of an otter, a horny beak resembling that of a duck, and webbed feet; the duck-bill, duck-mole, or water-mole.—**Ornithosaur**, or-nith'ō-sar, *n.* [Gr. *sauros*, a lizard.] A fossil reptile with bird-like characters.—**Ornithoscopy**, or-ni-thos'ko-pi, *n.* [Gr. *skopeō*, to view.] The practice or art of observing birds and their habits.

Orogeny, ō-roj'e-ni, *n.* [Gr. *oros*, mountain, and root *gen.* GENUS.] The origin and formation of mountains.

Orography, o-rog'ra-fi, *n.* [Gr. *oros*, a mountain, and *graphō*, to describe.] The science which describes or treats of the mountains and mountain systems of the globe; orology.—**Orographic, Orographical**, or-ō-graf'ik, or-ō-graf'i-kal, *a.* Relating to orography.—**Orographist**, o-rog'ra-fist, *n.* One versed in orography or the science of mountains.

Oroide, ō'roid, *n.* [Fr. *or*, gold, and Gr. *eidos*, resemblance.] An alloy resembling gold in appearance, and used in the manufacture of cheap watch-cases, trinkets, &c.—**Orology**, o-rol'o-ji, *n.* [Gr. *oros*, a mountain, and *logos*, discourse.] A description of mountains; orography.—**Orological**, or-ō-loj'i-kal, *a.* Pertaining to orology.—**Orologist**, o-rol'o-jist, *n.* A describer of mountains; one versed in orology.

Orotund, ō'rō-tund, *a.* [L. *os, oris*, the mouth, and *rotundus*, round, rotund.] *Rhet.* characterized by fulness, richness, and clearness; rich and musical: applied to the voice or manner of utterance.

Orphan, or'fan, *n.* [Gr. *orphanos*, orphaned; allied to L. *orbus*, bereaved.] A child bereft of both parents.—*a.* Being an orphan; bereaved of parents.—*v.t.* To reduce to the state of an orphan; to bereave of parents, children, or friends.—**Orphanage**, or'fan-āj, *n.* The state of an orphan; a home or institution for the care of orphans.—**Orphaned**, or'fand, *pp.* and *a.* Bereft of parents or, *fig.*, of friends.—**Orphanhood**, or'fan-hụd, *n.* The state of being an orphan.

Orphean, or-fē'an, *a.* Pertaining to *Orpheus*, the legendary poet and musician of ancient Greece; hence melodious.—**Orpheon**, or'fe-on, *n.* A kind of musical instrument.—**Orphic**, or'fik, *a.* Orphean.

Orpiment, or'pi-ment, *n.* [Fr. *orpiment*, from L. *auripigmentum—aurum*, gold, and *pigmentum*, a pigment.] A mineral substance, a compound of sulphur and arsenic, of a brilliant yellow colour, forming the basis of the yellow paint called *king's-yellow*.—*Red orpiment*, a name of *realgar*.

Orpin, or'pin, *n.* [Fr. *orpin—or*, gold, and *peindre*, to paint. ORPIMENT.] A yellow pigment of various degrees of intensity, approaching also to red.

Orpine, or'pīn, *n.* [Fr. *orpin.*] An herb of the stonecrop species, or sedum.

Orrery, or'e-ri, *n.* A machine that represents, by the movements of its parts, the motions and phases of the planets in their orbits, named after an Earl of *Orrery*.

Orris, or'is, *n.* [Fr. *or*, gold.] A sort of gold or silver lace; a pattern in which gold and silver lace is worked.

Orris, or'is, *n.* [Corruption of *iris.*] A plant from which is obtained orris-root.—**Orris-root**, *n.* The root of three species of iris which, in its dried state, is used as a pectoral and expectorant medicine.

Orsedew, Orsedue, or'se-dū, *n.* [Fr. *or*, gold, and *seduire*, to beguile, to seduce.] A sort of gold-leaf; Mannheim gold; Dutch gold.

Ort, ort, *n.* [L.G. *ort*, O.D. *oorete*, remnants of food; from *or*, as in *ordeal*, and verb to *eat* (D. *eten*).] A scrap of food left; a fragment; a piece of refuse; commonly in the plural.

Orthoceras, or-thos'ėr-as, *n.* [Gr. *orthos*, straight, and *keras*, a horn.] A genus of fossil shells, straight or slightly curved, of the nautilus family.—**Orthoceratite**, or-thō-ser'a-tīt, *n.* A fossil shell of this genus.

Orthoclase, or'thō-klāz, *n.* [Gr. *orthos*, straight, and *klasis*, fracture.] A kind of felspar with a straight flat fracture.

Orthodox, or'tho-doks, *a.* [Gr. *orthodoxos*, sound in the faith—*orthos*, right, and *doxa*, opinion (akin *dogma*).] Sound in opinion or doctrine; particularly, sound in religious opinions or doctrines: opposed to *heterodox*; in accordance with sound doctrine; sound; correct (an *orthodox* faith or proceeding).—**Orthodoxical**, or-tho-dok'si-kal, *a.* Pertaining to orthodoxy; orthodox.—**Orthodoxly**, or'tho-doks-li, *adv.* In an orthodox way; with soundness of faith.—**Orthodoxy**, or'tho-dok-si, *n.* [Gr. *orthodoxia.*] Soundness of faith; correctness of opinion or doctrine, especially in religious matters.

Orthodromy, or'thō-dro-mi, *n.* [Gr. *orthos*, right, and *dromos*, course.] The act or art of sailing on a great circle or in a straight course.—**Orthodromic**, or-thō-drom'ik, *a.* Pertaining to orthodromy.—**Orthodromics**, or-thō-drom'iks, *n.* The art of sailing in the arc of a great circle.

Orthoepy, or'thō-e-pi or or-thō'e-pi, *n.* [Gr. *orthoepeia—orthos*, right, *epos*, a word.] The art of uttering words with propriety; a correct pronunciation of words.—**Orthoepic, Orthoepical**, or-thō-ep'ik, or-thō-ep'i-kal, *a.* Pertaining to orthoepy.—**Orthoepically**, or-thō-ep'i-kal-li, *adv.* With correct pronunciation.—**Orthoepist**, or'-thō-ep-ist or or-thō'ep-ist, *n.* One who is skilled in orthoepy; one who writes on orthoepy.

Orthogamy, or-thog'a-mi, *n.* [Gr. *orthos*, straight, and *gamos*, marriage.] *Bot.* direct or immediate fertilization without the intervention of any mediate agency.

Orthogenesis, or'tho-jen"e-sis, *n.* [Gr. *genesis*, origin.] The view of evolution by which all variations follow a defined direction, and are not simply accidental.

Orthognathic, **Orthognathous**, or-thŏg-nath'ik, or-thog'na-thus, *a.* [Gr. *orthos*, straight, and *gnathos*, a jaw.] Having jaws that do not protrude; having a skull in which the forehead does not recede and the jaws project. PROGNATHIC.

Orthogon, or'thō-gon, *n.* [Gr. *orthos*, right, and *gōnia*, an angle.] A rectangular figure. — **Orthogonal**, or-thog'on-al, *a.* Right-angled. — **Orthogonally**, or-thog'on-al-li, *adv.* With or at right angles.

Orthography, or-thog'ra-fi, *n.* [Gr. *orthographia*—*orthos*, right, and *graphē*, writing.] The art of writing words with the proper letters; the way in which words are properly written; spelling; the part of grammar which treats of letters and spelling; a geometrical representation of an elevation or section of a building.—**Orthographer**, **Orthographist**, or-thog'ra-fėr, or-thog'ra-fist, *n.* One skilled in orthography.—**Orthographic**, **Orthographical**, or-thō-graf'ik, or-thō-graf'i-kal, *a.* Pertaining to orthography; *geom.* pertaining to right lines or angles.—*Orthographic projection*, a projection used in drawing maps, &c., the eye being supposed to be at an infinite distance from the object. — **Orthographically**, or-thō-graf'i-kal-li, *adv.* According to the rules of proper spelling; in the manner of the orthographic projection.—**Orthographize**,† or-thog'ra-fīz, *v.i.* To use true orthography; to spell correctly.

Orthometry, or-thom'et-ri, *n.* [Gr. *orthos*, right, and *metron*, a measure.] The art or practice of constructing verse correctly; the laws of correct versification.

Orthopedic, or-thō-pē'dik, *a.* [Gr. *orthos*, straight, and *pais*, a child.] Referring to the remedying of deformities; pertaining to orthopedics. — **Orthopedics**, or-thō-pē'diks, *n.* A branch of surgery dealing with the correction of deformities and with the treatment of chronic diseases of the joints and spine.—**Orthopedist**, *n.* A surgeon who practices orthopedics.

Orthophony, or-thof'o-ni, *n.* [Gr. *orthos*, straight, and *phōnē*, voice.] The art of correct speaking; systematic cultivation of the voice.

Orthopraxy, or'thō-prak-si, *n.* [Gr. *orthos*, straight, and *praxis*, a doing.] The treatment of physical deformities by mechanical agency.

Orthopter, **Orthopteran**, or-thop'tėr, or-thop'tėr-an, *n.* [Gr. *orthos*, straight, and *pteron*, a wing.] One of an order of insects which have four wings, the anterior pair being semi-coriaceous or leathery, the posterior pair folding longitudinally like a fan; such as the cockroaches, grasshoppers, and locusts. — **Orthopterous**, or-thop'tėr-us, *a.* Pertaining to the orthopterans.

Orthoscopic, or-thō-skop'ik, *a.* [Gr. *orthos*, straight, and *skopeō*, to see.] Pertaining to or giving correct vision.

Orthostichy, or'thō-sti"ki, *n.* [Gr. *orthos*, straight, *stichos*, a row.] A vertical row of leaves.

Orthotomous, or-thot'o-mus, *a.* [Gr. *orthos*, straight, and *temnō*, to cleave.] *Crystal.* having two cleavages at right angles with one another.

Orthotropal, **Orthotropous**, or-thot'ro-pal, or-thot'ro-pus, *a.* [Gr. *orthos*, straight, and *trepō*, to turn.] *Bot.* having an ovule with the foramen opposite the hilum, or an embryo with radicle next the hilum.

Ortive, or'tiv, *a.* [L. *ortivus*, from *ortus*, risen, *orior*, to rise. ORIENT.] Rising or eastern; relating to the rising of a star.

Ortolan, or'tō-lan, *n.* [It. *ortolano*, from L. *hortulanus*, from *hortus*, a garden; it frequents the hedges of gardens.] A European bird of the bunting family, much esteemed for the delicacy of its flesh.

Oryx, ō'riks, *n.* [L. and Gr.] A name for a species of antelope, a native of the countries on both sides of the Red Sea; also the gemsbok of South Africa.

Osage-orange, ō'sāj, *n.* A North American tree of the mulberry family, producing large yellow fruits resembling an orange, but not edible.

Oscan, os'kan, *n.* An ancient Italian language, of which a few fragments remain; allied to the Latin.

Oscillate, os'sil-lāt, *v.i.*—*oscillated*, *oscillating*. [L. *oscillo*, *oscillatum*, from *oscillum*, a little face or mask hung to a tree and swaying with the wind, dim. of *os*, the mouth, the face. ORACLE.] To swing; to move backward and forward; to vibrate; to vary or fluctuate between fixed limits.—**Oscillancy**, os'sil-lan-si, *n.* State of oscillating or swinging backwards and forwards. — **Oscillating**, os'sil-lāt-ing, *a.* Moving backward and forward; vibrating.—*Oscillating cylinder*, an engine cylinder which rocks on trunnions, and the piston-rod of which connects directly to the crank.—*Oscillating piston*, an engine piston which oscillates in a sector-shaped chamber.—**Oscillation**, os-sil-lā'shon, *n.* [L. *oscillatio*.] The act or state of oscillating or swinging backward and forward; vibration.—**Oscillative**, os'sil-lā-tiv, *a.* Having a tendency to oscillate.—**Oscillator**, os'sil-lā-tėr, *n.* One who or that which oscillates.—**Oscillatory**, os'sil-la-to-ri, *a.* Moving backward and forward like a pendulum.—**Oscillograph**, os-sil'lo-graf, *n.* [Gr. *graphein*, to write.] An instrument for indicating alternating-current wave forms.

Oscitancy, os'si-tan-si, *n.* [L. *oscito*, to yawn, from *os*, the mouth.] The act of gaping or yawning; sleepiness; drowsiness.—**Oscitant**, os'si-tant, *a.* Yawning; gaping; drowsy; sluggish.—**Oscitantly**, os'si-tant-li, *adv.* In an oscitant manner.—**Oscitate**, os'si-tāt, *v.i.* To yawn; to gape with sleepiness. — **Oscitation**, os-si-tā'shon, *n.* The act of yawning.

Osculate, os'kū-lāt, *v.t.*—*osculated*, *osculating*. [L. *osculor*, to kiss, from *osculum*, a kiss, dim. of *os*, the mouth. ORACLE.] To salute with a kiss; to kiss; *geom.* to touch, as one curve another.—*v.i.* To kiss one another; to kiss; *geom.* to touch at a point, as two curves coming in contact.—**Osculant**, os'kū-lant, *a.* Kissing; osculating; having features bordering on those of two groups of plants or animals.—**Osculating**, os'kū-lā-ting, *p.* and *a.* Kissing; *geom.* coming in contact so as merely to touch.—**Osculation**, os-kū-lā'shon, *n.* The act of osculating; a kissing; specifically, *geom.* the contact between any given curve and another curve.—*Point of osculation*, the point where the osculation takes place, and where the two curves have the same curvature.—**Osculatory**, os'kū-la-to-ri, *a.* Pertaining to osculation or kissing. — **Osculum**, os'kū-lum, *n.* pl. **Oscula**, os'kū-la. *Lit.* a little mouth; *zool.* one of the large exhalant apertures by which a sponge is perforated; one of the suckers of the tapeworms, &c.

Osier, ō'zhi-ėr, *n.* [Fr. *osier*, Fr. dial. *oisis*, Armor. *ozil*, *aozil*, an osier; comp. Gr. *oisos*, an osier.] The name of various species of willow, chiefly employed in basket-making. —*a.* Made of osier or twigs; like osier.—**Osiered**, ō'zhi-ėrd, *a.* Covered or adorned with osiers.—**Osiery**, ō'zhi-ėr-i, *n.* A place where osiers are grown.

Osiris, ō-sī'ris, *n.* The great Egyptian deity, the husband of Isis, and the personification of all physical and moral good.

Osmazome, os'ma-zōm, *n.* [Gr. *osmē*, odour, and *zōmos*, juice.] The matter in muscular fibre which gives the peculiar smell to boiled meat and flavour to soups.

Osmium, os'mi-um, *n.* [Gr. *osmē*, odour.] A bluish-white metal, very hard, and more infusible than any other metal, so called from its oxide possessing an extremely disagreeable odour. — **Osmic**, os'mik, *a.* Pertaining to or obtained from osmium.—**Osmious**, os'mi-us, *a.* Belonging to osmium.

Osmose, os'mōs, *v.t.* [Gr. *ōsmos*, an impulse, a pushing, from *ōtheō*, to push.] *Chem.* to subject to diffusion through a membrane.—**Osmosis**, os-mō'sis, *n.* The tendency of two solutions of different concentration, separated by a membrane with very fine pores, to pass through the membrane, mix with each other, and equalize their concentration. (The living cells of plant and animal tissues have such membranes and many of their activities depend upon osmosis.)—**Osmotic**, os-mot'ik, *a.* Pertaining to osmosis.—*Osmotic pressure*, pressure exerted on a membrane through which solutions of different density are diffusing, the pressure being in the direction of the less dense solution.—**Osmotically**, os-mot'i-ka-li, *adv.*

Osmund, os'mund, *n.* [Fr. *osmonde*.] Any fern of the genus *Osmunda*; especially the royal fern.

Osphradium, os-frad'i-um, *n.* [Gr. dim. of *osphra*, an odour.] In aquatic molluscs, a sense-organ connected with the gills, and perhaps serving to test the purity of the water.

Osprey, **Ospray**, os'prā, *n.* [Corrupted from *ossifrage*, L. *ossifraga*, lit. the bone-breaker—*os*, a bone, and *frango*, to break.] A well-known rapacious bird which feeds almost entirely on fish captured by suddenly darting upon them when near the surface.

Ossein, **Osseine**, os'sē-in, *n.* [From L. *osseus*, bony, from *os*, *ossis*, a bone; akin Gr. *osteon*, Skr. *asthi*, a bone.] Bone tissue; the soft glue-like substance of bone left after the removal of the earths.—**Osselet**, os'se-let, *n.* [Fr., a little bone, dim. of L. *os*, *ossis*, a bone.] A hard substance growing on the inside of a horse's knee; the internal bone of some cuttle-fishes.—**Osseous**, os'sē-us, *a.* [L. *osseus*.] Bony; resembling bone.—**Ossicle**, os'i-kl, *n.* [L. *ossiculum*, dim. from *os*, a bone.] A small bone; some of the small bones of the human skeleton, as those of the internal ear; a small hard structure in star-fishes, &c.—**Ossiculated**, os-sik'ū-lā-ted, *a.* Furnished with ossicles.—**Ossiferous**, os-sif'ėr-us, *a.* Producing or furnishing bones.—**Ossific**, os-sif'ik, *a.* Having power to ossify.—**Ossification**, os'si-fi-kā"shon, *n.* The act of ossifying; the change or process of changing into a bony substance.—**Ossifrage**, os'si-frāj, *n.* [L. *ossifraga*. OSPREY.] A name formerly given to the osprey or its young. — **Ossifragous**,† os-sif'ra-gus, *a.* Breaking or fracturing the bones.—**Ossify**, os'si-fī, *v.t.*—*ossified*, *ossifying*. [L. *os*, *ossis*, bone, and *facio*, to form.] To form into bone; to change from a soft animal substance into bone, or a substance of the hardness of bones.—*v.i.* To become bone or bony. — **Ossifying**, os'si-fī-ing, *p.* and *a.* Changing into bone; becoming bone.—**Ossivorous**, os-siv'o-rus, *a.* [L. *os*, *ossis*, bone, and *voro*, to eat.] Feeding on bones; eating bones.—**Ossuary**, os'sū-a-ri, *n.* [L. *ossuarium*.] A charnel-house; a place where the bones of the dead are deposited.

Osteal, os'tē-al, *a.* [Gr. *osteon*, a bone. OSSEIN.] Consisting of or pertaining to bone.

Osteine, os'tē-in, *n.* Same as *Ossein*.

Ostensible, os-ten'si-bl, *a.* [Fr. *ostensible*, from L. *ostendo*, *ostensum*, to show—*ob*, towards, and *tendo*, to hold out. TEND, TENT.] Put forth as having a certain character, whether worthy of it or not; hence, frequently, apparent and not real; having something of sham or pretence; pretended; professed. ∴ Syn. under COLOURABLE. — **Ostensibly**, os-ten'si-bli, *adv.* In an ostensible manner; professedly. —**Ostensibility**, os-ten'si-bil"i-ti, *n.* The state or quality of being ostensible.—**Ostensive**, os-ten'siv, *a.* [Fr. *ostensif*, from L. *ostendo*, to show.] Showing; exhibiting. —**Ostensively**, os-ten'siv-li, *adv.* In an ostensive manner.—**Ostentation**, os-ten-tā'shon, *n.* [L. *ostentatio*, from *ostento*, to show off, to display, intens. of *ostendo*.] Ambitious display; pretentious parade; display dictated by vanity, or to invite praise or flattery. — **Ostentatious**, os-ten-tā'shus, *a.* Characterized by ostentation; showy; intended for vain display.—**Ostentatiously**, os-ten-tā'shus-li, *adv.*

In an ostentatious manner. — **Ostentatiousness**, os-ten-tā'shus-nes, *n.* The state or quality of being ostentatious.

Osteocolla, os'tē-ō-kol''la, *n.* [Gr. *osteon*, a bone, and *kolla*, glue.] An inferior kind of glue obtained from bone; bone-glue.—**Osteodentine**, os'tē-ō-den''tin, *n.* [L. *dens, dentis*, a tooth.] A modification of dentine observed in the teeth of certain animals. — **Osteoblast**, os'tē-ō-blast, *n.* [Gr. *blastos*, a germ.] *Physiol.* a cell or corpuscle forming the germ from which osseous tissue is formed.—**Osteogenesis, Osteogeny**, os'tē-ō-jen''e-sis, os-tē-oj'e-ni, *n.* [Gr. *genesis*, origin.] The formation or growth of bone.—**Osteographer**, os-tē-og'ra-fėr, *n.* One who describes the bony parts of the body, or the skeleton.—**Osteography**, os-tē-og'ra-fi, *n.* A description of the bones; osteology. — **Osteolepis**, os-tē-ol'e-pis, *n.* [Gr. *lepis*, a scale.] A genus of ganoid fishes from the old red sandstone, with enamelled bony scales.—**Osteologic, Osteological**, os'tē-ō-loj''ik, os'-tē-ō-loj''i-kal, *a.* Pertaining to osteology.—**Osteologically**, os'tē-ō-loj''i-kal-li, *adv.* According to osteology. — **Osteologist, Osteologer**, os-tē-ol'o-jist, os-tē-ol'o-jėr, *n.* One versed in osteology; one who describes the bones of animals.—**Osteology**, os-tē-ol'o-ji, *n.* [Gr. *logos*, discourse.] That branch of anatomy which treats of bones and bone tissue.—**Osteomalacia**, os'tē-ō-ma-lā''si-a, *n.* [Gr. *malakia*, softness.] *Pathol.* a diseased softening of the bones. —**Osteopath, Osteopathist**, os'tē-ō-path, os-tē-op'a-thist, *n.* One who practices osteopathy.—**Osteopathy**, os-tē-op'a-thi, *n.* That system of the healing art which places the chief emphasis on the structural integrity of the body mechanism as the most important factor to maintain the organism in health. — **Osteoplasty**, os'tē-ō-plas-ti, *n.* [Gr. *plassō*, to form.] An operation by which the total or partial loss of a bone is remedied.—**Osteotomy**, os-tē-ot'o-mi, *n.* [Gr. *tomē*, a cutting.] The dissection of bones.

Ourang-outang, ō-rang'ō-tang", *n.* ORANGUTAN.

Ostiole, os'ti-ōl, *n.* [L. *ostiolum*, dim. of *ostium*, door.] A small orifice or opening, as in certain sacs or cells in plants.—**Ostiolar**, *a.* Of or pertaining to an ostiole.—**Ostiolate**, *a.* Furnished with an ostiole.

Ostitis, os-tī'tis, *n.* [Gr. *osteon*, a bone, and term. *-itis*.] Inflammation of a bone.

Ostler, os'lėr. HOSTLER.

Ostracean, os-trā'shē-an, *n.* [L. *ostrea*, an oyster.] A mollusc of the oyster family.

Ostracion, os-trā'shi-on, *n.* [Gr. *ostrakon*, a shell.] A fish with an external covering or case composed of plates firmly united to one another at their edges.

Ostracism, os'tra-sizm, *n.* [Gr. *ostrakismos*, from *ostrakon*, a shell, a voting tablet.] A political measure among the ancient Athenians by which persons considered dangerous to the state were banished by public vote for a term of years: so called because the votes were given on shells; banishment from society; expulsion.—**Ostracize, Ostracise**, os'tra-sīz, *v.t.*—*ostracized, ostracizing.* To exile by ostracism; to banish from society; to exclude from public or private favour.

Ostreaceous, os-trē-ā'shus, *a.* [L. *ostrea*, an oyster.] Of or belonging to the oyster family. — **Ostreaculture**, os'trē-a-kul''-tūr, *n.* The artificial cultivation or breeding of oysters.—**Ostreophagist**, os-trē-of'a-jist, *n.* [Gr. *phagō*, to eat.] One who feeds upon oysters; an oyster-eater.—**Ostriferous**, os-trif'ėr-us, *a.* Producing or containing oysters.

Ostrich, os'trich, *n.* [O.Fr. *ostruche, ostruce*, Fr. *autruche*, from L. *avis*, a bird, and *struthio*, Gr. *struthiōn*, an ostrich.] A large running bird inhabiting the sandy plains of Africa and Arabia, the largest of all existing birds, and whose wing and tail feathers form plumes of great beauty and value; an allied bird of S. America.

Ostrogoth, os'trō-goth, *n.* [L.L. *ostrogothus*, from *ostrus*, eastern (G. *ost*, east), and *Gothus*, a Goth.] One of the eastern Goths, as distinguished from the Visigoths or western Goths.—**Ostrogothic**, os-trō-goth'ik, *a.* Pertaining to the Ostrogoths.

Otacoustic, ō-ta-kous'tik, *a.* [Gr. *ous, ōtos*, an ear, and *akoustikos*, acoustic.] Assisting the sense of hearing.

Otalgia, Otalgy, ō-tal'ji-a, ō'tal-ji, *n.* [Gr. *ous, ōtos*, the ear, and *algos*, pain.] A pain in the ear; ear-ache.

Otary, ō'ta-ri, *n.* [Gr. *ōtaros*, large-eared, from *ous, ōtos*, an ear.] One of those seals that have projecting external ears, and yield the sealskin of commerce.

Other, uтн'ėr, *a.* and *pron.* [A.Sax. *ōther*, = D. and G. *ander*, Icel. *annar*, Dan. *anden*, Goth. *anthar*; cog. Lith. *antras*, L. *alter*, Skr. *anyatara* (compar. of *anya*)—other; all comparative forms.] Not the same; different; second of two; additional (get *other* knowledge as well); not this; opposite (the *other* side of the street); often used reciprocally with *each*, and applicable to any number of individuals (help *each other*). It is also used substantively, and may take the plural number and the sign of the possessive case, and frequently is opposed to *some, one, I*, or the like (*some* were right, *others* were wrong; the *one* and the *other*).—*The other day*, on some day not long past; quite recently. — *Every other*, every second (*every other* day, *every other* week).—**Otherness**, uтн'ėr-nes, *n.* The state or quality of being other.—**Otherwhere**, uтн'ėr-whār, *n.* In some other place; elsewhere.—**Otherwise**, uтн'ėr-wīz, *adv.* In a different manner; differently; not so; by other causes; in other respects.—*Rather . . . than otherwise*, rather than not (*rather* pleased *than otherwise*).—*conj.* Else; but for this; such not being the case.

Otic, ot'ik, *a.* [Fr. *otique*, from Gr. *ous, ōtos*, the ear.] Belonging or relating to the ear.

Otiose, ō'shi-ōs, *a.* [L. *otiosus*, from *otium*, leisure.] Idle; unemployed; useless; futile; needless.—**Otiosity**, ō-shi-os'i-ti, *n.* The state or quality of being otiose.

Otitis, ō-tī'tis, *n.* [Gr. *ous, ōtos*, the ear, and term. *-itis*, signifying inflammation.] Inflammation of the tympanic cavity of the ear, accompanied with intense pain.—**Otocrane**, ot'ō-krān, *n.* [Gr. *kranion*, the skull.] *Anat.* that part of the skull containing the internal ear.—**Otocyst**, ō'tō-sist, *n.* [Gr. *kystis*, a bladder.] In animals, a sense-organ in the form of a minute sac containing calcareous particles suspended in fluid. Probably concerned with space-perception and maintenance of equilibrium. —**Otography**, ō-tog'ra-fi, *n.* That branch of anatomy which describes the ear.—**Otolite, Otolith**, ō'tō-līt, ō'tō-lith, *n.* [Gr. *lithos*, a stone.] A name of small calcareous bodies contained in the ear-cavities of some of the lower animals.—**Otology**, ō-tol'o-ji, *n.* That branch of anatomy which concerns itself with the ear.—**Otopathy**, ō-top'a-thi, *n.* [Gr. *pathos*, a disease.] A diseased condition of the ear.—**Otorrhœa**, ō-tor-rē'a, *n.* [Gr. *rheō*, to flow.] A purulent discharge from the ears.—**Otoscope**, ō'to-skōp, *n.* *Surg.* an instrument for examining the interior of the ear.—**Otosteal**, ō-tos'tē-al, *n.* [Gr. *osteon*, a bone.] A bone of the ear.

Ottar, ot'tär, *n.* ATTAR.

Ottava-rima, ot-tä'va-rē-ma, *n.* [It., eighth or octuple rhyme.] An Italian form of versification consisting of eight lines, of which the first six rhyme alternately and the last two form a couplet.

Otter, ot'ėr, *n.* [A.Sax. *otter* = D. and G. *otter*, Dan. *odder*, Icel. *otr*; cog. Lith. *udra*, Rus. and Pol. *wydra*, same root as *water*.] A digitigrade carnivorous mammal of amphibious habits, there being several species; they feed on fish, and their fur is much prized. — **Otter-dog, Otter-hound**, *n.* A variety of dog employed in the chase of the otter.

Otto, ot'tō. ATTAR.

Ottoman, ot'tō-man, *a.* [From *Othoman* or *Osman*, the sultan who laid the foundation of the Turkish Empire in Asia.] Pertaining to or derived from the Turks.—*n.* A Turk; a kind of couch or sofa introduced from Turkey.

Oubliette, ö-blē-et', *n.* [Fr., from *oublier*, L. *obliviscor*, to forget. OBLIVION.] A dungeon with an opening only at the top for the admission of air, used for persons condemned to perpetual imprisonment, or to perish secretly, and existing in some old castles or other buildings.

Ouch, ouch, *n.* [For *nouch*, from O.Fr. *nouche, nosche*, O.H.G. *nusca*, a brooch.] The setting of a precious stone (O.T.); a jewel; a brooch.

Ought, ąt, *v. auxil.* [Originally the preterite of the verb *to owe*, A.Sax. *āgan*, to possess, but now used indifferently as a present and a past: *I ought, thou oughtest, he ought, we, ye, they ought*, to do or to have done. OWE.] To be held or bound in duty or moral obligation.

Ought, ąt, *n.* Aught; anything. AUGHT.

Ought, ąt, *n.* [A corruption of *nought*.] A vulgar name for a cipher.

Ouistiti, ö-is'ti-ti, *n.* [Imitative of its whistling cry.] A beautiful little monkey of tropical America.

Ounce, ouns, *n.* [From L. *uncia*, the twelfth part of anything; whence also *inch*.] A weight, the twelfth part of a pound troy, and the sixteenth of a pound avoirdupois.

Ounce, ouns. [Fr. *once*, Sp. *onza*, It. *lonza*, probably from Per. *youz*, an ounce.] A carnivorous animal resembling a small panther inhabiting the warmer parts of Asia; a name sometimes given to the American jaguar.

Our, our, *a.* [A.Sax. *ūre*, our, contr. for *ūser*, our, from *ūs*, us = G. *unser*, Goth. *unsar*, our. US.] Pertaining or belonging to us (*our* country; *our* rights). *Ours* is a later possessive form and is used in place of *our* and a noun (the book is *ours*).—**Ourself**, our'self, *pron.* Myself: used like *we* and *us* in the regal or formal style.—**Ourselves**, our'selvz, pl. of *ourself*. We or us, not others: often when used as a nominative added to *we* by way of emphasis or opposition; when in the objective often without emphasis and simply serving as the reflexive pronoun corresponding to *us*.

Ourang-outang, ō-rang'ō-tang", *n.* ORANG-OUTANG.

Ouranography. URANOGRAPHY.

Ourari, ö'ra-rē, *n.* CURARI.

Ouretic, ou-ret'ik, *a.* [Gr. *ouron*, urine.] Pertaining to or obtained from urine.

Ousel, Ouzel, ö'zl, *n.* [A.Sax. *ósle*, an ousel, akin to O.H.G. *amisala*, G. *amsel*, an ousel.] An old or poetical name for the blackbird; also applied with qualifications to other birds of the thrush family (*ring-ouzel, water-ouzel*).

Oust, oust, *v.t.* [O.Fr. *ouster*, Mod.Fr. *ôter*, supposed to be from L.L. *hausto, haustare*, to remove, a freq. from L. *haurio*, to draw out (as in *exhaust*).] To eject; to turn out; to dispossess.—**Ouster**, ous'tėr, *n.* *Law*, dispossession or ejection.

Out, out, *adv.* [A.Sax., O.Sax., O.Fris., Icel., and Goth. *ūt*, Sw. *ut*, Dan. *ud*, D. *uit*, G. *aus*, out; seen in *but, about, utter, utmost*.] On or towards the outside; not in or within; without: opposed to *in, into*, or *within*; not in-doors; abroad; beyond usual limits (he was *out* when I called); hence, engaged in a duel (he has been *out* several times); to call a person *out* = to challenge him; no longer concealed or kept secret; not in a state of obscurity; public (the secret is *out*); finished; exhausted; used up; deficient; having expended (*out* of money; extinguished; no longer burning (the candle or fire is *out*); not in employment; not in office; to an end or settlement (hear me *out*); loudly; in an open and free manner (to laugh *out*); not in the hands of the owner (*out* on loan); in an error; at a loss; in a puzzle; having taken her place as a woman in society (said of a young lady).—*Out at elbow, out at heels*, having the elbow or heels showing through the clothes; hence, in very poor circumstances. — *Out* is often used imperatively without a verb in the sense of begone, away; hence, as an interjection, expressive of anger, abhorrence, &c.: often with *on* or *upon* (*out* on you, *out upon* you). *Out* forms a prefix in many words, especially verbs, in which it usually expresses a greater measure or degree in doing something.—*n.* One who is out; especially one out of office, politically (chiefly in the plural); a nook or corner; a projecting angle (ins and *outs*); hence, the *ins and outs of a question*, all its details.—**Out of.** (Really a compound prep. like *into, upon.*) Proceeding from as source or origin; in consequence of; taken, extracted, or quoted from; from or proceeding from a place or the interior of a place; beyond (*out of* the power of fortune); not in; excluded from (*out of* favour; *out of* use); denoting deviation from what is common, regular, or proper (*out of* order); from, by way of rescue or liberation (to be delivered *out of* afflictions); not within the limits or scope of (*out of* hearing, *out of* sight, *out of* reach); denoting loss or exhaustion (*out of* breath).—*Out-of-door, a.*, out of the house; open-air (*out-of-door* exercise).—*Out-of-doors, adv.*, out of the house.—*Out of hand*, immediately; without delay.—*Out of print* denotes that a book is not on sale or to be purchased, the copies printed having been all sold.—*Out of sorts*, out of order; unwell.—*Out of temper*, in bad temper; irritated.—*Out-of-the-way, a.*, remote from populous districts; secluded; unfrequented; unusual; uncommon.—*Out of trim*, not in good order.—*Out of one's time*, having finished one's apprenticeship.—*Out of tune*, discordant; not harmonious. — **Out-and-out**, *adv.* Completely; thoroughly; without reservation. (*Colloq.*)—*a.* Thorough; thorough-paced; absolute; complete (an *out-and-out* swindle). (*Colloq.*)

Outargue, out-är′gū, *v.t.* To argue better than; to surpass in arguing.

Outbid, out-bid′, *v.t.* To bid more than; to go beyond in the offer of a price.—**Outblaze**, out-blāz′, *v.t.* To excel in blazing; to render comparatively obscure; to eclipse.—**Outblush**, out-blush′, *v.t.* To surpass in blushing; to exceed in rosy colour.—**Outboard**, out′bōrd, *a.* *Naut.* applied to anything that is on the outside of the ship (the *outboard* works, &c.).—**Outbrag**, out-brag′, *v.t.* To surpass in bragging, bravado, or ostentation.—**Outbrave**, out-brāv′, *v.t.* To surpass in braving; to bear down by more daring or insolent conduct.—**Outbrazen**, out-brā′zn, *v.t.* To exceed in brazening; to bear down with impudence.—**Outbreak**, out′brāk, *n.* A breaking out; a bursting forth; a sudden and violent manifestation (as of fever, anger, disease).—*v.i.* (out-brāk′). To break or burst forth.—**Outbreaking**, out′brāk-ing, *n.* The act of breaking out; an eruption.—**Outbreathe**, out-brēᴛʜ′, *v.t.* To breathe out.—**Outburst**, out′bėrst, *n.* A breaking or bursting out; an outbreak (an *outburst* of wrath).

Outcast, out′kast, *n.* One who is cast out or expelled; an exile; one driven from home or country.—*a.* Cast out; thrown away; rejected as useless.—**Outcome**, out′kum, *n.* That which comes out of or results from something; the issue; the result; the consequence.—**Outcrier, Outcryer**, out′krī-ėr, *n.* One who cries or proclaims; a public crier; an auctioneer.—**Outcrop**, out′krop, *v.i.* *Geol.* to crop out or appear above the surface of the ground: said of strata.—*n.* *Geol.* the exposure of an inclined stratum at the surface of the ground; the part so exposed; the basset.—**Outcry**, out′krī, *n.* A vehement or loud cry; cry of distress; clamour; noisy opposition; sale at public auction.—*v.t.* (out-krī′). To surpass or get the better of by crying; to cry louder than.

Outdare, out-dãr′, *v.t.* To dare or venture beyond.—**Outdazzle**, out-daz′l, *v.t.* To surpass in dazzling.—**Outdistance**, out-dis′tans, *v.t.* To excel or leave far behind in any competition or career.—**Outdo**, out-dö′, *v.t.* To excel; to surpass; to perform beyond another.—**Outdoor**, out′dōr, *a.* Being without the house; exterior; in the open air.—**Outdoors**, out-dōrz, *adv.* Abroad; out of the house; in the open air.—**Outdoor theater**, one situated in the open air without a roof.

Outer, out′ėr, *a.* [Compar. of *out.*] Being on the outside; external; opposed to *inner*; farthest or farther removed from a person or fixed point.—*n.* That part of a target beyond the circles surrounding the bull's-eye, and so nearer the outside; a shot which strikes that part.—**Outermost**, out′ėr-mōst, *a.* Being on the extreme external part; remotest from the midst; most distant of a series.

Outface, out-fās′, *v.t.* To brave; to bear down with an imposing front or with effrontery; to stare down.—**Outfall**, out′fal, *n.* The mouth of a river; the lower end of a water-course; the point of discharge for, or the embouchure of a drain, culvert, or sewer.—**Outfit**, out′fit, *n.* The act of fitting out for a voyage, journey, or expedition; articles for fitting out; the equipment of one going abroad.—**Outfitter**, out′fit-ėr, *n.* One who furnishes or makes outfits.—**Outfitting**, out′fit-ing, *n.* Equipment; outfit.—**Outflank**, out-flangk′, *v.t.* To go or extend beyond the flank or wing of; hence, to outmanœuvre; to get the better of.—**Outflow**, out′flō, *n.* The act of flowing out; efflux.—*v.i.* (out-flō′). To flow out.—**Outfly**, out-flī′, *v.t.* To fly faster than.—**Outfool**, out-föl′, *v.t.* To exceed in folly.—**Outfrown**, out-froun′, *v.t.* To frown down; to overbear by frowning.

Outgaze, out-gāz′, *v.t.* To surpass in sharpness of sight; to see farther than; to gaze longer than; to outstare.—**Outgeneral**, out-jen′ėr-al, *v.t.* To exceed in generalship; to gain advantage over by superior military skill.—**Outgive**, out-giv′, *v.t.* To surpass in giving.—**Outgo**, out-gō′, *v.t.* To advance before in going; to go faster than; to surpass; to excel.—*n.* (out′gō). That which goes out; specifically, expenditure.—**Outgoing**, out′gō-ing, *p.* or *a.* Going out; removing (an *outgoing* tenant).—*n.* The act of going out; outlay; expenditure.—**Outgrin**, out-grin′, *v.t.* To surpass in grinning.—**Outgrow**, out-grō′, *v.t.* To surpass in growth; to grow too great or too old for.—**Outgrowth**, out′grōth, *n.* That which grows out or proceeds from any body; an excrescence; *fig.* that which grows out of a moral cause; a result.—**Outgush**, out-gush′, *v.t.* To gush out; to flow forth suddenly.—*n.* (out′gush). A gush outward; an outburst.

Out-herod, out-her′od, *v.t.* To excel in resembling Herod; to go beyond in any excess of evil or enormity.—**Out-house**, out′hous, *n.* A small house or building near the main one.

Outing, out′ing, *n.* The act of going out; an excursion; an airing.

Outjuggle, out-jug′l, *v.t.* To surpass in juggling.

Outlandish, out-land′ish, *a.* [A.Sax. *ūtlændisc*, foreign, from *ut*, out, and *land*, land.] Belonging to or characteristic of a foreign country; foreign; not native: hence, strange; barbarous; uncouth; bizarre.—**Outlast**, out-last′, *v.t.* To last longer than; to exceed in duration; to outlive.—**Outlaugh**, out-laf′, *v.t.* To surpass in laughing; to laugh down; to discourage or put out of countenance by laughing.—**Outlaw**, out′la, *n.* [From *out* and *law*: A.Sax. *útlag, útlaga.*] A fugitive from justice, as a bandit, a murderer, &c.—*v.t.* To declare illegal; to taboo, as to outlaw war; to proscribe a person or a thing.—**Outlawry**, out′la-ri, *n.* The putting of a person out of the protection of law by legal means, or the process by which a man is deprived of that protection, being the punishment of a man who, when called into court, contemptuously refuses to appear.—**Outlay**, out′lā, *n.* A laying out or expending; that which is laid out or expended; expenditure.—*v.t.* (out-lā′). To lay or spread out; to expose; to display.—**Outlet**, out′let, *n.* The place or opening by which anything is let out, escapes, or is discharged; a means of egress; a place of exit; a vent.—*v.t.* To let forth; to emit.—**Outlier**, out′lī-ėr, *n.* A part lying without, or beyond the main body; *geol.* a portion of a rock, stratum, or formation detached, and at some distance from the principal mass.—**Outline**, out′līn, *n.* The line by which a figure is defined; the exterior line; contour; a drawing in which an object or scene is represented merely by lines of contour without shading; first general sketch of any scheme or design.—*v.t.* To draw in outline; to delineate.—**Outlinear**, out-lin′ē-ėr, *a.* Pertaining to or forming an outline.—**Outlive**, out-liv′, *v.t.* To live beyond; to survive.—**Outlook**, out′lök, *n.* A looking out or watching; vigilant watch (to be on the *outlook* for something); the place of watch; what lies before the eye; prospect; survey.—**Outlying**, out-lī′ing, *a.* Lying away from the main body or design; remote; being on the exterior or frontier.

Outmanœuvre, out-ma-nö′vėr or out-ma-nū′vėr, *v.t.* To surpass in manœuvring.—**Outmarch**, out-märch′, *v.t.* To march faster than; to march so as to leave behind.—**Outmeasure**, out-mezh′ūr, *v.t.* To exceed in measure or extent.—**Outmost**, out′mōst, *a.* [A superlative of *out.*] Furthest outward; most remote from the middle; outermost.

Outness, out′nes, *n.* The state of being out; externality; objectivity.—**Outnumber**, out-num′bėr, *v.t.* To exceed in number.

Outpace, out-pās′, *v.t.* To outrun; to leave behind.—**Out-patient**, *n.* A patient not residing in a hospital, but who receives medical advice, &c., from the institution.—**Outpost**, out′pōst, *n.* A post or station without the limits of a camp, or at a distance from the main body of an army; the troops placed at such a station.—**Outpour**, out-pōr′, *v.t.* To pour out; to send forth in a stream; to effuse.—*n.* (out′pōr). An outflow.—**Outprize**, out-prīz′, *v.t.* To exceed in value or estimated worth.—**Output**, out′put, *n.* The quantity of material put out or produced within a specified time, as coal from a pit or iron from a furnace, &c.

Outquarters, out′kwar-tėrz, *n.pl.* *Milit.* quarters away from the headquarters.

Outrage, out′rāj, *n.* [Fr. *outrage*, O.Fr. *oultrage*, from L.L. *ultragium*, L. *ultra*, beyond. Ultra.] Rude or injurious violence offered to persons or things; excessive abuse; an act of wanton mischief; an audacious transgression of law or decency.—*v.t.*—*outraged, outraging.* [Fr. *outrager.*] To treat with violence and wrong; to do violence to; to abuse; to maltreat; to commit a rape or indecent assault upon.—**Outrageous**, out-rā′jus, *a.* Characterized by outrage; violent; furious; turbulent; excessive; exceeding reason or decency; enormous; atrocious.—**Outrageously**, out-rā′jus-li, *adv.* In an outrageous manner.—**Outrageousness**, out-rā′jus-nes, *n.* The quality of being outrageous.—**Outrance**, ö′trañs, *n.* [Fr., from L. *ultra*, beyond. Outrage.] The last extremity.—**Outré**, ö-trā, *a.* [Fr., from *outrer*, to exaggerate, from L. *ultra*. Outrance.] Being out of the common course or limits; extravagant; exaggerated; bizarre.—**Outride**, out-rīd′, *v.t.* To pass by riding; to ride faster than.—**Outrider**, out′rī-dėr, *n.* A servant on horseback who precedes or accompanies a carriage.—**Outrigger**, out′rig-ėr, *n.* A structure of spars, &c., rigged out from the side of a sailing boat to steady it; an iron bracket on the outside of a boat, with the rowlock at the extremity; a light boat provided with such apparatus.—**Outright**, out-rīt′, *adv.* Completely; wholly; altogether (to kill him *outright*).—**Outrival**, out-rī′val, *v.t.* To surpass; to excel.—**Outroot**, out-röt′, *v.t.* To eradicate; to extirpate.—**Outrun**, out-run′, *v.t.* To excel in running; to leave behind; to exceed or go beyond.—**Outrush**, out-rush′, *v.t.* To rush or issue out rapidly or forcibly.—

n. (out'rush). A gushing or rushing out; an outflow.

Outsail, out-sāl', *v.t.* To leave behind in sailing. — **Outset**, out'set, *n.* A setting out; beginning; start.—**Outsettlement**, out'set-l-ment, *n.* A settlement away from the main settlement.—**Outsettler**, out'set-lėr, *n.* One who settles at a distance from the main body. — **Outshine**, out-shīn', *v.t.* To excel in lustre or excellence. —*v.i.* To shine out or forth.—**Outshipped goods**, out-ship't, *n.* (*Commercial.*) Goods refused, or left out, owing to absence of cargo-room on ship.—**Outshoot**, out-shöt', *v.t.* To excel in shooting; to shoot beyond. —**Outside**, out'sīd, *n.* The external outer or exposed parts or surface; superficial appearance; external aspect or features; space immediately without or beyond an inclosure; the farthest limit; the utmost; extreme estimate (with *the*).—*a.* Being on the outside; external; superficial.—*Outside broker*, a broker outside of the regular Stock Exchange. —**Outsider**, out'sī-dėr, *n.* One not belonging to a party, association, or set; unconconnected or not admitted.—**Outsit**, out-sit', *v.t.* To sit beyond the time of anything; to sit longer than.—**Outskirt**, out'-skėrt, *n.* Part near the edge or boundary of an area; border; purlieu.—**Outspan**, out-span', *v.t.* and *i.*—*outspanned, outspanning.* [E. *out*, and D. *spannen*, to yoke.] To unyoke (a team of oxen) from a wagon: correlative of *inspan.* (*South Africa.*)— **Outspeak**, out-spēk', *v.t.* To exceed in speaking; to say more than.—*v.i.* To speak out or aloud.—**Outspoken**, out'spō-kn, *a.* Free or bold of speech; candid; frank.— **Outspokenness**, out-spō'kn-nes, *n.* The character of being outspoken. — **Outspread**, out-spred', *v.t.* To spread out; to extend. — **Outstanding**, out-stand'ing, *a.* Not collected; unpaid (*outstanding* debts). —**Outstare**, out-stār', *v.t.* To stare out of countenance; to face down; to outface.— **Outstay**, out-stā', *v.t.* To stay longer than; to overstay.—**Outstep**, out-step', *v.t.* To step or go beyond; to exceed; to overstep. —**Outstretch**, out-strech', *v.t.* To extend; to stretch or spread out; to expand. —**Outstrip**, out-strip', *v.t.* To outrun; to advance beyond; to exceed.—**Outswear**, out-swār', *v.t.* To exceed in swearing.

Outtalk, out-tąk', *v.t.* To overpower by talking; to exceed in talking.

Outvalue, out-val'ū, *v.t.* To exceed in price or value.—**Outvie**, out-vī', *v.t.* To exceed or excel; to surpass. — **Outvote**, out-vōt', *v.t.* To exceed in the number of votes given; to defeat by plurality of votes.

Outwalk, out-wąk', *v.t.* To walk farther, longer, or faster than; to leave behind in walking.—**Outward**, out'wėrd, *a.* [A.Sax. *ūteweard*—*ūte*, out, and *weard*, denoting direction.] Forming the superficial part; exterior; external; visible; appearing; tending to the exterior; derived from without; not properly belonging; adventitious.—*adv.* Outwards; from a port or country.—**Outward-bound**, *a.* Proceeding from a port or country.—**Outwardly**, out'wėrd-li, *adv.* Externally; on the outside; in appearance only.—**Outwardness**, out'-wėrd-nes, *n.* State of being outward.— **Outwards**, out'wėrdz, *adv.* Towards the outer parts.—**Outwatch**, out-woch', *v.t.* To surpass in watching; to watch longer than.—**Outwear**, out-wār', *v.t.* To wear out; to last longer than.—**Outweigh**, out-wā', *v.t.* To exceed in weight or in value, influence, or importance.—**Outwit**, out-wit', *v.t.*—*outwitted, outwitting.* To defeat or frustrate by superior ingenuity; to prove too clever for; to overreach.—**Outwork**, out'wėrk, *n.* Part of a fortification distant from the main fortress or citadel.

Ouzel, *n.* Ousel.

Ova, ō'va, *n.* Plural of *ovum.*

Oval, ō'val, *a.* [Fr. *ovale*, from L. *ovum*, an egg; cog. Gr. *ōon*, an egg.] Of the shape of the outline of an egg; resembling the longitudinal section of an egg; elliptical.— *n.* A figure in the shape of the outline of an egg; an elliptical figure.—**Ovally**, ō'val-li, *adv.* In an oval form; so as to be oval.

Ovary, ō'va-ri, *n.* [Mod.L. *ovarium*, from L. *ovum*, an egg. Oval.] The female organ in which ova, reproductive germs or eggs, are formed and developed; *bot.* a case inclosing ovules or young seeds, and ultimately becoming the fruit. — **Ovarian**, **Ovarial**, ō-vā'ri-an, ō-vā'ri-al, *a.* Belonging to the ovary.—**Ovariotomist**, ō-va'-ri-ot''o-mist, *n.* One who practises ovariotomy. — **Ovariotomy**, ō-va'ri-ot''o-mi, *n.* The operation for removing a tumour in the ovary or the ovary itself.

Ovate, **Ovated**, ō'vāt, ō'vā-ted, *a.* [L. *ovatus.* Oval.] Egg-shaped; oval.

Ovation, ō-vā'shon, *n.* L. *ovatio*, from *ovare*, to exult.] A kind of triumph granted to ancient Roman commanders who could not claim the distinction of a full triumph; hence, any triumphal reception of a person or marks of respect publicly shown.

Oven, uv'n, *n.* [A.Sax. *ofen* = D. *oven*, Dan. *ovn*, Icel. *ofn*, G. *ofen*, Sw. *ugn*, Goth. *auhns.*] A closely-built recess for baking, heating, or drying any substance; a chamber in a stove or kitchen-range, or a portable apparatus of tinned iron used for baking, &c.

Over, ō'vėr, *prep.* [A.Sax. *ofer*, over, above, across = L., G., D., and Dan. *over*; Icel. *ofr*, *yfir*, G. *über*; cog. L. *super*, Gr. *hyper*, Skr. *upari*, above; a comparative form allied to *up.*] Above in place or position; rising to or reaching a height above; across (implying motion); upon the surface of; through the whole extent of; above in eminence or superiority; above in authority; with oversight or watchfulness in respect to (to keep guard *over*); denoting motive or occasion (to rejoice *over*); denoting superiority as the result of a struggle or contest; upwards of; more than.—*adv.* From side to side; in width; across; from one side to the other or to another (to roll *over*); on all the surface; above the top, brim, or edge; more than the quantity assigned; in excess; throughout; completely; having come to an end; past (till this heat be *over*); excessively; in a great degree.—*Over and over*, repeatedly; once and again.—*Over again*, once more; with repetition.—*Over and above*, besides; beyond what is supposed or limited.—*Over against*, opposite; in front of.—*Over the top*, or *over the lid* (to go), to leave the trench and take part in an attack on the enemy.— *To give over*, to cease from; to consider as in a hopeless state.—*To run over*, to run out over the brim; to take a rapid survey of.— *All over*, so as to affect the whole of a surface; in every part; completely.—*It is all over with* a person or thing, the person or thing is ruined or undone.—*To throw over*, to desert; to betray.—*a.* Upper; superior; covering; outer (*over*-shoes).—*Over* forms the first element in many compounds. Of these we can only give the principal.

Overact, ō-vėr-akt', *v.t.* To act or perform to excess.—*v.i.* To act more than is necessary.

Overalls, ō'vėr-ąls, *n. pl.* Loose trousers worn over others to protect them from being soiled.

Over-anxious, *a.* Anxious to excess.— **Over-anxiously**, *adv.* With excessive solicitude.

Overarch, ō-vėr-ärch', *v.t.* and *i.* To arch over; to cover with an arch.

Overawe, ō-vėr-ą', *v.t.* To restrain by awe, fear, or superior influence.

Overbalance, ō-vėr-bal'ans, *v.t.* To more than balance; to exceed in weight, value, &c.; to surpass; to destroy the balance or equilibrium of (used *refl.*). — *n.* Excess; something more than an equivalent.

Overbear, ō-vėr-bār', *v.t.* To bear down; to overpower; to overcome by argument, effrontery, or the like. — **Overbearing**, ō-vėr-bār'ing, *p.* and *a.* Haughty and dogmatical; given to effrontery.

Overboard, ō'vėr-bōrd, *adv.* Over the side of a ship; out of a ship or from on board. —*Thrown overboard* (*fig.*), discarded; deserted; betrayed.

Overbold, ō'vėr-bōld, *a.* Unduly bold; forward; impudent.

Overbright, ō'vėr-brīt, *a.* Bright to excess; too bright.

Overbrim, ō-vėr-brim', *v.i.* To flow over the brim or edge: said of a liquid; to be so full as to overflow: said of the vessel.

Overbuild, ō-vėr-bild', *v.t.* To build over; to build more than the area properly admits of, or than the population requires.—*v.i.* To build beyond the demand.

Overburden, **Overburthen**, ō-vėr-bėr'dn, ō-vėr-bėr'THn, *v.t.* To load with too great weight; to overload.

Overcanopy, ō-vėr-kan'ō-pi, *v.t.* To cover as with a canopy.

Overcast, ō-vėr-kast', *v.t.* To cloud; to obscure with clouds; to cover with gloom; to sew by running the thread over a rough edge.—*a.* Clouded.

Overcharge, ō-vėr-chärj', *v.t.* To charge or burden to excess; to fill too numerously; to make an excessive charge against; to charge at too high a sum or price; to exaggerate.—*n.* ō'vėr-chärj). An excessive charge; a charge of more than is just in an account.

Overcloud, ō-vėr-kloud', *v.t.* To cover or overspread with clouds.

Overcoat, ō'vėr-kōt, *n.* A coat worn over all the other dress; a top-coat or greatcoat.

Overcome, ō-vėr-kum', *v.t.* To conquer; to vanquish; to surmount; to get the better of.—*v.i.* To gain the superiority; to be victorious.

Over-confidence, *n.* Too great or excessive confidence. — **Over-confident**, *a.* Confident to excess. — **Over-confidently**, *adv.* In an over-confident manner.

Over-credulous, *a.* Credulous to excess.

Overcrowd, ō-vėr-kroud', *v.t.* To fill or crowd to excess, especially with human beings.

Overdaring, ō-vėr-dā'ring, *a.* Imprudently bold; foolhardy.

Overdo, ō-vėr-dö', *v.t.* To do to excess; to overact; to surpass or exceed in performance; to boil, roast, or otherwise cook too much.

Overdose, ō'vėr-dōs, *n.* Too great a dose. —*v.t.* (ō-vėr-dōs'). To dose excessively.

Overdraw, ō-vėr-dra', *v.t.* To draw upon for a larger sum than is standing at one's credit in the books of a bank, &c.; to exaggerate either in writing, speech, or a picture.

Overdress, ō-vėr-dres', *v.t.* and *i.* To dress to excess.

Overdrive, ō-vėr-drīv', *v.t.* To drive too hard or beyond strength.

Overdue, ō'vėr-dū, *a.* Not arrived at the proper date or assigned limit (an *overdue* ship); past the time of payment (an *overdue* bill).

Over-eager, *a.* Too eager; too vehement in desire.—**Over-eagerly**, *adv.* With excessive eagerness.—**Over-eagerness**, *n.*

Overeat, ō-vėr-ēt', *v.t.* To surfeit with eating: used *refl.* (to *overeat one's self*).

Over-estimate, *n.* An estimate or calculation that is too high.—*v.t.* To estimate too high; to overvalue.

Over-excited, *a.* Too much excited.— **Over-excitement**, *n.* The state of being over-excited.

Over-fatigue, *n.* Excessive fatigue.—*v.t.* To fatigue to excess.

Overfeed, ō-vėr-fēd', *v.t.* and *i.* To feed to excess.

Overfold, ō-vėr-fōld', *n.* A rock-fold which has been tilted over.

Overflow, ō-vėr-flō', *v.t.* (the pret. and pp. are properly *overflowed*, though the pp. *overflown* is sometimes used). To flow or spread over; to inundate; to fill and run over the brim of; to deluge; to overwhelm. —*v.i.* To swell and run over the brim or banks; to be so full that the contents run over; to abound.—*n.* (ō'vėr-flō). An inundation; a flowing over; superabundance.— **Overflowing**, ō-vėr-flō'ing, *a* Abundant;

exuberant.—**Overflowingly**, ō-vėr-flō′-ing-li, *adv.* Exuberantly; in great abundance.

Overgorge, ō-vėr-gorj′, *v.t.* To gorge or fill the stomach to excess; often *refl.*

Overgrow, ō-vėr-grō′, *v.t.* To cover with growth or herbage: generally in *pp.* (a ruin *overgrown* with ivy).—*v.i.* To grow beyond the fit or natural size.—**Overgrowth**, ō′vėr-grōth, *n.* Exuberant or excessive growth.

Overhand, ō′vėr-hand, *a.* and *adv.* With the hand over the object; with the knuckle upward.

Overhang, ō-vėr-hang′, *v.t.* To impend or hang over; to jut or project over.

Overhardy, ō-vėr-här′di, *a.* Excessively or unduly hardy or daring; foolhardy.

Overhaste, ō′vėr-hāst, *n.* Too great haste. —**Overhasty**, ō-vėr-hās′ti, *a.* Too hasty; rash; precipitate.

Overhaul, ō-vėr-hąl′, *v.t.* To turn over for examination; to examine thoroughly with a view to repairs; to re-examine (as accounts); to gain upon or overtake.—*To overhaul a ship*, to gain upon her in following; to search for contraband goods.—**Overhaul, Overhauling**, ō′vėr-hąl, ō′vėr-hąl-ing, *n.* Examination; inspection; repair.

Overhead, ō-vėr-hed′, *adv.* Aloft; in the zenith; above one's head.—*n.* (ō′vėr-hed). Expenses of a business, as rent, office expenses, taxes, depreciation, &c., which are not directly chargeable to production, as contrasted with direct charges, as wages and cost of materials.

Overhear, ō-vėr-hēr′, *v.t.* To hear though not intended or expected to hear.

Overhung, ō-vėr-hung′, *a.* Hung or covered over; adorned with hangings.

Overissue, ō′vėr-ish-ū, *n.* An excessive issue; an issue (as of coin or bank-notes) in excess of the conditions which should regulate or control it.—*v.t.* To issue in excess, as bank-notes or bills of exchange; to issue contrary to prudence or honesty.

Overjoy, ō-vėr-joi′, *v.t.* To give great or excessive joy to: generally in *pp.*

Over-king, *n.* A king holding sway over several petty kings or princes.

Overland, ō′vėr-land, *a.* Passing by land; made upon or across the land (an *overland* journey.

Overlap, ō-vėr-lap′, *v.t.* To lap or fold over; to extend so as to lie or rest upon.—*n.* The lapping of one thing over another; *geol.* the extension of a superior stratum over an inferior so as to cover and conceal it.

Overlay, ō-vėr-lā′, *v.t.*—pret. & pp. *overlaid.* To lay too much upon; to overwhelm; to cover or spread over the surface of; to coat or cover; to smother with close covering, or by lying upon; to obscure by covering.—**Overlaying**, ō′vėr-lā-ing, *n.* A superficial coating or covering.

Overleap, ō-vėr-lēp′, *v.t.* To leap over; to pass by leaping; *refl.* to leap too far.

Overlie, ō-vėr-lī′, *v.t.* pret. *overlay*, pp. *overlain.* To lie over or upon; to smother by lying on (to *overlie* a child; comp. OVERLAY).

Overlive, ō-vėr-liv′, *v.t.* To outlive; to survive.

Overload, ō-vėr-lōd′, *v.t.* To load with too heavy a burden or cargo; to overburden.

Overlook, ō-vėr-lųk′, *v.t.* To view from a higher place; to rise or be elevated above; to see from behind or over the shoulder of another; to inspect or superintend; to pass over indulgently; to omit to censure or punish (a fault); to slight.—**Overlooker**, ō-vėr-lųk′ėr, *n.* One that overlooks; an overseer.

Overlord, ō′vėr-lord, *n.* One who is lord over another; a feudal superior.

Overmasted, ō-vėr-mas′ted, *a.* Furnished with a mast or masts that are too long or too heavy.

Overmaster, ō-vėr-mas′tėr, *v.t.* To overpower; to subdue; to vanquish.

Overmatch, ō-vėr-mach′, *v.t.* To be too powerful for.—*n.* One superior in power; one able to overcome.

Overmodest, ō-vėr-mod′est, *a.* Modest to excess; bashful.

Overmuch, ō′vėr-much, *a.* Too much; exceeding what is necessary or proper.—*adv.* In too great a degree.—*n.* More than sufficient.

Overnice, ō-vėr-nīs′, *a.* Excessively nice; fastidious.—**Overnicely**, ō-vėr-nīs′li, *adv.* In an overnice manner; with too great fastidiousness or scrupulosity.

Overnight, ō′vėr-nīt, *adv.* Through or during the night; in the course of the night or evening; in the evening before.

Overpass, ō′vėr-pas, *n.* A section of a highway, &c., crossing over another road, railroad, &c.—*v.t.* (ō-vėr-pas′). To pass over; to cross.

Overpay, ō-vėr-pā′, *v.t.* To pay in excess; to reward beyond the price or merit.

Overpeople, ō-vėr-pē′pl, *v.t.* To overstock with inhabitants.

Overplus, ō′vėr-plus, *n.* [*Over*, and L. *plus*, more.] Surplus; that which remains after a supply, or beyond a quantity proposed.

Overpower, ō-vėr-pou′ėr, *v.t.* To vanquish by power or force; to subdue; to be too intense or violent for (his emotions *overpowered* him).—**Overpowering**, ō-vėr-pou′ėr-ing, *p.* and *a.* Bearing down by superior power; irresistible.—**Overpoweringly**, ō-vėr-pou′ėr-ing-li, *adv.* In an overpowering manner.

Overprize, ō-vėr-prīz′, *v.t.* To value or prize at too high a rate.

Over-production, *n.* Production of commodities in excess of demand.

Overrate, ō-vėr-rāt′, *v.t.* To rate at too much; to regard as having greater talents, abilities, or more valuable qualities than is really the case.

Overreach, ō-vėr-rēch′, *v.t.* To reach beyond; to rise above; to deceive by cunning, artifice, or sagacity; to cheat; to outwit.—**Overreacher**, ō-vėr-rē′chėr, *n.* One that overreaches.

Over-refinement, *n.* Excessive refinement; refinement with excess of subtlety or affectation of nicety.

Override, ō-vėr-rīd′, *v.t.* To ride over; hence, to trample down; to supersede; to annul—*To override one's commission*, to discharge one's office in too arbitrary a manner or with too high a hand.

Overripe, ō′vėr-rīp, *a.* Ripe or matured to excess.—**Overripen**, ō-vėr-rī′pn, *v.t.* To make too ripe.

Overrule, ō-vėr-röl′, *v.t.* To influence or control by predominant power; to set aside (objections) as not sufficiently weighty or convincing; *law*, to rule against or reject. —*v.i.* To govern; to exercise control.—**Overruler**, ō-vėr-röl′ėr, *n.* One who overrules.—**Overruling**, ō-vėr-röl′ing, *p.* and *a.* Exerting superior and controlling power; having effective sway.

Overrun, ō-vėr-run′, *v.t.* To run or spread over; to grow over; to cover all over (as with weeds); to harass by hostile incursions; to overcome and take possession of by an invasion; to outrun; to run faster and leave behind; *printing*, to carry over parts of lines or pages in correction, in the contraction or extension of columns, or when new matter has to be inserted.—**Overrunner**, ō-vėr-run′ėr, *n.* One that overruns.

Over-scrupulous, *a.* Scrupulous to excess.—**Over-scrupulousness**, *n.*

Oversea, ō′vėr-sē, *a.* Foreign; from beyond sea.—**Overseas**, ō′vėr-sēz, *adv.* Beyond or across the sea; abroad.

Oversee, ō-vėr-sē′, *v.t.* To superintend; to overlook; to take charge of.—**Overseer**, ō-vėr-sēr′, *n.* One who supervises; a superintendent; an officer who has the care or superintendence of any matter.—*Overseers of the poor*, officers in England who rate the inhabitants for the poor-rate, collect it, and apply it towards the relief of the poor.—**Overseership**, ō-vėr-sēr′ship, *n.* The office of an overseer.

Overset, ō-vėr-set′, *n.* An upsetting; an overturn.—*v.t.* To turn from the proper position; to turn upon the side, or to turn bottom upward (as a vehicle); to subvert; to overthrow.—*v.i.* To turn or be turned over.

Overshadow, ō-vėr-shad′ō, *v.t.* To throw a shadow over; to shelter or cover with protecting influence.

Overshoe, ō′vėr-shö, *n.* A shoe worn over another; an outer waterproof shoe.

Overshoot, ō-vėr-shöt′, *v.t.* To shoot over; to shoot beyond (a mark); to pass swiftly over.—*To overshoot one's self*, to venture too far.—**Overshot**, ō-vėr-shot′, *p.* and *a.* Shot over or beyond.—*Overshot water-wheel*, a wheel that receives the water *shot over* the top on the descent: opposed to *undershot.*

Oversight, ō′vėr-sīt, *n.* Superintendence; watchful care; a mistake of inadvertence; an overlooking; omission.

Oversleep, ō-vėr-slēp′, *v.t.* To sleep beyond or too long: often *refl.* (to *oversleep one's self*).

Oversman, ō′vėrz-man, *n.* An overseer; a superintendent; in Scotland, an umpire appointed to decide where two arbiters have differed in opinion.

Oversoon, ō-vėr-sön′, *adv.* Too soon.

Overspan, ō-vėr-span′, *v.t.* To reach or extend over; to extend from side to side of.

Overspread, ō-vėr-spred′, *v.t.* To spread over; to cover completely; to scatter over. —*v.i.* To be spread or scattered over.

Overstate, ō-vėr-stāt′, *v.t.* To exaggerate in statement; to state in too strong terms. —**Overstatement**, ō′vėr-stāt-ment, *n.* An exaggerated statement.

Overstay, ō-vėr-stā′, *v.t.* To stay too long for; to stay beyond the limits or duration of.

Overstep ō-vėr-step′, *v.t.* To step over or beyond; to exceed.

Overstock, ō-vėr-stok′, *v.t*, To stock to too great an extent; to fill too full; to supply with more than is wanted (the market with goods; a farm with cattle).

Overstrain, ō-vėr-strān′, *v.t.* and *t.* To strain to excess; to stretch too far; to exert too much.—**Overstrained**, ō′vėr-strānd, *a.* Stretched or strained beyond the limit of elasticity; exaggerated; overdone.

Overstrew, ō-vėr-strö′, *v.t.* To spread or scatter over; to cover by scattering.—**Overstrewn, Overstrown**, ō-vėr-strōn′, *pp.* Spread or scattered over.

Oversupply, ō′vėr-sup-plī, *n.* An excessive supply; a supply in excess of demand.

Overt, ō′vėrt, *a.* [O.Fr. *overt*, Fr. *ouvert*, O.Fr. *ovrir*, to open, from L. *aperire*, to open.] Open to view; public; apparent; *law*, not covert or secret; manifest.—**Overtly**, ō′vėrt-li, *adv.* In an overt manner; openly; publicly.

Overtake, ō-vėr-tāk′, *v.t.* To come up with in following; to follow and reach or catch; to come upon; to take by surprise.

Overtask, ō-vėr-task′, *v.t.* To impose too heavy a task or duty on.

Overtax, ō-vėr-taks′, *v.t.* To tax too heavily.

Overthrow, ō-vėr-thrō′, *v.t.* To overset; to turn upside down; to throw down; to demolish; to defeat, conquer, vanquish; to subvert or destroy.—*n.* (ō′vėr-thrō). The act of overthrowing; ruin; subversion; defeat.—**Overthrower**, ō-vėr-thrō′ėr, *n.* One that overthrows.

Overthwart, ō-vėr-thwąrt′, *prep.* Across; from side to side of.

Overtime, ō′vėr-tīm, *n.* Time during which one works beyond the regular hours.

Overtone, ō′vėr-tōn, *n.* Same as *Harmonic.*

Overtop, ō-vėr-top′, *v.t.* To rise above the top of; to excel; to surpass.

Overtrade, ō-vėr-trād′, *v.i.* To trade beyond capital or too rashly.

Overture, ō′vėr-tūr, *n.* [O.Fr. *overture*, Fr. *ouverture*, an opening, an overture. OVERT.] A proposal; something offered for consideration; a musical introduction to precede important compositions, as oratorios, operas, &c., written for a full orchestra.

Overturn, ō-vėr-tėrn′, *v.t.* To overset or overthrow; to turn or throw from a foundation; to subvert; to ruin.—*n.* (ō′vėr-tėrn). State of being overturned; overthrow.—**Overturner**, ō-vėr-tėr′nėr, *n.* One that overturns.

Overvalue, ō-vėr-val′ū, *v.t.* To set too great value on; to rate at too high a price.—**Overvaluation**, ō′vėr-val-ū-ā″shon, *n.* Too high valuation; an over-estimate.

Overween, ō-vėr-wēn′, *v.i.* To think too highly, arrogantly, or conceitedly.—**Overweening**, ō-vėr-wēn′ing, *p.* and *a.* Haughty; arrogant; proud; conceited.—**Overweeningly**, ō-vėr-wēn′ing-li, *adv.*

Overweigh, ō-vėr-wā′, *v.t.* To exceed in weight; to outweigh.

Overwhelm, ō-vėr-whelm′, *v.t.* To whelm entirely; to swallow up; *fig.* to bear down; to crush.—**Overwhelmingly**, ō-vėr-whel′ming-li, *adv.*

Overwind, ō-vėr-wīnd′, *v.t.* To wind too far (to *overwind* a watch).

Overwise, ō′vėr-wīz, *a.* Wise to affectation.—**Overwisely**, ō-vėr-wīz′li, *adv.* In an affectedly wise manner.

Overwork, ō-vėr-wėrk′, *v.t.* To work beyond strength; to cause to labour too much; often *refl.* (to *overwork one's self*).—*n.* (ō′vėr-wėrk). Excessive work or labour; work done beyond the amount required by stipulation.

Overworn, ō′vėr-wōrn, *p.* and *a.* Worn out; subdued by toil; spoiled by time; trite; threadbare.

Overwrought, ō-vėr-rat′, *p.* and *a.* Laboured to excess; worked all over; affected or excited to excess; tasked beyond strength.

Over-zealous, ō′vėr-zel-us, *a.* Too zealous; eager to excess.

Ovicell, ō′vi-sel, *n.* [L. *ovum*, an egg, *cella*, a cell.] Same as *Oocyst*.—**Ovicular**, ō-vik′ū-lėr, *a.* Pertaining to an egg.—**Oviduct**, ō′vi-dukt, *n.* [L. *ductus*, a duct.] A passage for the ovum or egg from the ovary of animals.—**Oviferous**, ō-vif′ėr-us, *a.* Carrying eggs: applied to organs of some crustaceans carrying the eggs after exclusion.—**Oviform**, ō′vi-form, *a.* Having the form or figure of an egg.—**Ovigerous**, ō-vij′ėr-us, *a.* Bearing ova or ovules; oviferous.

Ovine, ō′vīn, *a.* [L. *ovinus*, from *ovis*, a sheep.] Pertaining to sheep; consisting of sheep.

Oviparous, ō-vip′a-rus, *a.* [L. *ovum*, an egg, *pario*, to produce.] Producing eggs, especially eggs that are hatched after exclusion from the body (as opposed to *ovoviviparous*).

Oviposit, ō-vi-poz′it, *v.i.* [L. *ovum*, an egg, and E. *posit*.] To deposit eggs: said of insects.—**Oviposition**, ō′vi-pō-zish″on, *n.* The depositing of eggs by insects.—**Ovipositor**, ō-vi-poz′it-ėr, *n.* An organ at the extremity of the abdomen of many insects for depositing their eggs.

Ovisac, ō′vi-sak, *n.* [L. *ovum*, an egg, *saccus*, a sack.] The cavity in the ovary which immediately contains the ovum.

Ovoid, Ovoidal, ō′void, ō-voi′dal, *a.* [L. *ovum*, and Gr. *eidos*, form. OVAL] Having a shape resembling that of an egg.—**Ovolo**, ō′vō-lō, *n.* [It., from L. *ovum*.] *Arch.* a round moulding forming the quarter of a circle.—**Ovology**, ō-vol′o-ji, *n.* *Oology*.—**Ovoviviparous**, ō′vō-vī-vip″a-rus, *a.* [L. *ovum*, *vivo*, to live, *pario*, to produce.] Producing eggs which are hatched within the body (as is the case with vipers). OVIPAROUS.—**Ovulary**, ō′vū-la-ri, *a.* Pertaining to ovules.—**Ovulation**, ō-vū-lā′shon, *n.* The formation and discharge of ova or an ovum from the ovary.—**Ovule**, ō′vūl, *n.* A small vesicle; *bot.* a rudimentary seed; a small pellucid body borne by the placenta of a plant, and changing into a seed.—**Ovuliferous**, ō-vū-lif′ėr-us, *a.* Producing ovules.—**Ovulite**, ō′vū-līt, *n.* A fossil egg.—**Ovum**, ō′vum, *n.* pl. **Ova**, ō′va. A small vesicle within the ovary of a female animal, when impregnated becoming the embryo; an egg.

Owe, ō, *v.t.*—*owed*, *owing*. [From A.Sax. *āgan*, to own, to have (pret. *āhte*, whence *ought*; pp. *āgen*, whence *own*); Icel. *eiga*, Sw. *äga*, *ega*, O.H.G. *eigan*, Goth. *aigan*, to possess.] To possess or own‡; to be indebted in; to be bound to pay; to be obliged to ascribe; to be obliged for (he *owes* his safety to me); to be due or owing.—**Owing**, ō′ing, *ppr.* [Pres. part. used in passive sense of *owed*, *being due*.] Required by obligation to be paid; remaining as a debt; ascribable, as to a cause; due; imputable, as to an agent.

Owenism, ō′wen-ism, *n.* The Socialistic-philanthropical system of Robert Owen (d. 1858) established by him at the New Lanark Mills in Scotland.

Owl, oul, *n.* [A.Sax. *ūle* = D. *uil*, Icel. *ugla*, Dan. *ugle*, Sw. *uggla*, G. *eule*, names imitative of its cry; comp. L. *ululo*, to lament, E. *howl*.] One of the nocturnal birds of prey, well known for their somewhat cat-like heads and their harsh and screeching note.—**Owlery**, ou′lėr-i, *n.* An abode or haunt of owls.—**Owlet**, oul′et, *n.* [Dim. of *owl*.] An owl; a young owl.—**Owl-eyed**, *a.* Having eyes like an owl's, blinking in daylight.—**Owlish**, oul′ish, *a.* Resembling an owl.

Own, ōn, *a.* [A.Sax. *āgen*, pp. of *āgan*, to possess, like Dan. and Sw. *egen*, Icel. *eiginn*, D. and G. *eigen*, own. OWE.] Belonging to me, him, us, you, &c., distinctly and emphatically: always following a possessive pronoun, or a noun in the possessive, as *my own*, *his own*, *John's own*: sometimes used to impart tenderness to an expression (thine *own* true knight).—*To hold one's own*, to maintain one's own cause; not to lose ground.—*v.t.* [A.Sax. *āgnian* (from *āgen* = *own*, *a.*), Icel. *eigna*, Dan. *egne*, G. *eignen*, to own.] To have the right of property in; to hold or possess by right; to acknowledge or avow (*owned* him as his son); to concede; to admit to be true.—**Owner**, ō′nėr, *n.* One who owns; the rightful proprietor.—**Ownership**, ō′nėr-ship, *n.* The state of being an owner.

Ox, oks, *n.* pl. **Oxen**, ok′sn. [A.Sax. *oxa*, pl. *oxan* = Icel. *oxi*, Sw. and Dan. *oxe*, D. *os*, G. *ochs*, *ochse*, Goth. *auhsa*, *auhsus*, an ox; cog. L. *vacca*, a cow, Skr. *ukshā*, an ox.] The general name for any animal of the cow or bovine kind; especially, a male castrated, and full-grown, or nearly so.—**Ox-bow**, *n.* A curved piece of wood encircling an ox's neck when yoked; *arch.* an oval dormer-window.—**Ox-eyed**, *a.* Having large full eyes, like those of an ox.—**Ox-fly**, *n.* A species of bott hatched under the skin of cattle.—**Ox-gall**, *n.* The bitter fluid secreted by the liver of an ox, much used in the arts.—**Oxgang**, oks′gang, *n.* *Anc. law*, as much land as an ox can plough in a year, generally from 15 to 20 acres; in Scotland, termed *oxgate*.—**Oxlip**, oks′lip, *n.* A species of the primrose growing wild in Britain.

Oxalate, ok′sa-lāt, *n.* [Gr. *oxalis*, sorrel, from *oxys*, sharp, acid.] *Chem.* a combination of oxalic acid with a base.—**Oxalic**, ok-sal′ik, *a.* Pertaining to sorrel.—*Oxalic acid*, an acid obtained from sorrel, rhubarb, &c.; a violent poison. Erroneously called *salt of lemons*.—**Oxaluria**, ok-sa-lū′ri-a, *n.* [*Oxalic*, and Gr. *ouron*, urine.] A morbid state of the body in which oxalic acid is contained in the urine.

Oxford Clay, oks′ford, *n.* *Geol.* a bed of dark-blue clay between the lower and middle oolites, abounding in ammonites and belemnites.—**Oxford Mixture**, *n.* Woollen cloth of a very dark gray colour.—**Oxford Movement**, *n.* The Neo-Catholic movement of Newman, Keble, and Pusey, propagated by the *Tracts for the Times*.

Oxide, ok′sīd, *n.* [Gr. *oxys*, acid, sharp.] *Chem.* a compound of oxygen with another element (thus rust is *oxide* of iron).—**Oxidability**, ok′si-da-bil″i-ti, *n.* The capability of being converted into an oxide.—**Oxidable**, ok′si-da-bl, *a.* Capable of being converted into an oxide.—**Oxidate**, ok′si-dāt, *v.t.*—*oxidated*, *oxidating*. To oxidize.—*v.i.* To become oxidized.—**Oxidation**, ok-si-dā′shon, *n.* The operation or process of converting into an oxide.—**Oxidator**, ok′si-dā-tėr, *n.* A contrivance for throwing a stream of oxygen into the flame of a lamp.—**Oxidize**, ok′si-dīz, *v.t.* To cause to combine with oxygen; to convert into an oxide (which see).—**Oxidizer**, ok′si-dīz-ėr, *n.* That which oxidizes.—**Oxidizable, Oxidisable**, ok′si-dī-za-bl, *a.* Capable of being oxidized.—**Oxidizement**, ok′si-dīz-ment, *n.* Oxidation.—**Oxidulated**, ok-sid′ū-lā-ted, *a.* Containing oxygen as an ingredient.

Oxonian, ok-sō′ni-an, *n.* A native or inhabitant of Oxford; a member or a graduate of the University of Oxford.

Oxyacid, ok′si-as-id, *n.* An acid containing oxygen.

Oxygen, ok′si-jen, *n.* [Gr. *oxys*, acid, and root *gen*, to generate: so named because supposed to be present in all acids.] A gaseous element which, along with nitrogen, forms atmospheric air, and with hydrogen forms water, and which is essential to respiration (and therefore to animal life) and to combustion.—**Oxygenate**, ok′si-jen-āt, *v.t.* To unite or cause to combine with oxygen.—**Oxygenation**, ok′si-jen-ā″shon, *n.* Oxidation.—**Oxygenator**, ok′si-jen-āt-ėr, *n.* An oxidator.—**Oxygenizable**, ok′si-jen-ī-za-bl, *a.* Capable of being oxygenized.—**Oxygenize**, ok′si-jen-īz, *v.t.* To oxygenate (which see).—**Oxygenous**, ok-sij′en-us, *a.* Pertaining to or obtained from oxygen.

Oxyhydrogen, ok′si-hī″drō-jen, *a.* Formed by a mixture or combination of oxygen and hydrogen (*oxyhydrogen* gas); adapted to the combustion of oxygen and hydrogen in combination (*oxyhydrogen* blowpipe, lamp).—*Oxyhydrogen light*. LIME-LIGHT.

Oxymel, ok′si-mel, *n.* [Gr. *oxys*, acid, and *meli*, honey.] A mixture of vinegar and honey: used as an expectorant or demulcent.

Oxymoron, ok-si-mō′ron, *n.* [Gr. *oxymōron*, a smart saying which at first view appears foolish, from *oxys*, sharp, and *mōros*, foolish.] *Rhet.* a figure in which an epithet of a quite contrary signification is added to a word; as *cruel kindness*.

Oxyopia, Oxyopy, ok-si-ō′pi-a, ok′si-ō-pi, *n.* [Gr. *oxys*, acute, and *ōps*, the eye.] Acuteness of sight from increased sensibility of the retina.

Oxyphonia, Oxyphony, ok-si-fō′ni-a, ok-sif′ō-ni, *n.* [Gr. *oxys*, acute, and *phōnē*, voice.] Acuteness or shrillness of voice.

Oxytone, ok′si-tōn, *a.* [Gr. *oxys*, sharp, *tonos*, tone.] Having an acute sound; *Greek gram.* having the acute accent on the last syllable.

Oyer, ō′yėr, *n.* [Norm. *oyer*, Fr. *ouir*, L. *audire*, to hear.] *Law*, a hearing or trial of causes.—*Court of oyer and terminer* (to hear and determine), a court constituted to hear and determine felonies and misdemeanours.—**Oyes, Oyez**, ō′yes. ['Hear ye.'] The introduction to a proclamation made by a public crier, in order to secure silence and attention, and repeated three times.

Oyster, ois′tėr, *n.* [O.Fr. *oistre*, from L. *ostrea*, *ostreum*, from Gr. *ostreon*, an oyster, akin to *osteon*, a bone.] A well-known edible mollusc with a shell composed of two irregular valves, living in the sea and adhering to other objects.—**Oyster-bed**, *n.* A breeding place of oysters; a place where they are artificially or naturally reared.—**Oyster-catcher**, *n.* A British shore bird which feeds on small mollusca.

—**Oyster-dredge**, *n.* A drag-net for bringing up oysters from the water.—**Oysterling**, ois'tėr-ling, *n.* A young oyster.—**Oyster-patty**, *n.* A patty or small pie made with oysters.

Ozæna, ō-zē'na, *n.* [Gr. *ozaina*, from *ozō*, to smell.] A fetid ulcer in the nostril.

Ozocerite, Ozokerite, ō-zō'sē rīt, ō-zō-kē'rīt, *n.* [Gr. *ozō*, to smell, and *kēros*, wax.] A mineral wax or paraffin of a brown or brownish-yellow colour, made into candles.

Ozone, ō'zōn, *n.* [From Gr. *ozō*, to smell.] A modification of oxygen existing in the atmosphere to a minute extent, and produced when an electric machine is worked, and in other ways.—**Ozoniferous**, ō-zō-nif'ėr-us, *a.* Containing or furnishing ozone. **Ozonize**, ō'zon-īz, *v.t.* To charge or impregnate with ozone.—**Ozonometer**, ō-zō-nom'et-ėr, *n.* An apparatus for measuring the ozone in the atmosphere.—**Ozonometry**, ō-zō-nom'et-ri, *n.* The determination of ozone in the atmosphere. —**Ozonoscope**, ō-zō'nō-skōp, *n.* [E. *ozone*, and Gr. *skopeō*, I view.] A contrivance for showing the presence of ozone in the atmosphere, usually a test paper impregnated with iodide of potassium.

P

P, the sixteenth letter of the English alphabet.—*To mind one's P's and Q's*, to be very careful in behaviour—a colloquial phrase of unknown origin.

Pa, pä, *n.* A childish form of *Papa*.

Pabular, pab'ū-lėr, *a.* [L. *pabulum*, food, from *pasco*, to feed. PASTOR.] Pertaining to food or pabulum.—**Pabulum**, pab'ū-lum, *n.* Food; aliment; *fig.* food for the mind or intellect.

Paca, pä'ka, *n.* [Pg. *paca*, from *pak*, the native name.] A large rodent animal of South America and the West Indies, much esteemed for food.

Pacation,† pa-kā'shon, *n.* [L. *paco*, to calm or appease.] The act of pacifying or appeasing.

Pacchionian, pak-ki-ō'ni-an, *a.* After *Pacchioni*, an Italian anatomist.] A term applied to certain small bodies in the investing members of the brain.

Pace, pās, *n.* [Fr. *pas*, from L. *passus*, a step, from *pateo*, to lie open (whence *patent*), or from *pando*, *passum*, to stretch out. *Pass* has the same origin.] A step, or the space between the feet in walking (about 2½ feet); sometimes the distance from the place where either foot is taken up to that where the same foot is set down (this being the Roman pace); manner of walking; walk; gait (heavy, quick, or slow *pace*); degree of celerity; rate of progress (events followed at a great *pace*); a mode of stepping among horses.—*To keep* or *hold pace with*, to keep up with; to go or move as fast as: literally or figuratively.—*v.i.*—*paced*, *pacing*. To step; to walk; to step slowly or with measured tread; to stride.—*v.t.* To measure by steps; to walk over with measured paces.—**Paced**, pāst, *p.* and *a.* Having a particular gait (slow-*paced*); trained in paces, as a horse; broken in. — *Thorough-paced* (*lit.* thoroughly-trained), perfect in something bad; out-and-out (a *thorough-paced* scoundrel, &c.).—**Pacer**, pā'sėr, *n.* One that paces; a horse well-trained in pacing.

Pacha, pa-shä, *n.* [French spelling.] PASHA.

Pachymeter, pa-kim'et-ėr, *n.* [Gr. *pachys*, thick, and *metron*, a measure.] An instrument for measuring small thicknesses, as of glass or paper.—**Pachydactyl**, pak-i-dak'til, *n.* [Gr. *daktylos*, a toe.] A bird or other animal having thick toes.—**Pachydactylous**, pak-i-dak'ti-lus, *a.* Thick-toed.—**Pachyderm**, pak'i-dėrm, *n.* [Gr. *derma*, skin.] A non-ruminant hoofed animal; a member of an old mammalian order including the elephant, hippopotamus, horse, hog, &c. —**Pachydermatous**, pak-i-dėr'ma-tus, *a.* Belonging to the pachyderms; thick-skinned; hence *fig.* not sensitive to ridicule, sarcasm, or the like. — **Pachyopterous**, pak-i-op'tėr-us, *a.* [Gr. *pteron*, a wing.] Thick-winged.

Pacify, pas'i-fī, *v.t.*—*pacified*, *pacifying*. [Fr. *pacifier*, L. *pacificare*.] To appease; to cause to give up anger or excited feeling; to allay the agitation or excitement of; to calm; to restore peace to; to tranquillize.—**Pacifiable**, pas-i-fī'a-bl, *a.* Capable of being pacified.—**Pacific**, pa-sif'ik, *a.* [L. *pacificus*, from *pacifico*, to make peace—*pax*, *pacis*, peace, and *facio*, to make. PEACE.] Suited to make or restore peace; conciliatory; appeasing; pacifying; calm, peaceful, tranquil; not warlike (*pacific* disposition).—*Pacific Ocean*, *Pacific*, the ocean situated between the west coast of America and the shores of Asia and Australia. —**Pacifically**, pa-sif'i-kal-li, *adv.* In a pacific manner.—**Pacification**, pa-sif'i-kā"shon, *n.* The act of pacifying; state or condition of being pacified; appeasement; reconciliation.—**Pacificatory**, pa-sif'i-ka-to-ri, *a.* Tending to make peace; conciliatory.—**Pacifier**, pas'i-fī-ėr, *n.* One who pacifies; a device resembling a nipple, for a baby to suck.—**Pacifism**, pas'i-fizm, *n.* Opposition to war or the unrestricted use of military force; belief that all international disputes should be settled by arbitration.—**Pacifist**, pas'i-fist, *n.* One who favors or supports a policy of pacifism (also used as *a.*).

Pack, pak, *n.* [Either from D. *pak*, Dan. *pak*, *pakke*, G. *pack*, a pack or bundle; or from Armor., Ir., and Gael. *pac*, a pack.] A bundle made up to be carried; a bale; a budget; a collection; a complete set of playing cards; a number of hounds or dogs hunting or kept together; a number of persons united in a bad design or practice (a *pack* of rascals).—*v.t.* To put together for transportation or storage; to make up into a package, bundle, or bale; to stow; to fill methodically with contents (to *pack* a trunk); to assemble or bring together iniquitously and with a view to favor some particular side (to *pack* a jury; to *pack* a meeting); to dismiss without ceremony; to make begone; to make airtight by stuffing, as the piston of an engine; to stuff; to preserve in close vessels (to *pack* meat or fish).—*v.i.* To make up bundles or packs; to put up things for transportation; to depart in haste (with *off* or *away*); to gather together into flocks or bands (the grouse begin to *pack*).—**Package**, pak'āj, *n.* A bundle or bale; a packet; a parcel.—**Pack animal**, *n.* A beast of burden used on mountain and wilderness trails for transport of supplies and equipment. — **Pack drill**, pak'dril, *n.* Punishment of military offenses by compelling the offender to parade in full marching kit and order.—**Packer**, pak'ėr, *n.* One who packs; one who owns a meat-packing house; one who works in a meat-packing house.—**Packet**, pak'et, *n.* [Fr. *paquet*.] A small pack or package; a little bundle or parcel; a parcel of letters; a vessel employed in carrying mails, goods, and passengers on regular days of starting; also called *packet-boat*, *packet-vessel*. —**Packing**, pak'ing, *n.* Any material used for filling up empty spaces; stuffing; filling.—**Packing house**, *n.* An establishment where meats are packed for the market.—**Packing needle**, *n.* A strong needle for sewing packages.—**Packing press**, *n.* A powerful press, generally hydraulic, for compressing goods into small bulk for transport.—**Packman**, pak'man, *n.* One who carries a pack; a peddler.—**Packsaddle**, *n.* A saddle on which burdens are laid for conveyance by pack animals.—**Pack sheet**, pak'shēt, *n.* A strong coarse cloth for covering goods in bales.—**Pack thread**, pak'thred, *n.* Strong thread or twine used in tying up parcels.

Packfong, Paktong, pak'fong, pak'tong, *n.* A Chinese alloy of copper 40.4, zinc 25.4, nickel 31.6, and iron 2.6.

Paco, pä'kō, *n.* [Peruvian name.] The alpaca.

Pact, Paction, pakt, pak'shon, *n.* [Fr. *pacte*, L. *pactum*, a bargain (as in *compact*), from *paciscor*, *pactus*, to fix, bargain, covenant; same root as *pax*, peace. PEACE.] A contract; an agreement or covenant.—**Pactional**, pak'shon-al, *a.* By way of agreement.—**Pactitious**, pak-tish'us, *a.* Settled by agreement.

Pactolian, pak-tō'li-an, *a.* Pertaining to *Pactolus*, a river in Lydia, famous for its golden sands.

Pacul, pä'kul, *n.* One of the plants yielding Manilla hemp.

Pad, pad, *n.* [Origin uncertain; perhaps akin to *pod*.] A cushion, soft saddle, bolster, part of a garment, &c., stuffed with some soft material; a quantity of blotting-paper used for blotting or writing upon (a blotting or writing *pad*).—*v.t.*—*padded*, *padding*. To stuff so as to make a pad; to furnish with a pad.—**Padding**, pad'ing, *n.* The act of stuffing; the materials used for stuffing a saddle, bolster, &c.; literary matter inserted in a book, periodical, &c., merely to increase the bulk.

Pad, pad, *n.* [A form of *path*; comp. Prov. E. *pad*, Sc. *paad*, a path.] A robber that infests the road on foot; a footpad; an easy-paced horse.

Paddle, pad'l, *v.i.*—*paddled*, *paddling*. [A freq. and dim. from *pad*, to go = L.G. *paddeln*, to go with short steps, to paddle.] To play in the water with the hands or feet in swimming or sport; to use a paddle; to row with a paddle.—*v.t.* To propel by an oar or paddle.—*n.* A sort of short broad oar used in propelling and steering canoes and boats by a vertical motion; one of the float-boards placed on the circumference of the wheel of a steam-vessel; *zool.* the swimming apparatus of the turtles and certain other animals.—**Paddle-box**, *n.* The wooden covering of the paddle-wheel of a steamer.—**Paddler**, pad'l-ėr, *n.* One that paddles. — **Paddle-wheel**, *n.* A wheel with boards or floats on its circumference, driven by steam and propelling a steamship.

Paddock, pad'ok, *n.* [A.Sax. *pada*, a frog or toad (with dim. suffix *-ock*) = Icel. and Sw. *padda*, Dan *padde*, D. *pad*, *padde*, a frog or toad.] A toad or frog.—**Paddock-stool**, *n.* A mushroom; a toad-stool.

Paddock, pad'ok, *n.* [For *parrok*, A.Sax. *pearroc*. PARK.] A small field inclosed for pasture: ground adjacent to racecourse stables, used for the exercising of horses.

Paddy, pad'i, *n.* [Malay *padi*.] Rice in the husk whether in the field or gathered. (*East Indies*.)—**Paddy-bird**, *n.* The rice-bird.

Padella, pa-del'la, *n.* [It., from L. *patella*, dim. of *patera*, a cup. PATELLA.] A metal or earthenware cup or deep saucer containing fatty matter in which a wick is inserted, used in public illuminations, &c.

Pademelon, pad'e-mel-on, *n.* [Australian word.] A name of certain kangaroos that live in the bush.

Padishah, pä'di-shä, *n.* [Per. *pādishāh*, from *pād*, protector, master, and *shāh*, a king.] A title of the Turkish sultan and Persian shah.

Padlock, pad'lok, *n.* [Either from *pad*, a path, lit. a lock for a gate on a path, or from *pad* in the local sense of a pannier.]

A movable lock with a bow or semicircular link to be fastened through a staple.—*v.t.* To fasten or provide with a padlock or padlocks.

Padre, pa'drā, *n.* [It. *padre*, L. *pater*, father.] A title applied in Latin countries and in India to a minister of religion; and by British sailors and soldiers to a chaplain.

Paduasoy, Padesoy, pad'ū-a-soi, pad'ē-soi, *n.* [From *Padua*, in Italy, and Fr. *soie*, silk.] A particular kind of silk stuff.

Pæan, pē'an, *n.* [Gr.] An ancient Greek hymn in honour of Apollo, who was also called Pæan; a war-song before or after a battle; hence, a song of triumph generally; a loud and joyous song.

Pædagogics, Pædagogy, pē-da-goj'iks, pē'da-goj-i, *n.* PEDAGOGICS, PEDAGOGY.

Pædobaptism, pē-dō-bap'tizm, *n.* [Gr. *pais, paidos*, a child.] The baptism of infants or children.—**Pædobaptist**, pē-dō-bap'tist, *n.* One who holds to infant baptism.

Pædogenesis, pē'dō-jen"e-sis, *n.* [Gr. *pais, paidos*, a child, *genesis*, descent.] In animals, precocious sexual reproduction by immature individuals.

Pæon, pē'on, *n.* [Gr. *paeon.*] A metrical foot, consisting of four syllables, one long and three short.

Pagan, pā'gan, *n.* [L. *paganus*, a peasant, from *pagus*, a village or country district; comp. origin of *heathen*. Akin *peasant.*] One who worships false gods; one who is neither a Christian, a Jew, nor a Mohammedan; a heathen; an idolater.—*a.* Pertaining to pagans or heathens; heathenish; idolatrous. — **Paganish**, pā'gan-ish, *a.* Heathenish.—**Paganism**, pā'gan-izm, *n.* The worship of false gods; the religious opinions and worship of pagans; heathenism. — **Paganize**, pa'gan-īz, *v.t.*—*paganized, paganizing.* To render heathenish; to convert to heathenism.

Page, pāj, *n.* [Fr. *page*, It. *paggio*, a page, from L.L. *pagius*, a rustic, from L. *pagus*, a country district. PAGAN.] A young male attendant on kings, nobles, or other persons of distinction; a lad in the service of people of rank or wealth, whose duty it is to run errands, attend to the door, &c.—*v.t.*—*paged, paging.* To attend as a page.

Page, pāj, *n.* [Fr. *page*, from L. *pagina*, a page, from stem *pag*, seen in L. *pango*, Gr. *pēgnymi*, to fix; akin *compact* (*a.*), *pageant.*] One side of the leaf of a book; a writing or record (the *page* of history); *printing*, types set up for one side of a leaf.—*v.t. paged, paging.* To mark or number the pages of. —**Paginal**, paj'i-nal, *a.* Consisting of pages.—**Paginate**, paj'i-nāt, *v.t.*—*paginated, paginating.* To number the pages of; to page.—**Pagination**, paj-i-nā'shon, *n.* The act of paging; the marks or figures which indicate the number of pages.

Pageant, paj'ant or pā'jant, *n.* [Old forms *pagyn, pagen*, originally a scaffold or stage, from L. *pagina*, a slab, a page (of a book). PAGE.] A spectacle or entertainment; a great display or show, as at some public rejoicing; a theatrical exhibition; anything showy, without stability or duration. — **Pageantry**, paj'ant-ri, *n.* Pageants collectively; a showy exhibition or spectacle; splendid or ostentatious show.

Paginal, Pagination. Under PAGE.

Pagoda, pa-gō'da, *n.* [Fr. *pagode*, from Per. and Hind. *but-gadah* — *but*, an idol, and *gadah*, a house.] A Hindu temple in which idols are worshipped; a Buddhist temple in Siam, Burma, or China; a gold or silver coin of Hindustan, of a value of about two dollars.—**Pagoda-stone**, *n.* A limestone found in China, inclosing numerous fossil shells which present a resemblance to a pagoda. — **Pagodite**, pag'o-dit, *n.* Same as *Agalmatolite*.

Pagurus, pa-gū'rus, *n.* [Gr. *pagouros*—root *pag*, to fix, and *oura*, tail.] A genus of crabs which includes the hermit-crabs, &c. —**Pagurian**, pa-gū'ri-an, *n.* A crab of this genus or of the same family.

Pah, pä, *n.* In New Zealand, a fortified native camp.

Pah, pä, *interj.* An exclamation expressing contempt or disgust.

Paid, pād, pret. and pp. of *pay*.

Paideutics, pā-dū'tiks, *n.* [Gr. *paideutikē* (*technē*), education, from *paideuō*, to teach, from *pais*, a boy.] The science of teaching or of education.

Paigle, pā'gl, *n.* [Comp. W. *pigl*, a plant name.] The cowslip or primrose.

Pail, pāl, *n.* [O.Fr. *paile, paele*, from L. *patella*, a pan, from *pateo*, to lie open. PATENT.] A vessel of wood, or of tin or other metal, in which milk or water is commonly carried.—**Pailful**, pāl'ful, *n.* The quantity that a pail will hold.

Paillasse, pal-yas', *n.* [Fr., from *paille*, straw, L. *palea*, chaff.] An under bed of straw; an under mattress.

Pain, pān, *n.* [Fr. *peine*, O.Fr. *peine, paine*, &c., from L. *pœna*, punishment, and latterly pain, torment; akin *penal, penitence, pine* (verb), *punish*, &c.] Penalty; suffering annexed to the commission of a crime (under *pain* of death); an uneasy sensation in animal bodies; bodily distress; suffering; the throes of travail or childbirth (generally in plural); mental distress; careful labor; close application in working; trouble (chiefly in plural).—*v.t.* To give pain to; to cause to endure physical or mental suffering; to afflict; to distress. — **Painful**, pān'ful, *a.* Full of pain; giving or accompanied by pain; distressing; requiring labor or toil; difficult; executed with pains; attended with close and careful application or attention.—**Painfully**, pān'ful-li, *adv.* In a painful manner.—**Painfulness**, pān'-ful-nes, *n.* The state or quality of being painful.—**Painless**, pān'les, *a.* Free from pain.—**Painlessness**, pān'les-nes, *n.* The state of being painless. — **Painstaker**, pānz'tā-kėr, *n.* One who takes pains; a laborious person. — **Painstaking**, pānz'-tā-king, *a.* Taking or given to taking pains; giving close application; laborious and careful.—*n.* The taking of pains; careful labor.

Paint, pānt, *v.t.* [O.Fr. *paindre*, pp. *paint* (Fr. *peindre*), from L. *pingere, pictum*, to paint. PICTURE.] To lay color or colors on with a brush or otherwise; to diversify with hues; to color; to produce (a representation) in colors; to form a likeness or representation of in colors; to represent or exhibit to the mind; to describe vividly; to delineate; to depict.—*v.i.* To practice painting; to lay artificial color on the face.—*n.* A substance used in painting; a pigment; color laid on the face; rouge.—**Paint-box**, *n.* A color-box. Under COLOR.—**Painter**, pān'tėr, *n.* One whose occupation is to paint; an artist who represents objects by means of colors or pigments. — *Painter's colic*, a disease to which painters and others who work with poisonous preparations of lead are liable. —**Painting**, pān'ting, *n.* The act, art, or employment of laying on colors; the art of representing objects by means of figures and colors on a plane surface so as to produce the appearance of relief; a painted picture.

Painter, pān'tėr, *n.* [Ir. *painteir*, a snare, a net.] A rope used to fasten a boat to a ship or other object.—*To cut the painter*, to assert one's independence by severing a connection with a person or thing.

Pair, pār, *n.* [Fr. *paire*, from L. *par*, equal, whence also *parity, peer, compeer, disparage*, &c.] Two things similar in form and suited to each other or used together (a *pair* of gloves or stockings); a single thing composed of two pieces suiting each other (a *pair* of scissors or of trousers); two of a sort; a couple; a brace; distinctively, a man and his wife; in *parliament*, and similar bodies, two members who would vote on opposite sides and agree not to vote for a specified time. — *Pair* formerly often meant a set of things; hence, we speak of a *pair* of stairs for a flight of stairs or steps. —*v.i.* To join in pairs; to couple; to mate (as birds).—*To pair, to pair off*, to depart from a company in pairs or couples; to form a pair in the parliamentary sense.—*v.t.* To unite in pairs or couples; to assort in twos.—**Pairing-time**, *n.* The time when birds couple.—**Pair-royal**, *n.* Three similar things; three cards of a sort at certain games, as three kings, three queens, &c.—**Pairwise**, pār'wīz, *adv.* In pairs.

Pajamas, pa-jä'mas, *pl. n.* [Hindu.] A loose garment, usually including jacket and trousers, worn for sleeping, lounging, etc. (Seldom used in singular except attributively, as in *pajama*-coat.)

Pal, pal, *n.* [Of Gypsy origin.] Mate; partner; accomplice; chum. (*Slang.*)

Palace, pal'ās, *n.* [Fr. *palais*, from L. *Palatium*, the house of Augustus, on the hill at Rome, called by this name.] The house in which an emperor, a king, or other distinguished person resides; a splendid residence; a stately mansion.

Paladin, pal'a-din, *n.* [Fr. *paladin*, from L. *palatinus*, attached to the palace, from *palatium*. PALACE.] A knight attached to a sovereign's court; a knight-errant; a heroic champion; an eminent hero.

Palæarctic, pā-lē-ärk'tik, *a.* [Gr. *palaios*, ancient, and E. *arctic.*] Said of a region of the earth marked by a characteristic fauna, and embracing Europe, Africa north of the Atlas, and Northern Asia.—**Palæobotany**, pā'lē-ō-bot"a-ni, *n.* [Gr. *palaios*, and E. *botany.*] The study of the plants that are found in a fossil state.—**Palæocosmic**, pā'lē-ō-koz"mik, *n.* [Gr. *kosmos*, world.] Pertaining to the earth during former geological periods.—**Palæocrystic**, pā'lē-ō-kris"tik, *a.* [Gr. *kryos*, frost.] Frozen from of old; remaining frozen from antiquity: applied to the parts of the Arctic and Antarctic seas that are covered with ice of unknown ages, or to such ice. — **Palæoethnology**, pā'lē-ō-eth-nol"o-ji, *n.* [Gr. *ethnos*, a people.] The ethnology of the earliest times. — **Palæoethnological**, pā'lē-ō-eth-no-loj"i-kal, *a.* Pertaining to the science of palæoethnology.—**Palæoethnologist**, pā'lē-ō-eth-nol"o-jist, *n.* One versed in palæoethnology.—**Palæogean**, pā'lē-ō-jē"an, *a.* [Gr. *gē*, the earth.] Belonging to the former conditions of the earth's surface as distinct from the existing. —**Palæography**, pā-lē-og'ra-fi, *n.* [Gr. *graphō*, to write.] An ancient manner of writing; ancient writings collectively; the art of deciphering ancient documents or inscriptions.—**Palæograph**, pā'lē-ō-graf, *n.* An ancient manuscript.—**Palæographer, Palæographist**, pā-lē-og'ra-fėr, pā-lē-og'ra-fist, *n.* One skilled in palæography.—**Palæographic, Palæographical**, pā'lē-ō-graf"ik, pā'lē-ō-graf"i-kal, *a.* Pertaining to palæography. — **Palæoichthyology**, pā'lē-ō-ik-thi-ol"o-ji, *n.* [Gr. *ichthys*, a fish.] The science of fossil fishes. —**Palæolithic**, pā'lē-ō-lith"ik, *a.* [Gr. *lithos*, a stone.] *Arch.* belonging to the earlier stone period of prehistoric history.—**Palæolith**, pā'lē-ō-lith, *n.* An unpolished stone, implement, or other object belonging to the earlier stone age. — **Palæology**, pā-lē-ol'o-ji, *n.* [Gr. *logos*, discourse.] A discourse or treatise on antiquities, or the knowledge of ancient things; archæology. —**Palæologist**, pā-lē-ol'o-jist, *n.* One conversant with palæology; one of the Constantinople dynasty or family of the Palæologi.—**Palæontography**, pā'lē-on-tog"ra-fi, *n.* [Gr. *onta*, beings.] The description of fossil remains.—**Palæontographical**, pā-lē-on'tō-graf"i-kal, *a.* Relating to palæontography. — **Palæontology**, pā'lē-on-tol"o-ji, *n.* The science of the ancient life of the earth; that branch of biological science which treats of fossil organic remains.— **Palæontological**, pā'lē-on-tō-loj"i-kal, *a.* Relating to palæontology.—**Palæontologically**, pā'lē-on-tō-loj"i-kal-li, *adv.* In a palæontological sense or point of view. —**Palæontologist**, pā'lē-on-tol"o-jist, *n.* One who studies or is versed in palæontology. —**Palæophytology**, pā'lē-ō-fi-tol"o-ji, *n.* [Gr. *phyton*, a plant.] That branch of palæontology which treats of fossil plants or vegetable remains. — **Palæotherium**, pā'lē-ō-thē"ri-um, *n.* [Gr. *thērion*, a wild beast.] A sort of extinct pachyderms found in the eocene strata of Europe and America and holding a place intermediate between the rhinoceros, the horse, and the tapir.—**Palæotherian**, pā′lē-ō-thē″ri-an, *a.* Pertaining to the palæotherium.—**Palæozoic**, pā′lē-ō-zō″ik, *a.* [Gr. *zōē*, life.] *Geol.* applied to the lowest division of stratified groups, as distinguished from the *Mesozoic* and *Cainozoic*.—**Palæozoology**, pā′lē-ō-zō-ol″o-ji, *n.* [Gr. *zōon*, an animal.] That branch of biology which concerns itself with the fossil remains of animals.—**Palætiology**, pa-lē′shi-ol″o-ji, *n.* [Gr. *aitia*, a cause.] That mode of speculation or investigation which explains past conditions by reasoning from present conditions.—**Palætiological**, pa-lē′shi-ō-loj″i-kal, *a.* Belonging to palætiology.—**Palætiologist**, pa-lē′shi-ol″o-jist, *n.* An investigator by the method of palætiology.

Palanquin, Palankeen, pal-an-kēn′, *n.* [Fr. and Pg. *palanquin*, from Pali, *pālangki*.] A covered conveyance used in India, China, &c., borne by poles on the shoulder, and carrying a single person.

Palate, pal′at, *n.* [L. *palatum*, the palate.] The roof or upper part of the mouth; taste; relish; sometimes intellectual taste.—**Palatable**, pal′at-a-bl, *a.* Agreeable to the taste or palate; savoury.—**Palatableness**, pal′at-a-bl-nes, *n.* The quality of being palatable to the taste.—**Palatably**, pal′at-a-bli, *adv.* In a palatable manner.—**Palatal**, pal′at-al, *a.* Pertaining to the palate; uttered by the aid of the palate, as certain sounds.—*n.* A sound pronounced by the aid of the palate; as that of *ch* in *church*, and that of *j*.—**Palatalize**, pal′-a-tal-īz, *v.t.* To give a palatal sound to; to convert from guttural to palatal (*church* is palatalized compared with *kirk*).

Palatial, pa-lā′shal, *a.* [From L. *palatium*, palace. PALACE.] Pertaining to a palace; becoming a palace; magnificent.—**Palatine**, pal′a-tīn, *a.* [Fr. *palatin*, L. *palatinus*, from *palatium*, palace,] Pertaining to a palace; holding office in the king's palace; possessing royal privileges.—*County palatine* is a county over which an earl, bishop, or duke had a royal jurisdiction.—*n.* One invested with royal privileges and rights; a count palatine.—**Palatinate**, pa-lat′i-nāt, *n.* The province or seignory of a palatine.

Palaver, pa-lä′vėr, *n.* [Pg. *palavra*, Sp. *palabra*, a word, from L. *parabola*, a parable, in late times a word. PARABLE.] A talk or conference among some barbaric races; a conversation; superfluous or idle talk.—*v.t.* To flatter; to humbug by words.—*v.i.* To talk idly; to indulge in a palaver or palavers.—**Palaverer**, pa-lä′vėr-ėr, *n.* One who palavers; a flatterer.

Pale, pāl, *a.* [O.Fr. *pale* (Fr. *pâle*), from L. *pallidus*, pale. PALLID.] White or whitish; wan; not ruddy or fresh of colour; not bright; of a faint lustre; dim.—*v.t.*—*paled, paling.* To make pale; to diminish the brightness of.—*v.i.* To turn pale.—**Pale-ale**, *n.* A light-coloured pleasant bitter ale.—**Pale-face**, *n.* A name among the North American Indians for a white person.—**Palely**, pāl′li, *adv.* In a pale manner; wanly; not ruddily.—**Paleness**, pāl′nes, *n.* The quality or condition of being pale.—**Palish**, pāl′ish, *a.* Somewhat pale or wan.—**Paly**, pāl′i, *a.* Pale; wanting colour. (*Poet.*)

Pale, pāl, *n.* [A.Sax. *pal*, Fr. *pal*, from L. *palus*, a stake, from root seen in *page* (of a book), *pageant*, *pact*.] A pointed stake used in fencing or inclosing, fixed upright in the ground, or joined above and below to a rail; a picket; what surrounds and incloses; the space inclosed; an inclosure; an instrument for trying the quality of a cheese; in *her.* when a shield is divided into halves by a perpendicular line, it is said to be *palewise* or *per pale*.—*The Pale*, that portion of Ireland within which English rule was for some centuries confined after the conquests of Henry II.—*v.t.* To inclose with pales or stakes; to encompass.—**Paling**, pāl′ing, *n.* Pales in general, or a fence formed with pales.—**Paly**, pāl′i, *n.* The division of a shield into perpendicular bars of alternate tinctures and an even number of divisions.

Palea, pā′lē-a, *n.* pl. **Paleæ**, pā′lē-ē. [L. *palea*, chaff.] *Bot.* one of the bracts upon the receptacle of composite plants between the florets; one of the interior bracts of the flowers of grasses.—**Paleaceous**, pā-lē-ā′shus, *a.* *Bot.* consisting of chaff-like scales; covered with paleæ.

Paleography, Paleontology, &c. Under PALÆ-.

Palestine, pal′es-tīn, *n.* The land of Syria, extended from the original district peopled by the Philistines.

Palestra, pa-les′tra, *n.* [Gr. *palaistra*, from *palē*, wrestling.] A place appropriated to the exercise of wrestling or other athletic exercises; exercises of wrestling.—**Palestral, Palestrian, Palestric**, pa-les′-tral, pa-les′tri-an, pa-les′trik, *a.* Pertaining to the palestra or to wrestling.

Paletot, pal′e-tō, *n.* [Fr. *paletot*, *paletoque*, a paletot, an overcoat, from D. *paltsrok*, a pilgrim's coat.] A loose sort of man's coat or woman's long jacket; an overcoat.

Palette, pal′et, *n.* [Fr. *palette*, from L.L. *paleta*, dim. from L. *pala*, a spade or shovel.] A thin oval board or tablet, with a thumb-hole at one end, on which a painter lays the pigments with which he paints his pictures; a pallet.—**Palette-knife**, *n.* A sort of knife used by painters for mixing colours, and by druggists to mix salves.

Palewise. Under PALE.

Palfrey, pal′fri, *n.* [O.Fr. *palefrei*, from L.L. *parafredus*, L. *paraveredus*, an extra post-horse, from Gr. *para*, beside, and L. *veredus*, a post-horse (from *veho*, to carry, and *rheda*, a carriage).] An ordinary riding-horse, or a horse used by noblemen and others for state, distinguished from a war-horse; a small horse fit for ladies.

Pali, pä′lī, *n.* The sacred language of the Buddhists, a descendant of the Sanskrit, now used only in religious works.

Palichthyology, pa-lik′thi-ol″o-ji, *n.* PALÆOICHTHYOLOGY.

Palillogy, Palilogy, pa-lil′o-ji, *n.* [Gr. *palin*, again, and *legō*, to speak.] *Rhet.* the repetition of a word or words for the sake of greater energy.

Palimpsest, pā′limp-sest, *n.* [Gr. *palimpsēstos*, rubbed again—*palin*, again, and *psaō*, to rub.] A parchment or other piece of writing material from which one writing has been erased to make room for another, often leaving the first faintly visible, a process to which many ancient manuscripts were subjected.

Palindrome, pal′in-drōm, *n.* [Gr. *palindromos*, running back—*palin*, again, and *dromos*, a running.] A word, verse, or sentence that is the same when read backward or forward.—**Palindromic, Palindromical**, pal-in-drom′ik, pal-in-drom′i-kal, *a.* Belonging to or in the manner of a palindrome.

Paling. Under PALE.

Palingenesis, pal-in-jen′e-sis, *n.* [Gr. *palin*, again, and *genesis*, birth.] A transformation from one state to another; a metamorphosis as of insects; a great geological change on the earth.—**Palingenetic**, pal′in-je-net″ik, *a.* Pertaining to palingenesis.

Palinode, pal′i-nōd, *n.* [Gr. *palinōdia*—*palin*, again, and *ōdē*, a song.] Originally a poetical recantation; a piece in which a poet retracts the invectives contained in a former piece; hence, a recantation in general.—**Palinodial**, pal-i-nō′di-al, *a.* Relating to a palinode.—**Palinodist**, pal-i-nōd′ist, *n.* A writer of palinodes.

Palisade, pal-i-sād′, *n.* [Fr. *palissade*, from *palisser*, to pale, from *palis*, a pale. PALE (a stake).] A fence or fortification consisting of a row of strong stakes or posts set firmly in the ground; also applied to one of the stakes; a mass of rock, as the denuded face of a mountain.

Palisander, pal-i-san′dėr, *n.* [Fr. *palissandre*.] A continental name for rosewood.

Palish. Under PALE.

Palissy-ware, pal′is-i, *n.* A variety of pottery remarkable for its beauty: so called from its maker, Bernard *Palissy*, a French potter of the fifteenth century.

Palkee, pal′kē, *n.* [Hind.] A palanquin.

Pall, pal, *n.* [A.Sax. *pæll*, from L. *pallium*, a cloak, a pall.] An outer mantle of dignity; *eccles.* a vestment sent from Rome to patriarchs, primates, and metropolitans as an ensign of jurisdiction, and sometimes, as a mark of honour, to bishops; consisting of a band made of white lamb's wool, passing round the shoulders, and having a strip hanging down before and behind; a large black cloth thrown over a coffin at a funeral, or over a tomb; rich cloth of any kind, 'in purple and *pall*'.—*v.t.* To cover with a pall; to cover or invest; to shroud.—**Pall-bearer**, *n.* One of those who attend the coffin at a funeral.

Pall, pal, *v.i.* [W. *pallu*, to fail; *pall*, loss of energy, failure; the verb *appal* was probably to some extent affected by this word.] To become vapid; to become insipid; to become devoid of agreeableness or attraction (pleasures begin to *pall*).—*v.t.* To make vapid or insipid; to cloy; to dispirit or depress‡.

Palladian, pal-lā′di-an, *a.* Pertaining to Andrea *Palladio*, a celebrated Italian architect (1518–80).—*Palladian architecture*, a species of Italian architecture founded upon the Roman antique.

Palladium, pal-lā′di-um, *n.* [From Pallas or Athene, equivalent to the Latin *Minerva*.] A sacred statue or image of *Pallas*, the Greek goddess, on the preservation of which, according to ancient legend, was said to have depended the safety of Troy; hence, something that affords effectual defence, protection, and safety; a rare metal of a steel-gray colour, ductile and malleable, considerably harder and lighter than platinum.

Pallah, pal′la, *n.* A handsome species of antelope in South Africa.

Pallet, pal′et, *n.* [Fr. *palette*, from L.L. *paleta*, dim. from L. *pala*, a spade or shovel.] A palette; a wooden instrument used by potters, &c., for forming and rounding their wares; an instrument to take up and apply gold-leaf; pieces which receive the impulse from a pendulum or balance-wheel.

Pallet, pal′et, *n.* [From Fr. *paille*, straw; L. *palea*, chaff.] A small or rude bed.

Pallial, pal′i-al, *a.* [L. *pallium*, a mantle. PALL.] Pertaining to a mantle, especially the mantle of molluscs.—*Pallial impression*, the mark formed in a bivalve shell by the pallium or mantle.

Palliate, pal′i-āt, *v.t.*—*palliated, palliating.* [Fr. *pallier*, to cloak, palliate; from L. *pallium*, a cloak, whence also *pall* (*n.*).] To conceal the enormity of by excuses and apologies; to extenuate; to soften or tone down by favourable representations; to mitigate, lessen, or abate (to *palliate* a disease).—**Palliation**, pal-i-ā′shon, *n.* The act of palliating; what palliates or serves to excuse; extenuation; mitigating; alleviation.—**Palliative**, pal′i-ā-tiv, *a.* [Fr. *palliatif*.] Serving to palliate or extenuate; extenuating; mitigating.—*n.* That which palliates.—**Palliatory**, pal′i-a-to-ri, *a.* Palliative.

Pallid, pal′id, *a.* [L. *pallidus*, from *palleo*, to become pale. PALE, FALLOW.] Pale; wan; deficient in colour; not high coloured.—**Pallidity**, pa-lid′i-ti, *n.* Quality of being pallid; paleness; wanness.—**Pallidly**, pal′id-li, *adv.* Palely; wanly.—**Pallidness**, pal′id-nes, *n.* Paleness.

Pallium, pal′li-um, *n.* [L. *pallium*, whence *pall* (*n.*).] An ecclesiastical or other pall; the mantle of a mollusc.

Pallmall, pel-mel′, *n.* [O.Fr. *palemail*, from It. *pallamaglio*, from *palla*, a ball (akin E. *ball*), and *maglio*, L. *malleus*, a mallet.] An ancient game in which a ball was with a mallet or club struck through a ring elevated upon a pole; the alley or walk where the game was played (hence the street in London called *Pall Mall*).

Pallor, pal'or, *n.* [L. PALLID.] Paleness.

Palm, päm, *n.* [L. *palma*, the palm of the hand, a palm-tree (so named from the shape of its branches); cog. Gr. *palamē*, A.Sax. *folm*, O.H.G. *folma*, the palm of the hand.] The inner part of the hand; a lineal measure equal to 3 or 4 inches; a broad flat part, as of an anchor fluke; any of the plants of a well-known order of arborescent or tree-like endogens, chiefly inhabiting the tropics, of great value to man as affording food, &c.; a branch or leaf of the palm-tree anciently borne as a symbol of victory or triumph; hence, superiority, victory, triumph (to carry off the *palm*); a popular name for the bloom or a branch of the willow, carried on Palm-Sunday as a substitute for the Eastern palm branches.—*v.t.*—*palmed, palming.* To conceal in the palm of the hand, as jugglers or cheaters; to impose by fraud (to *palm off* trash *upon* the public).—*Palma Christi* (palm of Christ), a name for the castor-oil plant.—**Palmaceous**, pal-mā'shus, *a.* Belonging to the palm tribe.—**Palmar**, pal'mėr, *a.* [L. *palmaris.*] Pertaining to the palm of the hand; of the breadth of the hand.—**Palmarian**, **Palmary**, pal-mā'ri-an, pal'ma-ri, *a.* Worthy of obtaining the palm; of supreme excellence: 'a *palmary* emendation'.—**Palmate**, **Palmated**, pal'māt, pal'mā-ted, *a.* [L. *palmatus.*] Having the shape of the hand (*palmated* leaves); having the toes webbed (the *palmate* feet of aquatic birds).—**Palmately**, pal'māt-li, *adv.* In a palmate manner.—**Palmatifid**, pal-mat'i-fid, *a.* [L. *palmatus*, and *findo*, *fidi*, to split.] *Bot.* divided so as to resemble a hand.—**Palmatiform**, **Palmiform**, pal-mat'i-form, pal'mi-form, *a.* *Bot.* having a palmate form.—**Palmatilobate**, pal-mat'i-lō"bāt, *a.* *Bot.* palmate with the lobes divided to an uncertain depth.—**Palmatipartite**, pal-mat'i-pär"tīt, *a.* *Bot.* palmate with lobes deeply divided, but not to the midrib.—**Palmatisected**, pal'mat-i-sek"ted, *a.* [*Palmate*, and L. *sectus*, cut.] *Bot.* palmate with lobes divided to the midrib.—**Palm-bird**, *n.* A beautiful bird of West Africa, with bright orange and black plumage.—**Palm-butter**, *n.* Palm-oil.—**Palm cat.** See PARADOXURE.—**Palmer**, päm'ėr, *n.* A pilgrim that returned from the Holy Land with a branch of palm; one who palms or cheats, as at cards or dice.—**Palmer-worm**, *n.* A name for certain hairy caterpillars.—**Palmetto**, pal-met'tō, *n.* [Sp. *palmito.*] A name of several palms; the cabbage-palm of the West Indies and southern United States.—**Palm-house**, *n.* A glass-house for raising palms.—**Palmiferous**, pal-mif'ėr-us, *a.* Bearing or producing palms.—**Palmigrade**, pal'mi-grād, *a.* [L. *palma*, the palm, and *gradior*, to walk.] Plantigrade.—**Palmiped**, pal'mi-ped, *a.* [L. *palma*, the palm, and *pes*, *pedis*, a foot.] Web-footed.—*n.* A bird that has webbed feet.—**Palmister**, pal'mis-tėr, *n.* One who deals in palmistry.—**Palmistry**, pal'mis-tri, *n.* The art of telling fortunes by the lines and marks in the palm of the hand; manual dexterity (humorous).—**Palmitic**, pal-mit'ik, *a.* Pertaining to or obtained from palm-oil (*palmitic* acid).—**Palmitin**, **Palmitine**, pal'mi-tin, *n.* The principal solid ingredient of palm-oil.—**Palm-oil**, *n.* A fatty substance resembling butter obtained from palms, chiefly from the fruit of the African oil-palm, employed in the manufacture of soap and candles, for lubricating machinery, &c.; bribes; corruption; money in the palm. (*American.*)—**Palm-sugar**, *n.* Saccharine matter from the juice of palms.—**Palm-Sunday**, *n.* The Sunday next before Easter, commemorative of our Saviour's triumphal entry into Jerusalem, when the multitude strewed palm branches in the way.—**Palm-wine**, *n.* A liquor obtained by fermenting the juice of certain palms.—**Palmy**, pä'mi, *a.* Abounding in palms; worthy of the palm; flourishing; prosperous (the *palmy* days of Rome).

Palmyra, **Palmyra-palm**, pal-mī'ra, *n.* The most common palm of India, the wood, leaves, fruit, and juice of which are all of great value and use.

Palp, **Palpus**, palp, pal'pus, *n.* (pl. **Palpi**, pal'pi). [Mod.L. *palpus*, from L. *palpare*, to stroke, to feel.] A jointed sensitive organ on the head of an insect; a feeler.—**Palpiform**, pal'pi-form, *a.* Having the form of palpi or feelers.—**Palpigerous**, pal-pij'ėr-us, *a.* Bearing palpi.

Palpable, pal'pa-bl, *a.* [Fr. *palpable*, from L. *palpabilis*, from *palpo*, to touch; akin *palpitate.*] Perceptible by the touch; capable of being felt; easily perceived and detected; plain; obvious; easily perceptible.—*Palpable obscure*, darkness that may be felt. (*Mil.*)—**Palpableness**, **Palpability**, pal'pa-bl-nes, pal-pa-bil'i-ti, *n.* Plainness; obviousness.—**Palpably**, pal'pa-bli, *adv.* Plainly; obviously.—**Palpation**, pal-pā'shon, *n.* [L. *palpatio.*] The act of feeling; *pathol.* manual examination.

Palpebral, pal'pe-bral, *a.* [L. *palpebra*, an eyelid.] Pertaining to the eyelid or eyebrow.

Palpi. Under PALP.

Palpitate, pal'pi-tāt, *v.i.*—*palpitated, palpitating.* [L. *palpito*, *palpitatum*, freq. of *palpo*, to feel. PALPABLE.] To flutter or move with slight throbs; to throb; to pulsate violently: applied particularly to an abnormal movement of the heart, as from fright or disease; hence, to tremble; to quiver.—**Palpitation**, pal-pi-tā'shon, *n.* A violent and unnatural beating or pulsation of the heart, as from violent action, fright, or disease.

Palsgrave, pąlz'grāv, *n.* [G. *pfalzgraf*, from *pfalz* (contr. from L. *palatium*, palace), and *graf*, an earl.] A count palatine; a count with the superintendence of the king's palace.—**Palsgravine**, pąlz'gra-vin, *n.* The consort of a palsgrave.

Palstave, pąl'stāv, *n.* [Icel. *pálstafr*, a pole-staff.] An ancient axe-shaped weapon used by Celtic nations.

Palsy, pąl'zi, *n.* [A contr. of *paralysis*, Fr. *paralysie.*] Paralysis, especially in a limb or some of the superficial muscles.—*v.t.*—*palsied, palsying.* To affect with palsy or as with palsy; to paralyse.—**Palsied**, pąl'zid, *p.* and *a.* Affected with palsy.

Palter, pąl'tėr, *v.i.* [Of same origin as *paltry*, and originally having reference to the haggling of dealers in old clothes.] To act insincerely; to equivocate; to haggle; to shift; to dodge; to play tricks.—**Palterer**, pąl'tėr-ėr, *n.* One that palters; an insincere dealer; a shifter.

Paltry, pąl'tri, *a.* [Same as L.G. *paltrig*, *palterig*, ragged, from *palte*, Fris. *palt*, G. *palte*, Sw. *palta* (plur. *paltor*), Dan. *pialt*, a rag; akin *palter.*] Mean; vile; worthless; despicable. ∴ Syn. under CONTEMPTIBLE.—**Paltrily**, pąl'tri-li, *adv.* In a paltry manner.—**Paltriness**, pąl'tri-nes, *n.* The state of being paltry, vile, or worthless.

Paludal, pal'ū-dal, *a.* [L. *palus*, *paludis*, a marsh.] Pertaining to marshes; generated by marshes (*paludal* fever).

Paludamentum, pa-lū'da-men"tum, *n.* [L.] The cloak worn by an ancient Roman general commanding an army, and by his principal officers and personal attendants.

Paludine, **Palustral**, **Palustrine**, pal'ū-dīn, pa-lus'tral, pa-lus'trin, *a.* [L. *palus*, *paludis*, a pool, a marsh.] Pertaining to marshes; marshy.—**Paludose**, pal'ū-dōs, *a.* [L. *paludosus.*] *Bot.* growing in marshy places.

Paly. Under PALE.

Pam, pam, *n.* In five-card loo, the knave of clubs.

Pampas, pam'pas, *n. pl.* [Sp.-Amer.] The grassy treeless plains of South America, resembling the 'prairies' of North America; especially the immense plains in the southern portion of South America east of the Andes.—**Pampas-cat**, *n.* A species of leopard frequenting the Pampas.—**Pampas-grass**, *n.* A variety of grass with flower-stems 10 to 14 feet high growing on the pampas, introduced as an ornamental grass into Britain.—**Pampean**, pam-pē'an, *a.* Pertaining to the pampas.

Pamper, pam'pėr, *v.t.* [Probably akin to *pap* (with *m* inserted); comp. G. *pampen*, Bav. *pampfen*, to stuff, to cram with food.] To indulge with rich food; to feed luxuriously; to gratify to the full; to indulge to excess.—**Pampered**, pam'pėrd, *p.* and *a.* Fed luxuriously; spoiled by luxurious feeding or indulgence.—**Pamperedness**, pam'pėrd-nes, *n.*—**Pamperer**, pam'pėr-ėr, *n.* One who pampers.—**Pamperize**,† pam'pėr-īz, *v.t.* To pamper.

Pampero, pam-pē'ro, *n.* [Sp.-Amer. *pampas.*] The cold wind blowing from the Andes to the Atlantic.

Pamphlet, pam'flet, *n.* [Formerly *paunflet*, *pamfilet*, *pamflet*: of doubtful origin; perhaps from Sp. *papelete*, a written paper, with insertion of nasal, as in D. *pampier* (Fr. *papier*), paper. PAPER.] A small book consisting of a sheet of paper, or of a few sheets stitched together but not bound; a short treatise or essay published by itself.—**Pamphleteer**, pam-flet-ēr', *n.* A writer of pamphlets; a scribbler.—*v.i.* To write and issue pamphlets.

Pampiniform, pam-pin'i-form, *n.* [L. *pampinus*, a tendril.] Resembling a tendril.

Pampre, pam'pėr, *n.* [Fr., from L. *pampinus*, vine foliage.] *Arch.* an ornament consisting of vine leaves and grapes.

Pan, pan, *n.* [A.Sax. *panne*, D. *pan*, G. *pfanne*, all from L.L. *panna*, for *patna*, L. *patina*, a pan, from *pateo*, to be wide. PATENT.] A vessel of tin, iron, or other metal, often rather shallow; a vessel of various kinds used for domestic purposes; an open vessel for boiling or evaporating or other operations (a sugar-*pan*, a salt-*pan*, &c.); a pond for evaporating salt water to make salt; the part of a flint-lock which holds the priming; the skull or cranium (the brain-*pan*).—*Pan out*, to yield a good return = 'to cut-up' well: from the phrase of miners washing out the gravel of the gold in pans; to succeed; *agri.* HARD-PAN.—**Pancake**, *n.* A thin cake of batter fried or baked in a pan.

Pan, pan, *n.* [Hence *panic.*] *Greek myth.* the chief god of pastures, forests, and flocks.—**Pandean**, pan-dē'an, *a.* Pertaining to Pan.—*Pandean pipes*, *Pan's pipes*, a musical wind-instrument composed of reeds of different lengths tied together; a syrinx.

Panacea, pan-a-sē'a, *n.* [L., from Gr. *panakeia*, a universal remedy—*pan*, all, and *akeomai*, to cure.] A remedy for all diseases; a universal medicine or remedy.

Panada, **Panade**, pa-nā'da, pa-nād', *n.* [Fr. *panade*, from L. *panis*, bread.] A food made by boiling bread in water to the consistence of pulp.

Pan-Anglican, pan-ang'gli-kan, *a.* Representative of all who hold views similar to the Anglican Church.

Panary, pan'a-ri, *a.* [L. *panis*, bread.] Pertaining to bread (*panary* fermentation).

Pancake. Under PAN.

Pancarte, pan'kärt, *n.* [Fr.; L. *pancharta*—Gr. *pan*, all, and L. *charta*, a chart.] A royal charter confirming the enjoyment of all his possessions to a subject.

Pancratium, pan-krā'shi-um, *n.* [Gr. *pangkration*—*pan*, all, and *kratos*, strength.] A gymnastic contest of ancient Greece consisting of boxing and wrestling.

Pancreas, pan'krē-as, *n.* [Gr. *pan*, all, and *kreas*, flesh.] A large gland or organ of the body between the bottom of the stomach and the vertebræ of the loins: in cattle called the *Sweet-bread.*—**Pancreatic**, pan-krē-at'ik, *a.* Pertaining to the pancreas.

Panda, pan'dä, *n.* A carnivorous quadruped of the genus *Ailurus*, found in the Himalayas and Tibet, belonging to the raccoon family, whose fur is reddish-brown on the back and sides, and black on the underside and legs.—*Giant panda*, an animal of the genus *Ailuropoda*, which is related to and resembles the bear in form and disposition, is easily domesticated, and whose fur is white except for black patches around the eyes, and black collar, legs, and tail.

Pandect, pan'dekt, *n.* [Gr. *pandektēs*—*pan*, all, and *dechomai*, to contain.] A treatise which contains the whole of any science; *pl.* the digest or collection of Roman civil law, made by order of the emperor Justinian, and consisting of fifty books.

Pandemic, pan-dem'ik, *a.* [Gr. *pan*, all, and *dēmos*, people.] Incident to a whole people; epidemic.

Pandemonium, Pandæmonium, pan-dē-mō'ni-um, *n.* [Gr. *pan*, all, and *daimōn*, a demon.] The place or abode of demons or evil spirits—a name invented by Milton; hence, any lawless, disorderly place or assemblage.

Pander, pan'dėr, *n.* [From *Pandarus*, who performs the part of a pimp in the story of Troilus and Cressida.] A pimp; a procurer; a male bawd; hence, one who ministers to the gratification of any of the baser passions.—*v.i.* To act as agent for the lusts of others. — **Panderage**, pan'dėr-āj, *n.* The act of pandering. — **Panderess, Pandaress**, pan'dėr-es, *n.* A female pander; a procuress.—**Panderism**, pan'-dėr-izm, *n.* The employment of a pander; pimping.

Pandiculation, pan-dik'ū-lā"shon, *n.* [L. *pandiculor*, *pandiculatum*, to stretch one's self, from *pando*, to spread out.] The stretching of one's self, as when newly awaked from sleep; a morbid restlessness and stretching. — **Pandiculated**, pan-dik'ū-lā-ted, *a.* Stretched out; extended.

Pandit, pan'dit, *n.* PUNDIT.

Pandora, pan-dō'ra, *n.* [Gr., from *pan*, all, and *dōron*, a gift.] *Class. myth.* the name of the first woman on earth, on whom all the gods and goddesses bestowed gifts.—*Pandora's box*, a box Pandora received, containing all human ills, from which all escaped and spread over the earth, hope alone remaining.

Pandore, pan'dōr, *n.* A musical instrument of the lute kind; a bandore.

Pandour, pan'dör, *n.* [Croatian *bandur*, under a banner, later *pandur*, mounted policeman.] One of a body of Croatian foot soldiers, formerly dreaded for their savage mode of warfare.

Pandura, pan-dō'ra, *n.* [L. *pandura*, from Gr. *pandoura*.] A Neapolitan musical instrument, strung with eight metal wires, and played with a quill.

Pandurate, Panduriform, pan'dū-rāt, pan-dū'ri-form, *a.* *Bot.* shaped like a pandura; fiddle-shaped: applied to a leaf.

Pane, pān, *n.* [Fr. *pan*, a panel or definite portion of a surface, from L. *pannus*, a piece of cloth, a patch (whence also *panel*, *pawn*.] A distinct part of a flat surface‡; a plate of glass inserted in a window, door, &c.; a panel or division of a work; a sunken portion surrounded by a border.—**Paned**, pānd, *p.* and *a.* Provided with or composed of panes.

Panegyric, pan-e-jir'ik, *n.* [Gr. *panēgyrikos*, fit for a public assembly, from *panēgyris*, a public assembly—*pas*, *pan*, all, and *agyris*, an assembly.] A laudatory oration; a formal eulogy; an elaborate encomium; praise bestowed; laudation.—**Panegyric, Panegyrical**, pan-e-jir'i-kal, *a.* Containing praise or eulogy; encomiastic. — **Panegyrically**, pan-e-jir'i-kal-li, *adv.* By way of panegyric.—**Panegyrist**, pan-e-jir'ist, *n.* One who bestows praise; a eulogist.—**Panegyrize**, pan'e-ji-rīz, *v.t.* —*panegyrized*, *panegyrizing*. To write or pronounce a panegyric or eulogy on.—*v.i.* To indulge in panegyric; to bestow praises.

Panel, pan'el, *n.* [O.Fr. *panel*, dim. of *pan*, a pane, a panel. PANE.] A surface or compartment of a surface more or less distinct from others; an area on a wall sunk from the general surface; a similar portion fixed in the framing of a door, shutter, &c.; a piece of wood upon which a picture is painted; *law*, a document containing the names of persons summoned to serve upon a jury; the jury; *Scots law*, the accused person in a criminal action; of doctors in Insurance Act (which see). A list of registered doctors in any area accepting such medical practice.—*v.t.*—*panelled*, *panelling*. To form with panels.—**Panelling**, pan'el-ing, *n.* Panelled work.

Pang, pang, *n.* [Comp. W. *pang*, a pang, a convulsion.] A sudden paroxysm of extreme pain; a sudden spasm or throe.

Pangenesis, pan-jen'e-sis, *n.* [Gr. *pan*, *genesis*, descent.] A provisional theory, now abandoned, attributing the transmission of hereditary characters to living particles migrating into the sex-cells from all parts of the body.—**Pangenetic**, pan-je-net'ik, *a.* Pertaining to or relating to pangenesis.

Pan-Germanism, pan-jėr'man-ism, *n.* A movement aimed at keeping Germans, resident in any part of the world, conscious of their common cultural heritage.

Panhandle, pan'han-dl, *n.* A projection of land resembling a handle of a pan, in the N. W. section of Texas.—*v.t.* and *i.* To approach one on the street and beg.

Panhellenic, pan-hel-len'ik, *a.* [Gr. *pan*, all, and *Hellēnikos*, Greek, from *Hellēnes*, the Greeks.] Pertaining to all Greece.—**Panhellenism**, pan-hel'len-izm, *n.* The proposed union of all the Greeks into one political body.—**Panhellenist**, pan-hel'-len-ist, *n.* One who favours Panhellenism.

Panic, pan'ik, *n.* [From Gr. *panikos*, of or belonging to *Pan*, the god who was believed to inspire sudden fear, fear arising among people without visible cause.] A sudden fright, particularly without real cause; terror inspired by a trifling cause.—*a.* Extreme or causeless: applied to fright.—**Panicky**, pan'ik-i, *a.* Showing or inspired by panic. —**Panic-stricken Panic-struck**, *a.* Struck with a panic or sudden fear.

Panic, Panic-grass, pan'ik, *n.* [L. *panicum*, a kind of grass.] The name of several species of grass.

Panicle, pan'i-kl, *n.* [L. *panicula*, a panicle, dim. of *panus*, thread on the bobbin in a shuttle.] A branching form of inflorescence, as in the lilac or the oat.—**Panicled**, pan'i-kld, *a.* Furnished with panicles.—**Paniculate, Paniculated**, pa-nik'ū-lāt, pa-nik'ū-lā-ted, *a.* *Bot.* furnished with or arranged in a panicle; like a panicle.

Panification, pan'i-fi-kā"shon, *n.* L. *panis*, bread, and *facio*, to make.] The process of bread-making.

Panislamism, pan-iz'lam-izm, *n.* [Gr. *pan*, all, and E. *Islamism*.] A sentiment or movement in favour of a union or confederacy of the Mohammedan nations.

Pannage, pan'āj, *n.* [O.Fr. *panage*, from L. *panis*, bread.] An old term for the food of swine in the woods, as beech-nuts, acorns, &c.; money paid for this.

Pannel, pan'el, *n.* [PANEL.] In Scotland the accused person in a criminal trial.

Pannier, pan'i-ėr, *n.* [Fr. *panier*, from L. *panarium*, a bread-basket, from *panis*, bread. PANTRY.] A wicker-basket, primarily a bread-basket, but now one of two baskets slung across a beast of burden, in which things are carried; a part of a lady's dress attached to the back of the skirt; *arch.* a corbel.

Pannikin, pan'i-kin, *n.* A small pan or cup.—**Panning-out**, *n.* In *gold digging*, the washing process by which the grains of gold are separated from the dust.

Panoply, pan'ō-pli, *n.* [Gr. *panoplia*—*pan*, all, and *hopla*, arms.] Complete armor of defense; an elaborate covering.—**Panoplied**, pan'ō-plid, *a.* Having a panoply or full suit of armor.

Panopticon, pa-nop'ti-kon, *n.* [Gr. *pan*, all, and root *op*, to see.] Bentham's name for his proposed prison, in which each of the prisoners can be seen at all times; an exhibition of scientific or other novelties.

Panorama, pan-ō-rä'ma, *n.* [Gr. *pan*, all, and *horama*, view, from *horaō*, to see.] A picture in which all the objects of nature that are visible from a single point are represented on the interior surface of a round or cylindrical wall, the point of view being in the axis of the cylinder.—**Panoramic**, pan-ō-ram'ik, *a.* Pertaining to or like a panorama, or complete view.

Pan-Presbyterian, pan'pres-bi-tē"ri-an, *a.* Representative of those who hold Presbyterian views from all parts of the world (*pan-Presbyterian* synod).

Panslavic, pan-slav'ik, *a.* [Gr. *pan*, all, and E. *Slavic*.] Pertaining to all the Slavic races. — **Panslavism**, pan-slav'izm, *n.* The proposed amalgamation of all the Slavic races into one confederacy.

Panspermy, pan'spėr-mi, *n.* [Gr. *pan*, all, and *sperma*, seed, germ.] The doctrine that organic germs are everywhere diffused, and that all cases of so-called spontaneous generation are to be thus explained.

Pan's-pipes. Under PAN.

Panstereorama, pan-ster'ē-ō-rä"ma, *n.* [Gr. *pan*, all, *stereos*, solid, and *horaō*, to see.] A model, in rilievo, of a town or country in wood, cork, pasteboard, or other substance.

Pansy, pan'zi, *n.* [Fr. *pensée*, thought, heart's-ease, from *penser*, to think. PENSIVE.] A name applied to the garden varieties of violet; heart's-ease.

Pant, pant, *v.i.* [From or connected with O.Fr. *pantoier*, to pant, to gasp, *pantois*, a panting; Pr. *panteiar*, to be breathless.] To breathe quickly, as after exertion or from excited eagerness; to gasp; to throb or heave with unusual violence, as the heart or the breast after hard labour; to desire ardently.—*v.t.* To breathe forth; to gasp out.—*n.* A quick, short respiration; a gasp; a throb or palpitation.—**Pantingly**, pan'ting-li, *adv.* In a panting manner; with gasping or rapid breathing.

Pantagraph, pan'ta-graf, *n.* PANTOGRAPH.

Pantalets, pan'ta-lets, *n. pl.* [From *pantaloon*.] Loose drawers worn by females and children.

Pantaloon, pan-ta-lōn', *n.* [Fr. *pantalon*, lit. a Venetian, the Venetians being called *Pantalones*, after their patron saint *Pantalone* or *Pantaleon*.] An old kind of garment for males, consisting of breeches and stockings in one‡; a character in the Italian comedy: so called from his dress; in modern pantomimes, a character usually represented as a very fatuous old man, the butt of the clown; *pl.* a pair of trousers.

Pantechnicon, pan-tek'ni-kon, *n.* [Gr. *pan*, all, and *techē*, art.] A place where all kinds of manufactured articles are collected and exposed for sale.

Pantheism, pan'thē-izm, *n.* [Gr. *pan*, all, and *Theos*, God.] The doctrine that the universe, taken or conceived of as a whole, is God, or that all things are simply modes or manifestations of God.—**Pantheist**, pan'thē-ist, *n.* One that believes in pantheism. — **Pantheistic, Pantheistical**, pan-thē-is'tik, pan-thē-is'ti-kal, *a.* Pertaining to pantheism. — **Pantheistically**, pan-thē-is'ti-kal-li, *adv.* In the manner or from the point of view of a pantheist.—**Pantheology**, pan-thē-ol'o-ji, *n.* [Gr. *pan*, all, and E. *theology*.] A system of theology comprehending all religions, and a knowledge of all deities.—**Pantheologist**, pan-thē-ol'o-jist, *n.* One who is versed in pantheology.

Pantheon, pan'thē-on or pan-thē'on, *n.* [Gr. *pantheon*, *pantheion*—*pan*, all, and *theos*, a god.] A temple dedicated to all the gods, especially the building so called at Rome, now converted into a church; all the divinities collectively worshipped by a people.

Panther, pan'thėr, *n.* [L. *panthera*, Gr. *panthēr*; compr. Skr. *pundarīka*, a leopard.] A carnivorous animal of Asia and Africa, identical with or a variety of the leopard. —**Pantheress**, pan'thėr-es, *n.* A female panther. — **Pantherine**, pan'thėr-in, *a.* Belonging to the panther.

Pantile, pan'tīl, *n.* [*Pan* and *tile*.] A tile with a cross section resembling the letter S, overlapping the tile by its side as well as the one beneath.

Pantisocracy, pan-ti-sok'ra-si, *n.* [Gr.

pan, all, *isos*, equal, and *kratos*, power.] A utopian community in which all the members are equal in rank and social position; the principle of such a scheme or community.—**Pantisocratic**, pan-tis'o-krat"ik, *a.* Of or pertaining to pantisocracy.—**Pantisocratist**, pan-ti-sok'rat-ist, *n.* One who favours pantisocracy.

Pantofle, **Pantoffle**, pan'tofl, pan-tof'l, pan-tö'fl, *n.* [Fr. *pantoufle*.] A lounging slipper.

Pantograph, pan'tō-graf, *n.* [Gr. *pas*, *pantos*, all, and *graphō*, to write.] An instrument by means of which drawings, maps, plans, &c., can be copied mechanically on the original scale, or on one reduced or enlarged.—**Pantographic**, pan-tō-graf'ik, *a.* Pertaining to a pantograph.

Pantology, pan-tol'o-ji, *n.* [Gr. *pas*, *pantos*, all, and *logos*, discourse.] Universal knowledge; a systematic view of all branches of human knowledge. — **Pantological**, pan-tō-loj'i-kal, *a.* Relating to pantology.

Pantomime, pan'tō-mīm, *n.* [L. *pantomimus*, Gr. *pantomimos*—*pas*, *pantos*, all, and *mimos*, a mimic.] A player who acted, not by speaking, but wholly by gesticulations; a theatrical entertainment in dumb-show; hence, dumb-show generally; a popular stage entertainment usually produced about the Christmas season, the effects being heightened by gorgeous scenery and catching music. —**Pantomimic**, **Pantomimical**, pan-tō-mim'ik, pan-tō-mim'-i-kal, *a.* Pertaining to pantomime.—**Pantomimically**, pan-tō-mim'i-kal-li, *adv.* in the manner of pantomime.

Pantophagous, pan-tof'a-gus, *a.* [Gr. *pas*, *pantos*, all, and *phagō*, to eat.] Eating all kinds of food; omnivorous.

Pantry, pan'tri, *n.* [Fr. *paneterie*, a pantry, from L. *panis* (Fr. *pain*), bread, whence also *pannier*.] A room or closet for provisions, silverware, china, and glassware.

Pants, pants, *n.* Shortened form of pantaloons; trousers.

Panzer, pän'tsėr, *a.* [G.] Mechanized or armored, as a *panzer* division.

Pap, pap, *n.* [D. and Dan. *pap*, G. *pappe*, probable from an infantile cry. PAPA.] A kind of soft food for infants; the pulp of fruit.

Pap, pap, *n.* [Of similar origin to *pap*, food; comp. L. *papilla*, the nipple.] A nipple of the breast; a teat; a round hill resembling a pap.

Papa, pa-pä', *n.* [A reduplication of one of the earliest cries uttered by infants—Fr., G., D., and Dan. *papa*, L. *papa*, *pappa*, Gr. *pappa*; comp. *mama*, *mamma*.] Father: a word used by children.

Papacy, pā'pa-si, *n.* [L.L. *papatia*, the papacy, from L. *papa*, the pope, lit. father. PAPA, POPE.] The office and dignity of the pope; papal authority and jurisdiction; the popedom; the popes collectively. — **Papal**, pā'pal, *a.* Belonging to the pope or to popedom; proceeding from the pope. —**Papalize**, pā'pal-īz, *v.t.*—*papalized*, *papalizing*. To make papal. — *v.i.* To conform to popery.—**Papally**, pā'pal-li, *adv.* In a papal manner.

Papaveraceous, pa-pā'vėr-ā"shus, *a.* [L. *papaver*, a poppy.] Pertaining to the poppy family.

Papaw, pa-pa', *n.* [Sp. and Pg. *papaya*, a name brought from Malabar.] A tree indigenous to South America, but now widely cultivated in tropical countries; also its fruit; the juice of both fruit and tree renders tough meat tender.

Paper, pā'pėr, *n.* [Fr. *papier*, It. *papiro*, from L. *papyrus*, Gr. *papyros*, the papyrus, PAPYRUS.] A well-known substance used for writing and printing on, and for various other purposes, manufactured principally of vegetable fibre reduced to a pulp; a piece, leaf, or sheet of paper; a single sheet appearing periodically; a newspaper; a journal; an essay or article on some subject; any written or printed document; collectively, such documents as promissory notes, bills of exchange, &c.—*a.* Made of paper; appearing merely in certain documents without really existing (a *paper army*); thin; slight.—*v.t.* To cover with paper; to furnish with paper-hangings; to fold or inclose in paper.—**Papery**, pā'pėr-i, *a.* Like paper; having the thinness and consistency of paper —**Paper-clip**, *n.* A clip or contrivance for holding paper.—**Paper-cutter**, *n.* A paper-knife; a machine for cutting paper in piles, or for trimming the edges of books, &c.—**Paper-folder**, *n.* An instrument or machine for folding paper; a paper-knife. — **Paper-hanger**, *n.* One whose employment is to hang wallpaper —**Paper-hangings**, *n. pl.* Paper for covering and adorning the walls of rooms; wallpaper.—**Paper-knife**, *n.* An instrument of bone, ivory, &c., with an edge like a blunt knife used in cutting open the leaves of books, &c., or for folding paper. —**Paper-maker**, *n.* One that manufactures paper.—**Paper-making**, *n.* The art or process of manufacturing paper. —**Paper-mill**, *n.* A mill in which paper is manufactured —**Paper-money**, *n.* Bank-notes or the like circulated as the representative of coin.—**Paper-muslin**, *n.* Glazed muslin used for linings, &c.—**Paper-nautilus**, *n.* The paper-sailor or argonaut.—**Paper-reed**, *n.* The papyrus.—**Paper-sailor**, *n.* Same as *Paper-nautilus*.—**Paper-stainer**, *n.* A maker of paper-hangings. —**Paper-weight**, *n.* A small weight laid on loose papers to keep them in place.

Papeterie, päp-trē, *n.* [Fr., stationery or writing materials.] An ornamented case or box containing papers and other materials for writing.

Paphian, pā'fi-an, *a.* Pertaining to *Paphos*, a city of Cyprus sacred to Venus; hence, pertaining to Venus or her rites.

Papier-mâché, päp-yā-mä-shā, *n.* [Fr., lit masticated paper.] A material prepared by pulping different kinds of paper into a mass, which is moulded into various articles, dried, and japanned.

Papilionaceous, pa-pil'i-ō-nā"shus, *a.* [L. *papilio*, a butterfly.] Resembling the butterfly; *bot.* having the corolla shaped like a butterfly, such as the flower of the pea.

Papilla, pa-pil'la, *n.* pl. **Papillæ**, pa-pil'lē. [L.] A small pap or nipple; a little eminence on the surface of the skin, as on the tongue. — **Papillary**, pap'il-la-ri, *a.* Pertaining to or resembling the nipple; papillose. — **Papillate**, pap'il-lāt, *v.t.*—*papillated*, *papillating*. To grow into a nipple.—**Papillate**, **Papillated**, pap'-il-lā-ted, *a.* Covered with papillæ.—**Papilloma**, pap'il-ō"ma, *n.* [Gr *oma*, a tumour.] A benign tumour shaped like a papilla.—**Papillose**, pap'il-lōs, *a.* Papillary.—**Papillote**, pap'il-lōt, *n.* [Fr.] A curl paper.

Papingo, pa-ping'go. Also **Papejay**, **Papingoe** (POPINJAY), *n.* Parrot, as in Sir David Lindsay's 'Complaint and Epistle of the Papingo'. (*Scottish*.) 'To shoot at the *papingo*', old Scottish game of shooting at a stuffed figure on a pole, as in Scott's *Old Mortality*.

Papist, pā'pist, *n.* [Fr. *papiste*, from Fr. *pape*, L. *papa*, pope.] A Roman Catholic. —**Papistic**, **Papistical**, pā-pis'tik, pā-pis'ti-kal, *a.* Popish, pertaining to Popery. —**Papistically**, pā-pis'ti-kal-li, *adv.* In a papistic manner.—**Papistry**, pā'pist-ri, *n.* Popery

Papoose, **Pappoose**, pa-pös', pap-pös', *n.* Among the native Indians of North America, a babe or young child.

Pappus, pap'us, *n.* [L., from Gr. *pappos*, the down of plants.] *Bot.* the feathery appendage that crowns many single-seeded seed-vessels; a form of calyx in composite plants of a downy or hairy character.—**Pappose**, **Pappous**, pap'ōs, pap'us, *a.* Downy; furnished with pappus.

Papula, pap'ū-la, *n.* pl. **Papulæ**, pap'ū-lē. [L.] A pimple.—**Papular**, **Papulose**, pap'ū-lėr, pap'ū-lōs, *a.* Covered with pimples.—**Papulous**, pap'ū-lus, *a.* Papular.

Papyrograph, pa-pī'rō-graf, *n.* [Gr. *papyrus*, paper, *graphō*, to write.] An apparatus for producing a number of copies of a written document.

Papyrus, pa-pī'rus, *n.* [L. *papyrus*, Gr. *papyros*, probably of Egyptian origin. Hence *paper*.] A cyperaceous plant abundant in the valley of the Nile, the stems of which afforded the most ancient material for writing; a written scroll made of the papyrus (pl. **Papyri**, pa-pī'rī).—**Papyraceous**, **Papyrean**, pap-i-rā'-shus, pa-pir'ē-an, *a.* Made of or resembling papyrus or paper.—**Papyrine**, pap'i-rin, *n.* Parchment paper.

Par, pär, *n.* [L. *par*, equal, whence *pair* and *peer*; seen also in *compeer*, *disparage*, *umpire*, &c.] State of equality equality in circumstances or in value; the state of the shares of a public undertaking when they may be purchased at the original price, or *at par*—*Above par*, above the original price; at a premium.—*Below par*, below the original price, at a discount.—*Par of exchange*, the established value of the coin or of the standard value of one country expressed in the coin or standard value of another.

Para-, pär'ä. [Gr. *para-*, par, from *para*, beside.] A prefix meaning beside, with its variations: alongside, aside from, amiss, beyond as in parallel, paragraph, &c.

Para, pär'ä. [F. fr Ital. imper. of *parare*, to shield or defend.] To protect from, or that which shields, as in *parasol* and *parachute*.

Parable, par'a-bl, *n.* [Fr. *parabole*, from L. *parabola*, Gr *parabolē*, from *paraballō*, to throw beside, to compare—*para*, beside, and *ballō*, to throw Of same origin are *parley*, *parlour*, *parole*.] Originally, a comparison or similitude; now a fable or allegorical representation of something real in life or nature, from which a moral is drawn for instruction; *Scrip* a proverbial or notable saying, a thing darkly or figuratively expressed. — *v.t.* —*parabled*, *parabling*. To represent by a parable.—**Parabola**, pa-rab'ō-la, *n.* [Gr. *parabolē*, so called from its axis being parallel to the side of the cone.] A geometrical figure, one of the conic sections, shown when a cone is cut by a plane parallel to one of its sides; the curve which a projectile theoretically describes. — **Parabole**, pa-rab'ōl-ē, *n. Rhet.* similitude; comparison —**Parabolic**, par-a-bol'ik, *a.* Having the form of a parabola; pertaining to a parabola; pertaining to a parable.—**Parabolical**, par-a-bol'i-kal, *a.* Parabolic, of the nature of or having the character of a parable.—**Parabolically**, par-a-bol'i-kal-li, *adv.* By way of parable; in the form of a parabola. —**Paraboliform**, par-a-bol'i-form, *a.* Having the form of a parabola.—**Paraboloid**, pa-rab'ol-oid, *n.* The solid generated by the revolution of a parabola about its axis; a parabolic conoid.

Paracentesis, par'a-sen-tē"sis, *n.* [Gr *parakentēsis*—*para*, through, and *kenteō*, to pierce.] *Surg.* the perforation of a cavity of the body for the evacuation of any effused fluid; the operation of tapping.

Paracentric, **Paracentrical**, par-a-sen'trik, par-a-sen'tri-kal, *a.* [Gr. *para*, beyond, and *kentron*, centre.] Deviating from circularity; out of the strict curve which would form a circle.—**Parachordal**, par-a-kor'dal, *n.* [Gr. *para*, beside, and *chordē*, a chord.] One of the cartilaginous plates which form the first appearance of the skull in the embryo of vertebrates.

Parachronism, pa-rak'ron-izm, *n.* [Gr. *para*, beyond, and *chronos*, time.] An error in chronology by which an event is placed later than it should be.

Parachute, par'a-shöt, *n.* [Fr., from *parer*, to ward off, and *chute*, a fall.] *Aviation*, an apparatus of an umbrella shape with which aircraft are provided, for the purpose of enabling an aëronaut, in case of danger, to drop to the ground without sustaining injury, the umbrella shape affording great resistance to the air.

Paraclete, par'a-klēt, *n.* [Gr. *paraklētos*, from *parakaleō*—*para*, to, and *kaleō*, to call.] One called to aid or support; hence, a term applied to the Holy Spirit.

Parade, pa-rād', *n.* [Fr. *parade*, from Sp. *parada*, a parade, a place for the exercise of troops, from L. *paro*, *paratus*, to prepare. PARE, PREPARE.] Show; ostentation; display; a showy or pompous procession; a military display; the collection of troops for inspection or the like; the place where such display is held; a public walk or promenade.—*v.t.*—*paraded*, *parading*. To exhibit in a showy manner; to make a show of; to assemble and march in military order.—*v.i.* To assemble in military order; to go about in military procession; to walk about for show.

Paradigm, par'a-dim, *n.* [Gr. *paradeigma*—*para*, beside, and *deigma*, example, from *deiknumi*, to show.] An example; a model; *gram.* an example of a word, as a noun, adjective, or verb, in its various inflections.—**Paradigmatic, Paradigmatical**, par'a-dig-mat"ik, par'a-dig-mat"i-kal, *a.* Pertaining to a paradigm; suited for being an example; exemplary.—**Paradigmatically**, par'a-dig-mat"i-kal-li, *adv.* In the way of paradigm or example.

Paradise, par'a-dīs, *n.* [L. *paradisus*, from Gr. *paradeisos*, a garden—properly a Persian word.] The garden of Eden, in which Adam and Eve were at first placed; hence, a place of bliss; a region of supreme felicity; the abode of sanctified souls after death.—*Bird-of-paradise.* Under BIRD.—**Paradisaic, Paradisaical**, par'a-di-sā"ik, par'a-di-sā"i-kal, *a.* Pertaining to paradise.

Parados, par'a-dos, *n.* [Fr., from *parer*, to defend, *a*, for, and *dos*, L. *dorsum*, the back.] An elevation of earth behind a fortified place to protect it from attack.

Paradox, par'a-doks, *n.* [Gr. *paradoxon*, from *para*, beyond, and *doxa*, opinion. ORTHODOX.] A tenet or proposition contrary to received opinion; a statement which seems to be at variance with common sense, or to contradict some previously ascertained truth, though when properly investigated it may be perfectly well founded.—*Hydrostatic paradox.* HYDROSTATIC.—**Paradoxical**, par-a-dok'si-kal, *a.* Having the nature of a paradox; inclined to paradox.—**Paradoxically**, par-a-dok'si-kal-li, *adv.* In a paradoxical manner. — **Paradoxicalness**, par-a-dok'si-kal-nes, *n.*—**Paradoxy**, par'a-dok-si, *n.* The state of being paradoxical.

Paradoxure, par-a-doks'ūr, *n.* [*Paradox*, and Gr. *oura*, tail.] An animal of south-eastern Asia allied to the civet, living on the fruit of palms, and able to curl its tail into a tight spiral. Called also *Palm cat.*

Paraffin, Paraffine, par'a-fin, *n.* [L. *parum*, little, and *affinis*, akin, from its resistance to chemical reagents.] A fatty substance obtained from the dry distillation of wood, bituminous coal, wax, &c., largely used in the manufacture of candles.—**Paraffin-oil**, *n.* The oily matter which is given off in the destructive distillation of bituminous shale, the lighter oils being used for illuminating, the heavier for lubricating.

Paragenesis, par-a-jen'e-sis, *n.* [Gr. *para*, side by side with, and *genesis*, generation.] Origin of two things side by side; that state of minerals when they are made up of an aggregate of interblended crystals or crystals which have not assumed their normal structure (as in granite, &c.).—**Paragenic**, par-a-jen'ik, *a.* Characterized by or pertaining to paragenesis.

Paragoge, par'a-gō-ji, *n.* [Gr. *paragōgē*—*para*, beside, and *agō*, to lead.] The addition of a letter or syllable to the end of a word.—**Paragogic, Paragogical**, par-a-goj'ik, par-a-goj'i-kal, *a.* Pertaining to paragoge; lengthening a word by being affixed.

Paragon, par'a-gon, *n.* [Fr. *parangon*, from Sp. *paragon*, *parangon*, model, from the prepositions *para*, beside, and *con*, in comparison with.] A model or pattern, especially a model or pattern of superior excellence or perfection.—*v.t.* To compare; to rival; to form a rival or equal to.

Paragram, par'a-gram, *n.* [Gr. *paragramma*—*para*, beside, and *gramma*, a writing.] A play upon words, or a pun.

Paragraph, par'a-graf, *n.* [Gr. *paragraphē*, a marginal note—*para*, beside, and *graphō*, to write.] Originally a marginal note; hence the character ¶ used as a reference, or to mark a division in a written composition; a distinct part of a discourse or writing, consisting of one or several sentences; a portion or section which relates to a particular point, and is generally distinguished by a break in the lines; a brief notice, as in a newspaper.—**Paragraphic, Paragraphical**, par-a-graf'ik, par-a-graf'i-kal, *a.* Pertaining to a paragraph; exhibiting paragraphs. — **Paragraphically**, par-a-graf'i-kal-li, *adv.* By or with paragraphs.—**Paragraphist**, par'a-graf-ist, *n.* One who writes paragraphs.

Paraguay Tea, par'a-gwā, *n.* MATÉ.

Parakeet, par'a-ket, *n.* [Fr. *parroquet*, *perroquet*, a parakeet. PARROT.] The name given to various parrots of the eastern hemisphere, generally of small size and having very long tail-feathers.

Paraleipsis, Paralepsis, Paralipsis, par-a-lip'sis, par-a-lep'sis, par-a-lip'sis, *n.* [Gr. *paraleipsis*, omission—*para*, beside, and *leipō*, to leave.] *Rhet.* a pretended omission; a figure by which a speaker pretends to pass by what at the same time he really mentions.

Parallax, par'al-laks, *n.* [Gr. *parallaxis*, from *parallassō*, to vary, decline, or wander—*para*, beyond, and *allassō*, to change.] The apparent change of position of an object relatively to other objects when viewed from different places; *astron.* the difference between the position of any celestial object as viewed from the surface of the earth, and that which it would have when viewed from the centre of either the earth or the sun; *optics*, the non-coincidence of the cross fibres of a telescope with the focus of the eye-glass. — **Parallactic, Parallactical**, par-al-lak'tik, par-al-lak'ti-kal, *a.* Pertaining to parallax.

Parallel, par'al-lel, *a.* [Gr. *parallēlos*—*para*, side by side, and *allēlōn*, of one another.] Extended in the same direction, and in all parts equally distant; being exactly at an equal distance throughout their length or breadth (said of lines or surfaces); hence, having the same direction or tendency; running in accordance with something; equal in all essential parts, points, or features; exactly similar (a *parallel* passage or incident).—*Parallel forces*, forces which act in directions parallel to each other.—*Parallel lines*, *geom.* straight lines which are in the same plane, and being produced ever so far both ways, do not meet.—*Parallel motion*, a contrivance invented by Watt for converting a reciprocating circular motion into an alternating rectilinear motion, and applied in the steam-engine. — *Parallel roads*, a phenomenon observed in some valleys of the Scottish Highlands, consisting in a series of parallel and nearly horizontal lines running along the sides of the hills, supposed to have been formed by the action of a lake.—*Parallel rod*, in locomotive engines, a rod that connects the crank-pins of the driving-wheels. — *Parallel ruler*, a mathematical instrument for drawing parallel lines, formed of two equal rulers, connected by two cross-bars of equal length and movable about joints.—*Parallel sailing*, sailing on a parallel of latitude.—*n.* A line which throughout its whole extent is equidistant from another line; one of the circles on a sphere parallel to its equator; a line on a map marking latitude (called also a *parallel of latitude*); resemblance or conformity in essential points; likeness; comparison (to draw a *parallel* between two historians); one who corresponds essentially to another; a counterpart; *milit.* a trench cut before a fortress, parallel to its defences, for covering the besiegers from the guns of the place; *printing*, a mark of reference (thus ‖) used to direct attention to notes.—*v.t.*—*paralleled*, *paralleling* (also with *ll* in the second place); to make parallel; to form or serve as a parallel to; to match; to correspond to; to show or furnish an equal to; to compare. — **Parallelism**, par'a-lel-izm, *n.* State of being parallel; resemblance in a number of important particulars; correspondence; a comparison.—*Parallelism of the earth's axis*, that feature according to which the axis is always inclined at exactly the same slope.—**Parallelly**, par'a-lel-li, *adv.* In a parallel manner; with parallelism.—**Parallelogram**, par-a-lel'ō-gram, *n.* A four-sided figure composed of straight lines, and having its opposite sides parallel and equal; popularly, a quadrilateral figure of greater length than breadth. — *Parallelogram of forces*, the theorem in physics or natural philosophy that, if two forces acting at a point be represented in direction and magnitude by two sides of a parallelogram, the resulting force or resultant is represented by the diagonal through the point of intersection of these two sides.—**Parallelogrammatic**, par-a-lel'ō-gram-mat"ik, *a.* Relating to a parallelogram.—**Parallelogrammic**, par-a-lel'ō-gram"-ik, *a.* Having the properties of a parallelogram. — **Parallelepiped, Parallelepipedon**, par-a-lel'e-pī"ped, par-a-lel'e-pī"ped-on, *n.* [Gr. *parallēlepipedon* — *parallēlos*, parallel, and *epipedos*, plane, superficial — *epi*, upon, and *pedon*, the ground.] A solid body with six sides forming parallelograms; a solid in the shape of a brick.

Paralogism, pa-ral'ō-jizm, *n.* [Gr. *paralogismos*—*para*, beyond, and *logismos*, reasoning. LOGIC.] A fallacious argument; an instance of false reasoning.—**Paralogize**, pa-ral'ō-jīz, *v.i.*—*paralogized*, *paralogizing*. To reason falsely.

Paralysis, pa-ral'i-sis, *n.* [G. *paralysis*, from *paralyō*, to loosen—*para*, beside, and *lyō*, to loose.] A loss or diminution of the power of motion in some part of the body, arising from disease of the nerves; a loss of sensation in any part of the body; palsy. — **Paralyse**, par'a-līz, *v.t.* — *paralysed*, *paralysing*. To affect with *paralysis*; to destroy physical or mental energy in. — **Paralytic, Paralytical**, par-a-lit'ik, par-a-lit'i-kal, *a.* Pertaining to paralysis; affected with paralysis; inclined to paralysis. —**Paralytic**, *n.* A person affected with paralysis.

Paramagnetic, par'a-mag-net"ik, *a.* A term proposed by Faraday as a substitute for *magnetic* in contradistinction to *diamagnetic*.—**Paramagnetism**, par-a-mag'net-izm, *n.* Magnetism as opposed to *diamagnetism*.

Paramatta, par-a-mat'ta, *n.* A light twilled dress fabric, the weft of merino wool and the warp cotton: said to have been made originally with wool from *Paramatta* in Australia.

Parameter, pa-ram'et-ėr, *n.* [Gr. *para*, beside, and *metron*, measure.] *Geom.* a constant straight line belonging to each of the three conic sections; the constant quantity which enters into the equation of a curve.

Paramo, pä'rä-mo, *n.* In South America a mountainous district covered with stunted trees, and in which a damp cold perpetually prevails.

Paramount, par'a-mount, *a.* [O.Fr. *par* (L. *per*), through, completely, and *amont*, above. AMOUNT.] Superior in power or jurisdiction (lord *paramount*, the supreme lord of a fee or of lands, &c.); eminent; of the highest order; superior to all others.—*n.* Chief; highest in rank or order.—**Paramountcy**, par'a-mount-si, *n.* The condition of being paramount.

Paramour, par'a-mör, *n.* [Fr. *par amour*, with love — *par* = L. *per*, by, *amour*, L. *amor*, love.] A lover‡; a wooer‡; one who takes the place of a husband or wife without possessing the rights.

Paranoia, par'a-noi-a, *n.* [Gr. *para*, beside,

nous, mind.] A mental disease marked by delusions of one's importance and of being persecuted.—**Paranoiac**, par-a-noi'ak, *n.* A person affected by paranoia.—*a.* Pertaining to, or affected by, paranoia.—**Paranoid**, *a.* Resembling paranoia.

Paranymph, par'a-nimf, *n.* [Gr. *paranymphos—para*, by, and *nymphē*, a bride.] In ancient Greece, a bridesman.

Parapegm, par'a-pem, *n.* [Gr. *parapēgma—para*, beside, and *pēgnymi*, to fix.] A brazen tablet fixed to a pillar, on which proclamations, &c., were anciently engraved.

Parapet, par'a-pet, *n.* [Fr. *parapet*, It. *parapetto—parare* (Fr. *parer*, E. *parry*), to ward off, to guard, and *petto* (L. *pectus*), the breast.] *Lit.* a wall or rampart breast-high; *milit.* a wall or rampart to cover the soldiers from the attacks of the enemy in front; a breastwork; *arch.* a wall placed at the edges of platforms, sides of bridges, &c., to prevent people from falling over.—**Parapeted**, par'a-pet-ed, *a.* Furnished with a parapet.

Paraph, par'af, *n.* [Fr. *parafe*, *paraphe*, an abbreviation of *paragraph*.] The figure formed by the flourish of a pen at the conclusion of a signature.—*v.t.* To add a paraph to; to sign.

Paraphernalia, par'a-fér-nā"li-a, *n.pl.* [L.L. *paraphernalia*, from Gr. *parapherna*, what a bride has besides her dower—*para*, beyond, and *phernē*, a dowry.] The belongings of a wife over and above her dower or portion, as apparel and ornaments; personal attire of a showy or accessory description; also, fittings up, &c., of an apartment or house; appendages; ornaments; trappings.

Paraphrase, par'a-frāz, *n.* [Gr. *paraphrasis—para*, beside, and *phrasis*, phrase.] A restatement of a text, passage, or work, giving the sense of the original in other words; the setting forth in clearer and ampler terms of the signification of a passage or work; a sacred song or hymn based on a selected portion of Scripture.—*v.t.*—*paraphrased*, *paraphrasing*. To make a paraphrase of; to explain or translate with latitude.—*v.i.* To interpret or explain amply.—**Paraphrast**, par'a-frast, *n.* [Gr. *paraphrastēs*.] One who paraphrases.—**Paraphrastic, Paraphrastical**, par-a-fras'tik, par-a-fras'ti-kal, *a.* Having the character of a paraphrase; explaining in words more clear and ample than those of the author.—**Paraphrastically**, par-a-fras'ti-kal-li, *adv.* In a paraphrastic manner.

Paraplegia, Paraplegy, par-a-plē'ji-a, par'a-plē-ji, *n.* [Gr. *paraplēgia*, paralysis—*para*, beyond, and *plēgē*, stroke.] That kind of paralysis which affects the lower part of the body.

Parapodium, par-a-pō'di-um, *n.* pl. **Parapodia**. [Gr. *para*, beside, *pous*, *podos*, a foot.] A name for the rudimentary limbs of many worms.

Parapophysis, par-a-pof'i-sis, *n.* [Gr. *para*, beside, and *apophysis*, an apophysis.] The transverse process of an ideal typical vertebra; also, the name of the vertebral processes of fishes which extend outwards.

Parasang, par'a-sang, *n.* [Gr. *parasangēs*, from Per. *farsang*, a parasang.] An ancient Persian measure of length equal to 3¾ miles.

Parasceuastic, par'a-sū-as"tik, *a.* [Gr. *paraskeuastikos*, from prefix *para*, and *skeuē*, equipment.] Preparatory.

Paraselene, par'a-se-lē"nē, *n.* pl. **Paraselenæ**, par'a-se-lē"nē. [Gr. *para*, about, or near, and *selēnē*, the moon.] A mock moon; a luminous ring encompassing the moon, in which sometimes are other bright spots bearing some resemblance to the moon.

Parasite, par'a-sīt, *n.* [Fr. *parasite*, from L. *parasitus*, Gr. *parasitos*, one who eats at the table of another, a parasite, a toady—*para*, beside, and *sitos*, food.] One that frequents the tables of the rich and earns his welcome by flattery; a hanger-on; a sycophant; an animal that lives upon or in, and at the expense of, other animals; a plant which grows upon another plant, and feeds upon its juices.—**Parasitic, Parasitical**, par-a-sit'ik, par-a-sit'i-kal, *a.* Of the nature of a parasite; meanly dependent on others for support; *bot.* and *zool.* growing or living as a parasite.—**Parasitically**, par-a-sit'i-kal-li, *adv.* In the manner of a parasite.—**Parasiticide**, par-a-sit'i-sīd, *n.* [E. *parasite*, and L. *cædo*, to kill.] Any agent for destroying animal or vegetable parasites.—**Parasitism**, par'a-sīt-izm, *n.* The behaviour or manners of a parasite; the state of being a parasite.

Parasol, par'a-sol, *n.* [Fr. *parasol*, from It. *parasole*—*parare* (L. *parare*, to prepare), to ward off, and *sole* (L. *sol*), the sun. PARRY.] A small umbrella used by ladies to defend their faces from the sun's rays.

Parataxis, par-a-tak'sis, *n.* [Gr. *para*, beside, and *taxis*, arrangement.] *Gram.* the mere ranging of propositions one after another, without marking their dependence on each other by way of consequence or the like.—**Paratactic**, par-a-tak'tik, *a.* Pertaining to parataxis.

Parathesis, pa-rath'e-sis, *n.* [Gr. *para*, beside, and *thesis*, a placing.] *Gram.* apposition, or the placing of two or more nouns in the same case; *philol.* the expression of grammatical relations merely by the juxtaposition of roots.—**Parathetic**, par-a-thet'ik, *a.* Pertaining or relating to parathesis.

Parathyroid, par-a-thī'roid, *a.* Situated beside the thyroid gland.—*Parathyroid glands*, four small glands on the surface of the thyroid that control the calcium content of the blood and body.

Paratyphoid, par'a-tī"foid, *n.* [Gr. *para*, beyond, *typhoid*.] A bacterial disease with symptoms resembling typhoid fever.

Paravane, pa-ra-vān', *n.* A torpedo-shaped machine fitted with an apparatus for severing the moorings of sea-mines.

Parboil, pär'boil, *v.t.* [Fr. *parbouillir*—*part*, part, and *bouillir*, to boil; lit. to part-boil.] To boil in part; to boil in a moderate degree.

Parbuckle, pär'buk-l, *n.* A purchase formed by a single rope round a heavy object for hoisting or lowering, the object itself acting as a movable pulley.—*v.t.* To hoist or lower by means of a parbuckle.

Parcel, pär'sel, *n.* [Fr. *parcelle*, from a L.L. *particella*, equivalent to L. *particula*, dim. of *pars*, *partis*, a part. PART.] A portion of anything taken separately; a particle; a collection; a group; a lot; a quantity or number of things put up together; a bundle; a package; now the common meaning.—*v.t.* *parceled*, *parcelled*, *parceling*, *parcelling*. To divide or put up into parts or portions; to make up into a mass.—**Parcel-blind**, *a.* Half-blind; partially blind.—**Parcel-gilt**, *a.* Partially gilt.—**Parceling, Parcelling**, pär'sel-ing, *n.* A dividing into small parts, as a *parceling* of land; *naut.* long narrow slips of canvas daubed with tar and bound about a rope like a bandage.—**Parcel-office**, *n.* A place where parcels are received for delivery.—**Parcel-post**, *n.* The department of a post-office system by which parcels are sent.

Parcener, pär'sen-ėr, *n.* [O.Fr. *parçonnier*, from *parçon*, L. *partitio*, *partitionis*, a portion. PARTITION.] A coheir or coparcener.

Parch, pärch, *v.t.* [Perhaps from Fr. *percer*, Fr. dial. *percher*, to pierce, as if to pierce or penetrate with heat; or a corruption of L. *peraresco*, to grow very dry.] To burn the surface of; to scorch; to dry to extremity.—*v.i.* To become scorched or superficially burned; to become very dry.—**Parchedness**, pär'ched-nes, *n.* The state of being parched.—**Parchingly**, pär'ching-li, *adv.* In a parching manner; scorchingly.

Parchment, pärch'ment, *n.* [Fr. *parchemin*, from L. *pergamena*, *pergamina* (*charta*, paper, understood), lit. paper of Pergamus, from *Pergamus* in Asia Minor, where parchment was first brought extensively into use about B.C. 200.] The skin of a very young calf, sheep, or goat dressed or prepared and rendered fit for writing on.—*Parchment paper* or *vegetable parchment*, ordinary paper without size dipped in a liquid that gives it the appearance of parchment.

Parclose, pär'klōs, *n.* [Fr. *parclose*—*par*, by, and *clos*, close.] A screen or railing, such as to inclose a tomb, separate an altar, or the like.

Pard, pärd, *n.* [L. *pardus*, Gr. *pardos*, the leopard.] The leopard or panther.

Pardon, pär'dn, *v.t.* [O.Fr. *pardoner*, (Fr. *pardonner*), from L.L. *perdonare*, to pardon—L. *per*, through, quite, and *dono*, to give. DONATION.] To release from liability to suffer punishment for a crime or a fault; to forgive (an offender); to remit the penalty or punishment of; to forgive (the offence).—*Pardon me*, forgive me; excuse me: a phrase often used when a person means civilly to deny or contradict what another affirms. ∴ *Pardon* means strictly to remit the punishment or retaliation we were entitled to inflict; *forgive* implies that the party who has suffered injury entirely overlooks the offence, and cherishes no ill-feeling whatever against the offender.—*n.* Forgiveness of an offender or of his offence; a passing over without, or not visiting with, punishment; remission of penalty; forgiveness; an official warrant of penalty remitted.—**Pardonable**, pär'dn-a-bl, *a.* Capable of being pardoned or forgiven; excusable; venial.—**Pardonableness**, pär'dn-a-bl-nes, *n.* The quality of being pardonable.—**Pardonably**, pär'dn-a-bli, *adv.* In a manner admitting of pardon; excusably.—**Pardoner**, pär'dn-ėr, *n.* One who pardons; one licensed to sell the pope's indulgences.

Pare, pär, *v.t.*—*pared*, *paring*. [Fr. *parer*, to pare, to dress, to curry, from L. *parare*, to prepare, seen in a number of words, as *parade*, *parry*, *prepare*, *repair*, *separate*, &c.] To cut off, as the superficial substance or extremities of a thing; to shave off with a sharp instrument; to trim by shaving the surface; to diminish by little and little.—**Parer**, pär'ėr, *n.* One who or that which pares.—**Paring**, pär'ing, *n.* What is pared off; a piece clipped off; the rind.

Paregoric, par-e-gor'ik, *a.* [Gr. *parēgorikos*, soothing, from *parēgoreō*, to exhort, console, soothe—*para*, beside, and *agoreuō*, to speak in an assembly.] *Med.* mitigating or assuaging pain.—*Paregoric elixir*, a camphorated tincture of opium, flavoured by aromatics.—*n.* A medicine that mitigates pain; an anodyne.

Pareira brava, pa-rā'ra brä'va, brā'va, or **Pareira**, *n.* [Portuguese *parreira brava*, wild brier.] The roots of certain plants of Brazil employed in medical practice, as tonics and diuretics.

Parelectronomic, par'e-lek-tro-nom"ik, *a.* [Gr. *para*, against, *elektron*, amber, and *nomos*, law.] *Physiol.* not responding to the stimulation of an electric current.—*Parelectronomy*, par-e-lek-tron'o-mē, *n.* A condition in which the response of a muscle to the stimulation of an electric current is diminished.

Parencephalon, par-en-sef'al-on, [Gr. *para*, against, near, and *enkephalos*, brain.] *Anat.* the cerebellum.

Parella, Parelle, pa-rel'la, pa-rel', *n.* [Fr. *parelle*.] The name of lichens that produce archil.

Parenchyma, pa-ren'ki-ma, *n.* [Gr. *para*, beside, and *enchyma*, an infusion—*en*, in, and *cheō*, to pour.] *Anat.* the essential, functional tissue of the glands or other solid organs as distinct from the framework or supporting tissue, or stroma; *bot.* the pith or pulp of plants; the spongy and cellular tissue.—**Parenchymatous, Parenchymous**, par-en-kim'a-tus, pa-ren'ki-mus, *a.* Pertaining to or of the nature of parenchyma.

Parenesis,† pa-ren'e-sis, *n.* [Gr. *parain-*

esis = *paraineō*, to exhort.] Persuasion; exhortation. — **Parenetic, Parenetical**, par-e-net'ik, par-e-net'i-kal, *a*. Hortatory; persuasive.

Parent, pär'ent, *n*. [L. *parens*, *parentis*, from *pario*, *parere*, to bring forth; to beget; akin to *parēre*, to appear (APPEAR), *parare*, to prepare (PARE).] A father or mother; he or she that produces young; used of animals and plants as well as of man; one who or that which produces; cause; source.—**Parentage**, pär'en-tāj, *n*. Extraction; birth; origin; condition with respect to the rank or character of parents. —**Parental**, pa-ren'tal, *a*. Pertaining to parents; suited to or characteristic of parents.—**Parentally**, pa-ren'tal-li, *adv*. In a fatherly or parental manner.—**Parenthood**, pär'ent-hụd, *n*. The state of being a parent; the condition of a parent.—**Parenticide**, pa-ren'ti-sīd, *n*. [L. *parens*, and *caedo*, to kill.] One who kills a parent; the killing of a parent.—**Parentless**, pär'ent-les, *a*. Deprived of parents.

Parenthesis, pa-ren'the-sis, *n*. pl. **Parentheses**, pa-ren'the-sēz. [Gr. *parenthesis*—*para*, beside, *en*, in, and *thesis*, a placing, from *tithēmi*, to place.] An explanatory or qualifying sentence, or part of a sentence, inserted into the midst of another sentence, without being grammatically connected with it: generally marked off by upright curves ( ), but frequently by dashes — —, and even by commas; *printing*, the parenthetical sign ( ), including the words inserted.—**Parenthetic, Parenthetical**, par-en-thet'ik, par-en-thet'i-kal, *a*. Pertaining to a parenthesis; of the nature of a parenthesis; exhibiting parentheses. — **Parenthetically**, par-en-thet'i-kal-li, *adv*. In the manner or form of a parenthesis; by way of parenthesis.

Parergon, Parergy, par-ėr'gon, par'ėr-ji, *n*. [Gr. *para*, beside, and *ergon*, work.] A thing done incidentally; something subsidiary; a superfluity or superfluous detail.

Paresis, pä-rē'sis, par'e-sis, *n*. [Gr., from *pariēmi*, to relax.] *Pathol*. a slight incomplete paralysis, affecting motion but not sensation.

Parfait, pär-fā', *n*. A dessert made of beaten eggs and whipped cream, sweetened, flavored, and frozen without stirring.

Pargasite, pär'ga-sīt, *n*. [From the isle *Pargas*, in Finland.] Crystallized and granular hornblende of a high luster.

Parget, pär'jet, *n*. [O.E. *pariet*, O.Fr. *pariette*, from L. *paries*, *parietis*, a wall.] Plaster laid on roofs or walls.—*v.t.* To cover with plaster or parget; to ornament with parge work.—*v.i.* To plaster.—**Pargeting, Parge-work**, pär'jet-ing, pärj'wėrk, *n*. Plaster-work; plaster-work with patterns and ornaments raised or indented upon it, whether inside or outside a house.

Parhelion, pär-hē'li-on, *n*. pl. **Parhelia**, pär-hē'li-a. [Gr. *para*, near, and *hēlios*, the sun.] A mock sun, having the appearance of the sun itself, sometimes white and sometimes tinted with prismatic colors.—**Parhelic**, pär-hel'ik, *a*. Relating to parhelia.

Pariah, pä-rī'a, *n*. [A Tamil word.] One of a low caste of people in southern India; hence, one despised and contemned by society; an outcast.

Parian, pā'ri-an, *a*. Pertaining to *Paros*, an isle in the Ægean Sea.—*Parian marble*, a marble of Paros, chosen by the ancients for their choicest works.—*n*. A fine variety of porcelain or porcelain clay, of which statuettes, &c., are made, resembling Parian marble.

Parietal, pa-rī'et-al, *a*. [L. *parietalis*, from *paries*, *parietis*, a wall.] Pertaining to a wall; *anat*. pertaining to the walls of a cavity of the body, or to the bones which form the sides and upper part of the skull; *bot*. growing from the side of another organ.

Pari mutuel, par'i mū'tu-el, *n*. A plan of race-horse betting in which the total amount wagered on all of the horses in a race, less a small fee, is shared in proportion to amounts wagered by the betters who selected the win, place, and show horses.

Paripinnate, par-i-pin'āt, *a*. [L. *par*, equal, and *pinnatus*, *pinnate*.] *Bot*. equally pinnate; abruptly pinnate: said of a compound pinnate leaf ending in two leaflets.

Paris green, *n*. A poisonous, green-colored arsenic compound used as an insecticide.

Parish, par'ish, *n*. [Fr. *paroisse*, L.L. *paroecia*, from Gr. *paroikia*, a parish, a neighborhood, from *para*, beside, and *oikos*, a house (whence *economy*).] The district under the charge of a parson or other person having cure of souls therein; a subdivision of a county for civil purposes, especially for local government and taxation.—*a*. Belonging to a parish; parochial. —**Parishioner**, pa-rish'on-ėr, *n*. One that belongs to a parish.—**Parish-priest**, *n*. A parson; a minister who holds a parish as a benefice.—**Parish-register**, *n*. A book in which the births, deaths, and marriages that occur in a parish are registered.

Parisian, pa-riz'i-an, *a*. Of or pertaining to *Paris* or its inhabitants.—A native or resident of Paris.—**Parisienne**, pa-rē'zē-en", *n*. [Fr.] A female native or resident of Paris.

Parity, par'i-ti, *n*. [Fr. *parité*, L. *paritas*, from *par*, equal. PAIR.] The condition of being equal or equivalent; like state or degree; equality; close correspondence; analogy.

Park, pärk, *n*. [Either from Fr. *parc*, L.L. *parcus*, a park (from L. *parcere*, to spare), or from A.Sax. *pearruc*, a park (whence *paddock*).] A large piece of ground inclosed and set apart for beasts of chase; a piece of public ground in or near a large town, laid out and kept for the sole purpose of pleasure and recreation; in *Scot*. any field, as on a farm.—*Park of artillery*, the train of artillery, with ammunition, &c., which accompanies an army to the field; the space occupied by such a train. —*v.t.* To put or keep temporarily in a place, as to *park* a car.—**Park-keeper**, *n*. One who has the custody of a park.

Parkway, *n*. A wide street or thoroughfare lined with trees, shrubs, and turf; a driveway through a park.

Parlance, pär'lans, *n*. [O.Fr., from *parlant*, ppr. of *parler*, to speak. PARLEY.] Conversation; talk.

Parlay, pär'lā, *v.t.* and *i*. In horse racing, to place a bet on one horse, the proceeds of which are to be applied as a wager on a second horse.

Parley, pär'li, *v.t.* [Fr. *parler*, to speak, O.Fr. *paroler*, from L.L. *paraboiare*, to speak, from L. *parabola*, a comparison, later, a word. PARABLE.] To confer or speak with a person on some point of mutual concern; especially to confer with an enemy, as on an exchange of prisoners, a cessation of arms, &c.—*n*. Mutual discourse or conversation; a conference with an enemy in war.

Parliament, pär'li-ment, *n*. [Fr. *parlement*—*parler*, to speak, and term. *-ment*, as in *complement*, &c. PARLEY.] A meeting or assembly of persons for conference or deliberation; a supreme national or general council; the legislature of the three estates of the United Kingdom of Great Britain, the lords spiritual, lords temporal, and the commons; the general council of Great Britain constituting the legislature, summoned by the sovereign's authority to consult on the affairs of the nation, and to enact and repeal laws.—*Act of parliament*, a statute or law made by the sovereign, with the advice and consent of the lords temporal and spiritual and the commons in parliament assembled.—**Parliamentarian**, pär'li-men-tā"ri-an, *n*. One of those who adhered to the parliament in the time of Charles I; one thoroughly acquainted with the rules of order for group meetings, as public assemblies, clubs, or conventions.—**Parliamentary**, pär-li-men'ta-ri, *a*. Pertaining to parliament; enacted or done by parliament; according to the rules and usages of parliament, or similar legislative bodies.—*Parliamentary government*, a government whose legislature has complete power to make laws and control the administration of their enforcement.—*Parliamentary procedure*, the generally accepted rules and practices followed in conducting the business of a deliberative body so as to maintain order, determine the will of the majority, and insure the rights of the minority.

Parlor, pär'lėr, *n*. [Fr. *parloir*, from *parler*, to speak. PARLEY.] A room for familiar intercourse; the room commonly used by a family; an ordinary sitting room; also applied to a certain type of business, trade or amusement place.—**Parlor car**, a chair-fitted railroad car on which travelers pay extra fare.

Parlous, pär'lus, *a*. [For *perilous*.] Dangerous; risky; extreme or shocking (*colloq*.).

Parmesan, pär-me-zan', *a*. Pertaining to *Parma*, in Italy; name of a delicate sort of cheese made there. Used also as *n*.

Parnassian, pär-nas'i-an, *a*. Pertaining to *Parnassus*, the celebrated mountain in Greece sacred to Apollo and the Muses.

Parnellism, pär'nel-izm, *n*. The name of the policy of Charles Stewart Parnell, the Irish leader in the Commons of the Parliamentary Party.

Parochial, pa-rō'ki-al, *a*. [L. *parochia*, corruption from *paroecia*, a parish. PARISH.] Belonging to a parish; restricted to a parish; hence, limited in range or scope; narrow.—*Parochial school*, an elementary school maintained by a parish, usually adding religious instruction to secular subjects.—**Parochialism**, pa-rō'ki-al-izm, *n*. The state of being parochial; narrowness or contractedness of mind resulting from confining one's attention or interest to the affairs of one's parish or neighborhood.—**Parochialize**, pa-rō'ki-al-iz, *v.t.*—*parochialized*, *parochializing*. To render parochial; to form into parishes.—**Parochially**, pa-rō'ki-al-li, *adv*. In a parochial manner; in a parish; by parishes.

Parody, par'o-di, *n*. [Fr. *parodie*, from Gr. *parōdia*—*para*, beside, and *ōdē*, an ode.] A literary composition in which the form and expression of serious writings are closely imitated but adapted to a ridiculous subject or a humorous method of treatment; a burlesque imitation of a serious poem.—*v.t.*—*parodied*, *parodying*. To turn into a parody; to write a parody upon. —**Parodic, Parodical**, pa-rod'ik, pa-rod'i-kal, *a*. Pertaining to parody; after the manner of parody.—**Parodist**, par'o-dist, *n*. One who writes a parody.

Parole, pa-rōl', *n*. [Fr. *parole*, from L.L. *parabola*, a word, a parable. PARABLE.] Word of promise; word of honor; a promise given by a prisoner of war that he will not try to escape if allowed to go about at liberty, or not to bear arms against his captors for a certain period, or the like; *milit*. a sort of countersign given out every day; *penology*, release of a convict under supervision before he has served his full sentence and on promise of good conduct; a state or condition of one on parole.—*v.t.* To free for a parole period.—*To break parole*, to conduct one's self contrary to conditions of the parole.—**Parolee**, pa-rōl'ē, *n*. A person released on parole.

Paronymous, pa-ron'i-mus, *a*. [Gr. *parōnymos*—*para*, beside, and *onoma*, a name, a word.] Having the same or a like sound, but differing in orthography and signification, as *all*, *awl*; *ball*, *bawl*; having the same derivation, as *wise*, *wisely*, *wisdom*.—**Paronym**, par'ō-nim, *n*. A paronymous word.—**Paronymy**, pa-ron'i-mi, *n*. The quality of being paronymous.

Paroquet, par'ō-ket, *n*. PARAKEET.

Parotid, pa-rot'id, *a*. [Gr. *parōtis*, *parōtidos*—*para*, beside, and *ous*, *ōtos*, the ear.] *Anat*. a salivary gland on either side of the face, in front of the ear, and communicating with the mouth by a duct.—**Parotitis**, par-ō-tī'tis, *n*. Inflammation of the parotid gland; mumps.

Paroxysm, par'ok-sizm, *n*. [Gr. *paroxysmos*—*para*, in excess, and *oxynō*, to sharpen, from *oxys*, sharp.] A fit or period of great intensity of a disease; a sudden and violent access of feeling (as of rage); convulsion;

fit; *geol.* any sudden and violent effect of natural agency.—**Paroxysmic**, par-ok-siz'mik, *a.* Characterized or accompanied by paroxysm; spasmodic.—**Paroxysmal**, par-ok-siz'mal, *a.* Pertaining to or marked by a paroxysm.—**Paroxysmally**, par-ok-siz'mal-li, *adv.* In a paroxysmal manner; by paroxysms.

Paroxytone, pa-rok'si-tōn, *a.* and *n.* [Gr.] *Gram.* said of a word having the acute accent on the penultimate syllable.

Parquet, pär-kā', *n.* [Fr. *parquet*, dim. of *parc*, a park.] First floor in a theater or music-hall, frequently known as orchestra section.—*Parquet circle*, mezzanine balcony seats at rear of orchestra section.—*v.t.*—*parqueted, parqueting.* To form or ornament with parquetry.—**Parquetry**, pär'-ket-ri, *n.* [Fr. *parqueterie.*] Inlaid woodwork in geometric or other patterns, and generally of different colors.

Parr, pär, *n.* A small fish now known to be a young salmon at a certain stage.

Parrakeet, par'a-kēt, *n.* PARAKEET.

Parrel, Parral, par'el, par'al, *n.* [Abbrev. from *apparel.*] *Naut.* a band of rope, or now, more generally, an iron collar which confines a yard to the mast at the center. —*v.t.* and *i.* To make fast with a parrel. —**Parrel truck,** *n.* A wooden ball with a hole through the center, several of which are then strung on a parrel.

Parricide, par'ri-sīd, *n.* [L. *parricida*, the criminal, *parricidium*, the crime, from *pater*, father, and *cædo*, to kill.] A person who murders his father or mother; the murder of a parent.—**Parricidal**, par-ri-sī'dal, *a.* Pertaining to parricide; committing parricide.

Parrot, par'ot, *n.* [From Fr. *Perrot*, or *Perrette*, personal names from *Pierre*, Peter (like Fr. *pierrot*, a sparrow, from *Pierre*); comp. Sp. *Perico*, a dim. for *Pedro*, Peter, also a small parrot, *periquito*, a small parrot. Comp. such names as *Magpie, Jackdaw, Robin-redbreast*, &c.] A name common to a family of scansorial or climbing birds, including the parrakeets, macaws, lories, cockatoos, &c., or restricted to certain members of the family, all of which have hooked and rounded bills and fleshy tongues, some of them having the faculty of imitating the human voice in a high degree.—*v.t.* To repeat as a parrot; to repeat by rote.—**Parrot-coal**, *n.* A name given in Scotland to cannel-coal.—**Parrot-fish**, *n.* A fish of the wrass family, remarkable for the beak-like plates into which the teeth of either jaw are united, and for brilliancy of colour.

Parry, par'i, *v.t.*—*parried, parrying.* [Fr. *parer*, It. *parare*, to ward off, from L. *parare*, to prepare, keep off. PARE.] To ward off (a blow, a thrust); to stop or to put or turn aside; to prevent taking effect. —*v.i.* To put aside thrusts or strokes; to fence.

Parse, pärs, *v.t.* [L. *pars*, a part, *pars orationis*, a part of a speech: to *parse* a word is to tell what *part* of speech it is. PART.] *Gram.* to analyse or describe grammatically; to show the several parts of speech composing (a sentence) and their relation to each other by government or agreement.

Parsee, pär-sē', *n.* [Per. and Hind. *pârsî*, a Persian, a fire-worshipper.] One of the adherents of the Zoroastrian or ancient Persian religion in India, originally from Persia.—**Parseeism**, pär-sē'izm, *n.* The religion and customs of the Parsees.

Parsimony, pär'si-mo-ni, *a.* [Fr. *parsimonie*, from L. *parsimonia, parcimonia*, from *parco, parsum*, to spare.] Closeness or sparingness in the use or expenditure of money; niggardliness; miserliness.—*Law of parsimony*, in *logic*, also called 'Occam's Razor', the principle laid down by the Nominalist leader, William of Ockham (1270-1347), the Invincible Doctor, that entities, or supposed existences, must not be multiplied in a theory beyond what is strictly necessary.—**Parsimonious**, pär-si-mō'ni-us, *a.* Exhibiting or characterized by parsimony; niggardly; close-fisted.—**Parsimoniously**, pär-si-mō'ni-us-li, *adv.* In a parsimonious manner.—**Parsimoniousness**, pär-si-mō'ni-us-nes, *n.*

Parsley, pärs'li, *n.* [O.E. *persely, persylle*, &c., Fr. *persil*, from L. *petroselinum*, Gr. *petroselinon*, rock-parsley—*petra*, a rock, and *selinon* (*i* long), parsley.] A well-known garden herb, the leaves of which are used as a garnish to flavor soups.

Parsnip, pärs'nip, *n* [Corrupted from Fr. *pastinaque*, L. *pastinaca*, a parsnip, from *pastinum*, a kind of two-pronged dibble, and *nip, nep*, L. *napus*, a turnip.] An umbelliferous plant much cultivated for its edible roots.

Parson, pär'sn, *n.* [O.Fr. *persone*, from L.L *persona ecclesiæ*, the person of the church, L. *persona*, a person.] The priest or incumbent of a parish; one who has the parochial charge or cure of souls; a clergyman; a man that is in orders or has been licensed to preach.—**Parsonage**, pär'sn-āj, *n.* The official dwelling-house of a parson.—**Parson-bird**. POE-BIRD.

Part, pärt, *n.* [L. *pars, partis*, a part (whence also *particle, parcel, partial, party, partner, participate, apart*, &c.); same root as *parare*, to prepare, *portio*, a portion. PARE.] Any portion of a thing less than the whole; a piece or fragment separated from a whole thing; a portion or quantity not separated in fact, but considered as by itself; one of a number of equal portions or quantities that make up a whole; a constituent portion of a whole; a member of a whole; that which falls to each in division; share, portion, lot; concern or interest; side or party (to take one's *part*); allotted duty; particular office or business (to perform one's *part*); character assigned to an actor in a play or other like performance; *mus.* one of the different melodies of a concerted composition, which, heard in union, compose its harmony (the treble, tenor, or bass *part*); *pl.* qualities; powers; faculties; often excellent or superior endowments (a man of *parts*); *pl.* regions; districts; locality (well-known in these *parts*).—*For my* (*his, her*, &c.) *part*, so far as concerns me (him, her).—*For the most part*, commonly; oftener than otherwise. —*In part*, in some degree or extent; partly. —*In good part*, favourably; acceptably; in a friendly manner; not in displeasure.—*In ill part*, unfavourably; with displeasure. —*Part and parcel*, an essential portion; a part.—*Part of speech, gram.* a sort or class of words of a particular character as regards their meaning or relations to other words in a sentence.—*v.t.* [Fr. *partir*, to part, separate.] To divide; to separate or break into two or more pieces; to distribute; to share; to cause to sunder or go apart; to intervene betwixt; to interpose between; to separate, as combatants; *naut.* to break; to suffer the breaking of (the ship *parted* her cables).—*v.i.* To become separate or detached; to divide; to move apart; to go away from another or others; to quit each other; to take leave (to *part with* or *from* a person); to have a share; to share (O.T.); to break; to be torn asunder (the rope *parted*).—*To part with* a thing, to let it leave us; to resign it.—*adv.* Partly; in some measure.—**Partible, Partable**, pär'ti-bl, pär'ta-bl, *a.* Capable of being parted; divisible.—**Partibility, Partability**, pär-ti-bil'i-ti, pär-ta-bil'i-ti, *n.* The quality of being partible.—**Parter**, pär'tėr, *n.* One that parts.—**Parted**, pär'ted, *p.* and *a.* Divided; separated; *bot.* cleft into divisions.—**Parting**, pär'ting, *p.* and *a.* Serving to part; dividing; separating; given at separation (a *parting* kiss).—*n.* The act of dividing or separating; a division; a separation; leave-taking; *geol.* a fissure in strata.—**Partly**, pärt'li, *adv.* In part; in some measure or degree; not wholly: used in stating particulars that make up a whole. —**Part-song**, *n.* A song adapted to be sung in two or more distinct vocal parts; a harmonized or concerted song.

Partake, pär-tāk', *v.i.*—*partook* (pret.), *partaken* (pp.), *partaking* (ppr.). [*Part* and *take.*] To take a part, portion, or share in common with others; to have a share or part; to participate (to *partake* of a repast, *in* festivities); to have something of the character or nature of; to have features in common with: followed by *of*.—*v.t.* To have a part in; to share.—**Partaker**, pär-tā'kėr, *n.* One who partakes; a sharer, a participator: usually followed by *of* or *in*.

Parterre, pär-tār, *n.* [Fr., from *par*, on, by, and *terre*, earth, ground.] *Hort.* a system of flower beds, connected together with intervening spaces of gravel or turf for walking on; the pit of a French theatre.

Parthenogenesis, pär'the-nō-jen"e-sis, *n.* [Gr. *parthenos*, a virgin, and *genesis*, production.] *Zool.* the production of new individuals from imperfect females without the intervention of a male; the propagation by a plant or animal by any other method than impregnation.—**Parthenogenetic**, pär'the-nō-je-net"ik, *a.* Pertaining to, characterized by, or of the nature of parthenogenesis; born of a virgin.

Parthian, pär'thi-an, *a.* Pertaining to *Parthia* or its inhabitants.—*Parthian arrow*, a shaft aimed at an adversary while flying from or avoiding him; a parting shot; from the habit of the ancient Parthians in war.

Partial, pär'shal, *a.* [Fr. *partial*, from L. *pars, partis*, a part. PART.] Affecting a part only; not general or universal; not total; inclined to favour one party in a cause, or one side of a question more than the other; not indifferent; inclined to favour without principle or reason (a fond and *partial* parent); having a predilection; inclined or favourable: with *to*; *bot.* being one of several subordinates (a *partial* umbel, a *partial* peduncle).—**Partialism**, pär'shal-izm, *n.* The doctrine of the partialists.—**Partialist**, pär'shal-ist, *n.* One who is partial; *theol.* one who holds that the atonement was made only for a part of mankind, that is, for the elect.—**Partiality**, pär-shal'i-ti, *n.* The state or quality of being partial; unfair or undue bias; undue favour shown; a special liking or fondness.—**Partially**, pär'shal-li, *adv.* In a partial manner; with undue bias; in part; not totally; to some extent.

Partible. Under PART.

Participate, pär-tis'i-pāt, *v.i.*—*participated, participating.* [L. *participo, participatum*—*pars, partis*, a part, and *capio*, to take. PART, CAPABLE.] To partake; to take a part; to have a share in common with others: generally followed by *of* or *in*. —*v.t.* To partake, share, receive a part of.—**Participation**, pär-tis'i-pā"shon, *n.* The state of participating or sharing in common with others.—**Participative**, pär-tis'i-pā-tiv, *a.* Capable of participating.—**Participator**, pär-tis'i-pā-tėr, *n.* One who participates.—**Participable**, pär-tis'i-pa-bl, *a.* Capable of being participated or shared. —**Participant**, pär-tis'i-pant, *a.* Sharing; having a share or part.—*n.* One participating; a partaker.

Participle, pär'ti-si-pl, *n.* [L. *participium*, from *particeps*, partaking—*pars, partis*, a part, and *capio*, to take; comp. *principle*, from L. *principium*. PARTICIPATE.] *Gram.* a part of speech, so called because it partakes of the character both of a verb and an adjective, though it differs from the adjective chiefly in that it implies time, and therefore applies to a specific act, while the adjective designates a habitual quality or characteristic, without regard to time.—**Participial**, pär-ti-sip'i-al, *a.* Having the nature and use of a participle; formed from a participle (a *participial* noun).—*n.* A word formed from a verb, and having the nature of a participle.—**Participially**, pär-ti-sip'i-al-li, *adv.* In the sense or manner of a participle.

Particle, pär'ti-kl, *n.* [Fr. *particule*, L. *particula*, dim. of *pars, partis*, part. PART.] A minute part or portion of matter, the aggregation of which parts constitutes a whole mass; any very small portion or part; an atom; a jot; *gram.* a word that is not varied or inflected, as the preposition, conjunction, &c.; *physics*, a mass of matter conceived as a point, but yet possessing inertia and other properties of matter.

Parti-colored, pär'ti-kul-ėrd, *a.* Colored differently in different parts; of many colors.

Particular, pär-tik'ū-lėr, *a.* [Fr. *particulier*, L.L. *particularis*, from L. *particula*. PARTICLE.] Pertaining to one and not to more; special; not general; individual; considered separately; peculiar; personal; private (our own *particular* wrongs); not ordinary; notable (of no *particular* importance); minute; circumstantial (a full and *particular* account); singularly nice in taste; precise; fastidious.—*n.* A single instance; a single point; a distinct, separate, or minute part; a detail.—*In particular*, specially; particularly; to particularize.—**Particularity**, pär-tik'ū-lar"i-ti, *n.* The state or quality of being particular; that which is particular.—**Particularization**, pär-tik'ū-lėr-i-zā"shon, *n.* The act of particularizing.—**Particularize**, pär-tik'ū-lėr-īz, *v.t.*—*particularized*, *particularizing*. To specify or mention distinctly; to give the particulars of; to enumerate or specify in detail.—*v.i.* To mention or be attentive to single things or to small matters; to give full details.—**Particularly**, pär-tik'ū-lėr-li, *adv.* In a particular or especial manner; especially; chiefly.

Partisan, pär'ti-zan, *n.* [Fr., from *parti*, a party, from L. *pars*, *partis*, a part.] An adherent of a party or faction; one who is violently and passionately devoted to a party or interest.—*a.* Pertaining to a party or faction; biassed in favour of a party or interest.—**Partisanship**, pär'ti-zan-ship, *n.* The state or condition of being a partisan.

Partisan, pär'ti-zan, *n.* [Fr. *pertuisane*, Sp. *partesana*, It. *partigiana*; origin doubtful.] A kind of halbert or pike formerly in use; a baton; a truncheon; a quarter-staff.

Partite, pär'tīt, *a.* [L. *partitus*, pp. of *partio*, to divide. PART.] *Bot.* divided to the base (as a leaf).—**Partition**, pär-tish'-on, *n.* [L. *partitio*.] The act of parting, dividing, or separating into portions and distributing; division; separation; that by which different parts are separated; a wall separating apartments in a building; a division between the chambers or cells of a thing; *music*, SCORE.—*v.t.* To divide by walls or partitions; to divide into shares.—**Partitive**, pär'ti-tiv, *a.* *Gram.* denoting a part; expressing the relation of a part to a whole (a *partitive* genitive, 'the mountain's brow').—*n.* *Gram.* a word expressing partition.—**Partitively**, pär'ti-tiv-li, *adv.* In a partitive manner.

Partlet, part'let, *n.* [Fr. *Pertelote*, female proper name.] A hen.

Partly. Under PART.

Partner, pärt'nėr, *n.* [In part directly from *part*, partly from old *parcener*, O.Fr. *parçoner*, from L. *partitio*, a sharing. PARTITION.] One who partakes or shares with another; a partaker; an associate; one who has a share with another or others in some commercial, manufacturing, or other undertaking; a member of a partnership; one who dances with another, either male or female; a husband or wife.—**Partnership**, pärt'nėr-ship, *n.* The state or condition of being a partner; the association of two or more persons for the purpose of undertaking and prosecuting conjointly any business, occupation, or calling.

Partridge, pär'trij, *n.* [O.E. *partryke*, *partriche*, from O.Fr. *pertrix*, Fr. *perdrix*, from L. and Gr. *perdix*, a partridge.] Any of a number of rasorial birds similar to the grouse, especially game birds; in America, has particular reference to the ruffed grouse and the quail.

Part-song. Under PART.

Parturient, pär-tū'ri-ent, *a.* [L. *parturiens*, *parturientis*, ppr. of *parturio*, from *partus*, birth, from *pario*, to bear. PARENT.] Bringing forth or about to bring forth young.—**Parturition**, pär-tū-rish'on, *n.* [L. *parturitio*.] The act of bringing forth or being delivered of young.—**Parturitive**, pär-tū'ri-tiv, *a.* Pertaining or relating to parturition; obstetric.

Party, pär'ti, *n.* [Fr. *partie*, a party, side, faction, a suitor or litigant, &c., from Fr. *partir*, L. *partio*, to divide, from *pars*, *partis*, a part. PART.] A number of persons united in opinion or design, in opposition to others in the community; persons in a state united by certain political views; a faction; persons collected for a particular purpose, often an armed force; a detached portion of a larger body or company; a detachment; a select company invited to an entertainment (a tea *party*, an evening *party*); one of two litigants; one concerned or interested in an affair (a *party* to a scheme or plot); a single person distinct from or opposed to another; a person under special consideration; hence, a person in general; an individual (in this sense vulgar).—**Party-colored**, PARTI-COLORED. *a.* **Partyism**, pär'ti-izm, *n.* Devotion to party.—**Party line**, *n.* A single telephone circuit connecting several subscribers with the exchange; a boundary line.—**Partyman**, *n.* One of a party; a man of violent party principles; an abettor of a party.—**Party-spirit**, *n.* The spirit that supports a party.—**Party-spirited**, *a.* Having the spirit of party or of partisans.—**Party-wall**, *n.* A wall between buildings to separate them from each other; a wall separating adjoining tenements.

Parvanimity,† pär-va-nim'i-ti, *n.* [L. *parvus*, small, *animus*, mind; formed on type of *magnanimity*.] Littleness of mind; meanness.

Parvenu, pär've-nū, *n.* [Fr. *parvenu*, lit. one who has arrived, from *parvenir*, L. *pervenire*, to arrive.] An upstart, or one newly risen into notice.

Parvis, Parvise, pär'vis, *n.* [Fr. *parvis*, from L.L. *parvisius*, *paravisus*, from L. *paradisus*, paradise.] A name formerly given to the porch of a church, now applied to the area round a church.

Pas, pä, *n.* [Fr., from L. *passus*, a step, a pace. PACE.] A step; right of going foremost; precedence.

Pasch, pask, *n.* [L. and Gr. *pascha*, from Heb. *pascha*, passage, from *pâsach*, to pass over.] The passover; the feast of Easter.—**Paschal**, pas'kal, *a.* Pertaining to the passover or to Easter.

Pash,† pash, *v.t.* [Same as Sw. *paska*, Prov. G. *paschen*, to strike.] To strike violently; to dash or smash. (*Shak.*)

Pasha, pa-shä' or pash'ä, *n.* [Per. *pâshâh*, contr. from *pâdishâh*, protector or great king. PADISHAH.] In Turkey, a title formerly conferred upon military commanders and governors of provinces.—**Pashalic, Pachalic**, pa-shä'lik, pash'ä-lik, *n.* The jurisdiction of a pasha.

Pasigraphy, pa-sig'ra-fi, *n.* [Gr. *pas*, all, and *graphē*, writing.] A system of universal writing; a universal language. —**Pasigraphic, Pasigraphical**, pas-i-graf'ik, pas-i-graf'i-kal, *a.* Relating to pasigraphy.

Pasque-flower, pask, *n.* [O.Fr. *pasque*, Easter. PASCH.] A species of anemone with large handsome purple flowers, so named in consequence of its flowering about Easter.

Pasquil, Pasquinade, pas'kwil, pas'-kwi-nād, *n.* [From *Pasquino*, a witty and satirical tailor (or barber) of Rome, whose name after his death was bestowed upon a statue that had been dug up near his shop, and to which satirical placards were affixed at night.] A lampoon or short satirical publication.—*v.t.* and *i.*—*pasquilled*, *pasquilling*; *pasquinaded*, *pasquinading*. To lampoon; to satirize in writing.

Pass, pas, *v.i.* pret. & pp. *passed* or sometimes *past*. [Fr. *passer*, It. *passare*, from L. *passus*, a step, a pace. PACE.] To go; to proceed (to *pass* away, from, into, over, under, &c.); to go past a certain person or place (we saw him *pass*); to alter or change condition or circumstances; to undergo transition; to vanish, disappear, be lost; hence, to depart from life; to die; to elapse; to be spent; to receive the sanction of a legislative house or body by a majority of votes (the bill has *passed*); to be current; to gain reception or be generally received (bank-notes *pass* as a substitute for coin); to be regarded, held, or considered; to occur; to take place (what *passes* within one's own mind); to thrust; to make a push in fencing or fighting; to throw a ball, as a football or basketball; *Cards*, to decline a privilege, as of making a bid; to go unheeded or neglected; to be transferred from an owner; to go successfully through an inspection or examination.—*To come to pass*, to happen; to occur.—*To pass away*, to move from sight; to vanish; hence, to die; to be spent (as time, life).—*To pass by*, to move near and beyond a certain person or place.—*To pass into*, to unite and blend gradually.—*To pass on*, to continue to go forward; to proceed.—*To pass over*, to go or move to another side; to cross.—*To pass through*, to undergo; to experience.—*v.t.* To move near and go beyond; to move from side to side of; to live through; to spend (to *pass* the summer); to let go by without care or notice; to take no notice of; to transcend, exceed, excel, surpass; to transfer; to make to change hands; to hand over; to send; to circulate; to undergo successfully, as an examination, ordeal, or the like; to obtain the legislative or official sanction of; to be enacted by (the bill has *passed* the house); to give legal or official sanction to; to enact or ratify; to allow as valid or just; to give forth officially; to pronounce (to *pass* a sentence of death); to void, as faeces or other matter.—*To pass by*, to take no notice of; to overlook; to forgive; to neglect; to disregard.—*To pass the eyes over*, to glance over rapidly.—*To pass off*, to impose by fraud; to palm off.—*To pass over*, to let go by unnoticed; to disregard.—*n.* A passage; a way; a difficult or narrow way; a narrow road or defile between two mountains; permission to pass, or to go or come; a ticket of free transit or admission; a thrust or push in fencing;—*Baseball*, four balls pitched wide of the plate entitling the batter to proceed to first base; a movement of the hand over or along anything; a manipulation of a mesmerist; state or condition of things; an embarrassing situation; the successful or satisfactory standing or going through an examination.—**Passable**, pas'a-bl, *a.* Capable of being passed, traveled, traversed, penetrated, &c.; capable of being passed from person to person; current; receivable; tolerable; allowable; admissible; mediocre.—**Passably**, pas'a-bli, *adv.* Tolerably; moderately.—**Pass-book**, *n.* A book in which a shopkeeper makes an entry of goods sold on credit to a customer, for the information of the customer; also, a bank-book.—**Passer**, pas'ėr, *n.* One who passes; a passenger.—**Passer-by**, *n.* One who goes by or near.—**Passing**, pas'ing, *adv.* Surpassingly; wonderfully; exceedingly (*passing* fair, *passing* strange).—*prep.* Exceeding; beyond; over.—**Passing-bell**, *n.* The bell rung in former times at the time of a person's death, to admonish the living and call for their prayers for the dying.—**Passing-note**, *n.* *Music*, a note introduced between two others to form a transition, but not constituting an essential part of the harmony.—**Pass-key**, *n.* A key for opening several locks; a latch key.—**Pass-word**, *n.* A secret parole or countersign by which a friend may be distinguished from a stranger, and allowed to pass.

Passage, pas'āj, *n.* [Fr. *passage*, from *passer*, to pass. PASS.] The act of passing; transit from one place to another; a going by, through, over, or the like; transit by means of a conveyance; a journey by a conveyance, especially a ship; liberty of passing; access; entry or exit; way by which a person or thing may pass; avenue; way of entrance or exit; a gallery or corridor leading to the various divisions of a building; a part or portion quoted or referred to in a book, poem, &c.; the act of carrying through all the steps necessary to render valid (the *passage* of a bill or of a law); an encounter (a *passage* at arms, a *passage* of love).—*Birds of passage*, birds which migrate with the season from a colder to a warmer or from a warmer to a colder climate.

Passant, pas'ant, *a.* [Fr. *passant*, ppr. of *passer*, to pass. PASS.] *Her.* a term applied to an animal which appears to walk.

Passé, Passée, pas-ā, *a.* [Fr.] Past; faded; as applied to persons, past the heyday of life.

Passenger, pas'en-jėr, *n.* [O.E. *passager*, one who makes a passage; the *n* being an intrusive element, as in *messenger*.] One who passes or is on his way; a wayfarer; a travelet, one who travels, for payment, on a railway, steamboat, coach, or other conveyance.—**Passenger-pigeon**, *n.* A North American wild pigeon, great flocks of which once abounded, especially in the Mississippi valley. It was widely hunted, and is now extinct.—**Passenger-ship**, *n.* A ship having accommodation for passengers by sea.—**Passenger-train**, *n.* A railway train for the conveyance of passengers.

Passeres, pas'ėr-ēz, *n.pl.* [L., sparrows, so called because the bulk of them are small birds.] A name given to the extensive order of birds also called insessores or perchers.—**Passerine**, pas'ėr-īn, *a.* Pertaining to the order passeres.—*n.* A passerine bird.

Passible, pas'i-bl, *a.* [L. *passibilis*, from *patior*, *passus*, to suffer. PASSION.] Capable of feeling or suffering; susceptible of impressions from external agents.—**Passibility, Passibleness**, pas-i-bil'i-ti, pas'i-bl-nes, *n.* The quality of being passible.

Passim, pas'im, *adv.* [L.] Here and there in some book; in many different places or passages.

Passion, pash'on, *n.* [L. *passio*, *passionis*, from *patior*, *passus*, to bear, to suffer; allied to Gr. *pathos*, suffering; akin *patient*, *passive*, *compatible*, &c.] The suffering of bodily pangs; specifically, the last suffering of the Saviour; a strong feeling or emotion by which the mind is swayed, as ambition, avarice, revenge, fear, hope, joy, grief, love, hatred, &c.; a strong deep feeling; violent agitation or excitement of mind; violent anger; zeal, ardour, vehement desire (a *passion* for fame); love; ardent affection; amorous desire; a passionate display; an exhibition of deep feeling (a *passion* of tears); a pursuit to which one is devoted.—*v.i.* To bewail; to cry out in a passionate way or lament. (*Shak.*)—**Passional, Passionary**, pash'on-al, pash'on-a-ri, *n.* A book in which are described the sufferings of saints and martyrs.—**Passionate**, pash'on-āt, *a.* Characterized by passion; exhibiting or expressing passion; readily moved to anger; fiery; showing strong emotion; vehement; warm (*passionate* affection).—**Passionately**, pash'on-āt-li, *adv.* In a passionate manner; ardently; vehemently; angrily.—**Passionateness**, pash'on-āt-nes, *n.* State of being passionate.—**Passioned**, pash'ond, *p.* and *a.* Having passions; expressing passion.—**Passion-flower**, *n.* A genus of plants with showy flowers, chiefly natives of tropical South America, so called because in the anthers, styles, &c., was seen a resemblance to the symbols of our Lord's passion.—**Passionist**, pash'on-ist, *n.* The order of priests established by Paul Francis, 1694-1775, pledged to keep alive the memory of Christ's Passion, by preaching only Him and Him crucified.—**Passionless**, pash'on-les, *a.* Void of passion.—**Passion-play**, *n.* A mystery or miracle-play representing the different scenes in the passion of Christ.—**Passion-Sunday**, the fifth Sunday in Lent.—**Passion-Week**, the week before Holy Week, beginning with Passion-Sunday.

Passive, pas'iv, *a.* [L. *passivus*, from *patior*, *passus*, to suffer. PASSION.] Not active; inert; not acting, receiving, or capable of receiving impressions from external objects; unresisting; not opposing; receiving or suffering without resistance; *gram.* expressive of suffering or being affected by some action; expressing that the nominative is the object of some action or feeling (the *passive* voice, a *passive* verb or inflection).—**Passively**, pas'iv-li, *adv.* In a passive manner; without action; unresistingly; as a passive verb; in the passive voice.—**Passiveness**, pas'iv-nes, *n.* Quality of being passive.—**Passivity**, pas-iv'i-ti, *n.* Passiveness; the tendency of a body to continue in a given state till disturbed by another body; *chem.* the condition of a substance in which it has no disposition to enter into chemical combinations.

Passover, pas'ō-vėr, *n.* A feast of the Jews, instituted to commemorate the providential escape of the Hebrews in Egypt, when God, smiting the first-born of the Egyptians, *passed over* the houses of the Israelites, which were marked with the blood of the paschal lamb; the sacrifice offered at the feast of the passover; the paschal lamb.

Passport, pas'pōrt, *n.* [Fr. *passeport*, a safe-conduct, originally a permission to enter or leave a port. PASS, PORT.] A warrant of protection and authority to travel, granted to persons moving from place to place, by a competent authority; especially granted to persons travelling in a foreign country; something that enables one to pass with safety or certainty, or to attain any object or reach any end (the favour of the great was his *passport*); in *diplomacy, to demand a passport* is the request by an ambassador to leave a foreign country as a preliminary to war.—*To receive his passports*, is to be dismissed from an enemy country at the commencement of hostilities.

Past, past, *p.* and *a.* [A form of *passed*.] Gone by; belonging to a time previous to this; not present nor future; spent; ended; over; existing no more.—*n.* A past or former time or state; a bygone time; a state of matters no longer present.—*prep.* Beyond in time; after; having lost; no longer possessing (*past* sense of feeling); beyond; out of reach of; out of the scope or influence of (*past* help); beyond in position; further than.—*adv.* By.—**Past-master**, *n.* One who has occupied the office or dignity of master, especially in such bodies as Freemasons, &c.; *fig.* one who has experience in his particular craft or business.

Paste, pāst, *n.* [O.Fr. *paste*, Fr. *pâte*; from L. *pasta*, paste, from Gr. *pastē*, a mess of barley-porridge, from *passō*, to sprinkle.] A composition in which there is just sufficient moisture to soften without liquefying the mass; a mixture of flour with milk, water, &c., used in cookery, as for pies, pastry, &c.; a kind of cement variously compounded; a composition of pounded rock-crystal melted with alkaline salts, and coloured with metallic oxides, used for making imitation gems; *mineral.* the mineral substance in which other minerals are embedded.—*v.t.*—*pasted, pasting.* To unite or cement with paste; to fasten with paste.—**Pasteboard**, pāst'bōrd, *n.* A species of thick paper formed of several single sheets pasted one upon another, or by macerating paper and casting it in moulds, &c.; cardboard.—*a.* Made of pasteboard.—**Pastry**, pās'tri, *n.* Viands made of paste, or of which paste constitutes the principal ingredient; the crust or cover of a pie, tart, or the like.—**Pastry-cook**, *n.* One whose occupation is to make and sell pastry.—**Pasty**, pās'ti, *a.* Like paste; of the consistence of paste.—*n.* A meat-pie covered with a paste.

Pastel, pas'tel, *n.* [Fr. *pastel*, a pastel, woad, from L. *pastillus*, a little roll. PASTIL.] A colored crayon; also, any of a number of pale or faint colors.

Pastern, pas'tėrn, *n.* [O.Fr. *pasturon*, from *pasture*, a shackle for cattle at pasture, from L. *pasco*, *pastum*, to feed. PASTURE.] The part of a horse's leg between the joint next the foot and the coronet of the hoof; a shackle for horses while pasturing.—**Pastern-joint**, *n.* The joint in a horse's leg next the foot.

Pasteurism, past'ūr-izm, *n.* [Fr. *Pasteur*, scientist.] The theory of diseases aiming at their suppression by means of inoculations.—**Pasteurization**, past'ūr-i-zā"-shun. [After *Pasteur*.] Checking the activity of bacteria in milk, &c., by heating to 131°—158° F.—**Pasteurize**, pas'tūr-iz, *v.t.* To sterilize by Pasteur's method, by heating (milk).

Pasticcio, pas-tich'i-ō, *n.* [It.] A medley; an olio; a picture painted so as to show more than one painter's style and manner.

Pastil, Pastille, pas'til, pas'tēl, *n.* [Fr. *pastille*, L. *pastillus*, a little roll, from *pastus*, food, *pasco*, *pastum*, to feed. PASTOR.] A small roll of aromatic paste, composed of gum-benzoin, sandal-wood, spices, &c., for burning as a fumigator or disinfectant.—*v.t.*—*pastilled, pastilling.* To administer or fumigate with pastils.

Pastime, pas'tīm, *n.* [*Pass* and *time*.] That which amuses and serves to make time pass agreeably; sport; amusement.

Pastor, pas'tor, *n.* [L. *pastor*, a shepherd, from *pasco*, *pastum*, to feed; same root as W. *pasg*, a feeding, Armor. *paska*, to feed, Skr. *pâ*, to guard.] A shepherd‡; a minister of the gospel having the charge of a church and congregation.—**Pastoral**, pas'tor-al, *a.* [L. *pastoralis*.] Pertaining to shepherds; rustic; rural; descriptive of the life of shepherds or of a country life (a *pastoral* poem); relating to the cure of souls, or to the pastor of a church.—*Pastoral epistles*, epistles of St. Paul to Titus and Timothy dealing with the pastoral organization of their various spheres.—*Pastoral letter*, a letter or circular addressed by a bishop to the clergy and people of his diocese.—*Pastoral theology*, that part of theology which treats of the obligations of pastors and their relations towards their flocks.—*n.* A poem describing the life and manners of shepherds; a bucolic poem; a pastoral letter or address; *mus.* a simple melody in six-eight time in a rustic style; a symphony whose simple movements are designed to suggest pastoral scenes.—**Pastorale**, pas-tō-rä'le, *n.* [It.] *Mus.* a pastoral.—**Pastoralism**, pas'tor-al-izm, *n.* Pastoral character.—**Pastorally**, pas'tor-al-li, *adv.* In a pastoral or rural manner; in the manner of a pastor.—**Pastoral-staff**, *n.* The official staff of a bishop or abbot with a curved head. CROZIER.—**Pastorate**, pas'tor-āt, *n.* The office or jurisdiction of a pastor; a body of pastors—**Pastorless**, pas'tor-les, *a.* Having no pastor.—**Pastorly**, pas'tor-li, *a.* Becoming or suitable to a pastor.—**Pastorship**, pas'tor-ship, *n.* The office of a pastor.

Pastry. Under PASTE.

Pasture, pas'tūr, *n.* [O.Fr. *pasture* (Fr. *pâture*), from L. *pastura*, from *pasco*, to feed. PASTOR.] Grass for the food of cattle or other animals; ground covered with grass for the food of animals; a grazing ground.—*v.t.*—*pastured, pasturing.* To feed on growing grass, or to supply pasture for.—*v.i.* To graze.—**Pasturable**, pas'tūr-a-bl, *a.* Fit for pasture.—**Pasturage**, pas'tūr-āj, *n.* [O.Fr. *pasturage*.] The business of feeding or grazing cattle; grazing ground; growing grass on which cattle feed.—**Pasture-land**, *n.* Land appropriated to pasture.—**Pastureless**, pas'tūr-les, *a.* Destitute of pasture.

Pasty. Under PASTE.

Pat, pat, *v.t.*—*patted, patting.* [Imitative of the sound of a slight sharp blow; comp. W. *ffat*, a blow, and E. *tap*. *Patter* is a frequentative from this.] To strike gently with the fingers or hand; to tap.—*n.* A light quick blow with the fingers or hand; a small lump of butter molded or cut into shape.—*a.* Hitting the mark; apt; fit; convenient.—**Pat, Patly**, pat'li, *adv.* Fitly; conveniently; just in the nick; also unmoved, as to stand *pat*.

Patagium, pa-tā'ji-um, *n.* [L., the border of a dress.] The flying appendage or expansion of bats, flying-squirrels, &c.

Patamar, pat'a-mär, *n.* A kind of native vessel employed in the coasting trade of Bombay and Ceylon.

Patavinity, pat'a-vin"i-ti, *a.* [L. *Pata-*

vinitas.] Provincial characteristics of writing, like those professed to be found by Asinius Pollio in the work of the historian Livy, of *Patavium* or Padua.

Patch, pach, *n.* [Connected with Swiss *patschen*, to patch, to clap on a piece, *batsch*, a patch; also It. *pezza*, a patch, a piece.] A piece of cloth sewed on a garment to repair it; any similar piece; a small piece of silk formerly stuck on the face by way of adornment; a small piece of ground; a plot; the name of the clown in patchwork or motley; the mediæval fool; any sorry or poor creature.—*v.t.* To mend with patches or pieces; to repair clumsily; to adorn (the face) with a patch or with patches; to make up of pieces and shreds; *fig.* to make hastily or without regard to forms: usually with *up* (to *patch up* a quarrel). — **Patcher**, pach'ėr, *n.* One that patches.—**Patchery**, pach'ėr-i, *n.* Bungling work. — **Patchwork**, pach'wėrk, *n.* Work composed of various figures or colours sewed together; anything formed of ill-assorted parts.—**Patchy**, pach'i, *a.* Full of patches.

Patchouli, Patchouly, pa-chö'li, *n.* [An Indian name.] A plant of India and China, the leaves of which furnish an odorous oil; the perfume itself.

Pate, pāt, *n.* [Perhaps from Ir. *pata, pota*, Sc. *pat*, a pot, the radical meaning being the brain-pan or skull.] The head of a person; the top of the head.—**Pated**, pā'-ted, *a.* Having a pate: in composition (shallow-*pated*).

Patella, pa-tel'la, *n.* [L. dim. of *patera*, a cup, from *pateo*, to lie open. PATENT.] A small pan, vase, or dish; *anat.* the knee-pan. —**Patelliform**, pa-tel'li-form, *a.* Like the patella; of the form of a saucer.

Paten, pat'en, *n.* [L. *patina*, a pan, from *pateo*, to lie open. PATENT.] A metallic plate or flat dish; the round metallic plate on which the bread is placed in the sacrifice of the Lord's supper.

Patent, pat'ent, *a.* [From L. *patens, patentis*, ppr. of *pateo*, to lie open; same root as Gr. *petannymi*, to spread; *petalon*, a leaf; akin *pan, paten, patella*.] Open; spreading; expanded; open to the perusal of all (letters *patent*); secured by law as an exclusive privilege; patented (*patent* medicines); manifest to all; evident.—*n.* A document conferring a right; a privilege or license; a writing conveying to the individual or individuals specified therein the sole right to make, use, or dispose of some new invention or discovery for a certain limited period.—*v.t.* To make the subject of a patent; to secure by patent-right.—**Patentable**, pat'ent-ä-bl, *a.* Capable of being patented. — **Patentee**, pat'en-tē", *n.* One who holds a patent; one by whom a patent is secured.—**Patent leather**, *n.* A kind of leather to which a permanent polish is given by a process of japanning. —**Patent right**, *n.* An exclusive privilege in an invention, &c., granted by patent.—**Patent rolls**, *n.pl.* The records or registers of patents.

Patera, pat'e-ra, *n.* [L., from *pateo*, to be open. PATENT.] A shallow, circular saucer-like vessel used by the Greeks and Romans in their sacrifices, &c.; an architectural ornament of similar appearance.

Paterfamilias, pā'tėr-fa-mil"i-as, *n.* [L., from *pater*, father, and *familia*, a family.] The father or head of a family.

Paternal, pa-tėr'nal, *a.* [Fr. *paternel*, from L. *paternus*, from *pater*, father (FATHER); akin *parricide, patriarch, patrimony, patriot, patron, pattern*.] Pertaining to a father; fatherly; derived from the father; hereditary. — **Paternally**, pa-tėr'nal-li, *adv.* In a paternal manner.—**Paternity**, pa-tėr'ni-ti, *n.* [Fr. *paternité*.] Fatherhood; the relation of a father to his offspring; derivation from a father (the child's *paternity*); hence, origin; authorship.

Paternoster, pā'tėr-nos-tėr, *n.* [L., our Father, the two first words of the Lord's prayer in Latin.] The Lord's prayer; every tenth large bead in the rosary; the rosary itself.

Path, päth, *n.* pl. **Paths**, päTHz. [A.Sax. *pæth* = D. and L.G. *pad*, G. *pfad*, a path; perhaps from Gr. *patos*, a trodden way, *patein*, to walk.] A way beaten or trodden by the feet of man or beast, or made hard by wheels; a narrow or unimportant road; a footway; a way or route in general; the way or course which an animal or any object follows in the air, in water, or in space; *fig.* course of life; course of conduct or procedure. — **Pathless**, päth'les, *a.* Having no beaten way; untrodden.—**Pathway**, päth'wā, *n.* A path; a narrow way to be passed on foot; a way; a course of life.

Pathan, pat'han, *n.* A person of Afghan race settled in Hindustan; an Afghan.

Pathetic. Under PATHOS.

Pathogeny, pa-thoj'e-ni, *n.* [Gr. *pathos*, suffering, and root *gen*, to produce.] The doctrine or science of the generation and development of disease.—**Pathogenetic, Pathogenic**, path'ō-je-net"ik, path-ō-jen'ik, *a.* Relating to pathogeny; generating disease.—**Pathognomonic**, pa-thog'-nō-mon"ik, *a.* [Gr. *pathos*, suffering, and *gnōmōn*, one who knows, from *ginōskō*, to know.] *Med.* distinctive or characteristic of a disease; indicating a particular disease. —**Pathognomic**, path-og-nom'ik, *a.* Pertaining to pathognomy.—**Pathognomy**, pa-thog'no-mi, *n.* [Gr. *pathos*, passion, and *gnōmē*, signification.] Expression of the passions; the science of the signs by which human passions are indicated.

Pathology, pa-thol'o-ji, *n.* [Gr. *pathos*, suffering, and *logos*, discourse.] That part of medicine which explains the nature of diseases, their causes, and symptoms.—**Pathologic, Pathological**, path-ō-loj'ik, path-ō-loj'i-kal, *a.* Pertaining to pathology.—**Pathologically**, path-ō-loj'-i-kal-li, *adv.* In a pathologic manner.—**Pathologist**, pa-thol'o-jist, *n.* One versed in the nature of diseases.

Pathos, pā'thos, *n.* [Gr. *pathos*, passion, suffering, from stem of *pathein*, to suffer; same root as in *patient, passion*.] That quality, attribute, or element which awakens such tender emotions as pity, compassion, or sympathy; the quality that touches the heart; expression of strong or deep feeling; touching or affecting influence.—**Pathetic**, pa-thet'ik, *a.* [L. *patheticus*, Gr. *pathētikos*.] Full of pathos; moving the feelings; exciting pity, sorrow, or other tender emotion; affecting.—**Pathetical**, pa-thet'i-kal, *a.* Pathetic.—**Pathetically**, pa-thet'i-kal-li, *adv.* In a pathetic manner; affectingly.—**Patheticalness**, pa-thet'i-kal-nes, *n.*

Patience, pā'shens, *n.* [Fr. *patience*, from L. *patientia*, from *patiens*, patient. PASSION.] The quality of being patient; the power or capacity of physical endurance; the character or habit of mind that enables one to suffer afflictions, provocation, or other evil, with a calm unruffled temper; calmness; composure; quietness or calmness in waiting for something to happen; forbearance; long-suffering; constancy in labour or exertion; perseverance; a card game played by one person alone.—**Patient**, pā'shent, *a.* [L. *patiens, patientis*.] Physically able to support or endure; proof against (*patient of* labour or pain, heat, or cold); bearing pain or trial without murmuring; sustaining afflictions with fortitude, calmness, or submission; waiting with calmness; not hasty; long-suffering; persevering; calmly diligent.—*n.* One who or that which is passively affected; a sufferer from an ailment; a person who is under medical treatment. — **Patiently**, pā'shent-li, *adv.* In a patient manner; with patience; submissively; uncomplainingly.

Patin, pat'in, *n.* Same as *Paten*.

Patina, pat'i-na, *n.* [L. *patina*, a dish, a kind of cake, from *pateo*, to be open. PATENT, PAN.] The fine green rust with which ancient bronzes and copper coins and medals become covered by lying in particular soils; a bowl of metal or earthenware. — **Patine**, pat'in, *n.* A paten; a metal plate. (*Shak.*)

Patois, pat-wä, *n.* [Fr.] A dialect peculiar to the peasantry or uneducated classes; a provincial form of speech, the survival of a once literary dialect.

Patrial, pā'tri-al, *n.* and *a.* [L. *patrius*, belonging to a country, from *patria*. PATRIOT.] *Gram.* applied to words derived from the name of a country.

Patriarch, pā'tri-ärk, *n.* [L. *patriarcha*, from Gr. *patriarchēs* — *patria*, a family, from *patēr*, father, and *archē*, rule. PATERNAL.] The father and ruler of a family; generally applied to Abraham, Isaac, Jacob, and the sons of Jacob, or to the heads of families before the flood; hence, an aged venerable man; in the *Greek Church*, a dignitary superior to an archbishop.—**Patriarchal, Patriarchic**, pā-tri-är'-kal, pā-tri-är'kik, *a.* Belonging to patriarchs; subject to a patriarch.—**Patriarchate**, pā'tri-är-kāt, *n.* The office or jurisdiction of a patriarch.—**Patriarchism**, pā'tri-ärk-izm, *n.* Government by a patriarch. — **Patriarchship, Patriarchy**, pā'tri-ärk-ship, pā'tri-är-ki, *n.* A patriarchate.

Patrician, pa-trish'an, *a.* [Fr. *patricien*, from L. *patricius*, pertaining to the *patres*, senators or patricians, from *pater*, father. PATERNAL.] Pertaining to the senatorial order in ancient Rome; hence, of noble birth; not plebeian.—*n.* A person of patrician or noble birth; a nobleman. —**Patriciate**, pa-trish'i-āt, *n.* The aristocracy collectively.

Patricide, pat'ri-sīd, *n.* [L. *pater, patris*, father, and *cædo*, to kill.] The murder or murderer of a father; parricide.—**Patricidal**, pat-ri-sī'dal, *a.* Relating to patricide; parricidal.

Patrimony, pat'ri-mo-ni, *n.* [L. *patrimonium*, from *pater, patris*, father. PATERNAL.] A right or estate inherited from one's father or ancestors; heritage; a church estate or revenue.—**Patrimonial**, pat-ri-mō'ni-al, *a.* Pertaining to a patrimony; inherited from ancestors.—**Patrimonially**, pat-ri-mō'ni-al-li, *adv.* By way of patrimony or inheritance.

Patriot, pā'tri-ot, *n.* [Fr. *patriote*, from L. *patria*, one's native country, from *pater*, father. PATERNAL.] A person who loves his country, and zealously supports and defends it and its interests.—*a.* Patriotic. —**Patriotic**, pā-tri-ot'ik, *a.* Having the feelings of a patriot; inspired by the love of one's country; directed by zeal for the public safety and welfare.—**Patriotically**, pā-tri-ot'i-kal-li, *adv.* In a patriotic manner.—**Patriotism**, pā'tri-ot-izm, *n.* Love of one's country; the passion which leads a person to serve his country with zeal.

Patrist, pā'trist, *n.* [From L. *patres*, fathers.] One versed in the writings of the fathers of the Christian church.—**Patristic, Patristical**, pa-tris'tik, pa-tris'ti-kal, *a.* Pertaining to the ancient fathers of the Christian church. — **Patristically**, pa-tris'ti-kal-li, *adv.* In a patristic manner.—**Patristics**, pa-tris'tiks, *n.* That branch of historical theology which is devoted to the doctrines of the Christian fathers.

Patrol, pa-trōl', *n.* [Fr. *patrouille*, from *patrouiller*, to patrol, also to paddle with the feet, from *patte*, O.Fr. *pate*, a paw = G. *pfote*, D. *poot*, a paw.] *Milit.* the marching round of a guard in the night to secure the peace and safety of a camp or other place; the persons who go the rounds; a police constable who goes round a regular beat.—*v.i. patrolled, patrolling.* To go the rounds as a guard in a camp or garrison; to go the rounds in a city, as is done by a body of police. — *Patrol flotilla*, a flotilla or fleet of vessels acting by way of patrol, that is moving about and keeping guard against the approach of hostile craft and against attempts to break a blockade.—*v.t.* To pass through or perambulate in the capacity of a patrol.

Patron, pā'tron, *n.* [L. *patronus*, a protector or patron, from *pater*, a father. PATERNAL.] Among the ancient Romans, a master who had freed his slave, and still retained some rights over him; a man of distinction under whose protection another placed himself; hence, one who countenances, supports, or protects either a person or a work; a man of rank or standing who assists a person in an inferior position; a patron saint; one who has the gift and disposition of an ecclesiastical benefice.—*Patron saint*, any saint under whose special protection a church, a society, or a person is regarded as placed.—**Patronage**, pat′-ron-āj, *n.* The act of patronizing; protection; encouragement; guardianship, as of a saint; the right of presentation to a church or ecclesiastical benefice.—**Patroness**, pā′tron-es, *n.* A female patron.—**Patronize**, pat′ron-īz, *v.t.*—*patronized, patronizing.* To act as patron towards; to give support or countenance to; to favour; to assist; to assume the air of a patron or superior towards.—**Patronizer**, pat′ron-īz-ėr, *n.* One who patronizes.—**Patronizing**, pat′ron-īz-ing, *a.* Assuming the airs of a patron; having the style of one condescending to patronize or favour.—**Patronizingly**, pat′ron-īz-ing-li, *adv.*

Patronymic, pat-rō-nim′ik, *n.* [L. *patronymicus*, from Gr. *patēr, patros*, a father, and *onoma*, a name. PATERNAL.] A personal name derived from that of parent or ancestor (*Tydides*, the son of Tydeus; *Williamson*, the son of William); a family name; a surname.—**Patronymic, Patronymical**, pat-rō-nim′i-kal, *a.* Derived, as a name, from an ancestor.

Patten, pat′en, *n.* [Fr. *patin*, a clog, patten, from *patte*, the foot. PATROL.] A wooden shoe or sole, standing on an iron ring, worn to keep the shoes from the dirt or mud; *masonry*, the base of a column or pillar; the sole for the foundation of a wall.

Patter, pat′ėr, *v.i.* [Freq. from *pat*, to give a slight blow. PAT.] To strike, as falling drops of water or hail, with a quick succession of small sounds; to move with quick steps, making a succession of small sounds. —*n.* A quick succession of small sounds.

Patter, pat′ėr, *v.t.* [Perhaps from the *Paternoster*, or Lord's prayer, repeated in churches in a low tone of voice. Comp. also Icel. *pata*, to prattle, *pati*, a rumor.] To repeat in a muttering way; to mutter. —*n.* Rapid, routine talk used by magicians, comedians, &c.

Pattern, pat′ėrn, *n.* [Same word as *patron*, which has also the sense of *pattern* in French and Spanish, as has L.L. *patronus.*] An original or model proposed for imitation; that which is to be copied or imitated; a piece or part exhibited as a specimen of the whole; a design or figure corresponding in outline to an object that is to be fabricated, and serving as a guide for determining its shape and dimensions; an ornamental design on some woven fabric: the counterpart in wood of something that is to be cast in metal.—**Pattern-card**, *n.* A set of patterns attached to a card.—**Pattern-drawer**, *n.* One who designs patterns.

Patty, pat′i, *n.* [Fr. *pâté*, pie, pasty.] A little pie; a pasty.—**Patty-pan**, *n.* A pan to bake patties in.

Patulous, pat′ū-lus, *a.* [L. *patulus*, from *pateo*, to be open. PATENT.] Spreading slightly; expanded; opening widely; with a spreading aperture.

Paucity, pa̦′si-ti, *n.* [L. *paucitas*, from *paucus*, few; cog. with E. *few.*] Fewness; smallness of number; smallness or scantness of quantity.

Paul, pa̦l, *n.* PAWL.

Pauldron, pa̦l′dron, *n.* [O.Fr. *espalleron*, from *espalle*, shoulder, L. *spatula*, shoulder-blade. EPAULE.] A piece of armour covering the shoulder: 'splent on spauld'. (*Scottish.*)

Paulician, pa̦-lish′an, *n.* One of a sect who rejected most of the Bible except St. Paul's epistles.

Pauline, pa̦l′īn, *a.* Pertaining to St. *Paul*, or to his writings; a member of St. Paul's School in London.

Paulo-post-future, pa̦′lō-pōst-fū-tūr, *n.* [L. *paulo*, a little, *post*, after.] A tense of Greek verbs corresponding to the future perfect.

Paunch, pänsh, *n.* [O.Fr. *panche* (Fr. *panse*), from L. *pantex, panticis*, the belly.] The belly and its contents; the abdomen; the first and largest stomach in ruminating quadrupeds, into which the food is received before rumination.—**Paunchy**, pän′shi, *a.* Having a prominent paunch; big-bellied.

Pauper, pa̦′pėr, *n.* [L. *pauper*, poor (whence *poverty, poor, impoverish*); akin *paucus*, few. PAUCITY.] A poor person; one in a state of indigence; particularly, one who, on account of poverty, becomes chargeable to a parish.—**Pauperism**, pa̦′-pėr-izm, *n.* The state of being a pauper; a state of indigence in a community.—**Pauperization**, pa̦′pėr-i-zā″shon, *n.* The act of pauperizing.—**Pauperize**, pa̦′pėr-īz, *v.t.*—*pauperized, pauperizing.* To reduce to pauperism.

Pause, pa̦z, *n.* [Fr., from L. *pausa*, Gr. *pausis*, a stopping, from *pauō*, to stop; *pose* (seen in *compose, impose*, &c.) is of same origin.] A temporary cessation; an intermission of action, of speaking, singing, or the like; a short stop; cessation proceeding from doubt; suspense; a mark of suspension of the voice; a character marking a halt in music.—*v.i.*—*paused, pausing.* To make a pause or short stop; to intermit speaking or action; to wait; to forbear for a time; to hesitate; to hold back; to be intermitted (the music *pauses*).—**Pauser**, pa̦′zėr, *n.* One who pauses.—**Pausingly**, pa̦′zing-li, *adv.* By breaks or pauses.

Pave, pāv, *v.t.*—*paved* (pp. sometimes *paven*), *paving.* [Fr. *paver*, L.L. *pavare*, from L. *pavire*, to ram, to pave.] To make a hard level surface upon by laying with stones, bricks, &c.; to floor with brick, stone, or other material.—*To pave a way* (*fig.*), to prepare a way; to remove difficulties or obstacles beforehand.—**Pavement**, pāv′-ment, *n.* [L. *pavimentum.*] A paved path or road; a floor or surface that is trodden on, consisting of stones, bricks, &c.; the stones or other material with which anything is paved.—**Paver**, pā′vėr, *n.* One who paves; a pavior.—**Pavier**, pā′vi-ėr, *n.* A pavior.—**Paving**, pāv′ing, *n.* Pavement; the laying of floors, streets, &c., with pavement.—*Paving stones*, large prepared stones or slabs for paving.—**Pavior, Paviour**, pā′vi-ėr, *n.* One whose occupation is to pave; a slab or brick used for paving; a rammer for driving paving stones.

Pavid, pav′id, *a.* [L. *pavidus*, from *paveo*, to fear.] Timid; fearful.—**Pavidity**, pa-vid′i-ti, *n.* Timidity.

Pavilion, pa-vil′yon, *n.* [Fr. *pavillon*, L. *papilio, papilionis*, a butterfly, also a tent, from shape of latter.] A tent; particularly, a large tent raised on posts; a canopy; *arch.* a small building or a part of a building having a tent-formed roof.—*Pavilion roof*, a roof sloping or hipped equally on all sides. —*v.t.* To furnish with tents; to shelter with a tent.—**Pavilioned**, pa-vil′yond, *a.* Furnished with a pavilion; made in the form of a pavilion.

Pavise, pav′is, *n.* [O.Fr. *pavois.*] A large shield to rest on the ground, formerly in use.

Pavonine, pav′ō-nīn, *a.* [L. *pavoninus*, from *pavo*, a peacock.] Belonging to a peacock; resembling a peacock; exhibiting the brilliant hues of the tail of a peacock; iridescent: applied to ores, &c.—*n.* The iridescent lustre found on some ores and metallic products.

Paw, pa̦, *n.* [From the Celtic: W. *pawen*, Armor. *pav, pao*; comp. D. *poot*, G. *pfote*, a paw.] The foot of quadrupeds having claws.—*v.i.* To draw the fore-foot along the ground; to scrape with the fore-foot (as a horse does).—*v.t.* To scrape or strike with the fore-foot; to handle roughly.—**Pawed**, pa̦d, *a.* Having paws.

Pawky, pa̦′ki, *a.* Humorous, dry and satiric in tone.

Pawl, pa̦l, *n.* [W. *pawl*, akin to L. *palus*, a stake. POLE.] A short bar pivoted at one end, so as to catch in a notch of a revolving body and stop its motion; a click or detent which falls into the teeth of a ratchet-wheel.—*v.t.* To stop with a pawl.

Pawn, pa̦n, *n.* [Fr. *pan*, a piece of a garment, formerly also a pawn or pledge, from L. *pannus*, a cloth, a rag. PANE.] Some article or chattel given or deposited as security for money borrowed; a pledge. —*In pawn, at pawn*, in the state of being pawned or pledged.—*v.t.* To give or deposit in pledge; to pledge with a pawnbroker; to pledge for the fulfilment of a promise.—**Pawnable**, pa̦′na-bl, *a.* Capable of being pawned.—**Pawnbroker**, pa̦n′brō-kėr, *n.* A person licensed to lend money at a legally fixed rate of interest on goods deposited with him.—**Pawnbroking**, pa̦n′brō-king, *n.* The business of a pawnbroker.—**Pawnee**, pa̦-nē′, *n.* The person to whom a pawn is delivered as security.—**Pawner**, *n.* One that pawns.—**Pawn-ticket**, *n.* A ticket given by a pawnbroker to the pledger as an evidence of the transaction; a dated receipt for the article pledged.

Pawn, pa̦n, *n.* [O.Fr. *paon, poon, peon*, properly a foot-soldier. PEON.] A piece of the lowest rank at chess.

Pax, paks, *n.* [L. *pax*, peace.] In the Roman Catholic Church a small tablet engraved with sacred figures or emblems, which, having been kissed by the priest, was then kissed by others.

Pax-wax, paks′waks, *n.* [Also called *faxwax*, from A.Sax. *feax*, hair, and *weaxan*, to wax or grow.] A strong tendinous ligament strengthening the neck of the ox, sheep, &c.

Pay, pā, *v.t.*—pret. and pp. *paid.* [O.Fr. *paier, paer* (Fr. *payer*), to pay, originally to please, being from L. *pacare*, to pacify—*pax, pacis*, peace. PEACE.] To recompense for goods received or for service rendered; to discharge one's obligation to; to compensate, remunerate, reward, requite; to discharge (as a debt) by giving or doing that which is due; to give; to render or offer: without any sense of obligation (to *pay* attention, respect, court, a visit); *naut.* to cover or coat, as the bottom of a vessel, a mast, &c., with tar or pitch, &c.—*To pay off*, to recompense and discharge.—*To pay out* (*naut.*), to slacken or cause to run out (a rope).—*To pay one out*, to punish him thoroughly or adequately.—*v.i.* To make payment or requital; to be worth the pains or efforts spent; to be remunerative.—*To pay for*, to make payment for; to make amends for; to atone for; to be mulcted on account of.—*To pay off*, to pay wages and discharge; to fall to leeward, as the head of a ship.—*n.* An equivalent given for money due, goods purchased, or services performed. —**Payable**, pā′a-bl, *a.* Capable of being paid; suitable to be paid; justly due.—**Pay-bill**, *n.* A bill or statement specifying the amount of money to be paid, as to workmen, soldiers, and the like.—**Pay-clerk**, *n.* A clerk who pays wages.—**Pay-day**, *n.* The day when payment is regularly made; the day for paying wages.—**Payee**, pā-ē′, *n.* The person to whom money is to be paid.—**Payer**, pā′ėr, *n.* One that pays; the person named in a bill or note who has to pay the holder.—**Pay-list**, *n.* A payroll.—**Paymaster**, pā′mas-tėr, *n.* One from whom wages or reward is received; an officer in the army or navy who regularly pays the officers and men.—**Payment**, pā′ment, *n.* The act of paying; the discharge of a debt; the thing given in discharge of a debt; recompense; requital; reward.

Paynim, pā′nim, *n.* [O.Fr. *paienime*, *paienisme*, paganism, from *paien*, L. *paganus*, a pagan; *paynim* is thus a form of *paganism.* PAGAN.] A pagan; a heathen.

Pea, pē, *n.* [O.E. *pese, pees*, a pea, pl. *pesen*, *peses*, A.Sax. *pise*, from L. *pisum*, Gr. *pisos*, a pea. *Pea* is a false form, the *s* of the root being mistaken for the sign of the plural. In the plural we always write *peas* for the individual seeds, but often *pease* for an indefinite quantity (this form being the old singular): three or four *peas*, a bushel of *pease* (or *peas*).] A well-known plant with papilionaceous flowers, one of the most valuable of vegetables, cultivated in the garden and in the field; one of the seeds of the plant.—**Peanut**, *n.* An American plant, whose pods grow first above and then below ground; the nutlike seed of this plant.—**Peanut butter**, *n.* A paste made from crushed peanuts.—**Pea-ore**, *n.* An ore of iron occurring in spherical grains of the size of a pea.—**Pea-pod**, *n.* The pod or shell of a pea.—**Pease-pudding**, *n.* A pudding made chiefly of peas.—**Pea-soup Pease-soup**, *n.* Soup made from peas.—**Pea-stone**, *n.* Pisolite.

Peace, pēs, *n.* [From O.Fr. *pais* (Fr. *paix*), from L. *pax, pacis*, peace—root *pac*, seen in *paciscor*, to agree (whence *pact*); of same origin as *pay, appease*.] A state of quiet or tranquility; calm, quietness, repose; especially freedom from war; a cessation of hostilities; absence of strife; tranquility of mind; quiet of conscience; harmony; concord; public tranquility.—*At peace*, in a peaceful state.—*Breach of the peace*, a violation of public tranquility by riotous or other conduct.—*To hold one's peace*, to be silent; to suppress one's thoughts; not to speak.—*To make* a person's *peace*, with another, to reconcile the other to him.—*Peace establishment*, the reduced number of effective men in the army during time of peace.—*Commission of the peace*, a commission appointing justices of the peace, and by virtue of which the judges sit upon circuit.—*Justices of the peace.* JUSTICE.—**Peaceable**, pēs'a-bl, *a.* Tranquil; peaceful; disposed to peace; not quarrelsome. ∴ *Peaceable* usually refers to the character and disposition of men; *pacific* to designs and intentions; while *peaceful* refers to the state or condition of men or things.—**Peaceableness**, pēs'a-bl-nes, *n.* The state or quality of being peaceable.—**Peaceably**, pēs'a-bli, *adv.* In a peaceable manner.—**Peacebreaker**, *n.* One that violates or disturbs public peace.—**Peaceful**, pēs'fụl, *a.* Full of, possessing, or enjoying peace; tranquil; quiet; removed from noise or tumult; pacific.—**Peacefully**, pēs'fụl-li, *adv.* In a peaceful manner; quietly; tranquilly.—**Peacefulness**, pēs'fụl-nes, *n.* The state or quality of being peaceful.—**Peacemaker**, pēs'mā-kėr, *n.* One who reconciles parties at variance.—**Peace-offering**, *n.* Something offered to an offended person to procure peace; among the Jews, an offering to God for atonement and reconciliation.—**Peace pact**, *n.* A non-aggression agreement of limited duration, made between two or more nations.

Peach, pēch, *n.* [Fr. *pêche*, It. *pesca, persica*, from L. *persica, Persicum* (*malum*), the Persian apple.] A fruit tree of many varieties, grown in temperate climates; the fruit of the tree, a sweet, juicy drupe a little smaller than an apple, containing a stone; also, that which resembles a peach, as in beauty or goodness.—**Peach-blossom**, *n.* The delicate pink flower of the peach, which appears in early spring. —**Peach-color**, *n.* A pale red-yellow.—**Peach down**, *n.* The soft down of the peach skin.—**Peach-wood**, *n.* A dyewood yielding a peach color.—**Peachy**, pēch'i, *a.* Peachlike; pleasing, admirable, highly delightful (*Slang*).

Peacock, pē'kok, *n.* [*Pea* = A.Sax. *pawa*, from L. *pavo*, a peacock, the name being perhaps from the bird's cry.] A large and beautiful gallinaceous bird remarkable for the beauty of its plumage, properly the male of the species, the female being, for distinction's sake, called a *peahen*.—**Peachick**, *n.* The chicken or young of the peacock.—**Peacock-fish**, *n.* A fish of the Mediterranean and Indian Seas, showing brilliant green, yellow, and red hues.—**Pea-fowl**, *n.* The peacock or peahen.—**Peahen**, pē'hen, *n.* The hen or female of the peacock.

Pea-jacket, pē'jak-et, *n.* [*Pea* is from D. and L.G. *pije*, coarse, thick cloth, a warm jacket; akin to Goth. *paida*, a garment.] A thick loose woollen jacket worn by seamen, fishermen, &c.

Peak, pēk, *n.* [Fr. *pic*, a mountain peak, a pick, *pique*, a pike, from Armor. *pic*, W. *pig*, a point, a pike, a beak; akin *beak, pike, pick, peck*.] The top of a hill or mountain, ending in a point; a projecting point; a projecting portion on a head-covering (the *peak* of a cap); *naut.* the upper corner of a sail which is extended by a gaff or yard; also, the extremity of the yard or gaff.—**Peaked**, pēkt, *a.* Pointed; ending in a point.—**Peaky**, pēk'i, *a.* Consisting of peaks; resembling a peak.

Peak, pēk, *v.i.* [Perhaps from *peak*, *n.*, from the sharpened features of sickly persons.] To look sickly or thin; to be or become emaciated.—**Peakish**, pēk'ish, *a.* Of a thin and sickly cast of face.

Peal, pēl, *n.* [A mutilated form of *appeal*.] A succession of loud sounds, as of bells, thunder, cannon, shouts of a multitude, &c.; a set of bells tuned to each other; the changes rung on such bells.—*v.i.* To utter or give out a peal.—*v.t.* To cause to ring or sound; to utter loudly and sonorously.

Pean. PÆAN.

Pear, pār, *n.* [A.Sax. *peru*, Fr. *poire*, from L. *pirum*, a pear.] A fruit tree grown in temperate climates; the fruit itself, a sweet, fleshy pome.—*Alligator pear.* AVOCADO.—*Anchovy pear.* ANCHOVY.—*Prickly pear.* PRICKLY.—**Peariform**, pār'i-form, *a.* Pear-shaped.—**Pear-shaped**, *a.* Shaped like a pear, or somewhat like an egg.

Pearl, pėrl, *n.* [Fr. *perle*, from L.L. *perula, perla*, a pearl, either for *pirula*, from L. *pirum*, a pear, or for *pilula*, a pill, a globule.] A silvery or bluish-white, hard, smooth, lustrous body, of a roundish, oval, or pear-shaped form, produced by certain molluscs as the result of some abnormal or morbid process; poetically, something round and clear, as a drop of dew; a white speck or film growing on the eye; cataract; a small printing type, the smallest except diamond and brilliant; anything very valuable; what is choicest or best.—*a.* Relating to, made of pearl.—*v.t.* To set or adorn with pearls.—**Pearlaceous**, pėr-lā'shus, *a.* Resembling pearl or mother of pearl; of a pearly appearance.—**Pearlash**, pėrl'-ash, *n.* Commercial carbonate of potash.—**Pearl-barley**, *n.* The seed of barley ground into small round grains.—**Pearl-diver**, *n.* One who dives for pearl-oysters. —**Pearled**, pėrld, *a.* Set or adorned with pearls.—**Pearl-edge**, *n.* A narrow kind of thread edging for lace.—**Pearl-eye**, *n.* A white speck or film on the eye.—**Pearl-fishery**, *n.* A place where pearl-oysters are caught.—**Pearl-fishing**, *n.* The occupation of diving for or otherwise catching pearl-oysters.—**Pearliness**, pėr'li-nes, *n.* The state of being pearly.—**Pearl-mussel**, *n.* A fresh-water mussel which yields pearls.—**Pearl-nautilus**, *n.* The true nautilus as distinguished from the argonaut or paper-nautilus.—**Pearl-oyster**, *n.* A mollusc that yields pearls.—**Pearl-powder**, *n.* A sort of powder from bismuth, used as a cosmetic.—**Pearl-sago**, *n.* Sago in grains of the size of small pearls.—**Pearl-spar**, *n.* A variety of dolomite.—**Pearl-stone**, *n.* A kind of vitreous trachyte or lava.—**Pearl-white**, *n.* Pearl-powder.—**Pearly**, pėr'li, *a.* Containing pearls; resembling pearls; nacreous.

Peasant, pez'ant, *n.* [O.Fr. *païsant* (Fr. *paysan*), from *pais, pays*, L. *pagus*, a district of country (with *t* affixed as in *tyrant*). PAGAN, PAGE (boy).] A rustic or countryman; one occupied in rural labour.—*a.* Rustic; rural.—**Peasantry**, pez'ant-ri, *n.* Peasants collectively; the body of country people.

Pease, pēz, *n.* Under PEA.

Peat, pēt, *n.* [For *beat, bete*, from old *bete*, to mend a fire; A.Sax. *bétan*, to make better; akin *bette* boot.] A kind of turf used as fuel; the natural accumulation of vegetable matter, more or less decomposed, in hollows on land not in a state of cultivation; a small block of peat cut and dried for fuel.—**Peat-bog**, *n.* A bog or marsh containing peat.—**Peat-moss**, *n.* A moss producing peat.—**Peat-soil**, *n.* A soil mixed with peat.—**Peaty**, pēt'i, *a.* Resembling peat; abounding in peat; composed of peat.

Peba, pē'ba, *n.* A species of armadillo.

Pebble, peb'l, *n.* [A.Sax. *papolstán*, lit. pebble-stone; etym. unknown.] A small round stone; a stone worn and rounded by the action of water; a lapidary's name for agate; an optician's name for transparent colourless rock-crystal used as a substitute for glass in spectacles.—**Pebbled**, peb'ld, *a.* Abounding with pebbles.—**Pebbly**, peb'li, *a.* Full of pebbles.

Pébrine, pā-brēn, *n.* [Fr.] A very destructive epizoötic disease amongst silkworms.

Pecan, Pecan-nut, pē-kan', *n.* [Fr. *pacane*, Sp. *pacana*.] A species of hickory and its fruit.

Pecary, pek'a-ri, *n.* PECCARY.

Peccable, pek'a-bl, *a.* [L.L. *peccabilis*, peccable, from L. *pecco*, to sin.] Liable to sin; subject to transgress the divine law.—**Peccability**, pek-a-bil'i-ti, *n.* State of being peccable.—**Peccadillo**, pek-a-dil'ō, *n.* [Sp. *pecadillo*, dim. of *pecado*, L. *peccatum*, a sin, from *pecco*.] A slight trespass or offence; a petty crime or fault.—**Peccancy**, pek'an-si, *n.* State or quality of being peccant.—**Peccant**, pek'ant, *a.* [L. *peccans, peccantis*, ppr. of *pecco*.] Sinning; criminal; morbid; corrupt (*peccant* humours). —**Peccantly**, pek'ant-li, *adv.*

Peccary, pek'a-ri, *n.* [South American name.] A pachydermatous quadruped of America, representing the swine of the Old World, to which it is allied.

Peccavi, pek-kā'vi. [L., I have sinned, from *pecco*, to sin.] A word used to express confession or acknowledgment of an offence.

Pechblend, Pechblende, pek'blend, *n.* [G. *pech*, pitch.] PITCHBLEND.

Peck, pek, *n.* [Perhaps a form of *pack*; but comp. Fr. *picotin*, a peck; L.L. *picotus*, a liquid measure.] The fourth part of a bushel; a dry measure of 8 quarts.

Peck, pek, *v.t.* [A slightly different form of *pick*.] To strike with the beak; to pick up with the beak; to make by striking with the beak, or a pointed instrument (to *peck* a hole).—*v.i.* To make strokes with a beak, or a pointed instrument.—*To peck at*, to strike at with the beak; to attack with petty criticism.—**Pecker**, pek'ėr, *n.* One who or that which pecks.—**Peckish**, pek'ish, *a.* Inclined to eat; somewhat hungry. (*Colloq.*)

Pecten, pek'ten, *n.* [L. *pecten*, a comb, a kind of shell-fish, from *pecto, pexum*, to comb; root *pek*, also in Gr. *pekō*, to comb.] A genus of marine bivalves having a shell marked with diverging ribs and furrows.

Pectic, pek'tik, *a.* [Gr. *pēktikos*, curdling, from *pēgnymi*, to fix.] Having the property of forming a jelly: said of an acid found in fruits.—**Pectin, Pectine**, pek'tin, *n.* A principle which forms the basis of vegetable jelly.—**Pectinaceous**, pek-ti-nā'shus, *a.* Having the character of pectin.—**Pectose**, pek'tōs, *n.* A substance contained in fleshy fruits which certain agents change into pectin.—**Pectous**, pek'tus, *a.* Pertaining to pectin.

Pectinal, pek'ti-nal, *a.* [L. *pecten*, a comb. PECTEN.] Pertaining to a comb; resembling a comb.—**Pectinate, Pectinated**, pek'ti-nāt, pek'ti-nā-ted, *a.* [L. *pectinatus*.] Having resemblance to the teeth of a comb; toothed like a comb; serrated.—**Pectinately**, pek'ti-nāt-li, *a.* Like the teeth of a comb.—**Pectination**, pek-ti-nā'shon, *n.* The state of being pectinated; what is pectinated.—**Pectines**, pek'tin-ēz, *n.* In scorpions, a pair of comb-shaped appendages attached to the under side of the body.—**Pectinibranchiate**, pek-tin'i-brang"ki-āt, *a.* and *n.* Having pectinated gills, as certain molluscs; an animal of this kind.—**Pectiniform**, pek-tin'i-form, *a.* Resembling a comb in form.

Pectoral, pek'tō-ral, *a.* [L. *pectoralis*, from *pectus, pectoris*, the breast.] Pertaining to the breast.—*Pectoral fins*, the two fore fins of a fish, situated near the gills.—*Pectoral theology*, heartfelt, unctuous belief. —*Pectus theologum facit* (Augustine).—*n.* A covering or protection for the breast; a breastplate; the breastplate of the Jewish high-priest; a medicine for complaints of the chest; a pectoral fin.—**Pectoriloquism**, pek-to-ril'ō-kwizm, *n.* [L. *pectus*, and *loquor*, to speak.] A speaking from the chest.—**Pectoriloquy**, pek-to-ril'ō-kwi, *n.* A phase of disease in which the patient's voice seems to proceed from the point of the chest on which the ear or a stethoscope is placed, as in consumptive persons.

Pectose, Pectous. Under PECTIC.

Peculate, pek'ū-lāt, *v.i.*—*peculated, peculating.* [L. *peculor, peculatus*, to steal, from *peculium*, private property, from *pecu*, cattle, in which wealth originally consisted; cog. E. *fee*. PECULIAR, PECUNIARY.] To appropriate public money, or goods intrusted to one's care; to embezzle.—**Peculation**, pek-ū-lā'shon, *n.* The act of peculating; embezzlement.—**Peculator**, pek'-ū-lā-tėr, *n.* One who peculates.

Peculiar, pē-kūl'yėr, *a.* [L. *peculiaris*, one's own, peculiar, extraordinary, from *peculium*, one's own property. PECULATE.] One's own: of private, personal, or characteristic possession and use; specially belonging (*peculiar* to that part of the country); singular; striking; unusual; eccentric.—*n.* *England.* A parish or church which has ecclesiastical jurisdiction within itself.—**Peculiarity**, pē-kū'li-ar"i-ti, *n.* The quality of being peculiar; that which is peculiar to a person or thing; a special characteristic or feature.—**Peculiarize**, pē-kū'li-ėr-īz, *v.t.*—*peculiarized, peculiarizing.* To make peculiar; to set apart; to appropriate.—**Peculiarly**, pē-kū'li-ėr-li, *adv.* In a peculiar manner; especially; in a manner not common to others.—**Peculiarness**, pē-kū'li-ėr-nes, *n.*

Pecuniary, pē-kū'ni-a-ri, *a.* [Fr. *pecuniaire*, L. *pecuniarius*, from *pecunia*, money, from *pecu*, cattle. PECULATE.] Relating to or connected with money; consisting of money.—**Pecuniarily**, pē-kū'ni-a-ri-li, *a.* In a pecuniary manner.

Pedagogue, ped'a-gog, *n.* [Gr. *paidagōgos*—*pais, paidos*, a child, and *agō*, to lead.] A teacher of children; a schoolmaster: now generally by way of contempt.—**Pedagogic, Pedagogical**, ped-a-goj'ik, ped-a-goj'i-kal, *a.* Resembling or belonging to a pedagogue.—**Pedagogics**, ped-a-goj'iks, *n.* The science or art of teaching.—**Pedagogism**, ped'a-gog-izm, *n.* The business or manners of a pedagogue.—**Pedagogy**, ped'a-go-ji, *n.* The art or office of a pedagogue.

Pedal, ped'al, *a.* [L. *pedalis*, belonging to the foot, from *pes, pedis*, the foot, seen also in *pedestal, pedestrian, biped, quadruped, centipede, expedite, impede, dispatch*, &c. FOOT.] Pertaining to a foot (*pedal* digits); *mus.* relating to a pedal.—*n.* A lever to be pressed down by the foot; a sort of treadle; a part of a musical instrument acted on by the feet, as in the piano for strengthening or softening the sound; on the organ for opening additional sets of pipes; on the harmonium for working the bellows, &c.—*v.t.* To work the pedal of a bicycle, to increase or decrease the speed.—*v.i.* To advance or slow down on a bicycle.—**Pedal-bass**, *Mus.* ORGAN-POINT.—**Pedal-note**, *n.* *Mus.* a holding-note, generally the dominant.

Pedant, ped'ant, *n.* [Fr. *pédant*, It., Sp., and Pg. *pedante*, for *pedagogante*, from L. *pædagogans, pædagogantis*, ppr. of *pædagogo*, to educate. PEDAGOGUE.] A person who makes a vain display of his learning, or who prides himself on his book-learning but is devoid of taste; one devoted to a system of rules.—**Pedantic, Pedantical**, pē-dan'tik, pē-dan'ti-kal, *a.* Pertaining to a pedant or to pedantry.—**Pedantically**, pē-dan'ti-kal-li, *adv.* In a pedantic manner.—**Pedantry**, ped'ant-ri, *n.* The manners or character of a pedant; ostentation or boastful display of learning; obstinate adherence to rules or established forms.

Pedate, ped'āt, *a.* [L. *pedatus*, from *pes, pedis*, the foot. PEDAL.] Having divisions like toes; divided into distinct lobes; *bot.* applied to certain palmate leaves.—**Pedatifid**, pē-dat'i-fid, *a.* [L. *findo, fidi*, to divide.] *Bot.* divided in a pedate manner.

Peddle, ped'l, *v.i.*—*peddle, peddling.* [From Prov. E. *ped* or *pad*, a wicker basket, a pannier, akin to *pod*. Hence *pedlar*.] To travel about the country and retail small wares; to go about as a peddler; to be engaged in a small business; to trifle.—*v.t.* To sell or retail in small quantities while traveling about.—**Peddler**, ped'lėr, *n.* One who peddles. A hawker.

Pedestal, ped'es-tal, *n.* [Sp. *pedestal*, Fr. *piedestal*, It. *piedestallo*, from L. *pes, pedis*, the foot, and G. and E. *stall*.] A basement or support for a column, a statue, a vase, &c.

Pedestrian, pē-des'tri-an, *a.* [L. *pedestris*, from *pes, pedis*, the foot. PEDAL.] Going on foot; performed on foot; walking; in literary criticism, prosaic in tone.—*n.* One that walks or journeys on foot; a remarkable walker.—**Pedestrianism**, pē-des'-tri-an-izm, *n.* The practice of walking; the art of a professional walker.

Pediatrician, pē'di-a-trish"an, *n.* A physician specializing in pediatrics.

Pediatrics, pē-di-at'riks, *n.* The science which treats of the medical care and diseases of children.

Pedicel, ped'i-sel, *n.* [From *pedicellus*, a form equivalent to L. *pediculus*, dim. of *pes, pedis*, the foot. PEDAL.] *Bot.* the stalk that supports a single flower, leaf, &c.; any short small footstalk; *zool.* a foot-stalk by which certain animals of the lower orders, as zoophytes, &c., are attached.—**Pedicellate**, ped'i-sel-āt, *a.* Having a pedicel.—**Pedicle**, ped'i-kl, *n.* PEDICEL.—**Pedicellaria**, pl. **-ae**, pe-di-sel-lā'ri-a, *n.* [L. dim. of *pedica*, a trap.] In starfishes and sea-urchins, a spine ending in pincers.

Pedicular, Pediculous, pe-dik'ū-lėr, pe-dik'ū-lus, *a.* [L. *pediculus*, a louse.] Lousy; having the lousy distemper.

Pedicure, ped'i-kūr, *n.* [L. *pes, pedis*, foot, *cura*, care.] A person who practices the care-taking of other people's feet, cutting their nails, &c.

Pedigerous, pe-dij'ėr-us, *a.* [L. *pes, pedis*, a foot, and *gero*, to bear.] Having feet or legs; furnished with foot-like organs.

Pedigree, ped'i-grē, *n.* [O.Fr. *pedegru*, Fr. *pié de grue*, crane's foot; L. *pes*, foot, *de*, of, *grus*, crane.] A line of ancestors; lineage; a genealogy: a genealogical or family tree.

Pedimanous, pe-dim'a-nus, *a.* [L. *pes, pedis*, the foot, and *manus*, the hand.] Having the foot hand-shaped, as monkeys.

Pediment, ped'i-ment, *n.* [From L. *pes, pedis*, the foot.] *Arch.* the low triangular mass resembling a gable at the end of buildings in the Greek style, surrounded with a cornice, and often ornamented with sculptures; a small gable or triangular decoration like a gable over a window, a door, &c.—**Pedimental**, ped'i-men-tal, *a.* Relating to a pediment.

Pedipalp, ped'i-palp, *n.* [L. *pes, pedis*, a foot, *palpus*, a feeler.] In arachnids, one of the second pair of head-limbs.

Pedobaptism, pē-do-bap'tizm, *n.* PÆDOBAPTISM.

Pedometer, pe-dom'et-ėr, *n.* [L. *pes, pedis*, the foot, and Gr. *metron*, a measure.] An instrument (often resembling a watch) by which paces are numbered as a person walks, and the distance thus ascertained.—**Pedometric, Pedometrical**, pē-do-met'rik, pē-do-met'ri-kal, *a.* Pertaining to a pedometer.

Pedomotive, pē'do-mō-tiv, *a.* [L. *pes, pedis*, the foot, and E. *motive*.] Moved or worked by the foot or the feet.

Peduncle, pē-dung'kl, *n.* [From L. *pes, pedis*, a foot.] *Bot.* the stalk that supports the fructification of a plant, *i.e.* the flower and fruit; *zool.* the stem or stalk by which certain brachiopods, &c., are attached.—**Peduncular**, pē-dung'kū-lėr, *a.* Pertaining to a peduncle; growing from a peduncle.—**Pedunculate, Pedunculated**, pē-dung'kū-lāt, pē-dung'kū-lā-ted, *a.* Having a peduncle; growing on a peduncle.

Peek, pēk, *v.i.* To peep; to look or spy through half closed eyes.—*n.* A quick, secret glance.

Peel, Peel-tower, pēl, *n.* [W. *pill*, a tower, a fortress.] A name of certain strong square towers or strongholds common on the Scottish borders.

Peel, pēl, *v.t.* [O.Fr. *peiler* (Fr. *peler*), to peel, from L. *pellis*, the skin (cog. with E. *fell*, a skin), whence also *pellicle, peltry, pelisse*, &c.] To strip the skin, bark, or rind from; to strip by drawing or tearing off the skin; to decorticate; to strip (bark) from the surface.—*v.i.* To lose the skin or rind; to fall off (as bark or skin).—*n.* The skin or rind of anything.—**Peeler**, pēl'ėr, *n.* One that peels.

Peel, pēl, *n.* [Fr. *pelle*, from L. *pala*, a spade.] A wooden shovel used by bakers to put their bread in and take it out of the oven.

Peeler, pēl'ėr, *n.* *Eng. colloq.* A policeman.

Peen, pēn, *n.* The head of a sledge opposite the face.—*v. t.* To shape an object by striking it with the peen.

Peep, pēp, *v.i.* [Imitative of sound, like D. and G. *piepen*, Dan. *pippe*, L. *pipio*, Gr. *pippizō*, to chirp; the other meaning is supposed to have been suggested from the chicken's peep or chirp closely accompanying its peeping from the shell.] To cry, as chickens; to cheep; to chirp; to begin to appear; to look through a crevice; to look narrowly, closely, or slyly.—*n.* The cry of a chicken; a sly look, or a look through a crevice.—*Peep of day*, the dawn or day-break.—**Peeper**, pēp'ėr, *n.* One that peeps.—**Peep-hole, Peeping-hole**, *n.* A hole through which one may peep without being discovered.—**Peep-show**, *n.* A show of small pictures viewed through a hole fitted with a magnifying lens.

Peer, pēr, *n.* [Lit. an equal; O.Fr. *peer, per, par* (Fr. *pair*), from L. *par*, equal. PAIR.] One of the same rank, qualities, or the like; an equal; a match; a companion; a member of one of the five degrees of British nobility (duke, marquis, earl, viscount, baron); a nobleman.—*House of Peers*, the House of Lords.—**Peerage**, pēr'āj, *n.* The rank or dignity of a peer; the body of peers.—**Peeress**, pēr'es, *n.* The consort of a peer; a woman ennobled by descent, by creation, or by marriage.—**Peerless**, pēr'les, *a.* Unequaled; having no peer or equal.—**Peerlessly**, pēr'les-li, *adv.* In a peerless manner.—**Peerlessness**, pēr'les-nes, *n.*

Peer, pēr, *v.i.* [O.Fr. *perer, pareir*, from L. *pareo*, to appear; same as *-pear* in *appear*; or from L.G. *piren*, to peer.] To come just in sight; to appear (*Shak.*); to look narrowly; to pry; to peep.

Peevish, pē'vish, *a.* [Comp. Dan. *piæve*, to cry like a child; Sc. *pew, pyow*, a sound of complaint.] Apt to mutter and complain; easily vexed or fretted; fretful; querulous; self-willed; froward.—**Peevishly**, pē'vish-li, *adv.* In a peevish manner.—**Peevishness**, pē'vish-nes, *n.* The state or quality of being peevish; fretfulness.

Peewit, pē'wit, *n.* [From its cry.] The lapwing.

Peg, peg, *n.* [Comp. Dan. *pig*; a spike; W. *pig*, something sharp; allied probably to E. *peak, pick*.] A wooden pin used in fastening things, as a mark, or otherwise; one of the pins on a musical instrument for stretching the strings; a pin on which to hang anything.—*To take one down a peg*, to humiliate him.—*v.t.*—*pegged, pegging.* To put pegs into for fastening, &c.; to fasten on the sole of (a shoe) with pegs; to mark off by pegs.—*v.i.* To work diligently: generally followed by *away* or *on*. (*Colloq.*)—**Pegger**, peg'ėr, *n.* One that pegs.—**Peg-top**, *n.* A child's toy, a variety of top made to spin by a string.—**Pegtops**, *n.* Trousers wide at hips and narrow at the ankles. (*Colloq.*)

Pegasus, peg'a-sus, *n.* The winged horse of Greek mythology, often regarded as the horse of the Muses, and hence connected with poets and poetry.—**Pegasean**, pe-gă'sē-an, *a.* Pertaining to Pegasus; poetical.

Peirameter, pī-ram'et-ėr, *n.* [Gr. *peira*, a trial, and *metron*, a measure.] An instrument for ascertaining the resistance which the surfaces of roads offer to wheeled carriages, &c.—**Peirastic**, pī-ras'tik, *a.* [Gr. *peirastikos.*] Making trial; tentative.

Pejorative, pē'jor-ā-tiv, *a.* [L. *pejor*, worse.] Conveying a depreciatory meaning. —*n.* A word conveying such a meaning (*poetaster* is a *pejorative* of *poet*).

Pekan, pē'kan, *n.* A species of North American marten.

Pekoe, pē'kō, *n.* [Chinese, lit. white down.] A fine black tea.

Pelage, pel'āj, *n.* [Fr. *pelage*, hair of the hide, from L. *pilus*, hair. PILE.] *Zool.* the hairy covering of an animal.

Pelagian, pe-lā'ji-an, *n.* A follower of *Pelagius*, a British monk of the fourth century, who denied original sin, and asserted the doctrine of free-will and the merit of good works.—*a.* Pertaining to Pelagius and his doctrines.—**Pelagianism**, pe-lā'ji-an-izm, *n.* The doctrines of Pelagius.

Pelagic, pe-laj'ik, *a.* [Gr. *pelagos*, the ocean.] Belonging to the ocean; inhabiting the open ocean.

Pelargonium, pel-är-gō'ni-um, *n.* [From Gr. *pelargos*, a stork—from the shape of the capsules.] Stork's-bill, an extensive genus of highly ornamental plants, usually called *Geraniums*. GERANIUM.

Pelasgian, Pelasgic, pe-las'ji-an, pe-las'-jik, *a.* Pertaining to the Pelasgians or Pelasgi, prehistoric inhabitants of Greece, &c. —*Pelasgic architecture, Pelasgic building.* CYCLOPEAN.

Pelecan, pel'i-kan, *n.* PELICAN.

Pelecoid, pel'e-koid, *n.* [Gr. *pelekys*, axe.] A mathematical figure somewhat in the shape of the blade of a battle-axe.

Pelerine, pel'ėr-in, *n.* [Fr., from *pelerin*, a pilgrim. PILGRIM.] A lady's long cape or fur-tippet.

Pelf, pelf, *n.* [O.Fr. *pelfre*, spoil, booty, from L. *pilare*, to rob, and *facere*, to make. PILFER.] Money; riches; filthy lucre: a contemptuous term.

Pelican, pel'i-kan, *n.* [From L. *pelicanus*, Gr. *pelekanos*, a pelican, from *pelekys*, a hatchet—from shape of bill.] A web-footed bird, larger than the swan, with a very large bill, and beneath the under mandible a huge pouch for holding fish.

Pelisse, pe-lēs', *n.* [Fr. *pelisse*, from L. *pelliceus*, made of skins, from *pellis*, a skin. PEEL, *v.t.*] Originally a garment lined or trimmed with fur; now a robe of silk or other material worn by ladies.

Pell, pel, *n.* [L. *pellis*, a skin. PEEL, *v.t.*] A skin or hide; a roll of parchment. *Obs.*

Pellagra, pe-lā'gra, *n.* [It. *pellagra*, L. *pellis*, skin, and Gr. *agra*, seizure.] A disease affecting the skin, digestive system, and nervous system; it is caused by faulty diet due to vitamin deficiency; it is found in Italy and the southeastern U.S.A. —**Pellagrin**, *n.* One afflicted with pellagra.

Pellet, pel'et, *n.* [Fr. *pelote*, from L.L. *pilota*, *pelota*, dim. of L. *pila*, a ball. PILE (heap).] A little ball; one of the globules of small shot.—*v.t.* To form into pellets.—**Pelleted**, pel'et-ed, *p.* and *a.* Consisting of pellets; made of pellets.

Pellicle, pel'i-kl, *n.* [L. *pellicula*, dim of *pellis*, skin. PEEL, *v.t.*] A thin skin or film on a surface; *bot.* the outer cuticular covering of plants.—**Pellicular**, pel-lik'-ū-lėr, *a.* Pertaining to a pellicle; constituted by a pellicle or pellicles.

Pellitory, pel'i-to-ri, *n.* [A corruption of L. *parietaria*, lit. the wall plant, from *paries*, *parietis*, a wall.] A name of several plants of the nettle family; also, a number of European plants which are similar to yarrow.

Pell-mell, pel'mel, *adv.* [Fr. *pêle-mêle*, from *pelle* (L. *pala*), a shovel, and *mêler*, to mix (MEDLEY).] With confused violence; in a disorderly body; in utter confusion; at a wild speed.

Pellucid, pel-lū'sid, *a.* [L. *pellucidus*—*pel*, for *per*, through, and *lucidus*, bright. LUCID.] Transparent; admitting the passage of light; translucent; not opaque.—**Pellucidity, Pellucidness**, pel-lū-sid'i-ti, pel-lū'sid-nes, *n.* The state or quality of being pellucid.—**Pellucidly**, pel-lū'sid-li, *adv.* In a pellucid manner.

Peloponnesian, pel'ō-pon-nē"si-an, *a.* Belonging to *Peloponnesus*, or the southern peninsula of Greece.

Peloria, pē-lō'ri-a, *n.* [Gr. *pelōr*, a monster.] *Bot.* regularity of structure in the flowers of plants which normally bear irregular flowers. — **Peloric**, pē-lor'ik, *a.* Characterized by peloria.

Pelt, pelt, *n.* [Shortened from *peltry*, from L. *pellis*, a skin. PEEL, *v.t.*] The skin of a beast with the hair on it; a raw hide.—**Pelt-monger**, *n.* A dealer in pelts.—**Peltry**, pel'tri, *n.* [Fr. *pelletrie.*] Pelts collectively: usually applied to the skins of fur-bearing animals in the raw state.

Pelt, pelt, *v.t.* [O.E. *pulten*, probably from L. *pultare*, to strike or knock, from *pello*, to drive. PULSE.] To strike or assail with something thrown or driven; to drive by throwing something.—*v.i.* To throw missiles.—*n.* A blow or stroke from something thrown.—**Pelter**, pel'tėr, *n.* One who or that which pelts.

Peltate, Peltated, pel'tāt, pel'tā-ted, *a.* [L. *pelta*, a target.] Shield-shaped; *bot.* fixed to the stalk by the centre or by some point distinctly within the margin.—**Peltately**, pel'tāt-li, *adv.* In a peltate manner. — **Peltatifid**, pel-tat'i-fid, *a.* *Bot.* peltate and cut into subdivisions.—**Peltiform**, pel'ti-form, *a.* Shield-shaped.

Peltier Effect, pel-tē-ā', *n.* [After the physicist *Peltier.*] The evolution or absorption of heat at the junction of two metals traversed by an electric current.

Pelting, pel'ting, *a.* Paltry. (*Shak.*)

Pelton Wheel, pel'ton, *n.* A form of impulse water turbine, with double cup buckets at the rim.

Peltry, pel'tri, *n.* Under PELT, *n.*

Pelvis, pel'vis, *n.* [L. *pelvis*, a basin.] *Anat.* the bony cavity of the body constituting a framework for the lower part of the abdomen.—**Pelvic**, pel'vik, *a.* Pertaining to the pelvis.

Pemmican, pem'i-kan, *n.* [North Amer. Indian.] A North American Indian preparation consisting of the lean of venison dried, pounded into a paste, and pressed into cakes so that it will keep long; beef dried and similarly preserved.

Pemphigus, pem'fi-gus, *n.* [Gr. *pemphix*, *pemphigos*, a bubble.] A disease of the skin, consisting in an eruption of vesicles or pustules.

Pen, pen, *n.* [O.Fr. *penne*, a pen, a feather, from L. *penna*, a feather, for *pesna*, from root seen in Gr. *petomai*, to fly, and in E. *feather*. FEATHER.] A quill or large feather‡; an instrument used for writing by means of a fluid ink; formerly almost always made of the quill of some large bird, but now commonly of metal; a writer; a penman; style or quality of writing; the internal bone of some cuttle-fishes.—*v.t.*—*penned*, *penning.* To write; to compose and commit to paper.—**Pen-and-ink**, *a.* Literary; done with a pen and ink, as a drawing or sketch.—**Pen-case**, *n.* A case or holder for a pen.—**Pen-holder**, *n.* The stalk and attached appliance for holding pen-nibs. — **Penknife**, pen'nīf, *n.* A small pocket-knife, so called from its former use in making and mending quill-pens.—**Penman**, pen'man, *n.* pl. **Penmen**, pen'men. A calligrapher; an author; a writer.—**Penmanship**, pen'man-ship, *n.* The use of the pen; the art of writing; manner of writing.

Pen, pen, *v.t.*—*penned* or *pent*, *penning.* [Lit. to fasten with a *pin*; O.E. *pinne*, to bolt; A.Sax. *onpinnian*, to bolt in; L.G. *pinnen*, *pennen*, to shut, to bolt.] To shut in a small inclosure; to coop up; to encage. —*n.* A small inclosure, as for cows, sheep, fowls, &c.; a fold; a coop.

Penal, pē'nal, *a.* [Fr. *pénal*, from L. *pœnālis*, from *pœna*, pain, punishment. PAIN.] Pertaining to punishment; enacting punishment; inflicting punishment; incurring or entailing punishment.—*Penal code*, a code of laws relating to the punishment of crimes.—*Penal law*, a law prohibiting an act and imposing a penalty for commission of it.—*Penal servitude*, a punishment consisting in imprisonment, often with hard labor at some special establishment.—**Penalize**, pē'nal-iz, *v.t.* To make penal or subject to a penalty.—**Penally**, pē'nal-li, *adv.* In a penal manner.—**Penalty**, pen'al-ti, *n.* The punishment annexed to the commission of a crime, offense, or trespass; the suffering to which a person subjects himself by agreement, in case of non-fulfilment of stipulations; the sum forfeited for breaking an agreement.

Penance, pen'ans, *n.* [O.Fr. *penance*, *peneance*, from L. *pœnitentia*, repentance, from *pœnitens*, penitent; it is a doublet of *penitence*. PAIN.] An ecclesiastical punishment imposed for sin; the suffering to which a person subjects himself as an expression of repentance; a sacrament of the R. C. Church for remission of sin.

Penannular, pen-an'nū-lėr, *a.* [L. *pene*, almost, and *annulus*, a ring.] Nearly annular; having nearly the form of a ring.

Penates, pē-nā'tēz, *n.pl.* [L.] The household gods of the ancient Romans, including the lares.

Pence, pens, *n.* The plural of *penny*.

Penchant, pän-shän, *n.* [Fr., from *pencher*, to incline.] Strong inclination; decided taste; liking; bias.

Pencil, pen'sil, *n.* [O.Fr. *pincel*, a hair pencil, a brush; from L. *penicillus*, dim. of *penis*, a tail.] A small delicate brush used by painters for laying on their pigments; an instrument for marking, drawing, or writing, formed of graphite, coloured chalk, or the like; often a lead-pencil; *optics*, an aggregate of rays of light which converge to or diverge from the same point.—*v.t.*—*pencilled*, *pencilling.* To write or mark with a pencil. — **Pencilled**, pen'sild, *p.* and *a.* Painted, drawn, or marked with a pencil; delicately marked.

Pend, pend, *n.* [Scottish.] Alley, wynd, lane, or close.

Pendant, pen'dant, *n.* [Fr. *pendant*, hanging, what hangs, a counterpart, from *pendre*, L. *pendere*, to hang, which, with the allied *pendēre*, to weigh, appears in *pensile*, *pendulum*, *depend*, *impend*, *expend*, *compensation*, *compendium*, &c.] Anything hanging down by way of ornament, but particularly from the neck; *naut.* a flag borne at the mast-head of certain ships, of two kinds—the *long pendant*, and the *broad pendant*; an apparatus hanging from a roof or ceiling for giving light by gas; one of a pair of companion pictures, statues, &c.; an appendix or addition; *arch.* a hanging ornament used in the vaults and timber roofs of Gothic architecture. —**Pendency**, pen'den-si, *n.* State of being pendent or suspended; the state of being continued as not yet decided.—**Pendent**, pen'dent, *a.* [L. *pendens*, *pendentis*, hanging, ppr. of *pendere*, to hang.] Hanging; suspended; depending; overhanging; projecting.—*n.* Something pendent or hanging. —**Pendentive**, pen-den'tiv, *n.* [Fr. *pendentif.*] *Arch.* the part of a groined ceiling springing from one pillar or impost.—**Pendently**, pen'dent-li, *adv.* In a pendent or projecting manner.—**Pending**, pen'ding, *p.* and *a.* Depending; remaining undecided; not terminated.—*prep.* [A participle converted into a preposition, like *during.*] For the time of the continuance of; during.

Pendragon, pen-drag'on, *n.* [W. *pen*, a head, and *dragon*, a leader.] A chief leader, a title among the ancient British.

Pendulous, pen'dū-lus, *a.* [L. *pendulus*, from *pendeo*, to hang. PENDANT.] Hanging so as to swing freely; loosely pendent; swinging.—**Pendulousness**, pen'dū-lus-nes, *n.* The state of being pendulous.—**Pendulum**, pen'dū-lum, *n.* [Lit. what hangs down, from L. *pendulus.*] A body so suspended from a fixed point as to swing to and fro by the alternate action of gravity and momentum; the swinging piece in a clock serving as the regulating power, the wheel-work being attached to register the number of vibrations, and the weight or spring serving to counteract the effects of friction and resistance of the air.—*Compensation pendulum.* COMPENSATION.

Peneplain, pē'ni-plān, *n.* [L. *pæne*, almost.] A denuded area approximating to a plain.

Penetrate, pen'e-trāt, *v.t.* — *penetrated, penetrating.* [L. *penetro, penetratum*, to penetrate; root *pen*, denoting internality, and *tra*, to go.] To enter or pierce; to make way into the interior of; to pass into or affect the mind of; to touch; to pierce into by the intellect; to arrive at the inner meaning of; to understand.—*v.i.* To enter into or pierce anything; to pass or make way in.—**Penetrating**, pen'e-trāt-ing, *p.* and *a.* Having the power of entering or piercing; sharp; acute; discerning.—**Penetratingly**, pen'e-trāt-ing-li, *adv.* In a penetrating manner.—**Penetration**, pen-e-trā'shon, *n.* The act of penetrating; a seeing into something obscure or difficult; discernment; mental acuteness. —**Penetrative**, pen'e-trā-tiv, *a.* Sharp; subtle; acute; discerning. —**Penetrativeness**, pen'e-trā-tiv-nes, *n.*—**Penetrable**, pen'e-tra-bl, *a.* [L. *penetrabilis.*] Capable of being penetrated, entered, or pierced by another body; susceptible of moral or intellectual impression. —**Penetrableness, Penetrability**, pen'e-tra-bl-nes, pen'e-tra-bil"i-ti, *n.* State of being penetrable.—**Penetrably**, pen'e-tra-bli, *adv.* In a penetrable manner; so as to be penetrable. **Penetralia**, pen'e-trā"li-a, *n.pl.* [L., from *penetralis*, internal.] The inner parts of a building, as of a temple or palace; a sanctuary; hidden things.—**Penetrance, Penetrancy**, pen'e-trans, pen'e-tran-si, *n.* The quality of being penetrant.—**Penetrant**, pen'e-trant, *a.* Having the power to penetrate or pierce.

Penfold, pen'fōld, *n.* PINFOLD.

Penguin, pen'gwin, *n.* [From prov. E. *penwing* or *pinwing* (the wing bearing the *pens* or quills), the outer joint of the wing of a fowl, so that the name would mean a bird with a wing like this, or a wing that has the quills plucked out.] A name of swimming birds allied to the auks and guillemots, having rudimentary wings useless for flight, but effective in swimming.—**Penguinery**, pen-gwin'ėr-i, *n.* A colony of penguins.

Penicil, pen'i-sil, *n.* [L. *penicillus*, a pencil or small brush. PENCIL.] A tent or pledget for wounds or ulcers.—**Penicillate, Penicillated**, pen-i-sil'āt, pen-i-sil'ā-ted, *a. Bot.* consisting of a bundle of short, compact fibres or hairs; *zool.* supporting bundles of diverging hairs.

Peninsula, pe-nin'sū-la, *n.* [L., from *pene*, almost, and *insula*, an island.] A portion of land almost surrounded by water, and connected with the mainland by an isthmus. —*The Peninsula*, Spain and Portugal together. — **Peninsular**, pe-nin'sū-lėr, *a.* In the form of a peninsula; pertaining to a peninsula. — **Peninsulate**, pe-nin'sū-lāt, *v.t.*—*peninsulated, peninsulating.* To form into a peninsula.

Penis, pē'nis, *n.* [L.] The male organ of generation.

Penitence pen'i-tens, *n.* [Fr. *pénitence*, from L. *pœnitentia*, repentance. *Penance* is the same word. PENAL.] Sorrow for the commission of sin or offences; repentance; contrition.—**Penitency**, pen'i-ten-si, *n.* Penitence.—**Penitent**, pen'i-tent, *a.* [L. *pœnitens*, repentant.] Suffering sorrow of heart on account of sins or offences; contrite; sorry for wrong-doing and resolved on amendment.—*n.* One who is penitent; one under church censure, but admitted to penance.—**Penitential**, pen-i-ten'shal, *a.* Pertaining to, proceeding from, or expressing penitence.—*Penitential psalms*, the psalms numbered vi., xxxii., xxxviii., li., cii., cxxx., cxliii. of the authorized version of the Bible. —*n.* In the *R. Cath. Ch.* a book containing the rules which relate to penance.—**Penitentially**, pen-i-ten'shal-li, *adv.* In a penitential manner.—**Penitentiary**, pen-i-ten'sha-ri, *a.* Relating to penance.—*n.* A penitent; an official or office of the Roman Catholic Church connected with the granting of dispensations, &c.; a house of correction in which offenders are confined for punishment and reformation, and compelled to labour. — **Penitently**, pen'i-tent-li, *adv.* In a penitent manner.

Penknife, Penman, &c. Under PEN.

Pennant, pen'ant, *n.* [From *pennon*, but influenced by *pendant.*] A small flag; a pennon; a pendant.

Pennate, Pennated, pen'āt, pen'ā-ted, *a.* [L. *pennatus*, winged, from *penna*, a feather.] *Bot.* same as *Pinnate.*—**Penniform**, pen'i-form, *a.* Having the appearance of the barbs of a feather.—**Pennigerous**, pe-nij'ėr-us, *a.* Bearing feathers or quills.

Pennon, pen'on, *n.* [Fr. *pennon*, from L. *penna*, a feather, a plume. PEN.] A small pointed flag or streamer formerly carried by knights attached to their spear or lance, and generally bearing a badge or device; a pennant. — **Pennoncel, Pennoncelle**, pen'on-sel, *n.* A small pennon.

Penny, pen'i, *n.* pl. **Pennies** or **Pence**, pen'iz, pens. *Pennies* denotes the number of coins; *pence* the amount in value. [A. Sax. *penig, pening, pending* = D. *penning*, Dan. *penge*, Icel. *penningr*, O.H.G. *pfenting*, G. *pfennig*; perhaps of same origin as *pawn*, a pledge. PAWN.] A British coin, bronze, worth about two cents in U. S. money, twelve make a shilling; a cent in U. S. money, *Colloq.* Any small sum of money, as, to make an honest *penny.*—**Penniless**, pen'i-les, *a.* Moneyless; destitute of money; poor.—**Pennilessness**, pen'i-les-nes, *n.* The state of being penniless.—**Penny-a-liner**, *n.* A person who furnishes matter for public journals at a penny a line, or some such small price; any poor writer for hire.—**Penny-dog**, *n.* A kind of small shark or dog-fish.—**Pennyroyal**, pen'i-roi-al, *n.* An aromatic plant of the mint family.—**Pennyweight**, pen'i-wāt, *n.* A troy weight containing 24 grains—anciently the weight of a silver penny.—**Penny-wise**, *a.* Saving small sums at the hazard of larger; niggardly on unimportant occasions: generally in the phrase '*penny-wise* and pound-foolish'.—**Pennyworth**, pen'i-wėrth, *n.* As much as is bought for a penny; a purchase; a bargain.

Penology, pē-nol'o-ji, *n.* [Gr. *poinē*, punishment, and *logos*, discourse.] The science which treats of public punishments.

Pensile, pen'sil, *a.* [L. *pensilis*, from *pendeo*, to hang. PENDANT.] Hanging; suspended; pendulous.

Pension, pen'shon, *n.* [Fr. *pension*, from L. *pensio, pensionis*, a paying, from *pendo, pensum*, to weigh, to pay (whence *expend*, &c.). PENDANT.] A stated allowance to a person in consideration of past services; a yearly sum granted by government to retired public officers, to soldiers or sailors who have served a certain number of years or have been wounded, or others; a boarding-house or boarding-school on the Continent (in this sense pronounced päṅ-sē-oṅ, being French.)—*Old Age Pension.* A regular payment made by a government or institution to persons who have attained a certain age, usually 65 or over.—*v.t.* To grant a pension to.—**Pensionary**, pen'shon-a-ri, *a.* Receiving a pension; consisting in a pension.—*n.* A person who receives a pension; a pensioner.—*The Grand Pensionary of Holland*, the first minister of Holland: title from 1619 to 1794.—**Pensioner**, pen'shon-ėr, *n.* One in receipt of a pension; a dependant on the bounty of another; in the University of Cambridge, England, one who pays for his commons out of his own income, the same as a commoner at Oxford.

Pensive, pen'siv, *a.* [Fr. *pensif*, from *penser*, to think or reflect, from L. *pensare*, to weigh, to consider, a freq. from *pendo, pensum*, to weigh. PENDANT.] Thoughtful; employed in serious thought or reflection; thoughtful and somewhat melancholy; expressing thoughtfulness with sadness. —**Pensively**, pen'siv-li, *adv.* In a pensive manner. — **Pensiveness**, pen'siv-nes, *n.* The state or quality of being pensive.

Penstock, pen'stok, *n.* [*Pen*, an inclosure, and *stock.*] A trough, tube, or conduit of boards for conducting water; a sluice above a water-wheel.

Pent, pent, pp. of *pen.* Penned or shut up; closely confined.

Pentachord, pen'ta-kord, *n.* [Gr. *pente*, five, and *chordē*, a string.] An ancient Greek instrument of music with five strings.

Pentacle, pen'ta-kl, *n.* [L.L. *pentaculum*, from Gr. *pente*, five.] A figure consisting of five straight lines so joined and intersecting as to form a five-pointed star: formerly a mystic sign in astrology or necromancy.

Pentacoccous, pen-ta-kok'us, *a.* [Gr. *pente*, five, and L. *coccus*, a berry.] *Bot.* having or containing five grains or seeds.

Pentacrinite, pen-tak'ri-nīt, *n.* [Gr. *pente*, five, *krinon*, a lily.] A five-armed fossil encrinite.

Pentad, pent'ad, *n.* [Gr. *pente*, five.] An aggregate of five; a period of five years.

Pentadactylous, pen-ta-dak'ti-lus, *a.* [Gr. *pente*, five, and *daktylos*, a finger or toe.] Having five fingers or toes.

Pentadelphous, pen-ta-del'fus, *a.* [Gr. *pente*, five, and *adelphos*, brother.] *Bot.* having the filaments or stamens arranged in groups or divisions of five.

Pentaglot, pen'ta-glot, *n.* [Gr. *pente*, five, and *glōtta*, a tongue.] A work in five different languages.

Pentagon, pen'ta-gon, *n.* [Gr. *pente*, five, and *gōnia*, an angle.] *Geom.* a figure of five sides and five angles; if the sides and angles be equal it is a *regular* pentagon; otherwise, *irregular*; *fort.* a fort with five bastions.—**Pentagonal**, pen-tag'on-al, *a.* Having five corners or angles.—**Pentagonally**, pen-tag'on-al-li, *adv.* With five angles.

Pentagram, pen'ta-gram, *n.* [Gr. *pente*, five, and *grammē*, a line.] A pentacle.

Pentagyn, pen'ta-jin, *n.* [Gr. *pente*, five, and *gynē*, a female.] *Bot.* a plant having five styles.—**Pentagynian, Pentagynous**, pen-ta-jin'i-an, pen-taj'i-nus, *a. Bot.* having five styles.

Pentahedron, pen-ta-hē'dron, *n.* [Gr. *pente*, five, and *hedra*, a side or base.] A solid having five equal sides.—**Pentahedral**, pen-ta-hē'dral, *a.* Having five equal sides.

Pentamerous, pen-tam'ėr-us, *a.* [Gr. *pente*, five, and *meros*, a part.] Having or divided into five parts; *zool.* having five joints to the tarsus of each leg, a term applied to a family (Pentamera) of beetles. —**Pentameran**, pen-tam'ėr-an, *n.* A pentamerous beetle.

Pentameter, pen-tam'et-ėr, *n.* [Gr. *pente*, five, and *metron*, measure.] *Pros.* a verse of five feet, belonging more especially to Greek and Latin poetry, the two first feet being either dactyls or spondees; the Greek line whose first two feet may consist of either a dactyl or a spondee, followed by a cæsura, and followed in turn by two dactyls closed by a second cæsura.—*a.* Having five metrical feet.

Pentander, pen-tan'dėr, *n.* [Gr. *pente*, five, and *anēr*, a man or male.] A hermaphrodite plant having five stamens with distinct filaments not connected with the pistil. — **Pentandrous**, pen-tan'drus, *a. Bot.* having five stamens with distinct filaments not connected with the pistil.

Pentane, pent'ān, *n.* [Gr. *pente*, five.] Paraffin hydrocarbon occurring as a colourless fluid in petroleum and other oils.

Pentangular, pen-tang'gū-lėr, *a.* [Gr. *pente*, five, and E. *angular*.] Having five angles.

Pentapetalous, pen-ta-pet'a-lus, *a.* [Gr. *pente*, five, and *petalon*, a petal.] *Bot.* having five petals.

Pentaphyllous, pen-taf'i-lus, *a.* [Gr. *pente*, five, *phyllon*, a leaf.] *Bot.* having five leaves.

Pentarchy, pen'tär-ki, *n.* [Gr. *pente*, five, *archē*, rule.] A government in the hands of five persons.

Pentasepalous, pen-ta-sēp'a-lus, *a.* [Gr. *pente*, five, and E. *sepal*.] *Bot.* having five sepals.

Pentaspermous, pen-ta-spėr'mus, *a.* [Gr. *pente*, five, *sperma*, a seed.] *Bot.* containing five seeds.

Pentastich, pen'ta-stik, *n.* [Gr. *pente*, five, and *stichos*, a verse.] A composition consisting of five verses.

Pentastyle, pen'ta-stīl, *n.* and *a.* [Gr. *pente*, five, and *stylos*, a column.] *Arch.* applied to an edifice having five columns in front.

Pentateuch, pen'ta-tūk, *n.* [Gr. *pente*, five, and *teuchos*, a book.] A collective term for the first five books of the Old Testament.—**Pentateuchal**, pen-ta-tū'-kal, *a.* Relating to the Pentateuch.

Pentecost, pen'tē-kost, *n.* [Gr. *pentēkoste* (*hēmera*), the fiftieth (day), from *pentēkonta*, fifty, from *pente*, five.] A solemn festival of the Jews, so called because celebrated on the fiftieth day after the passover; Whitsuntide, which is fifty days after Easter.—**Pentecostal**, pen-tē-kos'-tal, *a.* Pertaining to Pentecost.

Pentegraph, pen'tē-graf, *n.* PANTOGRAPH.

Penthouse, pent'hous, *n.* [Formerly *pentice*, from Fr. *appentis*, a penthouse.—L. *ad*, to, and *pendeo*, to hang. PENDANT.] A roof sloping up against a wall; a shed standing aslope from a building; a dwelling or apartment situated on the roof of a larger building.

Pentile, pen'tīl, *n.* PANTILE.

Pent-roof, *n.* [From *pent* in *penthouse*.] A roof formed like an inclined plane, the slope being all on one side.

Penult, Penultima, pē'nult, pē-nul'-ti-ma, *n.* [L. *penultimus—pene*, almost, and *ultimus*, last.] The last syllable of a word except one. — **Penultimate**, pē-nul'ti-māt, *a.* The last but one.—*n.* The last syllable but one of a word.

Penumbra, pē-num'bra, *n.* [L. *pene*, almost, and *umbra*, shade.] The partial shadow outside of the total shadow caused by an opaque body intercepting the light from a luminous body, as in eclipses; *painting*, the boundary of shade and light, where the one blends with the other.—**Penumbral**, pē-num'bral, *a.* Pertaining to a penumbra.

Penury, pen'ū-ri, *n.* [Fr. *pénurie*, L. *penuria*, akin to Gr. *penia*, poverty.] Want of pecuniary means; indigence; extreme poverty.—**Penurious**, pē-nū'ri-us, *a.* Pertaining to penury; niggardly; parsimonious; sordid.—**Penuriously**, pē-nū'ri-us-li, *adv.* In a penurious manner.—**Penuriousness**, pē-nū'ri-us-nes, *n.* The quality of being penurious.

Peon, pē'on, *n.* [Sp. *peon*, a foot-soldier, a day-labourer, from L. *pes*, *pedis*, the foot. PAWN (at chess), PEDAL.] In Hindustan, a foot-soldier; a native constable; in Spanish America, a day-labourer; a farmer of Spanish descent; a kind of serf.—**Peonage**, **Peonism**, pē'on-āj, pē'on-izm, *n.* The state or condition of a peon.

Peony, pē'ō-ni, *n.* [L. *pæonia*, from Gr. *paiōnia*, from *Paiōn*, Apollo, who used this flower to cure the wounds of the gods.] A ranunculaceous genus of plants cultivated in gardens for their large gaudy flowers.

People, pē'pl, *n.* [O.E. *peple*, *puple*, &c., O.Fr. *pople*, *pueple*, Fr. *peuple*, from L. *populus*, people. POPULAR.] The body of persons who compose a community, race, or nation; a community; a body social (in this sense it admits the plural *peoples*); persons indefinitely; men (*people* may say what they please); with possessives, those who are closely connected with a person, as attendants, domestics, relatives, &c.—*The people*, the commonalty, as distinct from men of rank; the populace.—*v.t.*—*peopled*, *peopling*. To stock with people or inhabitants; to populate.

Peperine, Peperino, pep'e-rin, pep-e-rē'nō, *n.* [It. *peperino*, from L. *piper*, pepper.] A light porous species of volcanic rock.

Peplus, pep'lus, *n.* [Gr. *peplos*.] A large full upper robe anciently worn by Greek women.

Pepo, pē'pō, *n.* [L., a melon.] Any fruit of the type of the melon or gourd.

Pepper, pep'ėr, *n.* [A.Sax. *pipor*, *peppor*, from L. *piper*, Gr. *piperi*, *peperi*: a word of Oriental origin.] A plant and its fruit, which latter has an aromatic, extremely hot, pungent taste, and is used in seasoning, &c. — *Jamaica pepper*. PIMENTO.—*Guinea pepper*, *Cayenne pepper*, the produce of different species of capsicum.—*v.t.* To sprinkle with pepper; to pelt with shot or missiles; to cover with numerous sores; to drub thoroughly.—**Pepper-and-salt**, *a.* Of a light ground colour (as white, drab, gray, &c.) dotted with black, brown, or like dark colour.—**Pepper-box**, *n.* A small box with a perforated lid, for sprinkling pepper on food.—**Peppercorn**, pep'-ėr-korn, *n.* The berry or fruit of the pepper plant; hence, an insignificant quantity: something of inconsiderable value. — *Peppercorn rent*, a nominal rent.—**Peppermint**, pep'ėr-mint, *n.* A plant of the mint genus having a strong pungent taste, glowing like pepper, and followed by a sense of coolness; a liqueur prepared from the plant; a lozenge of sugar flavoured with peppermint.—**Pepper-pot**, *n.* A West Indian dish, the principal ingredient of which is cassareep, with flesh or dried fish and vegetables; a pepper-box; a kind of capsicum.—**Peppery**, pep'ėr-i, *a.* Having the qualities of pepper; choleric; irritable.

Pepperidge, pep'ėr-ij, *n.* PIPERIDGE.

Pepsin, Pepsine, pep'sin, *n.* [Gr. *pepsis*, digestion, from *peptō*, to digest.] A peculiar animal principle secreted by the stomach, the active principle of gastric juice.—**Peptic**, pep'tik, *a.* Promoting digestion, relating to digestion; digestive. — *n.* A medicine which promotes digestion.—**Peptics**, pep'tiks, *n.* The doctrine of digestion; as a plural, the digestive organs.—**Pepticity**, pep-tis'i-ti, *n.* The state of being peptic; good digestion.—**Peptone**, pep'-tōn, *n.* The substance into which the nitrogenous elements of the food are converted by the action of the gastric juice.

Per, pėr. A Latin preposition, denoting through, by, by means of, &c., occurring as a prefix in many English words, and also used separately in certain phrases.—*Per annum*, by the year; in each year; annually. So *per diem*, by the day, each day.—*Per centum*, by the hundred; commonly abbreviated to *per cent.*—**Percentage**, pėr-sen'tāj, *n.* The allowance, duty, rate of interest, or commission on a hundred.

Peradventure, pėr-ad-ven'tūr, *adv.* [Prefix *per*, by, and *adventure*, Fr. *par aventure*.] Perchance; perhaps; it may be. Sometimes used as a noun = doubt; question.

Perambulate, pėr-am'bū-lāt, *v.t.*—*perambulated*, *perambulating*. [L. *perambulo*—*per*, and *ambulo*, to walk. AMBLE.] To walk through or over; to survey the boundaries of (to *perambulate* a parish).—**Perambulation**, pėr-am'bū-lā"shon, *n.* The act of perambulating; a travelling survey or inspection; a walking through or over ground for the purpose of settling boundaries. — **Perambulator**, pėr-am'bū-lā-tėr, *n.* One who perambulates; a small carriage for a child, propelled from behind.

Perceive, pėr-sēv', *v.t.*—*perceived*, *perceiving*. [Fr. *percevoir*, L. *percipio*, to perceive, to comprehend—*per*, and *capio*, to take. CAPABLE.] To have or obtain knowledge of by the senses; to apprehend or take cognizance of by the organs of sense; to apprehend by the mind; to discern, know, understand. ∴ Syn. under SEE. — **Perceivable**, pėr-sē'va-bl, *a.* Capable of being perceived; perceptible. — **Perceivably**, pėr-sē'va-bli, *adv.* In a perceivable manner.—**Perceiver**, pėr-sē'vėr, *n.* One who perceives.—**Percept**, pėr'sept, *n.* That which is perceived.—**Perceptibility**, pėr-sep'-ti-bil"i-ti, *n.* The state or quality of being perceptible; perception; power of perceiving.—**Perceptible**, pėr-sep'ti-bl, *a.* Capable of being perceived.—**Perceptibly**, pėr-sep'ti-bli, *adv.* In a perceptible manner; so as to be perceived.—**Perception**, pėr-sep'shon, *n.* [L. *perceptio*, *perceptionis*.] The act of perceiving; that act or process of the mind which makes known an external object; the faculty by which man holds communication with the external world or takes cognizance of objects without the mind.—**Perceptive**, pėr-sep'tiv, *a.* Relating to the act or power of perceiving; having the faculty of perceiving.—**Perceptivity**, pėr-sep-tiv'i-ti, *n.* The quality of being perceptive; power of perception.

Percentage. Under PER.

Perch, pėrch, *n.* [Fr. *perche*, L. *perca*, from Gr. *perkē*, the perch, from *perkos*, dark-colored.] The popular name of acanthopterygious fishes, one species of which is found in rivers and lakes throughout the temperate parts of the United States.

Perch, pėrch, *n.* [Fr. *perche*, from L. *pertica*, a pole, a staff.] A measure of length containing 5½ yards; a pole or rod; a roost for birds; anything on which they light; hence, an elevated seat or position. — *v.i.* To sit or roost; to light or settle as a bird. —*v.t.* To place on a perch.—*Perched blocks*, blocks of stone that have been left by ancient glaciers high up on mountains.—**Percher**, pėrch'ėr, *n.* One that perches; a bird belonging to the order of insessores.

Perchance, pėr-chans', *adv.* [L. *per*, by, and E. *chance*.] Perhaps; peradventure.

Perchloric, pėr-klō'rik, *a.* Applied to an acid forming a syrupy liquid very explosive.—**Perchlorate**, pėr-klō'rāt, *n.* A salt of perchloric acid.

Percipient, pėr-sip'i-ent, *a.* [L. *percipiens*, ppr. of *percipio*. PERCEIVE.] Perceiving; having the faculty of perception.—*n.* One who perceives.—**Percipience, Percipiency**, pėr-sip'i-ens, pėr-sip'i-en-si, *n.* Act or power of perceiving; perception.

Perclose, pėr-klōz, *n.* [O.Fr. *perclose*.] PARCLOSE.

Percoid, pėr'koid, *a.* [Gr. *perkē*, perch, and *eidos*, form.] Resembling the perch; belonging to the perch family.

Percolate, pėr'kō-lāt, *v.t.*—*percolated*, *percolating*. [L. *percolo*—*per*, and *colo*, to strain, from *colum*, a sieve (whence *colander*).] To strain or filter.—*v.i.* To pass through small interstices or pores; to filter.—**Percolator**, pėr'kō-lā-tėr, *n.* One who or that which filters.—A kind of coffeepot in which boiling water is forced upward and filters down through the coffee.

Percurrent, pėr-kur'ent, *a.* [L. *per*, through, and *currens*, running.] Running through from top to bottom.

Percuss,† pėr-kus', *v.t.* [L. *percussus*, from *percutio*, *percussum* — *per*, through, and *quatio*, to strike (as in *concuss*). QUASH.] To strike against; to give a shock to.—**Percussion**, pėr-kush'on, *n.* [L. *percussio*.] The act of striking one body against another with some violence; forcible collision; the shock produced by the collision of bodies; the impression or effect of sound on the ear; *med.* the method of eliciting sounds by striking the surface of the body, for the purpose of determining the condition of the organs subjacent (as the lungs or heart).—**Percussion-cap**, *n.* A small copper cap or cup containing fulminating powder, used in a percussion-lock to explode gunpowder. — **Percussion-fuse**, *n.* A fuse in a projectile set in action by concussion when the projectile strikes the object. **Percussion-gun**, *n.* A gun discharged by a percussion-lock.—**Percussion-lock**, *n.* A lock for a gun, causing the ignition of the charge by the impact of a hammer or striker. — **Percussive**, pėr-kus'iv, *a.* Acting by percussion; striking against.—**Percutient**, pėr-kū'shi-ent, *n.* [L. *percutiens.*] That which strikes.

Perdition, pėr-dish'on, *n.* [L.L. *perditio*, from L. *perdo*, *perditus*, to destroy, to ruin —*per*, thoroughly, and *do*, a verb cog. with E. *do.*] Entire ruin; utter destruction; loss of final happiness in a future state; future misery or eternal death.

Perdu, Perdue, pėr'dū or per-dū', *a.* [Fr. *perdu*, lost, from *perdre*, to lose, L. *perdo.*] Hid; in concealment: generally in the phrase *to lie* or *to be perdu.*—**Perdus**, per'-dūs, *n.pl.* Soldiers sent to occupy a difficult post, regarded already as practically lost or destroyed men. (*Shak.*)

Perdurable, pėr'dū-ra-bl, *a.* [Fr., from L. *perduro*—*per*, intens., and *duro*, to last. DURABLE.] Very durable; lasting; continuing long. — **Perdurably**, pėr'dū-ra-bli, *adv.* In a perdurable manner; lastingly. —**Perduration, Perdurance**, pėr-dū-rā'shon, pėr-dū'rans, *n.* Long continuance. —**Perdure**, pėr-dūr', *v.i.* To endure or continue long.

Peregrinate, per'e-gri-nāt, *v.i.*—*peregrinated*, *peregrinating*. [L. *peregrinor*, from *peregrinus*, a traveller or stranger — *per*, through, and *ager*, land. PILGRIM.] To travel from place to place; to wander.—**Peregrination**, per'e-gri-nā"shon, *n.* A travelling, roaming, or wandering about; a journey. — **Peregrinator**, per'e-gri-nā-tėr, *n.* A traveller.—**Peregrine**, per'e-grin, *a.* [L. *peregrinus.*] Foreign; not native. — *Peregrine falcon*, a handsome species of European falcon.—*n.* A peregrine falcon.—**Peregrinity**,† per-e-grin'i-ti, *n.* Strangeness; foreignness.

Peremptory, per'emp-to-ri, *a.* [L. *peremptorius*, from *perimo*, *peremptus*, to destroy —*per*, thoroughly, and *emo*, to take, to buy (seen also in *exempt*, *example*, *prompt*).] Precluding debate or expostulation; decisive; authoritative; fully resolved; determined; positive in opinion or judgment; dogmatical; *law*, final; determinate. — **Peremptorily**, per'emp-to-ri-li, *adv.* In a peremptory manner. — **Peremptoriness**, per'emp-to-ri-nes, *n.*

Perennial, per-en'i-al, *a.* [L. *perennis*—*per*, through, and *annus*, a year.] Lasting or continuing without cessation through the year; continuing without stop or intermission; unceasing; never-failing; *bot.* continuing more than two years (a *perennial* stem or root).—*n.* A plant whose root remains alive more years than two, but whose stems flower and perish annually.—**Perennially**, per-en'i-al-li, *adv.* Continually; without ceasing. — **Perennibranchiate**, per-en'i-brang"ki-āt, *a.* Having the branchiæ or gills permanent, as certain amphibians. — *n.* An amphibian having permanent branchiæ.

Perfect, pėr'fekt, *a.* [L. *perfectus*, pp. of *perficio*, to complete or finish — *per*, thoroughly, and *facio*, to do. FACT.] Brought to a consummation or completion; having received and possessing all its parts; finished; completed; of the best, highest, or completest type; without blemish or defect; faultless; completely skilled (*perfect* in discipline). — *Perfect gas*, a theoretical gas which satisfies several conditions, and follows exactly the law of Boyle, that the volume varies inversely as the pressure when the temperature is constant. Actual gases at best only approximate to this perfectness.—*Perfect tense*, *gram.* a tense which expresses an act completed.—*v.t.* To finish or complete so as to leave nothing wanting; to make perfect; to instruct fully; to make fully skilful (often *refl.*).—**Perfectation**, pėr-fek-tā'shon, *n.* A bringing to perfection. —**Perfecter**, pėr'fek-tėr, *n.* One that makes perfect.—**Perfectibility**, pėr-fek'-ti-bil"i-ti, *n.* The quality of being perfectible; the capacity of becoming or being made morally perfect.—**Perfectible**, pėr-fek'ti-bl, *a.* Capable of becoming or being made perfect.—**Perfecting-press**, *n.* A press in which the paper is printed on both sides during one passage through the machine. — **Perfection**, pėr-fek'shon, *n.* [L. *perfectio*, *perfectionis.*] The state of being perfect or complete; supreme degree of moral or other excellence; a quality of the highest worth. — **Perfectionism**, pėr-fek'shon-izm, *n.* The doctrine of the Perfectionists.—**Perfectionist**, pėr-fek'-shon-ist, *n.* One who believes that some persons actually attain to moral perfection in the present life; one of an American sect of Christians founded on socialist principles.—**Perfective**, pėr-fek'tiv, *a.* Conducing to bring to perfection.—**Perfectively**, pėr-fek'tiv-li, *adv.* In a perfective manner.—**Perfectly**, pėr'fekt-li, *adv.* In a perfect manner; so as to reach perfection; completely; totally; thoroughly. — **Perfectness**, pėr'fekt-nes, *n.* The state or quality of being perfect.

Perfervid, pėr-fėr'vid, *a.* [L. *perfervidus* —*per*, intens., and *fervidus*, fervid.] Very fervid; very hot or ardent.

Perfidy, pėr'fi-di, *n.* [L. *perfidia*, from *perfidus*, faithless—prefix *per*, and *fidus*, faithful; *per* having the same force as in *perjure*, *pervert*. FAITH.] The act of violating faith or allegiance; breach of faith; treachery; faithlessness. — **Perfidious**, pėr-fid'i-us, *a.* Guilty of or involving perfidy or treachery; treacherous; consisting in breach of faith; traitorous.—**Perfidiously**, pėr-fid'i-us-li, *adv.* In a perfidious manner.—**Perfidiousness**, pėr-fid'i-us-nes, *n.* The quality of being perfidious.

Perfoliate, pėr-fō'li-āt, *a.* [L. *per*, through, and *folium*, a leaf.] *Bot.* applied to a leaf that has the base surrounding the stem, as if the stem ran through it.

Perforate, pėr'fo-rāt, *v.t.*—*perforated*, *perforating*. [L. *perforo*, *perforatus* — prefix *per*, through, and *foro*, to bore. BORE.] To bore through; to pierce with a pointed instrument; to make a hole or holes through by boring. — **Perforate, Perforated**, pėr'fo-rāt, pėr'fo-rā-ted, *a.* Bored or pierced through. — **Perforation**, pėr-fo-rā'shon, *n.* The act of perforating, boring, or piercing; a hole bored; a hole passing through anything. — **Perforative**, pėr'fo-rā-tiv, *a.* Having power to perforate or pierce.—**Perforator**, pėr'for-ā-tėr, *n.* One who or that which perforates.

Perforce, pėr-fōrs', *adv.* [Prefix *per*, through, by, and *force.*] By force or compulsion; of necessity.

Perform, pėr-form', *v.t.* [O.E. *parforme*, *parfourne*, from O.Fr. *parfournir*, to perform—prefix *par*, and *fournir*, to accomplish, to furnish. FURNISH.] To do; to execute; to accomplish; to fulfil, act up to, discharge (a duty); to act or represent as on the stage.—*v.i.* To act a part; to play on a musical instrument, represent a character on the stage, or the like.—**Performable**, pėr-for'ma-bl, *a.* Capable of being performed. — **Performance**, pėr-for'mans, *n.* The act of performing or condition of being performed; an action, deed, or thing done; a literary work; a composition; the acting or exhibition of character on the stage; an exhibition of skill and capacity; an entertainment provided at any place of amusement.—**Performer**, pėr-for'mėr, *n.* One who performs; an actor, musician, &c., who exhibits his skill. — **Performing**, pėr-for'ming, *p.* and *a.* Exhibiting performances or tricks (a *performing* dog).

Perfume, pėr'fūm or pėr-fūm', *n.* [Fr. *parfum*, from L. *per*, through, and *fumus*, smoke; lit. smoke or vapour that disseminates itself.] A substance that emits a scent or odour which affects agreeably the organs of smelling; the scent or odour emitted from sweet-smelling substances.—*v.t.* (pėr-fūm')—*perfumed*, *perfuming*. To fill or impregnate with a grateful odour; to scent.—**Perfumatory**, pėr-fū'ma-to-ri, *a.* Yielding perfume; perfuming.—**Perfumer**, pėr-fūm'ėr, *n.* One who perfumes; one whose trade is to sell perfumes.—**Perfumery**, pėr-fūm'ėr-i, *n.* Perfumes collectively; the art of preparing perfumes.

Perfunctory, pėr-fungk'to-ri, *a.* [L.L. *perfunctorius*—L. *per*, and *fungor*, *functus*, to perform, execute. FUNCTION.] Done in a half-hearted or careless manner, and merely for the sake of getting rid of the duty; careless, slight, or not thorough; negligent. — **Perfunctorily**, pėr-fungk'-to-ri-li, *adv.* In a perfunctory manner.—**Perfunctoriness**, pėr-fungk'to-ri-nes, *n.*

Pergameneous, Pergamentaceous, per-ga-mē'nē-us, pėr'ga-men-tā"shus, *a.* [L. *pergamena*, parchment. PARCHMENT.] Resembling parchment.

Pergola, per'go-la, *n.* [It.] A kind of arbour or bower on which plants may grow.

Pergunnah, per-gun'ä, *n.* In Hindustan, a district comprising a number of villages.

Perhaps, pėr-haps', *adv.* [L. *per*, by (as in *perchance*), and E. *hap.*] Peradventure; perchance; it may be; possibly.

Peri, pē'ri, *n.* [Per. *pari*, a fairy.] *Per. myth.* a sort of spiritual being or fairy, represented as a descendant of fallen angels, excluded from paradise till the accomplishment of a task imposed as a penance.

Periagua, per-i-ä'gwa, *n.* A sort of canoe; a pirogue.

Perianth, per'i-anth, *n.* [Gr. *peri*, about, and *anthos*, a flower.] *Bot.* a term for the floral envelope when the calyx and corolla are so combined that they cannot be satisfactorily distinguished from each other.

Periapt, per'i-apt, *n.* [Gr. *periapton*, *peri*, around, *haptō*, to fasten.] An armlet or necklet worn as a charm. (*Shak.*)

Periastral, per-i-as'tral, *a.* [Gr. *peri*, about, and *astron*, a star.] About or among the stars.

Periblem, per'i-blem, *n.* [Gr. *peri*, around, *blēma*, a coverlet.] *Bot.* embryonic tissue at a growing point from which cortex develops.

Pericardium, per-i-kär'di-um, *n.* [Gr. *perikardion*—*peri*, around, and *kardia*, the heart.] The membranous sac that incloses the heart.—**Pericardial, Pericardian, Pericardic, Pericardiac**, per-i-kär'di-al, per-i-kär'di-an, per-i-kär'dik, per-i-kär'di-ak, *a.* Relating to the pericardium. —**Pericarditis**, per'i-kär-dī"tis, *n.* [Term. *-itis*, signifying inflammation.] Inflammation of the pericardium.

Pericarp, per'i-kärp, *n.* [Gr. *peri*, about, and *karpos*, fruit.] The seed-vessel of a plant, or the shell of the seed-vessel; the part inclosing the seed. — **Pericarpial, Pericarpic**, per-i-kär'pi-al, per-i-kär'pik, *a.* Belonging to a pericarp.

Perichætium, per-i-kē'shi-um, *n.* [Gr. *peri*, around, and *chaitē*, foliage.] *Bot.* minute leaves round the stalk of the sporangium of mosses.

Perichondrium, per-i-kon'dri-um, *n.* [Gr. *peri*, around, and *chondros*, cartilage.] *Anat.* a synovial membrane which covers certain cartilages.

Pericladium, per-i-klā'di-um, *n.* [Gr. *peri*, around, and *klados*, a branch.] *Bot.* a petiole forming a sort of sheath.

Periclinal, per-i-klī'nal, *a.* [Gr. *peri*, around, and *klinō*, to bend.] Dipping on all sides from a central point or apex: applied to strata.—**Periclinium**, per-i-klī'-ni-um, *n.* *Bot.* the involucrum of composite plants.

Pericranium, per-i-krā'ni-um, *n.* [Gr. *peri*, about, and *kranion*, the skull.] The membrane that invests the skull.

Periderm, per'i-dėrm, *n.* [Gr. *peri*, around, and *derma*, skin.] A sort of outer layer or skin; *bot.* the outer layer of bark.

Peridot, per'i-dot, *n.* A precious stone of a yellowish-green colour.

Perigastric, per-i-gas'trik, *a.* [Gr. *peri*, around, and *gastēr*, the belly.] Surrounding the belly or stomach. — *Perigastric space*, the visceral cavity in the Polyzoa.

Perigee, per'i-jē, *n.* [Gr. *peri*, about, and *gē*, the earth.] That point of the moon's orbit which is nearest to the earth; formerly also this point in the orbit of any heavenly body. APOGEE. — **Perigean**, per-i-jē'an, *a.* Pertaining to the perigee.

Perigone, Perigonium, per-i-gōn, per-i-gō'ni-um, *n.* [Gr. *peri*, and *gonē*, generation.] *Bot.* a perianth, especially one that is herbaceous or not coloured.

Perigynous, pe-rij'i-nus, *a.* [Gr. *peri*, around, and *gynē*, a female.] *Bot.* having the ovary free, but the petals and stamens borne on the calyx.

Perihelion, per-i-hē'li-on, *n.* [Gr. *peri*, about, and *hēlios*, the sun.] That part of the orbit of a planet or comet in which it is at its least distance from the sun: opposed to *aphelion*.

Peril, per'il, *n.* [Fr. *péril*, from L. *periculum*, danger, from root seen in *perior*, *experior*, to try (whence *experiment*); same ultimate root as E. *fare*, *ferry*.] Danger; risk; hazard; jeopardy; exposure of person or property to injury, loss, or destruction. —*v.t.*—*perilled*, *perilling*. To hazard; to risk; to expose to danger. — **Perilous**, per'i-lus, *a.* Full of peril; dangerous; hazardous.— **Perilously**, per'i-lus-li, *adv.* In a perilous manner.—**Perilousness**, per'i-lus-nes, *n.*

Perimeter, pe-rim'et-ėr, *n.* [Gr. *peri*, about, and *metron*, measure.] *Geom.* the boundary of a body or figure, or the sum of all the sides.—**Perimetrical**, per-i-met'ri-kal, *a.* Pertaining to the perimeter.

Perimorph, per'i-morf, *n.* [Gr. *peri*, about, and *morphē*, form.] *Mineral.* a mineral or crystal inclosing other minerals or crystals. ENDOMORPH.

Perinæum, Perineum, per-i-nē'um, *n.* [Gr. *perinaion*, *perineon*.] *Anat.* the inferior surface of the trunk of the body, from the anus to the external organ of generation.—**Perineal**, per-i-nē'al, *a.* *Anat.* pertaining to the perinæum.

Period, pē'ri-od, *n.* [L. *periodus*, from Gr. *periodos* — *peri*, about, and *hodos*, way.] Originally a circuit; hence, the time taken up by the revolution of a heavenly body, or the time till it returns to the point of its orbit where it began; any round of time or series of years, days, &c., in which a revolution is completed, and the same course is to be begun; an indefinite portion of any continued state, existence, or series of events (the early *period* of life); the time in which anything is performed; termination or point of completion of any cycle or series of events; end; conclusion; limit; a complete sentence from one full stop to another; the point that marks the end of a complete sentence, or indicates an abbreviation, &c.; a full stop, thus (.).—**Periodic, Periodical**, pē-ri-od'ik, pē-ri-od'i-kal, *a.* Pertaining to a period or to periods; performed in a period or regular revolution; happening or returning regularly in a certain period of time; recurring; published at regular intervals, as a newspaper, magazine, &c. (in this sense *periodical* is the only form).—*Periodical diseases*, those of which the symptoms recur at stated intervals.—*Periodic law*, *chem.* the law determining the classification of elements into groups with comparable characters.—*Periodic system*, a classification of chemical elements according to their atomic weights, whereby they fall into groups having similar characters.—**Periodical**, *n.* A publication which appears in successive numbers at regular intervals, as a newspaper or magazine. — **Periodically**, pē-ri-od'i-kal-li, *adv.* In a periodical manner; at stated periods. — **Periodicity, Periodicalness**, pē'ri-o-dis''i-ti, pē-ri-od'i-kal-nes, *n.* The state or quality of being periodical.

Periœci, per-i-ē'si, *n.pl.* [Gr. *perioikoi*—*peri*, around, and *oikos*, a house.] Such inhabitants of the earth as have the same latitudes, but whose longitudes differ by 180°, so that when it is noon with one it is midnight with the other.

Periosteum, per-i-os'tē-um, *n.* [Gr. *peri*, about, and *osteon*, bone.] *Anat.* a vascular membrane immediately investing the bones of animals, and conducting the vessels by which the bone is nourished.—**Periosteal, Periosteous**, per-i-os'tē-al, per-i-os'tē-us, *a.* Belonging to the periosteum.—**Periostitis, Periosteitis**, per'i-os-tī''tis, per'i-os-tē-ī''tis, *n.* Inflammation of the periosteum.

Periostracum, per-i-os'tra-kum, *n.* [Gr. *peri*, around, and *ostrakon*, a shell.] The membrane which covers the shells of most molluscs.

Peripatetic, Peripatetical, per'i-pa-tet''ik, per'i-pa-tet''i-kal, *a.* [Gr. *peripatetikos*, from *peripateō*, to walk about—*peri*, about, and *pateō*, to walk. Aristotle taught his system of philosophy, and his followers disputed questions, *walking* in the Lyceum at Athens.] Walking about; itinerant; pertaining to Aristotle's system of philosophy; Aristotelian.—**Peripatetic**, *n.* One who walks; one who walks much; a follower of Aristotle.—**Peripateticism**, per'i-pa-tet''i-sizm, *n.* The philosophical system of the peripatetics.

Peripetia, per'i-pe-tī''a, *n.* [Gr. *peripeteia*.] That part of a drama in which the plot is unravelled; the dénouement.

Periphery, pe-rif'ėr-i, *n.* [Gr. *peri*, around, and *pherō*, to bear.] The outside or surface of a body; *geom.* the boundary line of a closed figure; the perimeter; in a circle, the circumference.—**Peripheric, Peripheral, Peripherical**, per-i-fer'ik, pe-rif'ėr-al, per-i-fer'i-kal, *a.* Pertaining to or constituting a periphery.

Periphrasis, pe-rif'ra-sis, *n.* pl. **Periphrases**, pe-rif'ra-sēz. [Gr. *periphrasis*—*peri*, about, and *phrazō*, to speak.] A roundabout phrase or expression; circumlocution; the use of more words than are necessary to express the idea. — **Periphrase**, per'i-frāz, *n.* A periphrasis.—*v.t.* —*periphrased*, *periphrasing*. To express by periphrasis or circumlocution.—*v.i.* To use circumlocution.— **Periphrastic, Periphrastical**, per-i-fras'tik, per-i-fras'ti-kal, *a.* Having the character of or characterized by periphrasis.—**Periphrastically**, per-i-fras'ti-kal-li, *adv.* In a periphrastic manner.

Periplus, per'i-plus, *n.* [Gr. *periplous*—*peri*, about, and *pleō*, to sail.] A circumnavigation or voyage round.

Peripneumonia, Peripneumony, per'ip-nū-mō''ni-a, per-ip-nū'mo-ni, *n.* [Gr. *peri*, about, and *pneumōn*, the lung.] Same as *Pneumonia*.

Peripteral, pe-rip'ter-al, *a.* [Gr. *peripteros*, from *peri*, around, and *pteron*, a wing, a row of columns.] *Greek arch.* surrounded by a single row of insulated columns.—**Peripteros**, pe-rip'ter-os, *n.* A peripteral edifice. — **Periptery**, pe-rip'ter-i, *n.* A surrounding row of columns.

Periscian, pe-rish'i-an, *a.* and *n.* [Gr. *periskios*—*peri*, around, and *skia*, a shadow.] Having the shadow, or one who has the shadow, moving all round in the course of the day: applied to the inhabitants of the polar circles.

Periscope, per'i-skōp, *n.* [Gr. *peri*, round, *skopeō*, to look.] An apparatus or structure rising above the deck of a submarine vessel, giving by means of mirrors, &c., a view of outside surroundings, though the vessel itself remains submerged, and enabling the crew to see how to direct torpedoes. A device of a similar kind is used on land in trenches or elsewhere.—**Periscopic, Periscopical**, per-i-skop'ik, per-i-skop'i-kal, *a.* Viewing on all sides: applied to spectacles having concavo-convex lenses for increasing the distinctness of objects when viewed obliquely; also to a kind of lens in microscopes.

Perish, per'ish, *v.i.* [Fr. *périr*, ppr. *périssant*, to perish, from L. *perio*, to perish—*per*, through, and *eo*, to go. ITINERANT.] To lose life or vitality in any manner; to die; to be destroyed; to pass away, come to nothing, be ruined or lost.—*v.t.* To cause to perish; to destroy.—**Perishable**, per'ish-a-bl, *a.* Liable to perish; subject to decay and destruction.—*Perishable goods*, goods which decay and lose their value if not consumed soon, such as fish, fruit, and the like.—**Perishability, Perishableness**, per'ish-a-bil''i-ti, per'ish-a-bl-nes, *n.* The state of being perishable.

Perisome, per'i-sōm, *n.* [Gr. *peri*, around, and *sōma*, body.] The coriaceous or calcareous integuments of echinoderms.

Perisperm, per'i-spėrm, *n.* [Gr. *peri*, around, and *sperma*, seed.] *Bot.* the part of the seed entirely or partially surrounding the embryo; the albumen; the external skin of a seed.—**Perispermic**, per-i-spėr'mik, *a.* *Bot.* pertaining to the perisperm.

Perispore, per'i-spōr, *n.* [Gr. *peri*, around, and E. *spore*.] *Bot.* the outer covering of a spore.

Perissad, pe-ris'sad, *a.* [Gr. *perissos*, odd, not even.] *Chem.* applied to an element which combines with odd numbers of atoms only.

Perissodactyle, Perissodactylous, pe-ris'ō-dak''til, pe-ris'ō-dak''ti-lus, *a.* [Gr. *perissos*, uneven, and *daktylos*, a finger or toe.] Having feet with toes odd in number; odd-toed: applied to a section of the ungulate or hoofed animals, including the rhinoceros, tapir, horse, &c.

Perissology,† per-is-sol'o-ji, *n.* [Gr. *perissologia*—*perissos*, redundant, *logos*, discourse.] Superfluity of words; macrology.

Peristaltic, per-i-stal'tik, *a.* [Gr. *peristaltikos*, from *peri*, around, and *stellō*, to place.] Contracting all round or in successive circles: applied to the peculiar worm-like motion of the intestines, by which their contents are gradually forced downwards. —**Peristaltically**, per-i-stal'ti-kal-li, *adv.* In a peristaltic manner.

Peristome, per'i-stōm, *n.* [Gr. *peri*, around, and *stoma*, a mouth.] *Bot.* a ring or fringe of bristles or teeth that close up the orifice of the seed-vessel in mosses; *zool.* a term used for the similar parts in sea-urchins, &c.—**Peristomial**, per-i-stō'mi-al, *a.* Pertaining to a peristome.

Peristrephic, per-i-stref'ik, *a.* [Gr. *peri*, around, and *strephō*, to turn.] Turning round; rotatory; revolving.

Peristyle, per'i-stīl, *n.* [Gr. *peri*, about, and *stylos*, a column.] *Arch.* a range of surrounding columns.

Perisystole, per-i-sis'tō-lē, *n.* [Gr. *peri*, about, and *systolē*, contraction.] The pause or interval between the systole or contraction and the dilatation of the heart.

Perithecium, per-i-thē'si-um, *n.* [Gr. *peri*, around, and *thēkē*, a theca or case.] *Bot.* the envelope surrounding the masses of fructification in some fungi and lichens.

Peritomous, pe-rit'ō-mus, *a.* [Gr. *peri*, around, and *temnō*, to cleave.] *Mineral.* cleaving in more directions than one parallel to the axis, the faces being all of one quality.

Peritoneum, Peritonæum, per'i-tō-nē''um, *n.* [Gr. *peritonaion*—*peri*, about, and *teinō*, to stretch.] A thin, smooth, serous membrane investing the whole internal surface of the abdomen, and more or less all the viscera contained in it.—**Peritoneal, Peritonæal**, per'i-tō-nē''al, *a.* Pertaining to the peritoneum. — **Peritonitis**, per'i-tō-nī''tis, *n.* Inflammation of the peritoneum.

Perityphlitis, pe'ri-tif-lī''tis, *n.* [Gr. *peri*, about, and *typhlos*, blind—in allusion to the blind gut or cæcum. Inflammation of the cæcum and surrounding tissues, an ailment akin to appendicitis and often fatal.

Perivisceral, per-i-vis'ėr-al, *a.* [Gr. *peri*, about, and L. *viscera*.] *Anat.* applied to the space surrounding the viscera.

Periwig, per'i-wig, *n.* [O.E. *perriwig*, *perewake*, *perwicke*, &c., corrupted from Fr. *perruque*. (PERUKE.) *Wig* is simply the final syllable of this word.] A small wig; a peruke. — *v.t.* — *periwigged*, *periwigging*. To dress with a periwig. — **Periwig-pated**, *a.* Having the pate or head covered with a periwig.

Periwinkle, per-i-wing'kl, *n.* [From A. Sax. *pinewincle*, from L. *pinna*, *vina*, a mussel, and A.Sax. *wincle*, a winkle or whelk.] A kind of edible sea snail abounding on the shores of the North Atlantic; the shell of this snail.

Periwinkle, per-i-wing'kl, *n.* [O.E. *pervinke*, *pervenke*, Fr. *pervenche*, from L. *pervinca*, the periwinkle.] The myrtle, a trailing herb with evergreen leaves and white, blue, or purple flowers; a related species, called the *large periwinkle*.

Perjure, pėr'jūr, *v.t.—perjured*, *perjuring*. [L. *perjuro—per*, and *juro*, to swear, *per* here conveying a bad sense as in *perfidia*, perfidy.] To cause to be false to oaths or vows; to swear falsely to an oath in judicial proceedings; to forswear: generally used *refl.* (the witness *perjured himself*).—**Perjured**, pėr'jūrd, *p.* and *a.* Having sworn falsely; guilty of perjury.—**Perjurer**, pėr'jūr-ėr, *n.* One that wilfully takes a false oath.—**Perjurious**, **Perjurous**, pėr-jū'ri-us, pėr'jū-rus, *a.* Guilty of perjury; containing perjury.—**Perjury**, pėr'jū-ri, *n.* The act of wilfully making a false oath; knowingly making a false oath in a judicial proceeding in a matter material to the issue or cause in question; the act of violating an oath or solemn promise.

Perk, pėrk, *a.* [W. *perc*, neat, trim, smart; comp. also *pert*, spruce, dapper.] Trim; smart; vain; pert.—*v.i.* To hold up the head pertly; to look narrowly or sharply.—*v.t.* To make trim or smart; to prank; to hold up (the head) pertly.—**Perking**, pėr'king, *a.* Scanning pertly and keenly; inquisitive.—**Perky**, pėr'ki, *a.* Perk; trim; saucy.

Perlaceous, pėr-lā'shus, *a.* [PEARL.] Resembling a pearl; pearly.—**Perlite**, pėr'-līt, *n.* The same as *Pearl-stone*.

Permanent, pėr'ma-nent, *a.* [L. *permanens*, permanent, from *permaneo*, to continue—*per*, through, and *maneo*, to remain. MANSION.] Continuing in the same state, or without any change that destroys the form or nature of the thing; remaining unaltered or unremoved; durable; lasting; abiding; fixed.—*Permanent way*, *rail.* the finished road-bed and track, including bridges, viaducts, crossings, and switches.—**Permanently**, pėr'ma-nent-li, *adv.* In a permanent manner.—**Permanence**, **Permanency**, pėr'ma-nens, pėr'ma-nen-si, *n.* The state or quality of being permanent; continuance; fixedness.

Permanganate, per-mang'ga-nāt, *n.* [L. *per*, intensive, and *manganese*.] A dark, purple, crystalline substance, containing potassium, manganese, and oxygen: used in solution as an oxidizer and disinfectant.

Permeate, pėr'mē-āt, *v.t.—permeated*, *permeating*. [L. *permeo*, *permeatum—per*, through, and *meo*, to flow or pass.] To pass through the pores or interstices of; to penetrate and pass through without rupture or displacement of parts: applied particularly to fluids which pass through substances of loose texture: also used *fig.*—**Permeable**, pėr'mē-a-bl, *a.* [L. *permeabilis*.] Capable of being permeated.—**Permeably**, pėr'mē-a-bli, *adv.* In a permeable manner.—**Permeability**, pėr'mē-a-bil"-i-ti, *n.* The quality or state of being permeable; in *magnetics*, the capacity or power of being traversed by magnetic lines of force; the unit of permeability is that of air.—**Permeation**, pėr-mē-ā'shon, *n.* The act of permeating.

Permian, pėr'mi-an, *a.* [From *Perm*, in Russia, or that part of Russia which formed the ancient kingdom of *Permia*, where the series is largely developed.] *Geol.* a term applied to a system of rocks lying beneath the triassic rocks, and immediately above the carboniferous system, and forming the uppermost of the palæozoic strata.—**Permo-carboniferous**, per'mō-kär-bon-if"-ėr-us, *a.* A series of strata of age intermediate between PERMIAN and CARBONIFEROUS (which see).

Permission, &c. Under PERMIT.

Permit, pėr-mit', *v.t.—permitted*, *permitting*. [L. *permitto*—prefix *per*, and *mitto*, to send. MISSION.] To allow by silent consent or by not prohibiting; to suffer without giving express authority; to grant leave or liberty to by express consent; to allow expressly; to give leave to do or be done.—*v.i.* To grant leave or permission; to allow (if circumstances *permit*).—*n.* (pėr'mit). A permission; a written permission given by officers of customs or excise, or other competent authority, for conveying spirits, wine, &c., from one place to another.—**Permissibility**, pėr-mis'i-bil"i-ti, *n.* The quality of being permissible.—**Permissible**, pėr-mis'i-bl, *a.* Proper to being permitted or allowed; allowable.—**Permissibly**, pėr-mis'i-bli, *adv.* In a permissible manner.—**Permission**, pėr-mish'on, *n.* [L. *permissio*.] The act of permitting or allowing; authorization; allowance; license or liberty granted; leave.—**Permissive**, pėr-mis'iv, *a.* Permitting; granting liberty; allowing.—*Permissive laws*, laws that permit certain persons to have or enjoy the use of certain things, or to do certain acts without enforcing anything.—**Permissively**, pėr-mis'iv-li, *adv.* By allowance; without prohibition or hindrance.—**Permittance**, pėr-mit'ans, *n.* Permission.—**Permittee**, pėr-mit-tē', *n.* One to whom anything is permitted; one to whom a permit is granted.—**Permitter**, pėr-mit'ėr, *n.* One who permits.

Permute, pėr-mūt', *v.t.—permuted*, *permuting*. [L. *permuto*—prefix *per*, and *muto*, to change. MUTABLE.] To interchange; to change as regards order or arrangement.—**Permutable**, pėr-mū'ta-bl, *a.* Capable of being permuted; exchangeable.—**Permutableness**, pėr-mū'ta-bl-nes, *n.*—**Permutably**, pėr-mū'-ta-bli, *adv.* In a permutable manner; by interchange.—**Permutation**, pėr-mū-tā'-shon, *n.* [L. *permutatio*.] Interchange; change among various things at once; *math.* change or combination in different order of any number of quantities; any of the different ways in which a set of quantities can be arranged.

Pernicious, pėr-nish'us, *a.* [L. *perniciosus*, from *pernicies*, destruction—*per*, thoroughly, and stem of *nex*, *necis*, death (as in *internecine*).] Having the effect of destroying or injuring; very injurious or mischievous; destructive; noxious; deadly; evil-hearted; wicked (*Shak.*).—**Pernicious anemia**, a chronic disease, often fatal, in which the red blood corpuscles become progressively fewer, treated by concentrated liver extract which contains an anti-pernicious anemia principle.—**Perniciously**, pėr-nish'us-li, *adv.*

Peroneal, per-o-nē'al, *a.* [Gr. *peronē*, a brooch, also a name of the fibula.] Pertaining to the fibula.

Peroration, per-ō-rā'shon, *n.* [L. *peroratio*, from *peroro*, to speak from beginning to end—*per*, through, and *oro*, to speak, to pray. ORATION.] The concluding part of an oration, in which the speaker recapitulates the principal points of his discourse or argument, and urges them with greater earnestness; a rhetorical passage at the conclusion of a speech.—**Perorate**, per'ō-rāt, *v.i.* To make a peroration; also, to speechify; to spout.

Peroxide, pėr-ok'sid, *n.* That oxide of a given base which contains the greatest quantity of oxygen.

Perpend, per-pend', *v.t.* [L. *perpendo*, to weigh carefully—*per*, intens., and *pendo*, to weigh. PENDANT.] To weigh in the mind; to consider attentively.

Perpend, **Perpender**, pėr'pend, pėr-pen'dėr, *n.* [Fr. *parpaing*, *parpain*, from *par*, through, and *pan*, the side of a wall.] A long stone reaching through the thickness of a wall so as to be visible on both sides; a bonder.

Perpendicular, per-pen-dik'ū-lėr, *a.* [L. *perpendicularis*, from *perpendiculum*, a plumb-line—*per*, intens., and *pendeo*, to hang. PENDANT.] Perfectly upright or vertical; extending in a straight line from any point toward the centre of the earth, or at right angles with the plane of the horizon; *geom.* falling directly on a line or surface at right angles; at right angles to a given line or surface or making a normal with a curved surface.—*Perpendicular style*, *arch.* the florid or Tudor style of Gothic; the latest style of purely English architecture.—*n.* A line at right angles to the plane of the horizon; a vertical line; *geom.* a line falling at right angles on another line or on a plane.—**Perpendicularity**, pėr-pen-dik'ū-lar"i-ti, *n.* The state of being perpendicular.—**Perpendicularly**, pėr-pen-dik'ū-lėr-li, *adv.* In a perpendicular manner; vertically.

Perpent-stone, pėr-pent, *n.* PERPEND.

Perpetrate, pėr'pe-trāt, *v.t.—perpetrated*, *perpetrating*. [L. *perpetro—per*, through, and *patro*, to finish or perform; same root as *pater*, father. PATERNAL.] To do, execute, or perform, generally in a bad sense; to be guilty of; to commit; also used humorously for to produce something execrable or shocking (to *perpetrate* a pun).—**Perpetration**, pėr-pe-trā'shon, *n.* The act of perpetrating; commission.—**Perpetrator**, pėr'pe-trā-tėr, *n.* One that perpetrates.

Perpetual, pėr-pet'ū-al, *a.* [Fr. *perpétuel*, L. *perpetualis*, from *perpetuus*, perpetual—*per*, through, and *peto*, to seek. PETITION.] Continuing or lasting for ever in future time; destined to be eternal; continuing or continued without intermission; uninterrupted. ∴ Syn. under CONTINUOUS.—*Perpetual curate*, a permanent holder of a curacy in which all the tithes are appropriated and no vicarage endowed.—*Perpetual motion*, motion that once originated generates a power of continuing itself for ever or indefinitely, by means of mechanism or some application of the force of gravity—such a motion being, however, impossible.—*Perpetual screw*, an endless screw. Under ENDLESS.—**Perpetually**, pėr-pet'ū-al-li, *adv.* In a perpetual manner; constantly; for ever.—**Perpetuable**, pėr-pet'ū-a-bl, *a.* Capable of being perpetuated.—**Perpetuate**, pėr-pet'ū-āt, *v.t.—perpetuated*, *perpetuating*. [L. *perpetuo*, *perpetuatum*.] To make perpetual; to cause to endure or to be continued indefinitely; to preserve from extinction or oblivion.—**Perpetuation**, pėr-pet'ū-ā"shon, *n.* The act of perpetuating or making perpetual.—**Perpetuity**, pėr-pe-tū'i-ti, *n.* [L. *perpetuitas*.] The state or quality of being perpetual; something of which there will be no end; duration to all futurity; exemption from intermission or ceasing.

Perplex, pėr-pleks', *v.t.* [From L. *perplexus*, entangled, intricate, involved—*per*, intens., and *plecto*, *plexum*, to twist; akin to Gr. *plekō*, L. *plico*, to fold. PLY.] To involve, entangle, make complicated or intricate; to puzzle; to tease with suspense, anxiety, or ambiguity.—**Perplexedly**, pėr-plek'sed-li, *adv.* In a perplexed or perplexing manner.—**Perplexing**, pėr-plek'-sing, *p.* and *a.* Embarrassing; difficult; intricate.—**Perplexity**, **Perplexedness**, pėr-plek'si-ti, pėr-plek'sed-nes, *n.* The state of being perplexed, puzzled, or at a loss; the state of being intricate or involved.

Perquisite, pėr'kwi-zit, *n.* [L. *perquisitum*, something sought out, from *perquiro—per*, intens., and *quæro*, to seek. QUERY.] Something obtained from a place or office over and above the settled wages or emoluments; something in addition to regular wages or salary.—**Perquisition**, pėr-kwi-zish'on, *n.* A thorough inquiry or search.

Perron, per'on, *n.* [Fr., from L.L. *petronus*, a perron, from L. and Gr. *petra*, a stone.] *Arch.* an external stair by which access is given to the entrance-door of a building.

Perroquet, per-o-ket', *n.* PARRAKEET.

Perruque, per-rūk, *n.* [Fr.] A peruke.—**Perruquier**, pe-rū'ki-ėr, *n.* A wig maker.

Perry, per'i, *n.* [Fr. *poiré*, perry, from *poire*, L. *pirum*, a pear.] A fermented liquor made from the juice of pears and resembling cider.

Perscrutation, pėr-skrö-tā'shon, *n.* [L. *perscrutatio—per*, thoroughly, and *scrutor*, to search.] A searching thoroughly; minute search or inquiry.

Persecute, pėr'se-kūt, *v.t.—persecuted, persecuting.* [Fr. *persecuter*, from L. *persequor*, *persecutus*, to persecute—*per*, intens., and *sequor*, to follow. SEQUENCE.] To harass or afflict with repeated acts of cruelty or annoyance; to afflict persistently; specifically, to afflict or punish on account of holding particular opinions or adhering to a particular creed or mode of worship.—**Persecuting**, pėr'se-kūt-ing, *a.* Given to persecution. — **Persecution**, pėr-se-kū'-shon, *n.* The act or practice of persecuting; the state of being persecuted.—**Persecutor**, pėr'se-kū-tėr, *n.* One who persecutes. —**Persecutrix**, pėr'se-kūt-riks, *n.* A female persecutor.

Perseides, pėr-sē'i-dēz, *n.pl.* A name given to the August meteors because they seem to radiate from the constellation *Perseus.*

Persevere, pėr-se-vēr', *v.i.—persevered, persevering.* [L. *persevēro*, from *perseverus*, very severe or strict—*per*, intens., and *severus*, severe, strict. SEVERE.] To continue resolutely in any business or enterprise undertaken; to pursue steadily any design or course commenced; not to give over or abandon what is undertaken. ∴ Syn. under PERSIST.—**Persevering**, pėr-se-vē'ring, *p.* and *a.* Steadfast in purpose; persisting in any business or course begun.—**Perseveringly**, pėr-se-vē'ring-li, *adv.* In a persevering manner. — **Perseverance**, pėr-se-vē'rans, *n.* [L. *perseverantia.*] The act or habit of persevering; persistence in anything undertaken.

Persian, pėr'shi-an, *a.* Pertaining to Persia, the Persians or their language.—*n.* A native of Persia; the language spoken in Persia; a thin silk formerly used for lining. —*Persian berries*, the berries of a species of buckthorn, used in dyeing yellow.—*Persian blinds*, jalousies; venetian blinds. —*Persian carpet*, a carpet made in one piece, instead of in breadths or strips to be joined.—*Persian wheel*, a large wheel fixed vertically with a series of buckets at its circumference, by which water is raised from a stream, well, &c.

Persiflage, per-sē-fläzh, *n.* [Fr., from *persifler* to quiz—L. *per*, and *sibilare*, to hiss.] Idle bantering talk; a frivolous or jeering talk regarding any subject, serious or otherwise.—**Persifleur**, per-sē-flėr, *n.* One who indulges in persiflage.

Persimmon, Persimon, pėr-sim'on, *n.* [Virginia Indian.] An American tree of the ebony family, and also its fruit, which is about the size of a small plum and has a very sweet pulp.

Persist, pėr-sist', *v.i.* [Fr. *persister*, L. *persisto*—*per*, through, and *sisto*, to stand. STATE, STAND.] To continue steadily and firmly in the pursuit of any business or course commenced; to continue in the face of some amount of opposition; to persevere; (of things) to continue in a certain state. ∴ *Persist* is nearly synonymous with *persevere*; but *persist* frequently implies more obstinacy than *persevere*, particularly in that which is evil or injurious to others. —**Persistence, Persistency**, pėr-sis'-tens, pėr-sis'ten-si, *n.* The state of persisting, or of being persistent; steady continuance in a course; perseverance, often in evil; *physics*, the continuance of an effect after the cause which first gave rise to it is removed, as the *persistence* of the impression of light on the retina after the luminous object is withdrawn.—**Persistent**, pėr-sis'tent, *a.* Inclined to persist; persevering; tenacious of purpose; *bot.* continuing without withering or falling off. — **Persistently**, pėr-sis'tent-li, *adv.* In a persistent manner.—**Persistive**, pėr-sis'tiv, *a.* Persevering; persistent. (*Shak.*)

Person, pėr'son, *n.* [L. *persona*, primarily a mask used by actors, hence, a character, a person, from *personare*, to sound through —*per*, through, and *sonare*, to sound.] An individual human being; a man, woman, or child; bodily form; human frame, with its characteristic appearance (to appear in *person*; cleanly in *person*); a human being, indefinitely; one; a man (a *person* would think so); a term applied to each of the three beings of the Godhead; *gram.* one of three relations in which nouns and pronouns are regarded as standing to the act of speaking, a pronoun of the *first person* denoting the speaker, the *second person* one who is spoken to, and the *third person* one who or that which is spoken of (thus including all nouns); one of the three corresponding inflections of a verb singular and plural.—*In person*, by one's self, not by representative.—**Personable**, pėr'son-a-bl, *a.* Having a well-formed body or person; of good appearance.—**Personage**, pėr'son-āj, *n.* A person; a man or woman of distinction (an illustrious *personage*); a being regarded as having an individuality like that of a human being (a divine or a mythological *personage*).—**Personal**, pėr'-son-al, *a.* [L. *personalis.*] Pertaining to a person as distinct from a thing; relating to or affecting some individual person; peculiar or proper to him or her, or to private actions or character; applying to the person, character, or conduct of an individual, generally in a disparaging manner (*personal* reflections or remarks); belonging to face and figure (*personal* charms); done in person, not by representative (a *personal* interview); *gram.* denoting or pointing to the person (a *personal* pronoun, as *I, we, thou, you, he, she, it, they*); having the modifications of the three persons. — *Personal identity, metaph.* sameness of being at every stage of life, of which consciousness is the evidence.—*Personal property, personal estate*, movables; chattels; things belonging to the person, as money, jewels, furniture, &c., as distinguished from *real* estate in land and houses. — **Personalism**, pėr'son-al-izm, *n.* State of being personal.—**Personality**, pėr-son-al'i-ti, *n.* The state of being personal; what constitutes an individual a distinct person; the state of existing as a thinking intelligent being; application or applicability to a person; an application of remarks to the conduct, character, or appearance of some person; a remark reflecting in some way on an individual (to indulge in *personalities*); *law*, personal estate; personalty.—**Personalize**, pėr'son-al-īz, *v.t.* —*personalized, personalizing.* To make personal. — **Personally**, pėr'son-al-li, *adv.* In a personal manner; in person; with respect to an individual; as regards one's personal existence or individuality.—**Personalty**, pėr'son-al-ti, *n. Law*, personal property, in distinction from *realty* or real property.—**Personate**, pėr'son-āt, *v.t.*—*personated, personating.* To assume the character or appearance of, whether in real life or on the stage; to represent by an assumed appearance; to act the part of; to assume or put on.—*a.* [L. *personatus*, masked.] *Bot.* a term applied to a gamopetalous corolla somewhat resembling an animal's mouth, as in the snapdragon.—**Personated**, pėr'son-ā-ted, *p.* and *a.* Counterfeited; feigned; pretended.—**Personation**, pėr-son-ā'shon, *n.* The act of counterfeiting the person or character of another.—*False personation*, the offence of personating another for the purpose of fraud. — **Personator**, pėr'son-ā-tėr, *n.* One who personates; one who assumes the character of another.—**Personification**, pėr-son'i-fi-kā"shon, *n.* The act of personifying; an embodiment; an impersonation; *rhet.* a species of metaphor, which consists in representing inanimate objects or abstract notions as endued with life and action, or possessing the attributes of living beings. — **Personify**, pėr-son'i-fī, *v.t.*—*personified, personifying.* [L. *persona*, and *facio*, to make.] To treat or regard as a person; to treat for literary purposes as if endowed with the characters of a rational being or person; to impersonate—**Personnel**, pėr-son-el', *n.* [Fr., from *personne*, a person.] The body of persons employed in any occupation: often opposed to *matériel.*

Perspective, pėr-spek'tiv, *a.* [Fr. *perspectif*, from L. *perspicio*, *perspectum*—*per*, through, and *specio*, to view. SPECIES.] Producing certain optical effects when looked through; optical (a *perspective* glass); pertaining to the art of perspective.—*n.* A telescope†; the art or science which teaches how to draw or paint objects or scenes so that they appear to have their natural dimensions, positions, and relations—*aerial* perspective dealing with light, shade, and colour, *linear* perspective with form and magnitude; a representation of objects in perspective; quality of a picture as regards perspective; view; vista.—**Perspectively**, pėr-spek'tiv-li, *adv.* According to the rules of perspective.

Perspicacious, pėr-spi-kā'shus, *a.* [L. *perspicax*, *perspicācis*, from *perspicio*, to look through. PERSPECTIVE.] Quick-sighted; quickly seeing through or understanding anything; of acute discernment.—**Perspicaciously**, pėr-spi-kā'shus-li, *adv.* In a perspicacious manner.—**Perspicaciousness, Perspicacity**, pėr-spi-kā'shus-nes, pėr-spi-kas'i-ti, *n.* The state or quality of being perspicacious; acuteness of discernment; penetration; sagacity.—**Perspicuity**, pėr-spi-kū'i-ti, *n.* [L. *perspicuitas.*] The quality of being perspicuous; easiness to be understood; freedom from obscurity or ambiguity.—**Perspicuous**, pėr-spik'ū-us, *a.* [L. *perspicuus.*] Clear to the understanding; not obscure or ambiguous; lucid. —**Perspicuously**, pėr-spik'ū-us-li, *adv.* In a perspicuous manner. — **Perspicuousness**, pėr-spik'ū-us-nes, *n.* Perspicuity.

Perspire, pėr-spīr', *v.i.*—*perspired, perspiring.* [L. *perspiro*—*per*, through, and *spiro*, to breathe. SPIRIT.] To give out watery matter through the pores of the skin; to sweat; to exude.—*v.t.* To emit through the excretories of the skin; to give out through pores. — **Perspirability**, pėr-spī'ra-bil"i-ti, *n.* The quality of being perspirable.—**Perspirable**, pėr-spī'ra-bl, *a.* Capable of being perspired.—**Perspiration**, pėr-spi-rā'shon, *n.* The act of perspiring; excretion of watery fluid (sweat) from the surface of the body (whether visibly or in the form of invisible vapour); matter perspired. — **Perspirative**, pėr-spī'ra-tiv, *a.* Performing the act of perspiration. — **Perspiratory**, pėr-spī'ra-to-ri, *a.* Pertaining to perspiration; causing perspiration; perspirative.

Perstringe, pėr-strinj', *v.t.*—*perstringed, perstringing.* [L. *perstringo*—*per*, and *stringo*, to graze or brush.] To touch upon in words; to criticise.

Persuade, pėr-swād', *v.t.*—*persuaded, persuading.* [L. *persuadeo*—*per*, effectively, and *suadeo*, to advise, urge. SUASION.] To influence by argument, advice, or expostulation; to argue or reason into a certain course of action; to advise; to try to influence; to convince by argument or reasons offered.—*v.i.* To use persuasion.—**Persuadable**, pėr-swā'da-bl, *a.* Capable of being persuaded.—**Persuadably**, pėr-swā'da-bli, *adv.* In a persuadable manner. —**Persuader**, pėr-swā'dėr, *n.* One who persuades.—**Persuasibility**, pėr-swā'zi-bil"i-ti, *n.* Capability of being persuaded.—**Persuasible**, pėr-swā'zi-bl, *a.* [L. *persuasibilis.*] Capable of being persuaded.—**Persuasibleness**, pėr-swā'zi-bl-nes, *n.* —**Persuasion**, pėr-swā'zhon, *n.* [L. *persuasio, persuasionis.*] The act of persuading; the state of being persuaded or convinced; settled opinion or conviction; a creed or belief; a sect or party adhering to a creed or system of opinions. ∴ Syn. under CONVICTION.—**Persuasive**, pėr-swā'ziv, *a.* Having the power of persuading; influencing to a course of action. — *n.* That which persuades; an incitement; an exhortation. — **Persuasively**, pėr-swā'ziv-li, *adv.* In a persuasive manner.—**Persuasiveness**, pėr-swā'ziv-nes, *n.* The quality of being persuasive.

Persulphate, pėr-sul'fāt, *n.* That sulphate of a metal which contains the greater relative quantity of acid.

Pert, pėrt, *a.* [Partly from O.Fr. *apert*, *appert* (as in *malapert*), from L. *apertus*, open (APERIENT); partly from W. *pert*, *perc*, trim, spruce (PERK).] Lively; brisk; dapper; smart; forward; saucy; indecorously free.—**Pertly**, pėrt'li, *adv.* In a pert manner; briskly; smartly; with indecorous boldness.—**Pertness**, pért'nes, *n.* The state or quality of being pert; smartness; sauciness; forward boldness.

Pertain, pėr-tān', *v.i.* [L. *pertineo—per*, intens., and *teneo*, to hold, whence also *tenant*, *contain*, *obtain*, *retain*, &c. TENANT.] To belong; to be the property, right, duty of; to appertain; to have relation or bearing: always followed by *to*.

Pertinacious, pėr-ti-nā'shus, *a.* [L. *pertinax—per*, intens., and *teneo*, to hold; PERTAIN.] Holding or adhering to any opinion, purpose, or design with obstinacy; obstinate; perversely persistent; resolute; constant.—**Pertinaciously**, pėr-ti-nā'shus-li, *adv.* In a pertinacious manner; persistently; obstinately.—**Pertinacity**, **Pertinaciousness**, pėr-ti-nas'i-ti, pėr-ti-nā'shus-nes, *n.* Firm or unyielding adherence to opinion or purpose; obstinacy; resolution; constancy.

Pertinent, pėr'ti-nent, *a.* [L. *pertinens*, ppr. of *pertineo*, to pertain. PERTAIN.] Related to the subject or matter in hand; just to the purpose; apposite; not foreign to the question.—**Pertinence**, **Pertinency**, pėr'ti-nens, pėr'ti-nen-si, *n.* The quality of being pertinent; justness of relation to the subject or matter in hand; fitness; appositeness.—**Pertinently**, pėr'ti-nent-li, *adv.* In a pertinent manner; appositely; to the purpose.—**Pertinentness**, pėr'ti-nent-nes, *n.* Pertinence.

Perturb, pėr-tėrb', *v.t.* [L. *perturbo—per*, intens., and *turbo*, to disturb, from *turba*, a crowd. DISTURB, TURBID.] To disturb; to agitate; to disorder; to confuse.—**Perturbability**, pėr-tėr'ba-bil"i-ti, *n.* The state or quality of being perturbable.—**Perturbable**, pėr-tėr'ba-bl, *a.* Capable of being perturbed or agitated.—**Perturbance**, pėr-tėr'bans, *n.* Perturbation.—**Perturbation**, pėr-tėr-bā'shon, *n.* [L. *pertubatio*.] The act of perturbing or state of being perturbed; disorder; especially, disquiet of mind; commotion of the passions; agitation; cause of disquiet.—*Perturbations of the planets*, their orbital irregularities or deviations from their regular elliptic orbits, arising from their attraction on one another.—**Perturber**, pėr-tėr'bėr, *n.* One who perturbs.

Pertuse, **Pertused**, pėr-tūs', pėr-tūsd', *a.* [L. *pertusus*, pp. of *pertundo*, to beat or bore through—*per*, through, and *tundo*, to beat. OBTUSE.] Pierced with holes; having holes or slits, as a leaf.—**Pertusion**, pėr-tū'zhon, *n.* The act of thrusting through with a pointed instrument; a hole made by punching; a perforation.

Pertussis, pėr-tus'is, *n.* [L. *per*, intens., and *tussis*, a cough.] *Med.* the whooping-cough.

Peruke, pe-rūk', *n.* [Fr. *perruque*, It. *perucca*, It. dial. *pilucca*, peruke, from L. *pilus*, hair. *Periwig* is a corruption of *perruque*, and its final syllable has become *wig*.] An artificial cap of hair; a periwig; a perruque.

Perule, per'ūl, *n.* [L. *perula*, a little bag, dim. of *pera*, a wallet.] *Bot.* the scaly covering of a leaf-bud; a sac formed in some orchids by the prolonged and united bases of two of the segments of their perianth; a perithecium.

Peruse, pe-rūz', *v.t.*—*perused*, *perusing*. [From prefix *per*, intens., and *use*.] To read through; to read with attention; to observe; to examine with careful survey.—**Peruser**, pe-rū'zėr, *n.* One who peruses.—**Perusal**, pe-rū'zal, *n.* The act of perusing or reading.

Peruvian, pe-rū'vi-an, *a.* Pertaining to *Peru* in South America.—*n.* A native of Peru.—**Peruvian-balsam**, *n.* A thick brown liquid, of a fragrant odour and a pungent and bitterish flavour, yielded by a tree of Peru.—**Peruvian-bark**, *n.* The bark of several species of Cinchona, trees of Peru, yielding quinine. CINCHONA, QUININE.

Pervade, pėr-vād', *v.t.*—*pervaded*, *pervading*. [L. *pervado*, to go through—*per*, through, and *vado*, to go (as in *invade*); cog. A.Sax. *wadan*, E. *wade*.] To pass or flow through; to extend through; to spread or be diffused through the whole extent of.—**Pervasion**, pėr-vā'zhon, *n.* The act of pervading.—**Pervasive**, pėr-vā'siv, *a.* Tending or having power to pervade.

Perverse, pėr-vėrs', *a.* [L. *perversus*, from *perverto*, to pervert, corrupt, overthrow—*per*, and *verto*, to turn. VERSE.] Turned aside from the right; turned to evil; obstinate in the wrong; froward; stubborn; intractable; cross; petulant; untoward.—**Perversely**, pėr-vėrs'li, *adv.* In a perverse manner; stubbornly; obstinately in the wrong.—**Perverseness**, pėr-vėrs'nes, *n.* The quality of being perverse; disposition to thwart or cross.—**Perversion**, pėr-vėr'shon, *n.* [L. *perversio*.] The act of perverting; a diverting from the true intent or object; sexual aberration.—**Perversity**, pėr-vėr'si-ti, *n.* [L. *perversitas*.] State or quality of being perverse; perverseness.—**Perversive**, pėr-vėr'siv, *a.* Tending or having power to pervert.—**Pervert**, pėr-vėrt', *v.t.* [L. *perverto*.] To turn from truth, propriety, or from its proper purpose; to distort from its true use or end; to misinterpret wilfully; to turn from the right; to corrupt.—**Pervert**, pėr'vėrt, *n.* One who has been perverted; an apostate; a degenerate; one who is sexually perverted; an invert.—**Perverter**, pėr-vėr'tėr, *n.* One that perverts; one that distorts, misinterprets, or misapplies.—**Pervertible**, pėr-vėr'ti-bl, *a.* Capable of being perverted.

Pervicacious, pėr-vi-kā'shus, *a.* [L. *pervicax*, headstrong.] Very obstinate; stubborn; wilfully contrary or refractory.—**Pervicaciously**, pėr-vi-kā'shus-li, *adv.* Stubbornly.—**Pervicacity**, pėr-vi-kas'i-ti, *n.* The state of being pervicacious; stubbornness.

Pervious, pėr'vi-us, *a.* [L. *pervius—per*, through, and *via*, a way. VOYAGE, WAY.] Capable of being penetrated by another body or substance; penetrable; allowing an entrance or a passage through; capable of being penetrated by the mental sight.—**Perviousness**, pėr'vi-us-nes, *n.* The quality of being pervious.

Pervis, pėr'vis, *n.* PARVIS.

Pes, pēz, *n.* [L. *pes*, the foot.] The foot; the part of any vertebrate corresponding to the human foot; any foot-like organ.

Pesade, pe-säd', *n.* [Fr. *pesade*, from *peser*, to weigh.] A technical term for the rearing of a horse.

Peshito, pesh-ē'tō, *a.* and *n.* [Syriac, single or true.] The Syrian translation of the Old and New Testaments (incomplete) made by a Christian in the second century.

Peso, pā'sō, *n.* [Sp.] A dollar; a term used in certain of the Central and South American countries.

Pessary, pes'a-ri, *n.* [Med. L. *pessarium*, from L. *pessum*, Gr. *pessos*, a small oval stone, a medicated plug.] A device introduced into the vagina to correct uterine displacement; a vaginal suppository.

Pessimism, pes'im-izm, *n.* [L. *pessimus*, the worst.] The belief or doctrine that man is imperfectible and that his life is essentially unhappy; the tendency to take the most unfavorable view of situations or actions: opposed to *optimism*.—**Pessimist**, pes'im-ist, *n.* One who believes in pessimism, also one who is inclined to take a desponding view of things.—**Pessimistic**, pes-si-mis'tik, *a.* Pertaining to pessimism.

Pest, pest, *n.* [Fr. *peste*, from L. *pestis*, a plague, a pest (whence *pestilent*, *pestiferous*); same root as *perdo*, to destroy (PERDITION).] A plague, pestilence, or deadly epidemic disease; anything very noxious, mischievous, or destructive; a mischievous or destructive person.—**Pest-house**, *n.* A hospital for persons infected with the plague or other pestilential disease.

Pestalozzian, pes-ta-lot'si-an, *a.* Pertaining to the system of elementary education instituted by a Swiss philanthropist named *Pestalozzi*, which is substantially the system now followed.

Pester, pes'tėr, *v.t.* [O.Fr. *empestrer*, originally to shackle the feet of a horse at pasture, from L.L. *pastorium*, foot-shackles, from L. *pastor*, a shepherd. PASTERN, PASTOR.] To encumber‡; to crowd or cram‡; to trouble; to disturb; to annoy with little vexations.—**Pesterer**, pes'tėr-ėr, *n.* One who pesters.

Pestiferous, pes-tif'ėr-us, *a.* [L. *pestis*, plague, and *fero*, to produce. PEST.] Pestilential; noxious to health; infectious; noxious in any manner; malignant.—**Pestiferously**, pes-tif'ėr-us-li, *adv.* In a pestiferous manner; pestilentially.

Pestilence, pes'ti-lens, *n.* [L. *pestilentia*, from *pestilens*, pestilent, from *pestis*, plague. PEST.] The disease called the plague or pest; any contagious and malignant disease that is epidemic and mortal; what is pestilential or pestiferous; something morally evil or destructive.—**Pestilent**, pes'ti-lent, *a.* [L. *pestilens*.] Pestilential; mischievous; noxious to morals or society; troublesome; corrupt.—**Pestilential**, pes-ti-len'shal, *a.* Having the nature of the plague or other infectious and deadly disease; producing or tending to produce infectious disease; destructive.—**Pestilentially**, pes-ti-len'shal-li, *adv.* In a pestilential manner.—**Pestilentialness**, pes-ti-len'shal-nes, *n.*—**Pestilently**, pes'ti-lent-li, *adv.* In a pestilent manner.—**Pestilentness**, pes'ti-lent-nes, *n.*

Pestle, pes'l, *n.* [O.Fr. *pesteil*, from L. *pistillum*, a pestle, from *pinso*, *pistum*, to bray, to pound; akin *pistil*, *piston*.] An instrument for pounding and breaking substances in a mortar.—*v.t.*—*pestled*, *pestling*. To break or pulverize with a pestle.

Pet, pet, *n.* [Possibly an abbreviated form of *petulant* or *petulance*.] A slight fit of peevishness or fretful discontent.—**Pettish**, pet'ish, *a.* Proceeding from or pertaining to a pet or peevish humour.—**Pettishly**, pet'ish-li, *adv.* In a pettish manner.—**Pettishness**, pet'ish-nes, *n.* Fretfulness; peevishness.

Pet, pet, *n.* [From Ir. *peat*, Gael. *peata*, a pet, or perhaps from *petty*, Fr. *petit*, little.] A fondling; a darling; a favourite child; an animal fondled and indulged.—*v.t.*—*petted*, *petting*. To treat as a pet; to fondle; to indulge.—*a.* Petted; favourite (a *pet* lamb, a *pet* theory).

Petal, pet'al, *n.* [From Gr. *petalon*, a leaf, from *petalos*, spread out, expanded; same root as in *patent*.] *Bot.* a flower leaf; one of the separate parts of a corolla.—**Petaled**, pet'ald, *a.* Having petals.—**Petaliform**, pe-tal'i-form, *a.* *Bot.* shaped like a petal; petaloid.—**Petaline**, pet'al-īn, *a.* *Bot.* pertaining to a petal.—**Petalite**, pet'al-īt, *n.* A mineral having a foliated structure, its colour being milk-white or shaded with gray, red, or green.—**Petaloid**, pet'al-oid, *a.* Having the form of a petal; resembling petals.—**Petalous**, pet'al-us, *a.* *Bot.* having petals; petaled.

Petard, pe-tärd', *n.* [Fr. *pétard*, from *péter*, to break wind, to bounce, from L. *pedo*, *peditum*, with same sense.] An engine of war made of metal, to be loaded with powder and fixed on a gate, barricade, &c., in order to break it down by explosion.—*Hoist with his own petard*, (*fig.*) caught in his own trap; involved in the danger he meant for others.—**Petardier**, pe-tär-dēr', *n.* One who manages a petard.

Petasos, **Petasus**, pet'a-sos, pet'a-sus, *n.* [Gr. *petasos*.] A broad-brimmed hat; the winged cap of Mercury.

Petechiæ, pe-tek'i-ē, *n.pl.* [L.L. *peteccia*, It. *petecchia*, from L. *petigo*, an eruption.] Purple spots which appear on the skin in malignant fevers.—**Petechial**, pe-tek'i-al, *a.* Having livid spots or *petechiæ*.—*Petechial fever*, a malignant fever accompanied with purple spots on the skin.

Peter, *n.*—*The Blue Peter*, the flag hoisted by a merchantman on the eve of leaving the docks.

Peterel, pet'ėr-el, *n.* A petrel.

Peter out, pē-tėr-out′, *v.i.* Said of a mine or vein of ore when it is exhausted and yields no return. (*Colloq.*)

Peter-pence, Peter's-pence, pē-tėr-pens′, *n.pl.* A tribute that used to be regularly offered to the popes (as the successors of St. Peter); a similar contribution still voluntarily given by some Roman Catholics.

Petersham, pē′tėr-sham, *n.* [After Lord *Petersham*, who set the fashion of wearing it.] A style of greatcoat formerly fashionable; the heavy, rough-napped woollen cloth of which such greatcoats were made.

Petiole, pet′i-ōl, *n.* [Fr., from L. *petiolus*, a dim. from *pes, pedis*, a foot.] *Bot.* a leaf-stalk; the stalk connecting the blade of the leaf with the branch or stem.—**Petiolar, Petiolary**, pet′i-ō-lėr, pet′i-ō-la-ri, *a. Bot.* pertaining to a petiole, or proceeding from it. — **Petiolate, Petioled**, pet′i-ō-lāt, pet′i-ōld, *a.* Having a petiole.—**Petiolule**, pet′i-ōl-ul, *n.* [A dim. of *petiole.*] *Bot.* a little or partial petiole, such as belong to the leaflets of compound leaves.—**Petiolulate**, pet-i-ol′ū-lāt, *a. Bot.* having a petiolule.

Petit, pet′i or pė-tē; **Petite** (feminine form), pė-tēt, *a.* [Fr.] Little; petty; small in figure.—*Petit juror*, a person serving on a petit jury.—*Petit jury*, a group of twelve persons impaneled as a jury to decide a case tried in a law court: distinguished from *grand jury*.

Petition, pē-tish′on, *n.* [L. *petitio, petitionis*, from *peto, petitum*, to seek, attack (seen in *appetite, competent, competition, impetus, petulant, repeat*).] An entreaty, supplication, or prayer, as one to the Supreme Being or a superior in rank or power; a particular request or article among several in a prayer; a formal written request; a written supplication from an inferior to a superior soliciting some favor, grant, right, or mercy; a written application in certain legal proceedings.—*v.t.* To make a petition, request, or prayer to; to solicit; to address a written or printed petition or supplication to (to *petition* government).—**Petitionary**, pē-tish′on-a-ri, *a.* Offering a petition; supplicatory; containing a petition or request.—**Petitioner**, pē-tish′on-ėr, *n.* One that presents a petition, either verbal or written.—**Petitio principii**, pe-tish′i-ō prin-sip′i-ī, [Latin.] The begging of the question; false reasoning in which something to be proved is assumed true. —**Petitory**, pet′i-to-ri, *a.* Petitioning; soliciting; begging.

Petralogy, pe-tral′o-ji, *n.* Same as *Petrology*.

Petrel, pet′rel, *n.* [Dim. of *Peter*, in allusion to St. Peter's walking on the sea, as the birds often seem to do.] The name of web-footed oceanic birds of several species, found at great distances from land, and generally in stormy weather: hence the name *stormy petrels*.

Petrescent, pe-tres′ent, *a.* [L. *petra*, from Gr. *petra*, a stone.] Changing into stony hardness.—**Petrescence**, pe-tres′ens, *n.* The process of changing into stone.

Petrify, pet′ri-fī, *v.t.*—*petrified, petrifying*. [L. *petra* (from Gr. *petra*), a stone or rock (seen also in *petroleum, pier*), and *facio*, to make.] To convert to stone or stony substance, as by the infiltration and deposition of mineral matter; to turn into a fossil; *fig.* to make callous or obdurate; to paralyse or stupefy with fear or amazement.—*v.i.* To become stone or of a stony hardness.—**Petrifaction**, pet-ri-fak′shon, *n.* The process of changing into stone; an organized body rendered hard by deposition of a stony substance in its cavities; a fossil; a state of being paralysed as with astonishment. — **Petrifactive**, pet-ri-fak′tiv, *a.* Having power to petrify or convert into stone.—**Petrifiable**, pet′ri-fī-a-bl, *a.* Capable of being petrified.—**Petrific**, pe-trif′ik, *a.* Petrifactive. (*Milton.*)

Petrine, pē′trīn, *a.* Relating to St. *Peter* (the *Petrine* epistles).

Petroglyphy, pet-rog′li-fi, *n.* [Gr. *petros*, a stone, and *glyphō*, to carve.] The art or operation of carving inscriptions and figures on rocks or stones.—**Petroglyphic**, pet-rō-glif′ik, *a.* Pertaining to this.

Petrography, pe-trog′ra-fi, *n.* [Gr. *petros*, a stone, and *graphō*, to write.] The study of rocks; a scientific description of rocks; petrology. — **Petrographer**, pe-trog′ra-fėr, *n.* One who studies petrography. — **Petrographic, Petrographical**, pet-rō-graf′ik, pet-rō-graf′i-kal, *a.* Pertaining to.

Petrol, pet′rol, *n.* Petroleum‡; in England, gasoline: used chiefly as motor fuel.

Petroleum, pe-trō′lē-um, *n.* [L. *petra*, rock, and *oleum*, oil.] A natural, oily liquid consisting chiefly of hydrocarbons which, by fractional distillation, yields such products as gasoline, kerosene, lubricating oils, fuel oils, &c.

Petrology, pe-trol′o-ji, *n.* [Gr. *petros*, a rock, and *logos*, a treatise.] The study of rocks; that branch of geology which determines the constitution of rocks by investigating the chemical composition of the separate mineral ingredients of which they consist. Spelled also *Petralogy*.—**Petrological**, pet-rō-loj′i-kal, *a.* Of or pertaining to petrology.—**Petrologist**, pe-trol′o-jist, *n.* One versed in petrology.

Petronel, pet′rō-nel, *n.* [O.Fr. *petrinal, poictrinal*, from L. *pectus, pectoris*, the breast, being discharged with the stock placed against the breast.] A kind of carbine or large horseman's pistol.

Petrosal, pe-trō′sal, *a.* and *n.* [L. *petrosus*.] Applied to the petrous portion of the temporal bone or to a homologous bone. PETROUS.

Petrosilex, pet-rō-sī-leks, *n.* [L. *petra*, a stone, and *silex*, flint.] Rock stone; rock flint or compact felspar.

Petrous, pē′trus, *a.* [L. *petrosus*, from *petra*, a stone.] Like stone; hard; stony; *anat.* applied to that portion of the temporal bone in which the internal organs of hearing are situated, from its hardness (known as the *petrosal portion*).

Pettichaps, pet′i-chaps, *n.* Same as *Pettychaps*.

Petticoat, pet′i-kōt, *n.* [From *petty*, short, small, and *coat*.] A loose under garment worn by females; hence, a woman.—*Petticoat government*, female government, either political or domestic.

Pettifog, pet′i-fog, *v.i.*—*pettifogged, pettifogging*. [*Petty* and Prov.E, *fog*, to seek gain by mean practices.] To act in mean or petty cases, as a lawyer.—**Pettifogger**, pet-i-fog′ėr, *n.* An inferior attorney or lawyer who is employed in mean business.—**Pettifoggery**, pet-i-fog′ėr-i, *n.* The practice of a pettifogger; tricks; quibbles.

Pettiness. Under PETTY.

Pettish. Under PET.

Pettitoes, pet′i-tōz, *n.pl.* [*Petty* and *toes*.] The toes or feet of a pig: sometimes used humorously for the human feet.

Petto, pet′tō, *n.* [It., from L. *pectus*, the breast.] The breast; hence, *in petto*, in secrecy; in reserve.

Petty, pet′i, *a.* [Fr. *petit*, little; small akin to W. *pitw*, small, *pid*, a point.] Small; little; trifling; inconsiderable; having little power or possessions; having little importance; inferior (a *petty* prince).—*Petty averages*, the accustomed duties of anchorage, pilotage, &c., which are paid by a vessel.—*Petty cash*, money kept on hand from which change is made and small bills are paid.—*Petty-cash book*, a book in which small receipts and payments are entered. —*Petty jury*, same as PETIT JURY.—*Petty officer*, an officer in the navy whose rank corresponds with that of a non-commissioned officer in the army.—**Pettily**, pet′i-li, *adv.* In a petty manner.—**Pettiness**, pet′i-nes, *n.* Smallness; littleness.

Pettychaps, pet′i-chaps, *n.* [From *petty*, small, and *chaps*, mandibles.] A name given to several species of warblers; notably, the chiffchaff and the garden warbler.

Petulant, pet′ū-lant, *a.* [L. *petulans, petulantis*, petulant, from *peto*, to attack. PETITION.] Manifesting pique, perversity, or fretfulness; saucy; pert; capricious.—**Petulance, Petulancy**, pet′ū-lans, pet′ū-lan-si, *n.* [L. *petulantia.*] Freakish passion; peevishness; pettishness; sauciness.—**Petulantly**, pet′ū-lant-li, *adv.* In a petulant manner; with saucy pertness.

Petunia, pē-tū′ni-a, *n.* [Brazil, *petun*, tobacco.] A genus of American herbaceous plants, nearly allied to the tobacco-plant, and much prized by horticulturists for the beauty of their flowers.

Petzite, pet′zīt, *n.* [From a chemist called *Petz.*] An ore of silver and tellurium.

Pew, pū, *n.* [O.Fr. *pui*, a raised place, from L. *podium*, a balcony, a front balcony in an amphitheatre, from Gr. *podion*, from *pous, podos*, the foot.] A fixed seat in a church, inclosed and separated from those adjoining by partitions; or an inclosure containing more than one seat.—*v.t.* To furnish with pews.—**Pew-fellow**, *n.* One who sits in the same pew; a companion (*Shak.*).—**Pew-opener**, *n.* An attendant in a church who opens the pew doors for the congregation.

Pewit, pē′wit, *n.* The peewit or lapwing.

Pewter, pū′tėr, *n.* [O.Fr. *peutre, piautre*, D. *peauter*, also, *speauter*, same as *spelter*.] An alloy of tin and lead, or of tin with such proportions of lead, zinc, bismuth, antimony, or copper as experience has shown to be most conducive to the improvement of its hardness and colour; a vessel, or vessels collectively, made of pewter.—*a.* Made of pewter.—**Pewterer**, pū′tėr-ėr, *n.* One whose occupation is to make articles of pewter.—**Pewtery**, pū′tėr-i, *a.* Belonging to or resembling pewter.

Peziza, pe-zī′za, *n.* [Gr. *pezis*, mushroom.] A generic name of numerous cup-shaped fungi.

Pfennig, pfen′ig, *n.* In Germany, the reichspfennig, a bronze coin worth 1/100 mark, or about ¼ of a cent.

Phacochere, Phacochœre, fak′o-kėr, *n.* [Gr. *phakos*, a lentil-shaped wart, from *phakē*, a lentil, and *choiros*, a hog.] The wart-hog of Africa, an animal akin to the swine, with a large wart-like excrescence on each side of the face.

Phænogam, fē′nō-gam, *n.* [Gr. *phainein*, to appear, and *gamos*, marriage.] A phanerogamous plant: opposed to *cryptogam*.—**Phænogamous**, fē-nog′a-mus, *a.* Having manifest flowers; phanerogamous.

Phænology, fēn-ol′o-jē, *n.* [Gr. *phainō*, I appear, *logos*, a discourse.] The study of times and seasons in relation to plants and animals as embodied in nature calendars.

Phænomenon, fē-nom′e-non. PHENOMENON.

Phaeton, fā′e-ton, *n.* [From Gr. *Phaethōn*, who obtained leave from his father Helios (the Sun) to drive the chariot of the sun, but as he was unable to restrain the horses Zeus dashed him with a thunderbolt headlong into the River Po.] An open four-wheeled carriage usually drawn by two horses.

Phagedena, Phagedæna, faj-ē-dē′na, *n.* [Gr. *phagedaina*, from *phagein*, to eat.] A spreading obstinate ulcer.—**Phagedenic, Phagedænic**, faj-ē-dē′nik, *a.* Pertaining to phagedena.—*n.* An application for phagedena or to destroy fungous or proud flesh.

Phagocyte, fag′o-sīt, *n.* [Gr. *phagein*, to eat, *kytos*, cell.] A white blood corpuscle that absorbs and destroys disease germs.—**Phagocytosis**, fag′ō-sīt-ō″sis, *n.* The destruction of disease germs and diseased products by phagocytes.

Phalange, fa-lanj′, *n.* [Gr. *phalanx, phalangos*, battle-array, a phalanx of soldiers, a bone of the fingers or toes.] *Anat.* one of the small bones of the fingers and toes; *bot.* a collection of several stamens joined more or less by their filaments.—**Phalangal, Phalangeal**, fa-lang′gal, fa-lan′jē-al, *a.* Belonging to the phalanges of the fingers and toes. — **Phalanger**, fa-lan′jėr, *n.* [From two of the toes being joined as far as the last *phalanges.*] An Australian marsupial animal of several species, nocturnal in habits and living in trees.—**Phalangial, Phalangian**, fa-lan′ji-al, fa-lan′ji-an, *a.* Same as *Phalangal.*—**Phalangite**, fal′an-jīt, *n.* [Gr. *phalangitēs.*] A soldier belonging to a phalanx.—**Phalanx**, fal′angks, *n.* pl. **Phalanges**, fa-lan′jēz, also, except in anatomy, **Phalanxes**, fal′angk-sēz. *Greek antiq.* the heavy-armed infantry of an army, especially when formed in ranks and files close and deep; a body of troops or men in close array; *anat.* one of the small bones of the fingers or the toes.

Phalanstery, fal′an-ste-ri, *n.* [Fr. *phalanstère*, from Gr. *phalanx*, a phalanx.] A socialistic community living together according to the system proposed by Fourier; the dwelling of such a community.

Phalarope, fal′a-rōp, *n.* [From Gr. *phalaros*, white, and *pous, podos*, a foot.] A lobe-footed grallatorial bird resembling the sandpiper.

Phallus, fal′lus, *n.* [Gr. *phallos*, the virile organ.] Image of the male organ of generation, symbolizing the power of fertility and reproductiveness in nature, as worshiped in some primitive systems of religion; in anatomy, the penis or clitoris.—**Phallic**, fal′lik, *a.* Pertaining to the phallus, or to the worship of the generative principle in nature.

Phanerogam, fan′ėr-o-gam, *n.* [Gr. *phaneros*, evident, and *gamos*, marriage.] *Bot.* a flowering plant or a plant with conspicuous flowers containing stamens and pistils: opposed to a *cryptogam.*—**Phanerogamic, Phanerogamous**, fan′ėr-o-gam″ik, fan-ėr-og′a-mus, *a.* *Bot.* belonging to the flowering plants, in contradistinction to *cryptogamic, cryptogamous.*

Phantasm, fan′tazm, *n.* [Gr. *phantasma*, from *phantazein*, to show, from the stem of *phainein*, to show. PHENOMENON.] A creation of the fancy; an imaginary existence which seems to be real; an apparition; a phantom; an idea; a notion; a fancy.—**Phantasmagoria**, fan-tas′ma-gō″ri-a, *n.* [Gr. *phantasma*, and *agora*, an assembly.] Any exhibition of images by means of shadows, as by the magic lantern; the apparatus used in such an exhibition; any mixed gathering of figures; illusive images. —**Phantasmagorial, Phantasmagoric**, fan-tas′ma-gō″ri-al, fan-tas′ma-gor″ik, *a.* Relating to a phantasmagoria.—**Phantasmal**, fan′taz-mal, *a.* Pertaining to or resembling a phantasm; spectral; illusive.

Phantasy, fan′ta-si, *n.* FANTASY.

Phantom, fan′tom, *n.* [Fr. *fantôme*, from L. *phantasma*; same word as *phantasm.* PHANTASM.] An apparition or spectre; a ghost; a fancied vision; a phantasm; something unreal. — **Phantomatic**, fan-to-mat″ik, *a.* Pertaining to or of the nature of a phantom.

Pharaoh, fā′rō, *n.* A name given by the Hebrews to the ancient monarchs of Egypt; a game at cards. FARO. — *Pharaoh's chicken*, the Egyptian vulture.—*Pharaoh's rat*, the ichneumon.—**Pharaonic**, fā-rā-on′ik, *a.* Pertaining to the Pharaohs, or to the old Egyptians.

Pharisee, far′i-sē, *n.* [Gr. *pharisaios*, from Heb. *pārash*, separated.] One of a sect among the Jews distinguished by their strict observance of rites and ceremonies and of the traditions of the elders, and who considered themselves as more righteous than other Jews; hence, a strict observer of the outward forms or ceremonies in religion, without the spirit of it; a hypocrite.—**Pharisaic, Pharisaical**, far-i-sā′ik, far-i-sā′i-kal, *a.* Pertaining to the Pharisees; resembling the Pharisees; addicted to external forms and ceremonies; making a show of religion without the spirit of it; hypocritical.—**Pharisaically**, far-i-sā′i-kal-li, *adv.* In a pharisaical manner; hypocritically.—**Pharisaicalness**, far-i-sā′i-kal-nes, *n.* — **Pharisaism**, far′i-sā-izm, *n.* The doctrines and conduct of the Pharisees, as a sect; rigid observance of external rites and forms of religion without genuine piety; hypocrisy in religion.

Pharmaceutic, Pharmaceutical, fär-ma-sū′tik, fär-ma-sū′ti-kal, *a.* [Gr. *pharmakeutikos*, from *pharmakeuein*, to administer medicine, from *pharmakon*, a drug.] Pertaining to the knowledge or art of pharmacy or preparing medicines. — *Pharmaceutical chemistry*, chemistry applied to those substances which are employed for the cure of diseases. — **Pharmaceutically**, fär-ma-sū′ti-kal-li, *adv.* In the manner of pharmacy.—**Pharmaceutics**, fär-ma-sū′tiks, *n.* The science of preparing medicines; pharmacy.—**Pharmaceutist**, fär-ma-sū′tist, *n.* One who prepares medicines; one who practises pharmacy; an apothecary.—**Pharmacist**, fär′ma-sist, *n.* One skilled in pharmacy; a druggist. — **Pharmacolite**, fär-mak′ō-līt, *n.* [Gr. *pharmakon*, poison, and *lithos*, a stone.] A mineral containing lime and arsenic, snow-white or milk-white in colour.—**Pharmacologist**, fär-ma-kol′o-jist, *n.* One who is skilled in pharmacology.—**Pharmacology**, fär-ma-kol′o-ji, *n.* [Gr. *pharmakon* and *logos.*] The science or knowledge of drugs, or the art of preparing medicines: a branch of materia medica; a treatise on preparing medicines.—**Pharmacopœia**, fär′ma-kō-pē″a, *n.* [Gr. *pharmakon*, and *poiein*, to make.] A book of directions for the preparation, &c., of medicines, generally published by authority.—**Pharmacopolist**, fär-ma-kop′o-list, *n.* [Gr. *pōlein*, to sell.] An apothecary. — **Pharmacosiderite**, fär′ma-kō-sid″ėr-īt, *n.* [Gr. *sidēros*, iron.] CUBE-ORE.—**Pharmacy**, fär′ma-si, *n.* [Fr. *pharmacie*, from Gr. *pharmakeia*, from *pharmakon.*] The art of preparing and compounding medicines, and of dispensing them according to the prescriptions of medical practitioners; the occupation of an apothecary.

Pharo, fā′rō, *n.* FARO.

Pharos, fā′ros, *n.* A lighthouse or tower which anciently stood on the isle of Pharos, at the entrance to the Port of Alexandria; hence, any lighthouse for the direction of seamen; a beacon.

Pharynx, far′ingks, *n.* [Gr. *pharynx, pharyngos*; akin to *pharanx*, a chasm.] The muscular sac which intervenes between the cavity of the mouth and the œsophagus, its contraction aiding in swallowing the food. —**Pharyngeal**, fa-rin′jē-al, *a.* Belonging to or affecting the pharynx.—**Pharyngitis**, far-in-jī′tis, *n.* Inflammation of the pharynx.—**Pharyngotomy**, far-in-got′o-mi, *n.* [Gr. *pharynx*, and *tomē*, a cutting.] The operation of making an incision into the pharynx to remove anything that obstructs the passage

Phascolotherium, fas-kol′ō-thē″ri-um, *n.* [Gr. *phaskōlos*, a pouch, and *thērion*, a wild beast.] A fossil marsupial animal remains of which have been found in the oolite.

Phase, fāz, *n.* [Fr. *phase*, from Gr. *phasis*, from *phainomai*, to appear. PHENOMENON.] One of the recurring appearances or states of the moon or a planet in respect to quantity of illumination or figure of enlightened disc; the particular state, at a given instant, of a continuously varying and periodic phenomenon (the *phases* of a tide, &c.); an aspect or appearance of that which presents various aspects; one of the various aspects in which a question presents itself to the mind; a turn or chance.—*Phase rule*, an equation $(c + 2 - p = F)$ expressing the relation between the solid, liquid, and gaseous states (phases) of substances in solution (c = components; p = number of phases; F = degrees of freedom).

Phasel, fā′zel, *n.* [Gr. *phasēlos*, a sort of bean.] The French bean or kidney-bean.—**Phaseolite**, fa-zē′o-līt, *n.* A fossil leguminous plant.

Phasis, fā′sis, *n.* pl. **Phases**, fā′sēz. *Astron.* a phase.

Pheasant, fez′ant, *n.* [L. *phasianus*, from Gr. *phasianos*, from *Phasis*, a river of Asia, near the mouth of which these birds are said to have been numerous.] A well-known and beautiful gallinaceous bird bred as a game bird, highly prized as a table delicacy; in the U. S., the ruffed grouse. The *golden* pheasant and the *silver* pheasant are natives of China.—**Pheasant-cuckoo**, *n.* An Australian bird of the cuckoo family.—**Pheasantry**, fez′ant-ri, *n.* A place for breeding, rearing, and keeping pheasants.

Phelloplastics, fel-lō-plas′tiks, *n.* [Gr. *phellos*, cork, and *plassein*, to form or fashion.] The art of modelling in cork.

Phenacetin, fē-nas′e-tin, *n.* A drug of coal-tar origin, used to relieve nervous headache, neuralgia, fever, &c.

Phenakistoscope, fen-a-kis′to-skōp, *n.* [Gr. *phenakistikos*, deceitful, *skopeō*, I view.] An optical toy which shows figures seemingly in actual motion, an effect due to the persistence of vision.

Phenician, fē-nish′i-an, *n.* and *a.* PHŒNICIAN.

Phenicine, fen′i-sin, *n.* [Gr. *phoinix*, purple.] A brown colouring matter used in dyeing.

Phenix, fē′niks, *n.* PHŒNIX.

Phenogam, fē′no-gam, *n.* A phanerogam.

Phenol, fē′nol, *n.* A name for *Carbolic Acid.*

Phenomenon, fē-nom′e-non, *n.* pl. **Phenomena**, fē-nom′e-na. [Gr. *phainomenon*, what appears, from *phainomai*, I appear.] A visible manifestation or appearance; a fact or occurrence presented to our observation either in the external world or in the human mind; an appearance produced by the action of the different forces upon matter; what strikes us as strange and uncommon; something extraordinary; an exceedingly remarkable thing or personage. —**Phenomenal**, fē-nom′e-nal, *a.* Connected with, relating to, or constituted by phenomena; so surprising or extraordinary as to arrest the attention; extremely remarkable or extraordinary; astounding.—**Phenomenalism**, fē-nom′e-nal-izm, *n.* That system of philosophy which inquires only into the causes of existing phenomena. — **Phenomenally**, fē-nom′e-nal-li, *adv.* In the manner of a phenomenon.—**Phenomenism**, fē-nom′en-izm, *n.* The doctrine or principles of the phenomenists.—**Phenomenist**, fē-nom′en-ist, *n.* One who believes only in phenomena, having no regard to their causes or consequences.

Pheon, fē′on, *n.* The barbed iron head of a dart or other weapon; a sort of barbed javelin.

Phial, fī′al, *n.* [L. *phiala*, from Gr. *phialē*, a phial. *Vial* is another form.] A glass vessel or bottle; especially, a small glass bottle used for holding liquors, and particularly liquid medicines.—*Leyden-phial*, a vessel used in electrical experiments. LEYDEN-PHIAL.—*v.t.*—*phialled, phialling.* To put or keep in a phial, or as in a phial.

Philabeg, Philibeg, fil′a-beg, fil′i-beg, *n.* FILLIBEG.

Philander, fi-lan′dėr, *v.i.* [From *Philander*, a virtuous youth in Ariosto's *Orlando Furioso*, between whom and a married lady there were certain tender passages.] To make love sentimentally to a lady; to flirt; to pretend admiration.

Philanthropy, fi-lan′thrō-pi, *n.* [Gr. *philanthrōpia*, from *philos*, loving, and *anthrōpos*, a man.] Love towards mankind; benevolence toward the whole human family.—**Philanthropic, Philanthropical**, fil-an-throp′ik, fil-an-throp′i-kal, *a.* [Gr. *philanthrōpikos.*] Pertaining to philanthropy; possessing general benevolence; entertaining good-will toward all men.—**Philanthropically**, fil-an-throp′i-kal-li, *adv.* In a philanthropic manner.—**Philanthropist**, fi-lan′throp-ist, *n.* One who evinces philanthropy; a person of general benevolence; one who exerts himself in doing good to his fellow-men.

Philately, fi-lat′e-li, *n.* [Fr. *philatélie*, a ridiculous compound of Gr. *philos*, loving, and *ateleia*, exemption from taxation.] The practice of collecting all sorts of postage stamps.—**Philatelist**, fi-lat'e-list, *n.* One who collects postage stamps.

Philharmonic, fil-här-mon'ik, *a.* [Gr. *philos*, loving, and *harmonia*, harmony.] Loving harmony; fond of harmony or music.

Philhellenist, Philhellene, fil-hel'len-ist, fil-hel'lēn, *n.* [Fr. *philhellène*, from Gr. *philos*, loving, and *Hellēn*, a Greek.] A friend of Greece; one who supports the cause and interests of the Greeks (Hellēnes); one who supported them in their successful struggle with the Turks for independence. —**Philhellenic**, fil-hel-len'ik, *a.* Loving the Greeks.—**Philhellenism**, fil-hel'len-izm, *n.* The principles of the philhellenists.

Philippian, fi-lip'i-an, *n.* A native or inhabitant of Philippi, a city of ancient Macedonia ('the Epistle of Paul to the *Philippians*').

Philippic, fi-lip'ik, *n.* One of a series of orations delivered by Demosthenes, the Grecian orator, against *Philip*, king of Macedon; any discourse full of acrimonious invective; a name given to the fourteen orations of Cicero against Mark Antony.—**Philippize**,† fil'ip-īz, *v.i.* — *philippized, philippizing.* To write or utter a philippic.

Philistine, fi-lis'tīn or fil'is-tin, *n.* An inhabitant of *Philistia*, now a portion of Syria; the English form of *Philister*, a term applied by German students to any one who has not been trained in a University; hence, a matter-of-fact, commonplace person deficient in liberal culture and large intelligence, and so wanting in sentiment and taste; a person of narrow views; a prosaic, practical man.—**Philistinism**, fil'is-tin-izm, *n.* Manners or modes of thinking of Philistines.

Phill-horse, fil'hors, *n.* A horse in the shafts: a corruption of *thill-horse*.

Philocalist, fi-lok'al-ist, *n.* [Gr. *philos*, loving, and *kalos*, beautiful.] A lover of the beautiful.

Philogyny, fi-loj'i-ni, *n.* [Gr. *philos*, loving, and *gynē*, a woman.] Fondness for women; uxoriousness.

Philology, fi-lol'o-ji, *n.* [Gr. *philologia*, from *phileō*, to love, and *logos*, a word.] The study of language and literature; the study of languages in connection with the whole moral and intellectual action of the peoples using them; the study of the classical languages, literature, and history; but the most common meaning now is the science of language; linguistic science; linguistics: often expressed by the qualified title of *comparative philology*.—**Philologist, Philologer, Philologian**, fi-lol'o-jist, fi-lol'o-jėr, fil-o-lō'ji-an, *n.* One versed in philology, or the study of language in a scientific manner.—**Philological, Philologic**, fil-ō-loj'i-kal, fil-ō-loj'ik, *a.* Pertaining to philology.—**Philologically**, fil-ō-loj'i-kal-li, *adv.* In a philological manner.

Philomath, fil'ō-math, *n.* [Gr. *philomathēs* — *philos*, a lover, and *math*, root of *manthanō*, to learn.] A lover of learning.—**Philomathic, Philomathical**, fil-ō-math'ik, fil-ō-math'i-kal, *a.* Pertaining to the love of learning.—**Philomathy**, fi-lom'a-thi, *n.* The love of learning.

Philomel, fil'ō-mel, *n.* [From *Philomela*, daughter of Pandion, king of Athens, who was changed into a nightingale.] The poetic name of the nightingale.

Philoprogenitiveness, fil'ō-prō-jen"i-tiv-nes, *n.* [Gr. *philos*, fond, and E. *progeny*.] The love of offspring, a term used chiefly by phrenologists.

Philosophe, fil-o-zof, *n.* [Fr.] A petty or puny philosopher.

Philosopher, fi-los'ō-fėr, *n.* [Gr. *philosophos*—*philos*, loving, and *sophos*, wise.] A person versed in or devoted to philosophy; one who devotes himself to the study of moral or intellectual science; one who conforms his life to the principles of philosophy; one who lives according to reason or the rules of practical wisdom.—*Philosophers' stone*, a stone or preparation which the alchemists formerly sought, as the instrument of converting the baser metals into pure gold.—**Philosophical, Philosophic**, fil-ō-sof'i-kal, fil-ō-sof'ik, *a.* Pertaining, suitable, or according to philosophy; characterized or constituted by philosophy; proceeding from philosophy; characteristic of a practical philosopher; based on the rules of practical wisdom; calm; cool; temperate.—**Philosophically**, fil-ō-sof'i-kal-li, *adv.* In a philosophical manner.—**Philosophicalness**,† fil-ō-sof'i-kal-nes, *n.* Quality of being philosophical.—**Philosophism**, fi-los'of-izm, *n.* [Fr. *philosophisme*.] Spurious or would-be philosophy; the affectation of philosophy.—**Philosophize**, fi-los'ō-fīz, *v.i.*—*philosophized, philosophizing.* To reason like a philosopher; to form or attempt to form a philosophical system or theory.—**Philosophizer**, fi-los'ō-fī-zėr, *n.* One who philosophizes.—**Philosophizing**, fi-los'ō-fīz-ing, *p.* and *a.* Searching into the reasons of things; reasoning like a philosopher.—**Philosophy**, fi-los'ō-fi, *n.* [Gr. *philosophia*, lit. love of wisdom, from *philos*, love, and *sophia*, wisdom.] The science which aims at an explanation of all the phenomena of the universe by ultimate causes; the knowledge of phenomena as explained by, and resolved into, causes and reasons, powers and laws; a particular philosophical system or theory; the calm and unexcitable state of mind of the wise man; practical wisdom; course of studies for the degree of 'Doctor of Philosophy' in Germany or elsewhere. — *Moral philosophy.* ETHICS. — *Mental philosophy.* METAPHYSICS.—*Natural philosophy.* PHYSICS.

Philotechnic, Philotechnical, fil-ō-tek'nik, fil-ō-tek'ni-kal, *a.* [Gr. *philos*, loving, *technē*, art.] Having an attachment to the arts.

Philter, Philtre, fil'tėr, *n.* [Fr. *philtre*, L. *philtrum*, from Gr. *philtron*, from *philos*, loving.] A potion supposed by the ancients, and even by the ignorant of the present day, to have the power of exciting love.—*v.t.*—*philtered, philtred; philtering, philtring.* To impregnate with a love potion; to administer a potion to.

Phiz, fiz, *n.* [A contr. of *physiognomy*.] The face or visage. (*Humorous.*)

Phlebitis, fle-bī'tis, *n.* [Gr. *phleps, phlebos*, a vein, and *-itis*, implying inflammation.] Inflammation of the inner membrane of a vein.—**Phlebology**, flē-bol'o-ji, *n.* [Gr. *phleps, phlebos*, and *logos*.] That branch of anatomy which treats of the veins. —**Phleborrhage, Phleborrhagia**, fleb'or-rāj, fleb-or-rā'ji-a, *n.* [Gr. *rhagē*, a rupture.] The rupture of a vein; venous hemorrhage.—**Phlebotomy**, flē-bot'ō-mi, *n.* [Gr. *phlebotomia*—*phleps, phlebos*, and *tomē*, a cutting.] The act or practice of opening a vein for letting blood.—**Phlebotomist**, flē-bot'ō-mist, *n.* One that opens a vein for letting blood; a blood-letter. — **Phlebotomize**, flē-bot'ō-mīz, *v.t.*—*phlebotomized, phlebotomizing.* To let blood from; to bleed by opening a vein.

Phlegm, flem, *n.* [Gr. *phlegma, phlegmatos*, a slimy humour, from *phlegō*, to burn. FLAME.] The thick viscid matter secreted in the digestive and respiratory passages, and discharged by coughing or vomiting; bronchial mucus; *fig.* coldness; sluggishness; indifference. — **Phlegmasia**, fleg-mā'si-a, *n.* [Gr., from *phlegō*, to burn.] An inflammation in the thigh or leg of lying-in women. — **Phlegmatic, Phlegmatical**, fleg-mat'ik, fleg-mat'i-kal, *a.* [Gr. *phlegmatikos*.] Abounding in phlegm; generating phlegm; cold or sluggish in temperament; not easily excited into action or passion; not mercurial or lively.—**Phlegmatically**, fleg-mat'i-kal-li, *adv.* In a phlegmatic manner; coldly; heavily.

Phleme, flēm, *n.* FLEAM.

Phloem, flō'em, *n.* [Gr. *phloios*, bark.] *Bot.* the liber or bast tissue in plants.

Phlogiston, flo-jis'ton, *n.* [Gr. *phlogistos*, burnt, from *phlogizō*, to burn, from *phlegō*, to burn.] According to an obsolete theory, the supposed principle of inflammability; a hypothetical element which was thought to be pure fire fixed in combustible bodies. —**Phlogistic**, flo-jis'tik, *a.* Pertaining to phlogiston; *med.* inflammatory.

Phlox, floks, *n.* [Gr. *phlox*, a flame, from the appearance of the flowers.] A North American genus of plants, with red, purple, or white flowers, cultivated in gardens.

Phlyctena, Phlyctaena, flik-tē'na, *n.* [Gr. *phlyktaina*.] A kind of watery pustule on the skin.—**Phlyctenula**, flik-ten'ū-la, *n.* [Dim. of *phlyctæna*.] A small transparent pustule; a phlyctena.—**Phlyctenular**, flik-ten'ū-lėr, *a.* Pertaining to phlyctenula.—*Phlyctenular ophthalmia*, inflammation of the eye, accompanied with phlyctena on the cornea.

Phobia, fō'bi-a, *n.* [Gr. *phobos*, fear.] Any persistent, morbid fear or dread.—**Phobic**, fō'bic, *a.*

Phocine, fō'sin, *a.* Pertaining to the seals.

Phœbus, fē'bus, *n.* [Gr. *Phoibos*, lit. the brilliant one.] A name of Apollo, often used in the same sense as Sol, the sun.

Phœnician, fē-nish'i-an, *a.* Pertaining to Phœnicia.—*n.* A native of ancient Phœnicia, the region between Lebanon and the Mediterranean; the language of the Phœnicians, an extinct Semitic tongue, akin to Hebrew.

Phœnix, fē'niks, *n.* [Gr. *phoinix*.] A bird of ancient legend said to be the only one of its kind and to live 500 or 600 years, at the end of which it built for itself a funeral pile, lighted it with the fanning of its wings, and rose again from its ashes; hence, an emblem of immortality; a paragon; a person of singular distinction or beauty.

Pholas, fō'las, *n.* pl. **Pholades**, fō'la-dēz. [Gr. *phōlas*, from *phōleō*, to lie concealed.] A genus of bivalve marine molluscs which pierce rocks, wood, &c., by rasping with certain projections on their shell.

Phonascetics, fō-nas-set'iks, *n.* [Gr. *phōnē*, the voice, and *askeō*, to practise.] Systematic practice for strengthening the voice.

Phonation, fō-nā'shon, *n.* [Gr. *phōnē*, voice.] The act of uttering vocal sounds.

Phonautograph, fō-na'tō-graf, *n.* [Gr. *phōnē*, sound, *autos*, self, and *graphō*, to write.] An instrument for automatically showing sound vibrations by waved lines.

Phone, fōn. Short for *Telephone*: used as noun and verb.

Phonetic, Phonetical, fō-net'ik, fō-net'i-kal, *a.* [Gr. *phōnētikos*, from *phōnē*, voice, sound.] Pertaining to the voice; pertaining to the representation of sounds; representing sounds. — *Phonetic spelling*, a system which aims at spelling words precisely according to their sound, and not in the loose manner in which English is spelled.—**Phonetically**, fō-net'i-kal-li, *adv.* In a phonetic manner.—**Phonetics**, fō-net'iks, *n.* The doctrine of sounds; the science which treats of the sounds of the human voice, and the art of representing them by writing.—**Phonic**, fō'nik, *a.* Pertaining to sound.—**Phonics**, fō'niks, *n.* The doctrine or science of sounds; phonetics.

Phonocamptic, fō-nō-kamp'tik, *a.* [Gr. *phōnē*, sound, and *kamptō*, to bend.] Having the power to inflect sound, or turn it from its direction.

Phonograph, fō'nō-graf, *n.* [Gr. *phōnē*, sound, and *graphō*, to write.] A type or character for expressing a sound; a character used in phonography; an instrument by means of which sounds can be permanently registered, and afterwards mechanically reproduced almost in the original tones from the register.—**Phonogram**, fō'nō-gram, *n.* A sound as reproduced by the phonograph. — **Phonographer, Phonographist**, fō-nog'raf-ėr, fō-nog'raf-ist, *n.* One versed in phonography; one who uses or is skilled in the use of the phonograph.—**Phonographic, Phonographical**, fō-nō-graf'ik, fō-nō-graf'i-kal, *a.* Pertaining to or based upon phonography; pertaining to the phonograph. — **Phonographically**, fō-nō-graf'i-kal-li, *adv.* In a phonographic manner.—**Phonography**, fō-nog'ra-fi, *n.* The description of sounds; the representation of sounds by characters, each of which represents one sound, and always the same sound; phonetic shorthand; the art of using the phonograph.

Phonolite, fō'nō-līt, *n.* [Gr. *phōnē*, sound, and *lithos*, stone.] Same as *Clink-stone.*

Phonology, fō-nol'o-ji, *n.* [Gr. *phōnē*, sound, voice, and *logos*, discourse.] The science or doctrine of the elementary sounds uttered by the human voice; phonetics.—**Phonologic, Phonological**, fō-nō-loj'ik, fō-nō-loj'i-kal, *a.* Pertaining to phonology. — **Phonologist**, fō-nol'o-jist, *n.* One versed in phonology.

Phonometer, fō-nom'et-ėr, *n.* [Gr. *phōnē*, sound, *metron*, a measure.] An instrument for ascertaining the number of vibrations of a given sound in a given time.

Phonoscope, fō'nō-skōp, *n.* [Gr. *phōnē*, a voice, a sound, and *skopeō*, to view.] An instrument for producing figures of light from vibrations of sound by means of an electric current.

Phonotypy, fō-not'i-pi, *n.* [Gr. *phōnē*, sound, and *typos*, type.] A method of representing each of the sounds of speech by a distinct printed character or letter; phonetic printing.—**Phonotype**, fō'nō-tīp, *n.* A type or character used in phonetic printing.—**Phonotypic**, fō-nō-tip'ik, *a.* Pertaining to phonotypy.

Phorminx, for'mingks, *n.* [Gr.] An ancient Grecian lute or lyre.

Phormium, for'mi-um, *n.* [From Gr. *phormos*, a basket—because it is made into baskets.] The generic name of New Zealand flax.

Phoronomics, for-ō-nom'iks, *n.* [Gr. *phoreō*, to bear or carry, and *nomos*, a law.] A name for kinematics.

Phosgene, fos'jēn, *n.* [Gr. *phōs*, light, and root *gen*, to produce.] A heavy, poisonous gas with a nauseating, choking smell, used in warfare, and in the making of dyes.

Phosphorus, fos'for-us, *n.* [L. *phosphorus*, Gr. *phōsphoros*, the morning-star, lit. light-bringer, from *phōs*, light (same root as in *phenomenon*), and *pherō*, to bring.] A solid non-metallic combustible elementary substance, at common temperatures a soft solid which undergoes slow combustion, an important constituent in animal and vegetable structures, and chiefly obtained from bones.—**Phosphate**, fos'fāt, *n.* A salt of phosphoric acid.—**Phosphatic**, fos-fat'ik, *a.* Partaking of the nature of a phosphate; containing a phosphate. — **Phosphide**, fos'fīd, *n.* A combination of phosphorus with a single element.—**Phosphite**, fos'fīt, *n.* A salt of phosphorous acid.—**Phosphorate**, fos'for-āt, *v.t.* —*phosphorated, phosphorating.* To combine or impregnate with phosphorus.—**Phosphor-bronze**, *n.* An alloy of copper, tin, and phosphorus, made into bearings for machinery, guns, cutlery, wire, sheathing for vessels, &c. — **Phosphoresce**, fos-fo-res', *v.i.*—*phosphoresced, phosphorescing.* To shine, as phosphorus, by exhibiting a faint light without sensible heat; to give out a phosphoric light.—**Phosphorescence**, fos-fo-res'ens, *n.* The state or quality of being phosphorescent; the property which certain bodies possess of becoming luminous without undergoing combustion, sometimes a chemical, sometimes a physical action.—**Phosphorescent**, fos-fo-res'ent, *a.* Shining with a faint light or luminosity like that of phosphorus; luminous without sensible heat.—**Phosphoric**, fos-for'ik, *a.* Pertaining to, obtained from, or resembling phosphorus; phosphorescent. —*Phosphoric acid*, an acid usually obtained by burning phosphuretted hydrogen in atmospheric air or oxygen.—**Phosphorite**, fos'for-īt, *n.* A species of calcareous earth; an amorphous phosphate of lime. — **Phosphoritic**, fos-fo-rit'ik, *a.* Pertaining to phosphorite.—**Phosphorize**, fos'for-īz, *v.t.*—*phosphorized, phosphorizing.* To combine or impregnate with phosphorus. — **Phosphorous**, fos'for-us, *a.* Pertaining to or obtained from phosphorus. — *Phosphorous acid*, an acid produced by exposing sticks of phosphorus to moist air, and in several other ways.—**Phosphuret**, fos'fū-ret, *n.* The name formerly given to phosphide.—**Phosphuretted**, fos'fū-ret-ed, *a.* Combined with phosphorus. — *Phosphuretted hydrogen*, a gas procured by boiling phosphorus in a solution of a caustic alkali.

Photics, fō'tiks, *n.* [Gr. *phōs*, *phōtos*, light.] That department of science which treats of light.

Photo, fō'tō, *n.* [Gr. *phōs*, *phōtos*, light.] A combining prefix meaning light.

Photochemistry, fō-tō-kem'ist-ri, *n.* [Gr. *phōs*, *phōtos*, light, and E. *chemistry*.] That branch of chemistry which treats of the chemical action of light, especially of solar light.—**Photochemical**, fō-tō-kem'i-kal, *a.* Pertaining to the chemical action of light.

Photochromy, fō-tok'ro-mi, *n.* [Gr. *phōs*, *phōtos*, light, and *chrōma*, color.] The art or operation of reproducing colors by photography.

Photo-electric cell, a vacuum tube in which the action of light produces, or changes the strength of, electric current.

Photo-electrotype, *n.* A process in which a photographic picture is produced in relief so as to afford, by electric deposition, a matrix for a cast, from which impressions in ink may be obtained.

Photo-engraving, *n.* A common name of many processes in which the action of light is used for obtaining a picture upon a plate or block for subsequent engraving.

Photogene, fō'tō-jēn, *n.* [Gr. *phōs*, *phōtos*, light, and root *gen*, to produce.] A more or less continued impression or picture on the retina.—**Photogenic**, fō-tō-jen'ik, *a.* Pertaining to photogenes or to photogeny.—**Photogeny**, fō-toj'e-ni, *n.* Photography.

Photoglyphy, fō-tog'li-fi, *n.* [Gr. *phōs*, *phōtos*, light, and *glyphō*, to engrave.] A method of engraving by which photographs and other transparent designs can be etched into steel, copper, or zinc plates by the action of light and certain chemicals.—**Photoglyphic**, fō-tō-glif'ik, *a.* Related to photoglyphy.

Photography, fō-tog'ra-fi, *n.* [Gr. *phōs*, *phōtos*, light, and *graphō*, to describe.] The art of obtaining accurate representations of scenes and objects by means of the action of light on substances treated with certain chemicals. — **Photograph**, fō'tō-graf, *n.* A picture obtained by means of photography. — *v.t.* To produce a likeness or representation of by photographic means.—**Photographer, Photographist**, fō-tog'raf-ėr, fō-tog'ra-fist, *n.* One who takes pictures by means of photography.—**Photographic, Photographical**, fō-tō-graf'ik, fō-tō-graf'i-kal, *a.* Relating to photography.—*Photographic printing*, the process of obtaining positives on sensitized paper from transparent negatives by exposure to light. — **Photographically**, fō-tō-graf'i-kal-li, *adv.* In a photographic manner; by means of photography.

Photogravure, fō'to-grav-ūr, *n.* [Gr. *phōs*, *phōtos*, light, Fr. *gravure*, engraving.] A process by which an engraving is produced on a metal plate by light acting on a sensitive surface.

Photo-lithograph, *n.* A picture produced by photo-lithography. — **Photo-lithography**, *n.* A mode of lithographing in which a photograph is transferred to a prepared lithographic stone.

Photology, fō-tol'o-ji, *n.* [Gr. *phōs*, *phōtos*, light, and *logos*, discourse.] The doctrine or science of light, explaining its nature and phenomena.—**Photologic, Photological**, fō-tō-loj'ik, fō-tō-loj'i-kal, *a.* Pertaining to photology.—**Photologist**, fō-tol'o-jist, *n.* One who devotes himself to the science of light.

Photometer, fō-tom'et-ėr, *n.* [Gr. *phōs*, *phōtos*, light, and *metron*, measure.] An instrument intended to measure the comparative intensity of different lights. — **Photometric, Photometrical**, fō-tō-met'rik, fō-tō-met'ri-kal, *a.* Pertaining to or made by a photometer.—**Photometry**, fō-tom'et-ri, *n.* The measurement of the relative amounts of light emitted by different sources.

Photo-micrography, *n.* [Gr. *phōs*, *phōtos*, light, *mikros*, small, and *graphō*, to write.] The art or process of photographing minute objects when magnified by means of the microscope.

Photophobia, fō-tō-fō'bi-a, *n.* [Gr. *phōs*, *phōtos*, light, and *phobia*, dread.] An intolerance or dread of light.

Photophone, fō'tō-fōn, *n.* [Gr. *phōs*, *phōtos*, light, and *phōnē*, a voice, a sound.] An instrument for reproducing sound in distant places by variations in the intensity of a beam of light.—**Photophonic**, fō-tō-fon'ik, *a.* Pertaining to or produced by the photophone. — **Photophony**, fō-tof'o-ni, *n.* The art or practice of using the photophone.

Photoplay, fō'tō-plā, *n.* A play reproduced by motion pictures; a motion picture.

Photopsia, Photopsy, fō-top'si-a, fō-top'si, *n.* [Gr. *phōs*, *phōtos*, light, and *opsis*, sight.] A disease of the eyes, in which lights seem to play before them.

Photosensitive, fō-tō-sen'si-tiv, *a.* Readily affected or changed by light or other radiant energy.

Photospectroscope, fō-tō-spek'trō-skōp, *n.* An instrument for photographing spectra.

Photosphere, fō'tō-sfēr, *n.* [Gr. *phōs*, *phōtos*, light, and E. *sphere*.] An envelope of light; the luminous envelope, supposed to consist of incandescent matter, surrounding the sun.

Photosynthesis, fō'tō-sin"the-sis, *n.* [Gr. *phōs*, *phōtos*, light, *synthēsis*, a putting together.] In green plants, the utilization by protoplasm of the energy of light, aided by the green pigment chlorophyll, for building up organic matter from water and carbonic acid gas.

Phototype, fō'tō-tīp, *n.* [Gr. *phōs*, *phōtos*, light, and *typos*, a type.] A plate produced from a photograph by a peculiar process, as by photoglyphy or photo-lithography, and from which copies can be printed.—**Phototypy**, fō-tot'i-pi, *n.* The art or process of producing phototypes.

Photo-xylography, *n.* [Gr. *phōs*, *phōtos*, light, *xylon*, wood, and *graphō*, to write.] A mode of wood-engraving where the picture is in the first place photographed on the block. — **Photo-zincography**, *n.* The process of printing from a prepared zinc plate on which a photograph has been taken.

Phragmacone, frag'ma-kōn, *n.* [Gr. *phragma*, a partition, and *kōnos*, a cone.] The internal chambered cone of the belemnite or other cuttle-fish.

Phrase, frāz, *n.* [Gr. *phrasis*, a phrase (seen also in *periphrasis*, *paraphrase*), from *phrazō*, I speak.] A brief expression; two or more words forming a complete expression by themselves or being a portion of a sentence; a peculiar or characteristic expression; an idiom; the manner or style in which a person expresses himself; diction; *music*, a short part of a composition usually occupying a distinct rhythmical period of from two to four bars. — *v.t.* — *phrased, phrasing.* To call; to style; to express.—**Phrase-book**, *n.* A book in which phrases or idioms of a language are collected and explained. — **Phraseogram**, frā'zē-ō-gram, *n.* A combination of shorthand characters to represent a phrase or sentence.—**Phraseologic, Phraseological**, frā'zē-ō-loj"ik, frā'zē-ō-loj"i-kal, *a.* Pertaining to phraseology; exhibiting idiomatic phrases.—**Phraseologist**, frā-zē-ol'o-jist, *n.* A stickler for a particular form of words or phraseology; a coiner of phrases. —**Phraseology**, frā-zē-ol'o-ji, *n.* Manner of expression; peculiar words or phrases used in a sentence; diction; a collection of phrases in a language. ∴ Syn. under DICTION.

Phrenetic, fre-net'ik, *a.* [L. *phreneticus*, from Gr. *phrenitikos*, suffering from *phrenitis* or inflammation of the brain, from *phrēn*, the mind, the midriff. FRANTIC.] Having the mind disordered; frantic; frenetic.—*n.* A frantic or frenzied person; one whose mind is disordered. — **Phrenetically**, fre-net'i-kal-li, *adv.* In a phrenetic manner.—**Phrenic**, fren'ik, *a.* [From Gr. *phrēn*, in sense of diaphragm.] *Anat.* belonging to the diaphragm.—**Phrenitis**, fre-nī'tis, *n.* [Gr., from *phrēn*, the mind, and *-itis*, term. denoting inflammation.] *Med.* an inflammation of the brain; delirium; phrensy or frenzy.

Phrenology, fre-nol'o-ji, *n.* [Gr. *phrēn*, *phrenos*, the mind, and *logos*, discourse.] A doctrine which professes to found a philosophy of the human mind upon a presumed knowledge of the functions of different portions of the brain obtained by comparing their relative forms and magnitudes in different individuals with the propensities and intellectual powers which these individuals are found respectively to possess.—**Phrenologic**, **Phrenological**, fren-ō-loj'ik, fren-ō-loj'i-kal, *a.* Pertaining to phrenology.—**Phrenologically**, fren-ō-loj'i-kal-li, *adv.* In a phrenological manner; according to the principles of phrenology.—**Phrenologist**, fre-nol'o-jist, *n.* One versed in phrenology.

Phrygian, frij'i-an, *a.* [From *Phrygia*, in Asia Minor.] Pertaining to Phrygia or to the Phrygians.—*Phrygian cap*, the red cap of Liberty worn by the leaders during the first French republic.—*Phrygian mode*, one of the modes in ancient music.

Phthalic acid, thal'ik, fthal'ik, one of three isomeric benzene-dicarboxylic acids, the most important of which is used in making synthetic dyes, resins, &c.

Phthiriasis, thi-rī'a-sis, *n.* [Gr. *phtheiriasis*, from *phtheir*, a louse.] The disease which consists in the multiplication of lice on the human body.

Phthisis, thī'sis, *n.* [Gr. *phthisis*, a wasting, from *phthiō*, to waste away.] A disease produced by tubercles in the lungs, and commonly known by the name of consumption; pulmonary consumption.—**Phthisic**, tiz'ik, *n.* A consumption or wasting away; a person affected with phthisis.—**Phthisical**, tiz'i-kal, *a.* [Gr. *phthisikos.*] Belonging to phthisis; affected by phthisis.

Phycography, fī-kog'ra-fi, *n.* [Gr. *phykos*, a sea-weed, and *graphē*, description.] A scientific description of algæ or sea-weeds.—**Phycology**, fī-kol'o-ji, *n.* [Gr. *phykos*, and *logos.*] That department of botany which treats of the algæ or sea-weeds.

Phylactery, fi-lak'tėr-i, *n.* [Gr. *phylaktērion*, from *phylassō*, to defend or guard.] An amulet worn as a preservative from danger or disease among the Jews; a strip of parchment inscribed with certain texts from the Old Testament, inclosed within a small leather case, and fastened on the forehead or on the left arm near the region of the heart.—**Phylacteric**, **Phylacterical**, fi-lak-ter'ik, fi-lak-ter'i-kal, *a.* Pertaining to phylacteries.

Phylarch, fī'lärk, *n.* [Gr. *phylē*, a tribe, and *archē*, rule.] The chief or governor of a tribe.—**Phylarchy**, fī'lär-ki, *n.* The office of a phylarch; government of a tribe.

Phylaxin, fī-laks'in, *n.* [Gr. *phylax*, a guardian.] A defensive proteid found in animals artificially immune to some infectious disease. A *mycophylaxin* destroys the disease germs, while a *toxophylaxin* counteracts the poison they produce.

Phyletic, fī-let'ik, *a.* [Gr. *phylē*, a tribe or race.] Pertaining to a race or tribe: applied especially in connection with the development of animal tribes.

Phyllary, fil'a-ri, *n.* [Gr. *phyllon*, a leaf.] *Bot.* one of the leaflets forming the involucre of composite flowers.

Phylloclade, fil'lō-klād, *n.* [Gr. *phyllon*, a leaf, *klados*, a branch. A CLADODE (which see).

Phyllode, fil'ōd, *n.* [Gr. *phyllon*, a leaf.] A flattened leaf-stalk which performs the functions of a leaf-blade.

Phyllodium, fil-ō'di-um, *n.* [Gr. *phyllon*, a leaf, and *eidos*, likeness.] *Bot.* a leaf-stalk developed into a flattened expansion like a leaf.—**Phylloid**, fil'oid, *a.* Leaf-like; shaped like a leaf.—**Phyllophagan**, fil-of'a-gan, *n.* [Gr. *phyllon*, and *phagō*, to eat.] An animal that feeds on the leaves of trees.—**Phyllophagous**, fil-of'a-gus, *a.* Leaf-eating.—**Phyllophore**, fil'o-fōr, *n.* [Gr. *phyllon*, and *phoros*, bearing.] *Bot.* the terminal bud or growing point in palms.—**Phyllophorous**, fil-of'o-rus, *a.* Leaf-bearing; producing leaves.—**Phyllopod**, fil'o-pod, *n.* [Gr. *phyllon*, and *pous*, *podos*, a foot.] One of those crustaceans that have limbs of leaf-like form for swimming.—**Phyllostome**, fil'o-stōm, *n.* [Gr. *stoma*, a mouth.] One of a family of bats that have a leaf-like appendage on the nose. — **Phyllotactic**, fil-o-tak'tik, *a.* Pertaining to phyllotaxis. — **Phyllotaxis**, **Phyllotaxy**, fil'o-tak-sis, fil'o-tak-si, *n.* [Gr. *taxis*, order.] *Bot.* the arrangement of the leaves on the axis or stem.—**Phylloxera**, fil-ok-sē'ra, *n.* [Gr. *phyllon*, a leaf, and *xeros*, parched.] An insect which infests the leaves and roots of the oak, vine, &c., one species of which has caused immense damage in some wine-producing countries.

Phylogenesis, **Phylogeny**, fī-lō-jen'e-sis, fī-loj'e-ni, *n.* [Gr. *phylē*, a tribe, and *genesis*, root *gen*, to produce.] *Biol.* the origin and history of races or types of animal forms.—**Phylogenetic**, fī'lō-je-net''ik, *a.* Pertaining to phylogenesis or phylogeny, or the race history of an animal.

Phylum, fī'lum, *n.* pl. **Phyla**. [Gr. *phylon*, a tribe.] One of the grand subdivisions of the animal or vegetable kingdom.

Phyma, fī'ma, *n.* [Gr. *phyma*, from *phyō*, to produce.] An imperfectly suppurating tumour, forming an abscess.

Physalia, fī-sā'li-a, *n.* [Gr. *physalis*, a bladder, from *physaō*, to puff.] A genus of Hydrozoa that float on the surface of the ocean and are remarkable for the brilliancy of their hues.

Physalite, fī'sa-līt, *n.* [Gr. *physaō*, to inflate, and *lithos*, a stone, from intumescing when heated.] A mineral of a greenish-white colour; a kind of topaz.

Physic, fiz'ik, *n.* [Gr. *physikos*, pertaining to nature, natural, from *physis*, nature, from *phyō*, to bring forth, to spring up; cog. with Skr. *bhû*, to be; E. to *be*. BE.] The science or knowledge of medicine; the art of healing; a medicine, popularly a medicine that purges; a purge; a cathartic. —*Physic garden*, an old name for a botanic garden.—*Physic nut*, the seed of one or two tropical plants (genus Jatropha), having strong purgative and emetic properties.—*v.t.*—*physicked*, *physicking*. To treat with physic; to purge with a cathartic; to remedy.—**Physical**, fiz'i-kal, *a.* Pertaining to nature; relating to what is material and perceived by the senses; pertaining to the material part or structure of an organized being, as opposed to what is mental or moral (*physical* force); material (the *physical* world); pertaining to physics or natural philosophy.—*Physical geography.* Under GEOGRAPHY. — *Physical science.* PHYSICS.—**Physically**, fiz'i-kal-li, *adv.* In a physical manner; as regards the material world; as regards the bodily constitution.—**Physician**, fi-zish'an, *n.* A person skilled in the art of healing; one whose profession is to prescribe remedies for diseases. — **Physicism**, fiz'i-sizm, *n.* The ascription of everything to merely physical or material causes.—**Physicist**, fiz'i-sist, *n.* One skilled in physics; a natural philosopher.—**Physico-mathematics**, fiz'i-kō, *n.* Mixed mathematics. — **Physico-philosophy**, *n.* The philosophy of nature. —**Physico-theology**, *n.* Theology illustrated or enforced by physics or natural philosophy. — **Physics**, fiz'iks, *n.* That branch of science which treats of the laws and properties of matter; the department of science that deals with mechanics, dynamics, light, heat, sound, electricity, and magnetism; natural philosophy.

Physiognomy, fiz-i-og'no-mi, *n.* [Properly *physiognomony*, from Gr. *physiognōmonia*—*physis*, nature, and *gnōmōn*, one who knows, from stem of *gignōskō*, to know.] The art of discerning the character of the mind from the features of the face; the face or countenance as an index of the mind; particular cast or expression of countenance. — **Physiognomic**, **Physiognomical**, **Physiognomonic**, fiz'i-og-nom''ik, fiz'i-og-nom''i-kal, fiz-i-og'no-mon''-ik, *a.* Pertaining to physiognomy.—**Physiognomist**, fiz-i-og'no-mist, *n.* One skilled in physiognomy.

Physiogony, fiz-i-og'o-ni, *n.* [Gr. *physis*, nature, and *gonē*, generation.] The production or generation of nature.

Physiography, fiz-i-og'ra-fi, *n.* [Gr. *physis*, nature, and *graphō*, to describe.] The science which treats of the earth's physical features, and the causes by which they have been modified, as well as of the climates, life, &c., of the globe; physical geography.—**Physiographical**, fiz'i-ō-graf''-i-kal, *a.* Pertaining to physiography.

Physiolatry, fiz-i-ol'a-tri, *n.* [Gr. *physis*, nature, and *latreia*, worship.] The worship of the powers or agencies of nature; nature worship.

Physiology, fiz-i-ol'o-ji, *n.* [Fr. *physiologie*, Gr. *physiologia*—*physis*, nature, and *logos*, discourse.] That science which has for its aim the study and elucidation of the phenomena of life in animals and plants.—**Physiologic**, **Physiological**, fiz'i-ō-loj''ik, fiz'i-o-loj''i-kal, *a.* Pertaining to physiology.—*Physiological selection*, partial or complete sterility of varying forms with the parent stock: a suggested cause of the isolation necessary for evolution of new species.—**Physiologically**, fiz'i-ō-loj''i-kal-li, *adv.* According to the principles of physiology.—**Physiologist**, fiz-i-ol'o-jist, *n.* One who is versed in or who treats of physiology.

Physique, fē-zēk', *n.* [Fr.] A person's physical or bodily structure or constitution.

Phytelephas, fī-tel'ē-fas, *n.* [From Gr. *phyton*, a plant, and *elephas*, ivory.] The plant that yields the ivory-nut.

Phytochemistry, fī-tō-kem'is-tri, *n.* [Gr. *phyton*, a plant.] Vegetable chemistry.—**Phytochemical**, fī-tō-kem'i-kal, *a.* Pertaining to phytochemistry.

Phytochlor, fī'tō-klor, *n.* [Gr. *phyton*, a plant, and *chlōros*, green.] CHLOROPHYLL.

Phytogenesis, **Phytogeny**, fī-tō-jen'e-sis, fī-toj'e-ni, *n.* [Gr. *phyton*, a plant, and *genesis.*] The doctrine of the generation of plants.

Phytogeography, fī'tō-jē-og''ra-fi, *n.* [Gr. *phyton*, a plant, and E. *geography.*] The geography or geographical distribution of plants.

Phytoglyphy, fī-tog'li-fi, *n.* [Gr. *phyton*, a plant, and *glyphō*, to engrave.] The art of taking impressions from plants on soft metal, from which copies can be taken by printing; nature-printing.—**Phytoglyphic**, fī-tō-glif'ik, *a.* Relating to phytoglyphy.

Phytography, fī-tog'ra-fi, *n.* [Gr. *phyton*, a plant, and *graphē*, description.] That branch of botany which concerns itself with the rules to be observed in describing and naming plants.—**Phytographical**, fī-tō-graf'i-kal, *a.* Pertaining to the description of plants.

Phytoid, fī'toid, *a.* [Gr. *phyton*, a plant, and *eidos*, likeness.] Plant-like.

Phytolithology, fī'tō-li-thol''o-ji, *n.* [Gr. *phyton*, plant, *lithos*, stone, *logos*, discourse.] That part of science which treats of fossil plants.—**Phytolithologist**, fī'tō-li-thol''-o-jist, *n.* One who is skilled in fossil plants.

Phytology, fī-tol'o-ji, *n.* [Gr. *phyton*, a plant, *logos*, discourse.] The science of plants, a name sometimes used as equivalent to botany.—**Phytological**, fī-tō-loj'i-kal, *a.* Relating to phytology.—**Phytologist**, fī-tol'o-jist, *n.* One versed in plants or skilled in phytology; a botanist.

Phyton, fī'ton, *n.* [Gr., a plant.] *Bot.* a rudimentary or embryo plant.

Phytonomy, fī-ton′o-mi, *n.* [Gr. *phyton*, a plant, and *nomos*, a law.] The science of the origin and growth of plants.

Phytopathology, fī′tō-pa-thol″o-ji, *n.* [Gr. *phyton*, a plant, *pathos*, disease, *logos*, treatise.] Scientific knowledge relating to the diseases of plants.

Phytophagous, fī-tof′a-gus, *a.* [Gr. *phyton*, a plant, *phagō*, to eat.] Eating or subsisting on plants.—**Phytophagy**, fī-tof′a-ji, *n.* The eating of or subsisting upon plants.—**Phytotomy**, fī-tot′o-mi, *n.* [Gr. *phyton*, a plant, and *tomē*, a cutting.] Vegetable anatomy.—**Phytotomist**, fī-tot′o-mist, *n.* One versed in phytotomy.

Phytozoa, fī-tō-zō′a, *n.pl.* [Gr. *phyton*, a plant, and *zōon*, an animal.] Same as *Zoophytes*.—**Phytozoon**, fī-tō-zō′on, *n.* One of the phytozoa; a zoophyte.

Piaba, pi-ä′ba, *n.* A small fresh-water fish of Brazil much esteemed for food.

Piacular, pī-ak′ū-lėr, *a.* [L. *piacularis*, from *piaculum*, expiation, from *pio*, to expiate, from *pius*, pious.] Expiatory; pertaining to expiation.

Pia-mater, pī′a-mā′tėr, *n.* [L., lit. pious mother.] *Anat.* a vascular membrane investing the whole surface of the brain. DURA-MATER.

Piano, pi-ä′nō, *a.* [It., soft, smooth, from L. *planus*, plain.] *Mus.* soft; a direction to execute a passage softly or with diminished volume of tone.—*n.* (pi-an′ō). A musical metal-stringed instrument with a keyboard, by means of which the metal strings are struck by hammers.—**Pianoforte**, pi-an′ō-for-tā, *n.* [It. *piano*, soft, smooth, and *forte* (L. *fortis*), strong.] A piano.—**Pianette**, **Pianino**, pi-a-net′, pi-ä-nē′nō, *n.* [Fr. and It. dim. of *piano*.] A small piano.—**Pianissimo**, pi-a-nis′i-mō. [It. superl. of *piano*, soft.] *Mus.* very soft; a direction to execute a passage in the softest manner.—**Pianist**, pi-an′ist, pi′an-ist, *n.* A performer on the piano.

Piarist, pī′ar-ist, *n.* [L. *pius*, pious.] One of a religious order who devote themselves to the gratuitous instruction of youth.

Piassava, pi-as′a-vä, *n.* [Pg. *piaçaba*.] The fibre of a Brazilian palm tree, extensively used in making brooms and brushes for street-sweeping.

Piaster, **Piastre**, pi-as′tėr, *n.* [Fr. *piastre*, It. and Sp. *piastra*, a thin plate of metal, a dollar, from L.L. *plastra*, L. *emplastrum*, Gr. *emplastron*, a plaster. PLASTER.] A denomination of money of various countries; the Egyptian piastre is worth about 5 cents; Spanish, about 96 cents; Turkish, approximately 4½ cents.

Piazza, pi-az′za, *n.* [It. *piazza*, open place, square, market-place. PLACE.] A rectangular open space surrounded by buildings or colonnades.

Pibroch, pē′broch, *n.* [Gael. *piobaireachd*, from *piobair*, a piper, *piob*, a pipe.] A wild irregular species of music performed on the bagpipe, and peculiar to the Highlands of Scotland.

Pica, pī′ka, *n.* [L. *pix*, *picis*, pitch: probably named from *litera picata* (pitch-black letter), a great black letter at the beginning of some new section in the liturgy.] Printing type of two sizes, *large pica* being 12 points, and *small pica*, 11 points.

Picador, pik-a-dor′, *n.* [Sp., from *pica*, a pike or lance.] One of the horsemen armed with a lance who excites and irritates the bull in a bull-fight.

Picaninny, pik′a-nin-i, *n.* PICKANINNY.

Picaroon, pik-a-rön′, *n.* [Sp. *picaron*, augmentative of *picaro*, a rogue.] A rogue or cheat; one that lives by his wits; an adventurer.—**Picaresque**, pik-a-resk′, *a.* [Fr.] Pertaining to rogues or picaroons; describing the fortunes of rogues.

Picayune, pik-a-yūn′, *n.* [Of Carib origin.] Formerly a small Spanish coin used in Louisiana and equal to 1/16 of a dollar; anything of little value.

Piccalilli, pik′a-lil-li, *n.* An imitation Indian pickle of various vegetables, with pungent spices.

Piccolo, pik′kō-lō, *n.* [It. *piccolo*, small.] A small flute, the tones of which range an octave higher than those of the ordinary orchestral flute; an octave flute.

Pice, pīs, *n. sing.* and *pl.* Small East Indian coin, value about ½ cent each.

Piceous, pis′ē-us, *a.* [L. *piceus*, from *pix*, *picis*, pitch.] Of or belonging to pitch; black as pitch.

Piciform, pī′si-form, *a.* [L. *picus*, woodpecker, and *forma*, form.] *Ornith.* having the form or characters of the woodpecker and kindred birds.

Pick, pik, *v.t.* [Allied to W. *pig*, a point, a pike; Gael. *pioc*, *piocaid*, a pick, a pickaxe; *pike*, *peak*, *peck*, *beak*; same root also in *spike*.] To strike at with anything pointed; to peck at, as a bird, with its bill; to pierce; to clean by removing with the teeth, fingers, claws, or a small instrument, something that adheres (to *pick* a bone, the teeth); to separate from other things; to select; to choose (to *pick* the best men); to pluck; to gather, as fruit or things growing; to gather up here and there; to collect (often with *up*); to snatch thievishly (a purse); to steal the contents of (to *pick* a pocket).—*To pick off*, to separate by the fingers or a small instrument; to separate by a sharp sudden movement (to *pick off* a leaf); to aim at and kill.—*To pick out*, to draw out by anything pointed; to select from a number or quantity; to relieve with figures or lines of a different colour.—*To pick up*, to take up with the fingers, or otherwise to snatch; to obtain by repeated effort or casually (to *pick up* a livelihood).—*To pick a hole in one's coat*, to find fault with one.—*To pick a lock*, to open it with some instrument other than the key.—*To pick oakum*, to make oakum by untwisting old ropes.—*To pick a quarrel*, to quarrel intentionally with a person.—*v.i.* To eat slowly or by morsels; to nibble; to pilfer.—*To pick up*, to acquire fresh strength, vigour, or the like. (*Colloq.*)—*n.* A heavy sharp-pointed iron tool, with a wooden handle, used for loosening hard earth, stones, &c., in digging, ditching, &c.; a sharp hammer used in dressing stones.—**Pickaxe**, pik′aks, *n.* [Apparently from *pick* and *axe*, but really a corruption of O.Fr. *picquois*, a pickaxe, from *picquer*, to pierce.] A pick with a sharp point at one end and a broad blade at the other; also, simply a pick.—**Picker**, pik′ėr, *n.* One who picks, culls, collects, or gathers (a rag-*picker*, a hop-*picker*); a name of tools or apparatus of many various shapes.—**Picking**, pik′ing, *n.* The act expressed by the verb to pick; perquisites not over honestly obtained; that which is left to be picked or gleaned; *pl.* the pulverized shells of oysters used in making walks.—**Picklock**, pik′lok, *n.* An instrument for picking or opening locks without the key.—**Pickpocket**, pik′pok-et, *n.* One who steals, or makes a practice of stealing, from people's pockets.—**Pickthank**, pik′thangk, *n.* One who is officious for the sake of gaining favour; a parasite; a toady.

Pickaback, pik′a-bak, *a.* or *adv.* [From the older form *pickapack*, a reduplication of *pack*.] On the back or shoulders like a pack. (*Colloq.*)

Pickaninny, pik′a-nin-i, *n.* [Sp. *pequeño niño*, little infant.] A negro or mulatto infant. (*Amer.*)

Pickerel, pik′ėr-el, *n.* [From *pike*.] A name applied to several small fresh-water fishes of the pike family.

Picket, pik′et, *n.* [Fr. *piquet*, a dim. of *pique*, a pike. PICK.] A stake sharpened or pointed, used in fortification and encampments; a narrow pointed board; *milit.* a detachment of troops in a camp kept equipped to protect the camp from surprise; a person posted, as by a labor union, before or near a place of business where the workers are on strike; a game at cards.—*v.t.*—*picketed*, *picketing*. To fortify with pickets or pointed stakes; to fence with narrow pointed boards or pales; to fasten to a picket or stake; to place or post as a guard of observation.—**Picket-fence**, *n.* A fence made of pickets or pales.—**Picket-guard**, *n.* *Milit.* a guard always in readiness in case of alarm.

Pickle, pik′l, *n.* [D. and L.G. *pekel*, G. *pökel*, *bökel*, brine.] A solution of salt and water in which flesh, fish, or other substance is preserved; brine; vinegar, in which vegetables, fish, oysters, &c., are preserved; a thing preserved in pickle; a state or condition of difficulty or disorder; a plight (*colloq.*); a troublesome child (*colloq.*).—*To have a rod in pickle for any one*, is to have a beating, flogging, or scolding in reserve for him. (*Colloq.*)—*v.t.*—*pickled*, *pickling*. To preserve in brine or pickle; to treat with pickle.—**Pickled**, pik′ld, *p.* and *a.* Preserved in brine or pickle.

Picnic, pik′nik, *n.* [Origin unknown.] A pleasure-party the members of which carry provisions along with them on an excursion to some place in the country: used also adjectively (a *picnic* party).—*v.i.*—*picnicked*, *picnicking*. To attend or take part in a picnic party.

Picotee, pik-ō-tē′, *n.* [Fr. *picotie*, from *Picot* de la Perousse, a French botanist.] A variety of carnation or clove-pink, having the dark colour only on the edge of the petals.

Picquet, pik′et, *n.* PIQUET.

Picra, pī′kra, *n.* [L., from Gr. *pikros*, sharp, bitter.] Powder of aloes with canella, a cathartic medicine.

Picric, pik′rik, *a.* [Gr. *pikros*, bitter, sharp.] Same as *Carbazotic*. Picric acid is now much used as an explosive, as, for instance, in Lyddite shells. MELINITE.

Picrotoxine, pik-rō-tok′sin, *n.* [Gr. *pikros*, bitter, and *toxicon*, poison.] The bitter poisonous principle which exists in the seeds of *Cocculus indicus*.

Pict, pikt, *n.* [From *Picti*, the name given them by Latin writers; of uncertain origin.] One of a race of people (probably Celts) who anciently inhabited the north-east of Scotland.—**Pictish**, pik′tish, *a.* Pertaining to the Picts.

Picture, pik′tūr, *n.* [L. *pictura*, from *pingo*, *pictum*, to paint. PAINT.] A painting, drawing, or engraving exhibiting the resemblance of anything; any resemblance or representation, either to the eye or to the mind; a likeness; an image; a representation or description in words.—*Picture hat*, a large-sized hat of the Duchess of Devonshire style; the style seen in the portraits by Sir Joshua Reynolds and Gainsborough.—*Picture house*, the place of entertainment devoted to cinemas or moving pictures.—*v.t.*—*pictured*, *picturing*. To draw or paint a resemblance of; to represent pictorially; to bring before the mind's eye; to form an ideal likeness of; to describe in a vivid manner.—**Picture-book**, *n.* A book for children, illustrated with pictures.—**Picture-cleaner**, **Picture-restorer**, *n.* One who restores the brightness of colour in old paintings.—**Picture-frame**, *n.* A case or border, more or less ornamented, which surrounds a picture and sets it off to advantage.—**Picture-gallery**, *n.* A gallery or large apartment in which pictures are hung up or exhibited.—**Pictorial**, pik-tō′ri-al, *a.* [L. *pictor*, a painter.] Pertaining to pictures; illustrated by pictures; constituting a picture.—**Pictorially**, pik-tō′ri-al-li, *adv.* In a pictorial manner; with pictures or engravings.—**Picturesque**, pik-tū-resk′, *a.* Forming or fitted to form a pleasing picture; expressing that peculiar kind of beauty which is agreeable in a picture; abounding with vivid and striking imagery; graphic in style of writing.—*The picturesque*, the quality that renders a scene suitable for making into a good picture.—**Picturesquely**, pik-tū-resk′li, *adv.* In a picturesque manner.—**Picturesqueness**, pik-tū-resk′nes, *n.*

Picul, pī′kul, *n.* In China, a weight of 133⅓ lbs.

Piddle, pid′l, *v.i.* [A form of *peddle*.] To deal in trifles; to attend to trivial concerns.

Piddock, pid′ok, *n.* The pholas.

Pidgin English, pij'in, *n.* The kind of mongrel dialect used for the transaction of '*business*' between English-speaking and Chinese traders.

Pie, pī, *n.* [From the Celtic; comp. Ir. *pighe*, a pie.] An article of food consisting of paste baked with something in it or under it; *print.* a mass of types confusedly mixed or unsorted.

Pie, pī, *n.* [Fr. *pie*, from L. *pica*, a magpie.] The magpie.

Piebald, pī'bald, *a.* [From *pie*, a magpie, and *bald*, spotted with white. BALD.] Having spots or patches of white and black or other colour; having patches of various colours; pied; diversified; mongrel.

Piece, pēs, *n.* [Fr. *pièce*, Pr. *peza*, It. *pezza*, from L.L. *petium*, a piece, probably from the Celtic: W. *peth*, Armor. *pez*, a piece.] A fragment or part of anything separated from the whole, in any manner (to tear in *pieces*); a part of anything, though not separated or separated only in idea; a portion; a definite quantity or portion of certain things (a *piece* of muslin, a *piece* of work); an artistic or literary composition (a *piece* of poetry or sculpture); a coin (a fourpenny *piece*); a gun or single firearm (a fowling *piece*).—*To work by the piece*, to work by the measure of quantity, and not by the measure of time.—*Of a piece*, of the same sort, as if taken from the same whole; alike.—*A piece of one's mind*, a colloquial phrase for blunt and uncomplimentary statements.—*v.t.*—*pieced*, *piecing.* To mend by the addition of a piece; to patch; to unite; to join; to cement.—*To piece out*, to extend or enlarge by addition of a piece or pieces.—**Piece-goods**, *n.pl.* Goods generally sold by the piece, as cottons, shirtings, &c.—**Piecemeal**, pēs'mēl, *adv.* [*Piece*, and suffix *-meal*, A.Sax. *maelum*, by parts.] In pieces; by pieces; by little and little in succession.—**Piecer**, pēs'ėr, *n.* One that pieces; a boy or girl employed in a spinning factory to join broken threads.—**Piecework**, pēs'wėrk, *n.* Work done and paid for by the measure of quantity.

Pied, pīd, *a.* [From *pie*, magpie.] Party-coloured; variegated with spots of different colours; spotted with larger spots than if speckled.—**Piedness**, pīd'nes, *n.* The state of being pied.

Piend, pēnd, *n.* [Dan. *pind*, a pin or peg; G. *pinne*, the piend of a hammer.] The sharp point or edge of a hammer.

Pier, pēr, *n.* [O.Fr. *pere*, *piere*, a stone (Fr. *pierre*), from L. and Gr. *petra*, a stone.] *Arch.* the solid parts between openings in a wall, as between doors or windows; the square or other mass or post to which a gate is hung; the solid support from which an arch springs; a large pillar or shaft; one of the supports of the arches of a bridge; a mole or jetty carried out into the sea, serving to protect vessels from the open sea, to form a harbour, &c.; a projecting quay, wharf, or landing-place.—**Pierage**, pēr'āj, *n.* Toll paid for using a pier.—**Pier-glass**, *n.* A mirror or glass hanging between windows.—**Pier-table**, *n.* A table placed between windows.

Pierce, pērs, *v.t.*—*pierced*, *piercing.* [Fr. *percer*, to pierce; origin uncertain.] To stab or transfix with a pointed instrument; to penetrate; to force a way into; to affect keenly; to move deeply; to penetrate into, as into a secret or purpose.—*v.i.* To enter, as a pointed instrument; to penetrate.—**Pierced**, pērst, *p.* and *a.* Penetrated; perforated with holes.—**Piercer**, pēr'sėr, *n.* An instrument that pierces; a person that pierces or perforates; that organ of an insect with which it pierces bodies; the ovipositor.—**Piercingly**, pēr'sing-li, *adv.* In a piercing manner.—**Piercingness**, pēr'sing-nes, *n.* The power of piercing or penetrating.

Pierides, pī-er'i-dēz, *n.pl.* [L.] A name of the Muses, from *Pieria*, where they were first worshipped among the Thracians.—**Pierian**, pī-ē'ri-an, *a.* Belonging to the Pierides.

Pierrot, pi'er-ō, *n.* [Fr. dim. of *Pierre*, Peter.] Itinerant minstrel or vocalist, generally at seaside places, with the dress of a clown in French pantomime.

Pietra-dura, pi-et'ra-dö'ra, *n.* [It., hard stone.] A kind of fine Florentine mosaic work executed in coloured stones.

Piety, pī'e-ti, *n.* [L. *pietas*, from *pīus*, pious. *Pity* is the same word.] Veneration or reverence of the Supreme Being and love of His character; the exercise of these affections in obedience to His will and devotion to His service; filial reverence; reverence towards parents or friends, with affection and devotion to them.—**Pietism**, pī'et-izm, *n.* The principles or practice of the pietists. — **Pietists**, pī'et-ists, *n. pl.* A religious party in Germany who proposed to revive declining piety in the Reformed Churches; hence, applied to one who makes a display of strong religious feelings.—**Pietistic**, **Pietistical**, pī-et-is'tik, pī-et-is'ti-kal, *a.*

Piezometer, pī-e-zom'et-ėr, *n.* [Gr. *piezō*, to press, *metron*, measure.] An instrument for measuring compressibility.

Piffle, pif'l, *n.* [Origin doubtful.] Silly spoken or written matter; trash.

Pig, pig, *n.* [A.Sax. *pecga*, akin to D. *big*, *bigge*, L.G. *bigge*, a pig.] A young swine, male or female; a swine in general; an oblong mass of unforged iron, lead, or other metal. ∴ In the process of smelting, the principal channel along which the metal in a state of fusion runs, when let out of the furnace, is called the *sow*, and the lateral channels or moulds are denominated *pigs*, whence the iron in this state is called *pig-iron*.—*v.t.* or *i.*—*pigged*, *pigging.* To bring forth pigs; to act as pigs; to live or huddle as pigs.—**Piggery**, pig'ėr-i, *n.* A place with sties and other accompaniments allotted to pigs.—**Piggish**, pig'ish, *a.* Relating to or like pigs; swinish.—**Pig-headed**, *a.* Having a head like a pig; stupidly obstinate.—**Pig-headedness**, *n.* The quality of being pig-headed or obstinately stupid.—**Pig-iron**, *n.* Iron in pigs.—**Pig-lead**, *n.* Lead in pigs, as when first extracted from the ore.—**Pig-nut**, *n.* The root of a plant. EARTH-NUT.—**Pig-skin**, *n.* The skin of a pig, especially when prepared for saddlery or other purposes.—**Pig-sty**, *n.* A sty or pen for pigs.—**Pig-tail**, pig'tāl, *n.* The tail of a pig; the hair of the head tied behind in a tail; tobacco twisted into a long rope.

Pigeon, pij'on, *n.* [Fr. *pigeon*, from L. *pipio*, *pipionis*, a chirping bird, from *pipio*, to peep, to chirp, an imitative verb; comp. E. *pipe*, *fife*.] A well-known bird of many varieties; a dove, as the stock-dove, the ring-dove, the turtle-dove; a simpleton; a gull; a person swindled by gamblers; hence, to *pluck a pigeon*, to strip a greenhorn of his money.—**Pigeon English**. PIDGIN.—**Pigeon-express**, *n.* Intelligence conveyed by means of a carrier-pigeon.—**Pigeon-hearted**, *a.* Timid; easily frightened.—**Pigeon-hole**, *n.* One of the holes in a dove-cot where the pigeons go in and out; a little compartment or division in a case for papers.—**Pigeon-house**, *n.* A dove-cot.—**Pigeon-livered**, *a.* Mild in temper; soft; gentle.—**Pigeonry**, pij'on-ri, *n.* A place for keeping pigeons; a dove-cot.

Piggin, pig'in, *n.* [Gael. *pigean*, Ir. *pigin*, an earthen pitcher.] A small wooden vessel with an erect handle.

Pigmean, pig-mē'an, *a.* PYGMEAN.

Pigment, pig'ment, *n.* [L. *pigmentum*, from the stem of *pingo*, to paint. PAINT.] Paint; any substance used by painters, dyers, &c., to impart colours to bodies; the colouring matter found in animal and plant bodies.—**Pigmental**, pig-men'tal, *a.* Pertaining to pigments.—**Pigment-cell**, *n.* A small cell of animals or plants containing colouring matter.

Pigmy, pig'mi, *n.* and *a.* PYGMY.

Pignon, pēn'yon, *n.* [Fr. *pignon*, from L. *pinus*, the pine.] An edible seed of the cones of certain pine-trees.

Pigotite, pig'ot-īt, *n.* [After the Rev. Mr. *Pigot*.] A brownish-yellow mineral containing alumina and organic matter, found encrusting certain caves.

Pika, pī'ka, *n.* A species of rodent allied to the hares that has a voice like that of a quail.

Pike, pīk, *n.* [Fr. *pique*, a pike; closely allied to *pick*, *peck*. PICK.] A military weapon, consisting of a long wooden shaft or staff with a flat pointed steel head; a pointed peak, hill, or mountain summit; a fresh-water fish, so named from its long shape or from the form of its snout; a turn-pike, or road on which a toll is charged; also, the toll; any main highway.—**Piked**, pīkt, *a.* Furnished with a pike.—**Pikeman**, pīk'man, *n.* A soldier armed with a pike.—**Pike-staff**, *n.* The shaft of a pike; a long staff with a sharp pike in the lower end of it.

Pilaster, pi-las'tėr, *n.* [Fr. *pilastre*, It. *pilastro*, from L. *pila*, a pile.] A square pillar projecting from a pier or from a wall to a short distance.—**Pilastered**, pi-las'tėrd, *a.* Furnished with pilasters.

Pilau, **Pilaw**, pī'la, *n.* PILLAU.

Pilch, pilch, *n.* [A.Sax. *pylca*, a furred garment, from L.L. *pellicea*. PELISSE.] A fur coat ‡; a flannel cloth for an infant.

Pilchard, pil'shärd, *n.* [Probably a Cornish word; comp. Ir. *pilseir*, a pilchard; W. *pilcod*, a minnow.] A fish resembling the herring, but smaller.

Pile, pīl, *n.* [Partly A.Sax. *pīl*, a heap, a stake, partly from Fr. *pile*, a heap, a pier, a voltaic pile; both from L. *pila*, a pier or mole.] A heap; a mass or collection of things in an elevated form; a collection of combustibles arranged for burning a dead body; a large building or mass of buildings; an edifice; *elect.* a series of plates of two dissimilar metals, such as copper and zinc, laid one above the other alternately, with cloth between each pair, moistened with an acid solution, for producing a current of electricity; a galvanic or voltaic battery; a beam pointed at the end, driven into the soil for the support of some superstructure or to form part of a wall, as of a coffer-dam or quay; a heraldic figure resembling a wedge.—*v.t.*—*piled*, *piling.* To lay or throw into a heap; to heap up; to accumulate; to drive piles into; to furnish or support with piles.—*To pile arms*, to place three muskets so that the butts remain firm upon the ground, and the muzzles close together.—**Pile-driver**, *n.* A workman whose occupation is to drive piles; a machine or contrivance worked by steam for driving in piles.—**Pile-dwelling**, *n.* A dwelling built on piles; a lake or lacustrine dwelling. LACUSTRINE.—**Pile-work**, *n.* A lacustrine dwelling.

Pile, pīl, *n.* [O.Fr. *peil*, from L. *pilus*, hair.] A hair; a fibre of wool, cotton, &c.; the nap or fine hairy or woolly surface of cloth; also, the shag or hair on the skins of animals.—**Pileous**, pil'ē-us, *a.* Pertaining to the hair; covered by or consisting of hair; pilose.

Pileate, **Pileated**, pī'lē-āt, pī'lē-ā-ted, *a.* [From L. *pileus*, a cap.] Having the form of a cap or cover for the head; *bot.* having a cap or lid like the cap of a mushroom.—**Pileiform**, pī'li-form, *a.* Resembling a cap; pileated.

Pileorhiza, pil'ē-ō-rī"za, *n.* [L. *pileus*, a cap, and Gr. *rhiza*, a root.] *Bot.* a cap or hood found at the end of some roots.

Pileous, pī'lē-us, *a.* Under PILE (nap).

Piles, pīlz, *n.pl.* [L. *pila*, a ball.] A disease originating in the morbid dilatation of the veins of the lower part of the rectum near the anus, the veins often forming bleeding enlargements and tumours; hemorrhoids.

Pileus, pī'lē-us, *n.* [L., a cap.] *Bot.* the cap or top of a mushroom, supported by the stalk.

Pilfer, pil'fėr, *v.i.* [O.Fr. *pelfrer*, to plunder, from *pelfre*, goods, spoil, booty. PELF.] To steal in small quantities; to practise petty theft.—*v.t.* To steal or gain by petty theft; to filch.—**Pilferer**, pil'fėr-ėr, *n.* One who pilfers.—**Pilferingly**, pil'fėr-ing-li, *adv.* In a pilfering manner.

Pilgarlic, pil-gär'lik, *n.* [*Peeled garlic.*] A poor bald-headed creature.

Pilgrim, pil'grim, *n.* [Same as D. *pelgrim*, Dan. *pilegrim*, Icel. *pilagrimr*, Fr. *pelegrin*, from L. *peregrinus*, a traveller, a foreigner —*per*, through, and *ager*, land (as in *agriculture*).] A wanderer; a traveller; one that travels to a distance from his own country to visit a shrine or holy place, or to pay his devotion to the remains of dead saints; *Scrip.* one who lives in the world, but is not of the world.—**Pilgrimage**, pil'gri-māj, *n.* A journey undertaken by a pilgrim; a journey to some place deemed sacred for a devotional purpose; the journey of human life.—**Pilgrim Fathers**, *n.* The Puritans who landed at Plymouth Rock, Massachusetts, in 1620, founding the first New England settlement.

Pili, pī'lī, *n. pl.* [L. *pilus*, a hair.] *Bot.* fine slender bodies, like hair, covering some plants.—**Piliferous**, pī-lif'ėr-us, *a.* Bearing or producing hairs, as a leaf.—**Piliform**, pī'li-form, *a.* Formed like or resembling down or hairs.

Pilidium, pl. **-a**, pī-lid'i-um, *n.* [Gr. *pilidion*, a little cap.] In some Nemertine worms, a free-swimming helmet-shaped larva.

Pill, pil, *n.* [Abbrev. of L. *pilula*, a dim. of *pila*, a ball (whence *pile*, a heap).] A little ball or small round mass of medicinal substance to be swallowed whole; something unpleasant that has to be metaphorically swallowed or accepted.—*v.t.* To dose with pills; to form into pills.—**Pill-box**, *n.* A box for holding pills; in military slang, a small concrete block-house, used in Europe as a machine-gun emplacement. —**Pillworm**, pil'wėrm, *n.* The millipede, which can roll itself into a ball.

Pill,‡ pil, *v.t.* [Fr. *piller*, to pillage, from L. *pilare*, to plunder.] To rob; to plunder; to peel; to strip bare.—**Pillage**, pil'āj, *n.* [Fr. *pillage*, from *piller*, to rob.] Plunder; spoil; that which is taken by open force, particularly from enemies in war; the act of plundering.—*v.t.—pillaged, pillaging.* To strip of money or goods by open violence, and usually by a number of persons; to plunder; to spoil.—**Pillager**, pil'āj-ėr, *n.* One who pillages.

Pillar, pil'ėr, *n.* [Fr. *pilier*, a pillar, from L.L. *pilare*, from L. *pila*, a column. PILE.] A column; a columnar mass or upright body; *fig.* a supporter; one who or that which sustains or upholds.—**Pillared**, pil'ėrd, *a.* Having pillars; supported by pillars; having the form of a pillar.—**Pillar-box**, *n.* In Great Britain, a mailbox fastened to a post.

Pillau, Pillaw, pil-lą', *n.* [Per. and Turk.] An oriental dish consisting of rice cooked with fat, butter, or meat. Spelled also *Pilau, Pilaw.*

Pillion, pil'yon, *n.* [From the Celtic; W. *pilyn*, Ir. *pillin*, Gael. *pillean*, a pillion, a pack-saddle, from root of L. *pilus*, hair (whence *pile*, of cloth).] A cushion for a woman to ride on behind a person on horseback; a pad; a low saddle; the pad of a saddle that rests on the horse's back.

Pillory, pil'o-ri, *n.* [Fr. *pilori*, a pillory, Pr. *espitlori*, L.L. *pilorium, spilorium*, a pillory; origin uncertain.] A frame of wood erected on a post or pole, with movable boards resembling those in the stocks, and holes through which were put the head and hands of an offender, who had to stand there by way of public punishment.—*v.t.—pilloried, pillorying.* To punish with the pillory; *fig.* to expose to ridicule, contempt, abuse, and the like.

Pillow, pil'ō, *n.* [O.E. *pilwe, pulwe*, from L. *pulvinus*, a cushion.] A long cushion to support the head of a person when reposing, filled with feathers, down, or other soft material; a supporting piece for an axle or shaft; a bearing.—*v.t.* To rest or lay on for support.—**Pillow-case, Pillow-slip**, *n.* The movable sack or case which is drawn over a pillow.—**Pillowed**, pil'ōd, *p.* and *a.* Provided with a pillow or pillows.—**Pillow-lace**, *n.* Hand-made lace worked on a small pillow or cushion.—**Pillowy**, pil'ō-i, *a.* Like a pillow; soft.

Pilose, pī'lōs, *a.* [L. *pilosus*, from *pilus*, hair (whence *pile*, of cloth).] Covered with, abounding in, or full of hairs; hairy.—**Pilosity**, pī-los'i-ti, *n.* Hairiness.

Pilot, pī'lot, *n.* [From O.D. *pijloot*, a pilot, from *pijlen*, to sound the depth, and *loot*, the sounding-lead.] A steersman (*Shak.*); a person qualified to conduct ships into and out of particular harbours, or along certain coasts, channels, &c.; a guide or director of the course of another person; one who has the conduct of any affair; in *aviation*, the man charged with operating the controls of an aeroplane or dirigible.—*v.t.* To act as pilot of; to guide through dangers or difficulties.—**Pilotage**, pī'lot-āj, *n.* The remuneration of a pilot; the guidance of a pilot.—**Pilot-balloon**, *n.* A balloon, the car of which carries only recording instruments; a small balloon sent up to ascertain the direction and strength of the wind.—**Pilot-boat**, *n.* A boat used by pilots for reaching ships near shore.—**Pilot-cloth**, *n.* A coarse stout blue cloth for overcoats, such as are worn by pilots.—**Pilot-engine**, *n.* A locomotive engine sent on before a train to clear the way.—**Pilot-fish**, *n.* A fish resembling the mackerel which attends ships at sea, and is in the habit of accompanying sharks.—**Pilot-jacket**, *n.* A pea-jacket, such as is worn by seamen.—**Pilot-star**, *n.* A guiding-star (*Tenn.*).

Pilous, pī'lus, *a.* PILOSE.

Pilular, pil'ū-lėr, *a.* [L. *pilula*, a pill.] Pertaining to pills.—**Pilule**, pil'ūl, *n.* A little pill.

Pimelite, pim'el-īt, *n.* [Gr. *pimelē*, fat, and *lithos*, stone.] A mineral of an apple-green colour, fat and unctuous to the touch; a variety of steatite.

Pimenta, Pimento, pī-men'ta, pī-men'tō, *n.* [Pg. *pimenta*, It. *pimento*, from L. *pigmentum*, paint, juice of plants. PIGMENT.] Allspice, the berry of a tree of the West Indies; Jamaica pepper. Under ALL.

Pimp, pimp, *n.* [A nasalized form of *pipe* (Pr. *pimpa*, a pipe), a pimp being as it were one who whistles for females like a call-bird.] One who provides gratifications for the lust of others; a procurer; a pander. —*v.i.* To pander; to procure lewd women for the gratification of others.

Pimpernel, pim'pėr-nel, *n.* [Fr. *pimprenelle*, It. *pimpinella.*] A little red-flowered prostrate annual found in cornfields.

Pimple, pim'pl, *n.* [A nasalized form of L. *papula*, a pimple; or from W. *pwmp*, *pwmpl*, a knob.] A small elevation of the skin, with an inflamed base, seldom containing a fluid or suppurating, and commonly terminating in scurf.—**Pimpled**, pim'pld, *a.* Having pimples on the skin; full of pimples.—**Pimply**, pim'pli, *a.* Full of pimples.

Pin, pin, *n.* [Same as D. *pin*, Dan. *pind*, G. *pinn*, W. *pin*, a pin, a peg, &c., from L. *penna* or *pinna*, a feather, a pen. PEN.] A piece of metal, wood, or the like, used for fastening separate articles together, or as a support from which a thing may be hung; a peg; a bolt; a small piece of wire pointed at one end and with a rounded head at the other, much used as a cheap and ready means of fastening clothes, &c.; a peg in stringed musical instruments for increasing or diminishing the tension of the strings; the centre of a target; a central part.—*v.t.—pinned, pinning.* To fasten with a pin or pins of any kind; to clutch; to hold fast.—*v.t.* To inclose; to confine; to pen or pound.—**Pincase**, pin'kās, *n.* A case for holding pins.—**Pin-cushion**, *n.* A small cushion or pad in which pins are stuck for preservation.—**Pinfeather**, pin'feтн-ėr, *n.* A small or short feather; a feather not fully grown.—**Pinfeathered**, pin'feтн-ėrd, *a.* Having the feathers only beginning to shoot.—**Pinhole**, pin'hōl, *n.* A small hole made by the puncture of a pin; a very small aperture.—**Pin-money**, *n.* An allowance made by a husband to his wife for her separate use, originally *to buy pins.*—**Pin-tail**, *n.* A variety of duck with a sharp-pointed tail.—**Pin-wheel**, *n.* A wheel of which the cogs are pins projecting outward.

Pina-cloth, pēn'ya or pī'na, *n.* [Sp. *piña*, the pine-apple.] A delicate, soft, transparent cloth made from the fibers of the pine-apple leaf.

Pinacotheca, pin'a-ko-thē''ka, *n.* [Gr. *pinax, pinakos*, a picture, and *thēkē*, a repository.] A picture-gallery.

Pinafore, pin'a-fōr, *n.* [Because it is or was *pinned* on *before.*] A sort of apron worn by children to protect the front part of their dress; a child's apron.

Pinang, pi-nang', *n.* The betel-nut.

Pinaster, pī-nas'tėr, *n.* [L., from *pinus*, pine.] A species of pine growing in the south of Europe.

Pincers, pin'sėrz, *n.pl.* [From Fr. *pincer*, to pinch (whence *pince*, pincers). PINCH.] An instrument by which anything is gripped in order to be drawn out, as a nail, or kept fast for some operation; the nippers of certain animals; prehensile claws. Sometimes called *Pinchers.*

Pinch, pinsh, *v.t.* [Fr. *pincer*, It. *pizzare*, Sp. *pizcar, pinchar*, to pinch; of doubtful origin.] To press hard or squeeze between the ends of the fingers, the teeth, claws, or with an instrument, &c.; to nip; to distress; to afflict; to nip with frost.—*v.i.* To act with pressing force; to press painfully; to be sparing or niggardly.—*To know* or *feel where the shoe pinches*, to have practical and personal experience as to where the cause of trouble in any matter lies.—*n.* A close compression, as with the ends of the fingers; a nip; a gripe; a pang; distress inflicted or suffered; straits; difficulty; a strong iron lever; a crowbar; as much as is taken by the finger and thumb; a small quantity generally of snuff.—**Pincher**, pinsh'ėr, *n.* One who or that which pinches. —**Pinchers**, pinsh'ėrz, *n.pl.* PINCERS.—**Pinchingly**, pinsh'ing-li, *adv.* In a pinching way.

Pinchbeck, pinsh'bek, *n.* [From the name of the inventor, a London watch-maker of the last century.] An alloy of copper and zinc, somewhat like gold in colour, and formerly much used for cheap jewelry. Hence, when used adjectively, sham; not genuine.

Pindaric, pin-dar'ik, *a.* After the style and manner of *Pindar.*—*n.* An ode in imitation of the odes of Pindar the Grecian lyric poet; an irregular ode.

Pine, pīn, *n.* [From L. *pinus*, a pine-tree; same root as *pix, picis*, pitch.] The name of a valuable genus of evergreen coniferous trees, of which about seventy species are known, furnishing timber, turpentine, pitch, and resin; the pine-apple; also the plant that produces it.—**Pineal**, pin'ē-al, *a.* [Fr. *pinéale*, from L. *pinea*, the cone of a pine, from *pinus*, a pine.] Resembling a pine-cone in shape.—*Pineal gland*, an internal part of the brain, about the size of a pea, considered by Descartes as the seat of the soul.—**Pine-apple**, *n.* A tropical fruit so called from its resemblance to the cone of the pine-tree; the plant itself.—*Pine-apple rum*, rum flavoured with sliced pine-apples.—**Pine-barren**, *n.* A tract of arid land producing pines. (*Amer.*)—**Pine-clad**, *a.* Clad with pines.—**Pine-cone**, *n.* The crown or strobilus of a pine-tree.—**Pine-crowned**, *a.* Crowned or surmounted with pine-trees.—**Pine-finch**, *n.* A bird nearly allied to the bull-finch.—**Pine-house**, *n.* A pinery.—**Pine-oil**, *n.* An oil resembling turpentine, used in making colours and varnishes.—**Pinery**, pī'nėr-i, *n.* A hothouse in which pine-apples are raised; a place where pine-trees grow.—**Pinetum**, pī-nē'tum, *n.* [L., a pine plantation.] A plantation or collection of growing pine-trees of different kinds, especially for ornamental or scientific purposes.—**Pine-wood**, *n.* A wood of pine-trees; pine timber.—**Pine-wool**, *n.* A fibrous substance obtained from the buds and leaves of pine-trees, and used for stuffing mattresses, for wadding, blankets, &c.—**Piney, Piny**, pī'ni, *a.* Pertaining to pines; abounding with pines. —**Piney tallow**, *n.* A kind of vegetable wax obtained from the fruit of an Indian tree (*Vateria Indica*).—**Piney varnish**, *n.* A resinous varnish obtained from the same tree.—**Pinic**, pī'nik, *a.* Pertaining to or derived from the pine-tree (*pinic* acid).

Pine, pīn, *v.i.*—*pined, pining.* [A.Sax. *pinian*, to pain, to pine; same word as *pain*.] To languish; to lose flesh or grow weakly under any distress or anxiety of mind; to languish with desire (to *pine for* a thing).—*v.t.* To pain or torment; to grieve for.—*n.* Pain; anguish; misery.

Pinfold, pin'fōld, *n.* [A.Sax. *pyndan*, to pound, to shut in, and *fold*. POUND.] A place in which cattle straying and doing damage are temporarily confined; a pound.

Ping, ping, *n.* [Imitative.] The sound made by a bullet, as from a rifle, in passing through the air. — **Ping-pong**, *n.* A trade-mark for a kind of tennis played on a table.

Pinion, pin'yon, *n.* [Fr. *pignon*, a pinion or small wheel; Sp. *piñon*, a joint of a bird's wing; from L. *pinna, penna*, a feather. PEN.] The joint of a fowl's wing remotest from the body; a wing; a small wheel which plays in the teeth of a larger.—*v.t.* To confine by binding the wings; to disable by cutting off the first joint of the wing; to bind the arms of; to shackle; to fetter.

Pink, pingk, *n.* [Comp. D. *pinken*, to twinkle with the eyes, to wink—some of them are marked with eye-like spots.] A name of various garden flowers, as the clove-pink or carnation and garden pink; a light red colour or pigment resembling that of the common garden pink; anything supremely excellent (the *pink* of perfection); a fish, the minnow: so called from the colour of its abdomen in summer.—*a.* Resembling in colour the most frequent hue of the pink.—**Pink-eye**, *n.* A sort of contagious fever affecting horses.

Pink, pingk, *v.i.* [D. *pinken*, to wink. See above.] To wink or blink.

Pink, pingk, *v.t.* [A nasalized form of *pick*.] To work in eyelet-holes; to ornament with holes, scollops, &c.; to stab; to wound with a sword or rapier.—**Pinked**, pingkt, *p.* and *a.* Pierced or worked with small holes.—**Pink-root**, *n.* The root of the Indian pink used as a vermifuge.

Pink, pingk, *n.* [D. and Dan.] A ship with a very narrow stern, a build now obsolete.—**Pink-sterned**, *a. Naut.* having a very narrow stern.

Pinna, pin'a, *n.* pl. **Pinnæ**, pin'ē. [L. *pinna, penna*, a feather, a wing, a fin.] *Zool.* the wing or feather of a bird; the fin of a fish; *anat.* the pavilion of the ear, that part which projects beyond the head; *bot.* a leaflet of a pinnate leaf.

Pinnace, pin'ās, *n.* [Fr. *pinasse*, Sp. *pinaza*, Pg. *pinaça*, It. *pinaccia, pinazza*, a pinnace, from L. *pinus*, a pine-tree.] A small vessel propelled by oars and sails, and having generally two masts rigged like those of a schooner: a boat usually rowed with eight oars.

Pinnacle, pin'a-kl, *n.* [Fr. *pinacle*, L.L. *pinnaculum*, from L. *pinna*, a feather. PINION.] A rocky peak; a sharp or pointed summit; *arch.* any lesser structure, whatever be its form, that rises above the roof of a building, or that caps and terminates the higher parts of other buildings.—*v.t.*—*pinnacled, pinnacling.* To put a pinnacle or pinnacles on; to furnish with pinnacles.

Pinnate, Pinnated, pin'āt, pin'ā-ted, *a.* [L. *pinnatus*, from *pinna*, a feather or fin. PEN.] *Bot.* shaped or branching like a feather; formed like a feather.—*Pinnate leaf, bot.* a compound leaf wherein a single petiole has several leaflets attached to each side of it; *zool.* having fins or processes resembling fins. — **Pinnately**, pin'āt-li, *adv.* In a pinnate manner.—**Pinnatifid**, pin-nat'i-fid, *a.* [L. *pinna*, and *findo*, to cleave.] *Bot.* said of a simple leaf divided transversely into irregular lobes. — **Pinnatipartite**, pin-nat'i-pär"tīt, *a.* [L. *partitus*, divided.] *Bot.* having the lobes of the leaf separated beyond the middle.—**Pinnatiped**, pin-nat'i-ped, *a.* [L. *pinna*, and *pes, pedis*, a foot.] Fin-footed; having the toes bordered by membranes, as certain birds.—*n.* A bird which has the toes bordered by membranes.—**Pinnatisect**, pin-nat'i-sekt, *a.* [L. *seco, sectum*, to cut.] *Bot.* having the lobes divided down to the mid-rib.

Pinners, pin'ėrz, *n.pl.* A female head-dress, having long flaps hanging down the sides of the cheeks, worn during the early part of the eighteenth century.

Pinniform, pin'i-form, *a.* [L. *pinna, penna*, a feather, and *forma*, form.] Having the form of a fin or feather. —**Pinnigrade**, pin'i-grād, *a.* [L. *pinna*, a fin, *gradior*, to go.] An animal, such as a seal, having limbs resembling paddles.—**Pinniped**, pin'i-ped, *n.* [L. *pinna*, and *pes, pedis*, a foot.] A fin-footed animal; a pinnigrade.

Pinnula, pin'ū-la, *n.* [L. *pinnula*, dim. of *pinna*, a feather.] *Zool.* one of the lateral processes of the arms of crinoids; the barb of a feather; *bot.* a leaflet.—**Pinnulate**, pin'ū-lāt, *a. Bot.* applied to a leaf in which each pinna is subdivided.—**Pinnule**, pin'ūl, *n.* A pinnula.

Pint, pīnt, *n.* [D. *pint*, Fr. and G. *pinte*, a pint, Sp. *pinta*, a mark, also a pint (a quantity marked), from L. *pingo, pinctum*, to paint. PICTURE.] A measure of capacity containing the eighth part of a gallon. —**Pint-pot**, *n.* A pot for holding just a pint.

Pintle, pin'tl, *n.* [Dim. of *pin*.] A pin or bolt; *artillery*, a long iron bolt to prevent the recoil of a cannon; *naut.* an iron bolt by which the rudder is hung to the stern-post; a pin passing through an axle to hold on a wheel.

Piny. Under PINE.

Pioneer, pī-o-nēr', *n.* [Fr. *pionnier*, O.Fr. *peonier*, from *peon*, It. *pedone*, a foot-soldier. PEON.] One whose business is to march with or before an army to repair the road or clear it of obstructions, work at intrenchments, &c.; any one that goes before to prepare the way for another (*pioneers* of civilization).—*v.t.* To go before and prepare a way for.—*v.i.* To act as pioneer; to clear the way.—**Pioneering**, pī-o-nēr'ing, *p.* and *a.* Pertaining to pioneers.

Piony, pī'o-ni, *n.* PEONY.

Pious, pī'us, *a.* [L. *pius*, pious, devout, kind, whence also *piety, pity*.] Having due respect and affection for parents or other relatives; more commonly, duly reverencing the Supreme Being; godly; devout; dictated by reverence to God; proceeding from piety; practised under the pretence of religion (*pious* frauds). — *Pious belief*, a Catholic opinion not of the importance of a dogma.—**Piously**, pī'us-li, *adv.* In a pious manner.—**Pious-minded**, *a.* Of a pious disposition.

Pip, pip, *n.* [D. *pip*, L.G. *pipp*, Fr. *pipie*, from L.L. *pipita*, for L. *pituita*, phlegm, the pip.] A disease of fowls, consisting in a secretion of thick mucus in the mouth by which the nostrils are stopped.

Pip, pip, *n.* [Fr. *pipin*, a kernel; derivation uncertain.] The kernel or seed of fruit; a spot on cards.

Pip, pip, *v.i.* [An imitative word, slightly differing in form from *peep* = Dan. *pipe*, Sw. *pipa*, G. *pipen*, to pip. PEEP, PIPE.] To cry or chirp, as a chicken.

Pipa, pī'pa, *n.* The toad of Surinam.

Pipe, pīp, *n.* [A.Sax. *pipe*, a pipe; D. *pijp*, Icel. *pipa*, Dan. *pibe*, G. *pfeife*; of imitative origin; comp. L. *pipo, pipio*, to cheep, chirp.] A wind-instrument of music, consisting of a tube of wood or metal; a long tube or hollow body made of various materials, such as are used for the conveyance of water, gas, steam, &c.; a tube of clay or other material with a bowl at one end, used in smoking tobacco, &c.; the windpipe; the sound of the voice; a whistle or call of a bird; a roll in the exchequer, so named from resembling a pipe; a wine measure, usually containing about 105 imperial or 126 wine gallons; *naut.* the boatswain's whistle used to call the men to their duties.—*v.i.*—*piped, piping.* To sound or play on a pipe; to have a shrill sound; to whistle.—*v.t.* To play on a pipe or other wind-instrument; to utter in a sharp or high tone; *naut.* to call by means of the boatswain's pipe or whistle.—**Pipe-clay**, *n.* The purest kind of potter's clay, manufactured into tobacco-pipes, and used by soldiers for cleaning belts, jackets, trousers, &c.—*v.t.* To whiten with pipe-clay.—**Piped**, pīpd, *a.* Formed with a pipe or tube; tubular.—**Pipe-fish**, *n.* A long and slender fish, the thickest part of whose body is only equal to a swan's quill.—**Pipe-layer**, *n.* A workman who lays gas mains, water or draining pipes.—**Piper**, pī'pėr, *n.* One who plays on a pipe; a bagpiper; a sea-urchin common in the northern seas.—*To pay the piper*, to be at the expense; to suffer or make good the loss.—**Pipette**, pi-pet', *n.* [Fr., a small pipe.] A small tube terminating in a perforated point, used by chemists for transferring liquids.—**Piping**, pī'ping, *p.* and *a.* Playing on a pipe; having or giving out a shrill whistling sound; accompanied by the music of the peaceful pipe (this *piping* time of peace); boiling; hissing with heat (*piping* hot).—*n.* Pipes, as for gas, water, &c., collectively; *hort.* a jointed stem used for propagating plants.—**Piping-crow**, *n.* A bird of New South Wales remarkable for its musical powers.—**Pipy**, pī'pi, *a.* Resembling a pipe; tubular.

Pip-emma. P.M. (of time). So called by signallers to prevent mistakes.

Piperaceous, pī-pėr-ā'shus, *a.* [L. *piper*, pepper.] Belonging to the pepper tribe of plants.—**Piperic**, pī-pėr'ik, *a.* Produced from plants of the pepper family or from piperin.—**Piperin, Piperine**, pī'pėr-in, *n.* A crystalline substance extracted from black pepper.

Piperidge, pī'pėr-ij, *n.* [Corruption of botanical name *berberis*.] The barberry.

Pipette. Under PIPE.

Pipi, pī'pi, *n.* The astringent pods of a leguminous plant used for tanning.

Pipistrel, Pipistrelle, pī-pis'trel, *n.* [Fr. *pipistrelle*, from L. *vespertilio*, a bat.] The common bat of Britain.

Pipit, pip'it, *n.* [Probably imitative of its cry.] A name of birds allied to the lark.

Pipkin, pip'kin, *n.* [Dim. of *pipe*.] A small earthen boiler.

Pippin, pip'in, *n.* [Perhaps because grown from the *pips* or seeds.] The name given to several kinds of apples.

Pip-squeak, pip-skwēk, *n.* In military slang a small high-explosive shell.

Piquant, pē'kant, *a.* [Ppr. of Fr. *piquer*, to prick, to be sharp, to pique; of same origin as *pick, pike, peak*, &c.] Making a lively, half-pleasing, half-painful impression on the organs of sense; sharp; racy; lively; sparkling; interesting; sharp or cutting to the feelings; pungent; severe.—**Piquantly**, pē'kant-li, *adv.* In a piquant manner; tartly. — **Piquancy**, pē'kan-si, *n.* The state or quality of being piquant; sharpness; pungency.

Pique, pēk, *n.* [Fr. PIQUANT.] An offence taken; slight anger at persons; feeling arising from wounded pride, vanity, or self-love.—*v.t.*—*piqued, piquing.* [Fr. *piquer*.] To nettle; to irritate; to sting (less strong than *exasperate*); to stimulate; to touch with envy, jealousy, or other passion; *refl.* to pride or value one's self.—*v.i.* To cause irritation.—**Piquet**, pik'et, *n.* [From Fr. *pique*, a pike, a lance, a spade at cards.] *Milit.* a picket; a game at cards played between two persons with thirty-two cards, the ace of spades being highest card. — **Pique-work**, pē'kā, *n.* A minute kind of buhl-work, employed to ornament snuff-boxes, card-cases, and the like.

Piracy. Under PIRATE.

Piragua, pi-rä'gwa, *n.* A rude canoe. PIROGUE.

Pirameter, pī-ram′et-ėr, *n.* [Gr. *peira*, a trial, and *metron*, measure.] An instrument for ascertaining the power required to draw carriages over roads.

Pirate, pī′rāt, *n.* [Fr. *pirate*, L. *pirata*, from Gr. *peiratēs*, from *peiraō*, to attempt, *peira*, a trial.] A robber on the high-seas; one that by open violence takes the property of another on the high-seas; an armed ship or vessel engaged in piracy; a publisher or compiler who appropriates the literary labours of an author without compensation or permission. —*v.i.* —*pirated*, *pirating*. To play the pirate; to rob on the high-seas.—*v.t.* To publish without right or permission.—**Piratic, Piratical**, pī-rat′ik, pī-rat′i-kal, *a.* [L. *piraticus*.] Having the character of a pirate; robbing or plundering by open violence on the high-seas; pertaining to or consisting in piracy.—**Piratically**, pī-rat′i-kal-li, *adv.* In a piratical manner; by piracy.—**Piracy**, pī′ra-si, *n.* The act, practice, or crime of robbing on the high-seas; the profession of pirate; literary theft; any infringement on the law of copyright.

Pirogue, pi-rōg′, *n.* [Fr. *pirogue*, Sp. *piragua*; originally a W. Indian word.] A kind of canoe made from a single trunk of a tree hollowed out.

Pirouette, pir′ö-et, *n.* [Fr.; origin unknown.] A rapid whirling on the point of one foot; the short turn of a horse so as to bring his head suddenly in the opposite direction to where it was before.—*v.i.*—*pirouetted*, *pirouetting*. To perform a pirouette, as in dancing.

Piscator, pis-kā′tor, *n.* [L., from *piscis*, a fish.] A fisherman; an angler.—**Piscatorial, Piscatory**, pis-ka-tō′ri-al, pis′ka-to-ri, *a.* [L. *piscatorius*.] Relating to fishermen or to fishing; pertaining to angling.—**Pisces**, pis′sēz, *n.pl.* [L. *piscis*, a fish.] *Astron.* the Fishes, the twelfth sign or constellation in the zodiac, next to Aries; the vertebrate animals of the class fishes. —**Piscicapture**, pis′i-kap-tūr, *n.* The taking of fish; angling, netting, &c. —**Piscicultural**, pis-i-kul′tū-ral, *a.* Connected with pisciculture.—**Pisciculture**, pis-i-kul′tūr, *n.* [L. *piscis*, a fish, and *cultura*, culture.] The breeding, rearing, preservation, feeding, and fattening of fish by artificial means; fish culture.—**Pisciculturist**, pis-i-kul′tūr-ist, *n.* One who practises pisciculture.—**Pisciform**, pis′i-form, *a.* Having the shape of a fish.—**Piscina**, pis-sī′na, *n.* [L., a cistern, a fish-pond.] A niche on the south side of the altar in churches, with a small basin and water-drain connected, into which the priest empties any water used.—**Piscine**, pis′sīn, *a.* Pertaining to fish or fishes.—**Piscivorous**, pis-siv′o-rus, *a.* [L. *piscis*, and *voro*, to eat.] Feeding or subsisting on fishes.

Pisé, pē-zā, *n.* [Fr., from L. *piso*, *pinso*, to bray, as in a mortar.] Stiff earth or clay used to construct walls, being rammed into moulds as it is carried up.

Pish, pish, *exclam.* A word expressing contempt.—*v.i.* To express contempt by *pish!*

Pisiform, pī′si-form, *a.* [L. *pisum*, a pea, and *forma*, form.] Having the form of a pea; having a structure resembling peas.

Pismire, pis′mīr, *n.* [E. *piss*, and *mire* = D. *mier*, Sw. *myra*, Icel. *maurr*, an ant; it discharges an irritant fluid vulgarly regarded as urine.] The ant or emmet.

Pisolite, pī′sō-līt, *n.* [Gr. *pison*, a pea, and *lithos*, a stone.] A carbonate of lime slightly coloured by the oxide of iron, occurring in little globular concretions of the size of a pea or larger, which usually contain each a grain of sand as a nucleus.—**Pisolitic**, pī-sō-lit′ik, *a.* Composed of, containing, or resembling pisolite.

Piss, pis, *v.i.* [Fr. *pisser*, D. and G. *pissen*, Sw. *pissa*, Dan. *pisse*, W. *pisaw*, to make water.] To discharge the fluid contained in the urinary bladder; to urinate.—*v.t.* To eject, as urine.—*n.* Urine.

Pissasphalt, Pissasphaltum, pis′as-falt, pis-as-fal′tum, *n.* [Gr. *pissasphalton*—*pissa*, turpentine, and *asphaltos*, asphalt.] A soft bitumen of the consistence of tar, black, and of a strong smell.

Pistachio, Pistachio-nut, pis-tā′shi-ō, *n.* [Sp. *pistacho*, L. *pistacium*, the fruit; *pistacia*, Gr. *pistakia*, the tree, from Per. *pista*, the pistachio-tree.] The nut of the pistachio-tree.—**Pistachio-tree**, *n.* A small tree cultivated over the south of Europe for its fruit.

Pistil, pis′til, *n.* [L. *pistillum*, a pestle, a dim. from *pinso*, *pistum*, to pound, to beat in a mortar; akin *pestle*, *piston*.] *Bot.* the seed-bearing organ of a flower, consisting of the ovary, the stigma, and often also of a style.—**Pistillary**, pis′til-la-ri, *a.* *Bot.* of or belonging to the pistil.—**Pistillate**, pis′til-lāt, *a.* Having a pistil.—**Pistillidia**, pis-til-lid′i-a, *n.pl.* [L. *pistillum*, and Gr. *eidos*, resemblance.] *Bot.* organs in cryptogamic plants having the apparent functions of pistils.—**Pistilliferous**, pis-til-lif′ėr-us, *a.* *Bot.* having a pistil without stamens, as a female flower.

Pistol, pis′tol, *n.* [Fr. *pistole*, from It. *pistola*, a pistol; originally a dagger made at *Pistola* or *Pistoia*, near Florence. From diminutive poniards the name came to be given to miniature firearms.] A small firearm, the smallest used, designed to be fired with one hand only.—*v.t.*—*pistolled*, *pistolling*. To shoot with a pistol.

Pistole, pis-tōl′, *n.* [Fr. *pistole*, same as *pistol*, so named as being originally a half-crown, a diminutive of the crown.] An old gold coin in Spain, France, &c., valued at about 4 dollars.

Piston, pis′ton, *n.* [Fr., from L. *pinso*, *pistum*, to beat, to pound. PISTIL.] *Mach.* a movable piece of a cylindrical form, which exactly fits a hollow cylinder, such as the barrel of a pump or the cylinder of a steam-engine, and capable of being driven alternately in two directions.—**Piston-rod**, *n.* A rod which connects a piston to a point outside the cylinder, and either moved by the piston or moving it.

Pit, pit, *n.* [A.Sax. *pyt*, pit = D. *put*, Icel. *pyttr*, a well; from L. *puteus*, a well.] A hollow or cavity more or less deep, either natural or made by digging in the earth; the shaft of a mine; a vat in tanning, bleaching, dyeing, &c.; *hort.* an excavation in the soil covered by a glazed frame, for protecting plants; a concealed hole in the ground for snaring wild beasts; any hollow, cavity, or depression in the flesh (the arm-*pits*); a place or area where cocks or dogs are brought to fight, or where dogs are trained to kill rats; part of a theatre on the floor of the house, and somewhat below the level of the stage.—*The pit* (*Scrip.*), the place of the dead or the abode of evil spirits.—The *bottomless pit*, hell (N.T.).—*v.t.*—*pitted*, *pitting*. To lay in a pit or hole; to mark with little hollows, as by the small-pox; to set in competition; to set against one another, as in combat (*lit.* like cocks in a *pit*).—**Pitfall**, pit′fal, *n.* A pit slightly covered over, forming a kind of trap.—**Pitman**, pit′man, *n.* One who works in a pit.—**Pit-saw**, *n.* A large saw worked by two men, one of whom stands in a pit below.—**Pitted**, pit′ed, *a.* Having little pits or hollows on the skin.

Pitapat, pit′a-pat, *adv.* [A reduplication of *pat*, a slight blow.] In a flutter; with palpitation or quick succession of beats.—*n.* A light quick step.

Pitch, pich, *n.* [A softened form of O.E. *pik*, A.Sax. *pic*, from L. *pix*, *picis*, pitch, akin to *pinus*, a pine (tree).] A thick, tenacious oily substance, commonly obtained from tar, and extensively used for closing up the seams of ships, for preserving wood from the effects of water, for coating iron-work, &c.; in *acoustics*, the quality of a sound which depends upon the number of vibrations per second.—*Jew's pitch*, *mineral pitch*, bitumen.—*v.t.* To smear or cover over with pitch.—**Pitch-blende**, *n.* A mineral which constitutes one of the most important sources of the metal uranium and its compounds.—**Pitch-coal**, *n.* A kind of bituminous coal; also a name given to *jet*.—**Pitch-dark**, *a.* Dark as pitch; very dark.—**Pitchiness**, pich′i-nes, *n.* State or quality of being pitchy.—**Pitch-mineral**, *n.* Bitumen or asphalt.—**Pitch-pine**, *n.* A pine abounding in resinous matter which yields pitch.—**Pitch-plaster**, *n.* A plaster of Burgundy pitch.—**Pitch-pot**, *n.* A large iron pot used for the purpose of boiling pitch.—**Pitch-stone**, *n.* The glassy form of felstone; retinite.—**Pitchy**, pich′i, *a.* Partaking of the qualities of pitch; like pitch; smeared with pitch; dark; dismal.

Pitch, pich, *v.t.* [O.E. *picche*, to pierce, to peck, to dart or throw, a softened form of *pick*, *pike*. PICK.] To fix or plant, as stakes or pointed instruments; to fix by means of such; hence, to set in array; to marshal or arrange in order (to *pitch* a tent, to *pitch* a camp); to fling or throw; to cast forward; to hurl; to toss, as *pitch* a baseball; to regulate or set the key-note of; to pave or face with stones, as an embankment.—*Pitched battle*, one in which the armies are previously drawn up in form, with a regular disposition of the forces.—*v.i.* To light; to settle; to come to rest from flight; to plunge or fall headlong; to fix choice: with *on* or *upon*; to fix a tent or temporary habitation; to encamp; *naut.* to rise and fall, as the head and stern of a ship passing over waves.—*n.* A point or degree of elevation or depression; height or depth; degree; rate; loftiness; the degree of slope or inclination (the *pitch* of a hill or roof); the rise of an arch; a throw; a toss; that part of a cricket-field where the wickets are put up; a cast or jerk of something from the hand; *music*, the relative height of a sound; in certain technical senses, a distance between two points (as the *pitch* of a screw, that is, the distance between its threads).—**Pitch circle, Pitch line**, *n.* The circle or line which would bisect all the teeth of two toothed wheels in gear.—**Pitcher**, pich′ėr, *n.* One who or that which pitches.—**Pitchfork**, pich′fork, *n.* A fork used in lifting or throwing hay or sheaves of grain; a tuning-fork.—*v.t.* To lift or throw with a pitch-fork; hence, to put suddenly or accidentally into any position.—**Pitch pipe**, *n.* A small flute or free-reed pipe used in regulating the *pitch* or elevation of the key or leading note of a tune.—**Pitch wheel**, *n.* One or two toothed wheels which work together.

Pitcher, pich′ėr, *n.* [O.Fr. *picher*, *pichier*, *pechier*, O.It. *pecchero*, from O.H.G. *pechar*, *behhar*, a beaker. BEAKER.] A vessel with a spout for holding liquors; an earthen or metallic vessel for holding water for domestic purposes; a water-pot, jug, or jar with ears.—**Pitcher-plant**, *n.* A name given to several plants from their pitcher-shaped leaves.

Piteous, &c. Under PITY.

Pitfall. Under PIT.

Pith, pith, *n.* [A.Sax. *pitha*, D. *pit*, marrow, pith, kernel.] A soft cellular substance occupying the centre of the root, stem, and branches of exogenous plants; the spinal cord or marrow of an animal; strength, vigour, or force; closeness and vigour of thought and style; cogency; condensed substance or matter; quintessence. —**Pithily**, pith′i-li, *adv.* In a pithy manner.—**Pithiness**, pith′i-nes, *n.* The state or quality of being pithy.—**Pithless**, pith′les, *a.* Destitute of pith.—**Pithy**, pith′i, *a.* Consisting of pith; containing pith; abounding with pith; terse and striking; forcible; energetic; uttering energetic words or expressions.

Pithecoid, pi-thē′koid, *a.* [Gr. *pithēkos*, an ape, and *eidos*, likeness.] Pertaining to apes; resembling an ape; ape-like.

Pitiable, Pitiful, Pitiless, &c. Under PITY.

Pittance, pit′ans, *n.* [Fr. *pitance*, a monk's mess, from L.L. *pietantia*, *pitantia*, a monk's allowance, from L. *pietas*, piety.] An allowance of food bestowed in charity;

a charity gift; a very small portion allowed or assigned.

Pittite, pit'īt, *n.* A follower of the Elder and Younger Pitt; a frequenter of the pit in a theatre.

Pituitary, pi-tū'i-ta-ri, *a.* [L. *pituita*, phlegm, rheum.] *Anat.* concerned in the secretion of phlegm or mucus (the *pituitary* membrane which lines the nostrils, the *pituitary* gland of the brain).—**Pituitous**, pi-tū'i-tus, *a.* [L. *pituitosus.*] Consisting of mucus; resembling mucus.

Pituitary gland, pi-tū'i-tėr-i, *n.* [L. *pituita*, slime.] A small gland attached to the under side of the brain, and producing an internal secretion governing obesity and bone length. See AKROMEGALY.

Pity, pit'i, *n.* [Fr. *pitié*, O.Fr. *pité*, from L. *pietas*, piety, from *pius*, pious. (PIOUS.) *Piety* is the same word.] The suffering of one person excited by the distresses of another: commiseration; compassion; mercy; the ground or subject of pity; cause of grief; thing to be regretted: in this sense it has a plural (it is a thousand *pities* he should fail).—*To have pity upon, to take pity upon*, generally to show one's pity towards by some benevolent act.—*v.t.*—*pitied, pitying.* [O.Fr. *pitoyer*, to pity.] To feel pity or compassion towards; to feel pain or grief for; to have sympathy for; to commiserate; to compassionate.—*v.i.* To be compassionate; to exercise pity.—**Pityingly**, pit'i-ing-li, *adv.* So as to show pity; compassionately.—**Piteous**, pit'ē-us, *a.* Fitted to excite pity; moving pity or compassion; mournful; affecting; lamentable.—**Piteously**, pit'ē-us-li, *adv.* In a piteous manner.—**Piteousness**, pit'ē-us-nes, *n.* The state of being piteous.—**Pitiable**, pit'i-a-bl, *a.* Deserving or exciting pity.—**Pitiableness**, pit'i-a-bl-nes, *n.* State of being pitiable.—**Pitiably**, pit'i-a-bli, *adv.* In a pitiable manner.—**Pitier**, pit'i-ėr, *n.* One who pities.—**Pitiful**, pit'i-ful, *a.* Full of pity; tender; compassionate; miserable; moving compassion; paltry; insignificant; contemptible. ∴ Syn. under CONTEMPTIBLE.—**Pitifully**, pit'i-ful-li, *adv.* In a pitiful manner.—**Pitifulness**, pit'i-ful-nes, *n.* The state or quality of being pitiful.—**Pitiless**, pit'i-les, *a.* Destitute of pity; hard-hearted; relentless; exciting no pity.—**Pitilessly**, pit'i-les-li, *adv.* In a pitiless manner.—**Pitilessness**, pit'i-les-ness, *n.* The state of being pitiless.

Pityriasis, pit-i-rī'a-sis, *n.* [Gr. *pityron*, bran.] A cutaneous disease consisting of irregular bran-like scaly patches.—**Pityroid**, pit'i-roid, *a.* Resembling bran; bran-like.

Pivot, piv'ot, *n.* [Fr. *pivot*, a pivot, from It. *piva*, a pipe (= Fr. and E. *pipe*).] A pin on which anything turns; a short shaft or point on which a wheel or other body revolves; *milit.* the officer or soldier upon whom the different wheelings are made in the various evolutions of the drill, &c.; that on which important results depend; a turning-point.—*v.t.* To place on a pivot; to furnish with a pivot.—**Pivotal**, piv'ot-al, *a.* Belonging to a pivot.—**Pivot-bridge**, *n.* A form of swing-bridge moving on a vertical pivot underneath it.—**Pivot-gun**, *n.* A gun set so that it can be turned about in any direction.—**Pivot industry**, *n.* — A branch of industry in which the national interests center and requiring to be controlled in totalitarian states; one forming an essential part (e.g. aniline dyes) of another great national industry, such as cotton.

Pix, piks, *n.* PYX.

Pixy, Pixie, pik'si, *n.* [Perhaps for *pucksy*, from *Puck.*] A sort of fairy.—**Pixy-ring**, *n.* A fairy ring.

Pizzicato, pit-si-kä'tō, *a.* [It., twitched.] *Mus.* to be plucked by the finger, and not played with the bow of the violin.

Placable, plak'a-bl or plā'ka-bl, *a.* [L. *placabilis*, from *placo*, to soothe, pacify; akin to *placeo*, to please. PLEASE.] Capable of being appeased or pacified; appeasable.—**Placability**, plak-a-bil'i-ti or plā-, *n.* The quality of being placable.—**Placate**, plā'kāt, *v.t.*—*placated, placating.* To appease, pacify, or conciliate.

Placard, plak'ärd or pla-kärd', *n.* [Fr., from *plaque*, a plate, from the Teutonic; comp. D. *plak*, a flat piece of wood, a slice, *plakbriefje*, a placard; L.G. *plakke*, a piece of turf.] A written or printed paper posted in a public place; a bill posted up to draw public attention; a poster.—*v.t.* To post placards on; to make known by placard.

Place, plās, *n.* [Fr. *place*, a place, post, position, an open space in a town; from L. *platea*, a street, an area, from Gr. *plateia*, from *platys*, flat, broad. PLATE.] A broad way or open space in a city; an area; a particular portion of space marked off by its use or character; a locality, spot, or site; position; a town or village; a fortified post; a passage in a book; point or degree in order of proceeding (in the first *place*); rank; order of priority, dignity, or importance; office; employment; official station; ground or occasion; room; station in life; calling; occupation; condition; room or stead, with the sense of substitution (to act in *place* of another); the position in the heavens of a heavenly body.—*To give place*, to make room or way; to retire in favour of another; to yield.—*To have place*, to have a station, room, or seat; to have actual existence.—*To take place*, to come to pass; to happen; to occur; to take the precedence or priority.—*v.t.*—*placed, placing.* To put or set in a particular place or spot; to set or put in a certain relative position; to locate; to appoint, set, induct, or establish in an office; to put or set in any particular rank, state, or condition; to set; to fix (to *place* confidence in a friend); to invest; to lend (to *place* money in the funds).—**Place-kick**, *n.* In football, the act of kicking the ball after it has been placed on the ground.—**Placeless**, plās'les, *a.* Having no place or office.—**Placement**, plās'ment, *n.* The act of placing or of putting in a certain spot or position.—**Place-name**, *n.* The name of a place or locality: in contradistinction to *personal* name.—**Placer**, plā'sėr, *n.* One who places.

Placenta, pla-sen'ta, *n.* [L., a cake.] The after-birth; a temporary organ developed in mammals during pregnancy, and forming a connection between the mother and the fœtus; *bot.* that part of a seed-vessel on which the ovules or seeds are placed.—**Placental**, pla-sen'tal, *a.* Pertaining to the placenta; possessing a placenta.—*n.* An animal that possesses a placenta.—**Placentary**, pla-sen ta-ri, *n.* *Bot.* a placenta bearing numerous ovules.—*a.* Having reference to the placenta.—**Placentation**, pla-sen-tā'shon, *n.* The disposition of the placenta, more especially in plants.—**Placentiferous**, pla-sen-tif'ėr-us, *a.* Bearing or producing a placenta; having a placenta.—**Placentiform**, pla-sen'ti-form, *a.* Shaped like a placenta.

Placer, plas'ėr, *n.* [Sp.] A gravelly place where gold occurs; a spot where gold-dust is found in the soil.

Placid, plas'id, *a.* [L. *placidus*, from *placeo*, to please. PLEASE.] Gentle; quiet; undisturbed; equable; serene; mild; unruffled.—**Placidity, Placidness**, pla-sid'i-ti, plas'id-nes, *n.* The state or quality of being placid.—**Placidly**, plas'id-li, *adv.* In a placid manner; calmly; quietly.

Plack, plak, *n.* [Fr. *plaque*, from Fl. *placke*, an ancient Flemish coin. PLACARD.] A small copper coin formerly current in Scotland equal to the third part of an English penny.

Placket, plak'et, *n.* [From the Fr. *plaquer*, to lay or clap on. PLACARD.] A petticoat; the opening or slit in a petticoat or skirt; a fent.

Placoid, plak'oid, *a.* [Gr. *plax, plakos*, something flat.] Applied to a certain class of fishes' scales, consisting of detached bony grains, tubercles, or plates.—*n.* A fish with such scales.

Placula, plak'ū-la, *n.* [Gr. dim. of *plakous*, a flat cake.] A plate-shaped BLASTULA (which see).

Plafond, pla-fond', *n.* [Fr., from *plat*, flat, and *fond*, bottom, back.] *Arch.* the ceiling of a room; the under side of a soffit.

Plagal, plā'gal, *a.* [Gr. *plagios*, oblique.] *Music*, applied to a cadence in which the chord of the subdominant is followed by that of the tonic.

Plagiary, plā'ji-a-ri, *n.* [L. *plagiarius*, a plagiary, a kidnapper, from *plagium*, man-stealing, kidnapping, from *plaga*, a snare.] One that steals or purloins the words or ideas of another and passes them off as his own; a literary thief; plagiarism.—**Plagiarism**, plā'ji-a-rizm, *n.* The act of plagiarizing; the crime of literary theft; that which is plagiarized.—**Plagiarist**, plā'ji-a-rist, *n.* One who plagiarizes.—**Plagiarize**, plā'ji-a-rīz, *v.t.* and *i.*—*plagiarized, plagiarizing.* To steal or purloin the thoughts or words of another in literary composition.

Plagioclase, plā'ji-ō-klāz, *n.* [Gr. *plagios*, oblique, and *klasis*, fracture.] A name of triclinic felspars, the two prominent cleavage directions in which are oblique to one another.—**Plagioclastic**, plā'ji-ō-klas"-tik, *a.* Of the nature of or containing plagioclase.

Plagiostome, plā'ji-ō-stōm, *n.* [Gr. *plagios*, transverse, and *stoma*, mouth.] One of a sub-order of cartilaginous fishes, including the sharks and rays, which have their mouth placed transversely beneath the snout.—**Plagiostomous**, plā-ji-os'-tō-mus, *a.* Of or belonging to the Plagiostomes.

Plague, plāg, *n.* [Same as D. *plaag*, Dan. and G. *plage*, Icel. *plaga*, Pr. *plaga*, O.Sp. *plaga*, the plague; all from L. *plaga*, a blow, stroke, calamity. PLAINT.] A blow or calamity; severe trouble or vexation; a pestilential disease; a malignant fever of the East eminently contagious, and attended by excessive debility, as also with carbuncles or buboes.—*Plague on* or *upon*, a kind of denunciation expressive of weariness or petty annoyance.—*v.t.*—*plagued, plaguing.* To vex; to tease; to harass; to trouble; to embarrass; to scourge with disease, calamity, or natural evil of any kind.—**Plaguer**, plā'gėr, *n.* One who plagues or vexes.—**Plague-sore**, *n.* A sore resulting from the plague.—**Plague-mark, Plague-spot**, *n.* A mark or spot of plague or foul disease; a deadly mark or sign.—**Plaguily**, plā'gi-li, *adv.* Vexatiously; in a manner to vex, harass, or embarrass. (*Colloq.*)—**Plaguy**, plā'gi, *a.* Vexatious; troublesome; tormenting; annoying; wearisome. (*Colloq.*)—*adv.* Vexatiously; deucedly. (*Colloq.*)

Plaice, Plaise, plās, *n.* [From L. *platessa*, a flat-fish, from Gr. *platys*, flat.] A well-known species of the flat-fish family, more flat and square than the halibut.

Plaid, plād or plad, *n.* [Gael. *plaide*, from *peallaid*, a sheepskin, from *peall*, a skin or hide. PELT.] A large rectangular outer garment or wrap, frequently of tartan, worn by the Highlanders and others in Scotland.—**Plaided**, plā'ded, *a.* Of the cloths of which plaids are made; tartan; wearing a plaid.—**Plaiden, Plaiding**, plā'den, plā'ding, *n.* A coarse woollen cloth, differing from flannel in being twilled. (*Scotch.*)

Plain, plān, *a.* [Fr. *plain*, Pr. *plan*, It. *piano*, from L. *planus*, plain (same root as *plango*, to beat). *Plan* and *plane* are the same word.] Without elevations and depressions; level; flat; even; smooth; void of ornament; without embellishment; simple; unadorned; without beauty; homely: sometimes used as a euphemism for *ugly*; artless; simple; unlearned; without disguise, cunning, or affectation; without refinement; unsophisticated; honestly undisguised; open; unreserved; mere; absolute; unmistakable; without difficulties or intricacies; evident to the understanding; clear; manifest; not obscure; not highly seasoned; not rich or luxurious (a *plain* diet).—*Plain clothes*, the ordinary dress of society; non-official dress: opposed to *uniform*.—*adv.* In a plain manner; plainly; frankly; bluntly.

—*n.* A piece of level land; a piece of ground with an even surface, or a surface little varied by inequalities; *geog.* the general term for all those parts of the dry land which cannot properly be called hilly or mountainous.—**Plain-clothes man**, *n.* A law officer who does not wear a uniform while on duty.—**Plain-dealing**, *a.* Dealing or communicating with frankness and sincerity.—*n.* A speaking or communicating with openness and sincerity.—**Plainly**, plān′li, *adv.* In a plain manner.—**Plainness**, plān′nes, *n.* The state or quality of being plain; evenness of surface; openness; candor; intelligibility.—**Plain-song**, *n. Music*, the simple, grave, and unadorned chant in which the services of the Roman Catholic Church have been rendered from a very early age; the simple notes of an air without ornament or variation; hence, a plain unexaggerated statement.—**Plain-speaking**, *n.* Plainness or bluntness of speech; candor; frankness. — **Plain-spoken**, *a.* Speaking with plain unreserved sincerity.

Plaint, plānt, *n.* [Fr. *plainte*, a complaint, from *plaindre*, to complain, from L. *plango, planctum*, to beat the breast, to lament, akin to *plaga*, a blow, Gr. *plēssō*, to strike. PLAGUE.] Lamentation; complaint; audible expression of sorrow; representation made of injury or wrong done.—**Plaintiff**, plān′tif, *n. Law*, the person who commences a suit before a tribunal for the recovery of a claim: opposed to *defendant*. — **Plaintive**, plān′tiv, *a.* Expressive of sorrow or melancholy; mournful; sad.—**Plaintively**, plān′tiv-li, *adv.* In a plaintive manner. — **Plaintiveness**, plān′tiv-nes, *n.* The quality or state of being plaintive.—**Plaintless**, plānt′les, *a.* Without complaint; unrepining.

Plait, plāt, plat, *n.* [O.Fr. *ploit, pleit*, from L. *plicatus*, folded, from *plicare*, to twist, whence *ply*.] A flattened gather or fold; a doubling of cloth or any similar tissue or fabric; a braid, as of hair, straw, &c.—*v.t.* To fold; to double in narrow strips; to braid; to interweave the locks or strands of (to *plait* the hair).—**Plaited**, plā′ted, *p.* and *a.* Braided; interwoven; *bot.* said of a leaf folded lengthwise like the plaits of a closed fan.—**Plaiter**, plā′tėr, *n.* One who or that which plaits.

Plan, plan, *n.* [Fr. *plan*, from L. *planus*, plain, flat, level. PLAIN.] The representation of anything drawn on a plane, and forming a map or chart (the *plan* of a town); the representation of a horizontal section of a building, showing the extent, division, and distribution of its area into apartments, passages, &c.; a scheme devised; a project; disposition of parts according to a certain design; a method or process; a way; a mode.—*v.t.*—*planned, planning.* To invent or contrive for construction; to scheme: to devise; to form in design.—**Planless**, plan′les, *a.* Having no plan.—**Planner**, plan′ėr, *n.* One who plans.

Planchette, plansbet′, *n.* [Fr. *planchette*. PLANK.] A small board, usually heart-shaped, resting on two castors and the point of a pencil; when the board is touched by the fingers, the pencil is said to trace words.

Planck's constant. [After the physicist Max *Planck*.] See QUANTUM THEORY.

Plane, plān, *a.* [From L. *planus*. PLAIN.] Without elevations or depressions; even; level; flat.—*n.* A smooth or perfectly level surface; a part of something having a level surface; the supporting surface of an aeroplane; a surface such that if any two points whatever in it be joined by a straight line, the whole of the straight line will be in the surface; an ideal surface, supposed to cut and pass through solid bodies or in various directions: frequently used in astronomy (the *plane* of the ecliptic, the *plane* of a planet's orbit); a joiner's tool, consisting of a smooth-soled stock, through which passes obliquely a piece of edged steel or a chisel, used in paring or smoothing boards or wood of any kind.—*v.t.*—*planed, planing.* To make smooth, especially by the use of a plane; to travel by aeroplane.—*Plane angle*, an angle contained between two straight lines meeting in a plane.—*Plane geometry*, the geometry of plane figures, in contradistinction to *solid geometry*, or the geometry of solids.—*Plane sailing*, the art of determining a ship's place, on the supposition that she is moving on a plane, or that the surface of the ocean is plane instead of being spherical.—*Plane trigonometry*, that branch of trigonometry which treats of triangles described on a plane.—**Planary**, plā′na-ri, *a.* Pertaining to a plane. — **Plane-iron**, *n.* The cutting iron of a plane. — **Planer**, plā′nėr, *n.* One who planes; a wooden block used to smooth the face of a form of type before printing; a planing-machine.—**Plane-stock**, *n.* The body of a plane in which the cutting-iron is fitted. — **Planing-machine**, *n.* A machine for planing wood; a machine-tool for planing metals.

Plane, Plane-tree, plān, *n.* [Fr. *plane, platane*, from L. *platanus*, the plane-tree.] A tree with a straight smooth branching stem and palmate leaves, used as a shade tree for lining avenues, roads, &c.; in Scotland, a name commonly given to the sycamore.

Planet, plan′et, *n.* [L. *planeta*, a planet, from Gr. *planētēs*, a wanderer, from *planaō*, to wander.] A celestial body (such as the earth) which revolves about the sun or other centre, whence it receives light. — *Primary planets*, those which revolve about the sun as their centre.—*Secondary planets*, those which revolve about other planets as their centre, and with them revolve about the sun; satellites or moons.—**Planetarium**, plan-e-tā′ri-um, *n.* An astronomical machine which, by the movement of its parts, represents the motions and orbits of the planets.—**Planetary**, plan′e-ta-ri, *a.* Pertaining to the planets; having the nature of a planet.—*Planetary years*, the periods of time in which the several planets make their revolutions round the sun. — **Planetesimals**, plan′et-es″im-als, *n.* [L.L. *planeta*, a wandering star.] Solid or liquid particles of which nebulæ are possibly composed. — **Planetoid**, plan′et-oid, *n.* One of a numerous group of very small planets revolving round the sun between the orbits of Mars and Jupiter; an asteroid. — **Planetoidal**, plan′et-oi-dal, *a.* Pertaining to the planetoids; relating to a planetoid.—**Planet-stricken, Planet-struck**, *a.* Affected by the influence of planets; blasted. — **Planet-wheel**, *n.* The exterior revolving wheel of the 'sun-and-planet' motion.

Plangent,† plan′jent, *a.* [L. *plangens, plangentis*, ppr. of *plango*, to beat.] Beating; dashing, as a wave.—**Plangency**,† plan′jen-si, *n.* The state or quality of being plangent.

Planifolious, Planipetalous, plā-ni-fō′li-us, plā-ni-pet′a-lus, *a.* [L. *planus*, plain, and *folium, petalon*, a leaf.] Applied to a flower made up of plane leaves or petals, set together in circular rows round the centre.

Planimeter, pla-nim′et-ėr, *n.* [L. *planus*, plain, and Gr. *metron*, a measure.] An instrument for measuring the area of any plane figure. — **Planimetric, Planimetrical**, plan-i-met′rik, plan-i-met′ri-kal, *a.* Pertaining to planimetry.—**Planimetry**, pla-nim′et-ri, *n.* The mensuration of plane surfaces.

Planish, plan′ish, *v.t.* [From *plane*.] To make smooth or plain, as wood; to condense, smooth, and toughen, as a metallic plate, by light blows of a hammer; to polish. —**Planisher**, plan′ish-ėr, *n.* A tool used by tinners and braziers for smoothing tin-plate and brass-work; a workman who smooths or planes.

Planisphere, plan′i-sfēr, *n.* [L. *planus*, plain, and E. *sphere*.] A sphere projected on a plane; a map exhibiting the circles of the sphere.—**Planispheric**, plan-i-sfer′ik, *a.* Pertaining to a planisphere.

Plank, plangk, *n.* [Fr. dial. *planke*, Pr. *planca, plancha*, Fr. *planche*, from L. *planca* (for *planica*), a board, slab, from L. *planus*, plain.] A broad piece of sawed timber, differing from a board only in being thicker; in political slang, one of the principles in the system adopted by a party. PLATFORM. —*v.t.* To cover or lay with planks.

Plankton, plangk′ton, *n.* [Gr. *plagkton*, wandering.] The mass of small organisms, plant or animal, floating or drifting in the ocean.

Planless, Planner. Under PLAN.

Plano-concave, plā′nō, *a.* Plane on one side and concave on the other.—**Plano-convex**, *a.* Plane or flat on one side and convex on the other.—**Plano-horizontal**, *a.* Having a level horizontal surface or position.—**Plano-orbicular**, *a.* Flat on one side and spherical on the other.— **Planometer**, plā-nom′et-ėr, *n.* A plane, hard surface used in machine-making as a gauge for plane surfaces.—**Planometry**, plā-nom′et-ri, *n.* The act of measuring or gauging plane surfaces; the art or act of using a planometer.

Plant, plant, *n.* [Fr. *plante*, a plant, from L. *planta*, a plant, a twig, the sole of the foot, from root of *planus*, plain.] One of the organisms which form the vegetable kingdom; a vegetable; an organized living body deriving its sustenance from the inorganic world, generally adhering to another body, and drawing from it some of its nourishment, and having the power of propagating itself by seeds or similar reproductive bodies; popularly the word is generally applied to the smaller species of vegetables; a collective term for the fixtures, machinery, tools, apparatus, &c., necessary to carry on any trade or mechanical business; a put-up game; a swindle. (*Colloq.*)—*v.t.* To put in the ground and cover, as seed for growth; to set in the ground for growth; to furnish with plants; to lay out and prepare with plants; to set upright; to set firmly; to fix; to set and direct or point (to *plant* cannon against a fort); to furnish the first inhabitants of; to settle (to *plant* a colony); to introduce and establish (to *plant* Christianity).—*v.i.* To perform the act of planting.—**Plantable**, plan′ta-bl, *a.* Capable of being planted.—**Plantation**, plan-tā′shon, *n.* [L. *plantatio*.] The act of planting or setting in the earth for growth; the place planted; a small wood; a grove; in the Southern states, a large estate cultivated chiefly by share croppers.—**Planter**, plan′tėr, *n.* One who plants, sets, introduces, or establishes; one who owns a plantation.— **Planticle**,† plan′ti-kl, *n.* A young plant, or plant in embryo (*Darwin*).—**Planting**, plant′ing, *n.* The art of forming plantations of trees; the act or art of inserting plants in the soil; a plantation.—**Plantless**, plant′les, *a.* Without plants; destitute of vegetation.—**Plantlet**, plant′let, *n.* A little undeveloped or rudimentary plant.—**Plant-louse**, *n.* An aphis.— **Plantule**, plant′ūl, *n.* The embryo of a plant.

Plantain, plan′tān, *n.* [Fr. *plantain*, from L. *plantago*, from *planta*, the sole of the foot, from a vague resemblance of the leaves to the foot.] A genus of perennial or annual herbs, found in all temperate regions. They are mostly roadside weeds with elliptic ribbed leaves and spikes of small greenish flowers.

Plantain, Plantain-tree, plan′tān, *n.* [Sp. *plantano, platano*, from L. *platanus*, a plane-tree.] A large herbaceous plant, with a soft succulent stem, sometimes attaining the height of 20 feet, the fruit of which is of great importance as an article of food in tropical climates.—**Plantain-eater**, *n.* An African scansorial bird of which plantains form the principal food.

Plantar, plan′tar, *a.* [L. *planta*, the sole of the foot.] *Anat.* relating or belonging to the sole of the foot.

Plantigrade, plan′ti-grād, *a.* [L. *planta*, the sole of the foot, and *gradior*, to walk.] Walking on the sole of the foot and not on the toes (digitigrade): applied to a section of carnivorous animals, including the bears.

Planula, plan′ū-la, *n.* [L. dim. of *planus*,

'a wanderer.] In sponges and zoophytes, an oval ciliated larva.

Plaque, plak, *n.* [Fr.] An ornamental plate; a brooch; the plate of a clasp; a flat plate of metal upon which enamels are painted.

Plash, plash, *n.* [D. *plasch*, *plas*, a puddle, perhaps from sound of splashing; comp. D. *plassen*, G. *platschen*, *platschern*, to paddle in water; L.G. *plasken*, E. to *splash*.] A small collection of standing water; a puddle; a pond; a splash.—*v.i.* To dabble in water; to fall with a dabbling sound; to splash. — **Plashy**, plash'i, *a.* Watery; abounding with puddles.

Plash, plash, *v.t.* [O.Fr. *plassier*, *plessier*, from L. *plexus*, pp. of *plecto*, to weave, to twist (as in *complex*). *Pleach* is a collateral form.] To bend down and interweave the branches or twigs of (to *plash* a hedge).

Plasma, plaz'ma, *n.* [Gr. *plasma*, something formed or moulded, from *plassō*, to form, whence *plastic*.] A siliceous mineral of a colour between grass-green and leek-green, used by the ancients for engraving upon; formless elementary matter; the liquid part of blood and lymph; specifically, *biol.* the simplest form of organized matter in the vegetable and animal body, out of which the several tissues are formed; the nearly colourless fluid in which the corpuscles of the blood are suspended. — **Plasmic, Plasmatic**, plaz'mik, plaz-mat'ik, *a.* Pertaining to plasma; having the character of a plasma.

Plasmodium, plaz-mōd'i-um, *n.* In slime fungi (Myxomycetes), a stage in the life-history consisting of a creeping mass of naked protoplasm.

Plaster, plas'tėr, *n.* [O.Fr. *plaster* (Fr. *plâtre*), from L. *emplastrum*, Gr. *emplastron*, plaster, from *emplassō*, to daub over —*en*, on, in, and *plassō*, to form, to shape (whence also *plastic*, *plasma*).] A composition of lime, water, and sand, with or without hair for binding, used for coating walls and partitions of houses; calcined gypsum, used, when mixed with water, for finishing walls, for casts, cement, &c.; *phar.* an external application of a harder consistence than an ointment, spread on linen, silk, &c.—*Plaster of Paris*, a composition of several species of gypsum, originally obtained from Montmartre near Paris, used for various purposes.—*Plaster cast*, a copy of an object obtained by pouring plaster of Paris mixed with water into a mould which forms a copy of the object in reverse.—*v.t.* To overlay or cover with plaster; to lay coarsely on; to bedaub.—**Plasterer**, plas'-tėr-ėr, *n.* One that overlays with plaster.—**Plastering**, plas'tėr-ing, *n.* The act or operation of overlaying with plaster; plaster-work; a covering of plaster.—**Plastery**, plas'tėr-i, *a.* Resembling plaster; containing plaster.

Plastic, plas'tik, *a.* [Gr. *plastikos*, from *plassō*, to form. PLASTER.] Having the power to give form or fashion to a mass of matter; capable of being molded into various forms; capable of change or modification; capable of receiving a new bent or direction (as the mind); applied to sculpture and the kindred arts, as distinguished from painting and the graphic arts.—*n.* Any synthetic nonmetallic compound, usually of organic composition, capable of being molded.—**Plasticity**, plas-tis'i-ti, *n.* The state or quality of being plastic.

Plastron, plas'tron, *n.* [Fr. *plastron*, a breastplate, same origin as *plaster*.] A piece of leather stuffed, used by fencers to defend the breast against pushes; *zool.* the lower or ventral portion of the bony case of tortoises and turtles.

Plat, plat, *v.t.*—*platted*, *platting*. [Same as *plait*.] To interweave; to plait.—**Platter**, plat'ėr, *n.* One who plats or forms by weaving.—**Platting**, plat'ing, *n.* Slips of cane, straw, &c., woven or plaited, for making into hats, &c.

Plat, plat, *n.* [Same word as *plot*; but probably affected by Fr. *plat*, *plate*, flat. PLATE.] A small piece of ground marked out and devoted to some special purpose; a plot of ground; a map or chart.

Platan, Platane, plat'an, plat'ān, *n.* [L. *platanus*.] The plane-tree.

Platband, plat'band, *n.* [Fr. *plate-bande* —*plat*, *plate*, flat, and *bande*, a band.] A border of flowers in a garden; *arch.* any flat rectangular moulding, the projection of which is much less than its width.

Plate, plāt, *n.* [From Fr. *plate*, a metal plate, a piece of plate-armour, and *plat*, a dish; from *plat*, *plate*, flat; perhaps (like *place*) from Gr. *platys*, broad, cog. with Skr. *prithu*, broad.] A flattened piece of metal with a uniform thickness; armour composed of broad pieces or plates; domestic vessels or utensils made of gold or silver; a small shallow vessel of metal, porcelain, or earthenware, from which food is eaten at table; a piece of timber laid horizontally in a wall to receive the ends of other timbers; a piece of metal on which anything is engraved for the purpose of being printed off on paper; a page of stereotype for printing.—*v.t.*—*plated*, *plating*. To cover with a plate or plates; to overlay with a thin coating of silver or other metal: used particularly of silver (*plated* vessels).—**Plate-armour**, *n.* Defensive armour consisting of plates of metal.—**Plate-glass**, *n.* A superior kind of thick glass used for mirrors, &c.—**Plate-iron**, *n.* Iron drawn into flat plates by being passed between cylindrical rollers; rolled iron.—**Plate-layer**, *n.* A workman on railways whose occupation is to lay down rails and fix them to the sleepers.—**Plate-mark**, *n.* A legal mark made on certain gold and silver articles for the purpose of indicating their degree of purity, &c.—**Plate-paper**, *n.* A heavy, spongy paper used for taking impressions from engraved plates.—**Plate-powder**, *n.* A composition for cleaning gold and silver plate. — **Plater**, plā'tėr, *n.* One who coats articles with gold or silver; horse of a poor quality competing for cups of gold or silver plate.—**Plate-rack**, *n.* A frame in a scullery, kitchen, or pantry for plates and dishes.—**Plate-warmer**, *n.* A case with shelves in which plates are warmed before the fire.—**Platey, Platy**, plā'ti, *a.* Like a plate; flat.—**Plating**, plā'ting, *n.* The art of covering articles with a thin coating of metal, especially of overlaying articles made of the baser metals with a thin coating of gold or silver; a thin coating of one metal laid upon another metal.

Plateau, pla-tō', *n.* pl. **Plateaux, Plateaus**, pla-tōz', *n.* [Fr., from *plat*, flat; akin to *plate*.] A broad, flat area of land in an elevated position; a tableland.

Platen, plat'en, *n.* [From Fr. *plat*, flat.] *Printing*, the flat part of a press by which the impression is made; the roller of a typewriter.

Platform, plat'form, *n.* [Fr. *plate-forme*—*plate*, flat, and *forme*, a form. PLATE.] Any flat or horizontal structure, especially if raised above some particular level; the flat roof of a building on the outside; the place where guns are mounted on a fortress or battery; the raised walk at a railway station for landing passengers and goods; a place raised above the floor of a hall set apart for the speakers at public meetings; the aggregate of principles adopted or avowed by any body of men, such as a political party; a declared system of policy (a political *platform*).

Platina, plat'i-na, *n.* [Sp. *platina*, from *plata*, silver; akin to *plate*.] The old name of platinum; twisted silver-wire.

Platinum, plat'i-num, *n.* [From *platina*.] A metal of a white colour very much like silver, but of inferior lustre, the heaviest of known metals, exceedingly ductile, malleable, tenacious, and difficult of fusion.—**Platinic**, pla-tin'ik, *a.* Pertaining to platinum.—**Platiniferous**, plat-i-nif'ėr-us, *a.* Producing platinum (*platiniferous* sand).—**Platinize**, plat'i-nīz, *v.t.* To combine or cover with platinum.—**Platinoid**, plat'-i-noid, *n.* [From *platinum*.] A metal of similar composition to German silver (which see), with an essential addition of 1 to 2 per cent of tungsten; any one of a series of metals allied to platinum.—**Platinotype**, plat'i-nō-tīp, *n.* [*Platinum* and *type*.] A permanent photographic print produced by a process in which platinum is used.—**Platinous**, plat'i-nus, *a.* Containing or consisting of platinum. — **Platinum-steel**, *n.* Steel alloyed with about 1/110th of platinum.

Platitude, plat'i-tūd, *n.* [Fr., from *plat*, flat.] Flatness; dulness; insipidity; a trite, dull, or stupid remark; a truism.—**Platitudinize**, plat-i-tū'di-nīz, *v.i.* To utter platitudes; to make stale or insipid remarks.

Platonic, Platonical, pla-ton'ik, pla-ton'i-kal, *a.* Pertaining to Plato the philosopher, or to his philosophy, his school, or his opinions.—*Platonic bodies*, the five regular geometrical solids. — *Platonic love*, a pure spiritual affection subsisting between the sexes, unmixed with carnal desires.—*Platonic year*, a period of time determined by the revolution of the equinoxes, which is accomplished in about 26,000 years.—*n.* A follower of Plato.—**Platonically**, pla-ton'i-kal-li, *adv.* In a Platonic manner.—**Platonism**, plā'ton-izm, *n.* The doctrines, opinions, or philosophy of Plato.—**Platonist**, plā'ton-ist, *n.* One who adheres to the philosophy of Plato.—**Platonize**, plā'ton-īz, *v.i.*—*platonized*, *platonizing*. To adopt the opinions or philosophy of Plato.

Platoon, pla-tön', *n.* [Fr. *peloton*, a ball of thread, a platoon, from *pelote*, a ball of thread, from L.L. *pelota*, *pilota*, from L. *pila*, a ball.] Formerly a small square body of soldiers; in present usage a body consisting of four sections and about forty men, commanded by a lieutenant, with a sergeant as second in command.—*Platoon firing*, firing by subdivisions.

Platter, plat'ėr, *n.* [From O.Fr. *platel*, dim. of *plat*, a plate. PLATE.] A plate; a large shallow dish for holding eatables.

Platter, Platting, *n.* Under PLAT.

Platycephalic, Platycephalous, plat'i-se-fal"ik, plat-i-sef'a-lus, *a.* [Gr. *platys*, broad, and *kephalē*, head.] Broad-headed; flat-headed.

Platycnemic, plā-tik-nem'ik, *a.* [Gr. *platys*, broad, and *knēmē*, a leg.] Broad-legged; having a flattened surface: said of some ancient human leg-bones.

Platypus, plat'i-pus, *n.* [Gr. *platys*, broad, and *pous*, a foot.] The original name of the ornithorhynchus.

Platyrhine, plat'i-rīn, *a.* [Gr. *platys*, broad, and *rhis*, *rhinos*, a nostril.] Having a broad nose: applied to a section of monkeys in which the nostrils are far apart.

Platysma, pla-tis'ma, *n.* [Gr. *platys*, broad.] A broad thin muscle on the side of the neck.

Plaudit, plą'dit, *n.* [L. *plaudite*, do you applaud, imper. of *plaudo*, *plausum*, to applaud, seen in *plausible*, *applause*, *explode*.] Applause; praise bestowed: usually in plural.—**Plauditory**, plą'di-to-ri, *a.* Applause; commending.

Plausible, plą'zi-bl, *a.* [L. *plausibilis*, from *plaudo*. PLAUDIT.] Praiseworthy‡; apparently worthy of praise; apparently right; specious; using specious arguments or discourse; fair-spoken. ∴ Syn. under COLOURABLE.—**Plausibility, Plausibleness**, plą-zi-bil'i-ti, plą'zi-bl-nes, *n.* The state or quality of being plausible; speciousness; superficial appearance of right. — **Plausibly**, plą'zi-bli, *adv.* In a plausible manner; speciously.—**Plausive**, plą'ziv, *a.* Applauding; manifesting praise.

Play, plā, *v.i.* [A.Sax. *plegian*, to play, from *plega*, play, pastime; connections doubtful.] To do something not as a task or for profit, but for amusement; to act wantonly or thoughtlessly; to dally, trifle, toy; to move irregularly; to flutter; to contend in a game; to gamble; to perform on an instrument of music; to act with free motion; to work freely (the lungs *play*); to act; to behave; to act a part on the stage; to personate a character.—*To play on or* *upon*, to make sport of; to trifle with; to delude; to give a humorous or fanciful turn to (to *play upon* words).—*v.t.* To perform in sport or for sport or for a prize; to make use of in a game (to *play* a trump card); to enter into a game with; to perform music on; to perform on a musical instrument (a tune); to act on the stage; to act or represent in general; to act like; to behave in the manner of (to *play* the fool); to perform; to execute (to *play* a trick).—*n.* Any exercise intended for pleasure, amusement, or diversion, as cricket, quoits, &c.; a game; amusement; sport; frolic; jest; not earnest; gaming; practice in any contest (sword-*play*); action; use; employment; practice; manner of acting or dealing (fair *play*); a dramatic composition; a comedy or tragedy; a dramatic performance; motion; movement, regular or irregular (the *play* of a wheel); hence, power or space for motion; liberty of action; scope; swing.—*To hold in play*, to keep occupied. —*Play of colours*, an appearance of several prismatic colours in rapid succession on turning an object, as a diamond.—*A play on words*, the giving of words a double signification; a pun.—**Play-actor**, *n.* A stage-player; an actor.—**Playbill**, plā'bil, *n.* A bill exhibited as an advertisement of a play, with the parts assigned to the actors. —**Playbook**, plā'bu̇k, *n.* A book of dramatic compositions.—**Playday**, plā'dā, *n.* A day given to play; a holiday.—**Played out**, *pp.* or *a.* Exhausted, from a game at cards which has been played to the last extremity or deal. — **Player**, plā'ėr, *n.* One who plays; an actor; a musician.—**Playfair**, plā'fār, *n.* A cipher sometimes employed when on active service.—**Playfellow**, plā'fel-ō, *n.* A companion in amusements or sports.—**Playful**, plā'fu̇l, *a.* Sportive; frolicsome; frisky; indulging in gambols; full of sprightly humour; pleasantly jocular or amusing.—**Playfully**, plā'fu̇l-li, *adv.* In a playful manner; sportively.—**Playfulness**, plā'fu̇l-nes, *n.* The state of being playful; sportiveness.—**Playgoer**, plā'gō-ėr, *n.* One who frequents plays.—**Playgoing**, plā'gō-ing, *a.* Frequenting the exhibitions of the stage.—**Playground**, plā'ground, *n.* A piece of ground set apart for open-air recreation, especially connected with a school, &c., for the pupils.—**Playhouse**, plā'hous, *n.* A theatre.—**Playmate**, plā'māt, *n.* A playfellow; a companion in diversions.—**Plaything**, plā'thing, *n.* A toy; anything that serves to amuse.—**Playwright**, plā'rīt, *n.* A maker of plays.

Plea, plē, *n.* [O.Fr. *plai, plaid, plait*, a suit, a plea; from L. *placitum*, an opinion, a determination, from *placeo*, to please. PLEASE.] That which is alleged by a party to a legal action in support of his demand; the answer of a defendant to the plaintiff's declaration; a suit or action; a cause in court; that which is alleged in support, justification, or defence; an excuse; a pleading.

Pleach,‡ plēch, *v.t.* [Akin to *plash*, to interweave.] To plash; to interweave.

Plead, plēd, *v.i.*—pret. and pp. *pleaded*, sometimes *pled.* [Fr. *plaider*, to plead, from L.L. *placitare*, from L. *placitum*. PLEA.] To argue in support of a claim, or in defence against the claim of another; to urge reasons for or against; to attempt to persuade one by argument or supplication; *law*, to present a plea; to present an answer to the declaration of a plaintiff; to deny the plaintiff's declaration and demand. —*To plead guilty* or *not guilty*, to admit or deny guilt.—*v.t.* To discuss, defend, and attempt to maintain by arguments or reasons (to *plead* one's cause); to allege or adduce in proof, support, or vindication; to offer in excuse (to *plead* poverty); to allege and offer in a legal plea or defence, or for repelling a demand in law.—**Pleadable**, plē'da-bl, *a.* Capable of being alleged in proof, defence, or vindication.—**Pleader**, plē'dėr, *n.* One who pleads; a lawyer who argues in a court of justice; one that forms pleas or pleadings (a special *pleader*). — **Pleading**, plē'ding, *n.* The act of advocating any cause; the act or practice of advocating clients' causes in courts of law; one of the written statements containing the subject-matter of a litigant's demand or claim, or of his defence or answer.—**Pleadingly**, plē'ding-li, *adv.* By pleading.

Pleasant, &c. Under PLEASE.

Please, plēz, *v.t.*—*pleased, pleasing.* [O.Fr. *plaisir, pleisir*, &c., Mod.Fr. *plaire*, from L. *placere*, to please; of similar origin are *placid, placable, plea, plead.*] To excite agreeable sensations or emotions in; to delight; to gratify; to satisfy; to content; to seem good to: in this sense used impersonally.—*To be pleased* to do a thing, to take pleasure in doing it; to think fit or condescend to do it.—*v.i.* To give pleasure; to gain approbation; to like; to choose; to prefer; to condescend; to be pleased; to be kind enough (do it, if you *please*).—**Pleaser**, plē'zėr, *n.* One that pleases; one that courts favour by pleasing. — **Pleasing**, plē'zing, *a.* Giving pleasure or satisfaction; agreeable; gratifying; delightful. — **Pleasingly**, plē'zing-li, *adv.* In a pleasing manner; in such a way as to give pleasure.—**Pleasingness**, plē'zing-nes, *n.*—**Pleasant**, plez'ant, *a.* [Fr. *plaisant*, ppr. of *plaire.*] Pleasing; agreeable; grateful to the mind or to the senses; cheerful; gay; lively; jocular.—**Pleasantly**, plez'ant-li, *adv.* In a pleasant manner; gaily; merrily; cheerfully.—**Pleasantness**, plez'ant-nes, *n.* State or quality of being pleasant or agreeable; cheerfulness; gaiety. — **Pleasantry**, plez'ant-ri, *n.* [Fr. *plaisanterie.*] Gaiety; merriment; a sprightly or humorous saying; a jest; raillery; lively talk; a laughable trick; a frolic. — **Pleasance**, plez'ans, *n.* [Fr. *plaisance.*] Pleasure; delight; a part of a garden or pleasure-grounds secluded by trees or hedges. (*Archaic.*) — **Pleasure**, plezh'ūr, *n.* [O.Fr. *plaisir, pleisir*, Mod.Fr. *plaisir*, from L. *placere*, to please: properly an infinitive but as in *leisure* the final syllable has been assimilated to that of nouns in *-ure*, L. *-ura*. PLEASE.] The gratification of the senses or of the mind; agreeable sensations or emotions; the feeling produced by enjoyment or the expectation of good; delight: opposed to *pain*; sensual or sexual gratification; vicious indulgence of the appetite; what the will dictates or prefers; choice; wish; desire; a favour; arbitrary will or choice (to go or stay at *pleasure*).—*To take pleasure in*, to have pleasure or enjoyment in.—*v.t.*—*pleasured, pleasuring.* To give or afford pleasure to; to please; to gratify.—**Pleasurable**, plezh'ūr-a-bl, *a.* Pleasing; giving pleasure.—**Pleasurableness**, plezh'ūr-a-bl-nes, *n.* The quality of being pleasurable or of giving pleasure.—**Pleasurably**, plezh'ūr-a-bli, *adv.* In a pleasurable manner.—**Pleasureless**, plezh'-ur-les, *a.* Devoid of pleasure; having no pleasure. — **Pleasure-ground**, *n.* A piece of ground laid out in an ornamental manner and appropriated to pleasure or amusement.

Pleat. PLAIT.

Plebeian, ple-bē'an, *a.* [L. *plebeius*, from *plebes, plebs*, the common people; same root as in PLENTY.] Pertaining to the common people; vulgar; common; belonging to the lower ranks. —*n.* One of the common people or lower ranks of men; originally applied to the common people of ancient Rome, or those free citizens who did not come under the class of the patricians. — **Plebeianism**, plē-bē'an-izm, *n.* The state or quality of being plebeian; vulgarity.—**Plebeianize**, plē-bē'-an-īz, *v.t.*—*plebeianized, plebeianizing.* To render plebeian or common.

Plebiscite, pleb'i-sit or pleb'i-sīt, *n.* [Fr., from L. *plebiscitum* — *plebis*, the people, and *scitum*, a decree.] A vote of a whole people or community; a decree of a country obtained by an appeal to universal suffrage.

Plectognathic, **Plectognathous**, plek-tog-nath'ik, plek-tog'na-thus, *a.* [Gr. *plekō*, to connect, and *gnathos*, a jaw.] Pertaining to an order of fishes which have the maxillary bones ankylosed to the sides of the intermaxillaries, which alone form the jaws.

Plectrum, plek'trum, *n.* [L. *plectrum*, from Gr. *plēktron*, from *plēssō*, to strike.] The small instrument of ivory, horn, or metal used for striking the strings of the lyre, or other stringed instrument.

Pled, pled. PLEAD.

Pledge, plej, *n.* [Fr. *pleige*, L.L. *plegius, plegium, plivium, pluvium*, pledge; origin uncertain.] *Law*, the transfer of a chattel by a debtor to a creditor in security of a debt; the thing pawned as security for the repayment of money borrowed or for the performance of some agreement or obligation; a pawn; anything given or considered as a security for the performance of an act; a guarantee; a promise; a surety; a hostage; the drinking of another's health; a health. —*To put in pledge*, to pawn.—*To hold in pledge*, to keep in security.—*To take the pledge*, a popular method of binding one's self to observe principles of total abstinence from intoxicating drink. — *v.t.* — *pledged, pledging.* To give as a pledge or pawn; to deposit in possession of a person as a security; to give as a guarantee or security; to gage (to *pledge* one's word or honour) to engage solemnly (to *pledge* one's self); to drink a health to; to drink to one's welfare. —**Pledgee**, plej-ē', *n.* The person to whom anything is pledged.—**Pledger**, plej'ėr, *n.* One who pledges or offers a pledge; one who drinks a health.

Pledget, plej'et, *n.* A compress or small flat mass of lint, laid over a wound to imbibe the matter discharged and keep it clean.

Pleiad, plī'ad, *n.* pl. **Pleiads, Pleiades**, plī'adz, plī'a-dēz. [Gr. *Pleiades*, the Pleiads, from *pleō*, to sail, as the rising of the seven stars indicated the time of safe navigation.] The Pleiads are a cluster of seven stars in the neck of the constellation Taurus; in *poetry*, a group of seven contemporaries in the reign of Ptolemy Philadelphus at Alexandria; seven poets in the reign of Henry III of France modelling their style on Latin and Greek work; seven poets in the reign of Louis XIII.

Pleiocene, plī'ō-sēn. PLIOCENE.

Pleiosaurus, plī-ō-sa̤'rus, *n.* [Gr. *pleiōn*, more, and *sauros*, a lizard.] An extinct marine saurian of gigantic dimensions, which seems to have been intermediate between the plesiosaurus and the ichthyosaurus. Written also *Pliosaurus*.

Pleistocene, plīs'tō-sēn, *n.* [Gr. *pleistos*, most, and *kainos*, recent.] *Geol.* the most recent or uppermost division of the tertiary formation, of which the fossil remains belong almost wholly to existing species. PLIOCENE.—*a.* Pertaining to this division.

Plenary, ple'na-ri, *a.* [L.L. *plenarius*, from L. *plenus*, full. PLENTY.] Full; entire; complete. — *Plenary inspiration*, in *theol.* that kind or degree of inspiration which excludes all mixture of error.—**Plenarily**, plē'na-ri-li, *adv.* In a plenary manner.—**Plenariness**, plē'na-ri-nes, *n.* The state of being plenary.—**Plenarty**, plē'när-ti, *n.* The state of an ecclesiastical benefice when occupied: opposed to *vacancy*.

Plenipotence, **Plenipotency**, ple-nip'-o-tens, ple-nip'o-ten-si, *n.* [L. *plenus*, full, and *potentia*, power. PLENTY, POTENT.] Fulness or completeness of power.—**Plenipotent**, ple-nip'o-tent, *a.* [L. *plenipotens.*] Possessing full power.—**Plenipotentiary**, plen'i-pō-ten"shi-a-ri, *n.* A person invested with full power to transact any business; particularly, an ambassador or envoy to a foreign court, furnished with full power to negotiate a treaty or to transact other business.—*a.* Invested with or containing full power.

Plenish, plen'ish, *v.t.* [L. *plenus*, full. REPLENISH.] To replenish.

Plenitude, plen'i-tūd, *n.* [L. *plenitudo*, from *plenus*, full.] The state of being full or complete; plenty; abundance; repletion.

Plenty, plen'ti, *n.* [O.Fr. *plenté*, from L.L. *plenitas*, fulness, abundance, from L. *plenus*, full, from root of *pleo*, to fill, which is seen also in Gr. *plērēs*, *pleos*, full, and also in E. *full*, *fill*.] Abundance; copiousness; a full or adequate supply; sufficiency; abundance of things necessary for man (a time of *plenty*). — *a.* Plentiful; being in abundance. (*Colloq.*)—**Plenteous**, plen'tē-us, *a.* Abundant; copious; sufficient for every purpose; yielding abundance; having an abundance. — **Plenteously**, plen'tē-us-li, *adv.* In a plenteous manner; plentifully.—**Plenteousness**, plen'tē-us-nes, *n.* The state of being plenteous.—**Plentiful**, plen'ti-fụl, *a.* Existing in great plenty; copious; abundant; ample; yielding abundant crops; fruitful.—**Plentifully**, plen'ti-fụl-li, *adv.* In a plentiful manner. — **Plentifulness**, plen'ti-fụl-nes, *n.*

Plenum, plē'num, *n.* [L. *plenus*, full.] That state of things in which every part of space is supposed to be full of matter: in opposition to a *vacuum*.

Pleochroic, plē'ō-krō-ik, *a.* [Gr. *pleion*, more, *chroa*, colour.] Of crystals which show different colours when viewed in different directions.

Pleomorphism, plē'ō-morf"ism, *n.* [Gr. *pleōn*, more, *morphē*, form.] In fungi, &c., the occurrence of more than one independent form in the life-history.

Pleonasm, plē'o-nazm, *n.* [Gr. *pleonasmos*, from *pleon*, *pleion*, more. PLENTY.] Redundancy of words in speaking or writing; the use of more words to express ideas than are necessary.—**Pleonast**, plē'o-nast, *n.* One guilty of pleonasm.—**Pleonastic**, **Pleonastical**, plē-o-nas'tik, plē-o-nas'ti-kal, *a.* Pertaining to pleonasm; redundant. —**Pleonastically**, plē-o-nas'ti-kal-li, *adv.* In a pleonastic manner.

Plesiomorphism, plē'si-ō-mor"fizm, *n.* [Gr. *plēsios*, near, and *morphē*, form.] A term applied to crystallized substances the forms of which closely resemble each other, but are not absolutely identical.—**Plesiomorphous**, plē'si-ō-mor"fus, *a.* Nearly alike in form.

Plesiosaur, **Plesiosaurus**, plē'si-ō-sạr, plē'si-ō-sạ"rus, *n.* [Gr. *plēsios*, near, and *sauros*, a lizard.] An extinct marine saurian, chiefly remarkable for its length of neck, nearly allied to the ichthyosaurus.

Plethora, pleth'ō-ra, *n.* [Gr. *plēthōra*, from *plēthō*, to be full, from *pleos*, full. PLENTY.] *Med.* over-fulness of blood; a redundant fulness of the blood-vessels; hence, overfulness in any respect; a superabundance.—**Plethoric**, **Plethorical**, plē-thor'ik, plē-thor'i-kal, *a.* Characterized by plethora; having a full habit of body.—**Plethorically**, plē-thor'i-kal-li, *adv.* In a plethoric manner.

Pleura, plụ'ra, *n.* [Gr. *pleuron*, a rib, pl. *pleura*, the side.] *Anat.* a thin membrane which covers the inside of the thorax, and also invests the lungs.—**Pleural**, plụ'ral, *a.* Pertaining to the pleura.—**Pleurisy**, **Pleuritis**, plụ'ri-si, plū-rī'tis, *n.* An inflammation of the pleura. — **Pleuritic**, **Pleuritical**, plụ-rit'ik, plụ-rit'i-kal, *a.* Pertaining to pleurisy; diseased with pleurisy.—**Pleurocarpous**, plụ-rō-kär'pus, *a.* [Gr. *pleuron*, a rib, and *karpos*, fruit.] *Bot.* having the fructification proceeding laterally from the axils of the leaves, as in some mosses.—**Pleurodynia**, plụ-rō-din'i-a, *n.* [Gr. *pleura*, and *odynē*, pain.] A spasmodic or rheumatic affection of the chest; pleuralgia. — **Pleuro-pneumonia**, plụ'rō-nū-mō"ni-a, *n.* [Gr. *pleura*, and *pneumōn*, the lungs.] An inflammation of the pleura and substance of the lungs; a combination of pleurisy and pneumonia. — **Pleurothotonos**, plụ-rō-thot'on-os, *n.* [Gr. *pleurothen*, from one side, and *teinō*, to stretch.] *Med.* tetanus of the lateral muscles. — **Pleuralgia**, plụ-ral'ji-a, *n.* [Gr. *pleura*, and *algos*, pain.] Pain of the side; pleurodynia. — **Pleurapophysis**, plụ-ra-pof'i-sis, *n.* pl. **Pleurapophyses**, plụ-ra-pof-i-sēz. [Gr. *pleuron*, a rib, and *apophysis*, a process.] One of the processes of a typical vertebra projecting from the side.

Plexiform, plek'si-form, *a.* [L. *plexus*, a fold, and *forma*, form.] In the form of network; complicated.

Pleximeter, **Plexometer**, plek-sim'et-ėr, plek-som'et-ėr, *n.* [Gr. *plēxis*, percussion, and *metron*, a measure.] *Med.* a small circular or ovoid plate, composed of ivory, india-rubber, or the like, placed in contact with the body in diagnosis of disease by percussion.

Plexure, plek'sūr, *n.* [L. *plexus*, an interweaving, from *plecto*, *plexum*, to interweave.] An interweaving; a texture; that which is woven together.—**Plexus**, plek'sus, *n.* [L.] *Anat.* a network of vessels, nerves, or fibres.

Pliable, plī'a-bl, *a.* [Fr. *pliable*, from *plier*, to bend, to fold, from L. *plico*, to fold, to bend.] Easy to be bent; flexible; pliant; flexible in disposition; easy to be persuaded. —**Pliability**, **Pliableness**, plī-a-bil'iti, plī'a-bl-nes, *n.* The quality of being pliable; flexibility; a yielding to force or to moral influence.—**Pliably**, plī'a-bli, *adv.* In a pliable manner.—**Pliant**, plī'ant, *a.* [Fr. ppr. of *plier*, to bend. PLY.] Capable of being easily bent; readily yielding to force or pressure without breaking; flexible; lithe; limber; plastic; easily yielding to moral influence; easy to be persuaded.—**Pliantly**, plī'ant-li, *adv.* In a pliant manner.—**Pliancy**, plī'an-si, *n.* The state or quality of being pliant; easiness to be bent; readiness to be influenced.

Plica, plī'ka, *n.* [L., a fold. PLY.] *Med.* a disease of the hair, peculiar to Poland and the neighbouring countries, in which the hair is vascularly thickened, matted, or clotted; *bot.* a diseased state in plants in which the buds, instead of developing true branches, become short twigs, the whole forming an entangled mass. — **Plicate**, **Plicated**, plī'kāt, plī'kā-ted, *a.* [L. *plicatus*, from *plico*, to fold, *plica*, a fold.] *Bot.* plaited; folded like a fan.—**Plicately**, plī'kāt-li, *adv.* In a plicate or folded manner.—**Plication**, plī-kā'shon, *n.* A folding or fold; *geol.* a bending back of strata on themselves.—**Plicature**, plī-kā'tūr, *n.* [L. *plicatura*.] A plication; a folding.

Pliers, plī'ėrz, *n.pl.* [Fr. *plier*, to bend. PLY.] A small pair of pincers adapted to handle small articles, and also for bending and shaping wire.

Plight, plīt, *v.t.* [A.Sax. *plihtan*, to pledge, to expose to danger, from *pliht*, a pledge, danger; D. *verpligten*, Dan. *forpligte*, G. *verpflichten*, to bind, oblige, or engage. See the noun.] To pledge, as one's word, hand, faith, honour; to give as a security for the performance of some act: never applied to property or goods, and therefore differing from *pledge*, which is applied to property as well as to word, honour, &c.—*n.* [A.Sax. *pliht*, a pledge, obligation, danger; D. and Dan. *pligt*, Sw. *pligt*, *plikt*, G. *pflicht*, duty.] A pledge or security‡; condition; state; predicament; generally, a risky or dangerous state; a distressed condition (to be in a wretched *plight*).—**Plighter**, plī'tėr, *n.* One who plights.

Plimsoll line or **mark**, plim'sol, the line on the hull of a British merchant ship, regulating the load carried, first proposed in the Merchant Shipping Act of 1876 by Samuel Plimsoll; since 1930, ships registered in the United States have been required to carry a similar line.

Plinth, plinth, *n.* [Gr. *plinthos*, a brick or tile; L. *plinthus*.] *Arch.* a flat square member, in form of a slab, which serves as the foundation of a column; the flat square table under the moulding of the base and pedestal, at the bottom of the order.

Pliocene, plī'ō-sēn, *a.* and *n.* [Gr. *pleiōn*, more, and *kainos*, recent.] A geological term applied to the most modern of the divisions of the tertiary epoch, the others being the eocene and miocene. The newer or more recent portion of the pliocene is sometimes called *pleistocene*.

Pliohippus, plī-ō-hip'us, *n.* [From *plio*, for *pliocene*, and Gr. *hippos*, a horse.] A fossil animal of the horse family.

Pliosaurus, plī-ō-sạ'rus, *n.* PLEIOSAURUS.

Plod, plod, *v.i.*—*plodded*, *plodding*. [Akin to Prov.E. *plowd*, to wade, *plodge*, to walk through mud or water; Ir. and Gael. *plod*, *plodach*, a puddle: the primary sense being to walk laboriously, as through mire.] To travel or work slowly, or with steady laborious diligence; to study dully but with steady diligence; to toil; to trudge; to moil. —*v.t.* To go or walk over in a heavy labouring manner; to accomplish by toilsome exertion. — **Plodder**, plod'ėr, *n.* A dull, heavy, laborious person. — **Plodding**, plod'ing, *p.* and *a.* Given to plod or work with slow and patient diligence; patiently laborious.—**Ploddingly**, plod'ing-li, *adv.* In a plodding manner.

Plot, plot, *n.* [A.Sax. *plot*, a spot of ground, a spot; Goth. *plats*, a patch. *Plat* is another form. *Plot* in sense of scheme is related to *plot*, piece of ground, as *plan*, a scheme, to *plan*, a design on a flat surface, only *plot* has generally the sense of ill design.] A plat or small extent of ground of a well-defined shape; *surv.* a plan or draught of a field, farm, estate, &c., on paper; a scheme, stratagem, or plan, usually a mischievous one; an intrigue; a conspiracy; the story of a play, poem, novel, or romance, comprising a complication of incidents; the intrigue.—*v.t.*—*plotted*, *plotting*. To make a plan of; to plan; to devise; to contrive.—*v.i.* To form a scheme of mischief against another, or against a government or those who administer it; to conspire; to contrive a plan.—**Plotter**, plot'ėr, *n.* One who plots; a conspirator.—**Plotting-scale**, *n.* A scale used in setting off the lengths of lines in surveying.

Plover, pluv'ėr, *n.* [O.Fr. *plovier*, Fr. *pluvier*, lit. the rain bird, from L. *pluvia*, rain, from *pluo*, to rain.] The common name of several species of grallatorial birds generally seen in meadows, on the banks of rivers, or on the seashore, including the golden plover, the dotterel, and the ring-plover. They are usually shorter billed and stouter built than the various sandpipers and snipes.

Plow, **Plough**, plou, *n.* [Same as Icel. *plógr*, Dan. *ploug*, *plov*, O.Fris. *plōch*, D. *ploeg*, G. *pflug*, a plough.] An agricultural implement for breaking and turning soil preparatory to planting seed, originally operated by hand, later drawn by oxen or horses, but in modern times generally drawn by a tractor; any of a variety of implements, tools, or instruments for cutting grooves; a carpenter's or joiner's tool for grooving; *astron.* Charles's Wain, otherwise known as the Dipper or the constellation Ursa Major.—*Ice plow*, a plow for cutting grooves in ice preparatory to its removal; an ice breaker.—*Rotary snow plow*, a snow plow equipped with a large rotary fan or propeller, which plows into the snow and clears the highway by blowing the snow to one side. —*Snow plow*, a device attached to the front of a locomotive, street car, automobile, or motor truck to remove snow from sidewalks, streets, and highways—*v.t.* To turn the soil; to turn the soil with a plow; to make furrows, grooves, or ridges; to *plow* under; to cut through water with a yacht, speedboat, or any other type of craft; to *plow* through water.—*v.i.* To do work with a plow; to admit of plowing, as dry snow *plows* easily. —**Plowable**, *a.* Readily plowed.—**Plowboy**, **Plowman**, *n.* A boy or man who operates or guides a plow; a rustic person; a farmer.—**Plowgang**, **Plowgate**, *n.* In Scotland, as much land as can be properly turned by one plow, in a normal planting season, which, according to some, is 13 acres, but the acreage varies.—**Plowland**, *n.* Land adaptable to cultivation.—**Plowshare**, *n.* That part of the plow which cuts and turns the soil.—**Plowed ground**, ground that has been plowed into furrows preparatory to seeding.

Pluck, pluk, *v.t.* [A.Sax. *pluccian*, to pluck = D. and L.G. *plukken*, Dan. *plukke*, Icel. *plokka*, *plukka*, G. *pflücken*.] To gather; to pick; to cull, as berries or flowers; to pull with sudden force or effort; to twitch; by a similar action to cause the string of a musical instrument to vibrate and produce a sound; to strip by plucking; to strip feathers from (to *pluck* a fowl); to rob (*slang*); to pull or draw, literally or figuratively.—*To pluck up courage*, to assume or resume courage.—**Plucker**, pluk'ėr, *n.*

Pluck, pluk, *n.* [Comp. Gael. and Ir. *pluc*, a lump, a knot, a bunch; as to the figurative sense compare a bold *heart*, a lily-*livered* rascal, a man of another *kidney*, *bowels* of compassion, &c.] The heart, liver, and lungs of a sheep, ox, or other animal of the butcher's market; courage or spirit (*colloq.*).—**Pluckily**, pluk'i-li, *adv.* In a plucky manner; spiritedly. (*Colloq.*)—**Pluckless**, pluk'les, *a.* Without pluck; faint-hearted. (*Colloq.*)—**Plucky**, pluk'i, *a.* Spirited; courageous. (*Colloq.*)

Plug, plug, *n.* [Same as D. *plug*, L.G. *pluck*, a block.] Any piece of wood or other material used to stop a hole; a stopper; a fitting in various electrical connections; a spark plug; a cake of tobacco, usually for chewing; that part of a cylindrical lock which is rotated by the key; a discharge pipe or hydrant for drawing water from a water main (a *water* plug); something wornout or inferior; especially a wornout horse (*slang*).—*v.t.* To insert a plug; to make tight by stopping a hole; to shoot (*slang*); to work steadily; to plod (*slang*).—**Plugger**, plug'ėr, *n.* One who works doggedly. (*Slang.*)

Plum, plum, *n.* [A.Sax. *plume*, L.G. *plumme*, G. *pflaume*, from L.L. *pruna* (Fr. *prune*), from L. *prunum*, a plum, from *prunus* = Gr. *prounos*, the plum-tree.] A well-known fleshy fruit containing a stone or kernel, and when dried being called a prune; also the tree producing it; a choice or lucrative thing.—**Plum-cake**, *n.* Cake containing raisins, currants, or other fruits.—**Plum-pudding**, *n.* Pudding containing raisins or currants.

Plumb, plum, *n.* [Fr. *plomb*, from L. *plumbum*, lead.] A plummet.—*a.* Standing according to a plumb-line; perpendicular.—*adv.* In a perpendicular direction.—*v.t.* To adjust by a plumb-line; to set in a perpendicular direction; to sound with a plummet; hence to ascertain the capacity of; to test.—**Plumbago**, plum-bā'gō, *n.* [L., from *plumbum*, lead.] Another name for *Graphite*.—**Plumbaginous**, plum-baj'i-nus, *a.* Resembling or consisting of plumbago.

Plumbean, Plumbeous, plum-bē'an, plum-bē'us, *a.* [L. *plumbum*, lead.] Consisting of lead; leaden.—**Plumber**, plum'ėr, *n.* One who fits and repairs water and gas pipes; originally a worker in lead.—**Plumber-block**, *n.* A metal box or case for supporting the end of a revolving shaft or journal.—**Plumbic**, plum'bik, *a.* Pertaining to lead; derived from lead.—**Plumbiferous**, plum-bif'ėr-us, *a.* Producing lead.—**Plumbing**, plum'ing, *n.* Plumber's trade or work: that which is installed by a plumber; the act of using a plumb.—**Plumbism**, plum'bizm, *n.* Poisoning by lead taken into the system.—**Plumb-line**, *n.* A line having a metal weight attached to one end, used to determine a perpendicular; a line perpendicular to the plane of the horizon.—**Plumb-rule**, *n.* A narrow board with a plumb-line attached, used by masons, bricklayers, &c., for determining a perpendicular.

Plume, plöm, *n.* [Fr., from L. *pluma*, the downy part of a feather, a small soft feather; cog. W. *pluf*, plumage; Skr. *plu*, to swim, to fly.] The feather of a bird, particularly a large or conspicuous feather; a feather or collection of feathers worn as an ornament; token of honor; prize of contest. *v.t.*—*plumed, pluming.* To pick and adjust the feathers of; to dress the feathers; to adorn with feathers or plumes; to pride; to boast: in this sense used reflexively.—**Plumage**, plö'māj, *n.* [Fr., from *plume*, a feather.] The feathers that cover a bird.—**Plumassier**, plu-mas'sēr, *n.* One who prepares or deals in ornamental plumes or feathers.—**Plumeless**, plöm'les, *a.* Without feathers or plumes.—**Plumelet**, plöm'let. *n.* A small plume.—**Plume moth**, a small moth with divided, plume-like wings.—**Plumery**, plö'mėr-i, *n.* Plumes collectively; a mass of plumes.—**Plumicorn**, plö'mi-korn, *n.* [L. *pluma*, feather, *cornu*, horn.] One of the so-called horns or ear-tufts of fowls.—**Plumiped**, plö'mi-ped, *n.* [L. *pluma*, and *pes, pedis*, a foot.] A bird that has its feet covered with feathers.—**Plumose, Plumous**, plö'mōs, plö'mus, *a.* [L. *plumosus*.] Feathery; resembling feathers; *bot.* consisting of long hairs which are themselves hairy (*plumose* bristle).—**Plumosity**, plö-mos'i-ti, *n.* The state of being plumose.—**Plumy**, plö'mi, *a.* Feathered; feathery; adorned with plumes.

Plummer, plum'ėr, *n.* PLUMBER.

Plummet, plum'et, *n.* [For *plumbet*, from *plumb*; O.Fr. *plummet*, Fr. *plomet*. PLUMB.] A piece of lead or other metal attached to a line, used in sounding the depth of water; a plumb-rule or plumb-line.—**Plumming**, plum'ing, *n.* *Mining*, the operation of finding by means of a mine dial the place at which to sink an air-shaft.

Plump, plump, *a.* [Allied to D. *plomp*, unwieldy, bulky; G., Dan., and Sw. *plump*, clumsy, massive, coarse; from a verbal root seen in E. *plim*, to swell.] Swelled with fat or flesh to the full size; fat or stout in person; fleshy; having a full skin; distended.—*v.t.* To make plump; to dilate; to fatten; to cause to fall suddenly and heavily.—*v.i.* [Perhaps an imitative word in first sense; as also in last sense above.] To plunge or fall like a heavy mass or lump of dead matter; to fall suddenly or at once; to grow plump.—*adv.* At once or with a sudden heavy fall; suddenly; heavily.—**Plumper**, plump'ėr, *n.* One who or that which plumps; a vote given to one candidate when more than one are to be elected, which might have been divided among the number to be elected; a person who gives such a vote.—**Plumply**, plump'li, *adv.* Fully; roundly; without reserve.—**Plumpness**, plump'nes, *n.* The state or quality of being plump; fullness of skin.—**Plumpy**, plump'i, *a.* Plump; fat; jolly.

Plumule, plö'mūl, *n.* [L. *plumula*, dim. of *pluma*, a feather. PLUME.] *Bot.* the growing point of the embryo, situated at the apex of the radicle, and at the base of the cotyledons, by which it is protected when young; the rudiment of the future stem of a plant.

Plunder, plun'dėr, *v.t.* [G. *plündern* (from *plunder*, baggage.) = D. *plunderen*, Sw. *plondra*, Dan. *plyndre*, to plunder. The word entered the English and other tongues about the time of the Thirty Years' War.] To take goods or valuables forcibly from; to pillage; to spoil; to rob in a hostile way; to take by pillage or open force.—*n.* The act of plundering; robbery; that which is taken from an enemy by force; pillage; spoil; that which is taken by theft; robbery, or fraud.—**Plunderer**, plun'dėr-ėr, *n.* One who plunders.

Plunge, plunj, *v.t.*—*plunged, plunging.* [From Fr. *plonger*, from hypothetical Latin *plumbicare*, from *plumbum*, lead; lit. to fall like lead or to fall plumb.] To thrust into water or other fluid substance, or into any substance easily penetrable; to immerse; to thrust; to thrust or drive into any state or condition (to *plunge* a nation into war); to baptize by immersion.—*v.t.* To thrust or drive one's self into water or other fluid; to drive or to rush in; to fall or rush into distress or any state or circumstances in which the person or thing is enveloped, inclosed, or overwhelmed (to *plunge* into war); to throw the body forward and the hind-legs up, as an unruly horse; to bet heavily and recklessly (*slang*).—*n.* A dive, rush, or leap into something; the act of pitching or throwing the body forward and the hind legs up, as an unruly horse; a place for diving, as a swimming tank or deep pool; a reckless speculation (*slang*).—**Plunger**, plun'jėr, *n.* One who plunges; a wild, reckless gambler, who 'plunges' into heavy bets; a cylinder sometimes used in force-pumps instead of the ordinary pistons or buckets.—*Plunger-pump*, a force pump.

Pluperfect, plö'pėr-fekt, *a.* and *n.* [L. *plus quam perfectum*, more than perfect.] *Gram.* applied to that tense of a verb which denotes that an action was finished at a certain period in the past; past or preterite perfect (he *had done* it).

Plural, plö'ral, *a.* [L. *pluralis*, from *plus*, *pluris*, more.] Containing more than one; consisting of two or more, or designating two or more; *gram.* the *plural number* is that number or form of a word which designates more than one.—*n.* A form of a word expressing more than one; the plural number.—**Pluralism**, plö'ral-izm, *n.* The quality of being plural; a philosophic doctrine which maintains that there are more than one (usually more than two) fundamental substances.—**Pluralist**, plö'ral-ist, *n.*—**Plurality**, plö-ral'i-ti, *n.* The state of being plural; an aggregate of two or more of the same kind; the greater number; the majority; in an election, the excess of votes of one candidate over those of any other candidate for the same office.—**Pluralization**, plö'ral-i-zā"shon, *n.* The act of pluralizing; the attributing of plurality to a person by the use of a plural pronoun.—**Pluralize**, plö'ral-īz, *v.t.*—*pluralized, pluralizing.* To make plural by using the termination of the plural number.—**Plurally**, plö'ral-li, *adv.* In a plural manner; in a sense implying more than one.

Pluriliteral, plö-ri-lit'ėr-al, *a.* [L. *plus*, *pluris*, more, and *litera*, a letter.] Containing more letters than three.

Plurilocular, plö-ri-lok'ū-lėr, *a.* [L. *plus, pluris*, more, and *loculus*, a cell.] *Bot.* multilocular.

Pluriparous, plö-rip'a-rus, *a.* [L. *plus*, *pluris*, more, and *pario*, to produce.] Producing several young ones at a birth.

Plus, plus. [L., more.] *Alg.* or *arith.* the name of a character marked thus +, which being placed between two numbers or quantities, signifies that they are to be added together; frequently used prepositionally, with the signification of in addition to (ability *plus* impudence).

Plush, plush, *n.* [Fr. *pluche, peluche*, It. *peluzzo*, from L. *pilus*, hair. PILE.] A textile fabric with a sort of velvet nap or shag on one side resembling short hairs.

Pluteus, plö'tē-us, *n.* [L.] A balustrade; a parapet; among the Romans a sort of wheeled shed covered with raw hides in which a besieging party made their approaches.—**Pluto**, plö'tō, *n.* In Greek mythology, the chief divinity of the lower regions; a planet of the solar system, the remotest known from the sun, visible only by telescope.

Plutocracy, plö-tok'ra-si, *n.* [Gr. *Ploutos*, the god of wealth, and *krateia*, rule, *archē*, power.] The power or rule of wealth.—**Plutocrat**, plö'to-krat, *n.* A person possessing power or influence solely or mainly owing to his riches.—**Plutocratic**, plö-to-krat'ik, *a.* Pertaining to or characteristic of a plutocracy or a plutocrat.

Plutonic, Plutonian, plö-ton'ik, plö-tō'ni-an, *a.* [From *Pluto*, the king of the infernal regions among the ancient Greeks.] Of or relating to Pluto or to the regions of fire; subterranean; dark.—*Plutonic action*, the influence of volcanic heat and other subterranean causes under pressure.—*Plutonic rocks*, unstratified crystalline rocks formed at great depth beneath the earth's surface.—*Plutonic theory*, that which ascribes the changes on the earth's surface to the agency of fire. NEPTUNIAN.—**Plutonist, Plutonian**, plö'ton-ist, plö-tō'ni-an, *n.* One who adopts the plutonic theory.

Pluvial, plö'vi-al, *a.* [L. *pluvialis*, from *pluvia*, rain, from *pluo*, to rain; same root as in *flow*.] Rainy; humid; relating to rain; *geol.* applied to results and operations which depend on or arise from the action of rain. — **Pluvious**, plö'vi-us, *a.* [L. *pluviosus*.] Rainy; pluvial.

Pluviometer, plö-vi-om'et-ėr, *n.* [L. *pluvia*, rain, and Gr. *metron*, measure.] A rain-gauge; an instrument for measuring rain-fall.—**Pluviometrical**, plö'vi-o-met"ri-kal, *a.* Pertaining to a pluviometer.

Ply, plī, *v.t.*—*plied*, *plying*. [From Fr. *plier* (also *ployer*), to fold, to bend, from L. *plicare*, to fold, coil, plait; same root as Gr. *plekō*, to plait. More or less closely akin are *apply*, *comply*, *imply*, *reply*, *deploy*, *employ*, *display*, *complicate*, *implicate*, *implicit*, *complex*, &c.] To employ with diligence (to *ply* a needle or an oar); to keep busy; to practise or perform with diligence; to busy one's self in; to press hard with blows or missiles; to assail briskly; to beset; to urge; to solicit, as for a favour.—*To ply with*, to present or offer to urgently and repeatedly; to press upon, especially with some ulterior object (to *ply* one *with* flattery). —*v.i.* To be steadily employed; to work steadily; to offer service; to run regularly between any two ports or places, as a vessel or vehicle; *naut.* to endeavour to make way against the wind.—*n.* A fold; a plait; a twist: often used in composition to designate the number of twists, &c. (a three-*ply* carpet); bent; turn; direction; bias.—**Plyer**, plī'ėr, *n.* One who or that which plies; *pl.* same as *Pliers*.

Plymouth Brethren, **Plymouthites**, plim'uth, plim'uth-īts, *n. pl.* A sect of Christians who first appeared at Plymouth, Eng., in 1830.—**Plymouth Rock**, the spot in Plymouth harbor, Mass., where the Pilgrims landed, Dec. 21, 1620; an American breed of chicken.

Pneumatic, **Pneumatical**, nū-mat'ik, nū-mat'i-kal, *a.* [Gr. *pneumatikos*, from *pneuma*, *pneumatos*, breath, spirit, from *pneō*, to breathe or blow.] Consisting of or resembling air; having the properties of an elastic fluid; pertaining to air, or to elastic fluids or their properties; moved or played by means of air; filled with or fitted to contain air; applied to numerous instruments, machines, apparatus, &c., for experimenting on elastic fluids, or for working by means of the compression or exhaustion of air (*pneumatic conveyors* and *pneumatic tools*, such as drills, hammers, grinders, rammers, diggers, pavement breakers, and hoists).—*Pneumatic philosophy*, a name formerly applied to the science of metaphysics.—**Pneumatics**, nū-mat'iks, *n.* That branch of physics which treats of the mechanical properties of elastic fluids, and particularly of atmospheric air.—**Pneumatology**, nū-ma-tol'o-ji, *n.* The branch of philosophy which treats of the nature and operations of mind or spirit; psychology. —**Pneumatological**, nū'ma-tō-loj"i-kal, *a.* Pertaining to pneumatology. — **Pneumatologist**, nū-ma-tol'o-jist, *n.* One versed in pneumatology.—**Pneumatometer**, **Pneumometer**, nū-ma-tom'et-ėr, nū-mom'et-ėr, *n.* An instrument for measuring the quantity of air inhaled into the lungs at each inspiration and given out at each respiration: a spirometer.

Pneumogastric, nū-mō-gas'trik, *a.* [Gr. *pneumōn*, a lung, and *gastēr*, the belly.] *Anat.* pertaining to the lungs and stomach. —*Pneumogastric nerves*, a pair of nerves extending over the viscera of the chest and abdomen.

Pneumometer. PNEUMATOMETER.

Pneumonia, nū-mō'ni-a, *n.* [Gr. *pneumōn*, a lung, from *pneō*, to breathe.] *Med.* an inflammation of the lungs. — **Pneumonic**, nū-mon'ik, *a.* Pertaining to the lungs; pulmonic. — **Pneumonitic**, nū-mō-nit'ik, *a.* Pertaining to pneumonitis.—**Pneumonitis**, nū-mō-nī'tis, *n.* Inflammation of the lungs; pneumonia.

Pneumoskeleton, nū-mō-skel'ē-ton, *n.* [Gr. *pneumōn*, a lung, and E. *skeleton*.] A hard structure connected with the breathing organs of certain animals, as the shell of a mollusc.

Poach, pōch, *v.t.* [From Fr. *pocher*, to poach eggs, from *poche* a pouch or pocket, the white of the egg forming a sort of pocket for the yolk. POUCH.] To cook (eggs) by breaking and pouring among boiling water; to cook with butter after breaking in a vessel.

Poach, pōch, *v.i.* [Either from the above word, meaning originally to pouch or pocket thievishly, or a softened form of *poke*, to push, to intrude.] To intrude or encroach on the property of another to steal or plunder; to steal game or carry it away privately; to kill or destroy game contrary to law.—**Poacher**, pōch'ėr, *n.* One who poaches or steals game; one who kills game unlawfully.

Poach, pōch, *v.t.* [A later and softened form of *poke*, to thrust. POKE.] To stab; to pierce; to spear (to *poach* fish); to force or drive into so as to penetrate; to tread, as snow or soft ground, so as to render it broken and slushy.—*v.i.* To become soft and slushy or miry; to be swampy. —**Poachiness**, pō'chi-nes, *n.* The state of being poachy.—**Poachy**, pō'chi, *a.* Wet and soft; easily penetrated, as by the feet of cattle: applied to land.

Pochard, poch'ärd, *n.* [Lit. the *poacher*, one that poaches or pokes.] The name of a genus of oceanic ducks, natives of the Arctic Seas.

Pock, pok, *n.* [A.Sax. *poc* or *pocc*, D. *pok*, G. *pok*, a vesicle or pustule; perhaps akin to *poke*, a bag. *Pox* = *pocks*.] A pustule raised on the surface of the body in an eruptive disease, as the small-pox.—**Pockiness**, pok'i-nes, *n.* The state of being pocky.—**Pock-mark**, pok'märk, *n.* Mark or scar made by the small-pox.—**Pock-pitted**, **Pock-pitten**, *a.* Pitted or marked with small-pox.—**Pocky**, pok'i, *a.* Having pocks or pustules.

Pocket, pok'et, *n.* [A dim. of *poke*, a pouch or bag.] A small bag inserted in a garment for carrying small articles; a small bag or net to receive the balls in billiards; a certain quantity, from 1½ to 2 cwt. (a *pocket* of hops); *mineral.* a small cavity in a rock, or on its surface, containing gold; a mass of rich ore.—*To be in pocket*, to have gain or profit from some transaction.—*To be out of pocket*, to expend or lose money.—*v.t.* To put or conceal in the pocket; to take clandestinely.—*To pocket an insult*, *affront*, *wrong*, or the like, to receive it without resenting it, or at least without seeking redress.—**Air-pocket**, *n.* A condition of the atmosphere met with by aviators in which the machine tends to drop as if into a 'pocket' empty of air, supposed to be due to a downward current at the point.—**Pocket-book**, *n.* A case used for carrying papers in the pocket.—**Pocket-borough**, *n.* A borough, the power of electing a member of parliament for which is in the hands of one or a few persons. (*British*.)—**Pocketful**, pok'et-ful, *n.* Enough to fill a pocket; as much as a pocket will hold.—**Pocket-handkerchief**, *n.* A handkerchief carried in the pocket for use.—**Pocket-knife**, *n.* A knife suited for carrying in the pocket with one or more blades which fold into the handle.—**Pocket-money**, *n.* Money for the pocket or for occasional expenses.—**Pocket-picking**, *n.* Act or practice of picking pockets; the trade of a pickpocket.—**Pocket-pistol**, *n.* A pistol to be carried in the pocket; a small flask of liquor for the pocket (*colloq.*).—**Pocket-volume**, *n.* A volume which can be carried in the pocket.

Pockmark, **Pocky**, &c. Under POCK.

Poco, pō'kō. [It.] *Music*, a little; a word frequently prefixed to another to lessen the strength of its signification (*poco largo*, a little slow). — **Pococurante**, pō'kō-kö-ran"tā, *n.* [It. *poco*, little, and *curo*, to care.] One who cares little; an apathetic, careless, indifferent person. — **Pococurantism**, pō'kō-kö-rant"izm, *n.* The character, disposition, or habits of a pococurante; extreme indifference, apathy, or carelessness.

Poculiform, pok'ū-li-form, *a.* [L. *poculum*, a cup, and *forma*, form.] Cup-shaped.

Pod, pod, *n.* [Probably connected with Dan. *pude*, Sw. *puta*, a pillow or cushion, as also with E. *pad*, a cushion.] A term applied to a number of different pericarps or seed-vessels of plants, such as the legume, the loment, the siliqua, the silicle, the follicle, &c. —*v.i.* —*podded*, *podding*. To swell and assume the appearance of a pod; to produce pods.

Podagra, pod'a-gra, *n.* [Gr., from *pous*, *podos*, the foot, and *agra*, a taking or seizure.] Gout in the foot.—**Podagral**, **Podagric**, pod'a-gral, pō-dag'rik, *a.* Pertaining to the gout; gouty; afflicted with the gout.

Podalgia, po-dal'ji, *n.* [Gr. *pous*, *podos*, a foot, *algos*, pain.] Pain in the foot, especially neuralgic pain.

Podarthrum, po-dar'thrum, *n.* [Gr. *pous*, *podos*, a foot, *arthron*, a joint.] *Ornith.* the foot joint; the joint uniting the toes to the rest of the leg.

Podesta, pō-des'ta, *n.* [It. *podestà*, a governor, from L. *potestas*, power.] A chief magistrate of the Italian republics of the middle ages.

Podgy, poj'i, *a.* Pudgy; fat and short.

Podium, pō'di-um, *n.* [L. *podium*, Gr. *pous*, *podos*, foot.] The low enclosure running all round the amphitheatre; *arch.* a continuous pedestal or low wall on which columns rest.

Podocarp, pod'o-kärp, *n.* [Gr. *pous*, *podos*, a foot, and *karpos*, fruit.] *Bot.* a stalk supporting the fruit.

Podocephalous, pod-o-sef'a-lus, *a.* [Gr. *pous*, *podos*, a foot, *kephalē*, the head.] *Bot.* having a head of flowers elevated on a long peduncle.

Podophthalmic, pod-of-thal'mik, *a.* [Gr. *pous*, *podos*, a foot, and *ophthalmos*, an eye.] Having the eyes borne at the end of long foot-stalks, as in certain crustacea.

Podophyllin, pod-o-fil'in, *n.* [Gr. *pous*, *podos*, a foot, and *phyllon*, a leaf.] A resin obtained from the root-stock of the may-apple, used in medicine as a purgative.—**Podophyllous**, pod-o-fil'us, *a.* *Entom.* having the feet or locomotive organs somewhat in the form of leaves.

Podosperm, **Podospermum**, pod'o-spėrm, pod-o-spėr'mum, *n.* [Gr. *pous*, *podos*, a foot, and *sperma*, a seed.] *Bot.* the umbilical cord of an ovule.

Poe-bird, pō'e-bėrd, *n.* A New Zealand bird of the honey-eater family, greatly valued for the fineness of its notes and its capability of speaking; the parson-bird.

Poem, pō'em, *n.* [Fr. *poème*, from L. *poema*, from Gr. *poiēma*, lit. the thing made, from *poieō*, to make. POET.] A metrical composition; a composition in which the verses consist of certain measures, whether in blank verse or in rhyme; a composition in which the language is that of excited imagination. — **Poematic**, pō-e-mat'ik, *a.* Relating to a poem; poetical. — **Poesy**, pō'e-si, *n.* [Fr. *poésie*, L. *poesis*, from Gr. *poiēsis*, the art of writing poems.] The art of or skill in composing poems; poetry; metrical composition; a short conceit engraved on a ring or other thing (*Shak.*). POSY.—**Poet**, pō'et, *n.* [Fr. *poète*, from L. *poeta*, Gr. *poiētēs*, lit. a maker, from *poieō*, to make. So in England poets were formerly often called 'makers'.] The author of a poem; the composer of a metrical composition; one skilled in making poetry, or who has a particular genius for metrical composition; one distinguished for poetic talents. — **Poetaster**, pō'et-as-tėr, *n.* [From *poet*, and the pejorative *-aster*; comp. *criticaster*, &c.] A petty poet; a pitiful rhymer or writer of verses.—**Poetess**, pō'et-es, *n.* A female poet.—**Poetic**, **Poetical**, pō-et'ik, pō-et'i-kal, *a.* [L. *poeticus*,

Gr. *poiētikos*.] Pertaining to poetry; suitable to poetry; expressed in poetry; having a metrical form; possessing the peculiar beauties of poetry.—*Poetical justice*, a distribution of rewards and punishments such as is common in poetry and works of fiction, but hardly in accordance with the realities of life.—*Poetic license*, a liberty or license taken by a poet with regard to matters of fact or language in order to produce a desired effect.—**Poetically**, pō-et′i-kal-li, *adv.* In a poetical manner.—**Poetics**, pō-et′iks, *n.* That branch of criticism which treats of the nature and laws of poetry.—**Poeticule**, pō-et′i-kūl, *n.* [A dim. of *poet*.] A poetaster.—**Poetize**, pō′et-īz, *v.i.* [Fr. *poétiser*.] To write as a poet; to compose verse.—**Poet-laureate**, *n.* Under LAUREATE.—**Poetry**, pō′et-ri, *n.* [O.Fr. *poeterie*, from *poete*, a poet.] That one of the fine arts which exhibits its special character and powers by means of language; the art which has for its object the creation of intellectual pleasure by means of imaginative and passionate language, generally in verse; the language of the imagination or emotions rhythmically expressed, or such language expressed in an elevated style of prose; especially that creative writing which is divided into lines, each containing a determined number of sounds, the sounds being accented according to a regular and determined rhythmical pattern; similar creative writing, of looser structure, in which the phrases flow in a cadenced pattern; in a wide sense whatever appeals to the emotions or the sense of beauty; verse; poems.

Pogrom, pog′rom, *n.* [Russian.] An organized massacre or attack on a party; e.g. Jews.

Poignant, poi′nant, *a.* [Fr. *poignant*, part. of *poindre*, from L. *pungere*, *pungo*, to prick. POINT.] Stimulating the organs of taste; piquant; pointed; keen; bitter; irritating; satirical; severe; piercing; very painful or acute. — **Poignantly**, poi′nant-li, *adv.* In a poignant manner.—**Poignancy**, poi′nan-si, *n.* The state or quality of being poignant.

Poikilitic, poi-ki-li′tik, *a.* [Gr. *poikilos*, variegated.] Of a variegated colour: said of certain rocks.

Poilu, pwa-lü, *a.* [Fr. 'hairy'.] A slang term, equivalent to the English 'Tommy', and applied to a soldier in French army: from the custom of letting the beard grow when on active service.

Poind, poind, *v.t.* [A.Sax. *pyndan*, to shut up. POUND (for cattle).] To inclose in a pound or pen; to distrain; to seize and sell a debtor's goods under proper warrant. (*Scotch*.)

Point, point, *n.* [Fr. *point*, a point, a spot, a matter, moment, &c., *pointe*, something sharp or pointed, wit or pungency, &c., the former from L. *punctum*, a puncture, from *pungo*, *punctum*, to puncture, the latter the fem. part of Fr. *poindre*, to prick, from same; akin *pounce*, *punch*, &c.] The mark made by the end of a sharp piercing instrument, such as a pin, a needle, or the like; hence, an indefinitely small space; *geom.* that which has neither length, breadth, nor thickness—that by the motion of which a line is considered to be produced; a mark of punctuation; a dot placed before a decimal fraction to show that it is a decimal; a division of the card of the mariner's compass, the card of which has its circumference divided into 32 equal spaces; north, south, east, and west, or any intermediate direction; any place marked in the heavens of importance in astronomical calculations; that which pricks, pierces, or punctures; particularly the sharp end of a thorn, pin, needle, knife, sword, and the like; a tool or instrument which pricks or pierces; a small cape or promontory; a lace, string, or the like, with a tag, formerly used for fastening articles of dress; lace worked by the needle; a lively turn of thought or expression which strikes with force or agreeable surprise; the sting of an epigram; hence, force or expression generally (his action gave *point* to his words); a salient trait of character; a peculiarity; a characteristic (the good or bad *points* of a man); a certain external peculiarity of an animal (the *points* of a horse or a dog); single thing or subject; matter (right in every *point*); particular thing desired or required; aim; purpose (to gain one's *point*); a single part of a complicated question, or of a whole; an indivisible part of time or space; the eve or verge (at the *point* of death); *pl.* the switches or movable guiding rails at junctions on railways (*Brit.*); a fielder in the game of cricket who stands a little to the off side of the batter's wicket, or the spot where he stands; a mark to denote the degree of success or progress one has attained in certain trials of skill and games, as in rifle-shooting, billiards, cards, and the like, a single point counting one.—*Acting point*, in *physics*, the exact point at which any impulse is given.—*Physical point*, the smallest or least sensible object of sight.—*Point of incidence*, that point upon the surface of a medium at which a ray of light falls.—*Point of reflection*, the point from which a ray is reflected.—*Point of sight*, that point of a picture which is determined by a line from the eye of the artist perpendicular to the perspective plane.—*Point of war*, a martial note on a trumpet or bugle.—*Vowel points*, in Hebrew, &c., certain marks representing the vowels, which precede or follow the consonant sounds.—*To stand upon points*, to be punctilious; to be nice or over-scrupulous.—*v.t.* To give a point to; to cut, forge, grind, or file to a point; to add to the force or expression of; to direct toward an object or place; to aim; to direct the eye or notice of; to indicate the purpose or point of; to punctuate; *masonry*, to fill the joints of with mortar, and smooth them with the point of a trowel.—*To point out*, to show by the finger or by other means.—*v.i.* To direct the finger for designating an object and exciting attention to it: with *at*; to indicate the presence of game by standing and turning the nose in its direction, as dogs do to sportsmen; to show distinctly by any means.—**Point-blank**, *a.* [This phrase has its origin in the directness with which an arrow is aimed at the white mark or blank in the centre of a butt.] In *gun.* having a horizontal direction; *fig.* direct; plain; explicit; express. As an adverb, horizontally; directly.—**Point d'appui**, pwaṅ-dä-pwē, *n.* [Fr.] Point of support; a fixed point at which troops form, and on which operations are based. — **Point-device**,† **Point-devise**,† *a.* [From *point*, condition, and *devise*, to imagine; lit. in as fine a condition as could be imagined.] Precise, nice, or finical to excess. (*Shak.*)—**Pointed**, poin′ted, *p.* and *a.* Having a sharp point; aimed at or expressly referring to some particular person (a *pointed* remark); epigrammatical; abounding in conceits or lively turns.—*Pointed style*, in *arch.* a name applied to several styles usually called *Gothic*.—**Pointedly**, poin′ted-li, *adv.* In a pointed manner.—**Pointedness**, poin′ted-nes, *n.* The state or quality of being pointed.—**Pointer**, poin′tėr, *n.* One who or that which points; a variety of dog remarkable for its habit of pointing at game.—**Pointers**, *n.* Two stars in the Great Bear, through which a straight line points to the Pole-star. — **Pointing**, poin′ting, *n.* Punctuation; marks or points made; the raking out of the mortar from between the joints of a stone or brick wall, and replacing the same with new mortar. — **Point-lace**, *n.* A fine kind of lace wrought with a needle.—**Pointless**, point′les, *a.* Having no point; blunt; obtuse; having no smartness or keenness.—**Point of view**, *n.* The position from which something is observed or considered; personal standpoint; attitude.

Poise, poiz, *v.t.*—*poised*, *poising*. [O.Fr. *poiser*, *peiser*, Fr. *peser*, from L. *penso*, to weigh out, from *pensus*, weighed, pp. of *pendo*, to weigh. PENDANT.] To balance in weight; to make of equal weight; to hold or place in equilibrium or equiponderance; to load with weight for balancing. —*v.i.* To be balanced or suspended; *fig.* to hang in suspense; to depend.—*n.* Weight; gravity; a thing suspended or attached as a counterweight; a counterpoise; hence, regulating power; that which balances; the weight used in weighing with steelyards, to balance the substance weighed; equipoise; balance; equilibrium.—**Poiser**, poi′zėr, *n.* One who or that which poises; *entom.* a balancer.

Poison, poi′zn, *n.* [Fr. *poison*, from L. *potio*, *potionis*, a drink, a draught, from *poto*, to drink. POTION.] Any agent capable of producing a morbid, noxious, dangerous, or deadly effect upon the animal economy, when introduced either by cutaneous absorption, respiration, or the digestive canal; that which taints or destroys moral purity or health.—*v.t.* To infect with poison; to put poison in or on; to add poison to; to attack, injure, or kill by poison; to taint; to mar, impair, vitiate, corrupt.—**Poisonable**, poi′zn-a-bl, *a.* Capable of being poisoned.—**Poisoner**, poi′zn-ėr, *n.* One who or that which poisons or corrupts.—**Poison-fang**, *n.* One of the upper teeth of certain serpents, having a channel in it through which a poisonous fluid is conveyed into the wound when they bite.—**Poison-gas**, *n.* Any noxious gas, such as chlorine or phosgene, especially when used against troops in warfare. —**Poison-gland**, *n.* A gland in animals and plants which secretes and contains poison.—**Poison-nut**, *n.* Nux-vomica.—**Poisonous**, poi′zn-us, *a.* Having the qualities of poison; containing poison; venomous; corrupting.—**Poisonously**, poi′zn-us-li, *adv.* In a poisonous manner. — **Poisonousness**, poi′zn-us-nes, *n.*

Poitrel, **Poitral**, poi′trel, poi′tral, *n.* [Fr. *poitrail*, from L. *pectorale*, from *pectus*, the breast.] Armour for the breast of a horse. —**Poitrine**, poi′trēn, *n.* The breast-plate of a knight.

Poize, poiz. POISE.

Poke, pōk, *n.* [O.D. a *poke*, a sack or bag; Icel. *poki*, a sack, a bag; *pouch* is a softened form of this, and *pocket* a diminutive.] A pocket; a pouch; a bag; a sack.—**Poke-bonnet**, *n.* A long, straight, projecting bonnet formerly worn by women.—**Poke-sleeve**, *n.* A kind of wide sleeve.

Poke, pōk, *v.t.*—*poked*, *poking*. [D. and L.G. *poken*, to poke; Sw. *pak*, a stick; comp. Ir. *poc*, a blow; Gael. *puc*, to push.] To thrust something long or pointed against, as the hand or a stick; hence, to feel or search, as in the dark or in a hole.—*To poke fun*, to joke; to make fun.—*To poke fun at*, to ridicule.—*v.i.* To grope; to search; to feel or push one's way, as in the dark; to busy one's self without a definite object: followed by *about*.—*n.* A gentle thrust; a jog; a sudden push.—**Poker**, pō′kėr, *n.* One who pokes; an iron or steel bar or rod used in poking or stirringthe fire when coal is used for fuel.—**Poker-picture**, *n.* A picture executed by singeing the surface of white wood with a heated poker.—**Poking-stick**, *n.* An instrument formerly used in adjusting the plaits of ruffs.—**Poky**, pō′ki, *a.* Narrow or confined as to space; close and musty.

Poker, pō′kėr, *n.* A gambling game played with cards.

Pokeweed, pōk′wēd, *n.* [Of American Indian origin.] A North American plant (genus Phytolacca) whose berries and roots have emetic and purgative qualities.

Polacca, **Polacre**, **Polaque**, pō-lak′a, pō-lak′ėr, pō-läk′, *n.* [It. *polacca*.] A vessel with three masts used in the Mediterranean.

Polar. POLE.

Polder, pol′dėr, *n.* [D.] In the Netherlands, a tract of land below the level of the sea or nearest river, which, being originally a morass or lake, has been drained and brought under cultivation.

Pole, pōl, *n.* [A.Sax. *pal*, a pole, a stake; collateral form of *pale*, L.G. and D. *paal*, from L. *palus*, a stake. PALE.] A long slender piece of wood; a tall piece of timber: frequently used in composition (a carriage-*pole*, a May-*pole*); a perch or rod, a measure of length containing 5½ yards.—*Under bare poles*, said of a ship when her sails are all furled.—*v.t.*—*poled, poling*. To furnish with poles for support; to bear or convey on poles; to impel by poles; to push forward by the use of poles.—**Pole-mast**, *n.* A mast composed of one single piece.

Pole, pōl, *n.* [Fr. *pôle*, L. *polus*, the pole of the heavens, the heavens, from Gr. *polos*, the axis of the sphere, the firmament, from *pelō*, to turn or move.] One of the two points in which the axis of the earth is supposed to meet the sphere of the heavens; the fixed point about which the stars appear to revolve; one of the extremities of the earth's axis; a point on the surface of any sphere equally distant from every part of the circumference of a great circle of the sphere; the pole-star; one of the points of a body at which its attractive or repulsive energy is concentrated, or in which a polar force is exerted; in *magnetism*, one of the two points at which the magnetic strength of a magnet is principally concentrated.—*Unit strength of pole*, or unit pole, is that pole which will attract or repel a pole of equal strength at a distance of one centimetre with unit force.—*The strength of a pole* is the force exerted between it and a unit pole at unit distance.—*Magnetic pole*, one of the points on the earth at which the dipping-needle is vertical, or the magnetic intensity greatest.—*Poles of a voltaic cell* or *battery*, the connections at which the current passes from the battery to the external circuit, and *vice versa*; the current leaving the battery at the *positive* pole, and entering it at the *negative* pole.—**Pole-star**, *n.* A star of the second magnitude, situated about 1° from the North Pole, round which it describes a small circle; *fig.* that which serves as a guide or director; a lode-star.—**Polar**, pō'lėr, *a.* [L.L. *polaris*, from L. *polus*, a pole.] Pertaining to a pole or the poles of a sphere; pertaining to one of the poles of the earth or of the heavens; proceeding from the poles of the earth; pertaining to a magnetic pole or poles; pertaining to the points of a body at which its attractive or repulsive energy is concentrated.—*Polar angle*, the angle at a pole formed by two meridians.—*Polar axis*, that axis of an equatorial which is parallel to the earth's axis.—*Polar bear*. Under BEAR.—**Polar bodies**, *n.* Two minute cells resulting from the last stages of the cell-divisions, which end in the production of an ovum (egg-cell).—*Polar circles*, the arctic and antarctic circles.—*Polar clock*, an apparatus whereby the hour of the day is found by means of the polarization of the scattered sunlight from the polar regions.—*Polar distance*, the angular distance of a heavenly body from the elevated pole of the heavens.—*Polar forces*, physical forces that are developed and act in pairs, with opposite tendencies, as in magnetism, electricity, &c.—*Polar lights*, the aurora borealis or australis.—*Polar star*, the pole-star.—**Polarimeter, Polariscope**, pō-lar-im'et-ėr, pō-lar'i-skōp, *n.* An optical instrument, various kinds of which have been contrived, for exhibiting the polarization of light.—**Polarimetry**, pō-lar-im'et-ri, *n.* The art of measuring or analysing the polarization of light.—**Polaristic**, pō-la-ris'tik, *a.* Pertaining to or exhibiting poles or polar characteristics; having a polar arrangement or disposition.—**Polarity**, pō-lar'i-ti, *n.* That quality of a body in virtue of which peculiar properties reside in certain points called poles.—**Polarizable**, pō'lėr-i-za-bl, *a.* Capable of being polarized.—**Polarization**, pō'lėr-i-zā"shon, *n.* The act of polarizing or giving polarity to a body; the state of being polarized or of having polarity; in a voltaic cell, the setting up of a back electromotive force owing to the deposition of gases on the electrodes.—*Polarization of light*, a change produced upon light by the action of certain media, by which it exhibits the appearance of having polarity or poles possessing different properties.—**Polarize**, pō'lėr-īz, *v.t.*—*polarized, polarizing*. To develop polarity in.—**Polarized**, pō'lėr-īzd, *p.* and *a.* Having polarity; affected by polarization.—**Polarizer**, pō-lėr-ī'zėr, *n.* That part of a polariscope by which light is polarized.

Pole, pōl, *n.* A native of Poland.

Pole-axe, *n.* [*Pole* may here be the long stick; but perhaps it is for *poll*, the head.] A kind of axe or hatchet.

Polecat, pōl'kat, *n.* [Supposed to be for *poult-cat*, that is, chicken or poultry cat, or abbrev. from *Polish-cat*.] An animal of the weasel family, about 17 inches in length excluding the tail, very destructive to poultry; also, a skunk.

Polemarch, pol'ē-märk, *n.* [Gr. *polemarchos*—*polemos*, war, and *archē*, rule.] A title of several officials in ancient Greek states.

Polemic, Polemical, pō-lem'ik, pō-lem'i-kal, *a.* [Gr. *polemikos*, from *polemos*, war.] Pertaining to polemics; given to controversy; engaged in supporting an opinion or system by controversy.—**Polemic**, *n.* A disputant; one who carries on a controversy; one who writes in support of an opinion or system in opposition to another.—**Polemics**, pō-lem'iks, *n.* The art or practice of disputation; controversy; controversial writings.

Polemoscope, pō-lem'ō-skōp, *n.* [Gr. *polemos*, war, and *skopeō*, to view—it was intended to be used in war.] A perspective glass fitted with a mirror at an angle of 45°, designed for seeing objects that do not lie directly before the eye.

Polenta, po-len'ta, *n.* [It., Sp., Pg., and Fr. *polenta*, from L. *polenta*, peeled barley.] A kind of pudding made in Italy from semolina, Indian corn, or maize meal; a thick porridge of chestnut-meal boiled in milk, used as an article of diet in France.

Police, pō-lēs', *n.* [Fr. *police*, from L. *politia*, from Gr. *politeia*, government, administration, from *polis*, a city.] The means instituted by a government or community to maintain public order, liberty, property, and individual security; the body of men by whom the municipal laws and regulations are enforced and public order maintained.—*Police commissioner*, one of a body of men, elected or appointed, whose duty it is to manage police affairs.—*Police court*, a court for the trial of offenders brought up on charges preferred by the police.—*Police magistrate*, a judge who presides at a police court.—*Police squad*, a group of policemen operating together.—*Police-squad car*, an automobile, equipped with one-way or two-way short-wave radio, in which police patrol.—*Police station*, the headquarters of the police or of a section of them.—**Policeman**, pō-lēs'man, *n.* An ordinary member of the police force, (if assigned to a beat, a *patrolman*).

Policy, pol'i-si, *n.* [L. *politia*, Gr. *politeia*, polity. POLICE.] The art or manner of governing a nation; the line of conduct which the rulers of a nation adopt on particular questions, especially with regard to foreign countries; the principles on which any measure or course of action is based; prudence or wisdom of governments or individuals in the management of their affairs public or private; dexterity of management; in Scotland, the pleasure-grounds around a gentleman's country residence. ∴ *Policy* is the course of conduct pursued, or the management of an affair, in certain circumstances; *polity*, the general principles on which such course of conduct is based.

Policy, pol'i-si, *n.* [Fr. *police*, from L.L. *poleticum*, a register, from L. *polyptychum*, Gr. *polyptychon*, an account-book—*polys*, many, and *ptychē*, a fold.] A written contract by which a corporation or other persons engage to pay a certain sum on certain contingencies, as in the case of fire or shipwreck, in the event of death, &c., on the condition of receiving a fixed sum or percentage on the amount of the risk, or certain periodical payments.—*Insurance policy*. Under INSURE.—**Policy-holder**, *n.* One who holds a policy or contract of insurance.

Polish, pō'lish, *a.* Pertaining to Poland or to its inhabitants.—*n.* The language of the Poles.

Polish, pol'ish, *v.t.* [Fr. *polir*, *polissant*, from L. *polio*, to smooth, whence also *polite*.] To make smooth and glossy, usually by friction; to burnish; to deprive of rudeness, rusticity, or coarseness; to make elegant and polite (to *polish* life or manners).—*v.i.* To become smooth; to take a smooth and glossy surface; to become refined.—*n.* A substance used to impart a gloss; a smooth glossy surface produced by friction; artificial gloss; refinement; elegance of manners.—**Polishable**, pol'ish-a-bl, *a.* Capable of being polished.—**Polished**, pol'isht, *p.* and *a.* Made smooth and glossy; refined.—**Polisher**, pol'ish-ėr, *n.* One who or that which polishes.—**Polishing-paste**, *n.* A kind of paste for polishing; blacking for harness and leather; a compound of oil, bees'-wax, and spirit varnish for imparting a gloss to furniture.—**Polishing-powder**, *n.* A preparation of plumbago for polishing iron articles.—**Polishing-slate**, *n.* A kind of gray or yellow slate, composed of microscopic infusoria, and used for polishing glass, marble, &c.

Polite, pō-līt', *a.* [L. *politus*, from *polio*, to polish. POLISH.] Polished or elegant in manners; refined in behaviour; well-bred; courteous; complaisant.—**Politely**, pō-līt'li, *adv.* In a polite manner.—**Politeness**, pō-līt'nes, *n.*

Politic, pol'i-tik, *a.* [L. *politicus*, Gr. *politikos*, from *polis*, a city. POLICE.] Consisting of citizens; constituting the state (the body *politic*); prudent and sagacious in devising and pursuing measures adapted to promote the public welfare; well devised and adapted to the public prosperity; ingenious in devising and pursuing any scheme of personal or national aggrandizement; cunning; artful; sagacious in adapting means to an end; well devised; adapted to its end, right or wrong.—**Political**, pō-lit'i-kal, *a.* Having a fixed or regular system or administration of government; relating to civil government and its administration; concerned in state affairs or national measures; pertaining to a nation or state, or to nations or states, as distinguished from *civil* or *municipal*; treating of politics or government.—*Political economy*, the science of the laws which regulate the production, distribution, and consumption of the products, necessary, useful, or agreeable to man, which it requires some portion of voluntary labour to produce, procure, or preserve.—*Political geography*. Under GEOGRAPHY.—*Political science*, that science which deals with the structure, organization and government of nations and their component parts.—**Politically**, pō-lit'i-kal-li, *adv.* In a political manner.—**Politician**, pol-i-tish'an, *n.* One versed in the science of government and the art of governing; one skilled in politics; one who occupies himself with politics.—**Politicly**, pol'i-tik-li, *adv.* In a politic manner.—**Politics**, pol'i-tiks, *n.* [Fr. *politique*, Gr. *politikē*.] The science of government; that part of ethics which relates to the regulation and government of a nation or state for the preservation of its safety, peace, and prosperity; political affairs, or the conduct and contests of political parties.—**Polity**, pol'i-ti, *n.* [Gr. *politeia*. POLICY.] The form or constitution of civil government of a nation or state; the constitution or fundamental principles of government of any body of citizens; the recognized principles on which any institution is based. ∴ Syn. under POLICY.

Polka, pōl'ka, *n.* A species of dance of Bohemian origin, the music to which is in 2-4 time, with the third quaver accented; an air appropriate to the dance.—**Polk**, pōlk, *v.i.* To dance a polka.—**Polka-jacket**, *n.* A knitted jacket worn by women.

Poll, pōl, *n.* [O.D. *pol*, *bol*, a ball, the head; L.G. *polle*, the head, the top of a tree; allied to *ball*, *bowl*: *pollard* is a derivative.]

The head of a person, or the back part of the head; a catalogue or register of heads, that is, of persons; the voting or registering of votes for candidates in elections (the close of the *poll*); the fish called a chub; the blunt end of a hammer, or the butt of an axe.—*v.t.* To remove the top or head of; to lop, clip, shear; to cut closely; to mow; to register or give a vote; to bring to the poll; to receive or elicit, as a number of votes or voters.—*v.i.* To vote at a poll; to record a vote, as an elector.—**Poll axe**, *n.* A pole axe; an axe with a hammer or stud for felling oxen.—**Poll book**, *n.* A register of persons entitled to vote at an election.—**Poll clerk**, *n.* An assistant clerk at an election. (*Brit.*)—**Polled**, pōld, *p.* and *a.* Deprived of the poll; lopped, as a tree having the top cut; having the hair cut; cropped; bald; having cast the horns, as a stag; hence, wanting horns (*polled* cattle).—**Poll evil**, *n.* A swelling or aposteme on a horse's head, or on the nape of the neck between the ears.—**Polling booth**, *n.* A temporary erection in which to record votes. (*Brit.*)—**Polling place**, *n.* A place for recording votes. (*Brit.*)—**Polling sheriff**, *n.* In Scotland, the presiding election officer.—**Poll tax**, *n.* A tax levied per head or person, usually on all males of mature years without regard to wealth or station.

Poll, pol, *n.* [Gr. *hoi polloi*, the many, the rabble.] At Cambridge University, England, one who receives no honors, but merely takes a degree.

Poll, pol, *n.* [A contr. of *Polly* for *Mary*.] A familiar name often applied to a parrot.

Pollack, pol'ak, *n.* [D. and G. *pollack*.] A species of marine fish belonging to the cod family.

Pollan, pol'an, *n.* [Ir. *pullog*, Gael. *pollag*. Akin to *pollack*.] An Irish species of freshwater herring.

Pollarchy, pol'är-ki, *n.* [Gr. *polloi*, many, and *archē*, rule.] The rule of the many; government by the mob or masses.

Pollard, pol'ärd, *n.* [From *poll*, the head, and affix *-ard*.] A tree with the head cut off at some height from the ground, for the purpose of inducing it to throw out branches all round the section where amputation has taken place; a stag that has cast his horns; also, a hornless ox; a coarse product of wheat, but finer than bran.—*v.t.* To make a pollard of; to convert into a pollard by cutting off the head.

Pollen, pol'en, *n.* [L. *pollen* and *pollis*, fine flour or dust.] The male element in flowering plants; the fine dust or powder which by contact with the stigma effects the fecundation of the seeds.—**Pollenarious**, pol-e-nā'ri-us, *a.* Consisting of meal or pollen.—**Polleniferous**, **Polliniferous**, pol-e-nif'ėr-us, pol-i-nif'ėr-us, *a.* Producing pollen.—**Pollenize**, pol'en-īz, *v.t.* To supply with pollen; to impregnate with pollen.—**Pollen-tube**, *n.* One of the tubular processes emitted by the pollen when it comes in contact with the stigma of a plant, and which are supposed to conduct the impregnating matter down the style into the ovules through the foramen.—**Pollinate**, pol'i-nāt, *v.t.* *Bot.* to convey pollen from the anther to the stigma of.—**Pollination**, pol-i-nā'shon, *n.* *Bot.* the conveyance of the pollen from the anther to the stigma.

Pollex, pol'leks, *n.* [L.] The thumb in man; a corresponding digit of other animals.

Pollicitation, pol-lis'i-tā"shon, *n.* [L. *pollicitatio*, from *pollicitari*, to promise.] A promise; a voluntary engagement.

Pollinium, pol-lin'i-um, *n.*; pl. **-ia**. [L. for *dust*.] An agglutinated mass of pollen-grains, as in orchids.

Pollute, pol-lūt', *v.t.*—*polluted, polluting*. [L. *polluo*, *pollutum*, from prep. *pol*, *por*, used in composition, and *luō*, to wash. LAVE.] To make foul or unclean; to render impure; to defile; to soil; to taint; to corrupt or defile in a moral sense; to impair; to profane.—**Pollutedly**, pol-lū'ted-li, *adv.* With pollution.—**Pollutedness**, pol-lū'ted-nes, *n.* The state of being polluted.—**Polluter**, pol-lū'tėr, *n.* One who pollutes or profanes.—**Pollution**, pol-lū'shon, *n.* [L. *pollutio*.] The act of polluting; the state of being polluted; defilement; uncleanness; impurity.

Polo, pō'lō, *n.* A game at ball resembling hockey, only that it is played on horseback.

Polonaise, pol-o-nāz', *n.* [Fr.] A robe or dress worn by ladies and adopted from the fashion of the Poles; a melody written in imitation of Polish dance tunes.

Polonium, pol-ō'ni-um, *n.* A radioactive chemical element, also called Radium F.

Polony, po-lō'ni, *n.* [Probably corrupted from *Bologna* sausage.] A kind of high-dried sausage made of partly-cooked pork.

Poltroon, pol-trön', *n.* [Fr. and Sp. *poltron*, from It. *poltrone*, from *poltro*, lazy, dastardly, from O.H.G. *polstar*, a pillow. BOLSTER.] An arrant coward; a dastard; a wretch; without spirit or courage.—*a.* Base; vile; contemptible.—**Poltroonery**, pol-trön'ėr-i, *n.* Cowardice; want of spirit.—**Poltroonish**, pol-trön'ish, *a.* Resembling a poltroon; cowardly.

Polverin, **Polverine**, pol'vē-rin, pol'vē-rin, *n.* [It. *polverino*, from L. *pulvis*, dust.] The calcined ashes of a plant, brought from the Levant and Syria, and used in the manufacture of glass.

Polyacoustic, pol'i-a-kous"tik, *a.* [Gr. *polys*, many, *akouō*, to hear.] Capable of multiplying or magnifying sound.

Polyadelph, pol'i-a-delf", *n.* [Gr. *polys*, many, *adelphos*, brother.] *Bot.* a plant having its stamens united in three or more bodies or bundles by the filaments.—**Polyadelphian**, **Polyadelphous**, pol'i-a-del"fi-an, pol'i-a-del"fus, *a.* *Bot.* having stamens united in three or more bundles.

Polyandrian, **Polyandrous**, pol-i-an'dri-an, pol-i-an'drus, *a.* [Gr. *polys*, many, *anēr*, *andros*, a male.] *Bot.* having many stamens, that is, any number above twenty, inserted in the receptacle.

Polyandry, pol-i-an'dri, *n.* [Gr. *polys*, many, *anēr*, *andros*, a man.] The practice of females having more husbands than one at the same time; plurality of husbands.

Polyanthus, pol-i-an'thus, *n.* [Gr. *polys*, many, *anthos*, a flower.] A garden variety of the oxlip primrose which has long been a favourite.

Polyarchy, pol'i-är-ki, *n.* [Gr. *polys*, many, and *archē*, rule.] The government of many, whether a privileged class (aristocracy) or the people at large (democracy).

Polyatomic, pol'i-a-tom"ik, *a.* [Gr. *polys*, many, E. *atomic*.] *Chem.* a term applied to elements or radicals which have an equivalency greater than one; polybasic.

Polybasic, pol-i-bā'sik, *a.* [Gr. *polys*, many, and E. *basic*.] *Chem.* of acids with more than one replaceable hydrogen atom.

Polycarpic, **Polycarpous**, pol-i-kär'pik, pol-i-kär'pus, *a.* [Gr. *polys*, many, and *karpos*, fruit.] *Bot.* having the carpels distinct and numerous, each flower bearing several fruits; also applied to a plant which bears fruit many times without perishing.

Polycephalous, pol-i-sef'a-lus, *a.* [Gr. *polys*, many, *kephalē*, head.] *Bot.* having a common support, capped by many like parts.

Polychromy, pol'i-krō'mi, *n.* [Gr. *polys*, many, and *chrōma*, colour.] The practice of colouring statues and the exteriors and interiors of buildings; architectural ornamentation in colours.—**Polychromatic**, **Polychromic**, pol'i-krō-mat"ik, pol'i-krō-mik, *a.* Exhibiting a play of colours.—**Polychrome**, pol'i-krōm, *a.* Having several or many colours; executed in the manner of polychromy.—*Polychrome printing*, the art of printing in one or more colours at the same time.

Polycotyledon, pol'i-kot-i-lē"don, *n.* [Gr. *polys*, many, *kotylēdon*.] *Bot.* a plant that has many or more than two cotyledons or lobes to the seed.—**Polycotyledonous**, pol'i-kot-i-lē"do-nus, *a.* Having more than two cotyledons.

Polycracy, po-lik'ra-si, *n.* [Gr. *polys*, many, and *krateia*, power.] Government by many rulers; polyarchy.

Polydactylism, pol-i-dak'til-izm, *n.* [Gr. *polys*, many, *daktylos*, a finger.] The condition of having several or many fingers or digits.—**Polydactylous**, pol-i-dak'ti-lus, *a.* Having many fingers or toes.

Polyembryony, pol-i-em'bri-o-ni, *n.* [Gr. *polys*, many, *embryon*, an embryo.] *Bot.* a phenomenon consisting in the existence of two or more embryos in the same seed of flowering plants.—**Polyembryonate**, **Polyembryonic**, pol-i-em'bri-on-āt, pol-i-em'bri-on"ik, *a.* *Bot.* consisting of or having several embryos.

Polyfoil, pol'i-foil, *n.* [Gr. *polys*, and L. *folium*, a leaf.] *Arch.* a leaf ornament of more than five divisions.

Polygamy, po-lig'a-mi, *n.* [Gr. *polys*, many, and *gamos*, marriage.] A plurality of wives or husbands at the same time, or the having of such plurality.—**Polygamous**, po-lig'a-mus, *a.* Relating to or characterized by polygamy (*polygamous* marriages); having a plurality of wives; *bot.* same as *Polygamian*.—**Polygamist**, po-lig'a-mist, *n.* A person who practises polygamy or who maintains its lawfulness.—**Polygam**, pol'i-gam, *n.* A polygamian plant.—**Polygamian**, pol-i-gā'mi-an, *a.* *Bot.* pertaining to a class of plants producing hermaphrodite flowers, with male or female flowers, or both.

Polygastric, pol-i-gas'trik, *a.* [Gr. *polys*, many, *gastēr*, a stomach.] Having or supposed to have many stomachs.—*n.* An animal having or appearing to have many stomachs.

Polygenesis, pol-i-jen'e-sis, *n.* [Gr. *polys*, many, and *genesis*.] The doctrine that beings have their origin in many cells or embryos of different kinds: opposed to *monogenesis*.—**Polygenetic**, pol'i-je-net"ik, *a.* Relating to polygenesis. MONOGENETIC.—**Polygenist**, pol-lij'e-nist, *n.* One who believes in polygenesis.

Polygenous, po-lij'e-nus, *a.* [Gr. *polys*, many, and *genos*, kind.] Consisting of many kinds.

Polyglot, pol'i-glot, *n.* [Gr. *polys*, many, *glōtta*, a language.] A book containing many languages, particularly a Bible that presents the Scriptures in several languages. Also used as an adjective.

Polygon, pol'i-gon, *n.* [Gr. *polys*, many, *gōnia*, an angle.] *Geom.* a plane figure of many angles and sides, or at least of more than four sides.—*Similar polygons* have their several angles equal each to each, and the sides about their equal angles proportionals.—**Polygonal**, **Polygonous**, po-lig'o-nal, po-lig'o-nus, *a.* Having the form of a polygon; having many angles. *Polygonal numbers*, the successive sums of a series of numbers in arithmetical progression.—**Polygonometry** pol'i-go-nom"et-ri, *n.* The doctrine of polygons, as trigonometry is the doctrine of triangles.

Polygram, pol'i-gram, *n.* [Gr. *polys*, many, *gramma*, a line.] A figure consisting of many lines.

Polygraph, pol'i-graf, *n.* [Gr. *polys*, many, *graphē*, a writing.] An instrument for multiplying copies of a writing.—**Polygraphic**, **Polygraphical**, pol-i-graf'ik, pol-i-graf'i-kal, *a.* Pertaining to polygraphy: done with a polygraph.—**Polygraphy**, po-lig'ra-fi, *n.* The art of writing in various ciphers, and of deciphering the same; the multiplication of copies of a writing.

Polygyn, pol'i-jin, *n.* [Gr. *polys*, many, and *gynē*, a female.] *Bot.* a plant having flowers with many pistils, more than twelve.—**Polygynian**, **Polygynous**, pol-i-jin'i-an, po-lij'i-nus, *a.* Having many pistils or styles; polygynic.—**Polygynic**, pol-i-jin'ik, *a.* Practising polygyny; polygynous.—**Polygynist**, po-lij'i-nist, *n.* One who practises polygyny.—**Polygyny**, po-lij'i-ni, *n.* The practice of having more wives than one at the same time.

Polyhalite, pol-i-hal'īt, *n.* [Gr. *polys*, many, *hals*, salt.] A mineral occurring in masses of a fibrous structure, of a brick-red colour.

Polyhedron, pol-i-hē'dron, *n.* [Gr. *polys*, many, *hedra*, a side.] *Geom.* a solid bounded by many faces or planes, and when all the faces are regular polygons the solid becomes a regular body; a multiplying glass with several plane surfaces; a polyscope.—**Polyhedrous, Polyhedral**, pol-i-hē'drus, pol-i-hē'dral, *a.* Forming a polyhedron; having many sides.

Polymath, pol'i-math, *n.* [Gr. *polys*, many, and *mathein*, to learn.] A man of various learning.

Polymeric, pol-i-mer'ik, *a.* [Gr. *polys*, many, *meros*, a part.] Pertaining to or characterized by polymerism.—**Polymeride**, po-lim'ėr-īd, *n.* A compound that exhibits polymerism.—**Polymerism**, po-lim'ėr-izm, *n.* *Chem.* the character in certain compound bodies, differing in chemical properties, of having the same chemical elements combined in the same proportions but with different molecular weights. ISOMERISM, METAMERISM.—**Polymerous**, po-lim'ėr-us, *a.* Composed of many parts, pertaining to polymerism.

Polymignite, pol-i-mig'nīt, *n.* [Gr. *polys*, many, and *mignymi*, to mix.] A mineral which occurs in small prismatic crystals of a metallic lustre, named from the variety of its constituent parts,

Polymorphism, pol-i-mor'fizm, *n.* [Gr. *polys*, many, *morphē*, form.] The property of existing in different forms; the property of crystallizing in two or more fundamental forms.—**Polymorphous, Polymorphic**, pol-i-mor'fus, pol-i-mor'fik, *a.* Having many forms; assuming many forms.

Polynesian, pol-i-nē'zhi-an, *a.* [Gr. *polys*, many, *nēsos*, an island.] Pertaining to *Polynesia*, the region of many islands in the Pacific.—*n.* A native or inhabitant of Polynesia.

Polynomial, pol-i-nō'mi-al, *n.* and *a.* MULTINOMIAL.

Polyonymous, pol-i-on'i-mus, *a.* [Gr. *polys*, many, and *onoma*, a name.] Having many names or titles.

Polyoptrum, Polyoptron, pol-i-op'trum, po-li-op'tron, *n.* [Gr. *polys*, many, and root *opt*, to see.] A glass through which, from the formation of its lens, objects appear multiplied but diminished.

Polyorama, pol'i-o-ra"ma, *n.* [Gr. *polys*, many, *horama*, a view.] A view of many objects; an optical apparatus presenting many views.

Polyoses, pol-i-ō'sēz, *n.* [Gr. *polys*, many.] Very complex CARBOHYDRATES (which see), such as starch and cellulose.

Polyp, Polype, pol'ip, *n.* [L. *polypus*, a polyp, a growth or tumour, from Gr. *polypous*—*polys*, many, *pous*, a foot.] A name loosely applied to what were once known as *radiate* animals, having the mouth surrounded by more or less numerous arms or tentacles, now commonly applied to the hydra or the sea-anemone; a zoophyte.—**Polypary**, pol'i-pa-ri, *n.* The horny envelope or case of polyps (Hydrozoa, Polyzoa, &c.).—**Polypean**, pol-i-pē'an, *a.* Pertaining to a polyp or a polypus.—**Polypidom**, po-lip'i-dom, *n.* [L. *polypus*, and *domus*, a house.] A stem or permanent fabric in which are the cells constituting the abodes of the polyps which fabricate it. —**Polypiferous**, pol-i-pif'ėr-us, *a.* Producing polyps.—**Polipier**, po-lēp-ē-ā, *n.* [Fr.] A polypary.—**Polypite**, pol'i-pīt, *n.* The fundamental portion of a hydrozoon. —**Polypoid**, pol'i-poid, *a.* Like a polyp.

Polyparous, po-lip'a-rus, *a.* [Gr. *polys*, many, and L. *pario*, to produce.] Producing many; bringing forth a great number.

Polypeptides, pol-i-pep'tīds, *n.* [Gr. *polys*, many, *peptō*, I digest.] Very complex synthetic compounds, resembling albuminoids in certain respects.

Polypetalous, pol-i-pet'a-lus, *a.* [Gr. *polys*, many, *petalon*, a petal.] *Bot.* having or consisting of many petals (a *polypetalous* corolla).

Polyphagous, po-lif'a-gus, *a.* [Gr. *polys*, many, *phagein*, to eat.] Eating or subsisting on many things or kinds of food.

Polyphase, pol'i-fāz", *n.* [Gr. *polys*, many, and *phasis*, appearance.] Of a combination of electric currents differing in their phases by constant amounts.

Polyphonic, pol-i-fon'ik, *a.* [Gr. *polys*, many, *phōnē*, sound.] Having or consisting of many voices or sounds; *music*, consisting of several parts progressing simultaneously according to the rules of counterpoint; contrapuntal.—**Polyphonism, Polyphony**, po-lif'on-izm, pō-lif'o-ni, *n.* Multiplicity of sounds or voices.—**Polyphonist**, po-lif'on-ist, *n.* One who can speak in different voices; a ventriloquist; a contrapuntist.

Polyphore, pol'i-fōr, *n.* [Gr. *polys*, many, and *phoros*, carrying.] *Bot.* a fleshy receptacle with numerous ovaries.

Polyphyllous, po-lif'i-lus, *a.* [Gr. *polys*, many, *phyllon*, a leaf.] *Bot.* many-leaved.

Polyphyodont, pol'ē-fī"od-ont, *a.* [Gr. *polus*, many, *phyō*, I produce, *odous*, *odontos*, a tooth.] Producing a continuous succession of teeth throughout life.

Polypi. POLYPUS.

Polypier, Polypite, &c. Under POLYP.

Polyplastic, pol-i-plas'tik, *a.* [Gr. *polys*, many, and *plastikos*, plastic.] Having or assuming many forms.

Polypode, pol'i-pōd, *n.* [Gr. *polys*, many, *pous*, *podos*, a foot.] An animal having many feet; the milliped or wood-louse.

Polypody, pol'i-po-di, *n.* [Gr. *polypodion*, from its spreading root-stock.] A name of various ferns, one of them common to Britain and North America.

Polyporous, pol-i-pō'rus, *a.* [Gr. *polys*, many, and *poros*, a pore.] Having many pores.

Polypous. Under POLYPUS.

Polyprismatic, pol'i-priz-mat"ik, *a.* [Gr. *polys*, many, E. *prismatic*.] *Mineral.* having crystals presenting numerous prisms in a single form.

Polypus, pol'i-pus, *n.* pl. **Polypi**, pol'i-pī. [POLYP.] A polyp; *pathol.* a pedunculated tumour in the mucous membrane, especially that of the nostrils and uterus.—**Polypous**, pol'i-pus, *a.* Pertaining to a polypus.

Polyrhizous, pol-i-rī'zus, *a.* [Gr. *polys*, many, *rhiza*, a root.] *Bot.* possessing numerous rootlets independently of those by which the attachment is effected.

Polyscope, pol'i-skōp, *n.* [Gr. *polys*, many, and *skopein*, to view.] A lens so constructed that an object seen through it appears multiplied.

Polysepalous, pol-i-sep'a-lus, *a.* [Gr. *polys*, many, and E. *sepal*.] *Bot.* a term applied to a calyx which has its sepals separate from each other.

Polyspermal, Polyspermous, pol-i-spėr'mal, pol-i-spėr'mus, *a.* [Gr. *polys*, many, *sperma*, seed.] Containing many seeds.

Polysporous, pol-i-spō'rus, *a.* [Gr. *polys*, many, and E. *spore*.] *Bot.* having many spores.

Polystyle, pol'i-stīl, *n.* [Gr. *polys*, many, and *stylos*, a column.] *Arch.* an edifice in which there are many columns. Also used as adj.

Polysyllable, pol'i-sil-la-bl, *n.* [Gr. *polys*, many, *syllabē*, a syllable.] A word of many syllables, that is, consisting of four or more syllables.—**Polysyllabic, Polysyllabical**, pol'i-sil-lab"ik, pol'i-sil-lab"i-kal, *a.* Consisting of many syllables or of more than three.

Polysyndeton, pol-i-sin'de-ton, *n.* [Gr., from *polys*, many, *syn*, together, *deō*, I bind.] A figure of rhetoric by which the copulative conjunction is often repeated.

Polysynthesis, pol-i-sin'the-sis, *n.* [Gr. *polys*, many, and *synthesis*, a putting together. SYNTHESIS.] A compounding of several elements; a polysynthetic structure.—**Polysynthetic, Polysynthetical**, pol'i-sin-thet"ik, pol'i-sin-thet"i-kal, *a.* *Philol.* compounded of an extraordinary number of elements or word forms, each retaining a kind of independence (a *polysynthetic* word); characterized by such compounds (a *polysynthetic* language).

Polytechnic, pol-i-tek'nik, *a.* [Gr. *polys*, many, and *technē*, art.] Of or designating an educational institution in which instruction is given in many technical arts and applied sciences.—*n.* A school of instruction in applied sciences; an exhibition of objects belonging to the industrial arts. —**Polytechnics**, pol-i-tek'niks, *n.* The science of the mechanical arts.

Polythalamous, pol-i-thal'a-mus, *a.* [Gr. *polys*, many, *thalamos*, a chamber.] Having many cells or chambers (*polythalamous* shells).

Polytheism, pol-i-thē'izm, *n.* [Gr. *polys*, many, *theos*, god.] The doctrine of a plurality of gods.—**Polytheist**, pol-i-thē'ist, *n.* A person who believes in a plurality of gods.—**Polytheistic, Polytheistical**, pol'i-thē-is"tik, pol'i-thē-is"ti-kal, *a.* Pertaining to polytheism; holding a plurality of gods.

Polytomous, po-lit'o-mus, *a.* [Gr. *polys*, many, *tomē*, a cutting.] *Bot.* a term applied to leaves subdivided into many distinct subordinate parts, which, however, are not jointed to the petiole.

Polyzoa, pol-i-zō'a, *n.pl.* [Gr. *polys*, many, *zōon*, an animal.] A class of animals, chiefly marine, forming compound groups or colonies, being the lowest members of the Mollusca, and generally known by the popular names of 'sea-mosses' and 'seamats'.—**Polyzoarium, Polyzoary**, pol'i-zō-ā"ri-um, pol-i-zō'a-ri, *n.* The dermal system of the colony of a polyzoon; a polypidom.—**Polyzoon**, pol-i-zō'on, *n.* One of the polyzoa.

Polyzonal, pol-i-zō'nal, *a.* [Gr. *polys*, many, *zōnē*, a zone.] Composed of many zones or belts; a term applied to burning lenses composed of pieces united in rings.

Pomace, pom'ās, *n.* [From L. *pomum*, an apple.] The substance of apples or of similar fruit crushed by grinding.—**Pomaceous**, pō-mā'shus, *a.* Like pomace; pertaining to the apple family of trees.

Pomade, pō-mād', *n.* [Fr. *pommade*, It. *pomada*, *pomata*, from L. *pomum*, an apple. Originally it was prepared from apples.] Perfumed ointment, especially ointment for the hair; pomatum.

Pomander, pō'man-dėr, *n.* [Fr. *pomme d'ambre*, apple or ball of amber.] A perfume ball, or a mixture of perfumes, formerly carried in the pocket or suspended from the neck or the girdle.

Pomatum, pō-mā'tum, *n.* [From L. *pomum*, an apple. POMADE.] A perfumed unguent used in dressing the hair; pomade.

Pome, pōm, *n.* [L. *pomum*, an apple.] *Bot.* a fleshy or pulpy pericarp without valves, containing a capsule or capsules, as the apple, pear, &c.

Pomegranate, pom'gra-nāt, *n.* [L. *pomum*, an apple, and *granatum*, grained, having many grains or seeds. GRAIN, GARNET.] A fruit as large as an orange, having a hard rind filled with a soft pulp and numerous grains or seeds; the fruit that produces pomegranates, supposed to be a native of Persia; an ornament on the robe and ephod of the Jewish high-priest.

Pomelo, pom'e-lō, *n.* The pompelmoose.

Pomeranian, pom'ėr-ā"ni-an, *n.* A small dog from Pomerania in Prussia.

Pomeroy, Pomeroyal, pom'roi, pom'-roi-al, *n.* [Fr. *pomme*, an apple, *roi*, king, *royal*, royal.] A particular sort of apple.

Pomiferous, pō-mif'ėr-us, *a.* [L. *pomum*, an apple, and *fero*, I produce.] Apple-bearing; an epithet applied to plants which bear the larger fruits (as melons, gourds, cucumbers, &c.).

Pommage, pom'āj, *n.* Same as *Pomace.*

Pommel, pum'mel, *n.* [O.Fr. *pommel*, from L. *pomum*, an apple or similar fruit.] A knob or ball; the knob on the hilt of a sword; the protuberant part of a saddle-bow; a round knob on the frame of a chair. —*v.t.* —*pommelled, pommelling.* To beat; to bruise. Spelled also *Pummel.*

Pomology, pō-mol'o-ji, *n.* [L. *pomum*, an apple, Gr. *logos*, discourse.] The branch of knowledge that deals with fruits; the cultivation of fruit-trees.—**Pomological**, pō-mo-loj'i-kal, *a.* Pertaining to pomology.—**Pomologist**, pō-mol'o-jist, *n.* One who is versed in pomology.

Pomp, pomp, *n.* [Fr. *pompe*, L. *pompa*, from Gr. *pompē*, a procession, from *pempō*, to send.] A procession distinguished by splendour or magnificence; a pageant; magnificence; parade; splendour; display. —**Pompous**, pom'pus, *a.* [Fr. *pompeux.*] Displaying pomp; splendid; showing self-importance; exhibiting an exaggerated sense of dignity; ostentatious.—**Pompously**, pom'pus-li, *adv.* In a pompous manner; ostentatiously.—**Pompousness, Pomposity**, pom'pus-nes, pom-pos'i-ti, *n.* Pompous display; show; ostentation.

Pompelmoose, pom'pel-mös, *n.* [Probably of Eastern origin.] The shaddock, or a large variety of that fruit.

Pompholyx, pom'fo-liks, *n.* [Gr. *pompholyx*, a bubble.] An eruption of deep-seated vesicles in the skin, especially of the palms and soles.

Pompion, pum'pi-on, *n.* [O.Fr, *pompon*; akin *pumpkin.*] A pumpkin.

Pom-pom, *n.* [From sound.] An automatic gun firing small shells.

Pompon, poṅ-poṅ, *n.* [Fr.] An ornament of feathers, artificial flowers, &c., for a bonnet or hat; a ball on a soldier's shako.

Pompous, Pompously, &c. Under POMP.

Poncho, pon'chō, *n.* [Sp.] In Spanish America a garment like a narrow blanket with a slit in the middle for the head to pass through.

Pond, pond, *n.* [A slightly different form of *pound*, A.Sax. *pund*, an inclosure.] A body of still water of less extent than a lake, either artificial or natural.—**Pond-lily**, *n.* The water-lily.—**Pond-weed**, *n.* A name of several British water-weeds.

Ponder, pon'dėr, *v.t.* [Fr. *ponderer*, from L. *pondero*, to weigh, from *pondus, ponderis*, weight.] To weigh carefully in the mind; to think about; to reflect upon; to examine carefully.—*v.i.* To think; to muse; to deliberate: with *on* or *over*.—**Ponderable**, pon'dėr-a-bl, *a.* [L. *ponderabilis.*] Capable of being weighed; having weight. —**Ponderability, Ponderableness**, pon'dėr-a-bil''i-ti, pon'dėr-a-bl-nes, *n.* That property of bodies by which they possess sensible weight.—**Ponderer**, pon'dėr-ėr, *n.* One that ponders.—**Ponderingly**, pon'dėr-ing-li, *adv.* In a pondering manner. —**Ponderous**, pon'dėr-us, *a.* [L. *ponderosus.*] Very heavy; of great weight; massive; weighty; forcible.—**Ponderously**, pon'dėr-us-li, *adv.* In a ponderous manner.—**Ponderousness, Ponderosity**, pon'dėr-us-nes, pon-dėr-os'i-ti, *n.* The state or quality of being ponderous; gravity; heaviness.

Pongee, pun'ji, *n.* [Chinese.] Soft unbleached Chinese silk employed in the construction of balloons.

Pongo, pong'gō, *n.* A name given to some of the large apes.

Poniard, pon'yärd, *n.* [Fr. *poignard*, from *poing*, L. *pugnus*, the fist.] A small dagger; a pointed weapon for stabbing.—*v.t.* To pierce with a poniard; to stab.

Pontage, pon'tāj, *n.* [L.L. *pontagium*, from L. *pons, pontis*, a bridge.] A toll or tax for the maintenance or repair of bridges.

Pontifex, pon'ti-feks, *n.* pl. **Pontifices**, pon-tif'i-sēz. [L. *pontifex, pontificis*, a high-priest, from *pons, pontis*, a bridge, and *facio*, to make.] The name by which the Romans designated the highest members of their great colleges of priests, the chief being termed *Pontifex Maximus.*—**Pontiff**, pon'tif, *n.* A high-priest; a designation of the pope.—**Pontific, Pontifical**, pon-tif'ik, pon-tif'i-kal, *a.* Relating to pontiffs or priests; relating to a pope; belonging to the pope; in a lofty manner, expressive of infallibility of speaker.—**Pontifical**, pon-tif'i-kal, *n.* A book containing rites and ceremonies ecclesiastical; *pl.* the dress and ornaments of, a pope, priest, or bishop. —**Pontifically**, pon-tif'i-kal-li, *adv.* In a pontifical manner.—**Pontificate**, pon-tif'i-kāt, *n.* [L. *pontificatus.*] The state or dignity of a high-priest; the office or dignity of the pope; the papacy; the reign of a pope. —**Pontifice**, pon'ti-fis, *n.* A bridge construction, on model of *edifice.* (*Mil.*, P.L., x. 348.)

Pontoon, Ponton, pon-tön', pon-ton', *n.* [Fr. *ponton*, from L. *pons, pontis*, a bridge.] A flat-bottomed boat, or any light framework or floating body used in the construction of a temporary military bridge over a river; a lighter, a low flat vessel resembling a barge, used in careening ships; a water-tight structure placed beneath a submerged vessel and then filled with air, to assist in refloating the vessel.—**Pontonier, Pontonnier**, pon-to-nēr', *n.* [Fr.] A soldier having the charge of pontoons; one who constructs pontoon-bridges.—**Pontoon-bridge**, *n.* A temporary military bridge supported on pontoons.—**Pontoon-train**, *n.* The carriages or wagons and materials carried with an army to construct bridges.—**Pont-volant**, pont-vō'-lant, *n.* [Fr. *pont*, bridge, and *volant*, flying.] *Milit.* a flying bridge, a kind of bridge used in sieges.

Pony, pō'ni, *n.* [Gael. *ponaidh*, Ir. *poni*, a pony.] A small variety of horse; a small liqueur glass; a printed or written translation used by students to avoid work.

Pood, pöd, *n.* A Russian weight, equal to 36.113 lbs.

Poodle, pö'dl, *n.* [Same as G. and Dan. *pudel*, D. *poedel*, L.G. *budel*, a poodle; akin to L.G. *pudeln*, to waddle.] A small variety of dog covered with long curling hair.

Pooh, pö, *interj.* Pshaw! pish! an expression of dislike, scorn, or contempt.—**Pooh-pooh**, *v.t.* To turn aside with a pooh; to express scorn or contempt for; to sneer at.

Pool, pöl, *n.* [A.Sax. *pól* = L.G. *pohl, pool*, Icel. *pollr*, D. *poll*, G. *pfuhl*, pool, fen; the word is also Celtic; W. *pwll*, a pool, a pit; perhaps akin to L. *palus*, a marsh.] A small collection of water or other liquid in a hollow place; a small piece of stagnant water; a hole in the course of a stream deeper than the ordinary bed.

Pool, pöl, *n.* [Fr. *poule*, a hen.] The receptacle for the stakes at certain games of cards, billiards, &c.; the stakes themselves; games played on a table similar to a billiard table but having six pockets, usually with fifteen object balls and one cue ball; a common fund or combination of properties and interests, often arranged for speculation in grain or commodity markets.—*v.t.* to combine interests or properties.

Poon, pön, *n.* [Indian name.] The name of several valuable trees of India (genus Calophyllum).

Poonac, pö'nak, *n.* [A Tamil word.] The substance left after the oil is expressed from cocoa-nuts, used for feeding stock and for manure.

Poop, pöp, *n.* [Fr. *poupe*, from L. *puppis*, the poop.] The highest and aftermost part of a ship's deck above the complete deck of the vessel.—*v.t. Naut.* to break heavily over the stern or quarter of; to drive in the stern of.

Poor, pör, *a.* [O.E. *poure*, O.Fr. *poure, povre*, Mod.Fr. *pauvre*, from L. *pauper*, poor, from *paucus*, few, and *pario*, to produce.] Destitute of riches; not having property sufficient for a comfortable subsistence; needy; wanting good or desirable qualities; having little value or importance; trifling; insignificant; paltry; mean; destitute of fertility; barren; destitute of intellectual or artistic merit (a *poor* discourse); wanting in spirit or vigour; weak; impotent; worthy of pity; ill-fated; a word of tenderness or endearment (*poor* thing); a word of slight contempt; wretched.—*The poor*, collectively, the indigent; the needy: opposed to the rich; those unable to support themselves, and who have to depend for support on the contributions of others.—*Poor in spirit*, humble; contrite. (N.T.)—**Poor-box**, *n.* A box to receive money for the poor.—**Poorhouse**, pör'hous, *n.* A residence for persons receiving public charity.—**Poor-john**, *n.* A fish of the cod family, formerly a cheap kind of food. (*Shak.*)—**Poor-law**, *n.* A law or the laws collectively established for the management of the funds for the maintenance of the poor. —**Poorly**, pör'li, *adv.* In a poor manner or condition; in indigence; with little or no success; in an inferior manner; insufficiently; defectively.—*a.* Somewhat ill; indisposed; not in health. (*Colloq.*)—**Poorness**, pör'nes, *n.* The state or quality of being poor; poverty.—**Poor-rate**, *n.* An assessment or tax imposed for the relief or support of the poor.—**Poor-spirited**, *a.* Of a mean spirit; cowardly.—**Poor-spiritedness**, *n.*—**Poor's Roll**, *n.* A roll or list of paupers, or persons entitled to or who have received parochial relief. (*Brit.*)

Pop, pop, *n.* [From the sound.] A small smart sound or report; a blow with a hatchet.—*v.i.*—*popped, popping.* To appear to the eye suddenly; to enter or issue forth with a quick, sudden motion; to dart; to start from a place suddenly.—*v.t.* To thrust forward, or offer suddenly; to thrust or push suddenly with a quick motion; to protrude (his eyes *popped*); to burst open.—*To pop corn*, to parch or roast Indian corn until it expands and 'pops' open.—*To pop the question*, in familiar language, to make an offer of marriage to a lady —*adv.* Suddenly; unexpectedly.—**Popcorn**, *n.* Corn or maize for parching; parched maize; popped-corn. —**Popgun**, *n.* A small gun or tube used by children for shooting pellets, which makes a 'pop' when the pellet is expelled.

Pope, pōp, *n.* [A.Sax. *pápa*, from L.L. *papa*, the pope, lit. father, same word as *papa*, the childish name for father. PAPA.] The Bishop of Rome, the head of the Roman Catholic Church; in the *Greek Church*, a priest or chaplain; the ruffe, a small fish closely allied to the perch.—*Pope's eye*, the gland surrounded with fat in the middle of the thigh of an ox or sheep, much prized for its delicacy.—**Popedom**, pōp'dum, *n.* The place, office, dignity, or jurisdiction of the pope.—**Pope-Joan**, *n.* A game of cards.—**Popery**, pō'pėr-i, *n.* The religion of the Church of Rome, comprehending doctrines and practice: a term offensive to Catholics.—**Popish**, pō'pish, *a.* Pertaining to the pope or the Roman Catholic Church: used with a shade of contempt.—**Popishly**, pō'pish-li, *adv.* In a popish manner; with a tendency to popery.

Popinjay, pop'in-jā, *n.* [O.E. *popingay*, Fr. *papegai*, Sp. and Pg. *papagayo*, L.Gr. *papagas*, from Ar. *babaghā, babbagā*, a parrakeet.] A parrot; a gay, trifling young man; a fop or coxcomb.

Poplar, pop'lär, *n.* [O.Fr. *poplier*, Mod.Fr. *peuplier*, from L. *pōpulus*, a poplar.] A common name of sundry well-known trees, of which there are numerous species, as the white poplar, gray poplar, trembling poplar or aspen, black poplar, &c.—**Poplared**, pop'lärd, *a.* Covered with or containing poplars.

Poplin, pop'lin, *n.* [Fr. *Popeline.*] Corded fabric of silk or worsted, originally made in the *papal* city of Avignon, and used especially for women's clothing.

Poppet, pop'et, *n.* [In first sense same as *puppet*; comp. Fr. *poupée*, a head of a lathe.] A term of endearment; a shore to support a ship in launching; one of the heads of a lathe.

Popple, pop'l, *v.i.* [Dim. and freq. of *pop*.] To move quickly up and down, as a cork dropped on water.

Poppy, pop'i, *n.* [A.Sax. *papig, popig*, from L. *papaver*, a poppy.] A gay flowering plant of many species, from one of which, the white poppy, is collected opium.—**Poppied**, pop'id, *a.* Grown over with poppies; mingled with poppies; made drowsy as with opium.—**Poppy-head**, *n.* A carved ornament on the end of a pew, desk, &c.—**Poppy-oil**, *n.* A bland, drying oil obtained from the seeds of the poppy, used in painting.

Populace, pop'ū-lās, *n.* [Fr. *populace*, It. *popolazzo*, from L. *populus*, the people (whence *popular, people*); the root is doubtful.] The common people; the vulgar; the multitude, comprehending all persons not distinguished by rank, education, office, or profession: usually with the definite article.—**Popular**, pop'ū-lėr, *a.* [L. *popularis*.] Pertaining to the common people; constituted by or depending on the people; suitable to common people; easy to be comprehended; plain; familiar; beloved by the people; pleasing to people in general.—**Popularity**, pop-ū-lar'i-ti, *n.* The state or quality of being popular, or esteemed by the people at large; good-will or favour proceeding from the people.—**Popularization**, pop'ū-lėr-i-zā"shon, *n.* The act of making popular.—**Popularize**, pop'ū-lėr-īz, *v.t.*—*popularized, popularizing.* To make popular; to treat in a popular manner, or so as to be generally intelligible; to spread among the people.—**Popularly**, pop'ū-lėr-li, *adv.* In a popular manner; so as to please the populace; among the people at large; currently; commonly.—**Populate**, pop'ū-lāt, *v.t.*—*populated, populating.* To furnish with inhabitants; to people.—**Population**, pop-ū-lā'shon, *n.* The act or process of populating or peopling; the whole number of people in a country, town, &c.; populousness.—**Populator**, pop'ū-lā-tėr, *n.* One who populates or peoples.—**Populist**, pop'ū-list, *n.* Member of a political party, formed in 1891, advocating an advanced program of national control and proprietorship of all natural means of production.—**Populous**, pop'ū-lus, *a.* [L. *populosus*.] Full of inhabitants; thickly peopled.—**Populously**, pop'ū-lus-li, *adv.* With many inhabitants in proportion to extent.—**Populousness**, pop'ū-lus-nes, *n.* The state of being populous.

Porbeagle, por'bē-gl, *n.* [Lit. hog-beagle—Fr. *porc*, a hog, and E. *beagle*, the latter term, like *dog* and *hound*, being applied to several sharks; comp. *porpoise*.] A species of shark.

Porcate, Porcated, por'kāt, por'kā-ted, *a.* [L. *porca*, a ridge.] Ridged; formed in ridges.

Porcelain, pōr'se-lan, *n.* [Fr. *porcelaine*, from It. *porcellana*, first a certain shell, then the nacre of the shell, and last porcelain, from L. *porcus*, a hog, from some fancied resemblance in the shell to a hog. PORK.] The finest species of pottery ware, originally manufactured in China and Japan, formed from the finest clays united with siliceous earths, which communicate a certain degree of translucency by means of their vitrification.—*a.* Belonging to or consisting of porcelain.—**Porcelain-clay**, *n.* KAOLIN.—**Porcelainized**, pōr'se-lan-īzd, *a.* Baked like potters' clay; *geol.* hardened and altered to resemble in texture porcelain.—**Porcellaneous**, pōr-sel-lā'nē-us, *a.* Pertaining to or resembling porcelain.—*Porcellaneous shells* are those which have a compact texture, an enamelled surface, and are generally beautifully variegated.—**Porcellanite**, pōr'sel-lan-īt, *n.* A siliceous mineral, a species of jasper, of various colours.

Porch, pōrch, *n.* [Fr. *porche*, It. *portico*, from L. *porticus*, a porch, from *porta*, a gate, entrance. PORT.] *Arch.* an exterior appendage to a building forming a covered approach or vestibule to a doorway; a covered walk or portico.—*The Porch*, a public portico in Athens, where Zeno, the philosopher, taught his disciples; hence, *the Porch* is equivalent to the *school of the Stoics*.

Porcine, pōr'sīn, *a.* [L. *porcinus*, from *porcus*, a hog. PORK.] Pertaining to swine; like a swine; hog-like.

Porcupine, por'kū-pīn, *n.* [O.Fr. *porc-espin*, lit. spine-hog; from L. *porcus*, a pig, and *spina*, a spine or thorn. PORK, SPINE.] A rodent quadruped covered with long spines mixed with bristly hairs, which the animal can erect at pleasure, and which serve for his defence.—**Porcupine-fish**, *n.* A fish covered with spines or prickles, and found in the tropical seas.—**Porcupine-wood**, *n.* The wood of the cocoa-nut palm, which when cut horizontally has markings like those of porcupine spines.

Pore, pōr, *n.* [Fr. *pore*, from L. *porus*, Gr. *poros*, a passage, a pore. PORT (a gate).] A small opening in a solid body, especially one of the minute openings on the surface of organized bodies through which fluids and minute substances are excreted or exhaled or by which they are absorbed; one of the small interstices between the molecules of matter which compose bodies.—**Porous, Pory**, pō'rus, pō'ri, *a.* Having many pores or minute openings or interstices; having the molecules separated by intervals or pores.—**Porously**, pō'rus-li, *adv.* In a porous manner.—**Porousness, Porosity**, pō'rus-nes, pō-ros'i-ti, *n.* The state or quality of being porous or of having pores.

Pore, pōr, *v.i.*—*pored, poring.* [O.E. *poure*; origin uncertain; possibly same as *pour*.] To look with steady continued attention or application; to read or examine anything with steady perseverance: generally followed by *on* (*upon*) or *over*.—**Porer**, pō'rėr, *n.* One who pores.

Porgee, por'jē, *n.* A coarse kind of India silk.

Porgy, Porgie, por'ji, *n.* [Origin doubtful.] The name given to a number of fishes, some of them used as food.

Porifera, pō-rif'ėr-a, *n.pl.* [L. *porus*, a pore, and *fero*, I bear.] An order of the Protozoa, including the marine and freshwater sponges.

Poriform, pō'ri-form, *a.* [L. *porus*, a pore, and *forma*, a shape.] Resembling a pore.

Porism, pōr'izm, *n.* [Gr. *porisma*, a corollary, from *porizō*, I gain.] *Geom.* a corollary; a proposition affirming the possibility of finding such conditions as will render a certain problem indeterminate or capable of innumerable solutions.—**Poristic, Poristical**, po-ris'tik, po-ris'ti-kal, *a.* Pertaining to a porism.

Porite, pō'rīt, *n.* [L. *porus*, a pore.] A coral of certain species having the surface covered with minute shallow pores or cells.

Pork, pōrk, *n.* [Fr. *porc*, from L. *porcus*, a swine, a pig (seen also in *porcupine, porpoise, porbeagle*). FARROW.] The flesh of swine, fresh or salted, used for food.—**Porker**, pōr'kėr, *n.* A hog; a pig; especially one fed for pork.—**Pork-butcher**, *n.* One who kills pigs or who deals in pork.—**Pork-chop**, *n.* A slice from the rib of a pig.—**Pork-pie**, *n.* A pie made of pastry and minced pork.—**Pork-sausage**, *n.* A sausage made of minced pork with various flavouring ingredients.

Pornography, por-nog'ra-fi, *n.* [Gr. *pornē*, prostitute, *graphō*, I write.] Literature in which prostitutes figure; obscene writing.—**Pornographer**, por-nog'ra-fėr, *n.* One who treats such subjects.—**Pornographic**, por-nō-graf'ik, *a.* Pertaining to the literary treatment of such subjects.

Porosity, Porous, &c. Under PORE.

Porphyrogenitus, por'fi-rō-jen"i-tus, *n.* [L. *porphyra*, purple, and *genitus*, begot, born.] A title given, especially by the Romans of the Eastern Empire, to such of the sovereign's sons as were born after his accession to the throne.

Porphyry, por'fi-ri, *n.* [Fr. *porphyre*, Pr. *porfiri*, from Gr. *porphyritēs*, lit. a purple-coloured rock, from *porphyra*, purple. PURPLE.] Originally, the name given to a very hard Egyptian stone containing crystals of rose-coloured felspar, partaking of the nature of granite, susceptible of a fine polish, and consequently much used for sculpture; also applied generally to any unstratified or igneous rock in which detached crystals of felspar or some other mineral are diffused through a compact base.—**Porphyritic, Porphyritical, Porphyraceous**, por-fi-rit'ik, por-fi-rit'i-kal, por-fi-rā'shus, *a.* Composed of, resembling, or containing porphyry.—**Porphyrization**, por'fi-ri-zā"shon, *n.* The act of porphyrizing.—**Porphyrize**, por'fi-rīz, *v.t.*—*porphyrized, porphyrizing.* To cause to resemble porphyry.

Porpoise, por'pus, *n.* [O.E. *porcpisce, porpesse*, &c., lit. swine-flesh, from L. *porcus*, a swine, and *piscis*, a fish. PORK.] A cetaceous mammal, rarely exceeding 5 feet in length, frequenting the Northern Seas, and frequently seen off the shores pursuing shoals of herring, mackerel, &c. Sometimes written *Porpus*.—**Porpoising**, por'pusing, *n.* In *aviation*, the movement of a seaplane on and off the water when an imperfect get-off or landing is made.

Porraceous, por-ā'shus, *a.* [L. *porrum*, a leek.] Of a leek-green colour.

Porridge, por'ij, *n.* [Perhaps from L. *porrum, porrus*, a leek, and meaning originally leek soup or broth; or a corruption of *pottage*.] A kind of food made by slowly stirring oatmeal, or other similar substance, amongst water or milk while boiling till a thickened mass is formed.—**Porringer**, por'in-jėr, *n.* [From *porridge*. The *n* has intruded as in *messenger*.] A porridge-dish; a small earthenware or tin vessel out of which children eat their food.

Porrigo, po-rī'go, *n.* [L.] Scald-head; scurf or scall in the head.

Port, pōrt, *n.* [A.Sax. *port*, a port, haven, harbour, from L. *portus*, a haven; akin to *porta*, a gate; same root as *fare*. It enters into many place-names, as *Port*land, *Ports*mouth, Brid*port*.] A natural or artificial harbour; a haven; any bay, cove, inlet, or recess of the sea, or of a lake, or the mouth of a river, which vessels can enter, and where they can lie safe from injury by storms.—**Port-bar**, *n.* A boom moored transversely across a port to prevent entrance or egress; an accumulated bank of sand, &c., at the mouth of a port or harbour.—**Port-charges, Port-dues**, *n.pl.* Charges or dues to which a ship or its cargo is subjected in a port or harbour.—**Portreeve, Portgrave**, pōrt'rēv, pōrt'grāv, *n.* The chief magistrate of a port or maritime town.—**Port-town**, *n.* A town having or situated near a port.

Port, pōrt, *n.* [Fr. *porte*, L. *porta*, a gate, from same root as Gr. *poros*, a passage, and E. to *fare*. See above.] A gate; an entrance; a passage-way in the side of a ship; an opening in the side of a ship of war, through which cannon are discharged: called also a port-hole; an aperture for the passage of steam or a fluid.—**Portal**, pōr'tal, *n.* [O.Fr. *portal*, L.L. *portale*, from L. *porta*, a gate.] A door or gate: a poetical or dignified term; *arch.* the lesser gate when there are two of different dimensions at the entrance of a building; a kind of arch over a door or gate, or the framework of the gate.—*a.* *Anat.* belonging to a vein forming a sort of entrance (*port*) to the liver.—*Portal circulation*, a special circulation of venous blood from the intestines, &c., through the liver.—**Porter**, pōr'tėr, *n.* [Fr. *portier*.] One who has charge of a door or gate; a doorkeeper; a waiter in a hall.—**Porteress, Portress**, pōr'tėr-es, pōr'tres, *n.* A female porter.—**Port-hole**, *n.* The port of a ship.

Port, pōrt, *v.t.* [Fr. *porter*, from L. *porto*, to carry (seen in *export, import, report, transport, sport*, &c.); same root as *portus*, a harbour, a port.] To carry in military fashion; to carry a weapon, such as a rifle, in a slanting direction, upwards towards the left, and across the body in front, as in the military command 'to *port* arms'.—*n.* [Fr. *port*, carriage, demeanour, from *porter*,

L. *porto*, to carry.] Carriage; air; mien; manner of movement or walk; demeanour; external appearance (the *port* of a gentleman). — **Portability, Portableness,** pōr-ta-bil'i-ti, pōr'ta-bl-nes, *n.* The state of being portable.—**Portable,** pōr'ta-bl, *a.* [L. *portabilis.*] Capable of being carried by the hand or about the person; capable of being carried or transported from place to place; easily carried; not bulky or heavy. —**Portage,** pōr'tāj, *n.* The act of carrying; the price of carriage; a break in a chain of water communication over which goods, boats, &c., have to be carried, as from one lake, river, or canal to another, or along the banks of rivers round waterfalls, rapids, &c.—**Porter,** pōr'tėr, *n.* [Fr. *porteur*, from *porter*, to carry.] A carrier; a person who carries or conveys burdens, parcels, or messages for hire; a dark-coloured malt liquor made wholly or partially with high-dried malt: so called from its having been originally the favourite beverage of *porters.*—**Porterage,** pōr'tėr-āj, *n.* Money charged or paid for the carriage of burdens or parcels by a porter.

Port, pōrt, *n.* [Etym. uncertain.] *Naut.* the larboard or left side of a ship.—*v.t.* and *i.* *Naut.* to turn or put to the left or larboard side of a ship: said of the helm.

Port, Port-wine, pōrt, *n.* [From *Oporto*, whence it is shipped; *Oporto* means the *port.*] A kind of wine made in Portugal.

Portage. Under PORT (to carry).

Portal. Under PORT (gate).

Portamento, por-ta-men'tō, *n.* [It.] *Mus.* the gliding from one note to another without a break.

Port-crayon, *n.* [From *port*, to carry.] A holder for chalks or crayons; a pencil-case.

Portcullis, pōrt-kul'is, *n.* [Fr. *porte*, a gate, and *coulisse*, groove, from *couler*, to slip or slide.] *Fort.* a strong grating of timber or iron, resembling a harrow, made to slide in vertical grooves in the jambs of the entrance-gate of a fortified place, to protect the gate in case of assault.

Porte, pōrt, *n.* [The chief office of the Ottoman Empire is styled *Babi Ali*, lit. the High Gate, from the gate (*bab*) of the palace at which justice was administered; and the French translation of this term being *Sublime Porte*, hence the use of this word.] The Ottoman court; the government of the Turkish Empire.

Porte-feuille, pōrt-fu-yé, *n.* [PORTFOLIO.] A portfolio; a pocket-book. — **Porte-monnaie,** pōrt-mon-nā, *n.* [Fr., from *porter*, to carry, and *monnaie*, money.] A small pocket-book for carrying money; a kind of purse.

Portend, por-tend', *v.t.* [L. *portendo*, to stretch forth, point out, portend—*por*, *pro*, forth or forward, and *tendo*, to stretch. TEND.] To foreshow ominously; to foretoken; to indicate something future by previous signs.—**Portent,** por'tent or portent', *n.* [L. *portentum.*] That which portends or foretokens; especially, an omen of ill.—**Portentous,** por-ten'tus, *a.* Of the nature of a portent; ominous; foreshowing ill; monstrous; prodigious; wonderful.—**Portentously,** por-ten'tus-li, *adv.* In a portentous manner.—**Portentousness,** por-ten'tus-nes, *n.*

Porter. Under PORT, a gate, and PORT, to carry.

Portfire, *n.* [*Port*, to carry.] A strong paper or cloth case, firmly packed with a composition of niter, sulphur, and mealed powder, used for firing mines.

Portfolio, pōrt-fō'li-ō, *n.* [In imitation of Fr. *porte-feuille*, a portfolio, the office of a minister—*porter*, to carry (L. *portare*), and *feuille*, a leaf, L. *folium.*] A portable case of the form of a large book, for holding loose drawings, prints, papers, &c.; the office and functions of a minister of state or cabinet member.

Portico, pōr'ti-kō, *n.* pl. **Porticoes;** pōr'ti-kōz. [It. and Sp. *portico*, from L. *porticus.* PORCH.] *Arch.* a kind of porch before the entrance of a building fronted with columns.—**Porticoed,** pōr'ti-kōd, *a.* Having a portico or porticoes.

Portion, pōr'shon, *n.* [L. *portio*, *portionis*, a portion; akin to *pars*, *partis*, a part. PART.] A part of anything separated from it; that which is divided off, as a part from a whole; a part, though not actually divided, but considered by itself; a part assigned; an allotment; fate; final state (N.T.).—*v.t.* To divide or distribute into portions or shares; to parcel out; to allot in shares; to endow with a portion or an inheritance.—**Portioner,** pōr'shon-ėr, *n.* One who divides or assigns in shares; *Scots law*, the proprietor of a small feu or portion of land; the sub-tenant of a feu; an under-feuar.—**Portionless,** pōr'shon-les, *a.* Having no portion.

Portland Cement, pōrt'land se-ment', [Called so because of its resemblance, when set, to a stone found on the Isle of Portland, in England.] A cement of superior quality, consisting of a mixture of clay and limestone, or two similar substances, which are first ground, then heated until they form clinker, then powdered, after which they harden into stone upon the addition of water or even when immersed in water.

Portlast, pōrt'last, *n.* The porpoise. (*Rare.*)

Portly, pōrt'li, *a.* [From *port*, carriage, mien, demeanour.] Grand or dignified in mien; stately; of a noble appearance and carriage; rather tall, and inclining to stoutness. — **Portliness,** pōrt'li-nes, *n.* The state or quality of being portly.

Portmanteau, pōrt-man'tō, *n.* [Fr. *portemanteau*, from *porter*, to carry, and *manteau*, a cloak or mantle.] A case or trunk, usually made of leather, for carrying apparel, &c., on journeys; a leather case attached to a saddle behind the rider.

Portrait, pōr'trāt, *n.* [Fr. *portrait*, pp. of *portraire*, to portray. PORTRAY.] A painted picture or representation of a person, and especially of a face drawn from the life: also used generally for engravings, photographs, crayon drawings, &c., of this character; a vivid description or delineation in words.—**Portrait-painter,** *n.* One whose occupation is to paint portraits.—**Portraiture,** pōr'trā-tūr, *n.* [Fr.] A portrait; the art or practice of drawing portraits, or of vividly describing in words.

Portray, pōr-trā', *v.t.* [Fr. *portraire*, to portray, to depict, from L. *portraho*, to draw forth—L. *por*, *pro*, forward, and *trahere*, to draw, whence *traction*, *abstract*, &c.] To paint or draw the likeness of; to depict; to describe in words.—**Portrayal,** pōr-trā'al, *n.* The act of portraying; delineation; representation. — **Portrayer,** pōr-trā'ėr, *n.* One who portrays.

Portreeve, pōrt'rēv, *n.* [*Port* and *reeve.*] The chief magistrate of a port or maritime town.

Portuguese, por'tū-gēz, *a.* Of or pertaining to Portugal. — *Portuguese hymn*, the hymn *Adeste Fideles*, 'O come all ye faithful'.—*Portuguese man-of-war*, a species of Physalia.—*n.* The language of Portugal; the people of Portugal.

Pory. Under PORE.

Pose, pōz, *v.t.*—*posed*, *posing.* [Fr. *poser*, to place, to put a question, from L. *pauso*, to halt, to stop, from *pausa*, a pause; but the meaning, as well as that of the compounds, has been influenced by *pono*, *positum*, to put, place, set, which gives *position*, &c. This word is seen in *compose*, *depose*, *dispose*, *repose*, &c. PAUSE.] To embarrass by a difficult question; to cause to be at a loss; to puzzle.—**Poser,** pō'zėr, *n.* One that poses or puzzles by asking difficult questions; something that puzzles, as a difficult question.

Pose, pōz, *n.* [Fr. *pose*, an attitude, from L. *pausa.* See above.] Attitude or position taken naturally, or assumed for effect; an artistic posture or attitude.—*v.i.*—*posed*, *posing.* [Fr. *poser.*] To attitudinize; to assume characteristic airs.—*v.t.* To cause to assume a certain posture; to place so as to have a striking effect.

Posit, poz'it, *v.t.* [L. *pono*, *positum*, to place. POSITION.] To lay down as a position or principle; to present to the consciousness as an absolute fact.

Position, pō-zish'on, *n.* [Fr. *position*, L. *positio*, from *pono*, *positum*, to place, set, which appears as *-pound* in *compound*, &c., as *-pone* in *postpone*, and is seen also in *deposit*, *opposite*, *positive*, *post*, *posture*, &c.] State of being placed; situation: generally with reference to other objects, or to different parts of the same object; relation with regard to other persons, or to some subject; manner of standing or being placed; attitude; that on which one takes one's stand; hence, principle laid down; predication; affirmation; place or standing in society; social rank; state; condition of affairs; *arith.* a mode of solving a question by one or two suppositions.

Positive, poz'i-tiv, *a.* [Fr. *positif*; L.L. *positivus*, from L. *pono*, *positum*. POSITION.] Definitely laid down or expressed; direct; explicit: opposed to *implied*; not admitting any condition or discretion; express; absolute; real; existing in fact; not negative; direct (*positive* proof); confident; fully assured; dogmatic; over-confident in opinion or assertion; demonstrable; distinctly ascertained or ascertainable; *photog.* having the lights and shades rendered as they are in nature: opposed to *negative.*—*Positive degree*, *gram.* is the form of an adjective which denotes simple or absolute quality, without comparison or relation to increase or diminution, as wise, noble.—*Positive electricity*, electricity produced by rubbing glass; vitreous electricity; as distinguished from *negative* or *resinous* electricity; also the electricity which a body contains above its natural quantity.—*Positive philosophy*, a philosophical system founded by Auguste Comte (1798-1857), which limits itself strictly to human experience, denies all metaphysics and all search for first or for final causes.—*Positive pole of a voltaic pile or battery.* Under POLE.—*Positive quantity*, in *alg.* an affirmative or additive quantity, which character is indicated by the sign + (plus) prefixed to the quantity, called in consequence the *positive sign.* — *Positive rays*, streams of positively charged atoms and molecules in the electric discharge tube.—*n.* *Gram.* the positive degree; *photog.* a picture in which the lights and shades are rendered as they are in nature: opposed to *negative.*—**Positively,** poz'i-tiv-li, *adv.* In a positive manner; absolutely; really; not negatively; expressly; with full conviction. — **Positiveness,** poz'i-tiv-nes, *n.* The state of being positive. — **Positivism,** poz'i-tiv-izm, *n.* The *positive philosophy.*—**Positivist,** poz'i-tiv-ist, *n.* One who maintains the doctrines of positive philosophy.

Posology, po-sol'o-ji, *n.* [Gr. *posos*, how much, and *logos*, discourse.] The doctrine of proportions; the science of quantity.—**Posologic, Posological,** pos-o-loj'ik, pos-o-loj'i-kal, *a.* Pertaining to posology. (*Bentham.*)

Posse, pos'sē. [L., to be able.] A number of people; a small body of men.—*Posse comitatus*, *lit.* the power of a county; *law*, the body of men which the sheriff is empowered to raise in case of riot, &c.

Possess, poz-zes', *v.t.* [L. *possideo*, *possessum*, to occupy, to possess—*pos* for *por*, before, near, and *sedeo*, to sit (as in *reside*, *preside*, &c.).] To occupy in person; to have and hold; to have as a piece of property or as a personal belonging; to be owner of; to own; to affect strongly (fear *possessed* them); to pervade; to fill or take up entirely; to have full power or mastery over; as, an evil spirit, evil influence, violent passion, &c. (*possessed* with a fury); to put in possession; to make master or owner: with *of* before the thing, and now generally in the passive or with reflexive pronouns (to be *possessed of* a large fortune; to *possess one's self of* another's property); to furnish or fill; to imbue or instil into: with *with* before the thing.—**Possession,** poz-zesh'on, *n.* The having or holding of property; the state of owning or having in one's hands or power; the thing possessed; land, estate, or goods owned; the state of being mastered by some evil spirit or influence.—*To take possession*, to enter on the possession of property; to assume ownership.—*To give possession*, to put in another's power or occupancy.—**Possessionary**, poz-zesh'on-a-ri, *a.* Relating to or implying possession.—**Possessive**, poz-zes'iv, *a.* [L. *possessivus.*] Pertaining to possession; expressing possession. —*Possessive case*, the genitive case, or case of nouns and pronouns which expresses possession, ownership (*John's* book), or some relation of one thing to another (*Homer's* admirers).—*Possessive pronoun*, a pronoun denoting possession or property, as *my, thy*, &c.—*n.* A pronoun or other word denoting possession.—**Possessively**, poz-zes'iv-li, *adv.* In a manner denoting possession.—**Possessor**, poz-zes'ėr, *n.* One who possesses.—**Possessory**, poz-zes'o-ri, *a.* Pertaining to possession.

Posset, pos'et, *n.* [Comp. W. *posel*, curdled milk, a posset, from *posiaw*, to gather.] A drink composed of hot milk curdled by some infusion, as wine or other liquor.—*v.t.* To curdle; to coagulate. (*Shak.*)

Possible, pos'i-bl, *a.* [L. *possibilis*, from *posse*, to be able, from *potis*, able, and *esse*, to be; akin *power.*] That may be or exist; that may be now, or may happen or come to pass; that may be done; not contrary to the nature of things; capable of coming to pass, but improbable.—**Possibly**, pos'i-bli, *adv.* In a possible manner; perhaps; perchance.—**Possibility**, pos-i-bil'i-ti, *n.* The state or condition of being possible; a chance of happening; a thing possible; that which may take place or come into being.

Post, pōst, *n.* [A.Sax. *post*, from L. *postis*, post, a door-post, from *pono, positum*, to place, set. POSITION.] A piece of timber, metal, or other solid substance set upright, and often intended to support something else.

Post, pōst, *n.* [From Fr. *poste* (masc.), a military post or station, an office, and *poste* (fem.), a letter-carrier, a post-house, a post-office, &c., both from L.L. *posta*, for *posita*, from L. *positum*, placed. POST, above.] The place at which some person or thing is stationed or fixed; a station or position occupied, especially a military station; the place where a single soldier or a body of troops is stationed; a bugle-call giving notice to soldiers to retire to their quarters for the night, sounded at tattoo, there being a first post and a last post, the latter sounded also at military funerals; an office or employment; an appointment; a berth; a messenger or a carrier of letters and papers; one that goes at stated times to convey the mails or despatches; a postman; an established system for the public conveyance of letters; the mail; a post-office; a size of writing and printing paper, measuring about 18¾ inches by 15¼.—*To ride post*, to be employed to carry despatches and papers; and as such carriers rode in haste, hence the phrase signifies to ride in haste, to pass with expedition. *Post* is thus used adverbially for swiftly, expeditiously, or expressly (to travel *post*).—*v.i.* [Fr. *poster*, to post.] To travel with post-horses; to travel with speed; to rise and sink on the saddle in accordance with the motion of the horse, especially when trotting.—*v.t.* To fix up in a public place, as a notice or advertisement; to expose to public reproach; to expose to opprobrium by some public action; to place; to station (to *post* troops on a hill); *book-keeping*, to carry (accounts or items) from the journal to the ledger; to make the requisite entries in, for showing a true state of affairs; to place in the post-office; to transmit by post (to *post* letters).—*To post up, in book-keeping*, to make the requisite entries in up to date; hence, to make one master of all the details of a subject.—**Postage**, pōs'tāj, *n.* The charge levied on letters or other articles conveyed by post.—**Postage-stamp**, *n.* An adhesive stamp of various values issued by the post-office department for affixing to letters, packets, &c., as payment of cost of transmission.—**Postal**, pōst'al, *a.* Relating to a post office or the carrying of mails.—**Postboy**, pōst'boi, *n.* A boy that carries letters; a boy or man that drives a post chaise.—**Post card**, *n.* Any card, to which a stamp may be affixed, transmitted through the mail; also, officially *Postal card*, a similar card, on which a stamp has been printed, issued by the government.—**Post chaise**, *n.* A chaise for conveying travelers from one station to another. (*Historical.*)—**Poster**, pōst'ėr, *n.* One who posts; a courier; a post horse; a large printed bill or placard posted for advertising.—**Poste restante**, post res-tänt', *n.* [Fr.] A department in a post office where letters so addressed are kept till the owners call for them.—**Postfree**, *a.* Franked; paying no postage.—**Posthaste**, *n.* Haste or speed in traveling, like that of a post or courier.—*adv.* With speed or expedition.—**Post horn**, *n.* A horn blown by drivers or guards of mailcoaches, &c.—**Post horse**, *n.* A horse for conveying travelers rapidly from one station to another, and let for hire.—**Post house**, **Posting house**, *n.* A house where relays of post horses are kept for the convenience of travelers.—**Postman**, pōst'man, *n.* A post or courier; a letter-carrier.—**Postmark**, pōst'märk, *n.* The mark or stamp of a post office on a letter.—**Postmaster**, pōst'mas-tėr, *n.* The officer who has the superintendence and direction of a post office.—**Postmaster general**, *n.* The chief executive head of a postal system; one of the members of the cabinet of the President of the United States of America, having charge of the Post Office Department.—**Post office**, *n.* An office or house where letters are received for transmission to various parts, and from which letters are delivered that have been received from places at home and abroad; a department of the government charged with the conveyance of letters, &c., by post.—*General post office.* Under GENERAL.—*Post-office order. Money order*, under MONEY.—**Postpaid**, *a.* Having the postage prepaid.—**Post road**, **Post route**, *n.* A road along which the mail is carried.—**Post town**, *n.* A town in which a post office is established.

Postdate, pōst'dāt, *v.t.*—*postdated, postdating.* [Prefix *post*, after, and *date.*] To affix a date to later than or in advance of the real time; to date so as to make appear earlier than the fact.

Postdiluvial, **Postdiluvian**, pōst-di-lū'vi-al, pōst-di-lū'vi-an, *a.* [L. *post*, after, and *diluvium*, the deluge.] Being or happening posterior to the flood in Noah's days. —**Postdiluvian**, *n.* A person who lived or has lived since the flood.

Posterior, pos-tē'ri-ėr, *a.* [L. *posterior*, compar. of *posterus*, from *post*, after.] Later or subsequent in time; opposed to *prior*; later in order; coming after; situated behind; hinder (the *posterior* portion of the skull); opposed to *anterior*.—*A posteriori.* A PRIORI.—**Posteriority**, pos-tē'ri-or"i-ti, *n.* The state of being later or subsequent.—**Posteriorly**, pos-tē'ri-ėr-li, *adv.* Subsequently in time; behind.—**Posteriors**, pos-tē'ri-ėrz, *n.pl.* The hinder part of an animal's body.—**Posterity**, pos-ter'i-ti, *n.* [L. *posteritas*, from *posterus*, later.] Descendants; the race that proceeds from a progenitor; succeeding generations.

Postern, pōs'tėrn, *n.* [O.Fr. *posterne*, from L.L. *posterna, posterula*, a secret means of exit, from L. *posterus*, behind, posterior, from *post*, behind.] Primarily, a back door or gate; a private entrance; hence, any small door or gate; *fort.* a covered passage leading under a rampart to the ditch in front.

Post-existence, pōst-eg-zis'tens, *n.* Subsequent or future existence.—**Post-existent**,† pōst-eg-zis'tent, *a.* Existing or living after.

Post-fix, pōst'fix, *n.* [Prefix *post*, after, and *fix.*] *Gram.* an affix or suffix.—*v.t.* To add or annex to the end of a word.

Postglacial, pōst-glā'shi-al, *a.* *Geol.* belonging to a section of the posttertiary deposits. GLACIAL.

Postgraduate, pōst-grad'ū-āt, *n.* One who engages in advanced academic studies after receiving a degree, usually bachelor's.—*a.* Pertaining to such a student or to such studies.

Posthumous, pos'tū-mus, *n.* [L. *postumus*, last, superl. of *posterus*, coming after, from *post*, behind.] Born after the death of the father; published after the death of the author (*posthumous* works); being or continuing after one's decease (*posthumous* fame).—**Posthumously**, pos'tū-mus-li, *adv.* After one's decease.

Postilion, **Postillion**, pōs-til'yon, *n.* [Fr. *postillon*, from *poste*, a post.] The rider of the near lead horse of a traveling or other carriage.

Postliminium, **Postliminy**, pōst-li-min'i-um, pōst-lim'i-ni, *n.* [L., from *post*, after, and *limen*, end, limit.] That right by virtue of which persons and things taken by an enemy in war are restored to their former state.

Postmeridian, pōst-me-rid'i-an, *a.* [L. *postmeridianus.* MERIDIAN.] Coming after the sun has passed the meridian; being or belonging to the afternoon.—*n.* The afternoon.

Post-mortem, pōst-mor'tem, *a.* [L. *post*, after, *mors*, death.] After death.—*Post-mortem examination*, an examination of a body made after death.

Post-natal, pōst-nā'tal, *a.* Subsequent to birth.

Post-nuptial, pōst-nup'shal, *a.* Being or happening after marriage.

Post-obit, pōst-ob'it, *n.* [L. *post obitum*, after death.] A bond given for the purpose of securing to a lender a sum of money on the death of some specified individual from whom the borrower has expectations.

Post-pleiocene, **Post-pliocene**, pōst-pli'ō-sēn, *n.* and *a.* *Geol.* PLEISTOCENE.

Postpone, pōst-pōn', *v.t.*—*postponed, postponing.* [L. *postpono*—*post*, after, and *pono*, to put. POSITION.] To put off; to defer to a future or later time.—**Postponement**, pōst-pōn'ment, *n.* The act of postponing or deferring to a future time.—**Postponer**, pōst-pō'nėr, *n.* One who postpones.

Post-position, pōst-pō-zish'on, *n.* The act of placing after; the state of being put behind; *gram.* a word or particle placed after or at the end of a word.—**Post-positional**, pōst-pō-zish'on-al, *a.* Pertaining to a post-position.—**Post-positive**, pōst-poz'i-tiv, *a.* Placed after something else as a word.

Post-prandial, pōst-pran'di-al, *a.* [L. *post*, after, and *prandium*, a dinner.] Happening after dinner.

Postscenium, pōst-sē'ni-um, *n.* [L., from *post*, behind, and *scena*, a scene.] *Arch.* the back part of a theatre behind the scenes.

Postscript, pōst'skript, *n.* [L. *post*, after, and *scriptum*, written.] A paragraph added to a letter after it is concluded and signed by the writer; any addition made to a book or composition after it had been supposed to be finished; something appended.

Post-tertiary, pōst-tėr'shi-a-ri, *a.* *Geol.* coming after the tertiary; a term applied to the various superficial deposits in which all the mollusca are of still living species.

Post-tonic, pōst-ton'ik, *a.* Following the tonic or accented syllable.

Postulate, pos'tū-lāt, *n.* [L. *postulatum*, a demand, from *postulo*, to demand, from *posco*, to ask.] A position or supposition of which the truth is demanded or assumed for the purpose of future reasoning; a necessary assumption; *geom.* something of the nature of a problem assumed or taken for granted; the enunciation of a self-evident problem.—*v.t.*—*postulated, postulating.* To beg or assume without proof; to regard as self-evident, or as too obvious to require further proof.—**Postulant**, pos'tū-lant, *n.* One who demands or requests; a candidate.—**Postulation**, pos-tū-lā'shon, *n.* The act of postulating or supposing without proof; supplication; intercession.—**Postulatory**, pos'tū-la-to-ri, *a.* Postulating; assuming or assumed without proof.

Posture, pos'tūr, *n.* [Fr. *posture*, from L. *positura*, a placing, from *pono*, *positum*, to place. POSITION.] The disposition of the several parts of the body with respect to each other, or with respect to a particular purpose; pose of a model or figure used by an artist; attitude; situation; condition; particular state with regard to something else (the *posture* of affairs).—*v.t.*—*postured*, *posturing*. To place in a particular posture. —*v.i.* To dispose the body in particular postures; to contort the body into artificial attitudes; to behave in an artificial manner.—**Posture-making**, *n.* The act or practice of posturing, or of making contortions of the body.—**Posturer**, **Posturist**, pos'tūr-ėr, pos'tūr-ist, *n.* One who postures; especially one who behaves and comports himself in a highly artificial manner. —**Postural**, pos'tū-ral, *a.* Pertaining or relating to posture.

Post-war, pōst-wạr', *a.* Belonging to the period after a war, especially the World War.

Posy, pō'zi, *n.* [Corrupted from *poesy*, being originally a piece of poetry.] A poetical quotation or motto attached to or inscribed on something, as on a ring; a motto or verse sent with a nosegay; hence, a bunch of flowers; sometimes a single flower, as for a button-hole.

Pot, pot, *n.* [A widely spread word, the origin of which is not clear = Fr. *pot*, D. *pot*, Dan. *potte*, Icel. *pottr*, W. *pot*, Ir. *pota*, a pot.] A hollow vessel more deep than broad, used for various domestic and other purposes (an iron *pot* for boiling meat or vegetables; an earthen *pot* for plants, called a *flower-pot*, &c.); a mug; a jug containing a specified quantity of liquor; the quantity contained in a pot; definitely, a quart (a *pot* of porter); a size of paper, 12½ inches by 15 inches the sheet: said to have had originally a pot as watermark; the metal or earthenware top of a chimney.—*To go to pot*, to be destroyed or ruined; to come to an ill end; the pot being here probably that in which old metal is melted down. (*Colloq.*) —*v.t.*—*potted*, *potting*. To put into pots; to preserve seasoned in pots (*potted* fowl and fish); to plant or cover in pots of earth. **Pot-ale**, *n.* The refuse from a grain distillery, used to fatten swine. — **Pot-bellied**, *a.* Having a prominent belly.—**Pot-belly**, *n.* A protuberant belly.—**Pot-boy**, pot'boi, *n.* A boy or man who carries pots of ale or beer for sale; a menial in a public-house.—**Pot-herb**, *n.* A herb for the pot and for cookery; a culinary plant.—**Pot-hole**, *n.* A circular cavity in the rocky beds of rivers formed by stones being whirled round by the action of the current. —**Pot-hook**, *n.* A hook on which pots and kettles are hung over the fire; a letter or character like a pot-hook, written by children in learning to write.—**Pot-house**, *n.* An ale-house; a tavern.—**Pot-hunter**, *n.* A sportsman who has more regard to winning prizes than to mere sport.—**Pot-lid**, *n.* The lid or cover of a pot.—**Pot-luck**, *n.* What may chance to be in the pot or provided for a meal.—*To take pot-luck*, is for an unexpected visitor to partake of the family meal, whatever it may chance to be. (*Colloq.*) — **Pot-metal**, *n.* An inferior kind of brass; a species of stained glass, the colours of which are incorporated within the glass when in the melting-pot in a state of fusion; a kind of cast-iron suitable for making hollow-ware. — **Pot-pourri**, pō-pō-rē, *n.* [Fr. *pot*, pot, and *pourrir*, to putrefy, to boil very much; from L. *putere*, to rot.] A dish of different kinds of meat and vegetables cooked together; hence, a miscellaneous collection; a medley.—**Pot-sherd**, pot'shėrd, *n.* [*Pot*, and *sherd* = *shard*, *shred*, a fragment.] A piece or fragment of an earthenware pot.—**Pot-stone**, pot'stōn, *n.* A coarsely granular variety of steatite or soapstone, sometimes manufactured into kitchen vessels (hence the name). —**Potter**, pot'ėr, *n.* [From *pot*.] One whose occupation is to make earthenware vessels or crockery of any kind; one who pots viands. — *Potters' clay*, a variety of clay of a reddish or gray colour which becomes red when heated.—*Potters' wheel*, an apparatus consisting of a vertical iron axis, on which is a horizontal disc made to revolve by treadles, the clay being placed on the disc.—**Pottery**, pot'ėr-i, *n.* The ware or vessels made by potters; earthenware glazed and baked; the place where earthen vessels are manufactured; the business of a potter. — **Pot-valiant**, *a.* Courageous over drink; heated to valour by strong drink.—**Pot-walloper**, **Pot-waller**, pot-wol'lop-ėr, pot'wol-ėr, *n.* [*Pot*, and *wallop*, to boil; akin to *gallop*.] A parliamentary voter in some English boroughs before 1832, who was admitted to vote on proof that he had boiled a pot within the borough bounds during the six months preceding the election.

Potable, pō'ta-bl, *a.* [L.L. *potabilis*, from L. *poto*, to drink, whence *potion*, *poison*.] Drinkable; suitable for drinking; capable of being drunk.—*n.* Something that may be drunk.—**Potableness**, pō'ta-bl-nes, *n.* The quality of being drinkable.—**Potation**, pō-tā'shon, *n.* The act of drinking; a drinking bout; a draught; a drink.—**Potatory**, pō'tā-to-ri, *a.* Relating to drinking.

Potamography, pot-a-mog'ra-fi, *n.* [Gr. *potamos*, a river, and *graphō*, to describe.] A description of rivers.—**Potamology**, pot-a-mol'o-ji, *n.* The science of rivers.

Potash, pot'ash, *n.* [*Pot*, and *ash*, from being prepared by evaporating the lixivium of wood-ashes in iron pots.] Alkali in an impure state, procured from the ashes of plants by lixiviation and evaporation, largely employed in the manufacture of flint-glass and soap, bleaching, making alum, &c.—*Potash water*, an aerated beverage consisting of carbonic acid water, to which is added bicarbonate of potash.

Potassa, pō-tas'sa, *n.* The older name for *Potash*.

Potassium, pō-tas'si-um, *n.* [A latinized term from *potash*.] The metallic basis of potash, a soft white metal resembling polished silver which rapidly oxidizes when exposed to the air.—**Potassic**, pō-tas'ik, *a.* Relating to potassium; containing potassium.

Potation. Under POTABLE.

Potato, pō-tā'tō, *n.* pl. **Potatoes**, pō-tā'tōz. [Sp. *patata*, *batata*; said to be a Haytian word.] Originally the plant called sweet-potato, but now transferred to the well-known esculent plant whose tubers constitute such cheap and nourishing food; a tuber of this plant.—*Potato beetle*, *potato bug*. COLORADO BEETLE.—*Potato disease*, *potato blight*, *potato murrain*, a disease caused by a microscopic fungus which affects potatoes.

Poteen, **Potteen**, **Potheen**, po-tēn', *n.* [From Ir. *potaim*, to drink.] Whisky illicitly distilled by the Irish peasantry; whisky generally. (*Irish.*)

Potent, pō'tent, *a.* [L. *potens*, powerful, pres. part. of *posse*, to be able, from *potis*, able (same root as E. *father*, L. *pater*), and *esse*, to be. *Potent* is seen in *impotent*, *omnipotent*. POWER.] Powerful, in a physical or moral sense; efficacious; having great authority, interest, or the like.—**Potency**, **Potentness**, pō'ten-si, pō'tent-nes, *n.* The state or quality of being potent.—**Potentate**, pō'ten-tāt, *n.* [Fr. *potentat*.] A person who possesses great power or sway; a prince; a sovereign; an emperor, king, or monarch.—**Potential**, pō-ten'shal, *a.* [L. *potentia*, power.] Being in possibility, not in actuality; latent; that may be manifested; in *electrostatics*, at a given point, the work required to bring a unit of positive electricity from an infinite distance to that point under given conditions of electrification.—*Potential energy*, energy of position, the energy of a system which is due only to the positions of its particles; the difference between total energy and kinetic energy.—*Potential mood*, that form of the verb which is used to express the power, possibility, liberty, or necessity of an action or of being (I *may go*; he *can write*).—*n.* Anything that may be possible; a possibility. — **Potentiality**, pō-ten'shi-al"i-ti, *n.* State of being potential; possibility, not actuality; inherent power or quality not actually exhibited.—**Potentially**, pō-ten'shal-li, *adv.* In a potential manner; in possibility, not in act. — **Potentiary**, pō-ten'shi-a-ri, *n.* One having or assuming power, authority, or influence.—**Potentiate**,† pō-ten'shi-āt, *v.t.* To give power to.—**Potentiometer**, pō-ten'shi-om"et-ėr, *n.* [From *potential*, and *meter*.] An electrical instrument which can be used to measure pressure, current, or resistance.—**Potentite**, pō'ten-tīt, *n.* [L. *potens*, powerful.] A powerful blasting substance.—**Potently**, pō'tent-li, *adv.* In a potent manner; powerfully.

Potentilla, pō-ten-til'la, *n.* [From L. *potens*, powerful, from the supposed medicinal qualities of some of the species.] An extensive genus of herbaceous perennials, of which one species is used in Lapland and the Orkney Islands to tan and dye leather.

Pother, poTH'ėr, *n.* [A different form of *bother* or of *potter*.] Bustle; confusion; tumult; flutter.—*v.i.* To make a pother or bustle; to make a stir.—*v.t.* To bother; to puzzle; to tease.

Potion, pō'shon, *n.* [L. *potio*, a drinking, a draught, from *poto*, to drink. *Poison* is the same word.] A draught; a liquid medicine; a dose to be drunk.

Potoroo, pot'o-rö, *n.* The native name of the bettong or kangaroo-rat.

Pot-pourri, **Potsherd**. Under POT.

Pott, pot, *n.* A size of paper. Under POT.

Pottage, pot'āj, *n.* [Fr. *potage*, lit. what one puts in the *pot*.] A species of food made of meat boiled to softness in water, usually with some vegetables; also, oatmeal or other porridge.

Potteen, *n.* POTEEN.

Potter, **Pottery**, &c. Under POT.

Potter, pot'ėr, *v.i.* [Comp. Sw. *pota*, D. *poteren*, *peuteren*, to poke or search with the finger or a stick; W. *pwtio*, to poke or thrust. PUT.] To busy or perplex one's self about trifles; to work with little energy or effect; to trifle.

Pottle, pot'l, *n.* [Fr. *potel*, a dim. of *pot*.] Originally a liquid measure of two quarts; hence, any large tankard; a vessel or small basket for holding fruit.

Potto, pot'tō, *n.* The kinkajou.

Pouch, pouch, *n.* [A softened form of *poke*, a bag, a pouch.] A small bag; a pocket; a bag or sac belonging to or forming an appendage of certain animals, as that of a marsupial animal.—*v.t.* To put into a pouch or pocket.—**Pouched**, poucht, *a.* Having a pouch; furnished with a pouch for carrying the young, as the marsupials.

Poulp, **Poulpe**, pölp, *n.* [Fr. *poulpé*, from L. *polypus*. POLYPUS.] An eight-footed cuttle-fish; an octopus.

Poulsen arc, poul'sen, *n.* [After *Poulsen*, Danish electrician.] A direct-current electric arc which generates high-frequency oscillations.

Poult, pōlt, *n.* [Fr. *poulet*, a dim. of *poule*, a hen. POULTRY.] A young chicken, partridge, grouse, &c.

Poultice, pōl'tis, *n.* [From L. *puls*, *pultis*, pottage, gruel, pap.] A soft composition of meal, bread, or the like mollifying substance, to be applied to sores, inflamed parts of the body, &c.; a cataplasm.—*v.t.* —*poulticed*, *poulticing*. To cover with a poultice; to apply a poultice to.

Poultry, pōl'tri, *n.* [A collective from *poult*, pullet, from Fr. *poulet*, a chicken, from *poule*, a hen, L. *pullus*, a young animal, a chicken; akin to Gr. *pōlos*, E. *foal*.] Domestic fowls which are reared for their flesh as an article of food, for their eggs, feathers, &c., such as cocks and hens, turkeys, ducks, and geese.—**Poultry-yard**, *n.*

A yard or place where fowls are reared.—**Poulterer**, pōl′tėr-ėr, *n.* One who makes it his business to sell fowls for the table.

Pounce, pouns, *n.* [Fr. *ponce*, It. *pomice*; from L. *pumex*, *pumicis*, a pumice-stone.] A fine powder, such as pulverized cuttle-fish bone, used to prevent ink from spreading on paper, but now almost entirely superseded by blotting-paper.—*v.t.*—*pounced, pouncing.* To sprinkle or rub with pounce.—**Pounce-box, Pouncet-box**, *n.* A small box with a perforated lid, used for sprinkling pounce on paper, or to hold perfume for smelling.

Pounce, pouns, *n.* [Ultimately from L. *pungo*, *punctum*, to prick or pierce; comp. Fr. *poinçon*, a bodkin; Sp. *punzar*, to prick, to pierce. PUNCTURE, PUNCH, POINT.] The claw or talon of a bird of prey.—*v.t.*—*pounced, pouncing.* To seize or strike suddenly with the claws or talons: said of birds of prey.—*v.i.* To fall on and seize with the claws or talons; to dart or dash on: with *on* or *upon*.—**Pounced**, pounst, *a.* Furnished with claws or talons.

Pound, pound, *n.* [A.Sax., Dan., Sw., Icel., and Goth. *pund*; G. *pfund*; from L. *pondo*, a pound, akin to L. *pondus*, a weight. PONDEROUS, PENDANT.] A standard weight consisting of 12 ounces troy, or 16 ounces avoirdupois; the British monetary unit consisting of 20 shillings, the equivalent (at par) of 4.86 American dollars. The *pound Scots* was only equal to a twelfth of the pound sterling, that is 1*s.* 8*d.*—**Poundage**, poun′dāj, *n.* A sum deducted from a pound, or a certain sum or rate per pound; payment rated by the weight of a commodity.—**Poundal**, poun′dal, *n.* In *physics*, the unit of force, equal to the force which in one second produces in one pound a velocity of one foot per second; equal to 1/gth of the pound weight.—**Pounder**, poun′dėr, *n.* A person or thing denominated from a certain number of pounds; often applied to pieces of ordnance along with a number to express the weight of the shell they fire (a 64-*pounder*, a cannon firing shells weighing 64 lbs.).

Pound, pound, *n.* [A.Sax. *pund*, an inclosure; a different form of *pond.*] An inclosure in which cattle are confined when taken in trespassing, or going at large in violation of law; a penfold or pinfold.—*v.t.* To shut up as in a pound; to confine in a public penfold; to impound.—**Poundage**, poun′dāj, *n.* Confinement of cattle in a pound; a mulct levied upon the owners of cattle impounded.

Pound, pound, *v.t.* [A.Sax. *punian*, to beat, bray; the *d* has become attached, as in *sound*, *compound*. Hence *pun.*] To beat; to strike repeatedly with some heavy instrument; to comminute and pulverize by beating; to bruise or break into fine parts by a heavy instrument.—**Pounder**, poun′dėr, *n.* One who or that which pounds.

Pour, pōr, *v.t.* [Perhaps from W. *bwrw*, to cast, to shed, as in *bwrw dagrau*, to shed tears; *bwrw gwlaw*, to rain.] To cause to flow, as a liquid, either out of a vessel or into it; to send forth in a stream or continued succession; to emit; to give vent to, as under the influence of strong feeling; to throw in profusion.—*v.i.* To flow; to issue forth in a stream; to gush; to rush in continued procession.—**Pourer**, pō′rėr, *n.* One who or that which pours.

Pourparler, pör-pär-lā, *n.* [Fr. from *pour*, for, and *parler*, to speak.] A preliminary conference tending to pave the way to subsequent negotiation.

Poursuivant. PURSUIVANT.

Pourtray, pör-trā′, *v.t.* PORTRAY.

Poussette, pö-set′, *n.* [Comp. Fr. *poussette*, a child's game with pins, from *pousser*, to push.] A figure executed by a couple who swing together in a country-dance.—*v.i.*—*poussetted, poussetting.* To swing round in couples, as in a country-dance.

Pout, pout, *v.i.* [From W. *pwtiaw*, to push, or from dial. Fr. *pout*, *potte*, Pr. *pot*, the lip.] To thrust out the lips, as in sullenness, contempt, or displeasure; hence, to look sullen; to swell out, as the lips; to be prominent.—*n.* A protrusion of the lips as in sullenness; a fit of sullenness.—**Pouter**, pout′ėr, *n.* One who pouts; a variety of pigeon, so called from its inflated breast.—**Poutingly**, pout′ing-li, *adv.* In a pouting or sullen manner.

Poverty, pov′ėr-ti, *n.* [Fr. *pauvreté*, L. *paupertas*, from *pauper*, poor. POOR.] The state of being poor or indigent; indigence; a deficiency of necessary or desirable elements; barrenness (*poverty* of soil); poorness; want of ideas or information; want or defect of words (*poverty* of language).—

Poverty-stricken, *a.* Reduced to a state of poverty; indigent.

Powan, pou′an, *n.* [A form of *pollan.*] The fresh-water herring of Loch Lomond.

Powder, pou′dėr, *n.* [Fr. *poudre*, O.Fr. *pouldre*, It. *polvēre*, from L. *pulvis*, *pulveris*, dust, powder.] Any dry substance composed of minute particles; a substance comminuted or triturated to fine particles; gunpowder; face-powder.—*v.t.* To reduce to fine particles; to pulverize; to sprinkle with powder or as with powder; to sprinkle with salt, as meat.—*v.i.* To fall to dust; to become like powder; to pat or rub powder on the face.—**Powder-box**, *n.* A box in which face-powder is kept.—**Powdered**, pou′dėrd, *p.* and *a.* Reduced to powder; sprinkled with powder.—**Powder blue**, *n.* Powdered smalt, as generally used in laundering; pale blue blended with gray.—**Powder-flask**, *n.* A flask in which gunpowder is carried.—**Powder-horn**, *n.* A horn in which gunpowder used to be carried by sportsmen before the introduction of cartridges.—**Powder-magazine**, *n.* A place where powder is stored; a bomb-proof building in fortified places.—**Powder-mill**, *n.* A mill in which gunpowder is made.—**Powder-room**, *n.* The apartment in a ship where gunpowder is kept.—**Powdery**, pou′dėr-i, *a.* Sprinkled or covered with powder; resembling powder; *bot.* having a surface covered with fine powder.

Power, pou′ėr, *n.* [O.Fr. *pooir* (Mod.Fr. *pouvoir*), from old infinitive *podir*, from L.L. *potēre*, to be able, used for L. *posse*, to be able, from *potis*, able, and *esse*, to be; akin *possible*, *potent*, &c. POTENT.] Ability to act; the faculty of doing or performing something; that in virtue of which one can; capability of producing an effect; strength, force, or energy manifested in action; capacity; susceptibility (great *power* of resistance); natural strength; animal strength; influence; prodominance (as of the mind, imagination); faculty of the mind as manifested by a particular mode of operation (the *power* of thinking); ability; capability; the employment of strength or influence among men; command; the right of governing or actual government; dominion; rule; authority; one who or that which exercises authority or control (the *powers* that be); a sovereign, or the sovereign authority of a state; a state (the great *powers* of Europe); a spirit or superhuman agent having a certain sway (celestial *powers*); legal authority; warrant; *mech.* that which produces motion or force, or that which may be applied to produce it; a mechanical agent; the moving force applied to produce the required effect; mechanical advantage or effect; force or effect considered as resulting from the action of a machine; rate of doing work; the unit for practical purposes in the U. S. is HORSE-POWER (which see); *arith.* and *alg.* the product arising from the multiplication of a number or quantity into itself; *optics*, the degree to which an optical instrument magnifies the apparent dimensions of an object.—*Power of attorney*, authority given to a person to act for another. ATTORNEY.—*European powers*, a term in modern diplomacy by which are usually meant Great Britain, France, Germany, Russia, and Italy.—**Powerful**, pou′ėr-ful, *a.* Having great power; able to produce great effects; strong; potent; energetic; efficacious.—**Powerfully**, pou′ėr-ful-li, *adv.* In a powerful manner; with great effect; forcibly.—**Powerfulness**, pou′ėr-ful-nes, *n.* The quality of being powerful.—**Powerless**, pou′ėr-les, *a.* Destitute of power; weak; impotent.—**Powerlessly**, pou′ėr-les-li, *adv.* In a powerless manner.—**Powerlessness**, pou′ėr-les-nes, *n.*—**Power-loom**, *n.* A loom worked by water, steam, or some mechanical power.

Powter, pout′ėr, *n.* POUTER.

Pow-wow, pou′wou, *n.* A priest or conjurer among the North American Indians; also, a public feast, festival, or conference.

Pox, poks, *n.* [A peculiar spelling of *pocks*, pl. of *pock*—used as a sing.] Eruptive pustules on the body; a disease characterized by pustules, the term being restricted to three or four diseases, as the small-pox, chicken-pox, &c.

Pozzuolana, Pozzolana, pot′zų-o-lä″na, pot-zo-lä′na, *n.* A volcanic product occurring near *Pozzuoli*, on the Gulf of Naples, largely employed in the manufacture of Roman or hydraulic cement.

Praam präm, *n.* [D.] PRAM.

Practicable, prak′ti-ka-bl, *a.* [From L.L. *practicare*, to transact, from L. *practicus*, active; Gr. *praktikos*, active, practical, from *prassō*, to do, to work.] Capable of being effected or performed by human means, or by powers that can be applied; feasible; capable of being passed or travelled over; passable; assailable.—**Practicability, Practicableness**, prak′ti-ka-bil″i-ti, prak′ti-ka-bl-nes, *n.* The quality of being practicable; feasibility.—**Practicably**, prak′ti-ka-bli, *adv.* In a practicable manner.—**Practical**, prak′ti-kal, *a.* [L. *practicus.*] Relating to practice, use, or employment; opposed to *speculative, ideal*, or *theoretical*; that may be turned to use; reducible to use in the conduct of life; given to or concerned with action or practice; capable of reducing knowledge or theories to actual use; educated by practice or experience; skilled in actual work (a *practical* gardener); derived from practice or experience.—*Practical joke.* Under JOKE.—**Practically**, prak′ti-kal-li, *adv.* In a practical manner; not merely theoretically; so far as actual results or effects are concerned; in effect.—**Practicality, Practicalness**, prak-ti-kal′i-ti, prak′ti-kal-nes, *n.* The quality of being practical.—**Practice**, prak′tis, *n.* [Formerly *practicke, practike*, from O.Fr. *practique*, from Gr. *praktikē*, practical knowledge.] A piece of conduct; a proceeding; a customary action; custom or habit; use or usage; state of being used; customary use; method or art of doing anything; actual performance (as opposed to *theory*); exercise of any profession (the *practice* of law); application of remedies; medical treatment of diseases; drill; exercise for instruction or discipline; skilful or artful management; stratagem; artifice: usually in a bad sense; a rule in arithmetic for expeditiously multiplying quantities expressed in different denominations.—**Practise**, prak′tis, *v.t.*—*practised, practising.* [From the noun.] To do or perform frequently, customarily, or habitually; to use for instruction or discipline, or as a profession or art (to *practise* law or medicine); to put into practice; to perform; to do; to teach by practice; to accustom; to train.—*v.i.*—*practised, practising.* To perform certain acts frequently or customarily, for instruction, profit, or amusement; to form a habit of acting in any manner; to use artifices or stratagems; to exercise some profession, as that of medicine or of law.—**Practised**, prak′tist, *p.* and *a.* Skilled through practice.—**Practiser**, prak′tis-ėr, *n.* One that practises.—**Practising**, prak′tis-ing, *a.* Engaged in the use or exercise of any profession.—**Practitioner**, prak-tish′on-ėr, *n.* One who is engaged in the exercise of any art or profession, particularly in law or medicine.—*A general practitioner*, one who practises both medicine and surgery.

Præcipe, prē′si-pe, *n.* [L., imper. of *præcipio*, I give precepts. PRECEPT.] *Law*, a writ commanding something to be done or requiring a reason for neglecting it.

Præcordia, prē-kor′di-a, *n.pl.* [L., from *præ*, before, and *cor, cordis*, the heart.] *Anat.* the forepart of the region of the chest; the thoracic viscera.—**Præcordial**, prē-kor′di-al, *a.* Pertaining to the præcordia.

Prædial, prē′di-al, *a.* PREDIAL.

Præ-molar. PRE-MOLAR.

Præmunire, prē-mū-nī′rē, *n.* [A corruption of L. *præmonere*, to pre-admonish, from the words of the writ.] *Law*, a name given to a species of writ, to the offence for which it is granted, and also to the penalty it incurs, this penalty being forfeiture of goods and imprisonment, and being attached in former times to the offences of asserting the jurisdiction of the pope, denying the sovereign's supremacy, &c.

Prætexta, prē-teks′ta, *n.* [L., from *præ*, before, on the edge, and *textus*, woven.] Among the ancient Romans, a white robe with a narrow scarlet border worn by a youth; the white outer garment bordered with purple of the higher magistrates.

Prætor, prē′tor, *n.* [L., from *præ*, before, and *eo*, I go.] In ancient Rome, a title originally of the consuls, in later times of two important magistrates of the city, and lastly of a number of magistrates who administered justice in the state.—**Prætorial, Prætorian**, prē-tō′ri-al, prē-tō′ri-an, *a.* Belonging to a prætor. — *Prætorian bands* or *guards*, bodies of troops originally formed by the emperor Augustus to protect his person and his power, and afterwards long maintained by successive Roman emperors; the household troops or body-guards of the emperors.—*n.* A soldier of the Prætorian guard.—**Prætorium**, prē-tō′ri-um, *n.* [L.] The official residence of a provincial governor among the ancient Romans; a hall of justice.—**Prætorship**, prē′tor-ship, *n.* The dignity of a prætor.

Pragmatic, Pragmatical, prag-mat′ik, prag-mat′i-kal, *a.* [L. *pragmaticus*, Gr. *pragmatikos*, from *pragma*, business, from *prassō*, I do. PRACTICE.] Skilled in business‡; active or diligent‡; forward to intermeddle; impertinently busy or officious in the concerns of others.—*The pragmatic sanction*, the instrument by which the German emperor Charles VI, being without male issue, endeavored to secure the succession to his female descendants.—**Pragmatically**, prag-mat′i-kal-li, *adv.* In a pragmatic manner; impertinently.—**Pragmaticalness**, prag-mat′i-kal-nes, *n.* —**Pragmatism**, prag′ma-tizm, *n.* A non-speculative system of philosophy, which regards the practical consequences and useful results of ideas as the test of their truthfulness, and which considers truth itself to be a process; especially the modern form of this philosophy, introduced by C. S. Pierce and William James.—**Pragmatist**, prag′ma-tist, *n.*

Prairie, prā′ri, *n.* [Fr., from L.L. *prataria*, from L. *pratum*, a meadow.] The extensive, mostly level tracts of land of the Middle West, including the Great Plains from the Mississippi to the Rockies, usually treeless and covered with coarse grass and flowering plants.—**Prairie-dog**, *n.* A small burrowing rodent allied to the marmot and squirrel, found on the prairies. —**Prairie-hen**, *n.* A species of grouse, much prized as a game bird.—**Prairie-squirrel**, *n.* A species of ground squirrel inhabiting the prairies; also called gopher. —**Prairie-wolf**, *n.* The small wolf of the prairies; the coyote.

Praise, prāz, *n.* [Formerly *preis, preys*, praise, price, value, from O.Fr. *pris, preis*, price, honour (Mod.Fr. *prix*), from L. *pretium*, price, value, reward; the same as *price* and to *prize*.] Commendation bestowed on a person; approbation; eulogy; laud; a joyful tribute of gratitude or homage paid to the Divine Being, often expressed in song; the ground or reason of praise; what makes a person worthy of praise.—*v.t.*—*praised, praising.* To commend; to applaud; to express approbation of; to extol in words or song; to laud or magnify, especially applied to the Divine Being.—**Praiseless**, prāz′les, *a.* Without praise or commendation.—**Praiser**, prā′zer, *n.* One who praises; a commender.—**Praiseworthy**, prāz′wėr-THi, *a.* Worthy or deserving of praise; commendable.—**Praiseworthily**, prāz′wėr-THi-li, *adv.* In a manner deserving of commendation. —**Praiseworthiness**, prāz′wėr-THi-nes, *n.* The quality of being praiseworthy.

Prakrit, prä′krit, *n.* [Skr. *prâkriti*, nature, hence that which is natural or vulgar.] A Hindu language or dialect based on the Sanskrit, and which has been the mother of various modern dialects.

Pram, präm, *n.* [D. *praam*, Dan. *pram*, Icel. *prámr*.] A flat-bottomed boat or lighter, used in Holland and the Baltic ports for loading and unloading merchant vessels. Written also *Praam.*

Prance, prans, *v.i.*—*pranced, prancing.* [A slightly different form of *prank*.] To spring or bound, as a horse in high mettle; to ride ostentatiously; to strut about in a showy manner or with warlike parade.—**Prancer**, prans′ėr, *n.* A prancing horse. —**Prancing**, prans′ing, *p.* and *a.* Springing; bounding; riding with gallant show.

Prandial, pran′di-al, *a.* [L. *prandium*, dinner.] Relating to a dinner, or meal in general.

Prank, prangk, *v.t.* [Allied to D. *pronk*, finery, *pronken*, to strut; Dan. *prange*, G. *prangen, prunken*, to make a show; comp. also G. *pracht*, D. and Dan. *pragt*, pomp.] To adorn in a showy manner; to dress up. —*v.i.* To have a showy or gaudy appearance.—*n.* A gambol or caper; a playful or sportive action; a merry trick; a mischievous act, generally rather for sport than injury.—**Prankish**, prangk′ish, *a.* Full of pranks.

Prase, prāz, *n.* [Fr., from Gr. *prason*, a leek.] A species of quartz of a leek-green colour.—**Prasinous, Prasine**, praz′i-nus, praz′īn, *a.* [L. *prasinus*.] Of a light-green colour, inclining to yellow.

Praseodymium, prā′sē-ō-dim″i-um, *n.* [Gr. *prasios*, leek-green, and *didymium*.] A chemical element, associated with neodymium in didymium.

Prate, prāt, *v.i.*—*prated, prating.* [Same as L.G. *praten*, Dan. *prate*, D. *praaten*, Icel. *prata*, to prate; probably of imitative origin.] To talk much and without weight; to chatter; to babble.—*v.t.* To utter foolishly.—*n.* Continued talk to little purpose; unmeaning loquacity.—**Prater**, prā′tėr, *n.* One that prates.—**Prating**, prā′ting, *p.* and *a.* Given to prate; loquacious.—**Pratingly**, prā′ting-li, *adv.* In a prating manner.

Pratincole, prat′in-kōl, *n.* [From L. *pratum*, a meadow, and *incola*, an inhabitant.] A graceful bird of a genus akin to the plovers, inhabiting the temperate and warmer parts of Europe, Africa, and Asia.

Pratique, prat′ēk, *n.* [Fr. *pratique*, practice, intercourse. PRACTICE.] A licence to a ship to hold intercourse and trade with the inhabitants of a place, after having performed quarantine: a term used particularly in the European ports of the Mediterranean.

Prattle, prat′l, *v.i.*—*prattled, prattling.* [Freq. and dim. of *prate*.] To talk much and idly; to be loquacious on trifling subjects; to talk like a child.—*n.* Puerile or trifling talk.—**Prattler**, prat′lėr, *n.* One who prattles.

Pravity, prav′i-ti, *n.* [L. *pravitas*, from *pravus*, crooked, evil.] Deviation from right; moral perversity; depravity.

Prawn, pran, *n.* [Etym. unknown.] A small crustaceous animal of the shrimp family, highly prized for food.

Praxis, prak′sis, *n.* [Gr., from *prassō*, I do. PRACTICE.] Use; practice; especially, practice or discipline for a specific purpose, as to acquire a specific art; an example or form to teach practice.

Pray, prā, *v.i.* [O.Fr. *preier* (Fr. *prier*), It. *pregare*, to pray, from L. *precari*, to pray (as in *deprecate, imprecate*), from *prex*, a prayer (whence also *precarious*); same root as Skr. *prach*, to demand, A.Sax. *frignan*, G. *fragen*, to inquire.] To ask something with earnestness or zeal; to supplicate; to beg (to *pray* for mercy); to make petition to the Supreme Being; to address the Supreme Being with confession of sins and supplication for benefits. — *Pray*, elliptically for *I pray you tell me*, is a common mode of introducing a question.—*v.t.* To make earnest request to; to entreat; to address with a prayer for something such as God may grant; to ask earnestly for; to beseech; to petition.—**Prayer**, prā′ėr, *n.* One who prays.

Prayer, prā′ėr or prār, *n.* [Not directly from *pray*, but from O.Fr. *proiere*, Fr. *prière*, a prayer, from L.L. *precaria*, a prayer, from L. *precarius*, obtained by begging. PRAY, PRECARIOUS.] The act of asking for a favor with earnestness; a petition, supplication, entreaty; a solemn petition for benefits addressed to the Supreme Being; the words of a supplication; a formula of church service or of worship, public or private; that part of a petition to a public body which specifies the thing desired to be done or granted.—**Prayer-book**, *n.* A book containing prayers, used by various churches.—**Prayerful**, prā′ėr-ful or prār′ful, *a.* Devotional; given to prayer.—**Prayerfully**, prā′ėr-ful-li or prār′ful-li, *adv.* In a prayerful manner.—**Prayerfulness**, prā′ėr-ful-nes or prār′ful-nes, *n.*—**Prayerless**, prā′ėr-les or prār′les, *a.* Habitually neglecting the duty of prayer.—**Prayerlessly**, prā′ėr-les-li or prār′les-li, *adv.* In a prayerless manner.—**Prayerlessness**, prā′ėr-les-nes or prār′-les-nes, *n.*—**Prayer-meeting**, *n.* A meeting for prayer; usually a mid-week devotional service.—**Prayer wheel**, *n.* *Lamaism.* An apparatus used mainly in Tibet: one of the commoner forms consists of a wheel to which a written prayer is attached, and each revolution of the wheel made by the devotee counts as an utterance of the prayer.

Preach, prēch, *v.i.* [O.Fr. *precher* (Fr. *prêcher*), from L. *prædicare*, to declare in public—*præ*, before, and *dico, dicatum*, I proclaim; closely akin to *dico, dictum*, I say. DICTION.] To pronounce a public discourse on a religious subject, or from a text of Scripture; to deliver a sermon; to give earnest advice; to discourse in the manner of a preacher.—*v.t.* To proclaim; to publish in religious discourses; to inculcate in public discourse; to deliver (a sermon).—**Preacher**, prēch′ėr, *n.* One who preaches.—**Preachership**, prēch′-ėr-ship, *n.* The office of a preacher.—**Preachify**, prēch′i-fī, *v.i.* To give a long-winded moral advice.—**Preaching-cross**, *n.* A structure formerly erected in a public place, at which the monks and others were wont to preach.—**Preachment**, prēch′ment, *n.* A discourse affectedly solemn: in contempt.

Preadamite, prē-ad′am-īt, *n.* [*Pre*, before, and *Adam*.] One of those inhabitants of the earth who are presumed by some to have lived before the time of Adam.—*a.* Prior to Adam; pertaining to the Preadamites.—**Preadamitic, Preadamic**, prē-ad′am-it″ik, prē-a-dam′ik, *a.* Existing before Adam; pertaining to the world before Adam.

Preamble, prē′am-bl, *n.* [Fr. *préambule*, from L. *prae*, before, and *ambulo*, I go about. AMBLE.] The introductory part of a discourse, statute, or written instrument, as the Constitution, usually beginning with *Whereas* and stating the nature and intent of the document.—*v.t.*—*preambled, preambling.* To preface; to introduce with previous remarks.

Preaudience, prē-a′di-ens, *n.* Right of previous audience or of being heard before another; precedence or rank at the bar among sergeants and barristers.

Prebend, pre′bend, *n.* [Fr. *prébende*, from L.L. *præbenda*, things to be supplied, from L. *præbeo*, to give, grant, furnish—*præ*, and *habeo*, to have. HABIT.] The stipend granted to a canon of a cathedral or collegiate church out of its estate.—**Prebendal**, prē-ben′dal, *a.* Pertaining to a prebend. — **Prebendary**, prē′ben-da-ri, *n.* An ecclesiastic who enjoys a prebend; a canon.—**Prebendaryship**, prē′ben-da-ri-ship, *n.* The office of a prebendary; a canonry.

Precambrian, prē-kam′bri-an, *n.* [L. *pre*, before, *Cambrian*.] The oldest known strata.

Precarious, prē-kā′ri-us, *a.* [L. *precarius*, primarily, depending on request, or on the will of another, from *precor*, I pray. PRAY, PRAYER.] Depending on or held at the will or pleasure of another; hence, held by a doubtful tenure; depending on unknown or unforeseen causes or events.—**Precariously**, prē-kā′ri-us-li, *adv.* In a precarious manner.—**Precariousness**, prē-kā′ri-us-nes, *n.* The state of being precarious.

Precative, **Precatory**, prē′ka-tiv, prē′ka-to-ri, *a.* [From L. *precor*, I pray. PRAY.] Suppliant; beseeching.

Precaution, prē-ka′shon, *n.* [L. *præcautio*, from *præcautus*—*præ*, before, and *caveo*, *cautum*, I take care. CAUTION.] Previous caution or care; a measure taken beforehand to ward off evil or secure good. —*v.t.* To warn or advise beforehand, for preventing mischief. —**Precautionary**, prē-ka′shon-a-ri, *a.* Containing previous caution; proceeding from precaution.

Precede, prē-sēd′, *v.t.*—*preceded*, *preceding*. [L. *præcedo*—*præ*, before, and *cedo*, I move. CEDE.] To go before in the order of time; to be previous to; to go before in place, rank, or importance.—**Precedence**, **Precedency**, prē-sē′dens, prē-sē′den-si, *n.* The act or state of preceding or going before; priority in time; the state of being before in rank or dignity; the right to a more honourable place; order or adjustment of place according to rank; the foremost place in a ceremony; superior importance or influence.—**Precedent**, prē-sē′dent, *a.* Going before in time; anterior; antecedent.—**Precedent**, pres′ē-dent, *n.* Something done or said that may serve or be adduced as an example or rule to be followed in a subsequent act of the like kind; *law*, a judicial decision, which serves as a rule for future decisions in similar or analogous cases.—**Precedented**, pres′ē-den-ted, *a.* Having a precedent; authorized by an example of a like kind.—**Precedently**, prē-sē′dent-li, *adv.* Beforehand, antecedently.

Precentor, prē-sen′tėr, *n.* [L.L. *præcentor* —L. *præ*, before, and *cantor*, a singer, from *cano*, *cantum*, I sing. CHANT.] The leader of the choir in a cathedral, usually a minor canon; a person whose duty it is to lead the psalmody of a Presbyterian or other congregation.—**Precentorship**, prē-sen′tėr-ship, *n.* The office of a precentor.

Precept, prē′sept, *n.* [Fr. *précepte*, L. *præceptum*, from *præcipio*, I teach, instruct—*præ*, before, and *capio*, to take. CAPABLE.] A commandment intended as an authoritative rule of action; a command respecting moral conduct; an injunction; *law*, a mandate in writing sent by a justice of the peace, &c., for bringing a person, record, &c., before him.—**Preceptive**, prē-sep′tiv, *a.* [L. *præceptivus*.] Giving or containing precepts for the regulation of conduct; admonitive; instructive.—**Preceptor**, prē-sep′tėr, *n.* [L. *præceptor*.] A teacher; an instructor; the head of a preceptory among the Knights Templars. —**Preceptorial**, prē-sep-tō′ri-al, *a.* Pertaining to a preceptor. — **Preceptory**, prē′sep-to-ri, *a.* Giving precepts.—*n.* A subordinate religious house where instruction was given; an establishment of the Knights Templars, the superior of which was called knight preceptor. — **Preceptress**, prē-sep′tres, *n.* A female teacher or preceptor.

Precession, prē-sesh′on, *n.* [Fr. *précession*, from L. *præcedo*, *præcessum*, I precede. PRECEDE.] The act of going before or forward.—*Precession of the equinoxes*, an astronomical phenomenon consisting in a slow movement of the equinoctial points (which see) from east to west, or contrary to the order of the zodiacal signs, thus causing the equinoxes to succeed each other in less time than they would otherwise do.

Precinct, prē′singt, *n.* [From. L. *præcingo*, *præcinctum*, I encompass — *præ*, before, and *cingo*, to gird. CINCTURE.] The boundary line encompassing a place; a limit; a part near a border; a district within certain boundaries; a minor territorial division.

Precious, presh′us, *a.* [Fr. *précieux*, from L. *pretiosus*, from *pretium*, price. PRAISE.] Of great price; costly; of great value or worth; very valuable; much esteemed; highly cherished; ironically, very great; rascally (a *precious* villain). — *Precious metals*, gold and silver.—*Precious stones*, jewels, gems. — **Preciously**, presh′us-li, *adv.* In a precious manner; at a great cost.—**Preciousness**, presh′us-nes, *n.*

Precipice, pres′i-pis, *n.* [Fr. *précipice*, from L. *præcipitium*, a falling headlong, a precipice, from *præceps*, headlong — *præ*, forward, and *caput*, head. CHIEF.] A headlong declivity; a bank or cliff extremely steep, or quite perpendicular or overhanging.—**Precipitate**, prē-sip′i-tāt, *v.t.*—*precipitated*, *precipitating*. [L. *præcipito*, from *præceps*, headlong.] To throw headlong; to cast down from a precipice or height; to urge or press with eagerness or violence; to hasten (to *precipitate* one's flight); to hurry blindly or rashly; to throw or cause to sink to the bottom of a vessel, as a substance in solution. —*v.i.* To fall to the bottom of a vessel, as sediment or any substance in solution.—*a.* Falling, flowing, or rushing with steep descent; headlong; overhasty; rashly hasty; adopted with haste or without due deliberation; hasty; hurried; headlong. — *n. Chem.* any matter which, having been dissolved in a fluid, falls to the bottom of the vessel on the addition of some other substance capable of producing a decomposition of the compound. ∴ Substances which fall or settle down, as earthy matter in water, are called *sediments*, the operating cause being mechanical and not chemical.—**Precipitately**, prē-sip′i-tāt-li, *adv.* In a headlong or precipitate manner; too hastily.—**Precipitable**, prē-sip′i-ta-bl, *a.* Capable of being precipitated.—**Precipitability**, prē-sip′i-ta-bil″i-ti, *n.* The state of being precipitable.—**Precipitance**, **Precipitancy**, prē-sip′i-tans, prē-sip′i-tan-si, *n.* The quality of being precipitate; rash haste; haste in resolving, forming an opinion, or executing a purpose. — **Precipitant**, prē-sip′i-tant, *a.* [L. *præcipitans*, *præcipitantis*, ppr. of *præcipito*.] Falling or rushing headlong; precipitate.—*n. Chem.* a substance which, when added to a solution, separates what is dissolved and makes it fall to the bottom in a concrete state.—**Precipitantly**, prē-sip′i-tant-li, *adv.* In a precipitant manner.—**Precipitation**, prē-sip′i-tā″shon, *n.* The act of precipitating, or state of being precipitated; a falling or rushing down with violence and rapidity; rash, tumultuous haste; *chem.* the process by which any substance is made to separate from another or others in a solution, and fall to the bottom. — **Precipitin**, prē-sip′it-in, *n.* [From *precipitate*.] A substance formed in the blood that precipitates disease material and renders it harmless.—**Precipitous**, prē-sip′i-tus, *a.* [L. *præceps*, *præcipitis*, headlong.] Very steep; like or forming a precipice; headlong in descent.—**Precipitously**, prē-sip′i-tus-li, *adv.* In a precipitous manner. — **Precipitousness**, prē-sip′i-tus-nes, *n.* Steepness of descent.

Précis, prā-sē, *n.* [Fr. *précis*, precise, also an abstract. PRECISE.] A concise or abridged statement; a summary; an abstract.

Precise, prē-sīs′, *a.* [L. *præcisus*, from *præcido*, to cut off—*præ*, before, and *cædo*, to cut (as in *concise*, *excision*).] Sharply or exactly limited or defined as to meaning; exact; definite, not loose, vague, or equivocal; exact in conduct; strict; formal; nice; punctilious. — **Precisely**, prē-sīs′li, *adv.* In a precise manner; exactly; accurately; with excess of formality.—**Preciseness**, prē-sīs′nes, *n.* Exactness; rigid nicety; excessive regard to forms or rules; rigid formality.—**Precisian**, prē-sizh′an, *n.* An over-precise person; one ceremoniously exact in the observance of rules. — **Precisianism**, prē-sizh′an-izm, *n.* The conduct of a precisian; excessive exactness.—**Precision**, prē-sizh′on, *n.* The state of being precise as to meaning; preciseness; exactness; accuracy.

Preclude, prē-klūd′, *v.t.*—*precluded*, *precluding*. [L. *præcludo*—*præ*, before, and *cludo*, *claudo*, to shut. CLOSE, *v.t.*] To shut up; to stop; to impede; to hinder; to hinder or render inoperative by anticipative action.—**Preclusion**, prē-klū′zhon, *n.* The act of precluding.—**Preclusive**, prē-klū′siv, *a.* Tending to preclude; hindering by previous obstacles.—**Preclusively**, prē-klū′siv-li, *adv.* In a preclusive manner.

Precocious, prē-kō′shus, *a.* [Fr. *précoce*, from L. *præcox*, *præcocis*, ripe early, precocious—*præ*, before, and *coquo*, to cook, to ripen. COOK.] Ripe before the proper or natural time; ripe in understanding at an early period; developed or matured early in life. — **Precociously**, prē-kō′shus-li, *adv.* In a precocious manner.—**Precociousness**, **Precocity**, prē-kō′shus-nes, prē-kos′i-ti, *n.* The state or quality of being precocious; early development of the mental powers.

Precognition, prē-kog-nish′on, *n.* [L. *præ*, before, and *cognitio*, knowledge.] Previous knowledge or cognition; *Scots law*, a preliminary examination of a witness or witnesses to a criminal act, in order to know whether there is ground of trial.—**Precognosce**, prē′kog-nos, *v.t. Scots law*, to take the precognition of.

Preconceive, prē-kon-sēv′, *v.t.*—*preconceived*, *preconceiving*. To form a conception or opinion of beforehand; to form a previous notion or idea of.—**Preconception**, prē-kon-sep′shon, *n.* The act of preconceiving; conception or opinion previously formed.

Preconcert, prē-kon-sėrt′, *v.t.* To concert beforehand; to settle by previous agreement.—*n.* (prē-kon′sėrt). A previous agreement. — **Preconcertedly**, prē-kon-sėr′ted-li, *adv.* In a preconcerted manner; by previous agreement or arrangement.

Preconize, **Præconize**, prē′kon-īz, *v.t.* [L. *præco*, a public crier.] To summon or proclaim publicly; to bestow excessive praise.

Preconscious, prē-kon′shus, *a.* Pertaining to or involving a state anterior to consciousness.

Preconsent, prē-kon-sent′, *n.* A previous consent.

Precontract, prē-kon′trakt, *n.* A contract or agreement previous to another.—*v.t.* and *i.* (prē-kon-trakt′). To contract or stipulate previously.

Precordia, prē-kor′di-a, *a.* PRÆCORDIA.

Precursor, prē-kėr′sėr, *n.* [L. *præcursor* —*præ*, before, and *cursor*, a runner, from *curro*, *cursum*, I run. CURRENT.] A forerunner; a harbinger; one who or that which precedes an event and indicates its approach. — **Precursory**, prē-kėr′so-ri, *a.* Preceding as the harbinger; forerunning.—**Precursive**, prē-kėr′siv, *a.* Precursory.

Predaceous, prē-dā′shus, *a.* [From L. *præda*, prey, spoil, plunder, &c. PREY.] Living by prey; given to prey on other animals.—**Predacean**, prē-dā′shan, *n.* A carnivorous animal.—**Predatory**, pred′a-to-ri, *a.* [L. *prædatorius*.] Plundering; pillaging; practising rapine.

Predate, prē-dāt′, *v.t.*—*predated*, *predating*. To date by anticipation; to antedate.

Predecease, prē-dē-sēs′, *v.t.*—*predeceased*, *predeceasing*. To die before.—*n.* The decease of one before another.

Predecessor, pre-dē-ses′ėr, *n.* [L. *prædecessor* — *præ*, before, and *decessor*, one who retires, from *decedo*, *decessum*, I depart

—*de*, from, and *cedo*, to go. CEDE.] One who precedes or goes before another in some position; one who has preceded another in any state, position, office, or the like.

Predeclare, prē-dē-klãr', *v.t.* — *predeclared, predeclaring.* To declare beforehand or previously.

Predella, pre-del'a, *n.* [It.] The basal part of an altar-piece; a sort of shelf or ledge at the back of an altar.

Predestinate, prē-des'ti-nāt, *v.t.* — *predestinated, predestinating.* [L. *prædestino, prædestinatum—præ*, before, and *destino*, I determine. DESTINE.] To predetermine or foreordain; to appoint or ordain beforehand by an unchangeable purpose. — *a.* Presdestinated; foreordained. — **Predestinarian**, prē-des'ti-nā"ri-an, *a.* Belonging to predestination.—*n.* One who believes in the doctrine of predestination.—**Predestinarianism**, prē-des'ti-nā"ri-an-izm, *n.* The system or doctrines of the predestinarians.—**Predestination**, prē-des'ti-nā"shon, *n.* The act of decreeing or foreordaining events; especially, *theol.* the doctrine that God has from eternity unchangeably appointed or determined whatever comes to pass; particularly that he has preordained men to everlasting happiness or misery. — **Predestinator**, prē-des'ti-nā-tėr, *n.* One that predestinates; a predestinarian. — **Predestine**, prē-des'-tin, *v.t.* — *predestined, predestining.* To decree beforehand; to foreordain.

Predetermine, prē-dē-tėr'min, *v.t.*—*predetermined, predetermining.* To determine beforehand; to doom by previous decree. —*v.i.* To make a determination beforehand. — **Predeterminate**, prē-dē-tėr'mi-nāt, *a.* Determined beforehand.—**Predetermination**, prē-dē-tėr'mi-nā"shon, *n.* Previous determination; purpose formed beforehand.

Predial, prē'di-al, *a.* [Fr. *prédial*, from L. *prædium*, a farm or estate.] Consisting of land or farms; landed; attached to land; derived from land (*predial* tithes).

Predicable, pred'i-ka-bl, *a.* [L. *prædicabilis*, from *prædico*. PREDICATE.] Capable of being affirmed of something; that may be attributed to something.—*n.* Anything that may be predicated or affirmed of another; *logic*, one of the five things which can be affirmatively predicated of several others, viz. genus, species, difference, property, and accident.—**Predicability**, pred'i-ka-bil"i-ti, *n.* The quality of being predicable.—**Predicament**, prē-dik'a-ment, *n.* [L.L. *prædicamentum*.] *Logic*, one of those general heads or most comprehensive terms under one or other of which every other term may be arranged, ten in number, according to Aristotle, viz. substance, quantity, quality, relation, action, passion, time, place, situation, and habit; hence, class or kind described by definite marks; condition; especially, a dangerous or trying condition or state. — **Predicamental**, prē-dik'a-men"tal, *a.* Pertaining to a predicament. — **Predicant**, pred'i-kant, *n.* [L. *prædicans*, ppr. of *prædico*.] One that affirms anything; a preaching friar; a Dominican. — *a.* Predicating; preaching.

Predicate, pred'i-kāt, *v.t.* — *predicated, predicating.* [L. *prædicare, prædicatum*, to affirm, to declare—*præ*, before, and *dicare*, to declare. PREACH.] To affirm as an attribute of something (to *predicate* whiteness of snow); to declare one thing of another.—*v.i.* To make an affirmation.—*n. Logic*, that which, in a proposition, is affirmed or denied of the subject; *gram.* the word or words in a proposition which express what is affirmed or denied of the subject.—**Predication**, pred-i-kā'shon, *n.* The act of predicating; affirmation; assertion.—**Predicative**, pred'i-kā-tiv, *a.* Expressing affirmation or predication.—**Predicatory**, pred'i-ka-to-ri, *a.* Affirmative; positive.

Predict, prē-dikt', *v.t.* [L. *prædico, prædictum—præ*, before, and *dicere*, to tell. DICTION.] To foretell; to prophesy; to declare to be to happen in the future.—**Prediction**, prē-dik'shon, *n.* The act of predicting; a foretelling; a prophecy.—**Predictive**, prē-dik'tiv, *a.* Foretelling; prophetic.

Predigest, prē'di-jest, *v.t.* To assimilate or digest previously.

Predilection, prē-di-lek'shon, *n.* [Fr. *prédilection*—L. *prae*, before, and *dilectio*, a choice, from *diligere*, to love. DILIGENT.] A previous liking; a prepossession of mind in favor of something.

Prediscover, prē-dis-kuv'ėr, *v.t.* To discover previously or beforehand.—**Prediscovery**, prē-dis-kuv'ėr-i, *n.* A discovery made previously.

Predispose, prē-dis-pōz', *v.t.*—*predisposed, predisposing.* To incline beforehand; to give a previous disposition or tendency to; to fit or adapt previously. — **Predisposing**, prē-dis-pō'zing, *p.* and *a.* Inclining or disposing beforehand; making liable or susceptible. — **Predisposition**, prē-dis'-pō-zish"on, *n.* The state of being previously disposed towards something; previous inclination or tendency; previous fitness or adaptation to any change, impression, or purpose.

Predominate, prē-dom'i-nāt, *v.t.* — *predominated, predominating.* [Fr. *prédominer* — L. *præ*, before, and *dominari*, to rule, from *dominus*, lord. DOMINATE, DAME.] To have surpassing power, influence, or authority; to have controlling influence among others.—*v.t.* To rule over; to master‡. —**Predominance**, **Predominancy**, prē-dom'i-nans, prē-dom'i-nan-si, *n.* Prevalence over others; superiority in power, influence, or authority; ascendency.—**Predominant**, prē-dom'i-nant, *a.* Prevalent over others; superior in strength, influence, or authority; ruling; controlling. —**Predominantly**, prē-dom'i-nant-li, *adv.* In a predominant manner.

Predoom, prē-döm', *v.t.* To doom or judge beforehand.

Pre-elect, prē-ē-lekt', *v.t.* To choose or elect beforehand.—**Pre-election**, prē-ē-lek'shon, *n.* Choice or election beforehand.

Pre-eminence, prē-em'i-nens, *n.* The state or quality of being notably eminent among others; superior or surpassing eminence; undoubted superiority, especially superiority in excellence.—**Pre-eminent**, prē-em'i-nent, *a.* Eminent above others; surpassing or highly distinguished in excellence, sometimes also in evil. — **Pre-eminently**, prē-em'i-nent-li, *adv.* In a pre-eminent manner or degree.

Pre-empt, prē-empt', *v.t.* and *i.* To acquire before others; to claim before others establish rights, as to *pre-empt* public lands.—**Pre-emption**, prē-em'shon, *n.* [L. *prae*, before, and *emptio*, a buying, from *emo*, to buy. EXEMPT.] The act or right of purchasing before others; the right of a settler to the first chance of buying land in or near which he has settled.—**Pre-emptive**, prē-em'tiv, *a.*

Preen, prēn, *v.t.* [O.E. *proine, proigne*, to prune, to preen. PRUNE.] To trim with the beak; to clean and dress: said of birds dressing their feathers.

Pre-engage, prē-en-gāj', *v.t.*—*pre-engaged, pre-engaging.* To engage by previous agreement; to engage or attach by previous influence; to preoccupy.—**Pre-engagement**, prē-en-gāj'ment, *n.* Prior engagement or attachment.

Pre-establish, prē-es-tab'lish, *v.t.* To establish or settle beforehand. — **Pre-establishment**, prē-es-tab'lish-ment, *n.* Settlement beforehand.

Pre-exist, prē-eg-zist', *v.i.* To exist beforehand or before something else.—**Pre-existence**, prē-eg-zis'tens, *n.* Existence previous to something else; existence in a previous state; existence of the soul before its union with the body.—**Pre-existent**, prē-eg-zis'tent, *a.* Existing beforehand; preceding in existence.

Preface, pref'ās, *n.* [Fr. *préface*, from L. *præfatio—præ*, before, and *fari, fatum*, to speak (whence also *fate, fame*).] Something spoken as introductory to a discourse, or written as introductory to a book or other composition.—*v.t.*—*prefaced, prefacing.* To introduce by preliminary remarks.—**Prefatory**, pref'a-to-ri, *a.* Having the character of a preface; pertaining to a preface.—**Prefatorily**, pref'a-to-ri-li, *adv.* By way of preface.

Prefect, prē'fekt, *n.* [L. *præfectus*, from *præficio—præ*, before, and *facio*, I make. FACT.] A governor, commander, chief magistrate, or the like; a name common to several officers, military and civil, in ancient Rome; an important functionary in France: a préfet, that is, an official who presides over and has extensive powers in a department. — **Prefectship**, **Prefecture**, prē'fekt-ship, prē'fek-tūr, *n.* The office or jurisdiction of a prefect; *prefecture* is also the official residence of a prefect.

Prefer, prē-fėr', *v.t.*—*preferred, preferring.* [L. *praefero*, to carry before, to present, to esteem more highly—*prae*, before, and *ferre*, to bear or carry. FERTILE.] To offer for one's consideration or decision; to present; said especially of petitions, prayers, &c.; to advance, as to an office or dignity; to raise; to exalt; to set above something else in estimation; to hold in greater favor or esteem; to choose rather (to *prefer* one *to* another).—**Preferable**, pref'ėr-a-bl, *a.* Worthy to be preferred; more eligible; more desirable.—**Preferableness**, **Preferability**, pref'ėr-a-bl-nes, pref'ėr-a-bil"i-ti, *n.* The quality or state of being preferable. —**Preferably**, pref'ėr-a-bli, *adv.* In or by preference.—**Preference**, pref'ėr-ens, *n.* The preferring of one thing before another; choice of one thing rather than another; higher place in esteem; the object of choice; choice.—**Preferred stock**, prē-fėrd', *n.* A form of capital stock given preference in payment of dividends (or other rights) over common stock.—**Preferential**, pref-ėr-en'shal, *a.* In a position to which some preference is attached.—**Preferment**, prē-fėr'ment, *n.* Advancement to a higher office, dignity, or station; promotion; a superior or valuable place or office, especially in the church.—**Preferrer**, prē-fėr'ėr, *n.* One who prefers.

Prefigure, prē-fig'ūr, *v.t.*—*prefigured, prefiguring.* To exhibit by antecedent representation or by types and similitudes. — **Prefiguration**, prē-fig'ū-rā"shon, *n.* The act of prefiguring; an antecedent similitude. — **Prefigurative**, prē-fig'ū-rā-tiv, *a.* Showing by previous figures, types, or similitudes.

Prefix, prē-fiks', *v.t.* [Fr. *préfixer*, L. *præfigo, præfixus—præ*, before, and *figere*, to fix. FIX.] To put or fix before or at the beginning of another thing (to *prefix* a syllable to a word, an advertisement to a book); to settle, fix, or appoint beforehand (to *prefix* the hour of meeting).—*n.* (prē'fiks.) A letter, syllable, or word put to the beginning of a word, usually to vary its signification. —**Prefixion**, prē-fik'shon, *n.* The act of prefixing.

Preformation, prē-for-mā'shon, *n.* The obsolete theory that development of an organism simply consists of increase in size. Cp. EPIGENESIS.

Preformative, prē-for'ma-tiv, *n.* A formative letter at the beginning of a word; a prefix.

Preglacial, prē-glā'shi-al, *a. Geol.* prior to the glacial or boulder-drift period.

Pregnable,† preg'na-bl, *a.* [Fr. *prenable* (with inserted *g*), from *prendre*, to take, L. *prehendo, prehensum.* PREHENSILE.] Capable of being taken or won by force; expugnable.

Pregnant, preg'nant, *a.* [L. *prægnans, prægnantis—præ*, before, and *gnans*, ppr. corresponding to *gnatus, natus*, born. NATAL, NATURE.] Being with young; great with child; gravid; full of important matter; abounding with results; full of consequence or significance (a *pregnant* argument).—**Pregnancy**, preg'nan-si, *n.* The state of being pregnant; time of going with child; the quality of being full of significance, or the like.—**Pregnantly**, preg'nant-li, *adv.* In a pregnant manner.

Prehensile, Prehensory, prē-hen'sīl, prē-hen'so-ri, *a.* [L. *prehendere, prehensus*, to lay hold of—*præ*, before, and *hendere*, to seize, as *apprehend, comprehend*, &c. PRIZE, PRISON.] Capable of or adapted to seize or grasp (a monkey's *prehensile* tail).—**Prehensible**, prē-hen'si-bl, *a.* Capable of being seized.—**Prehension**, prē-hen'-shon, *n.* A taking hold of; a seizing.—**Prehensor**, prē-hen'sėr, *n.* One who lays hold.

Prehistoric, prē-his-tor'ik, *a.* Relating to a period antecedent to that at which history begins.

Preinstruct, prē-in-strukt', *v.t.* To instruct previously or beforehand.

Preintimation, prē'in-ti-mā"shon, *n.* Previous intimation; a suggestion beforehand.

Prejudge, prē-juj', *v.t.*—*prejudged, prejudging.* [Fr. *préjuger.*] To judge before hearing, or before the arguments and facts are fully known; to decide by anticipation; to condemn beforehand or unheard.—**Prejudgment**, prē-juj'ment, *n.* The act of prejudging; judgment without a hearing or full examination.

Prejudicate, prē-jū'di-kāt, *v.t.*—*prejudicated, prejudicating.* [L. *præ*, before, and *judico*, to judge. Akin *prejudice.*] To prejudge; to determine beforehand, especially to disadvantage.—**Prejudication**, prē-jū'di-kā"shon, *n.* The act of prejudicating.

Prejudice, prej'ū-dis, *n.* [Fr. *préjudice*, from L. *præjudicium*, from *præ*, before, and *judicium*, a judgment, from *judex, judicis*, a judge. JUDGE.] A bias or leaning, favourable or unfavourable, without reason, or for some reason other than justice; a prepossession (when used absolutely generally with the unfavourable meaning of wrong or ignorant bias or view); mischief; damage; injury (without *prejudice* to one's interests). — *v.t.* — *prejudiced, prejudicing.* To implant a prejudice in the mind of; to bias by hasty and incorrect notions; to injure by prejudices; to hurt, damage, impair; to injure in general (to *prejudice* one's cause).—**Prejudicial**, prej-ū-dish'al, *a.* Hurtful; mischievous; injurious; detrimental.—**Prejudicially**, prej-ū-dish'al-li, *adv.* In a prejudicial manner.—**Prejudicialness**, prej-ū-dish'al-nes, *n.*

Preknowledge, prē-nol'ej, *n.* Prior knowledge; foreknowledge.

Prelate, prel'at, *n.* [Fr. *prélat*, from L.L. *prælatus*, from L. *prælatus*, pp. of *præfero, prælatum*—*præ*, before and *latus*, borne.] An ecclesiastic of the higher order having authority over the lower clergy, as an archbishop, bishop, or patriarch; a dignitary of the church.—**Prelacy**, prel'a-si, *n.* Episcopacy; the system of church government by prelates; prelates collectively.—**Prelateship**, prel'at-ship, *n.* The office of a prelate.—**Prelatic, Prelatical, Prelatial**, pre-lat'ik, pre-lat'i-kal, pre-lā'shi-al, *a.* Pertaining to prelates or prelacy.—**Prelatically**, pre-lat'i-kal-li, *adv.* In a prelatical manner.—**Prelatist**, prel'at-ist, *n.* An advocate for prelacy.

Prelect prē-lekt', *v.i.* and *t.* [L. *prælego, prælectus*—*præ*, before, and *lego*, I read. LEGEND.] To read a lecture or discourse in public.—**Prelection**, prē-lek'shon, *n.* A lecture or discourse read in public or to a select company.—**Prelector**, prē-lek'tor, *n.* A reader of discourses; a lecturer.

Prelibation, prē-lī-bā'shon, *n.* [L. *præ*, before, and *libo*, to taste. LIBATION.] Foretaste; a tasting beforehand; an effusion or libation previous to tasting.

Preliminary, prē-lim'i-na-ri, *a.* Fr. *préliminaire* — L. *præ*, before, and *limen*, threshold. LIMIT.] Introductory; preceding the main discourse or business; prefatory.—*n.* Something introductory or preparatory; something to be examined and determined before an affair can be treated of on its own merits; a preparatory act.—**Preliminarily**, prē-lim'i-na-ri-li, *adv.* In a preliminary manner.

Prelude, prē'lūd or prel'ūd, *n.* [Fr. *prélude*, from L. *præ*, before, and *ludus*, play. LUDICROUS.] Something preparatory or leading up to what follows; an introductory performance; *music*, a short introductory strain preceding the principal movement.—*v.t.* (prē-lūd')—*preluded, preluding.* To introduce with a prelude; to serve as prelude to.—*v.i.* To serve as a prelude.—**Preludial**, prē-lū'di-al, *a.* Pertaining to a prelude; introductory.—**Prelusive, Prelusory**, prē-lū'siv, prē-lū'so-ri, *a.* Having the character of a prelude; introductory.—**Prelusively, Prelusorily**, prē-lū'siv-li, prē-lū'so-ri-li, *adv.* By way of prelude.

Prelumbar, prē-lum'bär, *a.* [L. *præ*, before, and *lumbus*, a loin.] *Anat.* placed before the loins.

Premature, prē'ma-tūr, *a.* [L. *præmaturus*—*præ*, before, and *maturus*, ripe.] Happening, arriving, existing, performed, or adopted before the proper time; done, said, or believed too soon; too early; untimely. — **Prematurely**, prē-ma-tūr'li, *adv.* In a premature manner.—**Prematureness, Prematurity**, prē-ma-tūr'-nes, prē-ma-tū'ri-ti, *n.* The state of being premature.

Premaxillary, prē-mak'sil-la-ri, *n. Anat.* a bone of the upper jaw on either side anterior to the true maxillary bone.

Premeditate, pre-med'i-tāt, *v.t.* — *premeditated, premeditating.* [Fr. *préméditer*, L. *præmeditor*—*præ*, before, and *meditor*, I meditate.] To think on and revolve in the mind beforehand; to contrive and design previously.—*v.i.* To meditate beforehand.—**Premeditately**, prē-med'i-tāt-li, *adv.* With premeditation.—**Premeditation**, prē-med'i-tā"shon, *n.* The act of premeditating; previous deliberation; forethought; previous contrivance or design.

Premetallic, prē-me-tal'ik, *a.* Pertaining to that period during which men were ignorant of the art of working metals.

Premier, prē'mi-ėr, *a.* [Fr. *prémier*, from L. *primarius*, of the first rank, from *primus*, first. PRIME.] First; chief; principal; holding the most ancient title in any rank of the peerage (the *premier* earl).—*n.* The first or chief minister of state; the prime or premier minister. — **Premiership**, prē'mi-ėr-ship, *n.* The office of premier.

Premise, prē-mīz', *v.t.*—*premised, premising.* [From L. *præmitto, præmissum*—*præ*, before, and *mitto*, I send. MISSION.] To set forth or make known beforehand, as introductory to the main subject; to lay down as an antecedent proposition.—*v.i.* To make an antecedent statement. — *n.* (prem'is). [Fr. *prémisse*, a premise (in logic). L. *præmissum*, what is sent or put before.] A proposition laid down as a base of argument; *logic*, the name applied to each of the two first propositions of a syllogism, from which the inference or conclusion is drawn; *pl.* the beginning or early portion of a legal deed or document where the subject-matter is stated or described in full (lit. 'the things before mentioned'); hence, lands and houses or tenements; a house and the outhouses, &c., belonging to it. — **Premiss**, prem'is, *n. Logic*, a premise.

Premium, prē'mi-um, *n.* [L. *præmium*, a reward—*præ*, before, and *emo*, to take. PRE-EMPTION.] A reward or prize offered for some specific thing; a bonus; an extra sum paid as an incentive; a bounty; a fee paid for the privilege of being taught a trade or profession; a sum paid periodically to an office for insurance, as against fire or loss of life or property.—*At a premium*, above par, opposed to *at a discount*: said of shares or stock; hence, in high esteem.

Premolar, pre-mō'lėr, *n. Anat.* a tooth between the canine and the molars.

Premonish, prē-mon'ish, *v.t.* [Prefix *pre*, and *-monish*, as in *admonish.*] To forewarn; to admonish beforehand.—**Premonition**, prē-mo-nish'on, *n.* Previous warning, notice, or information.—**Premonitor**, prē-mon'i-tėr, *n.* One who or that which gives premonition. — **Premonitorily**, prē-mon'i-to-ri-li, *adv.* By way of premonition. — **Premonitory, Premonitive**, prē-mon'i-to-ri, prē-mon'i-tiv, *a.* Giving previous warning or notice.

Premorse, prē-mors', *a.* [L. *præmorsus*—*præ*, before, and *mordere*, to gnaw. MORDANT.] Bitten off; applied in *bot.* to a root or leaf terminating abruptly, as if bitten off.

Premosaic, prē-mō-zā'ik, *a.* Relating to the time before that of Moses.

Premotion, prē-mō'shon, *n.* Previous motion or excitement to action.

Premunire, prē-mū-nī'rē. *Præmunire.*

Prenominate, prē-nom'i-nāt, *v.t.*—*prenominated, prenominating.* To nominate or name previously or beforehand.—*a.* Forenamed. — **Prenomination**, prē-nom'i-nā"shon, *n.* The privilege of naming or being named first.

Prenotion, prē-nō'shon, *n.* A notion which precedes something else in time; previous notion or thought.

Prentice, pren'tis. A colloquial contraction of *Apprentice.* — **Prenticeship**, pren'tis-ship. A contraction of *Apprenticeship.*

Preoccupy, prē-ok'kū-pī, *v.t.* — *preoccupied, preoccupying.* To occupy or take possession of before another; to engage or occupy the attention of beforehand; to engross beforehand.—**Preoccupancy**, prē-ok'kū-pan-si, *n.* The act or right of taking possession before another. — **Preoccupant**, prē-ok'kū-pant, *n.* One who preoccupies.—**Preoccupation**, prē-ok'kū-pā"shon, *n.* An occupation or taking possession before another. — **Preoccupied**, prē-ok'kū-pīd, *p.* and *a.* Having the attention taken up previously; absorbed.

Preoperculum, prē-ō-pėr'kū-lum, *n.* A part of the gill-cover or operculum of a fish.

Preordain, prē-or-dān', *v.t.* To ordain or appoint beforehand; to predetermine.—**Preordination**, prē-or'di-nā"shon, *n.* The act of foreordaining.

Prepaid. PREPAY.

Prepare, prē-pār', *v.t.*—*prepared, preparing.* [Fr. *préparer*, L. *præparo, præparatum*—*præ*, before, and *parare*, to get ready. PARE.] To fit, adapt, or qualify for a particular purpose; to put into such a state as to be fit for use or application; to make ready; often, with a personal object, to make ready for something that is to happen; to give notice to (to *prepare* a person for ill news or calamity); to provide; to procure as suitable (to *prepare* arms, ammunition, &c., for troops). — *v.i.* To make ready; to put things in suitable order; to take the necessary previous measures; to make one's self ready.—**Preparation**, pre-pa-rā'shon, *n.* [L. *præparatio.*] The act of preparing; that which is prepared for a particular purpose; a substance compounded or made up for a certain use; the state of being prepared or in readiness.—**Preparative**, prē-par'a-tiv, *a.* [Fr. *préparatif.*] Tending or serving to prepare or make ready; preparatory.—*n.* That which is preparative or preparatory; that which is done to prepare. — **Preparatively**, prē-par'a-tiv-li, *adv.* In a preparative manner; by way of preparation.—**Preparatory**, prē-par'a-to-ri, *a.* Serving to prepare the way for some proceeding to follow; introductory; preparative.—**Preparedly**, prē-pārd'li, *adv.* With suitable previous measures.—**Preparedness**, prē-pārd'nes, *n.* The state of being prepared. — **Preparer**, prē-pā'rėr, *n.* One who or that which prepares.

Prepay, prē-pā', *v.t.*—*prepaid, prepaying.* To pay before obtaining possession of; to pay in advance; to pay before the payment falls due. — **Prepayment**, prē-pā'ment, *n.* Act of paying beforehand; payment in advance.

Prepense, prē-pens', *a.* [L. *præpensus*—*præ*, before, and *pendere, pensum*, to weigh. POISE.] Deliberated or devised beforehand; premeditated; aforethought: now scarcely used except in the phrase 'malice *prepense*'.—**Prepensely**, prē-pens'li, *adv.*

Preponderate, prē-pon′dėr-āt, *v.t.—preponderated, preponderating.* [L. *præpondero, præponderatum—præ*, before, and *ponderare*, to weigh, from *pondus, ponderis*, a weight. PONDER.] To outweigh; to have more weight or influence than.—*v.i.* To exceed in weight, influence, or power; to have the greater weight or influence; to have sway or power superior to others.—**Preponderance, Preponderancy**, prē-pon′dėr-ans, prē-pon′dėr-an-si, *n.* The state or quality of preponderating or being preponderant. — **Preponderant**, prē-pon′dėr-ant, *a.* Outweighing; superior in power, influence, or the like.—**Preponderantly, Preponderatingly**, prē-pon′dėr-ant-li, pre-pon′dėr-ā-ting-li, *adv.* In a preponderant manner.—**Preponderation**, prē-pon′dėr-ā″shon, *n.* The state of preponderating; preponderance.

Preposition, prep-ō-zish′on, *n.* [L. *præpositio.* POSITION.] *Gram.* a part of speech which is used to show the relation of one noun or pronoun to another in a sentence, and is usually placed before the word which expresses the object of the relation. —**Prepositional**, prep-ō-zish′on-al, *a.* Pertaining to or having the nature or function of a preposition.—**Prepositionally**, prep-ō-zish′on-al-li, *adv.* In a prepositional manner.—**Prepositive**, prē-poz′i-tiv, *a.* Put before.—*n.* A word or particle put before another word.

Prepossess, prē-poz-zes′, *v.t.* To take previous possession of; to preoccupy the mind or heart of; to fill or imbue beforehand with some opinion or estimate; to prejudice. ∴ *Prepossess* is more frequently used in a good sense than *prejudice.*—**Prepossessing**, prē-poz-zes′ing, *a.* Creating an impression favourable to the owner; engaging: said especially of the external characteristics of a person.—**Prepossession**, prē-poz-zesh′on, *n.* Prior possession; a preconceived opinion; an impression on the mind in favour or against any person or thing, especially in favour.

Preposterous, prē-pos′tėr-us, *a.* [L. *præposterus—præ*, before, and *posterus*, coming after. POSTERIOR.] Contrary to nature, reason, or common sense; utterly and glaringly foolish; totally opposed to the fitness of things; manifestly absurd.—**Preposterously**, prē-pos′tėr-us-li, *adv.* In a preposterous manner.—**Preposterousness**, prē-pos′tėr-us-nes, *n.* The state or quality of being preposterous; utter absurdity.

Prepotent, prē-pō′tent, *a.* [L. *præpotens —præ*, before, and *potens*, powerful. POTENT.] Very powerful; having a superiority of power or influence.—**Prepotency**, prē-pō′ten-si, *n.* Superior power; predominance.

Prepuce, prē′pūs, *n.* [L. *præputium*, the foreskin.] The foreskin. — **Preputial**, prē-pū′shal, *a.* Pertaining to the prepuce.

Pre-Raphaelite, prē-raf′a-el-īt, *n.* One who practises or favours the system or style of painting practised by the early painters before Raphael, or the modern revival of their style or system, said to be a rigidly faithful representation of natural forms and effects.—**Pre-Raphaelitism, Pre-Raphaelism**, prē-raf′a-el-it-izm, prē-raf′-a-el-izm, *n.* The style or practice of the pre-Raphaelites.

Prerequisite, prē-rek′wi-zit, *a.* Previously requisite; necessary to something subsequent. — *n.* Something that is prerequisite.

Prerogative, prē-rog′a-tiv, *n.* [L. *prærogativa*, from *prærogo*, to ask before—*præ*, before, and *rogare*, to ask (as in *interrogate, arrogate, derogate*, &c.).] An exclusive or peculiar privilege; a privilege belonging to one in virtue of his character or position; an official and hereditary right which may be asserted without question; a special right or privilege of a sovereign or other executive of a government; the name given to the century in the Roman Comitia that by lot was empowered to record its vote first, and so was believed to be divinely commissioned to determine the vote of the rest. — **Prerogatived**, prē-rog′a-tivd, *a.* Having prerogative. — **Prerogatively**, prē-rog′a-tiv-li, *adv.* By privilege or prerogative.

Presage, pres′ij or pre′sāj, *n.* [Fr. *présage*, L. *præsagium—præ*, before, and *sagire*, to perceive by the senses; allied to *sagacious*.] Something which portends or foreshows a future event; a prognostic; an omen; a foreboding or presentiment; a feeling that something is to happen; a prophecy; foreknowledge.—*v.t.* (pres-āj′)—*presaged, presaging.* To forebode; to foreshow; to foretell, predict, prophesy.—*v.i.* To form or utter a prediction.—**Presageful**, prē-sāj′-ful, *a.* Full of presages; ominous.—**Presagement**, prē-sāj′ment, *n.* A foreboding; a foretelling.—**Presager**, pre-sā′jėr, *n.* One who presages.

Presbyopia, pres-bi-ō′pi-a, *n.* [Gr. *presbys*, old, and *ōps*, the eye.] An imperfection of vision in which near objects are seen less distinctly than those at a distance, common in old age.—**Presbyope**, pres′bi-ōp, *n.* One affected with presbyopia.—**Presbyopic**, pres-bi-op′ik, *a.* Pertaining to presbyopia.

Presbyter, pres′bi-tėr, *n.* [L. *presbyter*, from Gr. *presbyteros*, compar. of *presbys*, old. *Priest* is the same word.] An elder or a person somewhat advanced in age, who had authority in the early Christian church; a priest; a parson.—**Presbyterian**, pres-bi-tē′ri-an, *a.* Pertaining to a presbyter; pertaining to ecclesiastical government by presbyteries, or to those who uphold such government.—*n.* A member of that section of the Christian church who vest church government in presbyteries or associations of ministers and elders, and have no bishops. — **Presbyterial**, pres-bi-tē′ri-al, *a.* Presbyterian. — **Presbyterianism**, pres-bi-tē′ri-an-izm, *n.* The doctrines, principles, and discipline or government of presbyterians.—**Presbytery**, pres′bi-te-ri, *n.* Presbyterianism; a judicatory consisting of presbyterian pastors of all the churches of any particular denomination within a given district, along with one ruling elder from each church-session.

Prescient, prē′shi-ent, *a.* [L. *præsciens, præscientis*, ppr. of *præscio*, to foreknow—*præ*, before, *scio*, to know. SCIENCE.] Foreknowing; having knowledge of events before they take place.—**Prescience**, prē′-shi-ens, *n.* [L. *prescientia.*] Foreknowledge; knowledge of events before they take place; foresight.

Prescientific, prē′sī-en-tif″ik, *a.* Anterior to the era of science.

Prescribe, prē-skrīb′, *v.t.—prescribed, prescribing.* [L. *præscribo—præ*, before, and *scribere*, to write. SCRIBE.] To lay down authoritatively for direction; to give as a rule of conduct; *med.* to direct to be used as a remedy.—*v.i.* To lay down rules or directions; to dictate; to write or give medical directions; to direct what remedies are to be used; *law*, to become extinguished or of no validity through lapse of time, as a right, debt, obligation, and the like.—**Prescriber**, prē-skrī′bėr, *n.* One that prescribes. — **Prescript**, prē′skript, *a.* Directed; set down as a rule; prescribed.—*n.* Direction; precept; model prescribed.—**Prescriptibility**, prē-skrip′ti-bil″i-ti, *n.* The quality of being prescriptible.—**Prescriptible**, prē-skrip′ti-bl, *a.* Suitable for being prescribed; depending or derived from prescription.—**Prescription**, prē-skrip′shon, *n.* The act of prescribing; what is prescribed; a direction; prescript; *med.* a written statement of the medicines or remedies to be used by a patient; a claim, right, or title based on long use or custom; the loss of a legal right by lapse of time and neglect.—**Prescriptive**, prē-skrip′tiv, *a.* Consisting in or acquired by prescription.

Presence. Under PRESENT.

Present, prez′ent, *a.* L. *præsens, præsentis*, from *præ*, before, and *sens, esens*, being, an old participle of *sum*, I am; comp. *absent.*] Being in a certain place: opposed to *absent*; being before the face or near; being in company; done on the spot; instant; immediate (*present* death); being now in view or under consideration; now existing, or being at this time; not past or future; ready at hand; quick in emergency. —*The present*, an elliptical expression for *the present time.*—*At present*, elliptically for *at the present time.*—*Present tense*, *gram.* the tense or modification of a verb which expresses action or being in the present time.—*v.t.* (prē-zent′). [Fr. *présenter*, L. *præsentare*, to present, lit. to make present.] To place or introduce into the presence or before the face of, especially of a superior; to make known; to offer for acquaintance; to exhibit or offer to view or notice (*presented* a wretched appearance); to bestow; to make a gift or donation of: generally to give formally and ceremoniously; to bestow a gift upon; to favour with a donation (to *present* a person *with* a thing); to nominate to an ecclesiastical benefice; to lay before a public body for consideration, as before a legislature, court, &c. (to *present* a memorial or the like); to point, level, aim, as a weapon, particularly some species of firearms.—*To present arms* (*milit.*), to put the arms or guns in a perpendicular position in front of the body, as in saluting a superior officer, or in token of respect.—*n.* (prez′ent). That which is presented or given; a gift; *pl.* (from the adj.), a term used in a legal deed to signify the document itself.—**Presence**, prez′ens, *n.* [L. *præsentia.*] The state of being present; the existence of a person or thing in a certain place: opposed to *absence*; the being in company with; personal attendance; the state of being within sight or call; the state of being in view of a superior; the person of a superior, as a sovereign; mien; air; personal appearance; demeanour. — *Presence of mind*, coolness and readiness of invention or resource in occasions of difficulty; quickness in devising expedients on pressing occasions.—**Presence-chamber**, *n.* The room in which a great personage receives company.—**Presentable**, prē-zen′-ta-bl, *a.* Capable of being presented; in such trim as to be able to present one's self without embarrassment; suitable to be exhibited or offered.—**Presentation**, prez-en-tā′shon, *n.* The act of presenting, or state of being presented; the act or right of presenting a clergyman or nominating a minister to a vacant parish.—**Presentative**, prē-zen′ta-tiv, *a.* Serving to present; presenting; *metaph.* applied to what may be apprehended directly, or to the faculty capable of apprehending directly.—**Presentee**, prez-en-tē′, *n.* One presented to a benefice.—**Presenter**, prē-zen′tėr, *n.* One who presents; one who leads or introduces. —**Presentive**, prē-zen′tiv, *a.* *Gram.* applied to words which present a definite conception of an object to the mind: opposed to *symbolic.*—*n.* A presentive word. —**Presentiveness**, prē-zen′tiv-nes, *n.*—**Presently**, prez′ent-li, *adv.* In a little time; soon; forthwith; immediately.—**Presentment**, prē-zent′ment, *n.* The act of presenting or state of being presented; representation or portrait (*Shak.*).—**Presentness**, prez′ent-nes, *n.* The state of being present; presence.

Presentiment, prē-sen′ti-ment, *n.* [*Pre*, before, and *sentiment*; O.Fr. *presentiment*, foreboding.] Previous conception, sentiment, or opinion; previous apprehension of something future; anticipation of impending evil; foreboding.

Preserve, prē-zėrv′, *v.t.—preserved, preserving.* [Fr. *préserver*, L.L. *præservo*—L. *præ*, before, and *servo*, I save. SERVE.] To keep or save from injury or destruction; to defend from evil; to save; to keep in the same state; to uphold, sustain, guard; to save from decay; to cause to remain good and wholesome for food by treating with salt, sugar, or otherwise (*preserved* meats or fruits); to prevent being hunted and killed, except at certain seasons or by certain persons, as game, salmon, &c.—*v.i.* To practise the art of seasoning fruits, &c., for preservation; to protect game for purposes of sport.—*n.* That which is preserved; fruit, &c., suitably seasoned, to keep from decay; a place set apart for the shelter and protection of game intended for sport.—**Preserver**, prē-zėr′vėr, *n.* A person or thing that preserves.—**Preservable**, prē-zėr′va-bl, *a.* Capable of being preserved.—**Preservation**, prez-ėr-vā′shon, *n.* The act of preserving; the state of being preserved; escape from danger; safety.—**Preservative**, prē-zėr′va-tiv, *a.* Having the power of keeping safe from injury, destruction, or decay; tending to preserve.—*n.* That which preserves or has the power of preserving; something that is preventive of injury or decay.—**Preservatory**, prē-zėr′va-to-ri, *a.* Having a tendency or power to preserve.

Preses, prē′ses, *n.* [L. *præses*, from *præ*, before, and *sedeo*, to sit.] A president; the chairman of a meeting. (*Scotch.*)

Preside, prē-zīd′, *v.i.*—*presided, presiding.* [Fr. *présider*, from L. *præsideo*—*præ*, before, and *sedeo*, I sit. SIT.] To be set over others; to have the place of authority over others, as a chairman or director: usually denoting temporary superintendence and government, as at a public meeting; to exercise superintendence; to watch over as inspector.—**Presidence**, pres′i-dens, *n.* Presidency.—**Presidency**, pres′i-den-si, *n.* Superintendence; inspection and care; the office of president; the term during which a president holds his office; the office of the president of the United States.—**President**, pres′i-dent, *n.* One who presides; an officer elected or appointed to preside over and control the proceedings of a number of persons; the chief officer of a corporation, company, society, &c.; the chief officer of some colleges or universities; the highest officer of state in a republic.—**Presidential**, pres-i-den′shal, *a.* Pertaining to a president.—**Presidentship**, pres′i-dent-ship, *n.* The office of president.

Presidio, prē-sid′i-ō, *n.* [Sp.] A fort or fortified station; a garrison town.

Presignify, prē-sig′ni-fī, *v.t.*—*presignified, presignifying.* To intimate or signify beforehand; to show previously.—**Presignification**, prē-sig′ni-fi-kā″shon, *n.* The act of signifying or showing beforehand.

Press, pres, *v.t.* [Fr. *presser*, from L. *presso*, a freq. of *premere, pressum*, to press; seen also in *compress, depress, express, impress, repress*, &c.] To act on with force or weight; to squeeze; to crush; to extract the juice of by squeezing; to squeeze for the purpose of making smooth (to *press* cloth or paper); to embrace closely; to constrain or compel; to urge by authority or necessity; to impose importunately (to *press* a gift on one); to straiten or distress (to be *pressed* with want); to urge or solicit with earnestness; to importune; to inculcate with earnestness; to enforce; to bear hard upon; to ply hard.—*v.i.* To exert pressure; to act with compulsive force; to bear heavily; to strain or strive eagerly; to go forward with impulsive eagerness or energetic efforts; to crowd; to throng; to force one's way; to urge.—*To press upon*, to urge with force; to attack closely.—*n.* [Fr. *presse*, a press, a crowd, a throng.] An instrument or machine by which any body is squeezed, crushed, or forced into a more compact form; a machine for printing; a printing press; (with *the*) printed literature in general, often restricted to the literature of newspapers; newspaper reporters; a printing or publishing establishment; also its personnel; a crowd; a throng; multitude of individuals crowded together; a wine-vat or cistern (O.T.); an upright cupboard in which clothes or other articles are kept; urgency; urgent demands of affairs.—*Freedom of the press*, the right to publish without political censorship.—*Press of sail* (*naut.*), as much sail as the state of the wind, &c., will permit.—**Press conference**, *n.* An assemblage of reporters invited to an interview and given information en masse.—**Presser**, pres′ėr, *n.* One who or that which presses.—**Pressing**, pres′ing, *p.* and *a.* Urgent; importunate; distressing.—**Pressingly**, pres′ing-li, *adv.* In a pressing manner.—**Pressman**, pres′man, *n.* One who works or attends to a printing press.—**Pressroom**, *n.* *Print.* the room where the printing presses are worked, as distinguished from a composing-room; a room where reporters assemble for a press conference.—**Pressure**, presh′ūr, *n.* [O.Fr. *pressure*, L. *pressura.*] The act of pressing; the state of being squeezed or crushed; the force of one body acting on another by weight or the continued application of power; a constraining force or impulse acting on the mind; severity of grievousness, as of personal circumstances; distress, strait, or difficulty; urgency; demand on one's time or energies (the *pressure* of business); force exerted upon a surface: also used to denote INTENSITY OF PRESSURE (which see).—*Pressure cooker*, an autoclave; an apparatus which may be sealed for cooking or sterilizing under high-pressure superheated steam.—**Presswork**, *n.* The operation of taking impressions from types, &c., by means of the press.

Press, pres, *v.t.* [Originally to *impress* or *imprest*. See IMPRESS (in this sense).] To force into service, especially into naval service; to impress.

Pressirostral, pres-i-ros′tral, *a.* [L. *pressus*, pressed, flattened, and *rostrum*, beak.] Having a compressed or flattened beak; applied to certain birds, as the plovers, &c.

Prester John, *n.* Priest John, the mythical or legendary Christian king, believed in the Middle Ages to be ruling in Abyssinia.

Prestidigitation pres′ti-dij′i-tā″shon, *n.* [L. *præsto*, at hand, ready, and *digitus*, a finger.] Skill in legerdemain; sleight of hand; juggling.—**Prestidigitator**, pres-ti-dij′i-tā-tėr, *n.* One who practises prestidigitation; a juggler.

Prestige, pres′tij or pres-tēzh′, *n.* [Fr., from L. *præstigium*, a delusion, a juggler's trick, from *præstinguo*, to obscure—*præ*, before, and *stinguo*, to extinguish. STIGMA.] Weight or influence derived from previous character, achievements, or associations, especially weight or influence derived from past success, on which a confident belief is founded of future triumphs.

Presto, pres′to, *adv.* [It. *presto*, quick, quickly, from L. *præsto*, at hand, ready—*præ*, before, and *sto*, to stand.] *Music*, a direction for a quick lively movement or performance; also used interjectionally for quickly, immediately, in haste.

Presume, prē-zūm′, *v.t.*—*presumed, presuming.* [Fr. *présumer*, from L. *præsumo*, to presume—*præ*, before, and *sumo*, to take, as in *assume, consume, resume*, &c. SUMPTUOUS.] To take for granted; to suppose on reasonable grounds.—*v.i.* To suppose or believe without examination; to infer; to venture without permission or beyond what is justifiable; to take the liberty; to make bold; to act on over-confident conclusions; to make unwarranted advances (to *presume upon* one's good nature); to act in a forward way; to go beyond the boundaries laid down by reverence, respect, or politeness.—**Presumable**, prē-zū′ma-bl, *a.* Capable of being presumed.—**Presumably**, prē-zū′ma-bli, *adv.* As may be presumed or reasonably supposed.—**Presumer**, prē-zū′mėr, *n.* One that presumes.—**Presumingly**, prē-zū′ming-li, *adv.* With presumption.—**Presumption**, prē-zum′shon, *n.* [L. *præsumptio.*] A supposition; a ground for presuming; a strong probability; that which is supposed to be true without direct proof; blind or headstrong confidence; unreasonable adventurousness; presumptuousness; arrogance; assurance; *law*, that which comes near to the proof of a fact, in greater or less degree.—**Presumptive**, prē-zum′tiv, *a.* Based on presumption or probability; proving circumstantially, not directly (*presumptive* evidence).—*Presumptive heir*, one whose right of inheritance may be defeated by any contingency, as by the birth of a nearer relative.—**Presumptively**, prē-zum′tiv-li, *adv.* In a presumptive manner.—**Presumptuous**, prē-zum′tū-us, *a.* Imbued with or characterized by presumption; taking undue liberties; given to presume or act in a forward manner; arrogant; over-confident.—**Presumptuously**, prē-zum′tū-us-li, *adv.* In a presumptuous manner.—**Presumptuousness**, prē-zum′tū-us-nes, *n.* The quality of being presumptuous.

Presuppose, prē-sup-pōz′, *v.t.* To suppose or imagine as previous; to cause to be taken for granted; to imply as antecedent; to require to exist previously.—**Presupposition, Presupposal**, prē-sup′pō-zish″on, prē-sup-pō′zal, *n.* The act of presupposing; that which is presupposed.

Presurmise, prē-sėr-mīz′, *n.* A surmise previously formed.

Pretend, prē-tend′, *v.t.* [L. *prætendo*, to hold out, pretend—*præ*, before, and *tendere*, to reach or stretch. TEND.] To hold out falsely; to allege falsely; to use as a pretext; to make false appearance or representation of; to feign or affect (to *pretend* zeal); to claim or put in a claim for.—*v.i.* To feign, make believe, or sham; to put in a claim, truly or falsely: usually with *to*.—**Pretender**, prē-ten′dėr, *n.* One who pretends; one who lays claim to anything; *Eng. hist.* a name applied to the son and grandson of James II, the heirs to the house of Stuart, who laid claim to the British crown, from which their house had been excluded by enactment of parliament.—**Pretense, Pretence**, prē-tens′, *n.* [From L. *prætentum*, later *prætensum*, pp. of *prætendo.*] The act of pretending; the presenting to others, either in words or actions, of a false or hypocritical appearance; false show or statement intended to mislead; a pretext; an excuse; a claim, true or false.—*Escutcheon of pretense* (heraldry), a small shield set in the center of a husband's arms, bearing those of his wife when she is an heiress or co-heiress in blood.—**Pretension**, prē-ten′shon, *n.* [Fr. *prétention.*] Claim true or false; a holding out the appearance of possessing a certain character; an alleged or assumed right.—**Pretentious**, prē-ten′shus, *a.* Full of pretension; attempting to pass for more than one is worth; pretending to a superiority not real.—**Pretentiously**, prē-ten′shus-li. *adv.* In a pretentious manner.

Preter-imperfect, prē′tėr-im-pėr″fekt, *a.* and *n.* [L. *præter*, beyond, and E. *imperfect.*] *Gram.* a term applied to a tense with time not perfectly past (he *was going*): generally called simply *Imperfect*.

Preterit, Preterite, pret′ėr-it, *a.* [L. *præteritus*, gone by, pp. of *prætereo*—*præter*, beyond, and *ire, itum*, to go. ITINERANT.] *Gram.* expressing past time; applied to the tense expressing action or existence perfectly past or finished; past (he *struck*); also used as equivalent to *perfect*.—*n. Gram.* the preterit tense.—**Preterition**, prē-tėr-ish′on, *n.* [L. *præteritio*, from *prætereo.*] *Rhet.* a figure by which, in pretending to pass over anything, we make a summary mention of it.—**Preteritive**, prē-tėr′i-tiv, *a.* *Gram.* an epithet applied to verbs used only or chiefly in the *preterit* or past tenses.

Pretermit, prē-tėr-mit′, *v.t.*—*pretermitted, pretermitting.* [L. *prætermitto*—*præter*, beyond, and *mittere*, to send.] To pass by; to omit.—**Pretermission**, prē-tėr-mish′on, *n.* A passing by; omission.

Preternatural, prē-tėr-nat′ū-ral, *a.* [L. *præter*, beyond, and E. *natural.*] Beyond what is natural, or different from what is natural, as distinguished from *supernatural*, above nature; and *unnatural*, contrary to nature.—**Preternaturally**, prē-tėr-nat′ū-ral-li, *adv.* In a preternatural manner.—**Preternaturalness, Preternaturalism**, prē-tėr-nat′ū-ral-nes, prē-tėr-nat′ū-ral-izm, *n.* A state of being preternatural.

Preterperfect, prē-tėr-pėr′fekt, *a.* and *n.* [L. *præter*, beyond, and E. *perfect.*] *Gram.* a term equivalent to *perfect*.—**Preterpluperfect**, prē-tėr-plö′pėr-fekt, *a.* and *n.* Same as *Pluperfect*.

Pretext, prē′tekst or prē-tekst′, *n.* [Fr. *prétexte*, from L. *prætextum*, from *prætexe*

—*præ*, before, and *texo*, to weave. TEXTURE.] An ostensible reason or motive assigned or assumed as a colour or cover for the real reason or motive; a pretence.

Pretor, prē′tor. PRÆTOR.

Pretty, prit′i, *a.* [O.E. *pretie*, *praty*, comely, clever; A.Sax. *prœtig*, crafty, from *prœt*, a trick; Icel. *prettugr*, tricky, *prettr*, a trick.] Having diminutive beauty; of a pleasing and attractive form without the strong lines of beauty, or without gracefulness and dignity; pleasing; neatly arranged; affectedly nice; foppish; ironically, nice; fine; excellent: meaning the opposite.—*adv.* In some degree; moderately; expressing a degree less than *very* (*pretty* well, large, sure, &c.).—**Prettily**, prit′i-li, *adv.* In a pretty manner; with prettiness; pleasingly. —**Prettiness**, prit′i-nes, *n.* State or quality of being pretty; diminutive beauty; beauty without stateliness or dignity; neatness and taste exhibited on small objects; affected niceness; foppishness.—**Prettyish**, prit′i-ish, *a.* Somewhat pretty.

Pretzel, pret′sel, *n.* [G. *bretzel.*] A crisp, glazed, salty, knotlike cracker.

Prevail, prē-vāl′, *v.i.* [Fr. *prévaloir*, from L. *prævaleo*—*præ*, before, and *valere*, to be strong. VALID.] To overcome; to gain the victory or superiority: often with *over* or *against*; to be in force; to have extensive power or influence (a disease, a custom *prevails* in a place); to have predominant influence; to succeed; to overcome or gain over by persuasion: with *on* or *upon* (they *prevailed on* him to go).—**Prevailing**, prē-vā′ling, *p.* and *a.* Predominant; having superior influence; prevalent; most common or general.—**Prevailingly**, prē-vāl′ing-li, *adv.* So as to prevail. —**Prevalence**, **Prevalency**, prev′a-lens, prev′a-len-si, *n.* The state or quality of being prevalent; superiority; general reception or practice; general existence or extension (the *prevalence* of vice or of a fashion).—**Prevalent**, prev′a-lent, *a.* Prevailing; predominant; most generally received or current; extensively existing. —**Prevalently**, prev′a-lent-li, *adv.* In a prevalent manner.

Prevaricate, prē-var′i-kāt, *v.i.* — *prevaricated*, *prevaricating*. [L. *prævaricor*, *prævaricatus*, to straddle, to shuffle—*præ*, before, and *varus*, straddling.] To act or speak evasively; to evade or swerve from the truth; to shuffle; to quibble in giving answers.—**Prevarication**, prē-var′i-kā″-shon, *n.* The act of prevaricating; a shuffling or quibbling to evade the truth or the disclosure of truth; *law*, a collusion between an informer and a defendant, in order to a feigned prosecution; the wilful concealment or misrepresentation of truth by giving evasive evidence.—**Prevaricator**, prē-var′i-kā-tėr, *n.* One who prevaricates; a shuffler; a quibbler.

Prevenient, prē-vē′ni-ent, *a.* [L. *præveniens.* PREVENT.] Going before; preceding; preventing; preventive. —*Prevenient grace*, *Theol.* term, the grace that precedes or anticipates repentance, but which disposes the heart of man to seek God.

Prevent, prē-vent′, *v.t.* [L. *prævenio*, *præventum*, to anticipate, to prevent—*præ*, before, and *venio*, to come (seen also in *advent*, *convent*, *circumvent*, *intervention*, &c.).] To anticipate‡; to forestall‡; to hinder by something done before; to stop or intercept; to impede; to thwart.—**Preventable**, prē-ven′ta-bl, *a.* Capable of being prevented or hindered.—**Preventer**, prē-ven′tėr, *n.* One who or that which prevents.—**Prevention**, prē-ven′shon, *n.* The act of preventing.—**Preventive**, prē-ven′tiv, *a.* Tending to prevent or hinder. —*Preventive medicine*, the branch of medical practice which seeks to guard against disease and its spread.—*n.* That which prevents; that which intercepts the access or approach of something; an antidote.—**Preventively**, prē-ven′tiv-li, *adv.* By way of prevention.

Previous, prē′vi-us, *a.* [L. *prævius*—*præ*, before, and *via*, a way. VOYAGE, WAY.] Going before in time; being or happening before something else; antecedent; prior. — *Previous question.* Under QUESTION.—**Previously**, prē′vi-us-li, *adv.* In time preceding; beforehand; antecedently. ∴ Syn. under FORMERLY. —**Previousness**, prē′vi-us-nes, *n.* Priority in time.

Previse, prē-vīz′, *v.t.*—*prevised*, *prevising.* [L. *prævisus*, pp. of *prævideo*—*præ*, before, and *video*, to see. VISION.] To foresee; to forewarn.—**Prevision**, prē-vizh′on, *n.* Foresight; foreknowledge; prescience.

Prey, prā, *n.* [O.E. *preie*, *praie*, O.Fr. *preie*, *praie* (Fr. *proie*), from L. *præda*, plunder, whence *predatory*, *depredation.*] Spoil; booty; goods taken from an enemy in war; anything taken by violence and injustice; a victim; that which is seized by carnivorous animals to be devoured. — *Beast of prey*, a carnivorous animal, or one that feeds on the flesh of other animals.—*v.i.* To take prey or booty; to feed by violence: with *on* or *upon* before the object of rapine; to rest heavily, as on the mind; to waste gradually (grief *preyed on* him).

Priapean, prī-ā′pē-an, *a.* Pertaining to the Roman deity *Priapus*, the god of procreation; grossly sensual; obscene.

Price, prīs, *n.* [O.Fr. *pris*, *preis*, Fr. *prix*, from L. *pretium*, a price; the same word as *praise*, and *prize*, to value.] The sum of money or the value which a seller sets on his goods in market; the current value of a commodity; the equivalent for which something is bought or sold; cost; value; worth (a pearl of great *price*); estimation. —*Price of money*, in *com.* the price of credit; the rate of discount at which capital may be lent or borrowed.—**Price-current**, *n.* A periodical account of the current value of merchandise, stocks, &c. Called also *Price-list.*—*v.t.*—*priced*, *pricing.* To set a price on; to value; to ask the price of.—**Priced**, prīst, *a.* Set at a value; having a price; mostly in composition (high-*priced*, low-*priced*).—**Priceless**, prīs′les, *a.* Invaluable; inestimable; too valuable to admit of a price being fixed.

Prick, prik, *n.* [A.Sax. *prica*, *pricu*, a point, a dot = D. *prik*, Dan. *prik*, Sw. *prick*, dot, prick; comp. W. *pric*, a skewer, Ir. *pricadh*, a goad.] A slender pointed thing hard enough to pierce the skin; a thorn; a skewer; a puncture or wound by a prick or prickle; a sting; *fig.* a stinging or tormenting thought; remorse; a dot or small mark (*Shak.*).—*v.t.* To pierce with something sharp pointed; to puncture; to erect (said of the ears, hence, *to prick up the ears*, to listen with eager attention); to fix by a sharp point; to designate or set apart by a puncture or mark (*pricked off* for duty); to spur; to goad; to incite: often with *on*; to sting; to trace by puncturing; to render acid or pungent to the taste (the wine is *pricked*).—*v.i.* To suffer or feel penetration by a point or sharp pain; to be punctured; to become acid; to spur on; to ride rapidly. —**Prick-eared**, *a.* Having pointed ears; having ears standing up prominently. —**Pricker**, prik′ėr, *n.* That which pricks; a sharp-pointed instrument; one who pricks; a light horseman; one who tested whether women were witches by sticking pins into them.—**Pricking**, prik′ing, *n.* The act of piercing with a sharp point; the act of driving a nail into a horse's foot so as to cause lameness; a feeling as from something sharp penetrating the flesh. — **Prickle**, prik′l, *n.* [Dim. of *prick.*] A little prick; a small sharp point; *bot.* a small pointed shoot or sharp process growing from the *bark*, and thus distinguished from the *thorn*, which grows from the *wood* of a plant; a sharp-pointed process or projection, as from the skin of an animal; a spine; a kind of basket. —*v.t.*—*prickled*, *prickling.* To prick slightly; to pierce with fine sharp points.—**Prickleback**, *n.* The stickleback. — **Prickly**, prik′li, *a.* Full of sharp points or prickles; armed with prickles; stinging in feeling.—**Prickliness**, prik′li-nes, *n.* The state of being prickly.—**Prickly-heat**, *n.* The popular name for a severe form of skin-disease known as *lichen.*—**Prickly-pear**, *n.* A variety of cactus covered with clusters of spines, and producing an edible fruit. —**Prickmadam**, prik′mad-am, *n.* A species of stonecrop.—**Prick-post**, *n.* Same as *Queen-post.* — **Prick-punch**, prik′-punsh, *n.* A pointed piece of steel used to prick marks on cold iron or other metal.

Pricket, pri′ket, *n.* A stag in the second year, bearing straight horns with no branches.

Pride, prīd, *n.* [A.Sax. *prýte*, pride, from *prút*, proud. PROUD.] The quality or state of being proud; inordinate self-esteem; an unreasonable conceit of one's own superiority over others; generous elation of heart; a noble self-esteem springing from a consciousness of worth; proud behaviour; insolence; that which is or may be a cause of pride; that of which men are proud; one who or that which gives rise to pride or glorification; highest pitch; splendid show; ostentation. — *v.t.* — *prided*, *priding.* To indulge in pride; to value one's self: used reflexively.—**Prideful**, prīd′ful, *a.* Full of pride; insolent; scornful.—**Pridefully**, prīd′ful-li, *adv.* In a prideful manner.—**Pridefulness**, prīd′ful-nes, *n.* The state or quality of being prideful.—**Prideless**, prīd′les, *a.* Destitute of pride.

Prie-dieu, prē-dyė, *n.* [Fr., pray God.] A kneeling desk for prayers.

Priest, prēst, *n.* [A.Sax. *preóst*, contr. from L. *presbyter.* PRESBYTER.] A clergyman of the Roman Catholic, Greek Catholic, Orthodox, or Episcopalian church; a person consecrated to the ministry of the gospel; a man who officiates in sacred offices; a minister of public worship; a minister of sacrifice or other mediatorial offices; among many non-Christian sects, the title of men selected and trained to perform sacred functions.—**Priestess**, prēs′tes, *n.* A woman who officiates in sacred rites.—**Priestly**, prēst′li, *a.* Pertaining to a priest or to priests; sacerdotal; becoming a priest.—**Priestliness**, prēst′li-nes, *n.* The quality of being priestly.—**Priestcraft**, prēst′kraft, *n.* Priestly policy or system of management based on temporal or material interest; policy of clergy to advance their own order.—**Priesthood**, prēst′hōd, *n.* The office or character of a priest; the order composed of priests; priests collectively.—**Priest-ridden**, *a.* Governed or entirely swayed by priests.

Prig, prig, *n.* [From *prick*, in old sense of to trim or dress up.] A pert, conceited, pragmatical fellow. — **Priggery**, **Priggism**, prig′ėr-i, prig′izm, *n.* The qualities of a prig; pertness; conceit.—**Priggish**, prig′-ish, *a.* Conceited; affected.—**Priggishly**, prig′ish-li, *adv.* In a priggish manner; pertly. — **Priggishness**, prig′ish-nes, *n.* The state or quality of being priggish.

Prig, prig, *n.* [O.Fr. *briguer*, to steal, to act the highwayman; akin *brigand.*] A thief; a low or mean thief.—*v.t.*—*prigged*, *prigging.* To filch; to steal. (A low word.)

Prim, prim, *a.* [O.Fr. *prim*, prime, first, also thin, slender, neat; from L. *primus*, first. PRIME.] Neat; formal; precise; affectedly nice; demure.—**Primly**, prim′-li, *adv.* In a prim or precise manner; with primness.—**Primness**, prim′nes, *n.* Affected formality; stiffness; preciseness.

Primacy. Under PRIMATE.

Prima Donna, prē′ma don′na. [It., first lady.] The first or chief female singer in an opera.—**Prima Facie**, prī-ma fā′shi-ē. [L. *primus*, first, and *facies*, face.] At first view or appearance.—*Prima facie evidence*, *law*, evidence having such a degree of probability that it must prevail unless the contrary be proved.

Primage, prī′māj, *n.* [From verb to *prime.*] A charge paid by the shipper or consigner of goods to the master and sailors for loading the same; the amount of water carried off in steam from the boiler.

Primal, prī′mal, *a.* [From L. *primus*, first. PRIME.] Primary; first in time, order, or importance; original.—**Primary**, prī′ma-ri, *a.* [L. *primarius.*] First in order of time; original; primitive; first; first in dignity or importance; chief; principal;

elementary; preparatory, or lowest in order (*primary* schools); first in intention; radical; original; as the *primary* sense of a word.—*Primary accent*, accent (ʹ) on the stressed syllable of a word.—*Primary cell*, *elect.* an ordinary voltaic cell. Comp. SECONDARY CELL, STORAGE BATTERY.—*Primary colors*. COLOR.—*Primary planets*. PLANET.—*Primary election, pol. sci.* election held to choose party candidates.—*Primary quills*, the largest feathers of the wings of a bird; primaries.—*Primary rocks*, *geol.* rocks of the palaeozoic group; former sense, primitive igneous rocks.—*n.* That which stands highest in rank or importance, as opposed to *secondary*.—**Primarily**, prīʹma-ri-li, *adv.* In a primary manner.—**Primariness**, prīʹma-ri-nes, *n.*

Primate, prīʹmāt, *n.* [Fr. *primat*; L.L. *primas*, *primatis*, from L. *primus*, first. PRIME.] The chief ecclesiastic in certain churches, as the Anglican; an archbishop. The Archbishop of York is entitled *primate* of England; the Archbishop of Canterbury, *primate* of *all* England.—*Primates*, the order of mammals consisting of man and the apes.—**Primateship**, **Primacy**, prīʹmāt-ship, prīʹma-si, *n.* The office or dignity of primate or archbishop.—**Primatial**, pri-māʹshi-al, *a.* Pertaining to a primate.

Prime, prīm, *a.* [L. *primus*, first; superl. of *prior*, former; same root as Skr. *pra*, Gr. and L. *pro*, before; E. *fore*, *first*, &c. PRINCE, PRIM, PRIMITIVE, &c.] First in order of time; primitive; original (*prime* cost); first in rank, degree, or dignity (*prime* minister); first in excellence, value, or importance; first-rate; capital; early; in the first stage. — *Prime conductor*, *elect.* the metallic conductor opposed to the glass plate or cylinder of an electrical machine. —*Prime cost*, first or original cost; the sum or expenditure for which an article can be made or produced.—*Prime minister*, in Great Britain, the first minister of state; the premier.—*Prime mover*, the initial force which puts a machine in motion; a machine which receives and modifies force as supplied by some natural source, as a water-wheel, a steam-engine, &c.—*Prime number*, *arith.* a number not divisible without remainder by any less number than itself except unity.—*Prime vertical*, in *astron.* a celestial great circle passing through the east and west points and the zenith.—*n.* The earliest stage or beginning of anything; the dawn; the morning; the spring of the year; the spring of life; youth; full health, strength, or beauty; the highest or most perfect or most flourishing condition; the best part; that which is best in quality; in *R. Cath. Ch.* the first canonical hour, succeeding to lauds.—*v.t.*—*primed*, *priming*. [Lit. to perform a *prime* or first operation with, to prepare.] To put into a condition for being fired: said of a gun, mine, &c.; to supply with powder for communicating fire to a charge; *painting*, to cover with a ground or first colour; to instruct or prepare a person beforehand what he is to say or do; to post up (to *prime* a witness).—**Primely**, prīmʹli, *adv.* In a prime manner or degree; most excellently.—**Primeness**, prīmʹnes, *n.* The quality of being prime; supreme excellence. — **Primer**, primʹėr or prīʹmėr, *n.* [Fr. *primaire*, elementary, from L. *primarius*, from *primus*, first.] A small elementary book for religious instruction or for teaching children to read; a book of elementary principles; *print.* a name given to two sizes of type, *longprimer* and *greatprimer*.—**Priming**, prīʹming, *n.* *Gun.* and *blasting*, the powder used to ignite the charge; *painting*, the first layer of paint or size laid on a surface which is to be painted; *steam-engine*, the carrying over of water spray with the steam from the boiler into the cylinder—a troublesome defect. — **Priming-valve**, *n.* A valve for the discharge of water carried into the cylinder of a steam-engine with the steam.

Primero, pri-mēʹro, *n.* [Sp. *primero*, first.] An old game at cards.

Primeval, prī-mēʹval, *a.* [L. *primævus*—*primus*, first, and *ævum*, age. PRIME, AGE.] Original; primitive; belonging to the first ages.—**Primevally**, prī-mēʹval-li, *adv.* In a primeval manner; in the earliest times.

Primigenial, prī-mi-jēʹni-al, *a.* [L. *primigenius*—*primus*, first, and root *gen*, to beget.] First-born; original; primary. Also **Primigenious**, **Primigenous**, prī-mi-jēʹni-us, prī-mijʹe-nus, *a.*

Primine, prīʹmin, *n.* [L. *primus*, first.] *Bot.* the outermost sac or covering of an ovule, the inner being termed *secundine*.

Primiparous, pri-mipʹa-rus, *a.* [L. *primus*, first, and *pario*, to bring forth.] Bearing young for the first time.

Primitiæ, prī-mishʹē-ē, *n.pl.* [L.] First-fruits.

Primitive, primʹi-tiv, *a.* [L. *primitivus*, earliest of its kind, from *primus*, first. PRIME.] Pertaining to the beginning or origin; original; first; old-fashioned; characterized by the simplicity of old times; *gram.* applied to a word in its simplest etymological form; not derived; radical; primary; *bot.* original, in opposition to forms resulting from hybridization.—*Primitive colours*. COLOUR.—*Primitive rocks*. PRIMARY. — *n.* An original or primary word; a word not derived from another: opposed to *derivative*. — **Primitively**, primʹi-tiv-li, *adv.* In a primitive manner; originally; primarily; in the ancient or antique style.—**Primitiveness**, primʹi-tiv-nes, *n.* State of being primitive.

Primly, Primness. Under PRIM.

Primogenial, prī-mō-jēʹni-al, *a.* PRIMIGENIAL.

Primogeniture, prī-mō-jenʹi-tūr, *n.* [Fr. *primogéniture*, from L. *primus*, first, and *genitūra*, a begetting, from *gigno*, *genitum*, to beget. GENDER, GENUS.] The state of being born first of the same parents; seniority by birth among children; the right or principle under which the eldest son of a family succeeds to the father's real estate, in preference to, and in absolute exclusion of the younger sons and daughters.—**Primogenitary**, prī-mō-jenʹi-ta-ri, *a.* Pertaining to primogeniture.—**Primogenitive**, prī-mō-jenʹi-tiv, *a.* Relating to primogeniture.—**Primogenitor**, prī-mō-jenʹi-tėr, *n.* [L. *primus*, and *genitor*, father.] The first father or forefather; an ancestor.

Primordial, prī-morʹdi-al, *a.* [L. *primordialis*, from *primordium*, beginning, origin—*primus*, first, and *ordior*, to commence. PRIME, ORDER.] First in order, original, existing from the beginning; *bot.* and *zool.* earliest formed.—*n.* A first principle or element. — **Primordially**, prī-morʹdi-al-li, *adv.* Under the first order of things; at the beginning.

Primp, primp, *v.t.* [From *prim*, or perhaps a form of *prink*.] To deck one's self in a stiff and affected manner.

Primrose, primʹrōz, *n.* [O.E. *primerole*, Fr. *primerole*, from L.L. *primula*, the primrose, from *primus*, first (as the first flower of spring); the last syllable was changed to *rose* to give the word an English appearance and a sort of meaning; comp. *barberry*, &c.] The common name for several beautiful herbaceous plants, both cultivated and wild, with flowers colored red, white, and yellow, and with each flower growing on a separate stem or peduncle rather than in clusters; a dye derived from coal-tar, pinkish-yellow in color; when referred to as a shade, it signifies a pale greenish-yellow tint.—*a.* Resembling a primrose in color; abounding with primroses; flowery; florid; excessively ornate.—**Primrose path**, *n.* The leading of a gay or merry life; indulgence in the showy and sensual pleasures of life.—**Primrose yellow**, *n.* A reddish-yellow color.

Primum mobile, prīʹmum mōʹbil-ē, *n.* [L.] The extreme or outmost sphere added in the earlier mediæval ages to the Ptolemaic system of astronomy, believed to circle the earth in twenty-four hours, and to carry along with it all the other contained spheres; any chief source of action or motion determining that of others.

Primus, prīʹmus, *n.* [L., first.] The first in dignity among the bishops of the Scottish Episcopal Church.

Prince, prins, *n.* [Fr., from L. *princeps*, *principis*, a prince, a chief—*primus*, first, and *capio*, to take. PRIME, CAPABLE.] A man holding the first or highest rank; a sovereign; a sovereign who has the government of a particular territory, but owes certain services to a superior; the son of a sovereign; a male member of a royal family; the chief of any body of men; a man at the head of any class, profession, &c. (a merchant *prince*).—**Princess**, prinʹses, *n.* A female of the same rank as a prince; a female sovereign; the consort of a prince. —**Princedom**, prinsʹdum, *n.* The jurisdiction, rank, or state of a prince. — **Princelike**, prinsʹlīk, *a.* Becoming a prince; like a prince.—**Princely**, prinsʹli, *a.* Pertaining to a prince; resembling a prince; noble; grand; august; magnificent. —*adv.* In a princelike manner.—**Princeliness**, prinsʹli-nes, *n.* The quality of being princely.—**Prince-royal**, *n.* The eldest son of a sovereign.—**Princess-royal**, *n.* The eldest daughter of a sovereign. — **Prince's-feather**, *n.* An annual plant of the amaranth kind.—**Prince's-metal**, *n.* A mixture of copper and zinc imitating gold; said to have been invented by Prince Rupert.

Principal, prinʹsi-pal, *a.* [L. *principalis*, from *princeps*, first in time or order, a chief. PRINCE.] Chief; highest in rank, character, authority, or importance; first; main; essential; most considerable.—*n.* A chief or head; one who takes a leading part; the chief executive of an educational institution, particularly, of an elementary or secondary public school; *law*, the actor or absolute perpetrator of a crime, or an abettor; one who engages another person to act as his representative or agent; *com.* a capital sum lent on interest, due as a debt, or used as a fund: so called in distinction to interest; *carp.* a main timber in an assemblage of pieces.—**Principality**, prin-si-palʹi-ti, *n.* [Fr. *principalité*.] Sovereignty; supreme power; a prince, or one invested with sovereignty; the territory of a prince, or the country which gives title to a prince.—**Principally**, prinʹsi-pal-li, *adv.* In the chief place; chiefly; above all.

Principate, prinʹsi-pāt, *n.* The name given to the rule of the early Roman emperors after Augustus, perpetuating the idea that the emperor was only the chief or *princeps* of the Roman Republic.

Principia, prin-sipʹi-a, *n.pl.* [L., pl. of *principium*. PRINCIPLE.] First principles; elements.

Principle, prinʹsi-pl, *n.* [Fr. *principe*, from L. *principium*, a beginning, origin, element, from *princeps*, *principis*. PRINCE. As to the insertion of the *l* comp. *participle*, *syllable*.] Beginning‡; commencement‡; a source of origin; the primary source from which anything proceeds; element; primordial substance; a general truth; a law comprehending many subordinate truths; a law on which others are founded or from which others are derived; an axiom; a maxim; a tenet; a governing law of conduct; a settled rule of action; a right rule of conduct; uprightness (a man of *principle*); ground of conduct; a motive; *chem.* a component part; an element; a substance on the presence of which certain qualities common to a number of bodies depend.—**Principled**, prinʹsi-pld, *a.* Holding certain principles; fixed in certain principles.

Prink, pringk, *v.i.* [A slightly modified form of *prank*.] To prank; to dress for show; to strut; to put on stately airs.—*v.t.* To deck; to adorn fantastically.

Print, print, *v.t.* [Shortened from *emprint*, *imprint*; Fr. *empreinte*, impression, stamp, from *empreindre*, to print, imprint, from L. *imprimo*, *impressum*, to impress. PRESS.] To impress; to imprint; to mark by pressing one thing on another; to take an impression of; to form by impression; to stamp; to fix deeply, as in the mind or memory; to form or copy by pressure, as from a stereotype plate, a form of movable types, engraved copper or steel plates, stone, &c.; to stamp or impress with coloured figures, as cotton cloth; *photog.* to take a positive picture of from a negative.—*v.i.* To use or practise the art of printing.—*n.* A mark made by impression; a stamp; printed letters; the impression of types in general; that which is produced by printing, especially an engraving; a newspaper or other periodical; printed cloth.—*In print*, in a printed form; issued from the press; published.—*Out of print*, said of a book of which there are no copies for sale, or none for sale by the publisher.—**Printer**, print′ėr, *n.* One who prints books, pamphlets, newspapers, &c.; one who prints cloth, or one who takes impressions from engraved plates, from stone, &c.—*Printer's devil*, the newest apprentice lad in a printing-office.—**Print-field**, *n.* An establishment for printing and bleaching calicoes.—**Printing**, print′ing, *n.* The art or practice of impressing letters, characters, or figures on paper, cloth, or other material; the business of a printer; typography. By the term *printing* what is called *letterpress printing* is commonly understood, that is, the method of taking impressions from letters and other characters cast or cut in relief, and whether directly from the type surface or from stereotype plates. In *photog.* the act or art of obtaining a positive photographic picture from a negative.—**Printing-frame**, *n.* In *photog.* a frame in which the negative is laid for printing photographs.—**Printing-ink**, *n.* Ink used by letterpress printers.—**Printing-machine**, *n.* A machine for taking impressions, used by printers, and of a great variety of forms.—**Printing-office, Printing-house**, *n.* A house or office where letterpress printing is executed.—**Printing-paper**, *n.* Paper to be used in printing books, pamphlets, &c., as distinguished from *writing-paper*, &c.—**Printing-press**, *n.* A press for the printing of books, &c.—**Printing-type**, *n.* Letterpress type used by printers for books, newspapers, &c.—**Print-room**, *n.* An apartment containing a collection of engravings.—**Print-seller**, *n.* One who sells prints or engravings.—**Print-shop**, *n.* A printing plant; a shop where prints or engravings are sold.—**Printworks**, *n.* A place for printing calicoes.

Prior, prī′or, *a.* [L. *prior*, a compar. to which *primus*, first, is the superl. PRIME.] Preceding, especially in the order of time; earlier; antecedent; anterior.—*adv.* Previously; antecedently (he had never been there *prior* to that time).—*n.* The superior of a priory or a monastery of lower than abbatial rank; a monk next in dignity to an abbot.—*Grand prior*, a title given to the commandants of the priories of the military orders of St. John of Jerusalem, of Malta, and of the Templars.—**Priorate, Priorship**, prī′or-āt, prī′or-ship, *n.* The dignity or office of a prior.—**Prioress**, prī′or-es, *n.* The female head in a convent of nuns, next in rank to an abbess.—**Priority**, prī-or′i-ti, *n.* The state of being prior or antecedent in time, or of preceding something else; precedence in place or rank.—**Priorly**, prī′or-li, *adv.* Antecedently.—**Priory**, prī′e-ri, *n.* A religious house of which a prior or prioress is the superior, in dignity below an abbey.

Prise, Prize, prīz, *n.* [From Fr. *prise*, a grasp, a taking, from *prendre*, L. *prehendere*. PRISON.] A lever.—*v.t.* To raise as by means of a lever; to force up.

Prism, prizm, *n.* [L. and Gr. *prisma*, lit. a sawn piece, from *prizō*, to saw.] A solid whose bases or ends are any similar, equal, and parallel plane figures, and whose sides are parallelograms; a bar of glass with a triangular section, used for decomposing light, as in spectrum analysis.—**Prismatic, Prismatical**, priz-mat′ik, priz-mat′i-kal, *a.* Resembling or pertaining to a prism; formed or exhibited by a prism.—*Prismatic colours*, the colours into which a ray of light is decomposed in passing through a prism, red, orange, yellow, green, blue, indigo, violet.—**Prismatically**, priz-mat′i-kal-li, *adv.* In the form or manner of a prism; by means of a prism.—**Prismatoidal**, priz-ma-toi′dal, *a.* Having a prism-like form.—**Prismoid**, priz′moid, *n.* A body that approaches to the form of a prism.—**Prismoidal**, priz-moi-dal, *a.* Having the form of a prismoid.

Prison, priz′on or priz′n, *n.* [Fr. *prison*, from L. *prehensio*, *prehensionis*, a capture, from *prehendo*, to seize (whence *prehensile*, &c.). APPREHEND.] A place of confinement or involuntary restraint; especially, a public building for the confinement or safe custody of criminals and others committed by process of law; a jail.—*v.t.* To shut up in a prison; to confine; to imprison.—**Prisoner**, priz′on-ėr, *n.* One who is confined in a prison; a person under arrest, whether in prison or not; a captive; one taken by an enemy in war; one whose liberty is restrained, as a bird in a cage.—**Prison-base, Prisoner's base**, *n.* A game consisting chiefly of running and being pursued from goals or bases.—**Prison-house**, *n.* A house in which prisoners are kept; a jail.—**Prison-ship**, *n.* A ship fitted up for receiving and detaining prisoners.—**Prison-van**, *n.* A close carriage for conveying prisoners.

Pristine, pris′tīn, *a.* [L. *pristinus*; same root as *prior*, *prime*, &c.] Belonging to a primitive or early state or period; original; primitive.

Pritch, prich, *n.* [A softened form of *prick*.] A sharp-pointed instrument; an instrument for making holes.

Prithee, priᴛʜ′ē, a corruption of *pray thee I pray thee.*

Private, prī′vat, *a.* [L. *privatus*, from *privo*, to separate, from *privus*, separate, peculiar (seen also in *deprive*, *privilege*).] Peculiar to one's self; belonging to or concerning an individual only; personal: opposed to *public* or *national*; not known, open, or accessible to people in general; secret; not invested with public office or employment; not having a public or official character; unconnected with others; solitary; participating in knowledge; privy; *milit.* said of a common soldier.—*Private hospital*, a hospital financed from private sources, rather than public agencies.—*Private nurse*, a nurse caring for one patient.—*In private*, not publicly or openly; secretly.—*n.* A common soldier; one of the lowest rank in the army.—**Privacy**, prī′va-si, *n.* A state of being private or in retirement; seclusion; secrecy; solitude; retirement.—**Privately**, prī′vat-li, *adv.* In a private or secret manner; not openly or publicly; in a manner affecting an individual; personally.—**Privateness**, prī′vat-nes, *n.* The state of being private.—**Privateer**, prī-va-tēr′, *n.* A vessel of war owned and equipped by one or more private persons, and licensed by a government to seize or plunder the ships of an enemy in war.—*v.i.* To cruise in a privateer.—**Privateersman**, prī-va-tērz′man, *n.* An officer or seaman of a privateer.—**Privation**, prī-vā′shon, *n.* [L. *privatio*, from *privo*, to bereave.] The state of being deprived; deprivation of what is necessary for comfort; destitution; want; the act of removing something possessed.—**Privative**, priv′a-tiv, *a.* Causing deprivation; *gram.* changing the sense from positive to negative.—*n.* A prefix to a word which gives it a contrary sense, as *un* and *in* in *unwise*, *inhuman*.—**Privatively**, priv′a-tiv-li, *adv.* In a privative manner.

Privet, priv′et, *n.* [Etym. unknown.] A shrub frequently planted to form ornamental hedges in gardens.

Privilege, priv′i-lej, *n.* [L. *privilegium*, an exceptional law, from *privus*, separate, peculiar, and *lex*, *legis*, a law. PRIVATE, LEGAL.] A right or advantage enjoyed by a person or body of persons beyond the common advantages of other individuals; a private or personal favour enjoyed; a peculiar advantage.—*Question of privilege*, in *parliament*, a question affecting the privileges appertaining to the members.—*v.t.* To grant some privilege, right, or exemption to; to invest with a peculiar right or immunity; to authorize†; to license.—**Privileged**, priv′i-lejd, *p.* and *a.* Invested with a privilege or privileges; enjoying some peculiar right, favour, or immunity.

Privy, priv′i, *a.* [Fr. *privé*, from L. *privatus*. PRIVATE.] Private; assigned to private uses; not public; secret; not seen openly; appropriated to retirement; sequestered (O.T.); privately knowing; admitted to the participation of knowledge with another of a secret transaction (*privy to* a thing).—*n.* A latrine or necessary-house.—*Gentlemen of the privy chamber*, officers of the royal household of Britain who attend on the sovereign at court, in progresses, &c.—**Privily**, priv′i-li, *adv.* In a privy manner; privately; secretly.—**Privity**, priv′i-ti, *n.* Privacy†; private knowledge; joint knowledge with another of a private concern: *pl.* secret parts; the genital organs.—**Privy-council**, *n.* The principal council of the English sovereign, the members of which are chosen at his or her pleasure.—**Privy-councillor**, *n.* A member of the privy-council.—**Privy-purse**, *n.* The income set apart for the sovereign's personal use.—**Privy-seal**, *n.* In England, the seal appended to grants which are afterwards to pass the great seal, and to documents of minor importance: the secretary of state who is intrusted with the privy-seal is called *lord privy-seal.*

Prize, prīz, *n.* [Fr. *prise*, a taking, capture, prize, from *prendre*, to take, from L. *prehendo*, to seize. PRISON.] That which is taken from an enemy in war, particularly a ship, with the property taken in it; that which is deemed a valuable acquisition; any gain or advantage; that which is obtained or offered as the reward of exertion or contest; that which is won in a lottery, or in any similar way.—**Prize-court**, *n.* A court which adjudicates on captures made at sea.—**Prize-fight**, *n.* A pugilistic encounter or boxing-match for a prize.—**Prize-fighter**, *n.* A professional pugilist or boxer.—**Prize-fighting**, *n.* Boxing in public for a reward.—**Prize-list**, *n.* A list of prizes gained in any competition, as a school examination or a cattle-show.—**Prizeman**, prīz′man, *n.* The winner of a prize.—**Prize-money**, *n.* Money distributed among the captors of a ship or place where booty has been obtained, in certain proportions according to rank, the money being realized from the sale of the prize or booty.—**Prize-ring**, *n.* A ring or inclosed place for prize-fighting; prize-fighters collectively (a member of the *prize-ring*).

Prize, prīz, *v.t.*—*prized*, *prizing*. [Fr. *priser*, to value, to set a price on, from L. *pretium*, a price. PRICE, PRECIOUS.] To set or estimate the value of; to rate; to value highly; to consider of great worth; to esteem.—*a.* Meriting award of a prize, as *prize* cattle.—**Prizable**, prīz′abl, *a.*

Prize, *v.t.* To force up. See PRISE.

Proa, prō′a, *n.* [Malay *prau*, *prahu.*] A kind of Malay vessel with one side flat, and an outrigger adjusted sometimes to the leeward side and sometimes to both sides, remarkable for swiftness.

Probable, prob′a-bl, *a.* [Fr. *probable*, from L. *probabilis*, that may be proved, probable, from *probo*, to prove. PROVE.] Supported by or based on evidence which inclines the mind to belief, but leaves some room for doubt; likely; rendering something probable (*probable* evidence).—**Probabilism**, prob′a-bil-izm, *n.* *R. Cath. theol.* a theory, which, when there are two contrary opinions on a point of morality, considers it lawful to adopt that which is the more in agreement with personal inclination, provided it be supported by some weighty authority.—**Probabilist**, prob′a-bil-ist, *n.* One who maintains the theory of probabilism.—**Probability**, prob-a-bil′i-ti, *n.* [Fr. *probabilité*, L. *probabilitas.*] The state or quality of being probable; likelihood; appearance of truth; anything that has the appearance of reality or truth (in this sense with a plural); *math.* the ratio of the number of chances by which an event may happen, to the number by which it may both happen and fail.—**Probably**, prob'a-bli, *adv.* In a probable manner; in all likelihood; as is probable; likely.

Probang, prō'bang, *n.* [Probably from *probe.*] *Surg.* a long slender elastic rod of whalebone, with a piece of sponge securely attached to one end, intended to push down anything stuck in the gullet.

Probate, prō'bāt, *n.* [L. *probatus*, from *probo*, to prove.] A proceeding before proper authorities by which a person's will or testament is established as such and registered.—**Probate court**, *n.* A court concerned with the probate of wills, and all matters relating thereto.

Probation, prō-bā'shon, *n.* [L. *probatio*, *probationis*, an approving. PROBABLE.] The act of proving; proof; any proceeding designed to ascertain character, qualifications, or the like; a preliminary or preparatory trial or examination; a period of time during which a delinquent must report at regular intervals to a probation officer. —**Probationer**, prō-bā'shon-ėr, *n.* One who is on probation or trial; a delinquent under the supervision of a probation officer; the designation given to a student nurse during her first year of training. —**Probation officer**, *n.* One to whom a probationer must report at regular intervals.—**Probative**, prō'ba-tiv, *a.* Serving for trial or proof.—**Probatory**, prō'ba-to-ri, *a.* Serving for trial; pertaining to or serving for proof.

Probe, prōb, *n.* [From L. *probo*, to test, to try, to prove. PROVE.] A surgeon's instrument for examining the depth or other circumstances of a wound, ulcer, or cavity; an investigation of any activity which may have a tendency to threaten the public welfare.—*v.t.*—*probed*, *probing*. To apply a probe to; to examine by a probe; *fig.* to search to the bottom; to examine thoroughly into.

Probity, prob'i-ti, *n.* [L. *probitas*, from *probus*, worthy, honest, good.] Tried virtue or integrity; strict honesty; rectitude; uprightness; high principle.

Problem, prob'lem, *n.* [Fr. *problème*, L. *problema*, from Gr. *problēma*—*pro*, before, and *ballō*, to throw.] A question proposed for solution, decision, or determination; a knotty point requiring to be cleared up; *geom.* a proposition requiring some operation to be performed, differing from a theorem in that the latter requires something to be proved. — **Problematic**, **Problematical**, prob-le-mat'ik, prob-le-mat'i-kal, *a.* Questionable; uncertain; disputable; doubtful.—**Problematically**, prob-le-mat'i-kal-li, *adv.* In a problematical manner.—**Problematist**,† prob'lem-a-tist, *n.* One who proposes problems.—**Problematize**, prob'lem-a-tīz, *v.t.* To propose problems.

Proboscis, prō-bos'sis, *n.* pl. **Proboscides**, prō-bos'si-dēz. [L. *proboscis*, from Gr. *proboskis*—*pro*, before, and *boskō*, to feed.] The snout or trunk projecting from the head of an elephant and other animals; the horny tube formed by the modified jaws of insects, used for sucking blood from animals or juice from plants; the nose: used humorously or in ridicule. — **Proboscidate**, **Proboscidial**, **Proboscidian**, prō-bos'si-dāt, prō-bos-sid'i-al, prō-bos-sid'i-an, *a.* Furnished with a proboscis; proboscidean. — **Proboscidean**, prō-bos-sid'ē-an, *a.* and *n.* Pertaining to, or one of, those mammals which have the nose prolonged into a prehensile trunk, as the elephant, &c. — **Proboscidiform**, prō-bos-sid'i-form, *a.* Having the form of a proboscis.

Pro-cathedral, prō-ka-thē'dral, *n.* A church that serves temporarily as a cathedral.

Proceed, prō-sēd', *v.i.* [Fr. *procéder*; L. *procedo*—*pro*, before, and *cedo*, to go. CEDE.] To move, pass, or go onward; to continue or renew motion or progress; to advance; to go on; to pass from one point, stage, or topic to another; to issue or come, as from an origin, source, or fountain; to set to work and go on in a certain way; to act according to some method; to begin and carry on a legal action.—**Procedure**, prō-sē'dūr, *n.* [Fr. *procédure.*] Manner of proceeding or acting; a course or mode of action; conduct; a step taken; a proceeding.—**Proceeder**, prō-sē'dėr, *n.* One who proceeds. — **Proceeding**, prō-sē'ding, *n.* The act of one who proceeds; a measure or step taken; a transaction; a mode of conduct; *pl.* the course of steps in the prosecution of actions at law; the record or account of the transactions of a society.—**Proceeds**, prō'sēdz, *n.pl.* The amount accruing from some transaction; the value of goods sold or converted into money.

Proceleusmatic, prō-sel'ūs-mat"ik, *a.* [Gr. *prokeleusmatikos*—*pro*, before, and *keleusma*, mandate, *keleuō*, to incite.] Inciting, animating, or encouraging†; *pros.* consisting of four short syllables: applied to a particular metrical foot.

Procere, prō-sēr', *a.* [L. *procerus*, tall.] Tall.—**Procerity**, prō-ser'i-ti, *n.* Tallness; height of stature. *Rare.*

Process, pros'es, *n.* [L. *processus*, from *procedo*, *processum*, to proceed. PROCEED.] A proceeding or moving forward; progressive course; way in which something goes on; gradual progress; course; series of actions or experiments (a chemical *process*); series of motions or changes going on, as in growth, decay, &c., in physical bodies; course; lapse; a passing or elapsing (the *process* of time); *law*, the whole course of proceedings in a cause; a projecting portion of something; especially, in *anat.* any protuberance or projecting part of a bone or other body; printing done from photo-engraved plates.—*Process printing*, *n.* A method of reproducing objects in natural colors, chiefly pictures, by means of three, four, or more photoengravings, each printing in a different color, and printed one over the other.—**Procession**, prō-sesh'on, *n.* [L. *processio.*] The act of proceeding or issuing forth; a train of persons walking, or riding on horseback or in vehicles, in a formal march.—**Processional**, prō-sesh'on-al, *n.* *R. Cath. Ch.* a prayer or hymn used for religious processions.—**Process server**, *n.* A bailiff or sheriff's officer.

Procès-verbal, prō-sā-ver-bäl, *n.* In *French law*, a detailed authentic account of an official proceeding; a statement of facts.

Prochronism, prō'kron-izm, *n.* [Gr. *pro*, before, and *chronos*, time.] The dating of an event before the time when it happened, or representing something as existing before it really did.

Procidence, prō'si-dens, *n.* [L. *procidentia*, from *pro*, forward, and *cado*, to fall.] *Med.* a falling down; a prolapsus.—**Procidnous**, prō-sid'ū-us, *a.* Falling from its proper place.

Proclaim, prō-klām', *v.t.* [L. *proclamo*—*pro*, before, and *clamo*, to cry out. CLAIM.] To make known by public announcement; to promulgate; to announce; to publish; to outlaw by public denunciation.—**Proclaimer**, **Proclaimant**, prō-klā'mėr, prō-klā'mant, *n.* One who proclaims. — **Proclamation**, prok-la-mā'shon, *n.* [L. *proclamatio.*] The act of proclaiming; an official public announcement or declaration; a published ordinance.

Proclitic, prō-klit'ik, *n.* [From Gr. *pro*, forward, and *klinō*, to lean.] *Greek gram.* a monosyllabic word so closely attached to a following word as to have no independent existence and therefore no accent.

Proclivity, prō-kliv'i-ti, *n.* [L. *proclivitas*, from *pro*, before, and *clivus*, a slope. ACCLIVITY.] Inclination; propensity; proneness; tendency; readiness.—**Proclivous**, prō-klī'vus, *a.* [L. *proclivus.*] Inclined; prone; tending by nature.

Procœlous, **Procœlian**, prō-sē'lus, prō-sē'li-an, *a.* [Gr. *pro*, before, and *koilos*, hollow.] A term applied to the vertebræ of certain animals, as the existing saurians, which have a cavity in front and a ball at the back part; having such vertebræ.

Proconsul, prō-kon'sul, *n.* [L., from *pro*, for, and *consul.*] In ancient Rome an officer who discharged the duties of a consul without being himself consul; generally one who had been consul. — **Proconsular**, **Proconsulary**, prō-kon'sul-ėr, prō-kon'sul-a-ri, *a.* Pertaining to a proconsul. — **Proconsulate**, **Proconsulship**, prō-kon'sul-āt, prō-kon'sul-ship, *n.* The office of a proconsul.

Procrastinate, prō-kras'ti-nāt, *v.t.*—*procrastinated*, *procrastinating*. [L. *procrastino*, *procrastinatus*—*pro*, forward, and *crastinus*, belonging to the morrow, from *cras*, to-morrow.] To put off from day to day; to delay; to defer to a future time.—*v.i.* To delay; to be dilatory.—**Procrastination**, prō-kras'ti-nā"shon, *n.* The act or habit of putting off to a future time; dilatoriness. — **Procrastinator**, prō-kras'ti-nā-tėr, *n.* One who procrastinates.—**Procrastinatory**, prō-kras'ti-na-to-ri, *a.* Pertaining to or implying procrastination.

Procreate, prō'krē-āt, *v.t.*—*procreated*, *procreating*. [L. *procreo*—*pro*, before, and *creo*, to create. CREATE.] To beget; to generate and produce; to engender.—**Procreation**, prō-krē-ā'shon, *n.* The act of procreating or begetting.—**Procreative**, prō'krē-ā-tiv, *a.* Having the power or function of procreating.—**Procreativeness**, prō'krē-ā-tiv-nes, *n.* — **Procreator**, prō'krē-ā-tėr, *n.* One that begets; a father or sire. — **Procreant**, prō'krē-ant, *a.* [L. *procreans*, *procreantis*, ppr. of *procreo.*] Procreating; producing young; assisting in producing young†. —*n.* One who or that which procreates.

Procrustean, prō-krus'tē-an, *a.* Pertaining to or resembling *Procrustes*, a robber of ancient Greece, who tortured his victims by placing them on a bed, and stretching or lopping off their legs to adapt the body to its length; hence, acting similarly; producing uniformity by deforming or mutilating.

Proctor, prok'tėr, *n.* [Contr. from *procurator*; comp. *proxy.*] A procurator; a person employed to manage another's cause in a court of civil or ecclesiastical law; an official in a university whose function is to see that good order is kept and that obedience is maintained.—**Proctorage**, prok'tėr-āj, *n.* Management by a proctor. —**Proctorial**, prok-tō'ri-al, *a.* Pertaining to a proctor.—**Proctorship**, *n.*

Procumbent, prō-kum'bent, *a.* [L. *procumbens*—*pro*, forward, and *cumbere*, to lie.] Lying down; prone; *bot.* trailing; prostrate; lying on the ground, but without putting forth roots (a *procumbent* stem).

Procurator, prok'ū-rā-tėr, *n.* [L., one who manages, an agent, from *procuro*. PROCURE.] The manager of another's affairs; one who undertakes the care of legal proceedings for another; a governor of a province under the Roman emperors. — **Procurator-fiscal**, *n.* The title of public officials in Scotland at whose instance criminal proceedings are instituted and carried on in inferior courts.—**Procuratorial**, prō-kū'ra-tō"ri-al, *a.* Pertaining to a procurator or proctor.—**Procuratorship**, prok'ū-rā-tėr-ship, *n.* The office of a procurator.—**Procuracy**, prok'ū-ra-si, *n.* The office or service of a procurator; the management of an affair for another. — **Procuration**, prō-kū-rā'shon, *n.* Management of another's affairs; the document by which a person is empowered to transact the affairs of another.

Procure, prō-kūr', *v.t.*—*procured*, *procuring*. [Fr. *procurer*, from L. *procurare*, to take care of, to attend to—*pro*, for, and *cura*, care. CURE.] To obtain, as by request, loan, effort, labour, or purchase; to get, gain, come into possession of; to bring on; to attract (modesty *procures* respect); to cause, bring about, effect, contrive.—*v.i.* To pimp.—**Procurable**, prō-kū'ra-bl, *a.* Capable of being procured; obtainable.—**Procurement**, prō-kūr'ment, *n.* The act of procuring or obtaining.—**Procurer**, prō-kū'rėr, *n.* One that procures; a pimp; a pander.—**Procuress**, prok'ū-res, *n.* A female pimp; a bawd.

Procurvation, prō-kėr-vā'shon, *n.* [L. *pro*, forward, and *curvatio*, a curving.] A bending forward.

Prod, prod, *n.* [A form of *brod, brad.*] A pointed instrument, as a goad or an awl; a stab.—*v.t.—prodded, prodding.* To prick with a pointed instrument; to goad.

Prodigal, prod'i-gal, *a.* [L.L. *prodigalis*, from L. *prodigus*, prodigal, from *pro*, forth, and *ago*, to drive. ACT.] Given to extravagant expenditure; expending wastefully; profuse; lavish; wasteful; lavishly bountiful.—*n.* One that expends money extravagantly; one that is profuse or lavish; a waster; a spendthrift. — **Prodigality**, prod-i-gal'i-ti, *n.* Extravagance in expenditure; profusion; waste; excessive or profuse liberality.—**Prodigally**, prod'i-gal-li, *adv.* In a prodigal manner; extravagantly; lavishly; wastefully; profusely.

Prodigious, prō-dij'us, *a.* [Fr. *prodigieux*; L. *prodigiosus*, strange, wonderful, from *prodigium*, a prodigy.] Of the nature of a prodigy‡; extraordinary; very great; huge; enormous; excessive; intense. — **Prodigiously**, prō-dij'us-li, *adv.* Enormously; astonishingly; excessively.—**Prodigiousness**, prō-dij'us-nes, *n.*—**Prodigy**, prod'i-ji, *n.* [L. *prodigium.*] Something extraordinary from which omens are drawn; a portent; anything very extraordinary; a wonder or miracle (he is a *prodigy* of learning); something out of the ordinary course of nature.

Produce, prō-dūs', *v.t.—produced, producing.* [L. *produco—pro*, before, forward, and *ducere*, to lead, bring. DUKE.] To bring forward; to bring or offer to view or notice; to exhibit; to bring forth; to give birth to; to bear, furnish, yield; to cause, effect, bring about; to make; to bring into being or form; to make accrue (money *produces* interest); *geom.* to draw out in length; to extend (to *produce* a line for a certain distance).—*v.t.* To bring forth or yield appropriate offspring, products, or consequences.

Produce, prō'dūs, *n.* A total produced, brought forth, or yielded; the outcome yielded by labor and natural growth; yield or production (the *produce* of a farm or of a country).—**Producer**, prō-dū'sėr, *n.* One who or that which produces; one who finances or supervises the making of motion pictures, plays, &c.—**Producers' goods**, *n.* Instruments of production; tools and raw materials; economic goods that benefit the consumer only indirectly. —**Producibility**, prō-dū'si-bil"i-ti, *n.* The capability of being produced.—**Producible**, prō-dū'si-bl, *a.* Capable of being produced.—**Product**, prod'ukt, *n.* [L. *productum.*] A thing which is produced by nature, as fruit, grain, or vegetables; that which is yielded by the soil; that which is produced by labor or mental application; a production; something resulting as a consequence; result; *math.* the result of, or quantity produced by, the multiplication of two numbers or quantities together.—**Productile**, prō-duk'til, *a.* [L. *productilis.*] Capable of being extended in length.—**Production**, prō-duk'shon, *n.* [L. *productio, productionis.*] The act or process of producing; *pol. econ.* the producing of articles having an exchange value; that which is produced or made (the *productions* of the earth, of art, of intellect).—**Productive**, prō-duk'tiv, *a.* Having the power of producing; fertile; producing good crops; bringing into being; causing to exist (an age *productive* of great men); *pol. econ.* producing commodities of great value; adding to the wealth of the world.—**Productively**, prō-duk'tiv-li, *adv.* In a productive manner.—**Productiveness**, prō-duk'tiv-nes, *n.* The quality of being productive.—**Productivity**, prō-duk-tiv'i-ti, *n.* Power of producing; state or quality of being productive.

Proem, prō'em, *n.* [Fr. *proème*, from L. *proœmium*, Gr. *prooimion—pro*, before, and *oimos*, way.] Preface; introduction; preliminary observations to a book or writing. —**Proemial**, prō-em'i-al, *a.* Having the character of a proem.

Profane, prō-fān', *a.* [Fr. *profane*, from L. *profanus*, profane, unholy—*pro*, forth from, and *fanum*, a temple. FANE.] Not sacred or devoted to sacred purposes; not possessing any peculiar sanctity; secular; irreverent towards God or holy things; speaking or spoken, acting or acted in contempt of sacred things or implying it; blasphemous; polluted.—*Profane history*, all history other than biblical.—*v.t.—profaned, profaning.* To treat as if not sacred or deserving reverence; to treat with irreverence, impiety, or sacrilege; to desecrate (to *profane* the name of God, or the Sabbath); to put to a wrong use; to employ basely or unworthily. — **Profanation**, prof-a-nā'shon, *n.* The act of profaning; the violating of sacred things, or the treating of them with contempt or irreverence; desecration; the act of treating with too little delicacy.—**Profanely**, prō-fān'li, *adv.* In a profane manner; impiously; blasphemously. — **Profaneness**, prō-fān'nes, *n.*—**Profaner**, prō-fā'nėr, *n.* One who profanes.—**Profanity**, prō-fan'i-ti, *n.* The quality of being profane; that which is profane; profane language or conduct.

Profess, prō-fes', *v.t.* [L. *profiteri, professus*, to declare, acknowledge, profess—*pro*, before, and *fateor*, to avow; same root as *fame, fable, fate.*] To make open declaration of; to avow, acknowledge, own; to acknowledge or own publicly to be; to lay claim openly to the character of; used *refl.* (to *profess one's self* a Christian); to make a show of; to make protestations or a pretence of; to pretend (to *profess* great friendship for a person); to declare one's self versed in (he *professes* surgery).—*v.i.* To declare openly; to make any declaration or assertion.—**Professedly**, prō-fes'ed-li, *adv.* By profession; avowedly.—**Profession**, prō-fesh'on, *n.* [L. *professio.*] The act of professing; a public avowal or acknowledgment of one's sentiments or belief; a declaration; a representation or protestation (*professions* of friendship or sincerity); a calling superior to a mere trade or handicraft, as that of medicine, law, architecture, &c.; a vocation; the collective body of persons engaged in such calling.—**Professional**, prō-fesh'on-al, *a.* Pertaining to a profession; engaged in a profession.—*n.* A member of any profession, but more often applied, in opposition to *amateur*, to persons who make their living by arts, &c., in which non-professionals are accustomed to engage.—**Professionally**, prō-fesh'on-al-li, *adv.* In a professional manner; in the way of one's profession or calling. — **Professor**, prō-fes'ėr, *n.* [L.] One who professes; one who publicly unites himself to the visible church; one who is visibly or ostensibly religious; one that publicly teaches any art, science, or branch of learning; particularly, an official in a university, college, or other seminary, whose business is to deliver lectures or instruct students. — **Professorial**, prō-fes-sō'ri-al, *a.* Pertaining to a professor in a college, &c.—**Professoriate** prō-fes-sō'ri-āt, *n.* A body of professors; the teaching staff of professors.—**Professorship**, prō-fes'ėr-ship, *n.* The office of a professor.

Proffer, prof'ėr, *v.t.* [Fr. *proférer*, from L. *proferre*, to bring forward—*pro*, before, and *ferre*, to bring. FERTILE, BEAR.] To hold out that a person may take; to offer for acceptance.—*n.* An offer made; something proposed for acceptance by another.—**Profferer**, prof'ėr-ėr, *n.* One who proffers.

Proficient, prō-fish'ent, *n.* [L. *proficiens*, from *proficio*, I advance, make progress, improve—*pro*, forward, and *facio*, to make. FACT.] One who has made considerable advances in any business, art, science, or branch of learning; an adept; an expert. —*a.* Well versed in any business or branch of learning; well qualified; competent.—**Proficiently**, prō-fish'ent-li, *adv.* In a proficient manner. — **Proficiency**, prō-fish'en-si, *n.* The state of being proficient; skill and knowledge.

Profile, prō'fīl, *n.* [Fr. *profil*, from It. *profilo*; from L. *pro*, before, and *filum*, a thread, line.] An outline or contour; especially an outline of the human face seen sideways; the side face or half face; the outline or contour of anything, such as a building, portion of country, &c., as shown by a section. Used also as adj.—*v.t.—profiled, profiling.* To draw in profile; to give a profile of.—**Profilist**, prō'fīl-ist, *n.* One who takes profiles.

Profit, prof'it, *n.* [Fr. *profit*, from L. *profectus*, progress, increase, from *proficio*, to advance, to improve. PROFICIENT.] Any advantage; an accession of good from labour or exertion; especially, the advantage or gain resulting to the owner of capital from its employment in any undertaking; the difference between the original cost and selling price of anything; pecuniary gain; emolument.—*Rate of profit*, the proportion which the amount of profit bears to the capital employed.—*v.t.* To benefit; to advantage; to be of service to; to advance.—*v.i.* To derive profit; to improve; to make progress intellectually or morally; to gain pecuniarily; to become richer; to be of use or advantage; to bring good.—**Profitable**, prof'i-ta-bl, *a.* Yielding or bringing profit or gain; gainful; lucrative; useful; advantageous.—**Profitableness**, prof'i-ta-bl-nes, *n.* The quality of being profitable. —**Profitably**, prof'i-ta-bli, *adv.* In a profitable manner; gainfully; advantageously.—**Profiteer**, prof-it-ēr', *n.* A trader who takes advantage of abnormal conditions, such as those which held during the Great War, to make excessive profit.—*v.i.* To make excess profits.—**Profitless**, prof'it-les, *a.* Void of profit, gain, or advantage. —**Profitlessly**, prof'it-les-li, *adv.*

Profligate, prof'li-gāt, *a.* [L. *profligatus*, pp. of *profligo*, to rout, to ruin—*pro*, intens., and *fligo*, to strike down; seen also in *conflict, inflict*, &c.] Ruined in morals; abandoned to vice; lost to virtue or decency; vicious; shameless in wickedness.—*n.* An abandoned person; one who has lost all regard to good principles, virtue, or decency. —**Profligately**, prof'li-gāt-li, *adv.* In a profligate manner.—**Profligacy, Profligateness**, prof'li-ga-si, prof'li-gāt-nes, *n.* The quality or condition of being profligate; a profligate or very vicious course of life; abandoned conduct.

Profound, prō-found', *a.* [Fr. *profond*, L. *profundus—pro*, forward, far, and *fundus*, bottom. FOUND, FUND.] Deep; descending or being far below the surface, or far below the adjacent places; having great depth; intellectually deep; deep in knowledge or skill (a *profound* scholar); characterized by intensity; far-reaching; deeply felt (*profound* grief); touching; bending low; humble; exhibiting or expressing humility (a *profound* bow, *profound* reverence).—*n.* The deep; the sea; the ocean (with *the*); an abyss; a deep immeasurable space.—**Profoundly**, prō-found'li, *adv.* In a profound manner.—**Profoundness**, prō-found'nes, *n.* Profundity; depth. — **Profundity**, prō-fun'di-ti, *n.* The quality or condition of being profound; depth of place, of knowledge, &c.

Profuse, prō-fūs', *a.* [L. *profusus*, from *profundo—pro*, forth, and *fundere*, to pour. FUSE.] Pouring forth lavishly; extravagant; lavish; liberal to excess; prodigal; poured forth lavishly; exuberant.—**Profusely**, prō-fūs'li, *adv.* In a profuse manner; lavishly; prodigally.—**Profuseness**, prō-fūs'nes, *n.* The state or quality of being profuse.—**Profusion**, prō-fū'zhon, *n.* [L. *profusio.*] Profuse or lavish expenditure; rich abundance; lavish supply; exuberant plenty.

Progeny, proj'e-ni, *n.* [Fr. *progénie*, L. *progenies*, from *pro*, forth, and root *gen*, to bring forth; seen also in *gender, generation, genus*, &c. GENUS.] Offspring collectively; children; descendants of the human kind, or offspring of other animals.—**Progenitor**, prō-jen'i-tėr, *n.* An ancestor in the direct line; a forefather; a parent.

Proglottis, prō-glot'tis, *n.* pl. **Proglottides**, prō-glot'ti-dēz. [Gr., the tip of the tongue.] *Zool.* the generative segment or joint of a tapeworm.

Prognathic, Prognathous, prog-nath'ik, prog-nā'thus, *a.* [Gr. *pro*, before, and *gnathos*, the cheek or jaw-bone.] Characterized by projecting jaws; applied to human skulls when the jaw slants forwards, making the lower part of the face very prominent. — **Prognathism**, prog-nā'thizm, *n.* The condition of being prognathic.

Prognosis, prog-nō'sis, *n.* [Gr. *prognōsis*, a foreknowing.] Foreknowledge; a forecast, especially of the probable course of a disease.

Prognostic, prog-nos'tik, *a.* [Gr. *prognōstikos*—*pro*, before, and *gignōskō*, to know. KNOW.] Foreshowing; indicating something future by signs or symptoms. — *n.* A sign by which a future event may be known or foretold; an omen; a token; a symptom; a foretelling; prediction.—**Prognosticable**, prog-nos'ti-ka-bl, *a.* Capable of being prognosticated. — **Prognosticate**, prog-nos'ti-kāt, *v.t.*—*prognosticated, prognosticating.* To foretell by means of present signs; to predict; to foreshow or foretoken; to indicate as to happen in the future.—*v.i.* To judge or pronounce from prognostics. — **Prognostication**, prognos'ti-kā"shon, *n.* The act of prognosticating; that which foreshows; a foretoken; previous sign.—**Prognosticative**, prognos'ti-kā-tiv, *a.* Having the character of a prognostic.—**Prognosticator**, prog-nos'ti-kā-tėr, *n.* One who prognosticates.

Program, Programme, prō'gram, *n.* [Fr. *programme*, from Gr. *programma*—*pro*, before, and *graphō*, to write.] A plan of proceedings sketched out beforehand: an outline or detailed sketch or advertisement of the order of proceedings or subjects embraced in any entertainment, performance, or public ceremony.

Progress, prog'res, *n.* [L. *progressus*, from *progredior*, I advance—*pro*, before, and *gradior*, to go, whence also *grade, gradual*, &c. GRADE.] A moving or going forward: a proceeding onward; a moving forward in growth; increase; advance in matters of any kind; course; intellectual or moral improvement; a passage from place to place; a journey.—*v.i.* (pro-gres'). To move forward or onward; to advance; to proceed in any course, to advance towards something better; to make improvement. —**Progression**, prō-gresh'on, *n.* [L. *progressio.*] The act of progressing, advancing, or moving forward; progress; advance; course; passage; *math.* regular or proportional advance in increase or decrease of numbers; continued proportion, arithmetical or geometrical (thus 2, 4, 6, 8, 10 are numbers in *arithmetical progression*; 2, 4, 8, 16, &c., in *geometrical progression.*— **Progressionist**, prō-gresh'on-ist, *n.* One who maintains that society is in a state of progress towards perfection —**Progressive**, prō-gres'iv, *a* Moving forward: proceeding onward; advancing, improving, in politics, one who advocates the passage of social and economic reform legislation. —**Progressively**, prō-gres'iv-li, *adv* — **Progressiveness**, prō-gres'iv-nes, *n* The state or quality of being progressive.

Prohibit, prō-hib'it, *v.t.* [L. *prohibeo, prohibitus*—*pro*, before, and *habeo*, I have, I hold. HABIT.] To forbid authoritatively; to interdict by authority (to *prohibit* a person from doing a thing; to *prohibit* the thing being done). to prevent; to preclude. —**Prohibition**, prō-hi-bish'on, *n.* The act of prohibiting; a declaration to hinder some action; interdict; the Eighteenth Amendment of the United States Constitution, in effect from 1919 to 1933, which forbade the manufacture, sale or transportation of intoxicating liquors for use as beverages. — **Prohibitionist**, *n.* — **Prohibitive, Prohibitory**, prō-hib'itiv, prō-hib'i-to-ri, *a.* Serving to prohibit; forbidding; implying prohibition.

Project, prō-jekt', *v.t.* [L. *projicio, projectum*, to cast forth, to cause to jut out—*pro*, forward, and *jacio*, to throw (as in *eject, reject*, &c.). JUT.] To throw out or forth; to cast or shoot forward; to scheme; to contrive; to devise; to exhibit or give a delineation of on a surface; to delineate. —*v.i.* To shoot forward; to extend beyond something else; to jut; to be prominent. —*n.* (pro'jekt). [O.Fr. *project*, Mod.Fr. *projet.*] That which is projected or devised; a plan; a scheme; a design.—**Projectile**, prō-jek'til, *a.* Impelling forward (a *projectile* force); caused by impulse (*projectile* motion).—*n.* A body projected or impelled through the air, as a stone thrown from the hand or a sling, a bullet discharged from a cannon. — **Projection**, prō-jek'shon, *n.* [L. *projectio.*] The act of projecting, throwing, or shooting forward; the state of projecting or jutting out; a part projecting or jutting out; a prominence; the act of projecting or scheming; the representation of something by means of lines, &c., drawn on a surface; especially the representation of any object on a perspective plane; the delineation of the earth's surface or a portion of it by a map. GNOMONIC, ORTHOGRAPHIC, STEREOGRAPHIC.—**Projector**, prō-jek'tėr, *n.* One who projects; one who forms a scheme or design.—**Projecture**, prō-jek'tūr, *n.* A jutting out; projection.

Prolapse, Prolapsus, prō-laps', prōlap'sus, *n.* [L. *prolapsus*—*pro*, forward, and *labor, lapsus*, to slip, fall. LAPSE.] *Med.* a falling down of some internal organ from its proper position; a falling down of the womb.—*v.i.*—*prolapsed, prolapsing.* To fall down or out; to suffer a prolapse.

Prolate, prō'lāt, *a.* [L. *prolatus*—*pro*, forth, and *latus*, carried.] Extended beyond the line of an exact sphere.—*Prolate spheroid*, a spheroid produced by the revolution of a semi-ellipse about its larger diameter; a sphere that projects too much at the poles OBLATE

Proleg, prō'leg, *n.* [L. *pro*, for, and E. *leg.*] One of the leg-like organs of certain larvæ, used in walking, but which disappear in the perfect insect.

Prolegomenon, prō-le-gom'e-non, *n.* pl. **Prolegomena** prō-le-gom'e-na. [Gr., from *pro*, before, and *legō*, to speak.] A preliminary observation; chiefly used in plural, and applied to an introductory discussion or discourse prefixed to a book or treatise.—**Prolegomenary, Prolegomenous**, prō-le-gom'e-na-ri, prō-legom'e-nus, *a.* Introductory.

Prolepsis, prō-lep'sis, *n.* [Gr. *prolēpsis*, preconception—*pro*, before, and *lambanō*, I take.] Something of the nature of an anticipation; *rhet.* a figure by which a thing is represented as already done, though in reality it is to follow as a consequence of the action which is described ('he washed himself *clean*'); a figure by which objections are anticipated; an anachronism.— **Proleptic, Proleptical**, prō-lep'tik, prō-lep'ti-kal, *a* Pertaining to prolepsis; anticipatory.—**Proleptically** prō-lep'tikal-li, *adv.* In a proleptic manner.

Proletarian, prō-le-tā'ri-an, *a.* [L. *proletarius*, a citizen of the lowest class, one useful to the state only by producing children, from *proles*, offspring, from *pro*, before, and *ol*, root of *adolesce* ADULT.] *n.* A member of the wage-earning class, a wage-earner who does not possess capital; formerly, one of the rabble, pertaining to the proletarians.—**Proletarianism**, prō-le-tā'ri-an-izm, *n.* The condition or political influence of the lower orders of the community.—**Proletariat**, prō-letā'ri-at, *n* Proletarians collectively; the lower classes.—**Proletary**, prol'e-ta-ri, *n.* One of the lower orders.

Proliferation, prō-lif'ėr-ā"shon, *n.* [L. *proles, prolis*, offspring, and *ferre*, to bear.] Reproduction by continued cell division or budding; the production of proliferous growths.—**Proliferous**, prō-lif'ėr-us, *a. Bot.* bearing or producing something abnormal or adventitious (as a flower within another flower).

Prolific, prō-lif'ik, *a.* [Fr. *prolifique*; L. *prolificus*—*proles*, offspring, and *facio*, to make. PROLETARIAN.] Producing young or fruit, especially in abundance; fruitful; productive; serving to give rise or origin; having the quality of generating abundantly (a topic *prolific* of controversy).— **Prolifically**, prō-lif'i-kal-li, *adv.* In a prolific manner.—**Prolificness**, prō-lif'ik-nes, *n.*

Proligerous, prō-lij'ėr-us, *a.* [L. *proles*, offspring, and *gero*, to produce. PROLETARIAN.] Productive of offspring.—*Proligerous disc*, the germ in an egg.

Prolix, prō-liks', *a.* [L. *prolixus*, extended, prolix—*pro*, forth, and root of *liqueo*, to flow. LIQUID.] Long and wordy; extending to a great length; diffuse; indulging in lengthy discourse; discussing at great length; tedious. — **Prolixity, Prolixness**, prō-lik'si-ti, prō-liks'nes, *n.* The state or quality of being prolix.—**Prolixly**, prō-liks'li, *adv.* In a prolix manner.

Prolocutor, prō-lok'ū-tėr, *n.* [L., from *proloquor*—*pro*, for, and *loquor, locutus*, to speak. LOQUACIOUS.] One who speaks for another†; the speaker or chairman of a convocation.—**Prolocutorship**, prōlok'ū-tėr-ship, *n.* The office of a prolocutor.

Prologue, prō'log, *n.* [Fr., *prologue*, L. *prologus*, from Gr. *prologos*—*pro*, before, and *legō*, to speak.] A preface or introduction; the discourse or poem spoken before a dramatic performance or play begins; the speaker of a prologue. — *v.t.* — *prologued, prologuing.* To introduce with a formal prologue; to preface. — **Prologize**, prō'log-īz, *v.i.*—*prologized, prologizing.* To deliver a prologue.

Prolong, prō-long', *v.t.* [Fr. *prolonger*—L. *pro*, forth, and *longus*. LONG.] To lengthen in time; to extend the duration of; to lengthen out; to put off to a distant time; to extend in space or length (to *prolong* a line).—*v.i.* To put off to a distant time.— **Prolongation**, prō-long-gā'shon, *n.* The act of prolonging; a part prolonged; an extension. — **Prolonger**, prō-long'ėr, *n.* One who or that which prolongs.—**Prolongment**, prō-long'ment, *n.* The act of.

Prolusion, prō-lū'zhon, *n.* [L. *prolusio*, a prelude—*pro*, before, and *ludo, lusum*, to play LUDICROUS.] A prelude or preliminary; a preliminary trial.

Promenade, prom-e-nad', *n* [Fr., from *promener*, from L. *pro*, forward, and *mināre*, to drive, from *mina*, a threat MENACE.] A walk for pleasure and show or exercise; a place for walking in public.—*v.i.*—*promenaded, promenading.* To walk for amusement, show, or exercise.—**Promenader**, prom-e-nā'dėr, *n.* One who promenades.

Promethean, prō-mē'thē-an, *a.* [From *Prometheus* of Greek mythology, lit. the forethinker, who stole fire from heaven and imparted it to mortals.] Pertaining to Prometheus; pertaining to fire or heat; hence, possessing life-giving qualities.

Prominence, Prominency, prom'i-nens, prom'i-nen-si, *n.* [L. *prominentia*, from *promineo*—*pro*, forward, and *minere*, to project EMINENT.] A standing out from the surface of something; that which juts out; protuberance; state of being distinguished among men; conspicuousness; distinction. — **Prominent**, prom'i-nent, *a.* [L. *prominens.*] Standing out beyond the line or surface of something; jutting; protuberant; distinguished above others (a *prominent* character); likely to attract special attention from size, position, &c.; striking; conspicuous. — **Prominently**, prom'i-nent-li, *adv.* In a prominent manner.

Promiscuous, prō-mis'kū-us, *a.* [L. *promiscuus*, from *promisceo*—*pro*, and *misceo*, to mix. MIX.] Consisting of individuals united in a body or mass without order; mingled indiscriminately; forming part of a confused crowd or mass; random; indiscriminate; not restricted to an individual. —**Promiscuously**, prō-mis'kū-us-li, *adv.*

In a promiscuous manner.—**Promiscuousness, Promiscuity**, prō-mis′kū-us-nes, prō-mis-kū′i-ti, *n.* The state of being promiscuous.

Promise, prom′is, *n.* [Fr. *promesse*, from L. *promissus*, put forward—*pro*, before, and *mittere*, to send. MISSION.] A declaration, written or verbal, made by one person to another, which binds the person who makes it to do or forbear a certain act specified; a declaration that something will be done or given for the benefit of another; ground or basis of expectation; earnest; pledge; that which affords a ground for expectation of future distinction (a youth of great *promise*).—*v.t.—promised, promising.* To make a promise of; to engage to do, give, grant, or procure for some one; to afford reason to expect (the year *promises* a good harvest).—*v.i.* To make a promise; to assure one by a promise; to afford hopes or expectations.—*I promise you*, I declare to you; I assure you.—**Promisee**, prom-is-ē′, *n.* The person to whom a promise is made.—**Promiser**, prom′is-ėr, *n.* One who promises.—**Promising**, prom′is-ing, *a.* Giving promise; affording reasonable ground of hope for the future; looking as if likely to turn out well.—**Promisingly**, prom′is-ing-li, *adv.* In a promising manner.—**Promissive**,† prō-mis′iv, *a.* Making or implying a promise.—**Promissorily**, prom′is-o-ri-li, *adv.* By way of promise.—**Promissory**, prom′is-o-ri, *a.* Containing a promise or binding declaration of something to be done or foreborne.—*Promissory note*, a writing which contains a promise of the payment of money to a certain person at a specified date.

Promontory, prom′on-tō-ri, *n.* [L. *promontorium*—*pro*, forward, and *mons*, *montis*, a mountain. MOUNT.] A high point of land or rock projecting into the sea beyond the line of coast; a headland.

Promote, prō-mōt′, *v.t.—promoted, promoting.* [L. *promotus*, pp. of *promovere*, to move forward—*pro*, forward, and *movere*, to move. MOVE.] To contribute to the growth, enlargement, increase, or power of; to forward; to advance; to help onward; to excite; to stir up (as strife); to exalt or raise to a higher post or position; to elevate.—**Promoter**, prō-mō′tėr, *n.* One who or that which promotes; an encourager; one that aids in promoting some financial undertaking; one engaged in getting up a joint-stock company.—**Promotion**, prō-mō′shon, *n.* The act of promoting; advancement; encouragement; exaltation in rank or honour; preferment.—**Promotive**, prō-mō′tiv, *a.* Tending to advance or promote.

Prompt, promt, *a.* [Fr. *prompt*, from L. *promptus*, brought out, ready, quick, from *promo*, *promptum*, to bring forth—*pro*, forth, and *emo*, to take. EXEMPT.] Ready and quick to act as occasion demands; acting with cheerful alacrity; ready and willing; performed without delay; quick; ready; not delayed.—*v.t.* To move or excite to action or exertion; to incite; to instigate; to assist a speaker when at a loss by pronouncing the words forgotten or next in order (to *prompt* an actor); to dictate; to suggest to the mind.—*n. Com.* an agreement in which one party engages to sell certain goods at a given price, and the other party to take them up and pay at a specified date.—**Prompt-book**, *n.* The book used by a prompter of a theatre.—**Prompter**, prom′tėr, *n.* One that prompts; specifically, one placed behind the scenes in a theatre, whose business is to assist the actors when at a loss by uttering the first words of a sentence or words forgotten.—**Promptitude**, prom′ti-tūd, *n.* Readiness; quickness of decision and action when occasion demands; readiness of will; cheerful alacrity.—**Promptly**, promt′li, *adv.* In a prompt manner.—**Promptness**, promt′nes, *n.* The state or quality of being prompt; promptitude.—**Promptuary**, prom′tū-a-ri, *n.* [L. *promptuarium*.] A storehouse; a magazine; a repository.

Promulgate, prō-mul′gāt, *v.t.—promulgated, promulgating.* [L. *promulgo*, *promulgatus*; origin unknown.] To make known by open declaration, as laws, decrees, tidings, &c.; to publish abroad; to announce; to proclaim.—**Promulgation**, prō-mul-gā′shon, *n.* The act of promulgating; publication; open declaration.—**Promulgator, Promulger**, prō′mul-gā-tėr or prō-mul′gā-tėr, prō-mul′jėr, *n.* One who promulgates or publishes abroad.—**Promulge**, prō-mulj′, *v.t.—promulged, promulging.* To promulgate.

Pronaos, prō-nā′os, *n.* [Gr. *pro*, before, and *naos*, a temple.] *Arch.* the space in front of the naos of a temple; a vestibule or portico.

Pronation, prō-nā′shon, *n.* [From L. *pronus*, prone, having the face downward. PRONE.] That motion of the arm whereby the palm of the hand is turned downward; position of the hand with the thumb toward the body and the palm downward.—**Pronator**, prō-nā′tėr, *n.* A muscle of the forearm which turns the palm downward.

Prone, prōn, *a.* [L. *pronus*, hanging or leaning forwards, prone, from *pro*, before, forward; cog. Gr. *prēnēs*, Skr. *pravana*, prone.] Bending forward; lying with the face downward; rushing or falling headlong or downward; sloping downward; inclined; inclined by disposition or natural tendency; propense; disposed: usually in a bad sense (men *prone* to evil, *prone* to strife).—**Pronely**, prōn′li, *adv.* In a prone manner or position.—**Proneness**, prōn′nes, *n.* The state of being prone; inclination; propensity; readiness.

Pronephros, prō-nef′ros, *n.* [L. *pro*, before, Gr. *nephros*, a kidney.] In vertebrates, the first of three successive renal organs; the 'head' kidney.

Prong, prong, *n.* [A nasalized form of prov.E. *prog*, to prod; W. *procio*, to thrust, to poke.] A sharp-pointed instrument; the spike of a fork or of a similar instrument; a pointed projection (the *prongs* of a deer's antlers).—*v.t.* To stab, as with a fork.—**Prong-buck, Prong-horn**, *n.* A species of hollow-horned antelope which inhabits the western parts of North America.—**Pronged**, prongd, *a.* Having prongs.

Pronominal, prō-nom′i-nal, *a.* [L. *pronomen*, a pronoun. PRONOUN.] Belonging to or of the nature of a pronoun.—**Pronominally**, prō-nom′i-nal-li, *adv.* With the effect of a pronoun.

Prononcé, prō-noṅ-sā, *a.* [Fr.] *Lit.* pronounced; hence, strongly marked or defined; decided, as in manners or character.

Pronoun, prō′noun, *n.* [From *pro*, for, and *noun*; L. *pronomen*, a pronoun—*pro*, for, and *nomen*, a name, a noun.] *Gram.* one of a certain class of words or generalized terms often used instead of a noun or name, to prevent the repetition of it: classified under the heads of *personal, relative, interrogative, possessive, demonstrative, distributive*, and *indefinite* pronouns, the last four classes being commonly called *adjective pronouns* or *pronominal adjectives*.

Pronounce, prō-nouns′, *v.t.—pronounced, pronouncing.* [Fr. *prononcer*, from L. *pronuntio*, *pronuntiatus*—*pro*, before, and *nuntio*, to declare. NUNCIO.] To form or articulate by the organs of speech; to utter; to speak; to utter formally, officially, or solemnly (the court *pronounced* sentence of death); to declare or affirm (he *pronounced* it a forgery).—*v.i.* To speak with confidence or authority; to utter an opinion; to use a certain pronunciation.—**Pronounceable**, prō-nouns′a-bl, *a.* Capable of being pronounced.—**Pronounced**, prō-nounst′, *a.* [Fr. *prononcé*, pronounced.] Strongly marked or defined; decided (a man of *pronounced* views).—**Pronouncement**, prō-nouns′ment, *n.* The act of pronouncing; a formal announcement.—**Pronouncer**, prō-nouns′ėr, *n.* One who pronounces.—**Pronouncing**, prō-nouns′ing, *a.* Pertaining to, indicating, or teaching pronunciation.—**Pronunciamento**, prō-nun′shi-ā-men″tō, *n.* [Sp.] A manifesto or proclamation; a formal announcement or declaration.—**Pronunciation**, prō-nun′si-ā″shon, *n.* [L. *pronunciatio*.] The act of pronouncing or uttering with articulation; the mode of uttering words or letters; utterance.—**Pronunciative, Pronunciatory**, prō-nun′si-a-tiv, prō-nun′si-a-to-ri, *a.* Serving to pronounce or declare; declaratory.

Pronucleus, prō-nū′klē-us, *n.* [L. *pro*, before, *nucleus*.] One of the two nuclei seen in the course of fertilization of an ovum, the *female pronucleus* belonging to the ovum itself, and the *male pronucleus* to the sperm.

Prony brake, prō′ni, *n.* [After Baron de *Prony*, French engineer.] A form of friction dynamometer, in which the friction is measured by balancing with a weighted lever.

Proof, prōf, *n.* [O.E. *profe*, Fr. *preuve*, L.L. *proba*. PROVE.] Any effort, process, or operation that ascertains truth or fact; a test; a trial; what serves as evidence; what proves or establishes; that which convinces the mind and produces belief; a test applied to certain manufactured or other articles; the act of testing the strength of alcoholic spirits; hence, also the degree of strength in spirit; *printing*, a rough impression of type, in which errors may be detected and marked for correction; *engr.* an impression taken from an engraving to prove the state of it; an early impression, or one of a limited number taken before the letters to be inserted are engraved on the plate; called a *proof-impression*, and considered the best, because taken before the plate is worn.—*a.* Impenetrable; able to resist, physically or morally (*proof against* shot, *against* temptation).—**Proofreader**, *n.* One who reads and marks corrections on printers' proofs.—**Proof sheet**, *n. Printing*, a rough impression of composed type, taken to see if any errors remain for correction.—**Proof spirit**, *n.* Alcoholic liquor of a certain standard strength, in U. S., 50% by volume.

Prop, prop, *n.* [Same as Ir. *propa*, Gael. *prop*, a prop.] That which sustains an incumbent weight; a fulcrum; a support; a stay.—*v.t.—propped, propping.* To support by placing something under or against; to support by standing under or against; to support or sustain, in a general sense.

Propædeutics, prō-pē-dū′tiks, *n.* [Gr. *propaideuō*, to instruct beforehand, from *pro*, before, and *paideuō*, to educate, from *pais*, *paidos*, a child.] The preliminary learning connected with any art or science.—**Propædeutic, Propædeutical**, prō-pē-dū′tik, prō-pē-dū′ti-kal, *a.* Pertaining to propædeutics; instructing beforehand.

Propaganda, prop-a-gan′da, *n.* [From the congregatio de *propaganda* fide, at Rome. PROPAGATE.] The dissemination and the defense of beliefs, opinions, or actions deemed salutary to the program of a particular group; the propagation of doctrines and tenets of special interests, as an effort to give credence to information partly or wholly fallacious. Originally, an institution of the Roman Catholic Church, established as a proselyting agency; now, generally an intensive undertaking of political partisans.—**Propagandist**, *n.* One who devotes himself to the spread of any system of principles or set of actions; publicity agent.—**Propagandize**, *v.t.* To present with propaganda.

Propagate, prop′a-gāt, *v.t.—propagated, propagating.* [L. *propagare*, *propagatus*, to peg down, to propagate—*pro*, before, and *pag*, root of *pango*, to fasten, fix, set, plant (seen in *paction, compact, impinge*, &c.).] To continue or multiply by generation or successive reproduction; to cause to reproduce itself: applied to animals and plants; to spread from person to person or from place to place; to diffuse; to generate, beget, produce, originate.—*v.i.* To have young or issue; to be reproduced or multiplied by generation, or by new shoots or plants.—**Propagation,** prop-a-gā'shon, *n.* The act of propagating; the multiplication of the kind or species by generation or reproduction; the spreading or extension of anything; diffusion. — **Propagative,** prop'a-gā-tiv, *a.* Having the power of propagation; propagating.—**Propagator,** prop'a-gā-tėr, *n.* One who propagates.—**Propagable,** prop'a-ga-bl, *a.* Capable of being propagated; capable of being spread, as doctrines or principles. — **Propagulum,** prō-pag'ū-lum, *n. Bot.* an offshoot or germinating bud attached by a thickish stalk to the parent plant.

Proped, prō'ped, *n.* [L. *pro*, for, and *pes, pedis*, a foot.] *Entom.* one of the false feet of certain larvæ.

Propel, prō-pel', *v.t.—propelled, propelling.* [L. *propello—pro*, forward, and *pello*, to drive, as in *compel, dispel, impel*, &c. PULSATE.] To drive forward; to urge or press onward by force.—**Propellent,** prō-pel'ent, *a.* Driving forward; propelling.—**Propeller,** prō-pel'ėr, *n.* One who or that which propels; a screw for propelling a motor-driven vessel; a rotary fan for propelling an aeroplane.

Propendent, prō-pen'dent, *a.* [PROPENSE.] *Bot.* hanging forward and downward.

Propense, prō-pens', *a.* [L. *propensus*, hanging forwards, projecting, from *propendeo—pro*, forward, and *pendeo*, to hang. PENDANT.] Leaning toward, in a moral sense; inclined; disposed, either to good or evil; prone.—**Propenseness, Propension,** prō-pens'nes, prō-pen'shon, *n.* The state of being propense; propensity.—**Propensity,** prō-pen'si-ti, *n.* Bent of mind, natural or acquired; inclination; natural tendency or disposition, particularly to evil.

Proper, prop'ėr, *a.* [Fr. *propre*, from L. *proprius*, one's own, peculiar, proper; allied to *prope*, near. PROPINQUITY.] Peculiar; naturally or essentially belonging to a particular individual or state; natural; particularly suited to or befitting; belonging to as one's own; *gram.* applied to a noun when it is the name of a particular person or thing: opposed to *common* (as Shakspere, London); fit; suitable; adapted; appropriate; correct; just; according to right usage; hence, properly so called; real; actual (the garden *proper*); *bot.* single, or connected with something single.—*Proper motion* (*astron.*), the real motion of the sun, planets, &c., as opposed to their apparent motions.—**Properly,** prop'ėr-li, *adv.* In a proper manner; fitly; suitably; rightly; in a strict sense; strictly.—**Properness,** prop'ėr-nes, *n.* The quality of being proper.—**Property,** prop'ėr-ti, *n.* [Fr. *propriété*, L. *proprietas*, from *proprius*, one's own.] A peculiar quality of anything; that which is inherent in a thing, or naturally essential to it; an attribute; the exclusive right of possessing, enjoying, and disposing of a thing; ownership; the subject of such a right; the thing owned; an estate, whether in lands, buildings, goods, money, &c.; in *theatres*, a stage requisite; any article necessary to be produced in some scene.—**Propertied,** prop'ėr-tid, *a.* Possessed of property.—**Property-man,** *n.* The man in charge of the properties or stage requisites of a theatre.—**Property-room,** *n.* The room in which stage properties are kept.—**Property-tax,** *n.* A direct tax imposed on property.

Prophecy, prof'e-si, *n.* [O.Fr. *prophecie, prophetie*, L. *prophetia*, from Gr. *prophēteia*, from *prophētēs*, a prophet—*pro*, before, and *phēmi*, to tell; same root as *fame.*] A foretelling; a declaration of something to come; especially, a foretelling inspired by God; a book of prophecies; *Scrip.* interpretation of Scripture; exhortation or instruction (O.T.).—**Prophesier,** prof'e-sī-ėr, *n.* One who predicts events. — **Prophesy,** prof'e-si, *v.t.—prophesied, prophesying.* To foretell; to predict.—*v.i.* To utter predictions; to make declaration of events to come; *Scrip.* to interpret or explain Scripture or religious subjects.—**Prophet,** prof'et, *n.* [L. *propheta*, from Gr. *prophētēs.*] One that foretells future events; a predictor; a foreteller; a person inspired or instructed by God to announce future events; *Scrip.* an interpreter.—*Minor prophets*, the authors of the twelve last books of the Old Testament, as opposed to Isaiah, Jeremiah, and Ezekiel.—**Prophetess,** prof'et-es, *n.* A female prophet.—**Prophetic, Prophetical,** prō-fet'ik, prō-fet'i-kal, *a.* Pertaining or relating to a prophet or prophecy; having the character of prophecy; containing prophecy. — **Prophetically,** prō-fet'i-kal-li, *adv.* In a prophetic manner; by way of prediction.

Prophylactic, prō-fi-lak'tik, *a.* [Gr. *prophylaktikos—pro*, before, and *phylassō*, to guard.] *Med.* preventive; defending from or warding off disease. — *n.* A medicine which preserves or defends against disease; a preventive.—**Prophylaxis,** prō-fi-lak'sis, *n.* [Gr.] Preventive or preservative treatment.

Propinquity, prō-pin'kwi-ti, *n.* [L. *propinquitas*, from *propinquus*, near, from *prope*, near; whence also (ap)*proach*. PROXIMITY.] Nearness in place; neighbourhood; nearness in time; nearness of blood; kindred.

Propitiate, prō-pish'i-āt, *v.t.—propitiated, propitiating.* [L. *propitio, propitiatum*, to propitiate, from *propitius*, propitious, from *pro*, foward, and *peto*, to seek, primarily referring to a bird whose flight is of happy augury. PETITION.] To appease and render favourable; to make propitious; to conciliate. — **Propitiation,** prō-pish'i-ā"shon, *n.* The act of propitiating; *theol.* the atonement or atoning sacrifice offered to God to assuage his wrath and render him propitious to sinners.—**Propitiator,** prō-pish'i-ā-tėr, *n.* One who propitiates. — **Propitiatorily,** prō-pish'i-a-to-ri-li, *adv.* By way of propitiation. — **Propitiatory,** prō-pish'i-a-to-ri, *a.* Having the power to make propitious; serving to propitiate.—*n. Jewish antiq.* the mercy-seat; the lid or cover of the ark of the covenant.—**Propitiable,** prō-pish'i-a-bl, *a.* Capable of being propitiated. — **Propitious,** prō-pish'us, *a.* Favourably disposed towards a person; disposed to be gracious or merciful; ready to forgive sins and bestow blessings; affording favourable conditions or circumstances (a *propitious* season).—**Propitiously,** prō-pish'us-li, *adv.* In a propitious manner.—**Propitiousness,** prō-pish'us-nes, *n.*

Proplasm, prō'plazm, *n.* [Gr, *proplasma—pro*, before, and *plassō*, to mould.] A mould; a matrix.—**Proplastic,** prō-plas'tik, *a.* Forming a mould or cast.—**Proplastics,** prō-plas'tiks, *n.* The art of making moulds for castings, &c.

Propodium, prō-pō'di-um, *n.* [Gr. *pro*, before, and *pous, podos*, a foot.] *Zool.* the anterior part of the foot in molluscs.

Propolis, prō'po-lis, *n.* [Gr. *pro*, before, and *polis*, city.] A substance having some resemblance to wax, used by bees to stop the holes and crevices in their hives.

Propone, prō-pōn', *v.t.* [L. *propono—pro*, before, and *pono*, to place. POSITION.] To propose; to propound.—**Proponent,** prō-pō'nent, *n.* One that makes a proposal, or lays down a proposition.

Proportion, prō-pōr'shon, *n.* [L. *proportio —pro*, before, and *portio*, part or share. PORTION.] The comparative relation of one thing to another in respect to size, quantity, or degree; suitable or corresponding degree; the relation of one part to another or to the whole, with respect to magnitude; relative size and arrangement of parts; symmetrical arrangement; the proper relation of parts in a whole; symmetry; that which falls to one's lot when a whole is divided according to rule; just or equal share; lot; *math.* the equality or similarity of ratios; *arith.* the rule of three, that rule which enables us to find a fourth proportional to three given numbers. — *Simple proportion*, the equality of the ratio of two quantities to that of two other quantities. — *Compound proportion*, the equality of the ratio of two quantities to another ratio, the antecedent and consequent of which are respectively the products of the antecedents and consequents of two or more ratios.—*Continued proportion*, a succession of several equal ratios, as 2, 4, 8, 16, &c.—*Harmonical* or *musical proportion.* HARMONICAL.—*Reciprocal* or *inverse proportion.* RECIPROCAL, INVERSE. —*v.t.* To adjust in a suitable proportion; to harmoniously adjust to something else as regards dimensions or extent; to form with symmetry.—**Proportionable,** prō-pōr'shon-a-bl, *a.* Capable of being proportioned; being in proportion; having a due comparative relation; corresponding; well proportioned; symmetrical.—**Proportionableness,** prō-pōr'shon-a-bl-nes, *n.*—**Proportionably,** prō-pōr'shon-a-bli, *adv.* In a proportionable manner; proportionally; correspondingly. — **Proportional,** prō-pōr'shon-al, *a.* Having a due proportion; being in suitable proportion or degree; *math.* having the same or a constant ratio (*proportional* quantities). — *Proportional parts*, parts of magnitude such that the corresponding ones, taken in their order, are proportional.—*n.* A quantity in proportion; *math.* one of the terms of a proportion. — *Mean proportional.* MEAN. — **Proportionality,** prō-pōr'shon-al"i-ti, *n.* The quality or state of being in proportion. — **Proportionally,** prō-pōr'shon-al-li, *adv.* In proportion; in due degree; with suitable comparative relation. — **Proportionate,** prō-pōr'shon-āt, *a.* Having due proportion or relation; proportional. — *v.t — proportionated, proportionating.* To make proportional; to adjust in due relation.—**Proportionately,** prō-pōr'shon-āt-li, *adv.* With due proportion. —**Proportionless,** prō-pōr'shon-les, *a.* Without proportion; without symmetry of parts.

Propose, prō-pōz', *v.t.—proposed, proposing.* [Fr. *proposer*, to purpose, to propose, from *pro* and *poser*. POSE, COMPOSE. *Purpose* is the same word.] To bring forward or offer for consideration or acceptance; to bring forward as something to be done, attained, or striven after: often governing an infinitive.—*v.i.* To form or declare an intention or design; to offer one's self in marriage (to *propose* to a lady). —**Proposal,** prō-pō'zal, *n.* That which is proposed or offered for consideration; a scheme or design, terms or conditions proposed (*proposals* of peace, of marriage).—**Proposer,** prō-pō'zėr, *n.* One that proposes. — **Proposition,** prō-pō-zish'on, *n.* [Partly from *propose*, partly from L. *propositio*, from *pro*, before, and *positio*, a placing. POSITION.] That which is proposed or offered for consideration, acceptance, or adoption; a proposal; term or offer advanced; *gram.* and *logic*, a form of speech in which something is affirmed or denied of a subject; *math.* a statement of either a truth to be demonstrated, or an operation to be performed.—**Propositional,** prō-pō-zish'on-al, *a.* Pertaining to a proposition; considered as a proposition.

Propound, prō-pound', *v.t.* [O.E. *propoune*, from L. *propono*, to put forth—*pro*, before, and *pono*, to place; as to form, comp. *compound, expound.* POSITION.] To offer for consideration; to propose; to put or set, as a question.—**Propounder,** prō-poun'dėr, *n.* One who propounds.

Proprætor, prō-prē'tor, *n.* [L. *proprætor —pro*, for, and *prætor.*] A Roman magistrate who, having discharged the office of prætor at home, was sent into a province to command there.

Proprietary, prō-prī'e-ta-ri, *n.* [Fr. *propriétaire*, a proprietor, from *propriété*, property. PROPERTY.] A proprietor; more commonly a body of proprietors collectively. —*a.* Belonging to a proprietor or owner; belonging to ownership. — **Proprietor,** prō-prī'e-tėr, *n.* An owner; the person who has the legal right or exclusive title to anything.—**Proprietorial,** prō-prī'e-tō"-ri-al, *a.* Proprietary.—**Proprietorship,** prō-prī'e-tėr-ship, *n.* The state or right of a proprietor. — **Proprietress,** prō-prī'e-tres, *n.* A proprietrix. — **Proprietrix,** prō-prī'e-triks, *n.* A female proprietor.—**Propriety,** prō-prī'e-ti, *n.* [L. *proprietas*, from *proprius*, one's own.] Property‡; possession‡; suitableness to an acknowledged or correct standard; consonance with established principles, rules, or customs; fitness; justness.—*pl.* *The proprieties*, conformity with established customs in social life.

Propulsion, prō-pul'shon, *n.* [From L. *propello*, *propulsum*. PROPEL.] The act of driving forward.—**Propulsive**, prō-pul'siv, *a.* Tending or having power to propel; driving or urging on.—**Propulsory**, prō-pul'so-ri, *a.* Propulsive.

Propylæum, pro-pi-lē'um, *n.* pl. **Propylæa**, prō-pi-lē'a. [Gr. *propylaion*, from *pro*, before, and *pylē*, a gate.] The porch, vestibule, or entrance of an edifice.—**Propylon**, prop'i-lon, *n.* A gateway before the entrance of an Egyptian temple.

Pro rata, prō rā'ta. Proportionately; in accordance with some determined standard, such as a share or liability.—**Prorate**, prō-rāt', *v.t.* and *i.* To distribute proportionately; to make a pro rata assessment.

Prorogue, prō-rōg', *v.t.*—*prorogued*, *proroguing*. [Fr. *proroger*, from L. *prorogare*, to prolong, continue—*pro*, before, and *rogo*, to ask. ROGATION.] To protract or prolong, to defer or delay‡; to adjourn a parliament for an indefinite period by royal authority. *British parl. practice.*—**Prorogation**, prō-rō-gā'shon, *n.* The act of proroguing.

Prosaic. Under PROSE.

Proscenium, prō-sē'ni-um, *n.* [L. *proscenium*, from Gr. *proskēnion*—*pro*, before, and *skēnē*, a scene. SCENE.] *Arch.* the part in a theatre from the curtain or drop-scene to the orchestra; the curtain and the ornamental framework from which it hangs. In the ancient theatre the proscenium comprised the whole stage.

Proscolex, prō-skō'leks, *n.* [L. *pro*, before, *skōlēx*, a worm.] In tapeworms, the bladder from which the 'head' is produced.

Proscribe, prō-skrīb', *v.t.* — *proscribed*, *proscribing*. [L. *proscribo*—*pro*, before, in public, and *scribo*, to write. SCRIBE.] Among the Romans, to publish the name of, as doomed to destruction and seizure of property; hence, to put out of the protection of the law; to outlaw; to reject utterly; to interdict, exclude, prohibit.—**Proscriber**, prō-skrī'bėr, *n.* One who proscribes. — **Proscription**, prō-skrip'shon, *n.* [L. *proscriptio*.] The act of proscribing; outlawry; exclusion; the dooming or denouncing of citizens to death and confiscation of goods as public enemies.—**Proscriptive**, prō-skrip'tiv, *a.* Pertaining to or consisting in proscription; proscribing.—**Proscriptively**, prō-skrip'tiv-li, *adv.* In a proscriptive manner.

Prose, prōz, *n.* [Fr. *prose*, from L. *prosa* for *prorsa* (*oratio*, speech, understood), from *prorsus*, forward, straight on—*pro*, forward, and *versus*, turned. VERSE.] The ordinary written or spoken language of man; language unconfined to poetical measure, as opposed to *verse* or *metrical composition*; hence, dull and commonplace language or discourse.—*a.* Relating to or consisting of prose; prosaic.—*v.i.*—*prosed*, *prosing*. To write in prose; to write or speak tediously.—**Prosaic**, **Prosaical**, prō-zā'ik, prō-zā'i-kal, *a.* In the form of prose; dull; uninteresting; commonplace.—**Prosaically**, prō-zā'i-kal-li, *adv.* In a prosaic manner.—**Prosaist**, prō-zā'ist, *n.* A writer of prose.—**Proser**, prō'zėr, *n.* One who proses.—**Prosy**, prō'zi, *a.* Like prose; dull; tedious.—**Prosily**, prō'zi-li, *adv.* In a prosy manner; tediously.—**Prosiness**, prō'zi-nes, *n.* State or quality of being prosy.—**Prosing**, prō'zing, *n.* Dull and tedious minuteness in speech or writing.—**Prosingly**, prō'zing-li, *adv.* In a prosing manner.

Prosecute, pros'e-kūt, *v.t.* — *prosecuted*, *prosecuting*. [L. *prosequor*, *prosecutus*—*pro*, before, and *sequor*, to follow. SEQUENCE. *Pursue* is the same word.] To pursue with a view to attain, execute, or accomplish; to apply to with continued purpose; to carry on; to continue; *law*, to seek to obtain by legal process; to pursue for redress or punishment before a legal tribunal.—*v.i.* To carry on a legal prosecution; to act as a prosecutor. — **Prosecutable**, pros-e-kū'ta-bl, *a.* Capable of being prosecuted; liable to prosecution. — **Prosecution**, pros-e-kū'shon, *n.* The act or process of prosecuting; the proceeding with or following up any matter in hand (the *prosecution* of a design, an inquiry, &c.); the carrying on of a suit in a court of law; the process of exhibiting formal charges against an offender before a legal tribunal; the party by whom criminal proceedings are instituted. — **Prosecutor**, pros'e-kū-tėr, *n.* One who prosecutes; the person who institutes and carries on proceedings in a court of justice.—**Prosecutrix**, pros'e-kūt-riks, *n.* A female prosecutor.

Proselyte, pros'e-līt, *n.* [Fr. *prosélyte*, from Gr. *prosēlytos*, one newly come—*pros*, towards, and root of *elthein*, to come.] A new convert to some religion or religious sect, or to some particular opinion, system, or party.—**Proselytism**, pros'e-līt-izm, *n.* The act or system of making proselytes; conversion to a system or creed.—**Proselytize**, pros'e-līt-īz, *v.t.*—*proselytized*, *proselytizing*. To make a proselyte or convert of.—*v.i.* To engage in making proselytes.—**Proselytizer**, pros'e-līt-ī-zėr, *n.* One who proselytizes.

Proseminary, prō-sem'i-na-ri, *n.* [Prefix *pro*, before, and *seminary*.] A seminary which prepares students to enter a higher.

Prosencephalon, pros-en-sef'a-lon, *n.* [Prefix *pros*, toward, and Gr. *encephalon*.] The fore-brain or anterior part of the brain.

Prosenchyma, pros-en'ki-ma, *n.* [Gr. *pros*, near, and *enchyma*, an infusion.] *Bot.* tissue of fusiform or fibriform cells, as of woody tissues.

Prosily, Prosiness. Under PROSE.

Prosobranchiate, prō-sō-brang'ki-āt, *a.* [Gr. *prosō*, in advance of, and *branchia*, gills.] Having the gills anterior to the heart: said of an order of gasteropodous molluscs.

Prosody, pros'o-di, *n.* [L. *prosodia*, from Gr. *prosōdia*, a song sung to music, prosody—*pros*, to, and *odē*, a song, an ode.] That part of grammar which treats of the quantity of syllables, of accent, and of the laws of versification; the rules of rhythm or versification. — **Prosodiacal**, pros-o-dī'a-kal, *a.* Pertaining to prosody.—**Prosodial**, **Prosodical**, pro-sō'di-al, pro-sod'i-kal, *a.* Pertaining to prosody; according to the rules of prosody.—**Prosodian**, **Prosodist**, pro-sō'di-an, pros'o-dist, *n.* One skilled in prosody.—**Prosodically**, pro-sod'i-kal-li, *adv.* In a prosodical manner.

Prosoma, prō-sō'ma, *n.* [Gr. *pro*, before, and *sōma*, the body.] *Zool.* the anterior portion of the body in cephalopods, comprising the head.

Prosopopeia, **Prosopopœia**, pros'o-pō-pē"ya, *n.* [Gr. *prosōpopoiia*—*prosōpon*, person, and *poieō* to make.] A figure in rhetoric by which things inanimate are spoken of as animated beings; personification.

Prospect, pros'pekt, *n.* [L. *prospectus*, from *prospicio*, to look forward—*pro*, forward, and *specio*, to see. SPECIES.] View of things within the reach of the eye; sight; that which is presented to the eye; the place and the objects seen; a looking forward; anticipation; expectation or ground of expectation (little *prospect* of success).—*v.i.* and *t.* (pros-pekt'). *Mining*, to make a search; to search for metal.—**Prospective**, pros-pek'tiv, *a.* Looking forward; being in prospect or expectation; looked forward to (*prospective* advantages).—**Prospectively**, pros-pek'tiv-li, *adv.* In a prospective manner.—**Prospectiveness**, pros-pek'tiv-nes, *n.* State of being prospective.—**Prospector**, pros'pek-tėr, *n.* One who searches for precious stones or metals as preliminary to settled or continuous operations. — **Prospectus**, pros-pek'tus, *n.* [L., prospect, sight, view.] A brief sketch issued for the purpose of making known the chief features of some commercial enterprise proposed, as the plan of a literary work, or the proposals of a new company or joint-stock association.

Prosper, pros'pėr, *v.i.* [Fr. *prospérer*, L. *prosperare*, from *prosperus*, favourable, fortunate, from *pro*, before, and *spes*, hope.] To be successful; to succeed; to advance in wealth or any good: said of persons; to be in a successful state; to turn out successfully: said of affairs; to be in a healthy growing state; to thrive: said of plants and animals.—*v.t.* To make prosperous; to render successful.—**Prosperity**, pros-per'i-ti, *n.* [L. *prosperitas*.] The state of being prosperous; good progress in any business or enterprise; success; attainment of the object desired; good fortune.—**Prosperous**, pros'pėr-us, *a.* [L. *prosperus*.] Making good progress in the pursuit of anything desirable; thriving; successful; favourable; favouring success. ∴ Syn. under FORTUNATE. — **Prosperously**, pros'pėr-us-li, *adv.* In a prosperous manner; successfully. — **Prosperousness**, pros'pėr-us-nes, *n.* Prosperity.

Prospicience, pros-pish'ens, *n.* [L. *prospicio*. PROSPECT.] The act of looking forward.

Prostate, **Prostatic**, pros'tāt, pros-tat'ik, *a.* [Gr. *prostatēs*, standing before—*pro*, before, and stem *sta*, to stand.] Applied to a gland situated just before the neck of the bladder in males.

Prosthesis, pros'the-sis, *n.* [Gr. *pros*, to, and *thesis*, a placing, from *tithēmi*, to place.] *Surg.* the addition of an artificial part to supply a defect of the body; *philol.* the adding of one or more letters to the commencement of a word (*be*loved). — **Prosthetic**, pros-thet'ik, *a.* Pertaining to prosthesis.

Prostitute, pros'ti-tūt, *v.t.* — *prostituted*, *prostituting*. [L. *prostituo*, *prostitutus*—*pro*, before, and *statuo*, to place. STATE.] To offer freely to a lewd use, or to indiscriminate lewdness for hire; to give up to any vile or infamous purpose; to sell to wickedness; to offer or expose upon vile terms or to unworthy persons.—*a.* Openly devoted to lewdness.—*n.* A female given to indiscriminate lewdness; a strumpet; a harlot; a base hireling.—**Prostitution**, pros-ti-tū'shon, *n.* The act or practice of yielding the body to indiscriminate intercourse with men for hire; the act of offering to an infamous employment.—**Prostitutor**, pros'ti-tū-tėr, *n.* One who prostitutes.

Prostomium, prō-stōm'i-um, *n.* [Gr. *pro*, in front of, *stoma*, a mouth.] In annelid worms, &c., the head-lobe.

Prostrate, pros'trāt, *a.* [L. *prostratus*, pp. of *prosterno*, *prostratum*, to lay flat—*pro*, before, and *sterno*, to strew. STRATUM.] Lying at length, or with the body extended on the ground; lying at mercy, as a suppliant; lying in the posture of humility or adoration; *bot.* lying flat and spreading on the ground without taking root. — *v.t.* — *prostrated*, *prostrating*. To lay flat or prostrate; *refl.* to throw one's self down as in humility or adoration; *fig.* to throw down; to overthrow; to ruin; to reduce to nothing (to *prostrate* one's strength). — **Prostration**, pros-trā'shon, *n.* The act of prostrating or laying flat; the act of falling down, or of bowing in humility or adoration; great depression or reduction (as of strength or spirits).

Prostyle, pros'tīl, *a.* [Gr. *pro*, in front, and *stylos*, a column.] *Arch.* having columns standing out quite free from the wall of the building; having pillars in front only.

Prosy. Under PROSE.

Protactic, prō-tak'tik, *a.* [Gr. *protaktikos*—*pro*, before, and *tassō*, to arrange.] Being placed at the beginning.

Protagonist, prō-tag'o-nist, *n.* [Gr. *prōtagōnistēs*—*prōtos*, first, and *agōnistēs*, an actor.] The leading character or actor in a Greek play; hence, a leading character generally.

Protandry, prō-tan'dri, *n.* [Gr. *prōtos*, first, and *anēr*, *andros*, a man, a male.] *Bot.*

the development of the stamens before the pistils. PROTERANDROUS.

Protasis, prō'ta-sis, *n.* [Gr. *protasis—pro*, before, and *teinō*, to stretch.] The first clause of a conditional sentence, being the condition on which the *apodosis* depends, as, if we run (*protasis*) we shall be in time (*apodosis*).—**Protatic**, prō-tat'ik, *a.* Pertaining to a protasis.

Protean. Under PROTEUS.

Protect, prō-tekt', *v.t.* [From L. *protectus*, pp. of *protego*, to protect—*pro*, before, and *tego*, to cover, from root seen also in E. *thatch.*] To cover or shield from danger or injury; to serve as a cover or shelter to; to defend; to guard.—**Protectingly**, prō-tek'ting-li, *adv.* In a protecting manner.—**Protection**, prō-tek'shon, *n.* The act of protecting, or state of being protected; defence; shelter from evil; that which protects or preserves from injury; a passport or other writing which secures from molestation; exemption, as from arrest in civil suits; an artificial advantage conferred by a legislature on articles of home production, usually by duties imposed on the same articles introduced from abroad.—**Protectionism**, prō-tek'shon-izm, *n.* The system of protection to commodities of home production.—**Protectionist**, prō-tek'shon-ist, *n.* One who favors the protection of some branch of industry by legal enactments; one opposed to free trade; tariff booster.—**Protective**, prō-tek'tiv, *a.* Affording protection; sheltering; defensive.—*Protective duties*, duties imposed on imports to prevent their obtaining an advantage in the market over commodities of home production.—*Protective substance*, an ANTITOXIN (which see).—**Protector**, prō-tek'tėr, *n.* One who or that which protects; a defender; a guardian.—*Eng. hist.* one who had the care of the kingdom during the king's minority; a regent; a title specifically applied to Oliver Cromwell, who assumed the title of *Lord Protector* in 1653.—**Protectorate**, prō-tek'tėr-āt, *n.* Government by a protector; the period in English history during which Cromwell was protector; the protection of a weaker country by a stronger.—**Protectorial**, prō-tek-tō'ri-al, *a.* Relating to a protector.—**Protectorship**, prō-tek'tėr-ship, *n.* The office of a protector.

Protégé, pro-tā-zhā, fem. **Protégée**, pro-tā-zhā, *n.* [Fr., one protected.] One under the care and protection of another.

Protein, prō'tē-in, *n.* [From Gr. *prōtos*, first.] One of a class of complex chemical compounds which contain carbon, hydrogen, nitrogen, oxygen, and sulphur, are essential constituents of living matter, and on decomposition yield various amino-acids.—**Proteic**, prō'tē-ik, *a.* Pertaining to protein.—**Proteid**, prō'tē-id, *n.* An older name for PROTEIN.

Protemporaneous,† prō-tem'pō-rā"nē-us, *a.* [L. *pro tempore*, for the time being.] For the time being; temporary. (*Thack.*)

Proteolytic, prō'tē-ō-lit"ik, *a.* [*Protein* and Gr. *lysis*, a solution.] Of an enzyme, converting ordinary proteins into peptones.

Proteose, prō'tē-ōs, *n.* [Gr. *prōtos*, first.] A class of products derived from proteins by hydrolysis.

Proterandrous, prot-ėr-an'drus, *a.* [Gr. *proteros*, before, and *anēr*, *andros*, a man, a male.] *Bot.* maturing the pollen before the female flowers on the plant are ready for fertilization.—**Proteranthous**, prot-ėr-an'thus, *a.* [Gr. *proteros*, and *anthos*, a flower.] *Bot.* having flowers appearing before the leaves; having the anthers matured before the stigma.—**Proterogynous**, prot-ėr-oj'i-nus, *a.* [Gr. *gynē*, a female.] *Bot.* having the stigmas matured before the pollen.

Protest, prō-test', *v.i.* [L. *protestor—pro*, before, and *testor*, to affirm, from *testis*, a witness. TEST.] To affirm with solemnity; to asseverate; to make a solemn or formal declaration (often in writing) expressive of opposition to something.—*v.t.* To make a solemn declaration or affirmation of; to assert.—*To protest a bill of exchange*, to mark or note it, through a notary public, for non-payment or non-acceptance.—*n.* (prō'test). A solemn declaration of opinion, commonly against some act; a formal statement (usually in writing), by which a person declares that he dissents from an act to which he might otherwise be deemed to have yielded assent; *law*, a formal declaration that acceptance or payment of a bill or promissory note has been refused.—**Protestant**, prot'es-tant, *n.* *Lit.* one who protests; a name given to the party who adhered to Luther at the Reformation in 1529, and protested against a decree of the Emperor Charles V and the diet of Spires; now applied to all those Christian denominations that differ from the Church of Rome, and that sprang from the Reformation.—*a.* Belonging to the religion of the Protestants.—**Protestantism**, prot'es-tant-izm, *n.* The principles or religion of Protestants.—**Protestantize**, prot'es-tan-tīz, *v.t.* To render Protestant; to convert to Protestantism.—**Protestation**, prot-es-tā'shon, *n.* [L. *protestatio.*] A solemn declaration; an asseveration; a solemn declaration of dissent; a protest.—**Protester**, prō-tes'tėr, *n.* One who protests; one who protests a bill of exchange.

Proteus, prō'tē-us, *n.* A marine deity of the ancient Greeks who had the faculty of assuming different shapes; hence, one who easily changes his form or principles; *zool.* a small amphibious animal with both lungs and gills, living in certain subterranean lakes, and having rudimentary eyes.—**Protean**, prō'tē-an, *a.* Readily assuming different shapes; exceedingly variable.

Prothallus, Prothallium, prō-thal'us, prō-thal'i-um, *n.* [Prefix *pro*, before, and *thallus.*] The first result of the germination of the spore in the higher cryptogams, as ferns, horse-tails, &c.

Prothesis, prō'the-sis, *n.* [Gr. *prothesis—pro*, forth, and *thesis*, a placing.] The place in a church on which the elements for the eucharist are put previous to their being placed on the altar; a credence.

Prothonotary, prō-thon'o-ta-ri, *n.* [L.L. *protonotarius*—Gr. *prōtos*, first, and L. *notarius*, a scribe. NOTARY. The insertion of *h* is a mistake.] A chief notary or clerk; in the *R. Cath. Ch.* a sort of registrar; one of twelve constituting a college, who receive the last wills of cardinals, &c.; in the *Eastern Church*, the chief secretary of the patriarch of Constantinople. In some states of the U. S. a chief clerk of a court.—**Prothonotaryship**, prō-thon'o-ta-ri-ship, *n.* The office of a prothonotary.

Prothorax, prō-thō'raks, *n.* [Gr. *pro*, before, and *thōrax.*] *Entom.* the first or anterior segment of the thorax in insects.

Protocercal, prō-tō-ser'kal. [Gr. *prōtos*, first, *kerkos*, a tail.] See DIPHYCERCAL.

Protococcus, prō-tō-kok'us, *n.* [Gr. *prōtos*, first, and *kokkos*, a berry.] A minute alga which produces the phenomenon of red snow.

Protocol, prō'tō-kol, *n.* [Fr. *protocole*, L.L. *protocollum*, the first leaf, the first sheet of a legal instrument glued to the cylinder round which the document was rolled—Gr. *prōtos*, first, *kolla*, glue.] The minutes or rough draft of some diplomatic document or instrument; a document serving as a preliminary to, or for the opening of, any diplomatic transaction; a record or registry.—*v.t.—protocolled, protocolling.* To make a protocol of.

Protogene, prō'tō-jēn, *n.* [Gr. *prōtos*, first, and root *gen*, to produce.] A species of granite composed of felspar, quartz, and talc or chlorite; so called because it was supposed to have been the first formed granite.—**Protogenic**, prō-tō-jen'ik, *a.* *Geol.* applied to crystalline rocks.

Protogyny, prō-toj'i-ni, *n.* [Gr. *prōtos*, first, *gynē*, a female.] *Bot.* the development of the pistils before the stamens. PROTEROGYNOUS.

Protomartyr, prō'tō-mär-tėr, *n.* [Gr. *prōtos*, first, and *martyr*, martyr.] The first martyr: a term applied to Stephen, the first Christian martyr; the first who suffers or is sacrificed in any cause.

Protomorphic, prō-tō-mor'fik, *a.* [Gr. *prōtos*, first, and *morphē*, shape.] In the earliest form or shape.

Protonema, prō-tō-nē'ma, *n.* [Gr. *prōtos*, first, *nēma*, a thread.] In mosses, a thread-like structure resulting from germination of a spore.

Protonotary, prō-ton'o-ta-ri, *n.* PROTHONOTARY.

Protophyte, prō'tō-fīt, *n.* [Gr. *prōtos*, first, and *phyton*, a plant.] A name given to the lowest organisms in the vegetable kingdom. Cp. METAPHYTE.

Protoplasm, pro'tō-plazm, *n.* [Gr. *prōtos*, first, and *plasma*, anything formed or moulded, from *plassō*, to mould.] A transparent substance, a complex and unstable mixture of proteins and other compounds, and constituting the basis of living matter in animal and plant structures.—**Protoplasmic**, prō-tō-plaz'mik, *a.* Pertaining to, resembling, or consisting of protoplasm.—**Protoplast**, prō'tō-plast, *n.* An original; a thing first formed, as a copy to be imitated.—**Protoplastic**, prō-tō-plas'tik, *a.* First formed.

Prototype, prō'tō-tīp, *n.* [Gr. *prōtotypos—prōtos*, first, and *typos*, type.] An original or model after which anything is formed; a pattern; archetype.

Protovertebra, prō-tō-vėr'tē-bra, *n.* [Gr. *prōtos*, first, and L. *vertebra.*] *Biol.* a structure in an embryo, afterwards developed into a vertebra.

Protoxide, prō-tok'sīd, *n.* [Gr. *prōtos*, first, and E. *oxide.*] That member of a series of oxides having the lowest proportion of oxygen.—**Protoxidize**, prō-tok'si-dīz, *v.t.*

Protozoa, prō-tō-zō'a, *n. pl.* [Gr. *prōtos*, first, and *zōon*, an animal.] A sub-kingdom including the most lowly organized members of the animal kingdom, and which may be defined to be animals composed of a nearly structureless jelly-like substance without a definite body cavity or trace of a nervous system.—**Protozoon, Protozoan**, prō-tō-zō'on, prō-tō-zō'an, *n.* A member of the Protozoa.—**Protozoic**, prō-tō-zō'ik, *a.* Belonging to the Protozoa; *geol.* applied to the rocks in which the earliest traces of organic life have been found.

Protract, prō-trakt', *v.t.* [From L. *protractus*, from *protraho—pro*, forward, and *traho*, to draw (whence *trace*, *traction*, *extract*, &c.).] To draw out or lengthen in time; to prolong; to lengthen out in space; to delay, defer, put off; *surv.* to draw to a scale.—**Protracted**, prō-trak'ted, *p.* and *a.* Prolonged; extending over a long time.—**Protractedly**, prō-trak'ted-li, *adv.* In a prolonged or protracted manner.—**Protracter**, prō-trak'tėr, *n.* One who protracts.—**Protractile**, prō-trak'tīl, *a.* Capable of being protracted, or thrust forward.—**Protraction**, prō-trak'shon, *n.* The act of protracting; *surv.* the act of laying down on paper the dimensions of a field, &c.—**Protractive**, prō-trak'tiv, *a.* Prolonging; continuing; delaying.—**Protractor**, prō-trak'tėr, *n.* One who protracts; *surv.* an instrument for laying down and measuring angles on paper; *anat.* a muscle which draws forward a part.

Protrude, prō-tröd', *v.t.—protruded, protruding.* [L. *protrudo—pro*, forth, forwards, and *trudo*, to thrust (seen in *obtrude*, *intrude*).] To thrust forward; to shoot forth or project, or cause to project.—*v.i.* To shoot forward; to stand out prominently.—**Protrudable**, prō-trö'da-bl, *a.* Capable of being protruded.—**Protrusile**, prō-trö'sil, *a.* Capable of being protruded and withdrawn.—**Protrusion**, prō-trö'zhon, *n.* The act of protruding.—**Protrusive**, prō-trö'ziv, *a.* Thrusting or impelling forward.—**Protrusively**, prō-trö'ziv-li, *adv.*

Protuberate, prō-tū'bėr-āt, *v.t.—protuberated, protuberating.* [L.L. *protubero*, *protuberatus*—L. *pro*, before, and *tuber*, a hump, a swell, akin to *tumeo*, to swell. TUMID.] To swell or be prominent beyond the adjacent surface; to bulge out.—**Protuberation**, prō-tū'bėr-ā"shon, *n.* The act of protuberating.—**Protuberance**, prō-tū'bėr-ans, *n.* A swelling or tumour; a prominence; a bunch or knob; anything swelled or pushed beyond the surrounding or adjacent surface.—**Protuberant**, prō-tū'bėr-ant, *a.* Swelling; prominent beyond the surrounding surface.—**Protuberantly**, prō-tū'bėr-ant-li, *adv.*

Protyle, prō'tīl, *n.* [Gr. *prōtos*, first.] A hypothetical substance supposed by Crookes to be the basis of all matter.

Proud, proud, *a.* [A.Sax. *prút*, proud, whence *prýte*, pride; cog. Dan. *prud*, stately, magnificent.] Possessing a high and often an unreasonable opinion of one's own excellence; filled with or showing inordinate self-esteem; possessing a praiseworthy self-esteem that deters from anything mean or base; haughty; arrogant; ready to boast; elated; priding one's self (*proud* of one's country); arising from pride; presumptuous; of fearless or untamable character; suggesting or exciting pride; ostentatious; grand; magnificent.—*Proud flesh*, an excessive development of granulations in wounds and ulcers.—**Proudly**, proud'li, *adv.* In a proud manner; haughtily; with lofty airs or mien.—**Proudness**, proud'nes, *n.* The state or quality of being proud.—**Proud-stomached**, *a.* Of a haughty spirit; haughty.

Prove, pröv, *v.t.*—*proved, proving.* [O.Fr. *prover, pruver*, Fr. *prouver*, from L. *probare*, to try, test, prove, lit. to test the good quality of, from *probus*, good (whence *probity*). *Proof* is a derivative.] To try or ascertain by an experiment; to test; to make trial of (to *prove* gunpowder); to establish the truth or reality of by reasoning, induction, or evidence; to demonstrate; to establish the authenticity or validity of; to obtain probate of (to *prove* a will); to gain personal experience of; *arith.* to show or ascertain the correctness of by a further calculation.—*The exception proves the rule*, lit. the exception tests or tries the rule.—*v.i.* To be found or ascertained by experience or trial; to turn out to be (the report *proved* to be false); to attain certainty.—**Provable**, prö'va-bl, *a.* Capable of being proved.—**Provableness**, prö'va-bl-nes, *n.* The state or quality of being provable.—**Provably**, prö'va-bli, *adv.* In a manner capable of proof.—**Proven**, prö'vn, *pp.* [A strong form for *proved*, the proper pp. Its usage in English is rare.] Proved.—*Not proven, Scots law*, a verdict given by a jury in a criminal case when, although there is a deficiency of evidence to convict the prisoner, there is sufficient to warrant grave suspicion of his guilt.—**Prover**, prö'vėr, *n.* One who or that which proves.

Proveditor, prō-ved'i-tėr, *n.* [It. *proveditore*, from *provedere*, to provide. PROVIDE.] A purveyor; one who procures supplies.

Provenance, pro've-nans, *n.* [Fr.—L. *pro*, and *venio*, to come.] Source or place of origin; quarter whence something is got.

Provençal, pro-väṅ-säl, *n.* A native of Provence, or Southern France; the Romance language of Provence.—**Provence-oil**, prov'ens, *n.* A fine kind of olive-oil.—**Provence-rose**, *n.* The cabbage-rose.

Provender, prov'en-dėr, *n.* [From Fr. *provende* (with *r* somewhat unaccountably added), from L. *præbenda*, things to be supplied. PREBEND.] Dry food for beasts, as hay, straw, and corn; provisions; food.

Proventriculus, prō'ven-trik"ū-lus, *n.* [Gr. *pro*, in front of, L. *ventriculus*, a stomach.] In birds, the first or chemical stomach.

Proverb, prov'ėrb, *n.* [Fr. *proverbe*, L. *proverbium*—*pro*, before, in public, and *verbum*, a word.] A short pithy sentence expressing a truth ascertained by experience or observation; a sentence which briefly and forcibly expresses some practical truth; a wise saw; an adage; a maxim; a short dramatic composition in which some proverb or popular saying is taken as the foundation of the plot; a by-word; a reproach or object of contempt; *Scrip.* a dark saying of the wise that requires interpretation.—**Proverbial**, prō-vėr'bi-al, *a.* Comprised in a proverb; used or current as a proverb; resembling a proverb.—**Proverbialism**, prō-vėr'bi-al-izm, *n.* A proverbial phrase or saying.—**Proverbialist**, prō-vėr'bi-al-ist, *n.* A composer, collector, or user of proverbs.—**Proverbialize**, prō-vėr'bi-al-īz, *v.t.*—*proverbialized, proverbializing.* To make or turn into a proverb.—**Proverbially**, prō-vėr'bi-al-li, *adv.* In a proverbial manner or style; by way of proverb.

Provide, prō-vīd', *v.t.*—*provided, providing.* [L. *provideo*, lit. to see before—*pro*, before, and *video, visum*, to see (whence *vision, visible, revise*, &c.).] To procure beforehand; to prepare (to *provide* warm clothing); to furnish; to supply (well *provided* with corn); to lay down as a previous arrangement; to make a previous condition or understanding.—*v.i.* To make provision; to take measures beforehand (we must *provide for* our wants, *against* mishaps).—**Provided**, prō-vī'ded, *conj.* [A conjunction only by ellipsis = it being provided that.] On condition; on these terms; this being conceded.—**Providence**, prov'i-dens, *n.* [L. *providentia.*] Foresight‡; timely care or preparation‡; prudence; the care of God over his creatures; divine superintendence; hence (with a capital letter), God, regarded as exercising forecast, care, and direction for and over his creatures; the divine being or power; something due to an act of providential intervention; a providential circumstance.—**Provident**, prov'i-dent, *a.* [L. *providens*, ppr. of *provideo*, I provide: the same word as *prudent*, as *providence* = *prudence.*] Foreseeing wants and making provision to supply them; prudent in preparing for future exigencies; frugal; economical.—**Providential**, prov-i-den'shal, *a.* Effected by the providence of God; referrible to divine providence.—**Providentially**, prov-i-den'shal-li, *adv.* In a providential manner.—**Providently**, *adv.* In a provident manner; with prudent foresight.—**Provider**, prō-vī'dėr, *n.* One who provides.

Province, prov'ins, *n.* [Fr., from L. *provincia*, a province—*pro*, before, and *vinco*, I conquer.] Originally, a region reduced under Roman dominion and subjected to the command of a governor sent from Rome; hence, a territory at some distance from the metropolis (*the provinces* being often thus used in contradistinction to the metropolis); a large territorial or political division of a state; in England, a division for ecclesiastical purposes under the jurisdiction of an archbishop, there being two *provinces*, that of Canterbury and that of York; *fig.* the proper duty, office, or business of a person; sphere of action; a division in any department of knowledge or speculation; a department.—**Provincial**, prō-vin'shal, *a.* Pertaining to a province; forming a province; exhibiting the manners of a province; characteristic of the inhabitants of a province; rustic; not polished; rude; pertaining to an ecclesiastical province or to the jurisdiction of an archbishop.—*n.* A person belonging to a province as distinguished from the metropolis; in some religious orders, a monastic superior in a given district.—**Provincialism**, prō-vin'shal-izm, *n.* A peculiar word or manner of speaking in a district of country remote from the principal country or from the metropolis.—**Provincialist**, prō-vin'shal-ist, *n.* A provincial; one who uses provincialisms.—**Provinciality**, prō-vin'shi-al"i-ti, *n.* The quality of being provincial.—**Provincially**, prō-vin'shal-li, *adv.* In a provincial manner.

Provision, prō-vizh'on, *n.* [L. *provisio, provisionis*, a foreseeing, foresight, purveying, from *providere, provisum*, to foresee. PROVIDE.] The act of providing or making previous preparation; a measure taken beforehand; provident care; accumulation of stores or materials beforehand; a store or stock; a stock of food provided; hence, victuals; food: usually in the plural; a stipulation or measure proposed in an enactment or the like; a proviso.—*v.t.* To provide with things necessary, especially victuals or food.—**Provisional**, prō-vizh'on-al, *a.* Provided for present need or for the occasion; temporarily established; temporary.—**Provisionally**, prō-vizh'on-al-li, *adv.* In a provisional manner; for the present exigency; temporarily.—**Provisionary**, prō-vizh'on-a-ri, *a.* Provisional; provident.

Proviso, prō-vī'zō, *n.* [L. *provisus*, pp. of *provideo*, ablative *proviso*, it being provided. PROVIDE.] An article or clause in any statute, agreement, contract, grant, or other writing, by which a condition is introduced; a conditional stipulation.—**Provisor**, prō-vī'zor, *n.* [Fr. *proviseur.*] A person appointed by the pope to a benefice before the death of the incumbent, and to the prejudice of the rightful patron.—**Provisory**, prō-vī'zo-ri, *a.* Temporary; provisional; conditional.—**Provisorily**, prō-vī'zo-ri-li, *adv.* In a provisory manner; conditionally.

Provoke, prō-vōk', *v.t.*—*provoked, provoking.* [Fr. *provoquer*, from L. *provoco*, I call forth, challenge, excite—*pro*, forth, and *voco*, to call. VOICE.] To challenge‡; to summon‡; to stimulate to action; to induce by motive; to excite or arouse (as hunger); to call forth; to instigate; to excite to anger or passion; to irritate; to enrage.—*v.i.* To produce anger.—**Provoker**, prō-vō'kėr, *n.* One who or that which provokes.—**Provoking**, prō-vō'king, *p.* and *a.* Having the power of exciting resentment; annoying; vexatious; exasperating.—**Provokingly**, prō-vō'king-li, *adv.* In a provoking manner; annoyingly.—**Provocation**, prov-ō-kā'shon, *n.* The act of provoking; anything that excites anger; cause of resentment; incitement; stimulus.—**Provocative**, prō-vō'ka-tiv, *a.* Serving to provoke; exciting; apt to incense or enrage.—*n.* Anything that tends to excite appetite or passion; a stimulant.

Provost, prov'ost, *n.* [O.Fr. *provost* (Fr. *prévôt*), from L. *praepositus*, one who is placed over others, from *praeponere*—*prae*, before, and *ponere*, to place. POSITION.] A superintendent; a university official directing educational activities; *British*, the heads of certain colleges; the chief dignitary of a cathedral or collegiate church; the chief magistrate of a Scotch burgh, corresponding to a mayor.—**Provost-court**, a military court for the trial of minor offenses.—**Provost-guard**, soldiers detailed for police duty.—**Provost-marshal**, *n.* *Milit.* an officer whose duty it is to attend to offenses committed against military discipline; *navy*, an officer who has the custody of prisoners at a court-martial.

Prow, prou, *n.* [Fr. *proue*, Sp. and Pg. *proa*, from L. *prora*, from Gr. *prōra*, a prow; akin to *pro*, before.] The forepart of a ship; the bow; the beak.

Prowess, prou'es, *n.* [Fr. *prouesse*, prowess, from O.Fr. *prou* (Fr. *preux*), brave; origin doubtful.] Bravery; valour; military bravery combined with skill; intrepidity and dexterity in war.

Prowl, proul, *v.i.* [Origin doubtful; older forms were *proule, prolle.*] To rove or wander stealthily, as a beast in search of prey.—*v.t.* To wander stealthily over.—**Prowler**, prou'lėr, *n.* One who prowls.—**Prowlingly**, prou'ling-li, *adv.* In a prowling manner.

Proximal, prok'si-mal, *a.* [L. *proximus*, nearest.] Nearest; applied to the extremity of a bone, limb, or organ of animals and plants nearest the point of attachment or insertion: opposed to *distal.*

Proximate, prok'si-māt, *a.* [L. *proximatus*, pp. of *proximo*, I come near, from *proximus*, nearest, superl. of *prope*, near. PROPINQUITY.] Nearest; next.—*Proximate cause*, that which immediately precedes and produces the effect, as distinguished from the *remote, mediate*, or *predisposing* *cause.*—*Proximate principles*, organic compounds which are the constituents of more complex organizations, and which exist ready formed in animals and vegetables, such as albumen, gelatine, gum, starch, &c. —**Proximately**, prŏk'si-māt-li, *adv.* In a proximate manner or position; immediately.—**Proximity**, prok-sim'i-ti, *n.* [L. *proximitas.*] The state of being proximate or next; immediate nearness, either in place, blood, or alliance. — **Proximo**, prok'si-mō, *a.* [L., on the next.] A Latin adjective used to mean in or of the next month (the 5th *proximo*). Often contracted *Prox.*

Proxy, prok'si, *n.* [Contr. from *procuracy* = L.L. *procuratia.* PROCURATOR.] The agency of a person who acts as a substitute for a principal; authority to act for another; the person deputed to act for another; a deputy; a writing by which one person authorizes another to vote in his place.—*v.i.*—*proxied, proxying.* To act by proxy.—**Proxyship**, prok'si-ship, *n.* The office or agency of a proxy.

Prude, pröd, *n.* [Fr. *prude*; probably from L. *prudens*, prudent.] A person, particularly a woman, affecting great reserve and excessive virtue or delicacy of feeling, or who pretends to great propriety of conduct.—**Prudery, Prudishness**, prö'dėr-i, prö'dish-nes, *n.* The conduct of a prude; affected delicacy of feeling; coyness.—**Prudish**, prö'dish, *a.* Pertaining to a prude; affecting excessive modesty or virtue; coy or reserved.—**Prudishly**, prö'dish-li, *adv.* In a prudish manner.

Prudent, prö'dent, *a.* [Fr. *prudent*, from L. *prudens, prudentis*, prudent, from *providens, providentis*, ppr. of *providere*, to foresee. PROVIDE.] Cautious or circumspect in determining on any action or line of conduct; careful of the consequences of enterprises, measures, or actions; dictated or directed by prudence (*prudent* behaviour); frugal; economical; correct and decorous in manner.—**Prudence**, prö'dens, *n.* [L. *prudentia* = *providentia.*] The state or quality of being prudent.—**Prudential**, prö-den'shal, *a.* Proceeding from prudence; dictated or prescribed by prudence; exercising prudence. — **Prudentialist**, prö-den'shal-ist, *n.* One who is governed by prudentiall motives. — **Prudentiality**, prö-den'shi-al''i-ti, *n.* The quality of being prudential. — **Prudentially**, prö-den'shal-li, *adv.* In conformity with prudence; prudently.—**Prudently**, prö'dent-li, *adv.* In a prudent manner; discreetly; cautiously; circumspectly.

Prud'homme, prü-dom, *n.* [Fr., from *prude*, grave, sober, and *homme*, man.] In France, the name of members of tribunals composed of masters and workmen whose principal office was to arbitrate in trade disputes.

Pruinate, Pruinose, Pruinous, prö'i-nāt, prö-in'ōs, prö'i-nus, *a.* [From L. *pruina*, hoar-frost.] Hoary; appearing as if frosted, from a covering of minute dust.

Prune, prön, *v.t.*—*pruned, pruning.* [Formerly *proine, proyne*, from Fr. *provigner*, dial. Fr. *preugner, progner*, from L. *propago, propaginis*, a slip or sucker. PROPAGATE.] To lop or cut off, as the superfluous branches of trees; to lop superfluous twigs or branches from; to trim with the knife; to clear from anything superfluous; to preen or trim, as the plumage of a bird.—**Pruner**, prö'nėr, *n.* One who prunes.—**Pruning-hook**, *n.* An instrument for pruning trees, shrubs, &c., with a hooked blade.—**Pruning-knife**, *n.* A kind of knife with a curved blade for pruning.—**Pruning-shears**, *n.pl.* Shears for pruning shrubs, &c.

Prune, prön, *n.* [Fr. *prune*, from L. *prunum*, a plum. PLUM.] A plum; specifically, a dried plum.—**Prune-tree**, *n.* A tree that bears prunes or plums.—**Pruniferous**, prö-nif'ėr-us, *a.* Bearing plums.

Prunella, prö-nel'a, *n.* [From Fr. *prunelle, brunelle*, from G. *bräune*, a disorder of the throat, which the plant was supposed to cure.] A European plant formerly used in popular medicine; a preparation of purified nitre in cakes or balls used to cure sore throats. Called also *Prunella Salt* and *Sal Prunella.*

Prunella, Prunello, prö-nel'a, prö-nel'ō, *n.* [Fr. *prunelle, prunella*, from its color resembling that of *prunes.* PRUNE.] A kind of woolen stuff of which clergymen's gowns were once made, afterwards used for the uppers of shoes; also, a twill.

Prurient, prö'ri-ent, *a.* [L. *pruriens*, from *prurire*, to itch or long for a thing, to be lecherous.] Itching after something; eagerly desirous; inclined or inclining to lascivious thoughts; having lecherous imaginations. — **Pruriently**, prö'ri-ent-li, *adv.* In a prurient manner; with a longing desire.—**Prurience, Pruriency**, prö'ri-ens, prö'ri-en-si, *n.* The state of being prurient; lascivious suggestiveness.

Prurigo, prö-rī'gō, *n.* [L., an itching, the itch.] An eruption of the skin in which the papules are diffuse and intolerably itchy. — **Pruriginous**, prö-rij'i-nus, *a.* Affected by prurigo; caused by prurigo.

Prussian, prush'an, *a.* Pertaining to Prussia.—*Prussian blue*, a cyanide of iron possessed of a deep-blue colour, much used as a pigment.—**Prussiate**, prus'i-āt or prus'i-āt, *n.* A compound of cyanogen with iron and potassium; a cyanide.—**Prussic-acid**, prus'ik or prus'ik, *a.* [Originally obtained from *Prussian* blue.] The common name for *Hydrocyanic Acid.* — **Prussine**, prus'in, *n.* CYANOGEN.

Pry, prī, *v.i.*—*pried, prying.* [A modification of O.E. *pire*, to peer. PEER.] To peep narrowly; to look closely; to attempt to discover something with scrutinizing curiosity; to open with a pry.—*n.* Narrow inspection; impertinent peeping; an instrument used for prying.—**Prying**, prī'ing, *p.* and *a.* Inquisitive; curious.—**Pryingly**, prī'ing-li, *adv.* In a prying manner.

Prythee, pri'THē. Same as *Prithee.*

Psalm, säm, *n.* [L. *psalmus*, a psalm, from Gr. *psalmos*, a twitching or twanging with the fingers, from *psallein*, to play a stringed instrument, to sing to the harp.] A sacred song or hymn; especially one of the hymns composed by King David and other Jewish writers, a collection of 150 of which constitutes a book of the Old Testament; also applied to versifications of the scriptural psalms composed for the use of churches.—**Psalmist**, säm'ist or sal'mist, *n.* A writer or composer of psalms. —**Psalmodic, Psalmodical**, sal-mod'ik, sal-mod'i-kal, *a.* Relating to psalmody. —**Psalmodist**, säm'od-ist or sal'mod-ist, *n.* One who writes psalms.—**Psalmody**, säm'o-di or sal'mo-di, *n.* The singing or writing of psalms; psalms collectively.—**Psalmography**, sä-mog'ra-fi or sal-mog'ra-fi, *n.* The act or practice of writing psalms.—**Psalmographer, Psalmographist**, sä-mog'ra-fėr or sal-mog'ra-fėr, sä-mog'ra-fist or sal-mog'ra-fist, *n.* A writer of psalms.

Psalter, sal'tėr, *n.* [L. *psalterium*, Gr. *psaltērion*, a kind of harp, from *psallō.* PSALM.] The Book of Psalms; a book containing the Psalms separately printed; a version of the Psalms used in religious services.—**Psalterium**, sal-tē'ri-um, *n.* A psalter; the third stomach of ruminants, called also the *Omasum* or *Manyplies.*—**Psaltery**, sal'tėr-i, *n.* An instrument of music used by the Hebrews, the form of which is not known; a form of dulcimer.

Psammite, sam'mīt, *n.* [Gr. *psammos*, sand.] *Geol.* a term used for fine-grained, fissile, clayey sandstones, in contradistinction, to those which are more siliceous and gritty.—**Psammitic**, sam-mit'ik, *a.* Pertaining to or containing psammite.

Psellismus, sel-iz'mus, *n.* [Gr. *psellizein*, to stammer.] A defect in enunciation; a lisping, stammering, or similar defect.

Pseudæsthesia, sū-dēs-thē'si-a, *n.* [Gr. *pseudēs*, false, and *aisthēsis*, perception.] Imaginary feeling; imaginary sense of touch in parts that have been long removed (as a leg that has been amputated).

Pseudo-, sū'dō. [Gr. *pseudos*, falsehood.] A Greek prefix, signifying false, counterfeit, or spurious, used in many compound words, often self-explanatory, and occasionally as an independent English word.—**Pseudobranchia**, *n.* *Zool.* a supplementary gill found in certain fishes.—**Pseudo-bulb**, *n.* *Bot.* an enlarged above-ground stem resembling a tuber, as in many orchids.—**Pseudograph, Pseudography**, sū'dō-graf, sū-dog'ra-fi, *n.* [Gr. *graphē*, writing.] False writing.—**Pseudo-hæmal**, *a.* [Gr. *haima*, blood.] A term applied to the vascular or circulatory system of annelids.—**Pseudo-membrane**, *n.* A false membrane resulting from inflammation.—**Pseudo-metallic**, *a.* Falsely or imperfectly metallic: applied to a kind of lustre in minerals.—**Pseudo-monocotyledonous**, *a.* *Bot.* having two or more cotyledons consolidated into a single mass. —**Pseudomorph**, sū'dō-morf, *n.* [Gr. *morphē*, shape.] A deceptive or irregular form; a mineral having a form belonging, not to the substance of which it consists, but to some other substance which has wholly or partially disappeared.—**Pseudomorphism**, sū-dō-mor'fizm, *n.* The state of being a pseudomorph.—**Pseudomorphous**, sū-dō-mor'fus, *a.* Not having the true form; having the character of a pseudomorph.—**Pseudonym**, sū'dō-nim, *n.* [Gr. *onoma*, a name.] A false or feigned name; a name assumed by a writer.—**Pseudonymity**, sū-dō-nim'i-ti, *n.* The state of being pseudonymous; writing under an assumed name. — **Pseudonymous**, sū-don'i-mus, *a.* [Gr. *pseudōnymous*—*pseudos*, and *onoma*, name.] Bearing a false name or signature; applied to an author who publishes a book under a feigned name; also to the book itself.—**Pseudopod**, sū'dō-pod, *n.* [Gr. *pous, podos*, foot.] An animal with pseudopodia. — **Pseudopodia**, sū-dō-pō'di-a, *n.pl.* *Zool.* the organs of locomotion characteristic of the lower Protozoa, consisting of threads or processes projected from any part of the body. — **Pseudopodial**, sū-dō-pō'di-al, *a.* Pertaining to pseudopodia.—**Pseudoscope**, sū'dō-skōp, *n.* [Gr. *pseudos*, and *skopeō*, to view.] An optical instrument somewhat on the principle of the stereoscope, but producing effects directly opposite, namely, reversing the reliefs. — **Pseudo-volcanic**, *a.* Pertaining to a pseudo-volcano.—**Pseudo-volcano**, *n.* A volcano that emits smoke and sometimes flame, but no lava. — **Pseudovum**, sū-dō'vum, *n.* pl. **Pseudova**, sū-dō'va. [L. *ovum*, an egg.] *Zool.* one of the egg-like bodies from which the young of the viviparous aphis are produced.

Pshaw, sha, *exclam.* An expression of contempt, disdain, or dislike.—*v.i.* To utter the interjection pshaw.

Psilanthropist, sī-lan'throp-ist, *n.* [Gr. *psilos*, bare, mere, and *anthrōpos*, man.] One who believes that Christ was a mere man; a humanitarian.—**Psilanthropic**, sī-lan-throp'ik, *a.* Pertaining to psilanthropy. — **Psilanthropism, Psilanthropy**, sī-lan'throp-izm, sī-lan'thro-pi, *n.* The doctrine or belief of the mere human existence of Christ.

Psilomelane, sī-lom'e-lān, *n.* [Gr. *psilos*, smooth, and *melas, melan*, black.] An ore of manganese having a colour nearly steel-gray.

Psittaceous, sit-tā'shus, *a.* [L. *psittacus*, from Gr. *psittakos*, a parrot.] Belonging to the parrot tribe.

Psoas, sō'as, *n.* [From Gr. *psoa*, a muscle of the loin.] The name of two inside muscles of the loins.—**Psoadic**, sō-ad'ik, *a.* *Anat.* connected with the psoas.

Psora, sō'ra, *n.* [Gr.] The itch.—**Psoriasis**, sō-rī'a-sis, *n.* [Gr.] A cutaneous affection, consisting of patches of rough, amorphous scales, generally accompanied by chaps and fissures; also, the itch. — **Psoric**, sō'rik, *a.* Relating to or connected with psora or the itch.—*n.* A medicine for the itch.

Psyche, sī'kē, *n.* [Gr. *psychē*, the soul.] The soul; a sort of mythical or allegorical personification of the human soul, as a beautiful maiden, beloved by Cupid.—**Psychiatrist**, sī-kī'a-trist, *n.* A physician specializing in psychiatry.—**Psychiatry**, sī-kī'a-tri, *n.* That field of scientific thought and practice in medicine and psychology which aims to discover and/or correct mental derangements.—**Psychic, Psychical, Psychal**, sī'kik, sī'ki-kal, sī'kal, *a.* [Gr. *psychikos.*] Belonging to the human soul, spirit, or mind; psychological; applied to that force by which spiritualists aver they produce 'spiritual' phenomena.—**Psychism**, sī'kizm, *n.* The doctrine which maintains the existence and efficacy of psychic force.—**Psychoanalysis**, sī'kō-a-nal"i-sis, *n.* That process of revealing the subconscious thoughts of an individual by inducing him to relate without restraint the complete details of his life's experiences, in order to detect hidden mental conflicts which may produce disorders of mind and/or body.—**Psychoanalyst**, sī'kō-an"a-list, *n.*—**Psychoanalyze**, (-līz), *v.t.*—**Psychogenesis**, sī-kō-jen'e-sis, *n.* [Gr. *psychē*, and *genesis*, origin.] The origin or generation of the mind as manifested by consciousness.—**Psychologic, Psychological**, sī-kō-loj'ik, sī-ko-loj'i-kal, *a.* Pertaining to psychology.—*Psychological moment*, the apparently predestined and inevitable moment: the absolute nick of time: by confusion with the 'moment' or momentum impelling the will to act, in a psychological sense.—**Psychologically**, sī-kō-loj'i-kal-li, *adv.* In a psychological manner.—**Psychologist**, sī-kol'o-jist, *n.* One who studies, writes on, or is versed in psychology.—**Psychology**, sī-kol'o-ji, *n.* [Gr. *psychē* and *logos.*] That branch of knowledge which deals with the human soul: that knowledge of the mind which we derive from a careful examination of the facts of consciousness: the natural history of the mind.—**Psychomachy**, sī-kom'a-ki. [Gr. *machē*, combat.] A conflict of the soul with the body.—**Psychomancy**, sī'kō-man-si, *n.* [Gr. *manteia*, prophecy.] Divination by consulting the souls of the dead; necromancy.—**Psychometry**, sī-kom'e-tri, *n.* [Gr. *psychē*, soul, *metron*, measure.] The estimation of the relative strength of mental faculties.—**Psychopathy**, sī-kop'a-thi, *n.* [Gr. *pathos*, suffering.] Mental disease.—**Psychophysical**, sī-kō-fiz'i-kal, *a.* Pertaining to psychophysics. — **Psychophysics**, sī-kō-fiz'iks, *n.* That branch of science which treats of the connection between nerve-action and consciousness; the doctrine or science of the physical basis of consciousness.—**Psychosis**, sī-kō'sis, *n.* Mental state or process; a mind disease.

Psychotherapy, sī-kō-ther'a-pi, *n.* [Gr. *therapeuō*, I attend medically.] That branch of psychiatry which prescribes and administers methods of treatment to eliminate maladjustments and to correct mental disorders.

Psychrometer, sī-krom'et-ėr, *n.* [Gr. *psychros*, cool, and *metron*, measure.] An instrument for measuring the tension of the aqueous vapor in the atmosphere; a form of hygrometer.—**Psychrometric Psychrometrical**, sī-krō-met'rik, sī-krō-met'ri-kal, *a.*—**Psychrometry**, sī-krom'-et-ri, *n.* The use of the psychrometer.

Ptarmic, tär'mik, *n.* [Gr. *ptairō*, to sneeze.] A sternutatory, or medicine which excites sneezing.

Ptarmigan, tär'mi-gan, *n.* [Gael. *termachan*, Ir. *tarmochan*, ptarmigan.] A bird of the grouse family, of a white color in winter, frequenting northern regions.

Pterichthys, te-rik'this, *n.* [Gr. *pteron*, a wing, and *ichthys*, a fish.] A fossil fish of the old red sandstone, protected anteriorly by large bony plates and having wing-like pectoral fins.

Pteridologist, ter-i-dol'o-jist, *n.* [Gr. *pteris*, *pteridos*, a fern, *logos*, discourse.] One versed in the botany of the ferns.—**Pteridology**, ter-i-dol'o-ji, *n.* The science of ferns.

Pteridophyte, ter'i-dō-fīt, *n.* [Gr. *pteris*, fern; *phuton*, plant.] One of the pteridophyta, the phylum of plants which includes the ferns and their allies; formerly called a vascular cryptogam.

Pterodactyl, Pterodactyle, ter-ō-dak'til, *n.* [Gr. *pteron*, a wing, and *daktylos*, a digit.] An extinct species of flying reptile belonging to the mesozoic period, and exhibiting affinities to mammals, reptiles, and birds. — **Pterodactylous**, ter-ō-dak'ti-lus, *a.* Pertaining to or resembling the pterodactyls.

Pteropod, ter'ō-pod, *n.* [Gr. *pteron*, a wing, and *pous*, *podos*, a foot.] One of a class of molluscs which have a swimming expansion on each side of the head.—**Pteropodous**, te-rop'o-dus, *a.* Belonging to the pteropods; wing-footed.

Pterosaur, ter'o-sar, *n.* [Gr. *pteron*, a wing, *sauros*, a lizard.] An extinct flying reptile, such as the pterodactyl.

Pterygoid, ter'i-goid, *a.* [Gr. *pteryx*, *pterygos*, a wing.] Wing-shaped; *anat.* applied to processes of the sphenoid bone which complete the osseous palate behind.

Pteryla, pl. **æ**, ter'i-la, *n.* [Gr. *ptĕron*, a plume.] In birds, a feathered tract of skin.

Pterylography, ter-i-log'ra-fi, *n.* [Gr. *pteron*, a feather, *hylē*, a wood, and *graphē*, a writing.] A description of the feathers of birds, more especially as regards the manner in which they are arranged in special tracts on their bodies.—**Pterylographic**, ter-il'ō-graf"ik, *a.* Pertaining to pterylography.

Pterylosis, ter-i-lō'sis, *n.* [Gr. *pteron*, wing, *hylē*, material.] *Ornith.* the peculiar disposition or arrangement of a bird's feathers on the different parts.

Ptisan, tī'san, *n.* [L. *ptisana*, from Gr. *ptisanē*, peeled barley, barley-water, from *ptissō*, to peel.] A decoction of barley with other ingredients; *med.* a drink containing little or no medicinal agent.

Ptolemaic, tol-ē-mā'ik, *a.* [From *Ptolemy*, the geographer and astronomer.] Pertaining to Ptolemy.—*Ptolemaic system*, that maintained by Ptolemy, who supposed the earth to be fixed in the centre of the universe, and that the sun and stars revolved around it.—**Ptolemaist**, tol-ē-mā'ist, *n.* A believer in the Ptolemaic system.

Ptomaine, tō'mān, *n.* [Gr. *ptōma*, a fall, a corpse, from *piptō*, to fall.] One of a class of alkaloids or organic bases which are generated in animal substances during putrefaction, or even it may be during life, some of them highly poisonous.

Ptyalin, tī'al-in, *n.* [Gr. *ptyalon*, saliva.] A ferment in saliva that converts starch into sugar.—**Ptyalism**, tī'al-izm, *n.* Salivation; a morbid and copious excretion of saliva.—**Ptyalogogue, Ptysmagogue**, tī-al'o-gog, tiz'ma-gog, *n.* [Gr. *ptyalon*, *ptysma*, saliva, and *agōgos*, leading, from *agō*, to induce.] A medicine which causes salivation or a flow of saliva.

Ptychode, tī'kōd, *n.* [Gr. *ptychē*, a fold.] *Physiol.* a coating of protoplasm lining the inside of the membrane of a cell.

Ptysmagogue. Under PTYALOGOGUE.

Puberty, pū'bėr-ti, *n.* [L. *pubertas*, from *puber* or *pubes*, *puberis*, of ripe age, adult, same root as *puer*, a boy, *pullus*, a chicken.] The period in both male and female marked by the functional development of the generative system; the age at which persons are capable of begetting or bearing children.—**Puberal**, pū'bėr-al, *a.* Pertaining to puberty.—**Puberulent**, pū-bėr'ū-lent, *a.* *Bot.* covered with fine down. — **Pubes**, pū'bēz, *n.* [L., the hair which appears on the body at puberty.] *Anat.* the middle part of the hypogastric region, so called because covered with hair at puberty; *bot.* the down or downy substance on plants; pubescence.—**Pubescence, Pubescency**, pū-bes'ens, pū-bes'en-si, *n.* The state of one who has arrived at puberty; puberty; *bot.* the downy substance on plants.—**Pubescent**, pū-bes'ent, *a.* Arriving at puberty; *bot.* covered with pubescence; *zool.* covered with very fine short hairs.—**Pubic**, pū'bik, *a.* Pertaining to the pubes.

Public, pub'lik, *a.* [Fr. *public* (masc.), *publique* (fem.), from L. *publicus*, for *populicus*, from *populus*, people, PEOPLE.] Not private; pertaining to the whole people; relating to, regarding, or affecting a state, nation, or community (the *public* service); proceeding from many or the many; belonging to people in general (a *public* subscription); open to the knowledge of all; general; common; notorious (*public* report); regarding not private interest, but the good of the community (*public* spirit); open to common use (a *public* road, a *public*-house). — *Public prosecutor*, one who originates and conducts prosecutions in the interests of the public. — *n.* The general body of mankind or of a nation, state, or community; the people, indefinitely: with *the*; the people who read an author's works; a public-house (*colloq.*).—*In public*, in open view; before the people at large; not in private or secrecy.—**Publican**, pub'li-kan, *n.* [L. *publicanus.*] Among the ancient Romans, a farmer of the public revenues: any collector of public dues or revenues (*Shak.*); the keeper of a public-house or a similar establishment. (*Brit.*)—**Publication**, pub-li-kā'shon, *n.* [L. *publicatio*, from *publico*, to make public.] The act of publishing or offering to public notice; notification to people at large; promulgation; the act of offering a book, map, print, or the like, to the public by sale or gratuitous distribution; a work printed and published.—**Public-house**, *n.* A shop for the retail of liquors, as beer, spirits. (*Brit.*)—**Publicist**, pub'li-sist, *n.* A writer on the laws of nature and nations; a writer on the current political topics of the time.—**Publicity**, pub-lis'i-ti, *n.* [Fr. *publicité.*] The state of being public or open to the knowledge of a community; notoriety.—**Publicly**, pub'lik-li, *adv.* In a public manner; openly; without concealment. — **Public-minded**, *a.* Disposed to promote the public interest.—**Publicness**, pub'lik-nes, *n.* The state of being public. — **Public-spirited**, *a.* Having or exercising a disposition to advance the interest of the community; dictated by a regard to public good.—**Public-spiritedness**, *n.* The quality or character of being public-spirited.—**Publish**, pub'lish, *v.t.* [Fr. *publier.*] To make public; to make known to people in general; to promulgate; to cause to be printed and offered for sale; to issue from the press to the public; to make known by posting, or by reading in a church (to *publish* banns of matrimony). — **Publishable**, pub'lish-a-bl, *a.* Capable of being published; fit for publication.—**Publisher**, pub'lish-ėr, *n.* One who publishes; especially, one who, as the first source of supply, issues books and other literary works, maps, engravings, &c., for sale.

Puce, pūs, *a.* [Fr. *puce*, from L. *pulex*, *pulicis*, a flea.] Dark-brown; reddish-brown; of a flea-colour.—**Puceron**, pū'sē-ron, *n.* [Fr., from *puce*, a flea.] The aphis, vine-fretter, or plant-louse.

Pucka, puk'a, *a.* [Hind. *pakka*, ripe.] Solid; substantial; permanent; genuine; an Anglo-Indian term.

Pucker, puk'ėr, *v.t.* [From *poke*, a bag or pocket; comp. to *purse* the lips.] To gather into small folds or wrinkles; to contract into ridges and furrows; to wrinkle.—*v.i.* To become wrinkled; to gather into folds.—*n.* A fold or wrinkle, or a collection of folds.—*To be in a pucker*, to be in a state of flutter or agitation (*colloq.*)—**Puckery**, puk'ėr-i, *a.* Full of puckers or wrinkles.

Puckish, puk'ish, *a.* [The name *Puck* is from W. *pwca*, Ir. *puca*, a goblin.] Resembling the fairy *Puck*; elvish; freakish.

Pudding, pud'ing, *n.* [From the Celtic; same as W. *poten*, Ir. *putag*, Gael. *putog*, a pudding; of the same root as *pod.*] An intestine; a gut of an animal; an intestine stuffed with meat, &c.; a sausage; a compound of flour or other farinaceous substance, with milk and eggs, sometimes enriched with raisins.—**Pudding-bag**, *n.* A bag in which a pudding is boiled.—**Pudding-faced**, *a.* Having a round meaningless face.—**Pudding-headed**, *a.* Dull; stupid.—**Pudding-pie**, *n.* A pudding with meat baked in it.—**Pudding-stone**, *n.* A term now considered synonymous with conglomerate, but originally applied to a mass of flint pebbles cemented by a siliceous paste.—**Puddingy**, pud'-ing-i, *a.* Resembling or suggestive of a pudding.

Puddle, pud'l, *n.* [Akin to L.G. *pudel*, pool; D. *poedelen*, to puddle; comp. Ir. and Gael. *plod*, a pool.] A small collection of dirty water; a small muddy pool; clay or earth tempered with water and thoroughly wrought so as to be impervious to water; puddling. — *v.t.* — *puddled, puddling.* To make turbid or muddy; to stir up the mud or sediment in; *fig.* to befoul; to render water-tight by means of puddle; to convert into wrought-iron by the process of puddling. —*v.i.* To make a dirty stir. — **Puddle-ball**, *n.* The lump of red-hot iron taken from the puddling-furnace to be hammered or rolled. — **Puddler**, pud'lėr, *n.* One who puddles; one who is employed at the process of turning cast-iron into wrought-iron.—**Puddling**, pud'ling, *n.* The operation of working plastic clay behind piling in a coffer-dam, or in other situations, to resist the penetration of water; the clay thus used; the process by which cast-iron is converted into malleable iron, consisting in working it in a special furnace, hammering and rolling.—*Puddling furnace*, a kind of reverberatory furnace for puddling iron. —**Puddly**, pud'li, *a.* Muddy; dirty.

Pudency,† pū'den-si, *n.* [L. *pudens, pudentis*; ppr. of *pudere*, to be ashamed (seen also in *impudent*)]. Modesty; shamefacedness.—**Pudenda**, pū-den'da, *n.pl.* [L., lit. things to be ashamed of.] The parts of generation.—**Pudendal**, pū-den'dal, *a.* Pertaining to the pudenda. — **Pudendous**,† pū-den'dus, *a.* [L. *pudendus*, shameful.] Shameful; disgraceful.—**Pudic, Pudical**, pū'dik, pū-dĭ'kal, *a.* [L. *pudicus* (*i* long), modest.] Pertaining to the pudenda. — **Pudicity**, pū-dis'i-ti, *n.* [L. *pudicitia*.] Modesty; chastity.

Pudgy, Pudsy, puj'i, pud'si, *a.* [Also *podgy*, probably akin to *pod, pad.*] Fat and short; thick; fleshy.

Puerile, pū'ėr-īl, *a.* [L. *puerilis*, from *puer*, a boy; same root as *pupus*, a boy, *pullus*, a chicken. PUPIL, PULLET.] Boyish; childish; trifling.—**Puerilely**, pū'ėr-īl-li, *adv.* In a puerile manner.—**Puerileness**, pū'ėr-īl-nes, *n.* Puerility. — **Puerility**, pū-ėr-il'i-ti, *n.* [L. *puerilitas*.] The state of being puerile; boyishness; that which is puerile; a childish or silly act, thought or expression; *civil law*, the period of life from the stage of infancy to puberty.

Puerperal, Puerperous, pū-ėr'pėr-al, pū-ėr'pėr-us, *a.* [L. *puerpera*, a lying-in-woman—*puer*, a boy, and *pario*, to bear.] Pertaining to childbirth.

Puff, puf, *n.* [From the sound; comp. G. *puff*, a puff, a thump; Dan. *puf*, W. *pwff*, a puff.] A sudden and single emission of breath from the mouth; a sudden and short blast of wind; a fungous ball filled with dust; a puff-ball; a substance of loose texture, used to sprinkle powder on the hair or skin; a swelling; a kind of pastry; a loose roll of hair.—*v.i.* To blow with single and quick blasts; to blow, as an expression of scorn or contempt; to breathe with vehemence, as after violent exertion; to be dilated or inflated; to assume importance.—*v.t.* To drive with a blast of wind or air; to inflate or dilate with air; to swell or inflate, as with pride or vanity: often with *up*; to praise with exaggeration.—**Puff-adder**, *n.* A South African snake, one of the most deadly in the world: so called from inflating the upper part of its body.—**Puff-ball**, *n.* A fungus in the form of a ball which bursts when ripe, and discharges its spores in the form of fine powder.—**Puff-bird**, *n.* A barbet: so called from puffing out the feathers.—**Puffer**, puf'ėr, *n.* One that puffs.—**Puffery**, puf'ėr-i, *n.* Act of puffing; extravagant praise.—**Puffin**, puf'in, *n.* [In allusion to its puffed-out beak.] The common name for a genus of marine diving birds of the auk family, characterized by a bill resembling that of a parrot.—**Puffiness**, puf'i-nes, *n.* State or quality of being puffy.—**Puffing**, puf'ing, *a.* Given to puff or praise in exaggerated terms.—**Puffingly**, puf'ing-li, *adv.*—**Puff-paste**, *n.* A rich dough for making the light friable covers of tarts, &c.—**Puffy**, puf'i, *a.* Swelled with air or any soft matter; tumid; turgid; bombastic (a *puffy* style).

Pug, pug, *n.* [A form of *Puck*, the fairy or hobgoblin (see PUCKISH); applied to a dog or monkey it means literally a goblin-like creature.] A monkey; a dwarf variety of dog; a pug-dog.—**Pug-dog**, *n.* A small dog which bears a miniature resemblance to the bull-dog.—**Pug-faced**, *a.* Having a monkey-like face.—**Pug-nose**, *n.* A snub-nose.—**Pug-nosed**, *n.* Snub-nosed.

Pugaree, pug'ar-ē, **Puggerie, Puggery**, pug'ėr-i, **Pugree**, pug'rē, *n.* [Hind. *pagri*, a turban.] A piece of muslin cloth wound round a hat or helmet to ward off the rays of the sun. (*Anglo-Indian*.)

Pugh, pö, *exclam.* A word used in contempt or disdain.

Pugilism, pū'jil-izm, *n.* [From L. *pugil*, a pugilist; same stem as *pugnus*, a fist, *pugna*, a fight. PUGNACIOUS.] The practice of boxing or fighting with the fists.—**Pugilist**, pū'jil-ist, *n.* A boxer.—**Pugilistic**, pū-jil-is'tik, *a.* Pertaining to boxing.

Pug-mill, pug, *n.* [Akin to Dan. *pukke*, to stamp or beat ore.] A machine for mixing and tempering clay for bricks or pottery. —**Pugging**, pug'ing, *n.* The process of mixing and working clay for bricks, &c.; a composition to prevent the transmission of sound through a floor or partition.

Pugnacious, pug-nā'shus, *a.* [L. *pugnax, pugnacis*, from *pugna*, a fight, from stem of *pugnus*, a fist; akin *impugn, oppugn, repugnant*, &c.] Disposed or inclined to fighting; quarrelsome.—**Pugnaciously**, pug-nā'shus-li, *adv.* In a pugnacious manner. — **Pugnaciousness, Pugnacity**, pug-nā'shus-nes, pug-nas'i-ti, *n.* Inclination to fight; quarrelsomeness.

Puisne, pū'nē, *a.* [O.Fr. *puisné*, from *puis*, L. *post*, after, and *né*, L. *natus*, born. (NATAL.) *Puny* is the same word.] *Law*, younger or inferior in rank; sometimes applied to certain judges.

Puissant, pū'is-ant or pū-is'ant, *a.* [Fr. *puissant*, powerful: formed as if from a participle *possens, possentis*, from L. *posse*, to be able. POTENT.] Powerful; strong; mighty; forcible. — **Puissantly**, pū'is-ant-li, *adv.* In a puissant manner; powerfully.—**Puissance**, pū'is-ans, *n.* Power; strength; might.

Puke, pūk, *v.i.*—*puked, puking.* [Akin G. *spucken*, to spit, E. *spew*.] To vomit; to retch; to be disgusted.—*v.t.* To vomit or eject from the stomach.

Pulchritude, pul'kri-tūd, *n.* [L. *pulchritudo*, from *pulcher*, beautiful.] Beauty; grace; comeliness.

Pule, pūl, *v.i.*—*puled, puling.* [Fr. *piauler*, to make the cry represented by the syllable *piau*, to pule; an imitative word; comp. Fr. *miauler*, to mewl, to mew.] To cry like a chicken; to cry as a complaining child; to whimper.—**Puler**, pū'lėr, *n.* One that pules.—**Puling**, pū'ling, *p.* and *a.* Crying like a chicken; whining; infantine; childish. —*n.* A cry as of a chicken; a whining.—**Pulingly**, pū'ling-li, *adv.* In a puling or whining manner.

Pulkha, pul'ka, *n.* A Laplander's travelling sledge.

Pull, pu̇l, *v.t.* [A.Sax. *pullian*, to pull; L.G. *pulen*, to pick, to pluck, to pull; connections doubtful.] To draw; to draw toward one or make an effort to draw; to tug; to haul: opposed to *push*; to pluck; to gather by the hand (to *pull* fruit); to tear, rend, draw apart: in this sense followed by some qualifying word or phrase (to *pull in pieces*, to *pull asunder* or *apart*); to impress by a printing-press; to move by drawing or pulling (to *pull* a bell, to *pull* a boat).—*To pull down*, to take down by pulling; to demolish (to *pull down* a house); to subvert. —*To pull off*, to separate by pulling; to pluck; also, to take off without force (to *pull off* a coat or hat).—*To pull on*, to draw on (to *pull on* boots). — *To pull out*, to draw out; to extract.—*To pull up*, to pluck up; to tear up by the roots; to apprehend or cause to be apprehended and taken before a court of justice (*colloq.*); to stop by means of the reins (to *pull up* a horse); hence, to stop in any course of conduct.—*To pull the long bow*, to exaggerate; to lie boastingly.—*To pull one through*, to help through a difficulty.—*v.i.* To give a pull; to tug; to exert strength in drawing.—*To pull through*, to get through any undertaking with difficulty.—*To pull up*, to draw the reins; to stop in riding or driving; to halt.—*n.* The act of pulling; an effort to move by drawing toward one; a pluck; a shake; a twitch; the act of rowing a boat. —**Pullback**, pu̇l'bak, *n.* That which keeps back or restrains; a drawback. —**Puller**, pu̇l'ėr, *n.* One who pulls.

Pullet, pu̇l'et, *n.* [Fr. *poulette*, dim. of *poule*, a hen, L.L. *pulla*, from L. *pullus*, a young animal. Of same origin are *poult, poultry*.] A young hen or chicken.

Pulley, pu̇l'i, *n.* pl. **Pulleys**, pu̇l'iz. [O.E. *poleyne*, a pulley, from Fr. *poulain*, a foal or colt, a slide for letting down casks into a cellar, a pulley rope, from L.L. *pullanus*, from L. *pullus*, the young of an animal. (PULLET.) The names of the horse, ass, goat, and other animals are given in different languages to various mechanical contrivances.] One of the simple machines or mechanical powers, used for raising weights, and consisting of a small wheel movable about an axle, and having a groove cut in its circumference over which a cord passes: used either singly or several in combination; a wheel placed upon a shaft and transmitting power to or from the different parts of machinery, or changing the direction of motion by means of a belt or band which runs over it.

Pullicate, pul'i-kat, *n.* [Probably of Indian origin.] A kind of coloured cotton handkerchief made originally in India.

Pullman car, pöl'man, *n.* The railway car adapted for sleeping in during journey, originally designed by G. M. *Pullman*.

Pulmobranchiate, Pulmonibranchiate, pul'mō-brang"ki-āt, pul'mon-i-brang"ki-āt, *n.* and *a.* [L. *pulmo*, a lung, and Gr. *branchia*, a gill.] One of or pertaining to an order of gasteropod molluscs in which the respiratory organ is adapted for aerial respiration, including the land-snails, &c.

Pulmonary, Pulmonic, pul'mon-a-ri, pul-mon'ik, *a.* [L. *pulmonarius*, from *pulmo, pulmonis*, a lung; akin to Gr. *pleumōn, pneumōn*, a lung.] Pertaining to the lungs; affecting the lungs. — **Pulmonary**, *n.* Lungwort.—**Pulmonate**, pul'mon-āt, *a.* Possessing lungs; having organs that act as lungs.—**Pulmonic**, *n.* A medicine for the lungs; a person affected with disease of the lungs. — **Pulmoniferous**, pul-mo-nif'ėr-us, *a.* Possessing lungs.

Pulp, pulp, *n.* [Fr. *pulpe*, from L. *pulpa*, fleshy substance, pulp.] Soft undissolved animal or vegetable matter; the soft, succulent part of fruit; material for making paper reduced to a soft uniform mass; the soft vascular substance in the interior of a tooth.—*v.t.* To make into pulp; to deprive of the pulp.—**Pulpiness**, pul'pi-nes, *n.* The state of being pulpy.—**Pulpous**, pul'-pus, *a.* Pulpy.—**Pulpousness**, pul'pus-nes, *n.*—**Pulpy**, pul'pi, *a.* Like pulp; soft; fleshy.

Pulpit, pu̇l'pit, *n.* [L. *pulpitum*, a scaffold, stage, desk.] An elevated place or inclosed stage in a church, in which the preacher stands; frequently used adjectively, and signifying belonging, pertaining, or suitable to the pulpit (*pulpit* eloquence, *pulpit* oratory).—*The pulpit*, preachers generally; the pulpit teaching in churches (the influence of *the pulpit*).—**Pulpiteer**, pul-pi-tēr′, *n.* A preacher, in contempt.—**Pulpitish**, pul-pit-ish, *a.* Smacking of the pulpit; like a pulpit performance.

Pulque, pul′kā, *n.* [Sp.] A vinous beverage obtained by fermenting the juice of various species of the agave or American aloe.

Pulsate, pul′sāt, *v.i.*—*pulsated, pulsating.* [L. *pulsare, pulsatum*, to beat, from *pellere, pulsum*, to drive (seen also in *expel, compel, impel, impulse, repel*, &c.).] To beat or throb.—**Pulsatile**, pul′sa-til, *a.* [L. *pulsatilis.*] Played on by beating; intended to be played on by beating; *med.* beating like the pulse; throbbing.—**Pulsation**, pul-sā′-shon, *n.* The beating or throbbing of the heart or of an artery; a beat of the pulse; a throb; a beat or stroke by which some medium is affected, as in the propagation of sound.—**Pulsative**, pul′sa-tiv, *a.*—Beating; throbbing.—**Pulsator**, pul′sā-tėr, *n.* A beater; a striker.—**Pulsatory**, pul′sa-to-ri, *a.* Capable of pulsating or beating; throbbing, as the heart and arteries.—

Pulse, puls, *n.* [Fr. *pouls*, L. *pulsus*, a beating, from *pello, pulsum.*] The beating or throbbing of the heart or blood-vessels, especially of the arteries; the pulsation of the radial artery at the wrist; pulsation; vibration.—*To feel one's pulse* (*fig.*), to sound one's opinion; to try or to know one's mind.—*v.i.*—*pulsed, pulsing.* To beat, as the arteries or heart.—**Pulseless**, puls′-les, *a.* Having no pulsation.—**Pulselessness**, puls′les-nes, *n.*—**Pulsific**,† pul-sif′-ik, *a.* [L. *pulsus*, and *facio*, to make.] Exciting the pulse; causing pulsation.—**Pulsimeter**, pul-sim′et-ėr, *n.* [L. *pulsus*, and Gr. *metron*, a measure.] An instrument for measuring the strength or quickness of the pulse.—**Pulsometer**, pul-som′et-ėr, *n.* A sort of pump which acts by the condensation of steam sent into a reservoir, the water rushing up into the vacuum formed by the condensation.

Pulse, puls, *n.* [From L. *puls*, pottage made of meal, pulse, &c.] Leguminous plants or their seeds; the plants whose pericarp is a legume, as beans, peas, &c.

Pulu, pū′lu, *n.* The silky fibres of tree-fern from the Sandwich Islands, used for stuffing mattresses, as a styptic, &c.

Pulverize, pul′vėr-īz, *v.t.*—*pulverized, pulverizing.* [Fr. *pulveriser*, from L. *pulvis, pulveris*, powder (whence *powder*).] To reduce to fine powder, as by beating, grinding, &c.—*v.i.* To become reduced to fine powder; to fall to dust.—**Pulverizable**, pul-vėr-ī′za-bl, *a.* Capable of being pulverized.—**Pulverizer**, pul′vėr-ī-zėr, *n.* One who or that which pulverizes.—**Pulverization**, pul′vėr-ī-zā″shon, *n.* The act of pulverizing.—**Pulveraceous**, pul-vėr-ā′-shus, *a. Bot.* having a powdery surface.—**Pulverate**,† pul′vėr-āt, *v.t.* To pulverize.—**Pulverous**, pul′vėr-us, *a.* Consisting of dust or powder.—**Pulverulence**, pul-vėr′ū-lens, *n.* Dustiness; abundance of dust or powder.—**Pulverulent**, pul-ver′-ū-lent, *a.* Dusty; consisting of fine powder; powdery.

Pulvilli, pul-vil′ī, *n.pl.* [L., little cushions, from *pulvinus*, a cushion.] A name for cushion-like masses on the feet of certain insects.—**Pulvinate, Pulviniform**, pul′vi-nāt, pul-vin′i-form, *a. Bot.* cushion-shaped.—**Pulvinated**, pul′vi-nā-ted, *a. Arch.* a term used to express a swelling in any portion of an order.—**Pulvinus**, pul′-vin-us, *n.* The thickened base of a leaf-stalk.

Puma, pū′ma, *n.* [Peruv.] The cougar or mountain lion. COUGAR.

Pumice, pu′mis, *n.* [L. *pumex, pumicis*, originally *spumex*, from *spuma*, foam, from *spuo*, to spit. *Pounce* (powder) is the same word.] A sort of porous stony substance frequently ejected from volcanoes, lighter than water, used for polishing ivory, wood, marble, metals, glass, &c.—**Pumiceous**, pu-mish′us, *a.* Pertaining to pumice; consisting of or resembling it.—**Pumice-stone**, *n.* PUMICE.—**Pumiciform**, pu-mis′i-form, *a.* Resembling or having the character of pumice.

Pummace, pum′ās, *n.* POMACE.

Pummel, pum′el. POMMEL.

Pump, pump, *n.* [Fr. *pompe*, a pump, from D. and L.G. *pomp*, G. *pumpe*, a pump; origin unknown.] An instrument or machine, consisting of a peculiar arrangement of a piston, cylinder, and valves, employed for raising water or other liquid to a higher level, or for exhausting or compressing air or other gases. AIR-PUMP.—*v.i.* To work a pump; to raise water with a pump.—*v.t.* To raise with a pump; to free from water or other fluid by a pump (to *pump* a ship); to put artful questions to for the purpose of extracting information (*colloq.*).—**Pump-barrel**, *n.* The cylinder which forms the body of a pump.—**Pump-box**, *n.* The piston of the common pump.—**Pump-chain**, *n.* The chain of the chain-pump.—**Pumper**, pump′ėr, *n.* One who pumps.—**Pump-handle**, *n.* The handle for moving the piston up and down.—**Pumping-engine**, *n.* A pump worked by steam, water, or wind.—**Pump-room**, *n.* A room connected with a mineral spring, in which the waters are drunk.—**Pump-stock**, *n.* The solid body of a pump.—**Pump-well**, *n.* A compartment round a ship's pumps.

Pump, pump, *n.* [Probably from being worn for *pomp* or ornament by persons in full dress.] A low, unfastened shoe holding to the foot only at toe and heel.

Pumpernickel, pum′pėr-nik-el, *n.* [G.] A species of coarse bread made from unbolted rye.

Pumpion, pum′pi-on, *n.* [PUMPKIN.] A pumpkin.

Pumpkin, pump′kin, *n.* [From Fr. *pompon*, from L. *pepo, peponis*, a pumpkin. from Gr. *pepōn*, a melon, lit. one thoroughly ripened, from root of *peptō* (akin to L. *coquo*), to cook. COOK.] A climbing plant and its fruit (which is large, and is eaten when cooked), originally from India.

Pun, pun, *n.* [From A.Sax. *punian*, to pound, to beat, the meaning of to *pun*, being lit. to *pound* words. to beat them into new senses. POUND, *v.t.*] A play on words that agree or resemble in sound but differ in meaning; an expression in which two different applications of a word present an odd or ludicrous idea.—*v.i.*—*punned, punning.* To play on words so as to make puns.—**Punning**, pun′ing, *p.* and *a.* Given to making puns.—**Punningly**, pun′ing-li, *adv.* In a punning manner.—**Punster**, pun′stėr, *n.* One skilled in or given to punning.

Punch, punsh, *n.* [Shortened from old *punchon*, a dagger, from O.Fr. *poinson*, a bodkin, from L. *punctio*, a puncturing. from *pungo, punctum*, to prick (whence *point, puncture, pungent*, &c.).] A tool employed for making apertures, as in plates of metal, in impressing dies, &c., usually made of steel, and operated by hammering: a blow, as with the fist, elbow, or knee.—*v.t.* To perforate with a punch; to give a blow or stunning knock to.—**Puncher**, punsh′ėr, *n.* One who or that which punches.

Punch, punsh, *n.* [Connected with *paunch* or with *bunch.*] A short-legged, barrel-bodied horse, an English draught-breed (a Suffolk *punch*); a short fat fellow.—**Punchy**, punsh′i, *a.* Short and fat.

Punch, punsh, *n.* [Contr. from *punchinello* (which see).] The chief character in a popular comic exhibition of puppets, who beats to death Judy his wife, belabours a police-officer, &c.

Punch, punsh, *n.* [From Hind. *panch*, Skr. *panchan*, five.] A beverage introduced from India, and so called from its being composed of the five ingredients, arrack, tea, sugar, water, and lemon-juice; in this country, a beverage made from spirits and water, and sweetened and flavoured with sugar and lemon-juice.—**Punch-bowl**, *n.* A bowl in which punch is made, or from which it is served to be drunk.

Puncheon, Punchion, punsh′on, *n.* [Fr. *poinçon*, a bodkin, a punch (see PUNCH, the tool); also O.Fr. *poinson*, Fr. *poinçon*, a wine-vessel—perhaps one stamped with a punch as of a certain capacity.] A perforating or stamping tool; a punch; *carp.* a short upright piece of timber in framing; a measure of liquids, or a cask containing from 84 to 120 gallons.

Punchinello, punsh-i-nel′lo, *n.* [Corrupted from It. *pulcinello*, from L. *pullus*, a chicken = my chicken.] A punch; a buffoon.

Punctate, Punctated, pungk′tāt, pungk′tā-ted, *a.* [From L. *punctum*, a point. POINT.] Ending in a point; pointed; *bot.* having dots scattered over the surface.

Punctilio, pungk-til′i-o, *n.* [From Sp. *puntillo* or It. *puntiglio*, a small point, a punctilio, from L. *punctum*, a point. POINT.] A nice point in conduct, ceremony, or proceeding; particularity or exactness in forms.—**Punctilious**, pungk-til′i-us, *a.* Attentive to punctilios; very nice or exact in the forms of behaviour; sometimes, exact to excess.—**Punctiliously**, pungk-til′i-us-li, *adv.* In a punctilious manner.—**Punctiliousness**, pungk-til′i-us-nes, *n.*

Punctual, pungk′tū-al, *n.* [Fr. *ponctuel*, from L. *punctum*, a point, from *pungo, punctum*, to prick. POINT, PUNCTURE, &c.] Observant of nice points‡; exact‡; exact in keeping an appointment; exact to the time agreed on; made at the exact time (*punctual* payment).—**Punctuality**, pungk-tū-al′i-ti, *n.* The state or quality of being punctual; adherence to the exact time of attendance or appointment.—**Punctually**, pungk′tū-al-li, *adv.* In a punctual manner; with scrupulous regard to time, appointments, promises, &c.—**Punctualness**, pungk′tū-al-nes, *n.* Punctuality.

Punctuate, pungk′tū-āt, *v.t.*—*punctuated, punctuating.* [Fr. *ponctuer*, from L. *punctum*, a point. PUNCTUAL, PUNCTURE.] To mark with the points or stops necessary in written or printed compositions; to separate into sentences, clauses, or other divisions by points.—**Punctuation**, pungk-tū-ā′shon, *n.* The act or art of punctuating or pointing a writing or discourse.—**Punctuator**, pungk′tū-ā-tėr, *n.* One who punctuates; a punctuist.—**Punctuist**, pungk′-tū-ist, *n.* One who understands the art of punctuation.

Puncture, pungk′tūr, *n.* [L. *punctura*, from *pungo, punctum*, to prick (whence *pungent, point*, and a *punch*).] The act of perforating with a pointed instrument, or a small hole thus made; a small wound, as by a needle. prickle, or sting.—*v.t.*—*punctured, puncturing.* To make a puncture in; to prick.

Pundit, pun′dit, *n.* [Skr. *pandita*, a learned man.] A learned Brahmin; one versed in the Sanskrit language, and in the science, laws, and religion of India; sometimes used ironically or contemptuously.

Pungent, pun′jent, *a.* [L. *pungens*, ppr. of *pungo, punctum*, to prick. whence also *point, puncture, compunction, expunge*, &c.] Affecting the tongue like small sharp points; biting; acrid; sharply affecting the sense of smell; affecting the mind similarly; caustic; racy; biting.—**Pungently**, pun′jent-li, *adv.* In a pungent manner; sharply.—**Pungency, Pungence**, pun′jen-si, pun′jens, *n.* The state or quality of being pungent; tartness; causticity.

Punic, pū′nik, *a.* [L. *punicus*, Carthaginian, from *Puni, Pœni*, the Carthaginians.] Pertaining to the Carthaginians; faithless; deceitful.—*n.* The language of the Carthaginians; Phœnician.

Punish, pun′ish, *v.t.* [Fr. *punir, punissant*, from L. *punire*, to punish, from *pœna*, punishment, penalty. PAIN.] To inflict a penalty on; to visit judicially with a penalty; to castigate; to chastise; to visit with pain or suffering inflicted on the offender (to *punish* murder or theft); to inflict pain on in a loose sense (*colloq.*).—**Punishable**, pun′ish-a-bl, *a.* Deserving punishment; liable to punishment; capable of being punished.—**Punishableness**, pun′ish-a-bl-nes, *n.*—**Punisher**, pun′ish-ėr, *n.* One that punishes.—**Punishment**, pun'ish-ment, *n.* The act of punishing; pain or penalty inflicted on a person for a crime or offence; a penalty imposed in the enforcement of law.—**Punitive**, pū'ni-tiv, *a.* Pertaining to or involving punishment; awarding or inflicting punishment.—**Punitory**, pū'ni-to-ri, *a.* Punishing or tending to punishment.

Punk, pungk, *n.* [Contr. from *spunk.*] Tinder made from a fungus; touchwood; spunk.

Punka, Punkah, pung'ka, *n.* A large fan slung from the ceilings of rooms in India to produce an artificial current of air.

Punster. Under PUN.

Punt, punt, *v.t.* [Fr. *punter*, It. *puntare*, from L. *punctum*, a point. PUNGENT.] *Football*, to drop and kick the ball before it touches the ground; to gamble for big stakes.—**Punter**, punt'ėr, *n.* One who punts; one who plays in games of chance against the banker or dealer.

a punt, a pontoon, from *pons, pontis*, a bridge. PONTOON.] A square flat-bottomed vessel without masts, used as a lighter for conveying goods, &c.; a small flat-bottomed boat used in fishing and wild-fowl shooting, &c.—*v.t.* To propel by pushing with a pole against the bed of the water; to convey in a punt.—**Punter**, punt'ėr, *n.* One who punts a boat; one who uses a punt.

Puny, pū'ni, *a.* [From Fr. *puisné*. PUISNE.] Puisne; imperfectly developed in size and vigour; small and weak; petty; insignificant.—**Puniness**, pū'ni-nes, *n.* The state or quality of being puny.

Pup, pup, *n.* [Abbrev. of *puppy.*] A puppy; a young seal.—*v.i.*—*pupped, pupping.* To bring forth whelps.

Pupa, pū'pa, *n.* pl. **Pupæ**, pū'pē. [L. *pupa*, a girl, a doll, fem. of *pupus*, a boy.] The chrysalis form of an insect.—**Pupal, Puparial**, pū'pal, pū-pā'ri-al, *a.* Pertaining to a pupa.

Pupil, pū'pil, *n.* [Fr. *pupille*, L. *pupilla*, a little girl, the apple of the eye, dim. of *pupa*, a girl; also *pupillus*, an orphan boy, dim. of *pupus*, a boy. PUPPET.] The round aperture in the middle of the iris through which the rays of light pass to reach the retina; a young person of either sex under the care of an instructor or tutor; a disciple; a ward; a young person under the care of a guardian.—**Pupilage**, pū'pil-āj, *n.* The state of being a pupil; the state or period of being a ward under the care of a guardian.—**Pupillary**, pū'pi-lėr-i, *a.* [L. *pupillaris.*] Pertaining to a pupil or ward; pertaining to the pupil of the eye.—**Pupil-teacher**, *n.* In Great Britain, one in apprenticeship as a teacher; a student-teacher.

Pupiparous, pū-pi'pa-rus, *a.* [L. *pupa*, and *pario*, to produce.] Producing pupæ from the eggs before they are excluded; said of certain insects.

Pupivorous, pū-piv'o-rus, *a.* [L. *pupa*, and *voro*,] Eating or living on the pupæ of other insects.

Puppet, pup'et, *n.* [O.E. *popet*, O.Fr. *poupette*, dim. from L. *pupa*, a doll, a puppet. PUPA, PUPIL.] A small figure in the human form, moved by cords or wires, in a mock drama; a marionette; one actuated by the will of another; a person who is a mere tool.—**Puppet-show**, *n.* A mock drama performed by puppets.

Puppy, pup'i, *n.* [Fr. *poupée*, a doll, a puppet, L. *pupa*. PUPA, PUPPET.] A whelp; a young dog not grown up; a conceited and insignificant fellow; a silly fop or coxcomb.—**Puppyism**, pup'i-izm, *n.* Empty conceit or affectation; silly foppery or coxcombry.

Purana, pū-rä'na, *n.* [Lit. *ancient*, from Skr. *purā*, before, past.] One of a class of sacred poetical writings in Sanskrit, which treat chiefly of the creation, the gods, heroes, &c.—**Puranic**, pū-ran'ik, *a.* Pertaining to the Purânas.

Purbeck, pėr'bek, *a.* Belonging to the peninsula of Purbeck in Dorsetshire.—*Purbeck beds, geol.* the uppermost members of the oolite proper, typically displayed at Purbeck.—*Purbeck marble*, an impure fresh-water limestone obtained from the Purbeck beds.

Purblind, pėr'blīnd, *a.* [From *pure* in sense of altogether, quite, and *blind.*] Near-sighted or dim-sighted; seeing obscurely.—**Purblindly**, pėr'blīnd-li, *adv.* In a purblind manner.—**Purblindness**, pėr'blīnd-nes, *n.* The state of being purblind; dimness of vision.

Purchase, pėr'chās, *v.t.*—*purchase, purchasing.* [Fr. *pourchasser*, O.Fr. *purchacer*, to pursue, to get—*pour, pur*, for, and *chasser*, to chase. CHASE.] To gain or acquire‡; to obtain by payment of money or its equivalent; to buy; to obtain by labour, danger, or other means.—*n.* Acquisition in general‡; the acquisition of anything by rendering an equivalent in money; buying; that which is purchased; any mechanical advantage (as is gained by a lever) used in the raising or removing of heavy bodies.—*To be worth so many years' purchase*, said of property that would bring in, in the specified time, an amount equal to the sum paid.—**Purchasable**, pėr'chās-a-bl, *a.* Capable of being purchased.—**Purchase-money**, *n.* The money paid or contracted to be paid for anything bought.—**Purchaser**, pėr'chās-ėr, *n.* One who purchases; a buyer.

Pure, pūr, *a.* [Fr. *pur*, from L. *purus*, pure (whence *purgo*, E. to *purge*); from root seen also in Skr. *pū*, to purify; and in *fire.*] Free from all heterogeneous or extraneous matter, especially from anything that impairs or pollutes; free from that which defiles or contaminates; innocent; spotless; chaste; stainless; genuine; ceremonially clean; unpolluted; mere; sheer; absolute (*pure* shame, hatred).—*Pure mathematics.* MATHEMATICS.—**Purely**, pūr'li, *adv.* In a pure manner; innocently; stainlessly; chastely; merely; absolutely.—**Pureness**, pūr'nes, *n.* The state or quality of being pure; purity.—**Purify**, pū'ri-fī, *v.t.*—*purified, purifying.* [Fr. *purifier*, from L. *purificare*—*purus*, and *facio*, to make.] To make pure or clear; to free from extraneous admixture; to free from pollution ceremonially; to cleanse from whatever renders unclean and unfit for sacred services; to free from guilt or the defilement of sin.—*v.i.* To grow or become pure or clear.—**Purification**, pū'ri-fi-kā"shon, *n.* [L. *purificatio.*] The act of purifying or making pure; the act of cleansing ceremonially by removing any pollution or defilement; lustration; a cleansing from guilt or the pollution of sin.—**Purificative, Purificatory**, pū-rif'i-kā-tiv, pū-rif'i-ka-to-ri, *a.* Having power to purify; tending to cleanse.—**Purifier**, pū'ri-fī-ėr, *n.* One who or that which purifies.—**Purist**, pū'rist, *n.* [Fr. *puriste*, from *pur*, pure.] One who scrupulously aims at purity, particularly in the choice of language; one who is a rigorous critic of purity in literary style.—**Puristic, Puristical**, pū-ris'tik, pū-ris'ti-kal, *a.* Pertaining or relating to purism.—**Purism**, pū'rizm, *n.* Affectation of rigid purity; excessive nicety as to the choice of words.—**Purity**, pū'ri-ti, *n.* [L. *puritas.*] The condition of being pure; freedom from foreign matter; cleanness; innocence; chastity; freedom from anything sinister or underhand; freedom from improper words or phrases.

Puree, pū'rā, *n.* [Fr. *purée*, from L. *porrum*, a leek.] Meat, fish, or vegetables boiled into a pulp and passed through a sieve.

Purfle, pėr'fl, *v.t.*—*purfled, purfling.* [O.Fr. *pourfiler*—*pour*, L. *pro*, for, before, and *fil*, L. *filum*, a thread. PROFILE.] To decorate with a wrought or flowered border; to border; to broider; to decorate richly.

Purge, pėrj, *v.t.*—*purged, purging.* [L. *purgare*, to cleanse, from *purus*, clean, and *agere*, to do. PURE.] To cleanse or purify by carrying off whatever is impure, foreign, or superfluous; to clear from moral defilement; to clear from accusation or the charge of a crime; to remove from a position of influence, in a political party or nation, persons considered harmful or disloyal; to evacuate the bowels; to operate on by means of a cathartic.—*v.i.* To produce evacuations by a cathartic.—*n.* The act of purging; anything that purges; a cathartic medicine; the act of removing from a position of influence, in a political party or nation, persons considered harmful or disloyal.—**Purgation**, pėr-gā'shon, *n.* [L. *purgatio.*] The act of purging; the act of carrying away impurities; purification; the act of cleansing from the imputation of guilt.—**Purgative**, pėr'ga-tiv, *a.* [Fr. *purgatif.*] Having the power of cleansing; having the power of evacuating the intestines; cathartic.—*n.* A medicine that evacuates the intestines; a cathartic.—**Purgatory**, pėr'ga-to-ri, *a.* [L. *purgatorius.*] Tending to cleanse; cleansing; expiatory.—*n.* According to R. Catholics and others, a place in which souls after death are purified from venial sins, and suffer punishment for mortal sins not atoned for; colloquially, any place or state of irritating temporary suffering.—**Purging**, pėr'jing, *n.* The process of cleansing; looseness of the bowels; diarrhea or dysentery.

Purify. Under PURE.

Purim, pu'rim, *n.* [Heb. *purim*, lots.] An annual festival among the Jews instituted to commemorate their preservation from the massacre with which they were threatened by the machinations of Haman.

Purine, pūr'in, *n.* [Gr. *pyr*, burning.] A nitrogenous excretory substance.

Purist. Under PURE.

Puritan, pū'ri-tan, *n.* [From L. *puritas*, purity.] The name by which the dissenters from the Church of England were generally known in the reign of Elizabeth and the first two Stuarts; given (probably in derision) on account of the superior purity of doctrine or discipline which they claimed as their own.—*a.* Pertaining to the Puritans.—**Puritanic, Puritanical**, pū-ri-tan'ik, pū-ri-tan'i-kal, *a.* Pertaining to the Puritans or their doctrines and practice; precise in religious matters; exact; rigid.—**Puritanically**, pū-ri-tan'i-kal-li, *adv.* In a puritanical manner.—**Puritanism**, pū'ri-tan-izm, *n.* The doctrines or practices of Puritans.

Purity. Under PURE.

Purl, pėrl, *n.* [Contracted form of *purfle.*] An embroidered border; an inversion of the stitches in knitting, giving a distinctive appearance.

Purl, pėrl, *v.i.* [Akin to Sw. *porla*, to purl; probably from the sound; comp. *purr.*] To murmur, as a shallow stream flowing among stones; to flow with a gentle murmur; to ripple.—*n.* A ripple; a murmuring sound, as of a shallow stream among stones; malt liquor flavoured with wormwood or aromatic herbs; now a name for beer flavoured with gin, sugar, and ginger.

Purlieu, pėr'lū, *n.* [From Norm. *purlieu*, *puraille*, O.Fr. *puralée*, perambulation, from *pur*, L. *per*, through, *alée*, a going. (ALLEY.) Both form and sense have been influenced by Fr. *lieu*, place.] A piece of land set apart from an ancient royal forest by perambulation of its boundaries; a part lying adjacent; the outer portion of any area; the environs.

Purloin, pėr'loin, *v.t.* [O.Fr. *porloignier*, *purloignier*, from L. *prolongare*, to prolong. PROLONG.] To steal; to filch; to take by plagiarism.—*v.i.* To practise theft.—**Purloiner**, pėr-loi'nėr, *n.* One who purloins; a thief; a plagiary.

Purple, pėr'pl, *a.* [Old form *purpre*, from L. *purpura*, purple, from Gr. *porphyra*, a kind of shell-fish that yielded a purple dye. Akin *porphyry.*] Of a colour composed of red and blue blended; imperial; regal—a sense derived from purple robes being formerly distinctive of great personages; bloody; dyed with blood.—*n.* A colour compounded by the union of blue and red; a purple robe or dress; hence, from a purple robe having been the distinguishing dress of emperors, &c., used typically of imperial or regal power.—*The purple*, the imperial dignity; also the dignity of a cardinal.—*Purple of Cassius*, a pigment used in painting on glass and porcelain. —*v.t.* —*purpled*, *purpling*. To dye or colour purple; to clothe with purple. —**Purple-fish**, *n.* A kind of mollusc that yields a purple dye.—**Purples**, pėr'-plz, *n.pl.* *Med.* spots of a livid red on the body, which appear in certain malignant diseases; a disease affecting the ears of wheat. EAR-COCKLE.—**Purple-heart**, **Purple-wood**, *n.* A handsome wood of a rich plum colour imported from Brazil.—**Purplish**, pėr'plish, *a.* Somewhat purple.

Purport, pėr'pōrt, *n.* [O.Fr. *purport*, from *pur*, Fr. *pour*, for, and *porter*, to bear. PORT (demeanour).] Meaning; tenor; import.—*v.t.* To convey, as a certain meaning; to import; to signify.—*v.i.* To have a certain purport or tenor.

Purpose, pėr'pos, *n.* [O.Fr. *pourpos*, Fr. *propos*, from L. *propositum*, from *propono*—*pro*, before, and *ponere*, *positum*, to place. POSITION.] That which a person sets before himself as an object to be reached or accomplished; end or aim; that which a person intends to do; design; plan; intention.—*Of purpose*, *on purpose*, with previous design; designedly; intentionally.—*To the purpose*, to the matter in question (to speak *to the purpose*).—*v.t.*—*purposed*, *purposing*. To intend; to resolve; to mean; to wish.—*v.i.* To have intention or design; to intend.—**Purposeless**, pėr'pos-les, *a.* Having no object or purpose.—**Purposely**, pėr'pos-li, *adv.* By purpose or design; intentionally. —**Purposer**, pėr'pos-ėr, *n.* One who purposes or intends.

Purpresture, pėr-pres'tūr, *n.* [From Fr. *pour*, for, and *prendre*, *pris*, to take, L. *prehendere*.] *Law*. an encroachment on something that belongs to another man, or to the public. Written also *Pourpresture*.

Purpura, pėr'pū-ra, *n.* [PURPLE.] A disease characterized by purple spots on the skin; the purples.—**Purpureal**, pėr-pū'rē-al, *a.* Purple.—**Purpurin**, pėr'pū-rin, *n.* A red colouring matter extracted from madder.

Purr, pėr, *v.i.* [Imitative of sound.] To utter a soft murmuring sound, as a cat when pleased.—*v.t.* To signify by purring. —*n.* The sound uttered by a cat when pleased.

Purr, **Purre**, pėr, *n.* DUNLIN.

Purse, pėrs, *n.* [From Fr. *bourse*, L.L. *bursa*, *byrsa*, a purse, from Gr. *byrsa*, a skin, a hide.] A small bag or case in which money is contained or carried in the pocket; a sum of money collected as a present; a specific sum of money, namely, in Turkey 500 piasters, or about $22.00; *fig.* a treasury; finances.—To have a *long* or *heavy purse*, to have plenty of money; to have a *short* or *light* one, to have little.—*v.t.*—*pursed*, *pursing*. To put in a purse; to contract into folds or wrinkles; to pucker.—**Purse-bearer**, *n.* One who carries a purse; a treasurer.—**Purseful**, pėrs'ful, *n.* As much as a purse will hold.—**Purse-net**, *n.* A net, the mouth of which may be drawn together like a purse.—**Purse-proud**, *a.* Proud of wealth; puffed up with the possession of riches.—**Purser**, pėr'sėr, *n.* A naval officer who keeps the accounts of the ship, has charge of the provisions, clothing, pay, &c.; also called a *paymaster*; the ticket officer on a steamer.

Pursiness, pėr'si-nes, *n.* PURSY.

Purslane, **Purslain**, pėrs'lān, *n.* [O.Fr. *porcelaine*, It. *porcellana*, from L. *porcilaca*, purslane.] An annual plant with fleshy succulent leaves, used in salads, as a pot-herb, in pickles, &c.

Pursue, pėr-sū', *v.t.*—*pursued*, *pursuing*. [O.Fr. *poursuir*, *porsuir* (Fr. *poursuivre*) —*pour*=L. *pro*, forward, and *suir*, *suivre*, to follow, L. *sequor*. SEQUENCE.] To follow with a view to overtake; to chase; to attend on (misfortune *pursues* him); to seek; to use measures to obtain; to prosecute, continue, or proceed in; to carry on; to follow up; to proceed along, with a view to some end or object; to follow (to *pursue* a course).—*v.i.* To go in pursuit; to proceed; *law*, to act as a prosecutor.—**Pursuer**, pėr-sū'ėr, *n.* One who pursues; *Scots law*, the party who institutes an ordinary action; the plaintiff.—**Pursuit**, pėr-sūt', *n.* [Fr. *poursuite*.] The act of pursuing or following with a view to overtake; a following with a view to reach or obtain; endeavour to attain; course of business or occupation; employment (mercantile *pursuits*).—**Pursuable**, pėr-sū'a-bl, *a.* Capable of being pursued.—**Pursuance**, pėr-sū'ans, *n.* A pursuing or carrying out (of a design); prosecution.—*In pursuance of*, in fulfilment or execution of; in carrying out.—**Pursuant**, pėr-sū'ant, *a.* [O.Fr. *porsuiant*, *poursuiant*.] Done in consequence of anything; agreeable; conformable: with *to*. —*adv.* Conformably: with *to*.—**Pursuantly**, pėr-sū'ant-li, *adv.* Pursuant; agreeably; conformably.

Pursuivant, pėr'swi-vant, *n.* [Fr. *poursuivant*, from *poursuivre*. PURSUE.] A state messenger; an attendant on heralds; one of the third and lowest order of heraldic officers, of whom there are four in England, named *Rouge Croix*, *Blue Mantle*, *Rouge Dragon*, and *Portcullis*.

Pursy, pėr'si, *a.* [O.Fr. *pourcif*, also *poulsif*, from *pourcer*, *pouiser* (Mod.Fr. *pousser*), to push, also to breathe or pant, from L. *pulsare*, to beat. PULSE, PUSH.] Short-winded; fat and short-winded; rank; wanton; self-indulgent. '*Pursy* times' (*Hamlet*).—**Pursiness**, pėr'si-nes, *n* A state of being pursy; shortness of breath.

Purtenance, pėr'te-nans, *n.* [Shortened from *appurtenance*.] Appurtenance; that which pertains or belongs to anything.

Purulent, pū'rụ-lent, *a.* [L. *purulentus*, from *pus*, *puris*, matter. Same root as in *putrid*.] Consisting of pus or matter; full of or resembling pus.—**Purulently**, pū'-rụ-lent-li, *adv.* In a purulent manner.—**Purulence**, **Purulency**, pū'rụ'lens, pū'rụ-len-si, *n.* The state of being purulent; pus.

Purvey, pėr-vā', *v.t.* [Fr. *pourvoir*, O.Fr. *proveoir*, *porveoir*, from L. *provideo*, to foresee, to provide. PROVIDE.] To provide, especially to provide provisions or other necessaries for a number of persons.—*v.i.* To purchase provisions, especially for a number.—**Purveyance**, pėr-vā'ans, *n.* Act of purveying; in England, the former royal prerogative of pre-emption of provisions and necessaries for the royal household.—**Purveyor**, pėr-vā'ėr, *n.* One who supplies eatables for a number of persons; in England, an officer who formerly exacted provision for the king's household.

Purview, pėr'vū, *n.* [O.Fr. *pourveu*, *purvieu*, Fr. *pourvu*, provided, from *pourvoir*, to provide. PURVEY.] *Law*, the body of a statute as distinguished from the *preamble*; the limit or scope of a statute; limit of sphere of authority; scope.

Pus, pus, *n.* [L. *pus*, *puris*, matter, from same root as in *putrid*, *putrefy*.] The white or yellowish matter found in abscesses; matter produced in a festering sore.

Puseyism, pū'zi-izm, *n.* The name given collectively to certain doctrines promulgated by Dr. *Pusey*, in conjunction with other divines of Oxford, in a series of pamphlets entitled 'Tracts for the Times'; tractarianism.—**Puseyite**, pū'zi-īt, *n.* An adherent of Puseyism; a Tractarian.

Push, pụsh, *v.t.* [O.E. *pusse*, from Fr. *pousser*, O.Fr. *poulser*, from L. *pulsare*, to beat, a freq. from *pello*, *pulsum*, to drive, whence *expel*, and other verbs in *-pel*. PULSATE.] To press against with force; to impel by pressure; to drive by steady pressure, without striking; opposed to *draw*; to press or urge forward; to advance by exertions (to *push* one's fortune); to enforce, as in argument; to press or ply hard (as an opponent in argument); to urge; to importune; to prosecute energetically (to *push* a trade).—*v.i.* To make a thrust; to make an effort; to press one's self onward; to force one's way.—*To push on*, to drive or urge one's course forward; to hasten.—*n.* The act of pushing; a short pressure or force applied; a thrust; a vigorous effort; an emergency; an extremity (to come to the *push*); persevering energy; enterprise. —**Pusher**, pụsh'ėr, *n.* One who pushes. —**Pushing**, pụsh'ing, *a.* Pressing forward in business; enterprising; energetic.—**Pushingly**, pụsh'ing-li, *adv.* In a pushing, energetic manner.

Pushtu, **Pushtoo**, push'tö, *n.* The language of the Afghans.

Pusillanimous, pū-sil-lan'i-mus, *a.* [L. *pusillanimis*, from *pusillus*, very little, from *pusus*, little (same root as in *puerile*), and *animus*, the mind. PUERILE, ANIMATE.] Destitute of strength and firmness of mind; being of weak courage; faint-hearted; cowardly. —**Pusillanimity**, pū'sil-la-nim"i-ti, *n.* Weakness of spirit; cowardliness; timidity.—**Pusillanimously**, pū-sil-lan'i-mus-li, *adv.* In a pusillanimous manner.—**Pusillanimousness**, pū-sil-lan'i-mus-nes, *n.* Pusillanimity.

Puss, pụs, *n.* [Same as D. *poes*, L.G. *puus*, Gael. and Ir. *pus*, a cat; perhaps imitative of the spitting of a cat. The hare is so called from resembling a cat.] A name for the cat and also for the hare; a sort of pet name sometimes applied to a child or young woman.—**Pussy**, pụs'i, *n.* Diminutive of *Puss*.

Pustule, pus'tūl, *n.* [Fr. *pustule*, L. *pustula*, a form of *pusula*, a blister or pimple.] *Med.* an elevation of the cuticle, with an inflamed base, containing pus; *bot.* a pimple or little blister.—**Pustular**, **Pustulous**, pus'tū-lėr, pus'tū-lus, *a.* Having the character of or proceeding from a pustule or pustules.—**Pustulate**, pus'tū-lāt, *v.t.*—*pustulated*, *pustulating*. To form into pustules or blisters.—*a.* *Bot.* covered with glandular excrescences like pustules.

Put, pụt, *v.t.*—pret. and pp. *put*, ppr. *putting*. [O.E. *putte*, A.Sax. *potian*, to thrust, to gore; Dan. *putte*, to put or set.] To place, set, or lay in any position or situation; to place in any state or condition (to *put* to shame, to death); to apply (to *put* one's hand, one's mind to a thing); to set before one for consideration; to propose (to *put* a case, a question).—*To put about*, to change the course of (a ship); to put to inconvenience.—*To put an end to*, to stop; to bring to a conclusion.—*To put away*, to renounce or discard; to divorce.—*To put back*, to hinder; to delay; to restore to the original place.—*To put by*, to turn away; to thrust aside; to place in safe-keeping.—*To put down*, to repress; to crush; to confute; to silence; to write down; to subscribe.—*To put forth*, to propose; to offer to notice; to stretch out; to shoot out, as leaves; to exert; to bring into action; to make known, as opinions; to publish, as in a book.—*To put in*, to introduce among others; to insert.—*To put in mind*, to remind.—*To put in practice*, to apply; to make use of.—*To put off*, to take from one's person; to lay aside; to turn aside from a purpose or demand; to delay; to postpone; to push from land.—*To put on*, to invest with as clothes or covering; to impute; to charge with (to *put* blame *on*); to assume (to *put on* a grave face); to impose; to inflict; to turn or let on; to set to work.—*To put out*, to eject; to drive out; to place (money) at interest; to extinguish; to shoot forth (to *put out* leaves); to extend; to reach out; to publish; to make public; to confuse; to disconcert; to dislocate.—*To put over*, to place in authority over; to defer; to postpone.—*To put to*, to add; to unite; to expose; to kill by; to punish by (to *put to* the sword).—*To put to it*, to press hard; to give difficulty to.—*To put the hand to*, to take hold; to begin; to undertake.—*To put this and that together*, to draw a conclusion from certain circumstances; to infer from given premises.—*To put to rights*, to arrange in an orderly condition; to set in proper order.—*To put to trial* or *on trial*, to bring before a court for examination and decision; to bring to a test; to try.—*To put up*, to offer publicly for sale; to hoard; to pack; to hide or lay aside; to put into its ordinary place when not in use; to give entertainment to; to accommodate with lodging.—*v.i.* Used only in certain phrases.—*To put in*, to enter a harbour; to offer a claim.—*To put in for*, to put in a claim for; to stand as a candidate for.—*To put off*, to sail from land.—*To put to sea*, to set sail; to begin a voyage.—*To put up*, to take lodgings; to lodge.—*To put up with*, to suffer without showing resentment; to pocket or swallow (an affront); to accept tamely; to overlook; to endure; to tolerate.—**Putter**, put'ér, *n.* One who puts.

Put, put, *v.t.*—*putted*, *putting*. [Akin to above.] To throw upwards and forwards from the shoulder.

Put, **Putt**, put, *n.* [W. *pwt*, a short, thick person.] A rustic; a clown; an odd fellow.—**Putamen**, pū-tā'men, *n.* [L., a shell.] *Bot.* the inner coat or shell of a fruit; the endocarp.

Putative, pū'ta-tiv, *a.* [Fr. *putatif*, L. *putativus*, from L. *puto*, to suppose (as in *compute*, *impute*, *dispute*, *repute*, &c., from *putus*, clean; akin to *purus*, pure.] Supposed; reputed (the *putative* father of a child).

Putid, pū'tid, *a.* [L. *putidus*, from *puteo*, to have an ill smell; root *pu*, as in *putrid*, *pus*.] Disgusting; vile; nasty; low or worthless.

Putlog, put'log, *n.* [From *put* and *log*.] *Carp.* one of the short pieces of timber used in building to carry the floor of a scaffold, having one end inserted in holes in the wall.

Putredinous, pū-tred'i-nus, *a.* [L. *putredo*, rottenness, PUTRID.] Having an offensive smell; rotten.

Putrefy, pū'trē-fī, *v.t.*—*putrefied*, *putrefying*. [Fr. *putrefier*, L. *putrefacio*—*putris*, putrid, *facio*, to make. PUTRID.] To render putrid; to cause to rot with an offensive smell; to make carious or gangrenous.—*v.i.* To become putrid; to rot.—**Putrefaction**, pū-trē-fak'shon, *n.* The act or process of putrefying; the decomposition of animal and vegetable substances, attended by the evolution of fetid gases; that which is putrefied.—**Putrefactive**, pū-trē-fak'tiv, *a.* Pertaining to putrefaction; tending to cause or causing putrefaction.—**Putrefactiveness**, *n.*

Putrescent, pū-tres'ent, *a.* [L. *putrescens*, ppr. of *putresco*, to rot. PUTRID.] Becoming putrid; growing rotten; pertaining to the process of putrefaction.—**Putrescence**, pū-tres'ens, *n.* The state of being putrescent; a putrid state.—**Putrescible**, pū-tres'i-bl, *a.* Capable of being putrefied; liable to become putrid.

Putrid, pū'trid, *a.* [Fr. *putride*, L. *putridus*, from *putris*, rotten, *putreo*, to rot, from *puteo*, to stink, from a root seen also in L. *pus*, Gr. *pyon*, matter; the same root producing also E. *foul*. PUS, FOUL.] In a state of decay or putrefaction; corrupt; rotten; proceeding from putrefaction or pertaining to it.—*Putrid fever*, typhus or spotted fever.—**Putridity**, **Putridness**, Pū-trid'i-ti, pū'trid-nes, *n.* The state of being putrid; corruption; rottenness.

Putt, put, *n.* A stroke made on a golf green, the object being to play the ball into the cup.—*v.t.* and *i.*—*putted*, *putting*. To tap a golf ball while on the golf green in the direction of the cup.—**Putter**, *n.* A short-shaft golf club with an almost perpendicular face, used for accurate play near the cup.—**Putting green**, *n.* Smooth turf surrounding the putting holes on a golf course.

Puttee, put'e, *n.* [Hind. *patti*.] Long roll of cloth wound round soldier's leg from ankle to knee as support and protection.

Puttock, put'tok, *n.* [From *pout*, *poult*, a chicken and *hawk*.] The common kite; the glead or gled.

Putty, put'i, *n.* [Fr. *potée*, calcined tin, brass, &c., putty powder, from *pot*, a pot, originally perhaps applied to a solder for pots.] A powder of calcined tin, used in polishing glass and steel; a kind of paste or cement compounded of whiting or soft carbonate of lime and linseed oil, used by glaziers for fixing in the panes or glass in window frames, &c.; a fine cement made of lime and stone dust; the mixture of ground materials in which earthenware is dipped for glazing.—*v.t.*—*puttied*, *puttying*. To cement with putty; to fill up with putty.—**Putty-faced**, *a.* Having a face resembling the colour of putty.—**Putty-knife**, *n.* A knife used by glaziers for laying on putty.

Puzzle, puz'l, *v.t.* — *puzzled*, *puzzling*. [Freq. from *pose*, to perplex with a question; or a form of *puddle*; comp. *muddle*, to make stupid.] To perplex; to nonplus; to put to a stand; to gravel; to make intricate; to entangle; with *out*, to discover or resolve by long cogitation.—*v.i.* To be bewildered; to be awkward.—*n.* Perplexity; embarrassment; a kind of riddle; a toy or contrivance which tries the ingenuity.—**Puzzle-headed**, *a.* Having the head full of confused notions.—**Puzzlement**, puz'l-ment, *n.* The state of being puzzled; bewilderment.—**Puzzler**, puz'lér, *n.* One who or that which puzzles.—**Puzzling**, puz'ling, *p.* and *a.* Such as to puzzle; perplexing; embarrassing; bewildering.—**Puzzle-monkey**, *n.* A popular name of the araucaria.

Puzzolana, **Puzzuolana**, **Puzzolite**, puz'zō-lä-na, puz'zū-ō-lä"na, puz'zo-līt. POZZOLANA.

Pyæmia, pī-ē'mi-a, *n.* [Gr. *pyon*, pus (PUTRID), and *haima*, blood.] Blood-poisoning, a dangerous disease resulting from the introduction of decaying animal matter, pus, &c., into the system.—**Pyæmic**, pī-ē'mik, *a.* Pertaining to pyæmia; characterized by or of the nature of pyæmia.

Pycnostyle, pik'nō-stīl, *n.* [Gr. *pyknos*, thick, and *stylos*, a column.] *Arch.* a colonnade where the columns stand very close to each other.

Pyebald, pī'bald, *a.* PIEBALD.

Pygarg, pī'gärg, *n.* [Gr. *pygargos*, lit. white-rump—*pygē*, a rump, and *argos*, white.] A species of antelope mentioned in the Bible, probably the addax; also, the sea-eagle or osprey.

Pygidium, pī-jid'i-um, *n.* [Gr. *pygē*, the posteriors.] The terminal division of the body of a trilobite, also of a flea.

Pygmy, pig'mi, *n.* [Fr. *pygmée*; L. *pygmæus*, from Gr. *pygmaios*, from *pygmē*, the fist, the distance from the elbow to the knuckles, about 13½ inches.] One of a fabulous race of dwarfs, first mentioned by Homer; a little or dwarfish person; a dwarf; also, anything little.—*a.* Pygmean; dwarfish; little.—**Pygmean**, pig-mē'an, *a.* Pertaining to a pygmy; dwarfish.

Pyjama, pī-jä'ma, *n.* PAJAMAS.

Pylon, pī'lon, *n.* [Gr. *pylōn*, from *pylē*, a gate.] The lofty massive doorway giving entrance to an Egyptian temple; a turning-point in aeroplane flights.

Pylorus, pī-lō'rus, *n.* [Gr. *pylōros*, from *pylē*, a gate, and *ouros*, a guard.] The outlet of the stomach, through which the food passes to the intestines.—**Pyloric**, pī-lor'ik, *a.* Pertaining to the pylorus.

Pyogenesis, **Pyogenia**, pī-ō-jen'e-sis, pī-ō-jē'ni-a, *n.* [Gr. *pyon*, pus, *genesis*, generation; root *gen*, to produce. PUS.] The generation or formation of pus.—**Pyogenic**, pī-ō-jen'ik, *a.* Having relation to formation of pus.—**Pyoid**, pī'oid, *a.* Partaking of the nature of pus.

Pyorrhea, pī'er-rē"a, *n.* [Gr. *pyon*, pus, *hroia*, a flow.] A suppurative inflammation in and about the sockets of the teeth which results in the loosening of the teeth, abscess formation in the gums, and, unless checked, inflammation of the jawbone.

Pyracanth, pir'a-kanth, *n.* [Gr. *pyrakantha*—*pyr*, fire, *akantha*, a thorn.] A kind of thorn found in southern Europe.

Pyracid, pī-ras'id, *n.* PYRO-ACID.

Pyramid, pir'a-mid, *n.* [Fr. *pyramide*; L. *pyramis*, from Gr. *pyramis*, *pyramidos*, a pyramid; probably an Egyptian word.] A solid structure whose base is a rectilineal figure, and whose sides are triangular and meet at a point; one of the ancient structures of this form erected in different parts of the world, the most noted being those of Egypt, to which the name was originally applied; *geom.* strictly a solid contained by a plane triangular, square, or polygonal base, and by other planes meeting in a point; *pl.* a game at billiards played with fifteen red balls and one white, the red balls being placed together in the form of a triangle or pyramid, and the players trying who will pocket the greatest number of balls.—**Pyramidal**, **Pyramidic**, **Pyramidical**, pi-ram'i-dal, pir-a-mid'ik, pir-a-mid'i-kal, *a.* Pertaining to a pyramid; having the form of a pyramid.—**Pyramidally**, **Pyramidically**, pi-ram'i-dal-li, pir-a-mid'i-kal-li, *adv.* In the form of a pyramid. — **Pyramidicalness**, pir-a-mid'i-kal-nes, *n.* — **Pyramidion**, pir-a-mid'i-on, *n.* *Arch.* the small pyramid which terminates the top of an obelisk.—**Pyramidoid**, **Pyramoid**, pi-ram'i-doid, pir'a-moid, *n.* A figure or solid resembling a pyramid.

Pyrargyrite, pīr-ar'ji-rīt, *n.* [Gr. *pyr*, fire, and *argyros*, silver.] An important ore of silver, chiefly sulphide of silver and antimony, with hexagonal crystallization.

Pyre, pīr, *n.* [L. *pyra*, from Gr. *pyra*, a pyre, from *pyr*, fire. FIRE.] A heap of combustible materials on which a dead body was laid to be burned; a funeral pile.—**Pyral**, pī'ral, *a.* Pertaining to a pyre.

Pyrene, pī-rēn', *n.* [Gr. *pyrēn*.] *Bot.* the stone found in the interior of fruits.

Pyrenean, pir-e-nē'an, *a.* Pertaining to the Pyrenees.—**Pyreneite**, pir-e-nē'īt, *n.* A mineral of a greyish-black colour, found in the Pyrenees; a variety of garnet.

Pyrenoid, pī'ren-oid, *n.* [Gr. *pyr*, fire, *eidos*, an appearance.] In green algæ, a starch-forming corpuscle.

Pyretic, pī-ret'ik, *n.* [Gr. *pyretos*, burning heat, fever, from *pyr*, fire. PYRE.] A medicine for the cure of fever.—**Pyretology**, pir-ē-tol'o-ji, *n.* The branch of medical science that treats of fevers.—**Pyrexia**, **Pyrexy**, pī-rek'si-a, pī-rek'si, *n.* [Fr. *pyrexie*, from Gr. *pyressō*, to be feverish.] Fever.—**Pyrexial**, **Pyrexical**, pī-rek'si-al, pī-rek'si-kal, *a.* Pertaining to fever; feverish.

Pyrheliometer, pīr-hē'li-om"et-ér, *n.* [Gr. *pyr*, fire, *hēlios*, the sun, *metron*, a measure.] An instrument for measuring the intensity of the heat of the sun.

Pyriform, pīr'i-form, *a.* [L. *pyrum*, a pear, and *forma*, shape.] Having the form of a pear.

Pyrites, pī-rī'tēz, *n.* [Gr. *pyritēs*, from *pyr*, fire. PYRE.] A term applied to yellow sulphide of iron, because it struck fire with steel; also applied to minerals in which sulphur exists in combination with copper, cobalt, nickel, &c.—*Arsenical pyrites*. MISPICKEL.—*White iron pyrites*. MARCASITE.—*Yellow* or *copper pyrites*, the sulphide of copper and iron, the most common ore of copper.—**Pyritic**, **Pyritical**, **Pyritous**, **Pyritaceous**, pī-rit'ik, pī-rit'i-kal, pīr'i-tus, pīr-i-tā'shus, *a.* Pertaining to pyrites; consisting of or resembling pyrites.—**Pyritiferous**, pīr-i-tif'ér-us, *a.* Containing or producing pyrites.—**Pyritize**, pir'i-tīz, *v.t.*—*pyritized*, *pyritizing*. To convert into pyrites.

Pyroacetic, pīr'ō-a-set"ik, *a.* [Gr. *pyr*, *pyros*, fire, and E. *acetic*.] Pertaining to or obtained from acetic acid when subjected to the action of heat.—**Pyro-acid**, *n.* A product obtained by subjecting certain organic acids to heat.

Pyro-electric, **Pyro-electricity**, pīr'ō-ē-lek"trik, pīr'ō-ē-lek-tris"i-ti. [Gr. *pyr*, *pyros*, fire, and E. *electric*.] THERMO-ELECTRIC, &c.

Pyrogenic, pīr-ō-jen'ik, *a.* and *n.* [Gr.

pyr, pyros, fire, and root gen, to produce.] Producing or that which tends to produce feverishness.—**Pyrogenous**, pi-roj'e-nus, *a.* Produced by fire; igneous.

Pyrognomic, pīr-og-nom'ik, *a.* [Gr. *pyr, pyros*, fire, and *gnōmōn*, an index.] Applied to certain minerals which, when heated to a certain degree, exhibit a glow of incandescence.

Pyrognostic, pīr-og-nos'tik, *a.* [Gr. *pyr, pyros*, fire, and *gignōskō*, to know.] *Mineral.* pertaining to the phenomena exhibited on the application of the blow-pipe.

Pyro-heliometer, pir'ō-hē-li-om"et-ėr, *n.* PYRHELIOMETER.

Pyrolatry, pī-rol'a-tri, *n.* [Gr. *pyr*, fire, and *latreia*, worship.] The worship of fire.—**Pyrolater**, pī-rol'a-tėr, *n.* A fire-worshipper.

Pyroleter, pī-rol'e-tėr, *n.* [Gr. *pyr, pyros*, fire, and *ollymi*, to destroy.] An apparatus for the extinction of fire.

Pyroligneous, Pyrolignic, Pyrolignous, pir-ō-lig'nē-us, pīr-ō-lig'nik, pir-ō-lig'nus, *a.* [Gr. *pyr*, fire, and L. *lignum*, wood.] Generated or procured by the distillation of wood.—*Pyroligneous acid*, impure acetic acid obtained by the distillation of wood.

Pyrology, pī-rol'o-ji, *n.* [Gr. *pyr*, fire, and *logos*, discourse.] The science of heat.—**Pyrologist**, pī-rol'o-jist, *n.* One versed in the science of heat.

Pyrolusite, pīr-ō-lū'sīt, *n.* [Gr. *pyr*, fire, and *louō*, I wash.] A black ore of manganese, much used in chemical processes.

Pyromagnetic, pīr'ō-mag-net"ik, *a.* [Gr. *pyr, pyros*, fire, and E. *magnetic*.] Having the property of becoming magnetic when heated.

Pyromancy, pīr'ō-man-si, *n.* [Gr. *pyr, pyros*, fire, and *manteia*, divination.] Divination by fire.—**Pyromantic**, pīr-ō-man'tik, *a.* Pertaining to pyromancy.—*n.* One who pretends to divine by fire.

Pyrometer, pī-rom'et-ėr, *n.* [Gr. *pyr, pyros*, fire, and *metron*, a measure.] A term applied to any instrument the object of which is to measure all gradations of temperature above those that can be indicated by the mercurial thermometer.—**Pyrometric, Pyrometrical**, pīr-ō-met'rik, pīr-ō-met'ri-kal, *a.* Pertaining to the pyrometer or its use.—**Pyrometry**, pī-rom'et-ri, *n.* The use of the pyrometer; the act or art of measuring high degrees of heat.

Pyromorphous, pīr-ō-mor'fus, *a.* [Gr. *pyr, pyros*, fire, and *morphē*, form.] *Mineral.* having the property of crystallization by fire.

Pyronomics, pīr-ō-nom'iks, *n.* [Gr. *pyr, pyros*, fire, and *nomos*, a rule, a law.] The science of heat.

Pyrope, pīr'ōp, *n.* [Gr. *pyr, pyros*, fire, and *ōps*, the face.] Fire-garnet or Bohemian garnet, a dark-red variety of garnet.

Pyrophanous, pī-rof'a-nus, *a.* [Gr. *pyr, pyros*, fire, and *phainō*; to show.] Rendered transparent by heat.

Pyrophone, pīr'ō-fōn, *n.* [Gr. *pyr, pyros*, fire, and *phonē*, sound.] A musical instrument in which the notes are produced by the burning of hydrogen gas within glass tubes of various sizes and lengths.

Pyrophorus, pī-rof'o-rus, *n.* [Gr. *pyr, pyros*, fire, and *phoros*, bearing.] Any substance which takes fire on exposure to air.—**Pyrophoric, Pyrophorous**, pīr-ō-for'ik, pi-rof'o-rus, *a.* Pertaining to or resembling pyrophorus.

Pyrophyllite, pīr-ō-fil'līt, *n.* [Gr. *pyr, pyros*, fire, and *phyllon*, a leaf.] A mineral of a foliated structure, resembling talc, and having a white, green, or yellow colour and pearly lustre.

Pyroscope, pīr'ō-skōp, *n.* [Gr. *pyr, pyros*, fire, and *skopein*, to view.] An instrument for measuring the intensity of heat radiating from a hot body.

Pyrosis, pī-rō'sis, *n.* [Gr. *pyrōsis*, a burning, from *pyr*, fire.] *Med.* a disease of the stomach attended with a burning sensation, accompanied with an eructation of watery fluid. WATER-BRASH.

Pyrosome, pīr'ō-sōm, *n.* [Gr. *pyr, pyros*, fire, and *sōma*, a body.] A molluscous animal forming compound organisms, composed of innumerable individuals, remarkable for their brilliant phosphorescent luminosity.

Pyrotechnic, Pyrotechnical, pīr-ō-tek'nik, pir-ō-tek'ni-kal, *a.* [Gr. *pyr, pyros*, fire, and *technē*, art.] Pertaining to fireworks or the art of forming them.—**Pyrotechnics, Pyrotechny**, pīr-ō-tek'niks, pir-ō-tek'ni, *n.* The art of making fireworks; the use of artificial fireworks; the management and application of fire in various operations.—**Pyrotechnist, Pyrotechnician**, pīr-ō-tek'nist, pīr'ō-tek-nish"an, *n.* One skilled in pyrotechny; a manufacturer of fireworks.

Pyrotic, pī-rot'ik, *a.* [Gr. *pyrōtikos*, from *pyr*, fire.] Caustic.—*n.* A caustic.

Pyroxene, pīr'ok-sēn, *n.* [Gr. *pyr, pyros*, fire, and *xenos*, a stranger.] Another name for the mineral augite; any of various minerals similar to augite.—**Pyroxenic**, pir-ok-sen'ik, *a.* Pertaining to pyroxene.

Pyroxylic, pīr-ok-sil'ik, *a.* [Gr. *pyr, pyros*, fire, and *xylon*, wood.] Applied to the crude liquid obtained by distilling wood in closed vessels.—**Pyroxyle, Pyroxyline**, pi-rok'sil, pi-rok'si-lin, *n.* Gun-cotton and other explosive substances obtained by immersing vegetable fibre in nitric or nitro-sulphuric acid.

Pyrrhic, pir'ik, *n.* [Gr. *pyrrhichē*, a war-like dance.] An ancient Grecian warlike dance; a metrical foot consisting of two short syllables.—*a.* Pertaining to the Greek martial dance; *pros.* consisting of two short syllables, or of feet of two short syllables.—*Pyrrhic victory*, a victory, as of those gained by King Pyrrhus of Epirus over the Romans, costing more to the victor than to the vanquished.

Pyrrhonism, pir'on-izm, *n.* [From *Pyrrho*, the founder of the Sceptics.] Scepticism; universal doubt.—**Pyrrhonean**, pi-rō'nē-an, *a.* Pyrrhonic.—**Pyrrhonic**, pi-ron'ik, *a.* Pertaining to Pyrrhonism.—**Pyrrhonist, Pyrrhonian**, pir'on-ist, pi-rō'ni-an, *n.* A sceptic, one who doubts of everything.

Pythagorean, Pythagoric, Pythagorical, pi-thag'ō-rē"an, pith-a-gor'ik, pith-a-gor'i-kal, *a.* Pertaining to Pythagoras or his system of philosophy, which taught the doctrine of the transmigration of souls, and resolved all philosophy into the relations of numbers.—*Pythagorean system, astron.* the system taught by Pythagoras, afterwards revived by Copernicus.—**Pythagorean, Pythagoric**, *n.* A follower of Pythagoras.—**Pythagoreanism, Pythagorism**, pi-thag'ō-rē"an-izm, pi-thag'or-izm, *n.* The doctrines or philosophy of Pythagoras.

Pythian, pith'i-an, *a.* [L. *Pythius*, Gr. *Pythios*, from *Pythō*, the older name of Delphi.] Pertaining to Delphi or to the priestess of Apollo at Delphi.—*Pythian games*, one of the four great national festivals of Greece, celebrated every fifth year in honour of Apollo near Delphi.—**Pythiad**, pith'i-ad, *n.* The period between the celebrations of the Pythian games.

Pythogenic, pī-thō-jen'ik, *a.* [Gr. *pythomai*, to rot, and root *gen*, to produce.] Engendered from filth: applied to diseases, as typhus, produced by filth or by a vitiated atmosphere.—**Pythogenesis**, pī-thō-jen'e-sis, *n.* Generation by means of filth.

Python, pī'thon, *n.* [Gr. *pythōn*, a great serpent slain by Apollo.] A genus of large non-venomous serpents, natives of the East Indies and elsewhere.

Pythoness, pī'thon-es, *n.* [Fr. *pythonisse*, from Gr. *Pythō*, old name of Delphi. PYTHIAN.] The priestess of Apollo at Delphi, who gave oracular answers; hence, any woman supposed to have a spirit of divination.—**Pythonic**, pī-thon'ik, *a.* Oracular; prophetic.—**Pythonism**, pī'thon-izm, *n.* The foretelling of future events.

Pyuria, pī-ū'ri-a, *n.* [Gr. *puon*, pus, *ouron*, urine.] *Pathol.* the presence of pus in the urine.

Pyx, piks, *n.* [Gr. *pyxis*, a box, especially of box-wood, from *pyxos*, the box-tree.] A covered vessel used in the Roman Catholic Church for holding the consecrated host; a box or chest in which specimen coins are deposited at the British Mint.—*Trial of the pyx*, the trial by weight and assay of the gold and silver coins of the United Kingdom, prior to their issue from the Mint; the assay of gold and silver plate at an assay office. Written also *Pix*.—*v.t.* To test by weight and assay.

Pyxidium, pik-sid'i-um, *n.* [Gr. *pyxis*, a box, and *eidos*, resemblance.] *Bot.* a capsule with a lid, as seen in the case of certain fruits; a term also applied to the theca of mosses.

Q

Q, the seventeenth letter of the English alphabet, a consonant having the same sound as *k* or hard *c*.

Qua, kwā, *adv.* [L.] In the quality or character of; as being; as.

Quack, kwak, *v.i.* [Formed from the sound, like D. *kwaaken, kwakken*, G. *quaken*, Dan. *qvække*, to croak, to quack; comp. Gr. *koax*, the croak of a frog.] To cry like the common domestic duck; to make vain and loud pretensions; to talk noisily and ostentatiously; to play the quack.—*n.* The cry of a duck; one who pretends to skill or knowledge which he does not possess; an empty pretender; a charlatan; especially, a pretender to medical skill.—*a.* Pertaining to or characterized by quackery (*quack* medicines, a *quack* doctor).—**Quackery**, kwak'ėr-i, *n.* The boastful pretensions or mean practice of a quack, particularly in medicine; humbug; imposture.—**Quackish**, kwak'ish, *a.* Like a quack or charlatan.—**Quacksalver**, kwak'sal-vėr, *n.* [D. *kwakzalver*, L.G. *kuaksalver*, G. *quacksalber*, lit. a *quack* that deals in *salves*.] A charlatan; a quack.

Quad, kwod, *n.* [Contr. for *quadrangle*.] The quadrangle or court, as of a college or jail; hence, a jail; quod.

Quadra, kwod'ra, *n.* pl. **Quadræ**, kwod'rē. [L., a square or plinth, a fillet.] *Arch.* a square frame or border inclosing a bas-relief; any frame or border.

Quadragenarian, Quadragenarious, kwod'ra-je-nā"ri-an, kwod'ra-je-nā"ri-us, *a.* [L. *quadragenarius*, from *quadrageni*, forty each, from *quadraginta*, forty.] Consisting of forty; forty years old.—**Quadragene**, kwod'ra-jēn, *n.* A papal indulgence for forty days.

Quadragesima, kwod-ra-jes'i-ma, *n.* [L. *quadragesimus*, fortieth, from *quadraginta*, forty, from *quatuor*, four.] Lent: so called because it consists of forty days.—*Quadragesima Sunday*, the first Sunday in Lent.—**Quadragesimal**, kwod-ra-jes'i-mal, *a.* Connected with the number forty; belonging to Lent.

Quadrangle, kwod-rang'gl, *n.* [L. *quadrus*=*quatuor*, four, and *angulus*, an angle.] A quadrilateral figure; a plain figure having four sides, and consequently four angles; a square or quadrangular court surrounded by buildings. — **Quadrangular**, kwod-rang'gū-lėr, *a.* Of a square shape; having four sides and four angles.—**Quadrangularly**, kwod-rang'gū-lėr-li, *adv.* In the form of a quadrangle.

Quadrant, kwod'rant, *n.* [L. *quadrans, quadrantis*, a fourth.] The quarter of a circle; the arc of a circle containing 90°; the space included between this arc and two radii drawn from the centre to each extremity; an instrument for measuring angular altitudes, in principle and application the same as the sextant, by which it is superseded. — **Quadrantal**, kwod-ran'tal, *a.* Pertaining to a quadrant.

Quadrat, kwod'rat, *n.* [L. *quadratum*, a square, from *quadrus*, square.] *Printing*, a piece of type-metal cast lower than a type, used for filling out spaces between letters, words, lines, &c., so as to leave a blank on the paper at the place.

Quadrate, kwod'rāt, *a.* [L. *quadratus*, squared, pp. of *quadro, quadratum*, to make square, from *quadrus*, square.] Square in form; square, by being the product of a number multiplied into itself.—*n.* A square surface or figure.—**Quadratic**, kwod-rat'ik, *a.* [Fr. *quadratique*.] Pertaining to, denoting, or containing a square; *alg.* involving the square or second power of an unknown quantity (a *quadratic* equation).—*n.* A quadratic equation; *pl.* that branch of algebra which treats of quadratic equations. — **Quadratrix**, kwod-rat'riks, *n.* [L. *quadro*, to square.] *Geom.* a curve employed for finding the quadrature of other curves. — **Quadrature**, kwod'rā-tūr, *n.* [L. *quadratura*.] *Geom.* the act of squaring; the reducing of a figure to a square; thus, the finding of a square which shall contain just as much area as a certain square or triangle, is the *quadrature* of that circle or triangle; *astron.* the position of one heavenly body in respect to another when distant from it 90°.

Quadrel, kwod'rel, *n.* [L.L. *quadrellus*, dim. of L. *quadrus*, a square.] A square stone, brick, or tile; sometimes restricted to a kind of artificial stone formed of a chalky earth moulded to a square form.

Quadrennial, kwod-ren'i-al, *a.* [From L. *quadriennium*, a space of four years—*quadrus* = *quatuor*, four, and *annus*, year.] Comprising four years; occurring once in four years.—**Quadrennially**, kwod-ren'i-al-li, *adv.* Once in four years.

Quadricapsular, kwod-ri-kap'sū-lėr, *a.* [L. *quadrus* = *quatuor*, four, and *capsula*, a capsule.] *Bot.* having four capsules.

Quadriceps, kwod'ri-seps, *n.* [L. *quadrus, quatuor*, four, *caput*, the head.] A large muscle in the front of the thigh.—**Quadricipital**, kwod-ri-sip'i-tal, *a.* Four-headed; belonging to the quadriceps.

Quadricornous, kwod-ri-kor'nus, *a.* [L. *quadrus*=*quatuor*, four, and *cornu*, a horn.] *Zool.* having four horns or antennæ.

Quadricostate, kwod-ri-kos'tāt, *a.* [L. *quadrus*=*quatuor*, four, and *costa*, a rib.] Having four ribs.

Quadridentate, kwod-ri-den'tāt, *a.* [L. *quadrus*=*quatuor*, four, and *dens, dentis*, a tooth.] *Bot.* having four teeth on the edge.

Quadridigitate, kwod-ri-dij'i-tāt, *a.* [L. *quatuor, digitus*, a finger.] Having four fingers or toes.

Quadrifarious, kwod-ri-fā'ri-us, *a.* [L. *quadrifarious*, fourfold, from *quadrus* = *quatuor*, four.] *Bot.* arranged in four rows or ranks.

Quadrifid, kwod'ri-fid, *a.* [L. *quadrus* = *quatuor*, four, and *findo, fidi*, to cleave.] Split or deeply cleft into four parts.

Quadrifoil, **Quadrifoliate**, kwod'ri-foil, kwod-ri-fō'li-āt, *a.* [L. *quadrus* = *quatuor*, four, and *folium*, a leaf.] *Bot.* having four leaves attached laterally to a common stalk.

Quadriform, kwod'ri-form, *a.* [L. *quatuor, forma*, shape.] Fourfold as regards form or shape.

Quadrifurcate, kwod-ri-fėr'kāt, *a.* [L. *quadrus*=*quatuor*, four, and *furca*, a fork.] Having four forks or branches.

Quadriga, kwod-rī'ga, *n.* pl. **Quadrigæ**, kwod-rī'jē. [L., contr. from *quadrijuga*—prefix *quadrus*, fourfold, and *jugum*, a yoke.] An ancient two-wheeled car or chariot drawn by four horses, harnessed all abreast.

Quadrigeminous, kwod-ri-jem'i-nus, *a.* [L. *quadrigeminous* — *quadrus* = *quatuor*, four, and *geminus*, double.] Fourfold; having four similar parts.

Quadrijugate, kwod-rij'ū-gāt, *a.* [L. *quadrus*=*quatuor*, four, and *jugum*, a yoke.] *Bot.* pinnate, with four pairs of leaflets.

Quadrilateral, kwod-ri-lat'ėr-al, *a.* [L. *quadrus*=*quatuor*, four, and *latus, lateris*, side.] Having four sides and consequently four angles.—*n.* A figure having four sides and four angles; the space inclosed between and defended by four fortresses, or the four fortresses collectively.—**Quadrilateralness**, kwod-ri-lat'ėr-al-nes, *n.*

Quadriliteral, kwod-ri-lit'ėr-al, *a.* [L. *quatuor, litera*, letter.] Consisting of four letters.

Quadrille, kwo-dril', *n.* [Fr. *quadrille*, Sp. *cuadrilla*, a group of four persons, *cuadrillo*, a small square, from L. *quadra, quadrum*, a square, from *quatuor*, four.] A game played by four persons with forty cards; a dance consisting generally of five figures or movements executed by four couples each forming the side of a square; the music for such a dance.

Quadrillion, kwod-ril'yon, *n.* [L. *quadrus* = *quatuor*, four, and E. *million*.] According to the United States and French system, a unit followed by fifteen ciphers; a million times a billion.

Quadrilocular, kwod-ri-lok'ū-lėr, *a.* [L. *quadrus*=*quatuor*, four, and *loculus*, a cell.] *Bot.* having four cells or compartments; four-celled.

Quadrinomial, kwod-ri-nō'mi-al, *a.* [L. *quadrus* = *quatuor*, four, and *nomen*, a name.] *Alg.* consisting of four denominations or terms.—*n.* *Alg.* a quantity consisting of four terms.

Quadripartite, kwod-ri-pär'tīt, *a.* [L. *quadrus* = *quatuor*, four, and *partitus*, divided.] Divided into four parts; *bot.* divided to the base into four parts (a *quadripartite* leaf).—**Quadripartitely**, kwod-ri-pär'tīt-li, *adv.* In a quadripartite manner. — **Quadripartition**, kwod'ri-pär-tish"on, *n.* A division by four or into four parts.

Quadripennate, kwod-ri-pen'āt, *a.* [L. *quadrus*=*quatuor*, four, and *penna*, a wing.] Having four wings: said of insects.

Quadriphyllous, kwod-ri-fil'lus, *a.* [L. *quadrus*=*quatuor*, and Gr. *phyllon*, a leaf.] *Bot.* having four leaves; four-leaved.

Quadriplicated, **Quadriplicate**, kwod-rip'li-kā-ted, kwod-rip'li-kāt, *a.* [L. *quadrus* = *quatuor*, four, and *plica*, a fold.] Having four plaits or folds.

Quadrireme, kwod'ri-rēm, *n.* [L. *quadriremis* — *quadrus* = *quatuor*, four, and *remus*, an oar.] A galley with four benches of oars, in use among the ancient Greeks and Romans.

Quadrisection, kwod-ri-sek'shon, *n.* [L. *quadrus*=*quatuor*, four, and *sectio*, a cutting.] A subdivision into four parts.

Quadrisulcate, kwod-ri-sul'kāt, *a.* [L. *quadrus*=*quatuor*, four, and *sulcus*, a furrow.] Having four furrows or clefts; *zool.* having the hoof divided into four.

Quadrisyllable, kwod-ri-sil'la-bl, *n.* [L. *quadrus* = *quatuor*, four, and E. *syllable*.] A word consisting of four syllables. — **Quadrisyllabic**, kwod'ri-sil-lab"ik, *a.* Consisting of four syllables.

Quadrivalent, kwod-riv'a-lent, *a.* [From L. *quadrus* = *quatuor*, four, and *valens, valentis*, ppr. of *valeo*, to be worth.] *Chem.* applied to an element one atom of which is equivalent in combination to four atoms of hydrogen; tetratomic.

Quadrivalve, **Quadrivalvular**, kwod'ri-valv, kwod-ri-val'vū-lėr, *a.* [L. *quadrus* = *quatuor*, four, and *valva*, a valve.] *Bot.* having four valves; four-valved.

Quadrivial, kwod-riv'i-al, *a.* [E. *quadrivium*—prefix *quadrus* = *quatuor*, four, and *via*, a way.] Having four roads meeting in a point.—**Quadrivious**, quod-riv'i-us, *a.* [L. *via*, way.] Literally, by all the four ways of the cross-roads; in all directions; 'they fled *quadrivious* or *septemvious*'. (*Charles Reade*.)—**Quadrivium**, kwod-riv'i-um, *n.* [L.L.] A collective term in the middle ages for the four lesser arts—arithmetic, music, geometry, and astronomy.

Quadroon, kwod-rön', *n.* [Sp. *cuarteron*, from L. *quartus*, fourth. QUARTER.] The offspring of a mulatto by a white person; a person who is one-fourth white.

Quadrumana, kwod-rụ'ma-na, *n.pl.* [From L. *quadrus* = *quatuor*, four, and *manus*, the hand.] An order of mammals comprising the apes, monkeys, baboons, lemurs, &c., usually characterized by all the four limbs terminating in prehensile hands. —**Quadrumane**, kwod'rụ-mān, *n.* One of the Quadrumana.—**Quadrumanous**, kwod-rụ'ma-nus, *a.* Pertaining to the order Quadrumana; four-handed.

Quadruped, kwod'rụ-ped, *n.* [L. *quadrupes, quadrupedis*—*quadrus*=*quatuor*, four, and *pes, pedis*, a foot.] An animal having four legs, usually restricted to four-footed mammals, though many reptiles have also four legs.—**Quadrupedal**, kwod-rụ'pe-dal, *a.* Belonging to a quadruped, having or walking on four feet.

Quadruple, kwod'rụ-pl, *a.* [L. *quadruplus*—*quadrus* = *quatuor*, four, and term. *-plus*, Gr. *ploos*. DOUBLE.] Fourfold; four times told. — *n.* Four times the sum or number. —*v.t.* — *quadrupled, quadrupling*. To make four times as much or as many; to multiply by four.—*v.i.* To become four times as much or as many.—**Quadruply**, kwod'rụ'pli, *adv.* In a quadruple or fourfold degree; to a fourfold quantity.

Quadruplicate, kwod-rụ'pli-kāt, *v.t.* [L. *quadruplico, quadruplicatum* — *quadrus* = *quatuor*, four, and *plico*, to fold.] To make fourfold; to double twice.—*a.* Fourfold; four times repeated (a *quadruplicate* ratio or proportion). — **Quadruplication**, kwod-rụ'pli-kā"shon, *n.* The act of making fourfold or four times as great.

Quæstor, kwes'tor. QUESTOR.

Quaff, kwäf, *v.t.* [From Ir. and Gael. *cuach*, Sc. *quaich, queff*, a drinking-cup.] To drink; to swallow in large draughts; to drink copiously.—*v.i.* To drink largely.—**Quaffer**, kwäf'ėr, *n.* One who quaffs.

Quagga, kwag'a, *n.* [Hottentot; name derived from its cry.] An animal of South Africa closely allied to the zebra.

Quagmire, kwag'mīr, *n.* [*Quag* for *quake*, and *mire*; lit. a mire or bog that quakes or shakes.] A piece of soft boggy land that trembles under the foot; a bog; a fen.—**Quaggy**, kwag'i, *a.* Trembling under the foot, as soft wet earth; boggy; spongy.

Quail, kwāl, *v.i.* [A.Sax. *cwelan*, to die = D. *quelen*, to pine away; O.H.G. *quelan*, to suffer torment. QUELL.] To have the spirits sink or give way, as before danger or difficulty; to shrink; to lose heart; to cower.

Quail, kwāl, *n.* [O.Fr. *quaille*, Fr. *caille*, It. *quaglia*, a quail—names derived from its cry. Comp. D. *kwakkel*, G. *wachtel*, and Armor. *coaill*, a quail.] A common name of certain birds nearly allied to the partridges, from which they differ chiefly in being smaller.

Quaint, kwānt, *a.* [O.E. *queint, coint*, from O.Fr. *coint*, neat, fine, dainty; from L. *cognitus*, known, the meaning having probably been influenced by L. *comptus*, trimmed, adorned. COGNITION, ACQUAINT.] Old and antique; singular; whimsical; curious; fanciful.—**Quaintly**, kwānt'li, *adv.* In a quaint manner; oddly; fancifully; singularly; whimsically. —**Quaintness**, kwānt'nes, *n.* The quality of being quaint; oddity and antiqueness.

Quake, kwāk, *v.i.*—*quaked, quaking.* [A. Sax. *cwacian*, same root as *quick*; comp. Prov. G. *quacken*, to waggle, to shake. QUICK.] To shake; to tremble; to shudder (to *quake* with fear); to be shaken with more or less violent convulsions (the earth *quakes*); to shake or tremble, as the earth under the feet, through want of solidity or firmness. — *n.* A shake; a trembling; a tremulous agitation.—**Quaker**, kwā'kėr, *n.* One that quakes; one of the religious sect called the *Society of Friends* (see under FRIEND).—**Quakeress**, kwā'kėr-es, *n.* A female Quaker. — **Quakerish**, kwā'kėr-ish, *a.* Relating to or resembling Quakers. —**Quakerism**, kwā'kėr-izm, *n.* The peculiar manners, tenets, or worship of the Quakers.—**Quakerly**, kwā'kėr-li, *a.* Resembling or characteristic of Quakers.—**Quakiness**, kwā'ki-nes, *n.* The state of quaking or shaking.—**Quaking-grass**, *n.* A genus of grasses of which the spikelets are always in tremulous motion, from the weakness of their footstalks. — **Quakingly**, kwā'king-li, *adv.* In a quaking or trembling manner. —**Quaky**, kwā'ki, *a.* Characterized by or prone to quaking; shaky.

Qualify, kwol'i-fī, *v.t.*—*qualified, qualifying.* [Fr. *qualifier*, from L.L. *qualificare*, from L. *qualis*, such, of such sort, and *facio*, to make.] To make such as is required; to fit for any place, office, or occupation; to furnish with knowledge, skill, &c., necessary for a purpose; to furnish with legal power or capacity (to *qualify* persons for the franchise); to limit or modify; to restrict; to limit by exceptions (to *qualify* a statement); to moderate, abate, soften; to modify the quality or strength of; to dilute or otherwise fit for taste (to *qualify* spirits with water).—*v.i.* To take the necessary steps for rendering one's self capable of holding any office or enjoying any privilege; to establish a right to exercise any function; followed by *for*.—**Qualifiable**, kwol'i-fī-a-bl, *a.* Capable of being qualified. — **Qualification**, kwol'i-fi-kā"shon, *n.* The act of qualifying, or the state of being qualified; that which qualifies or fits a person or thing for any use or purpose, as for a place, an office, an employment; legal power; ability; a qualifying or extenuating circumstance; modification; restriction; limitation; an abatement; a diminution.—**Qualificative**, kwol'i-fi-kā-tiv, *a.* Serving or having the power to qualify or modify. —*n.* That which serves to qualify; a qualifying term, clause, or statement.—**Qualified**, kwol'i-fīd, *p.* and *a.* Having a qualification; furnished with legal power or capacity; accompanied with some limitation or modification; modified; limited (a *qualified* statement). — **Qualifiedly**, kwol'i-fīd-li, *adv.* With qualification or limitation. — **Qualifiedness**, kwol'i-fīd-nes, *n.*—**Qualifier**, kwol'i-fī-ėr, *n.* One who or that which qualifies.

Quality, kwol'i-ti, *n.* [Fr. *qualité*, from L. *qualitas*, a quality or property, from *qualis*, such. QUALIFY.] That which makes or helps to make anything such as it is; a distinguishing property, characteristic, or attribute; a property; a trait; moral characteristic, good or bad; comparative rank; condition in relation to others; superior or high rank (ladies of *quality*).—*The quality*, persons of high rank collectively.—**Qualitative**, kwol'i-tā-tiv, *a.* Pertaining to quality; estimable according to quality.—*Qualitative analysis, chem.* the process of decomposing a compound substance with a view to determine what elements it contains. — **Qualitatively**, kwol'i-tā-tiv-li, *adv.* In a qualitative manner; as regards quality.

Qualm, kwäm, *n.* [A.Sax. *cwealm*, pestilence, death = D. *kwalm*, Dan. *qvalm*, qualm, vapour; O.H.G. *qualm*, death; from root of *quell, quail.*] A throe or throb of pain; a sudden feeling of sickness at the stomach; a sensation of nausea; a scruple or twinge of conscience; compunction. — **Qualmish**, kwäm'ish, *a.* Sick at the stomach; inclined to vomit; affected with nausea.—**Qualmishly**, kwäm'ish-li, *adv.* In a qualmish manner. — **Qualmishness**, kwäm'ish-nes, *n.* The state of being qualmish.

Quamash, kwa̤'mash, *n.* An American bulbous plant with roots which were much eaten by the Indians: the Camass.

Quandary, kwon-da'ri or kwon'da-ri, *n.* [Probably from Fr. *Qu'en dirai-je?* what shall I say of it?] A state of difficulty, perplexity, uncertainty, or hesitation; a pickle; a predicament.—*v.t. quandaried, quandarying.* To put into a quandary.

Quantity, kwon'ti-ti, *n.* [Fr. *quantité*, L. *quantitas*, quantity, extent, from *quantus*, how great, from *quam*, to what a degree.] That property in virtue of which a thing is measurable; greatness; extent; measure; size; any amount, bulk, or aggregate (a *quantity* of earth, a *quantity* of water); often a large or considerable amount (wheat shipped in *quantities*); *math.* anything which can be multiplied, divided, or measured; anything to which mathematical processes are applicable; *gram.* the measure of a syllable or the time in which it is pronounced; the metrical value of syllables as regards length or weight in pronunciation; *logic*, the extent in which the subject of a proposition is taken. — *Quantity of electricity*, measured practically in COULOMBS (which see). — *Quantity of heat*, the unit of quantity of heat is the quantity required to raise unit mass of water through one degree of temperature; according to the unit of mass and the scales employed there are the different units known as pound-degree F., pound-degree C., gramme-degree C. See CALORIE.—**Quantification**, kwon'ti-fi-kā"shon, *n.* The act or process of quantifying; the act of determining the quantity or amount. — **Quantify**, kwon'ti-fī, *v.t.*—*quantified, quantifying.* [L. *quantus*, how much, and *facio*, to make.] To determine the quantity of; to modify or qualify with regard to quantity: more especially a term in logic (to *quantify* the predicate, as by inserting 'all' in 'some men are (all) logicians'). — **Quantitative**, kwon'ti-tā-tiv, *a.* Estimable according to quantity; relating or having regard to quantity.—*Quantitative analysis, chem.* the process of decomposing a compound substance with a view to determine how much of each element it contains.—**Quantitatively**, kwon'ti-tā-tiv-li, *adv.* In a quantitative manner. — **Quantitive**, kwon'ti-tiv, *a.* Estimable according to quantity; quantitative.—**Quantitively**, kwon'ti-tiv-li, *adv.* So as to be measured by quantity; quantitatively. — **Quantivalence**, kwon-tiv'a-lens, *n.* [L. *quantus*, how much, and *valeo*, to have power.] *Chem.* the combination of elements in certain proportions.—**Quantum**, kwan'tum, *n.* [L., how much, as much as.] A quantity; an amount; a sufficient amount.

Quarantine, kwor'an-tēn, *n.* [O.Fr. *quarantaine*, It. *quarantana*, a space of forty days, from *quaranta*, from L. *quadraginta*, forty, from *quatuor*, four.] The period, originally of forty days, now of lesser but indeterminate length, during which a ship arriving in port is detained by health officers for investigation of the possible presence of contagious disease; a place where persons with contagious disease are detained; the place where ships are detained for inspection; the edict requiring one to be detained or the time required by health statutes for a person to be detained in his living quarters because of contagion. —*v.t. quarantined, quarantining.* To restrict the entrance to and exit from any place under observation for contagious disease.

Quarrel, kwor'el, *n.* [O.Fr. *querele*, Fr. *querelle*, a quarrel, from L. *querela*, a complaint, from *queror*, to complain; akin *querulous*, also *cry*.] A brawl; an angry dispute; a wrangle; an altercation; a breach of friendship or concord; open variance between parties; the basis or ground of being at variance with another; ill-will, or reason to complain; ground of objection.—*v.i.*—*quarreled, quarreling.* To dispute violently or with loud and angry words; to wrangle; to squabble: to fall out; to pick a quarrel; to get into hostilities; to find fault; to cavil.—**Quarreler**, kwor'el-ėr, *n.* One who quarrels.—**Quarrelous**,† kwor'el-us, *a.* Quarrelsome. (*Shak.*) — **Quarrelsome**, kwor'el-sum, *a.* Apt to quarrel; easily irritated or provoked to contest; irascible; choleric.—**Quarrelsomely**, kwor'el-sum-li, *adv.* In a quarrelsome manner.

Quarrel, kwor'el, *n.* [O.Fr. *quarrel* (Fr. *carreau*), dim. of L. *quadrum*, something square, from *quatuor*, four.] A bolt to be shot from a cross-bow, especially with a somewhat square-shaped head; a lozenge-shaped pane of glass in a window; a small paving-stone or tile of the square or lozenge form; a glazier's diamond; a kind of graver.

Quarry, kwor'i, *n.* [O.Fr. *quarriere* (Fr. *carrière*), lit. a place where stones are squared, from L. *quadro*, to square. QUADRAT, &c.] A place where stones are dug from the earth, or separated, as by blasting with gunpowder, from a large mass of rocks. —*v.t.*—*quarried, quarrying.* To dig or take from a quarry (to *quarry* marble).—**Quarriable**, kwor'i-a-bl, *a.* Capable of being quarried. — **Quarrier, Quarryman**, kwor'i-ėr, kwor'i-man, *n.* One who works in a quarry.

Quarry, kwor'i, *n.* [Fr. *curée*, the portion given to the dogs, wrapped in the skin of the beast killed, from L. *corium*, a hide, leather.] A part of the entrails of a beast of chase given to the dogs; a heap of game killed; any animal pursued for prey; the game which a hawk or hound pursues; object of chase or pursuit in general.

Quart, kwa̤rt, *n.* [Fr. *quarte*; lit. a fourth part, from L. *quartus*, fourth, from *quatuor*, four.] A unit of liquid measure (¼ of a gallon) or dry measure (⅛ of a peck); 2 pints; a container holding a quart.—**Quartan**, kwa̤r'tan, *a.* [L. *quartanus*, fourth.] Intermitting so as to occur every fourth day (a *quartan* fever).—**Quart-bottle**, *n.* A bottle containing, or nominally containing, the fourth part of a gallon.—**Quart-pot**, *n.* A pot or drinking vessel containing a quart.—**Quarte**, kärt, *n.* One of the four guards in fencing; a corresponding position of the body.

Quarter, kwa̤r'tėr, *n.* [O.Fr. *quarter*, *quartier* (Fr. *quartier*), a quarter, from L. *quartarius*, a fourth part, from *quartus*, fourth, from *quatuor*, four.] One of four parts into which anything is divided; a fourth part or portion; the fourth part of a hundredweight, that is, 25 lbs.; the fourth of a dollar, or twenty-five cents *U. S.*; the fourth part of the moon's period or monthly revolution; one of the four cardinal points; more widely, any region or point of the compass (from what *quarter* does the wind blow?); a particular region of a town, city, or country; a district; a locality (the Latin *quarter* of Paris; the Jews' *quarter* in Florence); the fourth part of the year; in schools, the fourth part of the teaching period of the year; the fourth part of the carcass of a quadruped, including a limb; *her.* one of the divisions of a shield when it is divided into four portions by horizontal and perpendicular lines meeting in the fesse-point; the piece of leather in a shoe which forms the side from the heel to the vamp; the part of a vessel's side which lies towards the stern; proper position; specific place; assigned or allotted position; the sparing of the life of a vanquished enemy; mercy shown by a conqueror (to give or show *quarter* to a person —perhaps originally to assign a lodging to, or to give a share of one's own quarters); *pl.* (in each of the following senses), temporary residence; shelter (to find *quarters* somewhere); a station or encampment occupied by troops (winter *quarters*); place of lodgment for officers and men; *naut.* the post allotted to the officers and men at the commencement of an engagement.—*On the quarter* (*naut.*), in a direction oblique to the ship's quarter.—*v.t.* To divide into four equal parts; to separate into parts; to cut to pieces; to furnish with lodgings or shelter, to find lodgings and food for (to *quarter* soldiers on the inhabitants); *her.* to add to other arms on the shield by dividing it into four or more compartments.—*v.t.* To be stationed; to lodge; to have temporary residence.—**Quarterback**, *n.* In football (*U. S.*) a player who calls signals while standing behind the center from whom he may receive the ball, either carrying it or passing it to another member of the team. —**Quarter-day**, *n.* One of the four days during the year on which payment of rent, interest, &c., is made.—**Quarter-deck**, *n.* *Naut.* that part of the upper deck which is abaft the mainmast.—**Quarter-face**, *n.* A countenance three parts averted.—**Quartering**, kwar'tėr-ing, *n.* *Her.* the conjoining of coats of arms in one shield to denote the alliances of one family with the heiresses of others; one of the compartments on such a shield.—**Quarterly**, kwar'tėr-li, *a.* Recurring at the end of each quarter of the year (*quarterly* payments of rent). —*adv.* Once in a quarter of a year.—*n.* A periodical publication issued once every three months.—**Quartermaster**, *n.* *Milit.* an officer who has charge of the quarters, barracks, tents, &c., and supplies all foodstuffs; *naut.* a petty officer who has charge of the stowage of ballast and provisions, and attends to the steering of the ship, &c.—**Quartermaster-general**, *n.* *Milit.* a staff officer of high rank, whose department is charged with all orders relating to the clothing, feeding and quartering of troops.—**Quartermaster-sergeant**, *n.* *Milit.* a non-commissioned officer whose duty it is to assist the quartermaster.—**Quarter note**, *n.* In music, the quarter part of a whole note.—**Quarter saw**, *v.t.* To saw timber into quarter sections, then into boards, so that when finished, the grain is attractive in appearance.—**Quarter section**, *n.* A system of land surveying used by the governments of the U. S. and Canada, whereby farm lands are accurately divided into sections one mile square (640 acres), half sections (320 acres), and quarter sections (160 acres).—**Quarter-staff**, *n.* A weapon formed of a stout pole about 6½ feet long, grasped by one hand in the middle, and by the other between the middle and the end.

Quartet, **Quartette**, kwar-tet', *n.* [It. *quartetto*, from L. *quartus*, fourth.] A piece of music arranged for four voices or four instruments; the persons who execute a quartet; a stanza of four lines.

Quartile, kwar'til, *n.* [L. *quartus*, fourth.] A point on a distribution curve indicating the division of that distribution into quarters or sections equivalent to 25% of the total number of units.

Quarto, kwar'tō, *n.* [L. *quartus*, fourth.] A book of the size of the fourth of a sheet; a size made by twice folding a sheet, which then makes four leaves: abbreviated thus, 4to.—*a.* Denoting the size of a book in which a sheet makes four leaves.

Quartz, kwarts, *n.* [From G. *quarz*, *quartz*, quartz, a word of unknown origin.] A name given to varieties of the native oxide of silicon occurring both crystallized and massive, and an important constituent of granite and the older rocks, varieties of it being known as rock crystal, flint, agate, amethyst, &c.—**Quartziferous**, kwart-sif'ėr-us, *a.* [*Quartz*, and L. *fero*, to bear.] Consisting of quartz, or chiefly of quartz; yielding quartz.—**Quartzite**, kwart'sit, *n.* A rock formed of granular quartz; quartz-rock.—**Quartz lamp**, *n.* A mercury lamp, used in physical therapy, which emits ultraviolet rays through a quartz lens.—**Quartzous**, kwart'sus, *a.* Containing quartz; composed of quartz; resembling quartz.—**Quartz-rock**, *n.* A stratified metamorphic rock consisting entirely, or almost entirely, of quartz.

Quash, kwosh, *v.t.* [O.Fr. *quasser*, Fr. *casser*, from L. *quassare*, to shake, shatter, shiver; intens. from *quatio*, *quassum*, to shake; seen also in *concussion*, *percussion*, *discuss*.] To subdue, put down, or quell; to extinguish; to put an end to (to *quash* a rebellion); *law*, to make void from insufficiency, or for other cause.

Quasi, kwā'si. [L.] As if; in a manner; sometimes forming compounds with English words, and generally implying that what it qualifies is in some degree fictitious or unreal, or only has certain features of what it professes to be (a *quasi-argument*, a *quasi-historical* account).—**Quasimodo**, kwas-i-mō'dō. [L. *quasi modo*, as if only, the words beginning the introit of the day.] A term applied to the first Sunday after Easter among Roman Catholics.

Quassia, kwas'i-a, *n.* [From *Quassy*, a negro who first made known the medicinal virtues of one species.] A genus of South American tropical trees containing an extremely bitter principle, having marked tonic properties, and used medicinally.—**Quassin**, **Quassite**, kwas'in, kwas'īt, *n.* The bitter principle of quassia.

Quatercentenary, kwot'ėr-sen-ten″ar-i, *n.* [L. *quatuor*, *centum*.] A four-hundredth anniversary.

Quaterfoil, kwa̤'tėr-foil. QUATREFOIL.

Quatern, kwat'ėrn, *a.* [L. *quaterni*, four each, from *quatuor*, four.] Consisting of four; growing by fours (*quatern* leaves).—**Quaternary**, kwa-tėr'na-ri, *a.* [L. *quaternarius*.] Consisting of four; arranged in fours; *geol.* a term applied to the strata above the tertiary; post-tertiary (which see); *chem.* applied to compounds which contain four elements.—**Quaternate**, kwa-tėr'nāt, *a.* Consisting of four.—*Quaternate leaf*, one that consists of four leaflets.

Quaternion, kwa-tėr'ni-on, *n.* [L. *quaternio*, a group of four, from *quatuor*, four.] A set or group of four; a term for a quantity employed in a method of mathematical investigation discovered by Sir W. R. Hamilton.

Quatrain, kwot'rān, *n.* [Fr., from *quatre*, L. *quatuor*, four.] A stanza of four lines rhyming alternately.

Quatrefoil, kä'tėr-foil or kwa̤'tėr-foil, *n.* [Fr. *quatre-feuille*—*quatre* (L. *quatuor*), four, and *feuille* (L. *folium*), a leaf.] *Arch.* an aperture or ornament somewhat resembling four leaves about a common centre; an opening showing four radiating cusps.

Quaver, kwā'vėr, *v.i.* [From older *quave*, to shake, akin to *quiver*; and to L.G. *quabbeln*, to quiver; perhaps also to *quake*.] To have a tremulous motion; to vibrate; to shake in vocal utterance; to sing with tremulous modulations of voice; to produce a shake on a musical instrument.—*v.t.* To utter with a tremulous sound.—*n.* A shake or rapid vibration of the voice, or a shake on an instrument of music; a note equal to half a crotchet or the eighth of a semibreve. —**Quaverer**, kwā'vėr-ėr, *n.* One that quavers.

Quay, kē, *n.* [From Fr. *quai*, a quay, a Celtic word=Bret. *cae*, W. *cae*, an inclosure.] A built landing-place along a line of coast or a river bank, or forming the side of a harbour, at which vessels are loaded and unloaded; a wharf.—*v.t.* To furnish with quays.—**Quayage**, kē'āj, *n.* Quay dues; wharfage.

Quean, kwēn, *n.* [A.Sax. *cwene*, a woman, a base woman. QUEEN.] A worthless woman; a slut; a strumpet.

Queasy, kwē'zi, *a.* [Allied to Icel. *kveisa*, pain in the stomach; N. *kveis*, sickness after a debauch.] Sick at the stomach; affected with nausea; qualmish; apt to cause nausea.—**Queasily**, kwē'zi-li, *adv.* In a queasy manner.—**Queasiness**, kwē'zi-nes, *n.* The state of being queasy; qualmishness; disgust.

Quebracho, ke-brä'chō, *n.* The name of South American timber trees, the bark of one of which is used in tanning, that of another in medicine.

Queen, kwēn, *n.* [A.Sax. *cwēn*, a queen, a wife (akin *quean*)=Goth. *qvens*, *qveins*; a woman; Icel. *kván*, a wife, *kona*, a woman; Dan. *qvinde*, a woman, *kone*, a wife; O.H.G. *quena*, a woman; Ir. and Gael. *coinne*, Gr. *gynē*, Skr. *jani*, a woman. From root *gan* Gr. and L. (*gen*), to produce. KIN, GENUS.] The consort of a king; a woman who is the sovereign of a kingdom; a female sovereign; a woman pre-eminent among others; the sovereign of a swarm of bees, or the female of the hive; a playing-card on which a queen is depicted; the most powerful of all the pieces in a set of chessmen; (*slang*) an extraordinarily attractive girl or young woman.—*Queen consort*, the wife of a king. *Queen dowager*, the widow of a deceased king.—*Queen mother*, a queen dowager who is also mother of the reigning sovereign.—**Queen-bee**, *n.* The only fully-developed and prolific female insect in a hive of bees. —**Queenly**, **Queenlike**, kwēn'li, kwēn'lik, *a.* Like a queen; becoming a queen.—**Queenliness**, kwēn'li-nes, *n.* The state of being queenly; queenly quality.—**Queen-of-the-May**, *n.* A girl crowned as queen to reign over the May-Day festivities.—**Queen of the prairie**, *n.* A perennial flower with pale-pink petals; found generally in clusters.—**Queen-post**, *n.* *Carp.* one of the two upright posts which connect two opposite rafters of a roof with the horizontal beam between them.—**Queen's-ware**, *n.* Glazed earthenware of a cream color.

Queen Anne style, *n.* A period of English architecture and furniture design in the reign of Queen Anne, during the 18th century. The buildings were ornamented by modified and simplified classic designs; the characteristic furniture of the time, largely influenced by the Dutch, emphasized comfort, upholstery of simple damask, and simple, curved lines.

Queer, kwēr, *a.* [From L.G. *quer*, *queer*, across=G. *queer*, *quer*, oblique, athwart, whence *querkopf*, a queer fellow.] Behaving or appearing otherwise than is usual; odd; singular; quaint.—**Queerish**, kwēr'ish, *a.* Somewhat queer; rather odd.—**Queerly**, kwēr'li, *adv.* In a queer manner.—**Queerness**, kwēr'nes, *n.* The state or quality of being queer; singularity.

Queest, kwēst, *n.* [From *cushat*.] The ringdove or wood-pigeon; the cushat.

Quell, kwel, *v.t.* [A.Sax. *cwellan*, to kill= Dan. *quæle*, to stifle, torment; Icel. *kvelja*, Sw. *qvälja*, G. *quälen*, to torment: same root as to *quail*.] To subdue; to cause to cease by using force; to crush (an insurrection or the like); to quiet; to allay.—**Queller**, kwel'ėr, *n.* One that quells or crushes.

Quench, kwensh, *v.t.* [A.Sax. *cwencan*, to quench, to extinguish; akin to *cwinan*, to dwindle; O.Fris. *kwinka*, to vanish.] To extinguish; to put out (fire); to allay; to slake (thirst); to suppress, stifle, check, repress.—*v.i.* To be extinguished; to go out; to lose zeal (*Shak.*).—**Quenchable**, kwensh'a-bl, *a.* Capable of being quenched. —**Quencher**, kwensh'ėr, *n.* One who or that which quenches.—**Quenchless**, kwensh'les, *a.* That cannot be quenched; inextinguishable.—**Quenchlessly**, kwensh'les-li, *adv.* In a quenchless manner.—**Quenchlessness**, kwensh'les-nes, *n.*

Quercitron, kwėr'sit-ron, *n.* [L. *quercus*, an oak, and *citrus*, the citron tree.] The black or dyer's oak, a large forest tree of N. America; the bark of this tree yielding a yellow dye; the dye-stuff itself.—**Quercitrin**, kwėr'sit-rin, *n.* The colouring principle of quercitron bark.

Querimonious, kwer-i-mō'ni-us, *a.* [L. *querimonia*, complaint, from *queror*, to complain. QUARREL.] Complaining; apt to complain; querulous.—**Querimoniously**, kwer-i-mō'ni-us-li, *adv.* Querulously.—**Querimoniousness**, kwer-i-mō'ni-us-nes, *n.*

Querist. Under QUERY.

Quern, kwėrn, *n.* [A.Sax. *cwyrn*, *cweorn*= D. *kweern*, Icel. *kvern*, Dan. *qvœrn*, Goth. *qvairnus*, a millstone, a quern; from root meaning to grind, same as in *corn*.] A stone hand-mill for grinding grain, still used to some extent by the Highlanders of Scotland.

Querulous, kwer'ū-lus, *a.* [L. *querulus*, from *queror*, to complain. QUARREL.] Complaining or habitually complaining; apt to murmur; peevish; expressing complaint. —**Querulously**, kwer'ū-lus-li, *adv.* In a querulous manner.—**Querulousness**, kwer'ū-lus-nes, *n.* Disposition to complain; peevishness.

Query, kwē'ri, *n.* [A modified form of L. *quære*, imper. of *quæro*, to ask, to inquire, to seek. QUEST.] A question; an inquiry to be answered or resolved; the mark or sign of interrogation (?). — *v.i. queried, querying.* To ask a question or questions. —*v.t.* To seek by questioning; to examine by questions; to doubt of; to mark with a query.—**Querist**, kwē'rist, *n.* One who puts a query; one who asks questions.

Quest, kwest, *n.* [O.Fr. *queste*, Fr. *quête*, from L. *quæsitus*, pp. of *quæro*, to seek, seen also in *question, query, inquest, request, inquire, require, conquer*, &c.] The act of seeking; search; pursuit; searchers collectively (*Shak.*); inquiry; examination.—*v.i.*† To make search or inquiry.—*v.t.*† To search or seek for.

Question, kwes'tyun, *n.* [Fr. *question*; L. *quæstio*, an inquiry, an investigation. QUEST.] An interrogation; something asked; an inquiry; a query; disquisition; discussion; the subject or matter of investigation or discussion; the theme of inquiry (foreign to the *question*); subject of debate; a point of doubt or difficulty; doubt; controversy (true beyond *question*); judicial trial (*Shak.*); *the question*, examination by torture.—*Question!* an exclamation used to recall a speaker to the subject under discussion; also used to express doubt as to the correctness of what a speaker is saying. —*Begging the question*, assuming something without proof; taking for granted what has to be proved.—*In question*, in debate; being at present dealt with (the point in *question*).—*To call in question*, to doubt; to challenge the truth or reality of.—*Out of question*, doubtless; undoubtedly.—*Out of the question*, not worthy of consideration; not to be thought of.—*Leading question.* Under LEADING.—*Previous question*, in *parliamentary practice*, the question whether a vote shall be come to on the main issue or not, brought forward before the main or real question is put, and for the purpose of avoiding, if the resolution is in the negative, the putting of this question. The motion is in the form, 'that the question be now put', and the mover and seconder vote against it.—*v.i.* To ask a question or questions; to debate; to doubt.—*v.t.* To inquire of by asking questions; to examine by interrogatories; to doubt of; to have no confidence in; to call in question; to challenge. —**Questionable**, kwes'tyun-a-bl, *a.* Capable of being questioned or inquired of; liable to question; suspicious; doubtful; uncertain; disputable.— **Questionableness**, kwes'tyun-a-bl-nes, *n.*—**Questionably**, kwes'tyun-a-bli, *adv.* In a questionable manner; doubtfully.—**Questionnaire**, kwes'tyun-ār", *n.* A systematic series of questions prepared for distribution for the purpose of gathering detailed information about an individual, or groups of persons, or social movements.—**Questioner**, kwes'tyun-ėr, *n.*

Questor, kwes'tor, *n.* [L. *quæstor*. QUEST.] The name of certain magistrates of ancient Rome whose chief office was the management of the public treasure; a receiver of taxes, tribute, &c. Also written *Quæstor*. —**Questorship**, kwes'tor-ship, *n.* The office of questor.

Queue, kū, *n.* [Fr., tail, from L. *cauda*, a tail. CUE.] The tail of a wig; a tail formed with a person's hair behind; a pigtail.

Quey, kwā, *n.* [Same as Icel. *kviga*, Sw. *quiga*, a quey.] A young cow or heifer; a cow that has not yet had a calf.

Quezal, **Quetzal**, kwē'zal, kwet'zal, *n.* [Native name.] A magnificent bird of Central America, one of the trogons.

Quib, kwib, *n.* [W. *gwib*, a quick turn; a form of *quip*.] A sarcasm; a taunt; a quip.

Quibble, kwib'l, *n.* [A freq. of *quib, quip*.] A turn of language to evade the point in question; an evasion; a prevarication; a pun; a low conceit.—*v.i.—quibbled, quibbling.* To evade the point in question by artifice, play upon words, or any conceit; to prevaricate; to pun.—**Quibbler**, kwib'lėr, *n.* One who quibbles; a punster.—**Quibblingly**, kwib'ling-li, *adv.* Evasively.

Quick, kwik, *a.* [A.Sax. *cwic*, living, lively = D. *kwik*, Icel. *kvikr*, Dan. *qvik*, Sw. *qvick*, L.G. *quick*, Goth. *qvius*; same root as L. *vivus*, living, Gr. *bios*, life, Skr. *jīv*, to live.] Alive; living (the *quick* and the dead); characterized by liveliness or sprightliness; nimble; brisk; speedy; rapid; swift; perceptive in a high degree (*quick* sight); sensitive; hasty; precipitate; irritable (*quick* of temper); pregnant (*Shak.*).—*adv.* In a quick manner; quickly. — *n.* A growing plant, usually hawthorn, for hedges; with *the*, the living flesh; sensible parts; hence, *fig.* that which is susceptible of or causes keen feeling (stung to the *quick*). —**Quicken**, kwik'n, *v.t.* To make alive; to revive or resuscitate; to cheer or refresh; to make quicker; to accelerate; to sharpen; to give keener perception to; to stimulate. —*v.i.* To become alive; to become quicker; to be in that state of pregnancy in which the child gives indications of life; to begin to give signs of life in the womb.—**Quickener**, kwik'n-ėr, *n.* One who or that which quickens.—**Quickens**, **Quickgrass**, kwik'enz, *n.* Same as *Couch-grass*. COUCH-GRASS.—**Quick-firing gun**, *n.* A gun or piece of ordnance that is loaded and fired with great rapidity. The projectile and powder are contained in a metallic cartridge case, and the carriage is furnished with a steel shield to protect the gunners. Not to be confounded with a machine-gun.—**Quick-hedge**, *n.* A fence or hedge of growing plants.—**Quicklime**, kwik'līm, *n.* [So called because of its active, burning properties.] Lime burned and not yet slaked with water.—**Quickly**, kwik'li, *adv.* Speedily; rapidly; nimbly; soon; without delay.—**Quick-match**, *n.* MATCH.—**Quickness**, kwik'nes, *n.* State of being quick or alive; speed; celerity; activity; briskness; acuteness of perception; keenness; sharpness.—**Quicksand**, kwik'-sand, *n.* A movable sandbank in the sea, a lake, or river, dangerous to vessels or to persons who trust themselves to it; *fig.* something deceptive or treacherous. —**Quick-scented**, *a.* Having an acute perception of smell. — **Quickset**, kwik'set, *n.* A living plant set to grow, particularly for a hedge; hawthorn planted for a hedge. —*a.* Made of quickset. — *v.t.* To plant with living shrubs for a hedge.—**Quick-sighted**, *a.* Of quick sight or acute discernment; quick to see or discern.—**Quick-sightedness**, *n.* Sharpness of sight.—**Quicksilver**, kwik'sil-vėr, *n.* [Living silver, so called from its fluidity.] Mercury, metal liquid at all ordinary temperatures. See MERCURY.—**Quicksilvered**, kwik'-sil-vėrd, *a.* Overlaid with quicksilver, or an amalgam of quicksilver and tinfoil.—**Quickstep**, *n.* A lively, spirited style of dancing. — **Quick-witted**, *a.* Having ready wit.

Quid, kwid, *n.* [A form of *cud*.] A piece of tobacco chewed and rolled about in the mouth.

Quiddity, kwid'i-ti, *n.* [Fr. *quiddité*, from L.L. *quidditas*, from L. *quid*, what.] An old philosophical term equivalent to essence, and comprehending both the substance and qualities; a trifling nicety; a quirk or quibble.

Quiddle, kwid'l, *v.i.—quiddled, quiddling.* [From L. *quid*, what. QUIDDITY.] To spend or waste time in trifling employments. —**Quiddle**, **Quiddler**, kwid'lėr, *n.* One who quiddles or busies himself about trifles.

Quidnunc, kwid'nungk, *n.* [L., what now?] One curious to know everything that passes; one who pretends to know all that goes on.

Quid pro quo, kwid-prō-kwō. Something in return for something; a fair requital.

Quiescent, kwī-es'ent, *a.* [L. *quiescens, quiescentis*, ppr. of *quiesco*, to keep quiet. QUIET.] Being in a state of repose; still; not moving; quiet; not excited; tranquil; *gram.* silent; not sounded (a *quiescent* letter).—**Quiescence**, **Quiescency**, kwī-es'ens, kwī-es'en-si, *n.* The state or quality of being quiescent; rest; repose.—**Quiescently**, kwī-es'ent-li, *adv.* In a quiescent manner.

Quiet, kwī'et, *a.* [Fr. *quiet*, L. *quietus*, from *quiesco*, to keep quiet, from *quies, quietus*, rest. *Coy, quit, quite*, have the same origin.] Not in action or motion; still; in a state of rest; free from alarm or disturbance; left at rest; tranquil; peaceable; not turbulent; free from emotion; calm; patient; retired; secluded; free from fuss or bustle; not glaring or showy (*quiet* colours).—*n.* Rest; stillness; tranquillity; repose; freedom from emotion of the mind; calmness. — *v.t.* To make or cause to be quiet; to calm; to pacify; to allay; to tranquillize; to bring to a state of rest.—*v.i.* To become quiet or still‡; to abate.—**Quieten**, kwī'tn, *v.t.* and *i.* To quiet; to pacify; to become quiet.—**Quieter**, kwī'-et-ėr, *n.* One who or that which quiets.—**Quietism**, kwī'et-izm, *n.* The absorption of the feelings or faculties in religious contemplation; the practice of a class of mystics who resigned themselves to mental inactivity in order to bring the soul into direct union with the Godhead.—**Quietist**, kwī'et-ist, *n.* One who believes in or practises quietism; especially applied to one of a sect of mystics originated by Molinos, a Spanish priest, in the latter part of the seventeenth century.—**Quietistic**, kwī-et-is'tik, *a.* Pertaining to a quietist or to quietism.—**Quietly**, kwī'et-li, *adv.* In a quiet state or manner; peaceably; calmly; patiently; in a manner to attract little or no observation.—**Quietness**, kwī'et-nes, *n.* The state of being quiet; tranquillity; calmness.— **Quietude**, kwī'e-tūd, *n.* [L. *quietudo*.] Rest; quiet; tranquillity. —**Quietus**, kwī-ē'tus, *n.* [L. *quietus*, quiet. *Quietus* or *quietus est* was a formula used in discharging accounts, equivalent to quit, discharged.] A final discharge of an account; a final settlement; a quittance.

Quill, kwil, *n.* [O.E. *quylle*, a cane or reed; from Fr. *quille*, a pin, a skittle, from G. *kiel*, a quill, a stalk, a pin, O.G. *kil*, a stalk.] One of the large, strong feathers of geese, swans, turkeys, crows, &c., used for pens, &c.; one of these made into an instrument of writing; the spine of a porcupine; a piece of small reed on which weavers wind the thread of the woof; a piece of quill attached to a slip of wood, by means of which certain stringed musical instruments were played; the fold of a plaited ruff or ruffle, about the size and shape of a goose-quill.—*v.t.* To plait with small ridges like quills.—**Quill-driver**, *n.* A contemptuous term for one who works with a quill or pen; a clerk.—**Quilled**, kwild, *a.* Furnished with quills. —**Quilling**, kwil'ing, *n.* A narrow bordering on a garment resembling a row of quills.

Quillet, kwil'et, *n.* [L. *quidlibet*, what you please.] A nicety or subtlety; a quibble.

Quilt, kwilt, *n.* [O.Fr. *cuilte, coutre, coultre*, from L. *culcitra, culcita*, a mattress, a pillow, a quilt. This word by corruption or confusion gave the *counter-* of *counterpane*.] A cover or coverlet made by stitching one cloth over another, with some soft substance between; any thick or warm coverlet.—*v.t.* To stitch together, as two pieces of cloth, with some soft substance between; to stuff in the manner of a quilt.—**Quilted**, kwilt'-ed, *p.* and *a.* Stitched in the manner of a quilt.—**Quilter**, kwilt'ėr, *n.* One who quilts.—**Quilting**, kwilt'ing, *n.* The act or operation of forming a quilt; the material used for making quilts; quilted work.

Quinary, kwī'na-ri, *a.* [L. *quinarius*, from *quini*, five each, from *quinque*, five.] Consisting of five or of a multiple of five; arranged by fives.—**Quinate**, kwī'nāt, *a.* *Bot.* applied to five similar parts arranged together, as five leaflets.

Quince, kwins, *n.* [From Fr. *coignasse*, a

kind of quince, from L. *cotonium, cydonium,* Gr. *kydōnion,* (*mēlon*), a quince, lit. Cydonian fruit, from *Cydonia,* a town in Crete.] A fruit and the tree that bears it, now widely cultivated, the fruit being golden yellow and much used in making preserves.—**Quince-wine**, *n.* A beverage made of the fermented juice of the quince.

Quincentenary, kwin-sen'tēn-a-ri, *n.* [L. *quinque, centum.*] The five-hundredth anniversary.

Quincunx, kwin'kungks, *n.* [L., from *quinque,* five, and *uncia,* ounce—a five-ounce weight being marked with five spots.] An arrangement of five objects in a square, one at each corner and one in the middle; an arrangement, as of trees, in such squares continuously.—**Quincuncial**, kwin-kun'shal, *a.* Having the form of a quincunx.—**Quincuncially**, kwin-kun'shal-li, *adv.* In a quincuncial manner.

Quindecagon, kwin-dek'a-gon, *n.* [L. *quinque,* five, Gr. *deka,* ten, and *gōnia,* angle.] *Geom.* a plane figure with fifteen sides and fifteen angles.

Quindecemvir, kwin-dē-sem'vėr, *n.* pl. **Quindecemviri**, kwin-dē-sem'vi-rī. [L., from *quinque,* five, *decem,* ten, and *vir,* man.] *Rom. antiq.* one of a body of fifteen magistrates who had charge of the Sibylline books.—**Quindecemvirate**, kwin-dē-sem'vėr-āt, *n.* The body or office of the Quindecemviri.

Quinine, kwin'īn, *n.* [Peruvian-Indian *kina, quina,* bark.] A most important vegetable alkali, obtained from the bark of several trees of the cinchona genus, extensively used in medicine as a febrifuge and tonic.—**Quininism**, kwin'īn-izm, *n.* CINCHONISM.—**Quinia, Quinina**, kwin'i-a, kwi-nī'na, *n.* Older names for *Quinine.*—**Quinic**, kwin'ik, *a.* Belonging to quinine: applied to a certain acid.—**Quinicine**, kwin'i-sīn, *n.* An alkaloid possessing febrifugal properties.—**Quinidine**, kwin'i-dīn, *n.* A substance in some cinchona barks, with acids forming salts having febrifugal properties.

Quinoa, kwi-nō'a, *n.* A South American cultivated plant the seeds of which are largely used as food.

Quinoline, kwin'ō-lēn, *n.* [From *quinine.*] A compound from which quinine is derived.

Quinquagesima, kwin-kwa-jes'i-ma, *n.* [L.] Fiftieth.—*Quinquagesima Sunday,* so called as being about the fiftieth day before Easter; Shrove Sunday.

Quinquangular, kwin-kwang'gū-lėr, *a.* [L. *quinque,* five, and *angulus,* angle.] Having five angles or corners.

Quinquarticular, kwin-kwär-tik'ū-lėr, *a.* [L. *quinque,* five, and *articulus,* joint, article.] Consisting of five articles, points, or statements.

Quinquecapsular, kwin-kwē-kap'sū-lėr, *a.* [L. *quinque,* five, and *capsula,* a little chest.] *Bot.* having five capsules.—**Quinquecostate**, kwin-kwē-kos'tāt, *a.* [L. *costa,* a rib.] *Bot.* five-ribbed.—**Quinquedentate**, kwin-kwē-den'tāt, *a.* [L. *dentatus,* toothed, from *dens, dentis,* a tooth.] *Zool.* or *bot.* having five teeth or indentations.—**Quinquefarious**, kwin-kwē-fā'ri-us, *a.* [From L. *quinque,* five.] *Bot.* opening into five parts.—**Quinquefid**, kwin'kwē-fid, *a.* [L. *findo, fidi,* to split.] *Bot.* five-cleft, as a leaf.—**Quinquefoliate**, kwin-kwē-fō'li-āt, *a.* [L. *folium,* leaf.] Having five leaves.—**Quinquelobate, Quinquelobed**, kwin-kwē-lō'bāt, kwin'kwē-lōbd, *a.* [L. *lobus,* lobe.] *Bot.* five-lobed.—**Quinquelocular**, kwin-kwē-lok'ū-lėr, *a.* [L. *loculus,* a cell.] *Bot.* five-celled.

Quinquennial, kwin-kwen'i-al, *a.* [L. *quinquennium,* a period of five years—*quinque,* five, and *annus,* year.] Occurring once in five years, or lasting five years.—**Quinquennium**, kwin-kwen'i-um, *n.* [L.] The space of five years. Also **Quinquenniad**,† kwin-kwen'i-ad. (*Tenn.*)

Quinquepartite, kwin-kwē-pär'tīt, *a.* [L. *quinque,* five, and *partitus,* divided.] Consisting of five parts; *bot.* divided into five parts almost to the base.

Quinquereme, kwin'kwē-rēm, *n.* [L. *quinqueremis,* from *quinque,* five, and *remus,* oar.] An ancient galley having five ranks of rowers.

Quinquevalent, Quinquivalent, kwin-kwev'a-lent, kwin-kwiv'a-lent, *a.* [L. *quinque,* five, and *valens, valentis,* ppr. of *valeo,* to be worth.] *Chem.* capable of being combined with or exchanged for five atoms of hydrogen.

Quinquevalvular, kwin-kwē-val'vū-lėr, *a.* [L. *quinque,* five, and *valva,* valve.] *Bot.* having five valves, as a pericarp.

Quinquina, kwin-kwī'na, *n.* [Sp. *quina quina,* from Indian *quina,* bark.] Peruvian bark.

Quinsy, kwin'zi, *n.* [From Fr. *esquinancie, squinancie,* from L. *cynanche,* Gr. *kynangchē,* a kind of sore throat, from *kyōn,* a dog, and *angchō,* to throttle—'dog' having a pejorative effect. CYNIC.] *Med.* an inflammation of the tonsils; any inflammation of the throat or parts adjacent.

Quint, kwint, *n.* [L. *quintus,* fifth.] A set or sequence of five, as in piquet.

Quintain, kwin'tān, *n.* [Fr. *quintaine,* L.L. *quintana,* a quintain, from L. *quintana,* a street or broad way in a camp (from *quintus,* fifth), hence a public place, and the exercise practised in such a place.] A figure or other object to be tilted at, often an upright post, on the top of which was a horizontal bar turning on a pivot, with a sand-bag attached to one end, on the other a broad board, it being a trial of skill to tilt at the broad end with a lance, and pass on before the bag of sand could whirl round and strike the tilter.

Quintal, kwin'tal, *n.* [Fr. *quintal,* from L. *centum,* a hundred, through the Sp. *quintal,* Ar. *kintār,* a weight of 100 lb.] A weight of 100 lb.

Quintan, kwin'tan, *a.* [L. *quintanus,* from *quintus,* fifth, from *quinque,* five.] Occurring or recurring every fifth day.—*n.* An intermittent fever the paroxysms of which recur every fifth day.

Quintessence, kwin-tes'ens, *n.* [L. *quinta, essentia,* fifth essence.] According to old notions the fifth or highest essence or most ethereal element of natural bodies; hence, an extract from anything, containing its virtues or most essential part in a small quantity; the best and purest part of a thing.—**Quintessential**, kwin-tes-sen'shal, *a.* Consisting of the quintessence.

Quintet, Quintette, kwin-tet', *n.* [Fr. *quintette,* from It. *quintetto,* from *quinto,* L. *quintus,* fifth.] *Music,* a vocal or instrumental composition in five parts.

Quintillion, kwin-til'yon, *n.* [L. *quintus,* fifth, and term. of E. *million.*] A number followed by eighteen zeros; a million raised to the fifth power.

Quintuple, kwin'tū-pl, *a.* [L. *quintuplus,* fivefold—*quintus,* fifth, and term. *-plus,* Gr. *ploos.* DOUBLE.] Fivefold; arranged in five or in fives; *music,* containing five notes of equal value in a bar.—*v.t.*—*quintupled, quintupling.* To make fivefold.

Quintuplet, kwin'tū-plet, *n.* A collection or mechanism for five of a kind; any one of five offspring born at the same birth.

Quip, kwip, *n.* [From W. *chwip,* a quick flirt or turn; *chwipiaw,* to move briskly, to whip (to *whip* round a corner).] A smart sarcastic turn; a sharp or cutting jest; a jibe.—*v.t.*—*quipped, quipping.* To utter quips on; to sneer at.—*v.i.* To use quips; to jibe.

Quipu-writing, kee'pö, kwi'pō, *n.* A Peruvian method of recording time by knotted threads of varying colours.

Quire, kwīr, *n.* [A different spelling of *choir.* CHOIR.] A body of singers; a chorus; the choir of a church.—*v.i.* To sing in concert or chorus; to chant or sing harmoniously. (*Shak.*).—**Quirister**,‡ kwir'is-tėr, *n.* A chorister.

Quire, kwīr, *n.* [O.Fr. *quayer;* Fr. *cahier,* from L.L. *quaternum,* a book of four leaves, from L. *quatuor,* four.] A collection of paper consisting of twenty-four sheets of equal size, and generally folded once.

Quirinal, kwir'i-nal, *n.* The Italian court, as opposed to the Papal court on the Vatican, at Rome.

Quirk, kwėrk, *n.* [Prov.E. *quirk,* to turn sharply; comp. W. *chwired,* a sudden start, craft, deceit.] An artful turn for evasion or subterfuge; a shift; a quibble; a quip: *arch,* an acute channel or recess; also, the hollow under the abacus.—**Quirked**, kwirkt, *a.* Having a quirk or quirks.—**Quirky, Quirkish**, kwėr'ki, kwėr'kish, *a.* Consisting of quirks; full of quirks; shifty; quibbling.

Quish, kwish, *n.* A cuish.

Quit, kwit, *a.* [From O.Fr. *quite,* Mod.Fr. *quitte,* discharged, freed, quit, from L. *quietus,* quiet. *Quiet* is thus the same word, as is also *quite.*] Discharged or released from a debt, penalty, or obligation; absolved; free; clear (with *of* before an object). It is often used in the form *quits,* as a kind of noun, to be *quits* with one, being to be on even terms, to have got even, with him, hence, as an exclamation, *quits!* equivalent to, we are even.—*v.t.*—*quitted, quitting.* [O.Fr. *quiter,* Fr. *quitter,* to leave, to abandon.] To discharge, as an obligation or duty; to meet and satisfy; to repay; to set free, absolve, acquit; to relieve; to rid; to discharge from; to meet expectations entertained of; to acquit: used *refl.* (to *quit one's self* like a man); to depart from; to leave; to resign; to give up; to abandon.—*To quit cost,* to pay expenses.—*To quit scores,* to make even.—**Quit claim**, *n.* The giving up of a claim; a deed or document resigning a claim in favor of another.—**Quit-rent**, *n.* A small rent once paid by freeholders and copyholders of a manor in discharge of other services.—**Quittance**, kwit'ans, *n.* Discharge from a debt or obligation; an acquittance; recompense; repayment.—**Quitter**, kwit'ėr, *n.* One who quits; one who withdraws under adverse circumstances.—**Quittor**, kwit'or, *n.* An ulcer between the hair and hoof of a horse's foot (for old *quitture,* a discharge of matter).—**Quittor-bone**, *n.* A hard round swelling on a horse's coronet.

Quitch, Quitch-grass, kwich, *n.* [A form of *quick-grass*—named from its vitality and vigorous growth.] A species of worthless grass; couch-grass.

Quite, kwīt, *adv.* [Old form of *quit,* that is, primarily, free or clear by complete performance. QUIT.] Completely; wholly; entirely; totally; altogether; to a great extent or degree; very (*quite* warm).

Quiver, kwiv'ėr, *v.i.* [Same as D. *quiveren,* to tremble, closely connected with *quaver,* and with old *quiver,* active, nimble, A.Sax. *cwifer,* perhaps also with *quick.*] To shake or tremble; to quake; to shiver; to show a slight tremulous motion; to be agitated.—*n.* The act or state of quivering; a tremulous motion; a shiver.—**Quiveringly**, kwiv'ėr-ing-li, *adv.* In a quivering manner; with quivering.

Quiver, kwiv'ėr, *n.* [O.Fr. *quivre, cuivre,* from O.H.G. *kohhar, kochar,* G. *köcher,* a quiver; cog. Dan. *koger,* D. *koker,* A.Sax. *cocer*—a case, a quiver.] A case or sheath for arrows.—**Quivered**, kwiv'ėrd, *a.* Furnished with a quiver; sheathed in a quiver.

Qui vive, kē vēv, *n.* [Fr., lit. who lives?] The challenge of the French sentries; equivalent to the English, 'Who goes there?' Hence, *to be on the qui vive,* is to be on the alert.

Quixotic, kwik-sot'ik, *a.* [From Don *Quixote,* the hero of Cervantes' celebrated romance, who is painted as a half-crazy reformer and champion, and is a caricature of the ancient knights of chivalry.] Romantic to extravagance; aiming at visionary ends; ideal; high-flown.—**Quixotically**, kwik-sot'i-kal-li, *adv.* In a quixotic or absurdly romantic manner.—**Quixotism, Quixotry**, kwik'sot-izm, kwik'sot-ri, *n.* Romantic and absurd notions.

Quiz, kwiz, *n.* [Said to have been originated simply to puzzle people, by Daly, the manager of a Dublin play-house, who had the letters *q u i z* put on all the walls of Dublin.] Something designed to puzzle; a hoax; a jest; one who quizzes; one liable to be quizzed; a brief, informal examination, as of a class.—*v.t.*—*quizzed, quizzing*. To puzzle; to banter; to make sport of by means of obscure questions; to look at through an eye-glass; to look at inquisitively; to question intensively with a view to obtaining information unwillingly revealed; curious, odd; mocking or teasing, as a *quizzical* remark.—**Quizzical**, kwiz'i-kal, *a.* Partaking of the nature of a quiz; addicted to quizzing.

Quod, kwod, *n.* [A form of *quad*, a contr. of *quadrangle*.] A jail. (*Slang.*)

Quodlibet, kwod'li-bet, *n.* [L., what you please.] A nice point; a subtlety.—**Quodlibetic**, **Quodlibetical**, kwod-li-bet'ik, kwod-li-bet'i-kal, *a.* Pertaining to quodlibets; discussed or debated for curiosity or entertainment.

Quoin, koin, *n.* [A slightly different spelling of *coin*; Fr. *coin*, a corner, a wedge, a quoin, a coin. COIN.] An external solid angle; the external angle of a building; a wedge-like piece of stone, wood, metal, or other material; *printing*, a wedge to wedge the types up within a chase; *gun.*, a wedge to raise a cannon to the desired elevation.

Quoit, koit, *n.* [Origin doubtful; comp. Prov.E. and Sc. *coit, quoit*, to throw; also O.D. *koot*, a die.] A flattish ring of iron, 8 or 9 inches in diameter and of some weight, convex on the upper side and slightly concave on the under side, to be thrown at a fixed mark on the ground at play; *pl.* the game played with such rings. —*v.t.* and *i.* To throw quoits; to play at quoits.

Quondam, kwon'dam, *a.* [L., formerly.] Having been formerly; former (one's *quondam* friend).

Quorum, kwō'rum, *n.* [Lit. 'of whom', being the genit. pl. of L. *qui*, who—from the phraseology of commissions, &c., written in Latin, certain persons being therein named generally, 'of whom' certain were specially designated as in all cases necessary and therefore constituted a quorum.] A selected group; an absolute majority unless specified to the contrary; such a number of the members of any body (a board of directors for instance) as is competent to transact business.

Quota, kwō'ta, *n.* [From L. *quotus*, which number in the series? QUOTE.] A proportional part or share; share or proportion assigned to each or which each of a number has to contribute.

Quote, kwōt, *v.t.*—*quoted, quoting*. [O.Fr. *quoter*, Fr. *coter*, from L.L. *quotare*, to give chapter and verse for, from L. *quotus*, which number in the series? from *quot*, how many?] To adduce from some author or speaker; to adduce by way of authority or illustration; to cite or cite the words of (to *quote* a passage, an author); *com.* to name, as the price of an article.—**Quoter**, kwō'tėr, *n.* One that quotes.—**Quotable**, kwō'ta-bl, *a.* Capable of or suitable for being quoted or cited.—**Quotability**, kwō-ta-bil'i-ti, *n.* Fitness for being quoted. —**Quotation**, kwō-tā'shon, *n.* The act of quoting; the passage quoted or cited; *com.* the current price of commodities or stocks published in prices-current, &c.

Quoth, kwoth, *v.t.* [A.Sax. *quœth*, pret. of *cwethan*, to speak, to say (whence with prefix *be*, the verb *bequeath*) = Icel. *kvetha* (pret. *kvath*), O.H.G. *quethan*, Goth. *quithan*, to speak.] Said; spoke: used generally in the first and third persons preterit tense, and followed instead of preceded by its nominative.—**Quotha**, kwoth'a, *interj.* [For *quoth I* or *quoth he*.] Forsooth! indeed!

Quotidian, kwō-tid'i-an, *a.* [L. *quotidianus*, from *quotidie*, daily—*quot*, how many? every, and *dies*, a day.] Daily; occurring or returning daily.—*n.* Anything that returns every day; a fever whose paroxysms return every day.

Quotient, kwō'shent, *n.* [Fr., from L. *quoties*, how often? QUOTE.] *Arith.* the number resulting from the division of one number by another, and showing how often a less number is contained in a greater.

Quotum,† kwō'tum, *n.* [Neut. of L. *quotus*, how much?] A quota; a share.

R

R, the eighteenth letter of the English alphabet.—*The three Rs*, a humorous and familiar designation for *Reading, (W)riting*, and *(A)rithmetic*.

Rabbet, rab'et, *v.t.* [From Fr. *raboter*, to plane—prefix *re*, again, and *abouter* = E. *abut*.] To cut the edge of (as of a board) in a sloping manner, so that it may join by lapping with another piece cut in a similar manner; also, to cut a rectangular groove along the edge of to receive a corresponding projection.—*n.* The cut or groove so made. Sometimes written REBATE.—**Rabbet-joint**, *n.* A joint formed by rabbetting.—**Rabbet-plane**, *n.* A plane for ploughing a groove along the edge of a board.

Rabbi, rab'bī, *n.* pl. **Rabbis, Rabbies**, rab'bīz. [Heb. *rabi*, my master, from *rab*, master.] A title of respect given to Jewish doctors or expounders of the law.—**Rabbin**, rab'bin, *n.* [A French form.] Same as *Rabbi*.—**Rabbinic, Rabbinical**, rab-bin'ik, rab-bin'i-kal, *a.* Pertaining to the rabbins, or to their opinions, learning, and language; pertaining to the later and non-canonical Hebrew writings.—**Rabbinic**, rab-bin'ik, *n.* The language or dialect of the rabbins; the later Hebrew.—**Rabbinism**, rab'bin-izm, *n.* A rabbinic expression or phraseology.—**Rabbinist, Rabbinite**, rab'bin-ist, rab'bin-īt, *n.* Among the Jews, one who adhered to the Talmud and the traditions of the rabbins.

Rabbit, rab'it, *n.* [O.E. *robbet*, akin to O.D. *robbe, robbeken*, a rabbit; connections doubtful.] A well-known rodent mammal which feeds on grass or other herbage, and burrows in the earth.—*Welsh rabbit*, a dish, variously made, of melted or toasted cheese, often mixed with milk, ale or beer, poured over buttered toast or crackers; sometimes called *Welsh rarebit*.—**Rabbit-fish**, *n.* The fish also called chimæra. CHIMÆRA.—**Rabbit-hutch**, *n.* A box for keeping tame rabbits in.—**Rabbit-warren**, *n.* A piece of ground fenced in for the preservation and breeding of rabbits.

Rabble, rab'l, *n.* [Comp. D. *rabbelen*, to gabble; G. *rabbeln, robbeln*, to chatter; perhaps imitative of noise.] A tumultuous crowd of vulgar, noisy people; a mob; with *the*; the lower class of people; the dregs of the people.—*v.t.*—*rabbled, rabbling*. To assault in a disorderly crowd; to mob.

Rabdoidal, Rabdomancy, rab-doi'dal, rab'dō-man-si. Same as *Rhabdoidal, Rhabdomancy*.

Rabelaisian, rab'el-ās-i-an, *a.* [Fr. *Rabelais*.] In the broad, indelicate style of the French author Francis Rabelais.

Rabid, rab'id, *a.* [L. *rabidus*, from *rabies*, madness, from *rabo*, to rave. RAGE.] Furious; raging; mad; affected with the distemper called *rabies*; excessively or foolishly enthusiastic; rampant; intolerant (a *rabid* Tory, a *rabid* teetotaller).—**Rabidity**, ra-bid'i-ti, *n.* The state of being rabid. —**Rabidly**, rab'id-li, *adv.* In a rabid manner; furiously.—**Rabidness**, rab'idnes, *n.* The state of being rabid.—**Rabies**, rā'bi-ēz, *n.* [L.] Hydrophobia; an infectious disease of small animals, particularly dogs, believed to be caused by a virus transmitted to man by the bite of infected animals, and invariably proving fatal unless the Pasteur treatment is instituted early in the incubation period.

Raccahout, rak'ka-höt, *n.* [Fr. *racahout*, from Ar. *rāqaut*.] A starch or meal prepared from the edible acorn of the Barbary oak.

Raccoon, ra-kön', *n.* [Corruption of the American Indian name, *arrathkune, arathcone*, formerly in use.] An American plantigrade carnivorous mammal about the size of a small fox, whose skin is valuable as a fur.

Race, rās, *n.* [Fr. *race*, It. *razza*, race, lineage, family; from O.H.G. *reiza*, a line; same root as *write* (comp. Fr. *ligne*, E. *line*, lineage as well as a line).] A class of individuals sprung from a common stock; a family, tribe, people, or nation believed or presumed to belong to the same stock; a breed or stock; a perpetuated variety of animals or plants.

Race, rās, *n.* [O.Fr. *raïs*, from L. *radix, radicis*, a root.] A root, as a *race* of ginger (*Shak.*); *race-ginger*, ginger in the root.

Race, rās, *n.* [A.Sax. *raes*, a rush; a rapid course, a stream; same as Icel. *rás*, a race.] A rapid course; career in life; a contest of speed, especially in running, but also in riding, driving, sailing, rowing, &c., in competition: *pl.* horse races (to go to the Santa Anita *races*); a strong or rapid current of water; a powerful current or heavy sea sometimes produced by the meeting of two tides; a canal or watercourse to and from a mill or water wheel; a strong tidal rush of water, as in the Bay of Fundy; the air stream delivered by the propeller of an air-machine.—*v.i.*—*raced, racing*. To run swiftly; to run or contend in running. —*v.t.* To cause to run; to cause to contend in running; to drive quickly in a trial of speed.—**Race horse**, *n.* A horse bred or kept for racing; a horse that runs in competition.—**Race track**, *n.* The place where races of horses, dogs, automobiles, &c., are held.—**Racer**, rā'sėr, *n.* One who races; a race horse.

Raceme, ras'ēm, *n.* [L. *racemus*, a cluster of grapes.] *Bot.* a species of inflorescence, in which a number of flowers with short and equal pedicels stand on a common slender axis, as in the currant.—**Racemed**, ras'ēmd, *a.* Having a raceme.—**Racemiferous**, ras-ē-mif'ėr-us, *a.* Bearing racemes.—**Racemose, Racemous**, ras'ē-mos, ras'ē-mus, *a.* [L. *racemosus*.] *Bot.* resembling a raceme; in the form of a raceme; bearing flowers in racemes.—**Racemule**, ras'ē-mūl, *n.* *Bot.* a small raceme. —**Racemulose**, ra-sem'ū-lōs, *a.* *Bot.* bearing racemules.

Rachis, rā'kis, *n.* [Gr. *rachis*, the spine.] The vertebral column of mammals and birds; something similar to this, as the shaft of a feather, the stalk of the frond in ferns, the common stalk bearing the alternate spikelets in some grasses.—**Rachidian**, ra-kid'i-an, *a.* Pertaining to a rachis; spinal; vertebral.—**Rachitic**, ra-kit'ik, *a.* Pertaining to rachitis; rickety.—**Rachitis**, ra-kī'tis, *n.* [Gr. *rachis*, and term. *-itis*, signifying inflammation.] Formerly inflammation of the spine, now applied to *rickets*; a disease characterized by softening and malformation of the bones.

Racial. Under RACE (family).

Racily, Raciness. Under RACY.

Rack, rak, *v.t.* [Closely allied to *reach*, Sc. *rax*, to reach; D. *rekken*, Dan. *række*, to stretch; G. *recken*, *racken*, to stretch, to torture, *reck-bank*, a rack. See also noun.] To stretch unduly; to strain vehemently (as in 'to *rack* one's brains', to strain or exercise his thoughts to the utmost); to twist; to wrest; to distort; to put a false meaning on; to punish on the rack; to heighten; to exaggerate (*Shak.*); to place on or in a rack or frame (to *rack* bottles).—*n.* [Comp. D. *rak*, *schotelrak*, a cupboard for dishes; G. *rack*, a rail, *recke*, a trestle, a frame, a rack for supporting things.] An appliance for straining or stretching; an instrument for the judicial torture of criminals and suspected persons, consisting of a framework on which the victim's limbs were strained by cords and levers; hence, torture; extreme pain; anguish; an open wooden framework above a manger to hold hay, grass, straw, &c., as fodder for horses and cattle; a framework on or in which articles are deposited; *mach.* a straight or very slightly curved bar, with teeth on one of its edges, adapted to work into the teeth of a wheel or pinion.

Rack, rak, *n.* [A.Sax. *hracca*, O.E. and Sc. *crag*, the neck.] The neck of a carcass of veal or mutton.

Rack, rak, *n.* [Icel. *rek*, *sky-rek*, drift, cloud motion; *reka*, to drive.] Thin flying broken clouds, or any portion of floating vapor in the sky.—*v.i.* To fly, as vapor or clouds.

Rack, rak, *v.t.* [From Fr. *raque*, mud, dregs.] To draw off from the lees; to draw off, as pure liquor from its sediments (to *rack* cider or wine).

Rack, rak, *n.* [Form of *wreck*.] Wreck; ruin; destruction: in the phrase *to go to rack and ruin*.

Racket, rak'et, *n.* [Probably onomatopoetic; comp. Gael. *racaid*, noise.] A confused, clattering noise; noisy talk; clamor; din.—*v.i.* To make a racket; to frolic.—*n.* Any of a number of methods, generally unlawful, for the purpose of extorting money or gaining advantages or control of businesses by violence or threats of physical violence.—**Racketeer**, rak-a-tēr', *n.* One who, alone or in company with others, under threats of violence extorts money or business advantages or otherwise controls business enterprises, frequently alleging to grant protection to a victim who subscribes or consents to the racketeer's demands.—**Rackety**, rak'et-i, *a.* Making a racket or tumultuous noise.

Racket, rak'et, *n.* [Fr. *raquette*, a racket; O.Fr. *rachete*, *rasquete*, the palm of the hand, from L.L. *racha*, the wrist, from an Arabic word.] The bat with which players at tennis or rackets strike the ball; *pl.* a modern variety of the old game of tennis.—*v.t.* To strike as with a racket; to toss.

Raconteur, ra-koṅ-tūr, *n.* [Fr.] Teller of a good story; conversationalist.

Racoon, ra-kön'. RACCOON.

Racquet, rak'et. RACKET.

Racy, rā'si, *a.* [Probably from *race*, lineage, lit. partaking strongly of its race; but comp. O.H.G. *rāzer*, racy, *rāzer win*, racy wine; Swiss *räss*, sharp, astringent.] Strong and flavorous (*racy* wine); having a strong distinctive character of thought or language; spirited; pungent; piquant (a *racy* style, a *racy* anecdote).—**Racily**, rā'si-li, *adv.* In a racy manner.—**Raciness**, rā'si-nes, *n.* The quality of being racy; peculiar and piquant flavor.

Raddle, rad'l, *v.t.*—*raddled*, *raddling*. [Perhaps a corruption from *hurdle* or *riddle*.] To interweave; to twist or wind together.—*n.* A hedge formed by interweaving the shoots and branches of trees or shrubs; *weaving*, a wooden bar with a row of upright pegs to keep the warp in trim.

Raddle, rad'l, *n.* [REDDLE.] A red pigment, chiefly used for marking sheep; reddle or ruddle.—*v.t.*—*raddled*, *raddling*. To paint, as with ruddle.

Radeau, rä'dō, *n.* [Fr., from L. *ratis*, a raft.] Beams bound together as a float; a raft for transporting goods or men.

Radial, rā'di-al, *a.* [From L. *radius*, a ray, a spoke. RADIUS, RAY.] Grouped or appearing like radii or rays; shooting out as from a center; pertaining to the radius, one of the bones of the human forearm (the *radial* artery or nerve).—**Radially**, rā'di-al-li, *adv.*—**Radiance, Radiancy**, rā'di-ans, rā'di-an-si, *n.* [From *radiant*.] Brightness shooting in rays or beams; hence in general, brilliant or sparkling luster.—**Radiant**, rā'di-ant, *a.* [L. *radians*, *radiantis*, ppr. of *radio*, to beam or shoot rays, from *radius*, a ray.] Radiating; giving out rays; darting, shooting, or emitting rays of light or heat; shining; beaming with brightness; emitting a vivid light or splendor.—**Radiantly**, rā'di-ant-li, *adv.*—**Radiate**, rā'di-āt,' *v.i.*—*radiated*, *radiating*. [L. *radio*, *radiatum*.] To issue and proceed in rays or straight lines from a point or surface, as heat or light; to beam forth; to emit rays.—*v.t.* To emit or send out in direct lines from a point or surface (a body *radiates* heat); to enlighten; to illuminate†.—*a.* Having rays; having lines proceeding as from a center like radii.—**Radiation**, rā-di-ā'shon, *n.* [L. *radiatio*, *radiationis*.] The act of radiating or state of being radiated; the divergence or shooting forth of anything from a point or surface, like the diverging rays of light (the *radiation* of heat, of sound, &c.).—**Radiator**, rā'di-ā-tėr, *n.* That which radiates; an appliance for heating a room by means of hot water, steam, gas, or electricity; in automobiles, the mechanism for cooling circulating water.

Radical, rad'i-kal, *a.* [Fr. *radical*, L. *radicalis*, from *radix*, *radicis*, a root (whence *radish*, *eradicate*); from root *vrad*, seen in E. *wort*; also in L. *radius*, a ray, *ramus*, a branch.] Pertaining to the root or origin; original; reaching to the principles; fundamental; thorough-going; extreme (a *radical* error, a *radical* cure or reform); implanted by nature; innate; native; *philol.* belonging to or proceeding directly from a root; (the *radical* signification of a word).—**Radicalism**, rad'i-kal-izm, *n.* The doctrine or principle of the radicals or advanced liberals.—**Radically**, rad'i-kal-li, *adv.* In a radical manner; in root or origin; fundamentally.—**Radicarian**, rad-i-kā'ri-an, *a.* *Philol.* pertaining to roots, or to the theory that roots are the basis of language.—**Radicate**, rad'i-kāt, *v.t.*—*radicated*, *radicating*. [L. *radicor*, *radicatus*.] To cause to take root; to plant deeply.—**Radicate, Radicated**, rad'i-kā-ted, *p.* and *a.* Deeply rooted; *bot.* rooted, or having taken root.—**Radication**, rad-i-kā'shon, *n.* The process of taking root deeply; *bot.* the disposition or character of the root of a plant.—**Radiciform**, ra-dis'i-form, *a.* *Bot.* being of the nature of a root.—**Radicle**, rad'i-kl, *n.* [L. *radicula*, dim. of *radix*, a root.] *Bot.* that part of the embryo or seed of a plant which, on vegetating, becomes the root; the fibrous parts of a root; *chem.* same as RADICAL.—**Radicose**, rad'i-kōs, *a.* *Bot.* having a large root.

Radio, rā'di-ō, *n.* pl. **Radios**, (rā'di-ōz) [L. *radius*, a ray.] The transmission or reception of electromagnetic waves without conducting wires intervening between transmitter and receiver.—*Compass radio*, *n.* A radio-telegraphic direction-finder for locating a transmitting station.—**Radioactive**, *a.* Emitting Becquerel rays; exhibiting the properties possessed by radium.—**Radio announcer**, *n.* One who broadcasts commercial advertising announcements and introduces and signs off radio programs.—**Radio antenna**, an-ten'a, *n.* pl. **Antennae**, an-ten'ē. An aerial; a system of wires completely insulated from earth, used in the radiation or reception of electromagnetic waves through space.—**Radio audition**, *n.* A trial to determine suitableness of a performance for radio broadcasting.—**Radiobroadcast**, *n.* The transmission of messages, music, speeches &c., by radio.—*v.t.*—**Radiochemistry**, *n.* That branch of chemistry which deals with radioactive bodies and radioactivity.—**Radio-conductor**, *n.* Any medium through which radio waves pass freely.—**Radio variable condenser**, *n.* A device in which two sets of aligned plates, separated from each other by air, are meshed together, thus varying their capacity, and used in the tuning of a circuit, consisting of capacity and inductance, to resonance at any desired frequency.—**Radioecholog**, rā'di-ō-ek"ō-log, *n.* An instrument for measuring the height of aircraft above the ground by recording the time required for a radio signal to reach the ground and reflect to a receiving device on the aircraft.—**Radio frequency**, *n.* A frequency higher than that corresponding to the normally audible vibrations and transmittible by electromagnetic waves.—**Radiogram**, *n.* A radio-telegraphic message.—**Radiograph**, rā'di-ō-graf, *n.* A picture obtained by means of radiography.—**Radiography**, rā-di-og'ra-fi, *n.* The process of producing X-ray pictures by the action of Roentgen rays upon photographic plates.—**Radiology**, rā-di-ol'ō-ji, *n.* The science of diagnostic medicine by means of radiographs.—**Radiometer**, rā-di-om'et-ėr, *n.* An instrument revolving in a vacuum, which, under the influence of light, demonstrates the energy of solar rays.—**Radiophone**, *n.* Radiotelephony.—**Radioscopy**, rā'di-os"kō-pi, *n.* A study of an object impervious to light, such as an Egyptian mummy, with the aid of X rays.—**Radiotelegram**, *n.* A radiotelegraphic message.—**Radio station**, *n.* A transmitting station from which radio waves emanate; in a broader sense, the broadcasting company, its entire personnel, and equipment.—**Radio studio**, *n.* A soundproof room where programs for broadcasting by radio originate.—**Radiotelegraphy**, rā'di-ō-te-leg"ra-fi, *n.* Wireless telegraphy; the art of sending coded electromagnetic waves through the air.—*Duplex radiotelegraphy*, *n.* A simultaneous sending and receiving without mutual interference.—**Radiotelephony**, rā'-di-ō-tel-lef"o-ni, *n.* Wireless telephony; telephoning through the air without wires.—**Radio television**, *n.* Vision of persons or objects at a distance projected and received by means of electromagnetic waves.—**Radiotherapy**, rā'di-ō-ther"a-pi, *n.* Treatment of diseases by radioactivity, as by the X ray, or by a radioactive element such as radium or thorium.—**Radiothorium**, rā'di-ō-thōr"i-um, *n.* A radioactive element.—**Radio tube**, *n.* An electronic valve generally consisting of an evacuated glass or metal shell, inclosing an electron-generating device, such as a heated filament, from which electrons are propelled by electrical attraction to an anode, or plate. In the valve type of tube a mesh of fine wires is placed in the electronic stream and by suitable charging with a control current, regulates the magnitude of the electrical current flowing between the filament and plate. The tube is used in radio receivers for the amplification and rectification of electromagnetic waves.—**Radio waves**, *n.* Electromagnetic waves generated and projected through space by a radio transmitter.—*Wave length*, *n.* The distance from crest to crest of the projected electromagnetic wave.—*Wave-train frequency*, *n.* The number of electromagnetic waves generated per second.

Radish, rad'ish, *n.* [Fr. *radis*, from L. *radix*, a root. RADICAL.] The name of cruciferous plants with lyre-shaped leaves, the young roots of which are eaten.—*Horse-radish*. Under HORSE.

Radium, rā'di-um, *n.* [RADIUS.] An intensely radioactive element extracted from pitchblende, and used medically in the treatment of tumors and cancer.

Radius, rā'di-us, *n.* pl. **Radii, Radiuses**, rā'di-ī, rā'di-us-ez. [L., a ray, a rod, a beam, a spoke. RADICAL, RAY.] *Geom.* a straight line extending from the center of a circle to its circumference.

moment of inertia with respect to the axis would remain unchanged. I = Mk^2, when I is the amount of inertia, M the mass, and *k* the radius of gyration. — *Radius vector*, pl. *radii vectores* (vek-tō'rēz). *Astron.* an imaginary straight line joining the centre of a planet or satellite to the sun or primary; *geom.* a straight line connecting any point with a fixed point round which it revolves.—*Radius bars, radius rods*, the guide-bars of the parallel motion of a steam-engine.

Radix, rā'diks, *n.* [L., a root.] A root (of a plant, of a word); *math.* any number which is arbitrarily made the fundamental number or base of any system, as 10 in decimals.

Radula, rad'ū-la, pl. -æ, *n.* [L. for a scraper.] In molluscs, a horny tooth-studded ribbon on the floor of the ODONTOPHORE (which see).

Raduliform, ra-dū'li-form, *n.* [L. *radula*, a scraper (from *rado*, to scrape), and *forma*, shape.] Rasp-shaped; specifically, said of the teeth of certain fishes.

Raff, raf, *n.* [O.E. *raff*, to sweep; Fr. *raffer*, from G. *raffen*, to sweep, to snatch; akin *raffle*.] Sweepings; refuse; a person of worthless character; the scum of society; the rabble: used chiefly in the reduplicated form *riff-raff*.—**Raffish**, raf'ish, *a.* Villainous; scampish; worthless.

Raffia, raf'i-a, *n.* [Name in Madagascar.] A fibrous substance obtained from a palm of Madagascar, and another of South America, used for agricultural tie-bands.

Raffle, raf'l, *n.* [Fr. *rafle*, O.Fr. *raffle*, a kind of game at dice, from G. *raffen*, *raffeln*, to sweep or snatch. RAFF.] A lottery in which several persons deposit a part of the value of something, the winner being determined by chance (as by the drawing of a lucky number)—*v.t.*—*raffled*, *raffling*. To engage in a raffle.—*v.t.* To dispose of by means of a raffle.

Rafflesia, raf-lē'si-a, *n.* [After Sir Stamford *Raffles*, the discoverer of the first known species.] A genus of parasitical plants, natives of Sumatra and Java, one of which is remarkable for its gigantic flower, about 3 feet in diameter.

Raft, räft, *n.* [Properly a float made of beams or rafters; Icel. *raptr* (pron. *raftr*), Dan. *raft*, a rafter. RAFTER.] A float of logs, planks, or other pieces of timber fastened together, for the convenience of transporting them by water; a floating structure used in shipwrecks, often formed of barrels, planks, spars, &c.; a floating mass of trees, branches, &c.—*v.t.* To transport on a raft.—**Raftsman**, räfts'man, *n.* A man who manages a raft.

Rafter, räf'tėr, *n.* [A.Sax. *ræfter* = Icel. *raptr* (pron. *raftr*), Dan. *raft*, a rafter, a beam.] One of the sloping timbers of a roof, which support the outer covering.—*v.t.* To furnish with rafters.

Rag, rag, *v.t.*—*ragged* (ragd), *ragging*. [Origin doubtful.] To torment, tease, or subject to annoyance, often petty or ludicrous.

Rag, rag, *n.* [Originally a tuft of rough hair; comp. Sw. and Dan. dial. *ragg*, rough hair; Icel. *rögg*, shagginess, a tuft; allied to *rug*.] Any piece of cloth torn from the rest; a tattered cloth, torn or worn; a fragment of dress; a shred; a tatter; *pl.* tattered garments or mean dress; a term for rock deposits consisting of hard irregular masses (coral-*rag*, Kentish-*rag*, &c.); ragstone. — **Ragamuffin**, rag-a-muf'in, *n.* [*Ragamofin* was the name of a demon in some old mystery-plays, perhaps from *rag*, and old *mof*, *muff*, a long sleeve, or from *rag*, and D. *muf*, musty.] A poorly-dressed youngster.—**Rag-bolt**, *n.* An iron pin with barbs on its shank to retain it in its place.—**Rag-carpet**, *n.* A carpet with a cotton or hempen warp and a weft of strips of rags or cloth.—**Ragged**, rag'ed, *a.* Rent or worn into rags or tatters; tattered; having broken or rough edges; jagged; rough with sharp or irregular points; wearing tattered clothes; shabby.—*On the ragged edge*, on the verge of misfortune, failure, or collapse.—**Raggedly**, rag'ed-li, *adv.* In a ragged condition.—**Raggedness**, rag'ed-nes, *n.* The state of being ragged.—**Ragman**, rag'man, *n.* A man who collects or deals in rags.—**Rag-picker**, *n.* A collector of rags, bones, &c., from streets, ash-pits, &c.; one who makes a living by scavenging.—**Ragstone**, *n.* A stone of the siliceous kind, so named from its rough fracture.—**Ragweed**, rag'wēd, *n.* A coarse, annual weed of the composite family, with some 15 species in North America, its pollen being extremely irritating to hay fever sufferers who are allergic to it.—**Rag-wheel**, *n.* A wheel having a notched or serrated margin.

Rage, rāj, *n.* [Fr. *rage*, from L. *rabies*, rage, madness (by a change similar to that seen in *abridge*); from *rabo*, to rave, to be mad; cog. Skr. *rabh*, to desire eagerly. RABID.] Violent anger accompanied with furious words, gestures, or agitation; anger excited to fury; vehemence or violent exacerbation (the *rage* of a fever, of hunger or thirst); fury; extreme violence (the *rage* of a tempest); violent desire.—*The rage*, the object of popular and eager desire; the fashion. (*Colloq.*) ∴ Syn. under ANGER. —*v.i.*—*raged*, *raging*. To be furious with anger; to be exasperated to fury; to be in a passion; to act or move furiously, or with mischievous impetuosity (the sea *rages*); to ravage; to prevail with fatal effect (the plague *rages*).—**Rageful**, rāj'fụl, *a.* Full of rage; violent; furious.—**Ragingly**, rā'jing-li, *adv.* In a raging manner; with fury.

Ragee, Raggee, rag'ē, *n.* [Indian word.] A grain plant of India and elsewhere.

Raglan, rag'lan, *n.* A type of coat or overcoat with sleeves (*raglan* sleeves) whose seams extend to the neckline, giving a slanting line to the shoulders.

Ragout, ra-gö', *n.* [Fr. *ragoût*, from L. *re*, again, *ad*, to, and *gustus*, a tasting.] A dish of stewed and highly seasoned meat.

Ragtime, rag'tīm, *n.* Syncopated music with a regularly accented accompaniment, being the earliest form of jazz and probably having its origin in Negro melodies.

Raid, rād, *n.* [From stem of *ride*; same as Icel. *reith*, a riding, a raid; akin to *road*.] A hostile inroad or incursion, especially one made suddenly by mounted men; a foray; an attack by violence; an unannounced entry or sudden attack by officers of the law in order to make seizures and arrests, &c.—*v.t.* To make a raid.—*v.i.* To take part in a raid.—**Raider**, rād'ėr, *n.*

Rail, rāl, *n.* [Same as L.G. and Sw. *regel*, G. *riegel*, a bar, a rail; akin G. *reihe*, a row.] A bar of wood or metal extending from one upright post to another, as in fences; a horizontal timber in any piece of framing or panelling; the upper pieces into which the balusters of a stair are mortised; a series of posts or balusters connected by cross-beams, bars, or rods, for inclosure; a railing; one of the parallel iron or steel bars forming a smooth track for the wheels of a locomotive and the cars which it draws, or for a streetcar, elevated, subway, &c.; a railroad (to travel or send goods by *rail*).—*v.t.* To inclose with rails; to send by rail, as goods, &c. —*v.i.* To ride or travel on a railroad.—**Railer**, rā'lėr, *n.* One who makes or furnishes with rails.—**Rail-fence**, *n.* A fence made of wooden rails.—**Railhead**, *n.* The most advanced point of a railroad under construction; the point at which goods are transferred from a railroad to some other means of transport.—**Railing**, rā'ling, *n.* A fence or barrier of wood or iron, constructed of posts and rails; rails in general, or the materials for rails.—**Railroad**, rāl'rōd, *n.* A permanent roadway consisting of one or more pairs of rails laid parallel to each other and several feet apart, making a track over which locomotives, freight or passenger cars, &c., may run; in an extended sense, the road and all the land, works, buildings, machinery, franchises, and other assets required for the support and use of the road. —*Railroad train*, locomotive and cars running on railroad tracks.—*v.t.* To transport or ship by railroad; to rush through forcefully and without careful consideration, especially a bill through a legislature (*colloq.*); to send a person to prison on a false charge (*slang*).—**Railroading**, rāl'rōd-ing, *n.* Construction or operation of railroads; employment on a railroad.—**Railway**, rāl'wā, *n.* A railroad (*British*); sometimes, a railroad built to carry light traffic; a small track in a store or factory.

Rail, rāl, *n.* [O.Fr. *rasle*, *raale*, a rail; same origin as *rattle*, being so called from its noisy cry.] The popular name of several grallatorial birds, inhabiting sedgy places, moist herbage, &c., and comprising the land-rail or corn-crake and the water-rail.

Rail, rāl, *v.i.* [Fr. *railler*, to banter; from L.L. *radiculare*, from L. *radere*, to scrape. RASE, RAZOR.] To utter reproaches; to use insolent and reproachful language; to scold.—**Railer**, rā'lėr, *n.* One who rails. —**Railing**, rā'ling, *a.* Expressing reproach; insulting.—**Railingly**, rā'ling-li, *adv.* In a railing manner. —**Raillery**, rā'lėr-i, *n.* [Fr. *raillerie*.] Good-humoured pleasantry or slight satire; satirical merriment; jesting language; banter.—**Railleur**, rä-yėr, *n.* [Fr.] One who turns what is serious into ridicule; a banterer; a mocker.

Raiment, rā'ment, *n.* [Contracted from obsolete *arrayment*. ARRAY.] Clothing in general; vestments; vesture; garments: now always in the *sing*.

Rain, rān, *n.* [A.Sax. *regn*, *rén* = Icel., Dan., and Sw. *regn*, D. and G. *regen*, Goth. *rign*; same root as L. *rigare*, to wet, whence *irrigate*. As to the disappearance of *g* compare *hail* and *flail*.] The descent of water in drops from the clouds; the water thus falling; the moisture of the atmosphere condensed and deposited in drops; a shower or pouring down of anything.—*v.i.* To fall in drops from the clouds, as water: used mostly with *it* for a nominative (*it rains*, *it* will *rain*); to fall or drop like rain (tears *rained* from their eyes).—*v.t.* To pour or shower down, like rain from the clouds; to pour or send down abundantly.—**Rain-band**, *n.* A dark line or band of atmospheric origin in the solar spectrum, caused by aqueous vapour, and of some importance as a weather predictor. —**Rainbow**, rān'bō, *n.* A bow or arc of a circle, consisting of all the prismatic colours, formed by the refraction and reflection of rays of light from drops of rain, appearing in the part of the heavens opposite to the sun. A *lunar rainbow*, or one produced by the moon's rays, fainter than that formed by the sun, is sometimes seen. —**Rain-cloud**, *n.* A ragged and hanging cloud which resolves itself into rain. —**Rain-drop**, *n.* A drop of rain.—**Rainfall**, rān'fạl, *n.* A fall of rain; the amount of water that falls as rain.—**Rain-gauge**, *n.* An instrument for measuring or *gauging* the quantity of rain which falls at a given place. — **Raininess**, rā'ni-nes, *n.* The state of being rainy.—**Rainless**, rān'les, *a.* Without rain (a *rainless* region).—**Rain-print**, *n.* *Geol.* the name given to marks found in aqueous rocks, and resulting from the action of rain-drops falling on the deposit when in a soft state.—**Rain-water**, *n.* Water that has fallen from the clouds in rain. — **Rainy**, rā'ni, *a.* Abounding with rain; wet; showery.—*A rainy day* (*fig.*), evil or less fortunate times.

Raise, rāz, *v.t.*—*raised*, *raising*. [A caus. of *rise*, but coming directly from a Scandinavian source; Icel. *reisa*, to raise, caus. of *risa*, to rise. RISE, REAR.] To cause to rise; to put, place, or remove higher; to lift upward; to elevate; to heave; to elevate in social position, rank, dignity, and the like; to increase the value or estimation of; to exalt, enhance, promote, advance; to increase the energy, strength, power, or vigour of; to excite; to heighten (to *raise* the courage, to *raise* the temperature of a room); to cause to appear from the world of spirits; to recall from death (to *raise* the dead); to cause to assume an erect position or posture; to set upright; to awaken; to rouse to action; to incite; to stir up (to *raise* the country, to *raise* a mutiny); to set into commotion (to *raise* the sea); to cause to arise or come into being; to build up; to erect; to construct; to bring or get together; to gather, collect, to levy (to *raise* money, to *raise* an army); to cause to be produced; to breed; to rear; to grow (to *raise* wheat, to *raise* cattle, sheep, &c.); to give rise to; to originate (to *raise* a false report); to give vent or utterance to (to *raise* a cry); to strike up (to *raise* the song of victory); to cause to appear; to call up (to *raise* a smile or a blush); to heighten or elevate in pitch (a sharp *raises* a note half a tone); to increase the loudness of (to *raise* the voice); *law*, to institute or originate (to *raise* an action); to cause to swell, as dough.—*To raise steam*, to produce steam enough to drive an engine.—*To raise a blockade*, to terminate or break it up.—*To raise a siege*, to relinquish the attempt to take a place by besieging it, or to cause the attempt to be relinquished.—*To raise the wind* (*fig.*), to obtain ready money by some shift or other.—*Raised beaches.* Under BEACH.—**Raisable**, rā'za-bl, *a.* Capable of being raised.—**Raiser**, rā'zėr, *n.* One who or that which raises.

Raisin, rā'zn, *n.* [Fr. *raisin*, a grape, from L. *racemus*, a cluster of grapes. RACEME.] A dried grape; a dried fruit of various species of vines.

Raisonné, rā'zo-nā, *a.* [Fr.] Supported by proofs, arguments, or illustrations; arranged and digested systematically.

Rajah, rā'jā or rä'jä, *n.* [Skr. and Hind. *râjâ*, a rajah; root in Skr. *râj*, to rule; cog. L. *rex* (for *regs*), a king, *rego*, to rule; Gael. and Ir. *righ*, a king; A.Sax. *rice*, dominion. REGAL, RICH.] In India, originally a title which belonged to princes of Hindu race who governed a territory; subsequently, a title given to Hindus of rank; a Hindu chief.—**Rajahship**, rā'jä-ship or rä'jä-ship, *n.* The dignity or principality of a rajah.

Rake, rāk, *n.* [A.Sax. *raca*, a rake; cog. Icel. *reka*, a shovel or spade; Sw. *raka*, an oven-rake; G. *rechen*, a rake; from root meaning to stretch. REACH.] An implement furnished with wooden or iron teeth, used for collecting hay or straw after mowing or reaping; and in gardening for smoothing the soil, covering the seed, &c.; a small implement like a hoe used for collecting the stakes on a gambling-table.—*v.t.* —*raked, raking.* To apply a rake to, or something that serves the same purpose; to gather with a rake; to smooth with a rake; to gather with labour or difficulty (to *rake* together wealth); to ransack; to pass swiftly over; to scour; *milit.* to enfilade; to cannonade so that the balls range the whole length.—*To rake up* (*fig.*), to bring up or revive, as quarrels, grievances, &c.—*v.i.* To use a rake; to seek by raking; to search with minute inspection into every part.—**Raker**, rā'kėr, *n.* One who or that which rakes; an implement for raking.—**Raking**, rā'king, *p.* and *a.* Enfilading; scouring from end to end.

Rake, rāk, *n.* [Shortened from O.E. *rakel*, *rakil*, rash (afterwards corrupted into *rakehell*), properly vagabond, wandering; comp. Prov. *rake*, to rove or ramble idly; Sw. *raka*, Icel. *reika*, to wander; Dan. *rækel*, a lout.] A loose, disorderly, vicious person; one addicted to lewdness; a libertine; a roué.—*v.i.* To play the part of a rake; to lead a dissolute debauched life; to fly wide of game: said of a hawk.—**Rakish**, rā'kish, *a.* Given to the practices of a rake; dissolute; debauched.—**Rakishly**, rā'kish-li, *adv.* In a rakish or dissolute manner.—**Rakishness**, rā'kish-nes, *n.* Dissolute practices.

Rake, rāk, *v.i.* [Same as Sw. *raka*, Dan. *rage*, to project, a Scandinavian verb = E. *reach.*] To incline; to slope; *naut.* to incline from a perpendicular direction (a mast *rakes* aft).—*n. Naut.* a slope or inclination; the projection of the stem or stern beyond the extremities of the keel; the inclination of a mast, funnel, &c., from a perpendicular direction.—**Rake-vein**, *n. Mining*, a fissure, generally vertical or highly inclined, cutting through strata.—**Raking**, rā'king, *p.* and *a.* Inclining from the horizontal.—**Rakish**, rā'kish, *a. Naut.* having a rake or inclination of the masts forward or aft.

Rakehell, rāk'hel, *n.* [This word should properly be *rakel.* See RAKE, a dissolute person.] A lewd dissolute fellow; a debauchee; a rake.—**Rakehell**, **Rakehelly**, rāk'hel-i, *a.* Dissolute; profligate.

Râle, räl, *n.* [Fr., O.Fr. *rasle*, a rattling sound. RATTLE.] *Pathol.* a noise or crepitation caused by the air passing through mucus in the bronchial tubes or lungs.

Rallentando, ral-len-tän'dō. [It.] *Music*, a term indicating that the time of the passage over which it is written is to be gradually decreased.

Ralline, ral'in, *a.* [Mod.L. *rallus*, a rail.] *Ornith.* pertaining to the rails.

Rally, ral'i, *v.t.*—*rallied, rallying.* [Fr. *rallier*, to rally—prefix *re*, and *allier*, E. *ally*, from L. *alligo*, I bind to—*ad*, to, and *ligo*, I bind. ALLY, LIGAMENT.] To collect and reduce to order, as troops dispersed or thrown into confusion; to bring together as for a fresh effort; to reunite.—*v.i.* To come back quickly to order; to reform themselves into an orderly body for a fresh effort; to resume or recover vigour or strength (the patient begins to *rally*).—*n.* A stand made by retreating troops; return of disordered troops to their ranks; the act of recovering strength; a mass meeting to arouse group enthusiasm.

Rally, ral'i, *v.t.*—*rallied, rallying.* [Fr. *railler*, to banter. RAIL (to banter).] To attack with raillery; to treat with good-humour and pleasantry, or with slight contempt or satire; to tease.—*v.i.* To use pleasantry or satirical merriment.—**Ralliance**, ral'i-ans, *n.* The act of rallying.—**Rallier**, ral'i-ėr, *n.* One who rallies.

Ram, ram, *n.* [A.Sax. *ram*, *ramm*, D. *ram*, G. *ramm*, a ram. Root uncertain.] The male of the sheep or ovine genus; a battering-ram (under BATTER); a steam ironclad ship-of-war, armed at the prow below the water-line with a heavy iron or steel beak intended to destroy an enemy's ships by the force with which it is driven against them; the loose hammer of a pile-driving machine; the piston of a hydraulic press.—*Hydraulic ram* or *water ram*, an automatic apparatus by which a descending stream of water is made to raise by its own momentum a portion of its mass to a required height.—*The Ram*, Aries, one of the signs of the zodiac.—*v.t.*—*rammed, ramming.* [From the noun, like G. *rammen*, Dan. *ramme*, to strike, to hit.] To strike with a ram; to drive a ram or similar object against; to batter; to force in; to drive down; to fill or compact by pounding or driving; to stuff; to cram.—*v.i.* To use a battering-ram or similar object.—*a.* Strong-scented; stinking (*ram* as a fox).—**Rammer**, ram'ėr, *n.* One who or that which rams or drives; a ramrod.—**Rammish**, ram'ish, *a.* Ramlike; hence, lascivious; rank; strong-scented.—**Rammishness**, ram'ish-nes, *n.* The state or quality of being rammish.—**Ramrod**, ram'rod, *n.* A rod for ramming down the charge of a gun or other firearm; a rammer.

Ramadan, **Ramadhan**, rä'ma-dan, *n.* [Ar., the hot month, from *ramida*, *ramiza*, to be hot.] The ninth month of the Mohammedan year; the great annual Mohammedan fast, kept throughout the entire month from sunrise to sunset.

Ramal, rā'mal, *a.* [L. *ramus*, a branch.] *Bot.* rameous.

Ramble, ram'bl, *v.i.*—*rambled, rambling.* [A dim. and freq. from *roam*; the *b* has crept in, as in *grumble*, *nimble*, *number*, &c.] To rove; to wander; to go from place to place without any determinate object in view; to think or talk in an incoherent manner; to grow without constraint.—*n.* A roving; an excursion or trip in which a person wanders from place to place; an irregular excursion.—**Rambler**, ram'blėr, *n.* One who rambles; a rover; a wanderer.—**Rambling**, ram'bling, *p.* and *a.* Roving; wandering; straggling; without method; confused in ideas or language.—*n.* A roving, irregular excursion.—**Ramblingly**, ram'bling-li, *adv.* In a rambling manner.

Ramee, ra-mē', *n.* [Malay.] Same as *Rhea-fibre.*

Ramenta, ra-men'ta, *n.pl.* [L. *ramentum*, a chip, shaving, scale, from *rado*, to scrape.] *Bot.* thin brown foliaceous scales on young shoots, and numerous on the backs of the fronds of ferns.—**Ramentaceous**, ram-en-tā'shus, *a.* Covered with ramenta.

Rameous, **Rameal**, rā'mē-us, rā'mē-al, *a.* [From L. *ramus*, a branch. RADIUS.] *Bot.* belonging to a branch; growing on or shooting from a branch.—**Ramification**, ram'i-fi-kā''shon, *n.* The act of ramifying; the process of branching out; a small branch or offshoot from a main stock or channel; a subordinate branch; a division or subdivision in a classification, or the like.—**Ramiform**, ram'i-form, *a. Bot.* resembling a branch.—**Ramify**, ram'i-fī, *v.t.* —*ramified, ramifying.* [Fr. *ramifier*—L. *ramus*, a branch, and *facio*, to make.] To divide into branches or parts.—*v.i.* To shoot into branches, as the stem of a plant; to branch out; to be divided or subdivided; to branch out, as a main subject or scheme.—**Ramiparous**, ra-mip'a-rus, *a.* [L. *ramus*, and *pario*, to bring forth.] Producing branches.—**Ramose**, **Ramous**, rā'mōs, rā'mus, *a.* [L. *ramosus.*] Branchy; full of branches; *bot.* branched, as a stem or root.

Rammer, **Rammish**. Under RAM.

Ramollescence, ram-o-les'ens, *n.* [From Fr. *ramollir*, to make soft—L. *re*, again, *ad*, to, and *mollio*, to soften.] A softening or mollifying.—**Ramollissement**, ra-mo-lēs-mon, *n.* [Fr.] *Pathol.* a softening, as of the brain.

Ramose. Under RAMEOUS.

Ramp, ramp, *v.i.* [Fr. *ramper*, to creep, to climb=It. *rampare*, to clamber, from the German; comp. Bav. *rampfen*, to snatch; a nasalized form corresponding to L.G. *rappen*, Sw. *rappa*, to snatch. *Romp* is the same word.] To climb, as a plant‡; to rear on the hind-legs; to assume a rampant attitude; to spring or move with violence; to rage; to bound; to romp.—*n.* A sloping platform serving as a way between different levels.—**Rampage**, ram'pāj, *v.i.* [From *ramp.*] To romp or prance about with unrestrained spirits; to rage and storm; to prance about with fury. (*Colloq.*)—*n.* A state of passion or excitement; violent conduct. (*Colloq.*)—**Rampageous**, **Rampacious**, ram-pā'jus, ram-pā'shus, *a.* Boisterous; unruly. (*Colloq.*)—**Rampant**, ram'pant, *a.* [Fr. *rampant*, ppr. of *ramper*, to clamber.] Springing or climbing unchecked; rank in growth; exuberant (*rampant* weeds); overleaping restraint or usual limits; excessively and obtrusively prevalent; predominant (*rampant* vice); *her.* standing upright upon his hind-legs (properly on one foot) as if attacking: said of a beast of prey, as the lion.—**Rampancy**, ram'pan-si, *n.* The state or quality of being rampant.—**Rampantly**, ram'pant-li, *adv.* In a rampant manner.

Rampart, ram'pärt, *n.* [Fr. *rempart*, a rampart, from *remparer*, to fortify a place—*re*, again, *em* for L. *in*, in, and *parer*, to defend, from L. *parare*, to prepare. PARE, PREPARE.] A bulwark; a defence; *fort.* an elevation or mound of earth round a place, capable of resisting cannon shot, and on which the parapet is raised; it also may include the parapet.—*v.t.* To fortify with ramparts.

Rampion, ram'pi-on, *n.* [A nasalized form from L. *rapum*, a turnip, rape.] A perennial plant of the bell-flower order, the root and leaves of which are used in salads.

Rampire,‡ ram'pīr, *n.* A rampart.

Ramrod. Under RAM.

Ramshackle, ram'shak-l, *a.* [Perhaps pp. of *ransackle*, *ransack.*] Ill-adjusted and threatening dissolution; carelessly constructed; rickety.

Ramson, Ramsons, ram′zon, ram′zonz, *n.* [A.Sax. *hramsa, hramse*, ramsons (pl. *hramsan*, so that *ramsons* is a double pl.); G. *rams, ramsel, ramsen*, Sw. *rams*, ramsons; allied to Gr. *kromyon*, an onion.] A species of garlic, having broad leaves and a bulbous root, sometimes used in salads.

Ramulose, Ramulous, ram′ū-lōs, ram′ū-lus, *a. Bot.* having many small branches.

Ran, ran, *pret.* RUN.

Ranch, Ranche, ranch, *n.* [Sp. *rancho*, a mess, a set of persons who eat and drink together, a messroom.] An establishment and tract of land for rearing and grazing horses, cattle, sheep, &c.; the buildings of such an establishment; any farm, as for dairying or fruit growing. (*Colloq.*) —**Rancher**, ran′chėr, *n.* One who owns or is employed on a ranch.—**Ranchero**, rän-chā′rō, *n.* A person employed on a ranch, or who owns and manages a ranch. (*Spanish Amer.*)—**Rancho**, rän′chō, *n.* Rude habitation for ranch or farm workers. (*Spanish Amer.*)

Rancid, ran′sid, *a.* [L. *rancidus*, from *ranceo*, to be rank (whence also *rancour*).] Having a rank smell; strong-scented, from turning bad with keeping: said of oils and fats, butter, &c.; musty. — **Rancidity, Rancidness**, ran-sid′i-ti, ran′sid-nes, *n.* The quality of being rancid.—**Rancidly**, ran′sid-li, *adv.* With a rancid unpleasant odour; mustily.

Rancor, rang′kėr, *n.* [L. *rancor*, an ill smell, rancor, from *ranceo*, to be rank or rancid (whence *rancid*).] The deepest malignity, enmity, or spite; deep-seated and implacable malice; inveterate enmity; malignity. — **Rancorous**, rang′kėr-us, *a.* Full of rancor; deeply malignant; intensely virulent. — **Rancorously**, rang′kėr-us-li, *adv.*

Random, ran′dum, *n.* [O.Fr. *randon*, an impetuous course or efflux, vivacity, violence; *à randon*, at random; *randoner, randir*, to run rapidly; from G. *rand*, edge, brim, the word originally having reference to the violence of a stream flowing full to the brim.] A roving motion or course without direction; want of rule or method; chance: used only in the phrase, *at random*, that is, in a haphazard or fortuitous manner; *mining*, the depth below a given plane.—*a.* Done at hazard or without settled aim or purpose; left to chance; fortuitous.—*Random courses, masonry* and *paving*, courses of stones of unequal thickness.—*Random shot*, a shot not directed to a point.—**Randomly**, ran′dum-li, *adv.* In a random manner; at hazard.

Ranee, ran′ē, *n.* [Hind. *rani*, queen.] The wife of a rajah, or queen in her own right, in native states.

Rang, rang, pret. of *ring.*

Range, rānj, *v.t.*—*ranged, ranging.* [From Fr. *ranger*, to range, from *rang*, O.Fr. *reng*, a rank; from the German. RANK.] To set in a row or in rows; to place in regular lines or ranks; to rank; to arrange systematically; to classify; to class; to rove through or over; to pass over.—*v.i.* To be placed in order; to be ranked; to rank; to rove at large; to wander without restraint; to pass from one point to another; to fluctuate (the price *ranges* between 50*s.* and 60*s.*); *gun.* to have range or horizontal direction. —*n.* A series of things in a line; a row; a rank (a *range* of mountains); space or room for excursion; the extent of country over which a plant or animal is naturally spread; compass or extent; discursive power; scope (a wide *range* of thought); the series of sounds belonging to a voice or a musical instrument; a kitchen grate and cooking apparatus; *gun.* the horizontal distance to which a shot or other projectile is carried; a place where gun or rifle practice is carried on.—**Range-finding**, *n.* The measurement of the distance in yards between a gun and the object of its aim, effected by means of instruments, the range-finder, the mekometer, &c. The term *range-taking* is used similarly but with wider meaning.—**Ranger**, rān′jėr, *n.* One who ranges; a member of a body of mounted, roving troops or police; a government official patrolling forest areas. — **Rangership**, rān′jėr-ship, *n.* The office of ranger.—**Ranging**, rān′jing, *n.* The process of finding the elevation which should be given to a gun in order that the projectile may hit the object aimed at.

Ranine, rā′nīn, *a.* [L. *rana*, a frog.] Relating to a frog or to frogs.—*Ranine artery*, an artery of the tongue.

Rank, rangk, *n.* [O.E. *ranc, renk*, from Fr. *rang*, O.Fr. *reng, renc*, a rank, row, range (whence also *range*), originally a circular row, from O.H.G. *hring, hrinc*, a ring, a circle. RING.] A row; a line; a tier; a range; *milit.* a line of soldiers; a line of men standing abreast or side by side: often used along with *file* (which see); hence in *pl.* the order of common soldiers (to reduce an officer to the *ranks*); an aggregate of individuals together; a social class; an order; a division; degree of dignity, eminence, or excellence; comparative station; relative place (a writer of the first *rank*); high social position; distinction; eminence (a man of *rank*). — *To fill the ranks*, to complete the whole number.—*To take rank of*, to enjoy precedence over. —*v.t.* To place abreast in a rank or line; to place in a particular class, order, or division; to class or classify; to range.—*v.i.* To be ranged, classed, or included, as in a particular class, order, or division; to have a certain rank; to occupy a certain position as compared with others; to put in a claim against the estate of a bankrupt.

Rank, rangk, *a.* [A.Sax. *ranc*, fruitful, rank, proud = Icel. *rakkr*, straight, bold; Dan. *rank*, erect; D. *rank*, slender; Prov. G. *rank*, slender, upright — all nasalized forms from same root as *rack, right, reach.*] Luxuriant in growth; causing vigorous growth; fertile; strong-scented; rancid; strong to the taste; high-tasted; raised to a high degree; excessive; utter (*rank* nonsense); gross; coarse; disgusting.—**Rankly**, rangk′li, *adv.* With vigorous growth; rancidly; coarsely; grossly. — **Rankness**, rangk′nes, *n.* The state or quality of being rank; vigorous growth; luxuriance; strength and coarseness in smell or taste.—**Rank-scented**, *a.* Having a coarse powerful odour.

Rankle, rang′kl, *v.i.*—*rankled, rankling.* To fester, as a sore or wound; to produce a painful sensation; *fig.* to produce bitterness or rancour in the mind; to continue to irritate.—*v.t.* To irritate; to inflame.

Rannee, ran-nē′, *n.* [Hind.] The wife of a rajah; a queen or princess.

Ranny, ran′i, *n.* [L. *araneus* (*mus*), the shrew-mouse, lit. spider-mouse, from *aranea*, a spider.] The shrew-mouse.

Ransack, ran′sak, *v.t.* [A Scand. word: Icel. *rannsaka*, Sw. *ransaka*, to search, as for stolen goods—Icel. *rann* (Goth. *razns*), a house, and *sækja*, to seek. SEEK.] To search thoroughly; to enter and search every place and part of; to rummage; to plunder; to strip by plundering.

Ransom, ran′sum, *n.* [Fr. *rançon*, O.Fr. *raenson, raanson*, &c., from L. *redemptio, redemptionis*, redemption, from *redimo*—*re*, back, and *emo*, I buy. (REDEEM.) The word is therefore *redemption* in another form.] Release from captivity, bondage, or the possession of an enemy by payment; the price paid for such release, or for goods captured by an enemy; price paid for the pardon of sins; redemption of sinners.—*v.t.* To pay a ransom for; to redeem from captivity, bondage, forfeit, or punishment; to deliver.—**Ransomer**, ran′sum-ėr, *n.* One who ransoms or redeems.—**Ransomable**, ran′sum-a-bl, *a.* Capable of being ransomed. —**Ransomless**, ran′sum-les, *a.* Free from ransom.

Rant, rant, *v.i.* [Same as O.D. *ranten*, to be enraged, G. *ranten, ranzen*, to move noisily, Prov.G. *rant*, noisy mirth.] To rave in violent or extravagant language; to be noisy and boisterous in words or declamation. — *n.* Boisterous, empty declamation; bombast. — **Ranter**, ran′tėr, *n.* One who rants; a noisy talker; a boisterous preacher; a name given by way of reproach to members of a denomination of Christians which sprang up in 1645; also vulgarly applied to the Primitive Methodists.

Rantipole, ran′ti-pōl, *a.* [From *rant*, and *pole, poll*, the head.] Wild; boisterous; rakish. — *n.* A rude, romping boy or girl. (*Colloq.*)

Ranunculus, ra-nun′kū-lus, *n.* [L. dim. of *rana*, a frog—a name first given to the aquatic ranunculus because it floats in marshes, ditches, &c.] The crow-foot genus, a genus of flowering plants almost exclusively inhabiting the northern hemisphere, possessing acrid properties, and widely distributed over the Temperate zone. — **Ranunculaceous**, ra-nun′kū-lā″shus, *a.* Of the ranunculus family.

Ranz-des-vaches, räṅz-dā-väsh, *n.* [Fr., lit. the ranks or rows of the cows, because on hearing it they move onwards in a row.] The name of certain simple melodies of the Swiss mountaineers, commonly played on a long trumpet called the *alpenhorn.*

Rap, rap, *n.* [Same as Sw. *rapp*, a blow, a stroke; Dan. *rap*, a rap; imitative of sound made by a blow; comp. *pat, tap.*] A quick smart blow; a knock.—*v.i.*—*rapped, rapping.* To strike with a quick sharp blow; to knock.—*v.t.* To strike with a quick blow; to give a knock (to *rap* one's knuckles).—*To rap out*, to utter with sudden violence (to *rap out* an oath).—**Rapper**, rap′ėr, *n.* One who raps or knocks; the knocker of a door.

Rap, rap, *v.t.*—*rapped, rapping.* [A Scandinavian word; Sw. *rappa*, Dan. *rappe*, to snatch; comp. Dan. *rap*, Sw. *rapp*, quick, brisk. *Rape* is closely allied; see also RAPT.] To affect with ecstasy or rapture; to snatch or hurry away; to seize by violence.

Rap, rap, *v.t.* To criticize or censure.—**Rap**, rap, *n.* (*Slang.*) A punishment (to take the *rap*).

Rap, rap, *n.* [Possibly derived from the name of a coin of slight value.] Something of trifling worth, chiefly used in such phrases as, *it isn't worth a rap.* (*Colloq.*)

Rapacious, ra-pā′shus, *a.* [L. *rapax, rapacis*, from *rapio*, I seize (whence also *rapine, rapture*); same root as *rapid.*] Given to plunder; accustomed to seize or take possession of property by violence; subsisting on prey or animals seized by violence; avaricious; grasping. — **Rapaciously**, ra-pā′shus-li, *adv.* In a rapacious manner; by rapine. — **Rapaciousness**, ra-pā′shus-nes, *n.* Disposition to plunder or to exact by oppression.—**Rapacity**, ra-pas′i-ti, *n.* [L. *rapacitas.*] The quality of being rapacious; ravenousness; the act or practice of extorting or exacting by oppressive injustice.

Rape, rāp, *n.* [From *rap*, to seize, to snatch, the meaning being influenced by L. *rapere, raptum*, to seize. RAP, to seize, RAPTURE.] The act of snatching by force; a seizing and carrying away by force or violence (the *rape* of Proserpine); *law*, the carnal knowledge of a woman forcibly and against her will; something seized and carried away.

Rape, rāp, *n.* [Fr. *râpe.*] Refuse stalks and skins of raisins used by vinegarmakers after the fruit has been employed in making wine.

Rape, rāp, *n.* [Icel. *hreppr*, a district, from *hreppa*, to obtain.] A division of the county of Sussex, England; a division containing three or four hundreds.

Rape, rāp, *n.* [From L. *rapa, rapum*, a turnip (whence also *rampion*).] A plant of the cabbage family, cultivated for its seeds, from which oil is extracted by grinding and pressure. — **Rape-cake**, *n.* A cake formed of the seed and husks of rape after the oil has been expressed, used for feeding oxen and sheep, and also as a manure.—**Rape-oil**, *n.* A thick yellow oil expressed from rape-seeds.

Raphaelite, raf′a-el-īt, *n.* An artist who adopts the principles of Raphael.

Raphe, rā'fē, *n.* [Gr. *raphē*, a seam or suture.] *Bot.* and *zool.* a term applied to parts which look as if they had been sewed or joined together; a suture or line of junction.—**Raphides**, raf'i-dēz, *n.pl.* [Pl. of Gr. *raphis*, a needle.] *Bot.* crystals of an acicular or needle-like form occurring in plant-cells.

Raphia, ra'fi-a, *n.* Same as *Raffia.*

Rapid, rap'id, *a.* [Fr. *rapide*, from L. *rapidus*, rapid, from *rapio*, to seize; same root as Gr. *harpazō*, to seize. (HARPY.) *Rapine*, *rapacious*, *ravish*, *rapture*, &c., are from the same L. stem.] Very swift or quick; moving with celerity; advancing with speed; speed in progression (*rapid* growth); quick or swift in performance.—*n.* A swift current in a river, where the channel is descending. — **Rapidity**, **Rapidness**, ra-pid'i-ti, rap'id-nes, *n.* [L. *rapiditas.*] The state or quality of being rapid; swiftness; celerity; velocity; haste in utterance; quickness.—**Rapidly**, rap'id-li, *adv.* In a rapid manner; with great speed.

Rapier, rā'pi-ėr, *n.* [Fr. *rapière*, lit. a rasper, from Sp. *raspar*, to rasp. RASP.] A sword used only in thrusting, and usually having a four-sided blade.—**Rapier-fish**, *n.* The sword-fish.

Rapil, **Rapillo**, rap'il, ra-pil'lō, *n.* [It. *rapillo.*] Pulverized volcanic substances.

Rapine, rap'in, *n.* [Fr., from L. *rapina*, from *rapio*, to seize. RAPID.] The act of plundering; the seizing and carrying away of things by force.

Rapparee, rap-a-rē', *n.* [Ir. *rapaire*, a noisy fellow, *rapach*, noisy, slovenly.] A wild Irish plunderer; a worthless fellow. (*Irish.*) Spelled also *Raparee.*

Rappee, rap-pē', *n.* [Fr. *râpé*, ppr. of *râper*, to rasp, lit. rasped or powdered tobacco.] A strong kind of snuff made from the darker and ranker kinds of tobacco.

Rappel, rap-el, *n.* [Fr., recall, from L. *re*, back, and *appello*, to call. APPEAL.] The roll or beat of the drum to call soldiers to arms.

Rapper. Under RAP.

Rapport, rap-pōrt', *n.* [Fr., from L. *re*, again, *ad*, to, and *portare*, to carry. PORTER.] A resemblance; a correspondence; harmony; affinity.

Rapscallion, rap-skal'yun, *n.* A modified form of *rascallion.*

Rapt, rapt, *p.* and *a.* [From *rap*, to snatch, but influenced by L. *raptus*, seized, from *rapio.* RAPTURE.] Snatched away; transported; enraptured; in an ecstasy; entirely absorbed.

Raptores, rap-tō'rēz, *n.pl.* [Pl. of L. *raptor*, a robber, from *rapio*, I seize.] The order of birds of prey.—**Raptorial**, rap-tō'ri-al, *a.* Pertaining to the Raptores or birds of prey; living by rapine or prey; adapted to the seizing of prey.

Rapture, rap'tūr, *n.* [From L. *rapere*, *raptum*, to seize and carry away; whence also *rapine*, &c. RAPID.] A seizing by violence†; a transport of delight; ecstasy; extreme joy or pleasure; enthusiasm.—**Raptured**, rap'tūrd, *a.* Inspired with rapture; transported.—**Rapturous**, rap'tū-rus, *a.* Ecstatic; transporting; ravishing.—**Rapturously**, rap'tū-rus-li, *adv.* With rapture; ecstatically.

Rare, rār, *a.* [Fr. *rare*, from L. *rarus*, thin, rare.] Thinly scattered; sparse; thin; porous; not dense or compact; uncommon; not frequent; possessing qualities seldom to be met with; excellent or valuable to a degree seldom found.—**Rarely**, rār'li, *adv.* In a rare degree or manner; seldom.—**Rareness**, rār'nes, *n.* The state of being rare; uncommonness; thinness; tenuity; value arising from scarcity.—**Rarity**, rā'ri-ti, *n.* [L. *raritas.*] The state or quality of being rare; a thing valued for its scarcity or excellence.—**Rarebit**, rar'bit, *n.* [A word made to account for the expression '*Welsh rabbit*'. RABBIT.] A dainty morsel; a Welsh rabbit.—**Rareeshow**, rā'rē-shō, *n.* A peep-show; a show carried about in a box. Such shows used to be chiefly exhibited by foreigners, and *raree* was the mode in which they pronounced the word *rare.*

Rarefy, rā're-fī, *v.t.*—*rarefied*, *rarefying.* [Fr. *raréfier*; L. *rarefacio*—*rarus*, rare, and *facio*, I make.] To make rare, thin, porous, or less dense; to expand by separation of constituent atoms or particles: opposed to *condense.*—*v.i.* To become rare, that is, not dense or less dense.—**Rarefiable**, rā-re-fi'a-bl, *a.* Capable of being rarefied. — **Rarefaction**, rā-re-fak'shon, *n.* The act of rarefying or state of being rarefied; expansion or distension by separation of constituent particles: chiefly used in speaking of the aëriform fluids, *dilatation* and *expansion* being used in speaking of solids and liquids: opposed to *condensation.*

Rarely, Rareness, Rarity. Under RARE.

Rascal, ras'kal, *n.* [Lit. scrapings or refuse; O.E. *rascall*, *rascayle*, the rabble, also a worthless deer; from a L.L. *rasicare*, from L. *rado*, *rasum*, to shave or scrape. RASE.] A lean beast, especially a lean deer, not fit to hunt or kill; a mean fellow; a trickish dishonest fellow; a rogue or scoundrel.—*a.* Worthless; mean; paltry; base.—**Rascaldom**, ras'kal-dum, *n.* The state of being a rascal; rascals collectively.—**Rascalism**, ras'kal-izm, *n.* Rascality.—**Rascality**, ras-kal'i-ti, *n.* Such qualities as make a rascal; mean trickishness or dishonesty.—**Rascallion**, ras-kal'yun, *n.* [From *rascal.*] A low mean wretch.—**Rascally**, ras'kal-li, *a.* Like a rascal; dishonest; vile; base; worthless.

Rase, rāz, *v.t.*—*rased*, *rasing.* [Fr. *raser*, from L.L. *rasare*, freq. of L. *rado*, *rasum*, to scrape, seen also in *erase*, *razor*, *rascal*, *abrade*, *rally*, to *rail.*] To touch superficially in passing; to graze; to erase; to level with the ground; to overthrow; to raze (RAZE).—**Rasure**, rā'zhūr, *n.* The act of scraping or erasing; an erasure.

Rash, rash, *a.* [Same as L.G., Dan., and Sw. *rask*, Icel. *röskr*, D. and G. *rasch*, rash; perhaps from same root as G. *rad*, a wheel, Skr. *ratha*, a chariot.] Hasty in counsel or action; precipitate; resolving or entering on a project without due deliberation and caution; uttered, formed, or undertaken with too little reflection. ∴ A *rash* man is one who undergoes risk from natural impulsiveness; a *foolhardy* man foolishly incurs danger in defiance of and not believing in evil consequences; a *reckless* man sees but disregards consequences.—**Rashly**, rash'li, *adv.* In a rash manner; precipitately; inconsiderately. — **Rashness**, rash'nes, *n.* Precipitation; inconsiderate readiness to decide or act; a rash act.

Rash, rash, *n.* [O.Fr. *rasche*, rash, scurf, itch; same origin as *rascal.*] An eruption on the skin, usually in the form of red spots or patches.

Rasher, rash'ėr, *n.* [Probably a piece hastily cooked, from *rash*, *a.*] *Cookery*, a slice of bacon for frying or broiling.

Rasores, ra-sō'rēz, *n.pl.* [Lit. scrapers or scratchers, from L. *rado*, *rasum*, to scrape. RASE.] Gallinaceous birds or scratchers, an order of birds of which the common domestic fowl may be regarded as the type. —**Rasorial**, ra-sō'ri-al, *a.* Pertaining to the Rasores.

Rasp, rasp, *v.t.* [O.Fr. *rasper*, Fr. *râper*, to scrape or rasp, from O.H.G. *raspôn*, to scrape together (D. *raspen*, Dan. *raspe*, Sw. *raspa*); akin to G. *raffen*, to sweep, E. *raff*, *raffle*, *rapier.*] To rub against with some rough implement; to file with a rasp; to grate; hence, *fig.* to grate harshly upon.—*v.i.* To rub or grate.—*n.* A coarse species of file with numerous separate projections or teeth; a raspberry.—**Rasper**, ras'pėr, *n.* One who or that which rasps; a scraper.—**Rasping**, ras'ping, *a.* Characterized by grating or scraping.—**Raspy**, ras'pi, *a.* Grating; harsh; rough.

Raspberry, raz'be-ri, *n.* [*Rasp* and *berry*; so named from the roughness of the fruit. Comp. G. *kratzbeere*—*kratzen*, to scratch, and *beere*, berry.] The well-known fruit of a plant extensively used by both the cook and the confectioner, and also in the preparation of cordials; also the plant itself; a derisive sound made by vibrating the tongue and lips (*slang*).

Rasse, ras, *n.* A carnivorous animal closely allied to the civet, a native of Asia.

Rasure. Under RASE

Rat, rat, *n.* [A.Sax. *ræt*, a rat = D. *rat*, G. *ratte* (whence Fr. *rat*), L.G. and Dan. *rotte*, Gael. *radan*, Armor. *raz*, rat; root probably in L. *rodo*, to gnaw.] Any of various long-tailed rodents resembling, and allied to, the mouse, but considerably larger, brown or gray in color, and infesting houses, barns, stables, and ships; a sneaky person; one who betrays or deserts his associates; in underworld jargon, a criminal who discloses the identity of his accomplices to the police; a section of false hair (*colloq.*). —*To smell a rat*, to be suspicious that all is not right.—*v.i.*—*ratted*, *ratting.* To catch or kill rats; to forsake one's associates. —**Rat-catcher**, *n.* One who makes it his business to catch rats.—**Rat-pit**, *n.* An inclosure into which rats are thrown, to ascertain how many a dog can kill in a given time, or to see which of two or more dogs will kill the most.—**Ratsbane**, rats'bān, *n.* [*Rat* and *bane.*] Poison for rats; arsenious acid.—**Rat-tail**, **Rat's-tail**, *n.* A disease in horses in which the hair of the tail is permanently lost.—**Ratter**, rat'ėr, *n.* One who rats: one whose business it is to catch rats; a terrier which kills rats. —**Rat-trap**, *n.* A trap for catching rats.

Ratafia, rat-a-fē'a, *n.* [Sp., from Malay *arak*, arrack, and *tafia*, a spirit distilled from molasses.] A spirituous liquor flavoured with the kernels of cherries, apricots, peaches, &c.; a kind of liqueur.

Ratan, ra-tan', *n.* RATTAN.

Ratany, rat'a-ni, *n.* [Peruv. *ratana.*] A shrubby plant found in Peru and Bolivia, having an excessively astringent root, sometimes used as an astringent medicine.

Ratch, rach, *n.* [A softened form of *rack.*] *Mach.* a bar having angular teeth into which a pawl drops, to prevent machines from being reversed in motion; a rack or rack-bar.—**Ratchet**, rach'et, *n.* [Dim. of *ratch.*] A piece one extremity of which abuts against the teeth of a ratchet-wheel; a click, pawl, or detent.—**Ratchet-wheel**, *n.* A wheel with pointed and angular teeth against which a ratchet abuts, used either for converting a reciprocating into a rotatory motion or for admitting of its motion in one direction only.

Rate, rāt, *n.* [O.Fr. *rate*, from L. *rata* (*pars*, part, understood), from *ratus*, reckoned, ppr. of *reor*, to reckon, to calculate; akin *ratio*, *reason*, *ratify.*] The proportion or standard by which quantity or value is adjusted; price or amount fixed on anything with relation to a standard; a settled proportion; comparative value or estimate; degree as regards speed; a tax or sum assessed on property for public use according to its income or value; a local tax; *navy*, the order or class of a ship according to its magnitude or force; the daily gain or loss of a chronometer or other timepiece. —*v.t.*—*rated*, *rating.* To settle or fix the value, rank, or degree of; to value or estimate; to fix the relative scale, rank, or position of (to *rate* a ship).—*v.i.* To be set or considered in a class.—**Rateable**, rā'ta-bl, *a.* Ratable. — **Ratable**, rā'ta-bl, *a.* Capable of being rated; reckoned according to a certain rate; liable by law to taxation. —**Ratability**, **Ratableness**, rā-ta-bil'i-ti, rā'ta-bl-nes, *n.* Quality of being ratable.—**Ratably**, rā'ta-bli, *adv.* By rate or proportion.—*Rate of exchange*, the price per unit of money at which the currency of one country may be exchanged for the currency of another.—**Rater**, rā'tėr, *n.* One who rates.—**Rating**, rā'ting, *n.* The act of estimating; a fixing in rank or place; rank, as the *rating* of men and the *rating* of ships in the navy.

Rate, rāt, *v.t.*—*rated*, *rating.* [Same word as Sw. *rata*, to blame; N. *rata*, to reject.]

To chide with vehemence; to reprove; to scold; to censure violently.

Ratel, rat′el, *n.* [Name in S. Africa, origin unknown.] A carnivorous quadruped of the badger family, a native of India and the Cape of Good Hope.

Rath, rath, *n.* [Ir.] A kind of prehistoric fortification in Ireland, consisting of a circular rampart of earth with a mound in the centre.

Rath, Rathe, rāth, rāth, *a.*† [A.Sax. *hrœth*, *hrœd*, quick, hasty, *hrathe*, quickly; Icel. *hrathr*, O.H.G. *hrad*, quick.] Early; coming before others, or before the usual time. —*adv.* Soon; betimes; early; speedily.—*Rath ripe*, early ripe.—**Rather**, rä′THėr, *adv.* [Compar. of *rath*, quickly; A.Sax. *hrathor*. So we use *sooner* in an equivalent sense.] More readily or willingly; with preference or choice; with better reason; more properly; more correctly speaking; to the contrary of what has been just stated (no better but *rather* worse); somewhat (*rather* pretty).—*The rather*, especially; for this particular cause.

Ratifia, rat-i-fē′a, *n.* RATAFIA.

Ratify, rat′i-fī, *v.t.*—*ratified, ratifying.* [Fr. *ratifier*—*ratus*, fixed by calculation, valid, firm (RATE), and *facio*, I make.] To confirm; to settle authoritatively; to approve and sanction; to make valid, as something done by a representative, agent, or servant. —**Ratifier**, rat′i-fī-ėr, *n.* One who ratifies. —**Ratification**, rat′i-fi-kā″shon, *n.* The act of ratifying or confirming; confirmation; authorization.

Rating, *n.* Under RATE.

Ratio, rā′shi-ō, *n.* [L. *ratio, rationis*, reckoning, calculation, from *reor, ratus*, to think or suppose. (RATE.) *Reason, ration* are from same word.] Relation or proportion which one thing has to another in respect of magnitude or quantity; in a narrower sense, the numerical measure which one quantity bears to another of the same kind, expressed by the number found by dividing the one by the other; thus the ratio of 3 to 4 is the same as of 6 to 8, each being equivalent to $\frac{3}{4}$; sometimes called *geometrical ratio*, in opposition to *arithmetical ratio* or the difference between two quantities.

Ratiocinate, rash-i-os′i-nāt, *v.i.*—*ratiocinated, ratiocinating.* [L. *ratiocinor, ratiocinatus*, from *ratio*, reason. RATIO.] To reason; to argue.—**Ratiocination**, rash-i-os′i-nā″shon, *n.* [L. *ratiocinatio.*] The act or process of reasoning, especially of reasoning deductively.—**Ratiocinative, Ratiocinatory**, rash-i-os′i-nā-tiv, rash-i-os′i-na-to-ri, *a.* Characterized by ratiocination; argumentative.

Ration, rā′shon, ra′shon, *n.* [Fr., from L. *ratio, rationis*, proportion. RATIO.] A daily allowance of provisions to soldiers and sailors; any fixed amount or quantity dealt out; allowance.—*v.t.* To supply with rations.

Rational, rash′on-al, *a.* [Fr. *rationnel*, L. *rationalis*, from *ratio, rationis*, proportion. RATIO, REASON.] Having reason or the faculty of reasoning; endowed with reason: opposed to *irrational*; agreeable to reason; not absurd, foolish, preposterous, or the like; acting in conformity to reason; judicious; *arith.* and *alg.* a term applied to an expression in finite terms, the opposite of a *surd* or *irrational* quantity.—**Rationale**, rash-o-nā′lē, *n.* [From L. *rationalis*, from *ratio, rationis*, in sense of reason, account, plan.] A statement of reasons; an account or exposition of the principles of some process, phenomenon, &c.—**Rationalism**, rash′on-al-izm, *n.* *Theol.* a system of opinions deduced from reason as distinct from inspiration or revelation, or opposed to it; the interpretation of Scripture statements upon the principles of human reason to the disregard of revelation or anything supernatural.—**Rationalist**, rash′on-al-ist, *n.* An adherent of rationalism; one who rejects the supernatural element in dealing with the Old and New Testaments, and disbelieves in revelation.—**Rationalistic**, rash′on-al-is″tik, *a.* Relating to or accordant with rationalism.—**Rationalistically**, rash′on-al-is″ti-kal-li, *adv.* In a rationalistic manner.—**Rationality**, rash-o-nal′i-ti, *n.* The quality of being rational; power of reasoning; possession of reason; reasonableness.—**Rationalize**, rash′on-al-īz, *v.t.* To explain or justify; *psych.* to devise logical or creditable motives for actions performed because of irrational, censorable, or unrecognized motives.—**Rationalization**, *n.*—**Rationally**, rash′on-al-li, *adv.* In a rational manner; reasonably; sensibly.

Ratite, rat′īt, *a.* [From L. *rates*, a raft.] Any of the division Ratitae with no ridge or keel on the sternum; birds such as the ostrich.

Ratline, Ratlin, rat′lin, *n.* [Probably from *rat* and *line*, perhaps because of the thickness of a rat's tail.] *Naut.* one of a series of small ropes or lines which traverse the shrouds horizontally, forming ladders for going aloft; also called *Ratling.*

Ratoon, ra-tön′, *n.* [Sp. *retono*, a sprout or shoot.] A sprout from the root of the sugar-cane which has been cut.

Ratsbane. Under RAT.

Rattan, rat-tan′, *n.* [Imitative.] The continuous beat or reverberation of a drum.

Rattan, rat′an or rat-tan′, *n.* [Malay *rotan.*] The commercial name for the long trailing stems of certain species of palm from India and the Eastern Archipelago, employed for walking-sticks, &c.; a cane or walking-stick made of rattan.

Rattany, rat′a-ni. RATANY.

Ratteen, ra-tēn′, *n.* [Fr. *ratine*, ratteen.] A thick woollen stuff quilled or twilled.

Ratten, rat′n, *v.t.* [Lit. to play a rat's trick upon, from prov. *ratten*, a rat.] To destroy or take away the tools or machinery of, a mischievous trick perpetrated upon those who work in defiance of trades-unions.

Ratter. Under RAT.

Rattle, rat′l, *v.i.*—*rattled, rattling.* [From an A.Sax. verb seen in *hrœtele*, rattlewort = L.G. *ratteln*, D. *ratelen*, G. *rasseln*, Dan. *rasle*, to rattle; all from a root probably onomatopoetic.] To make a quick sharp noise rapidly repeated, as by the collision of bodies not very sonorous; to clatter; to speak eagerly and noisily; to chatter fluently.—*v.t.* To cause to make a rapid succession of sharp sounds.—*n.* A rapid succession of sharp clattering sounds; loud rapid talk; an instrument with which a clattering sound is made, formerly used by watchmen; also a child's toy constructed to produce a rattling sound; one who talks rapidly and without constraint; a jabberer; the horny organ at the extremity of the tail of the rattlesnake; the peculiar sound heard in the throat which immediately precedes and prognosticates death; the death-rattle. —**Rattler**, rat′lėr, *n.* One who rattles or talks away without thought; a giddy noisy person.—**Rattling**, rat′ling, *p.* and *a.* Making a quick succession of sharp sounds; lively.—**Rattle-brained**, *a.* Giddy; wild; rattle-headed.—**Rattle-head**, *n.* A giddy person; a rattle-pate.—**Rattle-headed, Rattle-pated**, *a.* Noisy; giddy; unsteady.—**Rattle-pate, Rattle-skull**, *n.* A noisy empty fellow.—**Rattle-snake**, rat′l-snāk, *n.* A venomous American snake having the tail terminating in a series of articulated horny pieces, which the animal moves in such a manner as to make a rattling sound.—**Rattlesnake-root, Rattlesnake-weed**, *n.* Plants so named from being used as a cure for the bite of the rattlesnake.—**Rattle-trap**, *n.* A shaky rickety object. (*Colloq.*)—**Rattle-wort**, rat′l-wort, *n.* A name of certain plants the seeds of which rattle in the pods when shaken.

Raucous, ra̤′kus, *a.* [L. *raucus*, hoarse.] Hoarse; harsh, as the voice.—**Raucity**, ra̤′si-ti, *n.* Harshness of sound; rough utterance; hoarseness.

Ravage, rav′āj, *n.* [Fr. *ravage*, from *ravir*, to carry off, to ravish (which see).] Desolation or destruction by violence, either by men, beasts, or physical causes; devastation; ruin.—*v.t.*—*ravaged, ravaging.* [Fr. *ravager.*] To lay waste by force; to devastate; to pillage.—**Ravager**, rav′ā-jėr, *n.* One who ravages; a plunderer; a spoiler.

Rave, rāv, *v.i.*—*raved, raving.* [O.Fr. *raver*, to be delirious, from L. *rabies*, madness. RABID.] To wander in mind or intellect; to be delirious, wild, furious, or raging, as a madman; to talk with false enthusiasm; to speak enthusiastically.—*v.t.* To utter wildly and excitedly.—**Raver**, rā′vėr, *n.* One that raves or is furious.—**Raving**, rā′ving, *p.* and *a.* Furious with delirium; mad.—*n.* Furious exclamation; irrational incoherent talk.—**Ravingly**, rā′ving-li, *adv.* In a raving manner; with distraction.

Ravel, rav′el, *v.t.*—*ravelled, ravelling.* [Same as O.D. *ravelen*, D. *rafelen*, to disentangle; connections uncertain.] To untwist; to unweave; to disentangle; to entangle; to make intricate; to involve.—*v.i.* To become entangled; to fall into perplexity and confusion.—**Ravelling**, rav′el-ing, *n.* Anything, as a thread, detached in the process of untwisting.

Ravelin, rav′lin, *n.* [Fr. *ravelin*, from It. *ravellino, revellino*; probably from L. *re*, back, and *vallum*, a rampart.] A detached triangular work in fortification, with two embankments which form a projecting angle.

Raven, rā′vn, *n.* [A.Sax. *hrœfn* = Icel. *hrafn*, D. *raaf*, Dan. *ravn*, O.H.G. *hraban*, G. *rabe*. Like *crow*, ultimately from its cry.] A large bird of a black colour, of the crow family, noted for its hoarse cry and plundering habits; found in every part of the globe.—*a.* Resembling a raven, especially in colour; black (*raven* locks).

Ravin, Raven, rav′in, rav′en, *n.* [O.Fr. *ravine*, from L. *rapina*, rapine. RAVINE.] Prey; plunder.—*v.i.* To prey with rapacity; to show rapacity.—*v.t.* To devour; to eat with voracity. (O.T.)—**Ravener**, rav′en-ėr, *n.* One who ravens or plunders.—**Ravenous**, rav′en-us, *a.* Furiously voracious; hungry even to rage; eager for gratification (a *ravenous* appetite).—**Ravenously**, rav′en-us-li, *adv.* In a ravenous manner.—**Ravenousness**, rav′en-us-nes, *n.*

Ravine, ra-vēn′, *n.* [Fr. *ravine*, a ravine, from L. *rapina*, rapine, violence, from *rapio*, to seize, or carry away. RAPID.] A long deep hollow worn by a stream or torrent of water; any deep narrow gorge in a mountain, &c.; a gully.

Ravish, rav′ish, *v.t.* [Fr. *ravir, ravissant*, from L. *rapio, rapere*, to seize, to snatch. RAPID.] To seize and carry away by violence; to have carnal knowledge of a woman by force and against her consent; to commit a rape upon; to deflower or violate; to transport with joy or delight; to enrapture; to enchant.—**Ravisher**, rav′ish-ėr, *n.* One that ravishes.—**Ravishing**, rav′ish-ing, *p.* and *a.* Such as to ravish; delighting to rapture; transporting. —**Ravishingly**, rav′ish-ing-li, *adv.* In a ravishing manner.—**Ravishment**, rav′ish-ment, *n.* Ecstasy.

Raw, ra̤, *a.* [A.Sax. *hredw*, *hraew* = D. *raauw*, Dan. *raa*, Icel. *hrár*, O.H.G. *rão*, G. *roh*, raw; same root as L. *crudus*, raw, *cruor*, blood: Gr. *kreas*, flesh.] Not altered from its natural state by cooking; not roasted, boiled, or the like; not subjected to some industrial or manufacturing process; not manufactured (*raw* silk, *raw* hides); not mixed or diluted (*raw* spirits); not covered with the natural covering; having the flesh exposed; sore, as if galled; sensitive; immature; inexperienced; unripe in skill (*raw* soldiers); bleak; chilly; cold and damp (a *raw* day).—*n.* A raw, galled, or sore place, as on a horse.—**Raw-boned**, *a.* Having little flesh on the bones; gaunt; lean and large-boned.—**Rawhead**, ra̤′hed, *n.* A spectre mentioned to frighten children.—**Rawish**, ra̤′ish, *a.* Somewhat raw.—**Rawly**, ra̤′li, *adv.* In a raw manner; especially, in an ignorant or inexperienced manner.—**Rawness**, ra̤′nes, *n.* The state or quality of being raw; want of cooking; state of being inexperienced; chilliness; with dampness; bleakness.

Ray, rā, *n.* [O.Fr. *ray*, a sunbeam, from L. *radius*, a ray.] A line of light, one of the lines that make up a beam; *fig.* a beam of intellectual light; a gleam; one of a number of diverging radii; *bot.* the radiating part of a flower; the outer part or circumference of a compound radiate flower; *ich.* one of the radiating bony spines in the fins of fishes.—*Becquerel rays*, rays emitted by radio-active elements.—*Roentgen rays*, rent′gen, or *X-rays*, rays of intense penetrating power, enabling an operator to detect a body within an organism, much used for surgical, and to some extent for industrial, purposes.—*Ultraviolet rays*, invisible rays having a wave length between the violet end of the visible spectrum, and X-rays, used in physical therapy as a source of *Vitamin D*.—*Violet ray*, shortest of visible wave lengths of the spectrum.—*v.t.* To radiate; to shoot forth or emit rays; to cause to shine forth.—*v.t.* To shine forth or out, as in rays.

Ray, rā, *n.* [Fr. *raie*, from L. *raia*, a ray.] One of a genus of cartilaginous fishes, of which the skate is a well-known example, having a flattened body, with the pectoral fins extremely broad and fleshy.

Rayah, **Raia**, rä′yä, *n.* In Turkey, a person not a Mohammedan who pays the capitation tax.

Raze, rāz, *v.t.*—*razed, razing.* [Same word as *rase*, Fr. *raser*, to raze, to shave, to demolish, from L. *rado*, *rasum*, to scrape, RASE.] To graze; to subvert from the foundation; to overthrow; to demolish; to erase; to efface; to extirpate; to destroy.

Razor, rā′zor, *n.* [Fr. *rasoir*, from *raser*, to shave.] A keen-edged steel device used for shaving.—*Razorback*, *n.* A species of hog having long legs and a thin body; the rorqual whale. RORQUAL.—**Razorbill**, *n.* An aquatic bird, the common auk. AUK. —**Razor blade**, *n.* A thin, keen-edged piece of steel fitted into a holder for shaving. —**Razorstrop**, *n.* A strap for sharpening razors.

Razzia, räz′i-a, *n.* [Fr. *razzia*, Ar. *rhaziat*.] A raid or foray into a country for the purpose of carrying off cattle and destroying the standing crops, &c.

Re, rā. Shortened form of Latin legal expression *in re*, adopted in business correspondence: with reference to, in the matter of, a former communication or subject.

Re, rā, *n.* *Music*, the name given to the second of the syllables used in solmization.

Re-absorb, rē-ab-sorb′, *v.t.* To absorb or imbibe again. — **Re-absorption**, rē-ab-sorp′shon, *n.* The act of re-absorbing.

Reach, rēch, *v.t.* [A.Sax. *raecan*, O.Fris. *rēka*, G. *reichen*, to reach, to extend, to hold out; from same root as *rich*, *right*, *rack*, *rake*, &c.; L. *rego*, to govern, *rex*, a king, E. *regal*.] To extend or stretch out; to hold or put forth; to spread abroad: often followed by *out* and *forth*; to touch by extending the arm or something in the hand; to extend to; to stretch out as far, or as high as; to give with the hand (*reach* me a chair); to arrive at; to come to; to get as far as (the ship *reached* her port); to attain to by effort, labour, or study; to gain or obtain; to extend in action or influence to. —*v.i.* To extend in space (to *reach* to heaven); to extend in scope or power; to stretch out the hand in order to touch; to make efforts at attainment.—*To reach after*, to make efforts to attain to or obtain.—*n.* The act or power of reaching; distance to which one can reach; the sphere to which an agency or a power is limited; often the extent or limit of human faculties or attainments; scope; a stretch of water; a straight portion of a river between any two bendings.—**Reachable**, rēch′a-bl, *a.* Capable of being reached; within reach. —**Reacher**, rēch′ėr, *n.* One who reaches. —**Reachless**, rēch′les, *a.* Beyond reach; unattainable; lofty.

React, rē-akt′, *v.t.* To act or perform anew. —*v.i.* To return an impulse or impression; to resist the action of another body by an opposite force; to act in opposition; to act mutually or reciprocally upon each other, as two or more chemical agents.—**Reactance**, rē-ak′tans. [*Re*, back, and *act*.] In an electric circuit carrying alternating current, that part of the impedance which is due to induction and capacity.—**Reaction**, rē-ak′shon, *n.* The reciprocal action which two bodies or two minds exert on each other; action or tendency to revert from a present to a previous condition; in *politics*, a tendency to revert from a more to a less advanced policy; *physics*, the resistance made by a body to anything tending to change its state; *chem.* the mutual or reciprocal action of chemical agents upon each other; *pathol.* a vital phenomenon arising from the application of an external influence; depression or exhaustion consequent on excessive excitement or stimulation, or increase of activity succeeding depression.—*Reaction wheel*, a turbine wheel. — **Reactionary**, rē′ak′shon-a-ri, *a.* Pertaining to, proceeding from, or favouring reaction.—**Reactionary**, **Reactionist**, rē-ak′shon-ist, *n.* A favourer of reaction; one who attempts to check or reverse political progress.—**Reactive**, rē-ak′tiv, *a.* Having power to react; tending to reaction.—**Reactively**, rē-ak′tiv-li, *adv.* By reaction. — **Reactiveness**, rē-ak′tiv-nes, *n.*

Read, rēd, *v.t.* pret. & pp. *read* (red). [A Sax. *raedan*, to discern, to advise, to read; Icel. *rátha*, to advise, to read; D. *raden*, to advise, to interpret; G. *rathen*, O.H.G. *ratan*, to advise; same root as L. *reor*, *ratus*, to suppose (RATE). Akin *riddle*. It would have been better to have retained the old spelling *red* for the pret. & pp.; comp. *lead* and *led*.] To peruse; to go over and gather the meaning of (to *read* a book, an author); to utter aloud, following something written or printed; to reproduce in sound; to see through; to understand from superficial indications (to *read* one's face); to discover by marks; to study by reading (to *read* law); to explain; to interpret (to *read* a riddle). — *To read up*, to make a special study of.—*v.i.* To perform the act of perusing; to read many books; to study for a specific object; to stand written or printed (the passage *reads* thus); to have a certain effect when read; to be coherent; to make sense: said of a sentence.—*To read between the lines*, to perceive and appreciate the real motive or meaning of a writing or work, as distinguished from what is openly professed or patent.—*n.* A reading over; perusal.—*a.* (red). Instructed or knowing by reading: hardly used except with the adverb *well* (*well read* in history).—**Readable**, rē′da-bl, *a.* Capable of being read; legible; worth reading. — **Readability**, **Readableness**, rē-da-bil′i-ti, rē′da-bl-nes, *n.* The state of being readable. — **Readably**, rē′da-bli, *adv.* In a readable manner.—**Reader**, rē′dėr, *n.* One who reads or peruses; one who studies; one whose office it is to read prayers, lessons, lectures, and the like to others; a reading-book; one who corrects the errors in proof-sheets; a corrector of the press.—**Readership**, rē′dėr-ship, *n.* The office of a reader. —**Reading**, rē′ding, *n.* The act of one who reads; perusal; study of books (a man of extensive *reading*); a public recital or delivery of something written; a particular version of a passage; a lection; view or interpretation of an author's meaning or intention; reproduction in accordance with such interpretation; rendering; *legislation*, the formal recital of a bill by the proper officer before the house which is to consider it (the bill passed the second *reading*).—*Thought reading.* Under THOUGHT. — *a.* Addicted to the reading or study of books. —**Reading-book**, *n.* A school-book containing selections to be used as exercises in reading.—**Reading-desk**, *n.* A desk at which reading is performed. — **Reading-room**, *n.* A room furnished with books, newspapers, &c., to which persons resort for reading.

Readily, **Readiness**. Under READY.

Readjourn, rē-ad-jėrn′, *v.t.* To adjourn again or anew.—**Readjournment**, rē-ad-jėrn′ment, *n.* Adjournment anew.

Readjust, rē-ad-just′, *v.t.* To adjust or settle again; to put in order again.—**Re-adjustment**, rē-ad-just′ment, *n.* The act of readjusting.

Readmission, **Readmittance**, rē-ad-mish′on, rē-ad-mit′ans, *n.* The act of admitting again.—**Readmit**, rē-ad-mit′, *v.t.* To admit again.

Readorn, rē-a-dorn′, *v.t.* To adorn anew; to decorate a second time.

Readvance, rē-ad-vans′, *v.i.* To advance again or afresh.

Ready, red′i, *a.* [O.E. *redi*, *readi*, A.Sax. *raede*, ready = Dan. *rede*, Sw. *reda*, Icel. *reithr*, G. (*be*)*reit*, ready; perhaps from root of *ride*. *Array* is from this stem through the French.] Prepared at the moment; fit for immediate use; causing no delay from want of preparation; not slow, backward, dull, or hesitating (a *ready* apprehension); prompt; dexterous; not backward or reluctant; willing; inclined; offering itself at once; at hand; opportune, near, easy, convenient; on the point, eve, or brink: with *to*.—*Ready money*, means of immediate payment; cash.—*To make ready*, to make preparation; to get things in readiness.—**Readily**, red′i-li, *adv.* In a ready manner; quickly; promptly; cheerfully. — **Readiness**, red′i-nes, *n.* The state or quality of being ready; due preparation; aptitude; quickness; cheerfulness; alacrity. —**Ready-made**, *a.* Made or prepared beforehand, kept in stock ready for use or sale (*ready-made* clothes).—**Ready-reckoner**, *n.* A book of tabulated calculations, or tables to facilitate calculations.—**Ready-to-wear**, *n.* Ready-made clothes; clothes made beforehand in large quantities. — **Ready-witted**, *a.* Having quick wit.

Reaffirm, rē-af-fėrm′, *v.t.* To affirm again. —**Reaffirmance**, rē-af-fėr′mans, *n.* A second affirmation or confirmation.

Reagent, rē-a′jent, *n.* Generally, anything that produces reaction; *chem.* a substance employed to detect the presence of other bodies in a compound.

Reagree, rē-a-grē′, *v.i.* To agree again; to become reconciled.

Real, rē′al, *a.* [O.Fr. *real* (Fr. *réel*), L.L. *realis*, from L. *res*, a thing (whence *rebus*, *re-* of *republic*).] Actually being or existing; not fictitious or imaginary (*real* life); genuine; not artificial, counterfeit, or fictitious; not affected; not assumed (his *real* character); *law*, pertaining to things fixed, permanent, or immovable, as to lands and tenements (*real* estate); opposed to *personal* or *movable* (property).—*Real presence*, the alleged actual presence of the body and blood of Christ in the eucharist, or the conversion of the substance of the bread and wine into the real body and blood of Christ. —**Realism**, rē′al-izm, *n.* The doctrines or principles of a realist.—**Realist**, rē′al-ist, *n.* *Metaph.* as opposed to *idealist*, one who holds the doctrine that there is an immediate or intuitive cognition of external objects, that external objects exist independently of our sensations or conceptions; *scholastic philos.* one who maintains that things, and not words, are the objects of dialectics: opposed to *nominalist*; *fine arts* and *literature*, one who endeavours to reproduce nature or describes real life just as it appears to him.—**Realistic**, rē-al-is′tik, *a.* Pertaining to or characteristic of the realists; relating to realism.—**Realistically**, rē-al-is′ti-kal-li, *adv.* In a realistic manner.—**Reality**, rē-al′i-ti, *n.* [Fr. *réalité*.] The state or quality of being real; actual being or existence; actuality; truth; fact; that which is real as opposed to that which is imagination or pretence.—**Realizable**, rē′al-ī-za-bl, *a.* Capable of being realized.—**Realization**, rē′al-ī-zā″shon, *n.* The act of realizing.—**Realize**, rē′al-īz, *v.t.* —*realized, realizing.* [Fr. *réaliser*.] To make real; to bring into being or act (to *realize* a scheme or project); to feel as vividly or strongly as if real; to bring home to one's own case or experience; to acquire as the result of labour or pains; to gain (to *realize* profit from trade); to sell for or convert into money (to *realize* one's stock in a railway).—*v.i.* To turn any kind of property into money.—**Realizer**, rē'al-ī-zėr, *n.* One who realizes.—**Really**, rē'al-li, *adv.* In a real manner; in truth; actually; indeed; to tell the truth: often used familiarly as a slight corroboration of an opinion or declaration (well, *really*, I cannot say).—**Realness**, rē'al-nes, *n.* The quality of being real: reality.—**Real school**, rē'al sköl, *n.* [G. *realschule*, real or practical school.] The name of secondary schools in Germany where modern subjects are chiefly taught.—**Realty**, rē'al-ti, *n.* [A contr. of *reality*.] *Law*, the fixed or permanent nature of that kind of property termed *real*; real property.

Real, rē'al, *n.* [Sp. *real*, from royal.] A former Spanish coin worth about 12c.

Realgar, rē-al'gar, *n.* [Fr. *réalgar*, from Sp. *rejalgar*, from Ar. *rahj*, powder, *al*, the, and *ghār*, a mine.] A mineral consisting of sulphur and arsenic in equal equivalents: red sulphide of arsenic, a brilliant red pigment. ORPIMENT.

Realm, relm, *n.* [O.Fr. *realme* (Fr. *royaume*), from L. *regalis*, from *rex*, *regis*, a king. REGAL.] A kingdom; a king's dominions; hence, generally, region, sphere, domain.

Ream, rēm, *n.* [O.Fr. *raime*, from Sp. *resma*, a ream, from Ar. *rizmat*, a bale, a packet, a ream.] A bundle or package of paper, consisting generally of 20 quires of 24 sheets each: the *printer's ream* contains 21½ quires or 516 sheets.

Ream, rēm, *v.t.* [A.Sax. *rȳman*, to increase, to enlarge, from *rūm*, space. ROOM.] To bevel out, as a hole in metal; to enlarge, as the bore of a cannon; *naut.* to widen the seams between a vessel's planks for the purpose of caulking them.—**Reamer**, rē'mėr, *n.* An instrument for enlarging a hole.

Reanimate, rē-an'i-māt, *v.t.* To revive; to resuscitate; to restore to life or animation; to infuse new life or courage into.—**Reanimation**, rē-an'i-mā''shon, *n.* The act of reanimating.

Reannex, rē-an-neks', *v.t.* To annex again; to reunite.—**Reannexation**, rē-an'nek-sā''shon, *n.* The act of annexing again.

Reap, rēp, *v.t.* [A.Sax. *rípan*, to reap; closely allied to Goth. *raupjan*, to pluck; D. *rapen*, to gather; L.G. *rapen*, to pluck. *Ripe* is from same stem.] To cut with a sickle, scythe, &c., as a grain crop; to cut down and gather; to gather when ripe or ready; to cut down the crop on; to clear of a grain crop (to *reap* a field): hence, to shave (*Shak.*); to receive as a reward, or as the fruit of labour or of works: in a good or bad sense.—*v.i.* To perform the act or operation of reaping; to receive the fruit of labour or works.—**Reaper**, rē'pėr, *n.* One who reaps; a machine for cutting grain; a reaping-machine.—**Reaping-hook**, *n.* A curved cutting instrument used in reaping; a sickle.—**Reaping-machine**, *n.* A machine for cutting down standing corn, &c., and in many cases also for forming it into sheaves, moved by horses or motor tractors through the field.

Reappear, rē-ap-pēr', *v.i.* To appear again or anew.—**Reappearance**, rē-ap-pē'rans, *n.* A second or new appearance.

Reapply, rē-ap-plī', *v.t.* or *i.* To apply again.—**Reapplication**, rē-ap'pli-kā''shon, *n.* The act of applying again.

Reappoint, rē-ap-point', *v.t.* To appoint again.—**Reappointment**, rē-ap-point'ment, *n.* A renewed or second appointment.

Reapportion, rē-ap-pōr'shon, *v.t.* To apportion again.—**Reapportionment**, rē-ap-pōr'shon-ment, *n.* A renewed or second apportionment.

Reapproach, rē-ap-prōch', *v.i.* or *t.* To approach again or anew.

Rear, rēr, *n.* [O.F. *riere*, Pr. *reire*, from L. *retro*, behind—*re*, back, and suffix *tro*, denoting direction, from root corresponding to Skr. *tar*, to move. So *arrear*, from L. *ad*, to, and *retro*.] The part behind or at the back; the hind part; the background: generally with the definite article; specifically, the part of an army or a fleet which is behind the rest.—*a.* Pertaining to or in the rear; hindermost; last.—**Rear-admiral**, *n.* The third degree of the rank of admiral. ADMIRAL.—**Rear-guard**, *n.* The part of an army that marches in the rear of the main body to protect it and bring up stragglers.—**Rearmost**, rēr'mōst, *a.* Farthest in the rear; last of all.—**Rear-rank**, *n.* The rank of a body of troops which is in the rear.—**Rearward**, rēr'wạrd, *n.* The rear-guard; the latter part of anything.—*a.* At or towards the rear.

Rear, rēr, *v.t.* [A.Sax. *raeran*, for *raesan*, to raise, caus. of *risan*, to rise. RAISE. RISE.] To lift or set up; to erect; to raise; to bring up, as young; to foster; to educate; to breed, as cattle; to build up; to construct (to *rear* an edifice).—*v.i.* To rise on the hind-legs, as a horse; to assume an erect posture.

Reargue, rē-är'gū, *v.t.* To argue over again.

Rearrange, rē'a-rānj, *v.t.* To arrange again; to put in proper order again.—**Rearrangement**, rē-a-rānj'ment, *n.* A second or repeated arrangement.

Reason, rē'zn, *n.* [Fr. *raison*, O.Fr. *reson*, from L. *ratio*, *rationis*, reason, plan, account, from *reor*, *ratus*, to think, to calculate. RATE, RATIFY, RATIO.] A motive, ground, or cause acting on the mind; the basis for any opinion, conclusion, or determination; a ground or a principle; what accounts for or explains a fact or phenomenon; final cause; explanation; a faculty of the mind by which it distinguishes truth from falsehood, and which enables the possessor to deduce inferences from facts or from propositions, and to combine means for the attainment of particular ends; the act of deducing consequences from premises; ratiocination; justice; equity; fairness; that which is dictated or supported by reason; moderate demands; claims which reason and justice admit or prescribe (to bring one to *reason*).—*In reason, in all reason*, in justice; with rational ground.—*v.i.* To exercise the faculty of reason; to deduce inferences justly from premises; to argue; to ratiocinate; to discuss, in order to make something understood.—*v.t.* To examine or discuss by arguments; to debate or discuss (to *reason* the point); to persuade by reasoning or argument.—**Reasonable**, rē'zn-a-bl, *a.* Having the faculty of reason; rational; governed by reason; not given to extravagant notions or expectations conformable or agreeable to reason; not extravagant, excessive, or immoderate; fair; equitable (any *reasonable* demands); being in mediocrity; moderate; tolerable.—**Reasonableness**, rē'zn-a-bl-nes, *n.* The quality of being reasonable.—**Reasonably**, rē'zn-a-bli, *adv.* In a reasonable manner; in consistency with reason; moderately; tolerably.—**Reasoner**, rē'zn-ėr, *n.* One who reasons or argues.—**Reasoning**, rē'zn-ing, *n.* The act or process of exercising the faculty of reason; ratiocination; the arguments employed; the proofs or reasons when arranged and developed.—**Reasonless**, rē'zn-les, *a.* Destitute of reason; irrational; unreasonable.

Reassemble, rē-as-sem'bl, *v.t.* To collect or assemble again.—*v.i.* To assemble or meet together again.—**Reassemblage**, rē-as-sem'blāj, *n.* A renewed assemblage.

Reassert, rē-as-sėrt', *v.t.* To assert again.—**Reassertion**, rē-as-sėr'shon, *n.* A repeated assertion; the act of asserting anew.

Reassign, rē-as-sīn', *v.t.* To assign again.—**Reassignment**, rē-as-sīn'ment, *n.* A renewed or repeated assignment.

Reassimilate, rē-as-sim'i-lāt, *v.t.* To assimilate anew.—**Reassimilation**, rē-as-sim'i-lā''shon, *n.* A renewed assimilation.

Reassume, rē-as-sūm', *v.t.* To resume; to take again.—**Reassumption**, rē-as-sum'shon, *n.* A resuming.

Reassure, rē-a-shör', *v.t.* To assure anew; to restore courage to; to free from fear or terror; also, to reinsure.—**Reassurer**, rē-a-shö'rėr, *n.* One who reassures.—**Reassurance**, rē-a-shö'rans, *n.* Assurance or confirmation repeated; also reinsurance.

Reattach, rē-at-tach', *v.t.* To attach again.—**Reattachment**, rē-at-tach'ment, *n.* A second or repeated attachment.

Reattain, rē-at-tān', *v.t.* To attain again.

Reattempt, rē-at-temt', *v.t.* To attempt again.

Reaumur, rā'o-mer, *n.* [Inventor's name.] A thermometric scale on which the fixed points are 0° and 80°, answering respectively to 32° and 212° F.; denoted by R. See *Fahrenheit*.

Reave, rēv, *v.t.*—pret. & pp. *reaved* or *reft*; ppr. *reaving*. [A.Sax. *reáfian*, to seize, to rob, from *reáf*, clothing, spoil; akin to Icel. *raufa*, G. *rauben*, E. to rob. ROB.] To take away by stealth or violence; to bereave; to deprive (with *of*).—**Reaver**, rē'vėr, *n.* One who reaves; a robber.

Reavow, rē-a-vou', *v.t.* To avow again.

Reawake, rē-a-wāk', *v.i.* To awake again.

Rebaptize, rē-bap-tīz', *v.t.* To baptize a second time.—**Rebaptism**, rē-bap'tizm, *n.* A second baptism.

Rebarbarize, rē-bär'bär-īz, *v.t.* To reduce again to a state of barbarism.

Rebate, rē-bāt', *v.t.*—*rebated*, *rebating*. [O.Fr. *rebatre*—*re*, back, and *batre*, L. *batuere*, to beat; akin *battle*, *batter*, *abate*, &c.] To blunt; to diminish, reduce, abate; to deduct or make a discount from.—**Rebate**, **Rebatement**, rē-bāt'ment, *n.* Diminution; *com.* abatement in price; deduction.

Rebate, rē-bāt', *n.* RABBET.

Rebec, **Rebeck**, rē'bek, *n.* [Fr. *rebec*, *rebebe*, from Ar. *rabāb*, a kind of musical instrument.] A stringed instrument introduced by the Moors into Spain, somewhat similar to the violin, and played with a bow.

Rebeccaite, rē-bek'a-īt, *n.* A member of an anti-turnpike conspiracy commenced in Wales, in 1839, so called from a strange application of a passage in Gen. xxiv, 60.

Rebel, reb'el, *n.* [Fr. *rebelle*, from L. *rebellis*, making war again—*re*, again, and *bellum*, war. DUEL.] One who revolts from the government to which he owes allegiance; one who defies and seeks to overthrow the authority to which he is rightfully subject. ∴ Syn. under INSURGENT.—*a.* Rebellious; acting in revolt.—*v.i.* (rē-bel')—*rebelled*, *rebelling*. To revolt; to take up arms against the government of constituted authorities; to refuse to obey a superior; to shake off subjection; to turn with disgust or nausea; to conceive a loathing (his stomach *rebelled* at such food).—**Rebeller**, rē-bel'ėr, *n.* One that rebels; a rebel.—**Rebellion**, rē-bel'yon, *n.* [L. *rebellio*, *rebellionis*.] The act of rebelling; an armed rising against a government; the taking of arms traitorously to resist the authority of lawful government; open resistence to, or refusal to obey, lawful authority. ∴ Syn. under INSURRECTION.—**Rebellious**, rē-bel'yus, *a.* Engaged in, or characterized by, rebellion; mutinous.—**Rebelliously**, rē-bel'yus-li, *adv.* In a rebellious manner.—**Rebelliousness**, rē-bel'yus-nes, *n.*

Rebiting, rē-bīt'ing, *n.* *Engr.* the act or process of deepening or restoring worn lines in an engraved plate by the action of acid.

Rebloom, rē-blöm', *v.i.* To bloom or blossom again.

Reblossom, rē-blos'om, *v.i.* To blossom again; to rebloom.

Rebound, rē-bound', *v.i.* [Prefix *re*, and *bound*; Fr. *rebondir*, to rebound.] To spring or bound back; to fly back by elastic force after impact on another body.—*v.t.* To drive back; to cause to echo; to reverberate.—*n.* The act of flying back on collision with another body; resilience.

Rebuff, rē-buf′, *n.* [Prefix *re*, back, and old *buff*, a blow, from O.Fr. *buffe*, *bufe*, a blow. BUFFET.] A beating, forcing, or driving back; sudden check; a repulse; refusal; rejection of solicitation. —*v.t.* To beat back; to offer sudden resistance to; to repel the advances of.

Rebuild, rē-bild′, *v.t.* To build again; to build after having been demolished.—**Rebuilder**, rē-bil′dėr, *n.* One who rebuilds. —**Rebuilt**, rē-bilt′, *pp.* Built again; reconstructed.

Rebuke, rē-būk′, *v.t.*—*rebuked, rebuking.* [O.Fr. *rebouquer*, to dull, to blunt, to rebuff —*re* and *bouque*, an old and dialectic form of Fr. *bouche*, the mouth, from L. *bucca*, the mouth.] To check with reproof; to reprehend sharply and summarily; to reprimand; to reprove.—*n.* A direct and severe reprimand; reproof; reprehension; a chiding.—**Rebukable**, rē-bū′ka-bl, *a.* Worthy of rebuke or reprehension.—**Rebukeful**, rē-būk′fụl, *a.* Containing or abounding in rebukes.—**Rebuker**, rē-bū′kėr, *n.* One that rebukes.—**Rebukingly**, rē-bū′king-li, *adv.* In a rebuking manner; by way of rebuke.

Rebus, rē′bus, *n.* [L., ablative plural of *res*, a thing—lit. by things, because the meaning is indicated by things.] A set of words written by figures or pictures of objects whose names resemble in sound those words or the syllables of which they are composed; thus, 'I can see you' might be expressed by figures of an eye, a can, the sea, and a ewe; hence, a kind of puzzle made up of such figures or pictures.

Rebut, rē-but′, *v.t.*—*rebutted, rebutting.* [Fr. *rebuter*, *rebouter*, to put or thrust back —*re*, back, and *bouter*, to put, to thrust. BUTT.] To repel, as by counter evidence; to refute; *law*, to oppose by argument, plea, or countervailing proof.—**Rebuttal**, rē-but′al, *n.* The act of rebutting; refutation; confutation. — **Rebutter**, rē-but′ėr, *n.* *Law*, the answer of a defendant to a plaintiff's surrejoinder.

Recalcitrate, rē-kal′si-trāt, *v.i.*—*recalcitrated, recalcitrating.* [L. *recalcitro*, to kick back—*re*, back, and *calcitrare*, to kick, from *calx*, *calcis*, the heel.] To show repugnance or resistance to something; to be refractory. —**Recalcitration**, rē-kal′si-trā″shon, *n.* Act of recalcitrating; opposition; repugnance.—**Recalcitrant**, rē-kal′si-trant, *a.* Exhibiting repugnance or opposition; not submissive; refractory.

Recall, rē-ka̤l′, *v.t.* To call or bring back; to take back; to revoke; to annul by a subsequent act; to revive in memory; to order to come back from a place or mission (to *recall* a minister from a foreign court).—*n.* A calling back; revocation; the power of calling back or revoking; the removal of an official from office by a popular vote.

Recant, rē-kant′, *v.t.* and *i.* [L. *recantare*, to recant, to recall—*re*, back, and *canto*, freq. of *cano*, to sing. CHANT.] To retract; to unsay; to make formal contradiction of something which one had previously asserted.—**Recantation**, rē-kan-tā′shon, *n.* The act of recanting; retraction; a declaration that contradicts a former one.—**Recanter**, rē-kan′tėr, *n.* One who recants.

Recapitulate, rē-ka-pit′ū-lāt, *v.t.* — *recapitulated, recapitulating.* [Fr. *recapituler*, L.L. *recapitulo*, *recapitulatum*—prefix *re*, and *capitulum*, a head or heading. CAPITULATE.] To repeat or summarize, as the principal things mentioned in a preceding discourse; to give a summary of the principal facts, points, or arguments of.—*v.i.* To repeat in brief what has been said before. — **Recapitulation**, rē-ka-pit′ū-lā″shon, *n.* The act of recapitulating; a concise statement of the principal points in a preceding discourse, argument, or essay. —*Recapitulation theory*, the theory that ancestral stages are repeated in the life-history.—**Recapitulator**, rē-ka-pit′ū-lā-tėr, *n.* One who.—**Recapitulatory**, rē-ka-pit′ū-la-to-ri, *a.* Containing recapitulation.

Recapture, rē-kap′tūr, *n.* The act of retaking; the retaking of goods from a captor; a prize retaken.—*v.t.* To capture back; to retake.

Recast, rē-kast′, *v.t.* To cast or found again; to throw again; to mould anew; to throw into a new form.

Recede, rē-sēd′, *v.i.* — *receded, receding.* [L. *recedo*—*re*, back, and *cedere*, to walk. CEDE.] To move back; to retreat; to withdraw; to withdraw from a claim or pretension; to relinquish what had been proposed or asserted (to *recede* from a demand, from propositions).—*v.t.* (rē-sēd). To cede back; to grant or yield to a former possessor.

Receipt, rē-sēt′, *n.* [O.Fr. *recete*, *recepte* (Fr. *recette*), from L. *receptus*, pp. of *recipere*, to receive. RECEIVE.] The act of receiving (the *receipt* of a letter); that which is received; *pl.* money drawn or received; drawings (his *receipts* were $20 a day); a recipe; a prescription of ingredients for any composition, as of medicines, &c.; hence, *fig.* plan or scheme by which anything may be effected; a written acknowledgment of something received, as money, goods, &c.—*v.t.* To give a receipt for; to discharge, as an account.—**Receiptable**, rē-sēt′a-bl, *a.* Capable of being receipted. —**Receipt-book**, *n.* A book containing receipts.—**Receiptor**, rē-sēt′or, *n.* One who receipts; one who gives a receipt.

Receive, rē-sēv′, *v.t.*—*received, receiving.* [O.Fr. *recever*, *receveir*, Fr. *recevoir*, from L. *recipio*—*re*, again, and *capio*, to take. CAPABLE.] To get or obtain; to take, as a thing given, sent, paid, communicated, &c.; to accept; to take into the mind; to embrace; to allow or hold, as a belief, custom, tradition, &c.; to give acceptance to (a *received* belief); to allow to enter in an official capacity; to welcome as a guest; to entertain; to take in or on; to hold, admit, contain, have capacity for (a box to *receive* contributions); to be the object of; to suffer (to *receive* an injury); to take from a thief, knowing the thing to be stolen.—**Receivedness**, rē-sē′ved-nes, *n.* State of being received; general allowance or belief.—**Receivability**, rē-sē′va-bil″i-ti, *n.* Quality of being receivable.—**Receivable**, rē-sē′va-bl, *a.* Such as may be received, as in accounts *receivable*.—**Receivableness**, rē-sē′va-bl-nes, *n.* Capability of being received.—**Receiver**, rē-sē′vėr, *n.* One who receives; a person appointed by a court to manage the affairs of an enterprise in reorganization or liquidation; a person appointed in some business for the purpose of winding up the concern; one who takes stolen goods from a thief, knowing them to be stolen; *chem.* a vessel for receiving and containing the product of distillation; a vessel to receive gases.—**Receivership**, rē-sēv′ėr-ship, *n.* The legal status of an enterprise under jurisdiction of the court for the purpose of a trust, reorganization, or liquidation.—**Receiving**, rē-sē′ving, *p.* and *a.* Adapted to receive, take, hold, or contain.—**Receiving set**, *n.* A radio instrument, or set, used in the reception of radio programs or signals.

Recelebrate, rē-sel′ē-brāt, *v.t.* To celebrate again.—**Recelebration**, rē-sel′ē-brā″shon, *n.* The act of recelebrating.

Recense,† rē-sens′, *v.t.*—*recensed, recensing.* [L. *recensere*, to review or examine—*re*, again, and *censere*, to reckon. CENSOR.] To review; to revise.—**Recension**, rē-sen′shon, *n.* An examination; enumeration; a revision of the text of an author by a critical editor; an edited version.—**Recensionist**, rē-sen′shon-ist, *n.* One who revises.

Recent, rē′sent, *a.* [Fr. *récent*, from L. *recens*, *recentis*, recent; etym. unknown.] Of late origin, occurrence, or existence; new; not of remote date, antiquated style, and the like; modern; only made known or spoken of lately; fresh (*recent* intelligence); *geol.* applied to all accumulations and deposits whose remains belong exclusively to species still existing; occurring or formed since the glacial period.—**Recently**, rē′sent-li, *adv.* Newly; lately; freshly; not long since.—**Recentness**, **Recency**, rē′sent-nes, rē′sen-si, *n.* The state or quality of being recent.

Receptacle, rē-sep′ta-kl or res′ep-ta-kl, *n.* [L. *receptaculum*, from *recipio*, *receptum*, to receive. RECEIVE.] That which receives, admits, or contains things; a place or vessel in which anything is received and contained; a repository; *bot.* a general term given to a part which receives or bears other parts; as, that part of a flower upon which the carpels are situated; that part of the axis of a plant which forms a sort of disc, bearing the flowers.—**Receptacular**, rē-sep-tak′ū-lėr, *a.* Pertaining to a receptacle.

Reception, rē-sep′shon, *n.* [L. *receptio*, from *recipio*, to receive. RECEIVE.] A receiving or manner of receiving; receipt; treatment at first coming; welcome; entertainment; a formal occasion or ceremony of receiving guests, official personages, &c.; admission or credence, as of an opinion or doctrine; acceptance or allowance; in *radio*, the act or process of receiving programs or signals.—**Receptibility**, rē-sep′ti-bil″i-ti, *n.* The quality of being receptible; receivableness.—**Receptive**, rē-sep′tiv, *a.* Such as to receive readily (*receptive* of teaching); taking in; able to take in, hold, or contain.—**Receptivity**, **Receptiveness**, rē′sep-tiv″i-ti, rē-sep′tiv-nes, *n.* The state or quality of being receptive.

Recess, rē-ses′, *n.* [L. *recessus*, from *recedo*, *recessum*. RECEDE.] A withdrawing or retiring; a moving back (the *recess* of the tides); place of retirement or secrecy; private abode; the time or period during which public or other business is suspended (the Christmas *recess* of a school); a cavity, niche, or sunken space formed in a wall; an alcove or similar portion of a room.—*v.t.* To make a recess in; to put in a recess.—**Recessed**, rē-sest′, *a.* Having a recess or recesses.—*Recessed arch*, one arch within another.—**Recession**, rē-sesh′on, *n.* [L. *recessio*, *recessionis*, from *recedo*; in last sense directly from *re* and *cession*.] The act of receding; withdrawal; position relatively withdrawn; a cession or granting back; retrocession.—*Recession of the equinoxes*, the same as *Precession of the equinoxes*.—**Recessional**, *n.* Glacial deposit remaining after the ice sheet receded; hymn or other verses sung after service, when the choir and clergy withdraw from their places.—**Recessive**,† rē-ses′iv, *a.* Receding; going back.

Rechabite, rek′a-bīt, *n.* Among the ancient Jews, one of a family whom Jonadab, son of *Rechab*, bound to abstain from wine, from planting vines, &c., Jer. xxxv, 6; one of a benefit society of total abstainers.

Recharter, rē-chär′tėr, *v.t.* To charter again; to grant another charter to.

Rechauffé, rā-shō-fā, *n.* [Fr., from prefix *re*, and *chauffer*, to warm. CHAFE.] *Lit.* a warmed-up dish; hence, a concoction of old materials; old literary matter worked up into a new form.—**Rechauffage**, rā-shō-fäj, *n.* A working up of what is old.

Recheat, rē-chēt′, *n.* [Fr., *requête*, *requeste*, a recheat. REQUEST.] A call on a huntsman's horn to bring back hounds.

Recherché, rė-sher-shā, *a.* [Fr.] Much sought after; choice; rare; exquisite.

Recidivist, rē-sid′i-vist, *n.* [Fr. *récidiviste* —L. *re*, back, *cado*, to fall.] A relapsed criminal or one who returns to crime.

Recipe, res′i-pē, *n.* [L. *recipe*, take, receive, imper. of *recipio*, to take or receive RECEIVE.] The first word of a physician's prescription; hence the prescription itself; now applied to a receipt for preparing, mixing, or cooking food to produce a particular dish.

Recipient, rē-sip′i-ent, *n.* [L. *recipiens*, *recipientis*, ppr. of *recipio*. RECEIVE.] A person or thing that receives; one to whom anything is communicated.—*a.* Receiving. —**Recipience**, **Recipiency**, rē-sip′i-ens, rē-sip′i-en-si, *n.* A receiving; act or capacity of receiving; reception.—**Recipiomotor**, rē-sip′i-o-mō-tėr, *a.* Receptive of a nervous stimulus and giving rise to motion.

Reciprocal, rē-sip′rō-kal, *a.* [L. *reciprocus*, Fr. *réciproque*, alternating, reciprocal, probably connected with *re*, back, and *pro*, forward.] Acting with a backward and forward motion; moving backwards and forwards; reciprocating; done by each to the other; mutual; mutually interchangeable; *gram.* reflexive.—*Reciprocal* or *inverse proportion.* Under INVERSE.—*Reciprocal quantities, math.* quantities which, multiplied together, produce unity.—*Reciprocal ratio* is the ratio between the reciprocals of two quantities: thus the *reciprocal ratio* of 4 to 9 is that of 1-4th to 1-9th.—*n.* That which is reciprocal to another thing.—*Reciprocal of a quantity*, in *math.* the quotient resulting from the division of unity by the quantity; thus, the *reciprocal* of 4 is a ¼, and conversely the *reciprocal* of ¼ is 4.—**Reciprocally**, rē-sip′rō-kal-li, *adv.* In a reciprocal manner; mutually; interchangeably; inversely.—**Reciprocalness, Reciprocality**, rē-sip′rō-kal-nes, rē-sip′rō-kal″i-ti, *n.* The state or quality of being reciprocal. — **Reciprocate**, rē-sip′rō-kāt, *v.i.*—*reciprocated, reciprocating.* To move backwards and forwards; to have an alternate movement; to alternate.—*v.t.* To interchange; to give and return mutually; to give in requital (to *reciprocate* favours).—**Reciprocating**, rē-sip′rō-kāt-ing, *p.* and *a.* Alternating; moving backwards and forwards alternately.—*Reciprocating engine*, that form of engine in which the piston and piston-rod move back and forth in a straight line, absolutely, or relatively to the cylinder.—**Reciprocation**, rē-sip′rō-kā″-shon, *n.* The act of reciprocating; interchange of acts; a mutual giving and returning; alternation. — **Reciprocity**, res-i-pros′i-ti, *n.* The state or character of being reciprocal; reciprocal obligation or right; equal rights or benefits to be mutually yielded or enjoyed; especially equal commercial rights or privileges enjoyed mutually by two countries trading together.

Recision, rē-sizh′on, *n.* [L. *recisio*—*re*, back, and *cædo*, to cut. EXCISION.] The act of cutting off.

Recite, rē-sīt′, *v.t.*—*recited, reciting.* [Fr. *réciter*, from L. *recitare*—*re*, again, and *cito*, to cite. CITE.] To repeat, as something prepared, written down, or committed to memory beforehand; to rehearse, with appropriate gestures, before an audience; to tell over; to relate or narrate; to go over in particulars; to recapitulate. —*v.i.* To rehearse before an audience compositions committed to memory; to rehearse a lesson. —**Reciter**, rē-sī′tėr, *n.* One that recites or rehearses; a narrator.—**Recital**, rē-sī′tal, *n.* The act of reciting; the repetition of the words of another; narration; a telling of the particulars of an adventure or event; that which is recited; a story; a narrative; a musical entertainment given by a single performer (an organ *recital*). — **Recitation**, res-i-tā′shon, *n.* The act of reciting; the delivery aloud, with appropriate gestures, before an audience, of a composition committed to memory, as an elocutionary exhibition; the rehearsal of a lesson by pupils before their instructor. — **Recitative**, res′i-ta-tēv″, *n.* [It. *recitativo.*] *Music*, a species of vocal composition which differs from an air in having no definite rhythmical arrangement, and no strictly constructed melody; musical recitation or declamation; a piece of music to be sung recitatively.—**Recitatively**, res′i-ta-tēv″-li, *adv.* In the manner of recitative. — **Recitativo**, res′i-ta-tē″vō, *n.* [It.] Recitative.

Reck, rek, *v.i.* [A.Sax. *reccan, récan*, to reck, regard; cog. O.Sax. *rōkian*, Icel. *rækja*, O.H.G. *rōhhian, geruochen*, to reck or care; perhaps same root as *reckon.*] To care; to mind; to heed; to regard: often followed by *of.*—*v.t.*† To heed, regard, care for.—*It recks* (*impersonal*), it concerns (*it recks* me not).—**Reckless**, rek′les, *a.* Not recking; careless; heedless of consequences; mindless: with *of* before an object. ∴ Syn. under RASH. — **Recklessly**, rek′les-li, *adv.* In a reckless manner.—**Recklessness**, rek′les-nes, *n.* The state or quality of being reckless.

Reckling, rek′ling, *n.* [Probably from *reck*, lit. one that requires to be cared for.] The smallest and weakest in a brood of animals; hence, a helpless babe. (*Tenn.*)—*a.* Small; weak; helpless.

Reckon, rek′n, *v.t.* [O.E. *reknen, rekenen*, A.Sax. *gerecnian, recenian* = D. *rekenen*, Dan. *regne*, Icel. *reikna*, Sw. *räkna*, G. *rechnen*, to reckon, number, esteem; perhaps from same root as *reck* or *right.*] To count; to number; to tell one by one; to calculate; to estimate by rank or quality; to esteem, account, repute, hold.—*v.i.* To make computation; to compute; to calculate; to make up or render an account; to adjust relations of desert and penalty; to think, suppose, imagine (in this sense American rather than English). — *To reckon on* or *upon*, to count or depend upon.—*To reckon with*, to call to account; to exact penalty of. — **Reckoner**, rek′n-ėr, *n.* One who reckons; something that assists a person to reckon. READY-RECKONER. — **Reckoning**, rek′n-ing, *n.* The act of computing; calculation; a statement and comparison of accounts for adjustment; the charges made by a host in a hotel, tavern, &c. (to pay the *reckoning*); *naut.* the calculation of the position of a ship from the rate found by the log, and the course as determined by the compass.

Reclaim, rē-klām′, *v.t.* [*Re* and *claim*; Fr. *réclamer*, to claim back, to reclaim a hawk, to protest; L. *reclamo*—*re*, back, and *clamo*, to call. CLAIM.] To claim back; to demand to have returned; to call back; to bring a hawk to the wrist by a certain call; to reduce from a wild to a tame or domestic state; to tame; to rescue from being wild, desert, or waste; to bring under cultivation; to bring back from error; to reform.—*v.i.* To cry out; to exclaim against anything; *Scots law*, to appeal to the inner house of the Court of Session.—*n.* The act of reclaiming; reformation. — **Reclaimable**, rē-klā′ma-bl, *a.* Capable of being reclaimed. —**Reclaimably**, rē-klā′ma-bli, *adv.* So as to be capable of being reclaimed.—**Reclaimer**, rē-klā′mėr, *n.* One that reclaims. —**Reclaimless**, rē-klām′les, *a.* Incapable of being reclaimed; not to be reclaimed.—**Reclamation**, rek-la-mā′shon, *n.* The act of reclaiming; the act of bringing into cultivation; the bringing back of a person from evil courses; a demand; claim made; a remonstrance or representation.

Recline, rē-klīn′, *v.t.*—*reclined, reclining.* [L. *reclino*, to bend back—*re*, back, and *clino*, to bend (whence also *incline, decline*); root same as that of E. to *lean.*] To lean to one side or sidewise; to lay down to rest (to *recline* the head).—*v.i.* To rest or repose; to take a recumbent position.—**Recliner**, rē-klī′nėr, *n.* One who reclines.—**Reclining**, rē-klī′ning, *p.* and *a.* Leaning back or sidewise; lying in repose. — *Reclining dial*, a dial whose plane reclines from the perpendicular.—**Reclinate**, rē-klī′nāt, *a.* [L. *reclinatus.*] *Bot.* reclined, as a leaf; bent downward, so that the point is lower than the base.—**Reclination**, rēk-li-nā′-shon, *n.* The act of leaning or reclining; *surg.* one of the operations used for the cure of cataract.

Reclose, rē-klōz′, *v.t.* To close or shut again.

Reclothe, rē-klōᴛʜ′, *v.t.* To clothe again.

Recluse, rē-klös′, *a.* [Fr. *reclus*, fem. *recluse*, from L. *reclusus*, pp. of *recludo*, *reclusum*, to lay open, but in L.L. signifying to shut—*re*, again, back, and *claudere*, to shut. CLOSE.] Living shut up or apart from the world; retired; sequestered; solitary.—*n.* A person who lives in retirement or seclusion; a hermit; a religious devotee who lives in an isolated cell.—**Reclusely**, rē-klös′li, *adv.* In a recluse manner.—**Recluseness**, rē-klös′nes, *n.* The state of being recluse. — **Reclusion**, rē-klö′zhon, *n.* A state of retirement from the world; seclusion.—**Reclusive**, rē-klö′siv, *a.* Affording retirement from society; recluse.—**Reclusory**, rē-klö′so-ri, *n.* The abode of a recluse; a hermitage.

Recognize, rek′og-nīz, *v.t.*—*recognized, recognizing.* [From *recognisance* (which is older in English), O.Fr. *recognoissance*, from L. *recognosco*—*re* and *cognosco*. COGNITION, KNOW.] To recall or recover the knowledge of; to perceive the identity of, with a person or thing formerly known; to know again; to avow or admit a knowledge of; to acknowledge formally; to indicate one's notice by a bow or nod; *Parliamentary*, to give a speaker the floor in debate (by a presiding officer); to indicate appreciation of (to *recognize* services by a reward).—*v.i. Law*, to enter into recognizances.—**Recognition**, rek-og-nish′on, *n.* [L. *recognitio.*] The act of recognizing or state of being recognized; a perceiving as being known; avowal; notice taken; acknowledgment. — *Recognition markings*, in birds and mammals, conspicuous markings supposed to aid mutual recognition by members of a species.—**Recognitory**, rē-kog′ni-to-ri, *a.* Pertaining to recognition. — **Recognizable**, rek′og-nī″-za-bl, *a.* Capable of being recognized.—**Recognizance**, rē-kog′ni-zans or rē-kon′-i-zans, *n.* [Fr. *reconnaissance*, O.Fr. *recognoissance.*] Act of recognizing; recognition; mark or badge of recognition; token; *law*, an obligation which a man enters into before a proper tribunal, with condition to do some particular act, failure of which results in forfeiture.

Recoil, rē-koil′, *v.i.* [Fr. *reculer*, from L. *re*, back, and *culus*, the posteriors; same root as in Gael. *cul*, W. *cil*, the back.] To rebound; to fall back; to take a sudden backward motion after an advance; to be forced to retreat; to return after a certain strain or impetus (the gun *recoils*); to start or draw back as from anything repulsive, alarming, or the like; to shrink.—*n.* A starting or falling back; rebound; the rebound or resilience of a firearm when discharged.—**Recoiler**, rē-koi′lėr, *n.* One who recoils.

Recoin, rē-koin′, *v.t.* To coin again.—**Recoinage**, rē-koi′nāj, *n.* The act of coining anew.

Recollect, rek′ol-lekt, *v.t.* [Lit. to collect or gather again.] To recover or recall the knowledge of; to bring back to the mind or memory; to remember; *refl.* to recover resolution or composure of mind; to collect one's self. ∴ Syn. under REMEMBER.—**Recollection**, rek-ol-lek′shon, *n.* The act of recollecting or recalling to the memory; a bringing back to mind; remembrance; the power of recalling ideas to the mind, or the period over which such power extends; that which is recollected; something recalled to mind. ∴ Syn. under MEMORY.—**Recollective**, rek′ol-lek′tiv, *a.* Having the power of recollecting.

Recollect, rē-kol-lekt′, *v.t.* To collect or gather again; to collect what has been scattered.

Recollet, rek′o-lā, *n.* [Fr. *récollet*, L. *recollectus*, so called because they *recollected* and strictly observed all the rules of their order.] A monk of a reformed order of Franciscans.

Recolonize, rē-kol′on-īz, *v.t.* To colonize a second time. — **Recolonization**, rē-kol′o-ni-zā″shon, *n.* A second colonization.

Recombine, rē-kom-bīn′, *v.t.* To combine again.—**Recombination**, rē-kom′bi-nā″-shon, *n.* Combination a second time.

Recommence, rē-kom-mens′, *v.t.* and *i.* To commence again; to begin anew.—**Recommencement**, rē-kom-mens′ment, *n.* A commencement anew.

Recommend, rek-om-mend′, *v.t.* [*Re* and *commend*; Fr. *recommander*, to recommend, to commend, to intrust.] To commend to another's notice; to put in a favourable light before another; to commend or give favourable representations of; to make acceptable; to attract favour to; hence, to *recommend itself*, to make itself approved; to advise, as to an action, practice, measure, remedy, &c.; to set forward as advisable.—

Recommendable, rek-om-men'da-bl, *a.* Worthy of recommendation.—**Recommendation**, rek'om-men-dā"shon, *n.* The act of recommending; a favourable representation; that which procures favour or a favourable reception.—**Recommendatory**, rek-om-men'da-to-ri, *a.* Serving to recommend.—**Recommender**, rek-om-men'dėr, *n.* One who recommends.

Recommission, rē-kom-mish'on, *v.t.* To commission again.

Recommit, rē-kom-mit', *v.t.* To commit again (as persons to prison); to refer again to a committee.—**Recommitment**, **Recommittal**, rē-kom-mit'ment, rē-kom-mit'al, *n.* A second or renewed commitment; a renewed reference to a committee.

Recompense, rek'om-pens, *v.t.*—*recompensed, recompensing.* [Fr. *récompenser*, L.L. *recompenso*—L. *re*, again, and *compenso, compensatum*, to compensate. COMPENSATE.] To give or render an equivalent to, as for services, loss, &c.; to reward; to requite; to compensate; to return an equivalent for; to make amends for by anything equivalent; to make compensation for.—*n.* An equivalent returned for anything given, done, or suffered; compensation, reward; amends.—**Recompenser**, rek'om-pen-sėr, *n.* One who recompenses.

Recompile, rē-kom-pīl', *v.t.* To compile again or anew.—**Recompilation**, rē-kom'pi-lā"shon, *n.* A compiling anew.

Reconcile, rek'on-sīl, *v.t.*—*reconciled, reconciling.* [Fr. *réconcilier*, from L. *reconcilio*—*re*, again, and *concilio*, to conciliate. CONCILIATE.] To conciliate anew; to restore to union and friendship after estrangement; to adjust or settle (differences, quarrels); to bring to acquiescence or quiet submission (to *reconcile* one's self to afflictions); to make consistent or congruous: followed by *with* or *to*; to remove apparent discrepancies from; to harmonize.—*v.i.* To become reconciled.—**Reconciler**, rek'on-sīl-ėr, *n.*—One who reconciles.—**Reconcilement**, rek'on-sīl-ment, *n.* Reconciliation; renewal of friendship.—**Reconciliation**, rek'on-sil-i-ā"shon, *n.* [L. *reconciliatio*.] The act of reconciling parties at variance; renewal of friendship after disagreement or enmity; *Scrip.* atonement; expiation; the act of harmonizing or making consistent; agreement of things seemingly opposite or inconsistent.—**Reconciliatory**, rek-on-sil'i-a-to-ri, *a.* Able or tending to reconcile.—**Reconcilable**, rek-on-sī'la-bl, *a.* Capable of being again brought to friendly feelings; capable of being made to agree or be consistent; capable of being harmonized.—**Reconcilableness**, rek-on-sī'la-bl-nes, *n.*—**Reconcilably**, rek-on-sī'la-bli, *adv.*

Recondense, rē-kon-dens', *v.t.* To condense again.—**Recondensation**, rē-kon'den-sā"shon, *n.* The act of recondensing.

Recondite, rek'on-dīt or re-kon'dit, *a.* [L. *reconditus*, pp. of *recondo*—*re*, back, and *condo*, to conceal (as in *abscond*).] Hidden from the mental perception; abstruse; profound; dealing with things abstruse.

Reconduct, rē-kon-dukt', *v.t.* To conduct back or again.

Reconfirm, rē-kon-fėrm', *v.t.* To confirm anew.

Reconnaissance, re-kon'nā-sans, *n.* [Fr. RECONNOITRE.] The act or operation of reconnoitring; preliminary examination or survey of a territory or of an enemy's position, for the purpose of directing military operations.—*Reconnaissance in force*, a demonstration by a considerable body of men for the purpose of discovering the position or strength of an enemy.

Reconnoiter, **Reconnoitre**, rek-on-noi'tėr, *v.t.*—*reconnoitred, reconnoitring.* [O.Fr. *reconnoitre*, Fr. *reconnaître*, from L. *recognosco*—*re*, again, and *cognosco*. The elements of the word are same as in *recognize* (which see).] To make a preliminary survey of; to examine or survey, as a tract or region, for military or engineering purposes.

Reconquer, rē-kong'kėr, *v.t.* To conquer again; to recover by conquest; to recover; to regain.—**Reconquest**, rē-kong'kwest, *n.* A conquest again or anew.

Reconsecrate, rē-kon'sē-krāt, *v.t.* To consecrate anew.—**Reconsecration**, rē-kon'sē-krā"shon, *n.* A renewed consecration.

Reconsider, rē-kon-sid'ėr, *v.t.* To consider again; to turn over in the mind again; to take into consideration a second time, generally with the view of rescinding.—**Reconsideration**, rē'kon-sid-ėr-ā"shon, *n.* The act of reconsidering.

Reconstruct, rē-kon-strukt', *v.t.* To construct again; to rebuild.—**Reconstruction**, rē-kon-struk'shon, *n.* Act of constructing again; something reconstructed; *U. S. History*, the governmental reorganization of the seceded states after the Civil War.

Reconvene, rē-kon-vēn', *v.t.* To convene or call together again.—*v.i.* To reassemble.

Reconvert, rē-kon-vėrt', *v.t.* To convert again.—**Reconversion**, rē-kon-vėr'shon, *n.* A second or renewed conversion.

Reconvey, rē-kon-vā', *v.t.* To convey back or to its former place; to transfer back to a former owner.—**Reconveyance**, rē-kon-vā'ans, *n.* The act of reconveying; the act of transferring back to a former proprietor.

Record, rē-kord', *v.t.* [Fr. *recorder*, to get by heart, formerly also to record, from L. *recordor*, to remember—*re*, again, and *cor, cordis*, the heart.] To preserve the memory of by written or other characters; to register; to note; to write down or enter in order to preserve evidence; to cause to be inscribed on a wax cylinder or rubber disk for reproduction on the phonograph machine, as to *record* music; to imprint deeply on the mind or memory.—*n.* (rek'ord). Something set down in writing for the purpose of preserving the knowledge of it; a register; an authentic or official account of facts or proceedings, entered in a book for preservation; the book or document containing such; a public document; the known facts in a person's life, especially in that of a public figure; the best of recorded achievements in competitive sports as, the world's *record*.—*Court of record*, one of the higher courts in which the records of the suits are preserved.—*Phonograph record*, a hard-rubber disk upon which a transcription of sound has been made.—**Recorder**, rē-kor'der, *n.* One who records official transactions; in the United States, a judge with first jurisdiction in criminal cases, or a magistrate's jurisdiction; in England, the chief judicial officer of a borough or city; an old musical instrument, somewhat like a flageolet; a registering apparatus.—**Recordership**, rē-kor'der-ship, *n.* The office of a recorder.—**Recording**, rē-kor'ding, *n.* A transcription of sound made upon a phonograph record.

Recount, rē-kount', *v.t.* [Fr. *reconter*—*re*, and *conter*, to tell.] To relate in detail; to count again; to count ballots again when the result of the first count has been challenged by a defeated candidate.

Recoup, rē-köp', *n.* [From Fr. *recoupe*, cloth remaining after cutting out clothes, from *re*, back, and *couper*, to cut.] *Law*, a sum kept back; a deduction; discount.—*v.t. Law*, to keep back as a set-off or discount; hence, *refl.* to indemnify one's self for a loss or damage by a corresponding advantage.—**Recoupment**, rē-köp'ment, *n.* The act of recouping.

Recourse, rē-kōrs', *n.* [Fr. *recours*, from L. *recursus*, a running back, a return, from *recurro*, to run back—*re*, back, and *curro*, to run. COURSE.] A going to, as for help or protection; a recurrence in difficulty, perplexity, need, or the like.

Recover, rē-kuv'ėr, *v.t.* [O.Fr. *recovrer* (Fr. *recouvrer*), from L. *recuperare*, to recover; of doubtful origin.] To regain, to get or obtain after being lost; to get back; to restore from sickness, faintness, or the like; to revive; to cure; to heal; to retrieve; to make up for; to rescue; *law*, to gain as a compensation; to obtain in return for injury or debt; to obtain title to by judgment in a court of law.—*v.i.* To regain health after sickness; to grow well again; to regain a former state or condition, as after misfortune or disturbance of mind; to succeed in a lawsuit.—**Recoverable**, rē-kuv'ėr-a-bl, *a.* Capable of being regained or recovered; obtainable from a debtor or possessor.—**Recoverableness**, rē-kuv'ėr-a-bl-nes, *n.* The state of being recoverable.—**Recoverer**, rē-kuv'ėr-ėr, *n.* One who recovers.—**Recovery**, rē-kuv'ėr-i, *n.* The act or power of regaining or getting again; restoration from sickness or faintness; restoration from low condition or misfortune; *law*, the obtaining of right to something by a verdict and judgment of court from an opposing party in a suit.

Recreant, rek'rē-ant, *a.* [O.Fr. *recreant*, ppr. of *recroire*, L.L. *recredere*, to give in, to confess defeat—L. *re*, again, and *credo*, to believe. See MISCREANT.] Craven; yielding to an enemy; cowardly; mean-spirited; apostate; false.—*n.* One who basely yields; one who begs for mercy; a mean-spirited, cowardly wretch.—**Recreantly**, rek'rē-ant-li, *adv.* In a recreant manner; basely; falsely.—**Recreancy**, rek'rē-an-si, *n.* The quality of being recreant; cowardice.

Recreate, rek'rē-āt, *v.t.*—*recreated, recreating.* [L. *recreo, recreatum*—*re*, again, and *creo*, to create. CREATE.] To revive or refresh after toil or exertion; to reanimate; as languid spirits or exhausted strength; to amuse; to divert; to gratify.—*v.i.* To take recreation.—*v.t.* (rē-krē-āt'). [Directly from *re* and *create*.] To create or form anew.—**Recreation**, rek-rē-ā'shon, *n.* The act of recreating or the state of being recreated; refreshment of the strength and spirits after toil; amusement; entertainment.—**Recreative**, rek'rē-ā-tiv, *a.* Tending to recreate; refreshing; diverting.—**Recreatively**, rek'rē-ā-tiv-li, *adv.* In a recreative manner.—**Recreativeness**, rek'rē-ā-tiv-nes, *n.*

Recrement, rek'rē-ment, *n.* [L. *recrementum*, from *recerno*—*re*, back, and *cerno*, to separate. SECRET.] Superfluous matter separated from that which is useful; dross; scoria; spume.—**Recremental**, **Recrementitial**, **Recrementitious**, rek-rē-men'tal, rek'rē-men-tish"al, rek'rē-men-tish"us, *a.* Drossy; consisting of superfluous matter separated from that which is valuable.

Recriminate, rē-krim'i-nāt, *v.i.*—*recriminated, recriminating.* [L. *re*, again, and *criminor*, I accuse. CRIME.] To return one accusation with another; to charge an accuser with the like.—*v.t.* To accuse in return.—**Recrimination**, rē-krim'i-nā"shon, *n.* The act of recriminating; the return of one accusation with another; *law*, an accusation brought by the accused against the accuser upon the same fact; a counter-accusation.—**Recriminative**, **Recriminatory**, rē-krim'i-nā-tiv, rē-krim'i-na-to-ri, *a.* Recriminating or retorting accusation.—**Recriminator**, rē-krim'i-nā-tėr, *n.* One who recriminates.

Recross, rē-kros', *v.t.* To cross again.

Recrudescent, rē-krö-des'ent, *a.* [L. *recrudesco*—*re*, again, and *crudescere*, to become raw, from *crudus*, raw. CRUDE.] Recurring; renewing activity, as of an illness.—**Recrudes'cence**, **Recrudes'cency**, rē-krö-des'ens, rē-krö-des'en-si, *n.* The state of being recrudescent; *med.* increased severity of a disease after temporary remission.

Recruit, rē-kröt', *v.t.* [Fr. *recruter*, from *recrute*, a participial noun from O.Fr. *recroistre*, pp. *recrû*, from L. *recresco*—*re*, again, and *cresco*, to grow (seen in *crescent, increase*, &c.). CRESCENT.] To repair by fresh supplies; to restore the wasted vigour of; to renew the health, spirits, or strength of; to refresh; to supply with new men; to make up by enlistment (to *recruit* an army).—*v.i.* To gain new supplies of anything wasted; to gain flesh, health, spirits, &c.; to raise new soldiers.—*n.* A soldier newly enlisted.—**Recruiter**, rē-kröt'ėr, *n.* One who recruits.—**Recruiting-sergeant**, *n.* A sergeant deputed to enlist recruits.—**Recruitment**, rē-kröt'ment, *n.* The act of recruiting.

Recrystallize, rē-kris'tal-īz, *v.t.* To crystallize a second time.—**Recrystallization**, rē-kris'tal-i-zā"shon, *n.* The process of recrystallizing.

Rectal. Under RECTUM.

Rectangle, rek'tang-gl, *n.* [L. *rectangulus*—*rectus*, right, and *angulus*, an angle.] A right-angled parallelogram; a quadrilateral figure having all its angles right angles.—**Rectangular**, rek-tang'gū-lėr, *a.* Right angled; having an angle or angles of ninety degrees.—**Rectangularly**, rek-tang'gū-lėr-li, *adv.* In a rectangular manner; with or at right angles.

Rectify, rek'ti-fī, *v.t.*—*rectified*, *rectifying*. [Fr. *rectifier*, from L. *rectus*, right, and *facio*, to make.] To make or put right; to correct when wrong, erroneous, or false; to amend; to refine by repeated distillation or sublimation; to convert (alcohol) into gin, &c., by flavouring specially.—**Rectifiable**, rek'ti-fī-a-bl, *a.* Capable of being rectified or set right.—**Rectification**, rek'ti-fi-kā"shon, *n.* The act or operation of rectifying; the act of setting right that which is wrong; the process of refining or purifying by repeated distillation.—*Rectification of a globe*, the adjustment of it preparatory to the solution of a proposed problem.—**Rectifier**, rek'ti-fī-ėr, *n.* One who or that which rectifies; one who refines by repeated distillations; a device for obtaining direct electric current from alternating current. See THERMIONIC VALVE.

Rectilinear, Rectilineal, rek-ti-lin'ē-ėr, rek-ti-lin'ē-al, *a.* [L. *rectus*, right, and *linea*, a line.] Bounded by straight lines; consisting of a straight line or of straight lines; straight.—**Rectilinearity**, rek'ti-lin-ē-ar"i-ti, *n.* State of being rectilinear.—**Rectilineally, Rectilinearly**, rek-ti-lin'ē-al-li, rek-ti-lin'ē-ėr-li, *adv.* In a rectilinear manner; in a right line.

Rection,† rek'shon, *n.* [L. *rectio*, *rectionis*, from *rego*, *rectum*, to rule or govern.] *Gram.* same as *Government*.

Rectirostral, rek-ti-ros'tral, *a.* [L. *rectus*, straight, and *rostrum*, a beak.] Having a straight beak.

Rectiserial, rek-ti-sē'ri-al, *a.* [L. *rectus*, straight, and *series*, a row.] Disposed in a straight line or row.

Rectitude, rek'ti-tūd, *n.* [L. *rectitudo*, from *rectus*, pp. of *rego*, *rectum*, to keep or lead straight. REGENT.] Rightness of principle or practice; uprightness; integrity; honesty; probity; correctness.

Recto, rek'tō, *n.* [L. *rectus*, right.] The right-hand page of an open book; the right-hand side of a sheet of paper, as opposed to *verso*, on the reverse.

Rector, rek'tėr, *n.* [L. *rector*, a ruler, from *rego*, *rectum*, to rule, to keep right. RECTITUDE.] A clergyman of the Protestant Episcopal Church, elected by the vestrymen, who has charge of a parish, and to whom belong the parsonage and tithes; the chief elective officer of some universities, as in France and Scotland; in Scotland also the title of the head-master of an academy or important public school.—**Rectoral, Rectorial**, rek'tėr-al, rek-tō'ri-al, *a.* Pertaining to a rector or to a rectory.—*Rectorial tithes*, great or praedial tithes.—**Rectorship**, rek'tėr-ship, *n.* The office or rank of a rector.—**Rectory**, rek'to-ri, *n.* A parish church or parish held by a rector; a rector's mansion or parsonage-house.

Rectrix, rek'triks, *n.* pl. **Rectrices**, rek-trī'sēz. [L. *rectrix*, a female governor. RECTOR.] One of the long quill feathers in the tail of a bird, which like a rudder direct its flight.

Rectum, rek'tum, *n.* [L. *rectum*, straight, because once thought to be straight.] *Anat.* the third and last part of the large intestine opening at the anus.—**Rectal**, rek'tal, *a.* Relating to the rectum.

Recultivate, rē-kul'ti-vāt, *v.t.* To cultivate anew.—**Recultivation**, rē-kul'ti-vā"shon, *n.* The act of cultivating anew.

Recumbent, rē-kum'bent, *a.* [L. *recumbens*, *recumbentis*, ppr. of *recumbo*—*re*, back, and *cumbo*, to lie. INCUMBENT.] Leaning; reclining; lying down; reposing; inactive; *zool.* and *bot.* applied to a part that leans or reposes upon anything.—**Recumbency, Recumbence**, rē-kum'ben-si, rē-kum'-bens, *n.* The state of being recumbent; the posture of reclining, or lying; rest; repose; idle state.—**Recumbently**, rē-kum'-bent-li, *adv.* In a recumbent posture.

Recuperate, rē-kū'pėr-āt, *v.t.*—*recuperated*, *recuperating*. [L. *recupero*, *recuperatum*. RECOVER.] To recover; to regain.—*v.i.* To recover; to regain health.—**Recuperation**, rē-kū'pėr-ā"shon, *n.* [L. *recuperatio*.] Recovery.—**Recuperative, Recuperatory**, rē-kū'pėr-a-tiv, rē-kū'pėr-a-to-ri, *a.* Tending to recovery; pertaining to recovery.

Recur, rē-kėr', *v.i.*—*recurred*, *recurring*. [L. *recurro*—*re*, and *curro*, to run. CURRENT.] To return; to return to the thought or mind; to have recourse; to turn for aid; to occur again or be repeated at a stated interval, or according to some regular rule.—**Recurrence, Recurrency**, rē-kėr'-ens, rē-kėr'en-si, *n.* The act of recurring, or state of being recurrent; return; resort; recourse.—**Recurrent**, rē-kėr'ent, *a.* Returning from time to time; turned back in its course.—**Recurring**, rē-kėr'ing, *a.* Returning again.—*Recurring* or *circulating decimals*. CIRCULATING.

Recurvate, Recurved, rē-kėr'vāt, rē-kėrvd', *a.* [L. *re*, back, and *curvus*, bent.] *Bot.* bent, bowed, or curved backward or outward (a *recurvate* leaf, &c.).—**Recurvation, Recurvature**, rē-kėr-vā'shon, rē-kėr'va-tūr, *n.* A bending or flexure backward.—**Recurve**, rē-kėrv', *v.t.*—*recurved*, *recurving*. To bend back.—**Recurvirostral**, rē-kėr'vi-ros"tral, *a.* [L. *rostrum*, a beak.] *Ornith.* having the beak recurved or bent upwards, as an avoset.—**Recurvity**, rē-kėr'vi-ti, *n.* RECURVATION.—**Recurvous**, rē-kėr'vus, *a.* Bent backward.

Recusant, rek'ū-zant, *a.* [Fr. *récusant*, L. *recusans*, *recusantis*, ppr. of *recuso*, to refuse, to reject—*re*, back, and *causa*, cause.] Obstinate in refusal; refusing to acknowledge the supremacy of a sovereign, or to conform to the established rites of a church.—*n.* One obstinate in refusing; one who will not conform to general opinion or practice; specifically—*Eng. hist.* a nonconformist.—**Recusancy**, rek'ū-zan-si, *n.* The state of being a recusant; the tenets of a recusant; nonconformity.

Red, red, *a.* [A.Sax. *reád*, red; cog. Dan. and Sw. *röd*, Icel. *rauthr* (*raudr*), D. *rood*, G. *roth*, Goth. *rauds*; same root as in L. *rufus*, *ruber*, G. *erythros*, W. *rhwdd*, Ir. and Gael. *ruadh*, red; Skr. *rudhira*, blood. Akin are *ruddy*, *russet*, *ruby*, *rubric*, &c.] Of a bright warm color resembling blood; a general term applied to many different shades or hues, as crimson, scarlet, vermilion, &c.; often used in forming compound words which are self-explanatory (*red-backed*, *red-breasted*, *red-cheeked*, &c.).—*Red admiral*, a beautiful species of butterfly.—*Red cedar*, a species of North American and West Indian juniper, of which the heart-wood is in great demand for the manufacture of lead pencils.—*Red chalk*. REDDLE.—*Red cross*, the rectangular cross of St. George, the national saint of England.—*Red deer*, the common stag, a native of the forests of Europe and Asia; still plentiful in the Highlands of Scotland.—*Red gum*, an eruptive skin disease to which infants are subject.—*Red herring*, the common herring highly salted, dried, and smoked, so as to keep for a long time; something cast in the path as a means of diverting the attention of persons, or the scent of hounds, from the real object; something to sidetrack an issue. (*Colloq.*)—*Red Indian* or *Red man*, one of the copper-colored aborigines of America.—*Red ochre*, a name common to a variety of pigments.—*Red orpiment*. REALGAR.—*Red pine*, a species of pine, the *Scotch* or *Norway Pine*.—*Red republican*, an extreme republican, so called because in the first French revolution the extreme republicans were in the habit of wearing a red cap: often contracted into *red* (he is one of the *reds*).—*Red snow*. PROTOCOCCUS.—*n.* A red color; a color resembling that of arterial blood; one of the simple or primary colors; a red pigment; red hair; a red republican; one having radical political or social beliefs; a communist; an anarchist.—**Redbreast**, red'brest, *n.* A singing-bird so called from the color of its breast, also known as the *Robin redbreast*, or simply as the *Robin*.—**Redcoat**, red'kōt, *n.* A name formerly given to a British soldier because of his uniform.—**Red cross.** A rectangular red cross on a white background, as a symbol of mercy.—**Red Cross**, an international society organized to serve humanity in first aid, medical care, and relief of human suffering in times of catastrophe.—**Red deer**, *n.* See above.—**Redden**, red'n, *v.t.* To make red.—*v.i.* To grow or become red.—**Reddish**, red'ish, *a.* Somewhat red; moderately red.—**Reddishness**, red'ish-nes, *n.* The state or quality of being reddish.—**Red-hand, Red-handed**, *a.* With red or bloody hands; hence, in the very act, as if with red or bloody hands: said of a person caught in the perpetration of any crime.—**Red-hot**, *a.* Red with heat; heated to redness.—**Red-lattice**, *n.* A lattice-window painted red, formerly the customary badge of an inn or ale-house.—*Red-lattice phrases*, barroom talk.—**Red lead**, *n.* An oxide of lead much used as a pigment, and commonly known by the name of *Minium*.—**Red-letter**, *a.* Having red letters; marked by red letters.—*Red-letter day*, a fortunate or auspicious day; so called because the holidays or saints' days were marked in the old calendars with red letters.—**Redness**, red'nes, *n.* The quality of being red; red color.—**Redpole, Redpoll**, red'pōl, *n.* [From the red color of the *poll* or head.] A name given to several species of finches.—**Redshank**, red'-shangk, *n.* A grallatorial bird allied to the snipes, so called from its red legs.—**Redskin**, *n.* A red Indian; a North American Indian.—**Redstart**, red'stärt, *n.* [*Start* is from A.Sax. *steort*, a tail.] A species of American warbler; a singing-bird nearly allied to the redbreast, widely diffused over Europe, Asia, and North Africa.—**Redstreak**, red'strēk, *n.* A sort of apple so called from its red streaked skin.—**Red tape**, *n.* A sarcastic name for excessive regard to formality and routine without corresponding attention to essential duties: so named from the red tape used in tying up papers in government offices.—**Red-tapery, Red-tapism**, *n.* Excessive official routine; strict and pedantic adherence to official formalities.—**Red-water**, *n.* A disease of cattle, and occasionally of sheep, in which the urine becomes reddened with blood: called also *Hæmaturia*.—**Redwing**, red'wing, *n.* An American blackbird with a red spot on the wing.—**Redwood**, *n.* The name of various sorts of wood of a red color; an Indian dye-wood; a coniferous tree of California, often growing 300 feet high, and its cedar-like wood.

Redact, rē-dakt', *v.t.* [L. *redigo*, *redactum*, to reduce to order—*re*, again, and *ago*, to bring.] To give a presentable literary form to; to act as redactor or editor of.—**Redacteur, Redactor**, re-dāk'tėr, *n.* [Fr. *redacteur*.] One who redacts; an editor.—**Redaction**, rē-dak'shon, *n.* [Fr.] Preparation for publication.

Redan, rē-dan', *n.* [Fr. *redan*, O.Fr. *redent*, from *re*, back, and *dent*, L. *dens*, *dentis*, a tooth: from its shape.] *Field fort.* the simplest kind of work employed, consisting of two parapets of earth raised so as to form a salient angle, with the apex towards the enemy.

Redargue, red'ār-gū, *v.t.* [L. *redarguo*, to refute—*red*, *re*, back, and *arguo*, to argue.] To put down by argument; to refute.

Redd, red, *n.* A place where fish deposit their spawn.

Reddition, red-dish'on, *n.* [L. *redditio*, *redditionis*, from *reddere*, to give back—*red*, back, and *dare*, to give.] A returning or giving back of anything; restitution; explanation. — **Redditive**, red'i-tiv, *a.* *Gram.* answering to an interrogative; conveying a reply.

Reddle, red'l, *n.* [From *red*; comp. G. *röthel*, from *roth*, red.] Red chalk; a species of argillaceous ironstone ore used as a pigment and to mark sheep. Spelled also *Raddle*, *Ruddle*.

Rede, rēd, *v.t.* [A.Sax. *raedan*, to advise, to read.] To advise; to interpret.

Redecorate, rē-dek'ō-rāt, *v.t.* To decorate or adorn again.

Rededicate, rē-ded'i-kāt, *v.t.* To dedicate again or anew.

Redeem, rē-dēm', *v.t.* [Fr. *redimer*, L. *redimo*, to buy back, to ransom—*red*, *re*, back, and *emo*, to obtain or purchase. EXAMPLE, EXEMPT.] To buy back; to release from captivity or bondage, or from any obligation or liability to suffer or be forfeited, by paying an equivalent; to pay ransom or equivalent for; to ransom; to rescue; to perform, as a promise; to make good by performance; to make amends for; to atone for; to improve or employ to the best advantage ('*redeeming* the time'). — **Redeemability, Redeemableness**, rē-dē'ma-bil"i-ti, rē-dē'ma-bl-nes, *n.* The state of being redeemable. — **Redeemable**, rē-dē'ma-bl, *a.* Capable of being redeemed. — **Redeemer**, rē-dē'mėr, *n.* One who redeems or ransoms; the Saviour of the world, JESUS CHRIST.—**Redemption**, rē-dem'shon, *n.* [L. *redemptio*: a doublet of *ransom*.] The act of redeeming; the state of being redeemed; ransom; *theol.* the deliverance of sinners from the penalty of God's violated law by the sufferings and death of Christ.—**Redemptive**, rē-dem'tiv, *a.* Redeeming; serving to redeem.—**Redemptorist**, rē-dem'tor-ist, *n.* One of a religious congregation who devote themselves to the education of youth and the spread of Catholicism. — **Redemptory**, rē-dem'to-ri, *a.* Paid for ransom.

Redeliberate, rē-dē-lib'ėr-āt, *v.i.* and *t.* To deliberate again; to reconsider.

Redeliver, rē-dē-liv'ėr, *v.t.* To deliver back; to return to the sender; to liberate a second time. — **Redeliverance**, rē-dē-liv'ėr-ans, *n.* A second deliverance.

Redemand, rē-dē-mand', *v.t.* To demand back; to demand again.

Redemise, rē-dē-mīz', *v.t.* To demise back; to convey or transfer back, as an estate.—*n.* Reconveyance of an estate.

Redemonstrate, rē-dē-mon'strāt, *v.t.* To demonstrate again or afresh.

Redemption. Under REDEEM.

Redented, rē-den'ted, *a.* [L. *re*, back, and *dens*, a tooth.] Formed like the teeth of a saw; indented.

Redeposit, rē-dē-poz'it, *v.t.* To deposit again or anew.

Redescend, rē-dē-send', *v.i.* To descend again.—**Redescent**, rē-dē-sent', *n.* A descending or falling again.

Redia, pl. **-æ**, rē'di-a. [From *Redi*, an Italian naturalist.] In flukes, a cylindrical stage in the life-history.

Redigest, rē-di-jest', *v.t.* To digest or reduce to form a second time.

Redintegrate, rē-din'tē-grāt, *v.t.*—*redintegrated*, *redintegrating*. [L. *red*, again, and *integer*, whole. ENTIRE.] To make whole again; to restore to a perfect state.—**Redintegration**, rē-din'tē-grā"shon, *n.* The act of redintegrating; renovation; restoration to a whole or sound state.

Redisburse, rē-dis-bėrs', *v.t.* To repay or refund.

Rediscover, rē-dis-kuv'ėr, *v.t.* To discover again or afresh.

Redispose, rē-dis-pōz', *v.t.* To dispose or adjust again.

Redistribute, rē-dis-trib'ūt, *v.t.* To distribute again; to apportion afresh.—**Redistribution**, rē-dis'tri-bū"shon, *n.* A second or new distribution.

Redivide, rē-di-vīd', *v.t.* To divide again.

Redolent, red'ō-lent, *a.* [L. *redolens*, *redolentis*, ppr. of *redoleo*, to emit a scent—*red*, back, and *oleo*, to smell. ODOUR.] Having or diffusing a sweet scent; giving out an odour; odorous; fragrant: often with *of*. —**Redolently**, red'ō-lent-li, *adv.* In a redolent manner; fragrantly.—**Redolence, Redolency**, red'ō-lens, red'ō-len-si, *n.* The quality of being redolent; fragrance.

Redondilla, red-on-dēl'ya, *n.* [Sp.] A species of versification in Spanish poetry.

Redouble, rē-dub'l, *v.t.* [Prefix *re*, and *double*.] To multiply; to repeat often; to increase by repeated or continued additions. —*v.i.* To become twice as much; to become greatly or repeatedly increased.

Redoubt, rē-dout', *n.* REDOUT.

Redoubtable, rē-dout'a-bl, *a.* [O.Fr. *redoutable*, from *redoubter*, to fear—L. *re*, again, and *dubito*, to doubt. DOUBT.] Formidable; to be dreaded; terrible to foes; hence, valiant: often used in irony.—**Redoubted**, rē-dout'ed, *p.* and *a.* Redoutable; formidable; valiant.

Redound, rē-dound', *v.i.* [Fr. *redonder*, L. *redundo*, to overflow—*red*, back, and *undo*, to surge, from *unda*, a wave (seen also in *undulate*, *redundant*, *abound*).] To roll or flow back, as a wave; to conduce; to contribute; to result (this will *redound* to your benefit).—*n.* The coming back, as a consequence or effect; result.

Redout, Redoubt, rē-dout', *n.* [Fr. *redoute*, *reduit*, from L.L. *reductus*, a retired spot, from L. *reductus*, retired—*re*, back, and *duco*, to lead. DUKE.] *Fort.* a general name for nearly every class of works wholly inclosed and undefended by re-entering or flanking angles; a small inclosed temporary field-work.

Redraft, rē-draft', *v.t.* To draw or draft anew.—*n.* A second draft or copy; a second draft or order drawn for money.

Redraw, rē-dra', *v.t.* To draw again, as a second draft or copy.—*v.i.* *Com.* to draw a new bill of exchange.

Redress, rē-dres', *v.t.* [Fr. *redresser*, to straighten again, to put right. DRESS.] To remedy or put right, as a wrong; to repair, as an injury; to relieve of anything unjust or oppressive; to compensate; to make amends to. —*n.* Deliverance from wrong, injury, or oppression; undoing of wrong; reparation; indemnification.—**Redresser**, rē-dres'ėr, *n.* One who gives redress.—**Redressible**, rē-dres'i-bl, *a.* Capable of being redressed.—**Redressive**, rē-dres'iv, *a.* Affording redress; giving relief.—**Redressless**, rē-dres'les, *a.* Without redress or amendment; without relief.

Reduce, rē-dūs', *v.t.*—*reduced*, *reducing*. [L. *reduco*—*re*, back, and *duco*, to lead. DUKE.] To bring to any state or condition, good or bad; to bring (to power, to poverty, to order, &c.); to diminish in size, quantity, or value; to make less or lower; to bring to an inferior condition; to subdue; to bring into subjection; to bring under rules or within certain limits of description; to bring from a form less fit to one more fit for operation; *arith.* to change from one denomination into another without altering the value; *alg.* to bring to the simplest form with the unknown quantity by itself on one side, and all the known quantities on the other side; *metal.* to separate, as a pure metal from a metallic ore; *surg.* to restore to its proper place or state, as a dislocated or fractured bone.—*To reduce a design*, to make a copy of it smaller than the original.—*To reduce to the ranks*, to degrade for misconduct to the position of a private soldier.—**Reducent**, rē-dū'sent, *a.* [L. *reducens*.] Tending to reduce.—*n.* That which reduces.—**Reducer**, rē-dū'sėr, *n.* One that reduces.—**Reducible**, rē-dū'si-bl, *a.* Capable of being reduced; convertible. — **Reducibleness**, rē-dū'si-bl-nes, *n.* **Reducibly**, rē-dū'si-bli, *adv.* — **Reduction**, rē-duk'shon, *n.* [L. *reductio*.] The act of reducing; conversion into another state or form; diminution; conquest; subjugation; *arith.* the bringing of numbers of one denomination into another; the arithmetical rule by which this is done; *alg.* the process of bringing equations to their simplest forms with the unknown quantity alone on one side, and the known ones on the other; the act of making a copy of a map, design, &c., on a smaller scale, preserving the proper proportions; *surg.* the operation of restoring a dislocated or fractured bone to its former place; *metal.* the operation of obtaining pure metals from metallic ores.—**Reductive**, rē-duk'tiv, *a.* Having the power of reducing; tending to reduce.

Reductio ad absurdum, rē-duk'shi-ō ad ab-sėr'dum, *n.* [L.] A reduction to an absurdity, a species of argument which proves not the thing asserted, but the absurdity of everything which contradicts it.

Reduit, red-wē, *n.* [Fr.] A redoubt.

Redundant, rē-dun'dant, *a.* [L. *redundans*, *redundantis*, ppr. of *redundo*. REDOUND.] Superfluous; exceeding what is natural or necessary; superabundant; using more words than are necessary.—**Redundance, Redundancy**, rē-dun'dans, rē-dun'dan-si, *n.* The quality of being redundant; superfluity; superabundance; that which is redundant or superfluous.—**Redundantly**, rē-dun'dant-li, *adv.* In a redundant manner.

Reduplicate, rē-dū'pli-kāt, *v.t.*—*reduplicated*, *reduplicating*. [L. *reduplico*, *reduplicatum*—*re*, and *duplico*, to double. DUPLICATE.] To double again; to multiply; to repeat; *philol.* to repeat, as the initial syllable or the root of a word, for the purpose of marking past time.—*v.i.* *Philol.* to be doubled or repeated; to undergo reduplication. —*a.* Redoubled; repeated; *bot.* applied to a form of æstivation in which the edges of the sepals or petals are turned outwards. — **Reduplication**, rē-dū'pli-kā"shon, *n.* The act of doubling or reduplicating; *philol.* the repetition of a root or of the initial syllable (more or less modified), as in Gr. *pheugō*, to flee, perfect *pepheuga*; *did*, the reduplicated past of *do*; the new syllable formed by reduplication.

Redware, red'wãr, *n.* [*red* + *ware*, seaweed.] An edible brownish seaweed found off the coast of New England.

Redwing, Under RED.

Re-echo, rē-ek'ō, *v.t.* and *i.* To echo back; to reverberate again.—*n.* The echo of an echo; a second or repeated echo.

Reechy, rēch'i, *a.* [A form of *reeky*, from *reek*.] Smoky; sooty; foul. (*Shak.*)

Reed, rēd, *n.* [O.E. *rede*, A.Sax. *hreód* = O.Sax. *ried*, D. *riet*, *ried*, O.H.G. *hriot*, Mod.G. *riet*, *ried*; also Ir. *readan*, Gael. *ribhid*, a reed.] A name applied to tall broad-leaved grasses growing in marshy places, or to their hollow stems; a musical instrument made from a reed; a rustic or pastoral pipe; a little tube through which a hautboy, bassoon, or clarinet is blown; one of the thin plates of metal whose vibrations produce the notes of an accordion, harmonium, &c.; *weaving*, a frame of parallel flat strips of wood or metal for separating the threads of the warp, and for beating the weft up to the web.—**Reed-bird**. RICE-BIRD. — **Reed-bunting, Reed-sparrow**, *n.* One of the British buntings, a bird that frequents reeds, fens, &c.—**Reeded**, rēd'ed, *a.* Covered with reeds; abounding in reeds. — **Reeden**, rēd'n, *a.* Consisting of a reed or reeds; made of reeds.—**Reed-grass**, *n.* A name given to various large grasses. — **Reed-mace**, *n.* A British plant, tall, stout, and erect, with leaves used for making mats, &c. — **Reed-pipe**, *n.* A musical pipe made of reed; a pipe in an organ sounding by means of a reed. — **Reedy**, rēd'i, *a.* Abounding with reeds; resembling a reed;

applied to a voice or musical instrument having a thin, harsh tone.

Reef, rēf, *n.* [Same as D. *rif*, a reef; Icel. *rif*, Dan. *rev*, *riv*, Sw. *rev*, G. *riff*, reef; from root of *rive*.] A mass of rocks in the ocean lying at or near the surface of the water; among gold miners, a gold-bearing quartz vein.—**Reefy**, rēf'i, *a.* Full of reefs or rocks.

Reef, rēf, *n.* [From D. *reef*, a reef; L.G. *reff*, *riff*, Icel. *rif*, Dan. *rev*, *reb*, Sw. *ref*, reef; akin A.Sax. *reáf*, a garment. ROBE.] *Naut.* that part of a sail which can be drawn together by small cords, so as to contract the canvas in proportion to the increase of the wind.—*v.t.* *Naut.* to take in a reef or reefs in; to reduce the extent of a sail by folding a certain portion of it and making it fast to the yard.—**Reef-band**, *n.* A strong horizontal strip of canvas extending across a sail to strengthen it where the eyelet-holes are formed for the reef-points.—**Reefer**, rēf'ėr, *n.* One who reefs; a reefing-jacket.—**Reefing-jacket**, *n.* A close-fitting jacket of strong cloth.—**Reef-point**, *n.* One of the small pieces of line for tying up a sail to the yard when reefing it.

Reek, rēk, *n.* [A.Sax. *réc*, smoke, vapour; cog. O.Fris. *rēk*, Icel. *reykr*, D. and L.G. *rook*, Dan. *rōg*, Sw. *rōk*, G. *rauch*, Lith. *rukis*, smoke.] Vapour; steam; exhalation; fume; smoke.—*v.i.* To smoke; to steam; to exhale; to emit vapour.—**Reeky**, rēk'i, *a.* Giving out reek or fumes. (*Shak.*)

Reel, rēl, *n.* [A.Sax. *hreól*, *reól*, a reel; Icel. *hræll*, a weaver's rod or sley.] A roller or bobbin of wood, &c., for thread used in sewing; a machine on which yarn is wound to form it into hanks, skeins, &c.; a revolving frame on which the log-line is wound; a revolving appliance attached to the butt of a fishing-rod, and around which the line is wound; the photographic film of a motion-picture.—*v.t.* To wind upon a reel.—**Reel-stand**, *n.* In England, a holder for reels for ladies' use.

Reel, rēl, *n.* [Gael. *righil*, a reel.] A lively dance peculiar to Scotland; the music for this dance, generally written in common time of four crotchets in a bar, but sometimes in jig time of six quavers; also, the Virginia Reel.

Reel, rēl, *v.i.* [O.E. *reile*, *rele*, to roll, to reel; perhaps from *reel*, the implement.] To stagger or sway in walking; to whirl; to have a whirling or giddy sensation (my brain *reeled*).—*n.* A staggering motion, as that of a drunken man.

Re-elect, rē-ē-lekt', *v.t.* To elect again.—**Re-election**, rē-ē-lek'shon, *n.* Election for a second term to an office, or a repeated election, as, for instance, the re-election of a president of the United States at the termination of his first four years in office.

Re-embark, rē-em-bärk', *v.t.* and *i.* To embark or put on board again.—**Re-embarkation**, rē-em'bär-kā"shon, *n.* A putting on board or a going on board again.

Re-embody, rē-em-bod'i, *v.t.* To embody again.

Re-emerge, rē-ē-mėrj', *v.i.* To emerge after being plunged, obscured, or overwhelmed.—**Re-emergence**, rē-ē-mėr'jens, *n.* The act of emerging again.

Re-enact, rē-e-nakt', *v.t.* To enact again.—**Re-enactment**, rē-e-nakt'ment, *n.* The enacting or passing of a law a second time.

Re-encourage, rē-en-kur'āj, *v.t.* To encourage again.—**Re-encouragement**, rē-en-kur'āj-ment, *n.* Renewed or repeated encouragement.

Re-enforce, rē-en-fōrs', *v.t.* To enforce anew; to reinforce.

Re-engage, rē-en-gāj', *v.t.* and *i.* To engage a second time.—**Re-engagement**, rē-en-gāj'ment, *n.* Renewed engagement.

Re-enlist, rē-en-list', *v.t.* and *i.* To enlist a second time.—**Re-enlistment**, rē-en-list'ment, *n.* The act of re-enlisting.

Re-enter, rē-en'tėr, *v.t.* To enter again or anew; *engr.* to cut deeper, as the incisions of a plate which are too faint.—**Re-entering**, rē-en'tėr-ing, *p.* and *a.* Entering anew.—*Re-entering angle*, an angle pointing inwards; *fort.* the angle of a work whose point turns inwards towards the defended place.—**Re-entrance**, rē-en'trans, *n.* The act of entering again.—**Re-entry**, rē-en'tri, *n.* A new or second entry; *law*, the resuming or retaking possession of lands lately lost.

Re-erect, rē-ē-rekt', *v.t.* To erect again or anew.

Re-establish, rē-es-tab'lish, *v.t.* To establish anew.—**Re-establisher**, rē-es-tab'lish-ėr, *n.* One who re-establishes.—**Re-establishment**, rē-es-tab'lish-ment, *n.* The act of establishing again.

Reeve, rēv, *n.* [A.Sax. *geréfa*, a steward, a person in authority; origin doubtful; *sheriff* = *shire-reeve*.] In England a bailiff; a steward; a peace officer: now used only in such words as *borough-reeve*, *port-reeve*, &c.

Reeve, rēv, *n.* A bird, the female of the ruff.

Reeve, rēv, *v.t.* and *i.*—*reeve* or *rove*, *reeving*. [From *reef*, the nautical term.] *Naut.* to pass the end of a rope through any hole in a block, thimble, ring-bolt, &c.; to run or pass through such hole.

Re-examine, rē-eg-zam'in, *v.t.* To examine anew.—**Re-examination**, rē-eg-zam'i-nā"shon, *n.* A renewed or repeated examination.

Re-exhibit, rē-egs-hib'it, *v.t.* To exhibit again or anew.

Re-experience, rē-eks-pē'ri-ens, *n.* A renewed or repeated experience.—*v.t.* To experience again.

Re-export, rē-eks-pōrt', *v.t.* To export again; to export after having been imported.—*n.* (rē-eks'pōrt). Any commodity re-exported.—**Re-exportation**, rē-eks'pōr-tā"shon, *n.* The act of re-exporting.

Refashion, rē-fash'on, *v.t.* To fashion or form into shape a second time.

Refasten, rē-fas'n, *v.t.* To fasten again.

Refection, rē-fek'shon, *n.* [L. *refectio*, *refectionis*, from *reficio*, to restore, to refresh —*re*, again, and *facio*, to make.] Refreshment after hunger or fatigue; a repast.—**Refective**, rē-fek'tiv, *a.* Refreshing; restoring.—**Refectory**, rē-fek'to-ri, *n.* An eating-room; an apartment in convents where meals are taken.

Refer, rē-fėr', *v.t.*—*referred*, *referring*. [L. *refero*, *referre*, to bring back, to refer, &c.—*re*, back, and *fero*, to carry. FERTILE.] To trace back; to impute; to assign; to attribute to, as the cause, motive, or ground; to hand over, as to another person or tribunal for treatment, decision, &c. (to *refer* a matter to a third party); to appeal; to assign, as to an order, genus, or class; in all senses followed by *to*.—*v.i.* To respect; to have relation; to appeal; to have recourse; to apply; to consult (to *refer* to one's notes); to allude; to make allusion; to direct the attention. ∴ Syn. under ADVERT.—**Referee**, ref-ėr-ē', *n.* One to whom a matter in dispute has been referred for settlement or decision; an arbitrator.—**Reference**, ref'ėr-ens, *n.* The act of referring; the act of alluding; direct allusion; relation; respect, or regard (generally in the phrase *in* or *with reference to*); one of whom inquiries may be made in regard to a person's character, abilities, &c.; a passage or note in a work by which a person is referred to another passage.—*a.* Affording information when consulted.—*Reference Bible*, a Bible having brief explanations and references to parallel passages printed on the margin.—*Reference books*, books, such as dictionaries, &c., intended to be consulted as occasion requires.—*Reference library*, a library containing books which can be consulted on the spot.—**Referendum**, ref-ėr-en'dum, *n.* [L., a thing to be referred.] The reference to public vote, for final approval or rejection, of measures proposed or passed by a representative assembly; a means of consulting public opinion by popular vote when a public body is unable to make decisions or take on itself the responsibility for a measure.—**Referential**, ref-ėr-en'shal, *a.* Relating to or having reference.—**Referentially**, ref-ėr-en'shal-li, *adv.* By way of reference.—**Referment**, rē-fėr'ment, *n.* Reference for decision.

Refill, rē-fil', *v.t.* To fill again.

Refill, rē'fil, *n.* A product sold in a special container designed to be filled again when initial contents are consumed; the product made to fill again the container when original contents have been exhausted.

Refine, rē-fīn', *v.t.*—*refined*, *refining*. [Fr. *raffiner*, to refine—*re*, and *affiner*—*af* (for L. *ad*), to, and *fin*, fine. FINE.] To reduce to a pure state; to free from impurities; to purify; to reduce from the ore; to separate from other metals or from dross or alloy; to purify from what is coarse, inelegant, rude, and the like; to make elegant; to raise or educate, as the taste; to give culture to; to polish (to *refine* the manners, &c.).—*v.i.* To become pure or purer; to affect nicety or subtlety in thought or language.—**Refined**, rē-fīnd', *p.* and *a.* Polished or elegant in character; free from anything coarse or vulgar.—**Refinedly**, rē-fī'ned-li, *adv.* In a refined manner.—**Refinedness**, rē-fī'ned-nes, *n.* State of being refined.—**Refinement**, rē-fīn'ment, *n.* The act of refining or purifying, or state of being refined; the state of being free from what is coarse, rude, inelegant, or the like; elegance of manners, language, &c.; culture; a result of excessive elaboration, polish, or nicety; overnicety; an affected subtlety.—**Refiner**, rē-fī'nėr, *n.* One that refines liquors, sugar, metals, or other things; an improver in purity and elegance; one who is overnice in discrimination, argument, reasoning, &c.—**Refinery**, rē-fī'nėr-i, *n.* A place and apparatus for refining sugar, metals, or the like.

Refit, rē-fit', *v.t.*—*refitted*, *refitting*. To restore after damage or decay; to repair; to fit out anew.—*v.i.* To repair damages, especially to ships.—*n.* A repairing; the repair of a ship.—**Refitment**, rē-fit'ment, *n.* The act of refitting.

Refix, rē-fiks', *v.t.* To fix again; to re-establish.

Reflect, rē-flekt', *v.t.* [L. *reflecto*—*re*, back, and *flecto*, *flexum*, to bend, seen in *flexure*, *deflect*, *inflect*, *inflection*, &c. FLEX.] To bend back; to turn, cast, or direct back; to throw off after striking or falling on any surface, and in accordance with certain physical laws (to *reflect* light, heat, or sound); to give back an image or likeness of; to mirror.—*v.i.* To throw back light, heat, sound, or the like; to return rays or beams; to throw or turn back the thoughts upon anything; to think or consider seriously; to revolve matters in the mind; to bring reproach; to cast censure or blame (do not *reflect* on his errors).—**Reflected**, rē-flek'ted, *pp.* Cast or thrown back (*reflected* light); curved or turned back. See FLECTED.—**Reflectible**, rē-flek'ti-bl, *a.* Capable of being reflected.—**Reflecting**, rē-flek'ting, *p.* and *a.* Throwing back light, heat, &c., as a mirror or other polished surface does; given to reflection; thoughtful; meditative (a *reflecting* mind).—*Reflecting circle*, an instrument for measuring altitudes and angular distances, on the principle of the sextant.—*Reflecting telescope*, a form of telescope in which the image of the object to be viewed is produced by a concave reflector instead of a converging lens as in the *refracting telescope*.—**Reflectingly**, rē-flek'ting-li, *adv.* With reflection; censoriously.—**Reflection**, rē-flek'shon, *n.* The act of reflecting, or the state of being reflected; *physics*, the change of direction which light, heat, or sound experiences when it strikes upon a surface and is thrown back into the same medium from which it approached; that which is produced by being reflected; an image given back from a reflecting surface; attentive or continued consideration; meditation, contemplation, deliberation; a censorious remark or one attaching blame;

reproach cast; *anat.* the folding of a membrane upon itself.—**Reflective**, rē-flek′-tiv, *a.* Throwing back rays; reflecting; exercising reflection; *gram.* reflexive.—**Reflectively**, rē-flek′tiv-li, *adv.* In a reflective manner.—**Reflectiveness**, rē-flek′tiv-nes, *n.*—**Reflector**, rē-flek′tėr, *n.* One who reflects; that which reflects; a polished surface of metal or other suitable material for reflecting light, heat, or sound in any required direction; a reflecting telescope.

Reflex, rē′fleks, *a.* [L. *reflexus*, ppr. of *reflecto*, REFLECT.] Turned backwards; having a backward direction; reflective; introspective.—*Reflex actions*, those actions of the nervous system which are performed involuntarily, and often unconsciously, as the contraction of the pupil of the eye when exposed to strong light.—*n.* Reflection; image produced by reflection.—**Reflexed**, rē-flekst′, *a.* Turned or bent back.—**Reflexibility**, rē-flek′si-bil″i-ti, *n.* The quality of being reflexible.—**Reflexible**, rē-flek′si-bl, *a.* Capable of being reflected.—**Reflexion**, rē-flek′shon. REFLECTION.—**Reflexive**, rē-flek′siv, *a.* Reflective; bending or turning backward; having respect to something past; *gram.* having for its direct object a pronoun which stands for the agent or subject, said of certain verbs (I *bethought myself*, the witness *forswore himself*): also applied to pronouns of this class.—**Reflexively**, rē-flek′siv-li, *adv.* In a reflexive manner; after the manner of a reflexive verb or pronoun.—**Reflexly**, rē-fleks′li, *adv.* In a reflex manner.

Refluent, ref′lụ-ent, *a.* [L. *refluens*, *refluentis*—*re*, back, and *fluo*, to flow. FLUENT.] Flowing, surging, or rushing back; ebbing.—**Refluence**, **Refluency**, ref′lụ-ens, ref′lụ-en-si, *n.* A flowing back.

Reflux, rē′fluks, *n.* [Prefix *re*, back, and *flux*.] A flowing back (the flux and *reflux* of the tides).—*a.* Returning or flowing back.

Refold, rē-fōld′, *v.t.* To fold again.

Refoment, rē-fō-ment′, *v.t.* To foment anew; to excite anew.

Reforge, rē-forj′, *v.t.* To forge again or anew; to fabricate anew.

Reform, rē-form′, *v.t.* [Fr. *réformer*, to reform or amend, from L. *reformare*—*re*, again, and *formo*, to form, from *forma*, form. FORM.] To change from worse to better; to introduce improvement in; to amend; to bring from a bad to a good state; to remove or abolish for something better.—*v.i.* To abandon evil and return to good; to amend one's behavior.—*n.* A rearrangement which either brings back a better order of things or reconstructs the present order in an entirely new form; reformation; amendment of what is defective, vicious, corrupt, or depraved.—**Reformable**, rē-for′ma-bl, *a.* Capable of being reformed.—**Reformation**, ref-or-mā′shon, *n.* The act of reforming or state of being reformed; correction or amendment of life, manners, or of anything objectional or bad; the redress of grievances or abuses.—*The Reformation*, the name usually given to the religious revolution of the sixteenth century which divided the Western Church into the two sections known as Protestant and Roman Catholic.—**Reformatory**, rē-for′ma-to-ri, *a.* Tending to produce reformation.—*Reformatory*, a reform school.—*n.* An institution for the reception and reformation of juveniles who have already begun a career of criminality, and have been convicted.—**Reformed**, rē-formd′, *p.* and *a.* Corrected; amended; restored to a good state; having turned from evil courses (a *reformed* profligate); having accepted the principles of the Reformation and separated from the Church of Rome; especially those churches, such as the ones instituted in various parts of Europe by Zwingli, Calvin, and others, which also separated from Luther on various doctrines.—**Reformer**, rē-for′mėr, *n.* One who effects a reformation or amendment; one who promotes or urges political or social reform.

Re-form, rē-form′, *v.t.* [Directly from *re* and *form*.] To form again or anew; to give the same or another disposition or arrangement to (to *re-form* troops that have been scattered).—**Re-formation**, rē-for-mā′-shon, *n.* The act of forming anew; a second forming in order.

Refortify, rē-for′ti-fī, *v.t.* To fortify anew.—**Refortification**, rē-for′ti-fi-kā″-shon, *n.* A fortifying anew or a second time.

Refound, rē-found′, *v.t.* To found or cast anew; to found or establish again; to reestablish.—**Refounder**, rē-foun′dėr, *n.* One who refounds.

Refract, rē-frakt′, *v.t.* [Fr. *refracter*, from L. *refringo*, *refractum*, to break up—*re*, and *frango*, *fractum*, to break. FRACTION.] To bend back sharply or abruptly; especially, *optics*, to deflect (a ray of light) at a certain angle on passing from one medium into another of a different density.—**Refractable**, rē-frak′ta-bl, *a.* Capable of being refracted; refrangible.—**Refracted**, rē-frak′ted, *p.* and *a.* Turned from a direct course, as rays of light; *bot.* and *conch.* bent back at an acute angle.—**Refracting**, rē-frak′ting, *p.* and *a.* Serving or tending to refract; turning from a direct course.—*Refracting telescope*, a telescope in which the rays are refracted by an object-glass, at the focus of which they are viewed by an eye-piece.—**Refraction**, rē-frak′-shon, *n.* The act of refracting or state of being refracted; a deflection or change of direction impressed upon rays of light or heat passing from one transparent medium into another of different density, as from air into water or vice versa—or upon rays traversing a medium the density of which is not uniform, as the atmosphere.—*Astronomical* or *atmospheric refraction*, the apparent angular elevation of the heavenly bodies above their true places, caused by the refraction of the rays of light in their passing through the earth's atmosphere.—*Double refraction*, the separation of a ray of light into two separate parts by passing through certain transparent mediums, as Iceland-spar, causing objects to appear double.—**Refractive**, rē-frak′tiv, *a.* Pertaining to refraction; serving or having power to refract.—**Refractiveness**, rē-frak′tiv-nes, *n.*—**Refractometer**, rē-frak-tom′et-ėr, *n.* An instrument for exhibiting and measuring the refraction of light.—**Refractor**, rē-frak′tėr, *n.* A refracting telescope. Under REFRACTING.

Refractory, rē-frak′to-ri, *a.* [Fr. *refractaire*; from L. *refractarius*, stubborn, from *refringo*, *refractum*. REFRACT.] Sullen or perverse in opposition or disobedience; obstinate in non-compliance; stubborn and unmanageable (a *refractory* child); resisting ordinary treatment, as metals that are difficult of fusion.—*n.* A refractory person.—**Refractorily**, rē-frak′to-ri-li, *adv.* In a refractory manner; perversely; obstinately.—**Refractoriness**, rē-frak′to-ri-nes, *n.* The quality of being refractory.

Refragable, ref′ra-ga-bl, *a.* [L.L. *refragabilis*, from L. *refragor*, to oppose, to resist—*re*, back, and root of *frango*, to break. REFRACT.] Capable of being opposed or resisted; refutable.—**Refragability**, **Refragableness**,† ref′ra-ga-bil″i-ti, ref′ra-ga-bl-nes, *n.* The state of being refragable.

Refrain, rē-frān′, *n.* [Fr. *refrain*, from O.Fr. *refraindre*, L. *refringo*—*re*, again, and *frango*, to break. (REFRACT.) The *refrain*, therefore, is literally the break or interruption to the course of the piece.] The burden of a song; part of a poetic composition repeated at the end of every stanza; a kind of musical repetition.

Refrain, rē-frān′, *v.t.* [Fr. *refréner*, to bridle in, to repress, from L. *refrœno*—*re*, back, and *frœnum*, a bit.] To hold back; to restrain; to curb; to keep from action: often *refl.*—*v.i.* To forbear; to abstain; to keep one's self from action or interference: followed by *from*.—**Refrainer**, rē-frā′nėr, *n.* One who refrains.—**Refrainment**, rē-frān′ment, *n.* The act of refraining.

Reframe, rē-frām′, *v.t.* To frame or put together again.

Refrangible, rē-fran′ji-bl, *a.* [L. *re*, and *frango*, to break. REFRACT.] Capable of being refracted; subject to refraction, as rays of light.—**Refrangibility**, **Refrangibleness**, rē-fran′ji-bil″i-ti, rē-fran′ji-bl-nes, *n.* The state or quality of being refrangible; susceptibility of refraction.

Refresh, rē-fresh′, *v.t.* [O.Fr. *refreschir*, *refraischir* (Fr. *rafraîchir*), to refresh. FRESH.] To make fresh or vigorous again; to restore vigour or energy to; to give new strength to; to reinvigorate; to recreate or revive after fatigue, want, pain, or the like; to reanimate; to freshen.—**Refresher**, rē-fresh′ėr, *n.* One who or that which refreshes; among lawyers, an additional fee paid to counsel when the case is adjourned from one term or sittings to another.—**Refreshful**, rē-fresh′fụl, *a.* Full of refreshment; refreshing.—**Refreshing**, rē-fresh′ing, *p.* and *a.* Acting or operating so as to refresh; invigorating; reviving; reanimating.—*n.* Refreshment.—**Refreshingly**, rē-fresh′ing-li, *adv.* In a refreshing manner; so as to refresh.—**Refreshingness**, rē-fresh′ing-nes, *n.*—**Refreshment**, rē-fresh′ment, *n.* The act of refreshing; that which refreshes; that which gives fresh strength or vigour, as food, drink, or rest: in the plural almost exclusively applied to food and drink.

Refrigerate, rē-frij′ėr-āt, *v.t.*—*refrigerated*, *refrigerating*. [L. *refrigero*, *refrigeratum*, to refrigerate—*re*, again, and *frigus*, *frigoris*, cold. FRIGID.] To cool; to allay heat; to keep cool; to chill or freeze foods, &c., in order to preserve them.—**Refrigerant**, **Refrigerative**, rē-frij′ėr-ant, rē-frij′ėr-a-tiv, *a.* Cooling; allaying heat.—*n.* A cooling agency; ice, or gases used in mechanical refrigerators; a medicine which abates fever (*med.*).—**Refrigeration**, rē-frij′ėr-ā″shon, *n.* The abating of heat; the act or system of cooling or freezing foods, &c., in order to preserve them.—**Refrigerator**, rē-frij′ėr-a-tėr, *n.* That which refrigerates, cools, or keeps cool; a box or room in which materials (usually foods) are kept cool, either by the action of ice or by evaporation of various liquid gases, as sulphur dioxide or ammonia; an apparatus that cools hot liquids or vapors rapidly.—**Refrigeratory**, rē-frij′ėr-a-to-ri, *a.* Cooling; mitigating heat.

Refringent, rē-frin′jent, *a.* [L. *refringo*—*re*, back, and *frango*, to break. REFRACT.] Possessing the quality of refracting; refractive.—**Refringency**, rē-frin′-jen-si, *n.* Refringent or refractive power.

Reft, reft, pret. & pp. of *reave*. Bereft.

Refuge, ref′ūj, *n.* [Fr., from L. *refugium*, from *refugio*—*re*, again, and *fugio*, to flee (whence *fugitive*).] Shelter or protection from danger or distress; that which shelters or protects from danger, distress, or calamity; any place where one is out of the way of any evil or danger; an institution where the destitute or homeless find temporary shelter; a house of refuge; an expedient to secure protection or defence; a device, contrivance, shift.—*Cities of refuge*, among the Israelites, certain cities appointed to secure the safety of such persons as might unintentionally commit homicide.—*Harbours of refuge*, harbours which afford shelter to vessels in stress of weather.—*House of refuge*, an institution for the shelter of the homeless or destitute.—*v.t.*† To shelter; to protect.—*v.i.*† To take shelter.—**Refugee**, ref-ū-jē′, *n.* [Fr. *réfugié*.] One who flees for refuge; one who in times of persecution or political commotion flees to a foreign country for safety.

Refulgent, rē-ful′jent, *a.* [L. *refulgens*, *refulgentis*, ppr. of *refulgeo*—*re*, again, and *fulgeo*, to shine. FULGENT.] Casting a bright light; shining; splendid.—**Refulgently**, rē-ful′jent-li, *adv.* In a refulgent manner.—**Refulgence**, **Refulgency**, rē-ful′jens, rē-ful′jen-si, *n.* The state or quality of being refulgent; splendour; brilliancy.

Refund, rē-fund′, *v.t.* [L. *refundo*, to pour back, to restore—*re*, back, and *fundo*, to pour. FUSE.] To return in payment or compensation for what has been taken; to pay back; to restore; to reimburse.—**Refunder**, rē-fun'dėr, *n.* One who refunds.

Refurbish, rē-fėr'bish, *v.t.* To furbish a second time or anew.

Refurnish, rē-fėr'nish, *v.t.* To furnish anew; to resupply with furniture.

Refuse, rē-fūz', *v.t.*—*refused, refusing.* [Fr. *réfuser*, to refuse; Pr. *refusar*, Sp. *rehusar*; supposed to owe its origin partly to L. *recusare*, to refuse; partly to *refutare*, to refute.] To deny, as a request, demand, invitation, or command; to decline to do or grant: often with an infinitive as object (he *refused* to give me the book); to decline to accept; to reject (to *refuse* an office); to deny the request of; to say no to (I could not *refuse* him).—*v.i.* To decline a request; not to comply.—*a.* (ref'ūz). Rejected; worthless; left as of no value.—*n.* That which is rejected as useless; waste matter.—**Refusable**, rē-fū'za-bl, *a.* Capable of being refused.—**Refusal**, rē-fū'zal, *n.* The act of refusing; denial of anything demanded, solicited, or offered for acceptance; option of taking or buying; pre-emption.—**Refuser**, rē-fū'zėr, *n.* One who refuses.

Re-fuse, rē-fūz', *v.t.* To fuse or melt again.—**Re-fusion**, rē-fū'zhon, *n.* A renewed or repeated melting or fusion.

Refute, rē-fūt', *v.t.*—*refuted, refuting.* [Fr. *réfuter*, L. *refutare*—*re*, back, and old *futo*, to pour, from root of *fundo*, to pour. CONFUTE, FUTILE, FUSE.] To disprove and overthrow by argument, evidence, or countervailing proof; to prove to be false or erroneous; to confute; to prove to be in error.—**Refuter**, rē-fū'tėr, *n.* One who refutes.—**Refutability**, rē-fū'ta-bil"i-ti or ref'ū-ta-bil"i-ti, *n.* Capability of being refuted.—**Refutable**, rē-fū'ta-bl or ref'ū-ta-bl, *a.* Capable of being refuted.—**Refutation**, ref-ū-tā'shon, *n.* The act of refuting or proving to be false or erroneous; overthrow by argument or countervailing proof.—**Refutatory**, rē-fū'ta-to-ri, *a.* Tending to refute; containing refutation.

Regain, rē-gān', *v.t.* To gain anew; to recover what has been lost; to reach again (they *regained* the shore).

Regal, rē'gal, *a.* [L. *regalis*, from *rex*, *regis*, a king, from stem of *rego*, to rule, the same root being also seen in E. *right*. *Royal* is the same word; and *reign*, *regent*, &c., have the same origin, as also *-rect* in *correct*, *direct*, &c.] Pertaining to a king; kingly; royal. ∴ Syn. under ROYAL.—**Regalia**, rē-gā'li-a, *n. pl.* [L. *regalia*, royal or regal things, nom. pl. neut. of *regalis*, regal.] The ensigns or symbols of royalty; the apparatus of a coronation, as the crown, scepter, &c.; the insignia or decorations of some society; showy clothes.—**Regality**, rē-gal'i-ti, *n.* Royalty; sovereignty; kingship; sovereign right.—**Regally**, rē'gal-li, *adv.* In a regal or royal manner; royally.

Regale, rē-gāl', *v.t.*—*regaled, regaling.* [Fr. *régaler*, to regale—*re*, and an old verb *galer*, to rejoice, probably from root of Goth. *gailjan*, to rejoice. GALA.] To entertain sumptuously or with something that gives great pleasure; to gratify, as the senses; to delight; to feast.—*v.i.* To feast; to fare sumptuously.—*n.* A splendid repast; a treat.—**Regalement**, rē-gāl'ment, *n.* Entertainment; gratification.—**Regaler**, rē-gā'lėr, *n.* One who regales.

Regalia. Under REGAL.

Regard, rē-gärd', *v.t.* [Fr. *regarder*, to regard, to observe—*re*, back, and *garder*, to guard. GUARD.] To look upon; to observe; to notice with some care; to pay attention to; to observe a certain respect towards; to respect, reverence, honour, esteem; to mind; to care for; to have or to show certain feelings towards; to view in the light of; to put on the same footing as.—*As regards* (impers.), with regard to; as respects; as concerns (as *regards* that matter I am of your opinion).—*n.* Look or gaze; aspect directed to another (*Shak.*); attention or care; heed; consideration; that feeling which springs from estimable qualities in the object; respect, esteem, reverence; relation; respect; reference; view: often in the phrases, *in regard to*, *with regard to*; *pl.* respects; good wishes; compliments (give my *regards* to the family).—**Regardable**, rē-gär'da-bl, *a.* Worthy of notice; noticeable.—**Regardant**, rē-gär'dant, *a.* Regarding; watching; *her.* applied to an animal whose face is turned backwards in an attitude of vigilance.—**Regarder**, rē-gär'dėr, *n.* One that regards.—**Regardful**, rē-gärd'ful, *a.* Having or paying regard.—**Regardfully**, rē-gärd'ful-li, *adv.* In a regardful manner.—**Regarding**, rē-gär'ding, *prep.* [Like *concerning*, *during*, a participle, now established as a preposition.] Respecting; concerning; in reference to (to be at a loss *regarding* something).—**Regardless**, rē-gärd'les, *a.* Not having regard or heed; heedless; careless.—**Regardlessly**, rē-gärd'les-li, *adv.* In a regardless manner; heedlessly; carelessly.—**Regardlessness**, rē-gärd'les-nes, *n.* Heedlessness; negligence.

Regather, rē-gaᴛʜ'ėr, *v.t.* To gather or collect again.

Regatta, rē-gat'a, *n.* [It.] Originally a gondola race in Venice; now any sailing or rowing race in which a number of yachts or boats contend for prizes.

Regelation, rē-je-lā'shon, *n.* [L. *re*, again, and *gelatio*, *gelationis*, a freezing. CONGEAL.] The phenomenon presented by pieces of moist ice which when placed in contact with one another freeze together even in a warm atmosphere.

Regency. Under REGENT.

Regenerate, rē-jen'ėr-āt, *v.t.*—*regenerated, regenerating.* [L. *regenero*, *regeneratum*—*re*, again, and *genero*, to generate. GENERATE.] To generate or produce anew; to reproduce; *theol.* to cause to be born again; to change, as the heart and affections, from enmity or indifference to love of God.—*a.* Reproduced; *theol.* changed from a natural to a spiritual state.—**Regenerateness, Regeneracy**, rē-jen'ėr-āt-nes, rē-jen'ėr-a-si, *n.* The state of being regenerated.—**Regeneration**, rē-jen'ėr-ā"shon, *n.* The act of regenerating or producing anew; *theol.* that change by which love to God and his law is implanted in the heart.—**Regenerative**, rē-jen'ėr-ā-tiv, *a.* Producing regeneration; renewing.—**Regeneratively**, rē-jen'ėr-ā-tiv-li, *adv.*—**Regeneratory**, rē-jen'ėr-a-to-ri, *a.* Regenerative.—**Regenesis**, rē-jen'e-sis, *n.* [Prefix *re*, again, and *genesis*.] The state of being reproduced.

Regent, rē'jent, *a.* [L. *regens*, *regentis*, ppr. of *rego*, to rule; cog. Skr. *râj*, to rule; from same root also E. *right*. REGAL.] Ruling; governing; exercising vicarious authority.—*n.* A governor; a ruler; one who governs a kingdom in the minority, absence, or disability of the sovereign; one of a certain standing who taught in universities: the word formerly in use for a *professor*; in the English universities, one who has certain peculiar duties of instruction or government.—**Regentship**, rē'jent-ship, *n.* The office or dignity of a regent; regency.—**Regency**, rē'jen-si, *n.* Rule; government; the office or jurisdiction of a regent; a body of men intrusted with the power of a regent.

Regerminate, rē-jėr'mi-nāt, *v.i.* To germinate again.

Reget, rē-get', *v.t.* To get or obtain again.

Regicide, rej'i-sīd, *n.* [Fr. *régicide*, from L. *rex*, *regis*, a king, and *cædo*, to slay.] A king-killer; one who murders a king; the killing or murder of a king.—**Regicidal**, rej-i-sī'dal, *a.* Pertaining to regicide.

Regild, rē-gild', *v.t.* To gild anew.

Regime, rā-zhēm', *n.* [Fr. *régime*, from L. *regimen*, guidance, from *rego*, to govern.] Mode or system of management; government, especially as connected with certain social features; administration; rule.—*The ancient regime*, the political system which prevailed in France before the revolution of 1789.—**Regimen**, rej'i-men, *n.* Orderly government; the regulation of diet, exercise, &c.; *gram.* government of words.—**Regiminal**, re-jim'i-nal, *a.* Pertaining to regimen.

Regiment, rej'i-ment, *n.* [Fr. *régiment*, from L.L. *regimentum*, from L. *regimen*, rule, from *rego*, to rule. REGIME, REGENT.] An organization of troops under the command of a colonel, consisting of several battalions, squadrons, or batteries in those branches of the army designated respectively as the infantry, cavalry, or artillery.—*v.t.* To form troops into regiments; to assign soldiers to a regiment; to organize civilians into groups to control their actions and indoctrinate their minds.—**Regimentation**, rej-i-men-tā'shon, *n.* Strict control or uniformity imposed by external authority; the act of forming into groups.

Region, rē'jun, *n.* [Fr. *région*, from L. *regio*, *regionis*, from *rego*, to rule. REGAL.] A large division of any space or surface considered as apart from others; especially, a tract of land, sea, &c., of considerable but indefinite extent; a country; a district; a part or division of the body (the *region* of the heart).—**Regional**, rē'jun-al, *a.* Pertaining to a particular region; sectional.

Register, rej'is-tėr, *n.* [Fr. *registre*, L.L. *registrum*, *regestrum*, a book of records—*re*, back, and *gero*, *gestum*, to carry. GESTATION.] An official written account or entry in a book regularly kept for preservation or for reference; a record; a list; the book in which records are kept; a document issued by the customs authorities as evidence of a ship's nationality; a contrivance for regulating the passage of heat or air in heating or ventilation; a device for automatically indicating the number of revolutions made or amount of work done by machinery, recording pressure, &c.; *printing*, the agreement of two printed forms to be applied to the same sheet, either on the same side, as in colour printing, or on both sides as in a book or newspaper; *music*, the compass of a voice or instrument, or a portion of the compass; a stop or set of pipes in an organ.—*Lloyd's register.* Under LLOYD'S.—*Lord register*, or *lord clerk register*, a Scottish officer of state who has the custody of the archives.—*v.t.* To record; to enter in a register.—*v.i.* *Printing*, to correspond exactly, as columns or lines of printed matter on opposite sheets.—**Registered**, rej'is-tėrd, *p.* and *a.* Recorded in a register; enrolled.—*Registered company*, a joint-stock company entered in an official register, but not incorporated.—*Registered letter*, a letter the address of which is registered at a post-office, for which a special fee is paid in order to secure its safe transmission.—**Register-grate**, *n.* A grate with an apparatus for regulating the admission of air and the heat of the fire.—**Registering**, rej'is-tėr-ing, *p.* and *a.* Recording; indicating automatically.—**Register-office**, *n.* An office where registers or records are kept; a record-office.—**Registrar**, rej'is-trär, *n.* [L.L. *registrarius.*] One whose business it is to write or keep a register; a keeper of records.—**Registrar-general**, *n.* An officer who superintends a system of registration; in Britain an official who has the general superintendence of the system of registration of births, deaths, and marriages.—**Registrarship**, rej'is-trär-ship, *n.* The office of a registrar.—**Registration**, rej-is-trā'shon, *n.* The act of inserting in a register.—**Registry**, rej'is-tri, *n.* The act of entering in a register; the place where a register is kept; facts recorded; an entry.

Regium, Regius, rē'ji-um, rē'ji-us, *a.* [Neut. and masc. form of L. *regius*, royal. REGAL.] Royal.—*Regium donum* (royal grant), an annual grant of public money formerly given in aid of the income of the Presbyterian clergy in Ireland.—*Regius professors*, professors in the English universities whose chairs were founded by Henry VIII; in the Scottish universities, whose professorships were founded by the crown.

Reglet, reg'let, *n.* [Fr. *réglet*, from *règle*, rule, L. *regula*. REGULATE.] *Printing*, a strip of wood or metal used for separating pages in the chase, &c.; *arch.* a flat narrow molding between panels, &c.

Regnal, reg′nal, *a.* [From L. *regnum*, a kingdom. REIGN.] Pertaining to the reign of a monarch.—*Regnal year*, the year of a sovereign's reign (as given in an act of the British Parliament).

Regnant, reg′nant, *a.* [L. *regnans*, *regnantis*, ppr. of *regno*, to reign, from *regnum*, a kingdom.] Reigning as sovereign; predominant; prevalent.

Regorge, rē-gorj′, *v.t.* [Prefix *re*, and *gorge*.] To vomit up; to disgorge.

Regrade, rē-grād′, *v.t.* To grade again; to give a new grade; to degrade (*Obs.*).

Regraft, rē-graft′, *v.t.* To graft again.

Regrant, rē-grant′, *v.t.* To grant back.—*n.* The act of granting back; a new or fresh grant.

Regrass, rē-gras′, *v.t.* To plant again with grass.

Regrate, rē-grāt′, *v.t.*—*regrated*, *regrating*. [O.Fr. *regrater*, to scrape or scour old things for sale again, to *regrate*—*re*, and *grater*, to *grate*. GRATE.] To scrape off the outer surface of a wall in order to freshen it; to buy in large quantities and sell at retail (*Hist.*).

Regreet, rē-grēt′, *v.i.* To greet or salute again.

Regress, rē′gres, *n.* [L. *regressus*, from *regredior*, to go back—*re*, back, and *gradior*, to go. GRADE.] Passage back; return; power or liberty of returning or passing back.—*v.i.* (rē-gres′). To go back; to return to a former place or state.—**Regression**, rē-gresh′on, *n.* [L. *regressio.*] The act of passing back or returning; retrogression.—**Filial regression**. [L.L. *filialis*, relating to offspring.] In heredity, a tendency to return to the average.—**Regressive**, rē-gres′iv, *a.* Passing back; returning.

Regret, rē-gret′, *n.* [Fr. *regret*, regret, *regretter*, O.Fr. *regreter*, to regret; from *re*, again, and the Teutonic verb seen in Icel. *gráta*, A.Sax. *graetan*, Sc. *greet*, to weep.] Grief or trouble caused by the want or loss of something formerly possessed; sorrowful longing; pain of mind at something done or left undone; remorse.—*v.t.*—*regretted*, *regretting*. To lament the loss of, or separation from; to look back at with sorrowful longing; to grieve at; to be sorry for.—**Regretful**, rē-gret′ful, *a.* Full of regret.—**Regretfully**, rē-gret′ful-li, *adv.* With regret.—**Regrettable**, rē-gret′a-bl, *a.* Admitting of or calling for regret.

Regrowth, rē-grōth′, *n.* A growing again; a new or second growth.

Regula, reg′ū-la, *n.* [L., a rule.] *Arch.* a fillet or listel; a reglet.

Regular, reg′ū-lėr, *a.* [L. *regularis*, from *regula*, a rule, from *rego*, to rule. REGENT, REGAL.] Conformed to a rule; agreeable to a prescribed mode or customary form; normal; acting or going on by rule or rules; steady or uniform; orderly; methodical; unvarying; *geom.* applied to a figure or body whose sides and angles are equal, as a square, a cube, an equilateral triangle, an equilateral pentagon, &c.; *gram.* adhering to the common form in respect to inflectional terminations; *eccles.* belonging to a monastic order, and bound to certain rules; *bot.* symmetrical as regards figure and size and proportion of parts; colloquially, thorough, out-and-out, complete.—*Regular troops* or *regulars*, troops of a permanent army: opposed to *militia* or *volunteers*.—*Regular verb*, in English, one that forms the preterite and past participle in *d* or *ed*.—*n.* A monk who has taken the vows of some monastic order; a soldier belonging to a permanent army.—**Regularity**, reg-ū-lar′i-ti, *n.* The state or quality of being regular; agreeableness to rule or established order; conformity to the customary type; steadiness or uniformity in a course.—**Regularly**, reg′ū-lėr-li, *adv.* In a regular manner; in uniform order; at fixed intervals or periods; methodically; in due order.—

Regulate, reg′ū-lāt, *v.t.*—*regulated*, *regulating*. [L. *regulo*, *regulatum*, from *regula*, a rule.] To adjust by rule or established mode; to govern by or subject to certain rules or restrictions; to direct; to put or keep in good order; to control and cause to act properly.—**Regulation**, reg-ū-lā′shon, *n.* The act of regulating; a rule prescribed by a superior as to the actions of those under his control; a governing direction; a precept.—**Regulative**, reg-ū-lā′tiv, *a.* Regulating; tending to regulate.—**Regulator**, reg′ū-lā-tėr, *n.* One who or that which regulates; a device or contrivance of which the object is to produce uniformity of motion or action; the governor of a steam-engine.

Regulus, reg′ū-lus, *n.* [L., a petty king or sovereign, a dim. of *rex*, *regis*, a king. REGAL.] A name originally applied by the alchemists to antimony, from the facility with which it alloyed with gold (the *king* of metals), now applied to metals which still retain to a greater or less extent the impurities they contained in the state of ore; a fixed star of the first magnitude in the constellation Leo.

Regur, rē′gėr, *n.* The native name for the 'black cotton-soil' of Southern India, a soil of marvellous fertility.

Regurgitate, rē-gėr′ji-tāt, *v.t.*—*regurgitated*, *regurgitating*. [L.L. *regurgito*, *regurgitatum*—L. *re*, *back*, and *gurges*, *gurgitis*, a whirlpool. GORGE.] To pour or cause to rush or surge back; to pour or throw back in great quantity.—*v.i.* To be poured back; to rush or surge back.—**Regurgitation**, rē-gėr′ji-tā″shon, *n.* The act of regurgitating; *med.* the rising of some of the contents of the stomach into the mouth.

Rehabilitate, rē-ha-bil′i-tāt, *v.t.*—*rehabilitated*, *rehabilitating*. [Fr. *réhabiliter*—*re*, and *habiliter*, to qualify, from *habile*, qualified, able. ABLE.] To restore to a former capacity or position; to reinstate; to re-establish in the esteem of others.—**Rehabilitation**, rē-ha-bil′i-tā″shon, *n.* The act of rehabilitating.

Rehash, rē-hash′, *v.t.* To hash anew; to work up old material in a new form.—*n.* Something made up of materials formerly used.

Rehear, rē-hēr′, *v.t.* To hear again; *law*, to try a second time.

Rehearse, rē-hėrs′, *v.t.*—*rehearsed*, *rehearsing*. [O.E. *reherce*, *reherse*, from O.Fr. *rehercer*, *reherser*, to repeat over again—*re*, again, and *hercer*, *herser*, to harrow, from *herce*, *herse*, a harrow. HEARSE.] To repeat, as what has already been said or written; to recite; to narrate, recount, relate; to recite or repeat in private for experiment and improvement, before giving a public representation (to *rehearse* a tragedy).—*v.i.* To go through some performance in private preparatory to public representation.—**Rehearsal**, rē-hėr′sal, *n.* The act of rehearsing; narration; a telling or recounting; a trial performance (as of a play) made before exhibiting to the public.—**Rehearser**, rē-hėr′sėr, *n.* One who rehearses.

Rehypothecate, re-hī-poth′e-kāt, *v.t.* To hypothecate again; to give as security although already hypothecated as such; to redeposit collateral for a loan.

Reichsbank, rīchs′bänk, *n.* [G.] The state bank of Germany.

Reichsmark, rīchs′märk, *n.* [G.] The German monetary unit.

Reichstag, rīchs′täg, *n.* [G.] The German legislative assembly.

Reign, rān, *v.i.* [O.Fr. *reigner*, Fr. *régner*, from L. *regnare*, to rule, from *regnum*, a kingdom, from *rego*, to rule. REGAL.] To possess or exercise sovereign power or authority; to hold the supreme power; to rule; to be predominant; to prevail; to have superior or uncontrolled dominion.—*n.* [O.Fr. *reigne*, Fr. *règne*, L. *regnum*, a kingdom.] Royal authority; sovereignty; the time during which a king, queen, or emperor reigns; empire; kingdom; power; sway.

Reilluminate, rē-il-lū′mi-nāt, *v.t.* To illuminate or enlighten again.—**Reillumine**, rē-il-lū′min, *v.t.* To illumine again, to reilluminate.

Reimbark, rē-im-bärk′. RE-EMBARK.

Reimburse, rē-im-bėrs′, *v.t.*—*reimbursed*, *reimbursing*. [Fr. *rembourser*—*re*, again, *en*, in, and *bourse*, a purse. PURSE.] To replace in a treasury; to pay back; to refund; to pay back to; to render an equivalent to for money or other expenditure.—**Reimbursement**, rē-im-bėrs′ment, *n.* The act of reimbursing; repayment.—**Reimburser**, rē-im-bėr′sėr, *n.* One who reimburses.

Reimmerge, rē-im-mėrj′, *v.t.* To immerge again; to plunge afresh.

Reimplant, rē-im-plant′, *v.t.* To implant again.

Reimport, rē-im-pōrt′, *v.t.* To import again; to carry back to the country of exportation.—*n.* (rē-im′pōrt). Something reimported.—**Reimportation**, rē-im′pōr-tā″shon, *n.* The act of reimporting; that which is reimported.

Reimpose, rē-im-pōz′, *v.t.* To impose or levy anew.—**Reimposition**, rē-im′pō-zish″on, *n.* Act of reimposing.

Reimpress, rē-im-pres′, *v.t.* To impress anew.—**Reimpression**, rē-im-presh′on, *n.* A second impression; a reprint.

Reimprint, rē-im-print′, *v.t.* To imprint or print again.

Reimprison, rē-im-priz′on, *v.t.* To imprison again.—**Reimprisonment**, rē-im-priz′on-ment, *n.* The act of confining in prison a second time for the same cause, or after a release from prison.

Rein, rān, *n.* [Fr. *rêne*, O.Fr. *resne*, It. *redina*; from L. *retineo*, to retain. RETAIN.] The strap of a bridle, by which the rider or driver restrains and governs the horse, &c.; any thong or cord for the same purpose; *fig.* a means of curbing, restraining, or governing; restraint.—*To give the rein*, or *the reins*, to give licence; to leave without restraint.—*To take the reins*, to take the guidance or government.—*v.t.* To govern, guide, or restrain by a bridle; to restrain.

Reincarnation, rē-in-kär′na-shon, *n.* Belief that the soul returns after death to live in a new body.

Reindeer, rān′dēr, *n.* [Icel. *hrein-dýri*, Sw. *renagur*, Dan. *rensdyr*, a reindeer; said to be of Finnish or Lappish origin.] A deer of northern Europe and Asia, with broad branched antlers; used as a domestic animal among the Laplanders, to whom it furnishes food, clothing, and the means of conveyance.—**Reindeer-moss**, *n.* A lichen which constitutes almost the sole winter food for reindeer.

Reinduce, rē-in-dūs′, *v.t.* To induce again.

Reinflame, rē-in-flām′, *v.t.* To inflame anew; to rekindle.

Reinforce, rē-in-fōrs′, *v.t.* To strengthen; to strengthen with more troops, ships, &c.—*n.* An additional thickness given to any portion of an object in order to strengthen it; the part of a cannon nearest the breech.—*Reinforced concrete*, concrete in which steel bars are embedded, so as to increase the resistance of the structure to tension.—**Reinforcement**, rē-in-fōrs′ment, *n.* The act of reinforcing; additional troops or forces to augment an army or fleet.

Reinform, rē-in-form′, *v.t.* To inform again.

Reinfuse, rē-in-fūz′, *v.t.* To infuse again.

Reinhabit, rē-in-hab′it, *v.t.* To inhabit again.

Reinquire, rē-in-kwīr′, *v.t.* To inquire a second time.

Reins, rānz, *n.pl.* [Fr. *rein*, a kidney, *reins*, the loins, from L. *rens*, *renis*, the kidney.] The kidneys; the region of the kidneys; the lower parts of the back; the seat of the affections and passions, formerly supposed to be situated in that part of the body.

Reinsert, rē-in-sėrt′, *v.t.* To insert a second time.—**Reinsertion**, rē-in-sėr′shon, *n.* The act of reinsertion, or what is reinserted.

Reinspect, rē-in-spekt′, *v.t.* To inspect again.—**Reinspection**, rē-in-spek′shon, *n.* The act of inspecting a second time.

Reinspire, rē-in-spīr′, *v.t.* To inspire anew.

Reinspirit, rē-in-spir′it, *v.t.* To inspirit anew.

Reinstall, rē-in-stąl′, *v.t.* To install again.—**Reinstalment**, rē-in-stąl′ment, *n.* The act of reinstalling.

Reinstate, rē-in-stāt′, *v.t.* To instate again; to place again in possession or in a former state.—**Reinstatement**, rē-in-stāt′ment, *n.* The act of reinstating; reestablishment.

Reinstruct, rē-in-strukt′, *v.t.* To instruct anew.

Reinsurance, rē-in-shö′rans, *n.* A renewed or second insurance; a contract by which the first insurer relieves himself from the risks he had undertaken, and devolves them upon other insurers, called *reinsurers.* **Reinsure**, rē-in-shör′, *v.t.* To insure again.—**Reinsurer**, rē-in-shö′rėr, *n.* One who reinsures.

Reinter, rē-in-tėr′, *v.t.* To inter again.

Reinterrogate, rē-in-ter′ō-gāt, *v.t.* To interrogate again; to question repeatedly.

Reintroduce, rē-in′trō-dūs″, *v.t.* To introduce again.—**Reintroduction**, rē-in′trō-duk″shon, *n.* A second introduction.

Re-invest, rē-in-vest′, *v.t.* To invest anew.

Reinvestigate, rē-in-ves′ti-gāt, *v.t.* To investigate again.—**Reinvestigation**, rē-in-ves′ti-gā″shon, *v.t.* A second investigation.

Reinvigorate, rē-in-vig′o-rāt, *v.t.* To revive vigour in; to reanimate.

Reis, rēs, *n.* [Ar.] A head; a chief; a captain.—*Reis effendi*, one of the chief Turkish officers of state.

Reissue, rē-ish′ū, *v.i.* To issue or go forth again.—*v.t.* To issue, send out, or put forth a second time (to *reissue* bank-notes).—*n.* A second or renewed issue.

Reiterate, rē-it′ėr-āt, *v.t.*—*reiterated, reiterating.* [L. *re*, again, and *itero*, *iteratum*, to repeat, from *iterum*, again. ITERATE.] To repeat again and again; to do or say (especially to say) repeatedly.—*a.* Reiterated.—**Reiteratedly**, rē-it′ėr-ā-ted-li, *adv.* By reiteration; repeatedly.—**Reiteration**, rē-it′ėr-ā″shon, *n.* The act of reiterating; repetition.—**Reiterative**, rē-it′ėr-ā-tiv, *n.* A word or part of a word repeated so as to form a reduplicated word; *gram.* a word signifying repeated or intense action.

Reiver, *n.* REAVER.

Reject, rē-jekt′, *v.t.* [L. *rejicio*, *rejectum*, to reject—*re*, again, and *jacio*, to throw (whence also *eject*, *inject*, *project*, &c). JET.] To throw away as useless or vile; to cast off; to discard; to refuse to receive; to decline haughtily or harshly; to refuse to grant.—*n.*, rē′jekt, one who or that which is rejected.—**Rejecter**, rē-jek′tėr, *n.* One who rejects or refuses.—**Rejection**, rē-jek′shon, *n.* The act of rejecting; refusal to accept or grant.

Rejoice, rē-jois′, *v.i.*—*rejoiced, rejoicing.* [O.E. *rejoisse*, *rejoyse*, from O.Fr. *rejoir*, *rejoissant*, Fr. *réjouir*, *réjouissant*; prefix *re*, and *éjouir*, older *esjoïr*—L. *ex*, intens., and *gaudeo*, to rejoice. JOY.] To experience joy and gladness in a high degree; to be joyful; to exult: often with *at*, *in*, *on account of*, &c., or a subordinate clause.—*v.t.* To make joyful; to gladden.—**Rejoicer**, rē-jois′ėr, *n.* One that rejoices; one that causes to rejoice.—**Rejoicing**, rē-jois′ing, *n.* The act of expressing joy; procedure expressive of joy; festivity.—**Rejoicingly**, rē-jois′ing-li, *adv.* With joy or exultation.

Rejoin, rē-join′, *v.t.* To join again; to unite after separation; to join the company of again; to answer; to say in answer; to reply: with a clause as object.—*v.i.* To answer to a reply.—**Rejoinder**, rē-join′dėr, *n.* [An infinitive form: Fr. *rejoindre*, to rejoin. *Attainder*, *remainder* are similar forms.] An answer to a reply; *law*, the fourth stage in the pleadings in an action, being the defendant's answer to the plaintiff's replication.

Rejudge, rē-juj′, *v.t.* To judge again.

Rejuvenate, rē-jū′ven-āt, *v.t.*—*rejuvenated, rejuvenating.* [L. *re*, again, and *juvenis*, young. JUVENILE.] To restore to youth; to make young again.—**Rejuvenation**, rē-jū′ven-ā″shon, *n.* The act of rejuvenating.

Rejuvenescence, rē-jū′ven-es″ens, *n.* [L. *re*, and *juvenesco*, to grow young.] A renewing of youth; the state of being young again.—**Rejuvenescent**, rē-jū′ven-es″ent, *a.* Becoming or become young again.—**Rejuvenize**, rē-jū′ve-nīz, *v.t.* To render young again.

Rekindle, rē-kin′dl, *v.t.* To kindle again; to inflame again; to rouse anew.

Reland, rē-land′, *v.t.* To land again; to put on land after having been shipped or embarked.—*v.i.* To go on shore after having embarked.

Relapse, rē-laps′, *v.i.*—*relapsed, relapsing.* [L. *relabor*, *relapsus*, to slide back—*re*, back, and *labor*, *lapsus*, to slide. LAPSE.] To slip or slide back; to return to a former bad state or practice; to backslide; to fall back or return from recovery or a convalescent state.—*n.* A falling back into a former bad state, either of health or of morals.—**Relapsable**, rē-lap′sa-bl, *a.* Capable of relapsing or liable to relapse.—**Relapsed**, rē-lapst′, *a.* *R. Cath. Ch.* a term applied to a heretic who having abjured his errors has fallen back into them again.—**Relapser**, rē-lap′sėr, *n.* One that relapses.—**Relapsing**, rē-lap′sing, *p.* and *a.* Sliding or falling back; marked by a relapse or return to a former worse state.

Relate, rē-lāt′, *v.t.*—*related, relating.* [Fr. *relater*, to state, to mention; L. *refero*, *relatum*, to refer, to bring back—*re*, back, and *latus*, brought (as in *elate*, *oblate*, *translate*).] To tell; to recite; to recount; to narrate the particulars of; to ally by connection or kindred.—*v.i.* To have reference or respect; to regard; to stand in some relation: with *to* following.—**Related**, rē-lā′ted, *p.* and *a.* Allied; connected by blood or alliance, particularly by blood; standing in some relation or connection.—**Relater**, rē-lā′tėr, *n.* One who relates.—**Relation**, rē-lā′shon, *n.* [L. *relatio*, *relationis.*] The act of relating; that which is related or told; narrative; reference, respect, or regard: often in the phrase *in relation to*; connection perceived or imagined between things; a certain position of one thing with regard to another; the condition of being such or such in respect to something else; due conformity or harmony of parts; kinship; a kinsman or kinswoman; *math.* ratio; proportion; *logic*, one of the ten predicaments.—**Relational**, rē-lā′shon-al, *a.* Indicating or specifying some relation: used in contradistinction to *notional* (a *relational* part of speech, as the pronoun, preposition, and conjunction).—**Relationship**, rē-lā′shon-ship, *n.* The state of being related by kindred, affinity, or other alliance; kinship.—**Relative**, rel′a-tiv, *a.* [L. *relativus.*] Having relation to or bearing on something; close in connection; pertinent; relevant; not absolute or existing by itself; depending on or incident to something else; *gram.* applied to a word which relates to another word, sentence, or part of a sentence called the antecedent, applied especially to certain pronouns, as *who*, *which*, and *that.*—*Relative motion*, the change of the place of a moving body with respect to some other body also in motion.—*Relative terms*, terms which imply some relation, as *guardian* and *ward*, *master* and *servant*, &c.—*n.* Something considered in its relation to something else; a person connected by blood or affinity, especially one allied by blood; a kinsman or kinswoman; *gram.* a word which relates to or represents another word, called its antecedent, or refers back to a statement; a relative pronoun.—**Relatively**, rel′a-tiv-li, *adv.* In a relative manner; in relation to something else; not absolutely; comparatively; often followed by *to* (an expenditure large *relatively to* his income.)—**Relativeness, Relativity**, rel′a-tiv-nes, rel-a-tiv′i-ti, *n.* The state of being relative; a modern physical theory, based on the hypothesis that the distance between two points and the interval of time between two events are not absolute quantities, but have different values for different observers.—**Relator**, rē-lā′tėr, *n.* One who relates; *law*, an individual who furnishes information of an accusatory nature, or in whose behalf, or at whose instance, an information is filed, or a writ issued, as in the case of a quo warranto.

Relax, rē-laks′, *v.t.* [L. *relaxo*, to relax—*re*, back, and *laxo*, to loosen, from *laxus*, loose. LAX.] To slacken; to make less tense or rigid; to make less severe or rigorous; to remit in strictness; to remit or abate in respect to attention, effort, or labor.—*v.i.* To become loose, feeble, or languid; to abate in severity; to become more mild or less rigorous; to remit in close attention; to unbend; to rest or seek recreation.—**Relaxation**, rē-lak-sā′shon, *n.* [L. *relaxatio.*] The act of relaxing or state of being relaxed; a diminution of tension or firmness, remission of attention or application; recreation; an occupation giving mental or bodily relief after effort.

Relay, rē-lā′, rē′lā, *n.* [Fr. *relais*, a relay of horses; originally, relief or release, from L. *re*, and *laxus*, loose.] A supply of anything stored up for affording relief from time to time, or at successive stages; a supply of horses placed on the road to be in readiness to relieve others; a squad of men to take a spell or turn of work at stated intervals; a telegraphic apparatus which, on receiving a feeble electric current, sends on a much stronger current.—*v.t.* To carry or pass on by stages.—**Relay race**, a race between teams, in which each member of a team covers part of the total distance.

Release, rē-lēs′, *v.t.*—*released, releasing.* [From O.Fr. *relesser*, *relaisser*, to release, to relinquish—prefix *re*, and *laisser*, to leave, from L. *laxare*, to loosen, from *laxus*, loose, lax. *Release*, *relax* are thus doublets. LAX.] To let loose again; to set free from restraint or confinement; to liberate; to free from pain, grief, or any other evil; to free from obligation or penalty; *law*, to give up or let go, as a claim.—*n.* Liberation from restraint of any kind, as from confinement or bondage; liberation from care, pain, or burden; discharge from obligation or responsibility.—**Releasable**, rē-lēs′a-bl, *a.* Capable of being released.—**Releasement**, rē-lēs′ment, *n.* The act of releasing.—**Releaser**, rē-lēs′ėr, *n.* One who releases.

Re-lease, rē-lēs′, *v.t.* [Prefix *re*, and *lease.*] To lease again or anew.

Relegate, rel′e-gāt, *v.t.*—*relegated, relegating.* [L. *relego*, *relegatum*, to banish—*re*, back, and *lego*, to send. LEGATE.] To send away or out of the way; to consign to some obscure or remote destination; to banish.—**Relegation**, rel-ē-gā′shon, *n.* [L. *relegatio.*] The act of relegating; banishment; in ancient Roman law, banishment to a certain place for a certain time.

Relent, rē-lent′, *v.i.* [Fr. *ralentir*, to slacken, to abate—prefix *re*, back, *à*, to, and *lent*, L. *lentus*, pliant, slow. LENIENT.] To become less harsh, cruel, or obdurate; to soften in temper; to become more mild; to yield; to comply.—**Relentless**, rē-lent′les, *a.* Incapable of relenting; insensible to the distresses of others; merciless; implacable; pitiless.—**Relentlessly**, rē-lent′les-li, *adv.* In a relentless manner; without pity.—**Relentlessness**, rē-lent′les-nes, *n.* The quality of being relentless.

Relet, rē-let′, *v.t.* To let anew, as a house.

Relevant, rel′ē-vant, *a.* [Fr. *relevant*, ppr. of *relever*, to relieve, to help or aid. RELIEVE.] Lending aid or support†; to the purpose; pertinent; applicable; bearing on the matter in hand (arguments not *relevant* to the case).—**Relevantly**, rel'ē-vant-li, *adv.* In a relevant manner.—**Relevance, Relevancy**, rel'ē-vans, rel'ē-van-si, *n.* The quality of being relevant; pertinence.

Reliable, Reliance, Reliant, &c. Under RELY.

Relic, rel'ik, *n.* [Fr. *relique*, from L. *reliquiæ*, remains—*re*, back, and *linquo*, to leave (as in *delinquent, relinquish*; same root as *license*, Gr. *leipō*, to leave.] That which is left after the loss or decay of the rest; a remaining fragment; the body of a deceased person: usually in *pl.*; something preserved in remembrance; a memento, souvenir, or keepsake; a bone or other part of saints or martyrs, or some part of their garments, &c., preserved, and regarded as of extraordinary sanctity and often as possessing miraculous powers.

Relict, rel'ikt, *n.* [O.Fr. *relicte*, a widow, L. *relicta*, fem. of *relictus*, pp. of *relinquo*, to leave. RELIC.] A widow; a woman whose husband is dead.

Relief, rē-lēf', *n.* [Fr. *relief*, relief, a relieving, alleviation, also (like It. *rilievo*) artistic raised work, from *relever*. RELIEVE.] The removal of anything painful or burdensome by which some ease is obtained; ease from pain; alleviation; succor; what mitigates or removes pain, grief, or other evil; help given to the poor in the form of food, money, &c.; release from duty by a substitute or substitutes; *sculp., arch.*, &c., the projection or prominence of a figure above or beyond the ground or plane on which it is formed, being of three kinds: high-relief (*alto-rilievo*), low-relief (*basso-rilievo*), and middle or half relief (*mezzo-rilievo*), according to the degree of projection; hence, a piece of artistic work in one or other of these styles; *painting*, the appearance of projection and solidity in represented objects; hence, prominence or distinctness given to anything by something presenting a contrast to it; *phys. geog.* the undulations or surface elevations of a country; *fort.* the height of a parapet from the bottom of the ditch; *feudal law*, a payment by the heir of a tenant made to his lord for the privilege of taking up the estate.—**Relievable**, rē-lē'va-bl, *a.* Capable of being relieved; fitted to receive relief.—**Relieve**, rē-lēv', *v.t.*—*relieved, relieving.* [O.E. *releve*, from Fr. *relever*, to set up again, to release, to assist, from L. *relevare*, to lift up again—*re*, again, and *levare*, to raise, from *levis*, light. LEVITY.] To remove or lessen, as anything that pains or distresses; to mitigate) alleviate (pain, misery, wants); to free, wholly or partially from pain, grief, anxiety, or anything considered to be an evil; to help, aid, or succour (the poor, the sick, &c.); to release from a post or duty by substituting another person or party (to *relieve* a sentinel); to obviate the monotony of by the introduction of some variety; to make conspicuous; to set off by contrast; to give the appearance of projection to.—**Reliever**, rē-lē'vėr, *n.* One that relieves.—**Relieving**, rē-lē'ving, *p.* and *a.* Serving or tending to relieve.—*Relieving arch*, an arch in the substance of a wall to relieve the part below it from a superincumbent weight.—**Relieving tackle**, tackle fastened to the tiller when the steering gear has been broken, as in a gale or fight.

Relievo, rē-lē'vō or rel-ē-ā'vō, *n.* A form of *Rilievo.*

Relight, rē-līt', *v.t.* To light anew; to rekindle.

Religieux, rė-lēzh-ē-ė, *n. sing.* and *pl.* [Fr.] A member of a monastic order; a monk.—**Religieuse**, rė-lēzh-ē-ėz, *n.* [Fr.] A female religieux; a nun.

Religion, rē-lij'on, *n.* [Fr. *religion*, L. *religio, religionis*, probably from prefix *re*, and stem meaning to care for, to respect, allied to Gr. *alegō*, to heed.] The feeling of reverence which men entertain towards a Supreme Being; the recognition of God as an object of worship, love, and obedience; piety; any system of faith and worship (the *religion* of the Greeks, Jews, Hindus, Mohammedans, &c.)—*Established religion*, that form of religion in a country which is recognized and supported by the state.—*Natural religion*, the knowledge of God and of our duty which is derived from the light of nature.—*Revealed religion*, the knowledge of God and of our duty from positive revelation.—**Religionism**, rē-lij'on-izm, *n.* The outward practice of religion; affected or false religion.—**Religionist**, rē-lij'on-ist, *n.* A religious bigot; one who deals much in religious discourse; a partisan of a religion.—**Religionless**, rē-lij'on-les, *a.* Without religion; not having a religion.—**Religiosity**, rē-lij'i-os"i-ti, *n.* A natural tendency of mind towards religion.—**Religious**, rē-lij'us, *a.* [L. *religiosus.*] Pertaining or relating to religion; concerned with religion; set apart for purposes connected with religion; imbued with religion; pious; devout; devoted by vows to the practice of religion or to a monastic life (a *religious* order); bound by some solemn obligation; scrupulously faithful.—*n.* A religieux or religieuse.—**Religiously**, rē-lij'us-li, *adv.* In a religious manner; piously; reverently; strictly; conscientiously.—**Religiousness**, rē-lij'us-nes, *n.* The quality or state of being religious.

Relinquish, rē-ling'kwish, *v.t.* [O.Fr. *relinquir, relinquissant*, from L. *relinquo*, to leave. RELIC.] To give up the possession or occupancy of; to withdraw from; to leave; to abandon; to give up the pursuit or practice of; to desist from; to renounce a claim to.—**Relinquisher**, rē-ling'kwish-ėr, *n.* One who relinquishes.—**Relinquishment**, rē-ling'kwish-ment, *n.* The act of relinquishing; the renouncing a claim to.

Reliquary, rel'i-kwa-ri, *n.* [Fr. *reliquaire*, from L. *reliquiæ*, relics. RELIC.] A depositary for relics; a casket in which relics are kept; a shrine.—**Relique**, re-lēk' or rel'ik, *n.* A relic.

Reliquiæ, re-lik'wi-ē, *n.pl.* [L., remnants, remains. RELIC.] Relics; remains; fossil remains.

Relish, rel'ish, *v.t.* [O.Fr. *relêcher*, lit. to re-lick—*re*, again, and *lécher*, from O.H.G. *lecchon*, to lick. LICK.] To like the taste or flavor of; to be pleased with or gratified by; to have a liking for; to give an agreeable taste or flavor to; to savor or smack of.—*v.i.* To have a pleasing taste; to have a flavor.—*n.* The sensation produced by anything on the palate; savor; taste, commonly a pleasing taste; inclination; liking (a *relish for* something); delight given by anything; characteristic quality; savor or flavor; smack; a small quantity just perceptible; a pickled, spiced or glazed food served with the meat or fish course.—**Relishable**, rel'ish-a-bl, *a.* Capable of being relished.

Relisten, rē-lis'n, *v.i.* To listen again or anew.

Relive, rē-liv', *v.i.* To live again; to revive.

Reload, rē-lōd', *v.t.* To load again.

Relucent, rē-lū'sent, *a.* [L. *re*, back, and *luceo*, to shine. LUCID.] Throwing back light; luminous; shining; eminent.

Reluctant, rē-luk'tant, *a.* [L. *reluctans, reluctantis*, ppr. of *reluctor*, to struggle—*re*, back, and *luctor*, to struggle, *lucta*, a struggle.] Striving against doing something; unwilling to do what one feels called on to do; acting with repugnance; averse; loth; granted with unwillingness (*reluctant* obedience).—**Reluctantly**, rē-luk'tant-li, *adv.* In a reluctant manner; unwillingly.—**Reluctance, Reluctancy**, rē-luk'tans, rē-luk'tan-si, *n.* The state or quality of being reluctant; aversion; unwillingness; in magnetism, the resistance offered by a medium to the passage through it of lines of magnetic force; the reciprocal of permeability; also called magnetic resistance. Its unit is the ŒRSTED (which see).

Relume, Relumine, rē-lūm', rē-lū'min, *v.t.* [L. *re*, again, and *lumen*, light. LUMINARY.] To light anew; to illuminate again.

Rely, rē-lī', *v.t.*—*relied, relying.* [From Fr. *relier*, to bind, to attach—L. *re*, back, and *ligare*, to bind (hence *ligament*): formerly often used with reflexive pronouns (to *rely one's self upon*).] To rest with confidence, as when we are satisfied of the veracity, integrity, or ability of persons, or of the certainty of facts or of evidence; to have confidence; to trust: with *on* or *upon.*—**Reliable**, rē-lī'a-bl, *a.* [This word (introduced about 1800) has often been objected to as irregular in formation or for other reasons; but it has latterly come into good use.] Such as may be relied on; worthy of being relied on; to be depended on for support.—**Reliableness, Reliability**, rē-lī'a-bl-nes, rē-lī'a-bil"i-ti, *n.* The quality of being reliable.—**Reliably**, rē-lī'a-bli, *adv.* In a reliable manner; so as to be relied on.—**Reliance**, rē-lī'ans, *n.* The act of relying; dependence; confidence; trust; ground of trust.—**Reliant**, rē-lī'ant, *a.* Having reliance; confident; self-reliant.

Relier, rē-lī'ėr, *n.* One who relies.

Remade, rē-mād', pret. & pp. of *remake.*

Remain, rē-mān', *v.i.* [O.Fr. *remaindre*, to remain, from L. *remaneo*—*re*, back, and *maneo, mansi*, to stay. MANSION.] To continue in a place; to abide; to continue in an unchanged form or condition; to endure; to last; to stay behind after others have gone; to be left; to be left as not included or comprised; to be still to deal with.—*n.* That which is left; remainder; relic: chiefly used in the plural; specifically, *pl.*, that which is left of a human being after life is gone, that is the dead body; *pl.* the productions, especially the literary works, of one who is dead.—**Remainder**, rē-mān'dėr, *n.* [An infinitive form; comp. *rejoinder.*] That which remains; anything left after the removal of the rest; *arith.* &c., the sum or quantity that is left after subtraction or deduction; *law*, an estate limited so as to be enjoyed after the death of the present possessor or otherwise.—*a.* Remaining; left over.

Remake, rē-māk', *v.t.*—*remade, remaking.* To make anew; to make over again.

Remand, rē-mand', *v.t.* [Fr. *remander*, from L. *re*, and *mando*, to commit to one's charge. MANDATE.] To send, call, or order back; *law*, to send back to jail, as an accused party, in order to give time to collect more evidence.—*n.* The state of being remanded; the act of remanding.

Remanent, rem'a-nent, *a.* [L. *remanens, remanentis*, ppr. of *remaneo*. REMAIN.] Remaining.—**Remanence, Remanency**, rem'a-nens, rem'a-nen-si, *n.* The state of remaining; continuance; permanence.

Remark, rē-märk', *n.* [Fr. *remarque*—*re* and *marque*. MARK.] The act of observing or taking notice; notice or observation; a brief statement taking notice of something; an observation; a comment.—*v.t.* To observe; to note in the mind; to express, as a thought that has occurred to the speaker; to utter by way of comment or observation.—**Remarkable**, rē-mär'ka-bl, *a.* Observable; worthy of notice; extraordinary; unusual; striking; noteworthy; conspicuous; distinguished.—**Remarkableness**, rē-mär'ka-bl-nes, *n.*—**Remarkably**, rē-mär'ka-bli, *adv.* In a remarkable manner; singularly; surprisingly.—**Remarker**, rē-mär'kėr, *n.* One who remarks.

Re-mark, rē-märk', *v.t.* To mark anew or a second time.

Remarry, rē-mar'i, *v.t.* To marry again or a second time.—*v.i.* To be married again or a second time.—**Remarriage**, rē-mar'ij, *n.* Any marriage after the first; a repeated marriage.

Remast, rē-mast', *v.t.* To furnish with a second mast or set of masts.

Remasticate, rē-mas'ti-kāt, *v.t.* To chew or masticate again.—**Remastication**, rē-mas'ti-kā"shon, *n.* The act of remasticating.

Remblai, räṅ-blā, *n.* [Fr.] *Fort.* the earth used to form the whole mass of rampart and parapet.

Remead, Remede, re-mēd', *n.* Remedy; help. Written also *Remeed, Remeid.* (Old English or Scotch.)

Remeasure, rē-mezh'ūr, *v.t.* To measure anew.

Remedy, rem′e-di, *n.* [L. *remedium*, from *re*, again, and *medeor*, to heal. MEDICAL.] That which cures a disease; any medicine or application which puts an end to disease and restores health (a *remedy for* the gout); that which corrects or counteracts an evil of any kind; relief; redress; legal means for recovery of a right.—*v.t.*—*remedied, remedying.* To cure; to heal; to repair or remove, as some evil; to redress; to counteract.—**Remediable**, re-mē′di-a-bl, *a.* Capable of being remedied.—**Remediableness**, re-mē′di-a-bl-nes, *n.*—**Remediably**, re-mē′di-a-bli, *adv.*—**Remedial**, re-mē′di-al, *a.* [L. *remedialis.*] Affording a remedy; intended to remedy or cure something, or for the removal of an evil (*remedial* measures).—**Remedially**, re-mē′di-al-li, *adv.* In a remedial manner.—**Remediless**, rem′e-di-les, *a.* Not admitting a remedy; incurable; irreparable.—**Remedilessly**, rem′e-di-les-li, *adv.*—**Remedilessness**, rem′e-di-les-nes, *n.*

Remelt, rē-melt′, *v.t.* To melt again.

Remember, rē-mem′bėr, *v.t.* [O.Fr. *remembrer, se remembrer*, from L.L. *rememorare*—L. *re*, again, and *memorare*, to bring to mind, from *memor*, mindful. MEMOIR.] To have in the mind and capable of being brought back from the past; to bear or keep in mind; to be capable of recalling; not to forget; to put in mind; to remind; to think of; to keep in mind with gratitude, favour, affection, or other emotion.—*v.i.* To have something in remembrance; to recollect. ∴ *Remember* implies that a thing exists in the memory, but not that it is actually present in the thoughts at the moment. *Recollect* means that a fact, forgotten or partially lost to memory, is after some effort recalled. See also MEMORY.—**Rememberer**, rē-mem′bėr-ėr, *n.* One that remembers.—**Remembrance**, rē-mem′brans, *n.* [O.Fr. *remembrance.*] The keeping of a thing in mind; power or faculty of remembering; limit of time over which the memory extends; what is remembered; a memorial; a keepsake; state of being mindful; regard. ∴ Syn. under MEMORY.—**Remembrancer**, rē-mem′bran-sėr, *n.* One who reminds; an officer in the exchequer of England whose business is to record certain papers and proceedings, make out processes, &c.; a recorder; the name of an officer who collects debts due the sovereign.

Remerge, rē-mėrj′, *v.i.* To merge again.

Remiform, rē′mi-form, *a.* [L. *remus*, an oar.] Shaped like an oar.

Remiges, rem′i-jēz, *n. pl.* [L. *remex, remigis*, a rower, from *remus*, an oar.] The quill feathers of the wings of a bird.

Remigrate, rē-mī′grāt, *v.i.* To migrate again; to return.—**Remigration**, rē-mī-grā′shon, *n.* A migration to a former place.

Remind, rē-mīnd′, *v.t.* To put in mind; to cause to recollect or remember (to *remind* a person of his promise).—**Reminder**, rē-mīn′dėr, *n.* One who or that which reminds; a hint that serves to awaken remembrance.—**Remindful**, rē-mīnd′fųl, *a.* Tending or adapted to remind.

Reminiscence, rem-i-nis′ens, *n.* [Fr. *réminiscence*, L. *reminiscentia*, from *reminiscor*, to recall to mind—*re*, again, and *miniscor*, from root *men*, whence *mens*, the mind. MENTAL.] Recollection; that which is recollected or recalled to mind; a relation of what is recollected; a narration of past incidents within one's personal knowledge. ∴ Syn. under MEMORY.—**Reminiscent**, rem-i-nis′ent, *a.* Having remembrance; calling to mind.—*n.* One who calls to mind.—**Reminiscential**, rem′i-nis-en″shal, *a.* Pertaining to reminiscence.—**Reminiscentially**, rem′i-nis-en″shal-li, *adv.*

Remiped, rem′i-ped, *n.* [L. *remus*, an oar, and *pes, pedis*, a foot.] An aquatic animal whose feet serve as oars.

Remise, re-mēz′, *n.* [Fr., from *remettre*, L. *remitto.* REMISS.] *Law*, a granting back; a surrender; release, as of a claim.

Remiss, rē-mis′, *a.* [L. *remissus*, relaxed, languid, not strict, pp. of *remitto*—*re*, back, and *mitto*, to send. MISSION.] Not energetic or diligent in performance; careless in performing duty or business; negligent; dilatory; slack; wanting earnestness or activity.—**Remissibility**, rē-mis′i-bil″i-ti, *n.* Capability of being remitted.—**Remissible**, rē-mis′i-bl, *a.* Capable of being remitted or forgiven.—**Remission**, rē-mish′on, *n.* The act of remitting; diminution or cessation of intensity; abatement; moderation a giving up; the act of forgiving; forgiveness; pardon; a temporary subsidence of the force or violence of a disease or of pain.—**Remissive**, rē-mis′iv, *a.* Slackening; relaxing; forgiving; pardoning.—**Remissly**, rē-mis′li, *adv.* In a remiss or negligent manner; carelessly; slowly; slackly; not vigorously.—**Remissness**, rē-mis′nes, *n.* The state or quality of being remiss.—**Remissory**, rē-mis′o-ri, *a.* Pertaining to remission; serving or tending to remit.—**Remit**, rē-mit′, *v.t.*—*remitted, remitting.* [L. *remitto*, to send back, slacken, relax.] To relax in intensity; to make less intense or violent; to abate; to refrain from exacting; to give up in whole or in part (to *remit* punishment); to pardon; to forgive; to refrain from exacting punishment for (sins); to surrender; to resign; to send back; to put again into custody; *Scots law*, to transfer from one tribunal or judge to another; *com.* to transmit or send, as money, or other things in payment for goods received.—*v.i.* To slacken; to become less intense or rigorous; *med.* to abate in violence for a time (a fever *remits* at a certain hour every day); *com.* to transmit money, &c.—*n.* *Scots law*, the transferring of a cause from one tribunal or judge to another.

Remittal, rē-mit′al, *n.* A remitting; a sending money to a distant place.—**Remittance**, rē-mit′ans, *n.* The act of transmitting money, bills, or the like, to a distant place, in return or payment for goods purchased; the sum remitted.—**Remittee**, rē-mit′ē, *n.* A person to whom a remittance is sent.—**Remittent**, rē-mit′ent, *a.* [L. *remittens, remittentis*, ppr. of *remitto.*] Temporarily ceasing; having remissions from time to time.—*Remittent fever*, any fever which suffers a decided remission of its violence during the twenty-four hours, but without entirely leaving the patient.—*n.* A remittent fever.—**Remitter**, rē-mit′ėr, *n.* One who remits.

Remix, rē-miks′, *v.t.* and *i.* To mix again.

Remnant, rem′nant, *n.* [Contr. from *remanent.* REMANENT.] What remains after the removal of the rest of a thing; the remaining piece of a web of cloth after the rest is sold; that which remains after a part is done or past; a scrap, fragment, little bit.—*a.* Remaining; yet left.

Remodel, rē-mod′el, *v.t.*—*remodeled, remodeling.* To model or fashion anew.

Remodify, rē-mod′i-fī, *v.t.* To modify again; to shape anew.—**Remodification**, rē-mod′i-fi-kā″shon, *n.* The act of modifying again; a repeated modification.

Remold, Remould, rē-mōld′, *v.t.* To mold again or anew.

Remollient,† rē-mol′li-ent, *a.* [L. *remollio*, to soften.] Mollifying; softening.

Remonetize, rē-mon′e-tīz, *v.t.*—*remonetized, remonetizing.* [L. *re*, again, and *moneta*, money. MONEY.] To restore to circulation in the shape of money; to make again the legal or standard money of account.—**Remonetization**, rē-mon′et-i-zā″shon, *n.* The act of remonetizing.

Remonstrate, rē-mon′strāt, *v.i.*—*remonstrated, remonstrating.* [O.Fr. *remonstrer* (Fr. *remontrer*); L.L. *remonstro*—L. *re*, again, and *monstro*, to show. MONSTER.] To exhibit or present strong reasons against an act, measure, or any course of proceedings; to expostulate.—**Remonstrance**, rē-mon′strans, *n.* [O.Fr. *remonstrance.*] The act of remonstrating or expostulating; an expostulation; a strong statement of reasons, against something; a paper containing such a statement.—**Remonstrant, Remonstrative, Remonstratory**, rē-mon′strant, rē-mon′stra-tiv, rē-mon′stra-to-ri, *a.* Expostulatory; remonstrating.—**Remonstrant, Remonstrator**, rē-mon′strant, rē-mon′strā-tėr, *n.* One who remonstrates.

Remora, rem′o-ra, *n.* [L., from *re*, back, and *mora*, delay.] The sucking-fish, a fish with flattened, adhesive disc on the top of the head, by which it attaches itself firmly to other fishes or to the bottoms of vessels: fabled by the ancients to have miraculous powers of delaying ships.

Remorse, rē-mors′, *n.* [L.L. *remorsus*, a biting again, from L. *remordeo, remorsum*—*re*, again, and *mordeo*, to bite. MORSEL.] The keen pain or anguish excited by a sense of guilt; compunction of conscience for a crime committed; painful memory of wrong-doing.—**Remorseful**, rē-mors′fųl, *a.* Full of remorse; impressed with a sense of guilt.—**Remorsefully**, rē-mors′fųl-li, *adv.* In a remorseful manner.—**Remorsefulness**, rē-mors′fųl-nes, *n.* The state of being remorseful.—**Remorseless**, rē-mors′les, *a.* Without remorse; unpitying; cruel; insensible; pitiless.—**Remorselessly**, rē-mors′les-li, *adv.* In a remorseless manner; pitilessly.—**Remorselessness**, rē-mors′les-nes, *n.*

Remote, rē-mōt′, *a.* [L. *remotus*, from *removeo*, to remove—*re*, and *moveo, motum*, to move. REMOVE.] Distant in place; far off; not near; distant in time, past or future; not directly producing an effect; not proximate (the *remote* causes of a disease); distant in consanguinity or affinity (a *remote* kinsman); slight; inconsiderable (a *remote* resemblance).—*Remote control*, control from a point at some distance, as by a switchboard, by a movable actuating device electrically connected to a broadcasting station.—**Remotely**, rē-mōt′li, *adv.* In a remote manner; at a distance; slightly; not closely.—**Remoteness**, *n.*

Remount, rē-mount′, *v.t.* and *i.* To mount again.—*n.* A fresh horse to mount.

Remove, rē-möv′, *v.t.*—*removed, removing.* [O.Fr. *remouvoir*, from L. *removeo*, to remove—*re*, and *moveo*, to move. MOVE.] To shift from the position occupied; to put from its place in any manner; to displace from an office, post, or position; to take away by causing to cease; to cause to leave a person or thing; to put an end to; to banish (to *remove* a disease or grievance); to make away with; to cut off (to *remove* a person by poison).—*v.i.* To change place in any manner; to move from one place to another; to change the place of residence. ∴ *Move* is a generic term, including the sense of *remove*, but the latter is never applied to a mere change of posture without a change of place or position.—*n.* The act of removing; a removal; change of place; the distance or space through which anything is removed; an interval; stage; a step in any scale of gradation; a dish removed from table to make room for something else.—**Removability**, rē-mö′va-bil″i-ti, *n.* The capacity of being removable.—**Removable**, rē-mö′va-bl, *a.* Capable of being removed.—**Removal**, rē-mö′val, *n.* A moving from one place to another; change of place or site; the act of displacing from an office or post; the act of putting an end to (the *removal* of a grievance).—**Removed**, rē-mövd′, *p.* and *a.* Changed in place; displaced from office; remote; separate from others.—**Removedness**, rē-mö′ved-nes, *n.* State of being removed.—**Remover**, rē-mö′vėr, *n.* One who or that which removes, as paint *remover*.

Remugient, rē-mū′ji-ent, *a.* [L. *re*, again, and *mugio*, to bellow.] Rebellowing.

Remunerate, rē-mū′nėr-āt, *v.t*—*remunerated, remunerating.* [L. *remunero, remuneratum*—*re*, back, and *munus, muneris*, a present, gift.] To reward; to recompense; to requite, in a good sense; to pay an equivalent to for any service, loss, or sacrifice.—**Remunerability**, rē-mū′nėr-a-bil″i-ti, *n.* The capacity of being remunerated or rewarded.—**Remunerable**, rē-mū′nėr-a-bl, *a.* Capable of being remunerated.—**Remuneration**, rē-mū′nėr-ā″shon, *n.* The act of remunerating; what is given to remunerate.—**Remunerative**, rē-mū′nėr-ā-tiv, *a.* Affording remuneration; yielding a sufficient return.—**Remuneratory**, rē-mū'nėr-a-to-ri, *a.* Rewarding; requiting.

Remurmur, rē-mėr'mėr, *v.t.* and *i.* [L. *remurmuro.*] To murmur back; to return in murmurs; to repeat in low hoarse sounds.

Renaissance, ren'e-säns", *n.* [Fr. regeneration or new birth—*re*, again, and *naissance*, birth, L. *nascentia*, from *nascor, natus*, to be born. NATAL.] The revival of anything which has long been in decay or extinct; the transitional movement in Europe from the middle ages to the modern world; specially applied to the time of the revival of letters and arts in the fifteenth century.—*Renaissance style*, the style of building and decoration which succeeded the Gothic, and sought to reproduce the forms of classical ornamentation.—**Renaissant**, re-nā'sänt, *a.* Pertaining to the renaissance.—**Renascence**, re-näs'ens, *n.* The state of being renascent; also same as *Renaissance*.—**Renascency**, re-näs'en-si, *n.* Renascence; new birth.—**Renascent**, re-näs'ent, *a.* [L. *renascens.*] Rejuvenated.

Renal, rē'nal, *a.* [L. *renalis*, from *ren*, pl. *renes*, the kidneys. REINS.] Pertaining to the kidneys or reins.—*Renal glands*, two flat triangular bodies which cover the upper part of the kidneys.

Rename, rē-nām', *v.t.* To give a new name to.

Renard, ren'ärd, *n.* [Fr., from O.G. *Reinhard, Reginhart*, lit. strong in counsel, cunning—the name of a fox in a celebrated German epic poem.] A fox: a name used in fables, poetry, &c., also written *Reynard*.

Renavigate, rē-nav'i-gāt, *v.t.* To navigate again.

Rencounter, Rencontre, ren-koun'tėr, ren-kon'tėr, *n.* [Fr. *rencontre=re-encounter.*] An abrupt or chance meeting of persons; a meeting in opposition or contest; a casual combat or action, as between individuals or small parties; a slight engagement between armies or fleets.—*v.t.*† To meet unexpectedly.—*v.i.* To meet an enemy unexpectedly; to come in collision; to fight hand to hand.

Rend, rend, *v.t.*—pret. and pp. *rent.* [A.Sax. *rendan, hrendan*, to tear, to rend=O.Fris. *renda, randa*, N.Fris. *renne*, to cut, to rend; comp. W. *rhann*, Ir. *rann*, a part, Armor. *ranna*, to part, to separate.] To separate into parts with force or sudden violence; to tear asunder; to split; to take away with violence; to tear away.—*To rend the heart*, to affect with deep anguish or repentant sorrow.—*v.i.* To be or to become rent or torn; to split; to part asunder.—**Render**, ren'dėr, *n.* One who rends or tears by violence.—**Rendible**, ren'di-bl, *a.* Capable of being rent or torn asunder.

Render, ren'dėr, *v.t.* [Fr. *rendre*, from L. *reddo*, to restore, by the insertion of *n* before *d*—*re*, back, and *do*, to give.] To give in return; to give or pay back; to give, often officially, or in compliance with a request or duty; to furnish; to report (to *render* an account); to afford; to give for use or benefit (to *render* services); to make or cause to be so or so; to invest with qualities (to *render* a fortress more secure); to translate from one language into another; to interpret or bring into full expression to others; to reproduce (to *render* a piece of music); to boil down and clarify (to *render* tallow).—*v.i. Naut.* to yield or give way to force applied; to pass freely through a block: said of a rope.—*n.* A return; a payment, especially a payment of rent.—**Renderable**, ren'dėr-a-bl, *a.* Capable of being rendered.—**Renderer**, ren'dėr-ėr, *n.* One who renders.—**Rendering**, ren'dėr-ing, *n.* The act of one who renders; a version; a translation; *fine arts* and *drama*, interpretation; representation; exhibition.

Rendezvous, rän'de-vö, *n.* [Fr. *rendezvous*, lit. render yourselves, repair to a place. RENDER.] A place appointed for the assembling of troops; the port or place where ships are ordered to join company; an appointment; a place of meeting; a place at which persons commonly meet.—*v.t.*—*rendezvoused* (rän'de-vöd), *rendezvousing* (rän'de-vö-ing). To assemble at a particular place, as troops.

Rendition, ren-dish'on, *n.* [L. *redditio.* RENDER.] A rendering or giving the meaning of a word or passage; translation; the act of reproducing or exhibiting artistically; the act of rendering up or yielding possession; surrender.

Renegade, Renegado, ren'e-gād, ren-ē-gā'dō, *n.* [Sp. *renegado*, Fr. *renégat*, L.L. *renegatus*, one who denies his religion—L. *re*, back, and *nego, negatum*, to deny. NEGATION, RUNAGATE.] An apostate from a religious faith; one who deserts to an enemy or who deserts one party and joins another: a deserter.

Renege,‡ rē-nēg', *v.t.* and *i.* [L.L. *renego*, RENEGADE.] To deny; to renounce. (*Shak.*); to play a card of another suit when able to follow suit.

Renerve, rē-nėrv', *v.t.* To nerve again; to give new vigor to.

Renew, rē-nū', *v.t.* To make new again; to restore to former freshness, completeness, or perfection; to restore to a former state, or to a good state, after decay or impairment; to make again (to *renew* a treaty); to begin again; to recommence (*renew* a fight); to grant or furnish again, as a new loan or a new note for the amount of a former one (to *renew* a bill).—*v.i.* To become new; to grow afresh; to begin again; not to desist.—**Renewability**, rē-nū'a-bil"i-ti, *n.* The quality of being renewable.—**Renewable**, rē-nū'a-bl, *a.* Capable of being renewed.—**Renewal**, rē-nū'al, *n.* The act of renewing or of forming anew.—**Renewedly**, rē-nū'ed-li, *adv.* Again; anew; once more.—**Renewedness**, rē-nū'ed-nes, *n.* State of being renewed.—**Renewer**, rē-nū'ėr, *n.* One who renews.

Reniform, rē'ni-form, *a.* [L. *ren*, a kidney.] Having the form or shape of the kidneys.

Renitent, rē-nī'tent, *a.* [L. *renitens, renitentis*, ppr. of *renitor*—*re*, back, and *nitor*, to struggle.] Resisting pressure; acting against impulse; persistently opposed.—**Renitence, Renitency**, rē-nī'tens, rē-nī'ten-si, *n.* The state of being renitent.

Rennet, ren'et, *n.* [Also written *runnet*, and formed from the verb to *run*, O.E. *renne*; A.Sax. *rinnan*, to run, *gerinnan*, to curdle or coagulate; comp. G. *rennen*, to run, to curdle, *rennse*, rennet; D. *rinnen*, to curdle.] The prepared inner membrane of the calf's stomach, which has the property of coagulating milk.—**Renneted**, ren'et-ed, *a.* Treated with rennet.

Rennet, Renneting, ren'et, ren'et-ing, *n.* [Fr. *reinette*, dim. of *reine*, L. *regina*, a queen.] A kind of apple said to have been introduced in the reign of Henry VIII.

Rennin, ren'nin, *n.* A milk-curdling ferment contained in gastric juice.

Renounce, rē-nouns', *v.t.*—*renounced, renouncing.* [Fr. *renoncer*, from L. *renuncio*—*re*, back, and *nuncio, nuntio*, to tell. NUNCIO.] To disown, disclaim, abjure, forswear; to refuse to own or acknowledge as belonging; to cast off or reject.—*v.i. Card-playing*, not to follow suit when one has a card of the same sort; to revoke.—**Renouncement**, rē-nouns'ment, *n.* The act of disclaiming or rejecting; renunciation.—**Renouncer**, rē-noun'sėr, *n.* One who renounces.—**Renunciation**, rē-nun'si-ā"shon, *n.* The act of renouncing; a disowning or disclaiming; rejecting.

Renovate, ren'ō-vāt, *v.t.*—*renovated, renovating.* [L. *renovo, renovatum*—*re*, again, and *novo*, to make new, from *novus*, new. NOVEL.] To renew; to repair and render as good as new; to restore to freshness or to a good condition.—**Renovater, Renovator**, ren'ō-vā-tėr, *n.* One who or that which renovates.—**Renovation**, ren-ō-vā'shon, *n.* The act of renovating; renewal; repair; restoration.

Renown, rē-noun', *n.* [O.E. *renowne*, from Fr. *renom*, from L. *re*, and *nomen*, a name. NOUN.] The state of having a great or exalted name; exalted reputation derived from the widely spread praise of great achievements or accomplishments.—*v.t.* To make famous.—**Renowned**, rē-nound', *a.* Famous; celebrated for great and heroic achievements, for distinguished qualities, or for grandeur; eminent.—**Renownedly**, rē-noun'ed-li, *adv.* In a renowned manner; with fame or celebrity.

Rensselaerite, rens'sel-ār-īt, *n.* [After Van *Rensselaer.*] A steatitic mineral with a fine compact texture, worked into inkstands and other articles.

Rent, rent, pret. & pp. of *rend.*

Rent, rent, *n.* [From pp. of *rend.*] An opening made by rending or tearing; a break or breach; a hole torn; schism.

Rent, rent, *n.* [Fr. *rente*, It. *rendita*, that which is rendered or given up, from L.L. *rendo*, for L. *reddo*, to give up. RENDER.] A sum of money, or a certain amount of anything valuable, payable yearly for the use or occupation of lands or tenements; a compensation made to the owner by the user or occupier as a return for his occupancy.—*v.t.* To grant the possession and enjoyment of for a certain rent; to let on lease; to take and hold on the payment of rent.—*v.i.* To be leased or let for rent.—**Rentable**, rent'a-bl, *a.* Capable of being rented.—**Rental**, rent'al, *n.* A schedule or account of rents; rent-roll; the gross amount of rents drawn from an estate.—**Rent-day**, *n.* The day for paying rent.—**Renter**, rent'ėr, *n.* The lessee or tenant who pays rent.—**Rent-roll**, *n.* A rental; a list or account of rents of income.

Rente, räṅt, *n.* [Fr.] A public fund or stock bearing interest; French government stock.—**Rentier**, räṅ-tē-ā, *n.* [Fr.] One who has a fixed income, as from lands, stocks, &c.; a fund-holder.

Renter, rent'ėr, *v.t.* [Fr. *rentraire*—*re*, back, *en*, in, and *traire*, from L. *trahere*, to draw. TRACT.] To finedraw; to sew together, as the edges of two pieces of cloth.

Renuent, ren'ū-ent, *a.* [L. *renuens, renuentis*, ppr. of *renuo*—*re*, back, and *nuo*, to nod.] Throwing back the head: applied to two muscles.

Renumerate, rē-nū'mėr-āt, *v.t.* [L. *renumero, renumeratum.* NUMERATE.] To count or number again.

Renunciation. Under RENOUNCE.

Reoccupy, rē-ok'kū-pī, *v.t.* To occupy anew.

Reometer, rē-om'et-ėr, *n.* RHEOMETER.

Reopen, rē-ō'pen, *v.t.* To open again.—*v.i.* To be opened again; to open anew.

Reordain, rē-or-dān', *v.t.* To ordain again, as when the first ordination is defective.—**Reordination**, rē-or'di-nā"shon, *n.* A second or repeated ordination.

Reorganize, rē-or'gan-īz, *v.t.* To organize anew; to reduce again to an organized condition.—**Reorganization**, rē-or'gan-i-zā"shon, *a.* The act of organizing anew.

Reotrope, rē'ō-trōp, *n.* RHEOTROPE.

Reoxygenate, Reoxygenize, rē-ok'si-jen-āt, rē-ok'si-je-nīz, *v.t.* To unite or cause to combine with oxygen again or a second time.

Rep, Repp, rep, *n.* [Perhaps from *rib.*] A dress fabric having a ribbed or corded appearance, the ribs being transverse.

Repaid, rē-pād', pp. of *repay.*

Repaint, rē-pānt', *v.t.* To paint anew.

Repair, rē-pār', *v.t.* [Fr. *réparer*, from L. *reparo*—*re*, again, and *paro*, to get or make ready. PARE.] To execute restoration or renovation on; to restore to a sound or good state after decay, injury, dilapidation, or partial destruction; to make amends for, as for an injury, by an equivalent; to give indemnity for.—*n.* Restoration to a sound or good state; supply of loss; reparation; state as regards repairing (a building in good or bad *repair*).—**Repairable**, rē-pā'ra-bl, *a.* Capable of being repaired; reparable.—**Repairer**, rē-pā'rėr, *n.* One who repairs.—**Repairment**, rē-pār'ment, *n.* Act of repairing.—**Reparability**, rep′a-ra-bil″i-ti, *n.* The state or quality of being reparable.—**Reparable**, rep′a-ra-bl, *a.* [L. *reparabilis.*] Capable of being repaired, restored to a sound state, or made good.—**Reparably**, rep′a-ra-bli, *adv.* In a reparable manner.—**Reparation**, rep-a-rā′shon, *n.* The act of repairing; repair; what is done to repair a wrong; indemnification for loss or damage, as demanded of Germany by the Allies after the world war for property damage done in France; satisfaction for injury; amends.—**Reparative**, rē-par′a-tiv, *a.* Capable of effecting repair; tending to make good or amend defect.—*n.* That which restores to a good state; that which makes amends.

Repair, rē-pār′, *v.i.* [O.Fr. *repairer*, from L.L. *repatriare*—*re*, back, and *patria*, one's native country. PATRIOT.] To go to some place; to betake one's self; to resort.—*n.* The act of betaking one's self to any place; a resorting; haunt; resort.

Repand, rē-pand′, *a.* [L. *repandus*, bent backward, turned up.] *Bot.* having an uneven, slightly sinuous margin, as a leaf.

Repartee, rep-är-tē′, *n.* [Fr. *repartie*—*re*, back, and *partir*, from L. *partire*, to share, part, from *pars*, *partis*, a part. PART.] A smart, ready, and witty reply.

Repartition, rē-pär-tish′on, *n.* A fresh partition or division.

Repass, rē-pas′, *v.t.* To pass again; to pass or travel back over; to recross.—*v.i.* To pass or go back; to move back.

Repast, rē-past′, *n.* [O.Fr. *repast*, Fr. *repas*, from L. *re*, again, and *pasco*, *pastum*, to feed. PASTOR.] The act of taking food; a meal; food; victuals (*Shak.*).—*v.t.* To feed; to feast.—*v.i.* To take food; to feast.

Repatriate, rē-pā′tri-āt, *v.t.*—*repatriated*, *repatriating*. [L. *repatrio*, *repatriatum*—*re*, again, and *patria*, one's country. PATRIOT.] To restore to one's own country.—**Repatriation**, rē-pā′tri-ā″shon, *n.* Return or restoration to one's own country.

Repay, rē-pā′, *v.t.* To pay back; to refund; to make return or requital for.—*v.i.* To requite either good or evil.—**Repayable**, rē-pā′a-bl, *a.* Capable of being repaid; liable to be repaid or refunded.—**Repayment**, rē-pā′ment, *n.* The act of repaying or paying back; the money repaid.

Repeal, rē-pēl′, *v.t.* [Fr. *rappeler*—*re*, back, and *appeler*, L. *appello*, to call upon, speak to. APPEAL.] To recall, as a law or statute; to revoke; to abrogate by an authoritative act, or by the same power that made or enacted.—*n.* The act of repealing; revocation; abrogation.—**Repealability**, **Repealableness**, rē-pēl′a-bil″i-ti, rē-pēl′a-bl-nes, *n.* The quality or state of being repealable.—**Repealable**, rē-pēl′a-bl, *a.* Capable of being repealed.—

Repeat, rē-pēt′, *v.t.* [Fr. *répéter*, from L. *repeto*, to seek again, to repeat—*re*, again, and *peto*, to seek. PETITION.] To do or perform again (to *repeat* an attempt); to go over, say, make, &c., again; to iterate; to recite; to rehearse; to say over (to *repeat* a lesson).—*n.* The act of repeating; repetition; *music*, a sign that a movement or part of a movement is to be twice performed.—*v.i.* To strike the hours (a *repeating* watch). — **Repeatedly**, rē-pēt′ed-li, *adv.* With repetition; more than once; again and again.—**Repeater**, rē-pēt′ėr, *n.* One that repeats, as illegally voting a second time in an election; a gun with extra shells in a chamber to facilitate rapid firing; one returned to prison for a further crime, having served one or more previous sentences; one that recites or rehearses; a watch that strikes the hours, &c., on the compression of a spring; *arith.* an interminate decimal in which the same figure continually recurs.—**Repeating**, rē-pēt′ing, *p.* and *a.* Doing over again; producing a like result several times in succession (a *repeating* pistol, that is, a revolver).—**Repetend**, rep-ē-tend′, *n.* [L. *repetendum*, a thing to be repeated.] *Arith.* that part of a repeating decimal which recurs continually ad infinitum.—**Repetition**, rep-ē-tish′on, *n.* The act of doing or uttering a second time; the act of repeating or saying over; a reciting or rehearsing; what is repeated; something said or done a second time.—**Repetitious**, rep-ē-tish′us, *a.* Containing repetitions or statements repeated. — **Repetitive**, rē-pet′i-tiv, *a.* Containing repetitions.

Repel, rē-pel′, *v.t.*—*repelled*, *repelling*. [L. *repello*—*re*, back, and *pello*, to drive, as in *expel*, *compel*, *expulsion*, &c. PULSE.] To drive back; to force to return; to check the advance of; to repulse (to *repel* an enemy); to encounter with effectual resistance; to resist or oppose successfully (to *repel* an encroachment, an argument).—*v.i.* To cause repugnance; to shock; to act with force in opposition (electricity sometimes *repels*).—**Repellence**, **Repellency**, rē-pel′ens, rē-pel′en-si, *n.* The quality of being repellent; repulsion.—**Repellent**, rē-pel′ent, *a.* Having the effect of repelling; able or tending to repel; repulsive; deterring.—*n.* That which repels.—**Repeller**, rē-pel′ėr, *n.* One who or that which repels.

Repent, rē′pent, *a.* [L. *repens*, *repentis*, ppr. of *repo*, to creep.] Creeping (a *repent* root, a *repent* animal).

Repent, rē-pent′, *v.i.* [Fr. *repentir*—*se repentir*, to repent—L. *re*, and *pœnitere*, to repent, from *pœna*, pain. PENITENT, PAIN.] To feel pain, sorrow, or regret for something done or left undone by one's self; to experience such sorrow for sin as produces amendment of life; to be penitent.—*v.t.* To remember with compunction or self-reproach; to feel self-accusing pain or grief on account of (to *repent* rash words): frequently used in such phrases as I *repent me*, it *repented him* (impersonally).—**Repentance**, rē-pen′tans, *n.* The act of repenting; the state of being penitent; contrition for sin; such sorrow for past conduct as produces a new life.—**Repentant**, rē-pen′tant, *a.* Experiencing repentance; sorrowful for sin; expressing or showing sorrow for sin (*repentant* tears).—**Repentantly**, rē-pen′tant-li, *adv.* In a repentant manner. — **Repenter**, rē-pen′tėr, *n.* One that repents.—**Repentingly**, rē-pen′ting-li, *adv.* With repentance.—**Repentless**, rē-pent′les, *a.* Without repentance; unrepenting.

Repeople, rē-pē′pl, *v.t.* To people anew; to furnish again with a stock of people.

Repercuss, rē-pėr-kus′, *v.t.* [L. *repercutio*, *repercussum*. PERCUSS.] To beat or drive back (as sound or air); to make rebound.—**Repercussion**, rē-pėr-kush′on, *n.* The act of driving back; reverberation.—**Repercussive**, rē-pėr-kus′iv, *a.* Having the power of repercussion; causing to reverberate.

Repertoire, rep′ėr-twar, *n.* [Fr. *répertoire*. REPERTORY.] A list of dramas, operas, or the like, which can be performed by a dramatic or operatic company; those parts, songs, &c., that are usually performed by an actor, vocalist, &c.

Repertory, rep′ėr-to-ri, *n.* [L. *repertorium*, from *reperio*, to find again—*re*, again, and *pario*, to produce. PARENT.] What contains a store or collection of things; a treasury; a magazine; a repository.

Reperuse, rē-pėr-ūz′, *v.t.* To peruse again. —**Reperusal**, rē-pėr-ū′zal, *n.* A second or another perusal.

Repetition, &c. Under REPEAT.

Repine, rē-pīn′, *v.i.* — *repined*, *repining* [O.E. *repoyne*, Fr. *repoindre*, to prick again —L. *re*, again, and *pungo*, to prick (PUNCTURE), influenced by verb to *pine*.] To fret one's self; to feel inward discontent which preys on the spirits; to indulge in complaint; to murmur: with *at* or *against*. —**Repiner**, rē-pī′nėr, *n.* One that repines. —**Repiningly**, rē-pī′ning-li, *adv.* With murmuring or complaint.

Replace, rē-plās′, *v.t.* To put again in the former place; to repay; to refund; to fill the place of; to be a substitute for.—**Replacement**, rē-plās′ment, *n.* The act of replacing; that which replaces, as *pl.* soldiers assigned to a decimated company.

Replant, rē-plant′, *v.t.* To plant again; to reinstate. — **Replantable**, rē-plan′ta-bl, *a.* Capable of being planted again.—**Replantation**, rē-plan-tā′shon, *n.* The act of planting again.

Replead, rē-plēd′, *v.t.* or *i.* To plead again. —**Repleader**, rē-plē′dėr, *n.* *Law*, a second pleading or course of pleadings.

Repledge, rē-plej′, *v.t.* To pledge again.

Replenish, rē-plen′ish, *v.t.* [O.Fr. *replenir*, *replenissant*, from L. *re*, again, and *plenus*, full, from *pleo*, to fill. PLENARY, COMPLETE.] To fill again after having been emptied or diminished; hence, to fill completely; to stock with numbers or abundance.—**Replenisher**, rē-plen′ish-ėr, *n.* One who replenishes.—**Replenishment**, rē-plen′ish-ment, *n.* The act of replenishing.

Replete, rē-plēt′, *a.* [L. *repletus*, pp. of *repleo*, to fill again—*re*, again, and *pleo*, to fill. REPLENISH.] Completely filled; full; abounding; thoroughly imbued.—*v.t.* To fill to repletion or satiety.—**Repleteness**, **Repletion**, rē-plēt′nes, rē-plē′shon, *n.* The state of being replete or completely filled; superabundant fulness; surfeit. — **Repletive**, rē-plē′tiv, *a.* Tending to replete; causing repletion.—**Repletively**, rē-plē′tiv-li, *adv.* In a repletive manner.—**Repletory**, rē-plē′to-ri, *a.* Pertaining to repletion; tending to repletion.

Replevy, rē-plev′i, *v.t.*—*replevied*, *replevying*. [O.Fr. *replevir*.] *Law*, to recover possession of (as goods wrongfully seized) upon giving surety to try the right to them in court; to take back by writ of replevin.—**Replevlable**, **Replevisable**, rē-plev′i-a-bl, rē-plev′i-za-bl, *a.* *Law*, capable of being replevied.—**Replevin**, **Replevy**, rē-plev′in, *n.* *Law*, a personal action which lies to recover possession of goods or chattels wrongfully taken or detained. — **Replevisor**, rē-plev′i-sor, *n.* One who replevies.

Replica, rep′li-ka, *n.* [It. *replica*, a reply, a repetition—L. *re*, back, and *plica*, a fold. REPLY.] A copy of a picture or piece of sculpture made by the hand that executed the original.

Replicant, rep′li-kant, *n.* [L. *replicans*, *replicantis*, ppr. of *replico*, reply. REPLY.] One who makes a reply.—**Replication**, rep-li-kā′shon, *n.* An answer; a reply; a repetition; a copy; a replica.

Replicate, rep′li-kāt, *a.* [L. *re*, back, and *plico*, to fold. REPLY.] *Bot.* folded or bent back.

Replum, rē′plum, *n.* [L., the panel of a door.] *Bot.* the framework formed by the separation of the two sutures of a legume or silicule from its valves.

Replunge, rē-plunj′, *v.t.* To plunge again; to immerse anew.

Reply, rē-plī′, *v.i.*—*replied*, *replying*. [O.Fr. *replier* (Mod.Fr. *répliquer*), to reply, from L. *replico*, to fold back, to reply—*re*, back, and *plico*, to fold. PLY, APPLY, EMPLOY.] To make answer in words or writing, as to something said or written by another; to answer; to respond; to do or give something in return for something else; to answer by deeds; to meet an attack by fitting action. —*v.t.* To return for an answer: often with a clause as object.—*n.* That which is said or written in answer to what is said or written by another; an answer; that which is done in consequence of something else; an answer by deeds; a counter attack.—**Replier**, **Replyer**, rē-plī′ėr, *n.* One who replies; an answerer, a respondent; a replicant.

Repolish, rē-pol′ish, *v.t.* To polish again.

Repone, rē-pōn′, *v.t.*—*reponed*, *reponing*. [L. *repono*, to replace—*re*, again, and *pono*, to place. POSITION.] To replace; *Scots law*, to restore to a position or a situation formerly held.

Report, rē-pōrt′, *v.t.* [Fr. *reporter*, to carry back; *rapporter*, to carry back, relate, report; the former from L. *reporto*—*re*, and *porto*, to carry, the latter from *re*, *ad*, and *porto*. PORT (carriage).] To bear or bring back, as an answer; to relate, as what has been discovered by a person sent to examine or investigate; to give an account of;

to relate; to tell; to circulate publicly, as a story (as in the common phrase, it is *reported*, that is, it is said in public); to give an official or formal account or statement of; to give an account of for public reading; to write out or take down from the lips of the speaker (the debate was fully *reported*); to lay a charge or make a disclosure against (I will *report* you).—*To be reported of*, to be well or ill spoken of.—*To report one's self*, to make known one's whereabouts or movements to the proper quarter.—*v.i.* To make a statement of facts; to take down in writing speeches from a speaker's lips; to discharge the office of a reporter.—*n.* An account brought back; a statement of facts given in reply to inquiry; a story circulated; hence, rumour; common fame; repute; public character (a man of good *report*); an account of a judicial decision, or of a case argued and determined in a court of law, &c.; an official statement of facts; an account of the proceedings, debates, &c., of a legislative assembly or other meeting, intended for publication; an epitome or fully written account of a speech; sound of an explosion; loud noise (the *report* of a gun).—**Reportable**, rē-pōr'ta-bl, *a.* Fit to be reported.—**Reported**, rē-pōr'ted, *p.* and *a.* Told or made known by report.—**Reporter**, rē-pōr'tėr, *n.* One who reports; a member of a newspaper staff whose duty it is to give an account of the proceedings of public meetings and entertainments, collect information respecting interesting or important events, and the like.—**Reporting**, rē-pōr'ting, *p.* and *a.* Pertaining to a reporter or reports.—*n.* The act or system of drawing up reports.—**Reportorial**, rē-pōr'tō'ri-al, *a.* Relating to a reporter or reporters.

Repose, rē-pōz', *v.t.*—*reposed, reposing.* [Fr. *reposer*, to place again, to settle, to rest—*re*, again, and *poser*. POSE.] To lay at rest; to lay for the purpose of taking rest; to refresh by rest: frequently used reflexively; to lay, place, or rest in full reliance (to *repose* trust or confidence in a person).—*v.i.* To lie at rest; to sleep; to rest in confidence; to rely: followed by *on*.—*n.* [Fr. *repos.*] The act or state of reposing; a lying at rest; sleep; rest; quiet; rest of mind; tranquillity; settled composure; absence of all show of feeling; *painting*, an avoidance of obtrusive tints or of striking action in figures.—**Reposal**, rē-pō'zal, *n.* The act of reposing or resting with reliance. **Reposed**, rē-pōzd', *p.* and *a.* Exhibiting repose; calm; settled.—**Reposedly**, rē-pō'zed-li, *adv.* Quietly; composedly.—**Reposedness**, rē-pō'zed-nes, *n.*—**Reposeful**, rē-pōz'ful, *a.* Full of repose; affording repose or rest; trustful.—**Reposer**, rē-pō'zėr, *n.* One who reposes.

Reposit, rē-poz'it, *v.t.* [L. *repono, repositum*—*re*, back, and *pono*, to place. POSITION.] To lay up; to lodge, as for safety or preservation.—**Reposition**, rē-pō-zish'on, *n.* Act of repositing or laying up in safety.—**Repository**, rē-poz'i-to-ri, *n.* [L. *repositorium.*] A place where things are or may be deposited for safety or preservation; a depository; a storehouse; a magazine; a warehouse; a shop.

Repossess, rē-poz-zes', *v.t.* To possess again.—**Repossession**, rē-poz-zesh'on, *n.* The act or state of possessing again.

Repoussé, rė-pös-sā, *p.* and *a.* [Fr., pp. of *repousser*—*re*, back, and *pousser*, to push, to thrust. PUSH.] A term applied to a style of ornamentation in metal, effected by strokes of the hammer from behind until a rough image of the desired figure is produced, which is finished by chasing.

Reprehend, rep-rē-hend', *v.t.* [L. *reprehendo*—*re*, back, and *prehendo*, to lay hold of; seen also in *comprehend, apprehend, prehensile*, &c.] To charge with a fault; to chide sharply; to reprove; to take exception to; to speak of as a fault; to censure.—**Reprehender**, rep-rē-hen'dėr, *n.* One that reprehends; one that blames or reproves.—**Reprehensible**, rep-rē-hen'si-bl, *a.* Deserving to be reprehended or censured; blameworthy; censurable; deserving reproof.—**Reprehensibleness**, rep-rē-hen'si-bl-nes, *n.* The quality of being reprehensible.—**Reprehensibly**, rep-rē-hen'si-bli, *adv.* In a reprehensible manner; culpably.—**Reprehension**, rep-rē-hen'shon, *n.* [L. *reprehensio.*] The act of reprehending; reproof; censure; blame.—**Reprehensive, Reprehensory**, rep-rē-hen'siv, rep-rē-hen'so-ri, *a.* Containing reprehension or reproof.—**Reprehensively**, rep-rē-hen'siv-li, *adv.* With reprehension.

Represent, rep-rē-zent', *v.t.* [Fr. *représenter*, from L. *repræsento*,—*re*, again, and *præsento*, to present. PRESENT.] To exhibit the image or counterpart of; to typify; to portray by pictorial or plastic art; to act the part of; to personate; to exhibit to the mind in language; to bring before the mind; to give an account of; to describe; to supply the place of; to speak and act with authority on behalf of; to be a substitute or agent for; to serve as a sign or symbol of (words *represent* ideas or things).—**Representable**, rep-rē-zen'ta-bl, *a.* Capable of being represented.—**Representant**, rep-rē-zen'tant, *a.* Representing; having vicarious power.—*n.* A representative.—**Representation**, rep'rē-zen-tā"-shon, *n.* The act of representing, describing, exhibiting, portraying, &c.; that which represents; an image or likeness; a picture or statue; exhibition of a play on the stage, or of a character in a play; a dramatic performance; a statement of arguments or facts, &c.; sometimes a written expostulation; a remonstrance; the representing of a constituency in a legislative assembly (the *representation* of a county in parliament); delegates or representatives collectively.—**Representational**, rep'rē-zen-tā"shon-al, *a.* Pertaining to representation.—**Representative**, rep-rē-zen'ta-tive, *a.* Fitted to represent, portray, or typify; acting as a substitute for another or others; performing the functions of others (a *representative* body); conducted by the agency of delegates chosen by the people (a *representative* government); *nat. hist.* presenting the full characteristics of the type of a group (a *representative* genius).—*n.* One who or that which represents; that by which anything is represented; something standing for something else; an agent, deputy, or substitute who supplies the place of another or others, being invested with his or their authority; *law*, one that stands in the place of another as heir.—*House of Representatives*, the lower house of the supreme legislative body (Congress) in the United States.—**Representatively**, rep-rē-zen'ta-tiv-li, *adv.* In a representative manner.—**Representativeness**, rep-rē-zen'ta-tiv-nes, *n.*—**Representer**, rep-rē-zen'tėr, *n.* One who represents.

Re-present, rē-prē-zent', *v.t.* [Prefix *re*, and *present.*] To present anew.—**Re-presentation**, rē'prez-en-tā"shon, *n.* The act of presenting to the mind what was formerly present but is now absent.

Repress, rē-pres', *v.t.* [Prefix *re*, and *press*, L. *reprimo, repressum.* PRESS.] To press back or down effectually; to crush, quell, put down, subdue (sedition, a rising); to check; to restrain.—**Represser**, rē-pres'ėr, *n.* One who represses; one that crushes or subdues.—**Repressible**, rē-pres'i-bl, *a.* Capable of being repressed.—**Repressibly**, rē-pres'i-bli, *adv.* In a repressible manner.—**Repression**, rē-presh'on, *n.* The act of repressing, restraining, or subduing; check; restraint.—**Repressive**, rē-pres'iv, *a.* Having power to repress; tending to subdue or restrain.—**Repressively**, rē-pres'iv-li, *adv.* In a repressive manner.

Reprieve, rē-prēv', *n.* [From O.Fr. *reprover, repruver*, to blame, condemn, from L. *reprobare*, to reject, condemn, meaning originally the rejection of a sentence already passed. REPROBATE.] The suspension of the execution of a criminal's sentence; respite; interval of ease or relief.—*v.t.*—*reprieved, reprieving.* To grant a reprieve or respite to; to suspend or delay the execution of for a time.

Reprimand, rep'ri-mand, *n.* [Fr. *réprimande*, from L. *reprimenda*, a thing to be checked or repressed, from *reprimo, repressum*, to repress. REPRESS.] A severe reproof for a fault; a sharp rebuke; reprehension.—*v.t.* (rep-ri-mand'). To reprove severely; to reprehend; to reprove publicly and officially, in execution of a sentence.

Reprint, rē-print', *v.t.* To print again; to print a second or any new edition of; to renew the impression of.—*n.* (rē'print). A second or new impression of any printed work.

Reprisal, rē-prī'zal, *n.* [Fr. *représaille*, from It. *riprestaglia*, from L.L. *reprisaliæ*, from L. *reprehendo*, to take again; comp. *prize*, a capture, which is also from L. *prehendo.*] The seizure or taking of anything from an enemy by way of retaliation or indemnification; also, that which is so taken; any taking by way of retaliation; an act of severity done in retaliation.—*Letters of marque and reprisal.* MARQUE.

Reproach, rē-prōch', *v.t.* [Fr. *reprocher*, O.Fr. *reprochier*, Pr. *repropchar*, to reproach, from L.L. *repropiare*, from L. *re*, back, and *prope*, near; lit. to bring near or set before. APPROACH, PROPINQUITY.] To charge with a fault in severe language; to censure with severity, opprobrium, or contempt, or as having suffered wrong personally; to upbraid.—*n.* A severe or cutting expression of censure or blame; blame for something considered outrageous or vile; contumely; source of blame; shame, infamy, or disgrace; object of contempt, scorn, or derision.—**Reproachable**, rē-prō'cha-bl, *a.* Deserving reproach.—**Reproachableness**, rē-prō'cha-bl-nes, *n.* The state of being reproachable.—**Reproachably**, rē-prō'cha-bli, *adv.* In a reproachable manner.—**Reproacher**, rē-prō'chėr, *n.* One who reproaches.—**Reproachful**, rē-prōch'ful, *a.* Containing or expressing reproach or censure; upbraiding; scurrilous; opprobrious; worthy of reproach; shameful; infamous.—**Reproachfully**, rē-prōch'ful-li, *adv.* In a reproachful manner.—**Reproachfulness**, rē-prōch'ful-nes, *n.* Quality of being reproachful.—**Reproachless**, rē-prōch'les, *a.* Without reproach.

Reprobate, rep'rō-bāt, *a.* [L. *reprobatus*, disapproved, rejected, pp. of *reprobo*—*re*, denoting reverse, and *probo*, to approve. PROBABLE, REPRIEVE, REPROVE.] Abandoned in sin; morally abandoned; depraved; profligate; lost to virtue or grace.—*n.* One who is very profligate or abandoned; a person abandoned to sin; one lost to virtue; a wicked, depraved wretch.—*v.t.*—*reprobated, reprobating.* [L. *reprobo, reprobatum.*] To disapprove with detestation or marks of extreme dislike; to contemn strongly; to condemn; to reject.—**Reprobateness, Reprobacy**, rep'rō-bāt-nes, rep'rō-ba-si, *n.* The state of being reprobate.—**Reprobater**, rep'rō-bā-tėr, *n.* One who reprobates.—**Reprobation**, rep-rō-bā'shon, *n.* The act of reprobating; condemnation; censure; rejection.—**Reprobative, Reprobatory**, rep'rō-bā-tiv, rep'rō-ba-to-ri, *a.* Conveying reprobation.

Reproduce, rē-prō-dūs', *v.t.*—*reproduced, reproducing.* To produce again or anew; to renew the production of; to generate, as offspring; to portray or represent; to bring to the memory or imagination.—**Reproducer**, rē-prō-dū'sėr, *n.* One who or that which reproduces.—**Reproduction**, rē-prō-duk'shon, *n.* The act or process of reproducing; the process whereby new individuals are generated and the perpetuation of the species ensured; that which is produced or presented anew.—**Reproductive, Reproductory**, rē-prō-duk'tiv, rē-prō-duk'to-ri, *a.* Pertaining to reproduction; tending to reproduce.

Reprove, rē-pröv', *v.t.*—*reproved, reproving.* [Fr. *réprouver*, to blame, to censure; O.Fr. *reprover*, from L. *reprobare.* REPROBATE.] To charge with a fault to the face; to chide; to reprehend; to express disapproval of (to *reprove* sins); to serve to admonish.—**Reproof**, rē-pröf', *n.* The expression of blame or censure addressed to a person; blame expressed to the face; censure for a fault; reprehension; rebuke; reprimand.—**Reprovable**, rē-prö'va-bl, *a.*

Worthy of being reproved; deserving reproof or censure; blamable.—**Reprovableness**, rē-prö'va-bl-nes, *n.*—**Reprovably**, rē-prö'va-bli, *adv.* In a reprovable manner.—**Reproval**, rē-prö'val, *n.* Act of reproving; admonition; reproof.—**Reprover**, rē-prö'vėr, *n.* One that reproves. —**Reprovingly**, rē-prö'ving-li, *adv.* In a reproving manner.

Reprune, rē-prön', *v.t.* To prune or trim again.

Reptation, rep-tā'shon, *n.* [L. *reptatio, reptationis*, from *repto*, freq. of *repo*, to creep. REPTILE.] The act of creeping or crawling.—**Reptant, Reptatory**, rep'-tant, rep'ta-to-ri, *a.* Creeping; crawling.

Reptile, rep'tīl, *a.* [Fr. *reptile*, from L. *reptilis*, creeping, from *repo, reptum*, to creep; akin to *serpo*, to creep. SERPENT.] Creeping; moving on the belly, or with small, short legs; grovelling; low; mean; vile.—*n.* In a general sense, an animal that moves on its belly, or by means of small, short legs; a crawling creature; specifically, *zool.* an animal belonging to the class Reptilia; a grovelling, abject, or mean person.—**Reptilia**, rep-til'i-a, *n.pl.* A class of vertebrate animals intermediate between fishes and birds, comprising the snakes, lizards, crocodiles, tortoises, &c., breathing by lungs and having cold blood.—**Reptilian**, rep-til'i-an, *a.* Belonging to the class of reptiles.—*n.* An animal of the class Reptilia; a reptile.

Republic, rē-pub'lik, *n.* [Fr. *république*, L. *respublica*—*res*, an affair, interest, and *publica*, fem. of *publicus*, public. REAL, PUBLIC.] A commonwealth; a political community in which the supreme power in the state is vested either in certain privileged members of the community or in the whole community, and thus varying from the most exclusive oligarchy to a pure democracy. — *Federal republics*, of which the United States and Switzerland are examples, consist of a number of separate states bound together by treaty, so as to present the aspect of a single state with a central government, without wholly renouncing their individual powers of internal self-government.—**Republican**, rē-pub'li-kan, *a.* Pertaining to or having the character of a republic: consonant to the principles of a republic.—*n.* One who favors or prefers a republican form of government; a member of the Republican party in *U. S. politics*.—*Red Republican*. RED.—**Republicanism**, rē-pub'li-kan-izm, *n.* Republican system of government; principles and policies of the Republican party (*U.S.*); republican principles.

Republication, rē-pub'li-kā"shon, *n.* The act of republishing; a new publication of something before published.

Republish, rē-pub'lish, *v.t.* To publish anew; to publish again, as in a new edition. —**Republisher**, rē-pub'lish-ėr, *n.* One who republishes.

Repudiate, rē-pū'di-āt, *v.t.*—*repudiated, repudiating*. [L. *repudio, repudiatum*, to divorce, to cast off, from *repudium*, a casting off, a divorce.] To cast away; to reject; to discard; to disavow; to divorce; to refuse to acknowledge or to pay, as debt.—**Repudiable**, rē-pū'di-a-bl, *a.* Capable of being repudiated.—**Repudiation**, rē-pū'-di-ā"shon, *n.* [L. *repudiatio*.] The act of repudiating; rejection; disavowal; divorce; refusal on the part of a government to pay debts contracted by a former government. —**Repudiator**, rē-pū'di-ā-tėr, *n.* One who repudiates.

Repugnance, Repugnancy, rē-pug'-nans, rē-pug'nan-si, *n.* [Fr. *répugnance*; L. *repugnantia*, from *repugno*, to resist—*re*, against, and *pugno*, to fight. PUGNACIOUS.] The state of being opposed in mind; feeling of dislike to some action; reluctance; unwillingness; opposition in nature or qualities; contrariety.—**Repugnant**, rē-pug'nant, *a.* [L. *repugnans, repugnantis*, ppr. of *repugno*.] Standing or being in opposition; contrary; at variance: usually followed by *to* (a statement *repugnant to* common sense); highly distasteful; offensive (a course *repugnant to* him).—**Repugnantly**, rē-pug'nant-li, *adv.*

Repulse, rē-puls', *n.* [L. *repulsa*, from *repello, repulsum*—*re*, back, and *pello*, to drive. REPEL.] The condition of being repelled or driven back by force; the act of driving back; a check or defeat; refusal; denial.—*v.t.*—*repulsed, repulsing*. To repel; to drive back; to refuse; to reject.—**Repulser**, rē-puls'ėr, *n.* One that repulses.—**Repulsion**, rē-pul'shon, *n.* [L. *repulsio*.] The act of repelling; *physics*, a term often applied to the action which two bodies exert upon one another when they tend to increase their mutual distance.—**Repulsive**, rē-pul'siv, *a.* Acting so as to repel; exercising repulsion; tending to deter or forbid approach or familiarity; repellent; forbidding.—**Repulsively**, rē-pul'siv-li, *adv.* In a repulsive manner.—**Repulsiveness**, rē-pul'siv-nes, *n.*

Repurchase, rē-pėr'chās, *v.t.* To buy back; to regain by purchase.—*n.* The act of buying again; a new purchase.

Repute, rē-pūt', *v.t.*—*reputed, reputing*. [Fr. *réputer*, from L. *reputo*, to count over —*re*, and *puto*, to reckon, to estimate (as in *compute, impute*, &c.). PUTATIVE.] To hold in thought; to reckon, account, or consider as such or such; to deem.—*n.* Reputation; character, attributed by public report, especially good character; honourable name. —**Reputed**, rē-pū'ted, *p.* and *a.* Generally considered; commonly believed, regarded, or accounted.—**Reputedly**, rē-pū'ted-li, *adv.* In common opinion or estimation.—**Reputable**, rep'ū-ta-bl, *a.* Being in good repute; held in esteem; not mean or disgraceful.—**Reputableness**, rep'ū-ta-bl-nes, *n.* The quality of being reputable.—**Reputably**, rep'ū-ta-bli, *adv.* In a reputable manner.—**Reputation**, rep-ū-tā'shon, *n.* [L. *reputatio*.] Character by report; opinion of character generally entertained; character attributed; repute; in a good or bad sense; often favourable or honourable regard; good name.—**Reputeless**, rē-pūt'les, *a.* Not having good repute; inglorious. (*Shak.*)

Request, rē-kwest', *n.* [O.Fr. *requeste* (Fr. *requête*), from L. *requisita*, a thing required, a want, from *requiro, requisitum*—*re*, again, and *quæro, quæsitum*, to seek. QUEST.] The expression of desire to some person for something to be granted or done; an asking; a petition, prayer, entreaty; the thing asked for or requested; a state of being esteemed and sought after, or asked for (an article in much *request*). ∴ *Request* expresses less earnestness than *entreaty* and *supplication*; and supposes a right in the person requested to deny or refuse to grant, in this differing from *demand*.—*v.t.* To make a request for; to solicit or express desire for; to express a request to; to ask.—**Request-note**, *n.* An application to obtain a permit for removing excisable articles.

Requicken, rē-kwik'n, *v.t.* To reanimate; to give new life to.

Requiem, rē'kwi-em, *n.* [Acc. case of L. *requies*, rest, respite, relaxation—*re*, again, and *quies*, rest, repose.] A funeral dirge or service, containing the words '*Requiem æternam*', &c., sung for the rest of a person's soul; a grand musical composition performed in honour of some deceased person.

Require, rē-kwīr', *v.t.*—*required, requiring*. [O.Fr. *requerre, requierre, requirre* (Fr. *requérir*), from L. *requiro, requirere*, to ask for. REQUEST.] To demand; to ask as of right and by authority; to insist on having; to ask as a favour; to call upon to act; to request; to have need or necessity for; to need or want (the matter *requires* great care, we *require* food); to find it necessary; to have to: with infinitives (you will *require* to go).—**Requirable**, rē-kwī'ra-bl, *a.* Fit or proper to be demanded.—**Requirement**, rē-kwīr'ment, *n.* The act of requiring; demand; that which requires the doing of something; an essential condition; something required or necessary. — **Requirer**, rē-kwī'rėr, *n.* One who requires. —**Requisite**, rek'wi-zit, *a.* [L. *requisitus*, from *requiro*.] Required by the nature of things or by circumstances; necessary.—*n.* That which is necessary; something indispensable. — **Requisitely**, rek'wi-zit-li, *adv.* In a requisite manner; necessarily. —**Requisiteness**, rek'wi-zit-nes, *n.*—**Requisition**, rek-wi-zish'on, *n.* [L. *requisitio*.] An application made as of a right; a demand; a demand for or a levying of necessaries by hostile troops from the people in whose country they are; a written call or invitation (a *requisition* for a public meeting); state of being required or much sought after; request. — *v.t.* To make a requisition or demand upon.—**Requisitionist**, rek-wi-zish'on-ist, *n.* One who makes requisition. — **Requisitor**, re-kwiz'i-tėr, *n.* One empowered by a requisition to investigate facts.

Requite, rē-kwīt', *v.t.*—*requited, requiting*. [From *re*, back, and *quit*. QUIT.] To repay either good or evil: in a good sense, to recompense or reward: in a bad sense, to retaliate on. — **Requiter**, rē-kwī'tėr, *n.* One who requites.—**Requitable**, rē-kwī'-ta-bl, *a.* Capable of being requited.—**Requital**, rē-kwī'tal, *n.* Return for any office, good or bad; recompense; reward.

Re-read, rē-rēd', *v.t.* To read again or anew.

Reredos, rēr'dos, *n.* [Fr. *arrière dos*—*arrière*, behind, and *dos*, L. *dorsum*, the back. REAR, DORSAL.] The back of a fireplace; the decorated portion of the wall behind and rising above the altar in a church.

Re-refine, rē'rē-fīn, *v.t.* To refine anew or afresh.

Rere-mouse, rēr'mous, *n.* [A.Sax. *hrēre-mús*, from *hrēran*, to raise, to move, and *mús*, a mouse.] A bat. (*Shak.*)

Re-resolve, rē'rē-zolv, *v.t.* To resolve a second time.

Rerun, rē'run, *n.* An added running, as a later showing of a motion picture after its first run.—*v.t.* To again run.

Resail, rē-sāl', *v.t.* or *i.* To sail back.

Resale, rē'sāl, *n.* A sale at second hand; a second sale.

Resalute, rē-sa-lūt', *v.t.* To salute or greet anew.

Rescind, rē-sind', *v.t.* [Fr. *rescinder*, from L. *rescindo, rescissum*—*re*, again, and *scindo*, to cut (as in *concise, precise*, &c.).] To cut short‡; to abrogate; to revoke or annul by competent authority (to *rescind* a law, a judgment). — **Rescindment**, rē-sind'-ment, *n.* The act of rescinding.—**Rescission**, rē-sizh'on, *n.* [L. *rescissio, rescissionis*.] The act of rescinding; the act of abrogating or annulling.—**Rescissory**, rē-sis'o-ri, *a.* [L. *rescissorius*.] Having power to rescind, abrogate, or annul.

Rescript, rē'skript, *n.* [L. *rescriptum*, from *rescribo, rescriptum*, to write back—*re*, and *scribo*, to write. SCRIBE.] The answer or decision of a Roman emperor to some matter set before him; the decision by a pope of a question officially propounded; an edict or decree. — **Rescriptive**, rē-skrip'tiv, *a.* Pertaining to or having the character of a rescript.

Rescue, res'kū, *v.t.* — *rescued, rescuing*. [O.Fr. *rescovre, rescourre*, to rescue, from L. *re*, again, and *excutere*, to shake off — *ex*, away, and *quatio, quassum*, to shake. QUASH.] To free from confinement, danger, or evil; to withdraw from a state of exposure to evil; *law*, to take by forcible or illegal means from lawful custody.—*n.* The act of rescuing; deliverance from restraint or danger; *law*, a forcible taking out of the custody of the law.—**Rescuer**, res'kū-ėr, *n.* One that rescues.—**Rescuable**, res'-kū-a-bl, *a.* Capable of being rescued.

Research, rē-sėrch', *n.* [Prefix *re*, and *search*; Fr. *recherche*.] Diligent inquiry or examination in seeking facts or principles; laborious or continued search after truth; investigation.—*v.t.* To search again; to examine anew.—**Researcher**, rē-sėr'chėr, *n.* One engaged in research.

Reseat, rē-sēt', *v.t.* To seat or set again; to furnish with a new seat or seats.

Resect, rē-sekt′, *v.t.* [L. *reseco, resectum*, to cut off—*re*, back, and *seco*, to cut.] To cut or pare off.—**Resection**, rē-sek′shon, *n.* [L. *resectio*.] *Surg.* the removal of the articular extremity of a bone, or of the ends of the bones in a false articulation.

Reseek, rē-sēk′, *v.t.* and *i.* To seek again.

Reseize, rē-sēz′, *v.t.* To seize again; *law*, to reinstate (in such phrases as to be *reseized of* or *in*).—**Reseizer**, rē-sē′zėr, *n.* One who seizes again.—**Reseizure**, rē-sē′zūr, *n.* A second seizure.

Resell, rē-sel′, *v.t.* To sell again.

Resemble, rē-zem′bl, *v.t.*—*resembled, resembling*. [Fr. *ressembler*—*re*, and *sembler*, to seem, from L. *similare*, from *similis*, like. SIMILAR.] To be like to; to have similarity to in form, figure, or qualities; to liken; to compare.—**Resemblance**, rē-zem′blans, *n.* The state or quality of resembling; likeness; similarity either of external form or of qualities; something similar; a similitude.—*Resemblance, general*, in animals, a harmonizing with surroundings producing inconspicuousness. May be protective, aggressive (deceiving prey), or both. May be capable of adjustment, i.e. *variable*.—*Resemblance, special*, in animals, resemblance to some specific object in surroundings, causing inconspicuousness. May be protective, &c.—**Resemblant**, rē-zem′blant, *a.* Resembling.

Resend, rē-send′, *v.t.* To send again.

Resent, rē-zent′, *v.t.* [Fr. *ressentir*, from L. *re*, and *sentio*, to feel. SENSE.] To consider as an injury or affront; to be in some degree angry or provoked at; to take ill; to show such feeling by words or acts.—*v.i.* To be indignant; to feel resentment.—**Resenter**, rē-zent′ėr, *n.* One who resents.—**Resentful**, rē-zent′ful, *a.* Inclined or apt to resent; full of resentment.—**Resentfully**, rē-zent′ful-li, *adv.* In a resentful manner. — **Resentingly**, rē-zent′ing-li, *adv.* With resentment.—**Resentment**, rē-zent′ment, *n.* The act of resenting; the feeling with which one who resents is impressed; a deep sense of injury; anger arising from a sense of wrong; strong displeasure.

Reserve, rē-zėrv′, *v.t.*—*reserved, reserving*. [Fr. *réserver*, from L. *reservo*—*re*, back, and *servo*, to keep. SERVE.] To keep in store for future or other use; to withhold from present use for another purpose; to keep back for a time; to withdraw.—*n.* The act of reserving or keeping back; that which is reserved or retained from present use or disposal; something in the mind withheld from disclosure; a reservation; the habit of keeping back or restraining the feelings; a certain closeness or coldness towards others; caution in personal behavior; banking capital retained in order to meet average liabilities; a body of troops kept for an exigency.—*Federal Reserve Bank*, any of the 12 Federal banks which comprise the Federal Reserve System, and operate by the authority, and under the supervision, of the Federal Reserve Board. — **Reservation**, rez-ėr-vā′shon, *n.* The act of reserving or keeping back; concealment or withholding from disclosure; something not expressed, disclosed, or brought forward; a keeping over of part of the consecrated elements for the communion of the sick; a tract of the public land reserved for some special use, as for schools, the use of Indians, &c.; a reserve; the act of having reserved for oneself, in advance, accommodations in a public place, as a reservation in a hotel, bus, theater, ship, &c.—*Mental reservation*, an intentional reserving or holding back of some word or clause, the speaker thus intending to set his conscience at rest while being guilty of deceit, or to keep his real sentiments secret.—**Reserved**, rē-zėrvd′, *p.* and *a.* Kept for another or future use; showing reserve in behavior; distant; cold.—**Reservedly**, rē-zėr′ved-li, *adv.* In a reserved manner; with reserve.—**Reserver**, rē-zėr′vėr, *n.* One who reserves. — **Reservist**, rē-zėr′vist, *n.* A soldier of the reserve forces of an army, navy or militia organization.

Reservoir, rez′ėr-vwar, *n.* [Fr. RESERVE.] A place where anything is kept in store; a place where water is collected and kept for use; an artificial lake or pond from which pipes convey water to a town.

Reset, rē-set′, *n.* [O.Fr. *recepte, recette*, a receiving. RECEIPT.] *Scots law*, the receiving and harbouring of an outlaw or a criminal.—*Reset of theft*, the offence of receiving and keeping goods knowing them to be stolen.—**Resetter**, rē-set′ėr, *n.* *Scots law*, a receiver of stolen goods.

Reset, rē-set′, *v.t.* To set again (to *reset* a diamond); *printing*, to set over again, as a page of matter.—*n.* The act of resetting; *printing*, matter set over again.

Resettle, rē-set′l, *v.t.* and *i.* To settle again.—**Resettlement**, rē-set′l-ment, *n.* The act of resettling.

Reshape, rē-shāp′, *v.t.* To shape again.

Reship, rē-ship′, *v.t.* To ship again; to ship again what has been imported.—**Reshipment**, rē-ship′ment, *n.* The act of reshipping.

Reside, rē-zīd′, *v.t.*—*resided, residing*. [Fr. *résider*, from L. *resideo*—*re*, and *sedeo*, to sit, to settle down. SEDATE.] To dwell permanently or for a length of time; to have one's dwelling or home; to abide continuously; to abide or be inherent, as a quality; to inhere. — **Residence**, rez′i-dens, *n.* The act of residing or abiding; period of abode; the place where a person resides; a dwelling; a habitation; a mansion or dwelling-house.—**Residency**, rez′i-den-si, *n.* The domicile of the chief executive's governmental representative to a possession or mandated territory; a territory in a protected state governed by a resident agent. — **Resident**, rez′i-dent, *a.* [L. *residens, residentis*.] Dwelling or having an abode in a place for a continuance of time; residing.—*n.* One who resides or dwells in a place for some time; one residing; a public minister who resides at a foreign court: a kind of ambassador.—**Residential**, rez-i-den′shal, *a.* Relating or pertaining to residence or to residents. — **Residentiary**, rez-i-den′shė-ri, *a.* Having residence.—*n.* One who is resident; an ecclesiastic who keeps a certain residence.

Residue, rez′i-dū, *n.* [Fr. *résidu*, from L. *residuum*, what is left behind, from *residuus*, remaining, from *resideo*. RESIDE.] That which remains after a part is taken, separated, or dealt with in some way; that which is still over; remainder; the rest; *law*, the remainder of a testator's estate after payment of debts and legacies.—**Residual**, rē-zid′ū-al, *a.* Having the character of a residue or residuum; remaining after a part is taken or dealt with.—*Residual air*, the air which remains in the chest and cannot be expelled, variously estimated at from 80 to 120 cubic inches.—**Residuary**, rē-zid′ū-a-ri, *a.* Pertaining to a residue or part remaining; forming a residue or portion not dealt with.—*Residuary legatee*, the legatee to whom is bequeathed all that remains after deducting the debts and specific legacies.—**Residuum**, rē-zid′ū-um, *n.* [L.] That which is left after any process of separation or purification; a residue; the dregs or refuse; *law*, the part of an estate remaining after the payment of debts and legacies.

Resign, rē-zīn′, *v.t.* [Fr. *résigner*, L. *resigno*, to resign—*re*, and *signo*, to mark, from *signum*, to sign. SIGN.] To assign or give back; to give up, as an office or post, to the person or authority that conferred it; hence, to surrender or relinquish; to give over; to withdraw, as a claim; to submit, particularly to Providence. — **Resignation**, rez-ig-nā′shon, *n.* The act of resigning or giving up, as a claim, &c.; the state of being resigned or submissive; patience; quiet submission to the will of Providence; submission without discontent or repining.—**Resigned**, rē-zīnd′, *p.* and *a.* Surrendered; given up; feeling resignation; submissive; patient.—**Resignedly**, rē-zī′ned-li, *adv.* With resignation; submissively.—**Resigner**, rē-zī′nėr, *n.* One who resigns.

Resign, rē-sīn′, *v.t.* To sign again.

Resile, rē-zīl′, *v.i.*—*resiled, resiling*. [L. *resilio*, to leap or spring back—*re*, back, and *salio*, to leap. SALIENT.] To recede or withdraw from a purpose.—**Resilience, Resiliency**, rē-sil′i-ens, rē-sil′i-en-si, *n.* The act of resiling; the act of rebounding; rebound from being elastic; the quantity of work given out by a body, such as a spring, that is compressed and then allowed to resume its former shape.—**Resilient**, rē-sil′i-ent, *a.* Inclined to resile; rebounding.

Resin, rez′in, *n.* [Fr. *résine*, from L. *resina*, resin. *Rosin* is the same word.] An inflammable substance of sundry varieties found in most plants, and often obtained by spontaneous exudation, in some cases solid and brittle at ordinary temperatures, in others viscous or semi-fluid (in which case they are called *balsams*), valuable as ingredients in varnishes, and several of them used in medicine. *Rosin* is resin from coniferous trees.—*Fossil* or *mineral resins*, amber, petroleum, asphalt, bitumen, and other mineral hydrocarbons.—**Resiniferous**, rez-i-nif′ėr-us, *a.* Yielding resin.—**Resiniform**, rez′in-i-form, *a.* Having the form of resin.—**Resino-electric**, *a.* Containing or exhibiting negative electricity.—**Resinous**, rez′i-nus, *a.* Pertaining to or obtained from resin; partaking of the qualities of resin; like resin. — *Resinous electricity*, negative electricity, that kind of electricity which is excited by rubbing resinous bodies with a woollen cloth, in distinction from that excited by rubbing glass, &c., which is termed *vitreous* or *positive electricity*.—**Resinously**, rez′i-nus-li, *adv.* In the manner of a resinous body.—**Resinousness**, rez′i-nus-nes, *n.* — **Resiny**, rez′i-ni, *a.* Like resin, or partaking of its qualities.

Resist, rē-zist′, *v.t.* [Fr. *résister*, from L. *resisto*, to withstand — *re*, and *sisto*, to place, to stand, from *sto*, to stand. STATE, STAND.] To withstand so as not to be impressed by; to form an impediment to; to oppose, passively (certain bodies *resist* acids or a cutting tool); to act in opposition to; to strive or struggle against, actively.—*v.i.* To make opposition.—*n.* A sort of paste applied to calico goods to prevent colour or mordant from fixing on those parts not intended to be coloured. — **Resistance**, rē-zis′tans, *n.* The act of resisting, whether actively or passively; a being or acting in opposition; the quality or property in matter of not yielding to force or external impression; a force acting in opposition to another force so as to destroy it, or diminish its effect; in *elect.* the property of a body that limits the strength of an electric current in it by causing part of the electrical energy to be dissipated in the form of heat, &c.; measured practically in *ohms*.—*Unit of resistance*, the standard of measurement of electric resistance; an ohm.—**Resistant**, rē-zis′tant, *n.* One who or that which resists. — **Resistant, Resistent**, rē-zis′tent, *a.* Making resistance; resisting. — **Resister**, rē-zis′tėr, *n.* One who resists.—**Resistible**, rē-zis′ti-bl, *a.* Capable of being resisted.—**Resistibleness, Resistibility**, rē-zis′ti-bl-nes, rē-zis′ti-bil″i-ti, *n.* The quality of being resistible.—**Resistibly**, rē-zis′ti-bli, *adv.* In a resistible manner.—**Resistless**, rē-zist′les, *a.* Incapable of being resisted or withstood; irresistible; powerless to resist (*Keats*).—**Resistlessly**, rē-zist′les-li, *adv.* In a resistless manner; irresistibly.— **Resistlessness**, rē-zist′les-nes, *n.*

Resmooth, rē-smöᴛʜ′, *v.t.* To make smooth again.

Resolder, rē-sol′dėr, *v.t.* To solder again.

Resoluble, rez′o-lū-bl, *a.* [Fr. *résoluble*. RESOLVE.] Capable of being melted or dissolved.

Resolute, rez′o-lūt, *a.* [Fr. *résolu*, pp. of *résoudre*, L. *resolvere*, to resolve. RESOLVE.]

Having a fixed purpose; determined; steadfast; bold; firm.—**Resolutely**, rez'o-lūt-li, *adv.* In a resolute manner; with fixed purpose; determinedly; boldly.—**Resoluteness**, rez'o-lūt-nes, *n.* The quality of being resolute; unshaken firmness. — **Resolution**, rez-o-lū'shon, *n.* [Fr. *résolution*, L. *resolutio.*] The character of being resolute; a resolve taken; a fixed purpose or determination of mind; the character of acting with fixed purpose; firmness; determination; a formal decision of a legislative or other body; the operation of resolving or separating the component parts of a body; the act of unravelling a perplexing question or problem; solution; *music*, the succession of a concord immediately after a discord; *med.* a removal or disappearance, as the disappearance of a tumour.—*Resolution of an equation*, in *alg.* the bringing of the unknown quantity by itself on one side, and all the known quantities on the other. —*Resolution of forces*, in *dyn.* the dividing of any single force into two or more others, which shall produce the same effect. — **Resolutioner**, rez-o-lū'shon-ėr, *n.* One who joins in a resolution or declaration; *hist.* the party adhering to the resolution to admit into the army of Scotland the Engagers, Royalists, and Malignants during the Civil War; opposed by the *Protesters*, against the resolution adopted at Perth.—**Resolutive**, rez'o-lū-tiv, *a.* Having the power to dissolve or break up.

Resolve, rē-zolv', *v.t.*—*resolved, resolving.* [L. *resolvo*, to unloose, break up, dissolve, to do away with (hence, to determine, that is, to do away with doubts or disputes)—*re*, back or again, and *solvo*, to loose. SOLVE.] To separate the component parts of; to reduce to constituent elements; to reduce to simple parts; to analyse; to disentangle of perplexities; to clear of difficulties (to *resolve* doubts); to explain; to fix in determination or purpose; to determine (usually in pp.); to melt; to dissolve; to form or constitute by resolution (the house *resolved* itself into a committee); to determine on; to express by resolution and vote; *med.* to disperse or remove, as an inflammation or a tumour; *math.* to solve.—*v.i.* To form an opinion or purpose; to determine; to determine by vote; to melt; to become fluid; to become separated into its component parts or into distinct principles.—*n.* That which has been resolved on; fixed purpose of mind; a settled determination; a resolution.—**Resolved**, rē-zolvd', *p.* and *a.* Having the mind made up; determined.—**Resolvedly**, rē-zol'ved-li, *adv.* In a resolved manner; resolutely.—**Resolvedness**, rē-zol'ved-nes, *n.* Fixedness of purpose.—**Resolvent**, rē-zol'vent, *a.* Having the power to resolve; causing solution.—*n.* That which has the power of causing solution; *med.* a discutient. —**Resolver**, rē-zol'vėr, *n.* One who or that which resolves; one who determines.—**Resolvability, Resolvableness**, rē-zol'va-bil"i-ti, rē-zol'va-bl-nes, *n.* The property of being resolvable.—**Resolvable**, rē-zol'va-bl, *a.* Capable of being resolved or separated into constituent parts; capable of being solved.

Resonant, rez'o-nant, *a.* [L. *resonans*, *resonantis*, ppr. of *resono*—*re*, again, and *sono*, to sound. SOUND.] Capable of returning sound; resounding; full of sounds; echoing back.—**Resonantly**, rez'o-nant-li, *adv.* In a resonant manner.—**Resonance, Resonancy**, rez'o-nans, rez'o-nan-si, *n.* The state or quality of being resonant, the act of resounding.—**Resonator**, rez'o-nā-tėr, *n.* An instrument for facilitating the analysis of compound sounds.

Resorb, rē-sorb', *v.t.* [L. *resorbeo*—*re*, and *sorbeo*, to drink in.] To swallow up.—**Resorbent**, rē-sor'bent, *a.* Swallowing up.

Resort, rē-zort', *v.i.* [O.Fr. *resortir*, Fr. *ressortir*, to go out again, to resort, from prefix *re*, and *sortir*, to go out, from L. *sortiri*, to obtain, to acquire by lot, from *sors, sortis*, lot. SORT.] To have recourse; to betake one's self (to *resort* to force); to go (to *resort* to a place); to repair frequently. —*n.* A betaking one's self; recourse; the act of visiting or frequenting; a place frequented; a haunt.—**Resorter**, rē-zor'tėr, *n.* One who resorts.

Resound, rē-zound', *v.t.* [O.E. *resoune*, from L. *resono*, to resound—*re*, again, and *sono*, to sound. SOUND.] To sound again; to echo; to extol.—*v.i.* To be filled with sound; to echo; to reverberate; to sound loudly; to be echoed; to be much mentioned.—*n.* Return of sound; echo.

Resound, rē-sound', *v.t.* and *i.* To sound again.

Resource, rē-sōrs', *n.* [Fr. *ressource*, from O.Fr. *ressourdre*, to arise anew—*re*, again, and *sourdre*, L. *surgere*, to rise. SOURCE.] Any source of aid or support; an expedient; means yet untried; resort; *pl.* pecuniary means; funds; available means or capabilities of any kind.—**Resourceful**, rē-sōrs'ful, *a.* Capable of utilizing resources.

Resow, rē-sō', *v.t.* To sow again.

Respect, rē-spekt', *v.t.* [Fr. *respecter*, from L. *respicio*, *respectum*—*re*, back, and obs. *specio*, to look. SPECIES.] To regard, heed, or consider; to have reference or regard to; to relate to; to view with some degree of reverence.—*To respect persons*, to show undue bias towards them; to be more favourable to one than to another.—*n.* [L. *respectus.*] A respecting or noticing with attention; regard; attention; a holding in high estimation or honour; the deportment which proceeds from esteem, regard, or reverence; partial or undue regard; bias (*respect* of persons); *pl.* an expression of regard, esteem, or deference (give him my *respects*); a point or particular (wrong in many *respects*); relation; reference: especially in the phrase *in* or *with respect to*.—**Respectability**, rē-spek'ta-bil"i-ti, *n.* State or quality of being respectable. —**Respectable**, rē-spek'ta-bl, *a.* Worthy of respect; having an honest or good reputation; belonging to a fairly good position in society; mediocre; not despicable (a *respectable* number of citizens).—**Respectably**, rē-spek'ta-bli, *adv.* In a respectable manner; moderately; pretty well.—**Respecter**, rē-spek'tėr, *n.* One that respects. —**Respectful**, rē-spekt'ful, *a.* Marked by respect; showing respect or outward regard; ceremonious.—**Respectfully**, rē-spekt'ful-li, *adv.* In a respectful manner; with respect. — **Respectfulness**, rē-spekt'ful-nes, *n.* The quality of being respectful.—**Respecting**, rē-spek'ting, *ppr.* used as a *prep.* Regarding; in regard to; concerning.—**Respective**, rē-spek'tiv, *a.* Relating or pertaining severally each to each; severally connected or belonging; several (our *respective* places of abode); relative; not absolute.—**Respectively**, rē-spek'tiv-li, *adv.* In their respective relations; as each belongs to each.

Respire, rē-spīr', *v.i.*—*respired, respiring.* [Fr. *respirer*, from L. *respiro* — *re*, and *spiro*, to breathe. SPIRIT.] To breathe; to inhale air into the lungs and exhale it, for the purpose of maintaining animal life; to recover breath; to rest, as after toil or suffering.—*v.t.* To breathe in and out, as air; to inhale and exhale; to breathe out; to send out in exhalations.—**Respirable**, res'pi-ra-bl or rē-spī'ra-bl, *a.* Capable of or fit for being respired or breathed. — **Respirability, Respirableness**, rē-spī'ra-bil"i-ti, rē-spī'ra-bl-nes, *n.* The quality of being respirable.—**Respiration**, res-pi-rā'shon, *n.* [L. *respiratio.*] The act of respiring or breathing, in the higher animals performed by lungs and including inspiration or inhalation of air, and expiration or exhalation; in fishes performed by gills.—**Respirational**, res-pi-rā'shon-al, *a.* Relating to respiration.—**Respirator**, res'pi-rā-tėr, *n.* An appliance for breathing through, fitted to cover the mouth, or the nose and mouth, and used to exclude cold air, smoke, dust, &c.—**Respiratory**, re-spī'ra-to-ri, *a.* Pertaining to or serving for respiration.

Respite, res'pit, *n.* [O.Fr. *respit*, from L. *respectus*, respect. RESPECT.] A temporary intermission of labour or suffering; prolongation of time for the payment of a debt; *law*, a reprieve; temporary suspension of the execution of an offender.—*v.t.* —*respited, respiting.* To give or grant a respite to; to reprieve.

Resplendent, rē-splen'dent, *a.* [L. *resplendens, resplendentis*, ppr. of *resplendeo* —*re*, and *splendeo*, to shine. SPLENDID.] Very bright; shining with brilliant lustre.—*Resplendent felspar.* ADULARIA. — **Resplendently**, rē-splen'dent-li, *adv.* In a resplendent manner. — **Resplendence, Resplendency**, rē-splen'dens, rē-splen'-den-si, *n.* Brilliant lustre; splendour.

Respond, rē-spond', *v.i.* [O.Fr. *respondre* (Fr. *répondre*), *L. respondeo*—*re*, back, and *spondeo*, to promise solemnly. SPONSOR, SPOUSE.] To make answer; to give a reply in words; to answer or reply in any way; to answer by action; to correspond; to suit. —*n.* In religious services, a short anthem or versicle chanted at intervals; a response. **Respondence, Respondency**, rē-spon'dens, rē-spon'den-si, *n.* The state of being respondent; an answering. — **Respondent**, rē-spon'dent, *a.* [L. *respondens, respondentis.*] Answering; conformable; corresponding.—*n.* One who responds; one who answers in a lawsuit; one who maintains a thesis in reply. — **Respondentia**, rē-spon-den'shi-a, *n.* [L.] A loan advanced upon the cargo of a ship.—**Response**, rē-spons', *n.* [L. *responsum.*] The act of responding or replying; reply; answer; an oracular answer; the answer of the congregation to the priest in the litany and other parts of divine service; a reply to an objection in formal disputation. — **Responsibility**, rē-spon'si-bil"i-ti, *n.* The state of being responsible; that for which one is responsible; a trust, or the like, resting on a person; ability to answer in payment.—**Responsible**, rē-spon'si-bl, *a.* Accountable; answerable; able to respond to any claim; involving responsibility. —**Responsibly**, rē-spon'si-bli, *adv.* In a responsible manner. — **Responsions**, rē-spon'shonz, *n.* [L. *responsio*, an answering.] The first examination which the students at Oxford are obliged to pass before they can take any degree, familiarly called *Smalls.*—**Responsive**, rē-spon'siv, *a.* Answering; responding; correspondent; suited to something else. — **Responsively**, rē-spon'siv-li, *adv.* In a responsive manner. — **Responsiveness**, rē-spon'siv-nes, *n.*—**Responsory**, rē-spon'so-ri, *a.* Containing answer.—*n.* A response; an antiphonary.

Rest, rest, *n.* [A.Sax. *rest, ræst*, rest, repose=Dan., Sw., and G. *rast*, D. *rust*, rest, Goth. *rasta*, a stage or place of rest on the road; root seen in Goth. *razn*, a house.] A state of quiet or repose; cessation of motion, labour, or action of any kind; freedom from everything that disquiets; peace; tranquillity; sleep; figuratively, the last sleep; death; a place of quiet; that on which anything leans for support; an article or appliance for support; *music*, an interval of silence between one sound and another, or the mark or character denoting the interval.—*v.i.* [A.Sax. *restan*, to rest.] To cease from action, motion, or work of any kind; to stop; to be free from whatever harasses or disturbs; to be quiet or still; to lie for repose; to sleep; to sleep the final sleep; to die; to stand for support; to be supported; to be fixed in any state or opinion (to *rest* content); to rely (to *rest* on a man's promise); to be in a certain state or position, as an affair.—*To rest with*, to be in the power of; to depend upon (it *rests with* time to decide).—*v.t.* To lay at rest; to give rest or repose to; to quiet; to lay or place, as on a support.—*To rest one's self*, to take rest. — **Restful**, rest'ful, *a.* Full of rest; giving rest; quiet; being at rest.—**Restfully**, rest'ful-li, *adv.* In a state of rest or quiet.—**Restfulness**, rest'-ful-nes, *n.* State of being restful.—**Rest-house**, rest'hous, *n.* In India, an empty house for the accommodation of travellers. **Resting-place**, *n.* A place for rest; used poetically for the grave.—**Restless**, rest'les, *a.* Unresting; unquiet; continually moving; being without rest; unable to sleep; passed in unquietness; not satisfied to be at rest; unsettled; turbulent.—**Restlessly**, rest'les-li, *adv.* In a restless manner; unquietly. — **Restlessness**, rest'les-nes, *n.* Agitation; a state of disturbance or agitation, either of body or mind; inability to sleep or rest.

Rest, rest, *n.* [Fr. *reste*, from *rester*, to rest, to remain, from L. *resto—re*, back, and *sto*, to stand. STATE.] That which is left after the separation of a part, either in fact or in contemplation: used with *the*; the remainder; the others; those not before included (in this sense plural); a surplus fund held in reserve by a bank, or other such company, to fall back upon in any great emergency.—*v.i.* [Fr. *rester.*] To be left; to remain; to continue to be.—**Restant**, res'tant, *a. Bot.* remaining; not falling off.

Restate, rē-stāt', *v.t.* To state again.

Restaurant, res'tō-rant, *n.* [Fr.] A commercial establishment for the sale of refreshments; an eating-house.—**Restaurateur**, res-tō'ra-tėr, *n.* [Fr.] The keeper of a restaurant.

Restem, rē-stem', *v.t.* To stem again; to force back against the current.

Restharrow, rest'har-ō, *n.* [For *arrest-harrow.*] A European leguminous plant with pink flowers and long woody, tough roots, that arrest the harrow's prongs.

Restiform, res'ti-form, *a.* [L. *restis*, a cord, and *forma*, form.] In the form of a cord.

Restipulate, rē-stip'ū-lāt, *v.i.* To stipulate anew. — **Restipulation**, rē-stip'ū-lā"shon, *n.* The act of restipulating.

Restitution, res-ti-tū'shon, *n.* [L. *restitutio*, *restitutionis*, from *restituo*, to set up again—*re*, and *statuo*, to set. STATUTE.] The restoring of what is lost or taken away, especially taken away unjustly; amends; indemnification.

Restive, res'tiv, *a.* [O.Fr. *restif*, drawing backward, refusing to go forward, from *rester*, L. *restare*, to stay back, to remain. REST (to remain).] Unwilling to go forward‡; refusing to rest or stand still; constantly fidgeting or moving about: said of horses; hence, impatient under restraint or opposition: applied to persons.—**Restively**, res'tiv-li, *adv.* In a restive manner.—**Restiveness**, res'tiv-nes, *n.*

Restore, rē-stōr', *v.t.—restored, restoring.* [O.Fr. *restorer* (Fr. *restaurer*), to restore, repair, reinstall, from L. *restauro*, to restore, to repair—*re*, again, and *stauro*, to make strong. STORE.] To bring back to a former and better state; to repair; to rebuild; to heal; to cure; to revive; to re-establish after interruption (to *restore* peace); to give back; to return after having been taken away; to bring or put back to a former position; to recover or renew, as passages of an author defective or corrupted; *fine arts*, to bring back from a state of injury or decay (to *restore* a painting); to complete by adding the defective parts. —**Restorable**, rē-stō'ra-bl, *a.* Capable of being restored.—**Restorableness**, rē-stō'ra-bl-nes, *n.*—**Restoration**, res-tō-rā'shon, *n.* The act of restoring; replacement; renewal; re-establishment; the repairing of injuries suffered by works of art, buildings, &c.; recovery of health. — *The Restoration*, the return of King Charles II in 1660, and the re-establishment of the English monarchy. In French history the terms *first* and *second Restoration* are respectively applied to the return of the Bourbons after Napoleon's abdication and after Waterloo. — **Restorationists**, *n.* In *theol.* the followers of Origen, who maintained the restoration to divine favour and pardon of all persons, after a process of purgation proportioned to their merits and demerits. — **Restorative**, rē-stō'ra-tiv, *a.* Capable of restoring strength, vigour, &c.—*n.* A medicine efficacious in restoring strength and vigour. — **Restoratively**, rē-stō'ra-tiv-li, *adv.* In a restorative manner.—**Restorer**, rē-stō'rėr, *n.* One who restores.

Re-store, rē'stōr, *v.t.* To store anew.

Restrain, rē-strān', *v.t.* [O.Fr. *restraindre* (Fr. *restreindre*), from L. *restringo — re*, back, and *stringo*, to draw tight. STRAIN.] To hold back; to hold in; to check; to hold from action; to repress; to restrict.—**Restrainable**, rē-strā'na-bl, *a.* Capable of being restrained. — **Restrainedly**, re-strā'ned-li, *adv.* With restraint; with limitation.—**Restrainer**, rē-strā'nėr, *n.* One who or that which restrains.—**Restrainment**, rē-strān'ment, *n.* Act of restraining.—**Restraint**, rē-strānt', *n.* The act of restraining; a holding back or hindering from motion in any manner; hindrance of the will; a check to any tendency; abridgment of liberty; confinement; detention; that which restrains or hinders; a limitation.

Restrict, rē-strikt', *v.t.* [L. *restringo, restrictum—re*, back, and *stringo*. RESTRAIN.] To limit; to confine; to restrain within bounds. — **Restriction**, rē-strik'shon, *n.* The act of restricting, or state of being restricted; that which restricts; a restraint; reservation.—**Restrictive**, rē-strik'tiv, *a.* Having the quality of limiting or expressing limitation; imposing restraint. — **Restrictively**, rē-strik'tiv-li, *adv.* In a restrictive manner; with limitation. — **Restrictiveness**, rē-strik'tiv-nes, *n.* The state or quality of being restrictive.

Resubject, rē-sub-jekt', *v.t.* To subject again. — **Resubjection**, rē-sub-jek'shon, *n.* A second subjection.

Result, rē-zult', *v.i.* [Fr. *résulter*, to result, originally to rebound, from L. *resulto*, to rebound, from *resilio—re*, back, and *salio*, to leap. RESILE.] To proceed, spring, or rise, as a consequence, from facts, arguments, premises, combination of circumstances, &c.; to ensue; to accrue; to have an issue; to terminate: followed by *in* (this measure will *result in* good or evil).—*Resulting force.* RESULTANT.—*n.* Consequence; conclusion; outcome; issue; effect; product; that which proceeds naturally or logically from facts, premises, or the state of things.—**Resultance**, rē-zult'ans, *n.* The act of resulting; a result.—**Resultant**, rē-zult'ant, *a.* Following as a result or consequence; resulting from the combination of two or more agents.—*n. Physics*, the force which results from the composition of two or more forces acting upon a body; the single force, velocity, acceleration, &c., to which several forces, velocities, accelerations, &c., are together equivalent. —**Resultful**, rē-zult'ful, *a.* Having results; effectual.—**Resultless**, rē-zult'les, *a.* Without result; ineffectual.

Résumé, rā'zū-mā, *n.* [Fr. RESUME.] A summing up; a recapitulation; a condensed statement; a summary.

Resume, rē-zūm', *v.t.—resumed, resuming.* [Fr. *résumer*, from L. *resumo — re*, and *sumo*, to take (as in *assume, consume*, &c.). SUMPTUOUS.] To take again; to take back; to take up again after interruption; to begin again.—**Resumable**, rē-zū'ma-bl, *a.* Capable of being resumed.—**Resumption**, rē-zum'shon, *n.* The act of resuming, taking back, or taking again.—**Resumptive**, rē-zum'tiv, *a.* Taking back or again.

Resummon, rē-sum'on, *v.t.* To summon or call again; to recall; to recover.

Resupinate, Resupinated, rē-sū'pi-nāt, rē-sū'pi-nā-ted, *a.* [L. *resupinatus—re*, and *supinus*, lying on the back, supine.] Inverted; reversed; appearing as if turned upside down.—**Resupination**, rē-sū'pi-nā"shon, *n.* The state of being resupinate or reversed. — **Resupine**, rē-sū-pin', *a.* Lying on the back.

Resupply, rē-sup-plī', *v.t.* To supply again.

Resurge,† rē-sėrj', *v.i.* [L. *resurgo — re*, again, and *surgo*, to rise.] To rise again; to reappear, as from the dead.—**Resurgence**, rē-sėr'jens, *n.* The act of rising again; resurrection.—**Resurgent**, rē-sėr'jent, *a.* Rising again or from the dead.

Resurrect, rez'ėr-rekt', *v.t.* To raise from the dead; to restore to life or use.—**Resurrection**, rez-ėr-rek'shon, *n.* [L. *resurrectio*, from *resurgo*, *resurrectum—re*, again, and *surgo*, to arise. SOURCE.] A rising again to life; the rising of Christ after the crucifixion.—**Resurrectionist**, rez-ėr-rek'shon-ist, *n.* One who steals bodies from the grave for dissection.

Resurvey, rē-sėr-vā', *v.t.* To survey again or anew; to review.—*n.* (rē-sėr'vā). A new survey.

Resuscitate, rē-sus'i-tāt, *v.t.* — *resuscitated, resuscitating.* [L. *resuscito, resuscitatum—re*, again, and *suscito*, to rouse up—*sub*, and *cito*, to rouse, to summon, to cite. CITE.] To stir up anew; to revivify; to revive; particularly, to recover from apparent death.—*v.i.* To revive; to come to life again.—**Resuscitable**, rē-sus'i-ta-bl, *a.* Capable of being resuscitated.—**Resuscitant**, rē-sus'i-tant, *a.* Resuscitating.—*n.* One who or that which resuscitates.—**Resuscitation**, rē-sus'i-tā"shon, *n.* The act of resuscitating; revivification; the restoring to animation of persons apparently dead.—**Resuscitative**, rē-sus'i-tā-tiv, *a.* Tending to resuscitate. — **Resuscitator**, rē-sus'i-tā-tėr, *n.* One who resuscitates.

Ret, ret, *v.t.—retted, retting.* [D. *reten*; to ret flax; allied to *rot.*] To steep or macerate flax in water, in order to separate the fibre by incipient rotting.—**Rettery**, ret'ėr-i, *n.* A place where flax is retted.—**Retting**, ret'ing, *n.* The process of soaking flax in water.

Retable, rē-tā'bl, *n.* [For *rear-table.*] *Arch.* a shelf or ledge behind an altar for holding candles or vases.

Retail, rē-tāl, *v.t.* [Fr. *retail*, a piece cut off—*re*, again, and *tailler*, to cut, from L.L. *talea, talia*, a tally, L. *talea*, a stick (hence also *tailor, tally*). *Retail* is thus to sell by pieces cut off.] To sell in small quantities, or by the piece, in contradistinction to selling wholesale; to dispense in small quantities; to repeat a story to many persons.—*v.t.* To sell at retail, as, the coat *retails* for $50.—*n.* The sale of goods in small quantities.—*a.* Concerning the sale of anything in small quantities, as, a *retail* merchant, *retail* trade, &c. — **Retailer**, rē-tāl'er, *n.* One who engages in retail trade.

Retain, rē-tān', *v.t.* [Fr. *retenir*, L. *retineo —re*, back, and *teneo*, to hold. TENANT.] To hold or keep in possession; to keep from departure or escape; to detain; to keep; not to lose or part with; to engage by the payment of a preliminary fee (to *retain* counsel). — **Retainable**, rē-tā'na-bl, *a.* Capable of being retained. — **Retainer**, rē-tā'nėr, *n.* One who or that which retains; one who is kept in service; a dependant; a servant, not a domestic; *law*, a preliminary fee given to counsel to secure their services or prevent their being secured by others; a retaining fee.—**Retaining**, rē-tā'ning, *p.* and *a.* Keeping in possession; serving to retain.—*Retaining fee*, a retainer.—*Retaining wall*, a wall that is built to retain a bank of earth from slipping down; a revetment. — **Retainment**, rē-tān'ment, *n.* The act of retaining; retention.

Retake, rē-tāk', *v.t.* To take again; to recapture.

Retaliate, rē-tal'i-āt, *v.t.* — *retaliated, retaliating.* [L. *retalio, retaliatum*, to retaliate —*re*, in return, and noun *talio*, like for like, retaliation, from *talis*, such.] To return the like for (to *retaliate* injuries or wrongs); to pay or requite by an act of the same kind as has been received, in a bad sense; that is, to return evil for evil.—*v.i.* To return like for like; to do injuries in return for injuries.—**Retaliater**, rē-tal'i-ā-tėr, *n.* One who retaliates. — **Retaliation**, rē-tal'i-ā"shon, *n.* The act of retaliating; the return of like for like; requital of evil by evil; reprisal; revenge. — **Retaliative, Retaliatory**, rē-tal'i-ā-tiv, rē-tal'i-ā-to-ri, *a.* Returning like for like; consisting in retaliation.

Retard, rē-tärd', *v.t.* [Fr. *retarder*, from L. *retardo—re*, and *tardo*, to delay, from *tardus*, slow. TARDY.] To obstruct in swiftness of course; to keep delaying; to impede; to clog; to hinder.—*n.* Retardation. — **Retardation**, rē-tär-dā'shon, *n.* The act of retarding or delaying; *physics*, the act of hindering the free progress or velocity of a body; that which retards; an obstruction.—**Retardative**, rē-tär′da-tiv, *a.* Tending or having power to retard.—**Retarder**, rē-tär′dėr, *n.* One that retards. — **Retardment**, rē-tärd′ment, *n.* The act of retarding.

Retch, rech, *v.i.* [A.Sax. *hraecan*, to retch, to hawk; allied to *hraca*, the throat, a cough; Icel. *hrækja*, to spit, *hráki*, spittle.] To make an effort to vomit; to strain, as in vomiting.

Rete, rē′tē, *n.* [L., a net.] *Anat.* a vascular net-work or plexus of vessels.

Retell, rē-tel′, *v.t.* To tell again.

Retention, rē-ten′shon, *n.* [L. *retentio*, *retentionis*, from *retineo*, *retentum*. RETAIN.] The act of retaining or power of retaining; the faculty of remembering; power of memory; *med.* a morbid accumulation of matter in the body that should be evacuated.—**Retentive**, rē-ten′tiv, *a.* Characterized by retention; having strong power of recollecting.—**Retentively**, rē-ten′tiv-li, *adv.* In a retentive manner.—**Retentiveness**, rē-ten′tiv-nes, *n.* The quality of being retentive.

Retiary, rē′shi-a-ri, *a.* [From L. *rete*, a net.] Netlike; constructing or using a net or web to catch prey (*retiary* spiders).

Reticence, **Reticency**, ret′i-sens, ret′i-sen-si, *n.* [Fr. *réticence*, from L. *reticentia*, from *reticeo*, to be silent again—*re*, and *taceo*, to be silent. TACIT.] The quality of observing studied and continued silence; a refraining from talking; the keeping of one's counsel. — **Reticent**, ret′i-sent, *a.* Having a disposition to be silent; reserved; not apt to speak about or reveal any matters.

Reticular, re-tik′ū-lėr, *a.* [L. *reticulum*, dim. of *rete*, a net.] Having the form of a net or of net-work; formed with interstices. —**Reticularly**, re-tik′ū-lėr-li, *adv.* In a reticular manner.—**Reticulate**, **Reticulated**, re-tik′ū-lāt, re-tik′ū-lā-ted, *a.* [L. *reticulatus*, from *reticulum*.] Netted; resembling net-work; having distinct lines or veins crossing like net-work.—**Reticulation**, re-tik′ū-lā″shon, *n.* That which is reticulated; net-work; organization of substances resembling a net.—**Reticule**, ret′i-kūl, *n.* [Fr. *réticule*, L. *reticulum*, dim. of *rete*, a net.] A kind of bag, formerly of net-work, but now of every description of materials, used by ladies for carrying in the hand; a micrometer attached to a telescope, having a net-work of fine fibres crossing at right angles.—**Reticulum**, re-tik′ū-lum, *n.* [L.] The honey-comb bag, or second cavity of the complex stomach of ruminants.

Retiform, rē′ti-form, *a.* [L. *retiformis*—*rete*, a net, and *forma*, form.] Having the form of a net in texture; composed of crossing lines and interstices.

Retina, ret′i-na, *n.* [From L. *rete*, a net.] A membrane lining the interior of the eye behind, being a reticular expansion of the optic nerve, which receives the impressions from external objects.—**Retinal**, ret′i-nal, *a.* Pertaining to the retina.—**Retinitis**, ret-i-nī′tis, *n.* Inflammation of the retina. —**Retinoscopy**, ret-i-nos′ko-pi, *n.* Examination of the retina.

Retinervis, rē-ti-nėr′vis, *n.* [L. *rete*, a net, and *nervus*, a nerve.] *Bot.* having veins with the appearance of net-work.

Retinite, ret′i-nīt, *n.* [Fr. *rétinite*, from Gr. *rhētinē*, resin.] A translucent fossil resin; pitch-stone.—**Retinoid**, ret′i-noid, *a.* Resin-like; resembling a resin.

Retinue, ret′i-nū, *n.* [O.Fr. *retenue*, from *retenir*, to retain. RETAIN.] The attendants of a prince or other distinguished personage, chiefly on a journey or an excursion; a train of persons; a suite; a cortège.

Retire, rē-tīr′, *v.i.*—*retired*, *retiring*. [Fr. *retirer*—*re*, back, and *tirer*, to draw, a word of Teutonic origin = Goth. *tairan*, E. to *tear*.] To withdraw; to go back; to draw back; to go from company or from a public place into privacy; to retreat from action or danger (to *retire* from battle); to withdraw from business or active life; to recede; to be bent or turned back (the shore *retires* to form a bay).—*v.t.* To designate as being no longer qualified for active service (to *retire* a military officer); to withdraw from circulation by taking up and paying (to *retire* a bill).—**Retiral**, rē-tī′ral, *n.* The act of retiring or withdrawing; the act of taking up and paying a bill when due. —**Retired**, rē-tīrd′, *p.* and *a.* Secluded from much society or from public notice; apart from public view (a *retired* life, a *retired* locality); private; secret; withdrawn from business or active life; having given up business (a *retired* merchant); given to seclusion; inclining to retirement.—*Retired list*, a list on which superannuated and deserving naval or military officers are placed.—**Retiredly**, rē-tī′red-li, *adv.* In a retired manner; in solitude or privacy.—**Retiredness**, rē-tī′red-nes, *n.* A state of retirement. — **Retirement**, rē-tīr′ment, *n.* The act of retiring; state of living a retired life; seclusion; privacy; retired or private abode.—**Retirer**, rē-tī′rėr, *n.* One who retires.—**Retiring**, rē-tī′ring, *p.* and *a.* Withdrawing; retreating; reserved; not forward or obtrusive; granted to or suitable for one who retires, as from public employment or service (a *retiring* allowance).

Retold, rē-tōld′, pret. and pp. of *retell*.

Retort, rē-tort′, *v.t.* [L. *retorqueo*, *retortum*, to fling or cast back, to retort—*re*, back, and *torqueo*, *tortum*, to twist. TORTURE.] To return, as an argument, accusation, censure, or incivility (to *retort* the charge of vanity); to bend or curve back (a *retorted* line).—*v.i.* To return an argument or charge; to make a severe reply; to curl or curve back, as a line.—*n.* [The vessel is named from the neck being bent back or retorted.] A censure or incivility returned; a severe reply; a repartee; a flask-shaped vessel, to which a long neck is attached, employed for the purpose of distilling or effecting decomposition by the aid of heat; also applied to almost any apparatus in which solid substances, such as coal, wood, bones, &c., are submitted to destructive distillation (as *retorts* for producing coal-gas).—**Retorted**, rē-tor′ted, *p.* and *a.* Thrown back; bent back.—**Retorter**, rē-tor′tėr, *n.* One that retorts.—**Retortive**, rē-tor′tiv, *a.* Containing retort.

Retouch, rē-tuch′, *v.t.* To touch or touch up again; to improve by new touches; to revise.—*n.* A repeated touch; a revisal.

Retrace, rē-trās′, *v.t.* [Prefix *re*, back, and *trace*; Fr. *retracer*.] To trace or track back; to go over again in the reverse direction.—**Retraceable**, rē-trā′sa-bl, *a.* Capable of being retraced.

Retract, rē-trakt′, *v.t.* [Fr. *rétracter*, from L. *retracto*, freq. of *retraho*, *retractum*—*re*, back, and *traho*, to draw. TRACT.] To draw back; to draw in (to *retract* the claws); to rescind; to withdraw, as a declaration, words, or saying; to disavow; to recant.—*v.i.* To take back statements; to unsay one's words.—**Retractable**, rē-trak′ta-bl, *a.* Capable of being retracted.—**Retractation**, **Retraction**, rē-trak-tā′shon, rē-trak′shon, *n.* The act of retracting or drawing back; the act of recalling what has been said; recantation. — **Retractible**, **Retractile**, rē-trak′ti-bl, rē-trak′tīl, *a.* Capable of being drawn back.—**Retractive**, rē-trak′tiv, *a.* Tending or serving to retract. — **Retractively**, rē-trak′tiv-li, *adv.* By retraction or withdrawing.—**Retractor**, rē-trak′tėr, *n.* One who retracts; that which retracts or draws back; a muscle that draws back some part.

Retransform, rē-trans-form′, *v.t.* To transform anew; to change back again.—**Retransformation**, rē′trans-for-mā″shon, *n.* A second or repeated transformation.

Retranslate, rē-trans-lāt′, *v.t.* To translate again.

Retreat, rē-trēt′, *n.* [Fr. *retraite*, from *retraire*, to withdraw, from L. *retrahere*. RETRACT.] The act of retiring; a withdrawing from any place; state of privacy or seclusion; place of retirement or privacy; a refuge; a place of safety or security; a military operation, either forced or strategical, by which troops retire before an enemy; a period of retirement with a view to self-examination, meditation, and special prayer.—*v.i.* To make a retreat; to retire from any position or place; to withdraw; to take shelter; to retire before an enemy.

Retrench, rē-trensh′, *v.t.* [O.Fr. *retrencher* (Fr. *retrancher*)—*re*, and *trancher*, to cut. TRENCH.] To cut off, abridge, or curtail; to limit or restrict; *milit.* to furnish with a retrenchment.—*v.i.* To live at less expense; to practise economy.—**Retrenchment**, rē-trensh′ment, *n.* The removing of what is superfluous; the act of curtailing or lessening; *milit.* an interior rampart cutting off a portion of a fortress from the rest, and to which a garrison may retreat.

Retribute,† rē-trib′ūt, *v.t.*—*retributed*, *retributing*. [L. *retribuo*, *retributum*—*re*, back, and *tribuo*, to assign, bestow. TRIBUTE.] To pay back; to requite; to compensate. — **Retributer**, rē-trib′ū-tėr, *n.* One that makes retribution.—**Retribution**, ret-ri-bū′shon, *n.* The act of requiting actions, whether good or bad; a reward, recompense, or requital; especially, a requital or punishment for wrong or evil done; evil justly befalling the perpetrator of evil; the distribution of rewards and punishments in a future life.—**Retributive**, **Retributory**, rē-trib′ū-tiv, rē-trib′ū-to-ri, *a.* Making retribution; rewarding for good deeds and punishing for offences.

Retrieve, rē-trēv′, *v.t.*—*retrieved*, *retrieving*. [Fr. *retrouver*, O.Fr. *retreuver*, to find again, to recover—*re*, again, and *trouver*, to find. TROVER.] To get again; to regain; to recover; to restore from loss or injury (to *retrieve* the credit of a nation); to make amends for; to repair. — **Retrievable**, rē-trē′va-bl, *a.* Capable of being retrieved or recovered.—**Retrievableness**, rē-trē′va-bl-nes, *n.* State of being retrievable.—**Retrievably**, rē-trē′va-bli, *adv.* In a retrievable manner.—**Retrieval**, rē-trē′val, *n.* Act of retrieving. — **Retrievement**, rē-trēv′ment, *n.* Act of retrieving; retrieval.—**Retriever**, rē-trē′vėr, *n.* One who retrieves; a dog that goes in quest of game which a sportsman has shot.

Retriment, ret′ri-ment, *n.* [L. *retrimentum*.] Refuse; dregs.

Retroact, rē-trō-akt′ or ret′rō-akt, *v.i.* To act backward; to act in opposition or in return.—**Retroaction**, rē-trō-ak′shon or ret′, *n.* Action returned; reverse action; operation on something past or preceding. —**Retroactive**, rē-trō-ak′tiv or ret′, *a.* Designed to retroact; affecting what is past; retrospective.—**Retroactively**, rē-trō-ak′tiv-li or ret′, *adv.*

Retrocede, rē-trō-sēd′ or ret′rō-sēd, *v.i.* [L. *retro*, back, and *cedo*, to go. CEDE.] To go back; to give place; to retire.—*v.t.* To yield or cede back.—**Retrocedent**, rē-trō-sē′dent or ret′, *a.* Going back: applied to certain diseases which move from one part of the body to another.—**Retrocession**, rē-trō-sesh′on or ret′, *n.* The act of retroceding. — **Retrocessional**, rē-trō-sesh′on-al or ret′, *a.* Belonging to retrocession.

Retrochoir, rē′trō-kwīr or ret′, *n.* [Prefix *retro*, and *choir*.] That part of a church situated behind the choir, or on the other side of it from the body of the building.

Retroduction, rē-trō-duk′shon or ret′, *n.* [L. *retro*, back, and *duco*, *ductum*, to lead.] A leading or bringing back.

Retroflex, **Retroflected**, rē′trō-fleks, rē-trō-flek′ted or ret′, *a.* [L. *retro*, back, and *flexus*, bent, *flecto*, to bend.] Bent backwards.

Retrofract, **Retrofracted**, rē′trō-frakt, rē-trō-frak′ted or ret′, *a.* [L. *retro*, back, and *fractus*, pp. of *frango*, to break.] *Bot.* bent backward as it were by force.

Retrograde, rē′trō-grād or ret′, *n.* [L. *retro*, backward, and *gradior*, *gressus*, to go. GRADE.] Going or moving backward; specifically, *astron.* appearing to move from east to west in the sky: opposed to *direct*; declining from a better to a worse state.

v.i.—*retrograded, retrograding.* To go or move backward.—**Retrogradation**, rē-trō-gra-dā″shon or rēt′, *n.* The act of retrograding; the act of moving from east to west in the heavens; a decline in excellence. —**Retrogression**, re-trō-gresh′on or rēt′, *n.* [L. *retrogradior, retrogressus.*] The act of going backward; a backward movement; *astron.* retrogradation; *physiol.* development backward or to a less perfect form.—**Retrogressive**, re-trō-gres′iv or rēt′, *a.* Moving backward; declining from a more to a less perfect state.—**Retrogressively**, re-trō-gres′iv-li or rēt′, *adv.* In a retrogressive manner.

Retropharyngeal, re′trō-fa-rin″jē-al or rēt′, *a.* [L. *retro*, backwards, and *pharynx.*] Relating to parts behind the pharynx or upper part of the throat.

Retrorse, rē-trōrs′, *a.* [L. *retrorsus*, from *retro*, backward, and *versus*, turned.] *Bot.* turned backwards.—**Retrorsely**, rē-trōrs′li, *adv.* In a backward direction.

Retrospect, re′trō-spekt or rēt′, *n.* [L. *retro*, back, and *specio*, to look. SPECIES.] A looking back on things past; a review of past events. — **Retrospection**, re-trō-spek′-shon or rēt′, *n.* The act or faculty of looking back on things past.—**Retrospective**, re-trō-spek′tiv or rēt′, *a.* Looking back on past events; having reference to what is past; affecting things past.—**Retrospectively**, re-trō-spek′tiv-li or rēt′, *adv.* In a retrospective manner.

Retroversion, re-trō-vėr′shon or rēt′, *n.* [L. *retro*, backward, and *verto, versum*, to turn.] A turning or falling backward.—**Retrovert**, re′trō-vėrt or rēt′, *v.t.* To turn back.

Retrude, rē-tröd′, *v.t.*—*retruded, retruding.* [L. *retrudo*—*re*, back, and *trudo*, to thrust. INTRUDE.] To thrust back.—**Retrusion**, rē-trö′zhon, *n.* The act of retruding, or state of being retruded.

Rettery, Retting. Under RET.

Retund, rē-tund′, *v.t.* [L. *retundo*—*re*, back, and *tundo*, to beat.] To blunt or turn, as the edge of a weapon; to dull.

Return, rē-tėrn′, *v.i.* [Fr. *retourner*—*re*, back, and *tourner*, to turn. TURN.] To come back; to come or go back to the same place or state; to pass back; to come again; to reappear; to recur; to answer; to retort. —*v.t.* To bring, carry, or send back; to give back; to repay; to give in recompense or requital (to *return* good for evil); to give back in reply (to *return* an answer); to cast, throw, or hurl back; to render, as an account to a superior; to report officially; to transmit; to elect as a member of parliament.—*n.* The act of returning; the act of coming or going back (the *return* of a traveller, of the seasons); the act of giving or sending back; repayment; recompense; requital; restitution; that which is returned; the profit on labour, on an investment, undertaking, adventure, or the like; an account or official or formal report; *pl.* tabulated statistics for general information; also, a name for a light-coloured mild-flavoured kind of tobacco.—**Returnable**, rē-tėr′na-bl, *a.* Capable of being returned; *law*, legally required to be returned or delivered. —**Returner**, rē-tėr′nėr, *n.* One who returns; one who repays or remits money. —**Returning board**, an official body canvassing election returns.—**Returning officer**, *n.* One whose duty it is to make return of writs. (*Brit.*)—**Return match**, *n.* A subsequent match or trial by the same two contestants, sets of players, or clubs.—**Return ticket**, *n.* A ticket issued by a common carrier for passage to a given point and return within a specified time.

Re-turn, rē′tėrn, *v.t.* and *i.* To turn again.

Retuse, rē-tūs′, *a.* [L. *retusus*, pp. of *retundo*—*re*, back, and *tundo*, to hammer.] *Bot.* terminating in a rounded end, the centre of which is somewhat depressed.

Reunion, rē-ūn′yon, *n.* A second union; union after separation or discord; an assembly or festive gathering, as of friends, associates, &c.—**Reunite**, rē-ū-nīt′, *v.t.* To unite again; to join after separation; to reconcile after variance.—*v.i.* To be united again; to join and cohere again.

Reurge, rē-ėrj′, *v.t.* To urge again.

Reussin, Reussite, rois′in, rois′īt, *n.* [After *Reuss*, an Austrian mineralogist.] A salt occurring as an efflorescence in white acicular crystals at Seidlitz, in Bohemia.

Revaccinate, rē-vak′si-nāt, *v.t.* To vaccinate again.—**Revaccination**, rē-vak′si-nā″shon, *n.* A repeated vaccination.

Revalenta, rev′al-ent-a, *n.* [L. *ervum lens*, a lentil.] An invalid food made from lentil and barley flour.

Revaluation, rē-val′ū-ā″shon, *n.* A second valuation.—**Revalue**, rē-val′ū, *v.t.* To value again.

Revamp, rē-vamp′, *v.t.* To vamp or patch up again; to rehabilitate.

Reveal, rē-vēl′, *v.t.* [Fr. *révéler*, from L. *revelare*, to unveil—*re*, back, and *velo*, to veil. VEIL.] To make known, as something secret or concealed; to disclose; to divulge; to lay open; to betray; to make known by divine means; to communicate by supernatural revelation.—**Revealable**, rē-vē′la-bl, *a.* Capable of being revealed.—**Revealableness**, rē-vē′la-bl-nes, *n.* State or quality of being revealable.—**Revealer**, rē-vē′lėr, *n.* One who or that which reveals. —**Revealment**,† rē-vēl′ment, *n.* The act of revealing.—**Revelation**, rev-ē-lā′shon, *n.* [L. *revelatio.*] The act of revealing; that which is revealed or made known; the Apocalypse; the last book of the New Testament, containing the prophecies of St. John.—**Revelator**,† rev′ē-lā-tėr, *n.* One who makes a revelation; a revealer.—**Revelatory**, rev′ē-la-to-ri, *a.* Having the nature or character of a revelation.

Reveille, rev-e-lē′ or rev′e-lē, *n.* [From Fr. *réveiller*, to awake—L. *re*, and *vigilo*, to watch. VIGIL.] *Milit.* beat of drum, bugle call, or other signal given about daybreak to awaken soldiers.

Revel, rev′el, *n.* [O.Fr. *revel*, revelry, disorder, rebellion, from *reveler*, to rebel, from L. *rebellare*, to rebel. REBEL.] A feast with loose and noisy jollity; a festivity; a merry-making.—*v.i.*—*revelled, revelling.* To feast with boisterous merriment; to carouse; to indulge one's inclination or caprice; to wanton; to take one's fill of pleasure.—**Reveller**, rev′el-ėr, *n.* One who revels.—**Revelry**, rev′el-ri, *n.* The act of engaging in a revel; noisy festivity; clamorous jollity.

Revelation. Under REVEAL.

Revendicate, rē-ven′di-kāt, *v.t.* [Fr. *revendiquer*, from L. *re*, and *vindicare*, to vindicate. REVENGE.] To reclaim; to demand the surrender of, as of goods taken away or detained illegally.

Revenge, rē-venj′, *v.t.*—*revenged, revenging.* [O.Fr. *revenger, revengier* (Fr. *revancher*)—*re*, in return, and *vengier, venger*, to avenge, from L. *vindicare*, to vindicate. VINDICATE.] To take vengeance for or on account of; to exact satisfaction for, under a sense of wrong or injury; to exact retribution for or for the sake of; to avenge; to inflict injury for or on account of, in a spiteful, wrong, or malignant spirit, and in order to gratify one's bitter feelings. [From the use of the verb with reflexive pronouns the expression *to be revenged* often has the sense of *to revenge one's self*, to take vengeance.]—*v.i.* To take vengeance.—*n.* The act of revenging; the executing of vengeance; retaliation; the deliberate infliction of pain or injury in return for an injury received; the desire of inflicting pain on one who has done an injury.—*To give one his revenge*, to offer one a return-match after he has been defeated, as at chess or billiards. ∴ *Revenge* is the carrying into effect of a bitter desire to injure an enemy for a wrong done to one's self, or those closely connected with one's self, and is a purely personal feeling. *Vengeance* involves the idea of wrathful retribution, more or less just, and may arise from no personal feeling, but may be taken solely for another's wrong.—**Revengeful**, rē-venj′fųl, *a.* Full of revenge; harbouring revenge; vindictive. **Revengefully**, rē-venj′fųl-li, *adv.* In a revengeful manner; by way of revenge; vindictively.—**Revengefulness**, rē-venj′-fųl-nes, *n.*—**Revenger**, rē-ven′jėr, *n.* One who revenges.

Revenue, rev′e-nū, *n.* [Fr. *revenu*, lit. what comes back, from *revenir*, to return.] Income derived from an investment; receipts of a government from excise, taxes, imposts and duties, etc.—**Revenue agent**, *n.* A governmental agent whose function it is to seek out and apprehend tax evaders. —**Revenue collector**, *n.* A governmental agent whose function it is to collect customs and excise.—**Revenue cutter**, *n.* An armed vessel used to prevent smuggling and to enforce customhouse regulations.

Reverberate, rē-vėr′bėr-āt, *v.t.*—*reverberated, reverberating.* [L.L. *reverbero, reverberatum*—L. *re*, back, and *verbero*, to beat, from *verber*, a lash, a whip.] To return, as sound; to send back; to echo; to reflect, as heat or light; to repel from side to side (flame *reverberated* in a furnace).—*v.i.* To rebound; to be reflected, as rays of light; to echo; to resound.—**Reverberant**, rē-vėr′bėr-ant, *a.* Reverberating; returning sound; resounding. — **Reverberation**, rē-vėr′bėr-ā″shon, *n.* The act of reverberating; particularly, the act of reflecting or returning sound; a sound reverberated or echoed. — **Reverberative**, rē-vėr′bėr-ā-tiv, *a.* Reverberant. — **Reverberator**, rē-vėr′bėr-ā-tėr, *n.* That which reverberates.—**Reverberatory**, rē-vėr′bėr-a-to-ri, *a.* Producing reverberation, acting by reverberation; reverberating.—*Reverberatory furnace*, a furnace with a low roof, so that the flame in passing to the chimney is reflected down on the hearth, where the material (ores, metal, &c.) to be operated on can be heated without coming in direct contact with the fuel.

Revere, rē-vēr′, *v.t.*—*revered, revering.* [Fr. *révérer*, L. *revereor*—*re*, and *vereor*, to feel awe of, to fear; same root as in E. *wary.*] To regard with awe mingled with respect and affection; to venerate; to reverence. —**Reverence**, rev′er-ens, *n.* A feeling of deep respect and esteem mingled with affection; awe combined with respect; veneration; an obeisance; reverend character; a reverend personage; a common title of the clergy, used with the pronouns, *his, your*, &c.—*v.t.*—*reverenced, reverencing.* To regard with reverence. — **Reverencer**, rev′er-en-sėr, *n.* One that reverences. — **Reverend**, rev′er-end, *a.* [L. *reverendus*, to be revered.] Worthy of reverence; a title of respect given to clergymen or ecclesiastics, and sometimes to Jewish rabbis. In England deans are *very reverend*, bishops *right reverend*, and archbishops *most reverend*—**Reverent**, rev′er-ent, *a.* Expressing reverence or veneration; humble; impressed with reverence.—**Reverential**, rev-er-en′shal, *a.* Proceeding from reverence, or expressing it.—**Reverentially**, rev-er-en′shal-li, *adv.* In a reverential manner.—**Reverently**, rev′er-ent-li, *adv.* In a reverent manner.—**Reverer**, rē-vē′rėr, *n.* One who reveres.

Reverie, rev′ėr-i, *n.* [Fr. *rêverie*, from *rêver*, to dream; akin to *rave.*] A waking dream; a brown study; a loose or irregular train of thoughts occurring in musing or meditation.—**Reverist**, rev′ėr-ist, *n.* One who indulges in or gives way to reverie.

Reverse, rē-vėrs′, *v.t.*—*reversed, reversing.* [L. *revertor, reversus*—*re*, back, and *verto*, to turn. VERSE.] To turn or put in an opposite or contrary direction or position; to turn upside down; to alter to the opposite; to make quite the contrary, or have contrary bearings or relations; to make void; to annul, repeal, revoke (to *reverse* a judgment or decree); *mach.* to cause to revolve in a contrary direction; to change the motion of.—*n.* The side presented when anything is turned in a direction opposite to its natural position; a complete change or turn of affairs: generally in a bad sense; a change for the worse; a misfortune; a cessation of success; a check; a defeat; a back-handed stroke in fencing (*Shak.*); that which is directly opposite or contrary; the contrary; the opposite (with *the*); the back or undersurface, as of a leaf or of a coin (OBVERSE). — *a.* Opposite; turned backward; having a contrary or opposite direction.—*Reverse curve*, a double curve formed of two curves in opposite directions, like the letter S. — **Reversal**, rē-vėr'sal, *n.* The act of reversing. — **Reversed**, rē-vėrst', *p.* and *a.* Turned or changed to the contrary; made void or annulled, as a judgment, decree, &c.—**Reversedly**, rē-vėr'sed-li, *adv.* In a reversed manner.—**Reverseless**, rē-vėrs'les, *a.* Not to be reversed; irreversible. — **Reversely**, rē-vėrs'li, *adv.* In a reverse manner; on the opposite.—**Reverser**, rē-vėr'sėr, *n.* One who reverses.—**Reversibility**, rē-vėr'si-bil"i-ti, *n.* The quality of being reversible; the capability of being reversed.—**Reversible**, rē-vėr'si-bl, *n.* Capable of being reversed; capable of being turned outside in.—**Reversibly**, rē-vėr'si-bli, *adv.* In a reversible manner.—**Reversion**, rē-vėr'-shon, *n.* [L. *reversio.*] A reverting or returning; succession to a post or office after the present holder's term; *biol.* a return towards some ancestral type or character; atavism; *law*, the returning of an estate to the grantor or his heirs; a remainder.—**Reversionary**, rē-vėr'shon-a-ri, *a.* Involving or pertaining to a reversion.—**Reversioner**, rē-vėr'shon-ėr, *n.* One who has a reversion.—**Revert**, rē-vėrt', *v.t.* [L. *reverto—re*, back, and *verto*, to turn.] To turn or direct back; to reverse; to repel.—*v.i.* To return or come back to a former position; to turn back; to turn to something spoken of before; to go back to a former condition; *law*, to return to the possession of the donor, or of the former proprietor.—**Reverted**, rē-vėr'ted, *p.* and *a.* Reversed; turned back.—**Reverter**, rē-vėr'tėr, *n.* One who or that which reverts. —**Revertible**, rē-vėr'ti-bl, *a.* Capable of being reverted or returned.— **Revertive**, rē-vėr'tiv, *a.* Tending to revert; reversing. —**Revertively**, rē-vėr'tiv-li, *adv.* By way of reversion.

Revest, rē-vest', *v.t.* To reinvest; to vest again with possession or office.—*v.i.* To revert or return to a former owner.

Revet, rē-vet', *v.t.—revetted, revetting.* [Fr. *revêtir*, to reclothe; L.L. *revestio*—L. *re*, again, and *vestio*, to clothe.] *Fort.* and *civil engin.* to face, as an embankment, with mason-work or other material.—**Revetment**, rē-vet'ment, *n.* *Fort.* a facing to a wall or bank, as of a scarp or parapet; *civil engin.* a retaining or breast wall.

Revibrate, rē-vī'brāt, *v.i.* To vibrate in return or again. — **Revibration**, rē-vī-brā'shon, *n.* The act of revibrating.

Revictual, rē-vit'l, *v.t.* To victual again; to furnish again with provisions.

Review, rē-vū', *v.t.* [Prefix *re*, again, and *view.*] To view or behold again; to revise; to notice critically; to write a critical notice of, after an examination in order to discover excellences or defects (to *review* a newly published book); to inspect; to make a formal or official examination of the state of, as of troops (to *review* a regiment); to look back on.—*n.* A second or repeated view; a re-examination; a critical examination of a new publication, with remarks; a criticism; a critique; the name given to certain periodical publications, consisting of essays, with critical examinations of new publications; an official inspection of military or naval forces, which may be accompanied by manœuvres and evolutions.—*v.i.* To make reviews; to be a reviewer (he *reviews* for the *Times*). — **Reviewable**, rē-vū'a-bl, *a.* Capable of being reviewed.— **Reviewer**, rē-vū'ėr, *n.* One that reviews; a writer in a review; one who critically examines a new publication.

Revile, rē-vīl', *v.t.—reviled, reviling.* [*Re* and *vile.*] To assail with opprobrious and contemptuous language; to vilify; to speak evil of. — **Revilement**, rē-vīl'ment, *n.* The act of reviling.—**Reviler**, rē-vī'lėr, *n.* One who reviles.

Revindicate, rē-vin'di-kāt, *v.t.* To vindicate again; to reclaim.

Revise, rē-vīz', *v.t.—revised, revising.* [Fr. *reviser*; L. *reviso—re*, again, and *viso*, to look at attentively, intens. of *video*, *visum*, to see. VISION.] To examine or re-examine and make corrections on; to look over with care for correction; to review and amend.—*Revised Version of the Bible*, a modernized form of the Authorized Version, first published complete in 1885.—*n.* A revision; a re-examination and correction; *printing*, a second or further proof-sheet corrected.—**Reviser**, rē-vī'zėr, *n.* One that revises.—**Revisal**, rē-vī'zal, *n.* The act of revising; a revision.—**Revision**, rē-vizh'on, *n.* The act of revising; a re-examination for correction; that which is revised.—**Revisional**, **Revisionary**, rē-vizh'on-al, rē-vizh'on-a-ri, *a.* Pertaining to revision. — **Revisory**, rē-vī'zo-ri, *a.* Having power to revise; effecting revision.

Revisit, rē-viz'it, *v.t.* To visit again; to come to see again.—**Revisitation**, rē-viz'i-tā"shon, *n.* The act of revisiting.

Revitalize, rē-vī'tal-īz, *v.t.* To restore vitality to; to bring back to life.

Revive, rē-vīv', *v.i.* — *revived, reviving.* [Fr. *revivre*; L. *re*, again, and *vivo*, to live. VITAL.] To return to life; to recover life; to recover new life or vigour; to be reanimated after depression; to recover from a state of neglect, oblivion, obscurity, or depression.—*v.t.* To bring again to life; to reanimate; to raise from depression or discouragement; to quicken; to refresh; to bring again into notice or vogue (to *revive* a scheme); to renew in the mind or memory. — **Reviver**, rē-vī'vėr, *n.* One who or that which revives.—**Revivification**, rē-viv'i-fi-kā"shon, *n.* The act of recalling to life.—**Revivify**, rē-viv'i-fī, *v.t.* —*revivified, revivifying.* [Fr. *revivifier*—L. *re*, again, *vivus*, living, *facio*, to make.] To recall to life; to give new life or vigour to. — **Reviviscence**, **Reviviscency**, rev-i-vis'ens, rev-i-vis'en-si, *n.* The state of reviving; renewal of life.—**Reviviscent**, rev-i-vis'ent, *a.* [L. *reviviscens*, ppr. of *revivisco*, to come to life again.] Reviving; regaining or restoring life or action.—**Revivable**, rē-vī'va-bl, *a.* Capable of being revived.—**Revival**, rē-vī'val, *n.* The act of reviving, or the state of being revived; recovery from apparent death; return to activity from a state of languor or depression; recovery from a state of neglect; a renewed and more active attention to religion; an awakening among large numbers of men to their spiritual concerns.—**Revivalism**, rē-vī'val-izm, *n.* The spirit of religious revivals; excited feeling with respect to religion.—**Revivalist**, rē-vī'val-ist, *n.* One who promotes revivals of religion.

Revoke, rē-vōk', *v.t.* — *revoked, revoking.* [Fr. *révoquer*, from L. *revocare—re*, back, and *voco*, to call. VOICE.] To call back; to annul by recalling or taking back; to make void; to cancel; to repeal; to reverse. —*v.i.* *Card playing*, to neglect to follow suit when the player can follow.—*n.* *Card playing*, the act of renouncing or failing to follow suit.—**Revokement**, rē-vōk'ment, *n.* Revocation; reversal. — **Revocable**, rev'ō-ka-bl, *a.* [L. *revocabilis.*] Capable of being revoked.—**Revocableness**, **Revocability**, rev'ō-ka-bl-nes, rev'ō-kā-bil"-i-ti, *n.* The quality of being revocable. — **Revocably**, rev'ō-ka-bli, *adv.* In a revocable manner. — **Revocation**, rev-ō-kā'-shon, *n.* [L. *revocatio.*] The act of recalling, revoking, or annulling; reversal; repeal.—**Revocatory**, rē-vō'ka-to-ri, *a.* Tending to revoke.

Revolt, rē-vōlt', *v.i.* [Fr. *révolter*, from It. *rivoltare*, *revoltare*, to revolt—*re*, and *volte*, *volta*, a volt, bounding, turn, from L. *volvo*, *volutum*, to roll. REVOLVE, VOLT.] To desert or go over to the opposite side; to renounce allegiance and subjection; to rise against a government in rebellion; to rebel; to be grossly offended or disgusted: with *at.*—*v.t.* To repel; to shock.—*n.* The act of revolting; change of sides; a renunciation of allegiance and subjection to one's government; rebellion. ∴ Syn. under INSURRECTION.—**Revolter**, rē-vōl'tėr, *n.* One who revolts.—**Revolting**, rē-vōl'ting, *a.* Causing abhorrence or extreme disgust. — **Revoltingly**, rē-vōl'ting-li, *adv.* In a revolting manner.

Revolute, **Revolutive**, rev'ō-lūt, rē-vol'ū-tiv, *a.* [L. *revolutus*, from *revolvo.* REVOLVE.] Rolled or curled backwards or downwards; *bot.* rolled spirally back or toward the lower surface.

Revolution, rev-ō-lū'shon, *n.* [L. *revolutio*, *revolutionis*, a revolving, from *revolvo*, *revolutum*, to revolve. REVOLVE.] The act of revolving or rotating; rotation; the circular motion of a body on its axis; the course or motion of a body round a centre; one complete circuit made by a heavenly body round a centre; a cycle of time; a radical change of circumstances or of system; a sudden and violent change of government, or in the political constitution of a country, mainly brought about by internal causes; in *Amer. hist.* the Revolutionary War or War of Independence (1775-83); in *Eng. hist.* applied distinctively to the convulsion by which James II was driven from the throne in 1688; *French Revolution*, a term usually applied to the violent reaction against absolutism, which began in 1789.—**Revolutionary**, rev-ō-lū'shon-a-ri, *a.* Pertaining to a revolution in government; tending to produce a revolution.—*n.* A person disposed towards a revolution.—**Revolutionism**, rev-ō-lū'shon-izm, *n.* Revolutionary principles. — **Revolutionist**, rev-ō-lū'shon-ist, *n.* The favorer of a revolution. — **Revolutionize**, rev-ō-lū'shon-īz, *v.t.* To bring about a revolution in; to effect a complete change in.

Revolve, rē-volv', *v.i.—revolved, revolving.* [L. *revolvo—re*, again, and *volvo*, to roll (as in *convolve*, *devolve*, *evolve*, &c.). WALLOW.] To turn or roll round an axis; to rotate; to move round a centre; to circle; to move in an orbit; to pass away in cycles or periods (the years *revolve*).—*v.t.* To cause to turn round; to turn over and over in the mind; to meditate on.—**Revolver**, rē-vol'vėr, *n.* One who or that which revolves; a firearm (generally a pistol) having a revolving barrel or breech cylinder so constructed as to discharge several shots in quick succession without being reloaded.—**Revolving**, rē-vol'ving, *p.* and *a.* Turning; moving round. —*Revolving light*, in *lighthouses*, an arrangement such that there is exhibited once in one or two minutes a light gradually increasing to full strength, and then decreasing to total darkness; or a red and a white light may be exhibited alternately. —*Revolving storm*, a cyclone.

Revomit, rē-vom'it, *v.t.* To vomit or pour forth again; to reject from the stomach.

Revue, rē-vū', *n.* [Fr.] A loosely-constructed and spectacular theatrical exhibition of a topical character, depending on scenic and staging effects.

Revulsion, rē-vul'shon, *n.* [L. *revulsio*, from *revello*, *revulsum—re*, again, and *vello*, to pull.] A violent separation; a sudden and violent change of feeling; *med.* the diverting of a disease from an organ in which it seems to have taken its seat.—**Revulsive**, rē-vul'siv, *a.* Having the power of revulsion.—*n.* A medicine used for the power of revulsion.

Rewaken, rē-wā'kn, *v.t.* and *i.* To waken again.

Reward, rē-ward', *v.t.* [O.Fr. *rewarder*, from *re* and the Teutonic word *ward* = *guard*, so that *reward* = *regard.* WARD.] To give something to in return, either good or evil; to requite: commonly in a good sense; to bestow a recompense, remuneration, or token of favour upon: when evil is returned for injury *reward* signifies to punish.—*n.* That which is given in return for good or evil done or received, especially that which is in return for good; recompense; in a bad sense, punishment or requital of evil; the fruit of men's labour or works; a sum of money offered for taking or detecting a criminal, or for the recovery of anything lost.—**Rewardable**, rē-war'da-bl, *a.* Worthy of recompense.—**Rewarder**, rē-war'dėr, *n.* One who rewards. **Rewardless**, rē-ward'les, *a.* Having no reward.

Rewin, rē-win', *v.t.* To win again.

Rewrite, rē-rīt', *v.t.* To write a second time; to write over again.

Reynard, rā'närd. RENARD.

Rhabdoidal, rab'doi-dal, *a.* [Gr. *rhabdos*, a rod, *eidos*, resemblance.] Rodlike; in the shape of a rod.

Rhabdomancy, rab'dō-man-si, *n.* [Gr. *rhabdos*, a rod, and *manteia*, divination.] Divination by a rod or wand; the discovery of things concealed in the earth, as ores of metals and springs of water by a divining-rod.

Rhachitis, ra-kī'tis, *n.* The rickets.

Rhadamanthine, Rhadamantine, rad-a-man'thin, rad-a-man'tin, *a.* [From *Rhadamanthus*, one of the three judges of the lower world among the Greeks.] Severely or rigorously just.

Rhætian, rē'shi-an, *a.* and *n.* Pertaining to the ancient Rhæti, or their country Rhætia (Tyrol, Grisons); a native or inhabitant of Rhætia.—**Rhætic**, rē'tik, *a.* Belonging to the Rhætian Alps; the name of strata extensively developed in the Alps, and lying between the trias and lias. —**Rhæto-Romanic**, *n.* A Romance tongue spoken in South Switzerland.

Rhamadan, ram'a-dan, *n.* RAMADAN.

Rhaphe, rā'fē, *n.* *Bot.* same as *Raphe.*

Rhapsody, rap'sō-di, *n.* [Gr. *rhapsōdia*, —*rhaptō*, *rhapsō*, to sew, and *ōdē*, a song. ODE.] Originally, a short epic poem, or portion of a longer epic such as would be recited by a rhapsodist at one time; a spoken or written work of an ecstatic sort, depending less on logical structure than emotional appeal; a musical composition of irregular form, resembling an improvisation, usually instrumental.—**Rhapsodic Rhapsodical**, rap-sod'ik, rap-sod'i-kal, *a.* Pertaining to or consisting of rhapsody. —**Rhapsodically**, rap-sod'i-kal-li, *adv.* In the manner of rhapsody.—**Rhapsodist**, rap'so-dist, *n.* Among the ancient Greeks one who composed, recited, or sang poems; one whose profession was to recite or sing the verses of Homer and other poets; one who utters disconnected discourse.—**Rhapsodize**, rap'sō-diz, *v.t.* —*rhapsodized*, *rhapsodizing*.

Rhatany, rat'a-ni. RATANY.

Rhea, rē'a, *n.* The three-toed ostrich of S. America.

Rhea, Rhea-fibre, rē'a, *n.* [Name in Assam.] A valuable East Indian fibre, the produce of a species of nettle, used for textile purposes. Called also *Ramee, China Grass.*

Rhematic, rē-mat'ik, *a.* [Gr. *rhēma*, a word, a verb, from *rheō*, to speak.] Pertaining to verbs; verbal.

Rhenish, ren'ish, *a.* Pertaining to the River Rhine (*Rhenish* wine).—*n.* Rhenish wine or Rhine wine.

Rheochord, rē'ō-kord, *n.* [Gr. *rheō*, to flow, and *chordē*, a chord.] A metallic wire used in measuring the resistance, or varying the strength of an electric current.—**Rheometer**, rē-om'et-ėr, *n.* [Gr. *rheō*, to flow, and *metron*, measure.] Another name for the electrometer or galvanometer. —**Rheometric**, rē-ō-met'rik, *a.* Pertaining to a rheometer or its use —**Rheometry**, rē-om'et-ri, *n.* The use of the rheometer.—**Rheomotor**, rē'ō-mō-tėr, *n.* [Gr. *rheō*, and L. *motor*, a mover.] Any apparatus by which an electric current is originated.—**Rheoscope**, rē'ō-skōp, *n.* [Gr. *rheō*, and *skopeō*, to view.] An instrument by which the existence of an electric current may be ascertained.—**Rheostat**, rē'ō-stat, *n.* [Gr. *rheō*, and *statos*, standing.] An instrument for regulating the strength of an electric current by means of adjustable resistances. —**Rheotome**, rē'ō-tōm, *n.* [Gr. *rheō*, and *tomos*, cutting.] An instrument for interrupting a current.—**Rheotrope**, rē'ō-trōp, *n.* [Gr. *rheō*, and *tropos*, a turn.] An instrument for reversing a current. [Of these terms in *rheo-*, only *rheostat* is now in use.]

Rhesus, rē'sus, *n.* A small monkey held sacred in India.

Rhetoric, ret'o-rik, *n.* [Fr. *rhétorique*, L. *rhetorica*, from Gr. *hē rhētorikē* (*technē*, art, understood), from *rhētōr*, a public speaker, from *rheō*, to speak.] The art or branch of knowledge which treats of the rules or principles underlying all effective composition whether in prose or verse; the art which teaches oratory; the rules that govern the art of speaking with propriety, elegance, and force; rhetoric exhibited in language; eloquence, especially artificial eloquence; flashy oratory; declamation.—**Rhetorical**, re-tor'i-kal, *a.* Pertaining to, exhibiting, or involving rhetoric.—**Rhetorically**, re-tor'i-kal-li, *adv.* In a rhetorical manner; according to the rules of rhetoric. —**Rhetorician**, ret-o-rish'an, *n.* One who teaches the art of rhetoric; one well versed in the rules and principles of rhetoric; a declaimer.—**Rhetorize**, rē-tor-īz, *v.i.* To play the orator.

Rheum, rūm, *n.* [Gr. *rheuma*, a flowing, rheum, from *rheō*, to flow.] A thin serous fluid secreted by the mucous glands, &c., as in catarrh; humid matter which collects in the eyes, nose, or mouth.—**Rheumy**, rū'mi, *a.* Full of rheum or watery matter; causing rheum.—**Rheumatism**, rū'ma-tizm, *n.* [Gr. *rheumatismos*, from *rheuma* —the ancients supposing the disease to proceed from a defluxion of humours.] A painful inflammation affecting muscles and joints of the human body, attended by swelling and stiffness.—**Rheumatic, Rheumatical**, rū-mat'ik, rū-mat'i-kal, *a.* [L. *rheumaticus*.] Pertaining to rheumatism or partaking of its nature; affected with rheumatism.

Rhime, rīm. RHYME.

Rhinal, rī'nal, *a.* [Gr. *rhis*, *rhinos*, the nose.] Pertaining to the nose.—**Rhinencephalic**, rī-nen'sē-fal"ik, *n.* [Gr. *rhis*, *rhinos*, and *enkephalos*, the brain.] Pertaining to the nose and brain or to the portion of the brain from which rise the olfactory nerves.

Rhino, rī'nō, *n.* [Slang.] Money, cash.

Rhinoceros, rī-nos'e-ros, *n.* [L. *rhinoceros*; Gr. *rhinokerōs*, nose-horn—*rhis*, *rhinos*, the nose, and *keras*, a horn.] A large ungainly hoofed animal nearly allied to the hippopotamus, the tapir, &c., having a very thick skin which is usually thrown into deep folds, and deriving its name from the nasal bones usually supporting one or two horns, composed of matter somewhat analogous to that of hair.—**Rhinocerial**, rī-nō-sē'ri-al, *a.* Pertaining to the rhinoceros.

Rhinolith, rī'nō-lith, *n.* [Gr. *rhis*, *rhinos*, nose, *lithos*, stone.] A concretion formed in the nose.—**Rhinologist**, rī-nol'ō-jist, *n.* One with a special knowledge of diseases of the nose.

Rhinoplastic, rī-nō-plas'tik, *a.* [Gr. *rhis*, *rhinos*, the nose, and *plassō*, to form.] Forming a nose.—*Rhinoplastic operation*, a surgical operation for forming an artificial nose, or restoring a nose partly lost.

Rhinoscope, rī'nō-skōp, *n.* [Gr. *rhis*, *rhinos*, the nose, and *skopeō*, to view.] A small mirror for inspecting the passages of the nose.—**Rhinoscopic**, rī-nō-skop'ik, *a.* Pertaining to the rhinoscope.—**Rhinoscopy**, rī-nos'ko-pi, *n.* Use of the rhinoscope.

Rhizanth, rī'zanth, *n.* [Gr. *rhiza*, a root, and *anthos*, a flower.] A plant of a class destitute of true leaves, but with short amorphous stems, parasitical on roots.

Rhizocarpous, rī-zō-kär'pus, *a.* [Gr. *rhiza*, a root, and *karpos*, fruit.] *Bot.* having roots that endure many years, though the stems perish annually.

Rhizodont, rī'zō-dont, *n.* [Gr. *rhiza*, a root, and *odous*, *odontos*, a tooth.] A term applied to reptiles whose teeth, like those of the crocodiles, are planted in sockets.

Rhizogen, rī'zō-gen, *n.* [Gr. *rhiza*, a root, root *gen*, to produce.] A parasitic plant growing on the roots of others.

Rhizoid, rīz'oid, *n.* [Gr. *rhiza*, a root, *eidos*, form.] In mosses, &c., one of the hair-like structures acting as roots.

Rhizome, Rhizoma, rī'zōm or riz'om, rī-zō'ma, *n.* [Gr. *rhizōma*, a root from *rhiza*, a root.] *Bot.* a stem running along the surface of the ground, or partially subterranean, sending forth shoots at its upper end and decaying at the other, as in the ferns, iris, &c.

Rhizomorphous, rī-zō-mor'fus, *a.* [Gr. *rhiza*, a root, *morphē*, shape.] Rootlike in form.

Rhizophagous, rī-zof'a-gus, *a.* [Gr. *rhiza*, a root, and *phagō*, to eat.] Feeding on roots.

Rhizophorous, rī-zof'ō-rus, *a.* [Gr. *rhiza*, root, and *pherō*, to bear.] *Bot.* root-bearing.

Rhizopoda, rī-zop'o-da, *n.pl.* [Gr. *rhiza*, a root, and *pous*, *podos*, a foot.] The lowest class of the Protozoa; minute animals destitute of a mouth and capable of protruding rootlike or finger-shaped masses from any part of their substance.

Rhizotaxis, rī-zō-tak'sis, *n.* [Gr. *rhiza*, a root, and *taxis*, arrangement.] *Bot.* the arrangement of the roots.

Rhodesian skull, ro-dē'zi-an, *n.* A human skull of primitive type discovered in the Broken Hill Mine in Northern Rhodesia in November, 1921.

Rhodes-wood, rōdz, *n.* The wood of a West Indian tree. Called also *Candlewood.*

Rhodium, rō'di-um, *n.* [From Gr. *rhodon*, a rose, on account of the red colour of some of its salts when dissolved in water.] A rare metal found associated with palladium in the ore of platinum, which it resembles in its general and chemical properties.—**Rhodium oil**, *n.* A volatile rose-scented oil from plants of the convolvulus kind, used as a perfume; also a fragrant oil prepared artificially.

Rhododendron, rō-dō-den'dron, *n.* [Gr. *rhododendron*, lit. rose-tree—*rhodon*, a rose, and *dendron*, a tree.] A genus of highly-prized evergreen shrubs, with beautiful flowers disposed in corymbs, occurring both in the New and Old Worlds, especially in the Himalayas.

Rhodomontade, rod'ō-mon-tād, *n.* RODOMONTADE.

Rhomb, Rhombus, rom, rom'bus, *n.* [Fr. *rhombe*, L. *rhombus*, from Gr. *rhombos*.] A quadrilateral figure whose sides are equal and the opposite sides parallel, but the angles not right angles; a figure of a diamond or lozenge form; a solid bounded by six equal and similar rhombic planes; a rhombohedron.—**Rhombic**, rom'bik, *a.* Having the figure of a rhomb; in crystallography, the system of crystals having three unequal axes mutually at right angles. TRIMETRIC.—**Rhombohedral**, rom-bō-hē'dral, *a.* Relating to a rhombohedron.—**Rhombohedron**, rom-bō-hē'dron, *n.* [Gr. *rhombos*, and *hedra*, a side.] A solid bounded by six rhombic planes.—**Rhomboid**, rom'boid, *n.* A quadrilateral figure whose opposite sides and angles are equal, but which is neither equilateral nor equiangular; a solid having a rhomboidal form. —*a.* In the form of a rhomboid; rhomboidal; diamond-shaped.—**Rhomboidal**, rom-boi'dal, *a.* Having the shape of a rhomboid. **Rhomb-spar**, *n.* A mineral of a grayish white, occurring in rhomboids, embedded in chlorite slate, limestone, &c.

Rhonchus, rong'kus, *n.* [L., from Gr. *rhonchos*, a snoring sound.] *Med.* the deep snoring which accompanies inspiration in some diseases, particularly in apoplexy; stertor.—**Rhonchal**, rong'kal, *a.* Pertaining to rhonchus.

Rhopalocerous, rō-pa-los'ėr-us, *a.* [Gr. *rhopalon*, a club, and *keras*, a horn.] Having antennæ terminating with a small club, said of certain insects.

Rhubarb, rö'bärb, *n.* [Fr. *rhubarbe*; L.L. *rheubarbarum*; Gr. *rhēon barbaron*, from *Rha*, a name of the river Volga (where the plant is native), and *barbaron*, barbarian.] The common name of a large herbaceous plant which yields leaf-stalks used for making tarts, &c., and some species of which have roots used in medicine, being aperient, and at the same time tonic and astringent.

Rhumb, rum, *n.* [From *rhomb.*] *Navig.* a line which makes any given angle with the meridian; one of the thirty-two points of the compass; a rhumb-line.—**Rhumb-line**, *n.* *Navig.* a line described by the course of a ship sailing steadily in any one direction except towards any of the cardinal points; a loxodromic curve.

Rhusma, rus'ma, *n.* A mixture of caustic lime and orpiment, used in removing hair from hides.

Rhyme, rīm, *n.* [O.E. *ryme*, *rime*, from A.Sax. *rím*, number, rhyme = Icel. *rím*, D. *rijm*, Dan. *riim*, G. *reim*, rhyme. The proper spelling is *rime*; the *h* has been inserted by influence of L. *rhythmus*. Gr. *rhythmos*, rhythm.] A correspondence of sound in the final portions of two or more syllables, more especially the correspondence in sound of the terminating word or syllable of one line of poetry with the terminating word or syllable of another; poetry; metre; a composition in verse; a poem, especially a short one; a verse, word, or termination rhyming with another.—*Male* or *masculine rhymes*, rhymes in which only the final syllables agree, as *strain*, *complain*.—*Female* or *feminine rhymes*, rhymes in which the two final syllables agree, the first being accented, as *motion*, *potion*.—*Rhyme royal*, a stanza of seven ten-syllable lines in the formation *ababbcc*, possibly from its use by James I of Scotland in *The King's Quair*.—The words *rhyme* and *reason* are often used in combination and negatively to imply lack of common sense or irrational conduct; as to act without *rhyme* or *reason*, to act recklessly, or without due thought and consideration.—*v.i.*—*rhymed*, *rhyming*. To accord in the terminational sounds; to form a rhyme; to make verses. —*v.t.* To put into rhyme.—**Rhymeless**, rīm'les, *a.* Destitute of rhyme.—**Rhymer**, rī'mėr, *n.* One who makes rhymes; a poor poet.—**Rhymster**, rīm'stėr, *n.* A rhymer; a poor or mean poet.

Rhynchonella, rin-ko-nel'la, *n.* [A dim. from Gr. *rhynchos*, a beak.] An extensive genus of brachiopods, of which many are fossil, with an acutely beaked shell.

Rhysimeter, rī-sim'e-tėr, *n.* [Gr. *rhysis*, a flowing, and *metron*, a measure.] An instrument for measuring the velocity of fluids or the speed of ships.

Rhythm, Rhythmus, rithm, rith'mus, *n.* [L. *rhythmus*, from Gr. *rhythmos*, any regularly recurring vibratory motion, from root of *rheō*, to flow.] The measure of time or movement by regularly recurring impulses, sounds, &c., as in poetry, prose composition, and music, and by analogy, dancing; periodical emphasis; numerical proportion or harmony; rhyme; metre; verse; number.—**Rhythmic, Rhythmical**, rith'mik, rith'mi-kal, *a.* Pertaining to rhythm; having rhythm.—**Rhythmically**, rith'mi-kal-li, *adv.* In a rhythmical manner.—**Rhythmics**, rith'miks, *n.* That branch of music which treats of the length of sounds and of emphasis.—**Rhythmless**, rithm'les, *a.* Destitute of rhythm.—**Rhythmometer**, rith-mom'et-ėr, *n.* An instrument for marking time to movements in music. METRONOME.

Rial, rī'al, *n.* [An old form of *royal.*] A gold coin of varying value, formerly current in Britain. Spelled also *Ryal*.

Riant, rē-äṅ, *a.* [Fr. ppr. of *rire*, to laugh.] Laughing; gay; smiling.—**Riancy**, rē'an-si, *n.* Character of being riant; cheerfulness; gaiety.

Rib, rib, *n.* [A.Sax. *rib*, *ribb*=D. *rib*, *ribbe*, L.G. *ribbe*, Dan. *rib*, G. *rippe*, Icel. *rif*, a rib.] One of the curved bones springing from the vertebral column and inclosing a certain number of the important organs and viscera in man and other vertebrate animals; something resembling a rib in form, use, position, &c., as one of the bent timber or metallic bars which spring from the keel, and form or strengthen the side of a ship; a piece of timber or iron supporting an arched roof, as in domes, vaults, &c.; one of the principal veins or nerves in leaves of plants; one of the rods on which the cover of an umbrella is stretched; a prominent line or rising on cloth, as in corduroy.—*v.t.*—*ribbed*, *ribbing*. To furnish with ribs; to plough so as to leave riblike ridges somewhat apart.—**Ribbed**, ribd, *p.* and *a.* Furnished with ribs; inclosed as with ribs; marked with rising lines and channels.—**Ribbing**, rib'ing, *n.* An assemblage or arrangement of ribs, as of a vaulted ceiling, on cloth, &c.; a kind of imperfect ploughing, every alternate strip only being moved.—**Rib-grass**, *n.* A common British plant belonging to the plantain genus.—**Ribless**, rib'les, *a.* Having no ribs.

Ribald, rib'ald, *n.* [O.Fr. *ribauld*, *ribault*, *ribaud*, lecherous; It. *ribaldo*, a ribald person, from O.H.G. *hribâ*, *hripa*, a prostitute.] A low, vulgar, brutal wretch; a lewd, coarse fellow; a foul-mouthed fellow.—*a.* Low; mean; vile; obscene.—**Ribaldrous**, rib'ald-rus, *a.* Containing ribaldry. —**Ribaldry**, rib'ald-ri, n. The talk of a ribald; obscene language; indecency.

Riband, rib'and, *n.* RIBBON.

Ribbon, Riband, rib'on, rib'and, *n.* [O.E. *ribane*, *riban*, *ribant*, &c., from O. and Prov.Fr. *riban*, Mod.Fr. *ruban*, perhaps from the Celtic; comp. Gael. *ribean*, a ribbon, a fillet for the hair; *rib*, *ribe*, a hair; Ir. *ribin*, a ribbon.] A fillet of silk, satin, &c.; a narrow web of silk, satin, or other material, generally used for an ornament, or for fastening some part of female dress; what resembles a ribbon in some respects; a narrow, thin strip of anything; a shred (sails torn to *ribbons*).—*Blue ribbon* and *red ribbon*, often used to designate the orders of the Garter and Bath respectively, the badge of the former being supported by a blue ribbon, and that of the latter by a red ribbon. BLUE-RIBBON.—**Ribbon**, rib'on, *v.t.* To adorn or furnish with ribbons.—**Ribbon-fish**, *n.* A fish with a lengthened body much flattened on the sides.—**Ribbon-grass**, *n.* Canary-grass. —**Ribbonism**, rib'on-izm, *n.* The principles of a secret association of Irishmen, which had its origin about 1808, and was antagonistic to the Orangemen; so named from the piece of *ribbon* the members wore as a badge.—**Ribbon-jasper**, *n.* Jasper in which the colours are arranged in parallel layers or stripes, like ribbons.—**Ribbonman**, rib'on-man, *n.* An adherent of Ribbonism.—**Ribbon-saw**, *n.* BAND-SAW.—**Ribbon-worm**, *n.* A nemertid.

Ricardian, ri-car'di-an, *a.* Of or belonging to the doctrines of David Ricardo (1772-1823), political economist.

Rice, rīs, *n.* [O.Fr. *ris*, from L. *oryza*, from Gr. *oryza*, rice; of oriental origin.] A well-known cereal plant and its seed, probably a native of India, but now cultivated in all warm climates, the grain forming a large portion of the food of the inhabitants. —**Rice-bird**, *n.* A bird of the United States, allied to the buntings, so named from its feeding on rice. Called also *bobolink*, and *rice-bunting*.—**Rice-dust**, *n.* The refuse of rice which remains when it is cleaned for the market; rice-meal, a valuable food for cattle.—**Rice-flour**, *n.* Ground rice for making puddings, &c.—**Rice-milk**, *n.* Milk boiled and thickened with rice.—**Rice-paper**, *n.* Paper made from rice straw, used in Japan and elsewhere; also, a substance prepared from the pith of a certain plant, brought from China, where it is used for painting upon and for the manufacture of fancy and ornamental articles.—**Rice-pudding**, *n.* A pudding made of milk and rice, with eggs and sugar.

Rich, rich, *a.* [Partly from A.Sax. *rice*, rich, powerful, partly from Fr. *riche*, rich, the latter being from O.H.G. *rîche*, rich, which again is cog. with A.Sax. *rice*, Icel. *rikr*, Goth. *reiks*, rich, the root being that of E. *right*.] Having abundant material possessions; wealthy: opposed to *poor*; hence, generally, well supplied; abounding; producing ample supplies; productive; fertile; composed of valuable or costly materials or ingredients; sumptuous; highly valued; costly; abounding in nutritive or agreeable qualities; especially, as applied to articles of food and drink, sweet, luscious, or highly flavoured; largely gratifying the sense of sight; vivid; bright; agreeable to the sense of hearing; sweet; mellow; abounding in humour; highly provocative of amusement (a *rich* joke).—*The rich*, as a noun, rich men.—**Riches**, rich'ez, *n.* [Formerly *richesse*, from Fr. *richesse* (singular noun), from *riche*, rich.] That which makes rich; abundant possessions; wealth; affluence. This word is really in the singular number, but is very rarely so used, the apparently plural termination having caused it to be regarded as a plural.—**Richly**, rich'li, *adv.* In a rich manner; with riches; opulently; abundantly; splendidly; magnificently; highly.—**Richness**, rich'nes, *n.* The state or quality of being rich; opulence; productiveness; fertility; magnificence; costliness; lusciousness; brilliancy; sweetness.

Ricinine, ris'i-nīn, *n.* [From L. *ricinus*, the castor-oil plant.] An alkaloid contained in the seeds of the castor-oil plant.

Rick, rik, *n.* [A.Sax. *hreác*, a rick; cog. Icel. *hraukr*, a pile, W. *crug*, Ir. *cruach*, a heap, rick.] A stack or pile of corn or hay, the lower part generally of a cylindrical form, and the top part rounded or conical, and often thatched so as to protect the pile from rain.—*v.t.* To pile up in ricks.—**Rick-stand**, *n.* A frame of timber or iron on which ricks or stacks are built.

Rickets, rik'ets, *n.* [From old *wrick*, *wrikken*, to twist; allied to *wring*, *wriggle*.] A disease of children in which there is usually some distortion of the bones, due to faulty deposition of calcium, caused by vitamin-deficiency and lack of sunlight.—**Rickety**, rik'et-i, *a.* Affected with rickets; feeble or imperfect in general; shaky.

Rickshaw, rik'sha, *n.* See *Jinrikishaw*.

Ricochet, rik'o-shet, *n.* [Fr.; etym. unknown.] A rebounding from a flat surface, as of a stone from water or of a cannon-ball from the ground.—*Ricochet fire*, the firing of guns or mortars so as to cause balls or shells to roll or bound along.—*Ricochet battery*, a battery for firing in this manner.—*v.t.* (rik-o-shet')—*ricochetted*, *ricochetting*. To operate upon by ricochet firing.—*v.i.* To skim, as a stone, along the surface of water; to strike and fly onward, as a cannon-ball.

Rid, rid, *v.t.*—*rid* or *ridded* (pret. and pp.); *ridding*. [A.Sax. *hreddan*, to take or snatch; akin to Icel. *rydja* (*rythja*), Dan. *rydde*, to clear, to remove; D. *redden*, G. *retten*, to rescue.] To free; to deliver; to clear; to disencumber (to *rid* a person *of* pain, *of* a burden); to make away with†; to remove by violence (*Shak.*)†.—*pp.* or *a.* Free; clear (to be *rid* of trouble).—*To get rid of*, to free one's self from.—**Riddance**, rid'ans, *n.* The act of ridding; a clearing away; a getting rid of something.—*A good riddance*, fortunate relief from something disagreeable.

Ridden, rid'n, pp. of *ride*.

Riddle, rid'l, *n.* [A.Sax. *hridder*, a fan for winnowing; cog. O.H.G. *hritarâ*, a sieve; from same root as L. *cerno*, Gr. *krinō*, to separate, judge. CRITIC.] A kind of large sieve with coarse meshes, employed for separating coarser materials from finer.—*v.t.*—*riddled*, *riddling*. To pass through or separate with a riddle; to perforate with balls, so as to make like a riddle (a house *riddled* with shot).

Riddle, rid'l, *n.* [A.Sax. *raedels*, a riddle, from *raedan*, to read, discern, guess = D. *raadsel*, G. *räthsel*, a riddle. READ.] A proposition put in obscure or ambiguous terms to puzzle or exercise the ingenuity in discovering its meaning; something to be solved by conjecture; a puzzling question; an enigma; anything ambiguous or puzzling.—*v.t.*—*riddled*, *riddling.* To solve; to explain; to unriddle. —*v.i.* To speak ambiguously, obscurely, or enigmatically.

Ride, rīd, *v.i.*—*rode*, pret. *ridden*, pp. *riding*, ppr. [A.Sax. *rīdan*, to ride = L.G. *riden*, D. *rijden*, Icel. *rīda*, Dan. *ride*, G. *reiten*, O.G. *rītan*—to ride. *Raid* and *road*, as well as *ready*, are from this stem.] To travel or be carried on the back of an animal, as on a horse; to travel or be carried in a vehicle, as in a carriage or wagon; to be borne on or in a fluid (a ship *rides* at anchor); to have ability as an equestrian. —*To ride at anchor* (*naut.*), to lie at anchor; to be anchored.—*To ride to hounds*, to ride after hounds in fox-hunting.—*v.t.* To sit or be supported on, so as to be carried (to *ride* a horse); to go over in riding (he *rode* three miles); to tyrannize or domineer over (as in debt-*ridden*).—*To ride down*, to trample on, or drive over in riding; to treat with extreme roughness or insolence.—*To ride out*, to continue afloat during, and withstand the fury of, as a vessel does a gale.—*n.* An excursion on horseback or in a vehicle; a road cut in a wood or through pleasure-ground, for the amusement of riding.—**Ridable**, rī'da-bl, *a.* Capable of being ridden; passable on horseback.—**Rider**, rī'dėr, *n.* One who rides; one who breaks or manages a horse; formerly, a commercial traveler; any addition to a manuscript, or other document, inserted after its first completion; in legislative usage, a clause added to a bill, up for passage, often having nothing to do with the bill itself; certain mechanical parts, which overlie others or move along them. —**Riderless**, rī'dėr-les, *a.* Having no rider.—**Ridersbone**, *n.* A hard lump sometimes forming on the inside of the thigh of persons who ride much.—**Riding**, rī'ding, *p.* and *a.* Employed for riding on (a *riding* horse).—**Riding-habit**, *n.* A garment worn by females when they ride on horseback.—**Riding-hood**, *n.* A hood formerly used by females when they rode; a kind of cloak with a hood.—**Riding-master**, *n.* A teacher of the art of riding.—**Riding-school**, *n.* A place where the art of riding is taught.—**Riding-whip**, *n.* Whip used when riding.

Ridge, rij, *n.* [Softened form of older *rygge*, *rig*, from A.Sax. *hrycg*, *hrick*, a ridge, the back=Sc. *rig*, *rigg*, a ridge of land, Icel. *hryggr*, Dan. *ryg*, Sw. *rygg*, G. *rücken*, the back.] A long and narrow elevation on the earth's surface from which the ground slopes on either side; a long crest or summit (the *ridge* of a mountain, the *ridge* of a wave); a strip of ground thrown up by a plough or left between furrows; a strip of tilled land with a furrow on either side; the highest part of the roof of a building at the meeting of the upper end of the rafters. —*v.t.*—*ridged*, *ridging.* To form or make into a ridge; to furnish with a ridge or ridges.—*v.i.* To rise in ridges.—**Ridge-piece**, **Ridge-plate**, *n.* A piece of timber at the ridge of a roof against which the rafters abut.—**Ridge-roof**, *n.* A raised or peaked roof.—**Ridge-tile**, *n.* A convex tile made for covering the ridge of a roof.—**Ridged**, **Ridgy**, rijd, rij'i, *a.* Having a ridge or ridges; rising in a ridge.

Ridicule, rid'i-kūl, *n.* [Fr. *ridicule*, from L. *ridiculus*, laughable, from *rideo*, *risum*, to laugh (seen also in *deride*, *risible*).] Expression or action intended to convey contempt and excite laughter; contemptuous mockery or jesting; wit of that species which provokes contemptuous laughter; that species of writing which excites contempt with laughter.—*v.t.*—*ridiculed*, *ridiculing.* To treat with ridicule; to mock; to make sport or game of; to deride.—**Ridiculer**, rid'i-kū-lėr, *n.* One that ridicules.—**Ridiculous**, ri-dik'ū-lus, *a.* [L. *ridiculus*, *ridiculosus*.] Worthy of or fitted to excite ridicule; laughable and contemptible.—**Ridiculously**, ri-dik'ū-lus-li, *adv.* In a ridiculous manner.—**Ridiculousness**, ri-dik'ū-lus-nes, *n.*

Riding, rī'ding, *n.* [A.Sax. *thrithing*, a third part, from *thri*, three.] One of the three districts (North, East, and West Ridings) into which the county of York, in England, is divided.

Ridotto, ri-dot'tō, *n.* [It., from L. *reductus*, a retreat. REDOUBT.] In Italy, an entertainment consisting of singing and dancing.

Rifacimento, rē-fä'chē-men"tō, *n.* [It., from L. *re*, again, *facio*, to make.] A re-making or re-establishment: a term most commonly applied to the process of recasting literary works.

Rife, rīf, *a.* [A.Sax. *rȳf*, rife, prevalent= Icel. *rīfr* (allied to *reifa*, to enrich), O.D. *ryf*, *rijf*, plenteous.] Prevailing; prevalent; abundant; common; supplied or filled with in large numbers or great quantity; abounding in; replete.—**Rifely**, rīf'li, *adv.* In a rife manner; prevalently; frequently.—**Rifeness**, rīf'nes, *n.* The state of being rife; frequency; prevalence.

Riffraff, rif'raf, *n.* [A reduplication of *raff*, refuse.] Sweepings; refuse of anything; the rabble.

Rifle, rī'fl, *v.t.*—*rifled*, *rifling.* [O.Fr. *rifler*, *riffler*, to sweep away, a word of Germanic origin, the same stem being seen in *raff*, *raffle.*] To seize and bear away by force; to snatch away; to strip; to rob; to pillage; to plunder. —*v.i.* To rob; to pillage. —**Rifler**, rī'fl-ėr, *n.* One that rifles; one that pillages; a robber.

Rifle, rī'fl, *n.* [Lit. a grooved musket, being connected with Dan. *rifle*, a groove or fluting, *rifle*, to rifle a gun, *riffel*, a rifle; G. *riefeln*, to channel, *riefe*, a groove.] A gun the inside of whose barrel is grooved, or formed with spiral channels; *pl.* a body of troops armed with rifles.—*v.t.*—*rifled*, *rifling.* To groove; to channel.—*Rifled arms*, firearms in which spiral grooves, taking much less than one complete turn, are cut in the surface of the bore, thus giving the projectile greater accuracy and longer range.—**Rifle-ball**, *n.* A ball, generally cylindrical with a conoidal head, for firing with a rifle.—**Rifle-corps**, *n.* A body of soldiers armed with rifles.—**Rifleman**, rī'fl-man, *n.* A soldier armed with a rifle; a sharpshooter.—**Rifle-pit**, *n.* A pit in front of an army, fort, &c., to afford cover to a single skirmisher.

Rift, rift, *n.* [From *rive*; so Dan. *rift*, a rift, a rent.] A cleft; a fissure; an opening made by riving or splitting.—*v.t.* To cleave; to rive; to split.—*v.i.* To burst open; to split.

Rig, rig, *v.t.*—*rigged*, *rigging.* [Same as Dan. *rigge*, to rig; origin doubtful.] To dress; to clothe: generally with *out*, and used only colloquially; to furnish with apparatus or tackling; *naut.* to fit with shrouds, stays, &c.—*n.* Dress, usually gay or fanciful dress; *naut.* the peculiar style of the masts, sails, and rigging of any vessel.—**Rigger**, rig'ėr, *n.* One who rigs; one whose occupation is to fit the rigging of a ship.—**Rigging**, rig'ing, *n.* The ropes which support the masts, extend and contract the sails, &c., of a ship.

Rig, rig, *n.* [Origin doubtful; comp. Manx *reagh*, ruttish, wanton, *riggan*, to rut.] A wanton‡; a strumpet‡; a frolic; a trick.—*To run a rig*, to play a sportive or wanton trick.—*To rig the market*, to raise or lower prices artificially in order to one's private advantage.—**Riggish**, rig'ish, *a.* Wanton‡; lewd‡; frolicsome.

Rigadoon, rig-a-dön', *n.* [Fr. *rigadon*, *rigaudon*, from *Rigaud*, the inventor of the dance.] A gay brisk dance performed by one couple.

Riga-fir, rī'ga, *n.* A variety of the red or Scotch pine or fir, from *Riga*.

Rigescent, ri-jes'ent, *a.* [L. *rigescens*, ppr. of *rigesco*, from *rigeo*, to be stiff. RIGID.] Becoming stiff or rigid.

Right, rīt, *a.* [A.Sax. *riht*, right, true, just, straight=D. *regt*, G. *recht*, O.G. *reht*, Goth. *raihts*, Icel. *réttr*, Dan. *ret*; participial forms cognate with L. *rectus*, straight, pp. of *rego*, *rectum*, to rule, direct (REGENT, REGAL). *Reach* and *rich* are ultimately from same root.] In conformity with the rules which ought to regulate human action; in accordance with duty, truth, and justice, or the will of God; not wrong; just; equitable; fit; suitable; proper (the *right* man in the *right* place); real; true; not spurious (the *right* heir); not erroneous; according to fact or reality; not mistaken or wrong; not in error; not left, but its opposite; originally, no doubt, most useful or dexterous (the *right* hand); hence, being on the same side as the right hand (the *right* ear or eye); most favourable or convenient; opportune; properly done, made, placed, disposed, or adjusted; correct; to be placed or worn outward (the *right* side of cloth); straight; not crooked (a *right* line); hence, *math.* rising perpendicularly; having a perpendicular axis (a *right* cone); formed by one line or direction perpendicular to another (a *right* angle).—*At right angles*, so as to form a right angle or right angles; placed or standing perpendicularly.—*Right ascension.* Under ASCENSION.—*Right bank of a river*, the bank on the right hand of a person whose face is turned in the direction in which the water runs.—*adv.* [A.Sax. *rihte*, rightly.] In a right manner; justly; properly; correctly; in a great degree; very (*right* well; used especially in titles, as *right* honourable, *right* reverend; *right* noble); in a straight line; directly.—*Right and left*, to the right and to the left; in all directions. —*n.* What is right; the opposite of wrong; rectitude; a just claim (a *right* to fair play); legal or other claim or title; a prerogative; privilege belonging to one as member of a state, society, or community (natural, political, public *rights*); that which justly belongs to one; power of action; authority; legal power (a *right* to arrest malefactors); the side opposite to the left (on the *right*).—*Right of way*, the right of passing over land not one's own; the right of the public to a road or path over a certain piece of ground. —*Bill of rights*, the declaration delivered by the two houses of parliament to the Prince of Orange, Feb. 13, 1688, in which the rights and privileges of the people were asserted. —*By right*, *by rights*, rightfully; in accordance with right; properly.—*To be in the right*, to be not wrong or in error; to have justice on one's side.—*To set to rights* or *to put to rights*, to put into good order.—*In one's own right*, by absolute right (peeresses *in their own right*, that is, as opposed to peeresses by marriage).—*v.t.* To put right; to restore to the natural or proper condition; to make correct from being wrong; to do justice to; to relieve from wrong.—*v.i.* To resume a vertical position, as a ship in the water after having been listed over. —**Right-about**, *adv.* In an opposite direction: used substantively in the phrase *to send to the right-about*, to pack off; to dismiss; to cause to retreat.—**Right-angled**, *a.* Containing a right angle or right angles. —**Righter**, rīt'ėr, *n.* One who sets right; one who does justice or redresses wrong.—**Rightful**, rīt'ful, *a.* Having a right or just claim according to established laws (the *rightful* heir); being by right or by just claim (one's *rightful* property); just; consonant to justice (a *rightful* cause).—**Rightfully**, rīt'ful-li, *adv.* In a rightful manner. —**Rightfulness**, rīt'ful-nes, *n.* The state of being rightful.—**Right-hand**, *a.* Situated on the right hand, or in a direction from the right side; applied to one who is essential to another (our *right-hand* man).—**Right-handed**, *a.* Using the right hand more easily and readily than the left.—**Right-handedness**, *n.* The quality of being right-handed; hence, skill; dexterity. —**Rightly**, rīt'li, *adv.* According to right or justice; properly; fitly; suitably; according to truth or fact; not erroneously; correctly.—**Right-minded**, *a.* Having a right or honest mind; well-disposed. —**Right-mindedness**, *n.* The state of being right-minded.—**Rightness**, rīt'nes, *n.* The state or quality of being right; correctness; rectitude.—**Right-whale**, *n.* [That is, the proper one to be caught.] The common or Greenland whale, from whose mouth whalebone is obtained.

Righteous, rīt'yus, *a.* [A.Sax. *rihtwīs*, righteous—*riht*, right, and *wīs*, wise, prudent; similarly Icel. *rétt-víss*, righteous.] Upright; virtuous; acting in accordance with the dictates of religion or morality; free from guilt or sin; agreeing with right; just; equitable.—**Righteously**, rī'tyus-li, *adv.* In a righteous manner; uprightly; justly.—**Righteousness**, rī'tyus-nes, *n.* The quality of being righteous; *theol.* the state of being right with God; justification.

Rigid, rij'id, *a.* [Fr. *rigide*, L. *rigidus*, from *rigeo*, to be stiff or numb; allied to Gr. *rhigeō*, to shiver, *rhigos*, cold; Skr. *rij*, to be stiff.] Stiff; stiffened; not pliant; not easily bent; *physics*, theoretically such as to resist change of form when acted on by any force; strict in opinion, practice, or discipline; severe in temper: opposed to *lax* or *indulgent*; inflexible; unmitigated; severely just (a *rigid* law or rule).—**Rigidity, Rigidness**, ri-jid'i-ti, rij'id-nes, *n.* The quality of being rigid.—**Rigidly**, rij'-id-li, *adv.* In a rigid manner; stiffly; inflexibly; severely; strictly.—**Rigidulous**, ri-jid'ū-lus, *a.* *Bot.* rather stiff.

Rigmarole, rig'ma-rōl, *n.* [A corruption of *ragman-roll*.] A succession of confused or disjointed statements; an incoherent harangue; balderdash.

Rigour, rig'or, *n.* [L. *rigor*, from *rigeo*, to be stiff. RIGID.] Rigidity; severity of life; austerity; strictness; exactness without allowance, latitude, or indulgence (to enforce moral duties with *rigour*); sternness; harshness; intensity of atmospheric cold (the *rigour* of winter); *med.* same as *Rigor*.—**Rigorous**, rig'or-us, *a.* Characterized by rigour; severe; stringent; scrupulously accurate; very cold (*rigorous* weather).—**Rigorously**, rig'or-us-li, *adv.* In a rigorous manner.—**Rigorousness**, rig'or-us-nes, *n.* The state or quality of being rigorous.—**Rigor**, rig'or, *n.* *Med.* a sudden coldness, attended by a shivering more or less perfect: a symptom which ushers in many diseases.—*Rigor mortis*, the stiffening of the body after death.—**Rigorism, Rigourism**, rig'or-izm, *n.* Rigidity in principles or practice.—**Rigorist, Rigourist**, rig'or-ist, *n.* A person of severe or rigid principle or manners; a purist in style.

Rig Veda, *n.* [Sanskrit.] The chief Veda (which see) of the Hindus.

Rile, rīl, *v.t.* [A form of *roil*.] To stir to anger; to irritate. (*Colloq.*)

Rilievo, rē-lē'vō or rē-lē-ā'vō. [It.] Under RELIEF.

Rill, ril, *n.* [Same as L.G. *rille*, a brook, a furrow.] A small brook; a rivulet; a streamlet.—*v.i.* To run in a small stream or in streamlets.—**Rillet**, ril'et, *n.* [Dim. of *rill*.] A small stream; a rivulet.

Rim, rim, *n.* [A.Sax. *rima*, rim, edge, lip; perhaps a Celtic word; comp. W. *rhim*, Armor. *rim*, a rim, a border.] The border, edge, or margin of a thing; a brim; the lower part of the belly or abdomen (*Shak.*).—*v.t.*—*rimmed, rimming.* To be or to form a rim round.

Rime, rīm, *n.* The more correct spelling of *Rhyme*.

Rime, rīm, *n.* [A.Sax. *hrim*, rime = Icel. *hrím*, D. *rijm*, Dan. *riim*, Sw. *rim*—hoar-frost.] White or hoar frost; congealed dew or vapour.—*v.i.*—*rimed, riming.* To freeze or congeal into hoar-frost.—**Rimy**, rī'mi, *a.* Abounding with rime; frosty.

Rimose, Rimous, rī'mōs, rī'mus, *a.* [L. *rimosus*, from *rima*, a fissure or crack.] Full of chinks or fissures.—**Rimosity**, rī-mos'i-ti, *n.* The state of being rimose.

Rimple, rim'pl, *n.* [A.Sax. *hrympelle*, a fold, a rumple; D. *rimpel*, a wrinkle. RUMPLE.] A fold or wrinkle.—*v.t.* and *i.* — *rimpled, rimpling.* To rumple; to wrinkle.

Rind, rīnd, *n.* [A.Sax. *rind, hrind*, bark, crust = G. *rinde*, rind; same root as *rim*.] The outward coat or covering of trees, fruits, animals, &c.; bark; peel; husk; skin.—*v.t.* To take the rind from.

Rinderpest, rin'dėr-pest, *n.* [Gr. *rinder*, pl. of *rind*, a horned beast, and *pest*, a plague.] A most virulent and eminently contagious disease or plague, affecting ruminant animals, especially cattle.

Rinforzando, rin-for-tsan'dō. [It., strengthening.] *Music*, a direction to strengthen the power and emphasis.

Ring, ring, *n.* [A.Sax. *hring* = Icel. *hringr*, G., D., and Sw. *ring*, a ring. Akin are *range, rank, rink, harangue*, &c.] Anything in the form of a circular line or hoop; a circle of gold or other material worn on the fingers; a hoop of metal or other material used for a great variety of purposes; an area in which games or sports are performed; the arena of a hippodrome or circus; the inclosure in which pugilists fight; a space in which horses are exhibited or exercised; a circular group of persons; a combination of persons for a selfish end, as for controlling the market in stocks.—*The ring, the prize ring*, a term given to pugilism or those connected with pugilism. — *Fairy ring.* Under FAIRY.—*Saturn's rings*, rings surrounding and nearly in the planet's equatorial plane, probably composed of swarms of meteorites or minute satellites. — *v.t.* To encircle; to surround with a ring or as with a ring; to make a cutting circularly round (a tree or branch).—**Ring-armour**, *n.* Armour of ring-mail.—**Ring-bolt**, *n.* An iron bolt with an eye, to which is fitted a ring of iron, used in ships.—**Ring-bone**, *n.* A callus growing on the pastern of a horse. — **Ring-course**, *n.* The outer course of stone or brick in an arch.—**Ring-dove**, *n.* A species of pigeon (the cushat or wood-pigeon), so called from a circular marking on the neck.—**Ring-dropping**, *n.* A trick practised by rogues who pretend they have just found a valuable ring and offer to sell it for little, the article they offer being really worthless. — **Ringed**, ringd, *pp.* Surrounded with, or as with, a ring; having a ring or rings; encircled.—**Ringed-snake**, *n.* A harmless British snake. — **Ring-fence**, *n.* A fence continuously encircling an estate or some considerable extent of ground.—**Ring-finger**, *n.* The third finger of the left hand, on which the ring is placed in marriage. — **Ring-gauge**, *n.* A gauge in the form of a ring; a conical gauge, used by jewellers for measuring finger rings.—**Ringleader**, ring'lē-dėr, *n.* One who leads a ring, as of dancers‡; the leader of any association of men engaged in violation of law, or an illegal enterprise. — **Ringlet**, ring'let, *n.* [Dim. of *ring*.] A curl; particularly, a curl of hair.—**Ringleted**, ring'let-ed, *a.* Adorned with ringlets; wearing ringlets.—**Ring-mail**, *n.* Defensive armour made by sewing strong rings of steel edgewise upon leather or strong quilted cloth.—**Ring-master**, *n.* One who has charge of the performances in a circus ring.—**Ring-money**, *n.* Money consisting of rings, in use at an early stage of society.—**Ring-ousel, Ring-ouzel**, *n.* A British bird of the thrush kind, resembling the blackbird, but having a white ring or bar on the breast. — **Ring-sail**, *n.* *Naut.* same as RING-TAIL.—**Ring-tail**, *n.* The female of the hen-harrier; a sort of studding-sail set outside a spanker or a sloop's mainsail; a ring-sail.—**Ring-tailed**, *a.* Having a tail marked by rings or ringlike markings.—**Ringworm**, ring'wėrm, *n.* A contagious skin-disease appearing in the form of rings or patches on different parts of the body, but most frequently on the scalp.

Ring, ring, *v.t.*—pret. *rang* or *rung*, pp. *rung*. [A.Sax. *hringan*, to ring = Dan. *ringe*, Sw. *ringa*, Icel. *hringja*, O.D. *ringhen*, to ring.] To cause to sound, as a sonorous metallic body (to *ring* a bell); to repeat often, loudly, or earnestly; to sound (to *ring* one's praises); to attend on or celebrate by ringing.—*Ringing the changes*, a trick by which, in paying or receiving money, a rascal tries to confuse the person with whom he is dealing so that he may cheat him.—*v.i.* To sound, as a bell or other sonorous body; to resound; to have the sensation of sound continued; to tingle; to be filled with report or talk (the whole town *rings* with his fame).—*n.* The sound of a bell or other sonorous body; any loud sound continued, repeated, or reverberated; characteristic sound; a chime.—**Ringer**, ring'ėr, *n.* One who rings; one who rings chimes on bells.

Ringent, rin'jent, *a.* [L. *ringens, ringentis*, from *ringor*, to make wry faces, to gape.] *Bot.* labiated, with a space between the two lips like an open mouth.

Rink, ringk, *n.* [A form of *ring*, an area, or of *rank*, a row.] That portion of a sheet of ice on which the game of curling is played, also used for ice skating; the players that make up a side at the games of curling and bowling; a smooth flooring, generally under cover, on which people skate with roller-skates.

Rinse, rins, *v.t.*—*rinsed, rinsing.* [O.Fr. *rinser, reinser*, Fr. *rincer*, to rinse, to wash, from Icel. *hreinsa* (Dan. *rense*), from Icel. *hreinn* (= Dan. *reen*, D. and G. *rein*, Goth. *hrains*), clean.] To wash lightly; to wash by laving water over; to cleanse the inner surface of by the introduction of water or other liquid. — **Rinser**, rin'sėr, *n.* One who or that which rinses.

Riot, rī'ot, *n.* [O.Fr. *riote*, disturbance, combat, Fr. *rioter*, to make a disturbance; origin doubtful.] An uproar; a tumult; excessive and expensive feasting; wild and loose festivity; revelry; *law*, a tumultuous disturbance of the peace.—*To run riot*, to act or move without control or restraint; to grow wildly or in rank abundance.—*Riot act*, an act of parliament for the prevention of tumultuous disturbances, after the reading of which by a magistrate to a mob, those who do not disperse may be treated as felons.—*v.i.* To revel; to act in an unrestrained or wanton manner; to raise a riot, uproar, or sedition.—*v.t.*† To pass or spend in riot. (*Tenn.*)—**Rioter**, rī'ot-ėr, *n.* One who riots or engages in a riot.—**Riotous**, rī'ot-us, *a.* Indulging in riot or revelry; tumultuous; guilty of riot.—**Riotously**, rī'ot-us-li, *adv.* In a riotous manner; with revelry; tumultuously; seditiously.—**Riotousness**, rī'ot-us-nes, *n.* The state or quality of being riotous.

Rip, rip, *v.t.*—*ripped, ripping.* [Same as Dan. *rippe*, to rip, to tear; allied probably to *rive*.] To separate or divide by cutting or tearing; to tear or cut open; to take out by cutting or tearing.—*n.* A rent.—**Rip saw**, *n.* A saw used for cutting wood along the grain.—**Rip tide**, the clash of opposing tides or currents.

Rip, rip, *n.* [Comp. D. *rap*, scab; Dan. *ripsraps*, riffraff.] A base or worthless person; a contemptible creature; a scamp.

Riparian, ri-pā'ri-an, *a.* [L. *ripa*, a bank.] Pertaining to the bank of a body of water

Ripe, rīp, *a.* [A.Sax. *ripe*, ripe = L.G. *ripe*, D. *rijp*, G. *reif*, ripe; allied to *reap*.] Ready for reaping; brought to perfection in growth or to the best state; mature; advanced to the state of being fit for use; fully developed; maturated; complete; finished; consummate (a *ripe* scholar); ready for action or effect (*ripe* for a war).—*v.t.* and *i.* To mature; to ripen.—**Ripely**, rīp'li, *adv.* In a ripe manner; maturely; at the fit time.—**Ripen**, rī'pn, *v.i.* To grow ripe; to be matured, as grain or fruit; to approach or come to perfection.—*v.t.* To mature; to make ripe.—**Ripeness**, rīp'nes, *n.* The state of being ripe; maturity; perfection.

Riposte, rē-post, *n.* [Fr., from It. *riposta*.] *Fencing*, the thrust or blow with which one follows up a successful parry; hence, a smart reply or repartee.

Ripple, rip'l, *v.i.*—*rippled, rippling.* [A non-nasalized form corresponding to *rimple, rumple*.] To assume or wear a ruffled surface, as water when agitated or running over a rough bottom; to make a sound as of water running over a rough bottom.—*v.t.* To fret or dimple as the surface of water.—*n.* The fretting or ruffling of the surface of water; little curling waves.—**Ripple-mark**, *n.* The wavy or ridgy mark left on a beach by the ripples; *geol.* such marks preserved when the sand becomes hardened into rock.—**Ripple-marked**, *a.* Having ripple marks.—**Ripplingly**, rip'l-ing-li, *adv.* In a rippling manner.—**Ripply**, rip'l-i, *a.* Rippling; characterized by ripples.

Ripple, rip'l, *v.t.* [Dim. from *rip*; like L.G.

repeln, G. *riffeln*, to ripple.] To clean or remove the seeds or capsules from, especially from the stalks of flax.—*n.* A large comb or hatchel for separating the seeds or capsules from flax.

Riprap, rip′rap, *n.* [Same as *riffraff*, Dan. *ripsraps.*] A foundation of stones thrown together without order, as in deep water or on a soft bottom.

Ript, ript, pp. for *ripped.*

Ripuarian, rip′ū-ā″ri-an, *a.* Of or belonging to the division of Franks, opposed to the Salic, occupying the Rhine between the Moselle and the Meuse.

Rise, rīz, *v.i.*—*rose*, pret., *risen*, pp., *rising*, ppr. [A.Sax. *rísan*, to rise, pret. *rás*, rose, pp. *risen* = Icel. *rísa*, Goth. *reisan* (in *urreisan*), to rise. This is the intransitive form of which *raise* is the causal or transitive, as also *rear.*] To move or pass from a lower position to a higher; to move upwards; to ascend; to mount up; to change from a sitting, lying, or kneeling posture to a standing one; to become erect; to bring a sitting or a session to an end (the house *rose* at 11 p.m.); to get out of bed; to arise; to attain a height; to stand in height (a tree *rises* to 60 feet); to reach a higher level by increase of bulk or quantity (the tide *rises*); to swell or puff up in the process of fermentation, as dough and the like; to slope upwards; to have an upward direction; to seem to mount up; frequently, to appear above the horizon, as the sun, moon, stars, &c.; to become apparent; to come forth; to appear (an eruption *rises* on the skin); to become audible (there *rose* a shout); to come into existence; to be produced; to spring; to increase in force, value, intensity, degree, &c. (the wind *rises*, a price *rises*); to take up arms; to go to war; to rebel or revolt; to attain a higher social position or rank; to increase in power or interest: said of style, thought, or discourse.—*n.* The act of rising; ascent; the distance through which anything rises (a *rise* of 6 feet); elevation, or degree of ascent (a gradual *rise* in the land); spring; source; origin; beginning; appearance above the horizon (the *rise* of the sun or a star); increase; advance (a *rise* in the price of wheat); advance in rank, honour, property, or fame.—*Rise of strata*, *geol.* opposite of *dip of strata*. DIP.—**Riser**, rī′zėr, *n.* One that rises; the vertical face of a step of a stair.—**Rising**, rī′zing, *p.* and *a.* Increasing in wealth, power, or distinction (a *rising* man); advancing to adult years (the *rising* generation).—*n.* The act of one who or that which rises; the appearance of the sun or a star above the horizon; the act of reviving from the dead; resurrection; an insurrection; a mutiny; an eminence or prominence.

Risible, riz′i-bl, *a.* [Fr. *risible*, from L. *risibilis*, from *rideo*, *risum*, to laugh. RIDICULOUS.] Having the faculty or power of laughing; capable of exciting laughter; laughable; belonging to the phenomenon of laughter.—**Risibility**, **Risibleness**, riz-i-bil′i-ti, riz′i-bl-nes, *n.* The quality of being risible; proneness to laugh.—**Risibly**, riz′i-bli, *adv.* In a risible manner; laughably.—**Risorial**, ri-zō′ri-al, *a.* Causing laughter.

Risk, risk, *n.* [Fr. *risque*, from Sp. *risco*, a steep rock, from L. *reseco*, to cut off—*re*, and *seco*, to cut. SECTION.] Hazard; danger; peril; exposure to harm; *com.* the hazard of loss, either of ship, goods, or other property; the amount which may be lost, as in insurance.—*To run a risk*, to incur hazard; to encounter danger.—*v.t.* To hazard; to expose to injury or loss; to venture; to dare to undertake.—**Risker**, ris′kėr, *n.* One who risks.—**Riskful**, **Risky**, risk′ful, ris′ki, *a.* Dangerous; hazardous; full of risk.

Risque, rēs-kā′, *a.* [F. pp. of risquer.] Tending toward or verging on impropriety.

Rissole, ris′ōl, *n.* [Fr.] A dish consisting of minced meat or fish mixed with breadcrumbs and yolks of eggs wrapped in fine puff-paste, so as to resemble a sausage, and fried.

Risus, rī′sus, *n.* [L. See RISIBLE.] Laughter.—*Risus sardonicus*, sardonic laugh, a kind of convulsive grin, observed chiefly in cases of tetanus and inflammation of the diaphragm.

Ritardando, rē-tär-dan′dō, *a.* [It.] *Music*, retarding; a direction to sing or play slower and slower.

Rite, rīt, *n.* [Fr. *rite*, from L. *ritus*, a rite.] A formal act of religion or other solemn duty; a religious ceremony or usage; ceremonial.—**Ritual**, rit′ū-al, *a.* [L. *ritualis.*] Pertaining to rites; consisting of rites; prescribing rites (the *ritual* law).—*n.* A book containing the rites or ordinances of a church or of any special service; the manner of performing divine service; ceremonial.—**Ritualism**, rit′ū-al-izm, *n.* The system of rituals or prescribed forms of religious worship; observance of prescribed forms in religion; an excessive use of external forms in religion.—**Ritualist**, rit′ū-al-ist, *n.* One skilled in ritual; one of the party in favour of an elaborate ritual in the Church of England.—**Ritualistic**, rit′ū-al-is″tik, *a.* Pertaining to ritualism; characterized by the practices of the ritualists in the Church of England.—**Ritually**, rit′ū-al-li, *adv.* By ritual; by a particular rite.

Ritornelle, **Ritornello**, ri-tor-nel′, ri-tor-nel′lō, *n.* [Fr. *ritornelle*, It. *ritornello*, dim. of *ritorno*, return, *ritornare*, to return.] *Music*, a short repetition, such as of the concluding phrases of an air, especially if played whilst the principal voice pauses.

Rivage,† riv′āj, *n.* [Fr., from *rive*, L. *ripa*, a bank.] A bank, shore, or coast.

Rival, rī′val, *n.* [Fr. *rival*, from L. *rivalis*, pertaining to a brook, *rivales*, those who use the same brook, hence competitors, rivals; from *rivus*, a brook, whence *rivulet.*] One who is in pursuit of the same object as another; one striving to reach or obtain something which another is attempting to obtain, and which one only can possess; a competitor; one who emulates or strives to equal or exceed another in excellence.—*a.* Having the same pretensions or claims; standing in competition for superiority.—*v.t.*—*rivalled*, *rivalling*. To stand in competition with; to strive to equal or excel; to emulate.—**Rivalry**, rī′val-ri, *n.* The act of rivalling; competition; a strife or effort to obtain an object which another is pursuing; emulation. ∴ Syn. under COMPETITION.—**Rivalship**, rī′val-ship, *n.* The state or character of a rival; emulation; rivalry.

Rive, rīv, *v.t.*—pret. *rived*; pp. *rived* or *riven*; ppr. *riving*. [A Scandinavian word =Icel. *rífa*, Dan. *rive*, to rive, to tear; akin perhaps to *rip.*] To split; to cleave; to rend asunder by force.—*v.i.* To be split or rent asunder.—**Riven**, riv′n, pp. of *rive*. Split; rent or burst asunder.

Rivel, riv′l, *v.t.*—*rivelled*, *rivelling*. [A.Sax. (*ge*)*riflian*, to wrinkle; connections doubtful.] To contract into wrinkles; to corrugate; to shrink.

River, riv′ėr, *n.* [Fr. *rivière*, from L.L. *riparia*, a river, from L. *riparius*, pertaining to the banks of a river, from *ripa*, a bank.] A large stream of water flowing through a certain portion of the earth's surface and discharging itself into the sea, a lake, a marsh, or into another such stream.—**River-basin**, *n.* The region drained by all the rills, rivulets, streams, or rivers which ultimately gather to form one river.—**River-bed**, *n.* The bed or bottom of a river.—**River-craft**, *n.* Small vessels or boats which ply on rivers and do not put to sea.—**River-god**, *n.* A deity supposed to preside over a river.—**River-hog**, *n.* The water-hog or capybara.—**River-horse**, *n.* The hippopotamus.—**Riverine**, riv′ėr-īn, *a.* Belonging to a river; situated on a river.—**River-meadow**, *n.* A meadow on the bank of a river.—**River-side**, *n.* The bank of a river.—**River-wall**, *n.* A wall made to confine a river within definite bounds.—**River-water**, *n.* The water of a river as distinguished from *rain-water*, *spring-water*, &c.—**Rivery**,† riv′ėr-i, *a.* Pertaining to rivers; abounding in rivers.

Rivet, riv′et, *n.* [Fr. *rivet*, a clinch, a rivet; *river*, to rivet; origin doubtful, probably from the Teutonic; comp. Icel. *rífa*, to tack together, to sew together.] A short metallic pin or bolt passing through a hole and keeping two pieces of metal (or sometimes other substances) together; especially, a short bolt or pin of wrought iron formed with a head and inserted into a hole at the junction of two pieces of metal, the point after insertion being hammered broad so as to keep the pieces closely bound together.—*v.t.* To fasten with a rivet or with rivets; to clinch; *fig.* to fasten firmly; to make firm, strong, or immovable.—**Riveted**, riv′et-ed, *p.* and *a.* Fastened with rivets.—**Riveter**, riv′et-ėr, *n.* One who rivets.—**Riveting**, riv′et-ing, *p.* and *a.* Serving to rivet; used in clinching rivets.—*n.* The act of joining with rivets; a set of rivets taken collectively.

Rivose, rī′vōs, *a.* [L. *rivus*, a brook.] Marked with sinuous or wavy furrows.

Rivulet, riv′ū-let, *n.* [L. *rivulus*, dim. of *rivus*, a river (seen also in *derive*, *rival*).] A small stream or brook; a streamlet.

Rix-dollar, riks-dol′ėr, *n.* [Sw. *riksdaler*, Dan. *rigsdaler*, G. *reichsthaler*, lit. the dollar of the realm.] A silver coin formerly of Germany, Denmark, Sweden, &c., ranging in value between 60c and $1.00.

Roach, rōch, *n.* [A.Sax. *reohhe*; akin to D. *roch*, a skate, G. *roche*, a roach or ray.] A fish of the carp family, inhabiting lakes, ponds, and slow-running rivers of Europe.

Roach, rōch, *n.* The curve in the foot of a sail; also see COCKROACH.

Road, rōd, *n.* [A.Sax. *rád*, a riding, a journey on horseback, a road, from *rídan*, to ride. (RIDE.) *Raid* is a collateral form.] An open way or public passage; a piece of ground appropriated for travel, forming a line of communication between one city, town, or place and another for foot-passengers, cattle, vehicles, &c.; generally applied to highways, and as a generic term it includes highway, street, lane, &c.; a means or way of approach or access; a place where ships may ride at anchor at some distance from the shore.—*To take the road*, set out on a journey.—**Roadbed**, rōd′bed, *n.* The foundation and surfacing of a road, in railroads cross ties and rails being included.—**Road-hog**, *n.* A motorist who selfishly uses more than his share of the highway without regard for other motorists.—**Roadhouse**, rōd′hous, *n.* An inn, usually beside a highway.—**Road map**, *n.* A map, usually of a state, showing roads, towns, and points of interest.—**Road metal**, *n.* Broken stones used for macadamizing roads.—**Road scraper**, *n.* A machine for scraping or cleaning roads.—**Roadstead**, rōd′sted, *n.* A place where ships may ride at anchor off the shore.—**Roadster**, rōd′stėr, *n.* A horse well fitted for driving; an open-top automobile with one double seat.—**Roadway**, rōd′wā, *n.* A highway; the part of a road used by horses, carriages, &c.

Roam, rōm, *v.i.* [O.E. *rome*, also *rame*, to roam or rove; of doubtful connections; comp. O.H.G. *râmen*, to aim, to strive. *Ramble* is from this verb.] To wander; to ramble; to rove; to walk or move about from place to place without any certain purpose or direction.—*v.t.* To range; to wander over.—*n.* Act of wandering; a ramble.—**Roamer**, rō′mėr, *n.* One who roams; a vagrant.

Roan, rōn, *a.* [O.Fr. *roan*, Mod.Fr. *rouan*, It. *roano*, *rovano*, Sp. *ruano*, *roano*; origin unknown.] Applied formerly to a horse of a bay, sorrel, or dark colour, with numerous spots of gray or white; now generally applied to a colour having a decided shade of red.—*n.* A leather used largely in bookbinding to imitate morocco, prepared from sheep-skin; a horse of a roan colour; a roan colour.

Roan-tree, rōn, *n.* [ROWAN.] The mountain ash or rowan-tree.

Roar, rōr, *v.i.* [A.Sax. *rárian*, L.G. *râren*, D. *reeren*, Prov.G. *reren*, *rören*, to roar; akin perhaps to Dan. *röst*, Icel. *raust*, the voice.] To cry with a full, loud, continued sound; to bellow, as a beast; to cry aloud, as in distress or anger; to make a loud, continued, confused sound, as winds, waves, a multitude of people shouting together, and the like; to laugh out loudly and continuously.—*v.t.* To cry out aloud; to shout. —*n.* A full loud sound of some continuance; the strong loud cry of a beast; the loud cry of a person in distress, pain, anger; a loud, continued, confused sound; outcry of joy or mirth.—**Roarer**, rō'ėr, *n.* One who or that which roars; a broken-winded horse. —**Roaring**, rō'ring, *n.* A loud cry, as of a beast; a continuous roar; loud continued sound, as of the billows of the sea; a disease of the bronchial tubes in horses.—*p.* and *a.* Characterized by roars or noise; disorderly; riotous.

Roast, rōst, *v.t.* [O.Fr. *rostir* (Fr. *rôtir*), to roast, from O.H.G. *rostjan*, to roast (D. *roosten*, Sw. *rosta*, Dan. *riste*), or from the Celtic: Armor. *rosta*, W. *rhostiaw*, Gael. *roist*, to roast.] To cook or prepare for the table by exposure to the direct action of heat, on a spit, in an oven, or the like; to heat to excess; to dry and parch by exposure to heat; *metal.* to burn in a heap, as broken ore, in order to free it from foreign matters; colloquially, to banter severely.—*v.i.* To become roasted or fit for eating by exposure to fire.—*n.* That which is roasted, as a piece of beef; part of a slaughtered animal selected for roasting.—*a.* Roasted (*roast* beef).—**Roaster**, rōs'tėr, *n.* One who or that which roasts; an animal for roasting.—**Roasting-jack**, *n.* An apparatus for turning meat roasting before an open fire.

Rob, rob, *n.* [Fr. *rob*, from Sp. *rob*, from Ar. *robb*, a jelly of fruit.] The inspissated juice of ripe fruit, mixed with honey or sugar to the consistence of a conserve.

Rob, rob, *v.t.*—*robbed, robbing.* [O.Fr. *rober*, to steal, from O.H.G. *roubôn*, Goth. *raubon*, to rob, a verb akin to A.Sax. *reáfian*, E. to *reave*, D. *rooven*, G. *rauben*—to seize; the origin being O.G. *raub* (A.Sax. *reáf*), a garment, clothing, spoil. ROBE.] To plunder or strip by force or violence; to deprive of something by stealing; to deprive unlawfully; to deprive (to *rob* a person *of* his peace of mind).—**Robber**, rob'ėr, *n.* One who robs; one who commits a robbery.—**Robbery**, rob'ėr-i, *n.* The act or practice of robbing; a taking away by violence or wrong; the forcible and felonious taking of something from the person of another.

Roband, rob'and, *n.* *Naut.* a robbin or rope-band. ROBBIN.

Robbin, rob'in, *n.* [From *rope* and *band.*] *Naut.* a short flat plaited piece of rope, with an eye in one end, used in pairs to tie square sails to their yards.

Robe, rōb, *n.* [Fr. *robe*, from L.L. *rauba*, spoil, the taking of a man's garments, from O.G. *raub*, a garment, spoil (which in primitive times consisted chiefly of articles of dress). ROB.] A kind of gown or long loose garment worn over other dress; a gown or dress of a rich, flowing, or elegant style or make; a dressed buffalo (or bison) skin with the hair on.—*The robe*, or *the long robe*, the legal profession (gentlemen of *the long robe*).—*Master of the robes*, an officer in the royal household in England, whose duty consists in ordering the sovereign's robes; under a queen this office is performed by a lady, designated *Mistress of the robes.*—*v.t.*—*robed, robing.* To clothe in a robe; to attire; to invest.

Robin, rob'in, *n.* [A familiar form of *Robert*; comp. the personal names of *Mag* and *Jack* in *magpie, jackdaw.*] The well-known European bird called also *Redbreast* and *Robin-redbreast*; in America a species of thrush with a red breast.

Roborant, rob'o-rant, *a.* [L. *roborans, roborantis*, ppr. of *roboro*, to make strong, from *robur*, strength.] Strengthening.—*n.* A medicine that strengthens; a tonic.

Robot, rō'bot, *n.* [Czech *robotiti*, to work.] A mechanical device almost human in its functioning; an automaton; an unthinking but efficient person.

Roburite, rō'bur-īt, *n.* [L. *robur*, strength.] An explosive substance of recent introduction, having as its basis ammonium nitrate.

Robust, rō-bust', *a.* [L. *robustus*, from *robus, robur*, strength. LABOUR.] Possessed of or indicating great strength; strong; lusty; sinewy; muscular; vigorous. —**Robustly**, rō-bust'li, *adv.* In a robust manner; vigorously.—**Robustness**, rō-bust'nes, *n.* The quality of being robust; strength; vigour.—**Robustious**, rō-bust'-yus, *a.* Robust; sturdy; rough; boisterous.

Roc, rok, *n.* [Ar. *rukh.*] The well-known monstrous bird of Arabian mythology.

Rocambole, rok'am-bōl, *n.* [Fr., from G. *rockenbollen*—*rocken*, rye, and *bollen*, a bulb, because it grows amongst rye.] A kind of cultivated garlic.

Roccella, rok-sel'la, *n.* [From Pg. *roccha*, a rock, in allusion to its place of growth.] A genus of lichens used in dyeing; archil.

Roche-alum, roch, *n.* [Fr. *roche*, a rock, and E. *alum.* ROCK-ALUM.

Rochelle-salt, rō-shel', *n.* [From being first prepared at *Rochelle* in France.] The double tartrate of soda and potash, used as a mild cathartic.

Roche-moutonnée, rōsh-mö-ton-ā, *n.* [Fr.—*roche*, a rock, and *mouton*, a sheep.] The name given to rounded and smoothed humps of rock occurring in beds of ancient glaciers from their fancied resemblance to the backs of sheep.

Rochet, roch'et, *n.* [Fr. *rochet*, a blouse, a little jacket, from G. *rock*, O.H.G. *roch*, O.E. *rock*, a coat.] A sort of short surplice, with tight sleeves, and open at the sides, worn by bishops.

Rock, rok, *n.* [Same as Icel. *rokkr*, Dan. *rok*, Sw. *rock*, a distaff; akin to D. *rokken*, G. *rocken.*] A distaff used in spinning.

Rock, rok, *v.t.* [Same as Dan. *rokke*, to move, to shake; comp. G. *rücken*, to move.] To move backwards and forwards, as a body resting on a support beneath; to cause to reel or totter; to make to sway; to move backwards and forwards in a cradle, chair, &c.; to lull; to quiet, as if by rocking in a cradle.—*v.i.* To be moved backwards and forwards; to reel.—**Rocker**, rok'ėr, *n.* One who rocks anything, as a cradle; the curving piece of wood on which a cradle or rocking-chair rocks; a rocking-horse; a cradle or trough for washing ore by agitation.—**Rocking**, rok'ing, *n.* The act of one who or that which rocks; a social gathering for song and conversation, with women working at the rock or distaff. (*Burns.*) —**Rocking-chair**, *n.* An arm-chair mounted on rockers.—**Rocking-horse**, *n.* A wooden horse mounted on rockers; a hobby-horse.—**Rocking-stone**, *n.* A large block of stone poised (usually by natural causes) so nicely upon the point of a rock that a moderate force applied to it causes it to rock or oscillate.—**Rock-shaft**, *n.* *Steam-engines*, a shaft that oscillates or *rocks* on its journals instead of revolving.

Rock, rok, *n.* [Fr. *roc*, either from a form *rupicus*, from L. *rupes*, a rock; or of Celtic origin.] A large mass of stony matter; a large fixed stone or crag; the stony matter constituting the earth's crust, as distinguished from soil, mud, sand, gravel, clay, peat; *geol.* any natural deposit or portion of the earth's crust, whatever be its hardness or softness; *fig.* defence, means of safety; asylum; a cause or source of peril or disaster; a name for a kind of solid sweetmeat.—**Rocky**, rok'i, *a.* Full of rocks; hard; stony; obdurate.—**Rockiness**, rok'i-nes, *n.* State of being rocky.—**Rockery**, rok'ėr-i, *n.* An artificial mound formed of fragments of rock, earth, &c., for plants, as ferns.—**Rockless**, rok'les, *a.* Being without rocks.—**Rock-alum**, *n.* A reddish variety of native alum found in Italy.—**Rock-basin**, *n.* A basin or hollow of considerable size, surrounded by rocky walls, and often containing a lake; a basin-shaped cavity occurring in some rocks.—**Rock-bound**, *a.* Surrounded or hemmed in by rocks.—**Rock-butter**, *n.* A soft, yellowish, somewhat unctuous mineral substance oozing out of rocks containing alum.—**Rock-cod**, *n.* A cod taken on rocky sea-bottoms.—**Rock-cork**, *n.* Mountain-cork, a white or gray-coloured variety of asbestos.—**Rock-crowned**, *a.* Crowned or surmounted with rocks.—**Rock-crystal**, *n.* Crystallized quartz, found both colourless, and of various gradations of colour, as yellowish white, amber, purple, &c.—**Rock-leather**, *n.* ROCK-CORK.—**Rock-milk**, *n.* AGARIC MINERAL.—**Rock-moss**, *n.* The lichen which yields cudbear.—**Rock-oil**, *n.* Petroleum. —**Rock-pigeon**, *n.* A species of pigeon that builds its nest in rocks.—**Rock-rabbit**, *n.* The hyrax or 'coney' of Scripture.—**Rock-rose**, *n.* The plant cistus.—**Rock-ruby**, *n.* Garnet when of a strong but not deep red, with a cast of blue.—**Rock-salt**, *n.* Mineral salt; common salt found in masses or beds in the new red sandstone, as in Cheshire and elsewhere.—**Rock-soap**, *n.* A mineral of a pitch-black or bluish-black colour having a somewhat greasy feel, used for crayons and for washing cloth.—**Rock-wood**, *n.* Ligniform asbestos; a mineral of a brown colour, greatly resembling fossil wood.—**Rock-work**, *n.* Stones fixed in mortar in imitation of the asperities of rocks, forming a mound; a rockery.

Rocket, rok'et, *n.* [It. *rocchetta*, from *rocca*, a distaff, a rock; from the German.] A cylindrical tube of pasteboard or metal filled with a mixture of nitre, sulphur, charcoal, &c., which, on being ignited at the base, propels it forward by the action of the liberated gases against the atmosphere.

Rocket, rok'et, *n.* [Fr. *roquette*, It. *ruchetta*, from It. *ruca*, L. *eruca*, rocket.] A name applied to various plants, one of which is the common garden rocket.

Rococo, ro-kō'kō, *n.* [Fr., from *roc*, rock, from rockwork being a character of the style.] A debased variety of ornament of the time of Louis XIV and XV, characterized by meaningless scrolls and conventional shell-work; sometimes applied in contempt to anything bad or tasteless in decorative art.

Rocou, rō'kö. Same as *Annato.*

Rod, rod, *n.* [A.Sax. *ród*, a rod or beam, a rood or cross = D. *roede*, L.G. *rood, rode*, G. *ruthe*, rod; allied to L. *rudis*, a wand, from same root as Skr. *ruh*, to grow. *Rood* is a form of this word.] A shoot or slender stem of any woody plant; a wand; a straight slender stick; hence, an instrument of punishment or correction; a means of chastisement; a kind of sceptre or badge of office; a fishing-rod; an instrument for measuring; an enchanter's wand; a measure of length containing 5½ yards, or 16½ feet, often termed a *Pole* or *Perch.*

Rode, rōd, pret. of *ride.*

Rodent, rō'dent, *a.* [L. *rodens, rodentis*, ppr. of *rodo*, to gnaw (seen also in *erode, corrode*). Same root as *rudo*, to shave or scrape. RASE.] Gnawing; belonging or pertaining to the order of gnawing animals (Rodentia).—*n.* An animal that gnaws, as the squirrel, rat, mouse, &c.—**Rodentia**, rō-den'shi-a, *n.pl.* An order of mammals, including the squirrel, rat, mouse, hare, rabbit, beaver, &c., characterized by a single pair of chisel-like cutting teeth in each jaw, between which and the grinding teeth there is a wide gap.

Rodeo, rō'de-o, *n.* [Sp.] A cattle market place or roundup; an exhibition of lassoing, horse breaking, and steer riding.

Rodomont, rod'ō-mont, *n.* [Fr. *rodomont*, from It. *rodomonte*, a bully, from *Rodomonte*, the name of the brave but somewhat boastful leader of the Saracens against Charlemagne in Ariosto's *Orlando Furioso.*] A vain boaster; a bully.—**Rodomontade**, rod'ō-mon-tād", *n.* [Fr.] Vain boasting; empty bluster or vaunting; rant.

Roe, rō, *n.* [A.Sax. *rá, ráh*=Icel. *rá*, Dan. *raa*, D. *ree*, G. *reh*, roe, roebuck.] A roebuck; the female of the hart.—**Roebuck**, rō'buk, **Roedeer**, *n.* A species of European deer with erect cylindrical branched horns, of elegant shape and remarkably nimble.

Roe, rō, *n.* [Akin to Dan. *rogn*, Icel. *hrogn*, G. *rogen*, roe, spawn; Sc. *ran*, *rawn*, the female roe.] The sperm or spawn of fishes; the roe of the male being called *soft roe* or *milt*, that of the female *hard roe* or *spawn*. —**Roed**, rōd, *p.* and *a.* Filled or impregnated with roe.—**Roe-stone**, *n.* A name given to oolite, from its being composed of small rounded particles.

Rogation, rō-gā'shon, *n.* [L. *rogatio*, *rogationis*, an asking, from *rogo*, *rogatum*, to ask, seen also in *abrogate*, *derogate*, *interrogate*, *prerogative*, &c.] A supplication; a litany.—*Rogation days*, the Monday, Tuesday, and Wednesday before Ascension-day, the week in which they occur being called *Rogation week*, and the Sunday preceding *Rogation Sunday*: so called from the use of special prayers for an abundant supply of the fruits of the earth; in *Roman law*, a bill before the people waiting its sanction for conversion into a law.

Rogue, rōg, *n.* [Probably a Celtic word: comp. Ir. *roguire*, a rogue: Fr. *rogue*, arrogant, from Armor. *rog*, arrogant, proud.] A vagrant; a vagabond; a wandering knave; a dishonest person; a rascal: applied generally to males; a name of slight tenderness and endearment; a wag; a sly fellow.—*Rogue's gallery*, a collection of photographs, kept in police files, of known criminals.—*Rogue's march*, a tune played when a bad character is discharged with disgrace from a regiment or from a ship of war.—*Rogue's yarn* (*naut.*), a rope-yarn of special twist or a colored thread placed in cordage made for the British navy to distinguish it from other cordage.—**Roguery**, rō'gėr-i, *n.* Knavish tricks; dishonest practices; waggery; arch tricks; mischievousness.—**Roguish**, rō'gish, *a.* Knavish; fraudulent; dishonest; waggish; wanton; slightly mischievous.—**Roguishly**, rō'gish-li, *adv.*—**Roguishness**, rō'gish-nes, *n.*

Roil, roil, *v.t.* [From O.Fr. *roille* (Fr. *rouille*), rust, mildew, from L. *robigo*, rust. *Rile* is a slightly different form.] To render turbid by stirring; to annoy or anger.

Roister, rois'tėr, *v.i.* [From Fr. *rustre*, a boor, from L. *rusticus*, rustic; or connected with Sc. *roust*, to roar, Icel. *rosta*, a brawl, a riot.] To bluster; to swagger; to be noisy, vaunting, or turbulent.—**Roisterer**, rois'tėr-ėr, *n.* One who roisters; a blustering or turbulent fellow.

Rokambole, rok'am-bōl, *n.* Same as *Rocambole*.

Role, rōl, *n.* [Fr., a roll, scroll, character in a play, from L. *rotulus*, a wheel. ROLL.] A play or character represented by a stage-player; any conspicuous part or function performed by any one, as a leading public character.

Roll, rōl, *v.t.* [O.Fr. *roeler*, *roler* (Fr. *rouler*), to roll; Pr. *rolar*, *rotlar*; from L.L. *rotulare*, from L. *rotulus*, *rotula*, a little wheel, from *rota*, a wheel (whence also *rotary*, *rotate*).] To cause to revolve by turning over and over; to drive onward by turning on itself; to move in a circular direction; to whirl or wheel (to *roll* the eyes); to turn about, as in one's mind; to revolve; to wrap round on itself by turning; to bind or involve in a bandage or the like; to inwrap; to press or level with a roller.—*To roll a drum*, to beat it with rapid continuous strokes.—*v.i.* To move along a surface by revolving; to turn over and over; to rotate; to run on wheels; to move circularly; to be tossed about; to move, as waves or billows, with alternate swells and depressions; to tumble or fall over and over; to wallow; to sound with a deep prolonged sound.—*n.* The act of rolling; something made or formed by rolling; that which is rolled up; a scroll; an official document; a list of the names of persons, as of students or soldiers; a register; a catalogue; a quantity of cloth or paper wound up in a cylindrical form; a small piece of dough rolled up into a cake before baking; the beating of a drum with strokes so rapid as to produce a continued sound; a prolonged deep sound.—*Rolls of court, of parliament*, &c., the parchments on which were engrossed its acts and proceedings and which constitute its records.—*Master of the rolls*. MASTER. —**Roll-call**, *n.* The act of calling over a list of names, as of men who compose a military body.—**Roller**, rōl'ėr, *n.* One who or that which rolls; a cylinder which turns on its axis, used for various purposes, as smoothing, crushing, spreading out, and the like, in agriculture, gardening, road-making, &c.; that upon which something may be rolled up; that upon which a body can be rolled or moved along; a bandage; a long broad bandage used in surgery; a long, heavy, swelling wave, such as is seen setting in upon a coast after the subsiding of a storm.—**Roller-skate**, *n.* A skate mounted on small wheels or rollers, and used for skating upon asphalt or other smooth flooring.—**Rolling**, rōl'ing, *p.* and *a.* Revolving; making a continuous noise; undulating; rising and falling in gentle slopes (the *rolling* land of the prairies).—**Rolling-mill**, *n.* A combination of machinery consisting of one or more sets of rollers, between which heated metal is passed and thereby subjected to a strong pressure, to be reduced to plates, bolts, bars, &c.—**Rolling pin**, *n.* A cylindrical piece of wood with a handle on each end, for rolling dough or paste to a desired thickness.—**Rolling press**, *n.* A machine consisting of two or more cylinders, used by calenderers, bookbinders, &c.—**Rolling stock**, *n.* The freight cars, coaches, locomotives, &c., of a railroad.

Rolley, rol'i, *n.* A narrow-gauge car used in mines.—**Rolleyway**, *n.* A track for mine cars. (*England* and *Australia*.)

Rollick, rol'ik, *v.i.* [A sort of dim. from *roll*.] To move in a careless, swaggering manner; to be jovial in behavior.

Rollock, rol'ok, *n.* [For *row-lock*.] Same as *Row-lock*.

Roly-poly, rō'li-pō-li, *n.* [A jingling name derived from *roll*.] A sheet of paste spread with jam and rolled into a pudding; a short, plump child or person; a well-rounded thing.

Romaic, rō-mā'ik, *n.* [Mod.Gr. *Romaïkē*, from L. *Roma*, Rome.] The vernacular language of modern Greece; the language of the uneducated or peasantry, a corrupted form of ancient Greek.—*a.* Relating to the modern Greek vernacular.

Roman, rō'man, *a.* [L. *Romanus*, from *Roma*, Rome, the principal city of the Romans in Italy.] Pertaining to or resembling Rome or the Roman people; pertaining to or professing the Roman Catholic religion; applied to the common upright letter in printing, as distinguished from *italic*, and to numerals expressed by letters, and not in the Arabic characters. —*Roman candle*, a kind of firework, consisting of a tube which discharges upwards a stream of white or coloured stars.—*Roman Catholic*, of or pertaining to that branch of the Christian Church of which the pope or bishop of Rome is the head; hence, a *Roman Catholic* is a member of this church; and *Roman Catholicism* is a collective term for the principles, doctrines, rules, &c., of the Roman Catholic Church.—*Roman cement*, a dark-coloured hydraulic cement, which hardens very quickly, and is very durable.—*Roman law*, the civil law; the system of jurisprudence finally elaborated in the ancient Roman Empire. — *Roman order of architecture*. Same as *Composite Order*.—*n.* A native or citizen of Rome; one enjoying the privileges of a Roman citizen.—**Romanism**, rō'man-izm, *n.* The tenets of the Church of Rome.—**Romanist**, rō'man-ist, *n.* A Roman Catholic.—**Romanize**, rō'man-īz, *v.t.* —*romanized*, *romanizing*. To latinize; to convert to the Roman Catholic religion.—*v.i.* To use Latin words or idioms; to conform to Roman Catholic opinions, customs, or modes of speech.—**Romanizer**, rō'man-ī-zėr, *n.* One who romanizes.

Romance, rō-mans', *n.* [Fr. *romance*, from L.L. *Romanice* (*adv.*), 'in the Roman tongue' (that is in the provincial as opposed to the classical Latin), the adverb becoming a noun signifying a composition in this tongue.] Originally, a tale in verse, written in one of the Romance dialects; hence, any popular epic or any fictitious and wonderful tale in prose or verse; a kind of novel dealing with extraordinary and often extravagant adventures, or picturing an almost purely imaginary state or society; tendency of mind towards the wonderful and mysterious; romantic notions; something belonging rather to fiction than to everyday life; a fiction. ∴ Syn. under NOVEL.—*a.* A term applied to the languages which arose in the south and west of Europe, based on the Latin as spoken in the provinces, and including Italian, French, Provençal, Spanish, Portuguese, and Roumanian (which are therefore known as the *Romance* languages).—*v.i. romanced*, *romancing*. To devise and tell fictitious stories; to deal in extravagant stories.—**Romancer**, **Romancist**, rō-man'sėr, rō-man'sist, *n.* One who romances; a writer of romance.

Romanesque, rō-man-esk', *n.* [Fr., from L. *Romanus*, Roman.] The debased style of architecture and ornament that prevailed in the later Roman Empire.—*a.* Belonging to this style.—**Romanic**, rō-man'ik, *a.* Pertaining to the Romance languages or to the races speaking any of them; Romance.

Romanism, &c. Under ROMAN.

Romansch, **Roumansch**, rō-mansh', rö-mansh', *n.* [Lit. *Romanish*, or derived from *Rome*.] A dialect based on the Latin, spoken in the Grisons of Switzerland.

Romantic, rō-man'tik, *a.* [Fr. *romantique*. ROMANCE.] Pertaining to romance or romances; partaking of romance or the marvellous; fanciful, imaginative, or ideal; extravagant; chimerical; not belonging to real life; wildly picturesque; having striking natural features; full of wild or fantastic scenery. ∴ *Romantic* is used in relation to the imagination mainly, *sentimental* to the feelings. A *sentimental* person is given to displays of exaggerated feeling; a *romantic* person indulges his imagination in the creation and contemplation of scenes of an ideal life very different from the actual.—*Romantic school*, a term applied in literature and art to writers and critics who brought about a reaction from false classicalism, and strove to represent life in its actuality. —**Romantically**, rō-man'ti-kal-li, *adv.* In a romantic manner.—**Romanticism**, rō-man'ti-sizm, *n.* The state or quality of being romantic; a reaction in literature or art from classical to mediæval or modern forms; romantic feeling.—**Romanticist**, rō-man'ti-sist, *n.* One imbued with romanticism.—**Romanticness**, rō-man'tik-nes, *n.*

Romany, **Rommany**, rom'a-ni, *n.* A gypsy; the language spoken by the gypsies, a dialect brought from Hindustan and allied to the Hindustani.

Romaunt, rō-mạnt', *n.* [O.Fr.] A romantic ballad; a romance. (*Archaic*.)

Romepenny, **Romescot**, rōm'pen-i, rōm'skot, *n.* PETER-PENCE.

Romish, rōm'ish, *a.* [From *Rome*.] Belonging to the Roman Catholic Church: used with a slightly contemptuous feeling, hence not by Catholics themselves.

Romp, romp, *n.* [A slightly different form of *ramp*. RAMP.] A girl who indulges in boisterous play; energetic play or frolic. —*v.i.* To play boisterously; to leap and frisk about in play.—**Romper**, *n.* One who romps; a type of dress or suit worn by an infant.—**Rompingly**, romp'ing-li, *adv.* In a romping manner.—**Rompish**, romp'ish, *a.* Given to romp.

Rondeau, ron'dō, *n.* [Fr. *rondeau*, from *rond*, round.] A poem, commonly consisting of thirteen lines, of which eight have one rhyme and five another, and divided into three strophes, at the end of the second and third the beginning of the rondeau being repeated; a piece of music of three strains. Called also *Rondo*.

Rondo, ron'dō. RONDEAU.

Ronion, Ronyon, run'yun or ron'yon, *n.* [From Fr. *rogne*, itch, mange, from L. *robigo, robiginis*, rust.] A mangy, scabby animal; a scurvy person; a drab.

Röntgen, Roentgen, runt'gen, *a.* Pertaining to Konrad Röntgen or X rays, which he discovered.—*Röntgen rays*, *n.* X rays, which photograph through substances with varying degrees of clarity

Rood, röd, *n.* [The same word as *rod*, A.Sax. *ród*, a cross, a rod or pole; comp. D. *roede*, G. *ruthe*, a rod or switch and a measure of length.] A square measure, the fourth part of a statute acre, equal to 1210 square yards; a measure of 5½ yards in length; a rod, pole, or perch; also, a square pole, or 272¼ square feet, used in estimating mason work; a cross or crucifix; a large crucifix placed at the entrance to the chancel, often supported on the rood-beam or rood-screen.—**Rood-arch**, *n.* The arch in a church between the nave and chancel, so called from the rood being placed here. —**Rood-beam**, *n.* A beam across the entrance to the chancel of a church for supporting the rood.—**Rood-loft**, *n.* A gallery over the rood-screen in a church where the rood was placed. — **Rood-screen**, *n.* A screen or ornamental partition separating the choir of a church from the nave.

Roof, röf, *n.* [A.Sax. *hróf*, a roof; cog. Icel. *hróf*, a shed under which ships are built; *ráf*, a roof; D. *roef*, a cover, a cabin.] The cover of any house or building irrespective of the materials of which it is composed; that which corresponds with or resembles the covering of a house, as the arch or top of a vault, a furnace, the top of a carriage, &c.; a canopy; the palate; a house.—*v.t.* To cover with a roof; to inclose in a house; to shelter.—**Roofer**, röf'ér, *n.* One who roofs.—**Roofing**, röf'ing, *n.* The act of covering with a roof; the materials of which a roof is composed; the roof itself. **Roofless**, röf'les, *a.* Having no roof; having no house or home; unsheltered.— **Roof-tree**, *n.* A main beam in a roof.

Rook, ruk, *n.* [A.Sax. *hróc*, D. *roek*, L.G. *rôk*, Icel. *hrókr*, Sw. *roka*, O.H.G. *hruoh*, probably from the cry which the bird utters; comp. Gael. *roc*, to croak, L. *raucus*, hoarse.] A bird resembling the crow, but differing from it in not feeding on carrion but on insects and grain, also in having the root of the bill bare of feathers; a cheat; a trickish rapacious fellow.—*v.i.* and *t.* To cheat; to defraud.—**Rookery**, ruk'ér-i, *n.* A wood used for nesting-places by rooks; a neighborhood of poor mean dwellings; a squalid community; a resort of thieves, sharpers, &c. (*Brit.*).—**Rookie**, *n.* A raw army recruit.—**Rooky**, ruk'i, *a.* Inhabited by rooks.

Rook, ruk, *n.* [Fr. *roc*, It. *rocco*, Sp. *roque*, from Per. and Ar. *rokh*, the rook or castle at chess.] *Chess*, one of the four pieces placed on the corner squares of the board; also called a *Castle*.

Room, röm, *n.* [A.Sax. *rúm*=Icel. *rúm*, D. *ruim*, O.Sax., O.Fris., L.G., Sw., and Dan. *rum*, G. *raum*, room, space; Goth. *rums*, place, space; same root as L. *rus*, country. *Rummage* is a derivative.] Space; compass; extent of place, great or small; space or place unoccupied or unobstructed; fit occasion; opportunity; place or station once occupied by another; stead; an apartment in a house; any division separated from the rest by a partition; particular place or station (N.T.).—*To make room*, to open a way or passage; to remove obstructions.—**Roomer**, *n.* One who rents a room without board.—**Roomful**, röm'-ful, *n.* As much or as many as a room will hold.—**Roommate**, *n.* One who shares a room.—**Roomy**, röm'i, *a.* Having ample room; spacious.

Roorback, rör'bak, *n.* A false and malicious report circulated by a political candidate at the last moment.

Roost, röst, *n.* [A.Sax. *hróst*, D. *roest*, a roost: connections doubtful.] The pole or support on which fowls rest at night.—*At roost*, in a state of rest and sleep.—*v.i.* To occupy a roost; to lodge; to settle.— **Rooster**, rös'tér, *n.* The male of the domestic fowl; a cock. (*American.*)

Roost, *n.* The tidal race in the Orkney and Shetland Islands.

Root, röt, *n.* [From Icel. *rót*, Sw. *rot*, Dan. *rod*; connected with L. *radix* (whence *radical*), Gr. *rhiza*, root, E. *wort*.] That part of a plant which fixes itself in the earth, and by means of its radicles imbibes nutriment; a bulb, tuber, or similar part of a plant; that which resembles a root in position or function; the part of anything that resembles the root of a plant (the *root* of a tooth); foundation or base; the origin or cause of anything; that part of a word which conveys its essential meaning, as distinguished from the formative parts by which this meaning is modified; an ultimate form or element from which words are derived or regarded as having arisen; *math.* the root of any quantity is such a quantity as, when multiplied into itself a certain number of times, will exactly produce that quantity.—*To take root*, or *to strike root*, to become planted or fixed, or to be established.—*v.i.* To fix the root; to be firmly fixed; to be established.—*v.t.* To fix by the root; to plant and fix deep in the earth; to plant deeply; to impress deeply and durably (principles *rooted* in the mind).— **Root beer**, *n.* A nonalcoholic beverage made from various roots.—**Rooted**, röt'ed, *p.* and *a.* Having roots; firmly fixed; fixed in the heart (a *rooted* antipathy). —**Rootedly**, röt'ed-li, *adv.* In a rooted manner; deeply; from the heart.—**Rootedness**, röt'ed-nes, *n.* The state or condition of being rooted.—**Rootery**, röt'ér-i, *n.* A pile of roots used as an ornamental object in gardening.—**Root-house**, *n.* A house for storing potatoes, turnips, or other roots. —**Root-leaf**, *n.* A leaf growing immediately from the root.—**Rootless**, röt'les, *a.* Having no root.—**Rootlet**, röt'let, *n.* A radicle; a little root. — **Root-stock**, *n.* *Bot.* a prostrate rooting stem; a rhizome.— **Rooty**, röt'i, *a.* Full of roots.

Root, röt, *v.t.* [Formerly *wrote*, from A. Sax. *wrótan*, to root up, from *wrót*, Fris. *wrote*, a snout; D. *wroeten*, Icel. *róta*, Dan. *rode*, to root up as with the snout; akin G. *rüssel*, a snout.] To dig or burrow in with the snout; to turn up with the snout, as a swine; to tear up or out as if by rooting; to remove or destroy utterly; to exterminate: generally with *up*, *out*, *away*, &c.—*v.i.* To turn up the earth with the snout, as swine.

Ropalic, rō-pal'ik, *a.* [Gr. *hopalon*, a club.] Club-formed; swelling out toward the end.

Rope, rōp, *n.* [A.Sax. *ráp*, a rope=Icel *reip*, D *reep*, *roop*, G *reif*, Goth *raips*.] A cord of some thickness: a general name applied to cordage of greater circumference than string; a row or string of things tied together (a rope of onions).—*Rope's end*, a short piece of rope, or a hangman's noose; *fig.*, the end of one's opportunity.—*Rope of sand*, proverbially, a feeble union or tie; a band easily broken.—*To give a person rope*, to let him go on without check. —*v.i.—roped, roping.* To be formed into filaments from any glutinous or adhesive quality.—*v.t.* To fasten or tie with a rope or ropes; to pull by a rope. — **Rope-dancer**, *n.* One who dances or performs acrobatic feats on a rope extended at a greater or less height above the ground.— —**Rope-ladder**, *n.* A ladder made of ropes. — **Rope-maker**, *n.* One whose occupation is to make ropes or cordage.— **Rope-making**, *n.* The art or business of manufacturing ropes or cordage.—**Roper**, rō'pėr, *n.* A rope-maker; one who ropes goods. — **Ropery**, rō'pėr-i, *n.* A place where ropes are made; a rope-walk.— **Rope-spinner**, *n.* One that spins or makes ropes.—**Rope-walk**, *n.* A long covered walk or a long building where ropes are manufactured.—**Rope-yarn**, *n.* Yarn for ropes, consisting of a single thread which is twisted into strands.—**Ropy**, rō'pi, *a.* [Lit. like a rope, forming ropes.] Having such consistence that it may be drawn into viscous filaments; stringy; glutinous.—*Ropy wine*, wine showing a flaky sediment and oily appearance. — **Ropily**, rō'pi-li, *adv.* In a ropy or viscous manner.—**Ropiness**, rō'pi-nes, *n.* The state of being ropy.

Roquelaure, rō'ke-lōr, *n.* [From the Duke de *Roquelaure*.] A kind of short cloak used in the eighteenth century.

Roric, rō'rik, *a.* [L. *ros*, *roris*, dew.] Pertaining to or resembling dew; dewy.— **Roriferous**, rō-rif'ér-us, *a.* Generating or producing dew.

Rorqual, ror'kwal, *n.* A large whale of several species, not an object of capture, as it yields little oil or whalebone.

Rosace, rō-zäs', *n.* [Fr., from *rose*, a rose.] An ornamental piece of plaster-work in the centre of a ceiling.

Rosaceous, Rosary. Under ROSE.

Rose, rōz, *n.* [A.Sax. *rose*, Fr. *rose*, from L. *rosa*, a rose; allied to Gr. *rhodon*, a rose; probably from an Eastern source.] A well-known and universally cultivated plant and flower of many species and varieties, found in almost every country of the northern hemisphere, both in the Old and the New World; a knot of ribbon in the form of a rose, used as an ornament; a perforated nozzle of a pipe, spout, &c., to distribute water in fine shower-like jets; a popular name of the disease erysipelas: from its colour; a circular card or disc, or diagram with radiating lines, as the compass-card. — *Wars of the Roses*, the civil contest between the houses of York and Lancaster, the badge of the former house being a white, of the latter a red rose.— *Under the rose*, in secret; privately; in a manner that forbids disclosure.—*v.t.* To render rose-coloured; to cause to flush or blush. (*Poet.*)—**Rosaceous**, rō-zā'shus, *a.* [L. *rosaceus*.] Rose-like; composed of petals in a circular form (a *rosaceous* corolla); pertaining to the rose family of plants. — **Rosaniline**, rō-zan'i-lin, *n.* [That is, *rose-aniline*.] A substance obtained from aniline yielding a beautiful red dye. — **Rosary**, rō'za-ri, *n.* [Lit. a chaplet or garland of roses.] A chaplet; a garland; formerly often adopted as a title of books, consisting of pieces culled from various authors; a string of beads used by Roman Catholics, on which they count their prayers, there being so many small beads each for an Ave Maria, and so many large ones each for a Paternoster.—**Roseal**, rō'zē-al, *a.* Like a rose in smell or colour; roseate†. — **Rose-apple**, *n.* An Eastern tree and its fruit, the latter scented like the rose and flavoured like an apricot. —**Roseate**, rō'zē-āt, *a.* [L. *roseus*, rosy.] Full of roses; of a rose colour; blooming.— **Rosebud**, rōz'bud, *n.* The bud of a rose; the flower of the rose just appearing. — **Rose-carnation**, *n.* A carnation the ground colour of whose petals is striped with rose colour. — **Rose-colour**, *n.* The colour of the rose; *fig.* beauty; often fancied beauty or attractiveness. — **Rose-coloured**, *a.* Having the colour of a rose; highly alluring.—**Rose-diamond**, *n.* A diamond nearly hemispherical, cut with twenty-four triangular faces round a hexagonal centre.—**Rose-engine**, *n.* An appendage to the turning-lathe, by which a surface, such as a watch-case, is engraved with a variety of curved lines.—**Rose-gall**, *n.* An excrescence on the dog-rose.—**Rose-hued**, *a.* Of the hue or colour of the rose; rosy.—**Rose-lip**, *n.* A lip of a rosy colour. (*Tenn.*) — **Roselliate**, ro-zel'āt, *a.* *Bot.* applied to leaves when they are disposed like the petals of a rose.—**Rose-madder**, **Rose-lake**, *n.* A pigment of a rich red or rose colour.—**Rose-mallow**, *n.* Same as *Hollyhock*.—**Rose-noble**, *n.* An ancient English gold coin, stamped with the figure of a rose, current at 6*s.* 8*d.*—**Rose-pink**, *n.* A pigment having a rosy pink colour or hue.—*a.* Roseate; having a delicate bloom.—**Rose-quartz**, *n.* A variety of quartz which is rose-red.—**Rose-red**, *a.* Red as a rose.—**Rosery**, rō'zėr-i, *n.* A place where roses grow; a nursery of rose bushes.—**Rosette**, rō-zet', *n.* [Fr., a dim. of *rose*.] An imitation of a rose, as by ribbon, used as an ornament or badge; *arch.* a flower ornament of frequent use in decorations and in all styles.—**Rosetum**, rō-zē′tum, *n.* [L., from *rosa*, a rose.] A place devoted to the cultivation of roses.—**Rosewater**, *n.* Water tinctured with roses by distillation.—**Rose window**, *n.* *Arch.* a circular window divided into compartments by mullions or tracery radiating or branching from a center; called also *Catherine wheel* and *Marigold window*.—**Rosewood**, *n.* The wood of South American trees, so named because when freshly cut it has a faint agreeable odor of roses; in the highest esteem for cabinet-work.—**Rosolic acid**, rō-zol′ik, *n.* A dye-stuff akin to rosaniline.

Rosemary, rōz′ma-ri, *n.* [O.E. *rosmarine*, from L. *rosmarinus*, rosemary—*ros*, dew, and *marinus*, marine, from *mare*, the sea.] An evergreen shrub having a fragrant odor and a warm, pungent, bitterish taste.

Roseola, rō-zē′ō-la, *n.* [From L. *rosa*, a rose.] *Med.* a kind of rash or rose-colored efflorescence, occurring in connection with different febrile complaints.

Rosetta stone, rō-zet′a, *n.* A black basalt stele, with an inscription in hieroglyphics, demotic, and Greek, found in 1799 by Boussard, and important for having given Champollion a key for deciphering Egyptian hieroglyphics; it was acquired by the British in 1801, and is now in the British Museum.

Rosetta wood, rō-zet′a, *n.* A furniture wood of an orange-red color with dark veins, imported from the East Indies.

Rosicrucian, roz-i-krö′shi-an, *n.* [L. *rosa*, a rose, and *crux, crucis*, a cross, the name originating from that of the alleged founder *Rosenkreuz* (rosy cross).] One of a secret sect or society said to have originated in the fourteenth century, but brought into notice much more recently, whose members made great pretensions to a knowledge of the secrets of nature, and especially as to the transmutation of metals, the prolongation of life, &c., and were often known as Brothers of the Rosy Cross.—*a.* Pertaining to the Rosicrucians or their arts.—**Rosicrucianism**, roz-i-krö′shi-an-ism, *n.* The arts, practices, or doctrines of the Rosicrucians.

Rosin, roz′in, *n.* [Corruption of *resin*.] The name given to resin when it is employed in a solid state for ordinary purposes; obtained from turpentine by distillation, the volatile oil coming over and the rosin remaining behind.—*v.t.* To rub or cover over with rosin.—**Rosiny**, roz′i-ni, *a.* Resembling rosin; abounding with rosin.—**Rosin-oil**, *n.* An oil manufactured from pine-resin, used for machinery, &c.

Rosoglio, Rosolio, rō-zol′i-ō, *n.* [It. *rosolio*.] A red wine of Malta; a species of liqueur.

Rosset, ros′et, *n.* The kalong or flying-fox.

Rosso-antico, ros′ō-an-tē″kō, *n.* [It. *rosso*, red, and *antico*, ancient.] A technical name for the red porphyry of Egypt, used by the ancients for statuary purposes.

Rostel, ros′tel, *n.* [L. *rostellum*, dim. of *rostrum*, a beak. ROSTRUM.] *Bot.* any small beak-shaped process, as in the stigma of many violets.—**Rostellate**, ros′tel-āt, *a.* Having a rostel.—**Rostelliform**, ros-tel′i-form, *a.* Having the form of a rostel.

Roster, ros′tėr, *n.* [D. *rooster*, a thing for *roasting*, a gridiron, a table or list, a roster—the last meaning probably from perpendicular and horizontal lines of tabular statements giving a grated appearance. ROAST.] A list showing the rotation of those who relieve or succeed each other; a military list showing the rotation in which individuals, companies, regiments, &c., are called on to serve.

Rostrum, ros′trum, *n.* [L., the beak of a bird or other animal, the beak of a ship, from *rodo*, to gnaw. RODENT.] The beak or bill of a bird or other animal; the beak of a ship, especially of an ancient war galley; an elevated place in the forum at Rome where orations, funeral harangues, &c., were delivered (so called because adorned with the *rostra* of captured ships); hence, a platform from which any speaker addresses his audience.—**Rostral**, ros′tral, *a.* Pertaining to a rostrum; pertaining to the beak of a bird or other animal.—**Rostrate**, ros′trāt, *a.* Furnished or adorned with beaks; beak-shaped; having a process resembling the beak of a bird.—**Rostriform**, ros′tri-form, *a.* Having the form of a beak

Rosula, roz′ū-la, *n.* [Dim. of L. *rosa*, a rose.] A small rose; a rosette.—**Rosulate**, roz′ū-lāt, *a.* *Bot.* having the leaves arranged in little rose-like clusters.

Rosy. Under ROSE.

Rot, rot, *v.i.* — *rotted, rotting.* [A.Sax. *rotian*, to rot; D. *rotten*, Icel. *rotna*, to rot, *rotinn*, rotten (whence E. *rotten*, which is not used as the pp. of *rot*).] To decompose; to become putrid; to go to decay.—*v.t.* To make putrid; to cause to decompose; to bring to corruption; to expose to a process of partial rotting, as flax; to ret; used in the imperative as a sort of imprecation (*rot* it).—*n.* Putrefaction; a fatal distemper incident to sheep, caused by the liver-fluke; a disease very injurious to the potato; the potato disease.

Rota, rō′ta, *n.* [L. *rota*, a wheel.] An ecclesiastical court of Rome, composed of twelve prelates; a school roll or list; a roster.

Rotacism, rō′ta-sizm, *n.* [Gr. *rōtakismos*.] Faulty pronunciation of the letter R; burr.

Rotarian, rō-ta′ri-an, *n.* One who belongs to a world-wide organization, originating in America, having for its object the promotion of international fellowship and high ethical standards between business and professional men and members of various industries.

Rotary, rō′ta-ri, *a.* [From L. *rota*, a wheel; allied to G. *rad*, a wheel; W. *rhod*, a wheel, *rhedu*, to turn; Skr. *rathas*, a chariot. Ultimately from L. *rota* are E. *round, roll, rowel*, &c.] Turning, as a wheel on its axis; pertaining to rotation; rotatory.—*Rotary converter*, a machine for converting alternating electric current into direct current. — *Rotary engine*. ROTATORY. —**Rotate**, rō′tāt, *v.i.*—*rotated, rotating.* [L. *roto, rotatum*, to turn round, from *rota*, a wheel.] To revolve or move round a centre; to turn round as a wheel; to act in turn or rotation.—*v.t.* To cause to turn round like a wheel.—*a.* *Bot.* wheel-shaped; monopetalous, spreading nearly flat without any tube. —**Rotation**, rō-tā′shon, *n.* [L. *rotatio, rotationis*.] The act of rotating or turning; the motion of a solid body, as a wheel or sphere, about an axis; a return or succession in a series; established succession; the course in which persons leave their places or duties at certain times, and are succeeded by others; a recurring series of different crops grown on the same ground; the order of recurrence in cropping.—**Rotational**, rō-tā′shon-al, *a.* Pertaining to rotation. — **Rotator**, rō-tā′tėr, *n.* That which rotates or causes rotation; a muscle producing a rolling motion, as at the upper part of the thigh-bone.—**Rotatory**, rō′ta-to-ri, *a.* Pertaining to or consisting in rotation; exhibiting rotation; rotary. — *Rotatory* or *rotary steam-engine*, an engine in which a rotatory motion is produced by the direct action of the steam without the intervention of reciprocating parts.—*Rotatory muscle*, a rotator.—**Rotor**, rō′tor, *n.* [L. *rota*, a wheel.] The revolving part of an electric generator or motor.

Rotatoria, rō-tā-tō′ri-a, *n.pl.* Same as *Rotifera*.

Rotche, roch, *n.* [D. *rotje*, a petrel; comp. Prov.G. *rätsche*, a duck.] A bird of the auk family; the little auk.

Rote, rōt, *n.* [O.Fr. *rote*, a way, a *route*. ROUTE.] Repetition of words or sounds without attending to the signification; mere effort of memory: in the phrase *by rote*, by memory merely without intelligence.

Rotifers, Rotifera, rō′ti-ferz, rō-tif′ėr-a, *n.pl.* [L. *rota*, a wheel, and *fero*, to carry.] A class of animalcules, which, through the microscope, appear like revolving wheels, whence they have been called *wheel animalcules*.—**Rotiform**, rō′ti-form, *a.* Shaped like a wheel.

Rotor. ROTARY.

Rotten, rot′n, *a.* [A Scandinavian word= Icel. *rotinn*, Sw. *rutten*, rotten, a participle of an old verb akin to *rot*.] Putrid; decaying; decomposed by the natural process of decay; unsound; defective in principle; corrupt; fetid; ill-smelling.—*Rotten borough*, a name given to certain boroughs in England before the reform of 1832, which had fallen into decay and had a mere handful of voters, but which still retained the privilege of sending members to parliament.—**Rottenly**, rot′n-li, *adv.* In a rotten manner; putridly; unsoundly.—**Rottenness**, rot′n-nes, *n.* State of being rotten; putrefaction; unsoundness. — **Rotten-stone**, *n.* A soft stone much used for polishing household articles of brass or other metal, derived from the decomposition of siliceous limestones.

Rotund, rō-tund′, *a.* [L. *rotundus*, formed from *rota*, a wheel. *Round* is a form of the same word. ROTARY, ROUND.] Round; spherical; globular; *bot.* circumscribed by one unbroken curve, or without angles.—**Rotunda, Rotundo**, rō-tun′da, rō-tun′dō, *n.*. [It. *rotonda*. See above.] A round building; any building that is round both on the outside and inside.—**Rotundate**, rō-tun′dāt, *a.* Rounded off.—**Rotundity, Rotundness**, rō-tun′di-ti, rō-tund′nes, *n.* Sphericity; circularity.

Roturier, rō-tü-rē-ā, *n.* [Fr., a plebeian.] A plebeian; a man of mean extraction.

Rouble, rö′bl, *n.* [Rus.] The unit of the Russian money system before the World War, equal to about 50 cents, and divided into 100 kopecks. Written also *Ruble*.

Rouche, rösh, *n.* RUCHE.

Roué, rö-ā, *n.* [Fr. ppr. of *rouer*, to break on the wheel, from *roue*, L. *rota*, a wheel; lit. one worthy of suffering on the wheel. ROTARY.] A person devoted to a life of pleasure and sensuality; a rake.

Rouge, rözh, *n.* [Fr. *rouge*, from L. *rubeus*, red.] A cosmetic prepared from the dried flowers of the safflower, used to impart an artificial bloom to the cheeks or lips; a powder of a scarlet colour used for polishing gold, silver, &c.—*v.i.*—*rouged, rouging.* To paint the face, or rather the cheeks, with rouge.—*v.t.* To paint or tinge with rouge.—**Rouge-croix**, krwä, *n.* [Fr., red-cross.] **Rouge-dragon**, *n.* [Fr., red-dragon.] Names of two pursuivants of the Herald's College.—**Rouge-et-noir**, rözh-e-nwär, *n.* [Fr., red and black.] A game at cards played between a 'banker' and an unlimited number of persons, at a table marked with four spots of a diamond shape, two coloured black and two red.

Rough, ruf, *a.* [A.Sax. *rúh*, rough, shaggy; cog. D. *ruig*, *ruw*, L.G. *rug*, Dan. *ru*, G. *rauh, rauch*, rough; Lith. *raukas*, wrinkle.] Having prominences or inequalities; not smooth; having many irregularities of surface; harsh to the feel; unfinished; unpolished; shaggy; ragged; coarse; swelling into billows or breakers; stormy, as the sea or weather; not mild or gentle in character; boisterous; untamed; not mild or courteous; rude and brusque; harsh; severe; cruel; not refined or delicate; astringent; sour; harsh to the ear; grating; unharmonious; vague; crude (a *rough* guess).—*Rough diamond*, a diamond uncut; hence, *fig.* a person of genuine worth but rude and unpolished manners.—*Rough and ready*, of a hasty and unfinished sort; unpolished; unceremonious in manner, but reliable and always prepared for emergencies. — *v.t.* To give a rough appearance to; to make rough; to break in, as a horse; to shape out roughly, as a stone; to rough-hew.—*To rough it*, to submit to hardships; to put up for a time with rough accommodation.—*n.* The state of being coarse or in the original material: with *the* (materials or work in the *rough*); a rowdy; a rude coarse fellow; a bully.—

Rough-cast, *v.t.* To form in its first rudiments; to mould without nicety or elegance; to cover with a coarse sort of plaster composed of lime and gravel (to *rough-cast* a building).—*n.* The form of a thing in its first rudiments; a coarse kind of plastering for an external wall. — **Rough-draft, Rough-draught**, *v.t.* To draft or draw roughly; to make a rough sketch of.—*n.* A rough or rude sketch.—**Rough-draw**, *v.t.* To draw or delineate coarsely.—**Roughen**, ruf'n, *v.t.* To make rough.—*v.i.* To grow or become rough. — **Rough-footed**, *a.* Feather-footed. — **Rough-hew**, *v.t.* To hew coarsely without smoothing; to give the first form or shape to.—**Rough-hewn**, *p.* and *a.* Hewn coarsely without smoothing; rugged; unpolished; of coarse manners. **Roughish**, ruf'ish, *a.* In some degree rough.—**Roughly**, ruf'li, *adv.* In a rough manner; with uneven surface; harshly; severely; uncivilly; rudely; violently; not gently; boisterously; tempestuously. — **Roughness**, ruf'nes, *n.* The state or quality of being rough; harshness to the taste or ear; unevenness of surface; asperity of temper; coarseness of behavior or address. —**Roughrider**, *n.* One who breaks horses; in the Spanish-American War, a soldier of the 1st U. S. Volunteer Cavalry organized and later led by Theodore Roosevelt.— **Rough-shod**, *a.* Shod with shoes armed with points.—*To ride rough-shod, fig.* to pursue a violent or selfish course, regardless of others.

Roulade, rö-läd, *n.* [Fr., from *rouler*, to roll.] *Music*, a rapid run of notes, generally introduced as an embellishment.

Rouleau, rö-lō', *n.* pl. English **Rouleaus**, rö-lōz, French **Rouleaux**, rö-lō. [Fr., lit. a roll. ROLL.] A little roll; a roll of coin made up in paper.

Roulette, rö-let', *n.* [Fr., properly a little wheel, a castor, from *rouler*, to roll. ROLL.] A game of chance played with a ball at a table, in the centre of which is a cavity surmounted by a revolving disc having its circumference divided into compartments coloured black and red alternately, into any one of which the ball may drop; a tool furnished with a little toothed wheel, used by engravers for producing dotted work.

Roumansch, *n.* ROMANSCH.

Rounce, rouns, *n.* [Comp. D. *ronds*, wheel of a printing-press, from *rond*, round.] The handle of a printing-press that is worked by hand.

Round, round, *a.* [O.Fr. *roond*, round, Mod.Fr. *rond*, round, from L. *rotundus*, round, rotund, from *rota*, a wheel. ROTARY. *Rotund* is a doublet of this.] Having every part of the surface at an equal distance from the centre; spherical; globular; circular; cylindrical; having a curved form; swelling; plump; not given as extremely accurate (in *round* numbers); large; considerable (a good *round* sum); full in utterance; candid; free or plain in speech; without delicacy or reserve; without circumlocution; positive (a *round* assertion); smart or rapid (a *round* trot). — *Round dance*, a dance, as a polka, waltz, &c., in which the couples wheel round the room.— *Round game*, a game, as at cards, in which an indefinite number of players can take part, each on his own account. — *Round Table*, the table round which sat King Arthur and his knights.—*Round number*, a number that ends with a cipher, and may be divided by 10 without a remainder; a number not exact, but near enough the truth to serve the purpose.—*n.* That which is round, as a circle, a sphere, a globe; a series coming back to where it began (a *round* of toasts); a series of events or duties which come back to the point of commencement; the step of a ladder; a walk or circuit performed by a guard or an officer among sentinels; a short musical composition in which three or more voices starting at the beginning of stated successive phrases, sing the same music (in unison or octave) the combination of all the parts producing correct harmony; a dance in a ring; a general discharge of firearms by a body of troops, in which each soldier fires once; ammunition for firing once. — *A round of beef*, a cut of the thigh through and across the bone.—*adv.* On all sides; circularly; not in a direct line; through a circle, as of friends or houses.—*All round*, over the whole place; in every direction.— *To bring one round*, to restore one to health, composure, or the like; to cause one to alter his opinions. — *To come round*, to change one's opinions; to be restored to health, or the like.—*To turn round*, to turn one's self about; to change one's side; to desert one's party.—*prep.* On every side of; around; about, in a circular course. — *To come or get round one*, to gain advantage over one by flattery or deception.—*v.t.* To make round; to make full or complete; to make full, smooth, and flowing. — *v.i.* To grow or become round; to become complete or full; to develop into the full type.—*To round to* (*naut.*), to turn the head of the ship toward the wind.—**Roundabout**, round'a-bout, *a.* Indirect; going round; not straightforward. — *n.* A large horizontal wheel on which children ride; a merry-go-round; an arm-chair with a rounded back; a short close-fitting jacket; a circular dance. — **Round-backed, Round-shouldered**, *a.* Having a round or slightly raised back or shoulders. — **Rounder**, roun'dėr, *n.* One who makes the rounds of disreputable resorts; a dissolute spendthrift; a game played chiefly in England, somewhat resembling baseball.—**Round hand**. A style of penmanship in which the letters are round and full.—**Roundhead**, round'hed, *n.* A name given by the Cavaliers or adherents of Charles I to members of the Puritan or parliamentary party, from the latter having their hair closely cut, while the Cavaliers wore theirs long.—**Roundheaded**, round'hed-ed, *a.* Having a round head or top (*roundheaded* arches and windows).—**Roundhouse**, *n.* A circular building in which locomotives are repaired; a lock-up; a cabin on the after-part of the quarter-deck of a ship, having the poop for its roof.—**Roundish**, round'ish, *a.* Somewhat round.—**Roundly**, round'li, *adv.* In a round form; openly; plainly; without reserve; briskly; with speed; to the purpose; vigorously.— **Roundness**, round'nes, *n.* The quality of being round; circularity; sphericity; cylindrical form; fulness; smoothness of flow; plainness of speech; positiveness. — **Round robin**, [Fr. *rond*, round, and *ruban*, a ribbon.] A written petition, memorial, or remonstrance signed by names in a ring or circle that it may be impossible to ascertain who headed the list; a sport tournament arranged so that each contestant plays the same number of matches, resulting in the eventual elimination of the losers, an arrangement common in tennis.—**Round-shot**, *n.* A spherical solid shot of cast-iron or steel

Roundel, roun'del, *n.* [Fr. *rondelle*, from *rond*, round. ROUND.] Anything having a round form; a round figure; a circle; a roundelay (which see).

Roundelay, roun'de-lā, *n.* [O.Fr. *roundelet*, from Fr. *rond*, round. (ROUND.) The spelling has been influenced by *lay*, a song.] A sort of ancient poem, consisting of thirteen verses, of which eight are in one kind of rhyme and five in another; a song or tune in which the first strain is repeated; a dance in a circle.

Roup, roup, *n.* [O. and Prov.E. *roop*, *rope*, to cry, a cry, hoarseness; A.Sax. *hrópan*, Icel. *hrópa*, to cry.] In Scotland, a sale of goods by auction or outcry.

Roup, röp, *n.* A disease of poultry.

Rouse, rouz, *v.t.—roused, rousing.* [Connected with L.G. *ruse*, noise, disturbance; A.Sax. *hreósan*, to rush, to fall; O.H.G. *ruozjan*, to rouse, to move.] To wake from sleep; to excite to thought or action from a state of idleness, languor, or inattention; to put into commotion; to agitate; to startle; to surprise; to drive from a lurking-place or cover; a hunting term.—*v.i.* To awake from sleep or repose; to be excited to thought or action.—*n.* [Comp. D. *roes*, a bumper; G. *rausch*, drunkenness.] A carousal; a drinking frolic or festival. (*Tenn.*) — **Rousing**, rou'zing, *p.* and *a.* Having power to awaken or excite; stirring. — **Rousingly**, rou'zing-li, *adv.* In a rousing manner; excitingly.

Roussette, rö-set', *n.* [Fr., from *rousse*, red, from its colour.] A kind of bat of a rusty red colour.

Rout, rout, *n.* [O.Fr. *route*, a company, a band, a division; lit. a portion broken off or separated; from L.L. *rupta*, from L. *ruptus*, broken, pp. of *rumpo*, to break. RUPTURE.] A company of persons; a rabble or multitude; a fashionable assembly or large evening party; an uproar; a brawl; the breaking or defeat of troops; the disorder and confusion of troops thus defeated.—*v.t.* To break the ranks of and put to flight in disorder; to defeat and throw into confusion; to drive or chase away; to dispel.—**Routish**, rout'ish, *a.* Clamorous; disorderly.

Rout, röt, *v.t.* [Form of to *root*.] To turn up with the snout (as hogs); to root.

Route, röt, *n.* [Fr. *route*, O.Fr. *rote*, a rut, way, path, from L.L. *rupta*, a path, properly *rupta via*, a path broken through forests, &c., from L. *ruptus*, broken, pp. of *rumpo*, to break. ROUT, a company. RUPTURE.] The course or way which is travelled or passed, or to be passed; a passing; a course; a march.—*To get the route* (*milit.*), to receive orders to quit one station for another; *route march*, a march performed for exercise and training, by a body of troops in full equipment.

Routine, rö-tēn', *n.* [Fr., from *route*, a way: properly the way which one invariably takes through custom. ROUTE.] A round of business, amusements, or pleasure, daily or frequently pursued; a course of business or duties regularly returning; habit or practice adhered to by force of habit.—**Routinist**, rö-tēn'ist, *n.* One addicted to routine.

Rove, rōv, *v.i.—roved, roving.* [Originally to wander for plunder, a collateral form of *reave*, directly from the L.G. or D.; L.G. *roven*, D. *rooven*, Dan. *röve*, Sw. *röfva*, to rob; Icel. *ráfa*, *rápa*, to wander.] To wander; to ramble; to range; to go, move, or pass without certain direction in any manner.—*v.t.* To wander over.—**Rover**, rō'vėr, *n.* One who roves; one who rambles about; a fickle or inconstant person; a pirate; *in archery*, a mark chosen at will or at random, chiefly in the phrase, *to shoot at rovers*, equivalent to *to shoot at random*.— **Roving**, rō'ving, *n.* The act of rambling or wandering.—**Rovingly**, rō'ving-li, *adv.* In a roving or wandering manner.

Rove, rōv, *v.t.—roved, roving.* [Akin to *reeve* or to *ravel*.] To draw through an eye or aperture; to bring (wool or cotton) into that form which it receives before being spun into thread; to card into flakes, as wool, &c.—*n.* A roll of wool, cotton, &c., drawn out and slightly twisted.

Row, rō, *n.* [A.Sax. *ráw*, a row; perhaps from same root as *room*, and meaning originally the space or interval between rows.] A series of persons or things arranged in a continued line; a line; a rank; a file.

Row, rō, *v.t.* [A.Sax. *rówan*, to row=Icel. *róa*, Dan. *roe*, Sw. *ro*, D. *roeijen*, to row. *Rudder* is from same stem.] To impel along the surface of water by oars; to transport by rowing.—*v.i.* To labour with the oar; to be moved by means of oars.— *n.* An excursion taken in a boat with oars. —**Rower**, rō'ėr, *n.* One that rows or manages an oar in rowing.—**Rowlock**, rō'lok, *n.* A contrivance on a boat's gunwale on which the oar rests in rowing, formed with two upright pegs, or of a single peg or otherwise.

Row, rou, *n.* [Perhaps short for *rowdydow*, a word used as imitative of noise or disturbance; or from *rouse*, *n.*] A riotous noise; a turbulent, noisy disturbance; a riot. (*Colloq.*)—*v.t.* To scold. (*Colloq.*)

Rowan, rou'an, *n.* [Same as Dan. *rön*,

rönne-træ, Sw. *rönn*, the rowan; akin perhaps to old *roun*, *round*, to whisper, *rune*, A.Sax. *rún*, mystery, there being sundry superstitions connected with it.] MOUNTAIN-ASH.

Rowdy, rou'di, *n.* [From *rowdydow*. See ROW, a disturbance.] A riotous turbulent fellow; a rough. (*Colloq.*)—*a.* Disreputable; blackguard. (*Colloq.*)—**Rowdyish**, rou'di-ish, *a.* Belonging to a rowdy.—**Rowdyism**, rou'di-izm, *n.* The conduct of a rowdy; turbulent blackguardism.

Rowel, rou'el, *n.* [O.Fr. *rouelle*, dim. of *roue*, L. *rota*, a wheel. ROTARY.] The little wheel of a spur with sharp points for pricking the horse; a little flat ring or wheel on horses' bits; a roll of hair or silk passed through the flesh of horses, answering to a seton in surgery.—**Rowel-head**, *n.* The axis on which a rowel turns.

Rowen, rou'en, *n.* [From O.E. *row*, *rowe*, a form of *rough*.] The aftermath.

Royal, roi'al, *a.* [Fr. *royal*, from L. *regalis* from *rex*, *regis*, a king. REGAL.] Pertaining or belonging to a king; pertaining to the crown; regal; becoming a king; kingly; princely; noble; generous; founded or originated by, in the service of, under the patronage of, or receiving support from royalty (*royal* navy); a term for a large size of paper.—*Royal Academy*, an incorporated society in London established for the promotion of the fine arts and having forty-two members.—*Royal assent*. ASSENT.—*Royal grant*, a grant by letters patent from the crown.—*Royal Highness*, a title used in speaking to or of a prince or princess; also, the prince or princess thus referred to or addressed.—*Royal Standard*, a rectangular banner containing the Royal Arms. It is solely the prerogative of the sovereign, and may not be flown over any building in which the reigning monarch is not present.—*Royal Society*, a society incorporated by Charles II in 1660 for the study of physical science, and which still flourishes in London. ∴ *Royal* denotes what pertains to the king as an individual, or is associated with his person (the *royal* family). *Regal* is applied primarily to what pertains to a king in virtue of his office; hence, to what becomes a king, and is nearly synonymous with princely, magnificent (*regal* state). *Kingly* signifies literally, like a king, hence, proper to or becoming a king, and it has often, like *royal*, reference to personal qualities.—*n. Naut.* a square sail spread immediately above the top-gallant-sail; a gold coin formerly current in England.—**Royalism**, roi'al-izm, *n.* Attachment to a royal government.—**Royalist**, roi'al-ist, *n.* An adherent of a king, or one attached to a kingly government; *Eng. hist.* an adherent of Charles I and Charles II, opposed to *Roundhead* (which see).—**Royalize**, roi'al-īz, *v.t.*—*royalized*, *royalizing*. To make royal.—**Royally**, roi'al-li, *adv.* In a royal or kingly manner; like a king; as becomes a king.—**Royalty**, roi'al-ti, *n.* The state or quality of being royal; condition or status of a person of royal rank; the person of a king; majesty (to stand in the presence of *royalty*); a right or prerogative of a king; a tax paid to the crown or to a superior on the produce of a mine, or to an inventor for the use of his patent.—**Royal-yard**, *n. Naut.* the yard on which the sail called royal is set.

Roysterer, roi'stėr-ėr, *n.* ROISTERER.

Royston-crow, roi'ston, *n.* The common English name for what is otherwise called the hooded crow.

Rub, rub, *v.t.*—*rubbed*, *rubbing*. [Same word as Dan. *rubbe*, to rub, to scrub; akin also to W. *rhwb*, a rub, *rhwbiad*, a rubbing; Gael. *rub*, *rubadh*, Ir. *rubha*, a hurt, *rubadh*, attrition. *Rubbish*, *rubble* are derivatives.] To move along the surface of, or backwards and forwards upon, with friction; to apply friction to; to wipe; to clean; to scour; to smear all over; to gall or chafe; to gibe.—*To rub down*, to reduce to smaller dimensions by friction; to clean by rubbing, as a horse.—*To rub off*, to separate by friction.—*To rub out*, to erase; to obliterate.—*To rub up*, to burnish; to polish; to rouse to action.—*v.i.* To move along the surface of a body with pressure; to grate; to fret; to chafe; to get on or along with difficulty; usually with *on*, *along*, or *through* (to *rub through* the world).—*n.* An act of rubbing; something that renders motion or progress difficult; a difficulty or obstruction; a sarcasm; a gibe; something grating to the feelings; *bowling*, inequality of ground that hinders the motion of a bowl.

Rubber, rub'ėr, *n.* An elastic, resilient coherent solid made from the juice of certain trees and plants found chiefly in the tropics, and manufactured into tires, hose, water bottles, waterproofed fabrics, &c.; something made of this material, as an eraser, overshoe, &c.; a person who rubs, as a massager; a coarse file; a whetstone; *cards*, two games out of three, or a contest consisting of three games.—**Rubberize**, *v.t.*—*rubberized*, *rubberizing*. To coat or impregnate with rubber so as to make waterproof or airtight.—**Rubber-stamp**, *v.t.* To approve or endorse by printing with a stamping device; hence, to approve quickly without examination.

Rubasse, ru̦-bas', *n.* [Fr., from L. *rubeus*, red; akin *ruby*.] A lapidaries' name for a beautiful variety of rock-crystal, speckled in the interior with minute spangles of specular iron, which reflect a colour resembling that of the ruby.

Rubbish, rub'ish, *n.* [Influenced by *rub*, but from O.E. *robows*, *robeux*, *robrish*, a word of doubtful origin.] Refuse fragments of building materials; debris; waste or rejected matter; trash.—**Rubbishy**, rub'ish-i, *a.* Characterized by rubbish; trashy; worthless. (*Colloq.*)

Rubble, **Rubble-stone**, rub'l, *n.* [Akin to *rubbish*.] The upper fragmentary and decomposed portion of a mass of stone; stones of irregular shapes and dimensions, broken bricks, &c., used in coarse masonry, or to fill up between the facing courses of walls.—**Rubble-work**, *n.* Walls or masonry built of rubble-stones.—**Rubbly**, rub'l-i, *a.* Abounding in rubble.

Rubefacient, rö-bē-fā'shi-ent, *a.* [L. *rubefaciens*, *rubefacientis*—*rubeo*, to be red, and *facio*, to make.] Making red; producing redness on the skin.—*n. Med.* a substance for external application which produces redness of the skin, not followed by a blister.

Rubella, rö-bel'a, *n.* [L. *rubellus*, reddish, from *ruber*, red.] A disease resembling measles, accompanied by a reddish rash and other symptoms, but less serious than measles: called often *German Measles*.

Rubellite, rö'bel-īt, *n.* [L. *rubellus*, dim. of *ruber*, red.] Red tourmaline, a siliceous mineral of a red colour.

Rubeola, rö-bē'o-la, *n.* [From L. *ruber*, red.] A name of measles.—**Rubeoloid**, rö-bē'o-loid, *a.* Pertaining to or resembling rubeola.

Rubescent, rö-bes'ent, *a.* [L. *rubescens*, *rubescentis*, ppr. of *rubesco*, from *rubeo*, to be red, from *ruber*, red.] Growing or becoming red; tending to a red colour.

Rubicel, **Rubicelle**, rö'bi-sel, *n.* [L. *rubeo*, to be red.] A variety of ruby of a reddish colour, from Brazil.

Rubicon, rö'bi-kon, *n.* The river forming the southern boundary of Cæsar's province of Cisalpine Gaul, crossing which meant declaration of war. *Metaphorically*, to face any difficulty or crisis in a resolute manner.

Rubicund, rö'bi-kund, *a.* [L. *rubicundus*, from *rubeo*, to be red.] Inclining to redness; ruddy; blood-red: said especially of the face.—**Rubicundity**, rö-bi-kun'di-ti, *n.* The state of being rubicund; redness.

Rubidium, rö-bid'i-um, *n.* [From L. *rubidus*, red—from the nature of its spectrum.] A metal belonging to the group of elements which likewise includes lithium, sodium, potassium, and cæsium, found in mineral waters.

Rubific, rö-bif'ik, *a.* [L. *ruber*, red, and *facio*, to make.] Making red; colouring with red.

Rubigo, rö-bī'gō, *n.* [L. *rubigo*, rust, *rubeus*, red. RUBY, RUST.] A kind of rust on plants, consisting of a parasitic fungus; mildew.—**Rubiginous**, rö-bij'i-nus, *a.* Exhibiting or affected by rubigo; mildewed.

Ruble, rö'bl, *n.* Same as ROUBLE.

Rubric, rö'brik, *n.* [Fr. *rubrique*, from L. *rubrica* (*terra*), red earth, the title of a law in red, a law, from *ruber*, red. RUBY.] Some part of a manuscript or printed matter that is, or in former times usually was, coloured red, to distinguish it from other portions; in law books, the title of a statute, formerly written in red letters; in prayer-books, the directions and rules for the conduct of service, often printed in red; hence an ecclesiastical or episcopal rule or injunction; any formulated, fixed, or authoritative injunction of duty.—**Rubric**, **Rubrical**, rö'bri-kal, *a.* Pertaining to a rubric.—**Rubricate**, **Rubricated**, rö'bri-kāt, rö'bri-kā-ted, *a.* Marked with red.—**Rubrician**, **Rubricist**, rö-brish'an, rö'bri-sist, *n.* One versed in rubrics; an adherent or advocate for the rubric.

Ruby, rö'bi, *n.* [Fr. *rubis*, Sp. *rubi*, *rubin*, from L.L. *rubinus*, a carbuncle, from L. *rubeus*, red, reddish, *ruber*, red (akin *rubric*, *rust*).] A gem next to the diamond in hardness and value, of various shades of red, the most highly prized varieties being the crimson and carmine red; redness; red colour; something resembling a ruby; a blotch on the face; a carbuncle; *printing*, a type smaller than nonpareil and larger than pearl.—*Rock ruby*, the most valued species of garnet.—*v.t.*—*rubied*, *rubying*. To make red.—*a.* Of the colour of the ruby; red.—**Rubied**, rö'bid, *a.* Red as a ruby.

Ruche, **Rucheing**, rösh, rösh'ing, *n.* [Fr. *ruche*, a beehive. The stuff has its name from the quillings resembling honeycomb cells.] Quilled or goffered net, lace, silk, and the like, used as trimming for ladies' dress and bonnets. Spelled also *Rouche*.

Ruck, ruk, *v.t.* [Icel. *hrukka*, a wrinkle, a fold, *rykkja*, to draw into folds; comp. Gael. *roc*, a wrinkle, to become wrinkled.] To wrinkle; to crease.—*n.* A wrinkle; a crease.

Ruck, ruk, *n.* [Akin to *rick*, O.Sw. *ruka*, a heap.] An undistinguished crowd.

Ructions, ruk'shons, *n.* Disturbance; trouble. (*Colloq.*)

Rud, **Rudd**, rud, *n.* [A.Sax. *rudu*, redness.] Red ochre.

Rudd, rud, *n.* [From the *ruddy* colouring.] A European fresh-water fish, with sides and belly yellow, marked with red; ventral and anal fins and tail deep red.

Rudder, rud'ėr, *n.* [A.Sax. *róthor*, lit. rowing implement (the rudder being originally a kind of oar), from *rówan*, to row; D. *roeder*, Sw. *roder*, G. *ruder*, rudder. ROW, *v.t.*] The instrument by which a ship is steered; that part of the helm which consists of a piece of timber, broad at the bottom and attached to the stern-post by hinges, on which it turns; *fig.* that which guides or governs a course; in *aviation*, the subsidiary aerofoil (in an aeroplane more or less perpendicular to the main supporting surfaces) by means of which an air-craft is turned to left or right.—**Rudder-bands**, *n.pl.* The hinges of the rudder.—**Rudder-chains**, *n.pl.* Chains attached to the hinder part of the rudder to work it when the tiller is damaged.

Ruddle, rud'l, *n.* [Akin to *ruddy*, *red*.] A species of red earth colored by iron, used for marking sheep.—*v.t.* To mark with ruddle.

Ruddock, **Ruddoc**, rud'ok, *n.* [A.Sax. *rudduc*, a dim. akin to *ruddy*.] A bird, the European robin-redbreast.

Ruddy, rud'i, *a.* [From A. Sax. *rud*, red, *rudu*, redness. RED.] Of a red color, or of a color approaching redness; of a lively flesh-color, or the color of the Caucasian skin in high health; of a reddish shining color (*ruddy* gold).—*v.t.*—*ruddied*, *ruddy-*

ing. To make red or ruddy.—**Ruddily**, rud'i-li, *adv.* With a ruddy or reddish appearance.—**Ruddiness**, rud'i-nes, *n.* The state of being ruddy; that degree of redness which characterizes high health.

Rude, röd, *a.* [Fr. *rude*, from L. *rudis*, in a natural state, rough, wild.] Unformed by art, taste, or skill; rough; rugged; coarse; of coarse manners; ignorant; untaught; clownish; uncivil; uncourteous; violent; boisterous.—**Rudely**, röd'li, *adv.* In a rude manner; roughly; unskilfully; coarsely; uncivilly; violently; boisterously.—**Rudeness**, röd'nes, *n.* The state or quality of being rude.

Rudenture, rö'den-tūr, *n.* [Fr., from L. *rudens, rudentis*, a rope.] *Arch.* the figure of a rope with which the flutings of columns are sometimes filled.

Rüdesheimer, rü'des-hī-mėr, *n.* One of the white Rhine wines, made from grapes produced near *Rüdesheim.*

Rudiment, rö'di-ment, *n.* [L. *rudimentum*, from *rudis*, rude. RUDE.] That which is in an undeveloped state; an unformed or unfinished beginning; an element or first principle of any art or science; especially in plural, the introduction to any branch of knowledge; the elements or elementary notions.—**Rudimentary, Rudimental**, rö-di-men'ta-ri, rö-di-men'tal, *a.* Pertaining to rudiments; elementary; initial; in an undeveloped state; imperfectly developed; in the first stage of existence; embryonic. — *Rudimentary organ.* See VESTIGE.

Rue, rö, *v.t.—rued, ruing.* [A.Sax. *hreówan*, to rue = D. *rouwen*, G. *reuen*, to repent; same root as *crude*, L. *crudus*, raw, *cruel*, L. *crudelis.* Hence *ruth.*] To regret; to grieve for; to repent; to repent of and withdraw, or try to withdraw, from (to *rue* a bargain).—*v.i.* To have compassion; to become sorrowful, grieved, or repentant.—**Rueful**, rö'ful, *a.* Causing to rue or lament; mournful; sorrowful; expressing sorrow; suggesting sorrow or melancholy; pitiful.—**Ruefully**, rö'ful-li, *adv.* In a rueful manner.—**Ruefulness**, rö'ful-nes, *n.* The state of being rueful.

Rue, rö, *n.* [Fr. *rue*, from L. *ruta*, from Gr. *rutē*, rue.] A plant with evergreen leaves and greenish-yellow flowers, used as a sudorific and a vermifuge.

Rufescent, rö-fes'ent, *n.* [L. *rufescens*, from *rufus*, red.] Reddish; tinged with red.

Ruff, ruf, *n.* [Connected with Prov.Fr. *rufo*, a crease or wrinkle, Armor. *roufen*, a wrinkle, a fold; Sp. *rufo*, frizzled, curled; comp. also D. *ruif*, a fold.] A large muslin or linen collar plaited, crimped, or fluted, formerly an important ornament of dress among both sexes; a species of pigeon having feathers disposed round its neck in the form of a ruff; a male bird of the sandpiper family, having the feathers of the neck standing out like a ruff, the female being called *reeve*; a low vibrating beat of a drum; a ruffle.

Ruff, ruf, *n.* [Pg. *rufa*, a game with dice.] An old game at cards, the predecessor of whist; the act of trumping when you have no cards of the suit led.—*v.t. Card playing*, to trump instead of following suit.

Ruff, *n.* and *v.t.* A cry or sign of approbation or otherwise, distracting or encouraging a speaker.

Ruff, ruf, *n.* [Origin unknown.] A small European fish of the perch family.

Ruffian, ruf'i-an, *n.* [O.Fr. *rufien, ruffien*, a ruffian; Sp. *rufian*, a ruffian, a pimp; It. *ruffiano*, a pimp; probably of German origin.] A boisterous brutal fellow; a fellow ready for any desperate crime.—*a.* Like or belonging to a ruffian; brutal.—**Ruffianish**, ruf'i-an-ish, *a.* Having the qualities of a ruffian.—**Ruffianism**, ruf'i-an-izm, *n.* The character or manners of ruffians.—**Ruffianly**, ruf'i-an-li, *a.* Like a ruffian; bold in crimes; violent.

Ruffle, ruf'l, *v.t.—ruffled, ruffling.* [A freq. of *ruff*=D. *ruyffeln*, to wrinkle.] To disorder; to rumple; to derange; to disarrange; to disturb the surface of; to cause to ripple or rise in waves; to agitate; to disturb (to *ruffle* the mind); to furnish or adorn with ruffles; to contract into plaits or folds.—*To ruffle one's feathers*, to irritate one; to make one angry.—*v.i.* To grow rough or turbulent; to put on airs; to swagger: often with an indefinite *it.*—*n.* A strip of plaited cambric or other fine cloth attached to some border of a garment, as to the wristband or bosom; a frill; a state of being disturbed or agitated; a low vibrating beat of the drum. — **Ruffler**, ruf'l-ėr, *n.* A bully; a swaggerer.

Rufous, rö'fus, *a.* [L. *rufus*, red; allied to *ruber*, red (whence *rubric*).] Reddish; of a yellowish or brownish red.

Rug, rug, *n.* [Akin to Icel. *röggr*, a tuft, shagginess; Sw. *rugg, ragg*, rough hair. *Rugged* and *rag* are allied.] A floor covering of thick, heavy fabric with a nap or pile, mostly of wool, generally woven in one piece of a definite shape and design in distinction from a carpet; also a lap robe.

Rugate, rö'gāt, *a.* [L. *ruga*, a wrinkle.] Wrinkled; rugose.

Rugby, rug'bi, *n.* One of the two principal varieties of football, played by fifteen men a side, with an oval ball, handling being permitted.

Rugged, rug'ed, *a.* [Closely akin to *rug.*] Full of rough projections on the surface; broken into irregular points or prominences (a *rugged* mountain, a *rugged* road); rough; shaggy; rough in temper; hard; crabbed; austere; rough to the ear; harsh; grating (*rugged* prose).—**Ruggedly**, rug'ed-li, *adv.* In a rugged manner.—**Ruggedness**, rug'ed-nes, *n.* The quality or state of being rugged.

Rugose, Rugous, rö'gōs, rö'gus, *a.* [L. *rugosus*, from *ruga*, a wrinkle.] Wrinkled; full of wrinkles.—**Rugosity**, rö-gos'i-ti, *n.* A state of being rugose; a wrinkle; a pucker; a slight ridge.—**Rugulose**, rö'gū-lōs, *a. Bot.* finely wrinkled.

Ruin, rö'in, *n.* [Fr. *ruine*, from L. *ruina*, a falling down, downfall, ruin, from *ruo, rutum*, to fall, to rush down.] That change of anything which destroys it or entirely unfits it for use; destruction; overthrow; downfall; what promotes injury, decay, or destruction; bane; perdition; a building or anything in a state of decay or dilapidation; *pl.* the remains of a decayed or demolished city, house, fortress, &c.; the state of being destroyed or rendered worthless (to go to *ruin*).—*v.t.* To bring to ruin or destruction; to damage essentially; to destroy, defeat, demolish.—*v.i.* To fall into ruins; to run to ruin.—**Ruinable**, rö'in-a-bl, *a.* Capable of being ruined.—**Ruinate**, rö'i-nāt, *v.t.—ruinated, ruinating.* To ruin.—*a.* Brought to ruin; ruined; in ruins.—**Ruination**, rö-i-nā'shon, *n.* The act of ruinating; subversion; overthrow; demolition.—**Ruiner**, rö'in-ėr, *n.* One that ruins.—**Ruinous**, rö'i-nus, *a.* [L. *ruinosus.*] Fallen to ruin; dilapidated; composed of ruins; bringing or tending to bring ruin.—**Ruinously**, rö'i-nus-li, *adv.* In a ruinous manner; destructively.—**Ruinousness**, rö'i-nus-nes, *n.*

Rukh, ruk, *n.* The roc.

Rule, röl, *n.* [O.E. *reule, rewle*, from O.Fr. *reule, riule* (Fr. *règle*), from L. *regula*, a straight piece of wood, a ruler, a rule or pattern (whence *regular*), from *rego*, to keep straight, to govern. REGAL, RIGHT.] Government; sway; control; supreme command or authority; an established principle, standard, or guide for action; something settled by authority or custom for guidance and direction; a maxim, canon, or precept to be observed; the body of laws or regulations observed by a religious society and its members (the *rule* of St. Benedict); a point of law settled by authority; an instrument by which straight lines are drawn; an instrument for measuring short lengths, and performing various operations in mensuration; *arith.* a determinate mode prescribed for performing any operation and producing a certain result; *gram.* an established form of construction in a particular class of words, or the expression of that form in words.—*Rule of the road*, the regulation as to the side which drivers and equestrians are to keep in crossing or overtaking each other.—*Rule of thumb*, a rule suggested by a practical rather than a scientific knowledge.—*v.t.—ruled, ruling.* To govern; to exercise authority or dominion over; to control, conduct, guide; to mark with lines by a ruler; *law*, to establish by rule; to determine; to decide.—*v.i.* To have power or command; to exercise supreme authority: often followed by *over*; *com.* to stand or maintain a level (prices *rule* lower than formerly).—**Rulable**, röl'a-bl, *a.* Capable of being ruled; governable.—**Ruleless**, röl'les, *a.* Being without rule; lawless.—**Ruler**, röl'ėr, *n.* One that rules or governs; one that assists in carrying on a government; an instrument made of wood, brass, ivory, &c., with straight edges or sides, by which straight lines may be drawn on paper or other substance, by guiding a pen or pencil along the edge.—**Ruling**, röl'ing, *p.* and *a.* Governing; reigning; chief; prevalent; predominant.—*n.* A rule or point settled by a judge or court of law.—**Rulingly**, röl'ing-li, *adv.*

Rum, rum, *n.* [Perhaps of West Indian origin; or from an old cant word *rumbooze*, good drink. See RUM, *a.*] Spirit distilled from cane juice, or from treacle or molasses.—**Rummy**, rum'i, *a.* Pertaining to rum.—**Rum-shrub**, *n.* A liquor composed of rum, sugar, and lime or lemon juice.

Rum, rum, *a.* [From an old cant word *rum, rome*, great, good, used in a contemptuous sense, from *Rom*, applied by themselves to the gypsies.] Old-fashioned; odd; queer. (*Slang.*)

Rumble, rum'bl, *v.i.—rumbled, rumbling.* [Same as D. *rommelen*, Dan. *rumle*, G. *rummeln, rumpeln*, probably imitative of sound; comp. L. *rumor*, whence E. *rumour.*] To make a low, heavy, hoarse, continued sound.—*n.* A low, heavy, continuous sound; a rumbling; a seat for servants behind a carriage.—**Rumbler**, rum'blėr, *n.* The person or thing that rumbles.—**Rumbling**, rum'bling, *p.* and *a.* Making a low, heavy, continued sound (a *rumbling* noise).—*n.* A low, heavy, continued sound; a rumble.—**Rumblingly**, rum'bling-li, *adv.* In a rumbling manner.

Rumen, rö'men, *n.* [L.] The upper or first stomach of animals which chew the cud.

Ruminate, rö'mi-nāt, *v.i.—ruminated, ruminating.* [L. *rumino, ruminatum*, from *rumen*, the throat, the gullet.] To chew the cud; to chew again what has been slightly chewed and swallowed; to muse; to meditate; to think again and again; to ponder.—*v.t.* To chew over again; to muse or meditate on.—**Ruminant**, rö'mi-nant, *a.* [L. *ruminans, ruminantis*, ppr. of *rumino.*] Chewing the cud; characterized by chewing again what has been swallowed (*ruminant* animals).—*n.* A member of an order of herbivorous hoofed mammals that chew the cud, as the camel, deer, goat, ox, &c.—**Ruminantly**, rö'mi-nant-li, *adv.* In a ruminant manner; by chewing.—**Rumination**, rö-mi-nā'shon, *n.* The act of ruminating; the act of meditating; a musing or continued thinking.—**Ruminator**, rö'mi-nā-tėr, *n.* One that ruminates.

Rummage, rum'āj, *v.t.—rummaged, rummaging.* [Same as if *roomage*; originally a sea term signifying to stow goods in a ship's hold, or to remove them from the hold, from *rome*, an old form of *room*, or from D. *ruim*, the hold of a ship, a form of the same word. ROOM.] To search narrowly every place or part of, by looking into every corner and turning over goods or other things; to explore; to ransack.—*v.i.* To search a place narrowly by looking among things.—*n.* A searching carefully by looking into every corner and by tumbling over things.—**Rummager**, rum'āj-ėr, *n.* One who rummages.

Rummer, rum'ėr, *n.* [D. *roomer*, Sw. *remmer*, G. *römer*, a large drinking-glass; perhaps lit. a *Roman* glass.] A glass or drinking-cup.

Rummy. Under RUM.

Rumor, Rumour, rö'mėr, *n.* [Fr. *rumeur,* from L. *rumor,* common talk. RUMBLE.] Flying or popular report; the common voice; a current story passing from one person to another, without any known authority for the truth of it; a mere report. —*v.t.* To tell or circulate by report; to spread abroad; to report.

Rump, rump, *n.* [A Scandinavian word = Icel. *rumpr,* Sw. *rumpa,* D. *rompe,* G. *rumpf,* the trunk.] The end of the backbone of an animal, with the parts adjacent; the buttocks; *fig.* the fag-end of something which lasts longer than the original body; *Eng. hist.* the fag-end of the Long Parliament, after the expulsion of the majority of its members by Cromwell in 1648.—**Rump-steak,** *n.* A beef-steak cut from the thigh near the rump.

Rumple, rum'pl, *v.t.—rumpled, rumpling.* [Same as D. *rompelen,* to rumple; akin to O.L.G. *rumpele,* a wrinkle; G. *rumpfen, rümpfen,* to crimp, to wrinkle. *Rimple* is another form; comp. also *ripple.*] To wrinkle; to make uneven; to ruffle; to dishevel.—*n.* A fold or plait.—**Rumply,** rum'pli, *a.* Rumpled. (*Colloq.*)

Rumpus, rum'pus, *n.* [Perhaps imitative of a noise, like *rumble;* or allied to *romp.*] A riot; a great noise; disturbance. (*Colloq.*)

Run, run, *v.i.* pret. *ran* (*run* is now incorrect); pp. *run;* ppr. *running.* [A.Sax. *rinnan* (pret. *ran,* pl. *runnon,* pp. *runnen*); O.Sax., Goth., and O.H.G. *rinnan,* D. *rennen, rinnen,* Icel. *renna,* G. *rennen,* to run; same root as in Skr. *ri,* to go.] To pass over the ground by using the legs more quickly than in walking; to contend in a race; hence, to enter into a contest; to flee for escape; to retreat hurriedly; to steal away; to extend quickly; to spread (the fire *runs* over a field); to rush or be carried along with violence (a ship *runs* against a rock); to move on wheels or runners, as a locomotive or sledge; to sail, as a ship; to pass or go back and forth from place to place; to ply (ships, railway trains, stage-coaches, &c., between different places); to move or pass, as a fluid, the sand in an hour-glass, or the like; to be wet with a flowing liquid; to become fluid; to fuse; to melt; to spread on a surface; to spread and blend (colours *run* in washing; ink *runs* on damp paper); to discharge pus or other matter (an ulcer *runs*); to revolve on an axis or pivot; to turn, as a wheel; to continue going or in operation (an engine *runs,* the mills are *running*); to pass or proceed in thought or speech (to *run* from one topic to another); to pass from one state or condition to another (to *run* into error or into debt); to proceed or pass, as time; to have a certain course, track, or direction; to extend, stretch, lie (the street *runs* east and west); to have a certain written form; to read so or so to the ear (the lines *run* smoothly); to have a continued tenor or purport (the conversation *ran* as follows); to be popularly spread or received; to continue or be repeated for a certain time (the play *ran* for a hundred nights); to be carried to a pitch; to rise (debates *run* high); to grow exuberantly; to proceed or tend in growing; to continue in time before it becomes due and payable (a bill has ninety days to *run*).—*To run after,* to pursue or follow; to endeavour to obtain.—*To run against,* to come into collision with.—*To run at,* to attack with sudden violence; to rush upon.—*To run away,* to flee; to escape; to elope.—*To run away with,* to convey away in a hurried or clandestine manner; to join in eloping with; to bolt with; to start off with at a great pace (the horse *ran away with* the carriage).—*To run foul of,* to come into collision with.—*To run in* or *into,* to enter by running; to step in; to come or get into (to *run into* danger). —*To run on,* to be continued; to talk incessantly; to continue a course; *printing,* to be continued without a break or new paragraph.—*To run on all fours,* to run on hands and feet; to be coincident or concurrent; to be exactly analogous or similar to something else; to agree.—*To run out,* to stop after running to the end of its time, as a watch or sand-glass; to come to an end; to expire (a lease *runs out* at Michaelmas). —*To run over,* to overflow; to go over, examine, or recount cursorily (to *run over* all the particulars); to ride or drive over (to *run over* a child).—*To run through,* to spend quickly; to dissipate (he *ran through* his fortune).—*To run to seed,* said of herbaceous plants, which, instead of developing the produce for which they are valued, in a juicy state, shoot up, and yield, instead, flowers, and ultimately seed; hence, to become useless; to go to waste.—*To run up,* to rise; to grow; to increase (accounts *run up* very fast); to pass rapidly from bottom to top of (to *run up* a column of figures).—*v.t.* To cause to run or go quickly; to cause to be carried in a certain course (to *run* a ship aground); to cause to ply; to maintain in running (to *run* a stage-coach); to accomplish by running; to pursue, as a course; to incur; to encounter (to *run* the risk of being killed); to break through or evade (to *run* a blockade); hence, to smuggle; to import or export without paying duties; to push; to thrust; to pierce; to stab (to *run a* person through with a rapier); to pour forth in a stream; to melt; to melt and clarify; to form in a mould by melting; to carry on or conduct, as a hotel or other enterprise; to sew by passing the needle through and through in a continuous line. — *To run down,* to chase to weariness (to *run down* a stag); to run against and sink, as a vessel; to pursue with scandal or opposition. —*To run hard,* to press hard in a race or other competition; to come very near beating; to press with jokes, sarcasm, or ridicule.—*To run in,* to take into custody, as by a policeman; to lock up. (*Slang.*)—*To run on, printing,* to carry on or continue, as a line, without break or a new paragraph. — *To run riot.* Under RIOT. —*To run up,* to increase; to enlarge by additions (to *run up* a large account); to thrust up, as anything long and slender; to erect; especially, to erect hastily (to *run up* a block of buildings).—*To run the gantlet.* GANTLET.—*n.* The act of running; a course run (a long *run,* a quick *run*); a trip; a pleasure trip or excursion (*colloq.*); particular or distinctive course, progress, tenor, &c.; continued course (a *run* of ill luck); a general or uncommon pressure or demand, as on a bank or treasury for payment of its notes; the distance sailed by a ship; a voyage; a passage from one place to another; a pair of millstones; *cricket,* one complete act of running from one wicket to the other by the batsman; a place where animals run or may run; especially, a large extent of grazing ground, called variously a *Cattle-run,* a *Sheep-run,* &c., according to the animals pastured; *music,* a succession of notes, either ascending or descending, played or sung rapidly. —*The common run* (or simply *the run*), that which passes under observation as usual or most general; the generality.—*By the run,* suddenly; quickly; at once: said of a fall or sudden descent.—*In the long run,* in the final result; in the conclusion or end.—*a.* Liquefied; melted; clarified (*run* butter); run or conveyed ashore secretly; contraband (*run* brandy).—**Runaway,** run'a-wā, *n.* One that flies from danger or restraint; one that deserts lawful service; a fugitive. —*a.* Acting the part of a runaway; escaping or breaking from restraint; accomplished or effected by running away or eloping (a *runaway* match). —**Runnel,** run'l, *n.* A rivulet or small brook.—**Runner,** run'ėr, *n.* One who runs; a racer; a messenger; an old name for a criminal detective; a slender prostrate stem sending out leaves and roots, as in the strawberry; any bird of the order Cursores; that on which a thing runs or slides (the *runner* or keel of a sleigh or skate).—*Runner-up,* a term applied, chiefly in golfing, but occasionally in other sports, to the player who is next to the winner in a competition.—**Running,** run'ing, *p.* and *a.* Kept for racing (a *running* horse); in succession; without any intervening day, year, &c.: a semi-adverbial usage (to visit two days *running,* to sow land two years *running*); discharging pus or matter.—*Running fight,* a fight kept up by the party pursuing and the party pursued.—*Running fire,* a constant fire of musketry or artillery.—*Out of the running,* out of the race.—*Running hand,* the style of handwriting in which the letters are formed without the pen being lifted from the paper.—*Running rigging,* the ropes used for hoisting a ship's sails, moving the yards, and the like: in distinction from *standing rigging.*—*n.* The act of one who runs; a quantity run (the first *running* of a still).

Runagate, run'a-gāt, *n.* [Corruption of Fr. *renégat.* RENEGADE.] A fugitive; a vagabond; an apostate; a renegade.

Runcinate, run'si-nāt, *a.* [L. *runcina,* a plane.] In *bot.* having curved indentations and lateral lobes turned backwards, as in the dandelion leaf.

Rundle, run'dl, *n.* [For *roundle,* from *round.*] A round; a step of a ladder.

Rune, rön, *n.* [A.Sax. *rún,* a rune, a mysterious or magical character, a mystery, a whisper; from root meaning to whisper, as in L. *rumor,* a rumour.] One of a particular set of alphabetic characters peculiar to the ancient northern nations of Europe, all the runes being formed almost entirely of straight lines, either single or in composition.—**Runecraft,** rön'kraft, *n.* Knowledge of runes.—**Runic,** rön'ik, *a.* Pertaining to runes.—*Runic wand, runic staff,* a willow wand inscribed with runes, used for purposes of divination.—*Runic rhyme,* rhyme where the melody or rhyme follows readily, or in ranks, as in the runes. (*Poe.*) —**Runologist,** rö-nol'o-jist, *n.* One versed in runology; a student of runic remains.—**Runology,** rö-nol'o-ji, *n.* The study of runes.

Rung, rung, pp. of *ring.*

Rung, rung, *n.* [A.Sax. *hrung,* a pole, a beam; Icel. *röng,* a rib in a ship; O.D. *ronghe,* a prop; G. *runge,* a short piece.] A heavy staff; the round or step of a ladder.

Runlet, Rundlet, run'let, rund'let, *n.* [For *roundlet,* from *round.*] A small barrel of no certain dimensions.

Runnel. Under RUN.

Runnet, run'et, *n.* Same as *Rennet.*

Runrig, Rundale, run'rig, run'dāl, *n.* [*Rundale,* from *run,* and *dale* = *dole,* what is *dealt* or assigned, G. *teil.*] A system of holding land in which successive strips or *ridges* belong to different owners, an old custom in connection with villages in Scotland and Ireland.

Runt, runt, *n.* [Origin doubtful.] Any animal below the usual size of the breed; a variety of pigeon; a root of kale, colewort, or cabbage; a cudgel.

Rupee, rö-pē', *n.* [Hind. *rūpiyu,* a rupee, from Skr. *rûpya,* silver.] A silver coin the unit of value in British India: nearly equivalent to 50 cents at par.

Rupture, rup'tūr, *n.* [Fr. *rupture,* from L.L. *ruptura,* a breaking, from L. *rumpo, ruptum,* to break (seen also in *abrupt, corrupt, eruption, interrupt,* &c., and giving origin also to *route, rout,* &c.).] The act of breaking or bursting; the state of being broken or violently parted; *med.* same as hernia, especially hernia of the abdomen; a breach of concord either between individuals or nations; open hostility or war; a quarrel.—*v.t.—ruptured, rupturing.* To make a rupture in; to burst; to part by violence; to affect with or cause to suffer from rupture.—*v.i.* To suffer a breach or disruption.

Rural, rö'ral, *a.* [L. *ruralis,* from *rus, ruris,* the country (whence also *rustic*); same root as *room.*] Pertaining to the country, as distinguished from a city or town; suiting the country or resembling it; pertaining to agriculture or farming.—*Rural dean,* in the Church of England, an ecclesiastic under the bishop and the archdeacon, in charge of the clergy of a district. —**Ruralism,** rö'ral-izm, *n.* The state of being rural; an idiom peculiar to the speech of the country as opposed to the town.—**Ruralist**, rö'ral-ist, *n.* One that leads a rural life.—**Ruralize**, rö'ral-īz, *v.i.* —*ruralized, ruralizing.* To go into the country; to go to dwell in the country; to rusticate.—*v.t.* To render rural; to give a rural character to.—**Rurally**, rö'ral-li, *adv.* In a rural manner.—**Ruralness**, **Rurality**, rö'ral-nes, rö-ral'i-ti, *n.* The quality of being rural.—**Ruridecanal**, rö-ri-dē'kan-al, *a.* [L. *rus, ruris*, the country, and *decanus*, a dean.] Belonging to a rural dean.

Rusa, rö'za, *n.* [Malay *russa*, a stag.] A name of several species of Asiatic deer.

Ruse, röz, *n.* [Fr. *ruse*, from *ruser*, to dodge; O.Fr. *reüser*, to get out of the way, from L. *recusare*, to refuse. RECUSANT.] An artifice, trick, or stratagem; a wile.

Rush, rush, *n.* [O.E. *rishe, rusche*, from A.Sax. *risce, ricse*, a rush; D. *rusch*, G. *rausch*; probably from L. *ruscum*, butcher's-broom.] The common name of herbaceous plants, usually growing in damp meadows and swamps, having round erect stems which are sometimes used for plaiting into mats, chair-bottoms, &c., and which contain a large pith; used typically of anything weak or of trivial value; the merest trifle; a straw.—**Rush-bottomed**, *a.* Having a bottom or seat made with rushes (a *rush-bottomed* chair).—**Rush-candle**, *n.* A small taper made by the pith of a rush in tallow.—**Rushed**, rusht, *a.* Abounding with rushes; covered with rushes.—**Rush-light**, *n.* A rush-candle or its light; hence, any weak flickering light.—**Rush-mat**, *n.* A mat composed of rushes.—**Rush-nut**, *n.* A plant, a kind of cyperus, with edible tubers.—**Rushy**, rush'i, *a.* Abounding with rushes; made of rushes.

Rush, rush, *v.i.* [Akin to Dan. *ruske*, Sw. *ruska*, to shake; D. *ruischen*, G. *rauschen*, to rustle; O.G. *rûschen*, to rush, to roar; comp. also A.Sax. *hreósan*, to fall, to rush.] To move or drive forward with impetuosity, violence, and tumultuous rapidity; to enter with undue eagerness, or without due deliberation (to *rush* into a scheme).—*n.* A driving forward with eagerness and haste; a violent motion or course; an eager demand; a run.—**Rusher**, rush'ėr, *n.* One who rushes.

Rusk, rusk, *n.* [Perhaps akin to L.G. *rusken*, to crackle, as we have *cracknel*, a biscuit, from *crack*.] A kind of light hard cake browned in a moderately cool oven, and used as food for infants.

Russ, rus, *a.* Pertaining to the Russians. —*n.* The language of the Russians; *sing.* and *pl.* a native or the natives of Russia.—**Russia**, **Russia-leather**, rush'ya, *n.* A strong, pliant, and waterproof leather, having a peculiar penetrating odour, due to the oil of birch used in its preparation, specially useful in binding books, the oil repelling insects.—**Russian**, rush'yan, *a.* Pertaining to Russia.—*n.* A native of Russia; the language of Russia; Russ.—**Russophile**, **Russophilist**, rus'o-fil, rus-of'il-ist, *n.* [*Russ*, and Gr. *philos*, a friend.] One whose sympathies lie towards Russia or her policy.—**Russophobia**, rus-o-fō'bi-a, *n.* [*Russ*, and Gr. *phobos*, fear.] A fear of Russia or the Russians.—**Russophobist**, rus-of'ob-ist, *n.* One who fears or dislikes Russia.

Russet, rus'et, *a.* [O.Fr. *rousset*, from L. *russus*, red, akin to *ruber*, red.] Of a reddish-brown colour; coarse; homespun; rustic: from the general colour of homespun cloth.—*n.* A kind of apple of a russet colour and rough skin; a pigment of a rich transparent brown colour obtained from madder.—*v.t.* To give a russet hue to; to change into russet.

Rust, rust, *n.* [A.Sax. *rust*, rust=D. *roest*, Dan. *rust*, Sw. and G. *rost*, rust; so called from its *red* colour, the root being that of *red, ruddy*, L. *ruber*, red (RUBRIC); *russus*, reddish (RUSSET).] The red or orange-yellow coating (an oxide of iron) which is formed on the surface of iron when exposed to air and moisture; a composition of iron-filings and sal-ammoniac, with sometimes a little sulphur, moistened with water and used for filling fast joints; a parasitic fungus which attacks the leaves, glumes, stalks, &c., of cereals and grasses; any foul extraneous matter; corrosive or injurious accretion or influence.—*v.i.* To contract or gather rust; to be oxidized; to assume an appearance as if coated with rust; to degenerate in idleness or inaction.—*v.t.* To cause to contract rust; to impair by time and inactivity.—**Rustily**, rus'ti-li, *adv.* In a rusty state; in a manner to suggest rustiness.—**Rustiness**, rus'ti-nes, *n.* The state of being rusty.—**Rusty**, rus'ti, *a.* Covered or affected with rust; having the colour of rust; appearing as if covered with rust; impaired by inaction or neglect of use.

Rustic, rus'tik, *a.* [L. *rusticus*, from *rus*, the country. RURAL.] Pertaining to the country; living in or found in the country; rural; plain; simple; not elegant, refined, or costly.—*Rustic work*, masonry worked with grooves between the courses, to look like open joints; summer-houses, garden-seats, &c., made from rough limbs or branches of trees.—*n.* An inhabitant of the country; a clown; a swain.—**Rustically**, rus'ti-kal-li, *adv.* In a rustic manner.—**Rusticalness**, rus'ti-kal-nes, *n.*—**Rusticate**, rus'ti-kāt, *v.i.*—*rusticated, rusticating.* [L. *rusticor, rusticatus*.] To dwell or reside in the country.—*v.t.* To suspend from studies at a college or university and send away for a time by way of punishment.—**Rustication**, rus-ti-kā'shon, *n.* The act of rusticating or state of being rusticated.—**Rusticity**, rus-tis'i-ti, *n.* The state or quality of being rustic

Rustily, Rustiness, Rusty. Under RUST.

Rustle, rus'l, *v.i.*—*rustled, rustling.* [A. Sax. *hristlan*, to rustle, a dim. and freq. form corresponding to Icel. *hrista*, Dan. *ryste*, Sw. *rysta*, to shake, to tremble.] To make a quick succession of small sounds like the rubbing of silk cloth or dry leaves; to give out a slightly sibilant sound when shaken.—*v.t.* To cause to rustle; to steal (cattle); to do or get quickly and energetically.—*n.* A slight crackling sound as of dry leaves or silk.—**Rustler**, rus'l-ėr, *n.* One who steals cattle; one who rustles.

Rut, rut, *n.* [Fr. *rut*, O.Fr. *ruit*, the noise which deer make when they desire to come together, from L. *rugitus*, a roaring, from *rugio*, to roar, to bellow.] The time during which deer and some other animals are under the sexual excitement.—*v.i. rutted, rutting.* To desire to come together for copulation: said of deer.—*v.t.* To cover in copulation.—**Rutter**, rut'ėr, *n.* One that ruts.—**Ruttish**, rut'ish, *a.* Lustful; libidinous.—**Ruttishness**, rut'ish-nes, *n.* The state or quality of being ruttish.

Rut, rut, *n.* [Same word as *route, rote*.] The track of a wheel, a line cut on the soil with a spade.—*v.t.*—*rutted, rutting.* To make ruts in or on with cart-wheels; to cut a line on, as on the soil, with a spade.—**Rutty**, rut'i, *a.* Full of ruts; cut by wheels, as a road.

Rutabaga, rö-ta-bā'ga, *n.* [Origin doubtful.] The Swedish turnip.

Ruth, röth, *n.* [From *rue*, comp *truth*, from *true*.] Mercy; pity; tenderness; sorrow for the misery of another; sorrowful or tender regret. [*Mainly poet.*]—**Ruthless**, röth'les, *a.* Having no ruth or pity; cruel, pitiless; barbarous.—**Ruthlessly**, röth'-les-li, *adv.* In a ruthless manner.—**Ruthlessness**, röth'les-nes, *n.* Pitilessness.

Ruthenium, rö-thē'ni-um, *n.* [From *Ruthenia*, a Latin name for Russia, having been first obtained in ore from the Ural.] A hard rare metal of a grey colour occurring in platinum ore.

Rutherford atom, ru'THer-ford, *n.* The atom postulated in the theory of Sir E. Rutherford, consisting of a minute massive positively charged nucleus, surrounded by negative electrons.

Rutile, Rutilite, rö'til, rö'til-īt, *n.* [L. *rutilus*, red, inclining to yellow.] Native titanic oxide, an ore of titanium of a reddish-brown colour.

Ryal, rī'al, *n.* RIAL.

Rydberg's constant, rid'berg, *n.* In *physics*, a number which occurs as a factor in the expressions for the frequencies of the spectral lines of hydrogen.

Rye, rī, *n.* [A.Sax. *ryge*, Icel. *rúgr*, Dan. *rug*, Sw *rog*, D. *rogge*, G. *roggen, rocken*, cog. Gr. *oryza*, rice.] A cereal plant which bears naked seeds furnished with awns like barley, much cultivated for food and as a spring forage crop for livestock, the seeds of this plant; whiskey distilled from these seeds.—**Rye-grass**, *n.* The common name of a genus of esteemed fodder-grasses, of which there are several varieties, some annual, others perennial.

Ryot, rī'ot, *n.* [Ar. *ra'iyat*, a peasant.] A Hindu cultivator of the soil.

Rypeck, rī'pek, *n.* A pole used to moor a punt while fishing or the like.

S

S, the nineteenth letter of the English alphabet, a consonant representing a hissing sound.

Sabadilla, sab-a-dil'a. CEBADILLA.

Sabaism, sa-bā'izm, *n.* [Comp. Heb. *tsebâôth*, the heavenly host. SABAOTH.] The worship of the heavenly bodies, anciently practised in Western Asia.

Sabaoth, sa-bā'oth, *n.* [Heb. *tsebâôth*, armies, from *tsâbâ*, to assemble, to fight.] *Scrip.* armies; hosts.

Sabbath, sab'bath, *n.* [Heb. *shabbath*, rest, the day of rest.] The day which God appointed to be observed as a day of rest; originally the seventh day of the week, but in the Christian church the first day of the week is held sacred, in commemoration of the resurrection of Christ on that day; the Lord's-day; Sunday; intermission of pain or sorrow; time of rest; the sabbatical year among the Israelites (O.T.).—*Sabbath-day's journey*, the distance which the Jews were permitted to travel on the Sabbath-day, probably about an English mile. ∴ *Sabbath* is not strictly synonymous with *Sunday*. *Sunday* is the mere name of the day, *Sabbath* is the name of the institution. *Sunday* is the *Sabbath* of Christians, *Saturday* is the *Sabbath* of the Jews. But in the mouths of many it is equivalent to *Sunday*.—**Sabbatarian**, sab-ba-tā'ri-an, *n.* One who observes the Sabbath with extraordinary or unreasonable rigour; one careful to abstain from work or relaxation on Sunday. Used also *adjectively*.—**Sabbatarianism**, sab-ba-tā'ri-an-izm, *n.* The tenets of Sabbatarians.—**Sabbath-breaker**, *n.* One who profanes the Sabbath.—**Sabbath-breaking**, *n.* The act of breaking or profaning the Sabbath.—**Sabbathless**, sab'bath-les, *a.* Having no Sabbath; without intermission of labour.—**Sabbatic**, **Sabbatical**, sab-bat'ik, sab-bat'i-kal, *a.* [L. *sabbaticus*.] Pertaining to the Sabbath. —*Sabbatical year*, every seventh year, in which the Israelites were to allow their fields and vineyards to rest or lie without tillage; a period of absence, as granted a professor every seventh year.

Sabellian, sa-bel'i-an, *n.* A follower of

Sabellius, a philosopher of Egypt in the third century A.D., who taught that there is one person only in the Godhead.—*a.* Of or belonging to the group of early inhabitants in Italy, including Sabines, Samnites, Campanians, Lucanians, and others.

Saber, Sabre, sā'bėr, *n.* [Fr. *sabre*, from D., Dan., and Sw. *sabel*, G. *säbel*, a saber; ultimate origin unknown.] A sword with a broad and heavy blade, thick at the back and a little curved towards the point, specially adapted for cutting; a cavalry sword.—*v.t. sabered, sabering*, or *sabred, sabring*. To strike, cut, or kill with a saber.

Sabianists, sā'bi-an-ists, *n.* [Arab. *çabi*.] A class of believers mentioned in the Koran as followers of the true God, along with Jews, Christians, and others. Distinct from *Sabaism* (which see).

Sabicu, sab-i-kö', *n.* [Native name.] A tree of Cuba yielding timber used in shipbuilding, &c.

Sabine, sā'bin, *n.* [Fr. *sabine*, from L. *sabina* (*herba*), the Sabine herb, savin.] A plant. SAVIN.

Sabines, sā'binz, *n.* The tribe north of Rome, and one of the Sabellian family.—**Sabine**, *a.* Of or belonging to the Sabines, Horace's *Sabine* farm.

Sable, sā'bl, *n.* [O.Fr. *sable*, from Pol. *sabol*, Russ. *sobol*, a Slavonic word.] A digitigrade carnivorous animal nearly allied to the marten, found chiefly in the northern regions of Asia, and hunted for its black, lustrous fur; the fur of the sable; a black or mourning suit or garment; the heraldic name for black.—*a.* Of the color of the sable; black; dark.—*v.t.*—*sabled, sabling*. To make sable or dark in color.—**Sable-vested**, *a.* Clothed in sable garments.

Sabot, sä-bō', *n.* [Fr. Origin unknown.] A wooden shoe worn by the peasantry in France, Belgium, &c.

Sabotage, sa-bo-tazh, *n.* The practice of working in such a way as to slow up production or to injure the quality of the product.

Sabulous, sab'ū-lus, *a.* [L. *sabulosus*, from *sabulum*, sand.] Sandy; gritty.—**Sabulosity**, sab-ū-los'i-ti, *n.*

Sac, sak or säk, *n.* A member of the tribe of Algonquian Indians that once lived along the upper Mississippi River.

Sac, sak, *n.* [L. *saccus*, a bag. SACK.] A bag or cyst of an animal or plant; a pouch; a receptacle for a liquid (the lachrymal *sac*).—**Saccate**, sak'kāt, *a.* *Bot.* furnished with or having the form of a sac or pouch.—**Sacciform**, sak'si-form, *a.* Having the general form of a sac.—**Saccular**, sak'kū-lėr, *a.* Like a sac; sacciform.—**Sacculated**, sak'kū-lā-ted, *a.* Furnished with little sacs.—**Saccule**, sak'kūl, *n.* [L. *sacculus*.] A little sac or sack; a cyst; a cell.

Sacbut, sak'but. SACKBUT.

Saccade, sa-kād', *n.* [Fr.] A sudden violent check of a horse by drawing or twitching the reins.

Saccate. Under SAC.

Saccharic, sak-kar'ik, *a.* [L. *saccharum*, sugar, from Gr. *sakchar, sakcharon*, sugar, a word of oriental origin. SUGAR.] Pertaining to or obtained from sugar or allied substances.—**Sacchariferous**, sak-ka-rif'ėr-us, *a.* [L. *saccharum*, and *fero*, to produce.] Producing sugar.—**Saccharify**, sak-kar'i-fī, *v.t.*—*saccharified, saccharifying*. [Fr. *saccharifier*.] To convert into sugar.—**Saccharin, Saccharine**, sak'ka-rin, *n.* A substance, 300 to 500 times sweeter than cane sugar, derived from coal tar.—*a.* Pertaining to, or like sugar; sickeningly sweet.—**Saccharite**, sak'ka-rīt, *n.* A finely-grained variety of felspar, of a vitreous luster and white or greenish-white color.—**Saccharoid, Saccharoidal**, sak'ka-roid, sak'ka-roi-dal, *a.* Having a texture resembling that of loaf-sugar.—**Saccharometer, Saccharimeter**, sak-ka-rom'et-ėr, sak-ka-rim'et-ėr, *n.* An instrument for determining the quantity of saccharine matter in any solution.—**Saccharometry, Saccharimetry**, sak-ka-rom'et-ri, sak-ka-rim'et-ri, *n.* The operation of determining the quantity of sugar in any solution.

Sacciferous, Saccule, &c. Under SAC.

Sacellum, sa-sel'um, *n.* [L., dim. from *sacrum*, a sacred place.] A sanctuary consecrated to a deity; a small chapel.

Sacerdotal, sas-ėr-dō'tal, *a.* [L. *sacerdotalis*, from *sacerdos*, a priest. SACRED.] Pertaining to priests or the priesthood; priestly.—**Sacerdotally**, sas-ėr-dō'tal-li, *adv.* In a sacerdotal manner.—**Sacerdotalism**, sas-ėr-dō'tal-izm, *n.* Sacerdotal system or spirit; a tendency to attribute a lofty and sacred character to the priesthood; priestcraft.

Sachem, sā'chem, *n.* A chief among some of the early American Indian tribes.

Sachet, sä-shā, *n.* [Fr.] A small bag for containing odorous substances.

Sack, sak, *n.* [A.Sax. *sacc*, Dan. *säk*, D. *zak*, G. *sack*, Goth. *sakkus*, from L. *saccus*, Gr. *sakkos*, probably of Eastern origin, similar forms being also found in Hebrew and Coptic.] A bag, usually a large cloth bag, used for holding and conveying corn, wool, cotton, hops, and the like; a measure or weight which varies according to the article and country; a kind of loose gown or mantle formerly worn; a sacque.—*v.t.* To put in a sack or in bags.—**Sackcloth**, sak'kloth, *n.* Cloth of which sacks are made; coarse cloth worn in mourning, distress, or penance.—**Sackful**, sak'ful, *n.* As much as a sack will hold.—**Sacking**, sak'ing, *n.* A coarse fabric of which sacks are made.

Sack, sak, *v.t.* [Fr. *sac*, Sp. and Pg. *saco*, It. *sacco*, plunder; pillage; from the use of a *sack* in removing plunder. SACK, a bag.] To storm; to pillage; to devastate: usually said of a town; to dismiss an employee. (*Colloq.*).—*n.* The act of one who sacks; the storm and plunder of a town or city; also booty; spoil.—**Sackage**, sak'āj, *n.* The act of sacking.—**Sacker**, sak'ėr, *n.* One who sacks.

Sack, sak, *n.* [Fr. *sec*, dry, from L. *siccus*, dry.] Formerly, a general name for different sorts of dry wines, more especially the Spanish, which were first extensively used in England in the sixteenth century.

Sackbut, sak'but, *n.* [Fr. *saquebute*, from Sp. *sacabuche*, a kind of trumpet, from *sacar*, to draw, and *buche*, the stomach.] A musical instrument of the trumpet kind, so contrived that it can be lengthened or shortened according to the tone required, like the trombone; *Scrip.* a musical stringed instrument mentioned in Dan. iii., perhaps a kind of guitar.

Sackless, sak'les, *a.* [O.E. *sacléas*.] Harmless; innocent; feeble in mind.

Sacque, sak, *n.* [A form of *sack*, Fr. *sac*, a bag. SACK.] A kind of loose gown or upper robe worn by ladies in the seventeenth and eighteenth centuries.

Sacral. Under SACRUM.

Sacrament, sak'ra-ment, *n.* [L. *sacramentum*, a military oath of allegiance, an oath, from *sacer*, sacred (seen also in *sacrifice*, &c.). SACRED.] *Theol.* an outward and visible sign of inward and spiritual grace; a solemn religious ceremony enjoined by Christ, to be observed by his followers, by which their special relation to him is created, or their obligations to him renewed and ratified. In the *R. Cath. Ch.* and the *Greek Ch.* there are seven sacraments, viz. baptism, confirmation, the eucharist, penance, extreme unction, holy orders, and matrimony; but Protestants in general acknowledge but two sacraments, baptism and the Lord's supper. When used without any qualifying word by *sacrament* is meant the eucharist or Lord's supper.—**Sacramental**, sak-ra-men'tal, *a.* Constituting a sacrament or pertaining to it; having the character of a sacrament.—**Sacramentally**, sak-ra-men'tal-li, *adv.* After the manner of a sacrament.—**Sacramentarian**, sak'ra-men-tā"ri-an, *n.* A person holding some special view in regard to the sacraments.—**Sacramentary**, sak-ra-men'ta-ri, *a.* Pertaining to a sacrament or to sacraments.

Sacrarium, sa-krā'ri-um, *n.* [L., from *sacer*, sacred.] A chapel in the house of ancient Romans devoted to some particular divinity; the adytum of a temple; that part of a church where the altar is situated.

Sacre, sā'kėr. SAKER.

Sacred, sā'kred, *a.* [Pp. of old *sacre*, to set apart, to consecrate; Fr. *sacrer*, from L. *sacrare*, from *sacer*, sacred (seen also in *sacrilege, sacrifice, consecrate, desecrate*, &c.); same root as in *sanction, sanctify*.] Set apart by solemn religious ceremony; dedicated to religious use; holy; not profane or common; relating to religion or the services of religion; not secular; consecrated; dedicated; devoted: with *to* (*sacred to* one's memory); entitled to the highest respect or reverence; venerable; not to be profaned or violated; inviolable; inviolate (a secret kept *sacred*).—*Sacred College*, the college of cardinals at Rome.—*Sacred Majesty*, a title once applied to the kings of England.—**Sacredly**, sā'kred-li, *adv.* In a sacred manner; religiously; inviolably; strictly.—**Sacredness**, sā'kred-nes, *n.* The state of being sacred; holiness; sanctity; inviolableness.

Sacrifice, sak'ri-fīs, *n.* [Fr. *sacrifice*, from L. *sacrificium*, from *sacer*, sacred, and *facio*, to make. SACRED.] The offering of anything to God, or to a god; a consecratory rite; anything consecrated and offered to God or to a divinity; an immolated victim on an altar; surrender or loss made for gaining something else; a giving up of some desirable object in behalf of a higher object; the thing so devoted or given up; the selling of goods under cost price.—*v.t.*—*sacrificed, sacrificing*. To make an offering or sacrifice of; to consecrate or present to some divinity; to immolate on the altar of God either as an atonement for sin or to express gratitude; to destroy, surrender, or suffer to be lost for the sake of obtaining something else; to devote or give up with loss or suffering; to destroy; to kill.—*v.i.*—To offer up a sacrifice; to make offerings to God or to a deity by the slaughter and burning of victims, or some part of them, on an altar.—**Sacrificer**, sak'ri-fīs-ėr, *n.* One that sacrifices.—**Sacrificial**, sak-ri-fish'al, *a.* Pertaining to sacrifice; performing sacrifices; consisting in sacrifice.—**Sacrific, Sacrifical**, sa-krif'ik, sa-krif'i-kal, *a.* [L. *sacrificus*.] Employed in sacrifice.—**Sacrificant**, sa-krif'i-kant, *n.* [L. *sacrificans*, ppr. of *sacrifico*.] One that offers a sacrifice.

Sacrilege, sak'ri-lej, *n.* [Fr. *sacrilège*, from L. *sacrilegium*—*sacer*, sacred, and *lego*, to gather, to pick up.] The violation or profaning of sacred things; the alienating to common purposes what has been appropriated to religious uses; the stealing of goods out of any church or chapel.—**Sacrilegious**, sak-ri-lē'jus, *a.* Guilty of or involving sacrilege; violating sacred things; profane; impious.—**Sacrilegiously**, sak-ri-lē'jus-li, *adv.* In a sacrilegious manner.—**Sacrilegiousness**, sak-ri-lē'jus-nes, *n.* The quality of being sacrilegious.

Sacring, sā'kring, *n.* [Fr. *sacrer*, to make sacred.] Consecration. (*Tenn.*)—**Sacring-bell, Sanctus-bell**, (*n.*) *R. Cath. Ch.* the small bell rung at the *sanctus* and at the elevation of the host in high-mass.

Sacrist, sā'krist, *n.* [L.L. *sacrista*, from L. *sacer*, sacred. SACRED.] A sacristan; a person retained in a cathedral to copy out music for the choir and take care of the books.—**Sacristan**, sak'ris-tan, *n.* [L.L. *sacristanus*. *Sexton* is a contr. of this word.] An officer of the church who has charge of the sacristy and its contents.—**Sacristy**, sak'ris-ti, *n.* [Fr. *sacristie*.] A room in a church where sacred utensils and clerical vestments are deposited; the vestry.

Sacroiliac, sā-krō-il'i-ak, *a.* *Anat.* pertaining to both the sacrum and the ilium (*sacroiliac* ligaments).

Sacrosanct, sak'rō-sangkt, *a.* [L. *sacrosanctus* — *sacer*, sacred, *sanctus*, holy.] Sacred and inviolable; holy and venerable. —**Sacrosanctify**,† sac-rō-sangk'ti-fī, *v.t.* *-fied, -fying.* To render sacrosanct.

Sacrosciatic, sā'krō-sī-at''ik, *a.* [From *sacrum* and *sciatic.*] *Anat.* pertaining jointly to the sacrum and ischium.

Sacrum, sā'krum, *n.* [L. *os sacrum*, the sacred bone.] *Anat.* the bone which forms the basis or inferior extremity of the vertebral column, said to derive its name from its having been offered in sacrifice, and hence considered sacred.—**Sacral**, sā'-kral, *a.* Pertaining to the sacrum.

Sad, sad, *a.* [A.Sax. *sæd*, satisfied, sated, weary, sick; Icel. *saddr*, sated, full; Goth. *saths*, satiated, full; cog. with L. *satur*, full, *satis*, enough. SATE, SATISFY.] Serious‡; sedate or grave‡; sorrowful; melancholy; mournful; affected with grief; downcast; gloomy; having the external appearance of sorrow; afflictive; calamitous; causing sorrow; bad; naughty; wicked.—**Sadden**, sad'n, *v.t.* To make sad or sorrowful; to render melancholy or gloomy. — *v.i.* To become sad or sorrowful.—**Sadly**, sad'li, *adv.* In a sad manner; sorrowfully; grievously; calamitously.—**Sadness**, sad'nes, *n.* The state or quality of being sad; sorrowfulness; dejection.

Saddle, sad'l, *n.* [A.Sax. *sadel*, *sadol* = Dan. *saddel*, Icel. *söthull*, G. *sattel*, a saddle; perhaps from L. *sedile*, a seat, from *sedeo*, to sit. Same root as *seat*, *set*, *sit*.] A seat to be placed on an animal's back for the rider to sit on; a padded piece of harness on an animal's back supporting the shafts of a vehicle; something like a saddle in shape or use, as a rise and fall on the ridge of a hill; a technical name of various appliances.—*Saddle of mutton, venison*, &c., two loins of mutton, &c., cut together. —*To put the saddle on the right horse*, to impute blame where it is really deserved. —*v.t.—saddled, saddling.* To put a saddle on; to load; to burden (to *saddle* a person with expense).—**Saddle-back**, *n.* A hill or its summit when somewhat saddle-shaped; *geol.* a familiar name for anticlinal strata.—**Saddle-bag**, *n.* One of a pair of bags united by straps for carriage on horseback, one bag on each side. — **Saddle-bow**, *n.* The upper front part of a saddle, formed of two curved pieces united in an arch; a pommel.—**Saddle-cloth**, *n.* A cloth attached to a saddle, and extending over the loins of the horse; a housing.—**Saddle-girth**, *n.* The band or strap which passes under the horse's belly and serves to fasten the saddle. — **Saddle-horse**, *n.* A horse used for riding with a saddle.—**Saddler**, sad'lėr, *n.* One whose occupation is to make saddles or harness generally.—**Saddlery**, sad'lėr-i, *n.* The manufactures of a saddler; trade of a saddler.—**Saddle-tree**, *n.* The wooden frame of a saddle.

Sadducee, sad'dū-sē, *n.* [Gr. *saddoukaios*, Heb. *tsadûkim*, probably from *Zadok*, a distinguished priest in the time of David.] One of a sect or party among the ancient Jews, who denied the existence of any spiritual beings except God, believed that the soul died with the body, and therefore that there was no resurrection, and adhered to the written law alone.—**Sadduceeism, Sadducism**, sad'dū-sē-izm, sad'dū-sizm, *n.* The tenets of the Sadducees.—**Sadducaic, Sadducean**, sad-dū-kā'ik, sad-dū-sē'an, *a.* Pertaining to or characteristic of the Sadducees.

Safe, sāf, *a.* [O.E. *sauf*, from Fr. *sauf*, safe, from L. *salvus*, safe (whence also *salvation*); akin to *servus*, a slave, *servare*, to preserve, *solidus*, solid, Gr. *holos*, Skr. *sarva*, whole.] Free from or not liable to danger of any kind; free from or having escaped hurt, injury, or damage; not exposing to danger; securing from harm; no longer dangerous; placed beyond the power of doing harm; sound; whole (a *safe* conscience).—*n.* A box or chamber of great strength for preserving money, jewels, account-books, and other valuable articles from thieves or against the action of fire; a ventilated or refrigerated receptacle in which meat is kept.—**Safe-conduct**, *n.* A convoy or guard for a person travelling in a foreign or hostile country; a writing serving as a pass or warrant of security to a traveller.—**Safeguard**, sāf'gärd, *n.* One who or that which defends or protects; a defence; protection; a convoy or guard to protect a traveller; a passport; a warrant of protection to a traveller.—*v.t.* To guard; to protect.—**Safe-keeping**, *n.* The act of keeping in safety from injury or from escape; secure guardianship.—**Safe load**. The greatest dead load which a structure or material can safely be permitted to bear in practice.—**Safely**, sāf'li, *adv.* In a safe manner; without incurring danger; without hurt or injury; in safety; securely; carefully. —**Safeness**, sāf'nes, *n.* The condition or quality of being safe; freedom from danger. —**Safety**, sāf'ti, *n.* The state or quality of being safe; exemption from injury or loss; the state of not being liable to danger or injury; freedom from danger; preservation; the state or quality of not causing danger; close custody.—**Safety-belt**, *n.* A belt made of buoyant material or inflated to sustain a person in water; a life-belt.—**Safety-buoy**, *n.* A safety-belt; a life-buoy.—**Safety-fuse**, *n.* A fuse used in blasting operations, carefully made so as to burn at a certain known rate per minute.—**Safety-lamp**, *n.* A lamp for lighting coal-mines without exposing workmen to the explosion of fire-damp, the flame being enveloped in a cylinder of wire-gauze, and thus prevented from igniting the inflammable gas.—**Safety-match**, *n.* A match which will light only on being rubbed on a specially prepared friction substance.—**Safety-pin**, *n.* A pin for articles of dress having its point fitting into a kind of sheath, so that it may not be readily withdrawn or prick the wearer or others.—**Safety-plug**, *n.* A plug in a steam-boiler partly of fusible metal, which melts when the internal temperature becomes too high; a plug to prevent barrels from bursting with gases generated internally. — **Safety-valve**, *n.* A contrivance for obviating or diminishing the risk of explosions in steam-boilers, the principle of which consists in opposing the pressure within the boiler by such a force as will yield before it reaches the point of danger, and permit the steam to escape.—**Safe working stress**. The stress that may in practice be safely permitted upon a structure.

Safflower, saf'flou-ėr, *n.* [From *saffron* and *flower.*] Bastard saffron, a plant cultivated in the South of Europe, Egypt, &c., on account of its flowers, which in their dried state form the safflower of commerce, and afford two colouring matters (also called safflower), a yellow and a red.

Saffron, saf'ron, *n.* [Fr. *safran*, from Sp., Ar., and Per. *zaferân*, saffron.] A plant of the crocus genus with flowers of a purple colour, the dried stigmata of which form the saffron of the shops, a substance of a rich orange colour, used as a colouring and flavouring ingredient in culinary preparations, liqueurs, &c., and yielding an orange-red extract used in dyeing and painting.—*a.* Having the colour of saffron flowers; yellow.—*v.t.* To tinge with saffron; to make yellow; to gild.

Sag, sag, *v.i.—sagged, sagging.* [Allied to L.G. *sacken*, D. *zakken*, to sink; also perhaps to *sink*.] To incline or hang away owing to insufficiently supported weight; to sink in the middle; to hang off the perpendicular; to yield under the pressure of care, difficulties, or the like; to waver; *naut.* to incline to the leeward; to make leeway.—*v.t.* To cause to bend or give way. —*n.* The state or act of sagging.

Saga, sä'ga, *n.* [Icel. *saga*, a tale, a history; from *segja*, E. to *say*. SAY.] An ancient Scandinavian legend or tradition of considerable length relating either mythical or historical events; a tale.

Sagacious, sa-gā'shus, *a.* [L. *sagax*, *sagacis*, from *sagio*, to perceive keenly, from a root signifying to be sharp, seen in Gr. *sagaris*, a battle-axe, Skr. *saghnomi*, to kill.] Intellectually keen or quick; acute in discernment; discerning and judicious; shrewd; full of wisdom; sage; showing intelligence resembling that of man: said of the lower animals; quick of scent (*Milton*).—**Sagaciously**, sa-gā'shus-li, *adv.* In a sagacious manner. — **Sagaciousness**, sa-gā'shus-nes, *n.* The quality of being sagacious.—**Sagacity**, sa-gas'i-ti, *n.* [L. *sagacitas.*] The quality of being sagacious; quickness of discernment; readiness of apprehension with soundness of judgment; shrewdness and common sense; intelligence resembling that of mankind (the *sagacity* of a dog).

Sagamore, sag'a-mōr, *n.* Among some tribes of American Indians, a king or chief; a sachem.

Sagapen, Sagapenum, sag'a-pen, sag-a-pē num, *n.* [Gr. *sagapēnon.*] A fetid gum-resin brought from Persia and Alexandria, occasionally used in medicine.

Sagathy, sag'a-thi, *n.* [Fr. *sagatis*, from L. *sagum*, a blanket or mantle.] A mixed woven fabric of silk and cotton.

Sagbut,‡ sag'but, *n.* Same as *Sackbut*.

Sage, sāj, *n.* [Fr. *sauge*, from L. *salvia*, sage, from *salvus*, safe, sound; on account of the reputed virtues of the plant. SAFE.] A garden plant much used in cookery, and formerly also in great repute for its medicinal qualities.—*Sage apple*, an excrescence upon a species of sage caused by the puncture of an insect.—*Sage brush*, an American shrub of the wormwood family.—*Sage cheese*, a kind of cheese flavoured and coloured green with the juice of sage.—*Sage cock*, a species of grouse of the Rocky Mountain region, which feeds on the leaves of the sage brush.—**Sagy**, sā'ji, *a.* Full of sage; seasoned with sage.

Sage, sāj, *a.* [Fr. *sage*, from L. *sapius*, wise, from *sapio*, to be wise (whence *sapient*).] Wise; sagacious; proceeding from wisdom; well-judged; grave; serious.—*n.* A wise man; a man venerable for years, and of sound judgment and prudence; a grave philosopher.—**Sagely**, sāj'li, *adv.* In a sage manner; wisely.—**Sageness**, sāj'nes, *n.* Wisdom; sagacity.

Sagenite, saj'en-īt, *n.* [Fr. *sagénite*, from L. *sagena*, Gr. *sagēnē*, a large net.] Acicular rutile, or red oxide of titanium; the crystals cross each other, giving a reticulated appearance, hence the name.

Sagg, sag, *v.i.* Same as *Sag*.

Sagger, sag'ėr, *n.* A seggar. SEGGAR.

Saginate,† saj'i-nāt, *v.t.* [L. *sagino*, *saginatum*, to fatten.] To fatten.

Sagittal, saj'i-tal, *a.* [L. *sagittalis*, from *sagitta*, an arrow.] Pertaining to an arrow; resembling an arrow; *anat.* applied to the suture which unites the parietal bones of the skull.—**Sagittarius**, saj-i-tā'ri-us, *n.* [L., an archer.] One of the zodiacal constellations, which the sun enters Nov. 22; represented by the figure of a centaur in the act of shooting an arrow from his bow. —**Sagittary**, saj'i-ta-ri, *n.* An old name for a centaur.—*a.* Pertaining to an arrow. —**Sagittate**, saj'i-tāt, *a.* Shaped like the head of an arrow: used especially in *bot.*

Sago, sā'gō, *n.* [Malay and Javanese *sagu*, sago, from Papuan *sagu*, bread.] A kind of starch produced from the stem of several palms of the East Indies, forming light, wholesome, nutritious food.

Sagum, sā'gum, *n.* [L.] The military cloak worn by the Roman soldiers and inferior officers in war.

Sahib, sä'ib, *n.* [Hind., from Ar. *sahib*, lord, master.] A term of respect used by the natives of India or Persia in addressing or speaking of Europeans.

Sai, sä'i, *n.* A species of South American monkey.

Saic, sä'ik, *n.* [Fr. *saïque*, from Turk *shaïka*, a saic.] A variety of vessel common in the Levant.

Said, sed, pret. and pp. of *say*: so written for *sayed*. Declared; uttered; aforesaid; before mentioned.

Saiga, sä'ga, *n.* A species of antelope found on the steppes of Russia in Asia.

Sail, sāl, *n.* [A.Sax. *segel*, *segl*, a sail=Icel. *segl*, G. and Sw. *segel*, Dan. *seil*, D. *zeil*; probably from an Indo-European root (*sagh*) meaning to check, to resist (the wind).] A piece of cloth, &c., spread to the wind to cause a vessel to move through the water, usually made of canvas; that portion of the arm of a windmill which catches the wind; a ship or other vessel: used as a plural with the singular form (a fleet of twenty *sail*); an excursion upon water; a passage in a vessel. —*Full sail*, with all sails set.—*To loose sails*, to unfurl them.—*To make sail*, to extend an additional quantity of sail.—*To set sail*, to expand or spread the sails; and hence, to begin a voyage.—*To shorten sail*, to reduce the extent of sail or take in a part.—*To strike sail*, to lower the sails suddenly, as in saluting or in sudden gusts of wind. — *Under sail*, having the sails spread.—*v.i.* To be impelled by the action of wind upon sails, as a ship, or by steam, oars, &c.; to be conveyed in a vessel on water; to pass by water; to set sail; to begin a voyage; to glide through the air; to pass smoothly along; to glide; to float (the clouds *sail*).—*v.t.* To pass over by means of sails; to move upon or pass over, as in a ship (to *sail* the seas); to fly or glide through; to navigate; to direct or manage the motion of.—**Sail-boat**, *n.* A boat propelled by or fitted for a sail or sails.—**Sailborne**, sāl'bōrn, *a.* Borne or conveyed by sails.—**Sail-broad**, *a.* Spreading like a sail.—**Sail-cloth**, *n.* Canvas or duck used in making sails for ships, &c.—**Sailer**, sā'lėr, One that sails; a sailor†; a ship or other vessel with reference to her manner of sailing (a fast *sailer*).—**Sailing**, sā'ling, *n.* The act of one who or that which sails; the art of navigation.—**Sailless**, sāl'les, *a.* Destitute of sails.—**Sail-loft** *n.* A loft where sails are cut out and made.—**Sail-maker**, *n.* One whose occupation is to make, alter, or repair sails.—**Sailor**, sā'lėr, *n.* [Another spelling of *sailer*.] A mariner; a seaman.—**Sail-room**, *n.* An apartment in a vessel where spare sails are stowed away.—**Sail-yard**, *n.* The yard or spar on which a sail is extended.

Sain, sān, *v.t.* [O.E. *segnian*, G. *segnen*, bless.] To bless or protect by making the *sign* of the cross.

Sainfoin, Saintfoin, sān'foin, sānt'foin, *n.* [Fr. *sainfoin*, from *sain*, wholesome, and *foin*, hay, or from *saint*, holy, and *foin*.] A leguminous plant cultivated for supplying fodder for cattle either in the green state or when converted into hay.

Saint, sānt, *n.* [O.Fr., from L. *sanctus*, sacred, holy, pp. of *sancio*, to render sacred. SACRED.] A person sanctified; one eminent for piety and virtue; particularly applied to the apostles and other holy persons of early Christian times; one of the blessed in heaven; an angel (O. and N.T.); a person canonized by the Church of Rome: often contracted *St.* when coming before a personal name.—*St. Andrew's cross*, a cross shaped like the letter X.—*St. Anthony's fire*, erysipelas.—*St. Cuthbert's beads*, the detached and perforated joints of the fossil stems of encrinites.—*St. Elmo's light*, corposant. — *St. George's ensign*, the distinguishing badge of ships of the British navy, consisting of a red cross on a white field, with the union-flag in the upper quarter next the mast.—*St. Ignatius' bean*, the seed of a large climbing shrub nearly allied to that which produces nux-vomica. — *St. John's bread*, the carob tree or its fruit.—*St. Vitus' dance*. CHOREA.—*Saint's bell*. SACRING-BELL.—*v.t.*† To enrol among the saints; to canonize.—*v.i.* To act piously or with a show of piety. (*Shak.*)—**Saintdom**, sānt'dum, *n.* The state or condition of being a saint.—**Sainted**, sān'ted, *p.* and *a.* Canonized; holy; pious; entered into bliss; gone to heaven: often used as a euphuism for *dead*.—**Sainthood**, sānt'hōd, *n.* The character, rank, or position of a saint.—**Saintlike, Saintly**, sānt'līk, sānt'li, *a.* Resembling a saint; becoming a saint.—**Saintliness**, sānt'li-nes, *n.* The quality or state of being saintly.—**Saintship**, sānt'ship, *n.* The character or qualities of a saint.

Saint-Simonian, sānt-si-mō'ni-an, *n.* A partisan of the Count de *St. Simon*, who advocated a system of socialism.—**Saint-Simonianism**, sānt-si-mō'ni-an-izm, *n.* The doctrines of the Saint-Simonians.

Saitic, sa-it'ik, *a.* [*Sais*.] Of or belonging to the dynasties of Egyptian kings at Sais, in Lower Egypt.

Sake, sāk, *n.* [A.Sax. *sacu*, contention, a case or suit at law; Icel. *sök*, L.G. *sake*, G. *sache*, suit, affair, thing; akin to A.Sax. *sacan*, Icel. *saka*, to contend, accuse, &c.] Final cause; purpose; account; regard to any person or thing: always with *for* (*for* his *sake*).

Saker, sā'kėr, *n.* [Fr. *sacre*, a falcon, then a piece of ordnance; Sp. and Pg. *sacre*, from Ar. *saqr*, a sparrow-hawk.] A hawk; a species of falcon; formerly also a small piece of artillery.—**Sakeret**, sā'kėr-et, *n.* The male of the saker.

Saki, sä'ki, *n.* A name of American monkeys with non-prehensile bushy tails.

Sakieh, Sakia, sak'i-e, sak'i-a, *n.* A modification of the Persian wheel used in Egypt for raising water.

Sal, sal, *n.* [L. SALT.] Salt: a word much used by the older chemists and in pharmacy. —*Sal aeratus*. SALERATUS.—*Sal ammoniac* (am-mō'ni-ak), ammonium chloride, NH_4Cl, a salt much used in the arts and in pharmacy; a name derived from the temple of Jupiter *Ammon*, in Egypt, where it was originally made by burning camels' dung.—*Sal prunella*, nitrate of potash fused into cakes or balls and used for chemical purposes.—*Sal volatile*, (vo-lat'i-le), carbonate of ammonia; a spirituous solution of carbonate of ammonia flavoured with aromatics.

Sal, säl, *n.* [Native name.] One of the most valuable timber trees of India.

Salaam, sa-läm', *n.* [Per. and Ar. *salám*, Heb. *shalom*, peace.] A ceremonious salutation or obeisance among orientals.—*v.t.* and *i.* To perform the salaam; to salute with a salaam.

Salable, sā'la-bl, *a.* SALE.

Salacious, sa-lā'shus, *a*, [L. *salax*, *salacis*, salacious, from *salio*, to leap.] Lustful; lecherous. — **Salaciously**, sa-lā'shus-li, *adv.* Lustfully. — **Salaciousness, Salacity**, sa-lā'shus-nes, sa-las'i-ti, *n.* The quality of being salacious; lecherousness.

Salad, sal'ad, *n.* [Fr. *salade*, It. *salata*, a salted dish, from *salare*, to salt, from L. *sal*, salt.] A general name for certain vegetables prepared and served so as to be eaten raw; chiefly lettuce, endive, radishes, green mustard, cresses, celery, and young onions. — *Salad days*, green, unripe age; days of youthful inexperience.—*Salad oil*, olive-oil used in dressing salads.—**Salading**, sal'ad-ing, *n.* Vegetables for salads.

Sal-aeratus, sal'ā-ėr-ā"tus, *n.* SALERATUS.

Salam, sa-läm', *n.* SALAAM.

Salamander, sal-a-man'dėr, *n.* [L. and Gr. *salamandra*.] The name of harmless amphibian reptiles closely allied to the newts, formerly believed to be capable of living in fire; a kind of fire spirit or being supposed to live in fire; a large iron poker.—*Salamander's wool* or *hair*, fibrous asbestos.—**Salamandrine, Salamandroid**, sal-a-man'drīn, sal-a-man'droid, *a.* Pertaining to or resembling a salamander.

Salamstone, sa-läm'stōn, *n.* A variety of sapphire brought from Ceylon.

Salangane, sal'an-gān, *n.* [Of Eastern origin.] The species of swift which builds the edible nests prized by the Chinese.

Salary, sal'a-ri, *n.* [L. *salarium*, from *sal*, salt, originally salt money, money given to buy salt, as part of the pay of Roman soldiers; hence, stipend, pay. SALT.] The recompense or consideration stipulated to be paid to a person periodically for services, usually a fixed sum to be paid by the year, half-year, or quarter; stipend; wages.—*v.t.* —*salaried*, *salarying*. To pay or attach a salary or stipend to.

Sale, sāl, *n.* [Icel. *sal*, *sala*, sale; bargain; this word stands in same relation to *sell* as *tale* to *tell*.] The act of selling; the exchange or transfer of a commodity for an agreed on price in money; opportunity of selling; demand; market; public transfer to the highest bidder; exposure of goods in a market or shop; auction.—*On sale*, *for sale*, to be bought or sold; offered to purchasers.—**Salable**, sā'la-bl, *a.* Capable of being sold; finding a ready market; in demand. — **Salableness**, **Salability**, sā'la-bl-nes, sā-la-bil'i-ti, *n.* The state of being salable.—**Salably**, sā'la-bli, *adv.* In a salable manner.—**Sale-room**, *n.* A room in which goods are sold; an auction-room.—**Salesman**, sālz'man, *n.* One whose occupation is to sell goods or merchandise; a wholesale dealer, as, a cattle, butter, hay, fish, or other *salesman*.

Salep, Salop, sal'ep, sal'op, *n.* [Ar. *sahleb*, salep.] The dried tuberous roots of different species of orchis, much valued in the East for its supposed stimulant properties and esteemed as a nutritious food.

Saleratus, sal-e-rā'tus, *n.* [For *sal-aeratus*, lit. aerated salt.] The prepared carbonate of soda and salt used for mixing with the flour in baking.

Salic, sal'ik, *a.* [Fr. *salique*, from the *Salian* Franks, or Franks settled on the river *Sala*.] A term applied to a law by which in France females were excluded from the throne.

Salicaceous, sal-i-kā'shus, *a.* [L. *salix*, a willow.] Of or relating to the willow family of plants. — **Salicin, Salicine**, sal'i-sin, *n.* A bitter crystallizable substance extracted from willow bark and from that of the poplar, a valuable tonic.—**Salicylic**, sal-i-sil'ik, *a.* [L. *salix*, and Gr. *hylē*, matter.] A term for an acid used as an antiseptic and for other purposes.

Salient, sā'li-ent, *a.* [L. *saliens*, *salientis*, ppr. of *salio*, to leap (seen also in *sally*, *assail*, *assault*, *insult*, *result*, &c.).] Springing; shooting up or out; projecting outwardly (a *salient* angle); forcing itself on the notice or attention; conspicuous; prominent; a projecting angle or corner in a line of defence, forming a jumping-off place; *her.* animals jumping, with both hind feet on the ground, and fore paws in the air.—**Saliently**, sā'li-ent-li, *adv.* In a salient manner.—**Salience**, sā'li-ens, *n.* The quality of being salient; projection; protrusion.

Saliferous, sa-lif'ėr-us, *a.* [L. *sal*, salt, and *fero*, to produce.] Producing or bearing salt.—*Saliferous system*, an old geological term for the new red sandstone system, from salt being a characteristic of it.

Salify, sal'i-fī, *v.t.*—*salified*, *salifying*. [L. *sal*, salt, and *facio*, to make.] To form into a salt by combining an acid with a base.—**Salifiable**, sal'i-fī-a-bl, *a.* Capable of combining with an acid to form a salt.—**Salification**, sal'i-fi-kā"shon, *n.* The act of salifying.

Salimeter, sa-lim'et-ėr, *n.* [L. *sal*, *salis*, salt, and Gr. *metron*, a measure.] An instrument for measuring the amount of salt present in any given solution.

Salina, sa-lī'na, *n.* [Sp., from L. *sal*, salt. SALT.] A salt-marsh; a salt-pond inclosed from the sea; a place where salt is made from salt-water; a salt-work. — **Salination**, sal-i-nā'shon, *n.* The act of washing with or soaking in salt liquor.—**Saline**, sa-līn', *a.* [Fr. *salin*, from L. *sal*, salt.] Consisting of salt; partaking of the qualities of salt; salt.—*n.* [Fr. *saline*.] A salt spring, or a place where salt-water is collected in the earth.—**Salineness**, sa-līn'nes, *n.* State of being saline.—**Saliniferous**, sal-i-nif'ėr-us, *a.* Producing salt.—**Saliniform**, sa-lin'i-form, *a.* Having the form of salt.—**Salinity**, sa-lin'i-ti, *n.* The state of being salt; salineness.—**Salinometer**, sal-i-nom'et-ėr, *n.* An apparatus for indicating the density of brine in the boilers of marine steam-engines, and thus showing when they should be cleansed.

Salique, sal'ik or sa-lēk', *a.* SALIC.

Saliva, sa-lī'va, *n.* [L., akin to Gr. *sialon*, saliva; and to Gael. and Ir. *seile*, saliva, E. *slime*.] The fluid which is secreted by certain glands of the mouth and which serves to moisten the mouth and tongue and to make the food more fitted for digestion: when discharged from the mouth it is called *spittle*.—**Salival**, sa-lī'val, *a.* SALIVARY.—**Salivant**, sal'i-vant, *a.* Exciting salivation.—*n.* That which produces salivation.—**Salivary**, sal'i-va-ri, *a.* Pertaining to the saliva; secreting or conveying saliva (the *salivary* glands or ducts).—**Salivate**, sal'i-vāt, *v.t.*—*salivated, salivating.* [L. *salivare*.] To cause to have an unusual secretion and discharge of saliva, usually by mercury.—**Salivation**, sal-i-vā'shon, *n.* An excessive flow of saliva, often caused by mercury; ptyalism.

Sallow, sal'ō, *n.* [A.Sax. *sealh*=Sc. *saugh*, Icel. *selja*, Dan. *sœlje*, G. *sahl*; allied to L. *salix*, Gael. *seileach*, Ir. *sail*, a willow.] A shrub of the willow kind.

Sallow, sal'ō, *a.* [A.Sax. *salu*, *sealwe*, sallow, dark = Icel. *sölr*, D. *saluwe*, O.H.G. *salo*, pale.] Of a pale, sickly colour, tinged with a dark yellow: said especially of the skin or complexion.—*v.t.* To tinge with a sallow colour.—**Sallowness**, sal'ō-nes, *n.* The quality of being sallow.

Sally, sal'i, *n.* [Fr. *saillie*, from *saillir*, to leap, from L. *salire*, to leap. SALIENT.] A leaping forth; a rush of troops from a besieged place to attack the besiegers; a spring or flight of intellect, fancy or imagination (a *sally* of wit); an act of levity or extravagance; a piece of wild gaiety; a frolic.—*v.i.*—*sallied, sallying.* To make a sally; to leap or rush out; to issue suddenly from a fortified place, to attack besiegers.—**Sally-port**, *n.* *Fort.* a postern or passage to afford egress to troops in making a sally.

Salmagundi, Salmagundy, sal-ma-gun'di, *n.* [Fr. *salmigondis*.] A dish of chopped meat, eggs, anchovies, red pickled cabbage, &c.; a mixture of various ingredients; a miscellany.

Salmi, Salmis, säl'mē, *n.* [Fr.] A ragout of woodcocks, larks, thrushes, &c.

Salmiac, sal'mi-ak, *n.* A contraction of *Sal Ammoniac.*

Salmon, sam'un, *n. sing.* and *pl.* [L. *salmo*, *salmonis*, from *salio*, to leap.] A large marine food and game fish that breeds in fresh water. The adult is steel blue in color and has fat, pinkish-orange flesh when cooked. The Pacific salmon, now more important than the Atlantic salmon, is caught in enormous numbers from Oregon to Alaska, the two chief species being the Chinook King, or Columbia River Salmon, and the Blueback.—**Salmon-colored**, *a.* Pinkish-orange.—**Salmonet**, *n.* A little salmon; samlet.—**Salmonoid**, sam'un-oid, *a.* Belonging to the group of fishes of which the salmon is the type.—**Salmon peel**, or **peal**. A young salmon or grilse under 2 lbs.—**Salmon trout**. The European sea trout.

Salol, sal'ol, *n.* [L. *salix*, a willow.] Phenol salicylate, an antiseptic.

Salon, sa-lon', *n.* [Fr., see *Saloon*.] Any spacious apartment for the reception of guests or for showing works of art; a drawing room; a fashionable social gathering; an exhibition held every year in Paris for modern artists.

Saloon, sa-lön', *n.* [Fr. *salon*, It. *salone*, from O.H.G. *sal*, a house = A.Sax. *sœl*, a hall.] Any spacious apartment for the reception of company or for works of art; a large public room; an apartment for specific public use (the *saloon* of a steamer); in the United States, a shop where alcoholic beverages are sold and drunk.

Saloop, sa-lüp', *n.* [See SALEP.] The plant sassafras; a drink made from powdered salep, or from sassafras.

Salopian, sa-lōp'i-an, *n.* A native of Shropshire, England.—*a.* Pertaining to, or coming from, Shropshire, England.

Salsafy, sal'sa-fi. SALSIFY.

Salse, säls, *n.* [Fr. *salse*, from L. *salsus*, salt.] An eruption of hot acidulated mud from a small orifice, observed in volcanic regions.

Salsify, sal'si-fī, *n.* [Fr. *salsifis*, goat's-beard.] A plant, called also purple goat's-beard. GOAT'S-BEARD.

Salt, salt, *n.* [A.Sax. *sealt* (properly an adj.)=Fris., Dan., Sw., Icel., and Goth. *salt*, D. *zout*, G. *salz*; cog. W. *halen*, Gael. and Ir. *salann*, L. *sal* (Fr. *sel*), Gr. *hals* (= *sals*), salt.] A well-known substance in common use for seasoning and preserving food from the earliest ages, its chemical name being chloride of sodium, obtained from salt mines in the form of rock-salt, or from sea-water by simple evaporation; *chem.* a compound produced by the combination of a base (commonly a metallic oxide) with an acid; taste; smack; savour; wit; piquancy; pungency; sarcasm (Attic *salt*); a salt-cellar; an old sailor (*colloq.*).—*Salt of lemons*, a substance prepared from oxalic acid and potassium carbonate, used to remove ink-stains, &c.; also oxalic acid.—*Salt of Saturn*, acetate of lead; sugar of lead.—*Salt of soda*, carbonate of soda.—*Salt of sorrel*, oxalic acid; salt of lemons.—*Salt of tartar*, carbonate of potash.—*Salt of tin*, protochloride of tin, extensively used as a mordant in dyeing.—*Salt of vitriol*, sulphate of zinc.—*Spirit of salt*, muriatic or hydrochloric acid.—*To be worth one's salt*, to be worthy of one's hire.—*a.* Impregnated with salt; abounding in or containing salt; prepared with or tasting of salt; sharp; pungent.—*v.t.* To sprinkle, impregnate, or season with salt.—*To salt a mine*, to sprinkle it with a little of the precious metal in order to obtain a high price for the claim from an inexperienced person.—*To salt out*, to precipitate a substance from solution by the addition of ordinary, or other, salt.—**Saltbush**, *n.* The name for Australian plants of the orache genus, which flourish in dry regions, and are browsed by sheep.—**Salt butter**, *n.* Butter seasoned with salt to make it keep.—**Saltcellar**, *n.* [A tautological term, lit. a salt-salt-dish, *cellar* being = Fr. *salière*, a saltcellar, from L. *sal*, salt.] A small vessel used for holding salt on the table.—**Salter**, sạl'tėr, *n.* One who salts; one that sells salt; a drysalter.—**Saltern**, sạl'tėrn, *n.* A salt works; a building in which salt is made by boiling or evaporation.—**Saltish**, sạl'tish, *a.* Somewhat salt.—**Saltishly**, sạl'tish-li, *adv.* With a moderate degree of saltness.—**Saltishness**, sạl'tish-nes, *n.* The state of being saltish.—**Saltless**, *a.* Without salt; insipid.—**Salt lick**. A place where salt lies exposed and where animals come to lick it; a salt spring.—**Saltly**, sạlt'li, *adv.* In a salt manner; with the taste of salt.—**Salt marsh**. Land under pasture-grasses subject to be overflowed by sea water.—**Salt mine**. A mine where rock salt is obtained.—**Saltness**, sạlt'nes, *n.* The quality or state of being salt or impregnated with salt.—**Salt pan**. A large shallow pan or a shallow pond in which salt water or brine is evaporated to obtain salt.—**Saltpeter**, sạlt'pē-tėr. [*Salt* and L. *petra*, a stone.] A salt, called also *Niter* (which see).—**Salts**, sạlts, *n. pl.* Epsom salt or other salt used as medicine.—**Salt spring**. A spring of salt water; a brine spring.—**Salt water**. Water impregnated with salt; sea water.—**Saltworks**, *n.* A place where salt is made.—**Saltwort**, sạlt'wėrt. A name applied to several plants yielding kelp.

Saltant, sal'tant, *a.* [L. *saltans*, *saltantis*, ppr. of *salto*, to leap, from *salio*. SALIENT.] Leaping; jumping; dancing.—**Saltation**, sal-tā'shon, *n.* [L. *saltatio*.] A leaping or jumping; beating or palpitation.—**Saltatory**, sal'ta-to-ri, *a.* Leaping or dancing; adapted for leaping.

Saltarello, sal-ta-rel'lo, *n.* [It.] A brisk Neapolitan dance.

Saltigrade, sal'ti-grād, *a.* [L. *saltus*, a leap, *gradior*, to go.] Leaping; formed for leaping.

Saltimbanco,† sal'tim-bangk"ō, *n.* [It.] A mountebank (which see), quacksalver, charlatan. (*Sir T. Browne.*)

Salubrious, sa-lū'bri-us, *a.* [L. *salubris*, from *salus*, *salutis*, health, safety; akin to *salvus*, safe. SAFE, SALUTARY.] Favorable to health; healthful; conducive to health, as *salubrious* water or food.—**Salubriously**, sa-lū'bri-us-li, *adv.*—**Salubriousness, Salubrity**, sa-lū'bri-us-nes, sa-lū'bri-ti, *n.* The state or quality of being salubrious; healthfulness.

Saluki, sä-lu'ki, *n.* A swift, sharp-eyed, graceful hunting dog bred in the Near East and Egypt. It has a long, narrow head, long silky ears, widely set legs, and a long hairy tail. Height about two feet.

Salutary, sal'ū-ta-ri, *a.* [Fr. *salutaire*, L. *salutaris*, from *salus*, *salutis*, health. SALUBRIOUS.] Wholesome; healthful; promoting health; contributing to some beneficial purpose; advantageous; profitable.—**Salutarily**, sal'ū-ta-ri-li, *adv.* In a salutary manner.—**Salutariness**, sal'ū-ta-ri-nes, *n.* The quality of being salutary.

Salute, sa-lūt', *v.t.*—*saluted, saluting.* [L. *saluto*, from L. *salus*, *salutis*, health. SALUBRIOUS, SAFE.] To address with expressions of kind wishes, or in order to show homage or courtesy; to greet; to hail; to greet by some act, as by uncovering the head, a bow, &c.; in the *army* or *navy*, to honour by a salute (see the noun).—*v.i.* To perform a salutation; to greet each other.—*n.* A salutation; a greeting; a kiss; a bow, or the like; in an *army* or *navy*, a compliment paid to a royal or other distinguished personage when squadrons or other bodies meet, and on various ceremonial occasions, by firing cannons or small-arms, dipping colours or topsails, presenting arms, manning the yards, &c.—**Saluter**, sa-lū'tėr, *n.* One who salutes.—**Salutation**, sal-ū-tā'shon, *n.* [L. *salutatio*.] The act of saluting; that which is done or uttered in saluting; a greeting or salute.—**Salutatory**, sa-lū'ta-to-ri, *a.* Saluting; greeting.

Salvage. Under SALVE, *v.t.*

Salvation, sal-vā'shon, *n.* [O.Fr. *salvation*, from L. *salvo*, *salvatum*, to save, from *salvus*, safe, same root as *salus*, *salutis*, safety (whence *salute*). SAFE, SALUBRIOUS.] The act of saving; preservation from destruction, danger, or great calamity; the redemption of man from the bondage of sin and liability to eternal death and the conferring on him of everlasting happiness; that which saves; the cause of saving.—*Salvation Army*, a society organized for the religious revival of the masses, having its proceedings conducted by generals, majors, captains, &c., of either sex, and by military forms.—**Salvationist**, sal-vā'shon-ist, *n.* One of the Salvation Army.

Salve, salv, *v.t.* [From L. *salvo*, *salvatum*, to save, from *salvus*, safe. SALVATION.] To save a ship or goods from destruction, as by shipwreck or fire.—**Salvable**, sal'va-bl, *a.* Capable of being salved; admitting of salvation.—**Salvability**, sal-va-bil'i-ti, *n.* The state of being salvable.—**Salvage**, sal'vāj, *n.* [L.L. *salvagium*, from L. *salvus*.] The act of saving a ship or goods from extraordinary danger, as from the sea, fire, an enemy, or the like; an allowance to which persons are entitled by whose voluntary exertions ships or goods have been saved; property thus saved.—**Salvor**, sal'vor, *n.* One who saves a ship or goods from wreck or destruction.

Salve, säv or salv, *n.* [A.Sax. *sealf*, a salve, an ointment=D. *zalve*, Dan. *salve*, G. *salbe*, O.H.G. *salba*, salve, allied to Skr. *sarpis*, ghee or clarified butter.] An adhesive substance to be applied to wounds or sores; a healing ointment; help; remedy.—*v.t.*—*salved, salving.* To apply salve to; to remedy.—**Salver**, sä'vėr or sal'vėr, *n.* One who salves or cures.

Salver, sal'vėr, *n.* [Sp. *salva*, a salver, also the previous tasting of a great man's food by a servant to see that it is wholesome, from L. *salvus*, safe. SALVATION.] A kind of tray or waiter for table service, or on which anything is presented to a person.

Salvo, sal'vō, *n.* [From L. *salvo jure*, 'the right being intact', an expression used in reserving rights. SALVATION.] An exception or reservation; an excuse.

Salvo, sal'vō, *n.* [Fr. *salve*, It. and Sp. *salva*, a salvo, a salute, from L. *salve*, hail, from *salvus*, safe. SALVATION.] A general discharge of guns intended for a salute or for some special purpose; a shouting or cheering.

Sal-volatile. Under SAL.

Salvor, sal'vor, *n.* Under SALVE, to save.

Samara, sam'a-ra, *n.* [L. *samara*, the seed of the elm.] *Bot.* a fruit with wing-like expansions, as in the fruit or *key* of the ash tree, elm, maple.—**Samaroid**, sam'a-roid, *a.* Resembling a samara.

Samaritan, sa-mar'i-tan, *a.* Pertaining to *Samaria*, the principal city of the ten tribes of Israel; pertaining to the characters of a kind of ancient Hebrew writing probably in use before, and partly after, the Babylonish exile.—*n.* A native or inhabitant of Samaria; the language of Samaria; a Chaldean dialect; a charitable or benevolent person: in allusion to the 'good Samaritan' in the parable.

Samarium, sa-mā'ri-um, *n.* One of the chemical elements.

Sambo, sam'bō, *n.* The offspring of a black person and a mulatto.

Sam Browne, sam-broun, *n.* A belt with a shoulder-strap worn by military officers and first-class warrant officers.

Sambur, sam'bur, *n.* A kind of large deer of Northern India.

Same, sām, *a.* [A.Sax. *same*, Icel. *samr*, Dan. and Sw. *samme*, O.Sax. and Goth. *sama*; allied to L. *similis* (whence *similar*, *simulate*), like *simul*, together; Gr. *hama*, together, *homos*, same; Skr. *sama*, like.] Identical; not different or other (the *same* man); of the identical kind, species, or degree; exactly similar, though not the specific thing (the *same* error); just mentioned or denoted: always preceded by *the* or *this*, *that*, &c.—*All the same*, nevertheless; notwithstanding.—**Sameness**, sām'-nes, *n.* The state of being the same; identity; similarity; want of variety.

Samian, sā'mi-an, *a.* Pertaining to the isle of *Samos*.—*Samian earth*, an argillaceous earth found in Samos, and formerly used in medicine as an astringent.—*Samian letter*, the name of the Greek letter Y, selected by Pythagoras of Samos as the symbol of virtue, the stem representing the straight way, that ultimately divides towards virtue or vice on either hand.—*Samian ware*, an ancient kind of pottery made of Samian or other fine earth.—*n.* A native or inhabitant of Samos.

Samite, sā'mīt, *n.* [O.Fr. *samit*, from L.L. *samitum*, from Gr. *hexamiton*—*hex*, six, and *mitos*, a thread.] An old rich silk stuff interwoven with gold or embroidered.

Samlet, sam'let, *n.* [Dim. of *salmon*.] A name for the parr.

Samovar, sam'o-vär, *n.* [Russian.] A tea-urn used in Russia in which the water is heated by a tube passing through it containing live coals.

Samoyeds, sam'o-yeds, *n.* The Mongolian race in Siberia.

Samp, samp, *n.* In the United States, food composed of maize, broken or bruised, boiled, and mixed with milk.

Sampan, sam'pan, *n.* [Malay and Javanese.] A name applied to boats of various builds on the Chinese rivers, at Singapore, &c.

Samphire, sam'fīr, *n.* [Corruption of Fr. (*herbe de*) *Saint Pierre* (St. Peter's herb).] Sea-fennel, a genus of plants whose leaves are used in pickles and salads.

Sample, sam'pl, *n.* [O.Fr. *essample*, *example*, an example. EXAMPLE.] A pattern‡; an example‡; a small part or quantity of anything intended to be shown as evidence of the quality of the whole. ∴ Syn. under SPECIMEN.—*v.t.*—*sampled*, *sampling*. To take a sample of; to take a quantity from to serve as a sample (to *sample* sugar, &c.).—**Sampler**, sam'plėr, *n.* One who samples.

Sampler, sam'plėr, *n.* [From L. *exemplar*, a pattern, from *exemplum*, an example. SAMPLE, EXAMPLE.] A piece of fancy sewed or embroidered work done by girls for practice.

Samson's-post, sam'sonz-pōst, *n.* A strong pillar or a movable post used in a ship for various purposes.

Sanable, san'a-bl, *a.* [L. *sanabilis*, from *sano*, to heal, from *sanus*, sound. SANE.] Capable of being healed or cured; curable; —**Sanability, Sanableness**, san-a-bil'-i-ti, san'a-bl-nes, *n.* State of being sanable, curableness.—**Sanatarium**, san-a-tā'ri-um, *n.* Same as *Sanatorium*.—**Sanative**, san'a-tiv, *a.* Healing.—**Sanativeness**, san'a-tiv-nes, *n.* **Sanatorium**, san-a-tō'-ri-um, *n.* [Neut. of L.L. *sanatorius*.] A place to which people go for the sake of health; a military station on the mountains or table-lands of tropical countries, with climates suited to the health of Europeans. —*Sanatarium* and *Sanitarium* are less correct forms.—**Sanatory**, san'a-to-ri, *a.* [L.L. *sanatorius*, from L. *sano*, to heal.] Conducive to health; healing; curing: sometimes used as if the same as *sanitary*. See under SANITARY.

San-benito, san-be-nē'tō, *n.* [It. *sanbenito*, Sp. *sambenito*.] An upper garment painted with flames, figures of devils, &c., worn by persons going to the stake on the occasion of an *auto de fe*.

Sanctify, sangk'ti-fī, *v.t.*—*sanctified*, *sanctifying*. [Fr. *sanctifier*, L. *sanctifico*, from *sanctus*, holy (whence *saint*), and *facio*, to make.] To make holy or sacred; to set apart to a holy or religious use; to hallow; to purify from sin or sinful affections; to make the means of holiness; to celebrate or confess as holy.—**Sanctification**, sangk'-ti-fi-kā''shon, *n.* The act of sanctifying or state of being sanctified; the act of God's grace by which the affections of men are purified from sin; conformity to the will of God; consecration.—**Sanctifier**, sangk'-ti-fī-ėr, *n.* One who sanctifies.

Sanctimony, sangk'ti-mo-ni, *n.* [L. *sanctimonia*, from *sanctus*, holy. SAINT.] Piety‡, sanctity‡; the external appearance of devoutness; affected or hypocritical devoutness.—**Sanctimonious**, sangk-ti-mō'ni-us, *a.* Making a show of sanctity; affecting the appearance of sanctity.—**Sanctimoniously**, sangk-ti-mō'ni-us-li, *adv.* In a sanctimonious manner.—**Sanctimoniousness**, sangk-ti-mō'ni-us-nes, *n.*

Sanction, sangk'shon, *n.* [L. *sanctio*, from *sancio*, *sancire*, to render sacred or inviolable, whence *sanctus*, holy. SAINT.] An official act of a superior by which he ratifies and gives validity to the act of some other person or body; ratification or confirmation; authority; penalty incurred by the infringement of a command.—*Pragmatic sanction*. PRAGMATIC.—*v.t.* To give sanction to; to ratify; to give countenance to.

Sanctity, sangk'ti-ti, *n.* [L. *sanctitas*, from *sanctus*, holy. SANCTION, SAINT.] The state or quality of being sacred or holy; holiness; saintliness; sacredness; inviolability.

Sanctuary, sangk'tū-a-ri, *n.* [L. *sanctuarium*, from *sanctus*, sacred. SANCTITY.] A sacred or consecrated place; the temple at Jerusalem, particularly the most retired part of it, called the *Holy of Holies*; a house consecrated to the worship of God; a church; in the *R. Cath. Ch.* that part of a church where the altar is placed; the cella of an Egyptian, Greek, or Roman temple; a place of protection; a sacred asylum; right of affording such protection, a privilege attached to certain places in virtue of which criminals are protected from the law; refuge in a sacred place; shelter.—**Sanctum**, sangk'tum, *n.* A sacred place; A private retreat or room (an editor's *sanctum*).—*Sanctum sanctorum*, 'the holy of holies'; the innermost or holiest place of the Jewish temple.—**Sanctus**, sangk'tus, *n.* An anthem beginning with the Latin word *sanctus*, holy.—**Sanctus-bell**, *n.* Same as *Sacring-bell*.

Sand, sand, *n.* [A.Sax. *sand* = Dan., Sw., and G. *sand*, Icel. *sandr*, D. *zand*; probably from same root as L. *sabulum*, gravel.] Fine particles of stone, particularly of siliceous stone in a loose state, but not reduced to powder or dust, generally arising from disintegrated rock; *pl.* a tract of land consisting of sandy soil, like the deserts of Arabia; tracts of sand exposed by the ebb of the tide.—*v.t.* To sprinkle with sand; to drive upon a sandbank.—**Sandbag**, *n.* A bag filled with sand or earth, and used in a fortification or for other purposes.—**Sandbank**, *n.* A bank of sand; a bank of sand formed by tides or currents.—**Sand bath**, *n.* A bath of hot sand for the body; hot sand used as an equable heater for retorts, etc., in chemical processes.—**Sandblast**, *n.* A method used to engrave, clean, or abrade glass, rock, &c., by means of a stream of sand forced by compressed air or steam.—**Sand-blind**, *a.* [Corrupted from *sam-blind*, from A.Sax. *sām* (akin to L. *semi*), half.] Having imperfect sight.—**Sandbur, Sandburr**, *n.* A name for various weeds bearing prickly seed pods, growing in sandy places.—**Sand crack**. A crack in the hoof of a horse.—**Sand dollar**. A round, flat sea urchin found on sandy bottoms.—**Sanddrift**, *n.* Drifting or drifted sand; a mound of drifted sand.—**Sand dune**. A ridge or hill of sand, as along a shore, piled up by the wind.—**Sanded**, san'ded, *p.* and *a.* Sprinkled with sand; covered with drifted sand. —**Sand eel**. A name of certain small fishes that bury themselves in the sand, and are also known by the name of launce. —**Sanderling**, san'dėr-ling, *n.* [So called because it feeds among the moist sands of the shore.] A small wading bird which frequents the shores and feeds on small marine insects.—**Sand flea**. The beach flea, the chigoe, or other flea which lives in sandy places.—**Sand fly**. A minute dipterous insect whose bite is painful.—**Sandglass**, *n.* A glass that measures time by the running of sand from one division of it to the other.—**Sand grass**. Grass that grows on sandy soil.—**Sand grouse**, *n.* A genus of birds closely allied to the grouse, inhabiting arid sandy plains.—**Sand hill**. A hill of sand; a dune. —**Sandiness**, san'di-nes, *n.* The state of being sandy.—**Sand launce**. The sand eel.—**Sand lily**. A stemless plant of western U. S., bearing stalks of lily-shaped flowers.—**Sand lizard**. A common lizard of Europe.—**Sandman**, *n.* An imaginary person who puts sand into children's eyes to make them sleepy.—**Sand martin**. In England, the bank swallow.—**Sand mole**. The rat mole, a burrowing animal of South Africa.—**Sandpaper**, *n.* Paper covered on one side with a fine gritty substance for polishing woodwork.—**Sand pipe**, *Geol.* A rock crevice filled with sand or gravel.—**Sandpiper**, sand'-pī-pėr, *n.* A name of several grallatorial birds allied to the snipe, plover, &c.—**Sandstone**, sand'stōn, *n.* Stone composed of agglutinated grains of sand, which may be calcareous, siliceous, or of any other mineral nature, often known by the name of *freestone*.—**Sandstorm**, *n.* A windstorm which blows along great clouds of sand.—**Sand verbena**, A plant, similar to the verbena, that grows in the dry, sandy soil of the western U. S.—**Sand Wasp**, *n.* An insect resembling a wasp, the females of which burrow in sandy banks.—**Sandwort**, sand'wėrt, *n.* A name of several plants growing in sandy places.—**Sandy**, san'di, *a.* Consisting of or abounding with sand; resembling sand; of the color of sand; of a yellowish-red color.

Sandal, san'dal, *n.* [Fr. *sandale*, L. *sandalium*, from Gr. *sandalion*.] A kind of shoe, consisting of a sole fastened to the foot, generally by means of straps crossed over and worn round the ankle; a tie or strap for a shoe resembling that of a sandal.—**Sandaliform**, san'dal-i-form, *a.* shaped like a sandal or slipper.—**Sandaled**, san'dald, *p.* and *a.* Wearing sandals; shaped like a sandal.

Sandal-wood, *n.* [Ar. *sandal*, sandal-wood.] The wood of several trees of the East Indies and islands of the Pacific, with a strong scent which is very fatal to insects, and hence it is used for making cabinets, boxes, &c.—*Red sandal-wood*, the wood of a tree of India, used as a dye-wood.

Sandarach, san'da-rak, *n.* [L. *sandaracha*, from Gr. *sandarachē*, a word of Oriental origin.] A resin which exudes from the bark of a valuable timber tree of Morocco, used as incense and for making varnish.

Sanders, Sanders-wood, san'dėrz, *n.* Same as *Sandal-wood*.

Sanders-blue, san'dėrz-blū, *n.* Same as *Saunders-blue*.

Sandiver, Sandever, san'di-vėr, *n.* [A corruption of Fr. *sel de verre*, salt of glass.] The scum which is cast up from the materials of glass in fusion, and is used, when pulverized, as a polishing substance.

Sandix, Sandyx, san'diks, *n.* [Gr. *sandyx*, a bright red colour.] Red-lead prepared by calcining carbonate of lead.

Sandwich, sand'wich, *n.* [After an Earl of *Sandwich*, who brought it into fashion.] Two thin slices of bread with meat, fish, or the like, between.—**Sandwich-man**, *n.* A man carrying two advertising boards, one before and one behind.

Sandyx. SANDIX.

Sane, sān, *a.* [L. *sanus*, sound, whole, healthy (whence *sanatory, sanitary*); same root as Gr. *sōs*, safe.] Mentally sound; not deranged; having the regular exercise of reason and the other mental faculties.—**Saneness, Sanity**, sān'nes, san'i-ti, *n.* The state of being sane or of sound mind.

Sang, sang, pret. of *sing*.

Sangar, sang'ar, *n.* [Hindu *sunga.*] A stone breastwork or fortification.

Sangaree, sang'ga-rē, *n.* Wine and water sweetened and spiced, and sometimes iced; used as a refreshing drink.

Sang-froid, sang'frwạ, *n.* [Fr., cold-blood—*sang*, blood, and *froid*, cold.] Freedom from agitation or excitement of mind; coolness; calmness in trying circumstances.

Sangiac, san'ji-ak. SANJAK.

Sangreal, sang-rā'al, *n.* [The *san* is from L. *sanctus*, holy, and *greal* = *grail*.] The grail or holy vessel of mediæval legends. See GRAIL.

Sanguiferous, sang-gwif'ėr-us, *a.* [L. *sanguis*, blood, and *fero*, to carry.] Conveying blood, as the arteries and veins.

Sanguify, sang'gwi-fī, *v.i.* — *sanguified, sanguifying.* [L. *sanguis*, blood, and *facio*, to make.] To produce blood.—**Sanguification**, sang'gwi-fi-kā"shon, *n.* The production of blood.—**Sanguigenous**, sang-gwij'en-us, *a.* [L. *sanguis*, blood, and root *gen*, to produce.] Producing blood.

Sanguinary, sang'gwi-na-ri, *a.* [L. *sanguinarius*, from *sanguis*, blood; same root as *sucus* or *succus*, juice, *sugo*, to suck.] Consisting of blood; bloody; attended with much bloodshed; murderous; bloodthirsty.—**Sanguinarily**, sang'gwi-na-ri-li, *adv.* In a sanguinary manner.—**Sanguinariness**, sang'gwi-na-ri-nes, *n.*

Sanguine, sang'gwin, *a.* [Fr. *sanguin*, from L. *sanguineus*, from *sanguis*, blood. SANGUINARY.] Having the colour of blood; red; characterized by fulness of habit, vigour, activity of circulation, &c.; cheerful in temper; anticipating the best; not desponding; confident. — *n.* Blood colour; bloodstone. — **Sanguinely**, sang'gwin-li, *adv.* In a sanguine manner.—**Sanguineness**, sang'gwin-nes, *n.* The state or quality of being sanguine.—**Sanguineous**, sang-gwin'ē-us, *a.* [L. *sanguineus.*] Appertaining to the blood; of the colour of blood; sanguine; confident. — **Sanguinivorous, Sanguivorous**, sang-gwi-niv'o-rus, sang-gwiv'o-rus, *a.* [L. *sanguis*, and *voro*, to eat.] Eating or subsisting on blood.—**Sanguinolent**, sang-gwin'ō-lent, *a.* [L. *sanguinolentus.*] Tinged or mingled with blood; bloody.

Sanhedrim, san'he-drim, *n.* [Heb. *sanhedrin*, from Gr. *sunedrion*—*sun* (or *syn*), with, together, and *hedra*, seat.] The great council among the Jews of Maccabean and later times, consisting of a president (generally the high-priest) and seventy other members.

Sanicle, san'i-kl, *n.* [Fr. *sanicle*, from L. *sano*, to heal—from its supposed healing virtues.] An umbelliferous plant of several species, also called *Self-heal*.

Sanies, sā'ni-ēz, *n.* [L., bloody matter.] A thin reddish discharge from wounds or sores.—**Sanious**, sā'ni-us, *a.* [L. *saniosus.*] Pertaining to sanies, or partaking of its nature and appearance.

Sanitary, san'i-ta-ri, *a.* [Fr. *sanitaire*, from L. *sanitas*, health, from *sanus*, sound. SANE.] Pertaining to or designed to secure health; relating to the preservation of health; hygienic. ∴ *Sanitary* and *sanatory* are not unfrequently confounded. *Sanitary* (from L. *sanitas*, health) has the general meaning of pertaining to health, hygienic; *sanatory* (directly from L. *sano, sanatum*, to make healthy) means pertaining to healing or curing; tending to cure.—**Sanitarian**, san-i-tā'ri-an, *n.* A promoter of, or one versed in, sanitary measures.—**Sanitarium**, san-i-tā'ri-um, *n.* A health retreat; a sanitorium.—**Sanitation**, san-i-tā'shon, *n.* The adoption of sanitary measures for the health of a community; hygiene.

Sanity, san'i-ti, *n.* Under SANE.

Sanjak, san'jak, *n.* [Turk., a standard.] A minor province of Turkey.—**Sanjakate**, san'jak-āt, *n.* A sanjak.

Sank, sangk, pret. of *sink*.

Sanpan, san'pan, *n.* Same as *Sampan*.

Sans, sänz, *prep.* [Fr., from L. *sine*, without.] Without; deprived of.—**Sans-culotte**, sänz-kų-lot', *n.* [Fr., without breeches.] A fellow without knee-breeches, a name originally given in derision to the popular party by the aristocratical in the beginning of the French revolution of 1789; hence, a fierce republican of any country.—**Sans-culottic**, sänz-kų-lot'ik, *a.* Revolutionary; republican. — **Sans-culottism**, sänz-kų-lot'izm, *n.* Extreme republicanism.—**Sans-culottist**, sänz-kų-lot'ist, *n.* A sans-culotte; a rabid republican.

Sanskrit, Sanscrit, san'skrit, *n.* [Skr. *sanskrita*, perfectly formed—*sam* (= Gr. *syn*), with, and *krita*, made, perfected, from *kri*, to make.] The ancient language of the Hindus, being that in which most of their vast literature is written, one of the Aryan or Indo-European family of tongues. Also used as an adjective. — **Sanskritist, Sanscritist**, san'skrit-ist, *n.* A sanskrit scholar.

Santaline, san'ta-lin, *n.* [From *sandal*.] The colouring matter of red sandal or sanders-wood.

Santon, Santoon, san'ton, san'tön, *n.* An oriental priest regarded as a saint.

Santonin, Santonine, san'to-nin, *n.* [Gr. *santonion*, a kind of wormwood.] A substance obtained from the seeds of southern-wood, a most efficacious vermifuge.

Santorin, san'to-rin, *n.* An argillaceous mineral occurring on the island of *Santorin*, yielding an excellent cement.

Saouari, Souari-wood, sou-ä'rē, *n.* An excellent timber for ship-building, obtained from trees of tropical America, which yield also delicious nuts.

Sap, sap, *n.* [A.Sax. *sæp* = D. *sap*, L.G. *sapp*, juice; akin Dan. and G. *saft*, juice, sap.] The juice or fluid which circulates in all plants, being as indispensable to vegetable life as the blood to animal life; vital juice; blood; sap-wood; a stupid person.—*v.t.* To study. (*Colloq.*)—**Sapless**, sap'les, *a.* Destitute of sap; dry; withered. —**Sapling**, sap'ling, *n.* A young tree full of sap.—**Sappy**, sap'i, *a.* Abounding with sap; juicy; succulent; young; stupid.—**Sappiness**, sap'i-nes, *n.* The state or quality of being sappy; succulence; juiciness.—**Sap-color**, *n.* Vegetable juice inspissated and forming a pigment.—**Sap-green**, *n.* A pigment prepared from the juice of the berries of the buckthorn.—**Sap-sucker**, *n.* The name of several small woodpeckers.—**Sap-wood**, *n.* ALBURNUM.

Sap, sap, *v.t.*—*sapped, sapping.* [Fr. *saper*, from *sape*, L.L. *sapa*, a mattock.] To cause to fall, or to render unstable, by digging or wearing away the foundation; to undermine; to subvert; to destroy, as if by some secret, hidden, or invisible process. — *v.i.* To proceed by secretly undermining. — *n. Milit.* a ditch or trench by which approach is made to a fortress or besieged place within range of fire. — **Sapper**, sap'ėr, *n.* One who saps; a soldier of an engineer corps, or who is trained in fortification or siege works.

Sapadillo, sap-a-dil'ō, *n.* SAPODILLA.

Sapajou, Sajou, sap'a-jö, sä'jö, *n.* [Fr.] A name of certain South American prehensile-tailed monkeys, of small size.

Sapan-wood, sa-pan', *n.* SAPPAN-WOOD.

Saphena, sa-fē'na, *n.* [Gr. *saphēnēs*, visible.] One of two sub-cutaneous veins of the lower limb and foot.

Sapid, sap'id, *a.* [L. *sapidus*, from *sapio*, to taste. SAPIENT.] Possessing savour or relish; savoury.—**Sapidity, Sapidness**, sa-pid'i-ti, sap'id-nes, *n.* The quality of being sapid; savour; relish.

Sapient, sā'pi-ent, *a.* [L. *sapiens, sapientis*, wise, discreet, pp. of *sapio*, to taste, to know, to be wise; *sapid, insipid, savour, sage*, are of similar origin.] Wise; sage; knowing; discerning; proceeding from a wiseacre. (Now generally ironical, or used of affected wisdom.)—**Sapience**, sā'pi-ens, *n.* [L. *sapientia*, wisdom.] The quality of being sapient; wisdom; sageness.—**Sapiential**, sāp-i-ensh'al, *a.* *Sapiential books*, wisdom books: *Proverbs, Ecclesiastes, Ecclesiasticus, Song of Solomon*, &c.—*Sapiential orchard*, Garden of Eden. (*C. Lamb.*)—**Sapiently**, sā'pi-ent-li, *adv.* In a sapient manner; sagely.

Sapless, Sapling. Under SAP.

Sapodilla, sap-ō-dil'a, *n.* [Sp. *sapotilla*, from Mexican *zapotl.*] A large tree of the West Indies, yielding a fine fruit.

Saponaceous, sap-ō-nā'shus, *a.* [From L. *sapo, saponis*, soap.] Soapy; resembling soap; having the qualities of soap.—**Saponacity**, sap-ō-nas'i-ti, *n.* The state of being saponaceous.—**Saponify**, sa-pon'i-fī, *v.t.*—*saponified, saponifying.* [L. *sapo, saponis*, and *facio*, to make.] To convert into soap by combination with an alkali.—**Saponifiable**, sa-pon'i-fī-a-bl, *a.* Capable of being saponified. — **Saponification**, sa-pon'i-fi-kā"shon, *n.* Conversion into soap; the process in which fatty substances, through combination with an alkali, form soap.—**Saponine**, sap'o-nin, *n.* A vegetable principle found in the root of soapwort and many other plants, causing water to froth like soap on being agitated.—**Saponite**, sap'o-nīt, *n.* A silicate of magnesia and alumina, occurring in soft, soapy, amorphous masses.

Sapor, sā'por, *n.* [L. SAPID.] Taste; savour.—**Saporific**, sap-ō-rif'ik, *a.* Producing taste or relish.—**Saporosity**, sap-ō-ros'i-ti, *n.* Savouriness.—**Saporous**, sap'or-us, *a.* Having flavour or taste.

Sappadillo, sap-a-dil'ō. SAPODILLA.

Sappan-wood, sap'an or sa-pan', *n.* A dye-wood produced by a tree of Southern Asia, which yields a red colour.

Sappare, sap'pār, *n.* A mineral, called also *Kyanite*.

Sapper. Under SAP.

Sapphic, saf'ik, *a.* Pertaining to *Sappho*, a Grecian poetess; *pros.* applied to a kind of verse said to have been invented by Sappho.—*n.* A Sapphic verse.

Sapphire, saf'fīr, *n.* [L. *sapphirus*, Gr. *sappheiros*, of Eastern origin = Heb. *sappir*, Ar. *safīr*.] A precious stone, next in hardness to the diamond, belonging to the corundum class, and of various shades of blue colour; hence, a rich blue colour; blue.—*Green sapphire*, the emerald.—*Red sapphire*, the oriental ruby.—*Violet sapphire*, the oriental amethyst.—*White* or *limpid sapphire*, a colourless or grayish transparent or translucent variety, sometimes sold as diamond.—*Yellow sapphire*, the oriental topaz.—*a.* Resembling sapphire; blue.—**Sapphirine**, saf'fi-rin, *a.* Resembling sapphire; made of sapphire; of a rich blue.—*n.* A blue variety of spinel.

Sappy. Under SAP.

Saprolegnia, sap-ro-leg'ni-a, *n.* [Gr. *sapros*, rotten, *legnon*, edge,] The fungus which causes the well-known salmon disease.

Saprophagous, sa-prof'a-gus, *a.* [Gr. *sapros*, putrid, and *phagō*, to eat.] Feeding on substances in a state of decomposition.—**Saprophyte**, sap'rō-fīt, *n.* [Gr. *sapros*, and *phyton*, a plant.] A plant that grows on decaying vegetable matter.—**Saprophytic**, sap-rō-fit'ik, *a.* Pertaining to saprophytes.

Sapsago, sap'sa-gō, *n.* [Corruption of G. *schabzieger*.] A kind of hard cheese made in Switzerland.

Saque, sak, *n.* SACQUE.

Saraband, Sarabande, sar'a-band, *n.* [Fr. *sarabande*, Sp. *zarabanda*.] A dance used in Spain, derived from the Saracens; a piece of music adapted to the dance.

Saracen, sar'a-sen, *n.* [L. *Saracenus*, from Gr. *Sarakēnos*, Ar. *Sharkīīn*, orientals, easterns.] An Arabian or other Mussulman of the early and proselytizing period; by mediæval writers employed to designate the Arabs generally, and at a later time applied to any infidel nation against which crusades were preached.—**Saracenic, Saracenical**, sar-a-sen'ik, sar-a-sen'i-kal, *a.* Pertaining to the Saracens.

Sarcasm, sär'kazm, *n.* [L. *sarcasmus*, from Gr. *sarkasmos*, a bitter laugh, from *sarkazō*, to tear flesh like dogs, to speak bitterly, from *sarx*, *sarkos*, flesh.] A bitter cutting expression; a satirical remark; a bitter gibe; a taunt.—**Sarcastic, Sarcastical**, sär-kas'tik, sär-kas'ti-kal, *a.* Characterized by sarcasm; bitterly cutting.—**Sarcastically**, sär-kas'ti-kal-li, *adv.* In a sarcastic manner.

Sarcenet, särs'net, *n.* [O.Fr. *sarcenet*; L.L. *saracenicum*, lit. cloth made by *Saracens*.] A species of fine thin woven silk used for linings, &c.

Sarcocarp, sär'kō-kärp, *n.* [Gr. *sarx*, *sarkos*, flesh, and *karpos*, fruit.] *Bot.* the fleshy part of certain fruits, being the part which is usually eaten.

Sarcocol, Sarcocolla, sär'kō-kol, sär-kō-kol'la, *n.* [Gr. *sarx*, *sarkos*, flesh, and *kolla*, glue.] A medicinal gum-resin imported into India from Arabia, supposed to facilitate the consolidation of flesh.

Sarcode, sär'kōd, *n.* [Gr. *sarx*, *sarkos*, flesh, and *eidos*, form.] Structureless gelatinous matter forming the bodies of animals belonging to the Protozoa.

Sarcoderm, sär'kō-dėrm, *n.* [Gr. *sarx*, *sarkos*, flesh, and *derma*, skin.] *Bot.* the middle covering of the seed when it becomes succulent, placed between the episperm and the endosperm.

Sarcoid, sär'koid, *a.* [Gr. *sarx*, *sarkos*, flesh, and *eidos*, form.] Resembling flesh.

Sarcolemma, sär-kō-lem'ma, *n.* [Gr. *sarx*, *sarkos*, flesh, *lemma*, a sheath.] *Anat.* the tubular sheath enveloping the fibrils of muscle.

Sarcoline, sär'kō-lin, *a.* [Gr. *sarx*, *sarkos*, flesh.] Flesh-coloured.

Sarcolite, sär'kō-līt, *n.* [Gr. *sarx*, *sarkos*, flesh, and *lithos*, a stone.] A variety of analcime of rose-flesh colour.

Sarcolobe, sär'kō-lōb, *n.* [Gr. *sarx*, *sarkos*, flesh, and *lobos*, a lobe.] *Bot.* a thick fleshy cotyledon, as that of the bean or pea.

Sarcology, sär-kol'o-ji, *n.* [Gr. *sarx*, *sarkos*, flesh, and *logos*, discourse.] That part of anatomy which treats of the soft parts of the body.—**Sarcologic, Sarcological**, sär-kō-loj'ik, sär-kō-loj'i-kal, *a.* Pertaining to sarcology.

Sarcoma, sär-kō'ma, *n.* [Gr. *sarkōma*, from *sarx*, *sarkos*, flesh.] A fleshy growth; *bot.* a fleshy disc.—**Sarcomatous**, sär-kō'ma-tus, *a.* Relating to sarcoma.

Sarcophagous, sär-kof'a-gus, *a.* [Gr. *sarx*, *sarkos*, flesh; *phagein*, to eat.] Feeding on flesh; flesh-eating.—**Sarcophagus**, sär-kof'a-gus, *n.* pl. **Sarcophagi**, sär-kof'a-jī, also **Sarcophaguses**. [Gr. *sarkophagos*; it was originally the name of a species of stone used for making coffins, and believed to have the property of consuming the dead bodies.] A coffin or tomb of stone; a kind of stone chest, generally more or less ornamented, for receiving a dead body.

Sarcophile, sär'kō-fīl, *n.* [Gr. *sarx*, *sarkos*, flesh, and *phileō*, to love.] A flesh-eating animal.

Sarcosis, sär-kō'sis, *n.* [Gr. *sarkōsis*, from *sarx*, *sarkos*, flesh.] The formation of flesh in a wound; a fleshy tumour; sarcoma.

Sarcous, sär'kus, *a.* [Gr. *sarx*, *sarkos*, flesh.] Belonging to flesh or muscle.

Sard, särd, *n.* [Fr. *sarde*, from *Sardes*, the ancient capital of Lydia.] A variety of carnelian of a deep blood-red when held between the eye and the light.—**Sardachate**, sär'da-kāt, *n.* A kind of agate containing layers of sard.

Sardine, sär'dīn, *n.* [Fr. *sardine*, from L. *sardina*, so called because caught near *Sardinia*.] A small fish allied to the herring and pilchard, large quantities of which are preserved, salted, and hermetically sealed in tin boxes with olive-oil.

Sardius, sär'di-us, *n.* A sort of precious stone, probably sard or carnelian. (O.T.)

Sardoin, sär'doin, *n.* Same as *Sard*.

Sardonic, sär-don'ik, *a.* [Fr. *sardonique*, from L. *Sardonica herba*, the Sardinian herb, an herb said to cause a peculiar twitching of the face when eaten.] Not really proceeding from gaiety; forced; said of a laugh or smile; bitterly ironical; sarcastic; derisive and malignant: now the usual meaning.—**Sardonically**, *adv.* In a sardonic manner; grimly; viciously.—**Sardonicism**, *n.*

Sardonyx, sär'dō-niks, *n.* [Gr. *sardonyx*. SARD, ONYX.] A precious stone, a beautiful variety of onyx, consisting of alternate layers of sard and white chalcedony.

Saree, sä-rē', *n.* [Hind.] The chief garment of a Hindu woman, consisting of a long piece of cloth wound round the waist, with the one edge hanging down in front, the other taken up and thrown over the head.

Sargasso, Sargassum, sär-gas'ō, sär-gas'um, *n.* [Sp. *sargazo*, sea-weed.] Gulf-weed, floating on the surface of the sea, giving to part of the Atlantic the name *Sargasso Sea*.

Sark, särk, *n.* [A.Sax. *serce*, *syrce*=Icel. *serkr*, Dan. *særk*, a shirt.] A shirt. (*Scotch*.)—**Sarking**, sär'king, *n.* Thin boards for lining, &c.; in Scotland, the boarding on which slates are laid.

Sarmatian, Sarmatic, sär-mā'shi-an, sär-mat'ik, *a.* Pertaining to *Sarmatia* and its inhabitants, supposed to be the ancestors of the Russians and Poles.

Sarment, sär'ment, *n.* Same as *Sarmentum*.

Sarmentum, sär-men'tum, *n.* pl. **Sarmenta**, sär-men'ta. [L., for *sarpimentum*, from *sarpo*, to trim.] *Bot.* a runner; a running stem giving off leaves or roots at intervals.—**Sarmentose, Sarmentous**, sär-men'tōz, sär-men'tus, *a.* *Bot.* having sarmenta or runners; having the character of a runner.

Sarong, sä'rong, *n.* A garment used in the Indian Archipelago, consisting of a cloth wrapped round the lower part of the body.

Sarplar, sär'plėr, *n.* [Fr. *serpillière*, sack-cloth.] A sack or bale of wool weighing 2,240 pounds.—**Sarplier**, sär'plėr, *n.* Canvas; packing-cloth.

Sarsaparilla, sär'sa-pa-ril"la, *n.* [Sp. *zarzaparrilla*.] The rhizome of several plants of tropical America and the East Indies, yielding a medicine valued on account of its mucilaginous and demulcent qualities.

Sarsen, Sarsen-stone, sär'sen, *n.* One of the large flat blocks of sandstone found on the chalk flats or downs of Wiltshire, &c.

Sarsenet, särs'net, *n.* Same as *Sarcenet*.

Sartorious, sär-tō'ri-us, *n.* [From L. *sartor*, a tailor.] A muscle of the thigh, so called because used in crossing the legs in sitting as tailors do.—**Sartorial**, sär-tō'ri-al, *a.* Pertaining to a tailor.

Sarum, sārum, *n.* The Latin abbreviation of *Sarisburia*, Salisbury.—*Sarum use*, ecclesiastical phrase for the order of church service in the churches of Salisbury diocese before the Reformation.—In England, a rotten burgh, with a handful of voters.

Sarza, sär'za, *n.* Sarsaparilla.

Sash, sash, *n.* [Per. *shash*, a sash, scarf, or shawl.] A band or scarf worn over the shoulder or round the waist for ornament, usually of silk, variously made and ornamented.—*v.t.* To dress with a sash.

Sash, sash, *n.* [Fr. *châsse*, a frame, a sash, from L. *capsa*, a box, from *capio*, to take. CAPABLE.] The framed part of a window in which the glass is fixed; a similar part of a green-house, &c.; the frame in which a saw is fixed to prevent its bending when worked.—*v.t.* To furnish with sash windows.—**Sash-bar**, *n.* One of the vertical and transverse pieces in a window-frame.—**Sash-door**, *n.* A door with panes of glass in it.—**Sash-line**, *n.* The rope by which a window-sash is suspended in its frame.

Sasin, sä'sin, *n.* An antelope, remarkable for its swiftness and beauty, abundant in the plains of India.

Sasine, sā'sin, *n.* [Fr. *saisine*. SEIZIN.] *Scots law*, the act of giving legal possession of feudal property, or the instrument by which the fact is proved.

Sassaby, sas'a-bi, *n.* A handsome South African antelope.

Sassafras, sas'a-fras, *n.* [Fr. *sassafras*, from L. *saxifraga*—*saxum*, a stone, and *frango*, to break. SAXIFRAGE.] A kind of laurel, well-known on account of the medicinal virtues of its root; so named because formerly used to *break* or dissolve *stone* in the bladder.

Sassenach, sas'en-ach, *n.* A name applied by the Celts of the British Isles to persons of Saxon race; a Saxon; an Englishman.

Sassoline, sas'ō-lin, *n.* Native boracic acid, first discovered near *Sasso*, in North Italy, where it is deposited by hot springs.

Sassy, sas'i, *a.* A variation of *Saucy*. (U.S.).

Satan, sā'tan, *n.* [Heb., an adversary.] The devil or prince of darkness; the chief of the fallen angels; the archfiend.—**Satanic, Satanical**, sa-tan'ik, sa-tan'i-kal, *a.* Pertaining to Satan; resembling Satan; extremely malicious or wicked; devilish; infernal.—**Satanically**, sa-tan'i-kal-li, *adv.* In a satanic manner; diabolically.—**Satanism**, sā'tan-izm, *n.* The evil and malicious disposition of Satan.

Satchel, sach'el, *n.* [Also written *sachel*, a dim. of *sack*, the *k* sound having undergone the common softening to *ch*.] A little sack or bag; may be carried either by the hand or slung from the shoulder.

Sate, sat or sāt, a pret. of *sit*.

Sate, sāt, *v.t.*—*sated*, *sating*. [Perhaps from A.Sax. *sæd*, satisfied, satiated, the form having been influenced by *satisfy*, *satiate*. SATIATE, SAD.] To satisfy the appetite or desire of; to feed beyond natural desire; to glut; to satiate.—**Sateless**, sāt'les, *a.* Insatiable; not capable of being sated.

Sateen, sa-tēn', *n.* [From *satin*.] A kind of glossy fabric resembling satin, but having a woollen or cotton instead of a silken face.

Satellite, sat'el-līt, *n.* [Fr. *satellite*, from L. *satelles*, *satellitis*, one who guards the person of a prince.] An obsequious dependant; a subservient follower; a secondary planet or moon; a small planet revolving round a larger one.

Satiate, sā'shi-āt, *v.t.—satiated, satiating.* [L. *satio, satiatum*, to satisfy, to satiate, from *satis*, enough; akin to *satur*, full; akin *satisfy, saturate, satire.*] To satisfy the appetite or desire of; to feed or nourish to the full; to sate; to surfeit; to fill to repletion.—*a.* Filled to satiety; glutted; satiated†.—**Satiation**, sā-shi-ā'shon, *n.* The state of being satiated or filled.—**Satiable**, sā'shi-a-bl, *a.* Capable of being satiated or satisfied.—**Satiability, Satiableness**, sā'shi-a-bil"i-ti, sā'shi-a-bl-nes, *n.* The quality of being satiable or satisfied.—**Satiety**, sa-tī'e-ti, *n.* [L. *satietas.*] The state of being satiated; an excess of gratification which excites wearisomeness or loathing; a being surfeited.

Satin, sat'in, *n.* [Fr. *satin*, It. *setino*, probably of Oriental origin.] A species of glossy silk cloth of a thick, close texture with an overshot woof.—*a.* Belonging to or made of satin.—**Satin-bird**, *n.* An Australian bird, so called from the glossy dark-purple plumage of the male.—**Satin-de-laine**, sat'in-de-lān", *n.* [Fr., satin of wool.] A black cassimere manufactured in Silesia from wool.—**Satinet**, sat'i-net, *n.* [A dim. of *satin.*] A thin species of satin; a particular kind of twilled cloth, made of woollen weft and cotton warp, pressed and dressed to produce a glossy surface in imitation of satin.—**Satin-paper**, *n.* A fine kind of writing-paper with a satiny gloss.—**Satin-spar**, *n.* A fine fibrous variety of carbonate of lime, assuming a silky or pearly lustre when polished.—**Satin-wood**, *n.* The wood of an Indian tree of a deep yellow colour, heavy, and durable.—**Satiny**, sat'i-ni, *a.* Resembling satin; having a surface or texture like satin.

Satire, sat'īr or sat'ir, *n.* [L. *satira* (*i* short), or *satura*, a satire, a medley, an olio, lit. a full dish, from *satur*, full (whence *saturate*).] A poetical composition holding up vice or folly to reprobation; an invective poem; any literary production in which persons, manners, or actions are attacked with irony, sarcasm, or similar weapons; sarcastic ridicule; trenchant invective.—**Satiric, Satirical**, sa-tir'ik, sa-tir'i-kal, *a.* Belonging to satire; conveying or containing satire; given to satire; severe in language.—**Satirically**, sa-tir'i-kal-li, *adv.* In a satirical manner.—**Satiricalness**, sa-tir'i-kal-nes, *n.* Quality of being satirical. —**Satirist**, sat'ir-ist, *n.* One who satirizes; one who writes satire.—**Satirize**, sat'ir-īz, *v.t.—satirized, satirizing.* To assail with satire; to make the object of satire.

Satisfy, sat'is-fī, *v.t.—satisfied, satisfying.* [Fr. *satisfaire*, O.Fr. *satisfier*—L. *satis*, enough, and *facio*, to make. SATIATE.] To grant fully the wants, wishes, or desires of; to supply to the full extent with what is wished for; to make content; to comply with the rightful demands of; to give what is due to; to pay, liquidate, requite; to fulfil the conditions of; to answer; to free from doubt, suspense, or uncertainty; to set at rest the mind of.—*v.i.* To give satisfaction or content.—**Satisfying**, sat'is-fī-ing, *p.* and *a.* Giving satisfaction; setting doubts at rest.—**Satisfyingly**, sat'is-fī-ing-li, *adv.* In a manner tending to satisfy. —**Satisfier**, sat'is-fī-ėr, *n.* A person or thing that gives satisfaction.—**Satisfiable**, sat-is-fī'a-bl, *a.* Capable of being satisfied.—**Satisfaction**, sat-is-fak'shon, *n.* [L. *satisfactio.*] The act of satisfying, or state of being satisfied; gratification of appetite or desire; contentment in possession and enjoyment; settlement of a claim due; payment; that which satisfies; compensation; atonement; the opportunity of satisfying one's honour by a duel. ∴ Syn. under CONTENTMENT.—**Satisfactory**, sat-is-fak'to-ri, *a.* Giving or producing satisfaction; yielding content; relieving the mind from doubt or uncertainty; making amends or recompense; atoning.—**Satisfactorily**, sat-is-fak'to-ri-li, *adv.* In a satisfactory manner; so as to give satisfaction.—**Satisfactoriness**, sat-is-fak'to-ri-nes, *n.* The quality of being satisfactory.

Satrap, sā'trap, *n.* [Gr. *satrapēs*; borrowed from the Persian.] A governor of a province under the ancient Persian monarchy; a prince; a petty despot.—**Satrapal**, sā'trap-al, *a.* Pertaining to a satrap or a satrapy.—**Satrapy**, sā'trap-i, *n.* The government or jurisdiction of a satrap; a principality.

Saturate, sat'ū-rāt, *v.t.—saturated, saturating.* [L. *saturo, saturatum*, from *satur*, filled (whence *satire*); from root of *satis*, enough. SATE, SATIATE.] To cause to become completely penetrated, impregnated, or soaked; to fill fully; to imbue thoroughly; to impregnate or unite with till no more can be received (air *saturated* with moisture).—*a.* Being full; saturated.—**Saturable**, sat'ū-ra-bl, *a.* Admitting of being saturated.—**Saturant**, sat'ū-rant, *a.* Saturating; impregnating to the full.—*n.* A substance which neutralizes acid in the stomach.—**Saturation**, sat-ū-rā'shon, *n.* The act of saturation or state of being saturated; the combination of one body with another in such proportions as that they neutralize each other; solution continued till the solvent can contain no more.

Saturday, sat'ėr-dā, *n.* [A.Sax. *Sæterdæg, Sæterndæg*, lit. Saturn's day.] The seventh or last day of the week.

Saturn, sat'ėrn, *n.* [L. *Saturnus*, connected with *sero, satum*, to sow.] An ancient Italian deity, said to have instructed the people in agriculture, gardening, &c., and elevated them from barbarism to social order and civilization; one of the planets smaller than Jupiter, and more remote from the sun; *old chem.* an appellation given to lead.—**Saturnalia**, sat-ėr-nā'li-a, *n.pl.* [L.] In ancient Rome the festival of Saturn, celebrated as a period of unrestrained license and merriment; hence, any period of noisy license and revelry; unconstrained, licentious revelling.—**Saturnalian**, sat-ėr-nā'li-an, *a.* Pertaining to saturnalia or revels; loose; dissolute.—**Saturnian**, sa-tėr'ni-an, *a.* Pertaining to Saturn, whose age or reign was called 'the golden age'; hence, happy; distinguished by happiness and simplicity.—*Saturnian verse*, an ancient and peculiar metre used by the Romans, in which the oldest Latin poems were written.—**Saturnine**, sat'ėr-nīn, *a.* Supposed to be under the influence of the planet Saturn, which tended to make people morose; morose; of a gloomy temper; heavy; grave; phlegmatic.

Satyr, sat'ėr, *n.* [L. *satyrus*, from Gr. *satyros.*] A sylvan deity or demi-god of the Greeks and Romans, half man and half goat, the satyrs being common attendants on Bacchus, and distinguished for lasciviousness.—**Satyriasis**, sat-ėr-ī'a-sis, *n.* A diseased venereal appetite in males.—**Satyric**, sa-tir'ik, *a.* Pertaining to satyrs (a *satyric* drama).

Sauce, sąs, *n.* [Fr. *sauce*, O.Fr. *saulse*, from L.L. *salsa*, sauce, from L. *salsus*, salted. SALT.] A condiment or composition (usually liquid) to be eaten with food for improving its relish, for whetting the appetite, or aiding digestion; pertness; insolence; saucy language.—*v.t.—sauced, saucing.* To add a sauce to; to season; to treat with pert language; to be saucy to; to make to pay or suffer (*Shak.*).—**Sauce-boat**, *n.* A dish for holding sauce at table.—**Sauce-box**, *n.* A saucy, impudent fellow. (*Colloq.*) —**Sauce-pan**, *n.* Originally, a pan for cooking sauces; now, a metallic vessel for boiling or stewing generally.—**Sauce-tureen**, *n.* A tureen from which sauce is served at table.

Saucer, są'sėr, *n.* [Originally, a small pan or other vessel for sauce. SAUCE.] A piece of china or other ware in which a tea-cup or coffee-cup is set; something resembling a saucer; a kind of flat caisson used in raising sunken vessels.

Saucisse, Saucisson, są'sis, są'sis-son, *n.* [Fr. *saucisse*, a sausage, from *sauce*. SAUCE.] A long bag filled with powder to communicate fire to mines, &c., in war; a long bundle of fascines for raising batteries and other purposes.

Saucy, są'si, *a.* [From *sauce*, in the sense of pertness or impudence. SAUCE.] Showing impertinent boldness or impudent flippancy; treating superiors with impertinence; impudent; rude; pert; forward; expressive of impudence (a *saucy* eye).—**Saucily**, są'si-li, *adv.* In a saucy manner; pertly; impudently.—**Sauciness**, są'si-nes, *n.* The quality of being saucy.

Sauer-kraut, sour'krout, *n.* [G. *sauer*, sour, and *kraut*, herb, cabbage.] A German dish consisting of cabbage cut fine, pressed into a cask, with alternate layers of salt, and suffered to ferment.

Saul, sąl, *n.* Same as *Sal*, a tree.

Saunders-blue, sąn'dėrz, *n.* [Fr. *cendres bleues*, blue ashes.] An artificial blue prepared from carbonate of copper.

Saunter, sąn'tėr, *v.i.* [From Fr. prefix *es-* (L. *ex*), out, and *aventurer*, to adventure.] To wander idly; to walk leisurely along; to loiter; to linger; to dawdle.—*n.* A sauntering or place for sauntering.—**Saunterer**, sąn'tėr-ėr, *n.* One that saunters.

Sauria, są'ri-a, *n.pl.* [From Gr. *sauros*, a lizard.] The term by which the great order of lizards is sometimes designated.—**Saurian**, są'ri-an, *a.* Pertaining to the lizards; having lizard-like characters.—*n.* One of the order of scaly reptiles of which the lizard is a type.—**Sauroid**, są'roid, *a.* [Gr. *sauros*, a lizard, and *eidos*, form.] Resembling the lizards; having characters belonging to the lizards.—*n.* One of a group of fishes which present certain characters of reptiles, having teeth resembling those of crocodiles.—**Sauroidichnite**, są'roid-ik-nīt, *n.* The footprint or ichnite of a saurian.—**Sauropsida**, są-rop'si-da, *n.pl.* [Gr. *sauros*, a lizard, *opsis*, appearance.] A name for that section of vertebrates which comprises birds and reptiles together.—**Sauropterygian**, są'rop-tėr-ij"i-an, *n.* [Gr. *sauros*, and *pteryx, pterygos*, a wing, a fin.] An extinct reptile having paddles, such as the plesiosauros.

Saury-pike, są'ri-pīk, *n.* A fish having a greatly elongated body covered with minute scales, while the jaws are prolonged into a long sharp beak.

Sausage, są'sāj, *n.* [O.Fr. *sausisse*, Fr. *saucisse*; from L.L. *salsa*, sauce (which see).] An article of food, consisting of chopped or minced meat, variously seasoned with sage, and stuffed into properly cleaned entrails of the ox, sheep, or pig.—**Sausage-roll**, *n.* Meat minced and seasoned as for sausages, enveloped in paste.

Sauterne, sō-tėrn', *n.* [Fr.] A white Bordeaux wine made near *Sauternes*, department of Gironde.

Savable. Under SAVE.

Savage, sav'āj, *a.* [O.E. and O.Fr. *salvage* (Mod. Fr. *sauvage*), L.L. *salvaticus*, L. *silvaticus*, wild, from *silva*, a wood. SILVAN.] Pertaining to the forest or wilderness; wild; uncultivated; untamed; violent; brutal; uncivilized; untaught; rude; cruel; barbarous; inhuman.—*n.* A human being in his native state of rudeness; one who is untaught or uncivilized; a man of brutal cruelty; a barbarian.—**Savagely**, sav'āj-li, *adv.* In a savage manner; cruelly; inhumanly.—**Savageness**, sav'āj-nes, *n.* The quality of being savage; barbarism; cruelty; barbarousness.—**Savagery**, sav'āj-ri, *n.* The state of being savage; a wild, uncultivated condition; cruelty; barbarity. —**Savagism**, sav'āj-izm, *n.* The state of savages; savagery; barbarism.

Savanna, Savannah, sa-van'na, *n.* [Sp. *sabana*, properly a sheet for a bed, a plain, from L. *sabanum*, Gr. *sabanon*, a linen cloth.] An extensive open grassy plain or meadow in a tropical region: a word chiefly used in tropical America, though sometimes applied to any very large grassy plain or natural meadow.

Savant, sä-väṅ, *n.* [Fr., ppr. of *savoir*, L. *sapere*, to know.] A man of learning; a man of science; a man eminent for his acquirements.

Save, sāv, *v.t.—saved, saving.* [Fr. *sauver*, from L. *salvare*, to save, from *salvus*, safe. SAFE, SALVATION.] To preserve from destruction or evil of any kind; to snatch, keep, or rescue from impending danger; to rescue from sin and eternal death; to deliver; to keep clear; to rescue from the power or influence of; to spare; to keep from doing or suffering: with a double object (to *save* a person trouble); to hinder from being spent or lost (to *save* time); to hinder from being used; to reserve or lay by; to lay up or hoard.—*To save appearances*, to preserve a good outside; to do something to avoid exposure or embarrassment.—*v.i.* To be economical; to hinder expense.—*prep.* [Originally an imperative.] Except; not including.—**Savable**, sā'va-bl, *n.* Capable of being saved.—**Savableness**, sā'va-bl-nes, *n.* Capability of being saved.—**Saveall**, sāv'al, *n.* [*Save* and *all*.] A subordinate contrivance intended to save anything from being wasted.—**Saver**, sā'vėr, *n.* One that saves.—**Saving**, sā'ving, *p.* and *a.* Preserving from evil or destruction; frugal; not lavish; avoiding unnecessary expenses; incurring no loss, though not gainful (a *saving* voyage); reserving, as some title or right (a *saving* clause).—*n.* Something hoarded up; that which is saved: generally in plural.—*prep.* With exception; excepting.—**Savingly**, sā'ving-li, *adv.* In a saving manner; with frugality or parsimony.—**Savingness**, sā'ving-nes, *n.*—**Savings-bank**, *n.* A bank specially established for receiving and securely investing small savings, and for their accumulation at interest.

Saveloy, sav'e-loi, *n.* [Fr. *cervelas*, from *cervelle*, the brains, from L. *cerebellum*. CEREBELLUM.] A highly seasoned dried sausage, originally made of brains, now made of young salted pork.

Savin, Savine, sav'in, *n.* [Fr. *savinier*, *sabine*, from L. *Sabina* (*herba*), the Sabine herb, savin.] A coniferous tree or shrub of the juniper kind.

Savior, sāv'yėr, *n.* [O.Fr. *salveor* (Fr *sauveur*), from L. *salvator*, from *salvare*, to save, *salvus*, safe. SAVE.] One who saves, preserves, or delivers from destruction or danger; *Jesus Christ*, the Redeemer, who is called *the Savior* by way of distinction.

Savoir-faire, sa-vwär'fãr', *n.* [F.] The knowing how to act; tact; the appropriate or graceful thing.

Savor, sā'vėr, *n.* [O.Fr. *savor*, Mod. Fr. *saveur*, from L. *sapor*, from *sapio*, to taste. SAPIENT.] Flavor; taste; power or quality that affects the palate; odor (*Shak.*); characteristic property; distinctive quality.—*v.i.* To have a particular taste or flavor; to partake of the quality, nature, or appearance of something else; to smack; followed by *of* (his conduct *savors of* pride).—*v.t.* To like; to relish; to have the flavor or quality of.—**Savorily**, sā'vėr-i-li, *adv.* In a savory manner; with a pleasing relish.—**Savoriness**, sā'vėr-i-nes, *n.* The condition or quality of being savory; pleasing taste or smell.—**Savorless**, sā'vėr-les, *a.* Destitute of savor; insipid.—**Savory**, sā'vėr-i, *a.* Having savor or relish; pleasing to taste; palatable; hence, agreeable in general.

Savory, sā'vėr-i, *n.* [Fr. *savorée*, L. *satureia*, savory.] A European aromatic mint used as a culinary vegetable to flavor sauces and dishes.

Savory, sā'vėr-i, *a.* Having an appealing, delightful or appetizing flavor or aroma with reference to foods.

Savoy, sav'oi, *n.* [Because brought from *Savoy*.] A variety of cabbage much cultivated for winter use.—**Savoyard**, sa-voi'ärd, *n.* A native or inhabitant of Savoy.

Saw, sa, pret. of *see*.

Saw, sa, *n.* [A.Sax. *saga*, *sage*, a saw = Dan. *sav*, Icel. *sög*, D. *zaag*, O. *säge*; same root as L. *seco*, to cut (SECTION).] A cutting instrument consisting of a blade, band, or disc of thin iron or steel, with a dentated or toothed edge.—*v.t.*—pret. *sawed*, pp. *sawed* or *sawn*. To cut with a saw; to form by cutting with a saw; to move through, as in the act of sawing (to *saw* the air).—*v.i.* To use a saw; to cut with a saw.—**Saw-dust**, *n.* The small fragments of wood or other material produced by the cutting of a saw.—**Sawer**, sa'ėr, *n.* One that saws; a sawyer.—**Saw-file**, *n.* A file for sharpening saws.—**Saw-fish**, *n.* A fish allied to the sharks and rays; so called from the spines growing like teeth on both edges of its long bony snout.—**Saw-fly**, *n.* A hymenopterous insect, so called because the ovipositor of the females has serrated or toothed edges.—**Saw-frame**, *n.* The frame in which a saw is set or fixed for work.—**Saw-mill**, *n.* A mill for sawing timber.—**Saw-pit**, *n.* A pit over which timber is sawed.—**Saw-toothed**, *a.* Having teeth like a saw; serrated.—**Sawwort**, *n.* An English plant, so named from its serrated leaves; used for dyeing cloth yellow.—**Sawyer**, sa'yėr, *n.* [Formed like *lawyer*, *bowyer*.] One whose occupation is to saw timber into planks or boards, or to saw wood for fuel.

Saw, sa, *n.* [A.Sax. *sagu*, a saying, a saw, from stem of to *say*. SAY.] A saying; proverb; maxim.

Sawder, sa'dėr, *n.* Solder.—*Soft sawder*, flattering speeches.

Saxatile, sak'sa-til, *a.* [L. *saxatilis*, from *saxum*, a rock.] Pertaining to rocks; living among rocks.

Sax-horn, saks'horn, *n.* [After M. *Sax*, of Paris, the inventor.] A brass wind-instrument with a wide mouthpiece, and three, four, or five cylinders, much employed in military bands. Called also *Sax-cornet*.

Saxicavous, sak-sik'a-vus, *a.* [L. *saxum*, a rock, and *cavo*, to hollow.] A term applied to certain molluscs which make holes in the rocks.

Saxicolous, sax-sik'ō-lus, *a.* [L. *saxum*, a rock, and *colo*, to inhabit.] *Bot.* growing on rocks.

Saxifrage, sak'si-frāj, *n.* [L. *saxifraga*—*saxum*, a stone, and *frango*, to break. The name was originally given to a plant supposed to be beneficial in removing stone in the bladder; but the saxifrages seem to have got the name rather from growing among rocks. SASSAFRAS.] A popular name of various plants, which mostly inhabit the colder and temperate parts of the northern zone, and are mostly rock plants.—**Saxifragous**, sak-sif'ra-gus, *a.* Dissolving stone, especially in the bladder.

Saxon, sak'son, *n.* [L. *Saxo*, pl. *Saxones*, A.Sax. *Seaxa*, pl. *Seaxe*, *Seaxan*, usually derived from *seax*, O.H.G. *sahs*, a short sword; G. *Sachse*, a Saxon.] One of the people who formerly dwelt in the northern part of Germany, and who invaded and conquered England in the fifth and sixth centuries; a Saxon of England as opposed to an Angle or Anglian; an Anglo-Saxon; one of the English race; the language of the Saxons; Anglo-Saxon; a native or inhabitant of modern Saxony.—*a.* Pertaining to the Saxons, their country, or their language; Anglo-Saxon; pertaining to modern Saxony.—**Saxonism**, sak'son-izm, *n.* An idiom of the Saxon or early English language.—**Saxonist**, sak'son-ist, *n.* One versed in the Saxon language.

Saxophone, sak'sō-fōn, *n.* A tubular brass or silver wind musical instrument, with a reed mouthpiece like that of the clarinet, having tonal finger keys.

Say, sā, *v.t.* pret. & pp. *said*, ppr. *saying*. [A.Sax. *secgan*, to say = Icel. *segja*, D. *zeggen*, Dan. *sige*, G. *sagen*, to say.] To utter or express in words; to speak; to argue; to allege by way of argument; to give as an opinion; to repeat, rehearse, recite; to recite without singing; to answer; to utter by way of reply; to tell; to suppose; to assume; to take for granted: in this sense often elliptically (*say* 3000 men).—*It is said, they say*, it is commonly reported; people assert or maintain.—*To say nay*, to say no; to refuse.—*That is to say*, that is; in other words; otherwise. ∴ *Say* is especially common with a clause or words directly quoted after it, or with such objectives as *something, nothing, this, that*, &c.—*n.* What one has to say (he said his *say*); something said; a statement.—**Sayer**, sā'ėr, *n.* One who says.—**Saying**, sā'ing, *n.* That which is said; a sentence uttered; a proverbial expression; a maxim; an adage.

'Sblood, zblud, *inter.* An imprecation abbreviated from *God's blood*.

Scab, skab, *n.* [A.Sax. *scæb*, from L. *scabies*, scab, itch, from *scabo*, to scratch. Hence, *shabby*.] A sort of crust formed over a sore in healing; the mange in horses; a disease of sheep.—**Scab**, *n.* Blackleg; trade union term for non-unionist who takes the job of strikers.—**Scabby, Scabbed**, skab'i, skabd, *a.* Abounding with scabs; diseased with scabs; mean; vile; worthless.—**Scabbedness, Scabbiness**, skab'ed-nes, skab'i-nes, *n.* The state or quality of being scabbed or scabby.

Scabbard, skab'ärd, *n.* [Formerly *scaubert*, *scaberke*, *scaberge*, &c.; perhaps from A.Sax. *sceatha*, scathe, and *beorgan*, O.H.G. *bergan*, to protect (comp. *hauberk*), the scabbard being what prevents the weapon from doing harm when not in use.] The sheath of a sword or other similar weapon.—*v.t.* To put in a scabbard or sheath.

Scabble, skab'l, *v.t.* In *masonry*, to dress with a rough slightly furrowed surface.

Scabies, skā'bi-ēz, *n.* [L.] Scab; mange; itch.—**Scabious**, skā'bi-us, *a.* [L. *scabiosus*.] Consisting of scabs; rough; itchy; leprous.—*n.* The plant devil's-bit and allied species, named from being formerly deemed of efficacy against scabby eruptions of the skin.

Scabrous, skab'rus, *a.* [L. *scabrosus*, from *scaber*, rough, from *scabies*, scab.] Rough; having sharp points or little asperities.

Scad, skad, *n.* [Same as *shad*.] A member of the mackerel family; an important Atlantic coastal fish.—**Scads**. Large amounts or quantity of, as *scads* of money. (*Slang*.)

Scaffold, skaf'old, *n.* [O.Fr. *escafaut*, *eschafault* (Fr. *échafaud*); L.L. *scadafaltum*, from prep. *ex*, and *cadafaltum*, a scaffold, a catafalque. CATAFALQUE.] A temporary stage or platform; an elevated platform for the execution of a criminal; a temporary structure of timber for the workmen engaged in building or repairing houses, &c.—*v.t.* To furnish with a scaffold.—**Scaffolding**, skaf'old-ing, *n.* A temporary combination of timber-work for supporting workmen engaged on some building.

Scaglia, skal'yi-a, *n.* [It.] An Italian chalky rock of a red colour, and having a fissile structure.—**Scagliola**, skal-yi-ō'la, *n.* [It.] A composition of gypsum, splinters of marble, &c., imitative of marble, and used for enriching columns and internal walls of buildings.

Scalade, ska-lād', *n.* [Fr. *scalade*, from L. *scala*, a ladder.] An escalade.

Scalar, skā'lar, *n.* A quantity that has no direction, as opposed to *vector* (which see). Scalar quantities are compounded by addition and subtraction.

Scalariform, ska-lā'ri-form, *a.* [L. *scalaria*, a ladder, and *forma*, form.] Shaped like a ladder; resembling a ladder.—*Scalariform vessels*, certain tubes met with in plants.

Scald, skald, *v.t.* [O.Fr. *eschalder* (Fr. *échauder*), It. *scaldare*, to scald, from L. *ex*, intens., and *caldus*, *calidus*, hot. CALID, CALDRON.] To burn and injure with or as with hot liquid; to expose to a strong heat over a fire or in water or other liquid (to *scald* milk).—*n.* A burn or injury from scalding.—**Scalding**, skal'ding, *a.* So hot as to scald.

Scald, skald, *a.* [That is *scalled*, or affected with *scall*. SCALL.] Covered with scurf or scab; scabby; scurvy; paltry; poor.—**Scald-head**, *n.* A disease of the hairy scalp; favus.

Scald, Skald, skald, *n.* [Icel. *skáld*, Sw. *skald*.] An ancient Scandinavian poet, whose occupation was to compose poems in honour of distinguished men, and to recite and sing them on public occasions.—**Scaldic**, skal'dik, *a.* Pertaining to the scalds or Norse poets; composed by scalds.

Scale, skāl, *n.* [A.Sax. *scále*, *scálu*, the

dish of a balance = Icel. *skál*, Dan. *skaal*, D. *schaal*, G. *schale*, a dish, a balance. *Scale*, a thin lamina, is allied. See next art.] The dish of a balance; also the balance itself, or whole instrument: in this sense generally in the plural.—*v.t.* To weigh, as in scales. [*Shak.*]—**Scale-beam**, *n.* The beam or lever of a balance.

Scale, skāl, *n.* [A.Sax. *scale*, a shell, a husk = Dan. *skæl*, a scale; *skal*, rind, shell; Icel. *skel*, a shell; akin *shale*, *shell*, *skill*, *scull*, *skull*, and see above.] One of the overlapping plates on the exterior of certain animals; one of the thin, small plates which protect the skin of many fishes; one of the somewhat similar laminæ of reptiles; anything resembling the scale of a fish or other animal; a thin flake or lamina (a *scale* of bone, iron, and the like): *bot.* a rudimentary leaf on the exterior of a leaf-bud.—*v.t.*—*scaled*, *scaling*. To strip or clear of scales; to take off in thin laminae or scales: *gun.* to clean the inside of a cannon by exploding a little powder.—*v.i.* To come off in scales or thin layers.—**Scale-armor**, *n.* Armor consisting of small plates of steel partly overlapping each other like the scales of a fish.—**Scale-fern**, *n.* A fern, so called from the imbricated tawny scales at the back of the fronds.—**Scale-insect**, *n.* An insect, scale-like in form, injurious to plants.—**Scaleless**, skāl'les, *n.* Destitute of scales.—**Scale-moss**, *n.* The popular name given to plants resembling moss, which grow on the trunks of trees, &c., and have small scale-like leaves.—**Scaliness**, skā'li-nes, *n.* The state of being scaly.—**Scaly**, skā'li, *a.* Covered or abounding with scales; having the form of scales or thin laminæ.—**Scaling-hammer**, *n.* A hammer for removing incrustations from boilers, &c.

Scale, skāl, *n.* [L. *scala*, a ladder, from stem of *scando*, to mount; akin to Skr. *skand*, to ascend.] A ladder (*Milton*); anything graduated, especially when applied as a measure or rule; a mathematical instrument consisting of a slip of wood, ivory, &c., with spaces graduated and numbered on its surface, for measuring or laying off distances; any succession of ascending or descending steps or degrees; series of ranks; relative dimensions without difference in proportion of parts; a basis for a numerical system (the decimal *scale*); *music*, a succession of notes arranged in the order of pitch, and comprising the sounds that may occur in a piece of music written in a given key; the *diatonic scale*, having its eight notes ascending by five tones and two semitones; also the series of notes producible by voices or instruments (the *scale* of a violin).—*v.t.*—*scaled*, *scaling*. To climb, as by a ladder; to ascend by steps; to clamber up.—**Scaler**, skā'lėr, *n.* One who scales.—**Scaling-ladder**, *n.* A ladder made for the use of soldiers in scaling walls.

Scalene, ska-lēn', *a.* [Gr. *skalēnos*, limping, uneven.] A term applied to a triangle of which the three sides are unequal.—*n.* A scalene triangle.

Scaliola, skāl-yi-ō'la. SCAGLIOLA.

Scall, skąl, *n.* [Same as Dan. *skal*, peel, husk, whence *skaldet*, bald; Icel. *skalli*, a bald head; akin to *scale*.] Scab; scurf; scabbiness. (O.T.)—*Dry scall*, psoriasis or itch.—*Moist scall*, eczema.—**Scalled**, skąld, *a.* Scurfy; scabby; scald.

Scallawag, **Scalawag**, skal'a-wag, *n.* Underfed person; a worthless fellow. During the days of reconstruction after the Civil War, any white Southerner who espoused the radical Republican cause.

Scallion, skal'yun, *n.* [O.Fr. *escalogne*, It. *scalogno*, from L. (*caepa*) *Ascalonia*, the onion of *Ascalon*.] A kind of onion; a shallot; a leek.

Scallop, skal'op or skol'op, *n.* [O.Fr. *escalope*, from D. *schelp*, *schelpe*, shell, cockle-shell; akin *scalp*, *scale*, &c.] A marine bivalve of the oyster family, used for food, one species of which occurs in abundance on the coast of Palestine, and was formerly worn by pilgrims as a mark that they had been to the Holy Land; a kind of dish for baking oysters in; a curving on the edge of anything, like the segment of a circle. Written also *Scollop*.—*v.t.* To cut the edge or border of into scallops or segments of circles.—**Scalloped**, skal'opt or skol'opt, *p.* and *a.* Cut at the edge or border into scallops.—*Scalloped* or *scolloped oysters*, oysters cooked (originally in shells) with bread-crumbs, cream, &c.

Scalp, skalp, *n.* [Akin to *scale*, *shell*, *skill*, *scallop*; comp. D. *schelp*, *schulp*, a shell; Icel. *skálpr*, a sheath.] The skull (*Shak.*); the outer covering of the skull; the skin of the head, or part of it, with the hair on it, torn off by the American Indians as a mark of victory over an enemy; a bed of mussels or oysters.—*v.t.* To deprive of the scalp.—**Scalping-knife**, *n.* A knife used by the Indians of America in scalping their prisoners.

Scalpel, skal'pel, *n.* [L. *scalpellum*, dim. of *scalprum*, a knife, from *scalpo*, to cut, to scrape.] A knife used in anatomical dissections and surgical operations.—**Scalpelliform**, skal-pel'i-form, *a.* Having the form of a scalpel.—**Scalper**, **Scalping-iron**, skal'pėr, skal'ping, *n.* An instrument of surgery used in scraping foul and carious bones.—**Scalpriform**, skalp'ri-form, *n.* [L. *scalprum*, and *forma*, form.] Chisel-shaped; applied to the incisor teeth of rodent animals.

Scamble, skam'bl, *v.i.*—*scambled*, *scambling*. [Comp. O.D. *schampelen*, to deviate, to slip; D. *schommelen*, to stir, to shake.] To struggle; to be bold or turbulent; to shamble.

Scammony, skam'o-ni, *n.* [L. *scammonia*, from Gr. *skammōnia*, from the Persian.] A gum-resin of a bitter and acrid taste, obtained from a species of convolvulus, used in medicine as a drastic purge.

Scamp, skamp, *n.* [Originally one who decamps or runs off without paying debts. See SCAMPER.] A worthless fellow; a knave; a swindler; a mean villain; a rogue.—*v.t.* To execute, as a piece of work, in a slim, dishonest, or perfunctory manner.—**Scamper**, skam'pėr, *n.* One who scamps work.—**Scampish**, skam'pish, *a.* Pertaining to or like a scamp; knavish.

Scamper, skam'pėr, *v.i.* [From O.F. *escamper*, Pr. *escampar*, It. *scampare*, to save one's life, to escape; lit. to decamp, from L. *ex*, out of, and *campus*, a field. Hence *scamp*. CAMP.] To run with speed; to hasten away.—*n.* A hasty flight; a hurried run.

Scan, skan, *v.t.*—*scanned*, *scanning*. [Formerly *scand*, from Fr. *scander*, to scan verse, from L. *scando*, to climb, to scan (seen in *ascend*, *descend*); Skr. *skand*, to climb.] To examine by counting the metrical feet or syllables; to read so as to indicate the metrical structure; to examine minutely or nicely; to scrutinize.—**Scansion**, skan'shon, *n.* The act of scanning; the metrical structure of verse.

Scandal, skan'dal, *n.* [Fr. *scandale*, from L. *scandalum*, Gr. *skandalon*, a snare, a scandal. *Slander* is a different form of this word.] Offence given by the faults or misdeeds of another; public reproach or reprobation; opprobrium; shame; something uttered which is false and injurious to reputation; defamatory talk; slander.—*v.t.* To throw scandal on; to slander.—**Scandalize**, skan'dal-īz, *v.t.*—*scandalized*, *scandalizing*. To offend by some action considered very wrong or outrageous; to shock; to give offence to; to disgrace; to slander.—**Scandal-monger**, *n.* One who deals in or retails scandal.—**Scandalous**, skan'dal-us, *a.* Causing scandal or offence; shameful; disgraceful to reputation; libellous; slanderous.—**Scandalously**, skan'dal-us-li, *adv.* In a scandalous manner; disgracefully; shamefully.—**Scandalousness**, skan'dal-us-nes, *n.*—**Scandalum magnatum**, skan'da-lum mag-nā'tum. The offence of speaking evil of the great (magnates).

Scandent, skan'dent, *a.* [L. *scandens*, *scandentis*, ppr. of *scando*, to climb.] *Bot.* climbing.

Scandinavian, skan-di-nā'vi-an, *a.* Relating to Scandinavia.—*Scandinavian tongues*, Icelandic, Norwegian, Danish, Swedish.

Scandium, skan'di-um, *n.* A chemical element in the boron series.

Scansion. Under SCAN.

Scansores, skan-sō'rēz, *n.pl.* [Lit. the climbers, from L. *scando*, to climb.] The order of climbing birds, such as the cuckoos, woodpeckers, parrots, &c., having feet with two toes turned backwards and two forwards.—**Scansorial**, skan-sō'ri-al, *a.* Climbing or adapted to climbing; belonging to the Scansores.

Scant, skant, *a.* [Same as Icel. *skamt*, short, brief; akin to Norse *skanta*, exactly measured; comp. Prov.E. and Sc. *skimp* or *skemp*, to give short measure.] Scarcely sufficient; rather less than is wanted for the purpose; not enough; having a limited supply; scarce; short (with *of*).—*v.t.* To limit; to stint; to keep on short allowance; to afford or give out sparingly; to be niggard of; to grudge.—*adv.* Scarcely; hardly; not quite.—**Scantily**, **Scantly**, skan'ti-li, skant'li, *adv.* In a scant or scanty manner.—**Scantiness**, **Scantness**, skan'ti-nes, skant'nes, *n.* The state or condition of being scant or scanty.—**Scanty**, skan'ti, *a.* Wanting amplitude or extent; narrow; small; scant; not ample; hardly sufficient (a *scanty* supply).

Scantling, skant'ling, *n.* [O.Fr. *eschantillon*, Fr. *échantillon*, a specimen, a pattern, from prefix *ex*, and *cantel*, a cantle.] A quantity cut for a particular purpose; a sample; a pattern; a small quantity; the dimensions of timber, stones, &c., in length, breadth, and thickness; timber less than five inches square; a kind of trestle for supporting a cask.

Scape, skāp, *n.* [L. *scapus*, a stalk.] *Bot.* a radical stem bearing the fructification without leaves, as in the narcissus and hyacinth.—**Scapiform**, ską'pi-form, *a.* *Bot.* In the form of a scape.

Scape, skāp, *v.t.* and *i.* Short form of *escape*.—**Scapegoat**, skāp'gōt, *n.* Among the ancient Jews, a goat which was sent into the wilderness bearing the iniquities of the people, which were laid on him by the hands of the high-priest; hence, one made to bear the blame of others.—**Scapegrace**, skāp'grās, *n.* A graceless fellow; a careless, idle, hare-brained fellow.—**Scapement**, skāp'ment, *n.* Escapement.

Scaphite, skaf'īt, *n.* [L. *scapha*, Gr. *skaphē*, a skiff.] A fossil cephalopod, of a boat-shaped form, belonging to the family of ammonites.—**Scaphium**, skā'fi-um, *n.* *Bot.* the carina or keel of papilionaceous flowers.—**Scaphoid**, skaf'oid, *a.* Boat-shaped; resembling a boat; navicular.

Scapolite, skap'ō-līt, *n.* [Gr. *skapos*, a rod, and *lithos*, a stone.] A mineral, a silicate of alumina and lime, occurring often in long crystals.

Scapple, skap'l, *v.t.* To scabble.

Scapula, skap'ū-la, *n.* [L.] The shoulder-blade.—**Scapular**, skap'ū-lėr, *a.* Pertaining to the scapula or the shoulder.—**Scapular**, **Scapulary**, skap'ū-lėr, skap'ū-la-ri, *n.* A kind of ecclesiastical garment consisting of two bands of woollen stuff going over the shoulders, one in front the other behind; a kind of badge, consisting of two small squares of brown stuff, of the same colour as the Carmelite habit, connected by two lengths of tape, and worn in honour of the Virgin Mary; *surg.* a bandage for the shoulder-blade; *ornithol.* a feather on the shoulder of a bird.

Scapus, skā'pus, *n.* [L., a stalk.] *Ornith.* the stem of a feather; *arch.* the shaft of a column.

Scar, skär, *n.* [Fr. *escarre*, *escharre*, L. *eschara*, from Gr. *eschara*, a scar or scab on a wound caused by burning.] The mark of a wound or an ulcer remaining after healing; a cicatrix; a hurt; a wound; *bot.* a mark left after the fall of a leaf, or on a seed after the separation of its stem.—*v.t.*—*scarred*, *scarring*. To mark with a scar or scars; to wound; to hurt.—*v.i.* To be covered with a scar; to form a scar.—**Scarry**, skä'ri, *a.* Pertaining to scars; having scars or marks of old wounds.

Scar, skär, *n.* [Same as Icel. *skor*, a rift in a precipice, *sker*, a rocky islet; Dan. *skjær*, a cliff; root seen in *shear*, *short*.] A cliff; a naked detached rock; a bare and broken place on the side of a hill or mountain; a scaur.

Scar, skär, *n.* [L. *scarus*.] The parrot-fish. Under PARROT.

Scarab, Scarabee, skar'ab, skar'a-bē, *n.* [L. *scarabæus*, a beetle.] One of a group of beetles of which the sacred beetle of the Egyptians, so frequently figured on their monuments, is the best-known species; the figure of a beetle cut in hard stone, many of which are found in Egypt.

Scaramouch, skar'a-mouch, *n.* [Fr. *scaramouche*, It. *scaramuccia*, *scaramuccio*.] A buffoon in motley dress; a personage, in Italian comedy, whose character was compounded of traits of vaunting and poltroonery; any poltroon or braggadocio.

Scarce, skārs, *a.* [From O.Fr. *escars*, *eschars*, It. *scarso*, D. *schaars*, scarce, from L.L. *excarpsus*, *scarpsus*, for *excerptus*, pp. of L. *excerpo*, to pluck or cull out. EXCERPT.] Not plentiful or abundant; being in small quantity in proportion to the demand; deficient; seldom met with; rare; uncommon; unfrequent; scantily supplied; not having much: with *of*.—*To make one's self scarce*, to disappear voluntarily; to get out of the way.—**Scarce, Scarcely**, skārs'li, *adv.* Hardly; barely; scantly; but just; with difficulty.—**Scarceness, Scarcity**, skārs'nes, skär'si-ti, *n.* The state or condition of being scarce; dearth; want; famine.

Scare, skār, *v.t.*—*scared*, *scaring*. [Akin to Icel. *skjarr*, apt to flee, shy, *skirra*, to drive away, G. *scheren*, to drive away; same root as *shear*.] To fright; to terrify suddenly; to strike with sudden terror.—*n.* A sudden fright or panic; a sudden terror inspired by a trifling cause; a causeless alarm.—**Scarecrow**, skār'krō, *n.* Anything set up to frighten crows or other birds from crops; anything terrifying without danger; a person so meanly clad as to resemble a scarecrow.

Scarf, skärf, *n.* [Same as L.G. *scherf*, Dan. *skjærf*, *skierf*, G. *schärpe*, O.H.G. *scherbe*, originally a pocket, hence the band suspending the pocket, a scarf.] A sort of light shawl; an article of dress of a light and decorative character worn round the neck or loosely round the shoulders, or otherwise.—**Scarfed**, skärft, *a.* Wearing a scarf.—**Scarf-skin**, *n.* [Perhaps for *scurf-skin*.] The cuticle or epidermis; the outer thin integument of the body.

Scarf, skärf, *n.* [Same as Sw. *skarf*, a joint; akin Dan. *skarre*, to scarf; Sc. *skare*, a scarf, to scarf.] *Carp.* the joint by which the ends of two pieces of timber are united so as to overlap and form a continuous piece.—*v.t.* To cut a scarf on; to unite by means of a scarf.—**Scarf-joint**, *n.* A joint formed by scarfing.

Scarify, skar'i-fī, *v.t.*—*scarified*, *scarifying*. [Fr. *scarifier*, L. *scarifico*, from Gr. *skariphaomai*, to scratch open, from *skariphos*, a sharp-pointed instrument.] *Surg.* to make small cuts or incisions in the skin by means of a lancet or special instrument so as to draw blood without opening a large vein; to remove the flesh about a tooth in order to get a better hold of it; to stir the soil, as with a scarifier.—**Scarification**, skar'i-fi-kā"shon, *n.* *Surg.* the act of scarifying.—**Scarificator**, skar'i-fi-kā"tėr, *n.* An instrument used in scarification or cupping.—**Scarifier**, skar'i-fī-ėr, *n.* One who or that which scarifies; *agri.* an implement with prongs employed for stirring the soil without reversing its surface or altering its form.

Scarlatina, skär-la-tē'na, *n.* [From *scarlet*.] A serious contagious fever which especially attacks the young, accompanied by a scarlet eruption, sore throat, &c.; scarlet fever.—**Scarlatinous**, skär-la-tē'nus, *a.* Pertaining to scarlatina.

Scarlet, skär'let, *n.* [O.Fr. *escarlate*, Mod. Fr. *écarlate*, It. *scarlatto*, a word of Persian origin.] A beautiful bright-red color, brighter than crimson; cloth of a scarlet color; scarlet robe or dress.—*a.* Of the color scarlet; of a bright-red color; dressed in scarlet (*Shak.*).—*Scarlet bean*, *Scarlet Runner*, the kidney-bean.—*Scarlet fever*. SCARLATINA.—**Scarlet woman**, *n.* *Revelation* xvii. 4. A term applied by Protestants to Rome and Church of Rome.—**Scarlet-lake**, *n.* A red pigment prepared from cochineal.—**Scarlet-letter**, A scarlet "A" worn by women during Puritan times as a mark of adultery.

Scarp, skärp, *n.* [From Fr. *escarpe*, from It. *scarpa*, a scarp, a slope, from O.H.G. *scarp*, Mod.G. *scharf*, E. *sharp*—the scarp being cut sharp or steep.] *Fort.* the interior slope of the ditch next the place, at the foot of the rampart.—**Scarped**, skärpt, *p.* and *a.* Cut down like the scarp of a fortification; precipitous.

Scarred, Scarry, *a.* Under SCAR.

Scat, Scatt, skat, *n.* [A.Sax. *sceat*, a tax, a coin; Icel. *skattr*, Dan. *skat*.] A tax.

Scathe, Scaith, skāth, *n.* [A.Sax. *sceathan* = Icel. *skatha*, D. and G. *schaden*, to injure; Icel. *skathi*, Goth. *skathis*, D. and G. *schade*, injury.] Damage; injury; harm.—*v.t.*—*scathed*, *scathing*. To injure; to do damage to; to harm.—**Scatheful**, skāth'ful, *a.* Causing scathe; harmful.—**Scathing**, skā'thing, *p.* and *a.* Injuring; damaging; harming; blasting.—**Scatheless**, skāth'les, *a.* Without scathe or harm; unharmed.

Scatology, ska-tol'o-ji, *n.* [Gr. *skōr*, *skatos*, dung.] Knowledge of dung, or of savage practices in which dung or filth enters.

Scatter, skat'ėr, *v.t.* [A.Sax. *scaterian*, to scatter; same word as *shatter*; Gr. *skedannymi*, to scatter, is of kindred origin.] To throw loosely about; to sprinkle; to strew; to besprinkle; to disperse; to dissipate; to separate or remove to a distance from each other; to disunite; to frustrate, disappoint, and overthrow (to *scatter* hopes, &c.). ∴ Syn. under DISPERSE.—*v.i.* To disperse; to separate from each other; to straggle apart.—**Scatter-brain**, *n.* A thoughtless person; one incapable of concentration. (*Colloq.*)—**Scatter-brained**, *a.* Giddy; heedless; thoughtless. (*Colloq.*)—**Scattered**, skat'ėrd, *pp.* Sprinkled or thinly spread; loose and irregular in distribution.—**Scatteredly**,† skat'ėrd-li, *adv.* In a dispersed manner; separately.—**Scatterer**, skat'ėr-ėr, *n.* One who scatters.

Scaturient,†, ska-tū'ri-ent, *a.* [L. *scaturiens*, ppr. of *scaturio*, to gush forth.] Gushing forth as water from a spring. (*Lamb.*)

Scaup, skạp, *n.* [A form of *scalp*.] A bed of shell-fish (an *oyster-scaup*, a *mussel-scaup*); a species of duck which feeds on molluscs, &c.

Scaur, skạr, *n.* [SCAR.] A scar or precipitous bank; a cliff.

Scavenger, skav'en-jėr, *n.* [From *scavage*, L.L. *scavagium*, an old law term equivalent to *showage*, a duty on goods *shown*, from A.Sax. *sceawian*, to show. The scavenger was originally one who looked after the scavage. As to the insertion of *n* comp. *messenger*, *passenger*.] A person whose employment is to clean the streets of a city; a person similarly engaged.

Scena. Under SCENE.

Scene, sēn, *n.* [Fr. *scène*; L. *scena*, from Gr. *skēnē*, a covered place, a tent, a stage, from root of Skr. *sku*, to cover, E. *shade*.] A stage; that part of a theatre in which the acting is done; the imaginary place in which the action of a play is supposed to occur; the surroundings amid which anything is transacted; a whole series of actions and events connected and exhibited; an assemblage of objects displayed at one view; a place and objects seen together; a landscape; a view; one of the painted slides, hangings, or other devices used to give an appearance of reality to the action of a play; a part of a play, being a division of an act; an exhibition of strong feeling between two or more persons; a theatrical display of emotion; an artificial or affected action or course of action.—*Behind the scenes*, behind the scenery of a theatre, at the back of the stage; hence, specially acquainted with the motives influencing the actions of a party or an individual.—**Scena**, shā'na, *n.* [It.] *Mus.* a scene or portion of an opera; a solo for a single voice, in which various dramatic emotions are displayed.—**Scenario**, sē-nä'ri-ō; It. pron. she-nä'rē-ō, *n.* [It.] An abstract of the chief incidents in any dramatic work arranged according to act and scene, giving a sort of skeleton of the piece.—**Scene-painter**, *n.* One who paints scenery for theatres.—**Scenery**, sē'nėr-i, *n.* The paintings representing the scenes of a play; the general appearance or natural features of a place.—**Scene-shifter**, *n.* One who arranges the movable scenes in a theatre.—**Scenic, Scenical**, sē'nik or sen'ik, sē'nikal or sen'i-kal, *a.* Pertaining to the stage; dramatic; theatrical.—**Scenographic, Scenographical**, sē-nō-graf'ik, sē-nō-graf'i-kal, *a.* Pertaining to scenography; drawn in perspective.—**Scenographically**, sē-nō-graf'i-kal-li, *adv.* In a scenographic manner; in perspective.—**Scenography**, sē-nog'ra-fi, *n.* Representation or drawing according to the rules of perspective.

Scent, sent, *n.* [For *sent*, from Fr. *sentir*, to perceive, to smell, from L. *sentire*, to perceive by the senses. SENSE.] That which, issuing from a body, affects the olfactory nerves of animals; odour; smell; the power of smelling; odour left on the ground enabling an animal's track to be followed; hence, course of pursuit; track.—*v.t.* To perceive by the olfactory organs; to smell; to perfume.—**Scentful**, sent'ful, *a.* Odorous; having much scent.—**Scentless**, sent'les, *a.* Inodorous; destitute of smell.

Scepsis, sep'sis or skep'sis, *n.* [Gr. *skepsis*, doubt.] Scepticism; doubt.

Scepter, sep'tėr, *n.* [Fr. *sceptre*, L. *sceptrum*, from Gr. *skēptron*, a staff, from *skēptō*, to prop or lean.] A staff or baton borne by a monarch or other ruler as a symbol of authority.—*The scepter*, royal power or authority.—**Sceptered**, sep'tėrd, *a.* Bearing a scepter; invested with royal power; regal.—**Scepterless**, sep'tėr-les, *a.* Having no scepter.

Sceptic, skep'tik, *n.* [Fr. *sceptique*, from Gr. *skeptikos*, thoughtful, sceptic, from *skepsis*, speculation, doubt, from *skeptomai*, to examine critically; same root as L. *species*.] One who doubts the truth of any principle or system of principles or doctrines; one who disbelieves or hesitates to believe; a disbeliever; a person who doubts the existence of God or the truth of revelation; one who disbelieves in the divine origin of Christianity.—**Sceptical**, skep'ti-kal, *a.* Belonging to or characteristic of a sceptic or scepticism; holding the opinions of a sceptic.—**Sceptic**, skep'tik, *a.* Sceptical.—**Sceptically**, skep'ti-kal-li, *adv.* In a sceptical manner.—**Scepticalness**, skep'ti-kal-nes, *n.* The state or quality of being sceptical.—**Scepticism**, skep'ti-sizm, *n.* The doctrines or opinions of a sceptic; disbelief or inability to believe; doubt; incredulity; a doubting of the truth of revelation, or of the Christian religion.—**Scepticize**, skep'ti-sīz, *v.i.*—*scepticized*, *scepticizing*. To act the sceptic; to doubt.

Schedule, sked'ūl (English shed'ūl), *n.* [O.Fr. *schedule*, from L. *schedula*, dim. of *scheda*, a scroll, from Gr. *schedē*, a leaf, from root of *schizō*, L. *scindo*, to split.] A sheet of paper or parchment containing a written or printed list; a list annexed to a larger document, as to a will, lease, &c.—*v.t.*—*scheduled*, *scheduling*. To make a tabular statement of times of projected operations, as of a train.

Scheele's-green, shēlz, *n.* A green pigment containing arsenic and copper, first prepared by *Scheele*, a Swedish chemist.—**Scheeletine**, shēl'e-tin, *n.* A mineral of a green, yellow, brown; or red colour, consisting of tungstic acid and lead.

Scheik, shēk, *n.* Same as SHEIK.

Scheme, skēm, *n.* [Fr. *schème*, L. *schema*, from Gr. *schēma*, from *schein*, to hold, to keep.] A combination of things connected and adjusted by design; a system; a plan of something to be done; a project; the representation of any design or geometrical figure; a diagram.—*v.t.*—*schemed, scheming.* To plan, contrive, plot, project, design.—*v.i.* To form a plan; to contrive.—**Schematic**, skē-mat'ik, *a.* Pertaining to a scheme.—**Schematist**, skē'mat-ist, *n.* A projector; one given to forming schemes; a schemer.—**Schematize**, skē'ma-tīz, *v.t.*—*schematized, schematizing.* To form into a scheme or schemes.—**Schemeful**, skēm'-ful, *a.* Full of schemes or plans.—**Schemer, Schemist**, skē'mėr, skē'mist, *n.* One who schemes; a contriver; a plotter.—**Scheming**, skē'ming, *p.* and *a.* Given to forming schemes; artful; intriguing.—**Schemingly**, skē'ming-li, *adv.* By scheming or contriving.

Scheme-arch, *n.* [It. *arco scemo*, an incomplete arch.] An arch which forms a portion of a circle less than a semicircle.

Scherif, she-rif', *n.* SHEREEF.

Scherzando, skert-sän'dō, *adv.* [It.] *Mus.* in a playful or sportive manner.—**Scherzo**, skert'sō, *n.* [It.] A passage of a sportive character in musical pieces of some length, as in symphonies.

Schiedam, skē-dam', *n.* A name for Hollands gin, from *Schiedam*, in Holland, where it is largely manufactured.

Schiller-spar, shil'ėr-spär, *n.* [G. *schillern*, to change colour.] A mineral, a silicate of magnesia, comprising several varieties, of a pearly lustre and changeable hues.

Schiltron, shil'tron, *n.* [A.S. *scild-truma*, guard or troop of soldiers—*skild*, shield, and *truma*, troop, from *trum*, firm.] A hollow square, or 'Waterloo formation' of spearmen, presenting the appearance of a hedgehog, devised by Sir William Wallace, and imitated by European nations at the time and later.

Schism, sizm, *n.* [L. *schisma*; from Gr. *schisma*, from *schizō*, to divide; same root as L. *scindo*, to cut, A.Sax. *sceadan*, G. *scheiden*, to separate. SCHEDULE, SHED.] A split or division in a community; commonly, a division or separation in a church or denomination of Christians, occasioned by diversity of opinions; breach of unity among people of the same religious faith.—**Schismatic, Schismatical**, siz-mat'ik, siz-mat'i-kal, *a.* Pertaining to schism; partaking of the nature of schism; tending to schism.—**Schismatic**, *n.* One who takes part in a schism.—**Schismatically**, siz-mat'i-kal-li, *adv.* In a schismatical manner.—**Schismaticalness**, siz-mat'i-kal-nes, *n.*

Schist, shist, *n.* [Gr. *schistos*, divided, divisible, from *schizō*, to split. SCHISM.] A geological term applied to rocks which have a foliated structure and split in thin irregular plates; properly confined to metamorphic rocks (as gneiss) consisting of layers of different minerals.—**Schistic, Schistose, Schistous**, shis'tik, shis'tōz, shis'tus, *a.* Having the structure or character of schist.

Schizocarp, shiz'o-kärp, or skiz', *n.* [Gr. *schizō*, to split, *karpos*, fruit.] *Bot.* a dry fruit which splits at maturity into distinct one-seeded carpels.

Schizognathous, shi-zog'na-thus, or skiz'-, *a.* [Gr. *schizō*, and *gnathos*, jaw.] *Ornith.* having the bony palate cleft in a particular way.

Schizomycetes, shiz'o-mī-sē''tēz, *n.pl.* [Gr. *schizō*, and *mykēs*, fungus.] A division of minute vegetable organisms known as microbes, bacteria, &c.

Schizorhinal, shiz-ō-rī'nal, or skiz-, *a.* [Gr. *schizō*, and *rhis*, *rhinos*, nose.] *Ornith.* having the nasal bones cleft in a particular way.

Schnapps, Schnaps, shnaps, *n.* [G. *schnapps*, D. *snaps*, a dram.] A dram of Hollands gin or other ardent spirits.

Schneiderian, shnī-dē'ri-an, *a.* [From *Schneider*, who first described it.] A term applied to the lining membrane of the nostrils.

Scholar, skol'ėr, *n.* [O.Fr. *escolier* (Fr. *écolier*), from L.L. *scholaris*, from L. *schola*, a school. SCHOOL.] One who attends a school; one who learns of a teacher; a pupil; a disciple; a man of letters; a learned person; a person of high attainments in learning; one that learns anything; a pedant†; an undergraduate in an English university who receives a portion of its revenues to furnish him with the means of prosecuting his studies.—**Scholarly**, skol'-ėr-li, *a.* Like a scholar; becoming a scholar or man of learning.—**Scholarship**, skol'-ėr-ship, *n.* The character of a scholar; attainments in science or literature; erudition; learning; an exhibition or regularly settled allowance of money for a scholar at some educational institution; a foundation for the support of a student.—**Scholastic**, skō-las'tik, *a.* Pertaining to or suiting a scholar, school, or schools; characteristic of a scholar; pertaining to the schoolmen of the middle ages, or those philosophers and divines who adopted the system of Aristotle, and spent much time on points of nice speculation; hence, pedantic; formal.—*n.* One who adheres to the scholastic method; one of the schoolmen of the middle ages.—**Scholastically**, skō-las'ti-kal-li, *adv.* In a scholastic manner.—**Scholasticism**, skō-las'ti-sizm, *n.* The philosophy of the schoolmen of the middle ages.

Scholium, skō'li-um, *n.* pl. **Scholiums** or **Scholia**. [Gr. *scholion*, from *scholē*, leisure, lucubration. SCHOOL.] A marginal note, annotation, or remark; an explanatory comment, such as those annexed to the Latin and Greek authors by the early grammarians. **Scholiast**, skō'li-ast, *n.* [Gr. *scholiastēs*.] One who makes scholiums; an ancient grammarian who annotated the classics.—**Scholiastic**, skō-li-as'tik, *a.* Pertaining to a scholiast.

School, sköl, *n.* [A.Sax. *scól*, O.Fr. *escole*, from L. *schola*, from Gr. *scholē*, leisure, discussion, philosophy, a school.] A place in which persons are instructed in any species of learning; an educational establishment; a place in which instruction is imparted to the young; one of the seminaries of the scholastic philosophy of the middle ages; a body of pupils; the disciples or followers of a teacher; those who hold a common doctrine or accept the same teachings or principles (the Socratic *school*, painters of the Italian *school*); a system or state of matters prevalent at a certain time (the old *school*, the new *school*); any place of discipline or training.—*High School*, a school in which a superior education can be obtained; sometimes the chief public school in a town.—*Normal school.* NORMAL.—*a.* Relating to a school or to education; pertaining to the schoolmen; scholastic.—*v.t.* To instruct; to educate; to discipline; to chide and admonish; to reprove.—**School board**, an organized body of individuals appointed or elected to administer the affairs of the local public schools.—**Schoolbook**, *n.* A book used in schools; a textbook.—**Schoolboy**, *n.* A boy who attends school.—**School days**, the time of life during which children attend school.—**School district**, a local government, distinct from a township, chartered by the state for the administration of the public schools in a given area.—**Schoolfellow, Schoolmate**, *n.* An associate in school.—**Schoolgirl**, *n.* A girl who attends school.—**Schoolhouse**, *n.* A building appropriated for use as a school.—**Schooling**, sköl'ing, *n.* Instruction in school; tuition; cost of attending or maintaining a school; reproof; reprimand.—**Schoolman**, sköl'man, *n.* A man versed in the niceties of the school divinity of the middle ages; a scholastic.—**Schoolmaster**, sköl'mas-tėr, *n.* A man who presides over and teaches a school; a teacher, instructor, or preceptor of a school; one who or that which disciplines and instructs.—**Schoolmistress**, sköl'-mis-tres, *n.* The mistress of a school; a female who governs and teaches a school.—**Schoolroom**, *n.* A room for teaching.—**School-teacher**, *n.* One who gives regular instruction in a school.

School, sköl, *n.* [Same word as *shoal*.] A shoal or compact body (a *school* of fishes).

Schooner, skön'ėr, *n.* [Properly *scooner*, from a New England word *scoon*, to skim or skip upon the water, to make ducks and drakes, the first vessel of the kind having been built at Gloucester, Mass., about 1713. *Scoon* is the A.Sax. *scunian*, E. to *shun*. SHUN.] A vessel with two masts, and her chief sails fore and aft sails, her mainsail and foresail being both extended by a gaff and a boom; a measure of beer about two-thirds of a pint.

Schorl, Shorl, shorl, *n.* [G. *schörl*, Sw. *skörl*, Dan. *skjörl*; comp. Dan. *skjör*, brittle.] A mineral of a pitchy lustre and colour, brittle texture, and capable of being rendered electric by heat or friction, usually occurring in granitic rocks, and often embedded in felspar and quartz; tourmaline.—**Schorlaceous, Schorlous, Schorly**, shor-lā'shus, shor'lus, shor'li, *a.* Pertaining to or containing schorl; resembling schorl.

Schottische, shot-tish', *n.* [G. *schottische*, Scottish, lit. a Scottish dance.] A dance performed by a lady and gentleman, resembling a polka; the music suited for such a dance is 2-4 time.

Schweinfurth-green, shwīn'fụrt, *n.* A beautiful but highly poisonous pigment, prepared by boiling together solutions of arsenious acid and acetate of copper: so called from *Schweinfurth* in Bavaria, where it was first made.

Sciagraphy, sī-ag'ra-fi, *n.* [Gr. *skiagraphia*—*skia*, a shadow, and *graphō*, to describe.] The act or art of correctly delineating shadows; the art of sketching objects with correct shading.—**Sciagraph**, sī'a-graf, *n.* The section of a building to show its inside; an object shown by shadow, as by X rays.—**Sciagraphic, Sciagraphical**, *a.*

Sciamachy, sī-am'a-ki, *n.* [Gr. *skia*, a shadow, and *machē*, a battle.] A fight with a shadow; an imaginary or futile combat.

Sciatheric, sī-a-thē'rik, *a.* [Gr. *skiathēras*, a sun-dial, from *skia*, a shadow, and *thēra*, a catching.] Belonging to a sun-dial.

Sciatica, sī-at'i-ka, *n.* [L.L. *sciatica*, from Gr. *ischiadikos*, from *ischias*, a pain in the hip, from *ischion*, the hip.] Neuralgia of the sciatic nerve.—**Sciatic, Sciatical**, sī-at'ik, sī-at'i-kal, *a.* Pertaining to the hip (the *sciatic* artery or nerve).—**Sciatically**, sī-at'i-kal-li, *adv.* With sciatica.

Science, sī'ens, *n.* [Fr. *science*, from L. *scientia*, knowledge, from *scio*, to know (seen also in *conscious, conscience, nescience, sciolist*).] Knowledge; comprehension or understanding; knowledge co-ordinated, arranged, and systematized; hence, the knowledge regarding any one department of mind or matter co-ordinated, arranged, and systematized (the *science* of botany, of astronomy, &c.; mental *science*); art derived from precepts or built on principles; skill resulting from training; special skill.—*Applied science*, a science when its laws are employed and exemplified in dealing with concrete phenomena, as opposed to a *pure science*, as mathematics, when it treats of laws or general statements apart from particular instances.—*Natural science.* Under NATURAL.—*Physical science.* PHYSICS.—*Moral science*, moral philosophy or ethics.—*The seven sciences* of antiquity, grammar, logic, rhetoric, arithmetic, geometry, music, and astronomy.—**Scient**, sī'ent, *a.* [L. *sciens, scientis*, ppr. of *scio*, to know.] Skilful; knowing.—**Sciential**, sī-en'shal, *a.* Pertaining to science.—**Scientific**, sī-en-tif'ik, *a.* [L. *scientia*, knowledge, and *facio*, to make.] Pertaining to science; evincing or endowed with a knowledge of science; treating of science; well versed in science; according to the rules or principles of science.—**Scientifically**, sī-en-tif'i-kal-li, *adv.* In a scientific manner; according to the rules or principles of science.—**Scientism**,† sī'ent-izm, *n.* The views or practices of scientists.—**Scientist**, sī'ent-ist, *n.* A person versed in or devoted to science; a scientific man; a savant.

Scilicet, sī'li-set. [L.] To wit; videlicet; namely: abbreviated to *Scil.* or *Sc.*

Scimitar, Scimiter, sim'i-tėr, *n.* [O.Fr. *cimiterre*, It. *scimitarra*, from Per. *shemshir*, *shimshir*.] An oriental sword, the blade of which is single-edged, short, curved, and broadest at the point end.

Scincoid, sin'koid, *a.* Pertaining to the skink and allied animals.

Scintilla, sin-til'la, *n.* [L.] A spark; a glimmer; the least particle; a trace.—**Scintillant**, sin'til-lant, *a.* Sparkling.—**Scintillate**, sin'til-lāt, *v.i.*—*scintillated*, *scintillating*. [L. *scintillo*, *scintillatum*.] To emit sparks; to sparkle or twinkle, as the stars.—**Scintillation**, sin-til-lā'shon, *n.* The act of scintillating or sparkling; the twinkling of the stars.—**Scintillometer**, sin-til-lom'e-tėr, *Astron.* A telescope attachment which measures the intensity of the scintillation of a star.

Scintle, sin't'le, *v.t.* To arrange with air-spaces between, as freshly-made bricks; to arrange stones or bricks to make a rough surface.

Sciography, sī-og'ra-fi, *n.* SCIAGRAPHY.

Sciolist, sī'ol-ist, *n.* [L. *sciolus*, a smatterer, dim. of *scius*, knowing, from *scio*, to know. SCIENCE.] One who knows things superficially; a smatterer.—**Sciolistic**, sī-ol-is'tik, *a.* Pertaining to sciolism or a sciolist; superficial as to knowledge.

Sciomancy, sī'o-man-si, *n.* [Gr. *skia*, a shadow, and *manteia*, divination.] Divination by shadows.

Scion, sī'on, *n.* [Fr. *scion*, from L. *sectio*, *sectionis*, a cutting, from *seco*, to cut. SECTION.] A shoot or twig cut for the purpose of being grafted upon some other tree, or for planting; fig. a descendant; an heir.

Scioptic, Scioptric, sī-op'tik, sī-op'trik, *a.* [Gr. *skia*, a shadow, and *optomai*, to see.] Pertaining to the camera obscura, or to the art of exhibiting luminous images in a darkened room.

Sciotheric, sī-o-ther'ik, *a.* SCIATHERIC.

Scirocco, si-rok'ko, *n.* SIROCCO.

Scirrhus, Scirrhosis, skir'rus, skir-rō'sis, *n.* [L. *scirrus*, from Gr. *skirrhos*, a hardened swelling or tumour.] *Med.* a hard tumour usually proceeding from the induration of a gland, and often terminating in a cancer.—**Scirrhoid**, skir'roid, *a.* Resembling scirrhus.—**Scirrhosity**, **Scirrosity**, skir-ros'i-ti, *n.* The state of being scirrhous; also, a scirrhus or induration.—**Scirrhous**, skir'rus, *a.* Proceeding from or of the nature of scirrhus; indurated; knotty.

Scissel, Scissil, sis'sel, sis'sil, *n.* [From L. *scindo*, *scissum*, to cut.] Clippings of various metals; the remainder of a plate of metal after the planchets or circular blanks have been cut out for the purpose of coinage.—**Scissible, Scissile**, sis'si-bl, sis'sil, *a.* Capable of being cut.—**Scission**, sizh'on, *n.* [L. *scissio*, from *scindo*, to cut.] The act of cutting or dividing by an edged instrument; the state of being cut; division.

Scissors, siz'ėrz, *n.pl.* [From O.Fr. *cisoires*, *ciseaux*, from L. *cædo*, to cut (CHISEL); but influenced by *scissor*, one who cuts, from *scindo*, *scissum*, to cut.] A cutting instrument consisting of two blades movable on a pin in the centre, and which cut from opposite sides against an object placed between them: often spoken of as a *pair of scissors*.—**Scissor-bill**, *n.* A sea-bird also called *skimmer*.

Sciurine, sī-ū'rīn, *a.* [L. *sciurus*, a squirrel. SQUIRREL.] Having the characters of the squirrel tribe.

Sclav, sklav, *n.* SLAV.

Scleretinite, sklē-ret'i-nīt, *n.* [Gr. *sklēros*, hard, and *rētinē*, resin.] A black, hard, brittle mineral (or fossil) resin, nearly allied to amber.—**Sclerobasic**, sklē-rō-bā'sik, *a.* [Gr. *sklēros*, hard, and *basis*, a base.] Applied to a coral which forms a solid axis invested by the soft parts of the coral animals.—**Sclerodermic**, sklē-rō-dėr'mik, *a.* [Gr. *sklēros*, and *derma*, skin.] Having the skin covered with hard scales, as certain fishes; having the solid matter deposited between the tissues and each polyp with a skeleton of its own: said of coral animalcules.—**Sclerogen**, sklē'rō-jen, *n.* [Gr. *sklēros*, and root *gen*, to produce.] *Bot.* the ligneous matter deposited on the inner surface of the cells; lignin.—**Scleroid**, sklē'roid, *a.* *Bot.* having a hard texture.—**Scleroma, Sclerosis**, sklē-rō'ma, sklē-rō'sis, *n.* *Med.* induration of the cellular tissue.—**Sclerophthalmia**, sklē-rof-thal'mi-a, *n.* [Gr. *sklēros*, and *ophthalmos*, the eye.] A disease of the eye.—**Sclerosis**, skle-rō'sis. [Gr. *sklēros*, hard.] Hardening resulting from disease, especially of the nervous system and of arteries.—**Sclerotic**, sklē-rot'ik, *a.* [Gr. *sklērotēs*, hardness.] Hard; firm (the *sclerotic* coat of the eye).—*n.* The firm white membrane which covers the posterior part of the eye, the front being covered by the transparent *cornea*.—**Sclerotitis**, sklē-rō-tī'tis, *n.* Inflammation of the sclerotic.—**Sclerotium**, sklē'-rō-shum. [Gr. *sklērotēs*, hardness.] In fungi, a hard compact mass which germinates after a dormant period. See ERGOT.

Scobs, skobz, *n.* [L. *scobs*, saw-dust, scrapings, from *scabo*, to scrape.] Raspings of hard substances; saw-dust.—**Scobiform**, skob'i-form, *a.* Having the form of saw-dust or raspings.

Scoff, skof, *n.* [Same as O.Fris. *schof*, sport; Icel. *skop*, *skaup*, mockery, ridicule; O.H.G. *scoph*, sport.] An expression of derision, mockery, scorn, or contempt; a gibe; a flout; an object of derision.—*v.i.* To show insolent ridicule or mockery; to utter contemptuous language; to mock: with *at* before the object.—*v.t.* To mock at; to ridicule.—**Scoffer**, skof'ėr, *n.* One who scoffs; a mocker or scorner.—**Scoffingly**, skof'ing-li, *adv.* In a scoffing manner; by way of derision.

Scold, skōld, *v.i.* [Akin to Sc. *scald*, L.G. and D. *schelden*, Dan. *skielde*, G. *schelten*, to scold; Icel. *skjalla*, to clash; *skellr*, a crash; G. *schelle*, a bell.] To find fault in rude language; to utter harsh or rude rebuke; to make use of abuse or vituperation.—*v.t.* To chide with rudeness and ill-temper; to vituperate.—*n.* One who scolds; a noisy, foul-mouthed woman; a railing virago; a scolding; a brawl.—**Scolder**, skōl'-dėr, *n.* One that scolds.—**Scolding**, skōl'-ding, *n.* The act of one who scolds; a vituperative harangue; a rating.

Scolecida, skō-lē'si-da, *n.pl.* [From Gr. *skolēx*, an earthworm, a tape-worm.] The tape-worms and allied animals.—**Scolex**, skō'leks, *n.* pl. **Scolices**, skō'li-sēz. The larva of a tape-worm; a tape-worm embryo.

Scoliosis, skō-li-ō'sis, *n.* [Gr. *skolios*, crooked.] A distortion or curvature of the spine to one side.

Scolite, skō'līt, *n.* [Gr. *skolios*, tortuous.] *Geol.* one of the tortuous tubes found in rocks and supposed to be the burrows of annelids.

Scollop, skol'op, *n.* [SCALLOP.] A kind of shell-fish; a scallop; a curving indentation.—*v.t.* To form or cut with scollops.

Scolopendra, skol-o-pen'dra, *n.* [Gr. *skolopendra*, a milliped.] A venomous animal of the centiped or myriapod family.

Scomberoid, skom'bėr-oid, *n.* [Gr. *skombros*, a mackerel.] Any fish of the mackerel family.

Sconce, skons, *n.* [O.Fr. *esconce*, a shelter, a sconce; from L.L. *absconsa* (for *absconsa candela*, a hidden candle), a sconce, from L. *abscondo*, *absconsum*, to hide. ABSCOND.] A cover or screen; a cover or protection for a light; a case for a candle; the tube in a candlestick in which the candle is inserted; a fixed candlestick on a wall; a work for defence; a bulwark; a fort, as at a pass or river; a covering for the head; a helmet; a head-piece; the head itself; the skull: table fine for breach of etiquette, &c. and Cambridge, in the form of beer for the table.—*v.t.* To shelter; to ensconce.

Scone, skōn, *n.* A cake of flour bread.

Scoop, sköp, *n.* [Same as D. *schop*, *schup*, spade, shovel; Sw. *skopa*, a scoop; akin to Dan. *skuffe*, a shovel.] A thin metallic shovel with capacious sides for lifting grain; a similar but smaller utensil for lifting sugar, flour, &c.; a large ladle with a long handle for dipping in fluids; a spoon-shaped surgical instrument; a sort of pan for holding coals; the publication of news before a competitor; news so published.—*v.t.* To take out with a scoop or as with a scoop; to lade out; to empty as with a scoop; to hollow out; to excavate; to publish news before (a competitor).—**Scooper**, *n.*—**Scoop-net**, *n.* A net so formed as to sweep the bottom of a river.

Scooter, scöt'ėr, *n.* A child's vehicle with a board set between tandem wheels, the child standing with one foot on the board and pushing with the other; a flat-bottomed sailboat with a raised prow and steel runners, to sail on ice or water.

Scope, skōp, *n.* [It. *scopo*, mark, view, aim, L. *scopus*, Gr. *skopos*, a mark, aim, from Gr. *skeptomai*, to view.] A mark shot at†; an aim or end kept in view; ultimate design or purpose; intention; free or wide outlook or aim; amplitude of intellectual range; space; liberty; sweep.

Scorbutic, Scorbutical, skor-bū'tik, skor-bū'ti-kal, *a.* [Fr. *scorbutique*, from *scorbut*, the scurvy, from D. *scheurbuik*, G. *scharbock*, scurvy.] Pertaining to or affected with scurvy.—**Scorbutically**, *adv.*

Scorch, skorch, *v.t.* [O.Fr. *escorcher*, *escorcer* (Fr. *écorcher*), to strip off the skin; from L. *excorticare*—*ex*, and *cortex*, *corticis*, bark (whence *cork*).] To burn superficially; to subject to a degree of heat that injures the surface; to parch.—**Scorcher**, skorch'-ėr, *n.* That which scorches; a hot day; a sharp rebuke; a person who drives at an excessive speed.—*v.i.* To be burned on the surface; to be parched.—**Scorching**, skorch'ing, *a.* Such as to scorch.

Score, skōr, *n.* [A.Sax. *scor*, a score, a notch, from *sceran*, to shear (see SHEAR); Icel. *skor*, an incision, a tally, the number twenty; *skora*, to number by notches; akin *scar* or *scaur*, *share*, *sheer*, *shire*, *shore*, *short*.] A notch; a cut made on a tally for the purpose of keeping account of something; the number twenty, as being marked off by a special or larger score; among archers, twenty yards; an account or reckoning kept by notches, marks, or otherwise; an account of dues; hence, what is due; a debt; the number of points made by players in certain games; account, reason, ground (he declined on the *score* of illness); a line drawn; a long superficial scratch; *music*, the original draught, or its transcript, of a musical composition with the parts for all the different voices or instruments.—*To go off at score*, to start, as a pedestrian, from the score or scratch; hence, to start off, generally.—*To quit scores*, to pay fully; to make even by giving an equivalent.—*v.t.*—*scored*, *scoring*. To make scores or scratches on; to furrow; to set down, as in an account; to record; to mark; to note; to enter or register; to make a score of; to get for one's self, as points, hits, runs, &c., in certain games; *music*, to write out, as the different parts of a composition, in proper order and arrangement.—*v.i.* To make or keep a score; to make a point or hit, or a clever retort.—**Scorer**, skō'rėr, *n.* One who scores; one who keeps the score or tally at games, matches, &c.; an instrument used in marking numbers, &c., on timber.

Scoria, skō'ri-a, *n.* pl. **Scoriæ**, skō'ri-ē. [L. *scoria*, from Gr. *skōria*, from *skōr*, ordure.] The recrement of metals in fusion; the slag rejected after the reduction of metallic ores; dross; *pl.* the cinders of volcanic eruptions.—**Scoriaceous, Scorious**, skō-ri-ā'shus, skō'ri-us, *a.* Pertaining to scoria; partaking of the nature of scoria.—**Scorification**, skō'ri-fi-kā"shon, *n.* The act or operation of scorifying.—**Scorifier**, skō'ri-fī-ėr, *n.* A vessel use for the process of scorification in assaying silver.—**Scoriform**, skō'ri-form, *a.* Like scoria; in the form of dross.—**Scorify**, skō'ri-fī, *v.t.* To reduce to scoria or drossy matter; to separate the dross from the valuable metal.

Scorn, skorn, *n.* [O.Fr. *escorne*, affront, disgrace; *escorner*, It. *scornare*, to break off the horns, to affront, from L. *ex*, and *cornu*, a horn.] Extreme and passionate contempt; disdain springing from a person's opinion of the meanness and unworthiness of an object; the expression of this feeling; a scoff; a subject of extreme contempt or disdain.—*To think scorn*, to disdain; to despise.—*To laugh to scorn*, to deride; to make a mock of.—*v.t.* To hold in scorn; to despise; to disdain; to treat with scorn; to make a mock of.—*v.i.* To feel scorn or disdain; to show scorn.—**Scorner**, skor'nėr, *n.* One that scorns; a despiser; a scoffer; a derider; one who scoffs at religion.—**Scornful**, skorn'fu̧l, *a.* Full of scorn; contemptuous; disdainful.—**Scornfully**, skorn'fu̧l-li, *adv.* In a scornful manner; contemptuously.—**Scornfulness**, skorn'fu̧l-nes, *n.* The quality of being scornful.

Scorodite, skor'o-dīt, *n.* [Gr. *skorodon*, garlic; from its smell under the blowpipe.] A mineral consisting of arsenic acid and oxide of iron, having a leek-green or brownish colour.

Scorpio, skor'pi-ō, *n.* [L.] A constellation of the zodiac; the Scorpion.

Scorpion, skor'pi-on, *n.* [L. *scorpio, scorpionis*, from Gr. *skorpiōn*, a scorpion.] An animal belonging to the Arachnida (spiders, &c.) having a pair of large nipping claws and a long jointed tail terminating with a venomous sting; a kind of painful scourge or whip (O.T.); the eighth sign of the zodiac, which the sun enters about Oct. 23; an ancient military engine.—**Scorpioid, Scorpioidal**, skor'pi-oid, skor-pi-oi'dal, *a.* Scorpion-like; *bot.* said of a peculiar twisted inflorescence, curved or circinate at the end.—**Scorpion-fly**, *n.* An insect having a tail which resembles that of a scorpion.—**Scorpion-grass**, *n.* The old name of the well-known plant forget-me-not.—**Scorpion-shell**, *n.* A gasteropodous shell with projecting spines.—**Scorpion's-tail**, *n.* A plant having trailing stalks and long jointed pods.

Scorzonera, skor-zō-nē'ra, *n.* [It.] A genus of composite plants, one of which is cultivated for its carrot-shaped edible root.

Scot, skot, *n.* [A.Sax. *scot*, Icel. *skot*, D. and L.G. *schot*, G. *schoss*; from verb signifying to *shoot*, being a tax or contribution *shot* on along with others.] Formerly a payment of money; a tax or contribution.—*Scot and lot*, in England, parish payments imposed according to ability; obligations of any sort.—**Scot-free**, *a.* Free from payment or scot; untaxed; unhurt.

Scot, skot, *n.* [A.Sax. *Scotta*, a Scot, *Scottas*, the Scots, originally the inhabitants of Ireland; origin quite unknown.] A native of Scotland or North Britain.—**Scotch**, skoch, *a.* Pertaining to Scotland or its inhabitants; Scottish.—*Scotch fir*, the typical pine of Europe, especially of the northern and central parts, furnishing excellent timber, and turpentine, tar, resin, &c.—*Scotch mist*, a colloquial term for a wetting mist, like fine rain; or for a fine rain.—*Scotch pebble*, a name for varieties of agate, carnelian, &c.—*Scotch thistle*, a kind of thistle, so called because regarded as the national emblem of Scotland.—*n.* The dialect or dialects of English spoken in Scotland; collectively, the people of Scotland.—**Scotchman**, skoch'man, *n.* A native of Scotland; a Scot.—**Scots**, skots, *a.* Scotch (*Scots* law).—**Scotsman**, skots'man, *n.* SCOTCHMAN.—**Scottice**, skot'i-sē, *adv.* [L.] In the Scotch manner; in the Scotch language.—**Scotticism**, skot'i-sizm, *n.* An idiom or peculiar expression of the natives of Scotland.—**Scottish**, skot'ish, *a.* Pertaining to Scotland, its language, or its natives; Scotch.

Scotch, skoch, *v.t.* [Perhaps Celtic; comp. Gael. *sgoch*, a cut; or Fr. *coche*, a notch, might have given a verb *escocher*, whence this word.] To cut with shallow incisions; to notch; to chop.—*n.* A slight cut or shallow incision; a line drawn on the ground, as in hop-scotch.—**Scotch-collops**, *n.pl.* A dish consisting of slices of beef beaten and done in a stew-pan.—**Scotch-hop**, *n.* Same as *Hop-scotch*.—**Scotching**, skoch'ing, *n.* A method of dressing stone by pick-shaped chisels.

Scoter, skō'tėr, *n.* [Comp. Icel. *skoti*, a shooter: the name may mean diver or darter.] A diving duck found along the northern coasts of Europe and America.

Scotia, skō'ti-a, *n.* [Gr. *skotia*, lit. darkness.] A hollow moulding in the base of a column, so named from its surface being in shadow.

Scotist, skot'ist, *n.* One of the followers of Duns *Scotus*, one of the most celebrated scholastics of the fourteenth century.

Scotodinia, skot-ō-dī'ni-a, *n.* [Gr. *skotos*, darkness, and *dinos*, giddiness.] *Med.* giddiness, with imperfect vision.—**Scotograph**, skot'ō-graf, *n.* [Gr. *skotos*, and *graphō*, to write.] An instrument by which one may write in the dark, or for enabling the blind to write.—**Scotoma, Scotomy**, sko-tō'ma, skot'o-mi, *n.* [Gr. *skotoma*, from *skotos*, darkness.] Dizziness with dimness of sight.

Scotticism, Scottish. Under SCOT.

Scoundrel, skoun'drel, *n.* [Probably for *scounerel* or *scunerel*, one to be shunned or avoided, from A.Sax. *scunian*, to shun, an intermediate step being seen in Sc. *scunner*, *sconner*, to loathe, or as a noun, loathing; with *d* inserted as in *thunder*, *tender*.] A base, mean, worthless fellow; a rascal; a man without honour or virtue.—*a.* Belonging to a scoundrel; base; unprincipled.—**Scoundrelism**, skoun'drel-izm, *n.* The practices of a scoundrel; baseness; rascality.—**Scoundrelly**, skoun'drel-li, *a.* Characteristic of a scoundrel; base; villainous.

Scour, skour, *v.t.* [Same as Dan. *skure*, Sw. *skura*, G. *scheuern*, to scour; perhaps from O.Fr. *escurer*, from L. *excurare*—*ex*, intens., and *curare*, to clean, to care for. CURE.] To rub hard with something for the purpose of cleaning; to make clean or bright on the surface; to take grease or dirt out of the fabric of, by washing or chemical appliances; to cleanse away; to efface; to pass swiftly over; to brush along; to pass swiftly over in search of something or to drive away something; to overrun; to sweep clear.—*v.i.* To clean by rubbing; to take dirt or grease out of cloth; to rove or range; to run with celerity; to scamper.—*n.* A kind of diarrhœa or dysentery among cattle.—**Scourer**, skour'ėr, *n.* One who or that which scours.—**Scouring-ball**, *n.* A ball such as may be made of a combination of soap, ox-gall, and absorbent earth, used for removing stains of grease, paint, &c., from cloth.—**Scouring-drops**, *n.pl.* A mixture used to remove stains from cloth.

Scourge, skėrj, *n.* [Fr. *escourgée*, a scourge; L.L. *excorrigiata*, from L. *ex*, intens., and *corrigia*, a rein, a shoe-tie.] An instrument of the whip kind for the infliction of pain or punishment; a lash; a whip; hence a punishment; a vindictive affliction; one who greatly afflicts, harasses, or destroys; a whip for a top.—*v.t.*—*scourged, scourging.* To whip with a scourge; to whip severely; to lash; to chastise for correction; to afflict greatly; to harass.—**Scourger**, skėr'jėr, *n.* One who scourges.

Scout, skout, *n.* [O.Fr. *escoute*, a scout, from *escouter*, *escolter*, *esculter*, to hear, from L. *ausculto*, to listen. AUSCULTATION.] One sent out to gain and bring in information, especially to observe the motions and obtain intelligence regarding an enemy; a term at Oxford for a college servant or waiter; *cricket*, a fielder.—*v.i.* To act as a scout.—*v.t.* To watch closely; to observe the actions of.

Scout, skout, *v.t.* [Icel. *skúta*, a taunt; perhaps from root of *shoot*.] To treat with disdain and contempt; to reject with scorn.

Scow, skou, *n.* [D. *schouw*, a ferry-boat.] A kind of large flat-bottomed boat used chiefly as a lighter or a ferry-boat.

Scowerer, skou'ėr-ėr, *n.* [From *scour*.] The name of street ruffians, like the *Mohocks*, *Muns*, *Tityre Tus*, and other gangs infesting the London streets in the days of Queen Anne and earlier.

Scowl, skoul, *v.i.* [Same as Dan. *skule*, to scowl; comp. Icel. *skæla*, to make a wry face.] To wrinkle the brows, as in frowning or displeasure; to let the brows droop; to look sullen or angry; to look gloomy, dark, or tempestuous.—*n.* A deep angry frown by depressing the brows; dark or tempestuous aspect, as of the heavens; gloom.—**Scowling**, skoul'ing, *a.* Characterized by a scowl; frowning sullenly.—**Scowlingly**, skoul'ing-li, *adv.* In a scowling manner; with a sullen look.

Scrabble, skrab'l, *v.i.*—*scrabbled, scrabbling.* [A dim. of *scrape*; allied to *scribble* and *scramble*.] To make irregular, crooked marks; to scrawl; to scribble.—*v.t.* To mark with irregular lines or letters.—*n.* A scribble; a scrawl.

Scrag, skrag, *n.* [Comp. Gael. *screag*, parched, shrivelled; Icel. *skröggsligr*, scraggy, gaunt; Sc. *scrog*, a stunted bush.] Something thin or lean, with roughness.—*Scrag of mutton*, the bony part of the neck of a sheep's carcass.—**Scragged**, skrag'ed, *a.* Rough with irregular points; lean with roughness.—**Scraggedness**, skrag'ed-nes, *n.*—**Scraggily**, skrag'i-li, *adv.* In a scraggy manner.—**Scragginess**, skrag'i-nes, *n.* The state or quality of being scraggy; leanness; roughness.—**Scraggy**, skrag'i, *a.* Having an irregular broken surface; scragged; lean; bony.

Scramble, skram'bl, *v.i.*—*scrambled, scrambling.* [Akin to D. *scrammen*, to scratch; Dan. *skramle*, to ramble; Sw. *skramla*, to clatter; also to *scrabble*, *scrape*.] To move or climb by the aid of the hands; to move on all fours; to snatch eagerly at anything; to struggle to get before others.—*n.* The act of scrambling; an eager contest for something, in which one endeavours to get the thing before another.—**Scrambler**, skram'blėr, *n.* One who scrambles.—**Scrambling**, skram'bling, *p.* and *a.* Irregular; straggling; rambling.—**Scramblingly**, skram'bling-li, *adv.* In a scrambling manner; hurriedly.

Scrannel, skran'el, *a.* [Allied to Icel. *skran*, refuse.] Slight; thin; slender; miserable ('*scrannel* pipes of wretched straw'. *Mil.*).

Scrap, skrap, *n.* [Lit. what is *scraped*; same as Icel. *skrap*, scraps, trifles. SCRAPE.] A small piece; a detached, incomplete portion; a fragment; a fragment of something written or printed; a short or unconnected extract; a little picture suited to go along with others for ornamenting screens, boxes, &c.—*v.t.* To throw upon the *scrap-heap*: used of outworn or antiquated machinery plant rendered useless; to supersede.—**Scrap-book**, *n.* A book for the preservation of prints, engravings, &c., or of short pieces of poetry or other extracts from books; an album.—**Scrap-iron**, *n.* Fragments of iron accumulated for remelting or working up together.—**Scrap-metal**, *n.* Fragments of metal which are only of use for remelting.—**Scrappy**, skrap'i, *a.* Consisting of scraps; disconnected.

Scrape, skrāp, *v.t.*—*scraped, scraping.* [Same as Icel. *skrapa*, to scrape, to scratch; L.G. and D. *schrapen*, Dan. *skrabe*, to scrape; akin *scrap*, *scramble*, perhaps *sharp*.] To rub the surface of with a sharp or rough instrument, or with something hard; to deprive of the surface coating by a sharp instrument; to grate harshly over; to clean with something sharp; to erase; to collect by laborious effort; to acquire, save, or gather penuriously: usually with *together*.—*To scrape acquaintance* with a person, to make one's self acquainted, lit. by bowing or scraping; to insinuate one's self into a person's acquaintance.—*v.i.* To roughen or remove a surface by rubbing; to make a harsh noise by rubbing; to play awkwardly on a violin or such like instrument; to rub the feet on the ground; to make an awkward bow, with a drawing back of the foot. —*n.* A rubbing with something hard on a surface; an awkward bow accompanied with a scraping of the foot; a disagreeable predicament; a difficulty; perplexity; distress.—**Scraper**, skrā'pėr, *n.* One who or that which scrapes; an instrument with which anything is scraped; a metal instrument placed at or near the door of a house, upon which to scrape or clean the shoes.—**Scraping**, skrā'ping, *n.* What is scraped from a substance, or is collected by scraping.

Scratch, skrach, *v.t.* [O.E. *cratch*, to scratch; same as O.D. *kratsen*, Sw. *kratsa*, Dan. *kradse*, G. *kratzen*, to scratch, the *s* having been prefixed through the influence of *scrape*, &c.] To rub, tear, or mark the surface of with something sharp; to wound slightly by a point or points; to scrape with the nails so as not to wound; to write or draw awkwardly; to dig or excavate with the claws; to erase or blot out; to expunge; *horse-racing*, to erase from the list of horses that are to compete in the race.—*To scratch out*, to erase; to obliterate.—*v.i.* To use the nails, claws, or the like, in tearing a surface, or in digging.—*n.* A break in a surface made by scratching; a slight furrow; a score; a slight wound; a superficial laceration; a line up to which boxers are brought when they join fight; hence the vulgar phrase, to come up to the *scratch*, meaning to stand to the consequences, or appear when expected.—*a.* Taken at random or haphazard; heterogeneous; hastily collected (a *scratch* company of actors or of cricketers). —*Old Scratch*, the Devil; the *Skratti* of North European mythology. Akin to Bohemian *screti*, demon. — **Scratcher**, skrach'ėr, *n.* One who or that which scratches; a bird which scratches for food, as the common fowl. — **Scratchingly**, skrach'ing-li, *adv.* With the action of scratching.—**Scratch-weed**, *n.* A rough common weed, also called *Goose-grass*.—**Scratch-wig**, *n.* A kind of wig that covers only a portion of the head. — **Scratch-work**, *n.* A species of fresco consisting of a coloured plaster covered with a white one, through which a design is scratched.

Scrawl, skrąl, *v.t.* [A contracted form of *scrabble*; comp. D. *schravelen*, to scratch.] To draw or mark awkwardly and irregularly; to write awkwardly or imperfectly; to scribble; to make irregular lines or bad writing on.—*v.i.* To write unskilfully and inelegantly.—*n.* A piece of unskilful, hasty, or bad writing.—**Scrawl**, skrąl, *n.* [Perhaps from *scrawl*, form of *crawl*.] A young crab. (*Tenn.*) — **Scrawler**, skrą'lėr, *n.* One who scrawls.

Scrawny, skrą'ni, *a.* Thin; rawboned.—**Scrawnily**, *adv.*—**Scrawniness**, *n.*

Screak, skrēk, *v.i.* [A form of *screech*, *shriek* = Sw. *skrika*, Icel. *skrækja*, to screak.] To scream or screech; to creak.

Scream, skrēm, *v.i.* [Comp. Icel. *skramsa*, to scream; probably imitative, like *screech*, *shriek*, &c.] To cry out with a shrill voice; to utter a sudden, sharp outcry, as in a fright or in extreme pain; to shriek; to give out a shrill sound.—*n.* A shriek, or sharp shrill cry; a sharp, harsh sound.—**Screamer**, skrē'mėr, *n.* One that screams; a South American grallatorial bird, remarkable for its harsh discordant voice.—**Screaming**, skrē'ming, *p.* and *a.* Crying or sounding shrilly; causing screams of laughter (a *screaming* farce).

Screech, skrēch, *v.i.* [A softened form of *screak*, Icel. *skrækja*, Sw. *skrika*, Dan. *skrige*, to screech: an imitative word.] To cry out with a sharp, shrill voice; to shriek. —*n.* A sharp, shrill cry; a harsh scream; a sharp, shrill noise.—**Screech-owl**, *n.* An owl that screeches, in opposition to one that hoots.—**Screechy**, skrēch'i, *a.* Shrill and harsh; like a screech.

Screed, skrēd, *n.* [SHRED.] A shred or strip; a statement; a harangue or tirade.

Screen, skrēn, *n.* [O.Fr. *escren*, *escrein*, *escran*, Fr. *écran*, a screen, perhaps from O.H.G. *skranna*, a table.] A framework or curtain used to shut out the sun, rain, cold, or to conceal something from sight; that which shelters, protects, or conceals; a wire sieve for sifting sand, lime, &c.; a surface on which a stereoptican picture or motion picture is projected; hence, collectively, motion pictures; *arch.* an ornamental partition of wood, stone, or metal in a church.—*v.t.* To shelter or protect from inconvenience, injury, or danger; to cover; to conceal; to sift by passing through a screen.—**Screenings**, skrēn'ingz, *n. pl.* The refuse matter left after sifting coal, grain, &c.

Screes, skrēz, *n.pl.* [Comp. Icel. *skritha*, a landslip on a hill-side.] Debris of rocks; shingle; loose stones.

Screw, skrö, *n.* [Same as Dan. *skrue*, Sw. *skruf*, Icel. *skrúfa*, D. *schroef*, O.D. *schroeve*, L.G. *schruwe*, G. *schraube*, a screw.] A cylinder of wood or metal having a spiral ridge (the thread) winding round it in a uniform manner, so that the successive turns are all exactly the same distance from each other, and a corresponding spiral groove is produced: it forms one of the six mechanical powers, and is simply a modification of the inclined plane, the energy being transmitted by means of a hollow cylinder (the *female* screw) of equal diameter with the solid one (*male* screw), having a spiral channel cut on its inner surface so as to correspond exactly to the spiral ridge raised upon the solid cylinder; also, a screw-propeller or a screw-steamer; one who makes a sharp bargain; a skin-flint; a small quantity of tobacco twisted up in a piece of paper. — *Archimedean screw.* ARCHIMEDEAN.—*Endless screw.* ENDLESS.—*Right and left screw*, a screw of which the threads upon the opposite ends run in different directions.—*Screw propeller*, an apparatus which, being fitted to ships and driven by steam, propels them through the water, and which, in all its various forms, is a modification of the common screw. — *A screw loose*, something defective or wrong with a scheme or individual. — *To put on the screw*, to bring pressure to bear on a person, often for the purpose of getting money.—*To put under the screw*, to influence by strong pressure; to coerce.—*v.t.* To apply a screw to; to press, fasten, or make firm by a screw; to force as by a screw; to wrench; to twist; to rack; to oppress by exactions; to distort.—*To screw down*, to fasten down by means of screws.—*To screw in*, to force in by screwing or twisting round.—*To screw out*, to force out by turning; *fig.* to extort. —*To screw up*, to fix up by screws; *fig.* to raise extortionately.—**Screw-bolt**, *n.* A piece of iron, with a knob or flat head at one end and a screw at the other, used to join together pieces of timber, &c.—**Screw-driver**, *n.* An instrument resembling a blunt chisel for driving in or drawing out screw-nails.—**Screwer**, skrö'ėr, *n.* One who or that which screws.—**Screw-gun**, skrö'gun, *n.* A gun, designed for mountain warfare, which can be taken to pieces and conveyed in sections. — **Screw-jack**, *n.* A portable machine for raising great weights by the agency of a screw. JACK.—**Screw-key**, *n.* An implement for turning screws or nuts by catching them in its jaws.—**Screw-nail**, *n.* A nail the lower part of which forms a screw, and which has a notch across its head.—**Screw-picket**, skrö-pi'ket, *n.* An iron picket made to screw noiselessly into the ground, and used as the frame-work of a barbed-wire fence.—**Screw-pine**, *n.* The common name for useful trees which are natives of the East Indies, New Guinea, &c., and are remarkable for being supported above the ground by their aerial or adventitious roots.—**Screw-press**, *n.* A machine for communicating pressure by means of a screw or screws. — **Screw-propeller**, *n.* A ship's screw.—**Screw-steamer**, *n.* A steamship driven by a screw-propeller. — **Screw-valve**, *n.* A stop-cock with a valve opened and shut by a screw.—**Screw-wrench**, *n.* An implement for turning large screws; a screw-key.

Scribble, skrib'l, *v.t.*—*scribbled, scribbling.* [Based partly on *scrabble*, partly on L. *scribo*, to write; comp. O.H.G. *skribeln*, to scribble.] To write with haste, or without care; to fill with careless or worthless writing.—*v.i.* To scrawl; to write without care or beauty.—*n.* Hasty or careless writing; a scrawl.—**Scribbler**, skrib'lėr, *n.* One who scribbles or writes carelessly or badly; a petty author; a writer of no reputation.—**Scribbling**, skrib'ling, *a.* Fitted or adapted for being scribbled on.—*n.* The act of writing hastily and carelessly.

Scribble, skrib'l, *v.t.* [Sw. *skrubbla*, G. *schrubbeln*, to card, to scribble.] To card or tease coarsely; to submit, as cotton or wool, to a first rough teasing or carding. —**Scribbler**, skrib'lėr, *n.* The machine which scribbles or teases cotton or wool.

Scribe, skrīb, *n.* [Fr. *scribe*, from L. *scriba*, a clerk, a secretary, from *scribo*, *scriptum*, to write; seen also in *ascribe*, *describe*, *inscribe*, *subscribe*, *scripture*, *postscript*, &c.] One who writes; a penman; one skilled in penmanship; a secretary; an amanuensis; a notary; a copyist; a writer and doctor of the law among the ancient Jews; one who read and explained the law to the people. —*v.t.*—*scribed, scribing. Carp.* to mark by a rule or compasses; to mark for fitting accurately.—**Scriber**, skrīb'ėr, *n.* A tool used by joiners for marking lines on wood. —**Scribing-iron**, *n.* An iron-pointed instrument for marking casks or timber.

Scrimmage, **Scrummage**, skrim'āj, skrum'āj, *n.* [Corruption of *skirmish*.] A skirmish; a confused contest; a tussle; in *football*, a confused, close struggle round the ball.

Scrimp, skrimp, *v.t.* [Dan. *skrumpe*, Sw. *skrumpna*, L.G. *schrumpen*, to shrink, to shrivel; akin to A.Sax. *scrimman*, to wither or shrivel.] To make too small or short; to scant; to limit or straiten.—*a.* Scanty; deficient; contracted. — **Scrimpness**, skrimp'nes, *n.* Scantiness.

Scrip, skrip, *n.* [Same as Icel. *skreppa*, Dan. *skreppe*, L.G. *schrap*, Fris. *skrap*, a bag, a wallet; akin *scrap*.] A small bag; a wallet; a satchel.

Scrip, skrip, *n.* [For *script*, L. *scriptum*, something written, from *scribo*, to write. SCRIBE.] A small writing; a certificate or schedule; *com.* a certificate of stock subscribed to a bank or other company; an interim writing entitling a party to a share or shares in any company, exchanged after registration for a formal certificate; a certificate of indebtedness, in lieu of currency, at times issued by government or a business concern.

Script, skript, *n.* [L. *scriptum*, something written. SCRIP.] A typewritten or hand-written copy of a play showing the plot development usually by scenes and giving the directions for acting; a kind of hand-writing that resembles printed characters; *printing*, type resembling or in imitation of handwriting; *law*, the original or principa. document.

Scripture, skrip'tūr, *n.* [L. *scriptura*, a writing, from *scribo*, *scriptum*, to write. SCRIBE.] The books of the Old and New Testaments; the Bible: used by way of eminence and distinction, and often in the plural preceded by the definite article (*the Scriptures*); what is contained in the Scriptures; a passage or quotation from the Scriptures; a Bible text.—*a.* Relating to the Bible or the Scriptures; scriptural (*Scripture* history).—**Scriptural**, skrip'tūr-al, *a.* Contained in or according to the Scriptures; biblical.—**Scripturally**, skrip'tūr-al-li, *adv.* In a scriptural manner. — **Scripturalism**, skrip'tūr-al-izm, *n.* The quality of being scriptural; literal adherence to Scripture.—**Scripturalness**, skrip'tūr-al-nes, *n.* Quality of being scriptural.—**Scripturalist**, skrip'tūr-al-ist, *n.* One who adheres literally to the Scriptures. —**Scripture-reader**, *n.* One employed to read the Bible in private houses among the poor and ignorant. — **Scripturist**, skrip'tūr-ist, *n.* One well versed in the Scriptures.

Scrivener, skriv'nėr, *n.* [O.Fr. *escrivain* (with E. term. -*er* added), It. *scrivano*, from

L.L. *scribanus*, from L. *scribo*, to write. SCRIBE.] Formerly, a notary; a money-broker; a financial agent.

Scrobiculate, skrō-bik'ū-lāt, *a.* [L. *scrobiculus*, a little furrow, from *scrobs*, a furrow.] *Bot.* furrowed or pitted.

Scrofula, skrof'ū-la, *n.* [L. *scrofulae*, a swelling of the glands of the neck, scrofula.] A variety of consumption, characterized by tubercle formation in the glandular and bony tissues, and generally showing itself by hard indolent tumors of the glands, particularly in the neck, which after a time suppurate and degenerate into ulcers.—**Scrofulous**, skrof'ū-lus, *a.* Pertaining to scrofula; diseased or affected with scrofula.

Scroll, skrōl, *n.* [O.Fr. *eskrol*, *escrou* [Fr. *écrou*), a scroll, a register; probably from the Teutonic; comp. Icel. *skrá*, a scroll, Sw. *skra*, a short writing.] A roll of paper or parchment; a writing formed into a roll; a list or schedule; an ornament of a somewhat spiral form; the volute of the Ionic and Corinthian capitals; the curved head of instruments of the violin family; a kind of volute at a ship's bow; a flourish added to a person's name in signing.—**Scrolled**, skrōld, *a.* Inclosed in a scroll or roll; formed into a scroll; ornamented with scrolls.—**Scroll-head**, *n.* An ornament at the bow of a ship.—**Scroll saw**, A saw with a long, ribbon-like blade used to saw out curved shapes.

Scrophularia, skrof-ū-lā'ri-a, *n.* [Because used as a remedy for *scrofula*.] A genus of gamopetalous plants of wide distribution, type of a family containing the foxglove, antirrhinum, calceolaria, &c.

Scrotum, skrō'tum, *n.* [L.] The bag which contains the testicles.—**Scrotal**, skrō'tal, *a.* Pertaining to the scrotum.—**Scrotiform**, skrō'ti-form, *a.* *Bot.* formed like a double bag.—**Scrotocele**, skrō'tō-sēl, *n.* [*Scrotum*, and Gr. *kēlē*, a tumor.] A scrotal hernia.

Scrub, skrub, *v.t.*—*scrubbed*, *scrubbing*. [Same as Sw. *skrubba*, Dan. *skrubbe*, D. *schrobben*, L.G. *schrubben*, to scrub; allied to *scrape*, *scrabble*, or from *rub*, with initial *sc*, *sk*, intens.] To rub hard, as with a brush or with something rough, for the purpose of cleaning, scouring, or making bright; to scour by rubbing.—*v.i.* To be diligent and penurious.—*n.* A worn-out brush; a mean fellow; one that labours hard and lives meanly; something small and mean.—*a.* Mean; scrubby.—**Scrubbed**, skrub'ed, *a.* SCRUBBY.—**Scrubber**, skrub'ėr, *n.* One who or that which scrubs; a hard broom or brush.—**Scrubby**, skrub'i, *a.* Small and mean; insignificant; stunted in growth.

Scrub, skrub, *n.* [Same word as *shrub*, A.Sax. *scrob*, Dan. dial. *skrub*, a shrub.] Close, low, or stunted trees or brushwood; low underwood.—**Scrub-oak**, *n.* A stunted species of oak in America.

Scruff, skruf, *n.* The back of the neck: only in phrase, to take by the *scruff* of the neck.

Scrummage. SCRIMMAGE.

Scrunch, skrunsh, *v.t.* [From *crunch*, with *s* intens.] To crunch; to grind down.

Scruple, skrö'pl, *n.* [Fr. *scrupule*, a scruple, from L. *scrupulus*, lit. a little sharp stone (dim. of *scrupus*, a sharp stone), the twenty-fourth part of anything, a trifling matter causing doubt or anxiety, doubt, uneasiness.] A weight of 20 grains; the third part of a dram, or the twenty-fourth part of an ounce in the old apothecaries' measure; any small quantity (*Shak.*); hesitation as to action from perplexity; doubt; hesitation, or perplexity arising from motives of conscience; a point causing hesitation; dubiety.—*v.i.* *scrupled*, *scrupling*. To have scruples; to hesitate; to doubt: often followed by an infinitive.—**Scrupler**, skrö'plėr, *n.* One who scruples.—**Scrupulosity**, skrö-pū-los'i-ti, *n.* [L. *scrupulositas*.] Scrupulousness; nice regard to exactness and propriety; hesitation from fear of acting wrongly.—**Scrupulous**, skrö'pū-lus, *a.* [L. *scrupulosus*.] Full of scruples; hesitating to determine or to act; cautious in decision; careful; exact in regarding facts; precise; punctilious.—**Scrupulously**, skrö'pū-lus-li, *adv.* In a scrupulous manner; carefully; precisely.—**Scrupulousness**, skrö'pū-lus-nes, *n.* The state or quality of being scrupulous; scrupulosity; exactness; preciseness.

Scrutiny, skrö'ti-ni, *n.* [L. *scrutinium*, from *scrutor*, to search carefully, to rummage, from *scruta*, trash, frippery.] Close investigation or examination; a minute inquiry; a critical examination; an examination by a competent authority of the votes given at an election, for the purpose of correcting the poll.—**Scrutineer**, skrö-ti-nēr', *n.* One who scrutinizes; one who acts as an examiner of votes, as at an election, &c.—**Scrutinize**, skrö'ti-nīz, *v.t.*—*scrutinized*, *scrutinizing*. To subject to scrutiny; to investigate closely; to examine or inquire into critically.—*v.i.* To make scrutiny.—**Scrutinizer**, skrö'ti-nī-zėr, *n.* One who scrutinizes.—**Scrutinous**, skrö'-tin-us, *a.* Closely inquiring or examining.—**Scrutinously**, skrö'tin-us-li, *adv.* Searchingly.

Scrutoire, skrụ-twạr', *n.* An escritoire.

Scud, skud, *v.i.*—*scudded*, *scudding*. [Comp. Sw. *skutta*, to run quickly; akin perhaps to *shoot*.] To run quickly or with precipitation; to fly with haste; *naut.* to run before a tempest with little or no sail spread.—*n.* The act of scudding; loose vapoury clouds driven swiftly by the wind.—**Scudder**, skud'ėr, *n.* One who scuds.

Scudo, skö'dō, *n.* pl. **Scudi**, skö'dē. [It., lit. a coin marked with a shield, a crown-piece, from L. *scutum*, a shield.] An Italian silver coin of different value in the different states in which it was issued; the modern piece of 5 lire (about one dollar).

Scuffle, skuf'l, *v.i.*—*scuffled*, *scuffling*. [Freq. akin to A.Sax. *scúfan*, Sw. *skuffa*, to shove; same word as *shuffle*. SHOVE.] To struggle or contend with close grapple; to fight tumultuously or confusedly.—*n.* A struggle in which the combatants grapple closely; any confused quarrel or contest; a tumultuous fight.—**Scuffler**, skuf'lėr, *n.* One who scuffles.

Sculk, skulk, *v.i.* Same as *Skulk*.

Scull, skul, *n.* Same as *Skull*.

Scull, skul, *n.* [Origin uncertain; perhaps akin to *shell*.] An oar so short that one man can manage two, one on each side; an oar when used to propel a boat by being placed over the stern and worked from side to side.—*v.t.* To propel by sculls, or by moving and turning an oar over the stern.—**Sculler**, skul'ėr, *n.* One who sculls; a boat rowed by sculls.

Scullery, skul'ėr-i, *n.* [Perhaps from O.Fr. *escuelle*, *escuele*, a bowl, from L. *scutella*, dim. of *scutra*, a dish.] A place where culinary utensils are cleaned and kept; a back kitchen.

Scullion, skul'yon, *n.* [O.Fr. *escouillon*, a dish-clout, from L. *scopæ*, a broom.] A servant that does menial services in the kitchen or scullery; a low, mean, worthless fellow.—**Scullionly**, skul'yon-li, *a.* Base; low; mean.

Sculpin, skul'pin, *n.* A kind of small sea-fish.

Sculpture, skulp'tūr, *n.* [Fr. *sculpture*, from L. *sculptura*, from *sculpo*, *sculptum* (also *scalpo*), to grave or carve.] The art of carving, cutting, or hewing stone or other materials into images of men, beasts, &c.; the art of imitating natural objects in solid substances; statuary; carved work; a figure cut in stone or other solid substance, representing some real or imaginary object.—*v.t.*—*sculptured*, *sculpturing*. To represent in sculpture; to carve.—**Sculptor**, skulp'tor, *n.* One who sculptures; one who carves or hews figures.—**Sculptural**, skulp'tū-ral, *a.* Pertaining to sculpture.—**Sculpturally**, skulp-tū-ral-li, *adv.* By means of sculpture.—**Sculpturesque**, skulp'tū-resk, *a.* Possessing the character of sculpture; after the manner of sculpture.

Scum, skum, *n.* [Same as Sw. and Dan. *skum*, G. *schaum*, D. *schuim*, O.H.G. *scûm*, scum, from a root meaning to cover (seen in *sky*, &c.). *Skim* is a derivative verb.] The extraneous matter which rises to the surface of liquors in boiling or fermentation; the scoria of molten metals; refuse; recrement.—*v.t.*—*scummed*, *scumming*. To take the scum from; to clear off the impure matter from the surface.—*v.i.* To throw up scum; to be covered with scum.—**Scummer**, skum'ėr, *n.* One who or that which scums.—**Scummings**, skum'-ingz, *n. pl.* The matter skimmed from boiling liquors.—**Scummy**, skum'i, *a.* Covered with scum; like scum.

Scumble, skum'bl, *v.t.*—*scumbled*, *scumbling*. [Freq. of *scum*.] *Painting*, to cover thinly with semi-opaque colours to modify the effect.—**Scumbling**, skum'bling, *n.* The toning down of a picture by semi-transparent colours.

Scupper, skup'ėr, *n.* [Connected with *scoop*, or from O.Fr. and Sp. *escupir*, to spit; Armor. *skopa*, to spit.] A channel cut through the side of a ship for carrying off the water from the deck.—**Scupper-hole**, *n.* A scupper.—**Scupper-hose**, *n.* A leathern pipe attached to the mouth of the scuppers to prevent water from entering.

Scurf, skėrf, *n.* [A.Sax. *scurf*, scurf; Icel. *skurfur* (pl.), Dan. *skurv*, Sw. *skorf*, G. *schorf*, scurf; allied to *scrape*.] Matter composed of minute portions of the dry external scales of the cuticle, which is continually being detached from the surface of the body; a layer of matter adhering to a surface; *bot.* the loose scaly matter that is found on some leaves, &c.—**Scurfiness**, skėr'fi-nes, *n.* The state of being scurfy.—**Scurfy**, skėr'fi, *a.* Covered with scurf; resembling scurf.

Scurrile, skur'ril, *a.* [L. *scurrilis*, from *scurra*, a buffoon, a jester.] Such as befits a buffoon or vulgar jester; low; scurrilous.—**Scurrility**, skur-ril'i-ti, *n.* The quality of being scurrilous; that which is scurrilous; low, vulgar, abusive language; grossness of abuse or invective; obscene jests, &c.—**Scurrilous**, skur'ri-lus, *a.* Using low and indecent language; containing low abuse; foul; vile; obscenely jocular; opprobrious; abusive.—**Scurrilously**, scur'ri-lus-li, *adv.* In a scurrilous manner; with gross abuse.—**Scurrilousness**, skur'ri-lus-nes, *n.* The quality of being scurrilous; scurrility.

Scurry, skur'ri, *v.i.*—*scurried*, *scurrying*. [Comp. *scour*.] To run rapidly; to hurry.—*n.* Hurry; haste.

Scurvy, skėr'vi, *n.* [From *scurf*.] A disease characterized by livid spots and general bodily exhaustion, affecting persons who are deprived of fresh provisions and a due quantity of vegetable food, and which is successfully treated, both as a preventive and as a curative agent, by lime or lemon juice.—*a.* Vile; mean; low; mischievous; malicious.—**Scurvily**, skėr'vi-li, *adv.* Basely; meanly; with coarse and vulgar incivility.—**Scurviness**, skėr'vi-nes, *n.* Meanness; vileness.—**Scurvy-grass**, *n.* [A corruption of *scurvy-cress*, being used as a cure for *scurvy*.] The common name of several arctic species of cruciferous plants, with leaves that are eaten as a salad.

Scut, skut, *n.* [Comp. W. *cwt*, a tail.] A short tail such as that of a hare or deer.

Scutage, skū'tāj, *n.* [L.L. *scutagium*, from L. *scutum*, a shield.] A tax on feudal tenants holding lands by knight's service; escuage.—**Scutate**, skū'tāt, *a.* *Bot.* formed like an ancient round buckler; *zool.* protected or covered by large scales.

Scutch, skuch, *v.t.* [Perhaps same as *scotch*, to cut, to strike.] To dress by beating; to separate the woody parts of the stalks of flax by beating.—**Scutch**, **Scutcher**, skuch, skuch'ėr, *n.* An implement or machine for scutching.

Scutcheon, skuch'on, *n.* [A contr. of *escutcheon*.] A shield for armorial bearings; an escutcheon; the ornamental cover or frame to a key-hole.

Scute, skūt, *n.* [L. *scutum*, a buckler.] A scale, as of a reptile, especially a large scale. —**Scutel**, skū'tel, *n.* Same as *Scutellum.* —**Scutella**, skū-tel'la, *n.* pl. **Scutellæ**, skū-tel'lē. [L.] One of the plates on the feet of birds.—**Scutellate**, skū'tel-lāt, *a.* Formed like a plate; covered with scutellæ. —**Scutelliform**, skū-tel'li-form, *a.* Scutellate; saucer-shaped.—**Scutellum**, skū-tel'lum, *n.* pl. **Scutella**, skū-tel'la. [L. dim. of *scutum*, a shield.] *Bot.* the smaller cotyledon of wheat; the little cup or disc in lichens, containing tubes filled with sporules; *entom.* a part of the thorax of insects.—**Scutiform**, skū'ti-form, *a.* Having the form of a buckler or shield.

Scutter, skut'ėr, *v.i.* [Allied to *scud*; comp. *scuttle*, to run.] To run or scuttle away with short quick steps. (*Colloq.*)

Scuttle, skut'l, *n.* [A.Sax. *scutel*, from L. *scutella*, dim. of *scutra*, a dish or platter.] A broad shallow basket; a wide-mouthed metal pan or pail for holding coals.

Scuttle, skut'l, *n.* A square hole in the wall or roof of a house, with a lid; the lid itself; *naut.* a small hatchway with a lid for covering it; a hole in the side of a ship.—*v.t.*—*scuttled, scuttling.* *Naut.* to sink by making holes through the bottom.—**Scuttle-butt, Scuttle-cask**, *n.* A cask with a hole in it, covered by a lid, for holding fresh water for daily use in a ship.

Scuttle, skut'l, *v.i.*—*scuttled, scuttling.* [For *scuddle*, a freq. of *scud.*] To run with affected precipitation; to hurry.—*n.* A quick pace; a short run.

Scutum, skū'tum, *n.* pl. **Scuta**. [L., a shield.] A shield-shaped plate; a scute.

Scye, sī, *n.* [Akin *scion.*] The curve in a piece of a garment to receive the sleeve.

Scymetar, Scymitar, sim'i-tėr, *n.* A scimitar.

Scyphus, skī'fus, *n.* [Gr. *skyphos*, a cup or goblet.] *Bot.* the coronet or cup of such plants as narcissus.

Scythe, sīTH, *n.* [Better written *sithe*; A. Sax. *sithe* for *sigthe*, the older form = Icel. *sigth*; from root of *sickle.*] An instrument used in mowing or reaping, consisting of a long curving blade fixed to a handle, which is swung by both arms.—*v.t.*—*scythed, scything.* To mow; to cut with a scythe. —**Scythed**, sīTHd, *a.* Having scythes attached to the wheels, as ancient war chariots.—**Scytheman**, sīTH'man, *n.* One who uses a scythe.—**Scythe-stone**, *n.* A whetstone for sharpening scythes.

Scythian, sith'i-an, *a.* Pertaining to *Scythia*, the ancient name given to a vast territory north and east of the Black Sea, the Caspian, and the Sea of Aral.—*n.* A native of Scythia.

Sea, sē, *n.* [A.Sax. *sae*, sea or lake=D. *see, zee*, Dan. *sö*, Icel. *sær*, G. *see*, Goth. *saivs.*] The continuous mass of salt water which covers great parts of the earth; the ocean; some special portion of this (the Polar *Sea*, the Black *Sea*); a name of certain lakes, especially when large (the *Caspian Sea*, the *Sea of Galilee*); a large wave; a surge (the vessel shipped a *sea*); the swell of the ocean; set of the waves; any large quantity (a *sea* of difficulties); a flood.—*At sea*, on the open sea; out of sight of land; in a vague uncertain condition; wide of the mark.—*At full sea*, at high water; hence, at the height.—*Beyond the sea* or *seas*, out of the realm or country.—*Cross sea, chopping sea*, waves moving in different directions.—*The four seas*, the seas bounding Britain on the north, south, east, and west. —*To go to sea, to follow the sea*, to follow the occupation of a sailor.—*Half seas over*, half drunk.—*The high seas* or *main sea*, the open ocean.—**Sea-acorn**, *n.* A cirriped, called also *barnacle*.—**Sea-anemone**, *n.* The popular name given to the actiniæ.— **Sea-bear**, *n.* The white or Polar bear; a species of seal whose fur is of high value.— **Sea-beat, Sea-beaten**, *a.* Beaten by the sea; lashed by the waves.—**Sea-bird**, *n.* One of those birds that frequent the sea.—**Sea-blubber**, *n.* A jelly-fish.— **Sea-board**, *n.* [*Sea*, and *board*, Fr. *bord*, side.] The sea-coast; the country bordering on the sea.—*a.* Bordering on the sea.— **Sea-boat**, *n.* A vessel considered as regards her capacity of withstanding a storm or the force of the sea.—**Sea-born**, *a.* Born of the sea; produced by the sea.— **Sea-bream**, *n.* BREAM.—**Sea cabbage, Sea-kale**, *n.* A kind of cabbage found on sandy shores of the sea.—**Sea-calf**, *n.* The common seal.—**Sea-captain**, *n.* The captain of a ship.—**Sea-cat**, *n.* The wolf-fish.—**Sea-coal**, *n.* Coal brought by sea, a name formerly used for mineral coal in distinction from *charcoal.*— **Sea-coast**, *n.* The land immediately adjacent to the sea; the coast.—**Sea-cow**, *n.* A name given to the dugong and the manatee.—**Sea-cucumber**, *n.* A name given to several of the holothurians; the trepang or bêche-de-mer.—**Sea-devil**, *n.* The fishing-frog or toad-fish.—**Sea-dog**, *n.* The dog-fish; the common seal; a sailor who has been long afloat (*colloq.*).—**Sea-dragon**, *n.* A name given to the dragonets, fishes of the goby family.—**Sea-duck**, *n.* One of the ducks that frequent the sea.— **Sea-eagle**, *n.* The white-tailed eagle of Europe; the bald-eagle of America, found generally on the sea-coast, as it is a fish-loving bird; the eagle ray, a fish of the Mediterranean and warmer seas.—**Sea-ear**, *n.* The ear-shell.—**Sea-eel**, *n.* A conger or other eel of the sea.—**Sea-egg**, *n.* A sea-urchin.—**Sea-elephant**, *n.* A huge seal of the southern hemisphere that has the nose prolonged into a sort of proboscis.—**Seafarer**, sē'fār-ėr, *n.* A traveller by sea; a mariner.—**Seafaring**, sē'fār-ing, *a.* Following the business of a seaman.— **Sea-fennel**, *n.* Samphire.—**Sea-fight**, *n.* An engagement between ships at sea.— **Sea-fir**, *n.* A popular name applied to those hydrozoa that have a branching polypite somewhat resembling the fir.—**Sea-fish**, *n.* Any fish that lives usually in salt water.—**Sea-fowl**, *n.* Any bird that lives by the sea and procures its food from it.— **Sea-fox**, *n.* A kind of shark, 12 to 15 feet in length, and having the upper lobe of the tail remarkably long; called also *thresher*, because of lashing other animals with its tail.—**Sea-gage, Sea-gauge**, *n.* The depth that a vessel sinks in the water; an instrument for ascertaining the depth of the sea.—**Sea-gilliflower**, *n.* The sea-pink.—**Sea-girt**, *a.* Surrounded by the sea; forming an island.—**Sea-god**, *n.* A marine deity; a divinity supposed to preside over the ocean.—**Sea-goddess**, *n.* A female deity of the ocean.—**Sea-going**, *a.* Applied to a vessel which makes foreign voyages, as opposed to a coasting or river vessel.—**Sea-grass**, *n.* Grasswrack.— **Sea-green**, *a.* Having the green colour of sea-water; being of a faint green colour. —**Sea-gudgeon**, *n.* The rock-fish or black goby.—**Sea-gull**, *n.* A gull or bird of the gull kind.—**Sea-hare**, *n.* A marine molluscous animal having a fancied resemblance to a hare.—**Sea-hedgehog**, *n.* The sea-urchin.—**Sea-hog**, *n.* The porpoise.— **Sea-holly**, *n.* The plant eryngo.—**Sea-horse**, *n.* The walrus; a small lophobranch fish, related to the pipefish, with head and neck likened to a horse; a fabled animal, half horse and half fish.—**Sea-island**, *a.* Applied to a fine long-stapled variety of cotton grown on the islands off the coasts of South Carolina and Georgia.—**Sea-king**, *n.* A king of the sea; one of the piratical Northmen who infested the coasts of Western Europe in the eighth, ninth, and tenth centuries; a viking.—**Sea-legs**, *n. pl.* The ability to walk on a ship's deck when pitching or rolling.—**Sea-lemon**, *n.* A nudibranchiate gasteropodous mollusk of a lemon color.—**Sea-leopard**, *n.* A species of seal.—**Sea-level**, *n.* The level of the surface of the sea, usually taken as the point from which to measure heights or depressions of the land.—**Sea-lion**, *n.* A name of several large seals, the best known of which has a mane on the neck, is 10 to 15 feet long, and is found in the Pacific.— **Sea-louse**, *n.* A name common to various small crustacea.—**Seaman**, sē'man, *n.* A man whose occupation is to assist in the navigation of ships; a mariner; a sailor.— *Able seaman*, a sailor who is well skilled in seamanship, and classed in the ship's books as such.—*Ordinary seaman*, one less skilled than an able seaman.—**Seamanship**, sē'man-ship, *n.* The skill of a good seaman.— **Sea-mark**, *n.* Any elevated object on land which serves for a direction to mariners; a beacon.—**Sea-mew**, *n.* A gull; a sea-gull.—**Sea-mile**, *n.* A nautical mile, the sixtieth part of a degree of latitude. MILE. —**Sea-monster**, *n.* A huge, hideous, or terrible marine animal.—**Sea-mouse**, *n.* A marine dorsibranchiate annelid found on the sea-coast, splendidly coloured.—**Sea-needle**, *n.* GARFISH.—**Sea-nettle**, *n.* A kind of stinging medusa or jelly-fish.— **Sea-nymph**, *n.* A nymph or goddess of the sea.—**Sea-onion**, *n.* A plant. SQUILL. —**Sea-otter**, *n.* A marine mammal closely allied to the common otter, and yielding a valuable fur.—**Sea-parrot**, *n.* The puffin, so called from its bill.—**Sea-perch**, *n.* A marine fish closely allied to the perch, called also *bass*.—**Sea-pie**, *n.* A name of the oyster-catcher; a dish of paste and meat boiled together often used at sea.—**Sea-piece**, *n.* A picture representing a scene at sea.—**Sea-pike**, *n.* Another name for the garfish.—**Sea-pink**, *n.* A common British plant with pink flowers, growing on or near the sea-shore; called also *thrift*.— **Sea-plane**. See HYDROPLANE.—**Sea-porcupine**, *n.* A fish, the body of which is covered with spines.—**Seaport**, sē'pōrt, *n.* A port, or a town with a port, on or near the sea.—**Sea-reed**, *n.* A beach grass found on sandy sea-shores, where its roots assist in binding the shifting soil.—**Sea-risk**, *n.* Hazard or risk at sea; danger of injury by the sea.—**Sea-robber**, *n.* A pirate.—**Sea-rocket**, *n.* A cruciferous plant growing on the sea-shore in sand.—**Sea-room**, *n.* Sufficient room at sea for a vessel to make any required movement.—**Sea-salt**, *n.* Common salt obtained by evaporation of sea-water.— **Seascape**, sē'skāp, *n.* [Formed on the model of *landscape.*] A picture representing a scene at sea; a sea-piece.—**Sea-serpent**, *n.* A name common to a family of snakes which frequent the seas of warm latitudes; an enormous animal of serpentine form said to have been repeatedly seen at sea, but as to the real existence of which naturalists are generally sceptical.—**Sea-shark**, *n.* The white shark.—**Sea-shell**, *n.* The shell of a mollusc inhabiting the sea.—**Sea-shore**, *n.* The shore of the sea; *law*, the ground between the ordinary high-water mark and low-water mark.— **Sea-sick**, *a.* Affected with sickness or nausea from the pitching or rolling of a vessel.—**Sea-sickness**, *n.* A nervous affection attended with nausea and vomiting, produced by the rolling or pitching of a vessel at sea.—**Sea-side**, *n.* The land or country bordering on the sea.—**Sea-slug**, *n.* A marine mollusc destitute of a shell; also the trepang.—**Sea-snake**, *n.* A serpent that inhabits the sea.—**Sea-snipe**, *n.* The bellows-fish; also a bird, the dunlin.—**Sea-squirt**, *n.* An ascidian. —**Sea-swallow**, *n.* The common tern. **Sea-tangle**, *n.* The name of several species of sea-weeds.—**Sea-term**, *n.* A term used by seamen or peculiar to the art of navigation.—**Sea-toad**, *n.* The angler or fishing-frog.—**Sea-tossed**, *a.* Tossed by the billows of the sea.—**Sea-unicorn**, *n.* The narwhal.—**Sea-urchin**, *n.* A roundish spiny echinoderm; an echinus.—**Sea-wall**, *n.* A strong wall on the shore to prevent encroachments of the sea.—**Seaward**, sē'wėrd, *a.* Directed toward the sea.—*adv.* Toward the sea.— **Sea-ware**, *n.* The algæ thrown up by the sea, and made use of as manure, &c.— **Sea-water**, *n.* The salt water of the sea. **Sea-wax**, *n.* Maltha.—**Sea-way**, *n.* *Naut.* progress made by a vessel through the waves.—**Sea-weed**, *n.* A name given generally to any plant growing in the sea, but more particularly to members of the nat. order Algæ.—**Sea-wolf**, *n.* The wolf-fish.—**Sea-worn**, *a.* Worn or abraded by the sea.—**Sea-worthiness**, *n.* The state of being sea-worthy.—**Sea-worthy**, *a.*

Applied to a ship in good condition and fit for a voyage.—**Sea-wrack**, *n.* GRASS-WRACK.

Seal, sēl, *n.* [A.Sax. *seol, seolh*, Sc. *selch, silch*, Icel. *selr*, Dan. *sæl*, O.H.G. *selach*: origin doubtful.] A marine carnivorous mammal of numerous species, having both fore and hind feet forming a sort of swimming organs, largely hunted for their fur and blubber; the fur, which forms the valued 'seal-skin' of commerce, being obtained from some of the 'eared' species, or those that have external ears.—**Sealer**, sēl'ėr, *n.* A seaman or a ship engaged in the seal-fishery. — **Sealing, Seal-fishery, Seal-fishing**, *n.* The operation or occupation of catching seals.—**Seal-skin**, *n.* The skin of the fur-seal, which, with the fur on, is made into articles of clothing.

Seal, sēl, *n.* [O.Fr. *seel*, from L. *sigillum*, a seal, dim. of *signum*, a sign. SIGN.] A piece of stone, metal, or other hard substance on which is engraved some figure or inscription, used for making an impression on some soft substance, as on the wax that makes fast a letter, or is affixed to documents in token of authenticity; the wax or other substance so impressed; the wax, wafer, or similar fastening of a letter or other paper; that which authenticates, confirms, or ratifies; assurance; pledge; that which effectually shuts or secures; that which makes fast.—*Great seal*, a nation's official seal used to authenticate public documents and papers.—*Privy-seal, lord privy-seal.* See under PRIVY.—*To set one's seal to*, to give one's authority to; to give one's assurance of.—*v.t.* To affix a seal to, as a mark of authenticity; hence, to confirm or ratify; to establish; to settle; to fasten and mark with a seal; to fasten securely, as with a wafer or with wax; to close hermetically; to shut or keep close (to *seal* one's lips); to confine securely.—**Sealer**, *n.* A ship used in hunting seals.—**Sealing wax**, *n.* A composition of resinous materials used for fastening folded papers and envelopes, and capable of receiving impressions of seals.

Seam, sēm, *n.* [A.Sax. *seám*, a seam; Icel. *saumr*, Dan. and Sw. *söm*, D. *zoom*, G. *saum*, all from verb to *sew*. SEW.] A joining line formed by the sewing of two different pieces of cloth, &c., together; a suture; a scar or cicatrix; the line or space between planks joined together; *geol.* the line of separation between two strata; a thin layer or stratum, as of ore, coal, and the like, between two thicker strata.—*v.t.* To form a seam on; to unite with a seam; to mark with a cicatrix; to scar.—**Seamer**, sēm'ėr, *n.* One who or that which seams.—**Seamless**, sēm'les, *a.* Having no seam.—**Seamstress**, sēm'stres, *n.* [A.Sax. *seámestre*, with term. *-ess* added.] A woman whose occupation is sewing; a sempstress. — **Seamy**, sēm'i, *a.* Having a seam; containing seams or showing them, as the underside of a garment.—*Seamy side*, the darker side or hues of life, showing the evil side.

Seam, sēm, *n.* [A.Sax. *seam*, from L.L. *sauma, salma*, for L. *sagma*, Gr. *sagma*, a pack-saddle.] A measure of 8 bushels of corn, or the vessel that contains it.

Sean, sēn, *n.* A net. SEINE.

Seance, sā'ängs, *n.* [Fr. *séance*, from *séant*, sitting, L. *sedens, sedentis*, ppr. of *sedeo*, to sit. SEDATE.] A session, as of some public body; among spiritualists, a sitting with the view of evoking spiritual manifestations or holding intercourse with spirits.

Sear, sēr, *v.t.* [A.Sax. *seárian*, to parch, from *seár*, dry; akin to L.G. *soor*, O.D. *sore, soore*, D. *zoor*, dry.] To wither; to dry; to burn to dryness and hardness the surface of; to cauterize; to burn; to scorch; to make callous or insensible (a *seared* conscience); to brand.—*a.* [A.Sax. *seár.*] Dry; withered; no longer green and fresh (a *sear* leaf). Spelled also *Sere.*—**Searedness**, sērd'nes, *n.* The state of being seared; hardness; hence, insensibility.

Sear, sēr, *n.* [Fr. *serre*, a lock, a bar, from L. *sera*, a bolt or bar.] The pivoted piece in a gun-lock which enters the notches of the tumbler and holds the hammer at full or half cock.

Searce, sėrs, *n.* [Also *sarse*, from Fr. *sas*, O.Fr. *saas*, from L. *setaceus*, bristly, from *seta*, a bristle.] A kind of sieve or bolter.

Search, sėrch, *v.t.* [O.E. *serche, cerche*, O.Fr. *cercher, cerchier* (Fr. *chercher*), to search, from L.L. *cercare, circare*, to search, to run about, from L. *circus*, a circle. CIRCLE.] To look over or through, for the purpose of finding something; to examine; to explore; to probe (to *search* a wound); to put to the test.—*v.i.* To make search; to make inquiry; to inquire.—*n.* The act of seeking or looking for something; inquiry; quest.—*Right of search*, the right of a belligerent to enter merchant vessels of neutral nations on the high seas, to search for an enemy's property, articles contraband of war, &c.—**Searchable**, sėrch'a-bl, *a.* Capable of being searched.—**Searcher**, sėrch'ėr, *n.* One who searches; an examiner or investigator; a prison warden who searches new prisoners.—**Searching**, sėrch'ing, *p.* and *a.* Exploring; examining; investigating; penetrating; close; keen.—**Searchlight**, *n.* An apparatus pivoted so as to project a strong beam of light in any desired direction; also, the beam of light.—**Search warrant**, *n.* A warrant granted by a judge or magistrate to the police to enter premises in search of stolen goods or articles kept contrary to law.

Season, sē'zn, *n.* [O.E. *seson, sesoun*, O.Fr. *seson, seison*, Mod.Fr. *saison*, lit. time of sowing, from L. *satio, sationis*, a sowing, from *sero, satum*, to sow.] One of the periods into which the year is naturally divided, as marked by its temperature, moisture, &c. (as spring, summer, autumn, and winter; the wet and the dry *season* of tropical countries); a convenient or suitable time; a proper conjuncture; the right time; a period of time not very long; a while; a time; that time of the year when a particular locality is most frequented by visitors (the London *season*); that part of the year when a particular trade, profession, or business is in its greatest activity (the theatrical *season*); that which gives a relish to food‡; seasoning‡.—*v.t.* To render suitable; to fit; to fit for any use by time or habit; to accustom; to inure; to acclimatize; to bring to the best state for use by any process (to *season* timber by drying or hardening); to render palatable; to flavour; to give a relish or zest to; to temper; to qualify by admixture.—*v.i.* To become suitable by time; to grow fit for use.—**Seasonable**, sē'zn-a-bl, *a.* Suitable as to time or season; opportune; happening or being done in due season.—**Seasonableness**, sē'zn-a-bl-nes, *n.* The state or quality of being seasonable.—**Seasonably**, sē'zn-a-bli, *adv.* In due time; sufficiently early.—**Seasonal**, sē'zn-al, *a.* Pertaining to the seasons. — **Seasoner**, sē'zn-ėr, *n.* One who or that which seasons.—**Seasoning**, sē'zn-ing, *n.* That which is added to any species of food to give it a higher relish; something added to enhance enjoyment.—**Seasonless**, sē'zn-les, *a.* Without succession of seasons. — **Season-ticket**, *n.* A ticket which entitles its holder to certain privileges during a specified period of time, as a pass for travelling by railway, &c., issued at a cheap rate.

Seat, sēt, *n.* [Same as Icel. *sæti, set*, Sw. *säte*, a seat, from root of *sit*; so L.G. *sitt*, G. *sitz*. SIT.] The place or thing on which one sits; something made to be sat in or on, as a chair, throne, bench, stool, or the like; a regular place of sitting; hence, a right to sit; a sitting (a *seat* in a church); place of abode; residence; a mansion in the country; the place where anything is situated, fixed, settled, or established; station; abode (a *seat* of learning, the *seat* of war).—*v.t.* To place on a seat; to cause to sit down; to place in a post of authority or a place of distinction; to settle; to fix in a particular place or country; to situate; to locate; to fix; to set firm; to assign seats to; to accommodate with room to sit; to fit up with seats.

Sebaceous, sē-bā'shus, *a.* [L.L. *sebaceus*, from L. *sebum*, tallow.] Pertaining to tallow or fat; made of, containing, or secreting fatty matter; fatty; *bot.* having the appearance of grease or wax.—**Sebacic**, sē-bas'ik, *a.* *Chem.* pertaining to fat; obtained from fat (*sebacic* acid).—**Sebate**, sē'bāt, *n.* *Chem.* a salt formed by sebacic acid and a base.—**Sebiferous**, sē'bif'ėr-us, *a.* [L. *sebum*, and *fero*, to produce.] Producing fat or fatty matter.

Seborrhœa, sē-bō-rē'a, *n.* [L. *sebum*, tallow, Gr. *rheō*, to flow.] Excess of the fatty secretion of the skin.

Secant, sē'kant, *a.* [L. *secans, secantis*, ppr. of *seco*, to cut. SECTION.] Cutting; dividing into two parts.—*Secant plane*, a plane cutting a surface or solid.—*n.* *Geom.* a line that cuts another or divides it into parts; more especially, a straight line cutting a curve in two or more points; a straight line from the centre of a circle cutting the circumference and proceeding till it meets a tangent to the same circle.

Secco, sek'kō, *n.* [It., from L. *siccus*, dry.] A kind of fresco painting in which the colours have a dry appearance, owing to their being absorbed into the plaster.

Seccotine, sek'o-tēn, *n.* [Origin uncertain, but probably from Fr. *sec*, because it dries quickly.] A substitute for glue.

Secede, sē-sēd', *v.i.*—*seceded, seceding.* [L. *secedo*—*se*, apart, and *cedo*, to go. CEDE.] To withdraw from fellowship or association; to separate one's self; especially, to withdraw from a political or religious organization.—**Seceder**, sē-sē'dėr, *n.* One who secedes; one of those Presbyterians who seceded from the Established Church of Scotland in 1733; any Scotch Presbyterian outside the Scottish Church.—**Secession**, sē-sesh'on, *n.* [L. *secessio.*] The act of seceding; the act of withdrawing from a political or religious organization; the body of seceders from the Established Church of Scotland.—**Secessionism**, sē-sesh'on-izm, *n.* The principles of secessionists.—**Secessionist**, sē-sesh'on-ist, *n.* One who advocates or engages in a secession; one who supported the secession of the Southern States of America in their struggle to break away from the Northern States.

Secern, sē-sėrn', *v.t.* [L. *secerno, secretum* (whence *secret*)—*se*, apart, and *cerno*, to separate.] To separate; to distinguish; to secrete.—**Secernent**, sē-sėr'nent, *n.* That which promotes secretion; *anat.* a secreting vessel.—*a.* Having the power of secreting; secretory. — **Secernment**, sē-sėrn'ment, *n.* The process of secreting.

Secession. Under SECEDE.

Seclude, sē-klöd', *v.t.*—*secluded, secluding.* [L. *secludo*—*se*, apart, and *claudo*, to shut. CLAUSE, CLOSE.] To shut up apart from company or society, and usually to keep apart for some time; *refl.* to withdraw into solitude.—**Secluded**, sē-klö'ded, *p.* and *a.* Separated from others; living in retirement; unfrequented; retired.—**Secludedly**, sē-klö'ded-li, *adv.* In a secluded manner.—**Seclusion**, sē-klö'zhon, *n.* The act of secluding; the state of being secluded; retirement; privacy; solitude.—**Seclusive**, sē-klö'siv, *a.* Tending to seclude.

Secohm, sek'om, *n.* A former unit of electrical self-induction, now replaced by the *henry.*

Second, sek'und, *a.* [Fr. *second*, from L. *secundus*, second, from *sequor, secutus*, to follow. SEQUENCE.] Immediately following the first; next the first in order of place or time; repeated again; other; next to the first in value, power, excellence, or rank; inferior; secondary.—*n.* One next to the first; one who assists and supports another; one who attends another (his *principal*) in a duel and sees that his friend gets fair play; the sixtieth part of a minute of time or of that of a degree, that is, the second division next to the hour or degree; *music*, the difference between any sound and the next nearest sound above or below it, also a lower part added to a melody when arranged for two voices or instruments; *pl.* a coarse kind of flour.—*v.t.* To follow in the next place to; to follow up and support; to lend aid to; to assist; to promote; to encourage; to back; to support by one's voice or vote, as a motion or proposal brought forward in an assembly; to unite with in proposing some measure or motion.—**Secondarily**, sek'-un-da-ri-li, *adv.* In a secondary manner; secondly; in the second place.—**Secondariness**, sek'un-da-ri-nes, *n.* The state of being secondary.—**Secondary**, sek'un-da-ri, *a.* [L. *secondarius.*] Of second place, origin, rank, or importance; not primary; subordinate. — *Secondary circle*, in *geom.* and *astron.* a great circle passing through the poles of another great circle perpendicular to its plane. — *Secondary colours*, colours produced by the mixture of any two primary colours in equal proportions. — *Secondary fever*, a fever which arises after the crisis of some disease.—*Secondary planet*, a moon or satellite. — *Secondary strata, Secondary rocks, Secondary formation, geol.* the mesozoic strata.—*Secondary tints, painting*, those of a subdued kind, such as grays, &c.—*n.* One who acts in subordination to another; a term for the feathers growing on the second bone of a bird's wing; a secondary circle; a secondary planet.—**Second-best**, *a.* Next to the best; of second kind or quality.—*To come off second-best*, to be defeated; to get the worst of it.—**Second-cousin**, *n.* The son or daughter of a cousin-german. — **Seconder**, sek'un-dėr, *n.* One that seconds; one that supports what another attempts, or what he affirms, or what he moves or proposes. — **Second-flour**, *n.* Flour of a coarser quality; seconds. — **Second-hand**, *n.* Possession received from the first possessor or by transfer from a previous owner. — *At second hand*, not from the first source or owner; by transmission (a report received *at second hand*). —*a.* Not original or primary; received from another; not new; having been used or worn; dealing in second-hand goods (a *second-hand* bookseller).—**Secondly**, sek'-und-li, *adv.* In the second place.—**Second-rate**, *n.* The second order in size, quality, dignity, or value.—*a.* Of the second size, rank, quality, or value.—**Seconds-hand**, *n.* The hand of a watch that indicates seconds.—**Second-sight**, *n.* The power of seeing things future or distant; prophetic vision.

Secrecy. Under SECRET.

Secret, sē'kret, *a.* [Fr. *secret*, from L. *secretus*, pp. of *secerno*, *secretum*, to set apart —*se*, apart, and *cerno*, to sift, distinguish. CONCERN, DISCERN.] Apart from the knowledge of others; private; known only to one or to few; kept from general knowledge; not made public; affording privacy; retired; secluded (a *secret* spot); secretive; not inclined to betray confidence; occult; mysterious; not apparent; privy; not proper to be seen.—*n.* Something studiously concealed; a thing kept from general knowledge; what is not or should not be revealed; a thing not discovered or explained; a mystery.—*In secret*, in privacy or secrecy; privately.—**Secrecy**, sē'kre-si, *n.* A state of being secret or hidden; concealment from the observation of others; secret mode of proceeding; retirement; privacy; the quality of being secret; fidelity to a secret; the act or habit of keeping secrets.—**Secretary**, sek'rē-ta-ri, *n.* [L.L. *secretarius*, from L. *secretus*, secret; originally a confidant, one intrusted with secrets.] A person employed to write letters, draw up reports, records, and the like; one who carries on another's business correspondence or other matters requiring writing; a piece of furniture with conveniences for writing and for the arrangement of papers; an escritoire; an officer whose business is to superintend and manage the affairs of a particular department of government; a secretary of state.—**Secretary-bird**, *n.* An African bird of prey which renders valuable services by killing and eating serpents and other reptiles, so called from its long occipital plumes suggesting a secretary's quill behind his ear. —**Secretarial**, sek-rē-tā'ri-al, *a.* Pertaining to a secretary.—**Secretariate**, sek-rē-tā'ri-āt, *n.* The office of a secretary; the place where a secretary transacts business. — **Secretaryship**, sek'rē-ta-ri-ship, *n.* The office or post of a secretary.—**Secrete**, sē-krēt', *v.t.*—*secreted, secreting.* [L. *secerno*, *secretum*, to set apart.] To hide; to deposit in some secret place; *physiol.* to separate from the circulating fluid, as from the blood, sap, &c., and elaborate into a new product. —**Secretin**, se-krēt'in, *n.* [From *secretion.*] A HORMONE (which see) secreted by the lining of the small intestine which stimulates the activity of the pancreas.—**Secretion**, sē-krē'shon, *n.* The act or process of secreting; the physiological process by which there are separated from the blood substances differing from the blood itself or from any of its constituents, as bile, saliva, mucus, urine, &c.; the process by which substances are separated from the sap of vegetables; the matter so secreted. — **Secretitious**, sē-krē-tish'us, *a.* Separated by secretion. — **Secretive**, sē-krē'tiv, *a.* Causing or promoting secretion; given to secrecy or to keep secrets.—**Secretiveness**, sē-krē'tiv-nes, *n.* — **Secretly**, sē'kret-li, *adv.* In a secret manner.—**Secret Service**, *n.* In the U. S., a division in the Treasury Department, for the purpose of detecting persons engaged in violating the laws of the U. S. relating to the Treasury Department, especially counterfeiting; and for protecting the person of the president of the U. S.

Sect, sekt, *n.* [Fr. *secte*, from L. *secta*, from *seco*, *sectum*, to cut; or from *sequor*, *secutus*, to follow.] A body or number of persons who follow some teacher or leader, or are united in some settled tenets, chiefly in philosophy or religion; a school; a denomination.—**Sectarian**, sek-tā'ri-an, *a.* Pertaining to a sect or sects; strongly or bigotedly attached to a sect or religious denomination.—*n.* One of a sect; a strict member or adherent of a special denomination or party.—**Sectarianism**, sek-tā'-ri-an-izm, *n.* The principles of sectarians; a narrow-minded devotion to the interests of a party.—**Sectarianize**, sek-tā'ri-an-īz, *v.t.* To imbue with sectarian principles or feelings.—**Sectary**, sek'ta-ri, *n.* One that belongs to a sect; a schismatic; a sectarian.

Sectile, sek'til, *a.* [L. *sectilis*, from *seco*, *sectum*, to cut (seen in *bisect*, *dissect*, *intersect*, &c.); same root as *scythe*, *saw.*] Capable of being cut, as with a knife.—**Section**, sek'shon, *n.* [L. *sectio*, from *seco*, *sectum*, to cut.] The act of cutting; separation by cutting; a part cut or separated from the rest; a division; a portion; a distinct part or portion of a book or writing; the subdivision of a chapter; a paragraph; hence, the character §, often used to denote such a division; a distinct part of a country or people, community, class, &c.; a representation of a building or other object as it would appear if cut through by any intersecting plane, showing the internal structure; a small division of some military body, more especially the fourth part of a platoon, consisting of about ten men, commanded by a non-commissioned officer, and forming the normal fire-unit; there are sixteen sections in a company. A *cavalry section* consists of from four to eight men. An *artillery section* comprises two guns, with the necessary men, horses, ammunition wagons.—*Conic sections.* Under CONE. —**Sectional**, sek'shon-al, *a.* Pertaining to a section; composed of or made up in several independent sections. — **Sectionally**, sek'shon-al-li, *adv.* In a sectional manner. — **Sectionize**,† sek'shon-īz, *v.t.* To form into sections.—**Sective**, sek'tiv, *a.* SECTILE.—**Sector**, sek'tor, *n.* [L., a cutter.] *Geom.* a nearly triangular figure formed by two radii and the arc of a circle; a mathematical instrument so marked with lines of sines, tangents, chords, &c., as to fit all radii and scales, and useful in making diagrams, laying down plans, &c.; *milit.* an area of varying extent in war, over which operations are conducted.—*Dip sector*, an instrument used for measuring the dip of the horizon. — *Zenith sector.* ZENITH.—**Sectoral**, sek'tō-ral, *a.* Belonging to a sector.—**Sectorial**, sek-tō'ri-al, *a.* Adapted or intended for cutting, as the cutting teeth of certain animals.

Secular, sek'ū-lėr, *a.* [L. *sæcularis*, from *sæculum*, an age or generation, a century, the times, the world.] Coming or observed at long intervals; extending over, taking place in, or accomplished during a very long period of time (the *secular* refrigeration of the earth); pertaining to this present world or to things not spiritual or sacred; disassociated with religious teaching or principles; not devoted to sacred or religious use; temporal; profane; worldly (*secular* education, *secular* music); not bound by monastic vows or rules (a *secular* priest as opposed to a *regular*). — *n.* An ecclesiastic not bound by monastic rules; a secular priest. — **Secularism**, sek'ū-lėr-izm, *n.* Supreme or exclusive attention to the affairs of this life; the opinions or doctrines of the secularists. — **Secularist**, sek'ū-lėr-ist, *n.* One who theoretically rejects every form of religious faith and every kind of religious worship; also, one who believes that education and other matters should be conducted without the introduction of a religious element.—**Secularization**, sek'ū-lėr-ī-zā"shon, *n.* The act of secularizing or the state of being secularized.—**Secularize**, sek'ū-lėr-īz, *v.t.*—*secularized, secularizing.* To make secular; to convert from religious or ecclesiastical to secular or common use.—**Secularly**, sek'-ū-lėr-li, *adv.* In a secular or worldly manner. — **Secularness, Secularity**, sek'-ū-lėr-nes, sek-ū-lar'i-ti, *n.* The state or quality of being secular.

Secund, sē'kund, *a.* [L. *secundus*, second. SECOND.] *Bot.* applied to leaves or flowers which grow on one side of the stem; unilateral.—**Secundine**, sē'kun-dīn, *n.* *Bot.* the outermost but one of the inclosing sacs of the ovulum; *zool.* all that remains in the womb after the birth of the offspring; the after-birth: generally in the plural.

Secure, sē-kūr', *a.* [L. *securus*, without care, unconcerned, free from danger, safe —*se*, apart, and *cura*, care, cure. *Sure* is this word in a more modified form.] Free from fear or apprehension; confident of safety; careless; unsuspecting; free from or not exposed to danger; in a state of safety; safe: often followed by *against* or *from*; such as to be depended on; capable of resisting assault or attack; stable; certain, sure, or confident: with *of*; in safe custody.—*v.t.*—*secured, securing.* To make secure; to guard effectually from danger; to protect; to make certain; to put beyond hazard; to assure; to inclose or confine effectually; to guard effectually from escape; to seize and confine (to *secure* a prisoner); to make certain of payment; to warrant against loss; to make fast or firm (to *secure* a door); to get possession of; to make one's self master of (to *secure* an estate).—**Securable**, sē-kū'ra-bl, *a.* Capable of being secured.—**Securely**, sē-kūr'li, *adv.* In a secure manner; in security; safely.—**Secureness**, sē-kūr'nes, *n.* The feeling of security; the state of being secure; safety; security.—**Securer**, sē-kū'rėr, *n.* One who or that which secures.—**Security**, sē-kū'-ri-ti, *n.* [Fr. *sécurité*, L. *securitas.*] The state of being secure; freedom from apprehension; confidence of safety; sometimes, over-confidence; freedom from danger or risk; safety; that which secures or makes safe; something that secures against pecuniary loss; surety; a person who engages himself for the performance of another's obligations; an evidence of property, as a bond, a certificate of stock, or the like (government *securities*).

Securiform, sē-kū'ri-form, *a.* [L. *securis*, an axe or hatchet, and *forma*, form.] Having the form of an axe or hatchet.

Sedan, se-dan', *n.* Formerly, a covered chair or ornamental box for carrying one person, borne on poles by two men; a sedan chair; now, a type of automobile that holds from five to seven persons.

Sedate, sē-dāt', *a.* [L. *sedatus*, from *sedo*,

to calm or appease, to cause to subside, caus. of *sedeo*, to sit (seen also in *sedentary, sediment, session, preside, reside, supersede, assiduous*, &c.); same root as *sit*. SIT.] Calm or tranquil in feelings and manner; serene; unruffled by passion; staid; unmoved.—**Sedately**, sē-dāt'li, *adv.* In a sedate manner; calmly. — **Sedateness**, sē-dāt'nes, *n.* The state or quality of being sedate; composure of mind or manner; serenity; tranquillity.—**Sedative**, sed'a-tiv, *a.* Tending to calm or tranquillize; *med.* allaying irritability and irritation; assuaging pain. — *n.* A medicine which allays irritability and irritation, and which assuages pain.

Sedentary, sed'en-ta-ri, *a.* [L. *sedentarius*, from *sedens, sedentis*, ppr. of *sedeo*, to sit. SEDATE.] Accustomed to sit much; requiring much sitting (a *sedentary* occupation); passed for the most part in sitting.—**Sedentarily**, sed'en-ta-ri-li, *adv.* In a sedentary manner.—**Sedentariness**, sed'en-ta-ri-nes, *n.* The state of being sedentary.

Sederunt, se-dē'runt, *n.* [Third pers. pl. perf. indic. of *sedeo* to sit; lit. they sat.] A sitting or meeting of a court or other body of men; a more or less formal meeting of any association or company.

Sedge, sej, *n.* [A.Sax. *secg* = Sc. *segg*, L.G. *segge*, a reed, sedge; same root as in L. *seco*, to cut, being a plant with sword-like leaves.] The popular name of an extensive genus of grass-like plants growing mostly in marshes and swamps, and on the banks of rivers, distinguished from the grasses by having the stem destitute of joints.—**Sedge-bird, Sedge-warbler**, *n.* A species of warbler, a European bird that winters in Africa and frequents the sedgy banks of streams of Europe and Asia in summer.

Sedilia, se-dil'i-a, *n.pl.* [L. *sedile*, a seat.] *Arch.* stone seats in the south wall of the chancel of many churches and cathedrals.

Sediment, sed'i-ment, *n.* [L. *sedimentum*, from *sedeo*, to settle. SEDATE.] The matter which subsides to the bottom of water or any other liquid; settlings; lees; dregs. —**Sedimentary**, sed-i-men'ta-ri, *a.* Consisting of sediment; formed by sediment or matter that has subsided.—*Sedimentary rocks*, rocks which have been formed by materials deposited by water, and as a rule are stratified. — **Sedimentation**, sed'i-men-tā"shon, *n.* The disposition or accumulation of sediment.

Sedition, sē-dish'on, *n.* [L. *seditio, seditionis*, discord, sedition—*sed*, apart, and *itio, itionis*, a going, from *eo, itum*, to go. ITINERANT.] A factious commotion in a state, not amounting to an insurrection; the stirring up of such a commotion; such offences against the state as have the like tendency with, but do not amount to treason.—**Seditionary**, sē-dish'on-a-ri, *n.* An inciter or promoter of sedition. — **Seditious**, sē-dish'us, *a.* [L. *seditiosus.*] Pertaining to sedition; exciting or aiding in sedition; guilty of sedition.—**Seditiously**, sē-dish'us-li, *adv.* In a seditious manner.—**Seditiousness**, sē-dish'us-nes, *n.* The state or quality of being seditious.

Seduce, sē-dūs', *v.t.* — *seduced, seducing.* [L. *seduco*—*se*, apart, and *duco*, to lead. DUKE.] To draw aside or entice from the path of rectitude and duty; to lead astray; to corrupt; specifically, to entice to a surrender of chastity. — **Seducement**, sē-dūs'ment, *n.* The act of seducing; seduction; the means employed to seduce. — **Seducer**, sē-dū'sėr, *n.* One that seduces; one who by deception or the like persuades a female to surrender her chastity.—**Seducible**, sē-dū'si-bl, *a.* Capable of being seduced. — **Seducingly**, sē-dū'sing-li, *adv.* In a seducing manner.—**Seduction**, sē-duk'shon, *n.* [L. *seductio, seductionis.*] The act of seducing; the act or crime of persuading a female, by flattery or deception, to surrender her chastity. — **Seductive, Seducive**,† sē-duk'tiv, sē-dū'siv, *a.* Tending to seduce; apt to mislead by flattering appearances; alluring; enticing.—**Seductively**, sē-duk'tiv-li, *adv.* In a seductive manner.

Sedulous, sed'ū-lus, *a.* [L. *sedulus*, from *sedeo*, to sit; as *assiduous*, from *assideo*. SEDATE.] Assiduous; diligent in application; steady and persevering in endeavours to effect an object; steadily industrious.—**Sedulously**, sed'ū-lus-li, *adv.* In a sedulous manner; assiduously.—**Sedulousness, Sedulity**, sed'ū-lus-nes, se-dū'li-ti, *n.* The state or quality of being sedulous; assiduity.

See, sē, *v.t.*—pret. *saw*, pp. *seen*, ppr. *seeing.* [A.Sax. *seón*, to see=Icel. *sjá*, Dan. *see*, D. *zien*, Goth. *saihwan*, G. *sehen*—to see; same root as L. *sequor*, to follow.] To perceive by the eye; to behold; to perceive mentally; to form a conception or idea of; to understand; to comprehend; to give attention to; to examine; to attend or escort (to *see* a lady home); to have communication with; to meet or associate with; to visit (to go to *see* a friend); to experience; to know by personal experience (to *see* death). ∴ Simply to *see* is often an involuntary, and always a mechanical act; to *perceive* implies generally or always the intelligence of a prepared mind; to *observe* implies to look for the purpose of noticing. — *v.i.* To have the power or sense of sight; to perceive mentally; to discern; to understand; often with *through* or *into*; to examine or inquire; to consider; to be attentive; to take heed; to take care.—*To see to*, to be attentive to; to look after; to take care of.—*To see about a thing*, to pay some attention to it; to consider it.—*See to it*, look well to it; attend; consider; take care.—*Let me see, let us see*, phrases used to introduce the particular consideration of a subject. — *interj.* Lo! look! observe! behold!—**Seeing**, sē'ing, *conj.* Because; inasmuch as; since; considering; taking into account that.—**Seer**, sē'ėr or sēr, *n.* One who sees; one who foresees future events; a prophet.—**Seership**, sē'ėr-ship or sēr'ship, *n.* The office or quality of a seer.

See, sē, *n.* [From O.Fr. *se, sed*, from L. *sedes*, a seat, from stem of *sedeo*, to sit. SEDATE.] The seat of the power of a bishop; the diocese or jurisdiction of a bishop, archbishop, or, in Rome, of the pope.

Seed, sēd, *n.* [A.Sax. *saed*, from *sáwan*, to sow; Icel. *sæthi*, Dan. *sæd*, D. *zaat*, G. *saat*. SOW.] The impregnated and matured ovule of a plant, containing an embryo, which may be developed, and converted into an individual similar to that from which it derives its origin; one of the grains or fruits of wheat and many other plants, though sometimes the seed is contained in the fruit; the fecundating fluid of male animals; the semen; that from which anything springs; first principle; progeny; offspring; children; descendants.—*To run to seed.* Under RUN.—*v.i.* To produce seed; to shed the seed.—*v.t.* To sow; to supply with seed; to ornament with seed-like decorations. — **Seed-bed**, *n.* A piece of ground prepared for receiving seed.—**Seed-cake**, *n.* A sweet cake containing aromatic seeds. — **Seed-corn**, *n.* Corn or grain for seed.—**Seed-crusher**, *n.* An instrument for crushing seed and expressing oil.—**Seeded**, sē'ded, *p.* and *a.* Bearing seed; sown; sprinkled with seed.—**Seed-field**, *n.* A field for raising seed.—**Seediness**, sē'di-nes, *n.* State of being seedy; shabbiness. — **Seed-leaf**, *n.* *Bot.* the primary leaf developed from a cotyledon.—**Seedling**, sēd'ling, *n.* A plant reared from the seed, and not from a layer, bud, &c.—*a.* Produced from the seed (a *seedling* pansy).—**Seed-lobe**, *n.* *Bot.* a seed-leaf; a cotyledon.—**Seed-oil**, *n.* Oil expressed from seeds. —**Seed-pearl**, *n.* A small pearl resembling a grain or seed in size or form.—**Seedsman**, sēdz'man, *n.* A person who deals in seeds; one who scatters seed (*Shak.*).—**Seed-time**, *n.* The season proper for sowing.—**Seed-vessel**, *n.* *Bot.* the pericarp which contains the seeds.—**Seedy**, sē'di, *a.* Abounding with seeds; running to seed; worn-out; shabby; poor and miserable-looking; feeling or appearing wretched, as after a debauch (*colloq.*).

Seeing, *conj.* Under SEE.

Seek, sēk, *v.t.*—pret. and pp. *sought* (O.E. *seke*, A.Sax. *sécan*, to seek, pret. *sóhte*, pp. *sóht*; Icel. *sækja*, Dan. *søge*, Sw. *söka*, D. *zoeken*, G. *suchen*, Goth. *sokjan*; akin to *sake*. *Beseech* is from *seek*, with prefix *be-*.] To go in search or quest of; to look for; to search for; to take pains to find: often followed by *out*; to ask for; to solicit; to try to gain; to go to; to resort to; to have recourse to; to aim at; to attempt; to strive after (to *seek* a person's life or his ruin); to search.—*v.i.* To make search or inquiry; to endeavour; to make an effort or attempt; to try; to use solicitation.—*To seek after*, to make pursuit of; to attempt to find or take.—*To seek for*, to endeavour to find.—*To be to seek*, to require to be sought for; to be wanting or desiderated (the work is still *to seek*).—**Seeker**, sēk'ėr, *n.* One that seeks; an inquirer.

Seel, sēl, *v.t.* [Fr. *ciller, siller*, from *cil*, L. *cilium*, an eyelash.] To close the eyes of a hawk with a thread: a term of falconry; to blind; to hoodwink (*Shak.*).

Seem, sēm, *v.i.* [A.Sax. *séman*, to conciliate, to adjust, to seem, from root of *same*.] To appear; to present the appearance of being; to be only in appearance and not really; to show one's self or itself; hence, to assume an air; to pretend; to appear to one's opinion or judgment; to be thought; to appear to one's self; to imagine; to feel as if (I still *seem* to hear his voice).—*It seems*, it would appear; it appears.—*It seems to me*=I think; I am inclined to believe. ∴ Formerly *seem* was often used impersonally in such phrases as *me seems, him seemed*; hence *meseems* as a single word.—**Seemer**, sēm'ėr, *n.* One who seems; one who carries an appearance or semblance.—**Seeming**, sēm'ing, *p.* and *a.* Appearing; having the appearance or semblance, whether real or not; specious or plausible in appearance.—*n.* Appearance; show; semblance, especially a false appearance.—**Seemingly**, sēm'ing-li, *adv.* As it would seem; apparently; ostensibly; in appearance.—**Seemliness**, sēm'li-nes, *n.* The state or quality of being seemly.—**Seemly**, sēm'li, *a.* [Same as Icel. *sæmiligr*, from *sæmr*, fit, seemly.] Becoming; fitting.—*adv.* Becomingly.

Seen, sēn, pp. of *see*.

Seep, sēp, *v.i.* [A.Sax. *sipian*, to absorb; akin *sip*.] To percolate; to ooze.—**Seepage**, *n.* The act of seeping; also, the fluid that has seeped through.

Seer, under SEE.

See-saw, sē'sa̤, *n.* [A reduplicated form of *saw*, the motion resembling the act of sawing.] A game in which two children, one on each end of a long piece of timber balanced on a support, move alternately up and down; a motion or action resembling that in see-saw.—*a.* Moving up and down or to and fro.—*v.i.* and *t.* To move up and down, or back and forth.

Seethe, sēTH, *v.t.*—pret. *seethed*, pp. *seethed* or *sodden*, ppr. *seething.* [A.Sax. *seóthan*, to seethe; Icel. *sjótha*, G. *sieden*, to boil.] To boil; to prepare for food in boiling liquor; to soak; to steep and soften in liquor.—*v.i.* To be in a state of ebullition; to boil; to be hot.—**Seether**, sē'THėr, *n.* One who or that which seethes; a pot for boiling things.

Seggar, seg'är, *n.* [Prov.E. *saggard, saggar*, contr, for *safeguard.*] The case of fire clay in which fine stoneware is inclosed while being baked in the kiln. Also SAGGER.

Segment, seg'ment, *n.* [L. *segmentum*, from *seco*, to cut. SECTILE.] A part cut off or marked as separate from others; one of the parts into which a body naturally divides itself; a section; *geom.* a part cut off from any figure by a line or plane; the *segment of a circle*, being the part contained by an arc and its chord.—*v.i.* (seg-ment'). To divide or become divided up into segments.—**Segmental**, seg-men'tal, *a.* Pertaining to, consisting of, or like a segment. —**Segmentation**, seg-men-tā'shon, *n.* A division into segments; in animals (1), the division of the adult body into successive segments (rings, somites, and metameres), e.g. in crustacea. (2) See CLEAVAGE (3).—**Segment-saw**, *n.* A veneer saw whose active perimeter consists of segments attached to a disc; *surg.* a nearly circular saw used in operations on the bones of the cranium, &c.—**Segment-wheel**, *n.* A wheel a part of whose periphery only is utilized.

Segreant, *her.*, used in the place of *rampant* as applied to the griffin.

Segregate, seg'rē-gāt, *v.t.*—*segregated*, *segregating*. [L. *segrego*, *segregatum*—*se*, apart, and *grex*, *gregis*, a flock. GREGARIOUS.] To separate from others; to set apart.—*v.i.* To separate or go apart. — *a.* Separate; select.—**Segregation**, seg-rē-gā'shon, *n.* The act of segregating; separation from others; dispersion.

Seguidilla, seg-i-dēl'ya, *n.* A merry Spanish tune and dance.

Seidlitz-water, **Seidlitz**, sīd'lits, *n.* The aperient mineral water of *Seidlitz*, a village of Bohemia.—**Seidlitz-powder**, *n.* An aperient medicine composed of Rochelle-salt, bicarbonate of soda, and tartaric acid, taken while effervescing in water.

Seignior, **Seigneur**, sēn'yėr, *n.* [Fr. *seigneur*, It. *signore*, Sp. *señor*, Pg. *senhor*, titles or words of respectful address, equivalent to Sir, Mr., gentleman; from L. *senior*, elder.] *Feudal law*, the lord of a fee or manor. — *Grand Seignior*, a title sometimes given to the Sultan of Turkey.—**Seigneurial**, **Seigniorial**, sen-yō'ri-al, sēn-yō'ri-al, *a.* Pertaining to the lord of a manor; manorial. — **Seigniorage**, **Seignorage**, sēn'yėr-āj,*n.* Something claimed by the sovereign or by a superior as a prerogative; the profit derived from issuing coins at a rate above their intrinsic value, or by giving back rather less in coin than is received in bullion; a royalty or share of profit; the money received by an author from his publisher for copyright of his works.—**Seigniory**, **Seignory**, sēn-yėr-i, *n.* A lordship; power or authority as sovereign lord.

Seine, **Sein**, sēn, *n.* [Fr. *seine*, from L. *sagena*, Gr. *sagēnē*, a seine.] A large net for catching fish.—**Seine-boat**, *n.* A fishing-boat of about 15 tons, used on the west coast of England to carry the large seine.—**Seine-fisher**, **Seiner**, sēn'ėr, *n.* A fisher with a seine or net.

Seise, sēz, *v.t.* *Law*, see SEIZE.—**Seisin**, sē'zin, *n.* SEIZIN.

Seismic, **Seismal**, sīs'mik, sīs'mal, *a.* [Gr. *seismos*, an earthquake, from *seiō*, to shake.] Pertaining to earthquakes.—**Seismograph**, sīs'mō-graf, *n.* An electromagnetic instrument for registering the shocks and concussions of earthquakes.—**Seismographic**, sīs-mō-graf'ik, *a.* Pertaining to seismography or the seismograph. — **Seismography**, sīs-mog'ra-fi, *n.* A description or account of earthquakes.—**Seismologic**, sīs-mō-loj'ik, *a.* Pertaining to seismology.—**Seismologist**, **Seismologue**, sīs-mol'o-jist, sīs'mō-log, *n.* A student of, or one versed in seismology.—**Seismology**, sīs-mol'o-ji, *n.* The science of earthquakes; that department of science which treats of volcanoes and earthquakes. — **Seismometer**, **Seismoscope**, sīs-mom'et-ėr, sīs'mō-skōp, *n.* An instrument for measuring the direction and force of earthquakes and similar concussions. — **Seismometry**, sīs-mom'et-ri, *n.* The measurement of the force and direction of earthquakes, &c.; the art or practice of using the seismometer.

Seize, sēz, *v.t.*—*seized*, *seizing*. [Fr. *saisir*, to seize, from O.H.G. *sezzan*, *sazjan*, Goth. *satjan*, to set. SET.] To suddenly lay hold of; to gripe or grasp suddenly; to take possession by force, or by virtue of legal authority; to have a sudden and powerful effect on; to attack (a fever *seizes* a patient); to lay hold of by the mind; to comprehend; *naut.* to fasten two ropes, or different parts of one rope, together with a cord; *law*, to make possessed; to put in possession of: with *of* before the thing possessed. —*v.i.* With *on* or *upon*, to fall on and grasp; to take hold of; to take possession of.—**Seizable**, sē'za-bl, *a.* Capable of being seized; liable to be taken.—**Seizer**, sē'zėr, *n.* One who or that which seizes.—**Seizin**, sē'zin, *n.* [Fr. *saisine*, seizin, from *saisir*, to seize.] *Law*, possession; the act of taking possession; the thing possessed.—**Seizing**, sē'zing, *n.* *Naut.* the cord or cords used for fastening ropes together.—**Seizor**, sē'zor, *n.* *Law*, one who seizes or takes possession.—**Seizure**, sē'zūr, *n.* The act of seizing or taking sudden hold; a taking into possession; the thing seized or taken possession of; a sudden attack of some disease.

Sejant, **Sejeant**, sē'jant, *a.* [O.Fr., from L. *sedere*, to sit.] Sitting, a heraldic term applied to an animal in the position of a sitting cat. When the fore paws are raised off the ground, the term is *sejant erect*.

Sejoin, sē-join', *v.t.* [Prefix *se*, apart, and *join*.] To separate.

Selachian, sē-lā'ki-an, *n.* [Gr. *selachos*, a shark.] Any fish of the shark or dog-fish family.

Selah, sē'la, *n.* [Heb.] A note in the text of the Psalms, supposed to indicate a musical direction.

Seldom, sel'dom, *adv.* [A.Sax. *seldan*, *seldum* = Icel. *sjaldan*, Dan. *sielden*, D. *zelden*, G. *selten*; from A.Sax. *seld*, Goth. *sild*, rare.] Rarely; not often; not frequently.—*a.* Rare; unfrequent.—**Seldomness**, sel'dom-nes, *n.* Rareness; infrequency.

Select, sē-lekt', *v.t.* [L. *seligo*, *selectum*—*se*, from, and *lego*, to pick, cull, or gather. LEGEND.] To choose and take from a number; to take by preference from among others; to pick out; to cull. — *a.* Taken from a number by preference; picked out by reason of excellence; choice; picked.—**Selection**, sē-lek'shon, *n.* [L. *selectio*, *selectionis*.] The act of selecting; a taking by preference from a number; a thing or things selected from others. — *Natural selection*, that process in nature by which plants and animals best fitted for the conditions in which they are placed survive, propagate, and spread, while the less fitted die out and disappear; survival of the fittest.—**Selective**, sē-lek'tiv, *a.* Selecting; tending to select.—**Selectness**, sē-lekt'nes, *n.* The state or quality of being select.—**Selector**, sē-lek'tėr, *n.* One that selects.

Selenium, se-lē'ni-um, *n.* [From Gr. *selēnē*, the moon; so named from its being associated with *tellurium*, from L. *tellus*, the earth.] A non-metallic element, in general chemical analogies related to sulphur and tellurium, often occurring in iron pyrites, and when precipitated forming a red powder.—**Selenate**, sel'en-āt, *n.* A compound of selenic acid with a base.—**Selenic**, **Selenious**, se-len'ik, se-lē'ni-us, *a.* Pertaining to or obtained from selenium. —**Selenide**, sel'en-īd, *n.* A compound of selenium with one other element or radical. —**Seleniferous**, sel-e-nif'ėr-us, *a.* Containing selenium; yielding selenium.—**Selenite**, sel'en-īt, *n.* Foliated or crystallized sulphate of lime.—**Selenitic**, sel-e-nit'ik, *a.* Pertaining to selenite.—**Seleniuretted**, se-lē'nū-ret-ed, *a.* Containing selenium; combined with selenium.

Selenography, sel-ē-nog'ra-fi, *n.* [Gr. *selēnē*, the moon, and *graphō*, to describe.] A description of the moon and its phenomena; the art of picturing the face of the moon.—**Selenograph**, se-lē'nō-graf, *n.* A picture of the surface of the moon or part of it. — **Selenographer**, **Selenographist**, sel-ē-nog'ra-fėr, sel-ē-nog'ra-fist, *n.* One versed in selenography.—**Selenographic**, **Selenographical**, se-lē'nō-graf"ik, se-lē'nō-graf"i-kal, *a.* Belonging to selenography. — **Selenology**, sel-ē-nol'o-ji, *n.* [Gr. *selēnē*, and *logos*, description.] That branch of astronomical science which treats of the moon.—**Selenological**, se-lē'nō-loj"i-kal, *a.* Pertaining to selenology.

Self, self; pl. **Selves**, selvz. [A.Sax. *self*, *selfa* = D. *zelf*, Dan. *selv*, Icel. *sjálfr*, G. *selb*, Goth. *silba*.] A word affixed to certain personal pronouns to express emphasis or distinction; also when the pronoun is used reflexively. Thus for emphasis, I *myself* will write; I will examine for *myself*; thou *thyself* shalt go; thou shalt see for *thyself*. Reflexively, I abhor *myself*; he loves *himself*; we value *ourselves*. Sometimes *self* is separated from *my*, *thy*, &c., as *my* wretched *self*; and this leads to the similar use of *self* as a noun.—*n.* The individual as an object to his own reflective consciousness; one's individual person; personal interest; one's own private interest (he is always for *self*); a flower or blossom of a uniform colour (with pl. **Selfs**).—*Self* is the first element in innumerable compounds, generally of obvious meaning.—*a.*‡ Same; very same: still used in this sense in the compound *self-same*.—**Self-abasement**, *n.* Degradation of one's self by one's own act.—**Self-acting**, *a.* Acting of itself; applied to automatic contrivances for the manipulation of machines.—**Self-adjusting**, *a.* Adjusting itself by special mechanism. — **Self-aggrandizement**, *n.* The aggrandizement or exaltation of one's self. —**Self-asserting**, **Self-assertive**, *a.* Forward in asserting one's self, or one's rights and claims.—**Self-assertion**, *n.* The act of asserting one's self or one's own rights or claims; a putting one's self forward in an assuming manner.—**Self-assumed**, *a.* Assumed by one's own act or by one's own authority.—**Self-assured**, *a.* Self-confident; feeling secure in one's self.—**Self-begotten**, *a.* Begotten by one's self or one's own powers.—**Self-blinded**, *a.* Blinded by one's own actions or qualities. —**Self-centered**, *a.* Devoted to self; egocentric; self-adoring.—**Self-closing**, *a.* Closing of itself; closing or shutting automatically.—**Self-colored**, *a.* All of one color, as a blossom or piece of cloth.—**Self-command**, *n.* Command of feelings; presence of mind; coolness.—**Self-complacency**, *n.* Satisfaction with one's self or one's own doings.—**Self-complacent**, *a.* Pleased with one's self or one's own doings; self-satisfied. — **Self-conceit**, *n.* A high opinion of one's self; vanity. ∴ Syn. under EGOTISM.—**Self-conceited**, *a.* Having self-conceit; vain; having an over-weening opinion of one's own merits.—**Self-conceitedness**, *n.* The quality of being self-conceited.—**Self-condemnation**, *n.* Condemnation by one's own conscience.—**Self-confidence**, *n.* The state or quality of being self-confident.—**Self-confident**, *a.* Confident of one's own strength or powers; relying on the correctness of one's own judgment, or the competence of one's own powers, without other aid.—**Self-conscious**, *a.* Conscious of one's states or acts as belonging to one's self; conscious of one's self as an object of observation to others; apt to think of how one's self appears. — **Self-consciousness**, *n.* State of being self-conscious.—**Self-contained**, *a.* Wrapped up in one's self; reserved; not communicative; relying on no outside aid or relations; sufficient within itself, as of a large estate, or as of a political state, sometimes called autarchy.—**Self-contempt**, *n.* Contempt for one's self.—**Self-contradictory**, *a.* Contradicting itself. — **Self-control**, *n.* Control exercised over one's self; self-restraint; self-command.—**Self-convicted**, *a.* Convicted by one's own consciousness, knowledge, or avowal.—**Self-culture**, *n.* Culture, training, or education of one's self without the aid of teachers. — **Self-deceived**, *a.* Deceived or misled respecting one's self by one's own mistake or error.—**Self-deceit**, **Self-deception**, *n.* Deception concerning one's self, proceeding from one's own mistake.—**Self-defence**, *n.* Defence of one's own person, property, or reputation.—**Self-delusion**, *n.* The delusion of one's self; a delusion respecting one's self.—**Self-denial**, *n.* The act of being self-denying. — **Self-denying**, *a.* Denying one's self; forbearing to indulge one's own appetites or desires.—**Self-destroyer**, *n.* One who destroys himself.—**Self-destruction**, *n.* The destruction of one's self.—**Self-destructive**, *a.* Tending to the destruction of one's self.—**Self-devotion**, *n.* Sacrifice of one's own interests or happiness for the sake of others; self-sacrifice.—**Self-distrust**, *n.* Distrust of one's self or one's own powers.—**Self-**

educated, *a.* Educated by one's own efforts or without the aid of teachers.—**Self-elective**, *a.* Having the right to elect one's self, or, as a body, of electing its own members.—**Self-esteem**, *n.* The esteem or good opinion of one's self.—**Self-evident**, *a.* Evident without proof or reasoning; producing certainty or clear conviction upon a bare presentation to the mind.—**Self-evidently**, *adv.* By means of self-evidence. — **Self-existence**, *n.* The quality of being self-existent.—**Self-existent**, *a.* Existing by one's or its own nature or essence, independent of any other cause.—**Self-explanatory**, *a.* Capable of explaining itself; bearing its meaning on its own face; obvious.—**Self-feeding**, *a.* Capable of feeding one's self or itself; keeping up automatically a supply of anything of which there is a constant consumption (a *self-feeding* boiler, furnace, printing-press, &c.).—**Self-fertilization**, *n. Bot.* the fertilization of a flower by pollen from the same flower.—**Self-fertilized**, *p.* and *a. Bot.* fertilized by its own pollen.—**Self-governed**, *a.* Governed by one's self or itself.—**Self-government**, *n.* The government of one's self; self-control; a system of government by which the mass of a nation or people appoint the rulers.—**Self-help**, *n.* Assistance of or by one's self; the use of one's own powers to attain one's ends. — **Self-importance**, *n.* High opinion of one's self; pride. —**Self-important**, *a.* Important in one's own esteem; pompous.—**Self-imposed**, *a.* Imposed or voluntarily taken on one's self (a *self-imposed* task). — **Self-induction**. The production in a circuit of an induced current by the variation (especially starting or stopping) of the current in the same circuit; the unit is the *henry*.—**Self-indulgence**, *n.* Free indulgence of one's passions or appetites.—**Self-indulgent**, *a.* Indulging one's self; gratifying one's own passions, desires, or the like. —**Self-inflicted**, *a.* Inflicted by or on one's self.—**Self-interest**, *n.* Interest or concern for one's self; one's own advantage. —**Self-interested**, *a.* Particularly concerned for one's self; selfish. — **Self-invited**, *a.* Come without being asked. — **Self-involved**, *a.* Wrapped up in one's self or in one's thoughts. —**Selfish**, self'ish, *a.* Caring only or chiefly for self; regarding one's own interest chiefly or solely; proceeding from love of self; influenced solely by private advantage. — **Selfishly**, self'ish-li, *adv.* In a selfish manner.—**Selfishness**, self'ish-nes, *n.* The quality of being selfish; devotion to one's own interests with carelessness of others. — **Self-knowledge**, *n.* The knowledge of one's own real character, abilities, worth, or demerit. **Self-love**, *n.* The love of one's own person or happiness; the natural feeling which impels every rational creature to preserve his life and promote his own happiness.—**Self-luminous**, *a.* Luminous of itself; possessing in itself the property of emitting light. — **Self-made**, *a.* Made by one's self; having risen in the world by one's own exertions (a *self-made* man).—**Self-murder**, *n.* The murder of one's self; suicide. —**Self-murderer**, *n.* A suicide.—**Self-opinion**, *n.* Exalted opinion of one's self; self-conceit.—**Self-opinioned**, *a.* Valuing one's own opinion highly.—**Self-pollination**, self-pol'lin-a"shon. [From *pollen*.] Pollination of a flower by its own pollen.—**Self-possessed**, *a.* Composed; not excited or flustered; cool; not disturbed. — **Self-possession**, *n.* The possession of one's powers; presence of mind; calmness; self-command. — **Self-praise**, *n.* The praise of one's self; self-applause.—**Self-preservation**, *n.* The preservation of one's self from destruction or injury. —**Self-registering**, *a.* Registering automatically; an epithet applied to any instrument so contrived as to record its own indications of phenomena (a *self-registering* barometer, thermometer, or the like. —**Self-regulated**, *a.* Regulated by one's self or itself.—**Self-regulative**, *a.* Tending or serving to regulate one's self or itself. —**Self-reliance**, *n.* Reliance on one's own powers.—**Self-reliant**, *a.* Relying on one's self; trusting to one's own powers. —**Self-relying**, *a.* Depending on one's self.—**Self-renunciation**, *n.* The act of renouncing one's own rights or claims; self-abnegation.—**Self-reproach**, *n.* The reproach or censure of one's own conscience. —**Self-respect**, *n.* Respect for one's self or one's own character.—**Self-restrained**, *a.* Restrained by itself or by one's own power of will.—**Self-restraint**, *n.* Restraint or control imposed on one's self; self-command; self-control.—**Self-righteous**, *a.* Righteous in one's own esteem; deeming one's self righteous above others.—**Self-righteousness**, *n.* Reliance on one's own supposed righteousness; false or pharisaical righteousness. — **Self-sacrifice**, *n.* Sacrifice of one's self or of self-interest.—**Self-sacrificing**, *a.* Yielding up one's own interest, feelings, &c.; sacrificing one's self. — **Self-same**, *a.* The very same; identical.—**Self-satisfied**, *a.* Satisfied with one's self.—**Self-seeker**, *n.* One who seeks only his own interest. — **Self-seeking**, *a.* Seeking one's own interest or happiness; selfish.—**Self-styled**, *a.* Called or styled by one's self; called by a title assumed without warrant. — **Self-sufficiency, Self-sufficience**, *n.* The state or quality of being self-sufficient.—**Self-sufficient**, *a.* Independent of the aid of others; having undue confidence in one's own strength, ability, or endowments; conceited; overbearing.—**Self-taught**, *a.* Taught by one's self; educated without a teacher (a *self-taught* genius).—**Self-will**, *n.* Determination to have one's own way: wilfulness; obstinacy. —**Self-willed**, *a.* Governed by one's own will; wilful; not accommodating or compliant; obstinate.

Sell,‡ sel, *n.* [Fr. *selle*, L. *sella*, a seat, a saddle.] A saddle.

Sell, sel, *v.t.*—pret. and pp. *sold.* [A.Sax. *sellan, syllan*, to give, to deliver up; L.G. *sellen*, Icel. *selja*, to sell, to deliver; Goth. *saljan*, to offer; akin *sale*.] To transfer to another for an equivalent; to give up for a consideration; to dispose of for something else, especially for money; correlative to *buy*; to make a matter of bargain and sale of; to take a bribe for; to betray.—*To sell one's life dearly*, to cause great loss to those who take one's life.—*To sell a person up*, to sell his goods to pay his creditors.—*v.i.* To practice selling; to be sold; to fetch a price. —*To sell out*, to dispose of one's property completely; *v.t.*—to fool a person, as by a trick or hoax. (*Slang.*)—*n.* A deception, a hoax. (*Colloq.*)—**Seller**, sel'ėr, *n.* One who sells; a vender.

Sellanders, Sellenders, sel'an-dėrz, sel'en-dėrz, *n.* [Fr. *solandres*.] A skin disease in a horse's hock or pastern owing to a want of cleanliness.

Seltzer water, selt'sėr, *n.* Originally, a mineral water imported from Germany; a manufactured effervescent water.

Selvas, Silvas, sel'vaz, sil'vaz, *n. pl.* [L. *silva*, a wood.] The great forest plains of the Amazon.

Selvedge, Selvage, sel'vej, sel'vāj, *n.* [From *self* and *edge*; lit. an edge formed of the stuff itself; comp. D. *zelfkant, zelfegge*, G. *selbende*, lit. self-edge, self-end.] A woven border, or border of close work, on a fabric made of the threads of the fabric; a list.

Semantics, se-man'tiks, *n.* The science of meanings; the study of changes in the meaning of words in the matter of specialization or generalization.

Semaphore, sem'a-fōr, *n.* [Gr. *sēma*, a sign, and *pherō*, to bear.] A kind of telegraph or apparatus for conveying information by signals visible at a distance.—**Semaphoric, Semaphorical**, sem-a-for'ik, sem-a-for'i-kal, *a.* Relating to semaphores; telegraphic.—**Semaphorically**, sem-a-for'i-kal-i, *adv.* By means of a semaphore.—**Semaphorist**, se-maf'or-ist, *n.* One who has charge of a semaphore.

Sematology, sē-ma-tol'o-ji, *n.* [Gr. *sēma*, *sēmatos*, a sign, and *logos*, discourse.] The doctrine of signs; the science of language as expressed by signs.

Semblance, sem'blans, *n.* [Fr. *semblance*, from *sembler*, to seem, to appear, from L. *similare, simulare*, to make like, from *similis*, like. SIMILAR.] Similarity; resemblance; external figure or appearance; form; a form or figure representing something; likeness; image.

Semée, the heraldic term for powdered or sown, when used in connection with fleurs-de-lis.

Semeiography, sē-mī-og'ra-fi, *n.* [Gr. *sēmeion*, a sign, and *graphō*, to write.] The doctrine of signs; *pathol.* a description of the marks or symptoms of diseases. — **Semeiographic**, sē'mī-ō-graf"ik, *a.* Pertaining to semeiography. — **Semeiological**, sē'mī-ō-loj"i-kal, *a.* Pertaining to semiology.—**Semeiology**, sē-mī-ol'o-ji, *n.* [Gr. *sēmeion*, and *logos*, discourse.] The doctrine of signs; semeiotics.—**Semeiometer**, sē-mī-om'et-ėr, *n.* [Gr. *sēmeion*, and *metron*, measure.] A fanciful test invented to measure the relative greatness of miracles. (*Farrar*).—**Semeiotic**, sē-mī-ot'ik, *a.* Relating to semeiotics.—**Semeiotics**, sē-mī-ot'iks, *n.* The science of signs; the language of signs; *pathol.* that branch which teaches how to judge of symptoms in the human body.

Semen, sē'men, *n.* [L., from root of *sero*, to sow.] The seed or fecundating fluid of male animals; sperm.

Semese,† sem-ēs', *a.* [L. *semesus—semi*, half, and *esus*, eaten, from *edo, esum*, to eat.] Half-eaten.

Semester, se-mes'tėr, *n.* [L. *semestris*, half-yearly—*sex*, six, and *mensis*, month.] A period or term of six months.

Semi, sem'i. [L. *semi*, Gr. *hēmi*.] A prefix signifying half; half of; in part; partially. The compounds are generally of very obvious meaning if the latter parts be known, and we give only a certain number of them below.

Semi-Arian, sem-i-ā'ri-an, *n.* One of an ecclesiastical sect who acquiesced in some of the tenets of the Arians, but rejected others.

Semi-attached, sem'i-at-tacht", *a.* Partially attached or united. — *Semi-attached house*, one of two houses joined together, but both standing apart from others.

Semibreve, sem'i-brēv, *n.* [From *semi* and *breve*.] *Music*, a note of half the duration or time of the breve, equivalent to two minims, four crotchets, or eight quavers.

Semicircle, sem'i-sėr-kl, *n.* [L. *semicirculus*.] The half of a circle; the part of a circle comprehended between its diameter and half of its circumference; any body in the form of a half circle.—**Semicircular**, sem-i-sėr'kū-lėr, *a.* Having the form of a half circle.

Semi-circumference, sem'i-sėr-kum"-fėr-ens, *n.* Half the circumference.

Semicolon, sem'i-kō-lon, *n.* [*Semi* and *colon*.] The punctuation mark or point (;), marking a pause of less duration than the colon, and more than the comma: used to distinguish the conjunct members of a sentence.

Semi-columnar, sem'i-ko-lum"nėr, *a.* Like a half column; flat on one side and round on the other.

Semi-conscious, sem-i-kon'shus, *a.* Imperfectly conscious.

Semi-cylinder, sem-i-sil'in-dėr, *n.* Half of a cylinder that is cut longitudinally by a plane. — **Semi-cylindric, Semi-cylindrical**, sem'i-si-lin"drik, sem'i-si-lin"-dri-kal, *a.* In the form of a semi-cylinder.

Semi-detached, sem'i-dē-tacht", *a.* Partly separated: applied to one of two houses which are detached from other buildings, but joined together.

Semi-diameter, sem'i-dī-am"et-ėr, *n.* Half a diameter; a radius.

Semi-diurnal, sem'i-dī-ėr"nal, *a.* Pertaining to or accomplished in half a day; continuing half a day.

Semi-double, sem-i-dub'l, *a. Bot.* having the outermost stamens converted into petals while the inner ones remain perfect.

Semi-floscular, Semi-flosculous, Semi-flosculose, *a.* [*Semi*, and L. *flosculus*, a little flower.] *Bot.* having the corolla split and turned to one side, as in the ligule of composites.

Semi-fluid, sem-i-flū'id, *a.* Imperfectly fluid.

Semi-ligneous, sem-i-lig'nē-us, *a.* Partially ligneous or woody; *bot.* woody at the base and herbaceous at the top.

Semilor, sem'i-lor, *n.* [Prefix *semi*, half, and Fr. *l'or*, gold.] An alloy, consisting of five parts of copper and one of zinc, used for manufacturing cheap jewelry, &c.

Semi-lunar, sem-i-lū'nėr, *a.* [L. *semi*, half, and *luna*, the moon.] Resembling in form a half-moon.—*Semi-lunar valves*, *anat.* three valves at the beginning of the pulmonary artery and aorta.

Semi-metallic, sem'i-me-tal"ik, *a.* Partially metallic in character.

Semi-mute, sem'i-mūt, *a.* Applied to a person who, owing to losing the sense of hearing, has lost also to a great extent the faculty of speech.

Seminal, sem'i-nal, *a.* [L. *seminalis*, from *semen*, seed, from stem of *sero*, to sow. Sow.] Pertaining to seed or semen, or to the elements of reproduction; contained in seed; germinal; rudimentary.—**Seminarian, Seminarist**, sem-i-nā'ri-an, sem'i-na-rist, *n.* A member of a seminary; an English Roman Catholic priest educated in a foreign seminary. — **Seminary**, sem'i-na-ri, *n.* [L. *seminarium*, from *semen*, *seminis*, seed.] A seed plot‡; a nursery‡; a place of education; any school, college, or university in which persons are instructed. — *a.* Seminal; belonging to seed; trained or educated in a foreign seminary: said of a Roman Catholic priest.—**Semination**, sem-i-nā'shon, *n.* [L. *seminatio*.] *Bot.* the natural dispersion of seeds; the process of seeding.—**Seminiferous**, sem-i-nif'ėr-us, *a.* [L. *semen*, and *fero*, to produce.] Seed-bearing; producing seed. — **Seminific, Seminifical**, sem-i-nif'ik, sem-i-nif'i-kal, *a.* [L. *semen*, and *facio*, to make.] Forming or producing seed or semen.

Semi-nymph, sem'i-nimf, *n. Entom.* the nymph of insects which undergo a slight change only in passing to a perfect state.

Semiography, sē-mī-og'ra-fi, *n.* SEMEIOGRAPHY.—**Semiology**, sē-mī-ol'o-ji, *n.* SEMEIOLOGY. — **Semiotics**, sē-mī-ot'iks, *n.* SEMEIOTICS.

Semi-palmate, Semi-palmated, sem-i-pal'māt, sem-i-pal'mā-ted, *a. Zool.* having the feet webbed only partly down the toes.

Semiped, sem'i-ped, *n.* [*Semi*, and L. *pes*, *pedis*, a foot.] *Pros.* a half-foot.—**Semipedal**, sem-i-pē'dal, *a. Pros.* containing a half-foot.

Semi-Pelagian, sem'i-pē-lā"ji-an, *n. Eccles. hist.* a follower of John Cassianus, a monk who, about the year 430, modified the doctrines of Pelagius.—**Semi-Pelagianism**, sem'i-pē-lā"ji-an-izm, *n.* The tenets of the Semi-Pelagians.

Semi-plantigrade, sem-i-plan'ti-grād, *a. Zool.* applied to certain families of mammals, as the civets and weasels, in which a portion of the sole of the hind-feet at least is applied to the ground in walking.

Semiquaver, sem'i-kwā-vėr, *n. Music*, a note of half the duration of the quaver; the sixteenth of the semibreve.

Semite, sem'īt, *n.* [From *Sem* or *Shem*, eldest son of Noah.] A descendant of Shem; one of the Semitic races; a Shemite. —*a.* Belonging to Shem or his descendants. —**Semitic**, se-mit'ik, *a.* Relating to Shem or his descendants; pertaining to the Hebrew race or any of those kindred to it.—*Semitic* or *Shemitic languages*, an important group or family of languages, comprising the Hebrew, Phœnician, Arabic, Abyssinian, Chaldean, Assyrian, Babylonian. — **Semitism**, sem'it-izm, *n.* A Semitic idiom or word; the adoption of what is peculiarly Semitic.

Semitertian, sem-i-tėr'shi-an, *a. Med.* applied to a fever possessing both the characters of the tertian and quotidian intermittent.—*n.* A semitertian fever.

Semitone, sem'i-tōn, *n. Music*, half a tone; an interval of sound, as between *mi* and *fa* in the diatonic scale, which is only half the distance of the interval between *ut* (*do*) and *re*, or *sol* and *la*.—**Semitonic**, sem-i-ton'ik, *a.* Pertaining to a semitone.

Semi-transparent, sem'i-trans-pā"rent, *a.* Half or imperfectly transparent.

Semi-vocal, sem'i-vō-kal, *a.* Pertaining to a semi-vowel; imperfectly vocal.

Semi-vowel, sem'i-vou-el, *n.* A half-vowel; a sound partaking of the nature of both a vowel and a consonant, as *l*, *m*, *r*.

Semmet, sem'et, *n.* [Origin unknown.] Flannel shirt, underwear.

Semolina, Semola, sem-ō-lī'na, sem'ō-la, *n.* [It. *semolino*.] The large hard grains retained in the bolting-machine after the fine flour has been passed through it, or made separately, used for puddings.

Sempervirent, sem-pėr-vī'rent, *a.* [L. *semper*, always, and *virens*, *virentis*, flourishing.] Always fresh; evergreen.

Sempiternal, sem-pi-tėr'nal, *a.* [Fr. *sempiternel*, L. *sempiternus*—*semper*, always, and *eternus*, eternal.] Eternal in futurity; everlasting; having beginning, but no end; also, without beginning or end.—**Sempiternity**, sem-pi-tėr'ni-ti, *n.* Future duration without end; eternity.

Sempstress, semp'stres, *n.* [A.Sax. *seámestre*, a sempstress, with term. *-ess*, and inserted *p*. SEAM.] A woman who lives by needle-work.

Senarius, sē-nā'ri-us, *n.* The name of the iambic trimeter, of six feet.

Senary, sē'na-ri, *a.* [L. *senarius*, from *seni*, six each, from *sex*, six.] Of six; belonging to six; containing six.

Senate, sen'āt, *n.* [Fr. *sénat*, from L. *senatus*, from *senex*, old, aged; cog. with Goth. *sineigs*, Gr. *henos*, Skr. *sanas*, old. SENIOR, SIR.] Originally, in ancient Rome, a body of elderly citizens elected from among the nobles, and having supreme legislative power; hence, the upper branch of a legislature in various countries, as in France, the United States, &c.; in general, a legislative body; the legislative department of a government; the governing body of a university.—**Senate-house**, *n.* A house in which a senate meets, or a place of public council.—**Senator**, sen'a-tor, *n.* A member of a senate.—**Senatorial**, sen-a-tō'ri-al, *a.* Pertaining to a senator or senators; belonging to senators; in the United States, entitled to elect a senator.—**Senatorially**, sen-a-tō'ri-al-li, *adv.* In a senatorial manner. — **Senatorship**, sen'a-tor-ship, *n.* The office or dignity of a senator.

Senatus, se-nā'tus, *n.* [L.] A senate; a governing body in certain universities. — *Senatus academicus*, one of the governing bodies in Scotch universities, consisting of the principal and professors.

Send, send, *v.t.*—pret. and pp. *sent*. [A.Sax. *sendan* = Icel. *senda*, Dan. *sende*, D. *zenden*, G. *senden*, Goth. *sandjan*, to send; caus. of an old verb meaning to go.] To cause to go or pass from one place to another; to despatch; to cause to be conveyed or transmitted; to impel; to propel; to throw; to cast; to commission, authorize, or direct to go and act; to cause to befall; to inflict (to *send* destruction); before certain verbs of motion, to cause to do the act indicated by the respective verb (to *send* the enemy *flying* in all directions).—*To send down*, to rusticate, expel from college. (*Oxford and Cambridge use.*)—*To send forth* or *out*, to put or bring forth; to emit.—*v.i.* To despatch a message or a messenger for some purpose.—*To send for*, to request by message to come or be brought (to *send for* a physician).—**Sender**, sen'dėr, *n.* One that sends.

Sendal, sen'dal, *n.* [O.Fr. *cendal*, sendal; L.L. *cendalum*, from Gr. *sindōn*, a fine Indian cloth, from *Sindhu*, the river Indus.] A light thin stuff of silk or thread.

Seneca, sen'ē-kä, *n.* An Iroquois Indian tribe, formerly of western New York; the most warlike of the Five Nations.

Seneka, Senega, sen'ē-ka, sen'ē-ga, *n.* A drug consisting of the root of a plant of the United States, used in cough mixtures; the plant itself.

Senescence, sē-nes'ens, *n.* [L. *senesco*, from *senex*, old. SENATE.] The state of growing old.—**Senescent**, sē-nes'ent, *a.* Beginning to grow old.

Seneschal, sen'es-shal, *n.* [O.Fr. *seneschal*, L.L. *senescallus*, *senescalcus*, from O.G. *senescalh*—*sene*, old, cognate with L. *senex* (seen in *senate*), and *scalc*, *scalh*, a servant (seen also in *marshal*).] An officer in the houses of princes and dignitaries, who has the superintendence of feasts and domestic ceremonies; a steward.—**Seneschalship**, sen'es-shal-ship, *n.* The office of seneschal.

Sengreen, sen'grēn, *n.* [G. *singrün*, a plant—*sin*, signifying duration, and *grün*, green.] The house-leek.

Senile, sē'nīl, *a.* [L. *senilis*, from *senex*, old. SENATE.] Pertaining to old age; proceeding from age; characterized by the weakness of old age.—**Senility**, sē-nil'i-ti, *n.* The state of being senile; old age; dotage.

Senior, sēn'yėr, *a.* [L. *senior*, compar. of *senex*, old. (SENATE.) *Sir* is from *senior*.] More advanced in age; older; elder; being the elder of two persons of the same name (John Smith, *senior*); higher or more advanced in rank, office, or the like.—*n.* A person who is older than another (my *senior* by ten years); one that is older in office than another; one prior or superior in rank or office; an aged person; a student in the U. S. who is in his final year in college, a university, or high school.—**Seniority**, sēn-yor'i-ti, *n.* State of being senior; superior age; priority of birth; priority or superiority in rank or office, which presumes superior right to promotion.

Senna, sen'na, *n.* [Ar. *senā*, senna.] The leaves of various species of Cassia, used as a laxative medicine in constipation, dyspepsia, &c.

Sennit, sen'it, *n.* [From *seven* and *knit*.] *Naut.* a sort of flat braided cordage formed by plaiting rope-yarns or spun-yarn together.

Señor, sen-yōr', *n.* [L. *senior*.] A Spanish title or form of address, corresponding to the English Mr. or sir; a gentleman. — **Señora**, sen-yō'ra, *n.* The feminine of *Señor*; madame or Mrs.; a lady.

Sensation, sen-sā'shon, *n.* [Fr. *sensation*, L.L. *sensatio*, from L. *sentio*, *sensum*, to feel, to perceive. SENSE.] An impression made upon the mind through the medium of one of the organs of sense; feeling produced by external objects, or by some change in the internal state of the body; a feeling; the power of feeling or receiving impressions; feeling occasioned by causes that do not act on the senses; a purely spiritual or psychical affection (a *sensation* of awe, novelty, &c.); a state of some excitement (to create a *sensation*); what produces excited interest or feeling: often used as an adjective in the sense of causing excited interest or feeling (*sensation* novels, &c.).—*Sensation novels*, novels that produce their effect mainly by exciting and often improbable situations, as scenes of extreme peril, high-wrought passion, &c., depending but little on the delineation of character.—**Sensational**, sen-sā'shon-al, *a.* Relating to or implying sensation or perception by the senses; producing sensation or excited interest or emotion (a *sensational* novel, a writer of the *sensational* school); pertaining to sensationalism. — **Sensationalism**, sen-sā'shon-al-izm, *n. Metaph.* the theory or doctrine that all our ideas are solely derived through our senses; sensualism.—**Sensationalist**, sen-sā'shon-al-ist, *n. Metaph.* a believer in or upholder of the doctrine of sensationalism.—**Sensationary**, sen-sā′shon-a-ri, *a.* Relating to sensation; sensational.

Sense, sens, *n.* [L. *sensus*, sensation, a sense, from *sentio*, *sensum*, to perceive by the senses (seen in *scent*, *sensual*, *consent*, *dissent*, *assent*, *resent*, *sentence*, *sentiment*, &c.).] One of the faculties by which man and the higher animals perceive external objects by means of impressions made on certain organs of the body, the senses being usually spoken of as five, namely, sight, hearing, taste, smell, and touch; perception by the senses; sensation; feeling; apprehension through the intellect; discernment; appreciation (no *sense* of beauty); moral perception; consciousness (a *sense* of shame); faculty of thinking and feeling; sound perception and reasoning; good judgment; understanding (a man of *sense*); rationality; view or opinion held in common (to speak the *sense* of a public meeting); meaning; import; signification of language.—*Common sense*. COMMON.—*To be in our senses*, to be in a sound state of mind; to have possession of our mental faculties: the contrary being to be *out of our senses*.—**Senseless**, sens′les, *a.* Destitute of sense; having no power of sensation or perception; insensible; wanting feeling or sympathy; without sensibility; contrary to reason or sound judgment; unwise; foolish; nonsensical; wanting understanding; acting without judgment; stupid.—**Senselessly**, sens′les-li, *adv.* In a senseless manner; foolishly; stupidly.—**Senselessness**, sens′les-nes, *n.* The state or quality of being senseless; want of good sense; folly; stupidity.—**Sensibility**, sen-si-bil′i-ti, *n.* The state or quality of being sensible; capability of sensation; capacity to experience emotion or feeling; the capacity of being impressed with such sentiments as those of sublimity, awe, wonder, &c.; delicacy or keenness of feeling; quick emotion or sympathy; that quality of an instrument which makes it indicate very slight changes of condition; sensitiveness (the *sensibility* of a thermometer).—**Sensible**, sen′si-bl, *a.* [Fr. *sensible*, L. *sensibilis*, from *sensus*.] Capable of being perceived by the senses; capable of exciting sensation; perceptible; felt; capable of sensation or impression (the eye is *sensible* to light); capable of emotional influences; liable to impression or emotion; easily affected; perceiving or having perception either by the senses or the intellect; cognizant; persuaded; capable of indicating slight changes of condition; sensitive (a *sensible* thermometer); possessing or containing sense, judgment, or reason (a *sensible* remark); having good or sound sense; intelligent; reasonable; judicious.—**Sensibleness**, sen′si-bl-nes, *n.* The state or quality of being sensible; sensibility.—**Sensibly**, sen′si-bli, *adv.* In a sensible manner; perceptibly to the senses; with intelligence or good sense; judiciously.—**Sensific, Sensifacient**, sen-sif′ik, sen-si-fā′shi-ent, *a.* [L. *sensus*, and *facio*, to make.] Producing sensation.—**Sensificatory**, sen-sif′i-ka-to-ri, *a.* Sensifacient.—**Sensigenous**, sen-sij′e-nus, *a.* [L. *sensus*, and root *gen*, to beget.] Originating or causing sensation.—**Sensitive**, sen′si-tiv, *a.* [Fr. *sensitif*, L.L. *sensitivus*.] Having the capacity of receiving impressions from external objects; having feelings easily excited; readily and acutely affected; of keen sensibility; *physics*, easily affected, moved, or exhibiting change from some influence (a *sensitive* balance); *chem.* readily affected by the action of appropriate agents.—**Sensitively**, sen′si-tiv-li, *adv.* In a sensitive manner.—**Sensitiveness**, sen′si-tiv-nes, *n.* The state of being sensitive.—**Sensitive-plant**, *n.* A name given to several plants which display movements of their leaves in a remarkable degree under the influence of light and darkness, as also under mechanical and other stimuli.—**Sensitivity**, sen-si-tiv′i-ti, *n.* The state of being sensitive or readily affected by the action of appropriate chemical or other agents; readiness of muscle or nerves to respond to stimuli.—**Sensitize**, sen′si-tīz, *v.t.*—*sensitized*, *sensitizing*. To render capable of being acted on by the actinic rays of the sun or other means: a term in photography, &c.

Sensorium, sen-sō′ri-um, *n.* [From L. *sensus*, sense.] The brain or any part of it considered as the general receptacle of impressions derived from the external world; the central seat of consciousness; a nerve centre.—**Sensorial**, sen-sō′ri-al, *a.* Sensory.—**Sensory**, sen′so-ri, *a.* Relating to the sensorium; conveying sensation (*sensory* nerves).—The sensorium.

Sensual, sen′sū-al, *a.* [L. *sensualis*, from *sensus*, sense. SENSE.] Pertaining to the body, in distinction from the spirit; carnal; fleshly; pertaining to the gratification of the appetites; grossly luxurious; indulging in lust; voluptuous; pertaining to sensualism as a philosophical doctrine.—**Sensualism**, sen′sū-al-izm, *n.* *Metaph.* that theory which bases all our mental acts and intellectual powers upon sensation; sensationalism, opposed to *intellectualism*; a state of subjection to the appetites; sensuality.—**Sensualist**, sen′sū-al-ist, *n.* A person given to the indulgence of his appetites; a sensationalist in philosophy.—**Sensualistic**, sen′sū-a-lis″tik, *a.* Upholding the doctrine of sensualism.—**Sensuality**, sen-sū-al′i-ti, *n.* The quality of being sensual; devotedness to the gratification of the bodily appetites; indulgence in lust; carnality; fleshliness.—**Sensualize**, sen′sū-al-īz, *v.t.*—*sensualized*, *sensualizing*. To make sensual; to debase by carnal gratifications.—**Sensually**, sen′sū-al-li, *adv.* In a sensual manner.—**Sensualness**, sen′sū-al-nes, *n.* Sensuality.—**Sensuism**, sen′sū-izm, *n.* Sensualism.—**Sensuous**, sen′sū-us, *a.* Pertaining to the senses; appealing to the senses; readily affected through the senses; alive to the pleasure to be received through the senses.—**Sensuously**, sen′sū-us-li, *adv.* In a sensuous manner.—**Sensuousness**, sen′sū-us-nes, *n.*

Sent, sent, pret. and pp. of *send*.

Sentence, sen′tens, *n.* [L. *sententia*, an opinion, a judgment, a maxim, a sentence, from *sentio*, to perceive. SENSE.] A judgment; a decision; a judgment pronounced by a court or judge upon a criminal; a maxim (*Shak.*); *gram.* a number of words containing complete sense or a complete thought and followed by a full point.—*v.t.*—*sentenced*, *sentencing*. To pronounce sentence or judgment on; to condemn; to doom to punishment.—**Sentencer**, sen′ten-sėr, *n.* One who pronounces a sentence.—**Sentential**, sen-ten′shal, *a.* Comprising sentences; pertaining to a sentence or full period.—**Sententially**, sen-ten′shal-li, *adv.* In a sentential manner; by means of sentences.—**Sententious**, sen-ten′shus, *a.* [L. *sententiosus*, Fr. *sentencieux*.] Abounding in axioms or maxims; rich in judicious observations; having brevity and weight of meaning; pithy; terse.—**Sententiously**, sen-ten′shus-li, *adv.*—In a sententious manner.—**Sententiousness**, sen-ten′shus-nes, *n.* The quality of being sententious; brevity of expression combined with strength.

Sentient, sen′shi-ent, *a.* [L. *sentiens*, *sentientis*, ppr. of *sentio*, to perceive. SENSE.] Capable of perceiving or feeling; having the faculty of perception; *physiol.* a term applied to those parts which are more susceptible of feeling than others.—**Sentiently**, sen′shi-ent-li, *adv.* In a sentient or perceptive manner.—**Sentience, Sentiency**, sen′shi-ens, sen′shi-en-si, *n.* The state of being sentient; feeling.

Sentiment, sen′ti-ment, *n.* [Fr. *sentiment*, L.L. *sentimentum*, from L. *sentio*, to perceive. SENSE.] A thought prompted by feeling; a feeling respecting some person or thing; a particular disposition of mind in view of some subject; tendency to be swayed by feeling; emotion; sensibility; a thought or opinion; the thought or opinion contained in words, but considered as distinct from them; a thought expressed in striking words.—**Sentimental**, sen-ti-men′tal, *a.* Having sentiment; apt to be swayed by sentiment; manifesting an excess of sentiment; artificially or mawkishly tender; appealing to sentiment rather than to reason. ∴ Syn. under ROMANTIC.—**Sentimentalism**, sen-ti-men′tal-izm, *n.* Sentimentality.—**Sentimentalist**, sen-ti-men′tal-ist, *n.* One who affects sentiment; the character of being sentimental or swayed by sentiment.—**Sentimentality**, sen′ti-men-tal″i-ti, *n.* Affectation of fine feeling or exquisite sensibility; proneness to sentiment.—**Sentimentalize**, sen-ti-men′tal-īz, *v.i.* To affect exquisite sensibility.—**Sentimentally**, sen-ti-men′tal-li, *adv.* In a sentimental manner.

Sentinel, sen′ti-nel, *n.* [Fr. *sentinelle*; It. *sentinella*; origin doubtful.] One who watches or keeps guard to prevent surprise; especially, a soldier set to guard any place from surprise; a sentry.—*v.t.*—*sentinelled*, *sentinelling*. To watch over as a sentinel; to furnish with a sentinel or sentinels.—**Sentry**, sen′tri, *n.* [Corruption of *sentinel*.] A soldier placed on guard; a sentinel; guard; watch; duty of a sentinel.—**Sentry-box**, *n.* A small shed to cover and shelter a sentinel at his post.

Sepahi, sep′a-hi, *n.* A sepoy.

Sepal, sē′pal, *n.* [Fr. *sépale*, an invented term to correspond to *pétale*, a petal.] *Bot.* one of the separate divisions of a calyx when that organ is made up of various leaves.—**Sepaline**, sep′al-īn, *a.* *Bot.* relating to a sepal or sepals; having the nature of a sepal.—**Sepaloid**, sep′al-oid, *a.* Like a sepal.—**Sepalous**, sep′al-us, *a.* Relating to or having sepals.

Separate, sep′a-rāt, *v.t.*—*separated*, *separating*. [L. *separo*, *separatum*—*se*, apart, and *paro*, to put or place. PARE.] To disunite; to divide; to part, in almost any manner, either things naturally or casually joined; to set apart from a number; to make a space between; to sever, as by an intervening space; to lie between.—*v.i.* To go apart; to withdraw from each other; to cleave or split; to come apart.—*a.* [L. *separatus*, pp. of *separo*.] Divided from the rest; parted from another or others; disjoined; unconnected; not united; distinct; withdrawn; alone; without company.—**Separability**, **Separableness**, sep′a-ra-bil″i-ti, sep′a-ra-bl-nes, *n.* The quality of being separable; divisibility.—**Separable**, sep′a-ra-bl, *a.* [L. *separabilis*.] Capable of being separated or disjoined; divisible.—**Separably**, sep′a-ra-bli, *adv.* In a separable manner.—**Separately**, sep′a-rāt-li, *adv.* In a separate or unconnected state; apart; distinctly; singly.—**Separateness**, sep′a-rāt-nes, *n.* The state of being separate.—**Separation**, sep-a-rā′shon, *n.* [L. *separatio*.] The act of separating; the state of being separate; disjunction; disunion; disconnection; disunion of married persons; a cessation of conjugal cohabitation of man and wife.—*Judicial separation*, the separation of a husband and wife by decree of a court.—*Separation allowance*, provision made during war to the wives and relatives of soldiers and sailors on active service.—**Separatism**, sep′a-rāt-izm, *n.* The state of being a separatist; dissent.—**Separatist**, sep′a-rāt-ist, *n.* One who advocates separation; one who withdraws or separates himself from an established church; a dissenter.—**Separatistic**, sep′a-rā-tis″tik, *a.* Relating to or characterized by separatism; schismatical.—**Separator**, sep′a-rā-tėr, *n.* One who or that which separates; a name of several mechanical contrivances.—**Separatory, Separative**, sep′a-ra-to-ri, sep′a-rā-tiv, *a.* Causing or used in separation.—**Separatory**, *n.* A chemical vessel for separating liquors; a kind of surgical instrument.

Sepawn, se-pan′, *n.* [Of American Indian origin.] An American dish consisting of meal of maize boiled in water.

Sepia, sē′pi-a, *n.* [Gr. *sēpia*, the cuttle-fish or squid.] The cuttle-fish; a species of brown pigment prepared from a black juice secreted by certain glands of the cuttle-fish, and used in drawing.—**Sepic**, sē′pik, *a.* Pertaining to sepia; done in sepia, as a drawing.

Sepiment, sep′i-ment, *n.* [L. *sepimentum*, from *sepio*, to inclose.] A hedge; a fence; something that separates.

Sepiostaire, sē-pi-os'tār, *n.* [Gr. *sēpia*, a cuttle-fish, and *osteon*, a bone.] The cuttle-bone or internal shell of the cuttle-fish.

Sepon, se-pon', *n.* SEPAWN.

Sepoy, sē'poi, *n.* [Per. *sipahi*, a soldier.] A name given in Hindustan to the native soldiers in the British service.

Sepsis, sep'sis, *n.* [Gr. *sēpsis*, putrefaction, from *sēpō*, to rot.] A poisoned state of the system, due to putrefaction; poisoning resulting from infection.—*Intestinal sepsis*, food poisoning caused by the eating of spoiled foods.—*Puerperal sepsis*, poisoning due to infection after childbirth.

Septa, sep'ta, pl. of *septum*.

Septæmia, *n.* SEPTICÆMIA.

Septal. Under SEPTUM.

Septangle, sep'tang-gl, *n.* [L. *septem*, seven, and *angulus*, an angle.] *Geom.* a heptagon.

Septarium, sep-tā'ri-um, *n.* pl. **Septaria**, sep-tā'ri-a. [From L. *septum*, an inclosure, from *sepio*, to inclose.] A name given to spheroidal masses of calcareous marl, ironstone, or other matter, whose interior presents numerous fissures of some crystallized substance which divide the mass.

Septate. Under SEPTUM.

September, sep-tem'bėr, *n.* [L., from *septem*, seven.] The ninth month of the year, so called from being originally the seventh month from March, which was formerly the first month of the year.—**Septembrist**, *n.* One sharing as actor in the September massacres at Paris, in 1792, during the French Revolution.

Septempartite, sep-tem'pär-tīt, *a.* Divided nearly to the base into seven parts.

Septenary, sep'ten-a-ri, *a.* [L. *septenarius*, from *septeni*, seven each, from *septum*, seven.] Consisting of or relating to seven; lasting seven years; occurring once in seven years.—**Septenate**, sep'ten-āt, *a.* *Bot.* having seven parts, as a compound leaf with seven leaflets from one point.

Septennial, sep-ten'ni-al, *a.* [L. *septennis*—*septum*, seven, and *annus*, a year.] Lasting or continuing seven years; happening once in every seven years.—**Septennially**, sep-ten'ni-al-li, *adv.* Once in seven years.

Septentrion, sep-ten'tri-on, *n.* [L. *septentrio*, *septentrionis*, from *septentriones*, the seven stars of the Great Bear—*septem*, seven, and *triones*, ploughing oxen.] The north or northern regions.—**Septentrional**, sep-ten'tri-on-al, *a.* Northern.

Septet, **Septette**, sep-tet', *n.* [L. *septem*, seven.] *Music*, a composition for seven voices or instruments.

Sept-foil, sept'foil, *n.* [L. *septem*, seven, and *folium*, a leaf.] A figure of seven equal segments of a circle circularly disposed.

Septic, **Septical**, sep'tik, sep'ti-kal, *a.* [Gr. *sēptikos*, from *sēpō*, to putrefy.] Having power to promote putrefaction; causing putrefaction.—*n.* A substance causing putrefaction.—**Septically**, sep'ti-kal-li, *adv.* In a septic manner; by means of septics.—**Septicity**, sep-tis'i-ti, *n.* The quality of being septic.

Septicæmia, **Septæmia**, sep-ti-sē'mi-a, sep-tē'mi-a. *n.* [Gr. *sēptikos*, *sēptos*, putrefying, from *sēpō*, to putrefy, and *haima*, blood.] Blood-poisoning by absorption into the circulation of poisonous or putrid matter.

Septicidal, sep-ti-sī'dal, *a.* [L. *septum*, a partition, and *cædo*, to cut or divide. SEPTUM.] *Bot.* dividing or dehiscing at the septa or partitions.—**Septiferous**, sep-tif'ėr-us, *a.* [L. *septum*, an inclosure, and *fero*, to bear.] *Bot.* bearing septa.—**Septiform**, sep'ti-form, *a.* Resembling a septum or partition.—**Septifragal**, sep-tif'ra-gal, *a.* [L. *septum*, a partition, and *frango*, to break.] *Bot.* literally breaking from the partitions: applied to a mode of dehiscing in which the backs of the carpels separate from the dissepiments.

Septilateral, sep-ti-lat'ėr-al, *a.* [L. *septem*, seven, and *latus*, *lateris*, a side.] Having seven sides.

Septillion, sep-til'yon, *n.* [From L. *septem*, seven, with termination of E. *million*.] By the American numeration system, a number consisting of a unit followed by twenty-four ciphers.

Septisyllable, sep'ti-sil-a-bl, *n.* [L. *septem*, seven, and E. *syllable*.] A word of seven syllables.

Septuagenarian, sep'tū-a-je-nā"ri-an, *n.* [L. *septuagenarius*, consisting of seventy, *septuageni*, seventy each, from *septem*, seven.] A person seventy years of age.—**Septuagenary**, sep-tū-aj'e-na-ri, *a.* Consisting of seventy or of seventy years; pertaining to a person seventy years old.—*n.* A septuagenarian.

Septuagesima, sep'tū-a-jes"i-ma, *n.* [L. *septuagesimus*, seventieth.] The third Sunday before Lent, so called because it is about seventy days before Easter.—**Septuagesimal**, sep'tū-a-jes"i-mal, *a.* Consisting of seventy or of seventy years.

Septuagint, sep'tū-a-jint, *n.* [L. *septuaginta*, seventy, from *septem*, seven.] A Greek version of the Old Testament (usually denoted by the symbol LXX) executed for the Jews of Alexandria and said to have been the work of seventy translators who were employed by Ptolemy Philadelphus, king of Egypt, about 280 B.C.

Septum, sep'tum, *n.* pl. **Septa**, sep'ta. [L. a partition, from *sepio*, to hedge in, to fence.] A partition; a wall separating cavities in animals or plants, as the cartilage between the nostrils; one of the partitions of an ovary or fruit.—**Septulate**, sep'tū-lāt, *a.* *Bot.* applied to fruits having imperfect or false septa.—**Septal**, sep'tal, *a.* Belonging to or forming a septum.—**Septate**, sep'tāt, *a.* Partitioned off into compartments by septa.—**Septile**, sep'tīl, *a.* Belonging to septa or dissepiments.

Septuor, sep'tū-or, *n.* [Fr., from L. *septem*, seven.] A septet.

Septuple, sep'tū-pl, *a.* [L. *septuplus*, from *septem*, seven.] Sevenfold.—*v.t.* To make sevenfold.

Sepulcher, sep'ul-kėr, *n.* [L. *sepulchrum*, from *sepelio*, *sepultum*, to bury.] A tomb; a building, cave, &c., for interment; a burial vault; *eccles. arch.* a recess for the reception of the holy elements consecrated on Maunday Thursday till high-mass on Easter-day.—*v.t.*—*sepulchered*, *sepulchring*. To bury; to inter; to entomb.—**Sepulchral**, sē-pul'kral, *a.* [L. *sepulchralis*.] Pertaining to burial, to the grave, or to tombs; suggestive of a sepulcher; hence, deep, hollow in tone (a *sepulchral* tone of voice).—**Sepulture**, sep'ul-tūr, *n.* [L. *sepultura*, from *sepelio*, *sepultum*, to bury.] Burial; act of interment; a sepulcher.

Sequacious. sē-kwā'shus, *a.* [L. *sequax*, *sequacis*, from *sequor*, to follow. SEQUENCE.] Following; disposed to follow a leader; logically consistent; consecutive in development or transition of thought.—**Sequaciousness**, **Sequacity**, sē-kwā'shus-nes, sē-kwas'i-ti, *n.* State of being sequacious.

Sequel, sē'kwel, *n.* [L. *sequela*, sequel, result, consequence, from *sequor*, to follow. SEQUENCE.] That which follows and forms a continuation; a succeeding part; consequence; result; event.—**Sequela**, sē-kwē'la, *n.* pl. **Sequelæ**, sē-kwē'lē. [L., from *sequor*.] An adherent or band of adherents; a body of followers; *pathol.* the consequent of a disease; a morbid affection which follows another.

Sequence, sē'kwens, *n.* [Fr. *séquence*, L.L. *sequentia*, from L. *sequens*, *sequentis*, ppr. of *sequor*, *secutus*, to follow (seen also in *sequel*, *second*, *prosecute*, *execute*, *consequent*, *ensue*, &c.); root perhaps same as in to *see*.] A following or coming after; succession; a particular order or arrangement of succession; invariable order of succession; an observed instance of uniformity in following; a series of things following in a certain order; a set of playing cards immediately following each other, as king, queen, knave, &c.; *music*, the recurrence of a melodic figure in a different key to that in which it was first given; *R. Cath. Ch.* a hymn introduced into the mass on certain festival days, and coming immediately before the gospel.—**Sequent**, **Sequential**, sē'kwent, sē-kwen'shal, *a.* [L. *sequens*, *sequentis*.] Following; succeeding; following by logical consequence.—**Sequentially**, sē-kwen'shal-li, *adv.* By sequence or succession.

Sequester, sē-kwes'tėr, *v.t.* [L. *sequestro*, to put into the hands of an indifferent person, from *sequester*, a depositary or trustee.] To set apart or separate from other things; *refl.* to retire or withdraw into obscurity; to seclude one's self; *law*, to separate from the owner for a time; to set apart, as the property of a debtor, until the claims of creditors be satisfied.—**Sequestered**, sē-kwes'tėrd, *p.* and *a.* Secluded; private; retired; separated from others; *law*, seized and detained for a time to satisfy a demand.—**Sequestrable**, sē-kwes'tra-bl, *a.* Liable to sequestration.—**Sequestrate**, sē-kwes'trāt, *v.t.*—*sequestrated*, *sequestrating*. *Law*, to sequester; to take possession of for behoof of creditors, as of the estate of a bankrupt, with the view of realizing it and distributing it equitably.—**Sequestration**, sek-wes-trā'shon, *n.* Retirement; seclusion from society; *law*, the separation of a thing in controversy from the possession of those who contend for it; the act of taking property from the owner for a time till the profits from it satisfy a demand; *Scots law*, the seizing of a bankrupt's estate, by decree of a competent court, for behoof of the creditors.—**Sequestrator**, sek'wes-trā-tėr, *n.* One who sequesters or sequestrates.

Sequestrum, sē-kwes'trum, *n.* [From L. *sequestro*, to sever.] *Pathol.* the portion of bone which is detached in necrosis.

Sequin, sē'kwin, *n.* [Fr. *sequin*, from It. *zecchino*, from *zecca*, the mint, from Ar. *sikkah*, *sekkah*, a stamp, a die.] A gold coin first struck at Venice about the end of the thirteenth century, in value about $2.25.

Sequoia, sē-kwoi'a, *n.* [From *Sequoyah*, the inventor of the Cherokee alphabet.] The Wellingtonia genus of trees.

Seraglio, se-räl'yō, *n.* [It. *serraglio*, partly from Turk. *serai*, Per. *sarai*, a palace, partly from It. *serrare*, to shut up, from L. *sera*, a bar.] The palace of the Sultan of Turkey at Constantinople; a harem; a place for keeping wives or concubines.

Serai, se-rī', *n.* [Per. *serai*, a palace.] In Eastern countries, a place for the accommodation of travellers; a caravansary.

Serape, se-rä'pā, *n.* [A Mexican word.] A blanket or shawl worn as an outer garment by the Mexicans, &c.

Seraph, ser'af, *n.* pl. **Seraphs**, or **Seraphim**, ser'a-fim. [From Heb. *seraph*, to burn, to be eminent or noble.] An angel of the highest order.—**Seraphic**, **Seraphical**, se-raf'ik, se-raf'i-kal, *a.* Pertaining to a seraph; angelic; inflamed with holy love or zeal.—**Seraphically**, se-raf'i-kal-li, *adv.* In the manner of a seraph; angelically.—**Seraphina**, ser-a-fī'na, *n.* A keyed wind-instrument, the precursor of the harmonium.

Serapis, se-rā'pis, *n.* The Greek name of an Egyptian deity considered as a combination of Osiris and Apis.

Seraskier, se-ras'kēr, *n.* [Per. *serasker*—*ser*, *seri*, head, chief, and *asker*, an army.] A Turkish general or commander of land forces, especially a commander-in-chief and minister at war.—**Seraskierate**, se-ras'kēr-āt, *n.* The office of a seraskier.

Serb, sėrb, *n.* [Native form.] A native or inhabitant of Servia.

Serbonian, sėr-bō'ni-an, *a.* An epithet applied to a celebrated morass of ancient Egypt, fabled to have swallowed up whole armies; hence, *Serbonian bog* proverbially signifies a difficult or complicated state of matters; an inextricable mess.

Sere, sēr, *a.* Same as *Sear.*

Serenade, ser-ē-nād′, *n.* [Fr. *sérénade*, from It. *serenata*, a serenade, clear fine weather at night, from L. *serenus*, serene.] An entertainment of music given at night by a lover to his mistress under her window, or performed as a mark of esteem and good-will towards distinguished persons; also a piece of music characterized by soft repose in harmony with the stillness of night. — *v.t.* — *serenaded, serenading.* To entertain with a serenade.—*v.i.* To perform serenades or nocturnal music.—**Serenader**, ser-ē-nā′dėr, *n.* One who serenades.

Serene, sē-rēn′, *a.* [L. *serenus*, serene; allied to L. *sol*, the sun, Gr. *seirinos*, hot, scorching, *Seirios*, Sirius, Skr. *surya*, the sun.] Clear or fair, and calm; placid; quiet; unruffled; undisturbed; a form of address restricted to former sovereign princes of Germany, and the members of their families. —*v.t.*—*serened, serening.* To make serene. —**Serenely**, sē-rēn′li, *adv.* Calmly; quietly; with unruffled temper; deliberately.—**Sereneness**, sē-rēn′nes, *n.* The state of being serene; serenity.—**Serenity**, sē-ren′i-ti, *n.* [L. *serenitas.*] The quality or condition of being serene; clearness; calmness; quietness; stillness; peace.

Serf, sėrf, *n.* [Fr. *serf*, from L. *servus*, a slave. SERVE.] A villein; one of those who in the middle ages were attached to the land and transferred with it, and liable to the lowest services; a forced labourer attached to an estate, as formerly in Russia; a slave. — **Serfage**, **Serfdom**, **Serfhood**, **Serfism**, sėrf′āj, sėrf′dom, sėrf′hųd, sėrf′izm, *n.* The state or condition of a serf.

Serge, sėrj, *n.* [Fr. *serge*; origin doubtful, perhaps L. *serica*, a silken fabric. SILK.] A kind of twilled worsted cloth of inferior quality.

Serge, serj, *n.* [Fr. *cierge*, a wax taper, L. *cereus*, waxy, *cera*, wax.] A large wax candle burned before an altar.

Sergeant, sär-jant, *n.* [Also written *serjeant*; from Fr. *sergent*, O.Fr. *serjent*, originally a servant, from L. *serviens*, *servientis*, ppr. of *servio*, to serve. SERVE.] A non-commissioned officer in the army of the grade next above corporal; a police-officer in rank next below a captain; formerly in England, a lawyer of the highest rank; one of the servants of the British royal household. (In the last two meanings *serjeant* is the more usual spelling.)—**Sergeancy**, sär′jan-si, *n.* The office of a sergeant.—**Sergeant at arms.** An officer of a court, legislature, or other formal body, whose duty is to preserve order.—**Sergeant major**, in the U. S. Army, the highest non-commissioned officer who assists the commanding officers of a battalion or regiment in the clerical work and supervises personnel.—**Sergeantship**, *n.* The office of a sergeant.

Sericeous, sē-rish′us, *a.* [L. *sericeus*, from *sericum*, silk. SILK.] Pertaining to silk; consisting of silk; silky; *bot.* covered with very soft hairs pressed close to the surface. —**Sericulture**, sē′ri-kul-tūr, *n.* [L. *sericum*, silk, and *cultura*, cultivation.] The breeding and treatment of silkworms. — **Sericulturist**, sē-ri-kul′tū-rist, *n.* A cultivator of silkworms.

Series, sē′ri-ēz, *n. sing.* and *pl.* [L. *series*, same root as *sero*, to join, to weave together (seen also in *assert, insert, exert, desert*); Gr. *seira*, a cord; Skr. *sarat*, a thread.] A continued succession of similar things, or of things bearing a similar relation to each other; an extended rank, line, or course; a sequence; a succession; *geol.* a set of strata possessing some common mineral or fossil characteristic; *chem.* a group of compounds, each containing the same radical; *arith.* and *alg.* a number of terms or quantities in succession, each of which is related to the one before it according to a certain law.—**Series motor**, *n.* An electric motor in which the field magnet windings are connected in series with the armature winding, so that the same current flows in both sets of coils.—**Serial**, sē′ri-al, *a.* Pertaining to a series; consisting of or constituted by a series.—*n.* A tale or other composition running through successive numbers of a periodical work; a publication issued in successive numbers; a periodical.—**Seriality**, sē-ri-al′i-ti, *n.* The state or condition of following in successive order. — **Serially**, sēr′i-al-li, *adv.* In a series or in regular order.—**Seriate**, sē′ri-āt, *a.* Arranged in a series; pertaining to a series.— **Seriately**, sē′ri-āt-li, *adv.* In a regular series.—**Seriatim**, sē-ri-ā′tim, *adv.* [L.] In regular order; one after the other.

Serious, sē′ri-us, *a.* [Fr. *sérieux*, from L. *serius*, serious, earnest.] Grave in manner or disposition; solemn; not light, gay, or volatile; really intending what is said; being in earnest; not jesting; important; weighty; not trifling; attended with danger; giving rise to apprehension; deeply impressed with the importance of religion. —**Seriously**, sē′ri-us-li, *adv.* In a serious manner; earnestly; gravely; solemnly. — **Seriousness**, sē′ri-us-nes, *n.* The condition or quality of being serious; gravity; solemnity; earnest attention to religious concerns.—**Serio-comic**, **Serio-comical**, sē′ri-ō-kom″ik, sē′ri-ō-kom″i-kal, *a.* Having a mixture of seriousness and comicality.

Serjeant, sär′jant, *n.* [Fr. *sergent.* See SERGEANT.] A sergeant in the army or on a police force; in England, formerly a lawyer of the highest rank who acted for the king in trying cases.—*Serjeants of the household*, officers who execute several functions within the British royal household, as the *serjeant* surgeon, &c.—*Common serjeant*, a judicial officer connected with the City of London.—**Serjeant at arms**, *n.* In England, a title of officers who attend the lord-chancellor, the speaker of the House of Commons, and the Lord Mayor of London.—**Serjeantship**, sär′jant-ship, *n.* The office of a serjeant-at-law.—**Serjeantry**, **Serjeanty**, sär′jant-ri, sär′jan-ti, *n.* In feudal law, the tenure of land on condition of service, usually household or menial, due the king.

Sermon, sėr′mon, *n.* [L. *sermo*, *sermonis*, a speech or connected discourse, from *sero*, to join together. SERIES.] A discourse delivered in public, especially by a clergyman or preacher, for the purpose of religious instruction or the inculcation of morality, and grounded on some text or passage of Scripture; a similar discourse written or printed, whether delivered or not; a homily.—*v.t.* To tutor; to lesson; to lecture. —**Sermonist**, sėr′mon-ist, *n.* A writer of sermons.—**Sermonize**, sėr′mon-īz, *v.i.*—*sermonized, sermonizing.* To preach; to discourse.—*v.t.* To preach a sermon to.— **Sermonizer**, sėr′mon-ī-zėr, *n.* One who sermonizes; a preacher.

Seroon, **Seron**, se-rön′, se-ron′, *n.* [Sp. *seron*, a frail or basket.] A weight varying with the substance which it measures; a seroon of almonds being 87½ lb.; a bale or package for holding drugs, &c.; a ceroon.

Serosity. Under SERUM.

Serotinous, sē-rot′i-nus, *a.* [L. *serotinus*, from *serus*, late.] *Bot.* appearing late in a season.

Serous. Under SERUM.

Serpent, sėr′pent, *n.* [L. *serpens*, *serpentis*, from *serpo*, to creep; cog. Gr. *herpō*, to creep; Skr. *sarpa*, a serpent, from *srip*, to creep.] A reptile of an extremely elongated form, without feet, and moving by muscular contractions of the body; a snake; a powerful bass musical instrument, consisting of a conical tube of wood bent in a serpentine form; *fig.* a subtle or malicious person.—*Serpent stones* or *snake stones*, popular names sometimes applied to the ammonites. — **Serpent-charmer**, *n.* One who charms or professes to charm serpents; one who makes serpents obey his will.— **Serpent-eater**, *n.* The secretary-bird. —**Serpent-fence**, *n.* A zigzag fence made by placing the ends of the rails upon each other. —**Serpent-fish**, *n.* BAND-FISH.—**Serpentiform**, sėr-pen′ti-form, *a.* Having the form of a serpent; serpentine. — **Serpentigenous**, sėr-pen-tij′e-nus, *a.* Bred of a serpent.—**Serpentine**, sėr′pen-tīn, *a.* [L. *serpentinus.*] Pertaining to or resembling a serpent; having the qualities of a serpent; subtle; winding or turning one way and the other like a moving serpent; spiral; crooked.—*Serpentine verse*, a verse which begins and ends with the same word.—*n.* A rock, usually dark-coloured green, red, brown, or gray, with shades and spots resembling a serpent's skin; much used for the manufacture of various ornamental articles.—*v.i.*—*serpentined, serpentining.* To wind like a serpent; to meander.—**Serpentinely**, sėr′pen-tīn-li, *adv.* In a serpentine manner.—**Serpentinous**, sėr′pen-tī-nus, *a.* Of the nature of, or resembling serpentine.—**Serpent's-tongue**, *n.* A species of fern, so called from the form of its fronds; adder's-tongue.

Serpigo, sėr-pī′go, *n.* [L.L., from L. *serpo*, to creep.] A name for ringworm or similar skin-disease.—**Serpiginous**, sėr-pij′i-nus, *a. Med.* applied to certain affections which creep, as it were, from one part to another.

Serpolet, sėr′pō-let, *n.* [Fr.] Wild thyme.

Serpula, sėr′pū-la, *n.* pl. **Serpulæ**, sėr′pū-lē. [A dim. from L. *serpo*, to creep.] A genus of annelidans inhabiting tortuous calcareous tubes attached to rocks, shells, &c., in the sea. — **Serpulite**, sėr′pū-līt, *n.* Fossil remains of Serpula.

Serrate, **Serrated**, ser′rāt, ser′rā-ted, *a.* [L. *serratus*, from *serra*, a saw.] Notched on the edge like a saw; toothed.—**Serration**, ser-rā′shon, *n.* Formation in the shape of a saw.—**Serrature**, ser′ra-tūr, *n.* A notching in the edge of anything, like a saw.

Serricorn, ser′ri-korn, *n.* [L. *serra*, a saw, and *cornu*, a horn.] One of a family of coleopterous insects, which have serrated or saw-shaped antennæ.

Serrulate, **Serrulated**, ser′rū-lāt, ser′rū-lā-ted, *a.* [L. *serrula*, dim. of *serra*, a saw.] Finely serrate; having very minute notches.—**Serrulation**, ser-rū-lā′shon, *n.* A small notching; an indentation.

Serry,‡ ser′i, *v.t.* [Fr. *serrer*, to press, from L. *sero*, to lock, *sera*, a bolt or bar.] To crowd; to press together.—**Serried**, ser′id, *p.* and *a.* Crowded; compacted; in close order (*serried* ranks of soldiers).

Sertularia, sėr-tū-lā′ri-a, *n.* [L. *sertum*, a garland.] The genus of Hydrozoa commonly called *sea-firs.*—**Sertularian**, sėr-tū-lā′ri-an, *n.* A member of the sea-fir order.

Serum, sē′rum, *n.* [L. *serum*, whey, the watery portion of anything; akin to Gr. *oros*, whey, serum; Skr. *sâra*, water.] The thin transparent part of the blood, a liquid of a pale straw-coloured or greenish-yellow colour; the lymph-like fluid secreted by certain membranes in the human body, such as the pericardium, pleura, peritoneum, &c., thence denominated *serous membranes*; any clear fluid resembling blood serum, and containing cultures of bacteria or ANTIBODIES (which see), used in the treatment of many diseases.—*Serum treatment*, treatment of disease by the injection of ANTIBODIES (which see); the thin part of milk separated from the curd; whey.— **Serous**, sē′rus, *a.* Pertaining to serum; having the character of serum.—**Serosity**, sē-ros′i-ti, *n.* The state of being serous.

Serval, sėr′val, *n.* A South African carnivorous animal, a kind of small leopard with a bushy tail.

Serve, sėrv, *v.t.* — *served, serving.* [Fr. *servir*, from L. *servio*, *servire*, to serve, from *servus*, a servant, a slave; closely akin to *servo*, to preserve (as in *conserve, preserve, reserve*, &c.); same root in *solid, safe.*] To perform regular or continuous duties in behalf of; to be in the employment of, as a domestic, slave, hired assistant, &c.; to work for; to render spiritual obedience and worship to; to minister to; to wait on at table or at meals; to set or arrange on a table for a meal: generally with *up*; to conduce to; to be sufficient for; to promote;

to be of use to (to *serve* one's ends); to help by good offices; to administer to the wants of; to be in the place or instead of anything to; to be in lieu of (a sofa *served* him for a bed); to regulate one's conduct in accordance with the fashion, spirit, or demands of (to *serve* the time or the hour); to treat; to requite (he *served* me ill); to satisfy; to content (nothing would *serve* them but war); to handle, manage, or work (the guns were well *served*); *naut.* to protect from friction by winding something round; *law*, to deliver or transmit to; to present in due form. —*To serve out*, to deal out or distribute in portions.—*To serve one out*, to treat one according to his deserts; to take revenge on.—*To serve one right*, to treat one as he deserves.—*To serve the turn*, to meet the emergency; to answer the purpose.—*To serve a warrant*, to read it, and to seize the person against whom it is issued.—*To serve a writ*, to read it to the defendant, or to leave an attested copy at his usual place of abode.—*To serve an office*, to discharge the duties incident to it.—*v.i.* To be or act as a servant; to perform domestic offices; to discharge the requirements of an office; to act as a soldier, seaman, &c.; to answer a purpose; to be sufficient; to be of use; to suit (when occasion *serves*); to be convenient. —**Server**, sėr'vėr, *n.* One who serves; a salver or small tray.—**Servable**, sėr'va-bl, *a.* Capable of being served.—**Servant**, sėr'vant, *n.* [Fr. *servant*, from *servir*, L. *servire*, to serve; *servant* is a doublet of *sergeant*.] One who serves or does services; a person who is employed by another for menial offices or other labour, and is subject to his command; a subordinate assistant or helper: often applied distinctively to domestics or domestic servants, those who for the time being form part of a household (Mrs. Smith has four *servants*).—*Servants' hall*, the room in a house set apart for the use of the servants in common, in which they take their meals, &c.—*Your humble servant, your obedient servant*, phrases of civility used more especially in closing a letter.—*Servant of servants*, one debased to the lowest condition of servitude; a title (*servus servorum*) assumed by the popes.— **Servant-girl, Servant-maid**, *n.* A female or maid servant.—**Servant-man**, *n.* A male or man servant.—**Service**, sėr'vis, *n.* [Fr. *service*, from L. *servitium*.] The act of serving; the performance of labour or offices for another; menial duties; employment as a servant; menial employ or capacity (to be taken into a person's *service*); assistance or kindness rendered to another; kind office (has done me many *services*); duty performed; official function; especially military or naval duty; performance of the duties of a soldier or sailor (to see much *service* abroad); usefulness; benefit caused; profession of respect uttered or sent (my *service* to you); public religious worship or ceremony; religious rites appropriate to any event or ceremony (a marriage *service*); a set of dishes or vessels for the table (a tea *service*, a *service* of plate); the duty which a tenant owes to a lord for his fee.—*Service of a writ, process*, &c., the reading of it or due delivery of it to the person to whom notice is intended to be given.—**Serviceable**, sėr'vis-a-bl, *a.* Capable of rendering useful service; fit for using; useful; doing service; active; diligent. —**Serviceableness**, sėr'vis-a-bl-nes, *n.* The state of being serviceable.—**Serviceably**, sėr'vis-a-bli, *adv.* In a serviceable manner.—**Service-book**, *n.* A book used in church service; a prayer-book; a missal.—**Service-pipe**, *n.* A pipe for the supply of water, gas, and the like from the main to a building.—**Servile**, sėr'vīl, *a.* [L. *servilis*.] Pertaining to or befitting a servant or slave; slavish (*servile* fear); held in subjection; dependent; cringing; fawning; meanly submissive.—**Servilely**, sėr'vīl-li, *adv.* In a servile manner; slavishly. —**Servileness, Servility**, sėr'vīl-nes, sėr-vil'i-ti, *n.* The state or quality of being servile; mean submission; slavishness; slavish deference.—**Serving-maid**, *n.* A female servant.—**Serving-man**, *n.* A male servant; a menial.—**Servitor**, sėr'vi-tėr, *n.* [L.L., from L. *servio*, to serve.] A male servant; an attendant; a retainer; formerly, in Oxford University, a student aided by college funds and doing menial duties.—**Servitorship**, sėr'vi-tėr-ship, *n.* The office of a servitor.—**Servitude**, sėr'vi-tūd, *n.* [L. *servitudo*.] The condition of a menial, underling, or slave; involuntary subjection to a master; bondage; compulsory labour, such as a criminal has to undergo as a punishment (penal *servitude*); a state of slavish dependence. ∴ *Servitude* implies either the state of a voluntary servant or that of a slave; *slavery* is a stronger term, implying involuntary and compulsory servitude.—*a.* In *Scots law*, a right of way or otherwise over another's ground or property. EASEMENT.

Service-tree, sėr'vis, *n.* [A corruption of L. *sorbus*, the sorb or service tree.] A British and European tree of the pear family, yielding a hard-grained timber and a small fruit, which is only pleasant in an over-ripe condition.

Serviette, sėr-vi-et', *n.* [Fr.] A table-napkin.

Servile, Servitude, &c. Under SERVE.

Sesame, ses'a-mē, *n.* [Gr. *sēsamē, sēsamon*, L. *sesamum*.] An annual herbaceous plant, the seeds of which yield a bland oil of a fine quality, which will keep many years without becoming rancid.—*Open Sesame*, the charm by which the door of the robbers' dungeon, in the tale of *Ali Baba and the Forty Thieves*, flew open; hence, a specific for gaining entrance into any place, or means of exit from it.—**Sesamoid, Sesamoidal**, sē'sa-moid, sē'sa-moi-dal, *a.* Resembling the seeds of sesame in form.—*Sesamoid bones*, certain small bones formed at the articulations of the great toes, and occasionally the joints of the thumbs and in other parts.

Sesquialteral, Sesquialterate, ses-kwi-al'tėr-al, ses-kwi-al'tėr-āt, *a.* [L. prefix *sesqui*, one and a half, and *alter*, other.] *Math.* a term applied to a ratio where one quantity or number contains another once and a half as much more; thus the ratio 9 to 6 is *sesquialteral*.—**Sesquibasic**, ses'kwi-bā-sik, *a.* [L. *sesqui*, and *basis*, a base.] *Chem.* a term applied to a salt containing one and a half equivalents of the base for each equivalent of acid.—**Sesquiduplicate**, ses-kwi-dū'pli-kāt, *a.* [L. prefix *sesqui*, and *duplicatus*, double.] Designating the ratio of two and a half to one.—**Sesquioxide**, ses-kwi-ok'sīd, *n.* A compound of oxygen and another element in the proportion of three equivalents of oxygen to two of the other.—**Sesquipedalian, Sesquipedal**, ses'kwi-pē-dā"li-an, ses-kwip'ē-dal, *a.* [L. *sesquipedalis*—*sesqui*, and *pes, pedis*, a foot.] Containing or measuring a foot and a half: often humorously applied to long words, as translation of Horace's '*sesquipedalia verba*'.—**Sesquipedality, Sesquipedalianism**, ses'kwi-pē-dal"i-ti, ses'kwi-pē-dā"li-an-izm, *n.* The quality or condition of being sesquipedalian; the practice of using long words.—**Sesquiplicate**, ses-kwip'li-kāt, *a.* [Prefix *sesqui*, and *plicate*.] Designating the ratio of one and a half to one.—**Sesquisalt**, ses-kwi-salt', *n.* A salt consisting of three equivalents of one element to two of another.—**Sesquitertial, Sesquitertian**, ses-kwi-tėr'shi-al, ses-kwi-tėr'shi-an, *a.* [L. *sesqui*, and *tertius*, third.] Designating the ratio of one and one-third to one.

Sessile, ses'il, *a.* [L. *sessilis*, from *sedeo, sessum*, to sit. SEDATE.] *Zool.* and *bot.* attached without any sensible projecting support, a *sessile leaf* being one without a petiole or footstalk; a *sessile flower*, one having no peduncle; a *sessile gland*, one not elevated on a stalk.

Session, sesh'on, *n.* [Fr. *session*, from L. *sessio, sessionis*, from *sedeo, sessum*, to sit. SEDATE.] A sitting; the sitting of a court, academic body, council, legislature, &c., for the transaction of business; the time or term during which such body transacts business regularly without breaking up; in Scotland, the kirk-session, the lowest ecclesiastical court of the Presbyterian Church; *law*, generally in *pl.*, a sitting of a justice's court, as for granting local licenses, trying minor offenses, &c.—*Sessions of the peace*, in England, the sittings of the justice of the peace or magistrate.—*Petty sessions*, in England, the meeting of two or more justices for trying minor offenses without a jury.—*Quarter sessions*. Under QUARTER.—*Court of Session*, the supreme civil court of Scotland.—**Sessional**, sesh'on-al, *a.* Relating or belonging to a session or sessions.

Sess-pool, *n.* CESS-POOL.

Sesterce, Sestertius, ses'tėrs, ses-tėr'shē-us, *n.* [Fr. *sesterce*, L. *sestertius*, lit. what contains two and a half—*semis*, a half, and *tertius*, a third.] A Roman coin or denomination of money, originally containing two asses and a half, valued at about 2*d.* sterling.

Sestet, Sestette, ses'tet, ses-tet', *n.* [It. *sestetto*, from L. *sextus*, sixth, from *sex*, six.] *Music*, a composition for six voices or six instruments; the two concluding stanzas of a sonnet, consisting of three verses each; the last six lines of a sonnet.—**Sestetto**, ses-tet'tō. *n.* *Music*, same as *Sestet*.—**Sestine**, ses'tīn, *n.* *Pros.* a stanza of six lines; a sextain.

Set, set, *v.t.*—pret. and pp. *set*, ppr. *setting*. [Causative or factitive of *sit*; A.Sax. *settan*, to set, place, appoint, &c.; Icel. *setja*, Dan. *sette*, Goth. *satjan*, G. *setzen*, to set.] To make or cause to sit; to place in a sitting, standing, or any natural posture; to place upright (to *set* a box on its end or a table on its feet); to put, place, or fix; to put in a certain place, position, or station; to make or cause to be, do, or act; to put from one state into another (to *set* a person right, to *set* things in order); to fix as regards amount or value (to *set* a price on a house); to fix or settle authoritatively or by arrangement; to appoint; to assign (to *set* an hour for a journey); to estimate or rate (to *set* advice at naught); to regulate or adjust (to *set* a timepiece); to fit to music; to plant, as distinguished from *sowing*; to fix for ornament, as in metal (a diamond *set* in a ring); to adorn, as with precious stones; to intersperse; to stud; to reduce from a dislocated or fractured state (to *set* a joint); to fix mentally; to fix with settled purpose (to *set* the heart or affections); to stake at play (*Shak.*); to embarrass; to perplex; to pose (to be hard *set*); to put in trim for use (to *set* a razor or a saw); to apply or use in action; to employ: with *to* (to *set* spurs to one's horse); to incite; to instigate; to spur: often with *on*; to let to a tenant; *printing*, to place in proper order, as types; to compose; to put into type (to *set* a MS.: often with *up*); to make stiff or solid; to convert into curd (to *set* milk for cheese).—*To set against*, to oppose; to set in comparison.—*To set aside*, to omit for the present; to lay out of the question; to disregard; to abrogate (to *set aside* a verdict).—*To set at defiance*, to defy; to dare to combat.—*To set at ease*, to quiet; to tranquillize.—*To set at naught*, to regard as of no value or consideration; to despise. —*To set a trap* or *snare*, to prepare and place it so as to catch prey; to lay a plan to inveigle a person.—*To set at work*, to cause to enter on work or action.—*To set down*, to place upon the ground or floor; to enter in writing; to register.—*To set eyes on*, to fix the eyes in looking on; to behold.—*To set fire to*, to apply fire to; to set on fire.— *To set forth*, to present to view or consideration; to make known fully; to show; to promulgate; to publish.—*To set in order*, to adjust or arrange; to reduce to method. —*To set much* (*little*, &c.) *by*, to regard much; to esteem greatly.—*To set off*, to adorn; to decorate; to embellish; to show to the best advantage.—*To set* a person *on*, to instigate him; to prompt him to action. —*To set one's cap at*. Under CAP.—*To set one's self against*, to resist or oppose stubbornly; to be resolute against.—*To set one's teeth*, to press them close together.—*To set on fire*, to kindle; to inflame.—*To set on foot*, to start; to set agoing.—*To set over*, to appoint or constitute as supervisor, inspector, governor, or director.—*To set right*, to correct; to put in order.—*To set sail*. Under

SAIL.—*To set the teeth on edge.* Under EDGE.—*To set the fashion,* to establish the mode; to determine what shall be the fashion.—*To set up,* to erect; to institute; to establish; to enable to commence a new business; to utter loudly (to *set up* a loud cry); to propose (to *set up* a doctrine); to raise from depression or to a sufficient fortune.—*v.i.* To pass below the horizon; to sink; to decline; to congeal or concrete; to solidify; to have a certain direction in motion; to flow; to tend (the current *sets* westward); to point out game, as a sportsman's dog; to undertake earnestly; to apply one's self; to face one's partner in dancing.—*To set about,* to begin; to take the first steps in.—*To set forth* or *forward,* to move or march; to begin to march; to advance.—*To set in,* to begin (winter *sets in* about December); to flow towards the shore (the tide *sets in*).—*To set off,* to start; to enter on a journey.—*Offset, printing,* to employ the *offset* process, using intermediary smooth, rubber-surfaced cylinders that receive the impression from the plate and transfer the image to the paper instead of printing from the plate, thus permitting use of a variety of paper; the transfer from one sheet to another of printing ink before it has dried.—*Set up, p.* and *a.* Placed, put, fixed, &c.; regular; in due form; well arranged or put together (a *set* speech or phrase); fixed in opinion; determined; firm; obstinate; established; settled; appointed (*set* forms of prayer); predetermined; fixed beforehand (a *set* purpose); fixed; immovable.—*Set scene,* in theatres, a scene where there is a good deal of arrangement for the pose.—*n.* A collection of things of the same kind or to be used together, of which each is a complement of all the rest; a complete suit or assortment (a *set* of chairs, a *set* of tea dishes); a number of persons customarily or officially associated; a number of particular things united in the formation of a whole (a *set* of features); the five figures of a quadrille; the music for a quadrille; also, the number of couples required to execute the dance; the descent of the sun or other luminary below the horizon; an attitude, position, or posture; a permanent change of figure caused by pressure or being retained long in one position; a turn or bent; a direction or course (the *set* of a current).—*To make a dead set,* to make a determined onset, or an importunate application.—**Set-down,** *n.* A rebuff; an unexpected and overwhelming answer.—**Setness,**† set'nes, *n.* The state or quality of being set.—**Set-off,** *n.* That which is used to set off the appearance of anything; an ornament; a counter claim or demand; a cross debt; an equivalent; *printing,* an offset, the impression from a printed page, the ink on which is not dry, to an opposite page.—**Set-screw,** *n.* A screw screwed through one part tightly upon another to bring pieces into close contact.—**Setter,** set'ėr, *n.* One who or that which sets; a kind of sportsman's dog, named from its habit of *setting* or crouching when it perceives the scent of game, and which is also trained to mark game by standing.—**Setter-forth,** *n.* One who sets forth; a proclaimer.—**Setter-off,** *n.* One who or that which sets off or adorns.—**Setter-on,** *n.* One who sets on; an instigator.—**Setter-up,** *n.* One who sets up, establishes, makes, or appoints.—**Setting,** set'ing, *n.* The act of one who or that which sets; a sinking below the horizon; that in which something, as a jewel, is set (a diamond in a gold *setting*).—**Set-to,** *n.* A sharp contest; a fight at fisticuffs; a boxing-match; any similar contest, as with foils. (*Colloq.*)

Seta, sē'ta, *n.* pl. **Setæ,** sē'tē. [L., a bristle.] A bristle or sharp hair; especially a bristle or stiff hair-like appendage of plants and animals; the stalk that supports the theca, capsule, or sporangium of mosses.—**Setaceous,** sē-tā'shus, *a.* Bristly; set with bristles; having the character of setæ.—**Setiferous,** sē-tif'ėr-us, *a.* Producing or having bristles.—**Setiform,** sē'ti-form, *a.* Having the form of a bristle.—**Setigerous,** sē-tij'ėr-us, *a.* Covered with bristles; setiferous.—**Setireme,** sē'ti-rēm, *n.* [L. *seta,* and *remus,* an oar.] An insect's leg that has a dense fringe of hairs, enabling the animal to move on the water.

Seton, sē'ton, *n.* [Fr. *séton,* from L. *seta,* a bristle—hair or bristles having been originally used for the purpose.] *Surg.* a skein of silk or cotton, or similar material, passed under the skin in order to maintain an artificial issue.

Setose, Setous, sē'tōs, sē'tus, *a.* [L. *setosus,* from *seta,* a bristle.] *Bot.* bristly; having the surface set with bristles.

Sett, set, *n.* A small block of granite or other stone for paving streets.

Settee, set-ē', *n.* [From *set.*] A long seat with a back to it; a large sofa-shaped seat for several persons to sit in at one time.

Settee, set-ē', *n.* [Fr. *scétie, sétie.*] A vessel with a long sharp prow, carrying two or three masts with lateen sails; used in the Mediterranean.

Setter, &c. Under SET.

Settle, set'l, *n.* [A.Sax. *setl,* a seat, a stool, a settle; from *set.* Comp. L. *sella,* a seat, for *sedla,* from *sedeo,* to sit. SET, SIT.] A bench to sit on; a stool—*v.t.*—*settled, settling.* [From *set;* a freq. in form=A.Sax. *setlan,* to seat, to place.] To place in a fixed or permanent position; to establish or fix in any line of life, in an office, business, situation, &c.; to change from a disturbed or troubled condition to one of tranquillity; to quiet, still, calm, compose (to *settle* the mind when agitated); to clear of dregs or sediment by causing them to sink; to cause to sink to the bottom; to determine, as something which is exposed to doubt or question; to free from uncertainty or wavering; to confirm; to adjust, as something in controversy; to bring to a conclusion; to finish (to *settle* a dispute); to make secure formally or legally (to *settle* an annuity on a person); to liquidate; to pay; to square or adjust (to *settle* an account, claim); to plant with inhabitants; to people; to colonize.—*v.i.* To become fixed or permanent; to assume a lasting form or condition; to establish a residence; to take up a permanent abode; to quit an irregular and desultory for a methodical life; to enter the married state; to change from a disturbed or turbid state to the opposite; to become free from dregs by their sinking to the bottom; to sink or fall gradually; to subside, as dregs from a liquid; to become lowered, as a building, by the sinking of its foundation; to become calm; to cease from agitation; to adjust differences; to come to an agreement.—**Settled,** set'ld, *p.* and *a.* Established; stable; deep-rooted; unchanging (*settled* gloom, a *settled* conviction); orderly; methodical (a *settled* life).—**Settledness,** set'ld-nes, *n.*—**Settlement,** set'l-ment, *n.* The act of settling or state of being settled; establishment in life; the act of colonizing or peopling; colonization; a tract of country colonized; a colony in its earlier condition; the liquidation of a claim or account; adjustment; arrangement; a legal deed by which property is settled; right from a certain connection with a particular parish, town, or locality to maintenance there if a pauper.—**Settler,** set'lėr, *n.* One who settles; one who fixes his residence in a new colony; a colonist; that which settles or decides anything definitely (*colloq.*).—**Settling,** set'ling, *n.* The act of one who settles; *pl.* dregs; sediment.—**Settling-day,** *n.* A day set apart for the settling of accounts.

Setula, set'ū-la, *n.* pl. **Setulæ,** set'ū-lē. [L. dim. of *seta,* a bristle.] *Bot.* a small bristle or hair.—**Setule,** set'ūl, *n.* A small short bristle or hair.—**Setulose,** set'ū-lōs, *a.* Bearing or provided with setules.

Setwall, set'wąl, *n.* [O.Fr. *cetewale, citoual.*] A species of valerian once in use in medicine.

Seven, sev'n, *a.* [A.Sax. *seofan*=D. *zeven,* Goth. and O.H.G. *sibun,* G. *sieben,* Icel. *sjau,* Dan. *syv,* W. *saith,* Ir. *seacht,* Rus. *semj,* L. *septem,* Gr. *hepta* (for *septa*), Per. *haft* Skr. *saptan.*] One more than six or less than eight.—*n.* This number; a group of things amounting to this number; the symbol representing this number, as 7 or vii.—**Sevenfold,** sev'n-fōld, *a.* Repeated or multiplied seven times.—*adv.* Seven times as much; in the proportion of seven to one.—**Sevennight,** sev'n-nīt, *n.* The period of seven days and nights; a week. SE'NNIGHT.—**Seventeen,** sev'n-tēn, *a.* and *n.* Seven and ten added.—**Seventeenth,** sev'n-tēnth, *a.* Next in order after the sixteenth.—*n.* The next in order after the sixteenth; one of seventeen equal parts of a whole.—**Seventh,** sev'nth, *a.* Next after the sixth; being one of seven equal parts of a whole.—*n.* One next in order after the sixth; one of seven equal parts of a whole; *music,* the interval of five tones and a semitone, embracing seven degrees of the diatonic scale, as from C to B; the seventh note of the diatonic scale reckoning upwards; the B of the natural scale.—**Seventhly,** sev'nth-li, *adv.* In the seventh place.—**Seventieth,** sev'n-ti-eth, *a.* Next in order after the sixty-ninth.—*n.* One next after the sixty-ninth; one of seventy equal parts.—**Seventy,** sev'n-ti, *a.* and *n.* [A.Sax. *seofontig*—*seofon,* seven, and *tig,* ten.] Seven times ten; the number made up of seven times ten.

Sever, sev'ėr, *v.t.* [O.Fr. *sevrer, severer,* from L. *separare,* to separate. SEPARATE.] To part or divide by violence; to separate by cutting or rending; to part from the rest by violence; to disjoin, referring to things that are distinct but united by some tie (friends *severed* by death); to disunite.—*v.i.* To suffer disjunction; to be parted or rent asunder.—**Severable,** sev'ėr-a-bl, *a.* Capable of being severed.—**Severance,** sev'ėr-ans, *n.* The act of severing or state of being severed; separation; partition.

Several, sev'ėr-al, *a.* [O.Fr. *several,* from *severer.* SEVER.] Separate; distinct; not common to two or more: in this sense chiefly a law term; single; individual (each *several* thing); more than two, but not very many; divers: used with plural nouns.—*n.* A few separately or individually; a small number singly taken: with a plural verb.—**Severally,** sev'ėr-al-li, *adv.* Separately; distinctly; each by himself.—**Severalty,** sev'ėr-al-ti, *n.* A state of separation from the rest, or from all others.

Severe, sē-vēr', *a.* [Fr. *sévère,* from L. *severus,* serious, severe; seen also in *persevere, asseverate.*] Serious or earnest in feeling or manner; sedate; grave; austere; very strict in discipline or government; not indulgent; judging or criticising harshly; strictly regulated by rule; rigidly methodical; not allowing unnecessary or florid ornament or the like (the *severest* style of Greek architecture); afflictive; distressing; violent; extreme; intense (*severe* pain or cold); difficult to be undergone; rigorous (a *severe* test or examination).—**Severely,** sē-vēr'li, *adv.* In a severe manner; rigidly; strictly; rigorously; painfully.—**Severeness,** sē-vēr'nes, *n.* Severity.—**Severity,** sē-ver'i-ti, *n.* [L. *severitas.*] The quality or state of being severe; extreme strictness; rigour; harshness; intensity; extremity; keenness; extreme coldness or inclemency; cruel treatment; sharpness of punishment; strictness.

Sèvres, Sevres Ware, sā'vr, *n.* A kind of beautiful porcelain ware, manufactured at *Sèvres,* in France.

Sew, sō, *v.t.* [A.Sax. *siwian, seowian,* to sew=O.H.G. *siuwan,* Goth. *siujan,* Dan. *sye,* Icel. *sýja;* cog. L. *suo,* Skr. *siv,* to sew. *Seam* is from this stem.] To unite or fasten together with a needle and thread; to make or work by needle and thread.—*To sew up,* to close or unite by sewing.—*v.i.* To practice sewing; to join things with stitches.—**Sewer,** sō'ėr, *n.* One who sews. **Sewing,** sō'ing, *n.* The act of sewing; dress-goods that have been sewed.—**Sewing-machine,** *n.* A machine for sewing.

Sewage, sū'āj, *n.* [From old verb *sew,* to drain, from O.F. *essuier,* to drain, from L. *ex,* out, and *sucus* or *succus,* juice.] The filthy matter which passes through drains, conduits, or sewers, leading away from human habitations. — **Sewer,** sū′ėr, *n.* [O.Fr. *essuier, essuyer,* a drain, a conduit.] A subterranean channel or canal formed in towns and other places to carry off superfluous water, as well as excrementitious and other matters.—**Sewerage,** sū′-ėr-āj, *n.* The system of sewers; also, sewage.—*Sewerage* is generally applied to the system of sewers, and *sewage* to the matter carried off.

Sewer, sū′ėr, *n.* [From A.Sax. *seáw,* juice.] In medieval Europe, an officer who served up a feast and arranged the dishes.

Sex, seks, *n.* [Fr. *sexe,* from L. *sexus,* a sex, from *seco,* to cut. SECTION.] The distinction between male and female, or that property or character by which an animal is male or female; the structure of plants which corresponds to sex in animals; one or other of the divisions of males and females; by way of emphasis, womankind; the female sex: generally with *the.*—**Sexless,** seks′les, *a.* Having no sex.—**Sexual,** sek′sū-al, *a.* [L. *sexualis.*] Pertaining to sex or the sexes.—*Sexual system,* a system of classification founded on the distinction of sexes in plants.—**Sexually,** sek′sū-al-li, *adv.* In a sexual manner.—**Sexuality,** sek-sū-al′i-ti, *n.* The state or quality of being distinguished by sex.—**Sexualist,** sek′sū-al-ist, *n.* One who maintains the doctrine of sexes in plants.

Sexagenary, sek-saj′e-na-ri, *a.* [L. *sexagenarius,* from *sexaginta,* sixty, from *sex,* six.] Pertaining to the number sixty; composed of or proceeding by sixties.—*n.* A sexagenarian. — **Sexagenarian,** sek′sa-je-nā″ri-an, *n.* A person aged sixty or between sixty and seventy.—*a.* Sixty years old; sexagenary.

Sexagesima, sek-sa-jes′i-ma, *n.* [L. *sexagesimus,* sixtieth.] The second Sunday before Lent, so called as being about the sixtieth day before Easter. — **Sexagesimal,** sek-sa-jes′i-mal, *a.* Sixtieth; pertaining to the number sixty.—*Sexagesimal* or *sexagenary arithmetic,* a method of computation by sixties.—*Sexagesimal fractions,* or *sexagesimals,* fractions whose denominators are sixty or its multiple.

Sexangle, seks′ang-gl, *n.* [L. *sex,* six, and *angulus,* an angle.] *Geom.* a figure having six angles; a hexagon. — **Sexangular,** seks-ang′gū-lėr, *a.* Hexagonal.

Sexennial, sek-sen′ni-al, *a.* [L. *sex,* six, and *annus,* year.] Lasting six years, or happening once in six years.—**Sexennially,** sek-sen′ni-al-li, *adv.* Once in six years.

Sexisyllable, seks′i-sil-la-bl, *n.* [L. *sex,* six, and E. *syllable.*] A word having six syllables.

Sexlocular, seks-lok′ū-lėr, *a.* [L. *sex,* six, and *loculus,* a cell.] *Bot.* having six cells for seeds.

Sext, sext, *n.* [Fr. *sexte,* L. *sixtus.*] The office in the Roman Catholic Church recited at the sixth hour or noon.

Sextain, seks′tān, *n.* [From L. *sex,* six.] A stanza of six lines.

Sextan fever. A fever recurring every sixth day.

Sextant, seks′tant, *n.* [L. *sextans, sextantis,* a sixth part, from *sex,* six.] The sixth part of a circle contained by two radii and an arc; an improved form of quadrant, capable of measuring angles of 120° and having an arc embracing 60° of a circle, chiefly employed as a nautical instrument for measuring the altitudes of celestial objects and their angular distances.

Sextet, sex-tet′, *n.* A musical piece for six voices; the second part of the sonnet formation, opposed to the octave.

Sextile, sext′il, *n.* The aspect of two planets when distant from each other sixty degrees or two signs, marked *.

Sextillion, seks-til′yon, *n.* [From L. *sextus,* sixth, *sex,* six, and E. *million.*] In the American and French system, ten billion times one hundred billion, or a unit followed by twenty-one ciphers.

Sexto-decimo, seks-tō-des′i-mō, *n.* [L. *sextus decimus,* sixteenth — *sextus,* sixth, and *decimus,* tenth.] A book folded so that each sheet makes sixteen leaves; the size of the book thus folded. Usually indicated thus, 16mo (pron. as sixteen-mo).

Sexton, seks′ton, *n.* [Contr. from *sacristan* (which see).] An under officer of the church who takes care of the vessels, vestments, &c., and of the church generally, to which is added the duty of digging graves.—**Sextonship,** seks′ton-ship, *n.* The office of a sexton.

Sextuple, seks′tū-pl, *a.* [L.L. *sextuplus,* from L. *sextus,* sixth, *sex,* six, with term. *-ple.*] Sixfold; six times as much.

Sexual, Sexually, &c. Under SEX.

Sforzando, Sforzato, sfor-tsän′dō, sfor-tsä′tō. [It., forcing, forced.] A musical term written over a note or notes to signify that they are to be emphasized more strongly than they would otherwise be: generally contracted *sf.*

Sfumato, sfō-mä′tō, *a.* [It., smoky.] A term applied to a style of painting wherein the tints are so blended that outlines are scarcely perceptible.

Sgraffito, sgraf-fē′tō, *a.* [It., scratched.] Applied to a species of drawing in which a white coat is applied over dark stucco, and by an instrument the design is formed from the dark ground underneath.

Shabble, shabl, *n.* [G. *säbel,* sabre, Sw. *sabel.*] A sword.

Shabby, shab′i, *a.* [A softened form of *scabby*; Prov.E. *shabby,* itchy, mangy, from *shab,* itch. SCAB.] Threadbare or much worn; worn till no longer respectable; wearing much-worn clothes; mean; despicable. —**Shabbily,** shab′i-li, *adv.* In a shabby manner. — **Shabbiness,** shab′i-nes, *n.* The quality of being shabby.—**Shabby-genteel,** *a.* Retaining in present shabbiness traces of former gentility.

Shabrack, shab′rak, *n.* [G. *schabracke,* Fr. *chabraque,* from Hung. *csabrág,* Turk. *tshâprâk.*] The large saddle-cloth or housing of a cavalry officer's charger.

Shackle, shak′l, *n.* [A.Sax. *scacul, sceacul,* a shackle, probably originally a loose, dangling fastening, from *scacan, sceacan,* to shake.] A fetter, handcuff, or the like that confines the limbs so as to restrain the use of them; *fig.* that which obstructs or embarrasses free action: generally in pl. —*v.t.*—*shackled, shackling.* To fetter; to tie or confine the limbs of, so as to prevent free motion; *fig.* to bind or confine so as to embarrass action.—**Shackle-bolt,** *n.* A shackle; a gyve.

Shad, shad, *n. sing.* and *pl.* [A. Sax. *sceadd,* G. *schade,* a shad.] A fish of the herring family which inhabits the Atlantic Ocean near the mouths of rivers, and ascends them to spawn.

Shaddock, shad′ok, *n.* [After Captain *Shaddock,* who first brought it to the West Indies early in the eighteenth century.] A tree and its fruit, which is a large species of orange: a native of China. A small variety is called *grape-fruit.*

Shade, shād, *n.* [A.Sax. *scæd, sceadu,* shade. SHADOW.] A comparative obscurity, dimness, or gloom, caused by the interception of the rays of light; something that intercepts light, heat, dust, &c.; a cover for the flame of a lamp; a cover that confines the light of a lamp within a given area; a cover for the eyes; the dark or darker part of a picture; degree or gradation of light or brightness of colour; a small or scarcely perceptible degree or amount (a price a *shade* higher); a shadow (*poet.*); the soul after its separation from the body; a spirit; a ghost; hence, *the shades,* the abode of spirits; hades. ∴ *Shade* differs from *shadow,* as it implies no particular form or definite limit; whereas a *shadow* represents in form the object which intercepts the light.—*v.t.*—*shaded, shading.* To shelter or screen from light by intercepting its rays; to shelter from the light and heat of the sun; to cover with a shade or screen that intercepts light, heat, dust, &c.; to overspread with darkness or obscurity; to obscure; to shelter; to protect; *drawing* and *painting,* to put in darker colours to show where the light is less intense; to mark with gradations of colour.—**Shadeless,** shād′les, *a.* Without shade.—**Shader,** shā′dėr, *n.* One who or that which shades. — **Shady,** shā′di, *a.* Abounding with shade or shades; casting or causing shade; sheltered from the glare of light or sultry heat; dark; tricky; ignoble.—**Shadily,** shā′di-li, *adv.* In a shady manner; umbrageously. — **Shadiness,** shā′di-nes, *n.* The state of being shady; umbrageousness.—**Shading,** shā′ding, *n.* The effect of light and shade represented in a picture.

Shadoof, Shaduf, sha-dụf′, *n.* A contrivance employed in Egypt for raising water from the Nile, consisting of a long pole supported on an upright post and weighted at one end to serve as a counterpoise, the other end having a bucket or jar attached.

Shadow, shad′ō, *n.* [A.Sax. *sceadu,* a shadow, *scæd,* a shade; O.Sax. *scado,* Goth. *skadus,* D. *schaduw,* G. *schatten*; from a root *skad,* Skr. *chhad,* to cover; comp. Gr. *skotos,* darkness.] The figure of a body projected on the ground or other surface by the interception of the light; a portion of space from which light is intercepted by an opaque body (to be in *shadow*); darkness or obscurity from intercepted light; *fig.* the shelter, protection, or security afforded by some one; a dark part of a picture; anything unsubstantial or unreal, though having the appearance of reality; a spirit; a ghost; a shade; an imperfect and faint representation; adumbration; a dim bodying forth; an inseparable companion or one that follows like a shadow; a type or mystical representation; slight or faint appearance.—*The shadow of death,* the approach of death or dire calamity.—*v.t.* To overspread with obscurity or shade; to intercept light or heat from; to shade; to cloud; to darken; to throw a gloom over; to protect; to screen from danger; to mark with slight gradations of colour or light; to paint in obscure colours; to represent faintly or imperfectly; to represent typically: often followed by *forth*; to follow closely; to attend on like a shadow. —**Shadowiness,** shad′ō-i-nes, *n.* State of being shadowy or unsubstantial.—**Shadowing,** shad′ō-ing, *n.* Shade of gradation of light and colour; shading; the art of correctly representing the shadows of objects.—**Shadowless,** shad′ō-les, *a.* Having no shadow.—**Shadowy,** shad′ō-i, *a.* Full of shade or shadow; causing shade; gloomy; faintly representative; unsubstantial; unreal; dimly seen; obscure; dim; indulging in fancies or dreamy imaginations.

Shady. Under SHADE.

Shaft, shaft, *n.* [From G. *schacht,* the shaft of a mine.] A narrow deep pit made into the earth as the entrance to a coal or other mine or for its ventilation.

Shaft, shaft, *n.* [A.Sax. *sceaft,* a dart, arrow, spear, pole=Icel. *skaft, skapt,* Dan. *skaft,* D. and G. *schaft*; lit. the thing shaped or smoothed by shaving, from A. Sax. *scafan,* to shave; comp. L. *scapus,* a shaft; Gr. *skaptron, skēptron,* a staff.] An arrow; a spear or dart; the columnar part of anything; the body of a column between the base and the capital; the spire of a steeple; the handle of certain tools or instruments (the *shaft* of a hammer, axe, whip, &c.); a kind of large axle, as of a fly-wheel or the screw or paddles of a steamer; one of the bars between a pair of which a horse is harnessed to a vehicle; a thill; the pole of a carriage.—**Shafted,** shaf′ted, *a.* Having a shaft or shafts; ornamented with clustering pillars.—**Shaft-horse,** *n.* The horse that goes in the shafts of a carriage.—**Shafting,** shaf′ting, *n.* A system of shafts through which motion is communicated in machinery.

Shag, shag, *n.* [A.Sax. *sceacga,* coarse hair; akin to Icel. *skegg,* a beard, *skaga,* to stand out, *skagi,* a promontory.] Coarse hair or nap; rough woolly hair; a kind of cloth having a long coarse nap; a kind of tobacco cut into fine shreds; the crested or green cormorant.—*a.* Hairy; shaggy. (*Shak.*)—**Shaggy, Shagged,** shag'i, shag'ed, *a.* Rough with long hair or wool; rough; rugged.—**Shagginess,** shag'i-nes, *n.* The state of being shaggy.—**Shag-haired,** *a.* Having shaggy hair.

Shagreen, sha-grēn', *n.* [Fr. *chagrin,* Venetian, *sagrin,* from Turk. *sagri,* Per. *saghri,* shagreen. *Chagrin* is the same word.] A species of granulated leather prepared without tanning, from horse, ass, and camel skin, or made of the skins of the shark, sea-otter, seal, &c.

Shah, shä, *n.* [Per., a king, a prince (hence *chess, check*).] A title given by European writers to the monarch of Persia, who in his own country is designated by the compound appellation of *Padishah;* a chieftain or prince.

Shake, shāk, *v.t.*—pret. *shook;* pp. *shaken;* ppr. *shaking.* [A.Sax. *scacan, sceacan,* pret. *scóc,* pp. *scacen;* Icel. and Sw. *skaka,* to shake; allied to D. *schokken,* to shake; G. *schaukeln,* to swing. SHOCK.] To cause to move with quick vibrations; to make to tremble, quiver, or shiver; to agitate; to remove by agitating, or by a jolting, jerking motion: generally with *away, off, out,* &c.; to move from firmness; to threaten to overthrow; to cause to waver or doubt; to impair the resolution of; to depress the courage of; to give a tremulous sound to; to trill (a note in music).—*To shake hands,* to clasp right hands together mutually, as by two persons at meeting and parting, or to ratify or confirm an agreement.—*To shake hands with,* sometimes to take leave of; to give up; to take leave; to part.—*To shake off the dust from the feet,* a symbolic method of renouncing solemnly all intercourse or connection.—*To shake the head,* to express disapprobation, refusal, reproach, and the like.—*v.i.* To be agitated with a waving or vibratory motion; to tremble; to shiver; to totter.—*n.* A wavering rapid motion one way and the other; a shock or concussion; tremor; *mus.* a rapid reiteration of two notes; a trill, marked by the sign (*tr.,* abbreviation of *trill*) placed over the note; a crack or fissure in timber; *pl.* a trembling fit; specifically, ague; intermittent fever.—*Shake of the hand,* a friendly clasp of another's hand.—*No great shakes,* lit. no great windfall; hence, nothing extraordinary; of little value.—**Shake-down,** *n.* A temporary bed; money obtained by extortion (*Slang*).—**Shaken,** shā'kn, *p.* and *a.* Caused to shake; agitated; having the constitution or bodily health impaired; cracked or split (*shaken* timber).—**Shaker,** shā'kėr, *n.* A religious sect founded in Manchester about the middle of the eighteenth century, so called popularly from the agitations or movements in dancing which forms part of their ceremonial; now mostly confined to the United States of America.—**Shakerism,** shā'kėr-izm, *n.* The principles of the Shakers.—**Shakiness,** shā'ki-nes, *n.* State or quality of being shaky.—**Shaky,** shā'ki, *a.* Loosely put together; ready to come to pieces; unsubstantial; tottering; cracked or split, as timber.

Shakespearean, Shaksperian, shak-spē'ri-an, *a.* Relating to Shakespeare.—*n.* A scholar making Shakespeare's works his special field of study.

Shako, shak'ō, *n.* [Fr. *schako,* from Hung. *csákó,* a shako.] A kind of military cap somewhat resembling a truncated cone, with a peak in front.

Shale, shāl, *n.* [A form of *scale,* directly from G. *schale,* a shell, a thin layer. SHELL.] A shell or husk (*Shak.*); *geol.* a species of schist or schistous clay; a clayey rock having a slaty fracture, often found in strata in coal-mines; an important variety being impregnated with bitumen and yielding paraffin, while another yields alum.—*v.t.* and *i.* To peel.—**Shaly,** shā'li, *a.* Partaking of the qualities of shale.

Shall, shal, *auxiliary.* Pres. I *shall,* thou *shalt,* he *shall,* pl. 1, 2, and 3 *shall;* imperf. *should, shouldest* or *shouldst, should,* pl. *should.* [A.Sax. *sceal,* I shall, I have to, I ought; pl. *sculon,* pret. *sceolde, scolde,* inf. *sculan;* Icel. and Dan. *skal,* D. *zal,* G. *soll,* literal meaning seen in Goth. *skulan,* to owe, to have to pay.] In the first persons singular and plural it forms part of the future tense and future perfect, and simply foretells or declares what is to take place = am to, are to (I *shall* go, we *shall* go); in the second and third persons it implies control or authority on the part of the speaker, and is used to express a promise, command, or determination (you *shall* go, he *shall* go). Interrogatively, *shall* I go? *shall* we go? *shall* he go? *shall* they go? ask for direction or refer the matter to the determination of the person asked; *shall* you go? asks for information merely as to the future.—After *if,* &c., *shall,* in all persons, expresses simple futurity.—*Should,* though in form the past of *shall,* is not used to express simple past futurity unless in the indirect speech (I said I *should* go); it is very commonly used to express present as well as past duty or obligation (you *should* go, have gone).—It is also used to express a merely hypothetical case or a contingent future event, standing in the same relation to *would* that *shall* does to *will* (I *should* be glad if you *would* come).—Also often used in a modest way to soften a statement (I *should* think so).—*Shall* and *will* are often confounded by inaccurate speakers or writers. WILL.

Shalli, shal'i, *n.* [Connected with *shawl.*] A kind of twilled cloth made from the native goats' hair at Angora.

Shalloon, sha-lön', *n.* [Fr. *chalon,* a woollen stuff, said to be from *Châlons,* in France.] A slight woollen stuff.

Shallop, shal'op, *n.* [Fr. *chaloupe,* a form of D. *sloep,* E. *sloop.*] A large boat with two masts, rigged like a schooner; a small light vessel with a small mainmast and foremast, with lug-sails.

Shallot, sha-lot', *n.* [O.Fr. *eschalote,* from *Ascalon.*] A plant of the onion family having mild-flavored, clustered bulbs, and used in cooking and pickling; scallion.

Shallow, shal'ō, *a.* [Same word as Icel. *skjálgr,* wry, oblique, the water being shallow where the beach sinks obliquely downward; comp. also *shoal, shelf.*] Not deep; having the bottom at no great distance from the surface (*shallow* water); having sides not raised much above the bottom (a *shallow* trough); not intellectually deep; not profound; superficial; silly.—*n.* A place where the water is not deep; a shoal.—*v.t.* To make shallow.—**Shallow-brained,** *a.* Of no depth of intellect; empty-headed. **Shallow-hearted,** *a.* Incapable of deep feeling or affection.—**Shallowly,** shal'ō-li, *adv.* In a shallow manner; superficially.—**Shallowness,** shal'ō-nes, *n.* The state or quality of being shallow; superficialness of intellect.—**Shallow-pated,** *a.* Of weak mind; silly.

Shalm, sham, *n.* A shawm.

Shalt, shalt, second person singular of *shall.*

Sham, sham, *n.* [A form of *shame;* comp. Prov.E. *sham,* shame; *sham,* to blush for shame.] One who or that which deceives expectation; a trick or fraud; something counterfeit; an imposture.—*a.* False; counterfeit; pretended.—*v.t. shammed, shamming.* To make a pretence of in order to deceive; to feign (to *sham* illness).—*v.i.* To pretend; to make false pretences.—**Sham-fight,** *n.* A pretended fight or engagement; manœuvres of troops in imitation of a real fight.—**Shammer,** sham'ėr, *n.* One that shams; an impostor.

Shamanism, shā'man-izm, *n.* [Hind. and Per. *shaman,* an idolater.] An idolatrous religion of Northern Asia and elsewhere, consisting mainly in a belief in sorcery, and in demons who require to be propitiated by sacrifices and rites; a sort of fetishism.—**Shamanist,** shā'man-ist, *n.* A believer in Shamanism.—**Shaman,** shā'man, *n.* A priest or conjuror among those who profess Shamanism.—**Shamanic,** shā-man'ik, *a.* Pertaining to Shamanism.

Shamble, sham'bl, *v.i.*—*shambled, shambling.* [A form of *scamble* (which see).] To walk awkwardly and unsteadily, as if the knees were weak.—**Shambling,** sham'bling, *a.* Moving with an awkward, clumsy pace.—*n.* An awkward, clumsy, irregular pace or gait.

Shambles, sham'blz, *n.pl.* [A.Sax. *scamel,* a stool, a bench = Dan. *skammel,* Icel. *skemmill,* from L. *scamellum,* dim. of *scamnum,* a stool.] Originally tables or benches where butchers exposed meat for sale; hence, a slaughter-house: often treated as a singular; a place of indiscriminate slaughter or butchery; *mining,* shelves or benches on which ore is successively thrown in raising it.

Shame, shām, *n.* [A.Sax. *sceamu, scamu* = Icel. *skamm, skömm,* Dan. and Sw. *skam,* G. *scham,* O.H.G. *scama,* shame; probably from root meaning to cover. Hence *sham.*] A painful sensation excited by the exposure of that which nature or modesty prompts us to conceal, or by a consciousness of guilt, or of having done something which injures reputation; the cause or reason of shame; reproach; disgrace; contempt.—*For shame!* an interjectional phrase signifying you should be ashamed; shame on you!—*To put to shame,* to cause to feel shame; to inflict shame or dishonour on.—*v.t. shamed, shaming.* To make ashamed; to cause to feel shame; to cover with reproach or ignominy.—*v.i.* To be ashamed.—**Shamefaced,** shām'fāst, *a.* [Corrupted from *shamefast,* like *steadfast.*] Easily confused or put out of countenance; bashful; modest.—**Shamefacedly,** shām'fāst-li, *adv.* Bashfully; with excessive modesty.—**Shamefacedness,** shām'fāst-nes, *n.*—**Shameful,** shām'fųl, *a.* Bringing shame or disgrace; scandalous; disgraceful; raising shame in others; indecent.—**Shamefully,** shām'fųl-li, *adv.* In a shameful manner; disgracefully.—**Shamefulness,** shām'fųl-nes, *n.* The state or quality of being shameful; disgrace.—**Shameless,** shām'les, *a.* Destitute of shame; wanting modesty; brazen-faced; insensible to disgrace; done without shame; indicating want of shame.—**Shamelessly,** shām'les-li, *adv.* In a shameless manner; impudently.—**Shamelessness,** shām'les-nes, *n.* The state or quality of being shameless.—**Shamer,** shā'mėr, *n.* One who or that which makes ashamed.

Shammy, Shamoy, sham'i, sham'oi, *n.* [A corruption of *chamois,* the animal and its prepared skin.] The chamois; a kind of soft leather originally prepared from the skin of this animal, but now commonly made of the skin of the goat and sheep.

Shampoo, sham-pö', *v.t.* [Hind. *chāmpnā.*] To rub and squeeze the whole surface of the body of, stretching the limbs and joints, in connection with the hot bath, a practice introduced from the East; to rub the head vigorously with soap and water or some special cleansing preparation.—*n.* The act or operation of shampooing.

Shamrock, sham'rok, *n.* [Ir. *seamrog,* Gael. *seamrag,* trefoil, white clover.] A plant regarded as the national emblem of Ireland: generally supposed to be white clover or else wood-sorrel.

Shandry, Shandrydan, shan'dri, shan'-dri-dan, *n.* A one-horse Irish conveyance.

Shandygaff, shan'di-gaf, *n.* A mixture of beer and ginger-beer or lemonade.

Shank, shangk, *n.* [A.Sax. *scanca, sceanca,* the bone of the leg, the leg, *earm-scanca,* the arm-bone; Dan. and Sw. *skank;* G. and D. *schenkel,* the shank; akin perhaps *shin.*] The whole leg, or the part from the knee to the ankle; the tibia or shin-bone; the part of the foreleg of a horse between the knee and the fetlock; that part of a tool or other thing which connects the acting part with a handle; the stem of an anchor connecting the arms and the stock.—*v.i.* In *bot.* to be affected with disease of the footstalk; to fall by decay of the footstalk: often with *off.*—**Shanked,** shangkt, *p.* and *a.* Having a shank; *bot.* affected with disease of the footstalk.

Shanny, shan'i, *n.* [Origin unknown.] A small fish allied to the blenny.

Sha'n't, shänt. A colloquial contraction of *shall not.*

Shanty, shan'ti, *n.* [Ir. *sean*, old, and *tig*, a house.] A hut or mean dwelling; a slight temporary building.

Shape, shāp, *v.t.*—pret. *shaped;* pp. *shaped* or *shapen;* ppr. *shaping.* [A.Sax. *sceapan*, *scapan* = Goth. *skapjan*, Icel. *skapa*, Dan. *skabe*, O.H.G. *scafan*, G. *schaffen*, to shape, form, create; akin perhaps *shave.*] To form or create; to make; to mold or make into a particular form; to give form or figure to; to adapt to a purpose; to suit; to conceive or conjure up.—*v.i.* To square; to suit; to be adjusted.—*n.* External appearance of a body as determined by outlines or contours; make; figure; form; that which has form or figure; an appearance; a being; a pattern to be followed; a model; a mold; external manifestation of thought in words or action; *cookery*, a dish made of blancmange, rice, corn-flour, &c., which receives a particular form.—**Shapable**, shā'pa-bl, *a.* Capable of being shaped; shapely. —**Shapeless**, shāp'les, *a.* Destitute of regular form; wanting symmetry of dimensions. —**Shapelessness**, shāp'les-nes, *n.* The state of being shapeless.—**Shapeliness**, shāp'li-nes, *n.* The state of being shapely. —**Shapely**, shāp'li, *a.* Well formed; symmetrical.

Shard, shärd, *n.* [A.Sax. *sceard*, from *sceran*, to shear. SHARE, SHEAR.] A broken piece of an earthen vessel; a potsherd; a fragment in general; the wing-case of a beetle; the leaves of the artichoke and some other vegetables whitened or blanched. —**Shard-borne**, *a.* Borne along by its shards or scaly wing-cases. (*Shak.*)—**Sharded**, shär'ded, *a.* Having wings sheathed with a hard case.

Share, shãr, *n.* [A.Sax. *scearu*, a portion, lit. a *shearing*; *scear*, *scær*, that which shears or divides, the share of a plough, both from *sceran*, to cut. Akin *sheer*, *shire*, *shore*, *short*, *skirt.* SHEAR.] A certain allotted quantity; a part bestowed; a portion; a part or portion of a thing owned by a number in common (*shares* in a bank); the iron blade of a plough which cuts the bottom of the furrow-slice; a ploughshare. —*v.t.*—*shared*, *sharing.* To divide in portions; to part among two or more; to partake or enjoy with others; to seize and possess jointly or in common.—*v.i.* To have part; to get one's portion; to be a sharer.—**Share-beam**, *n.* That part of a plough to which the share is applied. —**Share cropper**, *n.* A tenant farmer who shares his crops with the owner of the land. —**Shareholder**, shãr'hōl-dėr, *n.* One that holds or owns a share or shares in a joint-stock company, or in some property. —**Share-list**, *n.* A list of the prices of shares of railroads, mines, banks, government securities, and the like. —**Sharer**, shã'rėr, *n.* One who shares; one who participates in anything with another.

Shark, shärk, *n.* [Origin uncertain; comp. D. *schrok*, a glutton, a greedy fellow.] A voracious carnivorous marine fish of which there are many species; a greedy, artful fellow; a sharper; a cheat.—*v.i.* To play the petty thief; to swindle.—*v.t.* To pick up hastily, slily, or thievishly; with *up.*—**Sharker**, shär'kėr, *n.* One who lives by sharking; an artful fellow.

Sharp, shärp, *a.* [A.Sax. *scearp*, from the root of *scrape*, and perhaps of *shear*; L.G. *scharp*, D. *scherp*, Icel. *skarpr*, G. *scharf*, sharp.] Having a very thin edge or fine point; not blunt; having a keen cutting edge; pointed; peaked; bent at or forming an acute angle; acute of mind; quick to discern or distinguish; ingenious; shrewd; subtle; keen as regards the organs of sense; quick of sight; vigilant; attentive; affecting the organs of taste like fine points; sour; acid; acrid; piercing to the ear; penetrating; shrill; acrimonious; severe; sarcastic; cutting (a *sharp* rebuke); severely rigid; severe; eager for food; feeling the calls of hunger; fierce; fiery; violent (a *sharp* contest); afflicting, distressing, or painful; biting; piercing (*sharp* frost); gritty (*sharp* sand) emaciated (a *sharp* visage); keenly alive to one's own interest; barely honest; *phonetics*, applied to a sound pronounced or uttered with breath and not with voice; surd; not sonant (the *sharp* mutes in *p*, *t*, *k*); *mus.* raised a semitone; too high; so high as to be out of tune or above true pitch.—*n. Mus.* a note artificially raised a semitone, marked by the sign (♯); the sign itself; *pl.* the hard parts of wheat which require grinding a second time.—*v.t.* To make sharp; to sharpen.—*adv.* Sharply; exactly; to the moment; not a minute behind.—**Sharp-cut**, *a.* Cut sharply and clearly, so as to present a sharp outline; well-defined.—**Sharpen**, shär'pn, *v.t.* To make sharp or sharper; to whet; to make more eager, active, intense, ingenious, &c.; to make more eager for any gratification; *mus.* to raise a semitone, or a little above the true pitch.—*v.i.* To grow or become sharp.—**Sharper**, shär'pėr, *n.* A tricky fellow; a cheat; one who lives by cheating. —**Sharp-ground**, *a.* Whetted till it is sharp; sharpened. —**Sharply**, shärp'li, *adv.* In a sharp or keen manner; severely; rigorously; acrimoniously; keenly; violently; vehemently; with keen perception; wittily; abruptly; steeply. —**Sharpness**, shärp'nes, *n.* The state or quality of being sharp; keenness of edge or point; pungency; acidity; keenness of appetite; severity of pain or affliction; severity of language; acuteness of intellect; quickness of sense or perception; keenness; severity (the *sharpness* of the air); keenness in transacting business; equivocal honesty.—**Sharp-set**, *a.* Eager in appetite; affected by keen hunger. —**Sharp-shooter**, *n.* A soldier or other person skilled in shooting with exactness.—**Sharp-sighted**, *a.* Having quick sight; having acute discernment.—**Sharp-visaged**, *a.* Having a sharp or thin face.—**Sharp-witted**, *a.* Having the mental faculties acute.

Shasta daisy, shas-tä dā'zi, *n. Chrysanthemum maximum*, a large-flowered species of the common or oxeye daisy.

Shatter, shat'ėr, *v.t.* [A softened form of *scatter*; to *shatter* is to smash into small pieces that scatter or fly apart.] To break at once into many pieces; to dash into splinters; to break up violently; to overthrow (a government, a person's intellect). —*v.i.* To be broken into fragments.—*n.* A fragment of many into which anything is broken.—**Shatter-brain**, *n.* A scatter-brain. —**Shattery**, shat'ėr-i, *a.* Brittle; easily falling into many pieces.

Shave, shāv, *v.t.*—pret. *shaved*; pp. *shaved* or *shaven*; ppr. *shaving.* [A.Sax. *scafan*, to shave, scrape, smooth = Icel. *skafa*, Dan. *skave*, D. *schaaven*, Goth. *skaban*, G. *schaben*; same root as Gr. *skaptō*, to dig; L. *scabo*, to scrape.] To pare off from the surface of a body by a razor or other edged instrument; to pare close; to remove the hair from by a razor or other sharp instrument; to skim along or near the surface of; to sweep along; to oppress by extortion; to fleece.—*v.i.* To use the razor.—*n.* A cutting off of the beard; a thin slice or shaving; the act of passing so closely as almost to graze; an exceedingly narrow miss or escape (*colloq.*).—**Shave-grass**, *n.* One of the plants called horsetail used for polishing.—**Shaver**, shā'vėr, *n.* One who shaves; one who is exacting and close in bargains or a sharp dealer; one who fleeces; a pillager; a youngster; a boy (*colloq.*).—**Shavetail**, *n.* A newly commissioned second lieutenant. —**Shaving**, shā'ving, *n.* The act of one who shaves; a thin slice pared off with a plane or other cutting instrument.—**Shaving-brush**, *n.* A brush used in shaving, for spreading the lather over the beard.

Shaw, sha, *n.* [A.Sax. *scaga*=Dan. *skov*, Icel. *skógr*, Sw. *skog*, a wood or grove.] A grove or thicket; a small wood.

Shawl, shal, *n.* [Fr. *châle*, from Ar. and Per. *shâl*, a shawl.] An article of dress of various textures, usually of a square or oblong shape, worn by persons of both sexes in the East, but in the West chiefly by females as a loose body or shoulder covering.—*v.t.* To cover with a shawl.

Shawm, Shalm, sham, *n.* [O.Fr. *chalemel*, Fr. *chalumeau*, a dim. of L. *calamus*, a reed, a reed-pipe.] An old wind instrument similar in form to the clarionet.

Shaya-root, shā'a, *n.* CHAYA-ROOT.

She, shē, *pron.*—possessive and dative *her*, objective *her*; pl. *they*, *their*, *them.* [A.Sax. *seó*, the, that, the nom. fem. of the def. art. = G. *sie*, D. *zij*, Icel. *sjá.*] The nominative feminine of the pronoun of the third person; occasionally used as a noun; used also as a prefix denoting of the female sex (*she*-bear, *she*-cat).

Shea, shē'a, *n.* A tree of tropical Asia and Africa, the trunk of which when pierced yields a copious milky juice, while a kind of vegetable butter is found in the nut. Called also *Butter-tree.*

Sheaf, shēf, *n.* pl. **Sheaves**, shēvz. [A. Sax. *sceaf*, a sheaf = L.G. *skof*, *schof*, D. *schoof*, Icel. *skauf*, G. *schaub*; from stem of *shove.*] A quantity of the stalks of wheat, rye, oats, or other plant, bound together; anything comparable to a sheaf of grain; a bundle of things tied together; a quiver full of arrows; a *sheaf catalogue*, a loose-leaf catalogue.—*v.t.* To collect and bind; to make sheaves of.—**Sheafy**, shēf'i, *a.* Pertaining to, consisting of, or resembling sheaves.

Shealing, Sheal, shēl'ing, shēl, *n.* [From Icel. *skjól*, a shelter.] A hut for shepherds or for fishermen, &c.; a shed for sheltering sheep during the night. Written also *Sheeling, Sheiling.*

Shear, shēr, *v.t.*—pret. *sheared* or *shore*; pp. *sheared* or *shorn*; pp. *shearing.* [A.Sax. *sceran*, to shear, to divide=D. *scheeren*, Icel. *skera*, Dan. *skjære*, G. *scheren*, to shear: from a root which appears without the initial *s* in Gr. *keirō*, Skr. *kar*, to cut. Akin *share*, *sheer*, *shire*, *shore*, *short.*] To cut or clip the wool from; to cut the nap from (to *shear* cloth); to separate by shears; to cut or clip from a surface; *fig.* to strip of property; to fleece; to cut with a sickle (*Scotch*).—*v.i.* To cut; to penetrate by cutting. —**Shearer**, shēr'ėr, *n.* One that shears.—**Shearing**, shēr'ing, *n.* A clipping by shears or by a machine; the result of the operation of clipping.—**Shearing stress**, *n.* That form of stress which tends to make one part of a body slide over the adjacent part.—**Shearling**, shēr'ling, *n.* A sheep that has been but once sheared.—**Shearman**, shēr'man, *n.* One whose occupation is to shear cloth. —**Shears**, shērz, *n.pl.* An instrument consisting of two movable blades with bevel edges, used for cutting cloth and other substances by interception between the two blades; something in the form of the blades of shears, as an apparatus for raising heavy weights. SHEERS. —**Shear-steel**, *n.* [From its value for shears, knives, &c.] Steel prepared by laying bars of common steel together, and heating them to the welding temperature, the bars being then beaten together and drawn out.—**Shear-tail**, *n.* A name of some species of humming-birds. —**Shear-water**, *n.* The name of several marine birds belonging to the petrel family, which skim over the waves.

Sheat-fish, shēt'fish, *n.* Same as *Silurus.*

Sheath, shēth, *n.* [A.Sax. *scaeth*=D. and L.G. *schede*, Dan. *skede*, Icel. *skeithir* (pl.), G. *scheide*, a sheath; akin to *shed*, A.Sax. *sceddan*, to divide.] A case for the reception of a sword or other long and slender instrument; a scabbard; any somewhat similar covering; a petiole or leaf that embraces the branch from which it springs; the wing-case of an insect. —**Sheathe**, shēᴛʜ, *v.t.*—*sheathed*, *sheathing.* To put into a sheath or scabbard; to cover with a sheath or case; to protect by a casing or covering, as of copper (to *sheathe* a ship).—*To sheathe the sword* (*fig.*), to put an end to war or enmity; to make peace. —**Sheathed**, shēᴛʜd, *p.* and *a.* Put in or covered with a sheath; covered with sheathing.—**Sheather**, shē'ᴛʜėr, *n.* One who sheathes.—**Sheathing**, shē'THing, *n.* The act of one who sheathes; that which sheathes; the covering of copper, or an alloy containing copper, to protect a wooden ship's bottom.—**Sheathless**, shēTH'les, *a.* Without a sheath or case for covering; unsheathed.—**Sheath-winged**, *a.* Having cases for covering the wings; coleopterous. —**Sheathy**, shēth'i, *a.* Forming or resembling a sheath or case.

Sheave, shēv, *n.* [Same as O.D. *schijve*, D. *schijf*, Icel. *skífa*, Dan. *skive*, G. *scheibe*, a slice, a disc; akin to *shift.*] A grooved wheel in a block, mast, yard, &c., on which a rope works; the wheel of a pulley; a sliding scutcheon for covering a keyhole.

Shebeen, shē-bēn', *n.* [Irish.] An Irish smuggler's hut; a low public-house; an unlicensed house where excisable liquors are sold.—**Shebeener**, shē-bēn'ėr, *n.* One who keeps a shebeen.—**Shebeening**, shē-bēn'ing, *n.* The act of keeping a shebeen.

Shechinah, Shekinah, shē-kī'na, *n.* [Heb. *shekinah*, from *shakan*, to rest.] The Jewish name for the symbol of the divine presence, which rested in the shape of a cloud or visible light over the mercy-seat.

Shed, shed, *v.t.*—pret. and pp. *shed*; ppr. *shedding*. [A.Sax. *sceddan*, to separate, to disperse; G. *scheiden*, Goth. *skaidan*, to part, to separate; allied to L. *scindo*, to cut.] To let flow out; to let fall in drops (to *shed* tears, to *shed* blood); to cast or throw off, as a natural covering (to *shed* the leaves); to emit or give out (flowers *shed* fragrance); to cause to flow off without penetrating (a sloping roof *sheds* the rain); to divide; to cast off or part with, as the hair.—*v.i.* To let fall seed, a covering or envelope, &c.—*n.* A parting of the streams of a district; a watershed; *weaving*, the interstice between the different parts of the warp of a loom through which the shuttle passes.—**Shedder**, shed'ėr, *n.* One who sheds.—**Shedding**, shed'ing, *n.* The act of one that sheds; that which is shed or cast off; a parting or branching off.

Shed, shed, *n.* [Perhaps originally a sloping roof or penthouse to *shed* off the rain.] A penthouse or covering of boards, &c., for shelter; a poor house or hovel; a hut; a large open structure for the temporary storage of goods, &c.

Sheen, shēn, *a.* [A.Sax. *scíne*, *scéne*, bright, beautiful, akin to G. *schön*, beautiful; from root of *show.*] Bright; shining; glittering; showy. (*Poet.*)—*n.* Brightness; splendour. —**Sheenly**, shēn'li, *adv.* Brightly. —**Sheeny**, shē'ni, *a.* Bright; shining; fair.

Sheep, shēp, *n.sing.* and *pl.* [A.Sax. *sceáp*, *scép*, sing. and pl.; L.G. and D. *schaap*, G. *schaf*, a sheep.] A ruminant animal nearly allied to the goat, and of great use to man both for its wool and its flesh; a silly fellow, the sheep being regarded as a stupid animal; leather prepared from sheep-skin.—**Sheep-cot, Sheepcote**, shēp'kot, shēp'kōt, *n.* A small inclosure for sheep; the cottage of a shepherd (*Shak.*).—**Sheep-dip**, *n.* A sheep-wash.—**Sheep-dog**, *n.* A dog for tending sheep; a collie.—**Sheep-fold**, shēp'fōld, *n.* A fold or pen for sheep.—**Sheepheaded**, shēp-hed'ed, *a.* Simple-minded; silly.—**Sheephook**, shēp'hök, *n.* A shepherd's crook.—**Sheepish**, shēp'ish, *a.* Like a sheep; foolishly bashful; over-modest; diffident.—**Sheepishly**, shēp'ish-li, *adv.* In a sheepish manner.—**Sheepishness**, shēp'ish-nes, *n.* The quality of being sheepish.—**Sheep-master**, *n.* An owner of sheep (O.T.).—**Sheep-pen**, *n.* An inclosure for sheep; a sheepfold.—**Sheep-run**, *n.* Originally an Australian name for a large tract of grazing country fit for pasturing sheep, more extensive than a sheep-walk.—**Sheep's-eye**, *n.* A modest, diffident look; a wishful glance; a leer.—*To cast a sheep's-eye*, to direct a wishful or leering glance.—**Sheep-shank**, *n.* *Naut.* a kind of knot made on a rope to shorten it temporarily.—**Sheep-shearer**, *n.* One that shears the wool from sheep.—**Sheep-shearing**, *n.* The act or the occasion of shearing sheep.—**Sheep-skin**, *n.* The skin of a sheep, or leather prepared from it.—**Sheep-stealer**, *n.* One that steals sheep.—**Sheep-stealing**, *n.* The act of stealing sheep.—**Sheep-tick**, *n.* A dipterous insect parasitic on sheep, the blood of which it sucks.—**Sheep-walk**, *n.* A tract of some extent where sheep feed.—**Sheep-wash**, *n.* A wash for sheep either to kill vermin or to preserve the wool.

Sheer, shēr, *a.* [A.Sax. *scír*, pure, clear, bright; Icel. *skírr*, *skœrr*, bright, clear; Goth. *skeirs*, clear, evident; G. *schier*, free from knots; probably from root of *shine.*] Pure or clear (*Shak.*)‡; simple; mere; downright (*sheer* falsehood or ignorance); straight up and down; perpendicular; precipitous.

Sheer, shēr, *v.i.* [A form of *shear*: so D. and G. *scheren*, to shear and to sheer.] To deviate from the line of the proper course; to slip or move aside: said especially of a ship.—*To sheer alongside*, to come gently alongside.—*To sheer off*, to move off or away.—*n.* The curve which the line of ports or of the deck presents to the eye when viewing the side of a ship; the sheer-strake of a vessel.—**Sheer-draught, Sheer-plan**, *n.* The plan or drawing showing the elevation of a ship.—**Sheer-hulk**, *n.* An old worn-out ship fitted with sheers to fix or take out masts, engines, &c., of other ships.—**Sheers**, shērz, *n.pl.* [Named from having some resemblance to *shears.*] A hoisting apparatus used in masting or dismasting ships, putting in or taking out boilers, &c., and consisting of two or more tall pieces of timber erected in an inclined position, and fastened together near the top, from which depends the necessary tackle for hoisting.—**Sheer-strake**, *n.* The uppermost line of plates or outer planking of a ship.

Sheet, shēt, *n.* [A.Sax. *scéte*, a sheet, a flap, also *sceát*, a nook, a projecting corner, part, region, from *sceótan*, to shoot, the root-meaning being something shot out or extended. SHOOT.] A broad, large, thin piece of anything, as paper, linen, iron, lead, glass, &c.; a large piece of linen or cotton cloth forming part of a set of bed-clothes; a broad piece of paper, either unfolded as it comes from the manufacturer, or folded into pages; a piece of writing paper folded in two leaves; anything expanded; a broad expanse or surface (a *sheet* of water or of ice); *naut.* a rope fastened to the lower corner of a sail to extend and retain it in a particular situation.—*Three sheets in the wind*, tipsy; intoxicated.—*Sheet* is often used in composition to denote that the substance to the name of which it is prefixed is in the form of sheets or thin plates; as *sheet*-lead, *sheet*-glass, &c.—*v.t.* To furnish with sheets; to fold in a sheet; to cover as with a sheet.—**Sheet-anchor**, *n.* [That is, the anchor *shot*, or thrown out for preservation.] The largest anchor of a ship, which is shot out in extreme danger; *fig.* the chief support; the last refuge for safety.—**Sheetful**, shēt'ful, *n.* As much as a sheet contains; enough to fill a sheet. —**Sheet-glass**, *n.* A kind of crown-glass blown at first in the form of a cylinder, which is afterwards opened out to form a sheet.—**Sheeting**, shēt'ing, *n.* Cloth for sheets.—**Sheet-iron**, *n.* Iron in sheets or broad thin plates.—**Sheet-lightning**, *n.* Lightning appearing in wide expanded flashes.

Sheik, shēk or shāk, *n.* [Ar., an old man, an elder.] A title of dignity properly belonging to the chiefs of the Arabic tribes or clans, but now widely used among Moslems as a title of respect or reverence.

Sheil, Sheiling, shēl, shēl'ing, *n.* SHEALING.

Shekarry, shē-kar'i, *n.* A name given in Hindustan to a hunter; a shikaree.

Shekel, shek'el, *n.* [Heb., from *shakal*, to weigh.] An ancient weight and coin among the Jews: the weight probably equaled 250 grains Troy, the value of the silver shekel was about 60 cents, that of the golden shekel about $11 in U. S. currency.

Shekinah, shē-kī'na, *n.* SHECHINAH.

Sheldrake, shel'drāk, *n.* [From *shield*, O.E. *sheld*, and *drake*, there being a somewhat shield-shaped chestnut patch on the breast.] A name of two species of European ducks, handsome birds that make their nests in rabbit-burrows.—**Shelduck**, shel'duk, *n.* The female of the sheldrake.

Shelf, shelf, *n.* pl. **Shelves**, shelvz. [A. Sax. *scelfe*, *scylfe*, a shelf; Icel. *skjálf*, a bench; comp. Sc. *skelb*, *skelve*, a splinter, a thin slice; akin to *shell*, *shale*, *scale.*] A board or platform of boards fixed horizontally to a wall for holding vessels, books, &c.; a ledge; a projecting ledge of rocks; a ledge of rocks in the sea; a shoal.—*To put or lay on the shelf*, to put aside or out of use; to lay aside, as from duty or active service.—*v.t.* To place on a shelf; to shelve.

Shelve, shelv, *v.t.*—*shelved*, *shelving*. To place on a shelf; hence, to put aside out of active employment, or out of use; to dismiss; to furnish with shelves.—*v.i.* To slope, like a shelf or sandbank; to incline; to be sloping.—**Shelving**, shel'ving, *p.* and *a.* Inclining; sloping; having declivity.—*n.* The shelves of a room, shop, &c., collectively.—**Shelvy**, shel'vi, *a.* Full of rocks or sandbanks; shallow.

Shell, shel, *n.* [A.Sax. *scel*, *scell* = Icel. *skel*, D. *schel*, G. *schale*, husk, shell, peel; same root as *shale*, *scale*, *skill.*] A hard outside covering, particularly that serving as a natural protection in certain plants and animals; the hard outside part of a nut; the hard covering or external skeleton of many invertebrate animals, as the crab, the oyster, &c.; the hard covering of some vertebrates, as the armadillo, tortoise, &c.; a carapace; the outside and calcareous layer of an egg; any outside framework; any slight hollow structure; a thin interior casket inclosed by a more substantial one which is called a vault; the outside plates of a boiler; a hollow projectile containing a bursting charge, which is exploded by a time or percussion fuse; a bomb. *Common* shells contain a charge of powder only. *High-explosive* shells are charged with *lyddite* or some similar substance, and act with tremendous power. *Armour-piercing* shells are used against armoured ships. See also *Shrapnel*; in *magnetism*, a thin lamina, either plane or curved, magnetized in directions everywhere normal to its surface.—*v.t.* To strip or break off the shell of; to take out of the shell; to throw bomb-shells into, upon, or among; to bombard (to *shell* a fort, a town, &c.).—*v.i.* To fall off, as a shell, crust, or exterior coat; to cast the shell.—**Shelled**, sheld, *p.* and *a.* Deprived of the shell; provided with a shell or shells.—**Shell-fish**, *n. sing.* and *pl.* A mollusc or a crustacean, whose external covering consists of a shell, as oysters, crabs, &c.—**Shell-jacket**, *n.* An undress military jacket reaching only to the waist.—**Shellac, Shell-lac**, shel'lak, *n.* Seed-lac melted and formed into thin cakes. LAC.—**Shell-lime**, *n.* Lime obtained by burning sea-shells.—**Shell-limestone**, *n.* A limestone largely consisting of shells; muschelkalk.—**Shell-marl**, *n.* A deposit of clay and other substances mixed with shells, which collects at the bottom of lakes. —**Shell-proof**, *a.* Proof against shells; impenetrable by shells; bomb-proof.—**Shell-sand**, *n.* The triturated shells of mollusca, constituting in a great measure the beach in some localities.—**Shell-shock**, *n.* Neurosis caused by shell-fire.—**Shell-work**, *n.* Work composed of shells or adorned with them.—**Shelly**, shel'i, *a.* Abounding with shells; covered with shells; consisting of a shell or shells.

Shellac. Under SHELL.

Shelter, shel'tėr, *n.* [A.Sax. *scild-truma*, a guard or troop of soldiers—*scild*, a shield, and *truma*, a troop, from *trum*, firm.] That which covers or defends from injury or annoyance; a protection; a refuge; a position affording cover or protection; a safe place; security.—*v.t.* To provide shelter for; to cover from violence, injury, annoyance, or attack; to protect; to place under cover; *refl.* to betake one's self to cover or a safe place.—*v.i.* To take shelter.—**Shelterless**, shel'tėr-les, *a.* Destitute of shelter.

Shelty, Sheltie, shel'ti, *n.* A small strong horse from *Shetland*.

Shelve. Under SHELF.

Shemite, shem'īt, *n.* [SEMITE.] A descendant of Shem.—**Shemitic**, shem-it'ik, *a.* Pertaining to Shem; Semitic.

Sheol, shē'ol, *n.* A Hebrew word in the Old Testament, rendered by the Authorized Version grave, hell, or pit.

Shepherd, shep'ėrd, *n.* [A.Sax. *sceáphirde* = *sheep-herd*.] A man employed in tending sheep in the pasture; one who exercises spiritual care over a community; a pastor. — *Shepherd kings*, the chiefs of a nomadic race from the East who conquered and ruled in Egypt in early times.—*Shepherd's crook*, a long staff having its upper end curved so as to form a hook, used by shepherds. — *Shepherd's dog*, a variety of dog employed by shepherds to assist them in looking after their flocks; a collie. — *Shepherd's* (or *shepherd*) *tartan*, a small black and white check pattern in cloth; cloth woven in this pattern. — **Shepherdess**, shep'ėr-des, *n.* A woman that tends sheep. — **Shepherd's-plaid**, *n.* Shepherd's tartan cloth. — **Shepherd's-purse, Shepherd's-pouch**, *n.* A common weed of world-wide distribution, having small white flowers, and small somewhat heart-shaped pods.

Sherardizing, sher-ard-īz'ing, *n.* [After *Sherard* Cowper-Coles, the inventor.] A process of galvanizing articles by heating them in closed retorts with zinc dust.

Sherbet, shėr'bet, *n.* [Ar. *sherbet*, from *sharaba*, to drink; akin *sirup*.] A favorite drink in the East, made of fruit juices, sweetened, and now usually frozen.

Sheriat, sher'i-at, *n.* The combined civil and religious law of Turkey.

Sherif, Shereef, she-rēf', *n.* [Ar.] A descendant of Mohammed through his daughter Fatima and Hassan Ibn Ali; a prince; the chief magistrate of Mecca.

Sheriff, sher'if, *n.* [A.Sax. *scīre-gerēfa*, a shire-reeve. SHIRE, REEVE.] The chief law enforcement officer of a county, usually elected for a term of years, who, with his appointed staff of deputy *sheriffs*, maintains law and order, executes mandates of the county court, maintains the jail and has custody of prisoners therein, and summons jurors to court sessions. In England, the chief officer of the crown in every county, whose duties are mainly honorary; in Scotland, the chief judge of a county, having under him one or more sheriffs-substitute, on whom falls the discharge of the greater part of the important duties of the office, all these judges being trained lawyers.

Sherry, sher'i, *n.* A species of wine, so called from *Xeres* in Spain, where it is made.—**Sherry-cobbler**, *n.* Sherry and fruit juices with iced water.

Shetland pony, shet'land pō'ni, *n.* A very small, hardy breed of pony originally bred in the Shetland Islands.

Shew, Shewed, shewn, shō, shōd, shōn. SHOW, SHOWED, SHOWN.

Shewbread, Showbread, shō'bred, *n.* Unleavened bread which the Jewish priest placed before the Lord. (*Bible*.)

Shiah, *n.* SHIITE.

Shibboleth, shib'ō-leth, *n.* [Heb.] A word made the test to distinguish the Ephraimites from the Gileadites (Judg. xii); hence, the watchword of any party; a pet phrase of a party; a party cry.

Shield, shēld, *n.* [A.Sax. *scild*, *scyld*, a shield, protection; Goth. *skildus*, Icel. *skjöldr*, G. *schild*; akin *shelter*.] A broad piece of defensive armour carried on the arm; a buckler, used in war for the protection of the body; anything that protects or defends; defence; protection; the person that defends or protects; *her.* the escutcheon or field on which are placed the bearings in coats of arms; *bot.* an apothecium. — *v.t.* To cover, as with a shield; to cover or protect from danger or anything hurtful or disagreeable, as a rubberized apron worn to *shield* the clothing; to defend; to protect.—**Shield-fern**, *n.* A common name for a genus of ferns, from the form of the indusium of the fructification.—**Shieldless**, shēld'les, *a.* Destitute of a shield or of protection. **Shieldlessly**, shēld'les-li, *adv.* In a shieldless manner.

Shieling, shēl'ing, *n.* SHEALING.

Shift, shift, *v.t.* [A.Sax. *scyftan*, to divide, to drive away = Dan. *skifte*, Icel. *skipta*, to divide, change, shift; akin to *shive*, *sheave*, or perhaps to *shove*.] To transfer from one place or position to another; to remove; to change; to substitute other clothes for; to dress in fresh clothes.—*v.i.* To change; to pass into a different form, state, or the like; to change place, position, or direction; to change dress, particularly the under garments; to resort to expedients; to adopt some course in a case of difficulty; to contrive.—*To shift about*, to turn quite round to a contrary side or opposite point; to vacillate.—*n.* A change, a substition of one thing for another; an expedient tried in difficulty; a contrivance; a resource; one thing tried when another fails; a mean or base refuge or resort; an artifice; a woman's under garment; a chemise; a squad of men to take a spell or turn of work at stated intervals; the working time of a squad or relay of men; the spell of work; *mus.* a complete change of four notes by changing the position of the left hand in violin playing.—*To make shift*, or *to make a shift*, to contrive; to find ways and means.—**Shiftable**, shif'ta-bl, *a.* Capable of being shifted or changed.—**Shifter**, shif'tėr, *n.* One who shifts (a scene-*shifter*); one who practises artifice.—**Shiftiness**, shif'ti-nes, *n.* The quality of being shifty.—**Shifting**, *p.* and *a.* Changing place or position.—*Shifting sand* or *sands*, loose moving sand; quicksand.—**Shiftingly**, shif'ting-li, *adv.* In a shifting manner; by shifts and changes. —**Shiftless**, shift'les, *a.* Destitute of expedients; not resorting to successful expedients.—**Shiftlessly**, shift'les-li, *adv.* In a shiftless manner.—**Shiftlessness**, shift'les-nes, *n.* A state of being shiftless. — **Shifty**, shif'ti, *a.* Full of shifts; fertile in expedients; especially fertile in evasions; given to tricks and artifices.

Shiite, Shiah, shē'īt, shē'ä, *n.* [Ar. *shīah*, a multitude following one another.] A member of one of the two great sects into which Mohammedans are divided, the other sect being the Sunnites or Sunnis: they consider Ali as being the only rightful successor of Mohammed.

Shikaree, shi-kä'rē, *n.* Same as *Shekarry*.

Shillelagh, shillalah, shi-lā'le, shi-lā'la, *n.* [From *Shillelagh*, a barony in Wicklow famous for its oaks.] An Irish name for an oaken sapling or other stick used as a cudgel.

Shilling, shil'ing, *n.* [A.Sax. *scylling* = O.Fris., O.Sax., Dan., and Sw. *skilling*, Goth. *skilliggs*, G. *schilling*.] A British coin equal to twelve pennies, or to one-twentieth of a pound sterling, or about 25c in U. S. currency.

Shilly-shally, shil'i-shal-i, *v.t.* [A reduplication of *shall I?* and equal to shall I or shall I not?] To act in an irresolute or undecided manner; to hesitate.—*n.* Foolish trifling; irresolution.

Shimmer, shim'ėr, *v.i.* [A.Sax. *scimrian*; freq. of *scimian*, to gleam; Dan. *skimre*, G. *schimmern*, to gleam.] To emit a tremulous light; to gleam; to glisten.—*n.* A tremulous gleam or glistening.

Shimmy, Shimmey, shim'i, *n.* A dance in which the muscles are made to quiver; short for chemise.—*v.i.* To shake and quiver, as in the dance, or in vibration of the front wheels of an auto.

Shin, shin, *n.* [A.Sax. *scin*, *scina*, the shin; D. *scheen*, the shin; Dan. *skinne*, the shin, a splint; G. *schiene*, a splint of wood, *schienbein*, the shin-bone.] The forepart of the leg between the ankle and the knee, particularly of the human leg.—*v.i.* and *t.* —*shinned, shinning*. To climb a tree by means of the hands and legs alone.—**Shin-bone**, *n.* The bone of the shin; the tibia.

Shindig, shin'dig, *n.* A merry, festive occasion, usually with dancing. (*Slang.*)

Shindy, shin'di, *n.* A row; a quarrel. (*Slang.*)

Shine, shīn, *v.i.*—*shone, shining*. [A.Sax. *scīnan* = D. *schijnen*, Icel. *skína*, Dan. *skinne*, Goth. *skeinan*, G. *scheinen*, to shine; same root as in *shimmer*, *sheer*.] To emit rays of light; to give light; to beam with steady radiance; to exhibit brightness or splendor; to glitter or be brilliant; to be splendid or beautiful (to *shine* in society); to be noticeably visible.—*v.t.* To cause or make to shine.—*n.* Fair weather (*shine* and storm); sunshine; brilliancy; brightness.—**Shiner**, shī'nėr, *n.* One who or that which shines; a black eye (*colloq.*); certain small fresh-water fish.—**Shining**, *p.* and *a.* Emitting light; gleaming, bright; splendid; radiant; illustrious; distinguished; *bot.* having a smooth polished surface, as certain leaves.—**Shiny**, shī'ni, *a.* Characterized by sunshine; bright; luminous; glossy; brilliant.

Shingle, shing'gl, *n.* [Corrupted from *shindle*, which, like G. *schindel*, was borrowed from L. *scindula*, a shingle, from L. *scindo*, to split.] A thin piece of wood, usually having parallel sides and thicker at one end than the other, used as a roof-covering; a short haircut; a small signboard, as of a doctor or lawyer (*colloq.*)—. *v.t.*—*shingled, shingling*. To cover with shingles; to perform the process of shingling on (to *shingle* iron).—**Shingling**, shing'gling, *n.* A covering of shingles; *iron manuf.* the process of expelling the impurities from iron.

Shingle, shing'gl, *n.* [Norweg. *singel*.] Round, water-worn, and loose gravel and pebbles.—**Shingly**, shing'gli, *a.* Abounding with shingle or gravel. (*Brit.*)

Shingles, shing'glz, *n. pl.* [From L. *cingulum*, a belt, from *cingo*, to gird.] A painful eruptive skin disease which spreads around the body somewhat like a girdle; herpes.

Shinny, Shinney, shin'i, *n.* Schoolboys' hockey; the curved stick used in playing the game.—*v.t.* and *i.* To climb, as a pole, with shins and arms (*colloq.*).

Shinto, Shintoism, shin'to, shin'to-izm, *n.* [Chinese *shin*, god or spirit, and *to*, way or law.] The ancient religion of Japan—originally a form of nature worship, it is now much changed by Confucianism and Buddhism from China and Korea. Among certain sects the religious element is strong, while with others it is essentially nationalism incorporating polytheism, the divine emperor being descended from the sun goddess. Reverence of ancestors and worship of the spirits of departed heroes are dominant elements, with intense loyalty to the god-emperor.—**Shintoist**, shin'to-ist, *n.* A believer in the Shinto religion.

Ship, ship, *n.* [A.Sax. *scip*, a ship = L.G. *schipp*, D. *schip*, Icel. and Goth. *skip*, Dan. *skib*, O.H.G. *scif*, G. *schiff*, a ship. *Skiff* is the same word.] A vessel of some size adapted to navigation; a general term for vessels of whatever kind, excepting boats; sometimes restricted to a three-masted, square-rigged vessel.—*Ship's papers*, certain papers or documents required to be carried by ships, as a certificate of registry, bills of lading, &c.—*Ship of the line*, a man-of-war large enough and of sufficient force to take its place in a line of battle.—*Ship of the desert*, a sort of poetical name for the camel.—*v.t.*—*shipped, shipping*. To put on board of a ship or vessel of any kind; to transport in a ship; to take for service on board ship; *naut.* to fix in its proper place (to *ship* the tiller, the rudder).—*To ship off*, to send away by sea.—*To ship a sea*, to have a wave come aboard; to have the deck washed by a wave.—*v.i.* To go on board a vessel to make a voyage with it; to embark; to engage for service on board a ship.—**Ship-biscuit**, *n.* Hard coarse biscuit prepared for long keeping, and for use on board a ship.—**Shipboard**, ship'bōrd, *n.*

The deck or the interior part of a ship: used only in the phrase *on shipboard*.—**Ship-boy**, *n.* A boy that serves on board of a ship.—**Ship-broker**, *n.* An agent engaged in buying and selling ships; a broker who procures insurance on ships.—**Ship-builder**, *n.* One whose occupation is to construct ships; a naval architect; a shipwright.—**Ship-building**, *n.* The art of constructing vessels for navigation.—**Ship-canal**, *n.* A canal through which vessels of large size can pass; a canal for sea-going vessels.—**Ship-captain, Ship-master**, *n.* The commander, captain, or master of a ship.—**Ship-carpenter**, *n.* A shipwright; a carpenter that works at ship-building.—**Ship-chandler**, *n.* One who deals in cordage, canvas, and other furniture of ships.—**Ship-chandlery**, *n.* The business and commodities of a ship-chandler.—**Shipful**, ship'fųl, *n.* As much or many as a ship will hold; enough to fill a ship.—**Ship-letter**, *n.* A letter sent by a common ship and not by mail.—**Ship-mate**, ship'māt, *n.* One who serves in the same ship with another; a fellow-sailor.—**Shipment**, ship'ment, *n.* The act of putting anything on board of a ship; the goods shipped or put on board.—**Ship-money**, *n.* An ancient imposition in England, levied for providing and furnishing certain ships for the king's service, revived by Charles I after having been long dormant.—**Ship-owner**, *n.* A person who owns a ship or ships, or any share therein.—**Shipped**, shipt, *p.* and *a.* Carried in a ship, as goods; furnished with a ship or ships.—**Shipper**, ship'ėr, *n.* One who places goods on board a vessel for transportation.—**Shipping**, ship'ing, *n.* Ships in general; the collective body of ships belonging to a country, port, &c.—*Shipping articles*, articles of agreement between the captain of a vessel and the seamen.—*a.* Relating to ships.—**Ship railway**, *n.* A railway for the transportation of ships by land from water to water.—**Ship-rigged**, *a.* Rigged like a ship, that is with square sails on all the masts.—**Ship-shape**, *a.* Having a seamanlike trim; hence, neat and trim; well arranged.—**Ship's-husband**, *n.* A person appointed to look after the repairs, equipment, provide stores, &c., of a ship while in port.—**Ship-worm**, *n.* The teredo, a mollusc very destructive to ships and submarine woodwork.—**Ship-wreck**, ship'rek, *n.* The wreck of a ship; the destruction or loss at sea of a ship; destruction; miscarriage; ruin.—*v.t.* To make to suffer shipwreck; to wreck; to cast away.—**Shipwright**, ship'rīt, *n.* A workman who builds ships; a ship-carpenter.—**Shipyard**, ship'yärd, *n.* A place near water in which ships are constructed.

Shippen, Shippon, ship'en, ship'on, *n.* [O.E. *schepne, schupne*, A.Sax. *scypen*, akin to *shop*.] A barn for cattle or sheep; a stable.

Shire, shīr, *n.* [A.Sax. *scire*, a division, from *sciran, sceran*, to *shear*, to divide. SHARE, SHEAR.] A name for the larger divisions into which Great Britain is divided, and practically corresponding to the term *county*.—*The shires*, those English counties the names of which terminate in 'shire', applied in a general way to the midland counties.—**Shire-town**, *n.* The chief town of a shire; a county town.

Shirk, shėrk, *v.t.* and *i.* [Probably a form of *shark*.] To avoid or get off unfairly or meanly; to seek to avoid the performance of duty.—*n.* One who seeks to avoid duty; the act of shirking.—**Shirker**, shėr'kėr, *n.* One who shirks duty or danger.—**Shirky**, shėr'ki, *a.* Disposed to shirk; characterized by shirking.

Shirred, shėrd, *a.* [Etymol. unknown.] Having cords or elastic threads inserted between two pieces of cloth or in the body of a fabric.

Shirt, shėrt, *n.* [From Icel. *skyrta*, Dan. *skiorte*, a shirt; lit. a garment shortened. SHORT.—*Skirt* is the same word.] A loose garment of linen, cotton, or other material, worn by men and boys under the outer clothes.—*v.t.* To put a shirt on; to clothe with a shirt.—**Shirt-front**, *n.* The part of a shirt which covers the breast; an article of dress made in imitation of this part.—**Shirting**, shėr'ting, *n.* Cloth suitable for shirts.—**Shirtless**, shėrt'les, *a.* Wanting a shirt.

Shist, shist. SCHIST.

Shittah-tree, shit'ta, *n.* [Heb. *shittâh*, pl. *shittim*.] A species of acacia which grows abundantly in the mountains of Sinai, and in some other Bible lands, and yields gum-arabic, and also a hard close-grained timber.—**Shittim-wood**, shit'tim, *n.* The wood of the shittah-tree.

Shive, shīv, *n.* [Same as Icel. *skífa*, a slice, Dan. *skive*, L.G. *schieve*, D. *schijf*, G. *scheibe*, a slice, a disk. SHEAVE.] A slice; a thin cut; a little piece or fragment.

Shiver, shiv'ėr, *v.t.* [Same root as above; comp. G. *schiefern*, to splinter; O.D. *scheveren*, to break in pieces.] To break into many small pieces or splinters; to shatter.—*v.i.* To fall at once into many small pieces or parts.—*n.* [Comp. G. *schiefer*, a splinter, slate.] A small fragment into which a thing breaks by sudden violence.

Shiver, shiv'ėr, *v.i.* [O.E. *chiver, chever*; comp. Prov.G. *schubbern*, to shiver; O.D. *schoeveren*, to shake; akin perhaps to *shift*.] To tremble, as from cold; to shake, as with ague, fear, horror, or excitement; to shudder; to quiver.—*n.* A shaking fit; a tremulous motion.—**Shiveringly**, shiv'ėr-ing-li, *adv.* With shivering or slight trembling.—**Shivery**, shiv'ėr-i, *a.* Pertaining to shivering; characterized by shivering.

Shoal, shōl, *n.* [A.Sax. *scolu, scalu*, a crowd, a shoal; perhaps same as *school*.] A great multitude assembled; a crowd; a throng.—*v.t.* To drive in shoals. (*Mil.*, *P. L.*, x, 288.)

Shoal, shōl, *n.* [Allied to *shallow*. SHALLOW.] A place where the water of a river, lake, or sea is shallow or of little depth; a sandbank or bar; a shallow.—*v.i.* To become more shallow (the water *shoals*).—*a.* Shallow; of little depth (*shoal* water).—**Shoaliness**, shō'li-nes, *n.* The state of being shoaly.—**Shoaling**, shō'ling, *p.* and *a.* Becoming shallow by being filled up with shoals.—**Shoaly**, shō'li, *a.* Full of shoals or shallow places.

Shock, shok, *n.* [Same as D. *schok*, a bounce, a jolt (but perhaps directly from the derived Fr. *choc*); O. and Prov.G. *schock*, a shock; allied to *shake*.] A violent collision of bodies; a concussion; a violent striking or dashing against; violent onset; hostile encounter; a strong and sudden agitation; any violent or sudden impression or sensation; a blow to the feelings; *elect.* the effect on the animal system of a discharge of electricity from a charged body; *med.* a violent and sudden disorganization of the system, with perturbation of body and mind.—*v.t.* [Fr. *choquer*, from D. *schokken*, to jog, to jolt.] To shake by sudden collision; to strike against suddenly; to strike, as with horror, fear, or disgust; to offend extremely; to disgust; to scandalize.—*v.i.* To come together with a shock; to meet in sudden encounter.—**Shocker**, *n.* A sensational novel. (*Colloq.*)—**Shocking**, shok'ing, *a.* Causing a shock of horror, disgust, or pain; causing to recoil with horror or disgust; extremely offensive or disgusting; very obnoxious or repugnant.—**Shockingly**, shok'ing-li, *adv.* In a shocking manner; disgustingly; offensively.—**Shockingness**, shok'ing-nes, *n.*

Shock, shok, *n.* [O.Sax. *scoc*, threescore, D. *schok*, G. *schock*, Dan. *skok*, a heap, threescore.] A group or pile of stalks, usually of grain, placed upright in a field to dry before removal.—*v.t.* To arrange or stack in shocks, as *to shock corn*.

Shock, shok, *n.* [Modified from *shag*.] A mass of close matted hair.—*a.* Shaggy; having shaggy hair.—**Shock-headed**, *a.* Having a thick and bushy head of hair.

Shod, shod, pret. and pp. of *shoe*.

Shoddy, shod'i, *n.* [From *shod*, a provincial pp. of *shed*—the original meaning being fluff thrown off, or *shed*, from cloth in weaving.] The fibre from old woollen or worsted fabrics torn up or devilled by machinery, and mixed with fresh but inferior wool, to be respun and made into cheap cloth, &c.; the coarse or inferior cloth made from this.—*a.* Made of shoddy; *fig.* of a trashy or inferior character (*shoddy* literature).—**Shoddy-mill**, *n.* A mill for the manufacture of yarn from old woollen cloths and refuse goods.

Shoe, shö, *n.* pl. **Shoes**, shöz, old pl. **Shoon**, shön. [A.Sax. *sceó, sceóh* = Dan. and Sw. *sko*, Icel. *skór*, Goth. *skohs*, G. *schuh*, a shoe; probably from root seen in Skr. *sku*, to cover, L. *scutum*, a shield, &c.] A covering for the foot, usually of leather, composed of a thick kind for the sole, and a thinner kind for the upper; a plate or rim of iron nailed under the hoof of an animal, as a horse, to defend it from injury; anything resembling a shoe in form or use.—*v.t.*—pret. and pp. *shod*, ppr. *shoeing*. To furnish with shoes; to put shoes on; to cover at the lower end.—**Shoeblack**, shö'blak, *n.* A person that cleans shoes.—**Shoe-buckle**, *n.* A buckle for fastening a shoe.—**Shoe-button**, *n.* A button for fastening a shoe.—**Shoe-horn**, *n.* A curved piece of polished horn (now also of sheet-metal) used to aid in putting on shoes.—**Shoe-lace**, *n.* A shoe-string.—**Shoe leather**, *n.* Leather for shoes.—**Shoeless**, shö'les, *a.* Destitute of shoes.—**Shoemaker**, shö'mā'kėr, *n.* One who makes or repairs shoes.—**Shoe-making**, shö'mā-king, *n.* The trade of making or repairing shoes.—**Shoer**, shö'ėr, *n.* One who puts shoes on horses.—**Shoe-string, Shoe-tie**, *n.* A ribbon for fastening a shoe in wearing it; a shoe lace.

Shog, shog, *n.* [A word originating partly in *jog*, partly in *shock*.] A sudden shake; a shock; concussion.—*v.t.* To move obliquely down a hillside (of the Scots army at Dunbar). (*Carlyle*.) To move; to quit: move on. (*Shak.*)

Shone, shōn, pret. and pp. of *shine*.

Shook, shųk, pret. of *shake*.

Shook, shųk, *n.* [A form of *shock*, a pile of sheaves.] The staves and headings sufficient for making one barrel, prepared for use and bound together.

Shoot, shöt, *v.t.*—pret. and pp. *shot*. [A. Sax. *sceótan*, to shoot, to dart; Icel. *skjóta*, Dan. *skyde*, D. *schieten*, G. *schiessen*, to shoot, dart, &c.; closely akin are *shut, sheet, shuttle, skittle, scuttle*, &c.] To let fly with force; to propel, as from a bow or firearm (to *shoot* an *arrow*, a *ball*); to discharge; to let off; to fire off (to *shoot off* a gun); to hit, wound or kill with a missile discharged from a weapon; to discharge or propel with force; to empty out with rapidity or violence (to *shoot* rubbish into a hole); to push or thrust forward; to dart forth; to protrude; to put forth by way of vegetable growth; to pass rapidly through, under, or over (to *shoot* a rapids or a bridge).—*To shoot craps* or *dice*, to participate in a game of craps; to throw or roll out the dice in order to make a point.—*v.t.* To perform the act of discharging a bullet, an arrow, or other missile from an engine or mark); to be emitted; to dart forth; to rush or move along rapidly; to dart along (*shooting* stars); to be felt as if darting through one (*shooting* pains); to sprout; to put forth buds or shoots; to increase in growth; to grow taller or larger; to push or be pushed out; to project; to jut.—*To shoot ahead*, to move swiftly away in front; to outstrip competitors in rapidity.—*n.* A young branch which shoots out from the main stock; an annual growth; a kind of sloping trough for conveying coal, grain, &c., into a particular receptacle; a place for shooting rubbish; a weft thread in a woven fabric.—**Shooter**, shöt'ėr, *n.* One that shoots; an implement for shooting; a ball shooting on the wickets at cricket.—**Shooting**, shöt'ing, *p.* and *a.* Pertaining to one who or that which shoots; connected with the killing of game by firearms (a *shooting* license, the *shooting* season).—*n.* The act of one who shoots; especially, the act or sport of killing game with firearms (to be fond of *shooting* and fishing); a tract of ground over which game is shot; sensation of a quick darting pain.—**Shooting-box**, *n.* A private lodge for the accommodation of a sportsman during the shooting season.—**Shooting-gallery**, *n.* A place, usually covered, for the practice of shooting at a mark; a covered shooting range.—**Shooting-star**, *n.* A meteor; a small celestial body passing with great velocity through the earth's atmosphere and becoming incandescent through friction with the resisting air.

Shoot, shöt, *n.* [Fr. *chute*, modified by the verb *to shoot*.] Same as *Chute*.

Shop, shop, *n.* [A.Sax. *sceoppa*, a booth, a storehouse; akin to O.D. *schop*, L.G. *schupp*, G. *schoppen*, *schuppen*, a shed, booth, &c.] A building or apartment in which goods are sold at retail, generally with a frontage to a street or road; a building in which workmen carry on their occupation (a joiner's *shop*, a machine *shop*).—*To talk shop*, to speak of one's calling or profession only.—*v.i.*—*shopped, shopping*. To visit shops for purchasing goods; used chiefly in ppr.—**Shop-boy**, *n.* A boy employed in a shop.—**Shop-girl**, *n.* A girl employed in a shop.—**Shopkeeper**, shop'-kēp-ėr, *n.* A trader who sells goods in a shop or at retail; a tradesman.—**Shop-keeping**, shop'kēp-ing, *n.* The business of keeping a shop.—**Shoplifter**, shop'lif-tėr, *n.* One who, under pretense of buying goods, steals anything in a shop.—**Shop-lifting**, shop'lif-ting, *n.* Larceny committed by a shoplifter.—**Shopman**, shop'-man, *n.* A petty trader; a shopkeeper; one who serves in a shop.—**Shoppish**, shop'-ish, *a.* Having the habits or manners of a shopman.—**Shop-steward**, *n.* A shop deputy appointed from among themselves, subject to the approval of their union, by the workmen in machine shops and similar shops, to take charge of their collective bargaining and to be the medium of complaints to the management.—**Shopwalker**, *n.* An attendant in a large shop who directs customers to the proper department; a floorwalker.—**Shopwindow**, *n.* A large window in a shop or store in which samples of the store's stocks are shown.—**Shop-woman**, *n.* A woman who serves in a shop.

Shore, shōr, *n.* [A.Sax. *score*, the shore, from *sceran*, *sciran*, to shear, to divide; O.D. *schoore*, *schoor*. SHEAR.] The land immediately adjacent to a great body of water, as an ocean or sea, or to a large lake or river; the land along the edge of the water.—**Shore-land**, *n.* Land bordering on a shore or sea-beach.—**Shoreless**, shōr'-les, *a.* Having no shore or coast; of indefinite or unlimited extent. — **Shoreward, Shorewards**, shōr'wėrd, shōr'-wėrdz, *adv.* Towards the shore.

Shore, shōr, *n.* [Lit. a piece *shorn* or cut to a certain length; same as D. and L.G. *schore*, *schoor*, Icel. *skortha*, a prop, a shore. SHEAR.] A prop; a piece of timber or iron for the temporary support of something, often resting obliquely against it.—*v.t.*—*shored, shoring*. To support by a shore or shores; to prop: usually with *up* (to *shore up* a building).—**Shoring**, shōr'-ing, *n.* A supporting with shores; a set of shores collectively.

Shore, shōr, *n.*† A sewer.

Shore, shōr, pret. of *shear*.

Shorl. SCHORL.

Shorling, shor'ling, *n.* [From *shear*, pret. *shore*.] A sheep of the first year's shearing; a shearling; a newly shorn sheep.

Shorn, shorn, pp. of *shear*. Cut off; having the hair or wool cut off; deprived (a prince *shorn* of his honours).

Short, short, *a.* [A.Sax. *sceort*, *scort*, short, from stem of *shear*; O.H.G. *scurz*, short, cut off; Icel. *skort*, scantily supplied. SHEAR.] Not long; not having great length or linear extension; not extended in time; not of long duration; not reaching a certain point; limited in quantity; insufficient; inadequate; scanty; deficient (a *short* supply, *short* weight); scantily supplied or furnished; not possessed of a reasonable or usual quantity or amount (to be *short of* money or means); not tenacious or retentive (a *short* memory); not containing many words; curt; brief; abrupt; sharp; severe; uncivil (a *short* answer); breaking or crumbling readily in the mouth; crisp; brittle; friable; not prolonged in sound (a *short* vowel or syllable); followed by *of*, less than; below; inferior to (his escape was nothing *short of* a miracle). [*Short* is used in the formation of numerous self-explaining compounds, as *short-armed, short-eared, short-legged, short-tailed*, &c.]—*adv.* In a short manner; abruptly; suddenly.—*To come short*, to be unable to reach a certain necessary point or standard; to fall below expectations; to fail: generally followed by *of*.—*To fall short*, to become inadequate or insufficient (provisions *fall short*); to fail to reach a certain standard.—*To stop short*, to stop suddenly or abruptly; to arrest the steps at once; not to go so far as intended; not to reach the point indicated.—*To turn short*, to turn abruptly on the spot occupied.—*n.* A summary account (the *short* of the matter).—*In short*, in few words; briefly; to sum up in few words.—*The long and the short*, a brief summing up in decisive, precise, or explicit terms.—**Shortage**, shor'-tāj, *n.* Amount short or deficient; an amount by which a sum of money is deficient.—**Short-bread, Short-cake**, *n.* A sweet and very brittle cake, in which butter or lard has been mixed with the flour.—**Short-coming**, short'kum-ing, *n.* A failing of the usual quantity or amount, as of a crop; a failure of full performance, as of duty.—**Short-drawn**, *a.* Drawn in without filling the lungs; imperfectly inspired.—**Shorten**, shor'tn, *v.t.* To make short or shorter; to abridge; to curtail; to lessen; to diminish in extent or amount.—*To shorten sail*, to reef some of the sails set.—*v.i.* To become short or shorter; to contract.—**Shortener**, shor'tn-ėr, *n.* One who or that which shortens.—**Shorthand**, short'hand, *n.* A general term for any system of contracted writing; stenography.—*Shorthand writer*, a reporter who takes down speeches, &c., in shorthand.—**Short-handed**, *a.* Not having the necessary or regular number of hands or assistants.—**Short-horn**, *n.* One of a valuable breed of cattle, having the horns shorter than in almost any other variety, and yielding flesh of excellent quality.—**Short-lived**, short'-livd, *a.* Not living or lasting long; being of short continuance.—**Shortly**, short'li, *adv.* In a short or brief time or manner; soon; in few words.—**Shortness**, short'nes, *n.* The quality of being short; briefness; brevity; conciseness; deficiency.—**Short-rib**, *n.* One of the lower ribs below the sternum; a false rib.—**Shorts**, shorts, *n.pl.* The bran and coarse part of meal in mixture; small-clothes; breeches; abbreviated trousers of athletes. — **Short-sight**, *n.* Near-sightedness; myopia; vision accurate only when the object is near.—**Short-sighted**, *a.* Not able to see far; myopic; near-sighted; not able to look far into futurity; not having foresight; characterized by a want of foresight (a *short-sighted* policy).—**Short-sightedness**, *n.* Myopia; defective intellectual vision.—**Short-winded**, *a.* Affected with shortness of breath.

Shot, shot, *n.* pl. **Shot** or **Shots**. [From *shoot* (which see); A.Sax. *gescot*, an arrow.] The act of shooting; a discharge of a firearm or other missile weapon; one who shoots; a marksman; a missile, particularly a ball or bullet for firing from ordnance; cannon balls collectively (comprising *round-shot, case-shot, grape-shot*, &c.); small globular masses of lead for use with fowling-pieces, &c.: in collective sense, often called distinctively *small shot*; the flight of a missile, or the range or distance through which it passes; range; reach; the whole sweep of a fisherman's nets thrown out at one time, also the number of fish caught in one haul of the nets; *weaving*, a single thread of weft carried through the warp at one run of the shuttle; *blasting*, a charge of powder or other explosive in a blast-hole, usually fired by a slow-match.—*v.t.*—*shotted, shotting*. To load with shot over a cartridge (to *shot* a cannon).—*p.* and *a.* Having a changeable colour, like that produced in weaving by all the warp threads being of one colour and all the weft of another; chatoyant (*shot*-silk); hence, interwoven; interspersed.—**Shot-belt**, *n.* A leathern belt or long pouch for shot worn by sportsmen.—**Shot-cartridge**, *n.* A cartridge containing small shot.—**Shot-gun**, *n.* A light, smooth-bored gun for firing shot at short range; a fowling-piece. — **Shot-pouch**, *n.* A pouch for carrying small shot, usually made of leather. — **Shot-proof**, *a.* Proof against shot; incapable of being damaged by shot. — **Shotted**, shot'ed, *p.* and *a.* Loaded with shot, as a cannon.—**Shot-tower**, *n.* A tower for making small shot by pouring melted lead through a colander from the summit, the lead forming into globules, which cool and harden as they fall.

Shot, shot, *n.* [A corruption of *scot* (which see).] A reckoning, or a person's share of a reckoning; share of expenses, as of a tavern-bill. — **Shot-free**, *a.* Free from shot or charge; exempted from any share of expense.

Shotten,‡ shot'n, *a.* [An old pp. of *shoot*.] Having ejected the spawn (a *shotten* herring). (*Shak.*)

Should, shųd. The pret. of *shall*.

Shoulder, shōl'dėr, *n.* [O.E. *shulder*, Sc. *shouther*, A.Sax. *sculdor* = Dan. *skulder*, Sw. *skuldra*, D. *schouder*, G. *schulter*, the shoulder, the shoulder-blade.] The joint by which the arm of a human being or the foreleg of a quadruped is connected with the body; the bones and muscles of this part together; the upper joint of the foreleg of an animal cut for the market; that which resembles a human shoulder; a prominent or projecting part (the *shoulder* of a hill); a projection on various implements and articles. — *Shoulder-of-mutton sail*, a triangular sail set on a boat's mast.—*The cold shoulder*, a cold or cool reception of a person (to give a person *the cold shoulder*). — *To put one's shoulder to the wheel*, to assist in overcoming a difficulty; to give effective help.—*Shoulder to shoulder*, a phrase expressive of united action and mutual co-operation and support. — *v.t.* To push or thrust with the shoulder; to push with violence; to take upon the shoulder or shoulders; *milit.* to carry vertically at the side of the body and resting against the hollow of the shoulder (to *shoulder* arms).—*v.i.* To push forward; to force one's way, as through a crowd.—**Shoulder-belt**, *n.* A belt that passes across the shoulder.—**Shoulder-blade**, *n.* The bone of the shoulder, or blade-bone, covering the hind part of the ribs; the scapula. — **Shoulder-bone**, *n.* The shoulder-blade.—**Shouldered**, shōl'dėrd, *a.* Having shoulders.—**Shoulder-knot**, *n.* An ornamental knot of ribbon or lace worn on the shoulder.—**Shoulder-strap**, *n.* A strap worn on or over the shoulder, either to support the lress or as a badge of distinction.

Shout, shout, *v.i.* [Perhaps a softened form of *scout*, or onomatopoetic.] To utter a sudden and loud cry, as in joy or exultation, or to call a person's attention.—*n.* A loud cry; a vehement and sudden outcry, particularly of a multitude of men, expressing joy, triumph, exultation, &c.—*v.t.* To utter with a shout.—**Shouter**, shout'ėr, *n.* One that shouts.

Shove, shuv, *v.t.*—*shoved, shoving*. [A.Sax. *scúfan* = O.Fris. *skuva*, Icel. *skýfa*, D. *schuiven*, Goth. *skiuban*, G. *schieben*, to shove; akin *shovel*, *scuffle*.] To force or push along, usually without a sudden impulse; to cause to slide by pushing; to press against; to jostle. — *To shove off*, to thrust or push away; to cause to move from shore by pushing with poles or oars.—*v.i.* To push or drive forward; to urge a course. — *To shove off*, to push a boat from shore.—*n.* An act of shoving; a push. — **Shove-board**, *n.* The game of shovel-board.

Shovel, shuv'el, *n.* [A. Sax. *scofl* (from *scúfan*, to shove) = D. *schoffel*, Dan. *skovl*, G. *schaufel*, a shovel, SHOVE.] An implement consisting of a broad and slightly hollow blade, or a shallow scoop, with a long handle, used for removing coal, sand, earth, or other loose matter.—*v.t.*—*shoveled, shovelled, shoveling, shovelling*. To take up and throw with a shovel.—**Shovelbill**, *n.* A variety of duck: a shoveler.—**Shovelboard**, *n.* SHUFFLEBOARD.—A kind of game played by pushing coins or the like along a board towards certain marks; a game played on board ships by shoving wooden disks with a cue so that they shall rest in one of nine squares chalked on the deck.—**Shoveler**, shuv'el-ėr, *n.* One who shovels; a species of duck.—**Shovel-hat**, *n.* A hat with a broad brim turned up at the sides, and projecting in front, worn by clergymen of the Church of England.—**Shovelhead**, *n.* A species of shark; also a subspecies of sturgeon.

Show, shō, *v.t.*—pret. *showed*; pp. *shown* or *showed*: also written *Shew, Shewed, Shewn*. [A.Sax. *sceáwian*, to behold, to show; D. *schouwen*, Dan. *skue*, G. *schauen*, Goth. *scavjan*; supposed to be from same root as L. *caveo*, to take care, *cautus*, E. *cautious*.] To exhibit or present to the view; to place in sight; to display; to let be seen; to communicate; to reveal; to make known; to make apparent or clear by evidence, reasoning, &c.; to teach; to direct; to guide or usher; to conduct; to bestow, confer, afford (mercy, &c); to explain or to expound; to indicate; to point out.—*To show forth*, to manifest; to publish.—*To show off*, to exhibit in an ostentatious manner.—*To show up*, to usher or conduct up a stair; to hold up to ridicule or to contempt.—*v.i.* To appear; to become visible; to look; to be in appearance.—*To show off*, to make a show: to display one's self.—*n.* The act of showing; exposure to view or notice; appearance, whether true or false; semblance; outward aspect assumed; pretext; ostentatious display; parade; pomp; an object attracting notice; a sight or spectacle; an exhibition; a motion picture or a stage performance; a collection of curiosities exhibited for money (a flower-*show*).—*A show of hands*, a raising of hands, as a means of voting.—**Showboat**, *n.* A river steamboat with stage and a troupe of actors, used as a floating theater.—**Show-bread**, *n.* SHEWBREAD.—**Show-case**, *n.* A case with glass on the top or front, within which articles are placed for sale or exhibition.—**Showdown**, *n.* A concluding disclosure of facts and conditions concerning a matter.—**Showily**, shō'i-li, *adv.* In a showy manner; with parade.—**Showiness**, shō'i-nes, *n.* State of being showy; great parade.—**Showing**, shō'ing, *n.* Exhibition.—**Showman**, shō'man, *n.* One who exhibits a show.—**Show-off**, *n.* Pretentious display; a person who shows off.—**Showroom**, *n.* A room in which a show is exhibited; an apartment where goods are displayed.—**Showy**, shō'i, *a.* Making a great show; gorgeous; gaudy.

Shower, shou'ėr, *n.* [A. Sax. *scúr* = Icel. *skúr*, D. *schoer*, Sw. *skur*, O.H.G. *scûr*, G. *schauer*, a shower.] A fall of rain of short duration; a fall of things in thick and fast succession (a *shower* of stones); a surprise party given to a woman at which those attending bring gifts for the guest of honor.—*v.t.* To pour down copiously and rapidly; to bestow liberally.—*v.i.* To rain in showers; to fall as a shower.—**Shower bath**, *n.* A bath in which water is showered upon the person from above; plumbing and equipment installed for such a bath.—**Showery**, shou'ėr-i, *a.* Raining in showers; abounding with falls of rain.

Shrapnel, shrap'nel, *n.* [After General *Shrapnel*, the inventor.] A shell filled with bullets and a small bursting charge just sufficient to split the shell open and release the bullets at any given point.

Shred, shred, *v.t.*—pret. and pp. *shred*; ppr. *shredding*. [A.Sax. *screddian*, to shred, from *screáde*, Sc. *screed*, a piece torn off; O.Fris. *skreda*, D. *schrooden*, O.H.G. *scrótan*, to tear. *Shroud* is akin.] To tear or cut into small pieces, particularly narrow and long pieces, as cloth or leather.—*n.* A piece torn or cut off; any torn fragment; a tatter; a fragment.

Shrew, shrö, *n.* [O. E. *shrewe*, wicked, a wicked person; hence, obsol. *shrews*, to curse, to (*be*)*shrew*, whence *shrewd*; A.Sax. *screáwa*, the shrewmouse, lit. the evil or venomous mouse.] An ill-tempered woman; a nagging, scolding woman; a virago; a termagant; a shrewmouse.—**Shrewish**, shrö'ish, *a.* Having the qualities of a shrew; vixenish.—**Shrewishly**, shrö'ish-li, *adv.* In a shrewish manner.—**Shrewishness**, shrö'ish-nes, *n.*—**Shrewmouse**, *n.* [So called because its bite was once thought venomous.] A small harmless mammal, of the genus *Sorex*, with a long pointed snout, small eyes, short tail and brownish velvety fur, somewhat resembling a mouse, but belonging to the insectivorous animals, while the mouse is a rodent.

Shrewd, shröd, *a.* [From old *shrewe*, to curse, *shrewe*, evil. SHREW.] Malicious or mischievous (*Shak.*)‡; astute; sagacious; discerning.—**Shrewdly**, shröd'li, *adv.* In a shrewd manner; astutely; sagaciously; of *wind*, 'biting *shrewdly*' (*Hamlet*), in original sense.—**Shrewdness**, shröd'nes, *n.* The quality of being shrewd; sagacity; acuteness of mind.

Shriek, shrēk, *v.i.* [A form of *screak* and *screech*.] To utter a sharp shrill cry; to scream, as in a sudden fright, horror, or anguish.—*n.* A sharp shrill cry or scream; a shrill noise.—*v.t.* To utter with a shriek.—**Shrieker**, shrēk'ėr, *n.* One who shrieks.—**Shriek-owl**, *n.* SCREECH-OWL.

Shrievalty, shrē'val-ti, *n.* [From obsol. *shrieve*, a sheriff.] The office or jurisdiction of a sheriff.

Shrift. Under SHRIVE.

Shrike, shrīk, *n.* [From its *shrieking* cry.] The name of certain dentirostral insessorial birds which feed on mice, insects, small birds, &c., and often impale their prey on thorns: called also butcher-birds.

Shrill, shril, *a.* [An imitative word akin to Sc. *skirl*, a screech, L.G. *skrell*, G. *schrill*, shrill.] Sharp or acute in tone; having a piercing sound; uttering an acute sound.—*v.i.* To utter an acute piercing sound.—*v.t.* To utter in a shrill tone.—**Shrillness**, shril'nes, *n.* The quality of being shrill; acuteness of sound.—**Shrilly**, shril'li, *adv.* In a shrill manner; with a sharp sound or voice.—*a.* (shril'i). Somewhat shrill.

Shrimp, shrimp, *n.* [Akin to Sc. *scrimp*, to deal out sparingly; A.Sax. *scrymman*, to wither, G. *schrumpfen*, to shrivel.] A small crustacean allied to the lobster and crayfish, which burrows in sand, and is esteemed as food; a dwarfish creature; a manikin.—**Shrimper**, shrimp'ėr, *n.* A fisherman who catches shrimps.—**Shrimp-net**, *n.* A bag-net mounted on a hoop and pole for catching shrimps.

Shrine, shrīn, *n.* [A.Sax. *scrín*, from L. *scrinium*, a box.] A box for holding the bones or other remains of departed saints; a reliquary; a tomb of shrine-like form; the mausoleum of a saint in a church; an altar; a place hallowed from its history or associations (a *shrine* of art).—*v.t.*—*shrined, shrining*. To place in a shrine; to enshrine.

Shrink, shringk, *v.i.*—pret. *shrank* and *shrunk*; pp. *shrunk, shrunken* (the latter now always an adjective). [A.Sax. *scrincan*, O.D. *schrincken*, to shrink; from root of *shrimp, shrug*.] To contract spontaneously, as woollen cloth in water; to draw or be drawn into less compass by an inherent quality; to shrivel; to become wrinkled; to draw back, as from danger; to decline action from fear; to recoil; to draw the body together as in fear or horror.—*v.t.* To cause to contract by immersing in water.—*n.* The act of shrinking.—**Shrinkage**, shringk'āj, *n.* The contraction of a material into less compass, as by soaking or by drying; hence, amount of depreciation in value, as of business assets; loss of weight, as of cotton in storage, &c.—**Shrunken**, shrungk'n, *p.* and *a.* Having shrunk; shriveled up; contracted.

Shrive, shrīv, *v.t.*—pret. *shrove* or *shrived*; pp. *shriven, shrived*; ppr. *shriving*. [A.Sax. *scrífan*, to shrive; perhaps borrowed from L. *scribo*, to write.] To hear or receive the confession of; to administer confession to, as a priest does; to confess and absolve.—**Shriven**, shriv'n, pp. of *shrive*.—**Shriver**, shrī'vėr, *n.* One who shrives; a confessor.—**Shriving**, shrī'ving, *n.* Shrift; confession taken.—**Shriving-pew**, *n.* A term sometimes applied to a confessional.—**Shrift**, shrift, *n.* [A.Sax. *scrift*; comp. *give* and *gift*.] Confession made to a priest; absolution.—**Shrift-father**, *n.* A father confessor.—*Short shrift*, the brief period between condemnation and execution.

Shrivel, shriv'el, *v.i.*—*shrivelled, shrivelling*. [Probably based partly on *rivel*, to shrivel, partly on *shrink*.] To contract or shrink; to draw or be drawn into wrinkles.—*v.t.* To contract into wrinkles.

Shroud, shroud, *n.* [A.Sax. *scrúd*, a garment, a shroud; Icel. *skrúd*, shrouds, tackle; Dan. *skrud*, dress; from root of *shred*.] That which clothes, covers, or conceals; a garment; a covering; the dress of the dead; a winding-sheet; *naut.* one of those large ropes that extend from the head of a mast to the right and left sides of the ship, to support the mast.—*v.t.* To envelop with some covering; to cover; to hide; to veil; to put a shroud or winding-sheet on.—*v.i.* To take shelter.—**Shroudless**, shroud'les, *a.* Without a shroud.

Shrove-tide, *n.* [*Shrove*, pret. of *shrive*, and *tide*, time, season.] The time when the people were shriven preparatory to the Lenten season; the few days before Ash-Wednesday.—**Shrove-Tuesday**, *n.* Confession-Tuesday; the Tuesday preceding the first day of Lent, or Ash-Wednesday.

Shrub, shrub, *n.* [A.Sax. *scrob*, a bush; perhaps from same root as *shrivel, shrimp*. *Scrub*, low shrubby trees, is the same word.] A low dwarf tree; a woody plant of a size less than a tree; or more strictly, a plant with several permanent woody stems dividing from the bottom.—**Shrubbery**, shrub'ėr-i, *n.* An ornamental plantation of shrubs; growing shrubs.—**Shrubby**, shrub'i, *a.* Full of shrubs; being or resembling a shrub; consisting of shrubs or brush.—**Shrubbiness**, shrub'i-nes, *n.* The quality of being shrubby.—**Shrubless**, shrub'les, *a.* Having no shrubs.

Shrub, shrub, *n.* [Ar. *shurb*, a drink; allied to *syrup, sherbet*.] A liquor composed of lime or lemon juice and sugar, with spirit (chiefly rum).

Shrug, shrug, *v.t.* and *i.*—*shrugged, shrugging*. [From root of *shrink*; allied to D. *schrikken*, G. *schrecken* to tremble.] To raise or draw up the shoulders, as in expressing dissatisfaction, aversion, &c.—*n.* A drawing up of the shoulders, a motion usually expressing dislike.

Shuck, shuk, *n.* [Comp. *chuck*, to throw, husks being thrown away.] A shell or husk, as of an ear of corn or of a nut.—*v.t.* To tear off the husk.

Shudder, shud'ėr, *v.i.* [Same as L.G. *schuddern*, O.D. *schudderen*, G. *schüttern*, to shake, to shiver, freq. forms from L.G. and D. *schudden*, G. *schütten*, O.H.G. *scutan*, to shake; allied to E. *shed*, to cast.] To be strongly agitated or shaken, as by a qualm; to tremble; to quake violently, as with great horror.—*To shudder at*, to feel violent aversion to; to be filled with disgust at, as to *shudder* at the thought of, to *shudder* to think of.—*n.* An agitation or shaking of the body, resembling shivering or trembling, caused by a strong feeling of horror or disgust.—**Shuddering**, shud'ėr-ing, *p.* and *a.* Trembling with fear or horror; quaking.

Shuffle, shuf'l, *v.t.*—*shuffled, shuffling*. [A dim. from *shove*, like L.G. *schuffeln*, to shuffle. *Scuffle* is another form.] To shove rapidly one way and the other; to mix together by pushing or shoving; to put into a fresh order at random, as playing-cards.—*To shuffle off*, to push off; to rid one's self of. — *To shuffle up*, to throw together in haste.—*v.i.* To change the position; to shift ground; to prevaricate; to shift; to move with an irregular dragging gait; to shove the feet noisily to and fro on the floor or ground, to scrape the floor in dancing.—*To shuffle off*, to take leave or to start off (*colloq.*).—*n.* The act of one who shuffles; an evasion; a trick; an artifice; *dancing*, a rapid scraping movement with the feet, also the *double shuffle*.—**Shuffleboard**, **Shovelboard**, *n.* A game played by pushing disks toward certain marks; a game played on board ship by shoving disks with a cue, so that they will rest in one of nine squares chalked on the deck.—**Shuffler**, shuf'lėr, *n.* One who shuffles; one who plays mean tricks.

Shumach, shū'mak. SUMAC.

Shun, shun, *v.t.*—*shunned*, *shunning*. [A. Sax. *scunian*, to shun; allied to D. *schuin*, oblique, *schuinen*, to slope. *Shunt* is from *shun*, as also *scoundrel*.] To keep clear of; to get out of the way of; to avoid; to eschew.—**Shunless**, shun'les, *a.* Not to be shunned; inevitable; unavoidable.

Shunt, shunt, *v.i.* [From *shun*.] *Railroads*, to switch from one line of rails to another. —*v.t.* To cause to turn from one line of rails to another; to turn into a siding; hence (*colloq.*), to shove off; to free one's self of.—**Shunter**, shunt'ėr, *n.* One who shunts.—**Shunt-gun**, *n.* A rifled cannon with two sets of grooves, down one of which the ball passes in loading, passing out by the other when fired.—**Shunt motor**, *n.* An electric motor in which the field coils are energized by being connected across the supply mains, forming a shunt or bypass to the main circuit through the armature.

Shut, shut, *v.t.*—pret. and pp. *shut*, ppr. *shutting*. [O.E. *shutte*, *shitte*, A.Sax. *scytian*, to bolt, to lock, to shoot the bolt, from *sceótan*, to shoot. (SHOOT.) A *shuttle* is what is *shot* or cast.] To close so as to prevent ingress or egress; to close up by bringing the parts together (a book, &c.); to forbid entrance into (to *shut* a port); to bar; to preclude; to exclude.—*To shut in*, to inclose; to confine; to cover or intercept the view of.—*To shut off*, to exclude; to intercept; to prevent the passage of.—*To shut out*, to preclude from entering; to exclude.—*To shut up*, to make fast the openings or entrances into; to inclose; to imprison; to lock or fasten in; to terminate or conclude; to cause to say nothing more (*colloq.*).—*v.i.* To close itself; to become closed.—*a.* Not resonant or sonorous; having the sound suddenly stopped by a succeeding consonant (as *o* in *got*).—*n.* The act of closing; close; a shutter.—**Shutter**, shut'ėr, *n.* One who or that which shuts; a movable covering for a window.

Shuttle, shut'l, *n.* [A.Sax. *scytel*, a shuttle, from *sceótan*, to shoot, because shot to and fro in weaving. SHOOT, SHUT.] An instrument used by weavers for passing the thread of the weft from one side of the web to the other between the threads of the warp; *sewing-machines*, the sliding thread holder which carries the lower thread between the needle and the upper thread to make a lock-stitch. —*v.i.* To scuttle; to hurry. (*Carl.*)—**Shuttle-cock**, *n.* [For shuttle-*cork*.] A cork stuck with feathers made to be struck by a battledore in play; also the play.—*v.t.* To throw or bandy backwards and forwards like a shuttle-cock.

Shwanpan, shwan'pan, *n.* A calculating instrument of the Chinese similar in shape and construction to the Roman abacus, and used in the same manner.

Shy, shī, *a.* [Same as Dan. *sky*, shy, skittish, G. *scheu*, shy, timid; akin to O.E. *schiech*, A.Sax. *sceóh*, Sc. *skiech*, Sw. *skygg*, shy. *Eschew* is akin to *shy*.] Keeping at a distance through caution or timidity; readily frightened; timid; sensitively timid; not inclined to be familiar; retiring; coy; reserved; cautious; wary; careful to avoid committing one's self: followed by *of*.—*v.i.*—*shied*, *shying*. To start away from an object that causes fear: said of a horse.—*v.t.* To throw (to *shy* a stone). (*Colloq.*)—**Shyly**, shī'li, *adv.* In a shy or timid manner; coyly; diffidently.—**Shyness**, shī'nes, *n.* The quality or state of being shy; reserve; coyness.

Shyster, shī'stėr, *n.* A tricky person; one without professional honor, especially an unethical lawyer.

Si, sē. *Mus.* a name given in some systems to the seventh note of the natural or normal scale.

Sialagogue, **Sialogogue**, sī-al'a-gog, sī-al'o-gog, *n.* [Gr. *sialon*, saliva, and *agōgos*, leading.] A medicine that promotes the salivary discharge.

Siamang, sī'a-mang, *n.* A quadrumanous animal, a kind of gibbon.

Siamese, sī-a-mēz', *n.* *sing.* and *pl.* A native or natives of Siam; the language of Siam.—**Siamese twins**, Eng and Chang, 1811-74, Chinese brothers, united from birth by a cartilaginous band; term used for any twins so united.

Sib, sib, *a.* Related by blood; akin to.

Siberian, sī-bē'ri-an, *a.* Pertaining to Siberia.—*Siberian crab*, a Siberian tree of the apple genus.—*Siberian dog*, a variety of the dog, in northern regions employed in drawing sledges over the frozen snow.

Sibilant, sib'i-lant, *a.* [L. *sibilans*, *sibilantis*, ppr. of *sibilo*, to hiss.] Hissing; making a hissing sound.—*n.* A letter that is uttered with a hissing of the voice, as *s* and *z*.—**Sibilance**, **Sibilancy**, sib'i-lans, sib'i-lan-si, *n.* The quality of being sibilant; a hissing sound as of *s*.—**Sibilate**, sib'i-lāt, *v.t.*—*sibilated*, *sibilating*. [L. *sibilo*, *sibilatum*, to hiss.] To pronounce with a hissing sound.—**Sibilation**, sib-i-lā'shon, *n.* The act of sibilating or hissing; a hissing sound; a hiss.—**Sibilatory**, **Sibilous**, sib'i-la-to-ri, sib'i-lus, *a.* Hissing; having a hissing sound.

Sibyl, sib'il, *n.* [Gr. *sibylla*.] A name common to certain women mentioned by Greek and Roman writers, and said to have been endowed with a prophetic spirit; hence, a prophetess; a sorceress; a fortune-teller; a witch.—**Sibylline**, sib'il-lin, *a.* Pertaining to the sibyls; like the productions of sibyls; prophetical. — *Sibylline books*, certain books, containing directions as to the worship of the gods, the policy that should be observed by the Romans, &c., purchased by Tarquin the Proud from the Cumæan Sibyl.

Sic, sik, *adv.* [L. *sic*, so.] Thus, or it is so: a word often used in quoting, and placed within brackets in order to call attention to the fact that the quotation is literally given, and that there is something peculiar about it.

Sicanian, sik-a'ni-an, *a.* Of or relating to the Sicani, the indigenous inhabitants of Sicily.

Sicca, sik'ka, *n.* An Indian jeweler's weight of 180 grains Troy.—*Sicca rupee*, a rupee which contained 176 grains of pure silver, and was equal to about 54 cents in U. S. currency.

Siccate, sik'āt, *v.t.*—*siccated*, *siccating*. [L. *sicco*, *siccatum*, to dry, from *siccus*, dry.] To dry very slowly for the purpose of preservation (*rare*).—**Siccation**, sik-kā'shon, *n.* The act or process of drying.—**Siccative**, sik'a-tiv, *a.* Drying; causing to dry by the slow elimination of moisture.—*n.* That which promotes the process of drying.—**Siccity**, sik'si-ti, *n.* Dryness.

Sicelian, si-kel'i-an, *a.* [Gr. *Sikeloi*, L. *Siculi*.] Of or relating to the Sicelians, the second inhabitants, migrating from the south of Italy.—**Siceliote**, si-kel'i-ōt, *n.* A Greek colonist in Sicily.

Sicilian, si-sil'i-an, *a.* Pertaining to Sicily. —*Sicilian Vespers*, the great massacre of the French in Sicily in 1282, on the evening of Easter Monday, the signal being the first stroke of the vesper-bell.—*n.* A native or inhabitant of Sicily.

Sick, sik, *a.* [A.Sax. *seóc* = Goth. *siuks*, L.G. *seek*, *siek*, D. *ziek*, Icel. *sjúkr*, G. *siech*, sick.] Affected with nausea; inclined to vomit; disgusted; feeling tedium; wearied (to be *sick of* flattery); affected with disease of any kind; not in health; ill; languishing; used by or set apart for sick persons (a *sick*-bed).—*The sick*, persons affected with disease.—**Sick-bay**, *n.* *Naut.* a portion of the main-deck partitioned off for invalids.—**Sick-bed**, *n.* A bed on which one is confined by sickness.—**Sick-berth**, *n.* An apartment for the sick in a ship.—**Sick-brained**, *a.* Disordered in the brain; distempered in mind. — **Sicken**, sik'n, *v.t.* To make sick; to disease; to make squeamish or qualmish; to disgust. —*v.i.* To become sick; to fall ill; to feel sick; to become distempered; to languish. —**Sickening**, sik'n-ing, *a.* Making sick; disgusting.—**Sickish**, sik'ish, *a.* Somewhat sick; indisposed; nauseating.—**Sickishly**, sik'ish-li, *adv.* In a sickish manner. —**Sickishness**, sik'ish-nes, *n.*—**Sickliness**, sik'li-nes, *n.* The state of being sickly; insalubrity; the disposition to generate disease (the *sickliness* of a climate). —**Sick-list**, *n.* A list containing the names of the sick.—**Sickly**, sik'li, *a.* Somewhat sick or ill; not healthy; attended with sickness; producing or tending to produce disease; faint; languid; appearing as if sick.—*adv.* In a sick manner or condition. —**Sickness**, sik'nes, *n.* The state of being sick; disease; ill health; a disease; a malady; a particular state of the stomach which occurs under the forms of nausea, retching, and vomiting; any disordered state.

Sickle, sik'l, *n.* [A.Sax. *sicel*, *sicol* = D. *sikkel*, G. *sichel*, Dan. *segel*, a sickle; a dim. form from root of *scythe*.] A reaping-hook; a curved blade or hook of steel with a handle, for use with one hand in cutting grain, grass, &c.—**Sickled**, sik'ld, *a.* Furnished with a sickle.—**Sickleman**, sik'l-man, *n.* One that uses a sickle; a reaper.

Side, sīd, *n.* [A.Sax. *side* = Dan. *side*, Icel. *sída*, G. *seite*, a side; akin to A.Sax. *síd*, Icel. *sídr*, long.] The broad or long surface of a solid body, as distinguished from the *end*, which is of less extent; the exterior line of anything considered in length; the margin, edge, border; the part of an animal between the hip and shoulder (the right or left *side*); the part of persons on the right hand or the left; the part between the top and bottom; the slope of a hill or mountain (the *side* of Mount Etna); one of two principal surfaces opposed to each other; part whichever way directed; quarter in any direction; any party or interest opposed to another (on the same *side* in politics); line of descent traced through one parent (by the father's *side*); *geom.* any line which forms one of the boundaries of a straight-lined figure; also, any of the bounding surfaces of a solid; swagger; pomposity. (*Colloq.*)—*By the side of*, near to; closely adjoining.—*Side by side*, close together and abreast.—*To choose sides*, to divide a group for competition in exercises of any kind.—*To take a side*, to embrace the opinions of a party in opposition to another.—*a.* Lateral; being on the side; being from the side or toward the side; oblique; indirect (a *side* view).—*v.t.*—*Sided*, *siding*. To embrace the opinions of one party when opposed to another party; to engage in a faction: often followed by *with*. —**Side arms**, *n. pl.* Arms carried at the side, as a revolver, sword, bayonet, &c.—**Sideboard**, sīd'bōrd, *n.* A piece of dining-room furniture, consisting of a kind of table with drawers or compartments used to hold dining utensils, &c.—**Sidecar**, *n.* A single-seated car attached to the side of a motorcycle with one wheel supporting the off side; an intoxicating drink (*colloq.*). —**Sided**, sī'ded, *a.* Having a side; used in composition (many-*sided*).—**Side dish**, *n.* A small extra dish or helping set beside one's plate.—**Side glance**, *n.* A glance to one side.—**Side light**, *n.* Light admitted laterally; indirect information.

upon a subject.—**Sideling**, sīd'ling, *adv.* SIDELONG. (*Swift.*)—**Sidelong**, sīd'long, *adv.* [*Side*, and term. *-long*, *-ling*, as in head*long*, dark*ling*.] Laterally; obliquely; in the direction of the side.—*a.* Lateral; oblique; not directly in front.—**Side-look**, *n.* An oblique look; a side-glance.—**Side-post**, *n.* *Carp.* one of a kind of truss-posts placed in pairs, for supporting the principal rafters, &c., in roofs.—**Sider**, sī'dėr, *n.* One that takes a side or joins a party.—**Side-saddle**, *n.* A saddle for a woman, in which the feet are both on one side.—**Side-slip**, *n.* A movement sideways of an aeroplane that may occur when the forward speed of the machine is unduly diminished.—**Sidesman**, sīdz'man, *n.* An assistant to the churchwardens.—**Side-view**, *n.* An oblique view; a side-look.—**Side-walk**, *n.* A raised walk for foot-passengers by the side of a street or road; a foot-way.—**Sideways**, sīd'wāz, *adv.* SIDEWISE.—**Side-wind**, *n.* A wind blowing laterally; *fig.* an indirect influence or means.—**Sidewise**, sīd'wīz, *adv.* Toward one side; laterally; on one side.—**Siding**, sī'ding, *n.* A short additional line of rails laid at the side of a main line for the purpose of shunting.

Sidereal, sī-dē'rē-al, *a.* [L. *sideralis*, *sidereus*, from *sidus*, *sideris*, a star (seen also in *consider*).] Pertaining to the stars; starry; measured or marked by the apparent motions of the stars (*sidereal* time).—*Sidereal clock*, a clock adapted to measure sidereal time.—*Sidereal day*, the time in which the earth makes a complete revolution on its axis in respect of the fixed stars, being 23 hours, 56 minutes, 4·092 seconds.—*Sidereal system*, the general system of stars of which the solar system is a member.—*Sidereal year*, the period in which the fixed stars apparently complete a revolution in the heavens, being the exact period of the revolution of the earth round the sun, and containing 366·25 sidereal days.

Siderite, sid'ėr-īt, *n.* [Gr. *sidēritēs*, from *sidēros*, iron.] Magnetic iron ore or loadstone; also native spathic iron ore, and a blue variety of quartz.—**Siderographic**, **Siderographical**, sid'ėr-ō-graf"ik, sid'ėr-ō-graf"i-kal, *a.* Pertaining to siderography.—**Siderographist**, sid-ėr-og'ra-fist, *n.* One who engraves steel plates.—**Siderography**, sid-ėr-og'ra-fi, *n.* [Gr. *sidēros*, steel or iron, and *graphō*, to engrave.] The art or practice of engraving on steel.—**Siderolite**, sid'ėr-ō-līt, *n.* [Gr. *sidēros*, and *lithos*, a stone.] A meteoric stone chiefly consisting of iron.—**Sideromancy**, sid'ėr-ō-man-si, *n.* [Gr. *sidēros*, and *manteia*, divination.] A species of divination performed by burning straws, &c., upon red-hot iron.—**Sideroscope**, sid'ėr-ō-skōp, *n.* [Gr. *sidēros*, and *skopeō*, to view.] An instrument for detecting small quantities of iron by magnetic needles.

Siderostat, sid'ėr-ō-stat, *n.* [L. *sidus*, *sideris*, a star, and Gr. *statos*, placed, standing, from *histēmi*, to stand.] An apparatus consisting of a mirror moved by clockwork and a fixed object-glass, for observing the light of the stars.

Sidle, sī'dl, *v.i.*—*sidled*, *sidling*. [From *side*.] To go or move side foremost; to move to one side.

Siege, sēj, *n.* [Fr. *siége*, from hypothetical L.L. *sedium*, *sidium*, from L. *sedeo*, to sit. SEDATE.] The investment of a fortified place by an army, and attack of it by passages and advance works that protect the besiegers; any continued endeavour to gain possession.—**Siege-train**, *n.* The artillery, carriages, ammunition, &c., carried with an army for attacking fortified places.

Sienite, sī'en-īt, *n.* SYENITE.

Sienna, **Sienna-earth**, sē-en'na, *n.* A ferruginous earth of a fine yellow colour, from *Sienna* in Italy, used as a pigment.

Sierra, sē-er'ra, *n.* [Sp. from L. *serra*, a saw.] A chain of hills or mountains with jagged or saw-like ridges.

Siesta, sē-es'ta, *n.* [Sp.] A sleep or rest in the hottest part of the day indulged in by the Spaniards and others.

Sieur, syėr, *n.* [Fr., abbrev. from *seigneur*.] A title of respect used by the French.

Sieve, siv, *n.* [A.Sax. *sife*, a sieve; L.G. *seve*, D. *zeef*, G. *sieb*; perhaps made originally of rushes; comp. Prov.E. *seave*, Dan. *siv*, a rush.] An instrument for separating the smaller particles of substances from the grosser, usually in the form of a shallow circular vessel having its bottom made of basket-work, interwoven wires, hair, canvas, net-work, &c., according to circumstances.

Sift, sift, *v.t.* [A.Sax. *siftan*, from *sife*, a sieve; L.G. *siften*, D. *ziften*, to sift. SIEVE.] To operate on by a sieve; to separate by a sieve, as the fine part of a substance from the coarse; to part, as by a sieve; to examine minutely or critically; to scrutinize.—**Sifter**, sif'tėr, *n.* One who sifts; that which sifts; a sieve.

Sigh, sī, *v.i.* [O.E. *syke*, A.Sax. *sícan*, Sc. *sic*, *sich*, Dan. *sukke*, to sigh; D. *zugt*, a sigh; probably imitative of sound; comp. *sough*, noise of the wind.] To make a deep single respiration, as the involuntary expression of sorrow or melancholy; to grieve; to give out a similar sound (the wind *sighs*).—*To sigh for*, to long or wish ardently for.—*v.t.* To emit in sighs; to mourn; to express by sighs.—*n.* A single deep involuntary respiration; a simple respiration giving involuntary expression of some depressing emotion, as sorrow, melancholy, anxiety, or the like.—**Sigher**, sī'ėr, *n.* One who sighs.—**Sighingly**, sī'ing-li, *adv.* With sighing.

Sight, sīt, *n.* [A.Sax. *gesiht*=G. *sicht*, Dan. and Sw. *sigte*; from stem of *see*; comp. *flight* and *flee*.] The act or power of seeing; perception of objects by the eye (to gain *sight* of land); the faculty of vision; range of unobstructed vision; open view (in *sight* of land); visibility; judgment or opinion from seeing; estimation (to find favour in one's *sight*); that which is beheld; a spectacle; particularly, something novel and remarkable; something worth seeing (the *sights* of a town); a great many individuals (*colloq.*); an appliance for guiding the eye in an optical instrument; a small elevated piece near the muzzle, or another near the breech, of a firearm, to aid the eye in taking aim.—*At sight*, *after sight*, terms applied to bills or notes payable on or after presentation.—*To take sight*, to take aim.—*v.t.* To get or catch sight of; to come in sight of; to see (to *sight* the land); to give the proper elevation and direction to by means of a sight (to *sight* a rifle or cannon).—**Sighted**, sī'ted, *a.* Seeing in a particular manner (short-*sighted*, quick-*sighted*); having a sight or sights (a rifle *sighted* for 1000 yards).—**Sight-hole**, *n.* A hole to see through.—**Sightless**, sīt'les, *a.* Wanting the power of seeing; blind.—**Sightlessly**, sīt'les-li, *adv.* In a sightless manner.—**Sightlessness**, sīt'les-nes, *n.* The state of being sightless; want of sight.—**Sightliness**, sīt'li-nes, *n.* The state of being sightly.—**Sightly**, sīt'li, *a.* Pleasing to the eye; striking to the view.—**Sight-seeing**, *n.* The act of seeing sights or visiting scenes of interest.—**Sight-seer**, *n.* One who goes to see sights or curiosities.

Sigillaria, sij-il-lā'ri-a, *n.* [L. *sigillum*, a seal, dim. of *signum*, a mark. SIGN.] The name given to certain large fossil plants of the coal formation, from the leaf-scars on their fluted stems resembling seal impressions.—**Sigillative**, sij'il-lā-tiv, *a.* Belonging to a seal.—**Sigillography**, sij-il-log'ra-fi, *n.* The science of seals on documents.

Sigmoid, **Sigmoidal**, sig'moid, sig-moi'dal, *a.* [From Gr. *sigma*, the letter Σ or C = S.] Curved like the letter sigma in its form C: applied in *anat.* to several parts, as the semilunar valves of the heart and the cartilages of the trachea.

Sign, sīn, *n.* [Fr. *signe*, from L. *signum*, a mark, a sign, whence *signal*, *signet*, *assign*, *consign*, *design*, *resign*, &c., also *seal* from the dim. *sigillum*.] That by which anything is made known or represented; anything visible that indicates the existence or approach of something else; a token; a mark; an indication; a motion or gesture by which a thought is expressed or intelligence communicated; a prodigy; an omen; a miracle; a wonder; any symbol or emblem; that which, being external, represents or signifies something internal or spiritual; something conspicuously placed on or near a house, indicating the occupation of the tenant or giving notice of what is sold or made within; a sign-board; *astron.* one of the twelve divisions of the ecliptic or zodiac, each containing 30 degrees, and named in succession Aries, Taurus, Gemini, Cancer, Leo, Virgo, Libra, Scorpio, Sagittarius, Capricornus, Aquarius, Pisces; *arith.* and *math.* a character indicating the relation of quantities, or an operation performed on them, as + (plus), − (minus), &c.; *mus.* any character, as a flat, sharp, dot, &c.—*v.t.* To express by a sign; to make known by gesture; to signify; to mark with a sign or symbol; to affix a signature to; to subscribe in one's own handwriting.—*v.i.* To make a sign or signal.—**Signable**, sī'na-bl, *a.* Capable of being signed; requiring to be signed.—**Sign-board**, *n.* A board carrying notice of one's occupation, business or goods for sale.—**Signer**, sī'nėr, *n.* One who signs or subscribes his name.—**Sign manual**, *n.* A signature; the subscription of one's own name to a document; a royal signature.—**Sign painter**, *n.* A painter of signs for tradesmen, &c.—**Signpost**, *n.* A post on which a sign hangs.

Signal, sig'nal, *n.* [Fr. *signal*, L.L. *signale*, from L. *signum*. SIGN.] A sign that is intended to communicate information, orders, or the like to persons at a distance, as by a motion of the hand, the raising of a flag, the showing of lights of various colors, &c.—*a.* Distinguished from what is ordinary; remarkable; notable; conspicuous: said of things.—*v.t.*—*signaled*, *signaling*. To communicate or make known by a signal or signals: to make signals to (the vessel *signaled* the forts).—*v.i.* To give a signal or signals.—**Signal box**, *n.* A small house in which railway signals are worked.—**Signal fire**, *n.* A fire intended for a signal.—**Signalize**, sig'nal-īz, *v.t.*—*signalized*, *signalizing*. To make remarkable; to render distinguished; to distinguish by some fact or exploit: often used reflexively.—**Signal lamp**, *n.* A railway lamp made to give out light of different colors as signals.—**Signaling coloration**, *n.* In gregarious animals, conspicuous color arrangements, e.g. white tail of rabbit, serving to give warning of danger.—**Signally**, sig'nal-li, *adv.* In a signal manner; eminently; remarkably; memorably.—**Signalman**, *n.* One who signals; specifically, an official on a railway who works the signals.—**Signal post**, *n.* A post or pole for displaying flags, lamps, &c., as signals.

Signatory, **Signatary**, sig'na-to-ri, sig'na-ta-ri, *a.* [L. *signatorius*, pertaining to signing, from *signator*, a signer, from *signum*, a mark. SIGN.] Relating to the signing of documents; setting a signature to a document; signing a public document, as a treaty.—*n.* One who signs; the representative of a state who signs a public document.

Signature, sig'na-tūr, *n.* [L.L. *signatura*, from L. *signo*, to sign. SIGN.] A stamp or mark impressed; the name of any person written with his own hand on a document; a sign-manual; *printing*, a letter or figure at the bottom of the first page of each sheet or half sheet of a book to indicate their order; *mus.* the sign placed at the commencement of a piece of music to indicate the time and key.

Signet, sig'net, *n.* [O.Fr. *signet*, dim. of *signe*, a sign. SIGN.] A seal; particularly, a seal for the authentication of royal grants or warrants.—*Writers to the signet*, a class of legal practitioners in Edinburgh who act generally as agents or attorneys in conducting causes before the Court of Session; originally they are said to have prepared writs for passing the royal signet.—**Signeted**, sig'net-ed, *a.* Stamped or marked with a signet.—**Signet-ring**, *n.* A ring containing a signet or private seal.

Signify, sig'ni-fī, *v.t.*—*signified, signifying.* [Fr. *signifier*, from L. *significo*—*signum*, a sign, and *facio*, to make. SIGN.] To make known by signs or words; to express or communicate to another by words, gestures, &c.; to give notice; to announce, declare, proclaim; to convey as its meaning; to mean; to import; to indicate; to matter or be of consequence: in particular phrases (it *signifies* much or little, it *signifies* nothing, what does it *signify*?).—**Significance, Significancy**, sig-nif'i-kans, sig-nif'i-kan-si, *n.* Meaning; import; that which is intended to be expressed; expressiveness; impressiveness; force; importance; moment.—**Significant**, sig-nif'i-kant, *a.* [L. *significans, significantis*, ppr. of *significo.*] Bearing a meaning; expressive in an eminent degree; expressive or suggestive of something more than what appears (a *significant* look); standing as a sign of something; important; momentous.—**Significantly**, sig-nif'i-kant-li, *adv.* In a significant manner; meaningly; expressively.—**Signification**, sig'ni-fi-kā"shon, *n.* [L. *significatio.*] The act of signifying; that which is signified or expressed by signs or words; meaning; import; sense; notion conveyed. — **Significative**, sig-nif'i-kā-tiv, *a.* [Fr. *significatif.*] Signifying; serving to signify; having meaning; expressive of a meaning.—**Significatively**, sig-nif'i-kā-tiv-li, *adv.* In a significative manner.—**Significativeness**, sig-nif'i-kā-tiv-nes, *n.* —**Significator**, sig-nif'i-kā-tėr, *n.* One who or that which signifies.—**Significatory**, sig-nif'i-kā-to-ri, *a.* Having signification or meaning.

Signior, Signore, sēn'yor, *n.* An English form of the Italian *Signor*, Spanish *Señor*, a title of respect equivalent to the English *Sir* or *Mr.*, the French *Monsieur*, and the German *Herr*. — **Signiory, Signory**, sēn'yo-ri, *n.* A principality; a province (*Shak.*); an estate; a manor; dominion; power; a governing body.—**Signora**, sēn-yō'ra, *n.* An Italian title of address or respect, equivalent to *Madam, Mrs.* — **Signorina**, sēn-yō-rē'na, *n.* An Italian title equivalent to *Miss* or the French *Mademoiselle*.

Signitary, sig'ni-ta-ri, *a.* SIGNATORY.

Sikh, sēk, *n.* One of an Indian community, half religious, half military, which founded a state in the Punjaub, annexed to British India in 1849.

Silence, sī'lens, *n.* [Fr. *silence*, from L. *silentium*, silence, from *sileo*, to be silent.] The condition prevailing when there is no noise; absence of sound; stillness; forbearance of speech; a holding of one's peace; taciturnity; a refraining from making known something; secrecy; absence of mention; oblivion.—*v.t.*—*silenced, silencing.* To put to silence; to oblige to hold the peace; to cause to cease speaking; to restrain in reference to liberty of speech; to cause to cease sounding; to stop the noise of; to still, quiet, or appease (to *silence* scruples); to make to cease firing, especially by a vigorous cannonade (to *silence* guns or a battery).—*interj.* Used elliptically for let there be silence, or keep silence.—**Silent**, sī'lent, *a.* [L. *silens, silentis*, ppr. of *sileo.*] Not speaking; mute; dumb; speechless; habitually taciturn; speaking little; not loquacious; not mentioning or proclaiming; making no noise or rumour; free from sound or noise; having or making no noise; having no sound in pronunciation (*e* is *silent* in *fable*).—**Silentious**, sī-len'shus, *a.* Habitually silent; taciturn.—**Silently**, sī'lent-li, *adv.* In a silent manner.—**Silentness**, sī'lent-nes, *n.* State of being silent; silence.

Silhouette, sil'ö-et, *n.* [Fr., from Etienne de *Silhouette*, French minister of finance in 1759, in derision of his excessive economy in regard to the finances.] A profile or shadow-outline portrait filled in with a black colour, the inner parts being sometimes indicated by lines of a lighter colour.

Silica, Silex, sil'i-ka, sī'leks, *n.* [L. *silex, silicis*, a flint.] Oxide of silicon, an important substance constituting the characteristic ingredient of a great variety of minerals, among which rock-crystal, quartz, chalcedony, and flint are nearly pure silica. —**Silicate**, sil'i-kāt, *n.* A compound of silica with certain bases, as alumina, lime, magnesia, potash, soda, &c.—*Silicate paint*, natural silica, when dried and forming an almost impalpable powder, mixed with colours and oil.—**Silicated**, sil'i-kā-ted, *a.* Coated, mixed, or impregnated with silica. — **Siliceous, Silicious**, si-lish'us, *a.* Pertaining to silica, containing it, or partaking of its nature.—**Silicic**, si-lis'ik, *a.* Pertaining to silica (*silicic* ether, *silicic* acid). — **Silicide**, sil'i-sīd, *n.* [L. *silex, silicis*, a flint.] A compound of silicon with a metal.—**Siliciferous**, sil-i-sif'ėr-us, *a.* [L. *silex*, and *fero*, to produce.] Producing silica; containing silica.—**Silicification**, si-lis'i-fi-kā"shon, *n.* Petrifaction; conversion into stone by siliceous matter.—**Silicify**, si-lis'i-fī, *v.t.*—*silicified, silicifying.* [L. *silex, silicis*, and *facio*, to make.] To convert into or petrify by silica.—*v.i.* To become impregnated with silica.—**Silicite**, sil'i-sīt, *n.* A variety of felspar. LABRADORITE.—**Silicon, Silicium**, sil'i-kon, si-lis'i-um, *n.* [From L. *silex, silicis*, a flint.] The non-metallic element of which silica is the oxide, the chief constituent of flint, and the most abundant of all the solid elements.

Silicle, Silicula, Silicule, sil'i-kl, si-lik'ū-la, sil'i-kūl, *n.* [L. *silicula*, dim. of *siliqua*, a pod.] *Bot.* a kind of seed-vessel differing from a siliqua in being as broad as it is long, or broader.—**Siliculose, Siliculous**, si-lik'ū-lōs, si-lik'ū-lus, *a.* Having silicles or pertaining to them. — **Siliqua**, sil'i-kwa, *n.* pl. **Siliquæ**, sil'i-kwē. [L. *siliqua*, a pod, also a very small weight.] *Bot.* the long pod or seed-vessel of crucifers (as wall-flower), dehiscing by two valves which separate from a central portion called the *replum*; a weight for gold and precious stones; a carat.—**Silique**, si-lēk', *n.* A siliqua.—**Siliquiform**, si-lik'wi-form, *a.* Having the form of a siliqua. —**Siliquose, Siliquous**, sil'i-kwōs, sil'i-kwus, *a.* *Bot.* bearing siliquæ.

Silicon. Under SILICA.

Silk, silk, *n.* [A.Sax. *seoloc*, silk, for *seric*, from L. *sericum*, Gr. *sērikon*, silk, lit. Seric stuff, from *Sēres*, the Greek name of the Chinese.] The fine, soft thread forming the cocoon of the larvæ of various species of moths, the most important of which is the common silk-worm moth, a native of the northern provinces of China; cloth made of silk; a garment made of this cloth. —*a.* Made of silk; silken.—*Silk gown*, the official robe of a queen's (or king's) counsel in England. — *To take silk*, to attain the rank of queen's counsel.—**Silk-cotton**, *n.* A silky fibre surrounding the seeds of several species of tropical American and Indian trees, used for stuffing mattresses, for covering hat bodies, &c. — **Silken**, sil'kn, *a.* Made of silk; like silk; silky.—**Silk-fowl**, *n.* A variety of the domestic fowl with silky plumage.—**Silkiness**, sil'ki-nes, *n.* The state or quality of being silky.—**Silk-man, Silk-mercer**, *n.* A dealer in silks.—**Silk-mill**, *n.* A mill or factory for reeling, spinning, and manufacturing silk. — **Silk-thrower, Silk-throwster**, *n.* One who twists or throws silk, to prepare it for weaving.—**Silk-tree**, *n.* A species of acacia, a native of the Levant.—**Silk-weaver**, *n.* One whose occupation is to weave silk stuffs.—**Silk-worm**, *n.* A worm which produces silk; the larva of various moths which spins a silken cocoon or case about the size of a pigeon's egg for the inclosure of the chrysalis. —**Silky**, sil'ki, *a.* Made of silk; like silk; soft and smooth to the touch; delicate; tender.

Sill, sil, *n.* [A.Sax. *syl, syll*, base, sill; Icel. *syll, svill*, Sw. *syll, swill*, G. *schwelle*, Goth. *sulja*, sill; perhaps from same root as L. *solum*, tho ground, a base.] A stone or a piece of timber on which a structure rests; the horizontal piece of timber or stone at the bottom of a door, window, or similar opening; *mining*, the floor of a gallery or passage in a mine.

Sillabub, sil'a-bub, *n.* [Origin doubtful.] A dish of wine or cider with cream or milk forming a soft curd.

Sillery, sil'ėr-i, *n.* [From *Sillery*, not far from Rheims in France.] A non-sparkling champagne wine of an esteemed kind.

Silly, sil'i, *a.* [O.E. *seely*, A.Sax. *saelig*, prosperous; blessed; Icel. *sælligr*, G. *selig*, happy; from A.Sax. *sæl*, Icel. *sæll*, Goth. *sels*, good, happy.] Happy‡; guileless or inoffensive; helpless‡; foolish; weak in intellect; witless; simple; characterized by weakness or folly; showing folly; unwise; stupid.—**Sillily**, sil'i-li, *adv.* In a silly manner; foolishly. — **Silliness**, sil'i-nes, *n.* The quality of being silly.

Silo, sī'lō, *n.* The pit in which green fodder is preserved in the method of ensilage. ENSILAGE.—*v.t.* To put into a silo.

Silt, silt, *n.* [From Prov.E. *sile*, Sw. *sila*, to strain or filter.] A deposit of mud or fine soil from running or standing water; fine earthy sediment.—*v.t.* To choke or fill with silt or mud: often with *up*.—*v.i.* To percolate through crevices; to ooze.—**Silty**, silt'i, *a.* Consisting of or resembling silt; full of silt.

Silurian, sī-lū'ri-an, *a.* Belonging to the *Silures*, an ancient people of South Wales. —*Silurian rocks, strata, system, geol.* the name given to a great succession of palæozoic strata intervening between the Cambrian formation and the base of the old red sandstone; so called from the district where the strata were first investigated.

Silurus, Silure, sī-lū'rus, sī-lūr', *n.* [L. *silurus.*] A malacopterygian fish of large size, found in the Danube and other rivers of Europe.

Silva, sil'va, *a.* SYLVA.

Silvanus, sil-vā'nus, *n.* A Roman rural deity, so called from L. *silva*, a wood.

Silvas. SELVAS.

Silver, sil'vėr, *n.* [A.Sax. *seolfer* = Icel. *silfr*, D. *zilver*, Dan. *sölv*, G. *silber*, Goth. *silubr*; cog. Rus. *srebro, serebro*, Lith. *sidabras*, Lett. *sudrabs*—silver. Root doubtful.] A precious metal which in its compact state is of a fine white colour and lively brilliancy, used for the purposes of coinage, and also for the construction of ornaments and jewellery; money; coin made of silver; plate made of silver. GERMAN-SILVER, NICKEL-SILVER. — *Silver* is used in the formation of many self-explanatory compounds, as *silver*-bright, *silver*-clear, *silver*-white, &c.—*a.* Made of silver; resembling silver; silvery.—*Silver age*, the second mythological period in the history of the world, following the golden age. The term is also applied to the period of Roman literature subsequent to the most brilliant period, from about A.D. 14 to A.D. 180.—*v.t.* To cover superficially with a coat of silver; to cover with tin-foil amalgamated with quicksilver (to *silver* glass); to give a silvery sheen or silver-like lustre to; to make hoary; to tinge with gray. — **Silver-beater**, *n.* One who beats silver into thin leaf or foil.—**Silver-fir**, *n.* A species of European fir growing to the height of 150 to 180 feet, and so called from two silvery lines on the under side of the leaves. — **Silver-fish**, *n.* A fish of a white colour with silvery lines, a variety of gold-fish.— **Silver-fox**, *n.* A fox of the northern parts of Asia, Europe, and America, with a valuable fur of a shining black colour, intermingled with white.—**Silver-glance**, *n.* A mineral, a native sulphuret of silver. —**Silver-grain**, *n.* The medullary rays in timber.—**Silver-gray**, *a.* Of a colour resembling silver. — **Silver-haired**, *a.* Having white or gray hair.—**Silvering**, sil'vėr-ing, *n.* The art of covering the surface of anything with silver, or with an amalgam of tin and mercury; the silver or amalgam laid on.—**Silverize**, sil'vėr-īz, *v.t.*—*silverized, silverizing.* To coat or cover with silver.—**Silver-leaf**, *n.* Silver foliated or beaten out into a thin leaf.—**Silverless**, sil'vėr-les, *a.* Having no silver; without money; impecunious.—**Silverly**, sil'vėr-li, *adv.* With a bright appearance, like silver.—**Silvern**, sil'vėrn, *a.* Made of silver.—**Silver nitrate**, *n.* A salt of silver dissolved in nitric acid, used in photography and as an antiseptic.—**Silver-plated**, *a.* Covered with a thin coating of silver.—**Silversmith**, sil'vėr-smith, *n.* One whose occupation is to work in silver.—**Silver-tongued**, *a.* Having a smooth tongue or speech.—**Silverware**, *n.* A collective name for tableware, dishes, and ornaments made of silver.—**Silvery**, sil'vėr-i, *a.* Like silver; containing silver; with luster.

Simian, **Simial**, **Simious**, sim'i-an, sim'i-al, sim'i-us, *a.* [L. *simia*, an ape, from *simus*, flat-nosed.] Pertaining to apes or monkeys; ape-like.—*n.* An ape or monkey.

Similar, sim'i-lėr, *a.* [Fr. *similaire*, from a hypothetical *similaris*, from L. *similis*, like; akin to *simul*, together, from root of E. *same*. *Dissemble*, *resemble*, *simulate*, &c., are akin.] Like; resembling; having a like form or appearance; like in quality; *geom.* having like parts and relations but not of the same magnitude.—*n.* That which is similar; something that resembles something else.—**Similarity**, sim-i-lar'i-ti, *n.* The state of being similar; close likeness; perfect or partial resemblance.—**Similarly**, sim'i-lėr-li, *adv.* In a similar or like manner; with resemblance in essential points.

Simile, sim'i-lē, *n.* [L., a like thing, from *similis*, like. SIMILAR.] *Rhet.* the likening together of two things which, however different in other respects, have some strong point or points of resemblance; a poetic or imaginative comparison. METAPHOR.—**Similitude**, si-mil'i-tūd, *n.* [L. *similitudo*.] Likeness; resemblance, in nature, qualities, or appearance; a comparison; a simile; a representation; a facsimile.

Simious. SIMIAN.

Simitar, sim'i-tėr. SCIMITAR.

Simmer, sim'ėr, *v.i.* [Probably imitative of the gentle murmuring sound made by liquids beginning to boil or boiling very slowly.] To boil or bubble gently, or with a gentle hissing.

Simnel cake, *n.* [O.Fr. *simenel*, L. *simila*, fine flour.] A kind of rich cake prepared at Easter, Christmas, and other days.

Simony, sim'o-ni, *n.* [Fr. *simonie*, L.L. *simonia*, from *Simon* Magus, who wished to purchase the power of conferring the Holy Spirit. Acts, viii.] The buying or selling of ecclesiastical preferment; the presentation of any one to an ecclesiastical benefice for money or reward.—**Simoniac**, si-mō'ni-ak, *n.* [Fr. *simoniaque*.] One who practises simony.—**Simoniacal**, sim-ō-nī'a-kal, *a.* Pertaining to, involving, or consisting of simony; guilty of simony.—**Simoniacally**, si-mō-nī'a-kal-li, *adv.* In a simoniacal manner.—**Simonious**, si-mō'ni-us, *a.* Simoniacal.

Simoom, si-mōm', *n.* [Ar. *samûm*, from *samma*, to poison.] An intensely hot suffocating wind, laden with dust and sand, that blows occasionally in Africa and Arabia, generated by the extreme heat of the parched deserts. Also SIMOON.

Simous, sī'mus, *a.* [L. *simus*.] Having a flat or snub nose.

Simper, sim'pėr, *v.i.* [Akin to Prov.G. *simpern*, to be affectedly coy; Dan. *semper*, *simper*, coy.] To smile in a silly, affected manner.—*n.* A smile with an air of silliness; an affected smile or smirk.—**Simperer**, sim'pėr-ėr, *n.* One who simpers.—**Simperingly**, sim'pėr-ing-li, *adv.* In a simpering manner.

Simplesometer, sim'pi-e-zom"et-ėr. SYMPIESOMETER.

Simple, sim'pl, *a.* [Fr. *simple*, from L. *simplex*, simple, from a root meaning one or unity (also in E. *same*), and that of *plica*, a fold (E. *ply*).] Not complex or compound; consisting of one thing or substance only; not complex or complicated; easily intelligible; clear; not given to deceit or duplicity; artless in manner; unaffected; inartificial; unadorned; plain; mere; being no more and no less (a *simple* knight); common; humble; weak in intellect; not wise or sagacious; silly; *bot.* consisting of one; not exhibiting divisions; *chem.* that has not been decomposed or separated into two or more elements; elementary.—*Simple interest.* Under INTEREST.—*n.* Something not mixed or compounded; a medicinal herb or a medicine obtained from a herb: so called because each vegetable was supposed to have one particular virtue.—**Simple-hearted**, *a.* Having a simple heart; single-hearted; ingenuous.—**Simple-minded**, *a.* Artless; undesigning; unsuspecting.—**Simple-mindedness**, *n.* The character of being simple-minded.—**Simpleness**, sim'pl-nes, *n.* The state or quality of being simple; simplicity.—**Simpleton**, sim'pl-ton, *n.* [From *simple*, with French term. *-ton*.] One who is very simple; a silly or foolish person; a person of weak intellect.—**Simplicity**, sim-plis'i-ti, *n.* [Fr. *simplicité*, L. *simplicitas*.] The state or quality of being simple, unmixed, uncompounded, or not complex; artlessness of mind; freedom from slyness or cunning; sincerity; freedom from artificial ornament; plainness; weakness of intellect; silliness.—**Simplification**, sim'pli-fi-kā"shon, *n.* The act of simplifying.—**Simplify**, sim'pli-fī, *v.t.*—*simplified*, *simplifying*. [Fr. *simplifier*, L.L. *simplificare*, L. *simplex*, and *facio*, to make.] To make simple; to bring to greater simplicity; to show an easier or shorter process for doing or making; to make plain or easy.—**Simply**, sim'pli, *adv.* In a simple manner; without art or subtlety; plainly; merely; solely; weakly; foolishly.

Simulacrum, sim-ū-lā'krum, *n.* pl. **Simulacra**, sim-ū-lā'kra. [L.] An unreal or mock image or likeness; a phantom; a hollow, pretentious person.

Simulate, sim'ū-lāt, *v.t.*—*simulated*, *simulating*. [L. *simulo*, *simulatum*, from *similis*, like. SIMILAR.] To assume the mere appearance or character of, without the reality; to counterfeit; to feign.—**Simulation**, sim-ū-lā'shon, *n.* The act of simulating or of feigning to be that which one is not. ∴ *Simulation* denotes the assuming of a false character; *dissimulation*, the concealment of the true character.—**Simulator**, sim'ū-lā-tėr, *n.* One who simulates.—**Simulatory**, sim'ū-la-to-ri, *a.* Consisting in or characterized by simulation.

Simultaneous, sī'mul-tā"nē-us, *a.* [L.L. *simultaneus*, from L. *simul*, at the same time, akin to *similis*, like, E. *same*.] Taking place or happening at the same time; done at the same time; coincident in time.—**Simultaneously**, sī'mul-tā"nē-us-li, *adv.* At the same time; together; in conjunction.—**Simultaneousness**, **Simultaneity**, sī'mul-tā"nē-us-nes, sī'mul-ta-nē"i-ti, *n.* The state or quality of being simultaneous; coincidence; concomitance.

Sin, sin, *n.* [A.Sax. *synn*, *sinn*, sin; Icel. and Dan. *synd*, O.D. *sunde*, G. *sünde*, sin; connected with L. *sons*, *sontis*, guilty.] The voluntary departure of a moral agent from a custom prescribed by society or by divine law or divine command; moral depravity; wickedness; iniquity; an offense in general; a transgression.—*v.i.*—*sinned*, *sinning*. To commit a sin, to violate any known rule of duty; to offend in general; to transgress; to trespass: with *against* (to *sin against* good taste).—*To sin one's mercies*, to be unmindful of the gifts of Providence.—**Sinful**, sin'ful, *a.* Tainted with, or full of sin; wicked; containing sin or consisting of sin.—**Sinfully**, sin'ful-li, *adv.* In a sinful manner; wickedly.—**Sinfulness**, sin'ful-nes, *n.* The quality of being sinful.—**Sinless**, sin'les, *a.* Free from sin; innocent.—**Sinlessly**, sin'les-li, *adv.* In a sinless manner.—**Sinlessness**, sin'les-nes, *n.* The state of being sinless.—**Sinner**, sin'ėr, *n.* One who sins; one who fails in any duty or transgresses any law; an offender.

Sinaic, **Sinaitic**, si-nā'ik, sī-nā-it'ik, *a.* Pertaining to Mount *Sinai*; given or made at Sinai.

Sinapism, sin'a-pizm, *n.* [Fr. *sinapisme*, L. *sinapismus*, from *sinapis*, Gr. *sinapi*, mustard.] A mustard poultice.

Since, sins, *adv.* [O.E. *sins*, *sinnes*, *sithens*, *sithence*, all genitive forms from A.Sax. *siththan*, lit. after that. Comp. the genitives *hence*, *whence*.] From that time; after that time; from then till now; in the interval; before this or now; ago.—*prep.* Ever from the time of; subsequently to; after.—*conj.* From the time when (*since* I saw you last); because that; seeing that; inasmuch as.

Sincere, sin-sēr', *a.* [L. *sincerus*, sincere, pure, unmixed.] Pure; unmixed; being in reality what it appears to be; not feigned or simulated; not assumed; real; genuine; undissembling; guileless; frank; true.—**Sincerely**, sin-sēr'li, *adv.* In a sincere manner.—**Sincereness**, **Sincerity**, sin-sēr'nes, sin-ser'i-ti, *n.* The quality of being sincere; freedom from hypocrisy; truthfulness; genuineness; earnestness.

Sinciput, sin'si-put, *n.* [L.] The fore part of the head, in contradistinction to the *occiput* or back part.—**Sincipital**, sin-sip'i-tal, *a.* Pertaining to the sinciput.

Sindoc, *n.* SINTOC.

Sine, sīn, *n.* [L. *sinus*, a bending, a curve, a bosom.] *Trigon.* the straight line drawn from one extremity of an arc perpendicular to the diameter passing through the other extremity.—*Versed sine* of an arc or angle, the segment of the diameter intercepted between the sine and the extremity of the arc.—**Sinical**, sin'i-kal, *a.* Pertaining to a sine.

Sinecure, sī'nē-kūr, *n.* [L. *sine*, without, and *cura*, cure, care.] An ecclesiastical benefice without cure of souls; any office which has revenue without employment.—*v.t.* To place in a sinecure.—**Sinecurism**, sī'nē-kūr-izm, *n.* The state of holding a sinecure.—**Sinecurist**, sī'nē-kūr-ist, *n.* One who holds a sinecure.—**Sinecural**, sī'nē-kū-ral, *a.* Relating to a sinecure; of the nature of a sinecure.

Sine qua non, sī'nē kwā non, *n.* [L., without which not.] Something absolutely necessary or indispensable.

Sinew, sin'ū, *n.* [A.Sax. *sinewe*, *sinu*; D. *zenuw*; G. *sehne*, Icel. *sin*, Dan. *sene*, a sinew.] The tough fibrous tissue which unites a muscle to a bone; a tendon; *fig.* that which gives strength or vigour; that in which strength consists.—*Sinews of war*, money as a means of carrying it on.—*v.t.* To knit or strengthen, as by sinews.—**Sinewed**, sin'ūd, *p.* and *a.* Having sinews; firm; vigorous; sinewy.—**Sinewiness**, sin'ū-i-nes, *n.* The quality of being sinewy.—**Sinewless**, sin'ū-les, *a.* Having no vigour.—**Sinewy**, sin'ū-i, *a.* Consisting of or resembling a sinew or sinews; well braced with sinews; strong; vigorous; firm.

Sinful, **Sinfulness**, &c. Under SIN.

Sing, sing, *v.i.*—pret. *sang* or *sung*; pp. *sung*. [A.Sax. *singan*, pret. *sang*, pp. *sungen*; = Icel. *singja*, Dan. *synge*, D. *zingen*, G. *singen*; comp. Gael. *seinn*, to ring as a bell, to sing.] To utter words or sounds with musical inflections or melodious modulations of voice; to utter sweet sounds, as birds; to give out a small shrill or humming sound (the kettle *sings*); to tell or relate something in poetry or verse.—*v.t.* To utter with musical modulations of voice; to celebrate in song; to give praises to in verse; to relate or rehearse in poetry; to act or produce an effect on by singing (to *sing* one to sleep).—**Singer**, sing'ėr, *n.* One who sings or whose occupation is to sing; a skilled or professional vocalist.—**Singing-bird**, *n.* A bird that sings; a song-bird.—**Singing-master**, *n.* A teacher of the art of singing.—**Sing-song**, *n.* A drawling or monotonous tone, or wearying succession of tones; repetition of similar words or tones.—*a.* Drawling; monotonous.

Singe, sinj, *v.t.*—*singed*, *singeing*. [A.Sax. *sengan*, to singe, lit. to cause to sing, a caus. of *singan*, to sing; so also G. *sengen*, to singe.] To burn slightly or superficially; to burn the surface, ends, or outside of; to scorch; to remove the nap from, as cloth, by passing it over a red-hot roller, through a gas flame, or the like.—*n.* A burning of the surface; a slight burn.—**Singer**, sin'-jėr, *n.* One who or that which singes.

Singhalese, sing-ga-lēz', *n. sing.* and *pl.* A native or natives of Ceylon; Cingalese.

Single, sing'gl, *a.* [L. *singulus*, single, from root seen in *simple.*] Consisting of one alone; not double or more (a *single* star, a *single* act); often emphatic, even one (I shall not give you a *single* farthing); individual; considered as apart; alone; having no companion or assistant; unmarried (a *single* man, a *single* life); performed by one person, or by one person only opposed to another (*single* combat); honest; unbiassed; sincere.—*Single blessedness*, the unmarried state; celibacy.—*Single entry*, a system of bookkeeping in which each entry appears only once on one side or other of an account. —*v.t.*—*singled, singling.* To select individually from among a number; to choose out separately from others: with *out* or similar words.—**Single-acting**, *a.* A term applied to a steam-engine in which steam is admitted to one side only of the piston.—**Single-breasted**, *a.* Applied to a coat or waistcoat which buttons only to one side.—**Single-handed**, *a.* Unassisted; by one's self; alone.—**Singleness**, sing'gl-nes, *n.* The state or quality of being single; oneness; sincerity; freedom from duplicity.—**Singles**, sing'glz, *n. pl.* The reeled filaments of silk twisted into a thread.—*Tennis, golf*, a game or match with only one player opposing another.—*Baseball, sing.*, a base hit.—**Single-phase**, *a. Elect.* Having an alternating current of one phase.—**Singlet**, sing'glet, *n.* A jersey or undershirt of wool or cotton; comp. *doublet.*—**Single tax**, a theory of tax on land values only for all revenue.—**Singleton**, *n. Cards*, an only card of a suit in a hand.—**Singletree**, *n.* A cross bar, pivoted at the center, to which one horse is hitched.—**Singly**, sing'gli, *adv.* Individually; separately; each alone; without partners; honestly; sincerely.

Singular, sing'gū-lėr, *a.* [L. *singularis*, from *singulus*, single. SINGLE.] Belonging to one; *gram.* denoting one person or thing (a *singular* noun); marked as apart from others; out of the usual course; odd (*singular* in his behavior); *gram.* the singular number; a word in this number.—**Singularity**, sing-gū-lar'i-ti, *n.*—**Singularly**, sing'gū-lėr-li, *adv.* In a singular manner; peculiarly; remarkably

Singultus, sin-gul'tus, *n.* [L.] *Med.* the hiccup.

Sinister, sin'is-tėr, *a.* [L., left, unlucky, bad; origin doubtful.] On the left hand or left side; left; *her.* the term which denotes the left side of the escutcheon, that is, the *right* side of a drawing of it; evil; bad; ill-intentioned; baneful; malign; unlucky; inauspicious.—**Sinisterly**, sin'is-tėr-li, *adv.* In a sinister manner.—**Sinistral**, sin'is-tral, *a.* Belonging to the left hand; inclining to the left.—**Sinistrorse**, sin'is-trors, *a.* [L. *sinistrorsus*, from *sinister*, left, and *vorsus, versus*, turned.] Directed to the left; turning or twining to the left: usually said of the stems of plants.—**Sinistrous**, sin'is-trus, *a.* Sinister; on the left side; inclined to the left.—**Sinistrously**, sin'is-trus-li, *adv.*

Sink, singk, *v.i.*—pret. *sunk* or *sank*; pp. *sunk* (*sunken* being used as a participial adj). [A.Sax. *sincan* = Dan. *synke*, D. *zinken*, G. *sinken*, Goth, *sigkvan*, to sink.] To fall by the force of gravity; to descend through a medium of little resisting power, as water; to go to the bottom; to fall as from want of bodily strength; to take a lower position to the eye; to decline below the horizon; to be overwhelmed or depressed; to enter the mind and be impressed; to decline in worth, strength, estimation, &c.; to fall off in value; to decay; to decrease and become less deep; to subside.—*v.t.* To cause to descend below the surface; to immerse in a fluid; to cause to fall or drop; to make by digging or delving (to *sink* a well); to depress; to degrade; to bring low; to ruin; to crush; to invest (money) more or less permanently in any undertaking or scheme.—*n.* A basin to receive dirty water and liquid waste, ordinarily with a drainpipe connected and usually with a fresh-water supply, as in a kitchen; a sewer; *fig.* a place where vice and filth abound.—**Sinker**, singk'ėr, *n.* One who or that which sinks; a weight, as on a fish-line or net, to sink it; a doughnut (*slang*).—**Sinkhole**, *n.* A place where drainage collects; a cesspool.—**Sinking**, singk'ing, *p.* and *a.* Falling; subsiding; declining.—*Sinking fund.* FUND.—**Sink-trap**, *n.* A trap for a kitchen sink, made by a bend in the drainpipe, to prevent a back flow of gases.

Sink-a-pace, *n.* A corruption of *Cinque-pace* (which see).

Sinless, Sinner, &c. Under SIN.

Sinn Fein, shin fān, *n.* [Irish, we ourselves.] An Irish Republican party, aiming at complete independence and separation, with the restoration of the old Irish tongue.

Sinologue, sin'o-log, *n.* [Fr. *sinologue*, from Gr. *Sina*, China, *Sinai*, the Chinese, and *logos*, discourse.] A student of the Chinese language, literature, history, &c.; one versed in Chinese.—**Sinology**, si-nol'o-ji, *n.* The knowledge of the Chinese language, &c.—**Sinological**, sin-o-loj'i-kal, *a.* Pertaining to sinology.—**Sinologist**, si-nol'o-jist, *n.* A sinologue.

Sinople, sī'no-pl, *n.* [Fr. *sinople*, Fr. *sinopis*, Gr. *sinōpis*, from *Sinōpē*, a town on the Black Sea.] Red ferruginous quartz, of a blood or brownish-red colour, sometimes with a tinge of yellow.—**Sinoper, Sinopite**, sī'no-pėr, sī'no-pīt, *n.* Same as *Sinople.*—**Sinopia, Sinopis**, sī-nō'pi-a, sī-nō'pis, *n.* A pigment of a red colour prepared from sinople.

Sinter, sin'tėr, *n.* A German name for a rock precipitated in a crystalline form from mineral waters.

Sintoc, Sindoc, sin'tok, sin'dok, *n.* The bark of a species of cinnamon-tree of Java.

Sintoo, Sintooism, sin'tö, sin'tö-izm, *n.* SHINTO, SHINTOISM.

Sinuate, sin'ū-āt, *v.t.* [L. *sinuo*, to curve or bend, from *sinus*, a curve or bend.] To bend or curve in and out; to wind; to turn. —**Sinuate, Sinuated**, sin'ū-ā-ted, *a.* Winding; sinuous; *bot.* having large curved breaks in the margin, as in the oak leaf, having a wavy margin.—**Sinuation**, sin-ū-ā'shon, *n.* A winding or bending in and out.—**Sinuose**, sin'ū-ōs, *a.* Sinuous.—**Sinuosity**, sin-ū-os'i-ti, *n.* The quality of being sinuous; a bending in and out; a bend in such a series; a wave line.—**Sinuous**, sin'ū-us, *a.* [L. *sinuosus.*] Bending or curving in and out; of an undulating form; winding; crooked.—**Sinuously**, sin'ū-us-li, *adv.* In a sinuous manner.

Sinus, sī'nus, *n.* [L., a bend, curve, bay, &c.] A curved opening; a bending inward; a bay; a recess or opening into the land; *anat.* a cavity; *surg.* a cavity containing air or fluid; *bot.* a curved hollow on a margin.—**Sinusitis**, sī'nus-ī"tis, *n.* Inflammation in a sinus.

Sinusoidal, sī-nus-oi'dl, *a.* Following a periodic course, like the curve of sines.

Sioux, sō or si-ö', *n. sing.* and *pl.* A classification of Indians in North America.

Sip, sip, *v.t.*—*sipped, sipping.* [A lighter form of *sup* = D. and L.G. *sippen*, to sip.] To imbibe or take into the mouth in small quantities by the lips; to drink in or absorb in small quantities; to draw into the mouth; to suck up.—*v.i.* To drink a small quantity; to take a fluid in small quantities with the lips.—*n.* A small draught taken with the lips.—**Sipper**, sip'ėr, *n.* One that sips.

Sipahi, sip'a-hē, *n.* A sepoy.

Siphon, Syphon, sī'fon, *n.* [Gr. *siphōn*, a hollow tube, a reed.] A bent tube whose legs are of unequal length, used for drawing liquid out of a vessel, the shorter leg being inserted in the liquid and the longer hanging down outside: when the air is sucked from the tube the pressure of the atmosphere causes the liquid to rise in it and flow over; *zool.* a tube in certain molluscs conveying water to or from the gills.—**Siphonage**, sī'fon-āj, *n.* The action or operation of a siphon.—**Siphonal**, sī'fon-al, *a.* Pertaining to or resembling a siphon. —**Siphon-barometer**, *n.* A barometer in which the lower end of the tube is bent upward.—**Siphon-bottle**, *n.* A bottle for aerated waters, which are discharged through a bent tube by the pressure of the gas.—**Siphon-gauge**, *n.* A glass pipe partially filled with mercury, for indicating some internal pressure.—**Siphonic**, sī-fon'ik, *a.* Pertaining to a siphon.—**Siphoniferous**, sī-fo-nif'ėr-us, *a.* Having a siphon, as the nautilus.—**Siphonobranchiate**, sī'fon-ō-brang"ki-āt, *a.* Having siphons conveying water to the gills, as certain gasteropodous molluscs.

Siphuncle, sī'fung-kl, *n.* [L. *siphunculus*, dim. from *siphon.*] A tube passing through the chambers of the shell of the nautilus and kindred animals.—**Siphuncular**, sī-fung'kū-lėr, *a.* Pertaining to a siphuncle. —**Siphunculated, Siphuncled**, sī-fung'kū-lā-ted, sī'fung-kld, *a.* Having a siphuncle.

Sippet, sip'et, *n.* [Dim. of *sip* or *sop.*] A small sip; a little bit of something eatable; a small piece of bread served along with soup, broth, &c.

Sir, sėr, *n.* [Fr. *sire*, from L. *senior*, an elder or elderly person. SENIOR.] A common mode of address now used without consideration of rank or status; a general title by which a speaker addresses the person he is speaking to; the title distinctive of knights and baronets, always prefixed to the Christian name; a title formerly given to clergymen ('*Sir* Hugh Evans').

Siraskier, si-ras'kēr, *n.* SERASKIER.

Sircar, sirk'ar, *n.* [Per. *sar*, head, *kar*, work.] The Government of India; native house steward, accountant.

Sirdar, sėr'där, *n.* [Hind. *sar-dār.*] A chieftain, captain, or head-man in Hindustan; the head of the Egyptian army.

Sire, sīr, *n.* [A form of *sir.*] A respectful title used in addressing a king or other sovereign prince; a father; a progenitor (used poetically); the male parent of a beast; particularly used of horses.—*v.t.*—*sired, siring.* To beget; to procreate: used especially of stallions.

Siren, sī'ren, *n.* [Gr. *seirēn*, a siren.] *Greek myth.* a name of several sea-nymphs, who by their singing fascinated those that sailed by their island, and then destroyed them; in works of art often represented as having partly the form of birds, sometimes only the feet of a bird; a charming, alluring, or enticing woman; a woman dangerous from her enticing arts; a genus of amphibians peculiar to the southern parts of the United States: called also *mud-eels*; an instrument for measuring the number of sound waves or vibrations; an instrument producing a loud piercing sound and used as a fog-signal. —*a.* Enticing; bewitching; fascinating (a *siren* song).—**Sirenia**, sī-rē'ni-a, *n.pl.* [From their fancied resemblance to mermaids or *sirens.*] An order of marine herbivorous mammals allied to the whales, and comprising the manatee and the dugong.—**Sirenian**, sī-rē'ni-an, *a.* and *n.* Belonging to, or one of, the Sirenia.

Siriasis, si-rī'a-sis, *n.* [Gr. *seiriasis*, from *seirios*, scorching.] A disease occasioned by the excessive heat of the sun; sunstroke.

Sirius, sir'i-us, *n.* [Gr. *Seirios*, from *seirios*, hot, scorching.] A large and bright star called also the Dog-star (which see).

Sirloin, sėr'loin, *n.* [Formerly *surloin*, from Fr. *surlonge, surlogne*, a sirloin—*sur*, over, upon, and *longe, logne*, a loin. LOIN.] The loin, or upper part of the loin, of beef, or the part covering either kidney.

Sirname, sėr'nām, *n.* A surname.

Sirocco, si-rok'kō, *n.* [It., from Ar. *shoruk*, from *shark*, the east.] An oppressive relaxing wind coming from Northern Africa to Italy, Sicily, &c.; a variety of the Simoom.

Sirrah, sir'a, *n.* [Icel. *síra*, sir, sirrah, from O.Fr. *sire*. SIRE.] A word of address, generally equivalent to fellow, or to sir, with an angry or contemptuous force added.

Sirup. Same as *Syrup*.

Sirvente, sēr-vạnt, *n.* [Fr., lit. a poem of service, being originally a poem in praise of some one, from L. *servio*, to serve.] In the literature of the middle ages, a species of poem in common use among the Troubadours and Trouveres.

Sisal-grass, Sisal-hemp, si-sal', *n.* The prepared fibre of the American aloe, used for cordage: from *Sisal*, in Yucatan.

Siskin, sis'kin, *n.* [Dan. *sisgen*, Sw. *siska*, G. *zeisig*.] A well-known European songbird of the finch family, of colour in general greenish.

Sissoo, sis-sö', *n.* [Hind.] A valuable timber tree of India.

Sist, sist, *v.t.* [L. *sistere*, to stop.] *Scots law*, to stop; to stay (to *sist* proceedings); also to cite or summon.

Sister, sis'tėr, *n.* [From Icel. *systir*, Sw. *syster*, a sister = D. *zuster*, A.Sax. *sweoster*, Goth. *swistar*, G. *schwester*, sister; cog. Rus. *sestra*, L. *soror*, Skr. *swasri*.] A female born of the same parents as another person; correlative to *brother*; a female fellow-Christian; a female belonging to the same community (as the nuns in a convent).—*Sisters of Mercy*. MERCY.—**Sisterhood**, sis'tėr-hụd, *n.* The state of being a sister; a society of females united in one faith or one community.—**Sister-in-law**, *n.* A husband's or wife's sister; also a brother's wife.—**Sisterless**, sis'tėr-les, *a.* Having no sister.—**Sisterly**, sis'tėr-li, *a.* Like a sister; becoming a sister.

Sistrum, sis'trum, *n.* [L., from Gr. *seistron*, from *seiō*, to shake.] A jingling instrument used by the ancient Egyptians in their religious ceremonies, consisting of a small metal frame with metal rods loosely inserted in it.

Sisyphean, sis-i-fē'an, *a.* [From *Sisyphus*, of *Greek myth.*; punished in the infernal world by having to roll to the top of a hill a huge stone which constantly rolled down again.] Entailing incessantly recurring toil; recurring unceasingly (a *Sisyphean* task).

Sit, sit, *v.i.*—pret. and pp. *sat*, ppr. *sitting*, [A.Sax. *sittan* = Icel. *sitja*, D. *zitten*, G. *sitzen*, Goth. *sitan*, to sit; from root seen also in L. *sedeo*, to sit, *sedes*, a seat (whence *sedentary*, *siege*, &c.); Skr. *sad*, to sit. *Set* is the causative of this verb; *seat* is also akin.] To rest upon the haunches; to repose on a seat; to remain, rest, abide; to lie, bear, or weigh (grief *sits* heavy on his heart); to have a seat or position; to be placed; to incubate; to cover and warm eggs for hatching; to be suited to one's person; to fit or suit when put on; to assume a position in order to have one's portrait taken or a bust modeled; to have a seat in Congress (he *sat* for Ohio); to be convened, as an assembly; to hold a session; to be officially engaged in public business.—*To sit down*, to place one's self on a seat; to begin a siege (the enemy *sat down* before the town).—*To sit out*, to sit till all is done.—*To sit under*, to attend church for the purpose of hearing; to be a member of the congregation of.—*To sit up*, to rise from a recumbent posture; to refrain from lying down; not to go to bed.—*v.t.* To keep the seat upon (he *sits* a horse well); to place on a seat: used with *one's self*, *me*, *thee*, &c.—**Sitter**, sit'ėr, *n.* One who sits; one who sits for his portrait.—**Sitting**, sit'ing, *p.* and *a.* Holding the position of one who sits; incubating; occupying a place in an official capacity; holding a court.—*n.* The act of one who sits; the occasion on which one sits for a portrait or a bust; a session; a business meeting; the time during which one sits, as at books, at cards or dice; the space occupied by one person in a church pew.—**Sitting-room**, *n.* Sufficient space for sitting in; an apartment for sitting in; a parlour.

Site, sīt, *n.* [L. *situs*, site, situation.] Situation, especially as regards relation to surroundings; local position; a plot of ground set apart for building.

Sitology, Sitiology, sī-tol'o-ji, sit-i-ol'o-ji, *n.* [Gr. *sitos*, *sition*, food, and *logos*, discourse.] That department of medicine which relates to the regulation of diet; dietetics.—**Sitophobia, Sitomania**, sī-tō-fō'bi-a, sī-tō-mā'ni-a, *n.* [Gr. *phobos*, fear, *mania*, madness.] Morbid repugnance to or refusal of food.

Situate, sit'ū-āt, *a.* [Fr. *situé*, situated, from L. *situs*, a site.] Placed with respect to any other object; permanently fixed; situated.—**Situated**, sit'ū-ā-ted, *a.* [A later form of *situate*, but now more common.] Having a site; placed or permanently fixed with respect to any other object; being in any state or condition with regard to men or things: circumstanced.—**Situation**, sit-ū-ā'shon, *n.* [Fr. *situation*.] Position or location in respect to physical surroundings; state, condition, or position with respect to society or circumstances; temporary state or position; place, post, or permanent employment.

Sitz-bath, sits, *n.* [G. *sitz-bad*—*sitz*, a seat, and *bad*, a bath.] A form of bath in which one can bathe sitting; a bath taken in a sitting posture.

Siva, sī'va, *n.* The name of the third god of the Hindu triad, in which he represents the principle of destruction.

Sivan, sī'van, *n.* The third month of the Jewish year, answering to part of May and part of June.

Sivatherium, sī-va-thē'ri-um, *n.* [From *Sivu*, the Indian deity, and Gr. *thērion*, a wild animal.] A large fossil ruminant with four horns, akin to the antelopes.

Six, siks, *a.* [A.Sax. *six*=Icel., Dan., and Sw. *sex*, D. *zes*, G. *sechs*, Goth. *saihs*, L. *sex*, Gr. *hex*, Per. *shesh*, Skr. *shash*, six.] Twice three; one more than five.—*n.* The number of six or twice three; a symbol representing this number, as 6.—*At sixes and sevens*, in disorder and confusion.—**Sixain**, sik'sān, *n.* A stanza of six verses.—**Sixfold**, siks'fōld, *a.* and *adv.* Six times repeated.—**Sixpence**, siks'pens, *n.* An English silver coin of the value of 25 cents.—**Sixpenny**, siks'pen-i, *a.* Worth sixpence; costing sixpence.—**Six-shooter**, *n.* A six-chambered revolver pistol.—**Sixteen**, siks'tēn, *a.* and *n.* [A.Sax. *sixtýne*.] Six and ten; consisting of six and ten.—**Sixteenmo**, siks'tēn-mō, *n.* SEXTODECIMO.—**Sixteenth**, siks'tēnth, *a.* Next in order after the fifteenth.—*n.* One of sixteen equal parts into which a thing is divided.—**Sixth**, siksth, *a.* The first after the fifth.—*n.* A sixth part; *mus.* an interval of two kinds, the *minor sixth*, consisting of three tones and two semitones, and the *major sixth*, composed of four tones and a semitone.—**Sixthly**, siksth'li, *adv.* In the sixth place.—**Sixtieth**, siks'ti-eth, *a.* Next in order after the fifty-ninth.—*n.* One of sixty equal parts of a thing.—**Sixty**, siks'ti, *a.* and *n.* [A.Sax. *sixtig*.] Ten times six; the sum of six times ten.

Sizar. See next art.

Size, sīz, *n.* [Contr. for *assize*, and meaning originally quantity or dimensions *assessed* or settled. ASSESS, ASSIZE.] Extent of volume or surface; dimensions great or small; comparative magnitude; bulk; a conventional relative measure of dimension, as of shoes, gloves, &c.—*v.t.*—*sized*, *sizing*. To adjust or arrange according to size; to fix the standard of.—*Size up*, to estimate, to value, take correct estimate of person or thing.—**Sizable**, sī'za-bl, *a.* Of considerable size; of suitable size; sometimes written *Sizeable*.—**Sized**, sīzd, *p.* and *a.* Having a particular magnitude; commonly used in compounds.—**Sizer**, sī'zėr, *n.* One who or that which sizes; a kind of gauge.—**Size-stick**, *n.* A shoemaker's measuring stick.—**Sizar**, sī'zär, *n.* [From *size*, the term at Cambridge for an allowance of food from the buttery.] One of a class of students in Cambridge University who get their commons or food free and receive certain emoluments, ranking below the ordinary students.—**Sizarship**, sī'zär-ship, *n.* The rank of a sizar.

Size, sīz, *n.* [It. *sisa*, *assisa*, a kind of glue, size, akin to *size* above, meaning a settling substance.] A kind of weak glue used by painters (to mix with colours), paper-manufacturers, &c.; a tenacious varnish used by gilders; matter resembling size.—*v.t.*—*sized*, *sizing*. To cover with size; to prepare with size.—**Siziness**, sī'zi-nes, *n.* The quality of being sizy.—**Sizing**, sī'zing, *n.* The act of covering with size; the coating of size.—**Sizy**, sī'zi, *a.* Containing or consisting of size; glutinous; adhesive.

Sizel, sī'zel, *n.* Same as *Scissel*.

Sjambok, zham'bok, *n.* [S.A. Dutch.] A long whip of rhinoceros hide.

Skain, skān, *n.* A skein.

Skald, skạld, *n.* An ancient Scandinavian poet; a scald.

Skat, skat, *n.* Same as *Scat*.

Skate, skāt, *n.* [From D. *schaats*, or Dan. *skœite*, a skate.] A contrivance consisting of a steel runner or ridge fixed to a wooden sole, or to a light iron framework, fastened under the foot, and used to enable a person to glide rapidly over ice.—*v.i.*—*skated*, *skating*. To slide or move on skates.—**Skater**, skā'tėr, *n.* One who skates.—**Skating-rink**, *n.* A prepared area for skating.

Skate, skāt, *n.* [Icel. *skata*, a skate; comp. L. *squatina*, the angel-fish.] A name for several species of the ray family of fishes, having the body flat, and more or less approaching to a rhomboidal form.

Skean, skēn, *n.* [Gael. *sgian*, Ir. *scian*, W. *ysgien*, a large knife.] A large knife used by the Irish and Highlanders of Scotland.—**Skean-dhu**, skēn'dū, *n.* [Gael. *sgian-dubh*, black knife.] The knife which, when the Highland costume is worn, is stuck in the stocking.

Skeet, skēt, *n.* Trapshooting, as of clay pigeons hurled into the air.

Skeg, skeg, *n.* [Icel. *skegg*, a beard, the cut-water of a ship.] The afterpart of a ship's keel.—*pl.* A kind of oats.

Skein, skān, *n.* [Fr. *escaigne*; of Celtic origin.] A small hank of thread; a certain quantity of yarn put up together.

Skeleton, skel'ē-ton, *n.* [Gr. *skeleton*, a dried body, a mummy, *skeletos*, dried up, from *skellō*, to dry.] The hard firm pieces constituting the framework which sustains the softer parts of any animal, in vertebrates consisting of bony pieces; the bones of an animal body separated from the flesh and retained in their natural position; the supporting framework of anything; an outline or rough draft; the heads and outline of a literary performance; a very thin or lean person.—*A skeleton in every house*, something to annoy and to be concealed in every family.—*a.* Containing mere outlines or heads (a *skeleton* sermon).—*Skeleton proof*, an early proof of an engraving with the inscription outlined in hair-strokes only.—*A skeleton regiment*, one the officers of which are kept up after the men are disbanded.—**Skeletonize**, skel'ē-ton-īz, *v.t.* To form into a skeleton; to make a skeleton of.—**Skeletal**, skel'ē-tal, *a.* Pertaining to a skeleton.—**Skeletology**, skel-ē-tol'o-ji, *n.* The branch of anatomical science that treats of the solid parts of the body.—**Skeleton-key**, *n.* A thin light key with nearly the whole substance of the bits filed away.

Skep, skep, *n.* [A.Sax. *scep*, a basket, chest, box.] A sort of basket, narrow at the bottom and wide at the top; in Scotland, a bee-hive.

Skeptic, Skeptical, &c. SCEPTIC, SCEPTICAL, &c.

Skerry, sker'i, *n.* [Icel. *sker*, a skerry, and *ey*, an island; akin Dan. *skar*, E. *scar*, *scaur*.] A rocky isle; an insulated rock.

Sketch, skech, *n.* [O.Fr. *esquiche*, Mod.Fr. *esquisse*, from It. *schizzo*, a sketch, from L. *schedius*, Gr. *schedios*, offhand, sudden.] An outline or general delineation of anything; a first rough or incomplete draught; a picture rapidly executed and intended to give the general features or characteristic aspect; the first embodiment of an artist's idea in clay, on canvas, or on paper.—*v.t.* To draw a sketch of; to make a rough draft of; to give the principal points or ideas of; to delineate.—*v.i.* To practise sketching.—**Sketcher**, skech'ėr, *n.* One who sketches.—**Sketchily**, skech'i-li, *adv.* In a sketchy manner. — **Sketchiness**, skech'i-nes, *n.* State of being sketchy.—**Sketchy**, skech'i, *a.* Possessing the character of a sketch; not executed with finish or carefulness of detail; unfinished.

Skew, skū, *a.* [Closely akin to Dan. *skiev*, Icel. *skeifr*, L.G. *schewe*, oblique, askew; allied to *shy*.] Having an oblique position; turned or twisted to one side.—*adv.* Awry; obliquely.—*v.t.* To put askew; to shape or form in an oblique way.—**Skew-arch**, *n.* An arch which is not at right angles to its abutments.—**Skew-bridge**, *n.* A bridge with skew-arch, set obliquely over a road.

Skewer, skū'ėr, *n.* [Prov.E. *skiver*, a skewer = *shiver*, a splinter.] A pin of wood or iron for fastening meat to a spit or for keeping it in form while roasting.—*v.t.* To fasten with skewers; to pierce or transfix.

Ski, skē, *n.* [O.N. *skidh*, snow-shoe.] A long, narrow snow-shoe for running or traveling over snow.—**Skijoring**, skē'jō-ring, *v.i.* Being drawn by a horse over snow or ice, wearing skis.—**Ski jump**, skē jump, *n.* A jump by a performer on skis from a take-off on a hillside.

Skid, skid, *n.* [Dan. and Sw. *skid*, Icel. *skith*, a billet of wood.] A fender for a ship's side; a log or something else forming an inclined plane in loading or unloading heavy articles from trucks, &c.; uncontrolled sliding, as by an automobile on a slippery pavement; a platform upon which paper is piled and shipped from the mill to facilitate handling.—*Aviation*, *Tail-skid*, part of the alighting-gear of an aircraft, arranged to slide along the ground.—*v.t.*—*skidded*, *skidding*. To check with a skid.—*v.i.* To slip, as a wheel, on a slippery surface without taking hold.—*Aviation*, sliding sideways in flight away from the center of the turn.

Skiff, skif, *n.* [Fr. *esquif*, from O.G. *scif*, Mod.G. *schiff*, a ship. SHIP.] A popular name for any small boat.

Skill, skil, *n.* [From Icel. *skil*, Dan. *skiel*, discrimination, discernment, from stem of Icel. *skilja*, A.Sax. *scylan*, to divide, to separate, to distinguish. *Scale*, *shell*, *scalp*, *scull*, *shale*, are akin.] Discernment; understanding; knowledge; wit; familiar knowledge of any art or science, united with readiness and dexterity in execution or performance; nice art in the application of knowledge of any kind; power to discern and execute; dexterity; aptitude. — **Skilful**, skil'fụl, *a.* Having skill; skilled; well versed in any art; dexterous; expert; displaying or done with skill; clever.—**Skilfully**, skil'fụl-li, *adv.* In a skilful manner; dexterously; expertly.—**Skilfulness**, skil'fụl-nes, *n.* The quality of being skilful.—**Skilled**, skild, *a.* Having skill or familiar knowledge, united with readiness and dexterity; expert; skilful.—**Skilless**, skil'les, *a.* Wanting skill.

Skillet, skil'et, *n.* [O.Fr. *escuellette*, dim. of *escuelle*, from L. *scutella*, a dish. SCUTTLE.] A kitchen pan with a long handle, used for frying and commonly called a frying pan.

Skilligalee, Skilligolee, skil'i-ga-lē", skil'i-gō-lē", *n.* Skilly. [Etym. doubtful.] A thin kind of broth or soup, such as is served out to prisoners, paupers, &c.

Skim, skim, *v.t.* — *skimmed*, *skimming*. [From *scum*, like *fill* from *full*.] To lift the scum from; to clear from any substance floating on the top; to take off from a surface; to pass near the surface of; to pass over lightly; to glance over in a superficial manner (to *skim* a newspaper article).—*v.i.* To pass lightly; to glide along.—**Skimmer**, skim'ėr, *n.* One who or that which skims; a flat dish or ladle for skimming liquors; an aquatic swimming bird, called also *scissor-bill*, from its peculiar bill. — **Skim-milk**, *n.* Milk from which the cream has been taken.—**Skimmingly**, skim'ing-li, *adv.* By gliding along a surface.

Skimble-skamble, *a.* Rambling, worthless stuff. (*Shak.*)

Skimp, skimp, *a.* *Skimp* measure, stinted. —*v.t.* To stint supplies.

Skin, skin, *n.* [Same as Icel. and Sw. *skinn*, Dan. *skind*, skin.] The external coating, layer, or tissue of most animals; a hide; a pelt; the skin of an animal separated from the body; the skin of an animal used as a vessel (wine-*skin*); any external covering resembling skin in appearance or use; the bark or husk of a plant; the exterior coat of fruits and plants.—*v.t.*—*skinned*, *skinning*. To strip the skin or hide from; to flay; to peel.—*v.i.* To become covered with skin (a wound *skins* over).—**Skin-deep**, *a.* Not penetrating beyond the skin; superficial; slight.—**Skinflint**, skin'flint, *n.* A very niggardly person.—**Skinful**, skin'fụl, *n.* As much as the stomach will hold.—**Skinless**, skin'les, *a.* Having no skin.—**Skinner**, skin'ėr, *n.* One who skins; one who deals in skins, pelts, or hides.—**Skinny**, skin'i, *a.* Consisting of skin, or of little more than skin; wanting flesh.—**Skinniness**, skin'i-nes, *n.* The quality of being skinny. — **Skin-wool**, *n.* Wool pulled from the dead skin.

Skink, skingk, *n.* [Gr. *skingkos*, a kind of lizard.] A small lizard of Egypt, &c.

Skink, skingk, *n.* The first cut off the ham or hough of an animal. — **Skink-soup**. Soup so prepared.

Skip, skip, *v.i.*—*skipped*, *skipping*. [Akin to Sw. *skimpa*, to run, *skumpa*, *skompa*, to skip.] To fetch quick leaps or bounds; to spring; to jump lightly; to pass without notice in reading; to make omissions in writing: often followed by *over*.—*v.t.* To pass with a bound; to pass over intentionally in reading.—*n.* A leap; a bound; a spring.—**Skip-jack**, *n.* An upstart; a name given to certain beetles, from their being able to spring into the air, and thus regain their feet when laid on their backs.—**Skipper**, skip'ėr, *n.* One who skips; the cheese maggot. — **Skipping**, skip'ing, *p.* and *a.* Given to skips; moving with leaps. —**Skippingly**, skip'ing-li, *adv.* By skips or leaps.—**Skipping-rope**, *n.* A small rope which young persons swing under their feet and over their heads in play.

Skip, skip, *n.* [A.Sax. *scep*, a box, basket, &c.] A box or basket for raising material from mines; a large basket on wheels.

Skip, skip, *n.* [Icel. *skipa*, to place in order, to arrange.] In the games of bowls and curling, an experienced player chosen by each of the rival sides as their director or captain.

Skipper, skip'ėr, *n.* [D. *schipper*, lit. a shipper, from *schip*, a ship. SHIP.] The master of a small trading or merchant vessel; a sea captain.

Skirmish, skėr'mish, *n.* [O.Fr. *eskermir*, to fence; It. *schermire*; from O.H.G. *skirman*, to fight, to defend one's self, from *skirm*, a shield.] A slight fight in war, especially between small parties; a short, desultory kind of engagement; a short contest of any kind; a contention.—*v.i.* To fight slightly or in small parties.—**Skirmisher**, skėr'mish-ėr, *n.* One that skirmishes.

Skirret, skir'et, *n.* [Contr. for *sugar-root*, the root containing much sugar.] An Asiatic plant, the water-parsnip, cultivated for its esculent tuberous root, somewhat resembling the parsnip.

Skirrhus, skir'rus, *n.* SCIRRHUS.

Skirt, skėrt, *n.* [The older form of *shirt*.] The lower and loose part of a coat or other garment; the edge of any part of dress; border; margin; extreme part; a woman's garment like a petticoat; the diaphragm or midriff in animals.—*v.t.* To border; to form the border or edge of; to run along the edge of.—*v.i.* To be on the border.—**Skirt dance**, *n.* A dance which the performer accompanies by waving her flowing skirts.—**Skirting**, skėr'ting, *n.* Material for making skirts; a skirting-board.—**Skirting-board**, *n.* The board placed round the bottom of the wall of a room.

Skit, skit, *n.* [From A.Sax. *scyte*, lit. a shooting, from *sceótan*, to shoot. SHOOT.] A satirical or sarcastic attack; a pasquinade; a squib. — **Skittish**, skit'ish, *a.* [Comp. Prov.E. *skit*, hasty.] Easily frightened; shy; wanton; volatile; changeable; fickle.—**Skittishly**, skit'ish-li, *adv.* In a skittish manner.—**Skittishness**, skit'ishnes, *n.* The quality of being skittish; shyness; fickleness; wantonness.

Skittles, skit'lz, *n.pl.* [From stem of A. Sax. *sceótan*, to shoot, because shot at. (SKIT, SHOOT.) *Shuttle* is the same word.] A game played with nine pins set upright at one end of a skittle-alley, the object of the player being to knock them over with as few throws as possible of a ball.—**Skittle-alley, Skittle-ground**, *n.* An oblong court in which the game of skittles is played.—**Skittle-ball**, *n.* A disc of hardwood for throwing at the pins in skittles.

Skiver, skī'vėr, *n.* [Akin to *shive*.] An inferior leather made of split sheep-skin.

Skonce, skons. SCONCE.

Skorodite, skor'ō-dīt, *n.* SCORODITE.

Skua, Skua-gull, skū'a, *n.* [N. *skua*, Icel. *skúfr*, the skua.] A powerful predatory bird of the gull family with strong hooked beak and claws.

Skulk, skulk, *v.i.* [Dan. *skulke*, to sneak, allied to *skiule*, Icel. *skjól*, a cover, a hiding-place.] To lurk; to keep in a place of concealment; to get out of the way in a sneaking manner; to shun doing one's duty. —**Skulk, Skulker**, skulk, skul'kėr, *n.* A person who skulks or avoids performing duties.—**Skulkingly**; skul'king-li, *adv.* In a skulking manner.

Skull, skul, *n.* [Same as Sw. *skull*, *skoll*, a bowl or drinking-cup; Dan. *skal*, a shell, *hjerneskal*, the skull (lit. brain-shell); the skull being so called from forming a kind of vessel. Allied to *scale* (of a balance) and to *shell*.] The cranium or bony case that forms the framework of the head and incloses the brain; the brain as the seat of intelligence.—**Skull-cap**, *n.* A cap fitting closely to the head or skull.—**Skulless**, skul'les, *a.* Having no skull.

Skulpin, skul'pin, *n.* SCULPIN.

Skunk, skungk, *n.* [Contr. from native American *seganku*.] An American carnivorous quadruped of the weasel family, provided with glands from which the animal can emit at pleasure an extremely fetid fluid; *metaphor.* a worthless, low fellow.

Skupshtina, sköpsh'tīn"a, *n.* [Servian.] The Parliament of Servia.

Skurry, skur'ri, *n.* and *v.* SCURRY.

Sky, skī, *n.* [Same as Icel. *ský*, Dan. and Sw. *sky*, a cloud; allied to A.Sax. *scúa*, a shade; also to E. *shade*. SHADE.] The apparent arch or vault of heaven; the firmament; that portion of the ethereal region in which meteorological phenomena take place; the region of clouds: the plural *skies* is often used in the same sense; weather; climate.—*Open sky*, open air; sky with no intervening cover or shelter.—*v.t.* *To sky a picture*, to give it a high position.—**Sky-blue**, *a.* Of the blue color of the sky.—**Sky-born**, *a.* Of heavenly birth.—**Sky-colored**, *a.* Like the sky in color; blue; azure.—**Skyey**, skī'i, *a.* Pertaining to the sky; ethereal.—**Sky-high**, *a.* High as the sky; very high.—**Skylark**, *n.* A lark that mounts and sings as it flies, the common lark of Europe.—**Skylarking**, *n.* Sportive gambols in the rigging of a ship; frolicking or tricks of various kinds. —**Skylight**, *n.* A window placed in the roof of a house, and having the same slope; a glazed aperture in a ship's deck.—**Sky line**, *n.* The horizon; a silhouette of trees or buildings against the sky.—**Sky pilot**, *n.* Minister, preacher. (*Colloq.*)—**Sky-rocket**, *n.* *Fireworks*, a rocket that ascends nigh and burns as it flies; a species of firework.—**Sky-sail**, *n.* A sail in a square-rigged vessel, next above the royal; sometimes called a *Sky-scraper* when it is triangular.—**Sky-scraper**, *n.* A high office building, characteristically American, which owes its origin to the lack of available land for building purposes.—**Skyward**, skī′wėrd, *a.* and *adv.* Toward the sky.—**Skywriting**, *n.* The writing in the air for advertising purposes done by means of oil vapors discharged from airplanes.

Slab, slab, *n.* [Perhaps for *sklab*, and allied to Sc. *skelb*, a thin slice, E. *shelf*.] A thin flat regularly shaped piece of anything, as of marble or other stone; an outside piece taken from round timber in sawing it into boards, planks, &c.

Slabber, slab′ėr, *v.i.* [Same as D. and L.G. *slabberen*, G. *schlabbern*, to slabber, freqs. of *slabben*, *schlabben*, to lap; *slaver* is akin.] To let the saliva fall from the mouth carelessly; to drivel; to slaver.—*v.t.* To sup up hastily, as liquid food; to beslobber; to besmear. — *n.* Slimy moisture from the

Slack, slak, *a.* [A.Sax. *sleac*, slack, slow = O.D. and L.G. *slakk*, Icel. *slakr*, Sw. *slak*; same root (with *s* prefixed) as L. *languidus*, languid, *laxus*, lax. LANGUISH.] Not tense or tightly drawn; loose; relaxed; backward; not using due diligence; not earnest or eager; not in a press of business; not busy; dull as regards trade; *pl.* loose trousers, usually worn in hot weather.—*Slack water*, the time when the tide runs slowly, between ebb and flow.—*adv.* In a slack manner.—*n.* The part of a rope that hangs loose; small coal screened from household or furnace coal of good quality.—**Slack, Slacken**, slak′n, *v.i.* To become less tense or tight; to become remiss or backward; to become less violent; to abate; to languish; to flag.—*v.t.* To lessen the tension of; to loosen; to relax; to remit for want of eagerness; to abate; to retard; to repress; to check.—**Slacker**, slak′ėr, *n.* One who performs his work or duties remissly; one who seeks to avoid duty, civil or military.—**Slackly**, slak′li, *adv.*—**Slackness**, slak′nes, *n.*

Slack, slak, *v.t.* and *i.* Same as *Slake*.

Slag, slag, *n.* [Same as Sw. *slagg*, G. *schlacke*, slag; comp. Icel. *slagna*, to flow over; *slag*, *slagi*, dampness.] The scoria from a smelting furnace or from a volcano; vitrified mineral matter removed in the reduction of metals; the fused dross of metal in a smelting furnace.—**Slaggy**, slag′i, *a.* Pertaining to or resembling slag.

Slain, slān, pp. of *slay*.

Slake, slāk, *v.t.*—*slaked*, *slaking*. [Icel. *slökva*, to slake; Sw. *släcka*, to quench thirst; akin to *slack*.] To quench (thirst, fire, rage); to extinguish; to abate; to reduce (quicklime) to the state of powder by mixing with water.—*v.i.* To be quenched; to become extinct; to slacken; to abate; to decrease.—**Slakeless**, slāk′les, *a.* Incapable of being slaked; quenchless.

Slam, slam, *v.t.*—*slammed*, *slamming*. [Same as Icel. *slæma*, *slamra*, to swing, to slam; comp. Sw. *slamra*, to jingle.] To close (a door, a lid) with force and noise; to shut with violence; to bang.—*v.i.* To shut or be closed violently or noisily, as a door.—*n.* A violent shutting of a door; at bridge, thirteen tricks is called a *grand slam*, and twelve, a *little slam*.

Slander, slan′dėr, *n.* [O.E. *sclaunder*, *esclaundre*, from Fr. *esclandre*, from L. *scandalum*, Gr. *skandalon*; so that this word is simply *scandal* in another form.] A false tale or report maliciously uttered, and tending to injure the reputation of another; the uttering of such reports; aspersion; defamation; detraction.—*v.t.* To defame by slander; to injure by maliciously uttering a false report respecting; to calumniate.—**Slanderer**, slan′dėr-ėr, *n.* One who slanders; a calumniator; a defamer.—**Slanderous**, slan′dėr-us, *a.* Given to slander; uttering slander; containing slander or defamation; calumnious.—**Slanderously**, slan′dėr-us-li, *adv.* In a slanderous manner; calumniously.—**Slanderousness**, slan′dėr-us-nes, *n.*

Slang, slang, *n.* [Connected with *sling*, being originally abusive language hurled at a person.] Colloquial language current among a certain class or classes, educated or uneducated, but having hardly the stamp of general approval, and often to be regarded as inelegant, incorrect, or even vulgar; often used adjectively (a *slang* word or expression).—*v.t.* To use slang; to engage in vulgar, abusive language.—*v t.* To address with slang or ribaldry; to abuse with vulgar language.—**Slangster**, *n.* A person who uses slang.—**Slangy**, slang′i, *a.* Of the nature of slang; addicted to the use of slang.

Slant, slant, *a.* [Akin to Prov.E. *slent*, to slope; Sw. *slinta*, to slide or glide down; perhaps also to *slide*.] Sloping; oblique; inclined from a direct line, whether horizontal or perpendicular.—*v.t.* To give a slant or sloping direction to.—*v.i.* To slope; to lie obliquely.—*n.* An oblique direction or plane; a slope.—**Slantingly**, slan′ting-li, *adv.* In a slanting manner.—**Slantly, Slantwise**, slant′li, slant′wīz, *adv.* Obliquely; in an inclined direction.

Slap, slap, *n.* [Same as L.G. *slappe*, G. *schlappe*, a slap, *slappen*, *schlappen*, to slap; probably from the sound.] A blow given with the open hand, or with something broad.—*v.t.*—*slapped*, *slapping*. To strike with the open hand, or with something broad.—*adv.* With a sudden and violent blow; plump.—**Slap-dash**, *adv.* All at once; in a careless manner; at random. (*Colloq.*)

Slash, slash, *v.t.* [O.Fr. *esclescher*, *esclischer*, from O.H.G. *slizan*, to split = E. to *slit*. SLIT.] To cut by striking at random; to cut with long incisions; to slit (to *slash* a garment).—*v.i.* To strike at random with an edged instrument.—*n.* A long cut; a cut made at random; a large slit in the thighs and arms of old dresses, to show a rich coloured lining through the openings.—**Slashed**, slasht, *p.* and *a.* Cut with a slash or slashes; gashed; having slashes or long narrow openings, as a sleeve, &c.—**Slashing**, slash′ing, *p.* and *a.* Cutting up, sarcastic, or severe (*slashing* criticism).

Slat, slat, *n.* [Perhaps akin to *slate* or *slit*.] A long narrow slip of wood, as in a venetian blind.—*v.i.* To strike against the mast with a flapping sound of the sails.

Slate, slāt, *n.* [O.E. and Sc. *sclate*, O.Fr. *esclat* (Fr. *éclat*), a splinter, from *esclater*, to fly in splinters, from O.H.G. *slizan*, to split (E. to *slit*).] A name common to such rocks as are capable of being split readily into thin laminae in accordance with the planes of cleavage; a slab or thin piece of smooth argillaceous stone, used for covering buildings; a tablet for writing upon, formed of slate, or of an imitation of slate; a group of candidates selected to run for political office.—*v.t.*—*slated*, *slating*. To cover with slates; to select a prospective candidate for an office or position.—**Slate-pencil**, *n.* A pencil of soft slate, used for writing on slate tablets in schools, &c.—**Slater**, slā′tėr, *n.* One whose occupation is to slate buildings; a popular name given to small crustaceous animals belonging to the isopods.—**Slatiness**, slā′ti-nes, *n.* The quality of being slaty; slaty character.—**Slaty**, slā′ti, *a.* Resembling slate, having the nature or properties of slate.—*Slaty cleavage*, cleavage of rocks into thin plates or laminae in planes oblique to the stratification

Slattern, slat′ėrn, *n.* [From Prov.E. *slatter*, to spill carelessly, to waste; akin to Icel. *sletta*, to squirt; or akin to G. *schlotterig*, negligent; D. *slodderen*, to hang and flap.] A woman who suffers her clothes and house to be in disorder; one who is not tidy; a slut.—*a.* Resembling a slattern; slovenly; slatternly.—**Slatternliness**, slat′ėrn-li-nes, *n.* State of being slatternly.—**Slatternly**, slat′ėrn-li, *a.* Pertaining to a slattern; sluttish.

Slaughter, sla̤′tėr, *n.* [From the stem of *slay*; same as Icel. *slátr*, raw flesh, *slátra*, to slaughter. SLAY.] The act of slaying or killing; great destruction of life by violent means; carnage; butchery; a killing of beasts for market.—*v.t.* To slay; to massacre; to butcher; to kill for the market.—**Slaughterer**, sla̤′tėr-ėr, *n.* One who slaughters; a person employed in slaughtering; a butcher.—**Slaughter-house**, *n.* A house where beasts are killed for the market; an abattoir.—**Slaughterous**, sla̤′tėr-us, *a.* Bent on killing; murderous.—**Slaughterously**, sla̤′tėr-us-li, *adv.* Murderously.

Slav, släv, *n.* One of a race of Eastern Europe, comprising the Russians, Bulgarians, Servians, Poles, Bohemians, &c.—**Slavic, Slavonic, Slavonian**, slav′ik, sla-von′ik, sla-vō′ni-an, *a.* Pertaining to the Slavs or Slavonians, or to their language.—*n.* The language of the Slavs, belonging to the family of Aryan tongues.

Slave, slāv, *n.* [Fr. *esclave*, from G. *sklave*, originally a Slavonian, a captive Slavonian.] A bond-servant; a person who is wholly subject to the will of another; a human being who is the property of another; one wholly under the dominion of any power (a *slave* to passion, to fear); an abject wretch; a drudge. (*Slave* is used in the formation of various self-explanatory compounds, as *slave-breeder*, *slave-catcher*, *slave-dealer*, *slave-market*, *slave-merchant*, *slave-owner*, &c.)—*v.i.*—*slaved*, *slaving*. To drudge; to toil; to labour as a slave.—**Slave-born**, *a.* Born in slavery.—**Slave-driver**, *n.* An overseer of slaves at their work; hence, a severe or cruel master.—**Slave-grown**, *a.* Grown or produced by slave labour.—**Slave-holder**, *n.* One who owns slaves.—**Slaver**, slā′vėr, *n.* A person engaged in the slave-trade; a slave-trader; a vessel engaged in the slave-trade.—**Slavery**, slā′vėr-i, *n.* The state or condition of a slave; bondage; complete subjection; the system of keeping or holding slaves; exhausting and mean labour; drudgery. ∴ Syn. under SERVITUDE.—**Slave-trade**, *n.* The business of purchasing or stealing men and women, and selling them for slaves.—**Slavish**, slā′vish, *a.* Pertaining to slaves; such as becomes a slave; servile; consisting in drudgery.—**Slavishly**, slā′vish-li, *adv.* In a slavish manner.—**Slavishness**, slā′vish-nes, *n.* The state or quality of being slavish.

Slaver, slav′ėr, *v.i.* [Icel. *slafr*, slaver, *slafra*, to slaver; akin to *slabber*, *slobber*.] To suffer the spittle to issue from the mouth; to be besmeared with saliva.—*v.t.* To smear with saliva.—*n.* Saliva drivelling from the mouth; drivel.—**Slaverer**, slav′ėr-ėr, *n.* One who slavers.

Slavonic. Under SLAV.

Slay, slā, *v.t.*—pret. *slew*; pp. *slain*. [A. Sax. *slahan*, or contr. *slean*, to beat, to slay; D. *slaan*, Icel. *slá*, Goth. *slahan*, G. *schlagen*; akin *slaughter*, *sledge* (-hammer).] To put to death in any violent or sudden manner; to kill; to destroy; to ruin.—**Slayer**, slā′ėr, *n.* One that slays; a killer; a murderer.

Slay, slā, *n.* A weaver's reed; a sley. SLEY.

Sleave, slēv, *n.* [Probably akin to *slip*; comp. G. *schleife*, a loop, a knot.] Soft floss or unspun silk used for weaving. (*Shak.*)

Sleazy, slē′zi, *a.* [Comp. G. *schleiszig*, worn out, thread-bare, from *schleiszen*, to split, to wear out. SLIT.] Thin; flimsy; wanting firmness of texture (*sleazy* silk or muslin).

Sled, sled, *n.* [D. *slede*, *sleede*, a sled; Dan. *slæde*, Icel. *sleði*; from stem of *slide*.] A sledge.—*v.t.*—*sledded*, *sledding*. To convey or transport on a sled.

Sledge, Sledge-hammer, slej, *n.* [A. Sax. *slecge*, a hammer, from *slahan*, *slagan*, to strike, to slay; so Icel. *sleggia*, a sledge-hammer. SLAY.] A large heavy hammer used chiefly by smiths.

Sledge, slej, *n.* [Formed from *sled*, or perhaps directly from D. *sleedie*, dim. of *sleede*, a sled.] A vehicle mounted on runners for the conveyance of loads over snow or ice, or the bare ground; a sled; a travelling carriage mounted on runners; a sleigh;

the hurdle on which traitors were formerly drawn to execution.—*v.t.* and *i.*—*sledged, sledging.* To convey or travel in a sledge or sledges.—**Sledge-chair**, *n.* A chair mounted on runners and propelled on the ice.

Sleek, slēk, *a.* [Icel. *slíkr*, smooth, sleek; connected with Icel. *sleikja*, Dan. *slikke*, to lick.] Having an even, smooth surface; having the hair smooth; glossy (*sleek* hair).—*v.t.* To make sleek; to render smooth, soft, and glossy; *fig.* to soothe; to calm.—**Sleekly**, slēk'li, *adv.* In a sleek manner; glossily.—**Sleekness**, slēk'nes, *n.* The quality of being sleek.—**Sleeky**, slēk'i, *a.* Of a sleek or smooth appearance.

Sleep, slēp, *v.i.*—pret. and pp. *slept.* [A. Sax. *slaepan, slépan*; D. and L.G. *slapen*, Goth. *slepan*, G. *schlafen*, to sleep; akin to *slip*, G. *schlaff*, loose, relaxed.] To be in that well-known state in which there is a suspension of the voluntary exercise of the powers of the body and mind, and which is periodically necessary to bodily health; to be dead; to lie in the grave; to be at rest; to be dormant or inactive (the question *sleeps* for the present); to assume a state as regards vegetable functions analogous to the sleeping of animals.—*v.t.* To pass in sleeping: with *away* (to *sleep away* the time); to get rid of, overcome, or recover from by sleeping: usually with *off* (to *sleep off* a fit of sickness).—*n.* A.Sax. *slaep*, D. *slaap*, Goth. *sleps*, G. *schlaf*.] That state in which the senses are more or less unaffected by external objects and the fancy or imagination only is active, and which is necessary to recruit both body and mind; slumber; death.—**Sleeper**, slēp'ėr, *n.* A person or an animal that sleeps; an animal that lies dormant; a piece of timber on which are laid the ground joists of a floor; a beam on or near the ground for the support of some superstructure; *rail.* a beam of wood, &c., embedded in the ground to sustain the rails.—**Sleepiness**, slēp'i-nes, *n.* The state or quality of being sleepy.—**Sleeping**, slēp'ing, *p.* and *a.* Reposing in sleep; pertaining to sleep.—*Sleeping partner*, a silent partner. Under DORMANT.—**Sleeping car**, *n.* A railroad car fitted up with berths for passengers during night travel.—**Sleeping sickness**, *n.* A disease prevalent in the African Congo and transmitted by the bite of the tsetse fly. Its victim becomes lethargic, soon sleeps all the time, becoming emaciated, and usually dies. Epidemic encephalitis: sleeping sickness of unknown etiology, believed to be caused by a virus infection; also called lethargic encephalitis.—**Sleepless**, slēp'les, *a.* Without sleep; wakeful; having no rest; never resting.—**Sleeplessly**, slēp'les-li, *adv.*—**Sleeplessness**, slēp'les-nes, *n.*—**Sleepwalker**, *n.* A somnambulist.—**Sleepwalking**, *n.*—**Sleepy**, slēp'i, *a.* Drowsy; inclined to or overcome by sleep; tending to induce sleep; heavy; inactive; sluggish.

Sleet, slēt, *n.* [Akin to N. *sletta*; Icel. *slydda*, Dan. *slud*, G. *schlosse*, sleet.] Rain mingled with hail or snow.—*v.i.* To snow or hail with a mixture of rain.—**Sleetiness**, slēt'i-nes, *n.* The state of being sleety.—**Sleety**, slēt'i, *a.* Consisting of sleet; characterized by sleet.

Sleeve, slēv, *n.* [A.Sax. *sléfe*, a sleeve; O.H.G. *slauf*, clothing; from root of *slip*.] The part of a garment that is fitted to cover the arm.—*To laugh in our sleeve*, to laugh privately or unperceived.—*v.t.*—*sleeved, sleeving.* To furnish with sleeves; to put in sleeves.—**Sleeve-button**, *n.* A button to fasten the sleeve or wristband.—**Sleeved**, slēvd, *a.* Having sleeves.—**Sleeveless**, slēv'les, *a.* Having no sleeves; wanting a cover, pretext, or palliation; resultless; bootless (a *sleeveless* errand).—**Sleeve-link**, *n.* A contrivance consisting of two buttons or studs connected by a link for fastening the sleeve or wristband.—**Sleeve valve**, *n.* Cylindrical tube or tubes with openings to register with those of the engine cylinder.

Sleeve, slēv, *n.* SLEAVE.

Sleezy, slē'zi, *a.* SLEAZY.

Sleigh, slā, *n.* [D. *sleê*, a contr. form of *sleede*, a sled. SLED.] A vehicle mounted on runners for transporting persons on the snow or ice, of a more elegant form than a sledge.—**Sleigh-bell**, *n.* A small bell attached to a sleigh or its harness to give notice of the vehicle's approach.

Sleight, slīt, *n.* [From O.E. *sleigh, sligh*, sly, like *height* from *high*; so Icel. *slœgth*, slyness, from *slœgr*, sly. SLY.] An artful trick; a trick or feat so dexterously performed that the manner of performance escapes observation; dexterous practice; dexterity.—*Sleight of hand*, legerdemain; prestidigitation.

Slender, slen'dėr, *a.* [Same as O.D. *slinder*, thin, slender; comp. D. *slinderen, slidderen*, to wriggle, L.G. *slindern*, to glide; akin *slide*.] Small in diameter or thickness compared with the length; not thick; slim; thin; weak; slight (*slender* hope); inconsiderable; insufficient; inadequate; meagre (*slender* means).—**Slenderly**, slen'dėr-li, *adv.* Slightly; feebly; inadequately; meagrely.—**Slenderness**, slen'dėr-nes, *n.* The state or quality of being slender; slimness; slightness; smallness.

Slept, slept, pret. and pp. of *sleep*.

Sleuth-hound, slöth'hound, *n.* [Icel. *slóth*, the slot or track of an animal. SLOT.] A blood-hound.

Slew, slū, pret. of *slay*.

Slew, slū, *v.t.* To slue.

Sley, slā, *n.* [A.Sax. *slae*, a sley; Icel. *slá*, a bar, bolt; akin verb to *slay*.] A weaver's reed.—*v.t.* To separate or part into threads.

Slice, slīs, *v.t.*—*sliced, slicing.* [O.Fr. *esclice*, a slice, a splinter, from O.H.G. *skleizan, slîzan*, G. *schleiszen*, to break, to split. Akin *slate, slit*.] To cut into thin pieces, or to cut off a thin broad piece from; to cut into parts; to cut off in a broad piece.—*n.* A thin broad piece cut off; that which is thin and broad like a slice; a broad thin knife for serving fish at table.—**Slicer**, slī'sėr, *n.* One who or that which slices.

Slick, slik, *a.* [L.G. *slick*, G. *schlich*.] Dexterous, bland, glib, smooth, smart; having a smooth, glassy surface, as ice.

Slicken-sides, slik'en-sīdz, *n.pl.* [From forming a *sleek* or smooth surface on the *sides* of cavities.] A variety of galena lining the walls of small fissures; *mining*, the polished striated surfaces of joints, beds, or fissures of rocks, glazed over with a film of calcareous or siliceous matter.

Slide, slīd, *v.i.*—pret. *slid*, sometimes *slided*, pp. *slid, slidden*, ppr. *sliding*. [A. Sax. *slidan*, to slide; O.G. *sliten*, to slide; G. *schlitten*, a sledge; Lith. *slidus*, slippery. *Sledge* (the vehicle) and *sled* are allied.] To move along a surface by slipping; to slip; to glide; to amuse one's self with gliding over a surface of ice; to pass along smoothly; to pass silently and gradually from one state to another, generally from a better to a worse.—*v.t.* To thrust smoothly along; to thrust or push forward by slipping; to pass or put imperceptibly; to slip.—*n.* A smooth and easy passage; a prepared smooth surface of ice for sliding on; an inclined plane for facilitating the descent of heavy bodies; that part of an instrument or apparatus which slides or is slipped into or out of place.—**Slider**, slī'dėr, *n.* One who or that which slides; the part of an instrument that slides.—**Slide-rest**, *n.* An appendage to the turning-lathe for holding and resting the cutting-tool, and ensuring accuracy in its motion.—**Slide-valve**, *n.* A kind of valve regulating the admission or escape of steam or water in machinery.—**Sliding**, slī'ding, *a.* Made so as to slide freely; fitted for sliding.—*n.* The act of one who slides; lapse; backsliding; the slipping of a body along a surface.—**Sliding-rule, Slide-rule**, *n.* A mathematical instrument, consisting of two parts, one of which slides along the other, and each having certain numbers engraved on it, such that when a given number on the one scale is brought to coincide with a given number on the other, the product of some other function of the two numbers is obtained by inspection.—**Sliding-scale**, *n.* A sliding-rule; a scale or rate of payment which varies under certain varying conditions; a scale to settle wages by the rise and fall of the market price of the product of labour.

Slight, slīt, *a.* [Same as O.L.G. *slight*, D. *slecht*, plain, common, mean; Icel. *sléttr*, smooth, common; G. *schlecht*, smooth; plain, bad; lit. perhaps 'beaten out smooth', the root being that of *slay*.] Not decidedly marked; small; trifling; insignificant (a *slight* difference); not strong or forcible (a *slight* impulse or effort); not severe or serious (a *slight* pain); not thorough or exhaustive (a *slight* examination); not firm or of strong construction; slim; slender; paltry; contemptible.—*n.* A moderate show of disrespect; contempt shown by neglect or inattention; intentional disregard.—*v.t.* To treat as unworthy of notice; to disregard intentionally; to treat with intentional neglect or superciliousness.—**Slighter**, slī'tėr, *n.* One who slights or neglects.—**Slightingly**, slī'ting-li, *adv.* In a slighting manner; with disrespect.—**Slightly**, slīt'li, *adv.* In a slight manner or measure; in a small degree; but little; somewhat.—**Slightness**, slīt'nes, *n.* The quality of being slight; smallness; weakness; want of strength; triviality.

Slily, slī'li, *adv.* SLYLY, under SLY.

Slim, slim, *a.* [Same as D. *slim*, L.G. *slimm*, Dan. and Sw. *slem*, Icel. *slœmr*, G. *schlimm*, all with the stronger sense of bad.] Slender; of small diameter or thickness in proportion to height; slight; unsubstantial; not executed with due thoroughness; cunning (S. Africa).—**Slimmish**, slim'ish, *a.* Somewhat slim.—**Slimness**, slim'nes, *n.* State or quality of being slim.

Slime, slīm, *n.* [A.Sax. *slim*, Icel. *slím*, D. *slijm*, G. *schleim*, slime, slimy matter, mucilage, &c.; allied to G. *schlamm*, mud, perhaps to *lime, loam*.] A soft, ropy, or glutinous substance; soft moist earth having an adhesive quality; viscous mud; asphalt or bitumen (O.T.); a mucous or viscous substance exuded from the bodies of certain animals; *fig.* anything of a clinging and offensive nature.—*v.t.*—*slimed, sliming.* To cover with slime; to make slimy.—**Slime-pit**, *n.* An asphalt or bitumen pit.—**Sliminess**, slī'mi-nes, *n.* The quality of being slimy; viscosity.—**Slimy**, slī'mi, *a.* Abounding with slime; consisting of slime; overspread with slime.

Sliness, slī'nes, *n.* SLYNESS, under SLY.

Sling, sling, *n.* [A.Sax. *slinge*, Sc. *slung*, Sw. *slunga*, Icel. *slanga*, O.G. *slinga*, a sling; G. *schlinge*, a noose or snare. See the verb.] An instrument for throwing stones or bullets, consisting of a strap or piece of leather to hold the missile and two strings attached to it; a sweep or swing; a sweeping stroke; a hanging bandage in which a wounded limb is sustained; a rope or chain specially arranged for raising or lowering heavy articles, as casks, bales, &c.; the strap to carry a rifle.—*Slings of a yard* (*naut.*), ropes or chains which suspend it by the middle.—*v.t.*—pret. and pp. *slung*. [A.Sax. *slingan*, to sling, to swing; Dan. *slynge*, Sw. *slinga*, Icel. *slyngva*, G. *schlingen*, to twist; same root as Icel. *slangi*, G. *schlange*, a serpent. *Slink* is akin.] To throw with a sling; to fling or hurl; to hang so as to swing; to place in slings in order to hoist or lower.—*v.i.* To move with long, swinging, elastic steps.—**Slinger**, sling'ėr, *n.* One who slings or uses a sling.

Sling, sling, *n.* [Comp. L.G. *slingen*, G. *schlingen*, to swallow.] A drink made of liquor or water, and served either hot (*hot toddy*) or iced.

Slink, slingk, *v.i.*—pret. and pp. *slunk* (pret. sometimes *slank*). [A.Sax. *slincan*, to slink, Sw. *slinka*; perhaps from root of *sling*.] To sneak; to creep away meanly; to steal away.—*v.t.* To cast prematurely: said of the female of a beast.—*a.* Born or cast prematurely, as a calf. — *n.* A sneaking fellow; a calf brought away prematurely.

Slip, slip, *v.i.*—*slipped* or *slipt, slipping.* [A.Sax. *slipan*, to slip, to guide; D. *slippen*, Dan. *slippe*, Icel. *sleppa*, G. *schleifen*, to slip.] To move smoothly along a surface; to slide; to glide; to have the feet slide; to fall by a false step; to depart or withdraw secretly; to sneak or slink: with *away*; to fall into error or fault; to err; to pass unexpectedly or imperceptibly; to glide; to enter by oversight: with *in* or *into* (some errors have *slipped in*); to escape insensibly, especially from the memory.—*To let slip*, to set free from the leash or noose, as a hound straining after a hare.—*v.t.* To put secretly or unobserved (*slipped* it into his pocket); to let loose (to *slip* the hounds); to disengage one's self from; to cast or suffer abortion of; to make a slip or slips of for planting.—*To slip off*, to take off noiselessly or hastily (to *slip off* one's shoes).—*To slip on*, to put on in haste or loosely.—*To slip a cable*, to let the end of it run out of the ship and sail without weighing anchor.—*n.* The act of slipping; an unintentional error or fault; a mistake inadvertently made (a *slip* of the pen); a departure from rectitude; a venial transgression; an indiscretion; a backsliding; a twig separated from the stock for planting or grafting; a scion (perhaps lit. a twig that can be *slipped* in); a leash or string by which a dog is held; a long narrow piece; a strip (a *slip* of paper); a child's pinafore; a loose covering or case (pillow-*slip*); a woman's fitted, dress-length undergarment with shoulder straps; an inclined plane upon which a vessel is supported while building or upon which she is hauled up for repair; also, a contrivance for hauling vessels out of the water for repairs, &c.; *pottery*, ground flint or clay mixed in water till of the consistence of cream for making porcelain; *geol.* a fault or dislocation of strata; *cricket*, one of the fielders who stands behind the wicket on the off side, and whose duty it is to back up the wicket-keeper; *pl.* that part of a theater at the sides of the stage where the flat-scenes are slipped on and off.—*To give a person the slip*, to escape or desert from him.—**Slipknot**, *n.* A knot which will not bear a strain, but slips.—**Slipped**, *a. Her.* applied to flowers, tree-branches, &c., when depicted with a shred of stalk remaining.—**Slipper**, slip′ėr, *n.* One who or that which slips or lets slip; loose, light footgear for household wear; a light shoe for formal evening wear.—**Slippered**, slip′ėrd, *a.* Wearing slippers.—**Slipperiness**, slip′ėr-i-nes, *n.* The state or quality of being slippery.—**Slippery**, slip′ėr-i, *a.* [A.Sax. *sliper*, slippery.] Allowing or causing anything to slip or slide readily; so smooth as to cause slipping; not affording sure footing; not to be trusted to; ready to use evasions or the like; unstable; changeable; uncertain.—**Slipshod**, slip′shod, *a.* Wearing slippers; wearing shoes down at heel; slovenly, especially with regard to literary qualities.—**Slip-on**, *n.* An overcoat or other loose garment that can be easily slipped on or off.

Slipslop, slip′slop, *n.* [A reduplication of *slop.*] Bad liquor; feeble composition. — *a.* Feeble; poor; jejune.

Slit, slit, *v.t.*—pret. and pp. *slit* or *slitted*, ppr. *slitting.* [A.Sax. *slitan*, to tear, to rend; Icel. *slíta*, Dan. *slide*, Sw. *slita*, G. *schleissen*, to slit, to split; akin *slate, slice, slash.*] To cut lengthwise; to cut into long pieces or strips; to cut a long fissure in (to *slit* the ear or tongue); to cut in general.—*n.* A long cut; a long narrow opening; a slash.—**Slitter**, slit′ėr, *n.* One who or that which slits.—**Slitting-mill**, *n.* A mill where iron bars or plates are slit into nail rods, &c.; a thin revolving iron disc used by lapidaries for slitting or cutting gems.

Sliver, sliv′ėr or slī′vėr, *v.t.* [A.Sax. *slifan*, to cleave, to split.] To cut into long thin pieces; to cut or rend lengthwise.—*n.* A long piece cut or rent off; a splinter; a small branch; *spinning*, a continuous strand of wool, cotton, or other fibre, in a loose untwisted condition.

Slob, slob, *n.* Mud; slime; a person (usually a woman) who is fat, untidy, and stupid.

Slobber, slob′ėr, *v.i.* [A form of *slabber.*] To drivel; to slaver; to slabber.—*v.t.* To beslaver.—*n.* Slaver; liquor spilled; slabber.—**Slobberer**, slob′ėr-ėr, *n.* One who slobbers.—**Slobbery**, slob′ėr-i, *a.* Moist; muddy; sloppy.

Sloe, slō, *n.* [A.Sax. *slá*, Sc. *slaé*, D. and L.G. *slee*, G. *schlehe*, from L.G. *slee*, D. *sleeuw*, G. *schleh*, sour, astringent.] An American wild plum shrub called also *Blackthorn*; also its fruit, which is black and very austere.—**Sloe gin**, *n.* An alcoholic beverage flavored with sloe plums.

Slogan, slō′gan, *n.* [From Gael. *sluaghghairm*, lit. an army cry.] The war-cry or gathering word or phrase of a Highland clan; hence, the watchword used by soldiers in the field; a catchword or phrase, as of a political party, or as in advertising.

Slokan, Sloke, slō′kan, slōk, *n.* A name given to some edible sea-weeds.

Sloop, slöp, *n.* [From D. *sloep*, L.G. *sluup*, *slupe*, a sloop; akin *shallop* (through the French).] A vessel with one mast, and often with nothing but fore-and-aft sails, the main-sail being extended by a gaff and a boom, and attached to the mast on its foremost edge.—*Sloop-of-war*, in the British navy, a vessel, of whatever rig, between a corvette and a gun-boat.

Slop, slop, *v.t.*—*slopped, slopping.* [Comp. Icel. *slöp*, offal of fish; Prov.G. *schloppen*, to swallow; E. *slobber, slabber*, also to *slip.*] To spill liquid upon; to soil by letting a liquid fall upon something.—*v.i.* To be spilled; to overflow, as some water has *slopped* on the floor.—*n.* A pool of spilled liquid, as produced by upsetting a cup or container of any kind; a quantity of water carelessly thrown about, as on a floor; *pl.* water that has been used for washing; liquid from utensils removed from bedrooms; swill or liquid garbage fed to swine; the clothes and bedding of a sailor.—**Slop pail**, *n.* A pail or bucket for holding the slops of a bedroom, &c.—**Sloppily**, *adv.* In a sloppy manner; carelessly.—**Sloppiness**, *n.* The state or condition of being sloppy (said of persons as well as things).—**Sloppy**, *a.* Of a thin, liquid, or watery consistency; soaked; covered with a liquid; muddy; apt to splash, as *sloppy* roads, *sloppy* food, &c.; carelessly put together or performed; lacking sound construction, as *sloppy* work, a *sloppy* style, &c.; lacking restraint or sincerity, as *sloppy* sentiment.

Slope, slōp, *n.* [From A.Sax. *slopen*, pp. of *slúpan*, to slip, akin to *slipan*, and D. *sluipen*, to slip. SLIP.] An oblique direction; a direction inclining obliquely downward; a declivity or acclivity; any ground whose surface forms an angle with the plane of the horizon.—*v.t.*—*sloped, sloping.* To form with a slope; to cause to slope; to direct obliquely; to incline.—*v.i.* To take an oblique direction; to descend in a slanting direction.—*To slope arms*, to place the rifle flat on the left shoulder, magazine outwards.—**Sloping**, slō′ping, *p.* and *a.* Oblique; inclining or inclined from a horizontal or other right line.—**Slopingly**, slō′ping-li, *adv.* In a sloping manner; obliquely.—**Slopy**, slō′pi, *a.* Sloping; having a gentle declivity.

Slot, slot, *n.* [Same as D. and L.G. *slot*, a lock, akin to D. *sluiten*, Dan. *slutte*, G. *schliessen*, to lock.] A bolt or bar; an oblong hole in a piece of metal, &c., as for the reception of a bolt; a trap-door in the stage of a theater.—**Slot machine**, an automatic mechanism, the operation of which is started by the insertion of coins; most frequently used for gambling purposes.

Slot, slot, *n.* [Same as Icel. *slóth*, a track or trail, *sleuth* in *sleuth*-hound.] The track of a deer, as followed by the scent or by the mark of the foot.—**Slot-hound**, *n.* A hound that tracks animals by the slot; a sleuth-hound.

Slote, slōt, *n.* A trap-door in the stage of a theatre. Written also *Slot.*

Sloth, slōth or sloth, *n.* [From *slow*, and equivalent to *slowth* (like *growth* from *grow*); A.Sax. *slaewth*, slowness, from *sláw*, slow. SLOW.] Slowness‡; disinclination to action; sluggishness; indolence; laziness; idleness; the name of two South American mammals, adapted for living in trees but moving with great slowness on the ground.—*Australian sloth*, the koala.—**Slothful**, slōth′ful or sloth′ful, *a.* Sluggish; lazy; indolent.—**Slothfully**, slōth′ful-li or sloth′ful-li, *adv.* In a slothful manner; sluggishly.—**Slothfulness**, slōth′ful-nes or sloth′ful-nes, *n.* The state or quality of being slothful; the habit of idleness.

Slouch, slouch, *n.* [Same as Icel. *slókr*, a dull inactive person; akin Sw. *sloka*, to droop, E. *slack, slug, sluggard.*] A stoop in walking; an ungainly clownish gait; an awkward clownish fellow; a depression or hanging down, as of the brim of a hat.—*v.i.* To have a downcast clownish gait or manner.—*v.t.* To depress; to cause to hang down.—**Slouch-hat**, *n.* A hat with a hanging brim.—**Slouching**, slouch′ing, *p.* and *a.* Hanging down; walking heavily and awkwardly.

Slough, slou, *n.* [A.Sax. *slóh*, a slough; allied to G. *schlauch*, an abyss, the gullet, *schlucken*, to swallow.] A place of deep mud or mire; a hole full of mire.—**Sloughy**, slou′i, *a.* Full of sloughs; miry.

Slough, sluf, *n.* [Sc. *sloch*, a husk; G. *schlauch*, the skin of an animal stripped off.] The cast skin of a serpent or other animal; *surg.* the dead part which separates from the living in mortification, or the part that separates from a foul sore.—*v.i.* To come off, as the matter formed over a sore; a term in surgery.—**Sloughy**, sluf′i, *a.* Pertaining to the dead matter which separates from flesh; having a slough.

Slovak, slō′vak, *a.* Of or belonging to the Slav race to the north of Hungary.

Sloven, sluv′n, *n.* [Akin to L.G. *sluf*, D. *slof*, careless; D. *sloffen*, to trail one's feet; *slip* is perhaps allied.] A man careless of his dress or habitually negligent of neatness and order; a lazy fellow. *Slut* is the corresponding feminine term. — **Slovenly**, sluv′n-li, *a.* Having the habits of a sloven; negligent of personal neatness; wanting neatness or tidiness; loose and careless (*slovenly* dress).—*adv.* In a slovenly manner.—**Slovenliness**, sluv′n-li-nes, *n.* The state or quality of being slovenly.

Slovene, slō-vēn′, *a.* Of or belonging to the Slav race in Styria, Carinthia, &c.

Slow, slō, *a.* [A.Sax. *sláw*, slow; Dan. *sløv*, Sw. *slö*, Icel. *sljór*, blunt, dull, slow. Hence *sloth.*] Moving a small distance in a long time; not swift; not quick in motion; extending over a long time; gradual; not ready; not prompt; inactive; tardy; dilatory; not hasty; acting with deliberation; indicating a time later than the true time (the clock is *slow*); dull; heavy; not lively; stupid.—*Slow coach*, a colloquial term for one who is slow in movement or deficient in quickness.—*Slow match.* Under MATCH.—*adv.* Slowly.—*v.t.* To delay; to retard; to slacken in speed.—*v.i.* To slacken in speed.—**Slowly**, slō′li, *adv.* In a slow manner; not rapidly; gradually; tardily; not hastily.—**Slowness**, slō′nes, *n.* Want of speed or velocity; tardiness; want of readiness or promptness; dulness; dilatoriness; sluggishness.

Slow-worm, slō′wėrm, *n.* [Not from *slow*, but from A.Sax. *slá-wyrm*, lit. slay-worm (from *slahan*, to slay), because it feeds on worms.] A name given to the blind-worm. BLIND-WORM.

Sloyd, sloid, *n.* [Sw. *slöjd*, akin to E. *sleight.*] A system of manual training for pupils in schools, originating in Sweden.

Slub, slub, *n.* [Perhaps akin to *slab*, *n.*] A roll of wool drawn out and slightly twisted by spinning machinery; a rove.—

v.t.—slubbed, slubbing. To form into slubs. —**Slubber**, slub'ėr, *n.* One who slubs; a slubbing-machine. —**Slubbing-billy, Slubbing-machine**, *n.* A machine that produces slubs.

Slubber, slub'ėr, *v.t.* [A form of *slabber, slobber.*] To daub; to besmear; to sully; to soil; to do lazily, or with careless hurry; to slur over†.

Sludge, sluj, *n.* [Also *slutch, slush, slich,* forms corresponding to L.G. *slick,* D. *slik; slijk,* dirt, mire, allied to E. *sleek.*] Mud; mire; soft mud.—**Sludge-door, Sludge-hole**, *n.* An opening in a steam-boiler to remove matter deposited at the bottom.—**Sludgy**, sluj'i, *a.* Miry; slushy.

Slue, slū, *v.t.—slued, sluing.* [Perhaps from Icel. *snúa,* to turn, to twist, with change of *n* to *l.*] To turn or swing round (as the yard of a ship).

Slug, slug, *n.* [Same as O.E. *slugge,* slow, sluggish. Akin to *slack* or *slouch.* As the name of an animal it is represented by D. *slak, slek,* a snail.] A slow, heavy, lazy fellow; a sluggard; in printing, a strip of metal used to space between lines; a line of type cast in one piece; a heavy blow delivered with a fist or weapon; a drink of whiskey (*Slang*).—**Sluggard**, slug'ärd, *n.* [From *slug,* and the suffix *-ard.*] A person habitually lazy and inactive.—*a.* Sluggish; lazy.—**Sluggish**, slug'ish, *a.* Habitually indolent; slothful; inactive; having little motion (a *sluggish* stream); inert.—**Sluggishness**, slug'ish-nes, *n.*

Slug, slug, *n.* [Akin to *slay;* comp. Prov.E. *slog,* to strike heavily.] A cylindrical, cubical, or irregularly shaped piece of metal used for the charge of a gun.

Sluice, slös, *n.* [Same as D. *sluys, sluis,* Dan. *sluse,* G. *schleuse,* O.Fr. *escluse,* Fr. *écluse,* from L.L. *exclusa,* from L. *excludo, exclusum,* to shut out, to exclude. EXCLUDE.] A contrivance for excluding or admitting the inflow of a body of water; a water-way provided with a gate by which the flow of water is controlled; a flood-gate; any vent for water; that through which anything flows.—*v.t.—sluiced, sluicing.* To let in a copious flow of water on; to wet or lave abundantly; to scour out or cleanse by means of sluices. —**Sluice-gate**, *n.* The gate of a sluice.

Slum, slum, *n.* [Comp. Dan. *slam,* mire, mud.] A neighborhood with dilapidated houses and tenement buildings.

Slumber, slum'bėr, *v.i.* [A.Sax. *slumerian,* from *sluma,* slumber; Dan. *slumre,* D. *sluimeren,* G. *schlummern,* to slumber. As to insertion of *b,* comp. *number, humble.*] To sleep lightly; to doze; to sleep; to be inert, or in a state of supineness or inactivity.—*n.* Light sleep; sleep not deep or sound; sleep; repose.—**Slumberer**, slum'bėr-ėr, *n.* One that slumbers. —**Slumbering**, slum'bėr-ing, *n.* State of sleep or repose.—**Slumberingly**, slum'bėr-ing-li, *adv.* In a slumbering manner. —**Slumberless**, slum'bėr-les, *a.* Without slumber; sleepless. —**Slumberous, Slumbrous**, slum'bėr-us, slum'brus, *a.* Inviting or causing sleep; soporific.

Slump, slump, *v.i.* [Comp. Dan. *slumpe,* to stumble or light upon, from *slump,* chance, hazard.] To sink in walking, as in snow; to walk with sinking feet.—*n.* A sudden fall in prices or values.

Slump, slump, *n.* [Same as Dan. *slump,* D. *slomp,* a lot, a heap; Sw. *slumpa,* to buy things in block.] The whole number taken in one lot; the gross amount (to take things in the *slump*).—*v.t.* To throw together into a single lot or mass.

Slung, slung, pret. and pp. of *sling.*

Slunk, slungk, pret. and pp. of *slink.*

Slur, slėr, *v.t.—slurred, slurring.* [From Prov.E. *slur,* thin mud; comp. Icel. *slor,* filth; L.G. *slurren,* to trail the feet, D. *sloren,* to drag.] To soil or sully; to disparage by insinuation or innuendo; to speak slightingly of; to traduce; to pass lightly over; to say little of; to pronounce in an indistinct or sliding manner; *mus.* to sing or perform in a smooth, gliding style; to run (notes) into each other.—*n.* A slight reproach or disgrace; a stigma; *mus.* the blending of two or more notes; a curved mark indicating this.

Slush, slush, *n.* [A form of *sludge.*] Sludge or watery mire; soft mud; wet, half-melted snow; a mixture of grease and other materials for lubrication; refuse fat or grease in ships; a mixture of white-lead and lime with which the bright parts of machinery are covered to prevent them rusting.—*v.t.* To cover or grease with slush.—**Slushy**, slush'i, *a.* Consisting of soft mud, or of snow and water; resembling slush.

Slut, slut, *n.* [Same as Dan. *slutte, slatte,* D. *slodde,* Prov.G. *schlutte,* a slut; comp. Dan. *slat,* loose, flabby.] A woman who is negligent of cleanliness and tidiness in her person, clothes, furniture, &c.; the correlative of *sloven;* a name of slight contempt for a woman.—**Sluttery**, slut'ėr-i, *n.* The practices of a slut; sluttishness.—**Sluttish**, slut'ish, *a.* Like a slut or what is characteristic of a slut; devoid of tidiness or neatness.—**Sluttishly**, slut'ish-li, *adv.* In a sluttish manner. —**Sluttishness**, slut'ish-nes, *n.* The qualities or practice of a slut; untidiness.

Sly, slī, *a.* [O.E. *slie, slee,* from Icel. *slœgr,* sly; akin L.G. *slou,* Dan. *slu,* G. *schlau,* sly. Hence *sleight.*] Meanly artful; crafty; cunning; proceeding by underhand ways; wily; cautious; shrewd; arch; knowing (a *sly* remark).—*On the sly,* in a sly or secret manner; secretly. —**Slyly, Slily**, slī'li, *adv.* In a sly manner; cunningly.—**Slyness, Sliness**, slī'nes, *n.* The quality of being sly; cunning; craftiness; archness.

Smack, smak, *v.i.* [A.Sax. *smæccan,* to taste, from *smæc,* smack, taste = D. *smaak,* Dan. *smag,* G. *geschmack,* taste; D. *smaken,* Dan. *smage,* G. *schmecken,* to taste.] To have a taste or flavour; to taste (it *smacks* of onions); to have a certain quality infused; to partake in character; to savour (it *smacks* of vanity).—*n.* A slight taste or flavour; savour; tincture; a slight or superficial knowledge; a smattering.

Smack, smak, *v.i.* [Same as Sw. *smacka,* to smack; D. *smakken,* to smack the lips: imitative of the sound made.] To make a sharp noise with the lips; to kiss so as to make a sound with the lips.—*v.t.* To kiss with a sharp noise; to make a sharp noise by opening the mouth; to make a sharp noise by striking; to crack; to give a sharp stroke to, as with the palm.—*n.* A loud kiss; a quick sharp noise, as of a whip; a quick smart blow, as with the flat of the hand; a slap.—*adv.* In a sudden and direct manner, as if with a smack or slap.—**Smacking**, smak'ing, *a.* Making a sharp brisk sound; brisk.

Smack, smak, *n.* [Same as D. and L.G. *smak,* Dan. *smakke,* G. *schmake,* a smack.] A large sloop with a gaff-topsail and a running bowsprit; a small sloop used in the fishing trade.

Small, smąl, *a.* [A.Sax. *smæl*=L.G. and D. *smal,* G. *schmal,* Goth. *smals,* Sc. *sma',* Dan. and Sw. *smaa,* Icel. *smá(r).*] Little in size; not great or large; of minute dimensions; little in degree, quantity, amount, duration, or number; of little moment; trivial; petty; trifling; of little genius or ability; insignificant; of little strength or force; weak; gentle; soft; not loud; characterized by littleness of mind or character; narrow-minded; ungenerous; mean.—*Small fruits,* fruits raised in market gardens, such as strawberries, raspberries, and the like. —*The small hours,* the early hours of morning. —*n.* The small or slender part of a thing; *pl.* small-clothes; breeches. —**Small-arms**, *n.pl.* A general name for rifles, carbines, pistols, &c., as distinguished from cannon. —**Small-beer**, *n.* A species of weak beer. —**Small-clothes**, *n.pl.* Breeches or trousers; smalls.—**Small-coal**, *n.* Coals not in lumps or large pieces. —**Small-craft**, *n.* A vessel, or vessels in general, of a small size.—**Small-fry**, *n.pl.* Small creatures collectively; young children; persons of no importance.—**Small-hand**, *n.* The style of writing commonly used, as distinguished from text or large hand.—**Smallish**, smąl'ish, *a.* Somewhat small. —**Smallness**, smąl'nes, *n.* The state or quality of being small; littleness of size, quantity, degree, or value.—**Small pica**, *n.* A size of type between longprimer and pica. —**Smallpox**, *n.* A disease characterized by fever and a cutaneous eruption, propagated by contagion, and very dangerous, especially in persons that have not been vaccinated.—**Small stuff**, *n.* A nautical term referring to spun yarn, marline, and other small rope of various threads.—**Small talk**, *n.* Light conversation; gossip. —**Small-town**, *a.* Pertaining to the customs and people of a small town in contradistinction to a metropolis.

Smallage, smąl'āj, *n.* [*Small* and Fr. *ache,* smallage, from L. *apium,* parsley.] A name for celery.

Smalt, smąlt, *n.* [It. *smalto,* from O.H.G. *smalzjan,* G. *schmelzen,* to melt, to *smelt.*] Glass tinged of a fine deep blue by the protoxide of cobalt, reduced to an impalpable powder, and employed as a pigment and colouring matter.—**Smaltine**, smąl'tin, *n.* Gray or tin-white cobalt, consisting of arsenic and cobalt.

Smaragd, smar'ag, *n.* [Gr. *smaragdos,* an emerald, a bright green stone.] An old name given to the emerald and other bright green transparent stones.—**Smaragdine**, sma-rag'din, *a.* Pertaining to emerald; of an emerald green. —**Smaragdite**, sma-rag'dīt, *n.* A mineral, called also *Green Diallage.*

Smart, smärt, *n.* [A.Sax. *smeortan,* to smart, to feel pain; D. *smart, smert,* Dan. *smerte,* G. *schmerz,* pain, ache; allied to Rus. *smert,* Lith. *smertis,* death, being from a root seen in L. *mors,* death (whence *mortal*).] A sharp quick pain; a pricking local pain; severe pungent pain of mind; smart-money (to pay the *smart*).—*v.i.* To feel a lively pungent pain; to be acutely painful; to feel sharp pain of mind; to suffer acute mental pain.—*a.* Causing a keen local pain; keen; severe; poignant; producing any effect with force and vigour; vigorous (a *smart* blow); sharp; severe (a *smart* skirmish); brisk; fresh (a *smart* breeze); acute and pertinent; witty; vivacious; lively; shrewd; fine in dress; spruce.—**Smarten**, smär'tn, *v.t.* To make smart; to render brisk, bright, or lively.—**Smartly**, smärt'li, *adv.* In a smart manner; keenly; painfully; briskly; sharply; wittily; sprucely. —**Smart-money**, *n.* Money paid by a person to buy himself off from some unpleasant engagement or painful situation; money paid by a recruit to be free of his engagement.—**Smartness**, smärt'nes, *n.* The quality of being smart; pungency; keenness; quickness; liveliness; briskness; vivacity; spruceness.

Smash, smash, *v.t.* [Perhaps formed from *mash* through the influence of *smite;* comp. G. *schmiss,* Sw. *smisk,* a dash, a blow.] To break in pieces by violence; to dash to pieces; to crush by a sudden blow.—*v.i.* To go to pieces; to go to utter wreck.—*n.* A breaking to pieces; ruin; bankruptcy.—**Smasher**, smash'ėr, *n.* One who or that which smashes.—**Smashing-machine**, *n.* A press used by bookbinders.

Smatter, smat'ėr, *v.i.* [For *smacker,* from *smack,* a taste or small quantity.] To have a slight superficial knowledge; to talk superficially.—*n.* Slight superficial knowledge.—**Smatterer**, smat'ėr-ėr, *n.* One who has only a smattering or slight superficial knowledge.—**Smattering**, smat'ėr-ing, *n.* [Formerly *smackering.*] A slight superficial knowledge; an insignificant degree of acquirement (a *smattering* of law).

Smear, smēr, *v.t.* [A.Sax. *smerian,* from *smeru,* grease; Icel. *smyrjan,* G. *schmieren,* to smear; D. *smeer,* Icel. *smjör,* Dan. *smör,* G. *schmeer,* grease.] To overspread with anything unctuous, viscous, or adhesive; to besmear; to daub; to soil.—*n.* A spot made as if by some unctuous substance; a stain; a blot or blotch.

Smectite, smek'tīt, *n.* [Gr. *smēktis*, fuller's-earth, from *smēchō*, to wipe.] An earth resembling fuller's-earth.

Smegmatic, smeg-mat'ik, *a.* [Gr. *smēgma*, soap, from *smēchō*, to wash off.] Soapy; cleansing; detersive.

Smell, smel, *v.t.*—pret. and pp. *smelled* or *smelt*. [Allied to L.G. *smellen, smelen*, to smoulder, to smoke; D. *smeulen*, to smoulder; Dan. *smul*, dust, powder. Akin *smoulder*.] To perceive by the nose; to perceive the scent of; to perceive as if by the smell; to detect by sagacity.—*To smell out*, to find out by sagacity.—*To smell a rat*. Under RAT.—*v.i.* To exercise the sense of smell; to give out odor or perfume; to affect the sense of smell; to have an odor or scent; to have a smack of any quality.—*n.* The sense or faculty of which the nose is the special organ; the faculty of perceiving by the nose; that which affects the olfactory organs; odor; scent.—**Smeller**, smel'ėr, *n.* One who smells; a nosy person (*colloq.*); a nose (*slang*).—**Smelling bottle**, *n.* A bottle containing smelling salts.—**Smelling salts**, *n. pl.* Ammonium carbonate, used for resuscitation and stimulation

Smelt, smelt, *n.* [A.Sax. and Dan. *smelt*.] A small edible fish allied to the salmon, inhabiting the salt water about the mouths of rivers.

Smelt, smelt, *v.t.* [Same as D. *smelten*, Dan. *smelte*, Icel. *smelta*, G. *schmelzen*, to melt, to liquefy; akin G. *schmelz*, fat. MELT.] To melt or fuse, as ore, for the purpose of separating the metal from extraneous substances.—**Smelter**, smel'tėr, *n.* One who smelts ore.—**Smeltery**, smel'tėr-i, *n.* A house or place for smelting ores.—**Smelting**, smel'ting, *n.* The process of obtaining metals from their ores by the action of heat, air, and fluxes. — **Smelting-furnace**, *n.* A furnace in which metals are separated from their ores; a blast-furnace.

Smew, smū, *n.* [Perhaps for *ice-mew*; comp. the German names *ice-diver* and *mew-diver*.] A swimming bird of the merganser family, frequenting the sea-shore, lakes, and ponds; also called *White Nun*.

Smile, smīl, *v.i.*—*smiled, smiling*. [Same as Dan. *smile*, Sw. *smila*, O.G. *smielen*, to smile; same root as Skr. *smi*, to smile.] To express pleasure or slight amusement by a special change of the features, especially the mouth: the contrary of to *frown*; to express slight contempt, sarcasm, or pity by a look; to sneer; to look gay and joyous (the desert *smiled*); to appear propitious or favourable.—*v.t.* To express by a smile (to *smile* content); to put an end to or dispel by smiling: with *away*.—*n.* A peculiar contraction of the features expressing pleasure, approbation, or kindness: opposed to *frown*; gay or joyous appearance; favour; countenance.—**Smiler**, smī'lėr, *n.* One who smiles.—**Smiling**, smī'ling, *p.* and *a.* Wearing a smile; gay or joyous in aspect.—**Smilingly**, smī'ling-li, *adv.* In a smiling manner.—**Smilingness**, smī'ling-nes, *n.*

Smirch, smėrch, *v.t.* [From stem of *smear*.] To stain; to smear; to smudge.

Smirk, smėrk, *v.i.* [A.Sax. *smercian, smearcian*, to smirk or smile; from stem of *smile*; comp. O.G. *smieren*, to smile.] To smile affectedly or wantonly; to look affectedly soft or kind. —*n.* An affected smile; a soft look.

Smite, smīt, *v.t.*—pret. *smote*; pp. *smitten* or *smit*; ppr. *smiting*. [A.Sax. *smītan*, to smite=D. *smijten*, Dan. *smide*, G. *schmeissen*, to strike, to cast or fling; originally to smear or defile; comp. Sc. *smit*, to communicate a disease to; akin are *smudge, smut*.] To strike; to give a blow with the hand, something in the hand, or something thrown; to slay; to kill; to assail or visit with something evil; to blast; to afflict, chasten, punish; to strike or affect with love or other feeling.—*v.i.* To strike; to knock. — **Smiter**, smī'tėr, *n.* One who smites. — **Smitten**, smit'n, pp. of *smite*. Struck; affected with some passion; excited by beauty or something impressive.

Smith, smith, *n.* [A.Sax. *smith*, a craftsman, a smith; Icel. *smithr*, Goth. *smitha*, D. *smid*, G. *schmidt*, a smith; not akin to *smooth*.] One who forges with the hammer; one who works in metals: often distinctively applied to a blacksmith. —*v.t.* To hammer into shape; to forge. —**Smithcraft**,† smith'kraft, *n.* The art or occupation of a smith.—**Smithery**, smith'ėr-i, *n.* A smithy; work done by a smith; the act or art of forging.—**Smithy**, smith'i, *n.* [A.Sax. *smiththe*, a smithy.] The workshop of a smith.

Smithereens, smiᴛʜ'er-ēnz", *n. pl.* [Perhaps from Ir. *smidirīn*, dim. of *smiodar*, fragment.] Small pieces; atoms; fragments, as *to blow, to smash, to smithereens*.

Smock, smok, *n.* [A.Sax. *smocc*=Icel. *smokkr*, a smock; Sw. *smog*, a garment; lit. a garment one creeps into; comp. A. Sax. *smúgan*, Icel. *smjúga*, to creep. SMUGGLE.] A loose outer garment, usually of knee length, worn to protect other garments, and to keep them from being soiled.—*v.t.* To gather by stitching through material, following a desired pattern; to dress in a smock.

Smoke, smōk, *n.* [A.Sax. *smoca*, smoke= D. and L.G. *smook*, Dan. *smög*, G. *schmauch*, smoke; comp. Gr. *smychō*, to burn slowly.] The exhalation or vaporous matter that escapes from a burning substance; especially the volatile particles expelled from burning vegetable matter; what resembles smoke; vapour; *fig.* idle talk; vanity; nothingness (it all ended in *smoke*); a continuous drawing in and puffing out of the fumes of burning tobacco.—*v.i.* —*smoked, smoking*. To emit smoke or vaporous matter; to give out visible vapour when heated; to inhale and exhale the fumes of burning tobacco; *fig.* to burn or rage (O.T.).—*v.t.* To apply smoke to; to foul by smoke; to hang in smoke; to fumigate; to drive out by smoke; to draw smoke from into the mouth and puff it out; to inhale the smoke of; to discover or find out; to make fun of (a person).—**Smoke-bell**, *n.* A glass bell suspended over a gas-light to intercept the smoke.—**Smoke-black**, *n.* Lampblack. —**Smoke-board**, *n.* A sliding board or plate to cause an increased draught in a chimney and prevent the smoke from coming out into the room.—**Smoke-box**, *n.* The part of a tubular steam-boiler into which the smoke is received before passing into the funnel.—**Smoke-dry**, *v.t.* To dry by smoke. — **Smoke-house**, *n.* A building employed for the purpose of curing flesh or fish by smoking.—**Smoke-jack**, *n.* A machine for turning a roasting-spit by means of a fly-wheel or wheels set in motion by the current of ascending air in a chimney. — **Smokeless**, smōk'les, *a.* Having no smoke.—**Smoker**, smō'kėr, *n.* One who smokes, especially tobacco; a place for smoking; a smoking concert.—**Smoke-stack**, *n.* In steam vessels a name common to the funnel and the several escape-pipes for steam beside it.—**Smoke-tight**, *a.* Impervious to smoke.—**Smokily**, smō'ki-li, *adv.* In a smoky manner. —**Smokiness**, smō'ki-nes, *n.* The state of being smoky. — **Smoking**, *p.* and *a.* Emitting smoke; used for smoking or having its smoke inhaled; set apart for the purpose of smoking in.—*n.* The act of one who or that which smokes; the act or practice of inhaling tobacco smoke from a pipe or cigar. —**Smoking-cap**, *n.* A light ornamental cap used by smokers and others for indoor wear. — **Smoky**, smō'ki, *a.* Emitting smoke, especially much smoke; resembling smoke; filled with smoke; tarnished with smoke.—*Smoky quartz*, a variety of quartz of a smoky brown colour, much the same as cairngorm.

Smolder, smōl'dėr, **Smoldering**, &c. SMOULDER.

Smolt, smōlt, *n.* [Comp. Gael. *smal*, a spot.] A salmon when a year or two old, and when it has acquired its silvery scales.

Smooth, smöᴛʜ, *a.* [A.Sax. *smoethe, smóthe*, also *sméthe*, smooth; root doubtful, perhaps that of Bohemian *smant*, cream.] Having a very even surface; free from asperities; not rough; evenly spread; glossy; gently flowing; not ruffled or undulating; falling pleasantly on the ear; not harsh or rugged; using language not harsh or rugged; bland; soothing; insinuating; without jolt or shock; equable as to motion.—*Smooth* is often used in the formation of self-explaining compounds, as *smooth*-haired, *smooth*-leaved, *smooth*-shaven, *smooth*-swarded, &c. —*n.* The act of making smooth; the smooth part of anything.—*v.t.* To make smooth; to make even on the surface by any means; to free from obstruction; to make easy; to palliate; to soften; to calm; to mollify; to allay.—**Smooth-bore**, *n.* A firearm with a smooth-bored barrel and not rifled.—**Smooth-bored**, *a.* Having a smooth bore; not rifled. — **Smooth-chinned**, *a.* Having a smooth chin; beardless. — **Smoothen**, smö'ᴛʜn, *v.t.* To make smooth; to smooth. —**Smoother**, smö'ᴛʜėr, *n.* One who or that which smooths. —**Smooth-faced**, *a.* Having a smooth face; beardless; having a fawning insinuating look.—**Smooth-grained**, *a.* Smooth in the grain, as wood or stone.—**Smoothing-iron**, *n.* An iron instrument with a flat polished face, used when heated for smoothing clothes, linen, &c.—**Smoothly**, smöᴛʜ'li, *adv.* In a smooth manner; evenly; not roughly or harshly; with bland, insinuating language. — **Smoothness**, smöᴛʜ'nes, *n.* The state or quality of being smooth; evenness of surface; easy flow of words; blandness of address.—**Smooth-spoken**, *a.* Speaking smoothly; plausible; flattering.—**Smooth-tongued**, *a.* Soft of speech; plausible; cozening.

Smorzando, smord-zän'dō. [Ital., dying away.] A word placed over a passage of music to indicate a decrease, or dying away of the sound.

Smote, smōt, pret. of *smite*.

Smother, smuᴛʜ'ėr, *n.* [For older *smorther, smurther*, from A.Sax. *smorian*, to suffocate.] Stifling smoke; a suffocating dust.—*v.t.* To suffocate or stifle; to suffocate by closely covering, and by the exclusion of air; to cover close up, as with ashes, earth, &c.; *fig.* to suppress; to hide from public view.—*v.i.* To be suffocated; to smoulder.—**Smother-fly**, *n.* A name given to the various species of aphis.—**Smotheriness**, smuᴛʜ'ėr-i-nes, *n.* State of being smothery. —**Smothery**, smuᴛʜ'ėr-i, *a.* Tending to smother; stifling; full of smother or dust.

Smoulder, smōl'dėr, *v.i.* [Perhaps from old *smorther*, and therefore the same word as *smother*; comp. also Dan. *smuldre, smulre*, to crumble, to moulder, from *smul*, dust.] To burn in a stifled manner; to burn and smoke without flame; *fig.* to burn inwardly, as a thought, passion, and the like; to exist in a suppressed state.

Smudge, smuj, *v.t.*—*smudged, smudging*. [A form of *smutch* (which see).] To smear or stain with dirt or filth; to blacken with smoke.—*n.* A foul spot; a stain; a smear; a smoldering fire used in an orchard to warm the air and protect the fruit from being destroyed by frost.

Smug, smug, *a.* [Same as L.G. *smuck*, Dan. *smuk*, G. *schmuck*, handsome, fine, neat; akin to *smock*.] Neat; trim; spruce; fine; affectedly nice in dress; self-satisfied.—*v.t.* —*smugged, smugging*. To make smug or spruce.—**Smug-faced**, *a.* Having a smug or precise face; prim-faced. — **Smugly**, smug'li, *adv.* In a smug manner; neatly; sprucely.—**Smugness**, smug'nes, *n.* The state or quality of being smug; neatness; spruceness.

Smuggle, smug'l, *v.t.* — *smuggled, smuggling*. [Same as L.G. *smuggeln*, Dan. *smugle*, G. *schmuggeln*, to smuggle, from stem of A. Sax. *smúgan*, Icel. *smjúga*, to creep. *Smock* is akin.] To import or export secretly and contrary to law; to manage, convey, or introduce clandestinely.—*v.i.*—To practise smuggling.—**Smuggler**, smug'lėr, *n.* One who smuggles; a vessel employed in smuggling goods.—**Smuggling**, smug'ling, *n.* The offence of importing or exporting prohibited goods or other goods without paying the legal duties.

Smut, smut, *n.* [Akin to *smudge, smutch*; being from stem of *smite*; comp. D. *smet*, a blot, a stain.] A spot made with soot or coal; or the foul matter itself; obscene and filthy language; a disease of cereals, the farina of the seed being converted into a black soot-like powder.—*v.t.*—*smutted, smutting.* To stain or mark with smut or other dirty substance; to affect with the disease called smut.—*v.i.* To gather smut; to give off smut.—**Smut-ball**, *n.* A fungoid disease analogous to smut; also, the fungus producing it.—**Smutty**, smut'i, *a.* Soiled with smut; affected with smut; obscene; not modest or pure.—**Smuttily**, smut'i-li, *adv.* In a smutty manner.—**Smuttiness**, smut'i-nes, *n.* The state or quality of being smutty.

Smutch, smuch, *v.t.* [Closely allied to *smut*; same as Sw. *smuds*, Dan. *smuts*, G. *schmutz*, filth, dirt. *Smudge* is another form. SMUT.] To blacken with smoke, soot, or coal; to smudge.—*n.* A foul spot; a smudge; a black stain.

Snack, snak, *n.* [Lit. a 'snatch' or morsel hastily taken. SNATCH.] A portion of food that can be eaten hastily; a slight, hasty repast; a share, as in the phrase, *to go snacks*, that is, to have a share.

Snaffle, snaf'l, *n.* [Comp. D. *snavel*, a snout or animal's muzzle.] A bridle, consisting of a slender bit with a single rein and without a curb; a snaffle-bit.—**Snaffle-bit**, *n.* A plain, slender bit having a joint in the middle.

Snag, snag, *n.* [Comp. Icel. *snagi*, a small stake or peg.] A small projecting stump of a branch; a branch broken from a tree; the trunk of a large tree stuck by chance in a river with one end projecting so that steamboats, &c., are liable to strike on it.—*v.t.*—*snagged, snagging.* To trim by lopping branches; to injure by a snag.—**Snaggy**, snag'i, *a.* Full of snags; having short stumps.

Snail, snāl, *n.* [A.Sax. *snæl*, contr. from *snægel*, *snægl* = Icel. *snigill*, Dan. *snegl*; dim. forms from root of *snake, sneak*, the name signifying creeping animal.] A slimy, slow-creeping, air-breathing mollusc differing from the slugs chiefly in having a spiral shell, but the latter are also sometimes popularly called *snails*; a slow-moving person; a sluggard; a drone; a piece of spiral machinery; a piece of metal forming part of the striking work of a clock.—**Snail-clover, Snail-plant, Snail-trefoil**, *n.* A papilionaceous plant with snail-like pods.—**Snail-paced**, *a.* Moving very slowly.—**Snail-shell**, *n.* The spiral shell of the snail.

Snake, snāk, *n.* [A.Sax. *snaca*; Icel. *snákr, snókr*, Sw. *snok*, Dan. *song*. Akin *sneak, snail*.] A limbless reptile having an elongated body, some species having poison glands and certain upper teeth modified as fangs; a treacherous person, as *a snake in the grass*.—**Snake-moss**, *n.* Common club-moss.—**Snake-root**, *n.* The popular name of various American plants reputed to be remedies for snake bites.—**Snake-stone**, *n.* An ammonite; a stone popularly believed to cure snake bites.—**Snake-weed**, *n.* The plant bistort.—**Snake-wood**, *n.* A tree of the East Indies supposed to be a remedy for the bite of the cobra; also a tree of Demerara, so called from the heart-wood being mottled with irregularly shaped dark spots.—**Snakish**, snā'kish, *a.* Having a snake-like form, habits, or qualities; snaky.—**Snaky**, snā'ki, *a.* Pertaining to a snake or to snakes; resembling a snake; serpentine; winding; cunning; insinuating.

Snap, snap, *v.t.*—*snapped, snapping.* [Same as L.G. and D. *snappen*, Dan. *snappe*, G. *schnappen*, to snap. *Snip* is a lighter form, and *snipe* is connected, probably also *neb*.] To bite suddenly; to seize suddenly with the teeth; to snatch suddenly or unexpectedly; to break upon suddenly with sharp, angry words: often with *up*; to crack; to make a sharp sound with (to *snap* the fingers); to shut with a sharp sound; to break with a sharp sound; to break short.—*To snap off*, to break or bite off suddenly.—*v.i.* To make a sudden effort to bite; to aim to seize with the teeth (to *snap at* a person's hand); to accept promptly (to *snap at* a proposal); to break short; to part asunder suddenly; to give a sharp cracking sound, such as that of the hammer of a firearm when it descends without exploding the charge; to utter sharp, angry words.—*n.* A sudden, eager bite; a sudden breaking or rupture of any substance; a sharp cracking sound: the spring catch of a purse, bracelet, and the like; a crisp kind of gingerbread nut or small cake.—*A cold snap*, a sudden severe time of cold weather.—**Snapdragon**, *n.* An antirrhinum; a play in which raisins are snatched from burning brandy and put into the mouth.—**Snaplock**, *n.* A lock that shuts with a catch or snap.—**Snapper**, snap'ėr, *n.* One that snaps.—**Snapping-turtle**, *n.* A large freshwater tortoise of the United States, which readily snaps at things.—**Snappish**, snap'ish, *a.* Apt to snap or bite; apt to use sharp words; sharp in reply; tart; crabbed.—**Snappishly**, snap'ish-li, *adv.* In a snappish manner; angrily; tartly.—**Snappishness**, snap'ish-nes, n. The quality of being snappish.—**Snap-shot**, *n.* A photograph taken instantaneously.

Snare, snār, *n.* [A.Sax. *snear*, a snare, a noose; Icel. *snara*, Dan. *snare*, a snare, D. *snaar*, a string; from a root meaning to twist, seen also in L. *nervus*. NERVE.] A noose or set of nooses by which a bird or other living animal may be entangled; a gin; *fig.* something that serves to entangle or entrap a person.—*v.t.*—*snared, snaring.* To catch with a snare; to catch or take by guile.—**Snarer**, snā'rėr, *n.* One who lays snares or entangles.—**Snary**, snā'ri, *a.* Of the nature of a snare; entangling; insidious.

Snarl, snärl, *v.i.* [A freq. corresponding to old *snar*=L.G. and O.D. *snarren*, G. *schnarren*, to snarl; akin to *snore, snort*.] To growl, as an angry or surly dog; to talk in rude, murmuring terms.—**Snarler**, snär'lėr, *n.* One who snarls.—**Snarling**, snär'ling, *p.* and *a.* Growling; snappish.

Snarl, snärl, *v.t.* [A freq. from *snare*.] To entangle; to involve in knots.—*n.* A knot; a complication; embarrassing difficulty.

Snarl, snärl, *v.t.* To raise hollow ornamental work in narrow metal vases by blows on a special instrument introduced.

Snatch, snach, *v.t.* [Softened form of O. and Prov.E. *snack*, to snatch; D. and L.G. *snakken, snacken*, to snatch: probably a parallel form of *snap*.] To seize hastily or abruptly; to seize without permission or ceremony; to seize and transport away.—*v.i.* To attempt to seize suddenly; to snap or catch, to *snatch* at a thing).—*n.* A hasty catch or seizing; a catching at or attempt to seize suddenly; a small piece or fragment (a *snatch* of a song).—**Snatch-block**, *n.* A block used in ships, having an opening in one side to receive the bight of a rope.—**Snatcher**, snach'ėr, *n.* One that snatches or takes abruptly.—**Snatchingly**, snach'ing-li, *adv.* By snatching; hastily; abruptly.—**Snatchy**, snach'i, *a.* Consisting of snatches or small pieces.

Sneak, snēk, *v.i.* [A.Sax. *snican*, to creep, to sneak; Dan. *snige*, to creep. SNAKE.] To creep or steal privately; to go furtively, as if afraid or ashamed to be seen; to slink; to behave with meanness; to truckle.—*n.* A mean fellow; a cowardly, mean, underhand fellow.—**Sneaker**, snē'kėr, *n.* One who sneaks; a kind of punch-bowl.—**Sneaking, Sneaky**, snē'king, snē'ki, *a.* Pertaining to a sneak; acting like a sneak; mean; underhand.—**Sneakingly**, snē'king-li, *adv.* In a sneaking manner.—**Sneakingness, Sneakiness**, snē'king-nes, snē'ki-nes, *a.* The quality of being sneaking.

Sneck, snek, *n.* A latch or catch in a door.

Sneer, snēr, *v.i.* [Same as Dan. *snærre*, to snarl; allied to *snarl*.] To show contempt by turning up the nose, or by a particular cast of countenance; to insinuate contempt in words; to speak derisively.—*v.t.* To treat with sneers; to utter with a sneer.—*n.* A look of contempt or disdain; an expression of contemptuous scorn; indirect expression of contempt.—**Sneerer**, snē'rėr, *n.* One that sneers.—**Sneeringly**, snē'ring-li, *adv.* In a sneering manner.

Sneeze, snēz, *v.i.*—*sneezed, sneezing.* [Same as *neese* with *s* prefixed; or modified from A.Sax. *fneósan*, D. *fniezen*, to sneeze.] To emit air through the nose audibly and violently by a kind of involuntary convulsive force, occasioned by irritation of the inner membrane of the nose.—*To sneeze at*, to show contempt for; to scorn.—*n.* The act of one who sneezes.—**Sneeze-wood**, *n.* A valuable timber tree of Cape Colony the dust of which causes sneezing.—**Sneezewort**, snēz'wėrt, *n.* A British composite plant: so called because the dried flowers and roots, when powdered, cause sneezing.—**Sneezing**, snē'zing, *n.* The act of ejecting air violently and audibly through the nose by a sudden and involuntary effort; sternutation.

Snick, snik, *n.* [Icel. *snikka*, to cut or work with a knife; D. *snik*, a chisel.] A small cut or mark.—*v.t.* To cut; to clip.—**Snickersnee**, snik'ėr-snē, *n.* [Comp. D. *snee*, a cut.] A large clasp-knife.

Snicker, snik'ėr, *v.i.* [Imitative of the sound.] To giggle; to snigger.

Snider, Snider-rifle, snī'dėr, *n.* A form of breech-loading rifle, so called from its inventor.

Sniff, snif, *v.i.* [A lighter form of *snuff*.] To draw air audibly up the nose, sometimes as an expression of scorn; to snuff.—*v.t.* To draw in with the breath through the nose; to snuff; to smell.—*n.* The act of sniffing; the sound so produced: that which is taken by sniffing (a *sniff* of fresh air).

Snigger, snig'ėr, *v.i.* [SNICKER.] To snicker; to giggle.—*n.* A suppressed laugh; a giggle.

Snip, snip, *v.t.*—*snipped, snipping.* [Closely allied to *snap*, and same as D. and L.G. *snippen*, G. *schnippen, schnipfen*, to snip.] To cut off at once with shears or scissors; to clip; to shred.—*n.* A cut with shears or scissors; a bit cut off; a small shred.

Snipe, snīp, *n.* [Same as Icel. *snípa*, a snipe; D. *snip*, L.G. *snippe*, Dan. *sneppe*, G. *schnepfe*, a snipe; akin to *snap, neb*, or *nib*.] A grallatorial bird frequenting marshy grounds, with a long straight bill, allied to the woodcock; a fool; a blockhead; a simpleton.—*v.t.* or *i.* To pick or snip off men with the rifle in war.—*Sea snipe*, the dunlin.—*Summer snipe*, the sand-piper.—**Snipe-fish**, *n.* The bellows-fish.—**Sniper**, *n.* A soldier who, from some unsuspected place of concealment, picks off those of the enemy that expose themselves to his fire.

Snippet, snip'et, *n.* [Dim. of *snip*, a part.] A small part or share.—**Snippety**, snip'et-i, *a.* Insignificant.

Snite, snīt, *v.t.*—*snited, sniting.* [Icel. *snýta*, D. *snuiten*, to blow the nose; akin *snout*.] To flip, so as to strike off; to clean the nose.

Snivel, sniv'el, *v.i.*—*snivelled, snivelling.* [Akin to *sniff, snuff*.] To run at the nose; to cry or fret, as children, with snuffing or snivelling; to whimper.—**Sniveller**, sniv'el-ėr, *n.* One who snivels or whines; one who weeps for slight causes.—**Snivelling**, sniv'el-ing, *n.* The act or the noise of one who snivels.—**Snivelly**, sniv'el-i, *a.* Running at the nose; pitiful; whining.

Snob, snob, *n.* [Origin unknown.] One who snubs people; one who deliberately ignores those whom he considers his social or intellectual inferiors; a smug, self-complacent individual; a person who apes gentility.—**Snobbery, Snobbishness**, snob'ėr-i, snob'ish-nes, *n.* The quality of being snobbish.—**Snobbish, Snobby**, snob'ish, snob'i, *a.* Belonging to or resembling a snob; vulgarly ostentatious.—**Snobbishly**, snob'ish-li, *adv.* In the manner of a snob.—**Snobbism**, snob'izm, *n.* The manners of a snob; snobbishness.

Snood, snöd, *a.* [A.Sax. *snód*, a snood;

comp. Icel. *snúa*, to twist.] A fillet or ribbon for the hair.

Snooze, snöz, *n.* [Imitative of the sound made in drawing the breath while asleep, and allied to *snore.*] A nap or short sleep. —*v.i.*—*snoozed, snoozing.* To slumber; to take a short nap. [*Colloq.*]

Snore, snōr, *v.i.*—*snored, snoring.* [A.Sax. *snora*, a snoring; L.G. *snoren*, D. *snorken*, Dan. *snorke*, G. *schnarchen*, to snore; imitative and akin to *snarl, snort.*] To breathe with a rough hoarse noise in sleep.—*n.* A breathing with a harsh noise through the nose and mouth in sleep.—**Snorer**, snō′rėr, *n.* One that snores.

Snort, snort, *v.i.* [Akin to *snore*, D. *snorken.*] To force the air with violence through the nose, so as to make an abrupt noise.—*n.* A loud short sound produced by forcing the air through the nostrils.—**Snorter**, snor′tėr, *n.* One who snorts.

Snot, snot, *n.* [Same as Dan. and D. *snot*, snot; akin *snite, snout.*] Mucus discharged from or secreted in the nose; *metaphor.* a fool, a dolt, a sniveller.—**Snottily**, snot′i-li, *adv.* In a snotty manner.—**Snottiness**, snot′i-nes, *n.* The state of being snotty. — **Snotty**, snot′i, *a.* Foul with snot; dirty; sneering or sarcastic. (*Colloq.*)

Snout, snout, *n.* [Same as L.G. *snute*, Sw. *snut*, Dan. *snude*, D. *snuit*, G. *schnautze*, a snout. *Snite* and *snot* are closely akin.] The long projecting nose of a beast, as that of swine; the nozzle or end of a pipe.—**Snouted**, snout′ed, *a.* Having a snout.—**Snouty**, snout′i, *a.* Resembling a beast's snout.

Snow, snō, *n.* [A.Sax. *snáw*, snow = D. *sneeuw*, L.G. and Dan. *snee*, Sw. *snö*, Icel. *snjór* (also *snær*), G. *schnee*, Goth. *snaivs*; cog. L. *nix*, Gr. *niphas* (without initial *s*).] Watery particles congealed into white crystals in the air, and falling to the earth in flakes.—*Red snow.* PROTOCOCCUS.—*v.i.* To fall in snow: used chiefly impersonally (it *snows*, it *snowed*). —*v.t.* To scatter or cause to fall like snow.—**Snow-ball**, *n.* A ball of snow; a round mass of snow pressed or rolled together.—*v.t.* To pelt with snow-balls. — *v.i.* To throw snow-balls.—**Snow-berry**, *n.* A name of certain shrubs bearing fruits consisting of snow-white berries.—**Snow-bird**, *n.* The snow-bunting. — **Snow-blind**, *a.* Affected with snow-blindness. — **Snow-blindness**, *n.* An affection of the eyes caused by the reflection of light from the snow.—**Snow-blink, Snow-light**, *n.* The peculiar reflection that arises from fields of ice or snow.—**Snow-broth**, *n.* Snow and water mixed.—**Snow-bunting, Snow-fleck**, *n.* A bird belonging to the bunting family, a winter visitant to Britain and other temperate regions.—**Snow-drift**, *n.* A driving snow; a bank of snow driven together by the wind.—**Snow-drop**, snō′drop, *n.* A well-known garden plant, bearing solitary, drooping, and elegant white flowers, which appear very early in the year. —**Snow-eyes**, *n. pl.* A sort of goggles used by the Eskimos as a preventive to snow-blindness.—**Snow-field**, *n.* A wide expanse of permanent snow.—**Snow-flake**, *n.* A flake of falling snow.—**Snow-hut**, *n.* A hut built of snow; a snow-house used by Eskimos; an igloo.—**Snow-line**, *n.* The line above which mountains are covered with perpetual snow, varying according to latitude and local circumstances, being highest near the equator and lowest near the poles.—**Snow-plant**, *n.* Red snow; protococcus.— **Snow-plow**, *n.* An implement for clearing away the snow from roads, railways, &c., moved by horses or a locomotive engine.—**Snow-shoe**, *n* A kind of flat framework worn on the feet, made of wood alone, or consisting of a light frame crossed and recrossed by thongs, the broad surface thus presented keeping the wearer from sinking in the snow —**Snow-slide**, *n.* A large mass of snow which slips down the side of a mountain.—**Snow-storm**, *n* A storm with falling snow (when accompanied by a strong wind, called a blizzard) **Snow-water**, *n.* Water produced from the melting of snow.—**Snow-white**, *a.* White as snow; very white. — **Snow-wreath**, *n.* An accumulation of drifted snow of some considerable length and height. — **Snowy**, snō′i, *a.* White like snow; abounding with snow; covered with snow; white; pure; spotless; unblemished.

Snow, snō, *n.* [D. *snaauw*, a kind of boat.] A vessel with two masts resembling the main and fore masts of a ship, and a third small mast just abaft and close to the main-mast, carrying a try-sail.

Snub, snub, *v.t.*—*snubbed, snubbing.* [Same as older English *snib*; Icel. *snubba*, to snub, to chide, Dan. *snubbe*, to snap or snip off; akin to *snap, snip.*] To nip or check in growth‡; to check, stop, or rebuke with a tart sarcastic reply or remark; to slight designedly; to treat with contempt or neglect, as a forward or pretentious person. —*n.* A check; a rebuke. — **Snubbish**, snub′ish, *a.* Tending to snub, check, or repress.—**Snub-nose**, *n.* A short or flat nose.—**Snub-nosed**, *a.* Having a short, flat nose.

Snuff, snuf, *v.t.* [Same as D. *snuffen*, to snuff; *snuf*, a sniffing; akin Dan. *snöfte*, G. *schnupfen*, to snuff; akin *sniff, snivel, snuffle.*] To draw in with the breath; to inhale; to scent; to smell; to crop the snuff of, as of a candle.—*To snuff out*, to extinguish by snuffing.—*v.i.* To inhale air with noise, as dogs and horses; to snort or sniff; to sniff contemptuously. —*n.* An inhalation by the nose; a sniff; resentment; huff, expressed by a snuffing of the nose; a powdered preparation of tobacco inhaled through the nose; that part of a candle wick which has been charred by the flame. —**Snuff-box**, *n.* A box for carrying snuff about the person.—**Snuffer**, snuf′ėr, *n.* One that snuffs; *pl.* an instrument for removing the snuff of a candle. — **Snuff-taking**, *n.* The act or practice of inhaling snuff into the nose.—**Snuffy**, snuf′i, *a.* Resembling snuff in colour; soiled with snuff, or smelling of it.

Snuffle, snuf′l, *v.i.* — *snuffled, snuffling.* [Freq. of *snuff*, and = L.G. *snuffeln*, D. *snuffelen*, Sw. *snufla*, to snuffle. SNUFF.] To speak through the nose or with a nasal twang; to breathe hard through the nose. —*n.* A sound made by the passage of air through the nostrils; a speaking through the nose; an affected nasal twang.—**Snuffler**, snuf′l-ėr, *n.* One who snuffles.—**Snuffles**, snuf′lz, *n.pl.* Obstruction of the nose by mucus; a malady of dogs.

Snug, snug, *a.* [Same as Icel. *snöggr*, short-haired, smooth; O.Dan. *snog*, Sw. *snygg*, neat, elegant; akin perhaps to *snag.*] Lying close and comfortable; neat, trim, and convenient.—*v.i.* — *snugged, snugging.* To lie close; to snuggle.—*v.t.* To put in a snug position; to place snugly.—**Snuggery**, snug′ėri, *n.* A snug, warm habitation or comfortable place. (*Colloq.*)—**Snuggle**, snug′l, *v.i.*—*snuggled, snuggling.* [A freq. and dim. from *snug.*] To lie close for convenience or warmth; to nestle.—**Snugly**, snug′li, *adv.* In a snug manner; closely; comfortably. — **Snugness**, snug′nes. *n.* The state or quality of being snug.

So, sō, *adv.* [A.Sax. *swá*, so, as; Icel. *svá*, *svo, so*, Goth. *sva, sve*, L.G. and G. *so*, D. *zoo.* It appears in *as, also, whosoever*, &c.] In this or that manner; to that degree (*so* long); thus (he does it *so*); in like manner or degree: after *as* (*as* thou art *so* were they); in such a manner; to such a degree: with *as* or *that* following (*so* fortunate *as* to escape); colloquially, extremely, very (it is *so* beautiful); as has been said or stated (it is *so*, do *so*); the case being such; accordingly; well (*so* you are here again, are you?); somewhere about this or that; thereby (a year or *so*); in wishes and asseverations (*so* help me Heaven! that is, may Heaven so help me as I speak truth). —*So forth, so on*, more of the same or a similar kind; et cetera.—*So so*, indifferent; middling; mediocre (a very *so so* affair).—*So, so*, an exclamation implying discovery or observation of some effect; ay, ay; well, well.—*So that*, to the end that; in order that; with the purpose or intention that; with the effect or result that.—*So then*, thus then it is that; the consequence is; therefore.—*conj.* Provided that; on condition that; in case that.—*interj.* Enough! that will do!—**So-and-so**, sō′and-sō. A certain person not mentioned by name; an indefinite person or thing. (*Colloq.*)

Soak, sōk, *v.t.* [Probably akin to *suck.*] To let lie in a fluid in order to imbibe what it can contain; to macerate in water or other fluid; to steep; to drench; to wet thoroughly; to draw in by pores; to penetrate or permeate by pores. —*v.i.* To lie steeped in water or other fluid; to steep; to enter into pores or interstices; to drink intemperately; to tipple constantly. — **Soakage**, sō′kāj, *n.* Act of soaking; fluid imbibed.—**Soaker**, sō′kėr, *n.* One who soaks; a constant drinker.—**Soaking**, sō′king, *p.* and *a.* Steeping; macerating; wetting thoroughly. — *n.* A wetting; a drenching.

Soap, sōp, *n.* [A.Sax. *sápe*=Sw. *sopa*, L.G. *sepe*, O.H.G. *seifa*, from same root as L. *sebum*, tallow.] A chemical compound of potash and soda with fat, soluble in water, and used for detergent or cleansing purposes; flattery (*slang*).—*v.t.* To rub or wash over with soap; to flatter (*slang*).—**Soap-boiler**, *n.* One whose occupation is to make soap.—**Soap-boiling**, *n.* The business of boiling or manufacturing soap.—**Soap-bubble**, *n.* A thin film of soap-suds inflated by blowing through a pipe, and forming a hollow globe with beautiful iridescent colours. —**Soap-plant**, *n.* A name common to several plants used in place of soap, being capable of raising a lather. — **Soap-stone**, *n.* A species of steatite.—**Soap-suds**, *n.pl.* Suds; water well impregnated with soap.—**Soapwort**, sōp′wėrt, *n.* A perennial plant common in gardens, the stems of which, upon being put in water, form a lather like soap.—**Soapy**, sō′pi, *a.* Resembling soap; having the qualities of soap; smeared with soap; *fig.* flattering; unctuous; oily: said of persons, language, &c. (*colloq.*).

Soar, sōr, *v.i.* [Fr. *essorer*, from L.L. *exaurare*, to take to the air—L. *ex*, out, and *aura*, the air.] To fly aloft, as a bird; to mount upward on wings or as on wings; to mount intellectually; to rise above what is prosaic or commonplace, &c.; to be transported with a lofty imagination, desires, &c.—*n.* A towering flight; ascent.

Sob, sob, *v.i.*—*sobbed, sobbing.* [Akin to A.Sax. *seófian*, to sigh; G. *seufzen*, to sigh; E. *sough.*] To weep with convulsive catching of the breath.—*n.* A convulsive catching of the breath excited by mental emotion of a painful nature; a short convulsive sigh.

Sober, sō′bėr, *a.* [Fr. *sobre*, from L. *sobrius*, sober, from *se*, apart, and *ebrius*, drunken.] Temperate in the use of intoxicating liquors; abstemious; not intoxicated; not drunk; not wild, visionary, or heated with passion; having the regular exercise of cool, dispassionate reason; dispassionate; calm; serious; grave; not bright, gay, or brilliant in appearance; dull-looking.—*v.t.* To make sober; to cure of intoxication; to make temperate, calm, or solemn.—*v.i.* To become sober, staid, or sedate: often with *down.*—**Soberize**, sō′bėr-īz, *v.i.* To become sober. —*v.t.* To make sober. — **Soberly**, sō′bėr-li, *adv.* In a sober manner; temperately; moderately; calmly; seriously; gravely.—**Sober-minded**, *a.* Having a calm and temperate disposition.—**Soberness**, sō′bėr-nes, *n.* The state or quality of being sober; sobriety; temperance; calmness.—**Sobriety**, sō-brī′e-ti, *n.* [L. *sobrietas.*] Temperance in the use of intoxicating liquors; abstemiousness; moderation; freedom from the influence of strong drink; calmness; coolness; seriousness; gravity.

Soboles, sob′o-lēz, *n.* [L.] *Bot.* a creeping underground stem.—**Soboliferous**, sob-ō-lif′ėr-us, *a.* *Bot.* producing young plants from a creeping underground stem.

Sobranje, sō-bran′yā, *n.* The Bulgarian Parliament.

Sobriquet, so-brē-kā, *n.* [Fr.] A nickname; a fanciful appellation.

Socage, **Soccage**, sok'āj, *n.* [L.L. *socagium*, socage; lit. the tenure of one over whom his lord had a certain jurisdiction, from A.Sax. *sóc*, the privilege of holding a court in a district.] A tenure of land in medieval England by the performance of certain and determinate service.—**Socman**, sok'man, *n.* One who holds lands or tenements by socage.

Soccer, sok'ėr, *n.* The popular name for Association football.

Sociable, sō'shi-a-bl, *a.* [Fr. *sociable*, L. *sociabilis*, from *socio*, to associate or unite, from *socius*, a companion, from the root of L. *sequor*, to follow (whence E. *sequence*, &c.).] Inclined to associate or join in friendly intercourse; fond of companions; companionable; conversible; social. — *n.* An open carriage with seats facing each other; a tricycle for carrying two persons abreast; a couch with a curved S-shaped back for two persons, who sit partially facing each other.—**Sociability, Sociableness**, sō'-shi-a-bil''i-ti, sō'shi-a-bl-nes, *n.* The quality of being sociable.—**Sociably**, sō'shi-a-bli, *adv.* In a sociable manner; conversibly; familiarly.—**Social**, sō'shal, *a.* [Fr. *social*, from L. *socialis*, from *socius*.] Pertaining to society; relating to men living in society, or to the public as an aggregate body; ready to mix in friendly converse; sociable; consisting in union or mutual converse; *bot.* growing naturally in large groups or masses; *zool.* living in communities, as wolves, deer, wild cattle, &c.; or as ants, bees, &c., which form co-operative communities. — *Social science*, the science dealing with all that relates to the social condition, or the relations and institutions which are involved in man's existence and his well-being as a member of an organized community; sociology.—*The social evil*, a term frequently applied to prostitution.—**Socialism**, sō'-shal-izm, *n.* The name applied to theories of social organization having for their aim the abolition of that individual action on which modern societies depend, and the substitution of a regulated system of cooperative action; especially, a system in which the government owns and controls the means of production and distribution. —**Socialist**, sō'shal-ist, *n.* One who advocates socialism.—**Socialite**, so'shal-īt, *n.* A man or woman well known in social circles. [*Colloq.*]—**Sociality, Socialness**, sō-shi-al'i-ti, sō'shal-nes, *n.* The quality of being social.—**Socialize**, sō'shal-īz, *v.t.*—*socialized, socializing.* To render social; to regulate according to socialism.—**Socially**, sō'shal-li, *adv.* In a social manner or way.—**Societarian, Societary**,† sō-sī'e-tā''ri-an, sō-sī'e-ta-ri, *n.* Pertaining to society.—**Society**, sō-sī'e-ti, *n.* [Fr. *société*, L. *societas*.] The relationship of men to one another when associated; companionship; fellowship; company; a body of persons united for the promotion of some object, either literary, scientific, political, religious, benevolent, convivial, or the like; an association for mutual profit, pleasure, or usefulness: the persons collectively who live in any region or at any period, viewed in regard to their manners and customs, civilization, moral or material condition; those who recognize each other as associates, friends, and acquaintances; the more cultivated portion of any community in its social relations and influences; those who give and receive formal entertainments mutually: used without the article.—*Society journal* or *newspaper*, a journal whose main object is to chronicle the sayings and doings of fashionable society.—*Society verses*, verses for the amusement of polite society; poetry of a light, entertaining, polished character.

Socinian, sō-sin'i-an, *a.* [From Lælius and Faustus *Socinus*, uncle and nephew, natives of Sienna, in Tuscany, the founders of the sect of Socinians in the sixteenth century.] Pertaining to Lælius or Faustus Socinus or their religious creed. — *n.* A follower of Socinus.—**Socinianism**, sō-sin'i-an-izm, *n.* The tenets of the Socinians; a belief akin to Unitarianism, rejecting the doctrine of the Trinity, the deity of Christ, the personality of the devil, and eternity of future punishment.

Sociology, sō-shi-ol'o-ji, *n.* [L. *socius*, a companion, and Gr. *logos*, discourse. SOCIABLE.] The science which investigates the laws that regulate human society in all its grades; the science which treats of the general structure of society, the laws of its development, and the progress of civilization. — **Sociologic, Sociological**, sō'shi-ō-loj''ik, sō'shi-ō-loj''i-kal, *a.* Pertaining to sociology. — **Sociologist**, sō-shi-ol'o-jist, *n.* One who treats of or devotes himself to the study of sociology.

Sock, sok, *n.* [A Sax. *socc*, from L. *soccus*, a kind of low-heeled shoe, especially worn by comic actors.] A knitted or woven covering for the foot, shorter than a stocking; the shoe worn by the ancient actors of comedy; hence, *the sock*, comedy in distinction from tragedy, which is symbolized by the buskin.—*v.t.* To strike violently, usually as with the fist, or with a bat in a game of baseball, as to *sock* the ball for a home run.

Socket, sok'et, *n.* [From *sock*, a shoe.] An opening or cavity into which anything is fitted endwise; a hollow which receives and holds something else (the *sockets* of the teeth or of the eyes).

Socle, sō'kl, *n.* [Fr. *socle*, *L. socculus*, dim. of *soccus*. SOCK.] *Arch.* a plain, low pedestal; also, a plain face or plinth at the lower part of a wall.

Socman. Under SOCAGE.

Socratic, Socratical, sō-krat'ik, sō-krat'-i-kal, *a.* Pertaining to *Socrates* the Grecian sage, or to his language or manner of teaching and philosophizing; reaching conclusions by means of question and answer.—**Socratically**, sō-krat'i-kal-li, *adv.* In the Socratic manner.—**Socratism**, sok'-rat-izm, *n.* The doctrines of Socrates.—**Socratist**, sok'rat-ist, *n.* A disciple of Socrates.

Sod, sod, *n.* [Same as L.G. and O.D. *sode*, D. *zode*.] The surface layer of the ground with the grass growing on it; a piece lifted from that surface; turf; sward.

Sod, sod, pret. and pp. of *seethe*.

Soda, sō'da, *n.* [Sp. Pg. and It. *soda*, glasswort, barilla.] A name for various compounds of sodium, as the oxide and hydroxide; popularly, *sodium carbonate* (*soda crystals* or *washing soda*), used in washing and in the manufacture of soap and glass, and extensively made from salt.—*Baking soda*, bicarbonate of soda.—*Caustic soda*, sodium hydroxide, having a corrosive effect on animal substances.—*Sulphate of soda*, glauber-salts.—**Soda fountain**, *n.* A store fixture so equipped as to serve ice cream, soft drinks, and generally light luncheons. —**Soda-water**, *n.* A refreshing and effervescent drink generally consisting of ordinary water into which carbonic acid has been forced under pressure.—**Sodium**, sō'di-um, *n.* [Named from its oxide *soda*.] A soft light silvery metallic element, of which soda is the oxide; never found in the uncombined state in nature, but existing in many minerals and in almost all vegetable and animal organisms. —**Sodium carbonate**, *n.* Salt of soda.

Sodality, sō-dal'i-ti, *n.* [L. *sodalitas*, from *sodalis*, a companion.] A fellowship or fraternity.

Sodden, sod'n, pp. of *seethe*. Boiled; seethed; soaked and softened, as in water; thoroughly saturated; not well baked; doughy.

Sodomite, sod'om-īt, *n.* An inhabitant of Sodom; one guilty of sodomy.—**Sodomitical**, sod-om-it'i-kal, *a.* Relating to sodomy. — **Sodomitically**, sod-om-it'i-kal-li, *adv.*—**Sodomy**, sod'omi, *n.* The sin attributed to the inhabitants of Sodom; a carnal copulation against nature.

Soever, sō-ev'ėr. A word compounded of *so* and *ever*: generally used in composition to extend or render emphatic the sense of such words as *who, what*, &c., in *whosoever, whatsoever*, &c., from which it is sometimes separated.

Sofa, sō'fa, *n.* [Fr. and Sp. *sofa*, a sofa, from Ar. *soffah*, a bench before a house.] A piece of upholstered furniture generally accommodating three or more people.—*Convertible sofa*, a sofa which may be converted into a bed.

Soffit, sof'it, *n.* [Fr. *soffite*, It. *soffitta*, from L. *sub*, under, and *figo*, to fasten.] *Arch.* the lower surface of an arch or of an architrave; the under part of an overhanging cornice, of a projecting balcony, &c.

Sofi, sō'fi, *n.* [Per.] A dervish.

Soft, soft, *a.* [A.Sax. *sófte*, softly; O.Sax. *saft*, O.D. *saeft*, *saft*; G. *sanft*, soft.] Easily yielding to pressure; easily impressible; yielding: the contrary of *hard*; not rough, rude, or violent; affecting the senses in a pleasant manner; delicate or pleasing to the touch; gentle or melodious to the ear; not glaring; not repelling or striking to the sight; easily yielding to persuasion or motives; facile, weak; not harsh, severe, or unfeeling; gentle; easily moved by pity; susceptible of tender affections; effeminate; not manly or courageous; foolish; simple; silly; quiet and refreshing (*soft* slumbers); readily forming a lather and washing well with soap (*soft* water); pronounced with more or less of a sibilant sound, as *c* in *cinder*, as opposed to *c* in *candle*; and *g* in *gin*, as opposed to *g* in *gift*.—*Soft goods*, textile goods; the wares of a draper or haberdasher.—*Soft palate*, that part of the palate which lies in the posterior part of the mouth.—*The softer sex*, the female sex. —*Soft soap*, a coarse kind of soap in a viscid form; as a *slang term*, flattery, blarney.—*adv.* Softly; gently; quietly.—*interj.* Be soft; hold; stop; not so fast.—**Soften**, sof'n, *v.t.* To make soft or more soft; to make less hard; to mollify; to make less implacable or angry; to make less severe, harsh, or strong in language; to alleviate; to tone down.—*v.i.* To become soft or less hard; to become less harsh or cruel; to become milder. — **Softener**, sof'n-ėr, *n.* One who or that which softens.—**Softening**, sof'n-ing, *n.* The act of making soft or softer.—*Softening of the brain*, an affection of the brain, in which it becomes pulpy or pasty, often causing death. — **Soft-headed**, *a.* Of weak or feeble intellect.—**Soft-hearted**, *a.* Having tenderness of heart.—**Soft-heartedness**, *n.* The quality of being soft-hearted.—**Softish**, sof'-tish, *a.* Somewhat soft; inclining to softness. — **Softly**, soft'li, *adv.* In a soft manner; not with force or violence; gently; not loudly; mildly; tenderly.—**Softness**, soft'nes, *n.* The quality of being soft; the opposite of *hardness*; penetrability; susceptibility of tender feeling; weakness of mind or will; mildness; gentleness.—**Soft-spoken**, *a.* Speaking softly; having a mild or gentle voice; mild; affable.

Softa, sof'ta, *n.* [Turk.] In Turkey, a person studying for the church, the law, the army, or the state; a student of the Koran.

Soho, sō'hō, *interj.* A word used in calling from a distant place.

Soi-disant, swą-dē-ząṅ, *a.* [Fr.] Calling himself; self-styled; pretended; would be.

Soil, soil, *v.t.* [O.Fr. *soillier* (Fr. *souiller*), to soil, lit. to act the pig, from L. *suillus*, pertaining to a swine, from *sus*, a swine. Sow, *n.*] To make dirty on the surface; to dirty; to defile; to tarnish; to sully; to dung; to manure.—*v.i.* To take on dirt; to take a soil or stain; to tarnish.—*n.* Foul matter upon another surface; stain; tarnish; defilement or taint.—**Soil-pipe**, *n.* A pipe for conveying from a house the foul or waste water, night-soil, &c.

Soil, soil, *n.* [O.Fr. *soil*, *soile* (Fr. *sol*), from L. *solum*, the soil. SOLID.] The upper stratum of the earth's crust; the mould, or that compound substance which furnishes nutriment to plants; earth; ground; land; country.

Soil, soil, *v.t.* [O.Fr. *saouler*, to satiate, from *saoul*, L. *satullus*, sated, dim. of *satur*, sated, full. SATURATE.] To feed (cattle or horses) in the house with fresh grass or green fodder instead of putting out to pasture.

Soirée, swa̤'rā, *n.* [Fr. *soirée*, evening, an evening party, from *soir*, evening, from L. *serus*, late.] Originally, an evening party; now usually a reunion or social meeting of some society or body, at which tea and other refreshments are introduced during the intervals of music, speech-making, &c.

Soixante-quinze, swa-sänt-kănz. [Fr.] The French field-gun of 75 mm. calibre.

Sojourn, sō-jėrn', sō'jėrn, *v.t.* [O.Fr. *sojorner*, from L. *sub*, under, and *diurnus*, diurnal. DIURNAL, DIARY.] To dwell for a time; to dwell as a temporary resident, or as a stranger, not considering the place a permanent habitation.—sō'jėrn, so-jėrn' —*n.* A temporary residence, as that of a traveler in a foreign land.—**Sojourner**, sō-jėrn'ėr, *n.*

Sol, sōl, *n.* *Music*, the fifth tone of the diatonic scale.

Sol, sol, *n.* [From *sol*ution.] A colloidal solution, composed of a liquid solvent and a liquid or very finely divided solid therein.

Sol, sol, *n.* [L.] The sun.

Sol, sol, *n.* A French coin no longer in use.

Sol, sōl, *n.* A Peruvian coin worth 28 cents.

Solace, sol'ās, *v.t.*—*solaced, solacing.* [O.Fr. *solace, solaz*, from L. *solatium*, from *solor, solatus*, to solace (seen in *console, disconsolate*).] To cheer in grief or under calamity; to relieve in affliction; to console; to comfort; to allay or assuage.—*n.* Comfort in grief; alleviation of grief or anxiety; what relieves in distress; recreation.—**Solacement**, sol'ās-ment, *n.* Act of solacing.

Solanaceous, sō-la-nā'shus, *a.* [L. *solanum*, nightshade.] Pertaining to plants of the nightshade family, which includes also the potato and tobacco.—**Solanine**, sō'la-nin, *n.* An alkaloid obtained from nightshade and allied plants, very bitter and highly poisonous.

Solander, sō-lan'dėr, *n.* [Fr. *soulandres.*] A disease in horses.

Solan-goose, sō'lan, *n.* [Icel. *súlan*, the gannet.] The gannet.

Solano, sō-lä'nō, *n.* [Sp., from L. *solanus* (*ventus*), easterly wind, from *sol*, the sun.] A hot oppressive south-east wind in Spain.

Solar, sō'lėr, *a.* [L. *solaris*, from *sol*, the sun; cog. Icel. *sól*, Goth. *sauil*, Ir. *sul*, the sun.] Pertaining to the sun; proceeding from, or produced by the sun; measured by the progress of the sun, or by its apparent revolution.—*Solar cycle*, a period of twenty-eight years. CYCLE.—*Solar day.* DAY.—*Solar flowers*, those which open and shut daily at certain determinate hours.—*Solar microscope*, a microscope in which the object is illuminated by the light of the sun concentrated upon it.—*Solar month*, the space of time in which the sun passes through one sign, or a twelfth part of the zodiac: 30 days, 10 hours, 29 minutes, 5 seconds.—*Solar spectrum*, the spectrum of sunlight.—*Solar spots*, dark spots that appear on the sun's disc, sometimes so large as to be seen by the naked eye, very changeable in their number, figure, and dimensions.—*Solar system*, the system of which the sun is the centre, and to which belong the planets, planetoids, satellites, comets, and meteorites, all directly or indirectly revolving round the central sun.—*Solar telegraph*, a telegraph in which the rays of the sun are projected from and upon mirrors.—*Solar time*, time as shown by a sun-dial, that is by the apparent motion of the sun.—*Solar year*, the time which the earth takes to go round the sun, 365 days, 5 hours, 48 minutes, 46 seconds.—*Arch.* a loft or upper room.

Solarium, sō-lâr'i-um, *n.* [L.] A room for the treatment of patients by exposure to the sun.

Solatium, sō-lā'shi-um, *n.* [L., consolation, solace. SOLACE.] Anything that alleviates or compensates for suffering or loss; a compensation in money.

Sold, sōld, pret. and pp. of *sell.*

Soldan,‡ sol'dan, *n.* A sultan.

Solder, sod'ėr, *v.t.* [O.Fr. *solder, solider* (Fr. *souder*); lit. to make solid, from L. *solidus*, solid. SOLID.] To unite by a metallic substance in a state of fusion, which hardens in cooling, and renders the joint solid: *fig.* to unite or combine in general; to patch up.—*n.* A metal or metallic composition used in uniting other metallic substances by being fused between them. *Hard solders* are such as require a red heat to fuse them. *Soft solders* melt at a comparatively low temperature.—**Solderer**, sod'ėr-ėr, *n.* One who solders.—**Soldering**, sod'ėr-ing, *n.* The act of one who solders.—**Soldering bolt**, **Soldering iron**, *n.* A tool consisting of a piece of copper with a handle, the copper being heated and used to melt the solder.

Soldier, sōl'jėr, *n.* [O.Fr. *soldier*, from L.L. *soldarius, solidarius*, from L. *soldus, solidus*, military pay; lit. a solid piece of money. SOLID.] A man who serves in an army; a common soldier or private; a man of military experience and skill, or a man of distinguished valour.—**Soldier-crab**, *n.* A name given to the hermit-crab, from its extreme combativeness.—**Soldiering**, sōl'jėr-ing, *n.* The occupation of a soldier.—**Soldierlike**, **Soldierly**, sōl'jėr-līk, sōl'jėr-li, *a.* Like or becoming a soldier; brave; martial; honourable.—**Soldiership**, sōl'jėr-ship, *n.* Military qualities or character; martial skill.—**Soldiery**, sōl'jėr-i, *n.* Soldiers collectively; a body of military men.

Sole, sōl, *n.* [Fr. *sole*, the sole of the foot, of a shoe, &c., the fish, from L. *solea*, a sandal, a sole, the fish, a sill, same origin as *solidus*, solid. SOLID, SOIL, *n.*] The under side of the foot; the bottom surface of a shoe or boot, or the piece of leather which constitutes the bottom; the part of anything that forms the bottom, and on which it stands; a marine fish belonging to the family of flat fishes, of an oblong form, probably so called from its shape.—*v.t.*—*soled, soling.* To furnish with a sole (to *sole* a shoe).—**Sole-leather**, *n.* Thick strong leather used for the soles of shoes.

Sole, sōl, *a.* [From L. *solus*, alone; which is of same origin as L. *salvus*, safe (whence *safe, salvation*), Gr. *holos*, entire, Skr. *sarva*, the whole. Akin *solitary, solitude, solemn, solid.*] Single; being or acting without another; alone in its kind; individual; *law*, single; unmarried (a femme *sole*).—**Solely**, sōl'li, *adv.* Singly; alone; only; without another.—**Soleness**, sōl'nes, *n.* The state of being sole; singleness.

Solecism, sol'e-sizm, *n.* [Gr. *soloikismos* from *Soloi*, in Cilicia, the Athenian colonists of which lost the purity of their language.] An impropriety in the use of language, arising from ignorance; a gross deviation from the idiom of a language, or a gross deviation from the rules of syntax; a violation of the rules of society.—**Solecist**, sol'e-sist, *n.* One who is guilty of a solecism.—**Solecistic**, **Solecistical**, sol-e-sis'tik, sol-e-sis'ti-kal, *a.* Pertaining to or involving a solecism.—**Solecistically**, sol-e-sis'ti-kal-li, *adv.*—**Solecize**, sol'e-sīz, *v.i.* To commit solecisms.

Solemn, sol'em, *a.* [L. *sollemnis, sollennis*, that occurs every year, festal, solemn—*sollus*, all, every, and *annus*, a year. SOLID.] Marked by religious rites or ceremonious observances; fitted to excite reverent or serious reflections; awe-inspiring; grave; impressive (a *solemn* silence); accompanied by seriousness or impressiveness in language or demeanour; earnest (a *solemn* promise); affectedly grave.—**Solemness**, sol'em-nes, *n.* The state or quality of being solemn; solemnity.—**Solemnity**, so-lem'ni-ti, *n.* The state or quality of being solemn; gravity; impressiveness; mock gravity; a solemn or reverent rite or ceremony; a proceeding adapted to impress awe or reverence.—**Solemnization**, sol'em-nī-zā"shon, *n.* The act of solemnizing, celebration.—**Solemnize**, sol'em-nīz, *v.t.* —*solemnized, solemnizing.* [O.Fr. *solemniser.*] To dignify or honour by ceremonies; to celebrate; to perform with ritual ceremonies or according to legal forms: used especially of marriage; to make grave, serious, and reverential.—**Solemnizer**, sol'em-nī-zėr, *n.* One who solemnizes.—**Solemnly**, sol'em-li, *adv.* In a solemn manner; with religious ceremonies; with impressive seriousness; with all due form.

Solen, sō'len, *n.* [Gr. *sōlēn*, a tube, the solen.] A genus of lamellibranchiate molluscs which burrow in the sand and have long bivalve shells.

Solenette, sōl-net', *n.* [Dim. of *sole.*] A small British fish allied to the sole.

Solenoid, sōl'en-oid, *n.* [Gr. *sōlēn*, channel.] A coil of wire wound in the form of a helix, which, when traversed by an electric current, acts like a magnet.

Solert, sol'ėrt, *a.* [L. *solers, solertis.*] Crafty; subtle.

Soleus, sō'lē-us, *n.* [L., from *solea*, a sole.] A muscle of the leg which serves to extend the foot, shaped like the sole-fish.

Sol-fa, sōl'fä, *v.i.* In *music*, to sing the notes of the scale in their proper pitch, using the syllables *do* (or *ut*), *re, mi, fa, sol, la, si.*—*v.t.* To sing to the syllables, *do, re, mi, fa, sol, la, si*, instead of to words.

Solfatara, sol-fä-tä'rä, *n.* [It., name of a volcano near Naples.] A volcanic vent emitting sulphureous, muriatic, and acid vapours or gases.

Solfeggio, sol-fej'i-ō, *n.* [It.] In *music*, a system of arranging the scale by the names *do* (or *ut*), *re, mi, fa, sol, la, si*; an exercise in scale singing; solmization.

Solferino, sol'fer-ī-nō, *n.* A red or purple colour made from rosaniline, discovered in 1859, the year of the battle of Solferino. MAGENTA.

Solicit, sō-lis'it, *v.t.* [Fr. *solliciter*, L. *sollicitare*, from *sollicitus*, solicitous, from *sollus*, whole, and *cieo, citum*, to agitate. SOLID, CITE.] To ask from with some degree of earnestness; to make petition to; to ask for with some degree of earnestness; to seek by petition; to awake or excite to action; to invite; to disturb or disquiet; to make anxious; *law*, to incite to commit a felony; to endeavor to influence by a bribe.—*v.t.* To make solicitation for some one or for a thing.—**Solicitant**, sō-lis'i-tant, *n.* One who solicits.—**Solicitation**, sō-lis'i-tā"shon, *n.* The act of soliciting; an earnest request; endeavor to influence to grant something by bribery; the offense of inciting a person to commit a felony.—**Solicitor**, sō-lis'i-tėr, *n.* One who solicits; an attorney; a law-agent; one who represents another in court.—**Solicitor general**, *n.* A law officer in the U. S. government, next in rank to the attorney-general, with whom he is associated in the management of the legal business of the nation.—**Solicitorship**, sō-lis'i-tėr-ship, *n.* The office of a solicitor.—**Solicitous**, sō-lis'i-tus, *a.* [L *sollicitus*, anxious, uneasy.] Anxious; concerned; apprehensive; disturbed; restless.—**Solicitously**, sō-lis'i-tus-li, *adv.* Anxiously; with care and concern.—**Solicitousness**, sō-lis'i-tus-nes, *n.*—**Solicitude**, sō-lis'i-tūd, *n.* The state of being solicitous; uneasiness of mind occasioned by fear of evil or desire for good; concern; anxiety. .: Syn. under CARE.

Solid, sol'id, *a.* [Fr. *solide*, from L. *solidus*, solid, firm, compact, from same root as *solum*, the soil (E. *soil*), *sollus*, whole (whence the *sol-* in *solicit, solemn*), *salvus*, safe (E. *safe*).] Possessing the property of excluding all other bodies from the space occupied by itself; impenetrable; firm; compact; opposed to *liquid* and *gaseous*; not hollow; full of matter; having all the geometrical dimensions—length, breadth, and thickness; cubic (a *solid* foot); strong; sound; substantial, as opposed to frivolous, fallacious, or the like; real; valid; financially sound or safe.—*Solid angle*, an angle formed by several planes or other surfaces meeting at one point; measured by the area intercepted on a sphere of unit radius with the point as centre.—*Solid square*, a square body of troops; a body in which the ranks and files are equal.—*n.* A firm compact body with the particles firmly cohering, and thus distinguished from a *liquid* or a *gas*, whose particles yield to the slightest impression; *geom.* a body or magnitude which has three dimensions — length, breadth, and thickness. — *Regular solids*, those which are bounded by equal and regular planes.—**Solidifiable**, so-lid'i-fī-a-bl, *a.* Capable of being solidified.—**Solidification**, so-lid'i-fi-kā"shon, *n.* The act or process of making solid; the passage of bodies from the liquid or gaseous to the solid state.—**Solidify**, so-lid'i-fī, *v.t.—solidified, solidifying.* [L. *solidus*, solid, and *facio*, to make.] To make solid or compact, to cause to change from a liquid or a gas to a solid.—*v.i.* To become solid or compact. —**Solidity**, so-lid'i-ti, *n.* [Fr. *solidité*, L. *soliditas*.] The state or quality of being solid; firmness; density; compactness; opposed to *fluidity*; strength or stability; massiveness; soundness; strength or validity as opposed to *weakness* or *fallaciousness*; the quantity of space occupied by a solid body; cubic content.—**Solidly**, sol'id-li, *adv.* In a solid manner; firmly; compactly; on firm grounds.—**Solidness**, sol'-id-nes, *n.* Solidity.

Solidarity, sol-i-dar'i-ti, *n.* [Fr. *solidarité*, from *solide*, solid.] Unity or communion of interests and responsibilities among nations or mankind in general.

Solidungulate, **Solidungulous**, sol-id-ung'gū-lāt, sol-id-ung'gū-lus, *a.* [L. *solidus*, solid, and *ungula*, a hoof.] Having hoofs that are whole or not cloven, as the horse, ass, zebra.—**Solidus**, an oblique stroke /, an abbreviation for *shilling*, also used in fractions, as 2/3 for ⅔.

Solifidian, sol-i-fid'i-an, *n.* [L. *solus*, alone, and *fides*, faith.] One who maintains that faith alone, without works, is necessary to justification.

Soliloquy, sō-lil'ō-kwi, *n.* [L. *soliloquium* —*solus*, alone, and *loquor*, to speak. SOLE, LOQUACIOUS.] A talking to one's self; a monologue; a discourse not addressed to any person. — **Soliloquize**, sō-lil'ō-kwīz, *v.i.—soliloquized, soliloquizing.* To utter a soliloquy; to talk to one's self.

Soliped, **Solipede**, sol'i-ped, sol'i-pēd, *n.* [L. *solus*, single, and *pes*, a foot.] An animal whose hoof is not cloven; a solidungulate.—**Solipedal**, **Solipedous**, so-lip'e-dal, so-lip'e-dus, *a.* Solidungular.

Solisequious, sō-li-sē'kwi-us, *a.* [L. *sol*, *solis*, the sun, and *sequor*, to follow.] Following the course of the sun.

Solitaire, sol'i-tār, *n.* [Fr. *solitaire*, from L. *solitarius*. SOLITARY.] An article of jewelry in which a single gem is set; a game for a single person played on a board indented with thirty-three or thirty-seven hemispherical hollows and an equal number of balls; a card game which one can play alone.

Solitary, sol'i-ta-ri, *a.* [Fr. *solitaire*; L. *solitarius*, from *solus*, alone (whence *sole*). SOLE, *a.*] Being or living alone; being by one's self; not much visited or frequented; retired; lonely (a *solitary* residence); passed without company; shared by no companions (a *solitary* life); single; individual (a *solitary* example).—*n.* One that lives alone or in solitude; a hermit; a recluse.—**Solitarily**, sol'i-ta-ri-li, *adv.* In a solitary manner; alone. — **Solitariness**, sol'i-ta-ri-nes, *n.* The state of being solitary or apart from others; the state of not being frequented; loneliness.

Solitude, sol'i-tūd, *n.* [Fr. *solitude*, from L. *solitudo*, from *solus*, alone. SOLITARY.] A state of being alone; loneliness; remoteness from society; destitution of inhabitants; a lonely place; a desert.

Sollar, sol'ėr, *n.* [L. *solarium*. SOLAR.] A loft or garret; the entrance to a mine.

Solmization, **Solmisation**, sol-mī-zā'-shon, *n.* [From the syllables *sol*, *mi*.] *Mus.* the act or art of giving to each of the seven notes of the scale its proper sound or relative pitch; solfeggio.

Solo, sō'lō, *n.* It. pl. **Soli**, sō'lē, Eng. pl. **Solos**, sō'lōz. [It., from L. *solus*, alone.] A tune, air, or strain to be played by a single instrument or sung by a single voice without or with an accompaniment.—**Solo flight**, sō'lō-flīt', *n.* An airplane trip made by a lone pilot.

Solstice, sol'stis, *n.* [From L. *solstitium*—*sol*, the sun, *sto*, to stand. SOLAR, STATE.] The time of the year at which, owing to the annual revolution of the earth, the sun is at its greatest distance north or south from the equator, and begins to turn back, which happens at midsummer and midwinter, or 21st June and 22nd December; either of the two points in the ecliptic at which the sun appears to be at these dates.—**Solstitial**, sol-stish'al, *a.* Pertaining to solstice; happening at a solstice.—*Solstitial points*, the two points in the ecliptic at which the sun arrives at the time of the solstices.—*Solstitial colure*, a great circle supposed to pass through the solstitial points.

Soluble, sol'ū-bl, *a.* [L. *solubilis*, from *solvo*, to melt. SOLVE.] Susceptible of being dissolved in a fluid; capable of solution; *fig.* capable of being solved or resolved, as a mathematical problem; capable of being cleared up or settled by explanation, as a doubt, question, &c.—**Solubility**, sol-ū-bil'i-ti, *n.* The quality of being soluble; susceptibility of being dissolved in a fluid; capability of being solved or cleared up.—**Solubleness**, sol'ū-bl-nes, *n.* The state or character of being soluble; solubility.

Solus, sō'lus, *a.* [L.] Alone: chiefly used in dramatic directions and the like (enter the king *solus*).

Solute, sol'ūt, *n.* [L. *solutio*, from *solvo*, to melt, dissolve. SOLVE.] A dissolved substance.—**Solution**, sō-lū'shon, *n.* The act of dissolving or state of being dissolved; the conversion of solid matter into liquid by means of a liquid (called the solvent); the combination of a liquid with a liquid or a gas to form a homogeneous liquid; the liquid thus produced; the preparation made by dissolving a solid in a liquid; the act of solving, clearing up, or explaining, explanation; *math.* the method of resolving a problem; *med.* the termination or the crisis of a disease. — *Chemical solution*, a perfect chemical union of a solid with a liquid.—*Mechanical solution*, the mere union of a solid with a liquid, without any alteration of the chemical properties of either.—*Solution of continuity*, a breach of continuity; a breach or rupture in a material substance.

Solutrean, solūt'ri-an, *a.* [From the *Solutré* cave, in France.] A culture stage of the upper Palæolithic age, after the Aurignacian, and before the Magdalenian.

Solvay process, sol'vā. [From *E. Solvay*, Belgian chemist.] A process for the manufacture of sodium carbonate, by the interaction of common salt, ammonia, and carbon dioxide.

Solve, solv, *v.t.—solved, solving.* [L. *solvo*, *solutum*, to loosen, release, solve, for *se-luo*, from *se*, apart, and *luo*, to loosen; *solvo* is seen also in *absolve*, *dissolve*, *resolve*, *soluble*, *dissolute*, *resolute*, &c.] To explain or clear up the difficulties in; to make clear; to remove perplexity regarding; to operate upon by calculation or mathematical processes so as to bring out the required result (to *solve* a problem).—**Solvency**, sol'ven-si, *n.* The state of being solvent; ability to pay all debts or just claims.—**Solvent**, sol'vent, *a.* [L. *solvens*, *solventis*, ppr. of *solvo*.] Having the power of dissolving; able to pay all just debts.—*n.* Any fluid or substance that dissolves or renders liquid other bodies; a menstruum.—**Solver**, sol'-vėr, *n.* One who or that which solves.—**Solvable**, sol'va-bl, *a.* Capable of being solved. — **Solvability**, sol-va-bil'i-ti, *n.* Capability of being solved.—**Solvableness**, sol'va-bl-nes, *n.*

Soma, sō'ma, *n.* A plant, and an intoxicating drink obtained from it, which played an important part in the great Vedic sacrifices of the ancient Hindus.

Soma, sō'ma, *n.* [Gr. for *body*.] The body of a plant or animal exclusive of the germ cells.—**Somatic**, **Somatical**, sō-mat'ik, sō-mat'ikal, *a.* [Gr. *sōmatikos*, from *sōma*, *sōmatos*, the body.] Corporeal; pertaining to a body.—**Somatics**, sō-mat'iks, *n.* Same as *Somatology*.—**Somatic variation**, *n.* Variation of the soma.—**Somatist**, sō'-mat-ist, *n.* One who denies the existence of spiritual substances; a materialist.—**Somatology**, sō-ma-tol'o-ji, *n.* The doctrine of bodies or material substances; that branch of physics which treats of matter and its properties. — **Somatome**, sō'ma-tōm, *n.* [Gr. *sōma*, and *tomē*, a cutting.] One of the sections into which an animal body is, or may be regarded as, divided.—**Somatoplasm**, sō-ma'tō-plasm, *n.* [Gr. *plasma*, something formed.] The protoplasm of the soma.

Somber, som'bėr, *a.* [Fr. *sombre*, somber; Sp. and Pg. *sombra*, a shade; from L. *sub*, under, and *umbra*, a shade. UMBRAGE.] Dark in hue or aspect; dusky; gloomy; dismal; melancholy.—*v.t.* To make somber, dark, or gloomy; to shade.—**Somberly**, som'bėr-li, *adv.* In a somber manner; darkly; gloomily.—**Somberness**, som'-bėr-nes, *n.* State or quality of being somber; gloominess.—**Sombrous**, som'brus, *a.* Somber.—**Sombrously**, som'brus-li, *adv.* Somberly.—**Sombrousness**, *n.*

Sombrero, som-brer'ō, *n.* [Sp. from *sombra*, a shade. SOMBRE.] A broad-brimmed hat.

Some, sum, *a.* [A.Sax. *sum*, some, one, a certain; Goth. *sums*, Icel. *sumr*, Dan. *somme* (pl.), some; perhaps akin to *same*.] Expressing a certain indeterminate quantity or number, sometimes expressive of a considerable quantity (situated at *some* distance); indicating a person or thing not definitely known, or not specific: often followed by *or other* (*some* person *or other*); used before a word or number, with the sense of *about* or *near* (a village of *some* eighty houses); applied to those of one party; certain, in distinction from others (*some* men believe one thing, *others* another). It is often used without a noun and often followed by *of* (*some of* us, *some of* our provisions).—**Somebody**, sum'bod-i, *n.* A person unknown or uncertain; a person indeterminate; a person of consideration. **Somehow**, sum'hou, *adv.* One way or other; in some way not yet known.—**Somesuch**, sum'such, *a.* Denoting a person or thing of that kind.—**Something**, sum'thing, *n.* An indeterminate or unknown event or thing; an indefinite quantity or degree; a little; a person or thing of importance.—*adv.* In some degree or measure; somewhat; rather.—**Sometime**, sum'tīm, *adv.* Once; formerly; at one time or other.—*a.* Having been formerly; former; late; whilom.—**Sometimes**, sum'-tīmz, *adv.* At times; at intervals; not always; now and then; once; formerly (*Shak.*). — **Somewhat**, sum'whot, *n.* Something, though uncertain what; more or less; a certain quantity or degree, indeterminate. — *adv.* In some degree or measure; rather; a little.—**Somewhere**, sum'whār, *adv.* In or to some place or other unknown or not specified; in one place or another.—**Somewhither**, sum'-whiᴛʜ-ėr, *adv.* To some indeterminate place.

Somersault, **Somerset**, sum'ėr-sạlt, sum'ėr-set, *n.* [Corrupted from O.Fr. *soubresault*, It. *soprassalto*, lit. an overleap; from L. *supra*, over, and *salio*, to leap.] A leap by which a person turns with the heels thrown over his head, completing a circuit, and again alights on his feet.

Somite, sō'mīt, *n.* [Gr. *sōma*, body.] One of the successive rings or segments making up the bodies of certain animals.

Sommer, sum'ėr, *n.* A summer or girder.

Somnambulate, som-nam'bū-lāt, *v.i.* [L. *somnus*, sleep, and *ambulo*, *ambulatum*, to walk.] To walk in sleep.—**Somnambulation**, som-nam'bū-lā"shon, *n.* The act of walking in sleep; somnambulism.—**Somnambulator**, som-nam'bū-lā-tėr, *n.* A somnambulist; a sleep-walker. — **Somnambulic**, som-nam'bū-lik, *a.* Pertaining to somnambulism. —**Somnambulism**, som-nam'bū-lizm, *n.* The act or practice of walking in sleep, resulting from a peculiar perversion of the mental functions during sleep. —**Somnambulist**, som-nam'bū-list, *n.* A person who walks in his sleep; a sleep-walker.—**Somnambulistic**, som-nam'bū-lis"tik, *a.* Pertaining to or affected by somnambulism.

Somniferous, som-nif'ėr-us, *a.* [L. *somnifer*—*somnus*, sleep, and *fero*, to bring.] Causing or inducing sleep; soporific. —**Somnific**, som-nif'ik, *a.* [L. *somnus*, and *facio*, to make.] Causing sleep.

Somniloquence, **Somniloquism**, som-nil'ō-kwens, som-nil'ō-kwizm, *n.* [L. *somnus*, sleep, and *loquor*, to speak.] The act or custom of talking in sleep.—**Somniloquist**, som-nil'ō-kwist, *n.* One who talks in his sleep.—**Somniloquous**, som-nil-ō-kwus, *a.* Apt to talk in sleep.—**Somniloquy**, som-nil'ō-kwi, *n.* A talking in sleep.

Somnolence, **Somnolency**, som'nō-lens, som'nō-len-si, *n.* [L. *somnolentia*, from *somnolentus*, sleepy, from *somnus*, sleep.] Sleepiness; drowsiness; inclination to sleep; *pathol.* a state intermediate between sleeping and waking. —**Somnolent**, som'nō-lent, *a.* Sleepy; drowsy; inclined to sleep. —**Somnolently**, som'nō-lent-li, *adv.* Drowsily.

Son, sun, *n.* [A.Sax. *sunu*=Icel. *sonr*, *sunr*, Sw. *son*, Dan. *sön*, Goth. *sunus*, G. *sohn*, Skr. *sūnu*, son; root seen in Skr. *su*, to beget.] A male child; the male issue of a parent, father, or mother: also used of animals; a male descendant; a term of affectionate address by an old man to a young one, a confessor to his penitent, a teacher to his disciple, &c.; a native of a country; a person strongly imbued by some quality (*sons* of light).—*The Son*, the second person of the Godhead; Christ: called also *Son of God* and *Son of Man*.—**Son-in-law**, *n.* A man married to one's daughter.—**Sonless**, sun'les, *a.* Having no son. —**Sonship**, sun'ship, *n.* The state of being a son.

Sonant, sō'nant, *a.* [L. *sonans*, ppr. of *sono*, to sound. SOUND.] Pertaining to sound; sounding; uttered with voice and not breath merely; voiced, as the letters, *b*, *d* compared with *p*, *t*.—*n.* A sonant letter.

Sonata, so-nä'ta, *n.* [It., from L. *sonare*, to sound.] A musical composition for solo instruments, consisting of several movements, the allegro, adagio, rondo, and minuetto or scherzo.

Song, song, *n.* [A.Sax. *sang*, *song*, from *singan*, to sing. SING.] That which is sung, whether by the human voice or a bird; a little poem to be sung; a vocal melody; an air for a single voice or several; a lay; a strain; poesy; verse.—*A mere song*, *an old song*, a trifle; an insignificant sum.—**Song-bird**, *n.* A bird that sings.—**Songless**, song'les, *a.* Destitute of the power of song; without song.—**Song-sparrow**, *n.* The hedge-sparrow.—**Songster**, song'stėr, *n.* One who sings; especially, a bird that sings.—**Songstress**, song'stres, *n.* [*Songster* and term. *-ess*.] A female singer.—**Song-thrush**, *n.* The mavis or throstle.

Soniferous, sō-nif'ėr-us, *a.* [L. *sonus*, sound, and *fero*, to bear.] Conveying sound; producing sound.

Sonnet, son'et, *n.* [Fr. *sonnet*, from It. *sonetto*, a dim. from L. *sonus*, a sound. SOUND.] A short poem of fourteen lines, forming two stanzas of four verses each and two of three each, the rhymes being adjusted by a particular rule; a short poem; a song.—**Sonneteer**, son-et-ēr', *n.* [Fr. *sonnetier*.] A composer of sonnets; a small poet: usually in contempt.—**Sonnetize**, son'et-īz, *v.t.* To make the subject of a sonnet; to celebrate in a sonnet.

Sonometer, sō-nom'et-ėr, *n.* [L. *sonus*, sound, and Gr. *metron*, a measure.] An apparatus for illustrating the phenomena and laws of the vibrations of tense strings or wires; an apparatus for testing the acuteness of a person's hearing.

Sonorous, sō-nō'rus, *a.* [L. *sonorous*, from *sonus*, sound. SOUND.] Giving sound. as when struck; resonant; sounding; giving a clear, loud, or full-volumed sound; high sounding.—**Sonorously**, sō-nō'rus-li, *adv.* In a sonorous manner.—**Sonorousness**, sō-nō'rus-nes, *n.* The state or quality of being sonorous.

Soochong, sö-shong', *n.* SOUCHONG.

Soodra, sö'dra, *n.* A person of the fourth or lowest caste into which the Hindus are divided. Written also *Sudra*.

Soon, sön, *adv.* [A.Sax. *sóna*, soon; O.Fris. *son*, *san*, Goth. *suns*, soon.] In a short time; shortly after any time specified or supposed; early; before any time supposed; quickly; speedily; readily; willingly; gladly (I would as *soon* do it).—*As soon as*, *so soon as*, immediately at or after another event. —*Sooner or later*, at some future time, near or remote.

Soosoo, **Soosook**, sö'sö, sö'sök, *n.* The dolphin of the Ganges.

Soot, söt, *n.* [A.Sax. *sót*, soot = Icel. *sót*, Dan. *sod*, L.G. *sott*, soot.] A black substance formed from fuel in combustion, rising in fine particles and adhering to the sides of the chimney or pipe conveying the smoke.—*v.t.* To cover or foul with soot.—**Soot-flake**, *n.* A flake or particle of soot; a smut. —**Sootiness**, söt'i-nes, *n.* The quality of being sooty.—**Sooty**, söt'i, *a.* Pertaining to, producing, covered with, or resembling soot; fuliginous; dusky; dark.

Sooterkin, söt'ėr-kin, *n.* [Comp. Prov.E. and Sc. *sotter*, Prov.G. *suttern*, to boil gently.] A kind of false birth fabled to be produced by the Dutch women from sitting over their stoves; an abortive proposal or scheme.

Sooth, söth, *n.* [A.Sax. *sóth*, true, truth = Dan. *sand*, Icel. *sannr*, Goth. *sunis*, true, corresponding to Skr. *sant*, being, and therefore meaning lit. 'being', or 'that is'.] Truth; reality: used frequently with *in* (*in sooth* I know not).

Soothe, sÖTH, *v.t.*—*soothed*, *soothing*. [Formerly to assent in a servile manner, to say yes to, from A.Sax. *gesóthian*, to confirm or show to be true, *sóth*, truth. SOOTH.] To please with blandishments or soft words; to cajole; to make less angry or violent; to pacify; to assuage; to mitigate, ease, or allay.—**Soother**, sö'THėr, *n.* One who or that which soothes.—**Soothing**, sö'THing, *p.* and *a.* Such as to soothe; assuaging.—**Soothingly**, sö'THing-li, *adv* In a soothing manner.

Soothsay, söth'sā, *v.i.* [From *sooth* and *say*.] To foretell; to predict. (N.T.)—**Soothsayer**, söth'sā-ėr, *n.* One who foretells or predicts; a prophet.—**Soothsaying**, söth'sā-ing. *n.* A foretelling; a prediction.

Sop, sop, *n.* [Same as Icel. *soppa*, a sop, a sup; Sw. *soppa*, broth, soup; D. *sop*, L.G. *soppe*, a sop. Closely connected with *sup*, *soup*.] Something dipped in broth or liquid food, and intended to be eaten; something given to pacify: so called from the sop given to Cerberus to pacify him, in the ancient story.—*v.t.*—*sopped*, *sopping*. To steep or dip in liquor.—**Soppy**, sop'i, *a* Sopped or soaked in liquid; like a sop.

Soph, sof, *n.* An abbreviation of *Sophister* and *Sophomore*.

Sophi, sō'fi, *n.* A title of the king of Persia.

Sophism, sof'izm, *n* [Fr. *sophisme*, from Gr *sophisma*, a trick, a quibble, a sophism, from *sophos*, clever, wise.] A specious proposition; a specious but fallacious argument; a fallacy designed to deceive. —**Sophist**, sof'ist, *n.* [Gr. *sophistēs*, a sophist.] One of a class of leading public teachers in ancient Greece during the fifth and fourth centuries B.C., many of whom were men who spent their time in verbal quibbles and philosophical enigmas, thus causing the term to take on a bad sense; a captious or fallacious reasoner; a quibbler.—**Sophister**, sof'is-tėr, *n.* A sophist; a quibbling disputant; a plausible fallacious reasoner; in the University of Cambridge, England, a student advanced beyond the first year of his residence; a soph.—**Sophistic**, **Sophistical**, sō-fis'tik, sō-fis'ti-kal, *n.* Fallaciously subtle; containing sophistry; quibbling. Syn. under FALLACIOUS.—**Sophistically**, sō-fis'ti-kal-li, *adv.* In a sophistical manner; fallaciously. —**Sophisticalness**, sō-fis'ti-kal-nes, *n.*—**Sophisticate**, sō-fis'ti-kāt, *v.t.*—*sophisticated*, *sophisticating*. To pervert; to wrest from the truth; to adulterate; to render spurious by admixture.—**Sophistication**, sō-fis'ti-kā"shon, *n.* The act of adulterating; adulteration; the act or art of quibbling; a quibble; artificial, narrow, complicated; of a person, worldly-wise; the process of disillusioning one.—**Sophistry**, sof'ist-ri, *n.* Fallacious reasoning; reasoning sound in appearance only and intended to mislead.

Sophomore, sof'ō-mōr, *n.* [From Gr. *sophos*, wise, and *mōros*, foolish.] In American colleges, a student belonging to the second of the four classes; one next above a freshman.

Sophta, sof'ta. SOFTA.

Soporiferous, sō-pō-rif'ėr-us, *a.* [L. *soporifer*—*sopor*, *soporis*, sleep (cog. with Skr. *svap*, to sleep, Gr. *hypnos*, sleep), and *fero*, to bring.] Causing or tending to cause sleep; soporific.—**Soporiferously**, sō-pō-rif'ėr-us-li, *adv.* In a soporiferous manner. —**Soporiferousness**, sō-pō-rif'ėr-us-nes, *n.* The quality of being soporiferous. —**Soporific**, sō-pō-rif'ik, *a.* [L. *sopor*, and *facio*, to make.] Causing sleep; tending to cause sleep.—*n.* A drug or other thing that has the quality of inducing sleep.

Soprano, sō-prä'nō, *n.* It. pl. **Soprani**, sō-prä'nē, E. pl. **Sopranos**, sō-prä'nōz. [It., from *sopra*, L. *supra*, above.] The highest quality of female voice, whose ordinary easy range is from C below the treble staff to G or A above it; equivalent to *Treble*, a term which is falling out of use.—**Sopranist**, sō-prä'nist, *n.*

Sorb, sorb, *n.* [Fr. *sorbe*, L. *sorbus*, the sorb.] The service tree or its fruit.—**Sorb-apple**, *n.* The fruit of the service tree.—**Sorbic**, sor'bik, *a.* Pertaining to the service tree.—**Sorbine**, sor'bin, *n.* A sugar existing in mountain-ash berries.

Sorbefacient, sor-bē-fā'shi-ent, *n.* [L. *sorbeo*, to absorb, and *facio*, to make.] *Med.* that which produces absorption.—*a.* *Med.* producing absorption.

Sorbonist, sor'bon-ist, *n.* A doctor of the *Sorbonne*, a celebrated institution founded in connection with the University of Paris in 1252 by Robert de *Sorbon*, chaplain and confessor of Louis IX.—**Sorbonical**, sor-bon'i-kal, *a* Belonging to a Sorbonist.

Sorcerer, sor'sėr-ėr, *n.* [Fr. *sorcier*, a sorcerer, from L.L. *sortiarius*, a caster of lots, from L. *sors*, *sortis*, a lot (whence also *sort*). As to the form of the word comp. *fruiterer*, Fr. *fruitier*.] A conjuror: an enchanter; a magician. —**Sorceress**, sor'sėr-es, *n.* A female sorcerer. —**Sorcery**, sor'sėr-i, *n.* [O.Fr. *sorcerie*.] Divination by the assistance or supposed assistance of evil spirits: magic; enchantment; witchcraft.

Sordes, sor'dēz, *n* [L.] Foul matter; excretions; dregs.

Sordid, sor'did, *a.* [Fr. *sordide*, L. *sordidus*, form *sordes*, filth.] Filthy‡; base; mean; meanly avaricious; covetous; niggardly.—**Sordidly**, sor'did-li, *adv* In a sordid manner; meanly; basely; covetously. —**Sordidness**, sor'did-nes, *n.* The state or quality of being sordid; niggardliness.

Sore, sōr, *a.* [A.Sax. *sár*, sore, a sore; Icel. *sárr*, sore, *sár*, a sore; Dan. *saar*, Goth. *sair*, a wound; G. *sehr*, very.] Painful; being the seat of pain; violent with pain; severe; distressing; tender, as the mind; easily annoyed or vexed; feeling aggrieved; galled. —*n.* A place in an animal body where the skin and flesh are ruptured or bruised, so as to be painful; a boil, ulcer, wound, &c.—*adv.* With painful violence; severely; sorely.—**Sorely**, sōr'li, *adv.* In a sore manner; grievously; greatly; severely. —**Soreness**, sōr'nes, *n.* The state of being sore.

Soredium, sō-rē'di-um, *n.* pl. **Soredia**,

sō-rē′di-a. [From Gr. *sōros*, a heap.] *Bot.* one of the little mealy patches scattered over the surface of the thallus in lichens. —**Sorediferous**, sō-rē-dif′ėr-us, *a.* *Bot.* bearing soredia.

Sorghum, sor′gum, *n.* [From *sorghi*, its Indian name.] A cereal plant, one species of which is cultivated for fodder, grain, and juice; a sirup or molasses, boiled down from the plant juice.

Sorites, sō-rī′tēz, *n.* [Gr. *sōreitēs*, from *sōros*, a heap.] *Logic*, a series of propositions so linked together that the predicate of each that precedes forms the subject of each that follows ($a = b$, $b = c$, $c = d$, therefore $a = d$); a logical sophism depending on numerical indetermination, the point at which a heap or other quantity precisely ceases to be such.

Sorn, sorn, *v.t.* [O.Fr. *sorner*, to play tricks, to jest, to cheat.] To obtrude one's self on another for bed and board. (*Scotch.*)

Sororal, sō-rō′ral, *a.* [L. *soror*, *sororis*, sister.] Pertaining to a sister or sisters; sisterly.—**Sororicide**, sō-rō′ri-sīd, *n.* [L. *soror*, and *cædo*, to kill.] The murder of a sister; the murderer of a sister.

Sorority, sō-ror′i-ti, *n.* A fraternal organization of women, usually of a social nature, to promote their mutual welfare.

Sorosis, sō-rō′sis, *n.* pl. **Soroses**, sō-rō′sēz. [From Gr. *sōros*, a heap.] *Bot.* a fleshy fruit composed of many flowers, seed-vessels, and receptacles consolidated, as the pineapple or mulberry.

Sorrel, sor′el, *a.* [A dim. from O.Fr. *sor*, *sore*, sorrel, from O.D. *soore*, akin to *sere.*] Of a reddish or yellowish brown colour.—*n.* A reddish or yellow-brown colour.

Sorrel, sor′el, *n.* [Fr. *surelle*, sorrel, from O.H.G. *sûr*, sour. SOUR.] The popular name of certain perennial plants, a common species being a succulent acid herb used as a salad and pot-herb.

Sorrel, so′rel, *n.* A buck of the third year.

Sorrow, sor′ō, *n.* [O.E. *sorwe*, A.Sax. *sorg*, *sorh*, care, sorrow; Icel., Dan., and Sw. *sorg*, G. *sorge*, Goth. *saurga*—sorrow.] Pain of mind from loss of or disappointment in the expectation of good; grief; regret; sadness; mourning. ∴ Syn. under AFFLICTION.—*v.i.* To be affected with sorrow; to feel sorry; to grieve; to be sad.—**Sorrowful**, sor′ō-fụl, *a.* Full of sorrow; exhibiting or producing sorrow; sad; mournful; dejected.—**Sorrowfully**, sor′ō-fụl-li, *adv.* In a sorrowful manner. — **Sorrowfulness**, sor′ō-fụl-nes, *n.*—**Sorrowless**, sor′ō-les, *a.* Without sorrow.

Sorry, sor′i, *a.* [Equivalent to *sore*, with term. *-y*; from A.Sax. *sârig*, from *sâr*, sore: influenced in spelling by *sorrow*. SORE.] Grieved for the loss of some good; pained at some evil experienced or committed; often slight or transient regret (I am *sorry* you cannot come); mean; vile; worthless; pitiful (a *sorry* excuse).—**Sorrily**, sor′i-li, *adv.* In a sorry or wretched manner. — **Sorriness**, sor′i-nes, *n.* Pitifulness; meanness; despicableness.

Sort, sort, *n.* [Fr. *sorte*, sort, kind, from L. *sors*, *sortis*, a lot, a condition (seen also in *assort*, *consort*, *resort*).] A kind, species, class, or order (a *sort* of men); manner; form of being or acting; degree (in some *sort*); a set; a suit.—*Out of sorts*, out of order; not in one's usual state of health; unwell.—*v.t.* To separate and arrange in distinct classes or divisions; to assort; to arrange; to reduce to order.—*v.i.* To consort; to associate; to suit; to agree.—**Sortable**, sor′ta-bl, *a.* Capable of being sorted. —**Sorter**, sor′tėr, *n.* One who sorts (a letter-*sorter*; a wool-*sorter*). — **Sortment**, sort′ment, *n.* The act of sorting; distribution into sorts; assortment.

Sortes, sor′tēz, *n.pl.* [L., pl. of *sors*, lot, decision by lot.] A kind of divination by the chance selection of a passage from an author's writings. In the Middle Ages, Virgil in particular was used for this purpose.

Sortie, sor′ti, *n.* [Fr., from *sortir*, to issue.] The issuing of troops from a besieged place to attack the besiegers; a sally.

Sortilege, sor′ti-lej, *n.* [L. *sortilegium*—*sors*, lot, and *lego*, to select.] The act or practice of drawing lots; divination by lots. —**Sortition**, sor-tish′on, *n.* [L. *sortitio.*] Selection or appointment by lot.

Sorus, sō′rus, *n.* pl. **Sori**, sō′rī. [Gr. *sōros*, a heap.] *Bot.* a cluster of spore-cases on the back of the fronds of ferns.

S.O.S. signal. A wireless telegraphic distress signal sent out by a ship at sea which has encountered serious trouble.

Sostenuto, sos-te-nö′to. [It., sustained.] *Mus.* a term implying that the note over which it is placed is to be held out its full length in an equal and steady manner.

Sot, sot, *n.* [Fr. *sot*, a fool, probably from the Celtic; comp. Ir. *suthan*, a blockhead, *sotaire*, a fop.] A stupid person; a dolt; a person stupefied by excessive drinking; a habitual drunkard. — *v.t.*† —*sotted*, *sotting*. To stupefy; to besot.—*v.i.* To tipple to stupidity.—**Sottish**, sot′ish, *a.* Pertaining to a sot; having the character of a sot.—**Sottishly**, sot′ish-li, *adv.* In a sottish manner. — **Sottishness**, sot′ish-nes, *n.* The quality of being sottish; drunkenness.

Soteriology, sō-tē′ri-ol″o-ji, *n.* [Gr. *sōtērios*, saving, salutary, and *logos*, discourse.] The science of health; the doctrine of salvation by Jesus Christ.

Sothiac, **Sothic**, soth′i-ak, soth′ik, *a.* [From *Sothis*, the dog-star, at whose heliacal rising the year was supposed to commence.] Pertaining to the dog-star.—*Sothic year*, the ancient Egyptian year of 365 days.

Sottish, Sottishness. Under SOT.

Sotto, sot′tō. [It., under, below, beneath.] *Mus.* a term signifying below or inferior. —*Sotto voce*, in an undertone.

Sou, sö, *n.* [Fr., from L. *solidus*, a coin, a solid piece.] An old French copper coin, twenty-four of which made a livre; a five-centime piece.

Souari, sou-ä′rē, *n.* SAOUARI.

Soubahdar, sö′ba-där, *n.* [From *soubah*, a province.] In India, the governor of a large province; a native sepoy officer with the same rank as a captain.

Soubrette, sö-bret′, *n.* [Fr.] A waiting-maid; the part of an intriguing servant-girl in a comedy.

Souce, sous, *n.* SOUSE.

Souchong, sö-shong′, *n.* [Chinese, little sprouts.] A kind of black tea.

Soufflé, söf-lā, *n.* [Fr., from *souffler*, to puff, *souffle*, a breath, a puff.] A light dish composed of white of eggs, variously flavoured and baked.

Sough, suf, *v.i.* [O.E. *swough*, from A.Sax. *swógan*, to sound.] To emit a rushing, moaning, or whistling sound, like that of the wind; to sound like the roar of the sea. —*n.* A sound of this kind; a rushing sound like that of the wind; a deep sigh.

Sought, sạt, pret. and pp. of *seek*.

Soul, sōl, *n.* [O.E. and Sc. *saul*, A.Sax. *sáwel*, *sáwl*; Icel. *sála*, Dan. *sjæl*, D. *ziel*, Goth. *saivala*, G. *seele*, the soul; perhaps connected with L. *sæculum*, an age.] The spiritual and immortal part in man; the immaterial spirit which inhabits the body; the moral and emotional part of man's nature; the seat of the sentiments or feelings; the animating or essential part; the vital principle; the essence (he is the very *soul* of honour); an inspirer or leader (the *soul* of an enterprise); courage or spirit; a spiritual being; a disembodied spirit; a human being; a person (not a *soul* present); a familiar term for a person (poor *soul*, he was a good *soul*).—*Cure of souls*, in the Church of England, an ecclesiastical charge. —*Soul* is used in many self-explanatory compounds; as *soul*-destroying, *soul*-entrancing, *soul*-felt, *soul*-stirring, *soul*-subduing, &c.—**Souled**, sōld, *a.* Having a soul; instinct with soul or feeling: often in composition (noble-*souled*, mean-*souled*). — **Soulless**, sōl′les, *a.* Without a soul; lifeless; spiritless; base.

Sound, sound, *a.* [A.Sax. *sund*, sound, healthy; L.G., Dan., and Sw. *sund*, G. (*ge*)*sund*, D. *zond*; from root of L. *sanus*, sound. SANE.] Healthy; not diseased; not being in a morbid state (a *sound* mind, a *sound* body); uninjured; unhurt (a *sound* limb); free from imperfection or defect (*sound* timber, *sound* fruit); founded in truth; valid; that cannot be refuted (*sound* reasoning); correct; free from error; orthodox; founded in right and law; just (a *sound* claim); profound, unbroken, undisturbed (a *sound* sleep); heavy; laid on with force (a *sound* beating).—**Soundly**, sound′li, *adv.* In a sound manner; healthily; validly; thoroughly; smartly (beat him *soundly*).—**Soundness**, sound′nes, *n.* The state of being sound.

Sound, sound, *n.* [A.Sax. *sund*, a strait, a sound; Icel., Dan., Sw., and G. *sund*, a sound; from root of *sunder*, or akin to *swim.*] A narrow passage or channel of water, as between the main land and an isle, or connecting two seas; a strait.

Sound, sound, *n.* [A.Sax. *sund*, a swimming, from *swimman*, to swim; it is also called the *swim.*] The air-bladder of a fish.

Sound, sound, *v.t.* [Fr. *sonder*, to sound; probably from the Teutonic *sund*, a strait. SOUND, a channel.] To measure the depth of; to fathom by sinking a plummet or lead attached to a line; *surg.* to examine by means of a probe; *fig.* to try or search out the intention, opinion, will, or desires of.—*v.i.* To use the line and lead in searching the depth of water.—*n.* *Surg.* any elongated instrument by which cavities of the body are sounded or explored. — **Soundable**, soun′da-bl, *a.* Capable of being sounded.—**Soundings**, sound′ingz, *n.pl.* The depths of water in rivers, harbours, along shores, and even in the open sea, which are ascertained by means of a sounding-line. — **Sounding-lead**, *n.* The weight used at the end of a sounding-line.—**Sounding-line**, *n.* A line for ascertaining the depth of water.—**Soundless**, sound′les, *a.* Unfathomable.

Sound, sound, *n.* [O.E. *soun*, *sowne*, from Fr. *son*, L. *sonus*, a sound (also in *consonant*, *dissonant*, *resonant*, *sonorous*, &c.), cog. Skr. *svan*, to sound. The *d* has been added, as in *round* (to whisper), *lend*, *hind* (a labourer).] That which is heard; the effect which is produced by the vibrations of a body affecting the ear; a noise; noise without signification; empty noise. —*v.i.* To make a noise; to give out a sound; to seem or appear when uttered; to appear on narration (this story *sounds* like a fiction); to be conveyed in sound; to be spread or published. —*v.t.* To cause to give out a sound; to play on; to utter audibly; to give a signal for by a certain sound (to *sound* a retreat); to publish or proclaim (to *sound* the praises of a great man).—**Soundable**, soun′da-bl, *a.* Capable of being sounded. —**Sound-bow**, *n.* The part of a bell on which the clapper strikes. —**Sounding**, soun′ding, *p.* and *a.* Causing sound; sonorous; having a lofty sound; bombastic (mere *sounding* phrases). —**Sounding-board**, **Sound-board**, *n.* A canopy over a pulpit, &c., to direct the sound of a speaker's voice towards the audience; a thin board over which the strings of a pianoforte, violin, guitar, &c., are stretched.—**Sounding-post**, **Sound-post**, *n.* A small post in a violin, set under the bridge for a support, and for propagating the sound.— **Soundless**, sound′les, *a.* Having no sound; noiseless; silent; dumb.

Soup, söp, *n.* [Fr. *soupe*, from G. *suppe*, D. *soep*, Dan. *suppe*, Icel. *súpa* — soup, broth, &c.: akin *sup*, *sip*, *sop.*] A kind of broth; a sort of food made generally by boiling flesh of some kind in water with various other ingredients. — **Soup-kitchen**, *n.* A charitable establishment for supplying soup to the poor.—**Soup-maigre**, söp-mā′gr, *n.* [Fr., lit. meagre soup.] Thin soup made chiefly from vegetables and a little butter.—**Soupy**, söp′i, *a.* Like soup.

Soupçon, söp-soṅ, *n.* [Fr., from O.Fr. *souspeçon*, a suspicion. SUSPICION.] A very small quantity; a taste.

Sour, sour, *a.* [A.Sax. *súr*, sour = Icel. *súrr*, Dan. *suur*, D. *zuur*, G. *sauer*; also found in Celtic: W. and Armor. *sur*—sour. SORREL.] Sharp to the taste; tart; acid; harsh of temper; crabbed; austere; morose; expressing discontent, displeasure, or peevishness (a *sour* word or look); become tart or acid by keeping, as milk.—*Sour grapes.* Under GRAPE.—*v.t.* To make acid or sour; to make cross, crabbed, or discontented (to *sour* the temper); to embitter.—*v.i.* To become acid; to acquire tartness; to become peevish, crabbed, or harsh in temper.—**Sour-crout, Sour-krout**, sour'krout, *n.* Same as *Sauer-kraut.*—**Sourish**, sour'ish, *a.* Somewhat sour; moderately acid. —**Sourly**, sour'li, *adv.* In a sour manner; acidly; morosely; peevishly, discontentedly. —**Sourness**, sour'nes, *n.* The state or quality of being sour; acidity; sharpness to the taste; asperity; harshness of temper.— —**Sour-sop**, *n.* A large succulent fruit closely allied to the custard-apple.

Source, sōrs, *n.* [Fr. *source*, O.Fr. *sorce*, from L. *surgo*, to rise, contr. for *surrigo*, for *sub-rego*—*sub*, under, and *rego*, to direct. SURGE, REGENT.] The spring or fountainhead from which a stream of water proceeds; one who or that which originates or gives rise to anything; first cause; origin.

Souse, sous, *n.* [A form of *sauce.*] Pickle made with salt; sauce; pickled meat; the ears, feet, &c., of swine pickled; a guzzler (*slang*).—*v.t.*—*soused, sousing.* To steep in pickle; to plunge into water.

Souse, sous, *v.i.* and *t.* [Comp. G. *sausen*, to rush.] To fall suddenly on; to guzzle, as liquor (*slang*).—*n.* A violent attack; a blow —*adv.* With sudden violence.

Soutane, sö-tän, *n.* [Fr., from L.L. *subtana*, from L. *subtus*, beneath.] A cassock, usually black, worn by Roman Catholic clergy.

South, south, *n.* [A.Sax. *súth*; Icel. *suthr*, *sunnr*, Dan. *syd*, *sönden*, O.H.G. *sund*, Mod. G. *süd*, south; allied to *sun*, being the region of the sun.] One of the four cardinal points of the compass, directly opposite to the north; the region or locality lying opposite to the north; the wind that blows from the south; [*cap.*] the section of the U. S. below Mason and Dixons line; the states of the cotton belt: Del., Md., Va., W. Va., N. C., S. C., Ky., Tenn., Fla., Ga., Ala., Miss., La., Tex., Okla., Ark., Mo.—*a.* Situated in the south, or in a southern direction; pertaining to the south; proceeding from the south.—*adv.* Toward the south; from the south

South-east, *n.* The point of the compass equally distant from the south and east.—*a.* Pertaining to the south-east.—**South-easter**, *n.* A wind from the south-east.—**South-easterly, South-eastern**, *a.* South-east.—**Southerliness**, suᴛʜ'ėr-li-nes, *n.* State of being southerly.—**Southerly**, suᴛʜ'ėr-li, *a.* Lying in the south; coming from the south. — **Southern**, suᴛʜ'ėrn, *a.* [A.Sax. *súthern*, from *súther*, *súth*, south.] Belonging to the south; lying on the south side of the equator; coming from the south.—*Southern Cross*, *n.* A bright constellation in the southern hemisphere, the principal stars of which form a cross.—**Southerner**, suᴛʜ'ėr-nėr, *n.* An inhabitant or native of the south.—**Southerniness**, suᴛʜ'ėrn-li-nes, *n.* State of being southerly.—**Southernly**, suᴛʜ'ėrn-li, *adv.* Toward the south.—**Southernmost**, suᴛʜ'ėrn-mōst, *a.* Furthest toward the south.—**Southernwood**, suᴛʜ'ėrn-wụd, *n.* A composite plant nearly allied to wormwood, formerly employed in medicine as a stomachic and stimulant.—**Southing**, south'ing, *n.* Motion to the south; the time at which the moon or other heavenly body passes the meridian of a place; *navig.* and *survey.* the difference of latitude southward from the last point of reckoning. NORTHING. — **Southmost**, south'mōst, *a.* Furthest towards the south. —**South Pole**, *n.* The southern end of the earth's axis.—**Southron, Southern**, suᴛʜ'ron, suᴛʜ'ėrn, *n.* A native or inhabitant of a southern country or region. —**Southward**, south'wėrd, *adv.* Toward the south.—*a.* Lying or situated toward the south; directed towards the south.—**South-west**, *n.* The point of the compass equally distant from the south and west.—*a.* Lying in the direction of the south-west; coming from the south-west.—**South-wester**, *n.* A strong south-west wind; a waterproof hat with a flap hanging over the neck, worn in bad weather: frequently contracted into *Sou'wester.* — **South-westerly**, *a.* In the direction of south-west; coming from the south-west. —**South-western**, *a.* Pertaining to the south-west.—**South-westward**, *a.* and *adv.* Towards the south-west.

Souvenir, sö-ve-nēr', *n.* [Fr., from L. *subvenire*, to occur to mind.] That which reminds or revives the memory of anything; a keepsake.

Sovereign, sov'ėr-in, *a.* [O.Fr. *soverain*, Mod.Fr. *souverain;* from L.L. *superanus*, from L. *super*, above, over. The *g* has been erroneously inserted.] Supreme in power; possessing supreme dominion; royal; princely; paramount; efficacious in the highest degree (a *sovereign* medicine).—*n.* A supreme ruler; the person having the highest power or authority in a state, as a king, queen, emperor, &c.; a monarch.—*a.* **Sovereignty**, sov'ėr-in-ti, *n.* The state of being a sovereign; the supreme power in a state; monarchical sway; supremacy; supreme excellence.

Soviet, sov'i-et, *n.* [Russian.] The form of communistic government established in Russia, in 1917, which provides for a hierarchy of local, provincial, national, and federal councils or assemblies composed of representatives of workers, peasants, and soldiers, and culminating in the *Union of Socialist Soviet Republics.*

Sow, sou, *n.* [A.Sax. *sugu*, *sú*, a sow=L.G. *suge*, O.D. *sowe*, G. *sau*, Dan. and Sw. *so*, sow; cog. L. *sus*, Gr. *hus*, sow; perhaps from root *su*, to bring forth (whence *son*).] The female of the swine; *founding*, the main channel into which metal is run from a smelting furnace. See under PIG.—*To have* or *get the right* (or *wrong*) *sow by the ear*, to pitch upon the right (or wrong) person or thing; to come to the right (or wrong) conclusion.

Sow, sou, *n.* A mediæval engine of attack, full of soldiers, covered at the top, and propelled against the walls of a town or fortress; when crushed from the side of the besieged it was said 'to farrow'.—**Sow-bread**, sou'bred, *n.* [From the roots being eaten by swine.] The common British species of cyclamen.—**Sow-thistle**, sou-this'l, *n.* A genus of composite plants in Britain, somewhat resembling thistles, and greedily eaten by various animals.

Sow, sō, *v.t.*—pret. *sowed*, pp. *sowed* or *sown.* [A.Sax. *sáwan* (pret. *seów*; pp. *sáwen*), to sow = Icel. *sá*, Dan. *saae*, G. *säen*, Goth. *saian*; same root as L. *sero*, *satum*, to sow (whence *season*). *Seed* is from this stem.] To scatter, as seed upon the earth, for the purpose of growth; to plant by strewing; to stock with seed; to spread abroad; to disseminate; to propagate (to *sow* discord). —*v.i.* To scatter seed for growth and the production of a crop.—**Sower**, sō'ėr, *n.* One who sows; a disseminator.

Soy, soi, *n.* A sauce prepared in China and Japan from a bean for fish, meat, &c. **Soybean**, soi'bēn, *n.* A leguminous plant and its seed high in protein value, rich in vegetable oil, useful for both human food and forage, and from which are made, by chemical processing, paints and plastics. The plant is cultivated in China, Japan, Manchuria, and the United States.

Spa, spạ, *n.* A mineral spring; a place to which people resort for its mineral waters; from *Spa*, a celebrated watering-place in Belgium.

Space, spās, *n.* [Fr. *espace*, from L. *spatium*, space, from root *spa*, to stretch, seen in *span.*] Extension, considered independently of anything which it may contain; extension in all directions; any portion of extension; the interval between any two or more points or objects; quantity of time; the interval between two points of time; *printing*, the interval between words in printed matter; also a kind of blank type for separating words; *mus.* one of the four intervals between the five lines of a staff.—*v.t.*—*spaced, spacing.* To arrange at proper intervals; to arrange the spaces in.—**Space-time**, *n.* The four-dimensional world of events, separable (according to the theory of Minkowski and Einstein) into three dimensions of length and one of time, but in different ways by different observers.—**Spacial**, spā'shi-al, *a.* Pertaining to space.—**Spacially**, spā'shi-al-li, *adv.* As regards or with reference to space.—**Spacious**, spā'shus, *a.* [L. *spatiosus.*] Inclosing an extended space; large in extent; wide extended; not contracted or narrow; roomy.—**Spaciously**, spā'shus-li, *adv.* In a spacious manner; widely; extensively.—**Spaciousness**, spā'shus-nes, *n.* The quality of being spacious.

Spadassin, spa-das'in, *n.* [Fr., from It. *spada*, L. *spatha*, a sword.] A swordsman; a bravo; a bully (*Carl.*).

Spade, spād, *n.* [A.Sax. *spada*=D., Dan., and Sw. *spade*, Icel. *spathi*, G. *spaten*; cog. Gr. *spathē*, any broad blade.] An instrument for digging, having a broad blade of iron and a stout handle, adapted to be used with both hands and one foot; *pl.* one of the four suits of playing cards.—*To call a spade a spade*, to call things by their proper names; to speak plainly and without mincing matters.—*v.t.* To dig with a spade; to pare the sward from with a spade.—**Spade-bone**, *n.* The shoulder-blade.—**Spadeful**, spād'fụl, *n.* As much as a spade will hold.—**Spade-guinea**, *n.* A guinea with a spade-formed shield bearing the coat of arms on the reverse.—**Spade-work**, *n.* Hard, preliminary, detailed work before the adoption of final measures. (*Rosebery.*)—**Spadille**, spa-dil', *n.* [Fr. *espadille.*] The ace of spades in playing ombre.

Spadix, spā'diks, *n.* [L., a palm branch with its fruit, as an *adj.* date-brown.] *Bot.* a form of inflorescence, in which the flowers are closely arranged round a fleshy radius, and the whole surrounded by a large leaf called a spathe, as in palms. — **Spadiceous**, spā-dish'us, *a.* *Bot.* growing within a spathe or spadix; forming a spadix. —**Spadicose**, spā'di-kōs, *a.* *Bot.* growing on a spadix.

Spado, spā'dō, *n.* [L.] A castrated animal; a gelding; an impotent person.

Spae, spā, *v.i.* and *t.* [Icel. *spá*, Dan. *spaa*, to foretell, to tell fortunes.] To foretell; to divine; to tell one's fortune.—*Spae-wife*, a fortune-teller. (*Scotch.*)

Spahi, spa'hē, *n.* [Hind. *sipahi*, sepoy.] Algerian cavalry serving with the French army.

Spaid, spād, *n.* A hart three years old.

Spake, spāk. One of the forms of the preterite of *speak*, the more commonly used form being *spoke.*

Spalpeen, spal'pēn, *n.* [Ir. *spailpin*, Gael. *spailpean.*] An Irish term for a mean or insignificant fellow.

Span, span, *n.* [A.Sax. *span*, a span (the measure), *spannan*, to bind; Icel. *spönn*, Dan. *spand*, D. *span*, G. *spanne*, a span; same root as L. *spatium*, space; Gr. *spaō*, to draw (whence *spasm*).] The space from the point of the thumb to that of the little finger when extended; nine inches; the eighth of a fathom; a short space of time; the spread or extent of an arch between its abutments; a pair of horses; a yoke of animals; a team.—*v.t.*—*spanned, spanning.* To measure by the hand with the fingers extended, or with the fingers encompassing the object; to measure or reach from one side of to the other.—**Spanless**, span'les, *a.* Incapable of being spanned or measured.—**Span-long**, *a.* Of the length of a span.—**Spanner**, span'ėr, *n.* One that spans; a screw-key.—**Span-roof**, *n.* A common roof formed by two meeting inclined planes.

Span, span, pret. of *spin*.

Spanæmia, spa-nē'mi-a, *n.* [Gr. *spanis*, scarcity, and *haima*, blood.] Poverty or thinness of blood.

Spandrel, span'drel, *n.* [From O.Fr. *esplanader*, to level or make even. ESPLANADE.] *Arch.* the irregular triangular space comprehended between the outer curve or extrados of an arch and a straight-sided figure surrounding it.

Spangle, spang'gl, *n.* [Dim. of O.E. *spang*, A.Sax. *spange*, a buckle, a clasp, &c.; D. *spang*, Icel. *spöng*, a spangle, a stud.] A small circular ornament of metal stitched on an article of dress; any little thing sparkling and brilliant; a small sparkling object.—*v.t.*—*spangled*, *spangling*. To set, sprinkle, or adorn with spangles.—*v.i.*† To glitter; to glisten.—**Spangler**, spang'glėr, *n.* One who or that which spangles. — **Spangly**, spang'gli, *a.* Like a spangle or spangles; glittering; glistening.

Spaniard, span'yėrd, *n.* A native of Spain.—**Spanish**, span'ish, *a.* Pertaining to Spain. — *n.* The language of Spain.— **Spanish-black**, *n.* A soft black, prepared by burning cork, used in painting.— **Spanish-broom**, *n.* A plant from which a good fibre is obtained. — **Spanish-brown**, *n.* A species of earth used in painting, having a dark reddish-brown colour.—**Spanish-chalk**, *n.* A variety of steatite or soap-stone.—**Spanish-fly**, *n.* CANTHARIDES.—**Spanish-grass**, *n.* Esparto. — **Spanish-juice**, *n.* The extract of the root of the liquorice.—**Spanish-red**, *n.* An ochre resembling venetian red.—**Spanish-soap**, *n.* CASTILE-SOAP. —**Spanish-white**, *n.* A pigment prepared from chalk which has been separated in an impalpable form by washing.

Spaniel, span'yel, *n.* [O.Fr. *espagneul*, Mod.Fr. *épagneul*, lit. a little Spanish dog, from Sp. *espana*, L. *Hispania*, Spain.] A name given to several kinds of dogs all more or less elegant, some of them used for sporting purposes, others kept merely as pets; also, a cringing fawning person.

Spank, spangk, *v.i.* [Same as Dan. *spanke*, to strut, to stalk; comp. Sc. *spang*, to leap.] To move with a quick lively step; to move or run along quickly.—*v.t.* To slap or smack, as with the open hand.—**Spanker**, spang'kėr, *n.* One that spanks; a fast-going or fleet horse (*colloq.*); *naut.* a large fore-and-aft sail set upon the mizzen-mast of a ship. — **Spanking**, spangk'ing, *p.* and *a.* Moving with a quick lively pace; dashing; free-going. (*Colloq.*)

Spanner, span'ėr, *n.* A tool with jaws or sockets at the end or ends of a lever: used for tightening nuts.

Span-new, span'nū, *a.* [Icel. *spán-nýr*, span-new, lit. chip-new, splinter-new, from *spánn*, G. *span*, a chip: in allusion to work fresh from the hands of the workman.] Quite new; bran-new.

Spar, spär, *n.* [A.Sax. *spær*, *spærstán*, a kind of stone.] A mineralogical term for various crystallized, earthy, and some metallic substances, which easily break into rhomboidal, cubical, or laminated fragments with polished surfaces, as calcareous-spar, fluor-spar, &c. — **Sparry**, spär'i, *a.* Resembling spar or consisting of spar; spathose; abounding with spar.—*Sparry iron*, a carbonate of iron; spathic or spathose iron; siderite.

Spar, spär, *n.* [Same as Icel. *sparri*, *sperra*, Dan. *sparre*, D. *spar*, G. *sparren*, a beam, a bar.] A long piece of timber of no great thickness; a piece of sawed timber; a pole; *naut.* a long beam: a general term for masts, yards, booms, and gaffs. — **Spar-deck**, *n.* *Naut.* a light deck fitted over the upper deck of a vessel.

Spar, spär, *v.i.*—*sparred*, *sparring*. [O.Fr. *esparer* (It. *sparare*), to fling out the hind-legs, to kick, from L. *ex*, out, and Fr. *parer*, to parry. PARRY.] To rise and strike with the feet or spurs: said of cocks; to move the arms in a way suitable for immediate attack or defence; to fight with boxing-gloves; to box.—*n.* A preliminary flourish of the fists; a boxing-match; a contest with boxing-gloves.

Sparable, spar'a-bl, *n.* [Corruption of *sparrow-bill*, from the shape.] A kind of nail driven into the soles of shoes and boots.

Spare, spār, *v.t.*—*spared*, *sparing*. [A.Sax. *sparian* = Icel. and Sw. *spara*, Dan. *spare*, G. and D. *sparen*, to spare: same root as L. *parco* (for *sparco*), to spare.] To use frugally; not to be profuse of; to part with; to do without; to dispense with; to omit; to forbear (in this sense often with an infinitive as object); to treat with pity, mercy, or forbearance; to forbear to afflict or punish; to forbear to inflict upon; to withhold from; to save, withhold, or gain, as from some engrossing occupation.—*v.i.* To be parsimonious or frugal; not to be liberal or profuse; to use mercy or forbearance.— *a.* [A.Sax. *spær*, moderate, spare.] Scanty; not plentiful or abundant; such as may be spared; over and above what is necessary; superfluous; held in reserve; not required for present use (a *spare* anchor, a *spare* bed); lean; wanting flesh; meagre; thin.— **Sparely**, spār'li, *adv.* In a spare manner; sparingly.—**Spareness**, spār'nes, *n.* State of being lean or thin; leanness.—**Sparer**, spā'rėr, *n.* One that spares.—**Sparerib**, spār'rib, *n.* [*Spare*, lean, and *rib*.] The piece of a hog taken from the side, consisting of the ribs with little flesh on them.— **Sparing**, spā'ring, *a.* Saving; parsimonious: chary (*sparing* of words).—**Sparingly**, spā'ring-li, *adv.* In a sparing manner; not abundantly; frugally; parsimoniously; not lavishly; seldom; not frequently. — **Sparingness**, spā'ring-nes, *n.*

Sparge, spärj, *v.t.* [L. *spargo*, to sprinkle. ASPERSE.] To dash or sprinkle; to throw water upon malt in a shower of small drops. —**Sparger**, spär'jėr, *n.* A sprinkler.

Spark, spärk, *n.* [A.Sax. *spearca* = L.G. *sparke*, D. *spark*, *sperk*, also *sprank*, a spark; same root as *spring*, *sprinkle*.] A small particle of fire emitted from bodies in combustion; a small shining body or transient light; the light accompanying electric discharge; a particle (a *spark* of life; of courage).—*v.i.* To emit particles of fire; to sparkle.—**Sparkle**, spär'kl, *v.i.*—*sparkled*, *sparkling*. [Freq. from *spark*.] To emit sparks; to shine as if giving out sparks; to glitter; to flash; to twinkle.—*v.t.* To emit with coruscations; to shine with. —*n.* A spark; a luminous particle; a scintillation; luminosity; lustre.—**Sparkler**, spärk'lėr, *n.* One who or that which sparkles.—**Sparkling**, spärk'ling, *p.* and *a.* Emitting sparks; glittering; brilliant; lively.—**Sparklingly**, spärk'ling-li, *adv.* In a sparkling manner. — **Sparklingness**, spärk'ling-nes, *n.*

Spark, spärk, *n.* [Same as Prov. E. *sprack*, lively, Icel. *sparkr*, sprightly; akin *spry*.] A brisk, showy, gay man; a lover; a gallant; a beau.—**Sparkish**, spär'kish, *a.* Having the style or character of a spark.

Sparrow, spar'ō, *n.* [A.Sax. *spearwa*, Goth. *sparwa*, Dan. *spurv*, Ital. *spörr*, G. *spar*, *sperling*, sparrow.] A well-known bird of the finch family, constantly seen in the vicinity of human dwellings, even in the midst of large cities. — **Sparrow-hawk**, *n.* A small European hawk, *Accipiter nisus*, very destructive to pigeons and small birds.

Sparrow-grass, *n.* A corruption of *Asparagus*.

Sparry. Under SPAR.

Sparse, spärs, *a.* [L. *sparsus*, pp. of *spargo*, to strew, to sprinkle (as in *asperse*, *disperse*, *intersperse*); akin to Gr. *speirō*, to sow.] Thinly scattered; set or planted here and there; not dense; *bot.* not in any apparent regular order. — **Sparsely**, spärs'li, *adv.* In a scattered or sparse manner; thinly.— **Sparseness**, spärs'nes, *n.* The state of being sparse; scattered state.

Spartacist, spar'ta-sist, *n.* A member of the extreme Anarchist party in the German revolution of 1918.

Spartan, spär'tan, *a.* Pertaining to ancient *Sparta*; hence, hardy; undaunted.

Spasm, spazm, *n.* [Fr. *spasme*, L. *spasmus*, from Gr. *spasmos*, from *spaō*, to draw, to wrench. SPAN.] *Med.* an abnormal, sudden, and more or less violent contraction of one or more muscles or muscular fibres, generally attended with pain. — **Spasmodic**, **Spasmodical**, spaz-mod'ik, spaz-mod'i-kal, *a.* [Gr. *spasmos*, and *eidos*, likeness.] Relating to spasm; consisting in spasm; convulsive; marked by strong effort, but of brief duration; violent and short-lived.—*Spasmodic school*, a name given in ridicule to certain modern authors whose writings were considered to be distinguished by an overstrained and unnatural style, e.g. Bailey, Dobell (*Aytoun*).—**Spasmodic**, *a.* Of the nature of a spasm; convulsive; taking place by fits and starts; intermittent, as *spasmodic* attempts. — **Spasmodically**, spaz-mod'i-kal-li, *adv.* In a spasmodic manner.—**Spastic**, spas'tik, *a.* [Gr. *spastikos*.] Relating to spasm; spasmodic. — **Spasticity**, spas-tis'i-ti, *n.* A state of spasm; tendency to or capability of spasm.

Spat, spat, pret. of *spit*.

Spat, spat, *n.* [Akin to verb to *spit*.] The spawn of shell-fish; the developing spawn of the oyster.

Spat, spat, *n.* [Abbrev. of *spatterdashes*?] Footwear round the ankles to keep the feet warm.

Spatangus, spa-tang'gus, *n.* [L., from Gr. *spatangos*, a sea-urchin.] A genus of sea-urchins, often called 'heart-urchins' from their shape.

Spatch-cock, *n.* [Perhaps for *despatch-cock* (*despatch* meaning haste), or for *spitstuck*. SPITCHCOCK.] A fowl killed, and immediately broiled, for some sudden occasion.

Spate, **Spait**, spāt, *n.* [Comp. Ir. *speid*, a flood in a river.] A sudden heavy flood, especially in mountain streams, caused by heavy rainfall.

Spatha, spā'tha, *n.* *Bot.* SPATHE.

Spathe, spāth, *n.* [L. *spatha*, from Gr. *spathē*, a broad blade, a spathe.] *Bot.* a large membranaceous bract situated at the base of a spadix, which it incloses as a sheath.—**Spathed**, spāthd, *a.* *Bot.* having a spathe.—**Spathaceous**, **Spathal**, spa-thā'shus, spā'thal, *a.* *Bot.* furnished with or formed like a spathe (*spathal* flowers).— **Spathella**, spa-thel'la, *n.* [Dim. of L. *spatha*.] *Bot.* another name for the *Glumella*.—**Spathose**, spath'ōs, *a.* *Bot.* spathaceous.

Spathic, spath'ik, *a.* [Fr. *spathique*, from *spath*, G. *spath*, spar.] Applied to minerals having an even lamellar or flatly foliated structure; sparry.—*Spathic iron*, carbonate of iron; an ore of iron of a foliated structure.—**Spathiform**, spath'i-form, *a.* Resembling spar in form.—**Spathose**, spath'ōs, *a.* Sparry; foliated in texture.

Spatial, **Spatially**. SPACIAL, SPACIALLY.

Spatter, spat'ėr, *v.t.* [Akin to *spit*, *spot*.] To scatter a liquid substance on; to sprinkle with anything liquid or semi-liquid that befouls; to bespatter; to throw out in drops; *fig.* to asperse; to defame. — **Spatterdash**, spat'ėr-dash, *n.* [*Spatter* and *dash*.] A covering of cloth or leather for the leg; a gaiter; a legging.

Spattle, spat'l, *n.* [A form of *spatula*.] A spatula; *pottery*, a tool for mottling a moulded article with colouring matter.

Spatula, spat'ū-la, *n.* [L., dim. of *spatha*, Gr. *spathē*, a broad flat instrument. SPADE.] A sort of knife with a thin flexible blade, used by druggists, painters, &c., for spreading plasters, working pigments, &c.; an instrument used in the kitchen for turning pancakes, spreading icing on a cake, &c.; *surg.* a flat instrument for depressing the tongue in operations about the throat.

Spavin, spav'in, *n.* [O.Fr. *espavent*; origin doubtful.] A disease of horses affecting the hock-joint, or joint of the hind-leg between the knee and the fetlock by which lameness is produced.—**Spavined**, spav'ind, *a.* Affected with spavin.

Spawl,† spal, *v.i.* [Contr. from A.Sax. *spátl*, spittle. SPIT.] To throw saliva from the mouth in a careless, dirty manner.—*n.* Saliva or spittle thrown out carelessly.

Spawn, span, *n.* [O.Fr. *espaundre*, to spawn, lit. to *expand*. EXPAND.] The eggs or ova of fishes, frogs, &c., when shed; the white fibrous matter from which fungi are produced; the mycelium of fungi; contemptuously, any offspring or product.—*v.t.* To deposit in the form of spawn; contemptuously, to bring forth or generate.—*v.i.* To deposit eggs, as fish, frogs, &c.—**Spawner**, spa'nėr, *n.* A female fish.

Spay, spā, *v.t.* [A Celtic word: Manx *spoiy*, Gael. *spoth*, to castrate.] To remove or destroy the ovaries of: a process applied to female animals, to incapacitate them for producing young.

Speak, spēk, *v.i.*—pret. *spoke* (*spake* archaic or poetical); pp. *spoken*. [O.E. *speken*, A. Sax. *specan*, *sprecan*; same as D. and L.G. *spreken*, G. *sprechen*, to speak.] To utter words; to express thoughts by words; to utter a speech, discourse, or harangue; to talk; to discourse; to make mention; to tell by writing; to communicate ideas in any manner; to be expressive.—*To speak for*, to argue in favour of; to plead the cause of; to urge the claims of; to be the representative or spokesman of; to ask in marriage. (*Scrip.*)—*To speak out*, to speak loud or louder; to speak boldly or unreservedly.—*To speak up*, to speak in a loud or louder tone; to express one's thoughts freely.—*To speak well for*, to be a favourable indication of.—*To speak with*, to converse with. ∴ A man may *speak* by uttering a single word, whereas to *talk* is to utter sentiments consecutively; so, a man may be able to *speak* though he is not able to *talk*. *Speak* is also more formal in meaning; as, to *speak* before a brilliant audience; while *talk* implies a conversational manner of speaking.—*v.t.* To utter with the mouth; to utter articulately; to say; to declare (to *speak* the truth); to proclaim; to talk or converse in (to *speak* French); to address; to accost; to express in any way (her eyes *spoke* love).—*To speak a ship*, to hail and speak to her captain or commander.—**Speakable**, spē'ka-bl, *a.* Capable of or fit for being spoken.—**Speaker**, spē'kėr, *n.* One who speaks; one that utters a speech in public, or one that practises public speaking; a person who is the mouthpiece or spokesman of another; a person who presides over a deliberative assembly, as of the House of Representatives.—**Speaking**, spē'king, *a.* Used for the purpose of conveying speech (a *speaking* trumpet); forcibly expressive (a *speaking* likeness); extending to mere phrases of civility (a *speaking* acquaintance).—**Speaking trumpet**, *n.* A trumpet-shaped instrument which enables the sound of the voice to be heard at a distance.—**Speaking tube**, *n.* A tube of gutta-percha or other material for communicating orally from one room to another.

Spear, spēr, *n.* [A.Sax. *spere*=D. and G. *speer*, Dan. *spær*, Icel. *spjör*; comp. L. *sparus*, a hunting spear; probably akin to *spar*.] A long pointed weapon used in war and hunting, by thrusting or throwing; a lance; a pointed instrument with barbs, for stabbing fish, &c.—*v.t.* To pierce with, or as with, a spear; to kill with a spear.—**Spearer**, spēr'ėr, *n.* One who spears.—**Spear-grass**, *n.* A name applied to various long sharp-leaved grasses.—**Spear-head**, *n.* The metal point of a spear.—**Spearman**, spēr'man, *n.* One who is armed with a spear.—**Spearmint**, spēr'-mint, *n.* An aromatic plant having spear-shaped leaves.

Spec, spek, *n.* A colloquial abbreviation of *Speculation* (as a commercial term).

Special, spesh'al, *a.* [Fr. *spécial*, from L. *specialis*, from *species*, kind (which see).] Pertaining to something distinct or having a distinctive character; distinctive; particular; peculiar; differing from others; designed for a particular purpose or occasion; having a distinct field or scope.—*Special case*, a statement of facts agreed to on behalf of parties, and submitted for the opinion of a court as to the law bearing on the facts.—*Special constable*, a person sworn to aid the constituted authorities in maintaining the public peace on occasions of exigency, as to quell a riot.—*Special correspondent*, a person specially appointed to give an account of some important event or series of events for a newspaper.—*Special creation*, the obsolete theory that all species of plants and animals were created independently.—*Special license*, a license obtained from the Archbishop of Canterbury, which enables a priest to marry the parties without banns, and at any time or place other than those necessary in ordinary cases.—*Special pleader*, a lawyer whose occupation it is to give opinions on matters submitted to him, and to draw pleadings.—*Special pleading*, the business of a special pleader; the specious but unsound or unfair argumentation of one whose aim is victory rather than truth.—*Special verdict*, a verdict in which the jury finds the facts proved, leaving the law bearing on them to be determined by the court.—*n.* Any person or thing appointed for a special purpose or occasion, as a constable, a railway train, &c.—**Specialism**, spesh'al-izm, *n.* A particular branch or department of knowledge, devotion to some one subject.—**Specialist**, spesh'al-ist, *n.* A person who devotes himself to a particular branch of a profession, art, or science; one who has a special knowledge of some particular subject.—**Speciality**, spesh-i-al'i-ti, *n.* That property by which a person or thing is specially characterized; that in which one is specially versed; a quality or attribute peculiar to a species.—**Specialization**, spesh'al-ī-zā"shon, *n.* The act of specializing or devoting to a particular use or function; special determination.—**Specialize**, spesh'al-īz, *v.t.*—*specialized*, *specializing*. To assign a specific use or purpose to; to devote or apply to a specific use or function.—**Specially**, spesh'al-li, *adv.* In a special manner; particularly; especially; for a particular purpose.—**Specialty**, spesh'al-ti, *n.* A particular point; that in which one is specially versed; a speciality; *law*, a special contract; an obligation or bond.

Specie, spē'shi, *n.* [The ablative of L. *species*, used as an English word from its occurrence in the phrase 'paid in *specie*', that is, in visible coin.] Gold or silver coined, and used as a circulating medium; coin: in contradistinction to paper-money.

Species, spē'shēz, *n.sing.* and *pl.* [L. *species*, appearance, shape, sort, kind, from *specio*, to behold; akin to Gr. *skeptomai*, Skr. *pash*, to see. English words in which L. *specio* appears are very numerous, as *specious*, *specimen*, *specify*, *spite*, *spice*, *despise*, *aspect*, *prospect*, *respect*, *spectacle*, &c.] A kind, sort, or variety; a class, collection, or assemblage of things or beings classified according to attributes which are determined by scientific observation; a group of animals or plants which bear a close resemblance to each other in the more essential features of their organization, and produce similar progeny, several species uniting to form a *genus*; *logic*, a group of individuals agreeing in common attributes and designated by a common name.

Specify, spes'i-fī, *v.t.*—*specified*, *specifying*. [Fr. *spécifier*, as if from a L. *specifico*—*species*, and *facio*, to make.] To mention or name distinctively; to designate in words, so as to clearly distinguish or limit.—**Specific**, spe-sif'ik, *a.* [Fr. *spécifique*.] Pertaining to, characterizing, or constituting a species; marking something as a distinct species; tending to specify or particularize; definite; precise; *med.* possessed of peculiar efficacy in the cure of a particular disease.—*Specific centre*, the locality where any species of animals or plants first appeared and from which it became diffused.—*Specific character*, that which distinguishes one species from every other species of the same genus; the essential character of a species.—*Specific gravity*, abbreviated *Sp. Gr.* or *S. G.*, the ratio of the weight of the given bulk of any substance to that of the same bulk of some standard substance, usually water for solids and liquids, air or hydrogen for gases; related to *relative density* as weight to mass, but represented by the same number in any case.—*Specific heat*, (S.H.), the ratio of the quantity of heat required to raise the temperature of a given mass of any substance through one degree to the quantity required to raise the same mass of a standard substance (water for solids and liquids, water or air for gases) through one degree. See ATOMIC HEAT.—*Specific inductive capacity*, for any substance, the ratio of the capacity of a condenser having that substance as a dielectric to the capacity of a similar condenser with air as the dielectric.—*Specific name*, the name which, appended to the name of the genus, constitutes the distinctive name of the species.—*Specific resistance*, for any substance, the resistance of a conductor of the substance of unit length and unit cross section.—*n.* A remedy which exerts a special action in the prevention or cure of a disease; an infallible or supposed infallible remedy; something certain to effect the purpose for which it is used; an unfailing agent.—**Specifically**, spe-sif'i-kal-li, *adv.* In a specific manner; so far as concerns the species; definitely; particularly.—**Specification**, spes'i-fi-kā"shon, *n.* The act of specifying; designation of particulars; particular mention; a statement describing the dimensions, details, &c., of any work about to be undertaken, as in building, engineering, &c.; an article, item, or particular specified.—**Specificness**, spe-sif'-ik-nes, *n.* The character of being specific.

Specimen, spes'i-men, *n.* [L. *specimen*, an example or specimen, from *specio*, to behold. SPECIES.] One of a number of similar things intended to show the character of the whole, or of others not exhibited; a portion exhibited; a sample. ∴ A *specimen* exhibits the nature or character of a whole without reference to the relative quality of individual portions; a *sample* is a portion taken out of a quantity, and implies that the quality of the whole is to be judged by it; in many cases, however, the words are used indifferently.

Specious, spē'shus, *a.* [Fr. *spécieux*, from L. *speciosus*, showy, beautiful, plausible, from *species*, show, appearance. SPECIES.] Pleasing to the eye†; superficially fair, just, or correct; plausible; appearing well at first view (a *specious* argument, a *specious* objection). ∴ Syn. under COLOURABLE.—**Speciously**, spē'shus-li, *adv.* In a specious manner; with show of right or reason.—**Speciousness**, spē'shus-nes, *n.* The quality of being specious; plausibility.—**Speciosity**, spē-shi-os'i-ti, *n.* The state of being specious; a specious show.

Speck, spek, *n.* [A.Sax. *specca*, a speck; akin L.G. *spaak*, a speck; *speckle* is a derivative.] A spot; a small discoloured place in anything; a stain; a blemish; a small particle or patch.—*v.t.* To spot; to mark with specks or spots.

Speck, spek, *n.* [D. *spek*, fat.] Blubber, the fat of whales and other mammalia.

Speckle, spek'l, *n.* [Dim. of *speck*.] A little spot in anything, of a different colour from that of the thing itself; a speck.—*v.t.*—*speckled*, *speckling*. To mark with small specks or spots.—**Speckled**, spek'ld, *p.* and *a.* Marked with specks or speckles; variegated with spots of a different colour from the ground or surface of the object.—**Speckledness**, spek'ld-nes, *n.* The state of being speckled.

Spectacle, spek'ta-kl, *n.* [Fr. *spectacle*, from L. *spectaculum*, from *specto*, to behold, freq. of *specio*, to see. SPECIES.] A show; a gazing-stock; something exhibited as worthy of being seen; a gorgeous or splendid show; anything seen; a sight; *pl.* an optical instrument used to assist or correct some defect in the organs of vision, consisting of two lenses mounted in a light frame, so constructed as to adhere to the nose and temples, and keep the lenses before the eyes.—**Spectacled**, spek'ta-kld, *a.* Furnished with or wearing spectacles.—**Spectacular**, spek-tak'ū-lėr, *a.* Pertaining to or of the nature of a show or spectacle; pertaining to spectacles.

Spectator, spek-tā′tor, *n.* [L., from *specto*, freq. of *specio*, to behold. SPECIES.] One who looks on; a beholder; one who is present at a play or spectacle.—**Spectatorial**, spek-ta-tō′ri-al, *a.* Pertaining to a spectator.—**Spectatress**, **Spectatrix**, spek-tā′-tres, spek-tā′triks, *n.* A female beholder or looker on.

Specter, spek′tėr, *n.* [Fr. *spectre*, from L. *spectrum*, an appearance, an apparition, from *specto*, to behold. SPECIES.] An apparition; the disembodied spirit of a person who is dead; a ghost; a phantom.—**Spectral**, spek′tral, *a.* Pertaining to a spectre; ghostlike; pertaining to spectra; pertaining to the solar or other spectrum.—**Spectrally**, spek′tral-li, *adv.* In a spectral manner; like a ghost or spectre.—**Spectroheliograph**, spek′trō-hēl″yō-graf, *n.* [L. *spectrum*, and Gr. *hēlios*, sun, and *graphō*, to write.] An instrument for photographing the sun by monochromatic light.—**Spectrology**, spek-trol′o-ji, *n.* [*Spectrum*, and Gr. *logos*, discourse.] That branch of science which treats of the characteristic spectra of bodies.—**Spectrological**, spek-trō-loj′i-kal, *a.* Pertaining to spectrology.—**Spectrometer**, spek-trom′et-ėr, *n.* [*Spectrum*, and Gr. *metron*, a measure.] An apparatus attached to a spectroscope for purposes of measurement.—**Spectroscope**, spek′trō-skōp, *n.* [*Spectrum*, and Gr. *skopeō*, to look at.] The instrument employed in spectrum analysis, which by means of a prism or train of prisms produces a magnified image of any spectrum.—**Spectroscopic**, **Spectroscopical**, spek-trō-skop′ik, spek-trō-skop′i-kal, *a.* Pertaining to the spectroscope or spectroscopy.—**Spectroscopically**, spek-trō-skop′i-kal-li, *adv.* By the use of the spectroscope.—**Spectroscopist**, spek-tro-skōp-ist, *n.* One who uses the spectroscope; one skilled in spectroscopy.—**Spectroscopy**, spek-tros′kō-pi, *n.* That branch of science which is concerned with the use of the spectroscope and with spectrum analysis.—**Spectrum**, spek′trum, *n.* pl. **Spectra**, spek′tra. A spectre‡; an image of something seen, continuing after the eyes are closed, covered, or turned away; the oblong figure or stripe, exhibiting the prismatic or rainbow colours or some of them, formed on a wall or screen by a beam of light, as of the sun, received through a small slit and refracted by being passed through a prism or series of prisms. The *solar spectrum* or spectrum of sunlight is coloured transversely throughout its length, the colours shading insensibly into one another from red at the one end, through orange, yellow, green, blue, indigo, to violet at the other, and it is also crossed by a number of black lines having definite positions. The moon and planets have spectra like that of the sun, while each fixed star has a spectrum peculiar to itself, and the incandescent vapour of each elementary substance has its characteristic spectrum.—*Spectrum analysis*, the art or operation of examining spectra, whether of the heavenly bodies or of substances heated to incandescence, by means of the spectroscope, a means of detecting the presence of substances otherwise undetected.

Specular. Under SPECULUM.

Speculate, spek′ū-lāt, *v.i.*—*speculated*, *speculating*. [L. *speculor*, *speculatus*, from *specula*, a look-out, from *specio*, to see. SPECIES.] To meditate; to consider a subject in its different aspects and relations; to theorize; to purchase goods, stock, or other things with the expectation of an advance in price and of selling the articles with a profit by means of such advance; to engage in speculation.—**Speculation**, spek-ū-lā′shon, *n.* Mental view of anything in its various aspects and relations; contemplation; a theory or theoretical view; the laying out of money or incurring of extensive risks with a view to more than the usual success in trade; a hazardous commercial or other business transaction entered into in the hope of large profits.—**Speculative**, spek′ū-lā-tiv. *a.* Given to speculation; contemplative; pertaining to, involving, or formed by speculation; theoretical; not verified by fact, experiment, or practice; pertaining to, or given to speculation in trade.—**Speculatively**, spek′ū-lā-tiv-li, *adv.* In a speculative manner.—**Speculativeness**, spek′ū-lā-tiv-nes, *n.* The state of being speculative.—**Speculator**, spek′ū-lā-tėr, *n.* One who speculates or forms theories; a theorizer; one who speculates in trade; one who incurs great risks in the hope of great gain.—**Speculatory**, spek′ū-la-to-ri, *a.* Speculative.

Speculum, spek′ū-lum, *n.* [L., a mirror, from *specio*, to look, to behold. SPECIES.] A mirror or looking-glass; *optics*, a reflecting surface, such as is used in reflecting telescopes, made of an alloy of copper and tin or of glass; *surg.* an instrument with a reflecting mirror attached for examining certain openings of the body.—*Speculum metal*, metal used for making the specula of reflecting telescopes—an alloy of two parts copper and one of tin.—**Specular**, spek′ū-lėr, *a.* [L. *specularis*.] Having the qualities of a mirror or looking-glass; having a smooth reflecting surface.—*Specular iron ore*, a hard, crystallized variety of hæmatite.

Speech, spēch, *n.* [A.Sax. *spaec*, *spraec*, specch, from *specan*, *sprecan*, to speak. SPEAK.] The faculty of expressing thoughts by words or articulate sounds; the power of speaking; language; a particular language; the act of speaking with another; conversation; anything spoken; a discourse, oration, or harangue.—**Speech-day**, *n.* Name for oral examination day in English schools.

—**Speechification**, spēch′i-fi-kā″shon, *n.* The act of speechifying.—**Speechifier**, spēch′i-fī-ėr, *n.* One who speechifies.—**Speechify**, spēch′i-fī, *v.i.*—*speechified*, *speechifying*. To make a speech; to harangue. (*Humorous or contemptuous.*)—**Speechless**, spēch′les, *a.* Destitute or deprived of the faculty of speech; dumb; mute; not speaking for a time; silent.—**Speechlessness**, spēch′les-nes, *n.* The state of being speechless; muteness.

Speed, spēd, *v.i.*—pret. and pp. *sped* or *speeded*. [A.Sax. *spédan*, to hasten, to prosper, from *spéd*, haste, prosperity, from *spówan*, to thrive, same as O.H.G. *spuôn*, to succeed.] To make haste; to move with celerity; to have success; to prosper; to succeed; to have any fortune good or ill; to fare.—*v.t.* To despatch or send away in haste; to hasten; to accelerate; to expedite; to help forward; to make prosperous; to cause to succeed; to dismiss with good wishes or friendly services; to kill or destroy: especially in pp. *sped* (*Shak.*).—*n.* Success; fortune; prosperity in an undertaking; swiftness; celerity; haste; impetuosity.—**God-speed.** Under GOD.—**Speeder**, spē′dėr, *n.* One who speeds; a kind of machine for forwarding things in manufacture.—**Speedful**, spēd′ful, *a.* Full of speed; successful; prosperous.—**Speedfully**, spēd′ful-li, *adv.* In a speedful manner; speedily; successfully.—**Speedy**, spē′di, *a.* Quick; nimble; rapid in motion; not dilatory or slow.—**Speedily**, spē′di-li, *adv.* In a speedy manner quickly; in a short time.—**Speediness**, spē′di-nes, *n.* The quality of being speedy; quickness; despatch.—**Speedless**, spēd′les, *a.* Having no speed; not prosperous; unsuccessful.—**Speedometer**, spēd-om′et-ėr, *n.* An instrument for indicating speed.—**Speedwell**, spēd′wel, *n.* [From growing on roadsides, and, as it were, cheering travellers on their way.] The common name of plants of the genus Veronica, a favourite species being the germander speedwell.

Speer, **Speir**, spēr, *v.t.* and *i.* [A.Sax. *spyrian*; Icel. *spyrja*, lit. to search out by the track or trace, from *spor*, D. *spoer*, G. *spur*, a track.] To ask; to inquire. (*Scotch.*)

Spelæan, spē-lē′an, *a.* [L. *spelæum*, from Gr. *spēlaion*, a cave.] Pertaining to a cave or caves; dwelling in a cave or caves.

Spelding, **Speldron**, spel′ding, spel′-dron, *n.* [Sc. *speld*, to spread out; akin to G. *spalten*, Sw. *spjäla*, to cleave to divide.] A small fish split and dried in the sun. (*Scotch.*)

Spell, spel, *n.* [A.Sax. *spell*, a saying, tale, charm; Icel. *spjall*, O.G. *spel*, Goth. *spill*, a tale. Hence the latter part of *gospel*.] A charm consisting of some words of occult power; an incantation; any charm.—*v.t.*—pret. and pp. *spelled* or *spelt*. [A.Sax. *spellian*, to say, speak, tell.] To repeat, point out, write, or print the proper letters of in their regular order; to form by letters; to read; to read with labour or difficulty: often with *out*; to act as a spell upon; to fascinate; to charm.—*v.i.* To form words with the proper letters, either in reading or writing; to read.—**Spellbound**, *a.* Bound as by a spell or charm.—**Speller**, spel′ėr, *n.* One that spells; a spelling-book.—**Spelling**, spel′ing, *n.* The act of one who spells; orthography.—**Spelling-bee**, *n.* An assemblage of persons met for the purpose of exercising themselves, or comparing their acquirements, in spelling.—**Spelling-book**, *n.* A book for teaching children to spell and read.

Spell, spel, *n.* [A.Sax. *spelian*, to supply the room of another; comp. D. and Sw. *spel*, G. *spiel*, play, game.] A piece of work done by one person in relief of another; a turn of work; a single period of labour; a period; a while or season.

Spell, spel, *n.* A splinter; a spill. SPILL.

Spelt, spelt, *n.* [A.Sax. *spelt*, L.G. and D. *spelt*, G. *spelz*, from root of *split*.] An inferior kind of wheat. Called also *German Wheat*.

Spelt, spelt. A pret. and pp. of *spell*.

Spelter, spel′tėr, *n.* [L.G. *spialter*, G. and D. *spiauter*, spelter, zinc; akin *pewter*.] A name often applied in commerce to zinc.

Spence, spens, *n.* [O.Fr. *despense*, a buttery, from *despendre*, L. *dispendere*, to dispense—*dis*, and *pendo*, to weigh.] A buttery; a place where provisions are kept; in Scotland, the apartment of a house where the family sit and eat.

Spencer, spen′sėr, *n.* An outer coat or jacket without skirts, named from an Earl *Spencer*, who first wore it.

Spencer, spen′sėr, *n.* [Perhaps akin to *spanker*.] *Naut.* a fore-and-aft sail with a gaff and boom set abaft the fore and main masts.

Spend, spend, *v.t.*—pret. and pp. *spent*. [A.Sax. *spendan*, borrowed from L. *expendo* or *dispendo*, to expend, to dispense. EXPEND, PENDANT.] To lay out (money); to part with in purchasing; to exhaust (to *spend* one's energies); to waste; to pass, as time; to suffer to pass away; to exhaust of force or strength; to waste (to *spend* efforts).—*v.i.* To make expense; to spend money.—**Spender**, spen′dėr, *n.* One that spends; a prodigal; a lavisher.—**Spendthrift**, spend′thrift, *n.* One who spends his means lavishly or improvidently; a prodigal: often used as an adjective (*spendthrift* ways).—**Spent**, spent, pret. and pp. of *spend*. Worn out; wearied; exhausted; having deposited the spawn: said of a herring.—*Spent ball*, a cannon or rifle ball which reaches an object without sufficient force to pass through it, or to wound otherwise than by a contusion.

Spenserian, spen-sē′ri-an, *a.* Pertaining to the poet *Spenser*; applied to the style of versification adopted by Spenser in his *Faëry Queen*.

Sperm, spėrm, *n.* [L. and Gr. *sperma*, *spermatos*, seed, from *speirō*, to sow.] The seminal fluid of animals; semen; spawn of fishes or frogs; a microscopic male cell, usually motile.—**Spermaceti**, spėr-ma-sē′ti, *n.* [Lit. sperm of whale; L. *sperma*, and *cetus*, a whale.] A fatty material obtained from a species of whale common in the Pacific.—**Spermarium**, **Spermary**, spėr-mā′ri-um, spėr′ma-ri, *n.* The organ in male animals in which spermatozoa are produced.—**Spermatheca**, spėr′ma-thē-ka, *n.* [Gr. *sperma*, and *thēkē*, case.] A cavity in certain female insects (e.g. queen-bees) in which the sperm of the male is received.—**Spermatic**, **Spermati-**

cal, spėr-mat'ik, spėr-mat'i-kal, *a.* Seminal; pertaining to the semen, or conveying it.—**Spermatism**, spėr'ma-tizm, *n.* The emission of sperm or seed.—**Spermatium, -ia**, spėr-mā'shum, *n.* [Gr. *sperma*, *spermatos*, seed.] In fungi, a free non-motile male cell.—**Spermatogenous**, spėr-ma-toj'en-us, *a.* [Gr. *sperma*, and root *gen*, to produce.] Sperm-producing. — **Spermatoid**, spėr'ma-toid, *a.* [Gr. *sperma*, and *eidos*, form.] Sperm-like; resembling sperm or semen.—**Spermatoon**, spėr'ma-tō-on, *n.* pl. **Spermatoa**, spėr'ma-tō-a. [Gr. *sperma*, and *ōon*, egg.] A cell constituting a nucleus of a sperm-cell. — **Spermatophyte**, spėr'ma-tō-fīt, *n.* [Gr. *sperma*, and *phyton*, plant.] The highest phylum of plants, the seed plants or flowering plants. —**Spermatorrhea**, spėr'ma-tō-rē"a, *n.* [Gr. *sperma*, and *rheō*, to flow.] Emission of the semen without copulation.—**Spermatozoon**, spėr'ma-to-zō"on, *n.* pl. **Spermatozoa**, spėr'ma-to-zō"a. [Gr. *sperma*, and *zōon*, a living being.] One of the microscopic animalcule-like bodies developed in the semen of animals and essential to impregnation.—**Sperm-cell**, *n.* A cell in which are developed spermatoa.—**Spermic**, spėr'mik, *a.* Pertaining to sperm or seed.—**Spermidium**, spėr-mid'i-um, *n.* [Gr. *sperma*, and *eidos*, resemblance.] *Bot.* a small seed-vessel, more commonly called an *Achene*. — **Spermoderm**, spėr'mo-dėrm, *n.* [Gr. *sperma*, and *derma*, skin.] *Bot.* the integuments of a seed in the aggregate.—**Sperm-oil**, *n.* The oil of the spermaceti whale.—**Spermotheca**, spėr'mo-thē-ka, *n.* [Gr. *sperma*, and *thēkē*, case.] *Bot.* the seed-vessel; the case in which seeds are contained.—**Sperm-whale**, *n.* The spermaceti whale or cachalot.

Spetches, spech'ez, *n.pl.* The offal of skin and hides, from which glue is made.

Spew, spū, *v.t.* [A.Sax. *spīwan*, to spew; D. *spouwen*, *spuwen*, G. *speien*, Icel. *spýja*, Goth. *speiwan*, to vomit; cog. L. *spuo*, to vomit. *Spit* is from same root.] To vomit; to eject from the stomach; to eject or to cast forth.—*v.i.* To vomit.—**Spewer**, spū'-ėr, *n.* One who spews.

Sphacelus, sfas'ē-lus, *n.* [Gr. *sphakelos*, from *sphazō*, to kill.] Gangrene; mortification of the flesh of a living animal; death or caries of a bone.—**Sphacel**, sfas'el, *n.* Gangrene. — **Sphacelate**, sfas'e-lāt, *v.i.* To mortify; to become gangrenous, as flesh; to become carious, as a bone.—*v.t.* To affect with gangrene.—**Sphacelate, Sphacelated**, sfas'ē-lāt, sfas'ē-lā-ted, *a.* *Bot.* decayed, withered, or dead. — **Sphacelation**, sfas-ē-lā'shon, *n.* The process of becoming or making gangrenous; mortification. — **Sphacelism, Sphacelismus**, sfas'e-lizm, sfas-e-liz'mus, *n.* A gangrene; an inflammation of the brain.

Sphærenchyma, sfē-reng'ki-ma, *n.* [Gr. *sphaira*, a sphere, and *enchyma*, anything poured in.] A name given to spherical or spheroidal cellular tissue, such as is found in the pulp of fruits.—**Sphæridium**, sfē-rid'i-um, *n.* pl. **Sphæridia**, sfē-rid'i-a. [Gr. *sphaira*, a sphere, and *eidos*, resemblance.] One of the curious stalked appendages with button-like heads, covered with cilia, carried on the tests of almost all sea-urchins. — **Sphæristerium**, sfē-ris-tē'ri-um, *n.* [Gr. *sphairistērion*, from *sphairistēs*, a ball-player, *sphaira*, a ball.] A building for playing at ball; a tennis-court. — **Sphæroblast**, sfē'rō-blast, *n.* [Gr. *sphaira*, and *blastos*, a sprout.] *Bot.* a cotyledon which rises above-ground, bearing at its end a spheroid tumour.—**Sphærosiderite**, sfē'rō-sid"ėr-īt. SPHEROSIDERITE. — **Sphærulite**, sfē'rū-līt. SPHERULITE.

Sphagnum, sfag'num, *n.* [Gr. *sphagnos*, a kind of moss.] An important genus of mosses; peat-moss, valuable for packing plants for transmission; much used in hospitals for dressing wounds.

Sphene, sfēn, *n.* [From Gr. *sphēn*, a wedge, from the shape of its crystals.] A mineral composed of silicic acid, titanic acid, and lime.

Sphenogram, sfē'nō-gram, *n.* [Gr. *sphēn*, *sphēnos*, a wedge, and *gramma*, a letter.] A wedge-shaped, cuneiform, or arrow-headed character. CUNEIFORM.—**Sphenography**, sfē-nog'ra-fi, *n.* The art of writing or of deciphering cuneiform writings. — **Sphenographer**, sfē-nog'raf-ėr, *n.* One versed in cuneiform writing. — **Sphenographic**, sfē-nō-graf'ik, *a.* Pertaining to sphenography.

Sphenoid, Sphenoidal, sfē'noid, sfē-noi'dal, *a.* [Gr. *sphēn*, a wedge, and *eidos*, form.] Resembling a wedge. — *Sphenoid bone*, a bone in the base of the skull, so named because it is wedged in amidst the other bones.—*n.* A wedge-shaped body; the sphenoid bone.—**Spheno-**. As a prefix in anatomical terms means pertaining to the sphenoid.

Sphenopteris, sfē-nop'tėr-is, *n.* [Gr. *sphēn*, *sphēnos*, a wedge, and *pteris*, a fern.] A genus of fossil ferns remarkable for the wedge-shaped divisions of their fronds.

Sphere, sfēr, *n.* [L. *sphæra*, from Gr. *sphaira*, a ball, a globe.] A globular body; an orb or globe; a planet, star, or sun; a solid body the surface of which in every part is equally distant from a point within it called its centre; the concave expanse of the heavens; circuit or range of action, knowledge, or influence; compass; province; rank or order of society.—*v.t.*—*sphered*, *sphering*. To place in a sphere or among the spheres; to form into a sphere. —**Spheral**, sfē'ral, *a.* Pertaining to the spheres or heavenly bodies; rounded like a sphere. — **Sphere-born**, *a.* Born among the spheres. — **Sphere-melody, Sphere-music**, *n.* The music, imperceptible to human ears, produced by the movements of the heavenly bodies, according to the hypothesis of Pythagoras. — **Spherical, Spheric**, sfer'i-kal, sfer'ik, *a.* [Fr. *sphérique*; L. *sphæricus*.] Having the form of a sphere; globular; pertaining or belonging to a sphere; relating to the orbs of the planets; planetary.—*Spherical angle*, an angle formed on the surface of a sphere by the intersection of two great circles.—*Spherical geometry*, that branch of geometry which treats of spherical magnitudes.—*Spherical triangle*, a triangle formed on the surface of a sphere by the mutual intersection of three great circles.—*Spherical trigonometry*, that branch of trigonometry which deals with spherical triangles.—**Spherically**, sfer'i-kal-li, *adv.* In the form of a sphere.—**Sphericity, Sphericalness**, sfe-ris'i-ti, sfer'i-kal-nes, *n.* The state or quality of being spherical; globularity; roundness.—**Sphericle**, sfer'i-kl, *n.* A small sphere.—**Spherics**, sfer'iks, *n.* *Geom.* the doctrine of the properties of the sphere.—**Spheroid**, sfē'roid, *n.* A body not perfectly spherical; *geom.* a solid generated by the revolution of an ellipse about one of its axes, being either *oblate* or *prolate*.—**Spheroidal**, sfē-roi'dal, *a.* Having the form of a spheroid; *crystal.* bounded by several convex faces.—*Spheroidal state*, the name given to the condition of a liquid when, on being placed on a red-hot plate, it assumes a spheroidal form and passes into the state of gas without boiling. —**Spheroidic, Spheroidical**, sfē-roi'dik, sfē-roi'di-kal, *a.* SPHEROIDAL. — **Spheroidicity**, sfē-roi-dis'i-ti, *n.* The quality of being spheroidal.—**Spherometer**, sfē-rom'et-ėr, *n.* An instrument for measuring the thickness of small bodies when great accuracy is required, as the curvature of optical glasses, &c.—**Spherosiderite**, sfē-ro-sid'ėr-īt, *n.* [Gr. *sphaira*, and *sidēros*, iron.] An ore of iron found in spheroidal masses.—**Spherula**, sfer'ū-la, *n.* [L. *sphærula*, a little sphere.] A spherule. —**Spherulate**, sfer'ū-lāt, *a.* Covered or studded with spherules.—**Spherule**, sfer'-ūl, *n.* A little sphere or spherical body.—**Spherulite**, sfer'ū-līt, *n.* [Gr. *sphaira*, and *lithos*, a stone.] A variety of obsidian found in rounded grains.—**Sphery**, sfē'ri, *a.* Belonging to the spheres; resembling a sphere or orb.

Sphincter, sfingk'tėr, *n.* [Gr. *sphingktēr*, from *sphingō*, to draw close.] *Anat.* a name applied to circular muscles or muscles in rings, which serve to close the external orifices of organs, as the sphincter of the mouth, of the anus, &c.

Sphinx, sfingks, *n.* pl. **Sphinxes**, sfingk'-sez. [L. *sphinx*, Gr. *sphingx*.] *Greek myth.* a she-monster often represented with the winged body of a lion and the breasts and head of a woman, said to have proposed a riddle to the Thebans and to have killed all who were not able to guess it, till Œdipus did so, whereupon the sphinx slew herself; hence, a person who puts puzzling questions; *Egyptian antiq.* a figure having the body of a lion and a human (male or female) or animal head, probably a purely symbolical figure, having no connection with the Greek fable; a name of the hawk-moths.

Sphragistics, sfra-jis'tiks, *n.* [Gr. *sphragis*, a seal.] The science of seals, their history, peculiarities, and distinctions.

Sphrigosis, sfri-gō'sis, *n.* [From Gr. *sphrigaō*, to be full of health and strength.] Over-rankness, a disease in plants, in which they tend to grow to wood or stem and leaves in place of fruit or bulb, &c.

Sphygmic, sfig'mik, *a.* [Gr. *sphygmos*, the pulse.] Of or pertaining to the pulse. — **Sphygmograph**, sfig'mō-graf, *n.* An instrument which, when applied over an artery, indicates the character of the pulse. **Sphygmographic**, sfig-mō-graf'ik, *a.* Of or pertaining to the sphygmograph.—**Sphygmometer**, sfig-mom'et-ėr, *n.* An instrument for counting the arterial pulsations; a sphygmograph.

Spicate, spī'kāt, *a.* [L. *spicatus*, from *spica*, a spike.] *Bot.* having a spike or ear; eared like corn.

Spice, spīs, *n.* [O.Fr. *espice* (Fr. *épice*), from L. *species*, species, kind, in late Latin, wares, spices, drugs, &c. SPECIES.] A vegetable production, fragrant, or aromatic to the smell and pungent to the taste, such as pepper, nutmeg, ginger, cinnamon, and cloves, used in sauces and in cookery; *fig.* a small admixture; a flavouring; a smack.—*v.t.*—*spiced*, *spicing*. To season with spice; to season, literally or figuratively.—**Spice-nut**, *n.* A ginger-bread nut. — **Spicer**, spī'sėr, *n.* One that seasons with spice; one who deals in spice.—**Spicery**, spī'sėr-i, *n.* Spices collectively; a repository of spices. **Spicily**, spī'si-li, *adv.* In a spicy manner; pungently; with flavour.—**Spiciness**, spī'-si-nes, *n.* Quality of being spicy.—**Spicy**, spī'si, *a.* Producing spice; abounding with spices; having the quality of spice; flavoured with spice; aromatic; *fig.* pungent; piquant; keen.

Spiciferous, spī-sif'ėr-us, *a.* [L. *spica*, an ear, and *fero*, to bear.] Bearing ears, as corn; spicated; eared.—**Spiciform**, spī'-si-form, *a.* *Bot.* spike-shaped.

Spick-and-span, spik'and-span, *a.* or *adv.* [*Spick*, a spike, and span, a chip, a splinter. SPAN-NEW.] In full use adverbially with *new* = quite new; bran-new; also used adjectively (a *spick-and-span* suit of clothes).

Spicose, Spicous, spīk'ōs, spik'us, *a.* [From L. *spica*, a spike or ear.] Having spikes or ears; eared like corn.—**Spicosity**, spī-kos'i-ti, *n.* The state of being spicose.

Spicula, spik'ū-la, *n.* pl. **Spiculæ**, spik'-ū-lē. [L. *spicula*, dim. of *spica*, a sharp point, a spike.] *Bot.* a small spike or spikelet; a pointed, fleshy, superficial appendage. —**Spicular**, spik'ū-lėr, *a.* Resembling a dart; having sharp points. — **Spiculate**, spik'ū-lāt, *a.* Covered with or divided into fine points. — **Spicule**, spik'ūl, *n.* [L. *spicula*.] A little spike; a little sharp needle-shaped body. — **Spiculiform**, spik'ū-li-form, *a.* Having the form of a spicule.

Spicy. Under SPICE.

Spider, spī'dėr, *n.* [For *spinder*, for *spinner*, one that spins; comp. G. *spinne*, a spider, from *spinnen*, to spin.] The common name of well-known animals of the class Arachnida, many of them remarkable for spinning webs for taking their prey and forming a convenient habitation; something supposed to resemble a spider, as a kind of grid-iron, or a trivet to support vessels over a fire. — **Spider-line**, *n.* One of the threads of a spider's web ingeniously substituted for wires in micrometer scales.—**Spider-monkey**, *n.* A name given to many species of New World monkeys.

Spiegeleisen, spē'gel-ī-zn, *n.* [G.—*spiegel*, a mirror, and *eisen*, iron: from its fracture showing large smooth shining surfaces.] A kind of cast-iron made from specular iron ore or hæmatite, containing much carbon and manganese, largely used in the Bessemer process of steel-making.

Spigot, spig'ot, *n.* [O.E. *spigotte*, *speget*, *spykette*, dim. forms from *spick* = *spike*.] A pin or peg used to stop a faucet, or a small hole in a cask of liquor; a faucet.

Spike, spīk, *n.* [Same word as *pike* with initial *s*; Icel. *spík*, Sw. *spik*, a spike; cog. L. *spica*, a sharp point, an ear of corn; W. *yspig*, a spike.] A large nail or pin; a piece of pointed iron like a long nail, as on the top of walls, gates, &c.; a nail or instrument with which the vents of cannon are filled up; an ear of corn or other grain; *bot.* a species of inflorescence in which the flowers are sessile along a common axis.—*v.t.*—*spiked*, *spiking*. To fasten with spikes or long nails; to set with spikes; to fix upon a spike.—*To spike a gun* or *cannon*, to fill up the touch-hole by driving a nail or steel pin with side springs forcibly into it, in order to render it unserviceable.—**Spikelet**, spīk'let, *n.* *Bot.* a small spike making a part of a large one.—**Spikenard**, spīk'närd, *n.* [The plant bears flowers in *spikes*. See NARD.] An aromatic herbaceous plant of the East Indies, the root of which is highly prized for its aromatic properties; a name given to several other plants, and to various fragrant essential oils.—**Spike-oil**, *n.* A volatile oil distilled from a species of lavender often called *Spikenard*.—**Spiky**, spī'ki, *a.* In the shape of a spike; set with spikes.

Spile, spīl, *n.* [Same as D. *spijl*, L.G. *spile*, a bar, a stake; G. *speil*, a skewer. SPILL, *n.*] A small peg or wooden pin used to stop a hole in a cask or barrel; a spigot.—*v.t.*—*spiled*, *spiling*. To supply with a spigot.—**Spile-hole**, *n.* A small aperture in a cask to let in air, so that the contained liquor may flow freely.

Spill, spil, *n.* [Same as D. *spil*, G. *spille*, a spindle, a peg; allied to *spile*, *spell*, Sc. *spale*, a chip.] A spigot; a spile; a small slip of wood or strip of paper rolled up, used to light a lamp, &c.

Spill, spil, *v.t.*—pret. and pp. *spilled* or *spilt*. [A.Sax. *spillan*, to spill; to ruin; L.G. and D. *spillen*, Icel. *spilla*, Dan. *spilde*, to spill, to waste; akin to *spill* above.] To suffer to fall or run out of a vessel: applied to fluids and to substances whose particles are small and loose; to suffer or cause to flow out; to shed (a man *spills* another's blood); to throw from a horse or carriage (*colloq.*).—*v.i.* To be shed; to be suffered to fall, to be lost, or wasted.—**Spiller**, spil'ėr, *n.* One who spills.—**Spillway**, *n.* In hydraulic engineering, a diversion for excess water from a river or reservoir; a gatelike mechanism of a dam to allow for the escape of superfluous water.

Spin, spin, *v.t.*—pret. *spun* or *span*; pp. *spun*; ppr. *spinning*. [A.Sax. *spinnan*=D. and G. *spinnen*, Goth. *spinnan*, Dan. *spinde*, Icel. and Sw. *spinna*—to spin; same root as *span* and Gr. *spaō*, to draw. Hence *spindle*, *spinster*, *spider*.] To draw out and twist into threads, either by the hand or machinery (to *spin* wool, cotton, or flax); to draw out tediously (to *spin* out a tale); to extend to a great length; to whirl rapidly; to cause to turn with great speed (to *spin* a top); to form by the extrusion of a viscid fluid from their body, as spiders, silkworms, &c.—*To spin a yarn*, to tell a long story: originally a seaman's phrase.—*v.i.* To perform the act of making threads; to work at drawing and twisting threads; to move round rapidly; to whirl, as a top or a spindle; to run or drive with great rapidity; to go quickly (*colloq.*).—*n.* The act of spinning; a rapid run; a race; the rotation of an elongated projectile (a shell) about its long axis imparted to it by the rifling of the gun. See TWIST.—**Spinner**, spin'ėr, *n.* One who or that which spins; a spider; a spinneret.—**Spinneret**, spin'ėr-et, *n.* One of the nipple-like organs with which spiders form their webs.—**Spinnerule**, spin'ėr-ūl, *n.* One of the numerous minute spinning tubes of spiders.—**Spinnery**, spin'ėr-i, *n.* A spinning-mill.—**Spinning-jenny**, *n.* The first spinning-machine by which a number of threads could be spun at once; invented about 1767 by James Hargreaves.—**Spinning-mill**, *n.* A mill or factory where spinning is carried on.—**Spinning-wheel**, *n.* A machine for spinning wool, cotton, or flax into threads by the hand.—**Spinster**, spin'stėr, *n.* [*Spin*, and double fem. ter. -*ster*, -*ess*.] A woman who spins; an unmarried woman; formerly, in England, an unmarried woman of the nobility from a viscount's daughter downward.

Spinach, **Spinage**, spin'āj, *n.* [O.Fr. *espinoche*, It. *spinace*, Sp. *espinaca*, from L. *spina*, a spine—being named from the prickles on its fruit.] An annual plant (*Spinacia oleracea*), with hollow stems and edible, fleshy leaves, used as a vegetable.—**Spinaceous**, spi-nā'shus, *a.* Pertaining to the spinach class of plants.

Spinal. Under SPINE.

Spindle, spin'dl, *n.* [A.Sax. *spindel*, lit. the instrument for spinning, from *spinnan*, to spin; so also, G., Sw., and Dan. *spindel*.] A slender rod by which the thread is twisted and wound in spinning; any slender pointed rod or pin which turns round or on which anything turns; an axis or arbour; a measure of yarn: in cotton, 15,120 yards; in linen, 14,400 yards.—*v.i.*—*spindled*, *spindling*. To shoot or grow in a long, slender stalk or body.—**Spindle-legs**, **Spindle-shanks**, *n.* Long slender legs, or a person having such.—**Spindle-tree**, *n.* A small tree (genus Euonymus) found wild in Britain.

Spindrift, spin'drift, *n.* [A form of *spoondrift*.] *Naut.* the blinding drift of salt water blown from the surface of the sea in hurricanes.

Spine, spīn, *n.* [L. *spina*, a thorn, the spine, from a root seen also in *spike*. From the Latin come also *spinach*, *spinet*, *spinney*.] The backbone of a vertebrated animal, so called from the thorn-like processes of the vertebræ; a thorn; a sharp process from the woody part of a plant; a stout, rigid, and pointed process of the integument of an animal; a ridge of mountains, especially a central ridge.—**Spinal**, spī'nal, *a.* Pertaining to the spine or backbone of an animal.—*Spinal column*, the backbone.—*Spinal cord*, *Spinal marrow*, the elongated mass of nervous matter contained in the osseous canal of the spine.—**Spinescent**, spī-nes'ent, *a.* [L. *spinesco*, to grow thorny.] *Bot* terminating in a spine; somewhat spinose.—**Spiniferous**, spī-nif'ėr-us, *a.* Producing spines; bearing thorns; thorny.—**Spiniform**, spī'ni-form, *a.* Having the form of a spine or thorn.—**Spinigerous**, spī-nij'ėr-us, *a.* Bearing a spine or spines.—**Spininess**, spī'ni-nes, *n.* The quality of being spiny.—**Spinosity**, spī-nos'i-ti, *n.* The state of being spinous or spinose.—**Spinous**, **Spinose**, spī'nus, spī'nōs, *a.* [L. *spinosus*.] Full of spines; armed with thorns; thorny.—**Spinule**, spī'nūl, *n.* [L. *spinula*, dim. of *spina*.] A minute spine.—**Spinulescent**, spī-nū-les'ent, *a.* *Bot.* somewhat thorny.—**Spinulose**, **Spinulous**, spī'nū-lōs, spī'nū-lus, *a.* *Bot.* covered with small spines.—**Spiny**, spī'ni, *a.* Full of spines; thorny; like a spine; slender; perplexed; troublesome.

Spinel, **Spinelle**, spi-nel', *n.* [Fr. *spinelle*, It. *spinella*, originally perhaps a mineral with spine-shaped crystals, from L. *spina*, a spine.] A species of corundum, which occurs in regular crystals and sometimes in rounded grains.

Spinet, spin'et, *n.* [O.Fr. *espinette*, from L. *spina*, a spine, because its strings were twitched by spine-like pieces of quill. SPINE.] A stringed musical instrument, which differed from the virginal only in being of a triangular form.

Spine-tail, *n.* A name of several birds having stiff pointed feathers in the tail.

Spiniferous. Under SPINE.

Spinifex, spin'i-feks, *n.* An excessively spiny grass, growing in tussocks, and covering large areas in Australia, where it forms a great impediment to travellers.

Spinnaker, spin'a-kėr, *n.* [From *spin*, in sense of to go rapidly.] A triangular racing sail carried by yachts when running before the wind, on the opposite side to the mainsail.

Spinner, **Spinneret**, &c. Under SPIN.

Spinney, **Spinny**, spin'i, *n.* [O.Fr. *espinaye*, from *espine*, a brier, from L. *spina*, a thorn.] A small wood with undergrowth; a clump of trees; a small grove.

Spinose, **Spinous**. Under SPINE.

Spinozism, spi-nō'zizm, *n.* A system of pantheistic philosophy propounded by Baruch *Spinoza*, who was born in Amsterdam in 1632 of a Jewish family, and died at the Hague in 1677.—**Spinozist**, spī-nō'zist, *n.* A believer in the doctrines of Spinoza.

Spinster. Under SPIN.

Spinthariscope, spin-thar'is-kōp, *n.* [Gr. *spinthēr*, a spark, *skopeō*, to view.] An instrument for demonstrating the physical properties of radium.

Spinule, **Spiny**. Under SPINE.

Spiracle, spī'ra-kl, *n.* [L. *spiraculum*, from *spiro*, to breathe. SPIRIT.] A breathing hole; an aperture for exhalation or inhalation; one of the breathing-pores or apertures of the breathing-tubes of insects.

Spiræa, spī-rē'a, *n.* [Gr. *speiraia*.] A genus of plants, order Rosaceæ, some of the species of which (as meadow-sweet) are esteemed for their flowers.

Spirant, spī'rant, *n.* [L. *spira*, to breathe.] A surd continuous consonant, as *h*, *th*, *f*, *s*, &c.

Spire, spīr, *n.* [L. *spira*, from Gr. *speira*, a spiral line, something twisted.] A winding line like the threads of a screw; a spiral; anything wreathed or contorted; a wreath; the convulutions of the spiral shell of a mollusc above the lowest or body whorl.—**Spiral**, spī'ral, *a.* Winding round a fixed point or centre, like a watch-spring; winding round a cylinder, and at the same time rising or advancing forward, like a cork-screw; pointed or shaped like a spire.—*Spiral nebula*, a nebula in the form of a double spiral, shining with white light, and supposed to be extremely remote.—*Spiral pump*, a form of the Archimedean screw.—*Spiral spring*, a coil whose rounds have the same diameter, and which is generally utilized by compression or extension in the line of its axis.—*n.* A curve which continually recedes from a center or fixed point while continuing to revolve about it; a helix or curve which winds round a cylinder like a screw.—*v.t.* *spiraled*, *spiralled*, *spiraling*, *spiralling*. To form, or move in, a spiral.—*v.t.* To arrange as, or form into, a spiral; to make, or cause, to spiral.—**Spiraling**, spī'raling, *n.* *Aviation*, the act of continuously turning and climbing or diving simultaneously, so that the path is a spiral or helical one.—**Spirally**, spī'ral-li, *adv.*—**Spiry**, spī'ri, *a.* Of a spiral form.

Spire, spīr, *n.* [A.Sax. *spir*, a spike or stalk; D. *spier*, a spire of grass; Dan. *spire*, a sprout, *spiir*, a spire; akin to *spear* and *spar*.] A body that shoots up to a point; the tapering portion of a steeple rising above the tower; a steeple; a stalk or blade of grass or other plant.—*v.i.*—*spired*, *spiring*. To shoot up pyramidically; to taper up.—**Spired**, spīrd, *a.* Having a spire.

Spirifer, spī'ri-fėr, *n.* [L. *spira*, a spiral, and *fero*, to bear.] A fossil genus of brachiopoda, having a shell with two internal, calcareous, spiral appendages.

Spirillum, spī-ril'um, *n.*; pl. **Spirilla**, spī-ril'a. [From its *spiral* growth.] A microscopic germ of the bacteria class.

Spirit, spir'it, *n.* [L. *spiritus*, breath, courage, the soul, life, from *spiro*, to breathe, seen also in *aspire, conspire, expire, inspire, respire*, &c. *Sprite* is the same word.] The intelligent, immaterial, and immortal part of man; the soul, as distinguished from the body which it occupies; a person considered with respect to his mental or moral characteristics; the human soul after it has quitted the body; an apparition; a spectre; a ghost; a supernatural being; an angel, fairy, elf, sprite, demon, or the like; vivacity, animation, ardour, enthusiasm, courage, or the like; emotional state; mood; humour: often in the plural (to be in high or low *spirits*); the vital or essential part of anything; inspiring or actuating principle; essence; real meaning; intent, as opposed to the letter or formal statement; a liquid obtained by distillation, especially alcohol; *pl.* brandy, gin, rum, whisky, or other distilled liquor containing much alcohol (a glass of *spirits*).—*Animal spirits*, liveliness of disposition; constitutional briskness and gaiety. — *Holy Spirit*, or *the Spirit*, the Spirit of God, or the third person of the Trinity.—*v.t.* To animate with vigour; to encourage; to convey away secretly, as if by the agency of a spirit; to kidnap.—**Spirited**, spir′it-ed, *a.* Animated; full of life; lively; full of spirit or fire (a *spirited* address); having a spirit of a certain character: used in composition (high-*spirited*, low-*spirited*). — **Spiritedly**, spir′it-ed-li, *adv.* In a spirited manner; with spirit; with courage.—**Spiritedness**, spir′it-ed-nes, *n.* The state.—**Spiriting**, spir′it-ing, *n.* The work of a spirit; work done as if by a spirit.—**Spirit-lamp**, *n.* A lamp in which alcohol is used instead of oil.—**Spiritless**, spir′it-les, *a.* Destitute of spirits; destitute of courage or fire; depressed; pusillanimous. — **Spiritlessly**, spir′it-les-li, *adv.* In a spiritless manner.—**Spiritlessness**, spir′it-les-nes, *n.* The state or quality of being spiritless. — **Spirit-level**, *n.* A glass tube nearly filled with spirit, for determining a line or plane parallel to the horizon, by the central position of an air-bubble on its upper side. —**Spiritoso**, spir-i-tō′sō. [It., spirited.] *Mus.* in a spirited manner.—**Spirit-rapper**, *n.* One who believes in or practises spirit-rapping.—**Spirit-rapping**, *n.* The name given to certain so-called spiritualistic manifestations, as audible raps or knocks on tables, table-turning, &c.—**Spiritual**, spir′it-ū-al, *a.* [L. *spiritualis.*] Pertaining to or consisting of spirit; not material; incorporeal; pertaining to the mind or intellect; mental; intellectual; pertaining to the soul or its affections as influenced by the Divine Spirit; proceeding from or controlled and inspired by the Holy Spirit; holy; sacred; divine; relating to sacred things; not lay or temporal; ecclesiastical.—**Spiritualism**, spir′it-ū-al-izm, *n.* The state of being spiritual; spiritual character; the doctrine of the existence of spirit as distinct from matter; that system of philosophy according to which all that is real is spirit, soul, or mind, matter or the external world being either a succession of notions impressed on the mind by the Deity, or else a mere educt of the mind itself; the belief that communication can be held with departed spirits by means of phenomena manifested through a person of special susceptibility, called a *medium*.—**Spiritualist**, spir′it-ū-al-ist, *n.* One whose state is spiritual; an adherent of spiritualism; one who believes that intercourse may be held with departed spirits through the agency of a *medium*; one who pretends to hold such intercourse.—**Spiritualistic**, spir′it-ū-a-lis″tik, *a.* Relating to spiritualism. — **Spirituality**, spir′it-ū-al″i-ti, *n.* The state or quality of being spiritual; spiritual character; immateriality; what belongs to the church or to religion, as distinct from *temporalities*: generally in plural.—**Spiritualization**, spir′it-ū-al-ī-zā″shon, *n.* The act of spiritualizing. — **Spiritualize**, spir′it-ū-al-īz, *v.t.*—*spiritualized, spiritualizing.* To make spiritual or more spiritual; to infuse spirituality or life into; to inform with life; to convert into spirit, or to impart the properties of spirit to. — **Spiritualizer**, spir′it-ū-al-ī-zėr, *n.* One who spiritualizes.—**Spiritually**, spir′it-ū-al-li, *adv.* In a spiritual manner.—**Spiritual-minded**, *a.* Having the mind set on spiritual things; having holy affections.—**Spiritualness**, spir′it-ū-al-nes, *n.* The state or quality of being spiritual; spirituality.—**Spirituous**, spir′it-ū-us, *a.* [Fr. *spiritueux.*] Containing spirit as the characteristic ingredient; alcoholic. — **Spirituousness**, spir′it-ū-us-nes, *n.*

Spiritus, spir′it-us, *n.* [L.] *Gram.* a breathing; an aspirate.—*Spiritus asper*, a rough breathing; in *Greek gram.* the mark (ʽ), indicating a sound like an aspirated *h* in English.—*Spiritus lenis*, a soft breathing; the mark (ʼ), denoting the absence of the rough breathing.

Spirochete, spī′rō-kēt, *n.* [Gr. *speira*, a coil, *chaitē*, a bristle.] Bacteria shaped like spiral threads.

Spirometer, spī-rom′et-ėr, *n.* [L. *spiro*, to breathe, and Gr. *metron*, a measure.] A contrivance for determining the capacity of the human lungs by breathing into it.

Spirt, spėrt, *v.t.* [Same as Icel. *spretta*, Sw. *spritta*, G. *spritzen*, to squirt, to spirt; A.Sax. *sprytan*, to sprout. *Spurt* is another form. SPROUT.] To throw or force out in a jet or stream (to *spirt* water from the mouth).—*v.i.* To gush or issue out in a small stream or jet.—*n.* A jet of water or other fluid.

Spiry. Under SPIRE.

Spissitude, spis′i-tūd, *n.* [L. *spissitudo*, from *spissus*, thick.] Thickness of soft or liquid substances; denseness.

Spit, spit, *n.* [A.Sax. *spitu*, a spit=D. *spit*, *spet*, Dan. *spid*, Icel. *spýta*, G. *spiess*, a spit, a pike; akin G. *spitz*, pointed; from a root seen also in *spike*.] A long pointed spike or prong of metal, on which meat is roasted; a small point of land running into the sea; a long narrow shoal extending from the shore.—*v.t.*—*spitted, spitting.* To thrust a spit through; to put upon a spit; to thrust through; to pierce.

Spit, spit, *v.t.*—pret. and pp. *spat* or *spit*, ppr. *spitting.* [A.Sax. *spittan*=Dan. *spytte*, Icel. *spýta*, to spit out; akin *spot, spatter*; same root as *spew*.] To eject from the mouth.—*v.i.* To throw out saliva from the mouth; to make a spitting or hissing noise as that of an angry cat.—*n.* What is ejected from the mouth; saliva.—**Spitfire**, spit′fīr, *n.* A violent or passionate person; one who is irascible or fiery. — **Spitter**, spit′ėr, *n.* One who spits. — **Spittle**, spit′l, *n.* The moist matter which is secreted by the salivary glands; saliva ejected from the mouth.—**Spittoon**, spit-tön′, *n.* A vessel to receive discharges of spittle.

Spital,‡ spit′al, *n.* [Corrupted from *hospital.*] A hospital.

Spitchcock, spich′kok, *v.t.* [From *spit* and *stuck*, or *spit* and *cook.*] To split an eel lengthwise and broil it. — *n.* An eel split and broiled.

Spite, spīt, *n.* [An abbreviated form of *despite* (which see).] A disposition to thwart and disappoint the wishes of another; a feeling of ill-will or malevolence; a manifestation of malevolence or malignity; chagrin; vexation.—*In spite of*, in defiance or contempt of; in opposition to all efforts of; notwithstanding.—*v.t.*—*spited, spiting.* To mortify; to thwart malignantly; to fill with spite or vexation.—**Spiteful**, spīt′ful, *a.* Filled with spite; having a malicious disposition; malignant; malicious.—**Spitefully**, spīt′ful-li, *adv.* In a spiteful manner.—**Spitefulness**, spīt′ful-nes, *n.* The state or quality of being spiteful.

Spitfire, Spittle, Spittoon. Under SPIT.

Spittle, spit′l. SPITAL.

Spitz-dog, spits, *n.* [G. *spitz*, lit. pointed, from its pointed muzzle and ears.] A small variety of the Pomeranian dog, which has become a favourite lap-dog.

Splanchnic, splangk′nik, *a.* [Gr. *splanchna*, the bowels.] Belonging to the entrails. —**Splanchnography**, splangk-nog′ra-fi, *n.* An anatomical description of the viscera. —**Splanchnology**, splangk-nol′o-ji, *n.* The doctrine of the viscera, or of diseases of the internal parts of the body. — **Splanchno-skeleton**, splangk′nō, *n.* The bones connected with the sense-organs and viscera.—**Splanchnotomy**, splangk-not′o-mi, *n.* [Gr. *splanchna*, and *tomē*, a cutting.] *Anat.* the dissection of the viscera.

Splash, splash, *v.t.* [A form of *plash*, with intens. *s* prefixed.] To spatter with water, or water and mud; to dash a liquid upon or over; to spatter; to cast or dash in drops. —*v.i.* To strike and dash about water, or something liquid.—*n.* A small quantity of water, or water and dirt, thrown upon anything; a stroke or fall of something in water; a noise from water dashed about; a spot of dirt or other discolouring matter; a blot; a daub.—**Splash-board**, *n.* A broad piece in front of a wheeled vehicle, to ward off mud thrown up from the horses' heels.—**Splasher**, splash′ėr, *n.* One who or that which splashes; a screen or guard placed over locomotive wheels.—**Splashy**, splash′i, *a.* Full of dirty water; wet and muddy.

Splatter, splat′ėr, *v.i.* [Probably formed from *spatter*, like *splutter* from *sputter.*] To make a noise, as in water.

Splay, splā, *v.t.* [Abbrev. from *display.*] To dislocate or break a horse's shoulder-bone; *arch.* to slope or form with an angle, as the jambs or sides of a window.—*n. Arch.* a sloped surface, as when the opening through a wall for a door, window, &c., widens inwards.—*a.* Spreading out; turned outward (a *splay*-foot).—**Splay-footed**, *a.* Having feet with the toes turned outward; having flat feet.—**Splay-foot**, *n.* A foot turning outward and with a flat under surface; a flat foot.—**Splay-mouth**, *n.* A wide mouth.

Spleen, splēn, *n.* [L. *splen*, Gr. *splēn*, the spleen.] A spongy glandular organ situated in the upper part of the abdomen, forming one of the ductless glands concerned in the elaboration of the blood; the milt; anciently, supposed to be the seat of melancholy, anger, or vexation; hence, anger; latent spite; ill-humour; malice (to vent one's *spleen*); melancholy; low spirits; vapours.—**Spleenful**, splēn′ful, *a.* Full of or displaying spleen; splenetic; fretful; melancholy.—**Spleenfully**, splēn′ful-li, *adv.* In a spleenful manner.—**Spleenish**, splēn′ish, *a.* Splenetic; affected with spleen.—**Spleenishly**, splēn′ish-li, *adv.* In a spleenish manner. — **Spleenishness**, splēn′ish-nes, *n.* — **Spleenwort**, splēn′wėrt, *n.* Any one of many tropical ferns, with long or linear sori on the upper side of a vein.—**Spleeny**, splēn′i, *a.* Characterized by spleen; splenetic; peevish; fretful.

Splendent, splen′dent, *a.* [L. *splendens*, *splendentis*, ppr. of *splendeo*, to shine.] Shining; resplendent; beaming with light; very conspicuous; illustrious.

Splendid, splen′did, *a.* [Fr. *splendide*, L. *splendidus*, from *splendeo*, to shine.] Magnificent; gorgeous; dazzling; sumptuous; illustrious; grand; heroic; brilliant; noble; glorious.—**Splendidly**, splen′did-li, *adv.* In a splendid manner; brilliantly; gorgeously; magnificently.—**Splendidness**, splen′did-nes, *n.* The quality of being splendid.—**Splendor, Splendour**, splen′dėr, *n.* [L. *splendor.*] Great brightness; brilliant luster; magnificence; pomp; parade; brilliance; glory; grandeur; eminence; *her. in splendor*, the sun when thus depicted is completely surrounded with rays alternately waved and straight—to represent light and heat—and shows a human face on the disk.

Splenetic, sple-net′ik or splen′e-tik, *a.* [L. *spleneticus*, from *splen*, the spleen. SPLEEN.] Affected with spleen; peevish; fretful.—*n.* A person affected with spleen.—**Splenetical**, sple-net′i-kal, *a.* Splenetic.—**Splenetically**, sple-net′i-kal-li, *adv.* In a splenetic manner.—**Splenic, Splenical**, splen′ik, splen′i-kal, *a.* [L. *splenicus.*] *Anat.* belonging to the spleen.—**Splenitis**, sple-nī′tis, *n.* [Term. *-itis*, signifying inflammation.] Inflammation of the spleen.—

Splenoid, splē′noid, *a.* [Gr. *splēn*, and *eidos*, resemblance.] Spleen-like; having the appearance of the spleen.—**Splenology**, splē-nol′o-ji, *n.* [Gr. *splēn*, liver, and *logos*, doctrine.] The knowledge or body of facts regarding the spleen. — **Splenotomy**, splē-not′o-mi, *n.* [Gr. *tomē*, cutting.] A cutting into, or anatomy of, the spleen.—**Splenule**, splen′ūl, *n.* A small or rudimentary spleen.

Splice, splīs, *v.t.*—*spliced*, *splicing*. [Same as Dan. *splisse*, *splidse*, D. *splitsen*, Sw. *splissa*, G. *splissen*, to splice. Closely akin to *split*, the ends of the rope being *split* in splicing.] To unite, as two ends of rope, by interweaving the strands of the ends; to unite by overlapping, as two pieces of timber; to unite in marriage (*slang*).—*n.* The joining of two ends of rope by interweaving the untwisted strands; the junction of two pieces of wood or metal by overlapping and fastening the ends.

Splint, splint, *n.* [A nasalized form of *split* = Dan., Sw., and G. *splint*, a splinter. *Splinter* is a derivative.] A splinter; *surg.* a thin piece of wood or other substance, used to confine a broken bone when set, or to maintain any part of the body in a fixed position; *farriery*, the splint-bone of a horse; a disease affecting the splint-bone. —*v.t.* To confine or support by means of splints.—**Splint-armor**, *n.* That kind of armor which was made of several overlapping plates.—**Splint-bone**, *n.* One of the two small bones extending from the knee to the fetlock of a horse, behind the shank-bone. — **Splint-coal**, *n.* A hard laminated variety of bituminous coal.

Splinter, splin′tėr, *n.* [Same as D. and G. *splinter*, a splinter; G. also *splitter*. SPLINT.] A fragment of anything split or shivered off; a thin piece of wood or other solid substance rent from the main body; a splint.—*v.t.* To split or rend into splinters or long thin pieces; to shiver; to support by a splint.—*v.i.* To be split or rent into long pieces; to shiver.—**Splinter-bar**, *n.* A cross-bar in front of a wagon or other vehicle which supports the springs; a whippletree.

Split, split, *v.t.*—pret. and pp. *split* (sometimes *splitted*); ppr. *splitting*. [Same as L.G. *splitten*, O.D. *splitten*, Dan. *splitte*, G. *spleiszen*; allied to *splice*; *splint*, *splinter*, are nasalized derivative forms.] To divide longitudinally or lengthwise; to separate or part in two from end to end by force; to rive; to cleave; to tear asunder by violence; to burst; to rend; to divide or break into parts as by discord; to separate into parts or parties. — *To split hairs*, to make too nice distinctions. — *To split the sides*, to burst with laughter.—*v.i.* To part asunder, especially lengthwise; to suffer disruption; to burst; to burst with laughter; to be dashed to pieces; to differ in opinion; to break up into parties; to inform upon one's accomplices or divulge a secret (*low*).—*n.* A crack, rent, or straight fissure; a division or breach, as in a party; a flat strip of steel, cane, &c.; a cleft twig of willow, &c., used in basket-weaving. — *p.* and *a.* Divided; cleft; rent in two. — *Split infinitive*, one with a word or words between 'to' and the verb.—**Split-peas**, *n.* Husked peas, split for cooking.—**Splitter**, split′ėr. *n.* One who or that which splits.

Splotch, sploch, *n.* [From *spot*, with inserted *l* (as in *spatter*, *splatter*, *sputter*, *splutter*), and term. borrowed from *blotch*.] A spot or stain; a daub; a smear.—**Splotchy**, sploch′i, *a.* Marked with splotches.

Splurge, splėrj, *n.* [Probably a coined word, suggested by *splash*, *surge*, or the like.] A showing off; great display or ostentation. (*Colloq.*)

Splutter, splut′ėr, *n.* [From *sputter*, with inserted *l*. SPLOTCH.] A bustle; a stir.—*v.i.* To speak hastily and confusedly; to sputter.—**Splutterer**, splut′ėr-ėr, *n.* One who splutters.

Spode, spōd, *n.* [Gr. *spodos*, ashes.] A material composed of calcined ivory, of which vases and ornaments are made.

Spodumene, spod′ū-mēn, *n.* [Gr. *spodoumenos*, converted into *spodos* or ashes.] A mineral, a silicate of aluminium and lithium, an emerald-green variety of which is used as a gem.

Spoil, spoil, *v.t.* [Fr. *spolier*, from L. *spoliare*, to plunder, from *spolium*, plunder.] To plunder; to strip by violence; to rob; to seize by violence; to corrupt or vitiate; to render useless; to injure fatally; to ruin; to destroy.—*v.i.* To practise plunder; to lose the valuable qualities; to be corrupted; *colloq.* to long for, as 'he is spoiling for a fight'. —*n.* That which is taken from others by violence; plunder; booty; the slough or cast skin of a serpent or other animal.—**Spoilable**, spoi′la-bl, *a.* Capable of being spoiled.—**Spoiled**, **Spoilt**, spoild, spoilt, *p.* and *a.* Deprived of its valuable qualities; rendered useless; vitiated; destroyed; ruined. — *Spoiled* or *spoilt child*, a child ruined by being petted or over-indulged.—**Spoiler**, spoi′lėr, *n.* One that spoils.—**Spoil-five**, *n.* A game of cards played with the whole pack, each player getting five cards; when no one takes three tricks the game is said to be spoiled.—**Spoils system**, *n.* The practice of removing political incumbents from office to make room for the supporters of the incoming administration; during Jackson's administration, the doctrine was expressed by the comment: "To the victor belong the spoils."

Spoke, spōk, pret. of *speak*.—**Spoken**, spō′kn, pp. of *speak*. Used adjectivally for oral, as opposed to *written*; also used as equivalent to *speaking* in such compounds as civil-*spoken*.—**Spokesman**, spōks′man, *n.* One who speaks for another or others.

Spoke, spōk, *n.* [A.Sax. *spáca* = Icel. *spóki*, D. *speek*, L.G. *speke*, G. *speiche*; same root as *spike*, *spigot*, *pike*.] The radius of a wheel; one of the bars which are inserted in the hub or nave, and which serve to support the rim; the round of a ladder; one of the handles jutting from the circumference of the steering-wheel of a vessel; a contrivance for fastening the wheel of a vehicle in order to prevent its turning when going down a hill.

Spoliate, spō′li-āt, *v.t.*—*spoliated*, *spoliating*. [L. *spolio*, *spoliatum*, to plunder. SPOIL.] To plunder; to pillage; to despoil.—*v.i.* To practise plunder; to commit robbery. —**Spoliation**, spō-li-ā′shon, *n.* The act of plundering; robbery; plunder.—**Spoliator**, spō′li-ā-tėr, *n.* One who commits spoliation.

Spondee, spon′dē, *n.* [L. *spondeus*, Gr. *spondeios*, from Gr. *spondē*, a solemn libation, such libations being accompanied by a slow and solemn melody.] A poetic foot of two long syllables, used in Greek and Latin poetry.—**Spondaic**, **Spondaical**, spon-dā′ik, spon-dā′i-kal, *a.* Pertaining to a spondee; composed of spondees.

Sponge, spunj, *n.* [O.Fr. *esponge* (Fr. *éponge*), from L. *spongia*, Gr. *spongia*, a sponge.] A name given to a class of animal growths or organisms belonging to the Protozoa, also to the framework or skeleton of these bodies, which is composed of horny elastic fibres, soft, light, and porous, easily compressible, readily imbibing fluids, and as readily giving them out again upon compression: in common domestic use; one who meanly lives upon others; a sycophantic or cringing dependant; a parasite; a kind of mop for cleaning cannon after a discharge; the extremity or point of a horse-shoe answering to the heel; *baking*, dough before it is kneaded and formed, when full of globules of carbonic acid, generated by the yeast; *metal*, iron in a soft or pasty condition, as delivered from the puddling furnace.—*To throw up the sponge*, to acknowledge that one is conquered or beaten; to submit; a phrase borrowed from the prize-ring.—*v.t.*—*sponged*, *sponging*. To cleanse or wipe with a sponge; to efface; to destroy all traces of; to gain by sycophantic or mean arts.—*v.i.* To imbibe, as a sponge; to live by parasitic arts.—**Sponge-cake**, *n.* A sweet-cake: so called from its light make. —**Spongeous**, spun′jus, *a.* Resembling a sponge; spongy.—**Sponger**, spun′jėr, *n.* One who sponges.—**Spongiform**, spun′ji-form, *a.* Resembling a sponge; soft and porous.—**Sponginess**, spun′ji-nes, *n.* The quality or state of being spongy.—**Sponging-house**, *n.* In England, a house where persons arrested for debt were kept for twenty-four hours, in order that their friends might have an opportunity of settling the debt: so called from the extortionate charges made.—**Spongiole**, spun′-ji-ōl, *n.* [Fr. *spongiole*, L. *spongiola*, dim. of *spongia*.] *Bot.* the extremity of the fibre of a root, presenting a spongy character.—**Spongiolite**, spon′ji-ō-līt, *n.* [Gr. *spongion*, a sponge, and *lithos*, a stone.] One of the minute siliceous spicules or needles found in sponges.—**Spongiose**, spun′ji-ōs, *a.* Sponge-like.—**Spongy**, spun′ji, *a.* Resembling a sponge; soft and full of cavities; of an open, loose, easily compressible texture.

Sponsal, spon′sal, *a.* [L. *sponsalis*, from *sponsus*, a spouse, from *spondeo*, *sponsum*, to promise. SPOUSE.] Relating to marriage or to a spouse.—**Sponsion**, spon′-shon, *n.* [L. *sponsio*, *sponsionis*, a solemn promise.] The act of becoming surety for another; an engagement made on behalf of a state by an agent not specially authorized.—**Sponsor**, spon′sor, *n.* [L. *sponsor*, a surety.] A surety; one who binds himself to answer for another, and is responsible for his default; one who is surety for an infant at baptism; a godfather or godmother. — **Sponsorial**, spon-sō′ri-al, *a.* Pertaining to a sponsor.

Spontaneous, spon-tā′nē-us, *a.* [L. *spontaneus*, from *sponte*, of free-will.] Proceeding from natural inclination and without constraint or external force; voluntary; acting by its own impulse, energy, or natural law; self-originated. — *Spontaneous combustion*. COMBUSTION. — *Spontaneous generation*. GENERATION. — **Spontaneously**, spon-tā′nē-us-li, *adv.* In a spontaneous manner. — **Spontaneity**, spon-ta-nē′i-ti, *n.* The quality of being spontaneous.

Spontoon, spon-tön′, *n.* [Fr. *sponton*, It. *spontone*, spontoon.] A kind of half-pike, formerly borne by officers of infantry, and used for signalling orders.

Spook, spök, *n.* [D. and L.G. *spook*.] A ghost or apparition.—**Spooky**, **Spookish**, spök′i, spök′ish, *a.* Pertaining to spooks; ghostly; haunted; unearthly.

Spool, spöl, *n.* [Same as D. *spoel*, Dan. and Sw. *spole*, G. *spule*, spool.] A piece of cane or reed, or a hollow cylinder of wood, &c., used to wind thread or yarn on.

Spoom, spöm, *v.i.* [Probably from *spume*, foam, to go foaming through the sea; comp. *skim*, *scum*.] *Naut.* to sail steadily and rapidly before the wind.

Spoon, spön, *n.* [A.Sax. *spón*, Icel. *spónn*, *spánn*, Dan. and D. *spaan*, G. *span*, a chip, a splinter, originally a chip of wood for supping up liquids, same as *span*, in *spannew*.] A small domestic utensil, with a bowl or concave part and a handle, used at table for taking up and conveying to the mouth liquids and soft food; a foolish fellow; a simpleton.—*v.t.* To take up or out with a spoon or ladle; *cricket*, to hit a ball softly with the bat, affording an easy catch.—*v.i.* To act like a spoon or spoony.—**Spoon-bill**, *n.* A grallatorial bird of the heron family, so called from the shape of the bill, which is somewhat like a spoon at the end. — **Spoonful**, spön′fụl, *n.* As much as a spoon contains. — **Spoonily**, spön′i-li, *adv.* In a spoony manner. — **Spoon-meat**, *n.* Food that is or must be taken with a spoon; liquid food. — **Spoon-net**, *n.* A form of angler's landing net.—**Spoony**, **Spooney**, spön′i, *a.* [Weak as a child fed on *spoon*-meat.] Soft; silly; weak-minded; weakly or foolishly fond; showing calf-love.—*n.* A stupid or silly fellow; a ninny; a spoon.

Spoon-drift, spön′drift, *n.* [For *spoom-drift*. SPOOM.] Fine spray from the tops of waves; spindrift.

Spoor, spör, *n.* [Borrowed from D. *spoor*,

a track; the same word as A.Sax. and Icel. *spor*, G. *spur*, a track.] The track or trail of a wild animal or animals; used originally by travellers in South Africa.

Sporadic, **Sporadical**, spō-rad'ik, spō-rad'i-kal, *a.* [Gr. *sporadikos*, from *sporas*, dispersed, from *speirō*, to sow, to scatter. SPORE.] Separate; single; scattered; occurring here and there in a scattered manner. — *Sporadic disease*, a disease which occurs in single and scattered cases, in distinction from *epidemic* and *endemic*.—**Sporadically**, spō-rad'i-kal-li, *adv.* In a sporadic manner.

Spore, spōr, *n.* [Gr. *sporos*, a seed, from *speirō*, to sow, whence also *sporadic*, *sperm*.] *Bot.* the reproductive germ of a cryptogamic plant, as distinguished from a true seed; *zool.* a minute germ of certain animal organisms, as Infusoria. — **Sporangium**, spō-ran'ji-um, *n.* pl. **Sporangia**, spō-ran'ji-a. [Gr. *sporos*, and *angeion*, a vessel.] *Bot.* the case in which the spores of cryptogams are formed.—**Spore-case**, *n.* *Bot.* the sporangium or covering of the spores of cryptogams. —**Sporidium**, spō-rid'i-um, *n.* pl. **Sporidia**, spō-rid'i-a. *Bot.* a name given to the spores of fungi and lichens when they are contained in asci or bags.—**Sporiferous**, spō-rif'ėr-us, *a.* *Bot.* bearing spores.—**Sporocarp**, spor'ō-karp, *n.* [Gr. *sporos*, and *karpos*, a fruit.] A spore-producing body in red seaweeds, certain fungi, and some lower fern-like plants.—**Sporocyst**, spō'rō-sist, *n.* *Bot.* the spore-case of algals.—**Sporoderm**, spō'rō-dėrm, *n.* [Gr. *derma*, a skin.] *Bot.* the skin of a spore.—**Sporogen**, spō'rō-jen, *n.* A plant producing spores instead of seed.—**Sporogonium**, spor'ō-gō"ni-um, *n.* [Gr. *sporos*, and *gonos*, offspring.] In mosses, the spore-producing 'fruit'.—**Sporophyte**, spor'ō-fit, *n.* [Gr. *sporos*, and *phyton*, a plant.] *Bot.* the asexual stage in the life-history.—**Sporozoa**, spor'ō-zō"a, *n.* [Gr. *sporos*, and *zōon*, an animal.] Animalcules, some disease-producing, which propagate by microscopic germs (spores) produced in a capsule. **Sporozoid**, spō-ro-zō'id, *n.* [Gr. *zōon*, an animal.] A moving spore furnished with cilia or vibratile processes. — **Sporule**, spor'ūl, *n.* *Bot.* a little spore; a distinct granule within a spore.—**Sporuliferous**, spor-ū-lif'ėr-us, *a.* *Bot.* bearing sporules.

Sporran, **Sporan**, spor'an, *n.* [Gael. *sporan*.] The pouch worn by Highlanders in full dress in front of the kilt, usually made of the skin of some animal with the hair on.

Sport, spōrt, *n.* [An abbrev. of *disport*. DISPORT.] A pastime or amusement in which a person engages; a game; a diversion; a merry-making; an out-of-door recreation such as grown men indulge in, more especially hunting or fishing, also horse-racing, &c.; such amusements collectively; amusement, fun, or enjoyment experienced; jest, as opposed to *earnest*; mockery; derision; object of mockery; any plant or animal deviating from the normal or natural condition or type; a monstrosity; a sportsman.—*In sport*, in jest; for play or diversion.—*v.t.* To divert; to make merry; used *refl.* (O.T.); to exhibit or wear in public (*colloq.*)—*v.i.* To play; to frolic; to make merry; to trifle.—**Sportful**, spōrt'ful, *a.* Full of sport; frolicsome; indulging in mirth or play; sportive; — **Sportfully**, spōrt'ful-li, *adv.* In a sportful manner.—**Sportfulness**, spōrt'ful-nes, *n.* The state of being sportful.—**Sporting**, spōr'ting, *p.* and *a.* Belonging to or practicing sport or sports.—*Sporting man*, one who practices field-sports; also, a horse-racer; one who patronizes pugilism, &c.—*Sporting chance*, or *offer*, an off chance, or offer made in a sporting spirit.—**Sporting-goods**, *n.* Merchandise and equipment specially suited for athletics, games, and sport activities of every kind.—**Sportive**, spōr'tiv, *a.* Engaging in sport; gay; frolicsome; playful; amorous; wanton.—**Sportively**, spōr'tiv-li, *adv.* In a sportive manner. — **Sportiveness**, spōr'tiv-nes, *n.* The state of being sportive; playfulness; frolicsomeness.—**Sports**, *n.* Athletic games.—**Sportsman**, spōrts'man, *n.* One who pursues the sports of the field; one skilled in hunting, shooting, fishing, &c.—**Sportsmanship**, spōrts'man-ship, *n.* The practice of sportsmen; skill in field-sports.

Sporule. Under SPORE.

Spot, spot, *n.* [Same as D. *spat*, Dan. *spætte*, a spot; Icel. *spotti*, *spottr*, a bit, a small piece; same root as *spit*, *spatter*.] A mark on a substance made by foreign matter; a speck; a place discoloured; a stain on character or reputation; disgrace; reproach; blemish; a locality; any particular place; a small part of definite shape and different colour from the ground on which it is.—*Upon the spot*, immediately; before moving. —*v.t.*—*spotted*, *spotting*. To make a spot, speck, or fleck upon; to stain; to tarnish; to mark with spots of colour different from the ground; to note something as peculiar to, in order to identify; to catch with the eye; to recognize (*colloq.*).—**Spot lens**, *n.* A lens having its central part obscured, so as to confine the light to an outside ring.—**Spotless**, spot'les, *a.* Free from spots; free from stain or impurity; pure; unspotted; immaculate. —**Spotlessly**, spot'les-li, *adv.* In a spotless manner. — **Spotlessness**, spot'les-nes, *n.* The state or quality of being spotless; freedom from spot or stain. — **Spotted**, spot'ed, *p.* and *a.* Marked with spots. — *Spotted fever*, a species of typhus fever accompanied by an eruption of red spots.—**Spottedness**, spot'ed-nes, *n.* The state of being spotted.—**Spotter**, *n.* An officer on board a ship who, by watching the fall of shells, helps to ascertain the range for which the guns shall be set.—**Spottiness**, spot'i-nes, *n.* The state or quality of being spotty.—**Spotty**, spot'i, *a.* Full of spots; marked with discoloured places; spotted.

Spouse, spouz, *n.* [O.Fr. *espouse*, from L. *sponsus*, betrothed, pp. of *spondeo*, to promise solemnly, to engage one's self. ESPOUSE.] One engaged or joined in wedlock; a married person, husband, or wife. — **Spouseless**, spouz'les, *a.* Destitute of a husband or wife; unmarried.—**Spousal**, spou'zal, *n.* Espousal: nuptials; generally in the plural.

Spout, spout, *n.* [From stem of *spit*, *spew*, perhaps directly from D. *spuit*, a spout, *spuiten*, to spout.] A nozzle or projecting mouth of a vessel, used in directing the stream of a liquid poured out; an ajutage; a pipe or conduit; a pipe for conducting water as from a roof; a water-spout.—*v.t.* To pour out in a jet and with some force; to throw out through a spout or pipe; to utter in the manner of a mouthing actor or orator; to mouth.—*v.i.* To issue in a strong jet; to run as from a spout; to spurt; to make a speech, especially in a pompous manner.—**Spouter**, spou'tėr, *n.* One who spouts; one who makes speeches in a pompous or affected manner. — **Spoutless**, spout'les, *a.* Having no spout.

Sprag, sprag, *n.* [Allied to *sprig*.] A billet of wood; a prop for preventing the roof of a mine from sinking. — *v.t.* — *spragged*, *spragging*. To prop by a sprag; to stop by putting a sprag in the spokes of a wheel.

Sprain, sprān, *v.t.* [O.Fr. *espreindre*, to force out, to strain, from L. *exprimere*, *expressum*, to press out. EXPRESS.] To overstrain, as the muscles or ligaments of a joint so as to injure them, but without dislocation. — *n.* A violent straining or twisting of the soft parts surrounding a joint, without dislocation.

Sprang, sprang, pret. of *spring*.

Sprat, sprat, *n.* [Formerly also *sprot*, from D. and L.G. *sprot*, G. *sprotte*, sprat; allied to *sprout*.] A small fish of the herring family found in great abundance on the British coasts, and excellent as food.

Sprawl, spral, *v.i.* [A contr. word allied to Sc. *sprattle*, *sprachle*, to scramble, Dan. *sprælle*, to sprawl; Sw. *sprattla*, to palpitate.] To spread and stretch the body carelessly in a horizontal position; to lie or crawl with the limbs stretched out or struggling; to grow or spread irregularly or ungracefully.

Spray, sprā, *n.* [Same as Dan. *sprag*, Sw. *spragg*, a spray; allied to *sprig* and *spring*.] A small shoot or branch (a *spray* of pearls, diamonds); the extremity of a branch; a twig; the small branches of a tree collectively.—**Spray-drain**, *n.* A drain formed by burying the spray of trees in a trench.—**Sprayey**, sprā'i, *a.* Full of or laden with sprays or twigs.

Spray, sprā, *n.* [A.Sax. *sprēgan*, to pour; D. *spreijen*, to scatter; akin *spring*, *sprinkle*.] Water flying in small drops or particles, as by the force of wind, or the dashing of waves, or from a waterfall; the vapour from an atomizer.

Spread, spred, *v.t.*—pret. and pp. *spread* (spred). [A.Sax. *spraedan*, to extend = L.G. *spreden*, D. *spreiden*, Dan. *sprede*, G. *spreiten*, to spread, to scatter.] To stretch or expand to a broader surface (a sheet, a carpet); to open out (the wings); to unfurl (a sail); to stretch; to cover by extending something; to overspread; to extend; to shoot to a greater distance in every direction (a tree *spreads* its branches); to put forth; to publish, as news or fame; to cause to be more extensively known; to propagate (a disease); to cause to affect greater numbers; to emit; to diffuse (perfume); to disperse; to scatter over a larger surface; to set and furnish with provisions.—*v.i.* To extend itself; to be extended or stretched; to be made known more extensively; to be propagated from one to another; to be diffused.—*n.* The act of spreading or state of being spread; extent; compass; a table, as spread or furnished with a meal; a feast (*colloq.*).—**Spread-eagle**, *n.* *Her.* an eagle having the wings and legs extended on each side of the body; also 'an eagle with two heads displayed'.—*a.* Pretentious; boastful; defiantly bombastic (a *spread-eagle* style).—**Spreader**, spred'ėr, *n.* One who or that which spreads.—**Spreadingly**, spred'ing-li, *adv.* In a spreading manner; increasingly.

Spree, sprē, *n.* [From Ir. *spre*, animation spirit, vigour; comp. *spry*.] A merry frolic, a drinking frolic; a carousal.

Sprengel pump, spreng'il, *n.* [After the German inventor.] An air pump which works by means of a stream of mercury.

Sprig, sprig, *n.* [A.Sax. *sprec*, a branch; allied to *spray*, a twig.] A small shoot or twig of a tree or other plant; a spray; an offshoot; a slip; a youth; a lad: used as a term of slight disparagement (a *sprig* of nobility); an ornament resembling a sprig; a small square brad or nail without a head. In *her.* a *sprig* has five leaves attached to it, whereas a *slip* has only three. — —**Sprigged**, sprigd, *a.* Marked with ornaments resembling sprigs; fastened with sprigs.—**Spriggy**, sprig'i, *a.* Full of sprigs or small branches.

Spright, sprīt, *n.* [Contr. for *spirit*, and spelled erroneously, *sprite* being the better spelling.] A spirit or sprite; an elf. The spelling *spright* is now obsolete or obsolescent, but *sprightly* and not *spritely* is still the common spelling.—**Sprightly**, sprīt'li, *a.* [Also written *spritely*.] Having the quality of a spirit or spright (*Shak.*); lively; spirited; brisk; airy; gay. — **Sprightliness**, sprīt'li-nes, *n.* The quality of being sprightly; liveliness; briskness; vivacity.

Spring, spring, *v.i.*—pret. *sprung* or *sprang* (sprung, sprang), pp. *sprung*. [A.Sax. *springan*, to spring, to leap = D. and G. *springen*, Sw. and Icel. *springa*, Dan. *springe*, from root seen also in *sprinkle*, *sprig*, *spray*.] To rise or come forth, as out of the ground; to shoot up, out, or forth; to begin to appear; to come to light; to issue into sight or knowledge; to take rise or origin; to issue or originate, as from ancestors, or from a country; to result, as from a cause, motive, principle, &c.; to leap; to jump; to fly back by elastic force; to start; to start or rise suddenly from a covert; to shoot; to issue with speed and violence; to warp or become warped; to become cracked (as a mast).—*To spring at*, to leap toward; to attempt to reach by a leap.—*To spring forth*, to leap out; to rush out.—*To spring in*, to rush in; to enter with a leap or in haste.—*To spring on* or *upon*, to leap on; to assault.—*v.t.* To start or rouse, as game; to cause to rise from a covert; to produce quickly or unexpectedly; to propose on a sudden; to crack; to weaken by a crack in the timber (to *spring* a mast); to pass by leaping; to jump over (to *spring* the fence).—*To spring a leak*, to have a leak open; to experience the opening of a leak.—*To spring a mine* (in the military sense), to cause it to explode: often used *fig.*—*n.* A leap; a bound; a flying back of a body by its elasticity; elastic power or force; an elastic body, made of various materials, as a strip or wire of steel coiled spirally, a steel rod or plate, &c., which, when bent or forced from its natural state, has the power of recovering it again in virtue of its elasticity; the springs of a railroad car or an automobile affording comfort in riding through their resiliency; Springs are used to check recoil or diminish concussion; elliptic springs for railroad cars or for carriages, semi-elliptic or cantilever springs in automobile construction, and coil springs, spiral springs, and flat springs in many other mechanical devices) *fig.* that by which action is induced; mainspring; a natural fountain of water, owing its origin to the water which falls upon the earth; an issue of water from the earth, or the basin of water at the place of its issue; any source of supply; that from which supplies are drawn; one of the four seasons of the year (so called because plants *spring* or grow then); the vernal season; *fig.* the first and freshest part of any state or time; a crack in a mast or yard running obliquely or transversely; a rope passed out of a ship's stern, and attached to a cable proceeding from her bow, when she is at anchor; *arch.* the point of an arch that rests on its support.—**Spring-balance**, *n.* A contrivance for weighing articles by observing the amount of deflection or compression which their weight produces upon a steel spring properly adjusted.—**Spring-board**, *n.* An elastic board used in vaulting, &c.—**Spring-bok**, *n.* [D., lit. the springing buck.] A species of antelope, nearly allied to the gazelle, very abundant in South Africa.—**Spring-carriage**, *n.* A wheel-carriage mounted upon springs.—**Spring-cart**, *n.* A light cart mounted upon springs.—**Springer**, spring'ėr, *n.* One who springs; *arch.* the lowest voussoir or bottom stone of an arch; the bottom stone of the coping of a gable; the rib of a groined roof or vault.—**Spring-grass**, *n.* Sweet vernal grass planted for its delicate fragrance.—**Spring-gun**, *n.* A gun so set that it may be unintentionally discharged by trespassers.—**Springlet**, spring'let, *n.* A little spring; a small stream.—**Spring-lock**, *n.* A lock that fastens with a spring.—**Spring-tide**, *n.* The tide which happens at or soon after the new and full moon, and which rises higher than common tides; the time or season of spring; spring-time.—**Spring-time**, *n.* The spring; the vernal season.—**Spring-water**, *n.* Water issuing from a spring.—**Spring-wheat**, *n.* A species of wheat to be sown in the spring.—

Springy, spring'i, *a.* Having elasticity like that of a spring; elastic; light (a *springy* step); abounding with springs or fountains.

Springal, spring'gal, *n.* [O.Fr. *espringale*, from G. *springen*, to spring.] An ancient warlike engine, used for shooting large arrows, &c.

Springe, sprinj, *n.* [From *spring*; comp. *swinge* from *swing*.] A noose attached to a spring or elastic body so as to catch a bird or other animal; a gin; a snare.—*v.t.* To catch in a springe; to ensnare.

Sprinkle, spring'kl, *v.t.*—*sprinkled*, *sprinkling*. [A dim. form from O.E. *sprinke*, A.Sax. *sprencan*, for *sprengan*, to sprinkle, caus. of *springan*, to spring; comp. D. *sprenkelen*, to sprinkle; G. *sprenkeln*, to speckle. SPRING.] To scatter in drops or particles; to cast or let fall in fine separate particles; to strew; to besprinkle; to bestrew; to bedrop.—*n.* A small quantity scattered; a sprinkling.—**Sprinkler**, springk'lėr, *n.* One who sprinkles; a device for sprinkling; a fire extinguisher.—**Sprinkling**, springk'ling, *n.* A small quantity falling in drops or particles; a small number or quantity scattered as if sprinkled.

Sprint, sprint, *n.* [Akin to *spurt*.] A short race or run at high speed.

Sprit, sprit, *n.* [A.Sax. *spreót*, a sprout, a shoot; D. *spriet*, a sprit, *boeysprit*, the bowsprit.] A sprout‡; a small boom or spar which crosses the sail of a boat diagonally and thus extends and elevates it; also, the bowsprit of a vessel.—**Sprit-sail**, *n.* A sail extended by a sprit; a sail, now disused, on a yard under a bowsprit.

Sprite, sprīt, *n.* A spirit or spright; commonly, a kind of fairy, elf, or goblin.

Sprocket-wheel, sprok'et, *n.* A wheel with cogs or sprockets to engage with the links of a chain.

Sprout, sprout, *v.i.* [Same as L.G. *spruten*, D. *spruiten*, to sprout; akin to A.Sax. *spreótan*, to sprout, whence *spreót*, a sprout. Akin *spirt*, *sprit*, *spurt*.] To shoot, as the seed of a plant; to germinate; to push out new shoots.—*n.* [D. *spruit*, a sprout.] The shoot or bud of a plant; a fresh outgrowth from a plant or tree; *pl.* young coleworts; Brussels-sprouts.

Spruce, sprös, *a.* [Lit. after the *Prussian* style, from *Spruce*, *Pruce*, formerly used for *Prussia*, *Prussian*.] Brisk‡; active (*Shak.*)‡; neat or smart in dress; trim; smug; dandified.—*v.t.*—*spruced*, *sprucing*. To trim or dress in a spruce manner.—*To spruce up*, to dress one's self sprucely or neatly.—**Spruce**, **Spruce-fir**, *n.* [So-called because the tree was first known as a native of Prussia.] The name given to several species of trees of the pine family, yielding valuable timber; as the Norway spruce-fir of Europe, and the white spruce, the black spruce, and the hemlock spruce of North America.—**Spruce-beer**, *n.* A fermented liquor made from sugar or molasses, and flavoured with sprouts of the spruce-fir.—**Sprucely**, sprös'li, *adv.* In a spruce manner; trimly; nattily.—**Spruceness**, sprös'nes, *n.* Trimness; nattiness.

Spruit, sproit, *n.* [D.] A brook; a small tributary stream: a S. African word.

Sprung, sprung, pret. and pp. of *spring*.

Spry, sprī, *a.* [Allied to *spree*; or to old *sprack*, N. *sprœk*, Sw. *spräk*, lively.] Nimble; active; vigorous; lively. (*Colloq.*)

Spud, spud, *n.* [A form of *spade*; or akin to Dan. *spyd*, Icel. *spjót*, a spear, E. a *spit*.] A straight narrow spade with a long handle for digging up weeds, &c.; also, a small spade with a short handle; (*slang*) potato.

Spue, spū, *v.t.* and *i.* Same as *Spew*.

Spume, spūm, *n.* [L. *spuma*, foam, from *spuo*, to spit out. SPEW.] Froth; foam; scum; frothy matter on liquors.—*v.i.* To froth; to foam; to spoom.—**Spumescence**, spū-mes'ens, *n.* Frothiness.—**Spumescent**, spū-mes'ent, *a.* [L. *spumesco*, to grow foamy.] Resembling froth or foam; foaming.—**Spumiferous**, spū-mif'ėr-us, *a.* Producing foam.—**Spuminess**, spū'mi-nes, *n.* Quality of being spumy.—**Spumous**, **Spumy**, spū'mus, spū'mi, *a.* [L. *spumosus*.] Consisting of froth or scum; foamy.

Spun, spun, pret. and pp. of *spin*.—**Spun-gold**, *n.* Flattened gold, or silver-gilt wire wound on a thread of silk.—**Spun-silk**, *n.* SILK.—**Spun-silver**, *n.* Flattened silver wire wound round a thread of silk.—**Spun-yarn**, *n.* *Naut.* a cord formed of two, three, or more rope-yarns twisted together.

Spunge, spunj. Same as *Sponge*.

Spunk, spungk, *n.* [Ir. *sponc*, Gael. *spong*, tinder, touchwood, sponge; from L. *spongia*, a sponge.] Touchwood; tinder; tinder made from a species of fungus; amadou; a quick, ardent temper; mettle; pluck.

Spur, spėr, *n.* [A.Sax. *spura*, *spora*, a spur; Icel. *spori*, Dan. *spore*, O.G. *spor*, Mod.G. *sporn*; from a root meaning to kick, seen also in *spurn*, *spurious*.] An instrument having a rowel or little wheel with sharp points, worn on horsemen's heels to prick the horses for hastening their pace; *fig.* an incitement or stimulus; a large or principal root of a tree; something that projects; a snag; the hard pointed projection on a cock's leg which serves as an instrument of offense and defense; *geog.* a mountain, or mountain mass, that shoots from another mountain mass and extends for some distance; a small sidetrack of a railroad; *bot.* any projecting appendage of a flower resembling a spur.—*v.t.*—*spurred*, *spurring*. To prick with spurs; to urge or encourage to action; to incite; to instigate; to impel; to stimulate; to put spurs on; to furnish with spurs.—*v.i.* To spur one's horse to make it go fast; to ride fast; to press forward.—**Spurgall**, spėr'gal, *v.t.* To gall or wound with a spur.—*n.* A place galled by the spur.—**Spur-gear**, **Spur-gearing**, *n.* Gearing in which spur-wheels are employed.—**Spurless**, spėr'les, *a.* Having no spurs.—**Spurred**, spėrd, *a.* Wearing spurs; having prolongations or shoots like spurs.—**Spurrer**, spėr'ėr, *n.* One who uses spurs; something that incites or urges on.—**Spurrier**, spėr'i-ėr, *n.* One whose occupation is to make spurs.—**Spur-wheel**, *n.* *Mach.* a wheel in which the teeth are perpendicular to the axis, and in the direction of radii.

Spurge, spėrj, *n.* [O.Fr. *espurge*, spurge, from L. *expurgare*, to purge—*ex*, out of, and *purgo*, to purge. PURGE.] The common name of certain *Euphorbia*, plants with an acrid milky juice powerfully purgative.—**Spurge-laurel**, *n.* A Eurasian shrub with oblong evergreen leaves and yellow flowers.

Spurious, spū'ri-us, *a.* [L. *spurius*, bastard, from same root as *sperno*, to despise. SPURN.] Not legitimate; bastard; not proceeding from the true source or from the source pretended; not genuine; counterfeit: adulterate.—*Spurious wing*, in *ornith.* the bastard wing.—**Spuriously**, spū'ri-us-li, *adv.* In a spurious manner; falsely.—**Spuriousness**, spū'ri-us-nes, *n.* The state or quality of being spurious.

Spurn, spėrn, *v.t.* [A.Sax. *spurnan*, to spurn; Icel. *sporna*, *spyrna*, O.H.G. *spurnan*, *spornan*, to kick; same root as *spur*, and L. *sperno*, to despise, *spurius*, spurious.] To drive back or away, as with the foot; to kick; to reject with disdain; to treat with contempt.—*v.i.* To kick or toss up the heels; to dash the foot against something; to manifest disdain or contempt in rejecting anything.—*n.* A kick†; disdainful rejection; contemptuous treatment.—**Spurner**, spėr'nėr, *n.* One who spurns.

Spurry, spėr'i, *n.* [D. and O.Fr. *spurrie*, G. *spurrey*, *spurre*.] A small herb of the chickweed family, one species of which is cultivated as food for cattle.

Spurt, spėrt, *v.t.* [A form of *spirt*; akin to *sprout*; comp. Icel. *spretta*, a spurt.] To throw out in a stream or jet, as water; to spout; to squirt.—*v.i.* To gush out; to spirt.—*n.* A forcible gush of liquid; a jet; a sudden extraordinary effort for an emergency; a short sudden act.

Sputter, sput'ėr, *v.i.* [Akin to *spout* or *spit*; same as L.G. *sputtern*; to sputter.] To emit saliva from the mouth in rapid speaking; to speak so rapidly as to emit saliva; to give out moisture (as green wood burning); to burn with some crackling or noise (as a candle).—*v.t.* To utter rapidly and with indistinctness; to jabber.—**Sputterer**, sput'ėr-ėr, *n.* One that sputters.

Sputum, spū'tum, *n.* pl. **Sputa**. [L. *sputum*, spittle, *spuo*, to spit.] Spittle; matter expectorated.

Spy, spī, *v.t.*—*spied*, *spying*. [O.Fr. *espier*, to spy, from O.H.G. *spehōn*, to search out or examine. Same root as in L. *specio*, to see, Skr. *spaç*, to look. SPECIES.] To gain sight of; to discover at a distance or in concealment; to espy; to gain a knowledge of by artifice; to explore; to view and examine secretly.—*v.i.* To search narrowly;

to scrutinize; to pry.—*n.* A person who keeps a constant watch on the actions, motions, conduct, &c., of others; a secret emissary sent into the enemy's camp or territory to bring back intelligence.—**Spy-glass**, *n.* A telescope, especially a small telescope.

Squab, skwob, *a.* [Akin Sw. *sqvabba*, a fat woman; Dan. *kvăbbet*, fat, squab.] Fat; short and stout; bulky; unfledged; unfeathered.—*n.* A young unfledged pigeon; a short fat person; a kind of sofa or couch; a soft cushion.—*v.i.* To fall plump.—**Squabby**, skwob'i, *a.* Thick; fat; squab.

Squabash, skwa-bash', *v.t.* To floor or defeat completely in a review, criticism, or argument. (*Colloq.*)

Squabble, skwob'l, *v.i.*—*squabbled, squabbling.* [Same as Sw. *sqvabbel*, a dispute; comp. L.G. *kabbeln*, to quarrel.] To engage in a noisy quarrel; to quarrel and fight noisily; to brawl; to wrangle; to debate peevishly; to dispute.—*v.t. Typog.* to put awry, as types that have been set up.—*n.* A scuffle; a wrangle; a petty quarrel.—**Squabbler**, skwob'lėr, *n.* One who squabbles.

Squad, skwod, *n.* [Abbrev. of *squadron.*] Any small party of men; *milit.* a small number of men assembled for drill or inspection.—*Awkward squad*, the recruits not yet fitted to take their place in the regimental line.

Squadron, skwod'ron, *n.* [O.Fr. *esquadron* (Fr. *escadron*), from It. *squadrone*, a squadron, from *squadra*, a square—L. prefix *ex*, and *quadra*, a square. SQUARE.] In the United States Army, a unit composed of two or more troops of cavalry. This is the normal command of a major. In the United States navy a squadron consists of one or more divisions of battleships, destroyers or aircraft, or it comprises a group of vessels assigned to a special duty. In the United States air fleet, three flights of from three to six airplanes each.—**Squadroned**, skwod'rond, *a.* Formed into squadrons.

Squalid, skwol'id, *a.* [L. *squalidus*, squalid, from *squaleo*, to be foul or filthy.] Foul; filthy; extremely dirty.—**Squalidly**, skwol'id-li, *adv.* In a squalid, filthy manner.—**Squalidity, Squalidness**, skwo-lid'i-ti, skwol'id-nes, *n.* The state of being squalid; filthiness.—**Squalor**, skwol'ėr, *n.* Foulness; filthiness; coarseness.

Squall, skwạl, *v.i.* [An imitative word: Icel. *skval*, a squall or scream, *skvala*, to scream; akin *squeal.*] To cry out; to scream or cry violently.—*n.* A loud scream; a harsh cry; a sudden and strong gust of wind; a sudden and vehement succession of gusts.—*A black squall*, one attended with dark clouds.—*A thick squall*, one accompanied with hail, sleet, &c.—*A white squall*, one which produces no diminution of light.—**Squaller**, skwạl'ėr, *n.* One who squalls.—**Squally**, skwạl-i, *a.* Abounding with sudden and violent gusts of wind; gusty.

Squaloid, skwā'loid, *a.* [L. *squalus*, a shark.] Like a shark, or resembling a shark.

Squalor. Under SQUALID.

Squama, skwā'ma, *n.* pl. **Squamæ**, skwā'mē. [L., a scale.] A scale or scaly part of plants; a horny scale on animals.—**Squamaceous**, skwa-mā'shus, *a.* SQUAMOSE.—**Squamate**, skwā'māt, *a.* Squamose; covered with small scale-like bodies.—**Squamella**, skwa-mel'la, *n.* [L.] A minute scale.—**Squamiform**, skwā'mi-form, *a.* Having the form or shape of scales.—**Squamigerous**, skwa-mij'ėr-us, *a.* [L. *squama*, and *gero*, to bear.] Bearing or having scales.—**Squamoid**, skwā'moid, *a.* Scaly; covered with scales.—**Squamous, Squamose**, skwā'mus, skwa-mōs', *a.* [L. *squamosus.*] Covered with or consisting of scales; resembling scales; scaly.

Squander, skwon'dėr, *v.t.* [Perhaps from A.Sax. *swindan, swand, swunden*, to waste away, vanish, with *q* inserted as in *squeamish* and vulgar *squim* for *swim*, &c.] To spend lavishly or profusely; to waste without economy or judgment.—**Squanderer**, skwon'dėr-ėr, *n.* One who squanders; a spendthrift.

Square, skwār, *a.* [O.Fr. *esquarre*, a square; from L. prefix *ex*, and *quadra*, a square, from *quadrus*, square, from *quatuor*, four.] Having four equal sides and four right angles; forming a right angle; having rectilineal and angular rather than curved outlines; fair, just, or honest; adjusted so as to leave no balance (to make accounts *square*).—*Square measures*, the squares of lineal measures; superficial (a *square* inch, a *square* foot, a *square* yard, &c.).—*Square number*, the product of a number multiplied into itself.—*Square root, arith.* and *alg.* that root which being multiplied into itself produces the given number or quantity; thus, 8 is the square root of 64.—*All square*, all arranged; all right. (*Colloq.*)—*n.* A four-sided plane rectilineal figure, having all its sides equal and all its angles right angles; what nearly approaches this shape; a square surface; an area of four sides with houses on each side or on at least three; an instrument used by artificers, draughtsmen, and others, for testing or describing right angles; *arith.* and *alg.* the number or quantity produced by multiplying a number or quantity by itself; *milit.* a body of infantry formed into a rectangular figure with several ranks or rows of men facing on each side.—*On* or *upon the square*, all right; not objectionable; fair and strictly honest.—*v.t.*—*squared, squaring.* To make square; to reduce or bring accurately to right angles and straight lines; to reduce to any given standard; to compare with a standard; to adjust, regulate, accommodate, fit; to make even so as to leave no difference or balance; to settle (to *square* accounts); *math.* to multiply by itself; *naut.* to place at right angles with the mast or keel (to *square* the yards).—*To square the circle*, to determine the exact area of a circle in square measure.—*v.i.* To suit; to fit; to accord or agree (the facts do not *square with* the theory).—**Square-built**, *a.* Of a square build or shape.—**Squarely**, skwār-li, *adv.* In a square form; fairly; honestly.—**Squareness**, skwār'nes, *n.* The state of being square; fairness in dealing.—**Squarer**, skwā'rėr, *n.* One who squares.—**Square-rigged**, *a. Naut.* a term applied to a vessel most of whose sails are of a square shape and extended by yards suspended by the middle.—**Square-sail**, *n. Naut.* a sail extended on a yard suspended by the middle.—**Square-toed**, *a.* Having the toes square.—**Square-toes**, *n.* A precise, formal, old-fashioned personage. (*Colloq.*)—**Squarish**, skwā'rish, *a.* Nearly square.

Squarrose, Squarrous, skwor'rōs, skwor'rus, *a.* [L. *squarrosus*, rough.] *Bot.* covered with processes or projecting points spreading at right angles or in a greater degree.—**Squarrulose**, skwor'ū-lōs, *a. Bot.* somewhat squarrose.

Squash, skwosh, *v.t.* [O.Fr. *esquacher*, to crush, from L. *ex*, intens., and *coactare*, to constrain, from *cogo, coactum*, to force (whence *cogent*). *Squat* is akin.] To crush; to beat or press into pulp or a flat mass.—*n.* Something soft and easily crushed; something unripe and soft; an unripe peapod; a sudden fall or shock of a heavy soft body.—**Squasher**, skwosh'ėr, *n.* One who squashes.—**Squashiness**, skwosh'i-nes, *n.* The state of being squashy.—**Squashy**, skwosh'i, *a.* Soft or pulpy and green; soft and wet; miry; muddy.

Squash, skwosh, *n.* [From American Indian name.] A plant, a kind of gourd, cultivated in America as an article of food; the flesh of this fruit boiled and mashed, served as a vegetable or used as a filling for pies; a drink, part of which is some fruit juice, e.g. *lemon squash.*—**Squash-gourd, Squash-melon**, *n.* The squash.

Squat, skwot, *v.i.*—*squatted, squatting.* [From O.Fr. *quatir*, to duck, to bend, with *es* = L. *ex.* intens. prefixed; same origin as *squash, v.t.*] To sit down upon the hams or heels; to sit close to the ground; to cower, as an animal; to settle on land, especially public lands, without any title or right.—*v.t.* To put on the hams or heels: used reflexively.—*a.* Sitting close to the ground; cowering; short and thick, like the figure of an animal squatting.—*n.* The posture of one who squats.—**Squatter**, skwot'ėr, *n.* One that squats; one that settles on unoccupied land, particularly public land, without a title.—**Squatting**, skwot'ing, *a.* Occupied by squatters.

Squaw, skwạ, *n.* [Amer. Indian.] Among American Indians, a female or wife.

Squawk, skwạk, *v.i.* [Akin to *squeak.*] To cry with a loud harsh voice.

Squawl, skwạl, *v.i.* To squall.

Squeak, skwēk, *v.i.* [Imitative; comp. *squawk*, G. *quieken*, to squeak; Sw. *sqväka*, to cry like a frog.] To utter a sharp, shrill cry; to cry with an acute tone, as a pig, a mouse, or the like; or to make a sharp noise, as a wheel, a door, &c.; to break secrecy.—*n.* A sharp shrill cry or noise.—**Squeaker**, swē'kėr, *n.* One that squeaks.

Squeal, skwēl, *v.i.* [A weaker form of *squall*, implying a shriller sound.] To cry with a sharp shrill voice, as certain animals do.—*n.* A shrill sharp cry; a squeak.

Squeamish, skwē'mish, *a.* [Prov.E. *sweamish*, O. and Prov. *sweam*, an attack of sickness, from A.Sax. *swíma*, a swimming or giddiness, or N. *sveim*, dizziness; akin to G. *schwindel*, dizziness. The *q* has been inserted partly through the influence of *qualmish.*] Having a stomach that is easily turned; excessively nice as to taste; fastidious; easily disgusted; scrupulous.—**Squeamishly**, skwē'mish-li, *adv.* In a squeamish or fastidious manner.—**Squeamishness**, skwē'mish-nes, *n.* The state or quality of being squeamish; fastidiousness.

Squeeze, skwēz, *v.t.*—*squeezed, squeezing.* [Formerly *squise, squize*, from A.Sax. *cwisan*, to squeeze (with additon of initial *s*); L.G. *quese*, a bruise; Sw. *qväsa*, to crush; G. *quetschen*, to squash.] To press between two bodies; to press closely; to crush; to clasp closely; to press lovingly; to oppress so as to make to give money; to harass by extortion; to force by pressure.—*v.i.* To press; to press among a number of persons; to pass by pressing.—*n.* An application of pressure; a compression; a hug or embrace.—**Squeezer**, skwē'zėr, *n.* One who or that which squeezes.—**Squeezing**, skwē'zing, *n.* Compression; that which is forced out by pressure.—**Squeezable**, skwē'za-bl, *a.* Capable of being squeezed.—**Squeezability**, skwē-za-bil'i-ti, *n.* The quality of being squeezable.

Squelch, skwelch, *v.t.* [From Prov.E. *quelch*, a blow (with prefixed *s* through influence of *squash*, &c.); allied perhaps to *quell.*] To crush; to destroy.—*v.i.* To be crushed.—*n.* A flat heavy fall.

Squib, skwib, *n.* [From O.E. *squippe*, for *swippe* (comp. *squeamish*), to move along swiftly; Icel. *svipa*, to dart; allied to *sweep* and *swoop.*] A little pipe or hollow cylinder of paper filled with gunpowder, which on being ignited flies along, throwing out a train of sparks and bursting with a crack; a petty lampoon.

Squid, skwid, *n.* [Probably from *squib*, from its squirting out black matter.] A popular name of certain cuttle-fishes, of which the most familiar are the calamaries.

Squill, skwil, *n.* [L. *squilla, scilla*, Gr. *skilla*, a squill (both plant and animal).] A plant allied to the hyacinths, onions, &c., with a bulbous root used in medicine as a diuretic and expectorant; a crustaceous animal; a kind of shrimp.

Squinch, skwinsh, *n. Arch.* a small arch (or several combined) formed across an angle, as in a square tower to support the side of a superimposed octagon.

Squint, skwint, *a.* [Comp. Prov.E. *squinny, squiny*, to squint; D. *schuinte*, a slope, *schuin, schuinsch*, sloping, oblique.] Looking obliquely or askance; not having the optic axes coincident: said of the eyes; having distorted sight.—*v.i.* To look obliquely with the eyes; to have the axes of the eyes not coincident; to be affected with strabismus; to have an indirect reference

—*v.t.* To turn (the eye) to an oblique position; to cause to be squint.—*n.* An oblique look; an affection of the eyes in which the optic axes do not coincide; *arch.* an oblique opening through the walls of old churches, to enable a person in the transepts or aisles to see the high altar.—**Squint-eyed**, *a.* Having eyes that squint; oblique; indirect.—**Squinting**, skwint'-ing, *n.* The act of looking squint; strabismus.—**Squintingly**, skwint'ing-li, *adv.* With squint look; by side glances.

Squire, skwīr, *n.* [Contr. of *esquire.*] The title of a gentleman next in rank to a knight; in America, a title of office and courtesy, often given to justices of the peace.—*v.t.*—*squired, squiring.* To attend on as squire.—**Squirehood, Squireship**, skwīr'hud, skwīr'ship, *n.* The rank and state of a squire.—**Squireling**, skwīr'ling, *n.* A small or petty squire.

Squirm, skwėrm, *v.t.* or *i.* [Perhaps a modification of *swarm*, to wriggle up a tree.] To move like a worm or eel, with writhing or contortions.—*n.* A wriggling motion.

Squirrel, skwir'el, *n.* [O.Fr. *esquirel, escurel* (Fr. *écureuil*), from L.L. *sciuriolus*, dim. of L. *sciurus*, Gr. *skiouros*, a squirrel—*skia*, shadow, and *oura*, tail.] A name common to various species of rodent mammals, mostly living in trees, and distinguished by their powers of leaping, and their usually long and bushy tails. Characteristic for the coniferous forests of North America are the red squirrels, while in the hardwood forests of the central and southern United States the gray and fox squirrels are at home. To the squirrel family belongs likewise the American ground squirrel or chipmunk, a burrowing rodent.—**Squirrel-corn**, *Dicentra canadensis*, one of the first spring flowers of the northern and eastern United States.—**Squirrel-monkey**, *n.* A monkey of Brazil, resembling a squirrel.

Squirt, skwėrt, *v.t.* [Prov. E. *swirt*, L.G. *swirtjen*, to squirt, the *q* being inserted as in *squeamish.* Comp. Icel. *skvetta*, to squirt.] To eject from a narrow pipe or orifice in a stream.—*v.t.* To be ejected in a rapid stream; to spurt or spirt.—*n.* An instrument with which a liquid is ejected in a stream; a syringe; a small jet.—**Squirter**, skwėr'tėr, *n.* One who squirts.

Stab, stab, *v.t.*—*stabbed, stabbing.* [Allied to *staff*; comp. Gael. *stob*, Ir. *stobaim*, to stab; Gael. and Sc. *stob*, a stake, a prickle; also Goth. *stabs*, a rod; G. *stab*, a staff.] To pierce or wound with a pointed weapon; to kill by a pointed weapon; to drive in; to pierce in a figurative sense; to inflict keen or severe pain on.—*v.i.* To aim a blow with a pointed weapon; to be extremely cutting.—*n.* The thrust of a pointed weapon; a wound with a sharp-pointed weapon; keen, poignant pain.—**Stabber**, stab'ėr, *n.* One who, or that which, stabs.

Stable, stā'bl, *a.* [L. *stabilis*, from *sto*, to stand. STAND.] Firmly established; not to be easily moved, shaken, or overthrown; firmly fixed or settled; steady in purpose; firm in resolution; not fickle or wavering; abiding; durable.—**Stabilify**, sta-bil'i-fī, *v.t.* To render stable.—**Stability, Stableness**, sta-bil'i-ti, stā'bl-nes, *n.* The state or quality of being stable or firm; strength to stand without being moved or overthrown; steadiness or firmness of character; a condition of equilibrium in which a body tends to return to its position of rest when disturbed.—**Stably**, stā'bli, *adv.* In a stable manner; firmly; fixedly; steadily.

Stable, stā'bl, *n.* [L. *stabulum*, a standing-place, a stable, from *sto*, to stand. STABLE, *a.*] A building constructed for horses (rarely beasts generally) to lodge and feed in, and furnished with stalls and necessary equipments; the racing horses of certain stables; the persons connected with the ownership, management, and operations of the stables, as, the Whitney *stables.*—*v.t.*—*stabled, stabling.* To put or keep in a stable.—*v.i.* To dwell or lodge in a stable; to dwell, as beasts; to kennel.—**Stable-boy, Stable-man**, *n.* A boy or man who attends at a stable.—**Stabler**, stā'bl-ėr, *n.* A stable keeper; one who stables horses.—**Stabling**, stā'bl-ing, *n.* A keeping in a stable; accommodation for keeping horses.

Stablish, stab'lish, *v.t.* [ESTABLISH.] To settle in a state for permanence; to establish.

Staccato, stak-kä'tō, *a.* [It., pp. of *staccare*, to separate.] *Mus.* a direction to perform the notes of a passage in a crisp, detached, distinct, or pointed manner.

Stack, stak, *n.* [Same as Icel. *stakk(r)*, Sw. *stack*, Dan. *stak*, a stack, a pile of hay; akin *stake, stick, stock.*] Corn in the sheaf, hay, pease, straw, &c., piled up in a regular form for keeping, and often thatched; a cord of wood containing 128 cubic feet in U. S.; a pile of indefinite quantity; a number of funnels or chimneys standing together; a single tall chimney; the funnel of a locomotive or steam-vessel; a high rock detached; a columnar rock rising out of the sea.—*v.t.* To pile or build into the form of a stack; to make into a large pile.—**Stack-stand**, *n.* A framework on which to build stacks of grain, &c., to keep them off the ground.—**Stack-yard**, *n.* A yard for stacks of hay or grain.

Stacte, stak'tē, *n.* [Gr. *staktē*, from *stazō*, to drop.] One of the sweet spices which composed the holy incense of the ancient Jews.

Staddle, stad'l, *n.* [A.Sax. *stathol, stathel*; akin to *stead, steady, stand.*] A stack-stand; a tree left uncut when others are cut down.

Stadium, stā'di-um, *n.* pl. **Stadia**, stā'-di-a. [L., from Gr. *stadion.*] A Greek measure equal to 606 ft. 9 in.; the course for foot-races in ancient Greece, flanked by terraced elevations with tiers of seats for spectators; a similar modern structure used for athletic games.

Stadtholder, stat'hōl-dėr, *n.* [D. *stadhouder*—*stad*, a city, and *houder*, holder.] Formerly, the chief magistrate of the United Provinces of Holland, also the governor or lieutenant-governor of a province.—**Stadtholdership**, stat'hōl-dėr-ship, *n.* The office of a stadtholder.

Staff, staf, *n.* pl. **Staves, Staffs**, stāvz, stafs (in last two senses always the latter). [A.Sax. *stæf*, a staff; D. and L.G. *staf*, Icel. *stafr*, Dan. *stav*, G. *stab*, a staff; same root as *stab, stem*, and Skr. *stabh, stambh*, to make firm.] A stick carried in the hand for support; a walking-stick; *fig.* that which props or upholds; a support; a stick used as a weapon; a straight stick used as symbol of office; a baton; a rod with a curved head belonging to a bishop; the long handle of an instrument or weapon; *surv.* a graduated stick used in leveling; *naut.* a light pole on which to hoist and display the colors; *mus.* the five parallel lines, and the four spaces between them, on which notes and other musical characters are placed; *milit.* a body of officers whose duties refer to an army or regiment as a whole, and who are not attached to particular subdivisions; a number of persons, considered as one body, assisting in carrying on any undertaking (the editorial *staff* of a newspaper, a hospital *staff*, &c.).—**Staff-officer**, *n.* An officer upon the staff of an army or regiment.—**Staff-sergeant**, *n.* A sergeant of a superior class on the staff of a regiment.

Stag, stag, *n.* [Same as O.E. *stag*, a young horse, a cock-turkey; Sc. *staig*, a stallion; Icel. *steggr*, a male animal; from stem of A.Sax. *stigan*, Icel. *stiga*, G. *steigen*, to mount; lit. the mounter. STAIR.] The male red-deer, or a generic name of the red-deer; the male of the hind; a hart: sometimes applied particularly to a hart in its fifth year; a man at a dance unaccompanied by a lady; a social gathering of men only.—**Stag-beetle**, *n.* One of the largest of American insects, distinguished by the enormous size of the horny and toothed mandibles in the males.—**Stag-hound**, *n.* A large and powerful kind of hound used in hunting deer.

Stage, stāj, *n.* [O.Fr. *estage* (Fr. *étage*), from hypothetical L. *staticum*, from *sto, statum*, to stand (whence *state, station*, &c.).] A floor or platform elevated above the ground or a common surface, as for an exhibition of something to public view; a scaffold; a staging; the raised platform or floor on which theatrical performances are exhibited; hence, *the stage*, the theatre, the dramatic profession, the drama; the scene of any noted action or affair; a place of rest on a journey, as where a relay of horses is taken; a station; the distance between two places of rest on a road (a *stage* of 15 miles); a single step of a gradual process; degree of advance or progression, an increase or decrease, in rising or falling; a coach or other carriage running regularly from one place to another; a stage-coach; a wooden landing-place at a quay or pier; a landing stage.—*v.t.* To put upon the theatrical stage.—**Stage-box**, *n.* A box in a theatre close to the stage.—**Stage-coach**, *n.* A coach that runs by stages; a coach that runs regularly between two places for the conveyance of passengers.—**Stage-coachman, Stage-driver**, *n.* A driver of a stage-coach.—**Stage-direction**, *n.* An instruction to the performers accompanying the text of a play.—**Stage-door**, *n.* The door giving access to the stage and the parts behind it in a theatre.—**Stage-effect**, *n.* Theatrical effect; effect produced artificially and designedly.—**Stage-manager**, *n.* One who superintends the production and performance of a play, and who regulates all matters behind the scenes.—**Stage-play**, *n.* A theatrical entertainment; a play adapted for representation on the stage.—**Stage-player**, *n.* An actor on the stage.—**Stager**, stā'jėr, *n.* One that has long acted on the stage of life; a person of experience, or of skill derived from long experience.—**Stage-struck**, *a.* Smitten with a love for the stage; seized by a passionate desire to become an actor.—**Stage-wagon**, *n.* A wagon for conveying goods and passengers at regularly appointed times.—**Stage-whisper**, *n.* A loud whisper; what is spoken on the stage in a subdued voice meant to indicate a whisper but loud enough to be heard by the audience; an aside.—**Stagey**, stā'ji, *a.* Pertaining to the stage; theatrical, in a depreciatory sense.—**Stageyness**, stā'ji-nes, *n.* The character or quality of being stagey; theatricality.—**Staging**, stā'jing, *n.* A temporary structure for support, as in building; scaffolding.

Staggard. Under STAG.

Stagger, stag'ėr, *v.i.* [From older *staker*, to stagger, from root of *stake*; comp. to *stick* fast = O.D. *staggeren*, Sc. *stacher, stacker*, Icel. *stakra*, to stagger.] To sway helplessly to one side and the other in standing or walking; to reel; to cease to stand firm; to hesitate; to become less confident or determined.—*v.t.* To cause to doubt and waver; to make to hesitate; to make less confident; to strike as incredible; to amaze.—*n.* A sudden swing or reel of the body, as if the person were about to fall; divergence from straightness, as when spokes or rivets are arranged on the two sides of a median line, or, in an aeroplane, when the leading edge of one plane falls behind that of the other; *pl.* a disease of horses and cattle attended with reeling or giddiness.—**Staggeringly**, stag'ėr-ing-li, *adv.* In a staggering manner.

Stagirite, staj'i-rīt, *n.* Aristotle, from Stagira in Macedonia, his birthplace.

Stagnate, stag'nāt, *v.i.*—*stagnated, stagnating.* [L. *stagno, stagnatum*, to stagnate (whence *stanch*), from *stagnum*, standing water, a pool (whence *stank, tank*).] To cease to run or flow; to have no current, as water; to become impure from want of current; to cease to be brisk or active; to become dull, quiet, or inactive (as trade).—**Stagnancy**, stag'nan-si, *n.* The state of being stagnant.—**Stagnant**, stag'nant, *a.* [L. *stagnans, stagnantis*, ppr. of *stagno.*] Not flowing; not running in a current or stream; standing, hence, impure from want of motion; inactive; dull; not brisk (trade is *stagnant*).—**Stagnantly**, stag'nant-li, *adv.* In a stagnant manner.—**Stagnation**, stag-nā'shon, *n.* The condition of being stagnant; the state of being without flow or circulation; the state of being very dull or inactive.

Staid, stād, *a.* [From *stay*, to stop, to steady.] Sober; grave; steady; sedate; not volatile, flighty, or fanciful.—**Staidly**, stād'li, *adv.* In a staid manner; sedately; soberly.—**Staidness**, stād'nes, *n.* Gravity; sobriety; sedateness.

Staid, stād, pret. and pp. of *stay*.

Stain, stān, *v.t.* [An abbrev. of *distain* (which see); comp. *sport*, from *disport*. TINGE.] To discolour by the application of foreign matter; to make foul; to spot; to colour, as wood, glass, &c., by a chemical or other process; to tinge with colours; to impress with figures or patterns in colours different from the ground (to *stain* paper for hangings); to soil or sully with guilt or infamy; to tarnish; to bring reproach on.—*v.i.* To take stains; to become stained or soiled; to grow dim.—*n.* A spot; discoloration from foreign matter; taint of guilt or evil; blot; blemish; disgrace; reproach; shame.—**Stained**, stānd, *p.* and *a.* Having a stain or stains; discoloured; tarnished; produced by staining.—*Stained glass*, glass painted with metallic oxides or chlorides ground up with proper fluxes, and fused into its surface at a moderate heat.—**Stainer**, stā'nėr, *n.* One who stains; a workman engaged in staining (paper-*stainer*).—**Stainless**, stān'les, *a.* Free from stains or spots; free from the reproach of guilt; unblemished; immaculate.—**Stainlessly**, stān'les-li, *adv.* In a stainless manner.

Stair, stār, *n.* [Lit. that by which a person mounts; A.Sax. *staeger*, from *stigan*, Icel. *stiga*, G. *steigen*, to mount, to climb, whence also *stag*, *stile* (on a fence), and the first part of *stirrup*.] A succession of steps rising one above the other arranged as a way between two points at different heights in a building, &c.: used often in plural in same sense, while the singular is also employed to mean a single step.—*Pair of stairs*, a set or flight of steps or stairs; more properly perhaps two flights.—*Flight of stairs*, a succession of steps in a continuous line or from one landing to another.—*Down stairs*, *below stairs*, in the basement or lower part of a house.—*Up stairs*, in the upper part of a house.—**Stair-carpet**, *n.* A carpet for covering stairs.—**Staircase**, stār'kās, *n.* The part of a building which contains the stairs.—**Stair-foot**, *n.* The bottom of a stair.—**Stair-head**, *n.* The top of a staircase.—**Stair-rod**, *n.* A metallic rod for holding a stair-carpet to its place.

Staith, stāth, *n.* [A.Sax. *stæth*, a shore, bank, a landing place; Icel. *stöth*; from root of *stead*, *stand*.] A landing place; an elevated wharf for shipping coal, &c.

Stake, stāk, *n.* [A.Sax. *staca*, a stake = L.G. *stake*, D. *staak*, Dan. *stage*; from the root of *stick*, *stock*.] A piece of wood sharpened at one end and set in the ground, or prepared for setting, as a support to something, as part of a fence, &c.; the post to which one condemned to die by fire was fastened (to suffer at *the stake*); that which is pledged or wagered; that which is laid down to abide the issue of a contest, to be gained by victory or lost by defeat; something hazarded; the state of being pledged or put at hazard: preceded by *at* (his honour is *at stake*).—*v.t.*—*staked*, *staking*. To set and plant like a stake; to fasten; support, or defend with stakes; to mark the limits of by stakes: with *out* (to *stake out* land); to pledge; to lay down as stake; to hazard upon the issue of a competition, or upon a future contingency.—**Stake-holder**, *n.* One who holds stakes, or with whom the stakes are deposited when a wager is laid.—**Stake-net**, *n.* A net for catching salmon, stretched upon stakes fixed into the ground in rivers or firths, where the sea ebbs and flows.

Stalactite, sta-lak'tīt, *n.* [From Gr. *stalaktos*, trickling or dropping, from *stalassō* or *stalazō*, to let fall drop by drop.] A mass of calcareous matter, usually in a conical or cylindrical form, pendent from the roofs of caverns, and produced by the filtration of water containing particles of carbonate of lime through fissures and pores of rocks.—**Stalactic**, **Stalactical**, **Stalactitic**, **Stalactitical**, sta-lak'tik, sta-lak'ti-kal, sta-lak-tit'ik, sta-lak-tit'i-kal, *a.* Pertaining to or having the character of stalactite; resembling a stalactite; containing stalactites.—**Stalactiform**, **Stalactitiform**, sta-lak'ti-form, sta-lak-tit'i-form, *a.* Having the form of a stalactite; like stalactite; stalactical.—**Stalagmite**, sta-lag'mīt, *n.* [Gr. *stalagmos*, a dropping, from *stalazō*, to drop.] A deposit of stalactitic matter on the floor of a cavern, sometimes rising into columns, which meet and blend with the stalactites above.—**Stalagmitic**, **Stalagmitical**, sta-lag-mit'ik, sta-lag-mit'i-kal, *a.* Relating to or having the form of stalagmite.—**Stalagmitically**, sta-lag-mit'i-kal-li, *adv.* In the form or manner of a stalagmite.

Stale, stāl, *a.* [Akin to *stall*, the meaning being from standing long; comp. O.D. *stel*, that remains standing, quiet, ancient. STALL.] Vapid or tasteless from age; having lost its life, spirit, and flavour from being long kept; not new; not freshly made (*stale* bread); out of regard from use or long familiarity; trite; common; musty.—*v.t.*—*staled*, *staling*. To make vapid, useless, cheap, or worthless; to wear out.—**Stalely**, stāl'li, *adv.* In a stale manner.—**Stale-mate**, *n.* *Chess-playing*, the position of the king when so situated that, though not in check, he cannot move without being placed in check, there being no other available move: in this case the game is drawn.—*v.t.* To subject to a stale-mate in chess; hence, to perplex completely; to nonplus.—**Staleness**, stāl'nes, *n.* The state of being stale.

Stale, stāl, *v.i.* [Same as D. and G. *stallen*, Dan. *stalle*, Sw. *stalla*, to make water, from G. *stall*, A.Sax. *stæl*, a stable. STALL.] To make water; to discharge urine, as horses and cattle.—*n.* Urine of horses and cattle.

Stale, stāl, *n.* [A.Sax. *stel*=L.G. and D. *steel*, G. *stiel*, a stalk, stock, handle.] A long handle, as of a rake.

Stalk, stąk, *n.* [Same as Dan. *stilk*, Icel. *stilkr*, a stalk. STALL.] The stem or main axis of a plant; the pedicel of a flower, or the peduncle that supports the fructification of a plant; anything resembling a stalk.—**Stalked**, stąkt, *a.* Having a stalk or stem.—**Stalk-eyed**, *a.* *Zool.* applied to crustacea such as the lobster, shrimp, and crab, which have the eyes set at the end of footstalks.—**Stalkless**, stąk'les, *a.* Having no stalk.—**Stalklet**, stąk'let, *n.* *Bot.* a secondary petiole; the stalk of a leaflet.—**Stalky**, stąk'i, *a.* Resembling a stalk.

Stalk, stąk, *v.i.* [A.Sax. *stælcan*, to go softly or warily; Dan. *stalke*, to stalk.] To walk softly or in a stealthy manner; to walk behind a stalking-horse; to pursue game by approaching softly and warily behind a cover; to walk in a lofty or dignified manner; to pace slowly.—*v.t.* *Sporting*, to pursue stealthily; to watch and follow warily for the purpose of killing.—*n.* A high, proud, stately step or walk.—**Stalker**, stą'kėr, *n.* One who stalks; a kind of fishing-net.—**Stalking**, stą'king, *n.* *Sporting*, the act of approaching game softly and warily, taking advantage of the inequalities of the ground, &c.—**Stalking-horse**, *n.* A horse behind which a fowler conceals himself from the sight of the game; *fig.* anything thrust forward to conceal a more important object; a mask; a pretence.

Stall, stąl, *n.* [A.Sax. *steall*, *stæl*, place, stall, stable; Icel. *stallr*, D. *stal*, G. *stall*, Dan. *stald*, a stall, a stable, &c.; akin *stale*, *a.* and *v.*, *stalwart*, *stalk*, *n.*, &c.; same root as in *stand*.] The place where a horse or an ox is kept and fed; the division or compartment of a stable or cow-house for one horse or ox; a bench or kind of table in the open air on which anything is exposed to sale; a small house or shed in which merchandise is exposed for sale or an occupation carried on (a butcher's *stall*); a fixed seat in the choir or chancel of a cathedral, church, &c., and mostly appropriated to some dignitary; a high-class seat in a theatre; *mining*, an opening made between pillars in the direction that the work is progressing or transversely.—*v.t.* To put into a stall or stable; to keep in a stall; to bring to a stand-still unintentionally, e.g. a horse, carriage, electric motor, or aeroplane.—*v.i.* To live as in a stall; to dwell.—**Stall-feed**, *v.t.* To fatten in a stall or stable (to *stall-feed* an ox).—**Stalling**, stąl'ing, *n.* Stabling (*Tenn.*).—**Stall plate**, *n.* *Her.* a rectangular plate of metal fixed above the stall of a knight in the Chapel of the Order to which he belongs, and bearing his arms emblazoned in full enamelled colours.

Stallion, stal'yun, *n.* [O.E. *stalon*, O.Fr. *estalon* (Fr. *étalon*), a stallion; from O.H.G. *stal*, E. *stall*; lit. the horse kept in the stall.] A horse not castrated; an entire horse.

Stalwart, **Stalworth**, stal'wėrt, stal'wėrth, *a.* [O.E. *stalword*, *stallworth*, from A.Sax. *stælweorth*, lit. worthy of place, from *stæl*, stall, place. STALL.] Brave; bold; redoubted; daring; tall and strong; large and strong in frame.—**Stalwartness**, **Stalworthness**, stal'wėrt-nes, stal'wėrth-nes, *n.* The state or quality of being stalwart.

Stamen, stā'men, *n.* pl. **Stamens**, stā'menz, or **Stamina**, stam'i-na. [L. *stamen*, pl. *stamina*, the warp of a web, a thread, the fibre of wood; from root *sta*, to stand.] *Bot.* the male organ of fructification in plants, situated immediately within the petals, and composed in most cases of three parts, the filament, the anther, and the pollen, of which the two latter are essential, the other not; pl. *stamina*, whatever constitutes the principal strength or support of anything; power of endurance; staying power; long lasting strength or vigour.—**Stamened**, stā'mend, *a.* Furnished with stamens.—**Staminal**, stam'i-nal, *a.* Pertaining to stamens or stamina; consisting in stamens or stamina.—**Staminate**, **Staminated**, stam'i-nāt, stam'i-nā-ted, *a.* Furnished with stamens.—**Stamineal**, **Stamineous**, sta-min'ē-al, sta-min'ē-us, *a.* [L. *stamineus*.] Consisting of stamens; possessing stamens; pertaining to the stamen.—**Staminiferous**, stā-mi-nif'ėr-us, *a.* Bearing or having stamens.—**Staminode**, stam'in-ōd, *n.* [From *stamen*.] A sterile stamen.

Stammer, stam'ėr, *v.i.* [A freq. form from a root *stam*; A.Sax. *stamor*, *stamer*, Icel. *stamr*, *stammr*, stammering, speaking with difficulty; L.G. *stammern*, D. *stameren*, *stamelen*, G. *stammeln*, Icel. *stamma*, to stammer; allied to *stumble*.] To make involuntary breaks or pauses in speaking; to hesitate or falter in speaking; to speak with stops and difficulty; to stutter.—*v.t.* To utter with hesitation or imperfectly: frequently with *out*.—*n.* Defective utterance; a stutter.—**Stammerer**, stam'ėr-ėr, *n.* One that stammers.—**Stammering**, stam'ėr-ing, *n.* The act of one who stammers; defective articulation.—*a.* Characterized by a stammer; stuttering.—**Stammeringly**, stam'ėr-ing-li, *adv.* With stammering.

Stamp, stamp, *v.t.* [Same as Sw. *stampa*, Dan. *stampe*, D. *stampen*, G. *stampfen*, to stamp, nasalized forms corresponding to Icel. *stappa*, D. *stappen*, G. *stapfen*, to step; akin *step*.] To strike or press forcibly by thrusting the foot downward; to impress with some mark or figure; to mark with an impression; to imprint; to fix deeply; to coin or mint; to affix a stamp (as a postage or receipt stamp) to; to cut out with a stamp; to crush by the downward action of a kind of pestle, as ore in a stamping-mill.—*To stamp out*, to extinguish, as fire, by stamping on with the foot; hence, to extirpate; to eradicate; to suppress at once by strong measures.—*v.i.* To strike the foot forcibly downward.—*n.* The act of stamping; an instrument for making impressions on other bodies; a mark imprinted; an official mark set upon things chargeable with some duty or tax showing that the duty is paid: often used as a means of raising revenue; a small piece of stamped paper used by government; a postage-stamp;

an instrument for cutting materials (as paper, leather, &c.) into various forms by a downward pressure; general character fixed on anything (bears the *stamp* of genius); sort or character (a man of the same *stamp*); *metal*, a kind of hammer for crushing or beating ores to powder.—**Stamp-act**, *n.* An act for regulating the imposition of stamp-duties; especially, an act of 1765 imposing a duty on all paper, vellum, and parchment used in the American colonies. It was repealed in March, 1766, as a result of the colonists' opposition.—*Stamp booklet*, a small book containing a few leaves of postage stamps of low denomination, bound in thin cardboard and separated by oiled paper.—**Stamp-collector**, *n.* One who collects stamps; a philatelist.—**Stamping ground**, a person's most familiar surroundings or usual place of activity (his *old stamping ground*) [*Slang*].—**Stamping-machine**, *n.* A machine for forming articles or impressions by stamping.—**Stamping-mill**, *n.* An engine by which ores are pounded by means of a stamp.

Stampede, stam-pēd', *n.* [Amer.Sp. *estampida*, a stampede; akin to *stamp*.] A sudden fright seizing upon large bodies of cattle or horses, on the prairies, and causing them to run for long distances.—*v.i.*—*stampeded, stampeding.* To take sudden flight, as if under the influence of panic terror.

Stanch, stänsh, *v.t.* [O.Fr. *estancher* (Fr. *étancher*), to stanch, from L.L. *stancare*, for L. *stagnare*, to make or be stagnant. STAGNATE.] To prevent the flow of, as of blood; to stop the flow of blood from; to dry up.—*v.i.* To stop, as blood; to cease to flow.—*a.* [Lit. made water-tight, and, as applied to a ship, not leaky.] Strong and tight; sound; firm in principle; steady; hearty; loyal (a *stanch* republican, a *stanch* friend).—**Stancher**, stänsh'ér, *n.* One who or that which stanches.—**Stanchless**, stänsh'les, *a.* Incapable of being stanched; insatiable.—**Stanchly**, stänsh'li, *adv.* In a stanch manner.—**Stanchness**, stänsh'nes, *n* The state or quality of being stanch; strongness and soundness; firmness in principle. Also written **Staunch, Staunchness**, &c.

Stanchion, stan'shon, *n.* [O.Fr. *estanson, estançon*, from *estance*, a support, from L.L. *stantia*, from L. *sto*, to stand. STAND.] A prop or support; a post or beam used for a support; an upright post or beam of different forms in ships.

Stand, stand, *v.i.*—pret. and pp. *stood* (stöd). [A.Sax. *standan*, to stand, pret. *stōd*, pp. *standen* = Icel. *standa*, O.H.G. *standan*, Goth. *standan*, D. *staan*, G. *stehen*; from root seen also in L. *sto*, Gr. (*hi*)*stanai*, Skr. *sthâ*; from same root are *stead, stall, still, stool*, &c., and through the French and Latin come *stage, state, station, stable*, &c.] To be stationary or at rest in an upright position; to be set upright; to be on end; to be as regards position or situation; to have its site or locality; to cease from progress; to come to a state of rest; to stop; to pause; to halt; to continue or remain without injury; to last; to endure; to maintain one's ground or position; to maintain a fixed or steady attitude; to persevere; to persist; to insist; to be placed as regards rank or order (*a stands* first); to be in a particular state or condition; to be (how *stands* the matter?); to be in the stead or place; to be equivalent (v *stands* for 5); to become a candidate; to hold a certain course, as a ship; to be directed towards any local point; to measure from feet to head, or from bottom to top; to stagnate; to be valid; to have efficacy.—[*Note. Stand* with many adverbs receives the sense of motion as previous to coming to rest, and becomes equivalent to to step, go, come; as, to *stand* aloof, to *stand* apart, to *stand* aside, to *stand* back, to *stand* forth, &c.]—*To stand against*, to resist; to oppose.—*To stand by* (with *by* the adverb), to be present; to be near; to be placed or left aside; (with *by* the preposition) to support; to defend; to assist; not to desert.—*To stand fast*, to be fixed; to be unshaken.—*To stand for*, to espouse the cause of; to represent; to take the place of; to offer one's self as a candidate; *naut.* to direct the course towards.—*To stand from* (*naut.*), to direct the course from.—*To stand in*, or *stand in for* (*naut.*), to direct a course toward land or a harbor.—*To stand off*, to keep at a distance.—*To stand off and on* (*naut.*), to sail toward land and then from it.—*To stand* or *stand in* (with personal objects, the person being really in the dative), to cost (that coat *stood* him ten dollars or *in* ten dollars).—*To stand out*, to project; to be prominent; to persist in opposition or resistance.—*To stand to*, to apply one's self to; to remain fixed in (a purpose or opinion); to abide by; to adhere, as to a contract, &c.; to be consistent or tally with (it *stands to* reason).—*To stand up*, to rise to one's feet; to rise to make a claim or a declaration; to rise in opposition; to rise and stand on end (as one's hair).—*To stand up against*, to place one's self in opposition to; to resist.—*To stand up for*, to rise in defense of.—*To stand upon*, to set value on; to insist on; to attach a high value to; to be a stickler for (to *stand upon* ceremony).—*To stand with*, to be consistent.—*v.t.* To place on end; to endure; to sustain; to bear; to await; to undergo.—*To stand it*, to be able to endure or bear something.—*To stand one's ground*, to keep the ground, the station one has taken; to maintain one's position.—*To stand fire*, to remain while being shot at by an enemy without giving way.—*To stand trial*, to sustain the trial or examination of a cause.—*n.* A cessation of progress, motion, or activity; a stop; a halt; a point or condition beyond which no further progress is made; a state of hesitation or perplexity; a place or post where one stands; a station; a halt made for the purpose of resisting an attack; a small table or frame, on or in which articles may be put for support (an umbrella *stand*), or on which goods may be exposed for sale (a fruit *stand*); a place in a town where automobiles stand ready for hire, a cabstand; an erection or raised platform for spectators at open-air gatherings.—*Grand stand*, tiers of seats at a base-ball, foot-ball, or other field.—*Stand of arms*, a musket or rifle with its usual appendages, as a bayonet, cartridge-box, &c.—**Stander-up**, *n.* One who takes a side.—**Standing**, stand'ing, *p.* and *a.* Permanent; not temporary; lasting; not transitory; stagnant; not flowing; fixed; not movable; remaining erect; not cut down; the relative position of a contestant in a tournament, or a team in a league, such as in base-ball.—*Standing orders*, regulations made by a deliberative assembly respecting the manner in which business shall be conducted in it.—*Standing rigging*, the ropes which sustain the masts and remain fixed in their position, as the shrouds and stays.—*n.* The act of one who stands; duration of existence (a custom of long *standing*); station; place to stand in; power to stand; condition in society; relative position; rank; reputation.—**Stand-point**, *n.* A fixed point or station; a basis or fundamental principle; a position or point of view from which a matter is considered.—**Stand-still**, *n.* A standing at rest; a stop.

Standard, stand'ärd, *n.* [From O.Fr. *estandart, estendart* (Fr. *étendard*), from the Teutonic verb to *stand* with suffix *-ard*.] A flag or ensign set up and round which men rally, or under which they unite for a common purpose; a flag or carved symbolical figure, &c., erected on a long pole or staff; a banner; the heraldic standard is a long, narrow pennant with a gold or parti-colored fringe; that which is established by competent authority as a rule or measure of quantity; a measure or weight by which others are to be regulated and adjusted; that which is established as a rule or model by public opinion, custom, or general consent; that which serves as a test or measure (a *standard* of morality, or of taste); *hort.* a tree or shrub which stands singly and not attached to any wall or support; *bot.* the upper petal or banner of a papilionaceous corolla; *carp.* any upright in a framing.—*a.* Serving as a standard; capable of satisfying certain conditions fixed by competent authority; fixed; settled; *hort.* not trained on a wall, &c.—**Standard-bearer**, *n.* One who bears a standard.—**Standardize**, stand'ärd-īz, *v.t.* To accept as a standard; to make in certain fixed or standard sizes, qualities, &c.

Stang, stang, *n.* [Same as D. *stang*, G. *stange*, Dan. *stang*, Icel. *stōng*, bar, beam, pole; from root of *sting, stick*.] A long bar; a pole; a shaft.—*To ride the stang*, to be carried on a pole in derision, a punishment inflicted in former times on wife or husband beaters and others.

Stanhope, stan'hōp, *n.* A light four-wheeled carriage without a top: with high seat and closed back; any high buggy of similar design.

Stank, stangk, *n.* [O.Fr. *estang*, Pr. *estanc*, from L. *stagnum*, a pool. STAGNATE.] A pool; a pond; a ditch.

Stank, stangk, old pret. of *stink*.

Stannary, stan'a-ri, *a.* [From L. *stannum*, tin.] Relating to tin-works.—*n.* A tin-mine; tin-works.—**Stannate**, stan'āt, *n.* A salt of stannic acid.—**Stannic**, stan'ik, *a.* Pertaining to tin; containing tin with valence four.—**Stannic oxide**, a white amorphous powder, used in making white enamels; also for polishing glass.—**Stanniferous**, stan-if'ér-us, *a.* Containing or affording tin.—**Stannotype**, stan'ō-tīp, *n.* *Photog.* a picture taken on a tin-plate.—**Stannous**, stan'us, *a.* Pertaining to, or containing tin; containing tin with valence two.

Stanza, stan'za, *n.* [It. *stanza*, a stanza, abode, stop, &c., from L. *stans, stantis*, ppr. of *sto*, to stand. STATE.] A number of lines of poetry connected with each other, and properly ending in a full point or pause; a part of a poem containing every variation of measure in that poem, and successively repeated.—**Stanzaic**, stan-zā'ik, *a.* Consisting of or relating to stanzas; arranged as a stanza.

Stapelia, sta-pē'li-a, *n.* [After *Stapel*, a Dutch botanist.] A genus of fleshy African plants with beautiful flowers, many of which have the odour of rotten flesh.

Stapes, stā'pēz, *n.* [L., a stirrup.] *Anat.* the innermost of the small bones of the ear, so called from its form.

Staphyline, staf'i-līn, *a.* [Gr. *staphylē*, a bunch of grapes.] *Mineral.* having the form of a bunch of grapes; botryoidal.—**Staphylococcus**, staf'il-ō-kok"us, *n.* [Gr. *staphylē*, and *kokkos*, a berry.] In bacteria, a form consisting of a cluster of cocci.—**Staphyloma, Staphylosis**, staf-i-lō'ma, staf-i-lō'sis, *n.* [Gr. *staphylē*.] *Pathol.* a tumour or bulging out of the eyeball in front.

Staphyloplasty, staf'il-o-plas-ti, *n.* [Gr. *staphylē*, the uvula, and *plassō*, to form.] *Surg.* the operation for replacing the soft palate when it has been lost.—**Staphyloplastic**, staf'il-o-plas"tik, *a.* Relating to staphyloplasty.—**Staphyloraphy**, staf-i-lor'a-fi, *n.* [Gr. *staphylē*, and *raphē*, a suture.] *Surg.* the operation of uniting a cleft palate.—**Staphylotome**, staf'il-o-tōm, *n.* *Surg.* a knife for operating upon the uvula or palate.—**Staphylotomy**, staf-i-lot'o-mi, *n.* [Gr. *staphylē*, and *tomē*, a cutting.] *Surg.* amputation of the uvula.

Staple, stā'pl, *n.* [Same as D. and G. *stapel*, a post, prop; so also Sw. *stapel*, Dan. *stabel*; same root as that of *stamp* and *step*.] According to old usage, a settled mart or market; an emporium; a town where certain commodities were chiefly taken for sale; hence, the principal commodity grown or manufactured in a country, district, or town; the principal element of or ingredient in anything; the chief constituent; the material or substance of anything; raw or unmanufactured material; the thread or pile of wool, cotton, or flax (wool of a long or coarse *staple*).—*a.* Pertaining to or being a mart or staple for commodities; mainly occupying commercial enterprise; established in commerce (a *staple* trade); chief; principal; regularly produced or made for market.—*v.t.*—*stapled, stapling.* To sort or adjust the different staples of, as wool.—**Stapler**, stā'pler, *n.* A dealer in staple commodities; one employed in assorting wool according to its staple; a contrivance that drives thin wire staples through paper and clinches them to bind the paper.

Staple, stā'pl, *n.* [A.Sax. *stapel*, a prop, trestle; really same as above word.] A loop of iron formed with two points to be driven into wood to hold a hook, pin, bolt, &c.

Star, stär, *n.* [A.Sax. *steorra*, Sc. *starn*, Icel. *stjarna*, Goth. *stairno*, D. *ster*, O.D. *sterne*, G. *stern;* cog. L. *stella* (*or sterula*), also *astrum*, Gr. *astēr*, Armor. *stéren*, Skr. *târâ* (for *stârâ*); from root of E. *strew*, Skr. *stri*, to strew, from scattering light.] Any celestial body except the moon, the planets, comets, meteors, and nebulae; more strictly, any of the bodies that shine by their own light, as the sun, situated at immense distances from us, and doubtless, like our sun, the centers of systems similar to our own, distinctively called *fixed stars*, as they apparently do not change their relative positions as do the planets, the wanderers among the stars; that which resembles a star; a figure with points radiating like the spokes of a wheel; an ornamental figure rayed like a star worn upon the breast to indicate rank or honor; a radiated mark in writing or printing; an asterisk, thus, *: used as a reference to a note in the margin or to fill a blank in writing or printing where letters or words are omitted; a person of brilliant qualities; a brilliant theatrical or operatic performer; a movie star. — *v.t.* — *starred, starring.* To set or adorn with stars; to bespangle.—*v.i.* To shine as a star; to appear as an actor in a provincial theater among inferior players. — **Star-anise**, *n.* A Chinese plant, the fruit of which is used as a condiment in the East.—**Star-apple**, *n.* A West Indian fruit somewhat resembling an apple. — **Star-fish**, *n.* A marine animal (one of the Echinodermata) which has the form of a star, with five or more rays radiating from a central disc.—**Star-gazer**, *n.* One who gazes at the stars; an astrologer. — **Star-gazing**, *n.* The act or practice of observing the stars with attention; astrology.—**Starless**, stär'les, *a.* Having no stars visible or no starlight. — **Starlight**, stär'līt, *n.* The light proceeding from the stars.—*a.* Lighted by the stars.—**Starlike**, stär'līk, *a.* Resembling a star; bright; lustrous. — **Starlit**, stär'lit, *a.* Lighted by stars.—**Star-nose**, *n.* A North American mole with star-like rays at the extremity of its muzzle. — **Starred**, stärd, *p.* and *a.* Studded or adorned with stars; influenced by the stars (ill-*starred*); marked with a star to indicate importance. — **Stars and Bars**, the first flag adopted by the "Confederate States of America," having three bars of red, white and red, and a blue union with seven white stars. — **Stars and Stripes**, the flag of the United States, consisting of 13 horizontal stripes, alternately red and white, and a union having in a blue field 48 white stars to represent the states. — **Star-Spangled Banner**, a patriotic poem by Francis Scott Key, adopted as the national anthem of the United States by act of Congress in 1931. — **Star-wort**, stär'wėrt, *n.* The popular name of the *Aster* family, fall-blooming plants, some of them of the chick-weed genus.

Starboard, stär'bōrd, *n.* [A.Sax. *steórbord*, that is, *steer-board*, from *steóran*, to steer, the old rudder being a kind of large oar used on the right side of the ship. STEER.] *Naut.* the right-hand side of a ship looking towards the stem or prow: opposed to *port* or old *larboard*.—*a.* Pertaining to the right-hand side of a ship; being or lying on the right side.

Starch, stärch, *n.* [A softened form of *stark*, stiff, strong; lit. stuff that makes stiff. STARK.] A substance universally diffused in the vegetable world, and forming the greater part of all farinaceous substances; this substance as prepared for commerce, chiefly extracted from wheat flour or potatoes, and employed for stiffening linen or other cloth; *fig.* stiffness of a person's behavior or manner.—*v.t.* To stiffen with starch. — **Starched**, stärcht, *p.* and *a.* Stiffened with starch; stiff; precise; formal. — **Starchedness**, stärcht'nes, *n.* **Starcher**, stärch'ėr, *n.* One who starches. — **Starchily**, stär'chi-li, *adv.* In a starchy manner; with stiffness of manner. — **Starchiness**, stär'chi-nes, *n.* Stiffness of manner; preciseness. — **Starch-sugar**, *n.* Glucose. — **Starchy**, stär'chi, *a.* Consisting of starch; resembling starch; stiff; formal in manner.

Stare, stār, *v.i.*—*stared, staring.* [A.Sax. *starian*, to stare, to gaze; D. and L.G. *staren*, G. *starren*, Icel. *stara*; lit. to look fixedly, the root being that of G. and Sw. *starr*, stiff, fixed, E. *stark*, stiff, strong.] To look with fixed eyes wide open; to gaze, as in admiration, surprise, horror, impudence, &c.—*v.t.* To affect or abash by gazing at; to look earnestly or fixedly at.—*To stare in the face*, (*fig.*) to be before the eyes, or undeniably evident.—*n.* The act of one who stares.—**Starer**, stā'rėr, *n.* One who stares or gazes. — **Staring**, stā'ring, *a.* Gazing fixedly; fixed.—*adv.* Staringly; so as to stare wildly (stark, *staring* mad). — **Staringly**, stā'ring-li, *adv.* In a staring manner; with fixed look.

Stare, stār, *n.* [A.Sax. *stær*, Icel. *starl*, Sw. *stare*, G. *staar.*] A starling.

Stark, stärk, *a.* [A.Sax. *stearc*, stiff, hard; G. and Sw. *stark*, D. *sterk*, Icel. *sterkr*; akin G. *starr*, stiff; E. *stare*. *Starch* is a softened form.] Stiff; rigid, as in death; strong; rugged; powerful; mere; pure; downright (*stark* nonsense).—*adv.* Wholly; entirely (*stark* mad, *stark* naked).—**Starkly**, stärk'li, *adv.* In a stark manner.

Starling, stär'ling, *n.* [Dim. of *stare*, a starling. STARE.] The birds of the family Icteridae are sometimes called American starlings; piles driven round piers of a bridge for its protection.

Start, stärt, *v.i.* [O.E. *sterte, sturte, stirte;* not in A.Sax. or Icel.; allied to D. *storten*, Dan. *styrte*, G. *stürzen*, to rush, to spring.] To move suddenly and spasmodically; to make a sudden and involuntary motion of the body, caused by surprise, pain, or any sudden feeling; to shrink; to wince; to make a sudden or unexpected change of place; to spring up; to change condition at once; to set out; to commence a course, as a race, a journey, or the like; to shift or spring from a fixed position; to be dislocated.—*To start after*, to set out in pursuit of; to follow.—*To start against*, to become a candidate in opposition to; to oppose.—*To start up*, to rise suddenly, as from a seat; to come suddenly into notice. — *v.t.* To rouse suddenly from concealment; to cause to flee or fly (to *start* a hare); to begin; to set agoing; to originate (to *start* an enterprise, a newspaper); to cause to jump from its place; to make to lose its hold (to *start* a nail); to dislocate.—*n.* A sudden involuntary twitch, spring, or motion, caused by surprise, fear, pain, &c.; a sudden change of place; a quick movement; a bursting forth; a sally; a spasmodic effort; a beginning of action or motion; the setting of something agoing; first motion from a place, first motion in a race; the outset.—*To get* or *have the start*, to be beforehand with another; to get ahead; with *of*. — **Starter**, stär'tėr, *n.* One who starts; one who sets out; one who sets persons or things in motion, as an official of a trolley line or a train dispatcher; *in automobile*, the electric motor that starts the gasoline engine; *at horse race*, one who starts as competitor in a race.—*Head start*, opposite of handicap, a favor, an advantage at a race for a supposedly inferior contestant.

Startle, stär'tl, *v.i.* — *startled, startling.* [Dim. of *start.*] To move with a start or spasmodically; to start.—*v.t.* To excite by sudden alarm, surprise, or apprehension; to alarm.—*n.* A start of alarm. — **Startling**, stärt'ling, *p.* and *a.* Such as to startle with fear or surprise; alarming; shocking.—**Startlingly**, stärt'ling-li, *adv.* In a startling manner.—**Start-up**,‡ *n.* An upstart. (*Shak.*)

Starve, stärv, *v.i.*—*starved, starving.* [A. Sax. *steorfan*, to perish of hunger or cold = L.G. *starven*, D. *sterven*, G. *sterben*, to die.] To perish with or suffer extremely from hunger; to suffer from want; to be hard put to it through want of anything.—*v.t.* To kill or distress with hunger; to subdue by famine; to destroy by want; to deprive of force or vigor. — **Starvation**, stär-vā'shon, *n.* [One of those words which have a Latin termination tacked on to an Anglo-Saxon base; comp. *flirtation, talkative, readable*, &c.] The state of starving or being starved; a suffering extremely from want of food.—**Starveling**, stärv'ling, *a.* Hungry; lean; pining with want.—*n.* An animal or plant that is thin and weak through want of nutriment.

Stasis, stā'sis, *n.* A stoppage of the normal flow of fluids in any organs of the body; a slackening of the blood current as in passive congestion.

Statant, stā'tant, *a.* Heraldic term applied to animals when standing still with all four feet on the ground.

State, stāt, *n.* [O.Fr. *estat*, state, condition, &c. (Fr. *état*); from L. *status*, state, position, from *sto*, to stand (seen also in *station, status, statue, stage, rest, arrest, constant, extant*, &c.). STAND.] Condition as determined by whatever circumstances; the condition or circumstances of a being or thing at any given time; situation; position; rank, condition, or quality; royal or gorgeous pomp; appearance of greatness; dignity; grandeur; a certain division of the community partaking in the government of their country; an estate (of the realm); a whole people united into one body politic; a commonwealth; the power wielded by the government of a country; the civil power (the union of church and *state*); one of the commonwealths or bodies politic which together make up a federal republic. —*v.t.*—*stated, stating.* To express the particulars of; to set down in detail; to explain particularly; to narrate; to recite.—**State-bank**, a bank chartered and controlled by the state. — **State-barge**, *n.* A royal barge; a barge of state.—**State-carriage**, *n.* The carriage of a prince or sovereign, used when he appears publicly in state.—**State-craft**, *n.* The art of conducting state affairs; statesmanship. — **State-criminal**, *n.* One who commits an offense against the state; a political offender. — **Stated**, stā'ted, *a.* Settled; established; fixed (stated hours or times). — **State Department**. The official name is the Department of State of the United States, at whose head is the Secretary of State, chief of the diplomatic and consular service. He issues passports and supervises the conduct of foreign relations. He also keeps the Great Seal of the United States and all important state documents. — **Statedly**, stā'ted-li, *adv.* At stated or settled times; at regular intervals.—**State-house**, *n.* The building in which the legislature of a state holds its sittings; the State Capitol. (*United States.*)—**Stateliness**, stāt'li-nes, *n.* The condition or quality of being stately; loftiness of mien; dignity. — **Stately**, stāt'li, *a.* August; lofty; majestic; magnificent. — **Statement**, stāt'ment, *n.* The act of stating; that which is stated; a narrative; a recital; the expression of a fact or of an opinion.—**State-paper**, *n.* A paper relating to the political interests or government of a state. — **State-prisoner**, *n.* One confined under the laws or authority of a state. — **Stater**, stā'tėr, *a.* One who states.—**State-room**, *n.* A magnificent room in a palace or great house; an elegantly fitted up cabin, generally for two persons, in a steamer. — **States-general**, *n. pl.* The legislative assemblies of France before the revolution of 1789, and those of the Netherlands. — **Statesman**, stāts'man, *n.* A man versed in the arts of government; a politician. — **Statesmanlike**, stāts'man-līk, *a.* Having the manner or wisdom of statesmen; worthy of or becoming a statesman.—**Statesmanship**, stāts'man-ship, *n.* The qualifications of a statesman; political skill.—**State-trial**, *n.* A trial of a person or persons for political offenses.

Statics, stat'iks, *n.* [Fr. *statique*, from Gr. *statikē*, statics, from *statikos*, causing to stop or stand; same root as *state*, *stand*.] That branch of dynamics which treats of the properties and relations of forces in equilibrium, the body upon which they act being in a state of rest. See DYNAMICS, MECHANICS.—**Static**, stat'ik, *a.* Statical; —*n.* Disturbance of radio reception caused by outside electrical interference. —**Statical**, stat'i-kal, *a.* Pertaining to bodies at rest or in equilibrium; acting by mere weight without producing motion (*statical* pressure).—*Statical electricity*, electricity produced by friction.

Station, stā'shon, *n.* [Fr. *station*, L. *statio*, *stationis*, from *sto*, to stand. STATE.] The spot or place where anything stands, particularly where a person habitually stands or is appointed to remain for a time; post assigned; situation; position or locality; condition of life; social position; the place where the police force of any district is assembled when not on duty; a building or buildings on a railway for the reception of passengers and goods intended to be conveyed, and where trains stop; *zool.* and *bot.* the peculiar locality where each species naturally occurs.—*Military station*, a place where troops are regularly kept in garrison. —*Naval station*, a harbour for war vessels, where there is a dockyard and every requisite for the repair of ships.—*v.t.* To assign a station or position to; to post; *refl.* to take up a post or position.—**Stational**, stā'shon-al, *a.* Pertaining to a station.—**Stationariness**, stā'shon-a-ri-nes, *n.* The quality of being stationary; fixity.—**Stationary**, stā'shon-a-ri, *a.* [L. *stationarius*.] Remaining in the same station or place; not moving; fixed; remaining in the same condition.—*Stationary engine*, a steam-engine in a fixed position; any steam-engine other than a locomotive.—**Station-clerk**, *n.* A clerk at a railway station.—**Stationer**, stā'shon-ėr, *n.* [From booksellers originally having a station or stall (L.L. *statio*) at fairs or in market-places.] One who sells paper, pens, pencils, ink, and various other materials connected with writing.—*Stationers' hall*, the hall of the London Stationers' Company. The Guild of Stationers (i.e. booksellers and publishers) of London was founded in 1403.—**Stationery**, stā'shon-ėr-i, *n.* The articles usually sold by stationers, as the various materials employed in connection with writing.—*Stationery office*, a public office in London which issues government stationery and publishes official documents.—**Station-house**, *n.* A place of arrest or temporary confinement; a police-station.—**Station-master**, *n.* The official in charge of a railway station.

Statistics, sta-tis'tiks, *n.* [Fr. *statistique*, from Gr. *statos*, fixed, settled, from stem *sta-*, to stand. STATE, STAND.] A collection of facts which admit of numerical statement and of arrangement in tables, especially facts illustrating the physical, social, moral, intellectual, political, industrial and economical condition of communities or classes of men; that department of political science which deals with such facts.—**Statist**, stat'ist, *n.* A statistician.—**Statistical**, **Statistic**, sta-tis'ti-kal, sta-tis'tik, *a.* Pertaining to statistics; containing statistics.—**Statistically**, sta-tis'ti-kal-li, *adv.* In a statistical manner. —**Statistician**, stat-is-tish'an, *n.* One versed in statistics.

Statoblast, sta'tō-blast, *n.* [Gr. *statos*, resting, *blastos*, a bud.] In freshwater polyzoa, an internally formed winter-bud.

Stator, stā'tor, *n.* The stationary part of an electric generator or motor.

Statoscope, stat'ō-skōp, *n.* [Gr. *statos*, standing, and *skopein*, to view.] An instrument for registering the rise or fall of a flying machine.

Statue, stat'ū, *n.* [Fr. *statue*, L. *statua*, from *statuo*, to set, to place, from stem of *sto*, to stand. STATE.] A lifelike representation of a human figure or animal in some solid substance, as marble, bronze, iron, wood; a sculptured cast or moulded figure of some size and in the round.—*Equestrian statue*, a statue in which the figure is represented as seated on horseback.—**Statued**, stat'ūd, *a.* Furnished with statues.—**Statuary**, stat'ū-a-ri, *n.* [L. *statuaria*, the art of statuary, *statuarius*, a statuary, from *statua*, a statue.] The art of carving or making statues, a branch of sculpture; statues regarded collectively; one that professes or practises the art of making statues.—**Statuesque**, stat-ū-esk', *a.* Partaking of or having the character of a statue.—**Statuesquely**, stat-ū-esk'li, *adv.* In a statuesque manner.—**Statuette**, stat-ū-et', *n.* [Fr.] A small statue; a statue smaller than nature.

Stature, stat'ūr, *n.* [L. *statura*, from *sto*, *statum*, to stand, STATE.] The natural height of an animal body; bodily tallness: generally used of the human body.

Status, stā'tus, *n.* [L. *status*, state. STATE.] Standing or position as regards rank or condition; position of affairs.—*Status quo*, the condition in which the thing or things were at first.

Statute, stat'ūt, *n.* [Fr. *statut*, L. *statutum*, from *statuo*, to set up, to fix, to determine, STATE.] A law proceeding from the government of a state; an enactment of the legislature of a state; especially one passed by a body of representatives; a written law; a permanent rule or law of a corporation.—*Statute law*, a statute; also, collectively, the enactments of a legislative assembly, in contradistinction to *common law*.—*v.i.* To ordain, of frequent occurrence in legal deeds. (*Scot.*)—**Statutable**, stat'ū-ta-bl, *a.* Made or introduced by statute; in conformity to statute.—**Statutably**, stat'ū-ta-bli, *adv.* In a manner agreeable to statute.—**Statute-book**, *n.* A register of statutes; *the statute-book*, the whole statutes of a country.—**Statute-roll**, *n.* An enrolled statute.—**Statutory**, stat'ū-to-ri, *a.* Enacted by statute; depending on statute for its authority.

Staunch, stänsh, STANCH.

Staurolite, sta'ro-līt, *n.* [Gr. *stauros*, a cross, and *lithos*, a stone.] CROSS-STONE.

Stave, stāv, *n.* [From *staff*, through influence of the plural *staves*.] A pole or piece of wood of some length; one of the thin narrow pieces of timber of which casks, tubs, buckets, &c., are made; a stanza; a verse; *mus.* the *staff*.—*v.t.*—*staved*, *staving*. To break in a stave or staves of, or to break a hole in (in this sense pret. and pp. may be *stove*); to furnish with staves or rundles. —*To stave off*, lit. to push off with a staff; hence, to put off; to delay.—**Staves**, stāvz, *n.* The plural of *staff* as well as of *stave*.

Stavesacre, stāvz'ā-kėr, *n.* [A corruption of Gr. *staphisagria*.] Lark-spur.

Stay, stā, *v.i.*—pret. *staid*, *stayed*; ppr. *staying*. [O.Fr. *estayer*, to prop, support, keep steady, from O.D. or Fl. *staeye*, *staede*, a prop, *staeden*, to establish; akin to E. *stead*, *steady*.] To remain, continue, or be in a place; to abide; to dwell; to delay; to tarry; to be steady or firm; to continue in a state; to remain; to wait; to forbear to act; to stop; to come to a stand.—*v.t.* To prop or support (O.T.); to make to stop; to stop; to cause to cease (to *stay* operations); to delay; to keep back; to abide; to wait for; to await.—*To stay the stomach*, to satisfy hunger; to satisfy a strong desire.—*n.* A continuance in a place; abode for a time; continuance in a state or condition; stand; stop; obstacle; obstruction; a prop; a support; a piece in some structure performing the office of a brace or tie; *pl.* a kind of waistcoat, stiffened with whalebone or other material, worn by females, sometimes by men; a bodice; a corset: so called from the support it gives to the body.—**Stayer**, stā'ėr, *n.* One who or that which stays; in sporting language, one who holds out long and steadily.—**Staylace**, stā'lās, *n.* A lace for fastening the stays or bodice in female dress.—**Staymaker**, stā'mā-kėr, *n.* One whose occupation is to make stays.—**Stay-rod**, *n.* A supporting or strengthening rod in a steam-boiler.

Stay, stā, *n.* [A.Sax. *stæg* = Icel., Dan., Sw., D., and G. *stag*, a stay.] *Naut.* a strong rope used to support a mast, and leading from the head of one mast down to some other, or to some part of the vessel.—*In stays*, the situation of a vessel when she is going about from one tack to the other.—*To miss stays*, to fail in the attempt to tack about.—**Stay-sail**, *n.* Any sail which hoists upon a stay.

Stead, sted, *a.* [A.Sax. *stede*=D. and L.G. *stede*, Dan. *sted*, Icel. *stathr*, Goth. *staths*, G. *statt*, place, stead; from root of *stand*; hence, *steady*, *steadfast*, *bestead*, *bedstead*, *roadstead*, *homestead*, &c.] Place or room which another had or might have; preceded by *in*, as, David died, and Solomon reigned *in* his *stead*: hence *instead*.—*To stand a person in stead*, to be of use or advantage to him.—*v.t.* To be of use to; to benefit.

Steadfast, sted'fast, *a.* [*Stead*, place, and *fast*; lit. firm in place.] Fast fixed; firm; constant or firm in resolution; resolute; not fickle or wavering. Written also *stedfast*.—**Steadfastly**, sted'fast-li, *adv.* In a steadfast manner; with fixed eyes; firmly. —**Steadfastness**, sted'fast-nes, *n.* The state of being steadfast; firmness of mind or purpose; constancy; resolution.

Steading, *n.* [*Stead*.] A farm building, a holding.

Steady, sted'i, *a.* [A.Sax. *stedig*, from *stede*, place (STEAD); D. and Dan. *stadig*, G. *stätig*, constant.] Firm in standing or position; firmly fixed; constant in mind or pursuit; not fickle; regular; constant; uniform.—*v.t.*—*steadied*, *steadying*. To make steady; to hold or keep from shaking, reeling, or falling; to support firmly.—*v.i.* To become steady; to regain or maintain an upright position.—**Steadily**, sted'i-li, *adv.* In a steady manner; firmly; steadfastly; assiduously; unwaveringly.—**Steadiness**, sted'i-nes, *n.* The state of being steady; firmness of mind or purpose; constancy; resolution.

Steak, stāk, *n.* [A Scandinavian word: Icel. *steik*, Sw. *stek*, a steak; perhaps akin to *stick*, as being *stuck* on a spit to roast.] A slice of beef, pork, venison, &c., broiled or cut for broiling.

Steal, stēl, *v.t.*—pret. *stole*, pp. *stolen* or *stole*. [A.Sax. *stelan*, to steal = D. *stelen*, Icel. *stela*, Goth. *stilan*, G. *stehlen*, to steal; same root as Gr. *stereō*, to deprive, Skr. *stenas*, a thief.] To take and carry away feloniously; to take clandestinely without right or leave; to gain or win by address or gradual and imperceptible means; to perform secretly; to try to accomplish clandestinely (to *steal* a look).—*To steal a march upon*, to gain an advantage over stealthily.—*v.i.* To practise or be guilty of theft; to withdraw or pass privily; to slip unperceived; to go or come furtively.—**Stealer**, stē'lėr, *n.* One that steals; a thief.—**Stealing**, stē'ling, *n.* The act of one who steals; theft.—**Stealth**, stelth, *n.* [Comp. *heal*, *health*; *till*, *tilth*.] The act of stealing†; a secret or clandestine method of procedure; a proceeding by secrecy.—**Stealthily**, stel'thi-li, *adv.* In a stealthy manner; by stealth.—**Stealthiness**, stel'thi-nes, *n.* The character of being stealthy. —**Stealthy**, stel'thi, *a.* Done by stealth; accompanied by efforts at concealment; done furtively; furtive; sly.

Steam, stēm, *n.* [A.Sax. *stedm*, steam, smoke; D. *stoom*, Fris. *stoame*, steam; akin L.G. *stäm*, drift of snow or rain.] The vaporous or gaseous substance into which water is converted under certain circumstances of heat and pressure; the elastic aeriform fluid generated by heating water to the boiling-point (212° F.); popularly, the visible moist vapour which rises from water, and from all moist and liquid bodies, when subjected to the action of heat.—*v.i.* To give out steam or vapour; to rise in a vaporous form; to pass off in visible vapour; to sail by the agency of steam.—*v.t.* To expose to steam; to apply steam to.—**Steam-boat**, *n.* A ship moved by the elastic power of steam acting upon machinery.—**Steam-boiler**, *n.* A strong metallic vessel of iron or steel plates riveted together, in which water is converted into steam for supplying steam-engines, &c.—**Steam-car**, *n.* A car drawn or driven by steam-power.—**Steam-carriage**, *n.* A locomotive engine adapted to work on common roads; a road-steamer.—**Steam-casing**, **Steam-jacket**, *n.* A vacuity surrounding any vessel, and into which steam may be admitted, to prevent loss of heat by radiation.—**Steam-chamber**, **Steam-room**, *n.* A division or compartment in the boiler of a steam-engine above the water, whence steam is conducted to the engine.—**Steam-chest**, **Steam-dome**, *n.* A box or chamber above a steam-boiler to form a reservoir for the steam, and from whence it passes to the engine.—**Steam-crane**, *n.* A crane worked by steam.—**Steam-engine**, *n.* An engine in which the elastic or expansive force of steam is made available as a source of motive power in the arts and manufactures, and in locomotion.—**Steamer**, stē′mėr, *n.* A steamship; a road-steamer; a fire-engine the pumps of which are worked by steam; a vessel in which articles are subjected to the action of steam.—**Steam-gauge**, *n.* A gauge attached to a boiler to indicate the pressure of steam; a pressure-gauge.—**Steam-governor**, *n.* The governor of a steam-engine.—**Steam-hammer**, *n.* A heavy hammer operated by steam.—**Steam-heat**, *n.* Heat, especially for an edifice, conducted from a steam-boiler by pipes and radiators.—**Steam-navigation**, *n.* The propulsion of boats and vessels by steam; the art of navigating steam-vessels.—**Steam-packet**, *n.* A packet or vessel propelled by steam, and running between certain ports.—**Steam-plough**, *n.* A plough or gang of ploughs worked by a steam-engine.—**Steam-power**, *n.* The power of steam mechanically applied.—**Steam-press**, *n.* A press actuated by steam-power; a printing-press worked by steam.—**Steam-propeller**, *n.* A screw-propeller.—**Steam-ship**, **Steam-vessel**, *n.* A ship propelled by steam.—**Steam-tilt**, *n.* A tilt-hammer driven by steam.—**Steam-tug**, *n.* A small steamer used for towing ships.—**Steam-turbine**, *n.* A machine for converting the energy of steam into mechanical energy of rotation, by causing the steam to impinge on blades fitted to a drum free to rotate.—**Steam-whistle**, *n.* A device connected with the boiler of a steam-engine, and made to sound by the steam passing through.—**Steamy**, stē′mi, *a.* Consisting of or abounding in steam; vaporous; misty.

Steapsin, stē-ap′sin, *n.* [Gr. *stear*, fat, *haptō*, I grasp.] A ferment in the gastric juice that acts on fats.

Stearin, **Stearine**, stē′a-rin, *n.* [Gr. *stear*, fat.] The chief ingredient of suet and tallow, or the harder ingredient of animal fats, oleine being the softer one.—**Stearic**, stē-ar′ik, *a.* Pertaining to stearine.—*Stearic acid*, a white, fatty acid.

Steatite, stē′a-tīt, *n.* [Fr. *stéatite*, from Gr. *stear*, *steatos*, fat, tallow.] A mineral consisting of magnesia and alumina, used in the manufacture of porcelain, in polishing marble, in the composition of crayons, &c.; soap-stone.—**Steatitic**, stē-a-tit′ik, *a.* Pertaining to steatite.

Steatoma, stē-a-tō′ma, *n.* [Gr., from *stear*, fat.] A wen or encysted tumour containing matter like suet.

Steatopygous, stē-a-top′i-gus, *a.* [Gr. *stear*, fat, and *pygē*, buttocks.] Having an accumulation of fat on the buttocks.

Stedfast, sted′fast. See Steadfast.

Steed, stēd, *n.* [A.Sax. *stēd*, *stēda*, a steed; akin to *stud*; from stem of *stand*.] A horse; a horse for state or war: a word used chiefly in poetry and poetical or picturesque prose.

Steel, stēl, *n.* [A.Sax. *stēl*, *stýle*, steel = L.G.D. and Dan. *staal*, Icel. *stál*, G. *stahl*, O.G. *stahal*; root probably that of *stick*, *stake*, *steak*, &c.] Iron combined with a small portion of carbon, capable of showing great hardness and elasticity, and used in forming various kinds of instruments, edge-tools, springs, &c., *fig.* a weapon, as a sword, spear, &c.; a kind of steel file for sharpening knives; a piece of steel for striking sparks from flint to ignite tinder or match; used to typify extreme hardness; sternness; rigour (a heart of *steel*).—*a.* Made of steel; resembling steel; unfeeling; rigorous.—*v.t.* To overlay, point, or edge with steel; to make hard or stubborn; to render insensible or obdurate (to *steel* one's heart against mercy).—**Steel-bronze**, *n.* An alloy of about 90 parts copper to 10 parts tin, used as a substitute for steel, especially in the manufacture of cannon.—**Steel-clad**, *a.* Clad with steel mail or armour.—**Steel-engraving**, *n.* The art of engraving upon steel-plates; an impression or print from an engraved steel-plate.—**Steeliness**, stēl′i-nes, *n.* The state of being steely; great hardness.—**Steeling**, stēl′ing, *n.* The welding of a piece of steel on that part of a cutting instrument which is to receive the edge; the covering of a metal plate (as an engraved copper-plate) with steel by voltaic electricity to render it more durable.—**Steel-pen**, *n.* A pen made of steel.—**Steel-plate**, *n.* A plate or broad piece of steel; a plate of polished steel on which a design is engraved; the print taken from such plate.—**Steely**, stēl′i, *a.* Made of or resembling steel; hard; stubborn.—**Steelyard**, stēl′yärd, *n.* [Apparently from *steel* and *yard*, but old forms of the name make this doubtful, though the real origin is not clear.] An instrument for weighing bodies, consisting essentially of a lever of unequal arms, the body to be weighed being applied at the shorter arm, while a weight is made to balance the body by being moved along the longer arm at a proper distance from the fulcrum.

Steenbok, stēn′bok or stān′bok, *n.* [D. *steen*, stone, and *bok*, a buck.] A species of antelope of South Africa.

Steenkirk, stēn′kirk, *n.* A kind of cravat, carelessly worn, to commemorate its hurried adoption by the French cavalry at the battle of Steenkirk in 1692.

Steep, stēp, *a.* [A.Sax. *steáp*, high, steep; Icel. *steypthr*, high; probably allied to *stoop*, and signifying literally sinking down abruptly. *Steeple* is a derivative.] Ascending or descending with great inclination (as a roof, a slope); precipitous (hill, rock, &c.).—*n.* A precipitous place; a bold projecting rock; a precipice.—**Steepen**,† stē′pn, *v.i.* To become steep.—**Steeply**, stēp′li, *adv.* In a steep manner; with steepness; precipitously.—**Steepness**, stēp′nes, *n.* The state of being steep; precipitousness.—**Steepy**,† stē′pi, *a.* Steep or precipitous.

Steep, stēp, *v.t.* [Same as D. and G. *stippen*, Fris. *stiepen*, to dip, to steep; perhaps connected with *steep*, adjective.] To soak in a liquid; to macerate; to extract the essence of by soaking: often used figuratively (*steeped* to the lips in misery).—*n.* Something that is steeped or used in steeping; that in which things are steeped.—**Steeper**, stē′pėr, *n.* One who steeps; a vessel in which things are steeped.

Steeple, stē′pl, *n.* [A.Sax. *stépel*, *stýpel*, a steeple, a tower; L.G. *stipel*, a pillar; Icel. *stöpull*, a steeple; allied to *steep*.] A lofty erection attached to a church, town-house, or other edifice, and generally intended to contain its bells; a tower surmounted by a spire.—**Steeple-chase**, *n.* A horse-race across country in which obstacles have to be jumped as they come in the way: so called because originally a church steeple or other conspicuous object served as a goal.—**Steeple-chaser**, *n.* One who rides, or the horse ridden, in steeple-chases.—**Steepled**, stē′pld, *a.* Furnished with a steeple; having steeples.—**Steeple-jack**, *n.* A man employed to repair steeples, tall chimneys, &c.

Steer, stēr, *n.* [A.Sax. *steór*=D. and G. *stier*, Icel. *stjórr*, Goth. *stiur*, a steer, a bull; same root as Skr. *sthûra*, strong, and akin to L. *taurus*, Gr. *tauros* (for *stauros*), a bull.] A young male of the common ox or ox kind.

Steer, stēr, *v.t.* [A.Sax. *steóran*, *stýran*, to rule, steer; Dan. *styre*, Icel. *stýra*, G. *steuern*, to steer; Goth. *stiurjan*, to establish; same root as Gr. *stauros*, a stake.] To direct and govern the course of, by the movements of the helm; to control or govern; to direct; to guide.—*v.i.* To direct a vessel by the helm; to direct one's course at sea; to take a course at the direction of the helm; *fig.* to take or pursue a course in life.—**Steerage**, stēr′āj, *n.* The steering of a ship; the hinder or stern part of a ship; that part of a ship allotted to the inferior class of passengers.—**Steerage-way**, *n.* *Naut.* that forward movement of a ship which enables the helm to act.—**Steering-wheel**, *n.* The wheel by which the rudder of a ship is governed.—**Steersman**, stērz′-man, *n.* One that steers; the helmsman of a ship.

Steeve, stēv, *v.i.* [Akin to *stiff*; comp. D. *stevig*, stiff, firm.] *Naut.* to project from the bows at an angle instead of horizontally: said of a bowsprit.—*n.* *Naut.* the angle which the bowsprit makes with the horizon.

Stefan's law. The law that the total radiation from a black body is proportional to the fourth power of the absolute temperature.

Steganographist, steg-a-nog′ra-fist, *n.* [Gr. *steganos*, secret, and *graphō*, to write.] One who practises the art of writing in cipher.—**Steganography**, steg-a-nog′ra-fi, *n.* The art of writing in cipher; cryptography.

Steganopodous, steg-a-nop′o-dus, *a.* [Gr. *stegnos*, covered, *pous*, *podos*, foot.] *Ornith.* having all four toes webbed, as the gannet and pelican.

Stegnosis, steg-nō′sis, *n.* [Gr. *stegnōsis*, from *stegnos*, tight, costive.] Constipation.—**Stegnotic**, steg-not′ik, *a.* Tending to render costive, or to diminish discharges.

Steinbock, stīn′bok, *n.* [That is, *stone buck*.] The German name of the ibex.

Stela, **Stele**, stē′la, stē′lē, *n.* pl. **Stelæ**, stē′lē. [Gr. *stēlē*, a post, an upright stone, from stem *sta*, to stand.] A small column without base or capital, serving as a monument, a milestone, and the like; a sepulchral slab or column.—**Stelene**, stē′lēn, *a.* Resembling or used as a stela; columnar.

Stell,† stel, *v.t.* [Same as D. and G. *stellen*, to set, to place; akin *stall*.] To fix; to set. (*Shak.*)—**Stell-net**, *n.* A net stretched out by stakes into, and sometimes quite across, the channel of a river. (*Scot.*)

Stellar, **Stellary**, stel′lėr, stel′lėr-i, *a.* [L. *stellaris*, from *stella*, a star. Star.] Pertaining to stars; starry; full of stars; set with stars.—**Stellate**, **Stellated**, stel′-lāt, stel′lā-ted, *a.* [L. *stellatus*.] Resembling a star; radiated; *bot.* arranged in the form of a star.—**Stelliferous**, stel-lif′ėr-us, *a.* Having or abounding with stars.—**Stelliform**, stel′li-form, *a.* Like a star; radiated.—**Stellular**, **Stellulate**, stel′-ū-lėr, stel′ū-lāt, *a.* [L. *stellula*, dim. of *stella*, a star.] Having the appearance of little stars; *nat. hist.* having marks resembling stars.

Stem, stem, *n.* [A.Sax. *stemn*, for *stæfn*, *stefn*, a stem; Icel. *stofn*, *stomn*, Dan. *stamme*, D. *stam*, G. *stamm*: ultimately from root of *stand*. *Stem*, of a ship, is closely allied.] The principal body of a tree, shrub, or plant of any kind; the firm part which supports the branches; the ascending axis, as opposed to the root or descending axis; the stalk; also, a peduncle, pedicel, or petiole or leaf-stem; the stock of a family; a race or generation of progenitors; anything resembling the stem of a plant; *mus.* the vertical line added to the head of a note.—**Stem-leaf**, *n.* A leaf growing from the stem.—**Stemless**, stem′-les, *a.* Having no stem; acaulous.—**Stemlet**, stem′let, *n.* A small or young stem.

Stem, stem, *n.* [Same as Icel. *stemni*, *stamn*, *stafn*, the stem of a ship; A.Sax. *stefn*, D. *steven*, a prow. See Stem above.] A curved piece of timber or combination of pieces to which the two sides of a ship are united at the fore end; the prow; the forward part of a vessel.—*From stem to stern*, from one end of the ship to the other.—*v.t.*—*stemmed, stemming.* To make way against by sailing or swimming; to press forward through; to dash against with the stem.

Stem, stem, *v.t.* [Icel. *stemma*, Sw. *stämma*, G. *stemmen*, to dam, to bank up; perhaps allied to *stamp*.] To dam up; to stop; to check, as a stream or moving force.

Stemmata, stem'a-ta, *n.pl.* [Gr. *stemma, stemmatos*, a wreath, a garland, from *stephō*, to encircle.] The ocelli, or simple eyes of insects, spiders, &c.

Stemple, stem'pl, *n.* [G. *stempel*; akin *step, stamp*.] *Mining*, one of the cross bars of wood in the shaft of a mine, in some places serving as ladders.

Stench, stensh, *n.* [A softened form of A.Sax. *stenc*, E. *stink*.] An ill smell; a stink.—**Stench-trap**, *n.* Same as *Stink-trap*.

Stencil, sten'sil, *n.* [Perhaps from O.Fr. *estance*, a support, a stencil forming a guide or support in making letters, &c., from L. *sto*, to stand.] A thin plate of metal, leather, or other material, which has a pattern cut through it, and which is laid flat on a surface and brushed over with colour so as to mark the surface below.—*v.t.* — *stencilled, stencilling.* To form by means of a stencil; to paint or colour with stencils.—**Stenciller**, sten'sil-ėr, *n.* One who works or paints in figures with a stencil.—**Stencil-plate**, *n.* A stencil.

Stenograph,† sten'ō-graf, *v.t.* [Gr. *stenos*, close, narrow, and *graphō*, to write.] To write or represent by shorthand. —*n.* A writing in shorthand. — **Stenographer, Stenographist**, ste-nog'ra-fėr, ste-nog'-ra-fist, *n.* One who is skilled in the art of shorthand writing. — **Stenographic, Stenographical**, sten-ō-graf'ik, sten-ō-graf'i-kal, *a.* Pertaining to stenography or shorthand; expressed in shorthand.—**Stenography**, ste-nog'ra-fi, *n.* A generic term which embraces every system of shorthand.

Stenophyllous, ste-nof'i-lus or sten-ō-fil'-us, *a.* [Gr. *stenos*, narrow, and *phyllon*, a leaf.] *Bot.* having narrow leaves.

Stenosis, sten-ō'sis, *n.* [Gr. *stenos*, narrow.] *Med.* the narrowing of a channel or aperture.

Stentorian, sten-tō'ri-an, *a.* [From *Stentor*, a Greek herald celebrated for his powerful voice.] Extremely loud or powerful (a *stentorian* voice); able to utter a very loud sound.

Step, step, *v.i.*—*stepped, stepping*, [A.Sax. *steppan*, to step; O.Fris. *steppa*, O.Sax. *stapan*, D. and L.G. *stappen*, to step; A.Sax. *stæpe*, D. *stap*, G. *stapfe*, a step. *Stamp* is allied, and *staple* is from same root.] To move the leg and foot in walking; to advance or recede by a movement of the foot or feet; to go; to walk; especially, to go a little distance and with a limited purpose (to *step* aside); to advance or come as it were by chance or suddenly (to *step* into an inheritance). — *To step aside*, to walk to a little distance; to deviate from the right path; to err.—*To step out*, to increase the length, but not the rapidity of the step.—*v.t.* To set (the foot)†; *naut.* to fix the foot of, as of a mast; to erect in readiness for setting sail.—*n.* A pace; an advance made by one removal of the foot in walking; one remove in ascending or descending a stair; the distance between the feet in walking or running; a small space or distance; a grade in progress or rank; a forward move; a higher grade of rank; print or impression of the foot; footprint; gait; manner of walking; sound of the feet; footfall; a proceeding; one of a series of proceedings; measure (to take *steps* in a matter); a foot-piece for ascending or descending from a carriage; the round of a ladder; *pl.* a self-supporting ladder with flat steps; a step-ladder: much used indoors; *naut.* a block or a solid piece supporting the heel of a mast.—*Step by step*, by a gradual and regular process; gradually; keeping pace.—**Step-ladder**, *n.* A portable ladder usually having flat steps, and its own means of support attached.—**Stepper**, step'ėr, *n.* One who steps; one that has a gait good or bad: often applied to a horse.—**Stepping-stone**, *n.* A raised stone in a stream or in a swampy place to keep the feet dry in crossing; an aid by which an end may be accomplished or an object gained; an assistance to progress.

Stepbrother, step'bruтн-ėr, *n.* [In this and following words *step-* is A.Sax. *steóp-*, Icel. *stjúp*, D. and G. *stief-*, a prefix of doubtful origin.] A brother by being a stepfather's or stepmother's son by a former wife or husband.—**Stepchild**, step'chīld, *n.* The child of a husband or wife by a former wife or husband.—**Stepdaughter**, step'da-tėr, *n.* The daughter of a husband or wife by a former wife or husband. — **Stepfather**, step'fä-тнėr, *n.* A mother's second or subsequent husband. — **Stepmother**, step'-muтн-ėr, *n.* A father's second or subsequent wife.—**Step-parent**, *n.* A stepfather or stepmother.—**Stepsister**, step'-sis-tėr, *n.* A stepfather's or stepmother's daughter by a former wife or husband.—**Stepson**, step'sun, *n.* The son of a husband or wife by a former wife or husband.

Steppe, step, *n.* [G. *steppe*, Rus. *stepy'*, a steppe.] A name applied to those extensive plains which stretch across the south-east of European Russia, round the shores of the Caspian and Aral Seas, and occupy the low lands of Siberia.

Stercoraceous, stėr-kō-rā'shus, *a.* [L. *stercus, stercoris*, dung.] Pertaining to dung, or partaking of its nature.—**Stercoration**, stėr-kō-rā'shon, *n.* [L. *stercoratio*.] The act of manuring with dung.

Stère, stār, *n.* [Fr. *stère*, from Gr. *stereos*, solid.] The French unit for solid measure, equal to a cubic metre, or 35·3156 cubic feet.

Stereo, ster'ē-ō, *n.* A contraction of *stereotype*; used also adjectively (a *stereo* plate).

Stereobate, ster'ē-ō-bāt, *n.* [Gr. *stereobates*—*stereos*, firm, *bainō*, to go.] *Arch.* a kind of continuous pedestal at the bottom of a wall.

Stereochemistry, ster'ē-ō-kem''ist-ri, *n.* [Gr. *stereos*, solid.] A branch of chemistry which deals with the geometrical arrangement of the atoms of a molecule.—**Stereochromy**, ster-ē-ok'ro-mi, *n.* [Gr. *stereos*, and *chrōma*, colour.] A method of wall-painting by which the colours are covered with a varnish of water-glass.—**Stereochrome**, ster'ē-ō-krōm, *n.* A stereochromic picture. — **Stereochromic**, ster'ē-ō-krom''ik, *a* Pertaining to stereochromy.—**Stereogram, Stereograph**, ster'ē-ō-gram, ster'ē-ō-graf, *n.* [Gr. *stereos*, and *graphō*, to write.] A diagram or picture which represents objects so as to give the impression of relief or solidity; a picture for a stereoscope.—**Stereographic, Stereographical**, ster'ē-ō-graf''ik, ster'ē-ō-graf''-i-kal, *a.* Made according to the rules of stereography; delineated on a plane. — *Stereographic projection*, the projection or delineation of the sphere upon the plane of one of its great circles, the eye being at the pole of that circle.—**Stereographically**, ster'ē-ō-graf''i-kal-li, *adv.* In a stereographic manner.—**Stereography**, ster-ē-og'ra-fi, *n.* The art of delineating solid bodies on a plane.—**Stereoisomer**, ster'-ē-ō-ī''sō-mer, *n.* [Gr. *stereos*, solid, *isos*, equal, *meros*, a part.] A chemical compound having the same composition as some other compound but with its atoms differently arranged.—**Stereometer**, ster-ē-om'et-ėr, *n.* [Gr. *stereos*, and *metron*, measure.] An instrument for measuring the contents of bodies or vessels; an instrument for determining the specific gravity of liquids, porous bodies, powders, &c.—**Stereometric, Stereometrical**, ster'-ē-ō-met''rik, ster'ē-ō-met''ri-kal, *a.* Pertaining to or performed by stereometry. — **Stereometry**, ster-ē-om'et-ri, *n.* The art of measuring solid bodies, &c.—**Stereopticon**, ster-ē-op'ti-kon, *n.* [Gr. *stereos*, firm, *optikos*, optic.] An apparatus in which two magic lanterns are combined.—**Stereoscope**, ster'ē-ō-skōp, *n.* [Gr. *stereos*, and *skopeo*, to view.] An optical instrument which enables us to look upon two pictures taken under a small difference of angular view, each eye looking upon one picture only, so that, as in ordinary vision, two images are conveyed to the brain as one, and the objects thus appear solid and real as in nature.—**Stereoscopic, Stereoscopical**, ster'ē-ō-skop''ik, ster'ē-ō-skop''i-kal, *a.* Pertaining to the stereoscope; adapted to the stereoscope. — **Stereoscopically**, ster'ē-ō-skop''-i-kal-li, *adv.* In a stereoscopic manner; by means of the stereoscope. — **Stereoscopist**, ster-ē-os'-ko-pist, *n.* One versed in the use of the stereoscope. — **Stereoscopy**, ster-ē-os'ko-pi, *n.* The art of using the stereoscope.—**Stereotrope**, ster'ē-ō-trōp, *n.* [Gr. *stereos*, and *tropē*, a turning.] An instrument by which an object is perceived as if in motion and with its natural solidity or relief.—**Stereotype**, ster'ē-ō-tīp, *n.* [Gr. *stereos*, and *typos*, type.] A metal plate, presenting on its upper surface a facsimile of a page of arranged types, being cast in a papier-maché, stucco, or other mould obtained from these types, and being used to print from in the same way, thus saving the types and allowing them to be used afresh at once.—*a.* Relating to the art of stereotyping or printing from stereotypes.—*v.t.*—*stereotyped, stereotyping.* To make a stereotype of; to prepare for printing by means of stereotype plates; *fig.* to fix firmly or unchangeably.—**Stereotyped**, ster'ē-ō-tīpt, *p.* and *a.* Made or printed from stereotype plates; formed in a fixed, unchangeable manner (*stereotyped* opinions). — **Stereotype-plate**, *n.* A stereotype; a sheet of metal, having a surface presenting a solid page of type, for printing.—**Stereotyper**, ster'ē-ō-tīp-ėr, *n.* One who stereotypes.—**Stereotypery**, ster'ē-ō-tīp''ėr-i, *n.* The art of making stereotype-plates; a stereotype foundry.—**Stereotypic**, ster'ē-ō-tip''-ik, *a.* Pertaining to stereotype-plates. — **Stereotypist**, ster'ē-ō-tīp-ist, *n.* A stereotyper. — **Stereotypographer**, ster'ē-ō-tī-pog''ra-fėr, *n.* A stereotype printer.—**Stereotypography**, ster'ē-ō-tī-pog''ra-fi, *n.* Printing from stereotype.—**Stereotypy**, ster'ē-ō-tī-pi, *n.* The art or business of making stereotype plates.

Sterile, ster'il, *a.* [Fr. *stérile*, from L. *sterilis*, barren, unproductive; cog. Gr. *steiros*, barren, *stereos*, stiff; Skr. *stari*, a barren cow; G. *starr*, stiff, rigid; E. to *stare*.] Unfruitful; not fertile; barren; producing no young; not germinating; barren of ideas; destitute of sentiment; *bot.* bearing only stamens; staminate.—**Sterility**, ste-ril'i-ti, *n.* [L. *sterilitas*.] The state of being sterile; unfruitfulness; barrenness.—**Sterilize**, ster'il-īz, *v.t.*—*sterilized, sterilizing.* To make sterile or barren; to destroy the germs or microbes in.

Sterlet, stėr'let, *n.* [Rus. *sterliad*.] A small species of sturgeon.

Sterling, stėr'ling, *a.* [From the *Esterlings* or *Easterlings*, the old name in England of traders from Germany (*east* from England), whose money was of peculiar purity; or from G. *sterling*, a coin.] An epithet by which English money is distinguished, signifying that it is of the standard value (a pound *sterling*); hence, genuine; undoubted; of excellent quality (a work of *sterling* merit).

Stern, stėrn, *a.* [A.Sax. *sterne, styrne*, stern; same root as to *stare*, and *stark*.] Severe, as regards facial expression; austere of aspect; gloomy; severe of manner; pitiless; harsh; rigidly steadfast; immovable.—**Sternly**, stėrn'li, *adv.* In a stern manner; with an austere or stern countenance.—**Sternness**, stėrn'nes, *n.* The state or quality of being stern; severity of look; severity or harshness of manner; rigour.

Stern, stėrn, *n.* [A.Sax. *steorn*, a helm; akin to *steer*.] The hind part of a ship or boat. — *By the stern*, *naut.* more deeply laden abaft than forward.—**Stern-board**, *n.* *Naut.* the backward motion of a vessel.—**Stern-chase**, *n.* A chase in which one vessel follows in the wake of the other.—**Stern-chaser**, *n.* A cannon placed in a ship's stern, pointing backward.—**Sterned**, stėrnd, *a.* Having a stern of this or that kind (square-*sterned*).—**Sternmost**, stėrn′-mōst, *a.* Farthest in the rear; farthest astern.—**Stern-port**, *n.* A port in the stern of a ship.—**Stern-post**, *n.* A principal piece of timber in a vessel's stern.—**Stern-sheets**, *n.* The after part of a boat, usually furnished with seats for passengers.—**Stern-way**, *n.* The movement of a ship stern foremost.—**Stern-wheeler**, *n.* A vessel driven by a paddle-wheel at the stern.

Sternal, stėrn′al, *n.* [L. *sternum*, breast-bone.] (1) In vertebrates, relating to the sternum. (2) In arthropods, the under side of the body. Cp. Tergal.—*a.* Pertaining to the sternum. — **Sterno-** is used as a prefix to mean connected with the sternum. —**Sternum**, stėr′num, *n.* The breast-bone.

Sternutation, stėr-nū-tā′shon, *n.* [L. *sternutatio*, from *sternuto*, freq. of *sternuo*, to sneeze.] The act of sneezing.—**Sternutative**, **Sternutatory**, stėr-nū′ta-tiv, ster-nū′ta-to-ri, *a.* Having the quality of exciting to sneeze.—*n.* A substance that provokes sneezing, as some kind of snuff.

Stertorous, stėr′to-rus, *a.* [From L. *sterto*, to snore.] Characterized by a deep snoring, such as frequently accompanies apoplexy (a *stertorous* breathing).

Stet, stet. [L., let it stand.] *Printing*, a word written upon proofs to signify that something which has been deleted is after all to remain.

Stethometer, ste-thom′et-ėr, *n.* [Gr. *stēthos*, the breast, and *metron*, a measure.] An instrument for measuring the external movement in the chest during respiration.—**Stethoscope**, steth′ō-skōp, *n.* [Gr. *stēthos*, and *skopeō*, to see.] An instrument of a tubular form used by medical men for listening to sounds within the thorax and other cavities of the body.—**Stethoscopic**, **Stethoscopical**, steth-ō-skop′ik, steth-ō-skop′i-kal, *a.* Pertaining to the stethoscope.—**Stethoscopically**, steth-ō-skop′-i-kal-li, *adv.* By means of a stethoscope.—**Stethoscopist**, steth′ō-skop-ist, *n.* A person versed in the use of the stethoscope. —**Stethoscopy**, ste-thos′ko-pi, *n.* The art of stethoscopic examination.

Stevedore, stē′ve-dōr, *n.* [Sp. *estivador*, a packer of wool, &c., from *estivar*, to stow; from L. *stipare*, to cram, to stuff.] One whose occupation is to stow goods, packages, &c., in a ship's hold; one who loads or unloads vessels.

Stew, stū, *v.t.* [From O.Fr. *estuver* (Fr. *étuver*), to stew, to bathe, from *estuve*, a stove; from O.H.G. *stupa*, a stove, a hot chamber. Stove.] To boil slowly in a moderate manner or with a simmering heat.—*v.i.* To be boiled in a slow gentle manner, or in heat and moisture.—*n.* A house furnished with warm baths; a bagnio; a brothel; a dish cooked by stewing; a state of agitation or excitement.—**Stew-pan**, *n.* A pan in which meat and vegetables are stewed.

Steward, stū′ėrd, *n.* [O.E. *styward*, A. Sax. *stiweard*, a steward, lit. a *styward*, from *stige*, a sty, a pen, and *weard*, a keeper. Originally one who took charge of the cattle, which constituted the chief wealth of a household.] A man employed on a large estate or establishment to manage the domestic concerns, superintend the other servants keep the accounts, &c.; one who has affairs to superintend for another; in hotels and restaurants, one who selects, buys, and superintends the preparation of food or liquors; an officer of state (the lord high *steward* of England, one of the ancient great officers of state); an officer on a vessel who distributes provisions to the officers and crew; in passenger ships, a man who superintends the provisions and liquors, waits at table, &c. —**Stewardess**, stū′ėrd-es, *n.* A female steward; a female who serves the passengers on an aeroplane, train, &c.—**Stewardship**, stū′ėrd-ship, *n.* The office or functions of a steward.

Sthenic, sthen′ik, *a.* [Gr. *sthenos*, strength.] *Med.* attended with morbid increase of vital energy and action in the heart and arteries.

Stibial, stib′i-al, *a.* [L. *stibium*, antimony.] Pertaining to or having the qualities of antimony; antimonial.—**Stibialism**, stib′i-al-izm, *n.* Antimonial intoxication or poisoning. — **Stibiated**, stib′i-ā-ted, *a.* Impregnated with antimony. — **Stibic**, stib′ik, *a.* Antimonic. — **Stibnite**, stib′-nīt, *n.* An ore of antimony of a lead-gray colour, yielding most of the antimony of commerce.

Stich, stik, *n.* [Gr. *stichos*, a line, a verse.] A verse, of whatever measure or number of feet; a line of writing.—**Stichic**, stik′ik, *a.* Consisting of lines or verses.—**Stichomancy**, stik′ō-man-si, *n.* [Gr. *stichos*, and *manteia*, divination.] Divination by lines or passages in books taken at hazard.—**Stichometrical**, stik-ō-met′ri-kal, *a.* Pertaining to stichometry. — **Stichometry**, sti-kom′et-ri, *n.* [Gr. *stichos*, and *metron*, measure.] Measurement of books or writings by the number of lines which each contains. — **Stichomythia**, stik-ō-mith′i-a, *n.* [Gr. *stichos* and *mythos*.] The conducting of dialogue in a Greek play in alternate lines of iambic trimeter.

Stick, stik, *n.* [A.Sax. *sticca*, a stick, stake, spike; Icel. *stika*, a stick; closely akin to *stick* (verb), *stake*, *steak*, *stock*.] A piece of wood of indefinite size and shape; a branch of a tree or shrub cut or broken off; a rod or wand; a staff; a walking-stick; anything shaped like a stick (a *stick* of sealing-wax); *printing*, a composing-stick. — *Gold-stick*, *Silver-stick*. See those headings.

Stick, stik, *v.t.*—pret. and pp. *stuck*. [A. Sax. *stician*, to stab, pierce, adhere; Dan. *stikke*, D. *steken*, to pierce; G. *stecken*, to thrust, to stand fast; from a root *stig*, seen also in L. *stinguo*, to quench (as in *extinguish*), *stimulus* (for *stigmulus*), Gr. *stizō*, to prick, E. *sting*. *Stitch* is a softened form, and *stick*, *n.*, *steak*, *stake*, *stock*, *ticket*, *etiquette*, &c., are akin.] To pierce or stab (*Shak.*); to thrust so as to wound or penetrate; to fasten by piercing (to *stick* a pin); to thrust in; to attach by causing to adhere to the surface; to fix; to set; to fix in; to set with something inserted; to fix on a pointed instrument.—*To stick out*, to project; to thrust out; to be prominent; to refuse to treat or surrender; to hold out (to *stick out* for more favourable terms).—*To stick one's self up*, to put on grand airs.—*v.i.* To cleave to the surface, as by tenacity or attraction; to adhere; to be fixed by being thrust in; to remain where placed; to cling; to be hindered from making progress; to be brought to a stop by some impediment; to scruple; to hesitate; often with *at*.—*To stick by*, to adhere closely to; to be constant to. — *To stick to*, to be persevering in holding to; to abide firmly and faithfully by.—*To stick up*, to have an upright position; to stand on end.—*To stick up for*, to espouse the cause of; to defend.—**Sticker**, stik′ėr, *n.* One who sticks (a bill-*sticker*).—**Stickiness**, stik′i-nes, *n.* The quality of being sticky; viscousness; glutinousness.—**Sticking-place**, *n.* Point of determination. (*Shak.*)—**Sticking-plaster**, *n.* An adhesive plaster for closing wounds; court-plaster. — **Stick-lac**. Lac. — **Sticky**, stik′i, *a.* Having the quality of adhering to a surface; gluey; viscous.

Stickle, stik′l, *v.i.* — *stickled*, *stickling*. [Modified by influence of *stick*, from O.E. *stihtle*, *stightle*, to rule, direct, from A.Sax. *stihtan*, to dispose, to govern.] To interpose between combatants and separate them‡; to arbitrate‡; to pertinaciously stick up for something, especially some trifle; to play fast and loose.—*v.t.* To arbitrate between or in‡.—**Stickler**, stik′lėr, *n.* One who stickles or pertinaciously insists; an obstinate contender about things of little consequence.

Stickleback, stik′l-bak, *n.* [O.E. *stickle*, a prickle, and *back*; from the spines on its back.] The popular name for certain very small British fishes found in ponds and streams, and having spines on their backs, remarkable for building nests.

Sticky. Under Stick, *v.*

Stiff, stif, *a.* [A.Sax. *stif*=O.Fris, *stef*, D. *stijf*, L.G. *stief*, G. *steif*; root in *stand*, Skr. *sthā*, to stand. Stand.] Not easily bent; not flexible; rigid; not liquid or fluid; thick and tenacious; inspissated; drawn very tight; tense; not supple; not working smoothly or easily (*stiff* joints); not natural and easy; cramped; constrained (a *stiff* style of writing); haughty and unbending; formal in manner; blowing strongly; violent; not easily subdued; obstinate; stubborn; containing a good deal of spirits (a *stiff* glass of grog); *naut.* bearing a press of canvas without careening much. — **Stiffen**, stif′n, *v.t.* To make stiff; to make less pliant or flexible.—*v.i.* To become stiff or stiffer; to become more rigid or less flexible; to become less susceptible of impression; to grow more obstinate.—**Stiffener**, stif′-n-ėr, *n.* One who or that which stiffens; a piece of stiff material inside a neckcloth.—**Stiffening**, stif′n-ing, *n.* The act of making stiff; something that is used to make a substance more stiff. — **Stiffish**, stif′ish, *a.* Somewhat stiff.—**Stiffly**, stif′li, *adv.* In a stiff manner; rigidly; unbendingly; obstinately; unyieldingly; in a constrained manner; formally.—**Stiff-neck**, *n.* A condition of the neck in which movement causes extreme pain, due to rheumatism of the muscles on the side of the neck. —**Stiff-necked**, *a.* Stubborn; inflexibly obstinate.—**Stiff-neckedness**, *n.* Stubbornness. — **Stiffness**, stif′nes, *n.* The state or quality of being stiff; want of pliableness, suppleness, or flexibility; rigidity; tension; viscidness; spissitude; stubbornness; formality or constraint of manner, expression, or writing.

Stifle, stī′fl, *v.t.* — *stifled*, *stifling*. [Icel. *stifla*, to dam up (akin to *stiff*), the sense being influenced by old *stive*, to stuff up, from Fr. *estiver*, L. *stipare*, to cram close.] To kill by impeding respiration; to suffocate or greatly oppress by foul or close air; to smother; to deaden (flame, sound); to suppress or conceal; to repress; to keep from being known.—*v.i.* To suffocate; to perish by suffocation.

Stifle, stī′fl, *n.* [Perhaps connected with *stiff*.] The joint of a horse next to the buttock, and corresponding to the knee in man.—**Stifle-bone**, *n.* A bone in the leg of a horse, corresponding to the knee-pan in man.

Stigma, stig′ma, *n.* pl. **Stigmas** or **Stigmata**, stig′ma-ta. [Gr. *stigma*, a prick with a pointed instrument, from *stizō*, to prick. Sting.] A brand impressed with a red-hot iron on slaves and others; any mark of infamy; a brand of disgrace which attaches to a person; a natural mark on the skin; *bot.* the upper extremity of the style, and the part which in impregnation receives the pollen; *entomol.* one of the apertures in the bodies of insects communicating with the air-vessels; *pl. stigmata*, marks said to have been supernaturally impressed upon the bodies of certain persons in imitation of the wounds on the crucified body of Christ (the *stigmata* of St. Francis). — **Stigmaria**, stig-mā′ri-a, *n.* A fossil of the coal formation, now ascertained to be the root of the Sigillaria (which see).—**Stigmatic**, **Stigmatical**, stig-mat′ik. stig-mat′i-kal, *a.* Marked with a stigma, having the character of a stigma; *bot.* belonging to the stigma. — **Stigmatic**, *n.* A person branded or marked with a natural stigma. (*Shak.*). — **Stigmatist**, stig′ma-tist, *n.* One on whom the marks of Christ's wounds, or stigmata, are said to be supernaturally impressed. — **Stigmatization**, stig′ma-tī-zā″shon, *n.* The impression on the bodies of certain individuals of the marks of Christ's wounds.—**Stigmatize**, stig′ma-tīz, *v.t.*—*stigmatized*, *stigmatizing*. [Fr. *stigmatiser*, Gr. *stigmatizō*, to brand.] To mark with a stigma or brand; to set a mark of disgrace on; to call or characterize by some opprobrious epithet. — **Stigmatose**, stig′ma-tōs, *a.* *Bot.* stigmatic.

Stilbite, stil′bīt, *n.* [Gr. *stilbō*, to shine.] A mineral of a shining pearly lustre; a kind of zeolite.

Stile, stīl, *n.* [See Style.] The gnomon on the face of a dial to form the shadow.—**Stilar**, stīl′ėr, *a.* Pertaining to the stile of a dial.

Stile, stil, *n.* [A.Sax. *stigel*, a step, a ladder, from *stigan*, to mount, which appears also in *stair, stirrup*, being same as Icel. *stiga*, G. *steigen*, Goth. *steigan*, Skr. *stigh*, to ascend.] A step or series of steps, or a frame of bars and steps, for ascending and descending in getting over a fence.

Stiletto, sti-let'tō, *n.* [It., dim. of *stilo*, a dagger, from L. *stilus*, a stile. STYLE.] A small dagger with a round pointed blade about 6 inches long; a pointed instrument for making eyelet-holes in working muslin. —*v.t.* To stab or pierce with a stiletto.

Still, stil, *a.* [A.Sax. *stille*, still, quiet, firm, fixed = D. *stil*, Dan. *stille*, G. *still*; from root of *stand*, seen also in *stall*, G. *stellen*, to place, &c. STAND.] Silent; noiseless; not loud; soft; low (a *still* small voice); quiet or calm; without agitation; motionless; not sparkling or effervescing.—*v.t.* [A.Sax. *stillan*.] To bring to silence; to make quiet; to check or restrain; to appease or allay.—*adv.* To this time; now no less than before; in future no less than formerly; always; time after time; continually; nevertheless; in spite of what has occurred; yet; in an increasing degree; even yet: very common with comparatives (*still* more).—*Still and anon*, at intervals and repeatedly.—**Still-birth**, *n.* State of being still-born.—**Still-born**, *a.* Dead at the birth; abortive; produced unsuccessfully.—**Stiller**, stil'ėr, *n.* One who stills or quiets.—**Still-life**, *n.* Inanimate objects, such as dead animals, furniture, fruits, &c., represented by the painter's art.—**Stillness**, stil'nes, *n.* The state or quality of being still; freedom from noise or motion; calmness; quiet; silence.—**Stilly**, stil'i, *a.* Still; quiet.—*adv.* (stil'li). Silently; without noise; calmly; quietly.

Still, stil, *n.* [Abbrev. from *distil*.] An apparatus for distilling or separating, by means of heat, volatile matters from substances containing them, and recondensing them into the liquid form; a distillery.—*v.t.* To distil.—**Still-burn**, *v.t.* To burn in the process of distillation. — **Still-house**, *n.* A building containing a still.—**Still-room**, *n.* An apartment for distilling; a domestic laboratory; an apartment where liquors, preserves, and the like are kept.

Stillicide, stil'i-sīd, *n.* [L. *stillicidium*—*stilla*, a drop, and *cado*, to fall.] *Law*, the right to have the rain from one's roof to drop on another's land or roof.—**Stilliform**, stil'i-form, *a.* [L. *stilla*, a drop, and *forma*, form.] Drop-shaped.

Stilt, stilt, *n.* [Same as Dan. *stylte*, Sw. *stylta*, L.G. and D. *stelt*, G. *stelze*, a stilt; root probably that of *stand*.] A long piece of wood with a rest for the foot, used in pairs for walking with the feet raised above the ground.—**Stilt-bird**, **Stilt-plover**, *n.* A wading bird of no great size having remarkably long slender legs, whence its name.—**Stilted**, stilt'ed, *p.* and *a.* Elevated as if on stilts; hence, pompous; inflated; stiff and bombastic: said of language.

Stilton, stil'ton, *a.* Applied to a well-known and highly esteemed solid, rich, white cheese, originally made at *Stilton*, Huntingdonshire, England, but now chiefly made in Leicestershire.—*n.* Stilton cheese.

Stimulate, stim'ū-lāt, *v.t.* — *stimulated, stimulating.* [L. *stimulo*, *stimulatum*, to prick, to urge on, from *stimulus*, a goad; root *stig*, as in Gr. *stizō*, to prick; allied to *stick, sting*.] To excite or animate to action by some pungent motive or by persuasion; to spur on; to incite, instigate, rouse; to excite greater vitality or keenness in; *med.* to produce a quickly diffused and transient increase of vital energy and strength of action in.—*v.i.* To act as a stimulus.—**Stimulation**, stim-u-lā'shon, *n.* The act of stimulating; the effect produced; *med.* a quickly diffused and transient increase of vital energy. — **Stimulative**, stim'ū-lā-tiv, *a.* Having the quality of stimulating.—*n.* That which stimulates.—**Stimulant**, stim'ū-lant, *a.* [L. *stimulans*, *stimulantis*, ppr. of *stimulo*.] Serving to stimulate.—*n.* That which stimulates; a stimulus; *med.* an agent which produces a quickly diffused and transient increase of vital energy in the organism or some part of it; often applied distinctively to some kind of alcoholic liquors.—**Stimulator**, stim'ū-lā-tėr, *n.* One that stimulates. — **Stimulose**, stim'ū-lōs, *a.* *Bot.* covered with stimuli.—**Stimulus**, stim'ū-lus, *n.* pl. **Stimuli**, stim'u-lī. [L.] Something that incites to action or exertion; an incitement; a stimulant; *bot.* a sting, as in the nettle.

Sting, sting, *v.t.*—pret. and pp. *stung*. [A. Sax. *stingan*, to pierce, to sting = Icel. and Sw. *stinga*, Dan. *stinge*, Goth. *stiggan* (i.e. *stingan*); nasalized forms corresponding to *stick*; akin also to *stink*; same root as in *stimulate*.] To pierce with the sharp-pointed organ with which certain animals and plants are furnished; to poison or goad with a sting; to give acute mental pain (*stung* with remorse or taunts).—*v.i.* To use a sting, as a bee.—*n.* [A.Sax. *sting*, Icel. *stingr*.] A sharp-pointed weapon which certain insects possess, and which they can thrust out from the hinder part of the body; a somewhat similar appendage of other animals, as scorpions; the thrust of a sting into the flesh; anything that gives acute pain; the biting, sarcastic, or cutting effect of words; the point, as in an epigram; that which gives acute mental pain; an impulse; a stimulus; *bot.* a hair which secretes a poisonous fluid, which, when introduced under the skin of animals, produces pain.—**Stinger**, sting'ėr, *n.* One who or that which stings.—**Stinging**, sting'ing, *p.* and *a.* Piercing with, or as with, a sting; goading; sharp; keen; *bot.* having hairs that sting, as in the nettle. — **Stingingly**, sting'ing-li, *adv.* With stinging. — **Stingless**, sting'les, *a.* Having no sting. **Sting-ray**, *n.* A fish allied to the rays having a sharp bony spine on its tail.—**Stingy**, sting'i, *a.* Having power to sting; stinging.

Stingo, sting'gō, *n.* [Probably from *sting*, alluding to the sharpness of the taste.] Pungent or strong ale; rare good liquor. (*Colloq.*)

Stingy, stin'ji, *a.* [Probably from *sting*; comp. *spring, springe*; *swing, swinge*.] Extremely close-fisted and covetous; meanly avaricious; niggardly; scanty.—**Stingily**, stin'ji-li, *adv.* In a stingy or niggardly manner; meanly; shabbily.—**Stinginess**, stin'ji-nes, *n.* The quality of being stingy; mean; covetousness; niggardliness.

Stink, stingk, *v.i.*—pret. and pp. *stank*, *stunk*. [A.Sax. *stincan*=D. and G. *stinken*, Dan. *stinke*, to stink; closely allied to *sting*, *stick*. *Stench* is a derivative form.] To emit a strong offensive smell; hence, *fig.* to be in bad odour; to have a bad reputation.—*v.t.* To annoy with an offensive smell.—*n.* A strong offensive smell; a stench.—**Stinkard**, stingk'ärd, *n.* A mean, paltry fellow.—**Stink-ball**, *n.* A ball of combustible materials used similarly to the stink-pot.—**Stink-pot**, *n.* An earthen pot filled with a stinking combustible mixture, formerly used in attacking an enemy's vessel at sea.—**Stink-stone**, *n.* Same as *Anthraconite*.—**Stink-trap**, *n.* A contrivance to prevent the escape of effluvia from the openings of drains.

Stint, stint, *v.t.* [A.Sax. *styntan*, to blunt or dull, from *stunt*, dull, stupid; akin Sw. *stunta*, Icel. *stytta*, to shorten. STUNT.] To restrict to a scanty allowance; to limit or make scanty.—*v.i.* To cease; to stop; to desist.—*n.* Limit or restraint set or observed; restriction as to quantity (to give money without *stint*). — **Stintedness**, stin'ted-nes, *n.* State of being stinted.—**Stinter**, stin'tėr, *n.* One who stints.

Stipe, Stipes, stīp, stī'pēz, *n.* [L. *stipes*, a stock, a trunk.] *Bot.* the petiole of the fronds of ferns; the stem of tree-ferns; the stem of certain fungi.—**Stipel**, stī'pel, *n.* *Bot.* a secondary stipule at the base of leaflets.—**Stipiform**, stī'pi-form, *n.* *Bot.* having the appearance of an endogenous trunk.—**Stipitate**, stī'pi-tāt, *a.* *Bot.* elevated on a stipe.

Stipend, stī'pend, *n.* [L. *stipendium*—*stips*, a donation, and *pendo*, to weigh out.] Any periodical payment or compensation for services rendered; salary.—**Stipendiary**, stī-pen'di-a-ri, *a.* [L. *stipendiarius*.] Receiving wages or salary; performing services for a stated compensation.—*Stipendiary magistrate*, in England, a paid magistrate acting in large towns.—*n.* One who performs services for a settled salary or stipend; a stipendiary magistrate.—**Stipendiarian**, stī-pen'di-ā"ri-an, *a.* Hired; stipendiary.

Stipes, Stipitate. Under STIPE.

Stipple, stip'l, *v.t.* — *stippled, stippling.* [From D. *stippelen*, dim. of *stippen*, to make dots or points, from *stip*, a dot, a point; akin *stab*.] To engrave by means of dots, in distinction from engraving in lines.—*n.* Engraving by means of dots.

Stiptic, stip'tik, *n.* and *a.* STYPTIC.

Stipulate, stip'ū-lāt, *v.i.*—*stipulated, stipulating.* [L. *stipulor*, *stipulatus*, to stipulate, from *stipulus*, firm; akin *stipes*, a tree trunk; same root as *step, stand*.] To make an agreement or covenant to do or forbear anything; to contract; to settle terms; to bargain.—**Stipulated**, stip'ū-lā-ted, *p.* and *a.* Agreed on; covenanted.—**Stipulation**, stip-ū-lā'shon, *n.* [L. *stipulatio*, *stipulationis*.] The act of stipulating; a contracting or bargaining; a point or matter settled by agreement; a particular article or item in a contract.—**Stipulator**, stip'ū-lā-tėr, *n.* One who stipulates.

Stipule, stip'ūl, *n.* [L. *stipula*, a stalk, a straw, dim. of *stipes*, a trunk. STIPULATE.] *Bot.* a small leaf-like appendage to a leaf commonly situated at the base of the petiole in pairs, either adhering to it or standing separate.—**Stipuled**, stip'ūld, *a.* *Bot.* furnished with stipules. — **Stipulaceous**, **Stipular**, stip-ū-lā'shus, stip'ū-lėr, *a.* *Bot.* belonging to, or standing in the place of stipules.—**Stipulary**, stip'ū-la-ri, *a.* *Bot.* stipular.—**Stipulate**, stip'ū-lāt, *a.* *Bot.* having stipules.

Stir, stėr, *v.t.*—*stirred, stirring.* [A.Sax. *styrian*, *stirian*, to stir, to move; allied to D. *storen*, Sw. *störa*. G. *stören*, to disturb; same root as *start, storm*.] To move or make to change place in any manner; to agitate the particles of; to bring into debate; to moot; to incite to action; to instigate; to excite; to awaken; to rouse, as from sleep.—*To stir up*, to incite; to instigate by inflaming passions; to excite; to give origin to (a mutiny, strife).—*v.i.* To move one's self; to change place; to be in motion; not to be still; to be on foot; to be already out of bed.—*n.* Agitation; tumult; bustle; public disturbance or commotion; excitement.—**Stirless**, stėr'les, *a.* Without stir.—**Stirrer**, stėr-ėr, *n.* One who stirs or is in motion; one who or that which puts in motion; an inciter or exciter; an instigator.—*Stirrer up*, an exciter; an instigator.—**Stirring**, stėr'ing, *p.* and *a.* Active in business; bustling; animating; rousing; exciting.

Stirk, stėrk, *n.* [A.Sax. *styrc*, *styric*, a dim. from *steor*, a steer.] A bullock or heifer between one and two years old.

Stirp theory, stirp thē'ō-ri, *n.* [L. *stirpo*, a stock.] Galton's theory attributing the phenomena of heredity to a material substance. See GERM-PLASM.

Stirrup, stėr'up, *n.* [A.Sax. *stigrāp*, *stirāp*, a stirrup, from *stigan*, to mount (O.E. *steye*, *stye*), and *rāp*, a rope; Icel. *stigreip*. STAIR, ROPE.] A strap hanging from a saddle, and having at its lower end a suitable appliance for receiving the foot of the rider, used to assist persons in mounting a horse; hence, anything resembling in shape and functions the stirrup of a saddle.—**Stirrup-cup**, *n.* A cup of liquor presented to a rider on having mounted his horse at parting.—**Stirrup-iron**, *n.* The iron portion of a stirrup.—**Stirrup-leather**, *n.* The leather portion of a stirrup.—**Stirrup-strap**, *n.* A stirrup-leather.

Stitch, stich, *v.t.* [Softened form of *stick*, Sc. *steke*, A.Sax. *stician*, to pierce; comp. G. *sticken*, to embroider, to stitch.] To sew; to sew by passing the needle through and through in a continuous line; to unite together by sewing.—*To stitch up*, to sew or unite with a needle and thread.—*v.i.* To practise stitching; to practise needlework.—*n.* A single pass of a needle in sewing; a single turn of the thread round a needle in knitting; *agri.* a furrow or ridge; a sharp pain in the side.—**Stitcher**, stich'ėr, *n.* One that stitches.—**Stitching**, stich'ing, *n.* The act of one who stitches; work done by stitching.

Stithy, stiTH'i, *n.* [Also *stiddy*, Sc. *studdy*, from Icel. *stethi*, an anvil; same root as *steady*, *stead*.] An anvil.

Stive, stīv, *n.* [Comp. G. *staub*, Dan. *stæv*, dust.] The floating dust in flour-mills.

Stiver, stī'vėr, *n.* [D. *stuiver*, Dan. *styver*.] An old Dutch coin and money of account, worth about two cents; used often as typical of insignificant value.

Stoa, stō'a, *n.* [Gr., a porch.] *Greek arch.* a porch or portico.

Stoat, stōt, *n.* [Armor. *stôt*, *staot*, urine of animals, from the fetid fluid secreted by the anal glands.] The ermine.

Stoccado, Stoccata, stok-kā'-dō, stok-kä'ta, *n.* [Sp. *estocada*, It. *stoccata*, from Sp. *estoque*, It. *stocco*, a rapier, from G. *stock*, a stick. STOCK.] A stab; a thrust with a rapier.

Stock, stok, *n.* [A. Sax. *stoc*, *stocc*, a stem, stick, block = D. and Dan. *stok*, Icel. *stokkr*, G. *stock*, stick, stock, block, &c., in the plural *stocks* (of a vessel): the root is that of *stick*, *v.* and *n.*, the primary notion being that which is stuck in and remains fast.] The stem or trunk of a tree or other plant; the stem in which a graft is inserted, or that furnishes grafts; a block; hence, what is lifeless and senseless (*stocks* and stones); a principal supporting or holding part in certain implements or tools; the wooden support to which the barrel, &c., of a rifle or like firearm is attached; the bar or cross-piece at the upper end of the shank of an anchor; the original race or line of a family; the progenitors and their direct descendants; lineage; family; the property which a merchant, tradesman, or company has invested in any business; capital invested in some commercial business or enterprise and contributed by individuals jointly; supply provided; store, provision, hoard; *agri.* the collective animals used or reared on a farm, or such animals collectively (prices of *stock* are low); a kind of stiff band or cravat worn round the neck; liquor in which meat, bones, vegetables, &c., have been boiled, used to form a foundation for soups and gravies; a cruciferous garden plant of various species, with a very sweet smell; *pl.* an instrument of punishment formerly used for petty offenders, consisting of a wooden frame in which their ankles or wrists were confined; *pl.* the frame of timbers on which a ship is supported while building.—*Stock in trade*, the goods kept for sale by a shopkeeper.—*To take stock*, to make an inventory of stock or goods on hand; hence, *to take stock of*, to make an estimate of or set a value on generally; to observe particularly for the purpose of forming an opinion.—*v.t.* To lay up in store; to put aside or accumulate for future use; to provide or furnish with stock; to supply with stock (to *stock* a farm, a warehouse).—*a.* Kept in stock; constantly ready for service; standing; permanent (a *stock* play, a *stock* jest).—*v.i.* To branch out into shoots or sprouts; applied to grasses or other plants.—**Stock-account**, *n.* The account in a ledger which deals with the invested capital.—**Stock-breeder**, *n.* A person who breeds live stock or domestic animals.—**Stock-broker**, stok'brō-kėr, *n.* A broker who purchases and sells stocks or shares for his customers.—**Stockbroking**, stok'brō-king, *n.* The business of a stockbroker.—**Stockcar**, *n.* An automobile such as is ordinarily carried in stock by dealers, as distinguished from one specially equipped for racing, &c.; run-of-the-factory car. **Stock-dove**, *n.* A wild pigeon of Europe, so called because it was believed to be the *stock* of the many varieties of the domestic pigeon.—**Stock-exchange**, *n.* The building, place, or mart where stocks or shares are bought and sold; an organized association of brokers or dealer in stocks.—**Stock-farmer**, *n.* A farmer who largely breeds live stock.—**Stockholder**, stok'hōl-dėr, *n.* One who is the recorded owner of shares of stock in a corporation. **Stockish**, stok'ish, *a.* Like a stock or block; stupid; blockish.—**Stock-jobber**, *n.* One who speculates or gambles in stocks, or whose occupation is to buy and sell stocks or shares.—**Stock-jobbery**, *n.* Speculation in stocks or shares.—**Stock-jobbing**, *n.* The practice of a stock-jobber.—**Stock-list**, *n.* A published record of stocks traded in on the exchange, with total number of shares sold, high and low prices, net change and other information.—**Stock-man**, *n.* One having the charge of stock, as on a large farm.—**Stock-pot**, *n.* *Cookery*, a pot in which stock for soups or gravies is boiled.—**Stock-still**, *a.* Still as a fixed post; perfectly still.—**Stock-taking**, *n.* A periodical examination and valuation of the stock or goods in a shop, warehouse, or other business premises

Stockade, stok-ād', *n.* [From *stock*, a stem or stake.] *Fort.* a fence or barrier constructed by planting upright in the ground trunks of trees or rough piles of timber; an inclosure made with posts.—*v.t.*—*stockaded*, *stockading*. To surround or fortify with sharpened posts fixed in the ground.

Stocking, stok'ing, *n.* [Formerly called *stocks* or *nether stocks*, as distinguished from the *upper stocks* or knee-breeches, *stock* here having the sense of stump or trunk, part of a body left when the limbs are cut off.] A close-fitting covering for the foot and leg, now usually knitted from woollen, cotton, or silk thread.—**Stockinger**, stok'ing-ėr, *n.* One who makes stockings.—**Stocking-frame**, *n.* A machine for weaving or knitting stockings or other hosiery goods.—**Stocking-loom**, *n.* A stocking-frame.—**Stocking-weaver**, *n.* One who weaves stockings.

Stodge, stoj, *v.t.* [Akin to *stock*, *stick*, *stoke*.] To stuff or cram.—**Stodgy**, *a.* Crude; indigestible.

Stœchiology, stē-ki-ol'o-ji, *n.* STOICHIOLOGY.

Stoic, stō'ik, *n.* [Gr. *Stōikos*, from *Stōa*, *Stoa*, a porch in Athens where the philosopher Zeno taught.] A disciple of the philosopher Zeno, who founded a sect about 308 B.C., teaching that men should strive to be free from passion, unmoved by joy or grief, and submit without complaint to the unavoidable necessity by which all things are governed, regarding virtue as the highest good; hence, an apathetic person, or one who is indifferent to pleasure or pain.—*a.* Pertaining to the Stoics or their teaching.—**Stoical**, stō'i-kal, *a.* Pertaining to the Stoics; able completely to repress feeling; manifesting or maintaining indifference to pleasure or pain.—**Stoically**, stō'i-kal-li, *adv* In the manner of a Stoic; without apparent feeling; with indifference to pain.—**Stoicalness**, stō'i-kal-nes, *n.*—**Stoicism**, stō'i-sizm, *n.* The opinions and maxims of the Stoics; indifference to pleasure or pain; endurance; insensibility. [When referring to the philosophical sect these words should have a capital letter.]

Stoichiology, stoi-ki-ol'o-ji, *n.* [Gr. *stoicheion*, an element or first principle, *logos*, discourse.] The science or doctrine of elements or first principles.—**Stoichiometry**, stoi-ki-om'et-ri, *n.* [Gr. *stoicheion*, an element.] A branch of chemistry which deals with atomic and molecular weights, or, more generally, with the relations of physical properties to composition.

Stoke, stōk, *v.t.*—*stoked*, *stoking*. [Same as D. *stoken*, *stooken*, to poke or kindle a fire, from *stok*, a stick; akin to *stick*, *stock*.] To supply a fire with fuel, and attend to its combustion.—*v.i.* To act as a stoker.—**Stoke-hole**, *n.* The mouth to the grate of a furnace.—**Stoker**, stō'kėr, *n.* [D. *stoker*.] One who feeds and trims a furnace or large fire.

Stola, stō'la, *n.* pl. **Stolæ**, stō'lē. [L., from Gr. *stolē*, equipment, a stola, from *stellō*, to array.] A long garment worn by Roman matrons over the tunic, fastened round the body by a girdle.—**Stole**, stōl, *n.* [O.Fr. *estole*, L. *stola*.] Originally, a garment resembling the stola; now a long narrow ornamental band or scarf with fringed ends, worn by ecclesiastics of the Roman and English churches, with the ends pendent in front to the knees.—*Groom of the stole*, the first lord of the bedchamber in the household of the English kings.—**Stoled**, stōld, *a.* Wearing a stole.

Stole, stōl, pret. of *steal*.

Stolen, stō'ln, pp. of *steal*.

Stolid, stol'id, *a.* [L. *stolidus*, dull, doltish; akin to *stultus*, foolish; probably from root of L. *sto*, E. *stand*.] Slow in intellect; dull; heavy; stupid.—**Stolidity, Stolidness**, sto-lid'i-ti, stol'id-nes, *n.* The state or quality of being stolid; dulness; stupidity.

Stolon, stō'lon, *n.* [L. *stolo*, *stolonis*, a sucker.] *Bot.* a sucker; a sucker taking root at intervals.—**Stoloniferous**, stō-lon-if'ėr-us, *a.* Producing suckers.

Stoma, stō'ma, *n.* pl. **Stomata**, stō'ma-ta. [Gr. *stoma*, the mouth.] *Bot.* a minute orifice or pore in leaves, &c., through which exhalation takes place; *zool.* a breathing-pore of insects.—**Stomate, Stomatous**, stō'māt, stom'a-tus, *a.* Having stomata.

Stomach, stum'ak, *n.* [L. *stomachus*, the gullet, the stomach, from Gr. *stomachos*, the gullet, from *stoma*, a mouth.] A membranous receptacle in animal bodies, which is the principal organ of digestion, and in which food is prepared for yielding its nourishment to the body; a specialized cavity for the digestion of food in some of the simpler forms of animals; the desire of food caused by hunger; appetite; inclination; liking.—*v.t.* To bear without open resentment or without opposition; to brook (to *stomach* an affront).—**Stomacher**, stum'ak-ėr, *n.* An ornamental covering for the breast, forming part of a lady's dress.—**Stomachic**, stō-mak'ik, *a.* Pertaining to the stomach; strengthening the stomach; exciting the action of the stomach.—*n.* A medicine that strengthens the stomach and excites its action.—**Stomachless**, stum'ak-les, *a.* Being without stomach or appetite.—**Stomach-pump**, *n.* A small pump used in medical practice for emptying the stomach.

Stomapod, stō'ma-pod, *n.* [Gr. *stoma*, a mouth, and *pous*, *podos*, a foot.] A member of an order of small crustaceans (generally called shrimps), having six to eight pairs of legs, mostly near the mouth (hence the name).—**Stomapodous**, stō-map'o-dus, *a.* Pertaining to the stomapods.

Stomata. Under STOMA.

Stomatic, stō-mat'ik, *n.* [Gr. *stoma*, the mouth.] A medicine for diseases of the mouth.—*a.* Pertaining to a stoma or to stomata.—**Stomatitis**, stom-a-tī'tis, *n.* *Pathol.* inflammation of the mouth.—**Stomatomorphous**, stom'a-tō-mor"-fus, *a.* [Gr. *morphē*, form.] *Bot.* mouth-shaped.

Stone, stōn, *n.* [A.Sax. *stán*, a stone, a rock = D. *steen*, Dan. and Sw. *sten*, Icel. *steinn*, G. *stein*, Goth. *stains*, stone; cog. Slav. *stjena*, Gr. *stia*, *stion*, a pebble. Probably from root *sta*, seen in *stand*.] A hard concretion of some species of earth or mineral matter, as lime, silex, clay, and the like—a *stone*, as distinguished from a *rock*, being usually a mass of no great size, and generally movable, whereas a *rock* is a solid and immovable portion of the earth's crust; the material obtained from stones or rocks; the kind of substance they produce (a house built of *stone*); *fig.* a type of hardness or insensibility (a heart of *stone*); a calculous concretion in the kidneys or bladder; the disease arising from such; a testicle; the nut of a drupe or stone fruit; a common measure of weight, the English standard stone being 14 lb. avoirdupois, though other values are in regular use;

printing, the imposing-stone. — *Meteoric stone*. Under METEOR. — *Philosopher's stone*. Under PHILOSOPHER.—*To leave no stone unturned*, to do everything that can be done; to spare no exertions.—*a*. Made of stone; like stone; pertaining to stone.—*v.t.—stoned, stoning*. To pelt with stones; to free from stones (to *stone* raisins). — **Stone-blind**, *a*. Blind as a stone; perfectly blind. — **Stone-borer**, *n*. One who or that which bores stones; a name of certain molluscs, which by rasp-like imbrications on their shell bore into rocks.—**Stone-broke**, *a*. *Colloq*. completely destitute of funds.—**Stone-cast, Stone's-cast, Stone's-throw**, *n*. The distance which a stone may be thrown by the hand. — **Stone-chat, Stone-chatter**, *n*. An insessorial bird of the family of warblers, common in Europe, and often seen about heaps of stone in waste places.—**Stone-color**, *n*. The color of stone; a grayish color.—**Stone-crop**, *n*. [A.Sax. *stán-crop, crop* meaning cluster.] A name of a genus of British plants that grow on rocks.—**Stone-cutter**, *n*. One whose occupation is to hew or cut stones for building, ornamental, or other purposes. — **Stone-cutting**, *n*. The business of a stone-cutter.—**Stone-dead**, *a*. As lifeless as a stone.—**Stone-deaf**, *a*. Deaf as a stone; totally deaf.—**Stone-dresser**, *n*. One who smooths and shapes stone for building purposes.—**Stone-falcon, Stone-hawk**, *n*. The merlin.—**Stone-fruit**, *n*. Fruit whose seeds are covered with a hard shell enveloped in the pulp, as peaches, cherries, plums, &c.; a drupe.—**Stone-hammer**, *n*. A hammer for breaking or rough-dressing stones; a hammer made of stone.—**Stone-hearted**, *a*. Hard-hearted. — **Stone-horse**, *n*. A horse not castrated. —**Stone-house**, *n*. A house built of stone.—**Stone-lily**, *n*. A fossil encrinite. —**Stone-mason**, *n*. One who dresses stones for building, or builds with them.—**Stone-pine**, *n*. A pine-tree common in the south of Italy. — **Stone-plover, Stone-curlew**, *n*. A species of European plover, a summer visitant in Britain; called also *Thick-knee*.—**Stoner**, stō′nėr, *n*. One who stones.—**Stone-still**, *a*. Perfectly still or motionless.—**Stone-wall**, *n*. A wall built of stones.—**Stone-ware**, *n*. A common species of glazed potter's ware made from a composition of clay and flint. —**Stone-work**, *n*. Work consisting of stone; mason's work of stone.—**Stonily**, stō′ni-li, *adv*. In a stony manner.—**Stoniness**, stō′ni-nes, *n*. The quality of being stony.—**Stony**, stō′ni, *a*. Pertaining to, abounding in, or resembling stone; pitiless; obdurate; with rigid features. — **Stony-hearted**, *a*. Hard-hearted.

Stood, stụd, pret. and pp. of *stand*.

Stook, stụk, *n*. [L.G. *stuke*, G. *stauch*, a heap of turf, flax, &c.] A shock of corn, consisting, when of full size, of twelve sheaves.—*v.t*. To set up in stooks.

Stool, stöl, *n*. [A.Sax. *stól*, a seat=D. *stoel*, Sw. and Dan. *stol*, Icel. *stóll*, G. *stuhl*, Goth. *stolls*; cog. Slav. *stul, stol*; root in *stand, stall, still*, &c.] A seat without a back and with three or four legs, intended as a seat for one person; the seat used in evacuating the bowels; hence, an evacuation; a discharge from the bowels; the stump of a timber-tree which throws up shoots; the cluster of shoots thus produced.—*Stool of repentance*, in Scotland, an elevated seat in the church on which persons in former times were made to sit during divine service as a punishment for fornication and adultery.

Stoop, stöp, *v.t*. [A.Sax. *stúpian*, to stoop = O.D. *stoepen, stuipen*, Icel. *stúpa*, to stoop; Dan. *stupe*, to fall; Sw. *stupa*, to incline; akin *steep*.] To bend down the head and upper half of the body; to have the back bowed or bent and the head forward; to yield or submit; to condescend; to lower one's self; to dart down on prey, as a hawk; to pounce; to sink when on the wing.—*v.t*. To bend or bow downward and forward; to bow down; to bend forward (to *stoop* a cask of liquor).—*n*. The act of stooping; a habitual bend of the back or shoulders; a condescension; fall of a bird on his prey; swoop.—**Stooper**, stöp′ėr, *n*. One who stoops.

Stoop, stöp, *n*. A vessel for liquor; a stoup. (*Shak*.)

Stoop, stöp, *n*. [D. *stoep* (pron. *stoop*); the word was brought to America by the Dutch.] The steps at the entrance of a house; also, a porch with seats.

Stop, stop, *v.t.—stopped, stopping*. [A.Sax. *stoppian*, to stop up; D. and L.G. *stoppen*, Dan. *stoppe*, Sw. and Icel. *stoppa*, to stop up; from L.L. *stuppo, stuppare*, to stop with tow, from L. *stuppa*, tow.] To close up by filling, stuffing, or otherwise; to fill up a cavity or cavities in (to *stop* a vent, the ears; to stanch or prevent from bleeding; to obstruct or render impassable (to *stop* a road or passage); to check, stay, arrest, impede, keep back, in a variety of usages; to regulate the sounds of with the fingers or otherwise (to *stop* a string); to retain or refuse to pay for some reason (to *stop* one's wages, an allowance of liquor). —*v.i*. To cease to go forward; to come to a stand-still; to cease from any motion, habit, practice, or course of action; to check one's self; to stay; to reside temporarily. — *n*. A cessation of progressive motion; a hindrance of progress or action; interruption; pause; that which hinders or obstructs; obstacle, impediment, hindrance; one of the vent-holes of a wind-instrument; a collection or series of pipes in an organ giving sounds of a distinctive tone and quality; a point or mark in writing, intended to distinguish the sentences, part of a sentence, or clauses.—**Stop-cock**, *n*. A cock or faucet used to turn off or regulate the supply of water, gas, &c. — **Stop-gap**, *n*. That which fills up a gap; a temporary expedient.—**Stopless**, stop′les, *a*. Not to be stopped.—**Stoppage**, stop′āj, *n*. The act of stopping; arrest of progress or motion; a halt; a deduction made from pay or allowances.—**Stopper**, stop′ėr, *n*. One who or that which stops; that which closes a vent or hole.—*v.t*. To close or secure with a stopper.—**Stopping**, stop′ing, *n*. The act of one who stops; that which stops or fills up.—**Stop-valve**, *n*. A valve which closes a pipe against the passage of fluid, steam, &c. — **Stop-watch**, *n*. A watch used in horse-racing, &c., in which one of the hands can be stopped at once so as to mark with accuracy the time occupied.

Stope, stōp, *n*. An excavation for the extraction of ore, the ore being cut so as to form a sort of staircase.

Stopple, stop′l, *n*. [Dim. of *stop*: same as L.G. *stöppel*, G. *stöpfel, stöpsel*, a stopple.] That which stops or closes the mouth of a vessel; a stopper.—*v.t.—stoppled, stoppling*. To close with a stopple.

Storax, stō′raks, *n*. [L. *storax, styrax*, from Gr. *styrax*, storax.] A resinous and odoriferous balsam formerly much employed in medicine, now used in perfumes.

Store, stōr, *n*. [O.Fr. *estore*, store, provisions, from *estorer*, to erect, store, from the L. verb *stauro*, seen in *instauro*, to erect, *restauro*, to restore, from root of *sto, stare*, E. to *stand*.] A quantity collected, hoarded, or massed together; a supply, stock, hoard; specifically, *pl*. supplies, as of provisions, ammunition, arms, clothing, and the like, for an army, a ship, &c.; a great quantity or a large number; abundance; a storehouse or warehouse; a place where goods are kept for sale either by wholesale or retail, as a department *store*, a book *store*, etc., a shop.—*In store*, in stock; on hand; ready to be produced.—*To set store by*, to set a great value on; to appreciate highly.—*a*. Kept in store; containing stores; obtained at a store, as *store* clothes purchased ready-made, as distinguished from clothes home-made or made-to-order.—*v.t.—stored, storing*. To collect or lay up in stock; to stock; to furnish or supply; to replenish (to *store* the mind with knowledge); to deposit in a warehouse.—**Storage**, stō′rāj, *n*. The act of storing; the act of depositing in a warehouse; a price for keeping goods in storage.—**Storage battery**, *n*. A group of electric cells which can be charged again and again by sending currents through them.—**Storehouse**, stōr′hous, *n*. A house in which things are stored; a magazine; a repository; a warehouse.—**Storekeeper**, *n*. One who has the care of stores or of a store or warehouse.—**Storer**, stō′rėr, *n*. One who lays up or forms a store.—**Storeroom**, *n*. A room for the reception of stores.—**Store-ship**, *n*. A vessel employed to carry stores for a fleet.

Storey, Storied. Under STORY, a stage or floor of a building.

Storied. Under STORY, a narrative.

Stork, stork, *n*. [A.Sax. *storc*=D., Dan., and Sw. *stork*, Icel. *storkr*, G. *storch*, stork; root meaning doubtful.] A genus of tall wading birds resembling the herons, found in the vicinity of marshes and rivers, where they feed on frogs, lizards, fishes, &c.

Storm, storm, *n*. [A.Sax., D., L.G., Dan., Sw., Icel. *storm*, G. *sturm*, storm, tempest, tumult; same root as in *stir, strew*. A violent commotion of the atmosphere, producing or accompanied by wind, rain, snow, hail, or thunder and lightning; a tempest; a heavy fall of rain or snow; a violent disturbance in human society; a civil, political, or domestic commotion; a tumult; *milit*. a violent assault on a fortified place or strong position.—*Magnetic storm*, a violent and unusual disturbance of the magnetism of the earth over a wide area.—*v.t*. *Milit*. to take by storm; to assault (to *storm* a fortified town).—*v.i*. To be a storm: used impersonally (it *storms*); to be in a violent agitation or passion; to fume.—**Storm-beat, Storm-beaten**, *a*. Beaten or impaired by storms. — **Storm-blast**, *n*. The blast of a tempest.—**Storm-cock**, *n*. The missel-thrush.—**Stormful**, storm′fụl, *a*. Abounding with storms.—**Stormfulness**, storm′fụl-nes, *n*.—**Storm-glass**, *n*. A weather-glass consisting of a tube containing a chemical solution sensible to atmospheric changes.—**Storminess**, stor′mi-nes, *n*. The state of being stormy; tempestuousness.—**Storming-party**, *n*. The party who make the first assault in storming a fortress.—**Stormless**, storm′les, *a*. Free from storms. — **Storm-sail**, *n*. A sail made of very stout canvas, of smaller size than ordinary, used in violent gales.—**Storm-signal**, *n*. A signal for indicating the probable approach of a storm. — **Storm-stayed, Storm-stead**, *a*. Stopped or interrupted on a journey by the inclemency of the weather.—**Storm-window**, *n*. An outer window to protect the inner from the weather. — **Stormy**, stor′mi, *a*. Characterized by storm or tempest; tempestuous; boisterous; characterized by violence of feeling; passionate; angry.—*Stormy petrel*. PETREL.

Storthing, stor′ting, *n*. [Dan. *stor*, great, and *thing*, court.] The parliament or supreme legislative assembly of Norway.

Story, stō′ri, *n*. [A short form of *history* (which see).] A narrative; an account of past events or transactions; history; an account of an incident or event; a short narrative about a matter or a person; a fictitious narrative less elaborate than a novel; a tale; a short romance; a lie; a falsehood (*euphemistic and colloq*.).—**Storied**, stō′rid, *a*. Adorned with historical paintings or designs; referred to or celebrated in story or history; having stories, tales, or legends associated with it.—**Story-book**, *n*. A book containing one or more stories; a book of short tales.—**Story-teller**, *n*. One who tells stories, true or fictitious; a writer of stories; a euphemism for a liar.—**Story-telling**, *n*. The act of relating stories; lying.

Story, Storey, stō′ri, *n*. [From O.Fr. *estorer*, to build. STORE.] A stage or floor of a building; a set of rooms on the same floor or level.—**Storied, Storeyed**, stō′rid, *a*. Having stories or stages (a four-*storied* building).

Stot, stot, *n*. [Same as Sw. *stut*, Dan. *stud*, a bull; N. *stut*, a bullock.] A young bullock or steer. (*Scotch*.)

Stound, stound, *n.* [A.Sax., Icel., Dan., Sw. *stund*, D. *stond*, G. *stunde*, a space of time, an hour.] A moment; an instant; a pang or throb of pain.

Stoup, stöp or stoup, *n.* [Same as Icel. *staup*, G. *stauf*, a pot, vessel, cup. See STOOP.] A basin for holy water placed in a niche at the entrance of Roman Catholic churches; a deep narrow vessel for holding liquids; a flagon.

Stout, stout, *a.* [From O.Fr. *estout*, from D. *stout*, L.G. *stolt*, G. *stolz*, bold, haughty; perhaps from same root as *stilt*.] Strong; vigorous; robust; bold; intrepid; firmly or strongly built; having strength; rather corpulent; bulky or thickset in body (*colloq.*)—The strongest kind of porter. —**Stout-hearted**, *a.* Having a stout or brave heart.—**Stoutly**, stout'li, *adv.* In a stout manner; boldly; strongly. —**Stoutness**, stout'nes, *n.* The quality of being stout; sturdiness; corpulence; bodily bulk.

Stovaine, stō-vā'in, *n.* A local anæsthetic.

Stove, stōv, *n.* [A.Sax. *stofe*, a stove; Icel. *stofa*, *stufa*, a bathing-room with a stove; D. *stoof*, a stove; G. *stube*, a room; akin *stew*.] An apparatus to contain a fire for warming a room or house, or for cooking or other purposes, usually consisting of an inclosure of metal, brick, or earthenware; a house or room artificially heated to a high temperature, and used for drying and other purposes; *hort.* a hothouse in which artificial heat is maintained at a constantly high temperature. —*v.t.* —*stoved*, *stoving*. To heat, as in a stove.

Stove, stōv, pret. of *stave*.

Stow, stō, *v.t.* [Lit. to put into its place, from A.Sax. *stow*, a place; comp. D. *stouwen*, Dan. *stuve*, to stow, to pack.] To put away in a suitable place; to lay up; to pack; to compactly arrange anything in; to fill by packing closely.—**Stowage**, stō'āj, *n.* The act of stowing; room for things to be stowed; money paid for stowing goods.—**Stowaway**, stō'a-wā, *n.* One who attempts to obtain a free passage by concealing himself aboard a ship.

Strabismus, stra-biz'mus, *n.* [Gr. *strabismos*, from *strabizō*, to squint, from *strabos*, squinting.] A defect in a person's eyes, rendering them incapable of looking exactly in the same direction, certain muscles not being of normal length; squinting.

Strabotomy, stra-bot'o-mi, *n.* [Gr. *strabos*, squinting, *tomē*, cutting.] A surgical operation to remedy squinting (*Strabismus*).

Strad, strad, *n.* [*Antonio Stradivarius*.] A Cremona violin, made by the celebrated maker there, in the eighteenth century.

Straddle, strad'l, *v.i.* — *straddle*, *straddling*. [For *stridle*, from *stride*.] To part the legs wide; to stand or walk with the legs far apart; to sit astride.—*v.t.* To stride over; to stand or sit astride of. — *n.* A standing or sitting with the legs far apart.—**Straddle-legged**, *a.* Having the legs wide apart.

Strafe, straf, *v.t.* [G. *strafen*.] To punish, from the cry of the German jingoes, *Gott strafe England*, May God punish England.

Straggle, strag'l, *v.i.*—*straggled*, *straggling*. [Freq. from O.E. *strake*, to wander, to stray, A.Sax. *strícan*, to go. STRIKE.] To wander from the direct course or way; to scatter in marching; to rove; to shoot too far in growth; to grow with long irregular branches; to occur at intervals or apart from one another; to occur here and there. —**Straggler**, strag'lėr, *n.* One who straggles, one who wanders from or is left behind by his fellows; something that stands apart from others.—**Straggling**, strag'ling, *p.* and *a.* Separated from the main body; spreading out irregularly; scattered; standing apart.

Straight, strāt, *a.* [The pp. of O E. *strecche*, *streke*, A.Sax. *streccan*, to stretch (STRETCH); distinct from *strait*.] Passing from one point to another by the nearest course; not curved, bent, or crooked; direct (a *straight* line); according with justice and rectitude; not deviating from truth or fairness; upright. — *adv.* Immediately; directly; in the shortest time; in a straight line. — *n.* Straight part; straight direction. —**Straight-edge**, *n.* A slip of wood or metal made perfectly straight on the edge, and used to test surfaces or for drawing straight lines.—**Straighten**, strā'tn, *v.t.* To make straight; to reduce from a crooked to a straight form.—**Straightener**, strā'-tn-ėr, *n.* One who or that which straightens. —**Straightforward**, strāt'for-wėrd, *a.* Proceeding in a straight course; not deviating; upright; honest; open.—**Straightforward**, **Straightforwards**, *adv.* Directly forward. — **Straightforwardly**, strāt'for-wėrd-li, *adv.* **Straightforwardness**, strāt'for-wėrd-nes, *n.* — **Straightly**, strāt'li, *adv.* In a straight line; not crookedly; directly.—**Straightness**, strāt'nes, *n.* The quality or state of being straight; directness. — **Straightway**, strāt'wā, *adv.* Immediately; forthwith; without delay.

Strain, strān, *v.t.* [From O.Fr. *estraindre*, *estreindre*, *streindre*, to strain, wring, &c. (Fr. *etreindre*), from L. *stringo*, *stringere*, to strain, to draw tight, pp. *strictus*. *Strict*, *strait*, *stringent* are from same verb; so *constrain*, *restrain*, *restrict*, *constriction*, &c.] To stretch or draw tightly; to make tighter; to squeeze or clasp in an embrace; to injure or weaken by stretching or overtasking: to subject to too great stress or exertion; to harm by a twist or wrench; hence, to sprain; to exert to the utmost; to push to the utmost strength or exertion; *fig.* to push beyond the due limit; to carry too far; to do violence to (to *strain* the meaning of a text); to squeeze out; to purify by filtration; to filter.—*To strain a point*, to make a special and often inconvenient effort; to exceed one's duty; to overstep one's commission.—*v.i.* To exert one's self; to make violent efforts; to filter or be filtered; to percolate.—*n.* A violent effort; an excessive exertion of the limbs or muscles, or of the mind; an injurious stretching of the muscles or tendons; a continued course of action; general bearing; a poem; a song; a lay; a tune; a melody or part of a melody; especially, a section of a melody ending with a cadence; the subject or theme of a poem, discourse, &c.; tenor of discourse; *mech.* a definite alteration of form or dimensions experienced by a solid under the action of a stress; sometimes, in older usage, stress or force.—**Strainable**, strā'na-bl, *a.* Capable of being strained. — **Strainer**, strā'nėr, *n.* One who strains; an instrument for filtration.

Strain, strān, *n.* [O.E. *strene*, *streen*, *stren*, A.Sax. *strýnd*, stock, race, from *strýnan*, *streónan*, to produce.] Race; stock in a genealogical sense; family blood; quality or line in regard to breeding; natural disposition; turn; tendency.

Strait, strāt, *a.* [From O.F. *estreit*, *estroit*, (Fr. *étroit*), narrow, from L. *strictus*, pp. of *stringo*, to draw tight. STRAIN, *v.t.*] Strict or rigorous‡; narrow; not wide.—*n.* A narrow pass or passage; a narrow passage of water between two seas or oceans (the plural is often used of one: the *Strait* or *Straits* of Gibraltar); distress; difficulty; distressing necessity.—**Straiten**, strā'tn, *v.t.* To make strait; to contract, confine, hem in, narrow; to make tense or tight; to distress; to press with poverty or other necessity; to put in pecuniary difficulties: used especially in pp.—**Strait-laced**, *a.* Having the stays or bodice tightly laced; constrained; strict in manners or morals; often excessively and puritanically strict.—**Straitly**, strāt'li, *adv.* In a strait manner.—**Straitness**, strāt'nes, *n.* The state or quality of being strait; narrowness; strictness. — **Strait-jacket**, **Strait-waistcoat**, *n.* A garment made of some strong material, with long sleeves, which are tied behind the body, used to restrain lunatics.

Strake, strāk, *n.* [A form of *streak*.] A continuous line of planking or plates on a ship's side, reaching from stem to stern.

Stramineous, stra-min'ē-us, *a.* [L. *stramineus*, from *stramen*, straw.] Strawy; consisting of straw; like straw.

Stramonium, stra-mō'ni-um, *n.* The thorn-apple (*Datura Stramonium*), and a drug obtained from it similar to belladonna.

Strand, strand, *n.* [A.Sax., D., Dan., Sw., and G. *strand*, Icel. *strönd*, strand, shore, coast; root meaning doubtful.] A shore or beach of the sea or lake.—*v.i.* To drift or be driven on shore; to run aground; to have progress interrupted; to come to a stand-still.—*v.t.* To drive or run aground on the sea-shore.

Strand, strand, *n.* [Same as D. *streen*, G. *strähne*, a skein, a strand.] One of the twists or parts of which a rope is composed.

Strange, strānj, *a.* [O.Fr. *estrange* (Fr. *étrange*), from L. *extraneus*, that is without, from *extra*, on the outside—*ex*, out, and affix *-tra* (as in *contra*). EXTERIOR.] Foreign; belonging to another country; not one's own; belonging to others; not before known, heard, or seen; new; wonderful; causing surprise; extraordinary; odd; unusual; not according to the common way; estranged; not familiar; unacquainted; not knowing. — *Strange sail* (*naut.*), an unknown vessel.—**Strangely**, strānj'li, *adv.* In a strange manner; surprisingly; wonderfully; remarkably; in a distant and reserved manner.—**Strangeness**, strānj'nes, *n.* The state or character of being strange.—**Stranger**, strān'jėr, *n.* [O.F. *estranger*.] A foreigner; one of another place; one unknown or at least not familiar; one not knowing; one ignorant or unacquainted (a *stranger* to the affair); a guest; a visitor; one not admitted to fellowship.

Strangle, strang'gl, *v.t.*—*strangled*, *strangling*. [O.Fr. *estrangler*, L. *strangulare*, to strangle, from Gr. *stranggalaō*, *stranggaloō*, to knot, *stranggō*, to tie tight; same root as E. *string*.] To destroy the life of by compressing the windpipe; to choke; *fig.* to suppress or stifle. — **Strangler**, strang'glėr, *n.* One who or that which strangles.—**Strangles**, strang'glz, *n.pl.* A disorder which attacks horses, consisting of an abscess between the branches of the lower jaw.—**Strangulated**, strang'gū-lā-ted, *a.* *Surg.* having the circulation stopped in any part by compression (*strangulated* hernia).—**Strangulation**, strang-gū-lā'-shon, *n.* [L. *strangulatio*.] The act of strangling; the state of being strangled; *med.* the state of a part too closely constricted, as the intestine in hernia.

Strangury, strang'gū-ri, *n.* [L. *stranguria*, Gr. *strangouria*—*stranx*, *strangos*, a drop, and *ouron*, urine.] A disease in which there is pain in passing the urine, which is given out by drops.—**Strangurious**, strang-gū'ri-us, *a.* Pertaining to strangury.

Strap, strap, *n.* [A collateral form of *strop*, from root of *stripe*, *strip*; or from L. *struppus*, a thong.] A long narrow slip of leather or other substance of various forms and for various uses, and often provided with a buckle; a plate, band, or strip of metal to connect or hold other parts together; a piece of leather for sharpening razors, &c.: in this sense often written *strop*.—*v.t.*—*strapped*, *strapping*. To chastise with a strap; to fasten or bind with a strap.—**Strapper**, strap'ėr, *n.* One who uses a strap.—**Strapping**, strap'ing, *a.* [Comp. *thumping*, *bouncing*, *thundering*, &c.] Tall and well made; handsome. (*Colloq.*)—**Strap-shaped**, *a.* *Bot.* ligulate.

Strappado, strap-pā'dō, *n.* [O.Fr. *strapade*, It. *strappata*, from *strappare*, to pull.] An old punishment, consisting in having the hands of the offender tied behind his back, drawing him up by them by a rope, and then suddenly letting him drop.

Strass, stras, *n.* [From the name of its German inventor.] A variety of flint-glass used in the manufacture of artificial gems.

Strata. See STRATUM.

Stratagem, strat'a-jem, *n.* [Fr. *stratagème*, from L. *strategema*, Gr. *stratēgēma*, from *stratēgos*, a general, from *stratos*, an army, *agō*, to lead.] An artifice in war; a plan or scheme for deceiving an enemy; a clever piece of generalship; any artifice; a trick to gain some advantage.—**Stratagemic,**† **Stratagemical,**† strat-a-jem′ik, strat-a-jem′i-kal, *a.* Containing stratagem or artifice.—**Strategic, Strategical,** stra-tej′ik, stra-tej′i-kal, *a.* Pertaining to strategy; effected by strategy.—*Strategic point,* any point in the theatre of warlike operations which affords to its possessor an advantage over his opponent. Also **Strategetic, Strategetical,** strat-ē-jet′ik, strat-ē-jet′i-kal.—**Strategically, Strategetically,** stra-tej′i-kal-li, strat-ē-jet′i-kal-li, *adv.* In a strategic manner. —**Strategist,** strat′ē-jist, *n.* One skilled in strategy.—**Strategy, Strategetics, Strategics,** strat′ē-ji, strat-ē-jet′-iks, stra-tej′iks, *n.* The science of forming and carrying out projects of military operations; generalship; the use of artifice or finesse in carrying out any project. ∴ *Strategy* refers to the operations or movements previous to a battle; *tactics* is the art of handling troops when in actual contact with the enemy.

Strath, strath, *n.* [Gael. *srath.*] In Scotland, a valley of considerable size, often having a river running through it, giving it its distinctive name (*Strathspey, Strathdon,* &c.]—**Strathspey,** strath-spā, *n.* In Scotland, a species of dance in duple time, resembling a reel, but slower; an air or piece of music for this dance.

Stratify, &c. Under STRATUM.

Stratoliner, stra′tō-lī′nėr, *n.* A type of large passenger airplane, designed and equipped for sustained and rapid flight at high altitudes.

Stratosphere, stra′tō-sfēr, *n.* [L. *stratus,* spread, Gr. *sphaira,* a ball.] An upper part of the atmosphere, in which temperature does not vary with height.

Stratum, strā′tum, *n.* pl. **Strata,** strā′ta. [L., what is spread or stretched out, from *sterno, stratum,* to strew (whence also *street*); the root is that of E. *straw,* to strew.] A layer or bed of matter spread out; *geol.* a layer of any substance, as sand, clay, limestone, &c., which is deposited over a certain surface by the action of water, especially such a layer when forming one of a number superposed.—**Stratify,** strat′i-fī, *v.t.*—*stratified, stratifying.* [Fr. *stratifier* —L. *stratum,* and *facio,* to make.] To form into strata or layers, as substances in the earth; to lay or arrange in strata.—**Stratification,** strat′i-fi-kā″shon, *n.* The process by which are formed strata; an arrangement in strata or layers.—**Stratified,** strat′i-fīd, *p.* and *a.* Arranged in layers or strata.—**Stratiform,** strat′i-form, *a.* In the form of strata.—**Stratigraphic, Stratigraphical,** strat-i-graf′ik, strat-i-graf′i-kal, *a.* [L. *stratum,* and Gr. *graphō,* to describe.] Relating to strata or their arrangement.—**Stratigraphically,** strat-i-graf′i-kal-li, *adv.* As regards stratigraphy or the disposition of strata.—**Stratigraphy,** stra-tig′ra-fi, *n.* That department of geology which treats of the arrangement of strata, or the order in which they succeed each other.

Stratus, strā′tus, *n.* [L. a strewing, a covering. STRATUM.] A low dense, horizontal cloud.

Straw, stra̤, *n.* [A.Sax. *streáw,* straw=Icel. *strá,* Dan. *straa,* D. *stroo,* G. *stroh,* straw; akin to *strew;* cog. L. *stramen,* straw, from *sterno,* to strew. STRATUM, STREW.] The stalk or stem of certain species of grain, pulse, &c.; such stalks collectively when cut, and after being thrashed (no plural in this sense); used proverbially as typical of worthlessness (I don't care a *straw*).—*Man of straw,* the figure of a man formed of a suit of old clothes stuffed with straw; hence, the mere resemblance of a man; a person of little or no means or substance; an imaginary person.—**Strawberry,** stra̤′be-ri, *n.* [A.Sax. *streáwberie, streów-berie,* from its habit of spreading or *strewing* itself along the ground.] A well-known fruit and plant, the fruit being succulent and bearing the seeds on its surface. —**Strawberry-tree,** *n.* The arbutus.—**Straw-board,** *n.* Thick paper board made altogether or principally from straw. —**Straw-bonnet,** *n.* A bonnet for females, made of plaited straw of some cereal plant.—**Straw-braid,** *n.* Straw-plait.—**Straw-built,** *a.* Built of straw.—**Straw-color,** *n.* The color of dry straw; a beautiful yellowish color.—**Straw-colored,** *a.* Of a light yellow. —**Straw-cutter,** *n.* An instrument to cut straw for fodder.—**Straw-hat,** *n.* A hat made of the plaited straw of cereals. —**Straw-paper,** *n.* Paper made wholly or principally from straw.—**Straw-plait,** *n.* A plait or braid formed of straws, generally wheat or rye, used to form ladies' bonnets, hats, &c.—**Strawy,** stra̤′i, *a.* Pertaining to, made of, or like straw.

Stray, strā, *v.i.* [O.Fr. *estrayer, extraier,* to wander, from O.Fr. *estrée,* It. *strada,* a road or street; from L.L. *strata,* a street, STREET.] To wander, as from a direct course; to go astray; *fig.* to wander from the path of duty or rectitude; to err; to roam or ramble; to run in a serpentine course; to wind.—*a.* Having gone astray; straggling.—*n.* Any domestic animal that wanders at large or is lost; an estray; *wireless,* random electromagnetic waves, which interfere with radio reception.—**Strayer,** strā′ėr, *n.* One who strays.

Streak, strēk, *n.* [A.Sax. *strica,* a line, a stroke=Icel. *stryk,* Dan. *streg,* D. *streek,* a stroke, streak, line; akin *strike.*] A line or long mark of a different color from the ground; a layer in a mine; a stripe; *naut.* a strake; *mineral,* the color and appearance of a mineral when scratched.—*To strike a streak of bad luck,* to experience continuous misfortunes.—*v.t.* To form streaks on; to variegate with lines of color.—**Streaked, Streaky,** strēkt, strē′ki, *a.* Having streaks; striped.

Stream, strēm, *n.* [A.Sax. *streám,* a stream, a river=D. *stroom,* Icel. *straumr,* Dan. and Sw. *ström,* G. *strom;* from root seen in Skr. *sru,* to flow (with *t* inserted).] Any river, brook, or course of running water; a flow or gush of any fluid substance; a flow of air or gas or of light; a steady current in the sea or in a river (the Gulf *Stream*); anything issuing as if in a flow (a *stream* of words); many individuals moving uniformly forward without interval.—*v.i.* To flow in a stream; to issue with continuance, not by fits; to issue or shoot in streaks or beams; to stretch in a long line; to float at full length in the air. —*v.t.* To send forth in a current or stream; to pour.—**Stream-anchor,** *n. Naut.* an anchor used for warping and like purposes.—**Streamer,** strē′mėr, *n.* A long narrow flag; a pennon; a stream of light shooting upward from the horizon, as in some forms of the aurora borealis.—**Stream-ice,** *n.* A line of pieces of drift ice in a current.—**Streamlet,** strēm′let, *n.* A small stream; a rivulet; a rill.—**Stream line.** The path of an individual particle of fluid in fluid motion.—**Stream-tin,** *n.* Tin ore found in alluvial ground in rounded particles and masses.—**Streamy,** strē′mi, *a.* Abounding with streams; having the form of a stream or beam of light.

Street, strēt, *n.* [A.Sax. *straet,* a street, from L. *strata* (*via*), a paved way, from *sterno, stratum,* to strew, to pave. STRATUM, STREW, STRAY.] A way or road in a city having houses on one or both sides, chiefly a main way, in distinction from a *lane* or *alley;* the houses as well as the open way.—**Street-arab,** *n.* A neglected street boy.—**Street-car,** *n.* A tramway-car which runs in a street.—**Street-door,** *n.* A door which opens upon a street.—**Street-sweeper,** *n.* One who sweeps the streets; a machine for sweeping the streets.—**Street-walker,** *n.* A common prostitute.—**Street-walking,** *n.* The practice of a street-walker.

Stremma, strem′ma, *n.* [Gr., a wrench, from *strephō,* to twist.] *Pathol.* a strain or sprain of the parts about a joint.

Strength, strength, *n.* [A.Sax. *strengthu,* strength, from *strang,* strong; comp. *length* and *long.* STRONG.] The muscular force or energy which an animal is capable of exerting; animal force; the quality of bodies by which they sustain the application of force without breaking or yielding; solidity or toughness (the *strength* of a bone); power or vigour of any kind; capacity for exertion (*strength* of mind, memory, evidence, argument, affection); power of resisting attacks; that on which confidence or reliance is placed; support; force or power in expressing meaning by words; vividness; intensity; intensity of some distinguishing or essential constituent; potency (*strength* of wine, poison, acid); legal or moral force or efficacy; force as measured or stated in figures; amount or numbers of an army, fleet, or the like; force proceeding from motion and proportioned to it; vehemence; impetuosity.—*On* or *upon the strength of,* in reliance upon the value of; on the faith of.—**Strengthen,** streng′then, *v.t.* To make strong or stronger; to add strength to; to confirm; to establish; to encourage; to fix in resolution; to make greater; to add intensity to.—*v.i.* To grow strong or stronger.—**Strengthener,** streng′then-ėr, *n.* One who or that which strengthens.—**Strengthless,** strength′les, *a.* Wanting strength.

Strenuous, stren′ū-us, *a.* [L. *strenuus,* vigorous, strenuous; allied to Gr. *strēnēs,* strong, hard.] Eager and constant in action; zealous; ardent; earnest.—**Strenuously,** stren′ū-us-li, *adv.* Ardently; actively.—**Strenuousness,** stren′ū-us-nes, *n.* Earnestness; active zeal.

Streptococcus, strep′tō-kok″us, *n.* [Gr. *streptos,* twisted, *kokkos,* a berry.] In bacteria, a form consisting of a chain of cocci.

Stress, stres, *n.* [O.Fr. *estrecer, estrecier* (Fr. *étrecir*), to straiten, to narrow, from L. *strictus,* pp. of *stringo, strictum,* to draw tight (whence *stringent, strain*). STRAIN.] Constraining, urging, or impelling force; pressure; urgency; violence (*stress* of weather); an effort or exertion; a strain; weight; any force tending to change the form or dimensions of a solid, that is, to produce a strain; also the reaction of the solid against the straining forces; importance or influence, imputed or ascribed (to lay *stress* on some point in argument); accent or emphasis; *mech.* force exerted in any direction or manner on bodies (*tensile* stress, &c.).

Stretch, strech, *v.t.* [A softened form from A.Sax. *streccan,* to stretch=D. *strekken,* G. *strecken,* Dan. *strække,* to stretch. *Straight* is a derivative, and *strake, streak, strike, string, strong* are connected.] To draw out; to extend in length; to draw tight; to make tense; to extend, spread, expand in any direction; to reach out; to hold forth; to extend or distend forcibly; to strain; to exaggerate; to extend too far (to *stretch* a prerogative).—*To stretch a point.* Same as *To strain a point.*—*v.i.* To extend; to reach; to be continuous over a distance; to bear extension without breaking; to attain greater length.—*n.* A stretching or the state of being stretched; an effort; a strain; utmost extent or reach; an extended portion; an expanse.—*On* or *upon the stretch,* in a continuous effort or strain; straining one's powers.—*At* or *on a stretch,* at one effort; at one time.—**Stretcher,** strech′ėr, *n.* One who or that which stretches; an instrument for widening gloves or for distending boots; a flat board on which corpses are laid out; a litter for carrying sick, wounded, or dead persons; *carp.* a tie-timber in a frame; *naut.* a narrow piece of plank placed across a boat for the rowers to set their feet against.

Strew, strö or strō, *v.t.*—pret. *strewed;* pp. *strewed* or *strewn.* [A.Sax. *streowian,* to scatter=Goth. *strawjan,* G. *streuen,* Icel. *strá,* Dan. and Sw. *strö;* same root as *straw, star,* L. *sterno, stratum* (E. *stratum*), Skr. *stri,* to strew.] To scatter or sprinkle: always applied to dry substances separable into parts or particles; to cover by scattering or being scattered over; to throw loosely apart; to spread abroad; to disseminate. Also written *Strow* and formerly *Straw.*

Stria, strī′a, *n.* pl. **Striæ,** strī′ē. [L.] A technical term for fine thread-like lines or streaks seen on the surface of shells, minerals, plants, &c.—**Striate, Striated,** strī'āt, strī'ā-ted, *a.* [L. *striatus.*] Marked with striæ.—*Striated fibre*, the fibre of the voluntary muscles or those that the will can influence. — **Striate**, *v.t.* — *striated, striating.* To mark with striæ.—**Striation**, strī-ā'shon, *n.* The state of being striated; striate markings; *geol.* the grooving of rock surfaces by masses of ice passing over them.

Stricken, strik'n, pp. of *strike.* Struck; smitten; advanced (as in age—'well *stricken* in years').

Strickle, strik'l, *n.* [From *strike.*] An instrument to strike grain to a level with the measure; an instrument for whetting scythes.

Strict, strikt, *a.* [L. *strictus*, pp. of *stringo*, to draw tight; whence also *stringent, strain.* STRAIN.] Carefully adhering to or governed by some rule; carefully observed; rigorously nice (*strict* watch); rigorous as to rules or conduct (*strict* in religious observances); definite as to terms; stringent; rigidly interpreted; not loose or vague (the *strict* sense of a word).—**Strictly**, strikt'li, *adv.* In a strict manner; with nice or rigorous accuracy; correctly; definitely; rigorously.—**Strictness**, strikt'nes, *n.* The state or quality of being strict; exactness in the observance of rules; rigorous accuracy; precision; severity; stringency.

Stricture, strik'tūr, *n.* [L. *strictura*, from *stringo, strictum*, to draw tight. STRICT.] A touch of sharp criticism; a censorious remark; censure; *med.* a morbid contraction of some mucous canal or duct of the body, especially the urethra.—**Strictured**, strik'tūrd, *a.* Affected with stricture.

Stride, strīd, *v.i.*—pret. *strode*; pp. *stridden*; ppr. *striding.* [A.Sax. *stridan*, to stride, to walk, *bestridan*, to bestride; L.G. *striden*, to stride; comp. Dan. *stritte*, to straddle; also G. *streiten*, to contend, *streit*, Dan. *strid*, contest.] To walk with long steps; to stand with the feet far apart; to straddle. —*v.t.* To pass over at a step; to bestride.—*n.* A long step; a measured or pompous step; a lofty gait; the space measured by the legs far apart.

Strident, strī'dent, *a.* [L. *stridens, stridentis*, ppr. of *strideo*, to creak.] Creaking; harsh; grating.—**Stridulation**, strid-ū-lā'shon, *n.* A small, harsh, creaking noise, as made by some insects.—**Stridulatory**, strid'ū-la-to-ri, *a.* Stridulous. — **Stridulous**, strid'ū-lus, *a.* [L. *stridulus.*] Making a small creaking sound.

Strife, strīf, *n.* [From Icel. *strīth*, war, strife; the *th* being changed to *f* by the influence of *strive*, O.Fr. *estriver.* STRIVE.] Exertion or contention for superiority; contest of emulation; emulation; contention in anger or enmity; discord; quarrel or war.—**Strifeful**, strīf'ful, *a.* Full of strife; contentious.

Strigil, strij'il, *n.* [L. *strigilis*, from *stringo*, to graze, to scrape.] An instrument used by the ancients for scraping the skin at the bath.

Strike, strīk, *v.i.*—pret. *struck*; pp. *struck, stricken*; ppr. *striking.* [A.Sax. *strican*, to go rapidly in a straight course; *āstrican*, to strike, to smite; D. *strijken*, to stroke; G. *streichen*, Icel. *strykja*, to stroke, to flog; cog. L. *stringo*, to strain, to touch lightly (STRAIN). *Stroke* is a derivative.] To pass or dart with rapidity (to *strike* into another path; the bullet *struck* through the door); to penetrate (the roots *strike* deep); to make a quick blow or thrust; to use one's weapons; to knock; to sound an hour (as a clock); to reach or act on by appulse (light *strikes* on the wall); to run or dash upon the shore, a rock, or bank; to be stranded; to lower a sail or a flag in token of respect, or to signify surrender (the ship *struck*); to yield; to quit work in order to compel an increase or prevent a reduction of wages, or for other reasons.—*To strike at*, to make or aim a blow at; to attack.—*To strike home*, to give an effective blow.—*To strike in*, to put in one's word suddenly; to interpose.—*To strike in with*, to conform to; to suit.—*To strike out*, to deliver a blow; to start to swim.—*To strike up*, to begin to play or sing.—*v.t.* To touch or hit with some force; to smite; to give a blow to; to give, deal, or inflict (with *blow* or similar word as object); to dash; to knock (with the instrument as object); to produce by a blow or blows (to *strike* fire); to stamp with a stroke; hence, to mint; to coin; to thrust in; to cause to enter or penetrate (a tree *strikes* its root deep); to cause to sound; to notify by sound; to impress (the mind) strongly; to affect sensibly with strong emotion (the scene *struck* him); to produce suddenly; to effect at once (to *strike* terror); to bring suddenly into some state or condition (to *strike* one dumb); to make and ratify (to *strike* a bargain); to lower, as the yards, flag, sails of a vessel.—*Well struck* or *stricken in years*, of an advanced age.—*To strike a balance*, in *bookkeeping*, to bring out the amount due on one or other of the sides of a debtor and creditor account; hence, in general, to ascertain on which side the preponderance is.—*To strike down*, to prostrate by a blow or illness; to fell.—*To strike off*, to separate by a blow; to erase from an account; to deduct; to impress; to print.—*To strike oil*, to find petroleum when boring for it; hence, to make a lucky hit (*colloq.*).—*To strike out*, to blot out; to efface; to erase; to plan or excogitate by a quick effort; to devise.—*To strike sail*, to lower or take in sail.—*To strike a tent*, to take it down.—*To strike up*, to drive up with a blow; to begin to play or sing.—*To strike work*, to cease work, especially till some dispute between employers and employed is settled.—*n.* An instrument for levelling a measure of grain, salt, &c.; a strickle; the act of a body of workmen discontinuing work with the object of compelling their employer to concede certain demands made by them; *geol.* the horizontal direction of the outcropping edges of tilted strata, running at right angles to the dip.—**Striker**, strī'kėr, *n.* One who or that which strikes.—**Striking**, strī'king, *a.* Such as to strike with surprise or other feeling; remarkable; forcible; impressive. — **Strikingly**, strī'king-li, *adv.* In a striking manner; remarkably; strongly; impressively. — **Strikingness**, strī'kingnes, *n.* The quality of being striking.

String, string, *n.* [A.Sax. *streng*=D. *streng*, Icel. *strengr*, Dan. and Sw. *sträng*, G. *strang*, string, cord; akin to *strong*, and to L. *stringo*, to draw tight (whence *strain, strict*), *strangulo*, to strangle.] A small rope, line, or cord used for fastening or tying things; a twine; a thread; a thread on which things are filed; and hence, a set of things on a line (a *string* of beads); the chord of a musical instrument which gives a sound by its vibrations; hence, *pl.* the stringed instruments of an orchestra; a line or chain of things following each other; a nerve or tendon of an animal body (the heart *strings*); a series of things connected or following in succession (a *string* of arguments).—*v.t.*—pret. and pp. *strung.* To furnish with strings; to put in tune the strings of; to put on a string (to *string* beads).—**String-band**, *n.* A band of musicians who play on stringed instruments. — **String-course**, *n.* A narrow moulding continued horizontally along the face of a building.—**Stringed**, stringd, *a.* Having strings; produced by strings. — **Stringer**, string'ėr, *n.* One who strings; an inside strake of plank or of plates in a ship; *carp.* a board that sustains some important part of a framework or structure.—**String-halt**, *n.* A twitching of the hinder leg of a horse, constituting a defect, being a convulsive motion of the muscles of the hough.—**Stringiness**, string'i-nes, *n.* The state of being stringy; fibrousness. — **Stringless**, string'les, *a.* Having no strings. —**Stringy**, string'i, *a.* Consisting of strings or small threads; fibrous; filamentous; ropy; sinewy; wiry.—**Stringy-bark**, *n.* A name of several Australian trees of the genus Eucalyptus.

Stringent, strin'jent, *a.* [L. *stringens, stringentis*, ppr. of *stringo*, to draw tight. STRICT, STRAIN.] Making strict claims or requirements; strict; rigid; making severe restrictions.—**Stringently**, strin'jent-li, *adv.* In a stringent manner.—**Stringency, Stringentness**, strin'jen-si, strin'jent-nes, *n.* State or character of being stringent; strictness.

Strip, strip, *v.t.*—*stripped, stripping.* [A. Sax. *strȳpan*, to strip, to spoil; L.G. *strippen, stripen, strepen*, D. *stroopen*, G. *streifen*, to strip; closely akin to *stripe.*] To pull or tear off (a covering); to deprive of a covering; to remove the clothes from; to skin; to peel (to *strip* a tree *of* the bark); to deprive; to bereave; to despoil; to tear off the thread of a screw or bolt; to milk dry; to unrig (to *strip* a ship).—*v.i.* To take off the covering or clothes.—*n.* A narrow piece comparatively long; a stripe. —**Stripper**, strip'ėr, *n.* One that strips.

Stripe, strīp, *n.* [Closely akin to *strip* and =L.G. *stripe*, D. *streep*, Dan. *stribe*, G. *streif*, a stripe.] A long narrow division of anything of a different colour from the rest; a streak; a strip or long narrow piece; a stroke made with a lash, rod, or scourge; a wale or weal.—*v.t.*—*striped, striping.* To make stripes upon; to form with lines of different colours. — **Striped**, strīpt, *a.* Having stripes of different colours.

Stripling, strip'ling, *n.* [From *strip, stripe*, with dim. term. *-ling*; primarily, a tall slender youth, one that shoots up suddenly; comp. *slip, scion.*] A youth in the state of adolescence, or just passing from boyhood to manhood; a lad.

Strive, strīv, *v.i.*—pret. *strove*, pp. *striven*, ppr. *striving.* [O.Fr. *estriver*, to strive, from O.H.G. *streban*, G. *streben*, Dan. *stræbe*, D. *streven*, to strive; or from Icel. *strīth*, strife.] To make efforts; to endeavour with earnestness; to try; to contend; to struggle in opposition; to fight; to quarrel or contend with each other; to be in dispute or altercation; to vie.—**Striver**, strī'vėr, *n.* One that strives.

Strobilus, Strobile, strō-bī'lus, strō'bil, *n.* [Gr. *strobilos*, a pine-cone.] *Bot.* a catkin the carpels of which are scale-like spread open, and bear naked seeds, as in the fruit of the pines; a pine-cone.—**Strobiliform, Strobilaceous**, strō-bī'li-form, strō-bi-lā'shus, *a.* Shaped like a strobile.—**Strobiline**, strō-bī'lin, *a.* Pertaining to a strobile; cone-shaped.—**Strobilite**, strō-bī'līt, *n.* [Gr. *strobilos*, and *lithos*, a stone.] A fossil coniferous cone.

Stroboscope, stro'bō-skōp, *n.* [Gr. *strobos*, a whirling, and *skopein*, to view.] An instrument for observing the succession of phases in a periodic motion by intermittent illumination.

Stroke, strōk, *n.* [From *strike.*] A blow; a knock; the striking of one body against another; a fatal assault or attack; a sudden attack of disease or affliction; a calamity; the striking of a clock; a dash in writing or printing; a line; the touch of a pen or pencil (a hair-*stroke*); a touch; a masterly effort (a *stroke* of genius); a successful attempt; the sweep of an oar; the stroke-oar or strokesman; *steam-engin.* the entire movement of the piston from one end to the other of the cylinder.—**Stroke-oar**, *n.* The aftmost oar of a boat; also, the man that uses it.—**Strokesman**, strōks'man, *n.* The man who rows the aftmost oar in a boat, and whose stroke is to be followed by the rest.

Stroke, strōk, *v.t.*—*stroked, stroking.* [A. Sax. *strácian*, to stroke = D. *strooken*, to stroke, to flatter; close akin to *strike.*] To rub gently with the hand in kindness or tenderness; to rub gently in one direction; to make smooth by gentle rubbing.—*n.* A caress; a gentle rubbing with the hand, expressive of kindness.—**Stroker**, strō'kėr, *n.* One who strokes.

Stroll, strōl, *v.i.* [Of doubtful origin: comp. Prov.G. *strolen, struolen*, to stroll.] To wander on foot slowly; to ramble idly or leisurely.—*Strolling player*, an inferior stage-player who goes about from place to place and performs wherever an audience can be obtained.—*n.* A walking idly and leisurely; a ramble.—**Stroller**, strōl'ėr, *n.* One who strolls; an itinerant player.

Stroma, strō'ma, *n.* [Gr. *strōma*, a bed, from *strōnnymi*, to spread out.] *Anat.* the bed or foundation texture of an organ, or of any deposit; the framework of an organ; *bot.* the fleshy substance in some fungous plants; a thallus.

Strombos horn, strom'bos horn, *n.* A horn worked by compressed air, used in the Great War as a warning against a German cloud-gas attack.

Strombus, strom'bus, *n.* [L. *strombus*, from Gr. *strombos*, a spiral shell, a top.] A genus of gasteropods having univalve spiral shells, one of them being the largest known.

Stromeyerite, strō-mī'ėr-īt, *n.* [After the chemist *Stromeyer*.] A steel-gray ore of silver, consisting of sulphur, silver, and copper.

Strong, strong, *a.* [A.Sax. *strang*, *strong*, strong, robust = Icel. *strangr*, Dan. and D. *streng*, strong; G. *streng*, strict; same root as *string*, and L. *stringo*, to draw tight (whence *strict*). *Strength* is a derivative.] Having physical power; having the power of exerting great bodily force; robust; muscular; able or powerful mentally or morally; of great power or capacity (a *strong* mind, memory, imagination); naturally sound or healthy; hale; not easily broken; firm; solid; compact; well fortified; not easily subdued or taken (a *strong* fortress or position); having great military or naval power or force; having great wealth or resources; having force from moving with rapidity; violent; impetuous; adapted to make a deep impression on the mind or imagination; effectual; cogent; ardent or zealous (a *strong* supporter); having a particular quality or qualities in a great degree (a *strong* decoction, *strong* tea), containing much alcohol; intoxicating; affecting the senses forcibly (a *strong* light, scent, flavour); substantial; solid, but not of easy digestion; well established; firm; not easily overthrown or altered; vehement; earnest (a *strong* affection); having great resources; powerful; mighty; having great force or expressiveness; forcibly expressed; (preceded by numerals); amounting to; powerful to the extent of (an army 10,000 *strong*); *com.* tending upwards in price; rising (a *strong* market); *gram.* applied to inflected words when inflection is effected by internal vowel change and not by adding syllables: *swim, swam, swum* is a *strong* verb (WEAK). *Strong* is used as an element in many self-explanatory compounds, as *strong*-backed, *strong*-bodied, *strong*-voiced, &c.—**Stronghold**, strong'hōld, *n.* A fastness; a fortified place; a place of security.—**Strongly**, strong'li, *adv.* In a strong manner; with strength, force, or power; firmly; forcibly; violently.—**Strong-minded**, *a.* Having a strong or vigorous mind; having a masculine rather than a feminine turn of mind; unfeminine: applied ironically to women claiming equality with men. —**Strong-room**, *n.* A fire-proof and burglar-proof apartment in which valuables are kept.—**Strong-waters**, *n.pl.* Distilled or ardent spirits.

Strontia, stron'shi-a, *n.* An oxide of strontium occurring at *Strontian*, in Argyleshire, whence its name, a grayish-white powder, closely resembling baryta. The *nitrate of strontia* is sometimes used in making fireworks, as it communicates a magnificent red colour to flame.—**Strontian**, stron'shi-an, *n.* A name given to strontia.—*a.* Pertaining to strontia; containing strontia. —**Strontianite**, stron'shi-an-īt, *n.* A mineral, native carbonate of strontia.—**Strontitic**, stron-tit'ik, *a.* Pertaining to strontia or strontium.—**Strontium**, stron'shi-um, *n.* The metal of which strontia is the oxide, of a whitish yellow colour, ductile and malleable, and somewhat harder than lead.

Strop, strop, *n.* [A.Sax. *stropp*, from L. *stroppus*, *struppus*, a thong.] A strip of leather, or a strip of wood covered with leather or other suitable material, used for sharpening razors; a razor-strop.—*v.t.* —*stropped*, *stropping*. To sharpen with a strop.

Strophanthin, strō-fan'thin, *n.* [From *Strophanthus*, the plant—Gr. *strephō*, to turn, twist, *anthos*, flower.] A drug obtained from the seeds of an African plant; a muscle poison, but used in heart disease.

Strophe, strō'fē, *n.* [Gr. *strophē*, from *strepho*, to turn.] The part of a Greek choral ode sung in turning from the right to the left of the orchestra, *antistrophe* being the reverse; hence, in lyric poetry, a term for the former of two corresponding stanzas, the latter being the *antistrophe*.—**Strophic**, strō'fik, *a.* Relating to or consisting of strophes.

Strophiole, strō'fi-ōl, *n.* [L. *strophiolum*, a chaplet, dim. of *strophium*, Gr. *strophion*, a wreath.] *Bot.* a little tubercular part near the hilum of some seeds; a caruncle. —**Strophiolate, Strophiolated**, strō'fi-o-lāt, strō'fi-o-lā-ted, *a.* *Bot.* having strophioles.

Strove, strōv, pret. of *strive*.

Strow, strō, *v.t.*—pret. *strowed*; pp. *strowed* or *strown*. Same as *Strew*.

Struck, struk, pret. and pp. of *strike*.

Structure, struk'tūr, *n.* [L. *structura*, from *struo*, *structum*, to build, seen in *construct*, *instruct*, *destruction*, *destroy*, *construe*, &c.] A building of any kind, but chiefly a building of some size or magnificence; an edifice; manner of building; make; construction; the arrangement of the parts in a whole (the *structure* of a sentence, rock of a columnar *structure*); manner of organization; mode in which different organs or parts are arranged.—**Structural**, struk'tū-ral, *a.* Pertaining to structure.—**Structured**, struk'tūrd, *a.* Possessing a regular organic structure.—**Structureless**, struk'tūr-les, *a.* Devoid of regular organic structure.

Struggle, strug'l, *v.i.* —*struggled*, *struggling*. [Formerly *stroggle*, *strogle*; of doubtful origin; comp. O.Sw. *strug*, a quarrel.] To make efforts with contortions of the body; to use great efforts; to labour hard; to strive.—*n.* A violent effort with contortions of the body; a contortion of distress; a forcible effort to attain an object; an effort to get on in the world; contest; strife. —**Struggler**, strug'lėr, *n.* One who struggles.

Struldbrugs, struld-brugz, *n.* The loathsome objects condemned to a deathless and lingering life in Swift's Luggnag, in *Gulliver's Travels*.

Strum, strum, *v.i.* [An imitative word.] To play unskilfully and coarsely on a stringed instrument; to thrum.—*v.t.* To play on unskilfully or noisily.

Struma, strö'ma, *n.* pl. **Strumæ**, strö'mē. [L., from *struo*, to build.] A scrofulous swelling or tumour; scrofula; sometimes goitre; *bot.* a swelling at the extremity of a petiole, next the lamina of a leaf.—**Strumatic**, strö-mat'ik, *a.* Strumose.—**Strumiform**, strö'mi-form, *a.* Having the appearance of a struma.—**Strumose, Strumous**, strö'mōs, strö'mus, *a.* Scrofulous; *bot.* having strumæ.—**Strumousness, Strumosity**, strö'mus-nes, strö-mos'i-ti, *n.*

Strumpet, strum'pet, *n.* [Origin doubtful; perhaps from O.Fr. *strupre*, *stupre*, L. *stuprum*, fornication, debauchery.] A prostitute; a harlot.—*v.t.* To debauch.

Strung, strung, pret. of *string*.

Strut, strut, *v.i.*—*strutted*, *strutting*. [O.E. *strut*, *strout*, to swell or bulge, to strut; akin Dan. *strutte*, to strut, to stick out; L.G. *strutt*, sticking out; G. *strotzen*, to teem.] To walk with a lofty, proud gait and erect head; to walk with affected dignity or pompousness.—*n.* A lofty, proud step or walk with the head erect; affectation of dignity in walking; *carp.* a strengthening piece obliquely or diagonally placed; a brace; a stretching-piece. —**Strutter**, strut'ėr, *n.* One who struts.—**Struttingly**, strut'ing-li, *adv.*

Strychnia, Strychnine, strik'ni-a, strik'nin, *n.* [Gr. *strychnos*, a name of several plants of the nightshade order.] A vegetable alkaloid obtained from certain East Indian trees and especially from the seeds of nux-vomica, a most energetic poison, yet in very small doses used as a remedy in paralysis.—**Strychnic**, strik'nik, *a.* Pertaining to strychnine.

Stub, stub, *n.* [A.Sax. *styb*, a stub = Icel. *stubbi*, *stubbr*, *stobbi*, a stump, Dan. *stub*, stump, stubble; L.G. *stubbe*, D. *stobbe*, a stump: *stubble*, *stump*, *stubborn* are akin.] The stump of a tree or that part which remains in the earth when the tree is cut down; a stub-nail.—*v.t.*—*stubbed*, *stubbing*. To grub up by the roots; to clear of roots. —**Stubby**, stub'i, *a.* Abounding with stubs; short and thick.—**Stubbiness**, stub'i-nes, *n.* The state of being stubby.—**Stub-iron**, *n.* Iron from stub-nails, used principally for making gun-barrels of superior quality.—**Stub-nail**, *n.* A nail broken off; a short thick nail.

Stubble, stub'l, *n.* [A dim. form from *stub*; Dan. and Sw. *stub*, stubble.] The stumps of corn left in the ground; the part of the stalk left in the ground by the scythe or sickle.—**Stubbled**, stub'ld, *a.* Covered with stubble.—**Stubble-fed**, *a.* Fed, as cows or geese, on the fine natural grass that grows among stubble.—**Stubble-goose**, *n.* A goose fed among stubble.—**Stubbly**, stub'li, *a.* Covered with stubble; resembling stubble; short and stiff (a *stubbly* beard).

Stubborn, stub'orn, *a.* [From *stub*, A.Sax. *styb*, lit. like a *stub*, blockish, obstinate, with A.Sax. adj. term. *-or* and *-n* added.] Unreasonably or perversely obstinate; not to be moved or persuaded by reason; inflexible; refractory; not easily worked (as soil; metal); stiff; not flexible. ∴ Syn. under OBSTINATE.—**Stubbornly**, stub'orn-li, *adv.* In a stubborn manner; obstinately. —**Stubbornness**, stub'orn-nes, *n.* Perverse obstinacy; inflexibility.

Stucco, stuk'kō, *n.* [It., from O.H.G. *stucchi*, a crust.] A kind of fine plaster, used for cornices, mouldings, &c., of rooms—a composition of fine sand, pulverized marble, and gypsum mixed with water; also, a popular name for plaster of Paris or gypsum.—*v.t.* To overlay with stucco.—**Stuccoer**, stuk'kō-ėr, *n.* One who stuccoes.—**Stucco-work**, *n.* Ornamental work of stucco, such as cornices, mouldings, &c.

Stuck, stuk, pret. and pp. of *stick*.—**Stuck-up**, *a.* Giving one's self airs of importance or superiority; aping the manners of one's superiors. (*Colloq.*)

Stud, stud, *n.* [A.Sax. *studu*, a prop, a stud; Icel. *stoð*, Dan. *stöd*, D. *stut*, a prop, support; from stem of *steady*.] A nail with a large head, inserted chiefly for ornament; an ornamental knob; an ornamental button for a shirt front, transferable from one shirt to another; a supporting beam; a post or prop.—*v.t. studded*, *studding*. To adorn with studs or knobs; to set thickly, as with studs.—**Studded**, stud'ed, *a.* Set with studs; thickly set or sprinkled (*studded* with stars).

Stud, stud, *n.* [A.Sax. *stód*, a stud (whence *stódhors*, a stallion); Icel. *stóð*, Dan. *stod*, a stud; akin *steed*.] A collection of breeding horses and mares; a person's horses collectively.—**Stud-book**, *n.* A book containing a genealogy or register of horses or cattle of particular breeds.—**Stud-horse**, *n.* A breeding-horse.

Studding-sail, stud'ing, stunsl, *n.* [From *stud*, a support, or altered from *steadying-sail*.] *Naut.* a sail set on the outer edge of any of the principal sails during a light wind.

Student, stū-dent, *n.* [L. *studens*, *studentis*, ppr. of *studeo*, to study.] A person engaged in learning something from books, or attending some educational institution, especially of the higher class; one studying anything; a scholar; a man devoted to books; a bookish man.—**Studentship**, stū'dent-ship, *n.* The state of being a student. —**Studied**, stud'id, *p.* and *a.* Made the subject of study; well considered; qualified by study; premeditated; deliberate (a *studied* insult).—**Studiedly**, stud'id-li, *adv.* In a studied manner.—**Studier**, stud'i-ėr, *n.* One who studies.—**Studio**, stū'di-ō, *n.* [It., from L. *studium*, study.]

The working room of a painter or sculptor.—**Studious**, stū-di-us, *a.* [Fr. *studieux*, L. *studiosus*.] Given to study; devoted to the acquisition of knowledge from books; eager to discover something or to effect some object; earnest; eager (*studious* to please); attentive; careful: with *of*; deliberate; studied.—**Studiously**, stū'di-us-li, *adv.* In a studious manner; with zeal and earnestness; diligently.—**Studiousness**, stū'di-us-nes, *n.* The quality of being studious.—**Study**, stud'i, *n.* [L. *studium*, zeal, study, from *studeo*, to study.] Application of mind to books, to arts or science, or to any subject for the purpose of learning what is not before known; earnest endeavour; diligence; a branch of learning studied; an object of study; a building or apartment devoted to study; a fit of thought; a reverie; *fine arts*, a work undertaken for improvement, or a preparatory sketch to be used in the composition of more finished works.—*v.i. studied, studying.* To apply the mind to books or learning; to dwell in thought; to ponder; to be zealous.—*v.t.* To apply the mind to for the purpose of learning; to consider attentively; to examine closely; to con over, or to commit to memory; to have careful regard to (one's interest, comfort, &c.); to be solicitous for the good of.

Stuff, stuf, *n.* [O.Fr. *estoffe* (Fr. *étoffe*), stuff, material, from L. *stuppa*, tow. STOP.] Substance or matter indefinitely; the matter of which anything is formed; material; furniture; goods (O.T.); refuse or worthless matter; hence, foolish or irrational language; trash; *com.* a general name for fabrics of silk, wool, hair, cotton, &c.; particularly woolen cloth of slight texture, for linings, &c.; a melted mass of turpentine, tallow, etc., with which ships are smeared for preservation.—*v.t.* [In this sense = G. *stopfen*, to stuff or cram; E. to *stop* up.] To fill by packing or crowding material into; to cram; to crowd in together; to fill or pack with material necessary to make complete (to *stuff* a cushion); to fill the skin of, as of a dead animal, for presenting and preserving its form; to fill mentally full; to put fraudulent ballots into; as, to *stuff* the ballot-box; to crowd with facts or idle tales or fancies; *cookery*, to fill with seasoning (to *stuff* a leg of veal).—*v.i.* To feed gluttonously.—**Stuffer**, stuf'ėr, *n.* One who stuffs; one who stuffs the skins of animals to preserve them as specimens.—**Stuffing**, stuf'ing, *n.* That which is used to fill something.—**Stuffing-box**, *n.* A box with packing that prevents leakage around a piston rod.

Stuffy, stuf'i, *a.* [O.Fr. *estouffer*, to stifle, from *estoffe*, stuff. STUFF.] Difficult to breathe in; close; stifling; said of a room.—**Stuffiness**, stuf'i-nes, *n.* The state of being stuffy; closeness; mustiness.

Stultify, stul'ti-fī, *v.t.—stultified, stultifying.* [L. *stultus*, foolish; and *facio*, to make.] To make foolish; to make a fool of; to cause to appear as a fool.—**Stultification**, stul'ti-fi-kā"shon, *n.* The act of stultifying.—**Stultifier**, stul'ti-fī-ėr, *n.* One who stultifies.—**Stultiloquence**, stul-til'o-kwens, *n.* [L. *stultus*, and *loquentia*, a talking.] Foolish talk; a babbling.

Stum, stum, *n.* [From D. *stom*, unfermented wine, must, from *stom*, G. *stumm*, Dan. and Sw. *stum*, dumb, mute.] Unfermented grape juice; must or new wine; wine made by must to ferment anew.—*v.t.—stummed, stumming.* To renew by mixing with must and fermenting anew.

Stumble, stum'bl, *v.i.—stumbled, stumbling.* [O.E. *stomble, stomel*; allied to E. *stammer*, Prov. E. *stummer*, Icel. *stumra*, to stumble, N. *stumle*, to totter, L.G. *stumpeln*, to walk heavily.] To trip in walking; to make a false step; to stagger; to walk unsteadily; to fall into crime or error; to err; to strike upon without design; to light by chance: with *on* or *upon*.—*v.t.* To cause to stumble; to puzzle.—*n.* The act of stumbling; a trip in walking or running; a blunder.—**Stumbler**, stum'blėr, *n.* One that stumbles.—**Stumbling-block**, **Stumbling-stone**, *n.* Any cause of stumbling; that which forms a difficulty in one's way or which causes offence: used in figurative sense.—**Stumblingly**, stum'-bling-li, *adv.*

Stump, stump, *n.* [A nasalized form of *stub*, and = Dan. *stump*, Icel. *stumpr*, D. *stomp*, G. *stumpf*, a stump. STUB.] The root part of a tree remaining in the earth after the tree is cut down; the part of a limb or other body remaining after the rest is cut off or destroyed (the *stump* of a tooth, of a lead pencil); one of the three posts constituting the wicket in a game of cricket.—*On the stump*, going through a district and making speeches. [Originally American; the stump of a tree being often used as a platform in lately cleared districts.]—*v.t.* To lop; to make a tour through delivering speeches for political or personal purposes (to *stump* the country); *cricket*, to put out of play by knocking down a stump or stumps whilst the batsman is out of the crease.—*v.i.* To walk stiffly, heavily, or noisily.—*To stump up*, to pay or hand over money. (*Colloq.*)—**Stumper**, stump'ėr, *n.* One who stumps.—**Stump-orator**, *n.* A man who harangues the populace from the stump of a tree; a frothy or bombastic speaker.—**Stump-oratory**, *n.* Oratory such as that of a stump-orator.—**Stump-speech**, *n.* A speech made from the stump of a tree or other improvised platform; a frothy or bombastic harangue.—**Stumpy**, stump'i, *a.* Full of stumps; short or stubby (*colloq.*).

Stun, stun, *v.t.—stunned, stunning.* [A.Sax. *stunian*, to stun, from *stun*, noise; same root as Skr. *stan*, to thunder. ASTONISH.] To overpower the sense of hearing of; to confound by loud noise; to render insensible or dizzy by force or violence; to render senseless by a blow; to surprise completely; to overpower.—**Stunner**, stun'-ėr, *n.* Something first-rate; a person or thing of very showy appearance. (*Slang.*)—**Stunning**, stun'ing, *a.* First-rate; excellent. (*Slang.*)

Stundist, stund'ist, *n.* [Gr. *stunde*, hour.] One of the Russian sect of peasants rejecting the doctrines of the Orthodox Church, and following the mystic ideas of German pietists.

Stung, stung, pret. and pp. of *sting*.

Stunk, stungk, pret. of *stink*.

Stunt, stunt, *v.t.* [From A.Sax. *stunt*, blunt, stupid; Sw. *stunt*, docked, short; akin Icel. *stuttr*, short, stunted; G. *stutzen*, to dock. STINT.] To hinder from free growth; to check in growth; to dwarf.—*n.* A check in growth.—**Stunted**, stunt'ed, *p.* and *a.* Checked in growth; of dwarfish growth.—**Stuntedness**, stunt'ed-nes, *n.* The state of being stunted.

Stunt, stunt, *n.* A remarkable feat of skill; any enterprise, task, or undertaking.

Stupa, stö'pa, *n.* [Skr. *stûpa*.] A Buddhist sacred monumental structure, commemorating some event or marking some spot.

Stupe, stūp, *n.* [L. *stupa*, tow.] Flannel, flax, or similar substance wrung out of hot water, plain or medicated, applied to a wound or sore.

Stupefy, stū'pē-fī, *v.t.—stupefied, stupefying.* [Fr. *stupéfier*, from L. *stupefacere*—*stupeo*, to be struck senseless, and *facio*, to make. STUPID.] To deprive of sensibility; to make dull or dead to external influences; to make torpid.—**Stupefacient**, **Stupefactive**, stū-pē-fā'shi-ent, stū-pē-fak'tiv, *a.* Having a stupefying power.—*n.* A medicine which produces stupor; a narcotic.—**Stupefaction**, stū-pē-fak'shon, *n.* The state of being stupefied or stunned; a senseless state; insensibility; torpor.—**Stupefier**, stū'pē-fī-ėr, *n.* One who or that which stupefies.

Stupendous, stū-pen'dus, *a.* [L. *stupendus*, amazing, from *stupeo*, to be astonished. STUPID.] Striking dumb by magnitude; great and wonderful; of astonishing magnitude or elevation; grand.—**Stupendously**, stū-pen'dus-li, *adv.* In a stupendous manner.—**Stupendousness**, stū-pen'dus-nes, *n.*

Stupeous, **Stupose**, stū'pē-us, stū'pōs, *a.* [L. *stupa*, tow.] Resembling tow; covered with filaments like tow.

Stupid, stū'pid, *a.* [L. *stupidus*, from *stupeo*, to be astonished or struck senseless (seen also in *stupefy, stupendous*); perhaps same root as *stand*.] Bereft of consciousness, sense, or feeling; in a state of stupor; insensible; stupefied; devoid of understanding; possessed of dull gross folly; extremely dull of perception or understanding; nonsensical.—**Stupidity**, **Stupidness**, stū-pid'i-ti, stū'pid-nes, *n.* [L. *stupiditas*.] The state or quality of being stupid; stupor; astonishment; extreme dulness of understanding; dull foolishness.—**Stupidly**, stū'pid-li, *adv.* In a stupid manner.—**Stupify**, stū'pi-fī, *v.t.* Same as *Stupefy*.—**Stupor**, stū'por, *n.* [L. *stupor*, from *stupeo*.] Great diminution or total suspension of sensibility; a state in which the faculties are deadened or dazed; torpor.

Stuprate, stū'prāt, *v.t.—stuprated, stuprating.* [L. *stupro, stupratum*, to defile, from *stuprum*, defilement.] To ravish; to debauch.—**Stupration**, stū-prā'shon, *n.* Rape; violation of chastity by force.

Sturdy, stėr'di, *a.* [O.Fr. *estourdi* (Fr. *étourdi*), stupid, inconsiderate, from L. *ex*, intens., and *torpidus*, torpid.] Stubborn‡; stiff-necked‡; exhibiting strength or force; forcible; vigorous; robust in body; strong; stout; vigorous and hardy.—**Sturdily**, stėr'di-li, *adv.* In a sturdy manner; stoutly; lustily.—**Sturdiness**, stėr'di-nes, *n.* The state or quality of being sturdy.

Sturdy, stėr'di, *n.* [Gael. *stuird, stuirdean*, vertigo, sturdy.] A disease in sheep, marked by staggering, vertigo, stupor, &c.

Sturgeon, stėr'jon, *n.* [Fr. *esturgeon*, from L.L. *sturio*, from O.H.G. *sturio*, A.Sax. *styria*, a sturgeon.] A genus of large fishes having a skin protected with rows of bony plates; flesh valuable as food; roes converted into caviare, and air-bladder into isinglass.

Stutter, stut'ėr, *v.i.* [Same as D. and L.G. *stotteren*, G. *stottern*, to stutter; freq. forms corresponding to Prov.E. *stut*, to stutter; Sc. *stot*, to rebound; Icel. *stauta*, to strike.] To stammer; to hesitate in uttering words.—*n.* A stammer; a hesitation in speaking.—**Stutterer**, stut'ėr-ėr, *n.* One who stutters; a stammerer.—**Stuttering**, stut'ėr-ing, *n.* A stutter or stammer.—**Stutteringly**, stut'ėr-ing-li, *adv.*

Sty, stī, *n.* [A.Sax. *stige*, a sty or pen = Icel. *stía*, Dan. *sti*, Sw. *stia*, O.H.G. *stiga*, a sty. The first part of *steward* is this word.] A pen or inclosure for swine; any filthy hovel or place; a place of bestial debauchery.—*v.t.—stied, stying.* To shut up in a sty.

Sty, **Styan**, stī, stī'an, *n.* Same as *Stye*.

Stye, stī, *n.* [A.Sax. *stigend*, a tumour on the eye, from *stigan*, to rise; akin *stair*.] A small inflammatory tumour on the edge of the eyelid, particularly near the inner angle of the eye. Written also *Sty*.

Stygian, stij'i-an, *a.* [L. *Stygius*, from *Styx*, Gr. *Styx, Stygos*, the Styx, from *stygeō*, to hate.] Pertaining to Styx, fabled by the ancients to be a river of hell over which the shades of the dead passed; hence, hellish; infernal.

Style, stīl, *n.* [Fr. *style*, from L. *stilus*, *stylus*, a stake, pointed instrument, style for writing, hence mode of expression; from root of *stimulus, stick, sting*. Spelling influenced by Gr. *stylos*, a pillar.] A pointed instrument used by the ancients for writing by scratching on wax tablets; anything of a similar kind; a pointed tool used in graving; a pointed surgical instrument; the pin or gnomon of a sundial; *bot.* the prolongation of the summit of the ovary which supports the stigma; manner of writing with regard to language; a distinctive manner of writing belonging to an author or body of authors; a characteristic mode of presentation in any of the fine arts; particular type of architecture pervading a building (the Gothic *style*); external manner, mode, or fashion; manner deemed elegant and appropriate; fashion (a person dressed in the *style*); a formal or official designation; title (a person's *style* and title); *chron.* a mode of reckoning time with regard to the Julian and Gregorian calendars. *Old Style* followed the Julian manner of computing the months and days, in which the year consists of 365 days and 6 hours, or something more than 11 minutes too much. The Gregorian or *New Style*, according to the calendar as reformed by Pope Gregory XIII in 1582, was adopted in England in 1752, and now almost everywhere prevails. ∴ Syn. under DICTION.—*v.t.*—*styled, styling.* To term; to name or call; to designate or denominate.—**Stylet**, stī'let, *n.* *Surg.* a probe.—**Stylar**, stī'lėr, *a.* Pertaining to a style.—**Stylate**, stī'lāt, *a.* *Bot.* having a persistent style.—**Styliform**, stī'li-form, *a.* Having the shape of or resembling a style; styloid.—**Styline**, stī'lin, *a.* *Bot.* pertaining to the style.—**Stylish**, stīl'ish, *a.* Being in fashionable form or in high style; being quite in the mode or fashion; showy.—**Stylishly**, stīl'ish-li, *adv.* In a stylish manner; showily.—**Stylishness**, stīl'ish-nes, *n.* The state or quality of being stylish; showiness.—**Stylist**, stīl'ist, *n.* A writer or speaker who is careful of his style; a master of style.—**Stylistic**, stī-lis'tik, *a.* Relating to style.—**Stylography**, stī-log'ra-fi, *n.* A method of writing or engraving with a style.—**Stylographic, Stylographical**, stī-lō-graf'ik, stī-lō-graf'i-kal, *a.* Pertaining to stylography.—**Styloid**, stī'loid, *a.* Having some resemblance to a style or pen.

Stylite, stī'līt, *n.* [Gr. *stylitēs*, from *stylos*, a pillar.] A pillar-saint, one of those ascetics who, by way of penance, passed the greater part of their lives on the top of high columns or pillars.

Stylobate, stī'lō-bāt, *n.* [L. *stylobates, stylobata*, from Gr. *stylobatēs*—*stylos*, a pillar, and *bainō*, to go.] *Arch.* a continuous and unbroken pedestal or elevation upon which a range of columns stands.

Stylography. Under STYLE.

Stylometer, stī-lom'et-ėr, *n.* [Gr. *stylos*, a column, and *metron*, a measure.] An instrument for measuring columns.—**Stylospore**, stī'lō-spōr, *n.* *Bot.* a spore in certain fungi at the tip of a short threadlike body.

Stylus, stī'lus, *n.* A style.

Stymie, stī'mi, *n.* The position in golf when the opponent's ball lies between the player's ball and the hole.

Styptic, Styptical, stip'tik, stip'ti-kal, *a.* [L. *stypticus*, from Gr. *styptikos*, from *styphō*, to contract.] Astringent‡; having the quality of stopping the bleeding of a wound.—**Styptic**, *n.* A substance that checks a flow of blood by application to the bleeding surface.—**Stypticity**, stip-tis'i-ti, *n.* The quality of being styptic.

Styrax, stī'raks, *n.* [L. and Gr. *styrax* or *storax*.] The genus of plants that yield storax.—**Styracin**, stī'ra-sin, *n.* A crystalline substance extracted from storax.—**Styrole, Styrol**, stī'rōl, *n.* Oil of storax.

Styx, *n.* Chief river in Hades or the lower world which had to be crossed by the dead.

Suasion, swā'zhon, *n.* [L. *suasio, suasionis*, from *suadeo, suasum*, to advise (as in *dissuade, persuade*).] The act of persuading.—**Suasive**, swā'ziv, *a.* Having power to persuade.—**Suasively**, swā'ziv-li, *adv.* In a manner tending to persuade.—**Suasory**, swā'zo-ri, *a.* [L. *suasorius.*] Tending to persuade.

Suave, swāv, *a.* [Fr. *suave*, sweet, pleasant, from L. *suavis*, sweet; same root as *suadeo*, to persuade, and as E. *sweet.*] Gracious or agreeable in manner: blandly polite; pleasant.—**Suavely**, swāv'li, *adv.* In a suave manner; blandly.—**Suavity**, swāv'i-ti, *n.* [Fr. *suavité*, L. *suavitas.*] The state or quality of being suave; graciousness and politeness of address; pleasantness.

Sub, sub, *n.* A colloquial contraction for Submarine; also *pref.* under; inferior; somewhat.

Subacid, sub-as'id, *a.* [L. *sub*, slightly.] Moderately acid or sour.—*n.* A substance moderately acid.

Subacrid, sub-ak'rid, *a.* [L. *sub*, slightly.] Moderately pungent or acrid.

Subacute, sub-a-kūt', *a.* [L. *sub*, slightly.] Acute or pointed in a modified degree.

Subaerial, sub-ā-ē'ri-al, *a.* [L. *sub*, under, *aer*, the air.] Under the air or sky; *geol.* used of phenomena taking place on the earth's surface under the open air: opposed to *subaqueous.*

Subah, sö'bä, *n.* [Per. and Hind., a province.] In India, a province or viceroyship.—**Subahdar, Subadar**, sö-bä-där', *n.* A ruler of a province.

Subalate, sub-ā'lāt, *a.* [L. *sub*, slightly.] *Bot.* slightly alate.

Subalpine, sub-al'pīn, *a.* [L. *sub*, under.] Belonging to a region on lofty mountains immediately below the Alpine.

Subaltern, sub'al-tėrn or sub-al'tėrn, *a.* [L. *subalternus*, subordinate—*sub*, under, *alter*, another.] Holding an inferior or subordinate position; in the army below the rank of a captain.—*n.* A commissioned military officer below the rank of captain.—**Subalternate**, sub-al-tėr'nāt, *a.* Subordinate; successive.—**Subalternation**, sub-al'tėr-nā"shon, *n.* State of inferiority or subjection.

Subangular, sub-ang'gū-lėr, *a.* [L. *sub*, slightly.] Slightly angular.

Subapical, sub-ap'i-kal, *a.* [L. *sub*, under.] Under the apex; pertaining to the part below the apex.

Subaquatic, Subaqueous, sub-a-kwat'ik, sub-ak'wē-us, *a.* [L. *sub*, under, and *aqua*, water.] Being under water; *geol.* formed under water; deposited under water.

Subarborescent, sub-är'bor-es"ent, *a.* [L. *sub*, slightly.] Having a somewhat treelike aspect.

Subarctic, sub-ärk'tik, *a.* [L. *sub*, slightly.] Applied to a region or climate next to the arctic; approximately arctic.

Subastringent, sub-as-trin'jent, *a.* [L. *sub*, slightly.] Astringent in a small degree.

Subaudition, sub-a-dish'on, *n.* [L. *subauditio*, from *subaudio*, to understand or supply a word omitted—*sub*, under, and *audio*, to hear.] The act of understanding something not expressed.

Subaxillary, sub-ak'sil-la-ri, *a.* [L. *sub*, under, and *axilla*, the arm-pit.] Under the arm-pit or the cavity of the wing; *bot.* placed under the axil.

Subbreed, sub'brēd, *n.* [L. *sub*, under.] A subdivision of a breed.

Subcalcareous, sub-kal-kā'rē-us, *a.* [L. *sub*, slightly.] Somewhat calcareous.

Subcartilaginous, sub-kär'ti-laj"i-nus, *a.* [L. *sub*, under or slightly.] Situated under or beneath cartilage; partially gristly.

Subcaudal, sub-ka'dal, *a.* [L. *sub*, under, *cauda*, a tail.] Lying or situated beneath the tail.

Subcentral, sub-sen'tral, *a.* [L. *sub*, under, slightly.] Being under the centre; nearly central.

Subcircular, sub-sėr'kū-lėr, *a.* [L. *sub*, slightly.] Somewhat or nearly circular.

Subclass, sub'klas, *n.* [L. *sub*, under.] A subdivision of a class, consisting of allied orders.

Subclavian, sub-klā'vi-an, *a.* [L. *sub*, under, and *clavis*, a key, used in sense of Gr. *kleis*, the collar-bone.] Situated under the clavicle or collar-bone.

Subcolumnar, sub-ko-lum'nėr, *a.* [L. *sub*, slightly.] *Geol.* approximately columnar.

Subcommittee, sub-kom-mit'ē, *n.* [L. *sub*, under.] An under committee; a part or division of a committee.

Subcompressed, sub-kom-prest', *a.* [L. *sub*, slightly.] Partially or somewhat compressed.

Subconcave, sub-kon'kāv, *a.* [L. *sub*, slightly.] Slightly concave.

Subconical, sub-kon'i-kal, *a.* [L. *sub*, slightly.] Slightly conical.

Subcontract, sub'kon-trakt, *n.* [L. *sub*, under.] A contract under a previous contract.—**Subcontractor**, sub-kon-trak'tėr, *n.* One who takes a portion of a contract from the principal contractor.

Subcontrary, sub-kon'tra-ri, *a.* [L. *sub*, under, slightly.] Contrary to an inferior degree; *geom.* applied to two similar triangles so placed as to have a common angle at their vertex, and their bases not parallel or coincident; *logic*, applied to the relation between two attributes which co-exist in such a way that the more there is of one the less there is of the other.

Subcordate, sub-kor'dāt, *a.* [L. *sub*, slightly.] Somewhat cordate; in shape somewhat like a heart.

Subcostal, sub-kos'tal, *a.* [L. *sub*, under, and *costa*, a rib.] Situated under or between the ribs.

Subcranial, sub-krā'ni-al, *a.* [L. *sub*, under.] Under the cranium or skull.

Subcrystalline, sub-kris'tal-īn, *a.* [L. *sub*, slightly.] Imperfectly crystallized.

Subcutaneous, sub-kū-tā'nē-us, *a.* [L. *sub*, under, *cutis*, skin.] Situated immediately under the skin.—*Subcutaneous syringe*, a syringe for injecting substances beneath the skin.—**Subcuticular**, sub-kū-tik'ū-lėr, *a.* Being under the cuticle or scarf-skin.

Subcylindrical, sub-si-lin'dri-kal, *a.* [L. *sub*, slightly.] Approximately or imperfectly cylindrical.

Subdeacon, sub'dē-kn, *n.* [L. *sub*, under.] In the *R. Cath. Ch.* an ecclesiastic subordinate to the deacon.—**Subdeaconry, Subdeaconship**, sub'dē-kn-ri, sub'dē-kn-ship, *n.* The office of a subdeacon.

Subdean, sub'dēn, *n.* [L. *sub*, under.] An under dean; a dean's substitute.—**Subdeanery**, sub'dē-nėr-i, *n.* The office and rank of subdean.—**Subdecanal**, sub-dek'a-nal, *a.* Relating to a subdean.

Subdialect, sub'dī-a-lekt, *n.* [L. *sub*, under.] An inferior or less important dialect.

Subdititious, sub-di-tish'us, *a.* [L. *subdititius*, from *subdo, subditum*, to substitute—*sub*, under, and *do*, to give.] Put secretly in the place of something else; foisted in.

Subdivide, sub-di-vīd', *v.t.*—*subdivided, subdividing.* [L. *subdivido*—*sub*, under, and *divido.* DIVIDE.] To divide the parts of into more parts; to part into subdivisions.—*v.i.* To be subdivided.—**Subdivisible**, sub-di-viz'i-bl, *a.* Susceptible of subdivision.—**Subdivision**, sub-di-vizh'on, *n.* The act of subdividing; one of the parts of a larger part.

Subdolous, sub'do-lus, *a.* [L. *subdolus*, cunning, sly—*sub*, slightly, and *dolus*, deceit.] Somewhat crafty; cunning; artful.

Subdominant, sub-dom'i-nant, *n.* [L. *sub*, under.] *Mus.* the fourth note of the diatonic scale lying a tone under the dominant or fifth of the scale.

Subduce, Subduct, sub-dūs', sub-dukt', *v.t.* [L. *subduco, subductum*—*sub*, under, and *duco*, to draw, to lead.] To withdraw; to take away; to subtract by arithmetical operation.—**Subduction**, sub-duk'shon, *n.* The act of subducting; subtraction.

Subdue, sub-dū', *v.t.*—*subdued, subduing.* [O.Fr. *subduzer*, to subdue, from L. *sub*, under, and *duco*, to lead. DUKE.] To conquer and bring into permanent subjection; to reduce under dominion; to overpower by superior force; to vanquish; to overcome by discipline; to tame; to prevail over by some mild or softening influence; to gain complete sway over; to melt or soften (the heart, opposition); to tone down or make less glaring. ∴ Syn. under CONQUER.—**Subdual**, sub-dū'al, *n.* The act of subduing.—**Subduable**, sub-dū'a-bl, *a.* Capable of being subdued.—**Subdued**, sub-dūd', *p.* and *a.* Vanquished; made mild or tractable; submissive; toned down or softened.—**Subduer**, sub-dū'ėr, *n.* One who subdues; a conqueror; a tamer.

Subduple, sub-dū'pl, *a.* [L. *sub*, under, and *duplus*, double.] Containing one part of two.—*Subduple ratio*, the ratio of 1 to 2.

Subduplicate, sub-dū-pli-kāt, *a.* [*Sub*, under, and *duplicate*.] *Math.* expressed by the square root.—*Subduplicate ratio* of two quantities, the ratio of their square roots.

Subeditor, sub-ed'i-tėr, *n.* [L. *sub*, under.] An assistant editor of a periodical or other publication.

Subepidermal, sub-ep-i-dėr'mal, *a.* [L. *sub*, under.] Lying immediately under the epidermis.

Subereous, Suberose, Suberous, sū-bē'rē-us, sū'bėr-ōs, sū'bėr-us, *a.* [L. *suber*, cork.] Of the nature of cork.—**Suberic**, sū-bėr'ik, *a.* Pertaining to cork.

Subfamily, sub'fam-i-li, *n.* [L. *sub*, under.] *Nat. hist.* a subdivision of a family; a subordinate family.

Subfeudatory, sub-fū'da-to-ri, *n.* [L. *sub*, under.] One who held a fief from a feudatory of the crown or other superior.

Subfossil, sub-fos'sil, *n.* and *a.* [L. *sub*, slightly.] Applied to remains only partially fossilized.

Subgenus, sub'jē-nus, *n.* [L. *sub*, under.] A subdivision of a genus comprising one or more species.—**Subgeneric**, sub-je-ner'ik, *a.* Pertaining to a subgenus.

Subglobular, sub-glob'ū-lėr, *a.* [L. *sub*, slightly.] Having a form approaching to globular.

Subgranular, sub-gran'ū-lėr, *a.* [L. *sub*, slightly.] Somewhat granular.

Subgroup, sub'gröp, *n.* [L. *sub*, under.] In scientific classifications, the subdivision of a group.

Subinfeudation, sub-in'fū-dā"shon, *n.* [L. *sub*, under.] The enfeoffment of a subordinate tenant by the holder of a fief.

Subjacent, sub-jā'sent, *a.* [L. *subjacens*, *subjacentis*, from *subjaceo*, to lie under—*sub*, under, and *jaceo*, to lie (as in *adjacent*, *circumjacent*).] Lying under or below; *geol.* applied to rocks, beds, or strata which lie under or are covered by others.

Subject, sub'jekt, *a.* [L. *subjectus*, pp. of *subjicio*, to place under—*sub*, under, and *jacio*, to throw (whence *object*, *eject*, *inject*, *jet*, &c.).] Placed under‡; being under the power and dominion of another; ruled by another state; liable, from extraneous or inherent causes; exposed (*subject to* headache). ∴ Syn. under LIABLE.—*n.* One who owes allegiance to a sovereign; one who lives under and owes allegiance to a government; a person as the recipient of certain treatment; that which is treated or operated on; a dead body for the purposes of dissection; that which is spoken of, thought of, treated of, or handled; matter dealt with; theme of discourse; *logic*, that term of a proposition of which the other is affirmed or denied; *gram.* that which is spoken of; the nominative of a verb; *philos.* the mind, soul, or personality of the thinker—the *Ego*; the thinking agent or principle, the *object*, which is its correlative, being anything or everything external to the mind; *mus.* the principal theme of a movement; *fine arts*, the incident chosen by an artist; the design of a composition or picture.—*v.t.* (sub-jekt'). To bring under; to subdue; to expose; to make liable; to cause to undergo; to expose, as in chemical or other operations: usually with *to* following in all senses (to *subject* a person to ridicule).—**Subjection**, sub-jek'shon, *n.* The act of subjecting or subduing; the state of being under the control and government of another; subjugation; enthralment.—**Subjective**, sub-jek'tiv, *a.* Relating to the subject, as opposed to the *object*; belonging to one's own mind and not to what is external; belonging to ourselves, the conscious *subject*; in *literature* and *art*, characterized by prominence of the personality of the author or artist (the writings of Shelley and Byron are *subjective*).—**Subjectively**, sub-jek'tiv-li, *adv.* In a subjective manner; as existing in thought or mind.—**Subjectiveness**, sub-jek'tiv-nes, *n.* Subjectivity.—**Subjectivism**, sub-jek'tiv-izm, *n.* *Metaph.* the doctrine that all human knowledge is merely relative.—**Subjectivity**, sub-jek-tiv'i-ti, *n.* The state of being subjective or in the mind alone; the character of exhibiting the individuality of an author or artist.—**Subject-matter**, *n.* The theme or matter discussed or spoken of.

Subjoin, sub-join', *v.t.* [L. *sub*, under, near.] To add at the end; to add after something else has been said or written.—**Subjoinder**, sub-join'dėr, *n.* A rejoinder.

Subjugate, sub'jū-gāt, *v.t.*—*subjugated*, *subjugating*. [L. *subjugo*, *subjugatum*—*sub*, under, and *jugum*, a yoke. JOIN, YOKE.] To subdue and bring under dominion; to conquer and compel to submit.—**Subjugation**, sub-jū-gā'shon, *n.* The act of subjugating; subjection.—**Subjugator**, sub'jū-gāt-ėr, *n.* One who subjugates.

Subjunctive, sub-jungk'tiv, *a.* [L. *subjunctivus*, from *subjungo*, *subjunctum*—*sub*, under, near, and *jungo*, to join.] Subjoined‡; *gram.* designating a mood or form of verbs expressing condition, hypothesis, or contingency, generally subjoined or subordinate to another verb, and preceded by a conjunction.—*n.* *Gram.* the subjunctive mood.

Subkingdom, sub'king-dum, *n.* [L. *sub*, under.] One of the great primary groups into which the animal kingdom is divided.

Sublapsarian, sub-lap-sā'ri-an, *n.* [L. *sub*, under, and *lapsus*, a sliding, a fall.] One who maintains the theological doctrine that God permitted the fall of man, and after it elected certain persons to salvation passing over others.

Sublease, sub'lēs, *n.* [L. *sub*, under.] *Law*, an under lease; a lease granted to a subtenant.—**Sublessee**, sub-les-sē', *n.* The receiver or holder of a sublease.

Sublet, sub-let', *v.t.* [L. *sub*, under.] To underlet; to let to another person, the party letting being himself lessee of the subject.

Sublibrarian, sub'lī-brā-ri-an, *n.* An under librarian; an assistant librarian.

Sublieutenant, sub'lef-ten-ant, *n.* An inferior or second lieutenant.

Sublimate, sub'li-māt, *v.t.*—*sublimated*, *sublimating*. [L. *sublimo*, *sublimatum*, to raise, elevate. SUBLIME.] To bring by heat from the solid state into the state of vapour, which on cooling again becomes solid; *fig.* to refine and exalt; to elevate.—*n.* What is produced by sublimation.—*Corrosive sublimate*. CORROSIVE.—*Blue sublimate*, a preparation of mercury with sulphur and sal ammoniac, used in painting.—**Sublimation**, sub-li-mā'shon, *n.* The process of sublimating; a process by which solids are by heat converted into vapour that again becomes solid.—**Sublimatory**, sub'li-ma-to-ri, *n.* A vessel used in sublimation.—*a.* Employed or used in sublimation.—**Sublimable**, sub-lī'ma-bl, *a.* Capable of being sublimated.

Sublime, sub-līm', *a.* [L. *sublimis*, elevated, exalted, lofty, sublime; origin doubtful.] High in place; elevated; high in excellence; elevated far above men in general by lofty or noble traits: said of persons; striking the mind with a sense of grandeur or power; calculated to awaken, or expressive of, awe, veneration, or lofty feeling; grand; noble: said of objects, of scenery, of an action or exploit, &c.—*The sublime*, what is sublime; sublimity; what is grand or lofty in style; the grand in the works of nature or art, as distinguished from the beautiful.—*v.t.*—*sublimed*, ppr. *subliming*. To exalt or render sublime; to dignify; to ennoble; to sublimate (which see).—*v.i.* To be susceptible of sublimation.—**Sublimely**, sub-līm'li, *adv.* In a sublime manner; grandly; majestically; loftily.—**Sublimeness**, sub-līm'nes, *n.* Sublimity.—**Sublimity**, sub-lim'i-ti, *n.* [Fr. *sublimité*; L. *sublimitas*.] The state or quality of being sublime; grandeur; loftiness of nature or character; moral grandeur; loftiness of conception, sentiment, or style; elevation, whether exhibited in the works of nature or of art; the emotion produced by what is sublime.

Subliminal, sub-lim'i-nal, *a.* [L.L. *sub*, under, *limen*, threshold.] Below consciousness; in the mind without our knowing it.

Sublineation, sub-lin'ē-ā"shon, *n.* [L. *sub*, under, *linea*, a line.] A line under a word or words.

Sublingual, sub-ling'gwal, *a.* [L. *sub*, under, *lingua*, the tongue.] Situated under the tongue.

Sublittoral, sub-lit'ō-ral, *a.* [L. *sub*, under, and *litus*, *littoris*, the shore.] Under or close to the shore.

Sublunary, sub'lū-na-ri, *a.* [L. *sub*, under, *luna*, the moon.] *Lit.* situated under the moon; hence, pertaining to this world; mundane; earthly; worldly.—**Sublunar**, sub-lū'nėr, *a.* Situated beneath the moon.

Subluxation, *n.* [L. *sub*, slightly.] *Surg.* an incomplete luxation or dislocation; a sprain.

Submammary, sub-mam'a-ri, *n.* [L. *sub*, under, *mamma*, the breast.] Situated under the mammæ or paps.

Submarginal, sub-mär'ji-nal, *a.* [L. *sub*, near.] *Bot.* situated near the margin.

Submarine, sub-ma-rēn', *a.* [L. *sub*, under, and *mare*, the sea. MARINE.] Situated, existing, acting, or growing at some depth in the waters of the sea; remaining at the bottom or under the surface of the sea (*submarine* plants).—*n.* A vessel that can be submerged at will and sail under the water. Submarines are chiefly intended to attack other vessels by means of torpedoes. They are driven by oil-engines when on the surface, and by electric motors when submerged.—*Submarine forest*, a collection of roots and stems of trees, &c., occupying the sites on which they grew, but now submerged by the sea.—*Submarine telegraph*, a telegraph cable laid along the bottom of the sea.

Submaxillary, sub-mak-sil'la-ri, *a.* [L. *sub*, under, and *maxilla*, the jaw.] Situated under the jaw.

Submediant, sub-mē'di-ant, *n.* [L. *sub*, under, *medius*, middle.] *Mus.* the sixth note of the diatonic scale, or middle note between the octave and subdominant.

Submental, sub-men'tal, *a.* [L. *sub*, under, and *mentum*, the chin.] *Anat.* situated under the chin.

Submerge, sub-mėrj', *v.t.*—*submerged*, *submerging*. [L. *submergo*—*sub*, under, and *mergo*, to plunge. MERGE.] To put under water; to plunge; to cover or overflow with water; to drown.—*v.i.* To plunge under water; to sink out of sight.—**Submergence**, sub-mėr'jens, *n.* Act of submerging.—**Submerse, Submersed**, sub-mėrs', sub-mėrst', *a.* *Bot.* being or growing under water.—**Submersible**, sub-mėr'si-bl, *n.* A submarine, especially one with projecting ballast tanks.—**Submersion**, sub-mėr'shon, *n.* [L. *submersio*, *submersionis*.] The act of putting or state of being put under water or other fluid; a dipping or plunging; a state of being overflowed.

Submetallic, sub-me-tal'ik, *a.* [L. *sub*, slightly.] Imperfectly or partially metallic.

Submit, sub-mit', *v.t.*—*submitted*, *submitting*. [L. *submitto*, to put under, submit—*sub*, under, and *mitto*, to send. MISSION.] To yield to the power or will of another: used *refl.*; to place under the control of another; to surrender; to leave to the discretion or judgment of another; to refer.—*v.i.* To yield one's person to the power of another; to surrender; to yield one's opinion; to acquiesce; to be submissive; to yield without murmuring.—**Submitter**, sub-mit'ėr, *n.* One who submits.—**Submission**, sub-mish'on, *n.* [L. *submissio*, *submissionis*.] The act of submitting, yielding, or surrendering; the state of being submissive; humble or suppliant behaviour; meekness; resignation; compliance with the commands of a superior; obedience.—**Submissive**, sub-mis'iv, *a.* Disposed, or ready to submit; compliant; obedient; humble; meek. — **Submissively**, sub-mis′iv-li, *adv.* In a submissive manner; meekly; humbly. — **Submissiveness**, sub-mis′iv-nes, *n.* The character of being submissive; ready compliance; meekness.

Submucous, sub-mū′kus, *a.* [L. *sub*, under.] *Anat.* lying under or pertaining to the parts under a mucous membrane.

Submultiple, sub-mul′ti-pl, *n.* [L. *sub*, under.] A number or quantity which is contained in another a certain number of times.

Submuscular, sub-mus′kū-lėr, *a.* [L. *sub*, under.] *Anat.* lying under or pertaining to parts under a muscle.

Subnarcotic, sub-när-kot′ik, *a.* [L. *sub*, slightly.] Moderately narcotic.

Subnascent, sub-nas′ent, *a.* [L. *sub*, under, *nascor*, to grow.] Growing underneath.

Subnormal, sub-nor′mal, *n.* [L. *sub*, under.] The portion of a diameter intercepted between the ordinate and the normal to any curve. Below normal.

Subnude, sub-nūd′, *a.* [L. *sub*, slightly, *nudus*, naked.] *Bot.* almost naked or bare of leaves.

Subobtuse, sub-ob-tūs′, *a.* [L. *sub*, slightly.] Somewhat or partially obtuse.

Suboccipital, sub-ok-sip′i-tal, *a.* [L. *sub*, under.] Being under the occiput.

Suboperculum, sub-ō-pėr′kū-lum, *n.* [L. *sub*, under, and *operculum.*] The lower part or section of the gill-covers of a fish. OPERCULUM. — **Subopercular**, sub-ō-pėr′kū-lėr, *a.* Pertaining to the suboperculum.

Suborbital, sub-or′bi-tal, *a.* [L. *sub*, under.] Beneath the orbital cavity; infraorbital.

Suborder, sub-or′dėr, *n.* [L. *sub*, under.] A subdivision of an order in classifications; a group of animals or plants greater than a genus and less than an order.

Subordinate, sub-or′di-nāt, *a.* [L. *sub*, under, and *ordinatus*, pp. of *ordino*, to set in order, from *ordo*, order. ORDER.] Placed in a low order, class, or rank; occupying a lower position in a scale; inferior in nature, power, importance, &c.—*v.t.*—*subordinated, subordinating.* To place below something else; to make or consider as of less value or importance; to make subject. —*n.* One inferior in power, rank, dignity, office, &c.: one below and under the orders of another.—**Subordinately**, sub-or′di-nāt-li, *adv.* In a subordinate manner; in a lower rank, dignity, &c. — **Subordination**, sub-or′di-nā″shon, *n.* The act of subordinating; gradation of ranks one below another; the state of being under control or government; subjection. — **Subordinative**, sub-or′di-nā-tiv, *a.* Tending to subordinate. — **Subordinacy, Subordinance**, sub-or′di-na-si, sub-or′di-nans, *n.* The state of being subordinate.

Suborn, sub-orn′, *v.t.* [Fr. *suborner*, from L. *suborno*, to prepare secretly, to suborn —*sub*, under, and *orno*, to equip, adorn. ORNAMENT.] To bribe to commit perjury; to induce to give false testimony or do some other wickedness. — **Subornation**, sub-or-nā′shon, *n.* The crime of suborning.— *Subornation of perjury*, the inducing of any person to commit perjury.—**Suborner**, sub-or′nėr, *n.* One who suborns.

Subovate, sub-ō′vāt, *a.* [L. *sub*, slightly.] Almost ovate; nearly in the form of an egg.

Subpellucid, sub-pel-lū′sid, *a.* [L. *sub*, slightly.] Nearly or almost pellucid.

Subperitoneal, sub-per′i-tō-nē″al, *a.* [L. *sub*, under.] *Anat.* situated under the peritoneum.

Subplinth, sub′plinth, *n.* [L. *sub*, under.] *Arch.* a second and lower plinth under the principal.

Subpœna, sub-pē′na, *n.* [L. *sub*, and *pœna*, pain, penalty.] *Law*, a writ or process commanding the attendance in a court of justice of the witness on whom it is served under a penalty.—*v.t.*—*subpœnaed, subpœnaing.* To serve with a writ of subpœna.

Subpolar, sub-pō′lėr, *a.* [L. *sub*, under.] Under or below the poles of the earth; adjacent to the poles.

Subprefect, sub-prē′fekt, *n.* [L. *sub*, under.] A subordinate or deputy prefect.

Subprior, sub′prī-or, *n.* [L. *sub*, under.] *Eccles.* the vicegerent of a prior.

Subpubic, sub-pū′bik, *a.* [L. *sub*, under.] *Anat.* situated under the pubes.

Subquadrate, sub-kwod′rāt, *a.* [L. *sub*, slightly.] Nearly quadrate or square.

Subreader, sub-rē′dėr, *n.* [L. *sub*, under.] An under reader in the inns of court. [Eng.]

Subrector, sub-rek′tėr, *n.* [L. *sub*, under.] A rector's deputy or substitute.

Subrigid, sub-rij′id, *a.* [L. *sub*, slightly.] Somewhat rigid or stiff.

Subsaline, sub-sa-līn′, *a.* [L. *sub*, slightly.] Moderately saline or salt.

Subsaturated, sub-sat′ū-rā-ted, *a.* [L. *sub*, slightly.] Not completely saturated.

Subscapular, sub-skap′ū-lėr, *a.* [L. *sub*, under.] Beneath the scapula or shoulder-blade.

Subscribe, sub-skrīb′, *v.t.* — *subscribed, subscribing.* [L. *subscribo*—*sub*, under, and *scribo*, to write. SCRIBE.] To write one's signature beneath; to sign with one's own hand; to consent or bind one's self to by writing one's name beneath; to attest by writing one's name; to promise to give by writing one's name (to *subscribe* money).— *v.i.* To promise along with others a certain sum by setting one's name to a paper; to give consent; to assent; to enter one's name for a newspaper, a book, &c.—**Subscriber**, sub-skrī′bėr, *n.* One who subscribes; one who admits, confirms, or binds himself to a promise or obligation by signing his name; one who contributes to an undertaking by paying or promising; one who enters his name for a newspaper, periodical, book, or the like.—**Subscribable**, sub-skrī′ba-bl, *a.* Capable or being subscribed. — **Subscript**, sub′skript, *a.* Underwritten; written below something.— **Subscription**, sub-skrip′shon, *n.* [L. *subscriptio.*] The act of subscribing or signing; the signature attached to a paper; a sum subscribed or promised by signature; a sum contributed along with other subscribers; the amount subscribed.

Subsection, sub′sek-shon, *n.* [L. *sub*, under.] Half an artillery section, that is, one gun with its complement of men, horses, and ammunition-wagons.

Subsellium, sub-sel′li-um, *n.* pl. **Subsellia**, sub-sel′li-a. [L. *subsellium*, a seat —*sub*, under, and *sella*, a seat.] A small projecting seat in the stalls of churches, made to turn up upon hinges, so as to be leant against in kneeling.

Subsensible, sub-sen′si-bl, *a.* [L. *sub*, under.] Deeper than the range of the senses; too profound for the senses to reach.

Subsequent, sub′sē-kwent, *a.* [L. *subsequens, subsequentis*, ppr. of *subsequor*, to follow close after—*sub*, under, near, and *sequor*, to follow. SEQUENCE.] Following in time; coming or being after something else at any time, indefinitely; following in the order of place or succession; succeeding. —**Subsequently**, sub′sē-kwent-li, *adv.* In a subsequent manner, time, or position; afterwards; later on. — **Subsequence, Subsequency**, sub′sē-kwens, sub′sē-kwen-si, *n.* The state of being subsequent.

Subserve, sub-sėrv′, *v.t.*—*subserved, subserving.* [L. *subservio* — *sub*, under, and *servio*, to serve. SERVE.] To serve or be of advantage to; to be of service to; to assist or promote.—*v.i.* To serve in an inferior capacity; to be subservient.—**Subservience, Subserviency**, sub-sėr′vi-ens, sub-sėr′vi-en-si, *n.* The state of being subservient. — **Subservient**, sub-sėr′vi-ent, *a.* [L. *subserviens*, ppr. of *subservio.*] Useful as an instrument to promote a purpose; serving to promote some end; acting as a subordinate instrument.—**Subserviently**, sub-sėr′vi-ent-li, *adv.* In a subservient manner.

Subside, sub-sīd′, *v.i.*—*subsided, subsiding.* [L. *subsido*—*sub*, under, and *sido*, to settle, akin to *sedeo*, to sit. SEDATE.] To sink or fall to the bottom; to settle, as lees; to sink or settle to a lower level, as a building; to fall into a state of quiet; to become tranquil; to abate.—**Subsidence**, sub-sī′dens, *n.* The act or progress of subsiding; a gradually settling lower; a sinking into the ground (the *subsidence* of ground).

Subsidiary, sub-sid′i-ar-ri, *a.* [L. *subsidiarius.* SUBSIDY.] Lending some aid or assistance; furnishing help; aiding or assisting; subordinate; contributory; pertaining to a subsidy.—*Subsidiary troops*, troops of one nation hired by another for military service.—*n.* One who or that which is subsidiary; an auxiliary; an assistant; a company controlled by another company by virtue of ownership of the controlling stock.

Subsidy, sub′si-di, *n.* [L. *subsidium*, from *sub*, under, *sedeo*, to sit; lit. that which is placed beneath as a support. SUBSIDE.] A sum of money granted for a purpose; an aid or tax formerly granted by parliament to the crown for urgent occasions of the realm; a sum paid by one government to another to meet the expenses of carrying on a war.—**Subsidize**, sub′si-dīz, *v.t.*— *subsidized, subsidizing.* To furnish with a subsidy; to purchase the assistance of by a subsidy.

Subsist, sub-sist′, *v.i.* [Fr. *subsister*, from L. *subsistere*—*sub*, under, and *sisto, sistere*, to stand, to be fixed, from *sto*, to stand. STATE.] To exist; to have continued existence; to continue to retain the present state; to be maintained with food and clothing; to be supported; to live; to inhere in something else.—*v.t.* To support with provisions.—**Subsistence**, sub-sis′tens, *n.* [Fr. *subsistance.*] Actual existence; that which furnishes support to animal life; means of support; support; livelihood; inherence in something else.—**Subsistent**, sub-sis′tent, *a.* [L. *subsistens, subsistentis.*] Having existence; inherent.

Subsoil, sub′soil, *n.* [L. *sub*, under.] The under-soil; the bed or stratum of earth or earthy matter which lies immediately under the surface soil.—*Subsoil plough*, a plough adapted to follow the common plough and loosen the subsoil.

Subspecies, sub′spē-shēz, *n.* [L. *sub*, under.] A subordinate species; a division of a species.

Substance, sub′stans, *n.* [Fr. *substance*, from L. *substantia*, substance, essence; from *substans, substantis*, ppr. of *substo*— *sub*, under, and *sto*, to stand. STATE.] That of which a thing consists or is made up; matter; material; a distinct portion of matter; a body; that which is real; that which constitutes a thing really a thing; the characteristic constituents collectively; the essential or material part; the purport; solidity; firmness; substantiality; material means and resources; goods; estate; *philos.* that which underlies all phenomena; that which exists independently and unchangeably, in contradistinction to *accident* or quality; *theol.* that in which the divine attributes inhere.—**Substantial**, sub-stan′shal, *a.* Actually existing; real; not seeming or imaginary; corporeal; material; firm in substance or material; strong; solid; possessed of considerable substance, goods, or estate; moderately wealthy.—**Substantiality**, sub-stan′shi-al″i-ti, *n.* The state of being substantial. — **Substantialize**, sub-stan′shal-īz, *v.t.* To render substantial. —**Substantially**, sub-stan′shal-li, *adv.* With reality of existence; strongly; solidly; in substance; in the main; essentially.— **Substantialness**, sub-stan′shal-nes, *n.* **Substantials**, sub-stan′shalz, *n.pl.* Essential parts.—**Substantiate**, sub-stan′shi-āt, *v.t.* — *substantiated, substantiating.* To make real or actual; to establish by proof or competent evidence; to verify; to make good; to prove.—**Substantiation**, sub-stan′shi-ā″shon, *n.* The act of substantiating or proving; evidence; proof.—**Substantival**, sub′stan-ti-val, *a.* Relating to or like a substantive. — **Substantive**, sub′stan-tiv, *a.* [L. *substantivus*, self-existent; *substantivum verbum*, the substantive verb.] Betokening or expressing existence;

depending on itself; independent. — *Substantive verb*, the verb *to be*.—*n. Gram.* a noun. — **Substantively**, sub'stan-tiv-li, *adv.* In a substantive manner; in substance; essentially; *gram.* as a substantive or noun (an adjective used *substantively*).

Substitute, sub'sti-tūt, *v.t.*—*substituted, substituting.* [L. *substituo, substitutum*—*sub*, under, and *statuo*, to place, to set (whence *statute*, &c.). STATE.] To put in the place of another; to put in exchange. —*n.* A person acting for or put in the room of another; a person who for a consideration serves in an army in the place of a conscript; one thing put in the place of another or serving the purpose of another.—**Substitution**, sub-sti-tū'shon, *n.* The act of substituting or putting in place of another; *alg.* the putting of one quantity in the place of another, to which it is equal but differently expressed.—**Substitutional**, sub-sti-tū'shon-al, *a.* Pertaining to or implying substitution.—**Substitutionary**, sub-sti-tū'shon-a-ri, *a.* Substitutional.

Substratum, sub-strā'tum, *n.* [L. *sub*, under, and *stratum*, something spread. STRATUM.] That which is laid or spread under something; a stratum lying under another; subsoil; *metaph.* matter or substance in which qualities inhere.

Substruction, sub-struk'shon, *n.* [L. *sub*, under, and *struo*, to build. STRUCTURE.] A mass of building below another; a foundation.—**Substructure**, sub-struk'tūr, *n.* An under structure; a foundation.

Subsultive, Subsultory, sub-sul'tiv, sub-sul'to-ri, *n.* [From L. *subsilio*, *subsultum*, to leap up—*sub*, under, and *salio*, to leap.] Moving by sudden leaps or starts; having a spasmodic character.—**Subsultus**, sub-sul'tus, *n. Med.* a twitching or convulsive motion.

Subsume, sub-sūm', *v.t.* [L. *sub*, under, and *sumo*, to take.] *Logic*, to include under a more general class or category.

Subtangent, sub'tan-jent, *n.* [L. *sub*, under.] *Math.* the part of a produced diameter or produced axis, intercepted between an ordinate and a tangent, both drawn from the same point in a curve.

Subtenant, sub-ten'ant, *n.* [L. *sub*, under.] The tenant under a tenant; one who rents land or houses from a tenant.

Subtend, sub-tend', *v.t.* [L. *subtendo*—*sub*, under, and *tendo*, to stretch.] To extend under or be opposite to: a geometrical term said of the side of a triangle opposite an angle.

Subterfuge, sub'tėr-fūj, *n.* [Fr. *subterfuge*, L.L. *subterfugium*, from L. *subter*, under, and *fugio*, to flee (whence *fugitive*, &c.).] A dishonest shift or expedient; a quirk, prevarication, or other artifice to escape censure or the force of an argument, or to justify opinions or conduct.

Subterranean, Subterraneous, sub-ter-rā'nē-an, sub-ter-rā'nē-us, *a.* [L. *subterraneus*—*sub*, under, and *terra*, the earth (whence *terrace, terrestrial, terrier*, &c.).] Being or lying at some depth in the earth; situated within the earth; underground.

Subtle, sut'l, *a.* [O.E. *sotel, sotil, subtil*, O.Fr. *sutil, soutil, subtil* (Fr. *subtil*), from L. *subtilis*, slender, delicate, subtle, from *sub*, under, and *tela*, for *textela*, a web, from *texo*, to weave (whence *texture*).] Thin or tenuous in substance; not gross or dense; rare; delicate in texture or workmanship; acute or penetrating in intellect; capable of drawing nice distinctions; sly in design; cunning; artful; insinuating; cunningly devised.—**Subtleness**, sut'l-nes, *n.* The quality of being subtle.—**Subtlety**, sut'l-ti, *n.* The quality of being subtle; cunning; craftiness; wiliness; acuteness of intellect; nicety of distinction or discrimination.—**Subtly**, sut'li, *adv.* In a subtle manner; artfully; cunningly; nicely; delicately; deceitfully; delusively.—**Subtile**, sub'til or sut'l, *a.* A spelling of *Subtle* now given up, as are also **Subtilely, Subtileness, Subtilty**.—**Subtilization**, sub'til-ī-zā"shon, *n.* The act of subtilizing; refinement in drawing distinctions, &c.—**Subtilize**, sub'til-īz, *v.t.*—*subtilized, subtilizing.* To make subtle; to refine; to spin into niceties.—*v.i.* To refine in argument; to make nice distinctions.

Subtonic, sub-ton'ik, *n.* [L. *sub*, under.] *Mus.* the semitone or note next below the tonic; the leading note of the scale.

Subtorrid, sub-tor'id, *a.* [L. *sub*, slightly.] Approximately torrid; bordering on the torrid zone.

Subtract, sub-trakt', *v.t.* [L. *subtraho, subtractum*—*sub*, under, and *traho*, to draw. TRACT.] To withdraw or take from a number or quantity; to deduct.—**Subtracter**, sub-trak'tėr, *n.* One who subtracts.—**Subtraction**, sub-trak'shon, *n.* The act or operation of subtracting; the taking of a lesser number from a greater.—**Subtractive**, sub-trak'tiv, *a.* Tending or having power to subtract.—**Subtrahend**, sub'tra-hend, *n.* [L. *subtrahendus*, that must be subtracted.] The sum or number to be subtracted from another, which is called the minuend.

Subtranslucent, sub-trans-lū'sent, *a.* [L. *sub*, slightly.] Imperfectly translucent.

Subtransparent, sub-trans-pā'rent, *a.* [L. *sub*, slightly.] Imperfectly transparent.

Subtropical, sub-trop'i-kal, *a.* [L. *sub*, near, slightly.] Adjoining the tropics; indigenous to or characteristic of the regions lying near the tropics.

Subtypical, sub-tip'i-kal, *a.* [L. *sub*, slightly.] Not quite true to the type; slightly aberrant.

Subulate, Subulated, Subuliform, sū'bū-lāt, sū'bū-lā-ted, sū'bū-li-form, *a.* [From L. *subula*, an awl, from *suo*, to sew. SEW.] Shaped like an awl; slender and gradually tapering toward the end or point.

Subungual, sub-ung'gwal, *a.* [L. *sub*, under, and *unguis*, a nail.] Under the nail.

Suburb, sub'ėrb, *n.* [L. *suburbium*—*sub*, under, near, and *urbs*, a city. URBAN.] An outlying part of a city or town; a part without the boundaries but in the vicinity of the town: often used in the plural to signify loosely some part near a city.—**Suburban**, sub-ėr'ban, *a.* Pertaining to the suburbs of a city.

Subvariety, sub'va-rī-e-ti, *n.* [L. *sub*, under.] A subordinate variety or division of a variety.

Subvene, sub-vēn', *v.i.*—*subvened, subvening.* [From L. *subvenio, subventum*, to come to one's assistance—*sub*, under, and *venio, ventum*, to come (as in *advent, prevent*, &c.).] To arrive or happen so as to obviate something or afford relief.—**Subvention**, sub-ven'shon, *n.* The act of coming to relieve or aid; a government grant or aid; pecuniary aid granted.

Subvert, sub-vėrt', *v.t.* [L. *subverto*, to overthrow—*sub*, under, and *verto*, to turn. VERSE.] To overthrow from the foundation; to ruin utterly; to destroy; to corrupt or pervert, as the mind.—**Subverter**, sub-vėr'tėr, *n.* One who subverts.—**Subvertible**, sub-vėr'ti-bl, *a.* Capable of being subverted.—**Subversion**, sub-vėr'shon, *n.* [L. *subversio*.] The act of subverting or overthrowing; overthrow; utter ruin; destruction.—**Subversive**, sub-vėr'siv, *a.* Tending to subvert, overthrow, or ruin.

Subway, sub'wā, *n.* [L. *sub*, under.] An underground way.

Succades, suk'kādz, *n.pl.* [L. *succus*, juice.] Fruits candied and preserved in syrup; sweetmeats.

Succedaneous, suk-sē-dā'nē-us, *a.* [L. *succedaneus*—*sub*, under, and *cedo*, to go. CEDE.] Supplying the place of something else; forming a substitute.—**Succedaneum**, suk-sē-dā'nē-um, *n.* pl. **Succedanea**, suk-sē-dā'nē-a. What supplies the place of or is used for something else; a substitute.

Succeed, suk-sēd', *v.t.* [Fr. *succéder*, from L. *succedo, successum*—*sub*, under, in place of, and *cedo*, to go. CEDE.] To take the place of in some post or position; to be heir or successor to; to come after; to be subsequent or consequent to. ∴ Syn. under FOLLOW.—*v.i.* To follow; to come next; to become heir; to ascend a throne after the removal or death of the occupant; to come down by order of succession; to devolve; to be fortunate or prosperous in any endeavour; to obtain the object desired; to turn out as wished; to have the desired result.—**Succeeder**, suk-sē'dėr, *n.* One who succeeds; a successor.—**Succeeding**, suk-sē'ding, *p.* and *a.* Following; coming next in order.—**Success**, suk-ses', *n.* [L. *successus*, from *succedo, successum*.] The termination or result of any affair, whether happy or unhappy; the issue; more especially, a favourable or prosperous termination of anything attempted; good hap or fortune.—**Successful**, suk-ses'fụl, *a.* Having or resulting in success; prosperous; fortunate. ∴ Syn. under FORTUNATE.—**Successfully**, suk-ses'fụl-li, *adv.* In a successful manner; prosperously; favourably.—**Successfulness**, suk-ses'fụl-nes, *n.*—**Succession**, suk-sesh'on, *n.* [L. *successio, successionis*, from *succedo, successum*.] A following of things in order, either in time or place; a series following one after the other; a series or line of descendants; successors collectively; a succession or coming to an inheritance; the act or right of entering upon an office, rank, &c., held by a predecessor.—*Law of succession*, or *law of descent*, the law according to which the inheritance of property is regulated, applied generally where the deceased party has died intestate, or in cases where the power of bequeathing property by will is limited by legislation.—*Apostolical succession*, the alleged transmission, through the episcopate, of the power and authority committed by Christ to his apostles for the guidance and government of the church.—**Successional**, suk-sesh'on-al, *a.* Relating to succession; consecutive.—**Successionist**, suk-sesh'on-ist, *n.* One who maintains the doctrine of apostolical succession.—**Successive**, suk-ses'iv, *a.* [L. *successivus*.] Following in an uninterrupted course or series, as persons or things, and either in time or place; coming one after another; consecutive.—**Successively**, suk-ses'iv-li, *adv.* In a successive manner; in a series one after another.—**Successiveness**, suk-ses'iv-nes, *n.*—**Successor**, suk-ses'or, *n.* [L.] One that succeeds or follows; one that takes the place which another has left: correlative to *predecessor*.

Succinct, suk-singkt', *a.* [L. *succinctus*, tucked or girded up, succinct—*sub*, up, and *cingo, cinctum*, to gird. CINCTURE.] Compressed into few words; characterized by verbal brevity; brief; concise. ∴ Syn. under CONCISE.—**Succinctly**, suk-singkt'li, *adv.* In a succinct manner; concisely.—**Succinctness**, suk-singkt'nes, *n.* The quality of being succinct; conciseness.

Succinic, suk-sin'ik, *a.* [L. *succinum*, amber.] Pertaining to amber; obtained from amber.—**Succinite**, suk'sin-īt, *n.* An amber-coloured variety of lime-garnet.—**Succinous**, suk'sin-us, *a.* Pertaining to or resembling amber.

Succory, suk'ko-ri, *n.* [A corruption of *chicory*.] Chicory.

Succotash, suk'kō-tash, *n.* [From American Indian name.] Green maize and beans boiled together. (*United States*.)

Succour, suk'ėr, *v.t.* [O.Fr. *sucurre, soucourre* (Fr. *secourir*), from L. *succurro*, to run up to the aid of—*sub*, under, and *curro*, to run. CURRENT.] To help when in difficulty or distress; to assist and deliver from suffering; to aid or relieve.—*n.* Aid; help; assistance; particularly, assistance in difficulty or distress; the person or thing that brings relief.—**Succourer**, suk'ėr-ėr, *n.* One who succours.—**Succourless**, suk'ėr-les, *a.* Destitute of succour, help, or relief.

Succulent, suk'kū-lent, *a.* [L. *succulentus*, from *succus*, juice.] Full of juice; juicy.—*Succulent plants*, plants remarkable for the thick and fleshy nature of their stems and leaves.—**Succulently**, suk'kū-lent-li, *adv.* In a succulent manner; juicily.—**Succulence, Succulency**, suk'kū-lens, suk'kū-len-si, *n.* The quality of being succulent; juiciness.

Succumb, suk-kum', *v.i.* [L. *succumbo*—*sub*, under, and *cumbo*, to lie down (seen also in *incumbent, concubine*).] To sink or give way without resistance; to yield; to submit.

Succursal, suk-kėr'sal, *a.* [Fr. *succursale*, from L.L. *succursus*, succour. SUCCOUR.] Serving as a chapel of ease: said of a church attached to a parish church.—*n.* A chapel of ease; also a branch establishment.

Succussion, suk'kush'on, *n.* [L. *succussio, succussionis*, a shaking—*sub*, under, and *quatio*, to shake.] The act of shaking; a shock; an aguish shaking.—**Succussive**, suk-kus'iv, *a.* Characterized by shaking.

Such, such, *a.* [Lit. so-like, from A.Sax. *swilc, swylc*, from *swá* = *so*, and *lic* = like; Icel. *slíkr*, G. *solch*, Goth. *swaleiks*. So *which* = who-like or why-like.] Of that or the like kind or degree; similar; like; the same as mentioned; so great (*such* baseness). *Such* is followed by *as* before the thing which is the subject of comparison; the article *a* or *an* is placed between it and the noun to which it refers (*such* a man), but *such* comes directly before nouns without the article (*such* weather).—*Such and such*, or *such or such*, used to represent an object generally or indefinitely, or to save particularizing.—*Such like*, of the like kind; similar persons or things; et cetera: used at the close of enumerations.—**Suchwise**, such'wīz, *adv.* In such a manner; so.

Suck, suk, *v.t.* [A.Sax. *súcan*, to suck, also *súgan*, like G. *saugen*, Icel. *sjúga, súga*, Dan. *suge*; cog. L. *sugo*, Gael. *sugaidh*, Ir. *suigim*, to suck.] To draw into the mouth by the action of the lips and tongue; to draw something from with the mouth; specifically, to draw milk from; to draw in or imbibe; to inhale; to absorb; to draw in as a whirlpool; to swallow up; to engulf.—*v.i.* To draw fluid into the mouth; to draw milk from the breast.—*n.* The act of drawing with the mouth; milk drawn from the breast by the mouth.—**Sucker**, suk'ėr, *n.* One who or that which sucks; an organ in animals for sucking; the piston of a suction-pump; a shoot or branch which proceeds from the roots or lower part of a stem; the sucking-fish; the lump-fish or lump-sucker; a toy consisting of a small piece of leather having a string attached to the centre of it, soaked in water and pressed firmly down on a substance, when the atmospheric pressure causes it to adhere through the vacuum made when the string is pulled.—**Sucking**, suk'ing, *p.* and *a.* Nourished by milk from the mother's breast; hence (*colloq.*) very young and inexperienced.—**Sucking-bottle**, *n.* An infant's feeding-bottle.—**Sucking-fish**, *n.* The remora.—**Sucking-pump**, *n.* The common or suction-pump.—**Suckle**, suk'l, *v.t.*—*suckled, suckling.* [Freq. from *suck*.] To give suck to; to nurse at the breast.—**Suckling**, suk'ling, *n.* [From *suck* and term. *-ling*.] A young child at the breast.

Suckatash, suk'a-tash, *n.* SUCCOTASH.

Sucrose, sū'krōs, *n.* [Fr. *sucre*, sugar.] A general name for the sugars identical with cane-sugar.

Suction, suk'shon, *n.* [O.Fr. *suction*, from L. *sugo, suctum*, to suck. SUCK.] The act of sucking; the sucking up of any fluid by the pressure of the external air when a vacuum is made.—**Suction-pump**, *n.* The common house or sucking pump as distinguished from the lifting or the force pump.—**Suctorial**, suk-tō'ri-al, *a.* Adapted for sucking; living by sucking; capable of adhering by sucking.

Sudamina, sū-dam'i-na, *n.pl.* [L. *sudo, sudare*, to sweat.] Minute vesicles appearing on the skin in certain cases.

Sudation, sū-dā'shon, *n.* [L. *sudatio, sudationis*, from *sudo*, to sweat. SWEAT.] A sweating.—**Sudatorium**, sū-da-tō'ri-um, *n.* [L.] A hot-air bath for producing perspiration.—**Sudatory**, sū'da-to-ri, *n.* A sudatorium.—*a.* Sweating; perspiring.

Sudd, sud, *n.* [Ar.] Floating vegetation obstructing boats in the Nile or other rivers.

Sudden, sud'en, *a.* [O.Fr. *sodain, sudain, soubdain* (Fr. *soudain*), from L.L. *subitanus*, from L. *subitus*, sudden, from *subeo, subitum*, to steal upon—*sub*, under, and *eo*, to go. ITINERANT.] Happening without or with scarcely a moment's notice; coming unexpectedly; hastily put in use, employed, or prepared; quick; rapid; hasty; violent; passionate.—*On a sudden, of a sudden*, all at once; hastily; unexpectedly. *On the sudden*, is also used.—**Suddenly**, sud'en-li, *adv.* In a sudden manner; unexpectedly; all at once.—**Suddenness**, sud'en-nes, *n.* State of being sudden.

Sudder, sud'ėr, *n.* [Ar. *sadr*, chief.] In India, chief, supreme, belonging to the capital, as distinguished from *moffussil*.

Sudoriferous, sū-do-rif'ėr-us, *a.* [L. *sudor*, sweat (akin to E. *sweat*), and *fero*, to bear.] Producing sweat; secreting perspiration.—**Sudorific**, sū-do-rif'ik, *a.* [L. *sudor*, and *facio*, to make.] Causing sweat.—*n.* A medicine that produces sweat; a diaphoretic.—**Sudoriparous**, sū-do-rip'a-rus, *a.* [L. *pario*, to produce.] Sweat-producing; secreting perspiration.

Sudra, sö'dra, *n.* [Hind.] A member of the lowest of the four great castes among the Hindus.

Suds, sudz, *n.pl.* [From stem of *seethe*; comp. G. *sud*, a seething, from *sieden*, to seethe.] A lye of soap and water, or water impregnated with soap, and forming a frothy mass.

Sue, sū, *v.t.*—*sued, suing.* [O.Fr. *suir, sewir, sivir* (Fr. *suivre*), from a form *sequere*, for L. *sequi*, to follow (whence *pursue, ensue, suit, suite*). SEQUENCE.] To ply with love; to seek in marriage; to seek justice or right from by legal process; to institute a process in law against.—*To sue out*, to petition for and take out (to *sue out* a pardon).—*v.i.* To play the lover; to woo or be a wooer; to prosecute; to make legal claim; to seek by request; to petition; to plead.—**Suability**, sū-a-bil'i-ti, *n.* Capability of being sued.—**Suable**, sū'a-bl, *a.* Such as may be sued.—**Suer**, sū'ėr, *n.* One who sues; a suitor.

Suet, sū'et, *n.* [O.Fr. *seu, sieu* (Fr. *suif*), from L. *sebum*, tallow, grease.] The fatty tissue situated about the loins and kidneys of the ox, sheep, deer, &c., and which is harder than the fat from other parts.—**Suety**, sū'et-i, *a.* Consisting of suet or resembling it.

Suffer, suf'ėr, *v.t.* [O.Fr. *suffrir, sofferre* (Fr. *souffrir*), from L. *sufferre*, inf. of *suffero*, to suffer—*sub*, under and *fero*, to bear. BEAR, FERTILE.] To feel or bear with painful, disagreeable, or distressing effects; to undergo (to *suffer* pain); to be affected by (to *suffer* change, a loss); not to forbid or hinder; to allow.—*v.i.* To feel or undergo pain of body or mind; to undergo punishment; to be capitally executed; to be injured; to sustain loss or damage.—**Sufferable**, suf'ėr-a-bl, *a.* Capable of being permitted or endured.—**Sufferableness**, suf'ėr-a-bl-nes, *n.* The character of being sufferable.—**Sufferably**, suf'ėr-a-bli, *adv.* In a sufferable manner.—**Sufferance**, suf'ėr-ans, *n.* The state of suffering; endurance; patient endurance; passive consent by not forbidding or hindering; toleration; permission.—*On sufferance*, by passive permission or consent; without being positively forbidden; tolerated.—**Sufferer**, suf'ėr-ėr, *n.* One who suffers; one who undergoes pain; one who sustains inconvenience or loss; one that permits or allows.—**Suffering**, suf'ėr-ing, *n.* The bearing of pain, inconvenience, or loss; pain endured; distress.

Suffetes, suf-fē'tez, *n.* [Heb. *shôphetîm*, judges.] The name of the two chief magistrates at Carthage.

Suffice, suf-fīs', *v.i.*—*sufficed, sufficing.* [O.E. *suffise*, from Fr. *suffire, suffisant*, L. *sufficio*, to be sufficient—*sub*, under, and *facio*, to make. FACT.] To be enough or sufficient; to be equal to the end proposed.—*v.t.* To satisfy; to be equal to the wants or demands of.—**Sufficient**, suf-fi'shent, *a.* [L. *sufficiens, sufficientis*, ppr. of *sufficio*.] Equal to the end proposed; adequate to wants; enough; of competent power or ability; qualified; capable.—**Sufficiently**, suf-fi'shent-li, *adv.* To a sufficient degree; well enough; adequately; to a considerable degree.—**Sufficiency**, suf-fish'en-si, *n.* The state of being sufficient or adequate; adequacy; capacity; adequate substance or means; a competence; a comfortable fortune; a supply equal to wants; self-conceit; self-confidence.

Suffix, suf'fiks, *n.* [L. *suffixus*, pp. of *suffigo, suffixum*, to affix—*sub*, under, near, and *figo, fixum*, to fix. FIX.] A letter or syllable added or annexed to the end of a word; an affix; a postfix.—*v.t.* To add or annex (a letter or syllable) to a word.—**Suffixion**, suf-fik'shon, *n.* The act of suffixing.

Sufflue, suf'flū, *n.* *Her.* a charge of unknown origin, supposed by some authorities to be a wind instrument.

Suffocate, suf'fō-kāt, *v.t.*—*suffocated, suffocating.* [L. *suffoco, suffocatum*—*sub*, under, and *faux, faucis*, the throat.] To choke or kill by stopping respiration; to stifle, as by depriving of air; to smother.—*v.i.* To become choked, stifled, or smothered.—**Suffocatingly**, suf'fō-kāt'ing-li, *adv.* So as to suffocate.—**Suffocation**, suf-fō-kā'shon, *n.* The act of suffocating; the condition of being suffocated, choked, or stifled.—**Suffocative**, suf'fō-kā-tiv, *a.* Tending or able to choke or stifle.

Suffolk-punch, suf'fok-punsh, *n.* A variety of English horse, strongly built, of a stout round shape.

Suffragan, suf'fra-gan, *a.* [Fr. *suffragant*, L. *suffragans, suffragantis*, ppr. of *suffragor*, to vote for, from *suffragium*, a vote.] Assisting in ecclesiastical duties: said of bishops.—*n.* A bishop consecrated to assist another bishop in a portion of his diocese; any bishop in relation to his archbishop.—**Suffraganship**, suf'fra-gan-ship, *n.* The office of suffragan.

Suffrage, suf'frāj, *n.* [Fr. *suffrage*, L. *suffragium*, a vote.] A vote given in deciding a question, or in choice of a person; an opinion expressed; one's voice given; right to vote; the parliamentary franchise.—**Suffragette**, suf-ra-jet', *n.* A female advocate of female suffrage.—**Suffragist**, suf'ra-jist, *n.* A supporter of some form of suffrage; a suffragette.

Suffrutescent, suf-frö-tes'ent, *a.* [L. *sub*, slightly, and *frutex*, a shrub.] Moderately shrubby.—**Suffruticose**, suf-frö'ti-kōs, *a.* In part shrubby; woody at the base.

Suffumigate, suf-fū'mi-gāt, *v.t.* [L. *suffumigo, suffumigare* — *sub*, under, *fumus*, smoke.] To apply fumes or smoke to, as in medical treatment.—**Suffumigation**, suf-fū'mi-gā"shon, *n.* The operation of suffumigating; fumigation.

Suffuse, suf-fūz', *v.t.*—*suffused, suffusing.* [L. *suffundo, suffusum*—*sub*, and *fundo*, to pour, to pour out. FUSE.] To overspread, as with a fluid or tincture; to fill or cover, as with something fluid (eyes *suffused* with tears, *suffused* with blushes).—**Suffusion**, suf-fū'zhon, *n.* The act of suffusing or state of being suffused; a spreading over.

Sufism, sū'fizm, *n.* [Ar. *sufiy*, intelligent.] The doctrine of the Sufis, or Mohammedan mystics, of a pantheistic nature.

Sugar, shu̧'gėr, *n.* [Fr. *sucre*, from Ar. *sukkar*, sugar, from Per. *shakhara*, Prakrit *sakkara*, Skr. *çarkarâ*, grains of sand, sugar.] A well-known sweet granular substance, prepared chiefly from the expressed juice of the sugar-cane, but obtained also from many other plants, as maple, beet, birch, parsnip, &c.; something resembling sugar in any of its properties; *fig.* honeyed or soothing words.—*Sugar of lead*, the acetate of lead, the crystals of which have a slight sweetness.—*Sugar of milk*, lactose.—*a.* Made of sugar.—*v.t.* To impregnate, season, sprinkle, or mix with sugar; *fig.* to sweeten, honey, or render acceptable.—**Sugar-baker**, *n.* One who refines sugar.—**Sugar-beet**, *n.* A species of beet from whose root sugar is largely manufactured.

—**Sugar-candy**, *n.* Sugar clarified and crystallized.—**Sugar-cane**, *n.* A plant from whose juice sugar is obtained, a tall handsome grass 18 to 20 feet high.—**Sugar-house**, *n.* A building in which sugar is refined.—**Sugariness**, shu̦'gėr-i-nes, *n.* The quality of being sugary.—**Sugaring**, shu̦'gėr-ing, *n.* A sweetening with sugar; the sugar thus used.—**Sugar-kettle**, *n.* A vessel for boiling down saccharine juice.—**Sugar-loaf**, *n.* A conical mass of refined sugar; anything shaped like a sugar-loaf.—**Sugar-maple**, *n.* A tree of North America, from the sap of which sugar is manufactured in considerable quantities in the United States and Canada.—**Sugar-mill**, *n.* A machine for pressing out the juice of the sugar-cane.—**Sugar-mite**, *n.* A species of mite found in raw or unrefined sugar.—**Sugar-nippers**, *n.pl.* A tool for cutting loaf-sugar into small lumps.—**Sugar-planter**, *n.* One who owns or manages land devoted to the growth of the sugar-cane.—**Sugar-plum**, *n.* A comfit or small sweet-meat made of boiled sugar, with flavouring and colouring ingredients.—**Sugar-refiner**, *n.* One who refines sugar.—**Sugar-refinery**, *n.* An establishment where sugar is refined; a sugar-house.—**Sugar-tongs**, *n.pl.* A small instrument of silver or plated metal for lifting lumps of sugar at table.—**Sugary**, shu̦'gėr-i, *a.* Resembling, containing, or composed of sugar; sweet; *fig.* honeyed.

Suggest, su-jest' or sud-jest', *v.t.* [L. *suggero, suggestum*, to put under, to suggest—*sub*, under, and *gero*, to bring. GESTURE.] To introduce indirectly to the mind or thoughts; to call up to the mind; to cause to be thought of; to recall; to propose with diffidence or modesty; to hint. ∴ Syn. under HINT.—*v.i.* To make suggestions of evil.—**Suggester**, su-jes'tėr or sud-jes'tėr, *n.* One that suggests.—**Suggestion**, su-jest'yon or sud-jest'yon, *n.* The act of suggesting, or that which is suggested; a hint; a prompting, especially a prompting to do evil; temptation; *philos.* same as *Association*.—*Principle of suggestion*, association of ideas.—**Suggestive**, su-jes'tiv or sud-jes'tiv, *a.* Calculated to suggest thoughts or ideas; suggesting what does not appear on the surface.—**Suggestively**, su-jes'tiv-li or sud-jes'tiv-li, *adv.* By way of suggestion.—**Suggestiveness**, su-jes'tiv-nes or sud-jes'tiv-nes, *n.* The state or quality of being suggestive.

Suicide, sū'i-sīd, *n.* [From L. *sui*, of himself, and *cædo*, to kill (as in *homicide, parricide*).] Self-murder; the act of designedly destroying one's own life; one guilty of self-murder; a person who intentionally kills himself; a felo de se.—**Suicidal**, sū-i-sī'dal, *a.* Pertaining to or of the nature of suicide.—**Suicidally**, sū-i-sī'dal-li, *adv.* In a suicidal manner.

Suit, sūt, *n.* [Fr. *suite*, succession, train, attendants, set, &c., from *suivre*, to follow. SUE.] A following†; pursuit†; the act of suing; a seeking for something by petition or entreaty; a request; a prayer; an attempt to win a woman in marriage; courtship; a set or number of things used together (a *suit* of curtains, a *suit* of clothes); a set of things of the same kind or stamp (a *suit* (or *suite*) of rooms); any of the four classes into which playing cards are divided; a retinue or train of attendants or followers (in this sense usually written *suite*); *law*, an action or process for the recovery of a right or claim.—*To follow suit*, to play a card of the same suit; hence, to do as another does.—*v.t.* To adapt; to make suitable; to become or be adapted to; to be suitable to; to fit; to be agreeable to; to fall in with the wishes or convenience of.—*v.i.* To agree; to correspond.—**Suitable**, sū'ta-bl, *a.* Suiting or being in accordance; fitting; accordant; proper; becoming.—**Suitableness, Suitability**, sū'ta-bl-nes, sū-ta-bil'i-ti, *n.* The state or quality of being suitable, fitted, or adapted; fitness.—**Suitably**, sū'ta-bli, *adv.* In a suitable manner; fitly.—**Suite**, swēt, *n.* [Fr.] A company or number of attendants or followers; a retinue; a train; a connected series forming one whole (a *suite* of rooms).—**Suitor**, sū'tor, *n.* A petitioner; an applicant; one who sues or entreats; one who solicits a woman in marriage; a wooer; a lover; *law*, a party to a lawsuit.

Sulcate, Sulcated, sul'kāt, sul'kā-ted, *a.* [L. *sulcatus*, from *sulcus*, a furrow.] Furrowed; grooved: applied especially to stems, leaves, &c., of plants; the surfaces of molluscous shells, &c.—**Sulcation**, sul-kā'shon, *n.* A channel or furrow.

Sulfanilamide, sul-fa-nil'a-mīd, *n.* A synthetic drug used for its therapeutic action in numerous bacterial infections, as in pneumonia, gonorrhea, etc.

Sulky, sul'ki, *a.* [A. Sax. *solcen*, sluggish, sulky, pp. of *seolcan*, to languish.] Sullen; morose; doggedly keeping up ill-feeling and repelling advances.—*n.* A light two-wheeled carriage for a single person.—**Sulkily**, sul'ki-li, *adv.* In a sulky manner; sullenly.—**Sulkiness**, sul'ki-nes, *n.* Sullenness; moroseness.—**Sulk**, sulk, *v.i.* To indulge in a sullen fit or mood.

Sullen, sul'en, *a.* [O.E. *solein, solain*, O.Fr. *solain*, from L.L. *solanus*, from L. *solus*, alone, sole. SOLE.] Gloomily angry and silent; morose; sour; sulky; dismal; of a threatening aspect; sombre.—**Sullenly**, sul'en-li, *adv.* In a sullen manner; sulkily; with gloomy moroseness.—**Sullenness**, sul'en-nes, *n.* The state or quality of being sullen; ill nature with silence.

Sully, sul'i, *v.t.*—*sullied, sullying.* [A.Sax. *solian, sylian*, to soil or sully; from *sol*, mud or mire = Dan. *söle*, to sully, *söl*, mud; Goth. *bi-sauljan*, to sully.] To soil; to spot; to tarnish; to dim; *fig.* to stain, tarnish, or pollute (character *sullied* by infamous vices).—*v.i.* To be soiled or tarnished.

Sulphate, sul'fāt, *n.* [From *sulphur*.] A salt of sulphuric acid or a compound of sulphuric acid and a base; as *sulphate* of copper, or blue vitriol; *sulphate* of iron, or green vitriol; *sulphate* of magnesium, or Epsom salts, &c.—**Sulphatic**, sul-fat'ik, *a.* Relating to, containing, or resembling a sulphate.—**Sulphide**, sul'fīd, *n.* A combination of sulphur with a metal or other element; a sulphuret.—**Sulphite**, sul'fīt, *n.* A salt composed of sulphurous acid with a base.

Sulphocyanic, sul'fō-sī-an-ik, *a.* [*Sulphur* and *cyanogen*.] Pertaining to, or containing sulphur and cyanogen.—*Sulphocyanic acid*, an acid occurring in the seeds and blossoms of cruciferous plants, and in the saliva of man and the sheep.—**Sulphocyanate, Sulphocyanide**, sul-fō-sī'an-āt, sul-fō-sī'an-īd, *n.* A salt of sulphocyanic acid.—**Sulphocyanogen**, sul'fō-sī-an"ō-jen, *n.* A compound of sulphur and cyanogen.

Sulphovinic, sul-fō-vin'ik, *a.* [From *sulphur*, and L. *vinum*, wine.] Containing sulphuric acid and spirits of wine or alcohol.—*Sulphovinic acid*, an acid produced by the action of sulphuric acid upon alcohol; now called ethyl hydrogen sulphate, or ethyl sulphuric acid.

Sulphur, sul'fėr, *n.* [L. *sulfur, sulphur*.] Brimstone, an elementary non-metallic substance of a greenish-yellow colour, occurring abundantly in the mineral, sparingly in the vegetable and animal kingdoms, nearly tasteless, readily melted, burning with a blue flame and then emitting suffocating fumes, largely used in the arts, as also in medicine.—*Flowers of sulphur*, sulphur in the form of a fine yellow powder.—*Roll* or *stick sulphur*, sulphur refined and cast in solid rolls.—**Sulphurate**, sul'fū-rāt, *v.t.* To impregnate or combine with sulphur; to subject to the action of sulphur.—**Sulphuration**, sul-fū-rā'shon, *n.* The subjection of a substance, such as straw-plait, silks, woollens, &c., to the action of sulphur for the purpose of bleaching.—**Sulphurator**, sul'fū-rā-tėr, *n.* An apparatus for fumigating or bleaching by the fumes of burning sulphur.—**Sulphureous**, sul-fū'rē-us, *a.* Consisting of or having the qualities of sulphur; sulphurous.—**Sulphureously**, sul-fū'rē-us-li, *adv.* In a sulphureous manner.—**Sulphureousness**, sul-fū'rē-us-nes, *n.*—**Sulphuret**, sul'fū-ret, *n.* A sulphide.—**Sulphuretted**, sul'fū-ret-ed, *a.* Having sulphur in combination.—*Sulphuretted hydrogen*, a compound of hydrogen and sulphur, a transparent colourless gas, recognized by its peculiar fetid odour, resembling that of putrid eggs, and very deleterious to animal life.—**Sulphuric**, sul-fū'rik, *a.* Pertaining to sulphur.—*Sulphuric acid*, oil of vitriol as it is called, from being first prepared from green vitriol (sulphate of iron), a compound of sulphur, oxygen, and hydrogen, colourless, oily, and strongly corrosive, used in the arts for innumerable purposes.—*Sulphuric ether*, an incorrect name for ordinary ether (which contains no sulphur).—**Sulphuring**, sul'fėr-ing, *n.* Sulphuration.—**Sulphur-ore**, *n.* Iron pyrites yielding sulphur and sulphuric acid.—**Sulphurous**, sul'fėr-us, *a.* Impregnated with sulphur; like sulphur; containing sulphur.—*Sulphurous oxide*, a gas formed by the combustion of sulphur in air or dry oxygen; also called *Sulphur dioxide*; when led into water it forms *sulphurous acid*.—**Sulphury**, sul'fėr-i, *a.* Partaking of sulphur; having the qualities of sulphur.

Sultan, sul'tan, *n.* [Ar. *sultân*.] The ordinary title of Mohammedan sovereigns, especially the ruler of Turkey, who assumed the title of Sultan of Sultans.—**Sultana**, sul-tä'na, *n.* The consort of a sultan; the empress of the Turks; a sultaness; a kind of large raisin.—**Sultanate**, sul'tan-āt, *n.* The rule or dominion of a sultan; sultanship.—**Sultaness**, sul'tan-es, *n.* A sultana.—**Sultanic**, sul-tan'ik, *a.* Belonging to a sultan.—**Sultanry**, sul'tan-ri, *n.* The dominions of a sultan.—**Sultanship**, sul'tan-ship, *n.* The office of a sultan.

Sultry, sul'tri, *a.* [A form of *sweltry*, O.E. *sweltrie*, sultry, from *swelter*. SWELTER.] Very hot, burning, and oppressive; very hot and moist, or hot, close, and heavy (a *sultry* atmosphere).—**Sultriness**, sul'tri-nes, *n.* The state of being sultry.

Sum, sum, *n.* [O.Fr. *sume, some* (Fr. *somme*), from L. *summa*, a sum, fem. of *summus*, highest, superl. of *superus*, that is above, from *super*, above. SUPER.] The aggregate of two or more numbers, magnitudes, quantities, or particulars; the amount or total of any number of things added together; the whole or totality; a quantity of money; any amount indefinitely; the principal points viewed or aggregated together; the essence; the substance; an arithmetical problem to be solved.—*v.t.*—*summed, summing.* To add into one whole; to cast up; to bring or collect into a small compass; to comprise in a few words (to *sum up* arguments).—*To sum up evidence*, to recapitulate to the jury the different facts and circumstances which have been adduced in the evidence: said of the presiding judge in a jury court.—**Sumless**, sum'les, *a.* Not to be summed up or computed.—**Summary**, sum'a-ri, *a.* Reduced into a narrow compass or into few words; succinct; concise; compendious; quickly executed; effected by a short way or method; *law*, said of proceedings carried on by methods intended to facilitate the despatch of business.—*n.* [L. *summarium*, a summary.] An abridged or condensed statement or account; an abridgment or compendium containing the sum or substance of a fuller statement.—**Summarily**, sum'a-ri-li, *adv.* In a summary manner; briefly; concisely; in a short way or method; without delay.—**Summarize**, sum'a-rīz, *v.t.*—*summarized, summarizing.* To make a summary or abstract of; to represent briefly.—**Summation**, sum-ā'shon, *n.* The act of forming a sum or total amount; an aggregate.

Sumac, Sumach, sū'mak, *n.* [Fr. *sumac*, Sp. *zumaque*, from Ar. *summâk*, sumach.] A genus of shrubs the leaves of which are much used for tanning; the leaves, shoots, &c., as forming an article of commerce. Written also *Shumach*.

Sumbul, sum'bul, *n.* An Eastern name for the root of an umbelliferous plant, used as an antispasmodic and tonic.

Summary, **Summation**, &c., Under SUM.

Summer, sum'ėr, *n.* [A.Sax. *sumor*, *sumer* = O.H.G. and Icel. *sumar*, G. and Dan. *sommer*, Sw. *sommar*, D. *somer*, *zomer*; root doubtful.] That season of the year when the sun shines most directly upon any region; the warmest season of the year, which, north of the equator, may be roughly said to include June, July, and August.—*All Saints' summer* (*Shak.*), about November 1st.—*Indian summer*, a period of the autumn season characterized by dry, hazy, windless days. *St. Martin's summer*, halcyon days (*Shak.*), about November 11th.—*a.* Relating to summer (*summer heat*).—*v.t.* To pass the summer or warm season.—**Summer-duck**, *n.* A very beautiful migratory duck.—**Summer-fallow**, *n.* A piece of land lying bare of crops in summer, but ploughed and tilled.—**Summer-house**, *n.* A small house or pavilion in a garden to be used in summer.—**Summer-time**, *n.* The summer season; a system of reckoning time in which clocks are kept one hour in advance of Standard time; Daylight Saving Time.—**Summer-wheat**, *n.* Wheat sown in spring.

Summer, sum'ėr, *n.* [Fr. *sommier*, a pack-horse, a rafter, from L. *sagmarius*, from Gr. *sagma*, a pack-saddle.] *Building*, a lintel; a girder; a supporting beam.

Summersault, sum'ėr-sạlt, *n.* SOMERSAULT.

Summerset, sum'ėr-set, *n.* SOMERSAULT.

Summit, sum'it, *n.* [Fr. *sommet*, dim. of O.Fr. *som*, a summit, from L. *summum*, highest part. SUM.] The top; the highest point; utmost elevation, as of rank; prosperity, &c. — **Summit-level**, *n.* The highest of a series of elevations over which a canal, railway, or the like, is carried.

Summon, sum'on, *v.t.* [O.E. *somone*, from O.Fr. *somoner* (Fr. *semondre*), from L. *summonere*, *submonere*—*sub*, under, privately, and *moneo*, to remind (whence *monition*, *monitor*, &c.).] To call or cite by authority to appear at a place specified; especially, to command to appear in a court of justice; to send for; to ask the attendance of; to call on; especially, to call upon to surrender; to call up; to excite into action or exertion: with *up* (*summon up* your courage). — **Summoner**, sum'on-ėr, *n.* One who summons; also, a former name for an apparitor.—**Summons**, sum'onz, *n.* [O.E. *somons*, *somounce*, O.Fr. *semonce*, *semonse*, a summons, fem. forms of *semons*, pp. of *semondre*.] A call by authority to appear at a place named, or to attend to some public duty; an invitation or asking to go to, or appear at, some place; *law*, a call by authority to appear in a court; also, the written or printed document by which such call is given; *milit.* a call to surrender.

Summum bonum, sum'mum bō'num, *n.* [L.] The highest good, the end pursued as the goal of an ethical or moral system.

Sump, sump, *n.* [L.G., Sw., and Dan. *sump*, D. *somp*, G. *sumpf*, a swamp, pool.] A pond of water for use in salt-works; a pit for receiving metal on its first fusion; a reservoir at the lowest point of a mine, from which is pumped the water that accumulates there. —**Sump-hole**, *n.* *Milit.* a pit dug in a trench for drainage purposes.

Sumpter, sump'tėr, *n.* [O.Fr. *sommetier*, a pack-horse driver; same origin as *summer*, a beam.] A horse that carries necessaries for a journey; a baggage-horse; a pack-horse.—*a.* Applied to a horse or mule that carries necessaries.—**Sumpter-saddle**, *n.* A pack-saddle.

Sumptuary, sump'tū-a-ri, *a.* [L. *sumptuarius*, from *sumptus*, expense, from *sumo*, *sumptum*, to use, spend—*sub*, under, and *emo*, to buy, to take (seen also in *exempt*, *prompt*, &c.).] Relating to expense; regulating expense or expenditure.—*Sumptuary laws*, laws made to restrain excess in apparel, food, or any luxuries.—**Sumptuous**, sump'tū-us, *a.* [L. *sumptuosus*, from *sumptus*, cost, expense.] Costly; expensive; hence, splendid; magnificent.—**Sumptuously**, sump'tū-us-li, *adv.* In a sumptuous manner; expensively; splendidly.—**Sumptuousness**, sump'tū-us-nes, *n.* Costliness; magnificence.

Sun, sun, *n.* [A.Sax. *sunne* (fem.) = Icel., O.H.G., and Goth. *sunna* (Goth. also *sunno*), G. *sonne*, L.G. *sunne*, D. *zon*; akin to Icel. *sól*, A.Sax. *sól*, L. *sol* (SOLAR); from a root meaning to shine.] The self-luminous orb which, being in or near the centre of our system of worlds, gives light and heat to the earth and other planets; the sunshine or sunlight (to lie in the *sun*); anything eminently splendid or luminous; that which is the chief source of light, honour, glory, or prosperity; the luminary which constitutes the centre of any system of worlds; a revolution of the earth round the sun; a year. — *Under the sun*, in the world; on earth; a proverbial expression. — *Sun of righteousness*, in *Scrip.* Christ. — *Sun and planet wheels*, a contrivance adopted by Watt in the steam-engine, equivalent to a crank, the planet wheel being a toothed wheel fixed to the end of the connecting-rod, and driving the fly-wheel by circling round a toothed-wheel at the end of the fly-wheel shaft.—*v.t.*—*sunned*, *sunning*. To expose to the sun's rays; to dry in the sun. —**Sunbeam**, sun'bēm, *n.* A ray of the sun. — **Sun-bear**, *n.* A species of bear that loves to bask in the sun.—**Sun-bird**, *n.* A name of small tropical insessorial birds, with plumage approaching in splendour that of the humming-birds. — **Sun-bonnet**, *n.* A lady's bonnet having a shade as a protection from the sun.—**Sun-bow**, *n.* An iris formed by the refraction of light on the spray of cataracts, or on any rising vapour. — **Sun-bright**, *a.* Bright as the sun.—**Sun-burn**, *v.t.* To discolour or scorch by the sun; to tan.—**Sunburnt**, sun'bėrnt, *a.* Discoloured by the heat or rays of the sun; tanned.—**Sun-burst**, *n.* A sudden flash of sunlight.—**Sun-clad**, *a.* Clothed in radiance; bright. —**Sun-dew**, *n.* A genus of plants, three of them British, which by a viscid substance entangle insects, and thus derive a certain amount of nutriment.—**Sun-dial**, *n.* An instrument to show the time of day by means of a shadow cast by the sun.—**Sun-dog**, *n.* A luminous spot of the nature of a halo.—**Sundown**, sun'doun, *n.* Sunset; sunsetting.—**Sun-dried**, *a.* Dried in the rays of the sun.—**Sun-fish**, *n.* A genus of large fishes, so called on account of the almost circular form and shining surface of the typical species. — **Sunflower**, sun'flou-ėr, *n.* A genus of plants, so named from the form and colour of the flower, or from its habit of turning to the sun. — **Sunless**, sun'les, *a.* Destitute of the sun or its rays; shaded.—**Sunlight**, sun'līt, *n.* The light of the sun; sunshine. — **Sun-light**, *n.* A large reflecting cluster of gas-burners in a ceiling.—**Sunlit**, sun'lit, *a.* Lit or lighted by the sun.—**Sunny**, sun'i, *a.* Like the sun; shining or dazzling with light or splendour; bright; exposed to the rays of the sun; lighted up or warmed by the direct rays of the sun.—**Sunniness**, sun'i-nes, *n.* State of being sunny.—**Sun-opal**, *n.* A variety of opal displaying bright yellow and red reflections.—**Sun-picture**, *n.* A photograph.—**Sunrise**, **Sunrising**, sun'rīz, sun'rīz-ing, *n.* The rising or appearance of the sun above the horizon; morning; the region where the sun rises; the east. — **Sunset**, **Sunsetting**, sun'set, sun'set-ing, *n.* The descent of the sun below the horizon; the time when the sun sets; evening; *fig.* close or decline; the region where the sun sets; the west. — **Sunshine**, sun'shīn, *n.* The light of the sun; sunlight; *fig.* an influence acting like the rays of the sun; warmth; pleasantness; brightness; cheerfulness. — *a.* Sunshiny. — **Sunshiny**, sun'shī-ni, *a.* Bright with the rays of the sun; bright like the sun.—**Sunstone**, sun'stōn, *n.* A popular name of various minerals, as cat's-eye. — **Sunstroke**, sun'strōk, *n.* A very serious affection of the nervous system frequent in tropical climates, and in temperate regions during very warm weather, generally caused by exposure of the head and neck to the direct rays of the sun.—**Sunward**, sun'wėrd, *adv.* Toward the sun.—**Sun-worship**, *n.* The worship or adoration of the sun.—**Sun-worshipper**, *n.* A worshipper of the sun.

Sun, **Sun-hemp**, sun, sun'hemp, *n.* SUNN.

Sunday, sun'dā, *n.* [A.Sax. *sunnan-dæg*, that is, day of the sun; G. *sonntag*, Dan. *söndag*, D. *zondag*; so called because this day was anciently dedicated to the *sun* or its worship.] The first day of the week; the Christian Sabbath; the Lord's-day. SABBATH.—*a.* Belonging to the Lord's-day or Christian Sabbath.—**Sunday-letter**, *n.* The dominical letter. DOMINICAL.—**Sunday-school**, *n.* A school for religious instruction held on the Lord's-day.

Sunder, sun'dėr, *v.t.* [A.Sax. *sundrian*, *syndrian*, from *sundor*, *sunder*, asunder, apart; similarly Icel. *sundra*, Dan. *söndre*, D. *zonderen*, G. *sondern*, to separate. Hence *sundry*, *asunder*. *Sound*, a channel, is closely allied.] To part; to divide; to disunite in almost any manner, as by rending, cutting, or breaking.—*v.i.* To part; to be separated. — *n.* A separation or division into parts: used chiefly, if not exclusively, in the phrase *in sunder*, in two.

Sundry, sun'dri, *a.* [A.Sax. *sundrig*, *syndrig*, from *sundor*, separate. SUNDER.] Several; more than one or two.—*All and sundry*, all both collectively and individually.—**Sundries**, sun'driz, *n.pl.* Various small things, too minute or numerous to be individually specified.

Sung, sung, pret. and pp. of *sing*.

Sunk, sungk, pret. and pp. of *sink*.—**Sunken**, sung'kn, *a.* Lying on the bottom of the sea or other water; low.—**Sunk-fence**, *n.* A ditch with a retaining wall on one side.

Sunn, **Sunn-hemp**, sun, *n.* An East Indian material similar to hemp, used for cordage, canvas, &c. Called also, *Sun*, *Sun-hemp*.

Sunnites, sụn'īts, *n.pl.* The orthodox Mohammedans who receive the *Sunna* or traditionary law as of equal importance with the Koran.

Sup, sup, *v.t.*—*supped*, *supping*. [A.Sax. *súpan*, to sup = Icel. *súpa*, L.G. *supen*, D. *zuipen*, O.G. *sufan*, G. *saufen*, to sip or sup. *Sip* is a lighter form of this, and *soup*, *sop*, are akin.] To take into the mouth with the lips, as a liquid; to imbibe; to sip; to have as one's lot; to be afflicted with (to *sup* sorrow).—*v.i.* To eat the evening meal. —*n.* A little taken with the lips; a sip.—**Supper**, sup'ėr, *n.* [O.E. *soper*, O.Fr. *soper*, *super*, Mod.Fr. *souper*, to sup, supper (the inf. used as a noun), from the Teutonic.] The evening meal; the last repast of the day.—*Lord's supper*, the eucharist. LORD. —*v.i.* To take supper; to sup.—*v.t.* To give supper to. — **Supperless**, sup'ėr-les, *a.* Wanting supper; being without supper.—**Supper-time**, *n.* The time when supper is taken; evening.

Supawn, su-pạn', *n.* In the United States, an Indian name for boiled Indian meal.

Super, sū'pėr, *n.* [L. *super*, above, beyond, besides (allied to E. *over*), whence *superus*, upper, comparative *superior*, superlative *supremus* or *summus* (whence *supreme*, *sum*, *summit*).] A contraction used colloquially for certain words of which it is the prefix; a supernumerary; specifically, a theatrical supernumerary.

Superable, sū'pėr-a-bl, *a.* [L. *superabilis*, from *supero*, to overcome.] Capable of being overcome or conquered. — **Superableness**, sū'pėr-a-bl-nes, *n.* The quality of being superable.—**Superably**, sū'pėr-a-bli, *adv.* So as may be overcome.

Superabound, sū'pėr-a-bound″, *v.t.* [Prefix *super*, and *abound*.] To abound above or beyond measure. — **Superabundance**, sū'pėr-a-bun″dans, *n.* More than enough; excessive abundance. — **Superabundant**, sū'pėr-a-bun″dant, *a.* Abounding to excess; being more than is sufficient. — **Superabundantly**, sū'pėr-a-bun″dant-li, *adv.* In a superabundant manner.

Superadd, sū-pėr-ad', *v.t.* [Prefix *super*,

and *add.*] To add over and above; to add or join in addition.—**Superaddition**, sū'pėr-ad-di"shon, *n.* The act of superadding; that which is superadded.

Superaltar, sū'pėr-al-tėr, *n.* [Prefix *super*, and *altar.*] A ledge or shelf over or at the back of an altar; a retable.

Superannuate, sū-pėr-an'nū-āt, *v.t.* — *superannuated, superannuating.* [Prefix *super*, above, beyond, and L. *annus*, a year.] To allow to retire from service on a pension, on account of old age or infirmity; to give a retiring pension to.—*v.i.* To retire on a pension when disabled by length of years. —**Superannuated**, sū-pėr-an'nū-ā-ted, *p.* and *a.* Disabled or impaired by old age; having received a retiring allowance for long service.—**Superannuation**, sū-pėr-an'nū-ā"shon, *n.* The state of being too old for office or business; retirement or removal from office with a pension, on account of long service or infirmity.

Superb, sū-perb', *a.* [Fr. *superbe*; L. *superbus*, proud, from *super*, above. SUPER.] Grand; august; stately; splendid; rich; sumptuous; showy; very fine; first-rate.—**Superbly**, sū-pėrb'li, *adv.* In a superb or splendid manner.—**Superbness**, sū-pėrb'nes, *n.*

Supercargo, sū-pėr-kär'gō, *n.* [Prefix *super*, and *cargo.*] *Lit.* a person over the cargo; a person in a merchant ship whose business is to manage the sales and superintend all the commercial concerns of the voyage.

Supercelestial, sū'pėr-sē-les"ti-al, *a.* [Prefix *super*, and *celestial.*] Situated above the firmament or great vault of heaven.

Superchery, sū-pėrch'e-ri, *n.* [Fr. *supercherie.*] Deceit; cheating; fraud.

Superciliary, sū-pėr-sil'i-ar-i, *a.* [L. *supercilium*, the eyebrow, also haughtiness or pride (as expressed by raising the brows) —*super*, above, and *cilium*, an eyelid.] Pertaining to the eyebrow; situated or being above the eyelid.—**Supercilious**, sū-pėr-sil'i-us, *a.* [L. *superciliosus.*] Having a haughty air or manner; acting as if others were our inferiors; haughty; over-bearing; arrogant.—**Superciliously**, sū-pėr-sil'i-us-li, *adv.* In a supercilious manner; with an air of contempt.—**Superciliousness**, sū-pėr-sil'i-us-nes, *n.* The state or quality of being supercilious; haughtiness.

Supercolumniation, sū'pėr-ko-lum-ni-ā"shon, *n.* [Prefix *super*, and *column.*] *Arch.* the placing of one order above another.

Superdominant, sū-pėr-dom'i-nant, *n.* [Prefix *super*, and *dominant.*] *Mus.* the note above the dominant; the sixth note of the diatonic scale.

Supereminent, sū-pėr-em'i-nent, *a.* [Prefix *super*, and *eminent.*] Eminent in a superior degree; surpassing others in excellence, power, authority, &c.—**Supereminence**, sū-pėr-em'i-nens, *n.* Eminence superior to what is common; distinguished eminence.—**Supereminently**, sū-pėr-em'i-nent-li, *adv.* In a supereminent manner.

Supererogation, sū-pėr-er'ō-gā-shon, *n.* [L. *supererogo, supererogatum*, to pay over and above—*super*, above, and *erogo*, to pay —*e, ex*, out, and *rogo*, to ask. ROGATION.] Performance of more than duty requires. —*Works of supererogation*, in the *R. Cath. Ch.* good works which are considered as not absolutely required of each individual for his salvation, and which it is believed God may accept in atonement for the defective service of another.—**Supererogatory**, sū'pėr-e-rog"a-to-ri, *a.* Partaking of supererogation.

Superexalt, sū'pėr-eg-zalt", *v.t.* [Prefix *super*, and *exalt.*] To exalt to a superior degree.—**Superexaltation**, sū'pėr-eg-zal-tā"shon, *n.* Elevation above the common degree.

Superexcellent, sū-pėr-ek'sel-lent, *a.* [Prefix *super*, and *excellent.*] Excellent in an uncommon degree.—**Superexcellence**, sū-pėr-ek'sel-lens, *n.* Superior excellence.

Superfecundation, sū'pėr-fē-kun-dā"-shon, *n.* [L. *super*, over, and *fecundus*, fruitful.] Superfetation.—**Superfecundity**, sū'pėr-fē-kun"di-ti, *n.* Superabundant fecundity.

Superfetate, sū-pėr-fē'tāt, *v.i.* [L. *superfeto*—*super*, over, after, and *feto*, to breed. FETUS.] To conceive after a prior conception.—**Superfetation, Superfœtation**, sū'pėr-fē-tā"shon, *n.* A second conception after a prior one, and by which two fetuses exist at once in the same womb.

Superficies, sū-pėr-fish'ēz, *n.* [L., from *super*, upon, and *facies*, face. (FACE.) *Surface* is another form of the same word.] The surface; the exterior part or face of a thing, consisting of length and breadth without thickness, and therefore forming no part of the substance or solid content of a body.—**Superficial**, sū-pėr-fish'al, *a.* [L. *superficialis.*] Lying on or pertaining to the surface; not penetrating the substance of a thing; not sinking deep; not deep or profound as regards knowledge; not learned or thorough; not going to the heart of things.—**Superficialist**, sū-pėr-fish'al-ist, *n.* A person of superficial attainments; a sciolist.—**Superficiality**, sū-pėr-fish'i-al"i-ti, *n.* The quality of being superficial; want of depth or thoroughness; shallowness; a superficial person or thing.—**Superficially**, sū-pėr-fish'al-li, *adv.* In a superficial manner; on the surface only; without going deep; slightly; not thoroughly.—**Superficialness**, sū-pėr-fish'al-nes, *n.* Superficiality; shallowness.

Superfine, sū-pėr-fīn', *a.* [Prefix *super*, and *fine.*] Very fine; surpassing others in fineness; excessively or faultily subtle.—**Superfineness**, sū-pėr-fīn'nes, *n.* Quality of being superfine.

Superfluity, sū-pėr-flū'i-ti, *n.* [Fr. *superfluité*, L. *superfluitas*, from *superfluus*, overflowing—*super*, above, and *fluo*, to flow. FLUENT.] A quantity that is over and above what is necessary; a greater quantity than is wanted; redundancy; something for show or luxury rather than use.—**Superfluous**, sū-pėr'flū-us, *a.* [L. *superfluus.*] Being more than is wanted or sufficent; unnecessary from being in excess; redundant.—**Superfluously**, sū-pėr'flū-us-li, *adv.* In a superfluous manner.—**Superfluousness**, sū-pėr'flū-us-nes, *n.*

Superfœtation, *n.* SUPERFETATION.

Superfrontal, sū-pėr-fron'tal, *n.* [Prefix *super*, and *frontal.*] The part of an altar-cloth that covers the top.

Superheat, sū'pėr-hēt, *v.t.* [Prefix *super*, and *heat.*] To heat to an extreme degree; specifically, to heat steam, apart from contact with water, until it resembles a perfect gas.

Superhuman, sū-pėr-hū'man, *a.* [Prefix *super*, and *human.*] Above or beyond what is human; hence, sometimes, divine.

Superimpose, sū'pėr-im-pōz", *v.t.* [Prefix *super*, and *impose.*] To lay or impose on something else.—**Superimposition**, sū-pėr-im'pō-zish"on, *n.* The act of superimposing or the state of being superimposed.

Superincumbent, sū'pėr-in-kum"bent, *a.* [Prefix *super*, and *incumbent.*] Lying or resting on something else.—**Superincumbence, Superincumbency**, sū'-pėr-in-kum"bens, sū'pėr-in-kum"ben-si, *n.* State of lying upon something.

Superinduce, sū'pėr-in-dūs", *v.t.* [Prefix *super*, and *induce.*] To bring in or on as an addition to something.—**Superinducement, Superinduction**, sū'pėr-in-dūs"ment, sū'pėr-in-duk"shon, *n.* The act of superinducing.

Superintellectual, sū'pėr-in-tel-lek"tū-al, *a.* [Prefix *super*, and *intellect.*] Being above intellect.

Superintend, sū'pėr-in-tend", *v.t.* [L. *superintendo*, to have the oversight of—*super* and *intendo.* INTEND.] To have the charge and oversight of; to oversee with the power of direction; to take care of with authority.—**Superintendence, Superintendency**, sū'pėr-in-ten"dens, sū'pėr-in-ten"den-si, *n.* The act of superintending; care and oversight for the purpose of direction, and with authority to direct.—**Superintendent**, sū'pėr-in-ten"dent, *n.* One who superintends or has the oversight and charge of something.—*a.* Overlooking others with authority.—**Superintender**, sū'pėr-in-ten"dėr, *n.* One who superintends.

Superior, sū-pē'ri-ėr, *a.* [L., compar. of *superus*, upper, high, from *super*, above. SUPER.] More elevated in place; higher; higher in rank, office, or dignity; higher or greater in excellence; being beyond some power or influence; too great or firm to be affected by (*superior* to revenge); *bot.* growing above or upon anything (as the ovary when growing above the origin of the calyx); next the axis.—*Superior courts*, the highest courts in a state.—*Superior planets*, those that are more distant from the sun than the earth, as Mars, Jupiter, Saturn, Uranus, and Neptune.—*n.* One who is superior to or above another; one who is higher or greater than another in social station, rank, power, excellence, or qualities of any kind; the chief of a monastery, convent, or abbey; *Scots law*, one who has certain rights of feu over a property.—**Superioress**, sū-pē'ri-ėr-es, *n.* A lady superior.—**Superiority**, sū-pē'ri-or"i-ti, *n.* The state or quality of being superior; pre-eminence; higher rank or excellency.—**Superiorly**, sū-pē'ri-ėr-li, *adv.* In a superior manner or position.—**Superiorness**, sū-pē'ri-or-nes, *n.* Superiority.

Superjacent, sū-pėr-jā'sent, *a.* [L. *super*, above, and *jacens, jacentis*, ppr. of *jaceo*, to lie.] Lying above or upon.

Superlative, sū-pėr'la-tiv, *a.* [L. *superlativus*, from *superlatus*—*super*, over, and *latus*, carried.] Of the highest pitch or degree; most eminent; surpassing all other (*superlative* wisdom or beauty); *gram.* applied to that form of an adjective or adverb which expresses the highest or utmost degree of the quality or manner.—*n.* That which is superlative; *gram.* the superlative degree of adjectives or adverbs; a word in the superlative degree.—**Superlatively**, sū-pėr'la-tiv-li, *adv.* In a superlative manner; in the highest or utmost degree.—**Superlativeness**, sū-pėr'la-tiv-nes, *n.* The state of being superlative.

Superlunar, Superlunary, sū-pėr-lū'-nėr, sū-pėr-lū'na-ri, *a.* [L. *super*, above, *luna*, the moon.] Being above the moon; not sublunary or of this world.

Superman, sū'pėr-man, *n.* The ideal superior man of the future in the philosophy of Nietzsche; also called *overman.*

Supermundane, sū-pėr-mun'dān, *a.* [Prefix *super*, and *mundane.*] Being above the world or mundane affairs.

Supernal, sū-pėr'nal, *a.* [L. *supernus*, from *super*, above. SUPER.] Being or situated above us; relating to things above; celestial; heavenly.

Supernatant, sū-pėr-nā'tant, *a.* [L. *super*, above, over, and *nato*, to swim.] Swimming above; floating on the surface.—**Supernatation**, sū'pėr-na-tā"shon, *n.* The act of floating on the surface of a fluid.

Supernatural, sū-pėr-nat'ū-ral, *a.* [Prefix *super*, and *natural.*] Being beyond or exceeding the powers or laws of nature; a term stronger than *preternatural*, and often equivalent to *miraculous.*—*The supernatural*, supernatural agencies, influence, phenomena, and so forth.—**Supernaturalism**, sū-pėr-nat'ū-ral-izm, *n.* The state of being supernatural; *theol.* the doctrine that religion and the knowledge of God require a revelation from God.—**Supernaturalist**, sū-pėr-nat'ū-ral-ist, *n.* One who upholds the principles of supernaturalism.—**Supernaturalize**, sū-pėr-nat'ū-ral-īz, *v.t.* To treat or consider as supernatural.—**Supernaturally**, sū-pėr-nat'ū-ral-li, *adv.* In a supernatural manner.—**Supernaturalness**, sū-pėr-nat'ū-ral-nes, *n.* The state or quality of being supernatural.

Supernumerary, sū-pėr-nū'me-ra-ri, *a.* [L. *super*, above, beyond, and *numerus*, a number.] Exceeding a number stated or prescribed; exceeding a necessary or usual number.—*n.* A person or thing beyond a certain number, or beyond what is necessary or usual; especially a person not formally a member of an ordinary or regular body or staff of officials or employees; *milit.* in drill, the N.C.O.'s, &c., forming the third rank.

Superordination, sū'pėr-or-di-nā"shon, *n.* [Prefix *super*, and *ordination.*] The ordination of a person to fill an office still occupied.

Superphosphate, sū-pėr-fos'fāt, *n.* [Prefix *super*, and *phosphate.*] A specially soluble phosphate of calcium, used as a fertilizer.

Superpose, sū-pėr-pōz', *v.t.*—*superposed, superposing.* [Fr. *superposer*, from prefix *super*, and *poser*, to lay. POSE.] To lay upon, as one kind of rock on another.—**Superposition**, sū'pėr-pō-zish"on, *n.* The act of superposing; a lying or being situated above or upon something; *geol.* the order in which mineral masses are placed upon or above each other, as more recent strata upon those that are older; *geom.* the process by which one magnitude may be conceived to be placed upon another.

Super-royal, sū-pėr-roi'al, *a.* [Prefix *super*, and *royal.*] Larger than royal; the name of a large species of printing paper.

Supersaturate, sū-pėr-sat'ū-rāt, *v.t.* [Prefix *super*, and *saturate.*] To saturate to excess.—**Supersaturation**, sū'pėr-sat-ū-rā"shon, *n.* Saturation to excess.

Superscribe, sū-pėr-skrīb', *v.t.* — *superscribed, superscribing.* [L. *superscribo*—*super*, over or above, and *scribo*, to write. SCRIBE.] To write on the top, outside, or surface; to put an inscription on; to write the name or address of one on the outside or cover of.—**Superscription**, sū-pėr-skrip'shon, *n.* The act of superscribing; what is written or engraved on the outside or above something else; especially, an address on a letter.

Supersede, sū-pėr-sēd', *v.t.*—*superseded, superseding.* [O.Fr. *superseder*, L. *supersedere*, to sit over, to refrain, omit—*super*, above, and *sedeo*, to sit. SEDATE.] To make void, inefficacious, or useless by superior power, or by coming in the place of; to set aside; to suspend; to come or be placed in the room of; to displace; to replace (one person *supersedes* another).—**Supersedure, Supersession**, sū-pėr-sē'dūr, sū-pėr-sesh'on, *n.* The act of superseding.

Supersensible, sū-pėr-sen'si-bl, *a.* [Prefix *super*, and *sensible, sensitive*, &c.] Beyond the reach of the senses.—**Supersensitiveness**, sū-pėr-sen'si-tiv-nes, *n.* Morbid sensitiveness or sensibility.—**Supersensual**, sū-pėr-sen'sū-al, *a.* Above or beyond the reach of the senses.—**Supersensuous**, sū-pėr-sen'sū-us, *a.* Supersensible; extremely sensuous.

Superstition, sū-pėr-stish'on, *n.* [L. *superstitio, superstitionis*, originally a standing still at, a standing in fear or amazement, hence superstition, from *supersto*, to stand over—*super*, over, and *sto*, to stand. STATE.] Belief in and reverence of things which are no proper objects of worship; a faith or article of faith based on ignorance of or on unworthy ideas regarding the Deity; a practice or observance founded on such a belief; credulity regarding the supernatural; belief in the direct agency of superior powers in certain affairs, as a belief in witchcraft or magic, or in supernatural phenomena, as apparitions, omens, &c.—**Superstitious**, sū-pėr-stish'us, *a.* Pertaining or addicted to superstition; credulous in regard to the supernatural; proceeding from superstition.—**Superstitiously**, sū-pėr-stish'us-li, *adv.* In a superstitious manner.—**Superstitiousness**, sū-pėr-stish'us-nes, *n.*

Superstratum, sū-pėr-strā'tum, *n.* [Prefix *super*, and *stratum.*] A stratum or layer above another, or resting on something else.

Superstructure, sū-pėr-struk'tūr, *n.* [Prefix *super*, and *structure.*] Any structure built on something else; anything erected on a foundation or basis.

Supersubtle, sū-pėr-sut'l, *a.* [Prefix *super*, and *subtle.*] Over-subtle; crafty in an excessive degree.

Super-tax, sūp'ėr-tax, *n.* [Prefix *super*, and *tax.*] An extra tax, usually graded, on incomes above some fixed amount.

Superterrestrial, sū'pėr-te-res"tri-al, *a.* [Prefix *super*, and *terrestrial.*] Being above the earth or terrestrial things.

Supertonic, sū-pėr-ton'ik, *n.* [Prefix *super*, and *tonic.*] *Mus.* the note next above the tonic or key-note; the second note of the diatonic scale.

Supervene, sū-pėr-vēn', *v.i.*—*supervened, supervening.* [L. *supervenio*—*super*, above, over, and *venio*, to come.] To come upon as something extraneous; to be added or joined; to take place; to happen.—**Supervenient**, sū-pėr-vē'ni-ent, *a.* Coming upon as something additional; added; arising or coming afterwards.—**Supervention**, sū-pėr-ven'shon, *n.* The act of supervening.

Supervise, sū-pėr-vīz', *v.t.* — *supervised, supervising.* [L. *super*, over, and *viso*, to look at, from *video, visum*, to see. VISION.] To oversee for direction; to superintend; to inspect.—**Supervisal**, sū-pėr-vī'zal, *n.* The act of supervising; inspection.—**Supervision**, sū-pėr-vizh'on, *n.* The act of supervising; superintendence; direction.—**Supervisor**, sū-pėr-vī'zėr, *n.* One who supervises; an overseer; an inspector; a superintendent.—**Supervisory**, sū-pėr-vī'zo-ri, *a.* Pertaining to or having supervision.

Supervolute, sū'pėr-vō-lūt", *a.* [L. *super*, upon, and *volutus*, rolled.] *Bot.* having one edge of the bud leaf rolled inwards, and enveloped by the opposite edge.

Supine, sū-pīn', *a.* [L. *supinus*, lying on the back, negligent, connected with *sub*, and Gr. *hypo*, under.] Lying on the back or with the face upward: opposed to *prone*; inclined or sloping; negligent; listless; indolent; inattentive.—*n.* (sū'pīn). [L. *supinum*; reason of the name not obvious.] A part of the Latin verb, really a verbal noun with two cases, an accusative in *-um*, and an ablative in *-u*.—**Supinely**, sū-pīn'li, *adv.* In a supine manner; carelessly; indolently; listlessly.—**Supineness**, sū-pīn'nes, *n.* Indolence; listlessness.—**Supination**, sū-pī-nā'shon, *n.* The position of the hand extended outwards with the palm upwards.—**Supinator**, sū-pī-nā'tėr, *n.* A muscle which aids in turning the hand upwards.

Supper. Under SUP.

Supplant, sup-plant', *v.t.* [Fr. *supplanter*, from L. *supplantare*, to trip up one's heels—*sub*, under, and *planta*, the sole of the foot. PLANT.] To trip up (*Mil.*)‡; to remove or displace by stratagem; to displace and take the place of.—**Supplantation**, sup-plan-tā'shon, *n.* The act of supplanting.—**Supplanter**, sup-plan'tėr, *n.* One who supplants.

Supple, sup'l, *a.* [Fr. *souple*, from L. *supplex*, suppliant, bending—*sub*, under, and *plico*, to fold. SUPPLICATE.] Pliant; flexible; easily bent; yielding; not obstinate; capable of moulding one's self to suit a purpose; flattering; fawning.—*v.t.*—*suppled, suppling.* To make supple or pliant; to make compliant, submissive, or yielding.—*v.i.* To become soft and pliant.—**Supple-jack**, *n.* A popular name given to various strong twining and climbing shrubs, the branches of which are imported into Europe from the West Indies for walking-sticks.—**Supplely**, sup'l-li, *adv.* In a supple manner.—**Suppleness**, sup'l-nes, *n.* The quality of being supple or easily bent; pliancy; readiness of compliance; facility.

Supplement, sup'lē-ment, *n.* [L. *supplementum*, from *suppleo*, to fill up, to make full—*sub*, and *pleo*, to fill. SUPPLY.] An addition to anything, by which it is made more full and complete, especially an addition to a book, to a periodical publication, &c.; *trigon.* the quantity by which an arc or an angle falls short of 180 degrees or a semicircle.—*v.t.* To increase or complete by a supplement.—**Supplemental, Supplementary**, sup-lē-men'tal, sup-lē-men'ta-ri, *a.* Of the nature of a supplement; serving to supplement; additional.—**Supplementation**, sup'lē-men-tā"shon, *n.* The act of supplementing.—**Suppletive, Suppletory**, sup'lē-tiv, sup'lē-to-ri, *a.* [From L. *suppleo, suppletum*, to supply.] Supplying deficiencies; supplemental.

Suppleness. Under SUPPLE.

Suppliant, sup'li-ant, *a.* [Fr. *suppliant*, ppr. of *supplier*, to entreat, from L. *supplico*, to *supplicate* (which see).] Entreating or begging earnestly; asking earnestly and submissively; supplicating; expressive of supplication.—*n.* A humble petitioner; one who entreats submissively.—**Suppliantly**, sup'li-ant-li, *adv.* In a suppliant manner.

Supplicate, sup'li-kāt, *v.t.*—*supplicated, supplicating.* [L. *supplico, supplicatum*, from *supplex, supplicis*, suppliant, lit. bending under (whence *supple*)—*sub*, under, and *plico*, to fold. PLY, *v.t.*] To entreat or beg humbly for; to seek by earnest prayer (to *supplicate* blessings); to address in prayer; to petition humbly (to *supplicate* God).—*v.i.* To petition with earnestness and submission; to implore; to beseech.—**Supplication**, sup-li-kā'shon, *n.* [L. *supplicatio.*] The act of supplicating; humble and earnest prayer in worship; a petition; an earnest request.—**Supplicator**, sup'li-kā-tėr, *n.* One who supplicates; a suplicant.—**Supplicatory**, sup'li-ka-to-ri, *a.* Containing supplication.—**Supplicant**, sup'li-kant, *n.* One who supplicates or humbly entreats; a humble petitioner; a suppliant.—*a.* Earnestly entreating; suppliant.—**Supplicantly**, sup'li-kant-li, *adv.* In a supplicant manner.

Supply, sup-plī', *v.t.*—*supplied, supplying.* [Fr. *suppléer*, to supply, from L. *supplere*, to fill up—*sub*, under, and *pleo*, to fill (seen also in *supplement, accomplish, complete, deplete, expletive, replete*, &c.). PLENTY.] To furnish with what is wanted (to *supply* a person *with* a thing); to afford or furnish a sufficiency for (to *supply* wants); to provide or furnish (to *supply* provisions); to serve instead of; to take the place of.—*n.* The act of supplying; a quantity supplied; a stock; a store; *pl.* the stores or articles necessary for an army or other great body of people; a grant of money provided by a national assembly to meet the expenses of government; the extent to which goods are produced to meet the demand.—**Supplier**, sup-plī'ėr, *n.* One who supplies.

Support, sup-pōrt', *v.t.* [Fr. *supporter*, to support, bear, endure, &c., from L. *supporto*, to convey—*sub*, under, and *porto*, to carry (as in *export, import, report*, &c.). PORT, to carry.] To bear, uphold, prop up; to keep from falling or sinking; to endure without being overcome; to bear; to undergo; to uphold by aid or encouragement; to further, second, aid, assist; to keep from sinking, failing, or declining (to *support* the courage); to represent in acting on the stage; to act (to *support* a part); to be able to supply funds for or the means of continuing; to be able to carry on or continue; to maintain with the means of living; to provide for; to keep up by nutriment; to sustain (to *support* life, to *support* combustion); to make good or substantiate (a statement, an accusation); to second, as a proposal or motion at a public meeting.—*n.* The act of supporting; that which upholds or keeps from falling; a base, prop, foundation of any kind; sustenance or what maintains life; maintenance; livelihood; one who furnishes another's livelihood; the act of assisting, maintaining, vindicating, &c.; aid; help; succour; assistance.—**Supportable**, sup-pōr'ta-bl, *a.* Capable of being supported; that may be tolerated; bearable; endurable.—**Supportableness**, sup-pōr'ta-bl-nes, *n.* The state of being supportable.—**Supportably**, sup-pōr'ta-bli, *adv.* In a supportable manner.—**Supporter**, sup-pōr'tėr, *n.* One who supports or maintains; a defender; advocate, vindicator, adherent; one who accompanies and aids another; that which supports or keeps up; a prop, a pillar, &c.; *her.* a figure on each side of a shield appearing to support it; a band or truss for the support of any part.—**Supportless**, sup-pōrt'-les, *a.* Having no support.

Suppose, sup-pōz', *v.t.*—*supposed, supposing.* [Fr. *supposer*—*sup* for *sub*, under, and *poser*, to place. POSE.] To lay down or regard as matter of fact for the sake of argument or illustration; to assume hypothetically; to take for granted; to imagine; to think to be the case; to require to exist or be true; to imply (creation *supposes* a creator).—*v.i.* To make or form a supposition; to think; to imagine.—**Supposer**, sup-pō'zėr, *n.* One who supposes.—**Supposable**, sup-pō'za-bl, *a.* Capable of being supposed or imagined.—**Supposal**, sup-pō'zal, *n.* A supposition.—**Supposition**, sup-pō-zish'on, *n.* The act of supposing; hypothesis; what is assumed hypothetically; an assumption; a conjecture. — **Suppositional**, sup-pō-zish'on-al, *a.* Based on supposition; hypothetical.—**Suppositive**, sup-poz'i-tiv, *a.* Including or implying supposition.—*n.* A word implying supposition, as *if.* — **Suppositively**, sup-poz'i-tiv-li, *adv.* With, by, or upon supposition.

Supposititious, sup-poz'i-tish"us, *a.* [L. *supposititius*, from *suppono, suppositum*—*sub*, under, and *pono*, to place. POSITION.] Put by trick in the place belonging to another; substituted falsely; not genuine; counterfeit; spurious. — **Supposititiously**, sup-poz'i-tish"us-li, *adv.* In a supposititious manner; spuriously. — **Supposititiousness**, sup-poz'i-tish"us-nes, *n.*

Suppress, sup-pres', *v.t.* [L. *supprimo, suppressum*—*sub*, under, and *premo, pressum*, to press. PRESS.] To overpower and crush; to put down; to quell; to destroy (a revolt, mutiny, or riot); to restrain from utterance or vent; to check or keep in (to *suppress* the breath); to conceal; not to tell or reveal; to retain without making public. —**Suppressible**, sup-pres'i-bl, *a.* Capable of being suppressed.—**Suppression**, sup-presh'on, *n.* The act of suppressing, crushing, or putting down; the act of retaining from utterance, vent, or disclosure; concealment; the retaining of anything from public notice; *gram.* omission or ellipsis.—**Suppressive**, sup-pres'iv, *a.* Tending to suppress.—**Suppressor**, sup-pres'ėr, *n.* One who suppresses.

Suppurate, sup'pū-rāt, *v.i.*—*suppurated, suppurating.* [L. *suppuro, suppuratum*—*sub*, and *pus, puris*, matter. PUS.] To generate pus or matter; to have a gathering of pus; to fester.—**Suppuration**, sup-pū-rā'shon, *n.* The process of forming pus, as in a wound or abscess.—**Suppurative**, sup'pū-rā-tiv, *a.* Tending to suppurate.—*n.* Something that promotes suppuration.

Supra-axillary, sū-pra-ak'sil-la-ri, *a.* [Prefix *supra*, above, and *axil.*] *Bot.* growing above the axil.

Supracostal, sū-pra-kos'tal, *a.* [Prefix *supra*, above, and *costa*, a rib.] Lying above or upon the ribs.

Supracretaceous, sū'pra-krē-tā"shus, *a.* [Prefix *supra*, above, and *cretaceous.*] *Geol.* a term applied to certain deposits lying above the cretaceous formation.

Suprafoliaceous, sū'pra-fō-li-ā"shus, *a.* [L. *supra*, above, *folium*, a leaf.] *Bot.* inserted in the stem above a leaf, petiole, or axil.—**Suprafoliar**, sū'pra-fō'li-ėr, *a.* *Bot.* growing upon a leaf.

Supralapsarian, sū'pra-lap-sā"ri-an, *n.* [L. *supra*, above, and *lapsus*, a fall.] One who maintains that God decreed or preordained the fall of man and all its consequences, determining to save some and condemn others. — **Supralapsarianism**, sū'pra-lap-sā"ri-an-izm, *n.* The doctrine of the Supralapsarians.

Supramundane, sū-pra-mun'dān, *a.* [L. *supra*, above, *mundus*, the world.] Being or situated above the world or above our system; celestial.

Supraoccipital, sū'pra-ok-sip"i-tal, *a.* [Prefix *supra*, above, and *occiput.*] *Anat.* above the occiput.

Supraorbital, sū-pra-or'bi-tal, *a.* [Prefix *supra*, above, and *orbit.*] *Anat.* being above the orbit of the eye.

Suprarenal, sū-pra-rē'nal, *a.* [L. *supra*, above, and *renes*, the kidneys.] *Anat.* situated above the kidneys.—*Suprarenal body.* See ADRENAL.

Suprascapulary, Suprascapular, sū-pra-skap'ū-la-ri, sū-pra-skap'ū-lėr, *a.* [Prefix *supra*, above, and *scapula.*] Being above the scapula.

Supraspinal, sū-pra-spī'nal, *a.* [Prefix *supra*, above, and *spine.*] *Anat.* situated above the spine.

Supreme, sū-prēm', *a.* [L. *supremus*, from *superus*, upper, higher, from *super*, above. SUPER.] Highest in authority; holding the highest place in government or power; highest as to degree; greatest possible; utmost; *bot.* situated at the highest part or point.—*The Supreme*, the most exalted of beings; the sovereign of the universe; God. —**Supremely**, sū-prēm'li, *adv.* With the highest authority; in the highest degree; to the utmost extent.—**Supremacy**, sū-prem'a-si, *n.* The state or character of being supreme; highest authority or power. —*Papal supremacy*, the supreme authority which the pope formerly exercised over the churches of England, Scotland, and Ireland, and which still continues to be more or less recognized in some countries.—*Regal supremacy*, the authority which the sovereign of England exercises over the Church of England, as being its supreme head on earth.—*Oath of supremacy*, in Great Britain, an oath denying the supremacy of the pope in ecclesiastical or temporal affairs in this realm.

Sura, sö'ra, *n.* [Ar.] A chapter of the Koran.

Sural, sū'ral, *n.* [L. *sura*, the calf of the leg.] Pertaining to the calf of the leg.

Surat, sö-rat', *n.* Coarse short cotton grown in the neighbourhood of *Surat*, in the Bombay presidency.

Surbase, sėr'bās, *n.* [Prefix *sur* (L. *super*), upon, and *base.*] *Arch.* the crowning moulding or cornice of a pedestal; a border or moulding above the base. — **Surbased**, sėr'bāst, *a.* *Arch.* having a surbase.

Surbed, sėr-bed', *v.t.* [Prefix *sur* (L. *super*), and *bed.*] To set edgewise, as a stone, that is, in a position different from what it had in the quarry.

Surcease, sėr-sēs', *v.i.*—*surceased, surceasing.* [Formerly *surcesse, sursease*, from Fr. *sursis*, pp. of *surseoir*, to intermit or leave off, from prefix *sur* (L. *super*), over, and *seoir*, L. *sedere*, to sit; the spelling being influenced by *cease.*] To cease; to leave off; to refrain finally.—*n.* Cessation; stop. (*Poetical.*)

Surcharge, sėr-chärj', *v.t.* [Prefix *sur* (L. *super*), over, and *charge.*] To overload: to overburden; to overcharge; to put an extra charge on.—*n.* An excessive or extra charge or burden; an overcharge.

Surcingle, sėr'sing-gl, *n.* [O.Fr. *sursangle*, from *sur*, L. *super*, upon, and *cingulum*, a belt.] A belt or girth fastening a saddle or anything else on a horse's back; the girdle round a clergyman's cassock.

Surcoat, sėr'kōt, *n.* [Prefix *sur* (L. *super*), over, and *coat.*] An outer garment formerly worn in a variety of forms; a loose sleeveless wrapper embroidered with the arms of a knight and girded round the waist with a sword belt, formerly worn by him over a coat of mail to protect it from wet.

Surculus, sėr'kū-lus, *n.* pl. **Surculi**, sėr'-kū-lī. [L.] *Bot.* any little branch or twig.

Surd, sėrd, *a.* [L. *surdus*, deaf, not sounding, stupid (seen also in *absurd*); allied to *sordid, swart.*] *Phonetics*, uttered with breath and not with voice; not sonant, as *t* compared with *d*, *p* with *b*, *f* with *v*; *math.* not capable of being expressed in rational numbers.—*n.* *Phonetics*, a non-sonant consonant; *math.* an irrational quantity; a quantity that cannot be expressed in finite terms, as the square root of 2.

Sure, shör, *a.* [Fr. *sûr*, O.Fr. *seur, seür*, Pr. *segur*, from L. *securus*, unconcerned, secure —*se*, apart, and *cura*, care. The same word as *secure.* CURE.] Perfectly confident; certainly knowing and believing; certain; fully persuaded; certain to find or retain (*sure* of success); to be depended on; unfailing; firm; stable; secure; infallible (a *sure* remedy).—*To make sure*, to make certain; to secure so that there can be no failure of the purpose or object.—*adv.* Certainly; without doubt. (*Colloq.*)—**Sure-footed**, *a.* Not liable to stumble, slip, or fall.—**Surely**, shör'li, *adv.* Certainly; undoubtedly; firmly; securely; verily.—**Sureness**, shör'nes, *n.* The state of being sure or certain; certainty. — **Surety**, shör'ti, *n.* Certainty; security; ground of security; security against loss or damage or for payment; *law*, one bound with and for another who is primarily liable, and who is called the principal; one who binds himself to stand good for another; a bail.—**Suretyship**, shör'ti-ship, *n.* The state of being a surety; the obligation of a person to stand good for another. Written also *Suretiship.*

Surf, sėrf, *n.* [For old *suffe*, the same as *sough*; or from O.Fr. *surflot*—*sur*, above, and *flot*, a wave.] The swell of the sea which breaks upon the shore, or upon sandbanks or rocks.—**Surfy**, sėr'fi, *a.* Abounding with surf; foamy.—**Surf-boat**, *n.* A strong and buoyant boat capable of passing with safety through surf.—**Surf-duck**, *n.* A species of duck frequent on the coasts of North America. Called also *Surf-scoter.*

Surface, sėr'fās, *n.* [Fr. *surface*, from *sur*, upon, and *face*, face; L. *super*, and *facies.*] The exterior part of anything that has length and breadth; one of the limits that terminates a solid; the superficies; outside; *fig.* outward or external appearance; what appears on a slight or casual view; *geom.* a superficies; that which has length and breadth only.—*A plane surface* is that in which any two points being taken the straight line between them lies wholly in that surface.—*a.* Pertaining to the surface; external; superficial. —*v.t.*—*surfaced, surfacing.* To give a particular surface to; to work over the surface of.—**Surface-gauge**, *n.* An instrument for testing the accuracy of plane surfaces. — **Surface-joint**, *n.* A joint uniting the edges of sheets or plates.—**Surfaceman**, sėr'fās-man, *n.* *Rail.* a person whose duty it is to keep the permanent way in order. — **Surface-tension**, *n.* Of a liquid, the condition of the surface layer, which behaves like a stretched film.—**Surface-water**, *n.* Water which collects on the surface of the ground from rain or snow.—**Surface-working**, *n.* Digging for gold or other minerals on the top soil.

Surfeit, sėr'fit, *n.* [O.Fr. *surfait*, excess—*sur* (L. *super*), over, and *fait*, pp. of *faire*, L. *facere*, to do. FACT.] An overloading of the stomach by excess in eating and drinking; a gluttonous meal that deranges the stomach and system; disgust caused by excess; satiety. —*v.t.* To derange the stomach by excess in eating; to overload the stomach of; to fill to satiety and disgust; to cloy.—*v.i.* To suffer from a surfeit. —**Surfeiter**, sėr'fit-ėr, *n.* One who surfeits; a glutton.

Surfy. Under *Surf.*

Surge, sėrj, *n.* [O.Fr. *surgeon, sourgeon*, a spring, a spouting up, from L. *surgere*, to rise, from *sub*, under, and *rego*, to direct. SOURCE.] A large wave or billow; a great rolling swell of water; a heaving or swelling up; an undulation.—*v.i.*—*surged, surging.* To swell; to rise high and roll, as waves.—**Surgeant**, sėr'jant, *a.* *Her.* the rising position as applied to birds.—**Surgeless**, sėrj'les, *a.* Free from surges; smooth; calm.—**Surgy**, sėr'ji, *a.* Rising in surges; billowy.

Surgeon, sėr'jun, *n.* [O.E. *chirurgeon*, O. Fr. *surgien*, contr. for *chirurgien*, from L. *chirurgus*, Gr. *cheirourgos*, a surgeon—*cheir*, the hand, and *ergon*, work.] A medical man whose profession is to cure diseases or injuries of the body by manual operation or by medical appliances employed externally or internally, as distinguished from a physician.—**Surgeoncy**, sėr'jun-si, *n.* The office of surgeon as in the army or navy.—**Surgeon-dentist**, *n.* A dental surgeon.—**Surgery**, sėr'jėr-i, *n.* [For *surgeonry*.] The operative branch of medicine; that branch of medical science and practice which involves the performance of operations on the human subject; a room where surgical operations are performed, or where medicines are prepared.—**Surgical**, sėr'-ji-kal, *a.* Pertaining to surgery; done by means of surgery.

Surgy. Under *Surge.*

Suricate, sū'ri-kāt, *n.* [South African name.] A carnivorous animal of South Africa, resembling the polecat or ferret, kept in houses like a cat.

Surloin, sėr'loin. SIRLOIN.

Surly, sėr'li, *a.* [Old form *sirly* or *syrly*; probably for *sir-like*, that is, magisterial, arrogant.] Arrogant‡; gloomily morose; sternly sour; cross and rude; churlish; rough or tempestuous.—**Surlily**, sėr'li-li, *adv.* In a surly manner.—**Surliness**, sėr'li-nes, *n.* The quality of being surly; gloomy moroseness; sour ill-nature.

Surmise, sėr-mīz', *n.* [O.Fr. *surmise*, accusation, from *surmettre*, pp. *surmis*, *surmise*, to accuse, from prefix *sur*, L. *super*, upon, above, and *mettre*, L. *mittere*, to send. MISSION.] A thought or supposition with little or no ground to go upon; a guess or conjecture.—*v.t. surmise, surmising.* To guess; to conjecture.—**Surmiser**, sėr-mī'-zėr, *n.* One who surmises.—**Surmising**, sėr-mī'zing, *n.* A surmise.

Surmount, sėr-mount', *v.t.* [Fr. *surmonter*—*sur*, above, and *monter*, to mount. MOUNT.] To mount or rise above; to conquer; to overcome; to surpass. — **Surmountable**, sėr-moun'ta-bl, *a.* Capable of being surmounted.—**Surmounted**, *a.* *Her.* a charge which has another charge placed upon it is said to be surmounted by that second charge.—**Surmounter**, sėr-moun'tėr, *n.* One who surmounts.

Surmullet, sėr'mul-et, *n.* [Fr. *surmulet*, for *sormulet*, from O.Fr. *sor*, reddish-brown, sorrel, and *mulet*, a mullet. SORREL, MULLET.] A name for a variety of fishes allied to the perch family, of which the red surmullet inhabits the Mediterranean, and was prized by the Romans.

Surname, sėr'nām, *n.* [Prefix *sur* (L. *super*), over and above, and *name*.] An additional name or appellation; a name or appellation added to the baptismal or Christian name, and which becomes a family name.—*v.t.* To give a surname to.

Surpass, sėr-pas', *v.t.* [Fr. *surpasser*—*sur*, over, and *passer*, to pass.] To exceed; to excel; to go beyond in anything good or bad. —**Surpassable**, sėr-pas'a-bl, *a.* Capable of being surpassed. — **Surpassing**, sėr-pas'ing, *p.* and *a.* Excellent in an eminent degree; exceeding others.—**Surpassingly**, sėr-pas'ing-li, *adv.* In a degree surpassing others.

Surplice, sėr'plis, *n.* [Fr. *surplis*, L.L. *superpellicium*, from L. *super*, over, and *pellicium*, a coat or tunic, lit. a skin coat, from *pellis*, a skin. PELL.] A white garment worn by priests, deacons, and choristers in the Anglican and Roman Catholic Churches over their other dress at religious services.—**Surpliced**, sėr'plist, *a.* Wearing a surplice.—**Surplice-fee**, *n.* A fee paid to the clergy for occasional duties, as on baptisms, marriages, funerals, &c.

Surplus, sėr'plus, *n.* [Fr. *surplus*, from *sur*, L. *super*, over and above, and *plus*, more.] That which remains when use or need is satisfied; more than suffices; overplus: often used adjectively (*surplus* population).—**Surplusage**, sėr'plus-āj, *n.* Surplus; something not necessary or relevant to any matter.

Surprise, sėr-prīz', *n.* [Fr. *surprise*, from *surpris*, pp. of *surprendre*, to surprise—prefix *sur* (L. *super*), over, and *prendre*, L. *prendere*, *prehendere*, to seize. PRIZE.] The act of coming upon unawares, or of taking suddenly and without preparation; an emotion excited by something happening suddenly and unexpectedly; wonder; astonishment. — *v.t.* — *surprised, surprising.* To fall upon suddenly and unexpectedly; to attack or take unawares; to confuse or perplex; to strike with wonder or astonishment; to astonish; to lead, bring, or betray unawares.—**Surprisal**, sėr-prī'zal, *n.* The act of surprising or taking unawares; a surprise.—**Surpriser**, sėr-prī'zėr, *n.* One who surprises.—**Surprising**, sėr-prī'zing, *p.* and *a.* Exciting surprise; wonderful; extraordinary. — **Surprisingly**, sėr-prī'-zing-li, *adv.* In a surprising manner; astonishingly.

Surrebutter, sėr-rē-but'ėr, *n.* [Prefix *sur*, over.] *Law*, the plaintiff's reply in pleading to a defendant's rebutter. — **Surrejoinder**, sėr-rē-join'dėr, *n.* *Law*, the answer of a plaintiff to a defendant's rejoinder.

Surrender, sėr-ren'dėr, *v.t.* [Fr. *surrendre* —*sur*, over, and *rendre*, to render. RENDER.] To yield to the power of another; to give or deliver up upon compulsion or demand; to resign in favour of another; to cease to claim or use; to relinquish; *refl.* to yield to any influence, passion, or power (to *surrender one's self* to grief).—*v.i.* To yield; to give up one's self into the power of another. —*n.* The act of surrendering; a yielding or giving up; the abandonment of an assurance policy by the party assured on receiving a portion of the premiums paid.

Surreptitious, sėr-rep-tish'us, *a.* [L. *surreptitius*, from L. *surrepo*, to creep stealthily —*sub*, under, secretly, and *repo*, to creep. REPTILE.] Done by stealth or without proper authority; made or produced fraudulently.—**Surreptitiously**, sėr-rep-tish'-us-li, *adv.* In an underhand way; fraudulently.

Surrogate, sur'rō-gāt, *n.* [L. *surrogatus*, substituted, pp. of *surrogo*, *surrogatum*, to put in another's place — *sub*, under, and *rogo*, to ask. ROGATION.] A deputy; the deputy of an ecclesiastical judge, most commonly of a bishop or his chancellor; in some states, a judicial officer corresponding to an ordinary judge.

Surround, sėr-round', *v.t.* [O.Fr. *suronder*, to overflow, from prefix *sur*, over, and L. *unda*, a wave (as in *abound*).] To encompass, environ, or inclose on all sides; to invest, as a city; to lie or be on all sides of; to form an inclosure round. —**Surrounding**, sėr-roun'ding, *n.* An encompassing; one of those things that surround or environ; an environment: generally in plural (a dwelling and its *surroundings*).

Surtax, sėr'taks, *n.* [Prefix *sur*, above, and *tax*.] A tax heightened for a particular purpose; an extra tax.

Surtout, sėr-tö', *n.* [Fr. *sur-tout*, over all —*sur* = L. *super*, over, and *tout* = L. *totus*, whole.] Originally, a man's coat to be worn over his other garments; in modern usage, an upper coat with long wide skirts; a frock-coat.

Surturbrand, sėr'tėr-brand, *n.* [Icel. *surtarbrand*—*svartr*, black, and *brand*, a firebrand.] Bituminous wood found in Iceland, resembling the black bog-oak.

Surveillance, sėr-vāl'yans, *n.* [Fr., from *surveiller*, to watch over, from *sur*, L. *super*, over, and *veiller*, L. *vigilare*, to watch. VIGILANT.] Watch kept over some person or thing; oversight; superintendence. — *Police surveillance*, for a fixed time during which prisoners, after their release, have to report themselves periodically, is sometimes added to sentences.—**Surveillant**,† sėr-vāl'yant, *a.* Watching over another or others.

Survey, sėr-vā', *v.t.* [O.Fr. *surveer*, *surveoir*—*sur* (L. *super*), over, and *veer*, *veoir* (Fr. *voir*), L. *videre*, to see. VISION.] To inspect or take a view of; to view as from a high place; to view with scrutinizing eye; to examine; to examine with reference to condition, situation, or value; to inspect for a purpose; to determine the boundaries, extent, position, natural features, &c., of, as of any portion of the earth's surface by means of measurements, and the application of geometry and trigonometry. — *n.* (sėr'vā or sėr-vā'). A general view; a look at or over; a close examination or inspection to ascertain condition, quantity, quality, &c.; the determination of dimensions and other topographical particulars of any part of the earth's surface; the plan or account drawn up of such particulars.—*Ordnance Survey.* Under ORDNANCE.— —*Trigonometrical survey.* TRIGONOMETRICAL.—**Surveying**, sėr-vā'ing, *n.* The act of one who surveys; the operation or art of making a survey of a portion of the earth's surface by means of measurements and calculations.—*Land surveying*, the determination of the area, shape, &c., of a tract of land, usually of no very great extent. —*Marine surveying* consists in determining the forms of coasts, the positions and distances of islands, rocks, shoals, the depth of water, nature of the bottom, &c.—**Surveyor**, sėr-vā'ėr, *n.* One who surveys; an overseer; one that views and examines for the purpose of ascertaining the condition or state of anything; one who practises the art of surveying.—**Surveyor-general**, *n.* A principal surveyor; a chief government surveyor.—**Surveyorship**, sėr-vā'-ėr-ship, *n.* The office of a surveyor.

Survive, sėr-vīv', *v.t.*—*survived, surviving.* [Fr. *survivre*, from L. *supervivo*—*super*, over, beyond, and *vivo*, *victum*, to live. VITAL. VIVACIOUS.] To outlive; to live beyond the life of; to live longer than; to live beyond (to *survive* one's usefulness).—*v.i.* To remain alive; to live after the death of another or after anything else.—**Survival**, sėr-vī'val, *n.* The act of surviving; a living beyond the life of another person, or beyond any event; any habit, usage, or belief remaining from ancient times and existing merely from custom.—*Survival of the fittest*, the principle in natural selection that the animals and plants best suited to their surroundings survive, while the others die out. SELECTION.—*Survival value*, of a biological character, value as being helpful in the struggle for existence.—**Surviving**, sėr-vī'ving, *p.* and *a.* Remaining alive; yet living.—**Survivor**, sėr-vī'vėr, *n.* One who lives after the death of another, or after some event or time; *law*, the longer liver of two persons who have a joint interest in anything. — **Survivorship**, sėr-vī'vėr-ship, *n.* The state of being a survivor.

Susceptible, sus-sep'ti-bl, *a.* [Fr. *susceptible*, from L. *suscipio*, *susceptum*—*sus* for *sub*, under, and *capio*, to take. CAPABLE.] Capable of being acted on or affected in any way; admitting any change (*susceptible* of pain, of alteration); capable of emotional impression; readily impressed; impressible; sensitive. — **Susceptibly**, sus-sep'ti-bli, *adv.* In a susceptible manner.—**Susceptibility, Susceptibleness**, sus-sep'ti-bil"i-ti, sus-sep'ti-bl-nes, *n.* The state or quality of being susceptible; sensitiveness; capacity for feeling or emotional excitement; sensibility; *magnetism*, the ratio between the intensity of magnetization in a magnetic substance and the magnetizing force producing it.—**Susceptive**, sus-sep'-tiv, *a.* Readily admitting or being affected by influence; susceptible.—**Susceptiveness, Susceptivity**, sus-sep'tiv-nes, sus-sep-tiv'i-ti, *n.* Susceptibility. — **Suscipient**, sus-sip'i-ent, *n.* One who receives or admits.

Suslik, sus'lik, *n.* [Rus.] A pretty little animal of the marmot kind found in Eastern Europe and Western Asia.

Suspect, sus-pekt', *v.t.* [L. *suspicio*, *suspectum*—*sus* for *sub*, under, and *specio*, to look. SPECIES.] To have a vague belief or fear of the existence of; to imagine as probably existing (to *suspect* danger); to mistrust; to imagine to be guilty, but upon slight evidence or without proof; to hold to be uncertain; to doubt.—*n.* A suspected person; one suspected of a crime, offence, or the like.—**Suspectedness**, sus-pek'-ted-nes, *n.* State of being suspected. — **Suspecter**, sus-pek'tėr, *n.* One who suspects.—**Suspectless**, sus-pekt'les, *a.* Not suspecting; unsuspicious; not suspected or mistrusted.—**Suspicion**, sus-pish'on, *n.* [L. *suspicio, suspicionis.*] The act of suspecting; the feeling of one who suspects; the thought that there is probably something wrong; a notion that something is so or so.—**Suspicious**, sus-pish'us, *a.* [L. *suspiciosus.*] Inclined to suspect; ready to entertain or entertaining suspicion; distrustful (*suspicious* of a person or his motives); indicating or exhibiting suspicion; adapted to raise suspicion (*suspicious* circumstances).—**Suspiciously**, sus-pish'us-li, *adv.* In a suspicious manner; so as to excite suspicion.—**Suspiciousness**, sus-pish'us-nes, *n.* The state or quality of being suspicious.

Suspend, sus-pend', *v.t.* [L. *suspendo*—*sus* for *sub*, under, and *pendo*, to hang. PENDANT.] To cause to hang; to hang up; to cause to cease for a time; to interrupt temporarily; to stay; to hold in a state undetermined (to *suspend* one's choice); to debar for a time from any privilege; to remove temporarily from an office; to cause to cease for a time from operation or effect.—*To suspend payment*, to formally stop paying debts from being insolvent.—*Suspended animation*, a temporary cessation of animation, especially from asphyxia.—*v.i.* To cease from operation; to stop payment or be unable to meet one's engagements.—**Suspender**, sus-pen'dėr, *n.* One that suspends; one of a pair of braces for the trousers.—**Suspense**, sus-pens', *n.* [L. *suspensus*, suspended.] The state of having the mind or thoughts uncertain; uncertainty, with more or less apprehension or anxiety; indetermination; indecision; *law*, a temporary cessation.—**Suspensible**, sus-pen'si-bl, *a.* Capable of being suspended.—**Suspension**, sus-pen'shon, *n.* [L. *suspensio, suspensionis.*] The act of suspending or hanging up; the act of delaying, interrupting, or stopping for a time; a cessation of operation; a stoppage; temporary abeyance; the state of being in the form of particles floating undissolved in a fluid.—*Suspension-bridge.* CHAIN-BRIDGE.—*Suspension of arms*, a short truce or cessation of operations during a war.—**Suspensive**, sus-pen'siv, *a.* In a suspense; uncertain; doubtful.—**Suspensor**, sus-pen'sor, *n.* Something which suspends; *bot.* the cord by which the embryo of some plants is suspended from the opening of the seed.—**Suspensory**, sus-pen'so-ri, *a.* Serving to suspend; suspending.

Suspicion, Suspicious, &c. Under SUSPECT.

Suspire, sus-pīr', *v.i.* [L. *suspiro*, to sigh—*sus* for *sub*, and *spiro*, to breathe. SPIRIT.] To fetch a long, deep breath; to sigh. (*Shak.*)—**Suspiration**, sus-pi-rā'shon, *n.* A sigh.

Sustain, sus-tān', *v.t.* [O.Fr. *sustenir, sostenir* (Fr. *soutenir*), from L. *sustinere*—*sus* for *sub*, under, and *teneo*, to hold (as in *contain, retain*, &c.). TENANT.] To rest under and bear up; to support; to hold suspended; to keep from sinking in despondence; to keep alive; to furnish sustenance for; to nourish; to aid effectually; to keep from ruin; to endure without failing or yielding; to bear up against; to suffer; to undergo; to allow (an action) to proceed before a court; to hold valid in law; to establish by evidence; to confirm or corroborate.—**Sustainable**, sus-tā'na-bl, *a.* Capable of being sustained.—**Sustained**, sus-tānd'. *p.* and *a.* Kept up to one pitch or level, especially a high pitch.—**Sustainer**, sus-tā'nėr, *n.* One who or that which sustains.—**Sustainment**, sus-tān'ment, *n.* The act of sustaining.—**Sustenance**, sus'ten-ans, *n.* [O.Fr. *sustenance.*] The act of sustaining; maintenance; subsistence; that which supports life; food; provisions.—**Sustentation**, sus-ten-tā'shon, *n.* [L. *sustentatio*, from *sustento*, intens. of *sustineo.*] Support; sustenance; support of life; the phenomenon of sustaining or supporting a heavier-than-air machine by the reaction of a deflected air stream; the flotation of a lighter-than-air machine by the displacement of an equal mass of air.—*Sustentation fund*, formerly a fund belonging to the Free Church of Scotland, now replaced by the Central Fund of the United Free Church, from which all clergymen are paid an equal sum annually.

Susurrus, sū-sur'rus, *n.* [L.] A soft, humming, murmuring sound; a whisper.—**Susurrant**, sū-sur'ant, *a.* [L. *susurro*, to hum.] Whispering; susurrous.—**Susurrous**, sū-sur'rus, *a.* Whispering; rustling.

Sutile, sū'til, *a.* [L. *sutilis*, from *suo, sutum*, to sew (whence also *suture*). SEW.] Done by stitching.

Sutler, sut'lėr, *n.* [O.D. *soeteler*, D. *zoetelaar*, a sutler, from *soetelen*, to perform menial offices or dirty work; allied to G. *sudeln*, to dabble, to do dirty work, and to E. *suds, seethe.*] A person who follows an army and sells to the troops provisions, liquors, or the like.—**Sutling**, sut'ling, *n.* The occupation of a sutler.

Sutra, sö'tra, *n.* [Skr., string.] A collection or string of aphorisms in the Sanskrit literature.

Suttee, sut-tē', *n.* [Skr. *sati*, from *sat*, good, pure; properly, a chaste and virtuous wife.] A Hindu widow who immolates herself on the funeral pile of her husband; the voluntary self-immolation by fire of a Hindu widow.—**Sutteeism**, suttē'izm, *n.* The practice of self-immolation among Hindu widows.

Suture, sū'tūr, *n.* [L. *sutura*, from *suo*, to sew. SUTILE.] The act of sewing; a seam; the line along which two things or parts are joined; *surg.* the uniting of the lips or edges of a wound by stitching; *anat.* one of the seams uniting the bones of the skull; *bot.* the seam of a dehiscent pericarp where the valves unite.—**Sutured**, sū'tūrd, *a.* Having sutures; united.—**Sutural**, sū'tū-ral, *a.* Relating to a suture; *bot.* taking place at a suture.

Suzerain, sö'ze-rān, *n.* [Fr. *suzerain*, from prefix *sus*, L. *sursum*, above, over, on type of *souverain*, from L. *super*, above.] A feudal lord or baron; a lord paramount.—**Suzerainty**, sö'ze-rān-ti, *n.* The office or dignity of a suzerain; paramount authority or command.

Swab, swob, *n.* [Same as Sw. *swab*, a mop; akin to D. *zwabber*, G. *schwabber*, Dan. *svabre*, a mop; comp. Prov. E. *swab*, G. *schwabbeln*, to splash; allied to *sweep.*] A mop for cleaning floors, ships' decks, and the like; a cleaner or sponge for the bore of a cannon; a term applied by sailors to an awkward clumsy fellow.—*v.t.*—*swabbed, swabbing.* To clean with a swab or mop.—**Swabber**, swob'ėr, *n.* An inferior officer in a warship whose business is to see that the ship is kept clean.

Swaddle, swod'l, *v.t.*—*swaddled, swaddling.* [From A.Sax. *swæthil, swethel*, a swaddling-band; same origin as *swathe.* SWATHE.] To bind as with a bandage; to swathe: used generally of infants.—*n.* A cloth band round the body of an infant.—**Swaddling-band, Swaddling-cloth**, *n.* A band or cloth wrapped round an infant.

Swadeshi, swa-desh'i, *n.* [Bengal. 'own country'. See SINN FEIN.] An Indian movement for boycotting British goods in order to secure political pressure and action.

Swag, swag, *v.i.* [A form of *sway*; hence *swagger.*] To move, as something heavy and pendent; to sway.—*n.* Plunder, booty (*colloq.*).—**Swag-bellied**, *a.* Having a prominent overhanging belly. (*Shak.*)

Swage, swāj, *n.* [Fr. *suage*, a tool of similar character; from *suer*, to sweat.] A tool used by blacksmiths, &c., for stamping or moulding heated metal into a required form.—*v.t.* To shape by means of a swage.

Swagger, swag'ėr, *v.t.* [A freq. from *swag*; comp. Swiss *schwaggeln*, to stroll about.] To boast noisily; to bluster; to hector; to strut with a defiant or insolent air.—*v.t.* To influence by blustering or threats; to bully.—*n.* A piece of bluster; bravado or insolence in manner; an insolent strut.—**Swaggerer**, swag'ėr-ėr, *n.* One who swaggers; a blusterer; a bully.—**Swaggering**, swag'ėr-ing, *p.* and *a.* Given to swagger; characterized by an insolent strut; blustering.

Swain, swān, *n.* [Same as Icel. *sveinn*, a youth, a servant; O. Sax. *swên*, Sw. *sven*, Dan. *svend*, A.Sax. *swān.*] A young man dwelling in the country; a peasant or rustic; a country gallant; a lover.

Swale, swāl. Same as *Sweal.*

Swallow, swol'ō, *n.* [A. Sax. *swalewe, swealwe* = D. *zwaluw*, Icel. and Sw. *svala*, Dan. *svale*, G. *schwalbe*, a swallow.] A name of certain insessorial birds remarkable for their extreme length of wing and velocity of flight, living on insects which they catch in the air, and in temperate climates coming in spring and departing when summer is over.—**Swallow-tail**, *n.* A plant, a species of willow; a swallow-tailed coat.—**Swallow-tailed**, *a.* Of the form of a swallow's tail; having tapering or pointed skirts (a *swallow-tailed* coat).—**Swallow-wort**, *n.* The common celandine.

Swallow, swol'ō, *v.t.* [A.Sax. *swelgan*, to swallow (pret. *swealg*, pp. *swolgen*) = L.G. *swalgen*, D. *zwelgen*, Dan. *svälge*, Icel. *svelgja*, G. *schwelgen*, to swallow.] To receive through the gullet into the stomach; to draw into an abyss or gulf; to ingulf; to absorb; to take into the mind readily; to receive or embrace, as opinions; to drink in; to occupy or take up (to *swallow* time); to exhaust or consume; to put up with; to bear or take patiently (to *swallow* an affront).—*n.* Capacity for swallowing; voracity.—**Swallower**, swol'ō-ėr, *n.* One who swallows.

Swam, swam, pret. of *swim.*

Swamp, swomp, *n.* [Closely akin to *sump*, a pond, and to A.Sax. *swamm*, Dan. and Sw. *svamp*, Icel. *svöppr*, G. *schwamm*, a sponge; from root of *swim.*] A piece of spongy land, or low ground saturated with water; a bog, fen, marsh, or morass.—*v.t.* To plunge or sink in a swamp, or as in a swamp; to plunge into inextricable difficulties; *naut.* to overset, sink, or cause to become filled, as a boat in water; to whelm.—**Swamp-oak**, *n.* An oak common on low ground in Canada and the United States.—**Swamp-ore**, *n.* Bog iron-ore.—**Swampy**, swom'pi, *a.* Consisting of swamp; low, wet, and spongy.

Swan, swon, *n.* [A.Sax. *swan* = D. *zwaan*, Icel. *svanr*, Sw. *svan*, Dan. *svane*, G. *schwan*; probably from same root as Skr. *svan*, L. *sono*, to sound.] A long-necked web-footed bird of several species, frequenting rivers and ponds of fresh water, of great size, very graceful in the water, and generally having plumage of snowy whiteness, though a black species exists in Australia.—**Swanherd**, swon'hėrd, *n.* One who tends swans.—**Swan-mark**, *n.* A mark made on a swan's beak to indicate the ownership.—**Swan-neck**, *n.* The end of a pipe curved or arched like the neck of a swan.—**Swannery**, swon'ėr-i, *n.* A place where swans are bred and reared.—**Swansdown**, swonz'doun, *n.* The down of the swan; a fine, soft, thick woollen cloth; also, a thick cotton cloth with a soft nap on one side.—**Swan-shot**, *n.* A large kind of shot used for swan-shooting.—**Swanskin**, swon'skin, *n.* The skin of a swan; a kind of fine twilled flannel.—**Swan-song**, swon-song, *n.* The last dying song or notes of a writer, from the fable of the dying swan.

Swank, swank, *n.* [Akin to *swagger.*] Conceit.—*v.i.* To act so.

Swap, swop, *v.t.*—*swapped, swapping.* [Allied to *sweep* and *swoop*; comp. G. *schwappen*, to strike, to swap; comp. *to strike a bargain.*] To strike with a sweeping stroke; to knock down; to swop; to barter; to exchange.—*n.* A blow; an exchange or barter.

Swape, swāp, *n.* [Collateral form of *sweep, swipe.*] A bucket hung to the end of a counterpoised lever for raising water from a well; a sweep or swipe; a long oar.

Sward, sward, *n.* [A.Sax. *sweard*, D. *zwoord*, Dan. *svær*, Icel. *svördr*, G. *schwarte*, all signifying the skin or rind of bacon, hence sward.] The grassy surface of land; turf; green-sward.—*v.t.* To cover with sward.—**Swarded**, swar'ded, *a.* Covered with sward.—**Swardy**, swar'di, *a.* Covered with sward or grass.

Sware, swār, old pret. *swear.*

Swarm, swarm, *n.* [A.Sax. *swearm*, swarm,

=Icel. *svarmr*, Dan. *sværm*, G. *schwarm*; from a root meaning to hum or buzz, seen in L. *susurrus*, a whisper; Skr. *svar*, to sound. SWEAR.] A large number or body of insects; the cluster of honey-bees which emigrate from a hive at once and seek new lodgings; any great number or multitude; a multitude of people in motion.—*v.i.* To depart from a hive in a swarm; to give out a swarm of bees; to throng in multitudes; to crowd; to be crowded or thronged with a multitude; to abound.

Swarm, swa̤rm, *v.i.* [Perhaps akin to *swerve* or to *squirm*.] To climb a tree, pole, or the like by embracing it with the arms and legs, and scrambling; to shin.

Swart, Swarth, swa̤rt, swa̤rth, *a.* [A.Sax. *sweart* = Goth. *svarts*, L.G. *swartr*, Icel. *svartr*, G. *schwarz*, D. *zwart*, black, dark; same root as L. *sordidus*, sordid, filthy.] Being of a dark hue; moderately black; swarthy: said especially of the skin.—*v.t.* To make tawny.—**Swarthy**, swa̤r'thi, *a.* Being of a dark hue or dusky complexion; tawny or black.—**Swarthily**, swa̤r'thi-li, *adv.* With a swarthy hue.—**Swarthiness**, swa̤r'thi-nes, *n.* The state of being swarthy; a dusky or dark complexion.—**Swartness, Swarthness**, swa̤rt'nes, swa̤rth'nes, *n.* The state of being swart or swarthy.

Swash, swosh, *n.* [Probably from sound of splashing water; comp. Sw. *swassa*, to bluster, to swagger; akin *swish*.] A dashing or splash of water; liquid refuse or filth.—*v.i.* To splash water; to bluster; to make a show of valour; to dash or strike.—**Swashbuckler**, *n.* A swaggering fellow; a bravo; a bully.—**Swasher**, swosh'ėr, *n.* A braggart; a bully.—**Swashing**, swosh'ing, *p.* and *a.* Like a swasher; swaggering; striking with great force; crushing.—**Swash-plate**, swosh-plāt, *n.* A revolving disc set obliquely on the end of a rotating shaft, to act as a cam and give longitudinal reciprocating motion to another shaft bearing on the disc.

Swath, swoth, *n.* [A.Sax. *swathu*, *swæth*, a track, path, swath; D. *zwaad*, *zwade*, G. *schwaden*, a swath; akin to *swaddle*.] A band or bandage‡; a line of grass or corn cut and lying: the reach or sweep of a scythe.—**Swathe**, swāᴛʜ, *v.t.*—*swathed*, *swathing*. [Icel. *svatha*, to swathe; A.Sax. *swethian*, to bind.] To bind with a band or bandage; to tie up in bundles or sheaves; to bind or wind about; to wrap.—*n.* A bandage.—**Swathing-clothes**, *n.pl.* Swaddling-clothes.

Sway, swā, *v.i.* [Same as Icel. *sveggja*, to make to sway, *sveigja*, to swerve; Dan. *svaie*, D. *swaaijen*, to swing; akin *swing*, *swag*.] To swing backwards and forwards; to be drawn to one side by weight; to incline or hang; to move or advance to one side; to have the judgment or feelings inclining one way; to have weight or influence; to bear rule; to govern.—*v.t.* To move backwards and forwards; to wield with the hand (a sceptre); to bias; to cause to incline to one side; to prejudice; to rule; to influence, govern, or direct.—*n.* A swing or sweep; power exerted in governing; rule; influence; weight or authority that inclines to one side.

Sweal, swēl, *v.i.* [A.Sax. *swēlan*, to burn slowly, from *swōl*, heat; L.G. *swelen*, G. *schwelen*, to burn slowly.] To blaze away; to gutter as a candle.—*v.t.* To singe.

Swear, swār, *v.t.*—pret. *swore* (formerly *sware*), pp. *sworn*. [A.Sax. *swerian*, to swear; same as the *swer* of *answer*; D. *zweren*, G. *schwören*, Goth. *svaran*, Icel. *sverja*, Sw. *swärja*, Dan. *sværge*, to swear; same root as in *swarm*.] To utter a solemn declaration, with an appeal to God for the truth of what is affirmed; to declare or affirm in a solemn manner; to promise upon oath; to give evidence on oath; to use profane language; to utter profane oaths.—*To swear by*, to treat as an infallible authority.—*v.t.* To affirm with an appeal to God; to utter on oath; to promise solemnly; to vow; to put to an oath; to bind by an oath; to utter in a profane manner.—**Swearer**, swā'rėr, *n.* One who swears.—**Sworn**, swōrn, *pp.* Bound by oath.—*Sworn brothers*, companions in arms bound together by an oath; very close intimates.—*Sworn enemies*, enemies who have taken an oath or vow of mutual hatred; hence, determined or irreconcilable enemies.—*Sworn friends*, friends bound to be true to each other by oath; hence, close or firm friends.

Sweat, swet, *n.* [A.Sax. *swaetan*, to sweat, from *swāt*, sweat = Icel. *sveiti*, Sw. *svett*, Dan. *sved*, L.G. *sweet*, D. *zweet*, G. *schweiss*, sweat; from same root as L. *sudor*, sweat; Skr. *svedas*, sweat.] The moisture which comes out upon the skin of an animal; perspiration; the state of one who sweats; moisture exuded from any substance.—*v.i.* pret. and pp. *sweat* or *sweated*. To have sweat exuding from the skin; to perspire; to toil; to drudge; to emit moisture, as green plants in a heap.—*v.t.* To cause to give out sweat; to emit from the pores; to exude.—*To sweat coins*, more especially gold coins, to shake a number of them together in a bag, so that a portion of the metal is worn off, being then fraudulently appropriated.—**Sweater**, swet'ėr, *n.* One who sweats; a grinding employer; thick jersey.—**Sweatily**, swet'i-li, *adv.* In a sweaty manner.—**Sweatiness**, swet'i-nes, *n.* The state of being sweaty.—**Sweating-bath**, *n.* A bath for putting a person in a sweat.—**Sweating-room**, *n.* A room for sweating persons; a room in which cheese is allowed to dry.—**Sweating-sickness**, *n.* An epidemic which made its appearance in England and on the Continent in the fifteenth and sixteenth centuries, characterized by profuse sweating, and frequently fatal in a few hours.—**Sweating-system**, *n.* The practice of employing poor people to make up clothes in their own houses at very low wages.—**Sweaty**, swet'i, *a.* Moist with sweat; having the character of sweat; consisting of sweat.

Swede, swēd, *n.* A native of Sweden; a Swedish turnip.—**Swedish**, swē'dish, *a.* Pertaining to Sweden or its inhabitants.—*Swedish turnip*, a hard sort of turnip, known by its glaucous leaves and somewhat elongated bulb.—*n.* The language of the Swedes.

Swedenborgian, swē-den-bor'ji-an, *a.* Relating to Emanuel *Swedenborg*, or to the doctrines taught by him.—*n.* One who holds the religious doctrines taught by Emanuel *Swedenborg*, a Swedish nobleman, born at Stockholm in 1688, who believed himself to have a divine revelation to found the New Jerusalem Church spoken of in the Apocalypse.—**Swedenborgianism**, swē-den-bor'ji-an-izm, *n.* The doctrines of the Swedenborgians.

Sweep, swēp, *v.t.*—pret. and pp. *swept*. [From A.Sax. *swāpan*, to sweep (pret. *sweóp*, pp. *swāpen*=Icel. *sópa*, also *sveipa*, Goth. *sveipan*, G. *schweifen*. SWOOP.] To rub over with a broom or besom, for removing loose dirt; to clean by brushing; to remove or strike by a brushing stroke; to carry along or off (the wind *sweeps* the snow, a river *sweeps* away a dam); to destroy or carry off at a blow; to rub or trail over (to *sweep* the ground); to pass over so as to clear (to *sweep* the seas of ships); to move swiftly over or along; to carry the eye over; to draw or drag something over.—*v.i.* To pass or flow with swiftness and violence; to pass or brush along with celerity; to pass with pomp; to take in a view with progressive rapidity; to range.—*n.* The act of sweeping; the reach or range of a continued motion or stroke; the compass or reach of anything flowing or brushing along; the direction or turn of a curve, as of a road; compass or extent of excursion; range; a rapid survey with the eye; *naut.* a large oar used in small vessels to aid their progress; one who sweeps chimneys; the depth of strata of air disturbed by an aeroplane in motion.—**Sweeper**, swē'pėr, *n.* One who sweeps.—**Sweeping**, swē'ping, *p.* and *a.* Including many individuals or particulars in a single act or assertion; wide and comprehensive (a *sweeping* charge).—*n.pl.* Things collected by sweeping; rubbish.—**Sweepingly**, swē'ping-li, *adv.* In a sweeping manner.—**Sweepingness**, swē'ping-nes, *n.*—**Sweep-net**, *n.* A large net for drawing over a wide compass.—**Sweepstake**, swēp'stāk, *n.* A gaming transaction in which a number of persons join in contributing a certain stake, which becomes the property of one or of several of the contributors under certain conditions; a prize made up of several stakes. Also called a *sweepstakes*.—**Sweepy**, swē'pi, *a.* Moving in sweeps; sweeping.

Sweet, swēt, *a.* [A.Sax. *swēte*=D. *zoet*, G. *süss*, Icel. *sætr*, *sōtr*, Goth. *sutis*; same root as L. *suavis* (for *suadvis*), whence *suave*; Skr. *svâdus*, sweet, *svad*, to taste.] Having a pleasant taste or flavour like that of sugar or honey: opposed to *bitter*; pleasing to the smell; fragrant; pleasing to the ear; soft; melodious; pleasing to the eye; beautiful; pleasing or grateful to the mind; mild; gentle; kind; obliging; bland; not salt or salted; not stale; not sour; not putrescent.—*Sweet herbs*, fragrant herbs cultivated for culinary purposes.—*A sweet tooth*, a great liking for sweet things or sweetmeats.—*n.pl.* Sweet things; sweetmeats; things that please (the *sweets* of domestic life).—**Sweet-bay**, *n.* A fragrant species of laurel.—**Sweet-bread**, *n.* The pancreas of an animal used as food.—**Sweet-brier, Sweet-briar**, *n.* A species of wild rose remarkable for the sweet smell of its leaves.—**Sweeten**, swē'tn, *v.t.* To make sweet to the taste; to make pleasing or grateful to the mind; to make mild or kind; to increase the agreeable qualities of; to make pure and wholesome; to make mellow and fertile; to restore to purity.—*v.i.* To become sweet.—**Sweetener**, swē'tn-ėr, *n.* One who or that which sweetens.—**Sweetening**, swē'tn-ing, *n.* The act of one who sweetens; that which sweetens.—**Sweet-flag**, *n.* SWEET-RUSH.—**Sweet-gale**, *n.* The plant gale.—**Sweetheart**, swēt'härt, *n.* [From *sweet* and *heart*.] A lover, male or female.—*v.t.* To act the part of a male lover to; to pay court to.—**Sweeting**, swē'ting, *n.* A sweet apple; a term of endearment.—**Sweetish**, swē'tish, *a.* Somewhat sweet.—**Sweetly**, swēt'li, *adv.* In a sweet manner; agreeably; harmoniously.—**Sweet-marjoram**, *n.* MARJORAM.—**Sweetmeat**, swēt'mēt, *n.* An article of confectionery made wholly or principally of sugar; fruit preserved with sugar.—**Sweetness**, swēt'nes, *n.* The quality of being sweet; fragrance; agreeableness to the ear; melody; gentleness; mildness; obliging civility.—**Sweet-oil**, *n.* Olive-oil.—**Sweet-pea**, *n.* An annual much cultivated in gardens for its showy sweet-scented flowers.—**Sweet-potato**, *n.* A tropical plant of the convolvulus family largely cultivated for its edible roots.—**Sweet-rush, Sweet-flag**, *n.* A plant of the arum family growing in wet places, the perennial rhizome of which is known as calamus, and is used in medicine, by confectioners, perfumers, &c.—**Sweet-scented**, *a.* Having a sweet smell; fragrant.—**Sweet-sop**, *n.* A fruit and tree allied to the custard-apple.—**Sweet-william**, *n.* A species of pink of many varieties, cultivated in gardens.

Swell, swel, *v.i.*—pret. *swelled*; pp. *swelled* or *swollen* (the latter more frequently an adjective). [A.Sax. *swellan*, to swell=Icel. *svella*, D. *zwellen*, G. *schwellen*, to swell; allied to L. *salum*, the sea, Gr. *salos*, surge.] To grow bulkier; to dilate; to increase in size or extent; to rise or be driven into billows; to protuberate; to bulge out; to rise in altitude; to be puffed up with some feeling; hence, to strut; to look big; to grow and increase in the mind; to become larger in amount; to increase in intensity or volume, as sound.—*v.t.* To increase the size of; to cause to dilate or increase; to aggravate; to heighten; to inflate; to puff up.—*n.* The act of swelling; gradual increase; an elevation of land; an undulation; a succession of long unbroken waves setting in one direction, as after a storm; a billow; a surge; a gradual increase and decrease in the volume of musical sound; an arrangement in an organ whereby the player can increase or diminish the intensity of the sound; a familiar word for a person of rank or high standing, or for a showy, fashionable person; a dandy, a fop, or the like.—

Swelling, swel'ing, *n.* A tumour; a protuberance.—*p.* and *a.* Turgid; bombastic; grand; pompous.—**Swell-mob**, *n.* The class of pickpockets who go about genteelly dressed.—**Swell-mobsman**, *n.* A member of the swell-mob.

Swelter, swel'tėr, *v.i.* [From A.Sax. *sweltan*, to die, Goth. *swiltan*, Icel. *svelta*, Sw. *svälta*, Dan. *sulte*, to die. Hence *sultry*, for *sweltery*.] To be overcome and faint with heat.—*v.t.* To oppress with heat.

Swept, swept, pret. and pp. of *sweep*.

Swerve, swėrv, *v.i.* — *swerved*, *swerving*. [A.Sax. *sweorfan*=Icel. *svarfa*, D. *zwerven*, L.G. *swarven*, O.H.G. *suerban*, Goth. *svairban*—used of movements of various kinds.] To wander from any line prescribed or from a rule of duty; to deviate; to turn to one side; to incline; to waver.

Swift, swift, *a.* [A.Sax. *swift*, from *swifan*, to move quickly, to revolve; Icel. *svifa*, to glide, G. *schweifen*, to sweep; same root as E. *sweep* and *swoop*.] Moving with great speed or rapidity; fleet; rapid; ready; prompt; coming suddenly or without delay; of short continuance; rapidly passing. —*adv.* In a swift or rapid manner; swiftly.—*n.* The name of birds of the family *Cypselidae*, which have an outward resemblance to the swallows, the common swift having great powers of flight; the common European newt. —**Swift-footed**, *a.* Fleet; swift in running.—**Swift-handed**, *a.* Prompt of action; ready to draw the sword.—**Swiftly**, swift'li, *adv.* In a swift or rapid manner; fleetly. —**Swiftness**, swift'nes, *n.* The state or quality of being swift; rapid motion; celerity; rapidity.

Swifter, swif'tėr, *n.* [Icel. *sviptingr*, a reefing rope.] *Naut.* a rope encircling a boat longitudinally to strengthen and defend her sides; one of a pair of shrouds above the others to strengthen the lower masts.

Swig, swig, *v.t.*—*swigged*, *swigging*. [Perhaps from A.Sax. *swilgan*, to swallow; comp. *bag* = *balg*. SWALLOW.] To drink by large draughts; to drink off rapidly and greedily.—*v.i.* To take deep draughts.—*n.* A large draught.

Swill, swil, *v.t.* [A.Sax. *swilian*, Sc. *sweel*, to wash; influenced by A.Sax. *swilgan*, to swallow. SWALLOW.] To wash (*Shak.*)‡; to drink grossly or greedily; to inebriate.—*v.i.* To drink greedily or to excess. — *n.* Drink taken in excessive quantities; the wash or mixture of liquid substances given to swine. Called also *Swillings*.—**Swiller**, swil'ėr, *n.* One who swills.

Swim, swim, *v.i.*—pret. *swam* or *swum*; pp. *swum*; ppr. *swimming*. [A.Sax. *swimman*, to swim=L.G. *swimmen*, Icel. *svimma*, G. *schwimmen* — to swim; connected with *swamp*.] To be supported on water or other fluid; to float; to move through water by the motion of the hands and feet, or of fins; to glide with a smooth motion; to be flooded; to be drenched; to overflow.—*v.t.* To pass or cross by swimming; to cause to swim or float.—*n.* The act of swimming; period or extent of swimming; a smooth, gliding motion; the air-bladder or sound of fishes.—**Swimmer**, swim'ėr, *n.* One who swims; a bird that swims, as the duck and goose. — **Swimming**, swim'ing, *n.* The act or art of sustaining and propelling the body in water.—**Swimming-bath**, *n.* A bath large enough for swimming in. —**Swimming-bell**, *n.* A nectocalyx.—**Swimming-belt**, *n.* An air-inflated belt worn as a support in the water.—**Swimmingly**, swim'ing-li, *adv.* In an easy gliding manner, as if swimming; smoothly; successfully. — **Swimming-pond**, *n.* An artificial pond in which the art of swimming is learned or practised.

Swim, swim, *v.i.*—pret. *swam* or *swum*; pp. *swum*, ppr. *swimming*. [Same as Icel. *svima*, to be dizzy, *svimi*, dizziness; A.Sax. *swima*, Dan. *svime*, a swoon; G. *schweimen*, to be dizzy. SQUEAMISH.] To be dizzy or giddy (the head *swims*). — **Swimming**, swim'ing, *n.* A dizziness or giddiness.

Swindle, swin'dl, *v.t.* — *swindled*, *swindling*. [Borrowed from G. *schwindeln*, to cheat, *schwindler*, a swindler, from *schwindel*, dizziness, infatuation.] To cheat and defraud grossly, or with deliberate artifice. —*n.* A fraudulent scheme intended to dupe people out of money; an act of cheatery; an imposition.—**Swindler**, swin'dlėr, *n.* One who swindles; a cheat.—**Swindlery**, swin'dlėr-i, *n.* The acts or practices of a swindler; roguery.

Swine, swīn, *n.sing.* and *pl.* [A.Sax. *swin*, =D. *zwijn*, G. *schwein*, Dan. *sviin*, Icel. *svin*, Goth. *svein*, Pol. *swinia*, Bohem. *swine*; same root as *sow*, L. *sus*. Sow.] A hoofed mammal, the female of which is the sow, and whose flesh is much eaten under the name of *pork*; a pig or hog.—**Swine-herd**, swīn'hėrd, *n.* A herd or keeper of swine. — **Swine-stone**, *n.* Stink-stone; anthraconite.—**Swine-sty**, *n.* A sty or pen for swine. — **Swinish**, swīn'ish, *a.* Befitting swine; like the swine in filthiness; hoggish.—**Swinishly**, swīn'ish-li, *adv.* In a swinish manner.—**Swinishness**, swīn'ish-nes, *n.* Quality of being swinish. — **Swinery**, swīn'ėr-i, *n.* A place where swine are kept.

Swing, swing, *v.i.*—pret. and pp. *swung*. [A.Sax. *swingan*, to dash, to scourge = L.G. *swingen*, Dan. *svinge*, Sw. *swinga*, G. *schwingen*. *Swinge*, *swingle* are derivatives, and *swink*, *sway* connected forms.] To move to and fro, as a body suspended in the air; to oscillate; to sway; to be carried to and fro while hanging on something.—*v.t.* To make to sway or oscillate loosely; to whirl in the air; to wave; to brandish.—*To swing a ship*, to bring her head to each point of the compass in succession, in order to correct the compass by ascertaining the amount of local deviation.—*n.* The act of swinging; an oscillation; the sweep of a moving body; an apparatus suspended for persons to swing in; free course of conduct; unrestrained liberty or license; a "hot" variation of folk music, deviating from main theme with counter rhythm, from "swing your partner." [*Colloq.*] — **Swing-bridge**, *n.* A bridge that may be moved by swinging, so as to afford passage for ships on a river, canal, at the mouth of docks, &c.—**Swinging**, swing'ing, *p.* and *a.* Moving to and fro: oscillating. — **Swinging-saw**, *n.* A saw swinging in an arc from an axis overhead. — **Swing-plough**, *n.* Any plough without wheels. — **Swing-tree**, *n.* A cross-bar by which a horse is yoked to a carriage, plough, &c., and to which the traces are fastened. Called also *Singletree*.—**Swing-wheel**, *n.* The wheel in a timepiece which drives the pendulum.

Swinge, swinj, *v.t.* — *swinged*, *swingeing*. [From *swing*; comp. *springe* from *spring*, *singe* from *sing*.] To beat soundly; to whip; to chastise. —**Swinge-buckler**, *n.* A swashbuckler, bravo. (*Shak.*).—**Swingeing**, swin'jing, *a.* Great; large; huge. (*Colloq.*). — **Swingeingly**, swin'jing-li, *adv.* Hugely; vastly. —**Swinger**, swin'jėr, *n.* One who swinges.

Swingle, swing'gl, *v.t.*—*swingled*, *swingling*. [A freq. of *swing*.] To scutch flax by beating it.—*n.* A swingle-staff.—**Swingle-staff**, *n.* An instrument formerly used for scutching flax; a scutcher. — **Swingle-tree**, *n.* SWING-TREE.

Swinish, **Swinishly**. Under SWINE.

Swink,‡ swingk, *v.i.* [A.Sax. *swincan*, to labour; akin *swing*.] To labour; to toil; to drudge. — **Swinked**, *a.* Tired, toilsome. (*Milton*, Comus, 293.)

Swipe, swīp, *v.t.* and *i.*—*swiped*, *swiping*. [Akin to *sweep*, *swoop*.] To strike with a sweeping blow; to strike or drive with great force.—*n.* A swape.

Swipe, swīp, *v.t.* — To strike with a sweeping motion; to wipe carelessly or quickly; to steal or snatch [*Slang*.]

Swipie, swip'l, *n.* [From *swipe*, to strike.] The effective end-piece of a flail.

Swirl, swėrl, *v.i.* [Akin to Dan. *svirre*, to whirl; same root as *swerve*.] To form eddies; to whirl in eddies.—*n.* A whirling motion; an eddy, as of water; a twist or curl in the grain of wood.

Swiss, swis, *n.sing.* and *pl.* A native or inhabitant (natives or inhabitants) of Switzerland.—*a.* Belonging to the Swiss or to Switzerland.—*Swiss muslin*, a fine open transparent cotton fabric. — *Swiss Guards*, Papal body-guard.

Switch, swich, *n.* [Same as O.D. *swick*, a switch; akin Icel. *svigi*, *sveigr*, a switch—from root of *swing* or *sway*.] A small flexible twig or rod; a movable piece of rail for turning a railway train from one line to another; a device for making or breaking an electric circuit or changing direction of current.—*v.t.* To strike with a switch; to lash; to transfer from one line of rails to another; to shunt; *elect.* to turn on or off or into a new circuit. —**Switchboard**, swich'bōrd, *n.* An apparatus consisting of a frame or panel on which are mounted switches for making electric-circuit connections, as for a series of lights in a building or theater; telephone wires in an exchange, &c.

Switzer, swit'zėr, *n.* A Swiss.

Swivel, swiv'el, *n.* [From A.Sax. *swifan*, to move quickly, to revolve; akin *swift*.] A fastening that allows the thing fastened to turn freely round on its axis; a link in a chain partly consisting of a pivot turning in a hole formed in the next link; a small cannon turning on a pivot. — **Swivel-eye**, *n.* A squint-eye. [*Colloq.*] — **Swivel-gun**, *n.* A swivel. — **Swivel-joint**, *n.* A joint with a swivel. — **Swiveled**, swiv'eld, *a.* Furnished or fastened with a swivel.

Swob, swob, *n.* A mop. SWAB.—**Swobber**, swob'ėr, *n.* A swabber.

Swollen, **Swoln**, swōln, *p.* and *a.* Swelled. SWELL.

Swoon, swön, *v.i.* [From A.Sax. *swógan*, to sound, to sigh, hence to faint; akin *sough*.] To faint; to sink into a fainting fit.—*n.* The state of one who swoons; a fainting fit.

Swoop, swöp, *v.t.* [From A.Sax. *swápan*, to sweep, to swoop. SWEEP.] To dash upon while on the wing; to take with a sweep.—*v.i.* To descend upon prey suddenly from a height, as a hawk; to stoop.—*n.* The sudden pouncing of a rapacious bird on its prey; a falling on and seizing, as of a bird on its prey.

Swop, swop, *v.t.* [SWAP.] To exchange; to swap.—*n.* An exchange; a barter.

Sword, sōrd, *n.* [A.Sax. *sweord*=D. *zwaard*, L.G. *sweerd*, Dan. *zværd*, Icel. *sverth*, G. *schwert*, a sword; allied to Skr. *çaru*, a dart or spear.] An offensive weapon having a long metal blade (usually steel), either straight and with a sharp point for thrusting, as the rapier; with a sharp point and one or two cutting edges for thrusting and striking, as the broadsword; or curved and with a sharp convex edge for striking, as the scimitar.—*The sword*, the emblem or symbol of justice, power, or authority, or of war, or used as equivalent to the military profession.—*Sword of state*, a sword borne before a king or other person of rank.—**Sword-arm**, *n.* The right arm. — **Sword-bayonet**, *n.* A short sword which can be attached to a rifle like a bayonet.—**Sword-bearer**, *n.* An attendant who bears or carries his master's sword; an official who carries a sword as an emblem on ceremonial occasions.—**Sword-belt**, *n.* A belt by which a sword is suspended and borne by the side.—**Sword-blade**, *n.* The blade or cutting part of a sword.—**Sword-cane**, *n.* A cane or walking-stick containing a blade, as in a scabbard.—**Sword-dance**, *n.* A dance by one performer over crossed swords among the Scotch Highlanders.—**Sworded**, sōr'ded, *a.* Wearing a sword.—**Sword-fight**, *n.* A combat or trial of skill with swords.—**Sword-fish**, *n.* A fish allied to the mackerel tribe, remarkable for its elongated upper jaw, which forms a sword-like weapon. —**Sword-hand**, *n.* The right hand.—**Sword-knot**, *n.* A ribbon or tassel tied to the hilt of a sword.—**Swordless**, sōrd'les, *a.* Destitute of a sword.—**Sword-**

lily, *n.* The gladiolus.—**Sword-play,** *n.* A combat or fencing match with swords; a sword-fight. — **Sword-player,** *n.* One who exhibits his skill in the use of the sword; a gladiator.—**Sword-shaped,** *a.* Shaped like a sword; ensiform.—**Swordsman,** sōrdz'man, *n.* A man who carries a sword; one skilled in the use of the sword. —**Swordsmanship,** sōrdz'man-ship, *n.* Skilful use of the sword.—**Sword-stick,** *n.* A walking-stick in which is concealed a sword.

Swore, swōr, pret. **Sworn,** swōrn, pp. of *swear.*

Swum, swum, pret. and pp. of *swim.*

Swung, swung, pret. and pp. of *swing.*

Sybarite, sib'a-rīt, *n.* [Fr. *Sybarite,* from L. *Sybarita,* Gr. *Sybaritēs,* an inhabitant of *Sybaris,* an ancient Greek city of southern Italy proverbial for the effeminacy and voluptuousness of its inhabitants.] A person devoted to luxury and pleasure; an effeminate person. — **Sybaritic, Sybaritical,** sib-a-rit'ik, sib-a-rit'i-kal, *a.* Luxurious; devoted to luxury or pleasure. — **Sybaritism,** sib'a-rīt-izm, *n.* Voluptuousness; devotion to pleasure.

Sycamine, sik'a-mīn, *n.* [Gr. *sykaminos.*] The mulberry. (N.T.)

Sycamore, sik'a-mōr, *n.* [Fr. *sycomore,* L. *sycomorus,* from Gr. *sykomoros,* the fig-mulberry—*sykon,* fig, *moron,* mulberry.] A fruit-tree of the fig family, common in Palestine, Arabia, &c.: also written *Sycomore*; a kind of maple, a well-known timber tree, long naturalized in England, and usually called *Plane-tree* in Scotland; a name frequently given in America to the plane-tree, button-wood, or cotton-wood.

Syce, sīs, *n.* A native groom in India.

Sycee, Sycee-silver, sī-sē, *n.* The fine silver of China cast into ingots weighing commonly rather more than a pound troy.

Sychnocarpous, sik-nō-kär'pus, *a.* [Gr. *sychnos,* frequent, *karpos,* fruit.] *Bot.* bearing fruit many times without perishing.

Sycoma, si-kō'ma, *n.* [Gr. *sykōma,* from *sykon,* a fig.] *Med.* a wart or excrescence resembling a fig.

Sycomore, sik'o-mōr, *n.* The sycamore of Scripture.

Syconus, si-kō'nus, *n.* [Gr. *sykon,* a fig.] *Bot.* a fleshy, hollow receptacle, containing numerous flowers which are combined in the fruit, as in the fig.

Sycophant, sik'ō-fant, *n.* [Gr. *sykophantēs,* a false accuser, slanderer—*sykon,* a fig, and *phainō,* to show; lit. a fig-shower; the reason for the name is unknown.] A parasite; a flatterer of princes and great men; a mean flatterer. — **Sycophancy,** sik'ō-fan-si, *n.* Obsequious flattery; servility.—**Sycophantic, Sycophantical,** sik-ō-fan'tik, sik-ō-fan'ti-kal, *a.* Belonging to or resembling a sycophant; obsequiously flattering. — **Sycophantish,** sik'ō-fant-ish, *a.* Sycophantic.—**Sycophantism,** sik'o-fant-izm, *n.* Sycophancy.

Sycosis, si-kō'sis, *n.* [Gr. *sykōsis,* from *sykon,* a fig.] A disease which consists of an eruption of tubercles on the bearded portion of the face and on the scalp.

Syenite, sī'en-īt, *n.* A granitic rock of a grayish colour, composed of quartz, hornblende, and felspar; so called because abundant near *Syene* (sī-ē'nē) in Upper Egypt.—**Syenitic,** sī-e-nit'ik, *a.* Containing or resembling syenite.—*Syenitic granite,* granite which contains hornblende.—*Syenitic porphyry,* fine-grained syenite containing large crystals of felspar.

Syllable, sil'a-bl, *n.* [Fr. *syllable,* L. *syllaba,* from Gr. *syllabē*—*syl* for *syn,* together, and root *lab,* to take; as to the termination comp. *participle, principle.*] A sound or combination of sounds uttered together, or at a single impulse of the voice, and constituting a word or part of a word; the least expression of language or thought; a particle. —*v.t.*—*syllabled, syllabling.* To utter; to articulate. — **Syllabarium, Syllabary,** sil-a-bā'ri-um, sil'a-ba-ri, *n.* A catalogue of the primitive syllables of a language. — **Syllabic, Syllabical,** si-lab'ik, si-lab'i-kal, *a.* Pertaining to a syllable or syllables; consisting of a syllable or syllables. — **Syllabically,** si-lab'i-kal-li, *adv.* In a syllabic manner.—**Syllabicate,** si-lab'i-kāt, *v.t.* To form into syllables.—**Syllabication,** si-lab'i-kā"shon, *n.* The act or method of dividing words into syllables.—**Syllabify,** si-lab'i-fī, *v.t.* To form into syllables.—**Syllabist,** sil'ab-ist, *n.* One versed in dividing words into syllables.

Syllabub, sil'a-bub, *n.* SILLABUB.

Syllabus, sil'a-bus, *n.* [L., from the same source as *syllable.*] A brief statement of the heads of a discourse, of a course of lectures, &c.; an abstract; *R. Cath. Ch.* a summary enumeration of points decided by ecclesiastical authority; a document issued by Pope Pius IX in 1864, condemning various doctrines, institutions, &c.

Syllepsis, sil-lep'sis, *n.* [Gr. *syllēpsis,* from *syl* for *syn,* with, and root *lab,* to take.] A figure of speech by which one word is referred to another in the sentence to which it does not grammatically belong.—**Sylleptic, Sylleptical,** sil-lep'tik, sil-lep'ti-kal, *a.* Relating to or implying syllepsis. — **Sylleptically,** sil-lep'ti-kal-li, *adv.* By way of syllepsis.

Syllogism, sil'ō-jizm, *n.* [L. *syllogismus,* from Gr. *syllogismos,* a syllogism, from *syl* for *syn,* with, and *logizomai,* to reckon, from *logos,* word, reason, &c.] *Logic,* a form of reasoning or argument, consisting of three propositions, of which the two first are called the *premises* (*major* and *minor*), and the last the *conclusion,* the conclusion necessarily following from the premises; thus: a plant has not the power of locomotion; an oak is a plant; therefore an oak has not the power of locomotion.—**Syllogistic, Syllogistical,** sil-ō-jis'tik, sil-ō-jis'ti-kal, *a.* Pertaining to a syllogism or to reasoning by syllogisms.—**Syllogistically,** sil-ō-jis'ti-kal-li, *adv.* In a syllogistic manner; by means of syllogisms.—**Syllogize,** sil'ō-jīz, *v.i.*—*syllogized, syllogizing.* To reason by syllogisms. —*v.t.* To put into the form of a syllogism.—**Syllogizer,** sil'ō-jī-zėr, *n.* One who syllogizes.

Sylph, silf, *n.* [Fr. *sylphe,* a sylph; a word coined by Paracelsus. GNOME.] An elemental spirit of the air, according to the system of Paracelsus, generally used as feminine, and often applied figuratively to a woman of graceful and slender proportions.—**Sylphid,** sil'fid, *n.* A diminutive of *sylph.*—**Sylphish,** silf'ish, *a.* Resembling a sylph.

Sylva, sil'va, *n.* [L. *sylva, silva,* a wood or forest.] The forest trees of any region or country collectively. Written also *Silva.*—**Sylvan,** sil'van, *a.* Pertaining to a wood or forest; abounding with trees; rural.—**Sylviculture,** sil-vi-kul'tūr, *n.* The culture of forest trees; arboriculture.

Symbiosis, sim-bi-ō'sis, *n.* [Gr. *syn,* together, *bios,* life.] A sort of parasitism in which two kinds of animals or plants, or a plant and animal, live in close relationship, the one being of service to the other for protection or food.

Symbol, sim'bol, *n.* [L. *symbolum,* from Gr. *symbolon,* a symbol, from *symballō,* to infer, conclude—*sym* for *syn,* with, and *ballō,* to throw or put.] An object animate or inanimate standing for or calling up something moral or intellectual; an emblem; a type (the olive branch is the *symbol* of peace); a letter or character which is significant; a sign (as in chemistry, astronomy, &c.); a distinctive mark or attribute of office or duty; *theol.* a creed or confession of faith.—*v.t.* To symbolize.—**Symbolatry, Symbololatry,** sim-bol'-at-ri, sim-bol-ol'at-ri, *n.* [Gr. *latreia,* service or worship.] The worship, extravagant reverence, or overestimation of symbols or types.—**Symbolic, Symbolical,** sim-bol'ik, sim-bol'i-kal, *a.* Pertaining to a symbol or symbols; of the nature of a symbol; representative; *gram.* said of a class of words, such as pronouns, prepositions, &c. PRESENTIVE.—**Symbolically,** sim-bol'-i-kal-li, *adv.* In a symbolical manner; by symbols; typically.—**Symbolics, Symbolic,** sim-bol'iks, *n.* The study of symbols; the study of Christian creeds and confessions of faith.—**Symbolism,** sim'bol-izm, *n.* The investing of objects or animals with a symbolic meaning; meaning expressed by symbols; symbols collectively.—**Symbolist,** sim'bol-ist, *n.* One who symbolizes.—**Symbolistic, Symbolistical,** sim-bol-is'tik, sim-bol-is'ti-kal, *a.* Characterized by the use of symbols.—**Symbolize,** sim'bol-īze, *v.t.*—*symbolized, symbolizing.* To represent by a symbol or by symbols; to serve as the symbol of; to regard or treat as symbolic. —*v.i.* To express or represent in symbols. — **Symbological,** sim-bo-loj'i-kal, *a.* Pertaining to symbology.—**Symbologist,** sim-bol'o-jist, *n.* One versed in symbology.—**Symbology, Symbolology,** sim-bol'o-ji, sim-bol-ol'o-ji, *n.* [Gr. *symbolon,* and *logos,* discourse.] The art of expressing by symbols; symbols collectively and their meaning and use.

Symmetry, sim'e-tri, *n.* [Gr. *symmetria,* —*sym* for *syn,* with, and *metron,* measure.] A due proportion in size and form of the parts of a body or structure to each other; such harmony of parts as produces a pleasing whole; the character of being well proportioned; *bot.* and *zool.* correspondence or similar distribution of parts in plants or animals; symmetrical disposition of organs. —**Symmetric,** sim-met'rik, *a.* Symmetrical; used chiefly in mathematics.—**Symmetrical,** sim-met'ri-kal, *a.* Possessing symmetry; well proportioned in all parts; handsome; finely made; *bot.* having the number of parts of one series corresponding with that of the other series (as, having five sepals, five petals, and five, or ten, or fifteen stamens); *math.* having corresponding parts or relations. — **Symmetrically,** sim-met'ri-kal-li, *adv.* In a symmetrical manner.—**Symmetricalness,** sim-met'-ri-kal-nes, *n.*—**Symmetrist,** sim'e-trist, *n.* One very studious of symmetry.—**Symmetrize,** sim'e-trīz, *v.t.* To make symmetrical.

Sympathy, sim'pa-thi, *n.* [Fr. *sympathie,* L. *sympathia,* from Gr. *sympatheia*—*syn,* with, and *pathos,* suffering. PATHOS.] Feeling corresponding to that which another feels; a feeling that enables a person to enter into and in part share another's feelings; fellow-feeling; compassion; commiseration; *physiol.* and *pathol.* that relation of the organs and parts of a living body to each other whereby a disordered condition of one part induces more or less disorder in another part.—**Sympathetic, Sympathetical,** sim-pa-thet'ik, sim-pa-thet'i-kal, *a.* Expressive of, produced by, or exhibiting sympathy; having sympathy or common feeling with another; feeling-hearted; *physiol,* produced by sympathy.—*Sympathetic ink,* ink which does not appear on the paper until exposed to heat or chemicals.—*Sympathetic nervous system,* a set of nerves or nervous masses in vertebrate animals, arranged along the spine. — *Sympathetic sounds,* sounds produced from bodies by the vibrations of some other sounding body.—**Sympathetically,** sim-pa-thet'i-kal-li, *adv.* In a sympathetic manner; with sympathy or fellow-feeling.—**Sympathize,** sim'pa-thīz, *v.i.*—*sympathized, sympathizing.* To have a common feeling, as of bodily pleasure or pain; to feel in consequence of what another feels; to have fellow-feeling; to be sorry for another's suffering; to condole; to agree; to harmonize.—**Sympathizer,** sim'pa-thī-zėr, *n.* One who sympathizes.

Symphony, sim'fō-ni, *n.* [L. *symphonia,* from Gr. *symphōnia*—*syn,* with, and *phōnē,* voice.] A consonance or harmony of sounds agreeable to the ear; harmony; *mus.* an elaborate composition for a full orchestra, consisting usually, like the sonata, of three or four contrasted but intimately related movements.—**Symphonic,** sim-fon'ik, *a.* Pertaining to a symphony.—**Symphonious,** sim-fō'ni-us, *a.* Agreeing in sound; harmonious.—**Symphonist,** sim'fo-nist, *n.* A composer of symphonies.

Symphyllous, sim-fil'lus, *a.* [Gr. *syn,* together, and *phyllon*, a leaf.] *Bot.* GAMOPHYLLUS.

Symphysis, sim′fi-sis, *n.* [Gr. *symphysis*, from *sym* for *syn*, together, and *phyō*, to grow.] *Anat.* a growing together; the union of bones by cartilage; the point of union between two parts; a commissure.

Sympiesometer, sim′pi-e-zom″et-ėr, *n.* [Gr. *syn*, together, *piezō*, to press, *metron*, a measure.] A kind of barometer for measuring the weight of the atmosphere by the compression of a column of gas.

Symposium, sim-pō′zi-um, *n.* pl. **Symposia**, sim-pō′zi-a. [Gr. *symposion*, from *syn*, with, *posis*, a drinking.] A feast where there is drinking; a convivial meeting; a discussion by writers in a periodical.—**Symposiac**, sim-pō′zi-ak, *a.* Pertaining to a symposium.—**Symposiarch**, sim-pō′zi-ärk, *n.* [Gr. *symposiarchēs*—*symposion*, and *archē*, rule.] The president or manager of a feast.—**Symposiast**, sim-pō′zi-ast, *n.* A sharer in a symposium.

Symptom, sim′tom, *n.* [Gr. *symptōma*—*syn*, together, with *piptō*, to fall.] Any sign or token; what serves as evidence of something not seen; *med.* an affection which accompanies a disease, and from which the existence and nature of a disease may be inferred. — **Symptomatic**, **Symptomatical**, sim-to-mat′ik, sim-to-mat′i-kal, *a.* Being or serving as a symptom; indicating the existence of something else.—*Symptomatic disease*, a disease which proceeds from some prior disorder, and opposed to *idiopathic disease*. — **Symptomatically**, sim-to-mat′i-kal-li, *adv.* By means of symptoms.—**Symptomatology**, sim′to-ma-tol″o-ji, *n.* That part of medicine which treats of the symptoms of diseases.

Synæresis, si-nē′re-sis, *n.* [Gr. *synairesis*—*syn*, together, and *hairō*, to take.] *Gram.* the contraction of two syllables into one.

Synagogue, sin′a-gog, *n.* [Fr. *synagogue*, Gr. *synagōgē*—*syn*, together, and *agō*, to bring.] A congregation of Jews met for the purpose of worship: a Jewish place of worship. — **Synagogal**, **Synagogical**, sin-a-gog′al, sin-a-goj′i-kal, *a.* Pertaining or relating to a synagogue.

Synallagmatic, sin-al′lag-mat″ik, *a.* [Gr. *synallagma*, a mutual agreement.] Applied to a contract or treaty imposing reciprocal obligations.

Synalœpha, sin-a-lē′fa, *n.* [Gr. *synaloiphē*, *synaleiphō*, to melt together—*syn*, together, and *aleiphō*, to smear.] A suppression of some vowel or diphthong at the end of a word before another vowel or diphthong.

Synantherous, sin-an′thėr-us, *a.* [Prefix *syn*, together, and *anther*.] *Bot.* having the anthers united so as to form a tube round the style.

Synanthous, sin-an′thus, *a.* [Gr. *syn*, with, together, and *anthos*, a flower.] *Bot.* exhibiting a union of several usually distinct flowers.—**Synanthy**, sin-an′thi, *n.* *Bot.* the union of flowers.

Synapsis, sin-ap′sis. [Gr. *synapsis*, union.] A stage in the development of a germ cell, at which the chromatins become reduced in number.

Synarthrosis, sin-är-thrō′sis, *n.* [Gr. *synarthrōsis*—*syn*, with, and *arthron*, a joint.] *Anat.* union of bones without motion.—**Synarthrodial**, sin-är-thrō′di-al, *a.* Pertaining to synarthrosis.

Syncarpium, sin-kär′pi-um, *n.* [Gr. *syn*, together, and *karpos*, fruit.] *Bot.* an aggregate fruit in which the ovaries cohere into a solid mass, with a slender receptacle, as in magnolia.—**Syncarpous**, sin-kär′pus, *n.* *Bot.* having the carpels completely united, as in the apple and pear.

Syncategorematic, sin-kat′ē-go-rē-mat″ik, *a.* [Gr. *syn*, together, and *katēgorēma*, a predicate.] *Logic*, applied to words which cannot singly express a term, as adverbs, prepositions, &c.

Synchondrosis, sin-kon-drō′sis, *n.* [Gr. *syn*, together, and *chondros*, a cartilage.] *Anat.* the union of bones by means of cartilage.

Synchronous, **Synchronal**, sin′kro-nus, sin′kro-nal, *a.* [Gr. *syn*, with, and *chronos*, time (whence also *chronic*, *chronicle*, &c.).] Happening at the same time; contemporaneous; simultaneous. — **Synchronism**, sin′kron-izm, *n.* Concurrence of two or more events or facts in time; simultaneousness; arrangement of contemporaneous events in tabular form.—**Synchronistic**, sin-kron-is′tik, *a.* Pertaining to synchronism.—**Synchronization**, sin′kron-ī-zā″shon, *n.* The act of synchronizing.—**Synchronize**, sin′kron-īz, *v.t.*—*synchronized*, *synchronizing*. To concur or agree in time.—*v.t.* To make to agree in time; to cause to indicate the same time, as one time-piece with another.—**Synchronizer**, sin′kron-ī-zėr, *n.* One who or that which synchronizes. — **Synchronously**, sin′kron-us-li, *adv.* Contemporaneously; at the same time.—**Synchrony**, sin′kro-ni, *n.* Contemporaneity in time.

Synclastic, sin-klas′tik, *a.* Of surfaces, bending away from a tangent plane towards the same side all round, like a ball. See ANTICLASTIC.

Synclinal, sin-klī′nal, *a.* [Gr. *syn*, together, and *klinō*, to incline or slope.] *Geol.* sloping downward in opposite directions so as to meet in a common point or line; dipping toward a common line or plane (*synclinal* strata); formed by or pertaining to strata dipping in such a manner (*synclinal* axis); opposed to *anticlinal*.—*n.* A synclinal line or axis.

Syncope, sin′ko-pē, *n.* [Gr. *synkopē*, from *synkoptō*, to beat together, to weary—*syn*, together, and *koptō*, to strike, to cut off.] A contraction of a word by elision in the middle, as in *ne'er* for *never*; a suspension or sudden pause; *med.* a fainting or swooning; *mus.* syncopation.—**Syncopate**, sin′ko-pāt, *v.t.*—*syncopated*, *syncopating*. To contract by syncope; *mus.* to treat with syncopation.—**Syncopation**, sin-ko-pā′shon, *n.* The contraction of a word by elision; *mus.* the alteration of rhythm by driving the accent to that part of a bar not usually accented, the accented part of a bar being usually the first note.—**Syncopize**, sin′ko-pīz, *v.t.*—*syncopized*, *syncopizing*. To contract by syncope.

Syncratism, sin′krat-izm, *n.* SYNCRETISM.

Syncretism, sin′kret-izm, *n.* [Gr. *synkrētismos*.] The attempted blending of irreconcilable principles or parties, as in philosophy or religion; opposed to *eclecticism*.—**Syncretist**, sin′kret-ist, *n.* One who attempts to blend incongruous tenets or doctrines into a system. — **Syncretistic**, sin-krē-tis′tik, *a.* Pertaining to syncretism.—**Syncretic**, sin-kret′ik, *a.* Pertaining to syncretism.

Syndactylic, **Syndactylous**, sin-dak-til′ik, sin-dak′ti-lus, *a.* [Gr. *syn*, together, *daktylos*, a finger or toe.] *Ornithol.* having the external toe nearly as long as the middle, and partly united to it, as in the bee-eater, kingfisher, &c.; or with some of the digits closely bound together.

Syndesmology, sin-des-mol′o-ji, *n.* [Gr. *syndesmos*, a ligament, from *syn*, together, *desmos*, a band.] The department of anatomy that deals with the ligaments.—**Syndesmosis**, sin-des-mō′sis, *n.* A connection of bones by a ligament.

Syndic, sin′dik, *n.* [Gr. *syndikos*, helping in a court of justice, an advocate—*syn*, with, and *dikē*, justice.] An officer of government, invested with different powers in different countries; a kind of magistrate; a person chosen to transact business for others.—**Syndicate**, sin′di-kāt, *n.* A body of syndics; the office of a syndic; an association of persons formed with the view of promoting some particular enterprise, financial scheme, or the like.—**Syndicalism**, sin′dik-al-izm, *n.* [Fr. *syndical*, a trades unionist.] A system through which, by strikes, general or sympathetic, and otherwise, workmen aim at the domination of industry and capital.

Syndrome, sin′drō-mē, *n.* [Gr. *syn*, with, and *dramein*, to run.] In medicine, concurrence of a group of symptoms.

Synecdoche, si-nek′do-kē, *n.* [Gr., from *syn*, with, *ek*, out, *dechomai*, to receive.] A figure of speech by which the whole of a thing is put for a part, or a part for the whole (as *hands* for *workmen*).—**Synecdochical**, sin-ek-dok′i-kal, *a.* Expressed by or implying synecdoche.

Synechia, sin-ē-kī′a, *n.* [Gr. *synecheia*, adherence, from *syn*, with, and *echō*, to hold.] A disease of the eye in which the iris adheres to the cornea, or to the capsule of the crystalline lens.

Synecphonesis, si-nek′fō-nē″sis, *n.* [Gr., from *syn*, with, *ek*, out, and *phōnē*, sound.] A contraction of two syllables into one; synæresis.

Syneresis, si-nē′re-sis. SYNÆRESIS.

Synergist, si-nėr′jist, *n.* [Gr. *syn*, with, and *ergon*, work.] One who maintains the co-operation of man with God in the conversion of sinners.

Syngenesian, **Syngenesious**, sin-je-nē′si-an, sin-je-nē′si-us, *a.* [Gr. *syn*, with, and *genesis*, generation.] *Bot.* having the anthers united at the edges so as to form a tube.

Synizesis, sin-i-zē′sis, *n.* [Gr., from *syn*, with, and *hizō*, to sit.] *Med.* an obliteration of the pupil of the eye; *gram.* synecphonesis.

Synocreate, si-nok′rē-āt, *a.* [Gr. *syn*, together, and L. *ocrea*, a greave.] *Bot.* said of stipules uniting together on the opposite side of the stem from the leaf.

Synod, sin′od, *n.* [Fr. *synode*, L. *synodus*, from Gr. *synodus*—*syn*, and *hodos*, a way, a journeying.] A council or meeting of ecclesiastics, especially bishops and clergy, to consult on matters of religion; among Presbyterians, a church court consisting of the members of several adjoining presbyteries; also, a meeting, convention, or council in general.—**Synodal**, sin′od-al, *a.* Pertaining to a synod; synodical.—**Synodic**, **Synodical**, si-nod′ik, si-nod′i-kal, *a.* Pertaining to a synod; transacted in a synod; *astron.* pertaining to a conjunction or two successive conjunctions of the heavenly bodies.—*Synodical month*, the period from one conjunction of the moon with the sun to another: called also a *Lunation*.—**Synodically**, si-nod′i-kal-li, *adv.* By the authority of a synod.—**Synodist**, sin′od-ist, *n.* One who adheres to a synod.

Synœcious, si-nē′shus, *a.* [Gr. *syn*, together, *oikos*, a house.] *Bot.* having male and female organs on the same head.

Synonym, **Synonyme**, sin′ō-nim, *n.* [Fr. *synonyme*, from Gr. *synōnymos*, having the same signification—*syn*, with, and *onoma*, a name.] A word having the same, or nearly the same, signification as another in the same language; one of two or more words in the same language which have the same meaning. — **Synonymic**, **Synonymical**, sin-ō-nim′ik, sin-ō-nim′i-kal, *a.* Synonymous. — **Synonymist**, si-non′im-ist, *n.* One who collects and explains synonyms.—**Synonymize**, si-non′im-īz, *v.t.*—*synonymized*, *synonymizing*. To express by words of the same meaning.—**Synonymous**, si-non′i-mus, *a.* Having the character of a synonym; expressing the same thing.—**Synonymously**, si-non′i-mus-li, *adv.* In a synonymous manner.—**Synonymy**, si-non′i-mi, *n.* The quality of being synonymous.

Synopsis, si-nop′sis, *n.* pl. **Synopses**, si-nop′sēz. [Gr., from *syn*, with, and *opsis*, a sight, view.] A summary or brief statement giving a general view of some subject, as by means of short paragraphs; a conspectus. — **Synoptic**, **Synoptical**, si-nop′tik, si-nop′ti-kal, *a.* Affording a synopsis or general view.—*Synoptic gospels*, a term for the gospels of Matthew, Mark, and Luke, which present a synopsis of the same series of events, whereas in John's gospel the narrative and discourses are different.—**Synoptic**, *n.* One of the synoptic gospels.—**Synoptically**, si-nop′ti-kal-li, *adv.* In a synoptical manner.—**Sy-**

noptist, si-nop'tist, *n.* One of the writers of the synoptic gospels.

Synosteosis, si-nos'tē-ō″sis, *n.* [Gr. *syn*, with, and *osteon*, a bone.]—*Anat.* unity by means of bone.

Synovia, si-nō'vi-a, *n.* [Gr. *syn*, with, and L. *ovum*, an egg.] A thick, viscid, yellowish-white fluid, somewhat resembling white of egg in appearance, secreted at the joints for the purpose of lubricating their surfaces. —**Synovial**, si-nō'vi-al, *a.* Pertaining to or consisting of synovia.—**Synovitis**, sin-ō-vī'tis, *n.* [The term. *-itis* denotes inflammation.] Inflammation of the synovial membrane.

Syntax, sin'taks, *n.* [Gr. *syntaxis*, arrangement, disposition, from *syn*, with, and *taxis*, order, from *tassō*, to put in order. TACTICS.] *Gram.* the construction of sentences; the due arrangement of words or members of sentences in their mutual relations according to established usage.—**Syntactic, Syntactical**, sin-tak'tik, sin-tak'ti-kal, *a.* Pertaining or according to the rules of syntax.—**Syntactically**, sin-tak'ti-kal-li, *adv.* As regards syntax; in conformity to syntax.

Synteresis, sin-te-rē'sis, *n.* [Gr., a watching closely, from *syn*, with, and *tēreō*, to watch.] *Med.* preservative or preventive treatment.—**Synteretic**, sin-tē-ret'ik, *a.* Preserving health; prophylactic.

Syntexis, sin-tek'sis, *n.* [Gr. *syntēxis*, from *syn*, with, and *tēkō*, to melt.] *Med.* a wasting of the body; a deep consumption.—**Syntectic, Syntectical**, sin-tek'tik, sin-tek'ti-kal, *a.* Relating to syntexis; wasting.

Synthesis, sin'the-sis, *n.* pl. **Syntheses**, sin'the-sēz. [Gr. *synthesis*, a putting together, from *syn*, with, and *tithēmi*, to place.] The putting of two or more things together to form a whole: opposed to *analysis*; *logic*, the combination of separate elements of thought into a whole; *surg.* the operation by which divided parts are united; *chem.* the uniting of elements into a compound; composition or combination. —**Synthetic, Synthetical**, sin-thet'ik, sin-thet'i-kal, *a.* Pertaining to synthesis; consisting in synthesis; made by mixing certain ingredients. — *Synthetic processes*, in chemistry, processes by which naturally occurring compounds are built up artificially from their elements, or from simpler constituents.—**Synthetically**, sin-thet'i-kal-li, *adv.* By sinthesis or composition.

Syntonin, sin'tō-nin, *n.* [Gr. *syntonos*, contracted.] A protein extracted from muscle.

Syphilis, sif'i-lis, *n.* [A name invented by the Italian Fracastoro, who wrote a Latin poem on this disease (published in 1530); perhaps from Gr. *syn*, with, and *phileo*, to love.] A contagious and hereditary venereal disease.—**Syphilitic**, sif-i-lit'ik, *a.* Pertaining to or infected with syphilis.— **Syphilize**, sif'i-līz, *v.t.* To inoculate with syphilis. — **Syphiloid**, sif'i-loid, *a.* Resembling or having the character of syphilis.

Syphon, *n.* SIPHON.

Syren, sī'ren. SIREN.

Syriac, sir'i-ak, *a.* [L. *Syriacus.*] Pertaining to Syria or its language.—*n.* The ancient language of Syria, a Semitic language differing little from Chaldee.

Syringa, sī-ring'ga, *n.* [Gr. *syrinx*, *syringos*, a pipe—pipes having been made from the plants.] A genus of plants of which the lilac is the type; also a name of the mock-orange.

Syringe, sir'inj, *n.* [From Gr. *syrinx*, *syringos*, a pipe, a tube.] A portable instrument of the pump kind employed to draw in fluid and to squirt it out again, consisting of a cylindrical tube with an air-tight piston fitted with a handle, used by surgeons, gardeners, &c. — **Syringe**, sir'inj, *v.t.* — *syringed*, *syringing*. To wash and cleanse or water by means of a syringe.

Syringotomy, sī-ring-got'o-mi, *n.* [Gr. *syrinx*, *syringos*, a tube, a fistula, and *tomē*, a cutting.] The operation of cutting for fistula.

Syrinx, sī'ringks, *n.* [Gr. *syrinx*, a pipe.] The Pandean or Pan's pipes.

Syrop, sir'op, *n.* SYRUP.

Syrt, Syrtis, sėrt, sėr'tis, *n.* [Fr. *syrte*, L. *syrtis*, Gr. *syrtis*, a sandbank.] A quicksand or sandbank.

Syrup, Sirup, sir'up, *n.* [Fr. *sirop*, It. *siroppo*, L.L. *syrupus*, from Ar. *sharāb*, beverage, syrup, whence also *sherbet* and *shrub.*] A saturated or nearly saturated solution of sugar in water; any sweet and somewhat viscous fluid; the uncrystallizable fluid finally separated from crystallized sugar in the refining process.— **Syrupy, Sirupy**, sir'up-i, *a.* Like syrup.

Systaltic, sis-tal'tik, *a.* [Gr. *systaltikos*—*syn*, with, and *stellō*, to put.] *Med.* having alternate contraction and dilatation, as the heart.

System, sis'tem, *n.* [L. *systema*, Gr. *systēma*, from *syn*, together, and *histēmi*, to set.] Any assemblage of things forming a regular and connected whole; things connected according to a scheme; a number of heavenly bodies acting on each other according to certain laws (the solar *system*); an assemblage or connected series of parts or organs in an animal body (the nervous *system*); also, the body itself as a functional unity or whole (to take poison into the *system*); a plan or scheme according to which things are connected into a whole (a *system* of philosophy); regular method or order (to have no *system* in working). —**Systematic, Systematical**, sis-te-mat'ik, sis-te-mat'i-kal, *a.* Pertaining to or consisting in system; methodical; proceeding according to system. — **Systematically**, sis-te-mat'i-kal-li, *adv.* In a systematic manner; regularly; methodically.— **Systematism**, sis'tem-at-izm, *n.* Reduction of facts to a system.—**Systematist**, sis'tem-at-ist, *n.* One who forms or who adheres to a system.—**Systematization**, sis'tem-at-ī-zā″shon, *n.* The act or process of reducing to system. — **Systematize**, sis'tem-a-tīz, *v.t.*—*systematized*, *systematizing*. To reduce to system or regular method. —**Systematizer**, sis'tem-a-tī-zėr, *n.* One who reduces things to system.—**Systematology**, sis'tem-a-tol″o-ji, *n.* Knowledge or information regarding systems. — **Systemic**, sis-tem'ik, *a.* Pertaining to a system; *physiol.* pertaining to the body as a whole (the *systemic* circulation of the blood); of hearts, containing pure blood only.— **Systemize**, sis'tem-īz, *v.t.* SYSTEMATIZE. **Systemless**, sis'tem-les, *a.* Without system; *biol.* not exhibiting structure characteristic of organic life.

Systole, sis'to-lē, *n.* [Gr. *systolē*, from *syn*, together, and *stellō*, to put.] The contraction of the heart and arteries for forcing the blood through the system and carrying on the circulation: opposite to *diastole*; *gram.* the shortening of a long syllable.— **Systolic**, sis-tol'ik, *a.* Relating to systole.

Systyle, sis'tīl, *a.* [Gr. *systylos*—*syn*, together, and *stylos*, a column.] *Arch.* having columns standing close together; having a row of columns set close together all round, as in the Parthenon.

Sythe, SĪTH. SCYTHE.

Syzygy, siz'i-ji, *n.* [Gr. *syzygia*—*syn*, together, and *zygon*, a yoke. YOKE.] *Astron.* the conjunction or opposition of a planet with the sun, or of any two of the heavenly bodies.

T

T, the twentieth letter of the English alphabet, closely allied to *d*, both being dentals. —*To a T*, exactly; with the utmost exactness (to suit *to a T*), the allusion being to a mechanic's T-square.

Taal, tal, *n.* [D. language.] Language of the Cape Dutch.

Tab, tab, *n.* [Akin to *tape.*] A strip, or insertion on dress, of cloth.

Tabard, tab'ärd, *n.* [Fr. *tabard*, Sp. and Pg. *tabardo*, It. *tabarro*, L.L. *tabarrus*, *tabardus*, a cloak; origin doubtful.] A garment open at the sides, with wide sleeves or flaps reaching to the elbows; now only worn by the Officers of Arms. The tabard of a King of Arms is of velvet, that of a Herald of figured silk, and that of a Pursuivant of damask.—**Tabarder**, tab'är-dėr, *n.* One who wears a tabard; senior scholar of Queen's College, Oxford.

Tabaret, tab'a-ret, *n.* [Probably connected with *tabby* or *tabard.*] A stout satin-striped silk used for furniture.

Tabasheer, tab-a-shēr', *n.* [Ar. *tabâshîr.*] A siliceous concretion found in the joints of the bamboo and other large grasses, highly valued in the East Indies as a tonic.

Tabbinet, tab'i-net, *n.* TABINET.

Tabby, tab'i, *n.* [Fr. *tabis*, Sp., Pg., and It. *tabi*, L.L. *attabi*, from Ar. *attābi*, watered silk, from the quarter of Bagdad where this stuff was manufactured, named after a prince *Attab.*] A kind of rich silk or other stuff watered or figured; a cat of a mixed or brindled colour; any cat; an ancient spinster. — *v.t.* — *tabbied*, *tabbying*. To water or cause to look wavy by the process of calendering (to *tabby* silk). — **Tabby-cat**, *n.* A brindled cat; a she-cat. —**Tabbying**, tab'i-ing, *n.* The watering of stuffs between engraved rollers.

Tabby, tab'i, *n.* [Perhaps from Ar. *tabāshēr*, tabasheer, lime, plaster.] A mixture of lime and water, with shells, gravel, &c., forming a hard mass when dry.

Tabefaction, ta-bē-fak'shon, *n.* [L. *tabes*, a wasting away, and *facio*, to make.] A wasting away; emaciation.

Tabernacle, tab'ėr-nak-l, *n.* [L. *tabernaculum*, a tent, a dim. from *taberna*, a hut, a tavern. TAVERN.] A slightly constructed temporary habitation; the human frame as the temporary abode of the soul; the movable building, so contrived as to be taken to pieces with ease, carried by the Jews during their wanderings in the wilderness; a temple; a place of worship; a small cell or repository for holy things; an ornamental chest on Roman Catholic altars for the consecrated vessels; *Goth. arch.* a canopied stall or niche; an arched canopy over a tomb; a tomb.—*Feast of tabernacles*, a festival of the Israelites to commemorate their dwelling in tents during their journeys in the wilderness, lasting eight days, during which the people dwelt in booths made of the branches of certain trees.—*v.i.* To sojourn.—**Tabernacular**, tab-ėr-nak'ū-lėr, *a.* Pertaining to a tabernacle; sculptured with delicate tracery work.

Tabes, tā'bēz, *n.* [L., from *tabeo*, to waste away.] A disease consisting in a gradual wasting away of the whole body, accompanied with languor and depressed spirits. — **Tabetic**, ta-bet'ik, *a.* Pertaining to tabes; consumptive.—**Tabid**, tab'id, *a.* [L. *tabidus.*] Relating to tabes; wasted by disease. — **Tabidly**, tab'id-li, *adv.* Consumptively. — **Tabidness**, tab'id-nes, *n.* Emaciation.

Tabinet, tab'i-net, *n.* [From a French Protestant refugee of this name who first made tabinet in Dublin.] A kind of taffety or tabby; a fabric of silk and wool used for curtains.

Tablature, tab'la-tūr, *n.* [Fr. *tablature*.

TABLE.] An old name for musical notation, especially for the manner of writing music by letters, &c., for certain instruments.

Table, tā'bl, *n.* [Fr. *table*, from L. *tabula*, a board, a painting, a tablet, &c., from root *ta*, to extend, and suffix *-bula* (as in *fabula*, a fable). Of allied origin are *tavern, tabernacle.*] An article of furniture consisting of a horizontal frame with a flat upper surface supported by legs; any detached flat surface, especially when horizontal; the fare or viands served on a table; the persons sitting at table; a thin piece of something for writing on; a tablet; a series of many items or particulars presented in one connected group, especially when the items are in lists or columns; a syllabus or index; a series of numbers which proceed according to some given law (*tables* of logarithms); *jewelry*, the upper and flat surface of a diamond or other precious stone; *pl.* an old name for the game of draughts or a similar game.—*The Lord's table*, the altar in a church; the sacrament of the Lord's supper.—*Round table.* ROUND.—*Twelve tables*, the tables containing a celebrated body of ancient Roman laws, which formed the basis of Roman jurisprudence.—*To lay on the table*, in parliamentary practice and in the usage of corporate and other bodies, to receive any document, as a report, motion, &c., but to agree to postpone its consideration indefinitely.—*To turn the tables*, to change the condition or fortune of contending parties, alluding to the vicissitudes of fortune in gaming.—*v.t.*—*tabled, tabling.* To form into a table or catalogue; to tabulate; to lay or place upon a table; to lay on the table in business meetings, whether public or private; to enter upon the record.—*a.* Appertaining to or provided for a table.—**Table-beer**, *n.* Beer of no great strength for the table or for common use.—**Table-bell**, *n.* A small bell used at table for calling servants.—**Table-book**, *n.* A book of tablets; a memorandum-book.—**Table-center**, *n.* A piece, usually of fancy-work, on which a vase with flowers, or a pot containing a plant, is placed in the middle of the table.—**Table-cloth**, *n.* A cloth, usually of linen, for covering a table before the dishes are set for meals.—**Table-cover**, *n.* An ornamental cloth of wool, flax, cotton, &c., laid on a table between meal-times.—**Table-d'hôte**, tä'bl-dōt, *n.* [Fr. *table d'hôte*, lit. table of the host or landlord.] A common table for guests at an hotel; an ordinary.—**Table-fruit**, *n.* Fresh fruit suitable for eating uncooked, as dessert.—**Table-knife**, *n.* An ordinary knife used at table.—**Table-land**, *n.* A stretch of elevated flat land; a plateau.—**Table-linen**, *n.* The linen used for and at the table; napery.—**Table-mat**, *n.* A mat, often of some thick stuff, but also of wood, cork, or asbestos, used for preventing hot dishes from spoiling the polish of the table.—**Table-money**, *n.* An allowance to general-officers in the army and flag-officers in the navy in addition to their pay.—**Table-napkin**, *n.* A linen cloth used as a protection for the clothes, at meals; a serviette.—**Table-spoon**, *n.* The ordinary large spoon used at table as distinguished from a tea-spoon.—**Table-spoonful**, *n.* As much as a table-spoon will hold.—**Table-talk**, *n.* Conversation at table; familiar conversation.—**Table-talker**, *n.* One who studies to shine in table-talk.—**Table-turning**, *n.* One of the alleged phenomena of spiritualism, consisting of certain movements of tables attributed to spirits or spiritual forces.

Tableau, tab-lō', *n.* pl. **Tableaux**, tab-lōz'. [Fr. *tableau*, from *table*, a table.] A picture; a striking representation; performers grouped in a dramatic scene, or any persons regarded as forming a dramatic group.—*Tableau vivant* (vē-vän), a group of persons so dressed and placed as to represent some historical or fictitious scene; *lit.* a living picture.

Tablet, tab'let, *n.* [Fr. *tablette*, dim. of *table.*] A small flat surface; a small flat piece of wood, metal, ivory, &c., for writing or drawing on; a slab of wood or stone, or a metal plate bearing some device or inscription; *pl.* a kind of pocket memorandum-book; a small flattish cake, as of soap.

Tablier, tab'li-ėr, *n.* [Fr.] Short apron in female dress.

Taboo, tä-bö', *n.* [Of Polynesian origin.] The setting of something apart and away from human contact, either as consecrated or accursed, practised among certain savage races; the state of being so set apart; prohibition of contact or intercourse.—*v.t.* To put under taboo; to interdict approach to or contact or intercourse with (a *tabooed* subject of conversation).

Tabor, Tabour, tā'bor, *n.* [O.Fr. *tabour*, Fr. *tambour*, Sp. and Pg. *tambor*, probably from Per. *tabīr*, a tabor.] A small drum beaten with one stick, used as an accompaniment to a pipe or fife.—*v.i.* To play the tabor.—**Taborer**, tā'bor-ėr, *n.* One who beats the tabor.—**Taboret, Tabouret**, tā'bor-et, *n.* A small tabor; a frame for embroidery, named from its shape.—**Taborine, Tabourine**, tā'bo-rēn, *n.* [Fr. *tabourin.*] A tabor; a tambourine.—**Tabret**, tā'bret, *n.* [A dim. form.] A tabor.

Tabu, tä-bö', *n.* TABOO.

Tabula, tab'ū-la, *n.* pl. **Tabulæ**, tab'ū-lē. [L. TABLE.] A table; a tablet; a flat portion of something; a horizontal plate across the cavity in certain corals.—**Tabular**, tab'ū-lėr, *a.* [L. *tabularis*, from *tabula*, a table.] In the form of a table; having a flat surface; having the form of laminæ or plates; set down in or forming a table or statement of items in columns; computed by the use of tables.—*Tabular spar*, silicate of lime, a mineral of a grayish-white colour, occurring either massive or crystallized, in rectangular tabular crystals.—**Tabularization**, tab'ū-lėr-ī-zā"shon, *n.* The act of tabularizing.—**Tabularize**, tab'ū-lėr-īz, *v.t.* To make tables of; to tabulate.—**Tabulate**, tab'ū-lāt, *v.t.*—*tabulated, tabulating.* To reduce to tables or synopses; to set down in a table of items.—*a.* Table-shaped; tabular.—**Tabulation**, tab-ū-lā'shon, *n.* The throwing of data into a tabular form.

Tacahout, tak'a-hut, *n.* [Ar.] The small gall formed on the tamarisk-tree. MAHEE.

Tacamahac, tak'a-ma-hak, *n.* A name of the balsam poplar of North America; a resin produced from a tree of Mexico and the West Indies.

Tach, Tache, tach, *n.* [A softened form of *tack.*] Something used for taking hold or holding; a catch; a loop; a button. (O.T.)

Tacheometer, tak-e-om'et-ėr, *n.* [Gr. *tachus*, swift, *metron*, measure.] An instrument used in rapid surveying.—**Tacheometry**, tak-e-om'et-ri, *n.* A system of rapid surveying, in which distances and bearings are determined by a modified form of theodolite, called a tacheometer or tachymeter.—**Tachometer**, ta-kom'et-ėr, *n.* An instrument for measuring velocity, as of running water; a contrivance for indicating small variations in the velocity of machines.

Tachycardia, tak'i-kard"i-a, *n.* [Gr. *tachys*, swift, *kardia*, heart.] Excessive rapidity of the heart's action.

Tachygraphy, ta-kig'ra-fi, *n.* [Gr. *tachys*, quick, and *graphō*, to write.] The art or practice of quick writing; shorthand; stenography.—**Tachygraphic, Tachygraphical**, tak-i-graf'ik, tak-i-graf'i-kal, *a.* Pertaining to tachygraphy or shorthand.

Tachylyte, tak'i-līt, *n.* [Gr. *tachys*, swift, *lūō*, to loose.] Vitreous basalt, quickly fused under blow-pipe.

Tacit, tas'it, *a.* [L. *tacitus*, silent, from *taceo*, to be silent; cog. with Goth. *thahan*, to be silent.] Implied but not expressed in words; silent (*tacit* consent, a *tacit* agreement).—**Tacitly**, tas'it-li, *adv.* Silently; by implication; without words.—**Taciturn**, tas'i-tėrn, *a.* [L. *taciturnus*, from *tacitus*, silent.] Habitually silent; not apt to talk or speak.—**Taciturnity**, tas-i-tėr'ni-ti, *n.* [L. *taciturnitas.*] The state or quality of being taciturn; habitual silence or reserve in speaking.—**Taciturnly**, tas'i-tėrn-li, *adv.* In a taciturn manner; silently.

Tack, tak, *n.* [Of Celtic origin; Ir. *taca* Armor. *tach*, a nail; seen also in *attach*, *attack, detach.*] A small, short nail, usually having a broad head; a slight fastening or connection, as by a few stitches; *naut.* a rope for pulling the foremost lower corners of certain sails; the part of the sail to which the tack is fastened; the course of a ship as regards having the wind impelling her on the starboard or the port side; *Scots law*, a lease.—*v.t.* To fasten; to attach; to unite in a slight or hasty manner; to add on as a supplement or addition; to append.—*v.i.* To change the course of a ship so as to have the wind act from the starboard instead of the port side, or vice versa.—**Tacket**, tak'et, *n.* A clout-nail or hob-nail. (*Scotch.*)—**Tacksman**, taks'-man, *n.* In Scotland, a person occupying a farm by a *tack* or lease.

Tackle, tak'l, *n.* [From the stem of *take*; L.G. and D. *takel*, Dan. *takkel*, Sw. *tackel*, tackle.] Apparatus, appliances, or equipment for various kinds of work; gear; one or more pulleys with a single rope, used for raising and lowering weights; the ropes and rigging, &c., of a ship; see also such compounds as GROUND-TACKLE, GUN-TACKLE, &c.—*v.t.*—*tackled, tackling.* To supply with tackle; to apply tackle to; to set vigorously to work upon; to attack for the purpose of controlling or mastering (*colloq.*).—*v.i.* To go vigorously to work; followed by *to.* (*Colloq.*)—**Tackling**, tak'-l-ing, *n.* Tackle; gear, rigging, &c.; instruments of action; harness, or the like.

Tact, takt, *n.* [Fr. *tact*, touch, feeling, tact, from L. *tactus*, touch, from *tango, tactum*, to touch, from which also *tactile, tangent, tangible*, &c. TANGENT.] Touch†; peculiar skill or faculty; skill or adroitness in doing or saying exactly what is required by circumstances; the stroke in beating time in music.

Tactics, tak'tiks, *n.* [Fr. *tactique*, Gr. *taktikē* (*technē*, art), the art of drawing up soldiers, from *tassō, taxō*, to arrange (seen also in *syntax, taxidermy*).] The science and art of disposing military or naval forces in order for battle, of manœuvring them in presence of the enemy or within the range of his fire, and performing military and naval evolutions. STRATEGY.—**Tactic**, tak'tik, *n.* System of tactics.—**Tactic, Tactical**, tak'tik, tak'ti-kal, *a.* Pertaining to tactics.—**Tactically**, tak'ti-kal-li, *adv.* According to tactics.—**Tactician**, tak-tish'an, *n.* One versed in tactics.

Tactile, tak'tīl, *a.* [Fr. *tactile*, from L. *tactilis*, from *tango*, to touch. TACT.] Capable of being touched or felt; tangible; pertaining to the sense of touch.—**Taction**,† tak'shon, *n.* [L. *tactio.*] The act of touching; touch.—**Tactual**, tak'tū-al, *a.* Pertaining to the sense of touch; consisting in or derived from touch.

Tadpole, tad'pōl, *n.* [Equivalent to *toad-poll*, that is toad with a big poll or head.] The young of the frog or allied animal in its first state from the spawn.

Tael, tāl, *n.* In China, a denomination of silver money now equal to about 3s. sterling; also, a weight of 1⅓ oz.

Ta'en, tān. Poetical contraction of *Taken*.

Tænia, tē'ni-a, *n.* [L. *tænia*, from Gr. *tainia*, a fillet or ribbon.] The tape-worm; *arch.* the fillet or band which separates the Doric frieze from the architrave; *surg.* a ligature.—**Tænioid**, tē'ni-oid, *a.* Ribbon-shaped; resembling or belonging to the tape-worm.

Tafferel, *n.* TAFFRAIL.

Taffeta, Taffety, taf'e-ta, taf'e-ti, *n.* [Fr. *taffetas*, It. *taffetà*, from Per. *tâftah*, pp. of verb *tâftan*, to weave.] A generic name for plain silk, shot-silk, glacé, and certain others; also applied to mixed fabrics of silk and wool.

Taffrail, Tafferel, taf'rāl, taf'e-rel, *n.* [D. *tafereel*, a panel, a picture, dim. of *tafel*, a table, a picture, from L. *tabula*, a table.

TABLE.] *Naut.* the rail over the heads of the stern-timbers; originally the upper flat part of a ship's stern.

Taffy, taf'i, *n.* [W. *David.*] A Welshman; kind of molasses candy; flattery, cajolery.

Tafia, ta'fi-a, *n.* [Fr. from Malay.] A variety of rum distilled from molasses.

Tag, tag, *n.* [Same as Sw. *tagg*, a point; akin, *tack, take.*] A metallic point to the end of a string; anything hanging loosely attached or affixed to another; the end or catchword of an actor's speech; something mean and paltry, as the rabble (*Shak.*); a young sheep of the first year.—*v.t.*—*tagged, tagging.* To fit with a tag or point; to fit one thing to another; to tack or join.—**Tagger**, tag'ėr, *n.* One who tags.—**Taglet**, tag'let, *n.* A little tag.—**Tag-rag**, *n.* The lowest class of people; the rabble.

Taglia, täl'ya, *n.* [It.] A set of pulleys in a fixed block and another set in a movable block used in combination.

Tagliacotian, tal'i-a-kō"shi-an. TALIACOTIAN.

Taglioni, täl-yō'nē, *n.* An overcoat; so named from a celebrated Italian family of professional dancers.

Taguan, tag'ū-an, *n.* The flying-squirrel of India.

Tail, tāl, *n.* [A.Sax. *tægel, tægl*, a tail = Icel. *tagl*, L.G. and Sw. *tagel*, O.H.G. *zagal*, originally hair, as seen from Goth. *tagl*, hair.] That part of an animal which consists of the projecting termination of the spinal column, and terminates its body behind; the hinder or inferior part of a thing, as opposed to the head; any long terminal appendage or anything resembling or suggesting the tail of an animal; the other side of a coin from that which bears the head; the reverse; *aviation*, the after part of an air-craft, usually carrying controlling organs, e.g. rudders, elevators, fins. —*To turn tail*, to run away; to shirk an encounter.—*v.i.* To follow, droop, or hang like a tail.—**Tail-board**, *n.* The movable board at the hinder end of a cart or wagon. —**Tail-dive**, *n.* A dive or sudden descent in the air with an aeroplane, the tail part of it being foremost.—**Tail-drain**, *n.* A drain receiving the water that runs out of the other drains of a field.—**Tailed**, tāld, *a.* Having a tail of this or that kind.—**Tail-end**, *n.* The latter end; the termination.—**Tailless**, tāl'les, *a.* Having no tail.—**Tail-piece**, *n.* A piece forming a tail; an end piece; an appendage; a small picture or ornamental design at the end of a chapter or section in a book; the piece at the lower end of instruments of the violin kind to which the strings are fastened.—**Tail-race**, *n.* The water which runs from the mill after it has produced the motion of the wheel.—**Tail-skid**, *n.* *Aviation*, alighting gear near the tail of an aeroplane, arranged to slide along the ground.—**Tail-slide**, *n.* The movement of an aeroplane rearwardly as a result of an attempted angle of climb too steep for the power of the engine to maintain.—**Tailspin**, *n.* Spinning fall of an aeroplane out of control.

Tail, tāl, *n.* [Fr. *taille*, a cutting, from *tailler*, to cut. TAILOR.] *Law*, limitation; abridgment.—*Estate tail*, or *estate in tail*, an entailed estate or estate limited to certain heirs.

Tailor, tā'lėr, n. [Fr. *tailleur*, from *tailler*, to cut, from L.L. *taliare, taleare*, to cut, from L. *talea*, a rod, slip, cutting (seen also in *detail, entail, retail, tally*).] One whose occupation is to cut out and make chiefly men's outer clothing, as coats, vests, trousers, &c.—*v.i.* To practice making men's clothes.—**Tailor-bird**, *n.* An East Indian bird of the warbler family, so called because it constructs its nest by sewing leaves together, using the bill as a needle and a fiber as thread.—**Tailor-made**, *a.* Garments made by or according to the style of a tailor.—**Tailoress**, tā'lėr-es, *n.* A female who makes garments for men.

Tailzie, Tailyie, tāl'yi, *n.* and *v.t.* [Fr. *tailler*, to cut off. TAILOR.] *Scots law*, an entail; to entail.

Taint, tānt, *v.t.* [O.Fr. *taindre*, pp. *taint*; (Mod.Fr. *teindre, teint*), from L. *tingere*, to wet or moisten; whence also *tinge, tincture, tint.*] To imbue or impregnate with something noxious or poisonous; to infect; to corrupt, as by incipient putrefaction; to sully or pollute.—*v.i.* To become infected or corrupted; to be affected with incipient putrefaction.—*n.* Something that infects or contaminates; infection; corruption; a stain; a blemish on reputation.—**Taintless**, tānt'les, *a.* Free from taint or infection; pure.—**Taintlessly**, tānt'les-li, *adv.* Without taint.—**Taint-worm**, *n.* A worm that taints; a destructive parasitic worm.

Taiping, tā-ping, *n.* [Chinese, *t'ai p'ing*, great peace.] One who took part in the Chinese Rebellion of 1850-64.

Take, tāk, *v.t.*—pret. *took*; ppr. *taking*; pp. *taken.* [From Icel. and O.Sw. *taka*, Sw. *taga*, Dan. *tage*, to take, to seize, &c.; same root as L. *tango, tactum*, to touch (whence *tangible, tact*, &c.) *Tackle* is akin.] To receive or accept; correlative to *give*, and opposed to *refuse* or *reject*; to lay hold of; to seize; to grasp (*took* him by the throat); to lay hold of and remove; to carry off; to abstract (to *take* one's goods); to catch suddenly; to entrap; to circumvent; to surprise; to make prisoner of; to capture; to obtain possession of by arms (to *take* a town); to captivate, attract, allure; to understand or comprehend; to receive with good or ill will; to feel concerning (*take* an act amiss); to look upon as; to suppose, regard, consider (I *take* this to be right); to avail one's self of; to employ; to use (precaution, advice, &c.); to require or render necessary (the journey *takes* a week); not to let slip; to choose and make one's own; to select; to have recourse to; to betake one's self to (to *take* a course, shelter); to form or adopt (a resolution, a plan); to put on; to assume (to *take* shape); to receive and swallow (food, medicine); to copy; to draw (a portrait, a sketch); to put into writing; to note down; to fasten on, attack, or assail, as by a blast, a disease or the like; to be infected or seized with (to *take* a cold); to experience, indulge, feel (comfort, pride); to bear or submit to; to put up with; to enter into possession of by renting or leasing; to conduct, guide, convey, carry (to *take* one home); to leap over; to clear; to place one's self in; to occupy (to *take* a seat).—*To take aback*, to surprise or astonish; to confound.—*To take advantage of*, to use any advantage or benefit offered by; to catch or seize by surprise or cunning. —*To take aim*, to aim.—*To take air*, to be divulged or disclosed.—*To take the air, to take an airing*, to walk or drive in the open air for refreshment.—*To take arms*, or *take up arms*, to commence war or hostilities.—*To take breath*, to stop in order to breathe or rest after exertion.—*To take care*, to be watchful, vigilant, or careful.—*To take care of*, to have the charge of; to keep watch over.—*To take down*, to remove to a lower position; hence, to humble; to abase; to pull to pieces; to put in writing; to write down.—*To take effect*, to produce the intended effect; to begin to act or come into operation.—*To take the field*, to commence the operations of a campaign.—*To take fire*, to become ignited or inflamed; *fig.* to become excited, as with anger or love.—*To take heart*, to become courageous or confident.—*To take to heart*, to be keenly or deeply affected by; to feel sensibly.—*To take heed*, to be careful or cautious.—*To take heed to*, to attend to with care.—*To take hold of*, to seize; to grasp; to lay hands on.—*To take horse*, to mount and ride.—*To take in*, to admit or bring into one's house; to encompass or embrace; to include; to comprehend; to draw into a less compass; to contract; to furl, as a sail; to receive into the mind; to admit the truth of; to circumvent; to cheat.—*To take in hand*, to undertake; to attempt to execute.—*To take in vain*, to use or utter unnecessarily, carelessly, or profanely.—*To take leave*, to bid farewell; to depart; to permit one's self; to use a certain license or liberty.—*To take notice of*, to regard or observe with attention; to pay some attention to; to make remarks on; to mention.—*To take oath*, to swear judicially or with solemnity.—*To take off*, to remove or lift from the surface, outside, or top; to divest one's self of; to remove to a different place; to kill; to make away with; to deduct; to withdraw; to call or draw away; to drink out; to mimic; to imitate, as in ridicule.—*To take on*, or *upon*, to undertake; to assume.—*To take out*, to remove from, within or from a number; to remove by cleansing or the like (to *take out* a stain).—*To take pains*, to use all one's skill, care, and the like.—*To take part in*, to share; to partake of.—*To take part with*, to join or unite with.—*To take one's part*, to espouse one's cause; to defend one.—*To take place*, to happen.—*To take root*, to strike a root; to put forth roots and grow; to become firmly fixed or established.—*To take time*, to act without haste or hurry; to be in no haste or excitement; to require or necessitate a portion or period of time.—*To take thought*, to be solicitous or anxious.—*To take up*, to lift; to raise; to obtain on credit; to begin where another left off (to *take up* a narrative); to occupy, engross, or engage; to arrest or apprehend; to charge one's self with (a friend's cause, a quarrel); to enter upon; to adopt (a trade or occupation); to pay and receive (a bill at a bank).—*v.i.* To direct one's course; to betake one's self; to turn in some direction; to suit the public taste; to please; to have the intended effect; to catch hold; to admit of being made a portrait of.—*To take after*, to learn to follow; to imitate; to resemble.—*To take from*, to derogate or detract from.—*To take on*, to be violently affected; to grieve; to fret. (*Colloq.*) —*To take to*, to become fond of; to resort to.—*To take up with*, to dwell with; to associate with.—*n.* The quantity of anything taken; the quantity of fish taken at one haul or upon one cruise.—**Taker**, tā'kėr, *n.* One that takes; one who catches; a captor.—**Taking**, tā'king, *p.* and *a.* Alluring; engaging.—*n.* A seizing; agitation or distress of mind.—**Takingly**, tā'king-li, *adv.* In a taking or attractive manner.

Talapoin, tal'a-poin, *n.* A Siamese bonze or priest of Buddha.

Talbot, tal'bot, *n.* [From the *Talbot* family, who bear the figure of a dog in their coat of arms.] A kind of hound with a broad mouth, deep chops, large pendulous ears, and usually pure white.

Talbotype, tal'bo-tip, *n.* [Inventor's name, W. H. Fox *Talbot*, 1839.] A photographic process.

Talc, talk, *n.* [Fr. *talc*, Sp. and Pg. *talco*, from Ar. *talq*, talc.] A magnesian laminated mineral, unctuous to the touch, of a shining lustre, translucent, and usually white, apple-green, or yellow, differing from mica in being flexible but not elastic. FRENCH-CHALK.—**Talcky, Talcose, Talcous**, tal'ki, tal'kōs, tal'kus, *a.* Like talc; consisting of talc; containing talc.—**Talc-schist**, *n.* A schistose foliated rock consisting of quartz and talc.—**Talc-slate**, *n.* A slaty rock consisting of talc and quartz in laminæ.

Tale, tāl, *n.* [A.Sax. *talu*, speech, number; Icel. *tal, tala*, a speech, a number; Dan. *tal*, number, *tale*, talk, to talk; D. *tal*, number, *taal*, speech; G. *zahl*, number; akin tell.] An oral relation; a piece of information; a narrative of events that have really happened or are imagined to have happened; a short story, true or fictitious; a number or quantity reckoned, estimated, or set down; especially a reckoning by counting or numbering.—**Tale-bearer**, *n.* A person who tells tales likely to breed mischief; one who carries stories and makes mischief by his officiousness.—**Tale-bearing**, *n.* The act of spreading stories officiously; communication of secrets maliciously.—**Tale-teller**, *n.* One who tells tales or stories; a tale-bearer.

Talegalla, tal-ē-gal'la, *n.* The native name of the brush-turkey.

Talent, tal'ent, *n.* [Fr. *talent*, L. *talentum*, from Gr. *talanton*, a thing weighed, a talent, from root *tal*, akin to Skr. *tul*, to lift up, L. *tollo*, to lift, O.E. and Sc. *thole*, to suffer.] An ancient weight and denomination of money; the Attic talent as a weight being about 56 lb.; as a denomination of silver money about $1,187; the Hebrew talent as a weight equal to 93¾ lb.; as a denomination of silver, variously estimated at from $1,655 to $1,900; a gift, endowment, or faculty (a *talent* for mimicry); mental endowments or capacities of a superior kind; general mental power. [In the latter senses probably borrowed from the Scriptural parable of the talents, Mat. xxv.] ∴ Syn. under GENIUS.—**Talented**, tal'ent-ed, *a.* Having superior capacities.

Tales, tā'lēz, *n.pl.* [L. *talis*, such, of like sort, pl. *tales*.] *Law*, suitable persons who happen to be in a court, and from whom certain may be selected to supply any deficiency in the required number of jurors.—*To pray a tales*, to pray that the number of jurymen may be thus completed.

Taliacotian, tal'i-a-kō"shi-an, *a.* Pertaining to *Taliacotius* or Tagliacozzi, an Italian anatomist.—*Taliacotian operation.* Same as *Rhinoplastic operation.*

Talion, tā'li-on, *n.* [Fr. *talion*, L. *talio*, from *talis*, such.] The law of retaliation, according to which the punishment inflicted is the same in kind and degree as the injury, as an eye for an eye, a tooth for a tooth, &c.

Talipat, Taliput, tal'i-pat, tal'i-put, *n.* [Singhalese name.] A palm of India, Ceylon, &c., the leaves of which are used for covering houses, making umbrellas, fans, as a substitute for writing paper, &c.

Talipes, tal'i-pes, *n.* [L. *talus*, ankle, *pes*, foot.] The deformity called clubfoot.

Talisman, tal'is-man, *n.* [Fr. and Sp. *talisman*, from Ar. *telsamān*, pl. of *telsam*, a magical figure, from Byzantine Gr. *telesma*, incantation, from Gr. *teleō*, to accomplish, from *telos*, an end.] A charm consisting of a magical figure cut or engraved on stone or metal, and supposed to preserve the bearer from injury, disease, or sudden death; hence, something that produces extraordinary effects; an amulet; a charm. —**Talismanic, Talismanical**, tal-is-man'ik, tal-is-man'i-kal, *a.* Having the properties of a talisman; preservative against evils; magical.

Talk, tąk, *v.i.* [A word related to *tale*, *tell*, in much the same way as *hark* to *hear*, *smirk* to *smile*, and *walk* to *well*, *wallow*.] To utter words; to speak; to converse familiarly; to hold converse; to prate; to confer; to reason.—*To talk to*, to remonstrate with; to reprove gently. ∴ Syn. under SPEAK.—*v.t.* To use as a means of conversation or communication (to *talk* French or German); to speak; to utter (to *talk* nonsense); to have a certain effect on by talking; *to talk one down*=to silence one with incessant talk; *to talk one out of*= to dissuade one from, as a plan, project, &c.; *to talk one over*= to gain one over by persuasion.—*To talk over*, to talk about; to discuss. —*n.* Familiar conversation; discourse; report; rumour; subject of discourse; a discussion.—**Talkative**, tą'ka-tiv, *a.* Apt to engage in conversation; freely communicative; chatty. (A hybrid word, E. with Latin termination, like *starvation*.)—**Talkatively**, tą'ka-tiv-li, *adv.* In a talkative manner. —**Talkativeness**, tą'ka-tiv-nes, *n.*—**Talker**, tą'kėr, *n.* One who talks; a loquacious person; a prattler. —**Talking**, tą'king, *a.* Given to talk; having the power of speech.

Tall, tal, *a.* [From W. *tâl*, tall, towering.] High in stature; long and comparatively slender: said of upright things; having height, great or small (how *tall* is he?); great; excellent; remarkable; extravagant; bombastic, as *tall* story, *tall* talk [*Colloq.*] —**Tallness**, tạl'nes, *n.* The state or quality of being tall.

Tallage, Talliage, tal'āj, tal'i-āj, *n.* [From Fr. *tailler*, to cut. TAILOR.] A term formerly applied to subsidies or taxes of various kinds.

Tallow, tal'ō, *n.* [Same as Dan., Sw., and G. *talg*, Icel. *tólg*, D. *talk*, tallow; comp. Goth. *tulgus*, firm.] The harder and less fusible fat of animals melted and separated from the fibrous or membranous matter; also a fat obtained from some plants.—*v.t.* To grease or smear with tallow —**Tallow-candle**, *n.* A candle made of tallow.—**Tallow-chandler**, *n.* One whose occupation is to make, or to make and sell, tallow candles.—**Tallow-chandlery**, *n.* The business or premises of a tallow-chandler. —**Tallower**, tal'ō-ėr, *n.* A tallow-chandler.—**Tallowy**, tal'ō-i, *a.* Greasy; having the qualities of tallow.

Tallow-tree, *n.* A tree yielding vegetable tallow, especially a Chinese tree, now grown in India and America.

Tally, tal'i, *n.* [Fr. *taille*, a tally, a cutting, from *tailler*, to cut. TAILOR.] A piece of wood on which notches or scores are cut, as marks of number, often split into two parts so that each part contained one half of every notch: formerly used so as to answer the double purpose of receipts and records; anything made to suit or correspond to another; a label of wood or metal used in gardens, &c., bearing the name of the plant with which it is connected.—*v.t.*—*tallied, tallying.* To make to correspond.—*v.i.* To correspond; to agree exactly (your information *tallies* with mine).—**Tallier**, tal'i-ėr, *n.* One who keeps a tally.—**Tallyman**, tal'i-man, *n.* One who carries on a tally-trade; one who keeps a tally or account. —**Tally-shop**, *n.* A shop at which goods are sold on the tally-system. —**Tally-system, Tally-trade**, *n.* A system of dealing in some large towns, by which shopkeepers furnish articles on credit, the stipulated price to be paid by weekly or monthly instalments.

Tally Ho, tal'i hō", *interj.* and *n.* The huntsman's cry to urge on his hounds.

Talmud, tal'mud, *n.* [Chal. *talmûd*, instruction.] The body of the Hebrew civil and canonical laws, traditions, and explanations, or the book that contains them.—**Talmudic, Talmudical**, tal-mud'ik, tal-mud'i-kal, *a.* Pertaining to the Talmud; contained in the Talmud.—**Talmudist**, tal'mud-ist, *n.* One versed in the Talmud. —**Talmudistic**, tal-mud-is'tik, *a.* Pertaining to the Talmud; Talmudic.

Talon, tal'on, *n.* [Fr. *talon*, the heel, from L. *talus*, the heel.] The claw of a bird of prey.

Talookdar, ta-lųk'där, *n.* In India, a native acting as the head of a revenue department (*talook*) under a superior; a petty zemindar.

Talus, tā'lus, *n.* [L. *talus*, the ankle.] *Anat.* the ankle bone or joint; *arch.* the slope or inclination of any work; *geol.* a sloping heap of broken rocks and stones at the foot of any cliff or rocky declivity.

Tamable, Tamableness. Under TAME.

Tamandua, ta-man'dū-a, *n.* A species of ant-eater.

Tamarack, tam'a-rak, *n.* The black or American larch; hackmatack.

Tamarin, tam'a-rin, *n.* [Native name in Cayenne.] A species of very small South American monkeys.

Tamarind, tam'a-rind, *n.* [It. and Sp. *tamarindo*, Fr. *tamarin*, from Ar. *tamr-hindi*, from *tamr*, fruit, date, and *hindi*, Indian.] A tropical leguminous tree, and also its seed-pods, the preserved pulp of which is imported into European countries, and frequently employed in medicine, in fevers, &c.

Tamarisk, tam'a-risk, *n.* [L. *tamariscus.*] A genus of shrubs or small trees belonging to Southern Europe and Asia, some of them yielding 'manna'.

Tambour, tam'bör, *n.* [Fr. *tambour*, a drum, a tabour. TABOUR.] A drum; *arch.* the naked part of Corinthian and Composite capitals, bearing some resemblance to a drum; the circular vertical part both below and above a cupola; a cylindrical stone as in the shaft of a column; a circular frame on which silk or other stuff is stretched to be embroidered. —*v.t.* and *i.* To embroider with a tambour; to work on a tambour frame. —**Tambourine**, tam-bų-rēn', *n.* [Fr. *tambourin*, from *tambour.*] A musical instrument formed of a hoop, over which parchment is stretched like one end of a drum, and having small pieces of metal called jingles inserted in the hoop.

Tame, tām, *a.* [A.Sax. *tam*, tame = D., Dan., Sw., and Goth. *tam*, Icel. *tamr*, G. *zahm*, tame; same root as in L. *domo*, to subdue, *dominus*, a lord; Skr. *dam*, to subdue. DAME.] Having lost its native wildness and shyness; accustomed to man; domesticated (a *tame* deer); wanting in spirit; submissive; spiritless; unanimated; without liveliness or interest; insipid; dull; flat (a *tame* poem, *tame* scenery); listless; cold; harmless or ineffectual (*Shak.*).—*v.t.* *tamed, taming.* To make tame; to reduce from a wild to a domestic state; to subdue; to crush; to depress. —**Tamableness, Tameableness**, tā'ma-bl-nes, *n.* The quality of being tamable.—**Tamability, Tameability**, tā-ma-bil'i-ti, *n.* Capability of being tamed; tamableness.—**Tamable, Tameable**, tā'ma-bl, *a.* Capable of being tamed or subdued; capable of being reclaimed from a wild or savage state. —**Tameless**, tām'les, *a.* Incapable of being tamed; untamable. —**Tamelessness**, tām'les-nes, *n.* The state or quality of being tameless; untamableness. —**Tamely**, tām'li, *adv.* In a tame manner; submissively; meanly; servilely; insipidly. —**Tameness**, tām'nes, *n.* The quality of being tame; domestication; want of spirit or liveliness; dulness; flatness.—**Tamer**, tā'mėr, *n.* One who tames.

Tamil, tam'il, *n.* One of a race of men inhabiting Southern India, and belonging to the Dravidian stock; a Dravidian language spoken in India.—**Tamilian**, ta-mil'i-an, *a.* Pertaining to the Tamils or their language.

Tamine, Taminy, tam'in, tam'i-ni, *n.* [Fr. *étamine*, from L. *stamen*, a thread. STAMEN.] A strainer or bolter of hair or cloth; a thin woollen or worsted stuff highly glazed.

Tamis, Tammy, tam'i, *n.* [Fr. *tamis*, from D. *tems*, A.Sax. *temes*, a sieve.] A sieve; a searce.

Tammany, tam'a-ni, *n.* [From a popular Indian chief of Revolutionary times.]—*Tammany Hall*, the headquarters and organization of a Democratic political faction in New York City.

Tam o' Shanter, tam-o-shant'ėr. [*Burns* character.] A loosely-woven round woollen cap worn by both sexes.

Tamp, tamp, *v.t.* [From Fr. *tamponner*; akin to *tampion.*] To ram tight with tough clay or other substance, as a hole bored for blasting, after the charge is lodged.—**Tamper**, tam'pėr, *n.* One who tamps; an instrument used in tamping.—**Tamping**, tam'ping, *n.* The operation of filling tight a blast-hole above the charge; the operation of stopping with clay the issues of a blast-furnace; the material used for these purposes.

Tamper, tam'pėr, *v.i.* [A form of *temper.*] To meddle or interfere; to try little experiments; to meddle so as to alter by corruption or adulteration; to influence towards a certain course by secret and unfair means: generally followed by *with* (to *tamper with* a document, a witness, &c.).—**Tamperer**, tam'pėr-ėr, *n.* One who tampers.

Tampion, tam'pi-on, *n.* [From Fr. *tampon*, a nasalized form from *tapon*, a bung, from D. *tap* = E. *tap*, a plug. TAP.] The stopper of a cannon or other piece of ordnance; a tompion; a plug.

Tam-tam, tam'tam, *n.* [Hind., from sound of drum.] A kind of native drum used in the East Indies; a Chinese gong.

Tan, tan, *v.t.*—*tanned, tanning.* [Fr. *tanner*, to tan, from *tan*, oak bark, from Armor. *tann*, oak; akin *tawny.*] To convert into leather, as animal skins, by steeping them in an infusion of oak or some other bark, by which they are rendered firm, durable, and in some degree impervious to water; to make brown by exposure to the rays of the sun; to make sunburnt; to beat, flog, or thrash (*colloq.*).—*v.i.* To become tanned (leather *tans* easily); to become tan-coloured or sun-burnt. —*n.* The bark of the oak, willow, or other trees, as broken by a mill, and used for tanning; a yellowish-brown colour like that of tan.—*a.* Of the colour of tan; resembling tan; tawny.—**Tan-balls**, *n.pl.* The spent bark of the tanner's yard pressed into balls or lumps and used for fuel.—**Tan-bed**, *n. Hort.* a bark bed or stove.—**Tannable**, tan'a-bl, *a.* Capable of being tanned.—**Tannage**, tan'āj, *n.* The operation of tanning.—**Tanner**, tan'ėr, *n.* One whose occupation is to tan hides.—**Tannery**, tan'ėr-i, *n.* A place where the operations of tanning are carried on; the art or process of tanning.—**Tannate**, tan'āt, *n.* A salt of tannic acid.—**Tannic**, tan'ik, *a.* Applied to an acid existing in oak, gall-nuts, &c., and forming the efficient substance in tanning leather.—**Tannin**, tan'in, *n.* Tannic acid.—**Tanning**, tan'ing, *n.* The operation and art of converting raw hides and skins of animals into leather; a brown colour produced on the skin by the sun.—**Tan-pit**, **Tan-vat**, *n.* A sunken vat in which hides are laid in tan; a bark-bed.—**Tan-yard**, *n.* A yard or inclosure where the tanning of leather is carried on.

Tanager, tan'a-jėr, *n.* [Altered from Brazilian *tanagra.*] A genus of tropical American birds of the finch family, remarkable for their bright colours.

Tandem, tan'dem, *adv.* [L., at length, that is, after some *time;* the English sense is by a pun or joke.] With two horses harnessed singly one before the other (to drive *tandem*).—*n.* A vehicle drawn by two horses harnessed one before the other; a cycle for two persons, one before the other.

Tang, tang, *n.* [Imitative of a sound, like *twang*, metaphorically transferred to a strong taste.] A twang or sharp sound (*Shak.*); a taste or flavour; characteristic flavour, quality, or property; a smack or taste.—*v.i.* To ring; to twang.

Tang, tang, *n.* [A modification of *tongue*, or allied to *tongs.*] A projecting part of an object which is inserted into and so secured to another; the part of a table-knife or tool which fits into the handle; the tongue of a buckle.

Tangent, tan'jent, *n.* [L. *tangens, tangentis*, ppr. of L. *tango, tactum*, to touch (whence also *contact, tact, tangible, taint, tax, task*, &c.; stem also in *contagion*).] *Geom.* a straight line which touches a circle or curve, and which being produced does not cut it; *trigon.* in a right-angled triangle, the tangent of an acute angle = opposite side ÷ adjacent side.—*To go* or *fly off at a tangent, fig.* to break off suddenly from one line of action, train of thought, or the like, and go on to something else.—*a.* Touching; forming a tangent.—**Tangence**, **Tangency**, tan'jens, tan'jen-si, *n.* State of being tangent; a contact or touching.—**Tangential**, tan-jen'shal, *a.* Pertaining to a tangent; in the direction of a tangent.—*Tangential force*, force acting on a body at its surface, in a line which touches or lies in the surface.—**Tangentially**, tan-jen'shal-li, *adv.* In the direction of a tangent.

Tangerine, tan'jer-ēn, *n.* [*Tangier.*] A small orange grown at Tangier.

Tanghin, tan'gin, *n.* A vegetable poison formerly employed in Madagascar as an ordeal.

Tangible, tan'ji-bl, *a.* [Fr. *tangible*, L. *tangibilis*, from *tango*, to touch. TANGENT.] Capable of being touched or grasped; perceptible by the touch; capable of being possessed or realized; real; actual; evident (*tangible* proofs).—**Tangibility**, **Tangibleness**, tan-ji-bil'i-ti, tan'ji-bl-nes, *n.* The quality of being tangible, or perceptible to the touch.—**Tangibly**, tan'ji-bli, *adv.* So as to be perceptible to the touch.

Tangle, tang'gl, *v.t.*—*tangled, tangling.* [Allied to Icel. *thöngull, thang*, Dan. and G. *tang*, tangle, sea-weed; hence *entangle.*] To knit together confusedly; to interweave or interlace so as to be difficult to unravel; to entangle or entrap; to involve; to complicate.—*n.* A knot of threads or other things confusedly interwoven; a perplexity or embarrassment; a name given to some species of sea-weed.—**Tangly**, tang'gli, *a.* Knotted; intertwined; intricate; covered with sea-weed or tangle.

Tanist, tan'ist, *n.* [Ir. and Gael. *tanaiste*, from *tan*, a region.] An elective prince or sovereign among the ancient Irish.—**Tanistry**, tan'ist-ri, *n.* An Irish custom of descent, according to which the tanist or prince was fixed by election, the right or succession not lying in the individual, but in the family to which he belonged.

Tank, tangk, *n.* [For *stank*, from O.Fr. *estanc* (Fr. *étang*), Sp. *estanque*, from L. *stagnum*, a pond or pool. STAGNANT.] A cistern or vessel of large size to contain liquids; a reservoir; a pond for storing water in India; *milit.* an armoured car with caterpillar wheels, protected by guns fired from inside, used for clearing trenches, destruction of iron barbed wire, &c.—**Tank car**, *n.* A railway car or wagon carrying a large tank for petroleum.—**Tank-worm**, *n.* A nematode worm abounding in the mud in tanks in India.

Tankard, tang'kärd, *n.* [O.Fr. *tanquart, tanquard*, O.D. *tanckaerd*, a tankard.] A rather large drinking vessel, with a cover, usually made of metal; a pitcher.

Tanner, Tannery, Tannic, Tannin, &c. Under TAN.

Tanrec, tan'rek, *n.* TENREC.

Tansy, tan'zi, *n.* [Fr. *tanaisie*, O.Fr. *tanasie*, tansy, from Gr. *athanasia*, immortality—because the dried flowers retain their natural appearance.] The popular name of a strongly-scented perennial herb with much-divided leaves, and yellow flowers, formerly in repute as a tonic and anthelmintic; a dish made of eggs, cream, sugar, the juice of herbs, &c.

Tantalite. Under TANTALUM.

Tantalize, tan'ta-līz, *v.t.*—*tantalized, tantalizing.* [From *Tantalus*, a mythical king of Lydia or Phrygia, who for divulging the secrets of his father Zeus was condemned to stand in water, which receded from him whenever he stooped to drink, while branches loaded with fruit, which always eluded his grasp, hung over his head.] To tease or torment by presenting something desirable to the view, but continually frustrating the expectations by keeping it out of reach; to excite by expectations or fears which will not be realized.—**Tantalism**,† tan'tal-izm, *n.* Tantalization.—**Tantalization**, tan'ta-lī-zā"shon, *n.* The act of tantalizing; the torment of expectations frustrated.—**Tantalizer**, tan'ta-lī-zėr, *n.* One that tantalizes.—**Tantalizing**, tan'ta-lī-zing, *p.* and *a.* Teasing or tormenting by presenting something unattainable.—**Tantalizingly**, tan'ta-lī-zing-li, *adv.* In a tantalizing manner.

Tantalum, tan'ta-lum, *n.* [Named from the *tantalizing* difficulties in analysing the ore.] A rare metallic element obtained as a black powder from several minerals.—**Tantalite**, tan'ta-līt, *n.* An ore of tantalum.

Tantalus, tan'ta-lus, *n.* A stand for spirit bottles which is provided with a lock, and so constructed that, whilst the bottles are plainly visible, their contents cannot be got at without unlocking the stand.

Tantamount, tan'ta-mount, *a.* [Fr. *tant*, L. *tantus*, so much, and E. *amount.*] Equivalent, as in value, force, effect, or signification.

Tantivy, tan-tiv'i, *n.* [Said to be from the note of a hunting horn.] A rapid, violent gallop, especially in hunting; in *politics*, a high Tory.

Tantra, tan'tra, *n.* [Skr.] A division, section, or chapter of certain Sanskrit sacred works.—**Tantrism**, tan'trizm, *n.* The doctrine of the tantras.

Tantrum, tan'trum, *n.* [Prov.E. *tantum*, from W. *tant*, a gust of passion, a whim.] A burst of ill-humour; a display of temper; an ill-natured caprice: used chiefly in plural.

Taoism, Taouism, tä'ō-izm, tä'ö-izm, *n.* [Chinese *tao*, way or path.] A Chinese religion, non-theistic, teaching a pure morality, but associated with belief in magic, &c.

Tap, tap, *v.t.*—*tapped, tapping.* [From Fr. *taper*, to tap, *tape*, a tap; from Prov.G. *tapp*, a blow, G. *tappen*, to grope; Icel. *tapsa*, to tap; imitative of sound, like *pat.*] To strike with something small, or to strike with a very gentle blow; to pat gently.—*v.i.* To strike a gentle blow.—*n.* A gentle blow; a slight blow with a small thing.

Tap, tap, *n.* [A.Sax. *tæppa* = L.G. *tappe*, D. and Dan. *tap*, Icel. *tappi*, G. *zapfen*, a tap, a faucet; akin *tip, top, tipple, tampion*, &c.] A pipe or hole through which liquor is drawn from a cask; a plug to stop a hole in a cask; a spigot; the liquor itself (*colloq.*); a tap-house or tap-room; *engin.* a small tool for forming threads in drilled holes.—*v.t.* [Same as L.G. and D. *tappen*, Icel. and Sw. *tappa*, G. *zapfen.*] To pierce so as to let out a fluid (to *tap* a cask); to treat in any analogous way for the purpose of drawing something from (to *tap* telegraph wires).—**Tap-house**, *n.* A house where liquors are retailed.—**Tapping**, tap'ing, *n.* The surgical operation of letting out a fluid by perforation, as in dropsy.—**Tap-room**, *n.* A room where beer is served from the tap; a common room for drinking in a tavern.—**Tap-root**, *n.* The main root of a plant, long and tapering, and penetrating the earth downwards.—**Tapster**, tap'stėr, *n.* A person employed in a tavern, &c., to tap or draw ale or other liquor.

Tape, tāp, *n.* [A.Sax. *tæppe*, a fillet; akin to *tapestry, tippet.*] A narrow fillet or band; a narrow woven band of cotton or linen, used for strings and the like.—**Tapeism**, tāp'izm, *n.* Same as *Red-tapery.*—**Tape-line, Tape-measure**, *n.* A tape painted to give it firmness and marked with inches, &c., used in measuring.—**Tape-worm**, *n.* The name of certain internal parasites composed of a number of flattened joints or segments, found in the intestines of warm-blooded vertebrates.

Taper, tā'pėr, *n.* [A.Sax. *tapor, taper*, a taper, from Ir. *tapar*, W. *tampr*, a taper; comp. Skr. *tap*, to burn.] A small candle; a long wick coated with wax or other suitable material; a small light; tapering form; gradual diminution of thickness in an elongated object.—*a.* Long and regularly becoming slenderer toward the point; becoming small toward one end (*taper* fingers).—*v.i.* To become gradually slenderer or less in diameter; to diminish; to grow gradually less.—*v.t.* To cause to taper.—**Tapering**, tā'pėr-ing, *a.* Becoming regularly smaller in diameter toward one end; gradually diminishing toward a point.—**Taperingly**, tā'pėr-ing-li, *adv.*

Tapestry, tap'es-tri, *n.* [Fr. *tapisserie*, tapestry, from *tapis*, tapestry, a carpet, from L. *tapes, tapete*, from Gr. *tapēs, tapētos*, a carpet, a rug.] A kind of woven hangings of wool and silk, often enriched with gold and silver, ornamented with figures of men, animals, landscapes, &c., and formerly much used for covering the walls and furniture of apartments, churches, &c.—*v.t.*—*tapestried, tapestrying.* To adorn with tapestry or as if with tapestry.

Taphrenchyma, taf-ren'ki-ma, *n.* [Gr. *taphros*, a pit, and *enchyma*, infusion, tissue.] *Bot.* bothrenchyma.

Tapioca, tap-i-ō'ka, *n.* [Native American name.] A farinaceous substance prepared from cassava meal, which, while moist or damp, has been heated for the purpose of drying it on hot plates.

Tapir, tā'pir, *n.* [From the native Brazilian name.] A South American hoofed animal allied both to the hog and to the rhinoceros, with a nose resembling a small proboscis.—**Tapiroid**, tā'pi-roid, *a.* Like or allied to the tapir family.

Tapis, tä-pē, *n.* [Fr., tapestry.] Carpeting or tapestry, formerly used to cover the table in a council chamber; hence, *to be on* or *upon the tapis*, to be under consideration, or on the table.

Tappet, tap'et, *n.* [A dim. from *tap*, to strike gently.] A small lever connected with the valve of the cylinder of a steam-engine; a small cam.

Tapster, Under TAP.

Taqua-nut, tak'wa, *n.* The ivory nut.

Tar, tär, *n.* [A.Sax. *taro*, *tero*, tar=D. *teer*, Icel. *tjaro*, G. *theer*, tar; allied to *tree*.] A thick, dark-coloured viscid product obtained by the destructive distillation of organic substances and bituminous minerals, as pine or fir, coal, shale, &c., used for coating and preserving timber and iron, for impregnating ships' ropes and cordage, &c.; a sailor, contraction of *tarpaulin* (which see) (*Macaulay, H.*, chap. ii).—*v.t.*—*tarred, tarring.* To smear with tar.—*To tar and feather* a person, to pour heated tar over him and then cover with feathers, as is sometimes done by mobs to obnoxious persons.—**Tar-water**, *n.* A cold infusion of tar, formerly a celebrated remedy for many chronic affections, especially of the lungs; the ammoniacal water obtained by condensation in gas manufacture.—**Tarry**, tär'i, *a.* Consisting of tar, or like tar; partaking of the character of tar; smeared with tar.

Tara fern, tä'ra, *n.* A New Zealand bracken fern with an edible rhizome.

Tarantass, tar-an-tas', *n.* A covered Russian carriage without springs.

Tarantula, ta-ran'tū-la, *n.* [It. *tarantola*, from L. *Tarentum*, now *Taranto*, in the south of Italy.] A kind of spider found in southern Italy, the bite of which was at one time supposed to be dangerous, and to cause the disease tarantism; the dance tarantella.—**Tarantella**, tar-an-tel'la, *n.* [It.] A swift, whirling Italian dance in six-eight measure; the music for the dance.—**Tarantism**, ta-ran'tizm, *n.* [It. *tarantismo*.] A fabulous dancing disease, said to be caused by the tarantula; a disease resembling St. Vitus's dance.

Taraxacum, ta-rak'sa-kum, *n.* [From Ar. or Per. *tarashagūn*, taraxacum.] Dandelion or its roots as used medicinally.

Tarboosh, **Tarbouche**, tär'bösh, *n.* [Ar. name.] A red woollen skull-cap worn by the Egyptians, Turks, and Arabs; a fez.

Tardenoisian, tard-nwa'zi-an, *a.* [From *Fère-en-Tardenois*, France.] A term indicating a stage of human culture intermediate between the Azilian and the Maglemosian, in the period of transition from the Palæolithic to the Neolithic age.

Tardigrade, tär'di-grād, *a.* [L. *tardus*, slow, *gradus*, step.] Slow-paced; moving or stepping slowly; pertaining to the tardigrades.—*n.* One of a family of edentate mammals comprising the sloths.

Tardy, tär'di, *a.* [Fr. *tardif*, tardy, as if from a form *tardivus*, from L. *tardus*, slow (seen in *retard*).] Moving with a slow pace or motion; slow; late; dilatory; not up to time; reluctant.—**Tardily**, tär'di-li, *adv.* In a tardy manner; with slow pace; slowly.—**Tardiness**, tär'di-nes, *n.* The state or quality of being tardy; slowness; dilatoriness; unwillingness; reluctance.

Tare, tär, *n.* [Probably from provincial *tare*, brisk, eager; comp. *quick-grass*.] A name of different species of leguminous plants, called also vetch.

Tare, tär, *n.* [Fr. *tare*, from Sp. *tara*, from Ar. *tarha*, waste, tare.] *Com.* a deduction from the gross weight of goods as equivalent to the weight of the package containing them.

Tare, tär, a pret. of *tear*.

Tarentula, ta-ren'tū-la, *n.* Same as *Tarantula*.

Target, tär'get, *n.* [A dim. from O.Fr. *targue*, *targe*, from O.H.G. *zarga*, G. *zarge*, a frame, border, &c.] A shield or buckler of a small kind, circular in form; the mark set up to be aimed at in archery, musketry, or artillery practice and the like.—**Targeted**, tär'get-ed, *a.* Furnished with a target.—**Targeteer**, **Targetier**, tär-get-ēr', *n.* One armed with a target.—**Targe**, tärj, *n.* A target or shield. (*Poetical.*)

Targum, tär'gum, *n.* [Chal. *targūm*, interpretation, from *targem*, to interpret; akin *dragoman*.] A translation or paraphrase of the Hebrew Scriptures in the Aramaic or Chaldee language, made after the Babylonish captivity, when Hebrew began to die out as the popular language.—**Targumist**, tär'gum-ist, *n.* The writer of a Targum; one versed in the Targums.

Tariff, tar'if, *n.* [Fr. *tarif*, Sp. *tarifa*, from the Ar. *tarif*, explanation, information, a list of fees to be paid, from *'arafa*, to inform.] A list of goods with the duties or customs to be paid for the same, either on importation or exportation; a table or scale of charges generally (a hotel *tariff*).

Tarlatan, tär'la-tan, *n.* [Milanese *tarlantanna*, linsey-woolsey.] A thin cotton stuff resembling gauze, used in costuming, &c.

Tarn, tärn, *n.* [Icel. *tjörn*, Sw. *tärn*, a tarn.] A small mountain lake or pool, especially one which has no visible feeders.

Tarnish, tär'nish, *v.t.* [Fr. *ternir*, ppr. *ternissant*, from O.H.G. *tarnjan*, to conceal; akin to A.Sax. *dernan*, Sc. *dern*, to hide.] To diminish or destroy the lustre of; to soil or sully; to cast a stain or disgrace upon.—*v.i.* To lose lustre; to become dull.—*n.* A spot; a blot; soiled state.—**Tarnisher**, tär'nish-ėr, *n.* One who or that which tarnishes.

Taro, tä'rō, *n.* [Native name.] A plant of the arum family, cultivated in the Pacific Islands for the sake of its esculent root.

Tarpan, tär'pan, *n.* The wild horse of Tartary.

Tarpaulin, **Tarpauling**, tär-pa̤'lin, tär-pa̤'ling, *n.* [*Tar*, and old *pauling*, a covering for a cart or wagon, equivalent to *palling*, from *pall*, a cover.] Tarred canvas used to cover the hatchways, &c., on shipboard, and to protect agricultural produce, goods, &c., from the weather; a sailor's hat covered with painted or tarred cloth.

Tarpeian, tar-pē'an, *a.* [L. *Tarpeius*.] Of the hill-side or rock from which in early Rome criminals were cast down.

Tarpon, **Tarpum**, tär'pon, tär'pum, *n.* [Origin unknown.] A fine large sea-fish of the Southern United States and West Indies, belonging to the herring family, and giving excellent sport to the angler.

Tarrace, **Tarrass**, tar'as, *n.* [G. *tarrass*, from Fr. *terrasse*, earthwork, from *terre*, L. *terra*, earth.] A kind of plaster or cement; trass.

Tarradiddle, ta-ra-did'l, *n.* A slight lie, fib, equivocation.

Tarragon, tar'a-gon, *n.* [Sp. *taragona*, It. *targone*, from L. *draco*, a dragon.] A plant used for perfuming vinegar.

Tarry, tar'i, *v.i.*—*tarried, tarrying.* [From A.Sax. *tergan*, *tyrgan*, to torment, to tease, hence to tire, to delay=D. *tergen*, G. *zergen*, to provoke; akin *tire*.] To stay; to abide; to remain behind; to wait; to put off going or coming; to delay; to linger.—*v.t.* To wait for.

Tarry, tar'i, *a.* Under Tar.

Tarsia, tär'si-a, *n.* [It.] A kind of Italian mosaic woodwork or marquetry.

Tarsier, tär'si-ėr, *n.* [Fr. *tarsier*, from the length of its *tarsus*.] A nocturnal animal of the lemur family inhabiting the Eastern Archipelago.

Tarsometatarsus, tär'sō-met-a-tär"sus, *n.* *Ornith.* same as *Tarsus*.

Tarsus, tär'sus, *n.* pl. **Tarsi**, tär'sī. [Gr. *tarsos*, the flat part of the foot.] *Anat.* that part of the lower limb which in man is known as the ankle; also the thin cartilage at the edges of the eyelids; *entom.* the last segment of the legs; *ornith.* that part of the leg (or properly the foot) of birds which extends from the toes to the first joint above; the shank.—**Tarsal**, tär'sal, *a.* Pertaining to the tarsus.

Tart, tärt, *a.* [A.Sax. *teart*, acid, sharp, from stem of *teran*, to tear.] Sharp tasting; severe; female of questionable morals.—**Tartish**, tär'tish, *a.* Somewhat tart.—**Tartly**, tärt'li, *adv.* In a tart manner; sharply.—**Tartness**, tärt'nes, *n.* Acidity; sharpness, asperity.

Tart, tärt, *n.* [Fr. *tarte*, *tourte*, Sp. *torta*, *tarta*, It. *torta*, a tart, from L. *tortus*, ppr. of *torqueo*, to twist, lit. a piece of pastry in a twisted form; comp. a *roll*, from being rolled. Torture.] A piece of pastry, consisting of fruit baked and inclosed in paste.—**Tartlet**, tärt'let, *n.* A small tart.

Tartan, tär'tan, *n.* [Fr. *tartane*, It., Sp., and Pg. *tartana*; of Eastern origin.] A vessel used in the Mediterranean, with a single mast bearing a large lateen sail, and with a bowsprit and fore-sail.

Tartan, tär'tan, *n.* [Fr. *tiretaine*, *tirtaine*, linsey-woolsey; of unknown origin.] A species of cloth, checkered or cross-barred in various colours.—*a.* Consisting of or resembling tartan.

Tartar, tär'tar, *n.* [Fr. *tartre*, It. and Sp. *tartaro*, L.L. *tartarum*, the hard deposit in wine casks; perhaps from Ar. *durd*, sediment, dregs.] A hard pink or red crust deposited from wines not completely fermented, a compound of tartaric acid and potassium, also called *argol*; also, a concretion which sometimes forms on the teeth.—*Cream of tartar*, purified tartar.—*Salt of tartar*, carbonate of potassium obtained by calcining cream of tartar.—*Tartar emetic*, a compound of tartaric acid, potassium, and antimony, used as an emetic, purgative, diaphoretic, sedative, &c.—**Tartareous**, tär-tā'rē-us, *a.* Consisting of tartar; resembling tartar.—**Tartaric**, tär-tar'ik, *a.* Pertaining to, or obtained from tartar.—*Tartaric acid*, the acid of tartar existing in grapes and other fruits, but principally in cream of tartar, used in calico-printing and in medicine, &c.—**Tartarize**, tär'tar-īz, *v.t.*—*tartarized, tartarizing.* To impregnate with tartar; to refine by means of the salt of tartar.—**Tartarous**, tär'tar-us, *a.* Consisting of tartar, or partaking of its qualities.—**Tartrate**, tär'trāt, *n.* A salt of tartaric acid.

Tartar, tär'tar, *n.* [A corruption of the native name *Tatar*.] A native of Tartary; a very irascible or rigorous person; as applied to a woman, a shrew; a vixen.—*To catch a tartar*, to assail a person who proves too strong for the assailant.—*a.* Pertaining to the Tartars.—**Tartaric**, tär-tar'ik, *a.* Pertaining to Tartary.

Tartarean, **Tartareous**. Under Tartarus.

Tartarus, tär'ta-rus, *n.* [Gr. *Tartaros*.] Among the Greeks and Romans a name for the lower world or infernal regions; hell.—**Tartarean**, **Tartareous**, tär-tā'rē-an, tär-tā'rē-us, *a.* Pertaining to Tartarus; infernal.

Tartlet. Under Tart, *n.*

Tartly, **Tartness**. Under Tart, *a.*

Tartuffe, tär-töf', *n.* [Fr.] Religious hypocrite or impostor, from the character in Molière's play of the name.

Tasco, tas'kō, *n.* A sort of clay for making melting-pots.

Tasimeter, ta-zim'et-ėr, *n.* [Gr. *tasis*, a stretching, from *teinō*, to stretch, and *metron*, a measure.] An instrument invented by Edison for measuring extremely slight variations of pressure, temperature, moisture, &c., by variations produced in the force of an electric current.—**Tasimetric**, taz-i-met'rik, *a.* Pertaining to the tasimeter.

Task, task, *n.* [O.Fr. *tasque*, *tasche*, (Fr. *tâche*), a task, from L.L. *tasca*, by metathesis from *taxa* (= *tacsa*), from L. *taxo*, to tax. Tax.] A labour or work imposed by another; a piece of work to be done; what duty or necessity imposes; a lesson to be learned; a portion of study imposed by a teacher; an undertaking; burdensome employment; toil.—*To take to task*, to reprove; to reprimand.—*v.t.* To impose a task upon; to oppress with severe labour.—**Tasker**, tas'kėr, *n.* One that imposes a task.—**Task-master**, *n.* One who imposes a task; one who assigns tasks to others.—**Task-work**, *n.* Work imposed or performed as a task.

Tasmanian, tas-mā'ni-an, *a.* Pertaining to Tasmania.—*Tasmanian devil*, the dasyure.—*Tasmanian wolf*, a carnivorous marsupial of Tasmania of nocturnal habits and very destructive to sheep.—*n.* A native or inhabitant of Tasmania.

Tass, Tasse, tas, *n.* [Fr. *tasse*, a cup.] A cup.

Tassel, tas'el, *n.* [O.Fr. *tassel*, a knob or knot, a button, from L. *taxillus*, a small cube or die, dim. of *talus*, a die, a small bone.] A pendent ornament, consisting generally of a roundish mold covered with twisted threads of silk, wool, &c., and having threads hanging down in a fringe; anything resembling a tassel.—*v.t. tasseled, tasseling.* To put forth a tassel or flower, as Indian corn.—*v.t.* To adorn with tassels.—**Tasseled**, tas'eld, *a.* Furnished or adorned with tassels.

Taste, tāst, *v.t.*—*tasted, tasting.* [O.Fr. *taster* (Fr. *tâter*), to handle, feel, taste, from hypothetical *taxitare*, freq. of L. *taxare*, to touch repeatedly, from *tango, tactum*, to touch (whence *tact*, &c.). TANGENT.] To try by the touch of the tongue; to perceive the relish or flavour of; to try by eating; to eat; to become acquainted with by trial; to experience (to *taste* death); to partake of (to *taste* happiness).—*v.i.* To eat or drink a little by way of trial; to have a smack or flavour; to have a particular relish or savour; to smack or savour (it *tastes* of garlic); to have experience or enjoyment.—*n.* The act of tasting; a particular sensation excited by certain bodies when applied to the tongue, palate, &c., and moistened with saliva; the sense by which we perceive this by means of special organs in the mouth; intellectual relish or discernment; appreciation and liking; nice perception; the faculty of discerning beauty, proportion, symmetry, congruity, or whatever constitutes excellence, particularly in the fine arts and literature; discernment of what is fit or becoming; manner or style as tested by this faculty; manner, with respect to what is pleasing (a work in good *taste*, a remark in bad *taste*); a small portion tasted; a small bit.—**Tastable**, tās'ta-bl, *a.* Capable of being tasted; savoury.—**Tasteful**, tāst'fu̧l, *a.* Having much flavour; savoury; possessing good taste; showing or produced in good taste.—**Tastefully**, tāst'fu̧l-li, *adv.* In a tasteful manner; with good taste.—**Tastefulness**, tāst'fu̧l-nes, *n.* The state or quality of being tasteful.—**Tasteless**, tāst'les, *a.* Having no taste; insipid; having no power of giving pleasure; stale; flat; void of good taste; showing or executed with bad taste.—**Tastelessly**, tāst'les-li, *adv.* In a tasteless manner.—**Tastelessness**, tāst'les-nes, *n.*—**Taster**, tās'tėr, *n.* One who tastes; one who tests food, provisions, or liquors by tasting samples; an instrument by which something is tasted in order to judge of its quality.—**Tastily**, tās'ti-li, *adv.* In a tasty manner.—**Tasty**, tās'ti, *a.* Palatable; good to the taste; tasteful; showing good taste.

Tat, tat, *v.t.* and *i.*—*tatted, tatting.* To make a type of lace by hand.—**Tatting**, tat'ing, *n.* A kind of lace woven or knitted from sewing-thread, with a somewhat shuttle-shaped implement; the act of making such lace.

Ta-ta, ta'ta, *n.* and *interj.* A familiar form of salutation at parting; good-bye.

Tatou, tat'ō, *n.* The giant armadillo of South America.

Tatter, tat'ėr, *n.* [Icel. *töturr, tötturr*, tatters, rags; akin to *totter*.] A rag or a part torn and hanging to the thing.—**Tatterdemalion**, tat'ėr-dē-mā"li-on, *n.* [E. *tatter*, Fr. *de*, from, and O.Fr. *maillon*, long clothes.] A ragged fellow.—**Tattered**, tat'ėrd, *p.* and *a.* Rent in tatters; hanging in rags; ragged.

Tattersalls, tat'ėr-salz, *n.* [*Tattersall*, name of head of firm.] The headquarters of the turf and horse-racing fraternity in London.

Tattle, tat'l, *v.i.*—*tattled, tattling.* [Like *titter*, an imitative word; comp. L.G. *tateln*, to gabble; G. *tattern*, to prattle.] To prate; to talk idly; to use many words with little meaning; to tell tales; to blab.—*v.t.* To utter in a prating way.—*n.* Idle talk or chat; trifling talk.—**Tattler**, tat'lėr, *n.* One who tattles.—**Tattling**, tat'ling, *a.* Given to idle talk; apt to tell tales.—**Tattlingly**, tat'ling-li, *adv.* In a tattling manner.

Tattoo, tat-tö', *n.* [Formerly *taptoo*, from D. *taptoe*, the tattoo—*tap*, a tap or spigot, and *toe* (pron. as E. *to*), to, being primarily the signal for the closing of drinking-houses.] A beat of drum and bugle-call at night, giving notice to soldiers to repair to their quarters.—*Devil's tattoo*, an idle drumming with the fingers upon a table, &c.

Tattoo, tat-tö', *v.t.* and *i.* [A Polynesian word.] To prick the skin and stain the punctured spots with a colouring substance, forming lines and figures upon the body.—**Tattooer**, tat-tö'ėr, *n.* One who tattoos.—**Tattooing**, tat-tö'ing, *n.* The act of one who tattoos; the design produced by a tattooer.

Taube, toub or toub'e, *n.* [G. *taube*, pigeon.] A German form of aeroplane.

Taught, ta̧t, pret. and pp. of *teach*.

Taunt, ta̧nt, *v.t.* [O.Fr. *tanter, tenter*, to tempt, to provoke, from L. *tentare, temptare*, to try. TEMPT.] To reproach with severe or insulting words; to twit scornfully or insultingly; to upbraid.—*n.* A bitter or sarcastic reproach; insulting invective.—**Taunter**, ta̧n'tėr, *n.* One who taunts.—**Tauntingly**, ta̧n'ting-li, *adv.* In a taunting manner; insultingly.

Taunt, ta̧nt, *a.* [O.Fr. *tant*, L. *tantus*, so great.] *Naut.* high or tall: said of masts.

Taupe, tōp, *n.* [Fr. mole.] A yellowish-gray color similar to that of the moleskin.

Taurus, ta̧'rus, *n.* [L., a bull; allied to E. *steer* (an ox). STEER.] The Bull, one of the twelve signs of the zodiac, which the sun enters about the 20th of April.—**Tauriform**, ta̧'ri-form, *a.* Having the form of a bull.—**Taurine**, ta̧'rin, *a.*

Taut, ta̧t, *a.* [A form of *tight* or closely allied to it.] Tight; not slack; applied to a rope or sail.

Tautochronous, ta̧-tok'ron-us, *a.* [Gr. *tautos*, the same, and *chronos*, time.] Performed in equal times; isochronous.

Tautog, tä-tog', *n.* [The plural of *taut*, the Indian name.] A fish of the wrasse family caught on the New England coasts.

Tautology, ta̧-tol'o-ji, *n.* [Gr. *tautologia*—*tautos*, the same, and *logos*, word.] A useless repetition of the same idea or meaning in different words; needless repetition.—**Tautologic, Tautological**, ta̧-tö-loj'ik, ta̧-tö-loj'i-kal, *a.* Involving tautology; repeating the same thing.—**Tautologically**, ta̧-tö-loj'i-kal-li, *adv.* In a tautological manner.—**Tautologist**, ta̧-tol'o-jist, *n.* One who uses tautology.—**Tautologize**, ta̧-tol'o-jīz, *v.i.*—*tautologized, tautologizing.* To repeat the same thing in different words.

Tautomerism, ta̧-tom'ėr-izm, *n.* [Gr. *tauto*, the same, *meros*, part.] *Org. chem.* property of a substance which in its reactions behaves sometimes like one of two isomeric forms, sometimes like the other.

Tautoüsian, Tautousian, ta̧-tō-ou'si-an, ta̧-tou'si-an, *a.* [Gr. *tautos*, the same, and *ousia*, being, essence.] *Theol.* having absolutely the same essence.

Tavern, tav'ėrn, *n.* [Fr. *taverne*, Pr., Sp., and It. *taverna*, from L. *taberna*, a shed, a tavern, from root of *tabula*, a board. TABLE.] A place where alcoholic drinks are sold and food may be served, the term displacing bar and saloon since repeal of the prohibition laws in the United States; a taproom; formerly an inn.

Tawdry, ta̧'dri, *a.* [From *St. Audrey*, otherwise called St. Etheldreda, at whose fair, held in the isle of Ely, laces and cheap gay ornaments are said to have been sold.] Fine and showy, without taste or elegance; tastelessly but showily ornamental.—**Tawdrily**, ta̧'dri-li, *adv.*—**Tawdriness**, ta̧'dri-nes, *n.*

Tawny, ta̧'ni, *a.* [O.Fr. *tané*, Fr. *tanné*, tanned, tawny, pp. of *tanner*, to tan. TAN.] Of a yellowish dark color, like things tanned, or persons who are sunburnt.—*v.t.* To make tawny; to tan.

Tax, taks, *n.* [Fr. *taxe*, from *taxer*, to tax, from L. *taxo, taxare*, to handle, to rate, to censure, from stem of *tango*, to touch (whence also *tangent, task, taste*, &c.).] A charge imposed by governmental authority upon property, individuals, or transactions to raise money for public purposes; a levy by civil authority on the property, real or personal, of an individual or corporation, or a levy on income, inheritance, or the purchase or holdings of commodities; *fig.* a strain, serious burden, or heavy demand, as *a tax on one's strength, one's endurance*, &c.—*v.t.* To impose a rate or duty upon for governmental purposes; to subject to a strain, to make heavy demands upon, as *to tax one's patience*; to accuse of, charge with, or impute to, as *to tax a man with rudeness*; *law*, to fix judicially and allow or disallow the items of charge or cost in any judicial matter.—*Capital stock tax*, a tax imposed upon a corporation, for the privilege of doing business, based upon the value of its capital stock.—*Direct tax*, a tax paid directly by the consumer such as on gasoline, theater tickets, &c.—*Franchise tax*, a tax on rights and privileges granted by a franchise.—*Hidden tax*, a tax paid indirectly by the consumer, frequently without his being aware of it.—*Income tax*, a graduated tax on the product or income derived from a person's property or business.—*Inheritance tax*, a tax on transfer of inherited wealth.—*Nuisance tax*, a small amount levied on miscellaneous transactions, such as theater tickets, and paid by the purchaser.—*Poll tax*, a head tax, usually on all adult males, but also frequently on women and children as well; a tax on a person without reference to property owned or business followed.—*Personal-property tax*, a levy on such movable things as chattels, mortgages, bonds, stocks, &c., as distinguished from real estate.—*Real-estate tax*, a direct tax on real property.—*Sales tax*, a small percentage tax imposed either on the person making the sale or on the purchaser.—*Social-security tax*, a tax paid in equal amounts by employers and employees to provide funds for old-age pensions of employees.—*Surtax*, an additional tax; a tax in excess of a normal tax.—**Taxability, Taxableness**, tak-sa-bil'i-ti, tak'sa-bl-nes, *n.* The state of being taxable.—**Taxable**, tak'sa-bl, *a.* Subject or liable to taxation.—**Taxably**, tak'sa-bli, *adv.* In a taxable manner.—**Taxation**, tak-sā'shun, *n.* [L. *taxatio, taxationis*.] The act of laying a tax or of imposing taxes by the proper authority; the raising of revenue required for public service by means of taxes; the aggregate of taxes.—**Tax appeal**, *n.* An appeal for adjustment of the amount of a tax regarded as excessive.—**Tax assessor**, *n.* The official who assesses taxes.—**Tax collector**, *n.* The official whose duty it is to collect taxes.—**Tax dodger**, *n.* One who evades taxes.—**Tax-exempt, Tax-free**, *a.* Exempt from taxation, as certain government bonds.—**Tax lien**, *n.* An encumbrance on property in favor of the government as a result of the non-payment of a tax.—**Taxpayer**, *n.* One who pays a tax; a small building or money-earning equipment on a valuable property to meet taxes on the land.—**Tax return**, *n.* An inventory of assets or income minus deductions, leaving a net amount upon which a tax is determined.—**Tax-anticipation warrant**, *n.* A warrant sold at a discount by proper authorities to raise revenue before taxes are due, redeemable for the full amount when taxes are collected.—**Tax stamp**, *n.* A stamp required to be placed on documents relating to real-estate transfers, capital-stock certificates, and other commercial transactions.

Taxidermy, tak'si-dėr-mi, *n.* [Gr. *taxis*, an arranging, order, *derma*, skin.] The art of treating the skins of animals so that they retain their natural appearance, and also of stuffing and mounting them.

Tchudi, chö'dē, *n.pl.* A name applied by the Russians to the Finnic races in the north-west of Russia.—**Tchudic**, chö'dik, *a.* Pertaining to the Tchudi or their language.

T-cloth, tē'kloth, *n.* A plain cotton cloth manufactured for the India and China market: so called from a large letter T being stamped on it.

Tea, tē, *n.* [Fr. *thé*, from Chinese *tha, the, tcha*, tea.] The dried leaves of a shrub extensively cultivated in China, India and Japan, &c.; the plant itself; a decoction or infusion of tea leaves in boiling water, used as a beverage; any similar infusion (sage *tea* or beef *tea*, &c.); the evening meal at which tea is usually served.—*Paraguay tea.* MATE.—*v.t.* To take tea. (*Colloq.*) —*v.t.* To serve with tea. (*Colloq.*)—**Tea caddy**, *n.* A small box for holding the tea used in a household.—**Teacake**, *n.* A light kind of cake eaten with tea.—**Tea canister**, *n.* A canister or box in which tea is kept.—**Tea chest**, *n.* A slightly formed box, lined with thin sheet-lead, in which tea is packed for shipping.—**Teacup**, *n.* A small cup for drinking tea from. —**Tea-dance**, *n.* An afternoon tea with dancing.—**Tea garden**, *n.* A garden, generally attached to a house of entertainment, where tea is served.—**Teakettle**, *n.* A portable-kettle in which water is boiled for making tea.—**Teapot**, *n.* A vessel with a spout in which tea is infused, and from which it is poured into teacups. —**Tea service**, *n.* A complete set of utensils required for the tea table.—**Tea set**, *n.* A tea service.—**Teaspoon**, *n.* A small spoon used in drinking tea.—**Teaspoonful**, *n.* As much as a teaspoon holds.—**Tea table**, *n.* A table at which tea is drunk.—**Tea taster**, *n.* A person employed to test teas by tasting their infusions.—**Tea things**, *n.pl.* Tea service. —**Tea tray**, *n.* A tray for a tea service. —**Tea urn**, *n.* A table urn to boil water.

Teach, tēch, *v.t.*—pret. and pp. *taught*. [From A.Sax. *taecan*. to teach, show, command; allied to *tihan*, to accuse; Goth. *teihan*, G. *zeigen*, to point out; cog. L. *dico*, to say (whence *diction*, &c.); Gr. *deiknȳmi*, Skr. *diç*, to point out. *Token* is akin.] To impart instruction to; to guide the studies of; to instruct; to impart the knowledge of; to instruct, train, or give skill in the use, management, or handling of; to let be known; to tell; to show how; to show.—*v.i.* To practise giving instruction; to perform the business of a preceptor.—**Teachable**, tēch'a-bl, *a.* Capable of being taught; apt to learn; docile.—**Teachableness**, tēch'a-bl-nes, *n.* The quality of being teachable; aptness to learn; docility.—**Teacher**, tēch'ėr, *n.* One who teaches or instructs; a preceptor; a tutor; a preacher; a minister of the gospel.—**Teaching**, tēch'ing, *n.* The act or business of instructing; instruction. —**Teachless**, tēch'les, *a.* Unteachable.

Teague, tēg, *n.* [Irish name.] A rough Irishman.

Teak, tēk, *n.* [Tamil name.] A tree growing in different parts of the East Indies, and yielding a strong, durable, and most valuable timber.

Teal, tēl, *n.* [Same as *tel* or *tal* in D. *teling, taling*, a teal; origin doubtful.] One of several short-necked fresh-water ducks, especially the blue-winged *teal* of America and the green-winged *teal* of Europe.

Team, tēm, *n.* [A.Sax. *teám*, offspring, a series, a row, whence *tȳman*, to teem; akin to O.Fris. *tam*, offspring; D. *toom*, a brood; from same stem as *tow, tug*.] A flock of young animals, especially young ducks; a brood; a number of animals in a line; two or more horses, oxen, or other beasts harnessed together for drawing; the persons forming one of the parties or sides in a game, match, or the like.—**Teamster**, tēm'stėr, *n.* [*Team* and suffix *-ster*.] One who drives a team.

Tear, tēr, *n.* [A.Sax. *teár*, a tear=Icel. *tár*, Dan. *taare*, G. *zähre*, Goth. *tagr*; cognate Gr. *dakry*, O.L. *dacryma*, L. *lacryma*, Ir. *dear*, W. *daigr*, Gael. *deur*; from a root meaning to bite.] A drop of the limpid fluid secreted by a special gland, and appearing in the eyes or flowing from them, especially through excessive grief or joy; any transparent drop of fluid matter; also a solid, transparent drop, as of some resins. —**Tear-drop**, *n.* A tear.—**Tearful**, tēr'ful, *a.* Abounding with tears; shedding tears.—**Tear gas**, *n.* A gas which causes temporary partial blindness, used by police and in war in tear shells, tear grenades, &c. —**Tear-stained**, *a.* Marked with tears; having traces of tears.

Tear, tãr, *v.t.*—pret. *tore* (formerly *tare*), pp. *torn*. [A.Sax. *teran*, to rend=Goth. (*ga*)*tairan*, to break; G. *zehren*, D. *teren*, Dan. *tære*, to consume; same root as Gr. *derō*, to flay; Skr. *dar*, to split. *Tire* is akin.] To separate the parts of by pulling; to pull apart by force; to form fissures or furrows in by violence; to lacerate; to wound; to divide by violent measures; to disturb, excite, or disorganize violently (*torn* by factions); to drag; to move or remove by pulling or violently; to cause or make by rending (to *tear* a hole).—*To tear up*, to remove from a fixed state by violence; to rend completely.—*To tear the hair*, to pull it in a violent or distracted manner; often as a sign of grief.—*v.i.* To be rent or torn; to rage; to act with turbulent violence.—*n.* A rent; a fissure.—*Tear and wear*, deterioration by long or frequent use. —**Tearer**, tãr'ėr, *n.* One who tears.—**Tearing**, tãr'ing, *p.* and *a.* Making a great noise or bustle; raving; clamorous (*colloq.*).

Tease, tēz, *v.t.*—*teased, teasing*. [A.Sax. *taesan*, to pluck, to tease=Dan. *tæse, tæsse*, to tease wool; D. *teezen*, to pick, to tease; akin G. *zausen*, to tug, tear. *Teasel* is from this, and *touse, tousy, tussle*, are allied.] To pull apart the adhering fibres of; to comb or card, as wool or flax; to vex with importunity; to annoy or irritate by petty requests or by raillery.—**Teasing**, tēz'ing, *a.* Vexing; irritating; annoying.

Teasel, Teazel, tē'zel, *n.* [A.Sax. *taesl*, teasel, from *taesan*, to tease. TEASE.] The fuller's thistle, cultivated for its heads or burrs, which have numerous hooked bracts, and are employed to raise the nap of woollen cloths; any contrivance similarly used in the dressing of woollen cloth.—*v.t.* To subject to the action of teasels.—**Teaseler**, tē'zel-ėr, *n.* One who uses the teasel.

Teat, tēt, *n.* [A.Sax. *tit, titt*, a teat=L.G. and O.D. *titte*, G. *zitze*, Ir. and Gael. *did*, a teat.] The projecting organ through which milk is drawn from the breast or udder of females; a nipple; a dug of a beast; a pap. —**Teated**, tēt'ed, *a.* Having teats.

Tebeth, tē'beth, *n.* [Heb.] The tenth month of the Jewish ecclesiastical year.

Techily, Techiness. Under TACHY.

Technical, tek'ni-kal, *a.* [L. *technicus*, from Gr. *technikos*, from *technē*, art.] Pertaining to the mechanical arts; specially appertaining to an art, science, profession, handicraft, business, or the like.—**Technic**, tek'nik, *n.* Method of manipulation in any art; artistic execution.—*a.* Technical.—**Technicality**, tek-ni-kal'i-ti, *n.* The character of being technical; a technical feature or peculiarity; a technical expression.—**Technically**, tek'ni-kal-li, *adv.* In a technical manner.—**Technicalness**, tek'ni-kal-nes, *n.* The quality of being technical.—**Technician**, tek-nish'an, *n.* One skilled in any technical art.—**Technique**, tek-nēk', *n.* Expert method of execution or manner of performance.—**Technological**, tek-nō-loj'i-kal, *a.* Pertaining to technology.—**Technologist**, tek-nol'o-jist, *n.* One versed in technology. —**Technology**, tek-nol'o-ji, *n.* [Gr. *technē*, art, and *logos*, discourse.] That branch of knowledge which deals with the various industrial arts;

Techy, Tetchy, tech'i, *a.* [From old *teche, tache*, a blemish, a vice, from Fr. *tache*, a spot.] Peevish; fretful; irritable; testy.—**Techily, Tetchily**, tech'i-li, *adv.* In a techy manner; peevishly.—**Techiness, Tetchiness**, tech'i-nes, *n.* The state or quality of being techy.

Tectibranchiate, tek-ti-brang'ki-āt, *a.* [L. *tectus*, concealed or covered, and *branchiæ*, gills.] A term designating a section of gasteropodous molluscs having the gills covered or partly covered by the mantle.

Tectonic, tek-ton'ik, *a.* [Gr. *tektonikos*, from *tektōn, tektonos*, a carpenter, a builder.] Pertaining to building or construction, or to the earth's structure.—**Tectonics**, tek-ton'iks, *n.* The art of constructing with utility as well as taste.

Tectrices, tek'tri-sēz, *n.pl.* [From L. *tego, tectum*, to cover.] *Ornith.* the feathers which cover the quill-feathers of the wing; the coverts.

Ted, ted, *v.t.*—*tedded, tedding*. [From W. *teddu*, to spread out.] *Agri.* to spread to the air after being mown; to turn and scatter new-mowed grass or hay.—**Tedder**, ted'ėr, *n.* One who teds; an implement that spreads newly-mown grass.

Te Deum, tē dē'um, *n.* [From the first words, *Te Deum laudamus*, 'We praise thee, O God'.] The title of a celebrated hymn of praise, usually ascribed to St. Ambrose, familiar from its translation in the *Book of Common Prayer*.

Tedium, tē'di-um, *n.* [L. *tædium*, from *tædet*, it wearies.] Irksomeness; wearisomeness.—**Tedious**, tēd'yus, *a.* [O.Fr. *tedieux*, L. *tædiosus*.] Involving or causing tedium; tiresome from continuance or slowness; wearisome; monotonous.—**Tediously**, tēd'yus-li, *adv.* In a tedious manner; so as to weary.—**Tediousness**, tēd'yus-nes, *n.* The quality of being tedious; wearisomeness.

Tee, tē, *n.* The umbrella-shaped structure as a termination or finial crowning the Buddhists' topes and Hindu pagodas.

Tee, tē, *n.* [Icel. *tjá*, to mark, to note.] A point of aim or starting-point in certain games, as quoits, curling, and golf; more particularly, the little heap of sand on which golfers set the ball for the first stroke towards each hole.—*v.t.* To set the ball in this position.—*Teeing ground*, the space within which the tee must be made and which is provided with a sand-box. (*Scotch.*)

Teel, tēl, *n.* [Indian name.] Indian sesame.

Teem, tēm, *v.t.*—[A.Sax. *teman, tyman*, to produce. TEAM.] to bring forth young; to be pregnant; to be stocked to overflowing; to be prolific or abundantly fertile.—*v.t.* To produce: to bring forth.—**Teeming**, *a.* Overflowing; crowded, as a *teeming* city.

Teen, Tene, tēn, *n.* [A.Sax. *teóna*, injury, vexation.] Grief; sorrow.

Teens, tēnz, *n.pl.* The years of one's age having the termination *-teen*, beginning with thir*teen* and ending with nine*teen*, during which period a person is said to be in his or her *teens*.

Teeth, tēth, pl. of *tooth*.—**Teethe**, tēTH, *v.i.* Under TOOTH.

Teetotal, tē'tō-tal, *a.* [Formed by reduplication of initial letter of *total*, for the sake of emphasis; comp. *tee-totum*.] Pertaining to total abstinence; totally abstaining from intoxicants.—**Teetotalism** tē'tō-tal-izm *n.* The principles or practice of teetotalers —**Teetotaler, Teetotaller**, tē'tō-tal-ėr *n.* One who binds himself to entire abstinence from intoxicating liquors, unless medically prescribed; a total abstainer

Tee-totum, tē-tō'tum, *n.* [That is *T-totum*, *totum* represented by T, from the T marked upon it and standing for L. *totum*, the whole, the whole stakes being won when T turns up; comp. *teetotal*.] A small four-sided toy of the top kind, made to spin by the fingers, and used by children in a game of chance, the result depending on which side turns up.

Teg, teg, *n.* A young sheep; a tag.

Tegmen, Tegumen, teg'men, teg'ū-men, *n.* pl. **Tegmina, Tegumina**, teg'mi-na, te-gū'mi-na. [L., from *tego*, to cover.] A covering or tegument; *bot.* the inner skin which covers the seed.—**Tegmentum**,

Tegmentum, teg-men′tum, teg-ū-men′-tum, *n.* pl. **Tegmenta**, **Tegumenta**, teg-men′ta, teg-ū-men′ta. [L.] *Bot.* the scaly coat which covers the leaf-buds of deciduous trees.

Teguexin, te-gek′sin, *n.* A large lizard of Brazil and Guiana.

Tegular, teg′ū-lėr, *a.* [L. *tegula*, a tile, from *tego*, to cover.] Resembling a tile; consisting of tiles.—**Tegulated**, teg′ū-lā-ted, *a.* Composed of plates or scales overlapping like tiles.

Tegument, teg′ū-ment, *n.* [L. *tegumentum*, from *tego*, to cover.] A cover or covering; a natural covering, as of an animal; an integument.—**Tegumentary**, teg-ū-men′ta-ri, *a.* Pertaining to teguments.

Tehee, tē-hē, *n.* A laugh, so named from the sound.—*v.i.*—*teheed*, *teheeing*. To laugh contemptuously; to titter.

Teil, **Teil-tree**, tēl, *n.* [Fr. *teil*, from L. *tilia*, a lime-tree.] The lime-tree.

Teind, tēnd, *n.* [Icel. *tiund*, a tenth, and hence a tithe, from *tíu*, ten; Sw. *tiende*, Goth. *taihunda*, the tenth.] In Scotland, a tithe; that portion of the annual value of land which is or may be assessed for the stipend of the clergy of the Established Church.

Teknonymy, tek-non′i-mi, *n.* [Gr. *teknon*, child, *onoma*, name.] The custom of naming a parent after his child, prevalent among some uncivilized peoples.—**Teknonymous**, tek-non′i-mus, *a.* Pertaining to or practising teknonymy.

Telamon, tel′a-mōn, *n.* pl. **Telamones**, tel-a-mō′nēz. [Gr. *telamōn*, a bearer.] *Arch.* the figure of a man employed as a column or pilaster. ATLANTES.

Telary, tē′la-ri, *a.* [L. *tela*, a web.] Pertaining to or having the character of a web; spinning webs (a *telary* spider).

Telautograph, te-la′tō-graf, *n.* [Gr. *tēle*, far, and E. *autograph*.] A telegraph that produces a facsimile of the person's handwriting who sends a message.

Teledu, tel′e-dö, *n.* [Native name.] A Javanese carnivorous animal allied to the skunk, and, like it, able to give out an abominable stench.

Telegony, te-leg′ō-ni, *n.* [Gr. *tēle*, far, *gonos*, offspring.] The hypothetical influence of a sire on subsequent offspring by a different sire.

Telegram, tel′e-gram, *n.* [Gr. *tēle*, far, and *gramma*, what is written, from *graphō*, to write.] A communication sent by telegraph; a telegraphic message or despatch.—**Telegrammic**, tel-e-gram′ik, *a.* Pertaining to a telegram; having the character of a telegram.—**Telegraph**, tel′e-graf, *n.* A general name for any apparatus for conveying intelligence beyond the limits of distance at which the voice is audible; now usually restricted to the electric telegraph, which consists essentially of a battery or other source of electric power, of a wire or conductor for conveying the electric current from one station to another, of the apparatus for transmitting the current, and of the indicator or signalling instrument; a telegraphic communication; a telegram.—*Telegraph cable*. Under CABLE.—*v.t.* To convey or announce by telegraph.—**Telegraphese**, te-leg′ra-fēz, *n.* [Modelled on *Carlylese*.] The curtest form of literary style, based on the jerky form of telegraph messages.—**Telegraphic**, **Telegraphical**, tel-e-graf′ik, tel-e-graf′i-kal, *a.* Pertaining to the telegraph; made by a telegraph; communicated by a telegraph.—**Telegraphically**, tel-e-graf′i-kal-li, *adv.* By means of a telegraph.—**Telegraphist**, tel′e-graf-ist, *n.* One who works a telegraph.—**Telegraphy**, te-leg′ra-fi, *n.* The art or practice of communicating by telegraph.

Telemeter, te-lem′et-ėr, *n.* [Gr. *tēle*, far, and *metron*, a measure.] An instrument used among artillery for determining the distance from the gun of the object fired at; an apparatus by which the variations recorded by any physical or other instrument can be shown at a distance by means of electricity.—**Telemetry**, te-lem′e-tri, *n.* Measurement or observation by means of a telemeter.

Teleology, tel-ē-ol′o-ji, *n.* [Gr. *telos*, *teleos*, an end, and *logos*, discourse.] The science or doctrine of final causes; the science treating of the end or design for which things were created.—**Teleological**, tel′ē-ō-loj″-i-kal, *a.* Pertaining to teleology.—**Teleologically**, tel′ē-ō-loj″i-kal-li, *adv.* In a teleological manner.—**Teleologist**, tel-ē-ol′o-jist, *n.* One versed in teleology; one who investigates the final cause or purpose of phenomena, or the end for which each has been produced.

Teleostean, tel-ē-os′tē-an, *a.* [Gr. *teleos*, *teleios*, complete, and *osteon*, a bone.] A term applied to an order of fishes having a well-ossified skeleton, and including almost all familiar food-fishes.—*n.* One of this division of fishes.

Telepathy, te-lep′a-thi, *n.* [Gr. *tēle*, far, *pathos*, feeling.] The communication of feelings or impressions between persons at a distance from each other.—**Telepathic**, tel-e-path′ik, *a.* Pertaining to telepathy.

Telephone, tel′e-fōn, *n.* [Gr. *tēle*, at a distance, and *phōnē*, sound.] Any instrument which transmits sound beyond its natural limits of audibility; more especially, an instrument transmitting sound and words uttered by the human voice by means of electricity and conducting wires, the vibrations of a metal plate that receives the sounds at one end of the wire giving rise to corresponding vibrations at the other end which reproduce the sound.—**Telephote**, tel′e-fōt, *n.* A telegraphic apparatus for reproducing pictures at a great distance.—**Telephotograph**, tel′e-fot″o-graf, *n.* A photograph reproduced by wire or wireless by means of a device using the scanning beam of a photoelectric cell on a sensitized medium.—**Telephotography**, tel′e-fo-tog″ra-fi, *n.* Process of photographing by means of the telephoto lens; also process of transmitting the telephotograph.—**Telephoto lens**, *n.* A compound telescopic lens for photographing objects at a distance.

Telerpeton, te-lėr′pē-ton, *n.* [Gr. *tēle*, far, and *herpeton*, a lizard.] A lizard-like reptile fossil found in triassic sandstones.

Telescope, tel′e-skōp, *n.* [Gr. *tēleskopos*, seeing afar, from *tēle*, at a distance, and *skopeō*, to view.] An optical instrument essentially consisting of a set of lenses fixed in a tube or a number of sliding tubes, by which distant objects are brought within the range of distinct, or more distinct vision.—*v.t.* To drive the parts of into each other, like the movable joints of a pocket telescope (the train was *telescoped* by the collision).—**Telescopic**, **Telescopical**, tel′e-skop-ik, tel′e-skop-i-kal, *a.* Pertaining to a telescope; performed by a telescope; seen only by a telescope; seeing at a great distance; having the power of extension by joints sliding one within another.—**Telescopically**, tel-e-skop′i-kal-li, *adv.* By the telescope.

Telespectroscope, tel-ē-spek′trō-skōp, *n.* A telescope and spectroscope combined.

Teletype, tel′ē-tīp, *n.* A system of communication by which messages may be sent by wire through an electrical sending device with keys similar to a typewriter, and transmitted to a receiving station which reproduces the typed message.

Television, tel″e-vizh′on, *n.* The transmission by wire or wireless of scenes or moving pictures by conversion of light rays to electrical waves, which are reconverted to reproduce the original image.

Telic, tel′ik, *a.* [Gr. *telos*, end.] *Gram.* denoting end or purpose.

Tell, tel, *v.t.*—pret. and pp. *told*. [A.Sax. *tellan*, to tell, announce, count = O.Fris. *tella*, D. *tellen*, Dan. *tælle*, Icel. *telja*, to tell, number, &c.; G. *zählen*, to number. Closely akin to *tale*.] To express in words; to say; to relate, narrate, rehearse (to *tell* a story); to make known by words; to disclose; to confess; to acknowledge (to *tell* a secret); to discern so as to be able to say (to *tell* one from another); to distinguish; to decide upon; to enumerate; to count; to inform; to give an order or request to.—*To tell off*, to count off; especially, to count off, detach, or select for some special duty.—*v.i.* To give an account; to make report; to play the informer; to blab; to take effect; to produce a marked effect (every shot *tells*).—*To hear tell*, to hear mention made; to learn by hearsay.—**Tellable**, tel′a-bl, *a.* Capable of being told.—**Teller**, tel′ėr, *n.* One who tells; one who numbers; one appointed to count votes, as in a lodge or public election; a functionary in a banking establishment whose business is to receive and pay money over the counter.—**Tellership**, tel′ėr-ship, *n.* The office or employment of a teller.—**Telling**, tel′ing, *p.* and *a.* Operating with great effect; highly effective; impressive (a *telling* speech).—*n.* The act of one that tells.—**Telltale**, *a.* Telling tales; officiously revealing; blabbing.—*n.* One who improperly discloses private concerns; one who tells that which prudence should suppress; an instrument or device of various kinds, usually automatic, for counting or registering.

Tellural, tel-ū′ral, *a.* [L. *tellus*, *telluris*, the earth.] Pertaining to the earth.—**Tellurate**, tel′ū-rāt, *n.* A salt of telluric acid.—**Telluretted**, tel′ū-ret-ed, *a.* Combined with tellurium.—**Tellurian**, tel-ū′-ri-an, *a.* Pertaining to the earth or to an inhabitant of the earth.—*n.* An inhabitant of the earth.—**Telluric**, tel-ū′rik, *a.* Pertaining to the earth or to tellurium.—*Telluric acid*, an oxyacid of tellurium.—**Telluret**, **Telluride**, tel′ū-ret, tel′ū-rīd, *n.* A compound of tellurium with an electro-positive element.—**Tellurion**, tel-ū′-ri-on, *n.* A kind of orrery showing the changes of the seasons, &c.—**Tellurium**, tel-ū′ri-um, *n.* A non-metallic element of a tin-white crystalline appearance, and closely resembling selenium and sulphur in its chemical relations.—**Tellurous**, tel-ū′rus, *a.* Pertaining to or obtained from tellurium.

Telotype, tē′lō-tīp, *n.* [Gr. *tēle*, far, and *typos*, impression.] A printing electric telegraph. See TELETYPE.

Telpherage, tel′fėr-āj, *n.* [Crude formation from *tēle*, far, *pherō*, to carry.] A system of transporting goods in a light car suspended from a cable and electrically propelled.—**Telpher-line**, **Telpher-railway**, *n.* A railway of this kind.

Telson, tel′son, *n.* [Gr., an extremity.] The last joint in the abdomen of crustacea.

Temblor, tem-blōr′, *n.* [Sp.] An earthquake.

Temerity, tē-mer′i-ti, *n.* [L. *temeritas*, rashness, from *temere*, rashly; same root as Skr. *tamas*, darkness, E. *dim*.] Heedlessness of consequences; extreme venturesomeness; recklessness; rashness.—**Temerarious**, tem-ē-rā′ri-us, *a.* [L. *temerarius*.] Rash; reckless; careless.

Temper, tem′pėr, *v.t.* [Fr. *tempérer*, from L. *temperare*, to regulate, mix properly, temper, from *tempus*, *temporis*, time. TEMPORAL.] To proportion duly as regards constituent parts; to mix or combine in due proportion; to mix and work up; to qualify by intermixture (to *temper* justice with mercy); to reduce the excess, violence, or severity of; to moderate; to calm; to form to a proper degree of hardness (to *temper* iron or steel).—*n.* Due mixture of different qualities; disposition or constitution of the mind, particularly with regard to the passions and affections; heat of mind; irritation; the state of a metal as to its hardness; middle character; mean or medium.—**Temperable**, tem′pėr-a-bl, *a.* Capable of being tempered.—**Temperament**, tem′pėr-a-ment, *n.* [L. *temperamentum*, admixture, moderation, &c., from *tempero*.] Due mixture of elements or qualities; adjustment of opposing influences; that individual peculiarity of physical organization by which the manner of acting, feeling, and thinking of each person is permanently affected (a person of a sanguine, or of a melancholy, *temperament*); *mus.* a certain adjustment of the tones or intervals of the scale of fixed-toned instruments, as the organ, piano, and the like, with the view of removing an apparent imperfection, and fitting the scale for use in all keys without offence to the ear.—**Temperance**, tem'pér-ans, *n.* [L. *temperantia*, moderation, sobriety, from *tempero*, to temper.] The observance of moderation; temperateness; moderation in regard to the indulgence of the natural appetites and passions; restrained or moderate indulgence; sobriety; sometimes loosely used to mean total abstinence from intoxicants.—**Temperate**, tem'pér-āt, *a.* [L. *temperatus.*] Moderate; showing moderation; moderate as regards the indulgence of the appetites or desires; abstemious; sober; not violent or excessive as regards the use of language; reasonable; calm; measured; not going beyond due bounds; moderate as regards amount of heat; not liable to excessive heats (a *temperate* climate).—*Temperate zones*, the spaces on the earth between the tropics and the polar circles, where the heat is less than in the tropics, and the cold less than in the polar circles.—**Temperately**, tem'pér-āt-li, *adv.* In a temperate manner or degree; moderately; soberly; calmly; sedately.—**Temperateness**, tem'pér-āt-nes, *n.* The quality of being temperate; moderation; reasonableness.—**Temperature**, tem'pér-a-tūr, *n.* [L. *temperatura*, due measure, temperature.] Constitution or temperament; the state of a body or of a region of the earth with regard to heat, the degree or intensity of the heat effects of a body.—**Tempered**, tem'pėrd, *a.* Having a certain disposition or temper; disposed: often used in composition (a good-*tempered*, bad-*tempered* man).—**Tempering**, tem'pér-ing, *n.* The process of giving the requisite degree of hardness or softness to a substance, as to iron or steel.

Tempera, tem'pe-ra, *n.* [It.] *Painting*, the same as *Distemper*.

Tempest, tem'pest, *n.* [O.Fr. *tempeste*, from L. *tempestas*, time, season, a tempest, from *tempus*, time. TEMPORAL.] An extensive current of wind rushing with great velocity and violence; a storm of extreme violence; a hurricane; a violent tumult or commotion.—**Tempestuous**, tem-pes'tū-us, *a.* [L. *tempestuosus.*] Belonging to a tempest; very stormy; blowing with violence; subject to fits of stormy passion.—**Tempestuously**, tem-pes'tū-us-li, *adv.* In a tempestuous manner.—**Tempestuousness**, tem-pes'tū-us-nes, *n.*

Templar. Under TEMPLE.

Template, *n.* TEMPLET.

Temple, tem'pl, *n.* [Fr. *temple*, from L. *templum*, a temple, originally a place marked or cut off, from root *tem* in Gr. *temnō*, to cut, whence Gr. *temenos*, a temple.] An edifice dedicated to the service of some deity or deities; originally, an edifice erected for some Roman deity; one of the three successive edifices at Jerusalem dedicated to the worship of Jehovah; an edifice erected among Christians as a place of public worship; a church; a semi-monastic establishment in London inhabited by the knights Templars and receiving its name from them; the buildings erected on this site and occupied by lawyers or students of law.—**Templar**, tem'plėr. *n.* One of a religious military order first established at Jerusalem about 1118 A. D. for the protection of pilgrims traveling to the Holy Land and of the Holy Sepulcher. and so named from their residence at Jerusalem being connected with the church and convent of the Temple: *Masonic order*, Knight Templar.—*Good-Templar*. Under GOOD.

Temple, tem'pl, *n.* [O.Fr. *temple* (Fr. *tempe*), the temple, from L. *tempus*, time, also a temple of the head. TEMPORAL.] The flat portion of either side of the head between the forehead and ear.

Templet, **Template**, tem'plet, tem'plāt, *n.* [Comp. Fr. *temple*, *templet*, a mechanical appliance of several kinds.] A flat thin board or piece of sheet-iron whose edge is shaped in some particular way, so that it may serve as a guide or test in making an article with a corresponding contour; a short piece of timber or a stone placed in a wall to support a girder, beam, &c.

Tempo, tem'pō, *n.* [It. *tempo*, time.] *Mus.* a word used to express the degree of quickness with which a piece of music is to be executed; musical time.

Temporal, tem'po-ral, *a.* [L. *temporalis*, from *tempus*, *temporis*, time, season, &c. (seen in *tense*, *n.*, *contemporary*, *extempore*), also one of the temples of the head; root *tan*, to stretch or extend, same as in E. *thin*. Akin *tempest*.] Pertaining to this life or this world; secular; opposed to *spiritual* and *ecclesiastical*; measured or limited by time, or by this life or state of things; having limited existence: opposed to *eternal*; *gram.* relating to a tense; pertaining to the temple or temples of the head.—*n.* Anything temporal or secular; a temporality.—**Temporality**, tem-po-ral'i-ti, *n.* The state or quality of being temporal; a secular possession; *pl.* revenues of an ecclesiastic from lands, tithes, &c.; opposed to *spiritualities*.—**Temporally**, tem'po-ral-li, *adv.* In a temporal manner; with respect to time or this life only.—**Temporalness**, tem'po-ral-nes, *n.* The state or quality of being temporal.—**Temporalty**, tem'po-ral-ti, *n.* The laity; secular people; a secular possession; a temporality.—**Temporarily**, tem'po-ra-ri-li, *adv.* In a temporary manner; for a time; provisionally.—**Temporariness**, tem'po-ra-ri-nes, *n.* The state of being temporary.—**Temporary**, tem'po-ra-ri, *a.* [L. *temporarius.*] Lasting for a time only; existing or continuing for a limited time; transient; provisional.—**Temporize**, tem'po-rīz, *v.i.*—*temporized*, *temporizing*. [Fr. *temporiser*, from L. *tempus*, *temporis*, time.] To comply with or humour the time or occasion; to try to suit both sides or parties; to trim; to use politic devices.—**Temporization**, tem'po-ri-zā"shon, *n.* The act of temporizing.—**Temporizer**, tem'po-rī-zėr, *n.* One who temporizes.—**Temporizing**, tem'po-rī-zing, *p.* and *a.* Inclined to temporize; time-serving.—**Temporizingly**, tem'po-rī-zing-li, *adv.*

Tempt, temt, *v.t.* [O.Fr. *tempter* (Fr. *tenter*), from L. *temptare*, *tentare*, to try, prove, test, incite, intens. of *tendo*, *tentum*, to stretch; same root as Gr. *teinō*, Skr. *tan*, to stretch. (TEND, THIN.) *Taunt* is of same origin.] To incite or solicit to an evil act; to entice to something wrong by some specious argument or inducement; to seduce; to invite; to try to induce; to try the patience of; to put to a test.—**Temptability**, tem-ta-bil'i-ti, *a.* Quality of being temptable.—**Temptable**, tem'ta-bl, *a.* Liable to be tempted.—**Temptation**, tem-tā"shon, *n.* The act of tempting or state of being tempted; enticement to evil; that which is presented as an inducement to evil; an enticement; an allurement to anything indifferent or even good (*colloq.*).—**Tempter**, tem'tėr, *n.* One who tempts; one who entices to evil.—**Tempting**, tem'ting, *a.* Adapted to entice or allure; attractive; seductive.—**Temptingly**, tem'ting-li, *adv.* In a tempting manner.—**Temptingness**, tem ting-nes, *n.*—**Temptress**, temt'res, *n.* A female who tempts or entices.

Temse, **Tems**, tems, *n.* [A.Sax. *temes*, a sieve; D. *tems*, a colander, a strainer.] A sieve; a searce; a bolter.

Temulence, **Temulency**, tem'ū-lens, tem'ū-len-si, *n.* [O.Fr. *temulence*, from L. *temulentia*, drunkenness, from *temulentus*, drunken. ABSTEMIOUS.] Intoxication; drunkenness.—**Temulent**, tem'ū-lent, *a.* Intoxicated; given to drink.

Ten, ten, *a.* [A.Sax. *tén*, *týn*=D. *tien*, Goth. *taihun*, G. *zehn*, Icel. *tiu*, Sw. *tio*, Dan. *ti*; cog. L. *decem*, Gr. *deka*, Skr. *daçan*; W. *deg*, Armor. *dek*, Ir. *deag*, Gael. *deich*.] Twice five; nine and one.—*n.* The number of twice five; a figure or symbol denoting ten units, as 10 or X; a playing card with ten spots.—**Tenth**, tenth, *a.* First after the ninth.—*n.* The tenth part; one of ten equal parts into which a whole is divided.—**Tenth meter**. ÅNGSTRÖM UNIT.—**Tenthly**, tenth'li, *adv.* In the tenth place.—**Tenfold**, ten'fōld, *a.* and *adv.* Ten times greater or more.

Tenable, ten'a-bl, *a.* [Fr. *tenable*, from *tenir*, L. *tenere*, to hold (seen also in *tenant*, *tenacious*, *tenement*, *tenor*, *tenure*, *abstain*, *contain*, *obtain*, *retain*, &c.); same root as in *tendo*, to stretch, *tempto*, to tempt. TEND, TEMPT.] Capable of being held, maintained, or defended against an assailant, or against attempts to take it.—**Tenability**, **Tenableness**, ten-a-bil'i-ti, ten'a-bl-nes, *n.* The state of being tenable.

Tenacious, te-nā'shus, *a.* [L. *tenax*, *tenacis*, from *teneo*, to hold. TENABLE.] Holding fast, or inclined to hold fast; inclined to retain: with *of* before the thing held; retentive; apt to retain long what is committed to it (a *tenacious* memory); apt to adhere to another substance; adhesive; tough; having great cohesive force among the constituent particles.—**Tenaciously**, te-nā'shus-li, *adv.* In a tenacious manner.—**Tenaciousness**, te-nā'shus-nes, *n.* The state or quality of being tenacious.—**Tenacity**, te-nas'i-ti, *n.* [Fr. *tenacité*, L. *tenacitas*.] The quality of being tenacious; adhesiveness; that property of material bodies by which their parts resist an effort to force or pull them asunder, or the measure of the resistance of bodies to tearing or crushing.

Tenaille, **Tenail**, te-nāl', *n.* [Fr. *tenaille*, from *tenir*, L. *tenere*, to hold. TENABLE.] *Fort.* an outwork or rampart in the main ditch immediately in front of the curtain, between two bastions.

Tenant, ten'ant, *n.* [Fr. *tenant*, holding, ppr. of *tenir*, L. *tenere*, to hold. TENABLE.] A person who holds or possesses lands or tenements by any kind of title, either in fee, for life, for years, or at will one who occupies lands or houses for which he pays rent; one who has possession of any place; a dweller; an occupant.—*v.t.* To hold or possess as a tenant.—*v.i.* To live as a tenant; to dwell.—**Tenancy**, ten'an-si, *n.* A holding or possession as tenant; period of occupancy as tenant; tenure.—**Tenantable**, ten'ant-a-bl, *a.* In a state of repair suitable for a tenant.—**Tenantableness**, ten'ant-a-bl-nes, *n.* State of being tenantable.—**Tenantless**, ten'ant-les, *a.* Having no tenant; unoccupied.—**Tenant-right**, *n.* A term for various rights or claims which tenants maintain against their landlords, as the right of the tenant to compensation for unexhausted improvements if he should be forced to leave the land.—**Tenantry**, ten'ant-ri, *n.* The body of tenants.

Tench, tensh, *n.* [O.Fr. *tenche* (Fr. *tanche*), from L. *tinca*, a tench.] A fish of the carp family inhabiting most of the lakes of Europe.

Tend, tend, *v.i.* [L. *tendo*, to stretch out, to extend, to bend one's footsteps (seen also in *attend*, *extend*, *contend*, *intend*, *superintend*, *tent*, &c.); same root as L. *teneo*, to hold, Gr. *teinō*, Skr. *tan*, to stretch. THIN, TENDER, *a.*, TENABLE.] To move in a certain direction; to be directed; to have influence towards producing a certain effect; to conduce or contribute.—**Tendency**, ten'den-si, *n.* [Fr. *tendance*.] An inclining or contributing influence; aptness to take a certain course; inclination; effect of giving a certain bent or direction.

Tend, tend, *v.t.* [Contr. from *attend*.] To accompany as an assistant or protector; to watch; to guard; to look after; to take care of; to attend to.—*v.i.* To attend; to wait, as attendants or servants; to attend as something inseparable; to be attentive (*Shak.*).—**Tendance**, ten'dans, *n.* Act of tending or attending.—**Tender**, ten'dėr, *n.* One that tends; *naut.* a small vessel attending a larger one with stores, or to convey intelligence; *rail.* a special car attached to a steam locomotive, for carrying the fuel, water, &c.

Tender, ten'dėr, *v.t.* [Fr. *tendre*, to reach or stretch out, from L. *tendo*, *tendere*, to stretch out. TEND, to move, &c.] To present for acceptance; to offer in payment or satisfaction of a demand.—*n.* An offer of money or any other thing in satisfaction of a debt or liability; any offer for acceptance; an offer in writing to execute some specified work, or to supply certain specified articles, at a certain rate; the thing offered.

Tender, ten'dėr, *a.* [Fr. *tendre*, from L. *tener*, tender, from same root as *tenuis*, thin, *tendo*, to stretch (whence *tend*), *teneo*, to hold (as in *tenable*), and E. *thin*. The *d* is inserted as in *gender*, *thunder*.] Easily injured; delicate; very sensible to pain; very susceptible of any sensation; not hardy; weak; easily affected by the distresses of another (a *tender* heart); sympathetic; affectionate; fond; pathetic; careful not to hurt or injure; gentle; unwilling to pain; apt to give pain or to annoy when spoken of (a *tender* subject).—*v.t.*‡ To hold dear; to esteem (*Shak.*).—**Tenderfoot**, *n.* *Amer.* A newcomer, one who is unaccustomed to the ways of a place; a Boy Scout beginner. —**Tender-hearted**, *a.* Very susceptible of the softer passions of love, pity, or kindness. — **Tenderloin**, *n.* The strip of meat along the backbone in beef, or pork; also, in cities, the section where vice abounds. — **Tenderly**, ten'dėr-li, *adv.* In a tender manner; with tenderness; mildly; gently; kindly; fondly; affectionately. — **Tenderness**, ten'dėr-nes, *n.* The state or character of being tender; delicacy; readiness to be hurt.

Tendon, ten'don, *n.* [Fr. *tendon*, from L. *tendo*, to stretch. TEND.] *Anat.* a hard, insensible cord or bundle of fibres by which a muscle is attached to a bone or other part which it serves to move.—*Tendon of Achilles*, the large tendon connecting the calf of the leg with the heel.—**Tendinous**, ten'di-nus, *a.* [Fr. *tendineux*.] Partaking of the nature of tendons; full of tendons; sinewy.

Tendril, ten'dril, *n.* [O.Fr. *tendrillon*, a tendril, from *tendre*, tender. TENDER.] *Bot.* a slender spiral shoot of a plant that winds round another body for the purpose of support. — **Tendrilled**, ten'drild, *a.* Furnished with tendrils.

Tenebrific, ten-ē-brif'ik, *a.* [L. *tenebræ*, darkness, and *facio*, to make.] Producing darkness.—**Tenebrosity**, ten-ē-bros'i-ti, *n.* Darkness; gloominess; gloom.—**Tenebrous, Tenebrose**, ten'ē-brus, ten'ē-brōs, *a.* [L. *tenebrosus*.] Dark; gloomy.

Tenement, ten'ē-ment, *n.* [O.Fr. *tenement*, L.L. *tenementum*, from L. *teneo*, to hold. TENABLE.] An abode; a habitation; a dwelling; an apartment or apartments in a building used by one family; *law*, any species of permanent property that may be held. — **Tenemental**, ten-ē-men'tal, *a.* Pertaining to a tenement or to tenements. —**Tenementary**, ten-ē-men'ta-ri, *a.* Capable of being leased; held by tenants.— **Tenement-house**, *n.* A house or block of building divided into dwellings for separate families.

Tenesmus, tē-nes'mus, *n.* [L., from Gr. *teinesmos*, from *teinō*, to stretch, to strain.] *Med.* a continual inclination to void the contents of the bowels, accompanied by straining, but without any discharge. — **Tenesmic**, tē-nes'mik, *a.* *Med.* pertaining to or characterized by tenesmus.

Tenet, ten'et, *n.* [L. *tenet*, he holds. TENABLE.] Any opinion, principle, dogma, or doctrine which a person believes or maintains as true.

Tenfold. Under TEN.

Tenioid, tē'ni-oid, *a.* Same as *Tænioid*.

Tennis, ten'is, *n.* [Said to be from Fr. *tenez*, take it (from *tenir*, L. *tenere*, to hold), a word which the French use when the ball is struck.] An ancient game in which players alternately drive a ball against a wall with rackets; short for *lawn tennis*, a game in which the ball must pass back and forth over a net and land within a marked court; the player failing to return the ball losing the point.—**Tennis-ball**, *n.* The ball used in tennis.—**Tennis-court**, *n.* An oblong court in which lawn tennis is played.

Tenon, ten'on, *n.* [Fr. *tenon*, from *tenir*, L. *tenere*, to hold. TENABLE.] A projecting piece on the end of a piece of wood fitted for insertion into a corresponding cavity or mortise in order to form a joint.—*v.t.* To fit with a tenon.—**Tenon-saw**, *n.* A small saw with a brass or steel back, used for cutting tenons.

Tenoplasty, ten'ō-plas-ti, *n.* [Gr. *tenōn*, a tendon, *plastos*, moulded.] *Surg.* tendon-grafting.

Tenor, ten'or, *n.* [L. *tenor*, a holding on, course, tenor, from *teneo*, to hold. TENABLE.] Prevailing course or direction; general course or drift of thought; general spirit or meaning; purport; substance (the *tenor* of a discourse); *mus.* the highest of the adult male chest voices: so called because in former times the leading melody was given to this voice; the part above the bass in harmonized music; one who sings a tenor part.—*a.* *Mus.* adapted for singing or playing the tenor.—*Tenor clef*, the C clef, placed on the fourth line.

Tenor-saw, ten'or, *n.* Corrupted from *Tenon-saw*.

Tenotomy, te-not'o-mi, *n.* [Gr. *tenōn*, a tendon, and *tomē*, a cutting.] *Surg.* the cutting or division of a tendon.

Tenrec, Tanrec, ten'rek, tan'rek, *n.* [Native Madagascar name.] An animal allied to the hedgehog, inhabiting Madagascar.

Tense, tens, *a.* [L. *tensus*, pp. of *tendo*, to stretch. TEND.] Stretched until tight; strained to stiffness; rigid; not lax.— **Tensely**, tens'li, *adv.* In a tense manner; with tension.—**Tenseness**, tens'nes, *n.* The state of being tense.—**Tensibility**, ten-si-bil'i-ti, *n.* The quality of being tensible.—**Tensible**, ten'si-bl, *a.* Capable of being extended.—**Tensile**, ten'sil, *a.* Pertaining to tension; capable of tension.— **Tensility**, ten-sil'i-ti, *n.* The quality of being tensile.—**Tension**, ten'shon, *n.* [L. *tensio*, *tensionis*.] The act of stretching or straining; the state of being stretched or strained to stiffness; tightness; mental strain; *mech.* the force by which a bar, rod, or string is pulled when forming part of any system; *elect.* intensity, or the degree to which a body is excited, as estimated by the electrometer; *physics*, elastic force.— *The tension of a gas*, the degree of pressure it exerts on the containing surface.— **Tensioned**, ten'shond, *a.* Subjected to tension.—**Tension-rod**, *n.* A rod in a structure holding together opposite parts.— **Tensity**, ten'si-ti, *n.* State of being tense; tenseness.—**Tensor**, ten'sor, *n.* *Anat.* a muscle that extends or stretches the part to which it is fixed.

Tense, tens, *n.* [O.Fr. *tens*, Mod.Fr. *temps*, time, from L. *tempus*, time. TEMPORAL.] *Gram.* one of the forms which a verb takes in order to express the time of action or of that which is affirmed.

Tensile, Tension, &c. Under TENSE, *a.*

Tent, tent, *n.* [Fr. *tente*, L.L. *tenta*, a tent, lit. something stretched out or extended, from L. *tendo*, *tentum*, to stretch. TEND.] A portable house consisting of some flexible covering, such as skins, matting, or canvas stretched and sustained by poles.—*v.i.* To lodge in a tent; to tabernacle.—**Tent-bed**, *n.* A bedstead having curtains in a tent form above.—**Tented**, tent'ed, *a.* Covered or furnished with tents.—**Tent-maker**, *n.* One who makes tents. (N.T.)

Tent, Tent-wine, *n.* [Sp. *tinto*, deep-coloured, from L. *tinctus*, pp. of *tingo*, to dye. TINGE.] A Spanish wine of a deep-red colour.

Tent, tent, *v.t.* [Fr. *tenter*, from L. *tentare*, to feel, to try. TEMPT.] To probe; to keep open with a tent or pledget.—*n.* *Surg.* a roll of lint or linen, &c., used to dilate an opening in the flesh, or keep open a sore from which matter is discharged.

Tentacle, ten'ta-kl, *n.* [L.L. *tentaculum*, from L. *tento*, to handle, to feel. TEMPT.] *Zool.* an elongated appendage on the head or cephalic extremity of many of the lower forms of animals, used as an instrument of prehension or as a feeler.—**Tentacled**, ten'ta-kld, *a.* Having tentacles. — **Tentacular**, ten-tak'ū-lėr, *a.* Of the nature of a tentacle.—**Tentaculated**, ten-tak'ū-lā-ted, *a.* Having tentacles.—**Tentaculiferous**, ten-tak'ū-lif"ėr-us, *a.* Bearing tentacles.

Tentative, ten'ta-tiv, *a.* [Fr. *tentatif*, from L. *tento*, *tentatum*, to try, to test. TEMPT.] Based on or consisting in trial or experiment; experimental; empirical.—*n.* An essay; a trial.—**Tentatively**, ten'ta-tiv-li, *adv.* By way of experiment or trial.

Tenter, ten'tėr, *n.* [From provincial *tent*, to tend or attend.] A person in a manufactory who looks after machines, so that they may be in proper order.

Tenter, ten'tėr, *n.* [From L. *tentus*, stretched, from *tendo*, *tentum*, to stretch. TEND.] A frame used in cloth manufacture to stretch the pieces of cloth, and make them set or dry even and square; a tenter-hook.—*On the tenters*, on the stretch; on the rack; in suspense.—*v.t.* To stretch on tenters.—**Tenter-hook**, *n.* A hook for stretching cloth on a tenter; *fig.* anything that painfully strains, racks, or tortures, chiefly used in the expression *to be on tenter-hooks*.

Tenth, Tenthly. Under TEN.

Tenuifolious, ten'ū-i-fō"li-us, *a.* [L. *tenuis*, thin, and *folium*, a leaf.] *Bot.* having thin or narrow leaves.

Tenuiroster, ten'ū-i-ros"tėr, *n.* [L. *tenuis*, thin, and *rostrum*, a beak.] A member of a suborder (Tenuirostres) of passerine or insessorial birds which have the beak long, slender, and tapering, as in the creepers, humming-birds, &c. — **Tenuirostral**, ten'ū-i-ros"tral, *a.* Slender-beaked; pertaining to the tenuirosters.

Tenuity, te-nū'i-ti, *n.* [L. *tenuitas*, from *tenuis*, thin, from root meaning to stretch, as in E. *thin*.] The state of being thin or fine; thinness; slenderness; rarity; thinness, as of a fluid.—**Tenuous**, ten'ū-us, *a.* Thin; slender; rare; subtle; not dense.

Tenure, ten'ūr, *n.* [Fr. *tenure*, L.L. *tenura*, from L. *teneo*, to hold. TENABLE.] The act, manner, or right of holding property, especially real estate; manner of holding or possessing in general; the terms or conditions upon which anything is held or possessed (life is held on a precarious *tenure*).

Teocalli, tē-o-kal'li, *n.* [Lit. God's house.] A temple among the aboriginal Indians of Mexico and Central America.

Tepee, tē'pē, tep'ē, *n.* [Amer. Ind.] The American Indian cone-shaped tent.

Tepefy, tep'ē-fi, *v.t.*—*tepefied*, *tepefying*. [L. *tepeo*, to be tepid, and *facio*, to make. TEPID.] To make tepid or moderately warm.—*v.i.* To become moderately warm.

Tepid, tep'id, *a.* [L. *tepidus*, warm, from *tepeo*, to be warm; same root as Skr. *tap*, to burn.] Moderately warm; lukewarm.— **Tepidness, Tepidity**, tep'id-nes, te-pid'i-ti, *n.* Moderate warmth; lukewarmness.

Teraph, ter'af, *n.* pl. **Teraphim**, ter'af-im. [Heb.] A household deity or image reverenced by the ancient Hebrews.

Terapin, ter'a-pin, *n.* TERRAPIN.

Teratology, ter-a-tol'o-ji, *n.* [Gr. *teras*, *teratos*, a prodigy, and *logos*, discourse.] That branch of biological science which treats of monsters or malformations in the vegetable and animal kingdoms.—**Teratological**, ter'a-tō-loj"i-kal, *a.* Pertaining to teratology.—**Teratologist**, ter-a-tol'o-jist, *n.* One versed in the study of teratology.

Terbium, tėr'bi-um, *n.* A rare element found along with erbium and yttrium at *Ytterby* in Sweden (whence the name).

Terce, tėrs, *n.* [TIERCE.] A tierce or cask of 42 gallons; *Scots law*, the right of a widow who has not accepted any special provision to a liferent of one-third of the heritage in which her husband died infeft.

Tercel, tėr'sel, *n.* TIERCEL.

Tercentenary, tėr-sen'ten-a-ri, *a.* [L. *ter*, thrice, and E. *centenary*.] Comprising three hundred years.—*n.* A festival in commemoration of some event that happened three hundred years before; the three-hundredth anniversary of any event.

Tercet, tėr'set, *n.* [Fr.] *Mus.* a third; *poetry*, a group of three rhyming lines; a triplet.

Terebinth, ter'ē-binth, *n.* [L. *terebinthus*, from Gr. *terebinthos*, the turpentine tree.] The turpentine tree; a name for various resinous exudations, both of fluid and solid. —**Terebinthine**, ter-ē-bin'thīn, *a.* Pertaining to turpentine.

Terebra, ter'ē-bra, *n.* pl. **Terebræ**, ter'ē-brē. [L., a boring tool, from *tero*, to pierce.] The borer of certain female hymenopterous insects for depositing their eggs.—**Terebrate**,† ter'ē-brāt, *v.t.*—*terebrated*, *terebrating*. [L. *terebro*, *terebratum*, to bore, from *terebra*, a borer.] To bore; to perforate.—**Terebration**,† ter-ē-brā'shon, *n.* The act of boring.—**Terebratula**, ter-ē-brat'ū-la, *n.* [A dim. form from L. *terebratus*, pp. of *terebro*, to bore—from its perforated valve.] A genus of brachiopod bivalve molluscs, one of the valves of which is perforated to permit the passage of a fleshy peduncle, by means of which the animal attaches itself.

Teredo, te-rē'dō, *n.* pl. **Teredos**. [L., from Gr. *terēdōn*, from *tereō*, to bore.] A worm-like molluscous animal, the ship-worm, well known on account of the destruction it causes by perforating submerged wood in order to form a habitation.

Terete, te-rēt', *a.* [L. *teres*, *teretis*, rounded off—properly, rubbed off—from *tero*, to rub.] Cylindrical and smooth; long and round; columnar, as some stems of plants.

Tergal. Under TERGUM.

Tergeminal, Tergeminate, Tergeminous, tėr-jem'i-nal, tėr-jem'i-nāt, tėr-jem'i-nus, *a.* [L. *tergeminus*—*ter*, thrice, and *geminus*, double.] Thrice double; three-paired; threefold; triple.

Tergiversate, tėr'ji-vėr-sāt, *v.i.*—*tergiversated*, *tergiversating*. [L. *tergiversor*, *tergiversatus*, from *tergum*, the back, and *versor*, to turn, from *verto*, to turn. VERSE.] To practise evasion; to make use of shifts or subterfuges.—**Tergiversation**, tėr'ji-vėr-sā"shon, *n.* The act of tergiversating; subterfuge; evasion; the act of changing or of turning one's back upon one's opinions; a turning against a cause formerly advocated.—**Tergiversator**, tėr'ji-vėr-sā-tėr, *n.* One who practises tergiversation.

Tergum, tėr'gum, *n.* [L., the back.] The convex upper plate of each segment of a crustacean.—**Tergal**, tėr'gal, *a.* *Anat.* pertaining to the back; dorsal.

Teribus, te'ri-bus, *interj.* [Perhaps an invocation to Tyr, one of the deities of the Goths.] This, according to local tradition, was the cry of the band which went from Hawick to the battle of Flodden; and it is still shouted by the inhabitants when they annually ride the marches.

Term, tėrm, *n.* [Fr. *terme*, an end, word, speech, period, &c., from L. *terminus*, a boundary (whence *terminal*, *terminate*, *determine*, &c.); akin Gr. *terma*, limit; same root as L. *trans*, E. *through*.] A limit; a bound or boundary; the time for which anything lasts; a time or period fixed in some way; a period during which instruction is regularly given to students in certain universities and colleges, there being three such—Michaelmas, Lent, and Easter (or Midsummer) at Cambridge, and four—Michaelmas, Hilary, Easter, and Trinity at Oxford; the time in which a superior law court is held or is open for the trial of causes (but the law terms of the superior courts in England are now called 'sittings'); a day on which rent or interest is regularly payable, such as Lady Day or Michaelmas Day; a word by which something fixed and definite is expressed; particularly, a word having a technical meaning; *pl.* in a general way, words or language (to speak in vague *terms*); *pl.* conditions or propositions stated and offered for acceptance (state your *terms*); *pl.* relative position or footing (on good *terms* with a person); *logic*, the expression in language of the notion obtained in an act of apprehension; the subject or the predicate of a proposition; *alg.* a member of a compound quantity connected with another or others by the signs of addition and subtraction.—*Terms of a fraction*, the numerator and denominator.—*To make terms*, to come to an agreement.—*To come to terms*, to agree.—*To bring to terms*, to reduce to submission or to conditions.—*v.t.* To name; to denominate.—**Termless**, tėrm'les, *a.* Having no term; boundless; endless.—**Termly**, tėrm'li, *a.* Occurring every term.—*adv.* Term by term.

Termagant, tėr'ma-gant, *n.* [O.Fr. *Tervagant*, It. *Tervagante*, *Trivagante*; probably a name of Eastern origin. Termagant was a fabled deity of the Mohammedans introduced into the old moralities or other shows, in which he figured as a most violent personage.] A brawling, turbulent woman; a virago.—*a.* Furious; scolding.

Termes, tėr'mēz, *n.* pl. **Termites**, tėr'mi-tēz. A termite or white-ant.

Terminate, tėr'mi-nāt, *v.t.*—*terminated*, *terminating*. [L. *termino*, *terminatum*, to bound, to terminate. TERM.] To bound; to limit; to form the extreme point or side of; to put an end to; to complete; to put the finishing touch to.—*v.i.* To be limited in space; to stop short; to end; to come to a limit in time.—*a.* Capable of coming to an end (a *terminate* decimal).—**Termination**, tėr-mi-nā'shon, *n.* The act of terminating; an ending or concluding; the end of a thing or point where it ends; limit in space; end in time; *gram.* a part annexed to the root or stem of an inflected word; the syllable or letter that ends a word; conclusion; issue; result.—**Terminational**, tėr-mi-nā'shon-al, *a.* Pertaining to or forming a termination.—**Terminative**, tėr'mi-nā-tiv, *a.* Terminating; definitive. —**Terminatively**, tėr'mi-nā-tiv-li, *adv.* —**Terminator**, tėr'mi-nāt-ėr, *n.* One who or that which terminates.—**Terminatory**, tėr'mi-na-to-ri, *a.* Bounding; terminating.—**Terminable**, tėr'mi-na-bl, *a.* Capable of being terminated; coming to an end after a certain term.—**Terminableness**, tėr'mi-na-bl-nes, *n.*—**Terminal**, tėr'mi-nal, *a.* Relating to or forming the end or extremity; placed at the end of something.—*n.* That which terminates; an extremity; the clamping-screw at each end of a voltaic battery for connecting it with the wires which complete the circuit.—**Terminer**, tėr'min-ėr, *n.* *Law*, a determining. OYER.—**Terminism**, tėr'min-izm, *n.* *Philos.* same as *Nominalism*; *theol.* the doctrine that God has assigned to every one a term of repentance during which his salvation must be wrought out.—**Terminist**, tėr'min-ist, *n.* An upholder of the doctrines of terminism.

Terminology, tėr-mi-nol'o-ji, *n.* [From L. *terminus*, with meaning of term or appelation, and Gr. *logos*, discourse.] The science of technical terms; theory regarding the proper use of terms; collectively, the terms used in any art, science, and the like; nomenclature. ∴ Syn. under NOMENCLATURE.—**Terminological**, tėr'min-ō-loj"i-kal, *a.* Of or pertaining to terminology.—**Terminologically**, tėr'min-ō-loj"i-kal-li, *adv.* In a terminological manner; in the way of terminology.

Terminus, tėr'mi-nus, *n.* pl. **Termini**, tėr'mi-nī. [L. TERM.] A boundary; a limit; a landmark; the extreme station at either end of a railway or important section of a railway.

Termite, tėr'mīt, *n.* [From L. *termes*, *termitis*, a wood-worm.] One of those neuropterous insects commonly called white ants which live in communities and build dwellings 10 to 12 feet high.—**Termitary**, tėr'mi-ta-ri, *n.* The dwelling of a community of termites.

Termless, Termly. Under TERM.

Tern, tėrn, *n.* [Dan. *terne*, Icel. *therna*, a tern.] A long-winged bird of the gull family, which, from its manner of flight, forked tail, and size, has received the name of *sea-swallow*.

Tern, tėrn, *a.* [L. *terni*, three each, from *ter*, thrice, *tres*, three.] Threefold; consisting of three.—**Ternary**, tėr'na-ri, *a.* [L. *ternarius*.] Proceeding by threes; consisting of three; arranged in order by threes. —**Ternate**, tėr'nāt, *a.* [L.L. *ternatus*.] Arranged in threes; *bot.* having three leaflets on a petiole.—**Ternately**, tėr'nāt-li, *adv.* In a ternate manner.

Terpsichore, tėrp-sik'o-rē, *n.* [Greek name, from *terpō*, (fut. *terpsō*), to delight, and *choros*, dancing.] *Greek myth.* one of the Muses, the inventress and patroness of the art of dancing and lyrical poetry.—**Terpsichorean**, tėrp'si-kō-rē"an, *a.* Relating to Terpsichore.—*The Terpsichorean art*, dancing.

Terra, ter'a, *n.* [L. *terra*, from a root meaning dry, seen also in *torridus*, torrid, being the root of E. *thirst*. Hence *terrace*, *terrestrial*, *terrier*, *tureen*, *inter*, &c.] Earth; the earth.—*Terra firma*, firm or solid earth; dry land, in opposition to water.—*Terra incognita* (in-kog'ni-ta), an unknown or unexplored region.—*Terra japonica* (ja-pon'i-ka), catechu, formerly supposed to be a kind of earth from Japan, hence the name. —**Terra-cotta**, *n.* [It., lit. baked or cooked earth.] A mixture of fine clay and fine-grained white sand with crushed pottery, first slowly air-dried, then baked in a kiln into the hardness of stone, much used for statues, figures, vases, &c.

Terrace, ter'ās, *n.* [Fr. *terrasse*, from L.L. *terracia*, from L. *terra*, earth. TERRA.] A raised level space or platform of earth, supported on one or more sides by masonry, a bank of turf, or the like; a level space on a sloping surface; a street or row of houses along the face or top of a slope: often applied arbitrarily.—*v.t.*—*terraced*, *terracing*. To form into a terrace; to cut into terraces.

Terra-cotta. Under TERRA.

Terrain, ter'ān, *n.* [Fr.] Land from a military point of view.

Terrapin, ter'a-pin, *n.* [Origin unknown.] A name of several species of fresh-water tortoises, whose flesh is much esteemed.

Terraqueous, ter-ak'wē-us, *a.* [From L. *terra*, land, and *aqua*, water. TERRA. Consisting of land and water, as the globe or earth.

Terras, ter'as, *n.* TRASS.

Terrene, ter-rēn', *a.* [L. *terrenus*, from *terra*, earth. TERRA.] Pertaining to the earth; earthy; terrestrial.

Terre-plein, ter'plān, *n.* [Fr.] *Fort.* that part of a rampart on which the guns are placed.

Terrestrial, ter-res'tri-al, *a.* [L. *terrestris*, from *terra*, the earth. TERRA.] Pertaining to the earth; existing on this earth; earthly: as opposed to *celestial*; pertaining to the world; mundane; pertaining to land as opposed to water; confined to or living on land: opposed to *aquatic*.—*Terrestrial magnetism*. MAGNETISM.—*n.* An inhabitant of the earth.—**Terrestrially**, ter-res'tri-al-li, *adv.* After a terrestrial or earthly manner.—**Terrestrialness**, ter-res'tri-al-nes, *n.*

Terrible, ter'ri-bl, *a.* [Fr. *terrible*, from L. *terribilis*, from *terreo*, to frighten; allied to Gr. *treō*, to tremble.] Adapted to excite fear, awe, or dread; dreadful; formidable; excessive; extreme.—**Terribleness**, ter'ri-bl-nes, *n.* The quality of being terrible.—**Terribly**, ter'ri-bli, *adv.* In a terrible manner; dreadfully; excessively.

Terricolous, ter-rik'o-lus, *a.* [L. *terra*, earth, *colo*, to inhabit.] Inhabiting the earth; living in the soil.

Terrier, ter'i-ėr, *n.* [In first sense from Fr. *terrier*, the hole of a rabbit, from *terre*, L. *terra*, the earth; equivalent therefore to burrow-dog; in second sense from Fr. *terrier*, lit. land-book.] A small and courageous variety of dog that follows animals into their burrows or holes; a book in which landed property is registered and described.

Terrify, ter'ri-fī, *v.t.*—*terrified*, *terrifying*. [L. *terreo*, to frighten, and *facio*, to make. TERRIBLE.] To frighten extremely; to alarm or shock with fear.—**Terrific**, ter-rif'ik, *a.* [L. *terrificus*.] Dreadful; terrifying; causing terror.—**Terrifically**, ter-rif'i-kal-li, *adv.* Terribly; frightfully.

Terrigenous, ter-rij'en-us, *a.* [L. *terra*, the earth, and root *gen*, to bring forth.] Earth-born; produced by the earth.

Territory, ter'ri-to-ri, *n.* [L. *territorium*, from *terra*, earth. TERRA.] Any separate tract of land as belonging to a state, city, or other body; a dominion; a region; a country; in the United States, a region not yet admitted as a state into the Union, but with an organized government.—**Territorial**, ter-ri-tō'ri-al, *a.* Pertaining to a territory; limited to a certain district.—*n.* A member of the Territorial Army.—*Territorial Army*, the force organized for home defence, levied in definite areas of territory.—**Territorially**, ter-ri-tō'ri-al-li, *adv.* In regard to territory.

Terror, ter'ror, *n.* [L. *terror*, from *terreo*, to frighten. TERRIBLE.] Fear that agitates the body and mind; dread; fright; the cause of extreme fear.—*King of terrors*, death.—*Reign of terror*, in the first French revolution, that period during which the rulers made the execution of all opponents the principle of their government, extending from April, 1793, to July, 1794.—**Terrorism**, ter'ror-izm, *n.* A system of government by terror; intimidation.—**Terrorist**, ter'ror-ist, *n.* One who rules by intimidation.—**Terrorize**, ter'ror-īz, *v.t.* To impress with terror; to repress or domineer over by means of terror.—**Terror-stricken**, **Terror-struck**, *a.*

Terry, ter'i, *n* [Fr. *tirer*, to draw.] A textile fabric with a long, smooth pile, such as plush or velvet.—**Terry cloth**, a cloth or fabric with this type of pile.

Terse, tėrs, *a.* [L. *tersus*, pp. of *tergo*, to rub or wipe.] Free from superfluity; neat and concise; pithy: said of style or language.—**Tersely**, tėrs'li, *adv.* In a terse manner; concisely.—**Terseness**, tėrs'nes, *n.* Neatness and conciseness of style.

Tertial, tėr'shal, *a.* and *n.* [L. *tertius*, third.] A term applied to the feathers growing on the innermost joint of a bird's wing.

Tertian, tėr'shan, *a.* [L. *tertianus*, from *tertius*, third.] *Med.* having its paroxysm every other day (a *tertian* fever).

Tertiary, tėr'shi-a-ri, *a.* [L. *tertiarius*, from *tertius*, third, from *ter*, thrice, *tres*, three.] Of the third order, rank, or formation; third.—*Tertiary colour*, a colour produced by the mixture of two secondary colours.—*Tertiary formation*, *geol.* the third great division of stratified rocks, lying immediately above the secondary and resting on the chalk, being followed by the post-tertiary.—*n.* *Geol.* the tertiary system of rocks; *ornith.* a tertial.

Terza-rima, tėr'tsa-rē'ma, *n.* [It.] The rhyming arrangement in triple lines adopted in Dante's *Divina Commedia*.

Terzetto, ter-tset'tō, *n.* [It.] *Mus.* a short composition for three performers.

Tesho-lama, tesh'o-lä-mä, *n.* One of the two popes of the Buddhists of Thibet, the other being the *Dalai-lama*.

Tessellated, Tesselated, tes'e-lā-ted, *a.* [L. *tessella*, a dim. of *tessera*, a square.] Formed by inlaying differently coloured materials in little squares, triangles, or other geometrical figures, or by mosaic work.—**Tessellation, Tesselation**, tes-e-lā'shon, *n.* The operation of making tessellated work.

Tessera, tes'e-ra, *n.* pl. **Tesseræ**, tes'e-rē. [L., a cube, a die.] A small cube of marble, precious stone, ivory, glass, wood, &c., used to form tessellated pavements and for like purposes; a small square of bone, wood, &c., used as a token or ticket in ancient Rome.—**Tesseral**, tes'e-ral, *a.* Pertaining to or containing tesseræ; cubical.

Test, test, *n.* [O.Fr. *test* (Fr. *têt*), from L. *testum*, an earthen vessel, from *testa*, a piece of earthenware, the shell of shell-fish. TESTY.] A vessel used in refining gold and silver; a cupel; examination by the cupel; hence, any critical trial and examination; means of trial; a touchstone; a standard; means of discrimination; *chem.* a substance which is employed to detect the presence of any ingredient in a compound, by causing it to exhibit some known property; a reagent.—*v.t.* To refine, as gold or silver, in a test; to bring to trial and examination; to prove by experiment or by some fixed standard; to try; *chem.* to examine by the application of some reagent.—**Tester**, tes'tėr, *n.* One who tests.—**Test-furnace**, *n.* A kind of refining furnace.—**Test-glass**, *n.* A glass to hold substances to be chemically tested.—**Test-paper**, *n.* A paper impregnated with some chemical reagent, and serving to detect the presence of certain substances by change of colour when they touch it.—**Test-plate**, *n.* A glass plate ruled with exceedingly fine and close lines to test the power of microscopes.—**Test-tube**, *n.* A glass tube to contain substances to be chemically tested.—**Testing-machine**, *n.* A machine for testing the strength of engineering materials.

Test, test, *n.* [L. *testa*, a shell, &c. See TEST above.] *Zool.* the outside hard covering of certain animals, as the shell of mollusca or of the sea-urchin; *bot.* the outer integument of a seed.—**Testacean**, tes-tā'shē-an, *n.* A testaceous animal; a mollusc with a shell.—**Testaceous**, tes-tā'shus, *a.* [L. *testaceus*.] Having a molluscous shell; having the character of a test or shell.

Test-act, *n.* [L. *testor*, to witness, *testis*, a witness. TESTAMENT.] *Eng. hist.* an act passed in the reign of Charles II, providing that all persons holding office from the crown should take oaths against popery; repealed in 1828.

Testacy. Under TESTAMENT.

Testament, tes'ta-ment, *n.* [L. *testamentum*, from *testor*, to be a witness, to make a will, from *testis*, a witness; similarly *testify*, *testimony*, *attest*, *contest*, &c.] *Law*, a duly executed document in writing, by which a person declares his will as to the disposal of his estate and effects after his death; a will; the name of each general division of the canonical books of the sacred Scriptures (the Old *Testament*, the New *Testament*): when used alone the word is often limited to the New Testament.—**Testamental**, tes-ta-men'tal, *a.* Relating to a testament or will.—**Testamentary**, tes-ta-men'ta-ri, *a.* Pertaining to a will or to wills; bequeathed or arranged by will.—**Testate**, tes'tāt, *a.* [L. *testatus*.] Having made and left a will.—**Testacy**, tes'ta-si, *n.* The state of being testate.—**Testator**, tes-tā'-tor, *n.* A man who makes and leaves a will at death.—**Testatrix**, tes-tā'triks, *n.* [L.] A woman who makes and leaves a will at death.

Tester, tes'tėr, *n.* [O.Fr. *testiere*, a head-piece, from *teste* (Fr. *tête*) a head, from L. *testa*, an earthen pot, the skull, the head. TEST.] The square canopy over a four-post bedstead; a flat canopy, as over a pulpit, tomb, and the like; an old French silver coin of the value of twelve cents, so named from the *teste* (head) upon it.

Testes, tes'tēz. *n.pl.* [L.] *Anat.* the testicles.

Testicle, tes'ti-kl, *n.* [L. *testiculus*, dim. of *testis*, a testicle.] One of the glands which secrete the seminal fluid in males.—**Testicular, Testiculate, Testiculated**, tes-tik'ū-lėr, tes-tik'ū-lāt, tes-tik'ū-lā-ted, *a.* *Bot.* shaped like a testicle.

Testify, tes'ti-fī, *v.i.*—*testified*, *testifying*. [O.Fr. *testifier*, from L. *testificari*—*testis*, a witness, and *facio*, to make. TESTAMENT.] To make a solemn declaration, verbal or written, to establish some fact; *law*, to give evidence under oath; to declare a charge.—*v.t.* To affirm or declare solemnly; *law*, to affirm under oath before a tribunal, for the purpose of proving some fact.—**Testification**, tes'ti-fi-kā"shon, *n.* [L. *testificatio*.] The act of testifying or giving evidence.—**Testifier**, tes'ti-fī-ėr, *n.* One who testifies.

Testily, Testiness. Under TESTY.

Testimony, tes'ti-mo-ni, *n.* [L. *testimonium*, from *testis*, a witness. TESTAMENT.] A solemn declaration or affirmation made for the purpose of establishing or proving some fact; evidence; declaration; attestation; witness; anything equivalent to a declaration or protest; divine revelation.—**Testimonial**, tes-ti-mō'ni-al, *n.* A certificate in favour of some one's character; a certificate of qualifications; a gift or token of appreciation raised by subscription in acknowledgement of an individual's services, or to show respect for his worth.

Teston, Testoon, tes'tön, *n.* [It. *testone*.] An early silver coin of several European countries, worth ten to thirty cents.

Testudo, tes-tū'dō, *n.* [L., from *testa*, a shell.] Among the ancient Romans a cover from missiles formed by soldiers holding their shields over their heads and standing close to each other; *zool.* the land-tortoise.—**Testudinal**, tes-tū'di-nal, *a.* Pertaining to the tortoise.—**Testudinarious**, tes-tū'di-nā"ri-us, *a.* Resembling a tortoise-shell in colour.—**Testudinate, Testudineous**, tes-tū'di-nāt, tes-tū-din'ē-us, *a.* Resembling the back of a tortoise; arched; vaulted.

Testy, tes'ti, *a.* [O.Fr. *testu* (Fr. *têtu*), headstrong, wilful, from *teste* (Fr. *tête*), the head, from L. *testa*, potsherd, shell. TEST, TESTER.] Fretful; peevish; easily irritated.—**Testily**, tes'ti-li, *adv.* In a testy manner; fretfully.—**Testiness**, tes'ti-nes, *n.* The state or quality of being testy.

Tetanus, tet'a-nus, *n.* [Gr. *tetanos*, tetanus, from *teinō*, to stretch. THIN.] Spasm with rigidity; a disease characterized by a more or less violent and rigid spasm of many or all of the muscles of voluntary motion, one form being lock-jaw.—**Tetanic**, te-tan'ik, *a.* Pertaining to tetanus.—*n.* A substance that tends to cause tetanus.—**Tetanoid**, tet'an-oid, *a.* Resembling tetanus.

Tetchy, tech'i. TECHY.

Tête-à-tête, tāt-ä-tāt, *adv.* [Fr., lit. head to head.] Face to face; in private; in close confabulation.—*n.* A private interview with no one present but the parties concerned.

Tête-de-pont, tāt-dė-poṅ, *n.* [Fr., lit. bridge-head.] *Fort.* a work that defends the head or entrance of a bridge nearest the enemy.

Tether, teтн'ėr, *n.* [Same as Icel. *tjóthr*, a tether, *tjóthra*, to tether; O.Fris. *tieder*, L.G. *tider*, O.Sw. *tiuther*, cord, tether; from same root as to *tie*.] A rope or chain by which a grazing animal is confined within certain limits; *fig.*, range of opportunity.—*v.t.* To confine with a tether.

Tetrabranchiate, tet-ra-brang'ki-āt, *a.* [Gr. *tetra-*, four, and *branchia*, gills.] Having four gills: applied to an order of cephalopods.

Tetrachord, tet'ra-kord, *n.* [Gr. *tetrachordon*—*tetra-*, four, and *chordē*, a chord.] A scale of four notes; half of the octave scale.

Tetrad, tet'rad, *n.* [Gr. *tetras*, *tetrados*, the number four.] The number four; a collection of four things.

Tetradactyl, tet'ra-dak-til, *n.* [Gr. *tetra-*, four, and *daktylos*, a finger or toe.] An animal having four toes on each foot.—**Tetradactylous**, tet-ra-dak'ti-lus, *n.* Having four toes on each foot.

Tetradrachm, Tetradrachma, tet'ra-dram, tet-ra-drak'ma, *n.* [Gr. *tetradrachmon*—*tetra-*, four, and *drachmē*, a drachm.] An ancient Greek silver coin worth 80c.

Tetradynamous, tet-ra-din'a-mus, *a.* [Gr. *tetra-*, four, and *dynamis*, power.] *Bot.* having hermaphrodite flowers with six stamens, four longer than the other two.

Tetragon, tet'ra-gon, *n.* [Gr. *tetragōnon*—*tetra-*, four, and *gōnia*, an angle.] *Geom.* a figure having four angles; a quadrangle, as a square, a rhombus, &c.—**Tetragonal**, te-trag'on-al, *a.* Having four angles or sides; of a system of crystals having all three axes equal, and two of them at right angles to each other.

Tetragyn, tet'ra-jin, *n.* [Gr. *tetra-*, four, and *gynē*, a female.] *Bot.* a monoclinous or hermaphrodite plant having four pistils.—**Tetragynous**, tet-raj'i-nus, *a.* *Bot.* having four carpels or four styles.

Tetrahedron, tet-ra-hē'dron, *n.* [Gr. *tetra-*, four, and *hedra*, a base.] A triangular pyramid having four equal and equilateral faces; a solid bounded by four equal triangles.—**Tetrahedral**, tet-ra-hē'dral, *a.* Having the form of a tetrahedron.—**Tetrahedrite**, tet-ra-hē'drīt, *n.* Fahlerz.

Tetrahexahedron, tet-ra-hek'sa-hē"-dron, *n.* [Gr. *tetra-*, four, *hex*, six, *hedra*, a base.] A solid bounded by twenty-four equal faces.

Tetralogy, te-tral'o-ji, *n.* [Gr. *tetralogia* —*tetra-*, four, and *logos*, discourse.] A collection of four dramatic compositions, three tragic and one satiric, which were exhibited together on the Athenian stage.

Tetramerous, te-tram'ér-us, *a.* [Gr. *tetra-*, four, and *meros*, a part.] Consisting of four parts; *bot.* having the parts in fours; *entom.* having four-jointed tarsi.

Tetrameter, te-tram'et-ėr, *n.* [Gr. *tetra-*, four, and *metron*, measure.] *Pros.* a verse consisting of four measures.

Tetrander, te-tran'dėr, *n.* [Gr. *tetra-*, four, and *anēr*, *andros*, a male.] *Bot.* a monoclinous or hermaphrodite plant having four stamens.—**Tetrandrian**, **Tetrandrous**, te-tran'dri-an, te-tran'drus, *a.* *Bot.* monoclinous or hermaphrodite and having four stamens.

Tetrapetalous, tet-ra-pet'al-us, *a.* [Gr. *tetra-*, four, and *petalon*, a leaf.] *Bot.* containing four distinct petals.

Tetraphyllous, te-traf'i-lus or tet-ra-fil'-us, *a.* [Gr. *tetra-*, four, *phyllon*, a leaf.] *Bot.* having four leaves or leaflets.

Tetrapla, tet'ra-pla, *n.* [Gr. *tetraploos*, fourfold, *tetra-*, four, and term. *-ploos*, akin to that of *double*.] An edition of the Bible arranged by Origen in four columns, containing four Greek versions; also a version in four languages.

Tetrapod, tet'ra-pod, *n.* [Gr. *tetra-*, four, and *pous*, *podos*, a foot.] A four-footed animal.

Tetrapteran, te-trap'tėr-an, *n.* [Gr. *tetra-*, four, and *pteron*, a wing.] An insect which has four wings.—**Tetrapterous**, te-trap'-tėr-us, *a.* Having four wings.

Tetraquetrous, tet-ra-kwe'trus, *a.* [Gr. *tetra-*, four, and L. *-quetrus*, angular.] *Bot.* having four very sharp angles or corners.

Tetrarch, tet'rärk, *n.* [Gr. *tetrarchēs*—*tetra-*, four, and *archē*, rule.] A Roman governor of the fourth part of a province; a petty king or sovereign.—**Tetrarchate**, **Tetrarchy**, tet'rär-kāt, tet'rär-ki, *n.* The office or jurisdiction of a tetrarch, or the district under his rule.—**Tetrarchical**, tet-rär'ki-kal, *a.* Pertaining to a tetrarch or tetrarchy.

Tetrasepalous, tet-ra-sep'al-us, *a.* [Gr. *tetra-*, four, and E. *sepal*.] *Bot.* applied to a calyx composed of four sepals.

Tetraspermous, tet-ra-spėr'mus, *a.* [Gr. *tetra-*, four, and *sperma*, seed.] *Bot.* having four seeds.

Tetraspore, tet'ra-spōr, *n.* [Gr. *tetra-*, four, and E. *spore*.] *Bot.* among the algæ a collection of spores, of which usually there are four.

Tetrastich, te-tras'tik, *n.* [Gr. *tetra-*, four, and *stichos*, verse.] A stanza or poem in four verses (or lines).

Tetrastyle, tet'ra-stīl, *a.* and *n.* [Gr. *tetra-*, four, and *stylos*, column.] Having or consisting of four columns; having a portico consisting of four columns.

Tetrasyllable, tet'ra-sil-a-bl, *n.* [Gr. *tetra-*, four, and *syllabē*, syllable.] A word consisting of four syllables.—**Tetrasyllabic**, **Tetrasyllabical**, tet'ra-si-lab"-ik, tet'ra-si-lab"i-kal, *a.* Consisting of four syllables.

Tetrathecal, tet-ra-thē'kal, *a.* [Gr. *tetra-*, four, and *thēkē*, a case.] *Bot.* having four cavities in the ovary.

Tetratomic, tet-ra-tom'ik, *a.* [Gr. *tetra-*, four, and E. *atomic*.] Such that one atom in composition is equivalent to four atoms of hydrogen.

Tetravalent, tet-ra-văl'ent, *a.* QUADRIVALENT.

Tetter, tet'ėr, *n.* [A.Sax. *tetr*, G. *zitter*, tetter; comp. Skr. *dadru*, tetter.] A vague name of several cutaneous diseases affecting man, as herpes, impetigo, &c.; a cutaneous disease of animals, which may be communicated to man.—**Tetterous**, tet'-ėr-us, *a.* Having the character of tetter.

Teutonic, tū-ton'ik, *a.* [L. *Teutones*, the Teutons; a Latinized form of their native name; akin *Dutch*.] Belonging to the Teutons or the peoples of Germanic origin in general; Germanic; pertaining to the languages spoken by these peoples, which include Gothic, Anglo-Saxon and English, Dutch, German, Icelandic, Norse, Danish, and Swedish.—*n.* The language or languages collectively of the Teutons.

Tew, tū, *v.t.* [Akin to *taw*.] To beat or press, as leather, hemp, and the like; to taw.

Tewel, tū'el, *n.* [O.Fr. *tuiel*, *tueil*, Fr. *tuyau*, a pipe, from L.L. *tubellus*, dim. of L. *tubus*, a pipe.] A pipe; a funnel, as for smoke; a tuyere.

Text, tekst, *n.* [Fr. *texte*, from L. *textus*, a tissue, a text, from *texo*, *textum*, to weave, seen also in *texture*, *textile*, *context*, *pretext*. Akin *tissue*, *toilet*.] A discourse or composition on which notes or a commentary is written; an author's own work as distinct from notes or annotations on it; a passage of Scripture, especially one selected as the theme of a sermon or discourse; any subject chosen to comment on; a topic; a kind of handwriting of a large size; a particular kind of letter or character (German *text*).—**Text-book**, *n.* A book used by students as a manual for a particular branch of study; a manual of instruction.—**Text-hand**, *n.* A large hand in writing.—**Textual**, teks'tū-al, *a.* Pertaining to or contained in the text.—**Textualist**, teks'tū-al-ist, *n.* One who can readily quote texts; one who adheres strictly to a text.—**Textually**, teks'tū-al-li, *adv.* In accordance with the text; placed in the text of a work.—**Textuary**, teks'tū-a-ri, *a.* Textual.

Textile, teks'tīl, *a.* [L. *textilis*, from *texo*, to weave. TEXT.] Woven or capable of being woven; formed by weaving.—*n.* A fabric made by weaving.—**Textorial**, teks-tō'ri-al, *a.* Pertaining to weaving.

Textual, &c. Under TEXT.

Texture, teks'tūr, *n.* [L. *textura*, from *texo*, *textum*, to weave. TEXT.] A fabric formed by weaving; the disposition or connection of threads or filaments interwoven; the disposition of the elementary constituent parts of any solid body; the grain or peculiar character of a solid.

Thalamus, thal'a-mus, *n.* pl. **Thalami**, thal'a-mī. [Gr. *thalamos*, a bed-room.] A part in the brain at the origin of the optic nerve; *bot.* the receptacle of a flower or part on which the carpels are placed.—**Thalamifloral**, thal'a-mi-flō"ral, *a.* [*Thalamus*, and L. *flos*, *floris*, a flower.] *Bot.* having the stamens rising immediately from the thalamus.

Thalassiophyte, tha-las'si-ō-fīt, *n.* [Gr. *thalassios*, marine, from *thalassa*, the sea, and *phyton*, a plant.] A sea-plant.

Thalassometer, thal-as-som'et-ėr, *n.* [Gr. *thalassa*, the sea, *metron*, a measure.] A tide-gauge.

Thaler, tä'lėr, *n.* [G. DOLLAR.] A German coin, value 3 marks.

Thalia, tha-lī'a, *n.* [Gr. *Thaleia*.] The Muse of comedy and the patroness of pastoral and comic poetry.

Thallium, thal'i-um, *n.* [Gr. *thallos*, a young green shoot—from the green line it gives in the spectrum.] A soft, heavy, grayish metal, resembling lead in appearance, discovered in 1861.—**Thallic**, **Thallous**, thal'ik, thal'i-us, *a.* *Chem.* pertaining to or containing thallium.

Thallophyte, thal'ō-fīt, *n.* [Gr. *thallos*, young shoot, *phyton*, plant.] The lowest phylum of plants, comprising the algæ and fungi; with some minor groups.

Thallus, thal'us, *n.* [Gr. *thallos*, a shoot, sprout, frond.] *Bot.* a solid mass of cells, or cellular tissue without woody fibre, forming the substance of the thallogens.—**Thalline**, thal'īn, *a.* *Bot.* pertaining to or of the character of a thallus.—**Thallogen**, **Thallophyte**, thal'ō-jen, thal'ō-fīt, *n.* [Gr. *thallos*, root, *gen*, to produce, *phyton*, a plant.] A stemless plant consisting only of expansions of cellular tissue; applied to all cryptogams with the exception of ferns and mosses.—**Thallogenous**, thal-loj'e-nous, *a.* Belonging to the thallogens.

Thammuz, tham'muz, *n.* [Heb.] The tenth month of the Jewish civil year, answering to part of June and part of July; a Syrian deity for whom the Hebrew idolatresses held an annual feast or lamentation; supposed identical with Adonis.

Than, THan, *conj.* [Originally same as *then*; 'this is better *than* that' is equivalent to 'this is better *then* that'.] A particle used after certain adjectives and adverbs which express comparison or diversity, such as *more*, *better*, *other*, *otherwise*, *rather*, *else*, &c., for the purpose of introducing the second member of the comparison: sometimes used to govern an objective like a preposition.

Thanatoid, than'a-toid, *a.* [Gr. *thanatos*, death, and *eidos*, resemblance.] Resembling death; death-like.—**Thanatology**, than-a-tol'o-ji, *n.* The doctrine of death.—**Thanatopsis**, than-a-top'sis, *n.* [Gr. *opsis*, a view.] A view or contemplation of death.

Thane, thān, *n.* [A.Sax. *thegen*, *thegn*, *thén*, a thane = Icel. *thegen*, a warrior; O.H.G. *degan*, G. *degen*, a warrior; akin to O.E. *thee*, A.Sax. *theón*, to thrive.] A title of honour among the Anglo-Saxons; an Anglo-Saxon baron; a landed proprietor.—**Thanage**, thā'nāj, *n.* The land of a thane; thanes collectively.—**Thanedom**, thān'-dum, *n.* The district or jurisdiction of a thane.—**Thanehood**, thān'hụd, *n.* The office of a thane; thanes collectively.—**Thaneship**, thān'ship, *n.* The dignity of a thane.

Thanks, thangks, *n.pl.* [A.Sax. *thanc*, thanks, also thought, mind, will; Goth. *thagks*, Icel. *thökk*, D. and G. *dank*, thanks; from stem of *think*.] Expression of gratitude; an acknowledgment made to express a sense of favour or kindness received or offered.—*Thanks!* a common contraction for *I give* (offer, render, &c.) *thanks*, or the like.—*v.t.* [A. Sax. *thancian*, to thank, from the noun.] To express gratitude to for a favour; to make acknowledgments to for kindness bestowed.—*I will thank you*, a phrase of civility introducing a request.—*Thank you*, a colloquial or informal contraction of the phrase *I thank you*.—**Thankful**, thangk'fụl, *a.* Impressed with a sense of kindness received and ready to acknowledge it; grateful; expressive of thanks.—**Thankfully**, thangk'fụl-li, *adv.* Gratefully.—**Thankfulness**, thangk'fụl-nes, *n.* Gratefulness; gratitude.—**Thankless**, thangk'les, *a.* Unthankful; ungrateful; not deserving or not likely to gain thanks (a *thankless* task).—**Thanklessly**, thangk'les-li, *adv.* In a thankless manner.—**Thanklessness**, thangk'les-nes, *n.*—**Thank-offering**, *n.* An offering made as an expression of gratitude.—**Thanksgiving**, thangks'giv-ing, *n.* The act of rendering thanks; a public celebration of divine goodness; a day set apart for such a celebration; a form of words expressive of thanks to God.—**Thankworthiness**, thangk'wėr-THi-nes, *n.*—**Thankworthy**, thangk'wėr-THi, *a.* Worthy of or deserving thanks; meritorious.

That, THat, *a.* and *pron.* pl. **Those**, THōz. [A.Sax. *thæt*, neut. of the demonstrative and def. art. *the* or *se* and = Goth. *thata*, Icel. *that*, D. *dat*, G. *das*, Skr. *tat*; akin *the*, *these*, *this*, *there*, &c. THE.] A word used as pointing to a person or thing before mentioned or supposed to be understood (*that* man, *that* city); frequently used in opposition to *this* (I will take *this* book, you can take *that* one): often used without a noun as a demonstrative pronoun, and also as a relative pronoun, in many cases equivalent to *who* or *which*; *who* being generally used for persons, *which* for things, and *that* for either. When governed by a preposition the latter is put at the end of the clause (the book *that* I read *from*).—*conj.* Introducing a reason: because (not *that* I care); introducing an end or purpose (speak *that* I may hear); introducing a result or consequence (so weak *that* he cannot stand); introducing a clause as the subject or object of the principal verb (we know *that* he is dead); used to introduce a wish (would *that* he were dead!).

Thatch, thach, *n.* [A.Sax. *thæc*, thatch, *theccan*, to thatch; Icel. *thak*, a roof, thatch; D. *dak*, G. *dach*, a roof; Dan. *dække*, D. *dekken*, G. *decken*, to cover; same root as L. *tego*, *tectum*, to cover, Gr. *tegos*, *stegos*, a roof, Skr. *sthag*, to cover. *Deck* is allied.] Straw, rushes, reeds, heath, &c., used to cover the roofs of buildings or stacks of hay or grain.—*v.t.* To cover with straw, reeds, or some similar substance.—**Thatcher**, thach′ėr, *n.* One who thatches.

Thaumatrope, tha̧′ma-trōp, *n.* [Gr. *thauma*, *thaumatos*, a wonder, and *trepō*, to turn.] An optical toy, which by revolving causes two pictures to seem connected.

Thaumaturgy, tha̧′ma-tėr-ji, *n.* [Gr. *thaumatourgia*—*thauma*, *thaumatos*, a wonder, and *ergon*, work.] The act of performing something wonderful; wonder-working; magic; legerdemain.—**Thaumaturge**, **Thaumaturgist**, tha̧′ma-tėrj, tha̧′ma-tėr-jist, *n.* A dealer in miracles; a miracle worker.—**Thaumaturgic**, **Thaumaturgical**, tha̧-ma-tėr′jik, tha̧-ma-tėr′ji-kal, *a.* Pertaining to thaumaturgy.—**Thaumaturgics**, tha̧-ma-tėr′jiks, *n.pl.* Feats of magic or legerdemain.—**Thaumaturgus**, tha̧′ma-tėr-gus, *n.* A miracle worker.

Thaw, tha̧, *v.i.* [A.Sax. *thâwan*, to thaw, Icel. *thá*, a thaw, *theyja*, to thaw; D. *dooi*, thaw, *dooijen*, to thaw; G. *thauen*, to melt, to thaw; comp. Gr. *tēkō*, to melt.] To melt, as ice or snow; to become so warm as to melt ice and snow: said of the weather, and used impersonally; *fig.* to become less cold, formal, or reserved; to become genial.—*v.t.* To melt ice or snow; to make less cold or reserved.—*n.* The melting of ice or snow; warmth of weather, such as liquefies ice.

The, ᴛʜē or ᴛʜi, *def. art.* or *definitive a.* [A.Sax. *the*, masc. nom. corresponding to *that*=O.Sax. and O.Fris. *the*, D. and L.G. *de*, Sw. and Dan. *den*, G. *der*. The *the* before comparatives represents the A.Sax. instrumental case *thí*, *thý*.] Used before nouns with a specifying or limiting effect (*the* laws of our country); used before a noun in the singular number to denote a species by way of distinction or a single thing representing the whole (*the* elephant is sagacious); prefixed to adjectives to give them the force of abstract nouns (a passion for *the* sublime and beautiful); used before adjectives and adverbs in the comparative degree it means by that; by how much; by so much (*the longer* we continue in sin *the more difficult* it is to reform).

Theanthropism, thē-an′thro-pizm, *n.* [Gr. *theos*, God, and *anthrōpos*, man.] A state of being God and man; a conception of God or of gods as possessing qualities essentially human.

Thearchy, thē′är-ki, *n.* [Gr. *theos*, God, and *archē*, rule.] Government by God; theocracy; a body of deities or divine rulers.

Theater, **Theatre**, thē′a-tėr, *n.* [Fr. *théâtre*, from L. *theatrum*, from Gr. *theatron*, from *theaomai*, to see, *thea*, a view.] A building for the representation of dramatic spectacles; a play-house; a room with seats rising stepwise for public lectures, anatomical demonstrations, &c.; the locality where events take place (the *theater* of war).—**Theatric**, **Theatrical**, thē-at′rik, thē-at′ri-kal, *a.* Pertaining to a theater or to scenic representations; calculated for display; meretricious; artificial; false.—**Theatricality**, thē-at′ri-kal″i-ti, *n.* Quality of being theatrical; something theatrical; theatrical display.—**Theatrically**, thē-at′ri-kal-li, *adv.* In a theatrical manner.—**Theatricals**, thē-at′ri-kalz, *n. pl.* A dramatic performance, especially in a private house.—**Theatrics**, thē-at′riks, *n.* *Plural in form but takes singular construction.* That skill which is involved in the writing, directing and staging of a dramatic presentation; stagecraft; dramaturgy.

Theban, thē′ban, *n.* An inhabitant of Thebes; 'learned Theban' ironically, of a Bœotian or proverbially dull person.—*Theban eagle*, Pindar.

Theca, thē′ka, *n.* pl. **Thecæ**, thē′sē. [L., from Gr. *thēkē*, a case.] A sheath or hollow case; *bot.* the spore-case of ferns, mosses, and other cryptogams.—**Thecal**, thē′kal, *a.* Pertaining to a theca.—**Thecaphore**, thē′ka-fōr, *n.* [Gr. *phoros*, bearing.] *Bot.* a surface or receptacle bearing thecæ.—**Thecasporous**, thē′ka-spō-rus, *a.* Having spores in thecæ.

Thecodont, thē′kō-dont, *n.* [Gr. *thēkē*, a case, *odous*, *odontos*, a tooth.] An extinct saurian reptile having the teeth in sockets.

Thee, ᴛʜē, *pron.* [A.Sax. *thé*, dat. and accus. of *thú*, thou.] The objective and dative case of *thou*.

Theft, theft, *n.* [A.Sax. *theófthe*, theft, from *theóf*, a thief. Final *th* became *t* as in *height*.] The wrongfully taking away the goods of another with intent to deprive him of them; the act of stealing.

Theine, **Thein**, thē′in, *n.* [From *Thea*, the generic name of the tea-plant.] A bitter principle found in tea, coffee, and some other plants; caffeine.

Their, ᴛʜār, *a.* [From Icel. *theirra*, their =A.Sax. *thaera*, of them: the genitive pl. of which *the*, *that*, are nominatives.] Pertaining or belonging to them.—**Theirs**, ᴛʜārz. A possessive or genitive, properly a double genitive of *they*, used without a noun following, either as a nominative, objective, or simple predicate.

Theism, thē′izm, *n.* [Fr. *théisme*, from Gr. *theos*, God, seen also in *theocracy*, *theology*, *atheism*, &c.] The belief or acknowledgment of the existence of a God, as opposed to *atheism*.—**Theist**, thē′ist, *n.* One who believes in the existence of a God. ∴ Syn. under Deist.—**Theistic**, **Theistical**, thē-is′tik, thē-is′ti-kal, *a.* Pertaining to theism or to a theist.

Them, ᴛʜem, *pron.* [Originally a dative corresponding to *their*=Icel. *theim*, A.Sax. *thâm*.] The dative and objective case of *they*; those persons or things; those.—**Themselves**, ᴛʜem-selvz′, *pron.* pl. of *himself*, *herself*, *itself*.

Theme, thēm, *n.* [Gr. *thema*, a proposition, a theme, a root word, from Gr. *tithēmi*, to place.] A subject or topic on which a person writes or speaks; a subject of discourse or discussion; a short dissertation composed by a student on a given subject; *philol.* the part of a noun or a verb unchanged in declension or conjugation; *mus.* a series of notes selected as the text or subject of a new composition; the leading subject in a composition or movement.—**Thematic**, thē-mat′ik, *a.* Relating to a theme or themes.—**Thematist**, thē′ma-tist, *n.* A writer of themes.

Theme, thēm, *n.* [Gr. *thema*.] One of the provinces, twenty-nine in number, of the old Byzantine Empire.

Themis, them′is, *n.* [Gr. *Themis*.] Greek goddess of law and justice.

Then, ᴛʜen, *adv.* [A.Sax. *thenne*, *thanne*, *thonne*, then, an acc. form belonging to the pronominal stem *the*, *thæt*; same word as *than*.] At that time, referring to a time specified, either past or future; soon afterward or immediately; at another time (now and *then*).—*By then*, by the time when or that.—*Till then*, until that time. Often used elliptically, like an adjective, for *then existing*; but this usage is discountenanced by careful writers.—*conj.* In that case; in consequence; therefore; for this reason.

Thenar, thē′nar, *n.* [Gr. *thenar*, from *thenō*, to strike.] *Anat.* the palm of the hand or the sole of the foot.—**Thenal**, thē′nal, *a.* Pertaining to the thenar.

Thence, ᴛʜens, *adv.* [O.E. *thens*, *thennes*, *thannes*, genitive forms from A.Sax. *thanan*, *thonon*, thence; comp. *hence*, *whence*.] From that place; from that time; for that reason; from this; out of this; not there; elsewhere; absent.—*From thence*, though pleonastic, is supported by custom and good usage.—**Thenceforth**, ᴛʜens′fōrth, *adv.* From that time forward.—**Thenceforward**, ᴛʜens′for-wėrd, *adv.* From that time or place onward.

Theobromine, thē-ō-brō′min, *n.* [From *Theobroma*, the generic name of the cacao tree—Gr. *theos*, God, and *brōma*, food.] A crystalline compound found in the seeds of cacao, analogous to theine.

Theocracy, thē-ok′ra-si, *n.* [Gr. *theokratia*—*theos*, God, and *kratos*, power.] Government of a state by the immediate direction of God; the state thus governed.—**Theocrat**, thē′ō-krat, *n.* One who lives under a theocracy.—**Theocratic**, **Theocratical**, thē-ō-krat′ik, thē-ō-krat′i-kal, *a.* Pertaining to a theocracy; administered by the immediate direction of God.

Theocrasy, thē-ok′ra-si, *n.* [Gr. *theos*, God, and *krasis*, mixture.] An intimate union of the soul with God in contemplation; a mixture of the worship of different gods.

Theodicy, thē-od′i-si, *n.* [Gr. *theos*, God, and *dikē*, justice.] A vindication of the ways of God with a theory as to the existence of evil; a doctrine as to the being, attributes, and government of God, and the immortality of the soul.—**Theodicean**, thē-od′i-sē″an, *a.* Pertaining to theodicy.

Theodolite, thē-od′o-līt, *n.* [Origin doubtful; perhaps from Gr. *thea*, a seeing, *hodos*, way, and *litos*, smooth.] A surveying instrument for measuring horizontal and vertical angles by means of a telescope the movements of which can be accurately marked on two graduated circles.—**Theodolitic**, thē-od′o-lit″ik, *a.* Pertaining to a theodolite; made by a theodolite.

Theogony, thē-og′o-ni, *n.* [Gr. *theogonia*—*theos*, a god, and *gonē*, generation.] A poem treating of the generation and descent of gods; doctrine as to the genealogy or origin of heathen deities.—**Theogonic**, thē-ō-gon′ik, *a.* Relating to theogony.—**Theogonist**, thē-og′on-ist, *n.* One versed in or a writer on theogony.

Theology, thē-ol′o-ji, *n.* [Gr. *theologia*—*theos*, God, and *logos*, discourse.] The science of divine things or of the Christian religion; the science which treats of God and man in all their known relations to each other.—**Theologian**, **Theologist**, thē-ō-lō′ji-an, thē-ol′o-jist, *n.* A person well versed in theology; a divine.—**Theologic**, **Theological**, thē-ō-loj′ik, thē-ō-loj′i-kal, *a.* Pertaining to theology.—**Theologically**, thē-ō-loj′i-kal-li, *adv.* In a theological manner; according to theology.—**Theologics**, thē-ō-loj′iks, *n.pl.* Theology.—**Theologize**, thē-ol′o-jīz, *v.i.*—*theologized*, *theologizing*. To theorize or speculate upon theological subjects.—**Theologizer**, thē-ol′o-jī-zėr, *n.* One who theologizes.

Theomachy, thē-om′a-ki, *n.* [Gr. *theos*, a god, and *machē*, combat.] A fighting against the gods; a strife or battle among the gods.

Theomancy, thē-om′an-si, *n.* [Gr. *theos*, God, and *manteia*, prophecy.] Divination from the responses of oracles, or persons supposed to be inspired by some divinity.

Theopathy, thē-op′a-thi, *n.* [Gr. *theos*, God, and *pathos*, passion.] Emotion excited by the contemplation of God; piety, or a sense of piety.—**Theopathetic**, **Theopathic**, thē′ō-pa-thet″ik, thē-ō-path′ik, *a.* Relating to theopathy.

Theophany, thē-of′a-ni, *n.* [Gr. *theos*, God, and *phainomai*, to appear.] A manifestation of God to man by actual appearance.—**Theophanic**, thē-ō-fan′ik, *a.* Relating to a theophany.

Theophilanthropist, thē′ō-fi-lan″-

throp-ist, *n.* [Gr. *theos*, God, *philos*, loving, *anthrōpos*, man.] One who practises or professes love to God and man; one of a society formed in the first French revolution, which had for its object to establish a new religion in place of Christianity.—**Theophilanthropic**, thē´o-fil-an-throp´´ik, *a.* Pertaining to theophilanthropy.—**Theophilanthropism, Theophilanthropy**, thē´ō-fi-lan´´throp-izm, thē´ō-fi-lan´´thrō-pi, *n.* Love to both God and man.

Theophilosophic, thē´ō-fil-ō-sof´´ik, *a.* [Gr. *theos*, God, and *philosophia*, philosophy.] Combining theism and philosophy.

Theopneusty, thē´op-nūs-ti, *n.* [Gr. *theopneustos*, inspired of God, from *theos*, God, and *pneō*, to breathe.] Divine inspiration. —**Theopneustic**, thē-op-nūs´tik, *a.* Given by inspiration of the Spirit of God; divinely inspired.

Theorbo, thē-or´bō, *n.* [It. *tiorba*, Fr. *téorbe.*] A musical instrument somewhat like a large lute, with two necks, to one of which the bass strings were attached.—**Theorbist**, thē-or´bist, *n.* One who played a theorbo.

Theorem, thē´ō-rem, *n.* [Gr. *theōrēma*, from *theōreō*, to look, to view. THEORY.] A position laid down as an acknowledged truth or established principle; *math.* a proposition to be proved by a chain of reasoning; *alg.* and *analysis*, a rule expressed by symbols or formulæ (the binomial *theorem*). —**Theorematic, Theorematical, Theoremic**, thē´ō-re-mat´´ik, thē´ō-re-mat´´i-kal, thē-ō-rem´ik, *a.* Pertaining to a theorem; comprised in a theorem.—**Theorematist**, thē-ō-rem´a-tist, *n.* One who forms theorems.

Theoric fund, thē-ō̆r´ik, *n.* [Gr. *theōreō*, to see.] The fund at Athens to enable the poorer classes to witness public spectacles of a dramatic or other nature.

Theory, thē´ō-ri, *n.* [L. *theoria*, a theory, from Gr. *theōria*, a looking at, theory, from *theōreō*, to see, from *theōros*, an observer.] A supposition explaining something; a doctrine or scheme of things resting merely on speculation; hypothesis; plan or system suggested; an exposition of the general or abstract principles of any science (the *theory* of music or of medicine); the science or rules of an art, as distinguished from the practice; a philosophical explanation of phenomena; a connected arrangement of facts according to their bearing on some real or hypothetical law or laws.—**Theoretic, Theoretical**, thē-ō-ret´ik, thē-ō-ret´i-kal, *a.* [Gr. *theōrētikos.*] Pertaining to theory; depending on theory or speculation; speculative; not practical.—**Theoretically**, thē-ō-ret´i-kal-li, *adv.* In or by theory; in speculation; speculatively; not practically.—**Theoretics**, thē-ō-ret´iks, *n.pl.* The speculative parts of a science; speculation.—**Theorist, Theorizer**, thē´ō-rist, thē´ō-rī-zėr, *n.* One who forms theories.—**Theorize**, thē´ō-rīz, *v.i.*—*theorized, theorizing.* To form a theory; to form opinions solely by theory; to speculate.

Theosophy, thē-os´o-fi, *n.* [Gr. *theosophia*, knowledge of divine things—*theos*, God, and *sophia*, wisdom, from *sophos*, wise.] Knowledge of divine things; a knowledge of the Divine Being obtained by spiritual ecstasy, direct intuition, or special individual relations.—**Theosophic, Theosophical, Theosophistical**, thē-ō-sof´ik, thē-ō-sof´i-kal, thē-os´o-fis´´ti-kal, *a.* Pertaining to theosophy.—**Theosophically**, thē-ō-sof´i-kal-li, *adv.* In a theosophical manner; with direct divine illumination.—**Theosophism**, thē-os´of-izm, *n.* Pretension to divine illumination.—**Theosophist, Theosopher**, thē-os´of-ist, thē-os´of-ėr, *n.* One who pretends to divine illumination, or to derive his knowledge from divine revelation.

Theotechnic, thē-ō-tek´nik, *a.* [Gr. *theos*, God, and *technē*, art.] Pertaining to the action or intervention of the gods.

Theotheca, thē´ō-thē-ka, *n.* [Gr. *theos*, God, and *thēkē*, a case.] Same as *Monstrance.*

Theow, thē-ou´, *n.* [A.Sax.] An Anglo-Saxon slave, serf, or bondman.

Therapeutic, Therapeutical, ther-a-pū´tik, ther-a-pū´ti-kal, *a.* [Gr. *therapeutikos*, from *therapeuō*, to nurse, serve, or cure.] Curative; pertaining to the healing art.—**Therapeutics**, ther-a-pū´tiks, *n.* That part of medicine which relates to the composition, application, and operation of remedies.—**Therapeutist**, ther-a-pū´tist, *n.* One versed in therapeutics.—**Therapy**, ther´a-pi, *n.* Therapeutics, as in *electrotherapy.*

There, ᴛʜār, *adv.* [A.Sax. *ther, thær*, there, a locative case of the pronominal stem *the, that, then,* &c. In *thereafter, thereby,* &c., the dative case fem. sing. of the definite article.] In that place; at that place: often opposed to *here, there* generally denoting the place most distant; in that object or matter; at that point; after going to such a length; into that place; to that place; thither; often used to begin sentences before a verb when there is an inversion of the subject (*there* came many strangers to the town).—*Here and there, neither here nor there.* Under HERE.—**Thereabout, Thereabouts**, ᴛʜār´a-bout, ᴛʜār´a-bouts, *adv.* Near that place; near that number, degree, or quantity.—**Thereafter**, ᴛʜār-af´tėr, *adv.* According to that; accordingly; after that; afterward. —**Thereat**, ᴛʜār-at´, *adv.* At that place; at that place or event; on that account.—**Thereaway**, ᴛʜār´a-wā, *adv.* Away in that place or direction.—**Thereby**, ᴛʜār-bī´, *adv.* By that; by that means; annexed or attached to that; by or near that place; near that number or quantity.—**Therefor**, ᴛʜār-for´, *adv.* For that or this or it.—**Therefore**, ᴛʜėr´for, *conj.* or *adv.* [*There*, the dat. sing. fem. of the old def. art., and *for.*] For that or this reason, referring to something previously stated; consequently; in return or recompense for this or that.—**Therefrom**, ᴛʜār-from´, *adv.* From this or that.—**Therein**, ᴛʜār-in´, *adv.* In that or this place, time, or thing; in that or this particular point or respect.—**Thereinto**, ᴛʜār-in-tö´, *adv.* Into that or this place.—**Thereof**, ᴛʜār-ov´, *adv.* Of that or this.—**Thereon**, ᴛʜār-on´, *adv.* On that or this; thereupon.—**Thereout**, ᴛʜār-out´, *adv.* Out of that or this.—**Thereto, Thereunto**, ᴛʜār-tö´, ᴛʜār-un-tö´, *adv.* To that or this.—**Theretofore**,† ᴛʜār-tö-fōr´, *adv.* Before that time; the counterpart of *heretofore.*—**Thereunder**, ᴛʜār-un´dėr, *adv.* Under that or this.—**Thereupon**, ᴛʜār-up-on´, *adv.* Upon that or this; in consequence of that; at once; without delay.—**Therewith**, ᴛʜār-with´, *adv.* With that or this.—**Therewithal**, ᴛʜār-with-al´, *adv.* With that or this; therewith.

Theriac, thē´ri-ak, *n.* [L. *theriaca*, Gr. *thēriakē*, from *thērion*, a wild beast.] A name given anciently to various substances esteemed efficacious against the effects of animal or other poison.—**Theriac, Theriacal, Therial**, thē´ri-ak, thē-rī´a-kal, thē´ri-al, *a.* Medicinal; serving as an antidote.

Theriomorphic, thē-ri-ō-mor´fik, *a.* [Gr. *thērion*, animal, *morphē*, shape.] Having the form of an animal.

Theriotomy, thē-ri-ot´o-mi, *n.* [Gr. *thērion*, a beast, and *tomē*, a cutting.] The anatomy of animals; zootomy.

Therm, therm, *n.* [Gr. *thermos*, hot.] A unit of heat, equal to 100,000 British thermal units.—**Thermal, Thermic**, thėr´mal, thėr´mik, *a.* Pertaining to heat; warm.—*Thermal springs, thermal waters*, hot springs.—*Thermal capacity.* See CAPACITY. —*Thermal efficiency*, in a heat engine, the ratio of the mechanical energy given out by the working substance to the heat energy supplied.—**Thermionic**, therm-ī-on´ik, *n.* [Gr. *thermos*, hot, and *iōn*, going.] Having reference to the ions or electrons given off by hot bodies.—*Thermionic valve*, an exhausted glass bulb with two or more, usually three, electrodes, viz. the metal plate, or anode, the grid, and filament. The filament when heated gives off electrons, which have a negative charge, so that a positive current of electricity can flow from plate to filament, but not in the reverse direction. The valve is of great importance in wireless telegraphy and telephony.—**Thermally**, thėr´mal-li, *adv.* In a thermal manner; with reference to heat. —**Thermite**, therm´it, *n.* [Gr. *thermos*, hot.] A mixture of aluminium powder with various oxides, used for generating intense heat.—**Thermo-chemistry**, *n.* That branch of chemistry in which heat is of importance.—**Thermo-current**, *n.* A current of thermo-electricity set up by heat. —**Thermo-dynamic**, *a.* Relating to thermo-dynamics.—**Thermo-dynamics**, *n.* That department of physics which deals with the conversion of heat into mechanical force or energy and vice versa. —**Thermo-electric**, *a.* Pertaining to thermo-electricity.—**Thermo-electricity**, *n.* Electricity produced at the junction of two metals, or at a point where a molecular change occurs in a bar of the same metal, when the junction or point is heated above or cooled below the general temperature of the conductor.—**Thermogene**, *n.* Cotton-wool, prepared to impart heat, as to the chest when affected by a cold, &c.—**Thermograph, Thermometrograph**, thėr´mō-graf, thėr-mō-met´rō-graf, *n.* An instrument for automatically recording variations of temperature.—**Thermo-magnetism**, *n.* Magnetism resulting from, or as affected by the action of heat.—**Thermometer**, thėr-mom´et-ėr, *n.* [Gr. *thermos*, warm, and *metron*, measure.] An instrument by which the temperatures of bodies are ascertained, usually a closed glass tube containing mercury or alcohol, which expands or contracts in accordance with the variations of temperature.—**Thermometric, Thermometrical**, thėr-mō-met´rik; thėr-mō-met´ri-kal, *a.* Pertaining to a thermometer; made by a thermometer.—**Thermometrically**, thėr-mō-met´ri-kal-li, *adv.* In a thermometrical manner.—**Thermometrograph**, thėr-mō-met´rō-graf, *n.* A self-registering thermometer.—**Thermo-pile**, *n.* An instrument for measuring very minute degrees of temperature.—**Thermoscope**, thėr´mō-skōp, *n.* An instrument by which changes of temperature are indicated and the effects of heat measured.—**Thermos-flask**, thėr´mos-flask, *n.* A flask with two walls separated by a vacuum, so that hot liquid in the inside receptacle remains hot for a considerable time.—**Thermostat**, thėr´mō-stat, *n.* [Gr. *statos*, standing.] A self-acting apparatus for regulating temperature.—**Thermotic, Thermotical**, thėr-mot´ik, thėr-mot´i-kal, *a.* [From Gr. *thermos*, warm.] Relating to heat; resulting from or dependent on heat.—**Thermotics**, thėr-mot´iks, *n.* The science of heat.

Thermidor, thėr´mi-dōr, *n.* [Gr. *thermos*, warm, *dōron*, gift.] The French Republican month from 19th July to 18th August. —**Thermidorian**, thėr-mi-dōr´i-an, *n.* One taking part in the *coup d'état* that brought on the fall of Robespierre, on the 9th Thermidor, in the second Republican year, 27th July, 1794.

Therology, thē-rol´o-ji, *n.* [Gr. *thēr*, *thēros*, a wild beast, and *logos*, discourse.] That branch of zoology which treats of the Mammalia.—**Therologist**, thē-rol´o-jist, *n.* One versed in therology.

Theromorph, thē´rō-morf, *n.* [Gr. *thēr*, beast, *morphē*, form.] An order of extinct reptiles of Permian and Triassic times, in some respects forerunners of mammals.

Thesaurus, thē-sa´rus, *n.* [L. *thesaurus*, from Gr. *thēsauros*, from (*ti*)*thēmi*, to place.] A treasury; a lexicon or treasury of words.

These, ᴛʜēz, *pron.* and *a.*, pl. of *this.*

Thesis, thē´sis, *n.* pl. **Theses**, thē´sēz. [L. *thesis*, Gr. *thesis*, a position, from (*ti*)*thēmi*, to set.] A position or proposition which a person advances and maintains; a subject propounded for a school or college exercise; the exercise itself; an essay or dissertation; *pros.* the part of a foot on which the depression of the voice falls: opposed to *arsis.*

Thespian, thes'pi-an, *a.* [From *Thespis*, who played an important part in the early history of the drama in Greece about B.C. 535.] Relating to Thespis, or to dramatic acting in general; hence, the *Thespian art* is equivalent to *the drama.*

Theurgy, thē'ėr-ji, *n.* [Gr. *theourgia*, from *theos*, a god, and *ergon*, work.] The working of some divine or supernatural agency in human affairs; a working or producing effects by spiritual means; magic.—**Theurgic, Theurgical**, thē-ėr'jik, thē-ėr'ji-kal, *a.* Pertaining to theurgy.—**Theurgist**, thē'ėr-jist, *n.* One who pretends to theurgy.

Thews, thūz, *n.pl.* [Perhaps same as A. Sax. *thedwas*, manners, habits.] Muscles, sinews, strength. — **Thewed**, thūd, *a.* Having thews, muscle, or strength. — **Thewy**, thū'i, *a.* Brawny; muscular.

They, ᴛʜā, *pron.*; poss. case *their*, obj. case *them*. [Partly from A.Sax. *thá*, nom. pl. of the def. art., partly from Icel. *their*, they, nom. pl. of the pers. pron.] The pl. form for *he, she*, or *it*, thus denoting more than one person or thing.

Thibet-cloth, ti-bet'kloth, *n.* A camlet or fabric of coarse goats' hair; a fine woollen cloth used for ladies' dresses.

Thick, thik, *a.* [A.Sax. *thicce* = O.Fris. *thikke*, Icel. *thykkr*, Dan. *tyk*, D. *dik*, G. *dick*, thick; probably akin to *thigh*, perhaps to *tight*.] Having more or less extent measured through and through or otherwise than in length or breadth: said of solid bodies; relatively of great dimensions when thus measured: opposed to *thin, slender, slim*; dense; having great consistence (*thick* fog or smoke); foggy or misty; close set or planted; closely crowded together; close; following each other closely (blows *thick* as hail); without due flexibility of articulation (*thick* utterance); stupid; gross; very friendly or familiar (*colloq.*).—*n.* The thickest part, or the time when anything is thickest.—*Thick and thin*, whatever is in the way; all obstacles or hindrances.—*adv.* In close succession one upon another; fast or close together.—**Thick-coming**, *a.* Coming or following in close succession; crowding one after another.—**Thicken**, thik'n, *v.t.* To make thick or thicker.—*v.i.* To become thick or thicker.—**Thickening**, thik'n-ing, *n.* Something put into a liquid or mass to make it more thick.—**Thicket**, thik'et, *n.* [Comp. G. *dickicht*, from *dick*, thick.] A wood or collection of trees or shrubs closely set. — **Thick-head**, *n.* A stupid fellow; a blockhead; a numskull.—**Thick-headed**, *a.* Dull; stupid.—**Thickish**, thick'ish, *a.* Somewhat dull.—**Thick-knee**, *n.* The stone-plover or stone-curlew.—**Thickly**, thik'li, *adv.* In a thick manner or condition; to considerable depth on a surface; closely. — **Thickness**, thik'nes, *n.* The state of being thick in any sense of the word; measure through from surface to surface; density; consistence; closeness or crowded state; clumsy indistinctness of speech.—**Thickset**, thik'set, *a.* Close set or planted; having a short thick body; thick; stout; stumpy.—*n.* A close or thick hedge; dense underwood.—**Thickskin**, thik'skin, *n.* A stolid person, not easily irritated by taunts or ridicule.—**Thick-skinned**, *a.* Having a thick skin or rind; not easily moved or irritated, as by taunts, ridicule, or the like.

Thief, thēf, *n.* pl. **Thieves**, thēvz. [A.Sax. *theóf*=Icel. *thjófr*, Sw. *tjuf*, D. *dief*, G. *dieb*, Goth. *thjubs*, thief; root doubtful.] A person who steals or is guilty of theft; one who deprives another of property secretly or without open force: as opposed to a *robber*, who openly uses violence.—*Thieves' Latin*, a jargon used by thieves.—**Thieve**, thēv, *v.i.*—*thieved, thieving.* To steal; to practise theft.—*v.t.* To take by theft; to steal.—**Thievery**, thē'vėr-i, *n.* The practice of stealing; theft.—**Thievish**, thē'vish, *a.* Given to stealing; of the nature of theft.—**Thievishly**, thē'vish-li, *adv.* In a thievish manner.—**Thievishness**, thē'vish-nes, *n.*

Thigh, thī, *n.* [A.Sax. *theóh*, the thigh = Icel. *thjó*, O.H.G. *dioh*, D. *dij*, O.D. *dygh*, thigh; probably allied to *thick*.] The thick fleshy portion of the leg between the knee and the trunk.—**Thigh-bone**, *n.* The bone of the thigh; the femur.

Thill, thil, *n.* [A.Sax. *thill, thille*, a stake, board; Icel. *thili, thil*, a deal, a plank; G. *diele*, a board; same root as Skr. *tala*, surface.] The shaft of a cart, gig, or other carriage.—**Thiller, Thill-horse**, thil'ėr, *n.* A horse going between shafts.

Thimble, thim'bl, *n.* [A.Sax. *thýmel*, a thimble, from *thúma*, thumb; having no doubt been first worn on the thumb, as the sailor's thimble still is. THUMB.] A metal cap or cover for the finger, used in sewing for driving the needle through; *naut.* an iron ring with a rope spliced round it.—**Thimble-case**, *n.* A case for holding a thimble.—**Thimbleful**, thim'bl-ful, *n.* As much as a thimble would hold; hence, a very small quantity. — **Thimblerig**, thim'bl-rig, *n.* [From *rig*, a trick.] A sleight-of-hand trick, played with three thimbles and a small ball or pea.—**Thimblerigger**, thim'bl-rig-ėr, *n.* One who practises the trick of thimblerig.

Thin, thin, *a.* [A.Sax. *thynne*, thin = Icel. *thunnr*, D. *dun*, Sw. *tunn*, G. *dünn*, cog. L. *tenuis*, Skr. *tanus*, thin; W. *tenau, teneu*, thin, rare; Ir. *tana*, thin, slender; all from root, *tan*, to stretch; seen also in L. *tendo*, to stretch, E. *tend*; Gr. *tonos*; G. *tonus*, E. *tone*; L. *tener*, E. *tender*, &c.] Not thick; having little extent from one surface to the opposite (a *thin* plate, a *thin* board); slight; flimsy (a *thin* veil); rare; not dense: said of aeriform fluids; deficient in body or substance: said of liquids or semi-liquids; not close or crowded; sparse; not abundant (*thin* grass); not numerously filled; slim; slender; lean; faint; feeble; destitute of fulness or volume, as sound; often used adverbially in composition as the first element in compounds (*thin*-clad).—*v.t.*—*thinned, thinning.* To make thin in all its senses. —*v.i.* To diminish in thickness; to grow or become thin: with *out, away*, &c.—**Thinly**, thin'li, *adv.* In a thin, loose, scattered manner.—**Thinner**, thin'ėr, *n.* One who thins or makes thin. — **Thinness**, thin'nes, *n.* The state of being thin. —**Thinnish**, thin'ish, *a.* Somewhat thin. —**Thin-skinned**, *a.* Having a thin skin; hence, unduly sensitive; easily offended; irritable.

Thine, ᴛʜīn, *pronominal adj.* [A.Sax. *thin*, thine, genit. of *thú*, thou. The loss of the *n* produced *thy*. THOU.] Thy; belonging to thee: used with or without a noun, and either for a nominative or objective or a predicate. ∴ *Thine*, like *thou*, is now used only in poetry or the solemn style, *your* and *yours* otherwise taking its place.

Thing, thing, *n.* [A.Sax. *thing*, a meeting, cause, affair, &c.; L.G. and G. *ding*, thing, matter, Dan. and Sw. *ting*, Icel. *thing*, a court, an assembly; root doubtful.] Whatever exists, or is conceived to exist, as a separate entity; whatever may be spoken or thought of; an inanimate object; a creature; applied to man and animals in pity, contempt, tenderness, or admiration; a transaction, matter, circumstance, event; *pl.* clothes, personal belongings, luggage. —*The thing*, as it ought to be: a colloquial phrase applied to an ideal or typical condition.

Think, thingk, *v.i.*—pret. and pp. *thought.* [A.Sax. *thincan, thencan*, to think = Goth. *thagkjan*, G. and D. *denken*, Icel. *thekkja*, Dan. *tænke*; allied to *thank*, and to A.Sax. *thyncan*, to seem, whence *methinks*.] To have the mind occupied on some subject; to revolve ideas in the mind; to perform any mental operation; to cogitate; to muse; to meditate; to consider; to deliberate; to judge, conclude, be of opinion (I *think* it will rain); to purpose, design, intend; to imagine, suppose, fancy.—*To think of*, to estimate; to esteem (to *think* little *of* a book).—*To think on* or *upon*, to meditate or muse on; to light on or discover by meditation (to *think on* an expedient).—*v.t.* To form in the mind; to imagine; to hold in opinion; to regard, consider, esteem; to form a conception of.—*To think scorn*, to disdain; to scorn.—*To think shame*, to feel shame; to be ashamed.—**Thinkable**, thingk'a-bl, *a.* Capable of being thought; conceivable; cogitable.—**Thinker**, thingk'ėr, *n.* One who thinks; one who reasons or meditates (a deep *thinker*); one who writes on speculative subjects.—**Thinking**, thingk'ing, *a.* Able to think; having the faculty of thought.—*n.* The act or state of one who thinks; thought; cogitation.—**Thinkingly**, thingk'ing-li, *adv.* By thought.

Thinly, Thinness, &c. Under THIN.

Thio, thī'ō, *n.* [Gr. *theion*, sulphur.] An adjective or combining form, indicating the presence of sulphur in a compound.

Thiosulphate, thī-ō-sul'fāt, *n.* Any salt of thiosulphuric acid, $H_2S_2O_3$, analogous to sulphuric acid, H_2SO_4.

Third, thėrd, *a.* [A.Sax. *thridda*; cog. Goth. *thridja*, Icel. *thrithi*, Sw. *tredje*, Dan. *tredie*, D. *derde*, G. *dritte*, Gr. *tritos*, L. *tertius*, Skr. *tritiya*, W. *trydy*, Gael. *treas*—all from words signifying *three*. THREE.] Next after the second; being one of three equal parts into which anything is divided. —*Third estate*, in Great Britain, the commonalty or commons, represented by the House of Commons.—*Third person, gram.* the person spoken of; *the third person* in the Trinity, the Holy Spirit.—*n.* The third part of anything; the sixtieth part of a second of time; *mus.* an interval consisting of three conjunct degrees of the scale; the upper of the two notes including this interval.—**Third-borough**,† *n.* An under-constable.—**Thirdly**, thėrd'li, *adv.* In the third place.—**Third-rate**, *a.* Next below second-rate; quite inferior; in the *navy*, applied to a certain class of men-of-war.

Thirst, thėrst, *n.* [A.Sax. *thyrst, thurst*, thirst = Sw. and Dan. *törst*, Icel. *thorsti*, D. *dorst*, G. *durst*, Goth. *thaurstei*, thirst; allied to Icel. *thurr*, G. *dürr*, dry, the root being that of L. *torridus*, torrid, *terra*, the earth, the dry land; Gr. *tersomai*, to be dry; Skr. *tarsh*, to thirst.] The desire, uneasiness, or suffering occasioned by want of drink; vehement desire for drink; a want and eager desire after anything (a *thirst* for knowledge).—*v.i.* [A.Sax. *thyrstan*, Icel. *thyrsta*.] To experience thirst; to have desire to drink; to have a vehement desire for anything.—**Thirster**, thėrs'tėr, *n.* One who thirsts.—**Thirsty**, thėrs'ti, *a.* [A.Sax. *thyrstig*.] Feeling a painful sensation for want of drink; having thirst; very dry; parched; having a vehement desire of anything.—**Thirstily**, thėrs'ti-li, *adv.* In a thirsty manner. — **Thirstiness**, thėrs'ti-nes, *n.* The state of being thirsty.

Thirteen, thėr'tēn, *a.* [A.Sax. *threótyne*, lit. three-ten.] Ten and three. — *n.* The number which consists of ten and three.—**Thirteenth**, thėr'tēnth, *a.* The third after the tenth; being one of thirteen equal parts of a thing.—*n.* One of thirteen equal parts of anything.

Thirty, thėr'ti, *a.* [A.Sax. *thrittig, thritig*, from *threó, thré*, three, and *-tig*, ten = L. *decem*, Gr. *deka*, ten.] Thrice ten; ten three times repeated. — *n.* The number which consists of three times ten.—**Thirtieth**, thėr'ti-eth, *a.* The next in order after the twenty-ninth; being one of thirty equal parts of a thing.—*n.* One of thirty equal parts of anything.

This, ᴛʜis, *a.* and *pron.* pl. **These**, ᴛʜēz, [A.Sax. masc. *thes*, fem. *theos*, neut. *this*, from the pronominal stem seen in *the, that, thither*, &c., and A.Sax. *se, sa*, he (=Skr. *sa*, he).] A demonstrative used with or without a noun to denote something that is present or near in place or time, or something just mentioned: often opposed to *that* (the latter referring to something more remote); applied to time, *this* may refer to the present time; now; to time next to come, or to time immediately ended; frequently used to signify present state, condition, &c.

Thistle, this'l, *n.* [A.Sax. *thistel*, a thistle =Icel. *thistill*, G. and D. *distel*, Sw. *tistel*, Sc. *thrissle*, thistle; origin doubtful.] The common name of a tribe of prickly plants of numerous species, most of them inhabitants of Europe; regarded as the national emblem of Scotland.—**Thistle-finch**, *n.* The goldfinch.—**Thistly**, this'l-i, *a.* Overgrown with thistles; resembling a thistle; prickly.

Thither, THITH'ėr, *adv.* [A.Sax. *thider*, Icel. *thathra*, thither, there; from demonstrative stem seen in *the*, *that*, and suffix *ther*=*tra* in Skr. *tatra*, there, from root *tar*, to go.] To that place: opposed to *hither*; to that end or result.—*Hither and thither*, to this place and that; one way and another. — **Thitherward**, THITH'ėr-wėrd, *adv.* Toward that place.

Thlipsis, thlip'sis, *n.* [Gr. *thlipsis*, pressure, from *thlibō*, to press.] *Med.* compression; constriction of vessels by an external cause.

Tho', THŌ. A contraction of *though*.

Thole, **Thole-pin**, thōl, *n.* [A.Sax. *thol*, a thole-pin = Icel. *thollr*, a thole-pin, a wooden peg; L.G. *dolle*, D. *dol*, a thole.] A pin inserted into the gunwale of a boat to serve as a fulcrum for the oar in rowing; often in pairs, the oar resting between; also written *Thowl*.

Thole, thōl, *v.t.*—*tholed*, *tholing*. [A.Sax. *tholian* = Goth. *thulan*, Icel. *thola*, to endure; same root as L. *tolerare*, to tolerate.] To bear; to endure; to undergo. (*Prov.*)

Tholobate, thol'ō-bāt, *n.* [Gr. *tholos*, a dome, and *basis*, basis.] *Arch.* the substructure on which a dome rests.

Thomist, tom'ist, *n.* A follower of the scholastic philosophy of *Thomas* Aquinas, in opposition to *Scotist*.

Thong, thong, *n.* [A.Sax. *thwang*, *thwong*, a thong; Icel. *thvengr*, a strap, a latchet.] A strap of leather used for fastening anything; a long narrow strip of leather or similar material.

Thor, thor, *n.* [Icel. *Thórr*, from older *Thonor*, equivalent to A.Sax. *thunor*, E. *thunder*. THUNDER.] The second principal god of the ancient Scandinavians, the god of thunder; son of Odin. *Thursday* is called after him.

Thorax, thō'raks, *n.* [Gr. *thōrax*, the chest, a breastplate.] The cavity of the body formed by the spine, ribs, and breast-bone, and containing the lungs, heart, &c.; the chest; the corresponding portion of animals; the portion of an insect between the head and abdomen.—**Thoracic**, thō-ras'ik, *a.* Pertaining to or contained in the thorax or chest.—*Thoracic duct*, *anat.* the vessel which receives the chyle conveyed by the lacteals, and carries it along the spine to the left subclavian vein, where it enters the blood.

Thorium, **Thorinum**, thō'ri-um, thō-rī'num, *n.* [From *Thor*, the Scandinavian deity.] A metal obtained as a gray powder which burns with great splendour.—**Thoria**, **Thorina**, thō'ri-a, thō-rī'na, *n.* An oxide of thorium.—**Thorite**, thō'rīt, *n.* A mineral found in Norway containing thorium.

Thorn, thorn, *n.* [A.Sax. *thorn*=Icel. *thorn*, Goth. *thaurnus*, Dan. *torn*, D. *doorn*, G. *dorn*; same word as Pol. *tarn*, Bohem. *trn*. Probably from a root meaning to pierce, seen also in *through*, *thrill*, &c.] A common name of trees and shrubs armed with spines or prickles, as the black-thorn, buckthorn, and especially the common hawthorn; any sharp-pointed spiny or prickly process growing on a plant; *fig.* anything that annoys or torments sharply; a care or trouble.—**Thorn-apple**, *n.* An annual plant of the potato family with narcotic properties, used medicinally. — **Thornback**, *n.* A species of skate with spines on its back and tail.—**Thorn-hedge**, *n.* A hedge of hawthorn.—**Thorny**, thor'ni, *a.* Full of thorns, spines, or prickles; prickly; vexatious; harassing.

Thorough, thur'ō, *a.* [Same word as *through*.] Going completely to the end; extending to all particulars; complete; perfect.—*Thorough bass*, the mode of expressing chords by means of figures placed over or under a given bass, such figures indicating the harmony *through* all the other parts; also sometimes used as equivalent to *harmony*.—**Thorough-bred**, *a.* Of pure or unmixed breed, bred from a sire and dam of purest blood; hence, high-spirited; mettlesome.—*n.* An animal, especially a horse, of pure blood.—**Thoroughfare**, thur'ō-fār, *n.* [A.Sax. *thurhfaru*.] An unobstructed way; especially an unobstructed road or street for public traffic. —**Thorough-going**, *a.* Going or ready to go all lengths; extreme.—**Thorough-lighted**, *a.* Having windows on opposite sides, the light not being intercepted by partitions.—**Thoroughly**, thur'ō-li, *adv.* In a thorough manner; fully; completely. —**Thoroughness**, thur'ō-nes, *n.*—**Thorough-paced**, *a.* *Lit.* trained to go through all the paces of a well-trained horse; hence, going all lengths; downright; consummate.

Thorp, **Thorpe**, thorp, *n.* [A.Sax. *thorp* =Icel. *thorp*, Sw. and Dan. *torp*, D. *dorp*, G. *dorf*, a village, a hamlet.] A group of houses standing together in the country; a hamlet; a village.

Those, THŌz, *a.* and *pron.* Historically the plural of *this*, being another form of *these*, but used as plural of *that*.

Thoth, thoth, *n.* An Egyptian divinity whom the Greeks considered to be identical with Hermes (Mercury).

Thou, THou, *pron.*; obj. and dat. *thee*, pl. *ye* or *you*. [A.Sax. *thú*, genit. *thín*, dat. and acc. *thé*, nom. pl. *gé*, genit. *eówer*, dat. and acc. *eów*; Icel. *thú*, Goth. *thu*, D., Dan., and G. *du*; L. *tu*, Gr. *su*, *tu*, Skr. *tvam*, Slav. *ti*, W. *ti*, Gael. *tu*, thou.] The second personal pronoun in the singular number: used to indicate the person spoken to; but in ordinary language the plural form *you* is now universally substituted, *thou* being used in the poetical or solemn style, as also among the Friends or Quakers.

Though, THŌ, *conj.* [A.Sax. *theáh*, though =Icel. *thó*, Dan. *dog*, D. and G. *doch*, Goth. *thauh*, though; from stem of *that*, *the*.] Granting or allowing it to be the fact that; notwithstanding that.—*As though*, as if.—*What though*, elliptically for what though the fact or case is so. . . Syn. under WHILE, ALTHOUGH.—*adv.* However; for all that.

Thought, that, pret. and pp. of *think*.

Thought, that, *n.* [A.Sax. *thoht*, *gethoht*, from *thencan*, to think, pret. *thohte*, pp. *gethoht*; Icel. *thótti*, G. *gedacht*. THINK.] The act or power of thinking; cogitation; meditation; that which is thought; an idea; a conception; a judgment; a fancy; a conceit; deliberation; reflection; solicitude. —*A thought*, a small degree or quantity. (*Colloq.*)—*Second thoughts*, maturer reflection; after-consideration.—**Thoughtful**, that'ful, *a.* Full of thought; contemplative; meditative; attentive; careful; mindful; full of anxiety; solicitous.—**Thoughtfully**, that'ful-li, *adv.* In a thoughtful manner. — **Thoughtfulness**, that'ful-nes, *n.* Serious attention; solicitude. — **Thoughtless**, that'les, *a.* Free from thought or care; heedless; negligent; light-minded. — **Thoughtlessly**, that'les-li, *adv.* Without thought; carelessly. — **Thoughtlessness**, that'les-nes, *n.* The quality of being thoughtless; heedlessness; inattention.—**Thought-reading**, *n.* A so-called psychical power by which it is claimed some persons are able to read the thoughts of others, or at least tell the object of their thoughts.—**Thought-reader**, *n.* One who possesses or pretends to possess the power of thought-reading.

Thousand, thou'zand, *n.* [A.Sax. *thúsend* = Icel. *thús-hund*, *thús-hundrath*, Dan. *tusind*, D. *duizend*, Goth. *thúsundi*, G. *tausend*.] The number of ten hundred; proverbially, a great number.—*a.* Denoting the number of ten hundred, or proverbially, a great number indefinitely.—**Thousandfold**, thou'zand-fōld, *a.* Multiplied by a thousand.—**Thousandth**, thou'zandth, *a.* Completing the number of a thousand; being one of a thousand equal parts of anything.—*n.* The thousandth part of anything.

Thowel, **Thowl**, thōl, *n.* THOLE.

Thrall, thral, *n.* [A.Sax. *thræl* = Icel. *thræll*, Sw. *träl*, Dan. *træl*, a serf, a slave.] A slave; a bondman.—**Thraldom**, thral'-dom, *n.* Slavery; bondage.

Thrap,† thrap, *v.t.* [Altered from *frap*.] *Naut.* to frap.

Thrash, **Thresh**, thrash, thresh, *v.t.* [A.Sax. *threscan*, *therscan*, to thrash (corn), to beat = Icel. *threskja*, Sw. *tröska*, Dan. *tærske*, D. *dorschen*, G. *dreschen*, Goth. *thriskan*; comp. Lith. *trasketi*, to rattle.] To beat out or separate the grain or seeds from by a flail or thrashing-machine, or by treading with oxen; to beat soundly with a stick or whip; to drub.—*v.i.* To drive out grain from straw.—**Thrasher**, **Thresher**, thrash'ėr, thresh'ėr, *n.* One who thrashes grain; a species of shark which uses its tail as a weapon.—**Thrashing**, **Threshing**, thrash'ing, thresh'ing, *n.* The operation by which grain is thrashed; a beating or drubbing.—**Thrashing-floor**, *n.* A floor or area on which grain is beaten out.—**Thrashing-machine**, **Thrashing-mill**, *n.* A machine for separating grain from the straw, and in which the moving power is that of horses, oxen, wind, water, or steam.

Thrasonical, thrā-son'i-kal, *a.* [From *Thraso*, a boaster in old comedy.] Given to bragging; boastful.—**Thrasonically**, thrā-son'i-kal-li, *adv.* Boastingly.

Thrave, thrāv, *n.* [Icel. *threfi*, a thrave; Dan. *trave*, a score of sheaves.] Two stooks or shocks of a grain crop of twelve sheaves each.

Thread, thred, *n.* [A.Sax. *thraed*, lit. what is twisted, from *thráwan*, to twist, to throw; similarly Icel. *thráðr*, Dan. *traad*, D. *draad*, G. *draht*, thread. THROW.] A fine cord, especially such as is used for sewing; the filaments of fibrous substances, such as cotton, flax, silk, or wool, spun out into a slender line; anything resembling this; any slender filament; continued course or tenor (the *thread* of a discourse); the prominent spiral part of a screw.—*v.t.* To pass a thread through the eye or aperture of; to pass or go through, as through a narrow way or any intricate course. — **Threadbare**, thred'bār, *a.* Having the nap worn off so as to show the separate threads; hence, trite; hackneyed; used till it has lost novelty or interest.—**Threadbareness**, thred'bār-nes, *n.*—**Thread-cell**, *n.* NEMATOCYST.—**Threader**, thred'ėr, *n.* One who threads. —**Threadiness**, thred'i-nes, *n.* The state of being thready.—**Thread-lace**, *n.* Lace made of linen thread.—**Thread-paper**, *n.* A thin strip of paper for wrapping up a skein of thread.—**Thready**, thred'i, *a.* Like thread; filamentous; containing thread.

Threat, thret, *n.* [A.Sax. *threát*, threat, punishment; from stem of A.Sax. *threótan*, to tire, harass; Goth. *thriutan*, G. (*ver*)*driessen*, to annoy; allied to L. *trudo*, to thrust (in *intrude*).] A menace; a declaration of an intention to inflict punishment, loss, or pain on another.—*v.t.* and *i.* To threaten. (*Shak.*)—**Threaten**, thret'n, *v.t.* To use threats towards; to declare an intention of injuring; to menace; to menace by action; to act as if intending to injure; to exhibit the appearance of bringing something evil or unpleasant on (the clouds *threaten* us with rain); to show to be impending (the sky *threatens* a storm).—*v.i.* To use threats or menaces.—**Threatener**, thret'n-ėr, *n.* One that threatens. — **Threatening**, thret'n-ing, *a.* Indicating a threat or menace; indicating something impending. — **Threateningly**, thret'n-ing-li, *adv.* In a threatening manner.

Threave, thrēv, *n.* Same as *Thrave*.

Three, thrē, *a.* [A.Sax. *thri*, *threó*=Goth. *threis*, Icel. *thrír*, Dan. *tre*, D. *drie*, G. *drei*; cog. W., Ir., and Gael. *tri*, Lith. *trys*, L. *tres*, Gr. *treis*, Skr. *tri*.] Two and one.—*Three-times-three*, three cheers thrice repeated.—*n.* The number which consists of two and one; a symbol representing this.—*Rule of three*, the arithmetical rule otherwise called *Proportion*. — **Three-cornered**, *a.* Having three corners or angles; triangular.—**Three-decker**, *n.* A vessel of war carrying guns on three decks.—**Threefold**, thrē'fōld, *a.* Consisting of three in one; triple.—*adv.* In a threefold manner; trebly.—**Three-foot**, *a.* Measuring three feet; as, a *three-foot* rule.—

Three-pence, *n.* A silver coin of Great Britain, with a value equivalent to six cents.—**Three-penny**, *a.* Worth three pence or six cents, hence, of little worth.—**Three-phase**, *a. Elect.* a system of alternating current supply, in which there are three circuits differing in phase by 120° from each other.—**Three-pile**, *n.* An old name for the finest and most costly kind of velvet.—**Three-ply**, *a.* Threefold; consisting of three strands, or three thicknesses, &c.

Threne, thrēn, *n.* [L. *threnus*, from Gr. *thrēnos*, lamentation.] A complaint or lamentation.—**Threnetic, Threnetical**, thrē-net'ik, thrē-net'i-kal, *a.* Sorrowful; mournful.—**Threnodial**, thrē-nō'di-al, *a.* Pertaining to a threnody; elegiac.

Thresh, *v.t.* To beat out grain by striking the stalks with a flail or by passing them through a threshing machine; to go over a matter again and again; to *thresh out* a subject. See THRASH.

Threshold, thresh'ōld, *n.* [A.Sax. *therscwald, therscold, therxold*, from *therscan*, to thrash or thresh, and apparently *wald*, a wood, timber, because this bar was thrashed or trod upon by the feet.] A door-sill; the stone or piece of timber which lies under a door; hence, entrance; beginning; outset (the *threshold* of an argument).—*Threshold of consciousness, psych.* the point at which a stimulus to the sensory organism is just sufficiently intense to be felt.

Threw, thrö, pret. of *throw*.

Thrice, thrīs, *adv.* [O.E. *thries, thryes*, from *thrie*, three, with genit. term., like *once, twice*.] Three times; also often used for emphasis or intensity (*thrice* blessed, &c.).

Thrift, thrift, *n.* [From Icel. *thrift*. THRIVE.] A thriving state or condition (*Shak.*)‡; economical management in regard to property; economy; frugality; a plant which grows on mountains and along the seacoasts of the North Temperate Zone.—**Thriftily**, thrif'ti-li, *adv.* In a thrifty manner; frugally.—**Thriftiness**, thrif'ti-nes, *n.* The quality of being thrifty; economy; frugality.—**Thriftless**, thrift'-les, *a.* Having no thrift; profuse; extravagant.—**Thriftlessly**, thrift'les-li, *adv.* Extravagantly.—**Thriftlessness**, thrift'-les-nes, *n.* The quality of being thriftless.—**Thrifty**, thrif'ti, *a.* Having thrift; careful in husbanding resources; frugal; economical.

Thrill, thril, *v.t.* [A.Sax. *thyrlian, thyrelian* (from *thirl, thyrel*, a hole = *tril* of nos*tril*), to pierce = D. *drillen*, to bore, to drill troops (whence E. to *drill*); same root as *through*.] To pierce in a figurative sense; to effect with a keen emotion, as of delight or excitement.—*v.i.* to penetrate, to produce a tingling sensation; to act tremulously, to vibrate; to feel a shivering sensation running through the body; to shiver; to quiver or move with a tremulous movement.—*n.* A warbling; a trill; a thrilling sensation.

Thrinax, thrī'naks, *n.* A kind of North American palm, the leaves of which are used for making fans and for the purpose of thatching.

Thrip, thrip, *v.t.* To make a snapping noise, as with the fingers. [*Obs.*].

Thrive, thrīv, *v.i.*—pret. *throve*; pp. *thriven* (thriv'n); ppr. *thriving*. [From Icel. *thrifask*, to thrive (a reflexive verb, *sk* meaning self, as in *bask*), whence also *thrift*, thrift; Dan. *trives*, to thrive.] To prosper or succeed; to be fortunate; to increase in goods and estate; to keep increasing one's acquisitions; to be marked by prosperity (a *thriving* business); to go on or turn out well; to have a good issue; to grow vigorously or luxuriantly; to flourish.—**Thriver**, thrī'vėr, *n.* One who thrives.—**Thriving**, thrī'ving, *a.* Being prosperous; advancing in wealth; flourishing.—**Thrivingly**, thrī'ving-li, *adv.* In a thriving or prosperous way.—**Thrivingness**, thrī'ving-nes, *n.*

Thro', thrö, *a.* Contraction of *Through*.

Throat, thrōt, *n.* [A.Sax. *throte*; akin G. *drossel*, the throat, the throttle; comp. D. *strot*, throat; hence *throttle*.] The anterior part of the neck of an animal, in which are the gullet and windpipe; the fauces; the pharynx; an opening or entrance somewhat resembling the throat (the *throat* of a valley); *bot.* the mouth of a monopetalous corolla; *arch.* the part of a chimney between the gathering and the flue; *fort.* same as *Gorge*.—*To lie in one's throat*, to lie outrageously.—**Throaty**, thrō'ti, *a.* Guttural; uttered back in the throat.

Throb, throb, *v.i.*—*throbbed, throbbing*. [O.E. *throbbe*; origin doubtful.] To beat, as the heart or pulse, with more than usual force or rapidity; to palpitate; to quiver or vibrate.—*Throbbing pain*, a pain augmented by the pulsation of the arteries.—*n.* A beat or strong pulsation; palpitation.—**Throbless**, throb'les, *a.* Not beating or throbbing.

Throe, thrō, *n.* [A.Sax. *threá*, affliction, from *threáwan*, to afflict; akin Icel. *thrá*, a throe, a hard struggle.] Extreme pain; agony; the anguish of travail in child-birth; a cleaving tool; a frow.

Thrombus, throm'bus, *n.* [L., from Gr. *thrombos*, a clot.] A fibrinous clot of blood which forms in and obstructs a blood-vessel.—**Thrombosis**, throm'bō-sis, *n.* [Gr.] *Pathol.* the obstruction of a blood-vessel by a thrombus.

Throne, thrōn, *n.* [O.Fr. *throne*, L. *thronus*, from Gr. *thronos*, a seat, chair.] An elevated and ornamental chair of state used by a king, emperor, pope, bishop, &c.; the official chair of a presiding official of certain societies; sovereign power and dignity; also, the wielder of that power: usually with *the*.—*v.t.*—*throned, throning*. To place on a royal seat; to enthrone; to exalt.—**Throneless**, thrōn'les, *a.* Without a throne; deposed.

Throng, throng, *n.* [A.Sax. *thrang, throng*, a crowd, from *thringan*, to crowd; Icel. *thröng*, G. *drang*, a crowd, distress; D. and G. *dringen*, to crowd; same root as L. *torqueo*, to twist (whence *torsion, torture*, &c.).] A multitude of persons pressed into a close body; a crowd; a great number; a number of things crowded or close together (a *throng* of words).—*v.i.* To crowd together; to come in multitudes.—*v.t.* To crowd or press; to annoy with a crowd of living beings; to fill with a crowd.

Thropple, throp'l, *n.* [Corrupted from *throttle*.] The windpipe; the throttle.

Throstle, thros'l, *n.* [A dim. corresponding to *thrush*; A.Sax. *throstle*, G. and Dan. *drossel*, a thrush. THRUSH.] The song-thrush or mavis; a machine for spinning wool, cotton, &c., from the rove.—**Throstle-cock**, *n.* The male thrush.

Throttle, throt'l, *n.* [From *throat*.] The windpipe or trachea; the throat (*colloq.*).—*v.t.*—*throttled, throttling*. To choke; to stop the breath of by compressing the throat; to strangle; to pronounce with a choking voice (*Shak.*).—**Throttler**, throt'-lėr, *n.* One who throttles.—**Throttle-valve**, *n.* *Steam-engines*, a valve which regulates the supply of steam to the cylinder.

Through, Thru, thrö, *prep.* [O.E. *thurgh, thurch*, A.Sax. *thurh*, G. *durch*, D. *door*, Goth, *thairh*; cog. W. *trw*, Armor, *tre*, through; L. *trans*, over, across; the root is Indo-European *tar*, Skr. *tri, tar*, to penetrate, seen also in E. *thrill, trite*, &c. *Thorough* is the same word.] From end to end or from side to side of; between the sides or walls of (to pass *through* a gate); by the agency of; by means of; on account of; over the whole surface or extent of; throughout; among or in the midst of, in the way of passage; among, in the way of experiencing; from beginning to end of.—*adv.* From one end or side to the other; from beginning to end; to the end; to completion.—*To carry through*, to complete; to accomplish.—*To fall through*, to come to an unsuccessful issue; to fail.—*To go through with* something, to prosecute it to the end.—*a.* Going with little or no interruption from one important place or center to another (a *through* passenger, a *through* journey).—**Through-carriage**, *n.* A carriage in a through-train.—**Throughly**,‡ thrö'li, *adv.* Completely; thoroughly.—**Throughout**, thrö-out', *prep.* Quite through in every part of: from one extremity to the other of.—*adv.* Everywhere; in every part.—**Through-service**, accommodations requiring no change of transportation.—**Through-ticket**, *n.* A ticket for the whole of a long journey.—**Through-traffic**, *n.* Traffic given right-of-way over other traffic.—**Through-train**, *n.* A train which goes the whole length of a railway, or a long route.

Throve, thrōv, pret. of *thrive*.

Throw, thrō, *v.t.*—*threw* (thrö), *thrown* (thrōn). [A.Sax. *thráwan*, to twist (as to *throw* silk), to throw; akin D. *draaijen*, G. *drehen*, to twist, to turn; same root as L. *torqueo*, to twist, to throw (whence *torture*). *Thread* is a derivative.] To fling or cast in any manner; to hurl, to dash: often *refl.* (*threw* himself on the enemy); to prostrate, as in wrestling; to overturn; to divest one's self of; to shed; to give violent utterance or expression to; to send (to *throw* defiance); to put on or over with haste or negligence; to wind or twist two or more filaments of, as of silk, so as to form one thread; *pottery*, to form or shape roughly on a wheel or throwing-engine.—*To throw away*, to cast away; to part with or bestow without compensation; to spend recklessly; to squander; to waste; to reject; to refuse.—*To throw back*, to cast or hurl back; to reject; to retort.—*To throw by*, to cast or lay aside as useless.—*To throw down*, to cast on the ground; to overturn; to subvert; to destroy.—*To throw in*, to cast or fling in or into; to put in or deposit along with others; to interpolate; to give or add to the bargain.—*To throw off*, to cast off or aside; to discard; to reject; to print at one impression.—*To throw one's self on* or *upon*, to resign one's self to the favour, benevolence, protection, &c., of.—*To throw open*, to open suddenly or widely; to give free or unrestricted admission to.—*To throw out*, to cast out; to eject; to reject or discard; to expel; to construct so as to project; to emit; to insinuate (to *throw out* a hint).—*To throw over*, to discard; to abandon.—*To throw up*, to erect or build rapidly; to resign; to abandon; to eject from the stomach; to vomit.—*v.i.* To perform the act of casting or flinging; to cast dice.—*n.* The act of one who throws; a cast; a cast of dice; hence, risk; venture; decision of fortune; *geol.* and *mining*, a dislocation of strata up or down.—**Thrower**, thrō'ėr, *n.* One who throws; a person who twists silk; a throwster.—**Throwing-engine, Throwing-wheel**, *n.* A potter's wheel.—**Thrown-silk**, *n.* Silk consisting of two or more singles twisted together like a rope.—**Throw-off**, *n.* A start in a hunt or race.—**Throwster**, thrō'stėr, *n.* One who throws or twists silk.

Thrum, thrum, *n.* [Allied to D. *dreum*, thrum; Icel. *thrömr*, margin, edge; same root as L. *terminus*, an end.] The end of a weaver's web; the fringe of threads by which it is fastened to the loom, and from which the cloth when woven has to be cut; coarse yarn.—**Thrummed-mat**, *n.* A mat or piece of canvas with short strands of yarn stuck through it: used in a vessel's rigging about any part, to prevent chafing.—**Thrummy**, thrum'i, *a.* Furnished with or resembling thrums.

Thrum, thrum, *v.i.*—*thrummed, thrumming*. [Akin to *drum*; comp. *strum*.] To play coarsely or unskilfully on a stringed instrument; to make a drumming noise.—*v.t.* To play roughly on with the fingers; to drum; to tap.

Thrush, thrush, *n.* [A.Sax. *thrisc*, a thrush; akin to Icel. *thröstr*, Sw. *trost*, Rus. *drozd*; same root as L. *turdus*, a thrush. *Throstle* is a dim. form.] A passerine bird of various species, including the song-thrush or mavis, the missel-thrush, &c., celebrated for their powers of song.

Thrush, thrush, *n.* [From Icel. *thurr*, dry,

and=Dan. *tröske*, Sw. *torsk*, the thrush; akin *thirst*.] *Pathol.* a disease characterized by vesicles of a pearl colour, affecting the lips and mouth; aphthæ; also an inflammatory and suppurating disease in the feet of the horse.

Thrust, thrust, *v.t.*—pret. and pp. *thrust*. [O.E. *thriste*, *threste*, from Icel. *thrýsta*, to thrust, probably same root as L. *trudo*, to thrust.] To push or drive with force; to impel: usually followed by *away*, *from*, *in*, *off*, &c.—*To thrust on*, to impel; to urge.—*To thrust through*, to pierce; to stab.—*To thrust out*, to expel; to push out or protrude.—*To thrust one's self in* or *into*, to obtrude; to intrude.—*v.i.* To make a push; to make a lunge with a weapon.—*n.* A violent push or drive, as with the hand or foot or with a pointed weapon; a lunge; a stab; *mech.* the force exerted by any body against another body, such as the force exerted by rafters or beams against the walls supporting them.—*Thrust of an arch*, the force by which it tends to press outwards the abutments from which it springs.—**Thruster**, thrus'tėr, *n.* One who thrusts.—**Thrust-hoe**, *n.* A hoe which is worked by pushing.

Thud, thud, *n.* [Imitative; comp. A.Sax. *thoden*, din.] The sound produced by a blow upon a comparatively soft substance; a blow causing a dull sound.

Thug, thug, *n.* [Hind.] A member of a peculiar association of robbers and assassins formerly prevalent in India, who strangled their victims partly from religious motives.—**Thuggee**, thug-gē', *n.* The profession and practices of the Thugs. Also **Thuggism**, **Thuggeeism**, thug'izm, thug'ē-izm.

Thule, thū'lē, *n.* The name given by the ancients to the most northern country which they knew of, supposed to have been Iceland, Norway, or the Shetland Islands; often spoken of by the Romans as *ultima Thule*, remotest Thule; hence, *fig.*, a farthest point or limit.—**Thulite**, thū'līt, *n.* A rare variety of the mineral epidote found in Norway.—**Thulium**, thū'li-um, *n.* A rare metallic element, found in gadolinite.

Thumb, thum, *n.* [A.Sax. *thuma*, the thumb=Dan. *tomme*, D. *duim*, G. *daumen*, from root seen in L. *tumeo*, to swell, whence *tumid*. *Thimble* is a derivative.] The short, thick finger of the human hand, or the corresponding member of other animals.—*Under one's thumb*, under one's power or influence.—*Rule of thumb*. RULE.—*v.t.* To soil or wear with the thumb or the fingers, or by frequent handling.—**Thumbed**, thumd, *a.* Having thumbs; soiled or worn with the thumb or the fingers.—**Thumbkins**, thum'kinz, *n.pl.* An instrument of torture for compressing the thumbs by means of screws. Called also *Thumb-screw*.—**Thumbless**, thum'les, *a.* Having no thumb; hence, clumsy.—**Thumb-mark**, *n.* A mark left by the thumb, as on the leaves of a book.—**Thumb-ring**, *n.* A ring formerly worn on the thumb.—**Thumb-screw**, *n.* A screw to be turned by the finger and thumb; the thumbkins.—**Thumb-stall**, *n.* A sheath of leather or other substance to be worn on the thumb by sail-makers and others.

Thummim, thum'im, *n.pl.* A Hebrew word denoting perfections. The *Urim* and *Thummim* were worn in the breastplate of the high-priest, but what they were is not known.

Thump, thump, *n.* [Allied to Dan. *dump*, a plunge, *dump*, dull, low; D. *dompen*, to plunge; perhaps of imitative origin; comp. *bump*, *plump*.] The sound made by the sudden fall of a heavy body; hence, a heavy blow given with anything that is thick.—*v.t.* To strike or beat with something thick or heavy.—*v.i.* To strike or fall with a heavy blow.—**Thumper**, thump'ėr, *n.* One who thumps; a person or thing which is huge or great (*colloq.*)—**Thumping**, thump'ing, *a.* Large; heavy. (*Colloq.*)

Thunder, thun'dėr, *n.* [From A.Sax. *thunor*, thunder (with insertion of *d*, as in *gender*, *jaundice*); D. *donder*, G. *donner*; cog. L. *tonitru*, Per. *tundur*; same root as L. *tonare*, to sound, E. *stun*, G. *stöhnen*, to groan, Gr. *stonos*, a groaning. THOR.] The sound which follows a flash of lightning; a report due to the sudden disturbance of the air produced by a violent discharge of atmospheric electricity or lightning; any loud noise (*thunders* of applause); an awful or startling denunciation or threat (the *thunders* of the Vatican).—*v.i.* To make thunder: often impersonal (it *thundered* yesterday); to make a loud noise, particularly a heavy sound of some continuance.—*v.t.* To emit as with the noise of thunder; to utter or issue by way of threat or denunciation.—**Thunderbolt**, thun'dėr-bōlt, *n.* A destructive flash of lightning, formerly supposed to be accompanied by the fall of a solid body; *her.* a charge consisting of a double twisted column of flame, having two rays or darts of lightning in saltire and two wings joined on to the centre; a dreadful threat, denunciation, or censure; a fulmination.—**Thunder-clap**, *n.* A clap or burst of thunder; a thunder-peal.—**Thunder-cloud**, *n.* A cloud that produces lightning and thunder, of dark and dense appearance.—**Thunderer**, thun'dėr-ėr, *n.* One who thunders; an epithet of Jupiter.—**Thunder-head**, *n.* A kind of cumulus cloud.—**Thundering**, thun'dėr-ing, *a.* Producing or characterized by a loud rumbling or rattling noise, as that of thunder or artillery; large or extraordinary (*colloq.*).—**Thunderous**, thun'dėr-us, *a.* Producing thunder; making a noise like thunder; giving a loud and deep sound.—**Thunder-peal**, *n.* A peal or clap of thunder.—**Thunder-shower**, *n.* A shower that accompanies thunder.—**Thunder-stone**, *n.* A thunderbolt (*Shak.*); a variety of crystalline iron pyrites; a belemnite; a flint arrow-head.—**Thunder-storm**, *n.* A storm accompanied with thunder.—**Thunderstruck**, thun'dėr-struk, *p.* and *a.* Astonished; amazed; struck dumb by something surprising or terrible suddenly presented.—**Thundery**, **Thundry**, thun'dėr-i, thun'dri, *a.* Accompanied with thunder.

Thurible, thū'ri-bl, *n.* [L. *thuribulum*, from *thus*, *thuris*, frankincense.] A kind of censer in the shape of a covered vase, perforated to allow the fumes of incense to escape.—**Thurifer**, thū'ri-fėr, *n.* *R. Cath. Ch.* the attendant who carries the thurible.—**Thuriferous**, thū-rif'ėr-us, *a.* [L. *thus*, and *fero*, to bear.] Producing or bearing frankincense.—**Thurification**, thū'ri-fi-kā"shon, *n.* [L. *thus*, and *facio*, to make.] The act of burning incense.—**Thurify**, thū'ri-fī, *v.t.* To perfume with incense; to cense.

Thursday, thėrz'dā, *n.* [That is, *Thor's day*, the day consecrated to Thor, the old Scandinavian god of thunder.] The fifth day of the week.

Thus, ᴛʜus, *adv.* [A.Sax. *thus*, akin to *thes*, *theos*, *this*, this. THIS.] In this way, manner, or state; accordingly; things being so; to this degree or extent; so (*thus* wise).—*Thus far*, *thus much*, to this point; to this degree.

Thus, thus, *n.* [L. *thus*, *tus*.] Frankincense; also the resin of the spruce-fir.

Thwack, thwak, *v.t.* [Modified from A.Sax. *thaccian*, to stroke gently; Icel. *thjökka*, to thwack. *Whack* is another form.] To strike, bang, beat, or thrash.—*n.* A heavy blow with something flat or heavy; a bang.

Thwart, thwart, *a.* [From Icel. *thvert*, transverse; Sw. *tvärt*, Dan. *tvert*, across; *tvär*, *tver*, cross; akin A.Sax. *thweorh*, across, perverse.] Transverse; being across something else.—*v.t.* To place or pass over†; to cross, as a purpose; to frustrate or defeat (a design, a person).—*n.* Opposition†; the seat of a boat placed athwart it.—**Thwarter**, thwart'ėr, *n.* One who thwarts.—**Thwartly**, thwart'li, *adv.* With opposition; crossly; perversely.—**Thwartness**, thwart'nes, *n.*—**Thwartship**, thwart'ship, *a.* *Naut.* lying across the vessel.—**Thwartships**, thwart'ships, *adv.* *Naut.* across the ship.

Thy, ᴛʜī, *pron.* [THINE.] Belonging or pertaining to thee: possessive pronoun of the second person singular.

Thyine, thī'in, *n.* [Gr. *thyinos*, pertaining to the tree *thyia*, *thya*, a tree with sweet-smelling wood.] An epithet for a precious wood, mentioned Rev. xviii. 12, supposed to be that of the white cedar or of the sandarach tree.

Thylacine, thī'la-sin, *n.* [Gr. *thylakos*, a pouch.] The Tasmanian wolf.

Thylacoleo, thī-la-kō'lē-ō, *n.* [Gr. *thylakos*, a pouch, and *leōn* (L. *leo*), a lion.] A remarkable extinct carnivorous marsupial, equalling a lion in size.

Thyme, tīm, *n.* [L. *thymum*, from Gr. *thymon*, thyme, from *thyō*, to smell.] A genus of small undershrubs, of which the common or garden thyme is a favourite on account of its aromatic odour.—**Thymol**, tīm'ol, *n.* [From *thyme*, *oleum*, oil.] A crystalline substance obtained from oil of thyme; a strong antiseptic and disinfectant, used as a gargle, for inhalation, in skin diseases, &c.—**Thymy**, tī'mi, *a.* Abounding with thyme; fragrant.

Thymus, thī'mus, *n.* [From Gr. *thymos*, thyme, being compared to the flower of this plant by Galen.] *Anat.* a glandular body situated behind the sternum or breastbone in children, often entirely disappearing in adults.

Thyroid, **Thyreoid**, thī'roid, thī'rē-oid, *a.* [Gr. *thyreos*, a shield, *eidos*, form.] Resembling a shield; applied to one of the cartilages of the larynx, to a gland situated near that cartilage, and to the arteries and veins of the gland.—**Thyroid gland**, *n.* A ductless gland attached to the front of the larynx. It produces an internal secretion that helps to regulate the nutrition of the body.

Thyrsus, thėr'sus, *n.* [L. *thyrsus*, from Gr. *thyrsos*, a thyrsus.] An attribute or emblem of Bacchus and his followers, consisting of a spear or staff wrapped round with ivy and vine branches, and often with a pine cone at the point; *bot.* a form of inflorescence resembling a panicle but denser and closer.—**Thyrsiform**, thėr'si-form, *a.* *Bot.* resembling a thyrsus.—**Thyrsoid**, **Thyrsoidal**, thėr'soid, thėr'soi-dal, *a.* *Bot.* having somewhat the form of a thyrsus.

Thyself, ᴛʜī-self', *pron.* A pronoun used after *thou*, to express distinction with emphasis; or used without *thou*, its usage being similar to that of *myself*, &c.

Ti, tē, *n.* A liliaceous plant of the Pacific islands, &c., with a highly nutritious root.

Tiara, tī-ā'ra, *n.* [L. and Gr. *tiara*, from the Persian.] An ornament or article of dress with which the ancient Persians covered their heads; a kind of turban; the pope's triple crown; hence, *the tiara*, the papal dignity.—**Tiaraed**, tī-ā'rad, *a.* Adorned with a tiara.

Tibia, tib'i-a, *n.* [L., a musical pipe, the large bone of the leg.] A kind of pipe, the commonest musical instrument of the Greeks and Romans; *anat.* the large bone of the lower leg; the shin-bone; *entom.* the fourth joint of the leg.—**Tibial**, tib'i-al, *a.* Pertaining to the tibia.

Tic, tik, *n.* [Fr. *tic*, spasm.] A convulsive twitching of certain muscles of the face; also tic-douloureux of facial neuralgia.—**Tic-douloureux**, tik-dö'lö-ru, *n.* [Fr. *douloureux*, painful.] A painful affection of a nerve, coming on in sudden attacks, usually in the head or face.

Tick, tik, *n.* [Contr. of *ticket*.] Credit; trust.—*To buy upon tick*=to buy on a *ticket* or note, or on credit.

Tick, tik, *n.* [L.G. *teke*, D. *teek*, G. *zecke*, a tick.] The name common to certain small parasitical arachnidans or mites which infest sheep, oxen, dogs, goats, &c.

Tick, tik, *n.* [Same as D. *tijk*, G. *zieche*, a cover, a tick, from L. *theca*, Gr. *thēkē*, a case, a cover.] The cover or case which contains the feathers, wool, or other materials of a bed; ticking.—**Ticking**, tik'ing, *n.* A strong striped linen or cotton fabric used for the ticks of beds, mattresses, &c.

Tick, tik, *v.i.* [From the sound; comp. D. *tikken*, to touch slightly and quickly, as with a pen, to dot.] To make a small noise by beating or otherwise, as a watch; to give out a succession of small sharp noises.—*n.* A small distinct noise, as that of a watch or clock; a small dot.—*v.t.* To mark with a tick or dot; to check by writing down a small mark: generally with *off*.—**Ticker**, tik'ėr, *n.* A device for facilitating detection of continuous waves; a telegraphic receiving instrument for the stock exchange that records quotations

Ticket, tik'et, *n.* [Fr. *étiquette*, O.Fr. *etiquet*, a bill, note, ticket, label, &c., from G. *stecken*, to stick, a ticket being something stuck on. STICK, ETIQUETTE.] A label stuck on the outside of anything to give notice of something concerning it; a small piece of paper, cardboard, or the like, with something written or printed on it, and serving as a notice, acknowledgment, &c.; a certificate or token of a share in a lottery or the like; a card or slip of paper given as a certificate of right of entry to a place of public amusement, or to travel in a railway or by other public conveyance.—*The ticket*, the right or correct thing. (*Slang*).—*Ticket of leave*, a license given to a convict before the expiry of his sentence to be, under certain restrictions, at large and labour for himself.—*v.t.* To distinguish by a ticket; to put a ticket on.—**Ticketed**, tik'et-ed, *p.* and *a.* Marked with a ticket.—**Ticket-porter**, *n.* A licensed porter who wears a badge or ticket. — **Ticket-writer**, *n.* One who writes or paints show-cards for shop-windows, &c.

Ticking. Under TICK (a cover).

Tickle, tik'l, *v.t.*—*tickled, tickling.* [A freq. of *tick*, to touch lightly; or by metathesis from A.Sax. *citelian* = Sc. *kittle*, D. *kittelen*, G. *kitzeln*, to tickle.] To touch lightly and cause peculiar thrilling sensation, which commonly causes laughter; to titillate; to please by slight gratification; to stir up to pleasure; to flatter; to cajole; to puzzle.—**Tickler**, tik'lėr, *n.* One who tickles or pleases; something that puzzles or perplexes (*colloq.*).—**Tickling**, tik'ling, *n.* A sensation similar to that produced by being tickled. — **Ticklish**, tik'lish, *a.* Easily tickled; in an unsteady or critical state; difficult; nice; critical.—**Ticklishly**, tik'lish-li, *adv.* In a ticklish manner.—**Ticklishness**, tik'lish-nes, *n.*

Tidbit, tid'bit, *n.* A titbit

Tide, tīd, *n.* [A.Sax. *tīd*, time, season, hour = Icel. *tīth*, Sw. and Dan. *tid*, D. *tijd*, G. *zeit*, time; same root as *time*. The tides are times of rising and falling of the sea. Hence *tidy, tidings, betide.*] Time; season; the alternate rising and falling of the waters of the ocean, and of bays, rivers, &c., connected therewith, depending on the relative position of the moon, and in a less degree of the sun; the whole interval between high and low water; a state of being at the height or acme (*Shak.*); stream; flow; current (a *tide* of blood); course or tendency of influences or circumstances; current. See also NEAP, SPRING, EBB, FLOOD.—*v.t.* or *i.*—*tided, tiding.* To drive with the tide or stream. — *To tide over*, to surmount by favourable incidents, by prudence, and management, or by aid from another.—**Tidal**, tī'dal, *a.* Pertaining to tides; showing tides.—*Tidal harbour*, a harbour in which the tide ebbs and flows, not having a dock with flood-gates.—*Tidal river*, a river up which the tide flows to a certain point in its course.—*Tidal train*, a railway train which runs in connection with a steamer, and whose running is therefore regulated by the state of the tide.—*Tidal-wave*, tide-wave.—**Tide-gate**, *n.* A gate through which water passes when the tide flows, and which is shut to retain it. — **Tide-gauge**, *n.* A gauge for ascertaining the rise and fall of the tide, thus indicating the depth of water at every instant during the day.—**Tide-lock**, *n.* A lock situated between the tide-water of a harbour and an inclosed basin, having double gates by which vessels can pass at all times of the tide.—**Tide-table**, *n.* A table showing the time of high-water at any place, or at different places, throughout the year.—**Tidal wave**, *n.* Great sea waves following earthquakes, or floods caused by the piling up of water in hurricanes; the daily tides caused by the gravitational attraction of the moon upon the earth; the spring tides at new and full moon, when earth, sun and moon are in a direct line.

Tidings, tī'dingz, *n.pl.* [Lit. events that happen or *betide*; Icel. *tīthindi* (pl.), tidings, news; Dan. *tidende*, D. *tijding*, G. *zeitung*. TIDE.] News; information; intelligence; account of what has taken place and was not before known.

Tidy, tī'di, *a.* [From *tide*, time, season; like D. *tijdig*, Dan. and Sw. *tidig*, G. *zeitig*, timely, seasonable. TIDE.] Seasonable†; arranged in good order or with neatness; dressed or kept with neatness; neat; trim; practising neatness; moderately large or great (*colloq.*).—*v.t.*—*tidied, tidying.* To make neat or tidy; to put in good order.—*n.* A piece of knitted or crotchet work for hanging over the back of a chair, the arms of a sofa, or the like.—**Tidily**, tī'di-li, *adv.* In a tidy manner.—**Tidiness**, tī'di-nes, *n.* The quality of being tidy.

Tie, tī, *v.t.*—*tied, tying.* [A.Sax. *týge*, a rope, from *teón*, to pull; akin *tug, tow.*] To fasten with a band or cord and knot; to bind; to fasten; to knit; to unite so as not to be easily parted; to limit or bind by authority or moral influence; to restrain; to confine; to oblige.—*To tie down*, to fasten so as to prevent from rising; to restrain, restrict, or confine; to impose stipulations on.—*To tie up*, to fasten up; to confine or restrain; to annex such conditions to that it cannot be sold or alienated.—*n.* Something used to fasten or bind; a fastening; an ornamental knot; a neck-tie; a bond; an obligation, moral or legal (the *ties* of blood or of friendship); *building*, a beam or rod which secures parts together and is subjected to a tensile strain; *mus.* a curved line written over or under notes of the same pitch to indicate that the sound is to be unbrokenly continued to the time value of the combined notes; a state of equality among competing or opposed parties, as in certain games, competitions among marksmen, &c.; a contest in which two or more competitors are equally successful.—*To play* or *shoot off a tie*, to go through a second contest (the first being indecisive) to decide who is to be the winner. — **Tie-beam**, *n.* The beam which connects the bottom of a pair of principal rafters in a roof.—**Tier**, tī'er, *n.* One who or that which ties.—**Tie-rod**, *n.* A wrought-iron bar or rod for bracing together the frames of steam-engines, roofs, &c.—**Tie-wig**, *n.* A wig having a queue tied with a ribbon.

Tier, tēr, *n.* [Fr. *tire*, from *tirer*, to draw, from German word = E. to *tear.*] A row; a rank, particularly when two or more rows are placed one above another.

Tierce, tērs, *n.* [Fr., a third, third part, from L. *tertius*, third, from *tres*, three.] Formerly a liquid measure equal to one-third of a pipe, or 42 wine gallons, equal to 35 imperial gallons; a cask for salt provisions, &c.; *mus.* a major or minor third; *fencing*, a position in which the wrist and nails are turned downwards, the weapon of the opponent being on the right of the fencer.

Tiercel, Tiercelet, tēr'sel, tērs'let, *n.* [Fr. *tiercelet*, tiercelet, a dim. from *tierce*, L. *tertius*, third—because said to be a third less than the female. TIERCE.] A male hawk or falcon.

Tiff, tif, *n.* [Originally a sniff; comp. N. *tæv, tæft*, scent.] A small draught of liquor; a pet or fit of peevishness; a slight altercation or quarrel.—*v.i.* To be in a pet.—*v.t.* To sip; to drink.

Tiffany, tif'a-ni, *n.* [O.Fr. *tiffer*, to adorn.] A species of gauze or very thin silk.

Tiffin, tif'in, *n.* [From Prov.E. *tiffing*, eating or drinking out of due season. TIFF.] In India a lunch or slight repast between breakfast and dinner.

Tiger, tī'gėr, *n.* [Fr. *tigre*, from L. and Gr. *tigris*, a tiger, from O.Per. *tigrâ*, an arrow.] A large and dreaded carnivorous mammal of the cat family found in Southern Asia, about the size of the lion, but more cat-like and having a striped body; it is usually driven out of its haunts by natives and shot by sportsmen seated on elephants.—**Tiger-beetle**, *n.* A name given to certain beetles that feed upon other insects.—**Tiger-cat**, *n.* A domestic cat having the striped appearance of a tiger.—**Tiger-flower**, *n.* A Mexican plant of the iris family with magnificent flowers.—**Tigerine, Tigrine, Tigerish, Tigrish**, tī'gėr-in, tī'grin, tī'gėr-ish, tī'grish, *a.* Resembling, pertaining to, or characteristic of a tiger. **Tiger-lily**, *n.* A garden lily with orange-colored flowers spotted with black.—**Tiger-moth**, *n.* A name of various moths having wings richly streaked.—**Tigress**, tī'gres, *n.* The female of the tiger.

Tight, tīt, *a.* [O.E. *thite, thiht, thyht*=Icel. *thēttr*, tight, Dan. *tæt*, tight, close, D. *digt*, G. *dicht*, thick, solid, dense; perhaps allied to *thick.*] Having the parts or joints so close as to prevent the passage of fluids; impervious to air, gas, water, &c.; compactly or firmly built or made; sound and strong; as applied to persons, well-knit, sinewy, strong; firmly packed or inserted; not loose; fitting too close to the body; tensely stretched or strained; taut; not slack (a *tight* rope); not easy to be obtained; not to be had on ordinary terms: said of money when capitalists are disinclined to speculate (*commercial slang*).—**Tighten**, tī'tn, *v.t.* To make tight; to draw tighter. —**Tightener, Tightner**, tī'tn-ėr, *n.* One who or that which tightens.—**Tightly**, tīt'li, *adv.* In a tight manner; closely; compactly.—**Tightness**, tīt'nes, *n.* The state or quality of being tight; closeness of parts; imperviousness; compactness; tenseness. — **Tight-rope**, *n.* A tightly stretched rope on which an acrobat performs feats.—**Tights**, tīts, *n.pl.* Tight-fitting breeches; a covering worn on the legs by acrobats, actors, dancers, and the like.

Tigress, Tigrine, &c. Under TIGER.

Tike, tīk, *n.* [Icel. *tík*, Sw. *tik*, a bitch, a cur.] A dog; a cur; a boor; a clown.

Tilbury, til'be-ri, *n.* [From the name of the inventor, a London coach-builder in the beginning of the present century.] A gig or two-wheeled carriage without a top or cover.

Til, tēl, *n.* Indian sesame.

Tilde, til'dā, *n.* [Sp.] The mark over the Spanish *n* when pronounced with a slightly added *y* sound, as in señor, cañon, &c.

Tile, tīl, *n.* [A.Sax. *tigel*, from L. *tegula*, a tile, from *tego*, to cover (seen also in *tegument, detect, protect*), from same root as E. *thatch, deck.*] A kind of thin slab of baked clay, used for covering the roofs of buildings, paving floors, lining furnaces and ovens, constructing drains, &c.; a tube or tunnel-shaped piece of baked clay for drains; a tall stiff hat (*slang*).—*Encaustic tiles.* Under ENCAUSTIC.—*v.t.*—*tiled, tiling.* To cover with tiles; *freemasonry*, to guard against the entrance of the uninitiated by placing the tiler at the closed door. — **Tile-drain**, *n.* A drain constructed with tiles.—**Tiler**, tī'lėr, *n.* A man who makes or who lays tiles; the doorkeeper of a freemasons' lodge.—**Tilery**, tī'lėr-i, *n.* A tile-work. — **Tile-work**, *n.* A place where tiles are made; a tilery.—**Tiling**, tī'ling, *n.* Covering a roof with tiles; tiles collectively.

Till, til, *n.* [Formerly a drawer in general, from A.Sax. *tyllan*, to draw; comp. D. *tillen*, O.Fris. *tilla*, to lift, to raise.] A money box in a shop, warehouse, &c.; a cash-drawer.

Till, til, *n.* [Comp. W. *tel*, compact.] A kind of hard clayey earth; boulder-clay; *geol.* unstratified boulder-clay or any unstratified alluvial formation of considerable thickness. — **Tilly**, til'i, *a.* Having the character of till or boulder-clay.

Till, til, *prep.* [Same as Icel. and Dan. *til*,

Sw. *till*; perhaps allied to G. *ziel*, end, aim.] To the time of; until (wait *till* next week); often used before verbs and clauses (I will wait *till* you arrive); also to, as far as, or up to.—*Till now*, to the present time.—*Till then*, to that time.

Till, til, *v.t.* [A.Sax. *tilian*, to labor, to till; lit. to make fit or good, from *til* (A.Sax. and Goth.), fit, good; allied to D. *telen*, to cultivate, to breed; O.G. *zilôn*, to cultivate. *Toil* is a closely allied form.] To plough and prepare for seed, and to dress the crops of; to cultivate; to labor.—**Tillable**, til′-a-bl, *a.* Capable of being tilled; arable.—

Tillage, til′āj, *n.* The operation or art of tilling land; cultivation; culture; husbandry.—**Tiller**, til′ėr, *n.* One who tills.—*Naut.* the bar or lever fitted to the head of a rudder to turn the helm of a ship or boat in steering.—**Tiller chain**, **Tiller rope**, **Tiller line**, *n.* A chain, rope or line from the tiller to the barrel of the steering-wheel.

Till, til, *n.* [From O.E. *tillen*, to draw; akin D. *tillen*, to lift.] A cash drawer, as in a store; a secret money compartment in a cabinet.

Tiller, til′ėr, *n.* [Comp. A.Sax. *telgor*, a plant, a shoot; akin D. *telen*, to breed.] The shoot of a plant springing from the root; a sucker.—*v.i.* To put forth shoots from the root.

Tilt, tilt, *n.* [A.Sax. *teld*, a tent=Dan. and L.G. *telt*, Icel. *tjald*, G. *zelt*, tent.] A tent‡; the cloth covering of a cart or wagon; a canopy or awning over the after part of a boat.—*v.t.* To cover with a tilt or awning.

Tilt, tilt, *v.t.* [From A.Sax. *tealt*, unsteady or unstable; comp. O.Fris. *tilla*, D. and L.G. *tillen*, to raise, to heave up; Sw. *tulta*, to waddle; Icel. *tölt*, an amble.] To raise one end of, as of a cask, for discharging liquor; to heave up at an angle; to hammer or forge with a tilt-hammer.—*To tilt up*, *geol.* to throw up abruptly at a high angle of inclination (the strata are *tilted up*).—*v.i.* To run or ride and thrust with a lance; to joust, as in a tournament; to fight similarly; to rush as in combat; to rise into a sloping position; to heel.—*n.* A thrust; a military exercise on horseback, in which the combatants attacked each other with lances; a tilt-hammer; inclination forward (the *tilt* of a cask); *geol.* the throwing up of strata at a high angle of inclination.—**Tilter**, til′tėr, *n.* One who tilts; one who jousts.—**Tilt-hammer**, *n.* A large hammer worked by steam or water power, lifted by a cam or projection on the axle of a wheel and again allowed to fall on the mass on the anvil.

Tilth, tilth, *n.* [A.Sax. *tilth*, culture, from *tilian*, to till; comp. *spilth*, from *spill*.] The operation of tilling; tillage; husbandry; the state of being tilled; tilled ground.

Timber, tim′bėr, *n.* [A.Sax. *timber*, timber, wood, structure = Icel. *timbr*, Dan. *tömmer*, D. *timmer*, G. *zimmer*; lit. building materials, the root being that of Gr. *demō*, to build, L. *domus*, a house (whence *domestic*, *domicile*, &c.).] Trees cut down and suitable for building purposes; trees felled and partly prepared for use; growing trees yielding wood suitable for constructive purposes; one of the main beams of a fabric; *naut.* a curving piece of wood forming the rib of a ship (with a plural in this and preceding sense).—*v.t.* To furnish with timber.—**Timbered**, tim′bėrd, *p.* and *a.* Furnished with timbers; covered with growing timber.—**Timber-merchant**, *n.* A dealer in timber.—**Timber-tree**, *n.* A tree yielding timber.—**Timber-yard**, *n.* A yard or place where timber is deposited.

Timbre, tim′br, or taṅ-br, *n.* [Fr., from L. *tympanum*, a drum.] *Mus.* the quality which distinguishes any given tone or sound of one instrument or voice from the same tone or sound of another instrument or voice, and which depends on the harmonics co-existing with the fundamental tone and their relative intensities.

Timbrel, tim′brel, *n.* [A dim. of Fr. *timbre*, a bell, originally a drum. See above.] A kind of drum or tabor; a tambourine.

Time, tīm, *n.* [A.Sax. *tíma*, time, hour, season; Icel. *tími*, Sw. and Dan. *time*; akin to *tide*, being from the same root but with a different termination.] The measure of duration; a particular portion or part of duration, whether past, present, or future, and either a space or a point, a period or a moment; occasion; season; moment; a proper occasion; opportunity (to bide our *time*); period at which any definite event occurred or person lived; an age (the *time* of James I); an allotted period of life; the present life; existence in this world; prevailing state of circumstances: generally in plural (good *times*, bad *times*); leisure (I have not *time* to speak with you); hour of death or of travail (his *time* was come); a performance or repetition among others; *mus.* the style of movement marked by the regular grouping of a certain and equal number of notes, or of more or less notes equal in time value to that certain number through all the bars of a movement; rhythm; the absolute velocity or rate of movement at which a piece is executed.—*At times*, at distinct intervals of duration.—*The time*, the present age; the present period (men of the *time*); also, any period definitely referred to.—*Absolute time*, time considered without relation to bodies or their motions; duration flowing on uniformly.—*Relative time*, the sensible measure of any portion of duration.—*Apparent time*, time regulated by the apparent motion of the sun; time as shown by a properly adjusted sun-dial; solar time.—*Astronomical time*, mean solar time reckoned through the twenty-four hours.—*Civil time*, mean time adapted to civil uses, and distinguished into years, months, days, &c.—*Common time*, *mus.* under COMMON.—*Equation of time*. Under EQUATION.—*In time*, in good season; at the right moment; sufficiently early; before it is too late; in the course of things; by degrees; eventually.—*Mean time*, or *mean solar time*, time regulated by the average or mean. Under MEAN.—*Nick of time*, the exact point of time required by necessity or convenience; the critical moment.—*Sidereal time*. Under SIDEREAL.—*Solar time*. Same as *Apparent time*.—*Time enough*, in season; early enough.—*Time out of mind*, or *time immemorial*, time beyond the memory of man; *law*, the time prior to the reign of Richard I, A.D. 1189.—*To kill time*, to occupy one's self so as to make it pass without too much tediousness.—*To lose time*, to fail to take full advantage of time or opportunity; to go too slow (as a watch or clock).—*v.t.*—*timed*, *timing*. To adapt to the time or occasion; to regulate as to time; to mark or ascertain the time or rate of.—*v.i.* To keep time; to harmonize.—**Time-ball**, *n.* A ball dropped down a staff at observatories to publish accurately certain preconcerted times, 1 P.M. being that in general use.—**Time-bargain**, *n.* A contract for the sale or purchase of merchandise, or of stock, at a certain time and price.—**Time-bill**, *n.* A time-table.—**Time-fuse**, *n.* A fuse arranged so as to explode a charge at a certain interval after ignition.—**Time-gun**, *n.* A gun fired exactly at the same time every day to announce publicly the correct time.—**Time-honoured**, *a.* Honoured for a long time; venerable and worthy of honour by reason of antiquity and long continuance.—**Time-keeper**, *a.* A clock, watch, or chronometer; a person who keeps or marks the time, as that during which a number of workmen work.—**Timeless**, tīm′les, *a.* Unseasonable; without end.—**Timeliness**, tīm′li-nes, *n.* The quality of being timely.—**Timely**, tīm′li, *a.* Seasonable; being in good time; sufficiently early.—**Timeous**, **Timous**, tī′mus, *a.* Timely; seasonable.—**Timeously**, **Timously**, tī′mus-li, *a.* Seasonably; in good time.—**Time-piece**, *n.* A clock, watch, or other instrument to measure time, especially a small portable clock.—**Time-server**, *n.* One who meanly and for selfish ends adapts his opinions and manners to the times; one who obsequiously complies with the ruling power.—**Time-serving**, *a.* Obsequiously complying with the humors of men in power.—*n.* The conduct of a time-server.—**Time-table**, *n.* A table or register of times, as of the hours to be observed in a school, of the departure and arrival of railroad trains, steamboats, &c.

Timid, tim′id, *a.* [L. *timidus*, from *timeo*, to fear, from same root as Skr. *tamas*, darkness.] Fearful; wanting courage to meet danger; timorous; not bold.—**Timidity**, **Timidness**, ti-mid′i-ti, tim′id-nes, *n.* The state or quality of being timid.—**Timidly**, tim′id-li, *adv.* In a timid manner; weakly; without courage.

Timocracy, tī-mok′ra-si, *n.* [Gr. *timokratia*—*timē*, honour, worth, and *krateō*, to rule.] A form of government in which a certain amount of property is requisite as a qualification for office.—**Timocratic**, tī-mō-krat′ik, *a.* Pertaining to timocracy.

Timorous, tim′or-us, *a.* [L.L. *timorosus*, from L. *timor*, fear, from *timeo*, to fear. TIMID.] Fearful of danger; timid; destitute of courage; indicating or marked by fear.—**Timorously**, tim′or-us-li, *adv.* In a timorous manner.—**Timorousness**, tim′or-us-nes, *n.* The state or quality of being timorous.

Timothy-grass, *n.* [First recommended by *Timothy* Hanson.] A kind of hard, coarse grass extensively cultivated for hay

Timous, Timeous. Under TIME.

Tin, tin, *n.* [A.Sax., D., Dan., and Icel. *tin*, Sw. *ten*, G. *zinn*; not connected with L. *stannum*, tin.] A valuable metal of a white colour tinged with gray, in hardness intermediate between gold and lead, and very malleable; thin plates of iron covered with tin; tin-plate; a cant name for money.—*v.t.*—*tinned*, *tinning*. To cover with tin, or overlay with tin-foil.—**Tin-foil**, *n.* Pure tin, or the metal alloyed with a little lead, beaten and rolled into thin sheets.—**Tin hat**, *n.* The British shrapnel helmet introduced in 1916.—**Tinman**, tin′man, *n.* A manufacturer of, or dealer in tinware.—**Tinner**, tin′ėr, *n.* One who works in a tin mine; a tinman.—**Tinning**, tin′ing, *n.* The act, art, or process of covering or coating other metals with a thin coat or layer of tin; the covering or layer thus put on.—**Tinny**, tin′i, *a.* Pertaining to, abounding with, or resembling tin.—**Tin-ore**, *n.* The ore of tin.—**Tin-plate**, *n.* Thin sheet-iron coated with tin, in order to protect it from oxidation or rust; white-iron.—**Tinsmith**, *n.* One who makes articles of tin or tin-plate.—**Tin-stone**, *n.* One of the principal ores of tin.—**Tinware**, tin′wār, *n.* Articles made of tinned iron.

Tinamou, tin′a-mö, *n.* [The native name.] A gallinaceous bird of South America, the species varying in size from a pheasant to a quail.

Tincal, ting′kal, *n.* [Malay *tingkal*, Hind. and Per. *tinkār*.] The commercial name of borax in its crude or unrefined state, employed in refining metals.

Tinchel, tin′shl, *n.* A Highland sporting drive, surrounding the deer or other animals, and gradually forcing them into a smaller ring.

Tinct, tingkt, *n.* A tint or tincture. (*Obsolete or poetical.*)

Tinctorial, tingk-tō′ri-al, *a.* [From L. *tinctor*, a dyer. TINCTURE.] Pertaining to colours or dyes.

Tincture, tingk′tūr, *n.* [L. *tinctura*, from *tingo*, *tinctum*. TINGE.] A tinge or shade of colour; slight taste superadded to any substance; slight quality added to anything; *med.* an extract or solution of the active principles of some substance in a solvent, the latter being often proof-spirit: so called from usually possessing colour; *tinctures* is the heraldic name for what are commonly called 'colours'. The 'metals' (gold and silver) are included in the 'tinctures' together with the five 'colours': red, blue, green, black, and purple.—*v.t.*—*tinctured*, *tincturing*. To tinge or impart a slight foreign colour to; to impregnate; to imbue.

Tinder, tin′dėr, *n.* [A.Sax. *tynder*, *tender*, from *tyndan*, *tendan*, to kindle (Dan. *tænde*,

G. *zünden*) = Sw. and L.G. *tunder*, Icel. *tundr*, D. *tonder*, G. *zunder*, tinder.] An inflammable substance generally composed of partially burned linen, used for kindling fire from a spark struck with a steel and flint. — *German tinder*. AMADOU.—**Tinder-box**, *n.* A box in which tinder is kept.—**Tindery**, tin'dėr-i, *a.* Like tinder; inflammable.

Tine, tīn, *n.* [O.E. *tinde*, A.Sax. *tind*=Icel. *tindr*, Dan. *tind*, *tinde*, L.G. and Sw. *tinne*; same root as *tooth*.] The tooth or spike of a fork; a prong; the tooth of a harrow; a point or prong of a deer's horn.—**Tined**, tīnd, *a.* Furnished with tines.

Tinea, tin'ē-a, *n.* [L., a gnawing worm, a bookworm, a moth.] A term for ringworm or similar diseases of the skin.

Ting, ting, *n.* [Imitative; comp. *tinkle*, *jingle*; L. *tinnio*, to tinkle.] A sharp sound, as of a bell; a tinkling.—*v.i.* To sound or ring.

Tinge, tinj, *v.t.*—*tinged*, *tinging*. [L. *tingo*, *tinctum*, to moisten, stain, dye (seen also in *tincture*, *tint*, *taint*, *distain*, whence *stain*); cog. Gr. *tenggō*, to wet.] To mix or imbue with some foreign substance so as to slightly affect or modify the colour, taste, or qualities of; to give a certain smack, flavour, or quality to; to colour.—*n.* A slight degree of colour, taste, flavour, or quality infused or added to something; tincture; tint; smack.

Tingle, ting'gl, *v.i.*—*tingled*, *tingling*. [A dim. from *ting*.] To feel a kind of thrilling sensation, as in hearing a small sharp ringing sound; to feel a sharp, thrilling pain; to have a thrilling, sharp, or penetrating sensation.—*v.t.* To cause to give a sharp ringing sound; to ring.—**Tingling**, ting'gl-ing, *n.* A thrilling, jarring, tremulous sensation.

Tinkal. TINCAL.

Tinker, ting'kėr, *n.* [From *tink*, *ting*, a sharp metallic sound.] A mender of kettles, pans, and the like; a repair; a cobbling or botching.—*v.t.* To mend like a tinker; to mend clumsily; to cobble; to botch.—*v.i.* To work at tinker's work; to cobble; to keep making petty repairs.

Tinkle, ting'kl, *v.i.*—*tinkled*, *tinkling*. [A freq. from *tink*, *ting*, imitative of sound.] To make small, quick, sharp sounds, as by striking on metal; to clink; to jingle; to resound with a small sharp sound; to tingle. —*v.t.* To cause to make sharp, quick, ringing sounds; to ring.—*n.* A small, quick, sharp, ringing noise.—**Tinkling**, tingk'-ling, *n.* A small, quick, sharp sound.

Tinner, &c. Under TIN.

Tinnitus, tin-nī'tus, *n.* [L., a ringing, a tingling, from *tinnio*, to ring.] *Med.* a ringing in the ears.

Tinsel, tin'sel, *n.* [Fr. *étincelle*, O.Fr. *estincelle*, from L. *scintilla*, a spark (whence also *scintillate*).] Thin shining metallic plate or foil for ornamental purposes; cloth or tissue of silk and silver threads; cloth overlaid with foil; something superficially showy, and more gay than valuable.—*a.* Consisting of tinsel; showy to excess; specious; superficial.—*v.t.*—*tinselled*, *tinselling*. To adorn with tinsel or with something showy and without value.

Tint, tint, *n.* [It. *tinta*, Fr. *teint*, from L. *tinctus*, pp. of *tingo*. TINGE.] A slight colouring or tincture distinct from the ground or principal colour; a hue; a tinge; degree of intensity of a colour.—*v.t.* To tinge; to give a slight colouring to.—**Tintless**, tint'les, *a.* Having no tint; colourless.—**Tint-tool**, *n.* A kind of engraving tool.

Tintamar, **Tintamarre**, tin-ta-mär', *n.* [Fr.] A hideous or confused noise.

Tintinnabular, **Tintinnabulary**, tin-tin-nab'ū-lėr, tin-tin-nab'ū-la-ri, *a.* [L. *tintinnabulum*, a bell, from *tintinno*, a freq. from *tinnio*, to ring, to jingle, a word imitative of sound.] Of or relating to bells or their sound.—**Tintinnabulation**, tin'-tin-nab-ū-lā''shon, *n.* A tinkling or ringing sound, as of bells.—**Tintinnabulous**, tin-tin-nab'ū-lus, *a.* Tintinnabular.

Tiny, tī'ni, *a.* [For *teeny*, from old *teen*, sorrow, A.Sax. *teóna*, vexation; lit. poor, sorry, insignificant.] Very small; little; puny.

Tip, tip, *n.* [Closely allied to *top*, and = Dan. and D. *tip*, L.G. and Sw. *tipp*, a tip; allied also to *tap*, to touch, and perhaps *tap*, spigot.] A small pointed or tapering end or extremity; a gentle stroke; a tap; a small present in money (*slang*); an item of private information, especially in regard to the chances of horses engaged for a race, for betting purposes (*slang*).—*v.t.*—*tipped*, *tipping*. To form the tip of; to cover the tip of; to cant up (a cart or wagon) so that a load may be discharged; to bestow a small money-gift or douceur upon; to give or hand over (*slang*).—*To tip over*, to turn over.—*To tip off*, to drink off.—*To tip up*, to raise up one end of.—*To tip the wink*, to direct a wink to another as a sign of caution or the like (*slang*.) — **Tip-and-run**, *n.* An informal kind of cricket in which the batsman is put out if he cannot make a run every time he strikes the ball, however slightly.—**Tip-cart**, *n.* A cart which can be canted up to empty its contents.—**Tip-cat**, *n.* A game in which a small pointed piece of wood called a cat is made to jump from the ground by being struck on the tip with a stick. — **Tip-cheese**. TIP-CAT. — **Tip-staff**, *n.* pl. **Tip-staves**. A staff tipped with metal; an officer who bears such a staff; a constable; a sheriff's officer.—**Tipster**, tip'-stėr, *n.* One who for a fee sends tips for betting purposes.—**Tiptoe**, tip'tō, *n.* The tip or end of the toe.—*To be* or *to stand on tiptoe*, *fig.* to be on the strain; to be interested or anxious.

Tippet, tip'et, *n.* [A.Sax. *tæppet*, a tippet, from L. *tapete*, cloth. TAPESTRY.] A sort of cape covering the shoulders, and sometimes descending as far as the waist.

Tipple, tip'l, *v.i.*—*tippled*, *tippling*. [Freq. and dim. from *tip*, to tilt or turn up; akin *tipsy*.] To drink spirituous or intoxicating liquors habitually; to drink frequently, but without getting drunk.—*v.t.* To drink, sip, or imbibe often.—*n.* Liquor taken in tippling; drink.—**Tippled**, tip'ld, *a.* Intoxicated; tipsy.—**Tippler**, tip'lėr, *n.* One who tipples; a toper; a soaker.

Tipsy, tip'si, *a.* [Connected with *tipple*; comp. Prov.G. *tips*, *tipps*, drunkenness.] Overpowered or muddled with strong drink; intoxicated, but not helplessly drunk; fuddled. — **Tipsily**, tip'si-li, *adv.* In a tipsy manner.—**Tipsiness**, tip'si-nes, *n.* The state of being tipsy.—**Tipsy-cake**, *n.* A cake composed of pastry saturated with Madeira.

Tiptop, tip'top, *a.* [From *tip* and *top*, or a reduplication of *top* (like *ding-dong*, *slip-slop*, &c.).] First-rate; excellent or perfect in the highest degree. (*Colloq.*)

Tirade, ti-rād, *n.* [Fr. *tirade*, from *tirer*, to draw, from the Germanic verb = E. to *tear*.] A long violent speech; a declamatory flight of censure or reproof; a series of invectives; a harangue.

Tirailleur, ti-rāl-yėr, *n.* [Fr.] In the French army, a skirmisher or a sharpshooter.

Tir de barrage, tēr-dė-băräj, *n.* [Fr., lit. 'barring fire'.] The same as *Curtain fire*.

Tire,† tīr, *n.* A row or rank; a tier (*Mil.*).

Tire, tīr, *n.* [Probably from *tiara*, influenced by *tire*, to adorn.] A head-dress; something that encompasses the head.

Tire,† tīr, *n.* [Contr. of *attire*.] Attire; furniture; apparatus. —*v.t.* To adorn; to attire.—**Tire-woman**, *n.* A woman who attends to the dressing of her mistress; a lady's-maid; a dresser in a theatre.—**Tiring-room**, *n.* The room where players dress for the stage.

Tire, tīr, *n.* [For *tier* from *tie*.] A band or hoop, as of steel or rubber (solid or pneumatic) forming the tread of a vehicle wheel.

Tire, tīr, *v.t.*—*tired*, *tiring*. [A.Sax. *teorian*, to tire; *tirian*, *tirigan*, to vex, annoy; akin to *teran*, to tear; Dan. *tirre*, D. *tergen*, to irritate.] To exhaust the strength of by toil or labour; to fatigue; to weary; to exhaust the attention or patience of, with dulness or tediousness. — *To tire out*, to weary or fatigue to excess; to exhaust.—*v.i.* To become weary; to have the patience exhausted.—**Tiredness**, tīrd'nes, *n.* The state of been wearied; weariness.—**Tiresome**, tīr'sum, *a.* Fitted or tending to tire; fatiguing; wearisome; tedious.—**Tiresomely**, tīr'sum-li, *adv.* In a tiresome manner.—**Tiresomeness**, tīr'sum-nes, *n.* Wearisomeness; tediousness.

Tiro, tī'rō, *n.* [L. *tiro*, a raw recruit, a novice.] A novice or mere beginner; a beginner in learning. Also written *Tyro*.

T-iron, tē'ī-ėrn, *n.* A kind of angle-iron having a flat flange and a web like the letter T.

'Tis, tiz. A common contraction of *It is*.

Tisan, tī'san. PTISAN.

Tisri, **Tizri**, tiz'ri, *n.* [Heb.] A Hebrew month answering to part of September and part of October.

Tissue, tish'ū, *n.* [Fr. *tissu*, woven, pp. of *tisser*, to weave, from L. *texere*, to weave. TEXT.] A woven or textile fabric; cloth interwoven with gold or silver, or with coloured figures; *fig.* a mass of connected particulars (a *tissue* of falsehood); *animal anat.* one of the primary layers composing any of the parts of animal bodies; *vegetable anat.* the minute elementary structures of which the organs of plants are composed.—**Tissued**, tish'ūd, *p.* and *a.* Clothed in or adorned with tissue; variegated.—**Tissue-paper**, *n.* A very thin, gauze-like paper, used for protecting engravings in books, wrapping delicate articles, &c.

Tit, tit, *n.* [Same as Icel. *tittr*, a small bird, a tit; Dan. *tite*, a sandpiper; N. *tite*, a titmouse; originally anything small.] A small bit; a morsel; a small horse; the titmouse; a contemptuous term for a woman.—*Tit for tat*, an equivalent in the way of revenge or repartee.

Titan, tī'tan, *n.* *Greek myth.* one of the twelve children of Heaven and Earth, said to have been of gigantic size and enormous strength, and to have been defeated by Zeus and thrown into Tartarus; poetical for the sun.—**Titaness**, tī'tan-es, *n.* A female Titan; a female personage of surpassing power. — **Titania**, tī-tā'ni-a, *n.* [Among the Romans a name of Diana.] The queen of Fairyland and consort of Oberon.—**Titanic**, tī-tan'ik, *a.* Pertaining to the Titans; enormous in size or strength; huge; vast.

Titanium, tī-tā'ni-um, *n.* [So called in fanciful allusion to the *Titans*.] A metallic element somewhat resembling tin. — **Titanate**, tī'tan-āt, *n.* A salt of titanic acid. —**Titanian**, **Titanitic**, tī-tan'i-an, tī-ta-nit'ik, *a.* Pertaining to titanium. — **Titanic**, tī-tan'ik, *a.* Pertaining to titanium. —*Titanic acid*, dioxide of titanium, called also) *Titanic oxide*. — **Titaniferous**, tī-tan-if'ėr-us, *a.* Producing titanium.

Titanotherium, tī'tan-ō-thē''ri-um, *n.* [Gr. *Titan*, *Titanos*, a Titan (in allusion to its size), and *thērion*, a wild beast.] A fossil herbivorous mammal, possibly twice the size of a horse, allied to the tapir.

Titbit, **Tidbit**, tit'bit, tid'bit, *n.* [From *tit*, anything small, and *bit*.] A small and delicious morsel; a particularly nice piece.

Tithe, tīTH, *n.* [O.E. *tethe*, *tiethe*, *teothe*, from A.Sax. *teótha* (for *teóntha*), the tenth. TEN.] The tenth part of anything; the tenth part of the profits of land and stock and the personal industry of the inhabitants, allotted to the clergy for their support; hence, any small part or proportion. —*Commutation of tithes*, the conversion of tithes into a rent-charge payable in money, and chargeable on the land.—*v.t.*—*tithed*, *tithing*. To levy a tithe on; to tax to the amount of a tenth.—*v.i.* To pay tithes.—**Tithable**, tī'THa-bl, *a.* Subject to the payment of tithes.—**Tithe-free**, *a.* Exempt from the payment of tithes.—**Tithe-gatherer**, *n.* One who collects tithes.—**Tithe-**

pig, *n.* One pig out of ten paid as a tithe or church-rate.—**Tithe-proctor**, *n.* A levier or collector of tithes or church-rates.—**Tither**, tī'THėr, *n.* One who collects tithes.—**Tithing**, tī'THing, *n.* The levying or taking of tithes; a tithe; formerly in England, a number or company of ten householders, who, dwelling near each other, were sureties or free pledges to the king for the good behaviour of each other.—**Tithing-man**, *n.* The chief man of a tithing; a headborough; a sort of peace officer or constable.

Tithonic, tī-thon'ik, *a.* [From Gr. *Tithōnos*, the consort of Aurora.] Pertaining to those rays of light which produce chemical effects; actinic.

Titillate, tit'i-lāt, *v.i.*—*titillated, titillating.* [L. *titillo, titillatum*, to tickle.] To tickle; to give a slight relish or pleasure to.—**Titillation**, tit-i-lā'shon, *n.* The act of tickling; any slight pleasure.—**Titillative**, tit'i-lā-tiv, *a.* Tending to titillate or tickle.

Titivate, Tittivate, tit'i-vāt, *v.t.* [Perhaps from *tidy.*] To put in order; to make look smart or spruce; to adorn. (*Slang.*)

Titlark, tit'lärk, *n.* [From *tit*, a small bird, and *lark.*] A common small bird somewhat resembling a lark; a pipit.

Title, tī'tl, *n.* [O.Fr. *title* (Fr. *titre*), from L. *titulus*, a title.] An inscription or superscription on anything as a name by which it is known; a label; the inscription at the beginning of a book or other composition, containing the subject of the work or its particular designation; a particular section or division of a writing, especially a chapter or section of a law-book; an appellation of dignity, distinction, or pre-eminence given to persons; the appellation or honour distinctive of a sovereign, prince, or nobleman; a name or appellation in general; a claim; a right; *law*, right of ownership, or the sources of such right; the instrument or document which is evidence of a right.—*v.t.*—*titled, titling.* To name; to call; to entitle.—**Titled**, tī'tld, *a.* Having a title; especially, having a title of nobility.—**Title-deed**, *n.* A writing evidencing a man's right or title to property.—**Title-page**, *n.* The page of a book which contains the title.—**Title-role**, *n.* The part in a play which gives its name to it, as Hamlet in the play of 'Hamlet'.

Titling, tit'ling, *n.* [A dim. of *tit*, something small.] The hedge-sparrow; the titlark.

Titmouse, tit'mous, *n.* pl. **Titmice**, tit'mīs. [From *tit*, a small thing, a small bird, and *mouse*, by corruption from A.Sax. *máse* (D. *mees*, G. *meise*), a titmouse.] A name of several common insessorial birds, small and active, feeding on seeds, insects, &c., with shrill, wild notes.

Titter, tit'ėr, *v.i.* [An imitative word, like *snigger, tattle*, &c.] To laugh with a stifled sound or with restraint.—*n.* A restrained laugh.—**Tittering**, tit'ėr-ing, *n.* Restrained laughter.

Tittle, tit'l, *n.* [O.Fr. *title*, a title, a tittle. TITLE.] A small particle; a jot; an iota.

Tittlebat, tit'l-bat, *n.* The stickleback.

Tittle-tattle, *n.* [A reduplication of *tattle*; an imitative word.] Idle trifling talk; empty prattle.—*v.i.* To talk idly; to prate.

Titubate,† tit'ū-bāt, *v.t.* and *i.* [L. *titubo, titubatum*, to stumble.] To stumble; to rock or roll, as a curved body on a plane.—**Titubation**, tit-ū-bā'shon, *n.* A stumbling; *med.* restlessness; fidgets.

Titular, tit'ū-lėr, *a.* [Fr. *titulaire*; from L. *titulus*, a title. TITLE.] Being such or such by title or name only; having the title to an office without the duties of it.—*n.* One who has merely the title of an office; one who may lawfully enjoy an ecclesiastical benefice without performing its duties.—**Titularity**, tit-ū-lar'i-ti, *n.* The state of being titular.—**Titularly**, tit'ū-lėr-li, *adv.* In a titular manner; by title only.—**Titulary**, tit'ū-la-ri, *a.* and *n.* Same as *Titular*.

Tiver, tī'vėr, *n.* [A.Sax. *teáfor*, a reddish colour.] A kind of ochre used in marking sheep.

Tizri, *n.* TISRI.

Tmesis, tmē'sis, *n.* [Gr. *tmēsis*, from *temnō*, to cut.] *Gram.* the division of a compound word into two parts, with one or more words between (of whom *be* thou *ware*).

To, tu̦, or when emphasized tö, *prep.* [A. Sax. *tó*, to, towards, for, &c. = D. *toe*, L.G. *to*, G. *zu*, Goth. *du*; cog. Ir. and Gael. *do*, Slav. *do.*] Denoting motion towards a place or thing (going *to* church); towards (point *to* the sky): opposed to *from*; indicating a point or limit reached (count *to* ten); denoting destination, aim, or design (born *to* poverty); denoting an end or consequence (*to* our cost); denoting addition, junction, or union (tied *to* a tree); compared with; often used in expressing ratios or proportions (three is *to* twelve as four is *to* sixteen); denoting opposition or contrast (face *to* face); often used in betting phrases (my hat *to* a halfpenny); according to; in congruity or harmony with (suited *to* his taste); denoting correspondency or accompaniment (dance *to* an air); in the character or quality of (took her *to* wife); for; denoting the relation of the dative in other languages (given *to* me); marking an object (a dislike *to* spirituous liquors); the sign of the infinitive mood of a verb, or governing the gerundial infinitive or gerund (slow *to* believe; we have *to* pay it).—*adv.* Forward; on; often denoting motion towards a junction, union, or closing (shut the door *to*).—*To and fro*, forward and backward; up and down.

Toad, tōd, *n.* [A.Sax. *tádie, tádige*, a toad: origin unknown. *Tad* in *tad*pole is this word.] A reptile somewhat resembling the frog, with a heavy bulky body; it leaps badly, and generally avoids the water.—*Surinam toad.* PIPA.—*Toad in the hole*, meat cooked in batter.—**Toad-eater**, *n.* [Originally a mountebank's attendant, who pretended to swallow toads, &c.] A fawning, obsequious parasite; a mean sycophant; a toady.—**Toad-eating**, *n.* Parasitism; sycophancy.—*a.* Pertaining to a toad-eater or his ways.—**Toad-fish**, *n.* A fish, the angler or fishing-frog.—**Toad-flax**, *n.* The name of several indigenous British plants allied to the antirrhinum.—**Toad-let**, tōd'let, *n.* A little toad.—**Toad-spit**, *n.* CUCKOO-SPIT.—**Toad-stone**, *n.* Bufonite.—**Toad-stool**, *n.* A popular name of fungi.—**Toady**, tō'di, *n.* [Short for *toad-eater.*] A base sycophant; a flatterer; a toad-eater.—*v.t.*—*toadied, toadying.* To fawn upon in a servile manner; to play the toady or sycophant to.—**Toadyism**, tō'di-izm, *n.* Mean sycophancy; servile adulation; nauseous flattery.

Toast, tōst, *v.t.* [O.Fr. *toster*, from L. *tostum*, pp. of *torreo*, to toast. TORRENT.] To dry and scorch (a piece of bread) by the heat of a fire; to warm thoroughly (to *toast* the feet); to drink to the success of or in honour of.—*n.* Bread scorched by the fire; a piece of such bread put in a beverage; a lady whose health is drunk in honour or respect; anyone or anything named in honour in drinking; a sentiment proposed for general acceptance in drinking.—**Toaster**, tōs'tėr, *n.* One who toasts; an instrument for toasting bread, cheese, &c.—**Toasting-fork, Toasting-iron**, *n.* A jocular name for a sword.—**Toast-master**, *n.* A person who at great entertainments announces the toasts.—**Toast-rack**, *n.* A stand for a table for slices of dry toast.

Tobacco, tō-bak'ō, *n.* A plant of the nightshade family, a native of the warmer parts of America, and now extensively cultivated in various regions; also the prepared leaves, used for smoking and chewing or in the form of snuff.—**Tobacconist**, tō-bak'ō-nist, *n.* A dealer in tobacco; a manufacturer of tobacco.—**Tobacco-pipe**, *n.* An implement used in smoking tobacco, consisting essentially of a bowl for the tobacco, and a stem through which the tobacco smoke is drawn into the mouth, varying in form and material.—**Tobacco-pouch**, *n.* A small pouch for holding tobacco.—**Tobacco-stopper**, *n.* A small implement for pressing down the tobacco as it is smoked in a pipe.

Tobine, tō'bin, *n.* [From G. *tobin*, D. *tabijn*; akin *tabby.*] A stout twilled silk, used for dresses.

Toboggan, tō-bog'an, *n.* [Corruption of Amer. Indian *odabagan*, a sled.] A kind of flat-bottomed sled turned up in front, used for sliding down snow-covered slopes.—*v.i.* To use such a sled; to fall rapidly, as stock prices (*Slang*).

Tocher, toch'ėr, *n.* [Gael. *tochradh*, Ir. *tochar*, a portion or dowry.] The dowry which a wife brings to her husband by marriage. (*Scotch.*)

Tocsin, tok'sin, *n.* [Fr. *tocsin*, O.Fr. *toquesin*; from *toque*, a stroke, and *sin, sein*, a bell, from L. *signum*, a sign. TOUCH, SIGN.] An alarm-bell; a bell rung as a signal or for the purpose of giving an alarm.

Tod, tod, *n.* [Icel. *toddi*, a tod of wool; akin G. *zote*, a lock of wool.] A bush, especially of ivy; a mass of growing foliage; an old weight used chiefly in buying wool, equal to 28 pounds; a fox, so named from his bushy tail.

To-day, tu̦-dā', *n.* [A.Sax. *tó-dæg*—*tó*, to, and *dæg*, day.] The present day; also, on this day, adverbially: seldom or never with *on* before it.

Toddle, tod'l, *v.i.*—*toddled, toddling.* [A freq. akin to *totter*; comp. G. *zotteln*, to toddle.] To walk with short steps in a tottering way, as a child or an old man.—*n.* A little toddling walk.—**Toddler**, tod'l-ėr, *n.* One who toddles; a young child.

Toddy, tod'i, *n.* [Hind.] The sweet juice of certain palms; palm-wine; also, a mixture of spirit and hot water sweetened.—**Toddy-ladle**, *n.* A sort of spoon with a deep circular bowl for filling a glass with toddy from the tumbler.

To-do, tu̦-dö, *n.* Ado; bustle; hurry; commotion. (*Colloq.*)

Tody, tō'di, *n.* [Probably from some Indian name.] A tropical passerine bird of gaudy plumage, allied to the king-fishers.

Toe, tō, *n.* [A.Sax. *tá*, toe=Icel. *tá*, Sw. *to*; Dan. *taa*, G. *zehe*, the toe.] One of the small members which form the extremity of the foot, corresponding to a finger on the hand; the fore part of the hoof of a horse or other hoofed animal; the member of an animal's foot corresponding to the toe in man.—*v.t.*—*toed, toeing.* To touch or reach with the toes.—**Toed**, tōd, *a.* Having toes: often used in composition (narrow-*toed*).

Toffee, Toffy, tof'i, *n.* [RATAFIA.] A kind of hard sweetmeat or candy composed of boiled sugar with a proportion of butter and flavoring matter.

Toft, toft, *n.* [A Scandinavian word; Icel. and Dan. *toft*, an inclosed field near a house.] A messuage; a house and homestead.

Toga, tō'ga, *n.* [L., from stem of *tego*, to cover.] The principal outer garment worn by males among the ancient Romans; a sort of loose robe.—**Togated**, tō'gā-ted, *a.* [L. *togatus.*] Dressed in a toga or gown.

Together, tu̦-geTH'ėr, *adv.* [A.Sax. *tógædere*—*tó*, to, *gador, geador*, at once. GATHER.] In company; unitedly; in concert; in the same place; at the same time; so as to be contemporaneous; the one with the other; mutually; into junction or a state of union; without intermission; on end.

Toggery, tog'ėr-i, *n.* [Perhaps humorously formed from L. *toga.*] Clothes; garments. (*Slang.*)

Toggle, tog'l, *n.* [Connected with *tag* or *tug.*] *Naut.* a pin through the bight or eye of a rope, or in a similar position, to prevent slipping.—**Toggle-joint**, *n.* A joint formed by two pieces jointed together endwise, or by two plates hinged edgewise; a knee-joint or elbow-joint.—**Toggle-press**, *n.* A kind of press in which the action of parts forming a toggle-joint is an important feature.

Toil, toil, *v.i.* [Perhaps from O.D. *teulen, tuylen*, to labour, *tuyl*, tillage, toil; O.Fris. *teula*, to labour, *teule*, labour; akin to *till*.] To exert strength continuously with pain and fatigue of body or mind, particularly of the body; to labour; to work; to drudge. —*v.t.* To labour on; to exhaust or overlabour.—*n.* Labour with pain and fatigue; labour that oppresses the body or mind.—**Toiler**, toi'lėr, *n.* One who toils.—**Toilful**, toil'ful, *a.* Full of toil; laborious.—**Toilsome**, toil'sum, *a.* Attended with toil; laborious; fatiguing.—**Toilsomely**, toil'sum-li, *adv.* In a toilsome manner.—**Toilsomeness**, toil'sum-nes, *n.* Laboriousness.—**Toil-worn**, *a.* Worn out or exhausted with toil.

Toil, toil, *n.* [Fr. *toile*, net, from L. *tela*, a web, from *texo*, to weave. TEXT.] A net or snare for taking prey.

Toilet, toi'let, *n.* [Fr. *toilette*, formerly a sort of wrapping cloth, from *toile*, cloth, L. *tela*, a web. TOIL, a net.] A cloth spread over a table in a bed-chamber or dressing-room; a dressing-table; lavatory; the act or process of dressing; also, the mode of dressing; style or fashion of dress; attire; dress.—*To make one's toilet*, to dress; to adjust one's dress with care. —**Toilet paper**, *n.* Thin paper for use in toilet rooms. —**Toilet-service**, **Toilet-set**, *n.* The collective earthenware and glass utensils necessary in a dressing-room. —**Toilet-table**, *n.* A dressing-table.

Toise, toiz, *n.* [Fr. *toise*, from L. *tensus*, stretched, tense.] An old measure of length in France, containing 6 French feet, or 6·395 English feet.

Tokay, tō-kā', *n.* A highly-prized wine produced at *Tokay* in Hungary, made of white grapes, and distinguished by its aromatic taste.

Token, tō'kn, *n.* [A.Sax. *tácen, tácn*, a token = Icel. *tákn, teiken*, D. *teeken*, G. *zeichen*, Goth. *taikns*—a sign, a token; akin to *teach*. TEACH.] Something intended or supposed to represent or indicate another thing or an event; a sign; a mark; indication; symptom; a memorial of friendship; a souvenir; a love-token; something that serves by way of pledge of authenticity, good faith, or the like; formerly a piece of money current by sufferance and not coined by authority; *printing*, ten and a half quires of paper.

Tolbooth, tōl'bōTH. TOLLBOOTH.

Told, tōld, pret. and pp. of *tell*.

Toledo, tō-lē'dō, *n.* A sword-blade of the finest temper, named from *Toledo* in Spain, formerly famous for its sword-blades.

Tolerate, tol'ėr-āt, *v.t.*—*tolerated, tolerating*. [L. *tolero, toleratum*, to bear or support, from root seen in *tollo*, to lift up, *tuli*, I have borne; Skr. *tul*, to bear; E. to *thole*.] To suffer to be or to be done without prohibition or hindrance; to allow or permit; to treat in a spirit of patience and forbearance; not to judge of or condemn with bigotry.—**Toleration**, tol-ėr-ā'shon, *n.* [L. *toleratis*.] The act of tolerating; allowance given to that which is not wholly approved; the recognition by the state of the right of private judgment in matters of faith and worship; a disposition to tolerate or not to judge or deal harshly in cases of difference of opinion or conduct; tolerance.—*Toleration Act*, the Act of 1689 releasing Dissenters in England from religious disabilities under certain conditions. —**Tolerator**, tol'ėr-ā-tėr, *n.* One who tolerates.—**Tolerable**, tol'ėr-a-bl, *a.* [L. *tolerabilis*.] Capable of being borne or endured; supportable, either physically or mentally; sufferable; moderately good or agreeable; not contemptible; passable; middling. —**Tolerableness**, tol'ėr-a-bl-nes, *n.* The state of being tolerable.—**Tolerably**, tol'ėr-a-bli, *adv.* In a tolerable manner; moderately well; passably.—**Tolerance**, tol'ėr-ans, *n.* [L. *tolerantia*.] The quality of being tolerant; the capacity or the act of enduring; a disposition to be patient and indulgent towards those whose opinions or practices differ from one's own; *engin.* the permitted amount of deviation from exact dimensions as specified.—**Tolerant**, tol'ėr-ant, *a.* [L. *tolerans, tolerantis*, ppr. of *tolero*.] Inclined or disposed to tolerate; favouring toleration; forbearing; able to endure or suffer.—**Tolerantly**, tol'ėr-ant-li, *adv.* In a tolerant manner.

Toll, tōl, *n.* [A.Sax. *toll*, tax or tribute = Icel. *tollr*, Sw. *tull*, Dan. *told*, D. *tol*, G. *zoll*, toll, duty, custom, from stem of *tell*, to count.] A tax or duty imposed for some liberty or privilege, as the sum charged for leave to offer goods in a market or fair; a fixed charge made by those intrusted with the maintenance of roads, streets, bridges, &c., for the passage of persons, goods, and cattle.—*v.i.*‡ To pay toll; to exact or levy toll.—**Tollable**, tōl'a-bl, *a.* Subject to toll.—**Tollage**, tōl'āj, *n.* Toll; payment of toll.—**Toll-bar**, *n.* A bar or gate to prevent persons or traffic passing without payment of toll.—**Tollbooth**, **Tolbooth**, tōl'bōTH, *n.* [*Toll*, and *booth*, originally a booth or slight structure where duties had to be paid and where defaulters were temporarily detained.] A place where duties or tolls are collected‡; the old Scotch name for a burgh jail, formerly used in England also.—**Toll-corn**, *n.* Corn taken at a mill in payment for grinding.—**Toll-gate**, *n.* A gate where toll is taken; a toll-bar.—**Toll-gatherer**, *n.* The man who takes toll.—**Toll-house**, *n.* A house placed by a road near a toll-gate, where the man who takes the toll is stationed.—**Toll-man**, *n.* A toll-gatherer; the keeper of a toll-bar.

Toll, tōl, *v.i.* [Probably from the sound.] To give out the slowly measured sounds of a bell when struck at uniform intervals, as at funerals.—*v.t.* To cause (a bell) to sound with strokes slowly and uniformly repeated; to indicate by tolling or striking; to draw attention to by slowly repeated sounds of a bell; to ring for or on account of.—*n.* The sounding of a bell with slow, measured strokes.

Tolmen, tol'men, *n.* A dolmen.

Tolu, tō'lö, *n.* A fragrant resin or balsam produced by a tree of South America, first brought from Santiago de *Tolu*, in New Granada, and used in coughs, &c.

Toluene, tol'ū-ēn, *n.* [From *tolu*.] A coal-tar product used in the preparation of trinitro-toluene, a high-explosive.

Tom, tom, *n.* A popular contraction of *Thomas*, used in slight contempt (a *tomfool*), or in the names of certain animals.—**Tomboy**, tom'boi, *n.* A rude boisterous boy; a wild, romping girl; a hoyden. —**Tom-cat**, *n.* A male cat, especially a full-grown male cat.—**Tomfool**, tom'föl, *n.* A great fool; a trifler.—**Tomfoolery**, tom-föl'ėr-i, *n.* Foolish trifling; ridiculous behaviour; silly trifles; absurd ornaments or knick-knacks. —**Tom-noddy**, *n.* A seabird, the puffin; a blockhead; a dolt; a dunce.—**Tomtit**, tom-tit', *n.* The titmouse.

Tomahawk, tom'a-hak, *n.* [From Virginian Indian *tamahaac, tamohake*, a hatchet.] An American Indian hatchet, used in the chase and in war, not only in close fighting, but by being thrown to a considerable distance.—*v.t.* To strike, cut, or kill with a tomahawk.

Toman, **Tomaun**, tō-män', tō-man', *n.* A Persian gold coin, at some places and times worth from 30*s.* to 35*s.*

Tomato, tō-mā'tō or tō-mä'tō, *n.* pl. **Tomatoes**. [Sp. *tomate*, from Mexican *tomatl*.] A tropical American plant of the potato family, and its wholesome and nutritious fruit, now much eaten, the plant being widely cultivated; called also *Love-apple*.

Tomb, töm, *n.* [Fr. *tombe*, It. *tomba*, L.L. *tumba*, from Gr. *tymba, tymbos*, a mound, from root of L. *tumeo*, to swell, *tumulus*, a mound.] A grave; a chamber or vault formed for the reception of the dead; a monument erected in memory of the dead; any sepulchral structure.—*v.t.* To bury; to entomb.—**Tombless**, töm'les, *a.* Without a tomb.—**Tombstone**, töm'stōn, *n.* A stone erected over a grave; a sepulchral stone.

Tombac, **Tombak**, tom'bak, *n.* [Fr. *tombac*, from Malay *tambaga*, copper.] An alloy of copper and zinc, used as an imitation of gold for cheap jewellery. When arsenic is added it forms *white tombac*.

Tombola, tom'bo-la, *n.* [It.] A kind of lottery, in which articles of various kinds are the prizes.

Tomboy, **Tom-cat**. Under TOM.

Tome, tōm, *n.* [Fr. *tome*, from L. *tomus*, a portion of a book, a book, from Gr. *tomos*, a section, from *temnō*, to cut.] A volume, forming part of a larger work; a book, usually a ponderous one.

Tomentose, **Tomentous**, tō-men'tōs, tō-men'tus, *a.* [L. *tomentum*, down.] Covered with hairs so close as scarcely to be discernible, or with a whitish down like wool; downy; nappy: used chiefly in botany.—**Tomentum**, tō-men'tum, *n.* Pubescence; downy matter.

Tomfool. Under TOM.

Tomin, tō'min, *n.* A jeweller's weight of 12 grains.

Tommy, tom'i, *n.* [From the name *Thomas Atkins*, used casually in specimen forms given in Army Regulations.] A private soldier in the British army.

Tommy, tom'i, *n.* (*Slang.*) A penny roll; bread; provisions; goods given to a workman in lieu of wages; the system of paying workmen in goods in place of money; the truck system. — **Tommy-shop**, **Tommy-store**, *n.* (*Slang.*) A shop or store conducted on the truck system; a truck-shop.

Tom-noddy. Under TOM.

To-morrow, tu-mor'ō, *n.* [*To* and *morrow*. Comp. *to-day, to-night*.] The day after the present; or, adverbially, on the day after the present; also used adjectively (*to-morrow* night).

Tompion, tom'pi-on, *n.* [Fr. *tampon*, a stopple. TAMPION.] The tampion or stopper of a cannon; the plug in a flute.

Tomtit. Under TOM.

Tomtom, tom'tom, *n.* Same as *Tam-tam*.

Ton, tun, *n.* [A.Sax. *tunne*, a butt, a large vessel. TUN.] A weight equal to 20 hundredweight or 2240 pounds avoirdupois; a certain weight or space (about 40 cubic feet) by which the burden of a ship is reckoned (a ship of 300 *tons*); a certain quantity of timber, as 40 feet of rough, and 50 feet of hewn.—**Tonnage**, tun'āj, *n.* The cubical content or burden of a ship in tons; the number of tons a ship can carry with safety; the ships of a port or nation collectively estimated by their burthen in tons; *hist. tonnage and poundage*, customs duties on the tun of wine and pound's worth of merchandise exported or imported, given as subsidies to the Crown, but levied illegally by Charles I.

Ton, ton, *n.* [Fr., TONE.] The prevailing fashion; high mode (ladies of *ton*).

Tone, tōn, *n.* [Fr. *ton*, tone, accent, style, manner, &c., L. *tonus*, a sound, a tone, from Gr. *tonos*, a stretching, a tone, note, strength, &c., from *teinō*, to stretch, cog. with L. *tendo*, to stretch, and E. *thin*. *Tune* is the same word.] Any sound considered with relation to its pitch, its quality or timbre, or its strength or volume; a modulation of the voice, as expressing some feeling; accent; a sing-song manner of speaking; a drawl; a musical sound; also one of the larger intervals between certain contiguous notes of the diatonic scale (known as *major* or *minor*); the peculiar quality of sound of any voice or instrument; timbre; that state of a living body in which all the parts and organs have due tension or are well-strung; healthy activity of the organs; state or temper of mind; mood; the general or prevailing character, as of morals, manners, or sentiments; *painting*, a harmonious relation of the colours of a picture in light and shade; the characteristic expression of a picture as distinguished by its colour.—*v.t.*—*toned, toning*. To give a certain tone to; to utter in an affected tone.—*To tone down*, to soften the colouring of; to give a lower tone to; to render less pronounced or decided (to *tone down* a statement); to soften.—**Toned**, tōnd, *a.* Having a certain tone.—**Toneless**, tōn′les, *a.* Having no tone; unmusical.—**Tonal**, tō′nal, *a.* Pertaining to tone.—**Tonality**, tō-nal′i-ti, *n.* *Mus.* the peculiarity characteristic of modern compositions due to their being written in definite keys, thereby conforming to certain defined arrangements of tones and semitones in the diatonic scale.—**Tonic**, ton′ik, *a.* [Fr. *tonique*, L. *tonicus*.] Relating to tones or sounds; *mus.* pertaining to or founded on the key-note; *med.* increasing the strength or tone of the animal system; obviating the effects of weakness or debility, and restoring healthy functions. — *Tonic spasm, pathol.* a steady and continuous spastic contraction enduring for a comparatively long time: opposed to a *clonic spasm.* — *n. Med.* any remedy which improves the tone or vigour of the stomach, or of the muscular fibres generally, as quinine, gentian, iron, &c.; *mus.* the key-note or fundamental note of a scale.—**Tonicity**, to-nis′i-ti, *n.* *Physiol.* the elasticity of living parts.—**Tonic Sol-fa**. A term applied to a system of writing and teaching music, the leading features of which are the substitution of letters denoting sounds, and of strokes, commas, and colons, denoting time, for the notes, &c., of the ordinary notation.—**Tonic-solfaist**, *n.* One who teaches or learns the tonic sol-fa notation.—**Tony**, *a.* Fashionable; smart. (*Colloq.*)

Tonga-bean, tong′ga-bēn, *n.* The tonka-bean.

Tongs, tongz, *n.pl.* [A.Sax. *tange*, pl. *tangan*, tongs = D. and Dan. *tang*, Icel. *töng*, G. *zange*, tongs; same root as Gr. *daknō*, to bite.] An instrument of metal, a kind of large nippers, used for handling things, particularly fire or heated metals.

Tongue, tung, *n.* [A.Sax. *tunge*, a tongue, speech = L.G. and Dan. *tunge*, Icel. and Sw. *tunga*, Goth. *tuggo*, G. *zunge*; cog. O.L. *dingua*, L. *lingua*, a tongue (whence *lingual*, *linguist*).] The fleshy movable organ within an animal's mouth, subserving the purposes of taste, prehension of food, swallowing, and in man of articulation or speech also; the instrument of speech (a bitter *tongue*); speech; the whole sum of words used by a particular nation; a language; a nation as distinguished by their language (O.T.); anything considered to resemble an animal's tongue; a point or strip of land running out into a sea or lake; a long low promontory; a tapering jet of flame; the pin of a buckle or brooch which pierces the strap, ribbon, or object to be fastened.—*To have on* (or *at*) *the tip* (or *end*) *of one's tongue*, to be on the point of uttering, telling, or speaking.—*To hold one's tongue*, to keep silence; to be silent.—*v.t.*—*tongued, tonguing.* To scold; *mus.* to modify with the tongue in playing, as in the flute.—**Tongued**, tungd, *a.* Having a tongue or voice.—**Tongueless**, tung′les, *a.* Having no tongue; speechless.—**Tonguelet**, tung′let, *n.* A little tongue; a little tongue-shaped process.—**Tonguester**, tung′stėr, *n.* [*Tongue*, and suffix *-ster*.] A talkative person; a babbler (*Tenn.*).—**Tongue-tied**, **Tongue-tacked**, *a.* Unable to articulate distinctly; having an impediment in the speech; unable to speak freely from whatever cause.

Tonic, &c. Under TONE.

To-night, tu̧-nīt′, *n.* [Comp. *to-day*, *to-morrow*.] The present night; or, adverbially, in the present night, or the night after the present day.

Tonite, tōn′īt, *n.* [L. *tono*, to thunder.] A very powerful explosive agent prepared from pulverized gun-cotton.

Tonka-bean, tong′ka-bēn, *n.* [From *tonka*, the name of the bean in Guiana.] The fruit of a shrubby leguminous plant of Guiana, containing a single seed, the odour of which is extremely agreeable.

Tonnage. Under TON.

Tonsil, ton′sil, *n.* [L. *tonsilla*, a tonsil, a mooring pole for a boat.] *Anat.* one of two oblong glands on each side of the throat or fauces, which secrete a mucous humour.—**Tonsillitis**, ton-sil-ī′tis, *n.* Inflammation of the tonsils; quinsy; malignant sore throat. — **Tonsillectomy**, ton′si-lek″tō-mē, *n.* A surgical operation for the removal of enlarged or inflamed tonsils.

Tonsile, ton′sīl, *a.* [L. *tonsilis*, from *tondeo*, *tonsum*, to clip or shear.] Capable of or fit to be clipped.—**Tonsor**, ton′sor, *n.* [L.] A barber; one that shaves. — **Tonsorial**, ton-sō′ri-al, *a.* Pertaining to a barber or to shaving. — **Tonsure**, ton′sūr, *n.* [L. *tonsura*, the act of shaving or clipping.] The act of clipping or shaving; the round bare place on the heads of the Roman Catholic priests and monks formed by shaving or cutting the hair.—**Tonsured**, ton′sūrd, *a.* Having a tonsure; hence, clerical.

Tontine, ton′tīn, *n.* [Fr. *tontine*, from its inventor *Tonti*, an Italian of the seventeenth century.] An annuity shared by subscribers to a loan, with the benefit of survivorship, the annuity being increased as the subscribers die, until at last the whole goes to the last survivor, or to the last two or three.

Too, tö, *adv.* [A form of *to*, the preposition; A.Sax. *tó*, meaning both *to* and *too*. Comp. G. *zu*, to and too.] Over; more than enough; denoting excess (*too* long, *too* short); sometimes with merely an intensive force = very, exceedingly (I should only be *too* glad); likewise; also; in addition; besides; over and above (a painter and a poet *too*). — *Too, too*, repeated, denotes excess emphatically.

Took, tu̧k, pret. of *take*.

Tool, töl, *n.* [A.Sax. *tól*, a tool, probably from stem of *tawian*, to make, to prepare. TAW.] Any implement used by a craftsman or labourer at his work; an instrument employed in the manual arts for facilitating mechanical operations; a person used by another as an instrument to accomplish certain ends: a word of reproach.—*Machine-tool.* Under MACHINE. ∴ A *tool* differs from an *implement* in being more general or less specific, and from an *instrument* in being always used in reference to the manual arts; agricultural *implements*; gardeners' *tools*; joiners' *tools*; surgical *implements*; mathematical *instruments*; musical *instruments*.—*v.t.* To shape with a tool; to drive, as a vehicle (*slang*).—**Tooling**, töl′ing, *n.* Skilled work with a tool; carving; ornamental embossing or gilding by heated tools upon the binding of books.

Toom, tu̧m, *a.* [Same as Icel. *tómr*, Dan. and Sw. *tom*, empty.] Empty. (*A provincial word.*)

Toon, Toona, tön, tö′na, *n.* The wood of an East Indian tree, highly valued as a furniture wood.

Toot, töt, *v.i.* [Same as D. *toeten*, G. *tuten*, Sw. *tuta*, to blow a horn, to toot; imitative of sound.] To make a noise like that of a pipe or horn.—*v.t.* To sound, as a horn. —*n.* A sound blown on a horn; a similar noise.—**Tooter**, tö′tėr, *n.* One who toots.

Tooth, töth, *n.* pl. **Teeth**, tēth. [A.Sax. *tóth*, pl. *tēth* (comp. *foot*, *feet*; *goose*, *geese*) = D., Sw., and Dan. *tand*, Icel. *tönn* (for *tönd*), G. *zahn*, Goth. *tunthus*; cog. W. *dant*, L. *dens*, *dentis*, Gr. *odous*, *odontos*, Skr. *danta*—tooth; from root meaning to divide, seen also in Gr. *daiō*, to divide.] One of the projecting bony growths in the jaws of vertebrate animals, serving as the instrument of mastication; taste; palate; any projection resembling the tooth of an animal in shape, position, or office; a small, narrow, projecting piece, usually one of a set (as of a comb, a saw, a rake, a wheel).—*Tooth and nail* (lit. by biting and scratching), with one's utmost power; by all possible means of attack and defence. — *To one's teeth*, in open opposition; directly to one's face.—*In the teeth of*, in direct opposition to.—*To cast* something *in one's teeth*, to taunt one with something; to retort reproachfully.—*In spite of one's teeth*, in open defiance of; in opposition to every effort.—*To show the teeth*, to threaten (like a snarling dog).—*To set the teeth on edge*, to cause a tingling or grating sensation in the teeth.—*v.t.* To furnish with teeth; to cut into teeth.—**Teethe**, tēᴛʜ, *v.i.*—*teethed, teething.* To have the teeth grow.—**Teething**, tē′ᴛʜing, *n.* The growth of the teeth in the young; dentition.—**Toothache**, töth′-āk, *n.* Pain in a tooth or in the teeth arising from decay. — **Toothbrush**, *n.* A small brush for cleaning the teeth. — **Toothed**, tötht, *p.* and *a.* Having teeth or cogs; having projecting points somewhat like teeth.—**Toothedge**, töth′ej, *n.* The sensation of having the teeth set on edge.—**Toothful**, töth′fu̧l, *n.* A small draught of any liquor. — **Toothless**, töth′les, *a.* Having no teeth; deprived of teeth.—**Tooth-ornament**, *n.* *Arch.* same as *Nailhead.* — **Toothpick**, töth′pik, *n.* A small instrument for picking substances from the teeth.—**Tooth-powder**, *n.* A powder for cleaning the teeth; a dentifrice.—**Tooth-rash**, *n.* A cutaneous disease of infants during the process of dentition.—**Toothsome**, töth′sum, *a.* Palatable; grateful to the taste.—**Toothsomeness**, töth′sum-nes, *n.* Pleasantness to the taste; palatableness.

Top, top, *n.* [A.Sax. *top*, top = D. and Dan. *top*, summit; Icel. *toppr*, a tuft or lock of hair, top; G. *zopf*, a tuft, a crest. *Tip*, *tap* (of a cask), *tuft*, are allied.] The highest part of anything; the most elevated or uppermost point; the summit; upper surface; the highest place or rank; the most honourable position; the utmost degree; the height; the crown of the head (from *top* to toe); the head or upper part of a plant; *pl.* top-boots; *woollen manuf.* the combed wool ready for the spinner; *naut.* a sort of platform surrounding the head of the lower masts, serving to extend the shrouds, and for the convenience of men aloft.—*The top of one's bent*, the utmost of one's inclination or liking (fooled to *the top of his bent*).—*a.* Being on the top or summit; highest (*top* speed).—*v.i.*—*topped, topping.* To rise aloft; to be eminent.—*v.t.* To cover on the top; to cap; to rise above; to surpass; to take off the top or upper part of; to rise to the top of.—*To top off*, to complete by putting on the top; hence, to finish; to complete.—**Top-boots**, *n.pl.* Boots having tops of light-coloured leather, used chiefly for riding.—**Top-coat**, *n.* An upper or over coat.—**Top-draining**, *n.* The act or practice of draining the surface of land.—**Top-dress**, *v.t.* To spread manure on the surface of.—**Top-dressing**, *n.* A dressing of manure laid on the surface of land.—**Topgallant**, top′gal-ant, *a.* *Naut.* being the third of the kind above the deck; above the topmast and below the royal mast (the *topgallant* mast, yards, &c.).—**Top-hamper**, *n.* *Naut.* any unnecessary weight either aloft or about the upper decks.—**Top-heavy**, *a.* Having the top or upper part too heavy for the lower.—**Top-knot**, *n.* An ornamental knot or bow worn on the top of the head, as by women; the crest of a bird.—**Topless**, top′les, *a.* Having no top; very lofty.—**Topmast**, top′-mast, *n.* *Naut.* the second mast from the deck, or that which is next above the lower mast, main, fore, or mizzen.—**Topmost**, top′mōst, *a.* Highest; uppermost.—**Topper**, top′ėr, *n.* One who tops or excels; anything superior. (*Colloq.*)—**Topping**, top′ing, *p.* and *a.* Rising aloft; pre-eminent; surpassing; fine; noble; gallant.—**Topsail**, top′sāl, *n.* *Naut.* the second sail above the deck on any mast (main, fore, or mizzen).—**Tops-and-bottoms**, *n.pl.* Small rolls cut in halves and browned in an oven.—**Top-sawyer**, *n.* The sawyer who takes the upper stand in a saw-pit; a first-rate man in any line (*slang*).—**Top-soil**, *n.* The upper part or surface of the soil.—**Top-soiling**, *n.* Removal of the top-soil before a canal, railway, &c., is begun.

Top, top, *n.* [D. *top*, G. *topf*—perhaps same word as above, being named from whirling round on its top or point.] A child's toy, shaped like a pear, made to whirl on its point by means of a string or a whip.

Toparch, top′ärk, *n.* [Gr. *toparchēs*, *toparchos*—*topos*, place, and *archē*, rule.] The principal man in a place or country; the governor of a toparchy.—**Toparchy**, top'-är-ki, *n.* A little state; a petty country governed by a toparch.

Topaz, tō'paz, *n.* [Fr. *topaze*, L. *topazus*, from Gr. *topazos*, the yellow or oriental topaz; comp. Skr. *tapus*, fire.] A gem harder than quartz, transparent or translucent, and having the colour yellow, white, green, or blue.—**Topazolite**, tō-paz'o-līt, *n.* [*Topaz*, and Gr. *lithos*, a stone.] A variety of precious garnet of a topaz-yellow colour.

Tope, tōp, *n.* [Originally a Cornish word.] A fish of the shark kind, attaining a length of six feet.

Tope, tōp, *n.* [Skr. *stûpa*, a tope.] A species of Buddhist monument occurring in India and South-eastern Asia, intended for the preservation of relics (DAGOBA) or the commemoration of some event (STUPA).

Tope, tōp, *v.i.* [From Fr. *toper*, to cover a stake in gaming, to accept an offer (hence, it might mean to vie in drinking); of German origin and akin to *tap*, to strike.] To drink hard; to drink strong or spirituous liquors to excess.—**Toper**, tō'pėr, *n.* One who drinks to excess; a drunkard; a sot.

Tophet, tō'fet, *n.* [Heb., lit. a place to be spit on.] A place near Jerusalem where the idolatrous Jews worshipped the fire-gods and sacrificed their children; hence, the place of torment in a future life.

Tophus, tō'fus, *n.* [L. *tophus*, tufa or tuff.] *Surg.* a soft tumour on a bone; also, a concretion in the joints.—**Tophaceous**, to-fā'shus, *a.* Pertaining to a tophus.

Topiary, tō'pi-a-ri, *a.* [L. *topiarius*, from *topia* (*opera*), ornamental gardening, from Gr. *topos*, a place.] Shaped by clipping, pruning, or training.—*Topiary work*, the trimming of thickets, trees, or hedges into fantastic shapes.—**Topiarian**, tō-pi-ā'ri-an, *a.* Pertaining to topiary work.

Topic, top'ik, *n.* [Fr. *topiques*, subjects of conversation, from L. *topica*, Gr. *topika* (pl.), the name of a work by Aristotle on *topoi* or commonplaces, from *topos*, a place, a commonplace, a topic.] Originally a general maxim or dictum regarded as being of use in argument or oratory; a general truth; in common usage, the subject of any discourse; any subject that is discussed or spoken of for the time being; the matter treated of.—**Topical**, top'i-kal, *a.* Pertaining to a topic; pertaining to a place or locality; local; *med.* pertaining to a particular part of the body (a *topical* application).—**Topically**, top'i-kal-li, *adv.* Locally; with limitation to a part.

Topography, to-pog'ra-fi, *n.* [Gr. *topos*, place (hence *topic*), and *graphō*, to describe.] The description of a particular place, city, town, parish, or tract of land; the detailed description of any country or region: distinguished from geography in dealing with the minuter features.—**Topographer**, **Topographist**, to-pog'raf-ėr, to-pog'raf-ist, *n.* One who deals with topography.—**Topographic**, **Topographical**, top-o-graf'ik, top-o-graf'i-kal, *a.* Pertaining to topography; descriptive of a place or country.—**Topographically**, top-o-graf'i-kal-li, *adv.* In the manner of topography.

Toponomy, to-pon'o-mi, *n.* [Gr. *topos*, a place, and *onoma*, a name.] The place-names of a country or district.

Topple, top'l, *v.i.*—*toppled*, *toppling*. [From *top*.] To fall forward, as something tall or high; to tumble down; to be on the point of falling.—*v.t.* To throw down.

Topsy-turvy, top'si-tėr-vi, *a.* or *adv.* [A word of uncertain origin.] In an inverted posture; with the top or head downward and the bottom upward.

Toque, tōk, *n.* [Fr., from Armor. *tôk*, W. *toc*, a hat or bonnet.] A kind of bonnet or head-dress.

Tor, tor, *n.* [W. *tor*, a bulge, a hill; allied to L. *turris*, a tower.] A high pointed rock or hill.

Torah, tō'ra, *n.* [Heb.] Mosaic law, the Pentateuch.

Torch, torch, *n.* [Fr. *torche*, It. *torcia*, from L.L. *tortia*, from L. *torqueo*, *tortus*, to twist, to turn (whence *torture*, &c.), because the torch was made of a twisted roll of tow and the like.] A light to be carried in the hand, formed of some combustible substance, as of twisted flax, hemp, &c., soaked with tallow; a flambeau.—**Torch-bearer**, *n.* One whose office is to carry a lighted torch.—**Torch-dance**, *n.* A dance with lighted torches.—**Torch-light**, *n.* The light of a torch or of torches.—*Torch-light procession*, a procession in which lighted torches are carried.—**Torch-race**, *n.* A race among the ancient Greeks in which the runners carried torches.

Tore, tōr, pret. of *tear*.

Toreador, tor'e-a-dor", *n.* [Sp., from *toro*, a bull.] A general name for a bull-fighter in Spain, especially one who fights on horse-back.

Toreutic, to-rū'tik, *a.* [Gr. *toreutikos*, from *toreutēs*, an embosser, from *toreuō*, to emboss, to work in relief.] Pertaining to carved or sculptured work, especially to work in relief.—**Toreumatology**, to-rū'ma-tol"o-ji, *n.* The art of sculpture.

Torfaceous, tor-fā'shus, *a.* [From *turf*, with Latin termination.] Growing in bogs or mosses: said of plants.

Torment, tor'ment, *n.* [O.Fr. *torment* (Fr. *tourment*), from L. *tormentum*, an engine for hurling missiles, a rack, torture, from *torqueo*, *tortum*, to twist. TORTURE.] Extreme pain; anguish of body or mind; torture; what causes such pain.—*v.t.* (tor-ment'). To put to extreme pain or anguish; to inflict excruciating pain on; to torture; to afflict; to tease, vex, or harass; to annoy.—**Tormenter**, tor-men'tėr, *n.* One who torments; a tormentor.—**Tormenting**, tor-men'ting, *p.* and *a.* Causing torment.—**Tormentor**, tor-men'tėr, *n.* One who or that which torments; a kind of harrow with wheels, used for breaking up stiff soils.

Tormentil, **Tormentilla**, tor'men-til, tor-men-til'a, *n.* [Fr. *tormentille*, from L. *tormentum*, pain—because said to allay the pain of toothache.] A common British weed with small yellow flowers, and large woody roots sometimes used in tanning.

Tormina, tor'mi-na, *n.pl.* [L. TORMENT.] Severe griping pains; gripes.

Torn, tōrn, pp. of *tear*.

Tornado, tor-nā'dō, *n.* pl. **Tornadoes**, tor-nā'dōz. [Sp. *tornada*, a return, from *tornar*, to turn. TURN.] A violent whirling wind; a whirlwind or tempest, usually accompanied with severe thunder, lightning, and torrents of rain; a typhoon or hurricane.

Torose, **Torous**, tō'rōs, tō'rus, *a.* [L. *torosus*, from *torus*, a protuberance.] *Bot.* and *zool.* protuberant; swelling in knobs.

Torpedo, tor-pē'do, *n.* pl. **Torpedoes**, tor-pē'dōz. [L., from *torpeo*, to be stiff, numb, or torpid.] A fish allied to the rays, noted for its power of discharging electric shocks when irritated; a cigar-shaped submarine missile about 21 feet in length, 21 inches in diameter, and weighing about 1½ tons, filled with an explosive which is discharged on impact, propelled and steered by its own mechanism, capable of traveling accurately a distance of 10,000 yards, stabilized by a gyroscope, used in naval warfare for destroying or damaging enemy ships at sea.—*v.t.* To sink by a torpedo.—**Torpedo boat**, *n.* A vessel specially intended to attack with torpedoes, and having one or more torpedo tubes.—**Torpedo net**, *n.* A strong steel net suspended vertically in the water by means of booms to intercept a torpedo aimed at a vessel.—**Torpedo tube**, *n.* A tube for the discharge of torpedoes.

Torpid, tor'pid, *a.* [L. *torpidus*, from *torpeo*, to be numb, motionless; same root as A.Sax. *theorf*, unfermented.] Having lost motion or the power of motion and feeling; numb; dull; sluggish; inactive.—**Torpidity**, **Torpidness**, tor-pid'i-ti, tor'pid-nes, *n.* The state of being torpid; numbness; insensibility; inactivity; sluggishness.—**Torpidly**, tor'pid-li, *adv.* In a torpid manner; numbly; dully.—**Torpescence**, tor-pes'ens, *n.* A becoming torpid or benumbed.—**Torpescent**, tor-pes'ent, *a.* [L. *torpesco*, to grow numb, from *torpeo*.] Becoming torpid or numb.—**Torpify**, tor'pi-fī, *v.t.*—*torpified*, *torpifying*. [L. *torpeo*, and *facio*, to make.] To make torpid.—**Torpor**, tor'por, *n.* [L.] Loss of motion or of sensation; torpidity; numbness; sluggishness.—**Torporific**, tor-po-rif'ik, *a.* [L. *torpor*, and *facio*, to make.] Tending to produce torpor.

Torque, tork, *n.* [From L. *torques*, a twisted neck-chain, from *torqueo*, to twist.] *Archæol.* a personal ornament, consisting of a stiff collar, formed of a number of gold wires twisted together, or of a thin twisted metal plate, worn round the neck as a symbol of rank by certain ancient nations, as by the ancient Britons, Gauls, and Germans.—*Mech.* a system of forces equivalent to a couple, and therefore having a twisting or turning effect.—**Torquated**, tor'kwāt-ed, *a.* Wearing a torque.

Torrefy, tor'e-fī, *v.t.*—*torrefied*, *torrefying*. [Fr. *torréfier*, from L. *torreo*, to roast, and *facio*, to make. TORRENT.] To dry, roast, scorch, or parch by a fire; *metal.* to roast, as metallic ores.—**Torrefaction**, tor-e-fak'shon, *n.* The operation of drying or parching by a fire.

Torrent, tor'ent, *n.* [Fr. *torrent*, from L. *torrens*, *torrentis*, a torrent, from *torrens*, burning, roaring, ppr. of *torreo*, *tostum*, to burn; same root as E. *thirst*. *Torrid*, *toast*, are of same origin.] A violent stream, as of water, lava, or the like; *fig.* a violent or rapid flow; a flood (a *torrent* of words or eloquence).—**Torrential**, **Torrentine**, tor-en'shal, tor-en-tīn, *a.* Pertaining to a torrent.

Torricellian, tor-i-sel'li-an or tor-i-chel'-li-an, *a.* Pertaining to *Torricelli*, an Italian physicist, who, in 1643, discovered the principle of the barometer.—*Torricellian tube*, a glass tube open at one end and hermetically sealed at the other, containing mercury, the essential part of the barometer.—*Torricellian vacuum*, the vacuum above the mercurial column in the barometer.

Torrid, tor'id, *a.* [L. *torridus*, from *torreo*, to roast. TORRENT.] Dried with heat; parched; violently hot; burning or parching.—*Torrid zone*, *geog.* the broad belt round the middle of the earth which is included between the tropics, and divided into two parts by the equator, and where the heat is always great.—**Torridity**, **Torridness**, tor-id'i-ti, tor'id-nes, *n.* The state of being torrid.

Torsion, tor'shon, *n.* [L.L. *torsio*, from L. *torqueo*, *torsi*, to twist. TORTURE.] The act of twisting; the twisting, wrenching, or straining of a body; *mech.* the force with which a body, such as a thread, wire, or slender rod, resists a twist, or the force with which it tends to return to its original state on being twisted; *surg.* the twisting of the cut end of a small artery for the purpose of checking hemorrhage.—*Torsion balance*, an instrument for estimating the intensity of a small force (as of electricity) by the force with which a thread or wire resists twisting, as observed by the angle made by an arm horizontally suspended from the thread or wire.—**Torsional**, tor'shon-al, *a.* Pertaining to torsion.—**Torsive**, tor'siv, *a.* *Bot.* twisted spirally.

Torsk, torsk, *n.* [Sw. and Dan. *torsk*, a codfish or torsk.] A European fish of the cod tribe, caught in great quantities and salted and dried as food.

Torso, tor'sō, *n.* [It., lit. a trunk or stump.] *Sculp.* the trunk of a statue lacking head and limbs; in anatomy, the human trunk minus head and limbs.

Tort, tort, *n.* [Fr., from L. *tortus*, twisted, from *torqueo*, to twist. TORTURE.] A legal term for any wrong or injury to person or property.—**Tortious**, tor'shus, *a.* Of the nature of or implying tort or injury.—**Tortiously**, *adv.*

Torteau, tor'tō, *n.* *Her.* a red sphere, or 'roundle gules'.

Tortile, **Tortive**, tor'til, tor'tiv, *a.* [From

L. *torqueo, tortum,* to twist. TORTURE.] Twisted; wreathed; coiled. — **Tortility,** tor-til'i-ti, *n.* The state of being twisted.

Tortilla, tor-tēl'yä, *n.* [Sp.] A large thin cake of maize, baked on a heated iron plate.

Tortoise, tor'tis, *n.* [Lit. twisted or distorted animal (referring to its peculiar limbs), from O.Fr. *tortis,* fem. *tortisse,* twisted, from L. *torqueo, tortum,* to twist. TORTURE.] A name common to a family of land reptiles covered with a flattened shell, a kind of bony box, from which the head and legs protrude. TURTLE.—**Tortoise-shell,** *n.* The shell, or more strictly the scutes or scales, of the tortoise and other allied reptiles, used in the manufacture of combs, snuff-boxes, &c., and in inlaying and other ornamental work.

Tortuous, tor'tū-us, *a.* [L. *tortuosus,* from *tortus,* twisted, pp. of *torqueo,* to twist. TORTURE.] Twisted; wreathed; winding; *fig.* proceeding in a circuitous and underhand manner; taking an oblique and deceitful course; not open and straightforward.—**Tortuously,** tor'tū-us-li, *adv.* In a tortuous or winding manner.—**Tortuousness,** tor'tū-us-nes, *n.* The state of being tortuous.—**Tortuose,** tor'tū-ōs, *a.* Tortuous; twisted; winding. — **Tortuosity,** tor-tū-os'i-ti, *n.* The state of being tortuose.

Torture, tor'tūr, *n.* [Fr. *torture,* from L. *tortura,* a twisting, torture, from *torqueo, tortum,* to twist, torture (seen also in *torment, torsion, tortoise, torch, truss, distort, extort,* &c.); same root as E. to *throw,* G. *drehen,* to turn.] Excruciating pain; extreme anguish of body or mind; agony; torment; severe pain inflicted judicially, either as a punishment for a crime or for the purpose of extorting a confession; the act of inflicting excruciating pain.—*v.t.*—*tortured, torturing.* To pain to extremity; to torment bodily or mentally; to punish with torture; to wrest greatly from the right meaning.—**Torturable,** tor'tūr-a-bl, *a.* Capable of being tortured.—**Torturer,** tor'tūr-ėr, *n.* One who tortures; a tormentor.

Torus, tō'rus, *n.* [L., a swelling or protuberance.] *Arch.* a large moulding used in the bases of columns, having a semicircular section; *bot.* the receptacle of a flower.—**Torulose, Torulous,** tor'ū-lōs, tor'ū-lus, *a.* [From L. *torulus,* dim. of *torus.*] *Bot.* cylindrical with several swells and contractions.

Tory, tō'ri, *n.* [From Irish *toruighe* or *toiridhe,* a pursuer, an Irish outlaw or plunderer.] A political party name first used in England about 1679, and applied originally in reproach to all supposed abettors of the imaginary Popish Plot; then to those who refused to concur in excluding a Roman Catholic prince (in the particular instance James II) from the throne; latterly it was generally applied to those adverse to changes in the constitution; in American history, a loyalist, one who during the War of Independence submitted to the claims of England against the colonies. — **Toryism,** tō'ri-izm, *n.* The principles or practices of the Tories.

Toss, tos, *v.t.* [Perhaps from W. *tosiaw,* to toss, from *tos,* a toss, a jerk.] To throw with the hand; to pitch; to fling; to cast; to throw up with a sudden or violent motion; to jerk (to *toss* the head); to dash about (to be *tossed* on the waves); to agitate; to make restless. — *To toss off,* to swallow at one gulp; to drink hastily.—*v.i.* To roll and tumble; to be in violent commotion; to writhe; to be flung or dashed about.—*To toss, to toss up,* to throw up a coin, and decide something by the side turned up when it falls.—*To toss oars,* to raise them perpendicularly with blades uppermost as a salute. — *n.* A throwing with a jerk; the act of tossing; a throw or jerk of the head; the tossing up of a coin to decide something.—**Tosser,** tos'ėr, *n.* One who tosses.—**Toss-pot,** *n.* A toper.—**Toss-up,** *n.* The throwing up of a coin to decide something; hence, an even chance or hazard.

Tot, tot, *n.* [Dan. *tot,* Icel. *tottr, tuttr,* applied to dwarfish persons; perhaps allied to *tit.*] Anything small or insignificant: used as a term of endearment; a young child; a small quantity of liquor.

Tot, tot, *v.t.*—*totted, totting.* [Abbrev. of *total.*] To sum: generally with *up.* (*Colloq.*)

Total, tō'tal, *a.* [L. *totalis,* from *totus,* whole; akin to *tot,* so many, *tam,* so, *tantus,* so great.] Pertaining to the whole; comprehending the whole; entire (the *total* sum); complete in degree; absolute (a *total* wreck); thorough. ∴ Syn. under COMPLETE.—*n.* The whole; the whole sum or amount; an aggregate.—**Totality,** tō-tal'i-ti, *n.* The whole or total sum; whole quantity or amount. — **Totally,** tō'tal-li, *adv.* **Totalitarian,** tō-tal'i-tār"i-an, *n.* Of or pertaining to a highly national socialistic state, or the philosophy of its government, headed by a political party whose control is omnipotent and absolute. — **Totalitarianism,** tō-tal'i-tār"i-an-izm, *n.* A national socialistic philosophy of government in which the state is omnipotent and absolute, superseding the welfare of its citizenry, the will of the state being expressed through a leader or a dictator.

Tother, tuтн'ėr. A colloquialism for *the other;* the initial *t* being the final *t* of *that* (old neuter article).

Totipalmate, tō-ti-pal'māt, *a.* and *n.* [L. *totus,* entire, and *palma,* a palm.] A term applied to swimming birds whose hind-toe is united with the others in a continuous membrane (as the pelican).

Totter, tot'ėr, *v.i.* [O.E. *toteren;* allied to *toddle,* and to G. *zotteln,* to trot; comp. also A.Sax. *tealtrian,* to totter, from *tealt,* unstable.] To appear as if about to fall when standing or walking; to walk unsteadily; to be on the point of falling; to threaten to topple down.—**Totterer,** tot'ėr-ėr, *n.* One who totters.—**Tottery,** tot'ėr-i, *a.* Unsteady; shaking.

Toucan, tö'kan, *n.* [Fr. *toucan,* Pg. and Braz. *tucano:* imitative of its cry.] The name of a family of scansorial birds of tropical America, distinguished by their enormous beak.

Touch, tuch, *v.t.* [Fr. *toucher,* O.Fr. *tucher, tocher, toquer* = Sp. and Pg. *tocar,* It. *toccare,* to touch, from O.H.G. *zuchon,* to draw, to pull; G. *zucken,* to twitch; E. to *tuck.*] To perceive by the sense of feeling; to come in contact with in any manner, but particularly by means of the hand, finger, &c.; to hit or strike against; to harm; to meddle or interfere with; hence, to taste or eat; to come to; to reach or arrive at; to relate to or concern (a person or thing); to mark or delineate slightly; to add a slight stroke or strokes to, as with a pen, pencil, brush, &c.; to handle in a skilful or special manner (as a musical instrument); to discourse of; to write about; to make a mere reference to; to move or strike mentally; to excite with compassion or other tender emotion; to melt or soften the heart of; to make an impression on physically; to act on; *geom.* to meet without cutting; to be in contact with.—*To touch off,* to sketch hastily; to finish by touches.—*To touch up,* to repair or improve by slight touches or emendations. — *v.i.* To be in contact; to take effect; to say a few words in discourse.—*Touch and go,* a phrase used either substantively or adjectively and applied to something, such as an accident, which had almost happened; a close shave. —*To touch at,* to come or go to in a voyage without staying.—*To touch on,* to mention slightly; to say very little about.—*n.* The act of touching, or the state of being touched; contact; the sense of feeling which resides in the nervous papillæ of the skin and forms one of the five senses; a state in which one or other of two parties has a knowledge of the other's position, opinions, &c.; a certain degree of some feeling, affection, or emotion (a *touch* of pity); a trait; a characteristic; a small quantity or degree; a smack; a little; a successful effort or attempt; a stroke (a *touch* of genius); a stroke of a pen, pencil, or the like; the act of the hand on a musical instrument; the peculiar handling usual to an artist, and by which his works may be known; the resistance of the keys of a musical instrument to the fingers.—**Touchable,** tuch'a-bl, *a.* Capable of being touched; tangible. —**Toucher,** tuch'ėr, *n.* One who touches. —**Touch-hole,** *n.* The vent of a cannon or other species of fire-arms, by which fire is communicated to the charge.—**Touching,** tuch'ing, *a.* Affecting; moving; pathetic.—*pp.* used as *prep.* Concerning; relating to; with respect to.—**Touchingly,** tuch'ing-li, *adv.* In a manner to touch the passions; pathetically; feelingly.—**Touch-me-not,** *n.* A plant the seed-vessel of which, being touched and irritated when ripe, projects the seeds to some distance; the disease lupus. — **Touch-needle,** *n.* A small bar of gold or silver, pure or alloyed, used along with the touchstone to test the quality of articles of gold and silver.—**Touch-paper,** *n.* Paper steeped in nitre so that it catches fire from a spark and burns slowly: used for firing gunpowder and the like.—**Touch-piece,** *n.* A coin given by the sovereigns of England to those whom they *touched* for the cure of scrofula or king's evil.—**Touchstone,** tuch'stōn, *n.* A hard black siliceous stone used in ascertaining the purity of gold and silver, the streak made by rubbing the article on it being compared with that made by the touch-needle, the quality of which is known; *fig.* any test or criterion by which the qualites of a thing are tried.—**Touchwood,** tuch'wụd, *n.* The soft white substance into which wood is converted by the action of several fungi, serving the purpose of tinder.

Touchy, tuch'i, *a.* [A form of *techy, tetchy,* brought into use by the influence of *touch.*] Apt to take offence; irritable; irascible; hence **Touchily, Touchiness.**

Tough, tuf, *a.* [A.Sax. *tóh,* tough; akin to D. *taai,* G. *zähe,* Prov.G. *zach,* tough.] Having the quality of flexibility without brittleness; yielding to force without breaking; having tenacity; tenacious; strong; able to endure hardship; viscous; durable; stubborn; unmanageable. — **Toughen,** tuf'n, *v.i.* To grow tough.—*v.t.* To make tough.—**Toughish,** tuf'ish, *a.* Tough in a slight degree.—**Toughly,** tuf'li, *adv.* In a tough manner.—**Toughness,** tuf'nes, *n.* The quality of being tough; flexibility with firm adhesion of parts; viscosity; tenacity; strength of constitution or texture.

Toupee, Toupet, tö-pē', tö'pā, *n.* [Fr. *toupet,* dim. from O.Fr. *toupe,* a tuft, from G. *zopf,* tuft. TOP.] A curl or artificial lock of hair; a small wig or upper part of a wig.

Tour, tör, *n.* [Fr. *tour,* a turn, trip, tour, &c.; same origin as *turn.*] A round or circuit; a journey in a circuit; a roving journey; a lengthy jaunt or excursion; turn or succession (a *tour* of duty): a military use of the word.—*v.i.* To make a tour. —**Tourist,** tör'ist, *n.* One who makes a tour; one who travels for pleasure.

Touraco, tö-rak'ō, *n.* An African insessorial bird of the family of plantain-eaters.

Tourbillion, tör-bil'yon, *n.* [Fr. *tourbillon,* a whirlwind.] An ornamental whirling firework.

Tourelle, tö-rel', *n.* [Fr., dim. of *tour,* a tower.] A small tower on a building.

Tourmalin, Tourmaline, tör'ma-lin, *n.* [A corruption of *tournamal,* a name given to it in Ceylon.] A mineral of various colours, frequently black or colourless, crystallized in three-sided or six-sided prisms, often found in granitic rocks and possessing strong electrical properties. Black tourmaline is schorl; red tourmaline, rubellite.

Tournament, tör'na-ment, *n.* [O.Fr. *tourneiment, tournoyement,* from *tourneier, tournoyer,* to turn or twirl about. TURN.] A martial sport or species of combat performed in former times by knights on horseback for the purpose of exercising and exhibiting their courage, prowess, and skill in arms; a tilting match; hence, any contest of skill in which a number take part (a chess *tournament*).—**Tourney**, tör'ne, *n.* [O.Fr. *tournei.*] A tournament.—*v.i.* To tilt; to engage in a tournament.

Tourniquet, tör'ni-ket, *n.* [Fr., from *tourner*, to turn.] A surgical bandage which is tightened by twisting with a stick or a pad tightened with a screw or elastic, to arrest hemorrhage.

Tournure, tör-nür, *n.* [Fr.] Contour; figure; shape.

Touse, touz, *v.t.*—*toused, tousing.* [Same as L.G. *tûsen*, G. *zausen*, to pull; akin to *tease.*] To pull or drag; to disorder the hair of; to tousle.—**Tousle**, tou'zl, *v.t.* To put into disorder; to dishevel; to rumple. (*Colloq.*)

Tout, tout, *v.i.* [Formerly *toot, tote*, to pry, peep, from A.Sax. *tótian*, to stick out or project.] To ply or seek for customers.—*n.* One who plies for customers, as for an inn or hotel; a person who clandestinely watches the trials of race-horses at their training quarters and for a fee gives information for betting purposes.—**Touter**, tout'ėr, *n.* A tout.

Tout-ensemble, tö-tan̄-san̄-bl, *n.* [Fr., all together.] The whole taken together; anything regarded as a whole; the general effect of a work of art.

Tow, tō, *v.t.* [From stem of A.Sax. *teóhan, teón*, to draw, to tug, whence *tohline*, a towing line; akin Icel. *toga*, G. *ziehen*, to draw; Scot. *tow*, Icel. *taug, tog*, D. *touw*, a rope or cord; cog. L. *duco*, to lead. Akin *tug, tie.*] To drag, as a boat or ship, through the water by means of a rope.—*n.* The state of being towed (to take a boat in *tow*).—**Towage**, tō'āj, *n.* The act of towing.—**Tow-boat**, *n.* A boat employed in towing a vessel; a boat that is towed.—**Towing-path**, *n.* A path used by men and horses in towing boats along a canal or river.—**Tow-line, Tow-rope**, *n.* A rope or hawser used to tow vessels.

Tow, tō, *n.* [A.Sax. *tow*, tow; akin Icel. *tó*, a tuft of wool; Dan. *tave*, a fibre, pl. *taver*, tow; same root as *tow*, above.] The coarse and broken part of flax or hemp separated from the finer part by the hatchel or swingle.

Toward, Towards, tō'ėrd, tō'ėrdz, *prep.* [A.Sax. *tóweard, tówеardes* — *tó*, to, and *-weard*, expressing direction. *Towards* is an adverbial genitive.] In the direction of; in regard or with respect to (well-disposed *toward* us); tending or contributing to; in aid of; for; nearly; about (*toward* three o'clock).—*Toward* was formerly sometimes divided by tmesis (*to* God*ward*).—*adv.* In a state of preparation; being carried on.—**Toward**, tō'wėrd, *a.* [Lit. bending or turned to; comp. *froward*, in the opposite sense.] Pliable; docile; ready to do or learn; apt.—**Towardliness, Towardness**, tō'wėrd-li-nes, tō'wėrd-nes, *n.* The quality of being toward; aptness; docility.—**Towardly**, tō'wėrd-li, *a.* Docile; tractable.

Towel, tou'el, *n.* [Fr. *touaille*, from O.H.G. *twahilla, dwahilla*, a towel, from *twahan*, A.Sax. *thweán* (for *thweahan*), Goth. *thvahan*, to wash.] A cloth or soft paper, for wiping the hands and face, especially after washing; a similar cloth for wiping in domestic use, as a *dish towel*.—**Towel rack**, *n.* A frame or stand to hold towels.—**Towelling**, tou'el-ing, *n.* Cloth or other material for towels, usually in narrow widths.—**Towel roller**, *n.* A revolving wooden bar for holding a looped towel.

Tower, tou'ėr, *n.* [O.E. *tour*, from Fr. *tour*, a tower, from L. *turris*, a tower; cog. Gr. *tyrris, tyrsis*, Ir. *túr*, W. *twr*, Gael. *torr*, a heap, a tower.] A lofty narrow building of a round, square, or polygonal form, either insulated or forming part of a church, castle, or other edifice; a tall, movable wooden structure anciently used in storming a fortified place; a citadel; a fortress.—*v.i.* To rise or fly high; to soar; to be lofty; to stand sublime.—**Towered**, tou'ėrd, *a.* Having towers; adorned or defended by towers. — **Towering**, tou'ėr-ing, *a.* Very high or lofty; extreme; violent; outrageous (a *towering* rage).—**Towery**, tou'ėr-i, *a.* Having towers.

Town, toun, *n.* [A.Sax. *tún*, inclosure, homestead, town = O.Sax. and Icel. *tún*, homestead, D. *tuin*, a fence; G. *zaun*, a hedge; allied to Celt. *dun*, fortress, town.] Originally a walled or fortified place; then houses inclosed with a wall; hence, any collection of houses larger than a village; a large assemblage of adjacent houses intersected by streets: often opposed to *country*; the metropolis, county town, or the particular city, &c., in or near which the speaker or writer is (to go to *town*, to be in *town*); the inhabitants of a town (all the *town* talks of it).—To *go to town*, to venture, especially when noted success is achieved (*slang*).—*a.* Pertaining to or characteristic of a town: urban.—**Town clerk**, *n.* The clerk of a municipal corporation, who keeps the records of the town and town council.—**Town council**, *n.* The elected governing body of a municipality.—**Town councillor**, *n.* A member of a town council.—**Town crier**, *n.* A public official who issues proclamations in a town, formerly by loud verbal announcement.—**Town hall**, *n.* A large hall or building belonging to a town or borough in which the town council holds its meetings, and offices are maintained for town officials and courts.—**Town house**, *n.* A town residence, usually of a family having a country home.—**Townsfolk**, tounz'fōk, *n. pl.* People of a town or city.—**Township**, toun'ship, *n.* *Brit.* A parish or division of a parish; *U.S.* An administrative division of a county, but varying in size and status in different states.—**Townsman**, tounz'man, *n.* An inhabitant of a town; one of the same town with another. — **Townspeople**, tounz'pē-pl, *n. pl.* The inhabitants of a town, especially as distinguished from country folk.—**Town talk**, *n.* The common topic of community talk among people of a town.

Tow-rope. Under Tow, *v.t.*

Toxic, Toxical, tok'sik, tok'si-kal, *a.* [Gr. *toxikon*, poison, originally for arrows, from *toxon*, a bow.] Pertaining to poisons; poisonous. — **Toxicant**, tok'si-kant, *n.* A poison of a stimulating, narcotic, or anæsthetic nature.—**Toxicological**, tok'si-ko-loj"i-kal, *a.* Pertaining to toxicology. — **Toxicologically**, tok'si-ko-loj"i-kal-li, *adv.* In a toxicological manner.—**Toxicologist**, tok-si-kol'o-jist, *n.* One who treats of poisons. — **Toxicology**, tok-si-kol'o-ji, *n.* [Gr. *toxikon*, poison, *logos*, discourse.] The doctrine of poisons; that branch of medicine which treats of poisons and their antidotes.

Toxophilite, tok-sof'i-līt, *n.* [Gr. *toxon*, a bow, and *philos*, loving.] A lover of archery.—*a.* Pertaining to archery.

Toy, toi, *n.* [Same as Dan. *töi*, D. *tuig*, G. *zeug*, as in Dan. *lege-töi*, D. *speel-tuig*, G. *spiel-zeug*, a plaything or toy; same root as *tug, tow.*] A plaything for children; a bauble; a thing for amusement and of no real value; a trifling object.—*v.i.* To dally amorously; to trifle; to play.—**Toyer**, toi'ėr, *n.* One who toys.—**Toyish**, toi'ish, *a.* Trifling; wanton.—**Toyman**, toi'man, *n.* One that deals in toys.—**Toyshop**, toi'shop, *n.* A shop where toys are sold.

Trace, trās, *n.* [Fr. *trace*, trace, track, outline, &c., from *tracer*, to trace, from L.L. *tractiare*, from L. *tractus*, pp. of *traho, trahere*, to draw; whence also *tract, tractable, train, trait, treat, abstract, detract, extract*, &c. In last sense directly from O.Fr. *trais*, pl. of *trait*, the trace of a carriage, from *traire*, L. *trahere*, to draw.] A mark left by anything passing; a track; any mark, impression, or appearance left when the thing itself no longer exists; visible evidence of something having been; token; vestige; a minute quantity or insignificant particle; one of the straps, chains, or ropes by which a carriage, wagon, &c., is drawn.—*v.t.*—*traced, tracing.* To follow by traces left; to track out; to follow by vestiges or indications; to draw or delineate with marks; to draw in outline; to copy, as a drawing or engraving, by following the lines and marking them on a sheet superimposed, through which they appear.—*v.i.* To walk; to travel.—**Traceable**, trās'a-bl, *a.* Capable of being traced.—**Traceableness**, trās'a-bl-nes, *n.* The state of being traceable. — **Traceably**, trās'a-bli, *adv.* So as to be traced. — **Tracer**, trās'ėr, *n.* One who or that which traces.—**Tracery**, trās'ėr-i, *n.* *Arch.* ornamental open-work in stone in the head of a Gothic window, showing curves and flowing lines intersecting in various ways and enriched with foliations; any similar ornamental work.—**Tracing**, trās'ing, *n.* The act of one who traces; a copy of an original design or drawing made by following its lines through a transparent medium.—**Tracing-paper**, *n.* Transparent paper which is laid on a drawing, so that the outlines of the original may be drawn on it.

Trachea, trā'kē-a, *n.* pl. **Tracheæ**, trā'kē-ē. [L. *trachia*, Gr. *tracheia*, from *trachys*, rough, from the inequalities of its cartilages.] The windpipe, a cartilaginous and membranous pipe through which the air passes into and out of the lungs; *bot.* one of the spiral vessels of plants; *zool.* one of those vessels in insects, &c., which receive air and distribute it to every part of the interior of the body.—**Tracheal**, trā'kē-al, *a.* Pertaining to the trachea.—**Tracheary**, trā'kē-a-ri, *a.* *Zool.* breathing by means of tracheæ.—**Tracheitis, Trachitis**, trā-kē-ī'tis, trā-kī'tis, *n.* Inflammation of the windpipe.—**Trachenchyma**, trā-ken'ki-ma, *n.* [*Trachea*, and Gr. *enchyma*, an infusion.] *Bot.* the vascular tissue of plants which consists of spiral vessels. — **Tracheocele**, trā-kē'o-sēl, *n.* [*Trachea*, and Gr. *kēlē*, a tumour.] Bronchocele or goitre. — **Tracheotome**, trā-kē-o-tōm, *n.* A surgical knife used in tracheotomy.—**Tracheotomy**, trā-kē-ot'o-mi, *n.* [*Trachea*, and Gr. *tomē*, a cutting, from *temnō*, to cut.] *Surg.* the operation of cutting into the trachea, as in cases of suffocation; bronchotomy; laryngotomy.

Trachyte, trā'kīt, *n.* [Gr. *trachys*, rough.] A felspathic rock abundant among the products of volcanoes, and often containing crystals of glassy felspar, with sometimes hornblende and mica.—**Trachytic**, trā-kit'ik, *a.* Pertaining to trachyte or consisting of it.

Track, trak, *n.* [O.Fr. *trac*, a track or course, from D. and L.G. *trek, treck*, a drawing, *trekken, trecken*, to draw.] A mark left by something that has passed along; a mark left by the foot of man or beast; a trace; a footprint; a road; a beaten path; course followed; path; the course of a railway; the permanent way.—*v.t.* To follow when guided by a track; to follow by tracks; *naut.* to tow by a line from the shore. — **Tracker**, trak'ėr, *n.* One who tracks; one who hunts by following the track.—**Trackless**, trak'les, *a.* Having no track; pathless; untrodden. — **Tracklessly**, trak'les-li, *adv.* So as to leave no track.—**Tracklessness**, trak'les-nes, *n.* The state of being without a track.—**Track-road**, *n.* A towing-path.

Tract, trakt, *n.* [L. *tractus*, a drawing, a district, from *traho, tractum*, to draw or drag; in second sense from *tractate*. TRACE.] A region or quantity of land or water of indefinite extent; a short dissertation; a short treatise, particularly on practical religion: in this sense often adjectivally used; as, a *tract* society, a society for the printing and distribution of tracts; a length or extent of time (a *tract* of dry weather).—**Tractarian**, trak-tā'ri-an, *n.* A term applied to the writers of the '*Tracts* for the Times', a series of papers published at Oxford between 1833 and 1841, written by Anglican scholars, and showing a considerable leaning towards Roman Catholicism; also a person who supports such opinions.—**Tractarianism**, trak-tā'ri-an-izm, *n.* The doctrines or teaching of the Tractarians.—**Tractate**,

trak'tāt, *n.* A treatise, a tract.
Tractable, trak'ta-bl, *a.* [L. *tractabilis*, from *tracto*, to handle, treat.] Capable of being easily trained or managed; very amenable to discipline; docile; governable. —**Tractableness, Tractability**, trak'-ta-bl-nes, trak-ta-bil'i-ti, *n.* The state or quality of being tractable; docility.—**Tractably**, trak'ta-bli, *adv.* In a tractable manner.
Tractarian. Under TRACT.
Traction, trak'shon, *n.* [Fr. *traction*, from L. *traho*, *tractum*, to draw. TRACT.] The act of drawing or pulling; the act of drawing a body along a plane, as when a vessel is towed in water or a carriage upon a road or railway.—**Traction-engine**, *n.* A steam locomotive engine for dragging heavy loads on common roads.—**Tractive**, trak'-tiv, *a.* Serving to pull or draw; drawing along.—**Tractor**, trak'tor, *n.* A vehicle driven by an internal-combustion engine, especially as used in agriculture.—*Tractor aeroplane*, an aeroplane in which the propeller is mounted in front of the main lifting surfaces. See PROPELLER.
Trade, trād, *n.* [TREAD.] Regular employment or way of life; the business which a person carries on for procuring subsistence or for profit; occupation; particularly a mechanical or mercantile employment or a handicraft, as distinguished from an art or profession; the business of exchanging commodities for other commodities or for money; commerce; traffic; collectively, those who are engaged in any trade; a trade-wind.—*Board of trade*, an organization for the advancement and protection of business interests; also the place where commercial exchange occurs. Commodities, bonds, or stocks are usually traded in a place of this kind.—*a.* Pertaining to trade or a particular trade.—*v.i. traded, trading,*. To barter or to buy and sell; to traffic; to carry on commerce; to engage in affairs generally; to deal or have dealings.—*v.t.* To sell or exchange in commerce; to barter.—**Trade-acceptance**, a bill of exchange, a promissory note originating from a merchandise transaction. —**Trade-allowance**, *n.* A discount allowed on articles to be sold again.—**Trade-journal**, a periodical devoted to news about a particular business.—**Trade-mark**, *n.* A distinctive mark or device adopted by a manufacturer or producer, and impressed on his goods, labels, &c., to distinguish them from those of others.—**Trade-name**, the name given to an article by traders, in distinction from its composition, chemical or otherwise.—**Trade-price**, *n.* The price charged to dealers for articles that are to be sold again.—**Trader**, trā'dėr, *n.* One engaged in trade or commerce; a vessel employed regularly in any particular trade.—**Trade school**, a school teaching the theory and practice of a trade.—**Tradesman**, trādz'man, *n.* A shopkeeper; a mechanic.—**Trades-union**, *n.* A combination of workmen of any particular trade or branch of manufacture to enable them all to secure the conditions most favorable for labor, and the redress of any of their grievances.—**Trades-unionism**, *n.* The principles or practices of trades-unions.—**Trades-unionist**, *n.* A member of a trades-union; one who favors the system of trades-unions.—**Trade-wind**, *n.* One of those constant winds which occur in all open seas on both sides of the equator, and to the distance of about 30° north and south of it, blowing always or for half the year in the same direction.—**Trading**, trā'ding, *a.* Carrying on commerce; engaged in trade; venal.—**Trading post**. A station of a trading company in sparsely settled regions, where trade is carried on with the natives, as the fur-trading posts of the Hudson's Bay Company.—**Trading stamp**. A printed stamp of a certain value, given by the dealer to the customer and redeemable by the dealer in the purchase of other merchandise.
Tradition, tra-dish'on, *n.* [Fr. *tradition*, from L. *trado*, to hand over, deliver.] The handing down of opinions, doctrines, practices, rites, and customs from father to son, or from ancestors to posterity by oral communication; that which is handed down from age to age by oral communication; a doctrine or statement of facts so handed down.—**Traditional**, tra-dish'on-al, *a.* Pertaining to or derived from tradition; communicated from ancestors to descendants by word only; transmitted from age to age without writing.—**Traditionalism**, tra-dish'on-al-izm, *n.* Adherence to or importance placed on tradition.—**Traditionalist**, tra-dish'on-al-ist, *n.* One who holds to tradition or traditionalism.—**Traditionally**, tra-dish'on-al-li, *adv.* By tradition; by oral transmission.—**Traditionarily**, tra-dish'on-a-ri-li, *adv.* In a traditionary manner; by tradition.—**Traditionary**, tra-dish'on-a-ri, *a.* Traditional.—**Traditionist**, tra-dish'on-ist, *n.* One who adheres to tradition.—**Traditive**,† trad'i-tiv, *a.* Pertaining to or based on tradition; traditional.
Traduce, tra-dūs', *v.t.*—*traduced, traducing.* [L. *traduco*, *traducere*, to lead along, exhibit, disgrace, defame—*trans*, over, and *duco*, to lead. DUKE.] To misrepresent wilfully; to defame; to calumniate; to vilify.—**Traducement**, tra-dūs'ment, *n.* The act of traducing; misrepresentation; calumny.—**Traducer**, tra-dū'sėr, *n.* One that traduces; a slanderer; a calumniator.—**Traducianism**, tra-dū'si-an-izm, *n.* The doctrine that the souls of children as well as their bodies are begotten from their parents. —**Traducible**, tra-dū'si-bl, *a.* Capable of being traduced.
Traffic, traf'ik, *n.* [Fr. *trafic*, It. *traffico*, Sp. *trafico*, *trafago*, traffic; origin doubtful.] An interchange of goods or merchandise between countries, communities, or individuals; trade; commerce; goods or persons passing along a road, railway, canal, steamboat route, &c., viewed collectively; dealings; intercourse.—*v.i.*—*trafficked, trafficking.* [Fr. *trafiquer*, Sp. *traficar* or *trafagar*.] To trade; to buy and sell wares; to carry on commerce; to have business or dealings; to deal; to trade meanly or mercenarily.—**Trafficker**, traf'-ik-ėr, *n.* One who traffics; a trader; a merchant.—**Trafficless**, traf'ik-les, *a.* Destitute of traffic.—**Traffic-manager**, *n.* The manager of the traffic on a railway, canal, and the like.—**Traffic-return**, *n.* A periodical statement of traffic on a railway, canal, &c.
Tragacanth, trag'a-kanth, *n.* [L. *tragacantha*, *tragacanthum*, from Gr. *tragakantha*—*tragos*, a goat, and *akantha*, a thorn.] Goat's-thorn, a leguminous plant yielding a gummy juice used in confectionery; a variety of gum familiarly termed gum-dragon or gum-tragacanth, used as a demulcent in coughs and for other purposes.
Tragedy, traj'e-di, *n.* [L. *tragœdia*, from Gr. *tragō(i)dia*, tragedy—*tragos*, a he-goat, and *ōdē*, *ō(i)dē*, a song, from *aeidō*, to sing; because, it is said, a goat was the prize of the early tragic choirs in Athens.] A dramatic poem representing an important event or a series of events in the life of some person or persons, in which the diction is elevated and the catastrophe melancholy; that kind of drama in which some fatal or mournful event is the main theme; a fatal and mournful event; any event in which human lives are sacrificed; a murderous deed.—**Tragedian**, tra-jē'di-an, *n.* [L. *tragœdus*.] A writer of tragedy; an actor of tragedy.—**Tragedienne**, tra-jē-di-en, *n.* [Fr. *tragédienne*.] A female actor of tragedy; a tragic actress.—**Tragic, Tragical**, traj'ik, traj'i-kal, *a.* [L. *tragicus*.] Pertaining to tragedy; of the nature or character of tragedy (in this sense *Tragic* is now the more common form); connected with or characterized by bloodshed or loss of life; murderous; dreadful; calamitous.—**Tragically**, traj'i-kal-li, *adv.* In a tragic or tragical manner.—**Tragicalness**, traj'-i-kal-nes, *n.*—**Tragi-comedy**, *n.* A kind of dramatic piece in which serious and comic scenes are blended, and of which the event is not unhappy.—**Tragi-comic, Tragi-comical**, *a.* Pertaining to tragi-comedy.—**Tragi-comically**, *adv.* In a tragi-comical manner.
Tragus, trag'us, *n.* [From Gr. *tragos*, a goat, being sometimes furnished with a tuft of hair suggesting the beard of a goat.] *Anat.* a small cartilaginous eminence at the entrance of the external ear.
Trail, trāl, *v.t.* [From old *traile*, a sledge, from L. *tragula*, a sledge, a drag-net, from *traho*, to draw. TRACE.] To draw behind or along the ground; to drag.—*v.i.* To sweep over a surface by being pulled or dragged; to grow with long slender and creeping shoots or stems, as a plant; to follow as a detective.—*To trail arms*, to carry the rifle horizontally at the full extent of the right arm.—*n.* A track followed by a hunter; anything drawn to length (a *trail* of smoke); the end of the stock of a gun-carriage which rests upon the ground when a gun is in position for firing.—**Trail-board**, *n.* A carved or ornamented board on each side of the stem of a vessel.—**Trailer**, trāl'ėr, *n.* One who trails; a plant which cannot grow upward without support; a car pulled by a motor vehicle; a house on wheels, attachable to an automobile and fitted with camping conveniences.—**Trailer camp**, parking grounds for trailers, public or private.—**Trailing-edge**, *n.* In an aeroplane, the rear edge of the wing.—**Trail-net**, *n.* A net trailed behind a boat; a drag-net.
Trail, trāl, *n.* [Abbrev. of *entrails*.] *Cookery*, intestines of certain birds and fishes, which are sent to the table without being extracted.
Train, trān, *v.t.* [Fr. *traîner*, O.Fr. *traïner*, *trahiner*, to draw, from L.L. *trahinare*, from L. *trahere*, to draw. TRACE.] To draw along‡; to trail‡; to draw by artifice; to entice; to educate; to rear and instruct: often followed by *up*; to form to any practice by exercise; to drill; to discipline; to break; to tame and reduce to docility; to teach to perform certain actions (to *train* dogs); to subject to proper regimen and exercise for the performance of some special exertion or feat (to *train* horses for the Derby); *gardening*, to form to a desired shape by growth and pruning, &c.—*v.i.* To undergo some special drill or discipline; to subject one's self to a special course of exercise and regimen for an athletic or other feat. —*n.* That which is drawn along behind; that part of a gown or robe which trails behind the wearer; the tail of a comet, meteor, &c.; the tail of a bird; the after part of a gun-carriage; a succession of connected things; a series; way or course of procedure; regular method; course; a number or body of followers or attendants; a retinue; a procession; a connected line of cars on a railroad together with the locomotive; a line of combustible material to lead fire to a charge or mine; a set of wheels, or wheels and pinions, as in a watch.—*Train of artillery*, a certain number of pieces, with attendants, carriages, &c., organized for a given duty.—**Trainable**, trān'a-bl, *a.* Capable of being trained. —**Train-band**, *n.* A band or company of militia.—**Train-bearer**, *n.* One who holds up a person's train or long state robe.—**Trained**, trānd, *p.* and *a.* Formed by training; exercised; educated; instructed; skilled by practice.—**Trainer**, trā'nėr, *n.* One who trains; one who prepares men, horses, &c., for the performance of certain feats, as a boxer for a prizefight, or a horse for racing.—**Training**, trān'ing, *p.* and *a.* Teaching and forming by practice.—*Training college*, a normal school.—*n.* The act of one who trains; the process of educating; education; drill; course of exercise and regimen.—**Training-ship**, *n.* A ship equipped with instructors, officers, &c., to train lads for the sea.
Train-oil, trān, *n.* [D. and L.G. *traan*, Dan. and Sw. *tran*, G. *thran*, train-oil; comp. D. *traan*, G. *thräne*, a tear, a drop.] The oil procured from the blubber or fat of whales.
Traipse, trāps, *v.i.* [Perhaps from O.Fr. *trespasser*, to pass across. TRAPE.] To walk sloppily or carelessly; *also* trapes.

Trait, trāt or trā, *n.* [Fr., a trait, a stroke, from L. *tractus*, a drawing. TRACT.] A stroke; a touch; a distinguishing or peculiar feature; a peculiarity.

Traitor, trā'tėr, *n.* [O.Fr. *traïtor* (Fr. *traître*), from L. *traditor*, from *trado*, to deliver up (whence *tradition*)—*trans*, over, and *do*, *datum*, to give.] One who violates his allegiance and betrays his country; one guilty of treason; one who, in breach of trust, plays into the hands of an enemy; one guilty of perfidy or treachery.—*a.* Traitorous. — **Traitorism**, trā'tėr-izm, *n.* Treachery. — **Traitorous**, trā'tėr-us, *a.* Acting the traitor; treacherous; perfidious; consisting in or partaking of treason. — **Traitorously**, trā'tėr-us-li, *adv.* In a traitorous manner. — **Traitorousness**, trā'tėr-us-nes, *n.* Treachery.—**Traitress**, trā'tres, *n.* A female traitor; a woman who betrays her country or her trust.

Traject, tra-jekt', *v.t.* [L. *trajicio*, *trajectum*—*trans*, across, over, and *jacio*, to throw. JET.] To throw, cast, or make to pass through. — **Trajection**, tra-jek'shon, *n.* The act of trajecting.—**Trajectory**, tra-jek'to-ri, *n.* The path described by a body, such as a planet, comet, projectile, &c., under the action of given forces.

Tralatitious, tral-a-tish'us, *a.* [L. *tralatitius*, *translatitious*. TRANSLATE.] Metaphorical; not literal. — **Tralatitiously**, tral-a-tish'us-li, *adv.* Metaphorically.

Tram, tram, *n.* [It. *trama*, from L. *trama*, weft.] A kind of doubled silk thread, in which two or more strands are twisted together.

Trammel, tram'el, *n.* [Fr. *tramail*, *trèmail*, a net, from L.L. *tramaculum*, *tremaculum*, a kind of fishing-net, from L. *tres*, three, and *macula*, a mesh.] A kind of net for catching birds or fish; a kind of shackles for regulating the motions of a horse and making him amble; whatever hinders activity, freedom, or progress; an instrument for drawing ovals, used by joiners and mechanics; a beam-compass.—*v.t.*—*trammeled*, *trammelled*, *trammeling*, *trammelling*. To confine; to hamper; to shackle. — **Trammeler**, **Trammeller**, tram'el-ėr, *n.* One who or that which trammels.—**Trammeled**, **Trammelled**, tram'eld, *p.* and *a.* Hampered; confined; shackled.

Tramontane, tra-mon'tān, *a.* [It. *tramontano*, from L. *transmontanus*—*trans*, beyond, and *mons*, mountain.] Lying or being beyond the mountains, originally applied by the Italians to those on the other side of the Alps; hence, foreign; barbarous.—*n.* A dweller in a tramontane region, especially the country north of the Alps mountains; so, a barbarian, a stranger.

Tramp, tramp, *v.t.* [Same as L.G. *trampen*, Dan. *trampe*, Sw. *trampa*, to tramp; nasalized forms corresponding to D. and G. *trappen*, to tread; akin *trap*, *trip*.] To tread under foot; to trample; to travel over on foot (to *tramp* a country).—*v.i.* To travel on foot; to hike.—*n.* A homeless vagrant who wanders along the roads from place to place, sleeps in the open, and lives by begging and by working occasionally for short periods; sound of a heavy tread, as of a regiment marching past; a cargo steamer making journeys to any port as the occasion arises, without having any regular ports of call, and without making any scheduled voyages; a flat plate of iron on a shoe or upper edge of a spade to protect the shoe when pressing the spade into the ground.—*To look like a tramp*, to present a dirty, disreputable, shabby appearance.—**Tramper**, tram'pėr, *n.* One who tramps.—**Trample**, tram'pl, *v.t.*—*trampled*, *trampling*. [A freq. from *tramp*; like D. *trampelen*, G. *trampeln*, to trample.] To tread under foot; to tread down; to prostrate by treading; to crush with the feet; to treat with pride, contempt, and insult.—*v.t.* To tread in contempt; to tread with force; to stamp.—**Trampler**, tram'pl-ėr, *n.* One who tramples. — **Tramp-pick**, *n.* A kind of pick or lever of iron which the foot helps to drive into the ground by means of a rest fixed on it, used for turning up very hard soils.

Trance, trans, *n.* [Fr. *transe*, from L. *transitus*, a passage, from *trans*, across, beyond, and *eo*, *itum*, to go; so that *trance* and *transit* are doublets.] An ecstasy; a state in which the soul seems to have passed out of the body, or to be rapt into visions; a state of insensibility to the things of this world; a state of perplexity or bewilderment; *med.* same as *Catalepsy*.—*v.t.*—*tranced*, *trancing*. To entrance; to place in or as in a trance; to charm; to enchant. —**Trancedly**, tran'sed-li, *adv.* In an absorbed or trance-like manner; like one in a trance.

Tranquil, tran'kwil, *a.* [Fr. *tranquille*, from L. *tranquillus*, quiet, calm.] Quiet; calm; undisturbed; peaceful; not agitated. —**Tranquility**, tran-kwil'i-ti, *n.* [L. *tranquillitas*.] The state of being tranquil; quietness; calmness; freedom from agitation. — **Tranquilize**, tran'kwil-īz, *v.t.* — *tranquilized*, *tranquilizing*. To render tranquil; to allay when agitated; to compose; to make calm and peaceful.—**Tranquilizer**, tran'kwil-ī-zėr, *n.* One who or that which tranquilizes. — **Tranquilly**, tran'kwil-li, *adv.* In a tranquil manner; quietly; peacefully.

Transact, tran-sakt', *v.t.* [L. *transigo*, *transactum* — *trans*, across, through, and *ago*, to lead, act.] To carry through, perform, or conduct (business affairs, &c.); to do; to perform; to manage; to complete; to carry through.—**Transaction**, tran-sak'shon, *n.* The doing or performing of any business; some piece of business; a proceeding; an affair; *pl.* reports containing papers or abstracts of papers, speeches, discussions, &c., read or delivered at the meetings of certain learned societies. — **Transactor**, tran-sak'tėr, *n.* One who transacts.

Transalpine, tran-sal'pīn, *a.* [L. *transalpinus*, from *trans*, beyond, and *Alpinus*, pertaining to the *Alps*.] Lying or being beyond the Alps: generally used in regard to Rome; opposed to *Cisalpine*.

Transatlantic, trans-at-lan'tik, *a.* [L. *trans*, beyond, and *Atlantic*.] Lying or being beyond the Atlantic; crossing the Atlantic (a *transatlantic* line of steamers).

Transcend, tran-send', *v.t.* [L. *transcendo* —*trans*, beyond, and *scando*, to climb (as in *ascend*, *descend*, &c.). SCAN.] To rise above or beyond; to be or go beyond the grasp or comprehension of; to surpass, outgo, excel, exceed.—**Transcendence**, **Transcendency**, tran-sen'dens, tran-sen'den-si, *n.* Superior excellence; supereminence. — **Transcendent**, tran-sen'dent, *a.* Superior or supreme in excellence; surpassing others; going beyond or transcending human experience. — **Transcendental**, tran-sen-den'tal, *a.* Transcendent; transcending the sphere of that knowledge which we acquire by experience; abstrusely speculative; beyond the reach of ordinary, everyday, or common thought and experience; *math.* applied to what cannot be represented by an algebraical expression of a finite number of terms, with numeral and determinate indexes. — **Transcendentalism**, tran-sen-den'tal-izm, *n.* The quality of being transcendental; a system of philosophy which claims to have a true knowledge of all things material and immaterial, human and divine, so far as the mind is capable of knowing them; sometimes used for that which is vague and illusive in philosophy.—**Transcendentalist**, tran-sen-den'tal-ist, *n.* One who believes in transcendentalism.—**Transcendentally**, tran-sen-den'tal-li, *adv.* In a transcendental manner. — **Transcendently**, tran-sen'dent-li, *adv.* Supereminently; by way of eminence.—**Transcendentness**, tran-sen'dent-nes, *n.*

Transcribe, tran-skrīb', *v.t.*—*transcribed*, *transcribing*. [L. *transcribo*—*trans*, over, and *scribo*, to write. SCRIBE.] To write over again or in the same words; to copy. —**Transcriber**, tran-skrī'bėr, *n.* One who transcribes; a copier or copyist.—**Transcript**, tran'skript, *n.* [L. *transcriptum*, from *transcriptus*, pp. of *transcribo*.] A writing made from and according to an original; a copy; an imitation.—**Transcription**, tran-skrip'shon, *n.* The act of transcribing or copying; a copy; a transcript; *mus.* the arrangement of a composition for some instrument or voice other than that for which it was originally composed.—**Transcriptive**, tran-skrip'tiv, *a.* Having the character of a transcript. — **Transcriptively**, tran-skrip'tiv-li, *adv.* By transcription; as a copy.

Transelementation, trans-el'e-men-tā"shon, *n.* [Prefix *trans*, and *element*.] The change of the elements of one body into those of another; transubstantiation.

Transept, tran'sept, *n.* [L. *trans*, across, and *septum*, an inclosure.] *Arch.* that portion of a church built in the form of a cross, which is between the nave and choir and projects externally on each side so as to form the short arms of the cross.

Transfer, trans-fėr', *v.t.* — *transferred*, *transferring*. [L. *transfero* — *trans*, and *fero*, to carry (as in *defer*, *confer*, &c.), *fero* being cognate with E. to *bear*. FERTILE.] To convey from one place or person to another; to transport or remove to another place or person; to make over the possession or control of; to convey, as a right, from one person to another; *lithography*, to produce a facsimile of on a prepared stone by means of prepared paper and ink.—*n.* (trans'fėr). The act of transferring; that which is transferred; *lithography*, a picture drawn or printed with a special ink on specially prepared paper, and transferred to the surface of a stone to be printed from.—**Transferability**, **Transferribility**, trans-fėr'a-bil"i-ti, trans-fėr'i-bil"-i-ti, *n.* Quality of being transferable. — **Transferable**, **Transferrible**, trans-fėr'a-bl or trans'fėr-a-bl, trans-fėr'i-bl, *a.* Capable of being transferred; capable of being legitimately passed into the possession of another.—**Transfer-book**, *n.* A register of the transfer of property, stock, or shares from one party to another. — **Transferee**, trans-fėr-ē', *n.* The person to whom a transfer is made.—**Transference**, trans'fėr-ens, *n.* The act of transferring; the act of conveying from one place, person, or thing to another; the passage of anything from one place to another. — **Transfer-paper**, *n.* Prepared paper used in lithography or copying-presses for transferring impressions.—**Transferrer**, trans-fėr'ėr, *n.* One who transfers.

Transfigure, trans-fig'ūr, *v.t.* — *transfigured*, *transfiguring*. [Fr. *transfigurer*, from L. *transfiguro*—*trans*, over, and *figura*, figure. FIGURE.] To change the outward form or appearance of; to transform in appearance; to give an elevated or glorified appearance to; to elevate and glorify; to idealize.—**Transfiguration**, trans-fig'ū-rā"shon, *n.* A change of form or figure; the supernatural change in the personal appearance of our Saviour on the mount; an ecclesiastical feast held on 6th August in commemoration of this.

Transfix, trans-fiks', *v.t.* [L. *transfigo*, *transfixum* — *trans*, through, and *figo*, to fix. FIX.] To pierce through as with a pointed weapon.—**Transfixed**, *a.* *Her.* when an animal is transfixed, the weapon is shown right through it, with the head or point protruding from the opposite side, otherwise it is only pierced. — **Transfixion**, trans-fik'shon, *n.* The act of transfixing.

Transfluent, trans'flu-ent, *a.* [L. *trans*, through, and *fluens*, *fluentis*, ppr. of *fluo*, to flow. FLUENT.] Flowing or running across or through.

Transform, trans-form', *v.t.* [Fr. *transformer*, from L. *transformare*—*trans*, across, and *forma*, form.] To change the form of; to give a new form to; to metamorphose; to change into another substance; to transmute; to change the character or disposition of.—*v.i.*† To be changed in form; to be metamorphosed.—**Transformable**, trans-for'ma-bl, *a.* Capable of being transformed. — **Transformation**, trans-for-mā'shon, *n.* The act or operation of transforming; the state of being transformed; an entire change in form, appearance, nature, disposition, &c.; a metamorphosis; false hair worn by women on the top and front of the head.—*Transformation scene*, a gorgeous scene at the end of the burlesque of a pantomime, in which the chief characters are supposed to be transformed into those that take part in the immediately following harlequinade.—**Transformative**, trans-for'ma-tiv, *a.* Having power or tendency to transform.—**Transformer**, trans-for'-mėr, *n.* *Elect.* an appliance for altering pressure in alternating current circuits.

Transfuse, trans-fūz', *v.t.* — *transfused, transfusing.* [Fr. *transfuser*, from L. *transfundo, transfusum—trans*, over, and *fundo, fusum*, to pour. FUSE.] To transfer by pouring; to cause to be instilled or imbibed; to instil; *surg.* to transfer (blood) from the veins or arteries of one animal to those of another. — **Transfusible**, trans-fū'zi-bl, *a.* Capable of being transfused. — **Transfusion**, trans-fū'zhon, *n.* The act of transfusing; *surg.* the transmission of blood from the veins of one creature to those of another, as from those of a man or one of the lower animals into a man, with the view of restoring vigour.—**Transfusive**, trans-fū'ziv, *a.* Tending or having power to transfuse.

Transgangetic, trans-gan-jet'ik, *a.* [Prefix *trans*, across, and *Ganges.*] On the opposite side of the Ganges; pertaining to countries beyond the Ganges.

Transgress, trans-gres', *v.t.* [Fr. *transgresser*, from L. *transgredior, transgressus — trans*, across, and *gradior*, to pass. GRADE.] To overpass, as some law or rule prescribed; to break or violate; to infringe. —*v.i.* To offend by violating a law; to sin.—**Transgressible**, trans-gres'i-bl, *a.* Liable to or capable of being transgressed.—**Transgression**, trans-gresh'on, *n.* The act of transgressing; the breaking or violation of any law; a trespass; an offence. —**Transgressional**, trans-gresh'on-al, *a.* Pertaining to transgression.—**Transgressor**, trans-gres'ėr, *n.* One who transgresses; an offender; an evil-doer.

Tranship, tran-ship', *v.t.* — *transhipped, transhipping.* To convey or transfer from one ship to another.—**Transhipment**, tran-ship'ment, *n.* The act of transhipping.

Transient, tran'shent, *a.* [L. *transiens*, ppr. of *transeo*, to pass away—*trans*, across, and *eo*, to go. Akin *transition, transit, trance.* ITINERANT.] Passing quickly away; of short duration; not permanent, lasting, or durable; momentary; passing. ∴ *Transient* implies shortness of duration; *transitory*, uncertainty of duration; while *fleeting* refers to something in the act of passing away.—**Transiently**, tran'shent-li, *adv.* In a transient manner.—**Transience**, **Transiency**, **Transientness**, tran'shens, tran'shen-si, tran'shent-nes, *n.* The state or quality of being transient; evanescence; fugitiveness.

Transit, tran'sit, *n.* [L. *transitus*, a passing across, from *transeo, transitum*, to go over. *Trance* is a doublet of this word. TRANSIENT.] The act of passing; a passing over or through; the process of conveying; passage; conveyance (the *transit* of goods through a country); *astron.* the passage of a heavenly body across the meridian of any place; the passage of one heavenly body over the disc of a larger one, as of the planets Mercury and Venus over the sun's disc; the transits of the latter being of great importance as affording the best known means of determining the sun's parallax, and consequently the dimensions of the planetary system.—**Transit-instrument**, *n.* An important astronomical instrument, which consists essentially of a telescope so fixed as to move in the plane of the meridian, the principal use of it being to determine the exact moment when a celestial body passes the meridian of the place of observation.—**Transition**, tran-sizh'-on or tran-zish'on, *n.* [L. *transitio.*] Passage from one place or state to another; change or process of change; *mus.* a change in the course of a composition from one key to another, or the passage from one major scale to another more or less related. —*Transition rocks, geol.* a name formerly given to the lowest uncrystalline stratified rocks, as marking the transition from the non-fossiliferous to the fossiliferous periods.—**Transitional**, **Transitionary**, tran-sizh'on-al, tran-sizh'on-a-ri, *a.* Containing or involving transition.—**Transitive**, tran'si-tiv, *a.* Having the power of passing or making transition; *gram.* taking an object after it; denoting action passing to an object that is expressed (a *transitive* verb). —*n.* A transitive verb. —**Transitively**, tran'si-tiv-li, *adv.* In a transitive manner. — **Transitiveness**, tran'si-tiv-nes, *n.* State of being transitive.—**Transitorily**, tran'si-to-ri-li, *adv.* In a transitory manner; with short continuance. — **Transitoriness**, tran'si-to-ri-nes, *n.* The state of being transitory.—**Transitory**, tran'si-to-ri, *a.* [L. *transitorius*, from *transeo.*] Passing away without continuance; unstable and fleeting; short and uncertain. ∴ Syn. under TRANSIENT. — **Transit-trade**, *n.* The trade arising from the passage of goods through one country to another.

Translate, trans-lāt', *v.t.* — *translated, translating.* [O.Fr. *translater*, from L. *translatus—trans*, across, and *latus*, borne or carried, for *tlatus*, from root seen also in *tolerate.*] To remove from one place to another†; to take up to heaven without dying (N.T.); to transfer from one office or charge to another; to remove a bishop from one see to another; in the Scotch Church, to transfer a minister from one parish to another; to transform (*Shak.*)‡; to render into another language; to interpret; to explain by using other words; to express in other terms.—*v.i.* To be engaged in or practise translation.—**Translatable**, trans-lā'ta-bl, *a.* Capable of being translated.—**Translation**, trans-lā'shon, *n.* The act of translating; a removal or motion from one place to another; the removal of a person from one office to another; especially the removal of a bishop from one see to another; also applied to the removal of the relics of a saint from one place to another; the removal of a person to heaven without subjecting him to death; the act of turning into another language; that which is produced by turning into another language; a version.—**Translation**, trans-lā'shon, *n.* [L. *translatus*, carried across.] That form of motion in which all the particles of a body move parallel to a fixed line with the same velocity. Comp. ROTATION and REVOLUTION. —**Translator**, trans-lā'tėr, *n.* One who translates.

Transliterate, trans-lit'ėr-āt, *v.t.*—*transliterated, transliterating.* [L. *trans*, across, over, and *litera*, a letter. LETTER.] To express or write in the alphabetic characters of another language; to spell in different characters intended to express the same sound. — **Transliteration**, trans-lit'ėr-ā"shon, *n.* The act of transliterating; a rendering in equivalent alphabetic characters.

Translucent, trans-lū'sent, *a.* [L. *translucens, translucentis—trans*, through, and *luceo*, to shine. LUCID.] Transmitting rays of light, but not so as to render the form or colour of objects beyond distinctly visible; transparent. — **Translucence**, **Translucency**, trans-lū'sens, trans-lū'-sen-si, *n.* The state of being translucent; tranparency.—**Translucently**, trans-lū'-sent-li, *adv.* In a translucent manner.—**Translucid**, trans-lū'sid, *a.* [L. *translucidus.*] Transparent; clear; translucent.

Translunar, **Translunary**, trans-lū'-nėr, trans'lū-na-ri, *a.* [L. *trans*, beyond, and *luna*, the moon. LUNAR.] Being beyond the moon: opposed to *sublunary.*

Transmarine, trans-ma-rēn', *a.* [L. *transmarinus—trans*, across, and *mare*, the sea. MARINE.] Lying or being beyond the sea.

Transmeate,† trans'mē-āt, *v.t.* [L. *transmeo, transmeatum—trans*, through, and *meo*, to pass.] To pass over or beyond.

Transmigrate, trans'mi-grāt, *v.i.*—*transmigrated, transmigrating.* [L. *transmigro, transmigratum—trans*, across, and *migro*, to migrate.] To migrate; to pass from one country or region to another; to pass from one animal body into another.—**Transmigration**, trans-mi-grā'shon, *n.* The act of transmigrating; the passing of a soul into another body after death; metempsychosis. —**Transmigrator**, trans'mi-grā-tėr, *n.* One who transmigrates.—**Transmigratory**, trans-mī'gra-to-ri, *a.* Passing from one place, body, or state to another.

Transmit, trans-mit', *v.t.* — *transmitted, transmitting.* [L. *transmitto, transmissum —trans*, across, through, and *mitto*, to send. MISSION.] To cause to pass or be conveyed from one point to another; to communicate by sending; to send from one person or place to another; to hand down; to suffer to pass through or form a medium or passage; to let penetrate.—**Transmitter**, trans-mit'ėr, *n.* One who or that which transmits; the sending or despatching instrument in telegraphy. — **Transmissibility**, trans-mis'i-bil"i-ti, *n.* The quality of being transmissible.—**Transmissible**, **Transmittible**, trans-mis'i-bl, trans-mit'i-bl, *a.* Capable of being transmitted. —**Transmission**, trans-mish'on, *n.* [L. *transmissio.*] The act of transmitting, or the state of being transmitted; transference; a passing through, as of light through glass or other transparent body; also **Transmittal**, **Transmittance**, trans-mit'al, trans-mit'ans. — **Transmissive**, trans-mis'iv, *a.* Transmitted; derived by transmission.

Transmogrify, trans-mog'ri-fī, *v.t.*—*transmogrified, transmogrifying.* [A fanciful formation from *trans.*] To transform into some other person or thing; to change entirely the appearance of. (*Humorous.*)—**Transmogrification**, trans-mog'ri-fi-kā"shon, *n.* A transformation. (*Humorous.*)

Transmute, trans-mūt', *v.t.*—*transmuted, transmuting.* [L. *transmuto—trans*, across, through, and *muto*, to change, from same root as *moveo*, to move. MOVE.] To change from one nature, form, or substance into another; to change into another thing or body; to metamorphose; to transform.—**Transmutability**, **Transmutableness**, trans-mū'ta-bil"i-ti, trans-mū'ta-bl-nes, *n.* The quality of being transmutable. — **Transmutable**, trans-mū'ta-bl, *a.* Capable of being transmuted. — **Transmutation**, trans-mū-tā'shon, *n.* [L. *transmutatio.*] The act of transmuting, or state of being transmuted; change into another substance, form, or nature; *alchemy*, the changing of base metals into gold or silver. —*Transmutation of energy*, in *physics*, the theory that any one of the various forms of energy may be converted into one or more of the other forms (as electricity into heat).—**Transmutationist**, trans-mū-tā'shon-ist, *n.* One who believes in transmutation.—**Transmuter**, trans-mū'tėr, *n.* One that transmutes.

Transom, tran'sum, *n.* [Short for *transommer, transummer*, from *trans*, across, and *summer*, a beam; or from L. *transtrum*, a transom.] A strengthening beam across the stern of a ship; a horizontal bar of stone or timber across a mullioned window; the cross-bar separating a door from the fanlight above it; the piece of wood or iron joining the cheeks of gun-carriages.

Transpadane, trans'pa-dān, *a.* [L. *transpadanus—trans*, across, and *Padus*, the Po.] Being beyond the river Po.

Transparent, trans-pā'rent, *a.* [Fr. *transparent*, from L. *trans*, across, through, and *parens, parentis*, ppr. of *pareo*, to appear (seen also in *apparent, appear*).] Having the property of transmitting rays of light so that bodies can be distinctly seen through; pervious to light; diaphanous; pellucid; *fig.* such as to be easily seen through; not sufficient to hide underlying feelings. — **Transparently**, trans-pā'-rent-li, *adv.* In a transparent manner;

clearly. — **Transparentness**, trans-pā'-rent-nes, *n.* Transparency. — **Transparency**, trans-pā'ren-si, *n.* The quality or condition of being transparent; perviousness to light; something transparent; a picture painted on transparent or semi-transparent materials, to be viewed by light shining through it.

Transpicuous, trans-pik'ū-us, *a.* [L. *trans*, through, and *specio*, to see.] Transparent; pervious to the sight.

Transpierce, trans-pērs', *v.t.* [Prefix *trans*, and *pierce*.] To pierce through.

Transpire, trans-pīr', *v.t.* — *transpired, transpiring.* [Fr. *transpirer*, from L. *trans*, across, and *spiro*, to breathe. SPIRIT.] To excrete through the pores of the skin; to send off in vapor; to perspire; to exhale. —*v.i.* To be emitted through the pores of the skin; to exhale; to pass off in insensible perspiration; to become public gradually; to come to light; to ooze out; to leak out; to take place; to happen.

Transpirable, trans-pī'ra-bl, *a.* Capable of being transpired. — **Transpiration**, trans-pī-rā'shon, *n.* The act or process of transpiring; exhalation of moisture through the skin; exhalation of watery vapour from the leaves of plants. — **Transpiratory**, trans-pī'ra-to-ri, *a.* Pertaining to transpiration; transpiring; exhaling.

Transplant, trans-plant', *v.t.* [Prefix *trans*, and *plant*; Fr. *transplanter*.] To remove and plant in another place; to remove from one place to another; to remove and settle or establish for residence in another place. — **Transplantation**, trans-plan-tā'shon, *n.* The act of transplanting; the shifting of a plant from one spot to another; *surg.* the removal of a part of the human body to supply a part that has been lost. — **Transplanter**, trans-plan'tėr, *n.* One who or that which transplants.

Transpontine, trans-pon'tīn, *a.* [L. *trans*, beyond, and *pons, pontis*, bridge.] Situated beyond the bridge; across the bridge; sensational, melodramatic, of the type of plays in London on the Surrey side of the Thames and London Bridge.

Transport, trans-pōrt', *v.t.* [Fr. *transporter*, from L. *transportare*—*trans*, across, and *porto*, to carry. PORT (to carry).] To carry or convey from one place to another; to hurry or carry away by violence of passion; to carry away or ravish with pleasure; to absorb.—*n.* (trans'pōrt). Transportation; conveyance; a vessel engaged in transporting goods and passengers; a ship employed for carrying soldiers, war equipment, &c.; a vehement emotion; passion; rapture; ecstasy. — **Transportability**, trans-pōr'ta-bil"i-ti, *n.* The capacity of being transported. — **Transportable**, trans-pōr'ta-bl, *a.* Capable of being transported.—**Transportal**,† trans-pōr'tal, *n.* The act of transporting; conveyance. (*Darwin.*) — **Transportation**, trans-pōr-tā'shon, *n.* The act of transporting; a conveyance from one place to another; a ticket purchased to travel on some public carrier such as a bus, train, &c. — **Transported**, trans-pōr'ted, *a.* Carried to ecstasy or rapture; ravished with delight.—**Transporting**, trans-pōr'ting, *a.* Ravishing with delight; ecstatic.—**Transport ship**, *n.* A vessel employed in conveying soldiers, military stores, &c.; a transport.

Transpose, trans-pōz', *v.t.* — *transposed, transposing.* [Fr. *transposer*, prefix *trans* and *poser*, to place. POSE, COMPOSE.] To change the place or order of by putting each in the place of the other; to cause to change places; *alg.* to bring, as any term of an equation, over from one side to the other side; *gram.* to change the natural order of words; *mus.* to change the key of.—**Transposer**, trans-pō'zėr, *n.* One who transposes. — **Transposable**, trans-pō'za-bl, *a.* Capable of being transposed.—**Transposal**, trans-pō'zal, *n.* The act of transposing; transposition. — **Transposition**, trans-pō-zish'on, *n.* The act of transposing or state of being transposed; *alg.* the bringing over of any term of an equation from one side to the other side; *rhet.* a change of the natural order of words for effect; *mus.* the change of a composition to a key either higher or lower than the original. — **Transpositional**, **Transpositive**, trans-pō-zish'on-al, trans-poz'i-tiv, *a.* Pertaining to transposition.

Trans-ship. TRANSHIP.

Transubstantiate, tran-sub-stan'shi-āt, *v.t.* [L. *trans*, over, and *substantia*, substance.] To change to another substance. —**Transubstantiation**, tran-sub-stan'-shi-ā"shon, *n.* Change of substance; *theol.* the conversion of the *substance* of the bread and wine in the eucharist into the *substance* of the body and blood of Christ, whilst the *accidents* remain unchanged, a belief held by Roman Catholics and others. — **Transubstantiator**, tran-sub-stan'shi-āt-ėr, *n.* One who maintains the doctrine of transubstantiation.

Transude, tran-sūd', *v.i.*—*transuded, transuding.* [L. *trans*, across, through, and *sudo*, to sweat; allied to E. *sweat*.] To pass or ooze through the pores of a substance.— **Transudation**, tran-sū-dā'shon, *n.* The act or process of transuding; osmose.— **Transudatory**, tran-sū'da-to-ri, *a.* Passing by transudation.

Transverberate, trans-vėr'bėr-āt, *v.t.* [L. *trans*, through, and *verbero*, to strike.] To beat or strike through.

Transverse, trans-vėrs' or trans'vėrs, *a.* [L. *transversus*—*trans*, across, and *versus*, turned. VERSE.] Lying or being across or in a cross direction; lying in a direction across other parts. — *Transverse axis* or *diameter*, in *conic sections*, the diameter which passes through the foci.—*Transverse stress*, that form of stress which bends a structure and tends to break it in pieces. — *Transverse vibrations*, vibrations executed in a direction perpendicular to that in which the undulation advances, e.g. those of light. — **Transversely**, trans-vėrs'li, *adv.* In a transverse manner; in a cross direction.—**Transversal**, trans-vėr'sal, *a.* Transverse; lying crosswise.— **Transversally**, trans-vėr'sal-li, *adv.* In a direction crosswise.

Trap, trap, *n.* [A.Sax. *træppe, treppe*, a trap = O.D. *trappe*, O.H.G. *trapo*, a trap; same root as *trip, tramp*, a trap often catching when trod upon.] A contrivance that shuts suddenly and often with a spring, used for taking game and other animals; any device or contrivance to betray or catch unawares; an ambush; a game, and also one of the instruments used in playing it, the others being a small bat and a ball; a drain-trap; a familiar name for a carriage, on springs, of any kind.—*v.t.*—*trapped, trapping.* To catch in a trap; to insnare; to take by stratagem.—*v.i.* To set traps for game.—**Trapper**, trap'ėr, *n.* One who sets traps to catch animals, usually for furs.

Trap, trap, *n.* [Dan. *trap*, Sw. *trapp*, G. *trapp*, the rock, from Dan. *trappe*, Sw. *trappa*, G. *treppe*, a stair, stairs; akin to *trap* above. The rock was named from the terraced or step-like arrangement seen in many of these rocks.] A kind of movable ladder or steps; a kind of ladder leading up to a loft; *geol.* a name applied to the multifarious igneous rocks of the palæozoic and secondary epochs that cannot be classed as either granitic or volcanic, comprising basalt, clinkstone, greenstone, felstone, &c. — **Trappean**, **Trappous**, **Trappy**, trap-ē'an, trap'us, trap'i, *a.* Pertaining to the rock known as trap; resembling trap.—**Trap-door**, *n.* A door in a floor or roof, with which when shut it is flush or nearly so.—**Trap-stair**, *n.* A narrow stair or kind of ladder surmounted by a trap-door.—**Trap-tufa**, **Trap-tuff**, *n.* *Geol.* a kind of sandstone composed of fragments and earthy materials from trap rocks cemented together.

Trap, trap, *v.t.*—*trapped, trapping.* [O.E. *trappe*, a horse-cloth; same word as Sp. *trapo*, L.L. *trapus*, cloth, Fr. *drap*, cloth; akin *drape*.] To adorn; to dress with ornaments. — **Trappings**, trap'ingz, *n.pl.* Ornamental accessories, as the ornaments put on horses; ornaments generally; dress; finery.—**Traps**, traps, *n.pl.* Small or portable articles for dress, furniture, &c.; goods; furniture; luggage.

Trapan, tra-pan', *v.t.* Same as *Trepan* (to insnare).

Trape, trāp, *v.i.*—*traped, traping.* [Comp. O.Fr. *treper*, to trip or skip; D. and G. *trappen*, to tread, to tramp; akin *tramp, trip.*] To walk carelessly and sluttishly; to run about idly; to traipse.—**Trapes**, trāps, *n.* [TRAIPSE.] A slattern; an idle sluttish woman.—*v.i.* To gad or flaunt about in a slatternly useless way.

Trapezium, tra-pē'zi-um, *n.* [L., from Gr. *trapezion*, a little table, dim. of *trapeza*, a table, for *tetrapeza*, lit. four-footed thing.] *Geom.* a plane figure contained by four straight lines, two of them parallel; *anat.* a bone of the wrist, so named from its shape.—**Trapezate**, trap'e-zāt, *a.* Having the form of a trapezium.—**Trapeze**, tra-pēz', *n.* A trapezium; *gymnastics*, a sort of swing, consisting of one or more crossbars suspended by two cords at some distance from the ground, on which various feats are performed.—**Trapeziform**, tra-pē'zi-form, *a.* Having the form of a trapezium. — **Trapezohedron**, tra-pē'zō-hē"dron, *n.* A solid bounded by twenty-four equal and similar trapezoidal planes.— **Trapezoid**, trap'e-zoid, *n.* *Geom.* a plane four-sided figure having two of its opposite sides parallel.—**Trapezoidal**, trap-e-zoi'dal, *a.* Having the form of a trapezoid.

Trapping. Under TRAP, to deck.

Trappist, trap'ist, *n.* [From the abbey of La *Trappe*, in Normandy, the headquarters of the order.] A member of a religious order of the Roman Catholic Church, founded in 1140, and remarkable for the austere life led by the monks.

Trash, trash, *n.* [Comp. Icel. *tros*, rubbish, leaves and twigs picked up for fuel.] Loppings of trees; sugar-canes from which the juice has been expressed; waste or worthless matter; rubbish; refuse; dross; dregs; a worthless person. — *v.t.* To free from superfluous twigs or branches; to lop.— **Trashily**, trash'i-li, *adv.* In a trashy manner. — **Trashiness**, trash'i-nes, *n.* The state or quality of being trashy.—**Trashy**, trash'i, *a.* Composed of or resembling trash, rubbish, or dross; waste; rejected; worthless; useless.

Trass, tras, *n.* [Prov.G. *trass, tarrass*, trass, from Fr. *terrasse*, earthwork, from L. *terra*, earth. TERRACE.] A volcanic production consisting of ashes and scoriæ, found near Coblentz, and used as a cement.

Trauma, trą'ma. [Gr. *trauma*, a wound.] A wound; mental instability due to shock. —**Traumatic**, trą-mat'ik, *a.* Pertaining to or applied to wounds; adapted to the cure of wounds.—*n.* A medicine useful in the cure of wounds.—**Traumatism**, trą'-mat-izm, *n.* *Pathol.* the condition of the system occasioned by a grave wound.

Travail, trav'āl, *v.i.* [From Fr. *travailler*, to labour, *travail*, labour, toil; originally an apparatus of bars to restrain a vicious horse, from L. *trabs*, a beam. (TRAVE.) *Travel* is the same word.] To toil‡; to suffer the pangs of childbirth.—*n.* Severe toil‡; parturition; childbirth.

Trave, trāv, *n.* [O.Fr. *traf, tref*, It. *trave*, a beam, from L. *trabs, trabis*, a beam. TRAVAIL.] A cross-beam‡; a wooden frame to confine an unruly horse while shoeing.

Travel, trav'el, *v.i.*—*travelled, travelling.* [A different orthography and application of *travail*.] To pass or make a journey from place to place on foot, on horseback, or in any conveyance; to visit distant or foreign places; to journey; to go from place to place for the purpose of obtaining orders for goods, collecting accounts, &c., for a commercial house; to proceed or advance in any way; to pass.—*v.t.* To journey over; to pass.—*n.* The act of travelling or journeying; journeying to a distant country or countries; *pl.* an account of occurrences and observations made during a journey. —**Traveled**, trav'eld, *p.* and *a.* Having made many journeys; hence, experienced. —**Traveler**, trav'el-ėr, *n.* One who travels; a wayfarer; one who visits foreign countries; one who explores regions more or less unknown; a person who goes from place to place to solicit orders for goods, collect accounts, and the like.—**Traveler's-joy**, *n.* A plant, lady's-bower. CLEMATIS.—**Traveler's-tree**, *n.* A characteristic tree of Madagascar belonging to the banana family, so named because the traveler may allay his thirst from water in the hollow at the base of the leaf-stalks.—**Traveling**, trav'el-ing, *a.* Pertaining to or used in travel; incurred by travel (*traveling* expenses).—**Traveling crane**, *n.* A crane fixed on a carriage which may be moved on rails. — **Travel-stained**, *a.* Having the clothes soiled by travel.

Traverse, trav'ėrs, *a.* [O.Fr. *travers, transvers*, from L. *transversus.* TRANSVERSE.] Transverse; being in a direction across something else.—*Traverse sailing*, where a ship makes several courses in succession, the track being zigzag, and the directions of its several parts lying more or less athwart each other. — *n.* A transverse piece; an untoward accident; *fort.* a portion of parapet thrown across the covered way at certain points; *naut.* the zigzag track described by a ship when compelled to sail on different courses; *arch.* a gallery or loft of communication in a church or other large building; *law*, a denial of what the opposite party has advanced in any stage of the pleadings; *surv.* a number of measured lengths and bearings forming a connected series.—*v.t.*—*traversed, traversing.* To cross; to lay in a cross direction; to thwart; to bring to nought; to wander over; to cross in travelling; *gun.* to turn and point in any direction; *carp.* to plane in a direction across the grain of the wood; *law*, to deny what the opposite party has alleged.—*v.i.* To use the motions of opposition in fencing (*Shak.*); to turn, as on a pivot; to swivel.—*adv.* Athwart; crosswise. —**Traversable**, trav'ėr-sa-bl, *a.* Capable of being traversed.—**Traverse-board**, *n.* *Naut.* a board for indicating a ship's course by pegs inserted in holes.—**Traverser**, trav'ėr-sėr, *n.* One who traverses; *rail.* a traverse-table.—**Traverse-table**, *n.* *Navig.* a table by means of which the dead-reckoning is worked out; *rail.* a movable platform with one or more tracks, for shifting carriages, &c., from one line of rails to another.—**Traversing-platform**, *n.* *Artillery*, a platform to support a gun and carriage which can be easily turned round.

Travertine, Travertin, trav'ėr-tin, *n.* [It. *travertino, tibertino, tiburtino*, L. *lapis Tiburtinus*, from being formed by the waters of the Anio at *Tibur*, now Tivoli.] A white concretionary limestone deposited from the waters of springs holding carbonate of lime in solution.

Travesty, trav'es-ti, *v.t.*—*travestied, travestying.* [Fr. *travestir*, to disguise, to travesty, from L. *trans*, over, and *vestio*, to clothe. VEST.] To give such a literary setting to as to render ludicrous after having been previously handled seriously; to burlesque.—*n.* A burlesque treatment or setting of a subject which had been originally handled in a serious or lofty manner.

Travis, trav'is, *n.* [Same origin as *trave.*] A partition between two stalls in a stable.

Trawl, tral, *n.* [From Fr. *trôler*, to lead, to drag. TROLL.] A long line from which short lines with baited hooks are suspended, used in sea-fishing; a trawl-net.—*v.i.* To fish with a trawl-net. —**Trawl-boat**, *n.* A boat used in fishing with trawls or trawl-nets.—**Trawler**, tra'lėr, *n.* One who trawls; a fishing vessel which uses a trawl-net.—**Trawling**, tra'ling, *n.* The act of fishing with a trawl-net.—**Trawl-net**, *n.* A long purse-shaped net for dragging behind a boat, employed in deep-sea fishing, being useful for taking fish which lie near or on the bottom.

Tray, trā, *n.* [A.Sax. *treg*, a tray; connected with *trough.*] A small shallow wooden vessel used for various domestic purposes, as kneading, mincing, &c.; a sort of salver or waiter on which dishes and the like are presented.

Tray, trā, *n.* [Fr. *trois*, three.] A projection on the antler of a stag.

Treacherous, trech'ėr-us, *a.* [O.Fr. *tricheor* (Fr. *tricheur*), a trickster, from O.Fr. *tricher, trecher*, to cheat, to trick; of Germanic origin, and akin to *trick.*] Characterized by treason or violation of allegiance or faith pledged; faithless; traitorous; deceptive; illusory. — **Treacherously**, trech'ėr-us-li, *adv.* In a treacherous manner; traitorously; faithlessly; perfidiously. —**Treacherousness**, trech'ėr-us-nes, *n.* The quality of being treacherous.—**Treachery**, trech'ėr-i, *n.* [Fr. *tricherie*, trickery.] Violation of allegiance or of faith and confidence; treason; perfidy.

Treacle, trē'kl, *n.* [O.Fr. *triacle*, corrupted from L. *theriaca*, from Gr. *thēriaka* (*pharmaka*, drugs, understood), antidotes against the bites of venomous animals, from *thērion*, a wild beast, dim. of *thēr*, an animal.] A medicinal compound of various ingredients, formerly believed to be capable of curing or preventing the effects of poison, particularly that of a serpent; the uncrystallizable matter separated from sugar in sugar-refineries; molasses; a saccharine fluid consisting of the inspissated juices of certain vegetables, as the sap of the birch, sycamore, &c.—**Treacly**, trē'kl-i, *a.* Composed of or like treacle.

Tread, tred, *v.i.*—pret. *trod*; pp. *trod, trodden.* [A.Sax. *tredan*, pret. *træd*, to tread =O.Fris. *treda*, D. and L.G. *treden*, Dan. *træde*, Icel. *trotha*, G. *treten*, Goth. *trudan*, to tread; root same as *tramp. Trade* is from this verb.] To set the foot down or on the ground; to press with the foot; to step; to walk with a more or less measured or cautious step; to copulate, as fowls.—*To tread on* or *upon*, to trample; to set the foot on in contempt.—*To tread upon the heels of*, to follow close upon.—*v.t.* To step or walk on; to beat or press with the feet; to perform by motions of the feet; to dance; to crush under the foot; to trample in contempt or hatred; to copulate with, as a male bird.—*To tread down*, to crush or destroy, as by tramping under foot.—*To tread out*, to press out with the feet; to destroy or extinguish, as by treading or trampling.—*To tread the stage* or *the boards*, to perform a part in a drama.—*n.* A step or stepping; way of walking; gait; the flat horizontal part of the step of a stair.—**Treader**, tred'ėr, *n.* One who treads.—**Treadle**, tred'l, *n.* The part of a loom or other machine which is moved by the foot; a treddle; the albuminous cords which unite the yoke of the egg to the white.—**Tread-mill**, *n.* A machine employed in prison discipline, the usual form of which is a wheel caused to revolve by the weight of the prisoners treading on steps on its periphery.—**Tread-wheel**, *n.* A wheel turned by men or animals such as that of a tread-mill.

Treason, trē'zon, *n.* [O.Fr. *traison* (Fr. *trahison*), from L. *traditio*, a delivering up, from *trado*, to deliver up—*trans*, over and *do*, to give. *Treason* and *tradition* are doublets. TRADITION.] A betrayal of trust; treachery; perfidy; disloyalty or treachery to one's country; any attempt to overthrow the government of a state to which one owes allegiance; the crime of giving aid and comfort to the enemies of one's country.—**Treasonable**, trē'zon-a-bl, *a.* Pertaining to or consisting of treason; disloyal; treacherous.—**Treasonableness**, trē'zon-a-bl-nes, *n.* Quality of being treasonable.—**Treasonably**, trē'zon-a-bli, *adv.* In a treasonable manner.

Treasure, trezh'ėr, *n.* [O.E. *tresoure*, Fr. *trésor*, L. *thesaurus*, from Gr. *thēsauros*, a store, treasure, from root of *tithēmi*, to put or place (whence also *thesis, theme*, &c.).] Wealth accumulated; particularly, a stock or store of money in reserve; a great quantity of anything collected for future use; something very much valued.—*v.t.*—*treasured, treasuring.* To hoard up; to collect for future use; to accumulate; to store; to retain carefully in the mind; to regard as precious; to prize.—**Treasure-house**, *n.* A house where treasures are kept.—**Treasurer**, trezh'ėr-ėr, *n.* One who has the care of a treasure or treasury; one who has the charge of collected funds, such as those belonging to incorporated companies or private societies; a public officer who receives and disburses the money collected from taxes, duties, imposts, &c.—**Treasurership**, trezh'ū-rėr-ship, *n.* The office of treasurer.—**Treasure-trove**, trōv, *n.* [O.Fr. *trovē*, Mod.Fr. *trouvé*, found. TROUBADOUR.] *Law*, money, gold, silver plate, or bullion found hidden in the earth or in any private place the owner of which is not known.—**Treasury**, trezh'ėr-i, *n.* A place or building where public revenues are deposited, and public debts discharged; that department of a government which has charge of the finances; the officials constituting such a department; one of the ten major departments of the executive branch of the U. S. Federal government, the head of which is a member of the Cabinet; *fig.* a collection of valuable information or facts.—*Secretary of the Treasury*, a member of the Cabinet who is responsible to the President and who supervises the collection of all Federal taxes, safeguards and expends public funds, and is in charge of such divisions as the Secret Service, Printing, Internal Revenue, Narcotics, Bureau of Engraving and Printing (where currency is made), the Mint, Public Health Service, and Bureau of the Budget.—**Treasury note**, trezh'ėr-i nōt, *n.* A demand note issued by the United States Treasury, and by law made a legal tender at its face value for all debts, public and private.

Treat, trēt, *v.t.* [Fr. *traiter*, O.Fr. *traicter*, to handle, to treat, from L. *tractare*, a freq. of *traho, tractum*, to draw (whence also *tract, trace, trait, train*, &c.). TRACE.] To behave to or towards; to act well or ill towards; to use in any manner; to handle in a particular manner, in writing or speaking, or by any of the processes of art; to entertain without expense to the guest; to give food or drink to; to manage in the application of remedies (to *treat* a patient); *chem.* to subject to the action of some other substance. — *v.i.* To discourse; to handle in writing or speaking: followed usually by *of*; to negotiate; to propose terms of accommodation.—*n.* An entertainment given as a compliment or expression of regard; anything which affords much pleasure; some unusual gratification. — *To stand treat*, to pay the expenses of an entertainment for another or others. — **Treater**, trē'tėr, *n.* One who treats.—**Treating**, trē'ting, *n.* The act of one who treats; bribing in parliamentary (or other) elections with meat and drink. — **Treatise**, trē'tiz, *n.* [O.Fr. *tretis, traitis.*] A written composition on some subject, in which the principles of it are discussed or explained; usually of considerable length. —**Treatment**, trēt'ment, *n.* The act or the manner of treating; management; manipulation; manner of dealing with substances; usage; good or bad behaviour towards a person; manner of applying remedies to cure.—**Treaty**, trē'ti, *n.* [Fr. *traité.*] The act of treating or negotiating for the adjustment of differences, or for forming an agreement; negotiation; an agreement, league, or contract between two or more nations or sovereigns.

Treble, treb'l, *a.* [O.Fr. *treble*, from L. *triplus*, triple. TRIPLE.] Threefold; triple; *mus.* pertaining to the highest or most acute sounds; playing or singing the highest part or most acute sounds.—*n.* The highest vocal or instrumental part in a concerted piece of music; a soprano voice; a soprano singer.—*v.t.*—*trebled, trebling.* To make thrice as much; to multiply by three; to triple.—*v.i.* To become threefold.—**Trebly**, treb'li, *adv.* In threefold number or quantity; triply.

Treddle, tred'l. Same as *Treadle*.

Tree, trē, *n.* [A.Sax. *treów*, *treó*, a tree = Icel. *tré*, Dan. *træ*, Sw. *träd*, O.D. *tree*, Goth. *triu*, tree, wood; cog. W. *derw*, an oak; Gr. *drus*, an oak, *doru*, a spear; Skr. *dru*, a tree. *Tar* is allied.] A perennial plant having a woody trunk of considerable size, from which spring branches, or, in the palms, fronds; something resembling a tree, consisting of a stem or stalk and branches; as, a genealogical *tree*; a generic name for many wooden pieces in machines or structures; as, axle-*tree*, saddle-*tree*, &c.—*Tree of life*, the tree which grew in the midst of the garden of Eden; also, arbor-vitæ. — *v.t.* — *treed*, *treeing*. To drive to a tree; to cause to take refuge in a tree (a dog *trees* a squirrel). —*v.i.* To take refuge in a tree, as a wild animal.—**Tree-fern**, *n.* The names given to ferns found in tropical countries which attain the size of trees.—**Tree-frog**, *n.* A variety of frog which climbs trees, and remains there all summer living upon insects.—**Treeless**, trē'les, *a.* Destitute of trees.—**Treenail**, trē'nāl, *n.* A cylindrical pin of hardwood used for securing the planking of wooden ships to the frames, or parts to each other.—**Tree-onion**, *n.* A species of onion the stalks of which produce small bulbs at the top.—**Tree-wool**, *n.* Pine-wool.

Trefoil, trē'foil, *n.* [O.Fr. *trefoil*, trefoil, from L. *tres*, three, and *folium*, a leaf.] A three-leaved plant, as the white and red clover, &c., so well known as fodder plants; an ornament used in Gothic architecture representing the form of a three-lobed leaf.

Trek, trek, *v.i.* — *trekked*, *trekking*. [D. *trekken*, to draw, to draw a wagon, to journey.] To travel by wagon. (*South Africa*.)

Trellis, trel'is, *n.* [Fr. *treillis*, lattice-work, from *treille*, an arbour, from L. *trichila*, a bower or arbour.] A structure or frame of cross-barred work or lattice-work, used for supporting plants; a kind of espalier for climbing plants or for training fruit-trees; a reticulated framing or lattice-work of wood or metal, for screens, doors, or windows.—**Trellised**, trel'ist, *a.* Furnished with a trellis. — **Trellis-work**, *n.* Lattice-work.

Trematode, **Trematoid**, trem'a-tōd, trem'a-toid, *a.* [Gr. *trēma*, *trēmatos*, a hole, a pore.] A term applied to certain annuloid parasitic worms living in the intestines of animals, some of them being called fluke-worms.

Tremble, trem'bl, *v.i.* — *trembled*, *trembling*. [Fr. *trembler*, from L. *tremulus*, trembling, from *tremo*, to tremble = Gr. *tremō*, to tremble. The *b* is inserted as in *number*. *Tremor*, *tremulous*, *tremendous* have same origin.] To shake involuntarily, as with fear, cold, weakness, &c.; to shudder: said of persons; to be moved with a quivering motion; to shake; to totter: said of things; to quaver, as sound.—*n.* The act or state of trembling; an involuntary shaking or shivering through cold or fear.—**Trembler**, trem'blėr, *n.* One who trembles.—**Trembling**, trem'bling, *p.* and *a.* Shaking, as with fear, cold, or weakness; quaking; shivering. — *Trembling poplar*, the aspen.—*n.* The act or state of shaking involuntarily; a tremor or quaking of the earth.—**Tremblingly**, trem'bling-li, *adv.* In a trembling manner.—**Tremefaction**, trem-i-fak'shon, *n.* [L. *tremo*, to tremble, and *facio*, to make.] Trembling; agitation.

Tremella, trē-mel'a, *n.* [From L. *tremo*, to tremble or shake.] A fungus of a gelatinous appearance.

Tremendous, trē-men'dus, *a.* [L. *tremendus*, lit. to be trembled at, from *tremo*, to tremble. TREMBLE.] Sufficient to excite fear or terror; terrible; awful; dreadful; hence, such as may astonish by magnitude, force, or violence. — **Tremendously**, trē-men'dus-li, *adv.* In a tremendous manner; dreadfully; terrifically. — **Tremendousness**, trē-men'dus-nes, *n.*

Tremolite, trem'ō-līt, *n.* [From Val *Tremola*, a valley in the Alps where it was discovered.] A mineral regarded as a variety of hornblende, found in dolomite, crystalline limestone, &c.

Tremolo, trem'o-lō, *n.* [It., from L. *tremulus*, tremulous.] *Mus.* a rapid quavering effect in playing or singing; a vibration of the voice in singing, suitable for the production of certain effects.

Tremor, trē'mor, *n.* [L., from *tremo*, to tremble. TREMBLE.] An involuntary trembling; a shivering or shaking; a quivering or vibratory motion.—**Tremulous**, trem'ū-lus, *a.* [L. *tremulus*, from *tremo*.] Trembling; affected with fear or timidity; shaking; shivering.—**Tremulously**, trem'ū-lus-li, *adv.* In a tremulous manner; tremblingly. —**Tremulousness**, trem'ū-lus-nes, *n.*

Trenail, trē'nāl. Same as *Treenail*.

Trench, trensh, *v.t.* [O.Fr. *trencher*, to cut off (Fr. *trancher*), perhaps from L. *truncare*, to lop, from *truncus*, a log, a trunk.] To cut or dig, as a ditch; to furrow deeply with the spade or plough; to break up and prepare for crops by deep digging; to fortify by a ditch and rampart of earth; to intrench. INTRENCH. — *v.i.* To encroach: with *on* or *upon*.—*n.* A long narrow cut in the earth; a ditch; *milit.* a deep ditch, with a parapet or breastwork, cut for defence (as in a siege or a position taken up) or to interrupt the approach of an enemy.—*To open the trenches*, to begin to dig or to form the lines of approach.—**Trenchant**, tren'shant, *a.* [O.Fr. *trenchant*.] Cutting; sharp; keen; unsparing; severe.—**Trencher**, tren'shėr, *n.* [In second sense, lit. that on which food is *trenched* or cut.] One who trenches or cuts; a wooden plate on which meat may be cut or carved, or on which it is eaten.—**Trencher-cap**, *n.* A cap having a flat square top like a square board set on it, such as that worn at universities.—**Trencher-man**, *n.* A hearty feeder; a table companion. — **Trench feet**, *n.* A condition of the feet resembling frost-bite, frequently terminating in gangrene, and caused by exposure to wet and cold.—**Trench fever**, *n.* An infectious disease with feverish symptoms, transmitted by vermin.—**Trench-plough**, *n.* A plough for opening land to a greater depth than common.

Trend, trend, *v.i.* [Lit. to bend circularly, from stem of A.Sax. *trendel*, *tryndel*, a circle; Fris. *trind*, *trund*, Dan. and Sw. *trind*, round; closely akin to *trundle*.] To extend or lie along in a particular direction; to stretch (the coast *trends* to the south).—*n.* Inclination of a coast or other line in a particular direction.

Trental, tren'tal, *n.* [From Fr. *trente*, L. *triginta*, thirty.] In the Roman Catholic Church, a series of thirty masses celebrated for thirty days successively for the repose of the soul of a person recently deceased; hence, a dirge; an elegy.

Trepan, trē-pan', *n.* [Fr. *trépan*, It. *trapano*, from Gr. *trypanon*, an auger, a surgical instrument, from *trypē*, a hole.] *Surg.* an instrument in the form of a crown-saw for removing portions of the bones of the skull, and thus relieving the brain from pressure.—*v.t.*—*trepanned*, *trepanning*. To operate on by the trepan.—**Trepanning**, trē-pan'ing, *n.* The operation of using the trepan.

Trepan, trē-pan', *v.t.*—*trepanned*, *trepanning*. [Formerly *trapan*, from O.Fr. *trappan*, from *trappe*, a trap. TRAP.] To ensnare or entrap; to inveigle in some deceitful manner.—*n.* A snare; a cheat; a deceiver.—**Trepanner**, trē-pan'ėr, *n.* One who trepans; a cheat.

Trepang, **Tripang**, trē-pang', *n.* [Malay name.] The sea-slug, 'sea-cucumber', or bêche-de-mer, found in the eastern seas, and used as food in China.

Trephine, tre-fīn' or tre-fēn', *n.* [Fr. *tréphine*, modified form of *trépan*.] An improved form of the trepan.

Trepidation, trep-i-dā'shon, *n.* [L. *trepidatio*, from *trepido*, to tremble, from *trepidus*, trembling, from obsolete *trepo*, to turn = Gr. *trepō*, to turn.] An involuntary trembling; a state of terror; a trembling of the limbs, as in paralytic affections; the oscillation of the ecliptic formerly assumed to account for the phenomenon of the procession of the equinoxes. (*Mil.*, *P. L.*, iii, 483.)—**Trepid**,† trep'id, *a.* Trembling; quaking with fear.—**Trepidity**,† tre-pid'-i-ti, *n.* The state of being trepid.

Trespass, tres'pas, *v.i.* [O.Fr. *trespasser*, from *tres* = L. *trans*, beyond, and *passer*, to pass. PASS.] To pass over a boundary line and enter unlawfully upon the land of another; to intrude; to encroach; to commit any offence; to transgress; to violate any divine law or any known rule of duty.—*n.* The act of one who trespasses; a violation of some law or rule laid down; any voluntary transgression of the moral law; sin; *law*, any transgression of the law not amounting to felony; especially wrong done by entering on the grounds of another. — **Trespasser**, tres'pas-ėr, *n.* One who commits a trespass. — **Trespass-offering**, *n.* An offering, among the Israelites, in expiation of a trespass.

Tress, tres, *n.* [Fr. *tresse*, It. *treccia*, a tress, plait of hair, from Gr. *tricha*, in three parts, from the usual mode of plaiting the hair; allied to *three*.] A lock or curl of hair; a ringlet.—**Tressed**, trest, *a.* Having tresses; formed into ringlets. — **Tressy**, tres'i, *a.* Pertaining to tresses; having the appearance of tresses.

Tressel, tres'l, *n.* Same as *Trestle*.

Trestle, tres'l, *n.* [O.Fr. *trestel* (Fr. *tréteau*), a trestle; from Armor. *treustel*, from *treust*, *trest*, W. *trawst*, a beam.] A sort of frame for supporting things; a frame with three or four legs attached to a horizontal piece. —**Trestle-board**, *n.* An architect's or draughtsman's designing board, formerly supported on trestles.—**Trestle-bridge**, *n.* A bridge in which the bed is supported upon framed sections or trestles.

Tret, tret, *n.* [Fr. *trait*, from O.Fr. *traire*, to draw, from L. *trahere*, to draw. TRACE.] An allowance of 4 lb. for every 104 to purchasers of certain goods for waste or refuse matter.

Trevet, trev'et, *n.* Same as *Trivet*.

Trews, trōz, *n.pl.* The tartan trousers of Highlanders or soldiers in Highland regiments.

Trey,† trā, *n.* [O.Fr. *trei*, Fr. *trois*, L. *tres*, three.] A three at cards or dice. (*Shak.*)

Triable. Under TRY.

Triachenium, trī-a-kē'ni-um, *n.* [Prefix *tri*, three, and *achenium*.] *Bot.* a fruit which consists of three achenia.

Triacontahedral, trī-a-kon'ta-hē"dral, *a.* [Gr. *triakonta*, thirty, and *hedra*, side.] Having thirty sides.

Triad, trī'ad, *n.* [Gr. *trias*, *triados*, from *treis*, *tria*, three.] A unity of three; three united; a trinity; *mus.* the common chord formed of three radical sounds, a fundamental note, its third, and its fifth; *chem.* an elementary substance, each atom of which will combine with three atoms of a monad.—**Triadic**, trī-ad'ik, *a.* Pertaining to a triad.

Triadelphous, trī-a-del'fus, *a.* [Gr. *treis*, three, and *adelphos*, a brother.] *Bot.* having the stamens combined into three masses by the filaments.

Trial. Under TRY.

Trialist, trī'al-ist, *n.* [Gr. *trias*, group of three.] An Austrian device to unite Austro-Hungary with Bohemia; an attempted union of the German, Magyar, Czech races.

Trialogue, trī'a-log, *n.* [Gr. *treis*, *tria*, three, and *logos*, discourse.] A colloquy of three persons.

Triander, trī'an-dėr, *n.* [Gr. *treis*, three, and *anēr*, *andros*, a male.] A monoclinous or hermaphrodite plant having three distinct and equal stamens.—**Triandrian**, **Triandrous**, trī-an'dri-an, trī-an'drus, *a.* Belonging to such plants.

Triangle, trī'ang-gl, *n.* [Fr. *triangle*, from L. *triangulum*—*tres*, *tria*, three, and *angulus*, an angle.] *Geom.* a figure bounded by three lines and containing three angles, the lines or sides being straight in a plane triangle, and parts of circles in spherical triangles; a musical instrument of percussion, made of a rod of steel bent into this shape, open at one of the angles; a three-cornered straight-edge, used by draughtsmen, &c.; a kind of gin for raising heavy weights; *milit.* three halberts stuck in the ground and united at the top, to which soldiers were bound when flogged.—**Triangular**, trī-ang'gū-lėr, *a.* Having three angles; having the form of a triangle; three-cornered. — *Triangular compass*, a compass having three legs by means of which any triangle or any three points may be taken off at once. — *Triangular pyramid*, a pyramid whose base is a triangle.—**Triangularity**, trī-ang'gū-lar''-i-ti, *n.* Quality of being triangular.—**Triangularly**, trī-ang'gū-lėr-li, *adv.* After the form of a triangle.—**Triangulate**, trī-ang'gū-lāt, *v.t.*—*triangulated, triangulating.* To make triangular; *surv.* to divide into triangles, or survey by dividing into triangles. — **Triangulation**, trī-ang'gū-lā''shon, *n.* The reduction of the surface of an area to triangles for the purpose of a trigonometrical survey.—**Trianguloid**, trī-ang'gū-loid, *a.* Somewhat triangular.

Triarchy, trī'är-ki, *n.* [Gr. *treis*, three, and *archē*, rule.] Government by three persons.

Trias, trī'as, *n.* [Gr. *trias*, the number three.] *Geol.* a name given to the upper new red sandstone, from its being composed in Germany of three well-marked groups, only the highest and lowest of which are known in England.—**Triassic**, trī-as'ik, *a.* Pertaining to or composed of trias.

Triatomic, trī-a-tom'ik, *a.* [Gr. *treis*, three, and *atomos*, an atom.] *Chem.* consisting of three atoms; having three atoms in the molecule.

Tribasic, trī-bā'sik, *a.* [Gr. *treis*, three, and *basis*, base.] *Chem.* applied to acids which combine with three equivalents of a base.

Tribe, trīb, *n.* [L. *tribus*, one of the three bodies into which the Romans were originally divided, from *tres*, three. THREE.] A division, class, or distinct portion of a people or nation; a family or race descending from the same progenitor, and kept distinct, as the twelve tribes of Israel; a nation or family of savages, forming a subdivision of a race; a number of persons of any character or profession: in contempt; a term used by some naturalists to denote a number of things having certain characters or resemblances in common (a *tribe* of plants); a division of animals or plants intermediate between order and genus.—**Tribal**, trī'bal, *a.* Belonging to a tribe; characteristic of a tribe.—**Tribalism**, trī'bal-izm, *n.* The state of existing in separate tribes; tribal feeling.

Triblet, trib'let, *n.* [Fr. *triboulet*; origin doubtful.] A mandrel used in forging tubes, nuts, and rings, and for other purposes; a mandrel for making lead-pipe.

Tribometer, tri-bom'et-ėr, *n.* [Gr. *tribō*, to rub, *metron*, measure.] An apparatus, resembling a sled, for measuring the force of friction in rubbing surfaces.

Triboulet, trib'ö-let, *n.* TRIBLET.

Tribrach, trī'brak, *n.* [Gr. *tribrachys*—*treis*, three, and *brachys*, short.] *Pros.* a poetic foot of three short syllables; a word of three short syllables.

Tribracteate, trī-brak'tē-āt, *a.* [Prefix *tri*, three, and *bracteate.*] *Bot.* having three bracts.

Tribulation, trib-ū-lā'shon, *n.* [Eccles. L. *tribulatio*, distress, from L. *tribulo*, *tribulatum*, to thrash, from *tribulum*, a thrashing-sledge for dragging over corn; akin *tero*, *tritum*, to rub (whence *trite*, *contrite* heart).] That which occasions affliction or distress; severe affliction; distress; trouble; trial.

Tribune, trī'būn or trib'ūn, *n.* [L. *tribunus*, a tribune, magistrate, or officer, from *tribus*, tribe; in latter senses short for *tribunal.*] An officer in ancient Rome who represented a tribe for certain purposes; an officer or magistrate chosen by the common people of Rome to protect them from the oppression of the patricians; also a military officer commanding a division or legion; a raised seat or stand; the throne of a bishop; a sort of pulpit or rostrum where a speaker stands to address an assembly. — **Tribunal**, trī-bū'nal, *n.* [L. *tribunal*, from *tribunus*, a tribune.] The seat of a judge; a bench for judges; a court of justice.—**Tribunate**, trī'bū-nāt, *n.* Tribuneship. —**Tribuneship**, trī'būn-ship or trib'ūn-ship, *n.* The office of a tribune.—**Tribunician**, **Tribunitial**, trib-ū-nish'an, trib-ū-nish'al, *a.* Pertaining to tribunes.

Tribute, trib'ūt, *n.* [Fr. *tribut*, L. *tributum*, from *tribuo*, to give, to bestow, perhaps from *tribus*, a tribe. TRIBE.] An annual or stated sum paid by one prince or nation to another, either as an acknowledgment of submission or by virtue of some treaty; the obligation of contributing; a personal contribution; anything done or given, as that which is due or observed (a *tribute* of respect).—**Tributary**, trib'ū-ta-ri, *a.* [L. *tributarius.*] Paying tribute to another; subject; subordinate; inferior; yielding supplies of anything; contributing.—*n.* An individual, government, or state that pays tribute; *geog.* an affluent; a stream which contributes water to another stream.—**Tributarily**, trib'ū-ta-ri-li, *adv.* In a tributary manner. — **Tributariness**, trib'ū-ta-ri-nes, *n.* The state of being tributary.—**Tribute-money**, *n.* Money paid as tribute.

Tricapsular, trī-kap'sū-lėr, *a.* [Prefix *tri*, and *capsule.*] *Bot.* having three capsules to each flower.

Trice, trīs, *v.t.*—*triced, tricing.* [Same as L.G. *trissen*, Dan. *tridse*, to hoist, *tridse*, a pulley; Sw. *trissa*, a pulley.] *Naut.* to haul or tie up by means of a small rope; to hoist.

Trice, trīs, *n.* [From Sp. *tris*, noise of breaking glass, a crack, an instant, a trice; *venir en un tris*, to come in a trice.] A very short time; a moment; now used only in the phrase *in a trice*, in an instant or moment.

Tricennial, trī-sen'ni-al, *a.* [L. *tricennium*, a space of thirty years, from *triginta*, thirty, *annus*, a year.] Belonging to thirty, especially thirty years; occurring once in every thirty years.

Tricentenary, trī-sen'te-na-ri, *n.* [L. *tricenti*, three hundred—prefix *tri*, three, *centum*, a hundred.] The space of three hundred years; the commemoration of any event which occurred three hundred years before. Called also *Tercentenary.*—*a.* Relating to three hundred years.

Triceps, trī'seps, *a.* and *n.* [L., from *tres*, three, and *caput*, head.] Three-headed: applied to certain muscles.

Trichina, tri-kī'na, *n.* pl. **Trichinæ**, tri-kī'nē. [From Gr. *thrix*, *trichos*, a hair.] A minute nematoid worm, the larva of which is found in the tissue of the muscles of man and several other mammals, giving rise to the disease trichiniasis.—**Trichiniasis**, **Trichinosis**, trik-i-nī'a-sis, trik-i-nō'-sis, *n.* A painful and frequently fatal disease produced by eating meat, especially pork, either raw or insufficiently cooked, infested with trichinæ.—**Trichinous**, tri-kī'nus, *a.* Connected with trichinæ or trichiniasis.

Trichocyst, trik'o-sist, *n.* [Gr. *thrix*, *trichos*, a hair, and *kystis*, a bag.] A cell capable of emitting thread-like filaments, found in infusoria.—**Trichogenous**, tri-koj'en-us, *a.* [Gr. *thrix*, *trichos*, and root *gen*, to produce.] Producing or encouraging the growth of hair.—**Trichogyne**, trī'kō-gin, *n.* [Gr. *thrix*, and *gynē*, a woman.] In red seaweeds, a receptive thread-like projection from the female organ.—**Trichoma**, tri-kō'ma, *n.* [Gr., from *thrix*, *trichos.*] *Bot.* the filamentous thallus of algals; *pathol.* an affection of the hair; plica.—**Trichomatose**, tri-kom'a-tōs, *a.* Affected with trichoma. — **Trichome**, trī-kōm, *n.* A hair or other outgrowth from the epidermis. — **Trichopteran**, tri-kop'tėr-an, *n.* [Gr. *thrix*, and *pteron*, a wing.] One of an order of insects comprising the caddice-flies, having hairy, membranous wings. — **Trichopterous**, tri-kop'tėr-us, *a.* Pertaining to the trichopterans.

Trichord, trī'kord, *n.* [Gr. *treis*, three, and *chordē*, a chord.] A musical instrument with three chords or strings.—*a.* Having three strings.—*Trichord pianoforte*, a pianoforte having three strings to each note for the greater part of its compass.

Trichotomy, trī-kot'o-mi, *n.* [Gr. *tricha*, thrice, and *tomē*, a cutting.] Division into three parts.—**Trichotomous**, trī-kot'o-mus, *a.* Divided or branching by threes; trifurcate.

Trichromatic, trī-krōm-at'ik, *a.* [Prefix *tri-*, and Gr. *chroma*, colour.] Pertaining to three colours, especially to red, green, and violet, which, according to the trichromatic theory, are fundamental in colour sensation; or to red, yellow, and blue, which are primary colours so far as regards mixtures of pigments.

Trick, trik, *n.* [Same as D. *trek*, a pull, stroke, dash, trick; *track*, *treachery*, are of same origin; akin *strike*, *stroke*, *s* having been lost.] An artifice; a stratagem; a fraudulent contrivance for an evil purpose; a cheat; a knack or art; a sleight-of-hand performance; the legerdemain of a juggler; a particular practice or habit; an action peculiar to a person (a *trick* of frowning); anything mischievously and roguishly done; a prank; a frolic; *card-playing*, all the cards played in one round; *naut.* a spell; a turn; the time allotted to a man to stand at the helm.—*v.t.* To deceive; to impose on; to defraud; to cheat; to draw in outline, as with a pen; to delineate without colour, as heraldic devices. [In last sense directly from D. *trekken*, to draw, to delineate.]—*v.i.* To live by deception and fraud.—**Tricker**, trik'ėr, *n.* One who tricks; a deceiver; a cheat; a trickster. —**Trickery**, trik'ėr-i, *n.* The practice of tricks; imposture; cheating; artifice.—**Trickiness**, trik'i-nes, *n.* The quality of being tricky.—**Trickish**, trik'ish, *a.* Given to tricks; artful; knavish.—**Trickishly**, trik'ish-li, *adv.* In a trickish manner.—**Trickishness**, trik'ish-nes, *n.*—**Tricksiness**, trik'si-nes, *n.* The quality of being tricksy; playfulness.—**Tricksome**, trik'-sum, *a.* Full of tricks.—**Trickster**, trik'stėr, *n.* One who practises tricks; a deceiver; a cheat.—**Tricksy, Tricksey**, trik'si, *a.* Full of tricks and devices; artful; given to pranks.—**Tricky**, trik'i, *a.* Trickish; mischievous.

Trick, trik, *v.t.* [From above word, or from W. *treciaw*, to trick out, from *trec*, harness, gear.] To dress; to decorate; to set off; to adorn fantastically: often followed by *out*. —**Tricking**, trik'ing, *n.* Dress; ornament.

Trickle, trik'l, *v.i.*—*trickled, trickling.* [Probably for *strickle*, from A.Sax. *strican*, to go. STRIKE.] To flow in a small gentle stream; to run down in drops.

Trick-track, trik-trak, *n.* A kind of backgammon.

Triclinic, trī-klin'ik, *a.* [Gr. *treis*, three, *klinō*, to incline.] *Crystal.* having three unequal axes intersecting obliquely. — **Triclinium**, trī-klin'i-um, *n.* [L., from Gr. *triklinion.*] Among the Romans, a couch running round three sides of a table, for reclining on at meals; the dining-room in which such a couch was laid.—**Triclinlary**, trī-klin'i-a-ri, *a.* Pertaining to.

Tricoccous, trī-kok'us, *a.* [Gr. *treis*, three, and *kokkos*, a berry.] *Bot.* having three cells with one seed in each.

Tricolor, Tricolour, trī'kul-ėr, *n.* [Fr *tricolore*, of three colors—L. *tres*, three, and *color*, color.] A flag having three colors; a flag having three colors arranged in equal stripes, adopted in France as the national ensign during the first revolution, the colors being blue, white, and red, divided vertically.—**Tricolored**, trī'kul-ėrd, *a.* Having three colors.

Tricorporal, Tricorporate, trī-kor'-po-ral, trī-kor'po-rāt, *a.* [L. *tricorpor*—*tri*

=*tres*, three, and *corpus, corporis*, a body.] Having three bodies united together.

Tricostate, trī-kos'tāt, *a.* [L. *tri=tres*, three, and *costa*, a rib.] *Bot.* having three ribs or ridges; three-ribbed.

Tricuspid, Tricuspidate, trī-kus'pid, trī-kus'pi-dāt, *a.* [L. *tri=tres*, three, and *cuspis, cuspidis*, a point.] Having three cusps or points; *bot.* three-pointed; ending in three points.

Tricycle, trī'si-kl, *n.* [Gr. *tri=treis*, three, and *kyklos*, a circle, a wheel.] A form of velocipede with three wheels, generally two driving wheels parallel to each other, and a steering wheel either in front or in the rear.—**Tricyclist**, trī-sik-list, *n.* One who rides on a tricycle.

Tridacna, trī-dak'na, *n.* [Gr. *tridaknos*, eaten at three bites—*tri=treis*, three, and *daknō*, to bite.] A genus of bivalve molluscs, some of them with shells of immense size.

Tridactylous, trī-dak'til-us, *a.* [Gr. *tri =treis*, three, and *daktylos*, a finger or toe.] Having three toes or three fingers.

Trident, trī'dent, *n.* [L. *tridens, tridentis*—*tri=tres*, three, and *dens, dentis*, a tooth.] Any instrument of the form of a fork with three prongs; the sceptre or spear with three barbed prongs with which Poseidon (Neptune), the sea-god, is represented.—**Tridentate, Tridentated**, trī-den'-tāt, trī-den'tā-ted, *a.* Having three teeth.—**Tridentiferous**, trī-den-tif'ėr-us, *a.* Bearing a trident.

Tridentine, trī-den'tīn, *a.* [L. *Tridentum*, Trent.] Pertaining to Trent, or to the celebrated ecumenical council which met in that city in 1545.

Tridimensional, trī-di-men'shon-al, *a.* [Prefix *tri*, three, and *dimension*.] Having three dimensions.

Tridodecahedral, trī-dō-dek'a-hē"dral, *a.* [Prefix *tri*, and *dodecahedral*.] *Crystal.* presenting three ranges of faces, twelve in each.

Triennial, trī-en'ni-al, *a.* [L. *triennium*, the space of three years—*tri=tres*, three; and *annus*, a year.] Continuing three years; happening every three years.—**Triennially**, trī-en'ni-al-li. *adv.* Once in three years.

Trier, trī'er, *n.* One who tries or attempts; one who tests or experiments; one who tests judicially; a judge.

Trierarch, trī'ėr-ärk, *n.* [Gr. *triērēs*, a trireme, and *archē*, rule.] The commander of a Greek trireme; also, one who was obliged to build ships and furnish them at his own expense.—**Trierarchy**, trī"ėr-är'-ki, *n.* The office or function of a trierarch.

Trifarious, trī-fā'ri-us, *a.* [L. *trifarius*, threefold—prefix *tri*, three, and term. *-farius*.] Arranged in three rows; threefold.

Trifid, trī'fid, *a.* [L. *trifidus*—*tri=tres*, three, and *findo, fidi*, to divide.] *Bot.* cut or divided half-way into three parts with straight margins; three-cleft.

Trifle, trī'fl, *n.* [O.E. *trifle, trofle, trufle*, a trifle, from O.Fr. *trufle, truffe*, mock, gibe; perhaps of Teutonic origin; comp. Icel. *truff*, trumpery.] A thing of very little value or importance; a paltry toy, bauble, or luxury; a silly or unimportant action, remark, or the like; a kind of light dish or fancy confection.—*v.i.*—*trifled, trifling.* To act or talk without seriousness or with levity; to indulge in light amusements.—*To trifle with*, to treat as a trifle; to make a toy or a fool of; to mock.—*v.t.* To waste to no good purpose; to spend: usually followed by *away*.—**Trifler**, trī'fl-ėr, *n.* One who trifles.—**Trifling**, trī'fl-ing, *p.* and *a.* Acting with levity; frivolous; being of small value or importance; trivial.—**Triflingly**, trī'fl-ing-li, *adv.* In a trifling manner.—**Triflingness**, trī'fl-ing-nes, *n.*

Trifloral, Triflorous, trī-flō'ral, trī-flō'rus, *a.* [L. *tri=tres*, three, and *flos, floris*, flower.] Three-flowered; bearing three flowers.

Trifoliate, Trifoliated, trī-fō'li-āt, trī-fō'li-ā-ted, *a.* [L. *tri=tres*, three, and *folium*, a leaf.] Having three leaves.—**Trifoliolate**, trī-fō'li-ō-lāt, *a.* Having three leaflets.

Triforium, trī-fō'ri-um, *n.* [L. *tri=tres*, three, and *foris*, pl. *fores*, a door.] *Gothic arch.* a gallery above the arches of the nave of a church, generally in the form of an arcade.

Triform, trī'form, *a.* [L. *triformis*—*tri=tres*, three, and *forma*, shape.] Having a triple form or shape.

Trifurcate, Trifurcated, trī-fėr'kāt, trī-fėr'kā-ted, *a.* [L. *tri=tres*, three, and *furca*, a fork.] Having three branches or forks; trichotomous.

Trig, trig, *v.t.*—*trigged, trigging.* [Comp. W. *trigaw*, to stay, to tarry; Pr. *trigar*, to stop.] To stop, as the wheel of a vehicle, by putting something down to check it.—*n.* A stone, wedge, &c., used for this purpose.

Trig, trig, *a.* [Sw. *trygg*, Dan. *tryg*, secure, safe.] Trim; spruce; neat. (Provincial.)

Trigamy, trig'a-mi, *n.* [Gr. *tri=treis*, three, and *gamos*, marriage.] The state of having three husbands or three wives at the same time.—**Trigamist**, trig'a-mist, *n.* One who has three husbands or wives at the same time.—**Trigamous**, trig'a-mus, *a.* Pertaining to trigamy; *bot.* having three sorts of flowers in the same head, male, female, and hermaphrodite.

Trigeminous, trī-jem'i-nus, *a.* [L. *tri=tres*, three, and *geminus*, double.] Being one of three born together; born three at a time; threefold.

Trigger, trig'ėr, *n.* [Older form *tricker*, from D. *trekker*, trigger, lit. a drawer, from *trekken*, to draw; allied to *trick, track*.] The catch or lever which, on being pulled back, liberates the hammer of the lock of a gun or pistol; any similar device.—**Trigger-fish**, *n.* The name of certain fishes which have a dorsal fin with a strong ray or spine in front, that cannot be pressed down till the second ray is depressed.

Triglyph, trī'glif, *n.* [Gr. *tri=treis*, three, and *glyphē*, sculpture.] *Arch.* an ornamental block in Doric friezes, repeated at equal intervals, having on its face two small perpendicular channels and a half channel on either side.—**Triglyphic, Triglyphical**, trī-glif'ik, trī-glif'i-kal, *a.* Pertaining to triglyphs.

Trigon, trī'gon, *n.* [Fr. *trigone*, L. *trigonum*, from Gr. *trigōnon*—*tri=treis*, three, and *gōnia*, an angle.] A triangle; *astrol.* the junction of three signs of the zodiac; an ancient triangular lyre.—**Trigonal, Trigonous**, trī'gon-al, trī'gon-us, *a.* Triangular; *bot.* having three prominent longitudinal angles, as a style or ovary.

Trigonometry, trig-o-nom'et-ri, *n.* [From Gr. *trigōnon*, a triangle (*treis*, three, and *gōnia*, an angle), and *metron*, a measure.] The measuring of triangles, or the science of determining the sides and angles of triangles by means of certain parts which are given, of high importance in astronomy, navigation, and surveying. It is of two kinds, *plane trigonometry*, treating of triangles described on a plane, and *spherical trigonometry*, of those described on the surface of a sphere.—**Trigonometric, Trigonometrical**, trig'o-no-met"rik, trig'o-no-met"ri-kal, *a.* Pertaining to trigonometry; performed by or according to the rules of trigonometry.—*Trigonometrical survey*, the survey of a country (such as the Ordnance Survey of Great Britain) carried on from a single base, which must be measured with the most extreme accuracy, by the computation of observed angular distances and careful geodetical operations.—**Trigonometrically**, trig'o-no-met"ri-kal-li, *adv.* In a trigonometrical manner; by trigonometry.

Trigram, Trigraph, trī'gram, trī'graf, *n.* [Gr. *tri = treis*, three, *gramma*, a letter, *graphē*, a writing.] A name given to three letters having one sound; a triphthong, as *eau* in *beau*.—**Trigrammatic, Trigrammic**, trī-gram-mat'ik, trī-gram'mik, *a.* Consisting of three letters, or three sets of letters.

Trigyn, trī'jin, *n.* [Gr. *tri = treis*, three, and *gynē*, a female.] *Bot.* a plant having three styles or pistils.—**Trigynian, Trigynous**, trī-jin'i-an, trī'ji-nus, *a.* *Bot.* having three styles.

Trihedron, trī-hē'dron, *n.* [Gr. *tri = treis*, three, and *hedra*, side.] A figure having three equal sides.—**Trihedral**, trī-hē-dral, *a.* Having three equal sides.

Trijugate, Trijugous, trī'jū-gāt, trī'jū-gus, *a.* [L. *tri = tres*, three, *jugum*, yoke.] *Bot.* in three pairs, as a pinnate leaf with three pairs of leaflets.

Trilateral, trī-lat'ėr-al, *a.* [L. *tri = tres*, three, *latus, lateris*, a side.] Having three sides, as a triangle.—**Trilaterally**, trī-lat'ėr-al-li, *adv.* With three sides.—**Trilateralness**, trī-lat'ėr-al-nes, *n.*

Trilinear, trī-lin'ē-ėr, *a.* [L. *tri = tres*, three, and *linea*, a line.] Composed of or consisting of three lines.

Trilingual, trī-ling'gwal, *a.* [L. *tri=tres*, three, and *lingua*, a tongue.] Consisting of three languages.

Triliteral, trī-lit'ėr-al, *a.* [L. *tri = tres*, three, and *litera*, a letter.] Consisting of three letters; combining three letters, as the roots in the Semitic family of tongues.—*n.* A word consisting of three letters.—**Triliteralness**, trī-lit'ėr-al-nes, *n.*

Trilithon, Trilith, trī'lith-on, trī'lith, *n.* [Gr. *tri=treis*, three, and *lithos*, a stone.] Three large blocks of stone placed together like door-posts and a lintel, and standing by themselves, as in sundry ancient monuments.—**Trilithic**, trī-lith'ik, *a.* Relating to a trilithon; consisting of three stones.

Trill, tril, *n.* [Perhaps imitative of sound = D. *trillen*, Dan. *trille*, to trill, to quaver; It. *trillo*, G. *triller*, a trill.] A warbling, quavering sound; a rapid, trembling series or succession of tones.—*v.t.* To sing with a quavering or tremulousness of voice; to sing.—*v.i.* To shake or quaver; to sound with tremulous vibrations; to sing with quavers; to pipe.

Trill, tril, *v.i.* [Comp. Sw. *trilla*, Dan. *trille*, to roll.] To flow in a small stream.

Trillion, tril'yon, *n.* [Formed from *tri-*, three, and *million*.] In the U. S. and France, a million times a million, or a thousand billions; a digit followed by twelve zeros (*1,000,000,000,000*).

Trilobate, Trilobed, trī-lō'bāt, trī'lōbd, *a.* [Gr. *tri = treis*, three, and *lobos*, a lobe.] Having three lobes.

Trilobite, trī'lō-bīt, *n.* [Gr. *tri = treis*, three, and *lobos*, a lobe.] One of an extinct and widely-distributed family of palæozoic crustacea abundant in the Silurian strata, having the body divided into three lobes, which run parallel to its axis.—**Trilobitic**, trī-lō-bit'ik, *a.* Pertaining to or resembling a trilobite.

Trilocular, trī-lok'ū-lėr, *a.* [L. *tri = tres*, three, and *loculus*, a cell, dim. of *locus*, a place.] *Bot.* three-celled; having three cells for seeds.

Trilogy, tril'o-ji, *n.* [Gr. *trilogia*, from *treis, tria*, three, and *logos*, speech, discourse.] A series of three dramas, each in a certain sense complete in itself, yet together forming one connected whole; a term especially relating to the Greek drama.

Triluminar, Triluminous, trī-lū'min-ėr, trī-lū'min-us, *a.* [L. *tri = tres*, three, and *lumen*, light.] Having three lights.

Trim, trim, *v.t.*—*trimmed, trimming.* [A. Sax. *trymian*, to prepare, to set in order, from *trum*, firm, strong; O.Sax. *trimm*, firm, L.G. *betrimmen*, to make firm.] To put in due order for any purpose; to adjust; to invest, embellish, or decorate, as with ribbons, braid, lace, &c. (to *trim* a gown); to bring to a neat or orderly condition by removing superfluous appendages or matter; to clip, pare, shave, prune, lop, or the like (to *trim* the hair, a hedge, or a tree); *carp.* to dress, as timber; *naut.* to adjust the weights in a ship or boat, so that it shall sit well on the water and sail well. —*v.i.* To hold a middle course or position between parties, so as to appear to favour each.—*a.* Being neat and in good order; properly adjusted; having everything appropriate and in its right place; tight; snug; neat; tidy; smart.—*n.* Dress; garb; state of preparation; order; condition; mood; disposition; the state of a ship by which she is well prepared for sailing.—**Trimly**, trim'li, *adv.* In a trim manner or condition.—**Trimmer**, trim'ėr, *n.* One who trims; a labourer who arranges the cargo of coal on board a ship; one who fluctuates between parties, especially political parties, or tries to keep on good terms with each. — **Trimming**, trim'ing, *n.* The act of one who trims; the act of one who fluctuates between parties; ornamental appendages to a garment; *pl.* the accessories to any dish or article of food (*colloq.*). —**Trimmingly**, trim'ing-li, *adv.* In a trimming manner.—**Trimness**, trim'nes, *n.* The state or quality of being trim.

Trimembral, trī-mem'bral, *a.* [Prefix *tri*, three, and *member.*] Having or consisting of three members.

Trimerous, trī'mėr-us, *a.* [Gr. *tri* = *treis*, three, and *meros*, a part.] *Bot.* consisting of three parts; *entom.* applied to beetles (Trimera) having three-jointed tarsi.

Trimester, trī-mes'tėr, *n.* [Fr. *trimestre*, from L. *trimestris*—prefix *tri*, three, and *mensis*, a month.] A term or period of three months.—**Trimestral**, **Trimestrial**, trī-mes'tral, trī-mes'tri-al, *a.* Pertaining to a trimester; occurring every three months; quarterly.

Trimeter, trim'et-ėr, *n.* [Gr. *tri* = *treis*, three, and *metron*, a measure.] A line or verse of poetry consisting of three measures (often of two iambic feet each).

Trimorphism, trī-mor'fizm, *n.* [Gr. *tri* =*treis*, three, and *morphē*, form.] The state or property of having three distinct forms; *crystal.* the property of crystallizing in three fundamentally different forms.—**Trimorphic**, **Trimorphous**, trī-mor'fik, trī-mor'fus, *a.* Characterized by trimorphism; having three distinct forms.

Trimurti, tri-mur'ti, *n.* [Skr., from *tri*, three, and *mûrti*, body.] The Hindu trinity, Brahma the creator, Vishnu the preserver, and Siva the destroyer, conceived as an inseparable unity.

Trinal, **Trine**, trī'nal, trīn, *a.* [L. *trinus*, threefold, from *tres*, three.] Threefold; triple.—**Trine**, *n.* The aspect of planets distant from each other 120 degrees; a triad.

Trinervate, **Trinerved**, **Trinerve**, trī-nėr'vāt, trī'nėrvd, trī'nėrv, *a.* [L. *tri* = *tres*, three, and *nervus*, a nerve.] *Bot.* having three unbranched vessels extending from the base to the apex: said of a leaf.

Tringle, tring'gl, *n.* [Fr.; origin unknown.] *Arch.* a little square member or ornament; a curtain-rod.

Trinitrotoluene, trī-nī'trō-tol''ū-ēn, *n.* [From *tri-*, *nitric*, and *toluene.*] A high explosive, made by treating toluene with nitric acid; also called T.N.T.

Trinity, trin'i-ti, *n.* [Fr. *trinité*, from L. *trinitas*, from *trinus*, threefold, from *tres*, three. THREE.] A union of three in one; the state of being three; *theol.* the union of three persons in one Godhead: the Father, the Son, and the Holy Spirit; a symbolical representation of the mystery of the Trinity frequent in Christian art.—*Trinity Sunday*, the Sunday next after Whitsunday, observed in honour of the Trinity.—*Trinity House*, an incorporation having its headquarters in London, intrusted with the regulation and management of the lighthouses and buoys of the shores and rivers of England, with supervision of those of Scotland and Ireland.—**Trinitarian**, trin-i-tā'ri-an, *a.* Pertaining to the trinity, or to the doctrine of the Trinity.—*n.* One who believes the doctrine of the Trinity.—**Trinitarianism**, trin-i-tā'ri-an-izm, *n.* The doctrine of trinitarians.

Trinket, tring'ket, *n.* [Probably a nasalized form of *tricket*, from *trick*, to dress out.] A small ornament, as a jewel, a ring, and the like; a thing of no great value; a trifle.—*v.i.* To hold secret communication; to intrigue; to traffic.—**Trinketer**, tring'ket-ėr, *n.* One who deals, traffics, or intrigues; a trafficker; an intriguer.—**Trinketry**, tring'ket-ri, *n.* Ornaments of dress; trinkets collectively.

Trinoctial, trī-nok'shal, *a.* [L. *tri* = *tres*, three, and *nox*, *noctis*, night.] Comprising three nights.

Trinomial, trī-nō'mi-al, *a.* [Gr. *tri*=*treis*, three, and *nomē*, a division.] *Alg.* consisting of three terms connected by the signs + or −.—*n.* *Alg.* a quantity of three terms.

Trio, trī'ō or trē'ō, *n.* [It., from L. *tres*, three.] Three united; *mus.* a composition for three voices or three instruments; the performers of a trio.

Triode, trī-ōd', *n.* [Prefix *tri-*, and Gr. *hodos*, way.] A thermionic valve with three electrodes.

Triolet, trī'o-let, trē'o-let, *n.* [Dim. of *trio.*] A stanza of eight lines in which the first line is repeated after the third, and the first and second lines after the sixth.

Trioses, trī-ō'sēz, *n.* [L. *tres*, three.] Sugars formed from three molecules of MONOSES (which see).

Trip, trip, *v.i.*—*tripped*, *tripping.* [A lighter and non-nasalized form akin to *tramp* and = Dan. *trippe*, Sw. *trippa*, D. *trippen*, G. *trippen*, *trippeln*, to trip. TRAMP, TRAP.] To run or step lightly; to move the feet nimbly, as in running, walking, dancing; to stumble and come near to fall; to make a false step; to lose the footing; to offend against morality, propriety, or rule; to err; to go wrong.—*v.t.* To cause to fall by striking the feet suddenly from under the person; to cause to stumble or make a false step: often followed by *up*; to catch in a fault or mistake (*Shak.*); *naut.* to loose (an anchor) from the bottom by its cable.—*n.* A light short step; a lively movement of the feet; a short journey or voyage; an excursion or jaunt; a causing to stumble or fall; a stumble; a false step; an error; a mistake.—**Trip-hammer**, *n.* A large hammer used in forges; a tilt-hammer.—**Tripper**, trip'ėr, *n.* One who trips or trips up; one who walks nimbly; a cheap tourist on an outing. — **Tripping**, trip'ing, *a.* Stepping quickly or lightly; quick; nimble.—**Trippingly**, trip'ing-li, *adv.* In a tripping manner; with rapid but clear enunciation; nimbly.

Tripaleolate, trī-pā'lē-ō-lāt, *a.* [L. *tri* =*tres*, three, and *palea*.] *Bot.* consisting of three pales or paleæ.

Tripang. TREPANG.

Tripartite, trip'ar-tīt, *a.* [L. *tripartitus*—*tri*=*tres*, three, and *partitus*, pp. of *partior*, to part. PART.] Divided into three parts; having three corresponding parts; made between three parties (a *tripartite* treaty); *bot.* divided into three parts down to the base, but not wholly separate.—**Tripartitely**, trip'ar-tīt-li, *adv.* In a tripartite manner.—**Tripartition**, trip-ar-tish'on, *n.* A division into three parts; a division by three.—**Tripartible**, trī-pär'ti-bl, *a.* Divisible into three parts.—**Tripartient**, trī-pär'shi-ent, *a.* Dividing into three equal parts.

Tripe, trīp, *n.* [Fr. *tripe*, Sp. and Pg. *tripa*, It. *trippa*, tripe; of Celtic origin; W. *tripa*, Ir. *triopas*, Armor. *stripen*, tripe.] The stomach of ruminating animals when prepared for food.—**Tripeman**, *n.* A man who sells tripe.—**Tripery**, trī'pėr-i, *n.* A place where tripe is prepared or sold.

Tripedal, trip'e-dal, *a.* [L. *tripedalis*—*tri* = *tres*, three, and *pes*, *pedis*, a foot.] Having three feet.

Tripe-de-roche, trēp-dė-rōsh, *n.* [Fr., lit. rock tripe.] A substance furnished by various species of lichen, used as food in the arctic regions of North America.

Tripennate, trī-pen'āt, *a.* *Bot.* tripinnate.

Tripersonal, trī-pėr'son-al, *a.* [Prefix *tri*, three, and *personal.*] Consisting of three persons. — **Tripersonalist**, trī-pėr'son-al-ist, *n.* A believer in the Trinity; a trinitarian. — **Tripersonality**, trī-pėr'son-al''i-ti, *n.* Trinity of persons in one Godhead.

Tripetaloid, trī-pet'al-oid, *a.* [Gr. *tri* = *treis*, three, *petalon*, a leaf.] *Bot.* appearing as if furnished with three petals.—**Tripetalous**, trī-pet'al-us, *a.* Having three petals.

Triphthong, trif'thong or trip'thong, *n.* [Gr. *tri*=*treis*, three, and *phthongē*, sound.] A combination of three vowels in a single syllable; three vowel characters representing a single sound (*eau* in *beau*); a trigraph. —**Triphthongal**, trif-thong'gal or trip-thong'gal, *a.* Pertaining to a triphthong; consisting of a triphthong.

Triphyllous, trī-fil'us, *a.* [Gr. *tri*=*treis*, three, and *phyllon*, a leaf.] *Bot.* three-leaved; having three leaves.

Tripinnate, trī-pin'āt, *a.* [Prefix *tri*, three, and *pinnate*, *pinnatifid*, *pinnatisect.*] *Bot.* trebly pinnate: said when the leaflets of a bipinnate leaf are themselves pinnate.—**Tripinnatifid**, trī-pin-nat'i-fid, *a.* *Bot.* pinnatifid with the segments twice divided in a pinnatifid manner. — **Tripinnatisect**, trī-pin-nat'i-sekt, *a.* In *bot.* parted to the base in a tripinnate manner, as a leaf.

Triple, trip'l, *a.* [Fr. *triple*, from L. *triplus*, threefold, triple, from *tres*, *tria*, three, and term. *-plus*, as in *double* (which see). *Treble* is a doublet of this.] Consisting of three united; threefold; three times repeated; treble.—*Triple crown*, the crown worn by the popes, consisting of three crowns placed one above another, surrounding a high cap or tiara.—*Triple time*, *mus.* time or rhythm of three beats, or of three times three beats, in a bar.—*v.t.*—*tripled*, *tripling.* To make threefold or thrice as much or as many; to treble.—**Triplet**, trip'let, *n.* [Dim. from *triple.*] A collection or combination of three of a kind, or three united; three verses or lines of poetry rhyming together; *mus.* a group of three notes of equal time value, to be performed in the time of two, indicated by a slur and the figure 3; a combination of three lenses; one of three children at a birth.—**Triply**, trip'li, *adv.* In a triple or threefold manner; trebly.

Triplicate, trip'li-kāt, *a.* [L. *triplicatus*, pp. of *triplico*, to triple—*tres*, three, and *plico*, to fold. PLY.] Made thrice as much; threefold.—*Triplicate ratio*, in *math.* the ratio which the cubes of two quantities bear to one another, compared with the ratio which the quantities themselves bear to each other.—*n.* A third thing corresponding to two others.—**Triplication**, trip-li-kā'shon, *n.* The act of trebling or making threefold.—**Triplicity**, tri-plis'i-ti, *n.* [From L. *triplex*, *triplicis*, triple.] The state of being triple or threefold.

Triploblastic, trip'lō-bläst''ik, *a.* [Gr. *triploos*, threefold, *blastos*, a bud.] In animals, forms in which the body consists essentially of three cellular layers.

Triply. Under TRIPLE.

Tripod, trī'pod, *n.* [Gr. *tripous*, *tripodos*—*tri* = *treis*, three, *pous*, *podos*, a foot.] A name for various ancient utensils or articles of furniture resting on three feet; the seat from which the priestesses at Delphi gave oracular responses; a three-legged frame or stand for supporting a theodolite, compass, &c.—**Tripod mast**, *n.* In a war-vessel, a great mast the lower part of which forms a tripod, and in which are stations for important officers, as a range-finder, a fire-control officer, search-light director, &c.

Tripoli, trip'o-li, *n.* A kind of siliceous rotten-stone, soft, and of a yellowish gray or white colour, composed of the shields of microscopic infusoria and diatomaceæ, originally brought from *Tripoli*, used in polishing metals, marbles, glass, &c. — **Tripoline**, trip'o-lin, *a.* Pertaining to tripoli.

Tripos, trī'pos, *n.* [Gr. *tripous*, a tripod. TRIPOD.] A tripod; in Cambridge University, the examination for honours at taking one's degree in any of the departments of mathematics, classics, moral sciences, &c., so called from the successful candidates being arranged in three classes or grades.

Trippant, trip'ant, *a.* *Her.* the term for passant, or walking, as applied to animals of the deer kind.

Tripper, Tripping, Under TRIP.

Tripterous, trip'tėr-us, *a.* [Gr. *tri=treis*, three, and *pteron*, a wing.] Three-winged: said of a leaf.

Triptich, Triptych, trip'tik, *n.* [Gr. *tri =treis*, three, and *ptychē*, a fold or folding.] A picture, carving, or other representation in three compartments side by side; most frequently such as is used for an altar-piece; a writing tablet in three parts, two of which might be folded over the middle part; hence, sometimes, a book or treatise in three parts or sections.

Triptote, trip'tōt. *n.* [L. *triptotum*, Gr. *triptōton—tri=treis*, three, and *ptōsis*, the case of a word.] In *gram.* a noun having three cases only.—**Triptotic**, trip-tot'ik, *a.* Pertaining to.

Triquetrous, trī-kwē'trus, *a.* [L. *triquetrus*, triangular, from *tres*, *tria*, three.] Three-sided; triangular; *bot.* having three acute angles with concave faces, as the stems of many plants; three-edged: three-cornered.

Triradiate, Triradiated, trī-rā'di-āt, trī-rā'di-ā-ted, *a.* [L. *tri = tres*, three, and *radius*, a ray.] Having three rays.

Trireme, trī'rēm, *n.* [L. *triremis—tri= tres*, three, and *remus*, an oar.] A galley or vessel with three benches or ranks of oars on a side, a common class of war-ship among the ancient Greeks, Romans, Carthaginians, &c.

Trisagion, Trishagion, tri-sā'gi-on, tris-hā'gi-on, *n.* [Gr. *trisagios*, thrice holy *—tris = treis*, three, and *hagios*, holy.] *Eccles.* the repetition of the words *Holy, Holy, Holy*, by the choir in certain parts of the liturgy.

Trisect, trī-sekt', *v.t.* [L. *tri = tres*, three, and *seco*, *sectum*, to cut. SECTION.] To cut or divide into three equal parts.—**Trisection**, trī-sek'shon, *n.* The division of a thing into three parts; particularly, in geometry, the division of an angle into three equal parts.

Trisepalous, trī-sep'al-us, *a.* [Prefix *tri*, and *sepal*.] *Bot.* having three sepals.

Triserial, Triseriate, trī-sē'ri-al, trī-sē'ri-āt, *a.* [Prefix *tri*, three, and *series*.] *Bot.* arranged in three rows, one beneath another.

Trismus, tris'mus, *n.* [Gr. *trismos*, gnashing of the teeth, from *trizō*, to gnash.] A species of tetanus affecting the under jaw with spastic rigidity; lock-jaw.

Trisoctahedron, tris-ok'ta-hē"dron, *n.* [Gr. *tris*, three times, *oktō*, eight, and *hedra*, face.] A solid bounded by twenty-four equal faces, three corresponding to each face of an octahedron.

Trispermous, trī-spėr'mus, *a.* [Gr. *tri = treis*, three, and *sperma*, seed.] *Bot.* three-seeded; containing three seeds.

Tristichous, trī'stik-us, *a.* [Gr. *tri = treis*, three, and *stichos*, a row.] *Bot.* arranged in three rows.

Trisulcate, trī-sul'kāt, *a.* [L. *trisulcus—tres*, three, *sulcus*, a furrow.] Having three forks or three furrows.

Trisyllable, tris'sil-a-bl, *n.* [L. *tri=tres*, three, and *syllaba*, syllable.] A word consisting of three syllables.—**Trisyllabic, Trisyllabical**, tris-si-lab'ik, tris-si-lab'i-kal, *a.* Pertaining to a trisyllable; consisting of three syllables.

Trite, trīt, *a.* [L. *tritus*, pp. of *tero*, *tritum*, to rub, to wear (seen also in *triturate*, *contrite*, *detritus*, &c.); root *tar*, *tra*, to pierce, &c., as in prep. *trans.* TRY.] Used till so common as to have lost its novelty and interest; commonplace; hackneyed; stale.—**Tritely**, trīt'li, *adv.* In a trite or commonplace manner; stalely.—**Triteness**, trīt'nes, *n.* The quality of being trite; commonness; staleness.

Triternate, trī-tėr'nāt, *a.* [Prefix *tri*, and *ternate*.] *Bot.* three times ternate.

Tritheism, trī'thē-izm, *n.* [Gr. *tri = treis*, three, and *Theos*, God.] The opinion that the Father, Son, and Holy Spirit are three beings or Gods.—**Tritheist**, trī'thē-ist, *n.* One who believes that there are three distinct Gods in the Godhead, that is, three distinct substances, essences, or hypostases.—**Tritheistic, Tritheistical**, trī-thē-is'tik, trī-thē-is'-ti-kal, *a.* Pertaining to tritheism.

Triton, trī'ton, *n.* [From *Triton*, the Greek sea deity, a son of Poseidon and Amphitrite.] One of certain subordinate sea deities among the Greeks and Romans, having their lower extremities fish-like; a genus of gasteropodous molluscs with trumpet-like shells; a genus of batrachian reptiles comprehending the newts.

Tritone, trī'tōn, *n.* [Gr. *tri = treis*, three, and *tonos*, a tone.] *Mus.* a dissonant interval consisting of three tones or of two major and one minor tone, or of two tones and two semitones.

Triturate, trit'ū-rāt, *v.t.—triturated*, *triturating.* [L.L. *trituro*, *trituratum*, to grind, from L. *tritus*, pp. of *tero*, to wear. TRITE.] To rub or grind to a very fine powder.—**Triturable**, trit'ū-ra-bl, *a.* Capable of being triturated.—**Trituration**, trit-ū-rā'shon, *n.* The act of triturating; levigation.—**Triturature**, trit'ū-rā-tūr, *n.* A wearing by rubbing or friction.

Triumph, trī'umf, *n.* [L. *triumphus*, a triumph; allied to Gr. *thriambos*, a festal song, a procession in honour of Bacchus.] *Rom. antiq.* a magnificent procession in honour of a victorious general, in which he entered the city riding in a chariot and followed by his army—the highest military honour which a general could obtain; hence, the state of being victorious; victory; conquest; joy or exultation for success; great gladness; rejoicing.—*v.i.* To enjoy a triumph; to celebrate victory with pomp; hence, to rejoice for victory; to obtain victory; to meet with success; to prevail; to exult upon an advantage gained; especially, to exult or boast insolently.—**Triumphal**, trī-um'fal, *a.* [L. *triumphalis.*] Pertaining to triumph; commemorating or used in celebrating a triumph or victory.—*Triumphal arch*, originally a temporary arch erected in connection with the triumph of a Roman general, and through which he and his army passed; afterwards a massive and ornamental permanent structure; a decorated temporary arch in public rejoicings.—**Triumphant**, trī-um'fant, *a.* [L. *triumphans*, *triumphantis*, ppr. of *triumpho*, to triumph.] Rejoicing for victory or as for victory; triumphing; exulting; victorious; graced with conquest.—**Triumphantly**, trī-um'fant-li, *adv.* In a triumphant manner; in the manner of a conqueror; with joy and exultation.—**Triumpher**, trī'umf-ėr, *n.* One who triumphs.

Triumvir, trī-um'vėr, *n.* [L. *tres*, genit. *trium*, three, and *vir*, man.] One of three men united in office.—**Triumvirate**, trī-um'vi-rāt, *n.* A coalition of three men in office or authority; in Roman history the coalition in 59 B.C. between Cæsar, Pompeius, and Crassus, and that in 43 B.C. between Antonius, Octavianus, and Lepidus; government by three men in coalition; a party of three men; three men in company or forming one company.

Triune, trī'ūn, *n.* [L. *tri=tres*, three, and *unus*, one.] Three in one: applied to express the unity of the Godhead in a trinity of persons.—**Triunity**, trī-ū'ni-ti, *n.* The state of being triune; trinity.

Trivalent, trī-vāl'ent or triv'a-lent, *a.* [Prefix *tri*, three, and L. *valeo*, to be worth.] Having a valency of three.

Trivalve, trī'valv, *n.* [Prefix *tri*, three, and *valve*.] Anything having three valves, especially a shell with three valves.—**Trivalvular**, trī-val'vū-lėr, *a.* Having three valves.

Trivet, triv'et, *n.* [Corruption of *three-feet* or *three-foot*, or of Fr. *trépied*, from L. *tripes*, *tripedis*, a three-footed stool—*tres*, three, and *pes*, *pedis*, a foot.] Anything supported by three feet; a kind of iron frame or stand whereon to place vessels for boiling, &c., or to receive something placed before the fire: frequently used as a proverbial comparison indicating stability, inasmuch as having three legs to stand on it is never unstable ('right as a *trivet*').

Trivial, triv'i-al, *a.* [Fr. *trivial*, from L. *trivialis*, belonging to the public streets, hence common, from *trivium*, a place where three roads meet, a cross-road—*tri = tres*, three, and *via*, a way, a road.] Commonplace; trifling; insignificant; of little worth or importance; inconsiderable; occupying one's self with trifles; trifling.—*Trivial name*, in *classification*, same as *specific name*; also used for the common English name.—**Trivialism**, triv'i-al-izm, *n.* A trivial matter or mode of acting.—**Triviality**, triv-i-al'i-ti, *n.* The state or quality of being trivial; a trivial thing; a trifle.—**Trivially**, triv'i-al-li, *adv.* In a trivial or trifling manner; lightly; inconsiderably; insignificantly.—**Trivialness**, triv'i-al-nes, *n.* The state of being trivial.—**Trivium**, triv'i-um, *n.* A collective term given in the schools of the middle ages to the first three liberal arts—grammar, rhetoric, and logic. QUADRIVIUM.

Tri-weekly, trī'wēk-li, *a.* Occurring or appearing once every three weeks; also, happening or appearing thrice a week.

Trocar, trō'kär, *n.* [Fr. *trocar*, from *trois*, three, and *carre*, a square, a face, the instrument having a triangular face.] A perforating surgical instrument used in cases of dropsy, &c., for drawing off the fluid.

Trochanter, trō-kan'tėr, *n.* [Gr. *trochantēr*, from *trochazō*, to run along, from *trechō*, to run.] *Anat.* a process of the upper part of the thigh-bone to which are attached the muscles which rotate the limb.

Trochar, trō'kär, *n.* Same as *Trocar*.

Troche, trō'kē, *n.* [Gr. *trochos*, something circular, a round ball or cake.] A small circular cake or lozenge made up of sugar, mucilage, and some drug, to be gradually dissolved in the mouth.

Trochee, trō'kē, *n.* [L. *trochæus*, Gr. *trochaios*, from *trechō*, to run.] *Pros.* a foot of two syllables, the first long and the second short.—**Trochaic**, trō-kā'ik, *a.* [L. *trochaicus.*] Pertaining to or consisting of trochees.—*n.* A trochaic verse.

Trochilus, trok'il-us, *n.* [L. *trochilus*, Gr. *trochilos.*] A small bird said in ancient legend to enter the crocodile's mouth and eat matters from among his teeth; also, *arch.* same as *Scotia*.

Trochite, trō'kīt, *n.* [Gr. *trochos*, a wheel.] A name once given to the wheel-like joints of the encrinite.

Trochlea, trok'lē-a, *n.* [L., a pulley, from Gr. *trochalia*, from *trochalos*, running, from *trechō*, to run.] A pulley-like cartilage connected with one of the superior muscles of the eye.—**Trochlear**, trok'lē-ėr, *a.* Pulley-shaped.—**Trochleary**, trok'lē-a-ri, *a.* Pertaining to the trochlea (the *trochleary* muscle).

Trochoid, trō'koid, *n.* [Gr. *trochos*, a wheel, and *eidos*, resemblance.] *Geom.* the curve otherwise called cycloid; *anat.* a trochoidal articulation.—**Trochoidal**, trō-koi'dal, *a.* Pertaining to a trochoid; *anat.* said of a species of joint in which one bone rotates upon another (as in the elbow).—**Trochosphere**, trō'kō-sfēr, *n.* [Gr. *trochos*, and *sphaira*, a globe.] In annelids, &c., an ovoid ciliated larva.

Trod, trod, pret. of *tread*.

Trodden, trod'n, pp. of *tread*.

Troglodyte, trō'glod-īt, *n.* [Gr. *trōglodytēs*, a troglodyte, from *trōglē*, a cavern, and *dyō*, to enter.] A cave-dweller; a name given by the ancient Greeks to the cave-dwellers on the coast of the Red Sea and on the Upper Nile; hence, one living in seclusion.—**Troglodytic**, trō-glo-dit'ik, *a.* Pertaining to troglodytes.

Trogon, trō'gon, *n.* [Gr. *trōgōn*, gnawing.] A name of certain tropical birds with long tail-plumes and most gorgeous plumage.

Trogonotherium, trō'gon-ō-thē"ri-um, *n.* [Gr. *trōgōn*, gnawing, and *thērion*, wild beast.] An extinct rodent allied to the beavers, but much larger.

Trojan, **Troic**, trō'jan, trō'ik, *a.* Pertaining to ancient Troy, a city in Asia Minor, the scene of a ten-year war, described in Homer's *Iliad*, which was caused by the kidnaping of Helen, wife of Menelaus, by Paris.—**Trojan**, *n.* A citizen of ancient Troy; a plucky, diligent, person.

Troll, trōl, *v.t.* [From the Celtic, partly through the French: W. *tròliaw*, to trundle, to roll; *trol*, a roller; Armor. *trôel*, a twining plant; Fr. *trôler*, to lead about, to drag. TRAWL.] To move in a circular direction; to roll (*Mil.*); to pass round or cause to circle, as a vessel of liquor at table; to sing the parts of in succession; also, to sing in a full, jovial voice; to angle in a certain way in or for.—*v.i.* To go round; to move round; to angle; to fish for pike by trolling.—*n.* The act of going or moving round; repetition; a song the parts of which are sung in succession; a round; a reel on a fishing-rod.—**Troller**, trōl'ėr, *n.* One who trolls.—**Trolling**, trōl'ing, *n.* The act of one who trolls; a certain method of fishing for pike with a rod and line, and with a dead bait which is dropped into holes and worked up and down.

Troll, trōl, *n.* [Icel. *troll*, Dan. and Sw. *trold*, L.G. *droll*; hence E. *droll.*] A name of certain supernatural beings in Scandinavian mythology and literature, dwelling in the interior of hills and mounds; described as in some respects obliging and neighbourly but also given to thieving.

Trolley, **Trolly**, trol'i, *n.* [Akin to *troll*, to roll.] A device so constructed as to run on an overhead rail or cable; a grooved wheel or bow-shaped device, mounted on electric trains and streetcars, for conducting electrical energy from an overhead wire.

Trollop, trol'op, *n.* [Comp. Sc. *trollop*, *trallop*, a loose hanging rag; Armor. *trul*, a rag or tatter, *trulen*, a slatternly woman; Ir. *troll*, corruption; Gael. *truaill*, to pollute; also G. *trulle*, a trull. *Trull* is allied.] A woman loosely dressed; a slattern; a draggle-tail; a drab.—**Trollopish**, **Trollopy**, trol'op-ish, trol'op-i, *a.* Like a trollop; slatternly.

Trombone, trom'bōn, *n.* [It., aug. of *tromba*, a trumpet. TRUMP.] A deep-toned instrument of the trumpet kind, consisting of three tubes of which the middle one is doubled and slides into the other two like the tube of a telescope.

Tromp, tromp, *n.* [Fr. *trompe*, a tube, a trumpet.] The blowing machine used in a certain process of smelting iron.

Tron, tron, *n.* [L.L. *trona*, from L. *trutina*, a balance.] A kind of steelyard or weighing-machine formerly used. — *Tron weight*, a system of weight once used in Scotland in which the pound was from 21 oz. to 28 oz.

Trona, trō'na, *n.* [An African word.] Same as *Natron*.

Troop, tröp, *n.* [Fr. *troupe*, It. *truppa*, Sp. *tropa*, from L.L. *troppus*, a troop; perhaps from L. *turba*, a crowd.] A collection of people; a number; a multitude; a body of soldiers; *pl.* soldiers in general, whether more or less numerous; a body of cavalry, usually sixty in number, forming the command of a captain; a band or company of performers; a troupe.—*v.i.* To collect in numbers; to gather in crowds; to march in a body or in company; to march in haste: often with *off*.—**Trooper**, tröp'ėr, *n.* A private soldier in a body of cavalry; a horse-soldier.—**Troop-ship**, *n.* A ship for the conveyance of troops; a transport.

Troopial, trö'pi-al, *n.* [From the great *troops* or flocks in which some of the species unite.] A name of certain passerine birds akin to the orioles and starlings.

Tropæolum, trō-pē'o-lum, *n.* [Gr. *tropaion*, a trophy, the leaves being shield-shaped, the flowers helmet-shaped.] A genus of South American trailing or climbing plants of the geranium family, some of them well known as Indian cress and nasturtium.

Trope, trōp, *n.* [Fr. *trope*, from L. *tropus*, from Gr. *tropos*, a trope or figure, a turn, from *trepō*, to turn. TROPHY, TROPIC.] *Rhet.* a figurative use of a word; a word or expression used in a different sense from that which it properly possesses; a figure of speech.—**Tropical**, trop'i-kal, *a.* Figurative; rhetorically changed from its original sense.—**Tropically**, trop'i-kal-li, *adv.* In a tropical manner.—**Tropism**, trōp'ism, *n.* The natural tendency of an organism to respond to an external stimulus.—**Tropist**, trōp'ist, *n.* One who deals in tropes.—**Tropology**, tro-pol'o-ji, *n.* [Gr. *tropos*, trope, *logos*, discourse.] A rhetorical mode of speech, including tropes.—**Tropologic**, **Tropological**, trop-o-loj'ik, trop-o-loj'i-kal, *a.* Varied or characterized by tropes; figurative.—**Tropologically**, trop'o-loj'i-kal-li, *adv.* In a tropological manner. —**Troposphere**, trop'ō-sfēr, *n.* [Gr. *tropos*, and *sphere.*] A lower part of the atmosphere, in which temperature falls with increasing height. See STRATOSPHERE.

Trophi, trō'fī, *n.pl.* [Gr. *trophos*, one who feeds, from *trephō*, to feed.] *Entom.* the parts of the mouth employed in the acquisition and preparation of food.

Trophy, trō'fi, *n.* [Fr. *trophée*, the spoil of an enemy, from L. *tropæum*, from Gr. *tropaion*, a trophy, from *tropē*, a putting to rout, lit. a turning, from *trepō*, to turn. TROPE.] Among the Greeks and Romans a monument or memorial in commemoration of some victory, consisting of arms and spoils of the vanquished enemy, hung on the trunk of a tree or on a pillar; hence, anything taken and preserved as a memorial of victory, as captured arms, standards, &c.; anything serving as an evidence of victory.—**Trophied**, trō'fid, *a.* Adorned with trophies.

Tropic, trop'ik, *n.* [Fr. *tropique*, L. *tropicus*, Gr. *tropikos*, turning, pertaining to a turn, from *tropē*, a turning, from *trepō*, to turn; the sun turns back at each tropic. TROPHY.] The name of two circles on the celestial sphere, distant from the equator each 23½° nearly, the northern one being called the *tropic of Cancer*, and the southern the *tropic of Capricorn*, bounding the sun's apparent annual path in the heavens; the name of two corresponding parallels of latitude or circles going round the globe at the same distance from the terrestrial equator, and including between them that portion of the globe called the torrid zone, having the equator for its central line; *pl.* the regions lying between the tropics or near them on either side. —*a.* Tropical; pertaining to the tropics. —**Tropical**, trop'i-kal, *a.* Pertaining to the tropics; being within the tropics; incident to the tropics (*tropical* diseases). See also under TROPE. —**Tropic-bird**, *n.* A tropical web-footed bird of the pelican family, wonderfully powerful on the wing.

Tropist, **Tropology**, &c. Under TROPE.

Trot, trot, *v.i.*—*trotted*, *trotting*. [Fr. *trotter*, It. *trottare*, from L. *tolutare*, to trot, modified into *tlutare*, *tlotare*, *trotare*.] To move faster than in walking; to walk or move fast; to run.—*n.* The pace of a horse or other quadruped more rapid than a walk; an endearing term used to a child; a contemptuous term for an old man or woman.—*v.t.* To cause to trot; to ride at a trot.—**Trotter**, trot'ėr, *n.* One who trots; a trotting horse; the foot of an animal, especially of a sheep.

Troth, troth, *n.* [A form of *truth.*] Truth; faith; fidelity; veracity. — *To plight one's troth*, to pledge one's faith; to betroth one's self. — **Troth-plight**, *n.* The act of betrothing or plighting faith.—**Troth-plighted**, *a.* Having fidelity pledged.—**Troth-ring**, *n.* A betrothal ring.

Troubadour, trö'ba-dör, *n.* [Fr. *troubadour*, from Pr. *trobador*, a troubadour (Sp. *trovador*, It. *trovatore*), from *trobar*, Fr. *trouver*, to find, originally to invent or compose new poems, from L.L. *tropare*, to sing, from L. *tropus*, a song, a trope. TROPE.] A name given to a class of early poets who first appeared in Provence, in France, and flourished from the eleventh to the latter part of the thirteenth century, their poetry being lyrical and amatory.

Trouble, trub'l, *v.t.*—*troubled*, *troubling*. [Fr. *troubler*, by metathesis and alteration from L. *turbula*, dim. of *turba*, a crowd, confusion; akin *turbid*, *turbulent*, *disturb*, *perturb*.] To put into confused motion; to agitate; to disturb; to annoy, fret, or molest; to afflict; to distress; to put to some slight labour or pains: used in courteous phraseology.—*n.* Distress of mind or what causes such; grief; great perplexity; affliction; anxiety; annoyance; pains; labour; exertion; *mining*, a fault or interruption in a stratum, especially a stratum of coal.—*To take the trouble*, to be at the pains; to give one's self inconvenience.—**Troubler**, trub'l-ėr, *n.* One who troubles or disturbs.—**Troublesome**, trub'l-sum, *a.* Giving or causing trouble; harassing; annoying; vexatious; importunate.—**Troublesomely**, trub'l-sum-li, *adv.* — **Troublesomeness**, trub'l-sum-nes, *n.* — **Troublous**, trub'lus, *a.* Full of civil commotion, disturbance, or disorder; unsettled (*troublous* times).

Trough, trof, *n.* [A.Sax. *trog*, *troh*=Icel., D., and G. *trog*, Dan. *trug*, a trough; akin *tray*.] A vessel of wood, stone, or metal, generally rather long and not very deep, for holding water, feeding-stuffs for animals, or the like; a channel or spout for conveying water; anything resembling a trough in shape, as a depression between two ridges or between two waves; a basin-shaped or oblong hollow.

Trounce, trouns, *v.t.*—*trounced*, *trouncing*. [O.Fr. *troncer*, *troncir*, to cut or break off or into pieces, from L. *truncus*, a trunk. TRUNK.] To punish or to beat severely; to castigate.

Troupe, tröp, *n.* [Fr.; same as *troop.*] A troop; a company; particularly, a company of players, dancers, acrobats, or the like.

Trous-de-loup, trö-dė-lö, *n.pl.* [Fr., lit. wolf holes—*trou*, a hole, and *loup*, a wolf.] *Milit.* holes or pits dug in the ground in the form of inverted cones or pyramids, in order to serve as obstacles to the advance of an enemy, each pit having a pointed stake in the middle.

Trousers, trou'zėrz, *n.pl.* [For older *trouses*, *trowses*, a kind of drawers, from O.Fr. *trousses*, a kind of hose, from *trousse*, a truss, case, or cover. TRUSS.] A garment worn by men and boys, extending from the waist to the ankles, covering the lower part of the trunk, and each leg separately. —**Trousered**, trou'zėrd, *a.* Wearing trousers.—**Trousering**, trou'zėr-ing, *n.* Cloth for making trousers.

Trousseau, trö-sō', *n.* [Fr., from *trousse*, a bundle, a truss. TRUSS.] The clothes and general outfit of a bride.

Trout, trout, *n.* [Fr. *truite*, from L.L. *trutta*, L. *tructa*, from Gr. *trōktēs*, a kind of fish, from *trōgō*, to gnaw.] The common name of various species of the salmon family, as the bull-trout, the salmon-trout, the common trout, &c., esteemed a delicacy.—**Trout-coloured**, *a.* White, with spots of black, bay, or sorrel. —**Troutlet**, **Troutling**, trout'let, trout'-ling, *n.* A small trout.—**Trout-stream**, *n.* A stream in which trout breed.

Trouvère, **Trouveur**, trö-vār, trö-vėr, *n.* [Fr. *trouver*, to find. TROUBADOUR.] A name given to the ancient poets of Northern France, corresponding to the *Troubadours* of Provence; but their productions partake of a narrative or epic character.

Trover, trō'vėr, *n.* [O.Fr. *trover*, Fr. *trouver*, to find. TROUBADOUR.] *Law*, the gaining possession of goods by finding or by other means than purchase; a form of action at law to recover goods or damages, now abolished.

Trow, trō, *v.i.* [A.Sax. *treówian, treówan*, to believe, lit. to believe to be *true*. TRUE.] To believe; to trust; to think or suppose.

Trowel, trou'el, *n.* [Fr. *truelle*, from L. *trulla*, a small ladle, dim. of *trua*, a stirring-spoon, a ladle.] A tool somewhat resembling a small spade, used for spreading and dressing mortar and plaster, &c.; a similar gardener's tool, used in taking up plants and for other purposes.—*To lay on* (flattery or the like) *with a trowel*, to lay it on thickly and coarsely.—*v.t.—trowelled, trowelling.* To dress or form with a trowel.

Trowsers, trou'zėrz. TROUSERS.

Troy, Troy-weight, troi, *n.* [From *Troyes*, in France.] A weight chiefly used in weighing gold and silver, divided into 12 ounces, each of 20 pennyweights, each of 24 grains. The pound troy=5760 grains; the pound avoirdupois 7000.

Truant, trö'ant, *n.* [O.Fr. *truant* (Fr. *truand*), a vagabond, from the Celtic; Armor. *truant*, vagabond, W. *truan*, wretched, Ir. and Gael. *truaghan*, poor.] One who shirks or neglects his duty; an idler; especially, a child who stays from school without leave.—*To play truant*, to stay from school without leave.—*a.* Shirking duty; wilfully absent from an appointed place; idle.—**Truantly**, trö'ant-li, *adv.* Like a truant.—**Truancy**, trö'an-si, *n.* The act of playing truant.

Truce, trös, *n.* [Properly a plural; O.E. *trews, trewse, trewis*, O.Fr. *trues* (pl.), a truce, from O.H.G. *triuwa, triwa*, G. *treue*, faith; akin *true, trust.*] *Milit.* a suspension of arms by agreement of the commanders of the opposing armies; an armistice; any temporary intermission or cessation; short quiet.—*Flag of truce.* FLAG.—**Truce-breaker**, *n.* One who violates a truce.—**Truceless**, trös'les, *a.* Without truce.

Truck, truk, *v.i.* [Fr. *troquer*, to truck, to barter, from Sp. *trocar*, to exchange; probably from Ar. *taraq*, to strike; comp. E. to *strike* a bargain.] To exchange commodities; to barter.—*v.t.* To exchange; to give in exchange; to barter; to put in a truck; to convey by truck.—*n.* Exchange of commodities; barter; payment of wages in goods; commodities appropriate for barter or for small trade.—*Truck system*, the practice of paying the wages of workmen in goods instead of money, which has prevailed particularly in the mining and manufacturing districts of Britain though prohibited by law.—**Truckage**, truk'āj, *n.* The practice of bartering goods.—**Trucker**, truk'ėr, *n.* One who trucks or traffics.

Truck, truk, *n.* [From L. *trochus*, a hoop, from Gr. *trochos*, a wheel, a disk, &c., from *trechō*, to run.] A small carriage or barrow with two low wheels, for heavy packages; an open wagon for the conveyance of goods on railways; a heavy motor vehicle used for transport; *gun.* a circular piece of wood like a wheel fixed on an axle-tree, for moving ordnance; *naut.* the small circular wooden cap at the extremity of a flagstaff or of a topmast.—**Truckage**, truk'āj, *n.* Money paid for conveyance of goods on a truck; freight.—**Truckle**, truk'l, *n.* [Dim. of *truck*, a wheel.] A small wheel or castor; a truckle-bed.—*v.t.* To move on rollers; to trundle.—**Truckle-bed**, *n.* A bed that runs on wheels and may be pushed under another; a trundle-bed.

Truckle, truk'l, *v.i.—truckled, truckling.* [Dim. of *truck*, to barter; or from *truckle-bed*, because inferiors slept in them.] To yield or bend obsequiously to the will of another; to cringe; usually with *to.*—**Truckler**, truk'lėr, *n.* One who truckles.—**Truckling**, truk'ling, *a.* Given to truckle; cringing; servile.

Truculent, truk'ū-lent, *a.* [L. *truculentus*, from *trux, trucis*, fierce, savage.] Fierce; savage; barbarous; inspiring terror; ferocious.—**Truculently**, truk'ū-lent-li, *adv.* In a truculent manner.—**Truculence, Truculency**, truk'ū-lens, truk'ū-len-si, *n.* [L. *truculentia.*] The quality of being truculent; savageness; fierceness.

Trudge, truj, *v.i.—trudged, trudging.* [Probably a modification of *tread*, through the influence of *drudge.*] To travel on foot with fatigue or more or less painful exertion; to travel or march with labour or effort.

True, trö, *a.* [A.Sax. *treówe* (whence *treówian*, to *trow*) = Icel. *trúr*, Dan. *tro*, D. *trouw*, G. *treu*, faithful, true; cog. Skr. *dhru*, to be fixed. Akin *truce, trust, troth.*] Conformable to fact; not false or erroneous; free from falsehood; truthful; genuine; not counterfeit, false, or pretended; firm or steady in adhering to promises, to friends, or the like; faithful; loyal; honest; exact; correct; right; conformable to law and justice; legitimate; rightful.—*True bill, law*, a bill of indictment endorsed by the grand-jury after evidence as containing a well-founded accusation.—*v.t.* To give a right form to; to make exactly straight, square, level, or the like: a workman's term.—**True-blue**, *a.* An epithet applied to a person of inflexible honesty and fidelity; stanch; inflexible.—*n.* A person of inflexible honesty or stanchness.—**True-born**, *a.* Of genuine birth; having a right by birth to any title.—**True-bred**, *a.* Of a genuine or right breed.—**True-hearted**, *a.* Being of a faithful heart; sincere; not deceitful.—**True-heartedness**, *n.* Fidelity; sincerity.—**True-love**, *n.* One truly loved or loving; one whose love is pledged to another; a sweetheart.—**Truelove-knot, True-lover's-knot**, *n.* A kind of double knot, made with two bows on each side interlacing each other and with two ends—the emblem of affection.—**Trueness**, trö'nes, *n.* The quality of being true; sincerity; genuineness; accuracy.—**Truepenny**, trö'pen-i, *n.* A familiar phrase for an honest fellow.—**Truism**, trö'izm, *n.* An undoubted or self-evident truth.—**Truly**, trö'li, *adv.* In a true manner; exactly; faithfully; honestly; legitimately; in reality; in fact.—**Truth**, tröth, *n.* [A.Sax. *treówthe*, from *treówe*, true. Formed similarly to *sloth, filth*, &c.] The state or quality of being true; conformity to fact or reality; veracity; purity from falsehood; fidelity; constancy; genuineness; that which is true; a true statement; fact; reality; verity; a verified fact.—*In truth*, in reality; in sincerity.—*Of a truth*, truly; certainly.—**Truthful**, tröth'fụl, *a.* Full of truth; loving and speaking the truth.—**Truthfully**, tröth'fụl-li, *adv.* In a truthful manner.—**Truthfulness**, tröth'fụl-nes, *n.* The state or character of being truthful.—**Truthless**, tröth'les, *a.* Wanting truth; faithless.—**Truth-lover**, *n.* One devoted to the truth.—**Truth-teller**, *n.* One who tells the truth.

Truffle, truf'l, *n.* [O.Fr. *trufle*, Fr. *truffe*; origin uncertain.] An edible and much-esteemed fungus growing a few inches beneath the surface of the ground, of a dark colour, of a roundish form, and without visible root.—**Truffled**, truf'ld, *a.* Cooked or stuffed with truffles.

Truism. Under TRUE.

Trull, trul, *n.* [Of similar origin with *trollop.*] A low vagrant strumpet; a drab.

Truly. Under TRUE.

Trump, trump, *n.* [Contr. from *triumph*, which formerly had sense of *trump*. See TRIUMPH.] A winning card; one of the suit of cards which takes any of the other suits; a good fellow; a person upon whom one can depend (*colloq.*).—*To put to one's trumps*, to reduce to the last expedient.—*v.t.* To take with a trump card; to put a trump card upon in order to win.

Trump, trump, *n.* [Fr. *trompe*, a trumpet or horn; Sp. and Pg. *trompa*, It. *tromba*, a trumpet; comp. O.H.G. *trumba, trumpa*, a drum; Lith. *truba*, a herdsman's horn. Akin *trombone*. Hence *trumpet.*] A wind-instrument of music; a trumpet.

Trump, trump, *v.t.* [Fr. *tromper*, to deceive, to dupe, probably from *trompe*, a trumpet, alluding to mountebanks or charlatans who summoned people by a trumpet.] To obtrude or impose unfairly.—*To trump up*, to devise; to forge (to *trump up* a story).—**Trumpery**, trum'pėr-i, *n.* [Fr. *tromperie*, fraud; trumpery is what deceives by false show.] Worthless finery; things worn out and of no value; rubbish.—*a.* Trifling; worthless.

Trumpet, trum'pet, *n.* [Fr. *trompette*, a dim. of *trompe*, a trumpet. TRUMP, a trumpet.] A wind-instrument of music made of brass or silver, having a clear ringing tone; one who praises or propagates praise. EAR-TRUMPET, SPEAKING-TRUMPET.—*Feast of trumpets*, a feast among the Jews, so called from the blowing of trumpets in the temple with more than usual solemnity.—*v.t.* To publish by sound of trumpet; hence, to blaze or noise abroad; to proclaim.—**Trumpeter**, trum'pet-ėr, *n.* One who sounds a trumpet; one who proclaims, publishes, or denounces; a variety of the domestic pigeon; a grallatorial bird of South America, called also *Agami*.—**Trumpet-fish**, *n.* The bellows-fish.—**Trumpet-flower**, *n.* A name applied to various large tubular flowers.—**Trumpet-major**, *n.* A head trumpeter in a band or regiment.—**Trumpetry**, trum'pet-ri, *n.* The sounding or sounds of a trumpet.—**Trumpet-shell**, *n.* A molluscous shell resembling a trumpet. TRITON.—**Trumpet-tongued**, *a.* Having a tongue vociferous as a trumpet. (*Shak.*)

Truncate, trung'kāt, *v.t.* [L. *trunco, truncatum*, to cut short, from *truncus*, mutilated, and as substantive, the trunk of a tree.] To shorten by cutting abruptly; to lop; to cut short.—*a.* Truncated; *bot.* appearing as if cut short at the tip (a *truncate* leaf).—**Truncated**, trung'kā-ted, *p.* and *a.* Cut short abruptly; having a part abruptly cut off, especially at the apex or top, or having the appearance of being so cut.—*A truncated cone* or *pyramid* is one whose vertex is cut off by a plane parallel to its base; *her.* a tree is truncated of a certain tincture when that tincture is different from the rest of the branches.—**Truncation**, trung-kā'shon, *n.* The act of truncating or state of being truncated; cutting off.

Truncheon, trun'shon, *n.* [O.Fr. *tronchon*, Fr. *tronçon*, from *tronche, tronce*, a trunk, staff, &c., L. *truncus*. TRUNK.] A short staff; a cudgel; a baton or staff of authority; a tree the branches of which have been lopped off to produce rapid growth.—*v.t.* To beat with a truncheon; to cudgel.—**Truncheoned**, trun'shond, *a.* Furnished with a truncheon.—**Truncheoner, Truncheoneer**, trun'shon-ėr, trun'shon-ēr, *n.* A person armed with a truncheon.

Trundle, trun'dl, *v.i.—trundled, trundling.* [A.Sax. *tryndel, trendel*, a circle, a wheel; akin Sw. and Dan. *trind*, round. TREND.] To roll, as on little wheels; to roll; to bowl along.—*v.t.* To wheel or move on wheels; to cause to roll (to *trundle* a hoop).—*n.* A little wheel; a castor; a small carriage with low wheels; a truck.—**Trundle-bed**, *n.* A truckle-bed.—**Trundle-tail**, *n.* A curled tail; a dog with a curled tail. (*Shak.*)

Trunk, trungk, *n.* [Fr. *tronc*, trunk or stem, main body, broken shaft of a column, a charity box; from L. *truncus*, mutilated, and as noun, trunk or stem, body, piece cut off, &c. (whence also *truncheon, truncate*). The elephant's *trunk* should have been *trump*, being from Fr. *trompe*, a trumpet, a proboscis, but the word was confused with this. TRUMP.] The woody stem of trees; that part which supports the branches; the body of an animal without the limbs, or considered as apart from the limbs; the main body of anything relatively to its branches or ramifications; a box or chest, often one covered with leather for containing clothes, &c.; the long snout or proboscis of an elephant; also, a similar organ of other animals, as the proboscis of an insect; a tube, usually wooden, to convey air, dust, broken matter, grain, &c.; a trough to convey water from a race to a water-wheel, &c.; a flume; a boxed passage for air to or from a blast apparatus or blowing-engine; *pl.* trunk-hose.—*Trunk road*, a highway or main road.—**Trunk-breeches**, *n.pl.* Trunk-hose.—**Trunked**, trungkt, *a.* Having a trunk.—**Trunk-fish**, *n.* OSTRACION.—**Trunk-hose**, *n.pl.* [Named probably from being *truncated* or cut short.] A kind of short wide breeches gathered in above the knees, or immediately under them, and worn during the reign of Henry VIII, Elizabeth, and James I.—**Trunk-line**, *n.* The main line of a railway, canal, &c.—**Trunk-sleeve**, *n.* A large white sleeve. (*Shak.*)

Trunnion, trun′yon, *n.* [Fr. *trognon*, a stump, from *tronc*, L. *truncus*, trunk of a tree. TRUNK.] A knob projecting on each side of a gun, mortar, &c., serving to support it on the carriage; *steam-engines*, a hollow gudgeon on each side of an oscillating cylinder to support it, and through which steam enters.—**Trunnioned**, trun′yond, *a.* Provided with trunnions.

Truss, trus, *n.* [Fr. *trousse*, a bundle, in pl. trunk-hose, breeches (whence E. *trousers*), from *trousser*, O.Fr. *trosser*, *trusser*, to tuck up, to pack; L.L. *tortiare*, to twist, from L. *torqueo*, *tortum*, to twist. TORTURE.] A bundle, especially a small hand-packed bundle of dry goods; a quantity, as of hay or straw tied together; *surg.* a bandage used in cases of rupture to keep up the parts or for other purposes; a tuft of flowers at the top of the main stalk of certain plants; an umbel; *building*, a combination of timbers, of iron, or of timbers and iron work, so arranged as to constitute an unyielding frame; *arch.* a large corbel or modillion supporting some object projecting from the face of a wall.—*v.t.* To put in a bundle; to pack up: often with *up*; to seize and carry off: said of birds of prey; to draw tight and tie the laces of, as of garments; to make fast, as the wings of a fowl to the body in cooking it; to skewer; to pull up by a rope or ropes; to hang.—**Trussed**, trust, *a.* Provided with a truss or trusses.—**Trussing**, trus′ing, *n.* The timbers, &c., which form a truss. —*a. Her.* applied to a bird of the eagle or falcon type preying upon anything.

Trust, trust, *n.* [From stem of *true*, *trow* =Icel. *traust*, trust, confidence; Dan. and Sw. *tröst*, G. *trost*, consolation, hope. TRUE.] A reliance or resting of the mind on the integrity, veracity, justice, friendship, &c., of another person; a firm reliance on promises or on laws or principles; confidence; confident expectation; assured anticipation; belief; hope; reliance or belief without examination (to take opinions on *trust*); the transfer of goods, property, &c., in confidence of future payment; credit; a person confided in and relied on; that which is committed or intrusted to one; something committed to one's care for use or for safe-keeping; the state of being confided to another's care and guard; safe-keeping; care; management; *law*, the conveying of property to one party (the *trustee*) in confidence that he will apply it for the benefit of a third party or to some specified purpose.—*v.t.* To place confidence in; to rely on; to depend upon; to believe; to receive as true; to rely on with regard to the care of; to intrust (to *trust* him *with* money); to commit, as to one's care; to leave to one's self or to itself without fear of consequences; to sell to upon credit or in confidence of future payment; to be confident; to hope confidently: followed by a clause.—*v.i.* To have trust or reliance; to confide readily; to practise giving credit; to sell in reliance upon future payment. —*To trust in*, to confide in; to rely on.—*To trust to*, to depend on; to have confidence in.—*a.* Held in trust (*trust* property). —**Trustee**, trus′tē, *n.* A person appointed to hold property, to take care of and apply the same for the benefit of those entitled to it.—**Trusteeship**, trus-tē′ship, *n.* The office of a trustee.—**Truster**, trus′tėr, *n.* One who trusts; one who relies; a believer. —**Trust-estate**, *n.* An estate held by a trustee or trustees.—**Trustful**, trust′ful, *a.* Full of trust; trusting; worthy of trust; trusty.—**Trustfully**, trust′ful-li, *adv.* In a trustful manner.—**Trustfulness**, trust′-ful-nes, *n.* The state or quality of being trustful.—**Trustily**, trus′ti-li, *adv.* In a trusty manner; faithfully.—**Trustiness**, trus′ti-nes, *n.* The quality of being trusty; fidelity; honesty.—**Trustless**, trust′les, *a.* Devoid of trust; not worthy of trust; unreliable.—**Trustlessness**, trust′les-nes, *n.* The quality of being trustless.—**Trustworthiness**, trust′wėr-THi-nes, *n.* The quality of being trustworthy.—**Trustworthy**, trust′wėr-THi, *a.* Worthy of trust or confidence.—**Trusty**, trus′ti, *a.* Admitting of being safely trusted; deserving confidence; fit to be confided in; not liable to fail a person (a *trusty* sword).

Truth, Truthful, &c. Under TRUE.

Truttaceous, trut-ā′shus, *a.* [From L. *trutta*, trout. TROUT.] Pertaining to the trout.

Try, trī, *v.t.*—*tried*, *trying*. [Fr. *trier*, to pick, cull, select; same as It. *triare*, *tritare*, to grind, bruise, examine; L.L. *tritare*, to thrash (corn), from L. *tritum*, pp. of *tero*, to rub, to cleanse corn by thrashing. TRITE.] To sift or pick out†; to purify, assay, or refine, as metals; to test or prove by experiment; to make experience of; to subject to some severe test or experience; to cause suffering or trouble to; to examine or inquire into, especially, to examine judicially; to subject to the examination and decision or sentence of a tribunal; to attempt; to undertake; to make experiment with; to see what will result from using or employing.—*To try on*, to put on, as a garment, to see if it fits.—*v.i.* To exert strength; to endeavour; to prove by a test.—*To try back*, to go back, as in search of a road that one has missed. —*n.* The act of trying; a trial; experiment. —**Tryable, Triable**, trī′a-bl, *a.* Capable of being tried; fit to be tried or stand trial.—**Trial**, trī′al, *n.* The act of trying or testing in any manner; an attempt; a test; experiment; a becoming acquainted by experience; that which tries or afflicts; that which tries the character or principle; affliction; temptation; the state of being tried; a process for testing qualification; an examination; *law*, the examination of a cause in controversy between parties before a proper tribunal.—**Trial-fire**, *n.* A fire for trying or proving; ordeal-fire.—**Trial-trip**, *n.* An experimental trip; especially, a trip made by a new vessel to test her sailing qualities, &c.—**Trier**, trī′ėr, *n.* One who tries.—**Trying**, trī′ing, *a.* Adapted to try; severe; afflictive.—**Try-sail**, *n. Naut.* a fore-and-aft sail set with a boom and gaff; a spanker or driver.

Trypanosome, trip′an-ō-sōm, *n.* A parasitic protozoan, infesting the blood of animals, including man, being usually introduced by the bite of an insect. It is the cause of various diseases, e.g. sleeping sickness.

Tryptophane, trip′tō-fān, *n.* [Gr. *truein*, to rub down, *phainein*, to show.] An amino acid, or an iodine derivative, supposed to be the active substance in the secretion of the thyroid gland.

Tryst, trīst, *n.* [Closely akin to *trust*; Icel. *treysta*, to trust.] An appointment to meet; a rendezvous; a market (Falkirk *Tryst*).—*v.i.* To agree to meet at any particular time or place.—**Trysting-day**, *n.* An appointed day of meeting or assembling.—**Trysting-place**, *n.* An arranged meeting-place.

Tsar, tsär, *n.* CZAR.—**Tsarina, Tsaritsa**, tsä-rē′na, tsä-rit′sa, *n.* CZARINA.

Tschudi, Tschudic. TCHUDI, TCHUDIC.

Tsetse, tset′sē, *n.* A South African two-winged fly, whose bite is often fatal to horses, dogs, and cattle, but is innoxious to man and wild beasts.

T-square, tē′skwār, *n.* An instrument used in drawing consisting of two slips of hard-wood of unequal length, the longer fixed into the shorter like a T, and both having their edges dressed exactly straight and parallel.

Tub, tub, *n.* [Same as L.G. *tubbe*, D. *tobbe*, a tub.] An open wooden vessel formed with staves, bottom, and hoops; a half barrel open above; a small cask or barrel for liquor; any wooden structure resembling a tub; *mining*, a corve or bucket for raising coal or ore from the mine.—*A tale of a tub*, an idle or silly fiction; a cock-and-bull story.—*v.t.*—*tubbed*, *tubbing*. To plant or set in a tub (to *tub* plants).—*v.i.* To wash; to make use of a bathing-tub.—**Tubbing**, tub′ing, *n.* Material for tubs; the lining of the shaft of a mine, of an artesian well, &c., to prevent falling in of the sides.—**Tubbish**, tub′ish, *a.* Like a tub; tubby.—**Tubby**, tub′i, *a.* Tub-shaped; round like a tub or barrel; having a dull sound.—**Tubful**, tub′ful, *n.* A quantity sufficient to fill a tub; as much as a tub will hold.—**Tub-wheel**, *n.* A horizontal water-wheel with a series of radial, spiral floats.

Tuba, tū′ba, *n.* [L. a trumpet.] A large musical instrument of brass, low in pitch, and resembling the bombardon.

Tube, tūb, *n.* [Fr. *tube*, from L. *tubus*, a tube, *tuba*, a trumpet.] A pipe; a hollow cylinder of wood, metal, glass, india-rubber, &c., used for the conveyance of fluids and for various other purposes; any similar object; a vessel of animal bodies or plants which conveys a fluid or other substance; *elec.* a hollow vessel, usually of glass, fitted with electrodes and various adjuncts, and containing air or other gas at a low or an adjustable pressure.—*Tube of force*, a tubular volume bounded on all sides by lines of electrical or magnetic force.—*v.t. tubed*, *tubing*. To furnish with a tube.—**Tube-mill**, *n.* A kind of mill used for grinding ore, &c.—**Tube-well**, *n.* A pointed iron tube with perforations immediately above the point, driven into the earth till water gathers, when a small suction-pump is applied and the water pumped up.—**Tubicolar, Tubicolous**, tū-bik′ō-lėr, tū-bik′-ō-lus, *a.* [L. *tubus*, and *colo*, to inhabit.] *Zool.* inhabiting a calcareous tube.—**Tubicole**, tū′bi-kōl, *n.* One of an order of annelids which live in calcareous tubes.—**Tubiform**, tū′bi form, *a.* Having the form of a tube; tubular.—**Tubing**, tūb′-ing, *n.* The act of making or providing with tubes; a series of tubes; material for tubes.—**Tubipore**, tū′bi-pōr, *n.* [L. *tubus*, and *porus*, a pore.] One of those corals that consist of a cluster of small tubes, each tube being the abode of a polyp.—**Tubular**, tū′bū-lėr, *a.* [From L. *tubulus*, dim. of *tubus*, a tube.] Having the form of a tube or pipe; consisting of a pipe; fistular. —*Tubular boiler*, a form of boiler in which the connection between the fire and the chimney is made by a large number of tubes surrounded by the water, which is heated by the gases, &c., passing through the tubes.—*Tubular bridge*, a bridge formed of a great rectangular iron or steel tube, through which the roadway or railway passes.—**Tubulated, Tubulate**, tū′bū-lā-ted, tū′bū-lāt, *a.* Made in the form of a small tube; furnished with a small tube.—**Tubulation**, tū-bū-lā′shon, *n.* The act of making tubular.—**Tubuliform**, tū′bū-li-form, *a.* Having the form of a small tube.—**Tubulose, Tubulous**, tū′bū-lōs, tū′bū-lus, *a.* Tubular.

Tuber, tū′bėr, *n.* [L., a swelling, tumour, protuberance; same root as *tumid*, *tumour*.] An underground fleshy stem or modification of the root of plants (as in the potato), roundish in shape, of annual duration, and with buds from which new plants are produced; *surg.* a knot or swelling in any part. —**Tubercle**, tū′bėr-kl, *n.* [L. *tuberculum*, dim. from *tuber*.] A small tuber; a little projecting knob; *anat.* a natural small rounded body or mass; *pathol.* one of certain small masses of morbid matter which may be developed in different parts of the body, but are most frequently observed in the lungs (in the disease consumption).—**Tubercled**, tū′bėr-kld, *a.* Showing tubercles; covered with tubercles.—**Tubercular**, tū-bėr′kū-lėr, *a.* Of the character of a tubercle; caused by tubercles; affected with tubercles.—**Tuberculate, Tuberculated, Tuberculose, Tuberculous**, tū-bėr′kū-lāt, tū-bėr′kū-lā-ted, tū-bėr′kū-lōs, tū-bėr′kū-lus, *a.* Affected with tubercles; having small knobs or pimples. —**Tuberculin**, tū-bėr′kū-lin, *n.* [From *tubercle.*] An extract from the bacilli of tuberculosis, used as a test for the presence of tuberculosis in domestic animals. —**Tuberculization**, tū-bėr′kū-lī-zā″shon, *n.* The formation of tubercles, as in the lungs. —**Tuberculosis**, tū-bėr′kū-lō″sis, *n.* A disease due to the formation of tubercles in various organs of the body; a consumptive state of the system.—**Tuberiferous**, tū-bėr-if′ėr-us, *a.* [L. *tuber*, and *fero*, to bear.] Producing tubers. —**Tuberiform**, tū′bėr-i-form, *a.* Tuber-shaped. —**Tuberosity**, tū-bėr-os′i-ti, *n.* State of being tuberous; something that is tuberous; a swelling or prominence.—**Tuberous, Tuberose**, tū′bėr-us, tū′bėr-ōs, *a.* Covered with knobby or wart-like prominences; knobbed; *bot.* having tubers; resembling a tuber.—**Tuberousness**, tū′bėr-us-nes, *n.* Quality of being tuberous.

Tuberose, tūb′rōz or tū′be-rōz, *n.* [From the Latin specific name *tuberosa*, which means simply 'tuberous'; so Fr. *tubéreuse*, Sp. *tuberosa*.] An odoriferous plant with a tuberous root, a favourite flower and much cultivated.

Tubicolous, Tubing, Tubular, &c. Under TUBE.

Tuck,† tuk, *n.* [From Fr. *estoc*, It. *stocco*, a rapier, from G. *stock*, a stick.] A rapier. (*Shak.*)

Tuck, tuk, *v.t.* [Same as L.G. *tucken*, G. *zucken*, Sw. *tocka*, to draw together, to contract; akin *tug, tow, touch.*] To put into smaller compass by folding; to fold in or under; to gather up; to gather the bed-clothes close around (to *tuck* a child into a bed).—*v.i.* To contract; to draw together.—*Tuck in*, to partake freely of food or dainties (*colloq.*).—*n.* A fold sewed in some part of a dress to shorten it, especially a horizontal fold made on a skirt.—*Tuck-shop*, a schoolboy name for the shop where pastry, confectionery, and the like are sold. —**Tucker**, tuk′ėr, *n.* One who or that which tucks; an ornamental frilling of lace or muslin round the top of a woman's dress.

Tuckahoe, tuk′a-hō, *n.* [American Indian word for bread.] A singular vegetable growth of the United States, found underground like the truffle, its exact nature being not ascertained.

Tucket, tuk′et, *n.* [From It. *toccata*, a prelude, from *toccare*, to touch. TOUCH.] A flourish on a trumpet; a fanfare. (*Shak.*) —**Tuck**, tuk, *n.* [From *tucket.*] The sound produced by beating a drum; beat.

Tucum, tö′kum, *n.* A South American palm, yielding a valuable fibre and oil.

Tudor, tū′dor, *a.* The dynasty and the style of architecture during the reigns of Henry VII, Henry VIII, Edward VI, Mary, Elizabeth, deriving from Owen Tudor, grandfather of Henry VII.—*Tudor rose*, *her.* a double rose, having a white centre with red petals, or vice versa, and intended to conjoin the emblems of the Houses of York and of Lancaster.

Tuesday, tūz′dā, *n.* [A.Sax. *Tiwesdæg*, that is, Tiw's day, the day of *Tiw*, the Northern Mars, or god of war; so Icel. *týsdagr, tyrsdagr*, Sw. *tisdag*, Dan. *tirsdag*, G. *dienstag*. Comp. *Thursday*=*Thor's* day.] The third day of the week.

Tufa, Tuff, tū′fa, tuf, *n.* [It. *tufa*, Fr. *tuf*, a kind of porous stone, from L. *tophus*, tuff, tufa.] *Geol.* a term originally applied to a light porous rock composed of cemented scoriæ and ashes, but now to any porous vesicular compound.—**Tufaceous**, tū-fā′shus, *a.* Pertaining to or resembling it.

Tuft, tuft, *n.* [From Fr. *touffe*, a tuft, a thicket, with addition of *t* (comp. *graft* and *graff*); from G. *zopf*, Icel. *toppr*, a tuft=E. *top*. TOP.] A collection of small flexible or soft things in a knot or bunch (a *tuft* of flowers, a *tuft* of feathers); a cluster; a clump (a *tuft* of trees); in English universities, a slang term for a young nobleman student: so called from the gold *tuft* on the cap formerly worn by him.—*v.t.* To adorn with or as with tufts or a tuft.—**Tufted**, tuf′ted, *p.* and *a.* Adorned with a tuft or tufts; growing in tufts or clusters.—**Tuft-hunter**, *n.* A hanger-on or toady in the society of titled persons.—**Tuft-hunting**, *n.* The practice of a tuft-hunter.—**Tufty**, tuf′ti, *a.* Abounding with tufts; growing in tufts.

Tug, tug, *v.t.* —*tugged, tugging.* [A.Sax. *teóhan, teón*, to tug or pull; pret. pl. *tugon*, pp. *togen*; Icel. *toga, tjúga*, to draw; G. *zug*, a pull; akin *tow*, to pull, *tuck, tie.*] To pull with effort; to haul; to strain at; to drag by means of a steam-tug.—*v.i.* To pull with great effort; to labour; to strive; to struggle.—*n.* A pull with the utmost effort; a supreme effort; the severest strain or struggle (the *tug* of war); a tug-boat.—*Tug-of-war*, a trial of strength between two parties at opposite ends of a rope, each striving to pull the other over a certain mark.—**Tug-boat**, *n.* A strongly built steam-boat used for towing sailing and other vessels.—**Tugger**, tug′ėr, *n.* One who tugs.

Tuition, tū-ish′on, *n.* [L. *tuitio, tuitionis*, guardianship, from *tueor, tuisus*, to see, to look to.] Guardianship or superintendence‡; instruction; tutorship; teaching. —**Tuitionary**, tū-ish′on-a-ri, *a.* Pertaining to tuition.

Tula-metal, tö′la, *n.* [From *Tula*, in Russia, where it is extensively made.] An alloy of silver, with small proportions of lead and copper.

Tulchan, tul′*ch*an, *n.* A stuffed calf-skin set against a cow to induce her to yield milk more freely.—*Tulchan bishops*, bishops in Scotland, soon after the Reformation, appointed to titular sees, the revenues of which were drawn by lay barons and others.

Tulip, tū′lip, *n.* [Fr. *tulipe*, from Sp. *tulipa, tulipan*, It. *tulipano*, a tulip, from Turk. *tolipend*, a turban, the name being given to the flower from its similarity. TURBAN.] A plant of the lily family of many species, much cultivated for the beauty of the flowers.—**Tulipist**, tū′lip-ist, *n.* A cultivator of tulips.—**Tulipomania**, tū′lip-ō-ma″ni-a, *n.* [*Tulip*, and L. *mania*, madness.] A violent passion for the cultivation or acquisition of tulips.—**Tulip-tree**, *n.* An American tree bearing flowers resembling the tulip, one of the most magnificent forest trees of temperate North America. —**Tulip-wood**, *n.* A beautiful striped, rose-coloured wood, the produce of a Brazilian tree, much used for inlaying.

Tulle, tųl, *n.* A kind of thin, open net, silk fabric, originally manufactured at *Tulle* in France, much used in female head-dresses, collars, &c.

Tulwar, tul′war, *n.* [Hind.] An East Indian sabre.

Tumble, tum′bl, *v.i.*—*tumbled, tumbling.* [From Dan. *tumle*, Sw. *tumla*, to tumble, allied to A.Sax. *tumbian*, to dance, D. *tuimelen*, to tumble, G. *taumeln*, to reel, to stagger.] To roll about by turning one way and the other; to toss the body about; to roll; to lose footing and fall; to be precipitated; to play acrobats' tricks.—*v.t.* To turn or throw about for examination or search; to toss over carelessly; to disorder; to rumple; to throw down; to precipitate. —*n.* A fall; a rolling over.—**Tumbler**, tum′blėr, *n.* One who tumbles; one who plays the tricks of an acrobat turning summersaults, &c.; a large drinking glass, originally one that had not a base that it could stand on; a variety of the domestic pigeon, so called from its practice of turning over in flight; a sort of spring-latch in a lock which detains the bolt until a key lifts it. —**Tumblerful**, tum′blėr-fųl, *n.* As much as a tumbler can contain.

Tumbrel, Tumbril, tum′brel, tum′bril, *n.* [O.Fr. *tumberel*, from *tomber*, to fall, because tilted up to be emptied; of Germanic origin and akin to *tumble*. TUMBLE.] A dung-cart; a low vehicle with two wheels used by farmers; a covered cart or carriage with two wheels, which accompanies troops for conveying the tools of pioneers, ammunition, &c.

Tumefy, tū′mi-fī, *v.t.*—*tumefied, tumefying.* [Fr. *tuméfier*, from L. *tumeo*, to swell, and *facio*, to make, TUMID.] To swell or cause to swell or be tumid.—*v.i.* To swell; to rise in a tumour.—**Tumefaction**, tū-mi-fak′shon, *n.* A swelling up; a tumour. —**Tumescence**, tū-mes′ens, *n.* The state of growing tumid; tumefaction.

Tumid, tū′mid, *a.* [L. *tumidus*, from *tumeo*, to swell, from root *tu*, producing also *tumulus, tumultus, tumor, tuber*, &c. (whence *tumult, tumor*, &c.) Akin *tomb*.] Being swelled, enlarged, or distended; swollen; protuberant; swelling in sound or sense; pompous; bombastic.—**Tumidity, Tumidness**, tū-mid′i-ti, tū′mid-nes, *n.* The state or quality of being tumid.—**Tumidly**, tū′mid-li, *adv.* In a tumid manner or form.—**Tumor, Tumour**, tū′mėr, *n.* [L. *tumor, tumoris*, from *tumeo*, to swell.] *Surg.* a morbid enlargement or swelling; more strictly, a permanent swelling occasioned by a new growth, and not a mere enlargement of a natural part.—**Tumored**, tū′mėrd, *a.* Having a tumor or tumors.

Tump, tump, *n.* [W. *twmp*, a round mass, a hillock; same root as *tumid.*] A little hillock.

Tumular, Tumulary. Under TUMULUS.

Tumult, tū′mult, *n.* [L. *tumultus*, from *tumeo*, to swell. TUMID.] The commotion, disturbance, or agitation of a multitude; an uproar; violent commotion or agitation, with confusion of sounds; irregular or confused motion.—**Tumultuarily**, tu-mul′tū-a-ri-li, *adv.* In a tumultuary manner.—**Tumultuariness**, tu-mul′tū-a-ri-nes, *n.* Disorderly or tumultuous conduct; turbulence.—**Tumultuary**, tu-mul′tū-a-ri, *a.* [L. *tumultuarius.*] Disorderly; promiscuous; confused; restless; agitated; unquiet. —**Tumultuous**, tu-mul′tū-us, *a.* [L. *tumultuosus.*] Full of tumult, disorder, or confusion; conducted with tumult; disorderly; agitated; disturbed, as by passion or the like; turbulent; violent.—**Tumultuously**, tu-mul′tū-us-li, *adv.* In a tumultuous manner; with turbulence. — **Tumultuousness**, tu-mul′tū-us-nes, *n.*

Tun, tun, *n.* [A.Sax. *tunne*, a butt=Icel., Sw., and O.H.G. *tunna*, L.G. *tunne*, D. *ton*, G. *tonne*, cask, tun; perhaps a Celtic word =Ir. and Gael. *tunna, tonna*; comp. W. *tynell*. *Ton* is the same word; *tunnel* is a derivative.] Originally any large cask or vessel for containing liquids; hence, a certain measure or quantity which contained 4 hogsheads or 252 gallons.—*v.t.*—*tunned, tunning.* To put into casks.

Tuna, tö′na, *n.* A prickly pear, genus *Opuntia*, native to Central America.

Tuna, tö′na, *n.* A large fish of the mackerel family, found in the warm-water regions of the Atlantic and Pacific oceans; a tunny.

Tundra, tun′dra, *n.* A term applied to the immense stretches of flat boggy country in the northern part of Siberia.

Tune, tūn, *n.* [A form of *tone*. TONE.] A rhythmical, melodious series of musical tones produced by one voice or instrument, or by several voices or instruments in unison; an air; a melody; correct intonation in singing or playing; adjustment of a musical instrument so as to produce its tones in correct key-relationship, or in harmony with other instruments; frame of mind; mood; temper for the time being.—*To the tune of*, to the sum or amount of. (*Colloq.*)—*v.t.*—*tuned, tuning.* To put into or cause to be in tune; to sing with melody or harmony; to attune; to put into the proper state; to adapt.—**Tunable**, tūn′a-bl, *a.* Capable of being put in tune or made harmonious; musical; tuneful.—**Tunableness**, tūn′a-bl-nes, *n.* The state or quality of being tunable.—**Tunably**, tūn′a-bli, *adv.* In a tunable manner; musically. —**Tuneful**, tūn′fųl, *a.* Harmonious; melodious; musical. —**Tunefully**, tūn′fųl-li, *adv.* In a tuneful manner; harmoniously; musically. —**Tunefulness**, tūn′fųl-nes, *n.* The state or quality of being tuneful.—**Tuneless**, tūn′les, *a.* Unmusical; unharmonious; not expressed musically; without voice or utterance.—**Tuner**, tūn'ėr, *n.* One who tunes; one whose occupation is to tune musical instruments.—**Tuning**, tūn'ing, *n.* The art or operation of adjusting a musical instrument so that the various sounds may be all at due intervals; *wireless*, adjusting some variable factor of a circuit, as its capacity, inductance, or resistance, so as to make its natural period of oscillation the same as that of some other circuit.—**Tuning-fork**, *n.* A steel instrument with two prongs, designed when set in vibration to give a musical sound of a certain fixed pitch.

Tungsten, tung'sten, *n.* [Sw. and Dan., from *tung*, heavy, and *sten*, stone, heavy stone, from the density of its ores.] A hard, grayish-white, brittle and heavy metal. Called also *wolfram*. — **Tungstenic, Tungstic**, tung-sten'ik, tung'-stik, *a.* Pertaining to or obtained from tungsten (*tungstic* acid).

Tungusic, tun-gụs'ik, *a.* A term applied to a group of Turanian tongues spoken by tribes in the north-east of Asia.

Tunic, tū'nik, *n.* [L. *tunica*, a tunic.] A very ancient form of under garment worn by both sexes, and fastened by a girdle or belt about the waist; at the present day a loose garment worn by women and boys drawn in at the waist and reaching not far below it; a military surcoat; the garment worn by a knight over his armour; the full-dress, short uniform coat worn by soldiers; *anat.* a membrane that covers or composes some part or organ (the *tunics* or coats of the eye, the *tunics* of the stomach, &c.); a natural covering; an integument; *bot.* any loose membranous skin not formed from epidermis; the skin of a seed.—**Tunicary**, tū'ni-ka-ri, *n.* One of the Tunicata.—**Tunicata**, tū-ni-kā'ta, *n.pl.* An order of molluscoida, or lower mollusca, which are enveloped in a coriaceous tunic or mantle; an ascidian or sea-squirt. — **Tunicate, Tunicated**, tū'ni-kāt, tū'ni-kā-ted, *a.* *Bot.* covered with a tunic or membranes; coated; *zool.* enveloped in a tunic or mantle.

Tunker, tung'kėr, *n.* [G. *tunken*, to dip.] DUNKER.

Tunnel, tun'el, *n.* [From Fr. *tonnelle*, an arbour, a tunnel, from *tonne*, L.L. *tunna*, a cask. TUN.] A subterranean passage cut through a hill, a rock, or any eminence, or under a river, a town, &c., to carry a canal, a road, or a railway in an advantageous course. — *v.t.* — *tunnelled, tunnelling.* To form or cut a tunnel through or under.—**Tunnel-net**, *n.* A net with a wide mouth at one end and narrow at the other. — **Tunnel-shaft**, *n.* A shaft sunk to meet a tunnel.

Tunny, tun'i, *n.* [It. *tonno*, Fr. *thon*, from L. *thynnus*, from Gr. *thynnos*, a tunny, from *thynō*, to dart.] A food fish of the mackerel family, attaining a length of from four to even twenty feet, and found in immense quantities in the Mediterranean, there being also an American species taken chiefly for the oil it yields.

Tup, tup, *n.* [Comp. L.G. *tuppen, toppen*, to push, to butt.] A ram.

Tupaia, tū-pī'a, *n.* The banxring.

Turanian, tū-rā'ni-an, *a.* [Persian *Turan*, a name for the Turks and kindred races.] A term applied to the Altaic family of languages, which includes the Ugrian or Finnish, Turkish, Mongolian, &c.

Turban, tėr'ban, *n.* [O.E. *turband, turbant, tulibant*, &c., Fr. *turban*, Sp. and It. *turbante*, from Turk. *tulbend, dulbend*, Per. *dulband*, turban. *Tulip* is a form of this word.] A form of head-dress worn by the Orientals, consisting of a cap without brim, and a sash, scarf, or shawl wound about it; a kind of head-dress worn by ladies.—**Turbaned**, tėr'band, *a.* Wearing a turban.

Turbary, tėr'ba-ri, *n.* [L.L. *turbaria*, from O.H.G. *turba*, E. *turf*.] A place where turf is cut; the right of cutting turf.

Turbellaria, tėr-bel-lā'ri-a, *n.pl.* [From L. *turba*, a crowd, a stir, from the currents caused by their moving cilia.] An order of annuloid animals nearly all aquatic and non-parasitic, including the nemertids and others.

Turbid, tėr'bid, *a.* [L. *turbidus*, from *turba*, a crowd, or *turbare*, to trouble (as in *disturb, perturb, turbulent*). TROUBLE.] Having the lees or sediment disturbed; muddy; foul with extraneous matter; not clear: said of liquids of any kind.—**Turbidity, Turbidness**, tėr-bid'i-ti, tėr'bid-nes, *n.* The state of being turbid. — **Turbidly**, tėr'bid-li, *adv.* In a turbid manner; muddily.

Turbinate, Turbinated, tėr'bi-nāt, tėr'bi-nā-ted, *a.* [From *turbo, turbinis*, a top.] Shaped like a whipping-top; *conch.* spiral or wreathed conically from a larger base to the apex like a top; *bot.* shaped like a top or cone inverted.—**Turbination**, tėr-bi-nā'shon, *n.* The act of spinning or whirling, as a top.

Turbine, tėr'bin, *n.* [L. *turbo, turbinis*, that which spins or whirls round, a top.] A kind of horizontal water-wheel, made to revolve by the escape of water through orifices, under the influence of pressure derived from a fall; an engine in which rotary motion is produced by the direct impact of steam, gas or vapor upon a series of projections on the circumference of a cylinder free to revolve.—**Turbo**, tur'bō. Contracted from *turbine* in compound words, meaning (*a*) coupled direct to a turbine, or (*b*) constructed like a turbine.—**Turbo-alternator**, *n.* A turbine-driven alternating-current electric generator.—**Turbo-blower**, *n.* A turbine-driven air compressor.—**Turbo-dynamo**, *n.* A turbine-driven direct-current electric generator.—**Turbo-generator**, *n.* A turbine-driven electric generator or a dynamo.—**Turbo-pump**, *n.* A rotary pump in which the pressure of the water is increased by stages.

Turbit, tėr'bit, *n.* A variety of the domestic pigeon remarkable for its short beak.

Turbot, tėr'bot, *n.* [Fr. *turbot*, O.D. *turbot*, perhaps from L. *turbo*, a whipping-top, like Gr. *rhombos*, which means both top and turbot, there being a supposed similarity in shape.] A well-known and highly esteemed species of flat-fish native to the North Atlantic Ocean, often weighing from 70 to 90 lb.

Turbulent, tėr'bū-lent, *a.* [L. *turbulentus*, from *turbare*, to disturb. TURBID.] Being in violent commotion; tumultuous; disposed to insubordination and disorder; riotous; disorderly.—**Turbulence, Turbulency**, tėr'bū-lens, tėr'bū-len-si, *n.* The state or quality of being turbulent; riotous disposition; unruliness. — **Turbulently**, tėr'bū-lent-li, *adv.* In a turbulent manner.

Turco, tür'ko, *n.* The name given by the French to Arab sharp-shooters in their army.

Turcoman, tụr'kō-man, *n.* TURKOMAN.

Tureen, tu-rēn', *n.* [From Fr. *terrine*, a tureen, lit. an earthen vessel, from *terre* = L. *terra*, earth. TERRA.] A rather large deep vessel for holding soup or other liquid food at the table.

Turf, tėrf, *n.* pl. **Turfs**, tėrfs, now seldom **Turves**, tėrvz. [A.Sax. *turf* = D. *turf*, Icel., Sw., and L.G. *torf*, Dan. *törv*, turf.] The surface or sward of grass lands; a piece of earth with the grass growing on it; a sod; a kind of peaty substance cut from the surface of the ground and used as fuel. —*The turf*, the race-course; and hence, the occupation or profession of horse-racing.—*v.t.* To cover with turf or sod. — **Turf-clad**, *a.* Covered with turf.—**Turfen**, tėr'fn, *a.* Made of turf; covered with turf. —**Turfiness**, tėr'fi-nes, *n.* The state or quality of being turfy.—**Turf-spade**, *n.* A spade for cutting turf, longer and narrower than the common spade.—**Turfy**, tėr'fi, *a.* Abounding or covered with turf; having the qualities or appearance of turf; connected with the turf or race-ground; characteristic of horse-racing; sporting.

Turgent, tėr'jent, *a.* [L. *turgens, turgentis*, ppr. of *turgeo*, to swell.] Swelling; tumid; turgid.—**Turgesce**,† tėr-jes', *v.i.* [L. *turgesco*, inceptive of *turgeo*, to swell.] To become turgid; to swell.—**Turgescence, Turgescency**, tėr-jes'ens, tėr-jes'en-si, *n.* The act of swelling or state of being swelled; inflation; bombast; *med.* superabundance of humours in any part of the body. — **Turgescent**, tėr-jes'ent, *a.* [L. *turgescens*.] Growing turgid; in a swelling state.—**Turgid**, tėr'jid, *a.* [L. *turgidus*, from *turgeo*.] Swelled; bloated; distended beyond its natural state; inflated; bombastic (a *turgid* style).—**Turgidly**, tėr'jid-li, *adv.* In a turgid manner; pompously.—**Turgidity, Turgidness**, tėr-jid'i-ti, tėr'jid-nes, *n.* The state or quality of being turgid; distention beyond its natural state; inflated manner of writing or speaking; bombast.

Turio, tū'ri-ō, *n.* pl. **Turiones**, tū-ri-ō'-nēz. [L.] *Bot.* the subterranean bud of a perennial herbaceous plant, annually developed, and producing a new stem.

Turk, tėrk, *n.* A native or inhabitant of Turkey; hence, a Mohammedan.†—**Turkey**, tėr'ki, *n.* [So called because it was erroneously believed to have come from *Turkey*.] A large gallinaceous bird native to America, including wild and domestic varieties; its flesh is a table delicacy.—**Turkey-buzzard, Turkey-vulture**, *n.* A common species of the vulture family having a distinct resemblance to a turkey. —**Turkey-carpet**, *n.* A carpet made entirely of wool, the loops being larger than those of Brussels carpets and always cut.—**Turkey-cock**, *n.* A male turkey.—**Turkey-red**, *n.* [Because originally produced by madder from Turkey.] A brilliant and durable red colour produced by madder or alizarine upon cotton cloth. — **Turkey-hone, Turkey-slate, Turkey-stone**, *n.* A very fine-grained siliceous slate originally brought from the Levant, used for sharpening small cutting instruments. — **Turkish**, tėr'kish, *a.* Pertaining to Turkey or to the Turks.

Turkis, Turkois, tėr'kis, tėr'koiz, *n.* Same as *Turquoise*.

Turko, tụr'ko, *n.* Same as *Turco*.

Turkoman, tụr'kō-man, *n.* One of a nomadic Tartar people of Asia, occupying a territory east and south-east of the Caspian Sea.

Turmeric, tėr'mer-ik, *n.* [Probably from Hind. *zurd*, yellow, and *mirch*, pepper.] A name of one or two East Indian plants of the ginger family, whose rhizomes are used as a condiment, a yellow dye, and as a chemical test for the presence of alkalies.

Turmoil, tėr'moil, *n.* [Origin doubtful; probably *turn* and *moil*.] Harassing labour; molestation by tumult; commotion; disturbance.—*v.t.* To harass with commotion; to trouble; to molest.—*v.i.* To be in commotion.

Turn, tėrn, *v.t.* [O.Fr. *turner, torner* (Fr. *tourner*), to turn, from L. *tornare*, to turn in a lathe, from *tornus*, a lathe, from Gr. *tornos*, a turner's chisel; same root as L. *tero, tritum* (E. *trite*), to grind, &c.; akin *tour, tournament, tornado, detour*, &c.] To cause to move round on a centre or axis, or as on a centre or axis; to put into circular motion; to rotate or revolve; to shape by means of a lathe; to direct or put into a different way, course, direction, or channel (to *turn* a person from a purpose, to *turn* the eyes towards); to apply or devote (to *turn* one's self to trade); to put to some use or purpose; to shift or change with respect to the top, bottom, front, back, sides, or the like; to reverse; to invert; to bring the inside of out; to change to another opinion or party; to convert; to translate; to alter into something else; to metamorphose; to transform, transmute, change; to revolve or ponder (*turn* the matter over); to consider and reconsider; to change from a fresh, sweet, or natural condition; to cause to ferment, become sour, or the like; to put, bring, or place in a certain state or condition (*turned* into ridicule).—*To turn adrift*, to expel from some place or office; to throw upon one's own resources.—*To turn against*, to direct towards or against; to use to one's disadvantage (his argument was *turned against* himself); to render unfavourable, hostile, or opposed to —*To turn aside*, to ward off; to avert (a blow).—*To turn away*, to dismiss, discharge, or discard; also, to avert.—*To turn back*, to cause to return the same way; to drive back —*To turn down*, to fold or double down; to reject (a proposal).—*To turn off*, to dismiss or put away; to discharge; to accomplish; to produce complete (the printer *turned off* 10,000 copies); to shut off, as a fluid, by means of a stopcock, valve, &c (to *turn off* the gas).—*To turn on*, to admit, as a fluid, by means of a stopcock or valve (to *turn on* the gas).—*To turn out*, to drive out; to expel; to put out to pasture; to produce as the result of labour; to furnish in a complete state (to *turn out* 1000 pieces of cloth); to bring the inside of out; to bring out to view.—*To turn over*, to change the position of the top, bottom, or sides of; to overturn; to transfer; to put into different hands; to do business, sell goods, or draw money to the amount of (he *turns over* $500 a week); to open and turn the leaves of as of a book.—*To turn over a new leaf*, to take a different and better line of conduct. —*To turn up*, to bring from below to the top, to dig up (to *turn up* the soil); to bring a different surface or side uppermost; to place with the face upward (to *turn up* a card); to tilt up; to bring the end, tip, or point uppermost (to *turn up one's nose*, an expression of contempt); to refer to in a book.—*To turn upon* (or *on*), to cause to operate on or against.—*To turn the back*, to turn away; to go off; to flee.—*To turn the back on* or *upon*, to withdraw one's favour, friendship, or assistance from. —*To turn a corner*, to go or pass round a corner.—*To turn the edge of*, to blunt or render dull. — *To turn an enemy's flank, line, position*, &c., to manœuvre so as to pass round his forces and attack him from behind or on the side.—*To turn one's hand*, to apply or adapt one's self.—*To turn one's head* or *brain*, to make one giddy or dizzy; to deprive of one's reason or judgment; to infatuate.—*To turn a penny*, or *the penny*, to keep one's money in brisk circulation; to increase one's capital by business.—*To turn the scale*, to make one side of the balance go down; *fig.* to decide in one way or another; to give superiority or success. —*To turn the stomach*, to cause nausea, disgust, or loathing.—*To turn the tables*, to overthrow a formerly victorious rival, antagonist, or the like.—*To turn tail*, to retreat with ignominy; to flee like a coward.—*v.i.* To have a circular or rotatory motion; to move round; to revolve or rotate; *fig.* to depend, as on the chief point for decision or the like; to hinge (the question *turns* upon this); to move the body, face, or head in another direction; to change the position or posture of the body, as in bed; to retrace one's steps; to go or come back; to return; to offer opposition; to show fight; to take an opposite or a new course; to be directed (the road *turns* to the right); to have recourse (knew not where to *turn*); to be transformed or transmuted; to be converted; in a general sense, to become; to grow (to *turn* pale); to change from a fresh or sweet condition; to become sour or spoiled, as milk, wine, cider; to become dizzy or giddy, as the head or brain; to reel; to become nauseated or qualmish, as the stomach; to become inclined in another direction; to change from ebb to flow or from flow to ebb, as the tide; to have a consequence, to result (to *turn* to account).—*To turn about*, to turn the face in another direction.—*To turn again*, to return.—*To turn against*, to become unfavourable, unfriendly, or hostile to. — *To turn aside*, to leave a straight course; to withdraw from the presence of others.—*To turn away*, to deviate; to move the face in another direction; to avert one's looks.—*To turn back*, to go or come back; to return.—*To turn in*, to bend or double or point inwards; to enter; to go to bed (*colloq.*).—*To turn off*, to diverge; to deviate from a course (the road *turns off* to the right).—*To turn on* or *upon*, to show sudden anger or hostility to; to confront in a hostile or angry manner; to depend or hinge.—*To turn out*, to bend or point outwards; to come abroad; to appear outside; to get out of bed; to prove in the result or issue; to terminate; to result (the affair *turned out* better).—*To turn over*, to move, shift, or change from side to side, or from top to bottom; to roll; to tumble. —*To turn to*, to apply or betake one's self to; to direct one's mind or attention to.—*To turn up*, to point upwards; to come to light; to occur; to appear.—*n.* The act of turning; a revolution or rotation; one round of a rope or cord; the point or place of deviation from a straight line; a winding; a bend; a flexure; an angle; a short walk, promenade, or excursion; alteration of course; new direction or tendency; change or alteration generally; vicissitude; opportunity enjoyed in alternation with another or others, or in rotation; due chance, time, or opportunity; occasion; occasional act of kindness or malice (a good or ill *turn*); purpose; requirement; use; exigence (to serve our *turn*); form, shape, or mould; manner; fashion; character or temper; a short spell or a little job (*colloq.*); a nervous shock, such as is caused by alarm or sudden excitement (*colloq.*); *mus.* the sign ~ indicating a certain way of playing a group of notes.—*By turns*, one after another; alternately; at intervals.—*In turn*, in due order of succession.—*To a turn*, to a nicety; exactly; perfectly.—*To take turns*, to take each other's place alternately.—*Turn of life*, the period of life in women between the ages of 45 and 50, when the menses cease naturally. — *Turn and turn about*, alternately; successively; by turns.—**Turn-coat**, *n.* One who forsakes his party or principles.—**Turn-cock**, *n.* The servant of a water company who turns on the water for the mains, regulates the fire-plugs, &c.—**Turn-down**, *a.* Folded or doubled down (a *turn-down* collar).—**Turner**, tėr′nėr, *n.* One who turns; one whose occupation is to form things with a lathe.—**Turnery**, tėr′nėr-i, *n.* The act of turning articles by the lathe; articles made by or formed in the lathe; a place where articles are turned.—**Turning**, tėr′ning, *n.* A bend or flexure; the place where a road or street diverges from another road or street; the art or operation of shaping articles in a lathe.—**Turning-lathe**, *n.* A lathe used by turners to shape their work. —**Turning-point**, *n.* The point where a thing or person turns back; the point at which a deciding change takes place, as from good to bad, increase to decrease, or the opposite.—**Turnkey**, tėrn′kē, *n.* [One who *turns* the *key* in locks.] A person who has charge of the keys of a prison for opening and fastening the doors.—**Turn-out**, *n.* A coming forth; a number of persons who have *come out* on some particular occasion (a great *turn-out* of spectators); that which is brought prominently forward or exhibited; hence, an equipage; a horse or horses and carriage; the net quantity of produce yielded.—**Turn-over**, *n.* The act or result of turning over; the amount of money turned over or drawn in a business, as in a retail shop, in a given time.—**Turnpike**, tėrn′pīk, *n.* [Originally a turning frame with *pikes* or *spikes* projecting.] A turnstile; a gate set across a road in order to stop traffic or travellers, till toll is paid; a toll-bar or toll-gate; a turnpike-road.—**Turnpike-road**, *n.* A road on which there are turnpikes or toll-gates.—**Turn-screw**, *n.* A screw-driver.—**Turn-sick**, tėrn′sik, *n.* A disease of sheep, gid or sturdy.—**Turnspit**, tėrn′spit, *n.* A person who turns a spit; a dog allied to the terrier, formerly employed to drive a wheel to turn the spit for roasting in kitchens. —**Turnstile**, tėrn′stīl, *n.* A post surmounted by four horizontal arms which move round as a person pushes by them. —**Turnstone**, tėrn′stōn, *n.* A bird of the plover family, so called from its practice of turning up small stones in search of worms, &c., on which it feeds.—**Turn-table**, *n.* A circular revolving platform used for shifting railway carriages from one line of rails to another, and for reversing engines on the same line of rails.

Turner, tėr′nėr, *n.* [Fr. *tournois.*] Old Scottish coin, bearing thistle, from French standard, like plack (Fr. *plaque*), groat (Fr. *gros*), and bawbee (Fr. *bas billon*), the reckoning in Scotland up to about 1760.

Turnip, tėr′nip, *n.* [The latter part is A.Sax. *naep*, Icel. *næpa*, Sc. *neip*, a turnip, from L. *napus*, a turnip; the first syllable is perhaps W. *tor*, something bulging.] A cruciferous, biennial plant, allied to the cabbage, with a solid bulbous root, much cultivated as food for sheep and cattle, especially in winter, and as a flavouring for soups, &c. — **Turnip-cutter**, *n.* A revolving machine for slicing turnips for cattle and sheep.—**Turnip-fly**, **Turnip-flea**, *n.* A small coleopterous insect, destructive to the seed-leaves of turnips.

Turnsole, **Turnsol**, tėrn′sōl, *n.* [Fr. *tournesol*, from *tourner*, to turn, and L. *sol*, the sun.] A plant whose flower is said to turn toward the sun; a leguminous plant the juice of which is rendered blue by ammonia and air, and which serves as a test for acids; the purple dye obtained from this plant.

Turpentine, tėr′pen-tīn, *n.* [D. *terpentijn*, O.Fr. *turbentine*, turpentine, from L.L. *terbentina*, turpentine, from L. *terebinthus*, Gr. *terebinthos*, the turpentine-tree.] An oleo-resinous substance flowing naturally or by incision from coniferous trees, as the pine, larch, fir, &c. See TURPS.—**Turpentine-tree**, *n* The name of certain trees which yield turpentine.

Turpeth, tėr′peth, *n.* [From Fr. *turbith*, *turbit*, Sp. *turbit*, from Per. *turbed*, *tirbid*, the plant, the name being given to the mineral on account of its medicinal properties and yellow colour like the roots of the plant.] The root of a convolvulus of Ceylon, Malabar, and Australia, which has cathartic properties; also, turpeth-mineral. —**Turpeth-mineral**, *n.* Yellow basic sulphate of mercury, a useful errhine in cases of headache.

Turpitude, tėr′pi-tūd, *n.* [L. *turpitudo*, from *turpis*, foul, base.] Inherent baseness or vileness of principle, words, or actions; shameful wickedness; moral depravity.

Turps, tėrps, *n.* A noun now often used as short for spirits of oil of turpentine, which is popularly, but incorrectly, called turpentine.

Turquoise, tėr′koiz, *n.* [Fr. *turquoise*, so called because brought originally from *Turkey*, Fr. *Turquie.*] A greenish-blue opaque precious stone, a favourite gem in rings and other articles of jewellery.

Turret, tur′et, *n.* [O.Fr. *tourette*, dim. of *tour*, a tower, from L. *turris*, a tower. TOWER.] A little tower on a building; an armoured shelter on a war-ship containing, and revolving with, a gun. Distinguished from BARBETTE.—**Turreted**, tur′et-ed, *p.* and *a.* Formed like a turret; furnished with turrets.—**Turret-ship**, *n.* An armour-plated ship of war having on the deck heavy guns mounted within one or more turrets, which are made to rotate, so that the guns may be brought to bear in any required direction.—**Turriculate**, **Turriculated**, tu-rik′ū-lāt, tu-rik′ū-lā-ted, *a.* Resembling a turret in shape.—**Turrilite**, tur′i-līt, *n.* [L. *turris*, a tower, and Gr. *lithos*, a stone.] A fossil cephalopod, the shells of which, spiral, turreted, chambered, occur in the cretaceous formations.—**Turritella**, tur-i-tel′la, *n.* [Dim. of L. *turris*, a tower.] A genus of gasteropods with elongated spirally striated shells.

Turtle, tėr′tl, *n.* [A.Sax. *turtle*, a corruption of L. *turtur*, a turtle-dove, whence also D. *tortel*, G. *turtel*, Icel. *turtil.*] A bird of the pigeon family, smaller than the ordinary domestic pigeon, celebrated for the constancy of its affection, and therefore much sung by poets and appealed to by lovers. Also called *Turtle-dove*.

Turtle, tėr′tl, *n.* [Probably a corruption of *tortoise*, or Sp. *tortuga*, a tortoise.] The name given to the sea-tortoise, found in warm climates, the most important species being the green turtle, the flesh of which is so much prized as a luxury at the tables of the rich.—**Turtle-soup**, *n.* A rich soup, the chief ingredient of which is turtle-meat.

Tuscan, tus'kan, *a.* Pertaining to *Tuscany*, in Italy.—*Tuscan order*, one of the five orders of architecture, devoid of ornaments, and having columns that are never fluted.—*n.* An inhabitant of Tuscany; *arch.* the Tuscan order.

Tush, tush, *interj.* An exclamation indicating rebuke, impatience, or contempt, and equivalent to pshaw!

Tush, tush, *n.* [A form of *tusk.*] A long pointed tooth; a tusk; applied especially to certain of the teeth of horses.—**Tushed**, tusht, *a.* Tusked.

Tusk, tusk, *n.* [A.Sax. *tusc*, *tux*, a tusk; probably for *twisc*, from *twá*, two.] The long, pointed, and often protruding tooth on each side of the jaw of certain animals, as in the elephant; the canine tooth of the boar, walrus, hippopotamus, &c.; the share of a plough, a harrow tooth, or the like.—**Tusked**, tuskt, *a.* Furnished with tusks. —**Tusker**, tus'kėr, *n.* An elephant that has its tusks developed.—**Tusky**, tus'ki, *a.* Furnished with tusks; tusked.

Tussac-grass, *n.* TUSSOCK-GRASS.

Tussah-silk, **Tusseh-silk**, tus'sa, tus'se, *n.* A strong, coarse, brown silk obtained from the cocoons of a wild Bengal silk-worm.

Tussilago, tus-i-lā'gō, *n.* [L. from *tussis*, a cough, for the cure of which the leaves have been employed.] Colt's-foot.

Tussle, tus'l, *n.* [A form of *tousle*, to pull about roughly.] A struggle; a conflict; a scuffle.—*v.i.*—*tussled*, *tussling.* To struggle; to scuffle.

Tussock, tus'ok, *n.* [Modified from older *tuske*, *tushe*, a tuft, a bush; Dan. *dusk*, a tuft, a tassel.] A clump, tuft, or small hillock of growing grass.—**Tussock-grass**, *n.* A large grass of the Falkland Islands, Patagonia, &c., which grows in great tufts or tussocks, and contains a large quantity of saccharine constituents, rendering it a useful food for cattle.—**Tussock-moth**, *n.* A light, brownish-gray moth, so called from the tufts of hair growing on the caterpillar. — **Tussocky**, tus'ok-i, *a.* Abounding in or resembling tussocks or tufts.

Tut, tut, *interj.* An exclamation used to check or rebuke, or to express impatience or contempt; synonymous with *tush.*

Tutelage, tū'tel-āj, *n.* [From L. *tutela*, protection, from *tueor*, to defend (whence also *tutor*, *tuition*).] Guardianship; protection bestowed; the state of being under a guardian; protection enjoyed.—**Tutelar**, **Tutelary**, tū'tel-ėr, tū'tel-a-ri, *a.* [L. *tutelaris.*] Having the guardianship or charge of protecting a person or a thing; guardian; protecting.

Tutenag, tū'te-nag, *n.* The Indian name of zinc or spelter; also an alloy of copper, nickel, and zinc, used for table ware, &c.

Tutor, tū'tor, *n.* [L., a defender or guardian, from *tueor*, to defend. TUTELAGE.] One who has the care of the education of another; a private instructor; a teacher or instructor in anything; in English universities, one of a body of selected fellows attached to the various colleges or halls, by whom the education of the students is chiefly conducted; *law*, a guardian.—*v.t.* To instruct; to teach; to train or discipline. —**Tutorage**, tū'tor-āj, *n.* The office of a tutor or guardian; guardianship.—**Tutoress**, tū'tor-es, *n.* A female tutor; an instructress. — **Tutorial**, tū-tō'ri-al, *a.* Belonging to a tutor or instructor.—**Tutorship**, tū'tor-ship, *n.* The office of a tutor; guardianship; tutelage.

Tutti, tụt'tē. [It., from L. *totus*, pl. *toti*, all.] *Mus.* all; a direction to every performer to take part in the execution of the passage or movement.

Tutty, tut'i, *n.* [Fr. *tutie*, Pg. *tutia*, from Ar. *tūtiya.*] An impure protoxide of zinc, collected from the chimneys of smelting furnaces, and used as a polishing powder.

Tuyere, twi-yār or tụ-yār, *n.* [Fr. *tuyère*, akin to *tuyau*, a pipe. TEWEL.] The nozzle of the pipe that introduces the blast of a blast-furnace; the blast-pipe itself, of which there are usually two.

Twaddle, twod'l, *v.i.*—*twaddled*, *twaddling.* [Older form *twattle*, also *twittle*, *twittle-twattle*; an imitative word like *tattle*, *twitter*, &c.] To talk in a weak, silly, or tedious manner; to prate!—*n.* Empty, silly talk; a twaddler.—**Twaddler**, twod'lėr, *n.* One who twaddles. — **Twaddling**, twod'ling, *n.* The act of one who twaddles; silly talk.—**Twaddly**, twod'li, *a.* Consisting of twaddle.

Twain, twān, *a.* [O.E. *tweyne*, *tweyen*, &c., A.Sax. *twegen*, from *twá*, two = O.Fris. *twêne*, Dan. *tvende*, G. *zween.* TWO.] Two. [Obsolete unless in poetry.]—*n.* A pair; a couple.

Twang, twang, *n.* [Imitative of a resonant sound; akin to *tang.*] A sharp quick sound; an affected modulation of the voice; a kind of nasal sound; after-taste; tang.—*v.i.* To sound with a quick sharp noise; to make the sound of a string which is stretched and suddenly pulled; to utter with a sharp or nasal sound.—*v.t.* To make to sound, as by pulling and letting go suddenly; to utter with a short, sharp sound.—*interj.* Imitative of a sharp, quick sound, as that made by a bowstring.—**Twangling**,† twang'gling, *a.* Twanging; shrill-sounding. (*Shak.*)

Twank, twangk, *v.t.* [Imitative of a more abrupt sound than *twang.*] To cause to make a sharp, twanging sound; to twang. —*n.* A twang.

Twankay, twang'kā, *n.* [Chinese.] A sort of green tea.

'Twas, twoz. A contraction of *It was.*

Twattle, twot'l, *v.i.* and *n.* An older form of *Twaddle.*

Tweak, twēk, *v.t.* [A.Sax. *twiccian*, to twitch=L.G. *twikken*, D. *zwikken*, G. *zwicken*; an older form of *twitch.*] To twitch; to pinch and pull with a sudden jerk.—*n.* A sharp pinch or jerk; a twitch.

Tweed, twēd, *n.* [Originally called *tweels*, that is *twills*, but this name was misread into *tweeds*, when the goods were sent to London, the idea being that they were so called from the river *Tweed.*] A twilled woollen fabric, principally for men's wear, the manufacture of which is largely carried on in the south of Scotland.

Tweedle, twē'dl, *v.t.* Same as *Twiddle.* **Tweedledum** and **Tweedledee**, *n.* The difference of nothing, between two trifles; adapted from lines by John Byrom (1692–1763) expressing the rivalry between the musical followers of Handel and Bononcini.

Tweel, twēl, *n.* Same as *Twill.*

'Tween, twēn, *prep.* A contraction of *Between.*

Tweer, twēr, *n.* Same as *Tuyere.*

Tweezers, twē'zėrz, *n.pl.* [Formerly *tweezes*, from *tweeze*, a surgeon's box of instruments, a case containing scissors, penknife, or similar articles, from Fr. *étuis*, pl. of *étui*, O.Fr. *estui*, a case or sheath (of Germanic origin).] Small pincers used to pluck out hairs, &c.; small forceps. —**Tweezer-case**, *n.* A case for carrying tweezers.

Twelve, twelv, *a.* [A.Sax. *twelf* = O.Sax. *twelif*, O.Fris. *twelef*, D. *twaalf*, Icel. *tólf*, Goth. *tvalif*, O.H.G. *zwelif*, Mod.G. *zwölf.* Formed similarly to *eleven*, the elements being *two*, A.Sax. *twá*, and a suffix = *ten.* ELEVEN.] The sum of two and ten; twice six; a dozen.—*Twelve tables.* Under TABLE. —*n.* The number which consists of ten and two: a symbol representing twelve units, as 12 or xii.—*In twelves*, in duodecimo.—*The Twelve*, the Apostles.—**Twelfth**, twelfth, *a.* The second after the tenth; the ordinal of twelve; being one of twelve equal parts of anything.—*n.* One of twelve equal parts of anything.—In music, (*a*) an interval of twelve diatonic degrees, the replicate of the fifth; (*b*) an organ-stop tuned twelve notes above the diapasons.—**Twelfth-cake**, *n.* A large cake, into which a bean was often introduced, prepared for Twelfth-night festivities. BEANKING.—**Twelfth-day**, *n.* The twelfth day after Christmas; the festival of the Epiphany.—**Twelfth-night**, *n.* The evening of the festival of the Epiphany.—**Twelvemo**, twelv'mō, *n.* and *a.* Duodecimo; contracted 12mo.—**Twelvemonth**, twelv'munth, *n.* A year.

Twenty, twen'ti, *a.* [A.Sax. *twéntig*, from *twegen*, two, *twain*, and *-tig*, ten; *-tig* being cog. with L. *decem*, ten; so D. and L.G. *twintig*, G. *zwanzig*, Goth. *twaitigjus.*] Twice ten; proverbially, an indefinite number. —*n.* The number of twice ten; a score; a symbol representing this, as 20 or xx.—**Twentieth**, twen'ti-eth, *a.* The ordinal of twenty; being one of twenty equal parts of anything. — *n.* One of twenty equal parts.—**Twenty-fold**, *a.* Twenty times as many.

Twibill, twī'bil, *n.* [A.Sax. *twibill*, from *twi*=*two*, and *bill*, *bil*, an axe, a bill.] A kind of double axe or mattock.

Twice, twīs, *adv.* [O.E. *twies*, from A.Sax. *twi*, *twý*, two or double—*twice* like *thrice*, being an adverbial genitive.] Two times; doubly.—**Twice-told**, *a.* Related or told twice.

Twiddle, twid'l, *v.t.*—*twiddled*, *twiddling.* [Perhaps akin to *twaddle* or *twitter.*] To twirl, in a small way; to touch lightly, or play with.—*v.i.* To play with a tremulous quivering motion.

Twig, twig, *n.* [A.Sax. *twig*, akin to *twá*, two, alluding to the bifurcation of the branch; L.G. *twieg*, D. *twijg*, G. *zweig*, a twig. TWO.] A small shoot or branch of a tree or other plant, of no definite length or size. — **Twiggen**, twig'en, *a.* Made of twigs; wicker. — **Twiggy**, twig'i, *a.* Pertaining to a twig; resembling a twig; having twigs.

Twig, twig, *v.t.*—*twigged*, *twigging.* [Ir. and Gael. *tuig*, to perceive, discern.] To take notice of; to observe keenly. (*Colloq.*)—*v.i.* To see; to apprehend or understand. (*Colloq.*)

Twilight, twī'līt, *n.* [From *twi*, double (as in *twibill*), A.Sax. *twi*, *twý*, akin to *twá*, *two*, and *light.*] The faint light which is reflected upon the earth after sunset and before sunrise; crepuscular light; usually applied to evening twilight, morning twilight being called *dawn*; a faint light in general; hence, a dubious or uncertain medium through which anything is seen or examined (the *twilight* of early history). —*a.* Imperfectly illuminated; seen, done, or appearing by twilight.

Twill, twil, *v.t.* [Same as L.G. *twillen*, to make double; akin G. *zwillich*, twill; akin to *twin*, *two*, and the prefix *twi* of *twilight*, *twibill.*] To weave in such a manner as to produce a kind of diagonal ribbed appearance upon the surface of the cloth.—*n.* A variety of textile fabric so woven as to have the appearance of parallel diagonal lines or ribs over the surface; the raised lines made by twilling.—**Twilled**, twild, *p.* and *a.* Woven so as to present the appearance of diagonal ribs on the surface.

Twin, twin, *n.* [A.Sax. *twin*, double, *getwinne*, twins, from *twi*, two; so Icel. *tvennr*, *tvinnr*, a pair; G. *zwilling*, a twin; akin *twill*, *two*, *twain*, &c.] One of two young produced at a birth by an animal that ordinarily bears but one; one very much resembling another. — *The Twins*, a constellation and sign of the zodiac; Gemini. —*a.* Applied to one or two born at a birth; very much resembling something else.—**Twin-born**, *a.* Born at the same birth with another.—**Twin-brother**, *n.* One of two brothers who are twins; hence, the facsimile of something else.—**Twin crystal**, a compound crystal made up (by *twinning*) of two simple crystals, or parts of these, in reversed positions.—**Twinling**, twin'ling, *n.* A twin lamb.—**Twinned**, twind, *a.* Produced at one birth, like twins. —**Twin-screw**, *a.* and *n.* A steam-vessel having two screw propellers on separate shafts and revolving in opposite directions so as to counteract the tendency to lateral vibration.—**Twin-sister**, *n.* One of two sisters who are twins.—**Twin-steamer**, *n.* A steam-vessel with two hulls.

Twine, twīn, *v.t.*—*twined, twining.* [A.Sax. *twinan*, from *twi*, two; so D. *twijnen*, Icel. *tvinna*, to double, to twine. TWIN.] To twist; to form by twisting two or more threads or fibres; to entwine; to encircle.—*v.i.* To wind circularly or spirally; to make flexures; to ascend or grow up in convolutions about a support (the plant *twines*).—*n.* A strong thread composed of two or three smaller threads or strands twisted together; a small cord or string.—**Twining**, twī'ning, *p.* and *a.* Twisting or winding round; *bot.* ascending spirally around a stem, branch, or prop.—**Twiningly**, twī'ning-li, *adv.* In a twining manner.

Twinge, twinj, *v.t.* — *twinged, twinging.* [Akin to Icel. *thvinga*, to weigh down, to oppress, Dan. *tvinge*, D. *zwingen*, to constrain.] To affect with a sharp, sudden pain; to torment with pinching or sharp pains; to pinch; to tweak.—*v.i.* To have a sudden, sharp, local pain.—*n.* A sudden, sharp pain; a darting, local pain of momentary continuance; a pinch; a tweak.

Twinkle, twing'kl, *v.i.*—*twinkled, twinkling.* [A.Sax. *twinclian*, to twinkle, a dim. and freq. corresponding to O.E. *twinken*, G. *zwinken*, to wink with the eyes; nasalized forms corresponding to *twitch.*] To open and shut the eyes rapidly; to gleam; to sparkle: said of the eyes; to flash at intervals; to shine with a tremulous, intermitted light; to scintillate.—*n.* A wink or quick motion of the eye; a gleam or sparkle of the eye or of a star; a twinkling.—**Twinkling**, twingk'ling, *n.* The act of that which twinkles; a quick movement of the eye; a wink; the time taken up in winking the eye; an instant.

Twirl, twėrl, *v.t.* [Allied to Fris. *twierren*, to whirl, D. *dwarl*, a whirling, *dwarlen*, to whirl, O.G. *twirel*, what turns rapidly; Swiss *zwirlen*, to twirl.] To cause to turn round with rapidity; to cause to rotate rapidly, especially with the finger. — *v.i.* To revolve with velocity; to be whirled round. — *n.* A rapid circular motion; a twist; a convolution.

Twist, twist, *v.t.* [A.Sax. *twist*, a cord, from stem of *twá*, two; hence allied to *twine, twill, twig*, &c.; similarly L.G. and D. *twist*, Dan. and Sw. *tvist*, G. *zwist*, discord, division in two parties.] To form by winding strands together; to twine; to form into a thread from many fine filaments; to contort: to crook spirally; to wreathe; to insinuate; to pervert; to turn from the true form or meaning.—*To twist round one's finger*, to completely control the opinions and actions of.—*v.i.* To be united by winding round each other; to be twisted.—*n.* The act of twisting; the result of the act; a convolution; a contortion; a flexure; what is formed by twisting, as a cord, thread, &c.; manufactured tobacco in the form of a thick cord; the spiral in the bore of a rifled gun.—**Twister**, twis'tėr, *n.* One that twists.—**Twisting-crook**, *n.* An agricultural implement used for twisting straw ropes.

Twit, twit, *v.t.*—*twitted, twitting.* [O.E. *atwite, atwiten*, A.Sax. *ætwitan*, to twit, reproach — *æt*, at, and *witan*, to blame; Sc. *wite*, blame; akin to Icel. *vita*, to fine.] To vex or annoy by bringing to remembrance a fault, imperfection, or the like; to taunt; to upbraid, as for some previous act.—**Twitter**, twit'ėr, *n.* One who twits or reproaches.

Twitch, twich, *v.t.* [A form of *tweak.*] To pull with a sudden jerk; to snatch.—*v.i.* To be suddenly contracted, as a muscle.—*n.* A pull with a jerk; a short quick pull; a short, spastic contraction of the muscles; a noose twisted around the upper lip of a horse to keep him quiet when shoeing.

Twitch-grass, twich'gras, *n.* COUCH-GRASS.

Twite, twīt, *n.* [From its cry.] A sort of finch, the mountain linnet.

Twitter, twit'ėr, *v.i.* [Imitative of sound, like G. *zwitschern*, D. *kwetteren*, to twitter.] To utter a succession of small, tremulous, intermitted notes, as certain birds do.—*n.* A small intermitted noise or series of chirpings, as the sound made by a swallow.—**Twittering**, twit'ėr-ing, *n.* A sharp, intermitted, chirping noise.

'Twixt, twikst. A contraction of *Betwixt*: used in poetry and colloquially.

Two, tö, *a.* [A.Sax. *twá*=Icel. *tveir, tvö*, Goth. *tvai*, D. *twee*, G. *zwei*, Rus. *dwa*, Lith. *du*, L. and Gr. *duo*, Ir. and Gael. *da, do*. Per. *do*, Hind. *do, doo*, Skr. *dvi, dvau*. *Twin, twine, twill, twain, twist*, &c., are connected.] One and one together: often used indefinitely for a small number (a word or *two, two* or three hours).—*In two*, into two parts; asunder.—*n.* The number which consists of one and one; the symbol representing it, as 2 or ii.—**Two-cleft**, *a.* Bifid.—**Two-decker**, *n.* A vessel of war carrying guns on two decks.—**Two-edged**, *a.* Having two cutting edges, one on each side.—**Two-faced**, *a.* Having two visages, like the Roman deity Janus; given to equivocation or double-dealing; insincere. —

Twofold, tö'fōld, *a.* Double; multiplied by two: *bot.* two and two together growing from the same place (*twofold* leaves).—*adv.* In a double degree; doubly.—**Two-handed**, *a.* Having two hands; requiring the two hands to grasp (a *two-handed* sword).—**Two-headed**, *a.* Having two heads.—**Twoness**, tö'nes, *n.* The state or condition of being two —**Twopence**, tup'-ens, *n.* In Great Britain, a small silver coin.—**Two-penny**, tup'en-i, *a.* Of the value of two-pence; hence, of little worth. —**Two-ply**, *a.* Having two strands, as cord, or two thicknesses, as cloth, carpets, &c.—**Two-stroke cycle**, *n.* The cycle in one type of internal combustion engine, completed in two strokes of the piston, or one revolution of the crank shaft.—**Two-tongued**, *a.* Double-tongued; deceitful.

Twybill, twī'bil, *n.* Same as *Twibill.*

Twy-natured, twī-nā'tūrd, *a.* Double-natured; having an animal and non-animal nature combined. (*Tenn.*)

Tyburn, tī'bėrn, *n.* The old place of the gallows in London.—**Tyburn-tree**, *n.* The gallows.—**Tyburnia**, tī-bėr'ni-a, *n.* The land of Thackeray's novels, selected by him specially for the fashionable and high-life quarters of Portman Square, Grosvenor Square, &c.

Tycoon, tī-kön', *n.* [Chinese *Tai-koon*, great lord.] The generalissimo of the Japanese army, and formerly virtual emperor and real ruler of the country. MIKADO.

Tyfoon, tī-fön', *n.* TYPHOON.

Tyke, tīk, *n.* [TIKE.] A dog; a base fellow. (*Shak.*)

Tyle, tīl, *v.t.* Same as *Tile* in freemasonry.

Tymbal, tim'bal, *n.* [Fr. *timbale*, It. *timballo, taballo*, from Ar. *thabal*, a tymbal.] A kind of kettle-drum.

Tympan, tim'pan, *n.* [Fr. *tympan*, L. *tympanum*, from Gr. *tympanon, typanon*, a drum, from *typtō*, to beat.] A drum†; *arch.* same as *tympanum*; *printing*, a frame attached to the hand-press or platen machine, and covered with parchment or cloth, on which the blank sheets are put in order to be laid on the form to be impressed.—**Tympanic**, tim-pan'ik, *a.* Like a tympanum or drum; *anat.* pertaining to the tympanum.—**Tympanites**, tim-pa-nī'tēz, *n.* *Med.* a distention of the abdomen from a morbid collection of air in the intestines.—**Tympanitic**, tim-pa-nit'ik, *a.* Relating to or affected with tympanites.—**Tympanitis**, tim-pa-nī'tis, *n.* Inflammation of the lining membrane of the middle ear or tympanum.—**Tympanum**, tim'pa-num, *n.* *Anat.* the drum of the ear, a cavity of an irregular shape, constituting the middle ear; *arch.* the triangular space in a pediment; *mach.* a drum-shaped wheel with spirally curved partitions, by which water is raised for the purposes of irrigation; *bot.* a membranous substance stretched across the theca of a moss.—**Tympany**, tim'pan-i, *n.* Tympanites; inflation of language; bombast.

Tynewald, tin'wald, *n.* [Norse *thing*, assembly, *völlr*, word. THING, HUSTINGS.] The legislative assembly of the Isle of Man. So *Standsting, Delting*, in Shetland; *Dingwall*, the farthest point in Ross reached by Norse invaders; *Tinwald Hill*, in Dumfries, from settlers pushing up the Solway.

Type, tīp, *n.* [Fr. *type*, from L. *typus*, from Gr. *typos*, a blow, an impression, a mark, a type, from root of *typtō*, to strike.] A distinguishing mark or stamp; an emblem; an allegorical or symbolic representation of some object, which is called the *antitype*; a symbol; what prefigures something else; an example of any class considered as eminently possessing the properties or characters of the class; the ideal representative of a group; distinctive plan of structure; the model or pattern which becomes the subject of a copy; *printing*, a rectangular piece of metal, wood, or other hard material having a raised letter, figure, or other character on the upper end, which, when inked, gives impressions on paper; such types collectively. —*In type*, set up, ready for printing.—*v.t.* To serve as type of; to typify; to type-write. —**Type-founder**, *n.* A person who makes type by casting.—**Type-founding, Type-casting**, *n.* The founding or casting of printing types. —**Type-foundry**, *n.* A place where types are cast.—**Type-metal**, *n.* An alloy of lead, antimony, and tin.—**Type-script**, *n.* Matter produced by a type-writer. —**Type-setter**, *n.* One who sets up type; a compositor; a type-setting machine. —**Type-setting**, *n.* The act or process by which type is set up to be printed from.—**Type-write**, *v.t.* To print by a type-writer. —**Type-writer**, *n.* A machine used as a substitute for the pen, the letters being produced by the impression of inked types; one who uses such machine. —**Typist**, tīp'ist, *n.* One who uses a type-writer.—**Typical, Typic**, tip'i-kal, tip'ik, *a.* Pertaining to a type; serving as or having the character of a type; emblematic; figurative. —**Typically**, tip'i-kal-li, *adv.* In a typical manner.—**Typicalness**, tip'i-kal-nes, *n.* —**Typification**, tip'i-fi-kā"-shon, *n.* The act of typifying.—**Typifier**, tip'i-fī-ėr, *n.* One who typifies.—**Typify**, tip'i-fī, *v.t.*—*typified, typifying.* To represent by an image or resemblance; to serve as the type of; to prefigure; to exemplify.—

Typographer, tī-pog'raf-ėr, *n.* A printer. —**Typographic, Typographical**, tip-o-graf'ik, tip-o-graf'i-kal, *a.* Pertaining to printing. —**Typographically**, tip-o-graf'i-kal-li, *adv.* By means of types; after the manner of printers.—**Typography**, tī-pog'ra-fi, *n.* [Gr. *typos*, and *graphō*, to write.] The art of printing; matter printed; style in which anything is printed.—**Typology**, tī-pol'o-ji, *n.* [Gr. *typos*, and *logos*, discourse.] The doctrine of types; a discourse on types, especially those of Scripture.

Typhlitis, tif-lī'tis, *n.* [Gr. *typhlos*, blind (referring to cæcum, from L. *cæcus*, blind), and term. -*itis*, denoting inflammation.] *Med.* inflammation of the cæcum or blind gut.

Typhomalarial, tī'fō-ma-lā"ri-al, *a.* *Med.* having the character both of typhus and malarial fever.

Typhoon, tī-fön', *n.* [Chinese *tai-fong*, great wind, influenced by Gr. *typhōn*, a whirlwind.] One of the violent hurricanes which rage on the coasts of China and Japan, from May to November.

Typhus, tī'fus, *n.* [Gr. *typhos*, stupor or coma.] A dangerous species of continued fever attended by great debility, contagious or infectious, and often epidemic; generally characterized by great depression of spirits, weariness, a frequent, small, and fluttering pulse, and an eruption of a deep livid colour on the skin; also known as hospital fever, jail-fever, &c.—**Typhoid**, tī'foid, *a.* Pertaining to or resembling typhus.—*Typhoid fever*, a continued fever, characterized by abdominal pains and diarrhœa, and analogous in many respects to eruptive fevers. Known also as *Enteric* and *Gastric Fever*.—**Typhomania**, tī-fō-mā'ni-a, *n.* The delirium which accompanies typhoid fever.—**Typhous**, tī'fus, *a.* Relating to typhus.

Typical, **Typography**, &c. Under TYPE.

Tyrant, tī'rant, *n.* [O.Fr. *tiran*, *tirant*, from L. *tyrannus*, from Gr. *tyrannos*, a lord, a despotic ruler. The final *t* has been added, as in *pheasant*, *peasant*, &c.] Originally, in ancient Greece, one who had usurped the ruling power without the consent of the people or at the expense of the existing government; a usurper; hence, a monarch or other ruler or master who uses power to oppress those under him; a cruel sovereign or master; an oppressor.—**Tyrannic**, tī-ran'ik, *a.* Tyrannical.—**Tyrannical**, tī-ran'i-kal, *a.* [Fr. *tyrannique*, Gr. *tyrannikos*.] Pertaining to or acting as a tyrant; unjustly severe in government; oppressive to subordinates; despotic; cruel.—**Tyrannically**, tī-ran'i-kal-li, *adv.* In a tyrannical manner; oppressively.—**Tyrannicalness**, tī-ran'i-kal-nes, *n.*—**Tyrannicidal**, tī-ran'i-sī"dal, *a.* Relating to tyrannicide.—**Tyrannicide**, tī-ran'i-sīd, *n.* [L. *tyrannus*, and *cædo*, to kill.] The act of killing a tyrant; one who kills a a tyrant.—**Tyrannize**, tir'an-īz, *v.i.*—*tyrannized*, *tyrannizing*. [Fr. *tyranniser*.] To act the tyrant; to exercise arbitrary power; to rule with unjust and oppressive severity.—**Tyrannous**, tir'an-us, *a.* Tyrannical; unjustly severe; oppressive.—**Tyrannously**, tir'an-us-li, *adv.* In a tyrannous manner.—**Tyranny**, tir'an-i, *n.* The rule of a tyrant; despotic exercise of power; cruel government; severity; oppression.

Tyre, tīr, *n.* See *Tire* (of wheel).

Tyrian, tir'i-an, *n.* A native of ancient Tyre, the famous Phœnician city.—*a.* Pertaining to Tyre; of a purple colour — *Tyrian purple*, a celebrated purple dye formerly prepared at Tyre from shell-fish.

Tyro, tī'rō, *n.* A bad spelling of *Tiro*.

Tyrolese, tī'rol-ēz or tir'ol-ēz, *a* Belonging or relating to the Tyrol or Tirol — *n. sing.* and *pl.* A native of the Tyrol; the people of the Tyrol.—**Tyrolienne**, tē-ro-lē-en, *n.* [Fr.] A Tyrolese popular melody, in which rapid alternation of the natural and falsetto voice is introduced.—**Tyrolite**, tī'rol-īt, *n.* A fine azure-blue or verdigris-green ore of copper.

Tzar, **Tzarina**, tsär, tsä-rē'na. Same as *Czar*, *Czarina*.

U

U. The twenty-first letter and the fifth vowel in the English alphabet.

Ubiety, ū-bī'e-ti, *n.* [From L. *ubi*, where.] The state of being somewhere.

Ubiquitous, ū-bik'wi-tus, *a.* [From L. *ubique*, everywhere.] Existing or being everywhere; omnipresent.—**Ubiquitously**, ū-bik'wi-tus-li, *adv.* In a ubiquitous manner.—**Ubiquity**, ū-bik'wi-ti, *n.* The state of being ubiquitous; existing everywhere at the same time; omnipresence.—**Ubiquitarian**, ū-bik'wi-tā"ri-an, *n.* A name of certain Lutherans, who maintained the omnipresence of Christ's body.

U-boat, ū-bōt, *n.* A German submarine (from German *unterseeischesboot*).

Udal, ū'dal, *a.* [Icel. *ódal*, ancestral possessions, allodium. ALLODIUM.] A term in Orkney and Shetland equivalent to allodial or freehold.—**Udaller**, **Udalman**, ū'dal-ėr, ū'dal-man, *n.* A freeholder without feudal superior.

Udder, ud'ėr, *n.* [A.Sax. *úder* = O.Fris. *uder*, O.H.G. *ûtar*, G. *euter*; cog. L. *uber*, Gr. *outhar*, Skr. *ûdhar*, an udder.] The glandular organ or bag of cows and other quadrupeds, in which the milk is secreted and retained for the nourishment of their young.—**Uddered**, ud'ėrd, *a.* Having an udder.

Udometer, ū-dom'et-ėr, *n.* [L. *udus*, moist, wet, and Gr. *metron*, measure.] A pluviometer; a rain-gauge.

Ugh, u, *interj.* An expression of horror or recoil: usually accompanied by a shudder.

Ugly, ug'li, *a.* [O.E. *uggely*, *uglike*, from Icel. *uggligr*, dreadful, terrible, from *uggr*, fear, and *-ligr* = E. *-like*, *-ly*; akin Icel. *ugga*, to fear, E. *awe*.] Possessing qualities opposite to beauty; offensive to the sight; deformed; morally repulsive; hateful.—*n.* A kind of sun-shade worn by ladies in front of their bonnets.—**Uglily**, ug'li-li, *adv.* In an ugly manner.—**Ugliness**, ug'li-nes, *n.* The quality of being ugly; want of beauty; deformity of person; moral repulsiveness.

Ugrian, ö'gri-an, *a.* [From name of a Finnish tribe.] Applied to the Finnic group of Turanian tongues and peoples, comprising the Lapps, Finns, and Magyars. By some used as equivalent to Turanian.

Uhlan, ö'lan, *n.* [G. *uhlan*, from Polish *ulan*, a lancer, from *ula*, a lance.] A name given to light cavalry soldiers in the Russian, Austro-Hungarian, and German armies. Written also *Ulan*.

Ukase, ū-kās', *n.* [Rus., from *kasati*, to show.] A Russian edict or order emanating from the government, and having the force of law.

Ulan, ö'lan, *n.* UHLAN.

Ulcer, ul'sėr, *n.* [Fr. *ulcère*, from L. *ulcus*, *ulceris*, an ulcer or sore, akin Gr. *helkos*, an ulcer or wound.] A sore in any of the soft parts of the body, and attended with a secretion of pus or some kind of discharge.—**Ulcerate**, ul'sėr-āt, *v.i.*—*ulcerated*, *ulcerating*. To be formed into an ulcer.—*v.t.* To affect with an ulcer or with ulcers.—**Ulceration**, ul-sėr-ā'shon, *n.* [L. *ulceratio*.] The process of becoming ulcerous; the state of being ulcerated; an ulcer.—**Ulcerative**, ul'sėr-ā-tiv, *a.* Pertaining to ulcers.—**Ulcered**, ul'sėrd, *a.* Ulcerated.—**Ulcerous**, ul'sėr-us, *a.* Having the nature or character of an ulcer; affected with an ulcer or with ulcers.—**Ulcerously**, ul'sėr-us-li, *adv.*—**Ulcerousness**, ul'sėr-us-nes, *n.*

Ule, ö'lē, *n.* A tree of tropical America yielding large quantities of rubber.

Ulema, ö'le-ma, *n.* [Ar. *ulemâ*, wise or learned men.] The collective name of the hierarchical corporation of learned men in Turkey, who have charge of the department of government relating to sacred matters; composed of the Imams, the Muftis, and the Cadis.

Uliginous, **Uliginose**, ū-lij'i-nus, ū-lij'i-nōs, *a.* [L. *uliginosus*, from *uligo*, *uliginis*, ooziness.] Muddy; oozy; slimy; *bot.* growing in swampy places.

Ullage, ul'āj, *n.* [O.Fr. *œillage*, the filling up of leaky wine vessels, from *œil*, the eye, the bunghole, from L. *oculus*, the eye. OCULAR.] The quantity that a cask wants of being full.

Ulmaceous, ul-mā'shus, *a.* [L. *ulmus*, an elm.] Belonging to the order of plants of which the elm is type.—**Ulmic**, ul'mik, *a.* Applied to an acid produced by decaying vegetable matter; humic.—**Ulmin**, ul'min, *n.* Same as *Humus*.

Ulna, ul'na, *n.* pl. **Ulnæ**, ul'nē. [L. *ulna*, elbow, arm, an ell. ELL.] The larger of the two bones of the forearm, reaching from the elbow to the wrist, its upper extremity forming the point of the elbow; *old law*, an ell.—**Ulnar**, ul'nėr, *a.* Pertaining to the ulna.

Ulodendron, ū-lō-den'dron, *n.* [Gr. *oulē*, a scar, and *dendron*, a tree.] A genus of fossil trees in the coal formation that show on their stems two rows of oval or circular scars (whence the name).

Ulotrichous, ū-lot'ri-kus, *a.* [Gr. *oulotrichos*, from *oulos*, crisp or curly, and *thrix*, *trichos*, hair.] Pertaining to the crisp- or woolly-haired races of man. LEIOTRICHOUS.

Ulster, ul'stėr, *a.* Pertaining to Ulster, the northern province of Ireland.—*n.* A long loose overcoat for either a male or a female, originally made of frieze cloth in Ulster.—**Ulster hand**, *n.* The bloody red hand, the badge of Baronets other than those of Nova Scotia.—**Ulster King**. The heraldic King of Ireland, king-at-arms.

Ulterior, ul-tē'ri-or, *a.* [L., compar. from *ulter*, beyond, further. ULTRA.] Being beyond or on the further side; not at present in view or consideration; more remote; distant (*ulterior* views or objects).—**Ulteriorly**, ul-tē'ri-or-li, *adv.* More distantly; remotely.

Ultima, ul'ti-ma, *n.* [L. *ultimus*, last, furthest, superl. of *ulter*, further. ULTERIOR.] *Gram.* the last syllable of a word —**Ultimate**, ul'ti-māt, *a.* Furthest; most remote in place; last or final; arrived at as a final result; such that we cannot go beyond incapable of further resolution or analysis — *Ultimate analysis*, *chem.* the resolution of a substance into its absolute elements, opposed to *proximate analysis*, or the resolution of a substance into its constituent compounds.—**Ultimately**, ul'ti-māt-li, *adv.* As an ultimate or final result; at last finally.—**Ultimatum**, ul-ti-mā'tum, *n.* pl **Ultimatums**, ul-ti-mā'tumz, or **Ultimata**, ul-ti-mā'ta. [A coined word.] Any final proposal or statement of conditions in diplomatic negotiations, the final terms offered by a negotiator or party.—**Ultimo** ul'ti-mō, *a.* [L. *ultimo mense*, in the last month.] Last, as distinguished from the current month and all others: usually contracted to *ult*.—**Ultimogeniture**, ul'ti-mo-jen"i-tūr, *n.* The custom or practice by which the youngest child succeeds to an inheritance, as *borough-English* in England opposed to *primogeniture*.

Ultra, ul'tra, *prefix*, *a.* and *n.* [L. *ultra*, beyond, from pronominal root seen in *ille*, that person, he, and *-tra*, as in *contra*, *intra*, &c. *Outrage* is from this word.] A Latin preposition used as a prefix, in sense of beyond; exceedingly; in a high degree (*ultra*-conservative, *ultra*-liberal); also as an independent adjective, to signify beyond due limit; extreme (*ultra* measures); and as a noun, to signify one who advocates extreme views or measures; an ultraist.—**Ultraism**, ul'tra-izm, *n.* The principles of men who advocate extreme measures.—**Ultraist**, ul'tra-ist, *n.* One who pushes a principle or measure to extremes; one who advocates extreme measures.—**Ultramarine**, ul'tra-ma-rēn", *a.* [L *ultra*, and *marinus*, marine.] Situated or being beyond the sea.—*n.* [From lapis-lazuli being brought from beyond sea.] A beautiful and durable sky-blue colour, formed of the mineral called lapis-lazuli.—**Ultramicroscope**, ul-tra-mī'krō-skōp, *n.* [L. *ultra*, beyond, and *microscope*.] An instrument which shows the presence of objects too small to be seen by an ordinary microscope.—**Ultramontane**, ul-tra-mon'tān, *a.* [L. *ultra*, and *mons*, mountain.] Being or lying beyond the mountains; tramontane; belonging to the Italian or ultra-papal party in the Church of Rome; holding the doctrines of ultramontanism.—*n.* One who belongs to the Italian or ultra-papal party in the Church of Rome; one holding the doctrines of ultramontanism.—**Ultramontanism**, ul-tra-mon'tān-izm, *n.* The views of that party in the Church of Rome who place an absolute authority in matters of faith and discipline in the hands of the pope.—**Ultramundane**, ul-tra-mun'dān, *a.* [L. *ultra*, and *mundus*, world.] Being beyond the world, or beyond the limits of our system.—**Ultra-red**, *a.* Belonging to that part of the solar spectrum which is continued beyond the red rays.—**Ultra-violet**, *a.* Said of the opposite end of the spectrum.—**Ultra-tropical**, *a.* Outside the tropics; extratropical; also, extremely tropical (of heat).—**Ultra-zodiacal**, *a.* Outside the zodiac; belonging to parts of the heavens beyond the zodiac.

Ultroneus, ul-trō′nē-us, *a.* [L. *ultroneus*, from *ultro*, of one's own accord; akin to *ultra*.] Spontaneous; voluntary.—**Ultroneously**, ul-trō′nē-us-li, *adv.* In an ultroneous manner; of one's own free-will.

Ululate, ul′ū-lāt, *v.i.* [L. *ululo*, *ululatum*, to howl.] To howl, as a dog or wolf.—**Ululant**, ul′ū-lant, *a.* Ululating; howling.—**Ululation**, ul-ū-lā′shon, *n.* A howling, as of the wolf or dog; a wailing.

Umbel, um′bel, *n.* [L. *umbella*, a little shade, dim. of *umbra*, a shade. UMBRAGE.] *Bot.* a particular mode of inflorescence, which consists of a number of flower-stalks or pedicels, nearly equal in length, spreading from a common centre, each bearing a single flower, as in the ivy, carrot, &c.—**Umbellal**, **Umbellar**, um-bel′al, um-bel′ėr, *a.* Pertaining to an umbel; having the form of an umbel.—**Umbellate**, **Umbellated**, um′bel-āt, um′bel-ā-ted, *a.* Bearing umbels; umbel-like.—**Umbellifer**, um-bel′i-fėr, *n.* A plant producing an umbel; a plant belonging to an extensive and nat. order, including many esculent plants, such as the carrot, parsnip, celery, &c., and some poisonous, as hemlock.—**Umbelliferous**, um-bel-lif′ėr-us, *a.* Producing umbels; bearing umbels.—**Umbellule**, um′bel-ūl, *n.* Dim. of *umbel*. *Bot.* a small or partial umbel.

Umber, um′bėr, *n.* [L. *umbra* a shade, or from *Umbria*, a district of Italy, where, according to some, it was first obtained.] A soft earthy combination forming a pigment of an olive-brown colour in its raw state, but much redder when burnt.—*v.t.* To colour with umber; to shade or darken.—**Umbery**, um′bėr-i, *a.* Pertaining to umber; dark brown; dark; dusky.

Umbilical, **Umbilic**, um-bil′i-kal or um-bi-lī′kal, um-bil′ik, *a.* [L. *umbilicus*, the navel; akin to G. *omphalos*, the navel.] Pertaining to the navel; formed in the middle like a navel; navel-shaped; central.—*Umbilical cord*, *anat.* a cord-like structure which passes from the navel of the fetus or embryo of the higher mammalia to the placenta; the navel-string.—**Umbilicate**, **Umbilicated**, um-bil′i-kāt, um-bil′i-kā-ted, *a.* Navel-shaped; *bot.* fixed to a stalk by a point in the centre.—**Umbilicus**, um-bi-lī′kus, *n.* [L.] *Anat.* the navel; *bot.* the part of a seed by which it is attached to the placenta; the hilum; *conch.* a circular depression in the lower whorl of many spiral univalves.

Umbles, um′blz, *n.pl.* [HUMBLES.] The humbles or entrails of a deer.—**Umble-pie**, um′bl-pī, *n.* Humble-pie. Under HUMBLES.

Umbo, um′bō, *n.* [L. *umbo*, a boss on a shield, any boss or knob.] The boss or protuberant part of a shield; *bot.* the knob in the centre of the pileus or hat of the fungus tribe; *conch.* the projection of a bivalve shell situated immediately above the hinge.—**Umbonate**, **Umbonated**, um′bō-nāt, um′bō-nā-ted, *a.* Bossed; knobbed in the centre; *bot.* round with a projecting point in the centre.—**Umbonulate**, um-bon′ū-lāt, *a.* *Bot.* terminated by a very small boss.

Umbra, um′bra, *n.* [L., a shadow.] *Astron.* the total shadow of the earth or moon in an eclipse, or the dark cone projected from a planet or satellite on the side opposite to the sun, as contrasted with the *penumbra*; the dark central portion of a sun-spot surrounded by a brighter annular portion.

Umbraculiferous, um-brak′ū-lif″ėr-us, *a.* [L. *umbraculum*, a sort of umbrella, dim. of *umbra*, a shade, and *fero*, to bear.] *Bot.* bearing a body in the form of an expanded umbrella. **Umbraculiform**, um-brak′ū-li-form, *a.* Umbrella-shaped.

Umbrage, um′brāj, *n.* [O.Fr. *umbrage*, Fr. *ombrage*, from L. *umbra*, a shade (whence also *umbel*, *umbrella*, *adumbrate*).] A shade; shadow; shade caused by foliage; hence, the feeling of being overshadowed; jealousy of another, as standing in one's light or way; suspicion of injury; offence; resentment.—**Umbrageous**, um-brā′jus, *a.* [Fr. *ombrageux*.] Shading; forming a shade; shady; shaded (an *umbrageous* garden).—**Umbrageously**, um-brā′jus-li, *adv.* In an umbrageous manner.—**Umbrageousness**, um-brā′jus-nes, *n.*

Umbrella, um-brel′la, *n.* [It. *ombrella*, an umbrella, dim. of *ombra*, a shade, from L. *umbra*, a shade. UMBRAGE.] A portable shade, screen, or canopy of silk, cotton, &c., extended on an expanding frame composed of bars of steel, cane, &c., inserted in, or fastened to a rod or stick, and carried in the hand for sheltering the person from the rays of the sun, or from rain or snow.—**Umbrella-tree**, *n.* The magnolia tree with umbrella-like leaves at end of branches.

Umbrian School. The followers in painting of Raphael and Perugino.

Umbriferous, um-brif′ėr-us, *a.* [L. *umbra*, a shade, and *fero*, to bear. UMBRAGE.] Casting or making a shade.—**Umbriferously**, um-brif′ėr-us-li, *adv.* So as to make or cast a shade.

Umiak, ö′mi-ak, *n.* [Eskimo.] A flat-bottomed skin boat rowed by women.

Umlaut, öm′lout, *n.* [G., from prefix *um*, indicating alteration, and *laut*, sound = change of sound.] *Philol.* the change of a vowel in one syllable through the influence of one of the vowels, *a*, *i*, *u*, in the syllable immediately following—a common feature in several of the Teutonic tongues; mutation.

Umpire, um′pīr, *n.* [From O.E. *noumpere*, *nowmpere*, *nompere*, and with loss of initial *n* (as in *apron*), *owmper*, &c., from O.Fr. *nonper*, not equal, odd—L. *non*, not, and *par*, equal, a pair. PAIR. Lit. an odd person, in addition to a pair.] A person to whose sole decision a controversy or question between parties is referred; one agreed upon as arbiter of decisions in baseball and other sports events.—**Umpirage**, um′pīr-āj, *n.* The post of umpire; the act of one who arbitrates as umpire; arbitrament.—**Umpireship**, um′pīr-ship, *n.* The office of an umpire.

Umpteen, ump-tēn, *a.* An indefinite number.

Un-. A prefix derived from two sources and with two uses, viz. those of negation and those of reversal or undoing. As expressive of simple negation it is A.Sax. *un-* (Goth. *un-*, G. *un-*, D. *on-*, L. *in-*, all signifying not): and in this sense it is used chiefly before adjectives, past participles passive, and present participles used adjectively, being also prefixed to some nouns as in *un*truth, *un*dress, *un*rest, *un*wisdom, &c. Before some words of Latin origin it may be used alternatively with *in* or *non*; thus *un*alterable, *in*alterable; *un*elastic, *in*elastic, and *non*-elastic. As expressing reversal it represents A.Sax. *on-*, *ond-*, *and-*, *an-* in *answer* (Icel. and Goth. *and-*, G. *ant-*, L. *ante*, before), and is generally prefixed to active transitive verbs, as, *un*do, *un*learn, *un*lock, *un*make, &c. As adjectives and participles with the prefix *un-*, simply in the sense of not, are almost unlimited in number, and their meaning generally quite obvious, many of them are omitted from this work. When such words, however, have a special signification or usage of their own, and are not simply to be explained as equivalent to 'not' and their latter element, they are here given (as, for instance, *unaccountable*, *unruly*, *unconscionable*, *unparalleled*, &c.). Verbs and nouns with the other *un* as a prefix are also carefully defined.

Unabashed, un-a-basht′, *a.* Not abashed or daunted; not put to shame or confusion.

Unabated, un-a-bāt′ed, *a.* Not diminished in strength or violence.

Unable, un-ā′bl, *a.* Not able; not having sufficient ability; not equal for some task. ∴ Syn. under INCAPABLE.

Unabolished, un-a-bol′isht, *a.* Not abolished, repealed, or annulled; remaining in force.

Unabridged, un-a-brijd′, *a.* Not abridged; not shortened.

Unaccented, un-ak-sent′ed, *a.* Not accented; having no accent.

Unacceptable, un-ak-sep′ta-bl, *a.* Not acceptable or pleasing; not welcome; not such as will be received with pleasure.

Unaccommodating, un-ak-kom′mo-dāt-ing, *a.* Not ready to accommodate or oblige.

Unaccompanied, un-ak-kum′pa-nid, *a.* Having no attendants, companions, or followers; *mus.* performed or written without an accompaniment.

Unaccomplished, un-ak-kom′plisht, *a.* Not accomplished; not performed completely; not having accomplishments.

Unaccountable, un-ak-koun′ta-bl, *a.* Not to be accounted for; not explicable; such that no reason or explanation can be given.—**Unaccountableness**, un-ak-koun′ta-bl-nes, *n.*

Unaccredited, un-ak-kred′it-ed, *a.* Not accredited; not authorized.

Unaccustomed, un-ak-kus′tumd, *a.* Not accustomed; not habituated.

Unacknowledged, un-ak-nol′ejd, *a.* Not acknowledged or recognized; not owned, confessed, or avowed.

Unacquainted, un-ak-kwān′ted, *a.* Not having formed an acquaintance; not having knowledge: followed by *with*.

Unacted, un-akt′ed, *a.* Not acted; not performed on the stage; not executed.

Unadjusted, un-ad-just′ed, *a.* Not adjusted, settled, or regulated.

Unadmired, un-ad-mīrd′, *a.* Not regarded with admiration.

Unadmonished, un-ad-mon′isht, *a.* Not cautioned, warned, or advised.

Unadored, un-a-dōrd′, *a.* Not adored or worshipped.

Unadorned, un-a-dornd′, *a.* Not adorned; not decorated; not embellished.

Unadulterated, un-a-dul′tėr-āt-ed, *a.* Not adulterated; genuine; pure.

Unadvisable, un-ad-vī′za-bl, *a.* Not advisable; not to be recommended; not expedient; not prudent.—**Unadvised**, un-ad-vīzd′, *a.* Done without due consideration; rash.—**Unadvisedly**, un-ad-vī′zed-li, *adv.* Imprudently; indiscreetly.—**Unadvisedness**, un-ad-vī′zed-nes, *n.*

Unaffected, un-af-fek′ted, *a.* Not having the feelings moved; not showing affectation; natural; not artificial; simple; not hypocritical; sincere.—**Unaffectedly**, un-af-fek′ted-li, *adv.* In an unaffected manner; naturally; simply; sincerely.

Unaided, un-ād′ed, *a.* Not aided; not assisted.

Unalienable, un-āl′yen-a-bl, *a.* Not alienable; inalienable (which is more common).

Unallied, un-al-līd′, *a.* Having no alliance or connection, either by nature, marriage, or treaty.

Unalloyed, un-al-loid′, *a.* Not alloyed; having no admixture of alloy; without disturbing elements (*unalloyed* happiness or satisfaction).

Unalterable, un-ąl′tėr-a-bl, *a.* Not alterable; unchangeable; immutable.—**Unalterableness**, **Unalterability**, un-ąl′tėr-a-bl-nes, un-ąl′tėr-a-bil″i-ti, *n.*—**Unalterably**, un-ąl′tėr-a-bli, *adv.*—**Unaltered**, un-ąl′tėrd, *a.* Not altered or changed.

Unambiguous, un-am-big′ū-us, *a.* Not of doubtful meaning; plain; clear; certain.

Unambitious, un-am-bi′shus, *a.* Free from ambition; not affecting show; not showy or prominent.

Unamiable, un-ā′mi-a-bl, *a.* Not amiable or lovable, not adapted to gain affection.

Unaneled,† un-a-nēld′, *a.* or *pp.* [From *un*, not, old *an-* for *on*, and A.Sax. *elan*, to oil, from *ele*, oil.] Not having received extreme unction. (*Shak.*)

Unanimous, ū-nan′i-mus, *a.* [L. *unanimus*, of one mind—*unus*, one, and *animus*, mind. ANIMAL.] Being of one mind;

agreeing in opinion or determination; formed by unanimity (a *unanimous* vote).—**Unanimously**, ū-nan'i-mus-li, *adv.* With entire agreement of minds.—**Unanimity**, ū-na-nim'i-ti, *n.* The state of being unanimous.

Unanswerable, un-an'sėr-a-bl, *a.* Not to be satisfactorily answered; not capable of refutation. — **Unanswerableness**, un-an'sėr-a-bl-nes, *n.*—**Unanswerably**, un-an'sėr-a-bli, *adv.* So as to be beyond refutation.

Unanticipated, un-an-tis'i-pā-ted, *a.* Not anticipated.

Unapostolic, **Unapostolical**, un'ap-os-tol''ik, un'ap-os-tol''i-kal, *a.* Not apostolic; not agreeable to apostolic usage.

Unappalled, un-ap-pąld', *a.* Not appalled or daunted; not impressed with fear.

Unappealable, un-ap-pēl'a-bl, *a.* That cannot be carried to a higher court by appeal; not to be appealed from.

Unappeasable, un-ap-pēz'a-bl, *a.* Not to be appeased or pacified.

Unapprehensive, un-ap'prē-hen''siv, *a.* Not apprehensive; not fearful or suspecting; not quick of apprehension or understanding.

Unapprised, un-ap-prīzd', *a.* Not apprised; not previously informed.

Unapproachable, un-ap-prō'cha-bl, *a.* That cannot be approached; inaccessible; not to be equalled.

Unappropriate, un-ap-prō'pri-āt, *a.* Not appropriate; inappropriate. — **Unappropriated**, un-ap-prō'pri-ā-ted, *a.* Not appropriated; not applied to any specific object; not granted to any person, company, or corporation (*unappropriated* lands).

Unapproved, un-ap-prövd', *a.* Not having received approbation.

Unapt, un-apt', *a.* Not apt; dull; not ready to learn; unfit; unsuitable (*Shak.*).

Unarmed, un-ärmd', *a.* Not having on arms or armour; not equipped.

Unarrayed, un-a-rād', not arrayed; not dressed; not disposed in order.

Unasked, un-askt', *a.* Not asked; not invited; unsolicited; not sought by entreaty or care.

Unaspirated, un-as'pi-rā-ted, *a.* Having no aspirate; pronounced or written without an aspirate.

Unaspiring, un-as-pīr'ing, *a.* Not aspiring; not ambitious.

Unassailable, un-as-sā'la-bl, *a.* Incapable of being assailed; not to be moved or shaken from a purpose.

Unassimilated, un-as-sim'i-lā-ted, *a.* Not assimilated; *physiol.* not taken into the system by way of digestion.

Unassuming, un-as-sūm'ing, *a.* Not assuming; not bold or forward; not arrogant; modest.

Unattached, un-at-tacht', *a.* Not attached; *law*, not taken on account of debt; *milit.* not belonging to any one company or regiment, or on half-pay: said of officers.

Unattainable, un-at-tā'na-bl, *a.* Not to be gained or obtained.

Unattempted, un-at-temp'ted, *a.* Not attempted; not tried; not essayed.

Unattended, un-at-tend'ed, *a.* Not accompanied; having no retinue or attendance.

Unau, ö'nou, *n.* [South American.] The two-toed sloth of Brazil.

Unauthentic, un-ą-then'tik, *a.* Not authentic; not genuine or true.—**Unauthenticated**, un-ą-then'ti-kā-ted, *a.* Not attested; not shown to be genuine.

Unauthorized, un-ą'thor-īzd, *a.* Not warranted by proper authority; not duly commissioned.

Unavailing, un-a-vā'ling, *a.* Not having the effect desired; of no avail; ineffectual; useless; vain.

Unavenged, un-a-venjd', *a.* Not avenged; not having obtained revenge or satisfaction; not punished; not atoned for.

Unavoidable, un-a-voi'da-bl, *a.* Not avoidable; not to be shunned; inevitable.—**Unavoidably**, un-a-voi'da-bli, *adv.* Inevitably.

Unawakened, un-a-wāk'nd, *a.* Not roused from sleep; not roused from spiritual slumber or to a sense of sin.

Unaware, un-a-wãr', *a.* Not aware; not knowing; not cognizant. Sometimes used adverbially for *unawares.* — **Unawares**, un-a-wãrz', *adv.* [An adverbial genitive, like *betimes*, &c.] Unexpectedly; without previous preparation; inadvertently. — *At unawares*, unexpectedly.

Unawed, un-ąd', *a.* Not awed; not restrained by fear; undaunted.

Unbalanced, un-bal'anst, *a.* Not balanced; not in equipoise; not brought to an equality of debit and credit.

Unbar, un-bär', *v.t.* To remove a bar or bars from; to unfasten; to unlock.

Unbearable, un-bãr'a-bl, *a.* Not to be borne or endured; intolerable. — **Unbearably**, un-bãr'a-bli, *adv.* In an unbearable manner; intolerably.

Unbecoming, un-bē-kum'ing, *a.* Not becoming; improper; indecorous. — **Unbecomingly**, un-bē-kum'ing-li, *adv.* Indecorously.

Unbefitting, un-bē-fit'ing, *a.* Not fitting or suitable; unsuitable; unbecoming.

Unbefriended, un-bē-fren'ded, *a.* Not supported by friends; having no friendly aid.

Unbegot, **Unbegotten**, un-bē-got', un-bē-got'n, *a.* Not begot; having never been generated; having always been self-existent.

Unbelief, un-bē-lēf', *n.* Incredulity; the withholding of belief; infidelity; disbelief of divine revelation; disbelief of the truths of the gospel. — **Unbelievable**, un-bē-lē'va-bl, *a.* Such as cannot be believed; impossible to believe.—**Unbeliever**, un-bē-lē'vėr, *n.* One who does not believe; an infidel; one who discredits revelation, or the mission and doctrines of Christ.—**Unbelieving**, un-bē-lē'ving, *a.* Incredulous; infidel; discrediting divine revelation.

Unbend, un-bend', *v.i.* To become relaxed or not bent; to rid one's self of constraint; to act with freedom; to give up stiffness or austerity of manner.—*v.t.* To free from bend or flexure; to relax; to set at ease for a time (to *unbend* the mind); *naut.* to unfasten from the yards and stays, as sails.—**Unbending**, un-ben'ding, *p.* and *a.* Unyielding; resolute; inflexible. — **Unbendingly**, un-ben'ding-li, *adv.* Obstinately.

Unbeneficed, un-ben'e-fist, *a.* Not enjoying or having a benefice.

Unbeseeming, un-bē-sēm'ing, *a.* Unbecoming; not befitting.

Unbias, un-bī'as, *v.t.* To free from bias, prejudice, or prepossession.—**Unbiased**, un-bī'ast, *a.* Free from bias, undue partiality, or prejudice; impartial.

Unbidden, un-bid'n, *a.* Not commanded; spontaneous; uninvited; not requested to attend.

Unbind, un-bīnd', *v.t.* To untie; to unfasten; to loose; to set free from shackles.

Unbishop, un-bish'up, *v.t.* To divest of the rank of bishop.

Unbleached, un-blēcht', *a.* Not bleached; not whitened by bleaching.

Unblemished, un-blem'isht, *a.* Not blemished; free from turpitude or reproach; untarnished; pure; spotless (*unblemished* reputation).

Unblest, un-blest', *a.* Not blest; excluded from benediction; hence, cursed; wretched; unhappy.

Unblown, un-blōn', *a.* Not blown; not having the bud expanded.

Unblushing, un-blush'ing, *a.* Not blushing; destitute of shame; impudent.—**Unblushingly**, un-blush'ing-li, *adv.* In an unblushing or shameless manner.

Unbolt, un-bōlt', *v.t.* To remove a bolt from; to unfasten; to open.—**Unbolted**, un-bōlt'ed, *p.* and *a.* Freed from fastening by bolts; (in this sense of different origin) not bolted or sifted (*unbolted* meal).

Unborn, un-born', *a.* Not yet born; future; to come; never born or brought into existence.

Unbosom, un-bö'zum, *v.t.* To reveal in confidence; to disclose, as one's secret opinions or feelings: often used with reflexive pronouns (to *unbosom himself*).

Unbought, un-bąt', *a.* Not bought; obtained without money or purchase.

Unbound, un-bound', *a.* Not bound; loose; not tied; not bound by a bookbinder; not bound by obligation or covenant; also, pret. of *unbind.*

Unbounded, un-boun'ded, *a.* Having no bound or limit; unlimited in extent; very great; excessive. — **Unboundedly**, un-boun'ded-ly, *adv.*

Unbrace, un-brās', *v.t.* To remove the braces from; to free from tension; to loosen; to relax.

Unbridle, un-brī'dl, *v.t.* To free from the bridle; to let loose.—**Unbridled**, un-brī'dld, *p.* and *a.* Loosed from the bridle; hence, unrestrained; unruly; violent; licentious.

Unbroken, un-brō'kn, *a.* Not broken; not violated; not subdued; not tamed and rendered tractable; not interrupted.

Unbuckle, un-buk'l, *v.t.* To loose from buckles; to unfasten the buckle or buckles of.

Unbuilt, un-bilt', *a.* Not yet built; not erected.

Unburden, un-bėr'dn, *v.t.* To rid of a load or burden; to relieve the mind or heart of, as by disclosing what lies heavy on it: with reflexive pronouns (to *unburden oneself*).

Unburied, un-ber'id, *a.* Not buried; not interred.

Unburned, **Unburnt**, un-bėrnd', un-bėrnt', *a.* Not burned; not consumed or injured by fire; not hardened in fire, as brick.

Unbutton, un-but'n, *v.t.* To loose the buttons of.

Uncalled, un-kąld', *a.* Not called; not summoned; not invited. — *Uncalled for*, not required; not needed or demanded; improperly brought forward. Also written *Uncalled-for.*

Uncanny, un-kan'i, *a.* [Scotch and occasional in English.] Not canny; eerie; mysterious; not of this world; of evil and supernatural character.

Uncared, un-kãrd', *a.* Not regarded; not heeded: with *for.*

Uncase, un-kās', *v.i.* To disengage from a case or covering.

Unceasing, un-sēs'ing, *a.* Not ceasing; not intermitting; continual.—**Unceasingly**, un-sēs'ing-li, *adv.* In an unceasing manner; without intermission; continually.

Unceremonious, un-sėr'e-mō''ni-us, *a.* Not using ceremony or form; not ceremonious; familiar. — **Unceremoniously**, un-sėr'e-mō''ni-us-li, *adv.* In an unceremonious manner; without ceremony; informally.

Uncertain, un-sėr'tin, *a.* Not certain; doubtful; not certainly known; ambiguous; not having certain knowledge; not sure; unreliable; not to be depended on; undecided; not having the mind made up; not steady; fitful; fickle; inconstant; capricious. —**Uncertainly**, un-sėr'tin-li, *adv.* In an uncertain manner. — **Uncertainty**, un-sėr'tin-ti, *n.* The quality or state of being uncertain; want of certainty; doubtfulness; state of doubting; dubiety; hesitation; something not certainly and exactly known; a contingency.

Unchain, un-chān', *v.t.* To free from chains or slavery; to let loose.

Unchallenged, un-chal'enjd, *a.* Not challenged or called to account; not objected to; not called in question.

Unchangeable, un-chān'ja-bl, *a.* Not capable of change; immutable; not subject to variation.—**Unchangeableness**, un-chān′ja-bl-nes, *n.* The state or quality of being unchangeable.—**Unchanging**, un-chān′jing, *a.* Suffering no alteration; unalterable.

Uncharitable, un-char′i-ta-bl, *a.* Not charitable; ready to think evil or impute bad motives; harsh; censorious; severe in judging.—**Uncharitableness**, un-char′i-ta-bl-nes, *n.* The quality of being uncharitable. — **Uncharitably**, un-char′i-ta-bli, *adv.* In a manner contrary to charity.

Unchaste, un-chāst′, *a.* Not chaste; not continent; libidinous; lewd.—**Unchastity**, un-chas′ti-ti, *n.* The quality of being unchaste; incontinence; lewdness.

Unchristian, un-kris′tyan, *a.* Contrary to the laws or opposed to the spirit of Christianity.

Uncial, un′shi-al, *a.* [From L. *uncia*, an inch, the letters being about an inch long. OUNCE.] A term applied to letters of a large size used in ancient Latin and Greek manuscripts.—*n.* An uncial letter.

Unciform, un′si-form, *a.* [L. *uncus*, a hook, and *forma*, form.] Hook-like; having a curved or hooked form.—**Uncinate**, un′si-nāt, *a.* [L. *uncinatus*.] *Bot.* hooked at the end, as an awn.

Uncircumcised, un-sėr′kum-sīzd, *a.* Not circumcised. — **Uncircumcision**, un-sėr′kum-si″zhon, *n.* Absence or want of circumcision.

Uncivil, un-siv′il, *a.* Not courteous; ill-mannered; rude; coarse.—**Uncivilized**, un-siv′il-īzd, *a.* Not civilized or reclaimed from savage life; rude; barbarous; savage.

Unclaimed, un-klāmd′, *a.* Not claimed; not demanded; not called for.

Unclasp, un-klasp′, *v.t.* To loose or undo the clasp of; to open what is clasped.

Uncle, ung′kl, *n.* [O.Fr. *uncle* (Fr. *oncle*), from L. *avunculus*, an uncle, a dim. of *avus*, a grandfather.] The brother of one's father or mother; also applied to the husband of one's aunt; pawnbroker (*colloq.*).

Unclean, un-klēn′, *a.* Not clean; foul, dirty; filthy; morally impure; foul with sin; wicked; evil; ceremonially impure according to the Jewish law. — **Uncleanly**, un-klen′li, *a.* Foul; filthy; dirty; indecent; unchaste; obscene.—**Uncleanness**, un-klēn′nes, *n.* The state of being unclean.

Unclerical, un-kler′i-kal, *a.* Not clerical; not befitting the clergy.

Uncloak, un-klōk′, *v.t.* To deprive of the cloak; to tear the disguise from; to unmask.

Unclose, un-klōz′, *v.t.* To open; to disclose; to lay open.—**Unclosed**, un-klōzd′, *p.* and *a.* Not closed or shut; open; opened.

Unclothe, un-klōᴛʜ′, *v.t.* To strip of clothes; to make naked; to divest of covering.—**Unclothed**, un-klōᴛʜd′, *p.* and *a.* Stripped of clothing; not clothed; wanting clothes.

Unclouded, un-kloud′ed, *a.* Free from clouds; free from gloom; clear.

Uncock, un-kok′, *v.t.* To let down the cock of, as of a gun.

Uncoil, un-koil′, *v.t.* and *i.* To unwind or open, as the turns of a rope or a spiral spring; to open out its coils, as a snake.

Uncoined, un-koind′, *a.* Not coined or minted.

Uncollected, un-kol-lek′ted, *a.* Not collected; not received; not having one's thoughts collected.

Uncolored, un-kul′ėrd, *a.* Not colored; not heightened in description.

Uncomely, un-kum′li, *a.* Not comely; wanting grace; unbecoming. — **Uncomeliness**, un-kum′li-nes, *n.* Want of comeliness.

Uncomfortable, un-kum′fėr-ta-bl, *a.* Affording no comfort; causing bodily discomfort; giving uneasiness; uneasy; ill at ease. —**Uncomfortableness**, un-kum′fėr-ta-bl-nes, *n.* The state of being uncomfortable. — **Uncomfortably**, un-kum′fėr-ta-bli, *adv.* In an uncomfortable manner.

Uncommissioned, un-kom-mish′ond, *a.* Not commissioned or duly appointed; not having a commission.

Uncommitted, un-kom-mit′ed, *a.* Not committed or done; not referred to a committee; not pledged by anything said or done.

Uncommon, un-kom′on, *a.* Not common; infrequent; rare; remarkable; extraordinary.—**Uncommonly**, un-kom′on-li, *adv.* Rarely; not usually; remarkably.

Uncommunicable, un-kom-mū′ni-ka-bl, *a.* Not communicable; incommunicable.

Uncommunicative, un-kom-mū′ni-kā-tiv, *a.* Not apt to communicate to others; reserved. — **Uncommunicativeness**, un-kom-mū′ni-kā-tiv-nes, *n.*

Uncompanionable, un-kom-pan′yon-a-bl, *a.* Not companionable or sociable.

Uncomplaining, un-kom-plā′ning, *a.* Not complaining; not disposed to murmur or complain.

Uncompromising, un-kom′prō-mī-zing, *a.* Not accepting of any compromise; not agreeing to terms; inflexible.

Unconcern, un-kon-sėrn′, *n.* Want of concern; freedom from solicitude; cool and undisturbed state of mind.—**Unconcerned**, un-kon-sėrnd′, *a.* Feeling no concern or solicitude; easy in mind; having or taking no interest; not affected.—**Unconcernedly**, un-kon-sėrnd′li, *adv.* In an unconcerned manner; without anxiety; coolly.—**Unconcernedness**, un-kon-sėrnd′nes, *n.*

Unconditional, un-kon-dish′on-al, *a.* Not limited by any conditions; absolute; unreserved. — **Unconditionally**, un-kon-dish′on-al-li, *adv.* Without terms or conditions.—**Unconditioned**, un-kon-dish′ond, *a.* *Metaph.* a word employed to designate that which has neither conditions, relations, nor limitations either as regards space or time: used commonly in the noun-phrase *the unconditioned*, that is, the absolute, the infinite.

Unconfined, un-kon-fīnd′, *a.* Not confined; free from restraint or control; not having narrow limits; wide and comprehensive.

Unconfirmed, un-kon-fėrmd′, *a.* Not firmly established; not strengthened or established by additional testimony; not confirmed according to the church ritual.

Unconformable, un-kon-for′ma-bl, *a.* Not consistent; *geol.* applied to strata whose planes do not lie parallel with those of the strata above or below but have a different inclination. — **Unconformability**, un-kon-for′ma-bil″i-ti, *n.* — **Unconformably**, un-kon-for′ma-bli, *adv.*

Unconnected, un-kon-nek′ted, *a.* Not connected; separate; not coherent; not joined by proper transitions or dependence of parts; loose; rambling.

Unconquerable, un-kong′kėr-a-bl, *a.* Not conquerable; not to be overcome in contest; incapable of being subdued or brought under control; insuperable.—**Unconquerably**, un-kong′kėr-a-bli, *adv.* Invincibly; insuperably.

Unconscionable, un-kon′shon-a-bl, *a.* Not conscionable; exceeding the limits of any reasonable claim or expectation; inordinate; unreasonable (an *unconscionable* demand or claim). — **Unconscionableness**, un-kon′shon-a-bl-nes, *n.* — **Unconscionably**, un-kon′shon-a-bli, *adv.*

Unconscious, un-kon′shus, *a.* Not conscious; devoid of consciousness; having no mental perception; not knowing; not perceiving. — *Unconscious mind*, that part of the mind whose states and activity remain permanently out of consciousness; distinguished from conscious mind and sub-conscious mind.—**Unconsciously**, un-kon′shus-li, *adv.* In an unconscious manner; without perception. — **Unconsciousness**, un-kon′shus-nes, *n.* The state of being unconscious; want of perception.

Unconstitutional, un-kon′sti-tū″shon-al, *a.* Not agreeable to the constitution of a country; contrary to the principles of the constitution. — **Unconstitutionally**, un-kon′sti-tū″shon-al-li, *adv.*

Unconstrained, un-kon-strānd′, *a.* Free from constraint; voluntary; having no feeling that checks one's words or actions.—**Unconstrainedly**, un-kon-strā′ned-li, *adv.* Without constraint; spontaneously.—**Unconstraint**, un-kon-strānt, *n.* Freedom from constraint; ease.

Uncontested, un-kon-test′ed, *a.* Not contested; not disputed.

Uncontrollable, un-kon-trōl′a-bl, *a.* That cannot be controlled, ruled, or restrained; ungovernable. — **Uncontrollably**, un-kon-trōl′a-bli, *adv.*

Uncontroverted, un-kon′trō-vėr-ted, *a.* Not controverted; not disputed or called in question.

Unconverted, un-kon-vėr′ted, *a.* Not converted; not turned from one faith to another.

Unconvinced, un-kon-vinst′, *a.* Not convinced; not persuaded.—**Unconvincing**, un-kon-vin′sing, *a.* Not sufficient to convince.

Uncord, un-kord′, *v.t.* To loose from cords; to unfasten the cord or cords of.

Uncork, un-kork′, *v.t.* To draw the cork from.

Uncorrected, un-ko-rek′ted, *a.* Not corrected; not revised; not reformed or amended; not chastised.

Uncorrupted, un-ko-rup′ted, *a.* Not corrupted; not depraved.

Uncouple, un-ku′pl, *v.t.* To loose, as dogs coupled together; to disjoin.

Uncourteous, un-kōr′tē-us, *a.* Not courteous; uncivil; unpolite.—**Uncourteously**, un-kōr′tē-us-li, *adv.* Uncivilly; unpolitely. — **Uncourtly**, un-kōrt′li, *a.* Not courtly; not bland or polite of manner; blunt; uncivil. — **Uncourtliness**, un-kōrt′li-nes, *n.* The quality of being uncourtly.

Uncouth, un-köth′, *a.* [A.Sax. *uncúth*, unknown—*un*, not, and *cúth*, pp. of *cunnan*, to know. CAN.] Strange; odd in appearance; awkward; ungainly.—**Uncouthly**, un-köth′li, *adv.* Oddly; strangely; awkwardly.—**Uncouthness**, un-köth′nes, *n.* Oddness; strangeness.

Uncovenanted, un-kuv′e-nan-ted, *a.* Not promised by covenant; not proceeding from the covenant made between God and his people through Christ; a theological term, as in the phrase *uncovenanted mercies*; that is, such mercies as God may be pleased to show to those not sharing in the covenant.

Uncover, un-kuv′ėr, *v.t.* To remove a cover or covering from; to divest of a cover or covering; hence, to lay bare; to disclose.—*v.i.* To bare the head; to take off one's hat. —**Uncovered**, un-kuv′ėrd, *p.* and *a.* Deprived of a cover; not provided with a cover or covering; bare; naked.

Uncreated, un-krē-ā′ted, *p.* and *a.* Not yet created; not produced by creation.

Uncrippled, un-krip′ld, *a.* Not crippled or lamed; not having the powers of motion, activity, usefulness, &c., impaired.

Uncritical, un-krit′i-kal, *a.* Not critical; wanting in critical powers; not according to the rules of criticism.

Uncropped, un-kropt′, *a.* Not cropped; not bearing a crop.

Uncrossed, un-krost′, *a.* Not crossed; not traversed; not thwarted.

Uncrown, un-kroun′, *v.t.* To deprive of a crown; to dethrone.

Unction, ungk′shon, *n.* [L. *unctio*, *unctionis*, from *ungo*, *unctum*, to anoint (whence *unguent*, *ointment*, *anoint*); same root as Skr. *anj*, to anoint.] The act of anointing or rubbing with an unguent, ointment, or oil; an unguent; a salve; *fig.* something soothing or lenitive; that quality in language, mode of address, or manner, which excites devotion or sympathy; religious fervour; sham devotional fervour; oiliness. —*Extreme unction.* Under EXTREME.—**Unctuous**, ungk′tū-us, *a.* Of an oily or greasy character; fat and clammy; soapy; greasy or soapy to the feel when rubbed or touched by the fingers, a characteristic of steatite and other minerals; nauseously bland, sympathetic, devotional, or the like; oily; fawning. — **Unctuously**, ungk'tū-us-li, *adv.* In an unctuous manner. — **Unctuousness, Unctuosity**, ungk'tū-us-nes, ungk-tū-os'i-ti, *n.* The state or quality of being unctuous.

Uncultivated, un-kul'ti-vā-ted, *a.* Not cultivated or tilled; rough or rude in manners; not improved by labour, study, care, or the like.

Uncurl, un-kėrl', *v.t.* To straighten out, as something curled.—*v.i.* To fall from a curled state, as ringlets; to become straight. —**Uncurled**, un-kėrld', *a.* Not curled.

Uncut, un-kut', *a.* Not cut; not cut open at the edges, as the leaves of a book.

Undamaged, un-dam'ājd, *a.* Not damaged; not made worse.

Undated, un'dā-ted, *a.* [L. *undatus*, from *unda*, a wave. UNDULATE.] Rising and falling in waves towards the margin, as a leaf; waved.

Undated, un-dā'ted, *a.* Not dated; having no date.

Undaunted, un-dąn'ted, *a.* Not daunted; not depressed by fear; fearless; intrepid.— **Undauntedly**, un-dąn'ted-li, *adv.* In an undaunted manner; boldly; intrepidly.— **Undauntedness**, un-dąn'ted-nes, *n.* Boldness; intrepidity.

Undé, undy, *a.* *Her.* wavy.

Undecagon, un-dek'a-gon, *n.* [L. *undecim*, eleven, and Gr. *gōnia*, an angle.] A hendecagon.

Undecaying, un-dē-kā'ing, *a.* Not decaying; lasting for ever; undying.

Undeceive, un-dē-sēv', *v.t.* To free from deception, misapprehension, or mistake, whether caused by others or by ourselves; to open one's eyes.

Undecennial, un-dē-sen'ni-al, *a.* [L. *undecim*, eleven, and *annus*, a year.] Belonging to a period of eleven years.

Undecided, un-dē-sī'ded, *a.* Not decided or determined; not settled; not having the mind made up; hesitating; irresolute.

Undecked, un-dekt', *a.* Not having a deck (an *undecked* vessel).

Undeclinable, un-dē-klī'na-bl, *a.* Not to be declined; *gram.* indeclinable.

Undecomposable, un-dē'kom-pō"za-bl, *a.* Not admitting of decomposition; indecomposable.

Undefended, un-dē-fen'ded, *a.* Not defended; being without works of defence; *law*, not characterized by a defence being put forward.

Undefinable, un-dē-fī'na-bl, *a.* Not definable; indefinable.—**Undefined**, un-dē-fīnd', *a.* Not defined; not having its limits distinctly marked or seen.

Undemonstrative, un-dē-mon'stra-tiv, *a.* Not demonstrative; not apt to let the feelings betray themselves; reserved; cold in manner.

Undeniable, un-dē-nī'a-bl, *a.* Incapable of being denied; indisputable; evidently true.—**Undeniably**, un-dē-nī'a-bli, *adv.* Indisputably.

Under, un'dėr, *prep.* [A.Sax. *under*, under, among=Sw. and Dan. *under*, Icel. *undir*, D. *onder*, G. *unter*, Goth. *undar*; cog. L. *inter*, Skr. *antar*, in the midst, under. The term. *-ter*, *-dar*, *-tar* is the compar. suffix, and the root portion is akin to the prepositions *in*, *on*.] In a lower place or position than; so as to be overtopped, overhung, or covered by; beneath; denoting a state of being loaded, oppressed, or distressed by; subject to the government, direction, instruction, or influence of; in a state of liability or limitation with respect to; inferior to in rank, social position, &c.; inferior to or less than with respect to number, quantity, value, &c.; falling short of; included in; in the same category, division, class, &c., as; with the character, pretext, or cover of; being the subject of (*under* discussion). — *Under arms*, fully armed and equipped so as to be ready for action.—*Under fire*, exposed to the enemy's shot; taking part in a battle or engagement.—*Under ground*, below the surface of the ground.—*Under one's hand, signature, seal*, or the like, attested or confirmed by writing one's name, or by affixing a seal.— *Under sail*, having the sails unfurled or spread out to catch the wind; hence, in motion.—*Under the breath*, with a low voice; in a whisper; very softly.—*Under the rose*, in secret.—*Under water*, below the surface of the water.—*Under way*, *naut.* having just weighed anchor or left moorings and making progress through the water.— *adv.* In a lower or subordinate condition or degree (to keep a person *under*).—*To knock under*. KNOCK. — *Under*, with its adverbial force, is frequently used as the first element of a compound with verbs and adjectives, when it denotes not sufficiently or imperfectly (*under*bred, *under*done); or it may have reference to literal inferiority of place (to *under*mine, &c.).—*a.* Lower in position, rank, or degree; subject; subordinate (*under* sheriff). *Under*, in this sense, is often used with nouns as the first element of a compound.

Underagent, un-dėr-ā'jent, *n.* A subordinate agent.

Underbid, un-dėr-bid', *v.t.* To bid less than, as in auctions; to offer to execute work or the like at a lower price than.

Underbrace, un-dėr-brās', *v.t.* To bind, fasten, or tie together below.

Underbred, un'dėr-bred, *a.* Of inferior breeding or manners; vulgar.

Underbrush, un'dėr-brush, *n.* Shrubs and small trees in a wood, growing under large trees; undergrowth.

Underbuy, un-dėr-bī', *v.t.* To buy at a lower price than.

Undercharge, un-dėr-chärj', *v.t.* To charge less than a fair price for; to take too low a price from.—*n.* (un'dėr-chärj). Too low a charge or price.

Underclay, un'dėr-klā, *n.* A layer of clay underlying another deposit; a layer of clay underlying the tilled soil; a stratum of clay underlying a seam of coal.

Undercliff, un'dėr-klif, *n.* A terrace along the sea-shore at the base of a cliff, formed by materials falling from the cliff.

Underclothes, Underclothing, un'dėr-klōTHz, un'dėr-klōTH-ing, *n.* Clothes worn under others or next the skin.

Undercoat, un'dėr-kōt, *n.* A coat worn under another.

Undercroft, un'dėr-kroft, *n.* [*Under*, and *croft*, a corruption of *crypt*.] A vault under the chancel of a church.

Undercurrent, un'dėr-kur-ent, *n.* A current below the surface of the water; *fig.* an influence at work out of sight or not readily apparent.

Underdo, un-dėr-dö', *v.t.* To do less thoroughly than is requisite; to cook insufficiently (the beef was *underdone*).

Underdrain, un'dėr-drān, *n.* A drain below the surface of the ground.—*v.t.* (un-dėr-drān'). To drain by cutting a channel below the surface.

Underdressed, un-dėr-drest', *a.* Not well or sufficiently dressed; underdone, as meat.

Underestimate, un-dėr-es'ti-māt, *v.t.* To estimate at too low a rate.—*n.* An estimate at too low a rate.

Undergird, un-dėr-gėrd', *v.t.* To gird round the bottom. (N.T.)

Undergo, un-dėr-gō', *v.t.* To bear up against; to endure with firmness; to suffer; to pass through; to be subjected to; to experience (to *undergo* changes).

Undergraduate, un-dėr-grad'ū-āt, *n.* A student or member of a university or college who has not taken his first degree.

Underground, un'dėr-ground, *a.* Being below the surface of the ground.—*adv.* Beneath the surface of the earth.

Undergrowth, un'dėr-grōth, *n.* That which grows under something else; shrubs or small trees growing among large ones.

Underhand, un'dėr-hand, *adv.* [The opposite of *above-board*, and borrowed from the gaming table.] By secret means; in a clandestine manner and often with a bad design.—*a.* Working by stealth; clandestine: usually implying meanness or fraud, or both; sly and sinister.—*Underhand bowling*, with the knuckles turned under and the palm turned up.—**Underhanded**, un'dėr-han-ded, *a.* Kept secret; underhand.

Underhung, un'dėr-hung, *a.* Projecting beyond the upper jaw: applied to the under jaw.

Under-keeper, *n.* A subordinate or assistant warder, gamekeeper, or the like.

Underlaid, un-dėr-lād', *p.* and *a.* Having something lying or laid beneath (sand *underlaid* with clay).

Underlay, un-dėr-lā', *v.t.* To lay beneath; to put under; to support by laying something under.

Under-lease, *n.* *Law*, a sublease,

Underlet, un-dėr-let', *v.t.* To let below the value; to sublet.

Underlie, un-dėr-lī', *v.t.*—pret. *underlay*, pp. *underlain*, ppr. *underlying*. To lie beneath; to be situated under; to be at the basis of; to form the foundation of; to be subject or liable to.—*v.i.* To lie beneath. —**Underlying**, un-dėr-lī'ing, *a.* Lying beneath or under; *geol.* applied to rocks or strata lying below others.

Underline, un'dėr-līn, *v.t.* To mark underneath or below with a line; to underscore.

Underling, un'dėr-ling, *n.* [*Under*, and term. *-ling*.] An inferior person or agent; a mean sorry fellow.

Undermaster, un'dėr-mas-tėr, *n.* A master subordinate to the principal master.

Undermine, un-dėr-mīn', *v.t.* To form a mine under; to sap; to make an excavation beneath, especially for the purpose of causing to fall, or of blowing up; *fig.* to subvert clandestinely; to injure by secret or dishonourable means. — **Underminer**, un-dėr-mī'nėr, *n.* One who undermines.

Undermost, un'dėr-mōst, *a.* Lowest in place, rank, or condition.

Underneath, un-dėr-nēth', *adv.* [*Under*, and *-neath*, as in *beneath*. NETHER.] Beneath; in a lower place.—*prep.* Under; beneath.

Underpay, un-dėr-pā', *v.t.* To pay insufficiently.

Underpeopled, un'dėr-pē-pld, *a.* Not fully peopled.

Underpin, un-dėr-pin', *v.t.* To pin or support underneath; to place something under for support or foundation when a previous support is removed. — **Underpinning**, un-dėr-pin'ing, *n.* The act of one who underpins; the solid building or other supports introduced beneath a wall, &c., already constructed.

Underplot, un'dėr-plot, *n.* A plot subordinate to another plot, as in a play or a novel; an underhand clandestine scheme.

Underprop, un-dėr-prop', *v.t.* To prop from beneath; to uphold.

Underrate, un-dėr-rāt', *v.t.* To rate too low; to undervalue.

Underscore, un-dėr-skōr', *v.t.* To underline or draw a line or lines under.

Under-secretary, *n.* A secretary subordinate to the principal secretary.

Undersell, un-dėr-sel', *v.t.* To sell cheaper than.

Under-servant, *n.* An inferior or subordinate servant.

Under-sheriff, *n.* A sheriff's deputy.

Undershoot, un'dėr-shöt, *v.t.* To shoot short of; to fail to reach in aiming at.— **Undershot**, un'dėr-shot, *a.* Moved by water passing under, or acting on the lowest part: said of a water-wheel, and opposed to *overshot*.

Undershrub, un'dėr-shrub, *n.* A plant of shrubby habit, but scarcely attaining the dimensions of a shrub.

Underside, un′dėr-sīd, *n.* The lower side or side underneath.

Undersign, un-dėr-sīn′, *v.t.* To write one's name at the foot or end of; to subscribe.—**Undersigned**, un-dėr-sīnd′, *p.* and *a.* Subscribed at the bottom or end. —*The undersigned*, the person or persons signing any document; the subscriber or subscribers.

Undersized, un′dėr-sīzd, *a.* Being of a size or stature less than common; dwarfish.

Undersoil, un′dėr-soil, *n.* Soil beneath the surface; subsoil.

Undersong, un′dėr-song, *n.* The burden or accompaniment of a song; a subordinate strain.

Understand, un-dėr-stand′, *v.t.*—pret. and pp. *understood*, formerly sometimes incorrectly *understanded*. [A.Sax. *understandan*, to understand, lit. to stand under—*under*, and *standan*, to stand; so O.Fris. *understonda*, Icel. *undirstanda*.] To apprehend or comprehend fully; to know or apprehend the meaning of; to perceive or discern by the mind; to have just and adequate ideas of; to comprehend; to see through; to be informed; to learn: governing a clause; to suppose to mean; to interpret (how do you *understand* it?); to take as meant or implied; to infer; to assume; to supply or leave to be supplied mentally; to recognize as implied or meant although not expressed. —*To give to understand, to let understand, to make understand*, to tell; to inform; to let know. —*v.i.* To have the use of the intellectual faculties; to have understanding; to be informed by another; to learn.—**Understanding**, un-dėr-stan′ding, *a.* Knowing; skilful; intelligent.—*n.* The act of one who understands or comprehends; comprehension; apprehension and appreciation; discernment; intelligence between two or more persons; anything mutually understood or agreed upon; that power by which we perceive, conceive, and apprehend; that mental faculty which comprehends the just import, relations, and value of all notions and ideas, however derived; the faculty of forming judgments on the communications made through the senses; in a more popular sense, clear insight and intelligence in practical matters; wisdom and discernment.

Understate, un-dėr-stāt′, *v.t.* To state or represent less strongly than the truth will bear; to state too low. —**Understatement**, un-dėr-stāt′ment, *n.* The act of understating; a statement under the truth.

Understock, un-dėr-stok′, *v.t.* To supply insufficiently with stock (a farm).

Understrapper, un′dėr-strap-ėr, *n.* [Comp. *strapper*, in local sense of groom.] A petty fellow; an inferior agent.

Understratum, un′dėr-strā-tum, *n.* A substratum; subsoil.

Understroke, un-dėr-strōk′, *v.t.* To underline; to underscore.—*n.* (un′dėr-strōk). A stroke or line under.

Understudy, un′dėr-stu-di, *n.* A player who makes a study of a theatrical part so as to be able to take it in the absence of the regular performer.

Undertake, un-dėr-tāk′, *v.t.*—pret. *undertook*, pp. *undertaken*, ppr. *undertaking*. To take on one's self; to lay one's self under obligations to perform or execute; to pledge one's self to do: often with infinitives; to engage in; to take in hand; to set about; to attempt; to warrant; to answer for; to guarantee: often governing a clause (*undertook* that he would go). —**Undertaker**, un-dėr-tā′kėr, *n.* One who undertakes any business.—(un″dėr-tāk′ėr). One who directs and provides things necessary for a funeral; one who has an undertaking establishment; a mortician.—**Undertaking**, un-dėr-tāk′ing, *n.* That which a person undertakes; an enterprise; a promise; an engagement.—(un″dėr-tāk′ing). The business of an undertaker.

Undertenant, un′dėr-ten-ant, *n.* The tenant of a tenant; one who holds lands or tenements of a tenant.

Undertone, un′dėr-tōn, *n.* A low or subdued tone; a tone lower than is usual, as in speaking.

Undertow, un′dėr-tō, *n.* A current of water below the surface in a different direction from that at the surface; the backward flow of a wave breaking on a beach.

Undervalue, un-dėr-val′ū, *v.t.* To value or estimate below the real worth; to esteem lightly; to despise; to hold in mean estimation. —**Undervaluation**, un-dėr-val′ū-ā″shon, *n.* The act of undervaluing.—**Undervaluer**, un-dėr-val′ū-ėr, *n.* One who undervalues.

Underwear, un′dėr-wār, *n.* A wearing under the outer clothing.

Underwent, un-dėr-went′, pret. of *undergo*.

Underwood, un′dėr-wụd, *n.* Small trees and bushes that grow among large trees; coppice; underbrush.

Underwork, un′dėr-wėrk, *v.t.* To work against or destroy by clandestine measures; to do like work at a less price than.

Underworld, un′dėr-wėrld, *n.* The lower world; the place of departed souls; Hades; the criminal element.

Underwrite, un-dėr-rīt′, *v.t.* To write below or under; to subscribe; to subscribe or set one's name to a policy of insurance along with others, for the purpose of becoming answerable for loss or damage to a certain amount; to issue insurance on life, fire, theft, &c.—**Underwriter**, un′dėr-rīt-ėr, *n.* A marine insurer; a person who practices the business of insuring anything, so called because he writes his name at the foot of the policy of insurance; one who insures subscriptions to stocks, bonds, &c.—**Underwriting**, un′dėr-rīt-ing, *n.*

Undescribable, un-dē-skrī′ba-bl, *a.* Incapable of being described; indescribable.

Undeserved, un-dē-zėrvd′, *a.* Not deserved; not merited.—**Undeservedly**, un-dē-zėr′ved-li, *adv.* Not according to merit or desert.—**Undeserving**, un-dē-zėr′ving, *a.* Not deserving; not having merit.

Undesigned, un-dē-zīnd′, *a.* Not intended; unintentional.—**Undesignedly**, un-dē-zīn′ed-li, *adv.* Without design or intention.—**Undesigning**, un-dē-zīn′ing, *a.* Not having any underhand design; not having any hidden motive.

Undesirable, un-dē-zī′ra-bl, *a.* Not desirable; not to be wished.

Undetermined, un-dē-tėr′mind, *a.* Not determined; not decided, fixed, or settled.

Undeviating, un-dē′vi-ā-ting, *a.* Not departing from a rule, principle, or purpose; steady; regular.

Undid, un-did′, pret. of *undo*.

Undigested, un-di-jes′ted, *a.* Not digested; not acted on or prepared by the stomach; not properly prepared or arranged; crude.

Undignified, un-dig′ni-fīd, *a.* Not dignified; not consistent with dignity.

Undiluted, un-di-lū′ted, *a.* Not diluted or mixed with water; not tempered with any admixture.

Undine, un-dēn′, *n.* [From L. *unda*, a wave.] A water-spirit of the female sex, resembling in character the sylphs or spirits of the air, and corresponding somewhat to the naiads of classical mythology.

Undiscernible, un-diz-zėr′ni-bl, *a.* That cannot be discerned or discovered; invisible.—**Undiscerning**, un-diz-zėr′ning, *a.* Not discerning; wanting judgment or discrimination.

Undischarged, un-dis-chärjd′, *a.* Not discharged; not freed from obligation.

Undisciplined, un-dis′si-plind, *a.* Not disciplined; not properly trained; raw.

Undiscoverable, un-dis-kuv′ėr-a-bl, *a.* That cannot be discovered or found out.—**Undiscovered**, un-dis-kuv′ėrd, *a.* Not discovered; not laid open to view; lying hid.

Undiscriminating, un-dis-krim′i-nā-ting, *a.* Not discriminating or distinguishing; disregarding or not perceiving differences.

Undisguised, un-dis-gīzd′, *a.* Not disguised; not covered with a mask; hence, open; candid; artless.

Undishonored, un-dis-on′ėrd, *a.* Not dishonored; not disgraced.

Undismayed, un-dis-mād′, *a.* Not dismayed; not disheartened by fear; undaunted.

Undisposed, un-dis-pōzd′, *a.* Not set apart; not allocated; not appropriated: with *of* (goods *undisposed of*).

Undisputed, un-dis-pū′ted, *a.* Not disputed; not called in question.

Undissolvable, un-diz-zol′va-bl, *a.* Incapable of being dissolved or melted; incapable of being loosened or broken.—**Undissolved**, un-diz-zolvd′, *a.* Not dissolved; not melted; not loosened, broken, &c.

Undistinguishable, un-dis-ting′gwish-a-bl, *a.* Incapable of being distinguished by the eye; not to be distinctly seen; not to be known or distinguished by the intellect by any peculiar property. —**Undistinguishably**, un-dis-ting′gwish-a-bli, *adv.* So as not to be distinguished. —**Undistinguished**, un-dis-ting′gwisht, *a.* Not having any distinguishing mark; not treated with any particular respect; not famous; not distinguished by any particular eminence.

Undisturbed, un-dis-tėrbd′, *a.* Free from interruption; not molested or hindered; calm; tranquil; not agitated.—**Undisturbedly**, un-dis-tėr′bed-li, *adv.* Calmly; peacefully.

Undiversified, un-di-vėr′si-fīd, *a.* Not diversified or varied; uniform.

Undiverted, un-di-vėr′ted, *a.* Not diverted; not turned aside; not amused.

Undivided, un-di-vī′ded, *a.* Not divided; unbroken; whole (one's *undivided* attention).

Undo, un-dö′, *v.t.*—pret. *undid*; pp. *undone*. [With *un-* in sense of reversal. UN-.] To reverse, as something which has been done; to annul; to untie or unfasten; to unravel; to open out; to bring ruin or distress upon; to ruin the morals, reputation, or prospects of; to destroy; to impoverish.—**Undoer**, un-dö′ėr, *n.* One who undoes; one who reverses what has been done; one who ruins. —**Undoing**, un-dö′ing, *n.* The reversal of what has been done; ruin; destruction. —**Undone**, un-dun′, *pp.* Untied or unfastened; reversed; ruined.

Undo, un-dö′, *v.t.* [With *un-*, not.] To leave unperformed.—**Undone**, un′dun, *pp.* Not done or performed.

Undoubted, un-dou′ted, *a.* Not doubted; not called in question; indubitable; indisputable. —**Undoubtedly**, un-dou′ted-li, *adv.* Without question; indubitably. —**Undoubting**, un-dou′ting, *a.* Not doubting; not hesitating respecting facts; not fluctuating in uncertainty. —**Undoubtingly**, un-dou′ting-li, *adv.* Without doubting.

Undraw, un-dra̤′, *v.t.* To draw aside or open. —**Undrawn**, un-dra̤n′, *p.* and *a.* Not drawn; not pulled; not portrayed; drawn aside.

Undreamed, Undreamt, un-drēmd′, un-dremt′, *a.* Not dreamed; not thought of; not imagined; often followed by *of*.

Undress, un-dres′, *v.t.* To divest of clothes; to strip; to disrobe; to take the dressing or bandages from.—*v.i.* To take off one's dress or clothes.—*n.* (un′dres). A loose negligent dress; also, ordinary dress, as opposed to full dress or uniform.—**Undressed**, un-drest′, *p.* and *a.* Divested of dress; not attired; not prepared; in a raw state.

Undrinkable, un-dring′ka-bl, *a.* Not drinkable; not fit for drinking.

Undue, un-dū′, *a.* Not due; not yet demandable by right (a debt, money); not right; not lawful; improper; unworthy; erring by excess; excessive; inordinate (an *undue* attachment to forms). —**Unduly**, un-dū′li, *adv.* Improperly; unlawfully; unwarrantably; inordinately.

Undulate, un′dū-lāt, *v.i.*—*undulated, undulating*. [L.L. *undulo, undulatum*, from L. *undula*, a little wave, dim. of *unda*, a wave (seen also in *inundate, abundant, abound, redundant*, &c.); from a root seen also in E. *water*.] To have a wavy motion; to rise and fall in waves; to move in curving or bending lines; to wave.—*v.t.* To cause to wave, or move with a wavy motion.—**Undulate, Undulated**, un′dū-lāt, un′dū-lā-ted, *a.* Wavy; having a waved surface.—**Undulating**, un′dū-lā-ting, *p.* and *a.* Waving; rising and falling like waves; in form resembling a series of waves; wavy.—**Undulatingly**, un′dū-lā-ting-li, *adv.* In an undulating manner. — **Undulation**, un-dū-lā′shon, *n.* The act of undulating; a waving motion; a wavy form; *physics*, a vibratory motion transmitted through some fluid medium by impulses communicated to the medium; any one vibration of such fluid. — **Undulatory**, un′dū-la-to-ri, *a.* Having an undulating character; moving in the manner of waves; pertaining to such a motion. — *Undulatory theory*, the theory which regards light as the effect on the eye of vibrations propagated from a luminous source by undulations in the subtle medium (ether) presumed to pervade all space.

Unduly. Under UNDUE.

Undutiful, un-dū′ti-ful, *a.* Not dutiful; not performing or not in accordance with duty; disobedient; rebellious; irreverent.—**Undutifully**, un-dū′ti-ful-li, *adv.* In an undutiful manner.—**Undutifulness**, un-dū′ti-ful-nes, *n.*

Undying, un-dī′ing, *a.* Not dying; not subject to death; immortal.

Unearned, un-ėrnd′, *a.* Not merited by labour or services.—*Unearned increment*, the increase in the value of land not due to any expenditure on the part of the owner, as when it arises from growth of population.

Unearth, un-ėrth′, *v.t.* To drive or bring forth from an earth or burrow; to bring to light; to discover or find out. — **Unearthly**, un-ėrth′li, *a.* Not earthly; not terrestrial; supernatural; weird.

Uneasy, un-ē′zi, *a.* Feeling some degree of pain either mental or physical; unquiet; troubled; anxious; constrained; cramped; stiff; awkward; causing constraint, discomfort, or want of ease; irksome.—**Uneasily**, un-ē′zi-li, *adv.* In an uneasy manner.—**Uneasiness**, un-ē′zi-nes, *n.* The state of being uneasy; want of ease or comfort, physical or mental.

Uneatable, un-ē′ta-bl, *a.* Not eatable; not fit to be eaten.

Uneclipsed, un-ē-klipst′, *a.* Not eclipsed; not dimmed or lessened in brightness or splendour.

Unedified, un-ed′i-fīd, *a.* Not edified.—**Unedifying**, un-ed′i-fī-ing, *a.* Not edifying; not improving to the mind.

Uneducated, un-ed′ū-kā-ted, *a.* Not educated; illiterate.

Unembarrassed, un-em-bar′ast, *a.* Not embarrassed; not perplexed or put to some confusion of feeling; free from pecuniary difficulties.

Unembellished, un-em-bel′isht, *a.* Not embellished.

Unembodied, un-em-bod′id, *a.* Free from a corporeal body; disembodied; not embodied; not collected into a body (*unembodied* militia).

Unemotional, un-ē-mō′shon-al, *a.* Not emotional; free from emotion or feeling; impassive.

Unemphatic, Unemphatical, un-em-fat′ik, un-em-fat′i-kal, *a.* Not emphatic; having no emphasis or stress of voice.—**Unemphatically**, un-em-fat′i-kal-li, *adv.* In an unemphatic manner; with no emphasis.

Unemployed, un-em-ploid′, *n.* Not employed; having no work or occupation; at leisure; not being in use.—*The unemployed*, work-people who are out of work.

Unending, un-en′ding, *a.* Not ending; having no end; perpetual; eternal.

Unendowed, un-en-doud′, *a.* Not endowed; not furnished; having no endowment or settled fund.

Unendurable, un-en-dū′ra-bl, *a.* Not to be endured; intolerable.

Unenfranchised, un-en-fran′chīzd, *a.* Not having the franchise or right to vote; disfranchised.

Unengaged, un-en-gājd′, *a.* Not engaged; free from obligation to any person; free from attachment that binds; disengaged; unoccupied; not busy.

Unenglish, un-ing′glish, *a.* Not English; not characteristic or worthy of Englishmen; opposed in character or feeling to what is English.

Unenjoyed, un-en-joid′, *a.* Not enjoyed; not experienced with pleasure; not obtained; not possessed.

Unenlightened, un-en-lī′tend, *a.* Not enlightened; not mentally or morally illuminated.

Unenlivened, un-en-lī′vend, *a.* Not enlivened; not rendered, gay, cheerful, or animated.

Unenterprising, un-en′tėr-prī-zing, *a.* Not enterprising; not adventurous.

Unentertaining, un-en′tėr-tā-ning, *a.* Not entertaining or amusing.

Unenviable, un-en′vi-a-bl, *a.* Not enviable; not to be envied or viewed with envy (an *unenviable* notoriety).—**Unenvied**, un-en′vid, *a.* Not envied; exempt from envy.

Unequable, un-ē′kwa-bl, *a.* Not equable; not uniform; changeful; fitful.

Unequal, un-ē′kwal, *a.* Not equal; not of the same size, length, breadth, quantity, quality, strength, talents, age, station; inadequate; insufficient; not equable or uniform. — **Unequaled**, un-ē′kwald, *a.* Not to be equaled; unparalleled; unrivalled.—**Unequally**, un-ē′kwal-li, *adv.* In an unequal manner or degree.

Unequivocal, un-ē-kwiv′ō-kal, *a.* Not equivocal; not doubtful; clear; evident; not ambiguous.—**Unequivocally**, un-ē-kwiv′ō-kal-li, *adv.* In an unequivocal manner.

Unerring, un-er′ing, *a.* Committing no mistake; incapable of error; incapable of missing the mark; certain.—**Unerringly**, un-er′ing-li, *adv.* In an unerring manner.

Unessential, un-es-sen′shal, *a.* Not essential; not constituting the real essence; not absolutely necessary; not of prime importance.—*n.* Something not essential or of absolute necessity.

Uneven, un-ē′vn, *a.* Not level, smooth, or plain; rough; not straight; crooked; not uniform or equable; changeable; not fair, just, or true; *arith.* odd; not divisible by 2 without a remainder.—**Unevenly**, un-ē′vn-li, *adv.* In an uneven manner.—**Unevenness**, un-ē′vn-nes, *n.* The state or quality of being uneven; inequality of surface; want of uniformity; variableness.

Unexamined, un-eg-zam′ind, *a.* Not interrogated judicially; not submitted to inquiry, investigation, discussion, or the like.

Unexceptionable, un-ek-sep′shon-a-bl, *a.* Not liable to any exception or objection; unobjectionable; faultless; excellent; admirable. — **Unexceptionably**, un-ek-sep′shon-a-bli, *adv.* In an unexceptionable manner; perfectly; admirably.

Unexecuted, un-ek′sē-kū-ted, *a.* Not executed; not performed; not having the proper attestations or forms that give validity.

Unexhausted, un-egz-has′ted, *a.* Not exhausted; not spent or used up; not worn out with fatigue.

Unexpected, un-eks-pek′ted, *a.* Not expected; not looked for; unforeseen; sudden.—**Unexpectedly**, un-eks-pek′ted-li, *adv.* At a time or in a manner not expected or looked for; suddenly.

Unexpired, un-eks-pīrd′, *a.* Not having come to an end or termination; not having reached the date at which it is due (an *unexpired* promissory note or bill).

Unexplored, un-eks-plōrd′, *a.* Not explored; not examined by any traveller.

Unexposed, un-eks-pōzd′, *a.* Not exposed; not laid out or open to view; sheltered.

Unfading, un-fā′ding, *a.* Not liable to fade; not losing strength or freshness of colouring; not liable to wither or to decay.

Unfailing, un-fā′ling, *a.* Not liable to fail; ever fulfilling a hope, promise, or want; sure; certain.

Unfair, un-fār′, *a.* Not fair; not honest; not impartial; disingenuous; using trick or artifice; proceeding from trick or dishonesty.—**Unfairly**, un-fār′li, *adv.* In an unfair or unjust manner.—**Unfairness**, un-fār′nes, *n.* The character of being unfair; injustice; bias.

Unfaithful, un-fāth′ful, *a.* Not observant of promises, vows, allegiance, or duty; faithless; violating trust or confidence; violating the wedding vow. — **Unfaithfully**, un-fāth′ful-li, *adv.* In an unfaithful manner.—**Unfaithfulness**, un-fāth′fulnes, *n.* The quality of being unfaithful.

Unfamiliar, un-fa-mil′yėr, *a.* Not familiar; not well known by frequent use; having an element of strangeness.—**Unfamiliarity**, un-fa-mil′i-ar″i-ti, *n.* The state of being unfamiliar.

Unfashionable, un-fash′on-a-bl, *a.* Not according to the prevailing fashion or mode; not complying in dress or manners with the reigning custom.

Unfasten, un-fas′n, *v.t.* To loose; to unbind; to untie.

Unfathered, un-fä′ᴛʜėrd, *a.* Having no father; fatherless; having no acknowledged father. — **Unfatherly**, un-fä′ᴛʜėr-li, *a.* Not becoming to a father; unkind.

Unfathomable, un-faᴛʜ′um-a-bl, *a.* Incapable of being fathomed or sounded; too deep to be measured.

Unfavorable, un-fā′vėr-a-bl, *a.* Not favorable; not propitious; discouraging; giving an adverse judgment or opinion; somewhat prejudicial.—**Unfavorably**, un-fā′vėr-a-bli, *adv.* In an unfavorable manner; adversely; with some censure.

Unfeeling, un-fē′ling, *a.* Devoid of feeling; insensible; without sensibility; devoid of sympathy with others; hard-hearted.—**Unfeelingly**, un-fē′ling-li, *adv.* In an unfeeling or cruel manner.

Unfeigned, un-fānd′, *a.* Not feigned; not counterfeit; not hypocritical; real; sincere.—**Unfeignedly**, un-fā′ned-li, *adv.* In an unfeigned manner.

Unfelt, un-felt′, *a.* Not felt; not perceived.

Unfeminine, un-fem′in-in, *a.* Not feminine; not according to the female character or manners.

Unfenced, un-fenst′, *a.* Having no fence.

Unfermented, un-fėr-men′ted, *a.* Not fermented; not having undergone fermentation, as liquor; not leavened or made with yeast, as bread.

Unfetter, un-fet′ėr, *v.t.* To loose from fetters; to unchain; to unshackle; to free from restraint; to set at liberty.—**Unfettered**, un-fet′ėrd, *a.* Unshackled; free from restraint; unrestrained.

Unfilial, un-fil′i-al, *a.* Unsuitable to a son or daughter; not becoming a child.

Unfinished, un-fin′isht, *a.* Not finished; not complete; imperfect; wanting the last hand or touch.

Unfit, un-fit′, *a.* Not fit; improper; unsuitable; unbecoming: said of things; wanting suitable qualifications, physical or moral; not suited or adapted; not competent: of persons. — *v.t.* To render unfit; to make unsuitable; to deprive of the strength, skill, or proper qualities for anything.—**Unfitly**, un-fit′li, *adv.* In an unfit manner; not properly; unsuitably.—**Unfitness**, un-fit′nes, *n.* The quality of being unfit.—**Unfitted**, un-fit′ed, *p.* and *a.* Rendered or being unfit; unsuitable.—**Unfitting**, un-fit′ing, *a.* Improper; unbecoming.

Unfix, un-fiks′, *v.t.* To make no longer fixed or firm; to loosen from any fastening; to detach; to unsettle.—**Unfixed**, un-fikst′, *p.* and *a.* Not fixed; loosened; erratic; inconstant; irresolute; undetermined.—**Unfixedness**, un-fik′sed-nes, *n.* The state of being unfixed or unsettled.

Unflagging, un-flag′ing, *a.* Not flagging; not drooping; maintaining strength or spirit.

Unflattering, un-flat′ėr-ing, *a.* Not flattering; not colouring the truth to please; not affording a favourable prospect.

Unfledged, un-flejd′, *a.* Not yet furnished with feathers; not having attained to full growth or experience.

Unflinching, un-flinch′ing, *a.* Not flinching; not shrinking.

Unfold, un-fōld′, *v.t.* To open the folds of; to expand; to spread out; to lay open to view or contemplation; to disclose; to reveal. — *v.i.* To become gradually expanded; to open out; to become disclosed or developed; to develop itself.

Unforbidden, Unforbid, un-for-bid′n, un-for-bid′, *a.* Not forbidden; not prohibited; allowed; permitted.

Unforced, un-fōrst′, *a.* Not forced or compelled; not constrained; not feigned; not artificially assumed or heightened; not strained; easy; natural.

Unforeseen, un-fōr-sēn′, *a.* Not foreseen; not foreknown.—*The unforeseen*, that which is not foreseen or expected.

Unforgivable, un-for-giv′a-bl, *a.* Incapable of being forgiven; unpardonable.—**Unforgiven**, un-for-giv′n, *a.* Not forgiven; not pardoned. — **Unforgiving**, un-for-giv′ing, *a.* Not forgiving; not disposed to overlook or pardon offences; implacable.

Unforgotten, Unforgot, un-for-got′n, un-for-got′, *a.* Not forgot; not lost to memory; not overlooked; not neglected.

Unformed, un-formd′, *p.* and *a.* Not having been formed; not fashioned; not moulded into regular shape.

Unfortified, un-for′ti-fīd, *a.* Not fortified; not having fortifications; not strengthened by means of adventitious spirit, as wine.

Unfortunate, un-for′tū-nit, *a.* Not successful; not prosperous; unlucky; unhappy. —*n.* One who is unfortunate; a woman who has lapsed from virtue; a prostitute.—**Unfortunately**, un-for′tū-nāt-li, *adv.* In an unfortunate manner; by ill fortune; unhappily.

Unfounded, un-foun′ded, *a.* Having no real foundation; groundless; idle; baseless.

Unfranchised, un-fran′chīzd, *a.* Not franchized; disfranchised.

Unfree, un-frē′, *a.* Not free; in bondage.

Unfrequent, un-frē′kwent, *a.* Not frequent; infrequent.—**Unfrequented**, un-frē-kwen′ted, *a.* Rarely visited; seldom resorted to by human beings; solitary.

Unfriended, un-fren′ded, *a.* Wanting friends; not countenanced or supported.—**Unfriendliness**, un-frend′li-nes, *n.* The quality of being unfriendly; want of kindness; disfavour.—**Unfriendly**, un-frend′li, *a.* Not friendly; not kind or benevolent; not favourable.—*adv.* In an unkind manner; not as a friend.

Unfrock, un-frok′, *v.t.* To deprive or divest of a frock; hence, to deprive of the character and privileges of a priest or clergyman.

Unfruitful, un-fröt′ful, *a.* Not producing fruit or offspring; barren; unproductive; not fertile (an *unfruitful* soil); not productive of good (an *unfruitful* life); fruitless; ineffectual. — **Unfruitfulness**, un-fröt′ful-nes, *n.* The quality of being unfruitful.

Unfulfilled, un-ful-fild′, *a.* Not fulfilled; not accomplished.

Unfunded, un-fun′ded, *a.* Not funded; having no permanent fund established for the payment of its interest: said of government debt when it exists in the form of treasury notes or the like.

Unfurl, un-fėrl′, *v.t.* To loose from a furled state; to expand to the wind.

Unfurnish, un-fėr′nish, *v.t.* To strip of furniture; to strip in general. — **Unfurnished**, un-fėr′nisht, *a.* Not furnished; not supplied with furniture; unsupplied; unprovided in general.

Ungainly, un-gān′li, *a.* [From *un-*, not, and old *gainly*, *geinly*, from Icel, *gegn*, ready, serviceable; akin to *-gain* in *again.*] Clumsy; awkward; uncouth; ill-shaped in person.—**Ungainliness**, un-gān′li-nes, *n.* The state or character of being ungainly; clumsiness; awkwardness.

Ungallant, un-gal′ant, *a.* Not gallant; uncourtly to ladies.

Ungathered, un-gaтн′ėrd, *a.* Not gathered; not culled; not picked.

Ungenerous, un-jen′ėr-us, *a.* Not generous; not showing generosity or liberality of mind or sentiments; illiberal; mean.—**Ungenerously**, un-jen′ėr-us-li, *adv.* In an ungenerous manner; illiberally.

Ungenteel, un-jen-tēl′, *a.* Not genteel; unpolite; rude: of persons or manners.—**Ungenteelly**, un-jen-tēl′li, *adv.* In an ungenteel manner.

Ungentle, un-jen′tl, *a.* Not gentle; harsh; rude.

Ungentlemanlike, un-jen′tl-man-līk, *a.* Not like or becoming a gentleman.

Ungentlemanly, un-jen′tl-man-li, *a.* Not becoming a gentleman; such as no gentleman would do.

Ungifted, un-gif′ted, *a.* Not gifted; not endowed with peculiar faculties.

Ungird, un-gėrd′, *v.t.* To loose or free from a girdle or band; to divest of a girdle or what is girt on; to unbind.

Unglazed, un-glāzd′, *a.* Not furnished with glass (as windows); wanting glass windows; not covered with vitreous matter (*unglazed* pottery).

Unglove, un-gluv′, *v.t.* To take off the glove or gloves from.

Unglue, un-glö′, *v.t.* To separate, as anything that is glued or cemented.

Ungodly, un-god′li, *a.* Not godly; careless of God; godless; wicked; impious; sinful.—**Ungodliness**, un-god′li-nes, *n.* Impiety; wickedness.

Ungovernable, un-guv′ėr-na-bl, *a.* Incapable of being governed, ruled, or restrained; refractory; unruly; wild; unbridled.—**Ungovernableness**, un-guv′ėr-na-bl-nes, *n.* — **Ungovernably**, un-guv′ėr-na-bli, *adv.* In an ungovernable manner.—**Ungoverned**, un-guv′ėrnd, *a.* Not governed; unbridled; licentious.

Ungraceful, un-grās′ful, *a.* Not graceful; wanting grace and elegance; inelegant; clumsy. — **Ungracefully**, un-grās′ful-li, *adv.* In an ungraceful manner; awkwardly; inelegantly. — **Ungracefulness**, un-grās′ful-nes, *n.* The quality of being ungraceful.

Ungracious, un-grā′shus, *a.* Unmannerly; rude; not well received; not favoured.—**Ungraciously**, un-grā′shus-li, *adv.* In an ungracious manner.—**Ungraciousness**, un-grā′shus-nes, *n.* State of being ungracious.

Ungrammatical, un-gram-mat′i-kal, *a.* Not according to the rules of grammar.—**Ungrammatically**, un-gram-mat′i-kal-li, *adv.* In a manner contrary to the rules of grammar.

Ungrateful, un-grāt′ful, *a.* Not grateful; not feeling thankful or showing gratitude; making ill returns for kindness; unpleasing; unacceptable; disagreeable; harsh.—**Ungratefully**, un-grāt′ful-li, *adv.* In an ungrateful manner.—**Ungratefulness**, un-grāt′ful-nes, *n.* The state or character of being ungrateful; ingratitude. — **Ungratified**, un-grat′i-fīd, *a.* Not gratified; not satisfied; not indulged.

Ungrounded, un-groun′ded, *a.* Having no foundation or support; groundless; baseless; unfounded.

Ungrudging, un-gruj′ing, *a.* Not grudging; freely giving; liberal; hearty.—**Ungrudgingly**, un-gruj′ing-li, *adv.* In an ungrudging manner.

Ungual, ung′gwal, *a.* [From L. *unguis*, a nail, claw, or hoof.] Pertaining to a nail, claw, or hoof; having a nail, claw, or hoof. —**Unguicular**, ung-gwik′ū-lėr, *a.* [L. *unguiculus*, dim. of *unguis.*] Pertaining to a claw or nail.—**Unguiculate, Unguiculated**, ung-gwik′ū-lāt, ung-gwik′ū-lā-ted, *a.* Clawed; having claws. — **Unguiferous**, ung-gwif′ėr-us, *a.* [L. *unguis*, and *fero*, I bear.] Producing, having, or supporting nails or claws. — **Unguiform**, ung′gwi-form, *a.* Claw-shaped.

Unguarded, un-gär′ded, *a.* Not guarded; having no guard or watch; not being on one's guard; not attentive to danger; not cautious; negligent; not done or spoken with caution. — **Unguardedly**, un-gär′ded-li, *adv.* In an unguarded manner.—**Unguardedness**, un-gär′ded-nes, *n.* State of being unguarded.

Unguent, ung′gwent, *n.* [L. *unguentum*, from *ungo*, to anoint. UNCTION.] Any soft composition used as an ointment, or for the lubrication of machinery.

Unguicular, Unguiferous, &c. Under UNGUAL.

Unguided, un-gī′ded, *a.* Not guided, led, or conducted; not regulated; ungoverned.

Unguinous, ung′gwi-nus, *a.* [L. *unguinosus*, from *unguen*, *unguinis*, fat, from *ungo*, to anoint. UNCTION.] Oily; unctuous; fatty; greasy.

Unguis, ung′gwis, *n.* pl. **Ungues**, ung′gwēz. [L., nail or claw.] A nail, claw, or hoof of an animal. *Bot.* a claw-like portion of a petal.

Ungula, ung′gū-la, *n.* [L. *ungula*, a hoof, dim. of *unguis*, a nail or claw. UNGUAL.] A hoof, as of a horse; *geom.* a part cut from a cylinder, cone, &c., by a plane passing obliquely through the base and part of the curved surface: so named from its shape.—**Ungulata**, ung-gū-lā′ta, *n.pl.* The hoofed quadrupeds, a large and important order of the mammalia, including the pig, horse, rhinoceros, &c., in one section; and the ox, sheep, deer, and all other ruminants in another. ARTIODACTYLE, PERISSODACTYLE.—**Ungulate**, ung′gū-lāt, *n.* A hoofed quadruped; one of the order Ungulata or hoofed animals.—*a.* Hoof-shaped; having hoofs.—**Unguled**, *a.* *Her.* an adjective applied to the hoofs of animals to signify that they are of a different tincture from the rest of the body.

Unhackneyed, un-hak′nid, *a.* Not hackneyed; not stale, flat, or commonplace from frequent use or repetition.

Unhallowed, un-hal′ōd, *a.* Not hallowed, consecrated, or dedicated to sacred purposes; unholy; profane; impious.

Unhampered, un-ham′pėrd, *a.* Not hampered, hindered, or restricted.

Unhand, un-hand′, *v.t.* To take the hand or hands from; to release from a grasp; to let go.

Unhandily, Unhandiness. Under UNHANDY.

Unhandled, un-han′dld, *a.* Not handled; not touched; not treated or managed.

Unhandsome, un-hand′sum, *a.* Not handsome; not well-formed; not beautiful; not generous or liberal; unfair; mean; unbecoming. — **Unhandsomely**, un-hand′sum-li, *adv.* In an unhandsome manner. — **Unhandsomeness**, un-hand′sum-nes, *n.*

Unhandy, un-han′di, *a.* Not handy; not dexterous; not skilful and ready in the use of the hands; not convenient; awkward. —**Unhandily**, un-han′di-li, *adv.* In an unhandy manner. — **Unhandiness**, un-han′di-nes, *n.*

Unhanged, Unhung, un-hangd′, un-hung′, *a.* Not hung or hanged; not punished by hanging.

Unhappy, un-hap′i, *a.* Not happy; not cheerful or gay; in some degree miserable or wretched; marked by ill fortune or mishap; ill-omened; evil. — **Unhappily**, un-hap′i-li, *adv.* In an unhappy manner; unfortunately; by ill fortune; as ill luck would have it.—**Unhappiness**, un-hap′i-nes, *n.* The state of being unhappy; misfortune; ill luck.

Unharbor, un-här'bėr, *v.t.* To drive from harbor or shelter; to dislodge.

Unharmed, un-härmd'. *a.* Not harmed or injured.

Unhat, un-hat', *v.t.* and *i.* To take off the hat, as in respect or reverence.

Unhealthy, un-hel'thi, *a.* Wanting health; not sound and vigorous of body; habitually weak or indisposed; wanting vigour of growth; unfavourable to the preservation of health (an *unhealthy* season or city); adapted to generate disease; unwholesome; insalubrious (an *unhealthy* climate); not indicating health; resulting from bad health; morbid. — **Unhealthily**, un-hel'thi-li, *adv.* In an unwholesome or unsound manner.—**Unhealthiness**, un-hel'thi-nes, *n.* The state or quality of being unhealthy.

Unheard, un-hėrd', *a.* Not heard; not perceived by the ear; not admitted to audience. —*Unheard-of*, unprecedented; such as was never known before; not known to fame; not celebrated.

Unhedged un-hejd', *a.* Not surrounded by a hedge; not shut in or inclosed.

Unheeded, un-hē'ded, *a.* Not heeded; disregarded; neglected; unnoticed.—**Unheededly**, un-hē'ded-li, *adv.* Without being noticed.—**Unheedful**, un-hēd'ful, *a.* Not heedful; unheeding; not cautious; inattentive; careless; inconsiderate.—**Unheedfully**, un-hēd'ful-li, *adv.* In an unheedful manner. — **Unheeding**, un-hē'ding, *a.* Not heeding; careless; negligent.

Unhesitating, un-hez'i-tā-ting, *a.* Not hesitating; not remaining in doubt; prompt; ready. — **Unhesitatingly**, un-hez'i-tā-ting-li, *adv.* Without hesitation.

Unhinge, un-hinj', *v.t.* To take from the hinges; to unsettle; to render unstable or wavering; to discompose or disorder (the mind, opinions); to put quite out of sorts; to incapacitate by disturbing the nerves.

Unhit, un-hit', *a.* Not hit; not receiving a stroke or blow.

Unhitch, un-hich', *v.t.* To disengage from a fastening.

Unholy, un-hō'li, *a.* Not holy; not sacred; not hallowed or consecrated; impious; wicked.—**Unholily**, un-hō'li-li, *adv.* In an unholy manner. — **Unholiness**, un-hō'li-nes, *n.* The quality or state of being unholy.

Unhonored, un-on'ėrd, *a.* Not honored; not regarded with veneration; not celebrated.

Unhook, un-hök', *v.t.* To loose from a hook; to undo the hook or hooks of.

Unhoped, un-hōpt', *a.* Not hoped for; not so probable as to excite hope.—*Unhoped-for*, unhoped; not hoped for.—**Unhopeful**, un-hōp'ful, *a.* Not hopeful; hopeless.

Unhorse, un-hors', *v.t.* To throw or strike from a horse; to cause to fall from the saddle; to remove the horse or horses from.

Unhouse, un-houz', *v.t.* To drive from the house or habitation; to deprive of shelter.—**Unhoused**, un-houzd', *p.* and *a.* Having no house or home; deprived of a house, home, roof, or shelter.

Unhouseled,‡ **Unhouselled**,‡ un-hou'-zeld, *a.* [HOUSEL.] Not having received the sacrament. (*Shak.*)

Unhurt, un-hėrt', *a.* Not hurt; not harmed; free from wound or injury.—**Unhurtful**, un-hėrt'ful, *a.* Not hurtful.

Unhusk, un-husk', *v.t.* To deprive of husks.

Uniat, ū'ni-at, *n.* One of the Oriental Christian Churches, which, while having its own religious forms, recognizes unity under Papal supremacy.

Uniaxial, **Uniaxal**, ū-ni-ak'si-al, ū-ni-ak'-sal, *a.* [L. *unus*, one, and *axis*.] Having but one axis.

Unicameral, ū-ni-kam'ėr-al, *a.* [L. *unus*, one, *camera*, a chamber.] Consisting of a single chamber: said of a legislative body.

Unicellular, ū-ni-sel'ū-lėr, *a.* [L. *unus*, one, and E. *cellular*.] Consisting of a single cell; exhibiting only a single cell.

Unicity, ū-nis'i-ti, *n.* [L. *unicus*, single, from *unus*, one.] The state of being unique, or of forming one individual.

Uniclinal, ū-ni-klī'nal, *a.* [L. *unus*, one, and *clino*, to slope.] Inclined in one direction only; *geol.* applied to a bend or inclination of a stratum either up or down: opposed to *anticlinal* and *synclinal*.

Unicorn, ū'ni-korn, *n.* [L. *unicornis*, one-horned—*unus*, one, and *cornu*, horn.] An animal with one horn; a fabulous animal having the head, neck, and body of a horse, the legs of a deer, the tail of a lion, and a long horn growing out of the forehead.—*Sea unicorn*, the narwal or narwhal. — **Unicornous**, ū-ni-kor'nus, *a.* Having only one horn.

Unicostate, ū-ni-kos'tāt, *a.* [L. *unus*, one, and *costa*, a rib.] *Bot.* having one large vein running down the centre, called the *midrib*.

Unifacial, ū-ni-fā'shi-al, *a.* [L. *unus*, one, and *facies*, a face.] Having but one front surface.

Unific, ū-nif'ik, *a.* [L. *unus*, one, and *facio*, to make.] Making one; forming unity.—**Unification**, ū'ni-fi-kā"shon, *n.* The act of uniting into one.

Unifilar, ū-ni-fī'lėr, *a.* [L. *unus*, one, and *filum*, a thread.] Having only one thread: applied to a magnetometer consisting of a magnetic bar suspended by a single thread.

Uniflorous, ū-ni-flō'rus, *a.* [L. *unus*, one, and *flos*, *floris*, flower.] *Bot.* bearing one flower only.

Uniflow-engine, ū'ni-flō, *n.* A type of steam-engine in which expansion takes place in a single cylinder, having inlet ports at each end, and the exhaust port in the middle, thus minimizing condensation of the entering steam.

Uniform, ū'ni-form, *a.* [Fr. *uniforme*, L. *uniformis*—*unus*, one, and *forma*, form.] Having always the same form; not changing in shape, appearance, character, &c.; not varying in degree or rate; equable; invariable; of the same kind or matter all through; homogeneous; consistent at all times; conforming to one rule or mode. —*n.* A dress of the same kind, fabrics, fashion, or general appearance as others worn by the members of the same body, whether military, naval, or any other, intended as a distinctive costume.—**Uniformitarian**, ū-ni-for'mi-tā"ri-an, *n.* One who upholds a system or doctrine of uniformity; one who maintains that all geologic changes and phenomena are due to agencies working uniformly and uninterruptedly, and of the same character as those we still see in operation, as opposed to a *catastrophist*.—*a.* Pertaining to uniformity or some doctrine of uniformity. — **Uniformitarianism**, ū-ni-for'mi-tā"ri-an-izm, *n.* The doctrine of continuity as regards the action of geological agents.—**Uniformity**, ū-ni-for'mi-ti, *n.* The state or character of being uniform; a state of matters in which sameness is exhibited; freedom from variation or difference; conformity to one type. — *Act of uniformity*, in *Eng. hist.* an act of parliament passed in the reign of Charles II (1662) regulating the form of worship to be observed in all the churches.—**Uniformly**, ū'ni-form-li, *adv.* In a uniform manner; invariably. — **Uniformness**, ū'ni-form-nes, *n.* State of being uniform; uniformity.

Unify, ū'ni-fi, *v.t.* [L. *unus*, one, and *facio*, to make.] To form into one; to reduce to unity; to view as one.—**Unification**, ū'ni-fi-kā"shon, *n.* The act of unifying.

Unigeniture, ū-ni-jen'i-tūr, *n.* [From L. *unigenitus*, only begotten—*unus*, one, and *genitus*, pp. of *gigno*, *genitum*, to beget.] The state of being the only begotten. — **Unigenitus**, ū'ni-gen"i-tus, *n.* The Papal Bull of 1713 issued by Clement XI against Quesnel's *Nouveau Testament... avec des Réflexions Morales*, supposed to favour Jansenism: so styled from the opening phrase, *Unigenitus Filius Dei*, the Only-Begotten Son of God.—**Unigenous**, ū-nij'-e-nus, *a.* [L. *unus*, one, and root *gen*, to beget.] Of one kind; of the same genus.

Unilateral, ū-ni-lat'ėr-al, *a.* [L. *unus*, one, and *latus*, *lateris*, side.] One-sided; pertaining to one side; *bot.* growing chiefly to one side.

Uniliteral, ū-ni-lit'ėr-al, *a.* [L. *unus*, one, and *litera*, a letter.] Consisting of one letter only.

Unilluminated, un-il-lū'mi-nā-ted, *a.* Not illuminated; not enlightened; dark: ignorant.

Unilocular, ū-ni-lok'ū-lėr, *a.* [L. *unus*, one, and *loculus*, cell, dim. of *locus*, a place.] Having one cell or chamber only; not divided into cells (a *unilocular* pericarp).

Unimaginable, un-im-aj'i-na-bl, *a.* Not capable of being imagined, conceived, or thought of; inconceivable.—**Unimaginableness**, un-im-aj'i-na-bl-nes, *n.*—**Unimaginably**, un-im-aj'i-na-bli, *adv.* — **Unimagined**, un-im-aj'ind, *a.* Not imagined, conceived, or formed in idea.

Unimpaired, un-im-pārd', *a.* Not impaired; not diminished; not enfeebled by time or injury.

Unimpassioned, un-im-pash'ond, *a.* Not impassioned; not moved or actuated by passion; calm; tranquil; not violent.

Unimpeachable, un-im-pēch'a-bl, *a.* Not impeachable; not to be called in question; blameless; irreproachable.—**Unimpeachableness**, un-im-pēch'a-bl-nes, *n.*—**Unimpeached**, un-im-pēcht', *a.* Not impeached; not called in question.

Unimportance, un-im-por'tans, *n.* Want of importance or consequence.—**Unimportant**, un-im-por'tant, *a.* Not important; not of great moment.

Unimposing, un-im-pō'zing, *a.* Not imposing; not commanding respect or awe.

Unimpressible, un-im-pres'i-bl, *a.* Not impressible; not sensitive; apathetic.

Unimproved, un-im-prövd', *a.* Not made better or wiser; not used for a valuable purpose; not tilled; not cultivated.

Unimpugnable, un-im-pū'na-bl, *a.* Not capable of being impugned; unimpeachable.

Unimuscular, ū-ni-mus'kū-lėr, *a.* [L. *unus*, one, and *musculus*, a muscle.] Having one muscle only and one muscular impression: said of bivalve molluscs.

Uninclosed, un-in-klōzd', *a.* Not inclosed; not surrounded by a fence, wall, &c.

Unincorporated, un-in-kor'po-rā-ted, *a.* Not incorporated; not mixed or united in one body; not associated or united in one body politic.

Uninhabitable, un-in-hab'i-ta-bl, *a.* Not inhabitable; unfit to be the residence of men.—**Uninhabitableness**, un-in-hab'i-ta-bl-nes, *n.*—**Uninhabited**, un-in-hab'i-ted, *a.* Not inhabited; having no inhabitants.

Uninjured, un-in'jurd, *a.* Not injured; not hurt; suffering no harm.

Uninspired, un-in-spīrd', *a.* Not having received any supernatural instruction or illumination; not produced under the direction or influence of inspiration.

Uninstructed, un-in-struk'ted, *a.* Not instructed or taught; not educated; not furnished with instructions. — **Uninstructive**, un-in-struk'tiv, *a.* Not serving to instruct or improve the mind.

Unintelligent, un-in-tel'i-jent, *a.* Not having reason or understanding; not having the mental faculties acute; not showing intelligence; dull. — **Unintelligibility**, un-in-tel'i-ji-bil"i-ti, *n.* The quality of being not intelligible.—**Unintelligible**, un-in-tel'i-ji-bl, *a.* Not intelligible; not capable of being understood; meaningless.—**Unintelligibly**, un-in-tel'i-ji-bli, *adv.* In an unintelligible manner.

Unintentional, un-in-ten'shon-al, *a.* Not intentional; done or happening without design. — **Unintentionally**, un-in-ten'-shon-al-li, *adv.* Without design or purpose.

Uninterested, un-in'tėr-es-ted, *a.* Not interested; not personally concerned; not having the mind or feelings engaged.—**Uninteresting**, un-in′tėr-es-ting, *a.* Not capable of exciting an interest, or of engaging the mind or passions.

Unintermitted, un-in′tėr-mit″ed, *a.* Not intermitted; not suspended for a time; continuous.—**Unintermittedly**, un-in′-tėr-mit″ed-li, *adv.* Uninterruptedly.—**Unintermitting**, un-in′tėr-mit″ing, *a.* Not intermitting; not ceasing for a time; incessant.

Uninterrupted, un-in′tėr-rup″ted, *a.* Not interrupted; unintermitted; incessant.—**Uninterruptedly**, un-in′tėr-rup″ted-li, *adv.* Without interruption.

Uninvited, un-in-vī′ted, *a.* Not having received an invitation: unbidden.

Union, ūn′yon, *n.* [Fr. *union*, from L. *unio*, *unionis*, oneness, unity, later a union, from *unus*, one (seen also in *unit, unity, unique, universal*, &c.); allied to E. *one*. ONE.] The act of joining two or more things into one, and thus forming a compound body; the state of being united; junction; coalition; concord; agreement and conjunction of mind, will, affections, or interest; that which is formed by a combination of individual things or persons; a combination; a confederation; a confederacy; two or more parishes united into one whole for better administration, as Union Methodist Church; a permanent combination among workmen engaged in the same occupation or trade; a trade-union; a joint, screw, &c., uniting parts of machinery, or the like; a kind of coupling; a mixed fabric of cotton, flax, jute, silk, wool, &c. —**Unionism**, ūn′yon-izm, *n.* The principle of union, attachment to the federal union of the United States.—*Trade-unionism*, designed to unite all workers into organizations for improving working conditions, *e.g.* the A. F. of L. (American Federation of Labor) and the C. I. O. (Congress of Industrial Organization).—**Unionize**, to form into a union, as the employees of a factory.—**Union Jack**, U. S. Navy, a pilot flag hoisted at the bow of a ship.

Uniparous, ū-nip′a-rus, *a.* [L. *unus*, one, *pario*, to bear.] Producing one at a birth; *bot.* having but one peduncle.

Uniped, ū′ni-ped, *n.* [L. *unus*, one, *pes*, *pedis*, a foot.] An animal having only one foot.

Unipersonal, ū-ni-pėr′son-al, *a.* [L. *unus*, one, *persona*, a person.] Having but one person; existing in one person, as the Deity; *gram.* used only in one person: said chiefly of impersonal verbs.—**Unipersonalist**, ū-ni-pėr′son-al-ist, *n.* One who believes there is but a single person in the Deity.

Unipetalous, ū-ni-pet′a-lus, *a.* [L. *unus*, one, and E. *petal*.] Having the corolla exhibiting one petal only.

Unipolar, ū-ni-pō′lėr, *a.* [L. *unus*, one, *polus*, a pole.] Having but one pole; capable of receiving only one kind of electricity.

Unique, ū-nēk′, *a.* [Fr. *unique*, from L. *unicus*, from *unus*, one. UNION.] Without a like or equal; unmatched; unequalled; single in its kind of excellence.—**Uniquely**, ū-nēk′li, *adv.* So as to be unique.—**Uniqueness**, ū-nēk′nes, *n.*

Uniseptate, ū-ni-sep′tāt, *a.* [L. *unus*, one, *septum*, a partition.] *Bot.* having but one septum or partition.

Uniserial, ū-ni-sē′ri-al, *a.* [L. *unus*, one, *series*, a row.] Having only one row or series.

Unisexual, ū-ni-sek′sū-al, *a.* [L. *unus*, one, *sexus*, a sex.] Having one sex only; *bot.* applied to plants having separate male and female flowers.

Unison, ū′ni-son, *n.* [L. *unus*, one, and *sonus*, sound. UNION, SOUND.] *Mus.* the state of sounding at the same pitch; the combination of two or more sounds equal in pitch, or at one or more octaves apart; hence, accordance; harmony.—**Unisonance**, ū-nis′ō-nans, *n.* Accordance of sounds; unison.—**Unisonant, Unisonous**, ū-nis′ō-nant, ū-nis′ō-nus, *a.* Being in unison; concordant.

Unit, ū′nit, *n.* [E. *unitas*, unity, from *unus*, one. UNION.] A single thing or person regarded as having oneness for the main attribute; a single one of a number; an individual; *arith.* one, the least whole number; *math.* and *physics*, any known determinate quantity by the constant repetition of which any other quantity of the same kind is measured (as a footpound, a gramme, a dyne); *war*, any self-contained portion of a military force, comprising men, horse, vehicles, &c., ready to act or to be employed together. There may be fighting, medical, transport, &c., units.

Unitarian, ū-ni-tā′ri-an, *n.* [From L. *unitas*, unity, from *unus*, one. UNION.] One who ascribes divinity to God the Father only; one of a religious sect distinguished by the denial of the received doctrine of the Trinity; also, a monotheist. —*a.* Pertaining to Unitarians or their doctrines.—**Unitarianism**, ū-ni-tā′ri-an-izm, *n.* The doctrines of Unitarians.

Unite, ū-nīt′, *v.t.*—*united, uniting.* [L. *unio, unitum*, from *unus*, one. UNION.] To combine or conjoin, so as to form one; to incorporate in one; to associate by some bond, legal or other; to join in interest; affection, or the like; to ally; to couple; to cause to adhere; to attach.—*v.i.* To become one; to become incorporated; to coalesce; to commingle; to join in an act; to concur.—**Unitable**, ū-nī′ta-bl, *a.* Capable of being united.—**United**, ū-nī′ted, *p.* and *a.* Joined or combined; made one. —*United Brethren*, a religious community commonly called Moravians. MORAVIAN. —*United Presbyterians*, the Presbyterian church formed in Scotland by the union in 1847 of certain bodies who had seceded from the Established Church.—**Unitedly**, ū-nī′ted-li, *adv.* In a united manner; jointly; amicably.—**Uniter**, ū-nī′tėr, *n.* The person or thing that unites.—**Unitive**, ū-ni-tiv, *a.* Having the power of uniting.

Unity, ū′ni-ti, *n.* [L. *unitas*, from *unus*, one. UNION.] The property of being one; oneness; concord; agreement; oneness of sentiment, affection, and the like; the principle by which a uniform tenor of story and propriety of representation are preserved in literary compositions; *math.* any definite quantity taken as one, or for which 1 is made to stand in calculation. —*The unities* (of *time, place*, and *action*), formerly deemed essential to a classical drama, demanded that there should be no shifting of the scene from place to place, that the whole series of events should be such as might occur within the space of a single day, and that nothing should be admitted irrelevant to the development of the single plot.

Univalent, ū-ni-vā′lent, *a.* [L. *unus*, one, *valere*, to be strong.] Having a valency of one, like a hydrogen atom.

Univalve, ū′ni-valv, *a.* [L. *unus*, one, and E. *valve*.] Having one valve only, as a shell or pericarp.—*n.* A shell having one valve only; a mollusc with a shell composed of a single piece, usually of a conical and spiral form.—**Univalved, Univalvular**, ū′ni-valvd, ū-ni-val′vū-lėr, *a.* Having one valve only; univalve.

Universal, ū-ni-vėr′sal, *a.* [L. *universalis*, from *universus*, universal, lit. turned into one—*unus*, one, and *versus*, turned. UNION, VERSE.] Extending to or comprehending the whole number, quantity, or space; pervading all or the whole; all-embracing; all-reaching; total; whole; comprising all the particulars.—*Universal church*, the church of God throughout the universe.—*Universal joint*, a form of joint or coupling allowing free swivelling in any direction.—*Universal proposition*, *logic*, one in which the subject is taken in its widest extent and the predicate applies to everything which the subject can denote.—*n.* A general notion or idea; a predicable; a universal proposition.—**Universalism**, ū-ni-vėr′sal-izm, *n.* *Theol.* the doctrine of the Universalists.—**Universalist**, ū-ni-vėr′sal-ist, *n.* One who holds the doctrine that all men will finally be saved, in opposition to the doctrine of eternal punishment.—**Universality**, ū′ni-vėr-sal″i-ti, *n.* The state of being universal.—**Universally**, ū-ni-vėr′sal-li, *adv.* In a universal manner; with extension to the whole; without exception.—**Universe**, ū′ni-vėrs, *n.* [L. *universum*, the universe, neut. of the adj. *universus*.] The general system of things; all created things viewed as constituting one system or whole; the world. ∴ *World* properly signifies this globe and everything inhabiting it. *Universe* designates the entire mass of worlds, with everything associated with them.—**University**, ū-ni-vėr′si-ti, *n.* [L. *universitas*, the whole of anything; the universe; later, an association, corporation, company, &c.] An establishment or corporation for the purposes of instruction in all or some of the most important branches of science and literature, and having the power of conferring certain honorary dignities, termed *degrees*, in several faculties, as arts, medicine, law, and theology.

Universology, ū′ni-vėr-sol″o-ji, *n.* [L. *universum*, the universe; and Gr. *logos*, discourse.] The science of the universe; a science covering the whole ground of philosophy and the sciences in their general aspects.—**Universological**, ū-ni-vėr′sō-loj″i-kal, *a.* Pertaining to universology.

Univocal, ū-niv′ō-kal, *a.* [L. *unus*, one, and *vox, vocis*, a voice, a word.] Having one meaning only; not equivocal; having unison of sounds.—*n.* A word having only one meaning.—**Univocally**, ū-niv′ō-kal-li, *adv.* In one sense; not equivocally.

Unjointed, un-join′ted, *p.* and *a.* Having no joints; disconnected; incoherent.

Unjust, un-just′, *a.* Not just; not acting according to law and justice; contrary to justice and right.—**Unjustly**, un-just′li, *adv.* In an unjust manner; wrongfully.

Unjustifiable, un-jus′ti-fī″a-bl, *a.* Not justifiable; not to be vindicated or defended. —**Unjustifiably**, un-jus′ti-fī″a-bli, *adv.* In a manner that cannot be justified.

Unkempt, un-kemt′, *a.* Uncombed; hence, rough; slovenly dressed; untidy; unpolished; unrefined.

Unkennel, un-ken′el, *v.t.* To drive or force from a kennel; to rouse from secrecy or a close retreat.

Unkind, un-kīnd′, *a.* Wanting in kindness, affection, or the like; harsh; cruel.—**Unkindliness**, un-kīnd′li-nes, *n.* Unkindly conduct.—**Unkindly**, un-kīnd′li, *a.* Unkind; ungracious.—*adv.* In an unkind manner; without kindness or affection; harshly.—**Unkindness**, un-kīnd′nes, *n.* The quality of being unkind; want of kindness or affection; unkind conduct; an unkind act.

Unknit, un-nit′, *v.t.* To separate so as to be no longer knit; to smooth out (the brow).

Unknowable, un-nō′a-bl, *a.* Incapable of being known or discovered.—**Unknowing**, un-nō′ing, *a.* Not knowing; ignorant. —**Unknowingly**, un-nō′ing-li, *adv.* Without knowledge or design.—**Unknown**, un-nōn′, *a.* Not known; not discovered or found out; not ascertained: often used adverbially in the phrase *unknown to* = without the knowledge of (he did it *unknown to* me).

Unlace, un-lās′, *v.t.* To loose the lacing or fastening of; to unfasten by untying the lace of.

Unlade, un-lād′, *v.t.* To take out the cargo of; to remove, as a load; to discharge.

Unlamented, un-la-men′ted, *a.* Not lamented; whose loss is not deplored.

Unlatch, un-lach′, *v.i.* To open by lifting the latch.

Unlawful, un-la̦′fu̦l, *a.* Contrary to law; illegal; begotten out of wedlock; illegitimate.—**Unlawfully**, un-la̦′fu̦l-li, *adv.* In an unlawful manner; illegally; illegitimately.—**Unlawfulness**, un-la̦′fu̦l-nes, *n.* The quality of being unlawful; illegality.

Unlearn, un-lėrn′, *v.t.* To divest one's self of the acquired knowledge of; to forget the knowledge of.—**Unlearned**, un-lėr′-ned, *a.* Not learned or erudite; ignorant; illiterate; inexperienced. — *a.* (un-lėrnd′). Not made known by study; not known.

Unleash, un-lēsh′, *v.t.* To free from a leash; to let go.

Unleavened, un-lev′nd, *a.* Not leavened; not raised by leaven or yeast.

Unless, un-les′, *conj.* [For *on less* (than), the older forms being *onles*, *onlesse* = on lower terms, on any lower condition.] If it be not that; if . . . not; supposing that . . . not; except; excepting. By omission of a verb *unless* may have the force of a preposition = except, but for.

Unlettered, un-let′ėrd, *a.* Unlearned; untaught; ignorant.

Unlicensed, un-lī′senst, *a.* Not having a license or legal permission; done or undertaken without due license.

Unlike, un-līk′, *a.* Not like; having no resemblance. — *Unlike quantities, math.* quantities expressed by different letters or by the same letters with different powers. — *Unlike signs*, the signs *plus* (+) and *minus* (−).—**Unlikelihood, Unlikeliness**, un-līk′li-hụd, un-līk′li-nes, *n.* The state of being unlikely; improbability.—**Unlikely**, un-līk′li, *a.* Such as cannot be reasonably expected; improbable; not holding out a prospect of success; likely to fail; unpromising.—**Unlikeness**, un-līk′-nes, *n.* Want of resemblance; dissimilarity.

Unlimber, un-lim′bėr, *v.t.* To take off the limbers; to prepare for action.

Unlimited, un-lim′i-ted, *a.* Not limited; boundless; indefinite; unconfined; not restrained.

Unlink, un-lingk′, *v.t.* To separate the links of; to loose, as something fastened by a link.

Unload, un-lōd′, *v.t.* To take the load from; to discharge or disburden; to remove from a vessel or vehicle; *fig.* to relieve from anything onerous or troublesome; to withdraw the charge from (to *unload* a gun).

Unlock, un-lok′, *v.t.* To unfasten something which has been locked; to open, in general: to lay open.

Unlooked-for, un-lökt′for, *a.* Not looked for; not expected; not foreseen.

Unloose, un-lös′, *v.t.* To loose; to untie; to undo; to set free from hold or fastening; to set at liberty.

Unlovely, un-luv′li, *a.* Not lovely; tending rather to repel; not beautiful or attractive.

Unlucky, un-luk′i, *a.* Not lucky or fortunate; not successful in one's undertakings; resulting in failure, disaster, or misfortune; ill-omened; inauspicious. — **Unluckily**, un-luk′i-li, *adv.* In an unlucky manner; unfortunately; by ill luck. — **Unluckiness**, un-luk′i-nes, *n.* The state of being unlucky; ill fortune.

Unmaidenly, un-mā′dn-li, *a.* Not becoming a maiden; wanting maidenly modesty.

Unmake, un-māk′, *v.t.* To destroy the essential form and qualities of; to cause to cease to exist.—**Unmade**, un-mād′, *p.* and *a.*

Unman, un-man′, *v.t.* To deprive of the character or qualities of a man; to deprive of manly courage and fortitude; to dishearten; to overpower with womanish weakness; to emasculate —**Unmanly**, un-man′li, *a.* Not manly, or the reverse of manly; effeminate; womanish; childish; unbecoming in a man; cowardly. — **Unmanliness**, un-man′li-nes, *n.* State of being unmanly; effeminacy.—**Unmanned**, un-mand′, *p.* and *a.* Deprived of the qualities of a man; rendered effeminate or weak.

Unmanageable, un-man′āj-a-bl, *a.* Not manageable; not easily restrained or directed; not controllable; beyond control.

Unmannerly, un-man′ėr-li, *a.* Not mannerly; not having good manners; rude; ill-bred.—**Unmannerliness**, un-man′ėr-li-nes, *n.* Want of good manners; rudeness of behaviour.

Unmanufactured, un-man′ū-fak″turd, *a.* Not manufactured; not wrought into the proper form for use.

Unmarketable, un-mär′ket-a-bl, *a.* Not fit for the market; not saleable.

Unmask, un-mask′, *v.t.* To strip of a mask or of any disguise; to lay open to view. —*v.i.* To put off a mask.

Unmatched, un-macht′, *a.* Matchless; having no equal.

Unmeaning, un-mēn′ing, *a.* Having no meaning or signification; mindless; senseless.

Unmeasured, un-mezh′ūrd, *a.* Not measured; plentiful; beyond measure; immense; infinite; excessive; immoderate.

Unmeet, un-mēt′, *a.* Not meet or fit; not worthy or suitable.—**Unmeetly**, un-mēt′-li, *adv.* Not fitly; not suitably.—**Unmeetness**, un-mēt′nes, *n.*

Unmelodious, un-me-lō′di-us, *a.* Not melodious, wanting melody; harsh.

Unmentionable, un-men′shon-a-bl, *a.* Incapable of being mentioned; unfit for being mentioned or noticed.—*n.pl.* Articles of dress not to be mentioned in polite circles. (*Colloq. and humorous.*)

Unmerciful, un-mėr′si-fụl, *a.* Not merciful; cruel; inhuman; merciless; unconscionable. — **Unmercifully**, un-mėr′si-fụl-li, *adv.* In an unmerciful manner; cruelly. — **Unmercifulness**, un-mėr′si-fụl-nes, *n.*

Unmerited, un-mer′i-ted, *a.* Not merited or deserved; obtained without service or equivalent; not deserved through wrong-doing.

Unmindful, un-mīnd′fụl, *a.* Not mindful; not heedful; regardless.—**Unmindfully**, un-mīnd′fụl-li, *adv.* Carelessly; heedlessly.—**Unmindfulness**, un-mīnd′fụl-nes, *n.* Heedlessness; inattention.

Unmistakable, un-mis-tāk′a-bl, *a.* Not capable of being mistaken or misunderstood; clear; evident.

Unmitigable, un-mit′i-ga-bl, *a.* Not capable of being mitigated, softened, or lessened.—**Unmitigated**, un-mit′i-gā-ted, *a.* Not mitigated; not softened or toned down; perfect in badness; having no redeeming feature (an *unmitigated* scoundrel).

Unmixed, Unmixt, un-mikst′, *a.* Not mixed; pure; unadulterated; unalloyed.

Unmolested, un-mō-les′ted, *a.* Not molested or disturbed; free from disturbance.

Unmoor, un-mör′, *v.t.* *Naut.* to loose from anchorage or moorings.

Unmotherly, un-muᴛʜ′ėr-li, *a.* Not resembling or not becoming to a mother.

Unmoved, un-mövd′, *a.* Not moved; not changed in place; not changed in purpose or resolution; unshaken; firm; not touched by passion or emotion; calm; cool.

Unmuffle, un-muf′l, *v.t.* To uncover by removing what muffles or conceals.

Unmurmuring, un-mėr′mėr-ing, *a.* Not murmuring or given to murmur; uncomplaining.

Unmusical, un-mū′zi-kal, *a.* Not musical; not melodious.

Unmutilated, un-mū′ti-lā-ted, *a.* Not mutilated; not deprived of a member or part; entire.

Unmuzzle, un-muz′l, *v.t.* To remove a muzzle from; to free from restraint.

Unnamable, un-nām′a-bl, *a.*—Incapable of being named; indescribable. — **Unnamed**, un-nāmd′, *a.* Not having received a name; not mentioned.

Unnatural, un-nat′ū-ral, *a.* Not natural; contrary to the laws of nature; contrary to the natural feelings; acting without the affections of our common nature; not representing nature; forced; affected; artificial. — **Unnaturally**, un-nat′ū-ral-li, *adv.* In an unnatural manner; in opposition to natural feelings and sentiments.—**Unnaturalness**, un-nat′ū-ral-nes, *n.*

Unnavigable, un-nav′i-ga-bl, *a.* Incapable of being navigated.

Unnecessary, un-nes″e-ser′i, *a.* Not necessary; needless, not required by the circumstances of the case. — **Unnecessarily**, un-nes″e-ser′i-li, *adv.* In an unnecessary manner; needlessly.—**Unnecessariness**, un-nes″e-ser′i-nes, *n.*

Unneighborly, un-nā′bėr-li, *a.* Not neighborly; not suitable to the duties of a neighbor; not kind and friendly.

Unnerve, un-nėrv′, *v.t.* To deprive of nerve, force, or strength; to enfeeble; to deprive of coolness or composure of mind.

Unnoted, un-nō′ted, *a.* Not noted; not observed; not heeded or regarded.

Unnoticed, un-nō′tist, *a.* Not observed; not regarded; not treated with the usual marks of respect.

Unnumbered, un-num′bėrd, *a.* Not numbered; innumerable; indefinitely numerous.

Unobjectionable, un-ob-jek′shon-a-bl, *a.* Not liable to objection; incapable of being condemned as faulty, false, or improper; unexceptionable.

Unobscured, un-ob-skūrd′, *a.* Not obscured; not darkened or overcast.

Unobservable, un-ob-zėr′va-bl, *a.* Not observable; not discoverable. — **Unobservant, Unobserving**, un-ob-zėr′vant, un-ob-zėr′ving, *a.* Not observant; not attentive; heedless. — **Unobserved**, un-ob-zėrvd′, *a.* Not observed, noticed, or regarded; not heeded. — **Unobservedly**, un-ob-zėr′ved-li, *adv.* Without being observed.

Unobstructed, un-ob-struk′ted, *a.* Not obstructed; not filled with impediments; not hindered.

Unobtrusive, un-ob-trö′siv, *a.* Not obtrusive; not forward; modest.—**Unobtrusively**, un-ob-trö′siv-li, *adv.* Not forwardly.

Unoccupied, un-ok′kū-pīd, *a.* Not occupied; not possessed; not employed or taken up in business or otherwise.

Unoffending, un-of-fen′ding, *a.* Not giving offence; harmless; innocent; inoffensive.

Unofficial, un-of-fish′al, *a.* Not official; inofficial.

Unopposed, un-op-pōzd′, *a.* Not opposed; not resisted; not meeting with any obstruction or opposition.

Unorganized, un-or′gan-īzd, *a.* Not organized; inorganic.

Unorthodox, un-or′tho-doks, *a.* Heterodox; heretical.

Unostentatious, un-os′ten-tā″shus, *a.* Not ostentatious; not making show and parade; modest; not glaring or showy.—**Unostentatiously**, un-os′ten-tā″shus-li, *adv.* Without show or ostentation.

Unowned, un-ōnd′, *a.* Having no known owner; not acknowledged as one's own.

Unpack, un-pak′, *v.t.* To take from a package; to remove a wrapper from; to unload.

Unpaid, un-pād′, *a.* Not paid; not discharged, as a debt; not having received what is due; not receiving a salary or wages.—*Unpaid for*, not paid for; taken on credit.

Unpalatable, un-pal′a-ta-bl, *a.* Not palatable; disgusting to the taste; not such as to be relished; disagreeable to the feelings.

Unparagoned, un-par′a-gond, *a.* Unequalled; matchless.

Unparalleled, un-par′a-leld, *a.* Having no parallel or equal; unequalled; matchless; such that nothing similar was ever seen.

Unpardonable, un-pär′dn-a-bl, *a.* Not to be forgiven; incapable of being pardoned.

Unparliamentary, un-pär′li-men″ta-ri, *a.* Contrary to the usages or rules of proceeding of parliamentary bodies; not such as can be used or uttered in a parliamentary assembly, unseemly, as language.

Unpathed, un-päthd′, *a.* Not trodden; trackless.

Unpatriotic, un-pā′tri-ot″ik, *a.* Not patriotic.

Unpatronized, un-pat'ron-īzd, *a.* Not having a patron; not supported by friends.

Unpaved, un-pāvd', *a.* Not paved; having no pavement.

Unpensioned, un-pen'shond, *a.* Not pensioned; not having a pension.

Unpeople, un-pē'pl, *v.t.* To deprive of inhabitants; to depopulate; to dispeople.

Unperceivable, un-pėr-sē'va-bl, *a.* Incapable of being perceived; not perceptible.

Unperformed, un-pėr-formd', *a.* Not performed; not done; not fulfilled.

Unperturbed, un-pėr-tėrbd', *a.* Not perturbed; not disturbed.

Unperverted, un-pėr-vėr'ted, *a.* Not perverted; not wrested or turned to a wrong sense or use.

Unphilosophic, Unphilosophical, un-fil'ō-sof''ik, un-fil'ō-sof''i-kal, *a.* Not philosophic; the reverse of philosophic; not according to the principles of sound philosophy.

Unpin, un-pin', *v.t.* To loose from pins; to unfasten or undo what is held together by a pin or pins.

Unpitied, un-pit'id, *a.* Not pitied; not regarded with sympathetic sorrow.—**Unpitying**, un-pit'i-ing, *a.* Having no pity; showing no compassion.

Unplagued, un-plāgd', *a.* Not plagued, harassed, or tormented.

Unplanted, un-plan'ted, *a.* Not planted; of spontaneous growth.

Unpleasant, un-plez'ant, *a.* Not pleasant; not affording pleasure; disagreeable.—**Unpleasantly**, un-plez'ant-li, *adv.* In a manner not pleasing.—**Unpleasantness**, un-plez'ant-nes, *n.* Disagreeableness.—**Unpleasing**, un-plē'zing, *a.* Unpleasant; offensive; disagreeable.—**Unpleasingly**, un-plē'zing-li, *adv.*

Unpliable, Unpliant, un-plī'a-bl, un-plī'ant, *a.* Not pliable; not easily bent; not readily yielding the will.

Unplumbed, un-plumd', *a.* Not plumbed or measured by a plumb-line; unfathomed.

Unpoetic, Unpoetical, un-pō-et'ik, un-pō-et'i-kal, *a.* Not poetical; not having poetical qualities; not proper to or becoming a poet.—**Unpoetically**, un-pō-et'i-kal-li, *adv.* In an unpoetic manner.

Unpolished, un-pol'isht, *a.* Not polished; not made smooth or bright by rubbing; not refined in manners; rude; plain.

Unpolite, un-pō-līt', *a.* Impolite; uncivil; rude.—**Unpolitely**, un-pō-līt'li, *adv.* In an uncivil manner. See IMPOLITE.

Unpolluted, un-pol-lū'ted, *a.* Not polluted or defiled; pure.

Unpopular, un-pop'ū-lėr, *a.* Not popular; not having the public favour.—**Unpopularity**, un-pop'ū-lar''i-ti, *n.* The state of being unpopular.—**Unpopularly**, un-pop'ū-lėr-li, *adv.* Not popularly.

Unpractical, un-prak'ti-kal, *a.* Not practical; impractical.

Unpractised, un-prak'tist, *a.* Not having been taught by practice; raw; unskilful.

Unprecedented, un-pres'ē-den-ted, *a.* Having no precedent; not matched by any other instance; unexampled.—**Unprecedentedly**, un-pres'ē-den-ted-li, *adv.* Without precedent; exceptionally.

Unprejudiced, un-prej'ū-dist, *a.* Not prejudiced; free from undue bias or prepossession; unbiassed; impartial.

Unpremeditated, un-prē-med'i-tā-ted, *a.* Not previously meditated or prepared in the mind; not previously purposed or intended; not done by design.

Unprepared, un-prē-pārd', *a.* Not prepared; not fitted or made suitable or ready; not brought into a right or suitable condition in view of a future event, contingency, danger, or the like.—**Unpreparedly**, un-prē-pā'red-li, *a.* Without due preparation.—**Unpreparedness**, un-prē-pā'red-nes, *n.*

Unprepossessed, un-prē'poz-zest'', *a.* Not biassed by previous opinions; not prejudiced.—**Unprepossessing**, un-prē'poz-zes''ing, *a.* Not having a prepossessing or winning appearance; not attractive or engaging.

Unpresentable, un-prē-zen'ta-bl, *a.* Not fit for being presented to company or society.

Unpresuming, un-prē-zū'ming, *a.* Not presuming; modest; humble.—**Unpresumptuous**, un-prē-zum'tū-us, *a.* Not presumptuous.

Unpretending, un-prē-ten'ding, *a.* Not pretending to any distinction; making no pretensions to superiority; unassuming.

Unprincipled, un-prin'si-pld, *a.* Not having settled principles; destitute of virtue; profligate; immoral; iniquitous; wicked.

Unprivileged, un-priv'i-lejd, *a.* Not enjoying a particular privilege or immunity.

Unproductive, un-prō-duk'tiv, *a.* Not productive; not producing large crops; not making profitable returns for labour; not producing profit or interest; not producing articles for consumption or distribution; not producing any effect.—**Unproductiveness**, un-prō-duk'tiv-nes, *n.* The state of being unproductive.

Unprofessional, un-prō-fesh'on-al, *a.* Not pertaining to one's profession; contrary to the rules or usages of a profession; not belonging to a profession.

Unprofitable, un-prof'i-ta-bl, *a.* Not profitable; bringing no profit; serving no useful end; useless; profitless.—**Unprofitableness**, un-prof'i-ta-bl-nes, *n.* Uselessness.—**Unprofitably**, un-prof'i-ta-bli, *adv.* Without profit, advantage, or use; to no good purpose.

Unprohibited, un-prō-hib'i-ted, *a.* Not forbidden; lawful.

Unprolific, un-prō-lif'ik, *a.* Barren; not producing young or fruit.

Unpromising, un-prom'is-ing, *a.* Not affording a favourable prospect of success, of excellence, of profit, &c.—**Unpromisingly**, un-prom'is-ing-li, *adv.*

Unpronounceable, un-prō-noun'sa-bl, *a.* Incapable of being pronounced; unfit for being named; unmentionable.

Unpropitious, un-prō-pish'us, *a.* Not propitious or favourable; inauspicious.

Unprosperous, un-pros'pėr-us, *a.* Not attended with success; unfortunate.—**Unprosperously**, un-pros'pėr-us-li, *adv.* Unsuccessfully; unfortunately.

Unprotected, un-prō-tek'ted, *a.* Not protected or defended; without protector or guardian.

Unproved, un-prövd', *a.* Not tested or known by trial; not established as true by proof.

Unprovided, un-prō-vī'ded, *a.* Not provided; not supplied.

Unprovoked, un-prō-vōkt', *a.* Not provoked; not proceeding from provocation or just cause.

Unpublished, un-pub'lisht, *a.* Not made public; not published or issued from the press to the public, as a manuscript or book.

Unpunctual, un-pungk'tū-al, *a.* Not punctual; not exact as to time.

Unpunished, un-pun'isht, *a.* Suffered to pass with impunity.

Unpurchased, un-pėr'chāst, *a.* Not bought.

Unqualified, un-kwol'i-fīd, *a.* Not having the requisite qualifications; without sufficient talents, abilities, or accomplishments; not legally competent to act; not having passed the necessary examinations and received a diploma or license; not modified by conditions or exceptions (*unqualified* praise).

Unquenchable, un-kwensh'a-bl, *a.* Incapable of being quenched, extinguished, or the like.—**Unquenchably**, un-kwensh'a-bli, *adv.* In an unquenchable manner.

Unquestionable, un-kwes'tyun-a-bl, *a.* Not to be doubted or called in question; indubitable; certain.—**Unquestionably**, un-kwes'tyun-a-bli, *adv.* Without doubt; indubitably.—**Unquestioned**, un-kwes'tyund, *a.* Not called in question; not doubted; not interrogated.

Unquiet, un-kwī'et, *a.* Not calm or tranquil; restless; agitated; disturbed.—**Unquietly**, un-kwī'et-li, *adv.* In an unquiet manner; in an agitated state.—**Unquietness**, un-kwī'et-nes, *n.* Agitation; uneasiness; restlessness.

Unravel, un-rav'el, *v.t.* To disentangle; to disengage or separate; to clear from complication or difficulty; to unriddle; to unfold or bring to a denouement, as the plot or intrigue of a play.—*v.i.* To be unfolded; to be disentangled.

Unread, un-red', *a.* Not perused; not instructed by books.—**Unreadable**, un-rē'da-bl, *a.* Incapable of being read or deciphered; illegible; not worth reading; so dull or ill-written as to repel readers.

Unready, un-red'i, *a.* Not prepared; not fit; not prompt.—**Unreadiness**, un-red'i-nes, *n.* Want of promptness or of preparation.

Unreal, un-rē'al, *n.* Not real; not substantial; having appearance only.—**Unreality**, un-rē-al'i-ti, *n.* Want of real existence; that which has no reality.

Unreason, un-rē'zn, *n.* Want of reason; folly; absurdity.—**Unreasonable**, un-rē'zn-a-bl, *a.* Not agreeable to reason; not guided by reason; exceeding the bounds of reason; exorbitant; immoderate; unconscionable.—**Unreasonableness**, un-rē'zn-a-bl-nes, *n.* The state or quality of being unreasonable.—**Unreasonably**, un-rē'zn-a-bli, *adv.* In an unreasonable manner; excessively; immoderately.—**Unreasoning**, un-rē'zn-ing, *a.* Not having reasoning faculties; characterized by want of reason; not taking a reasonable view.

Unreckoned, un-rek'nd, *a.* Not computed, counted, or summed up.

Unreclaimed, un-rē-klāmd', *a.* Not brought to a domestic state; not tamed; not brought into tillage; not reformed; not called back from vice to virtue.

Unrecognizable, un-rek'og-nī''za-bl, *a.* Incapable of being recognized; irrecognizable.

Unrecommended, un-rek'om-men''ded, *a.* Not favourably mentioned.

Unrecompensed, un-rek'om-penst, *a.* Not rewarded or requited.

Unreconciled, un-rek'on-sīld, *a.* Not reconciled; not made consistent; not restored to friendship or favour; still at enmity.

Unrecorded, un-rē-kor'ded, *a.* Not recorded or registered; not kept in remembrance by public monuments.

Unredeemed, un-rē-dēmd', *a.* Not redeemed; not ransomed; not recalled into the treasury or bank by payment of the value in money (*unredeemed* bills); not having any countervailing quality; unmitigated.

Unredressed, un-rē-drest', *a.* Not redressed; not having received redress; not removed or reformed.

Unrefined, un-rē-fīnd', *a.* Not purified; not polished in manners, taste, or the like.

Unreformed, un-rē-formd', *a.* Not reclaimed from vice; not corrected or amended.

Unregarded, un-rē-gär'ded, *a.* Not heeded; neglected; slighted.

Unregeneracy, un-rē-jen'ėr-a-si, *n.* State of being unregenerate.—**Unregenerate, Unregenerated**, un-rē-jen'ėr-āt, un-rē-jen'ėr-ā-ted, *a.* Not regenerated or renewed in heart; remaining at enmity with God.

Unregistered, un-rej'is-tėrd, *a.* Not entered in a register.

Unrelated, un-rē-lā'ted, *a.* Not connected by blood or affinity; having no connection of any kind.

Unrelenting, un-rē-len'ting, *a.* Not becoming lenient, gentle, or merciful; relentless; hard; pitiless.

Unreliable, un-rē-lī′a-bl, *a.* Not reliable; not to be relied or depended on.—**Unreliableness**, un-rē-lī′a-bl-nes, *n.* The character of being unreliable.

Unrelieved, un-rē-lēvd′, *a.* Not eased or delivered from pain; not succoured; not delivered from distress; not released from duty.

Unremembered, un-rē-mem′bėrd, *a.* Forgotten.

Unremitted, un-rē-mit′ed, *a.* Not remitted; not forgiven; not having a temporary relaxation.—**Unremitting**, un-rē-mit′ing, *a.* Not abating; not relaxing for a time; incessant; continued.

Unremovable, un-rē-mö′va-bl, *a.* Fixed; irremovable; immovable.

Unrenewed, un-rē-nūd′, *a.* Not made anew; not regenerated.

Unrepaid, un-rē-pād′, *a.* Not compensated; not requited.

Unrepealed, un-rē-pēld′, *a.* Not repealed, revoked, or abrogated; remaining in force.

Unrepentant, un-rē-pen′tant, *a.* Not penitent; not contrite for sin.—**Unrepented**, un-rē-pen′ted, *a.* Not repented of.

Unrepining, un-rē-pī′ning, *a.* Not peevishly murmuring or complaining.

Unrepresented, un-rep′rē-zen″ted, *a.* Not represented; not having a representative or person to act in one's stead; not yet put on the stage.

Unrequited, un-rē-kwī′ted, *a.* Not requited; not recompensed; not reciprocated.

Unreserved, un-rē-zėrvd′, *a.* Not reserved or restricted; not withheld in part; full; entire; open; frank; concealing nothing.—**Unreservedly**, un-rē-zėr′ved-li, *adv.* Without limitation or reservation; frankly; without concealment.—**Unreservedness**, un-rē-zėr′ved-nes, *n.*

Unresisted, un-rē-zis′ted, *a.* Not resisted or opposed.—**Unresisting**, un-rē-zis′ting, *a.* Not making resistance; submissive.

Unresolved, un-rē-zolvd′, *a.* Not determined; not solved; not cleared.

Unrest, un-rest′, *n.* Disquiet; want of tranquillity; uneasiness; unhappiness.—**Unresting**, un-res′ting, *a.* Never resting or ceasing; continually in motion.

Unrestored, un-rē-stōrd′, *a.* Not given back; not restored to a former and better state.

Unrestrained, un-rē-strānd′, *a.* Not restrained or controlled; not limited; uncontrolled; licentious; loose.—**Unrestraint**, un-rē-strānt′, *n.* Freedom from restraint.

Unrestricted, un-rē-strik′ted, *a.* Without restriction; not limited or confined.

Unrevenged, un-rē-venjd′, *a.* Not having obtained revenge; not having taken vengeance; remaining without vengeance taken.

Unrewarded, un-rē-wạr′ded, *a.* Not having received a reward; not compensated by reward bestowed; unrequited.

Unriddle, un-rid′l, *v.t.* To solve or explain; to interpret.

Unrighteous, un-rī′chus, *a.* Not righteous; not just; wicked; not honest and upright; of persons or things.—**Unrighteously**, un-rī′chus-li, *adv.* Unjustly; wickedly.—**Unrighteousness**, un-rī′chus-nes, *n.* Injustice; a violation of the principles of justice and equity; wickedness

Unripe, un-rīp′, *a.* Not ripe; not mature; not fully prepared; not completed.—**Unripeness**, un-rīp′nes, *n.* Want of ripeness; immaturity.

Unrivaled, un-rī′vald, *a.* Having no rival or equal; peerless; incomparable.

Unrobe, un-rōb′, *v.t.* To strip of a robe; to undress; to disrobe.

Unroll, un-rōl′, *v.t.* To open out, as something rolled or convolved; to lay open or display.—*v.i.* To unfold; to uncoil.

Unromantic, un-rō-man′tik, *a.* Not romantic; not given to romantic fancies; having nothing of romance connected with it.

Unroof, un-röf′, *v.t.* To strip off the roof or roofs of.

Unroot, un-röt′, *v.t.* To tear up by the roots; to extirpate; to eradicate.

Unruffled, un-ruf′ld, *a.* Calm; tranquil; not agitated; not disturbed.

Unruly, un-rö′li, *a.* [From O.E. *unroo*, unrest, from *un*, not, and O.E. *roo*, *ro*, rest, quietness (with term. *-ly*), from A.Sax. *rów*, Icel. *ró*, D. *roe*, G. *ruhe*, rest. *Rule* has influenced the meaning.] Disregarding restraint; disposed to violate laws; turbulent; ungovernable; disorderly.—**Unruliness**, un-rö′li-nes, *n.* Disregard of restraint; turbulence.

Unsaddle, un-sad′l, *v.t.* To take the saddle from.

Unsafe, un-sāf′, *a.* Not affording or accompanied by complete safety; not free from danger; perilous; hazardous.—**Unsafely**, un-sāf′li, *adv.* Not without danger.

Unsaid, un-sed′, *a.* Not spoken; not uttered.

Unsaintly, un-sānt′li, *a.* Not like a saint; unholy.

Unsalable, un-sā′la-bl, *a.* Not salable; not meeting a ready sale; that cannot find a purchaser.

Unsanctified, un-sangk′ti-fīd, *a.* Unholy; profane; wicked; not consecrated.

Unsatisfactory, un-sat′is-fak″to-ri, *a.* Not satisfactory; not satisfying; not giving satisfaction.—**Unsatisfactoriness**, un-sat′is-fak″to-ri-nes, *n.*—**Unsatisfied**, un-sat′is-fīd, *a.* Not having enough; not gratified to the full; not content; not pleased; not convinced or fully persuaded; unpaid.—**Unsatisfying**, un-sat′is-fī-ing, *a.* Not affording full gratification; not convincing the mind.

Unsavory, un-sā′vėr-i, *a.* Not savory; tasteless; insipid; disagreeable to the taste or smell; unpleasing; offensive.—**Unsavorily**, un-sā′vėr-i-li, *adv.*—**Unsavoriness**, un-sā′vėr-i-nes, *n.*

Unsay, un-sā′, *v.t.* To recant or recall after having been said; to retract; to take back.

Unscathed, un-skāᴛʜd′, *a.* Not scathed or injured; without scathe; uninjured.

Unschooled, un-sköld′, *a.* Not schooled; not taught; illiterate.

Unscrew, un-skrö′, *v.t.* To draw the screws from; to unfasten by screwing back.

Unscriptural, un-skrip′tū-ral, *a.* Not agreeable to the Scriptures; not warranted by the authority of the Word of God.—**Unscripturally**, un-skrip′tū-ral-li, *adv.* In a manner not according with the Scriptures.

Unscrupulous, un-skrö′pū-lus, *a.* Having no scruples; regardless of principle.—**Unscrupulously**, un-skrö′pū-lus-li, *adv.* In an unscrupulous manner.—**Unscrupulousness**, un-skrö′pū-lus-nes, *n.* Want of scrupulousness.

Unseal, un-sēl′, *v.t.* To open after having been sealed.—**Unsealed**, un-sēld′, *p.* and *a.* Not stamped with a seal; not ratified or sanctioned.

Unsearchable, un-sėr′cha-bl, *a.* Incapable of being discovered by search; inscrutable; mysterious.—**Unsearchableness**, un-sėr′cha-bl-nes, *n.*

Unseasonable, un-sē′zn-a-bl, *a.* Not seasonable; not agreeable to the time of the year; ill-timed; untimely; not suited to the time or occasion.—**Unseasonableness**, un-sē′zn-a-bl-nes, *n.* The quality of being unseasonable.—**Unseasonably**, un-sē-zn-a-bli, *adv.* Not seasonably; not at the most suitable time.—**Unseasoned**, un-sē′znd, *a.* Not seasoned; not kept and made fit for use; not inured; not flavoured with seasoning.

Unseat, un-sēt′, *v.t.* To remove from a seat; to throw from one's seat on horseback; to depose from a seat in the House of Representatives or the Senate.

Unseaworthy, un-sē-wėr′ᴛʜi, *a.* Not fit for a voyage: said of ships not in a fit state to encounter the ordinary perils of a sea voyage.—**Unseaworthiness**, un-sē-wėr′ᴛʜi-nes, *n.*

Unseconded, un-sek′un-ded, *a.* Not supported; not assisted; without any one to second.

Unsectarian, un-sek-tā′ri-an, *a.* Not sectarian; not characterized by any of the peculiarities of a sect; not belonging to any one sect.

Unseeing, un-sē′ing, *a.* Wanting the power of vision; blind.

Unseemly, un-sēm′li, *a.* Not seemly; not becoming; indecorous; indecent.—*adv.* Indecently; unbecomingly.—**Unseemliness**, un-sēm′li-nes, *n.* Uncomeliness; indecency; indecorum.

Unseen, un-sēn′, *a.* Not seen; invisible.—*The unseen*, that which is unseen; especially, the world of spirits; the hereafter.

Unselfish, un-sel′fish, *a.* Not selfish or unduly attached to one's own interest.

Unsent, un-sent′, *a.* Not despatched; not transmitted.—*Unsent for*, not called to attend.

Unsentenced, un-sen′tenst, *a.* Not having received sentence.

Unsentimental, un-sen′ti-men″tal, *a.* Not apt to be swayed by sentiment; matter-of-fact.

Unserviceable, un-sėr′vis-a-bl, *a.* Not bringing advantage, use, profit, or convenience; useless.

Unsettle, un-set′l, *v.t.* To change from a settled state; to unhinge; to make uncertain or fluctuating; to disorder the mind of; to derange.—**Unsettled**, un-set′ld, *p.* and *a.* Not fixed in resolution; unsteady or wavering; disturbed or troubled; not calm or composed; having no fixed place of abode; apt to change one's abode or occupation; displaced from a fixed or permanent position; not adjusted; unpaid; not occupied by permanent inhabitants.—**Unsettledness**, un-set′ld-nes, *n.*

Unsex, un-seks′, *v.t.* To deprive of the qualities of sex; to transform in respect to sex; usually, to deprive of the qualities of a woman.

Unshackle, un-shak′l, *v.t.* To unfetter; to set free from restraint.

Unshaken, un-shā′kn, *a.* Not shaken; not agitated; not moved in resolution; firm; steady.

Unshamed, un-shāmd′, *a.* Not ashamed; not abashed.

Unshaped, **Unshapen**, un-shāpt′, un-shā′pn, *a.* Shapeless; misshapen; deformed.—**Unshapely**, un-shāp′li, *a.* Ill formed.

Unsheathe, un-shēᴛʜ′, *v.t.* To draw from the sheath or scabbard.—*To unsheathe the sword*, often equivalent to to make war.

Unshed, un-shed′, *a.* Not shed; not spilt.

Unshielded, un-shēl′ded, *a.* Not protected; exposed.

Unship, un-ship′, *v.t.* To take out of a ship or other water craft; *naut.* to remove from the place where it is fixed or fitted.

Unshod, un-shod′, *a.* Having no shoes.

Unshorn, un-shorn′, *a.* Not sheared; not clipped.

Unshot, un-shot′, *v.t.* To take or draw the shot or ball out of; not shot.—**Unshotted**, un-shot′ed, *a.* Not loaded with shot.

Unshrinking, un-shringk′ing, *a.* Not withdrawing from danger or toil; not recoiling.

Unshroud, un-shroud′, *v.t.* To remove the shroud from; to uncover; to disclose.

Unsifted, un-sif′ted, *a.* Not separated by a sieve; not critically examined.

Unsightly, un-sīt′li, *a.* Disagreeable to the eye; repulsive; ugly; deformed.—**Unsightliness**, un-sīt′li-nes, *n.* Repulsiveness; deformity; ugliness.

Unsinking, un-singk′ing, *a.* Not subsiding; not failing.

Unsinning, un-sin′ing, *a.* Untainted with sin.

Unsisterly, un-sis′tėr-li, *a.* Not like or becoming a sister.

Unsized, un-sīzd′, *a.* Not sized or stiffened; not made with size (*unsized* paper).

Unskilful, un-skil′fụl, *a.* Not skilful; having no or little skill; wanting knowledge and dexterity.—**Unskilfully**, un-skil′fụl-li, *adv.* Without skill or dexterity; clumsily.—**Unskilfulness**, un-skil′fụl-nes, *n.* The quality of being unskilful; want of skill.—**Unskilled**, un-skild′, *a.* Destitute of skill or practical knowledge.—*Unskilled labour*, labour not requiring special skill or training; simple manual labour.

Unslaked, un-slākt′, *a.* Not slaked or quenched; not mixed with water and so reduced to powder (*unslaked* lime).

Unsleeping, un-slēp′ing, *a.* Never sleeping; ever wakeful.

Unsling, un-sling′, *v.t.* *Naut.* to release from slings.

Unsmirched, un-smėrcht′, *a.* Not stained or soiled.

Unsociable, un-sō′shi-a-bl, *a.* Not sociable; not suitable for society; not inclined for society; not free in conversation; not companionable.—**Unsociableness**, **Unsociability**, un-sō′shi-a-bl-nes, un-sō′shi-a-bil″i-ti, *n.* The state or quality of being unsociable.—**Unsociably**, un-sō′shi-a-bli, *adv.*—**Unsocial**, un-sō′shal, *a.* Not social; not adapted to society; not caring to mix with one's fellows.

Unsoiled, un-soild′, *a.* Not soiled; unpolluted; pure.

Unsold, un-sōld′, *a.* Not sold; not transferred for a consideration.

Unsolicited, un-sō-lis′i-ted, *a.* Not solicited; not applied to or petitioned; not asked for; not eagerly requested.

Unsolved, un-solvd′, *a.* Not explained or cleared up.

Unsophisticated, un-sō-fis′ti-kā-ted, *a.* Not sophisticated; not adulterated; unmixed; pure; in the natural and simple state; natural; void of the conventionalities or artificialities of polite society.

Unsought, un-sạt′, *a.* Not searched for; unasked for; unsolicited.

Unsound, un-sound′, *a.* Not sound or healthy; corrupt; decayed; not solid, firm, or the like; not founded on truth or correct principles; not valid; erroneous; not orthodox.—**Unsoundly**, un-sound′li, *adv.* In an unsound manner.—**Unsoundness**, unsound′nes, *n.* Want of soundness; want of strength or solidity; weakness; erroneousness; defectiveness.

Unsoured, un-sourd′, *a.* Not made sour, morose, or crabbed.

Unsowed, **Unsown**, un-sōd′, un-sōn′, *a.* Not sowed; not planted with seed; not scattered on land for growth; not propagated by seed scattered.

Unsparing, un-spā′ring, *a.* Not parsimonious; profuse; not merciful or forgiving; severe; rigorous in treatment.

Unspeakable, un-spē′ka-bl, *a.* Incapable of being spoken or uttered; unutterable; ineffable.—**Unspeakably**, un-spē′ka-bli, *adv.* Unutterably.

Unspecified, un-spes′i-fīd, *a.* Not specified or particularly mentioned.

Unspent, un-spent′, *a.* Not spent; not used or wasted; not exhausted.

Unspiritual, un-spir′i-tū-al, *a.* Carnal; worldly.

Unspoken, un-spō′kn, *a.* Not spoken or uttered.

Unspotted, un-spot′ed, *a.* Free from spots; free from moral stain; untainted with guilt; unblemished; faultless; pure.

Unstable, un-stā′bl, *a.* Not stable; inconstant; irresolute; wavering.—**Unstableness**, un-stā′bl-nes, *n.* Instability.

Unstaid, un-stād′, *a.* Not staid or steady; not settled in judgment; volatile.—**Unstaidness**, un-stād′nes, *n.*

Unstained, un-stānd′, *a.* Not stained; not polluted, tarnished, or dishonoured.

Unstamped, un-stampt′, *a.* Not having a stamp impressed or affixed (an *unstamped* receipt or letter).

Unsteady, un-sted′i, *a.* Not steady; shaking; staggering; reeling; wavering; fluctuating; not constant in mind; fickle; unsettled; not regular, equable, or uniform; varying.—**Unsteadily**, un-sted′i-li, *adv.* In an unsteady manner; without steadiness; waveringly; totteringly; restlessly; inconsistently.—**Unsteadiness**, un-sted′i-nes, *n.* Want of firmness, fixedness, or stability; restlessness; inconstancy.

Unstinted, un-stin′ted, *a.* Not stinted; bestowed abundantly; rather profuse or lavish.

Unstop, un-stop′, *v.t.* To free from a stopper, as a bottle or cask; to free from obstruction.

Unstormed, un-stormd′, *a.* Not assaulted; not taken by assault.

Unstrained, un-strānd′, *a.* Not purified by straining; not forced; easy or natural.

Unstratified, un-strat′i-fīd, *a.* Not consisting of a series of strata or layers (as is the case with rocks deposited by water), but forming amorphous masses.

Unstring, un-string′, *v.t.* To deprive of strings; to relax or untune the strings of; to take from a string; to relax the tension of; to loosen or relax (the nerves).—**Unstrung**, un-strung′, *pp.* Deprived of strings; having the nerves shaken.

Unstudied, un-stud′id, *a.* Not studied; not premeditated; not laboured; easy; natural; ignorant; unskilled.

Unsubdued, un-sub-dūd′, *a.* Not brought into subjection; not conquered.

Unsubstantial, un-sub-stan′shal, *a.* Not substantial or solid; not real; not having substance.—**Unsubstantiality**, un-sub-stan′shi-al″i-ti, *n.* The state or quality of being unsubstantial; want of substance or reality.

Unsuccessful, un-suk-ses′fụl, *a.* Not successful; having met with no success; not fortunate in the result or issue.—**Unsuccessfully**, un-suk-ses′fụl-li, *adv.* Without success; unfortunately.—**Unsuccessfulness**, un-suk-ses′fụl-nes, *n.*

Unsuitable, un-sū′ta-bl, *a.* Not suitable, fit, or adapted; unfit; improper.—**Unsuitableness**, un-sū′ta-bl-nes, *n.* Unfitness.—**Unsuitably**, un-sū′ta-bli, *adv.* Unfitly; inadequately.—**Unsuited**, un-sū′ted, *a.* Not suited or adapted; unfit.

Unsullied, un-sul′id, *a.* Not sullied; not stained or tarnished; free from imputation of evil; pure; stainless.

Unsung, un-sung′, *a.* Not sung; not celebrated in song.

Unsupplied, un-sup-plīd′, *a.* Not supplied; not provided; not furnished.

Unsupported, un-sup-pōr′ted, *a.* Not supported; not upheld; not sustained; not countenanced; not aided.

Unsuppressed, un-sup-prest′, *a.* Not suppressed; not subdued or put down.

Unsurpassable, un-sėr-pas′a-bl, *a.* Not capable of being surpassed, excelled, or exceeded.—**Unsurpassed**, un-sėr-past′, *a.* Not excelled, exceeded, or outdone.

Unsusceptible, un-sus-sep′ti-bl, *a.* Not susceptible; insusceptible.

Unsuspected, un-sus-pek′ted, *a.* Not suspected; not an object of suspicion.—**Unsuspecting**, un-sus-pek′ting, *a.* Not imagining that any ill is designed; free from suspicion.—**Unsuspicious**, un-sus-pish′us, *a.* Not inclined to suspect or to imagine evil; unsuspecting.

Unswathe, un-swāᴛʜ′, *v.t.* To take a swathe from; to relieve from a bandage or bandages.

Unswayed, un-swād′, *p.* and *a.* Not biassed or influenced.

Unswept, un-swept′, *a.* Not swept; not cleaned by sweeping; not passed over by a sweeping motion.

Unswerving, un-swėr′ving, *a.* Not deviating from any rule or standard; unwavering; firm.

Unsworn, un-swōrn′, *a.* Not bound by an oath; not having taken an oath.

Unsymmetrical, un-sim-met′ri-kal, *a.* Wanting symmetry or due proportion of parts.

Unsystematic, **Unsystematical**, un′-sis-te-mat″ik, un′sis-te-mat″i-kal, *a.* Not systematic; wanting a proper system.

Untainted, un-tān′ted, *a.* Not tainted; not impregnated with foul matter; not putrescent; not sullied; unblemished.

Untaken, un-tā′kn, *a.* Not taken; not seized or captured.

Untamable, **Untameable**, un-tā′ma-bl, *a.* Not capable of being tamed.—**Untamed**, un-tāmd′, *a.* Not reclaimed from wildness; not domesticated; not subdued or brought under control.

Untarnished, un-tär′nisht, *a.* Not soiled or tarnished; unstained; unblemished.

Untasted, un-tās′ted, *a.* Not tried by the taste; not experienced or enjoyed.

Untaught, un-tạt′, *a.* Not instructed or educated; unlettered; unskilled; unschooled; not made the subject of teaching.

Untaxed, un-takst′, *a.* Not charged with or liable to pay taxes; not charged with any fault.

Unteach, un-tēch′, *v.t.* To cause to forget, disbelieve, or give up what has been taught.—**Unteachable**, un-tē′cha-bl, *a.* That cannot be taught; indocile.

Untempered, un-tem′pėrd, *a.* Not tempered; not duly mixed; not regulated, moderated, or controlled.

Untenable, un-ten′a-bl, *a.* Not tenable; that cannot be held in possession; that cannot be maintained by argument; not defensible.

Untenantable, un-ten′an-ta-bl, *a.* Not capable of being tenanted; uninhabitable.—**Untenanted**, un-ten′an-ted, *a.* Not occupied by a tenant; not inhabited.

Unthanked, un-thangkt′, *a.* Not having received thanks; not repaid with acknowledgments.—**Unthankful**, un-thangk′-fụl, *a.* Ungrateful; not making acknowledgments for good received.

Untheological, un-thē′ō-loj″i-kal, *a.* Not according to sound theology.

Unthinkable, un-thingk′a-bl, *a.* That cannot be made an object of thought; incogitable.—**Unthinking**, un-thingk′ing, *a.* Not heedful; inconsiderate; not indicating thought or reflection.—**Unthinkingly**, un-thingk′ing-li, *adv.* Without reflection; thoughtlessly.—**Unthought**, un-thạt′, *a.* Not imagined or conceived; not considered; often followed by *of*.

Unthread, un-thred′, *v.t.* To draw or take out a thread from.

Unthrift, un′thrift, *n.* A prodigal.—**Unthriftiness**, un-thrif′ti-nes, *n.* The state of being unthrifty; prodigality.—**Unthrifty**, un-thrif′ti, *a.* Prodigal; profuse; lavish; wasteful.

Untie, un-tī′, *v.t.* To loosen, as a knot; to undo; to unfasten; to unbind; to set loose.

Until, un-til′, *prep.* [From a prefix *und-* (seen in O.Fris., O.Sax., O.Goth.), and *till*, the prefix itself meaning till or to, and occurring also in *unto*.] Till; to: used before nouns of time; preceding a sentence or clause: till the time that; till the point or degree that.

Untillable, un-til′a-bl, *a.* Incapable of being tilled; barren.—**Untilled**, un-tild′, *a.* Not cultivated.

Untimely, un-tīm′li, *a.* Not timely; not done or happening in the right season; inopportune; premature.—*adv.* Before the natural time; unseasonably.

Untinctured, un-tingk′tūrd, *a.* Not tinctured; not tinged, mixed, or imbued.

Untinged, un-tinjd′, *a.* Not tinged, stained, or discoloured.

Untiring, un-tī′ring, *a.* Not becoming tired or exhausted; unwearied.

Untitled, un-tī'tld, *a.* Having no title of rank; not belonging to the nobility.

Unto, un'tö, *prep.* [Prefix *und* and *to.* UNTIL.] To. *Unto* is now antiquated, though still sometimes used in the solemn or elevated style.

Untold, un-tōld', *a.* Not told; not related; not revealed; not numbered.

Untouched, un-tucht', *a.* Not hit; not meddled with; uninjured; not mentioned; not affected; not affected emotionally.

Untoward, **Untowardly**, un-tō'ėrd, un-tō'ėrd-li, *a.* Froward; perverse; not easily guided or taught; awkward; inconvenient; vexatious.—*adv.* In an untoward manner; perversely.—**Untowardness**, un-tō'ėrd-nes, *n.* Frowardness; perverseness.

Untraceable, un-trās'a-bl, *a.* Incapable of being traced or followed.

Untracked, un-trakt', *a.* Not tracked; not marked by footsteps.

Untractable, un-trak'ta-bl, *a.* Not tractable; intractable; refractory.

Untrained, un-trānd', *a.* Not trained; not disciplined; not instructed.

Untrammeled, un-tram'eld, *a.* Not trammeled or fettered; free to act.

Untransferable, un-trans-fer'a-bl, *a.* Incapable of being transferred or passed from one to another.

Untranslatable, un-trans-lā'ta-bl, *a.* Not capable of being translated or rendered into another language.

Untraveled, un-trav'eld, *a.* Not traversed by passengers; not having gained experience by travel.

Untried, un-trīd', *a.* Not tried; not attempted; not showing capabilities by trial or proof given; not having passed trial; not heard and determined in a court of law.

Untrod, **Untrodden**, un-trod', un-trod'n, *a.* Not having been trod; not marked by the feet; unfrequented.

Untroubled, un-trub'ld, *a.* Free from trouble; not disturbed by care, sorrow, or business; not agitated or ruffled; not raised into waves.

Untrue, un-trö', *a.* Not true; false; contrary to the fact; not faithful to another; not to be trusted; inconstant in love.—**Untruly**, un-trö'li, *adv.* Falsely; not according to reality.

Untrustworthy, un-trust'wėr-THi, *a.* Not worthy of being trusted; not deserving of confidence.

Untruth, un-tröth', *n.* The quality of being untrue; contrariety to truth; want of veracity; want of fidelity; a false assertion; a lie.—**Untruthful**, un-tröth'ful, *a.* Wanting in truth or veracity.

Untunable, un-tū'na-bl, *a.* Not capable of being tuned; discordant; not musical.—**Untune**, un-tūn', *v.t.* To put out of tune; to disorder; to confuse.

Untutored, un-tū'tord, *a.* Untaught; uninstructed; rude.

Untwine, un-twīn', *v.t.* To untwist; to open or separate after having been twisted; to cause to cease winding round and clinging.—*v.i.* To become untwined.

Untwist, un-twist', *v.t.* To separate and open, as threads twisted; to turn back from being twisted.—*v.i.* To become untwisted.

Unurged, un-ėrjd', *a.* Not urged; not pressed with solicitation; unsolicited.

Unused, un-ūzd', *a.* Not employed; disused; that has never been used; not accustomed.

Unusual, un-ū'zhö-al, *a.* Not usual; not common; rare.—**Unusually**, un-ū'zhö-al-i, *adv.* In an unusual manner; not commonly.

Unutterable, un-ut'ėr-a-bl, *a.* Incapable of being uttered or expressed; ineffable; inexpressible.—**Unutterably**, un-ut'ėr-a-bli, *adv.* Inexpressibly.—**Unuttered**, un-ut'ėrd, *a.* Not uttered or spoken.

Unvalued, un-val'ūd, *a.* Not valued or prized; neglected.

Unvanquished, un-vang'kwisht, *a.* Not conquered; not overcome.

Unvaried, un-vā'rid, *a.* Not varied; not altered; not diversified; always the same.—**Unvarying**, un-vā'ri-ing, *a.* Not altering; uniform.

Unvarnished, un-vär'nisht, *a.* Not overlaid with varnish; *fig.* not artfully embellished; plain.

Unveil, un-vāl', *v.t.* To remove a veil from; to disclose to view.—*v.i.* To remove one's veil.

Unventilated, un-ven'ti-lā-ted, *a.* Not ventilated; not purified by a free current of air.

Unveracious, un-ve-rā'shus, *a.* Not veracious; untruthful.—**Unveracity**, un-ve-ras'i-ti, *n.* Want of veracity; untruthfulness.

Unversed, un-vėrst', *a.* Not versed or skilled; unacquainted.

Unviolated, un-vī'ō-lā-ted, *a.* Not violated; not injured; inviolate.

Unvoiced, un-voist', *a.* Not spoken; unuttered; *phonetics*, not uttered with voice as distinct from breath.

Unwakened, un-wā'knd, *a.* Not roused from sleep or as from sleep.

Unwarlike, un-war'līk, *a.* Not warlike; not used to or fond of war; not military.

Unwarned, un-warnd', *a.* Not warned or cautioned; not previously admonished of danger.

Unwarped, un-warpt', *a.* Not warped; not biassed; impartial.

Unwarrantable, un-wor'an-ta-bl, *a.* Not defensible; not justifiable; improper.—**Unwarrantably**, un-wor'an-ta-bli, *adv.* In a manner that cannot be justified; unjustifiably.—**Unwarranted**, un-wor'an-ted, *a.* Not authorized; not assured or certain; not guaranteed.

Unwary, un-wā'ri, *a.* Not wary or vigilant against danger; not cautious; unguarded.—**Unwarily**, un-wā'ri-li, *adv.* Without vigilance and caution; heedlessly.—**Unwariness**, un-wā'ri-nes, *n.* Want of caution; heedlessness.

Unwashed, un-wosht', *a.* Not washed; not cleansed by water; filthy.—*The great unwashed*, a phrase first applied by Burke to the artisan class, now used to designate the lower classes generally; the mob; the rabble.—**Unwashen**, un-wosh'n, *a.* Unwashed. (N.T.)

Unwasted, un-wās'ted, *a.* Not wasted or lavished away; not consumed or diminished by time or other means.

Unwatchful, un-woch'ful, *a.* Not vigilant.

Unwavering, un-wā'vėr'ing, *a.* Not wavering; not unstable; fixed: steadfast.

Unwearied, un-wē'rid, *a.* Not tired; not fatigued; indefatigable; assiduous.—**Unweariedly**, un-wē'rid-li, *adv.* Indefatigably.—**Unweariedness**, un-wē'rid-nes, *n.*

Unweave, un-wēv', *v.t.* To undo what has been woven; to disentangle.

Unwed, un-wed', *a.* Unmarried.

Unwedgeable, un-wej'a-bl, *a.* Not to be split with wedges. (*Shak.*)

Unweeded, un-wē'ded, *a.* Not cleared of weeds.

Unweighed, un-wād', *a.* Not having the weight ascertained; not deliberately considered and examined.

Unwelcome, un-wel'kum, *a.* Not welcome; not pleasing or grateful; not well received.

Unwell, un-wel', *a.* Indisposed; not in good health; ailing.

Unwept, un-wept', *a.* Not wept for; not lamented; not mourned.

Unwholesome, un-hōl'sum, *a.* Not wholesome; unfavourable or prejudicial to health; insalubrious; causing sickness; not sound; diseased.—**Unwholesomeness**, un-hōl'sum-nes, *n.* State of being injurious to health; insalubrity.

Unwieldy, un-wēl'di, *a.* [From *un*, not, and old *weldy*, *wieldy*, active. WIELD.] Movable with difficulty; too bulky and clumsy to move or be moved easily; unmanageable from weight; ponderous.—**Unwieldily**, un-wēl'di-li, *adv.* Cumbrously.—**Unwieldiness**, un-wēl'di-nes, *n.* Heaviness; difficulty of being moved.

Unwilling, un-wil'ing, *a.* Not willing; loath; disinclined; reluctant.—**Unwillingly**, un-wil'ing-li, *adv.* Against one's will; reluctantly.—**Unwillingness**, un-wil'ing-nes, *n.* Loathness; disinclination; reluctance.

Unwind, un-wīnd', *v.t.* To wind off; to disentangle.—*v.i.* To admit of being unwound.

Unwinking, un-wingk'ing, *a.* Not winking; not shutting the eyes; not ceasing to wake or watch.

Unwisdom, un-wiz'dom, *n.* Want of wisdom; foolishness; unwise conduct or speech.—**Unwise**, un-wīz', *a.* Not wise; defective in wisdom; foolish; injudicious.—**Unwisely**, un-wīz'li, *adv.* Foolishly; injudiciously; indiscreetly.

Unwished, un-wisht', *a.* Not wished or desired; unwelcome.

Unwitnessed, un-wit'nest, *a.* Not witnessed; not attested by witnesses.

Unwitting, un-wit'ing, *a.* Not knowing; unconscious; unaware.—**Unwittingly**, un-wit'ing-li, *adv.* Without knowledge or consciousness; inadvertently.

Unwomanly, un-wu'man-li, *a.* Unbecoming a woman.

Unwonted, un-wun'ted, *a.* Not wonted; not common; unusual; infrequent; unaccustomed.—**Unwontedly**, un-wun'ted-li, *adv.* In an unaccustomed manner.—**Unwontedness**, un-wun'ted-nes, *n.* Uncommonness; rareness.

Unwooed, un-wöd', *a.* Not wooed or courted.

Unworldly, un-wėrld'li, *a.* Not influenced by worldly or sordid motives.—**Unworldliness**, un-wėrld'li-nes, *n.* State of being unworldly.

Unworn, un-wōrn', *a.* Not worn; not impaired by wearing.

Unworshiped, un-wėr'shipt, *a.* Not adored.

Unworthy, un-wėr'THi, *a.* Not deserving; not worthy (*unworthy of* confidence): worthless; vile; base; beneath the character (work *unworthy of* the man).—**Unworthily**, un-wėr'THi-li, *adv.* Not according to desert.—**Unworthiness**, un-wėr'THi-nes, *n.* Want of worth or merit.

Unwounded, un-wön'ded, *a.* Not hurt; not injured in body.

Unwrap, un-rap', *v.t.* To open or undo, as what is wrapped up; to take off a wrapper from.

Unwreathe, un-rēTH', *v.t.* To untwist or untwine.

Unwritten, un-rit'n, *a.* Not reduced to writing; oral; not written upon; blank.—*Unwritten law*, a law not formulated in any written document.

Unwrought, un-rat', *a.* Not manufactured; not worked up.

Unwrung, un-rung', *a.* Not pinched or galled.

Unyielding, un-yēl'ding, *a.* Unbending; unpliant; stiff; firm; obstinate.

Unyoke, un-yōk', *v.t.* To loose from a yoke.

Up, up, *adv.* [A.Sax. *up*, *upp*, up=D. and Dan. *op*, Icel. *upp*, Sw. *up*, *upp*, Goth. *iup*, G. *auf*; akin to *over*.] The opposite of *down*; to a higher place or position; from a lower to a higher place; on high; aloft; raised; upright; erect; no longer in bed; in a state of action; in commotion, excitement, insurrection, or the like; higher or advanced in price, rank, social standing, &c.; to a more complete or mature condition; reaching a certain point; as far as: with *to* (*up to* the roof); not below or inferior: with *to* (*up to* one's expectations); denoting approach or arrival (to bring *up* troops); quite; thoroughly: often used to intensify a verb (to eat *up* all the food); in a place where it is kept when not used; in a state of being brought together or into close compass; often used elliptically for rise up, go up, &c.; followed by *with* in this elliptical use it signifies set up, erect, raise (*up with* the flag, he *up with* his hand).—*All up*, all over; completely done or ruined; come to an end (it is *all up* with him).—*To come up with*, to overtake. —*The time is up*, the allotted time is past. —*To have one up* or *pull one up*, to bring one before a magistrate or court of justice. —*Up and down*, here and there; hither and thither; from one place to another.—*prep.* From a lower to a higher place or point on; at or in a high or higher position on; towards the interior (generally the more elevated part) of a country; in a direction from the coast, or towards the head or source of a stream.—*n.* Used in the phrase *ups and downs*, rises and falls; alternate states of prosperity and the contrary; vicissitudes.—It is also used adjectively in such expressions as the *up* line of a railway. See compounds below.—**Uppish**, up′ish, *a.* Proud; arrogant; putting on airs.—**Uppishness**, up′ish-nes, *n.* The quality of being uppish.

Upas, ū′pas, *n.* [Malay *upas*, poison.] A tree of Java and the neighbouring islands yielding a poison, concerning the deadly properties of which exaggerated stories were formerly current, its exhalations being said to be fatal to both animal and vegetable life at several miles' distance.

Upbear, up-bār′, *v.t.* To bear or raise aloft; to elevate; to sustain aloft; to support.—**Upbind**, up-bīnd′, *v.t.* To bind up.—**Upbraid**, up-brād′, *v.t.* [From *up*, and *braid*, in old sense of to scold. Braid.] To cast some fault or offence in the teeth of; to charge reproachfully: followed by *with* or *for* before the thing imputed; to reprove with severity; to chide; to be a reproach to.—**Upbraiding**, up-brā′ding, *n.* Reproach; reproof.—**Upbreak**, up′brāk, *n.* A breaking or bursting up.—**Upbringing**, up′bring-ing, *n.* The process of bringing up; training; education; breeding.—**Upcast**, up′kast, *a.* Cast up; thrown or turned upward; directed up.—*n.* The ventilating shaft of a mine up which the air passes after circulating in the mine. — **Upcoil**, up-koil′, *v.t.* or *i.* To make or wind up into a coil.—**Upcurl**, up-kėrl′, *v.t.* To curl or wreathe upwards. — **Upgather**, up-gaᴛʜ′ėr, *v.t.* To gather up together.—**Upgaze**, up-gāz′, *v.i.* To gaze upwards.—**Upgrow**, up-grō′, *v.i.* To grow up.—**Upheaval**, up-hē′val, *n.* The act of upheaving; *geol.* a lifting up of a portion of the earth's crust by some expansion or elevating power from below.—**Upheave**, up-hēv′, *v.t.* To heave or lift up from beneath; to raise up or aloft.—**Upheld**, up-held′, pret. and pp. of *uphold*.—**Uphill**, up′hil, *a.* Leading or going up a rising ground; attended with exertion; difficult; fatiguing.—**Uphold**, up-hōld′, *v.t.* To raise on high; to keep elevated; to keep erect; to support; to sustain; to keep from declining.—**Upholder**, up-hōl′dėr, *n.* A supporter; a defender.

Upholsterer, up-hōl′stėr-ėr, *n.* [Lengthened from older *upholster* to resemble *fruiterer*, *poulterer*; lit. an *upholder*. Comp. *undertaker* as to similar specialized meaning.] One who furnishes houses with curtains, carpets, cushions for chairs and sofas, &c.—**Upholster**, up-hōl′stėr, *v.t.* To furnish with upholstery. — **Upholstery**, up-hōl′stėr-i, *n.* The business or goods of an upholsterer.

Upkeep, up′kēp, *n.* Maintenance in a state of efficiency.—**Upland**, up′land, *n.* The higher ground of a district; ground elevated above meadows and valleys; slopes of hills, &c.—*a.* Pertaining to uplands or higher grounds. — **Uplander**, up′land-ėr, *n.* An inhabitant of the uplands.—**Uplandish**, up-land′ish, *a.* Pertaining to uplands; rustic.—**Uplift**, up-lift′, *v.t.* To raise aloft; to elevate. — **Up-line**, *n.* A line of railway which leads to the metropolis or to a main terminus from the provinces in England.—**Upmost**, up′mōst, *a.* Highest; topmost; uppermost.

Upon, up-on′, *prep.* [A.Sax. *uppon*, upon —*upp*, up, and *on*, on. Up, On.] On; especially, resting on; at or in contact with the upper or outer part of a thing; resting, lying, or placed in contact with: all but synonymous with *on*, though sometimes rather more emphatic.

Upper, up′ėr, *a.* [Compar. from *up*.] Higher as contrasted with *lower*; higher in place; superior in rank or dignity.— *Upper case*, the capital letters, named after the top case used by compositors to hold capital letters, reference marks, and other less-used type.— *Upper House*, in Congress, the Senate as distinguished from the House of Representatives or "*Lower House*." — *Upper ten thousand*, the leading classes in society; the aristocracy: *the upper ten*.—*n.* An abbreviation of *Upper-leather*. — **Upper-hand**, *n.* Superiority; advantage. — **Upper cut**, *n.* An upward blow in boxing. — **Upper-leather**, *n.* The leather for the vamps and quarters of shoes. — **Upper-most**, up′ėr-mōst, *a.* Highest in place; highest in power or authority.—**Upper-world**, *n.* The heavens; the earth, as opposed to the *infernal regions*.

Uppish. Under Up.

Upraise, up-rāz′, *v.t.* To raise or lift up.

Uprear, up-rēr′, *v.t.* To rear up; to raise.

Upright, up′rīt, *a.* [That is *right*, or directly, *up*.] Erect; perpendicular; erect on one's feet; pricked up; shooting directly from the body; adhering to rectitude; of inflexible honesty; conformable to rectitude. — *n.* Something standing erect; a vertical piece in some structure. —**Uprightly**, up′rīt-li, *adv.* In an upright manner; perpendicularly; honestly; justly. —**Uprightness**, up′rīt-nes, *n.* The quality or condition of being upright; honesty; integrity; probity.

Uprise, up-rīz′, *v.i.*—pret. *uprose* (sometimes in poetry *uprist*), pp. *uprisen.* To rise up, as from bed or from a seat; to ascend above the horizon; to slope upwards.—**Uprising**, up-rī′zing, *n.* The act of rising up; rise; an ascent or declivity; a riot; a rebellion.

Uproar, up′rōr, *n.* [From D. *oproer*, uproar, tumult = Dan. *uprör*, Sw. *upror*, G. *aufruhr*, from *op*, *up*, *auf*, up, and D. *roeren*, Dan. *röre*, Sw. *röra*, G. *ruhren*, to stir; the spelling being affected by *roar*.] A violent disturbance and noise; bustle and clamour; a noisy tumult.—**Uproarious**, up-rō′ri-us, *a.* Making an uproar or tumult; tumultuous.—**Uproariously**, up-rō′ri-us-li, *adv.* With great noise and tumult. —**Uproariousness**, up-rō′ri-us-nes, *n.*

Uproot, up-röt′, *v.t.* To tear up by the roots, or as if by the roots; to eradicate.—**Uprouse**, up-rouz′, *v.t.* To rouse up; to awake. —**Uprush**, up′rush, *n.* A rush upward.—**Upset**, up-set′, *v.t.* To overturn; to overthrow; to overset; to put out of one's normal state; to discompose completely.—*n.* (up′set). The act of upsetting.—*a.* Fixed; determined. — *Upset price*, the price at which anything is exposed to sale by auction.—**Upshoot**, up-shöt′, *v.i.* To shoot or grow up.—**Upshot**, up′shot, *n.* Final issue; conclusion.—**Upside**, up′sīd, *n.* The upper side.—*Upside down*, the upper part undermost; hence, in complete disorder.—**Upspring**, up-spring′, *v.i.* To spring up.—**Upstairs**, up′stārz, *a.* Pertaining or relating to an upper story or flat.—*adv.* In or towards an upper story. — **Upstart**, up-stärt′, *v.i.* To start or spring up suddenly. —*n.* (up′stärt). One that suddenly rises from a humble position to wealth, power, or consequence; a parvenu.—**Up-stroke**, *n.* An upward line made by the pen or pencil in writing.—**Upthrow**, up-thrō′, *v.t.* To throw up; to elevate.—*n.* (up′thrō). *Geol.* a lifting up of a portion of the earth's crust; an upheaval. — **Up-train**, *n.* A railway train on an up-line.—**Upturn**, up-tėrn′, *v.t.* To turn up; to throw up; to furrow.—**Upward, Upwards**, up′wėrd, up′wėrdz, *adv.* [A.Sax. *upweard*, *upweardes*, the latter being an adverbial genitive, like *towards*, &c.] Toward a higher place; in an upward direction; toward heaven and God; with respect to the higher part; toward the source or origin.—*Upwards of*, *upward of*, more than; above.—**Upward**, *a.* Directed or turned to a higher place.

Uræmia, u-rē′mi-a, *n.* [Gr. *ouron*, urine, and *haima*, blood.] A condition of the blood in which it contains urine or urea.

Uralic, Uralian, ū-ral′ik, ū-rā′li-an, *a.* Pertaining to the *Ural* Mountains or that region; Finnish.—**Uralo-Altaic**, ū-ral′ō-al-tā″ik, *a.* Same as *Turanian*.

Urania, ū-rā′ni-a, *n.* [L. *Urania*, Gr. *Ourania*, lit. 'the Heavenly', from *ouranos*, heaven.] The muse of astronomy, generally represented holding in her left hand a celestial globe.—**Uranic**, ū-ran′ik, *a.* Pertaining to the heavens; celestial; pertaining to uranium.—**Uraninite**, ū-ran′-in-īt, *n.* [From *uranium*.] A mineral closely allied to *pitchblende*, which is considered to be a massive and altered form. These minerals consist largely of uranium, and also contain cerium and thorium, but are chiefly important as sources of radium. —**Uranite**, ū′ran-īt, *n.* An ore of uranium, of a green or yellow colour.—**Uranium**, ū-rā′ni-um, *n.* A rare metal, of a colour resembling that of nickel or iron, forming several oxides, which are used in painting on porcelain.—**Uranography**, ū-ra-nog′ra-fi, *n.* [Gr. *ouranos*, heaven, and *graphō*, to describe.] The determination of the positions of the heavenly bodies, the construction of celestial maps and globes, &c.—**Uranous**, ū′ra-nus, *a.* Pertaining to the metal uranium.—**Uranus**, ū′ra-nus, *n.* [The Greek name of heaven.] A deity of Greek mythology, father of Kronos or Saturn; *astron.* one of the primary planets, the most distant of all except Neptune, possessing several satellites.

Urari, u̦′ra-rē, *n.* Curari.

Urban, ėr′ban, *a.* [L. *urbanus*, from *urbs*, a city (seen also in *suburb*).] Belonging to or included in a town or city (*urban* population).—**Urbane**, ėr-bān′, *a.* [Same word used differently.] Courteous; polite; sauve; elegant or refined.—**Urbanity**, ėr-ban′i-ti, *n.* That civility or courtesy of manners which is acquired by associating with well-bred people; politeness; courtesy.

Urceolate, Urceolar, ėr′sē-o-lāt, ėr′sē-o-lėr, *a.* [From L. *urceolus*, dim. of *urceus*, a pitcher.] *Bot.* shaped like a pitcher; swelling or bulging out like a pitcher.

Urchin, ėr′chin, *n.* [Prov. Fr. *hurchon*, *hirchon*, Fr. *hérisson*, O.Fr. *eriçon*, from L.L. *ericio*, *ericionis*, from L. *ericius*, a hedgehog, from *er* = Gr. *chēr*, hedgehog.] A hedgehog; a familiar, half-chiding name sometimes given in sport to a child; a sea-urchin.

Urdu, u̦r′du̦, *n.* [Hind. camp.] The Hindustani language springing from the union of the Mohammedan invaders with their various camp-followers.

Urea, ū′rē-a, *n.* [From the *ur* of *urine*.] A crystalline compound which exists in healthy urine, and may also be prepared artificially.—**Ureter**, ū-rē′tėr, *n.* [Gr. *ourētēr*, from *oureō*, to make water.] The duct or tube that conveys the urine from the kidney to the bladder.—**Urethra**, ū-rē′thra, *n.* [Gr. *ourēthra*.] The canal by which the urine is conducted from the bladder and discharged.—**Urethral**, ū-rē′thral, *a.* Pertaining to the urethra.—**Uretic**, ū-ret′ik, *a.* Relating to or promoting the flow of urine.

Uredo, ū-rē′dō, *n.* [L. blight of plants, from *uro*, to burn.] A genius of parasitic fungi, causing such diseases in plants as smut, rust, &c.

Uredospore, ū-rē′dō-spōr, *n.* [Gr. *eurēdō*, blight, *sporos*, fruit.] In rust-fungi, a one-celled stalked summer-spore.

Urge, ėrj, *v.t.*—*urged*, *urging*. [L. *urgeo*, *urgere*, to press, push, urge; same root as A.Sax. *wrecan*, to wreak.] To press, impel, or force onward; to press the mind or will of; to serve as a motive or impelling cause; to stimulate; to press or ply hard with arguments, entreaties, or the like;

to importune; to solicit earnestly; to press upon attention; to insist on (to *urge* an argument).—*v.i.* To press forward.—**Urgency**, ėr'jen-si, *n.* The state or character of being urgent; importunity; earnest solicitation; pressure of necessity. — **Urgent**, ėr'jent, *a.* [L. *urgens, urgentis.*] Pressing; necessitating or calling for immediate action; eagerly soliciting; pressing with importunity. — **Urgently**, ėr'jent-li, *adv.* In an urgent manner; with pressing importunity; vehemently.

Urginea, ėr-jin'ē-ä, *n.* A genus of herb, native to the Old World.

Urheen, ör'hēn', *n.* A Chinese musical instrument having two strings.

Uric, ū'rik, *a.* [From *ur* in *urine.*] Pertaining to or obtained from urine; applied to an acid which is a main constituent of guano.

Urim, ū'rim, *n.* [Heb. *urîm*, lights or flames, pl. of *ûr*, flame.] A kind of ornament or appendage belonging to the habit of the Jewish high-priest in ancient times, along with the Thummim, in virtue of which he gave oracular answers to the people.

Urinant, ū'rin-ant, *a.* *Her.* applied to a fish, swimming or diving, head downwards, with the belly opposite the sinister side of the shield.

Urine, ū'rin, *n.* [Fr. *urine*, from L. *urina*, allied to Gr. *ouron*, urine; Skr. *vâri*, water; A.Sax. *ûrig*, humid; Icel. *ûr*, drizzling rain.] An animal fluid secreted by the kidneys, whence it is conveyed into the bladder by the ureters, and through the urethra discharged.—**Urinal**, ū'ri-nal, *n.* [L. *urinal.*] A vessel for receiving urine in cases of incontinence; a convenience, public or private, for the accommodation of persons requiring to pass urine.—**Urinalysis**, ū-ri-nal'i-sis, *n.* The act of analyzing the chemical elements of urine.—**Urinary**, ū'ri-na-ri, *a.* Pertaining to urine or to the organs connected with its secretion and discharge.— *Urinary organs*, the kidneys, the ureters, the bladder, and the urethra.—*n.* A reservoir for the reception of urine, &c., for manure.—**Urinate**, ū'ri-nāt, *v.i.* To discharge urine.—**Urinogenital**, ū'ri-nō-jen"i-tal, *a.* Pertaining to the urinary and genital organs.—**Urinometer**, *n.* An instrument for ascertaining the specific gravity of urine.

Urn, ėrn, *n.* [L. *urna*, from *uro*, to burn, as being made of burned clay.] A kind of vase — a term somewhat loosely applied; a rather large vessel with a foot or pedestal, and a stop-cock, employed to keep hot water at the tea-table; a tea-urn; a vessel in which the ashes of the dead were formerly kept; a cinerary urn; *bot.* the spore-case of mosses.—**Urnful**, ėrn'fụl, *n.* As much as an urn will hold.

Urodela, ū-rō-dē'la, *n.pl.* [Gr. *oura*, a tail, and *dēlos*, evident.] The tailed amphibians, such as the newt.—**Urodele**, ū'rō-dēl, *n.* and *a.* One of, or pertaining to, the Urodela.

Urogenital, ū-rō-jen'i-tal, *a.* Urinogenital.

Uropod, ū'ro-pod, *n.* [Gr. *oura*, tail, *pous*, *podos*, foot.] A name of certain posterior appendages of the abdomen in crustaceans, serving as feet.

Uropygium, ū-rō-pij'i-um, *n.* [Gr. *ouropygion.*] *Ornith.* the rump of birds.—**Uropygial**, ū-rō-pij'i-al, *a.* Pertaining to the uropygium.

Uroscopy, ū-ros'ko-pi, *n.* [Gr. *ouron*, urine, and *skopeō*, to view.] The judgment of diseases by inspection of the urine.

Ursa, ėr'sa, *n.* [L., a she-bear, a constellation.] A name of two constellations: *Ursa Major*, the Great Bear, one of the most conspicuous of the northern constellations, situated near the pole, and popularly called *Charles's Wain* or the *Plough*; and *Ursa Minor*, the Little Bear, the constellation which contains the pole-star.—**Ursiform**, ėr'si-form, *a.* Having the shape of a bear. —**Ursine**, ėr'sin, *a.* [L. *ursinus.*] Pertaining to or resembling a bear.

Urson, ėr'son, *n.* [Same as *urchin*, Fr. *hérisson.*] CAWQUAW.

Ursuline, ėr'sū-lin, *a.* Applied to an order of nuns who took their name from St. *Ursula*, and who devote themselves to the succour of poverty and sickness, and the education of female children.

Urticaceous, ėr-ti-kā'shus, *a.* [L. *urtica*, a nettle, from *uro*, to burn.] *Bot.* pertaining to plants of the nettle family.—**Urticaria**, ėr-ti-kā'ri-a, *n.* Nettle-rash.—**Urticating**, ėr'ti-kā-ting, *p.* and *a.* Stinging like a nettle; pertaining to urtication.—**Urtication**, ėr-ti-kā'shon, *n.* The stinging of nettles or a similar stinging; the whipping of a benumbed or paralytic limb with nettles, in order to restore its feeling.

Urubu, ụ-rö'bụ, *n.* The black vulture or zopilote, resembling the turkey-buzzard.

Urus, ū'rus, *n.* [L.] The mountain-bull or *Bos urus*, described by Caesar, which ran wild in Gaul in the period of the Roman invasion, probably now extinct though relationship is claimed for an English species.

Us, us, *pron.* [A.Sax. *ús*, acc. and dat.; Goth. *unsis*, *uns*, G. *uns*, us.] The objective or accusative case of *we*; the dative of *we*, used after certain verbs, such as verbs of *giving*.

Usage, Usance. Under USE.

Use, ūs, *n.* [O.Fr. *us*, use, from L. *usus*, use, a using, service, need, from *utor*, *usus*, to use (whence also *utility*, *utensil*, *usury*, *abuse*, &c.).] The act of employing anything, or the state of being employed; employment; conversion to a purpose (*to make use of*, that is, to use or employ); the quality that makes a thing proper for a purpose; utility; service; convenience; need for employing; exigency (I have no *use* for it); continued or repeated practice; wont; usage; a liturgical form of service for use in a diocese (the *Sarum use*). — *Use and wont*, the common or customary practice. —*v.t.* (ūz)—*used*, *using*. [Fr. *user*, from L.L. *usare*, to use, from *usus*, pp. of L. *utar*, to use.] To employ or make use of; to act with or by means of; to do work with; to consume or exhaust by employment (to *use* flour for food); to practise or employ (to *use* treachery); to make a practice of; to act or behave towards; to treat (to *use* one ill); to accustom; to render familiar by practice. —*To use up*, to consume entirely by using; to exhaust or wear out the strength of.—*v.i.* To be accustomed; to be in the habit; to be wont.—**Usable**, ū'za-bl, *a.* Capable of being used.—**Usage**, ū'zāj, *n.* [Fr. *usage*, from *user*, to use.] Treatment; behaviour of one person towards another; long-continued practice; customary way of acting; custom; practice; established mode of employing some particular word.—**Usance**, ū'zans, *n.* [Fr. *usance*, from *user*, to use.] Usury; interest paid for the loan of money; the time which in certain countries is allowed by custom or usage for the payment of bills of exchange drawn on those countries.—**Useful**, ūs'fụl, *a.* Valuable for use; suited or adapted to the purpose; beneficial; profitable.—**Usefully**, ūs'fụl-li, *adv.* In a useful manner; profitably; beneficially.—**Usefulness**, ūs'fụl-nes, *n.* The state or quality of being useful; profitableness.—**Useless**, ūs'les, *a.* Having no use; unserviceable; producing no good end; not advancing the end proposed.—**Uselessly**, ūs'les-li, *adv.* Without profit or advantage. —**Uselessness**, ūs'les-nes, *n.* Unfitness for any valuable purpose or for the purpose intended.—**User**, ū'zėr, *n.* One who uses.—**Usual**, ū'zhū-al, *a.* [L. *usualis*, Fr. *usuel.*] In common use; customary; ordinary; frequent. — **Usually**, ū'zhū-al-li, *adv.* Customarily; ordinarily.—**Usualness**, ū'zhū-al-nes, *n.* Commonness; frequency.

Ushas, Ushasa, ụ'shas, ụ-shä'sa, *n.* [From Skr. *ush*, to shine.] The Hindu goddess of dawn.

Usher, ush'ėr, *n.* [O.Fr. *ussier*, *uissier*, *hussier*, Fr. *huissier*, a door-keeper, from O.Fr. *uis*, *huis*, from L. *ostium*, a door.] An officer or servant who had care of the door of a court, hall, chamber, &c.; hence, an officer whose business is to introduce strangers or to walk before a person of rank; an under-teacher or assistant to a schoolmaster or principal teacher. — *v.t.* To act as an usher towards; to introduce, as forerunner or harbinger: generally followed by *in*, *forth*, &c.—**Ushership**, ush'ėr-ship, *n.* Office of an usher.

Usquebaugh, us'kwē-bạ, *n.* [Ir. and Gael. *uisge-beatha*, whisky, lit. water of life. WHISKY.] Whisky.

Ustulate, us'tū-lāt, *a.* [L. *ustulatus*, pp. of *ustulo*, dim. of *uro*, *ustum*, to burn.] *Bot.* blackened as if burned.—**Ustulation**, us-tū-lā'shon, *n.* The act of burning or searing; the operation of expelling a substance by heat, as sulphur from ores.

Usual, Usually, &c. Under USE.

Usucaption, ū-zū-kap'shon, *n.* [L. *usus*, use, and *capio*, *captum*, to take.] In *civil law*, the acquisition of property by uninterrupted undisputed possession of it for a certain term.

Usufruct, ū'zū-frukt, *n.* [L. *usufructus*—*usus*, use, and *fructus*, fruit.] *Law*, the use and enjoyment of lands or tenements without the right to alienate such.

Usurp, ū-zėrp', *v.t.* [Fr. *usurper*, from L. *usurpare*, from *usus*, use, and *rapio*, to seize. USE, RAPID.] To seize and hold possession of by force or without right; to appropriate or assume illegally or wrongfully (a throne, power, or rank).—*v.i.* To be or act as a usurper; to encroach.—**Usurpation**, ū-zėr-pā'shon, *n.* The act of usurping; the seizing or occupying the place or power of another without right; especially, the unlawful occupation of a throne; an encroaching. — **Usurpatory**, ū-zėr'pa-to-ri, *a.* Characterized or marked by usurpation; usurping. — **Usurper**, ū-zėr'pėr, *n.* One who usurps; one who seizes power or position without right.—**Usurping**, ū-zėr'ping, *p.* and *a.* Characterized by usurpation.—**Usurpingly**, ū-zėr'ping-li, *adv.* By usurpation.

Usury, ū'zhụ-ri, *n.* [O.E. *usure*, later, *usurie*, from Fr. *usure*, L. *usura*, interest for money lent, lit. a using, from *utor* to use. USE.] Interest for money†; an excessive or inordinate premium for the use of money borrowed; extortionate interest; the practice of taking exorbitant or excessive interest.—**Usurer**, ū'zhụr-ėr, *n.* Formerly, any person who lent money on interest; now, one who lends money at an exorbitant rate of interest. — **Usurious**, ū-zhū'ri-us, *a.* Pertaining to or practising usury; taking exorbitant interest for the use of money. — **Usuriously**, ū-zhū'ri-us-li, *adv* In a usurious manner.—**Usuriousness**, ū-zhū'ri-us-nes, *n.* The state or quality of being usurious.

Ut, ut, *n.* The first or key note in the musical scale of Guido d'Arezzo (being the initial word in a Latin hymn, from the first syllable of each of the succeeding lines of which the names of the other notes were also taken), now superseded by *do*.

Utensil, ū-ten'sil or ū'ten-sil, *n.* [Fr. *utensile*, from L. *utensilis*, fit for use, from *utor*, to use. USE.] An implement; an instrument; particularly, an instrument or vessel used in domestic business.

Uterine, ū'tėr-in, *a.* [L. *uterinus*, from *uterus*, the womb.] Pertaining to the womb; born of the same mother but by a different father.

Utility, ū-til'i-ti, *n.* [L. *utilitas*, from *utilis*, useful, from *utor*, to use. USE.] The state or quality of being useful; usefulness.—**Utilitarian**, ū-til'i-tā"ri-an, *a.* [From *utility.*] Consisting in or pertaining to utility; holding forth utility as a standard in ethics or politics.—*n.* One who holds the doctrine of utilitarianism.—**Utilitarianism**, ū-til'i-tā"ri-an-izm, *n.* The doctrine that the greatest happiness of the greatest number should be the end and aim of all social and political institutions; or the doctrine that utility is the standard of morality, that actions are right in proportion as they tend to promote happiness, wrong as they tend to produce the reverse of happiness.—**Utilization**, ū'til-i-zā"shon, *n.* The act of utilizing or turning to account.—**Utilize**, ū'til-īz, *v.t.*—*utilized, utilizing*. [Fr. *utiliser*, from *utile*, L. *utilis*, useful.] To turn to profitable account or use; to make useful; to adapt to some useful purpose.

Utmost, ut'mōst, *a.* [A.Sax. *útemest*, uttermost, outmost, a double superlative, being from *utema*, which itself is a superlative, and *-est*, also a superlative termination; similarly *aftermost*. *Outmost* is another form; *utter* is the comparative.] Being at the farthest point or extremity; farthest out; most distant; extreme; being in the greatest or highest degree: often used substantively, signifying the most that can be; greatest power, degree, or effort (strained to *the utmost*, try *your utmost*).

Utopia, ū-tō'pi-a, *n.* [Lit. the land of No-place, from Gr. *ou*, not, and *topos*, a place.] A name invented by Sir Thomas More, and applied by him to an imaginary island which he represents as enjoying the utmost perfection in laws, politics, &c., as contrasted with the defects of those which then existed; hence, a place or state of ideal perfection.—**Utopian**, ū-tō'pi-an, *a.* Pertaining to Utopia; founded upon or involving imaginary or ideal perfection.—*n.* An inhabitant of Utopia; an ardent but impracticable reformer.

Utraquists, ū'tra-kwists, *n.* [L. *utraque specie*.] The followers of John Huss, claiming for the laity the sacrament in both kinds.

Utricle, ū'tri-kl, *n.* [L. *utriculus*, dim. of *uter*, *utris*, a bottle of hide or skin.] A little bag or reservoir; a microscopic cell in an animal or vegetable structure; any thin bottle-like or bladder-like body in plants.—**Utricular, Utriculate**, ū-trik'-ū-lėr, ū-trik'ū-lāt, *a.* Having utricles; resembling a utricle or bag.—**Utriculiform, Utriculoid**, ū-trik'ū-li-form, ū-trik'ū-loid, *a.* Shaped like a bladder or bottle.

Utter, ut'ėr, *a.* [A.Sax. *útor*, *úttor*, compar. of *út*, out. *Outer* is the same word. OUT, UTMOST.] Outer‡; situated at or beyond the limits of something‡; complete; total; entire; perfect. — *v.t.* [From the above word; comp., as also from comparatives, the verbs to *lower*, to *better*.] To put into circulation, as money, notes, base coin, &c.; to give expression to; to give vent to by the vocal organs; to pronounce; to speak. —**Utterable**, ut'ėr-a-bl, *a.* Capable of being uttered, pronounced, or expressed.—**Utterance**, ut'ėr-ans, *n.* The act of uttering; manner of speaking; expression; circulation, as of money.—**Utterer**, ut'ėr-ėr, *n.* One who puts into circulation; one who pronounces, speaks, discloses, or publishes.—**Utterless**,† ut'ėr-les, *a.* That cannot be uttered; unutterable. — **Utterly**, ut'ėr-li, *adv.* To the full extent; fully; perfectly; totally. — **Uttermost**, ut'ėr-mōst, *a.* Extreme; being in the furthest, greatest, or highest degree; utmost: used also substantively, like *utmost*.

Uvea, ū'vē-a, *n.* [From L. *uva*, a grape—from resembling a grape skin.] *Anat.* the black layer on the back part of the iris.—**Uveous**, ū'vē-us, *a.* Resembling a grape or a bunch of grapes.

Uvula, ū'vū-la, *n.* [L., dim. of *uva*, a grape, the uvula.] The small conical fleshy substance which hangs from the soft palate over the root of the tongue.—**Uvular**, ū'-vū-lėr, *a.* Pertaining to the uvula.

Uxorious, ug-zō'ri-us, *a.* [L. *uxorius*, from *uxor*, *uxoris*, a wife.] Excessively or foolishly fond of one's wife; doting on one's wife.—**Uxoriously**, ug-zō'ri-us-li, *adv.* In an uxorious manner. — **Uxoriousness**, ug-zō'ri-us-nes, *n.* The state or quality of being uxorious.—**Uxorial**†, ug-zō'ri-al, *a.* Pertaining to a wife or married woman.—**Uxoricide**, ug-zor'i-sīd, *n.* [L. *uxor*, and *cædo*, to kill.] The murder of a wife by her husband; a husband who murders his wife.

V

V, the twenty-second letter of the English alphabet, formerly, as a character, used indiscriminately with *u*.

Vacant, vā'kant, *a.* [L. *vacans*, *vacantis*, ppr. of *vaco*, to be empty, to have leisure (from same stem, *vacuity*, *vacuum*).] Having no contents; empty; unfilled; void; not occupied or filled by an incumbent, possessor, or official; unoccupied; unemployed; not required to be spent in work; leisure; free (*vacant* hours); free from thought; not given to thinking, study, reflection, or the like; wanting intelligent facial expression; inane.—**Vacancy**, vā'kan-si, *n.* The quality or state of being vacant; empty space; vacuity; a space between objects; an unoccupied space; an unoccupied interval of time; an unoccupied post, position, or office, a situation or office destitute of a person to fill it; vacuity or inanity.—**Vacate**, va-kāt', *v.t.*—*vacated, vacating*. To make vacant; to quit the occupancy or possession of; to leave empty or unoccupied; to make void or of no validity.—**Vacation**, va-kā'shon, *n.* [Fr. *vacation*, L. *vacatio*.] The act of vacating; the act of leaving without an occupant; a stated interval in a round of duties; holidays; the time when a post has no occupant.

Vaccinate, vak'si-nāt, *v.t.* — *vaccinated, vaccinating*. [L. *vaccinus*, pertaining to a cow, from *vacca*, a cow.] To inoculate with the cow-pox by means of matter or lymph taken directly from the cow or from a person previously treated, for the purpose of procuring immunity from small-pox or of mitigating its attack.—**Vaccination**, vak-si-nā'shon, *n.* The act of vaccinating; the art or practice of inoculating persons with the cow-pox, by lymph taken from a pustule caused by previous vaccination in a healthy child. *Inoculation* is artificial communication of the small-pox itself.—**Vaccine**, vak'sīn, *a.* [L. *vaccinus*.] Pertaining to cows or to cow-pox.—*Vaccine matter*, the lymph contained in the pustules produced by vaccination or derived from cow-pox vesicles.

Vacillate, vas'i-lāt, *v.i.*—*vacillated, vacillating*. [L. *vacillo*, *vacillatum*, to sway to and fro; perhaps allied to E. *wag*.] To waver; to move one way and the other; to fluctuate in mind or opinion; to be unsteady or inconstant. — **Vacillating**, vas'i-lā-ting, *p.* and *a.* Moving so as to vacillate; unsteady in opinion or resolution; wavering. —**Vacillatingly**, vas'i-lā-ting-li, *adv.* In a vacillating manner.—**Vacillation**, vas-i-lā'shon, *n.* [L. *vacillatio*.] The act of vacillating; a wavering; vacillating conduct; fluctuation of mind; unsteadiness; change from one object to another; inconstancy.

Vacuity, Vacuousness, va-kū'i-ti, vak'-ū-us-nes, *n.* [L. *vacuitas*, from *vacuus*, empty. VACANT.] The state of being empty or unfilled; emptiness; a space unfilled or unoccupied, or occupied with an invisible fluid only; a vacuum; freedom from mental exertion; absence of thought; absence of intelligence in look; vacant expression.—**Vacuole**, vak'ū-ōl, *n.* [A dim. from *vacuum*.] A minute cell or cavity in the tissue of organisms, as in the Protozoa.—**Vacuous**, vak'ū-us, *a.* [L. *vacuus*.] Empty; unfilled; void; vacant.—**Vacuum**, vak'ū-um, *n.* [L., an empty space, neut. sing. of *vacuus*, empty.] Space empty, or space devoid of all matter or body; an inclosed space from which air is more or less completely removed, as from the receiver of an air-pump, a portion of a barometric tube, &c.—**Vacuum-brake**, *n.* A steam brake for railway carriages, &c., in which the power employed is the pressure of the atmosphere produced by creating a vacuum.—**Vacuum-gauge**, *n.* A gauge for indicating to what extent a vacuum is produced. —**Vacuum-pan**, *n.* A vessel for boiling saccharine juices in a partial vacuum in sugar-making. — **Vacuum-tube**, *n.* A tube employed to examine the effects of a discharge of electricity through air or gas rarefied or exhausted to a certain degree.

Vade-mecum, vā-dē-mē'kum, *n.* [L. *vade mecum*, go with me.] A book or other thing that a person constantly carries with him; a manual; a pocket companion.

Vagabond, vag'a-bond, *a.* [Fr. *vagabond*, from L. *vagabundus*, wandering, from *vagor*, to wander; from *vagus*, wandering, whence E. *vague*.] Wandering; going from place to place without settled habitation; pertaining to a vagrant or idle stroller.—*n.* An idle worthless stroller from place to place without fixed habitation or visible means of earning an honest livelihood; an idle, worthless fellow; a scamp; a rascal.—**Vagabondage**, vag'a-bon-dāj, *n.* The state or condition of a vagabond.—**Vagabondism**, vag'a-bond-izm, *n.* The ways or habits of a vagabond; vagabondage.

Vagary, va-gā'ri, *n.* [From It. *vagare*, to wander, or directly from L. *vagari*, to wander (whence *vagabond*, &c.).] A wandering of the thoughts; a wild freak; a whim; a whimsical purpose.

Vagina, va-jī'na, *n.* [L., a sheath.] *Bot.* and *anat.* a name for any part having the character of a sheath; the canal in females leading from the exterior to the womb.—**Vaginal**, va-jī'nal or vaj'i-nal, *a.* Pertaining to or resembling a sheath; pertaining to the vagina.—**Vaginate, Vaginated**, va-jī'nāt, va-jī'nā-ted, *a.* *Bot.* sheathed; invested by the tubular base of the leaf.—**Vaginopennous**, va-jī'nō-pen"us, *a.* [L. *penna*, a feather.] Sheath-winged; coleopterous.

Vagrant, vā'grant, *a.* [Formerly *vagarant*, same origin as *vagary*.] Wandering without any settled habitation; pertaining to one who wanders; unsettled; moving without any certain direction.—*n.* A wanderer; one without a settled home or habitation; an idle wanderer or stroller; a vagabond; a tramp; *law*, a term for various minor offenders, such as beggars, prostitutes, fortune-tellers, and other impostors. — **Vagrancy**, vā'gran-si, *n.* A state of wandering without settled home; the condition of being a vagrant.

Vague, vāg, *a.* [Fr. *vague*, from L. *vagus*, wandering. VAGABOND.] Wandering‡; vagabond‡; unsettled as regards meaning, scope, or the like; indefinite; hazy; uncertain; doubtful; proceeding from no known authority; of uncertain origin or foundation (a *vague* report).—**Vaguely**, vāg'li, *adv.* In a vague, uncertain, unsettled manner. — **Vagueness**, vāg'nes, *n.* The character of being vague; want of clearness; haziness.

Vagus or **Vagus nerve**, vā'gus, *n.* Same as Pneumogastric Nerve.

Vail, vāl, *n.* and *v.* Same as *Veil*.

Vail,‡ vāl, *v.t.* [Abbrev. from O.E. *avale*, *avail*, from Fr. *avaler*, to let down, from L. *ad*, to, and *vallis*, a valley. VALLEY.] To let down; to lower; to let fall. (*Shak.*)

Vail, vāl, *v.i.* [An abbrev. of *avail*.] To profit. (*Poet.*)—*n.* Money given to servants by a visitor on going away, formerly regarded by domestics as a perquisite which they might demand: a term now disused.

Vain, vān, *a.* [Fr. *vain*, vain, empty, vainglorious, &c., from L. *vanus*, empty, void (whence also *vanish*, *evanescent*); same root as to *wane*, *want*.] Having no real value or importance; unsubstantial; empty; idle; worthless; unsatisfying; producing no good result; fruitless; ineffectual; light-minded; foolish; silly; proud of petty things or of trifling attainments; having a foolish craving for the admiration or applause of others; puffed up; inflated; conceited.—*In vain*, to no purpose; without effect; ineffectually.—

To take the name of God in vain, to use the name of God with levity or profaneness.—**Vainglorious**, vān-glō′ri-us, *a.* Feeling or proceeding from vainglory; vain to excess of one's own achievements; boastful.—**Vaingloriously**, vān-glō′ri-us-li, *adv.* With vainglory or empty pride.—**Vainglory**, vān-glō′ri, *n.* Glory, pride, or boastfulness that is vain or empty; tendency to unduly exalt one's self or one's own performances; vain pomp or show.—**Vainly**, vān′li, *adv.* In a vain manner; without effect; to no purpose; in vain; in a conceited manner; foolishly.—**Vainness**, vān-nes, *n.* The state of being vain; empty pride; vanity.—**Vanity**, van′i-ti, *n.* [Fr. *vanité*. L. *vanitas*.] The quality or state of being vain; worthlessness; falsity; unrealness; want of substance to satisfy desire; the desire of indiscriminate admiration; empty pride, inspired by an overweening conceit of one's personal attainments or decorations; ambitious display; anything empty, visionary, or unsubstantial. ∴ Syn. under EGOTISM.—*Vanity Fair*, the vain show of this world, sketched in Bunyan's *Pilgrim's Progress*, and in Thackeray's novel of the name.

Vair, vār, *n.* [O.Fr. *vair*, from L. *varius*, various, variegated.] An old name for a kind of fur, said to have been the skin of a species of squirrel with a gray back and white belly; *her.* one of the furs represented by little pieces like shields alternately silver and blue.—**Vairée**, *a.* Applied to an heraldic field, signifies that it is divided up in vair fashion, but any two tinctures may be used.

Vaisya, vis′ya, *n.* A member of the third caste among the Hindus, comprehending merchants, traders, and cultivators.

Vakeel, va-kēl′, *n.* In the East Indies, an ambassador or agent; a native attorney; a native law-pleader.

Valance, **Valence**, val′ans, val′ens, *n.* [From Norm. *valaunt*, O.Fr. *avalant*, descending, hanging down, from *avaler*, to let down. VAIL (to let down).] The drapery hanging round a bed, from the head of window curtains, from a couch, &c.

Vale, vāl, *n.* [Fr. *val*, from L. *vallis*, a valley. VALLEY.] A tract of low ground between hills; a valley: more poetical and less general than *valley*; *fig.* a state of decline or wretchedness.

Vale, vā′lē, *n.* [L., imper. of *valere*, to be well, to be strong. VALID.] Farewell; adieu.—**Valediction**, va-le-dik′shon, *n.* [L. *valedico, valedictum*—*vale*, and *dico*, to say.] A farewell; a bidding farewell.—**Valedictory**, va-le-dik′to-ri, *a.* Bidding farewell; pertaining to a leave-taking; farewell.

Valence, **Valency**, vā′lens, vā′len-si, *n.* [L.L. *valentia*, strength, *valeo*, to be strong. VALID.] *Chem.* the combining strength or capacity of atoms, referred to hydrogen as a standard; the force which determines with how many atoms of an element an atom of another element will combine.

Valenciennes, vä-lań-sē-en, *n.* A rich variety of lace made at *Valenciennes* in France.

Valentine, val′en-tīn, *n.* A sweetheart selected or got by lot on St. *Valentine's* Day, 14th February; a letter or missive of an amatory or satirical kind, sent by one young person to another on St. Valentine's Day.

Valerian, va-lē′ri-an, *n.* [Supposed to be from the Emperor *Valerianus*, who had benefited from it.] The common name of a genus of perennial herbs, having small red or white flowers, which are collected for their medicinal properties.—*Valerian oil*, an aromatic essential oil obtained from the root of the great wild valerian.

Valet, val′et, *n.* [Fr. *valet*, O.Fr. *varlet*, *vaslet*, a lad, a servant; dim. of *vassal*. VASSAL. *Varlet* is the same word.] A man-servant who attends on a gentleman's person.

Valetudinarian, val-ē-tū′di-nā″ri-an, *a.* [L. *valetudinarius*, from *valetudo*, good or ill health, from *valeo*, to be well. VALID.] Sickly; in a poor state of health; infirm; seeking to recover health.—*n.* A person of an infirm or sickly constitution; one who is seeking to recover health.—**Valetudinarianism**, val-ē-tū′di-nā″ri-an-izm, *n.* A state of feeble health; infirmity.—**Valetudinariness**, val-ē-tū′di-na-ri-nes, *n.* State of being valetudinary.—**Valetudinarious**, val-ē-tū′di-nā″ri-us, *a.*—**Valetudinary**, val-ē-tū′di-na-ri, *n.* and *a.* Same as *Valetudinarian*.

Valhalla, val-hal′la, *n.* [Icel. *valhöll*, the hall of the slain—*valr*, slaughter, and *höll*, a hall.] In the Scandinavian mythology the palace of immortality, inhabited by the souls of heroes slain in battle; *fig.* any edifice which is the final resting-place of many of the heroes or great men of a nation.

Valiant, val′yant, *a.* [Fr. *vaillant*, from *valoir*, L. *valere*, to be strong. VALID.] Brave; courageous; intrepid in danger; puissant; performed with valour; heroic.—**Valiantly**, val′yant-li, *adv.* In a valiant manner.—**Valiantness**, val′yant-nes, *n.* The quality of being valiant; valour.

Valid, val′id, *a.* [Fr. *valide*, L. *validus*, strong, powerful, from *valeo*, to be strong, to be well (seen also in *value*, *valiant*, *valour*, *valetudinary*, *avail*, *prevail*, &c.); perhaps from a root meaning to cover or protect, same as in *valley*, *wool*.] Sufficiently supported by actual fact; well grounded; sound; just; good; not weak or defective; having sufficient legal strength or force; good or sufficient in point of law.—**Validate**, val′i-dāt, *v.t.* To make valid; to confirm.—**Validity**, **Validness**, va-lid′i-ti, val′id-nes, *n.* The state or quality of being valid; strength or cogency from being supported by fact; justness; soundness; legal strength or force; sufficiency in point of law.—**Validly**, val′id-li, *adv.* In a valid manner; so as to be valid.

Valise, va-lēs′, *n.* [Fr.] A small leather bag or case for holding a traveller's equipment; a portmanteau.

Valkyr, **Valkyria**, väl′kēr, väl-kē′ri-a, *n.* [Icel. *valkyrja*—*valr*, the slain, and *kjósa*, to select.] One of the sisters of Odin, who led to Valhalla the souls of those who fell in battle, where they ministered at their feasts.—**Valkyrian**, väl-kē′ri-an, *a.* Of or relating to the Valkyrs or Valkyrias.

Vallar, **Vallary**, val′ėr, val′ėr-i, *a.* [L. *vallaris*, from *vallum*, a rampart.] Pertaining to a rampart or palisade.

Valley, val′i, *n.* [Fr. *vallée*, O.Fr. *valee*, from *val*, a vale, from L. *vallis*, a valley. VALID.] Any hollow or surface depression of some width bounded by hills or mountains, and usually traversed by a stream or river; a vale; the internal angle formed by the meeting of the two inclined sides of a roof.

Vallisneria, val-is-nē′ri-a, *n.* [*Vallisneri*, Italian naturalist.] A genus of plants that grow at the bottom of water.

Vallum, val′lum, *n.* [L. *vallum*, from *vallus*, a stake.] A rampart; a palisaded rampart, such as that with which the Romans inclosed their camps.

Valonia, va-lō′ni-a, *n.* [It. *vallonia*, from Mod.Gr. *balania*, the holm-oak, from Gr. *balanos*, an acorn, an oak.] The acorn-cups of a species of oak exported from the Levant for the use of tanners and dyers.

Valor, val′or, *n.* [O.Fr. *valor*, Mod.Fr. *valeur*, L.L. *valor*, worth, from L. *valeo*, to be strong. VALID.] That quality which enables a man to encounter danger with firmness; personal bravery, especially as regards fighting; intrepidity; prowess.—**Valorous**, val′or-us, *a.* Brave; courageous; valiant; intrepid.—**Valorously**, val′or-us-li, *adv.* In a valorous manner; valiantly.

Value, val′ū, *n.* [O.Fr. *value*, the fem. of *valu*, pp. of *valoir*, from L. *valere*, to be strong, to be worth. VALID.] Worth; that property or those properties of a thing which render it useful or estimable; the degree of such property or properties; utility; importance; what makes a person of some account, estimation, or worth; estimate of worth; price equal to the worth; market price; the money for which a thing is sold or will sell; equivalent in the market; import; precise signification (the *value* of a word or phrase); *mus.* the relative length or duration of a tone or note.—*v.t.*—*valued*, *valuing*. To estimate the worth of; to rate at a certain price; to appraise; to consider with respect to importance; to rate, whether high or low; to have in high esteem; to prize; to regard; to hold in respect and estimation.—**Valued**, val′ūd, *p.* and *a.* Regarded as of high value; highly esteemed.—**Valueless**, val′ū-les, *a.* Being of no value; having no worth; worthless.—**Valuer**, val′ū-ėr, *n.* One who values; an appraiser.—**Valuable**, val′ū-a-bl, *a.* Having value or worth; having a high value; having qualities which are useful and esteemed; precious.—*n.* A thing, especially a small thing, of value; a choice article of personal property: usually in the plural.—**Valuableness**, val′ū-a-bl-nes, *n.* The quality of being valuable; preciousness.—**Valuation**, val-ū-ā′shon, *n.* The act of valuing; the act of setting a price; appraisement; estimation; value set upon a thing; estimated worth.—**Valuator**, val′ū-ā-tėr, *n.* One who sets a value; an appraiser.

Valve, valv, *n.* [Fr. *valve*, from L. *valvæ*, folding doors, from same root *volvo*, to roll (whence *voluble*, &c.).] One of the leaves of a folding door; a kind of movable lid or partition adapted to a tube or orifice, and so formed as to open communication in one direction and to close it in the other, used to regulate the admission or escape of water, gas, or steam; *anat.* a partition within the cavity of a vessel opening to allow the passage of a fluid in one direction, and shutting to prevent its return (the *valves* of the heart); *bot.* one of the divisions of any dehiscent body; *conch.* one of the separable portions of the shell of a mollusc; *wireless tel.* see THERMIONIC VALVE.—**Valvate**, val′vāt, *a.* Having or resembling a valve.—**Valved**, valvd, *a.* Having valves or hinges; composed of valves.—**Valve-gear**, **Valve-motion**, *n.* The combination of mechanical devices for working a valve in steam-engines.—**Valve set**, *n.* *Wireless tel.* receiving apparatus which includes one or more thermionic valves for rectification, amplification, or both. The phrase is also applied to transmitting apparatus.—**Valvular**, val′vū-lėr, *a.* Containing valves; having the character of or acting as a valve.—**Valvule**, **Valvelet**, val′vūl, valv′let, *n.* [Dim. from *valve*.] A little valve.

Vambrace, vam′brās, *n.* [Also *vantbrace*, *vantbras*—Fr. *avant*, before, and *bras*, arm. VAN (front).] The piece of plate armour which covered the forearm.—**Vambraced**, *a.* *Her.* applied to indicate that the arm is entirely covered with armour.

Vamoose, va-mōs′, *v.t.* or *i.* [Sp. *vamos*, let us go.] To quit, to depart.

Vamp, vamp, *n.* [Formerly *vampey*, from Fr. *avant-pied*—*avant*, before, and *pied*, the foot. VAN (front).] The upper leather of a boot or shoe; any piece or patch intended to give an old thing a new appearance; a piece added for appearance sake; *mus.* an improvised accompaniment.—*v.t.* To put a new vamp or upper leather on; to furbish up; to give a new appearance to; to patch.

Vamp, vamp, *n.* (*Slang.*) Short for VAMPIRE.—*v.t.* and *i.* To beguile men; to act the part of a vampire.

Vampire, vam′pīr, *n.* [Fr., from G. *vampyr*, from Serv. *vampir*, *vampira*, a vampire.] A kind of spectral being or ghost still possessing a human body, believed to leave the grave during the night and suck the blood of living men and women while they are asleep; an adventuress; a woman who uses her physical charms in such a manner as to allure or debase a man; a siren; an extortioner.—**Vampire bat**, *n.* A bloodsucking bat of South America of several species, with long sharp teeth.

Van, van, *n.* [Abbrev. from *vanguard*, from Fr. *avant-garde*—*avant*, before, and *garde*, guard. AVAUNT, GUARD.] The front of an army, or the front line or foremost division of a fleet.—**Vanguard**, van'gärd, *n.* The troops who march in the van of an army; the advance guard; the van.

Van,‡ van, *n.* [Fr. *van*, from L. *vannus*, a van or fan for winnowing. FAN.] A fan or any contrivance for winnowing grain; a wing.

Van, van, *n.* [Abbrev. from *caravan.*] A caravan; a covered vehicle used by tradesmen and others for carrying goods; a close railway-carriage for carrying luggage or for other purposes.

Vanadium, va-nā'di-um, *n.* [From *Vanadis*, a surname of the Scandinavian goddess Freyja, from its being discovered in a Swedish ore.] A silvery brittle metal of rare occurrence discovered in 1830 in Swedish iron.—**Vanadic, Vanadous**, va-nad'ik, van'a-dus, *a.* Pertaining to vanadium.

Vandal, van'dal, *n.* [L. *Vandali, Vinduli, Vindili*, the Vandals.] One of a Teutonic race who pillaged Rome in the fifth century, and unsparingly destroyed the monuments of art and the productions of literature; hence, one who wilfully or ignorantly destroys any work of art, literature, or the like.—**Vandal, Vandalic**, van-dal'ik, *a.* Pertaining to or resembling the Vandals.—**Vandalism**, van'dal-izm, *n.* Wilful or ignorant destruction of works of art or literature; hostility to art or literature.

Vandyke, van-dīk', *n.* A pointed collar of lace or sewed work worn by both sexes during the reign of Charles I, and to be seen in portraits painted by Vandyke; a pointed beard.—*Vandyke brown*, a pigment obtained from a kind of peat or bog-earth, of a fine, deep, semi-transparent brown color.

Vane, vān, *n.* [O.E. *fane*, a banner, a weathercock, from A.Sax. *fana* = O.H.G. *fano*, G. *fahne*, D. *vaan*, a flag; Goth. *fana*, cloth; cog. L. *pannus*, cloth.] A weathercock, arrow, or thin slip of metal, wood, &c., placed on a spindle at the top of a spire, tower, &c., for the purpose of showing by its turning and direction which way the wind blows; any somewhat similar device or contrivance; the broad part of a feather on either side of the shaft; one of the plates or blades of a windmill, a screw-propeller, &c.

Vanessa, va-nes'sa, *n.* A genus of brightly-coloured butterflies, including the tortoise-shell butterfly, the peacock butterfly, &c.

Vang, vang, *n.* [D. *vangen*, G. *fangen*, to catch.] *Naut.* a steadying-rope from a gaff to the ship's side.

Vanguard. Under VAN.

Vanilla, va-nil'a, *n.* [From Sp. *vainilla*, dim. of *vaina*, a scabbard, from L. *vagina*, a scabbard; the pod resembles a scabbard.] A genus of orchidaceous plants, natives of tropical America, the fleshy pod-like fruit of several species of which is remarkable for its fragrant odour and is used in medicine, confectionery, and perfumery.

Vanish, van'ish, *v.i.* [From L. *vanesco*, *evanesco*, to vanish, to pass away (through the old French), from *vanus*, vain. VAIN.] To disappear; to pass from a visible to an invisible state; to pass beyond the limit of vision; to be annihilated or lost; to be no more; *math.* to become less and less till the value is nothing, or is denoted by 0.—*Vanishing point*, the point in a view or picture at which all parallel lines in the same plane tend to meet when correctly represented in a picture.

Vanity. Under VAIN.

Vanquish, vang'kwish, *v.t.* [From Fr. *vaincre*, pret. *vainquis*, subj. *vainquisse*, O.Fr. *veinquir*, from L. *vincere*, to conquer. VICTOR.] To conquer, overcome, or subdue in battle; to defeat in any contest; to get the better of; to confute; to overpower; to prostrate; to be too much for. .˙. Syn. under CONQUER.—**Vanquishable**, vang'kwish-a-bl, *a.* Capable of being vanquished; conquerable.—**Vanquisher**, vang'kwish-ėr, *n.* A conqueror; a victor.

Vantage, van'tāj, *n.* [Fr. *avantage*. ADVANTAGE.] Advantage; vantage-ground.—**Vantage-ground**, *n.* Superiority of position or place; the place or condition which gives one an advantage over another; favourable position.

Vapid, vap'id, *a.* [L. *vapidus*, vapid, having lost spirit, same root as *vapour*.] Having lost its life and spirit; insipid; dead; flat; dull; unanimated; spiritless.—**Vapidly**, vap'id-li, *adv.* In a vapid manner.—**Vapidity, Vapidness**, va-pid'i-ti, vap'id-nes, *n.* The state or quality of being vapid; deadness; flatness; dulness; want of life or spirit.

Vapor, Vapour, vā'por, *n.* [L. *vapor*, steam; vapor; akin to *vapidus*, vapid, having lost flavor, *vappa*, vapid wine.] An exhalation or fume; a gaseous substance; visible steam; the gaseous form which any solid or liquid substance assumes when heated; also specifically used of a gas below its critical temperature; any visible diffused substance floating in the atmosphere, as fog or mist; hazy matter; something unsubstantial, fleeting, or transitory; a mental fume; a vain imagination; an unreal fancy; *pl.* an old name for a nervous hypochondriacal or hysterical affection; the blues.—*Vapor density*, the density of a substance in the state of vapor, referred to air or hydrogen as the standard; of importance in chemistry in determining the molecular weight.—*v.i.* To boast or vaunt with ostentatious display; to bully; to hector; to brag; to bounce.—**Vapor-bath**, *n.* The application of vapor or steam to the body in a close place; the place or bath itself.—**Vaporer**, vā'por-ėr, *n.* One who vapors, brags, or bullies; a braggart, bully, or boaster.—**Vaporing**, vā'por-ing, *p.* and *a.* Boasting; given to boast or brag.—*n.* Boastful or windy talk.—**Vaporish**, vā'porish, *a.* Affected by vapors; hypochondriac; whimsical; fanciful.—**Vaporishness**, vā'por-ish-nes, *n.*—**Vapory**, vā'por-i, *a.* Vaporous; full of vapors.—**Vaporability**, vā'por-a-bil"i-ti, *n.* The quality of being vaporable.—**Vaporable**, vā'por-a-bl, *a.* Capable of being converted into vapor.—**Vaporiferous**, vā-por-if'ėr-us, *a.* [L. *vapor*, and *fero*, to bear.] Conveying or producing vapor.—**Vaporific**, vā-por-if'ik, *a.* [L. *vapor*, and *facio*, to make.] Forming vapor; converting into steam, or into a volatile form.—**Vaporizable**, vā'por-ī-za-bl, *a.* Capable of being vaporized.—**Vaporization**, vā'por-ī-zā"shon, *n.* The act of vaporizing; conversion into vapor.—**Vaporize**, vā'por-īz, *v.t.*—*vaporized, vaporizing.* To convert into vapor by the application of heat or artificial means; to cause to evaporate; to sublimate.—*v.i.* To pass off in vapor.—**Vaporizer**, vā'por-īz'ėr, *n.* In oil engines, a contrivance for converting the oil fuel into fine spray.—**Vaporose**, vā'por-ōs, *a.* Vaporous.—**Vaporous**, vā'por-us, *a.* Being in the form of, or having the character of vapor; full of vapors or exhalations; promoting exhalation or effluvia; unsubstantial; vainly imaginative or soaring; whimsical.

Vaquero, vä-kār'ō, *n.* [Sp., a cowherd, from *vaca*, L. *vacca*, a cow.] In Mexico and the western United States, a herdsman, a cowboy.

Varangian, va-ran'ji-an, *n.* [Icel. *Væringjar*, lit. confederates or sworn men, from *várar*, an oath.] One of those Scandinavians, Anglo-Saxons, &c., who entered the service of the Byzantine emperors and became the Imperial Guard.

Variable, Variance, &c. Under VARY.

Varicella, var-i-sel'la, *n.* [Dim. of *variola*, the small-pox.] The chicken-pox.

Varicocele, var'i-kō-sēl, *n.* [L. *varix*, a dilated vein, and Gr. *kēlē*, a tumour.] A varicose enlargement of the spermatic veins, or the veins of the scrotum.

Varicose, var'i-kōs, *a.* [L. *varicosus*, from *varix*, a varicose vein.] Exhibiting a morbid enlargement or dilation, knotty and irregular in shape, as often seen in the veins of the lower extremities, which sometimes burst with considerable hemorrhage.—**Varicosity**, var-i-kos'i-ti, *n.* The state of being varicose.

Variegate, vā'ri-e-gāt, *v.t.*—*variegated, variegating.* [L. *variego, variegatum*, to variegate, from *varius*, various, and term. from *ago*, to do. VARY.] To diversify by means of different tints or hues.—**Variegated**, vā'ri-e-gā-ted, *p.* and *a.* Diversified with tints or hues; *bot.* irregularly marked with spots of a light colour: said of leaves.—**Variegation**, vā'ri-e-gā"shon, *n.* The state of being variegated; diversity of colours, especially on the leaves or petals of plants.

Variety. Under VARY.

Variola, va-rī'ō-la, *n.* [Fr. *variole*, Mod.L. *variola*, small-pox, from L. *varius*, spotted.] The small-pox.—**Variolar, Variolic, Variolous**, va-rī'ō-lėr, vā-ri-ol'ik, va-rī'ō-lus, *a.* Pertaining to or designating the small-pox.—**Variolite**, va-rī'ō-līt, *n.* [Gr. *lithos*, stone.] A porphyritic rock in which the embedded substances are imperfectly crystallized, or are rounded, giving a spotted appearance.—**Variolitic**, va-rī'ō-lit"ik, *a.* Pertaining to variola; thickly marked with small round specks or dots; spotted.—**Varioloid**, va-rī'ō-loid, *a.* Resembling variola; spotted.

Variorum, va-ri-ō'rum, *a.* [From L. *editio cum notis variorum*, an edition with the notes of various persons.] A term applied to an edition of some work in which the notes of different commentators are inserted (a *variorum* edition of Shakspere).

Various. Under VARY.

Varix, vā'riks, *n.* pl. **Varices**, var'i-sēz. [L.] A varicose vein. VARICOSE.

Varlet, vär'let, *n.* [O.Fr. *varlet, vaslet*, VALET.] Anciently, a page or knight's follower; an attendant on a gentleman; hence, a term of contempt for one in a subordinate or menial position; a low fellow; a rascal.—**Varletry**, vär'let-ri, *n.* The rabble; the crowd.

Varnish, vär'nish, *n.* [From Fr. *vernis*, varnish, *vernisser, vernir*, to varnish, from L. *vitrinus*, glassy, from *vitrum*, glass—varnish giving a glassy surface. VITREOUS.] A solution of resinous matter, forming a clear limpid fluid, used by painters, cabinet-makers, &c., for coating the surface of their work in order to give it a shining, transparent, and hard surface, capable of resisting the influences of air and moisture; what resembles varnish either naturally or artificially; a glossy or lustrous appearance; outside show; gloss.—*v.t.* To lay varnish on; to give an improved appearance to; to give a fair colouring to; to gloss over.—**Varnisher**, vär'nish-ėr, *n.* One who varnishes; one who gives a fair external appearance.—**Varnish-tree**, *n.* The name of certain trees found chiefly in India, Burmah, and China, which exude resinous juices employed as varnishes.

Varsovienne, var-sō'vi-en, *n.* [Fr.] A dance, named from *Warsaw*, in Poland, where it probably originated.

Varus, va'rus, *a.* [L. *varus*.] Knock-kneed, in-kneed.

Vary, vā'ri, *v.t.*—*varied, varying.* [Fr. *varier*, from L. *variare*, to vary, from *varius*, variegated, diverse, various.] To alter in form, appearance, substance, or position; to make different by a partial change; to change; to diversify; *mus.* to embellish, as a melody or theme with passing notes, arpeggios, &c.—*v.i.* To alter or be altered in any manner; to suffer change; to appear in different forms; to differ or be different; to be unlike or diverse; to change, as in purpose, opinion, or the like; to deviate; to swerve; to alternate; to disagree; to be at variance; *math.* to be subject to continual increase or decrease.—**Variable**, vā'ri-a-bl, *a.* Capable of varying, changing, or altering; liable to change; often changing; changeable (*variable* winds); fickle; unsteady; inconstant; capable of being varied or changed.—*Variable quantities, math.* quantities subject to continual increase or diminution.—*Variable stars*, stars which undergo a periodical increase and diminution of their lustre.—*n.* That which is variable; a variable quantity; a shifting wind as opposed to a trade-wind; hence *the variables*, the region between the north-east and the south-east trade-winds. — **Variableness, Variability**, vā'ri-a-bl-nes, vā'ri-a-bil''i-ti, *n.* The state or quality of being variable.—**Variably**, vā'ri-a-bli, *adv.* In a variable manner; changeably; mutably; inconstantly.—**Variance**, vā'ri-ans, *n.* Difference that produces dispute or controversy; disagreement; dissension; discord.—*At variance*, in disagreement; in a state of dissension; in enmity.—**Variant**, vā'ri-ant, *a.* Different; diverse; variable; varying.—*n.* Something that is really the same, though with a different form; a different reading or version. — **Variation**, vā-ri-ā'shon, *n.* [L. *variatio.*] The act or process of varying; partial change in the form, position, state, or qualities of the same thing; alteration; mutation; change; modification; the extent to which a thing varies; the amount or rate of change; the act of deviating; deviation; *gram.* change of termination of words; inflection; *astron.* any deviation from the mean orbit or mean motion of a heavenly body occasioned by another disturbing body; *physics* and *navig.* same as *declination*; *mus.* one of a series of ornamental changes or embellishments in the treatment of a tune, movement, or theme during several successive repetitions. — *Calculus of variations*, a branch of analysis, the chief object of which is to find what function of a variable will be a maximum or minimum on certain prescribed conditions. — **Varied**, vā'rid, *p.* and *a.* Altered; changed; characterized by variety; diversified; consisting of various kinds or sorts differing from each other; diverse; various.—**Variedly**, vā'rid-li, *adv.* Diversely.—**Varier**, vā'ri-ėr, *n.* One who varies. (*Tenn.*) — **Varietal**, va-rī'e-tal, *a.* Pertaining to a variety, as distinguished from an individual or a species. —**Variety**, va-rī'e-ti. *n.* [L. *varietas*, from *varius.*] The state or quality of being varied or various; intermixture or succession of different things, or of things different in form; diversity; multifariousness; many-sidedness; a collection or number of different things; a varied assortment; something different from others of the same general kind; a sort; a kind; in scientific classifications, a subdivision of a species of animals or plants; according to the evolution theory, a species in process of formation.—*Theatre of Varieties, Variety Entertainment*, a light, mixed theatrical show.— **Variform**, vā'ri-form, *a.* Having different shapes or forms. — **Variformed**, vā'ri-formd, *a.* Formed with different shapes. —**Variometer**, vā-ri-om'etėr, *n.* [From *vary*, and Gr. *metron*, a measure.] *Wireless tel.* an inductance coil whose inductance can be varied by moving a part of the coil with reference to the remainder.—**Various**, vā'ri-us, *a.* [L. *varius.*] Differing from each other; different; diverse; manifold; divers; several; exhibiting different characters; multiform.—**Variously**, vā'ri-us-li, *adv.* In various or different ways; with diversity; diversely; multifariously.

Vascular, vas'kū-lėr, *a.* [L. *vasculum*, a vessel, dim. of *vas*, a vessel.] Pertaining to the vessels or tubes connected with the vital functions of animals or plants, and especially making up the circulatory system; consisting of, containing, or operating by means of animal or vegetable vessels. — *Vascular plants*, flowering plants and ferns, as contrasted with *cellular* plants.— *Vascular tissue*, tissue composed of small vessels like the woody tissue or substance of flowering plants: used in contradistinction to *cellular*. — *Vascular system*, *anat.* the system formed by all the blood-vessels, lacteals, &c.—**Vascularity**, vas-kū-lar'i-ti, *n.* The state or quality of being vascular. —**Vasculose**, vas'kū-lōs, *a.* *Bot.* same as *Vascular*.—*n.* The substance constituting the principal part of the vessels of plants.— **Vasculum**, vas'kū-lum, *n.* A botanist's case for carrying specimens as he collects them; *bot.* a pitcher-shaped leaf.

Vase, vāz or väz, *n.* [Fr. *vase*, from L. *vasum* (rarely used for *vas*), a vessel; akin *vessel, vascular.*] A vessel of some size of various materials, forms, and purposes, often merely serving for ornament, *arch.* a sculptured ornament representing the vessels of the ancients, as incense-pots, flower-pots, &c.; the body of a Corinthian or Composite capital. — **Vasiform**, vā'si-form, *a.* [L. *vas*, a vessel, and *forma*, a shape.] In the form of a vase.—*Vasiform tissue.* Same as *Bothrenchyma*. — **Vasomotor**, vas-ō-mō'tėr, *a.* [L. *vas*, a vessel, and *motor*, a mover.] Applied to the system of nerves distributed over the muscular coats of the blood-vessels.

Vase-painting, väz-pānt'ing, *n.* The embellishment of vases with pigments: a term especially applied to the ornamentation of ancient Greek pottery.

Vassal, vas'al, *n.* [Fr. *vassal*, L.L. *vassallus*, a vassal, dim. of *vassus*, a domestic, from Armor. *gwaz*, W. *gwas*, a youth, a servant. Of same origin are *valet*, *varlet*.] A feudal tenant holding lands under a lord, and bound by his tenure to feudal services; a subject; a dependant; a retainer; a servant; a bondman; a slave.—*a.* Servile; subservient.—**Vassalage**, vas'al-āj, *n.* The state of being a vassal; servitude; dependence; slavery.—**Vassalry**, vas'al-ri, *n.* A body of vassals.

Vast, vast, *a.* [Fr. *vaste*, from L. *vastus*, waste, desert, vast, huge (hence, *vasto*, to lay waste, to *devastate*); allied to G. *wüste*, a desert. WASTE.] Waste or desert‡; lonely‡; of great extent; boundless; huge in bulk and extent; immense; very great in numbers or amount; very great as to degree or intensity.—*n.* A boundless waste or space; immensity. (*Poetical.*) — **Vastly**, vast'li, *adv.* Very greatly; to a vast extent or degree. — **Vastness**, vast'nes, *n.* The quality of being vast; great extent; immensity; greatness in general. — **Vasty**,‡ vas'ti, *a.* Vast; boundless; very spacious. (*Shak.*)

Vat, vat, *n.* [Also *fat*, a vat, from A.Sax. *fæt*, a vat=D. *vat*, Icel. and Sw. *fat*, a vat, G. *fass*, a cask.] A large vessel for holding liquors; a large vessel of the tub kind; a tun; a wooden tank or cistern.—*v.t.*—*vatted, vatting.* To put in a vat.—**Vatful**, vat'fụl, *n.* As much as a vat will hold; the contents of a vat.

Vatic,† vat'ik, *a.* [L. *vates*, a prophet.] Pertaining to a prophet; oracular; inspired.

Vatican, vat'i-kan, *n.* A most extensive palace at Rome upon the Vatican hill, the residence of the pope; hence, the *Vatican* is equivalent to the papal power or government. — *Vatican Council*, the Ecumenical Council which met in the Vatican in 1870, and declared the infallibility of the pope to be a dogma of the church.— **Vaticanism**, vat'i-kan-izm, *n.* The doctrines and tenets promulgated by the Vatican; ultramontanism.

Vaticinate, vā-tis'i-nāt, *v.i.*—*vaticinated, vaticinating.* [L. *vaticinor*, *vaticinatus*, to prophesy, from *vates*, a prophet.] To prophesy; to practise prediction.—*v.t.* To prophesy; to foretell. — **Vaticination**, vā-tis'i-nā''shon, *n.* A prediction; a prophecy. — **Vaticinator**, vā-tis'i-nā-tėr, *n.* One who vaticinates or predicts.

Vaudeville, vōd'vēl, *n.* [Fr. *vaudeville*, from O.Fr. *Vau de Vire*, *Val de Vire*, the valley of the Vire, in Normandy—originally applied to songs of Oliver Basselin, who lived there.] A French name for a light, gay song, consisting of several couplets and refrain or burden, sung to a familiar air; in the U.S. various types of entertainment, as song and dance acts, humorous skits, comic dialogues, and juggling acts.

Vaudois, vōd-wa, *n.* [*Vaud* in Switzerland.] An inhabitant of the Pays de Vaud, a Waldense.

Vault, vạlt, *n.* [O.Fr. *vaulte*, *voulte* (Fr. *voûte*) from L.L. *volta*, *voluta*, a vault, from L. *volvo*, *volutum*, to turn round, to roll. VOLUBLE.] An arched roof; a concave roof or roof-like covering (the *vault* of heaven); *arch.* a continued arch; an arched apartment, a compartment built of steel or fire-proof brick for the storing of valuables; a safe.—*v.t.* To form with a vault or arched roof; to arch.—**Vaulted**, vạl'ted, *p.* and *a.* Arched; concave; covered with an arch or vault.—**Vaulting**, vạl'ting, *n.* Vaulted work; vaults collectively.

Vault, valt, *n.* [Fr *volte*, from It *volta*, a turn, a leap or vault, from *volvo*, *volutum*, to roll, to turn. Hence this word is a doublet of *Vault* above.] A leap or spring, a bound; a leap by means of a pole, or assisted by resting the hand or hands on something. — *v.i.* To leap; to bound, to spring; to exhibit equestrian or other feats of tumbling or leaping.—**Vaulter**, vạl'ter, *n.* One that vaults; a leaper; a tumbler.— **Vaulting**, vạl'ting, *n.* The art or practice of a vaulter.

Vaunt, vạnt, *v.i.* [From Fr. *vanter*, to vaunt, from L.L. *vanitare*, to boast, from L. *vanus*, vain. VAIN.] To boast; to talk with ostentation; to brag, to glory; to exult. — *v.t.* To boast of; to magnify or glorify with vanity; to display or put forward boastfully. — *n.* A boast; a brag.— **Vaunter**, vạn'tėr, *n.* A boaster; a man given to vain ostentation. — **Vaunting**, vạn'ting, *n.* Vain boasting; bragging. — **Vauntingly**, vạn'ting-li, *adv.* Boastfully; with vain ostentation.

Vautin process, vō'tin, *n.* An electrical method of preparing caustic soda.

Vavasor, vav'a-sor, *n.* [O Fr *vavassor*, L.L. *vavassor*, *vasvassor*, probably a contr of *vassus vassorum*, the vassal of vassals. VASSAL.] A principal vassal not holding immediately of the sovereign but of a great lord, and having himself vassals.

Vaward,‡ vā'wạrd, *n.* [From *van* and *ward*, for *vanward* = *vanguard.*] The van or vanguard.

Veal, vēl, *n.* [O.Fr. *veel* and *vedel*, from L. *vitellus*, dim. of *vitulus*, a calf; from root of L. *vetus*, *veteris*, old (whence *veteran*, Gr. (*v*)*etos*, a year).] The flesh of a calf killed for the table.

Vector, vek'tor, *n.* [L., a bearer or carrier, from *veho*, to carry.] A quantity, such as a velocity or a force, which has direction as well as magnitude, and is compounded by the parallelogram law; also a radius vector. RADIUS.

Veda, vā'dä or vē'da, *n.* [Skr., from *vid*, to know; cog. L. *video*, E. *wit*, to know WIT.] The general name for the body of ancient Sanskrit hymns, with accompanying comments, believed by the Hindus to have been revealed by Brahma, and on which the Brahmanical system is based.—**Vedanta**, ve-dän'ta, *n.* A system of philosophy among the Hindus founded on the Vedas. —**Vedic**, vē'dik, *a.* Relating to a Veda or the Vedas.

Vedette, Vidette, vē-det', vi-det', *n.* [Fr. *vedette*, from It. *vedetta*, a vedette, from *vedere*, L. *videre*, to see. VISIBLE.] A sentinel on horseback stationed on an outpost or elevated point to watch an enemy and give notice of danger; a picket or outpost.

Veer, vēr, *v.i.* [Fr. *virer*, to turn, veer, tack, &c.; from L.L. *virare*, to turn, from L. *viria*, a ring, a bracelet; akin *environ.*] To shift or change direction, as the wind; to go round; to change the direction of its course by turning (as a ship); to turn round, vary, be otherwise minded: said in regard to persons, feelings, intentions.—*v.t.* *Naut.* to direct into a different course; to wear or cause to change a course by turning the stern to windward, in opposition to *tacking*. —**Veering**, vē'ring, *p* and *a.* Turning; changing; shifting. — **Veeringly**, vē'ring-li, *adv.* Changingly; shiftingly.

Vegetable, vej'e-ta-bl, *a.* [Fr *végétable*, from L. *vegetabilis*, enlivening, from *vegeto*, to enliven, from *vegetus*, lively, from *vegeo*, to rouse, excite; from root seen also in *vigour*, *vigilant.*] Belonging, pertaining, or peculiar to plants; having the characteristics of a plant or plants.—*Vegetable ivory.* IVORY-NUT. — *Vegetable marrow.* MARROW. — *Vegetable mould*, mould consisting wholly or chiefly of humus.—*n.* A plant; often distinctively, a plant used for culinary purposes, or used for feeding cattle and sheep or other animals.—**Vegetal**, vej'e-tal, *a.* Having the characteristics or nature of a plant; pertaining to that class of vital phenomena common to plants and animals.—*n.* A plant; a vegetable. (*Johnson.*)—**Vegetality**, vej-e-tal'i-ti, *n.* The property of being vegetal; those vital phenomena which constitute plant life.—**Vegetarian**, vej-e-tā'ri-an, *n.* One who abstains from animal food, and maintains that vegetable food is the only kind proper for man. —*a.* Belonging to the diet or system of the vegetarians.—**Vegetarianism**, vej-e-tā'-ri-an-izm, *n.* The theory and practice of living solely on vegetable food.—**Vegetate**, vej'e-tāt, *v.i.* — *vegetated, vegetating.* [In form from L. *vegeto, vegetatum*, to enliven, but in meaning from *vegetable.*] To grow in the manner of plants; hence, to live a monotonous, useless life; to have a mere existence.—**Vegetation**, vej-e-tā'shon, *n.* The process of growing exhibited by plants; vegetable growth; vegetables or plants in general or collectively.—**Vegetative**, vej'-e-tā-tiv, *a.* Growing as plants; having the power to produce or support growth in plants. — **Vegetativeness**, vej'e-tā-tiv-nes, *n.* The quality of being vegetative.—**Vegeto - animal**, vej'e-tō-an-i-mal, *a.* Partaking of the nature both of vegetable and animal matter.

Vehement, vē'he-ment, *a.* [Fr. *véhément*, from L. *vehemens, vehementis*, eager, vehement, lit. carried out of one's mind, from *veho*, to carry, and *mens, mentis*, the mind. VEHICLE, MENTAL.] Proceeding from or characterized by strength or impetuosity of feeling; very eager or urgent; fervent; passionate; acting with great force or energy (*vehement* wind, fire); energetic; violent; very forcible. — **Vehemently**, vē'he-ment-li, *adv.* With great force and violence; urgently; passionately.—**Vehemence**, vē'he-mens, *n.* [Fr. *véhémence*, L. *vehementia.*] The character or quality of being vehement; violent ardour; fervour; impetuosity; fire; impetuous force; boisterousness; violence.—**Vehemency**, vē'he-men-si, *n.* Vehemence.

Vehicle, vē'hi-kl, *n.* [L. *vehiculum*, a vehicle, a carriage, from *veho*, to carry (seen also in *inveigh, vehement*), from a root seen also in E. *wagon, way.*] Any kind of carriage moving on land; a conveyance; that which is used as the instrument of conveyance, transmission, or communication (language is the *vehicle* for conveying ideas), a substance in which medicine is taken; a menstruum or medium in which paints, gums, varnishes, &c., are dissolved and prepared for use.—**Vehicled**, vē'hi-kld, *p.* and *a.* Conveyed in or by a vehicle.—**Vehicular, Vehiculary**, vē-hik'ū-lėr, vē-hik'ū-la-ri, *a.* Pertaining to a vehicle; of the nature of a vehicle.

Vehmgerichte, fām'ge-rēch-te, *n.pl.* [G.] A system of secret tribunals widely spread over Germany in the middle ages. — **Vehmic**, vē'mik, *a.* Pertaining to the vehmgerichte.

Veil, vāl, *n.* [O.Fr. *veile, vaile* (Fr. *voile*), from L. *velum*, a sail, a veil, from root seen also in *veho*, to carry, and in E. *way, wagon.*] Something hung up or spread out to intercept the view; a screen; a curtain; especially, a more or less transparent piece of dress worn to conceal, shade, or protect the face; *fig.* anything that prevents observation; a covering, mask, disguise, or the like; *anat.* the soft palate. — *To take the veil*, to assume the veil on becoming a nun; to retire to a nunnery.—*v.t.* To cover or conceal with a veil; to enshroud; to envelop; to keep from being seen; to conceal from view; to conceal, figuratively; to mask; to disguise.—**Veilless**, vāl'les, *a.* Destitute of a veil.

Vein, vān, *n.* [Fr. *veine*, from L. *vena*, a vein, also natural bent, genius, same root as *veho*, to carry. VEHICLE, VEIL.] One of a system of membranous canals or tubes distributed throughout the bodies of animals for the purpose of returning the impure blood from the extremities, surfaces, and viscera to the heart and lungs; a tube or an assemblage of tubes through which the sap of plants is transmitted along the leaves; a crack or fissure in a rock, filled up by substances different from the rock, and which may either be metallic or non-metallic; a streak or wave of different colour appearing in wood, in marble, &c.; disposition or cast of mind; particular mood, humour, or disposition for the time being.—*v.t.* To fill or furnish with veins; to streak or variegate with veins.—**Veined**, vānd, *a.* Full of veins; streaked; variegated; *bot.* having vessels branching over the surface, as a leaf.—**Veining**, vā'ning, *n.* A streaked appearance as if from veins. —**Veinless**, vān'les, *a.* Destitute of veins. —**Veinlet**, vān'let, *n.* A vein branching off from a larger vein.—**Veiny**, vā'ni, *a.* Full of veins.

Velar, vē'lėr, *a.* [L. *velum*, a veil. VEIL.] Pertaining or relating to a veil; pertaining to the veil of the palate.—**Velarium**, vē-lā'ri-um, *n.* An awning stretched over an ancient Roman theatre or amphitheatre, these buildings being open to the sky.—**Velate**, vē'lāt, *a.* *Bot.* having a veil; veiled.

Veld, felt, *n.* [D. *veld*, a field=E. *field.*] A term in S. Africa for open uninclosed country.

Veliger, vē'li-jėr, *n.* [L. *velum*, a sail, *gero*, I carry.] In molluscs, a shell-bearing larva which swims by means of a large ciliated head-flap.

Velitation, vel'i-tā"shon, *n.* [L. *velites*, light-armed soldiers.] A preliminary skirmish, a slight controversy.

Velleity, vel-lē'i-ti, *n.* [Fr. *velléité*, from L. *velle*, to will.] *Philos.* volition in the weakest form; an indolent or inactive wish or inclination towards a thing.

Vellicate, vel'i-kāt, *v.t.* [L. *vellico, vellicatum*, from *vello*, to pull.] To twitch.—**Vellication**, vel-i-kā'shon, *n.* A twitching; a convulsive twitching of muscles.

Vellum, vel'um, *n.* [Fr. *vélin*, from L. *vitulinus*, pertaining to a calf, from *vitulus*, a calf. VEAL.] A fine kind of parchment made of calf's skin, and rendered clear, smooth, and white for writing on.—**Vellumy**, vel'um-i, *a.* Resembling vellum.

Velo, vē'lō, *n.* [L. *velox*, swift.] A proposed name for 1 ft. per sec. as the unit of velocity. See CELO.

Velocipede, ve-los'i-pēd, *n.* [From L. *velox*, and *pes, pedis*, a foot.] A light vehicle or conveyance consisting mainly of wheels and driven or impelled by the feet of the rider or pair of riders; a bicycle or tricycle. — **Velocipedist**, ve-los'i-pēd-ist, *n.* One who uses a velocipede.

Velocity, ve-los'i-ti, *n.* [Fr. *vélocité*, from L. *velocitas, velocitatis*, from *velox, velocis*, swift, rapid.] Quickness or speed in motion or movement; swiftness; rapidity; not applied to the movements of animals, or but rarely; *physics*, rate of motion, differing from speed in involving direction as well as magnitude.—*Velocity potential*, in the theory of fluid motion, a quantity varying from point to point of space, and having the property that its rate of change per unit length in any direction gives the component velocity in that direction.—*Virtual velocity*, an infinitesimal displacement of the point of application of a force measured in the direction of the force.

Velour, vel'ör, *n.* [Fr. *velours*, L. *villosus.*] A substance of felt or other velvety combinations, much used in the construction of silk hats, woman's hats, &c.

Velum, vē'lum, *n.* [L., a veil.] *Bot.* the horizontal membrane connecting the margin of the pileus of a fungus with the stipes; *anat.* the veil of the palate.

Velumen, ve-lū'men, *n.* [L., a cover, a fleece.] *Bot.* the velvety coating of leaves.

Velutinous, ve-lū'ti-nus, *a.* [From It. *veluto*, velvet. VELVET.] Resembling velvet; velvety.

Velvet, vel'vet, *n.* [O.E. *velouette, velwet, vellute*; L.L. *velluetum, vellutum*; It. *veluto*, from L. *villus*, shaggy hair.] A rich silk stuff, covered on the outside with a close, short, fine, soft shag or nap; a cotton stuff manufactured in the same way, distinctively called *velveteen* or *cotton velvet*; a delicate hairy integument covering a deer's antlers in the first stages of growth.—*a.* Made of velvet; soft and delicate like velvet.—**Velveteen**, vel-ve-tēn', *n.* A cloth made of cotton in imitation of velvet; cotton velvet. —**Velveting**, vel'vet-ing, *n.* The fine nap or shag of velvet.—**Velvet-pile**, *n.* A kind of carpet with a long soft nap.—**Velvety**, vel've-ti, *a.* Made of or resembling velvet; smooth, soft, or delicate in surface.

Vena, vē'na, *n.* [L.] *Anat.* a vein.—*Vena cava* (the hollow vein) the largest vein in the body, which receives blood from the other parts and transmits it to the right auricle of the heart.—*Vena contracta*, the most contracted part of a jet of fluid issuing from an orifice.—*Vena portæ* (the vein of the entrance), the great vein situated at the entrance of the liver, which receives the blood from the abdominal viscera, and carries it into the liver, where it is utilized in the formation of bile.

Venal, vē'nal, *a.* [L. *venalis*, venal, for sale, from *venum*, sale; akin *vend.*] Ready to sell one's self for money or other consideration and entirely from sordid motives; ready to accept a bribe; mercenary.—**Venality**, vē-nal'i-ti, *n.* Prostitution of talents, offices, or services for money or reward; mercenariness.

Venation, vē-nā'shon, *n.* [From L. *vena*, a vein.] *Bot.* the manner in which the veins of leaves are arranged.

Vend, vend, *v.t.* [From L. *vendo*, to sell, from *venum*, sale, and *do*, to give. VENAL.] To sell.—**Vendee**, ven-dē', *n.* The person to whom a thing is sold: opposed to *vendor*. —**Vender**, ven'dėr, *n.* One who vends or sells.—**Vendible**, ven'di-ble, *a.* Capable of being sold; saleable; marketable.—**Vendibleness, Vendibility**, ven'di-bl-nes, ven-di-bil'i-ti, *n.* The state of being saleable.—**Vendibly**, ven'di-bli, *adv.* In a saleable manner.—**Vendor**, ven'dor, *n.* A seller.

Vendace, ven'dās, *n.* [O.Fr. *vendese*, Fr. *vandoise*, the dace; origin unknown.] A fish of the salmon family found only in a few British lakes, and in some of the rivers and lakes of Sweden; very delicate eating.

Vendean, vaṅ'dē-an, *a.* [Fr. *Vendéen.*] Of or belonging to the province of Vendée in western France; royalist of the 1793 party.

Vendemiaire, vaṅ-dā-myer, *n.* [Fr. *Vendémiaire.*] The wine or vintage month from 22nd September to 21st October, in the French Republican Calendar.

Vendetta, ven-det'tä, *n.* [It., from L. *vindicta*, revenge. VINDICTIVE.] A blood-feud; the practice of the nearest of kin executing vengeance on the murderer of a relative, as among the Corsicans, Arabs, &c.

Vendue,† ven'dū, *n.* [O.Fr. *vendue*, from *vendre*, to sell. VEND.] A sale by auction.

Veneer, ve-nēr', *n.* [From G. *furnier*, a veneer, *furnieren*, to veneer, from Fr. *fournir*, to furnish (which see).] A thin piece of wood (sometimes ivory or other substance) laid upon another of a less valuable sort, so that the whole article appears to be of the more valuable sort.—*v.t.* To overlay or face over with veneer; *fig.* to put a fine superficial show on; to gild.—**Veneering**, ve-nēr'ing, *n.* The act of one who veneers; the material laid on; *fig.* superficial show.

Venerate, ven'ėr-āt, *v.t.*—*venerated, venerating.* [L. *veneror, veneratus*, to venerate, from the stem of *Venus, Veneris*, Venus, love; allied to Skr. *van*, to worship, to love. VENUS.] To regard with respect and reverence; to reverence; to revere; to regard as hallowed. — **Veneration**, ven-ėr-ā'shon, *n.* [L. *veneratio.*] The highest degree of respect and reverence; a feeling or sentiment excited by the dignity, wisdom, and goodness of a person, or by the sacredness of his character, and with regard to place, by whatever makes us regard it as hallowed. —**Venerator**, ven'ėr-ā-tėr, *n.* One who venerates. — **Venerable**, ven'ėr-a-bl, *a.* [L. *venerabilis.*] Worthy of veneration; deserving of honour and respect; to be regarded with awe and reverence; hallowed by associations.—**Venerableness**, ven'-ėr-a-bl-nes, *n.* The state or quality of being venerable.—**Venerably**, ven'ėr-a-bli, *adv.* So as to excite veneration or reverence.

Venereal, ve-nē'rē-al, *a.* [L. *venereus*, from *Venus, Veneris.*] Pertaining to sexual love or its indulgence; relating to or arising from sexual intercourse.—**Venery**, ven'ėr-i, *n.* Sexual intercourse.

Venery, ven'ėr-i, *n.* [Fr. *vènerie*, from O.Fr. *vener*, L. *venari*, to hunt, whence also *venison.*] The act or exercise of hunting; the sports of the chase.

Venesection, ven-e-sek'shon, *n.* [L. *vena*, vein, and *sectio*, a cutting.] The operation of opening a vein for letting blood; blood-letting; phlebotomy.

Venetian, vē-nē'shi-an, *a.* Pertaining to Venice in Northern Italy.—*Venetian blind*, a blind made of thin narrow transverse slips of wood, so connected as to overlap each other when closed, and to show a series of open spaces for the admission of light and air when in the other position. [In this usage the capital letter need not be employed.]—*Venetian chalk, Venetian talc.* Same as *French Chalk.*—*Venetian door*, a door with long narrow side lights.—*Venetian red*, a burnt ochre which owes its colour to the presence of an oxide of iron.—*Venetian white*, a carefully prepared carbonate of lead.—*n.* A native of Venice; a venetian blind.

Vengeance, ven'jans, *n.* [Fr. *vengeance*, from *venger*, to revenge, from L. *vindicare*, to avenge. VINDICATE.] Punishment inflicted in return for an injury or an offence, generally implying indignation on the part of the punisher and more or less justice in the nature of the punishment. ∴ Syn. under REVENGE. The word is often used in curses or imprecations (a *vengeance* on you!); the phrase *with a vengeance!* is expressive of excess in degree, vehemence, violence, and the like (a forced march, *with a vengeance!*).—**Vengeful**, venj'fụl, *a.* Vindictive; retributive; revengeful.—**Vengefully**, venj'fụl-li, *adv.* In a vengeful manner; vindictively.

Venial, vē'ni-al, *a.* [L. *venialis*, from L. *venia*, pardon; akin to *Venus* (which see).] That may be forgiven; pardonable; not deeply sinful; excusable; that may pass without censure.—**Venialness, Veniality**, vē'ni-al-nes, vē-ni-al'i-ti, *n.* Quality of being venial.—**Venially**, vē'ni-al-li, *adv.* In a venial manner; pardonably.

Venison, ven'zn or ven'i-zn, *n.* [O.Fr. *venison* (Fr. *venaison*), from L. *venatio*, a hunting, from *venari*, to hunt (whence *venery*, hunting).] The flesh of such wild animals as are taken in the chase and used as human food; in modern usage restricted to the flesh of animals of the deer kind.

Vennel, ven'l, *n.* [Fr. *venelle.*] A lane; a narrow alley.

Venom, ven'om, *n.* [O.E. *venim, venime*, O.Fr. *venim, venin*, Mod.Fr. *venin*, from L. *venenum*, poison.] The poisonous fluid secreted by certain animals and introduced into the bodies of other animals by biting, as in the case of serpents, and stinging, as in the case of scorpions, bees, &c.; hence, spite; malice; malignity; virulency.—**Venomous**, ven'om-us, *a.* Full of venom; noxious to animal life from venom; poisonous; malignant; spiteful; malicious.—**Venomously**, ven'om-us-li, *adv.* In a venomous manner; malignantly; spitefully.—**Venomousness**, ven'om-us-nes, *n.*

Venous, vē'nus, *a.* [L. *venosus*, from *vena*, a vein. VEIN.] Pertaining to a vein or to veins; contained in veins (*venous* blood, distinguishable from arterial blood by its darker colour); consisting of veins; *bot.* veined or venose.—**Venose**, vē'nōz, *a.* *Bot.* having numerous branched veins, as leaves.—**Venosity**, vē-nos'i-ti, *n.* The state or quality of being venous or venose.

Vent, vent, *n.* [From Fr. *vent*, wind, air, from L. *ventus*, wind (in *ventilate*), so that the original meaning would be air-hole; or same as *fent.*] A small aperture or opening; the priming and firing aperture of a gun; the touch-hole; the anus; the opening at which the excrements of birds and fishes are discharged; the flue or funnel of a chimney; an outlet; means of outward manifestation or expression (a *vent* for one's feelings); utterance; expression.—*To give vent to*, to suffer to escape; to keep no longer pent up (anger or the like).—*v.t* To let out; to give passage to; to emit; to keep no longer pent up in one's mind; to pour forth; to utter; to publish.

Vent, vent, *n.* [Fr. *vente*, sale, a market, from L. *vendo, venditum*, to sell. VEND.] A selling; sale; market.

Ventage, ven'tāj, *n.* [From Fr. *vent*, L. *ventus*, wind. VENTILATE.] A small hole, as of a flute.—**Ventail**, ven'tāl, *n.* [Fr. *ventail*, L.L. *ventaculum*, from L. *ventus.*] The movable front of a helmet.

Venter, ven'tėr, *n.* [L., the belly.] *Anat.* the abdomen or lower belly; the belly of a muscle; *law*, the womb.

Ventilate, ven'ti-lāt, *v.t.*—*ventilated, ventilating.* [L. *ventilo, ventilatum*, to winnow, to ventilate, from *ventus*, wind; same root as Skr. *vâ*, to blow, E. *wind.*] To expose to the free passage of air or wind; to supply with fresh and remove vitiated air; to expose to common talk or consideration; to let be freely discussed.—**Ventilation**, ven-ti-lā'shon, *n.* [L. *ventilatio.*] The act of ventilating; the replacement of vitiated air by pure fresh air; the art or operation of supplying buildings, mines, and other confined places with a necessary quantity of fresh air; public examination or discussion of questions or topics.—**Ventilative**, ven'ti-lā-tiv, *a.* Belonging to ventilation.—**Ventilator**, ven'ti-lā-tėr, *n.* One who ventilates; a contrivance for keeping the air fresh in any close space.

Ventrad, vent'rad, *a.* [From L. *venter, ventris*, the belly, and *ad*, towards.] Towards the ventral surface.—**Ventral**, ven'-tral, *a.* Belonging or pertaining to the belly, or to the surface of the body opposite to the dorsal side or back.—**Ventricle**, ven'tri-kl, *n.* [L. *ventriculus*, dim. of *venter*, belly.] A small cavity in an animal body serving some function.—*Ventricles of the heart*, two cavities of the heart (distinguished as *right* and *left*), which propel the blood into the arteries.—**Ventricous, Ventricose**, ven'tri-kus, ven'tri-kōs, *a.* [L. *ventricosus.*] Swelled out; *bot.* swelling out in the middle.—**Ventricular**, ven-trik'ū-lėr, *a.* Pertaining to a ventricle; distended in the middle.—**Ventriloquism**, ven-tril'ō-kwizm, *n.* [L. *ventriloquus*, a ventriloquist—*venter*, and *loquor*, to speak, the notion being that the voice proceeded from the belly.] The act, art, or practice of speaking or uttering sounds by employing the vocal organs in such a manner that the voice appears to come, not from the person, but from some distance, as from the opposite side of the room, from the cellar, &c.—**Ventriloquist**, ven-tril'ō-kwist, *n.* One who practises or is skilled in ventriloquism.—**Ventriloquize**, ven-tril'ō-kwīz, *v.i.* To practise ventriloquism.—**Ventrilocution**, ven'tri-lo-kū''shon, *n.* Ventriloquism.—**Ventriloquial, Ventriloquous**, ven-tri-lō'kwi-al, ven-tril'ō-kwus, *a.* Pertaining to ventriloquism.

Venture, ven'tūr, *n.* [Abbrev. of *aventure*, old form of *adventure*, from Fr. *aventure*, L. *ad*, to, and *venturus*, about to come, from *venio*, to come (seen also in *advene, advent, convene, convent, covenant, event, invent, prevent, revenue*, &c.). COME.] An undertaking of chance or danger; the risking or staking of something; a hazard; a scheme for making gain by way of trade; a commercial speculation; the thing put to hazard; something sent to sea in trade; chance; luck; contingency.—*At a venture*, at hazard; without seeing the end or mark, or without foreseeing the issue.—*v.i.*—*ventured, venturing.* To dare; to have courage or presumption to do, undertake, or say something; to run a hazard or risk; to risk one's self.—*v.t.* To expose to hazard; to risk; to expose one's self to.—**Venturer**, ven'tūr-ėr, *n.* One who ventures.—**Venturesome**, ven'tūr-sum, *a.* Inclined to venture; venturous.—**Venturesomely**, ven'tūr-sum-li, *adv.* In a venturesome manner.—**Venturesomeness**, ven'tūr-sum-nes, *n.*—**Venturous**, ven'tū-rus, *a.* Daring; bold; intrepid; adventurous.—**Venturously**, ven'tū-rus-li, *adv.* Daringly; fearlessly; boldly.—**Venturousness**, ven'tū-rus-nes, *n.*

Venturine, ven'tū-rīn, *n.* [Same as *aventurine, aventurine.*] Powdered gold used in japanning to cover varnished surfaces.

Venue, ven'ū, *n.* [Fr. *venue*, a coming, from *venir*, L. *venire*, to come. VENTURE.] *Fencing*, a coming on; an onset; a bout; a turn; a thrust; *law*, a locality; the place where an action is laid, or the trial of a cause takes place.

Venule, ven'ūl, *n.* [L. *venula*, a small vein. VEIN.] A small vein.

Venus, vē'nus, *n.* [L. *Venus, Veneris* (hence *venereal*), cog. with A.Sax. *wine*, Icel. *vinr*, O.G. *wini*, a friend, Skr. *van*, to love, to worship. VENERATE, VENIAL.] The goddess of beauty and love among the Romans, often identified with the Greek *Aphrodite*; a planet having its orbit between Mercury and the earth, the most brilliant of all the planetary bodies, sometimes the morning, sometimes the evening star.

Veracious, ve-rā'shus, *a.* [L. *verax, veracis*, from *verus*, true. VERY.] Observant of truth; habitually disposed to speak truth; characterized by truth; true.—**Veraciously**, ve-rā'shus-li, *adv.* In a veracious manner; truthfully.—**Veracity**, ve-ras'i-ti, *n.* The state or quality of being veracious or true; regard to or observance of truth; truthfulness; truth; agreement with actual fact.

Veranda, Verandah, ve-ran'da, *n.* [Pg. *varanda*, from Skr. *varanda*, a veranda, from *vri*, to cover.] A kind of open portico, or a sort of light external gallery attached to the front of a building, with a sloping roof supported on slender pillars.

Veratrin, Veratrine, vē-rā'trin, *n.* [L. *veratrum*, hellebore.] A vegetable alkaloid found in plants of the hellebore genus, used as external application in neuralgia and rheumatism.

Verb, vėrb, *n.* [Fr. *verbe*, from L. *verbum*, a word, a verb; same root as E. *word.*] *Gram.* that part of speech whose essential function is to predicate or assert something in regard to something else (the subject or thing spoken of), divided into *active* and *neuter, transitive* and *intransitive*, &c.—**Verbal**, vėr'bal, *a.* [L. *verbalis.*] Spoken; expressed to the ear in words; oral; respecting words only and not things; literal; having word answering to word (a *verbal* translation); *gram.* derived from a verb (a *verbal* noun).—*n. Gram.* a noun derived from a verb.—**Verbalism**, vėr'bal-izm, *n.* Something expressed orally.—**Verbalist**, vėr'bal-ist, *n.* One who deals in words merely; a literal adherent to, or a minute critic of words.—**Verbality**, vėr-bal'i-ti, *n.* The state or quality of being verbal.—**Verbalization**, vėr'bal-ī-zā''shon, *n.* The act of verbalizing.—**Verbalize, Verbify**, vėr'bal-īz, vėr'bi-fī, *v.t.* To convert into a verb; to use as a verb.—*v.i.* To use many words; to be verbose or diffuse.—**Verbally**, vėr'bal-li, *adv.* In a verbal manner; by words uttered; orally; word for word.—**Verbarian**, vėr-bā'ri-an, *n.* A word-coiner; a verbalist.—**Verbatim**, vėr-bā'tim, *adv.* [L.] Word for word; in the same words (to tell a story *verbatim*).—*Verbatim et literatim* (lit-ėr-ā'tim), word for word, and letter for letter.—**Verbiage**, vėr'bi-āj, *n.* [Fr.] Verbosity; use of many words without necessity; wordiness.—**Verbose**, vėr-bōs', *a.* [L. *verbosus.*] Abounding in words; using or containing more words than are necessary; wordy; prolix.—**Verbosely**, vėr-bōs'li, *adv.* In a verbose manner; wordily.—**Verboseness, Verbosity**, vėr-bōs'nes, vėr-bos'i-ti, *n.* The state or quality of being verbose; wordiness; prolixity.

Verbena, vėr-bē'na, *n.* [L. *verbena*, any green bough used in sacred rites.] A genus of plants, mostly American, though one species, common vervain—formerly supposed to possess remarkable virtues—is common in Britain, while others are cultivated for the great beauty of their flowers.

Verbiage, Verbose, &c. Under VERB.

Verdant, vėr′dant, *a.* [From Fr. *verdir,* to grow green, O.Fr. *verd,* green, from L. *viridis,* green.] Green with herbage or foliage covered with growing plants or grass; green in knowledge; simple by reason of inexperience (*colloq.*).—**Verdancy,** vėr′dan-si, *n.* Greenness; rawness inexperience.—**Verdantly,** vėr′dant-li, *adv.* In a verdant manner.—**Verd-antique,** vėrd-an-tēk′, *n.* [Fr., from *verd,* green, *antique,* ancient.] The green incrustation seen on ancient coins, brass or copper; *mineral.* an aggregate of serpentine and white crystallized marble, having a greenish colour; also, a green porphyry used as marble.—**Verderer, Verderor,** vėr′dėr-ėr, vėr′dėr-or, *n.* [Fr. *verdier,* L.L. *viridarius.*] An official having charge of the trees, &c., in a royal forest.

Verdict, vėr′dikt, *n.* [L.L. *verdictum, veredictum,* from L. *vere,* truly, and *dictum,* something declared, from *dico, dictum,* to say. VERY, DICTION.] The answer of a jury given to the court concerning any matter of fact in any cause committed to their trial and examination; hence, a decision, judgment, or opinion pronounced in general.

Verdigris, vėr′di-gris, *n.* [O.Fr. *verd-de-gris,* verdigris, apparently from *verd,* green, *de,* of, *gris,* gray; but rather from *verd de Grèce,* lit. green of Greece. VERDANT.] A substance obtained by exposing copper to the air in contact with acetic acid, used as a pigment, as a mordant, and otherwise.

Verditer, vėr′di-tėr, *n.* [Fr. *verd-de-terre,* green of earth. VERDANT.] A blue or bluish-green pigment, generally prepared by decomposing nitrate of copper with chalk.

Verdure, vėr′dūr, *n.* [Fr. *verdure,* greenness, green vegetation, from *verd, vert,* green, from L. *viridis,* green. VERDANT.] Greenness or freshness of vegetation; green plants or foliage.—**Verdured,** vėr′dūrd, *a.* Covered with verdure.—**Verdurous,** vėr′dūr-us, *a.* Covered with verdure; verdant.

Verge, vėrj, *n.* [Fr. *verge,* a rod, mace, ring, or hoop, from L. *virga,* a rod.] A rod or staff of office; a mace; a ring or circle (*Shak.*)‡; compass; space; room; scope; the extreme side or edge of anything; the brink, border, margin, limit.—**Verger,** vėr′jėr, *n.* One who carries a verge; an officer who bears the verge or staff of office before a bishop, dean, or other dignitary; the official who takes care of the interior of the fabric of a church.

Verge, vėrj, *v.i.*—*verged, verging.* [L. *vergo,* to turn, to incline.] To tend downward; to bend; to slope; to tend; to incline; to approach; to border.—**Vergency,** vėr′jen-si, *n.* The act of verging, tending, or inclining.

Veridical,† ve-rid′i-kal, *a.* [L. *veridicus*—*verum,* truth, and *dico,* to say. VERDICT.] Truth-telling; veracious.

Verify, ver′i-fī, *v.t.*—*verified, verifying.* [Fr. *vérifier,* from L. *verus,* true, and *facio,* to make. VERY.] To prove to be true; to confirm; to establish the truth, correctness, or authenticity of.—**Verifiable,** ver′i-fī-a-bl, *a.* Capable of being verified.—**Verification,** ver′i-fi-kā″shon, *n.* The act of verifying; authentication; confirmation.—**Verificative,** ver′i-fi-kā″tiv, *a.* Serving to verify.—**Verifier,** ver′i-fī-ėr, *n.* One who or that which verifies.

Verily, ver′i-li, *adv.* [From *very.*] In truth; in very truth or deed; in fact; certainly; really; in sincere earnestness.

Verisimilar, ver-i-sim′i-lėr, *a.* [L. *verisimilis*—*verus,* true, and *similis,* like. VERY, SIMILAR.] Having the appearance of truth; probable; likely.—**Verisimilitude,** ver′i-si-mil″i-tūd, *n.* [L. *verisimilitudo.*] The appearance of truth; probability; likelihood.

Verity, ver′i-ti, *n.* [Fr. *vérité,* from L. *veritas,* from *verus,* true. VERY.] The quality of being true or real; true or real nature; reality; truth; fact; a true assertion or tenet; a truth.—*Of a verity,* in very truth or deed; of a truth; certainly.—**Veritable,** ver′i-ta-bl, *a.* [Fr. *véritable.*] True; agreeable to truth or fact; real; actual.—**Veritably,** ver′i-ta-bli, *adv.* In a veritable or true manner; truly.

Verjuice, vėr′jūs, *n.* [Fr. *verjus,* from *verd, vert,* L. *viridis,* green, and *jus,* juice. VERDANT, JUICE.] An acid liquor expressed from crab-apples, unripe grapes, &c., used for culinary and other purposes; *fig.* sourness or acidity of temper, manner, or expression.

Vermeil, vėr′mil, *n.* [Fr. *vermeil.* VERMILION.] Vermilion; a bright, beautiful red, the colour of vermilion (*poet.*); silver or bronze gilt; a liquid applied to a gilded surface to give lustre to the gold.

Vermes, vėr′mēz, *n.pl.* [L.] Worms: the name given by Linnæus to all animals which could not be arranged among vertebrates and insects.

Vermicelli, vėr-mi-chel′li, *n.* [It., lit. little worms, pl. of *vermicello,* from L. *vermiculus,* dim. of *vermis,* a worm. VERMIN.] An Italian food preparation of flour, yolks of eggs, sugar, and saffron, in the form of long, slender tubes or threads.

Vermicide, vėr′mi-sīd, *n.* [L. *vermis,* a worm, and *cædo,* to kill. VERMIN.] A substance which destroys intestinal worms; a worm-killer.

Vermicular, vėr-mik′ū-lėr, *a.* [From L. *vermiculis,* a little worm, dim. of *vermis,* a worm. VERMIN.] Pertaining to worms; resembling a worm; particularly resembling the motion of a worm; peristaltic.—*Vermicular* or *vermiculated work,* mosaic work showing knots or windings resembling the tracks of worms; a species of rusticated masonry appearing as if eaten into or formed by the tracks of worms.—**Vermiculate,** vėr-mik′ū-lāt, *a.* Wormlike in shape or appearance; crawling or creeping like a worm.—**Vermiculated,** vėr-mik′ū-lā-ted, *p.* and *a.* Formed with a worm-like pattern.—**Vermiculation,** vėr-mik′ū-lā″shon, *n.* Motion in the manner of a worm; a worm-like ornament or body of any kind; the state of being worm-eaten.—**Vermicule,** vėr′mi-kūl, *n.* A little worm.—**Vermiculite,** vėr-mik′ū-līt, *n.* [L. *vermiculus,* and Gr. *lithos,* a stone.] *Geol.* a short worm-track seen on the surface of many flagstones.—**Vermiculose, Vermiculous,** vėr-mik′ū-lōs, vėr-mik′ū-lus, *a.* [L. *vermiculosus.*] Containing worms or grubs; resembling worms.—**Vermiform,** vėr′mi-form, *a.* [L. *vermis,* and *forma,* form.] Having the form or shape of a worm or of its motions.—**Vermifugal,** vėr-mif′ū-gal, *a.* [L. *vermis,* and *fugo,* to expel.] Tending to prevent or destroy worms; anthelmintic.—**Vermifuge,** vėr′mi-fūj, *n.* A medicine or substance that destroys or expels intestinal worms; an anthelmintic.

Vermilion, vėr-mil′yon, *n.* [Fr. *vermillon,* from *vermeil,* vermilion, red, from L. *vermiculus* (dim. of *vermis,* a worm), a little worm, the kermes insect, hence a scarlet colour such as that obtained from the kermes insect. This colour was formerly called *worm-dye.* VERMIN.] The red sulphide of mercury or cinnabar; a bright red pigment formed of this, or artificially prepared from a preparation of sulphur and mercury; a colour such as that of the above pigment; a beautiful red colour.—*v.t.* To colour with vermilion; to cover with a delicate red.

Vermin, vėr′min, *n. sing.* and *pl.*: used chiefly in plural. [Fr. *vermine,* vermin, parasitic insects, from L. *vermis,* a worm (seen also in *vermicular, vermilion, vermicelli,* &c.) cog. E. *worm.* WORM.] A name given to the smaller mammalia or certain birds which damage man's crops or other belongings, and to noxious or destructive insects or the like; also used of noxious human beings.—**Verminate,** vėr′mi-nāt, *v.i.* [L. *vermino, verminatum.*] To breed vermin.—**Vermination,** vėr-mi-nā′shon, *n.* The breeding of parasitic vermin; a gripping of the bowels.—**Vermin-killer,** *n.* A poisonous substance intended to kill mice or other vermin.—**Verminous,** vėr′mi-nus, *a.* Caused by or arising from the presence of vermin on the body.—**Vermiparous,** vėr-mip′a-rus, *a.* [L. *vermis,* and *pario,* to bear.] Producing or bearing worms.—**Vermivorous,** vėr-miv′o-rus, *a.* [L. *vermis,* and *voro,* to devour.] Devouring worms; feeding on worms.

Vermuth, vėr′mut, *n.* [Fr. *vermout, vermouth,* from G. *wermuth,* absinthe. WORMWOOD.] A liquor compounded of white wine, absinthe, angelica, and other aromatics, used to excite the appetite.

Vernacular, vėr-nak′ū-lėr, *a.* [L. *vernaculus,* domestic, indigenous, from *verna,* a slave born in his master's house, a native.] Belonging to the country of or place of one's birth; belonging to the speech that we all naturally acquire, or more particularly to the everyday idiom of a place.—*n.* One's mother-tongue; the native idiom of a place.—**Vernacularism,** vėr-nak′ū-lėr-izm, *n.* A vernacular idiom.—**Vernacularly,** vėr-nak′ū-lėr-li, *adv.* In agreement with the vernacular manner.

Vernal, vėr′nal, *a.* [L. *vernalis,* from *ver,* spring; cog. Icel. *vár,* Dan. *vaar,* the spring; from root signifying to be bright, to burn, seen in *Vesta, Vesuvius,* &c.] Belonging to the spring; appearing in spring; belonging to youth; the spring of life.—*Vernal equinox.* Under EQUINOX.—**Vernation,** vėr-nā′shon, *n.* [L. *verno, vernatum,* to be spring-like.] *Bot.* the disposition of the nascent leaves within the bud.

Vernier, vėr′ni-ėr, *n.* [From the inventor, Peter *Vernier,* of Brussels, who died 1637.] A small sliding-scale parallel with the fixed scale of a barometer, theodolite, or other instrument, used for measuring fractional parts of the divisions on the fixed graduated scale.

Vernility,† vėr-nil′i-ti, *n.* [L. *vernilitas,* from *vernilis,* slavish, servile, from *verna,* a slave.] Servility; fawning behaviour like that of a slave.

Veronal, ver′ō-näl, *n.* A white, crystalline substance used as a hypnotic.

Veronica, vē-ron′i-ka, *n.* [From a supposed female saint of the name of *Veronica.*] A genus of plants including the various species of speedwell.

Verrel, Verrule, ver′el, ver′ūl, *n.* A ring at the end of a cane, &c.; a ferrule.

Verrucose, Verrucous, ver′ū-kōs, ver′ū-kus, *a.* [L. *verrucosus,* warty, from *verruca,* a wart.] Warty; having little knobs or warts on the surface.—**Verruculose,** ve-rū′kū-lōs, *a.* Having minute wart-like prominences.

Versant, vėr′sant, *n.* [Fr. *versant,* a mountain slope, from *verser,* to shed, to pour, from L. *versare,* to turn, freq. of *verto.* VERSE.] All that part of a country which slopes or inclines in one direction; general slope of surface; aspect.

Versatile, vėr′sa-til, *a.* [L. *versatilis,* from *verso,* to turn, freq. of *verto, versus,* to turn. VERSE.] Capable of being moved or turned round; turning with ease from one thing to another; readily applying one's self to a new task or to various subjects; many-sided; *bot.* turning like the needle of a compass; fixed but freely movable.—**Versatilely,** vėr′sa-til-li, *adv.* In a versatile manner.—**Versatility, Versatileness,** vėr-sa-til′i-ti, vėr′sa-til-nes, *n.* The state or quality of being versatile; the faculty of easily turning one's mind to new tasks or subjects; facility in taking up various intellectual pursuits.

Verse, vėrs, *n.* [L. *versus,* a row, a line in writing, a verse, from *verto, versum,* to turn; seen also in *advert, convert, revert, adverse, converse, inverse, version, vertex,* &c.; same root as E. *worth* (verb).] A line of poetry consisting of a certain number of metrical feet; poetry; metrical language; poetical composition; versification; a short division of the chapters in the Scriptures;

a short division of a poetical composition; a stanza.—**Versicle**, vėr'si-kl, *n.* [L. *versiculus*, dim. of *versus*.] A little verse; a short verse in a church service spoken or chanted by the priest or minister alternately with a response by the people.—**Versicular**, vėr-sik'ū-lėr, *a.* Pertaining to verse or verses.—**Versification**, vėr'si-fi-kā"shon, *n.* The act or practice of composing poetic verse; a turning into verse; the construction of poetry; metrical composition.—**Versifier, Versificator**,† vėr'si-fī-ėr, vėr'si-fi-kā-tėr, *n.* One who versifies; one who makes verses; one who converts into verse.—**Versify**, vėr'si-fī, *v.i.*—*versified, versifying.* [Fr. *versifier*, L. *versificare*—*versus*, a verse, and *facio*, to make.] To make verses.—*v.t.* To relate in verse; to treat as the subject of verse; to turn into verse.

Versed, vėrst, *a.* [Fr. *versé*, from L. *versatus*, pp. of *versor*, to turn about frequently, to be engaged, from *verto*. VERSE.] Thoroughly acquainted; practised; skilled: with *in*.—*Versed sine.* Under SINE.

Versiform, vėr'si-form, *a.* [L. *versiformis*, from *verto*, *versum*, to turn, and *forma*, shape.] Varied in form; changing form.

Version, vėr'shon, *n.* [From L. *verto*, *versum*, to turn, change, translate, &c. VERSE.] The act of translating from one language into another†; a translation; that which is rendered from another language (the revised *version* of the Scriptures); a statement or account of incidents or proceedings from some particular point of view; a school exercise consisting of a translation of one language into another.

Verst, vėrst, *n.* A Russian measure of length, containing 1166⅔ yards, or two-thirds of a mile.

Versus, vėr'sus, *prep.* [L., against, turned in the direction of. VERSE.] Against; used chiefly in legal phraseology (Doe *versus* Roe) and in sports (Yale *vs.* Brown).

Vert, vėrt, *n.* [Fr. *vert*, green, from Latin *viridis*, green. VERDANT.] *Forest law*, everything within a forest that grows and bears a green leaf; *her.* a green color, expressed in engraving by diagonal lines drawn downward from left to right.

Vert, vėrt, *n.* One who goes over from one church or sect to another.

Vertebra, vėr'te-brä, *n*, pl. **Vertebræ**, vėr'te-brē. [L. *vertebra*, a joint, a joint or vertebra of the spine, from *verto*, to turn. VERSE.] One of the bones of which the spine or backbone of an animal consists; *pl.* the spine.—**Vertebral**, vėr'te-bral, *a.* Pertaining to the vertebræ (the *vertebral* column, that is, the spine); vertebrate.—*n.* A vertebrate animal.—**Vertebrata**, vėr-te-brā'ta, *n.pl.* The highest division of the animal kingdom, consisting of those animals which possess a backbone, including the fishes, amphibians, birds, reptiles, quadrupeds, and man.—**Vertebrate**, vėr-te-brāt, *n.* *Zool.* a member of the Vertebrata.—**Vertebrate, Vertebrated**, vėr'te-brā-ted, *a.* Having a spine or vertebral column.

Vertex, vėr'teks, *n.* pl. **Vertexes**, vėr'-tek-sez, or **Vertices**, vėr'ti-sēz. [L. *vertex*, an eddy, top, summit, lit. a turning-point, from *verto*, to turn. VERSE.] The highest or principal point; apex; top; crown; summit; *math.* the point in any figure opposite to and most distant from the base; the point of a conic section where the axis meets the curve.—**Vertical**, vėr'-ti-kal, *a.* Relating to the vertex; situated at the vertex; directly overhead; in a position perpendicular to the plane of the horizon; upright; plumb.—*Vertical angles*, the opposite angles made by two straight lines which intersect each other.—*Vertical circle*, *astron.* a great circle passing through the zenith and the nadir.—*Vertical plane*, a plane perpendicular to the plane of the horizon.—*Vertical steam-engine*, an engine in which the piston moves vertically, or straight up and down.—*n.* A vertical circle, plane, or line.—*Prime vertical*, *astron.* that vertical circle which passes through the zenith and the east and west points of the horizon.—**Vertically**, vėr'ti-kal-li, *adv.* In a vertical manner, position, or direction.—**Verticalness, Verticality**, vėr'ti-kal-nes, vėr-ti-kal'i-ti, *n.* The state of being vertical.

Verticil, Verticel, vėr'ti-sil, vėr'ti-sel, *n.* [L. *verticillus*, dim. of *vertex*, a whirl. VERTEX.] *Bot.* a mode of inflorescence in which the flowers surround the stem in a kind of ring; a whorl.—**Verticillate, Verticillated**, vėr-tis'i-lāt, vėr-tis'i-lā-ted, *a.* *Bot.* growing in a whorl, or on the same plane round the axis.

Vertigo, vėr-tī'go or vėr'ti-go, *n.* [L. *vertigo*, from *verto*, to turn. VERSE.] Dizziness or swimming of the head; giddiness arising from some disorder of the system.—**Vertiginous**, vėr-tij'i-nus, *a.* [L. *vertiginosus*.] Affected with vertigo; giddy; apt to make one giddy.—**Vertiginously**, vėr-tij'i-nus-li, *adv.* In a vertiginous manner.—**Vertiginousness**, vėr-tij'i-nus-nes, *n.* Giddiness.

Vertu, vėr'tu̧, It. pron. ver-tö', *n.* [It. *vertù*, *virtù*, virtue, goodness, excellence, &c.] Excellence in objects of art or curiosity; objects of art, antiquity, or curiosity taken collectively.

Vertumnus, ver-tum'nus, *n.* [L. *vertumnus*, from *verto*, to turn.] The Latin god of the changing seasons of the year, husband of Pomona.

Vervain, vėr'vān, *n.* [Fr. *verveine*, from L. *verbena*. VERBENA.] The popular name of some plants of the genus Verbena, formerly believed to have medicinal properties.

Verve, verv, *n.* [Fr.] Poetical or artistic rapture or enthusiasm; great spirit; energy; rapture; enthusiasm.

Vervels, vėr'vels (Fr. *vervelle*), *n.pl.* The rings attached to the ends of the thongs or jesses of a hawk.

Very, ver'i, *adv.* [O.E. *verri*, *veray*, *verray*, *verrei*, from O.Fr. *verai*, Fr. *vrai*, true, from a L.L. form *veracus*, from L. *verax*, veracious, from *verus*, true (seen also in *verify*, *verity*, *aver*, *verdict*, &c.); cog. D. *waar*, G. *wahr*, true.] In a high degree; to a great extent; extremely; exceedingly.—*a.* Veritable; real; true; actual; often placed before substantives to indicate that they must be understood in their full, unrestricted sense (my *very* heart-strings); to denote exact conformity with what is expressed by the word, or to express identity (the *very* words); to give emphasis or force generally (even your *very* eyes). [*Very* is sometimes met with in the comparative and superlative.]

Very light, ve-ri lit, *n.* [After Lieut. *Very*, the inventor.] The commonest make of British star-shell, used for purposes of observation and signalling.

Vesical, ves'i-kal, *a.* [L. *vesica*, a bladder.] Pertaining to the bladder.—**Vesicate**, ves'-i-kāt, *v.t.*—*vesicated, vesicating.* To raise vesicles or blisters on; to blister.—**Vesication**, ves-i-kā'shon, *n.* The process of blistering.—**Vesicant**, ves'i-kant, *n.* A blistering application or agent.—**Vesicatory**, ves'i-ka-to-ri, *a.* Having the property, when applied to the skin, of raising a blister; blistering.—*n.* A blistering agent.—**Vesicle**, ves'i-kl, *n.* [Fr. *vésicule*, L. *vesicula*, a little bladder, dim. of *vesica*.] Any small bladder-like structure, cavity, cell, or the like in a body; a little sac or cyst; a small blister or pustule on the skin.—**Vesicular, Vesiculose, Vesiculous**, ve-sik'ū-lėr, ve-sik'ū-lōs, ve-sik'ū-lus, *a.* Pertaining to or consisting of vesicles; bladdery; cellulose; full of interstices.—**Vesiculate**, ve-sik'ū-lāt, *a.* Full of vesicles; vesicular.

Vesper, ves'pėr, *n.* [L., akin to Gr. *Hesperos*, the evening, the evening-star; same root as *west*.] The evening-star; hence, the evening; *pl.* the time of evening service in some churches; *pl.* evening worship or service.—*Sicilian vespers.* Under SICILIAN.—*a.* Relating to the evening or to vespers.—**Vesper-bell**, *n.* The bell that summons to vespers.—**Vespertine**, ves'pėr-tin, *a.* [L. *vespertinus*.] Pertaining to the evening, of flowers opening in evening, of stars sinking to horizon at evening, of birds that fly in the evening.

Vespiary, ves'pi-a-ri, *n.* [From L. *vespa*, a wasp. WASP.] A nest or colony of wasps, hornets, &c.

Vessel, ves'el, *n.* [O.Fr. *vessel*, *veissel* (Fr. *vaisseau*), from L. *vascellum*, a dim. of *vas*, a vessel. VASE.] A utensil proper for holding liquors and other things, as a barrel, kettle, cup, dish, &c.; a ship; a craft of any kind, but usually one larger than a mere boat; *anat.* any tube or canal in which the blood or other humours are contained, secreted, or circulated; *bot.* a canal or tube in which the sap is contained and conveyed; *fig.* in scriptural phraseology, a person into whom anything is conceived as poured or infused (a chosen *vessel*, *vessels* of wrath).—*The weaker vessel*, applied in a jocular way to a woman, a usage borrowed from 1 Pet. iii. 7.

Vest, vest, *n.* [Fr. *veste*, from L. *vestis*, a garment, a vest (whence also *vesture*, *vestry*, *vestment*, *invest*, *divest*); cog. Gr. (*v*)*esthēs*, dress; Skr. *vas*, to put on; Goth. *vasjan*, to clothe.] A garment or dress; a short sleeveless garment worn by men under the coat, covering the upper part of the body; a waistcoat.—*v.t.* To clothe; to invest or clothe, as with authority; to endow; to confer upon (*vested with* power); to confer possession or enjoyment of (to *vest* dominion *in* a person).—*v.i.* To devolve; to take effect, as a title or right (the estate *vests in* the heir).—**Vested**, ves'ted, *p.* and *a.* Clothed; habited; *law*, not in a state of contingency or suspension; fixed (*vested* rights or interests in property).—**Vesting**, ves'ting, *n.* Cloth for vests.

Vesta, ves'ta, *n.* [L.] One of the great divinities of the ancient Romans, the virgin goddess of the hearth, in honour of whom a sacred fire was kept constantly burning under the charge of six stainless virgins; *astron.* one of the asteroids; a wax match which ignites by friction.—**Vestal**, ves'tal, *a.* [L. *vestalis*.] Pertaining to Vesta; pure; chaste.—*n.* Among the ancient Romans, a virgin consecrated to Vesta; hence, a virgin or woman of spotless chastity; a nun.

Vestibule, ves'ti-būl, *n.* [Fr. *vestibule*, from L. *vestibulum*, a vestibule, from same root as Skr. *vas*, to dwell; E. *was*.] A passage, hall, or ante-chamber next the outer door of a house; a lobby; a hall; *anat.* a cavity belonging to the labyrinth of the ear.—**Vestibular**, ves-tib'ū-lėr, *a.* Pertaining to or resembling a vestibule.

Vestige, ves'tij, *n.* [L. *vestigium*, a footprint (seen also in *investigate*).] A footprint‡; a trace, mark, or appearance of something which is no longer present or in existence; remains of something long passed away; in plants and animals, structures which have been reduced as a result of adaptation.

Vestment, vest'ment, *n.* [O.Fr. *vestement*, [L. *vestimentum*, from *vestio*, to clothe. VEST.] A covering or garment; some part of clothing or dress; especially, some part of outer clothing.—*Ecclesiastical* or *sacerdotal vestments*, articles of dress or ornament worn by clergymen in the celebration of divine service.

Vestry, ves'tri, *n.* [Fr. *vestiaire*, L. *vestiarium*, a wardrobe, from *vestis*, a garment. VEST.] A place or room appendant to a church, where the ecclesiastical vestments are kept, and where the clergy robe themselves; in *England*, a parochial assembly, so called from its meetings being held in the vestry; a select number of ratepayers elected to carry on the local government of a parish.—**Vestry-man**, *n.* One of a vestry-board.

Vesture, ves'tūr, *n.* [O.Fr. *vesture*. VEST.] A garment or garments generally; clothing; apparel; dress; that which invests or covers; envelope; integument.—**Vestured**, ves'-tūrd, *a.* Clothed; enveloped.

Vesuvian, vē-sū'vi-an, *a.* Pertaining to *Vesuvius*, a volcano near Naples.—*n.* The mineral idocrase; a kind of match for lighting cigars, &c.

Vetch, vech, *n.* [O.Fr. *veche, vesse*, Mod. Fr. *vesce*, It. *veccia*, from L. *vicia*, a vetch, cog. Gr. *bikos*, a vetch. *Fitch* is another form.] The popular name of plants allied to the bean, some of them, as the common tare, cultivated for fodder to cattle. — **Vetchling**, vech'ling, *n.* [Dim. of *vetch.*] A name for various vetch-like plants. — **Vetchy**, vech'i, *a.* Consisting of or abounding with vetches.

Veteran, vet'e-ran, *a.* [L. *veteranus*, from *vetus, veteris*, old; same root as Gr. (*v*)*etos*, a year, seen also in L. *vitulus*, a calf. VEAL.] Having been long exercised in anything; long practiced or experienced in war and the duties of a soldier. In the U. S. a soldier who survived the Civil War, the Spanish-American War, or the World War.

Veterinary, vet'e-ri-na-ri, *a.* [L.L. *veterinarius*, pertaining to beasts of burden, from L. *veterinæ*, beasts of burden.] Pertaining to the art or science of treating the diseases of domestic animals (a *veterinary* surgeon, a *veterinary* college or school).

Veto, vē'tō, *n.* [L. *veto*, I forbid.] The power which one branch of a legislature has to negative the resolutions of another branch; the power of governors and of the president of the U. S. to interdict a measure passed by the legislature.—*v.t.*—*vetoed, vetoing*. To put a veto on; to forbid; to interdict.

Vex, veks, *v.t.* [Fr. *vexer*, to vex, from L. *vexare*, to vex, a freq. or intens. of *veho, vectum*, to carry. VEHICLE.] To excite slight anger or displeasure in; to trouble by petty or light annoyances; to irritate, fret, plague, annoy; to make sorrowful; to grieve or distress. — **Vexation**, vek-sā'shon, *n.* The act of vexing or state of being vexed; irritation; annoyance; cause of irritation; affliction. — **Vexatious**, vek-sā'shus, *a.* Causing vexation; annoying; mortifying. — **Vexatiously**, vek-sā'shus-li, *adv.* In a vexatious manner.—**Vexatiousness**, vek-sā'shus-nes, *n.*—**Vexed**, vekst, *p.* and *a.* Annoyed; troubled; much disputed or contested; causing contention (a *vexed* question).—**Vexer**, vek'sėr, *n.* One who vexes.

Vexillum, vek'sil-um, *n.* [L., a dim. of *vellum*, a veil. VEIL.] The standard of the cavalry of ancient Rome; *bot.* the standard or fifth petal placed at the back of a papilionaceous corolla. — **Vexillar, Vexillary**, vek'sil-ėr, vek'si-la-ri, *a.* Pertaining to an ensign or standard; *bot.* pertaining to or having a vexillum.—**Vexillary**, *n.* A standard-bearer.

Via, vī'a, *prep.* [L., a way or road. WAY.] By way of (to send or travel *via* airplane).

Viable, vī'a-bl, *a.* [Fr., likely to live, from *vie*, L. *vita*, life. VITAL.] Capable of sustaining independent life, said of a new-born child.—**Viability**, vī-a-bil'i-ti, *n.* The state of being viable.

Viaduct, vī'a-dukt, *n.* [L. *via*, way, and *ductus*, a leading, a duct. WAY, DUKE.] A long bridge or series of arches conducting a railway or road over a valley or district of low level.

Vial, vī'al, *n.* [A modification of *phial.*] A small glass vessel or bottle; a phial.

Viand, vī'and, *n.* [Fr. *viande*, viands, food, from L.L. *vivanda*, provisions, from L. *vivo*, to live. VITAL.] Meat dressed; food; victuals: used chiefly in the plural.

Viaticum, vī-at'i-kum, *n.* [L. *viaticus*, pertaining to a way or road, from *via*, way. VOYAGE.] Provisions for a journey; *R.Cath. Ch.* the communion or eucharist given to a dying person.

Vibrate, vī'brāt, *v.i.*—*vibrated, vibrating.* [L. *vibro, vibratum*, to vibrate, brandish, shake.] To swing; to oscillate; to move one way and the other; to play to and fro; to produce a vibratory or resonant effect; to quiver.—*v.t.* To move or wave to and fro; to oscillate; to cause to quiver; to measure by vibrating or oscillating (a pendulum which *vibrates* seconds).—**Vibraculum**, vī-brak'ū-lum, *n.* pl. **Vibracula**, vī-brak'ū-la. A long filamentous appendage in polyzoa.—**Vibrant**, vī'brant, *a.* L. *vibrans, vibrantis*, ppr. of *vibro.*] Vibrating; tremulous; resonant.—**Vibratile**, vī'bra-til, *a.* Adapted to or used for vibratory motion; vibratory.—**Vibratility**, vī-bra-til'i-ti, *n.* The quality of being vibratile.—**Vibrating**, vī'brā-ting, *p.* and *a.* Vibratory.—**Vibration**, vī-brā'shon, *n.* [L. *vibratio, vibrationis.*] The act of vibrating; an oscillation or swing of a pendulum or similar body; one of a series of rapid tremulous motions produced in a body or substance; the tremulous motion of a sonorous body.—**Vibratory**, vī'bra-to-ri, *a.* Consisting in or belonging to vibration; causing to vibrate; vibrating.

Vibrio, vī'bri-ō, *n.* [From *vibrate.*] A genus of bacteria, having the form of curved filaments, with a wavy motion.

Vibrissæ, vī-bris'sē, *n.pl.* [L. *vibrissæ*, the hairs in the nostrils.] The stiff, long bristles on the head in many mammals; the hairs about the mouth of certain birds, as the fly-catchers.

Vicar, vik'ėr, *n.* [Fr. *vicaire*, from L. *vicarius*, forming a substitute, from *vicis*, change (whence prefix *vice* in *viceroy*, &c., *vicissitude*).] A substitute in office; a representative; the priest of a parish in England who receives only the smaller tithes or a salary.—**Vicarage**, vik'ėr-āj, *n.* The benefice of a vicar; the house or residence of a vicar. — **Vicar-apostolic**, *n.* *R. Cath. Ch.* a bishop who possesses no diocese, but who exercises jurisdiction over a certain district by direct authority of the pope.—**Vicar-general**, *n.* The official assistant of a bishop or archbishop. — **Vicarial, Vicariate**, vī-kā'ri-al, vī-kā'ri-āt, *a.* Pertaining to a vicar; vicarious; delegated.—**Vicarious**, vī-kā'ri-us, *a.* [L. *vicarius.*] Belonging to a deputy or substitute; delegated; filling the place of another; performed or suffered for, or instead of, another.—**Vicariously**, vī-kā'ri-us-li, *adv.* In the place of another; by substitution.—**Vicarship**, vik'ėr-ship, *n.* The office of a vicar.

Vice, vīs, *n.* [Fr. *vice*, from L. *vitium*, vice, blemish, fault, error, crime, from root *vi*, to twist (as in *withe, wine*, and in *vice*, the instrument. See below).] A defect, fault, or blemish; a fault or bad trick in a horse; any immoral or evil habit or practice; a moral failing; a particular form of wickedness or depravity; the indulgence of impure or degrading appetites or passions; depravity or corruption of manners (an age of *vice*); the character in the old Morality Plays, dressed in the habit of a fool, furnished with a dagger of lath, whose chief employment was to belabour the devil.—**Vicious**, vish'us, *a.* [Fr. *vicieux*, L. *vitiosus*, from *vitium*, vice.] Characterized by vice; faulty; defective; imperfect; addicted to vice; depraved; wicked; contrary to morality; evil; bad (*vicious* examples); not genuine or pure; faulty; incorrect (a *vicious* style in language); addicted to bad tricks (a *vicious* horse). — **Viciously**, vish'us-li, *adv.* In a vicious manner.—**Viciousness**, vish'us-nes, *n.* The quality or state of being vicious.

Vice, vīs, *n.* [Fr. *vis*, a screw, from L. *vitis*, a vine (from twining of vine tendrils); root *vi*, to twist. See above.] An instrument with a pair of iron jaws brought together by means of a screw, so that they can take a very fast hold of anything placed between them. Spelled *Vise* in America.

Vice, vī'sē, *prep.* [L. *vice*, in the room of, ablative of *vicis*, change, turn, &c., the stem being seen also in *vicar, vicissitude.*] In place of; in room of (A.B. appointed to be captain *vice* C.D. promoted).—**Vice versa**, *adv.* [L.] Contrariwise; the reverse; the terms or the case being reversed.

Vice, vīs. [Fr. *vice-*, from L. *vice.* See above.] A prefix denoting position second in rank: sometimes used by itself as a noun, the context making the intended meaning clear.—**Vice-admiral**, *n.* An officer next in rank and command to the admiral.—**Vice-admiralty**, *n.* The office of a vice-admiral.—**Vice-chancellor**, *n.* An officer next to a chancellor; a judge in the chancery division of the High Court of Justice in England; an officer of a university who discharges certain duties of the chancellor.—**Vice-consul**, *n.* One who acts in the place of a consul; a consul of subordinate rank.—**Vicegerency**, vīs-jē'ren-si, *n.* The office of a vicegerent.—**Vicegerent**, vīs-jē'rent, *n.* [Fr. *vicegerent*—*vice*, and L. *gerens, gerentis*, ppr. of *gero*, to act. GESTURE.] An officer who is deputed to exercise the powers of another; a substitute; one having a delegated power. — **Vice-presidency**, *n.* The office of vice-president. — **Vice-president**, *n.* An office-bearer next in rank below a president.—**Vice-regal**, *a.* Pertaining to a viceroy.—**Viceroy**, vīs'roi, *n.* [Fr. *viceroi*—*vice*, in the place of, and *roi*, L. *rex*, a king. REGENT.] One who rules in the name of the king (or queen) with regal authority.—**Viceroyalty, Viceroyship**, vīs-roi'al-ti, vīs'roi-ship, *n.* The dignity or jurisdiction of a viceroy.

Vicenary, vis'e-na-ri, *a.* [L. *vicenarius*, from *viceni*, twenty.] Belonging to or consisting of twenty.

Vicennial, vi-sen'ni-al, *a.* [L. *viceni*, twenty, and *annus*, a year.] Lasting or continuing twenty years.

Vice-regal, Viceroy, &c. Under VICE (prefix).

Vicinage, vis'in-āj, *n.* [O.Fr. *veisinage* (Fr. *voisinage*), neighbourhood, from L. *vicinus*, neighbouring, from *vicus*, a village, akin to Gr. (*v*)*oikos*, Skr. *veça*, a house.] Neighbourhood; the place or places adjoining or near; the vicinity.—**Vicinity**, vi-sin'i-ti, *n.* [L. *vicinitas*, from *vicinus*, neighbouring.] The quality of being near; propinquity; proximity; nearness in place; neighbourhood; the adjoining district, space, or country.

Vicious, &c. Under VICE.

Vicissitude, vi-sis'i-tūd, *n.* [L. *vicissitudo*, from *vicis*, a change. VICAR.] A passing from one state or condition to another; change, especially in regard to the affairs of life or the world; mutation.—**Vicissitudinary**, vi-sis'i-tū"di-na-ri, *a.* Subject to vicissitudes. — **Vicissitudinous**, vi-sis'i-tū"di-nus, *a.* Full of vicissitude; characterized by changes.

Vickers gun, vik'ėrs, *n.* The chief machine gun used in the British army, an improved form of the Maxim gun.

Victim, vik'tim, *n.* [Fr. *victime*, from L. *victima*, a victim, lit. a well-grown beast; same root as *vigour, wax* (to grow).] A living being sacrificed to some deity, or in the performance of a religious rite; a person or thing destroyed; a person sacrificed in the pursuit of an object; a person who suffers severe injury from another; one who is cheated or duped; a gull.—**Victimize**, vik'tim-īz, *v.t.*—*victimized, victimizing*. To make a victim of; to make the victim of a swindling transaction.

Victor, vik'tėr, *n.* [L. from *vinco, victum* to conquer (seen also in *convince, evince, invincible, vanquish*).] One who wins or gains the advantage in a contest; especially, one who conquers in war.—*a.* A Victorious.—**Victoress**, vik'tėr-es, *n.* A victress.—**Victoria**, vik-tō'ri-a, *n.* [L. *victoria*, victory, hence the name of the British queen.] A kind of four-wheeled carriage, with a calash top, seated for two persons, and with an elevated driver's seat in front.—*Victoria cross*, a British naval and military decoration granted for bravery, and securing to the recipient a pension of £10 a year.—*Victorian Order*, order of knighthood founded in 1896 by Queen Victoria, conferred usually for some personal service rendered to the sovereign. — **Victorine**, vik'to-rēn, *n.* A small fur tippet worn by ladies; a variety of peach.—**Victorious**, vik-tō'ri-us, *a.* [Fr. *victorieux*, from L. *victoriosus.*] Having conquered in battle or contest; being victor; conquering; associated with victory; indicating victory.—**Victoriously**, vik-tō'ri-us-li, *adv.* In a victorious manner; with conquest; triumphantly.—**Victory**, vik'to-ri, *n.* [L. *victoria.*] The defeat of an enemy in battle, or of an antagonist in a contest; the superiority gained in any contest (as over passions, temptations, &c.).—**Victress**, vik'tres. *n.* A female that conquers.

Victual, vit'l. *n.* [O.Fr. *vitaille*. Mod.Fr. *victuaille*. from L.L. *victualia*, provisions, *victualis*, pertaining to food, from L. *victus*, food, from *vivo*, *victum*, to live. VITAL.] Provision of food: provisions: now generally in plural, and signifying food for human beings, prepared for eating.—*v.t. victualed, victualing.* To supply or store with victuals; to provide with stores of food.—**Victualer**, vit'l-ėr. *n.* One who furnishes victuals; a tavern-keeper; one who keeps a house for selling intoxicating liquors by retail.—**Victualing-ship**, *n.* A ship which conveys provisions to the navy.—**Victualing-yard**, *n.* A place where provisions are deposited for supplying war-vessels and transports.

Vicugna, Vicuna, vi-kön'ya, *n.* [Sp. *vicuña*, from native name.] A South American animal of the camel family, closely allied to the llama, yielding short, soft, silken fur used for making delicate fabrics.

Vide, vī'dē. [L., imper. of *video*, to see.] See: a word indicating reference to something stated elsewhere.

Videlicet, vī-del'i-set, *adv.* [L., contr. for *videre licet*, it is permitted to see, one may see.] To wit; that is; namely: most frequently met with in its contracted form, *Viz.*

Vidette, vi-det', *n.* VEDETTE.

Vidimus, vī'di-mus, *n.* [L., we have seen.] An examination or inspection (a *vidimus* of accounts); an abstract or syllabus of the contents of a document, book, and the like.

Vie, vī, *v.i.* [Contr. from old *envie*, *envye* (accent on last), from Fr. *envier*, to invite, to vie in games, from L. *invitare*. INVITE.] In old games of cards, to wager on one's hand against an opponent; hence, to strive for superiority; to contend: followed by *with* and said of persons or things.

Vielle, vē-el', *n.* [Fr. *vielle*, akin to *viol*.] A hurdy-gurdy.

Viennese, vē-en-ēz'. *n. sing.* and *pl.* A native of *Vienna*: natives of Vienna.

View, vū, *n.* [O.Fr. *veue* (Fr. *vue*), from *veu*, *veu*, L.L. participle *vidutus*, from L. *video*, *videre*, to see. VISION.] The act of looking, seeing, or beholding; survey; look; sight; a mental survey; consideration; range of vision; power of seeing or perception, either physical or mental; that which is viewed, seen, or beheld; a sight or spectacle presented; scene; prospect; a scene portrayed; a representation of a landscape or the like; manner or mode of looking at things; judgment; opinion; way of thinking; something looked towards or forming the subject of consideration; intention; purpose (to act with a *view* to happiness).—*Field of view*, the whole region or space within the range of vision.—*Point of view*, the direction from which a thing is seen; hence, *fig.* the particular mode or manner in which a subject is considered; standpoint.—*On view*, open or submitted to public inspection; exhibited to the public. —*v.t.* To see; to look on; to examine with the eye; to inspect; to survey; to survey intellectually; to consider.—*v.i.* To look: to take a view.—*In view of*, considering the consequences of.—*With a view to*, for the purpose of.—**Viewless**, vū'les, *a.* Not capable of being viewed or seen; invisible. —**Viewfinder**, *n.* In photography, a camera attachment that indicates, on a small mirror, the extent of view that is to be projected on the photographic plate or film.

Vigesimal, vī-jes'i-mal, *a.* [L. *vigesimus*, twentieth, from *viginti*, twenty.] Twentieth.

Vigil, vij'il, *n.* [Fr. *vigile*, vigil, from L. *vigilia*, a watch, from *vigil*, watchful, from *vigeo*, to be vigorous, from root seen in E. *wake*. VIGOUR, WAKE.] The act of keeping awake; forbearance from sleep; a period of sleeplessness; a watch or watching; a devotional watching; devotions performed during the customary hours of sleep; *eccles.* the eve or evening or whole day preceding a festival, as Christmas, Easter, or some principal saint's day.—**Vigilance**, vij'i-lans, *n.* The state or quality of being vigilant; watchfulness; circumspection; *her.* a crane *in its vigilance* is depicted standing on one leg and clasping a stone in the talons of the other foot.—**Vigilant**, vij'i-lant, *a.* [L. *vigilans*, *vigilantis*, ppr. of *vigilo*, to watch.] Watchful; ever awake and on the alert; circumspect.—**Vigilantly**, vij'i-lant-li, *adv.* Watchfully; circumspectly.

Vigneron, vēn-ye-roṅ, *n.* [Fr. *vigne*, vine.] A vine-grower; a wine-grower.

Vignette, vin-yet' or vi-net', *n.* [Fr., dim. of *vigne*, L. *vinea*, a vine.] An ornament representing vine-leaves, tendrils, and grapes, such as those with which capital letters in ancient manuscripts were often surrounded; hence, flowers, head and tail pieces, &c., in printed books; any woodcut or engraving not inclosed within a definite border; a small photographic portrait.

Vigor, vig'or, *n.* [L. *vigor*, vigor, from *vigeo*, to be strong: from root also seen in *vigil*, *vegetable*, *victim*.] Active strength or force of body in animals; physical strength; strength of mind; intellectual force; energy; strength in animal or vegetable nature or action.—**Vigorous**, vig'or-us, *a.* Possessing vigor or physical strength; strong; lusty; exhibiting or resulting from vigor, energy, or strength of either body or mind; powerful; energetic.—**Vigorously**, vig'or-us-li, *adv.* In a vigorous manner; forcibly; with active exertions.—**Vigorousness**, vig'or-us-nes, *n.* Strength; force; energy.

Viking, vik'ing, *n.* [Icel. *víkingr*, lit. one who frequents bays and fiords—*vík*, a bay, and term. *-ing*, one who belongs to or is descended from (*r* being the masc. art.).] A rover or sea-robber belonging to the predatory bands of Northmen who infested the European seas during the eighth, ninth, and tenth centuries.

Vilayet, vil-ā'yet, *n.* [Turk.] Any province of the Turkish Empire.

Vile, vīl, *a.* [Fr. *vil*, *vile*, from L. *vilis*, worthless, vile.] Worthless; despicable; morally base; depraved; bad; wicked; villainous.—**Vilely**, vīl'li, *adv.* Basely; shamefully; odiously; worthlessly.—**Vileness**, vīl'nes, *n.* The state or quality of being vile; moral or intellectual baseness; degradation; sinfulness; extreme badness.—**Vilify**, vil'i-fī, *v.t.*—*vilified*, *vilifying*. [L. *vilifico* —*vilis*, vile, and *facio*, to make.] To attempt to degrade by slander; to defame; to traduce.—**Vilifier**, vil'i-fī-ėr, *n.* One who defames or traduces.—**Vilification**, vil'i-fi-kā"shon, *n.* The act of vilifying or defaming.

Vilipend, vil'i-pend, *v.t.* [L. *vilipendo*, to hold in slight esteem—*vilis*, worthless, vile, and *pendo*, to weigh, to value. VILE, PENDANT.] To express a disparaging or mean opinion of; to slander.

Villa, vil'a, *n.* [L. *villa*, a country house, farm, villa, a contr. of *vicula*, from *vicus*, a village. VICINAGE, VILLAIN.] A country residence, usually of some size and pretension; a rural or suburban mansion. —**Village**, vil'āj, *n.* [Fr. *village*, from L. *villa*.] An assemblage of houses smaller than a town or city and larger than a hamlet.—*a.* Pertaining to a village; hence, rustic.—**Villager**, vil'a-jėr, *n.* An inhabitant of a village.

Villain, vil'in, *n.* [O.Fr. *villain*, *villein*, *vilein* (Fr. *vilain*), from L.L. *villanus*, a farm-servant, from *villa*, a country house. VILLA.] A feudal serf; a man of the lowest grade in feudal times; hence, a boor, peasant, or clown; latterly, a man extremely depraved, and capable or guilty of great crimes; a vile, wicked person.—**Villainous**, vil'in-us, *a.* Pertaining to a villain; very wicked or depraved; vile; proceeding from depravity; sorry; mean.—**Villainously**, vil'in-us-li, *adv.* In a villainous manner.—**Villainy**, vil'in-i, *n.* The quality of being villainous; extreme depravity; great wickedness; a villainous act; a crime; an action of deep depravity.

Villanelle, vē'la-nel, *n.* [Fr.] A French two-rhyme measure of nineteen lines.

Villein, vil'en, *n.* [O.Fr. *villein*. VILLAIN.] A feudal tenant of the lowest class.—**Villenage, Villeinage**, vil'en-āj, *n.* A feudal tenure of lands and tenements by base services, and at the will of a lord.

Villi, vil'lī, *n.pl.* [Pl. of L. *villus*, hair.] *Anat.* fine small fibres like the pile of velvet, as on the internal coat of the intestinal canal; *bot.* long, straight, and soft hairs covering fruit, flowers, &c.—**Villiform**, vil'i-form, *a.* Having the form or character of villi.—**Villosity**, vil-los'i-ti, *n.* The state of being villous.—**Villous, Villose**, vil'lus, vil'lōs, *a.* [L. *villosus*, from *villus*, hair.] Abounding with villi; having the surface covered with fine hairs or woolly substance.

Vim, vim, *n.* [L. acc. of *vis*, strength.] Vigour, energy. (*Colloq.*)

Vimen, vī'men, *n.* [L. *vimen*, *viminis*, from *vieo*, to weave.] *Bot.* a long and flexible shoot of a plant.—**Viminal**, vim'i-nal, *a.* Pertaining to twigs.

Vinaceous, vī-nā'shus, *a.* [L. *vinaceus*, from *vinum*, wine.] Belonging to wine or grapes; of the colour of wine.

Vinaigrette, vin-ā-gret', *n.* [Fr., from *vinaigre*, vinegar.] A small box of gold, silver, &c., with perforations, for holding aromatic vinegar (in a sponge) or smelling-salts: used like a smelling-bottle.

Vincible, vin'si-bl, *a.* [From L. *vinco*, to conquer. VICTOR.] Capable of being conquered or subdued.

Vinculum, ving'kū-lum, *n.* [L., from *vincio*, to bind.] A bond of union; a bond or tie; *alg.* a line over a quantity of several terms in order to connect them together as one quantity.

Vindemial, vin-dē'mi-al, *a.* [L. *vindemialis*, from *vindemia*, vintage, from *vinum*, wine, and *demo*, to take away.] Belonging to a vintage or grape harvest.—**Vindemiation**, vin-dē'mi-ā"shon, *n.* The operation of gathering grapes.

Vindicate, vin'di-kāt, *v.t.*—*vindicated*, *vindicating*. [L. *vindico*, *vindicatum*, to lay claim to, to avenge or revenge, from *vindex*, *vindicis*, one who lays claim, perhaps from root meaning desire, love (in *Venus*), and *dico*, to declare. Of same origin are *vengeance*, *avenge*, *revenge*.] To assert a right or claim to†; to prove (a claim) to be just or valid; to maintain the cause or rights of; to deliver from wrong, oppression, or the like; to support or maintain against denial, censure, or objections; to defend (to *vindicate* a theory); to justify.—**Vindicable**, vin'di-ka-bl, *a.* That may be vindicated.—**Vindication**, vin-di-kā'shon, *n.* [L. *vindicatio*, *vindicationis*.] The act of vindicating; justification against censure, objections, or accusations; the proving of anything to be just; defence from wrong or oppression, by force or otherwise.—**Vindicator**, vin'di-kā-tėr, *n.* One who vindicates.—**Vindicatory**, vin'di-ka-to-ri, *a.* Tending to vindicate; justificatory.—**Vindictive**, vin-dik'tiv, *a.* [L. *vindicta*, revenge.] Revengeful; given to revenge.—**Vindictively**, vin-dik'tiv-li, *adv.* By way of revenge; revengefully.—**Vindictiveness**, vin-dik'tiv-nes, *n.* Revengeful spirit; revengefulness.

Vine, vīn, *n.* [O.Fr. *vine* (Fr. *vigne*), a vine; from L. *vinea*, a vine, from *vineus*, adj. from *vinum*, wine. WINE.] A well-known climbing plant with a woody stem, producing the grapes of commerce; the trailing or climbing stem of a plant.—**Vine-clad**, *a.* Clad or covered with vines.—**Vine-disease**, *n.* A disease affecting the vine. OIDIUM, PHYLLOXERA.—**Vine-dresser**, *n.* One who trims or prunes vines.—**Vine-fretter**, *n.* A small insect that injures vines.—**Vinery**, vī'nėr-i, *n.* A kind of greenhouse where vines are cultivated by artificial heat.—**Vineyard**, vin'yärd, *n.* A plantation of vines producing grapes.—**Vinosity**, vī-nos'i-ti, *n.* State or quality of being vinous.—**Vinous, Vinose**, vī'nus, vī'nōs, *a.* [L. *vinosus*, from *vinum*, wine.] Having the qualities of wine. —*Vinous fermentation*, the fermentation that produces wine from grape juice.

Vinegar, vin′e-gėr, *n.* [Fr. *vinaigre*, from *vin*, L. *vinum*, wine, and *aigre*, L. *acer*, sharp, sour. WINE, EAGER.] Dilute and impure acetic acid, usually obtained by the souring or acetification of fermented fruit juices, or an infusion of malt; anything really or metaphorically sour; sourness of temper.—*Aromatic vinegar*, a vinegar holding camphor and essential oils in solution. —*Wood vinegar.* PYROLIGNEOUS ACID.—**Vinegar Bible**, *n.* The Oxford 1717 Clarendon Press edition, bearing the misprint of *vinegar* for *vineyard* in the headline of *Luke*, xx. — **Vinegar-cruet**, *n.* A small glass bottle for holding vinegar.—**Vinegarette**, vin′e-gėr-et, *n.* A vinaigrette. — **Vinegar-plant**, *n.* A fungus found on decaying substances, and in fluids in a state of acetification.

Vinery, Vineyard. Under VINE.

Vingt-un, vańt-uń, *n.* [Fr., twenty-one.] A game at cards in which the object is to get points as near as possible in number to twenty-one without exceeding it.

Vin-ordinaire, vań-or-dē-nār, *n.* [Fr., ordinary wine.] A cheap claret much drunk in France.

Vinous. Under VINE.

Vintage, vin′tāj, *n.* [Partly from *vintner*, partly from Fr. *vendange*, vintage, from L. *vindemia*, the vintage — *vinum*, wine, and *demo*, to take away. VINE.] The gathering of a crop of grapes; the crop produced; the wine from the crop of grapes in one season.—**Vintager**, vin′ta-jėr, *n.* One engaged in the vintage.

Vintner, vint′nėr, *n.* [O.E. *viniter*, O.Fr. *vinetier*, from L.L. *vinitarius*, from L. *vinum*, wine. VINTAGE.] One who deals in wine; a wine-seller; a licensed victualler; a taverner. — **Vintnery**, vint′nėr-i, *n.* The trade or occupation of a vintner. — **Vintry**, vin′tri, *n.* A place where wine is stored or sold; the ward in London occupied by the wine merchants of Bordeaux, on the banks of the Thames.

Viol, vī′ol, *n.* [Fr. *viole*, It. *viola*, Pr. *viola*, *viula*, L.L. *vidula*, a viol, from L. *vitulari*, to celebrate a festival (probably by killing a calf—*vitulus*, a calf).] An ancient stringed musical instrument of much the same form as the violin.—**Viola**, vī′o-la, *n.* [It.] A large kind of violin, to which the part between the second violin and the bass is generally assigned.—**Violist**, vī′ol-ist, *n.* A player on the viol or viola.

Viola, vī′o-la, *n.* [L.] The violet, an extensive genus of plants. — **Violaceous**, vī-ō-lā′shus, *a.* [L. *violaceus.*] Pertaining to the violet family; resembling the violet in colour. — **Violascent**, vī-ō-las′sent, *a.* Approaching a violet in colour.

Violable. Under VIOLATE.

Violate, vī′ō-lāt, *v.t.*—*violated*, *violating.* [L. *violo*, *violatum*, to violate; akin to *vis*, force.] To treat roughly and injuriously; to do injury to; to outrage; to break in upon; to disturb; to desecrate; to treat with irreverence; to profane or profanely meddle with; to infringe; to sin against; to transgress; to ravish; to commit rape on.—**Violable**, vī′ō-la-bl, *a.* Capable of being violated.—**Violation**, vī-ō-lā′shon, *n.* The act of violating; desecration; profanation; infringement; transgression. — **Violator**, vī′ō-lā-tėr, *n.* One who violates; one who infringes or transgresses; one who profanes or desecrates.—**Violence**, vī′ō-lens, *n.* [L. *violentia*, from *violentus*, violent.] The quality of being violent; vehemence; intensity of action or motion; highly excited feeling; impetuosity; injury done to anything which is entitled to respect or reverence; profanation; violation; unjust force; outrage; attack; assault.—**Violent**, vī′ō-lent, *a.* [L. *violentus*, violent; akin *violate.*] Characterized by the exertion of force accompanied by rapidity; impetuous; furious; effected by violence; not coming by natural means (a *violent* death); acting or produced by unlawful, unjust, or improper force; unreasonably vehement; passionate; severe; extreme; sharp or acute (*violent* pains).—**Violently**, vī′ō-lent-li, *adv.* In a violent manner; by violence; forcibly; vehemently.

Violet, vī′ō-let, *n.* [Fr. *violet*, *violette*, from *viole*, L. *viola*, a violet; allied to Gr. (*v*)*ion*, a violet.] The common name of a genus of plants that includes the pansy and other well-known species.—*Violet powder*, starch reduced to a very fine powder, and perfumed, used for nursery and other purposes.

Violin, vī′ō-lin, *n.* [It. *violino*, a dim. of *viola.* VIOL.] A well-known musical instrument of wood, having four catgut strings stretched by means of a bridge over a hollow body, and played with a bow; a fiddle.—**Violinist**, vī′ō-lin-ist, *n.* A person skilled in playing on a violin.

Violoncello, vē′ō-lon-chel″ō, vi′ō-lon-sel″ō, *n.* [It., a dim. of *violone*, which is an augmentative of *viola*, a viol. VIOL.] A powerful and expressive bow instrument of the violin kind, held by the performer between the knees, and filling a place between the violin and double-bass.—**Violoncellist**, vē′ō-lon-chel″ist, vi′ō-lon-sel″-st, *n.* A performer on the violoncello.

Viper, vī′pėr, *n.* [Fr. *vipère*, from L. *vipera*, from *vivus*, alive, and *pario*, to bring forth, as bringing forth its young alive.] A name of certain poisonous serpents, one of them the common viper or adder found in Britain; a mischievous or malignant person.—**Viperine**, vī′pėr-īn, *a.* [L. *viperinus.*] Pertaining to a viper or to vipers.—**Viperish**, vī′pėr-ish, *a.* Inclining to the character of a viper.—**Viperous**, vī′pėr-us, *a.* Having the qualities of a viper; malignant; venomous.

Virago, vi-rā′gō, *n.* [L., a heroic maiden, a heroine, a female warrior, from *vir*, a man. VIRILE.] A manlike woman; a bold, impudent, turbulent woman; a termagant.

Virelai, vir′e-lā, *n.* [Fr. *virelai*, from *virer*, to turn, to *veer*, and *lai*, a lay.] A short poem with a refrain, based throughout on two rhymes.

Virescent, vī-res′sent, *a.* [L. *virescens*, *virescentis*, ppr. of *viresco*, to grow green, incept. verb from *vireo*, to be green.] Slightly green; beginning to be green.

Virgate, vėr′gāt, *a.* [From L. *virga*, a rod.] Having the shape of a rod or wand.—*n.* [L. *virga*, a rod, in L.L. a measure of land, like *rod*, *pole*, or *perch.*] A yard-land.

Virgilian, vėr-jil′i-an, *a.* Pertaining to *Virgil*, the Roman poet; resembling the style of Virgil.

Virgin, vėr′jin, *n.* [O.Fr. *virgine*, L. *virgo*, *virginis*, a virgin, from same root as *virga*, a rod or twig, Gr. *orgaō*, to swell.] A woman who has had no carnal knowledge of man; a maiden of inviolate chastity; a man who has preserved his chastity; the sign or the constellation Virgo.—*a.* Pertaining to a virgin; maidenly; modest; chaste; untouched; fresh; unsullied.—**Virginal**, vėr′jin-al, *n.* [Fr. *virginal*, from being commonly played by young ladies or virgins.] An obsolete keyed musical instrument resembling the spinet. — **Virginity**, vėr-jin′i-ti, *n.* [L. *virginitas.*] The state of being a virgin; perfect chastity.—**Virgin's-bower**, *n.* A plant of the Clematis genus.—**Virgo**, vėr′gō, *n.* One of the twelve signs of the zodiac, which the sun enters about the 22nd of August.

Viridity, vi-rid′i-ti, *n.* [L. *viriditas*, from *viridis*, green. VERDANT.] Greenness; verdure.

Virile, vir′īl or vir′il, *a.* [Fr. *viril*, from L. *virilis*, from *vir*, a man; cog. A.Sax. *wer*, Icel. *verr*, a man; Gr. *hērōs*, a hero; Skr. *vira*, a hero. From L. *vir* comes also *virtus*, E. *virtue.*] Pertaining to a man as opposed to a woman; masculine; not puerile or feminine.—**Virility**, vi-ril′i-ti, *n.* [Fr. *virilité*, L. *virilitas.*] Manhood; the power of procreation; masculine conduct or action.

Virose, vī′rōs, *a.* [L. *virosus*, from *virus*, poison.] Poisonous; *bot.* emitting a fetid odour.

Virtu, vėr-tö′, *n.* [It. *virtù.*] Same as *Vertu.*

Virtue, vėr′tū, *n.* [Fr. *vertu*, virtue, goodness, power, efficacy, from L. *virtus*, *virtutis*, properly manliness, bravery, hence worth, excellence, virtue, from *vir*, a man. VIRILE.] Moral goodness; uprightness; morality: the opposite of *vice*; a particular moral excellence (the *virtue* of temperance); specifically, female purity; chastity; any good quality, merit, or accomplishment; an inherent power or property (the medicinal *virtues* of plants); efficacy; active, efficacious power.—*By virtue of*, *in virtue of*, by or through the efficacy or authority of. — *Cardinal virtues.* CARDINAL.—*Theological virtues*, the three virtues, Faith, Hope, and Charity.—**Virtual**, vėr′tū-al, *a.* [Fr. *virtuel.*] Being in essence or effect, not in fact; not actual but equivalent, so far as result is concerned (a *virtual* denial of a statement).—**Virtually**, vėr′tū-al-li, *adv.* In a virtual manner; in efficacy or effect if not in actuality.—**Virtueless**, vėr′tū-les, *a.* Destitute of virtue.—**Virtuous**, vėr′tū-us, *a.* Imbued with or proceeding from virtue; morally good; practising the moral duties and abstaining from vice; often specifically, chaste; pure: applied to women.—**Virtuously**, vėr′tū-us-li, *adv.* In a virtuous manner.

Virtuoso, vėr-tū-ō′sō, *n.* pl. **Virtuosi**, vėr-tū-ō′sī. [It. VERTU.] One skilled in or having a taste for artistic excellence; one skilled in antiquities, curiosities, and the like.

Virulent, vir′ū-lent, *a.* [Fr. *virulent*, from L. *virulentus*, poisonous, from *virus*, poison. VIRUS.] Extremely poisonous or venomous; very actively injurious to life; very noxious or baneful; very bitter in enmity; malignant.—**Virulently**, vir′ū-lent-li, *adv.* With malignant activity; with bitter spite.—**Virulence**, vir′ū-lens, *n.* [Fr. *virulence*, L. *virulentia.*] The quality of being virulent; intensity of destructive quality; acrimony of temper; rancour or malignity.

Virus, vī′rus, *n.* [L., poison; allied to Gr. *ios* (for *vios*, *visos*), Skr. *visha*, Ir. *fi*, poison.] Contagious poisonous matter, as of smallpox, cholera, hydrophobia, &c.; *fig.* extreme acrimony or bitterness; malignity.

Vis, vis, *n.* [L., pl. *vires.*] Force; power; energy.—*Vis inertiæ*, lit. force of inertia. INERTIA. — *Vis mortua* (mor′tū-a), dead force; force doing no work, but merely producing pressure.—*Vis viva* (vī′va), living force, the force of a body moving against resistance, or doing work.

Visage, viz′āj, *n.* [Fr. *visage*, from L. *visus*, a look, from L. *video*, *visum*, to see. VISION.] The face, countenance, or look of a person or of other animal: chiefly applied to human beings.—**Visaged**, viz′ājd, *a.* Having a visage of such or such kind.

Visard, viz′ärd, *n.* A mask. VISOR.

Vis-à-vis, vē-zä-vē, *adv.* [Fr., lit. face to face, from O.Fr. *vis*, a visage, L. *visus*, a look. VISAGE.] In a position facing each other; standing or sitting face to face.—*n.* One who is face to face with another; one person who faces another in certain dances; a light town carriage for two persons, who are seated facing each other.

Viscera, vis′e-ra, *n.pl.* [L. *viscera*, pl. of *viscus*, *visceris*; akin to *viscid.*] The entrails; the bowels.—**Visceral**, vis′e-ral, *a.* Pertaining to the viscera.—*Visceral arches and clefts*, in vertebrates, thickenings and slits on the side of the throat in the neck. The latter place the cavity of the throat in communication with the exterior.—**Viscerate**, vis′e-rāt, *v.t.* To deprive of the entrails or viscera; to eviscerate.

Viscid, vis′sid, *a.* [L.L. *viscidus*, clammy, from L. *viscum*, the mistletoe, bird-lime.] Sticking or adhering, and having a ropy or glutinous consistency; semi-fluid and sticky. — **Viscidity**, vis-sid′i-ti, *n.* The state or quality of being viscid; glutinousness; stickiness.—**Viscosity**, vis-kos′i-ti, *n.* The quality of being viscous; stickiness; glutinousness; viscidity. — **Viscous**, vis′-

kus, *a.* [L. *viscosus.*] Glutinous; sticky; adhesive; tenacious.

Viscount, vī'kount, *n.* [Lit. a vice-count; O.E. *viconte*, O.Fr. *viceconte*, *viscomte*, Fr. *vicomte*. VICE, COUNT.] A degree or title of nobility next in rank to an earl, and above that of baron.—**Viscountess**, vī'kount-es, *n.* The wife of a viscount, or a lady having equal rank.—**Viscountship, Viscounty**, vī'kount-ship, vī'koun-ti, *n.* The quality or rank of a viscount.

Viscous. Under VISCID.

Viscus, vis'kus, *n.* [L. See VISCERA.] One of the viscera; one of the organs (as the heart, liver, &c.) contained in the larger cavities of the body.

Visé, vē-zā, *n.* [Fr. *visé*, pp. of *viser*, to put a visé to, from L. *visus*, seen, *video*, *visum*, to see. VISION.] An indorsation made upon a passport, denoting that it has been examined and found correct.

Vishnu, vish'nö, *n.* [Skr. *Vishnu*, from *vish*, to pervade.] The Hindu deity, called 'the Preserver', who, with Brahma and Siva, forms the *trimurti*, or trinity.

Visible, viz'i-bl, *a.* [L. *visibilis*, from *video*, *visum*, to see. VISION.] Perceivable by the eye; capable of being seen; in view; apparent.—*Visible church*, the whole body of professed believers in Christ on earth.—*Visible speech*, a system of alphabetical characters designed to represent every possible articulate utterance of the organs of speech, each organ and every mode of action having its appropriate and suggestive symbol.—**Visibility, Visibleness**, viz-i-bil'i-ti, viz'i-bl-nes, *n.* The state or quality of being visible; condition of the atmosphere with reference to the ease with which objects can be seen through it: chiefly used in aviation, and with such adjectives as good, low, poor, moderate. — **Visibly**, viz'i-bli, *adv.* Perceptibly to the eye; manifestly; obviously.

Visier, vi-zēr'. VIZIER.

Visigoth, viz'i-goth, *n.* One of the Western Goths, as distinguished from the *Ostrogoths*, or Eastern Goths. GOTH, OSTROGOTH.—**Visigothic**, viz-i-goth'ik, *a.* Pertaining to the Visigoths.

Vision, vizh'on, *n.* [Fr. *vision*, from L. *visio*, *visionis*, from *video*, *visum*, to see, from root seen also in Gr. (*v*)*idein*, to see, (*v*)*oida*, I know; Skr. *vid*, to know; E. *wit*, *wot*. The Latin verb is seen also in *visual*, *visible*, *visit*, *visage*, *vista*, *advise*, *evident*, *provide*, Fr. *vue*, E. *view*, &c.] The act or faculty of seeing; the power or faculty by which we perceive the forms and colours of objects; sight; that which is seen; an object of sight; something supposed to be seen otherwise than by the ordinary organs of sight; something seen in a dream, trance, or the like; an apparition; a phantom; a mere creation of fancy; fanciful view.—**Visional**, vizh'on-al, *a.* Pertaining to a vision.—**Visionariness**, vizh'on-a-ri-nes, *n.* The quality of being visionary.—**Visionary**, vizh'on-a-ri, *a.* [Fr. *visionnaire.*] Apt to behold visions of the imagination; given to indulging in day-dreams, fanciful theories, or the like; not real; having no solid foundation; imaginary.—*n.* One who sees visions or unreal sights; one who forms impracticable schemes.

Visit, viz'it, *v.t.* [Fr. *visiter*, from L. *visitare*, a freq. from *viso*, to go to see, from *video*, *visum*, to see. VISION.] To go or come to see (a person or thing); to make a call upon; to proceed to in order to view; to come or go to generally; to afflict; to overtake or come upon: said especially of diseases or calamities; to send a judgment upon; to inflict punishment for.—*v.i.* To practise going to see others; to make calls.—*n.* The act of visiting; a going to see a person, place, or thing; a short stay of friendship, ceremony, business, curiosity, &c.; a call.—**Visitant**, viz'i-tant, *n.* One who visits; a visitor.—**Visitation**, viz-i-tā'shon, *n.* [L. *visitatio.*] A visit; a formal or judicial visit by a superior, superintending officer, &c.; a special dispensation or judgment from heaven; communication of divine favor or goodness, more usually of divine indignation and retribution.—**Visitatorial**, viz'i-ta-tō"ri-al, *a.* Pertaining to a judicial visitor or visitation.—**Visitor, Visiter**, viz'i-tor, viz'i-tėr, *n.* One who visits; a caller; a guest.—**Visiting**, viz'it-ing, *a.* Pertaining to visits; authorized to visit and inspect.—*n.* The act or practice of paying visits or making calls; prompting; influence (*Shak.*)—**Visiting-card**, *n.* A small card bearing one's name, &c., to be left in making calls or paying visits.

Visor, Vizor, viz'ėr, *n.* [Fr. *visière*, a visor, from O.Fr. *vis*, the face or visage. VISAGE.] A mask used to conceal the face or disguise the wearer; the movable face-guard of a helmet; a shield worn above the eyes to protect them from glare.

Vista, vis'ta, *n.* [It., sight, view, from L. *video*, *visum*, to see. VISION.] A view or prospect through an avenue, as between rows of trees; the trees that form the avenue.

Visual, vizh'ū-al, *a.* [Fr. *visuel*, L.L. *visualis*, from L. *visus*, sight. VISION.] Pertaining to sight; used in sight; serving as the instrument of seeing.—*Visual angle*, the angle formed at the eye by the rays of light from the extremities of the object.—*Visual education*, a modern method of teaching by presenting objects or pictures to supplement that which is being taught.—*Visual purple*, a rose-colored substance, sensitive to light, found in the retina of the eye. Its decomposition by light is supposed to be an essential step in the process which leads to the sensation of vision.—**Visualize**, vizh'ū-al-īz, *v.t.*—*visualized*, *visualizing*. To form a mental picture of anything.

Vital, vī'tal, *a.* [Fr. *vital*, from L. *vitalis*, vital, pertaining to life, from *vita* (for *vivita*), life, from stem of *vivus*, living, *vivo*, *victum*, to live (whence also *vivid*, *vivacity*, *victual*, *viand*, &c.); from a root seen also in E. *quick*.] Pertaining to life, either animal or vegetable; contributing to life; necessary to life; being the seat of life; being that on which life depends (a *vital* part); hence, absolutely necessary; essential; indispensable.—*Vital functions*, those functions on which life immediately depends, as the circulation of the blood, respiration, digestion, &c.—**Vitality**, vī-tal'i-ti, *n.* The state of showing vital powers; the principle of life; animation; manifestation of life or of a capacity for lasting.—**Vitalization**, vī-tal-ī-zā"shon, *n.* The act of vitalizing. — **Vitalize**, vī'tal-īz, *v.t.*—*vitalized*, *vitalizing*. To give life to; to furnish with the vital principle.—**Vitally**, vī'tal-li, *adv.* In a vital manner; essentially (*vitally* important).—**Vitals**, vī'talz, *n.pl.* Internal parts or organs of animal bodies essential to life; the part of a complex whole essential to its life, existence, or to a sound state.

Vitamin, vī'ta-min, *n.* [L. *vita*, life, and *amine.*] One of several substances necessary for animal nutrition, and occurring in minute quantities in natural foods.

Vitellus, vī-tel'us, *n.* [L., the yoke of an egg.] The yoke of an egg; a membrane inclosing the embryo in some plants.—**Vitelline**, vī-tel'lin, *n.* A substance consisting of casein and albumen in the yolk of birds' eggs.

Vitiate, vish'i-āt, *v.t.*—*vitiated*, *vitiating*. [L. *vitio*, *vitiatum*, from *vitium*, a fault, vice. VICE.] To render faulty or imperfect; to injure the quality or substance of; to impair; to spoil; to render invalid or of no effect; to invalidate.—**Vitiation**, vish-i-ā'shon, *n.* The act of vitiating.

Viticulture, vit'i-kul-tūr, *n.* [L. *vitis*, a vine, and *cultura*, culture.] The culture or cultivation of the vine.

Vitreous, vit'rē-us, *a.* [L. *vitreus*, from *vitrum*, glass; same root as *video*, to see. VISION.] Pertaining to or obtained from glass; consisting of glass; resembling glass (the *vitreous* humour of the eye, a transparent gelatinous fluid occupying the posterior of the globe).—*Vitreous electricity*, that produced by rubbing glass, as distinguished from *resinous electricity*.—**Vitreousness**, vit'rē-us-nes, *n.* The quality of being vitreous. — **Vitrescence**, vi-tres'sens, *n.* The quality of being vitrescent.—**Vitrescent**, vi-tres'sent, *a.* Turning into glass; tending to become glass.—**Vitrescible**, vi-tres'si-bl, *a.* Capable of being vitrified.—**Vitric**, vit'rik, *a.* Of a glassy nature.—**Vitrifaction, Vitrification**, vit-ri-fak'shon, vit-rif'i-kā"shon, *n.* The process or operation of vitrifying.—**Vitrifacture**, vit'ri-fak-tūr, *n.* The manufacture of glass.—**Vitrifiable**, vit'ri-fī-a-bl, *a.* Capable of being vitrified.—**Vitrified**, vit'ri-fīd, *p.* and *a.* Converted into glass.—*Vitrified forts*, a class of prehistoric hill fortresses, the walls of which are wholly or partially vitrified or transformed into a kind of glass.—**Vitriform**, vit'ri-form, *a.* Having the form or resemblance of glass.—**Vitrify**, vit'ri-fī, *v.t.*—*vitrified*, *vitrifying*. [L. *vitrum*, and *facio*, to make.] To convert into glass by fusion or the action of heat.—*v.i.* To become glass; to be converted into glass.—**Vitrine**, vit'rin, *n.* A glass showcase for articles requiring protection.

Vitriol, vit'ri-ol, *n.* [Fr. *vitriol*, L.L. *vitriolum*, vitriol, from L. *vitrum*, glass. VITREOUS.] The common name of sulphuric acid and of many of its compounds, which, in certain states, have a glassy appearance.—*Blue vitriol* or *copper vitriol*, sulphate of copper. — *Green vitriol*, copperas. — *Lead vitriol*, sulphate of lead.—*Oil of vitriol*, concentrated sulphuric acid.—*Red vitriol*, a sulphate of cobalt; also, red sulphate of iron. — *White vitriol*, sulphate of zinc.—**Vitriolate, Vitriolize**, vit'ri-ō-lāt, vit'ri-ōl-īz, *v.t.* To convert into a vitriol.—**Vitriolation, Vitriolization**, vit'ri-ō-lā"shon, vit'ri-ol-i-zā"shon, *n.* The act of conversion into a vitriol.—**Vitriolic**, vit-ri-ol'ik, *a.* Pertaining to vitriol; having the qualities of vitriol.

Vitruvian, vi-trö'vi-an, *a.* [*Vitruvius*, Latin writer on architecture.] Of or relating to Vitruvius and his work.—*Vitruvian scroll*, a kind of decoration in a frieze.

Vitta, vit'a, *n.* pl. **Vittæ**, vit'ē. [L.] A headband, fillet, or garland; *bot.* a name given to the receptacles of oil in the fruits of umbelliferous plants, as anise, fennel, caraway, &c.—**Vittate**, vit'āt, *a.* Filleted; *bot.* striped lengthwise.

Vituline, vit'ū-līn, *a.* [L. *vitulinus*, from *vitulus*, a calf. VEAL.] Belonging to a calf or to veal.

Vituperate, vī-tū'pe-rāt, *v.t.*—*vituperated*, *vituperating*. [Fr. *vituperer*, from L. *vitupero*, *vituperatum*—*vitium*, a vice, a fault, and *paro*, to prepare. VICE, PARE.] To blame with abusive language; to abuse; to rate; to objurgate.—**Vituperable**, vī-tū'pe-ra-bl, *a.* Deserving vituperation; censurable. — **Vituperation**, vī-tū'pe-rā"shon, *n.* [L. *vituperatio.*] The act of vituperating; abuse; railing.—**Vituperative**, vī-tū'pe-rā-tiv, *a.* Containing or expressing abusive censure; abusive. — **Vituperatively**, vī-tū'pe-rā-tiv-li, *adv.* With vituperation; abusively. — **Vituperator**, vī-tū'pe-rāt-ėr, *n.* One who vituperates.

Vitus dance, vī'tus. [*St. Vitus.*] A spasmodic dancing mania, of a semi-religious nature, appearing at various times in mediæval Europe, called after St. Vitus, the supposed patron of nerve and hysterical affections. See CHOREA.

Viva, vē'vā, *interj.* [It. VIVE.] An Italian exclamation of applause or joy, corresponding to the French *vive*, long live.

Vivace, vē-vä'chā, *a.* or *adv.* [It.] *Mus.* vivacious; brisk; in a brisk, lively manner.

Vivacious, vī-vā'shus, *a.* [L. *vivax*, *vivacis*, from *vivus*, alive. VITAL.] Lively; active; sprightly in temper or conduct; proceeding from or characterized by sprightliness.—**Vivaciously**, vī-vā'shus-li, *adv.* With vivacity, life, or spirit.—**Vivaciousness**, vī-vā'shus-nes, *n.* Vivacity; liveliness.—**Vivacity**, vī-vas'i-ti, *n.* [L. *vivacitas.*] Liveliness of manner or character; sprightliness of temper or behaviour; animation; briskness; cheerfulness; spirit.

Vivandière, vē-väṅ-dē-ār, *n.* [Fr. VIAND.] A female attached to French and other continental regiments, who sells provisions and liquor.

Vivarium, vī-vā'ri-um, *n.* pl. **Vivaria**, vī-vā'ri-a. [L., from *vivus*, alive. VITAL.] A place artificially prepared for keeping animals alive, in as nearly as possible their natural state.

Viva voce, vī'va vō'sē, *adv.* [L., by the living voice.] By word of mouth; orally; sometimes used adjectively (a *viva voce* examination).

Vive, vēv, *interj.* [Fr., from *vivre*, L. *vivere*, to live. VITAL.] Long live; success to (*vive le roi*, long live the king).

Vivid, viv'id, *a.* [L. *vividus*, from *vivus*, alive. VITAL.] Exhibiting the appearance of life or freshness; bright; clear; lively; fresh (*vivid* colours); forming brilliant images or painting in lively colours; realistic.—**Vividly**, viv'id-li, *adv.* In a vivid or lively manner; with strength or intensity; in bright or glowing colours; with animated exhibition to the mind.—**Vividness, Vividity**, viv'id-nes, vi-vid'i-ti, *n.* The quality of being vivid; liveliness; brightness.

Vivify, viv'i-fī, *v.t.*—*vivified, vivifying.* [Fr. *vivifier*, L. *vivificare*—*vivus*, alive, and *facio*, to make.] To endue with life; to animate; to make to be living.—*v.i.* To impart life or animation.—**Vivific**,† **Vivifical**,† vi-vif'ik, vi-vif'i-kal, *a.* [L. *vivificus.*] Giving life; reviving; enlivening; vivifying.—**Vivification**,† viv'i-fi-kā"shon, *n.* The act of vivifying.

Viviparous, vi-vip'a-rus, *a.* [L. *vivus*, alive, and *pario*, to bear.] Producing young in a living state, as distinguished from *oviparous*, producing eggs.—**Viviparously**, vi-vip'a-rus-li, *adv.* In a viviparous manner.—**Viviparity, Viviparousness**, viv-i-par'i-ti, vi-vip'a-rus-nes, *n.* State or character of being viviparous.

Vivisection, viv-i-sek'shon, *n.* [From L. *vivus*, alive, and *sectio*, *sectionis*, a cutting.] The dissection of, or otherwise experimenting on, a living animal, for the purpose of ascertaining or demonstrating some fact in physiology or pathology.—**Vivisector**, viv'i-sek-tėr, *n.* One who practises vivisection.

Vixen, vik'sen, *n.* [A.Sax. *fixen, fyxen*, a she-fox, fem. of *fox* (with change of *f* to *v*); comp. G. *füchsinn*, a she-fox, *fuchs*, a fox.] A she-fox; a froward, turbulent, quarrelsome woman; a scold; a termagant.—**Vixenish**, vik'sen-ish, *a.* Pertaining to a vixen.—**Vixenly**, vik'sen-li, *a.* Having the qualities of a vixen.

Viz. A contraction of L. *videlicet*, meaning namely, to wit, and read as so.

Vizier, viz'i-ėr or vi-zēr', *n.* [Fr. *vizir*, from Ar. *wazir*, a vizier, lit. a bearer of burdens, a porter, from *wazara*, to bear a burden.] The title of high political officers in the Turkish Empire and other Mohammedan states; a minister of state.—*Grand vizier*, the president of the divan; the prime minister.—**Vizierate**, viz'i-ėr-āt or vi-zēr'-āt, *n.* The office, state, or authority of a vizier.—**Vizierial**, vi-zē'ri-al, *a.* Pertaining to a vizier.

Vizor, viz'or, *n.* VISOR.

Vlach, vlak, *a.* and *n.* [Bohemian.] Of or relating to Wallachia; a native of Wallachia.

Vlej, Vlei, vlī or flī, *n.* [D.] In South Africa a name for a swampy hollow or pool that dries up at certain seasons.

Vocable, vō'ka-bl, *n.* [L. *vocabulum*, from *voco*, to call. VOICE.] A word; a term; a word without regard to its meaning.—**Vocabulary**, vō-kab'ū-la-ri, *n.* [Fr. *vocabulaire*, from L. *vocabulum.*] A list or collection of words arranged in alphabetical order and briefly explained; a word-book; sum or stock of words employed; range of language (a limited *vocabulary*).

Vocal, vō'kal, *a.* [L. *vocalis*, from *vox*, voice. VOICE.] Pertaining to the voice or speech; uttered or modulated by the voice; endowed or as if endowed with a voice; *phonetics*, voiced or sonant: said of certain sounds; having a vowel character.—*Vocal chords*, two elastic membranous folds so attached to the cartilages of the larynx and to muscles that they may be stretched or relaxed, so as to modify the sounds produced by their vibration.—**Vocalist**, vō'kal-ist, *n.* A vocal musician; a singer.—**Vocality, Vocalness**, vō-kal'i-ti, vō'kal-nes, *n.* The quality of being vocal.—**Vocalization**, vō'kal-ī-zā"shon, *n.* Act of vocalizing; the state of being vocalized.—**Vocalize**, vō'kal-īz, *v.t.*—*vocalized, vocalizing.* To form into voice; to make vocal; to utter with voice and not merely breath; to make sonant.—**Vocally**, vō'kal-li, *adv.* In a vocal manner; with voice; verbally.

Vocation, vō-kā'shon, *n.* [Fr. *vocation*, from L. *vocatio*, from *voco*, *vocatum*, to call. VOICE.] A calling or designation to a particular state or profession; a summons; a call; employment; calling; occupation; trade.—**Vocative**, vok'a-tiv, *a.* [L. *vocativus*, from *voco*, to call.] Relating to calling or addressing by name: applied to the grammatical case in which a person or thing is addressed.—*n.* The vocative case.

Vociferate, vō-sif'ėr-āt, *v.i.*—*vociferated, vociferating.* [L. *vocifero*, *vociferatum*—*vox*, *vocis*, the voice, and *fero*, to bear. VOICE, FERTILE.] To cry out with vehemence; to exclaim.—*v.t.* To utter with a loud voice or clamorously; to shout.—**Vociferation**, vō-sif'ėr-ā"shon, *n.* The act of vociferating; a violent outcry; clamour; exclamation.—**Vociferous**, vō-sif'ėr-us, *a.* Making a loud outcry; clamorous; noisy.—**Vociferously**, vō-sif'ėr-us-li, *adv.* In a vociferous manner.—**Vociferousness**, vō-sif'ėr-us-nes, *n.*

Vodka, vod'ka, *n.* An intoxicating spirit distilled from rye, and much used in Russia.

Voe, vō, *n.* [Icel. *vör*, a voe.] An inlet, bay, or creek. (*Orkneys* and *Shetland.*)

Vogue, vōg, *n.* [Fr. *vogue*, fashion, lit. rowing of a ship, from It. *voga*, a rowing, from G. *wogen*, to wave, akin E. *wag*, *wave.*] The prevalent mode or fashion; popular repute or estimation: now almost exclusively used in the phrase *in vogue*, that is, in fashion, held in esteem for the time being.

Voice, vois, *n.* [O.E. *voys*, O.Fr. *vois*, Mod. Fr. *voix*, from L. *vox*, *vocis*, voice, a word, from stem of *vocare*, to call (seen also in *vocation, vocative, vocal, vowel, advocate, convoke, invoke*, &c.); allied to Skr. *vach*, to speak.] The sound uttered by the mouths of living creatures, whether men or animals; especially, human utterance in speaking, singing, or otherwise; the sound made when a person speaks or sings; the faculty of uttering audible sounds; the faculty of speaking; language; a sound produced by an inanimate object; sound emitted; the right of expressing an opinion; vote; suffrage (you have no *voice* in the matter); *phonetics*, sound uttered with resonance of the vocal chords, and not with breath merely; sonant utterance; *gram.* a form of verb inflection (active *voice*, middle *voice*, passive *voice*).—*v.t.*—*voiced, voicing.* To utter, declare, or proclaim.—**Voiced**, voist, *a.* Furnished with a voice; *phonetics*, sonant.—**Voiceful**, vois'ful, *a.* Having a voice; vocal.—**Voiceless**, vois'les, *a.* Having no voice, utterance, or vote.

Void, void, *a.* [O.Fr. *voide*, *vuide* (Fr. *vide*), empty, void, from L. *viduus*, widowed, bereaved; allied to E. *widow*. Hence also *avoid, devoid.*] Empty or not containing matter; having no holder or possessor; vacant; unoccupied; devoid; destitute (*void of* learning); not producing any effect; ineffectual; in vain; having no legal or binding force; null (a deed not duly signed and sealed is *void*).—*n.* An empty space; a vacuum.—*v.t.* [O.Fr. *voidier*, to empty.] To make or leave vacant; to quit or vacate; to emit, throw, or send out; to evacuate from the bowels.—**Voidable**, voi'da-bl, *a.* Capable of being voided.—**Voidance**, voi'dans, *n.* The act of voiding; ejection from a benefice; vacancy, as of a benefice.—**Voided**, *a.* *Her.* a charge is voided when the centre is cut out and only a framework left round the edge.—**Voider**, voi'dėr, *n.* One who voids.

Volant, vō'lant, *a.* [Fr. *volant*, flying, from *voler*, L. *volare*, to fly.] Flying; nimble; rapid; *her.* represented as flying.—**Volar**,† vō'lėr, *a.* Pertaining to flight; used in flying (the *volar* membranes of bats).—**Volplane**, vol'plān, *n.* and *v.* *Aviation;* to alight with a long glide downwards.

Volapuk, vō'la-pük, *n.* [An invented name based on the words *world* and *speak*: world speech.] An artificial language intended for universal use, its vocables being based on English and other words, changed so as to be easily uttered, and its grammar or syntax of the simplest and most regular kind.

Volar, vō'lėr, *a.* [L. *vola*, palm.] Relating to the palm or sole of foot.

Volatile, vol'a-til, *a.* [Fr. *volatil*, from L. *volatilis*, from *volo*, *volatum*, to fly.] Having the quality of passing off by spontaneous evaporation; diffusing more or less freely in the atmosphere; passing off insensibly in vapour; of a lively, brisk, or gay temperament; fickle; apt to change.—**Volatility, Volatileness**, vol-a-til'i-ti, vol'a-til-nes, *n.* The quality of being volatile; capability of evaporating or dissipating; flightiness; fickleness.—**Volatilizable**, vol'a-til-ī-za-bl, *a.* Capable of being volatilized.—**Volatilization**, vol'a-til-ī-zā"shon, *n.* The act or process of volatilizing.—**Volatilize**, vol'a-til-īz, *v.t.*—*volatilized, volatilizing.* [Fr. *volatiliser.*] To cause to exhale or evaporate; to cause to pass off in vapour or invisible effluvia.

Volcano, vol-kā'nō, *n.* pl. **Volcanoes**, vol-kā'nōz. [It. *volcano, vulcano*, Fr. *volcan*, from L. *Vulcanus*, the god of fire; cog. Skr. *ulkā*, fire.] A hill or mountain more or less perfectly cone-shaped, with a circular cup-like opening or basin (called a *crater*) at its summit, from which are sent out clouds of vapour, gases, showers of ashes, hot fragments of rocks, and streams of lava.—**Volcanic**, vol-kan'ik, *a.* Pertaining to volcanoes; changed or affected by the heat of a volcano.—*Volcanic foci*, subterranean centres of igneous action, from which minor exhibitions diverge.—*Volcanic glass*, obsidian.—*Volcanic rocks*, rocks which have been formed by volcanic agency.—**Volcanicity, Volcanism**, vol-ka-nis'i-ti, vol'kan-izm, *n.* State of being volcanic; volcanic power.—**Volcanist**, vol'kan-ist, *n.* One versed in volcanoes; a vulcanist.—**Volcanite**, vol'kan-īt, *n.* Same as *Augite*.—**Volcanization**, vol'kan-ī-zā"shon, *n.* The process of volcanizing.—**Volcanize**, vol'kan-īz, *v.t.*—*volcanized, volcanizing.* To subject to volcanic heat and modify by its action.

Vole, vōl, *n.* [Fr., from *voler*, to fly.] A deal at cards that draws all the tricks.

Vole, vōl, *n.* [Also called *vole-mouse*, perhaps for *wold-mouse.*] A name of several rodent animals, resembling, and in many cases popularly bearing the names of rats and mice, as the short-tailed field-mouse, the water-rat, &c.

Volition, vō-lish'on, *n.* [L. *volitio*, from *volo*, to will; same root as E. *will*. VOLUNTARY.] The act of willing; the exercise of the will; the power of willing; will.—**Volitional**, vō-lish'on-al, *a.* Pertaining to volition.—**Volitive**, vol'i-tiv, *a.* Having the power to will; originating in the will; *gram.* used in expressing a wish or permission (a *volitive* proposition).

Volksraad, volks'rät, *n.* [D.] The Legislative Assembly of the former South African Republic and Orange Free State.

Volley, vol'i, *n.* [Fr. *volée*, a flight, from *voler*, L. *volare*, to fly. VOLATILE.] A flight of missiles, as of shot, arrows, &c.; a simultaneous discharge of a number of missile weapons, as small-arms; in tennis, a return of the ball before it touches the ground.—*v.t.*—*volleyed, volleying.* To discharge with a volley, or as if with a volley.—*v.i.* To be discharged at once or with a volley; to sound like a volley of artillery.

Volplane, *n.* and *v.* See VOLANT.

Volt, volt, *n.* [Fr. *volte*, from L. *volvo*, *volutum*, to turn. VAULT.] A bound or spring; *fencing*, a sudden movement or leap to avoid a thrust.

Volt, volt, *n.* [From *Volta*, the discoverer of voltaism.] The practical unit of electromotive force, equal to 10^8 absolute electromagnetic units of *e.m.f.* The *e.m.f.* of a standard Clark cell at 15° C. is taken as 1·434 volts.—**Voltage**, *n.* Electromotive force as measured in volts. — **Voltaic**, vol-tā'ik, *a.* Pertaining to ordinary current electricity or galvanism. — *Voltaic battery*, an apparatus consisting of a combination of voltaic cells.—*Voltaic cell*, a contrivance for producing electric current, consisting in its simplest form of a jar containing an electrolyte, such as dilute sulphuric acid, and two metals, such as copper and zinc. When the metals are joined by a wire a current flows. See GALVANIC. — *Voltaic electricity*, current electricity, produced chemically.—**Voltaism**, vol'ta-izm, *n.* Voltaic electricity; galvanism. — **Voltameter**, vol-tam'et-ėr, *n.* [*Voltaic*, and Gr. *metron*, measure.] An electrolytic means for measuring the strength of a current.—**Volt-meter**, volt'mē-tėr, *n.* [After A. *Volta*, Gr. *metron*, a measure.] An instrument for measuring electrical pressure, or difference of potential, in volts.

Volte-face, volt-fās, *n.* [Fr.] A wheel about; a sudden change in speaking, acting, &c.

Voltigeur, vol'ti-zhėr, *n.* [Fr., from *voltiger*, to vault.] Formerly, a special variety of infantry soldier in a French regiment.

Voluble, vol'ū-bl, *a.* [Fr. *voluble*, L. *volubilis*, revolving, fluent, voluble, from *volvo*, *volutum*, to roll (whence also *vault, volume, revolve, involve, convolution*, &c.); cog. E. *wallow, walk*.] Having a great flow of words or glibness of utterance; speaking with over great fluency; over fluent; *bot.* twisting: applied to stems which twist or twine round other bodies.—**Volubly**, vol'ū-bli, *adv.* In a voluble or fluent manner. —**Volubility, Volubleness**, vol-ū-bil'i-ti, vol'ū-bl-nes, *n.* [Fr. *volubilité*, L. *volubilitas*.] The quality of being voluble in speech; over great fluency or readiness of the tongue; unchecked flow of speech.

Volume, vol'ūm, *n.* [Fr. *volume*, from L. *volumen*, a roll, a roll of manuscript, a book, from *volvo*, to roll. VOLUBLE.] A roll of manuscript, such as anciently formed a book; a book; a tome; a part or portion of an extended work that is bound up together in one cover; something of a convolved, rounded, or swelling form; a coil; a convolution; a wreath (*volumes* of smoke); the bulk or solid content of a body, measured e.g. in cubic feet or cubic centimetres; a quantity as having a certain bulk (a *volume* of a gas); *mus.* quantity, fulness, power, or strength of tone or sound.—**Volumed**, vol'ūmd, *a.* Having the form of volumes or rounded masses; consisting of rolling masses. — **Volumenometer**, vol'ū-men-om"e-tėr, *n.* [L. *volumen*, a volume, and Gr. *metron*, a measure.] An instrument for measuring the volume of a solid body; a stereometer.—**Volumetric**, vol-ū-met'rik, *a.* *Chem.* pertaining to estimation by measured volumes of standard solutions of reagents.—*Volumetric analysis*, a method of chemical analysis in which the quantity of a substance present in a solution is estimated by the amount of a standard solution required to produce a certain reaction.—*Volumetric efficiency* (*aviation*), the ratio of the volume of charge or mixture induced into the cylinder of a gasoline engine to the volume which would completely fill the cylinder. — **Volumetrically**, vol-ū-met'ri-kal-li, *adv.* By volumetric analysis.

Voluminous, vō-lū'mi-nus, *a.* [Fr. *volumineux*, from L. *volumen*, *voluminis*, a volume. VOLUME.] Consisting of many coils or complications (*Mil.*); of great volume; bulky; having written much; producing books that are bulky or writing many of them (a *voluminous* writer).—**Voluminously**, vō-lū'mi-nus-li, *adv.* In a voluminous manner.—**Voluminousness**, vō-lū'mi nus-nes, *n.*

Voluntary, vol'un-ta-ri, *a.* [L. *voluntarius*, from *voluntas*, will, choice, from *voluns*, for *volens*, part. pres. of *volo*, *velle*, to will (whence *volition*, (*bene*)*volence*, (*male*)*volence*); cog. E. *will*.] Proceeding from the will; done of one's own accord or free choice; spontaneous; not prompted or suggested by another; of one's or its own accord or choice; subject to or controlled by the will; regulated by the will; endowed with free-will; pertaining to the doctrines of the voluntaries (a *voluntary* church).—*n.* A person who maintains that churches should be supported entirely by voluntary contributions, and should be quite free from connection with the state; *mus.* an organ solo performed at the beginning, during, or at the end of a church service.—**Voluntarily**, vol'un-ta-ri-li, *adv.* In a voluntary manner; spontaneously. — **Voluntariness**, vol'un-ta-ri-nes, *n.* The character of being voluntary; spantaneity. — **Voluntaryism**, vol'un-ta-ri-izm, *n.* The principle of supporting religion by voluntary effort and association.—**Volunteer**, vol-un-tēr', *n.* [Fr. *volontaire*.] A person who enters into any service of his own free-will; a person who of his own free-will offers the state his services in a military capacity without the stipulation of a substantial reward; a person belonging to one of the corps of riflemen, artillery, engineers, &c., in Britain, who voluntarily undergo a military training for home defence (absorbed by the Territorials since 1907). — *v.t.* To offer or bestow voluntarily.—*v.i.* To enter into any service of one's free-will.

Voluptuary, vō-lup'tū-a-ri, *n.* [L. *voluptuarius*, from *voluptas*, pleasure, akin to *volo*, to wish. VOLUNTARY.] A man wholly given up to luxury or the gratification of the appetite and sensual pleasures; a sensualist. — **Voluptuous**, vō-lup'tū-us, *a.* [L. *voluptuosus*.] Pertaining to sensual pleasure; gratifying the senses; exciting or tending to excite sensual desires; sensual. — **Voluptuously**, vō-lup'tū-us-li, *adv.* In a voluptuous manner; luxuriously; sensually. — **Voluptuousness**, vō-lup'tū-us-nes, *n.* The state or quality of being voluptuous.

Volute, vō-lūt', *n.* [L. *voluta*, a volute, from *volutus*, pp. of *volvo*, *volutum*, to roll. VOLUBLE.] *Arch.* a kind of spiral scroll used in the Ionic, Corinthian, and Composite capitals, of which it is a principal ornament.—**Voluted**, vō-lūt'ed, *a.* Having a volute or volutes.—**Volution**, vō-lū'shon, *n.* A spiral turn; a convolution.

Volva, vol'va, *n.* [L., a wrapper.] *Bot.* a wrapper or bag that envelops certain fungi when young.

Vomer, vō'mėr, *n.* [L., a ploughshare.] *Anat.* the slender thin bone between the nostrils.—**Vomerine**, vō'mėr-īn, *a.* Pertaining to the vomer.

Vomic-nut. NUX-VOMICA.

Vomit, vom'it, *v.t.* [From L. *vomo*, *vomitum*, to vomit; allied to Gr. *emō* (for *vemō*), Skr. *vam*, to vomit.] To throw up or eject from the stomach; to belch forth; to emit. —*v.i.* To eject the contents of the stomach by the mouth; to spew.—*n.* The matter ejected from the stomach; an emetic.—*Black vomit*, dark coloured matter ejected from the stomach in the last stage of yellow fever; hence, yellow fever. — **Vomiting**, vom'it-ing, *n.* That which is vomited; vomit. — **Vomitory**, vom'i-to-ri, *n.* [L. *vomitorius*, causing vomiting, *vomitoria*, passages for exit in a theatre.] An emetic; *arch.* an opening or door in an ancient theatre and amphitheatre which gave ingress or egress to the people.

Voodoo, vö-dö, *n.* [Perhaps of African origin.] Among the West Indies and some Southern States Negroes, a person who professes to be a sorcerer, or to possess mysterious powers; such mysterious and malign powers collectively; an evil spirit. Also used adjectively.—**Voodooism**, vö-dö-izm, *n.* Voodoo beliefs or practices.

Voracious, vō-rā'shus, *a.* [L. *vorax*, *voracis*, from *voro*, to devour; same root as Gr. *bora*, food; Skr. *gar*, to swallow.] Greedy for eating; eating food in large quantities; rapacious; ready to devour or swallow up.—**Voraciously**, vō-rā'shus-li, *adv.* In a voracious manner; ravenously. — **Voraciousness, Voracity**, vō-rā'shus-nes, vō-ras'i-ti, *n.* The quality of being voracious.

Vortex, vor'teks, *n.* pl. **Vortices**, vor'ti-sēz, or **Vortexes**, vor'tek-sez. [L., from *verto*, anciently *vorto*, to turn. VERSE.] A whirling or gyratory motion in any fluid, whether liquid or aeriform; a whirlpool or a whirlwind; an eddy. — *Vortex ring*, a ring of fluid matter, which may be regarded as composed of rotating circles placed side by side, like beads on a string, as the singular smoke-rings which are sometimes produced in smoking tobacco.—**Vortical, Vorticose**, vor'ti-kal, vor'ti-kōs, *a.* Pertaining to a vortex; whirling; turning.—**Vortically**, vor'ti-kal-li, *adv.* In a vortical manner; whirlingly.

Votary, vō'ta-ri, *n.* [From L. *votum*, a vow. VOTE.] One devoted, consecrated, or engaged by a vow or promise; a person devoted, given, or addicted to some particular service, worship, study, or state of life.—**Votarist**, vō'ta-rist, *n.* A votary.—**Votaress**, vō'ta-res, *n.* A female devoted to any service, worship, or state of life.

Vote, vōt, *n.* [Fr. *vote*, a vote, from L. *votum*, a vow, wish, will, from *voveo*, *votum*, to vow (seen also in *devote, devout*). VOW.] The expression of a desire, preference, or choice in regard to any measure proposed, in which the person voting has an interest in common with others; a suffrage; that by which will or preference is expressed in elections or in deciding proposals; a ballot, a ticket, &c.; a thing conferred by vote; a grant. — *v.i.* — *voted, voting*. To give a vote; to express or signify the mind, will, or preference in electing men to office or the like.—*v.t.* To elect by some expression of will; to enact, establish, or grant by vote.—**Voter**, vō'tėr, *n.* One who votes or has a legal right to vote; an elector.—**Voting-paper**, *n.* A ballot by which a person casts his vote.—**Votive**, vō'tiv, *a.* [L. *votivus*, from *votum*, a vow.] Given, paid, or consecrated, in consequence of some vow. — *A votive offering*, a tablet, picture, &c., dedicated in consequence of the vow of a worshiper.—**Votively**, vō'tiv-li, *adv.* In a votive manner; by vow.

Vouch, vouch, *v.t.* [O.Fr. *vocher*, from L. *vocare*, to call; hence *avouch*. VOICE.] To declare, assert, affirm, or attest; to maintain by affirmations; to warrant; to answer for.—*v.i.* To bear witness; to give testimony or attestation; to maintain; to assert; to aver.—**Voucher**, vouch'ėr, *n.* One who vouches; a paper or document which serves to confirm and establish facts of any kind; the written evidence of the payment of a debt, as a discharged account or the like.

Vouchsafe, vouch-sāf', *v.t.*—*vouchsafed*, *vouchsafing*. [From *vouch* and *safe*, to vouch or attest as safe; formerly often as two words.] To condescend to grant; to concede (to *vouchsafe* an answer).—*v.i.* To condescend; to deign; to yield.—**Vouchsafement**, vouch-sāf'ment, *n.* The act of vouchsafing.

Voussoir, vös'war, *n.* [Fr., akin in origin to *vault*.] One of a series of stones, &c., shaped like truncated wedges, with which an arch is constructed, the uppermost or middle one of which is called the keystone.

Vow, vou, *n.* [O.Fr. *vou*, Mod.Fr. *vœu*, a vow, from L. *votum*, a vow; hence really the same word as *vote*. *Avow* is a derivative.] A solemn promise; an engagement solemnly entered into; an oath made to God, or to some deity, to perform some act on the fulfilment of certain conditions; a promise to follow out some line of conduct, or to devote one's self to some act or service.—*v.t.* To promise solemnly; to give, consecrate, or dedicate by a solemn promise, as to a divine power; to threaten solemnly or upon oath (to *vow* vengeance). —*v.i.* To make vows or solemn promises.—**Vowed**, vou'd, *p.* and *a.* Devoted; confirmed by oath; sworn; inveterate. — **Vower**, vou'ėr, *n.* One who makes a vow.

Vowel, vou'el, *n.* [Fr. *voyelle*, from L. *vocalis*, vocal, lit. a vocal letter, from *vox*, *vocis*, the voice. VOICE.] A sound uttered by opening the mouth and giving vent to voice; a sound uttered when the vocal organs are in an open position, as the sound of *a* or *o*; the letter or character which represents such a sound.—*a.* Pertaining to a vowel; vocal.—*Vowel points.* Under POINT.—**Vowelism**, vou'el-izm, *n.* The use of vowels.—**Voweled**, vou'eld, *a.* Furnished with vowels.

Vox-humana, voks-hū-mā'na, *n.* [L., human voice.] A reed-stop in an organ, so called from its resemblance to the human voice.

Voyage, voi'āj, *n.* [Fr. *voyage*, a journey; It. *viaggio*, Sp. *viage*; from L. *viaticum*, from *viaticus*, pertaining to a journey, from *via*, a way (seen also in *viaduct, deviate, obviate, obvious, previous, convey*, &c.); same root as E. *way*.] Formerly, a journey by sea or by land; now, a journey by sea from one place, port, or country to another, especially a journey by water to a distant place or country.—*v.i.*—*voyaged, voyaging.* To take a journey or voyage; to sail or pass by water.—*v.t.* To travel; to pass over.—**Voyageable**, voi'āj-a-bl, *a.* Navigable.—**Voyager**, voi'āj-ėr, *n.* One who makes a voyage.—**Voyageur**, vwą-yä-zhėr, *n.* [Fr., lit. a traveller.] The Canadian name of a class of men employed in the fur trade, &c., in transporting goods by land or water.

Vraisemblance, vrā-saṅ-blaṅs, *n.* [Fr.] The appearance of truth.

V-shaped depression, vē-shāpt dē-pre'-shon, *n.* A special distribution of low barometric pressure, in which the isobars have a shape resembling the letter V.

Vulcan, vul'kan, *n.* [L. *Vulcanus* or *Volcanus* (hence *volcano*); akin Skr. *ulkā*, a fire.] The Roman deity who presided over fire and the working of metals; the name given in 1859 to a hypothetical intra-Mercurial planet, now considered to have no existence.—**Vulcanian**, vul-kā'ni-an, *a.* Pertaining to Vulcan, or to works in iron, &c.; volcanic; *geol.* pertaining to vulcanism.—*Vulcanian theory*, the Plutonic theory. Under PLUTONIC.—**Vulcanic**, vul-kan'ik, *a.* Volcanic.—**Vulcanicity**, vul-ka-nis'-i-ti, *n.* Volcanic power or action; volcanicity.—**Vulcanism**, vul'kan-izm, *n.* The phenomena due to the internal heat of the earth, as volcanoes, hot springs, &c.—**Vulcanist**, vul'kan-ist, *n.* One who supports the Vulcanian theory.—**Vulcanite**, vul'kan-īt, *n.* A kind of vulcanized caoutchouc differing from ordinary vulcanized caoutchouc in containing a larger proportion of sulphur, and in being made at a higher temperature, used for combs, brooches, bracelets, &c.; ebonite; a name for pyroxene, from its being found in ejected blocks and lavas.—**Vulcanization**, vul'kan-ī-zā"shon, *n.* A method of combining caoutchouc or india-rubber with sulphur and other ingredients to effect certain changes in its properties, and yield a soft (*vulcanized india-rubber*) or a hard (*vulcanite*) product.—**Vulcanize**, vul'kan-īz, *v.t.*—*vulcanized, vulcanizing.* To subject to the process of vulcanization.—**Vulcanologist**, vul-ka-nol'o-jist, *n.* A student of vulcanology.—**Vulcanology**, vul-ka-nol'o-ji, *n.* The science of volcanic phenomena.

Vulgar, vul'gėr, *a.* [Fr. *vulgaire*, from L. *vulgaris*, from *vulgus*, the common people, the crowd; same root as *urgeo*, E. to *urge*. URGE.] Pertaining to the common people or the multitude; plebeian; common; ordinary; in general use; hence, national; vernacular (the *vulgar* tongue); pertaining to the lower or less refined class of people; hence, somewhat coarse; rude; boorish; low.—*Vulgar fractions.* Under FRACTION.—*The vulgar*, the common people collectively; the uneducated, uncultured class of people.—**Vulgarian**, vul-gā'ri-an, *n.* A vulgar person.—**Vulgarism**, vul'gėr-izm, *n.* Vulgarity; a vulgar phrase or expression.—**Vulgarity**, vul-gar'i-ti, *n.* The quality of being vulgar; coarseness or clownishness of manners or language; an act of low manners.—**Vulgarize**, vul'gėr-īz, *v.t.*—*vulgarized, vulgarizing.* To make vulgar or common.—**Vulgarly**, vul'gėr-li, *adv.* In a vulgar manner; commonly; by popular usage; coarsely; clownishly.—**Vulgarness**, vul'gėr-nes, *n.* Vulgarity.—*The Vulgate* (L. *vulgata editio*, the edition made public or given to all), the authorized Latin version of the Scriptures in the Roman Catholic Church.

Vulned, vul'ned, *a.* [L. *vulnus*, a wound.] *Her.* wounded but not pierced through, the latter being indicated by *transfixed* (which see).

Vulnerable, vul'nėr-a-bl, *a.* [Fr. *vulnerable*, from L. *vulnero*, to wound, from *vulnus, vulneris*, a wound; from a root meaning to tear, whence also *wolf*.] Capable of being wounded; liable to injury; subject to be affected injuriously.—**Vulnerability, Vulnerableness**, vul'nėr-a-bil"i-ti, vul'nėr-a-bl-nes, *n.* The quality of being vulnerable.—**Vulnerary**, vul'nėr-a-ri, *a.* [L. *vulnerarius*.] Useful in healing wounds.—*n.* Any plant, drug, or composition useful in the cure of wounds.

Vulpine, vul'pīn, *a.* [L. *vulpinus*, from *vulpes*, a fox.] Pertaining to the fox; resembling the fox; cunning.—**Vulpicide**, vul'pi-sīd, *n.* [L. *vulpes*, and *cœdo*, to kill.] The practice of killing foxes; a fox-killer.

Vulpinite, vul'pin-īt, *n.* [From *Vulpino*, in Italy, where it is found.] A variety of gypsum sometimes employed for small statues and other ornamental work.

Vulture, vul'tūr, *n.* [O.Fr. *vultor*, L. *vultur*, same root as *vulnerable*.] The name of well-known raptorial birds which live chiefly on carrion.—**Vulturine**, vul'tū-rīn, *a.* [L. *vulturinus*.] Having the qualities of or resembling the vulture. Also **Vulturish, Vulturous.**

Vulva, vul'va, *n.* [L. *vulva, volva*, a wrapper, the womb, from *volvo*, to roll.] *Anat.* the opening of the external parts of generation in the female.—**Vulvo-uterine**, *a.* Pertaining to the vulva and the uterus.

Vying, vī'ing, *p.* and *a.* Competing; emulating. VIE.

W

W is the twenty-third letter of the English alphabet, taking its form and name from the union of two V's or U's.

Waacs, waks, *n.* [From the initials.] Members of the Women's Army Auxiliary Corps in the World War.

Wabble, wob'l, *v.i.*—*wabbled, wabbling.* [WOBBLE.] To vacillate; to wobble.—*n.* A rocking unequal motion, as of a top imperfectly balanced.—**Wabbly**, wob'li, *a.* Inclined to wabble; unsteady.

Wacke, wak'e, *n.* [G. *wacke, grauwacke*, wacke, graywacke.] A soft earthy variety of trap-rock, generally of a grayish-green colour, and usually containing crystals.

Wad, wod, *n.* [Same word as Sw. *vadd*, Dan. *vat*, G. *watte*, wad.] A soft mass of fibrous material, as cotton-wool or the like, used for stuffing, stopping an aperture, &c.; a little mass of some soft or flexible material, used for stopping the charge of powder in a gun and pressing it close to the shot.—*v.t.*—*wadded, wadding.* To furnish with a wad; to stuff or line with wadding, as a garment.—**Wadding**, wod'-ing, *n.* A fabric of cotton fibre or the like, used for stuffing various parts of articles of dress; material for ramming down above the charge of firearms.

Wad, Wadd, wod, *n.* An earthy ore of manganese; also, a name of plumbago or black-lead.

Waddle, wod'l, *v.i.*—*waddled, waddling.* [A dim. and freq. formed from *wade*.] To sway or rock from side to side in walking; to walk in a tottering or vacillating manner; to toddle.—**Waddler**, wod'lėr, *n.* One who waddles.—**Waddlingly**, wod'ling-li, *adv.* With a vacillating gait.

Wade, wād, *v.i.*—*waded, wading.* [A.Sax. *wadan*, to go, to wade = L.G. *waden*, Icel. and Sw. *vada*, D. *waden*, G. *waten*, to wade; same root as L. *vado*, to go. INVADE.] To walk through any substance that impedes or hinders the free motion of the limbs (as long grass or snow); to move stepwise through a fluid; to move or pass with difficulty or labour.—*v.t.* To pass or cross by wading; to ford.—**Wader**, wā'dėr, *n.* One who wades; specifically, the name applied to such birds as the heron, snipe, rail, &c. GRALLATORES.

Wadi, Wady, wod'i, *n.* [Ar. *wâdi*.] The channel of a water-course which is dry, except in the rainy season; a water-course; a term used chiefly in the topography of certain Eastern or North African countries.

Wadmal, Wadmoll, wad'mal, wad'mol, *n.* [Icel. *vad-mál*, Sw. *vadmal*, Dan. *vadmel*.] A coarse cloth formerly manufactured.

Wafer, wā'fėr, *n.* [O.Fr. *waufre* (Fr. *gaufre*), wafer, from G. *waffel*, D. *wafel*, a thin cake, a wafer.] A small thin sweet cake; a thin circular portion of unleavened bread, used in the Roman Church in the celebration and administration of the eucharist; a small thin disc of dried paste used for sealing letters, &c.

Waffle, wof'l, *n.* [D. *wafel*, G. *waffel*. WAFER.] A kind of thin cake.

Waft, wäft, *v.t.* [Closely akin to *wave*, and to Sw. *vefta*, to waft, Dan. *vifte*, to waft, to fan; *vift*, a puff.] To convey through water or air; to make to sail or float; to buoy up; to keep from sinking.—*v.i.* To sail or float.—*n.* The act of one who or that which wafts; a sweep; a breath or current, as of wind.—**Waftage**, wäf'tāj, *n.* The act of wafting or state of being wafted.—**Wafter**, wäf'tėr, *n.* One who wafts.

Wag, wag, *v.t.*—*wagged, wagging.* [A.Sax. *wagian*, to wag, to shake; Sw. *vagga*, to wag, Icel. *vaga*, to wag, to waddle, D. *waggelen*, to stagger, G. *wackeln*, to waggle; akin *wagon, wain, weigh, way, wave*.] To cause to move backwards and forwards, or from side to side alternately; to cause to oscillate or vibrate slightly; to wave.—*v.i.* To move backwards and forwards; to hang loosely and shake; to oscillate; to sway; to be in motion or action; to move off or away; to be gone.—*n.* [Most likely a shortening of the old term *waghalter*, one likely to *wag* in a *halter* or gallows. Comp. Sc. *hempie*, a gallows bird, a frolicsome fellow, lit. one fitted for the hempen rope.] A person who is fond of making jokes; one who is full of frolicsome tricks; a humorist; a wit; a joker.—**Waggery**, wag'ėr-i, *n.* The manner, action, or pranks of a wag; jocular sayings; pleasantry.—**Waggish**, wag'ish, *a.* Belonging to a wag; full of sportive or jocular tricks, antics, sayings, &c.; frolicsome.—**Waggishly**, wag'ish-li, *adv.* In a waggish manner; in sport.—**Waggishness**, wag'ish-nes, *n.*

Wage, wāj, *v.t.*—*waged, waging.* [O.Fr. *wager*, to pledge, to promise (hence, to pledge one's self to combat), Fr. *gager*, to stake, to pledge, from L.L. *vadium, wadium*, Goth. *wadi*, a pledge, same word as A. Sax. *wed*, a pledge. WED. *Gage* is another form of this word.] To engage in (a contest); to carry on (war); to undertake.—*n.* A gage or pledge; hire; wages.—**Wages**, wā'jez, *n.pl.* [O.Fr. *wage, gage*, a pledge; *wages* are what the person hiring another has pledged himself to give.] The payment given for services performed; the price paid for labour; hire; recompense. Though a plural, *wages* sometimes has a verb in the singular.

Wager, wā'jėr, *n.* [O.Fr. *wageure, gageure*, from L.L. *vadiatura*, from *wadium*, a pledge. WAGE.] An occasion on which two parties bet; a bet; the stake laid; the subject of a bet.—*Wager of battle*, the legal trial of a cause by combat either between the parties themselves or their champions, formerly in practice in England.—*v.t.* To hazard on the issue of some question that is to be decided; to bet; to stake.—*v.i.* To make a bet; to bet.—**Wagerer**, wā'jėr-ėr, *n.* One who wagers.

Wages. Under WAGE.

Waggle, wag'l, *v.i.*—*waggled, waggling.* [A freq. and dim. from *wag.*] To move with a wagging motion; to sway or move from side to side.—*v.t.* To cause to wag frequently and with short motions.

Wagon, Waggon, wag'on, *n.* [From D. *wagen*, rather than from A.Sax. *wægen*, a wagon (whence *wain*); Icel. and Sw. *vagn*, Dan. *vogn*, G. *wagen*; lit. what carries, from stem of *weigh*; cog. Skr. *vah*, L. *veho*, to carry (whence *vehicle*); akin also *way, wag*, &c.] A four-wheeled vehicle for the transport of heavy loads; an open four-wheeled vehicle for the conveyance of goods on railways.—*v.t.* To transport or carry in a wagon.—**Wagonage**, wag'on-āj, *n.* Money paid for conveyance by wagon.—**Wagoner**, wag'on-ėr, *n.* One who drives a wagon; the constellation Charles's Wain or Ursa Major.—**Wagonette**, wag-on-et', *n.* [Dim. of *wagon.*] An open four-wheeled pleasure vehicle of light construction, seated for six or eight persons.

Wagtail, wag'tāil, *n.* A small bird of several species, distinguished by its brisk and lively motions, as well as by the length of its tail, which it jerks up and down incessantly, hence the name; a pert person.

Wahabee, Wahabi, wa-hä'bē, *n.* [From Abdel *Wahab*, a reformer of Mohammedanism about 1760.] A member of a very strict sect of Mohammedans in Arabia.

Waif, wāf, *n.* [O.Fr. *waif, gaif*, a waif; of Scandinavian origin, like E. *waive.*] A stray or odd article; an article that no one claims; goods found of which the owner is not known; a wanderer; a neglected, homeless wretch.

Wail, wāl, *v.t.* [From Icel. *væla, vála*, to wail or lament; perhaps connected with *woe.*] To lament; to bewail.—*v.i.* To express sorrow audibly; to lament.—*n.* Loud weeping; violent lamentation.—**Wailing**, wāl'ing, *n.* Cries of sorrow.

Wain, wān, *n.* [A.Sax. *waen*, a contracted form of *wægen*, a wagon, from *wegan*, to carry. WAGON, WEIGH.] A four-wheeled vehicle for the transportation of goods; a wagon; a constellation, Charles's Wain.

Wainscot, wān'skot, *n.* [From D. *wagenschot*, wainscot, for *wageschot*, from *waeg*, a wall, and *schot*, boarding, a covering of boards.] A wooden lining or boarding of the walls of rooms, usually made in panels.—*v.t.* To line with wainscot.—**Wainscoted**, wān'skot-ed, *p.* and *a.* Covered with wainscot.—**Wainscoting**, *n.* Wainscot, or the material used for it.

Waist, wāst, *n.* [A.Sax. *wæstm*, growth, stature, form, from stem of *wax*, to grow.] That part of the human body which is immediately below the ribs or thorax, or between the thorax and hips; the middle part of a ship, or that part between the fore- and main-masts.—**Waistband**, wāst'band, *n.* A band round the waist; the band at the top of a pair of trousers round the waist.—**Waistcoat**, wāst'kōt, *n.* A garment without sleeves, under the coat, covering the chest and waist; a vest.

Wait, wāt, *v.i.* [O.Fr. *waiter* (Fr. *guetter*), to watch or lie in wait, from *waite*, a watchman or sentinel, from O.H.G. *wahta*, a watchman; akin E. *watch, wake.*] To stay or rest in expectation or patience; to perform the duties of a servant or attendant; to serve at table.—*To wait on* or *upon*, to attend upon; to perform menial services for; to visit on business or for ceremony; to attend or follow, as a consequence; to accompany.—*v.t.* To stay or wait for; to await.—*n.* The act of waiting; a waiting in concealment; ambush; a musician who with others promenades the streets in the night about Christmas time, performing music appropriate to the season.—*To lie in wait*, to lie in ambush; hence, *fig.* to lay snares or make insidious attempts.—**Waiter**, wā'tėr, *n.* One who waits; a male attendant on the guests in an hotel, inn, or similar place; a salver or small tray.—**Waiting**, wā'ting, *n.* The act of staying in expectation; attendance.—*In waiting*, in attendance (lords *in waiting*, certain officers of the royal household).—**Waiting-maid, Waiting-woman**, *n.* A female servant who attends a lady.—**Waitress**, wāt'res, *n.* A female attendant in a restaurant, &c.

Waive, wāv, *v.t.* [The verb corresponding to the noun *waif*; lit. it would seem to mean, to leave loose or unregarded; comp. Icel. *veifa*, to swing loosely, to vibrate. WAIF.] To relinquish or give up; not to insist on or claim; to forego.

Waiwode, wā'wōd. WAYWODE.

Wake, wāk, *v.i.* pret. and pp. *woke* or *waked*; ppr. *waking.* [A.Sax. *wacan*, also *wacian*, to arise, to wake, to be awake; Icel. *vaka*, D. and L.G. *waken*, Goth. *vakan*, G. *wachen*, to wake; cog. with L. *vigil*, watchful (whence *vigilant*). Hence *waken*, *watch.*] To be awake; to continue awake; not to sleep; to cease to sleep; to be aroused; to be excited from a torpid or inactive state; to be put in motion; to revel or carouse late at night.—*v.t.* To rouse from sleep; to excite or stir; to put in motion or action: often with *up*; to hold a wake for.—*n.* [A.Sax. *wacu*, a watching, a vigil.] Vigils; the feast of the dedication of a parish church, formerly kept by watching all night; a merry-making; a festive gathering (*Shak.*); the watching of a dead body prior to burial by the friends and neighbours of the deceased.—**Waking**, wā'king, *p.* and *a.* Being awake; rousing from sleep; exciting.—*Waking hours*, the hours when one is awake.—**Wakeful**, wāk'ful, *a.* Keeping awake after going to bed; watchful; vigilant.—**Wakefully**, wāk'ful-li, *adv.* In a wakeful manner.—**Wakefulness**, wāk'ful-nes, *n.* The state of being wakeful; indisposition to sleep.—**Waken**, wā'kn, *v.i.* [A.Sax. *wacnan*, to become awake, from *wacan*, to wake.] To wake; to cease to sleep.—*v.t.* To excite or rouse from sleep; to awaken; to excite to action; to rouse; to stir; to produce; to call forth (to *waken* love or fear).—**Wakener**, wā'kn-ėr, *n.* One who or that which wakens.—**Wakening**, wā'kn-ing, *n.* The act of one who wakens; a ceasing from sleep.—**Waker**, wā'kėr, *n.* One who wakes.—**Wake-robin**, *n.* A plant, the arum.

Wake, wāk, *n.* [Same as Prov.E. *wake*, a row of grass; Icel. *vök*, a channel for a vessel in ice.] The track which is left by a ship in the water, and which may be seen to a considerable distance behind.

Waldenses, wal'den-sēz, *n.* [From Peter *Waldo* or *Waldus*, the founder of the sect in the twelfth century.] A sect of Christians in Northern Italy whose faith is substantially that of the Reformed churches, formerly much persecuted.

Wale, wāl, *n.* [A.Sax. *walu*, a wale = O. Fris. *walu*, Icel. *völr*, Goth. *walus*, a rod, a staff. Hence *wale* in *gunwale.*] A streak or stripe produced by the stroke of a rod or whip on animal flesh; a weal; a plank from one end of a ship to another a little above the water-line.—*v.t.*—*waled, waling.* To mark with wales or stripes.

Walhalla, wal-hal'la, *n.* VALHALLA.

Walk, wak, *v.i.* [A.Sax. *wealcan*, to roll, to turn about, to rove (whence *wealcere*, a fuller, origin of the name *Walker*) = Icel. *válka*, Dan. *valke*, G. *walken*, to full; same root as *wallow, well*, L. *volvo*, to roll (whence *voluble*, &c.).] To step along; to advance by alternate steps, lifting one foot past the other without running; to go or travel on foot; to go or come, as used in the ceremonious language of invitation (*walk* in); to haunt or show itself in some place, as a spectre; to conduct one's self; to pursue a particular course of life.—*v.t.* To pass over or through on foot; to cause to walk or step slowly.—*To walk over*, to win a race without having to run, owing to the absence of a competitor; to be unopposed at an election; to win easily.—*To walk the hospitals*, to attend the medical and surgical practice of hospitals for instruction.—*To walk the plank*, a method used by pirates to dispose of captives by compelling them to walk blindfolded along a plank overhanging the sea.—*n.* The act of one who walks; the pace of one who walks; a short excursion on foot, for pleasure or exercise; manner of walking; gait; a place in which one is accustomed to walk; an avenue, promenade, or the like; sphere of action; a department, as of art, science, or literature; way of living; a tract or piece of ground in which animals graze; a sheep-walk; a district habitually served by an itinerant vendor of any commodity.—**Walker**, wa'kėr, *n.* One who walks; a pedestrian.—**Walking-beam**. Same as WORKING-BEAM.—**Walking-gentleman**, *n.* An actor who fills subordinate parts requiring a gentlemanly appearance.—**Walking-leaf**, *n.* LEAF-INSECT.—**Walkingstick**, wa'king-stik, *n.* A staff or stick carried in the hand in walking.

Wall, wal, *n.* [A.Sax. *weall*, a wall, a rampart = O.Sax., O.Fris., and D. *wal*, Dan. *val*, Sw. *vall*, G. *wall*, a rampart; from L. *vallum*, a fence of stakes, a rampart (seen also in *interval*), from *vallus*, a stake.] A structure of stone, brick, or other materials, of some height and breadth, serving to inclose a space, form a division, support superincumbent weights, &c.; the side of a building or room; a solid and permanent inclosing fence; a rampart; a fortified enceinte or barrier; in this sense often spoken of as plural; means of security or protection; *mining*, the rock inclosing a vein.—*To go to the wall*, to get the worst of a contest; to be overpowered.—*To push* or *thrust to the wall*, to crush by superior power.—*v.t.* To inclose with a wall; to defend by walls; to fill up with a wall.—**Walled**, wald, *p.* and *a.* Provided with a wall or walls; fortified.—**Waller**, wal'ėr, *n.* One who builds walls.—**Wallflower**, wal'flou-ėr, *n.* The name of a cruciferous plant—a biennial or perennial herb or undershrub—which exhales a delicious odour, and is a great favourite in gardens; so called because in its wild state it grows on old walls and in stony places.—**Wall-fruit**, *n.* Fruit grown on trees trained against a wall.—**Walling**, wal'ing, *n.* Walls in general; materials for walls.—**Wall-paper**, *n.* Paper for covering room-walls; paper-hangings.—**Wall-plate**, *n.* A piece of timber fixed horizontally in or on a wall, under the ends of girders, joists, and other timbers.—**Wall-saltpeter**, *n.* NITRO-CALCITE.—**Wall-tree**, *n.* A fruit-tree nailed to a wall for the better exposure of the fruit to the sun, &c

Wallaby, wol'a-bi, *n.* [Native Australian.] The name of several varieties of the Australian Kangaroo.

Wallace's Line, *n.* The boundary between the Oriental and Australian regions.

Wallachian, wal-lak'yan, *a.* Pertaining to *Wallachia*, its language, or inhabitants.—*n.* A native of Wallachia; the language, one of the Romance family of tongues, spoken in Roumania (Wallachia and Moldavia) and adjoining regions.

Wallah, wol'la, *n.* [Anglo-Indian.] Person employed about or concerned with something.—*Competition-wallah*, Indian civil servant appointed by examination.

Wallet, wol'et, *n.* [Probably a corruption

of old *watel*, a bag. WATTLE.] A bag or sack for containing articles which a person carries with him; a knapsack; a pack, bundle, or bag.

Wall-eye, *n.* [Icel. *vagl-eygr*, wall-eyed, from *vagl*, a beam or defect in the eye.] An eye in which the iris is of a very light gray or whitish colour: said commonly of horses.—**Wall-eyed**, *a.* Having such an eye: said of horses; glaring-eyed; fierce-eyed (*Shak.*).

Walloon, wal-lön′, *n.* [From a Teutonic word meaning foreign, seen also in *walnut*, *Welsh*.] One of the descendants of the old Gallic Belgæ who occupy part of Belgium and north-eastern France, speaking a French dialect containing Gallic and Low German words; the language of the Walloons.

Wallop, wal′op, *v.t.* To thrash; beat soundly. (*Colloq.*)

Wallow, wol′ō, *v.i.* [A.Sax. *wealwian*, to roll; akin to E. to *well* up; same root as L. *volvo*, to roll. VOLUBLE.] To roll one's body on the earth, in mire, or in other substance; to tumble and roll in anything soft; to live in filth or gross vice.—**Wallower**, wol′ō-ėr, *n.* One who wallows.

Walnut, wąl′nut, *n.* [A.Sax. *wealh-hnut*, a walnut, lit. a foreign nut—*wealh*, foreign, and *hnut*, nut; so G. *wallnuss*, D. *walnoot*. WELSH.] A large handsome tree and its fruit, a native of Persia, yielding timber of great value as a cabinet and furniture wood.—**Walnut-oil**, *n.* A bland oil obtained from the walnut fruit and much used by painters.

Walrus, wol′rus, *n.* [From D. *walrus*, a walrus, lit. a whale-horse—*wal*, a whale, and *ros*, a horse; so G. *wallross*, Dan. *valros*, Sw. *vallross*, A.Sax. *hors-hwæl*, Icel. *hross-hvalr*, horse-whale.] A large marine carnivorous mammal of the Arctic regions allied to the seal; also known as the morse, sea-horse, and sea-cow; hunted for its oil and for the ivory of its tusks.

Walschaert gear, wąl-shėrt, *n.* In locomotive engines, a reversing valve gear.

Waltz, wąlts, *n.* [Short for G. *walzer*, from *walzen*, to roll, to waltz; akin to *welter*.] A dance performed by two persons, who, almost embracing each other, swing round the room with a whirling motion; the music composed for the dance.—*v.i.* To dance a waltz.—**Waltzer**, wąlt′sėr, *n.* A person who waltzes.

Wamble, wom′bl, *v.i.* [Same as Dan. *vamle*, to nauseate; akin Icel. *væma*, to loathe, *væma*, nausea.] To be disturbed with nausea: said of the stomach.

Wampum, wom′pum, *n.* [American Indian; said to mean white.] Small beads made of shells, used by the American Indians as money, or wrought into belts, &c., as an ornament.

Wan, won, *a.* [A.Sax. *wan*, *won*, *wann*, dark, dusky.] Having a pale or sickly hue; languid of look; pale; gloomy: often applied to water.—*v.i.* To grow or become wan. (*Poetical.*)—**Wanly**, won′li, *adv.* In a wan manner; palely.—**Wanness**, won′nes, *n.* Paleness; a sallow, dead colour.—**Wannish**, won′ish, *a.* Somewhat wan.

Wand, wond, *n.* [Same as Dan. *vaand*, O.Sw. *wand*, Icel. *vöndr*, Goth. *wandus*, a twig, a wand; probably akin to *wind* (*v.*), from its flexibility.] A long slender stick; a rod; a rod or similar article, having some special use or character; a staff of authority; a rod used by conjurors or diviners.

Wander, won′dėr, *v.i.* [A.Sax. *wandrian*, to wander = O.D. *wanderen*, Dan. *vandre*, Sw. *vandra*, G. *wandern*, to wander; freq. forms akin to *wend*. WEND, WIND (verb).] To ramble here and there without any certain course or object in view; to roam; to stroll; to leave home; to go through the world; to deviate; to err; to be delirious; not to be under the guidance of reason.—*v.t.* To travel over without a certain course; to traverse.—**Wanderer**, won′dėr-ėr, *n.* One who wanders.—**Wandering**, won′dėr-ing, *p.* and *a.* Given to wander; roaming; unsettled.—*n.* A travelling without a settled course; peregrination; aberration; deviation; mental aberration.—**Wanderingly**, won′dėr-ing-li, *adv.* In a wandering manner.

Wanderoo, won-de-rö′, *n.* A monkey inhabiting the East Indies.

Wane, wān, *v.i.*—*waned*, *waning*. [A.Sax. *wanian*, to diminish, become less, from *wan*, deficient; akin *want*.] To diminish; to decrease or grow less: particularly applied to the illuminated part of the moon, as opposed to *wax*; to decline; to approach its end (the autumn *wanes*).—*n.* Decrease of the illuminated part of the moon to the eye of the spectator; decline (his fortunes were on the *wane*).

Wangle, wang′gl, *v.* To gain one's ends by devious or unscrupulous methods.

Wanion,† won′yon, *n.* [Connected with *wane*; perhaps the old infinitive *wanian*, to wane.] A misfortune or calamity; mischief: used chiefly as an imprecation in the phrases, '*with a wanion*', '*wanion on you*', &c.

Wanly, Wanness, &c. Under WAN.

Want, wont, *n.* [From Icel. *vant*, neut. of *vanr*, lacking, wanting, *vanta*, to be lacking; akin *wane*, *wan-* in *wanton*.] The state of not having; absence or scarcity of what is needed or desired; lack; need; necessity (to supply one's *wants*); poverty; indigence; lack of the necessaries of life (to suffer from *want*).—*v.t.* To be without; not to have; to lack; to have occasion for; to require; to need; to feel a desire for; to long for.—*v.i.* To be deficient; to be lacking; to be absent or not present where required or expected; to be in want.—**Wanter**, won′tėr, *n.* One who wants.

Wanton, won′ton, *a.* [O.E. *wantowen*, *wantoun*, undisciplined, dissolute, from *wan*, prefix denoting want or deficiency (A. Sax. *wan*, lacking), and *towen*, A.Sax. *togen*, pp. of *teón*, to draw, to educate. WANT, TUG.] Indulging the natural impulses or appetites without restraint; licentious; lustful; unrestrained in various ways, as in gaiety or sport; playful; frolicsome; sportive; playing freely or without constraint (*wanton* ringlets); unrestrained in growth); growing too luxuriantly; arising from recklessness or disregard of right or consequences; unprovoked (*wanton* mischief).—*n.* A lascivious man or woman; a pampered, petted creature.—*v.i.* To revel; to frolic unrestrainedly; to sport or dally in lewdness.—**Wantonly**, won′ton-li, *adv.* In a wanton manner; without cause or provocation. — **Wantonness**, won′ton-nes, *n.* The state or quality of being wanton; lewdness; negligence of restraint; sportiveness.

Wap, wop, *v.t.* To beat; to whop. (*Colloq.*)

Wapenshaw, Wapinschaw, wä′pn-shä, wä′pin-shą, *n.* [Lit. a *weapon-show*.] In Scotland, a review of persons under arms, made formerly at certain times in every district; afterwards applied in some quarters to the periodical gatherings of the volunteer corps of a district.

Wapentake, wä′pn-tāk, *n.* [Lit. a *weapon-taking* or weapon-touching—from the men of a district touching the arms of a superior in token of fealty.] The name formerly given in some of the northern shires of England, and still given in Yorkshire, to a division of the county, corresponding to a *hundred*.

Wapiti, wap′i-ti, *n.* [Indian name.] The North American stag, closely resembling the European red-deer, though larger.

War, wąr, *n.* [A.Sax. *war*, O.D. *werre*, O.H.G. *werra*, war (whence Fr. *guerre*, war); akin to G. *wirren*, to embroil, confuse; D. *war*, entanglement; perhaps allied to *worse*.] A contest between nations or states (*international war*), or between parties in the same state (*civil war*), carried on by force of arms; the profession of arms; art of war; a state of violent opposition or contest; hostility; enmity (feelings at *war* with each other).—*Articles of war*. Under ARTICLE.—*Council of war*. Under COUNCIL.—*v.i.*—*warred*, *warring*. To make or carry on war; to carry on hostilities; to contend; to strive; to be in a state of opposition.—**War-cry**, *n.* A cry or phrase used in common by a body of troops or the like in charging an enemy.—**War-dance**, *n.* A dance engaged in by savage tribes before a warlike excursion; a dance simulating a battle.—*War department*, in the U. S. one of the ten divisions of the executive branch of the national government, presided over by the secretary of war.—**Warfare**, wąr′fār, *n.* Military service; military life; hostilities; war.—*v.i.* To carry on warfare; to engage in war; to contend; to struggle.—**War-horse**, *n.* A horse used in war; a trooper's horse; a charger.—**Warlike**, wąr′līk, *a.* Fit for war; disposed or inclined for war; military; pertaining to war; having a martial appearance; having the qualities of a soldier.—**War-paint**, *n.* Paint put on the face and other parts of the body by savages before going to war.—**War-path**, *n.* The route or path taken on going to war; a warlike expedition or excursion: used chiefly in regard to the American Indians.—**Warring**, wąr′ing, *a.* Adverse; conflicting; antagonistic; hostile.—**Warrior**, wąr′i-ėr, *n.* A soldier; a man engaged in military life; a brave soldier.—**War-ship**, *n.* A ship constructed for engaging in naval warfare; a man-of-war.—**War-whoop**, *n.* A cry American Indians gave when they entered battle.

Warble, wąr′bl, *v.t.*—*warbled*, *warbling*. [O.Fr. *werbler*, from O.H.G. *hwerbalôn*, G. *wirbeln*, to whirl, to warble, WHIRL.] To sing in a trilling, quavering, or vibrating manner; to modulate with turns or variations; to sing or carol generally; to utter musically.—*v.i.* To have a trilling, quavering, or vibrating sound; to carol or sing with smoothly gliding tones; to trill.—*n.* A soft, sweet flow of melodious sounds, a trilling, flexible melody; a carol; a song.—**Warbler**, wąr′blėr, *n.* One who warbles; a song-bird; the popular name given to members of a dentirostral family of birds comprising most of the small woodland songsters of Europe and North America.

Warble, wąr′bl, *n.* [Perhaps from D. *var*, ox, and *bol*, ball, bulb.] A small tumour on the backs of cattle, containing the maggot or larva of a fly.

Ward, wąrd, *v.t.* [A.Sax. *weardian* to guard, from *weard*, a guard, a watch; G. *wart*, Icel. *vörthr*, Goth. *vards*, guard. From the G. are Fr. *garder*, E. *guard*, *regard*, *reward*. Akin to *wary*.] To fend off; to keep from hitting; to turn aside, as anything mischievous that approaches; often followed by *off*.—*n.* [Partly from A. Sax. *weard*, a guard, partly from the verb.] The act of guarding; guard (to keep watch and *ward*); a defensive motion or position in fencing or the like; the state of being under a guard; confinement; custody; guardianship; one who is guarded; specifically, a minor who is under guardianship; a certain division or section of a town or city, such as is constituted for the convenient transaction of local public business; one of the apartments into which an hospital is divided; a curved ridge of metal inside a lock to oppose the passage of a key which has not a corresponding notch; the notch in the key.—**Warden**, wąr′den, *n.* [O.Fr. *wardein*, *gardein*—a Germanic word with a Latin termination=-*anus*.] A guard or watchman; an officer of rank in charge of something; a keeper; the title given to the head of some colleges and to the superior of some conventual churches.—*Warden of a church*. CHURCHWARDEN, under CHURCH.—**Wardenship, Wardenry**, wąr′den-ship, wąr′den-ri, *n.* The office of a warden.—**Warder**, wąr′dėr, *n.* One who guards or keeps; a keeper; a guard; a truncheon or staff of authority.—**Wardrobe**, wąrd′rōb, *n.* A place in which clothes are kept, often a piece of furniture resembling a press or cupboard; wearing apparel in general.—**Ward-room**, *n.* The mess-room of the chief officers in a warship.—**Ward-ship**, wąrd′ship, *n.* The office of a ward or guardian; guardianship; also pupilage.

Ware, wār, *a.* [A.Sax. *wær*, wary = Icel. *varr*, Dan. and Sw. *var*, wary, aware.

WARY.] On one's guard; aware, conscious, assured. (*Poet.*)—*v.t.* To take heed of; to beware of.

Ware, wār, *n.* [A.Sax. *waru* = D. *waar*, Icel. *vara*, Dan. *vare*, G. *waare*, ware, merchandise; perhaps connected with *worth* (value), *wary*.] Articles of merchandise; goods; commodities; manufactures of a particular kind: properly a collective noun, as in the compounds china*ware*, hard*ware*, tin*ware*, &c., but generally used in the plural form when articles for sale of different kinds are meant.—**Warehouse**, wār'hous, *n.* A house in which wares or goods are kept; a building for storing imported goods on which customs dues have not been paid; a store for the sale of goods wholesale; also a building for storage purposes.—*v.t.* To deposit or secure in a warehouse.—**Warehouseman**, wār'hous-man, *n.* One who keeps a warehouse; one who is employed in a warehouse.

Ware, wār, *n.* [A.Sax. *wár*, sea-weed; akin D. *wier*, sea-weed.] A name of various sea-weeds, employed as a manure, in the manufacture of kelp, &c.

Warfare. Under WAR.

Warily, Wariness. Under WARY.

Warlike. Under WAR.

Warlock, wạr'lok, *n.* [Icel. *varthlokur*, *varthlokkur*, lit. weird songs or spells, the name being transferred from the things to the person who used them, or O.E. *waerloga*, deceiver.] A male witch; a wizard or sorcerer.

Warm, wạrm, *a.* [A.Sax. *wearm*, warm = O.Sax., G., and D. *warm*, Icel. *varmr*, Dan. and Sw. *varm*, warm; comp. O.L. *formus*, Gr. *thermos*, warm.] Having heat in a moderate degree; not cold; having the sensation of heat; feeling hot; flushed; subject to heat; having prevalence of heat (a *warm* climate); full of zeal, ardour, or affection; zealous; ardent (a *warm* friend); somewhat ardent or excitable; irritable (a *warm* temper); somewhat excited; nettled; brisk; keen (a *warm* contest); wealthy; moderately rich; well-off (*colloq.*).—*Warm colours*, such as have yellow or yellow-red for their basis: opposed to *cold colours*, such as blue and its compounds.—*Warm tints*, *cold tints*, modifications of the preceding. —*v.t.* To make warm; to communicate a moderate degree of heat to; to interest; to excite ardour or zeal in; to animate; to inspirit; to give life to; to flush; to cause to glow. — *v.i.* To become moderately heated; to become ardent or animated.—*n.* A warming; a heating. (*Colloq.*)—**Warm-blooded**, *a.* Having warm blood: *zool.* said of mammals and birds, in contradistinction to fishes, amphibians, and reptiles, or cold-blooded animals.—**Warm-hearted**, *a.* Having warmth of heart; cordial; sincere; hearty.—**Warm-heartedness**, *n.* Warmth or kindness of heart; cordiality.—**Warming-pan**, *n.* A covered pan with a long handle for warming a bed with ignited coals.—**Warmly**, wạrm'li, *adv.* In a warm manner; with warmth or heat; with warmth of feeling; eagerly; ardently; hotly. — **Warmth, Warmness**, wạrmth, wạrm'nes, *n.* The quality or state of being warm; the sensation of heat; gentle heat; hearty kindness or good feeling; ardour; zeal; fervour; earnestness; slight anger or irritation; *painting*, that glowing effect which arises from the use of warm colours.

Warn, wạrn, *v.t.* [A.Sax. *warnian*, *wearnian*, to warn, to take heed, from *wearn*, refusal, denial; Icel. and Sw. *varna*, G. *warnen*, to warn; of same origin as *ware*, *wary*.] To give notice of approaching or probable danger or evil, that it may be avoided; to caution against anything that may prove injurious; to advise; to expostulate with; to inform previously; to give notice to.—**Warner**, wạr'nėr, *n.* One who warns.—**Warning**, wạr'ning, *n.* Caution against danger, or against faults or evil practices which incur danger; previous notice; a notice given to terminate the relation of master and servant or landlord and tenant.—*Warning coloration*, in animals, conspicuous marks and colours that indicate the presence of obnoxious qualities.—**Warningly**, wạr'ning-li, *adv.* In a warning manner.

Warp, wạrp, *v.t.* [From A.Sax. *weorpan*, pret. *wearp*, to throw, to cast; Icel. *verpa*, to throw, and reflexively, to warp or shrink, also *varpa*, to throw; Dan. *varpe*, to warp a vessel; Goth. *vairpan*, G. *werfen*, to throw. Akin *wrap*. As to first meaning comp. *cast* in sense of twist.] To turn or twist out of shape, or out of a straight direction, by contraction (the heat of the sun *warps* boards); to turn aside from the true direction; to pervert (the mind or judgment); *naut.* to tow or move, as a ship into a required position, by means of a rope attached to something; *agri.* to fertilize by artificial inundation from rivers which hold large quantities of earthy matter in suspension.—*v.i.* To twist, or be twisted from straightness; to turn from a straight, true, or proper course; to deviate; to swerve; to wind yarn off bobbins to form the warp of a web; *naut.* to work forward by means of a rope.—*n.* [A.Sax. *wearp*, the warp of cloth, from *weorpan*, to cast; so D. *werp*, O.H.G. *warf*, warp.] *Weaving*, the threads which are extended lengthwise in the loom and crossed by the woof; *naut.* a rope used in moving a ship by attachment to an anchor, post, &c.; a towing-line; *agri.* an alluvial deposit of water artificially introduced upon low lands; a tidal deposit of marine silt; the twist of wood in drying.—**Warped**, wạrpt, *p.* and *a.* Twisted by shrinking; perverted; unnatural—**Warper**, wạr'pėr, *n.* One who warps; one who or that which prepares warp for weaving.—**Warping**, wạrp'ing, *v.* *Aviation*, moving the control lever sideways so as to change the angle of incidence on a wing with a view to raising or lowering it.—**Warping-machine, Warping-mill**, *n.* A machine for laying out the threads of a warp and dividing them into two sets.

Warrant, wor'ant, *v.t.* [O.Fr. *warantir*, *garantir* (Fr. *garantir*), to warrant, *warant*, *garant*, a warrant, from O.H.G. *warjan*, to give bail for, to defend; G. *gewähren*, to warrant; akin *wary*, *ward*.] To give an assurance or surety to; to guarantee; to give authority or power to do or forbear anything; to justify, sanction, support, allow; to give one's word for or concerning; to assert as undoubted; to furnish sufficient grounds or evidence to; to give a pledge or assurance to or in regard to (to *warrant* goods to be as said).—*n.* An authority granted by one person to another to do something which he has not otherwise a right to do; a document or anything that authorizes an act; security; guarantee; pledge; a voucher; an attestation; a document or negotiable writing authorizing a person to receive money or other thing; an instrument giving power to arrest or execute an offender; *army* and *navy*, a writ or authority inferior to a commission.—**Warrantable**, wor'ant-a-bl, *a.* Justifiable; defensible; lawful. — **Warrantableness**, wor'ant-a-bl-nes, *n.*—**Warrantably**, wor'ant-a-bli, *adv.* Justifiably; legally.—**Warranter**, wor'ant-ėr, *n.* One who warrants.—**Warrant-officer**, *n.* An officer in the army or navy next below a commissioned officer, acting under a warrant from a department of state, and not under a commission.—**Warranty**, wor'an-ti, *n.* A legal deed of security; any promise from a vendor to a purchaser, that the thing sold is such as represented; *insur.* an absolute condition, non-compliance with which voids the insurance.

Warren, wor'en, *n.* [O.Fr. *warene*, *warenne*, of similar origin to *warrant*.] A piece of ground appropriated to the breeding and preservation of game or rabbits; a preserve for keeping fish in a river.—**Warrener**, wor'en-ėr, *n.* The keeper of a warren.

Warrior. Under WAR.

Warrison, war'i-son, *n.* [*War-sound*.] An improper formation ('sound the warrison') by Scott in the *Lay*, iv, 418. Rightly means 'reward'.

Wart, wạrt, *n.* [A.Sax. *wearte*, a wart = Icel. *varta*, Dan. *vorte*, D. *wrat*, G. *warze*; same root as L. *verruca*, a wart.] A small dry hard growth in the skin, most common on the hands; a spongy excrescence on the hinder pasterns of a horse; a roundish glandule on the surface of plants.—**Wart-hog**, *n.* A species of swine found in Africa notable for its large tusks and warty growths or excrescences on the cheeks.—**Warty**, wạr'ti, *a.* Covered with warts; of the nature of warts.

Wary, wā'ri, *a.* [Formed from *ware*, wary, aware (the *-ware* of *a-ware*, *be-ware*), from A.Sax. *wær*, cautious = Icel. *varr*, Dan. and Sw. *var*, Goth. *vars*; from root of L. *vereor*, to regard, to dread. (REVERE.) Of kindred origin are *warn*, *warrant*, *ward*, *guard*, &c.] Carefully watching against deception, artifices, and dangers; ever on one's guard; cautious; circumspect; prudent; careful, as to doing or not doing something.—**Warily**, wā'ri-li, *adv.* In a wary manner; cautiously.—**Wariness**, wā'ri-nes, *n.* The quality or state of being wary.

Was, woz. [A.Sax. *ic wæs*, I was, *hé wæs*, he was, *thú waere*, thou wert, pl. *waeron*, were; inf. *wesan*, to be; Icel. *vesa* or *vera*, to be; G. *wesen*, to be, *war*, I was; Dan. *være*, Sw. *vara*, to be; allied to Goth. *visan*, to dwell, to be; Skr. *vas*, to dwell. See also AM, BE.] The past tense of the verb to be; as, I *was*, thou *wast* or *wert*, he *was*; we, you, or they *were*. The subjunctive is seen in if I *were*, or *were* I to go; if thou *wert*; *wert* thou; *were* they, &c.

Wash, wosh, *v.t.* [A.Sax. *wascan*, to wash = L.G. *wasken*, Dan. *vaske*, Sw. *vaska*, G. *waschen*; same root as *water*.] To apply water or other liquid to, for the purpose of cleansing; to scour, scrub, or the like, with water or other liquid; to cover with water or other liquid; to overflow or flow along; to wet copiously; to remove by ablution, literally or figuratively: with *away*, *off*, *out*, &c.; to sweep away by a rush of water (a man *washed* overboard); to cover with a watery or thin coat of colour; to tint lightly or thinly; to overlay with a thin coat of metal; to separate from earthy and lighter matters by the action of water (to *wash* gold, to *wash* ores).—*v.i.* To perform the act of ablution on one's own person; to perform the business of cleansing clothes in water; to stand the operation of washing without being injured, spoiled, or destroyed; hence, to stand being put to the proof; to stand the test (*colloq.*).—*n.* The act of washing; the clothes washed on one occasion; the flow or sweep of water; a piece of ground sometimes overflowed; a shallow; waste liquor containing the refuse of food, such as is often given to pigs; swill or swillings; the fermented wort from which spirit is extracted; a liquid used for toilet purposes, such as a liquid dentifrice, a hair-wash, &c.; a lotion; a thin coat of colour spread over surfaces; a thin coat of metal.—**Washable**, wosh'a-bl, *a.* Capable of being washed.—**Wash-ball**, *n.* A ball of soap, to be used in washing the hands or face.—**Wash-board**, *n.* A board with a ribbed surface for washing clothes on; a broad thin board on the edge of a boat to prevent the sea from breaking over; a board round the bottom of the walls of a room.—**Washer**, wosh'ėr, *n.* One who or that which washes; an annular disc or flat ring of metal, leather, or other material, used to reduce friction, form an air-tight or water-tight packing, &c.—**Washerwoman**, wosh'ėr-wụm-an, *n.* A woman that washes clothes for hire.—**Washhand-basin**, *n.* A basin for washing the hands in.—**Washhand-stand**, *n.* A stand for holding one or more wash-hand-basins, &c.—**Wash-house, Washing-house**, *n.* A house, generally fitted with boilers, tubs, &c., for washing clothes, &c.—**Washiness**, wosh'i-nes, *n.* The quality of being washy.—**Washing**, wosh'ing, *n.* A cleansing with water; ablution; clothes washed at one time; a wash.—**Washing-machine**, *n.* A machine for washing clothes.—**Wash-leather**, *n.* A kind of soft leather, usually from split sheepskins, used for domestic purposes, as cleaning glass or plate, polishing, &c.—

Wash-out, *n.* The washing out or away of earth by rain or a flood; a complete failure or defeat.—**Wash-pot**, *n.* A vessel in which anything is washed. (O.T.)—**Wash-tub**, *n.* A tub in which clothes are washed.—**Washy**, wosh'i, *a.* Watery; too much diluted; thin; feeble; worthless.

Wasp, wosp, *n.* [A.Sax. *wæsp*, by metathesis for *wæps*; D. *wesp*, G. *wespe*; cog. L. *vespa* (for *vepsa*), a wasp, Lith. *wapsa*, a gad-fly.] The common name applied to various hymenopterous insects which live in societies, and consist of males, females, and neuters, the latter two classes being armed with powerful and in some cases highly venomous stings; *fig.* a person characterized by ill-nature, irritability, or petty malignity.—**Waspish**, wos'pish, *a.* Resembling a wasp in form; having a wasp-like waist; snappish; irritable; irascible.

Wassail, wos'el, *n.* [A.Sax. *wes hael*, *wæs hael*, be hale, that is, health be to you, an old pledge or salutation in drinking—*wes*, imper. of *wesan*, to be. WAS, HALE.] A festive occasion where drinking and pledging of healths are indulged in; a drinking bout; a carouse; the liquor used on such occasions, especially about Christmas or the New Year.—*v.i.* To hold a merry drinking meeting.—**Wassail-bowl**, *n.* A large bowl in which wassail was mixed and set before a festive company.—**Wassailer**, wos'el-ėr, *n.* One who takes part at a wassail or drinking feast; a reveler.

Wassermann test, väs'er-män, *n.* A serum reaction used for the detection of syphilis; named after August Wassermann, a German bacteriologist (1866-1925).

Waste, wāst, *v.t.*—*wasted*, *wasting*. [O.Fr. *waster*, to waste, lay waste (later *gaster*, Mod.Fr. *gâter*, to spoil), from O.H.G. *wasten*, from L. *vastare*, to lay waste, *vastus*, vast, waste. VAST.] To bring to desolation; to devastate; to desolate; to ravage; to wear away gradually; to spend uselessly, vainly, or foolishly; to squander; *law*, to damage, injure, or impair, as an estate, voluntarily, or by allowing the buildings, fences, or the like, to go to decay.—*v.i.* To decrease gradually; to be consumed; to dwindle.—*a.* Resembling a desert or wilderness; desolate; not cultivated; producing no crops nor timber; rendered unfit for its intended use; spoiled in making or handling; refuse.—*To lay waste*, to render desolate; to devastate.—*n.* The act of wasting or process of being wasted; lavish expenditure; gradual decrease in quantity, strength, value, &c.; a desert region; a wilderness; a tract of land not in cultivation, and producing little or no herbage or wood.—*To run to waste*, to become useless, exhausted, or spoiled from want of proper attention, care, or skill.—**Wastage**, wās'tāj, *n.* Loss by use, decay, leakage, and the like.—**Waste-basket**, *n.* A basket used in offices, &c., to hold waste papers.—**Waste-book**, *n.* Same as *Day-book*.—**Wasteful**, wāst'fụl, *a.* Causing waste; grossly thriftless; ruinous; lavish; prodigal.—**Wastefully**, wāst'fụl-li, *adv.* In a wasteful manner.—**Wastefulness**, wāst'fụl-nes, *n.* Lavishness; prodigality.—**Wasteness**, wāst'nes, *n.* The state of being waste; desolation.—**Waste-paper**, *n.* Spoiled or used paper.—**Waste-pipe**, *n.* A pipe for waste water, &c.; an overflow pipe.—**Waster**, wās'tėr, *n.* One who wastes; a squanderer; a prodigal; a growth in the snuff of a candle causing it to waste; an article spoiled in the making.—**Wasting**, wās'ting, *p.* and *a.* Desolating; laying waste; sapping the bodily strength (a *wasting* disease).—**Wastrel**, wās'trel, *n.* An idle, worthless fellow; a waster.

Watch, woch, *n.* [A.Sax. *wæcce*, a watch, a watching, from stem of *wacan*, to wake. WAKE.] A keeping awake for the purpose of attending, guarding, preserving, or the like; a vigil; vigilant attention; vigilance; a guard or number of guards; a watchman or body of watchmen; the time during which a person or body of persons are on guard; a division of the night, when the precautionary setting of a watch is most generally necessary; *naut.* the period of time occupied by each part of a ship's crew alternately while on duty; a certain part of the officers and crew of a vessel who together attend to working her for an allotted time; a small time-piece, now universally circular in shape, to be carried in the pocket or about the person.—*v.i.* To be or continue without sleep; to keep vigil; to be attentive, circumspect, or vigilant; to be closely observant; to give heed; to act as a watchman, guard, sentinel, or the like; to look forward with expectation; to be expectant; to wait.—*To watch over*, to be cautiously observant of; to guard from error and danger.—*v.t.* To look with close attention at or on; to keep a sharp look-out on or for; to regard with vigilance and care; to have in keeping; to tend; to guard; to look for; to wait for.—**Watch-dog**, *n.* A dog kept to watch or guard premises and property.—**Watcher**, woch'ėr, *n.* One who watches.—**Watch-fire**, *n.* A fire kept up in the night as a signal or for the use of a guard.—**Watchful**, woch'fụl, *a.* Careful to observe; observant; giving wary attention; vigilant.—**Watchfully**, woch'fụl-li, *adv.* Vigilantly; heedfully.—**Watchfulness**, woch'fụl-nes, *n.* Vigilance; heedfulness; wary attention.—**Watch-glass**, *n.* A concavo-convex glass for covering the dial of a watch.—**Watch-guard**, *n.* A chain, cord, ribbon, &c., by which a watch is attached to the person.—**Watch-house**, *n.* A house in which a watch or guard is placed; a guard-house; a lock-up.—**Watch-key**, *n.* A small key by which a watch is wound up.—**Watch-maker**, *n.* One whose occupation is to make and repair watches.—**Watch-making**, *n.* The art of making watches; the business of a watch-maker.—**Watchman**, woch'man, *n.* A person set to pay heedful attention over something; one who holds a post of observation; a guard; a sort of night policeman; the care-taker of a building by night.—**Watch-pocket**, *n.* A small pocket for carrying a watch.—**Watch-spring**, *n.* The mainspring of a watch.—**Watch-tower**, *n.* A tower on which a sentinel is placed to watch for enemies.—**Watchword**, woch'wėrd, *n.* The word given to sentinels and such as have occasion to visit guards, as a token by which a friend is known from an enemy; a countersign; a password, motto, or maxim.

Watchet, wochet, *n.* or *a.* [Origin doubtful.] Light blue; pale blue; sky-blue.

Water, wạ'tėr, *n.* [A.Sax. *wæter*, water = O.Sax. *watar*, D. and L.G. *water*, G. *wasser*; akin to Icel. *vatn*, Sw. *vatten*; Goth. *wato*, water; from root seen also in L. *udus*, wet, *unda*, a wave (whence *undulate*); Gr. *hydōr*, Skr. *udan*, water. Akin *wet*, *otter*.] A compound substance, consisting of hydrogen and oxygen in the proportion of 2 volumes of the former gas to 1 volume of the latter; a fluid covering about three-fifths of the entire surface of the earth, and forming an essential constituent of vegetable and animal organisms; this fluid as opposed to *land* (to travel by *water*); any natural collection of it; sometimes used of other fluids, humours, &c.; urine; the colour or lustre of a diamond or other precious stone (a diamond of the first *water*, that is, perfectly pure and transparent).—*Water of crystallization*, the water which unites chemically with many salts during the act of crystallizing.—*Water-vascular system*, in echinoderms, a set of tubes containing sea-water: concerned with breathing and locomotion.—*To hold water*, to be able to retain water without leaking; hence, *fig.* to be correct, valid, or well-grounded: said of arguments, theories, &c.—*v.t.* To irrigate; to overflow or wet with water; to supply with water or streams of water (a country well *watered*); to supply with water for drink (to *water* horses); to subject to a calendering process, as silk, &c., in order to make it exhibit a variety of undulated reflections and plays of light.—*v.i.* To shed water or liquid matter (his eyes *water*); to take in water (the ship put into port to *water*); to gather saliva as a symptom of appetite; to have a longing desire (his mouth *watered*).—**Water-bailiff**, *n.* A custom-house officer in a port for searching ships; one who watches a salmon river to prevent poaching.—**Water-bath**, *n.* A bath of water; *chem.* a bath of water at a certain temperature, in which vessels may stand for heat or evaporation.—**Water-bed**, *n.* A bed composed of india-rubber cloth inflated with water on which a patient rests; a hydrostatic bed.—**Water-boatman**, *n.* The boat-fly.—**Water-bottle**, *n.* A bottle for holding drinking water.—**Water-butt**, *n.* A large open-headed cask as a reservoir for rain-water.—**Water-carriage**, *n.* Conveyance by water.—**Water-cart**, *n.* A cart carrying water for sale or for watering streets, gardens, &c.—**Water-cask**, *n.* A strong barrel in ships for holding water for those on board.—**Water-cement**, *n.* A cement which hardens under water.—**Water-clock**, *n.* A clepsydra.—**Water-closet**, *n.* A privy in which the discharges are removed by means of water through a waste-pipe.—**Water-color**, *n.* A pigment or color carefully ground up with water and isinglass or other mucilage instead of oil.—*Water-color painting*, painting in which water-colors are used instead of oil-colors; a painting done in water-colors.—**Water-course**, *n.* A stream of water; a channel.—**Watercress**, *n.* An aquatic plant much used as a salad.—**Water-cure**, *n.* Hydropathy.—**Water-dog**, *n.* A dog having remarkable swimming powers.—**Watered**, wạ'tėrd, *a.* Having a wavy appearance on the surface (*watered* silk or paper).—**Waterfall**, wạ'tėr-fạl, *n.* A fall or perpendicular descent of the water of a river or stream; a cascade; a cataract.—**Water-flag**, *n.* A plant, a species of iris.—**Water-flea**, *n.* A minute animal belonging to the entomostraca.—**Water-fowl**, *n.* A bird that lives about rivers, lakes, or on or near the sea; an aquatic fowl; such birds collectively; wild-fowl.—**Water-frame**, *n.* Arkwright's frame for spinning cotton, at first driven by water; a throstle.—**Water-gall**, *n.* [O.E. *galle*, Icel. *galli*, G. *galle*, fault, flaw, imperfection.] An appearance in the sky known to presage rain; a rainbow-coloured spot; a weather-gall.—**Water-gas**, *n.* An illuminating gas obtained by decomposing water.—**Water-gauge**, **Water-gage**, *n.* An instrument for measuring or ascertaining the depth or quantity of water, as in the boiler of a steam-engine.—**Water-glass**, *n.* A soluble alkaline silicate made by boiling silica in an alkali, as soda or potash, used to give surfaces, as of walls, a durable covering resembling glass.—**Water-god**, *n.* A deity that presides over the water.—**Water-gruel**, *n.* A liquid food composed of water and a small portion of meal or other farinaceous substance boiled and seasoned.—**Water-hammer**, *n.* The concussion of moving water against the sides of a pipe, especially a steam pipe.—**Water-hen**, *n.* The gallinule or moor-hen.—**Water-hog**, *n.* A South American rodent mammal of aquatic habits; the capybara; also, an animal allied to the wart-hog.—**Wateriness**, wạ'tėr-i-nes, *n.* The state of being watery.—**Watering**, wạ'tėr-ing, *n.* The act of supplying with water; the process of giving a wave-like appearance or ornamentation whereby an article is made to exhibit a wavy lustre and different plays of light; tabbying.—**Watering-place**, *n.* A place where water may be obtained, as for a ship, for cattle, &c.; a place to which people resort at certain seasons in order to drink mineral waters, or for bathing, &c., as at the sea-side.—**Watering-can**, **Watering-pot**, *n.* A hand vessel for sprinkling water on plants.—**Watering-trough**, *n.* A trough in which cattle and horses drink.—**Water-jacket**, *n.* An outer casing containing cooling water, e.g. in an internal-combustion engine.—**Waterless**, wạ'tėr-les, *a.* Destitute of water.—**Water-level**, *n.* A levelling instrument in which water is employed, consisting of a bent glass tube open at both ends, and having the ends turned up.—**Water-lily**, *n.* The common name of several genera of aquatic plants distinguished for their beautiful flowers and large floating leaves.—**Water-line**, *n.* The line of floatation in a ship; one of those horizontal lines supposed to be described by the surface of the water on the bottom or side of a ship.—**Water-logged**, *a.* Lying like a log on the water: applied to a ship when by leaking and receiving a great quantity of water into her hold she has become so heavy as to be nearly or altogether unmanageable, though still keeping afloat.—**Waterman**, wą'tėr-man, *n.* A boatman; a ferryman; one who plies for hire on rivers, &c.—**Water-mark**, *n.* The mark indicating the rise and fall of water; any distinguishing device or devices indelibly stamped in the substance of a sheet of paper during the process of manufacture.—**Water-meadow**, *n.* A meadow that may be kept in a state of fertility by being overflowed with water at certain seasons.—**Water-melon**, *n.* A plant and its fruit extensively cultivated in dry hot parts of the world, the fruit abounding with a sweetish refreshing liquor, and the pulp remarkably delicious.—**Water-meter**, *n.* An instrument that measures the quantity of water that passes through it, as a gas-meter measures gas.—**Water-mill**, *n.* A mill whose machinery is moved by water.—**Water-mole**, *n.* The duck-mole or ornithorhynchus.—**Water-murrain**, *n.* A disease among cattle.—**Water-newt**, *n.* A name of two newts from their frequenting ponds, ditches, &c.—**Water-ousel**, *n.* The dipper, a European bird of the thrush family that can walk about under the surface of water.—**Water-parsnip**, *n.* Skirret.—**Water-parting**, *n.* A watershed.—**Water-pipe**, *n.* A pipe for the conveyance of water.—**Water-pitcher**, *n.* A pitcher for holding water; a pitcher-plant.—**Water-plane.** See HYDROPLANE.—**Water-plant**, *n.* Any plant that lives entirely in water, or requires a great deal of water for its existence.—**Water-pot**, *n.* A vessel for holding water; a watering-pot.—**Water-power**, *n.* The power of water employed or capable of being employed as a prime mover in machinery.—**Water-pox**, *n.* A variety of chicken-pox.—**Water-privilege**, *n.* The right to use running water to turn machinery.—**Waterproof**, wą'tėr-pröf, *a.* Impervious to water; so firm and compact as not to admit water.—*n.* Cloth rendered waterproof; an over-coat or other article of dress made of such cloth.—*v.t.* To render impervious to water, as cloth, leather, &c.—**Water-rail**, *n.* A bird, a species of rail, the only one found in Europe.—**Water-ram**, *n.* Same as *Hydraulic ram.* Under RAM.—**Water-rat**, *n.* A rodent animal of the vole genus which lives in the banks of streams or lakes.—**Water-rate**, *n.* A rate or tax for the supply of water.—**Water-sapphire**, *n.* A transparent precious stone of an intense blue colour found in Ceylon.—**Watershed**, wą'tėr-shed, *n.* [*Shed* has sense of parting.] An imaginary line which runs along the ridge of separation between adjacent seas, lakes, or river-basins, and represents the limit from which water naturally flows in opposite directions.—**Water-side**, *n.* The bank or margin of a stream or lake; the sea-shore.—**Water-snake**, *n.* A snake or serpent that lives in water; a sea-snake.—**Water-spaniel**, *n.* The name of two varieties of the spaniel, excellent swimmers.—**Water-spout**, *n.* A meteorological phenomenon frequently observed at sea, and consisting of a pillar of dark cloud caused to revolve by a whirlwind and forming a vast funnel, which descends to the surface of the sea and draws up a certain quantity of spray or water; a water-spout (so-called) on land is merely a very heavy shower.—**Water-supply**, *n.* The amount of water supplied to a community.—**Water-tap**, *n.* A tap or cock by which water may be drawn from any supply.—**Water-tight**, *a.* So tight as to retain or not to admit water; stanch.—**Water-twist**, *n.* A kind of cotton twist, first made by the water-frame.—**Water-vole**, *n.* A water-rat.—**Water-wagtail**, *n.* A wagtail.—**Water-way**, *n.* That part of a river, arm of the sea, &c., through which vessels enter or depart; the fair-way; also, a name given to the thick planks along the scuppers of a ship.—**Water-wheel**, *n.* A kind of wheel for raising water in large quantities, as the Persian wheel; a wheel moved by water, and employed to turn machinery.—**Water-works**, *n.pl.* The aggregate of constructions and appliances for the collection, storage, and distribution of water for the use of communities.—**Water-worn**, *a.* Worn by the action of water; smoothed by the action of running water.—**Watery**, wą'-tėr-i, *a.* Pertaining to water; resembling water; thin or transparent, as a liquid; consisting of water; abounding in, filled with, or containing water; wet; moist; tasteless; insipid; vapid; spiritless.—**Water-yam**, *n.* The lattice-plant of Madagascar.

Watt, wot, *n.* [After James *Watt*.] The practical unit of power, or rate of conveying energy, used in electricity: the power of a current of one ampere driven by an electrical pressure of one volt, viz. 10^7 ergs per second.—**Wattmeter**, wot'mē-tėr, *n.* [*Watt*, Gr. *metron*, a measure.] An instrument for measuring the energy per second developed in a given part of an electric current.

Wattle, wot'l, *n.* [A.Sax. *watel*, *watul*, a wattle, a hurdle, &c.] A hurdle made of interwoven rods or wands; the fleshy lobe that grows under the throat of the domestic fowl, or any appendage of the like kind.—*v.t.*—*wattled*, *wattling*. To twist, interweave, or interlace (twigs or branches); to plat (to *wattle* a hedge); to form by platting twigs.—**Wattled**, wot'ld, *a.* Furnished with wattles, as a cock or turkey; in *her.* the term indicates that the wattles of a cock or cockatrice are of a different tincture from the rest of the body.—**Wattle-turkey**, *n.* Same as *Brush-turkey*.—**Wattling**, wot'ling, *n.* A wattled structure.

Wattle, Wattle-tree, wot'l, *n.* A name in Australia for various species of acacia, some of them with beautiful flowers.

Wattle-bird, wot'l, *n.* A name of certain Australian birds of the honey-eater family, having wattles hanging below the ear.

Wave, wāv, *v.i.*—*waved*, *waving*. [From A.Sax. *wafian*, to waver or hesitate through astonishment; Icel. *veifa*, to wave, to vibrate; O.G. *waben*, to fluctuate. *Waver*, *waft*, are derivative forms.] To move loosely backwards and forwards; to float or flutter; to undulate; to be moved as a signal; to beckon.—*v.t.* To move one way and the other; to brandish; to signal to by waving the hand or the like; to beckon.—*n.* [O.E. *wawe*, a wave of the sea, from A.Sax. *wæg*, a wave (akin to *wag*); modified by the verb above.] A swell or ridge on the surface of water or other liquid resulting from the oscillatory motion of its component particles, when disturbed from their position of rest by any force; especially, a swell or surge on the surface of the sea or other large body of water by the action of the wind; a billow; *physics*, a vibration propagated from one set of particles of an elastic medium to the adjoining set, and so on; anything resembling a wave; one of a series of undulating inequalities on a surface; an undulation; a swelling outline; that which advances and recedes, rises and falls, comes and goes, &c., like a wave; the undulating line or streak of lustre on cloth watered and calendered; a signal made by waving the hand, a flag, or the like.—**Wave-length**, *n.* The distance between the crests of or hollows between two adjacent waves.—**Waveless**, wāv'les, *a.* Free from waves.—**Wavelet**, wāv'let, *n.* A small wave; a ripple on water.—**Wave-worn**, *a.* Worn by the waves.—**Waviness**, wā'vi-nes, *n.* The state or quality of being wavy.—**Wavy**, wā'vi, *a.* Rising or swelling in waves; full of waves; *bot.* undulating on the border or on the surface.

Wave, wāv, *v.t.* Same as *Waive*.

Wavellite, wā'vel-īt, *n.* [From Dr. *Wavel*, the discoverer.] A mineral, a phosphate of aluminium.

Waver, wā'vėr, *v.i.* [A freq. corresponding to the verb to *wave*, to fluctuate = Icel. *vafra*, to hover.] To play or move to and fro; to flutter; to be unsettled in opinion; to be undetermined; to fluctuate: to vacillate; to hesitate; to be in danger of falling or failing; to totter; to reel.—**Waverer**, wā'vėr-ėr, *n.* One who wavers; one who is unsettled in doctrine, faith, or opinion.—**Waveringly**, wā'vėr-ing-li, *adv.* In a wavering, doubtful, or fluctuating manner.—**Waveringness**, wā'vėr-ing-nes, *n.*

Wavy, wā'vi, *n.* [American-Indian *wawa*.] The snow-goose.

Wax, waks, *n.* [A.Sax. *weax*, wax = G. *wachs*, Icel. and Sw. *vax*, Dan. *vox*, D. *vas*; cog. Pol. *vosk*, Rus. *voska*, Lith. *waszkas*, wax.] A thick, viscid, tenacious substance, excreted by bees from their bodies, and employed in the construction of their cells; any substance resembling this in appearance or properties; a vegetable product which may be regarded as a concrete fixed oil; vegetable wax; a tenacious substance excreted in the ear; ear-wax; a substance used in sealing letters; sealing-wax; a thick resinous substance used by shoemakers for rubbing their thread.—*v.t.* To smear or rub with wax.—**Wax-candle**, *n.* A candle made of wax.—**Wax-cloth**, *n.* A popular but erroneous name for *Floor-cloth*.—**Wax-doll**, *n.* A child's doll made or partly made of wax.—**Waxen**, wak'sn, *a.* Made of wax; resembling wax; covered with wax.—**Wax-end, Waxed-end**, *n.* A thread pointed with a bristle and covered with shoemakers' *wax*, used in sewing boots and shoes.—**Waxiness**, wak'si-nes, *n.* The state or quality of being waxy.—**Wax-light**, *n.* A taper made of wax.—**Wax-modelling**, *n.* The art of forming models and figures in wax; ceroplastic.—**Wax-myrtle**, *n.* The candle-berry tree.—**Wax-palm**, *n.* A species of S. American palm, which exudes a thick secretion, consisting of resin and wax.—**Wax-wing**, *n.* The name of a dentirostral bird, so called because it has small, oval, horny appendages on the secondaries of the wings of the colour of red sealing-wax.—**Wax-work**, *n.* Work in wax; figures formed of wax in imitation of real beings; a place where a collection of such figures is exhibited.—**Waxy**, wak'si, *a.* Resembling wax; made of wax; abounding in wax.

Wax, waks, *v.i.*—pret. *waxed*; pp. *waxed* or *waxen* (the latter now only poetical). [A.Sax. *weaxen*, to grow, to become = Icel. *vaxa*, Dan. *voxe*, Sw. *växa*, G. *wachsen*, D. *wassen*, to wax; allied to L. *augeo* (whence *augment*), Skr. *vakshāmi*, to increase, to wax; from a root seen also in L. *vigor*, E. *vigour*, *vegetable*, &c.] To increase in size; to grow; to become larger or show a larger disc (as the moon); to become (to *wax* strong).

Way, wā, *n.* [A.Sax. *weg*, a way, road, passage=Dan. *vei*, Sw. *väg*, Icel. *vegr*, D. and G. *weg*, Goth. *vigs*, way; from a root meaning to move, go, take, carry, seen also in E. *wagon*, *weigh*, *wain*, L. *via*, a way (in *viaduct*), *veho*, to carry (whence *vehicle*), *velum*, a sail (E. *veil*), *vehemens*, E. *vehement*, &c.] A track or path along or over which one passes or journeys; a path, route, or road of any kind; distance (a good *way* off); path or course in life; direction of motion; means by which anything is accomplished; scheme; device; plan; method or manner of proceeding; mode; style; usual or habitual mode of acting or behaving; plan or mode of action selected; course approved of as one's own; sphere of observation (to come in one's *way*); *naut.* progress or motion through the water; *pl.* the timbers on which a ship is launched.—*To give way*, to break or fall, as under pressure or a strain; to make room for another person passing; to yield; to submit.—*To go one's way* or *ways*, to take one's departure; to set out.—*To go the way of all the earth*, to die. (O.T.)—*To lead the way*, to go in front; to act the part of a leader, guide, &c.—*To make way*, to give room for passing; to stand aside; to give place.—*To make one's way*, to find and keep a successful career; to advance in life by one's own exertions.—*To take one's way*, to follow one's own settled opinion, inclination, or fancy.—*By the way*, in the course of the journey; in passing; without necessary connection with the main subject; parenthetically.—*By way of*, as being; to serve as or in lieu of.—*In the way*, in a position or of such a nature as to obstruct or impede.—*In the way of*, in a favourable position for doing or getting.—*On the way*, in going or travelling along; advancing towards completion.—*Out of the way*, not in the proper course or position; not where it can be found or met with; concealed or lost; out of the beaten track; hence, extraordinary; striking.—*Milky Way*. GALAXY.—*Right of way*, in *law*, a privilege which a person or persons have of going over another's ground.—*Ways and means*, methods; resources; facilities; means for raising money for governmental purposes; resources of revenue. — **Way-bill**, *n.* A list of passengers or goods carried by rail or other public conveyance.—**Wayfarer**, wā'fā-rėr, *n.* One who journeys or travels; a traveller; a passenger.—**Wayfaring**, wā'fā-ring, *a.* Being on a journey; travelling.—**Waylay**, wā-lā' or wā'lā, *v.t.*—pret. and pp. *waylaid*; ppr. *waylaying*. [*Way* and *lay*.] To watch insidiously in the way, with a view to seize, rob, or slay; to beset in ambush.—**Waylayer**, wā-lā'ėr or wā'lā-ėr, *n.* One who waylays. — **Wayleave**, wā'lēv, *n.* Permission, or right, to cross land.—**Wayless**, wā'les, *a.* Pathless; trackless.—**Wayside**, wā'sīd, *n.* The side, border, or edge of a road or highway.—*a.* Growing, situated, &c., by or near the side of the way (*wayside* flowers). — **Way-warden**, *n.* The surveyor of a road.—**Way-worn**, *a.* Worn or tired by travel.

Wayward, wā'wėrd, *a.* [For *awayward*; comp. *froward, toward*.] Full of peevish caprices or whims; froward; perverse.—**Waywardly**, wā'wėrd-li, *adv.* Frowardly; perversely. — **Waywardness**, wā'wėrd-nes, *n.* Frowardness; perverseness.

Waywode, Waiwode, wā'wōd, *n.* [Pol. and Rus. *woyewoda*.] A name originally given to military commanders in various Slavonic countries, and afterwards to governors of towns and provinces.

We, wē, *pron.*, pl. of *I*. [A.Sax. *wē*, O.Sax. *we, wi*, Icel. *vér, vær*, Dan. and Sw. *vi*, D. *wij*, G. *wir*, Goth. *weis*; cog. Skr. *vayam*, we.] I and another or others; I and he or she, or I and they. *We* is frequently used by individuals, as editors, authors, and the like, when alluding to themselves, in order to avoid the appearance of egotism; and the plural style is also used by kings and otherwise heads of countries.

Weak, wēk, *a.* [Same as Icel. *veikr, veykr*, Sw. *vek*, Dan. *veg*, L.G. and D. *week*, G. *weich*, pliant, soft, weak, the A.Sax. form being *wác*; allied to Gr. (*v*)*eikein*, to yield. *Wick, wicker*, are from same root.] Not strong; wanting physical strength; feeble; infirm; not able to sustain a great weight or strain; easily broken; brittle; frail; wanting in ability to perform functions or office (a *weak* stomach, *weak* eyes); deficient in force of utterance (a *weak* voice); unfit for effective attack or defence (a *weak* fortress or body of troops); deficient in essential or characteristic ingredients (*weak* tea, &c.); deficient in intellectual power or judgment; silly; not decided or confirmed (*weak* faith); vacillating; wanting resolution; easily moved or worked upon; facile; wanting moral courage; not supported by the force of reason or truth (*weak* arguments); ineffective; not founded in right or justice; deficient in force of expression; not affecting the mind or the senses strongly; slight; *gram.* a term applied when inflection is effected by adding a letter or syllable (*love, loved* as compared with *rise, rose*): distinguished from *strong*. — *Weak side*, that side of a person's character on which he is most easily influenced or affected.—**Weaken**, wē'kn, *v.t.* To make weak or weaker; to enervate; to enfeeble.—*v.i.* To become weak or weaker. — **Weakener**, wē'kn-ėr, *n.* One who or that which weakens.—**Weakening**, wē'kn-ing, *p.* and *a.* Having the quality of reducing strength.—**Weak-headed**, *a.* Having a weak mind or intellect.—**Weakish**, wē'kish, *a.* Somewhat weak.—**Weakling**, wēk'ling, *n.* A feeble creature.—**Weakly**, wēk'li, *adv.* In a weak manner; with little physical strength; faintly; not forcibly; with feebleness of mind or intellect; injudiciously.—*a.* Not strong of constitution; infirm.—**Weakness**, wēk'nes, *n.* The state or quality of being weak; want of physical, mental, or moral strength; feebleness; want of strength of will or resolution; want of cogency; a defect; a failing.—**Weak-spirited**, *a.* Having a weak or timorous spirit; pusillanimous.

Weal, wēl, *n.* [A.Sax. *wela*, prosperity, lit. the state of being well, from *wel*, well; Dan. *vel*, Sw. *väl*. WELL.] A sound, healthy, prosperous state; welfare; prosperity; happiness. — The *public, general*, or *common weal*, the interest, well-being, prosperity of the community, state, or society. — **Wealth**, welth, *n.* [From *well*, and suffix *th*; comp. *health, sloth*, &c.] Well-being or welfare†; a collective term for riches; material possessions in all their variety; affluence; opulence; profusion; abundance; *pol. econ.* all and only such objects as have both utility and can be appropriated in exclusive possession, and therefore exchanged. —**Wealthy**, wel'thi, *a.* Having wealth; having large possessions in lands; affluent; rich; opulent; large in point of value; ample.—**Wealthily**, wel'thi-li, *adv.* In a wealthy manner; richly.—**Wealthiness**, wel'thi-nes, *n.* State of being wealthy; richness.

Weal, wēl, *n.* The mark of a stripe. WALE.

Weald, wēld, *a.* [A.Sax. *weald*, a forest tract; akin G. *wald*, a wood or forest. It is a form of *wold*.] A piece of open forest land; a wold: as a proper name applied to the tract of country lying between the North and South Downs of Kent and Sussex.—**Weald-clay**, *n.* The upper portion of the Wealden formation, composed of beds of clay, sandstone, &c.—**Wealden**, wēl'den, *a.* Pertaining to a weald; belonging to the Weald of Sussex and Kent.—*Wealden formation, group*, or *strata, geol.* a series of fresh-water strata belonging to the lower cretaceous epoch, and occurring between the uppermost beds of the oolite and the lower ones of the chalk formation. —*n.* The Wealden group or formation.

Wealth, Wealthy, &c. Under WEAL.

Wean, wēn, *v.t.* [A.Sax. *wenian*, to accustom, whence *áwenian*, to wean; Icel. *venja*, to accustom; Dan. *vænne*, to accustom, *vænne fra brystet*, to wean, lit. to accustom from the breast; from stem seen in *wont*. WONT.] To accustom to do without the mother's milk as food; to reconcile to the want of the breast; to detach or alienate, as the affections, from any object of desire; to reconcile to the want or loss of something; to disengage from any habit. — **Weanling**, wēn'ling, *n.* A child or other animal newly weaned.

Weapon, wep'on, *n.* [A.Sax. *waepen*, a weapon = Icel. *vápn*, Dan. *vaaben*, Sw. *vapen*, D. *wapen*, G. *waffe*, a weapon, Goth. *wepna* (pl.), arms.] Any instrument of offence or defence; an instrument for contest or for combating enemies; an instrument that may be classed among arms; *bot.* a thorn, prickle, sting, or the like, with which plants are furnished for defence.—**Weaponed**, wep'ond, *a.* Armed; furnished with weapons. — **Weaponless**, wep'on-les, *a.* Unarmed. — **Weaponschaw**, wep'on-sha, *n.* WAPENSHAW.

Wear, wār, *v.t.*—pret. *wore*, pp. *worn*. [A. Sax. *werian*, to wear (on the body); O.H.G. *werian*, to put on; Icel. *verja*, Goth. *wasjan*, to clothe; same root as in L. *vestis*, a garment. VEST.] To carry covering or appendant to the body, as clothes, weapons, ornaments, &c.; to have on; to deteriorate or destroy (clothes, &c.) by frequent or habitual use; to waste or impair by rubbing or attrition; to destroy by degrees; to produce by constant rubbing or attrition (to *wear* a channel); to have or exhibit an appearance of; to exhibit; to show (to *wear* a glad face).—*To wear away*, to impair or destroy by gradual or imperceptible action. —*To wear off*, to remove or diminish by attrition.—*To wear out*, to wear till useless; to waste by degrees; to tire or harass completely; to waste the strength of.—*v.i.* To be undergoing gradual impairment or diminution; to waste gradually; to pass away, as time; to make gradual progress (winter *wore* over).—*To wear well* or *ill*, to be wasted away slowly or quickly; to be affected by time or use with difficulty or easily.—*To wear off*, to pass away by degrees.—*n.* The act of wearing; the state of being worn; diminution by friction, use, time, or the like; style of dress; fashion or vogue in costume.—*Wear and tear*, loss or deterioration by wearing or ordinary use; tear and wear.—**Wearable**, wār'a-bl, *a.* Capable of being worn.—**Wearer**, wār'ėr, *n.* One who wears.—**Wearing**, wār'ing, *a.* Applied to what is worn (*wearing* apparel).

Wear, wār, *v.t.* [A form of *veer*.] *Naut.* to bring on the other tack by turning the vessel round, stern towards the wind.

Wear, wēr, *n.* WEIR.

Weary, wē'ri, *a.* [A.Sax. *wérig*, weary, perhaps from *wór*, a swampy place, the word originally having reference to the fatigue of walking on wet ground.] Having the strength much exhausted by toil or violent exertion; tired; fatigued; impatient of the continuance of something painful, irksome, or the like; sick; disgusted (*weary* of life); tiresome; irksome. —*v.t.*—*wearied, wearying*. To make weary; to tire; to fatigue; to exhaust the patience of; to harass by anything irksome.—*v.i.* To become weary; to tire.—**Wearily**, wē'ri-li, *adv.* In a weary manner; like one fatigued.—**Weariness**, wē'ri-nes, *n.* The state of being weary or tired; lassitude or exhaustion of strength induced by labour; fatigue; tedium; ennui; languor.—**Wearisome**, wē'ri-sum, *a.* Causing weariness; tiresome; irksome; monotonous.—**Wearisomely**, wē'ri-sum-li, *adv.* Tediously.—**Wearisomeness**, wē'ri-sum-nes, *n.* Tiresomeness; tediousness.

Weasand, wē'zand, *n.* [A.Sax. *wásend*, the windpipe; O.Fris. *wasende*, O.H.G. *weisunt*; perhaps named from the *wheezing* sound made in breathing. WHEEZE.] The windpipe. Written also *Wesand, Wezand*, and *Weazand*.

Weasel, wē'zl, *n.* [A.Sax. *wesle*=D. *wezel*, Dan. *væsel*, G. *wiesel*, weasel; perhaps akin to G. *wiese*, a meadow.] A small carnivorous animal distinguished by the length and slenderness of its body, feeding on mice, rats, moles, and small birds; a lean, mean, sneaking fellow.—**Weasel-faced**, *a.* Having a thin sharp face like a weasel.

Weather, weᴛʜ'ėr, *n.* [A.Sax. *weder*=D. and L.G. *weder*, Icel. *vethr*, Sw. *väder*, G. *wetter*; supposed to be from same root as *wind*. *Wither* is a derivative.] The atmospheric conditions at any particular time; the state of the atmosphere with respect to its temperature, pressure, humidity, motions, or any other meteorological phenomena.—*v.t.* To bear up against and come through, though with difficulty (to *weather* a gale); hence, to bear up against and overcome, as danger or difficulty; *naut.* to sail to the windward of.—*v.i.* *Geol.* to suffer change, disintegration, or waste, by exposure to the weather, as a rock or cliff. —*a. Naut.* toward the wind; windward: opposite of *lee*.—**Weather-beaten**, *a.* Beaten or harassed by the weather; seasoned by exposure to every kind of weather.—**Weather-board**, *n.* That side of a ship which is toward the wind; the windward side; one of a set of overlapping boards on a roof.—**Weather-boarding**, *n.* Overlapping boards nailed on roofs, &c. — **Weather-bound**, *a.* Delayed by bad weather. — **Weather-bow**, *n.* The side of a ship's bow that is to windward. — **Weather-cock**, weᴛʜ'ėr-kok, *n.* A vane or figure on the top of a spire, which turns with the wind and shows its direction: so called from the figure of a cock being a favorite form of vane; a fickle, inconstant person.—**Weathered**, weᴛʜ'ėrd, *p.* and *a.* Wasted, worn, or discolored by exposure to atmospheric influences: said of stones or rock surfaces.—**Weather-eye**, *n.* The eye that looks at the sky to forecast the weather.—*To keep one's weather-eye open* or *awake*, to be vigilantly on one's guard.—**Weather-gauge**, *n.* *Naut.* the situation of one ship to the windward of another; hence, advantage of position; superiority.—**Weather-gall**, *n.* Same as *Water-gall*.—**Weather-glass**, *n.* An instrument to indicate the state of the atmosphere; a term popularly applied to the barometer.—**Weather-gleam**, *n.* A peculiar clear sky near the horizon.—**Weathering**, weᴛʜ'ėr-ing, *n.* *Geol.* the action of the elements in altering rocks.—**Weatherly**, weᴛʜ'ėr-li, *a.* *Naut.* applied to a ship that makes very little leeway, but keeps close to the wind.—**Weather-molding**, *n.* A dripstone or canopy over a door or window, intended to throw off the rain.—**Weather-proof**, *a.* Proof against rough weather.—**Weather-prophet**, *n.* One skilled in foreseeing the changes or state of the weather.—**Weather-side**, *n.* *Naut.* that side of a ship under sail which is to windward.—**Weather-worn**, *a.* Worn by the action of the weather; weathered.

Weave, wēv, *v.t.*—pret. *wove*, ppr. *weaving*, pp. *woven*: pret. and pp. formerly often *weaved*. [A.Sax. *wefan*, to weave = D. *weven*, Icel. *vefa*, Dan. *væve*, G. *weben*, to weave; cog. Skr. *vabh*, to weave. Akin *web*, *weft*, *woof*.] To form by interlacing anything flexible, such as thread, yarn, filaments, or strips of different materials; to form by a loom; to form a tissue with; to entwine into a fabric; to unite by intermixture or close connection; to work up into one whole (to *weave* incidents into a story); to contrive or construct with design (to *weave* a plot).—*v.i.* To work with a loom; to become woven.—**Weaver**, wē'vėr, *n.* One who weaves or whose occupation is to weave; an aquatic insect, the whirlwig beetle; a weaver-bird.—**Weaver-bird**, *n.* An insessorial tropical bird, so called from its nest being woven of various vegetable substances.—**Weaver-fish**, *n.* WEEVER.—**Weaving**, wē'ving, *n.* The act of one who weaves; the act or art of producing cloth or other textile fabrics.

Weazen, wē'zn, *a.* [Icel. *visinn*, wizened, withered. WIZEN.] Thin; lean; wizened.

Web, web, *n.* [A.Sax. *web*, *webb*, from stem of *weave*. WEAVE.] That which is woven; the whole piece of cloth woven in a loom; something resembling this; a large roll of paper such as is used for newspapers and the like; the blade of a saw; a flat portion of various things; the membrane which unites the toes of many water-fowl; the threads or filaments which a spider spins; a cobweb; *fig.* anything carefully contrived and put together, as a plot or scheme.—**Webbed**, webd, *a.* Having the toes united by a membrane or web.—**Webbing**, web'ing, *n.* A strong fabric of hemp, 2 or 3 inches wide, for supporting the seats of stuffed chairs, sofas, &c.—**Webby**, web'i, *a.* Relating to a web; resembling a web.—**Web-eye**, *n.* A disease of the eye produced by a film.—**Web-fingered**, *a.* Having the fingers united by webs of skin.—**Web-foot**, *n.* A foot whose toes are united by a web or membrane.—**Web-footed**, *a.* Having web-feet; palmiped.

Weber, vā'ber, *n.* [From Wilhelm Edouard *Weber*, a German physicist.] The unit of magnetic flux; practically obsolete, the name *Gauss* or *Maxwell* being used.

Wed, wed, *v.t.*—*wedded*, *wedding*; *wed* as pret. and pp. also occurs. [A.Sax. *weddian*, to engage, to pledge, from *wed*, a pledge; similarly Goth. (*ga*)*wadjan*, to pledge, to betroth, from *wadi*, a pledge. Akin *gage*, *wage*, *wager*.] To marry; to take for husband or for wife; to join in marriage; to unite closely by passion or prejudice; to unite inseparably.—*v.i.* To marry; to contract matrimony.—**Wedded**, wed'ed, *a.* Pertaining to matrimony (*wedded* life); intimately connected or joined together.—**Wedding**, wed'ing, *n.* Marriage; nuptial ceremony; nuptial festivities.—*Silver wedding*, *golden wedding*, *diamond wedding*, the celebrations of the twenty-fifth, the fiftieth, and the seventy-fifth anniversaries of a wedding. ∴ Syn. under MARRIAGE.—*a.* Pertaining to a wedding.—**Wedding-cake**, *n.* A richly decorated cake to grace a wedding.—**Wedding-card**, *n.* One of a set of cards sent by a newly-married couple to friends to announce the event.—**Wedding-day**, *n.* The day of marriage.—**Wedding-dower**, *n.* A marriage portion.—**Wedding-favor**, *n.* A rosette or bunch of white ribbons worn by males attending a wedding.—**Wedding-feast**, *n.* A feast prepared for the guests at a wedding.—**Wedding-ring**, *n.* A ring, usually gold, placed by the bridegroom on the third finger of the bride's left hand at the marriage ceremony.—**Wedlock**, wed'lok, *n.* [A.Sax. *wedlác*, a pledging, from *wed*, a pledge, and *lác*, sport, a gift, latterly used as a mere termination of abstract nouns.] MARRIAGE.

Wedder, wed'ėr, *n.* A wether.

Wedding. Under WED.

Wedge, wej, *n.* [A.Sax. *wecg*, a wedge = Icel. *veggr*, Dan. *vægge*, Sw. *vigg*, D. *wig*, G. *weck*, wedge; perhaps akin to *wag*, *way*, *weigh*, and signifying lit. the mover.] A piece of wood or metal, thick at one end and sloping to a thin edge at the other, used in splitting wood, rocks, &c.; one of the mechanical powers, a mass of metal, especially if resembling a wedge in form; anything in the form of a wedge.—*The thin* or *small end of the wedge*, is used figuratively of an initiatory move of small apparent importance, but calculated to produce ultimately an important effect.—*v.t.*—*wedged*, *wedging*. To split with a wedge or with wedges; to rive; to drive as a wedge is driven; to crowd or compress closely; to fasten with a wedge or with wedges; to fix in the manner of a wedge.

Wedgwood-ware, wej'wụd, *n.* [After Josiah *Wedgwood* (1730-1795) of Etruria, Staffordshire, the inventor.] A superior kind of semivitrified pottery capable of taking on the most brilliant and delicate colours, and much used for ornamental ware, as vases, &c.

Wedlock. Under WED.

Wednesday, wenz'dā, *n.* [A.Sax. *Wódnesdæg*, that is Woden's day. Woden is the same as Odin. ODIN.] The fourth day of the week; the next day after Tuesday.

Wee, wē, *a.* [A form of *way*, its present meaning being due to its frequent usage in the phrase 'a little *we*' (or *wea*) = a little way, a little bit.] Small; little. (*Colloq.*)

Weed, wēd, *n.* [A.Sax. *weód*, a weed; D. *wiede*, weeds; affinities doubtful.] The general name of any plant that is useless or troublesome; a plant such as grows where it is not wanted, and is either of no use to man or injurious to crops; a sorry, worthless animal; a leggy, loose-bodied horse; a cigar.—*v.t.* To free from weeds or noxious plants; to take away, as noxious plants; to extirpate; to free from anything hurtful or offensive.—**Weeder**, wēd'ėr, *n.* One that weeds; a weeding-tool.—**Weed-grown**, *a.* Overgrown with weeds.—**Weeding-tool**, *n.* An implement for pulling up, digging up, or cutting weeds.—**Weedless**, wēd'les, *a.* Free from weeds.—**Weedy**, wēd'i, *a.* Consisting of weeds; abounding with weeds; worthless for breeding or racing purposes (a *weedy* horse).

Weed, wēd, *n.* [A.Sax. *waed*, *waede*, a garment; O.Fris. *wede*, D. (*ge*)*waad*, Icel. *váð*; from same root as Goth. *ga-widan*, to bind, and as E. *withy*.] A garment†; *pl.* mournings, especially the mourning dress of a widow.

Week, wēk, *n.* [A.Sax. *wice*, a week = D. *week*, Icel. *vika*, a week; akin G. *woche*, a week; root doubtful.] The space of seven days; the space from one Sunday to another.—*This* (*that*) *day week*, the same day a week afterwards; the corresponding day in the succeeding week.—**Week-day**, *n.* Any day of the week except Sunday.—**Weekly**, wēk'li, *a.* Pertaining to a week or week-days; lasting for a week; happening or done once a week.—*adv.* Once a week.—*n.* A periodical, as a newspaper, appearing once a week.

Ween, wēn, *v.i.* [A.Sax. *wénan*, to ween, from *wén*, Icel. *ván*, Goth. *wens*, expectation, hope. WIN.] To be of opinion; to have the notion; to think; to imagine.

Weep, wēp, *v.i.*—pret. and pp. *wept*. [A.Sax. *wépan*, to weep, from *wóp*, clamour, outcry; O.Sax. *wopian*, Goth. *wopjan*, to cry; cog. Rus. *vopit*, Lith. *vapiti*, to weep; L. *vox*, voice; Skr. *vach*, to speak.] To manifest grief or other strong passion by shedding tears; to drop or flow like tears; to let fall drops; to rain; to give out moisture; to have the branches drooping or hanging downwards; to droop.—*v.t.* To lament, bewail, or bemoan; to shed tears for; to shed or let fall drop by drop; to pour forth in drops, as if tears; to get rid of by weeping: followed by *away*, *out*, &c.—**Weeper**, wē'pėr, *n.* One who weeps; a sort of white linen cuff or band on a dress, worn as a badge of mourning.—**Weeping-ash**, *n.* A variety of ash which has its branches arching downwards instead of upwards.—**Weeping-birch**, *n.* A variety of the birch with drooping branches.—**Weeping-elm**, *n.* An elm with pendulous branches.—**Weepingly**, wē'ping-li, *adv.* With weeping; tearfully.—**Weeping-willow**, *n.* A species of willow whose long and slender branches hang down almost perpendicularly.

Weever, wē'vėr, *n.* [O.Fr. *wivre*, *guivre*, from L. *vipera*, a viper; akin *wyvern*.] An edible fish of the North Atlantic Ocean which inflicts wounds with the spines of its first dorsal fin.

Weevil, wē'vil, *n.* [A.Sax. *wifel*, L.G. and D. *wevel*, G. *wiebel*; cog. Lith. *wabalas*, a beetle.] The name applied to various insects of the beetle family, distinguished by the prolongation of the head, so as to form a sort of snout or proboscis; dangerous enemies to the agriculturist, from destroying grain, fruit, &c.—**Weeviled**, **Weevily**, wē'vild, wē'vil-i, *a.* Infested by weevils.

Weft, weft, *n.* [A.Sax. *weft*, the woof, from *wefan*, to weave; so Icel. *veftr*. WEAVE.] The woof of cloth; the threads that are carried in the shuttle and cross the warp.

Weigh, wā, *v.t.* [A.Sax. *wegan*, to lift, to weigh, to move; *wæg*, a balance, a pair of scales; D. *wegen*, to weigh; Icel. *vega*, to bear, lift, move; G. *wiegen*, to rock; same root as *way*, *wain*, *wag*, &c.] To raise or bear up; to lift so that it hangs in the air (to *weigh* anchor); to examine by the balance so as to ascertain how heavy a thing is; to pay, allot, or take by weight; to consider for the purpose of forming an opinion or coming to a conclusion; to estimate; to balance; to compare.—*To weigh down*, to preponderate over; to oppress with weight or heaviness; to overburthen.—*v.i.* To have weight; to be equal in weight to (to *weigh* a pound); to be considered as important; to have weight in the intellectual balance; to bear heavily; to press hard.—*n.* A wey; *naut.* a corruption of *way*, used only in the phrase *under weigh*.—**Weighable**, wā'a-bl, *a.* Capable of being weighed.—**Weighage**, wā'āj, *n.* A rate or toll paid for weighing goods.—**Weigh-bridge**, *n.* A machine for weighing carts, wagons, &c., with their load.—**Weigher**, wā'ėr, *n.* One who or that which weighs.—**Weigh-house**, *n.* A building at or in which goods are weighed.—**Weighing**, wā'ing, *n.* The act of ascertaining weight.—**Weighing-machine**, *n.* Any contrivance by which the weight of an object may be ascertained; generally applied only to contrivances employed for ascertaining the weight of heavy bodies.—**Weight**, wāt, *n.* [O.E. *weght*, *wight*, A.Sax. *wiht*.] That property of bodies by which they tend toward the centre of the earth; the measure of the force of gravity as determined for any particular body; the amount which anything weighs; a certain mass of brass, iron, or other substance to be used for determining the weight of other bodies (a pound *weight*); a heavy mass; something heavy; in clocks, one of the two masses of metal that by their weight actuate the machinery; pressure; burden (the *weight* of grief); importance; influence; efficacy; consequence; moment; impressiveness; *med.* a sensation of oppression or heaviness.—*Dead weight*, a heavy and oppressive burden.—*v.t.* To add or attach a weight or weights to; to add to the heaviness of. — **Weightily**, wā'ti-li, *adv.* In a weighty manner; heavily; ponderously; with force or impressiveness. —**Weightiness**, wā'ti-nes, *n.* Ponderousness; gravity; force; importance. — **Weightless**, wāt'les, *a.* Having no weight. —**Weighty**, wā'ti, *a.* Having great weight; heavy; ponderous; important; momentous; grave; adapted to turn the balance in the mind, or to convince; cogent; grave or serious.

Weir, wēr, *n.* [A.Sax. *wær*, *wer*, a fence, an inclosure for fish; G. *wehr*, weir, dam; lit. a fence or defence, being akin to *ward*, *ware*, *wary*, *warren*.] A dam across a stream to stop and raise the water, for the purpose of conveying water to a mill for irrigation, &c.; a fence of twigs or stakes set in a stream for catching fish.

Weird, wērd, *n.* [A.Sax. *wyrd*, *wird*, fate, destiny, from stem of *weorthan*, G. *werden*, Goth. *wairthan*, to become, to be. WORTH, *v.*] Destiny; a person's allotted fate.—*a.* Connected with fate or destiny; able to influence fate; partaking of the supernatural; unearthly; suggestive of unearthliness.—**Weirdness**, wērd'nes, *n.*

Weismannism, vis'män-iz'm, *n.* A theory of heredity propounded by the German biologist, August Weismann (1813-1914), which regards the germ plasm as the basis of heredity and denies the possibility of the transmission of acquired characteristics.

Welcome, wel'kum, *a.* [Equivalent to *well come*.] Received with gladness; admitted willingly to one's house and company; producing gladness on its reception; grateful; pleasing; free to have or enjoy: in phrases of courtesy.—*n.* Salutation of a newcomer; kind reception of a guest or newcomer. — *To bid welcome*, to receive with professions of friendship, kindness, or gladness.—*v.t.*—*welcomed*, *welcoming*. To salute a newcomer with kindness; to receive hospitably and cheerfully; to accept or meet with gladness (to *welcome* death).—**Welcomer**, wel'kum-ėr, *n.* One who welcomes.

Weld, **Wold**, weld, wōld, *n.* [O.E. *welde*, *wolde*, Sc. *wald*; origin unknown.] An annual herb (*Reseda luteola*) from which a yellow dye is obtained.

Weld, weld, *v.t.* [O.E. *welle*, Sc. *waul* (the final *d* has been added) = G. and D. *wellen*, to boil, to weld; Sw. *välla*, to weld; same word as *well*, to boil, to bubble up.] To unite or join together into firm union, as two pieces of metal, by heating until brought to a semiliquid or liquid state and then allowing them to run together; *fig.* to unite very closely (*welded* by affection).—*n.* A junction of two pieces of metal by welding.—**Weldable**, wel'da-bl, *a.* Capable of being welded.—**Welder**, wel'dėr, *n.* One who welds.

Welfare, wel'fār, *n.* [Lit. a state of *faring well*. WELL, FARE.] A state of exemption from misfortune, calamity, or evil; the enjoyment of health and the common blessings of life; well-being; prosperity.

Welk, welk, *v.i.* [Same as D. and G. *welken*, to wither, to fade.] To fade; to decay.

Welkin, wel'kin, *n.* [O.E. *welkne*, *wolkne*, A.Sax. *wolcen*, *wolcn*, a cloud, pl. the sky; G. *wolke*, O.H.G. *wolchan*, a cloud.] The sky; the vault of heaven. (*Poetical.*)

Well, wel, *n.* [A.Sax. *well*, *wella*, a well, fountain, *weallan*, to well up, to boil; Icel. *vell*, a boiling, D. *wel*, a spring, Dan. *væld*, a spring, G. *welle*, a wave, *wallen*, to boil; from root of *walk*, *wallow*, L. *volvo*, to roll (whence *volume*, &c.).] A spring; a fountain; an artificial structure from which water is obtained, often a round pit sunk perpendicularly into the earth to reach a supply of water; a compartment at the bottom of certain things; a compartment in a fishing-vessel having holes to let in water so that fish may be kept alive; *arch.* the space in a building in which winding stairs are placed; *fig.* a spring, source, or origin.—*v.i.* To spring or issue forth, as water from the earth; to flow; to bubble up. — **Well-sinker**, *n.* One who digs wells.—**Well-sinking**, *n.* The operation of sinking or digging wells.—**Well-room**, *n.* A room into which the water of a mineral spring is conducted.—**Well-spring**, *n.* A fountain; a source of continual supply.

Well, wel, *a.* [A.Sax. *wel*, well, enough, much=D. *wel*, Icel. and Dan. *vel*, Sw. *väl*, Goth. *waila*, G. *wohl*, well; of same origin as *will*, and meaning originally according to one's *will*. Akin *weal*, *wealth*.] Not ill; in accordance with wish or desire (the business turned out *well*); satisfactory: often in impersonal usages (it is *well*); being in health; not ailing or sick; having recovered; comfortable; being in favour; favoured (to be *well* with the king); just; right; proper (was it *well* to do this?). ∴ This word is almost always used predicatively, not attributively. — *To let well alone*, not to try and improve what is already well.—*adv.* In a proper manner; justly; rightly; not ill or wickedly; in a satisfactory manner; skilfully; with due art (the work is *well* done); sufficiently; very much (I like it *well*); to a degree that gives pleasure; with praise; commendably (to speak *well* of one); conveniently; suitably (I cannot *well* go); easily; fully; adequately; thoroughly; considerably; not a little (*well* advanced in life). This word is often merely expletive or used to avoid abruptness (*well*, the work is done; *well*, let us go; *well*, *well*, be it so). — *As well*, rather right, convenient, or proper than otherwise (it may be *as well* to inform you before you go).—*As well as*, together with; and also; not less than; one as much as the other (a sickness long *as well as* severe).—*Well enough*, in a moderate degree; so as to give satisfaction, or so as to require no alteration.—*Well nigh*, nearly; almost.—*To be well off*, to be in a good condition, especially as to property.—**Well-appointed**, *a.* Fully furnished and equipped.—**Well-behaved**, *a.* Of good conduct or behaviour.—**Well-being**, wel'-bē-ing, *n.* Welfare; happiness; prosperity. —**Well-born**, *a.* Born of a noble or respectable family; not of mean birth. — **Well-bred**, *a.* Of good breeding; polite; cultivated; refined; of good breed, stock, or race. — **Well-conducted**, *a.* Properly led on; of good conduct; well-behaved.— **Well-doing**, *n.* Performance of duties; upright conduct. — **Well-educated**, *a.* Having a good education; well-instructed. — **Well-favored**, *a.* Handsome; well-formed; pleasing to the eye. — **Well-founded**, *a.* Founded on good and valid reasons.—**Well-informed**, *a.* Well furnished with information; intelligent. — **Well-knit**, *a.* Firmly compacted; having a strong bodily frame.—**Well-known**, *a.* Fully known; generally known or acknowledged.—**Well-meaning**, *a.* Having a good intention.—**Well-meant**, *a.* Rightly intended; sincere; not feigned.—**Well-met**, *interj.* A term of salutation denoting joy at meeting.—**Well-off**, *a.* In comfortable circumstances; having a good store of wealth; fortunate.—**Well-ordered**, *a.* Rightly regulated or governed. — **Well-proportioned**, *a.* Having good proportions; well-shaped.—**Well-read**, *a.* Having read a great deal; conversant with books. — **Well-regulated**, *a.* Having good regulations; well-ordered. — **Well-spent**, *a.* Spent or passed in virtue; spent to the best advantage.—**Well-spoken**, *a.* Spoken well or with propriety; speaking well; fair-spoken; civil; courteous.—**Well-timed**, *a.* Done at a proper time; opportune.—**Well-to-do**, *a.* Being in easy circumstances; well-off; prosperous.—**Well-wisher**, *n.* One who wishes the good of another.—**Well-won**, *a.* Honestly gained; hardly earned.—**Well-worn**, *a.* Much worn or used.

Welladay, wel'a-dā, *interj.* [A corruption of *welaway*, from A.Sax. *wá*, *lá*, *wá*, woe! lo! woe!] Welaway! alas! lackaday!

Wellington, wel'ing-ton, *n.* A kind of long-legged boot, worn by men, named after the Duke of *Wellington*: used also adjectively. — **Wellingtonia**, wel-ing-tō'ni-a, *n.* A name popularly given to a genus of trees (Sequoia) comprising the mammoth trees of America. Under MAMMOTH.

Welsbach burner, wels'bak, *n.* [After A. von *Welsbach*, the inventor.] A gas burner in which air is admitted into the stream of gas, and combustion of the mixture raises an incandescent mantle to white heat.

Welsh, welsh, *a.* [A.Sax. *welisc*, *wælisc*, lit. foreign, from *wealh*, a foreigner; similarly G. *wälsch*, *welsch*, is foreign, especially French or Italian, and *Wälschland* is Italy. So *wal*nut is the welsh or foreign nut. Akin *Walloon*, Corn*wall*.] Pertaining to Wales or to its people; Cymric.—*Welsh rabbit*. Under RABBIT.—*n.* The language of Wales, a member of the Celtic family, forming with the Breton and now extinct Cornish the Cymric group; the inhabitants of Wales.—**Welshman**, **Welshwoman**, welsh'man, welsh'wụm-an, *n.* A native of the principality of Wales.

Welsher, welsh'ėr, *n.* [Yorkshire *welch*, a failure, a form of *welk*, to fail, to fade = D. and G. *welken*, to fade.] One who makes a bet and does not pay if he loses (*slang*).

Welt, welt, *n.* [Probably from W. *gwald*, a hem, a welt.] A border; a kind of hem or edging; a strip of leather sewed round the edge of the upper of a boot or shoe and the inner sole, and to which the outer sole is afterwards fashioned; an inflamed stripe raised on the skin by a blow; a wale.—*v.t.* To furnish with a welt; to raise welts on the skin by striking or thrashing.

Welter, wel'tėr, *v.i.* [From A.Sax. *wealtan*, to roll; L.G. *weltern*, Sw. *vältra*, G. *wälzen*, to roll, to wallow, to welter; same root as *walk*, *wallow*. Akin *waltz*.] To wallow; to tumble about; to roll or wallow in some foul manner; to rise and fall, as waves.

Wen, wen, *n.* [A.Sax. *wenn*, D. *wen*, L.G. *ween*, Prov.G. *wenne*, a swelling, a wart.] A tumour without inflammation or change of colour of the skin. — **Wennish**, **Wenny**, wen'ish, wen'i, *a.* Having the nature of a wen.

Wench, wensh, *n.* [O.E. *wenche*, from *wenchel*, a child, A.Sax. *wencel*, weak; allied to G. *wanken*, to totter. WINK.] A familiar expression applied to a woman, especially a young woman, in any variation of tone between tenderness and contempt; in a bad sense, a young woman of loose character.—*v.i.* To frequent the company of women of ill fame.—**Wencher**, wensh'ėr, *n.* One who wenches; a lewd man.

Wend, wend, *v.i.*—pret. and pp. *wended*. *Went*, which is really the pret. of this verb, is now detached from it and used as pret. of *go*. [A.Sax. *wendan*, to turn, to go=Icel. *venda*, Dan. *vende*, D. and G. *wenden*, to change, to turn: a caus. of the verb to *wind*, to turn, to twist. WIND.] To go; to pass to or from a place; to travel.—*v.t.* To go; to direct: in the phrase *to wend one's way*; also used reflexively (*wend thee* homewards).

Went, went, old pret. and pp. of *wend*: now used as the pret. of *go*, or vulgarily as its pp.

Wept, wept, pret. and pp. of *weep*.

Were, wer. [See WAS.] The indicative past tense plural of the verb to *be*, and the past or imperfect subjunctive—*wert* being used as second person singular.

Werewolf, wēr'wụlf, *n.* A werwolf.

Wergild, **Weregild**, wer'gild, wēr'gild, *n.* [A.Sax. *wergild*—*wer*, man, and *gild*, *geld*, a payment.] Formerly a fine of varying amount for manslaughter and other crimes against the person, by paying which the offender got rid of every further obligation or punishment.

Wernerian, wėr-nē′ri-an, *a.* Pertaining to *Werner*, a celebrated German mineralogist and geologist, or to his theory of the earth, which was also called the *Neptunian Theory*. Under NEPTUNE.

Wert, wėrt. See WERE.

Wertherian, wėr-tē′ri-an or vėr-tē′ri-an, *a.* [After the hero of Goethe's work.] Sentimental; namby-pambyish.

Werwolf, wer′wulf, *n.* [A.Sax. *werewulf*, lit. man-wolf, from *wer* (Icel. *verr*, Goth. *wair*), a man, and *wulf*, wolf; *wer* is cog. with L. *vir*, a man. VIRILE.] A man transformed for a time or periodically into a wolf; a man by day and a wolf by night; a lycanthrope.

Wesleyan, wes′li-an, *a.* Pertaining to John *Wesley*, or the religious sect (the Methodists) established by him about 1739. —*n.* One who adopts the principles and doctrines of Wesleyanism.—**Wesleyanism**, wes′li-an-izm, *n.* The system of doctrines and church polity of the Wesleyan Methodists.

West, west, *n.* [A.Sax. *west*, west, westward = D. *west*, Icel. *vestr*, Dan. and Sw. *vest*, G. *west* (whence Fr. *ouest*); probably from a root *vas*, to dwell, as the home of the sun. WAS.] That point of the horizon where the sun sets at the equinox, and midway between the north and south points; the region of the heavens near this point; the region or tract lying opposite the east, or nearer the west point than another point of reckoning.—In the U. S. the whole region west of the Mississippi River, the land of unlimited possibilities. —*a.* Being in the west or lying towards the west; western; coming or moving from the west or western region.—*adv.* To the western region; at the westward; more westward:—*v.t.*—To pass to the west; to assume a westerly direction.—**Westering**, wes′tėr-ing, *p.* and *a.* Passing to the west. (*Poet.*)—**Westerly**, wes′tėr-li, *a.* Being toward the west; situated in the western region; coming from the westward.—*adv.* Tending, going, or moving toward the west.—**Western**, wes′tėrn, *a.* Being in the west, or in the direction of west; moving or directed to the west; proceeding from the west (a *western* breeze).—**Westerner**, wes′tėr-nėr, *n.* A native or inhabitant of the west.—**Westernmost**, wes′tėrn-mōst, *a.* Farthest to the west; most western.—**Westing**, wes′ting, *n.* Space or distance westward; space reckoned from one point to another westward from it.—**Westmost**, west′mōst, *a.* Farthest to the west.—**Westward**, **Westwards**, west′wėrd, west′wėrdz, *adv.* [A. Sax. *west*, and *-weard*, denoting direction. *Westwards* is an adverbial genitive.] Toward the west.

Wet, wet, *a.* [O.E. and Sc. *weet*, A.Sax. *wæt*, Icel. *vátr*, Dan. *vaad*, wet; akin to *water*.] Containing water; soaked with water; having water or other liquid upon the surface: rainy; drizzly; very damp (*wet* weather).—*n.* Water or wetness; moisture or humidity in considerable degree; rainy weather: rain.—*v.t.*—pret. and pp. *wet* or *wetted* (the latter regularly in the passive to avoid confusion with the adjective *wet*), ppr. *wetting*. To make wet; to moisten, drench, or soak with water or other liquid; to dip or soak in liquor.—**Wet-dock**, *n.* Under DOCK. — **Wetness**, wet′nes, *n.* The state of being wet; a watery or moist state of the atmosphere; moisture.—**Wet-nurse**, *n.* A woman who suckles and nurses a child not her own: opposed to *dry-nurse*.—**Wetshod**, wet′shod, *a.* Wet over the shoes.—**Wettish**, wet′ish, *a.* Somewhat wet; moist; humid.

Wether, weᴛʜ′ėr, *n.* [A.Sax. *wether*, a ram; a word common to the Teutonic tongues, and allied to L. *vitulus*, a calf, lit. a yearling. VEAL.] A castrated ram.

Wey, wā, *n.* [A.Sax. *waege*, a weight. WEIGH.] In Britain a certain weight or measure: of wool, 182 lbs.; of wheat, 5 quarters; of cheese, 224 lbs.

Whack, whak, *v.t.* [THWACK.] To thwack; to give a hearty or resounding blow to. (*Colloq.*)—*v.i.* To strike or continue striking anything with smart blows. (*Colloq.*)

Whale, whāl, *n.* [A.Sax. *hwæl*, a whale; Icel. *hvalr*, Sw. and Dan. *hval*, *hvalfish* (whalefish), D. *walvisch*, G. *wallfisch*; perhaps connected with A.Sax. *hwelan*, to roar, to bellow, from the noise they make in blowing.] The common name given to the larger mammals of the order Cetacea; the typical representative being the common or Greenland whale, so valuable on account of the oil and whalebone which it furnishes.—**Whale-boat**, *n.* A strong carvel-built boat from 23 to 28 feet in length, rounded at both ends, used in hunting whales.—**Whale-bone**, *n.* A well-known elastic horny substance which adheres in thin parallel plates to the upper jaw of certain species of whales; baleen.—**Whale-fishery**, *n.* The fishery or occupation of taking whales.—**Whale-fishing**, *n.* The employment of catching whales. — **Whaler**, whā′lėr, *n.* A person or ship employed in the whale-fishery.—**Whaling**, whā′ling, *a.* Pertaining to the capture of whales.

Whall, whal, *n.* [Probably for *wall*, in *wall*-eyed.] A disease of the eyes; glaucoma. —**Whally**, whal′i, *a.* Having greenish-white eyes.

Whap, whop, *v.t.* Same as WHOP.

Wharf, wharf, *n.* pl. **Wharfs**, wharfs, or **Wharves**, wharvz. [A.Sax. *hwerf*, *hwearf*, a turning, a bank, a wharf; O.Sw. *hwarf*, a turning, a wharf; Icel. *hvarf*, a turning, a shelter; D. *werf*, a wharf, a yard, a turn. Perhaps originally an embankment or dam that turns the course of a stream; from A.Sax. *hweorfan*, Icel. *hverfa*, to turn.] A quay of wood or stone on a roadstead, harbour, or river, alongside of which ships are brought to load or unload.—*v.t.* To place or lodge on a wharf.—**Wharfage**, whar′fāj, *n.* Money paid for using a wharf; a wharf or wharfs collectively.—**Wharfinger**, whar′fin-jėr, *n.* [For *wharfager*, the *n* being inserted as in *messenger*, *passenger*.] A person who owns or who has the charge of a wharf.

What, whot, *pron.* [A.Sax. *hwæt*, what, also, why, lo, &c., neut. of *hwá*, who. WHO.] An interrogative pronoun used in asking questions as to things, and corresponding in many respects to *who*, but used adjectively as well as substantively (*what's* the matter? I do not know *what* the matter is; *what* stuff is this?). Used alone in introducing a question it has an emphatic force, or is almost an interjection, equivalent to is it possible that? really? (*what*, do you believe that?); hence, such expressions as, *what if*=what would be the consequence if? what will it matter if? *what of*=what follows from? why need you speak of? *what though*=what does it matter though? granting or admitting that. Used to introduce an intensive or emphatic phrase or exclamation, and when employed adjectively it is equivalent to how great . . .! how remarkable . . .! how extraordinary . . .! (*what* a season it has been!). It often has the force of a compound relative pronoun: when used substantively=the thing (or things) which; that which (I know *what* you mean): when used adjectively=the . . . which; the sort or kind of . . . which; such . . . as (*what* money I have is my own). It also stands for whatever or whoever; whatsoever or whosoever (come *what* will). In such phrases as, *I tell you what, I'll tell you what*, &c., *what* is used to lay some stress on what is about to be stated.—*What's his (its) name? what do you call it?* &c., colloquial phrases generally signifying that the speaker cannot supply a definite name or word.—*What not*, is used in concluding an enumeration of several articles or particulars, and is equivalent to something more which I need not mention; et cetera.—*To know what's what*, to know the nature of things; to be knowing.—*What ho!* an exclamation of calling.—*What with* (repeated), partly by or in consequence of (*what with* one thing *what with* another the scheme miscarried).—**Whatever**, whotev′ėr, *pron.* Anything soever that; be it what it may that; all that: used substantively; of any kind soever; be what may the: used adjectively. Often contracted to **Whate'er**, whot-ār′.—**What-not**, *n.* A stand or piece of household furniture having shelves for papers, books, &c.—**Whatsoe'er**, **Whatsoever**, whot-sō-ār′, whot-sō-ev′ėr, *pron.* No matter what thing or things: more emphatic that *whatever*.

Wheal, whēl, *n.* [Corn. *huel*, a mine.] A mine, particularly a tin-mine.

Wheal, whēl, *n.* [In first meaning from A.Sax. *hwele* (?), putrefaction.] A pimple or pustule; a wale or weal.

Wheat, whēt, *n.* [A.Sax. *hwaete* = Sc. *white*, Icel. *hveiti*, Sw. *hvete*, Dan. *hvede*, D. *weit*, Goth. *hwaiteis*, G. *weizen*. Lit. the *white* grain. WHITE.] A plant belonging to the grass family, of several varieties; the seeds collectively of the plant, a well-known grain which furnishes a white nutritious flour.—**Wheat-ear**, *n.* An ear of wheat. — **Wheat-eel**, *n.* A disease in wheat, called also *Ear-cockle*.—**Wheaten**, whē′tn, *a.* Made of wheat.—**Wheat-fly**, **Wheat-midge**, *n.* A small two-winged fly, the maggots of which destroy the flower of the plant. HESSIAN-FLY.—**Wheat-moth**, *n.* The grain-moth.

Wheatear, whēt′ēr, *n.* [A.Sax. *hwít*, white, *ærs*, posteriors.] A bird akin to the stone-chat, a common summer visitant to Britain, having a conspicuous white patch at the base of the tail.

Wheatstone's bridge, whēt′stōnz, *n.* [After Sir Charles *Wheatstone*, inventor.] *Elec.* an instrument for measuring the resistance of an electrical conductor.

Wheedle, whē′dl, *v.t.*—*wheedled*, *wheedling*. [Probably from W. *chwedla*, to talk, to gossip, from *chwedl*, a story, discourse.] To entice by soft words; to gain over by coaxing and flattery; to cajole; to procure by coaxing.—*v.i.* To flatter; to coax.—**Wheedler**, whēd′lėr, *n.* One who wheedles. —**Wheedling**, whēd′ling, *a.* Coaxing; flattering.

Wheel, whēl, *n.* [A.Sax. *hweól*, contr. from *wheowol*; akin D. *wiel*, Dan. *hjul*, Icel. *hjól*, *hvél*; connections doubtful.] A circular frame or solid disc turning on an axis; as applied to carriages, a wheel usually consists of a nave, into which are inserted radiating spokes connecting it with the periphery or circular ring; any apparatus or machine the essential feature of which is a wheel (a spinning-*wheel*, a potter's *wheel*); a circular frame with projecting handles and an axle on which are wound the ropes or chains connecting it with the rudder for steering a ship; an instrument of torture formerly used, the victim being fastened on it and his limbs broken by successive blows; a whirling round; a revolution or rotation; circumgyration.—*Wheel and axle*, one of the mechanical powers, an application of the general principle of the lever, consisting of a cylindrical axle on which a wheel is firmly fastened, power being applied to the wheel and a weight raised by a rope coiled round the axle.—*Wheels within wheels*, a complication of circumstances, motives, influences, or the like.—*To put one's shoulder to the wheel*. Under SHOULDER.—*Wheel of life*. ZOETROPE.—*v.t.* To cause to turn round or revolve; to give a circular motion to; to rotate; to whirl; to convey in a wheeled vehicle; to give a circular direction or form to.—*v.i.* To turn on an axis or as on an axis; to revolve; to rotate; to turn round; to make a circular flight; to roll forward or along; to march, as a body of troops, round a point that serves as a pivot.—**Wheel-animal**, **Wheel-animalcule**, *n.* A rotifer.—**Wheel-barometer**, *n.* A barometer in which the motion of the mercury is communicated to a hand that shows the variations on a dial.—**Wheel-barrow**, *n.* A frame or box with a wheel in front and two handles behind, rolled by a single individual.—**Wheel bug**, *n.* An insect of North America which feeds upon the blood of other insects.—**Wheel chair**, *n.* A chair mounted on wheels and used by invalids.—**Wheeled**, whēld, *a.* Having wheels: often in composition (a two-*wheeled* carriage).—**Wheeler**, whē'lėr, *n.* One who wheels; a maker of wheels; a wheel-horse, or one next the wheels of the carriage.—**Wheel-horse**, *n.* WHEELER.—**Wheel-house**, *n. Naut.* a kind of house built over the steering-wheel in large ships.—**Wheel-lock**, *n.* A kind of old musket lock with a wheel which revolved against a flint, for producing sparks.—**Wheelman**, whēl'-man, *n.* One who uses a bicycle or tricycle or similar conveyance.—**Wheel-plough**, *n.* A plough with a wheel or wheels regulating the depth of the furrow.—**Wheel-race**, *n.* The place in which a water-wheel is fixed.—**Wheel-window**, *n.* A circular Gothic window with radiating mullions.—**Wheel-work**, *n.* The combination of wheels which communicate motion to one another in machinery.—**Wheel-wright**, *n.* A man whose occupation is to make wheels.

Wheel, whēl, *n.* Same as *Wheal*, a mine.

Wheeze, whēz, *v.i.*—*wheezed*, *wheezing.* [A.Sax. *hwēsan*, *hwaesan*, to wheeze; Dan. *hvæse*, Icel. *hvæsa*, to hiss: an imitative word, akin to *whisper*, *whistle.*] To breathe hard and with an audible sound, as persons affected with asthma.—**Wheezy**, whē'zi, *a.* Affected with or characterized by wheezing.

Whelk, whelk, *n.* [A.Sax. *weolc*, *weluc*, allied to *wealcan*, to turn; lit. a twisted shell. WALK.] An edible mollusk with a spiral shell, used for food in Europe.

Whelk, whelk, *n.* [Dim. from *wheal*, a pustule.] A pustule or pimple. (*Shak.*)

Whelm, whelm, *v.t.* [Apparently modified from old *whelve*, *whelfe*, to overturn, to cover over, from A.Sax. *hwylfan*, to vault over, from *hwealf*, a vault or arch = Icel. *hválf*, Sw. *hvalf*, a vault.] To throw over so as to cover‡; to engulf; to swallow up; to ruin or destroy by overpowering disaster.

Whelp, whelp, *n.* [A.Sax. *hwelp*=D. *welp*, G. *welf*, Dan. *hvalp*, Icel. *hvelpr*, a whelp.] The young of the canine species, and of several other beasts of prey; a puppy; a cub; a son; a young man: in contempt or sportiveness.—*v.i.* To bring forth whelps.—*v.t.* To bring forth, as a bitch does; hence to give birth to or originate: in contempt.

When, when, *adv.* [A.Sax. *hwænne*, *hwonne*, O.Fris. *hwenne*, G. *wann*, *wenn*, Goth. *hwan*, when; akin to *who.* Comp. L. *quum*, *quando*, when, *qui*, who.] At what or which time: used interrogatively (*when* did he come?); at the time that; at or just after the moment that: used relatively (he came *when* I went); at which time; at the same time that; while; whereas (you were absent *when* you should have been present); which time; then; preceded by *since* or *till.*—**Whene'er**, when-ãr'. Contracted form of *Whenever.*—**Whenever**, when-ev'ėr, *adv.* At whatever time.—**Whensoever**, when-sō-ev'ėr, *adv.* At whatever time.

Whence, whens, *adv.* [O.E. *whennes*, from *when* by affixing a genitive termination, as in *hence*, *thence*, *twice*, &c.] From what place; from what or which source, origin, premises, antecedents, principles, facts, and the like; how: used interrogatively (*whence* and what art thou?); from which: referring to place, source, origin, facts, arguments, &c., and used relatively (the place *whence* he came).—*From whence*, although a pleonastic mode of expression, is used by good writers.—**Whencesoever**, whens-sō-ev'-ėr, *adv.* From whatsoever place or cause or source.

Where, whãr, *adv.* [A.Sax. *hwær*, akin to *who*, *what*, like *there* and *that.*] At or in what place; in what position, situation, or circumstances: used interrogatively; at or in the place in which; in which case, position, circumstances, &c.: used relatively; to which place; whither: used both interrogatively and relatively.—**Whereabout**, whãr-a-bout', *adv.* Near what or which place; the place near which; concerning or about which: also frequently used as a noun (a notice of your *whereabout*).—**Whereabouts**, whãr-a-bouts', *adv.* Near what or which place; whereabout: often used substantively (I do not know his *whereabouts*).—**Whereas**, whãr-az', *conj.* The fact or case really being that; when in fact; the thing being so that; considering that things are such that.—**Whereat**, whãr-at', *adv.* At which: used relatively; at what: used interrogatively.—**Whereby**, whãr-bī', *adv.* By which: used relatively; by what: used interrogatively.—**Wherefore**, whãr'for, *adv.* and *conj.* For which reason: used relatively; why; for what reason: used interrogatively.—**Wherein**, whãr-in', *adv.* In which; in which thing, time, respect, &c.: used relatively; in what thing, time, &c.: used interrogatively.—**Whereinto**, whãr-in'tö, *adv.* Into which: used relatively; into what: used interrogatively.—**Whereness**, whãr'nes, *n.* The state or quality of having a place or position; ubiety.—**Whereof**, whãr-ov', *adv.* Of which: used relatively; of what: used interrogatively.—**Whereon**, whãr-on', *adv.* On which: used relatively; on what: used interrogatively.—**Whereso'er**, **Wheresoever**, whãr-sö-ãr', whãr-sō-ev'ėr, *adv.* In what place soever; in whatever place.—**Wherethrough**, whãr'thrö, *adv.* Through which; by reason of which.—**Whereto**, whãr-tö', *adv.* To which: used relatively; to what; to what end: used interrogatively.—**Whereupon**, whãr-up-on', *adv.* Upon which; upon what; immediately after and in consequence of which.—**Where'er**, **Wherever**, whãr-ãr', whãr-ev'ėr, *adv.* At whatever place.—**Wherewith**, **Wherewithal**, whãr-with', whãr-with-al', *adv.* With which: used relatively; with what: used interrogatively.—*The wherewith*, *the wherewithal*, a sufficiency of resources or money.

Wherry, wher'i, *n.* [Perhaps akin to Icel. *hverfr*, crank, said of vessels, and to A.Sax. *hweorfan*, to turn. WHARF.] In England, a light shallow boat, seated for passengers, and plying on rivers.—**Wherryman**, wher'i-man, *n.* One who rows a wherry.

Whet, whet, *v.t.*—pret. and pp. *whetted* or *whet*, ppr. *whetting.* [A.Sax. *hwettan*, to whet, from *hwæt*, sharp, keen, bold; so Icel. *hvetja*, from *hvatr*, bold; D. *wetten*, G. *wetzen*, to whet.] To sharpen by rubbing on or with a stone; to sharpen in general; to make keen, or eager; to excite; to stimulate (to *whet* the appetite); to provoke.—*n.* The act of sharpening; something that provokes or stimulates the appetite.—**Whet-stone**, *n.* A stone for sharpening cutlery or tools by friction.—**Whetter**, whet'ėr, *n.* One who or that which whets or sharpens.

Whether, wheᴛʜ'ėr, *pron.* [A. Sax. *hwæther*, which of two, also conj.; O.H.G. *hwedar*, Goth. *hwathar*; from the interrogative *who*, and comparative suffix *-ther*, as in *hither*, *other*, &c.] Which of two; which one of the two: used interrogatively and relatively.—*conj.* Which of two or more alternatives: used to introduce the first of a series of alternative clauses, the succeeding clause or clauses being connected by *or* or by *or whether.*—*Whether or no*, in either alternative; in any case.

Whew, whū, *v.i.* [Imitative.] To whistle with a shrill pipe, as plovers.—*interj.* A sound expressing astonishment, aversion, or contempt.

Whey, whā, *n.* [A.Sax. *hwaeg*=D. *wei*, *hui*, L.G. *wey*, whey.] The watery part of milk separated from the more coagulable part, particularly in the process of making cheese.—**Wheyey**, whā'i, *a.* Partaking of or resembling whey.—**Whey-face**, *n.* A face white or pale, as from fear.—**Whey-faced**, *a.* Having a white or pale face; pale-faced.—**Wheyish**, whā'ish, *a.* Wheyey; thin; watery.

Which, which, *pron.* [A.Sax. *hwilc*, *hwylc*, contr. from *hwilic*, lit. *why-like*, from *hwi*, instrumental case of *whā*, who, *whæt*, what, and *lic*, like; so Icel. *hvilíkr*, Dan. *hvilken*, Goth. *hveleiks*, D. *welk*, G. *welch.* Comp. *such* = *so-like.* Like *who*, *which* was originally an interrogative; as such it is of any gender, but as a relative it is now only neuter. It is both singular and plural.] An interrogative pronoun, by which one or more among a number of persons or things (frequently one of two) is inquired for: used adjectively or substantively (*which* man is it? *which* are the articles you mean?); a relative pronoun, serving as the neuter of *who*: often used adjectively, the relative coming before the noun by a kind of inversion (within *which* city he resides); used as an indefinite pronoun, standing for any one which (take *which* you will).—**Whichever**, **Whichsoever**, which-ev'ėr, which-sō-ev'ėr, *pron.* No matter which; anyone: used both as an adjective and as a noun.

Whiff, whif, *n.* [Imitative of the sound of blowing; comp. *puff*, W. *chwif*, a whiff, a puff, *chwaf*, a quick gust.] A sudden expulsion of air, smoke, or the like from the mouth; a puff; a gust of air conveying some smell.—*v.t.* To puff; to throw out in whiffs; to smoke.—*v.i.* To emit puffs, as of smoke; to puff; to smoke.—**Whiffle**, whif'l, *v.i.* [Probably from *whiff*; but comp. D. *weifelen*, to waver; Icel. *veifla*, to shake often.] To veer about, as the wind; to change from one opinion or course to another; to use evasions; to prevaricate.—**Whiffler**, whif'lėr, *n.* One who whiffles; a piper or fifer; hence, a harbinger (*Shak.*).

Whig, whig, *n.* [From the name *whiggamores* applied to a body of Covenanters who marched from the southwest of Scotland to Edinburgh in 1648, said to be from *whiggam*, a word used in Southwestern Scotland in driving horses; akin to Sc. *whig*, to jog along briskly, the connections of this being doubtful.] A name once given to the members of a political party in Britain: opposed to *Tory*; later applied to the more conservative section of the Liberal party, and opposed to *Radical*; one who sympathized with the American Revolution in contradistinction to the *Royalists* and *Tories* who favored allegiance to the King; a political party in the United States (1834-1854) that favored a protective tariff, and was succeeded by the present Republican party.

While, whīl, *n.* [A.Sax. *hwīl*, a time, a space of time; D. *wijl*, *wijle*, Goth. *hweila*, G. *weile*, a time; Icel. *hvíla*, a place of rest; Dan. *hvile*, rest; allied to L. *quies*, rest. QUIET.] A time; a space of time; especially, a short space of time during which something happens or is to happen or be done.—*The while*, in the meantime.—*Worth while*, worth the time which it requires; worth the time and pains, or the trouble and expense.—*conj.* During the time that; as long as; at the same time that. ∴ *While* implies less of contrast in the parallel than *though*, sometimes, indeed, implying no contrast at all (*while* I admire his bravery, I esteem his moderation; but *though* I admire his courage, I detest his cruelty).—*v.t.*—*whiled*, *whiling.* To cause to pass pleasantly and without irksomeness, languor, or weariness; usually with *away* (to *while away* time).—**Whilst**, whīlst, *conj.* [From *whiles*, an adverbial genitive, with *t* added as in *amongst*, *amidst*, *betwixt.*] The same as *while*, but less commonly used.

Whilom,‡ whī'lom, *adv.* or *adj.* [A.Sax. *hwilum*, dat. pl. of *hwil*, a time. WHILE.] Formerly; once; quondam.

Whim, whim, *n.* [Probably akin to Icel. *hvima*, to wander with the eyes; Sw. *hvimsa*, to be unsteady; Dan. *vimse*, to skip about. Comp. also W. *chwim*, motion.] A sudden turn of the mind; a freak; a capricious notion; a kind of large capstan worked by horse-power or steam for raising ore, water, &c., from the bottom of a mine.—**Whimsey**, whim'zi, *n.* A whim; a freak; a capricious notion.—**Whimsical**, whim'-zi-kal, *a.* [From *whimsey.*] Full of whims; freakish; capricious; odd in appearance; fantastic.—**Whimsicality**, **Whimsicalness**, whim-zi-kal'i-ti, whim'zi-kal-nes, *n.* The state or quality of being whimsical; an oddity; a whim.—**Whimsically**, whim'zi-kal-li, *adv.* Freakishly.

Whimbrel, whim'brel, *n.* [Perhaps from its cry resembling a *whimpering.*] A British bird closely allied to the curlew, but considerably smaller.

Whimper, whim'pėr, *v.i.* [Akin to G. *wimmern*, to whimper, and to *whine*, both being imitative words.] To cry with a low, whining, broken voice.—*v.t.* To utter in a low, whining, or crying tone.—*n.* A low, peevish, broken cry.—**Whimperer**, whim'-pėr-ėr, *n.* One who whimpers.—**Whimpering**, whim'pėr-ing, *n.* A whimper.

Whimsey. Under WHIM.

Whin, whin, *n.* [W. *chwyn*, weeds.] Gorse; furze. FURZE.—**Whin-chat**, *n.* A passerine bird visiting Britain in summer, and commonly found among broom and furze. —**Whinny**, whin'i, *a.* Abounding in whins.—**Whinstone**, whin'stōn, *n.* [Probably first given to the blocks of whinstone often found lying in waste places.] A name for greenstone, and also applied to any dark-coloured and hard unstratified rock.

Whine, whīn, *v.i.—whined, whining.* [A. Sax. *hwinan*, to whiz; Icel. *hvina*, Dan. *hvine*, to whiz; imitative words like *whiz*, *whir*, &c.] To express distress or complaint by a plaintive drawling cry; to complain in a mean or unmanly way; to make a similar noise, as dogs or other animals. —*n.* A drawling plaintive tone; a mean or affected complaint. — **Whiner**, whī'nėr, *n.* One who whines.—**Whiningly**, whī'ning-li, *adv.* In a whining manner.

Whinny, whin'i, *v.i.—whinnied, whinnying.* [Imitative and akin to *whine*; comp. L. *hinnio*, to whinny.] To neigh.—*n.* The neigh of a horse; a low neigh.

Whip, whip, *v.t.—whipped, whipping.* [Allied to D. *wippen*, to skip, to toss; *wip*, a swing, a swipe; O.D. *wippe*, a whip; L.G. *wippen*, Dan. *vippe*, to see-saw; G. *wippen*, to rock, to see-saw, &c.; comp. also W. *chwip*, a quick turn; *chwipiaw*, to move briskly.] To take or seize with a sudden motion; to carry or convey suddenly and rapidly: with *away*, *out*, *up*, and the like; to sew slightly; to form into gathers; to overlay, as a rope or cord, with a cord, twine, or thread going round and round; to strike with a lash or with anything tough and flexible; to lash; to flog; to drive with lashes; to make to spin round with lashes (to *whip* a top); to lash in a figurative sense; to treat with cutting severity; to fish in with rod and line; to beat into a froth, as eggs, cream, &c.—*To whip in*, to keep from scattering, as hounds in a hunt; hence, to bring or keep the members of a party together.—*v.i.* To start suddenly and run; to turn and run, with *away*, *round*, &c.—*n.* An instrument for driving horses, cattle, &c., or for correction, consisting commonly of a handle, to which is attached a thong of plaited leather; a lash; a coachman or driver of a carriage (a good *whip*); a member of parliament or other legislative body who secures the attendance of as many members as possible at important divisions; a call made upon members to be in their places at a certain time.—**Whip-cord**, *n.* A hard-twisted cord of which lashes for whips are made.—**Whip-hand**, *n.* The hand that holds the whip in riding or driving.—*To have the whip-hand of*, to have an advantage over.—**Whip-lash**, *n.* The lash or striking end of a whip.—**Whipper**, whip'ėr, *n.* One who whips.—**Whipper-in**, *n.* One who keeps hounds from wandering, and *whips* them *in*, if necessary.—**Whipper-snapper**, *n.* A diminutive, insignificant person; a whipster.—**Whipping**, whip'ing, *n.* Punishment with a whip; flagellation.—**Whipping-boy**, *n.* A boy educated with a prince and punished in his stead.—**Whipping-post**, *n.* A post to which offenders were tied when whipped.—**Whip-poor-will**, *n.* The popular name of an American bird, allied to the European goat-sucker or night-jar, so called from its cry.—**Whip-saw**, *n.* A thin, narrow saw set in a frame.—**Whipster**, whip'stėr, *n.* A nimble little fellow; a sharp shallow fellow: used with some degree of contempt.

Whippet, whip'et, *n.* A breed of dog resembling the greyhound but smaller, used chiefly for coursing and racing; *milit.* a light tank which can move quickly.

Whir, whėr, *v.i.* [From the sound, partly influenced in meaning by *whirl*; comp. *whiz.*] To whiz; to fly, dart, revolve, or otherwise move quickly with a whizzing or buzzing sound. —*n.* The buzzing or whirring sound made by a quickly revolving wheel, a partridge's wings, and the like.—**Whirring**, whėr'ing, *n.* The sound of something that whirs; the sound of a partridge's or pheasant's wings.

Whirl, whėrl, *v.t.* [A freq. corresponding to A.Sax. *hweorfan*, to turn (whence *wharf*); equivalent to Icel. and Sw. *hvirfla*, Dan. *hvirvle*, O.D. *wervelen*, G. *wirbeln*, similar frequentatives.] To turn round or cause to revolve rapidly; to turn with velocity; to carry away by means of something that turns round.—*v.i.* To turn round rapidly; to revolve or rotate swiftly; to move along swiftly as in a wheeled vehicle.—*n.* A turning with velocity; rapid rotation; something that moves with a whirling motion; a hook used in twisting, as in a rope machine; *bot.* and *conch.* same as *Whorl*. — **Whirl-about**, *n.* Something that whirls with velocity; a whirligig.—**Whirl-blast**, *n.* A whirlwind.—**Whirler**, whėr'lėr, *n.* One who or that which whirls.—**Whirligig**, whėr'li-gig, *n.* [*Whirl* and *gig.*] A toy which children spin or whirl round. — **Whirlpool**, whėrl'pöl, *n.* A circular eddy or current in a river or the sea produced by the configuration of the channel, by meeting currents, by winds meeting tides, &c.—**Whirlwig**, whėrl'wig, *n.* [*Whirl*, and A.Sax. *wicga*, *wigga*, a beetle or similar insect; comp. *earwig.*] A beetle which may be seen circling round on the surface of ponds, &c., with great rapidity.—**Whirlwind**, whėrl'wind, *n.* A whirling wind; a violent wind moving in a circle, or rather in a spiral form, as if moving round an axis, this axis having at the same time a progressive motion.

Whisk, whisk, *v.t.* [Same as Dan. *viske*, to wipe, from *visk*, a wisp, a bunch; Icel. *visk*, a wisp; Sw. *viska*, to wipe; akin to *wash.*] To sweep, brush, or agitate with a light, rapid motion; to move with a quick, sweeping motion.—*v.i.* To move nimbly and with velocity.—*n.* A rapid, sweeping motion, as of something light; a sudden puff or gale; a wisp or small bunch; a brush or small besom; *cookery*, an instrument for rapidly agitating certain articles, as cream, eggs, &c. — **Whisker**, whis'kėr, *n.* One who or that which whisks; the hair growing on the cheeks of a man, formerly also the hair on the upper lip, the moustache; the bristly hairs growing on the upper lip of a cat or other animal at each side.—**Whiskered**, whis'kėrd, *a.* Having whiskers; formed into whiskers.

Whiskey, whis'ki, *n.* [From *whisk*, because it whisks along rapidly.] A kind of one-horse chaise. Sometimes called *Tim-whiskey*.

Whisky, Whiskey, whis'ki, *n.* [Ir. and Gael. *uisge-beatha*, whisky, usquebaugh, lit. water of life—*uisge*, water, *beatha*, life. *Whisky*, therefore, means simply water.] An ardent spirit distilled generally from barley, but sometimes from wheat, rye, sugar, &c.; there being two chief varieties —viz. malt-whisky and grain-whisky, the former of finer quality, and made from malted grain.—**Whiskeyfied, Whiskified**, whis'ki-fīd, *a.* Affected with whisky; intoxicated.

Whisp, whisp, *n.* Same as *Wisp*.

Whisper, whis'pėr, *v.i.* [A.Sax. *hwisprian*, to whisper, an imitative word, like G. *wispern*, O.D. *whisperen*, and Icel. *hviskra*, to whisper. Comp. *whistle*, *whist*, *whizz*, &c.] To speak with a low, hissing, or sibilant voice; to speak softly or without sonant breath; to make a low, sibilant sound, as the wind.—*v.t.* To say in a whisper or under the breath.—*n.* A low, soft, sibilant voice; the utterance of words with the breath merely; what is uttered by whispering; a low, sibilant sound, as of the wind.—**Whisperer**, whis'pėr-ėr, *n.* One who whispers; one who tells secrets. —**Whispering**, whis'pėr-ing, *p.* and *a.* Speaking in a whisper; making secret insinuations of evil; backbiting; making a low, sibilant sound.—*Whispering gallery* or *dome*, a gallery or dome in which the sound of words uttered in a low voice or whisper is communicated to a greater distance than under ordinary circumstances. — **Whisperingly**, whis'pėr-ing-ly, *adv.* In or with a whisper.

Whist, whist, *interj.* [Akin to *hush*, *hist.*] Silence! hush! be still!—*a.* Silent; still. —*n.* A well-known game at cards, played by four persons and with the full pack, said to be so called because the parties playing it have to be *whist* or silent.

Whistle, whis'l, *v.i.—whistled, whistling.* [A.Sax. *hwistlian*, to whistle, to pipe; Dan. *hvisle*, Sw. *hvissla*, to whistle; Icel. *hvísla*, to whisper; all imitative words like *whisper*, *wheeze*, *whizz*, &c.] To utter a kind of musical sound by pressing the breath through a small orifice formed by contracting the lips; to utter a sharp or piercing tone, or series of tones, as birds; to pipe; to produce a shrill sound; to sound with a loud shrill wind-instrument; to sound shrill or like a pipe.—*v.t.* To utter or modulate by whistling; to call, direct, or signal by a whistle. —*To whistle off*, to send off by a whistle; to send from the fist in pursuit of prey: a term in falconry.—*n.* The sound produced by one who whistles; any similar sound; the shrill note of a bird; a sound of this kind from an instrument; an instrument or apparatus for producing such a sound; the instrument sounded by escaping steam used on railway engines, steam-ships, &c.; the mouth or throat (in the colloquial phrase *to wet one's whistle*=to take a drink or dram).—*To pay for one's whistle*, or *to pay dear for one's whistle*, to pay a high price for something one fancies; to pay dearly for indulging one's taste or wish.—**Whistler**, whis'lėr, *n.* One who whistles.

Whit, whit, *n.* [By metathesis from A.Sax. *wiht*, a creature, a wight, a whit. WIGHT.] The smallest part or particle imaginable; an iota; a tittle: used generally with a negative (not a *whit* better).

White, whīt, *a.* [A.Sax. *hwít*, white = D. *wit*, Icel. *hvítr*, Dan. *hvid*, Sw. *hvit*, G. *weiss*, Goth. *hveits*; cog. Skr. *çveta*, white, *çvit*, to shine. Hence *wheat*, the *white* grain.] Being of the colour of pure snow; not tinged or tinted with any of the proper colours or their compounds; snowy; the opposite of black or dark; pale; pallid; bloodless, as from fear or cowardice; pure and unsullied; gray, grayish-white or hoary, as from age, grief, fear, &c. (*white* hair); lucky; favourable (a *white* day).—*n.* The colour of snow; the lightest colouring matter or pigment, or the hue produced by such; a part of something having the colour of snow; the central part of the butt in archery; the albumen of an egg; that part of the ball of the eye surrounding the iris or coloured part; a member of the white race of mankind.—*v.t.* To make white; to whiten. — **White-ant**, *n.* A termite.—**White-arsenic**, *n.* Arsenious oxide.—**White-bait**, *n.* A very small fish of the herring kind, abounding in the Thames, and much prized as a delicacy.—**White-bear**, *n.* The polar bear.—**Whiteboy**, whīt'boi, *n.* A member of an illegal association formed in Ireland about 1760. —**Whitechapel-cart**, *n.* [From *White-chapel* in London.] A light, two-wheeled spring-cart. Often called *Chapel-cart*. —**White-clover**, *n.* A small species of perennial clover bearing white flowers.—**White-copper**, *n.* Same as *Packfong* and *Tutenag*.—**White-crop**, *n.* A grain crop: in contradistinction to *green-crop*, *root-crop*, &c.—**White-faced**, *a.* Having a white or pale face.—**White-feather**, *n.* The symbol of cowardice, a term introduced from cock-fighting, a game-cock having no white feathers; generally used in such phrases as *to show the white-feather*= to show cowardice, to behave like a coward.

—**White-fish**, *n.* A general name for whitings and haddocks.—**White-friar**, *n.* A friar of the Carmelite order, from their white cloaks.—**White-gum**, *n.* A species of rash, in which the pimples are whitish.—**White-heat**, *n.* That degree of heat at which iron becomes glowing white.—**White-herring**, *n.* A herring salted but not smoked.—**White-iron**, *n.* Thin sheet-iron covered with a coating of tin; tinplate.—**White-lead**, *n.* A carbonate of lead much used in painting; ceruse. Under LEAD.—**White-leather**, *n.* Leather prepared with alum and salt, and therefore of a white colour.—**White-leg**, *n.* PHLEGMASIA.—**White-lie**, *n.* A lie for which some kind of excuse can be offered; a harmless or non-malicious falsehood.—**White-light**, *n.* The light which comes directly from the sun; a whitish light produced artificially. — **White-livered**, *a.* [From an old notion that pusillanimous persons had pale-coloured or bloodless livers.] Cowardly; dastardly. — **White-metal**, *n.* A general name for any alloy in which zinc, tin, nickel, or lead is used in such quantity as to give it a white colour, as Britannia-metal, German-silver, queen's-metal, &c. — **White-money**, *n.* Silver coin. — **Whiten**, whī'tn, *v.t.* To make white; to bleach; to blanch.—*v.i.* To grow white; to turn or become white.—**Whitener**, whī'tn-ėr, *n.* One who or that which whitens.—**Whiteness**, whīt'nes, *n.* The state of being white; want of blood in the face; paleness; purity; cleanness.—**White-nun**, *n.* A name of the smew.—**White-pine**, *n.* A valuable pine of Canada and the northern United States. — **White-poplar**, *n.* A poplar that has the under side of the leaves white.—**White-precipitate**, *n.* A white mercurial preparation used in medicine as an outward application.—**White-pyrites**, *n.* An iron ore of a tin-white colour, passing into a brass-yellow or steel-gray.—**Whites**, whīts, *n.pl.* A superior kind of flour made from white wheat; cloth goods of a plain white colour; also leucorrhœa.—**White-smith**, whīt'smith, *n.* A tinsmith; a worker in iron who finishes or polishes the work.—**White-spruce**, *n.* A species of spruce. —**White-squall**, *n.* Under SQUALL.—**White-swelling**, *n.* A popular name for severe diseases of the joints which are the result of chronic inflammation, the knee, ankle, wrist, and elbow being the joints most subject to white-swellings. — **White-thorn**, *n.* The common hawthorn.—**White-throat**, *n.* A small British bird of the warbler family.—**White-vitriol**, *n.* A name for sulphate of zinc, employed in medicine as an emetic and tonic. — **Whitewash**, whīt'wosh, *n.* A wash or liquid for whitening something; a composition of lime and water, or of whiting, size, and water, for whitening walls, ceilings, &c. — *v.t.* To cover with whitewash; hence, *fig.* to clear from imputations; to restore the reputation of; colloquially, to clear from the effects of bankruptcy by passing through a judical process. — **Whitewasher**, whīt'wosh-ėr, *n.* One who whitewashes.—**White-wine**, *n.* Any wine of a clear transparent colour. —**White-witch**, *n.* A witch of a beneficent disposition.—**White-wood**, *n.* A name applied to a number of trees. — **Whitish**, whī'tish, *a.* Somewhat white.

Whither, whiᴛʜ'ėr, *adv.* [A.Sax. *hwider*, whither, from stem of *who*, *what*, and suffix *-ther*; closely akin to *whether*.] To what place: used interrogatively; to which place: used relatively. *Where* has now to a considerable extent taken the place of *whither*. —**Whithersoever**, whiᴛʜ'ėr-sō-ev-ėr, *adv.* To whatever place.

Whiting, whī'ting, *n.* [From *white*; in first meaning with dim. term. *-ing*; in second with term. of verbal noun.] A small fish of the cod tribe which abounds on all the British coasts, and forms a delicate article of food; chalk pulverized and freed from impurities, used in whitewashing, for cleaning plate, &c.—**Whiting-pollack**, *n.* The pollack.—**Whiting-pout**, *n.* A British fish of the cod family; called also *Bib.*

Whitlow, whit'lō, *n.* [A corruption of *whickflaw* for *quick-flaw*, lit. *flaw* or sore of the *quick*.] An inflammation affecting one or more of the joints of the fingers, generally terminating in an abscess; an inflammatory disease of the feet in sheep.

Whitsunday, whit'sun-dā, *n.* [Lit. white Sunday. The name was given because Pentecost was formerly a great season for christenings, in which white robes are a prominent feature.] The seventh Sunday after Easter; a festival of the church in commemoration of the descent of the Holy Spirit on the day of Pentecost; in Scotland, a term-day (May 15, or May 26 Old Style).—**Whit-Monday**, *n.* The Monday following Whitsunday; in England generally observed as a holiday.—**Whitsun**, whit'sun, *a.* Pertaining to Whitsuntide.—*Whitsun Monday, Tuesday*, &c., the Monday, Tuesday, &c., following Whitsunday.—**Whitsuntide**, whit'sun-tīd, *n.* [*Whitsun*, and *tide*, time, season.] The season of Pentecost.

Whittle, whit'l, *n.* [O.E. *thwitel*, dim. from A.Sax. *thwītan*, to cut; O.E. and Sc. *white*, to cut with a knife.] A knife: rarely now used except in provincial English or Scotch.—*v.t.*—*whittled, whittling.* To cut or dress with a knife.

Whiz, whiz, *v.i.*—*whizzed, whizzing.* [An imitative word; comp. *wheeze, whistle, whir*, &c.] To make a humming or hissing sound, like an arrow or ball flying through the air. — *n.* A sound between hissing and humming.

Whizz-bang, whiz-bang, *n.* In the European War, a small high-velocity shell which burst before the report of the gun was heard.

Who, hö, *pron. relative*; possessive **Whose**, höz; objective **Whom**, höm. [A.Sax. *hwá*, who, masc. and fem., *hwæt*, what, neut.: always an interrogative; Icel. *hver, hvat*, Dan. *hvo, hvad*, D. *wie, wat*, G. *wer, was*, Goth. *hvas, hvo, hvata*; cog. L. *qui*, W. *pwy*, Gael. and Ir. *co*, Per. *ki*, Skr. *kas*, who. Akin are *when, where, whither, which*, &c. WHY, HOW.] A relative and interrogative pronoun always used substantively (that is, not joined with a noun), and with relation to a person or persons; used interrogatively who = what or which person or persons? of what personality (*who* is he? I do not know *who* he is); used relatively = that; which person; sometimes used elliptically for *he, they*, or *those, who* or *whom*.—*As who should say*, as one who should say; as if he should say. ∴ *Who, Which, That.* These agree in being relatives, *who* being used for persons, *which* for things, and *that* for either; but *that* has often more preciseness, and in some cases it cannot be used for *who* ('James *who*', not 'James *that*').—**Whoever**, hö-ev'ėr, *pron.* Any person whatever; no matter who.—**Whoso**, hö'sō, *pron.* Whosoever; whoever. — **Whosoever**, hö-sō-ev'ėr, *pron.* Whoever; whatever person. — **Whosesoever**, höz-sō-ev'ėr, *pron.* Of whatever person: the possessive or genitive case of *whosoever.*

Whoa, whō'a, *exclam.* Stop! stand still!

Whole, hōl, *a.* [O.E. *hole, hool* (the *w* being erroneous, as in *whore*), from A.Sax. *hál*, whole, sound, safe; D. *heel*, Icel. *heill*, G. *heil*, Goth. *hails*, healthy, sound, whole. HALE, HEAL, HOLY.] In a healthy state; sound; well; restored to a sound state; healed; unimpaired; uninjured; not broken or fractured; not defective or imperfect; entire; complete; comprising all parts, units, &c., that make up an aggregate; all the; total (the *whole* city).—*Whole number*, an integer, as opposed to a fraction. ∴ Syn. under COMPLETE.—*n.* An entire thing; a thing complete in itself; the entire or total assemblage of parts; a complete system; a regular combination of parts. — *Upon the whole*, all circumstances being considered; upon a review of the entire matter. — **Whole-length**, *n.* A portrait or statue exhibiting the whole figure.—**Wholeness**, hōl'nes, *n.* The state of being whole, entire, or sound; entireness; totality.—**Wholesale**, hōl'sāl, *n.* Sale of goods by the entire piece or large quantity, as distinguished from *retail.*—*a.* Pertaining to the trade by wholesale; dealing by wholesale; *fig.* in great quantities; extensive and indiscriminate.—**Wholesome**, hōl'sum, *a.* [*Whole*, and affix *-some.*] Tending to promote health; good for the bodily system; nourishing; healthful; favourable to morals, religion, or prosperity; salutary.—**Wholesomely**, hōl'sum-li, *adv.* In a wholesome manner. —**Wholesomeness**, hōl'sum-nes, *n.* The quality of being wholesome; salutariness.—**Wholly**, hōl'li, *adv.* [For *whole-ly.*] Entirely; completely; perfectly; totally; exclusively.

Whoop, whöp, *v.t.* [Perhaps from Fr. *houper*, to whoop, an imitative word; comp. *hoot.* Hence *whooping-cough.*] To shout with a loud, clear voice.—*n.* A shout; a loud clear call.—**Whooping-cough**, *n.* A disease, *esp.* of children, characterized by paroxysms of coughing ending in prolonged crowing or respiratory whoop.

Whoot, whöt, *v.i.* The same as *Hoot.*

Whop, whop, *v.t.* — *whopped, whopping.* [W. *chwapiaw*, to strike, from *chwap*, a stroke.] To strike; to beat. (*Colloq.*) — **Whopper**, whop'ėr, *n.* [The idea of greatness or bulk is often associated with that of a blow; thus a *striking* likeness is an impressive likeness.] Anything uncommonly large; a manifest lie. (*Colloq.*)

Whore, hōr, *n.* [A.Sax. *hóre*, Icel. *hóra*, Dan. *hore*, D. *hoer*, G. *hure*, a whore; same root as L. *carus*, dear; Skr. *kâma*, love. The *w* has intruded as in *whole.*] A woman who prostitutes her body for hire; a harlot; a prostitute; a lewd woman.—*v.i.* —*whored, whoring.* To have to do with prostitutes. — *v.t.* To corrupt by lewd intercourse. — **Whoredom**, hōr'dum, *n.* Fornication; idolatry (O.T.). — **Whoremonger**, hōr'mung-gėr, *n.* One who has to do with whores; a fornicator; a lecher. —**Whoreson**, hōr'sun, *n.* A bastard: a term of contempt or abuse.—*a.* Bastard-like; scurvy.—**Whorish**, hō'rish, *a.* Incontinent; unchaste.—**Whorishly**, hō'rish-li, *adv.* In a whorish manner.—**Whorishness**, hō'rish-nes, *n.*

Whorl, whorl, *n.* [A form of *whirl*, which is also used in same sense.] A ring of leaves or other organs of a plant all on the same plane; a verticil; a turn of the spire of a univalve cell; the fly of a spindle, generally made of wood, sometimes of hard stone.—**Whorled**, whorld, *a.* Furnished with whorls; verticillate.

Whortleberry, whor'tl-be-ri, *n.* [From A.Sax. *wyrtil*, a small shrub, dim. of *wort*, a wort. WORT.] The bilberry and its fruit.—**Whort**, whort, *n.* The fruit of the Whortleberry or the shrub itself.

Whose, Whoso, &c. Under WHO.

Why, whī, *adv.* [A.Sax. *hwí, hwý*, the instrumental case of *hwá*, who, *hwæt*, what. *How* is a form of the same word. WHO.] For what cause, reason, or purpose; wherefore: interrogatively (direct or indirect); for what reason or cause; for what; wherefore: used relatively.—*Why so*, for what reason; wherefore. *Why* is sometimes used substantively (the how and the *why*). — *interj.* Used emphatically or to enliven the speech or to draw attention.

Wick, wik, *n.* [A.Sax. *weoca, wecca*, a wick; D. *wiek*, a wick, a tent for a wound; Sw. *veke*, Dan. *væge*, a wick; allied to *weak* (being pliant) and to *wicker.*] A sort of loose spongy string or band which draws up the oil in lamps or the melted tallow or wax in candles to be burned.

Wicked, wik'ed, *a.* [From old *wicke, wikke*, wicked (comp. *wretched*), apparently from A.Sax. *wicca*, a wizard, *wicce*, a witch. WITCH.] Evil in principle or practice; doing evil; sinful; bad; wrong; iniquitous; mischievous; prone or disposed to mischief, often good-natured mischief; roguish. — **Wickedly**, wik'ed-li, *adv.* In a wicked manner; viciously; corruptly; immorally.—**Wickedness**, wik'ed-nes, *n.* The state or quality of being wicked; depravity; sinfulness; vice; crime; sin; a wicked act.

Wicker, wik'ėr, *a.* [O.E. *wikir, wiker*, a

withy, from stem of *weak*; comp. Sw. *wika*, to plait, to bend; Dan. *vegre*, a withy, G. *wickel*, a roll. WEAK, WICK.] Made of plaited twigs or osiers; covered with such plaited work.—*n.* A small pliant twig; a withe; a basket.—**Wickered**, wik'ėrd, *a.* Made of or covered with wickers or twigs.—**Wicker-work**, *n.* A texture of twigs; basket-work.

Wicket, wik'et, *n.* [O.Fr. *wiket* (Fr. *guichet*), from Icel. *vikja*, to turn, to bend, same word as A.Sax. *wican*, to yield. WEAK.] A small gate or doorway, especially a small door forming part of a larger one; a hole in a door; *cricket*, the object at which the bowler aims, consisting of three upright rods, having two small pieces lying in grooves along their tops; the ground on which the wickets are set.

Wide, wīd, *a.* [A.Sax. *wíd*, wide, broad, extensive = D. *wijd*, Icel. *víðr*, Sw. and Dan. *vid*, G. *weit*, wide; connections doubtful.] Having a great or considerable distance or extent between the sides; broad: opposed to *narrow*; having a great extent every way; vast; extensive; *fig.* not narrow or limited; enlarged; liberal; broad to a certain degree (three feet *wide*); failing to hit a mark; hence, remote or distant from anything, as truth, propriety, or the like.—*adv.* To a distance; to a considerable extent or space; far; far from the mark or from the purpose; astray.—**Wide-awake**, *a.* On the alert; ready prepared; knowing. (*Colloq.*)—*n.* [So called because worn greatly by smart sporting men.] A species of soft felt hat with a broad brim turned up all round.—**Widely**, wīd'li, *adv.* In a wide manner or degree; with great extent each way; very much; greatly; far.—**Widen**, wī'dn, *v.t.* To make wide or wider; to extend the breadth of.—*v.i.* To grow wide or wider; to extend itself.—**Wideness**, wīd'nes, *n.* The state or quality of being wide; breadth; large extent in all directions.—**Wide-spread**, *a.* Spread to a great distance; extending far and wide.—**Width**, width, *n.* [Comp. *breadth*, *length*.] Breadth; wideness.

Widgeon, wij'on, *n.* [Fr. *vigeon*, *vingeon*, names of ducks; comp. L. *vipio*, *vipionis*, a small crane.] A migratory bird allied to the duck family, which breeds in high northern latitudes.

Widow, wid'ō, *n.* [A.Sax. *widuwe*, *wuduwe*, a widow = D. *weduwe*, L.G. *wedewe*, G. *wittwe*, Goth. *widuwo*; cog. Rus. *vdova*, L. *vidua*, from *viduus*, deprived (VOID); Skr. *vidhavâ*, a widow.] A woman who has lost her husband by death, and who remains still unmarried: also used adjectively (a *widow* lady).—*v.t.* To reduce to the condition of a widow; to bereave of a husband or mate; to strip of anything good.—**Widower**, wid'ō-ėr, *n.* A man who has lost his wife by death.—**Widowhood**, wid'ō-hųd, *n.* The state of a man or woman whose husband or wife is dead, and who has not married again; the state of being a widow.

Width. Under WIDE.

Wield, wēld, *v.t.* [O.E. *welden*, A.Sax. (*ge*)*weldan*, (*ge*)*wyldan*, from *wealdan*, to rule; Icel. *valda*, G. *walten*, to rule; Goth. *valdan*, to govern; same root as L. *valeo*, to be strong. VALID.] To use in the hand or hands with full command or power; to hold aloft or swing freely with the arm; to use or employ with the hand; to manage, employ, or have full control over.—*To wield the sceptre*, to govern with supreme command.—**Wieldable**, wēl'da-bl, *a.* Capable of being wielded.—**Wielder**, wēl'dėr, *n.* One who wields.—**Wieldy**, wēl'di, *a.* Capable of being wielded; wieldable.

Wien's Law, vēn, *n.* [After W. *Wien*, German physicist.] *Physics*, the law that the wave-length of the dominant radiation from a black body is inversely as the absolute temperature.

Wier, wēr, *n.* Same as *Weir*.

Wife, wīf, *n.* pl. **Wives**, wīvz. [A.Sax. *wíf*, a woman, a wife = D. *wijf*, Icel. *víf*, Dan. *viv*, G. *weib*, a woman; root doubtful. This word gives the first syllable of *woman*.] Originally, any woman of mature age; still so used in compounds (ale-*wife*, fish-*wife*); a woman or female of any age who is united to a man in wedlock: the correlative of *husband*.—**Wifehood**, wīf'hųd, *n.* State and character of a wife.—**Wifeless**, wīf'les, *a.* Without a wife; unmarried.—**Wifelike**, wīf'līk, *a.* Resembling or pertaining to a wife or woman.—**Wifely**, wīf'li, *a.* Like a wife; becoming a wife.

Wig, wig, *n.* [The final syllable of *periwig*.] An artificial covering of hair for the head, used generally to conceal baldness, but formerly worn as a fashionable means of decoration.—**Wig-block**, *n.* A block or shaped piece of wood for fitting a wig on.—**Wigged**, wigd, *a.* Having the head covered with a wig.—**Wiggery**, wig'ėr-i, *n.* The work of a wigmaker; false hair.—**Wigging**, wig'ing, *n.* A rating; a scolding. (*Colloq.*)—**Wigless**, wig'les, *a.* Without a wig.

Wigan, wig'an, *n.* [From *Wigan* in Lancashire.] A stiff, open canvas-like fabric, used for stiffening and protecting the lower inside surface of skirts, &c.

Wight, wīt, *n.* [A.Sax. *wiht*, *wuht*, a creature, a thing; D. *wicht*, a baby; G. *wicht*, creature, fellow; Goth. *waihts*, *waiht*, a thing, a whit; originally 'moving creature'; allied to *wag*, *weigh*. *Whit* is the same word, and it is also contained in *aught*, *naught* or *nought*.] A being; a human being; a person either male or female.

Wight, wīt, *a.* [Icel. *vígr*, neut. *vígt*, warlike, fit for war, from *víg* (A.Sax. *wíg*), war; akin Sw. *vig*, agile, nimble.] Having warlike prowess; strong and active; agile. (*Poet.*)

Wigwam, wig'wam, *n.* [A native Indian term.] An Indian cabin or hut, so called in North America.

Wild, wīld, *a.* [A.Sax. *wild*, wild, not tame; savage = Sc. *will*, Icel. *villr*, wild, astray, bewildered; Dan. and Sw. *vild*, D. *wild*, G. *wild*, Goth. *wiltheis*, wild; akin to *will*, an animal that is wild, also wandering at its will. WILL.] Living in a state of nature; roving at will; not tame; not domestic; savage; uncivilized; ferocious; sanguinary; growing or produced without culture; not cultivated; desert; uncultivated; as left by nature (a *wild* scene); turbulent; tempestuous; stormy; furious: in both a physical and moral sense; violent; unregulated; passionate (a *wild* outbreak of rage); disorderly in conduct; frolicsome; wayward; reckless; rash; not based on reason or prudence; wanting order or regularity; extravagant; fantastic; indicating strong emotion or excitement; excited; bewildered; distracted (a *wild* look); excessively eager; ardent to pursue, perform, or obtain.—*To run wild*, to take to a wild life, or to a loose way of living; to escape from cultivation and grow in a wild state.—*n.* A desert; an uninhabited and uncultivated tract or region.—**Wild-basil**, *n.* Basil-weed.—**Wild-beast**, *n.* An untamed or savage animal.—**Wild-boar**, *n.* An animal of the hog kind, the ancestor of the domesticated swine.—**Wildcat**, *n.* A ferocious animal closely akin to the domestic cat, but larger and has a shorter, bushier tail, formerly abundant in Europe.—**Wild duck**, *n.* A web-footed bird, the stock of the common domestic duck; the mallard.—**Wildfire**, wīld'fīr, *n.* A composition of inflammable materials readily catching fire and hard to be extinguished; a kind of lightning unaccompanied by thunder; a name for erysipelas; also a name for an eruptive disease, a species of lichen.—**Wildfowl**, *n.* A name given to various birds pursued as game, but ordinarily restricted to waterfowl.—**Wild goose**, *n.* A migratory North American game bird that breeds in the cold regions, and is usually gray and brown in color.—*Wild-goose chase*, the pursuit of anything in ignorance of the direction it will take; a foolish pursuit or enterprise.—**Wilding**, wīl'ding, *n.* A plant that grows wild or without cultivation.—**Wildish**, wīl'dish, *a.* Somewhat wild.—**Wildly**, wīld'li, *adv.* In a wild state or manner; savagely; with disorder, perturbation, or distraction; extravagantly; irregularly.—**Wildness**, wīld'nes, *n.* The state of being wild; desert or uncultivated state; savageness; fierceness; distraction; great perturbation of look.—**Wild oats**, *n.* Weeds and grass of the genus *Avena*; youthful excesses or indiscretions.—*To sow one's wild oats*, to indulge in youthful excesses, dissipations, or follies; *to have sown one's wild oats*, to have given up youthful dissipation; to have settled down.—**Wildwood**, Belonging to wild or unfrequented woods.

Wilder, wil'dėr, *v.t.* [From the *wilder-* of *wilderness*; hence *bewilder*.] To cause to lose the way or track; to puzzle with mazes or difficulties; to bewilder.—**Wilderedly**, wil'dėrd-li, *adv.* In a wildered manner.—**Wilderment**, wil'dėr-ment, *n.* Bewilderment.

Wilderness, wil'dėr-nes, *n.* [Formed with suffix *-ness* from older *wilderne*, a wilderness, from A.Sax. *wilder*, a wild animal, from *wild*, wild, *deór*, an animal; comp. D. *wildernis*, G. *wildniss*, wilderness.] A desert; a tract of land or region uncultivated and uninhabited by human beings, whether a forest or a wide barren plain, a portion of a garden set apart for things to grow in unchecked luxuriance.

Wile, wīl, *n.* [A.Sax. *wíle*, *wíl*, wile; Icel. *vél*, *vœl*, artifice, craft, trick; connections doubtful. *Guile* is the same word, but has come to us directly from the French. GUILE.] A trick or stratagem practised for insnaring or deception; a sly, insidious artifice.—*v.t.*—*wiled*, *wiling*. To draw or turn away, as by diverting the mind; to cajole or to wheedle (Sc.).—**Wileful**, wīl'fųl, *a.* Full of wiles; wily; tricky.—**Wilily**, wī'li-li, *adv.* In a wily manner; insidiously; craftily; cunningly.—**Wiliness**, wī'li-nes, *n.* The character of being wily; cunning; guile.—**Wily**, wī'li, *a.* Capable of using wiles; full of wiles; subtle; cunning; crafty.

Wilful. Under WILL.

Will, wil, *n.* [A.Sax. *willa*, will, from *willan*, to desire, and = D. *wil*, Icel. *vili*, Dan. *villie*, Sw. *vilja*, G. *wille*, will. See the verb.] That faculty or power of the mind by which we determine either to do or not to do something; the power of control which the mind possesses over its own operations; volition; power of resisting impulse; determination; the determination or choice of one possessing authority; wish or pleasure of a superior; strong wish or inclination (it is against my *will*); *law*, the legal declaration of a man's intentions as to what he wishes to be performed after his death in relation to his property; a testament; the written paper containing such a disposition of property. GOOD-WILL, ILL-WILL.—*At will*, at pleasure; as one wishes.—*With a will*, with willingness and pleasure; heartily.—*v. aux.*, pres. I *will*, thou *wilt*, he *will*; past *would*; no past participle. [A.Sax. *willan*, pret. *wolde*; D. *willen*, Icel. *vilja*, Dan. *ville*, to will; G. *will*, I will, infin. *wollen*, to be willing; cog. L. *volo*, I will, *velle*, to will (VOLITION); Gr. *boulomai*, I will. Akin *well*, *weal*, *wild*.] A word denoting either simple futurity or futurity combined with volition according to the subject of the verb. In the first person it expresses willingness, consent, intention, or promise; and when emphasized, determination or fixed purpose (I *will* go); simple futurity with the first person being expressed by *shall* (SHALL). In the second and third persons *will* expresses only a simple future or certainty, the idea of volition, purpose, or wish being then lost.—**Would**, wųd, past tense of *will*, stands in the same relation to *will* that *should* does to *shall*, being seldom or never a preterite indicative pure and simple, but mainly employed in subjunctive, conditional, or optative senses, in the latter case having often the force of an independent verb.—*v.t.* [From the noun rather than from the auxiliary verb. In this use the conjugation is regular, pres. ind. I *will*, thou *willest*, he *wills*, &c., pret. and pp. *willed*.]

To determine by an act of choice (a man may move if he *wills* it); to ordain; to decree; to desire or wish; to intend; to dispose of by testament; to give as a legacy; to bequeath.—*v.i.* [From the noun.] To form a volition; to exercise an act of the will; to desire; to wish; to determine; to decree.—**Willing**, wil'ing, *a.* Ready to do or grant; having the mind inclined; not averse; desirous; ready; borne or accepted voluntarily; voluntary.—**Willing-hearted**, *a.* Having a readily consenting heart or disposition.—**Willingly**, wil'ing-li, *adv.* In a willing manner; with one's free choice or consent; without reluctance; voluntarily; readily; gladly.—**Willingness**, wil'ing-nes, *n.*—**Wilful**, wil'ful, *a.* Governed by one's own will without yielding to reason; not to be moved from one's notions or inclinations; obstinate; refractory; wayward; done by design; intentional (*wilful* murder).—**Wilfully**, wil'ful-li, *adv.* In a wilful manner; waywardly; obstinately; by design; intentionally.—**Wilfulness**, wil'ful-nes, *n.* Obstinacy; stubbornness; perverseness; intention; character of being done by design.

Will-o'-the-wisp, *n.* IGNIS FATUUS.

Willow, wil'ō, *n.* [A.Sax. *welig*, *wilig*, D. *wilg*, L.G. *wilge*, a willow.] A name for numerous well-known species of plants of a tree-like or shrubby habit, valuable for a variety of purposes, including basket-making; an instrument for opening and disentangling locks of wool previous to manufacture. — **Willow pattern**, *n.* A well-known design on stoneware and porcelain dishes, in imitation of a Chinese design: so called from a willow tree (or what may pass for one) which is a prominent object in it.—**Willow herb**, *n.* An herb with pinkish-purple flowers and long leaves like those of the willow. — **Willowy**, wil'ō-i, *a.* Abounding with willows; resembling a willow; slender and graceful.

Wilt, wilt, *v.i.* [Akin *welk.*] To fade.

Wilton-carpet, *n.* [Made originally at *Wilton.*] A variety of Brussels carpet in which the loops are cut open into an elastic velvet pile.

Wily. Under WILE.

Wimble, wim'bl, *n.* [Same (with inserted *b*) as Sc. *wimmle* or *wummle*, Dan. *vimmel*, an auger; akin D. *wemelen*, to bore, *weme*, an auger; Sw. *wimla*, G. *wimmeln*, to be in tremulous movement. *Gimlet* is a dim. form. GIMLET.] An instrument of the gimlet, auger, or brace kind used for boring holes.

Wimple, wim'pl, *n.* [A.Sax. *winpel*, a wimple = D. *wimpel*, Icel. *vimpill*, Dan. *vimpel*, G. *wimpel*, a pennon; perhaps akin to *whip*, *gimp.*] A former female head-dress laid in plaits over the head and round the chin, sides of the face, and neck, still worn by nuns. —*v.t.*—*wimpled*, *wimpling*. To cover, as with a wimple or vail; hence, to hoodwink.—*v.i.* To resemble or suggest wimples; to undulate; to ripple (a brook that *wimples* onwards).

Win, win, *v.t.*—pret. and pp. *won* (wun), ppr. *winning*. [A.Sax. *winnan*, to strive, labour, fight, struggle = D. *winnen*, Icel. *vinna*, Dan. *vinde*, G. (*ge*)*winnen*, to fight, strive, win, &c., Goth. *winnan*, to endure; from root meaning to desire eagerly, seen also in the name of the goddess *Venus*; akin *wean*, *wont.*] To gain by proving one's self superior in a contest; to be victorious in; to gain as victor; to gain possession of by fighting; to get into one's possession by conquest (to *win* a fortress); to gain, procure, or obtain in a general sense, but especially implying labour, effort, or struggle; to allure to kindness or compliance; to gain or obtain, as by solicitation or courtship; to gain to one's side or party, as by solicitation or other influence.—*v.i.* To be superior in a contest or competition; to be victorious; to gain the victory.—**Winner**, win'ėr, *n.* One who wins.—**Winning**, win'ing, *a.* Attracting; adapted to gain favour; charming (a *winning* manner).—*n.* The sum won or gained by success in competition or contest: usually in the pl.—**Winningly**, win'ing-li, *adv.* In a winning manner; charmingly.—**Winning-post**, *n.* A post or goal in a race-course, the order of passing which determines the issue of the race.

Wince, wins, *v.i.*—*winced*, *wincing*. [Formerly also *winch*, from O.Fr. *guinchir*, *guenchir*, *winchir* (?), from O.G. *wenken*, to start aside. Akin to *wink.*] To twist or turn, as in pain or uneasiness; to shrink; to start back. — *n.* The act of one who winces; a start, as from pain.—**Wincer**, win'sėr, *n.* One that winces.

Wincey, win'si, *n.* [Probably a corrupted contr. of *linsey-woolsey*, the steps being *linsey-winsey*, then simply *wincey*. The word was originally Scotch.] A strong and durable cloth, plain or twilled, composed of a cotton warp and a woollen weft.

Winch, winsh, *n.* [A.Sax. *wince*, a winch, a reel for thread; akin *wince*, *wink*, *winkle.*] The crank for turning an axle; a hoisting machine in which an axis is turned by a crank-handle, and a rope or chain wound round it so as to raise a weight.

Wind, wind, in poetry often wīnd, *n.* [A. Sax. *wind*=D. and G. *wind*, Dan. and Sw. *vind*, Icel. *vindr*, Goth. *winds*; cog. L. *ventus*, W. *gwynt*, wind. The root is in Goth. *waian*, Skr. *vâ*, to blow. *Weather* is from same root.] Air naturally in motion with any degree of velocity; a current of air; a current in the atmosphere, as coming from a particular point; a point of the compass, especially one of the cardinal points (O.T.); air artificially put in motion (the *wind* of a cannon-ball); breath modulated by the respiratory organs or by an instrument; power of respiration; lung power; breath; empty or unmeaning words; idle or vain threats; gas generated in the stomach and bowels; flatulence. — *Between wind and water*, in that part of a ship's side which is frequently brought above the water by the rolling of the vessel.—*How the wind blows* or *lies*, the direction of the wind; *fig.* position or state of affairs; how matters stand. —*In the wind's eye*, *in the teeth of the wind*, directly towards the point from which the wind blows; right against the wind.— *Something in the wind*, something within the region of suspicion or surmise, without being acknowledged or announced (*colloq.*). —*To get* (*take*) *wind*, to become public; to be disclosed; to become generally known.— *To get the wind up*, to become nervous and excited.—*To raise the wind*, to obtain the necessary supply of cash (*colloq.*).—*To sail close to the wind*, to sail as much against the direction of the wind as possible. — *v.t.* (wīnd). Pret. and pp. generally *wound*, sometimes *winded*. [From *wind*, the above noun, pronounced as wīnd; the strong conjugation has been introduced through confusion with *wind*, to twist.] To blow; to sound by blowing.—*v.t.* (wind). [From *wind*, *n.*, pronounced wind.] To perceive or follow by the scent; to nose (hounds *wind* an animal); to expose to the wind; to render scant of wind by riding or driving (a horse); to let rest and recover wind.— **Windage**, win'dāj, *n.* *Gun.* the difference between the diameter of the bore of a firearm and that of the ball or shell; the influence of the wind in deflecting a missile; the extent of such deflection. — **Wind-bag**, *n.* A bag filled with wind; a man of mere words; a noisy pretender.—**Wind-bound**, wind'bound, *a.* Prevented from sailing by a contrary wind.—**Wind-chest**, *n.* The chest or reservoir in an organ or harmonium for storing the wind produced by the bellows.—**Wind-egg**, *n.* An egg surrounded only by a membrane.—**Wind-fall**, wind'fal, *n.* Fruit blown from a tree; timber blown down; an unexpected legacy; any unexpected piece of good fortune.— **Wind - flower**, *n.* The anemone. — **Wind-gall**, *n.* A soft tumour on the fetlock joints of a horse; a streak of light on the edge of a cloud, reckoned a sign of approaching stormy weather. — **Wind-gauge**, *n.* An instrument for ascertaining the velocity and force of wind; an anemometer.—**Wind-hover**, *n.* A name of the kestrel.—**Windiness**, win'di-nes, *n.* The state of being windy.—**Wind-instrument**, *n.* An instrument of music, played by breath or wind, as the flute, horn, organ, harmonium, &c.—**Wind-jammer**, wind'-jam-ėr, *n.* A merchant sailing ship or one of its crew.—**Windless**, wind'les, *a.* Free from wind; calm; unruffled.—**Windmill**, wind'mil, *n.* A mill driven by the force of the wind, and used for grinding corn, pumping water, &c.—**Windpipe**, wind'pīp, *n.* The passage for the breath to and from the lungs; the trachea.—**Wind-rose**, *n.* A card with lines corresponding to the points of the compass showing the connection of the wind with the barometer, &c.—**Wind-row**, *n.* A row or line of hay racked together for the purpose of being rolled into cocks or heaps.—**Wind-sail**, *n.* A tube or funnel of canvas used to convey air into the lower apartments of a ship; one of the vanes or sails of a windmill.—**Windward**, wind'wėrd, *n.* The point from which the wind blows.—*a.* On the side toward which the wind blows.—*adv.* Toward the wind.— **Windy**, win'di, *a.* Consisting of wind; formed by gales; tempestuous; boisterous; exposed to the wind; resembling the wind; as empty as the wind; flatulent.

Wind, wīnd, *v.t.* —pret. and pp. *wound* (occasionally *winded*). [A.Sax. *windan*, to wind, twist, twine=D. and G. *winden*, Icel. and Sw. *vinda*, Goth. *windan*; akin *wand*, *wend*, *wander.*] To coil round something; to form into a ball or coil by turning; to turn by shifts and expedients; *refl.* to insinuate; to bend or turn to one's pleasure: to enfold or encircle.—*To wind off*, to unwind; to uncoil.—*To wind up*, to coil up into a small compass; to bring to a conclusion, as a speech or operation; to make a final settlement of; to coil anew the spring or draw up the weights of (a watch or clock). —*v.i.* To turn around something; to have a spiral direction; to have a course marked by bendings; to meander; to make one's way by bendings.—*To wind up*, to come to a conclusion; to conclude; to finish. — **Winder**, wīn'dėr, *n.* One who or that which winds yarn or the like; an instrument or machine for winding.—**Winding**, wīn'-ding, *a.* Bending; having curves or bends; spiral.—*n.* A turn or turning; a bend.— **Windingly**, wīn'ding-li, *adv.* In a winding form.—**Winding-engine**, *n.* A hoisting engine for mines. — **Winding-machine**, *n.* A twisting or warping machine. —**Winding-sheet**, *n.* A sheet in which a corpse is wrapped; a piece of tallow or wax hanging down from a burning candle: regarded as an omen of death.—**Wind-up**, *n.* The conclusion or final settlement of any matter; the closing act; the close.

Windlass, wind'las, *n.* [Partly from D. *windas*, or Icel. *vindáss*, lit. winding-beam; partly from old *windle*, a wheel or reel, a dim. from the verb to *wind.*] A modification of the wheel and axle, consisting of a horizontal barrel turned by a winch or by levers, for raising a weight that hangs at the end of a rope or chain wound on to a barrel.

Windlestraw, win'dl-stra, *n.* [A.Sax. *windelstreow*, properly straw for plaiting, from *windel*, a basket, from *windan*, to wind. WIND.] A name given to various species of grasses; a stalk of grass.

Window, win'dō, *n.* [O.E. *windoge*, *windohe*, from Icel. *vindauga*, a window, lit. a wind-eye—*vindr*, wind, and *auga*, an eye. WIND, EYE.] An opening in the wall of a building for the admission of light or of light and air when necessary; an opening resembling or suggestive of a window; the sash or other thing that covers the aperture. —**Window-blind**, *n.* A blind, screen, or shade for a window.—**Window-curtain**, *n.* A curtain, usually decorative, hung over the window inside a room. — **Window dressing**, *n.* Merchandise attractively displayed in a shop window; an exaggerated statement made with the intention of giving unfavorable facts an attractive appearance.—**Windowed**, win'-dōd, *p.* and *a.* Having a window or windows.—**Window frame**, *n.* The frame of a window which receives the sashes. — **Window glass**, *n.* Glass for windows, of an inferior quality to plate glass.—**Windowless**, win'dō-les, *a.* Without windows.

Windsor-chair, *n.* A kind of strong, plain, polished chair, made entirely of wood, seat as well as back.—**Windsor-soap**, *n.* A kind of fine-scented soap, the chief manufacture of which was once confined to Windsor.

Wine, wīn, *n.* [A.Sax. *win*, borrowed (like D. *wijn*, Icel. *vín*, G. *wein*) from L. *vinum*, wine, akin to *vitis*, the vine, the twining plant (cog. with E. *withy*), the root being seen also in E. to *wind*, *wire*, &c.] An alcoholic liquor obtained by the fermentation of the juice of the grape or fruit of the vine; also, the juice of certain fruits prepared in imitation of this (currant *wine*, gooseberry *wine*). — *Quinine wine*, sherry with sulphate of quinine in solution.—*Spirit of wine*, alcohol.—**Wine-bibber**, *n.* One who drinks much wine.—**Wine-biscuit**, *n.* A light biscuit served with wine.—**Wine-cellar**, *n.* An apartment or cellar for stowing wine.—**Wine-coloured**, *a.* Approaching the colour of red wine. — **Wine-cooler**, *n.* A vessel for cooling wine before it is drunk.—**Wine-fat**, *n.* The vat into which the liquor flows from the wine-press.—**Wine-glass**, *n.* A small glass in which wine is drunk. — **Wine-grower**, *n.* One who cultivates a vineyard and makes wine.—**Wine-measure**, *n.* An old English measure for wines and spirits, in which the gallon was to the imperial gallon as 5 to 6 nearly.—**Wine-merchant**, *n.* A merchant who deals in wines.—**Wine-palm**, *n.* A palm from which palm-wine is obtained. — **Wine-press**, *n.* An apparatus in which the juice is pressed out of grapes.—**Wine-taster**, *n.* A person employed to taste and judge of wine for purchasers.—**Wine-vault**, *n.* A vault or cellar for wine; a name frequently assumed by a public-house or tavern. — **Winy**, wī'ni, *a.* Having the taste or qualities of wine.

Wing, wing, *n.* [Same as Sw. and Dan. *vinge*, Icel. *vængr*, a wing; probably akin to *wag*.] One of the anterior limbs in birds, specially modified and provided with feathers, in most cases serving as organs of flight; an organ used for flying by some other animals, as insects and bats; act of flying; flight (to take *wing*); that which moves or acts like a wing, as the sail of a windmill, of a ship, &c.; a projection of a building on one side of the central or main portion; a lateral extension of anything; a leaf of a gate or double door; one of the sides of the stage of a theatre; also, one of the long narrow scenes which fill up the picture on the side of the stage; the half of a regiment or larger body, termed 'right' and 'left' when in line, 'leading' and 'rear' when in column.—*On the wing*, flying (to shoot wild fowl *on the wing*); speeding to its object; on the road.—*v.t.* To furnish with wings; to enable to fly; to transport by flight (to *wing* me home); to move in flight through; to traverse by flying (to *wing* the air); to wound in the wing; to disable a wing or limb of.—*To wing a flight* or *way*, to proceed by flying; to fly. — **Wing-case**, *n.* The hard case which covers the wings of beetles, &c.; the elytron. —**Winged**, wingd, *a.* Having wings; swift; rapid; passing quickly; *bot.* and *conch.* same as *Alate*.—**Wingless**, wing'les, *a.* Having no wings. — **Winglet**, wing'let, *n.* A little wing; the bastard wing of a bird.

Wink, wingk, *v.i.* [A.Sax. *wincian*, to wink; akin to *wancol*, unsteady; D. *winken*, *wenken*, Icel. *vanka*, to wink; Dan. *vinke*, Sw. *vinka*, to wink or nod; G. *winken*, to beckon; root perhaps same as in *weak*, G. *weichen*, to yield or turn aside. Akin *wince*, *winch*.] To close and open the eyelids quickly and involuntarily; to blink; to nictitate; to give a significant hint by motion of the eyelids; to twinkle; to connive; to seem not to see; to shut the eyes wilfully: with *at* (to *wink at* faults). —*n.* The act of closing the eyelids quickly; no more time than is necessary to shut the eyes; a hint given by shutting the eye with a significant cast.—**Winker**, wing'kėr, *n.* One who winks; one of the blinds of a horse; a blinker.

Winkle, wing'kl, *n.* A common abbreviation of *Periwinkle*.

Winner, **Winning**, &c. Under WIN.

Winnow, win'ō, *v.t.* [A.Sax. *windwian*, to winnow, from *wind*, the wind. (WIND.) Comp. L. *ventilare*, to winnow, from *ventus*, the wind.] To drive the chaff from by means of wind; to fan; *fig.* to examine, sift, or try, as for the purpose of separating falsehood from truth. — *v.i.* To separate chaff from corn.—**Winnower**, win'ō-ėr, *n.* One who or that which winnows.

Winsey, win'si, *n.* Same as *Wincey*.

Winsome, win'sum, *a.* [A.Sax. *wynsum*, pleasant, delightful, from *wynn*, delight, joy (akin to *win*), and term. *-sum*, later *-some*.] Attractive; agreeable; engaging.—**Winsomeness**, win'sum-nes, *n.* Attractiveness; engaging manner or appearance.

Winter, win'tėr, *n.* [A.Sax. *winter*, winter = D. and G. *winter*, Sw. and Dan. *vinter*, Icel. *vetr*, *vitr* (for *vintr*), Goth. *vintrus*; allied to *wind* or to *wet*.] The cold season of the year, which in northern latitudes may be roughly said to comprise December, January, and February; a year: the part being used for the whole; also often used as an emblem of any cheerless situation.—*a.* Belonging to winter.—*v.i.* To pass the winter; to hibernate.—*v.t.* To keep, feed, or manage during the winter (to *winter* cattle). — **Winter-apple**, *n.* An apple that keeps well in winter, or that does not ripen till winter. — **Winter-barley**, *n.* A kind of barley which is sowed in autumn. — **Winter-cress**, *n.* A name of two British cruciferous plants, one of them bitter and sharp to the taste, and sometimes used as a salad.—**Winter-green**, *n.* The common name of certain perennial plants allied to the heaths, some of which are medicinal, whilst an American species yields an oil, used in confectionery and to disguise the taste of disagreeable medicines. **Winterly**,† win'tėr-li, *a.* Wintery; cheerless.—**Winter-moth**, *n.* A moth which appears in its perfect state in the beginning of winter.—**Winter-quarters**, *n.pl.* The quarters of an army during the winter; a winter residence or station.—**Winter's-bark**, *n.* [From Captain John *Winter*, who introduced it to notice.] A South American plant or its bark, which has an aromatic taste, and is sometimes used as a stimulant tonic.—**Winter-tide**, *n.* The winter season. — **Winter-wheat**, *n.* Wheat sown in autumn.—**Wintry**, **Wintery**, win'tri, win'tėr-i, *a.* Suitable to winter; brumal; cold; bleak and cheerless.

Winy. Under WINE.

Winze, winz, *n.* [Icel. *vinza*, to winnow, from *vindr*, wind.] A small shaft in a mine sunk from one level to another, for ventilation or communication.

Wipe, wīp, *v.t.*—*wiped*, *wiping*. [A.Sax. *wipian*, to wipe; akin to L.G. *wiep*, G. *wif*, a wisp of straw, and to *whip* and *wisp*.] To rub with something soft for cleaning; to clean by gentle rubbing; to strike or brush gently: often with *off*, *up*, *away*, &c. —*To wipe away*, to remove by gentle rubbing; *fig.* to remove or take away in general (to *wipe away* a reproach).—*To wipe out*, to efface; to obliterate.—*n.* The act of one who wipes; a rub for the purpose of cleaning; a gibe; a jeer.—**Wiper**, wī'pėr, *n.* One who wipes; something used for wiping; *mach.* a piece projecting from an axle for raising stampers or pistons, and letting them fall.

Wire, wīr, *n.* [A.Sax. *wir*=L.G. *wire*, Icel. *virr*, Dan. *vire*, wire; allied to L. *viriæ*, bracelets; of same root as *wind*, to twist, *withe*.] A thread of metal; a fine or slender metal rod of uniform diameter; such metallic threads collectively; a telegraph wire; hence, the telegraph.—*v.t.*—*wired*, *wiring*. To bind with wire; to apply wire to; to snare by means of a wire; to send by telegraph.—*v.i.* To communicate by means of the telegraph. — **Wire-bridge**, *n.* A bridge suspended by cables formed of wire. —**Wire-cloth**, *n.* A texture of wire intermediate between wire-gauze and wire-netting.—**Wiredraw**, wīr'dra, *v.t.* To form into wire by forcibly pulling through a series of holes; to draw or spin out to great length and tenuity.—**Wiredrawer**, wīr'dra-ėr, *n.* One who draws metal into wire. —**Wiredrawing**, wīr'dra-ing, *n.* The act or art of extending ductile metals into wire; the drawing out of an argument or discussion to prolixity by useless distinctions, disquisitions, &c.—**Wire-fence**, *n.* A fence made of parallel wires attached to upright posts.—**Wire-gauze**, *n.* A kind of stiff close fabric made of fine wire.—**Wire-grub**, *n.* The wire-worm.—**Wire-guard**, *n.* Wire-netting placed in front of a fire.—**Wire-gun**, *n.* A gun which is greatly strengthened by having layers of flattish steel wire wound tightly round an inner tube.—**Wireless**, wīr'les, *n.* Wireless telegraphy or telephony; communication between distant places by means of electromagnetic waves, without the use of wires.—**Wire-netting**, *n.* A texture of wire used for light fencing, &c.—**Wire-puller**, *n.* One who pulls the wires of puppets; hence, one who instigates the actions of others without his influence appearing; an intriguer.—**Wire-pulling**, *n.* The procedure of a wire-puller.—**Wire-rope**, *n.* A strong rope made of iron or steel wire twisted together.—**Wire-work**, *n.* Some kind of fabric made of wire.—**Wire-worker**, *n.* One who manufactures articles from wire.—**Wire-worm**, *n.* A name for several kinds of larvæ or grubs very destructive to crops, the name being given from the cylindrical form and hardness of these grubs. — **Wire-wove**, *n.* Applied to a paper of fine quality and glazed.—**Wiry**, wī'ri, *a.* Made of wire; like wire; tough; lean and sinewy.—**Wiriness**, wī'ri-nes, *n.* The state or quality of being wiry.

Wise, wīz, *a.* [A.Sax. *wis*, wise, prudent= D. *wijs*, Icel. *viss*, Dan. *viis*, G. *weise*, wise; from same root as *wit*, *wot*, L. *video*, to see (VISION). The wise man is therefore the man that sees and knows. WIT.] Having the power of discerning and judging correctly; possessed of discernment, judgment, and discretion; prudent; sensible; sage; judicious; experienced; skilled; *Scrip.* godly; pious.—*Wise man*, a man skilled in hidden arts; a sorcerer.—*Wise woman*, a witch; a fortune-teller.—**Wisdom**, wiz'dom, *n.* [A. Sax. *wisdóm*, from *wis*, and term. *-dóm*= Icel. *visdómr*, Sw. *visdom*, Dan. *viisdom*.] The quality of being wise; the power or faculty of forming the fittest and best judgment in any matter presented for consideration; sound judgment and sagacity; prudence; discretion; sound common sense: often opposed to *folly*; *Scrip.* right judgment concerning religious and moral truth; godliness.—**Wisdom-tooth**, *n.* A large back double-tooth, so named because not appearing till a person is grown up.—**Wisely**, wīz'li, *adv.* In a wise manner; judiciously; discreetly.—**Wiseness**, wīz'nes, *n.* Wisdom.

Wise, wīz, *n.* [A.Sax. *wise*, manner = D. *wijs*, Icel. *vís*, *vísa*, Dan. *viis*, G. *weise*; originally, knowledge or known way; akin to the adjective *wise*. *Guise* is the same word.] Manner; mode: now used only in such phrases as *in any wise*, *in no wise*, &c., or in composition, as in like*wise*, length*wise*, &c., having then much the same force as *-ways* in length*ways*, &c.

Wiseacre, wīz'ā-kėr, *n.* [Corrupted from G. *weissager*, a soothsayer, from O.H.G. *vizzago*, *vizago*, a seer = A.Sax. *wítega*, a seer, lit. one who is wise or knowing; akin to *wit* and *wise*.] One who makes pretensions to great wisdom; a would-be wise person.

Wish, wish, *v.i.* [O.E. *wische*, *wusche*, A. Sax. *wýscan*, to wish, from *wúsc*, a wish; D. and G. *wunsch*, a wish; allied to Skr. *van*, to love, *vanchh*, to desire, L. *Venus*, the goddess, *veneror*, to venerate. WIN, VENERATE.] To have a desire; to long: with *for* before the object.—*v.t.* To desire; to long for: often governing an infinitive or a clause; to frame or express desires concerning; to desire to be (with words completing the sense: to *wish* one well, to *wish* himself rich); to imprecate; to invoke (to *wish* one evil).—*n.* A desire; a longing; an expression of desire; a request; a petition; the thing desired.—**Wish-bone, Wishing-bone,** *n.* A fowl's merry-thought.—**Wisher,** wish'ėr, *n.* One who wishes or expresses a wish.—**Wishful,** wish'fu̇l, *a.* Having a desire; desirous: with *of* before an object; showing desire; longing.—**Wishfully,** wish'fu̇l-li, *adv.* Longingly; wistfully.—**Wishfulness,** wish'fu̇l-nes, *n.* —**Wishing-cap,** *n.* The cap of Fortunatus, in the fairy tale, upon putting on which he obtained whatever he wished for.

Wish-wash, wish'wosh, *n.* [A reduplication of *wash,* thin or waste liquor.] Any sort of weak, thin drink.—**Wishy-washy,** wish'i-wosh'i, *a.* Very thin and weak; diluted; hence, feeble; wanting in substantial qualities.

Wisp, wisp, *n.* [O.E. *wispe, wesp, wips*; akin to L.G. *wiep, vippa,* a wisp, also to *whip.*] A bundle of straw or other like substance; a bunch of fibrous matter; a whisk or small broom; an ignis-fatuus or will-o'-the-wisp.

Wist, wist, pret. of *wit.*

Wistful, wist'fu̇l, *a.* [Modified from old *wistly,* observantly, from *wist,* known, pp. of *wit,* to know.] Anxiously observant; pensive from the absence or want of something; earnest from a feeling of desire; longing.—**Wistfully,** wist'fu̇l-li, *adv.* In a wistful manner; pensively; longingly.—**Wistfulness,** wist'fu̇l-nes, *n.*

Wistiti, wis'ti-ti, *n.* [Native name.] The marmoset.

Wit, wit, *v.t.* and *i.*; present tense, I *wot,* thou *wottest* or *wotst,* he *wots* or *wot*; pl. *wot*; pret. *wist* in all persons; ppr. *witting,* also *wotting.* [A.Sax. *witan,* to know; pres. *ic wát,* I wot; pl. *witon,* pret. sing. *wiste,* pl. *wiston,* pp. *wist*; D. *weten,* pret. *wist*; Icel. *vita,* pret. *vissa*; Dan. *vide,* pret. *vidste*; Goth. *witan,* pret. *wissa*; G. *wissen,* pret. *wusste*; cog. L. *video, visum,* to see (VISION), Gr. *(v)idein,* to see, *(v)eidenai,* to know, Skr. *vid,* to know, to perceive. Hence *wit,* the noun, *witness.* Akin are *wise, wizard.*] To know; to be or become aware; to learn. *To wit* is now used parenthetically to call attention to something particular, or as introductory to a detailed statement of what has been just before mentioned generally, and is equivalent to namely, that is to say.—**Wittingly,** wit'ing-li, *adv.* Knowingly; not inadvertently or ignorantly.

Wit, wit, *n.* [A.Sax. *wit, gewit,* knowledge, mind, understanding; Icel. *vit,* Dan. *vid,* G. *witz,* understanding, wit. See WIT, *v.*] Intellect, understanding or mental powers collectively; a faculty or power of the mind (he has all his *wits* about him); wisdom; sagacity; the faculty of associating ideas in a new and ingenious, and at the same time natural and pleasing way exhibited in apt language; a quality or faculty akin to humour, but depending more on point or brilliancy of language; facetiousness; a person possessing this faculty; one distinguished for bright or amusing sayings; a humorist.—*The five wits,* the five senses.—*At one's wits' end,* at a loss what further steps or measures to adopt; unable to think further.—*To live by one's wits,* to live by shifts or expedients, as one without a regular means of living.—**Witless,** wit'les, *a.* Destitute of sense or understanding; silly; senseless; foolish.—**Witlessly,** wit'les-li, *adv.* Sillily; foolishly.—**Witlessness,** wit'les-nes, *n.*—**Witling,** wit'ling, *n.* [Dim. from *wit.*] A person who has little wit; a pretender to wit.—**Witted,** wit'ed, *a.* Having wit or understanding: used chiefly in composition (a quick-*witted* boy).—**Witticism,** wit'i-sizm, *n.* [From *witty*; comp. such words as *Atticism, Gallicism.*] A witty sentence, phrase, or remark; an observation characterized by wit.—**Witty,** wit'i, *a.* [A.Sax. *witig.*] Possessed of wit; smartly or cleverly facetious; bright and amusing.—**Wittily,** wit'i-li, *adv.* In a witty manner; with wit.—**Wittiness,** wit'i-nes, *n.* The quality of being witty.

Witch, wich, *n.* [A.Sax. *wicce,* a witch, *wicca,* a wizard; origin doubtful, perhaps akin to *wit.* Hence *wicked.*] Formerly a person of either sex given to the black art; now a woman supposed to have formed a compact with the devil or with evil spirits, and by their means to operate supernaturally; one who practises sorcery or enchantment; a bewitching or charming young woman.—*Witches' Sabbath,* a grand meeting of witches and devils at night accompanied by obscene revels.—*v.t.* To bewitch; to fascinate; to enchant.—**Witchcraft,** wich'kraft, *n.* The practices of witches; sorcery; power more than natural; enchantment; fascination.—**Witch-elm.** WYCH-ELM.—**Witchery,** wich'ėr-i, *n.* Witchcraft; fascination; entrancing influence.—**Witch-finder,** *n.* A professional discoverer of witches; one whose services were taken advantage of formerly when the persecution of so-called witches was in vogue.—**Witch-hazel.** WYCH-HAZEL.—**Witching,** wich'ing, *a.* Bewitching; suited to enchantment or witchcraft.—**Witch-meal,** *n.* The powdery pollen of club-moss, so rapidly inflammable that it is used in theatres to represent lightning; lycopode.—**Witch-tree,** *n.* The rowan-tree or mountain-ash.

Witenagemot, wit'en-a-ge-mot, *n.* [A. Sax. *witena,* gen. pl. of *wita,* a wise man, *(ge)mót,* a meeting, a moot. WIT, MEET.] Among the Anglo-Saxons, the great national council or parliament, consisting of athelings or princes, nobles or ealdormen, the large landholders, principal ecclesiastics, &c.

With, wiᴛʜ, *prep.* [A.Sax. *with,* near, by, against, towards; Icel. *vith,* against, towards, along with; Dan. *ved,* near, with, against. The A.Sax. *wither,* opposite, against (seen in *withers*), is a comparative from this; like Icel. *vithr,* D. *weder,* G. *wieder.* Hence *withal, within, without, withdraw, withhold,* &c.] Against; competing against (to fight, contend, or vie *with*); not apart from; in the company of; on the side of or in favour of; in the estimation, consideration, or judgment of (*with* you art is useless); having as a concomitant, consequence, or appendage (*with* a blush); so as to contrast or correspond; immediately after (*with* that he left); correspondence; through or by, as means, cause, or consequence (pale *with* fear).—*With child,* pregnant; in the family way.

With, with, *n.* A withe.

Withal, wiᴛʜ-a̤l', *adv.* [*With* and *all.*] With the rest; together with that; likewise. —*prep.* With: used after relatives or equivalent words, and transposed to the end of a sentence or clause.

Withdraw, wiᴛʜ-dra̤', *v.t.*—pret. *withdrew*; pp. *withdrawn.* [Prefix *with,* against, opposite to, and *draw.*] To draw back or in a contrary direction; to lead, bring, or take back; to recall; to retract.—*v.i.* To retire from or quit a company or place; to go away; to retreat.—**Withdrawal,** wiᴛʜ-dra̤'al, *n.* Act of withdrawing or taking back; a recalling.—**Withdrawment,** wiᴛʜ-dra̤'ment, *n.* Withdrawal; a recalling.

Withe, Withy, with or wiᴛʜ, with'i, *n.* [A.Sax. *withig,* a willow, a withe; Icel. *vithja, vith,* a withy, a withe; Dan. *vidie,* Sw. *vide, vidja,* G. *weide,* a willow; allied to Gr. *itea* (for *vitea*), a willow; from a root meaning to twist or bend, seen also in L. *vimen,* a withe, *vitis,* a vine. WINE.] A willow or osier; a willow or osier twig; a flexible twig used to bind something; a fastening of plaited or twisted twigs.

Wither, wiᴛʜ'ėr, *v.i.* [Lit. to *weather,* to suffer from or expose to the weather. WEATHER.] To dry and shrivel up, as a plant; to lose freshness and bloom; to fade; to become dry and wrinkled, as from the loss of animal moisture; to lose pristine freshness, bloom, or vigour; to decline; to pass away.—*v.t.* To cause to fade; to make sapless and shrunken; to cause to lose bloom; to shrivel; to blight, injure, or destroy, as by some malign or baleful influence.—**Witheredness,** wiᴛʜ'ėrd-nes, *n.* The state of being withered.—**Witheringly,** wiᴛʜ'ėr-ing-li, *adv.* In a manner tending to wither.

Withers, wiᴛʜ'ėrz, *n.pl.* [Lit. the parts that act against or resist, from A.Sax. *wither,* against, from prep. *with,* against.] The junction of the shoulder-bones of a horse, forming an elevation at the springing of the neck.—**Wither-band,** *n.* A piece of iron laid under a saddle near a horse's withers to strengthen the bow.—**Wither-wrung,** *a.* Injured or hurt in the withers.

Withhold, wiᴛʜ'hōld', *v.t.*—pret. and pp. *withheld.* [*With,* in sense of against, and *hold.*] To hold back; to restrain; to keep from action; to retain; to keep back; not to grant.—**Withholder,** wiᴛʜ-hōl'dėr, *n.* One that withholds.

Within, wiᴛʜ-in', *prep.* [A.Sax. *withinnan* —*with,* against, towards, and *innan,* within, inwardly, from *in,* in.] In the inner or interior part or parts of; inside of: opposed to *without*; in the limits, range, reach, or compass of; not beyond; inside or comprehended by the scope, limits, reach, or influence of; not exceeding, not overstepping, &c.—*adv.* In the interior or centre; inwardly; internally; in the mind, heart, or soul; in the house or dwelling; indoors; at home.—*From within,* from the inside; from within doors, &c.

Without, wiᴛʜ-out', *prep.* [A.Sax. *withutan,* without—*with,* towards, against, and *ut,* out.] On or at the outside or exterior of; out of: opposed to *within*; out of the limits, compass, range, or reach of; beyond; not having or not being with; in absence or destitution of; deprived of; not having.—*conj.* Unless; except: now rarely used by correct speakers and writers.—*adv.* On the outside; outwardly; externally; out of doors.—*From without,* from the outside: opposite to *from within.*

Withstand, wiᴛʜ-stand', *v.t.*—pret. and pp. *withstood.* [*With,* in sense of against, and *stand.*] To resist, either with physical or moral force; to oppose.—*v.i.* To resist; to make a stand.—**Withstander,** wiᴛʜ-stan'dėr, *n.* One that withstands; an opponent.

Withy. Under WITHE.

Witless, Witling, &c. Under WIT, *n.*

Witness, wit'nes, *n.* [A.Sax. *witnes,* testimony, lit. what one knows, from *witan,* to know. WIT.] Attestation of a fact or event; testimony; that which furnishes evidence or proof; a person who knows or sees anything; one personally present: *law,* one who sees the execution of an instrument, and subscribes it for confirmation of its authenticity; a person who gives testimony or evidence in a judicial proceeding.—*With a witness,*‡ effectually; with a vengeance; so as to leave some mark as a testimony behind.—*v.t.* To attest; to testify; to see or know by personal presence; to be a witness of; to give or serve as evidence or token of; to subscribe as witness. —*v.i.* To bear testimony; to give evidence. —**Witnesser,** wit'nes-ėr, *n.* One who witnesses.

Witticism, Wittily, &c. Under WIT, *n.*

Wittingly. Under WIT, *v.*

Wittol,‡ wit'ol, *n.* [Probably for *wittal, witwal, woodwale,* old names for a bird in whose nest the cuckoo's eggs were sometimes laid; comp. the origin of the term *cuckold.*] A cuckold; a man who knows his wife's infidelity and submits to it.

Witty. Under WIT, *n.*

Witwal, Witwall, wit'wa̤l, *n.* [A form akin to *woodwale* (which see).] A name formerly given to the greenfinch or other bird, now generally applied to the green woodpecker.

Wive,‡ wīv, *v.i.* and *t.* [From *wife.*] To marry; to provide with a wife; to take for a wife.—**Wives,** wīvz, pl. of *wife.*

Wizard, Wisard, wiz'ėrd, *n.* [From *wise,* and term. *-ard.*] Originally, a wise man; a sage; latterly, an adept in the black art; a sorcerer; an enchanter; a magician; a conjurer.

Wizen, wiz'n, *a.* [A.Sax. *wisnian,* to become dry, akin to Icel. *visna*, to wither, from *visinn*, withered, palsied.] Hard, dry, and shrivelled; withered; weazen.—**Wizen-faced**, *a.* Having a thin, shrivelled face.

Wo, wō, *n.* A spelling of *Woe.*

Woad, wōd, *n.* [A.Sax. *wád*, D. *weede*, Dan. *vaid, veid*, G. *waid, weid*, woad; connected with L. *vitrum*, woad.] A cruciferous plant, the pulped and fermented leaves of which yield an excellent blue dye.—**Woaded**, wōd'ed, *a.* Dyed or coloured blue with woad.—**Woad-mill**, *n.* A mill for bruising and preparing woad.

Wobble, wob'l, *v.i.*—*wobbled, wobbling.* [Also *wabble*; akin to L.G. *wabbeln*, G. *wabern, weibeln, weiben*, to move to and fro.] To move unsteadily in rotating or spinning; to rock; to vacillate.

Woden, wō'den, *n.* [Akin to A.Sax. *wód*, mad; G. *wuth*, rage; or to *wind.*] The Anglo-Saxon form of the name of the deity called by the Norse Odin. *Wednes*day derives its name from him.

Woe, wō, *n.* [A.Sax. *wá*: often as an interjection, as in *wá lá wá*, woe lo woe! wellaway! D. *wee*, Icel. *vei*, Dan. *vee*, G. *weh*, Goth. *vai*; a natural sound of grief, like L. *væ!* Gr. *ouai!* alas.] Grief; sorrow; misery; heavy calamity. *Woe* is frequently used in denunciations either with a verb or alone; it is also used in exclamations of sorrow, a pronoun following being then in the dative (*woe* is me). The phrase '*Woe worth* the day', means *woe be to* the day. WORTH, *v.i.*—**Woebegone**, wō'bē-gon, *a.* [That is, surrounded or overwhelmed with woe, *begone* being from A.Sax. *begán*, to surround —*be*, by, and *gán*, to go.] Overwhelmed with woe; immersed in grief and sorrow.—**Woeful, Woful**, wō'fụl, *a.* Full of woe; afflicted; sorrowful; expressing woe; doleful; distressful; piteous; wretched.—**Woefully, Wofully**, wō'fụl-li, *adv.* Sorrowfully; lamentably; wretchedly; miserably; extremely.—**Woefulness, Wofulness**, wō'fụl-nes, *n.*

Wold, wōld, *n.* [A.Sax. *wald, weald*, a wood; O.Sax., O.Fris., and G. *wald*, a wood or forest. *Weald* is the same word, which is also seen in *threshold.*] A wood; a forest; a weald or open country; a low hill; a down: in the plural, a hilly district or a range of hills.

Wold, wōld, *n.* A plant. WELD.

Wolf, wụlf, *n.* pl. **Wolves**, wụlvz. [A.Sax. *wulf*=D. and G. *wolf*, Icel. *úlfr*, Dan. *ulv*, Sw. *ulf*, Goth. *wulfs*; cog. L. *lupus*, Gr. *lukos*, Skr. *vrika*, a wolf: traced to a root meaning to tear.] A carnivorous quadruped belonging to the dog family, and closely related to the dog, swift of foot, crafty, and rapacious, but, in general, cowardly and stealthy; hence, a term for a person considered ravenous, cruel, cunning, or the like; *mus.* a jarring discordant sound produced by instruments tuned to unequal temperament.—*To cry wolf*, to raise a false alarm: in allusion to the shepherd-boy in the fable.—*To keep the wolf from the door*, to keep away hunger or want.—**Wolf-dog**, *n.* A large kind of dog kept to keep off or destroy wolves.—**Wolf-fish**, *n.* An edible fish of the British seas, 6 or 7 feet long, so called from its ferocious aspect and habits. Called also *Sea-cat, Sea-wolf.*—**Wolfish**, wụlf'ish, *a.* Like a wolf; savage.—**Wolfishly**, wụlf'ish-li, *adv.* In a wolfish manner.—**Wolfkin**, wụlf'kin, *n.* A young or small wolf.—**Wolf's-bane**, *n.* A poisonous plant of the aconite kind, yielding the virulent poison aconitin; monk's-hood or aconite.

Wolffian body. See MESONEPHROS.

Wolfram, wol'fram, *n.* [G. *wolfram*—*wolf*, wolf, *ram, rahm*, froth, cream, soot.] A native tungstate of iron and manganese; the ore from which tungsten is usually obtained; a name of the metal tungsten.

Wollastonite, wol'as-ton-īt, *n.* Same as *Tabular spar.*

Wolverine, wụl'vėr-ēn, *n.* A carnivorous mammal, the glutton. The state of Michigan is called the Wolverine State.

Woman, wụm'an, *n.* pl. **Women**, wim'en. [A.Sax. *wifman*, later *wimman*, from *wif*, wife, and *man*, in its primitive sense of human being, person. WIFE, MAN.] The female of the human race; an adult or grown-up female, as distinguished from a girl; a female attendant on a person of rank.—**Womanhood**, wụm'an-hụd, *n.* The state, character, or collective qualities of a woman.—**Womanish**, wụm'an-ish, *a.* Suitable to a woman; feminine; effeminate: often in a contemptuous sense.—**Womanishly**, wụm'an-ish-li, *adv.* Effeminately.—**Womanishness**, wụm'an-ish-nes, *n.* State or quality of being womanish.—**Womankind**, wụm'an-kīnd, *n.* Women in general; the female sex.—**Womanliness**, wụm'an-li-nes, *n.* Quality of being womanly.—**Womanly**, wụm'an-li, *a.* Becoming or suiting a woman; feminine, in the praiseworthy sense; not masculine.

Womb, wöm, *n.* [A.Sax. *wamb, womb*, the belly=D. *wam*, Icel. *vömb*, Dan. *vom*, G. *wamme, wampe*, Goth. *wamba*, the belly.] The belly or stomach‡; the uterus of a female; something likened to this; any large or deep cavity that receives or contains anything.

Wombat, wöm'bat, *n.* [Corruption of the native name *womback* or *wombach.*] A marsupial mammal of Australia and Tasmania, about the size of a badger; it inhabits a burrow and feeds on roots.

Women, pl. of *woman.*

Won, wun, pret. and pp. of *win.*

Wonder, wun'dėr, *n.* [A.Sax. *wundor*=D. *wonder*, G. *wunder*, Icel. *undr*, Sw. and Dan. *under*; perhaps akin to *wind* (*v.*), *wend*, a prodigy being such as to turn a person away through awe.] That emotion which is excited by something new, strange, and extraordinary, or that arrests the attention by its novelty, grandeur, or inexplicableness: a feeling less than *astonishment*, and much less than *amazement*; a cause of such feeling; a strange or extraordinary thing; a prodigy.—*A nine days' wonder*, something that causes a sensation or astonishment for a short time.—*v.i.* To be struck with wonder; to marvel; to be amazed; to look with or feel admiration; to entertain some doubt and curiosity; to be in a state of expectation, mingled with doubt and slight anxiety: followed by a clause.—**Wonderer**, wun'dėr-ėr, *n.* One who wonders.—**Wonderful**, wun'dėr-fụl, *a.* Adapted to excite wonder; strange; astonishing; marvellous.—**Wonderfully**, wun'dėr-fụl-li, *adv.* In a wonderful manner; surprisingly; strangely; colloquially often equivalent to very.—**Wonderfulness**, wun'dėr-fụl-nes, *n.* The state or quality of being wonderful.—**Wonderingly**, wun'dėr-ing-li, *adv.* With wonder.—**Wonderland**, *n.* A land of wonders or marvels.—**Wonderment**, wun'dėr-ment, *n.* Wonder; surprise; astonishment.—**Wonderstruck**, wun'dėr-struk, *a.* Struck with wonder or surprise.—**Wonderwork**, *n.* A prodigy; a miracle.—**Wonderworker**, *n.* One who performs wonders.—**Wondrous**, wun'drus, *a.* Such as to excite wonder; wonderful; marvellous; strange.—*adv.* In a wonderful degree; remarkably; exceedingly (*wondrous* wise).—**Wondrously**, wun'drus-li, *adv.* In a strange or wonderful manner or degree.

Won't, wōnt. A contraction for *will not.*

Wont, wunt, *a.* [For older *woned*, a participle or participial adjective, from A.Sax. *wuna, gewuna*, custom, habit, or from the kindred *wunian*, to dwell; akin Icel. *vani*, custom, *vanr*, accustomed. WEAN, WIN.] Accustomed; having a certain habit or custom; using or doing customarily.—*n.* [From old *wone*, A.Sax. *wuna*, habit, custom, through the influence of *wont*, adjective.] Custom; habit; use.—*v.i.* pret. *wont*; pp. *wont, wonted.* [For old *wone*, to be accustomed, to dwell. The pret. and pp. *wont* are thus put for *woned*, and *wonted* is a doubled form.] To be accustomed or habituated; to use; to be used.—**Wonted**, wun'ted, *p.* and *a.* Customary or familiar from use or habit; usual; accustomed; made or having become familiar by using, frequenting, &c.

Woo, wö, *v.t.*—*wooed, wooing.* [A.Sax. *wógian*, to woo, from *wóh*, genit. *wóges*, bent, bending; the meaning is therefore to bend or incline another towards one's self.] To court; to solicit in love; to invite; to seek to gain or bring about; to court (to *woo* destruction).—*v.i.* To make love.—**Wooer**, wö'ėr, *n.* One who woos; one who courts or solicits in love; a suitor.—**Wooing**, wö'ing, *n.* Courtship; time of courtship.

Wood,‡ wöd, *a.* [A.Sax. *wód*, Sc. *wud*, Goth. *wods*, mad, furious; G. *wuth*, rage, fury.] Mad; furious; frantic. (*Shak.*)

Wood, wụd, *n.* [A.Sax. *wudu*, a wood, timber; akin O.D. *wede*, Icel. *vithr*, Dan. and Sw. *ved*, wood, a tree; comp. W. *gwydd*, trees, shrubs.] A large collection of growing trees; a forest; the substance of trees or their trunks; timber; *pl.* wind-instruments in an orchestra, such as the flute, clarionet, oboe, &c.—*v.i.* To take in or get supplies of wood.—*v.t.* To supply with wood, or get supplies of wood for.—**Wood-acid**, *n.* Same as *Wood-vinegar.*—**Wood-ashes**, *n.pl.* The remains of burned wood or plants.—**Woodbine, Woodbind**, wụd'bīn, wụd'bīnd, *n.* [BINE.] The wild honeysuckle; formerly the bindweed.—**Wood-carving**, *n.* The art of carving wood into figures or ornamental forms; a device or figure carved on wood.—**Wood-chat**, *n.* A species of butcher-bird or shrike.—**Wood-chuck**, *n.* A species of marmot common in the United States and Canada; the ground-hog.—**Wood-coal**, *n.* Charcoal; also lignite or brown coal.—**Wood-cock**, wụd'kok, *n.* A bird allied to the snipe but with a more robust bill and shorter legs, a winter visitant to Britain, where it sometimes breeds; esteemed for the table.—**Wood-cracker**, *n.* The nuthatch.—**Wood-craft**, wụd'kraft, *n.* Skill in anything which pertains to woods or forests; skill in hunting deer, &c.—**Wood-cut**, *n.* An engraving on wood, or a print from such engraving.—**Wood-cutter**, *n.* A person who cuts wood; an engraver on wood.—**Wood-cutting**, *n.* The act or employment of cutting wood; wood-engraving.—**Wooded**, wụd'ed, *a.* Supplied or covered with wood (land well *wooded*).—**Wooden**, wụd'n, *a.* Made of wood; consisting of wood; ungainly; awkward; without spirit or expression.—**Wood-engraver**, *n.* An artist who engraves on wood.—**Wood-engraving**, *n.* The art of engraving on wood, or of producing by special cutting tools a design or picture in relief on the surface of a block of wood (generally box), from which impressions can be taken by means of an ink or pigment.—**Woodenly**, wụd'n-li, *adv.* In a wooden manner; stiffly; clumsily; awkwardly.—**Wood-grouse**, *n.* The capercailzie.—**Woodiness**, wụd'i-nes, *n.* State or quality of being woody.—**Woodland**, wụd'land, *n.* Land covered with wood.—*a.* Relating to woods; sylvan.—**Wood-lark**, *n.* A small species of lark which usually sings perched on the branch of a tree.—**Wood-louse**, *n.* An insect, the oniscus or slater, a flattish insect of a slaty colour frequenting rotten wood, &c.—**Woodman**, wụd'man, *n.* A forester; one who fells timber.—**Wood-mite**, *n.* A small insect found in old wood.—**Wood-mouse**, *n.* The long-tailed field-mouse.—**Wood-nymph**, *n.* A goddess of the woods; a dryad.—**Wood-oil**, *n.* A balsamic substance obtained from trees in the Eastern Archipelago.—**Wood-opal**, *n.* A striped variety of opal, having the form and texture of wood.—**Woodpecker**, wụd'pek-ėr, *n.* [So called from pecking or tapping with the bill on trees.] The name for certain climbing birds which feed on insects and their larvæ that they find on trees.—**Wood-pigeon**, *n.* The ring-dove or cushat.—**Wood-pile**, *n.* A stack of piled-up wood for fuel.—**Wood-pulp**, *n.* Pulp from wood widely used in making paper.—**Woodruff, Woodroof**, wụd'ruf, wụd'röf, *n.* [A.Sax. *wuderofe, wudurofe*, the latter part of doubtful meaning.] A well-known plant found in Britain in woods and shady places, and cultivated in gardens for the beauty of its whorled leaves and simple white blossoms, but chiefly for the fragrance of its leaves.—**Wood-rush**, *n.* The common name of several species of rush.—**Wood-sage**, *n.* A species of germander, extremely bitter, and sometimes used as a substitute for hops.—**Wood-screw**, *n.* An iron screw suited for joining pieces of wood in carpenter or joiner work. —**Wood-shock**, *n.* A species of marten; the pekan.—**Wood-sorrel**, *n.* A small species of sorrel, supposed by some to be the Irish shamrock.—**Wood-spirit**, *n.* A crude spirit obtained by distilling wood in closed vessels.—**Wood-spite**, *n.* [*Spite* =G. *specht*, woodpecker.] The green woodpecker.—**Wood-swallow**, *n.* A bird of Australia and the East Indies, much resembling swallows in habit.—**Wood-tin**, *n.* A fibrous nodular variety of oxide of tin.—**Wood-vinegar**, *n.* A sort of vinegar obtained by the distillation of wood.—**Woodwale**, wụd'wāl, *n.* [Latter part of doubtful origin.] An old name of a bird; the witwall.—**Wood-warbler**, *n.* A small bird visiting England in summer.—**Wood-wasp**, *n.* A species of solitary wasp.—**Wood-work**, *n.* Work formed of wood; the part of any structure that is made of wood.—**Woody**, wụd'i, *a.* Abounding with wood; consisting of wood; ligneous; pertaining to woods.—*Woody tissue*, that which constitutes the basis of the wood in trees.—**Woody-nightshade**, *n.* Same as *Bitter-sweet*.

Wooer. Under Woo.

Woof, wöf, *n.* [O.E. *oof*, *owef*, from A.Sax. *ówef*, from prefix *ó*, for *on*, and *wefan*, to weave. WEAVE.] The threads that cross the warp in weaving; the weft; texture.

Wool, wụl, *n.* [A.Sax. *wull*, *wul*,=D. *wol*, G. *wolle*, Goth. *wulla*, Icel. and Sw. *ull*, Dan. *uld*; allied to L. *villus*, shaggy hair, *vellus*, a fleece; from a root signifying to cover, seen also in L. *vallis*, a valley, and in *valeo*, to be strong. VALID.] That soft species of hair which grows on sheep and some other animals; the fleecy coat of the sheep; also applied to other kinds of hair, especially short, crisped, and curled hair like that of a negro; any fibrous or fleecy substance resembling wool.—**Wool-comber**, *n.* One whose occupation is to comb wool.—**Wool-combing**, *n.* The act or process of combing wool, generally of the long-stapled kind, for the purpose of worsted manufacture.—**Wool-dyed**, *a.* Dyed in the form of wool or yarn before being made into cloth.—**Woolen**, wụl'en, *a.* Made of wool; consisting of wool; pertaining to wool.—*n.* Cloth made of wool, such as blanketings, serges, flannels, tweeds, broad-cloth, and the like.—**Wool-gathering**, *n.* The act of gathering wool; usually applied figuratively to the indulgence of idle fancies; a fruitless pursuit.—**Wool-grower**, *n.* A person who raises sheep for the production of wool.—**Woolliness**, wụl'i-nes, *n.* The state of being woolly.—**Woolly**, wụl'i, *a.* Consisting of wool; resembling wool; clothed or covered with wool; *bot.* covered with a pubescence resembling wool.—**Woolly-bear**, *n.* In the European War, a large shrapnel-shell which emitted a cloud of brown smoke on bursting.—**Wool-mill**, *n.* A mill for manufacturing wool and woollen cloth.—**Woolpack**, wụl'pak, *n.* A bag of wool; a bundle or bale weighing 240 lb.—**Woolsack**, wụl'sak, *n.* A sack or bag of wool; the seat of the lord-chancellor in the House of Lords, a large square bag of wool, without back or arms, covered with red cloth.—**Wool-sorter**, *n.* One who sorts wools according to their qualities. —**Wool-stapler**, *n.* A dealer in wool; a sorter of wool.—**Woolward**, wụl'wėrd, *adv.* [*Wool* and *-ward*, that is, with the skin next or toward the wool.] In wool or woollen underclothing.

Woorali, wụ'ra-li, *n.* CURARI.

Wootz, wụts, *n.* A very superior kind of steel made in the East Indies, and imported into Europe and America for making the finest edge-tools.

Wop, wop, *v.t.* To whop; to give a beating to. (*Colloq.*)

Word, wėrd, *n.* [A.Sax. *word*, a word=D. *woord*, G. *wort*, Icel., Sw., and Dan. *ord*, Goth. *waurd*; cog. Lith. *vardas*, name; L. *verbum*, a word (whence *verb*); from a root meaning to speak, seen in Gr. (*v*)*eirō*, to speak.] A single articulate sound, or a combination of articulate sounds or syllables, uttered by the human voice, and by custom expressing an idea or ideas; a vocable; a term; speech exchanged; conversation; talk: in this sense plural; information; tidings: in this sense without an article and only as a singular (to send *word* of one's safe arrival); a watchword; a password; a motto; a term or phrase of command; an injunction; an order; an assertion or promise; an affirmation on honour; a declaration: with possessives (to take him at his *word*); terms or phrases interchanged in contention, anger, or reproach: in plural, and often qualified by *high*, *hot*, *harsh*, *sharp*, &c.—*The Word*, the Scriptures, or any part of them; the second person of the Trinity; the Logos.—*Word for word*, in the exact words or terms; verbatim; exactly.—*By word of mouth*, by actual speaking; orally.—*Good word*, expressed good opinion; a recommendation (to speak a *good word* for a person).—*In word*, in mere phraseology.—*In a word*, *in one word*, briefly; to sum up; in short.—*To eat one's words*, to retract what one has said.—*A word and a blow*, a threat and its immediate execution.—*v.t.* To express in words; to phrase. —**Word-book**, *n.* A vocabulary; a dictionary; a lexicon.—**Wordily**, wėr'di-li, *adv.* In a wordy manner.—**Wordiness**, wėr'di-nes, *n.* The quality of being wordy; verbosity.—**Wording**, wėr'ding, *n.* Expression in words; form of expression.—**Wordless**, werd'les, *a.* Not speaking; silent.—**Word-painter**, *n.* A writer who has the power of peculiarly graphic or vivid description; one who affects great picturesqueness of style.—**Word-painting**, *n.* The act or art of a word-painter.—**Word-picture**, *n.* A vivid description of any scene or event.—**Wordy**, wėr'di, *a.* Using many more words than are necessary; verbose; consisting of words; verbal.

Wore, wōr, pret. of *wear*.

Work, wėrk, *n.* [A.Sax. *worc*, *weorc* = D. *werk*, Icel. and Sw. *verk*, Dan. *værk*, G. *werk*, work; from same root as Gr. (*v*)*ergon*, work.] Exertion of energy, physical or mental; effort directed to some purpose or end; toil; labour; employment; the matter upon which one is employed, engaged, or labouring; that which engages one's time or attention; an undertaking; an enterprise; a task; that which is done; performance; deed; feat; achievement; goings-on; that which is made or produced; a product of nature or art; a literary or artistic performance; a composition; some extensive structure, as a dock, bridge, fortification, &c.; any establishment where labour is carried on extensively (an iron *work*), the plural being often applied to one such establishment; *mech.* the overcoming of resistance; the act of producing a change of configuration in a system in opposition to a force which resists that change.—*Unit of work*, a foot-pound. Under FOOT.—*v.i.*—pret. and pp. *wrought* or *worked*. [From the noun; A.Sax. *wircan*, *wyrcan*; pret. *worhte*, pp. *geworht*.] To make exertion for some end or purpose; to be engaged or employed on some task, labour, duty, or the like; to labour; to toil; to be engaged in an employment or occupation; to perform the duties of a labourer, workman, man of business, &c.; to be in motion, operation, or activity (the machine *works* well); to act; to operate; to have or take effect; to exercise influence; to tend or conduce (things *work* to some end); to be tossed or agitated, as the sea; to be in agitation; to boil (passion *works* in him); to make way laboriously and slowly; to act as a purgative or cathartic; to ferment, as liquors.—*To work against*, to act in opposition to; to oppose actively.—*To work on* or *upon*, to act on; to influence.—*v.t.* To bestow manual labour upon; to carry on the operations of (to *work* a mine or quarry); to bring about; to effect, perform, do (to *work* mischief); to keep at work; to keep busy or employed (he *works* his horses, his servants); to bring by action to any state (to *work* one's self out); to make or get by labour or exertion (to *work* one's way); to make into shape; to fashion; to mould; to embroider; to operate on, as a purgative; to purge; to cause to ferment, as liquor.—*To work a passage*, to give one's work or services as an equivalent for passage-money. —*To work in* or *into*, to intermix gradually, as in the process of manufacture; to cause to enter or penetrate by repeated efforts; to introduce artfully; to insinuate (he *works* himself *into* favour).—*To work off*, to get rid of by some gradual process; to produce, as separate articles of the same kind from a machine or the like.—*To work out*, to effect by continued labour or exertion; to solve, as a problem; to exhaust by drawing all the useful material (to *work out* a mine).—*To work up*, to stir up; to excite; to agitate; to use up in the process of manufacture or the like; to elaborate (to *work up* a story or article).—**Workable**, wėr'ka-bl, *a.* That can be worked or that is worth working.—**Workaday**, wėr'ka-dā, *a.* Working-day; everyday; toiling.—**Work-bag**, *n.* A small bag used by ladies for containing needle-work, &c.; a reticule. —**Work-box**, *n.* A small box for holding needle-work, &c.—**Worker**, wėr'kėr, *n.* One who works; a laborer; a toiler; a performer; a working bee; sterile or neuter bees, ants, and other insects that work.—**Workhouse**, wėrk'hous, *n.* A house of correction where petty offenders are incarcerated and put to work.—**Working**, wėr'king, *p.* and *a.* Engaged in bodily toil; laborious; industrious; taking an active part in a business (a *working* partner).—*n.* The act of labouring; fermentation; movement; operation.—**Working-beam**, *n.* The oscillating lever of a steam-engine forming the medium of communication between the piston-rod and the crank-shaft; a walking-beam.—**Working-class**, *n.* A collective name for those who earn their bread by manual labour: generally used in the plural.—**Working-day**, *n.* Any day on which work is ordinarily performed, as distinguished from Sundays and holidays; such part of the day as is devoted or allotted to work.—*a.* Relating to days on which work is done; plodding; laborious.—**Working load**. Same as SAFE LOAD.—**Working stress**. Same as SAFE WORKING STRESS.—**Workman**, wėrk'man, *n.* Any man employed in work, especially manual labour; a labourer; a toiler; a worker; a skilful artificer or operator.—**Workmanlike**, wėrk'man-līk, *a.* Skilful; well performed.—**Workmanly**, wėrk'man-li, *a.* Skilful; workmanlike.—**Workmanship**, wėrk'man-ship, *n.* The art or skill of a workman; the style or character of work performed on anything; operative skill; the result or objects produced by a workman, artificer, or operator.—**Work-people**, *n.* People engaged in labour, particularly manual labour.—**Workshop**, wėrk'shop, *n.* A shop or building where any work or handicraft is carried on.—**Workwoman**, wėrk'wụm-an, *n.* A woman who performs any work.

World, wėrld, *n.* [A.Sax. *world*, *worold* = O.Sax. *werold*, D. *wereld*, Icel. *veröld*, Sw. *verld*, O.H.G. *weralt*, G. *welt*; lit. manage, age of man, age, hence, course of time, world; from A.Sax. *wer*, a man (cog. with L. *vir*, whence *virile*, *virtue*), and *eld*, *yld*, age, akin to *old*.] The earth and all created things thereon; the terraqueous globe; the universe; any celestial orb or planetary body; a large portion or division of our globe (the Old *World*, or eastern hemisphere; the new *World*, or western hemisphere; the Roman *world*); the earth as the scene of human existence and action; any state or sphere of existence (a future *world*); a domain, region, or realm (the *world* of dreams, of art); the human race; the aggregate of humanity; the public; the people among whom one lives; the life of humanity at large; the people united by a common faith, aim, pursuit, &c. (the religious *world*, the heathen *world*); the people exclusively interested in secular affairs; the unregenerate or ungodly part of humanity. It is sometimes used to signify a great multitude or quantity; a great degree or measure (a *world* too large); it is also used in emphatic phrases expressing perplexity or surprise (what in the *world* am I to do?).—*World without end*, to all eternity; eternally; unceasingly.—*For all the world*, exactly; precisely; entirely.—*The world's end*, the remotest part of the earth.—**Worldliness**, wėrld'li-nes, *n.* The state of being worldly.—**Worldling**, wėrld'ling, *n.* One who is devoted exclusively to the affairs and interests of this life.—**Worldly**, wėrd'li, *a.* Belonging to the world or present state of man's existence; temporal; secular; desirous of temporal benefit or enjoyment merely; earthly as opposed to heavenly or spiritual; carnal; sordid.—**Worldly-minded**, *a.* Devoted to worldly aims.—**Worldly-mindedness**, *n.*—**World-wide**, *a.* Wide as the world; extending over all the world.

Worm, wėrm, *n.* [A.Sax. *wyrm*, a worm, a serpent = D. *worm*, G. *wurm*, Goth. *waurms*, Icel. *ormr*, Dan. and Sw. *orm*; cog. L. *vermis*, a worm (whence *vermicular* and *vermin*).] A term loosely applied to many small creeping animals, entirely wanting feet or having but very short ones; any somewhat similar creature; an intestinal parasite of lengthened form; *pl.* the disease due to the presence of such parasites; a maggot; a canker; an epithet of scorn, disgust, or contempt; anything vermicular or spiral; the thread of a screw; the spiral pipe of a still placed in a vessel of cold water, and through which the vapour of the substance distilled is conducted to cool and condense it; a small vermicular ligament under the tongue of a dog, often cut out to prevent the young dog from gnawing things.—*v.i.* To advance by wriggling; *refl.* to insinuate one's self; to work gradually and secretly.—*v.t.* To effect by slow and stealthy means; to extract or get at slily or cunningly (to *worm* a secret out of a person); to cut the worm from a dog.—**Worm-cast**, *n.* A small mass of fine earth voided by the earthworm after all the nutritive matter has been extracted from it.—**Worm-eaten**, *a.* Gnawed by worms; having a number of internal cavities made by worms.—**Wormed**, wėrmd, *a.* Bored or penetrated by worms; injured by worms.—**Worm-fever**, *n.* A popular name for infantile remittent fever.—**Worming**, wėr'ming, *n.* *Naut.* yarn wound round ropes between the strands.—**Wormling**, wėrm'ling, *n.* A minute worm.—**Worm-seed**, *n.* The seed of a species of wormwood brought from the Levant, and used as an anthelmintic.—**Worm-wheel**, *n.* A wheel which gears with an endless screw.—**Wormy**, wėr'mi, *n.* Containing a worm or worms; earthy; grovelling.

Wormwood, wėrm'wụd, *n.* [A corruption of a name having no connection with *worm* or *wood*; A.Sax. *wermód*, D. *wermoet*, G. *wermuth*; lit. *ware-mood*, mind-preserver (from some old notion as to its virtues), the *wer* being akin to *ware* (in *beware*), *wary*. (WARY, MOOD.) The plant was used as a remedy for worms, hence the corruption.] A well-known plant, celebrated for its intensely bitter, tonic, and stimulating qualities; bitter feeling; mortification (*gall and wormwood*).

Worn, wōrn, pp. of *wear*.—**Worn-out**, *a.* Destroyed or much injured by wear; wearied; exhausted with toil.

Worry, wur'i, *v.t.*—pret. and pp. *worried*. [O.E. *wirie*, *wurie*, *worowe*, &c.; from A.Sax. *wyrgan*, seen in *á-wyrgan*, to strangle, to injure; D. *worgen*, *wurgen*, G. *würgen*, to strangle; akin to *wring*, *wrong*, nasalized forms.] To seize by the throat with the teeth; to tear with the teeth, as dogs when fighting; to harass with importunity or with care and anxiety; to plague, tease, bother, vex, persecute.—*v.i.* To be unduly careful and anxious; to be in solicitude or trouble; to fret.—*n.* The act of worrying or mangling with the teeth; perplexity; trouble; anxiety; harassing turmoil.—**Worrying**, wur'i-ing, *p.* and *a.* Troubling; harassing; fatiguing.—**Worryingly**, wur'i-ing-li, *adv.* Teasingly; harassingly.—**Worrier**, wur'i-ėr, *n.* One that worries.—**Worriment**, wur'i-ment, *n.* Worry; anxiety.—**Worrisome**, wur'i-sum, *a.* Causing worry.—**Worrit**, wur'it, *v.t.* [A colloq. or provincial word.] To worry; to harass; to annoy.—*n.* Worry; annoyance; vexation.

Worse, wėrs, *a.* [A.Sax. *wyrsa*, adj., *wyrs*, adv.; Icel. *verr*, *verri*, Dan. *værre*, Goth. *wairs*, adv., *wairsiza*, adj.; same root as G. *wirren*, to entangle, E. *war*. *Worse* and *worst* are used as comparative and superlative to *ill* and *bad*.] Bad or ill in a greater degree; less good or perfect; of less value; inferior; more unwell; more sick; in poorer health; in a less favourable situation; more ill off; also used substantively, often with *the*; loss; defeat; disadvantage; something less good or desirable (*worse* remains behind).—*adv.* In a manner more evil or bad; in a smaller or lower degree; less (it pleases him *worse*); in a greater manner or degree: with a notion of evil (he hates him *worse*).—**Worsen**,† wėr'sn, *v.i.* To grow worse; to deteriorate.—**Worser**, wėr'sėr, *a.* and *adv.* A redundant comparative of *worse*, sometimes used by good writers.—**Worst**, wėrst, *a.* Bad in the highest degree, whether in a moral or physical sense.—*n.* The most evil, aggravated, or calamitous state or condition: usually with *the*.—*adv.* Most ill or extreme; most intensely (he hates us *worst*).—*v.t.* To get the advantage over in conquest; to defeat; to overthrow.

Worship, wėr'ship, *n.* [From *worth*, and term. *-ship*; A.Sax. *weorthscipe*, honour.] Excellence of character‡; worth‡; honour‡; a title used in addressing certain magistrates and others of rank or station; the performance of devotional acts in honour of a deity; the act of paying divine honours to the Supreme Being; religious exercises; reverence; submissive respect; loving or admiring devotion.—*v.t.*—*worshipped*, *worshipping*. To pay divine honours to; to reverence with supreme respect and veneration; to perform religious service to; to adore; to idolize.—*v.i.* To perform acts of adoration; to perform religious service.—**Worshipful**, wėr'ship-fụl, *a.* Worthy of honor; honorable; a term of respect especially applied to magistrates and corporate bodies.—**Worshipfully**, wėr'ship-fụl-li, *adv.* Respectfully; honorably.—**Worshipfulness**, wėr'ship-fụl-nes, *n.*—**Worshiper**, **Worshipper**, wėr'ship-ėr, *n.* One who worships; one who pays divine honors to any being; one who adores.

Worst. Under WORSE.

Worsted, wụs'ted, *n.* [From *Worsted*, in Norfolk, where it was first manufactured.] A variety of woollen yarn or thread, spun from long-staple wool, used in knitting stockings, &c.

Wort, wėrt, *n.* [A.Sax. *wyrt*, a plant = G. *wurz*, Goth. *waurts*, Icel. and Dan. *urt*. This word is contained in *orchard*, and is of same root as *root*, *radical* (which see).] A plant; a herb: now used chiefly in compounds (liver*wort*, spleen*wort*).

Wort, wėrt, *n.* [A.Sax. *wyrte*, wort, must; Icel. *virtr*, O.D. *wort*, G. *würze*, wort; probably akin to above word.] New beer unfermented or in the act of fermentation; the sweet infusion of malt.

Worth, wėrth, *v.i.* [A.Sax. *weorthan*, to be or to become = Icel. *vertha*, Dan. *vorde*, D. *worden*, G. *werden*, Goth. *wairthan*; same root as in L. *verto*, to turn, whence E. *verse* (which see).] To be; to become; to betide: now used only in the phrases woe *worth* the day, woe *worth* the man, &c., equivalent to woe *be to* the day, &c.

Worth, wėrth, *n.* [A.Sax. *weorth*, *wurth*, price, value, honour, or as an adj. valuable, honorable, with similar forms in the other Teutonic languages; perhaps from root meaning to guard, as in *wary*, *beware*.] That quality of a thing which renders it valuable; value; money value; price; rate; value in respect of mental or moral qualities; desert; merit; excellence.—*a.* Equal in value or price to; deserving of (a cause *worth* defending); having estate to the value of; having a fixed or specified value.—*Worth while*. Under WHILE.—**Worthily**, wėr'THi-li, *adv.* In a worthy manner; suitably; excellently; deservedly; justly; according to merit.—**Worthiness**, wėr'THi-nes, *n.* The state or quality of being worthy or well-deserved; excellence; dignity; virtue.—**Worthless**, wėrth'les, *a.* Having no value; having no dignity or excellence; mean; contemptible; unworthy; not deserving.—**Worthlessly**, wėrth'les-li, *adv.* In a worthless manner.—**Worthlessness**, wėrth'les-nes, *n.* The state of being worthless.—**Worthy**, wėr'THi, *a.* Having worth; excellent; deserving praise; valuable; estimable; applied to persons and things; such as merits; deserving (*worthy* of love or hatred); suitable; proper; fitting.—*n.* A person of worth or distinguished for estimable qualities; a local celebrity; a character (a village *worthy*).

Would, wụd, pret. of *will*. Under WILL.—**Would-be**, *a.* Wishing to be; vainly pretending to be (a *would-be* philosopher).—*n.* A vain pretender.

Wound, wönd, *n.* [A.Sax. *wund*, a wound; also, as an adjective, wounded, from *winnan*, to fight; D. *wonde*, Icel. *und*, Dan. *vunde*, G. *wunde*, a wound. WIN.] A cut, breach, or rupture in the skin and flesh of an animal caused by violence; an injury in a soft part of the body from external violence; a similar injury to a plant; any injury, hurt, or pain, as to the feelings.—*v.t.* To inflict a wound on; to cut, slash, or lacerate; to hurt the feelings of; to pain.—*v.t.* To inflict hurt or injury.—**Woundable**, wön'da-bl, *a.* Capable of being wounded; exposed to harm; vulnerable.—**Wound chevron**, *n.* In the U. S. Army, a small stripe of gold braid worn on the right forearm, denoting that the soldier has been wounded in action.—**Wound fever**, *n.* Fever resulting from an infected wound.—**Woundless**, wönd'les, *n.* Unwounded; unharmed; invulnerable.

Wound, wound, pret. and pp. of *wind*.

Wourali, wö'ra-li, *n.* CURARI.

Wove, wōv, pret. and sometimes pp. of *weave*.—*Wove* or *woven paper*, writing paper made with a surface of uniform appearance, without water-mark or lines.—**Woven**, wō'vn, pp. of *weave*.

Wrack, rak, *n.* [A form of *wreck*; the seaweed is so called as being cast up by the waves. Comp. Dan. *vrag*, wreck, *vrage*, to reject, Sw. *vrak*, wreck, refuse, *vraka*, to reject. WRECK.]. A popular name for seaweeds generally, but more especially when thrown ashore by the waves; also, a wreck‡; ruin‡.—*v.t.*‡ To wreck; to destroy.—**Wrack-grass**, *n.* Same as *Grasswrack*.

Wrack, rak, *n.* [RACK.] A thin, flying cloud; a rack.

Wraith, rāth, *n.* [Gael. and Ir. *arrach*, a specter or apparition.] An apparition in the exact likeness of a person, supposed to be seen before or soon after the person's death; an apparition.

Wrangle, rang'gl, *v.i.*—*wrangled*, *wrangling*. [A freq. from *wring*, A.Sax. *wringan*, pret. *wrang*, to press.] To dispute angrily; to brawl; to altercate; to engage in discussion and disputation; to argue; to debate.—*n.* An angry dispute; a noisy quarrel.—**Wrangler**, rang'glėr, *n.* One who wrangles; an angry or noisy disputant; a cowboy or herdsman; in Cambridge University, Eng., the name given to those who attain first class in the public examination for honors in mathematics.—*Senior wrangler*, formerly the student who took firstplace in the examination.—**Wranglership**, rang'glėr-ship, *n.* The honor of being a wrangler (*Cambridge*).—**Wrangling**, rang'gling, *n.* Angry disputation or altercation.

Wrap, rap, *v.t.*—*wrapped, wrapping.* [O.E. *wrappe*, formed by metathesis from *warp*, in old sense of to throw, hence to throw clothes or the like round. WARP, LAP (to fold), ENVELOP.] To fold together; to arrange so as to cover something; to envelop or muffle; to cover up or involve generally. —*To be wrapped up in*, to be bound up with or in; to be involved in; to be engrossed in or entirely devoted to (*wrapped up* in his studies).—*n.* An outer article of dress for warmth; a wrapper.—**Wrappage**, rap′āj, *n.* That which wraps; covering.—**Wrapper**, rap′ėr, *n.* One who wraps; that in which anything is wrapped; an outer covering; a loose upper garment; a lady's dressing-gown or the like.—**Wrapping**, rap′ing, *a.* Used for wrapping (*wrapping* paper).—*n.* That in which anything is wrapped; a wrapper.—**Wrap-rascal**, *n.* A colloquial term for a coarse upper coat.

Wrasse, ras, *n.* [W. *wrach.*] A genus of prickly-spined, edible fish (*Labridae*), with oblong scaly bodies and a single dorsal fin, related to the parrot fish, and inhabiting temperate waters.

Wrath, räth, *n.* [A.Sax. *wraeththo*, wrath, from *wráth*, wrathful, wroth; Icel. *reithi*, wrath, from *reithr*, wroth, from *ritha*, for *vritha*, to writhe or twist; Sw. and Dan. *vrede*, wrath; akin to *writhe, wreathe, wrest.*] Violent anger; vehement exasperation; indignation; rage. ∴ Syn. under ANGER.—**Wrathful**, räth′fųl, *a.* Full of wrath; wroth; greatly incensed; raging; furious; impetuous.—**Wrathfully**, räth′-fųl-li, *adv.* In a wrathful manner.—**Wrathfulness**, räth′fųl-nes, *n.* Vehement anger.

Wreak, rēk, *v.t.* [A.Sax. *wrecan*, to punish, to revenge, originally to banish or drive away = D. *wreken*, to avenge or revenge; Icel. *reka*, to repel; G. *rächen*, to revenge; Goth. *wrikan*, to persecute; same root as L. *urgeo*, E. to *urge. Wretch, wreck*, are closely akin.] To revenge or avenge; to inflict or cause to take effect (to *wreak* vengeance, rage, &c.).

Wreath, rēth, *n.* [A.Sax. *wraeth*, from *writhan*, to twist. WRITHE.] Something twisted or curled; a twist or curl; a garland; a chaplet; an ornamental twisted bandage to be worn on the head.—**Wreathe**, rēth, *v.t.*—*wreathed, wreathing.* To form into a wreath; to make or fashion by twining or twisting the parts together; to entwine; to intertwine; to surround with a wreath; to twine round; to encircle.—*v.i.* To twine circularly; to be interwoven or entwined.—**Wreathen**, rē′THn, an old *pp.* Wreathed; twisted.—**Wreathless**, rēth′les, *a.* Destitute of a wreath.—**Wreathy**, rē′thi, *a.* Forming a wreath; twisted; spiral.

Wreck, rek, *n.* [Same as A.Sax. *wræc*, exile, punishment (from *wrecan*, to *wreak*, originally to drive), the special meaning of shipwreck being seen in D. *wrak*, a wreck; Dan. *vrag*, O.Dan. *vrak*, a wreck, Icel. *rek* for *vrek*, Sw. *wrak*, what is drifted ashore. *Wrack*, sea-weed cast up, is the same word. WRACK, WREAK.] The destruction of a vessel by being driven ashore, dashed against rocks, or the like; shipwreck; the ruins of a ship stranded or floating about; goods which, after a shipwreck, have been thrown ashore by the sea; destruction or ruin generally; a person whose constitution is quite ruined; the remains of anything destroyed, ruined, or fatally injured.—*v.t.* To cause to become a wreck; to cast away, as a vessel, by violence, collision, or otherwise· to cause to suffer shipwreck; to ruin or destroy generally, physically or morally.—**Wreckage**, rek′āj, *n.* The act of wrecking; the remains of a ship or cargo that has been wrecked; material or parts recovered from any demolished building or structure.—**Wrecker**, rek′ėr, *n.* One who plunders the wrecks of ships; one whose occupation is to recover cargo or goods from wrecked vessels; one engaged in the business of tearing down buildings and removing the debris; a demolisher.

Wren, ren, *n.* [A.Sax. *wrenna*, a wren; allied perhaps to *wræne*, lascivious.] A name of various small birds; more especially a well-known insessorial little bird, of brisk and lively habits, with a comparatively strong and agreeable song.

Wrench, rensh, *n.* [Same as A.Sax. *wrence*, *wrence*, deceit, fraud (a figurative meaning); allied to G. *renken*, to sprain, to wrench; O.D. *wronck*, contortion; akin *wring, wrong, wrinkle.*] A violent twist, or a pull with twisting; a sprain; an injury by twisting, as in a joint; an instrument consisting essentially of a bar of metal having jaws adapted to catch upon the head of a bolt or a nut to turn it; a screw-key; the combination of a single force and a couple in a plane at right angles to its line of action. Any system of forces whatever can be reduced to a wrench.—*v. t.* To pull with a sudden, sharp, violent jerk (*to wrench a plant out of the ground; to wrench a box open*); to twist, jerk, or tear from the normal position, as a tendon, ligament, &c. of the body; to distort the meaning of what is said.

Wrest, rest, *v.t.* [A.Sax. *wraestan*, to writhe, to twist; Icel. *reista* (for *vreista*), Dan. *vriste*, to wrest, to twist; akin to *writhe, wreathe, wrist*; *wrestle* is a derivative.] To twist; to wrench; to apply a violent twisting force to; to extort or bring out, as by a twisting, painful force; to force, as by torture; to turn from truth or twist from the natural meaning by violence; to pervert.—*n.* A wrench or twist; an instrument of the wrench or screw-key kind; a key to tune stringed musical instruments with.—**Wrester**, res′tėr, *n.* One who wrests.

Wrestle, res′l, *v.i.*—*wrestled, wrestling.* [A freq. of *wrest*; A.Sax. *wraestlian*, D. *wrastelen, worstelen*, to wrestle.] To contend by grappling, and trying to throw down; to struggle, strive, or contend.—*v.t.* To contend with in wrestling.—*n.* A bout at wrestling; a wrestling match.—**Wrestler**, res′lėr, *n.* One who wrestles, or is skilful in wrestling.

Wretch, rech, *n.* [A.Sax. *wræcca*, an outcast, an exile, from *wrecan*, to banish, to wreak. WREAK, WRECK.] A miserable person; one sunk in the deepest distress; one who is supremely unhappy; a worthless mortal; a mean, base, or vile person; often used by way of slight or ironical pity or contempt, like *thing* or *creature.*—**Wretched**, rech′ed, *a.* [From *wretch*; similar in formation to *wicked.*] Miserable or unhappy; sunk into deep affliction or distress; calamitous; very afflicting; worthless; paltry; very poor or mean; despicable.—**Wretchedly**, rech′ed-li, *adv.* In a wretched manner; miserably; meanly; contemptibly.—**Wretchedness**, rech′ed-nes, *n.* The state or quality of being wretched.

Wretchless,‡ rech′les, *a.* [A form of *reckless.*] Reckless.

Wriggle, rig′l, *v.i.*—*wriggled, wriggling.* [Freq. from older *wrig, wrigge*, to wriggle; so D. *wriggelen*, to wriggle, a freq. from *wrikken*, Dan. *vrikke*, to wriggle; akin *wry, wrench, wring, wrong.*] To move the body to and fro with short motions like a worm or an eel; to move with writhing or twisting of the body; hence, to proceed in a mean, grovelling manner; to work by paltry shifts or schemes (to *wriggle* into one's confidence).—*n.* The motion of one who wriggles; a quick twisting motion like that of a worm or an eel.—**Wriggler**, rig′lėr, *n.* One who wriggles.

Wright, rīt, *n.* [A.Sax. *wyrhta*, a worker, a maker, from *wyrht*, a work, from *wyrcan*, to work. WORK.] An artisan or artificer; a worker in wood; a carpenter: now chiefly used in compounds, as in ship*wright*, wheel*wright*, also play*wright*.

Wring, ring, *v.t.*—pret. and pp. *wrung.* [A.Sax. *wringan*, to wring, strain, press = L.G. and D. *wringen*, Dan. *vrænge*, Sw. *vränga*, G. *ringer* to wring, twist, &c., all nasalized forms of stem seen in *wriggle*, and in A.Sax. *wrigian*, to bend (whence *wry*), and akin to *wrong.*] To twist and squeeze or compress; to pain, as by twisting, squeezing, or racking; to torture; to distress (to *wring* one's heart); to squeeze or press out; hence, to extort or force (to *wring* a confession or money from a person).—*To wring off*, to force off by wringing or twisting.—*To wring out*, to squeeze out by twisting; to free from a liquor by wringing.—*v.i.* To writhe; to twist, as with anguish.—**Wringer**, ring′ėr, *n.* One who wrings; an apparatus for forcing water from clothes, after they have been washed, by compression between rollers.

Wrinkle, ring′kl, *n.* [A.Sax. *wrincle*, a wrinkle = O.D. *wrinckle*, a wrinkle; a dim. form corresponding to Dan. *rynke*, Sw. *rynka*, a wrinkle; akin to *wring, wrench*, &c.] A small ridge or a furrow, formed by the shrinking or contraction of any smooth substance; a crease; a fold.—*v.t.*—*wrinkled, wrinkling.* To contract into wrinkles or furrows; to furrow; to crease.—*v.i.* To become contracted into wrinkles.—**Wrinkly**, ring′kli, *a.* Somewhat wrinkled; puckered; creasy.

Wrinkle, ring′kl, *n.* [Dim. from A.Sax. *wrenc, wrence*, a trick. WRENCH.] A valuable hint; a new or good idea; a notion; a device. (*Colloq.*)

Wrist, rist, *n.* [A.Sax. *wrist, handwrist*, the wrist; lit. the turning joint, from *writhan*, to twist; Dan. and Sw. *vrist*, Icel. *rist* (for *vrist*), the instep; G. *rist*, the wrist, the instep. WRITHE, WREST.] The joint by which the hand is united to the arm, and by means of which the hand moves on the forearm; the carpus.—**Wristband**, rist′band, *n.* The band or part of a sleeve, especially of a shirt sleeve, which covers the wrist.—**Wristlock**, rist′lok, *n.* A hold upon a wrestler's wrist which makes use of his arms and hands impossible.

Writ, rit, *n.* [A.Sax. *writ, gewrit*, a writing, a writ; from *wrītan*, to write.] That which is written, particularly applied to the Scriptures (holy *writ*, sacred *writ*); a formal document or instrument in writing; *law*, a precept issued by competent authority commanding a person to do a certain act therein specified.

Write, rīt, *v.t.*—pret. *wrote* (formerly also *writ*); pp. *written*; ppr. *writing.* [A.Sax. *wrītan*, pret. *wrát*, pp. *writen*, to write = Icel. *rita*, to scratch, write; Sw. *rita*, to draw, to trace; D. *rijten*, G. *reissen*, to tear. Originally it meant to scratch marks with something sharp.] To form or trace by a pen, pencil, graver, or other instrument; to produce by tracing legible characters expressive of ideas; to set down in letters or words; to inscribe; to cover with characters or letters; to make known or express by means of characters formed by the pen, &c.; to compose and produce as author; to style in writing; to entitle; *fig.* to impress deeply or durably.—*To write down*, to trace or form with a pen, &c., the words of; to put an end or stop to by writing unfavourably of.—*To write off*, to note or record the deduction or cancelling of.—*To write out*, to make a copy or transcription of; *refl.* to exhaust one's ideas or literary faculties by too much writing.—*To write up*, to heighten the reputation of by written reports or criticisms; to give the full details of in writing; *book-keeping*, to make the requisite entries in up to date; to post up.—*v.i.* To trace or form characters with a pen, pencil, or the like, upon paper or other material; to be engaged in literary work; to be an author; to conduct epistolary correspondence; to convey information by letter or the like.—**Writer**, rī′tėr, *n.* One who writes; a penman; a scribe; a clerk; a title given to clerks in the service of the late East India Company; a member of the literary profession; in Scotland, a law-agent, solicitor, attorney, or the like.—*Writer to the Signet.* SIGNET.—*Writer's cramp*, a spasmodic affection frequently attacking persons (generally middle-aged) who have been accustomed to employ the pen much.—**Writership**, rī′tėr-ship, *n.* The office of writer.—**Writing**, rī′ting, *n.* The act or art of setting down words or characters on paper or other material, for the purpose of recording ideas; anything written; a literary or other composition; a manuscript; a book; an inscription.—**Writing-book**, *n.* A copy-book.—**Writing-chambers**, *n.pl.* Apartments occupied by lawyers and their clerks, &c.—**Writing-desk**, *n.* A desk with a sloping top used to write on.—**Writing-master**, *n.* One who teaches the art of penmanship.—**Writing-paper**, *n.* Paper finished with a smooth surface for writing, generally sized.—**Writing-table**, *n.* A table used for writing, having commonly a desk part, drawers, &c.—**Written**, rit'n, *p.* and *a.* Reduced to writing: as opposed to *oral* or *spoken.*—*Written law*, law contained in a statute or statutes.—**Write-up**, *n.* A story, especially one written for a newspaper; copy (*slang*).

Writhe, rīтн, *v.t.*—*writhed, writhing.* [A. Sax. *writhan*, to writhe, wreath, twist = Icel. *ritha* (for *vritha*), Dan. *vride*, Sw. *vrida*, to writhe; from same root as *worth* (verb), L. *verto*, to turn [VERSE). Akin *wrath, wreath, wrist, wrest.*] To twist with violence (to *writhe* the body); to distort; to wrest.—*v.i.* To twist the body about, as in pain.

Wrong, rong, *a.* [A participial form from *wring*; Dan. *vrang*, Icel. *rangr*, *vrangr*, wrong; D. *wrang*, sour, harsh (lit. twisting the mouth). WRING.] Not right; not fit or suitable; not according to rule, wish, design, or the like; not what ought to be; not according to the divine or moral law; deviating from rectitude; not according to facts or truth; inaccurate; erroneous; holding erroneous notions; being in error; mistaken.—*n.* What is not right, especially morally; a wrong, unfair, or unjust act; a breach of law to the injury of another; an injustice; any injury, hurt, pain, or damage.—*In the wrong*, holding a wrong or unjustifiable position as regards another person; blamable towards another.—*adv.* In a wrong manner; erroneously; incorrectly.—*v.t.* To treat with injustice; to deal harshly or unfairly with; to do injustice to by imputation; to think ill of unfairly.—**Wrong-doer**, *n.* One who does wrong or evil.—**Wrong-doing**, *n.* The doing of wrong; evildoing.—**Wrongful**, rong'fụl, *a.* Injurious; unjust; illegal; criminal; contrary to moral law or justice; unfair.—**Wrongfully**, rong'fụl-li, *adv.* In a wrongful manner; unjustly.—**Wrongfulness**, rong'fụl-nes, *n.* Injustice.—**Wronghead**, rong'hed, *n.* A person who takes up wrong ideas and obstinately sticks to them.—**Wrongheaded**, rong'hed-ed, *a.* Perversely wrong; having a perverse understanding.—**Wrongheadedly**, rong'hed-ed-li, *adv.* Obstinately; perversely.—**Wrongheadedness**, rong'hed-ed-nes, *n.*—**Wrongly**, rong'li, *adv.* Unjustly; amiss.—**Wrongness**, rong'nes, *n.* The state or condition of being wrong.—**Wrongous**, rong'us, *n.* [O.E. *wrongwis*, that is *wrongwise*, the opposite of *rightwise* or righteous.] *Scots law*, unjust; illegal (*wrongous* imprisonment).

Wroth, rąth, *a.* [A.Sax. *wrāth*, angry, enraged (whence *wrath*), lit. twisted, from *writhan*, to twist or writhe. WRATH, WRITHE.] Very angry; much exasperated; wrathful.

Wrought, rąt, pret. and pp. of *work.*—*Wrought iron.* Under IRON.

Wrung, rung, pret. and pp. of *wring.*

Wry, rī, *a.* [A.Sax. *wrigian*, to bend, to turn, to incline; akin to *wriggle* (which see).] Abnormally bent or turned to one side; twisted; distorted; crooked.—**Wryly**, rī'li, *adv.* In a wry, crooked, or distorted manner.—**Wryneck**, rī'nek, *n.* A twisted or distorted neck; a small European bird allied to the woodpeckers: so called from the singular manner in which it twists its neck.

Wyandot, wī'an-dot, *n.* A member tribe of the Iroquois Indians.

Wyandotte, wī'an-dot, *n.* A breed of domestic fowls.

Wych-elm, wich, *n.* [O.E. *wiche, wyche*, A.Sax. *wice*, a name applied to various trees; allied to *wicker.*] A variety of elm with large leaves and sometimes pendulous branches, forming a 'weeping' tree. —**Wych-hazel**, *n.* An American shrub with yellow flowers grown in gardens or shrubberies.

Wye, wī, *n.* The letter Y.

Wyvern, wī'vėrn, *n.* [O.Fr. *wivre, vivre* (with *n* added as in *bittern*), a viper, a dragon, from L. *vipera*, a viper. VIPER, WEEVER.] A heraldic monster, a sort of dragon, with two wings, two legs, and a tapering body.

X

X, the twenty-fourth letter of the English alphabet, representing the sounds *ks, gz, z, ksh, gzh.*

Xanthic, zan'thik, *a.* [Gr. *xanthos*, yellow.] Tending towards a yellow colour; yellowish.—*Xanthic flowers*, flowers which have yellow for their type, and which are capable of passing into red or white, but never into blue.—**Xanthin, Xanthine**, zan'thin, *n.* A name of certain yellow colouring matters.—**Xanthite**, zan'thīt, *n.* A mineral of a yellowish colour, a variety of vesuvian.

Xanthippe, zan-tip'ē, *n.* [Wife of Socrates.] A shrew.

Xanthochroi, zan-thok'ro-ī, *n.pl.* [Gr. *xanthochroos*, yellow-skinned, from *xanthos*, yellow, and *chroa*, colour.] One of the five groups into which Huxley classifies man, comprising the fair whites.—**Xanthochroic**, zan-tho-krō'ik, *a.* Pertaining to this group.

Xanthophyll, zan'tho-fil, *n.* [Gr. *xanthos*, yellow, *phyllon*, a leaf.] The yellow colouring matter of withering leaves.

Xanthous, zan'thus, *a.* [Gr. *xanthos*, yellow.] Of the fair-haired type; having brown, auburn, yellow, flaxen, or red hair.

Xebec, zē'bek, *n.* [Sp. *xabeque*, from Turk. *sumbeki*, a xebec; Ar. *sumbūk*, a small vessel.] A small three-masted vessel having both square and lateen sails, used in the Mediterranean.

Xenogenesis, zen-o-jen'e-sis, *n.* [Gr. *xenos*, strange, and *genesis*, birth.] Heterogenesis, the production of offspring entirely unlike their parents.—**Xenogenetic**, zen'o-je-net"ik, *a.* Pertaining to xenogenesis.

Xenon, zen'on, *n.* [Gr. *xenos*, stranger.] An inert gaseous element present in the atmosphere in the minute proportion of 5 parts in a hundred million by volume.

Xerasia, zē-rā'si-a, *n.* [From Gr. *xēros*, dry.] A disease of the hair, which becomes dry and ceases to grow.—**Xeroderma**, zē-rō-dėr'ma, *n.* [Gr. *derma*, skin.] A morbid dryness of the skin, in its severest form constituting fish-skin disease.—**Xerophthalmy, Xerophthalmia**, zē'-rof-thal-mi, zē-rof-thal'mi-a, *n.* [Gr. *ophthalmos*, the eye.] A dry, red soreness or itching of the eyes.—**Xerotes**, zē'rō-tēz, *n.* [Gr. *xērotēs*, dryness.] A dry habit of the body.

Xerophyte, zē'rō-fīt, *n.* [Gr. *xēros*, dry, *phyton*, a plant.] A plant adapted to live in surroundings where water is scarce (deserts) or difficult to absorb (moors).

Xiphoid, zif'oid, *a.* [Gr. *xiphos*, a sword, and *eidos*, likeness.] Shaped like or resembling a sword.

Xmas, *n.* (*X*, symbol for Christ; *mas*, contraction of Mass.) Christmas (*Colloq.*).

X rays, or **Röntgen rays**, eks-rāz, rent'-gen, *n.* [From discoverer's name.] Rays generated by the impact of high-speed electrons on a metal target. They are electromagnetic waves of high frequency, very penetrating, and able to affect a photographic plate, so that they are of great value in medical diagnosis.—**X-ray spectrum**, *n.* The assemblage of wave lengths in the characteristic radiation of a substance, especially an element, in the X-ray region of frequencies. Its relation to atomic number is fundamental in modern atomic theory.—**X-ray therapy**, *n.* Treatment of certain diseases as cancer, by the use of X rays.—**X-ray tube**, *n.* A discharge tube containing a metal target, by impact of electrons on which X rays are produced.

Xylem, zī'lem, *n.* Woody tissue, in botany opposed to *phloem.*

Xylene (Xylol), zī'lēn (zī'lol), *n.* [Gr. *xylon*, wood.] A transparent liquid distilled from coal-tar, and used in microscopic work as a solvent.

Xylite, zī'līt, *n.* [Gr. *xylon*, wood.] Ligniform asbestos, mountain wood, or rock-wood.—**Xylocarp**, zī'lō-kärp, *n.* [Gr. *xylon*, and *karpos*, fruit.] *Bot.* a hard and woody fruit.—**Xylocarpous**, zī-lō-kär'-pus, *a.* Having fruit which becomes hard or woody.—**Xylograph**, zī'lō-graf, *n.* [Gr. *xylon*, and *graphō*, to write or engrave.] A wood-engraving.—**Xylographer**, zī-log'ra-fėr, *n.* One who engraves on wood.—**Xylographic, Xylographical**, zī-lō-graf'ik, zī-lō-graf'i-kal, *a.* Relating to xylography.—**Xylography**, zī-log'ra-fi, *n.* Wood-engraving; a process of decorative painting on wood.—**Xyloid**, zī'loid, *a.* [Gr. *xylon*, and *eidos*, form.] Having the nature of wood; resembling wood.—**Xyloidine**, zī-loi'din, *n.* An explosive compound produced by the action of strong nitric acid upon starch or woody fibre.—**Xylophagous**, zī-lof'a-gus, *a.* [Gr. *phagō*, to eat.] Eating or feeding on wood.—**Xylophilous**, zī-lof'i-lus, *a.* [Gr. *philos*, loving.] Growing upon or living in wood.—**Xylophone**, zī'lo-fōn, zil'o-fōn, *n.* [Gr. *xylon*, wood, *phōnē*, sound.] A musical instrument using wooden bars graduated to produce the notes of the scale when struck with a small wooden hammer.—**Xylopyrography**, zī'lō-pi-rog"ra-fi, *n.* [Gr. *pyr, pyros*, fire.] The art of producing a picture on wood by charring it with a hot iron.—**Xyloretine**, zī'lō-rē-tin, *n.* [Gr. *rhetinē*, resin.] A resinous substance found in connection with the pine-trunks of certain peat-mosses.

Y

Y, the twenty-fifth letter of the alphabet, sometimes a vowel, sometimes a consonant.

Yacca-wood, yak'a, *n.* [Of West Indian origin.] A brownish cabinet wood of the West Indies, yielded by a large tree belonging to the yew family.

Yacht, yot, *n.* [From O.D. *jacht*, Mod.D. *jagt*, a yacht, a chase, from *jagen*, G. *jagen*, Dan. *jage*, to hunt.] A light and elegantly fitted up vessel, used for either pleasure trips or racing, or as an off-shore residence.

now usually motor-powered.—*v.i.* To sail or cruise in a yacht.—**Yacht-club**, *n.* A club or union of yacht-owners for racing purposes, &c.—**Yachter**, yot'ėr, *n.* One who commands a yacht; one who sails in a yacht.—**Yachting**, yot'ing, *a.* Belonging to a yacht or yachts.—**Yachtsman**, yots'man, *n.* One who keeps or sails a yacht.

Yaffle, Yaffingale, yaf'l, yaf'in-gāl, *n.* [From its cry.] The green woodpecker.

Yager, yä'gėr, *n.* [G. *jäger*, lit. a huntsman, from *jagen*, to hunt. YACHT.] A soldier in certain regiments of light infantry in the armies of various German states.

Yahoo, yä'hö, *n.* [Coined by Swift.] A name given by Swift, in *Gulliver's Travels*, to a race of brutes having the form of man and all his degrading passions; hence, a rude, boorish, uncultivated character.

Yahveh, ya'wā, *n.* [Heb.] Jehovah.

Yak, yak, *n.* [Thibetan.] A kind of ox with long silky hair, a bushy mane, and horse-like tail, inhabiting Thibet and the Himalayas.

Yam, yam, *n.* [Pg. *inhame*, a yam; origin unknown.] A large esculent tuber or root produced by a genus of tropical plants, forming a wholesome and nutritious food.

Yankee, yang'kē, *n.* [Probably a corrupt pronunciation of *English* or Fr. *Anglais* formerly current among the American Indians.] A cant name for a citizen of New England; in Britain often applied more widely to natives of the United States.—**Yankee-Doodle**, *n.* A famous air, now regarded as American and national. —**Yankeeism**, yang'kē-izm, *n.* An idiom or practice of the Yankees.

Yap, yap, *v.i.* [Imitative of sound.] To yelp; to bark.—*n.* The cry of a dog; a bark; a yelp.

Yapock, yap'ok, *n.* An opossum of Brazil and Guiana, aquatic in its habits and resembling a small otter.

Yard, yärd, *n.* [A.Sax. *gyrd*, *gird*, a rod, a yard measure = D. *garde*, G. *gerte*, a rod, a twig; Goth. *gazds*, a goad; cog. with L. *hasta*, a spear.] The British and American standard measure of length, equal to 3 feet or 36 inches, the foot being practically the unit; also 9 square feet and 27 cubic feet (the square and cubic yard); a long cylindrical piece of timber in a ship, slung crosswise to a mast, and supporting and extending a sail.—**Yard-arm**, *n.* The end of a ship's yard.—*Yard-arm and yard-arm*, the situation of two ships lying alongside of each other so near that their yard-arms cross or touch.—**Yardmaster**, yärd"-mas'tėr, *n.* One in charge of a lumber yard or a railroad yard.—**Yard-stick**, *n.* A stick, 3 feet in length, used as a measure of cloth, &c.

Yard, yärd, *n.* [A.Sax. *geard*, a yard, a court, &c.; Icel. *garthr*, an inclosure (E. *garth*); Dan. and D. *gaard*, a garden; G. *garten*, a garden; same root as L. *hortus*, a garden. Akin *garden*, *gird*, to surround. *Orchard* contains this word.] A small piece of inclosed ground adjoining a house; an inclosure within which any work or industry is carried on (a brick-*yard*, a dock-*yard*, &c.).—*v.t.* To inclose or shut up in a yard, as cattle.

Yare, yãr, *a.* [A.Sax. *gearu*, prepared, ready, yare; akin *garb*, *gear*.] Ready; quick; dexterous.

Yark, yärk, *v.t.* Same as *Yerk*.

Yarn, yärn, *n.* [A.Sax. *gearn*, yarn = D. *garen*, Icel. Sw. Dan. and G. *garn*, yarn; comp. Icel. *garnir*, intestines; Gr. *chordē*, a chord, an intestine.] Any kind of thread prepared for weaving into cloth; one of the threads of which a rope is composed; *fig.* a long story or tale (*colloq.*).

Yarrow, yar'ō, *n.* [A.Sax. *gearwe*, D. *gerw*, G. *garbe*, O.G. *garwe*, yarrow.] An odorous herb, also called *Milfoil*.

Yataghan, yat'a-gan, *n.* [Turk.] A dagger-like sabre about 2 feet long, the handle without a cross-guard, worn in Mohammedan countries.

Yaw, ya̤, *v.i.* [Comp. prov. G. *gagen*, to rock, to move unsteadily.] To steer wild; to deviate from the line of her course in steering: said of a ship.—*n.* A temporary deviation of a ship or vessel from the line of her course.

Yawl, ya̤l, *n.* [From D. *jol*, a yawl, a skiff; Sw. *julle*, Dan. *jolle*, a jolly-boat, a yawl. *Jolly* in *jolly-boat* is this word.] A small ship's boat, usually rowed by four or six oars; a jolly-boat; the smallest boat used by fishermen.

Yawl, ya̤l, *v.i.* [Akin to *yowl*, *yell*.] To cry out; to howl; to yell.

Yawn, ya̤n, *v.i.* [A.Sax. *gánian*, to yawn, to gape; akin Sc. *gant*, to yawn; Gr. *gähnen*, to yawn; from root seen in Gr. *chainō*, L. *hio*, to gape; also in G. *gans*, E. *gander*, *goose*. From same root are *chasm*, *chaos*.] To have the mouth open involuntarily through drowsiness or dulness; to gape; to open wide; to stand open, as a chasm or gulf, or the like.—*n.* An involuntary opening of the mouth from drowsiness; a gaping or opening wide.—**Yawningly**, ya̤'ning-li, *adv.* In a yawning manner.

Yaws, ya̤z, *n.* [African *yaw*, a raspberry.] A contagious disease of the African races characterized by cutaneous tumours, growing to the size of a raspberry.

Yclept, Ycleped, i-klept', i-klēpd', *pp.* [A. Sax. *ge-clypod*, pp. of *ge-clypian*, to call.] Called; named. (*Archaic.*)

Ye, yē, *pron.* [A.Sax. *gé*, ye, you, nom. pl. corresponding to *thú*, thou; D. *gij*, Dan. and Sw. *i*, Goth. *jus*. YOU.] Properly the nominative plural of the second personal pronoun, but in later times also used as an objective; now used only in the sacred and solemn style, in common discourse and writing *you* being exclusively used.

Yea, yā, *adv.* [A.Sax. *geá*, yea, indeed= Icel. *já*, D. Dan. Sw. and G. *ja*, Goth. *ja*, *jai*, yea, yes; allied to Goth. *jah*, and; L. *jam*, now. YES.] Yes: the opposite of *nay*; also used like nay=not this alone, not only so but also.

Yean, yēn, *v.t.* and *i.* [A.Sax. *eánian*, *eácnian*, from *eácen*, gravid, lit. increased, being pp. of *eacan*, to increase, to *eke*. EKE.] To bring forth young, as a goat or sheep; to lamb.—**Yeanling**, yēn'ling, *n.* A lamb; an eanling.

Year, yēr, *n.* [A.Sax. *geár*, *gér*=D. *jaar*, L.G. *jör*, G. *jahr*, Goth. *jēr*, Icel. *ár*, Dan. *aar*; cog. Slav. *jaro*, spring; Zend *yâre*, a year. Perhaps from root *i*, to go, seen in L. *eo*, *ire*, to go.] The period of time during which the earth makes one complete revolution in its orbit, comprehending what are called the twelve calendar months, or 365 days from 1st January to 31st December; *pl.* age or old age.—*Anomalistic year*. ANOMALISTIC.—*Civil year*, the tropical or solar year.—*Common year*, a year of 365 days, as distinguished from *leap year*.—*Ecclesiastical year*, from Advent to Advent.—*Gregorian year*, *Julian year*. GREGORIAN, JULIAN, STYLE. — *Leap year*. LEAP.—*Lunar year*, a period of 12 lunar months, or 354 days.—*Sidereal year*. SIDEREAL. — *Tropical* or *solar year*, the period from the time the sun is on one of the tropics till its return again to it, being 365 days, 5 hours, 48 minutes, 46 seconds.—*Year of grace*, any year of the Christian era.—**Year-book**, *n.* A book published every year, each issue supplying fresh information on matters in regard to which changes are continually taking place. —**Yearling**, yēr'ling, *n.* An animal one year old or in the second year of his age.—*a.* Being a year old.—**Yearly**, yēr-li, *a.* Annual; happening every year. — *adv.* Annually; once a year.

Yearn, yėrn, *v.i.* [A.Sax. *geornian*, *gyrnan*, to yearn, from *georn*, desirous; Icel. *gjarn*, eager, whence *girna*, to desire; Goth. *gairns*, desirous, *gairnjan*, to long for; Dan. *gierne*, D. *gaarne*, G. *gern*, willingly.] To feel mental uneasiness from longing desire; to be filled with eager longing; to have a wistful feeling.—**Yearning**, yėr'ning, *p.* and *a.* Longing; having longing desire.—*n.* The feeling of one who yearns; a strong feeling of tenderness, pity, or longing desire.—**Yearningly**, yėr'ning-li, *adv.* With yearning.

Yeast, yēst, *n.* [O.E. *yeest*, A.Sax. *gist*, *gyst* = Icel. *jast*, *jastr*, D. *gest*, *gist*, G. *gäscht*, yeast; from a verb signifying to ferment seen in O.H.G. *gesan*, *jesan*, G. *gähren*, *gischen*, Sw. *gäsa*, to ferment, to froth; allied to Gr. *zeō*, to boil, *zēlos*, E. *zeal*.] Barm; ferment; the yellowish substance of vegetable nature produced during the vinous fermentation of saccharine fluids; foam of water; froth. — *German yeast*, common yeast collected, drained, and pressed till nearly dry.—*Patent yeast*, yeast collected from a wort of malt and hop, and treated similarly to German yeast.—*Artificial yeast*, a dough of flour and a small quantity of common yeast made into small cakes and dried, which, if kept free from moisture, long retains its fermentative property.—**Yeasty**, yēs'ti, *a.* Resembling or containing yeast; frothy; foamy.—**Yeastiness**, yēs'ti-nes, *n.* The state or quality of being yeasty.

Yelk, yelk, *n.* The yolk of an egg.

Yell, yel, *v.i.* [A.Sax. *gellan*, *gyllan*, to yell = Icel. *gella*, *gjalla*, D. *gillen*, to yell; G. *gellen*, to resound; allied to A.Sax. *galan*, to sing, whence -*gale* in *nightingale*.] To cry out with a sharp, disagreeable noise; to shriek hideously; to cry or scream as with agony or horror.—*n.* A sharp, loud, harsh outcry; a scream or cry of horror, distress, or agony.—**Yelling**, yel'ing, *n.* The act or the noise of one who or that which yells.

Yellow, yel'ō, *a.* [A.Sax. *geolo*, *geolu*, yellow; akin D. *geel*, G. *gelb*, Icel. *gulr*, Dan. and Sw. *guul*, yellow; from same root as *gold* and *green*; Gr. *chloē*, green herb, *cholē*, bile (cog. with E. *gall*).] Being of a pure bright golden color, or of a kindred hue; traitorous, cowardly (*slang*).—*Yellow berries*, called also *French berries*, the fruit of a species of buckthorn, used by dyers and painters for staining yellow.—*Yellow journalism*, a type of writing and press reporting which stresses sensational and unpleasant or horrifying aspects and details.—*Yellow ocher*, an earthy pigment colored by the oxide of iron.—*Yellow soap*, a common soap composed of tallow, resin, and soda, to which some palm-oil is occasionally added.—*n.* One of the prismatic colors, a bright golden color, the type of which may be found in the field buttercup. United with blue it yields *green*, with red it produces *orange*.—*v.t.* To render yellow.—*v.i.* To grow yellow.—**Yellow-bunting**, *n.* The yellow-hammer.—**Yellow-fever**, *n.* An infectious febrile disease common in the West Indies and neighboring regions, attended with yellowness of the skin, caused by a filterable virus and transmitted by the bite of the female *Stegomyia* mosquito.—**Yellow-hammer**, *n.* [A.Sax. *amore*, G. *ammer*, the yellow-hammer.] A passerine song-bird of Europe, called also *Yellow Bunting*, from the predominance of yellow in its plumage.—**Yellow-jacket**, *n.* A wasp common to America, having bright yellow stripes.—**Yellow-metal**, *n.* A sheathing alloy of copper and zinc; Muntz's metal.—**Yellow-pine**, *n.* A North American tree, the wood of which is largely employed and is extensively exported.—**Yellows**, yel'ōz, *n.* A kind of jaundice which affects horses, cattle, and sheep, causing yellowness of the eyes; a disease of peach trees.—**Yellow-throat**, *n.* A small North American singing-bird, a species of warbler.—**Yellow-top**, *n.* A variety of turnip, so called from the color of the bulb.

Yelp, yelp, *v.i.* [O.E. *yelpen*, *gelpen*, A.Sax. *gilpan*, to boast; Icel. *gjálpa*, to yelp; allied to *yell*.] To utter a sharp or shrill bark; to give a sharp, quick cry, as a dog, either in eagerness or in pain or fear.—*n.* A sharp bark or cry caused by fear or pain.

Yen, yen, *n.* A piece of Japanese money worth approximately fifty cents; an urgent desire (*slang*).

Yeoman, yō'man, *n.*pl. **Yeomen**, yō'men. [O.E. *yeman, yoman*; supposed to be equivalent to Fris. *gaman, gamon*, a villager, a man of a *ga* or village, from *ga* = G. *gau*, Goth. *gawi*, a district.] In England a man of small estate in land, not ranking as one of the gentry; one who farms his own land; a farmer; a member of the yeomanry cavalry.—*Yeoman of the guard*, in England, a bodyguard of the sovereign, habited in the costume of Henry VIII's time, and commanded by a captain and other officers. BEEF-EATER.—**Yeomanry**, yō'man-ri, *n.* Yeomen collectively.

Yerba, Yerba-mate, yer'ba, yer-ba-mä'tā, *n.* [*Yerba* (Sp., from L. *herba*, herb) is the proper name; *mate* is a cup, the cup or dish from which the tea is drunk.] A name given to Paraguay tea. PARAGUAY TEA.

Yerk, yėrk, *v.t.* [See JERK.] To throw or kick out, as a horse; to lash.—*v.i.* To kick with both hind legs.—*n.* A sudden kick of a horse; a blow.

Yes, yes, *adv.* [A.Sax. *gese, gise*, from *ged*, yea, and *sí, sý*, be it so, let it be, 3d sing. pres. subj. of the substantive verb in A. Sax.=G. *sei*, let it be; akin to L. *sim*, may it be; from root *as*. YEA, AM, ARE.] A word which expresses affirmation or consent: opposed to *no*.

Yest, yest, *n.* Same as *Yeast*.

Yester, yes'tėr, *a.* [A.Sax. *geostra, giestra, gystra*, yesterday's, *geostran dæg*, yesterday; *gystran niht*, yesternight; D. *gisteren*, G. *gestern*, yesterday; Goth. *gistra, gistra dagis*, to-morrow. These are comparative forms, applied to L. *hesternus*, of yesterday, and to Gr. *chthes*, Skr. *hyas*, yesterday.] Belonging to the day preceding the present; next before the present: mostly in composition.—**Yesterday**, yes'tėr-dā, *n.* The day next before the present; often used for time not long gone by. *Yesterday, yesternight*, &c., are used without the preposition *on* or *during*.—**Yestereve, Yestereven**, yes'tėr-ēv, yes-tėr-ē'vn, *n.* The evening last past.—**Yestermorn, Yestermorning**, yes'tėr-morn, yes-tėr-mor'ning, *n.* The morn or morning last past.—**Yesternight**, yes'tėr-nīt, *n.* The night last past.

Yesty, yes'ti, *a.* Yeasty.

Yet, yet, *adv.* [A.Sax. *get, git*, yét, still; equivalent etymologically to *yea to* or *yea too*.] In addition; over and above; further; still: used especially with comparatives (*yet* more surprising); at this or at that time, as formerly; now or then, as at a previous period (while *yet* young); at or before some future time; before all is done (he'll suffer *yet*); thus far; hitherto (a letter not *yet* sent off): often accompanied by *as* in this sense (I have not met him *as yet*); though the case be such; nevertheless.—*conj.* Nevertheless; notwithstanding; however.

Yew, yū, *n.* [A.Sax. *iw*, the yew; O.H.G. *iwa*, G. *eibe*, D. *ijf*, Icel. *ýr*; cog. W. *yw, ywen*, Armor. *ivin*, Corn. *hivin*, the yew.] An evergreen tree allied to the conifers and indigenous in Europe and Asia, yielding a hard and durable timber used for cabinet work and formerly for making bows; frequently planted in churchyards, and thus associated with death, perhaps from its poisonous leaves.

Yex, yeks, *n.* [A.Sax. *geocsa*, a sobbing; Sc. *yisk*, the hiccup.] The hiccup.—*v.i.* To hiccup.

Yield, yēld, *v.t.* [A.Sax. *gildan, gieldar*, to yield, pay, render = Icel. *gjalda*, Dan. *gjelde*, to yield, Sw. *gälla*, to be of consequence; D. *gelden*, G. *gelten*, to be worth, to avail, &c.; akin *guild*.] To pay‡; to requite‡; to give in return or by way of recompense; to produce as return for labour or capital; to produce generally; to bring forth, give out, or furnish (trees *yield* fruit); to afford; to grant or give (to *yield* consent); to give up, as to superior power; to relinquish; to surrender: in this sense often followed by *up*.—*To yield up the ghost* or *life*, to die.—*v.i.* To give way, as to superior force; to submit; to surrender; to give way, as to entreaty, argument, &c.; to comply; to consent; to give place, as inferior in rank or excellence.—*n.* Amount yielded; product; return; particularly product resulting from growth or cultivation.—**Yielder**, yēl'dėr, *n.* One who yields.—**Yielding**, yēl'ding, *a.* Ready to submit, comply, or yield; compliant; unresisting.—**Yieldingly**, yēl'ding-li, *adv.* With compliance.—**Yieldingness**, yēl'ding-nes, *n.*

Yodel, Yodle, yō'dl, *v.t.* and *i.* [German Swiss.] To sing like the Swiss and Tyrolese mountaineers, by suddenly changing from the natural voice to the falsetto, and vice versâ.

Yoicks, yo'iks, *interj.* An old fox-hunting cry.

Yoke, yōk, *n.* [A.Sax. *geoc, ioc*, a yoke = D. *juk, jok*, G. *joch*, Goth. *juk*, Icel. and Sw. *ok*, Dan. *aag*; cog. L. *jugum*, Gr. *zygon*, Skr. *yuga*, a yoke, from a root meaning to join, seen in Skr. *yuj*, to join; L. *jungo*, to join. JOIN.] A part of the gear or tackle of draught animals, particularly oxen, passing across their necks and so that two are connected for drawing; a pair of draught animals, especially oxen, yoked together; something resembling a yoke in form or use; a frame to fit the shoulders and neck of a person for carrying pails or the like; *fig.* servitude, slavery, or burden imposed; something which couples or binds together; a bond of connection; a tie.—*v.t.*—*yoked, yoking*. To put a yoke on; to join in a yoke; to couple; to join with another.—*v.i.* To be joined together.—**Yoke-fellow**, *n.* One associated with another in labour; one connected with another by marriage; a partner; a mate.—**Yoke-mate**, *n.* Same as *Yoke-fellow*.

Yokel, yō'kl, *n.* [Perhaps from *yoke* = one who drives yoked animals, or akin to *gawk*.] A rustic or countryman; a country bumpkin; a country lout.

Yolk, yōk, *n.* [A.Sax. *geoleca*, lit. the yellow of the egg, from *geolu*, yellow. YELLOW.] The yellow part of an egg; the vitellus; the yelk; the unctuous secretion from the skin of sheep which renders the pile soft and pliable.—**Yolk-bag**, *n.* The sac or membranous bag which contains the yolk of an egg.

Yon, yon, *a.* [A.Sax. *geon*, yon, that; Goth. *jains*, G. *jener*, that; of pronominal origin, and akin to Skr. *yas*, who, also to *yea* and *yes*.] That; those: referring to an object at a distance; yonder; now chiefly used in the poetic style.—**Yonder**, yon'dėr, *a.* [A compar. form from *yon*; comp. Goth. *jaindre*, there.] Being at a distance within view; that or those, referring to persons or things at a distance.—*adv.* At or in that place there.

Yoni, yō'ni, *n.* Among the Hindus, the female power in nature, or a symbol of it in the form of an oval.

Yore, yōr, *adv.* [A.Sax. *gedra*, formerly of old, originally genit. pl. of *gear*, a year, being thus an adverbial genitive of time, like *twice, thrice*, &c.] In time long past; long since; in old time. Now used only in the phrase *of yore*, that is, of old time; long ago (in days *of yore*).

You, yö, *pron.* [A.Sax. *eów*, dat. and acc. pl. of the pronoun of the second person, *ye* being properly the nom. pl.; O.Sax. *iu*, D. *u*, you, *gij*, ye; O.H.G. *iu*, you, *iuwar*, your; cog. Skr. *yuyam*, you. YE.] The nominative and objective plural of *thou*: also commonly used when a single person is addressed (*you are, you were*, &c., being said of one person).

Young, yung, *a.* [A.Sax. *geong, giung, iung*=D. *jong*, G. *jung*, Goth. *juggs*, Icel. *ungr, jungr*, Dan. and Sw. *ung*; cog. L. *juvenis* (whence *juvenile*), Skr. *juvan*, young.] Being in the first or early stage of life or growth; not yet arrived at maturity; not old; being in the early part of existence; not yet far advanced; having the appearance of early life; fresh or vigorous; having little experience; raw; green; pertaining to one's early life.—*n.pl.* The offspring of an animal collectively.—*With young*, pregnant; gravid.—**Younger**, yung'gėr, *n.* One who is not so old as another; a junior.—**Young-eyed**, *a.* Having the fresh bright eyes or look of youth.—**Youngish**, yung'ish, *a.* Somewhat young.—**Youngling**, yung'ling, *n.* An animal in the first part of life; also, a young person.—**Youngly**, yung'li, *adv.* In a young manner.—**Youngness**, yung'nes, *n.* The state of being young.—**Youngster**, yung'ster, *n.* A young person; a lad.—**Younker**, yung'kėr, *n.* [From Du. *jonker, jonkheer*, lit. young sir (*heer*=G. *herr*, sir, gentleman).] A young fellow; a lad; a youngster. JUNKER.

Your, yör, *a.* [A.Sax. *eówer*=D. *uwer*, G. *euer*; the possessive corresponding to *ye, you*, and therefore properly plural (*thy* being the singular), but now like *you* used as singular or plural.] Pertaining or belonging to you.—**Yours**, yörz, *poss. pron.* A double possessive of *you*; that or those which belong to you; belonging to you: used with or without direct reference to a preceding noun; your property; your friends or relations.—*Yours truly, yours faithfully*, &c., phrases preceding the signature at the end of a letter; hence, sometimes used playfully by a speaker in alluding to himself.—**Yourself**, yör-self', *pron.* pl. **Yourselves**, yör-selvz'. You, not another or others; you, in your own person or individually: used distinctively or reflexively.

Youth, yöth, *n.* [A.Sax. *geóguth*, for *geonguth* (=*youngth, young* and *-th*), from *geong*, young. YOUNG.] The state or quality of being young; youthfulness; the part of life between childhood and manhood; a young man; a stripling or lad; young persons collectively.—**Youthful**, yöth'ful, *a.* Being in the early stage of life; young; pertaining to the early part of life; suitable to the first part of life; fresh or vigorous, as in youth.—**Youthfully**, yöth'ful-li, *adv.* In a youthful manner.—**Youthfulness**, yöth'ful-nes, *n.* The state or quality of being youthful.

Yowl, youl, *v.i.* [Akin to *yell*.] To give a long distressful or mournful cry, as a dog.—*n.* A long distressful or mournful cry, as that of a dog.

Yperite, ēp'ėr-īt, *n.* [After the Belgian town of *Ypres*.] Mustard gas.

Yttria, it'ri-a, *n.* A metallic oxide or earth, having the appearance of a white powder; the protoxide of yttrium, discovered in 1794 in a mineral found at *Ytterby* in Sweden, whence the name.—**Yttrious**, it'ri-us, *a.* Pertaining to yttria or yttrium.—**Yttrium**, it'ri-um, *n.* A rare metal found in Sweden of a scaly texture, a grayish black colour, and a perfectly metallic lustre. Written also *Ittrium*.

Yucca, yuk'ka, *n.* [From some American tongue.] A genus of American plants of the lily family, of considerable size, with white flowers in large panicles, and long rigid, pointed leaves, cultivated in British gardens.

Yule, yöl, *n.* [A.Sax. *geól, giúl, iúl, geóhol*, Christmas; Icel. *jól*, Dan. *juul*, Sw. *jul*; originally a pagan festival; etymol. doubtful. *Jolly* is from this through the French.] The Old English and still the Scotch and Northern English name for Christmas.—**Yule-log, Yule-block**, *n.* A large log of wood forming the basis of a Christmas fire in the olden time.—**Yule-tide**, *n.* The time or season of Yule or Christmas.

Y-wis,‡ *adv.* [A.Sax. *gewis, gewiss*, certain, sure = D. *gewis*, G. *gewiss*, certainly; from root of *wit*, with prefix *ge*.] Certainly; verily; truly.

Z

Z, the last letter of the English alphabet, equivalent to the *s* in *wise, ease,* &c.

Zabaism, Zabism, za-bā'izm, zab'izm. Same as *Sabaism.*

Zaffer, zaf'ėr, *n.* [Fr. *zafre, safre, saffre,* Sp. *zafre*; probably of Arabic origin.] Impure oxide of cobalt; the residuum of cobalt after the sulphur, arsenic, and other volatile matters have been expelled by calcination, much used by enamelers and porcelain manufacturers as a blue color.

Zambo, zam'bō, *n.* [Sp. *zambo,* bandy-legged, a zambo.] The child of a mulatto and a negro, also sometimes of an Indian and a negro.

Zamia, zā'mi-a, *n.* [L. *zamia,* a fir cone.] A genus of plants of the cycad order, the stem of some of which yields a starchy pith used for food.

Zamindar, zam-in-där', *n.* Same as *Zemindar.*

Zante, zan'tā, *n.* A species of sumach from *Zante,* in the Mediterranean, used for dyeing.

Zany, zā'ni, *n.* [Fr. *zani,* from It. *zanni, zane,* a zany or clown; originally simply a familiar and abbreviated pronunciation of *Giovanni,* John.] A buffoon or merry-andrew.—**Zanyism**, zā'ni-izm, *n.* The character or practice of a zany; buffoonery.

Zareba. Same as ZEREBA.

Zarnich, zär'nik, *n.* [From Ar. *az-zernikh,* from Gr. *arsenikos,* arsenical. ARSENIC.] A name given to the native sulphurets of arsenic, sandarach or realgar, and orpiment.

Zax, zaks, *n.* [A.Sax. *seax,* Icel. *sax,* a knife or short sword.] An instrument used by slaters for cutting and dressing slates.

Zeal, zēl, *n.* [Fr. *zèle,* from L. *zelus,* Gr. *zēlos,* zeal; from stem of *zeō,* to boil, which is akin to E. *yeast.* JEALOUS.] Passionate ardour in the pursuit of anything; eagerness in any cause or behalf, good or bad; earnestness; fervency; enthusiasm.—**Zealot**, zel'ot, *n.* [Fr. *zélote,* L. *zelotes,* from Gr. *zēlōtēs.*] One who is zealous or full of zeal; one carried away by excess of zeal; a fanatical partisan.—**Zealotism**, zel'ot-izm, *n.* The character or conduct of a zealot.—**Zealotry**, zel'ot-ri, *n.* Behaviour of a zealot; excessive zeal; fanaticism.—**Zealous**, zel'us, *a.* [From *zeal. Jealous* is really the same word.] Inspired with zeal; warmly engaged or ardent in the pursuit of an object; fervent; eager; earnest.—**Zealously**, zel'us-li, *adv.* In a zealous manner.—**Zealousness**, zel'us-nes, *n.* The quality of being zealous; zeal.

Zebec, Zebeck, zē'bek, *n.* Same as *Xebec.*

Zebra, zē'bra, *n.* [A native African word.] A quadruped of southern Africa allied to the horse and ass, nearly as large as a horse, white, striped with numerous brownish-black bands.—**Zebra-opossum, Zebra-wolf**, *n.* The thylacine or Tasmanian wolf.—**Zebra-wood**, *n.* A South American wood somewhat resembling the skin of a zebra in colour, used by cabinet-makers.—**Zebrine**, zē'brīn, *a.* Pertaining to the zebra.

Zebu, zē'bū, *n.* [The Indian name.] A species of ox found extensively in India, and regarded with veneration by the Hindus, having one, or more rarely two, humps of fat on the shoulders.

Zechin, zek'in, *n.* [It. *zecchino,* Fr. *sequin.* SEQUIN.] A sequin.

Zedoary, zed'ō-a-ri, *n.* [Sp. and Pg. *zedoaria,* from Ar. and Pers. *zedwār,* zedoary.] An Asiatic root used for similar purposes as ginger.

Zeeman effect, zē'man, *n.* [After the Dutch physicist, P. *Zeeman.*] The splitting up of a spectral line into polarized components, when produced in a magnetic field.

Zemindar, zem-in-där', *n.* [Per. *zemindâr,* a landholder—*zemin,* land, and *dâr,* holding, a holder.] In India, a landholder or landed proprietor, subject to the payment of the land-tax or government land-revenue.—**Zemindary**, zem'in-da-ri, *n.* The position of a zemindar; the land possessed by a zemindar.

Zenana, ze-nä'na, *n.* [Hind. *zananah,* from Per. *zan,* a woman.] The portion of a house exclusively for the females in a family of good caste in India.

Zend, zend, *n.* An ancient Iranian language belonging to the Aryan family, and closely allied to Sanskrit, in which are composed the sacred writings of the Zoroastrians.—**Zend-Avesta**, zend-a-ves'ta, *n.* The collective name for the sacred writings of the Parsees, ascribed to Zoroaster.

Zenith, zē'nith, *n.* [Fr. *zenith,* from Sp. *zenit, zenith,* a corruption of Ar. *samt, sent,* abbreviated for *samt-ur-ras, samt-er-ras,* way of the head, zenith, *samt* being a way (*ras,* head). Akin *azimuth.*] The vertical point of the heavens at any place, or point right above a spectator's head; the upper pole of the celestial horizon; *fig.* the highest point of a person's fortune; culminating point.—*Zenith distance,* the arc intercepted between a heavenly body and the zenith.—**Zenithal**, zē'nith-al, *a.* Pertaining to the zenith.

Zeolite, zē'ō-līt, *n.* [Gr. *zeō,* to boil, *lithos,* stone: so named from boiling and swelling when heated by the blow-pipe.] A generic name of hydrated double silicates in which the principal bases are aluminium and calcium.—**Zeolitic**, zē-ō-lit'ik, *a.* Pertaining to zeolite; consisting of zeolite or resembling it.—**Zeolitiform**, zē-ō-lit'i-form, *a.* Having the form of zeolite.

Zephyr, Zephyrus, zef'ėr, zef'i-rus, *n.* [L. *zephyrus,* from Gr. *zephyros,* allied to *zophos,* darkness, gloom, the west.] The west wind; and poetically, any soft, mild, gentle breeze.

Zeppelin, zep'el-in, *n.* [From the inventor, Count *Zeppelin.*] A German air-ship.

Zereba, ze-rē'ba, *n.* A temporary camping-place surrounded by a fence of bushes, stones, &c., used in the Sudan.

Zero, zē'rō, *n.* [Fr. *zéro,* It. and Sp. *zero,* by contraction from Ar. *sifr,* a cipher; the same word as *cipher.*] No number or quantity; number or quantity diminished to nothing; a cipher; nothing; *physics,* the point of a graduated instrument at which its scale commences; the starting-point on a graduated scale, generally represented by the mark 0. In thermometers the zero of the Centigrade and Réaumur scales is the freezing-point of water; in Fahrenheit's scale, 32° below the freezing-point of water, temperatures being counted upwards and downwards from this.

Zest, zest, *n.* [Fr. *zeste,* the peel of an orange or lemon; from L. *schistus,* Gr. *schistos,* split, divided, from *schizō,* to split (whence also *schism, schist*).] Originally, a piece of orange or lemon peel, used to give flavour to liquor; hence, that which serves to enhance enjoyment; a relish; keen enjoyment; gusto.

Zetetic, zē-tet'ik, *a.* [Gr. *zētētikos,* from *zēteō,* to seek.] Proceeding by inquiry; seeking.—*n.* One who seeks or investigates.

Zeuglodon, zū'glo-don, *n.* [Gr. *zeuglē,* the loop of a yoke, and *odous, odontos,* a tooth, lit. *yoke-tooth*: so called from the peculiar form of its molar teeth.] An extinct genus of marine mammals, belonging to the eocene and miocene, and attaining a length of 70 feet.

Zeugma, zūg'ma, *n.* [Gr. *zeugma,* from *zeugnymi,* to join, same root as E. *yoke.*] A figure in grammar in which two nouns are joined to a verb suitable to only one of them, but suggesting another verb suitable to the other noun; or in which an adjective is similarly used with two nouns.—**Zeugmatic**, zūg-mat'ik, *a.* Pertaining to zeugma.

Zeus, zūs, *n.* The supreme divinity among the Greeks: generally treated as the equivalent of the Roman Jupiter.

Zibet, zib'et, *n.* [CIVET.] An animal closely akin to the civet.

Zigzag, zig'zag, *n.* [Fr. *zig-zag,* from G. *zick-zack,* reduplicated from *zacke,* a tooth or sharp point.] Something that consists of straight lines or pieces with short sharp turns or angles; a zigzag moulding; a chevron.—*a.* Having sharp and quick turns or flexures.—*v.t.*—*zigzagged, zigzagging.* To move or advance in a zigzag fashion; to form zigzags.—**Zigzaggy**, zig'zag-i, *a.* Having sharp a quick turns; zigzag.

Zimb, zim, *n.* [Ar. *zimb,* a fly.] A fly of Abyssinia, resembling the tsetse in being destructive to cattle.

Zinc, zingk, *n.* [Fr. *zinc,* G., Sw., and Dan. *zink*; allied to G. *zinn,* tin.] A metal frequently called *spelter,* having a strong metallic lustre and a bluish-white colour, brittle at low or high degrees of heat, but between 250° and 300° F. both malleable and ductile, so that it may be rolled or hammered into thin sheets and drawn into wire; also used in brass and other alloys.—*v.t.*—*zinked, zinking.* To coat or cover with zinc.—**Zinc-blende**, *n.* Native sulphide of zinc, a brittle transparent or translucent mineral.—**Zinc-bloom**, *n.* A mineral of the same composition as calamine.—**Zinciferous, Zinckiferous**, zing-kif'ėr-us, *a.* [*Zinc,* and L. *fero,* to bear.] Producing zinc.—**Zincite**, zingk'īt, *n.* Native oxide of zinc.—**Zincky**, zingk'i, *a.* Pertaining to zinc; containing zinc; having the appearance of zinc.—**Zincode**, zingk'ōd, *n.* [*Zinc,* and Gr. *hodos,* a way.] The positive pole of a galvanic battery.—**Zincographer**, zing-kog'ra-fėr, *n.* One who practises zincography.—**Zincographic, Zincographical**, zing-kō-graf'ik, zing-kō-graf'i-kal, *a.* Relating to zincography.—**Zincography**, zing-kog'ra-fi, *n.* An art similar to lithography, the stone printing surface of the latter being replaced by that of a plate of polished zinc.—**Zincoid**, zingk'oid, *a.* Resembling zinc; pertaining to zinc.—**Zincous**, zingk'us, *a.* Pertaining to zinc, or to the positive pole of a voltaic battery.—**Zinc-white**, *n.* Oxide of zinc, a pigment now largely substituted for white-lead as being more permanent and not poisonous.

Zingiberaceous, Zinziberaceous, zin'ji-bėr-ā"shus, zin'zi-bėr-ā"shus, *a.* [L. *zingiber, zinziber,* ginger.] Pertaining to ginger, or to the order of plants of which ginger is the type.

Zionism, zī'on-ism, *n.* [From *Mount Zion,* in Jerusalem.] A Jewish national movement for the re-establishment of the Jews in Palestine.

Zipper, zip'per, *n.* Trade name for a device used on openings in place of buttons or other fasteners.

Zircon, zėr'kon, *n.* [Singhalese.] A mineral, one of the gems, originally found in Ceylon, and appearing in colorless or colored specimens, jargon being also a name of it.—**Zirconia**, zėr-kō'ni-a, *n.* An oxide of the metal zirconium discovered in the zircon of Ceylon.—**Zirconium**, zėr-kō'ni-um, *n.* The metal contained in zirconia.

Zither, Zithern, tsit'ėr, tsit'ėrn, *n.* [G., from L. *cithara.* CITHARA.] A flat, stringed musical instrument consisting of a sounding-box with thirty-one strings, played with the right hand, the strings being stopped with the left.

Zoæa, pl. -æ, zō'ē-a, *n.* [Gr. *zōia,* life.] In higher crustacea, a large-headed larva, swimming by its foot-jaws and devoid of abdominal limbs.

Zoantharia, zō-an-thā'ri-a, *n.pl.* [Gr. *zōon*, an animal, and *anthos*, a flower.] A division of the actinozoa, including sea-anemones, &c.

Zodiac, zō'di-ak, *n.* [Fr. *zodiaque*, L. *zodiacus*, the zodiac, from Gr. *zōdiakos* (*kyklos*, circle, understood), from *zōdion*, dim. of *zōon*, an animal.] An imaginary belt or zone in the heavens, extending about 8° on each side of the ecliptic, within which the motions of the sun, moon, and principal planets are confined.—*Signs of the zodiac.* Under SIGN.—**Zodiacal**, zō-dī'a-kal, *a.* Pertaining to the zodiac.—*Zodiacal light*, a luminous tract lying nearly in the ecliptic, its base being on the horizon, seen at certain seasons either in the west after sunset or in the east before sunrise.

Zoetrope, zō'ē-trōp, *n.* [Gr. *zōē*, life, and *tropē*, a turning.] An optical contrivance which has figures painted in its interior, and these, from the persistence of vision, produce the appearance of natural motion when the instrument is made to revolve.

Zoilism, zō'il-izm, *n.* [After *Zoilus*, a grammarian who criticised Homer, Plato, &c., with exceeding severity.] Liberal or carping criticism; unjust censure.—**Zoilean**, zō-i-lē'an, *a.* Bitterly or malignantly critical.

Zollverein, tsol'ver-īn, *n.* [G. *zoll*, toll, custom, and *verein*, union.] The German customs union, established in order that there might be a uniform rate of customs duties throughout the various states.

Zone, zōn, *n.* [L. *zona*, a belt or girdle, a zone of the earth, from Gr. *zōnē*, a girdle, from *zōnnymi*, to gird.] A girdle or belt; any well-marked band or stripe running round an object; *geog.* one of the five great divisions of the earth, bounded by circles parallel to the equator, named according to the temperature prevailing in each, the *torrid zone*, two *temperate zones*, and two *frigid zones*; *nat. hist.* any well-defined belt within which certain forms of plant or animal life are confined.—**Zoned**, zōnd, *a.* Wearing a zone; having zones or bands resembling zones.—**Zonular**, zō'nū-lėr, *a.* Zone-shaped.—**Zonule, Zonulet**, zō'nūl, zō'nū-let, *n.* A little zone, band, or belt. —**Zonal**, zō'nal, *a.* Having the character of a zone or belt.—**Zonar, Zonnar**, zō'nar, zon'ar, *n.* [Gr. *zōnarion*, dim. of *zōnē*, a girdle.] A belt or girdle which native Christians and Jews in the East were obliged to wear to distinguish them from Mohammedans.—**Zonate**, zō'nāt, *a.* *Bot.* marked with zones or concentric bands of colour.

Zoogloea, zō'o-glē"a, *n.* [Gr. *zōon*, an animal, *gloia*, glue.] In bacteria, a slimy colony.

Zoogony, Zoogeny, zō-og'o-ni, zō-oj'en-i, *n.* [Gr. *zōon*, an animal, and roots *gon-*, *gen-*, to produce.] The doctrine of the formation of living beings.

Zoography, zō-og'ra-fi, *n.* [Gr. *zōon*, an animal, and *graphō*, to describe.] A description of animals, their forms and habits.—**Zoographer, Zoographist**, zō-og'ra-fėr, zō-og'ra-fist, *n.* One who describes animals.—**Zoographic, Zoographical**, zō-o-graf'ik, zō-o-graf'i-kal, *a.* Pertaining to zoography.

Zooid, zō-oid, *a.* [Gr. *zōon*, an animal, and *eidos*, likeness.] Resembling or pertaining to an animal.—*n.* An organic body, as a cell or a spermatozoön, in some respects resembling a distinct animal; one of the more or less completely independent organisms produced by gemmation or fission, as in polyzoa, tapeworms, &c.

Zoolatry, zō-ol'a-tri, *n.* [Gr. *zōon*, an animal, and *latreia*, worship.] The worship of animals.

Zoolite, zō'ol-īt, *n.* [Gr. *zōon*, an animal, and *lithos*, stone.] An animal substance petrified or fossil.

Zoology, zō-ol'o-ji, *n.* [Gr. *zōon*, an animal, and *logos*, discourse.] That science which treats of the natural history of animals, or their structure, physiology, classification, habits, and distribution.—**Zoological**, zō-o-loj'i-kal, *a.* Pertaining to zoology.—*Zoological garden*, a garden in which a collection of living animals is kept. —**Zoologically**, zō-o-loj'i-kal-li, *adv.* In a zoological manner.—**Zoologist**, zō-ol'o-jist, *n.* One who studies or is well versed in zoology.

Zoom, zöm, *v.i.* In aviation, to increase suddenly the upward slope of the flight path.—*n.* The act of zooming.

Zoomorphic, zō-o-mor'fik, *a.* [Gr. *zōon*, an animal, *morphē*, shape.] Pertaining to animal forms; exhibiting animal forms.—**Zoomorphism**, zō-o-mor'fizm, *n.* The state of being zoomorphic.

Zoonomy, zō-on'o-mi, *n.* [Gr. *zōon*, an animal, and *nomos*, law.] The laws of animal life, or the science which treats of the phenomena of animal life.

Zoophagous, zō-of'a-gus, *a.* [Gr. *zōon*, an animal, and *phagō*, to eat.] Feeding on animals; carnivorous; taking living prey.

Zoophile, Zoophilist, zō'o-fil, zō-of'i-list, *n.* [Gr. *zōon*, an animal, *philos*, love.] A lover of animals.—**Zoophily**, zō-of'i-li, *n.* Love of animals.

Zoophyte, zō'o-fīt, *n.* [Gr. *zōon*, an animal, *phyton*, a plant.] A name loosely applied to many plant-like animals, as sponges, corals, sea-anemones, sea-mats, and the like.—**Zoophytic**, zō-o-fit'ik, *a.* Relating to zoophytes.—**Zoophytoid**, zō-of'i-toid, *n.* Like a zoophyte.—**Zoophytological**, zō'o-fit-o-loj"i-kal, *a.* Pertaining to zoophytology.—**Zoophytology**, zō'o-fi-tol"o-ji, *n.* The natural history of zoophytes.

Zoosperm, zō'os-pėrm, *n.* [Gr. *zōon*, an animal, and *sperma*, seed.] One of the spermatozoa of animals.

Zoospore, zō'os-pōr, *n.* [Gr. *zōon*, an animal, *spora*, a sowing, seed.] A spore of algæ, fungi, &c., which can move spontaneously to some extent by its cilia or long filiform processes.—**Zoosporic**, zō-os-por'ik, *a.* Pertaining to zoospores.

Zootheca, zō-o-thē'ka, *n.* [Gr. *zōon*, an animal, *thēkē*, a case.] *Bot.* a cell containing a spermatozooid.

Zootomy, zō-ot'o-mi, *n.* [Gr. *zōon*, an animal, and *tomē*, a cutting, from *temnō*, to cut.] The anatomy of the lower animals; that branch of anatomical science which relates to the structure of the lower animals. —**Zootomical**, zō-o-tom'i-kal, *a.* Pertaining to zootomy.—**Zootomist**, zō-ot'o-mist, *n.* One who dissects animals.

Zoroastrian, zor-o-as'tri-an, *a.* Pertaining to *Zoroaster*, whose system of religion was the national faith of ancient Persia, and is embodied in the Zend-Avesta.—*n.* A believer in this religion.—**Zoroastrianism**, zor-o-as'tri-an-izm, *n.* The religion founded by Zoroaster, one feature of which was a belief in a good and an evil power or deity perpetually striving against each other.

Zouave, zwäv, *n.* [Fr., from the name of a tribe inhabiting Algeria.] A soldier belonging to certain light-infantry corps in the French army, originally organized in Algeria, and having a dress of a somewhat Turkish fashion.

Zounds, zoundz. An exclamation contracted from '*God's wounds*', formerly used.

Zulu, zö'lö or zu-lö', *n.* A member of a warlike branch of the Kafir race dwelling north of Natal.

Zumbooruk, zum-bö'ruk, *n.* In the East a small cannon fired from a camel's back.

Zygapophysis, zig-a-pof'i-sis, *n.* [Gr. *zygon*, a yoke, and *apophysis*.] *Anat.* one of the processes by which the vertebræ articulate with each other.

Zygodactylic, Zygodactylous, zī'gō-dak-til"ik, zī-gō-dak'til-us, *a.* [Gr. *zygon*, what joins, and *daktylos*, a finger or toe.] Having the toes disposed in pairs, as the parrots; scansorial.

Zygoma, zī-gō'ma, *n.* [Gr. *zygōma*, from *zygon*, a yoke.] *Anat.* the prominence of the the cheek-bone, or the part that joins it with the cranium.—**Zygomatic**, zī-gō-mat'ik, *a.* Pertaining to the cheek-bone.

Zygomorphic, zī'gō-mor"fik, *n.* [Gr. *zeugos*, a pair, *morphē*, form.] Of flowers, with bilateral symmetry (irregular).

Zygospore, zī'gō-spōr, *n.* [Gr. *zeugos*, a pair, *sporos*, fruit.] *Bot.* a spore formed by union of two gametes.

Zygote, zī'gōt, *n.* [Gr. *zeugos*, a pair.] *Biol.* the product of fusion of two gametes.

Zymic, zim'ik, *a.* [Gr. *zymē*, leaven.] Pertaining to a ferment or to fermentation; causing fermentation.—**Zymologic, Zymological**, zī-mō-loj'ik, zī-mō-loj'i-kal, *a.* Pertaining to zymology.—**Zymologist**, zī-mol'o-jist, *n.* One skilled in zymology.—**Zymology**, zī-mol'o-ji, *n.* The doctrine of ferments and fermentation.—**Zymometer**, zī-mom'e-tėr, *n.* An instrument for ascertaining the degree of fermentation of a fermenting liquor.—**Zymosis**, zī-mō'sis, *n.* [Gr., fermentation.] Fermentation; a zymotic disease; the origin or production of such diseases.—**Zymotic**, zī-mot'ik, *a.* [Gr. *zymōtikos*, from *zymoō*, to ferment, from *zymē*, ferment.] Pertaining to or produced by fermentation.—*Zymotic diseases*, epidemic, endemic, contagious, or sporadic diseases, supposed to be produced by some morbific principle acting on the system like a ferment. GERM-THEORY.—**Zymotically**, zī-mot'i-kal-li, *adv.* In a zymotic manner. **Zymurgy**, zī'mėr-ji, *n.* [Gr. *zymē*, and *ergon*, work.] That part of chemistry which treats of the principles of wine-making, brewing, distilling, and the preparation of yeast and vinegar.

SUPPLEMENT

Abreaction, ab'rē-ak''shon, *n.* [L. *ab*, away, and *reaction*.] *Psych.* getting rid of a past disagreeable experience by living it through again in speech or action in the course of treatment.

Abscissa, ab-sis'sa, *n.* pl. **abscissæ**. [L. *abscissus*, cut off.] *Co-ordinate geometry*, the *x* of a point, or distance of the point from the *y*-axis, measured parallel to the *x*-axis.—**Abscission**, ab-sis'shon, *n.* [L. *abscissio*, a cutting off.] In plants, the natural cutting off of members, e.g. leaves, by a specially-formed layer of cork.—**Absciss-layer**, ab'sis, *n.* [L. *abscissio.*] Special layer of cork. See ABSCISSION.

Absolute temperature. Temperature measured from the absolute zero (−273° C.), or, practically, on the scale of the air-thermometer.

Absorption bands. Dark bands in a spectrum, usually due to selective absorption by liquids or solids. A cluster of absorption lines closely grouped is also called an absorption band.—**Absorption lines**. Dark lines in a spectrum, due to the selective absorption of the light, usually by gases or vapours.

Acceleration, ak-sel'ėr-ā''shon, *n.* [L. *accelero*, I hasten.] Rate of change of velocity in magnitude, direction, or both: the ordinary units of uniform acceleration in a straight line (*a*) are one foot per second per second (1 ft./sec.^{2}) and one cm. per sec. per sec. See also ANGULAR ACCELERATION.

Accommodation, ak-kom'mō-dā''shon, *n.* Adjustment of the individual plant or animal to its surroundings.

Accrescent, ak-kres'ent, *a.* [L. *accrescere*, to increase.] Of parts of flowers, continuing to grow after flowering.

Ac-emma, ak'-em''a, *n.* The letters A.M. So called by signallers to avoid confusion in telephoning.

Acetone, as'e-tōn, *n.* [L. *acetum*, vinegar.] A liquid of pungent odour, the lowest of the ketones, and related to acetic acid.

Acheulian, a-shöl'i-an, *a.* [From St. Acheul in the Somme valley, France.] Of a culture stage or epoch of the Lower Palæolithic age, between the Chellean and the Mousterian.

Achromatin, ȧ-krō'ma-tin, *n.* [Gr. *a*, without, *chrōma*, colour.] The part of the nucleus of a cell which is not readily stained by dyes. See CHROMATIN.

Acidophile, as'id-ō-fīl, *a.* [From *acid*, and Gr. *philos*, loving.] In microscopy, with affinity for acid stains.

Acquired character. A character acquired by an individual plant or animal in adaptation to its surroundings; also, psychologically, the acquisition of mental traits.

Acriflavine, ak'ri-flav-ēn'', *n.* [L. *acer*, sharp, *flavus*, yellow.] An antiseptic dye.

Acromegaly, ak'rō-meg''a-lē, *n.* [Gr. *akros*, an extremity, *megalē*, large.] A rare disease, associated with overgrowth of bone, especially in the jaws, hands, and feet.

Acrophobia, ak'rō-fō''bi-a, *n.* [Gr. *akron*, a height, *phobos*, fear.] Morbid fear of being at a great height.

Actinomorphic, ak'tin-ō-mor''fik, *a.* [Gr. *aktis*, *aktinos*, a ray, *morphē*, form.] Of flowers, possessing radial symmetry, star-shaped (regular).

Action, ak'shon, *n.* *Physics*, twice the time-integral of the kinetic energy of a system. See LEAST ACTION.

Adaptation, a-dap-tā'shon, *n.* Of organisms, adjustment to surroundings by structural modifications.

Adhesion, ad-hē'zhon, *n.* [L. *adhæsio*, *-onis*, a sticking together.] Of flowers, the union of unlike parts, as stamens with petals. *Phys.* the attractive force between two bodies of different kinds in close contact. *Med.* the abnormal union of two surfaces as the result of inflammation.

Adipoma, a-dip-ō'ma, *n.* [L. *adiposus*, fat, and Gr. *-ōma*, a tumour.] A fatty tumour.

Adrenal bodies, ad-rēn'al. [L. *ad*, near, *renes*, the kidneys.] Two small, ductless, glandular bodies, one close to each kidney, which produce important internal secretions.—**Adrenalin**, ad-ren'al-in, *n.* [L. *ad*, *renes*.] The active principle of the internal secretion produced by the adrenal bodies, which seems to affect the muscular and circulatory systems. The extract is used in medicine as a circulatory stimulant, an astringent, and as a hemostatic.

Adsorption, ad-sorp'shon, *n.* [L. *ad*, to, and *sorbeo*, I drink in.] Condensation of gases or dissolved substances on the surfaces of solids.

Adventitious, ad-ven-ti'shus, *a.* [L. *adventicius*, accessory.] *Bot.* arising out of order or from less usual place, as roots from stems.

Æcidium, ē-sid'i-um, *n.* [Gr. *oikidion*, a small house.] In certain rust-fungi, a little spore-producing cup ('cluster cup').

Aerial, ā'ri-al, *n.* [Gr. *aēr*, air.] The overhead structure of a wireless station, used for transmitting and receiving electrical oscillations; any wire erection, similarly used.

Aerobus, ā'ėr-ō-bus, *n.* A flying machine for transport of passengers or goods.—**Aerofoil**, ā'ėr-ō-foil, *n.* The cambered lifting surfaces of an aeroplane, i.e. the planes or wings, and stabilizers.

Agglutinin, ag-glụt'in-in, *n.* [L. *agglutino*, I fasten together.] A substance existing dissolved in the blood, which checks the action of disease germs by causing them to form motionless aggregates.

Agoraphobia, ag-o-ra-fō'bi-a, *n.* [Gr. *agora*, a market-place, *phobos*, fear.] A morbid fear of open spaces.

Air pocket. A current or aerial disturbance that causes an airplane to drop suddenly a considerable distance.—**Airship**, ār'ship, *n.* A lighter-than-air vessel for navigating the air, driven by mechanical power, and depending on gas for flotation.

Akinesia, a-ki-nē'si-a, *n.* [Gr. *a*, without, *kinēsis*, movement.] Motor paralysis.

Alæ, ā'lē, *n.pl.* [L. for wings.] In a papilionaceous flower (e.g. pea), the two side petals.

Algesia, al-je'zi-a, *n.* [Gr. *algēsis*, pain.] Sensitiveness to pain.

Algol variable. A star which fluctuates in brightness, like the star Algol.

Aliphatic compounds, al-i-fat'ik. [Gr. *aleiphar*, oil.] *Chem.* open-chain carbon compounds, e.g. the fats and many of their derivatives.

Alkyl, al'kil, *n.* [See ALCOHOL.] *Organic chem.* a radical of the methane series, as methyl, ethyl, propyl, butyl.

Allanite, al'an-īt, *n.* [From the name of the discoverer.] A brown or black mineral containing cerium, and allied to epidote.

Alliance, al-lī'ans, *n.* *Bot.* a group of allied families or orders.

Alpha rays. Rays emitted by radium and other radio-active substances. They consist of positively charged atoms of helium.

Alternating current, ạlt'ėr-nāt-ing. *Elect.* a current which changes periodically in magnitude and direction.

Alternation of generations. In organisms, alternation of sexual and asexual stages in the life-history.

Alternator, ạlt'ėr-nāt-or, *n.* An electric generator for producing alternating currents.

Altimeter, al-tim'et-ėr, *n.* [L. *altus*, high, Gr. *metron*, measure.] An instrument for taking altitudes, as a sextant or a quadrant; an instrument for indicating the height of an aeroplane above the ground.

Amatol, am'at-ōl, *n.* A high explosive, a mixture of ammonium nitrate and trinitrotoluene.

Amidogen, a-mī'dō-jen, *n.* [*Amide*, and Gr. *gennaō*, I produce.] *Chem.* the radical NH_2, the characteristic part of amides and amines.

Amino acid, am'in-ō, am-ēn'ō. *Chem.* an acid derived from a fatty or dibasic acid by exchanging one or more hydrogen atoms of the hydrocarbon radical or radicals for the amino group (NH_2).

Amitosis, a'mi-tōs''is, *n.* [Gr. *a*, without, *mitos*, a thread.] Simple or direct cell-division.

Ammeter, am'met-ėr, *n.* [From *Ampère*, and Gr. *metron*, a measure.] An instrument for measuring an electric current (in AMPERES).

Ammocoetes, am-mō-sēt'iz, *n.* [Gr. *ammos*, sand, *koitē*, bed.] Larva of the lamprey.

Ammonal, am'ō-nal, *n.* A blasting explosive, a mixture of ammonium nitrate, powdered aluminium, and charcoal.

Amœboid movement, a-mēb'oid. [Gr. *eidos*, form, *amoeba* (*amoibē*, change), the Proteus animalcule.] Creeping movement of naked protoplasm, as in colourless blood-corpuscles.

Ampere turn. *Elect.* a practical unit of magnetomotive force. In terms of this unit, the magnetomotive force of a solenoid is the product of the number of turns by the current in amperes.

Amphigastria, am'fi-gas''trē-a, *n.* [Gr. *amphi*, on both sides, *gastrion*, a little stomach.] In liverworts, pairs of small scale-like leaves on the under side.

Amphimixia, am'fi-miks''i-a, *n.* [Gr. *amphi*, on both sides, *mixis*, a mixing.] In sexual reproduction, the mixing of germ-plasm from the two reproductive cells involved.

Amphoteric, am'fō-ter''ik, *a.* [Gr. *amphoteros*, both.] *Chem.* both basic and acid.

Amplifier, am'pli-fī-ėr, *n.* *Wireless Tel.* an instrument for increasing the strength of weak received signals by using them to tap a local source of energy. The best example is the triode valve.

Amplitude, am'pli-tūd, *n.* The maximum value of the excess of a periodically varying quantity over its mean value.

Amylolytic, a-mi'lo-lit''ik, *a.* [Gr. *amylon*, starch, *lysis*, solution.] *Physiol.* of the conversion of starch into sugar by enzyme action during digestion.

Amylopsin, am'il-ops''in, *n.* [Gr. *amylon*, starch, *opsis*, an appearance.] Diastase, an enzyme in the pancreatic juice by which starch is converted into sugar.

Anabolism, an-ab'ol-izm, *n.* [Gr. *anabolē*, an ascent.] Up-building chemical changes in living bodies.

Anaerobic, an-ā-ėr-ō'bik, *a.* [Gr. *an*, without, *aēr*, air, *bios*, life.] Of bacteria, only active in the absence of oxygen.

Analysis, an-al'i-sis, *n.* That one of the two great branches of mathematics—the other being geometry—which is based on arithmetic and algebra.

Angle, ang'gl, *n.* The inclination to each other of two straight lines in one plane, denoted by θ, ω, ϕ, a, β, &c.; measured in terms of either sexagesimal units (see DEGREE), or centesimal units (see GRADE), or circular units (see RADIAN). See also SOLID ANGLE.—**Angle of friction.** See ANGLE OF REPOSE.—**Angle of incidence.** *Aviation*, the angle that the chord of a wing makes with the direction of motion relative to the air.—**Angle of repose.** The angle of inclination to the horizontal of an inclined plane when the force of gravity is just sufficient to overcome friction: its tangent is the *coefficient of friction*.

Angström unit, ong'strum. A minute unit of length equal to the hundred millionth part (10^{-8}) of a centimetre, used in the measurement of wave-lengths of light.

Angular acceleration. Rate of change of angular velocity, measured in degrees, or grades, or radians, per sec. per sec.—**Angular velocity** (ω). The number of units of angle passed through in unit time by a plane forming part of a revolving body, the axis of revolution being a fixed line in the plane.

Anhydride, an-hīd'rīd, *n.* [See ANHYDROUS.] *Chem.* a compound derived from another by the abstraction of water.

Anlage, an'lä-ge, *n.* [Gr. for *foundation.*] In embryos, a mass of cells constituting the beginning of some special structure or organ.

Anode. See ELECTRODE.—**Anode rays.** A stream of charged atoms and molecules given off at the anode of an electric discharge tube.

Anoia, an-oi'a, *n.* [Gr. for *idiocy.*] Idiocy.

Anopheles, an-ŏf'el-ēz, *n.* [Gr. *anōphelēs*, harmful.] The genus containing the species of mosquito by which malarial germs are distributed.

Antenna, an-ten'na, *n.* [L. *antenna*, a sail-yard.] *Wireless Tel.* same as AERIAL.

Antheridium, an'ther-id''-i-um, *n.* [Dim. of *anther.*] In lower plants, a male sexual organ, usually producing motile male cells.

Anti-bodies, an'ti-bod'is, *n.pl.* [Gr. *anti*, against, and *bodies.*] *Med.* substances formed in the blood which combat disease germs.

Anticlastic, an-ti-klast'ik, *a.* [Gr. *antiklaō*, I bend back.] Of a surface curved in opposite directions, like a saddle; contrasted with *synclastic*.

Anti-node, an'ti-nōd, *n.* [Gr. *anti*, and *node.*] *Vibrations*, see LOOP.

Antipodal cells, an-tip'o-dal. [From *antipodes.*] In angiospermous plants, three minute cells in the base of the embryo-sac.

anti-serum, an'ti-sē''rum, *n.* [Gr. *anti*, against, and *serum.*] *Med.* a blood-preparation containing an anti-body, and employed as a hypodermal injection in the treatment of bacterial diseases, e.g. diphtheria.

Antivenin, an'ti-ven''in, *n.* [Gr. *anti*, against, L. *venenum*, poison.] *Med.* an ANTI-SERUM, used in cases of snake-poisoning.

Aortic arches. Arteries traversing the VISCERAL ARCHES of vertebrates.

Aphoria, a-fō'ri-a, *n.* [Gr. *a*, not, *pherō*, I bear.] Sterility.

Apteria, ap-tē'ri-a, *n.pl.* [Gr. *a*, without, *pterylon*, a feather.] Bare patches of a bird's skin.

Arabinose, a-rab'in-ōz, *n.* A sugar derived from cherry gum.

Archæozoic, ar'kē-ō-zō''ik, *a.* [Gr. *archaios*, ancient, *zōē*, life.] *Geol.* the era, or part of the era, of the most ancient rocks, preceding the palæozoic.

Archenteron, ark-en'ter-on, *n.* [Gr. *archē*, a beginning, *enteron*, an intestine.] Digestive cavity of a GASTRULA.

Archesporium, ar'kē-spō''ri-um, *n.* [Gr. *archē*, a beginning, *sporos*, seed.] *Bot.* a cell or cells from which spore mother-cells are produced.

Archie, ar'chi, *n.* An anti-aircraft gun, or its shell.

Area of distribution. Area inhabited by a species or other group of plants or animals. It is *discontinuous* when consisting of two or more isolated parts; e.g. tapirs live in tropical America and the Malay region.

Armature, är'ma-tūr, *n.* *Elect.* that part of a dynamo or motor which carries the conductors in which the generation of electricity takes place, or in which the main currents act.

Army Medical Corps. The main body of the medical service of the army, in time of peace employed at home; in time of war divided among the different bodies of troops employed. The officers hold rank corresponding with those of the combatant ranks.—**Army Service Corps.** A branch of the army employed in connection with providing food, transport, &c., for the troops (*British*).

Aromatic compounds. *Organic Chem.* benzene derivatives and other closed chain compounds, many of which occur in odorous resins and balsams.

Arthrology, ar-throl'o-ji, *n.* [Gr. *arthron*, joint, *logos*, discourse.] The section of anatomy relating to the joints.

Artifact, ar'ti-fakt, *n.* [L. *arte*, by art, *factum*, made.] In microscopic preparations, a space or appearance caused artificially.

Artifact, ar'ti-fakt, *n.* *Archæology*, a product of human workmanship.

Artificial selection. Production of breeds or races (e.g. of pigeons and cereals) by human agency.

Aryl, ar'il, *n.* A certain type of univalent aromatic hydrocarbon radical such as phenyl (C_6H_5).

Ascospore, as'kō-spōr, *n.* [Gr. *askos*, a bag, *sporos*, seed.] One of a set of spores contained in an ASCUS.

Aseptic, a-sep'tik, *a.* [Gr. *a*, without, *sēptos*, putrefying.] Free from disease germs; especially in *aseptic surgery*.

Astronomical unit. A unit of length used in astronomy, equal to the mean distance of the earth from the sun.

Astro-physics, ast'rō-fiz''iks, *n.* [Gr. *astron*, star, *physis*, nature.] The science which treats of the physics and chemistry of the heavenly bodies.

Atmospherics, at-mos-fer'iks, *n.pl.* *Wireless Tel.* disturbances, resembling actual signals, produced in the receiving circuits by electrical action in the atmosphere or in the earth's crust.

Atomic heat. The product of the specific heat and atomic weight of an element, equal to about 6.4 for practically all elements.—**Atomic number.** *Phys. and Chem.* a number marking the place of an element in the periodic table, and having important relations to the properties of the element. It is supposed to be the net number of unit positive charges in the nucleus of the atom. See RUTHERFORD-BOHR ATOM.—**Atomic volume.** *Chem.* the number obtained by dividing the atomic weight of an element by its density.

Atoxyl, a-toks'il, *n.* [Gr. *a*, not, *toxikon*, a poison.] An arsenical drug employed in cases of sleeping sickness.

Attenuation, at-ten'ū-ā''shon, *n.* [L. *attenuo*, *attenuatus*, I make thin.] Of disease bacteria, diminution of virulence by successive cultures or other laboratory methods.

Aura, ą'ra, *n.* [Gr. *aura*, a breath.] The symptoms immediately preceding attacks of certain diseases, especially epilepsy and hysteria.

Aurignacian, ō-ri-nyā'shi-an, *a.* [From the cave of Aurignac, in France.] Of an early culture stage of the Upper Palæolithic age.

Australian region. Australia and adjacent islands, with eastern part of E. Indies and Polynesia.

Autoclave, ą'tō-klāv, *n.* [Gr. *autos*, self, L. *clavis*, a key.] A strong metallic vessel, used for heating liquids under high pressure.

Autocoid, ą'tō-koid, *n.* [Gr. *autos*, self, *eidos*, form.] *Physiol.* the name given by Schafer to the internal secretions (usually all called HORMONES) of the ductless glands; those secretions which excite metabolic processes being called *hormones*, and those which depress them *chalones*.

Autogamy, ą-tog'a-mi, *n.* [Gr. *autos*, self, *gamos*, marriage.] SELF-POLLINATION.

Autosuggestion, ą'tō-suj-jest''yon, *n.* [Gr. *autos*, self, and suggestion.] *Psych.* suggestion, akin to hypnotic suggestion, made to oneself with a view to producing a desired frame of mind or bodily condition. The practice may be almost unconscious, and either beneficial or harmful.

Auxanometer, ąks'an-om''et-ėr, *n.* [Gr. *auxanō*, I cause to grow, *metron*, a measure.] An instrument for measuring the growth of plants.

Auxospore, ąks'ō-spōr, *n.* [Gr. *auxō*, I make grow, *sporos*, seed.] In diatoms, a reproductive cell.

Avogadro's Law, av-ō-gad'roz. [After the Italian scientist *Avogadro.*] The law that equal volumes of all gases and vapours, at the same temperature and pressure, contain an equal number of molecules.

Azilian, a-zil'i-an, *a.* [From the cavern of Mas d'Azil, in the Pyrenees.] Of a late culture stage of the Palæolithic age, in the period of transition to the Neolithic.

Azo dyes, ā'zō. [See AZOTE.] Synthetic organic colouring compounds, containing nitrogen combined in a special way.

Baffle, baf'l, *n.* *Engin.* a plate or wall for deflecting or checking the flow of gases or liquids.

Ball bearing. A bearing in which the revolving part turns upon loose hardened steel balls rolling in a race.

Ballistite, bal'ist-īt, *n.* [Gr. *ballō*, I throw.] A smokeless powder, composed of equal parts of nitro-glycerine and soluble nitro-cotton.

Balmer series. A series of lines in the spectrum of hydrogen, with wave-lengths given by a simple algebraical formula discovered by Balmer in 1885, the earliest example of a SPECTRAL SERIES.

Banket, bang'ket, *n.* A gold-bearing conglomerate.

Bar, bär, *n.* [Gr. *baros*, weight.] A standard unit of barometric pressure, equal to a million dynes per square centimetre.

Barb, bärb, *n.* [L. *barba*, a beard.] One of the flattened branches of a feather.

Barretter, bar'et-ėr, *n.* A device for detecting electrical oscillations, depending on their heating effect on a fine wire.

Basedow's disease, bas'dō. [After

Basedow, German physician (1799-1854).] EXOPHTHALMIC GOITRE.

Basidiomycetes, bas-id′i-ō-mī-sē″tēz, *n. pl.* [From *basidium* and Gr. *mykēs*, a fungus.] Fungi, such as mushrooms and toadstools, producing spores from BASIDIA (which see).

Basidiospore, bas-id′i-ō-spōr, *n.* [Gr. from *basidium*, and *sporos*, seed.] A spore produced by a BASIDIUM.

Basophile, bā′sō-fil, *a.* [*Base* and Gr. *philos*, loving.] In microscopy, with affinity for basic stains.

Bearing stress. The stress of a body pressing against another in such a way as to tend to produce indentation or cutting: resolvable into compression and shearing stresses.

Bedplate, bed′plāt, *n.* *Engin.* a foundation plate of an engine or other machine.

Behaviorism, be-hāv′yėr-ism, *n.* *Psych.* A theory which views the organism in terms of muscular and glandular responses.

Bending moment. For a particular section of a given beam under a load of specified magnitude and distribution, is the sum of the moments round the section of all the forces acting upon either of the two parts into which the beam is divided at the section.

Benthos, ben′thos, *n.* [Gr. *benthos*, depth.] The assemblage of organisms inhabiting the depths of the sea. Opposed to PLANKTON and NEKTON.

Benzaldehyde, benz-al′dē-hīd, *n.* A coal-tar product used to replace the oil of bitter almonds.

Benzene, ben′zēn, *n.* [BENZOIN.] A colourless liquid obtained in the destructive distillation of coal, a hydrocarbon (C_6H_6) important in organic chemistry as the basis of numerous compounds.

Benzene ring. *Chem.* a closed circuit of six carbon atoms, each united to one hydrogen atom, supposed to exist in the molecule of benzene and other aromatic compounds.

Benzine, ben′zēn, *n.* [From *benzoin.*] An inflammable liquid derived by distillation from crude petroleum, and distinct from coal tar benzene.

Bertha, Big. A long-range German gun, especially one of those which bombarded Paris in 1918. Named after Frau Krupp von Bohlen of Essen.

Beta rays. [From Greek letter *beta.*] Penetrating rays emitted by radium and other radio-active substances. They consist of electrons moving at high speed. See CATHODE RAYS.

Binaural, bin-a̧′ral, *a.* [L. *bini*, two by two, *auris*, ear.] Involving the use of both ears.

Bio-chemistry, bī′ō-kem″ist-ri, *n.* [Gr. *bios*, life.] The study of chemical processes taking place in organisms.

Biometrics, bī′ō-met″riks, *n.* [Gr. *bios*, life, *metron*, a measure.] The application of mathematics to biology.

Bionomics, bī′ō-nom″iks, *n.* [Gr. *bios*, life, *nomos*, law.] The study of the relation of plants and animals to their surroundings or environment.

Biophore, bī′ō-fōr, *n.* [Gr. *bios*, life, *pherō*, I bear.] One of the ultimate constituents of GERM-PLASM. A physiological unit.

Bio-physics, bī′ō-fiz″iks, *n.* [Gr. *bios*, life.] Physiological physics, especially as regards muscles and nerves.

Bioses, bī-ō′sēz, *n.pl.* [L. *bis*, twice.] Sugars formed from monoses by combination of molecules with elimination of water. Examples are cane-sugar, maltose, and milk-sugar.

Bivalent, bī-vāl′ent, *a.* DIVALENT.

Black body. *Phys.* an ideal body with surface so constituted as to absorb all the radiation which falls on it, without reflecting any.

Blastogenesis, blas′tō-jen″e-sis, *n.* [Gr. *blastos*, a bud, *genesis*, production.] The theory of heredity by means of GERM-PLASM. See PANGENESIS. — **Blastomere**, blas′tō-mēr, *n.* [Gr. *blastos*, a bud, *meros*, a part.] One of the cells into which a fertilized ovum divides.—**Blastopore**, blas′tō-pōr, *n.* [Gr. *blastos*, a germ, *poros*, a passage.] The mouth of a GASTRULA.

Blueprint. A print obtained by the action of light on prepared paper over which a transparent drawing is laid. The exposed part of the paper becomes covered with blue, and the drawing is shown in white.

Board of Education. A department of municipal governments, with an elected or appointed membership, charged with the maintenance and administration of the public school system.—**Board of Trade.** An association of businessmen for the purpose of increasing and improving trade relationships.—**Board of Trade unit.** A British unit of electrical energy, equal to a kilowatt-hour.

Bohr atom. RUTHERFORD-BOHR ATOM.

Bolometer, bō-lom′eter, *n.* [Gr. *bolē*, stroke, *metron*, measure.] An instrument for measuring radiant heat, dependent on change of electrical resistance with temperature.

Bond, bond, *n.* *Chem.* a unit of combining power, such as is possessed by the hydrogen or other univalent atom; represented in formulæ by a short line or dash.

Bonnet, bon′et, *n.* *Engin.* a metal covering for a valve or other part; the metal shield over the engine of a motor-car.

Bornite, bor′nīt, *n.* [After *Born*, Australian mineralogist.] A sulphide of copper and iron, crystals of which are used as detectors of electromagnetic waves.

Bourdon gauge, bōr′don. [After L. Bourdon, the inventor.] An instrument for measuring the pressure of steam or other gas, consisting of a blind metal tube, the bending of which when the gas is admitted actuates a pointer.

Bowden wire, bou′den. A mechanism capable of transmitting force by a tortuous route. It consists of a practically inextensible wire threaded through a closely coiled and practically incompressible spiral wire, the latter being usually anchored at both ends.

Box respirator, *n.* An improved type of gas-helmet, in which the air is drawn through a box containing chemicals and acting as a filter. It was first issued in 1916, and was several times re-issued with improvements.

Boyle and Mariotte's Law. The law that at any given temperature the volume of a given mass of gas varies inversely as the pressure.

Brass hat. A staff-officer.

Breaking load. The dead load which just produces fracture in a material or structure.—**Breaking stress.** The stress under which a material will just give way.

Bridge, brij, *n.* A game of cards resembling whist. In the variety called *auction* bridge, the declaration goes to the player engaging to score the highest number of points.

Bridging train. A body of engineer troops specially instructed in the making of temporary bridges.

Brinell hardness number. [Introduced by J. A. Brinell in 1900.] An index of hardness obtained by pressing a hardened steel ball under a known pressure into the substance to be tested. The quotient of the pressure in kilograms by the spherical area of the indentation in square millimetres is the hardness number.

Brin's process. A process for making oxygen by converting barium monoxide into barium dioxide by heating in air, and then decomposing the dioxide by further heating.

British thermal unit. A unit of heat, being the quantity of heat required to raise the temperature of one pound of water near its point of maximum density by one degree Fahrenheit.—**British warm.** The short warm coat worn by British officers during the European War.

Broadcasting, bra̧d′kast-ing, *n.* *Wireless Tel.* a system by which listeners provided with suitable receivers can hear items of music and speech transmitted at definite wave-lengths from certain central stations.

Brownian movements. [After the Scottish botanist, Dr. Robert Brown, who discovered them in 1827.] Rapid oscillatory motions, visible under the microscope, of minute particles suspended in liquids.

Brush, brush, *n.* *Elect.* in an electric generator, a block of carbon or other suitable material, bearing upon a commutator or slip ring, and thus collecting the current from the revolving part.

Bryophyte, brī′ō-fīt, *n.* [Gr. *bryon*, moss, *phyton*, plant.] A member of the phylum of plants Bryophyta, comprising the mosses and liverworts.

Butane, bū′tane, *n.* *Chem.* a colourless, inflammable gas (C_4H_{10}) of the methane series.

Buzzer, buz′ėr, *n.* *Elect.* an apparatus for producing high-frequency interruptions of current, e.g. the trembler of an induction coil.

Bye, bī, *n.* The odd man in a game where the players pair off in couples. In *golf*, the holes remaining after match is decided.

By-pass, bī′pas, *n.* A secondary channel or outlet for a liquid or gas flowing through a pipe.—*By-pass burner*, a gas burner which is kept always lit, so that the main burner can be lit from it as required.

Calcium carbide. A compound of calcium and carbon (CaC_2), made by heating lime and carbon together in the electric furnace, and used for generating acetylene.

Caliche, kal-ē′chā, *n.* Chile saltpetre, an impure sodium nitrate found in great deposits in Chile.

Calorific value. The quantity of heat obtained from the complete combustion of a given weight of a fuel.

Calorifier, kal-or′i-fī-er, *n.* [L. *calor*, heat, *facio*, I make.] An apparatus for heating air.

Cantaloupe, kan′ta-lōp, *n.* [From Castle of Cantalupo, in Italy.] A round, ribbed variety of musk melon, with reddish flesh of delicate flavour.

Capital levy. A levy or tax on capital distinct from income taxes or any other taxes. The nature of the levy makes it a general property tax.

Carbonyl, car′bon-il, *n.* *Chem.* a divalent organic radical (CO) found only in combination.

Carburet, car′bū-ret, *v.t.* [From *carbon.*] To impregnate a gas with volatilized hydrocarbons, so as to increase its illuminating power.

Cardan shaft, car′dan. [After the Italian mathematician Cardan.] A shaft with a universal joint at each end.

Carnot cycle, car′nō. [After N. L. S. Carnot, French physicist.] *Thermodynamics*, a process through which the working fluid in an ideal heat-engine is imagined to pass in four stages, two isothermal and two adiabatic, the fluid returning finally to its initial state.

Carotid body, Carotid gland, ca-rot′id. A body consisting of nervous tissue, a reflex center influencing pulse, blood pressure and respiration.

Carpogonium, kar′pō-gon″i-um, *n.* [Gr. *karpos*, a fruit, *gonos*, offspring.] In red seaweeds, the female organ.

Cataphoresis, ka-ta-fo-rē′sis, *n.* [Gr. *kata*, down, *phorēsis*, a bearing.] Migration of colloidal particles towards one or other electrode in a solution through which an electric current is passing.

Caterpillar, kat′ėr-pil-ėr, *n.* *Engin.* a traction device consisting of an endless chain encircling the wheels of the tractor.

Cathode. See ELECTRODE. — **Cathode**

rays, cath'ōd. [Gr. *kata*, down, *hodos*, way.] A stream of electrons passing from cathode to anode of a discharge tube in action. The current is carried by the electrons, which can be deflected by an electric or a magnetic field. See BETA RAYS.

Cat's whisker. *Wireless Tel.* a thin wire, usually in the form of a spiral, which makes contact with the crystal in a crystal DETECTOR.

Cell. See VOLTAIC CELL.

Censorship, sen'sėr-ship, *n. Psych.* according to Freud, the mental agency which represses unpleasant memories, or prevents them from being consciously recalled.

Central exhaust engine. See UNIFLOW ENGINE.

Center of curvature. Of a curve at a given point, the center of the circle which touches the curve most closely at the point. The radius of the circle is called the *radius of curvature*.—**Center of inertia.** CENTER OF MASS.

Centroid, sen'troid, *n.* Centre of inertia.

Cepheid, sef'ē-id, *n.* [After a star in the constellation Cepheus.] A type of giant stars, the light from which varies in a regular periodic way, suggesting dilation and contraction of the star itself.

Chalcopyrite, kalk'ō-pīr″īt, *n.* [Gr. *chalkos*, copper, and *pyrites*.] An important ore of copper, a sulphide of copper and iron.

Chalones, kal-ō'nēs, *n.pl.* [Gr. *chalaō*, I slacken.] See AUTOCOID.

Chamber process. A method of manufacturing sulphuric acid. Sulphur dioxide is made to combine with oxygen from the air in lead chambers, with the help of steam in presence of oxides of nitrogen.

Chellean, shel'lē-an, *a.* [From *Chelles*, France.] Of the earliest, or a very early, epoch of the palæolithic age of human culture.

Chemotaxis, kem'ō-tax″is, *n. Biol.* movement of a free-swimming cell or organism induced by a chemical stimulus.

Chemotropism, kem-ot'rō-pism, *n.* [From *chem-* of *chemistry*, Gr. *tropē*, a turning.] *Bot.* curvature of a plant organ, due to unequal growth induced by a chemical stimulus.

Chloramine T, klōr-am'ēn, *n.* [From *chlorine*, and *amine*.] An antiseptic organic solution containing chlorine.

Choking coil. *Elect.* a coil of small resistance but large inductance, used to impede an alternating current, with little loss of energy; also called a reactance coil.

Chromaffin, krō-maf'in, *a.* [Gr. *chrōma*, color, L. *affinis*, having affinity for.] Of cells which stain strongly when chrome salts are applied. It refers to those cells which are found in the carotid, adrenal, and coccygeal glands.

Chromatic aberration. Dispersion of light by a lens, a beam of white light from a point source being split up into its coloured constituents, which converge to different foci.

Chromosome, krō'mō-sōm, *n.* [Gr. *chrōma*, colour, *sōma*, body.] One of the minute fragments into which the CHROMATIN of a cell breaks up during indirect division.

Chuck, chuk, *n. Engin.* a contrivance to hold work or a tool in a machine, especially in a lathe.

Cinema, sin'e-ma, *n.* [Gr. *kinēma*, motion.] A picture-house, or theatre, for the exhibition of moving pictures.

Civvies, siv'is, *n.pl.* Civilian clothes, as opposed to a uniform.

Closed chain. *Organic chem.* in a graphic formula, a group of atoms forming a complete ring.

Clutch, kluch, *n. Engin.* a coupling between two working parts of a machine or engine, allowing these parts to be thrown into or out of gear with each other.

Coefficient of elasticity. MODULUS OF ELASTICITY.—**Coefficient of mutual induction.** The number of lines of force due to unit current in one circuit which are embraced by another circuit.—**Coefficient of self-induction.** The flux of induction through a circuit due to unit current in it.

Coherer, kō-hēr'ėr, *n.* A detector of electromagnetic waves, consisting of metal filings between two metal plugs, and showing the waves by increase of electrical conductivity.

Cohort, kō'hort, *n.* [L. *cohors*, *cohortis*, a company of soldiers.] *Bot.* an ALLIANCE.

Coke oven. A retort, usually vertical, for the manufacture of coke by the carbonization of coal.

Collimator, kol'im-āt-ėr, *n.* A tube with a convex lens at one end and a slit at the other end, exactly at the focus of the lens; used in spectroscopy to produce parallel light.

Color filter. In photography, a screen of colored glass or liquid, allowing only certain colors to pass.

Compensator. An electrical transformer so constructed that the primary and secondary form a single coil.

Complex, kom'pleks, *n.* [L. *complector*, *complexus*, I weave together.] In PSYCHO-ANALYSIS, a series of emotionally accentuated ideas in a repressed state.—*Electra complex*, an excessive attachment (in Freud's nomenclature) of a female child to her father.—*Œdipus complex*, a similar attachment of a boy to his mother.

Complex number. *Math.* an expression of the form $a + \sqrt{-1}\, b$, where a and b are ordinary, or *real* numbers.

Component, kom-pō'nent, *n.* [L. *compono*, I construct.] The effective part of a force, velocity, &c., in a given direction; one of any number of constituent forces, velocities, &c., of which the given force, velocity, &c., is the resultant.

Compression, kom-pre'shon, *n.* One of the forms of stress, or more strictly of strain, consisting in a crushing action.

Conchy, con'shi, *n.* A conscientious objector; one who, during the World War, attributed to conscience his unwillingness to fight (*Eng. slang*).

Condenser, con-dens'ėr, *n. Elect.* an instrument for obtaining large electrical charges at comparatively small differences of potential. It consists essentially of two conducting surfaces insulated from each other at a very small distance apart.

Conductivity, kon-duk-tiv'i-ti, *n. Elect.* the reciprocal of RESISTANCE.

Conflict, kon'flikt, *n. Psych.* antagonism between motives, e.g. between primitive instincts and acquired ideals.

Congruent, Congruous, kong'grụ-ent, kong'grụ-us, *a. Math.* of geometrical figures, superposable so as to be coincident.

Conservation of energy. The leading doctrine of modern physics, according to which the total energy of the universe is a constant quantity. It implies the doctrine of the correlation of different types of energy, according to which the various forms of energy are mutually transformable in definite quantitative relations.

Contact process. *Chem.* any catalytic process (see CATALYSIS), more especially a method of manufacturing sulphuric acid, in which sulphur dioxide and oxygen are combined in the presence of finely divided platinum.

Continuous current. *Elect.* an electric current in one direction only; sometimes implying steadiness and freedom from pulsation. See DIRECT CURRENT, ALTERNATING CURRENT.

Contour map. A map showing elevations above sea level by means of curves (*contour lines*) drawn through places of equal elevation.

Conversion, kon-vėr'shon, *n. Psych.* a process by which a repressed idea is supposed to give rise to a hysterical symptom corresponding to it.

Converter. See ROTARY CONVERTER.

Coolidge tube. An instrument for generating X-rays, consisting of a highly exhausted tube, from the independently heated cathode of which a stream of electrons issues, producing the rays by impact against a target of tungsten.

Coronium, kor-ō'ni-um, *n.* An element supposed on spectroscopic evidence to exist in the sun's corona. Its spectrum contains a bright green line.

Costing, kos'ting, *n.* Preliminary estimate of the total cost of manufacture of an article (*Brit.*).

Crater, krā'tėr, *n.* The hole made by the explosion of a large shell or mine.

Creatine, krē'at-in, *n.* [Gr. *kreas*, *kreatos*, flesh.] A nitrogenous compound contained in meat. When treated with acid it loses water and yields *creatinine*, which is an invariable constituent of urine.

Cresol, krē'sol, *n.* [From CREOSOT.] One of three colourless, oily liquids or solids obtained from wood-tar or coal-tar, similar to phenol, and used as disinfectants.

Crystal detector. *Wireless Tel.* a detector of electromagnetic waves which depends on the property some crystals, such as carborundum, have of rectifying an oscillating current, by allowing it to pass more readily in one direction than the other.

Crystal set. *Wireless Tel.* an apparatus for receiving wireless communications, especially broadcasting, the rectifying agent being a crystal detector.

Curie, kū'ri, *n.* [After Madame *Curie*.] A standard of radio-activity, being the quantity of radium emanation in equilibrium with 1 gm. of radium.

Current, ku'rent, *n. Elect.* often used for strength, amount, or intensity of current, denoting the quantity of electricity which passes any particular section in unit time; the unit of current is the AMPERE.

Cutout, kut'out, *n. Elect.* a device to break the electrical continuity of a circuit when the current is excessive.

Cyanamide, sī'an-am″id, *n.* [CYANOGEN, AMIDE.] A compound of calcium, produced by heating calcium carbide strongly in nitrogen, and used as a fertilizer.

Cyanide process. A method of extracting gold from its ores by treatment with dilute potassium cyanide.

Cycle, sī'kl, *n. Elect.* and *engin.* A set of changes after which initial conditions are restored. In any alternating phenomenon, the number of cycles (per second) is the number of periods per second, called the frequency.

Dakin's fluid. An antiseptic fluid containing sodium hypochlorite.

Damping, damp'ing, *p.a. Phys.* causing the gradual decay of an oscillation: said of frictional forces and other energy-dissipating agencies.

Deflation, dē-flā'shon, *n.* Contraction of the amount of money in circulation, tending to lower prices and wages: the opposite of INFLATION.

Delta metal. An alloy consisting chiefly of copper, zinc, and a little iron.

Denature, dē-nāt'ūr, *v.t.* To render unfit for eating or drinking by the addition of some undesirable substance, e.g. of methyl alcohol or pyridine to spirits.

Departure, dē-par'tūr, *n. Navig.* the distance sailed east or west from a given meridian; the position in latitude and longitude of the starting point of a voyage.

Depression, dē-pre'shon, *n. Meteor.* a state of the atmosphere associated with low barometer and wet, stormy weather. In a depression, which is also called a *cyclone*, the pressure is lowest at the centre; in an *anticyclone*, it is highest there.

Depth charge. A charge of explosive which is detonated on reaching a certain depth, used against submarines.

Desmid, des'mid, *n.* [Gr. *desmos*, chain.]

A unicellular alga, of frequent occurrence in fossil form, differing from a diatom in having no siliceous skeleton.

Desmotropism, des-mot′rop-ism, *n.* [Gr. *desmos*, bond, *tropē*, a turning.] *Chem.* TAUTOMERISM.

Detector, dē-tek′tėr, *n.* *Wireless Tel.* an instrument for converting the received high-frequency currents into currents capable of affecting an indicating instrument, such as a telephone. See CRYSTAL DETECTOR.

Diazo compounds, dī′az″ō. *Chem.* organic substances containing the active azo group (N_2), and important as intermediate products in many reactions. See AZOTE, AZO DYES.

Dibasic, dī-bās′ik, *a.* [*Di*, double, and *basic*.] *Chem.* of acids, containing two hydrogen atoms capable of being replaced by a base in forming salts, e.g. sulphuric acid, H_2SO_4; of salts, containing two equivalents of a base.

Dictaphone, dik′ta-fōn, *n.* [L. *dico*, I speak; Gr. *phōnē*, voice.] The trade name of an instrument similar to the phonograph, into which correspondence is dictated, to be transcribed afterwards.

Diesel engine, dē′zel. [After Rudolph *Diesel*, the inventor.] An oil engine in which the vaporized oil is burned by being sprayed into air whose temperature has been raised by high compression.

Differential gear. *Mech.* an arrangement of gear wheels connecting two axles in one line, permitting one wheel to revolve faster than the other when necessary, as when a vehicle turns a corner.

Diffusion, di-fū′zhon, *n.* The tendency of two different gases or miscible liquids to become uniformly intermingled.

Diode, dī-ōd′, *n.* [Gr. *dis*, twice, *hodos*, way.] The original form of the THERMIONIC VALVE, with two electrodes, the grid being absent.

Direct current. *Elect.* an electric current flowing always in one direction, as distinguished from an alternating current. See CONTINUOUS CURRENT.

Discharge tube. *Physics.* See TUBE; X-RAY TUBE.

Displacement current. *Elect.* a hypothetical rate of change of electrical displacement in the ether, equivalent in magnetic effects to a current, the basis of *Clerk Maxwell's* electromagnetic theory of light and electric waves.

Distinguished Service Cross. A bronze cross instituted by Act of U. S. Congress April 6, 1917 as an award for heroism on the battlefield.—**Distinguished Service Medal.** A bronze medal instituted by Act of U. S. Congress April 6, 1917 as an award for meritoriously performing a responsible duty in wartime.

Divalent, dī-vāl′ent, *a.* [Gr. *dis*, twice; L. *valeo*, I am strong.] *Chem.* having a valency of two, i.e. capable of uniting with, or taking the place of, two hydrogen atoms, or any two univalent atoms, or another divalent atom or radical.

Dole, dōl, *n.* In Great Britain, a maintenance allowance made by the State under certain conditions to unemployed persons, and distributed at the Employment Exchanges.

Dope, dōp, *v.t.* To drug; to dose.—*n.* A preparation used for painting the wings of airplanes; a stupid person (*slang*); inside information (*slang*).

Doppler effect, or **Doppler principle**, dop′ler. *Phys.* the alteration of period of a wave motion, such as sound or light, when the emitting body is approaching, or receding from, the observer.

Duck-boards, duk′bōrds, *n.pl.* Boards used as the flooring of a trench; used also to form a path across a muddy piece of open country.

Ductless glands. Glands of internal secretion, also called *endocrine* organs, the material secreted by which is not conveyed away by a duct, but through the veins. The chief examples are: the adrenal, thyroid, parathyroid, and pineal glands, and the pituitary body or gland.

Dud, dud, *n.* A shell which fails to explode; hence an incompetent person or a defective thing.

Duplex telegraphy. The simultaneous transmission of signals over a single wire, without mutual interference.

Dwarf star. A star in the dense, feebly luminous stage of its evolution, when its maximum temperature is long past. See GIANT STAR.

Earth, erth, *n.* *Elect.* the earth or ground considered as a conductor at zero potential. *To ground* a conductor is to connect it to the ground.

Echelon grating. [See ECHELON.] *Optics*; a diffraction grating of high resolving and dispersive power, formed of parallel plates, each of which very slightly overlaps the one beneath.

Ecology, ē-kol′ō-ji, *n.* BIONOMICS. See ŒCOLOGY.

Elan vital, ā-lan vit-al′. [Fr.] The vital impulse, or will to live, a prominent idea in the philosophy of Henri Bergson.

Electrode, ē-lek′trōd, *n.* [Gr. *electron*, amber, *hodos*, way.] *Elect.* a conducting terminal by which an electric current enters or leaves an instrument, or a special part of the circuit, e.g. a discharge tube or an electrolytic cell. The current enters by the *anode*, and leaves by the *cathode*.

Electromagnetic theory of light. A theory advanced by James Clerk Maxwell, Scottish physicist. The theory attributes the phenomena of light to periodic changes in the electrical and magnetic condition of the ether, propagated with finite velocity as electromagnetic waves.—**Electromagnetic waves**. Waves of alternating electric and magnetic force in the ether; the means, according to modern physical theory, whereby light and electrical influences are transmitted through space.—**Electromagnetism**, ē-lek′trō-mag″net-ism, *n.* That branch of electrical science which deals with the relations between electricity and magnetism, as shown, for example, in the action of dynamos and electric motors.

Electron, ē-lek′tron, *n.* [Gr. *electron*, amber.] A particle carrying a charge of negative electricity of definite amount, $4{\cdot}774 \times 10^{-10}$ electrostatic units, and having a mass about 1/1840 of the mass of the hydrogen atom. All charges of negative electricity are made up of these electrons. See CATHODE RAYS, RUTHERFORD-BOHR ATOM.

Electro-therapeutics, ē-lek′trō-the-ra-pū″iks, *n.* The treatment of disease by electricity.

Elevator, el′ē-vā-tėr, *n.* One of the small planes attached to the main planes of an aeroplane, that can be tilted up or down so as to cause the machine to rise or fall.

Emanation. See RADIUM EMANATION.

E.M.F. See ELECTROMOTIVE FORCE.

Empirical formula. *Phys.* a formula devised by trial so as to suit some series of experimental results, and not deduced mathematically from any assumed theory of the phenomenon.

Employment Exchange. An employment agency.

Endocrine, Endocrinal, end′ō-crīn, end′ō-crīn-al, *a.* [Gr. *endon*, within, *krinō*, I separate.] *Physiol.* of, or relating to, the DUCTLESS GLANDS.

Enhanced spectral lines. *Phys.* lines of a spectrum which only appear, or are intensified, when the spectrum is produced under the influence of the electric spark. They are supposed to occur when atoms are ionized.

Entropy, en′trop-i, *n.* [Gr. *en*, in, *tropē*—transformation.] The entropy of a physical or chemical system is a quantity which increases by an amount Q/T, when Q units of heat are added, under certain conditions, at absolute temperature T. In a system left to itself, the entropy tends to increase, and the energy of the system to become less *available* for conversion into mechanical energy.

Enzyme, en′zīm, *n.* [Gr. *en*, in, *zymē*, leaven.] An unorganized ferment, one of a group of complex nitrogenous substances similar to albumen, which break up complex molecules and render food-stuffs soluble and digestible. Examples are *pepsin, trypsin, diastase, sucrase, thrombase.*

Ester, est′er, *n.* [Coined word.] A compound in which all or part of the replaceable hydrogen of an organic or inorganic acid is replaced by a hydrocarbon radical, e.g. ethyl acetate $CH_3CO_2\,(C_2H_5)$ is the ethyl ester of acetic acid CH_3CO_2H. Fats are glyceryl esters of the fatty acids.

Ethiopian region. South Arabia with Africa south of the Sahara.

Euclidean, ū-klid′i-an, *a.* Having reference to the geometer Euclid, or to his system of geometry.

Euclidean space. Space considered as according with the more or less hypothetical laws laid down by Euclid, especially on the subject of parallel straight lines. See NON-EUCLIDEAN.

Eusol, ū′sol, *n.* An antiseptic fluid containing hypochlorous acid.

Eusporangiate, ū-spōr-anj′i-āt, *a.* [Gr. *eu*, well. SPORANGIUM.] Of a type of ferns, mostly extinct, in which the sporangium is a massive organ arising from several cells. See LEPTOSPORANGIATE.

Eutectic, ū-tek′tik, *a.* [Gr. *eu*, well, *tēkein*, to melt.] Most easily fusible; said of an alloy of proportions giving the lowest melting-point for the given components.

Exhibitionism, eks-i-bish′on-ism, *n.* *Psych.* a perverted mental condition in which pleasure is derived from immodest exposure of the body.

Exophthalmic goiter, eks-of-thal′mik. [Gr. *ex*, out of, *ophthalmos*, the eye.] A disease characterized by enlargement of the thyroid gland, protrusion of the eyeballs, and abnormal heart action. Also called Basedow's disease and Graves' disease.

Exothermic, eks-ō-ther′mik, *a.* [Gr. *exō*, outside, *thermos*, heat.] Of a chemical reaction, in which heat is given out; or of the compound so formed. See ENDOTHERMIC.

Factor, fak′tėr, *n.* GENE.

Farad, far′ad, *n.* [From *Faraday*.] *Elect.* the unit of capacity, equal to the capacity of a condenser which requires one coulomb to charge it to one volt potential; equal to 10^{-9} of the absolute electromagnetic unit of capacity. See MICROFARAD.

Fatty acids. *Chem.* a series of monobasic saturated organic acids, including formic and acetic acids, &c.; also palmitic and stearic acids, which occur in oils and fats.

Fehling's solution. *Chem.* a blue solution obtained by mixing an alkaline solution of Rochelle salt with a solution of copper sulphate. It is used as a test for sugar.

Ferric, fer′ik, *a.* Of compounds in which iron appears with valency 3, as in ferric chloride, $FeCl_3$.—**Ferri-cyanide**, fer′i-sī″an-īd, *n.* *Chem.* one of a series of salts, double cyanides of ferric iron and another base, used in preparing paper for blue prints, in pigment manufacture, and in dyeing.—**Ferro-cyanide**, fer′o-sī″an-īd, *n.* *Chem.* a double cyanide containing ferrous iron, used for silk dyeing, for Prussian blue manufacture, and for case-hardening iron.—**Ferro-silicon**, fer′ō-sil″ik-on, *n.* A compound or mixture of silicon and iron, added to molten iron to increase its content of silicon.—**Ferrous**, fer′us, *a.* Of compounds in which iron appears with valency 2, as in ferrous sulphide, FeS.

Field, fēld, *n.* *Phys.* a region of space,

considered as the scene of certain physical phenomena; that part of an electrical generator which carries the magnetizing or field coils.—*Field strength* or *intensity*, the force exerted on a unit mass, electric charge, or magnetic pole placed at the point where the strength is measured, according as the field is gravitational, electrostatic, or magnetic. The region in which these forces are exerted is called the *field of force*.

Filament, fil'a-ment, *n.* *Wireless Tel.* the fine wire fitted into a THERMIONIC VALVE, which, when heated by the current from the filament battery, gives off electrons, which carry the current in the main circuit.

Filariasis, fil-ar-ī'a-sis, *n.* A disease caused by thread-worms of the genus Filaria, parasitic in man and other animals, especially in tropical countries.

Film, film, *n.* A thin, flexible, celluloid sheet, sensitive to light, made into a roll or film pack, and used in photography.

Filter, fil'tėr, *n.* A device, such as a piece of coloured glass, which allows rays of a certain colour to pass, but stops other rays.

Flair, flār, *n.* [O.Fr. and Fr. *flair*, odour.] Scent; keen instinctive discernment.

Flame arc. An arc lamp in which the carbons have been impregnated with metallic salts, usually fluorides. — **Flame spectrum.** *Phys.* a spectrum of a substance obtained by volatilizing it in a Bunsen flame.

Fluoride, flö'or-īd, *n.* A compound of FLUORINE with another element or a radical; a salt of hydrofluoric acid.

Fluorine, flö'or-ēn, *n.* [From *fluor-spar.*] A chemical element, found in fluorite and cryolite. See HALOGEN.

Flux. See MAGNETIC FLUX.

Flying boat. An aeroplane capable of alighting upon, travelling on, and rising from water.

Flying Corps. A body of military aviators operating aircraft in cooperation with the land and sea forces of a nation.

Foot poundal. The absolute unit of work or energy; the work done by a force of one poundal when its point of application moves through a distance of one foot; equal to $1/g$ of the foot-pound, when g is the acceleration due to gravity.

Formaldehyde, form-al'de-hīd, *n.* [From *formic acid* and *aldehyde.*] A gaseous organic compound, H·CHO, obtained from methyl alcohol. It is supposed to be produced in growing plants by reduction of carbonic acid. See FORMALIN.

Formalin, for'ma-lin, *n.* A liquid used as an antiseptic and disinfectant, a 40 per cent solution of FORMALDEHYDE in water.

Four-stroke cycle. See OTTO CYCLE.

Frequency, frē'kwen-si, *n.* *Phys.* in any form of periodic change, the number of complete periods which take place per sec. See CYCLE.

Freudian, froid'i-an, *a.* Of the theories of Sigmund Freud, Austrian neurologist, on hysteria, dreams, and psychoanalysis.

Fundamental, fun-da-men'tl, *n.* *Phys.* in any system capable of periodic changes, the natural vibration of lowest frequency.

Fuse, fūz, *n.* *Elect.* a wire or strip of metal of low melting-point, which melts, and thus interrupts the circuit, if the current becomes too great for safety.

Gabbro, gab'rō, *n.* [It.] Any coarsely crystalline igneous rock consisting of a pyroxene and a lime-soda or lime felspar.

Gametophyte, gam-ēt'ō-fīt, *n.* [From *gamete*, and Gr. *phyton*, a plant.] In the life history of plants, that stage or generation in which sexual organs are developed, e.g. the prothallus of a fern, or the moss-plant.

Gamma rays. [From the Greek letter.] *Phys.* penetrating rays emitted by radioactive substances, of the same vibrational nature as X-rays, but with higher frequencies.

Gay-Lussac tower, gā-lüs'ak. [After the French physicist.] In the CHAMBER PROCESS for sulphuric acid, a tower in which the spent nitrous fumes are absorbed.

Gel, jel, *n.* [From *gelatine.*] A colloidal substance in a coagulated condition. See SOL.

Gene, jēn, *n.* [Gr. *genos*, race.] An independent unit (more commonly called a *factor*) in the germ, corresponding definitely (according to Mendel's theory of heredity) to a character of the developed organism.

Generator, jen'ėr-āt-or, *n.* *Elect.* a machine for generating electric current. A direct-current generator is usually called a *dynamo*; an alternating-current generator, an *alternator*.

Genetics, jen-et'iks, *n.* The branch of biology which deals with heredity.

Geophone, jē'ō-fōn, *n.* [Gr. *gē*, earth, *phōnē*, sound.] An instrument for finding the direction of sounds proceeding through the earth.

Giant star. A star in a comparatively early stage of its evolution, with density small, and temperature rising. See DWARF STAR.

Gland, gland, *n.* *Engin.* the part of a stuffing-box which is movable, and compresses the packing.

Glider, glīd-er, *n.* A modification of the aeroplane, which can travel through the air for a certain time without engine power.

Globular cluster. *Astron.* extremely remote clusters of stars, of a symmetrical and condensed appearance. One such cluster is estimated to be 200,000 light years distant from the earth.

Glover tower. In the manufacture of sulphuric acid by the chamber process, a tower lined with lead and filled with flints, through which the hot sulphurous gases pass, meeting a stream of crude acid with dissolved oxides of nitrogen.

Glucase, glök-āz', *n.* An enzyme which converts maltose into glucose.

Glyceride, glis'er-īd, *n.* A natural or artificial ESTER of the radical *glyceryl*, C_3H_5, of which *glycerine*, $C_3H_5(HO)_3$, is the hydroxide.

Glycol, glī-kol, *n.* A thick, sweet, liquid organic compound, intermediate between ordinary alcohol and glycerine.

Gonad, gon'ad, *n.* [Gr. *gonē*, that which generates.] A germ gland; a reproductive gland in a rudimentary state.

Gram molecule. *Chem.* of any substance, a weight of it equal to its molecular weight in grams.

Grating, grāt'ing, *n.* *Phys.* a polished surface ruled with a great number of fine parallel lines, usually many thousands to the inch, used for producing spectra by diffraction, and thence for determining wave-lengths of light.

Graves' disease. EXOPHTHALMIC GOITRE.

Grid, grid, *n.* *Wireless Tel.* a spiral of wire, or a cylinder of wire gauze, round the FILAMENT of a THERMIONIC VALVE.

Group velocity. Of waves whose velocity varies with the wave-length, the velocity of a group as distinguished from the velocity of individual waves.

Guild socialism. A theory for the reorganization of society, based on communal ownership, with administration vested in trade-unions or guilds.

Gyro compass or **gyrostatic compass**, jī'rō, jī'rō-stat''ik. An instrument containing a flywheel in rapid rotation, used at sea for the same purpose as the magnetic compass.

Haber process, häb'er. [After the German chemist Haber.] A process for producing ammonia by the combination of nitrogen and hydrogen at a high temperature and pressure in presence of activated iron as a catalyst.

Hafnium, haf'ni-um, *n.* A chemical element, of atomic number 72, discovered by Coster and Hevesy at Copenhagen in 1922, by X-ray spectrum analysis.

Half-tone, haf-tōn, *n.* An illustration printed from a block obtained by photographing an original through a screen formed by two plates of glass ruled in perpendicular directions with fine parallel lines, the original being thus broken up into dots of varying size, according to the depth of tone.

Half-watt lamp. A metallic filament electric lamp, the globe of which is filled with nitrogen or other inert gas.

Halide, hal'īd, *n.* A general term for chlorides, bromides, iodides, and fluorides. See HALOGEN.

Hamiltonian, ham-il-tō'ni-an, *a.* Pertaining to the discoveries of the mathematician Sir William Rowan Hamilton, as the Hamiltonian equations in dynamics.

Heidelberg man. An extinct variety of the human family, supposed to be revealed by the discovery near Heidelberg in 1908 of a very massive and chinless jaw.

Helical gear. Gearing in which the teeth of the gear-wheels wind round the cylinder on which they are formed in the shape of a spiral or helix.

Helium, hē'li-um, *n.* [Gr. *hēlios*, sun.] A gas present in the air in small quantities, the lightest element next to hydrogen, one of the inert elements.

Henry, hen'ri, *n.* [After the natural philosopher *Henry.*] The practical electric unit of self induction and mutual induction. A circuit has an INDUCTANCE of 1 henry when a rate of change of current of 1 ampere per second induces an E.M.F. of one volt.—**Henry's law.** Of solubility of gases, the law that, in the absence of chemical action, a solvent will dissolve the same volume of compressed gas as of gas under ordinary pressure.

Herd instinct. The unreflective tendency towards uniformity of social conduct.

Hertzite, hert'zīt, *n.* A crystal used as a detector in wireless telegraphy.

Heterocyclic, het'ėr-ō-sīk''lik, *a.* [Gr. *heteros*, other, *kyklos*, circle.] *Chem.* of a ring containing atoms of different kinds.

Heterodyne, het''er-ō-dīn', *a.* [Gr. *heteros*, other, *dynamis*, force.] *Wireless Tel.* of the production of beats by reaction between locally generated oscillations and those received.

Hexagonal, heks-ag'ō-nal, *a.* *Crystal.* of a system of crystals (sometimes divided into two, hexagonal and trigonal) which may be referred to 4 equal axes, three equal and equally inclined in one plane, the fourth at right angles to that plane.

Hexose, heks'-ōz, *n.* [Gr. *hex*, six.] A sugar containing six carbon atoms in the molecule, as glucose and fructose.

High frequency. *Wireless Tel.* of alternations having a frequency of over 10,000 per second.

Hippuric acid, hip-ū'rik. [Gr. *hippos*, horse, *ouron*, urine.] A white, crystalline, nitrogenous acid, present in small quantities in urine.

Hooke's joint. [After Robert Hooke, English physicist.] UNIVERSAL JOINT.

Hormones, hor-mō'nēs, *n.pl.* [Gr. *hormao*, I set in motion.] Products of the ductless glands, affecting other organs by way of the blood stream. See AUTOCOID.

Horse latitudes. Two regions in latitudes 30° N. and S., where atmospheric pressure is high, and winds are light and variable.

Horst, horst, *n.* [G.] *Geol.* a part of the earth's crust separated by faults from, and higher than, surrounding parts.

Humors, hū'mėrz or ū'mėrz, *n.* Animal fluids by the preponderance of one of which a person was melancholic, phlegmatic, sanguine, choleric. The theory regulated Ben Jonson's plan of dramatic representation, each one being shown in his prevailing mood, passion or temperament.

Hydrazine, hīd'ra-zēn, *n.* [Gr. *hydōr*, water, *a*, not, *zōē*, life.] A colorless gas, NH_2 NH_2, with an irritating odor.

Hydriodic, hīd'ri-od"ik, *a.* [From *hydrogen* and *iodine*.] Of an acid, HI, formed by union of hydrogen and iodine, the salts of which are the iodides.

Hydrobromic, hīd'rō-brom"ik, *a.* [From *hydrogen* and *bromine*.] Of an acid, HBr, composed of hydrogen and bromine, the salts of which are the bromides.

Hydrogenation, hīd'rō-jen-ā"shon, *n.* *Chem.* treatment of a substance so as to cause it to combine with hydrogen.

Hydroglider, hīd'rō-glīd"er, *n.* A type of flat-bottomed boat driven by an air-screw.

Hydrolysis, hīd-rol'is-is, *n.* [Gr. *hydōr*, water, *lyō*, I loose.] *Chem.* the resolution of a compound into two products, with the introduction of the hydrogen and hydroxyl groups of water into those products.

Hydroplane, hī'drō-plān, *n.* A fin-like plane which governs the vertical course of a submarine; a plane used to raise surface-boats partially in the water; a very light motor-boat, driven either by submerged screws or aerial propellers.

Hydroquinone, hīd'rō-kwin"on. See Quinol.

Hydrosphere, hīd'rō-sfēr, *n.* The aqueous envelope of the earth, including oceans, lakes, rivers, &c.; the aqueous vapour in the atmosphere; the combination of these two.

Hydroxylamine, hīd-roks'il-am"ēn, *n.* [From *hydroxyl* and *amine*.] A nitrogenous base, NH_2OH, resembling ammonia, a strong reducing agent. See Oxime.

Hyposulphite, hī'pō-sul"fīt, *n.* The name of certain substances containing sulphur, of which the hyposulphite of sodium is used in medicine and the arts. They are salts of thiosulphuric acid ($H_2S_2O_3$), formerly called hyposulphurous acid.

Idols, ī'dolz, *n.* The idols in Baconian Philosophy—the idols, phantoms, or false prepossessions 'of the cave', 'tribe', 'market-place', 'theatre'.

Igneous rocks, ig'nē-us rocks. Rocks that have been formed by solidification from a molten state; formerly called Plutonic rocks, and now often divided into two groups, *plutonic* and *volcanic*.

Imaginary number. Complex Number.

Impedance, im-pēd'ans, *n.* [From *impede*.] *Elect.* the ratio of root-mean-square voltage to root-mean-square current in a conductor carrying alternating current. Impedance is compounded of Resistance and Reactance.

Incandescent mantle. A network hood for a Welsbach burner, of cotton, artificial silk, or other fabric, saturated with the nitrates of thorium and cerium in definite proportions, and giving off a bright, white light when heated to a high temperature.

Indicator, ind'i-kāt-ėr, *n.* *Chem.* a substance used to indicate by changes of colour the condition of a solution as to acidity and alkalinity. Examples are *litmus, phenol phthalein, methyl orange*.

Inductance, in-dukt'ans, *n.* [From *induction*.] *Elect.* of an electric circuit, the Linkage of Magnetic Flux with the circuit, when unit current is flowing; this is equal to the E.M.F. induced in the circuit when the current is changing at unit rate. See Henry. Also called coefficient of self-induction. The inductive part of the Reactance is sometimes called the inductance.

Induction motor. An electric motor in which the currents in the rotor winding are *induced* by the action of the rotating magnetic field set up by the stator currents.

Inert elements. *Chem.* a group of elements, probably all monatomic, including helium, argon, neon, krypton, xenon. They are gases at ordinary temperatures, and form no compounds.

Inevitable, in-ev'i-ta-bl, *a.* In artistic and literary criticism, the pat word or style, the use of the word that seems inevitably to be adapted to the expression of an idea.

Inflation, in-flā'shun, *n.* Over-issue of currency, tending to cause a general rise in prices.

Infra-red, in'fra-red, *a.* [L. *infra*, below.] The part of the spectrum lying beyond the visible spectrum on the side of the red.

Inhibit, in-hib'it, *v.t.* *Physiol.* and *Psych.* to check or stop one mental or nervous process by another opposing process.—**Inhibition**, in-hi-bish'on, *n.* *Physiol.* and *Psych.* the act or process of inhibiting; the restraint of will over impulse.

Insulation, in-su-lā'shon, *n.* *Elect.* the substance or material used for the purpose of insulating.

Insulin, ins'u-lin, *n.* [L. *insula*, island, after the *islets of Langerhans* in the pancreas.] A substance extracted from the pancreas of animals, and found beneficial in diabetes.

Intelligentsia, in-tel-li-jent'sē-a, *n.* [Russian.] The educated classes.

Interferometer, int'ėr-fēr-om"e-tėr, *n.* [From *interfere* and Gr. *metron*, a measure.] An instrument for measuring small distances or dimensions with the help of the fringes produced by optical interference.

International, in-tėr-nä'shon-al, *n.* The International Congress of Socialistic Workers. The first International was dissolved in 1876; the second is still adhered to by the more moderate socialists; the third was founded at Moscow in 1919.

Invertase, in-vert'ās, *n.* *Chem.* an enzyme capable of changing cane sugar into the mixture of grape sugar and fruit sugar called invert sugar.

Invigilate, in-vij'il-āt, *v.i.* [L. *in*, in, *vigilare*, to watch.] To watch diligently; to supervise an examination.

Ion, ī'on, *n.* [Gr. *iōn*, going.] *Phys.* one of the substances appearing at the electrodes in electrolysis; one of the electrified particles into which the molecules of an electrolyte are supposed to be dissociated in solution; one of the electrified particles into which the molecules of a gas are broken up by ionizing agencies, such as ultra-violet or alpha rays.—**Ionization**, ī'on-īz-ā"shon, *n.* [See Ion.] *Phys.* the process by which a gas becomes a conductor of electricity through the production of ions which carry the current.—**Ionization potential**. *Phys.* the energy necessary to produce an ion in the process of ionization of a gas, expressed as the number of volts through which an electron must fall to attain this energy.—**Ionized**, ī-on-īz'd, *a.* [See Ion.] *Phys.* of a liquid or gas, containing ions, and therefore capable of conducting an electric current.

Isentropic, īs-ent-rop'ik, *a.* [Gr. *isos*, equal, and *entropy*.] *Phys.* a curve in an indicator diagram, passing through points representing states of equal entropy.

Isostasy, īs-os'ta-si, *n.* [Gr. *isos*, equal, *stasis*, position.] *Geol.* a theory of the equilibrium of the earth's crust, according to which mountains are masses of smaller density supported by the lateral thrust of lower and denser layers.

Isotope, īs'ō-tōp, *n.* [Gr. *isos*, equal, *topos*, place.] *Chem.* an element having the same place in the periodic table as another element. Isotopes are elements which have the same atomic number and the same chemical properties but different atomic weights. Many substances treated by chemists as elements are really mixtures of two or more isotopes.

Jamming, jam'ing, *p.* and *n.* *Wireless Tel.* interference with signals from one wireless station to another, by signals or noises from a third station.

Kame, kām, *n.* [Celtic for *ridge*.] Esker.

Keel-surface, kēl'sėr'fās, *n.* The side surface of an aeroplane, as opposed to the head-on surface.

Keep, kēp, *v.* To lodge, have rooms in college. (*Cambridge use*.)

Keltium, kelt'i-um, *n.* The name originally given to the chemical element now called Hafnium.

Ketone, kē'tōn, *n.* [From Acetone.] *Chem.* one of a class of compounds, containing the carbonyl group (CO) united to two univalent hydrocarbon radicals.

Key, kē, *n.* *Elect.* a lever, or other device, for closing and opening an electric circuit.

Kieselguhr, kēz'el-gör, *n.* [G.] Diatomite.

Kilowatt, kil'ō-wot, *n.* *Elect.* a unit of power equivalent to 1,000 watts, or 1.34 horse power.—**Kilowatt-hour**, kil'ō-wot-our', *n.* *Elect.* a unit of electrical energy equal to the work done by one kilowatt in one hour.

Kinetic theory of gases. *Phys.* the kinetic molecular theory which maintains that the molecules of a gas are continually moving in a straight line, and it is the frequency of their impact against the walls of a container that determines the pressure.

Krypton, krip'ton, *n.* [Gr. *krypto*, I hide.] An inert gaseous element, occurring in minute quantities in the atmosphere.

Lagging, lag'ing, *n.* [From *lag*, a stave.] A covering of non-conducting material used to reduce loss of heat from a boiler or other hot body.

Lattice, lat'is, *n.* *Crystal.* in crystals, the regular linear geometrical form in which the particles are grouped in space.

Least action. *Phys.* a general principle, or law of motion, viz. that the *action* (i.e. the time-integral of the kinetic energy) is less in the actual motion of a system between two given configurations than it is in any hypothetical possible motion between these configurations, subject to the constancy of the total energy.

Leptosporangiate, lep'tō-spō-ranj"i-āt, *a.* [Gr. *leptos*, thin.] Of ferns, those in which the sporangia are small and delicate, each arising from a single superficial cell. See Eusporangiate.

Light year. A unit of distance used in astronomy, being the distance which light can travel in a year, or about 63,000 times the distance from the earth to the sun.

Lindé process, lin'dā. A process for manufacturing oxygen by the fractional distillation of liquid air.

Line squall. A long, narrow region of instability in the atmosphere, travelling at a rate of 20 to 50 miles per hour, its passage being accompanied by violent and sudden wind changes, thunder, and hail.

Linkage, ling'kaj, *n.* *Elect.* the linking together of lines of magnetic force and the turns of an electric circuit through which the lines pass; numerically, the product of the magnetic flux and the number of turns of wire surrounding it.

Lipase, lip'āz, *n.* [Gr. *lipos*, fat.] An enzyme which splits up fats into glycerine and fatty acids.

Listening-in. *Wireless Tel.* listening to speech or music transmitted by Broadcasting.

Literal, lit'ėr-al, *n.* *Print.* misprint.

Lithosphere, lith'ō-sphēr, *n.* [Gr. *lithos*, stone.] The solid part of the earth, contrasted with the atmosphere and the hydrosphere.

Load factor. *Engin.* the ratio of the average power to the maximum capability of a machine, plant, or system.

Longeron, lon'zhėr-on, *n.* *Aviation*; one of the main longitudinal spars of the fuselage.

Long Tom, *n.* A long gun used on naval vessels.

Loop, lụp, *n.* *Phys.* in vibratory or wave

motion, a point where the disturbance considered (e.g. displacement, pressure) is a maximum. See NODE.

Loud speaker. *Wireless Tel.* a special telephone, with a horn attached, used when the sounds received are to be heard by an audience not using head-phones.

Low frequency. *Elect.* of alternating current, not over 25 cycles per second. *Wireless Tel.* of alternations, not over 1000 cycles per second.

Low temperature carbonization. A process of heating coal to a temperature of 500° or 600° C., so as to extract hydrocarbons yielding fuel oil and motor spirit, and to leave a residue suitable as a smokeless domestic fuel.

Luminescence, lū'min-es"ens, *n.* Emission of light due to some other cause than incandescence, e.g. the glow of the firefly, the glow in electric discharge tubes, fluorescence, and phosphorescence.

Lutein, lū'te-in, *n.* [From *corpus luteum,* the reddish-yellow mass found in Graafian follicles of the ovary of mammals.] Any of a class of pigments, usually yellowish, found in yolk of egg, blood serum, *corpus luteum,* &c.

Lyman series, lī-man. [After T. Lyman, physicist.] A series of lines in the hydrogen spectrum, in the far ultra-violet.

Magdalenian, mag'da-lē"ni-an, *a.* [From La Madeleine, in France.] Of the latest stage of Palæolithic culture.

Maglemosian, mag'le-mōz"i-an, *a.* [From Maglemose, in Denmark.] Of a stage of human culture, late in the period of transition from the Palæolithic to the Neolithic.

Magnetic field. See FIELD.—**Magnetic flux.** The total amount of MAGNETIC INDUCTION through a circuit, measured by the number of lines of induction linked with the circuit.—**Magnetic induction.** A vector quantity found by multiplying the magnetic intensity, or field strength, by a coefficient called the *permeability* of the medium. See FIELD.

Magneto, mag-nē'to, *n.* A type of combined dynamo and transformer used in internal combustion engines to generate electrical pressures sufficient to cause a spark across the gap of a sparking plug.

Magnetomotive force, mag-nē'to-mō"-tiv. The difference of magnetic potential between two points of a magnetic circuit. It is regarded as the cause of magnetic induction. See AMPERE TURN.

Mail, māl, *n.* [L. *macula,* mesh.] *Weaving;* a glass or metal ring or eye through which the warp thread passes.

Martensite, mar'tens-īt, *n.* [After A. Martens, German metallurgist.] A very hard form of steel, containing less than two per cent of carbon, obtained by quenching from a high temperature.

Marxian, märks'i-an, *a.* Of the socialistic theories of the German writer Karl Marx.

Masochism, mas'ō-kism, *n.* [After Masoch, Austrian novelist.] Pathological sexual condition, in which pleasure is derived from cruel treatment by the associate.

Mass spectrum. *Phys.* a register of the mass of atoms obtained on a sensitive plate by subjecting swiftly moving atoms in a discharge tube to electric and magnetic forces; used by the English physicist F. W. Aston in his researches on ISOTOPES.

Mendelism, men'del-izm, *n.* [From *Mendel,* an Austrian abbot.] A system of numerical laws of inheritance, determined by crossing allied plants or animals differing in some easily recognized character, and by observing the distribution of the character among the offspring of several generations.

Metallography, met'al-og"ra-fi, *n.* A branch of metallurgy, dealing with the microscopic structure and physical properties of metals and alloys.

Michelson - Morley Experiment. *Phys.* an attempt to show the motion of the earth relative to the surrounding ether by an optical effect arising from the difference in the velocity of rays of light across, and in the line of, the relative stream of ether. The effect expected was not found.

Microcosmic salt, mīk'rō-kos"mik. *Chem.* hydrogen sodium ammonium phosphate, a substance which becomes glassy on heating, and is used in testing for metals with the blowpipe.

Microphone, mīk'rō-fōn, *n.* [Gr. *mikros,* small, *phōnē,* sound.] An instrument for converting sound waves into electrical impulses.—A component of the transmitting apparatus of a modern telephone. Its action depends on the effect of sound waves in changing the electrical resistance between conductors in loose contact, called carbon transmitter.

Millibar, mil'i-bar, *n.* [L. *mille,* a thousand, Gr. *baros,* weight.] *Meteor.* a pressure of 1000 dynes per sq. cm. See BAR.

Mohs' scale of hardness, mōz. A list of substances arranged in order of increasing hardness, viz. 1, talc; 2, gypsum; 3, calcite; 4, fluorite; 5, apatite; 6, orthoclase; 7, quartz; 8, topaz; 9, corundum; 10, diamond. The hardness of any other substance is indicated by a whole number with a decimal, as 7·5.

Molecular pump. *Phys.* an air-pump for producing very high vacua.

Mond gas, mond. [After Ludwig *Mond,* chemist.] A kind of WATER-GAS.

Monobasic, mon'ō-bās"ik, *a. Chem.* having only one hydrogen atom, replaceable by a basic atom or radical; having one hydrogen atom replaced, of several originally replaceable.

Motor-bicycle, -bus, -cab, -car, -cycle, -truck, &c. Various vehicles driven by motors, usually either electrical or of the INTERNAL COMBUSTION type.

Mould-loft, mōld'loft, *n.* A loft, or room, in a ship-yard, where sections are drawn full size, and wooden moulds of the plates are prepared.

Mousterian, mụs-tēr'i-an, *a.* [From the *Moustier* cave, in France.] Of an intermediate stage of palæolithic culture.

Mustard gas. A poisonous liquid, dichlorethyl sulphide, also called yperite, much used in the World War. It evaporates very slowly, and produces serious effects on skin, eyes, and lungs.

Mutation, mū-tā'shon, *n. Biol.* a VARIATION which appears suddenly.

Nacelle, nā-sel', *n.* [L. *navicella,* little ship.] *Aviation;* the cabin, or accommodation for crew and passengers, as distinguished from the fuselage, &c.

Narcissism, nar-sis'ism, *n.* [From the legend of *Narcissus.*] *Psych.* gratification arising from self-admiration.

Neanderthal man, ne-and'er-tal. A type of mankind supposed to have inhabited Europe in Mousterian times, and represented by a skull found in a cave at Neanderthal in 1857.

Nebulium, neb-ū'li-um, *n.* [From *nebula.*] A chemical element supposed to exist in nebulæ, the evidence being the presence of two characteristic green lines in their spectra.

Nekton, nek'ton, *n.* [Gr. *nēkton,* swimming.] The actively swimming fishes and other organisms living near the surface of the ocean. See PLANKTON.

Neo-realists, nē'ō-rē"al-ists, *n.pl.* A modern school of philosophers, prominent in the United States, insisting on the independent reality of physical phenomena, apart from a knowing subject.

Niton, nē'ton, nī'ton, *n.* RADIUM EMANATION, considered as a chemical element.

Nitriles, nī-trils', *n.* [From *nitre.*] *Chem.* compounds which may be regarded as esters of hydrocyanic acid, as $CH_3 \cdot CN$, acetic nitrile. They are mostly pleasant-smelling, colourless liquids.

Nitrogen fixation. The process of building up nitrogenous compounds by causing free atmospheric nitrogen to combine with other elements; carried out by bacteria in the soil, and also on the manufacturing scale by modern synthetic methods.

Nitrolim, Nitrolime, nīt'rō-lim, -līm, *n.* [From *nitre* and *lime.*] Trade name for calcium CYANAMIDE.

Node, nōd, *n.* [L. *nodus,* a knot.] *Phys.* in oscillatory or wave motion, a point where the disturbance considered vanishes. See LOOP.

Nomogram, nom'ō-gram, *n.* [Gr. *nomos,* law, *gramma,* something drawn.] A figure of straight lines or curves, the points of which are marked with numbers according to some law. The figure is constructed once for all for a given type of problem with variable numerical data, and gives the solution by simple manipulations.

Nomography, nom-og'ra-fi, *n.* The art of making and using nomograms (see above).

Non-euclidean, non-ū-klid'i-an, *a.* Of a system of geometry, or a type of space, in which the definitions and axioms of Euclid do not hold good.

Nordhausen acid, nord-hous'en. [After Nordhausen, Germany.] Fuming sulphuric acid, being ordinary acid containing dissolved sulphur trioxide.

Nova, nō'va, *n.* [L. *novus,* new.] A new star, shining for a time, and then disappearing.

Nucleic acids, nū-klē'ik. A class of organic compounds, important in physiological chemistry, containing phosphoric acid and a carbohydrate united with nitrogenous bases.

Nucleus, nūk'li-us, *n. Phys.* the central part of the RUTHERFORD-BOHR ATOM, containing a certain number of protons with a smaller number of binding electrons.

Observant, ob-zer'vant, *n.* A member of the Franciscan Order, bound to the strict observance of the rules of his fraternity.

Ohmic, ōm'ik, *a.* Relating to the OHM.—*Ohmic drop,* in a wire carrying electric current, the fall of potential between two points, due to the resistance between these points.

Ohmmeter, ōm'mē"tėr, *n.* An electrical instrument for measuring resistance. See OHM.

Old Age Pension. A sum of money paid periodically, by a government according to law, to persons attaining a certain age, usually sixty years or over in some countries irrespective of the applicant's financial status.

Opisometer, op-is-om'e-tėr, *n.* [Gr. *opisō,* backwards.] An instrument for measuring the lengths of curved lines, consisting essentially of a wheel which is rolled along the curve, and then backwards along a straight scale.

Orthorhombic, or-thō-rom'bik, *a.* [Gr. *orthos,* perpendicular, *rhombos,* a rhomb.] *Crystal.* that system of crystals in which the three axes are unequal, and mutually at right angles.

Osmotic pressure, os-mot'ik. [Gr. *ōsmos,* impulse.] The pressure, analogous to gaseous pressure, which gives rise in liquids to diffusion and osmosis or OSMOSE.

Osteopathy, os-te-op'a-thi, *n.* That system of the healing art which places the chief emphasis on the structural integrity of the body mechanism, as being the most important single factor to maintain the well-being of the organism in health and disease.

Otto cycle, ot'ō. [After the German inventor A. N. *Otto.*] The four-stroke cycle used on the Otto gas engine, consisting of intake, compression and ignition, expansion, exhaust. See TWO-STROKE CYCLE.

Oximes, oks'ēms, *n.pl. Chem.* organic compounds containing the group CNOH, obtained by the action of hydroxylamine on aldehydes and ketones.

Palingenesis, pal′in-jen″e-sis, *n.* [Gr. *palin*, again, *genesis*, production.] Recapitulation of ancestral stages in the life-history.

Pancake, pan′kāk, *n.* *Aviation*, an abrupt landing in which the airplane drops vertically instead of on a sloping angle.

Panchromatic, pan-krō-mat′ik, *a.* [Gr. *pan*, all, *chrōma*, colour.] Of a photographic plate, sensitive to all the colours of the spectrum in proportion to their intensity, as judged by the eye.

Pan-German, pan-jer′man, *a.* Used to designate the policy of those Germans whose object was to achieve the political union, and as a consequence to establish the supremacy, not only of countries where the population is preponderatingly German, but also of those of which the inhabitants are of Teutonic origin.—*n.* One who favoured this policy.

Paracusis, pa-ra-kū′zis, *n.* [Gr. *para*, beside, *akousis*, hearing.] Any disorder of hearing.

Paraffin, pa′ra-fin, *n.* [L. *parum*, little, *affinis*, akin.] *Chem.* any of the methane series of hydrocarbons, CH_4, C_2H_6, &c., called saturated hydrocarbons.

Parallel, pa′ra-lel, *n.* *Elect.* an arrangement of part of an electric circuit, such that the conductors in that part form distinct branches, each of which carries a fraction of the total current.

Parathyroid, par′a-thī″roid, *a.* [Gr. *para*, beside, and *thyroid*.] Of the four small glands situated next to the thyroid gland. They are believed to regulate the tone of the skeletal muscles.

Park, *v.t.* Said of motor-cars, to draw them up and leave them for a time in an enclosed space, or at the side of a road.

Parodos, par′o-dos, *n.* [Gr.] In a Greek play, the anapæstic march of the chorus into the orchestra, followed by a lyric ode.

Parsec, par′sek, *n.* [From *parallax* and *second*.] A unit of astronomical distance, viz. the distance of a star whose annual parallax is 1 second, or a distance at which a radius of the earth's orbit subtends an angle of 1 second.

Paschen series. A series of spectral lines in the infra-red in the spectrum of hydrogen.

Pearlite, perl′īt, *n.* A form in which steel and carbon combine, with a laminated structure, containing 0.9 per cent of carbon.

Pentose, pent′ōs, *n.* [Gr. *pente*, five.] Any of a class of sugars having five carbon atoms in the molecule ($C_5H_{10}O_5$), e.g. *arabinose* and *xylose*.

Phase, fāz, *n.* [Gr. *phasis*, aspect.] *Phys.* in alternating or periodic phenomena, the fraction of the complete period (usually represented by 360°) which has elapsed since the last occurrence of some assigned state or condition, e.g. since the last maximum. —*In phase*, said of two varying magnitudes of equal periods when their maxima occur simultaneously.—*Out of phase*, not *in phase*. —*Opposite in phase*, having phases differing by half a period, or 180°. See THREE PHASE.

Phenyl, fēn-il, *n.* [PHENOL.] A univalent aromatic hydrocarbon radical C_6H_5, of which *benzene* is the hydride, and *phenol* a hydroxyl derivative.

Phobia, fōb′i-a, *n.* [Gr. *phobeō*, I fear.] *Psych.* a morbid fear dominating the mind.

Photogrammetry, fō′tō-gram″et-ri, *n.* [Gr. *phōs*, light, *gramma*, a writing, *metron*, a measure.] A method of surveying by means of photography.

Photomechanical, fō′tō-mek-an″ik-al, *a.* Of any process of producing pictures from a plate obtained with the help of photography.

Pickering series, pik′er-ing. A series of spectral lines found by the physicist Pickering in a star of the constellation Puppis, and now recognized as belonging to the ENHANCED spectrum of helium.

Pictures, pikt′ūrz, *n.pl.* In the phrase 'the pictures', the moving photographs shown in motion picture theaters.

Piezo-electricity, pī′e-zō-ē-lek-tris′i-ti, *n.* [Gr. *piezo*, I press.] Electricity due to pressure, especially in crystals.

Piltdown skull, pilt′doun. A human skull found at Piltdown, Sussex, in 1912, supposed to represent a very primitive race of mankind.

Pinacoid, pin′a-koid, *n.* [Gr. *pinax*, a tablet, and *-oid*.] *Crystal.* a crystal form in which certain faces are parallel to two of the axes.

Pineal body, **Pineal gland**, pin′e-al. [L. *pinea*, a pine-cone.] A small, reddish-grey gland-like body found behind the third ventricle of the brain. It is supposed to be a remnant of an ancient organ.

Pineapple, pīn′apl, *n.* A light German trench-mortar.

Pipe-line, pīp′līn, *n.* A line of pipes with apparatus for conveying liquids, e.g. petroleum.

Pitch, pich, *n.* In a toothed wheel, the distance from centre to centre of two adjacent teeth, measured along either a circular arc (*pitch circle*) or the straight chord.

Pitot tube, pē′tō. [After H. Pitot, French engineer.] A tube with a bend at one end, placed in a moving stream to determine its velocity from the height the fluid rises in the tube.

Planck's constant, plangk. [After the physicist Max *Planck*.] See QUANTUM THEORY.

Plane-tabling, plān-tāb′ling, *p.n.* A method in surveying, in which points are determined graphically by the use of a flat table standing on a tripod.

Plug. See SPARK PLUG.

Pocket, pok′et, *n.* A depressed area in warfare, often dangerous to the troops in it who seek to extricate themselves. (*Recent.*)

Poliomyelitis, pol′i-ō-mī-el-ī″is, *n.* [Gr. *polios*, gray, and *myelitis*.] Inflammation of the gray matter of the spinal cord, as in infantile paralysis.

Polybasic, pol′i-bās″ik, *a.* [Gr. *polys*, many, and *basic*.] *Chem.* of substances in which the molecule contains two or more hydrogen atoms capable of replacement by basic atoms or radicals.

Power factor. *Elect.* in alternating-current measurement, the factor by which the apparent watts (i.e. product of root-mean-square current and voltage, as read from ammeter and voltmeter) must be multiplied to give the true watts.

Pressure. *Elect.* practical electrician's term for electromotive force.

Pre-war, prē-war′, *a.* [L. *prae*, before.] Belonging to the period before the World War, 1914-18.

Process block. A piece of wood or metal on which is mounted a printing surface obtained from a photograph by means of a resist and etching process.

Prohibition, prō-hib-ish′on, *n.* The forbidding by law of the manufacture, importation, or sale of alcoholic liquors for ordinary use.

Propellant, prō-pel′ant, *n.* A propelling agent, such as the explosives nitrocotton and nitroglycerine.

Proportional representation. A system of voting in elections to representative bodies, designed to secure equitable representation of minorities.

Proterozoic, prot′ėr-ō-zō″ik, *a.* [Gr. *proteros*, former, *zōē*, life.] The geological era preceding the Cambrian.

Proton, prō′ton, *n.* [Gr. *prōtos*, first.] The elementary positive charge of electricity, corresponding, and equal except for sign, to the negative *electron*; the nucleus of the hydrogen atom.

Provided, prō-vīd′ed, *a.* Of a public elementary school, provided by the local authority. (*Brit.*)

Psychasthenia, sīk′as-thēn″ia, *n.* [Gr. *psychē*, soul, *asthenēs*, weak.] Mental weakness, or mental fatigue.—**Psychometry**, sī- or psī-kom′e-tri, *n.* [Gr. *psychē*, soul, *metron*, measure.] The science of measurement of psychophysical processes, especially in their time relations.—**Psychoneuroses**, sīk′ō-nūr-ōz″es, *n.pl.* [Gr. *psychē*, soul, *neuron*, a nerve.] Mental disorders, such as hysteria, which affect the emotions rather than the reasoning powers.—**Psychosis**, sī-kō′sis, *n.* [Gr. *psychē*, the mind.] A disease of the mental functions, resulting, according to Freud, from the inability of a repressed desire to find an outlet in action.

Push, push, *n.* An attack on a large scale; an offensive.

Pusher, pōsh′ėr, *n.* *Aviation*, an aeroplane in which the propeller is fitted behind the main planes.

Pyridine, pir′i-dēn, *n.* [Gr. *pyr*, fire.] A pungent liquid C_5H_5N, obtained by distilling bone oil or coal tar, used in denaturing alcohol and as a disinfectant. It has numerous derivatives.

Pyrogallic acid, **Pyrogallol**, pīr′ō-gal″ik, -gal″ol. [Gr. *pyr*, fire, and *gallic*.] An organic compound, used as a developer in photography, and as a solvent for oxygen in gas analysis.

Quadrature, kwad′ra-tūr, *n.* *Phys.* two alternating quantities of equal periods, as pressure and current in an electric circuit, are said to be in quadrature when their phases differ by a quarter-period, or 90°. *Maths.* integration.

Quai d'Orsay, kā-dor-sā, *n.* The French Foreign Office.

Quantum, kwon′tum, *n.* [L. *quantus*, how great.] *Phys.* a certain discrete amount of energy; pl. **Quanta**. See QUANTUM THEORY.

Quantum theory. A modern physical theory which asserts that radiant energy is transferred in bundles, or *quanta*, each *quantum* containing hn ergs, where n is the frequency of the wave, and h is a universal constant, called *Planck's* constant, equal to 6.55×10^{-27} erg-seconds.

Quenched spark. *Wireless Tel.* a method of exciting electrical oscillations in which the spark in the primary circuit is quickly extinguished.

Quinol, kwin′ōl, *n.* [From *quina*, Peruvian bark.] A white crystalline substance, $C_6H_4(OH)_2$, used as a developer in photography, and as an antiseptic. Also called *hydroquinone*. —**Quinoline**, kwin′ō-lēn, *n.* [From *quinine*.] An organic compound, C_9H_7N, which is obtained from coal-tar and bone-oil as a colourless, pungent liquid. One of its derivatives occurs in quinine.

Racemic acid, ra-sēm′ik. [L. *racemus*, a bunch of berries.] An optically inactive form of tartaric acid, found in grapes.

Radiation, rā′di-ā″shon, *n.* That which is radiated; light, heat, and electromagnetic action transmitted through space. — *Corpuscular radiation*, alpha and beta rays.—**Radiator**, rā′di-ā-tėr, *n.* A nest of tubes for cooling circulating water, as in a motor-car engine.

Radio, rād′i-ō. [L. *radius*, ray.] A combining form, used in compound words as equivalent to *wireless*; also used as a noun for the wireless system of transmission.—**Radioactive**, rād′i-ō-akt″iv, *a.* [L. *radius*, ray, and *active*.] Of substances which spontaneously emit rays, either charged atoms of helium (*alpha* rays), electrons (*beta* rays), or electromagnetic waves of higher frequency than light or than ultra-violet rays (*gamma* rays). — **Radiogram**, rā′di-ō-gram, *n.* [L. *radius*, a ray, Gr. *gramma*, a picture.] A radio-telegram.—**Radiology**, rād′i-ol″ō-ji, *n.* The science of X-rays, and of the rays emitted by radioactive bodies, with special reference to their use in medicine.—**Radiotelephony**, răd′i-ō-tel-ef″-ō-ni, *n.* Wireless telephony.—**Radiotherapy**, răd′i-ō-ther″a-pi, *n.* The use of X-rays and the rays from radium, &c., in medicine.

Radium emanation. A radioactive inert gaseous element, produced from radium by the loss of an *alpha* particle from a radium atom. Also called *niton*, and *radon*.

Radius of curvature. See CENTRE OF CURVATURE.

Radon, rā′don, *n.* Niton, or RADIUM EMANATION.

Raidisseur, red′iss-ėr, *n.* [French word from *raidir*, to tighten, stiffen.] An apparatus for tightening the wires of the espaliers or trellis-work on which the branches of fruit trees or vines are extended.

Rand, rand, *n.* [D. *rand*, bank.] The land on either side of a river valley, e.g. at Johannesburg, South Africa.

Rankine cycle, rang′kin. [After W. J. MacQuorn *Rankine*, Scottish engineer.] *Thermodynamics*; a theoretical reversible cycle, roughly equivalent to the actual cycle which the water and steam pass through in a steam engine. It is used as a standard for estimating the efficiency of an engine.

Rare earths. *Chem.* a series of oxides of metallic elements occurring in certain rare minerals.

Rationalization of industry. A system or principle under which employers and employees in a particular industry or group of industries combine to eliminate wasteful methods and promote efficiency.

Reaction, Reaction coil. *Wireless Tel.* a reaction coil is a coil in the plate or the grid circuit of a valve, used to reinforce received oscillations, or to produce oscillations. This use of a coil is described as *use of reaction*. See CHOKING COIL.

Recessive, rē-ses′iv, *a.* In Mendel's theory of heredity, one of the two types of sex-cells concerned in crossing may be able to impose its character on all the offspring of the first generation; this character is then called *dominant* to the character of the second type, which is called *recessive*.

Regiment, rej′i-ment, *n.* Government, rule (obs.); 'The Monstrous Regiment of Women' (*Knox*).

Relay, rē-lā′, rē′lā, *v.t.* Of broadcasting, to retransmit by wireless items received from a distance by land telephone.

Remainder, rē-mān′dėr, *n.* In bookselling trade, the copies of a book which are left unsold when the demand or sale has fallen off, and which are then issued or sold at a reduced price.

Reparations, re-pa-rā′shons, *n.pl.* Compensation, to an amount fixed by the peace treaties after the World War, or to some modified amount, for damage done in invaded countries by the defeated powers.

Repression, rē-presh′on, *n.* *Psych.* deliberate avoidance of unpleasant memories. See CENSORSHIP.

Retroaction, ret′rō-ak″shon, *n.* REACTION.

Root-mean-square, röt′mēn′skwār″, *n.* In electrical and statistical calculations, the square root of the average of the squares of a number of quantities, often written *r.m.s.*

Rosolic acid, rō-zol′ik, *n.* A dye-stuff akin to rosaniline.

Ruhmkorff coil, rụm′korf. [After the manufacturer of the machine.] INDUCTION COIL.

Rush, *v.t.* To carry with violence, with a rush; to rush a platform, a meeting, a fortified place.

Sabotage, sä-bo-täzh, *n.* Malicious destruction of property or plant in order to weaken one's opponent, as in a strike, a war, &c.

Sadism, sad′ism, *n.* [After the Marquis *de Sade*.] *Psych.* a form of sexual perversion, in which pleasure is taken in the cruel treatment of the companion.

Saint, sānt, *n.*—*St. Andrew's Day*, November 30; *St. Bartholomew's*, hospital in London; *St. Bartholomew's massacre*, on St. Bartholomew's Day, of Huguenots, on August 24, 1572; *Little and Great St. Bernard*, Alpine passes into Italy; *St. David's Day*, of Wales, March 1; *St. George's Day*, April 23; *St. Genevieve*, patron saint of Paris, 'burghers of St. Genevieve' (Macaulay, *Ivry*); *St. Gothard*, railway and Alpine pass; *St. Helena*, place of Napoleon's banishment; *St. James's*, the Court of Britain, as opposed to other European Courts; *St. Mark's*, the great church in Venice to the patron saint, the Evangelist; *St. Martin's*, the London Post Office; *St. Patrick's Day*, March 17; *St. Paul's*, church of St. Paul's, London; *St. Peter's*, at Rome; *St. Sophia*, at Constantinople; *St. Stephen's*, chapel at Westminster, House of Commons.

Salvarsan, sal-var′san, *n.* A derivative of arseno-benzene, introduced by Ehrlich as a cure for syphilis; also known as 606.

Saturated steam. Steam the temperature of which is the boiling-point temperature corresponding to its pressure.

Sausage, sos′āj, *n.* An observation balloon.

Schlick controller. A gyrostatic device for steadying a ship at sea.

Schupo, shö′pō, *n.* A French abbreviation of Schutzpolizei, the name of an armed police force formed in Germany after the World War.

Scooter, sköt′er, *n.* A child's toy consisting of an elongated roller-skate on which one foot rests, while the other is used to propel it. Also a two-wheeled motor-driven vehicle of similar appearance.

Scourer, skou′rėr, *n.* [From *scour*.] The name of street ruffians, like the *Mohocks*, *Muns*, *Tityre Tus*, and other gangs infesting the London streets in the days of Queen Anne and earlier.

Secant, sē′kant, *n.* *Trigon.* in a right-angled triangle, the secant of an acute angle = hypotenuse ÷ adjacent side.

Secondary cell. An electric cell which after discharge can be charged afresh from any suitable source of power.

Segregation, se′grē-gā″shon, *n.* In Mendel's theory of heredity, a process occurring in crossbreds, whereby sexual cells, of two different types with respect to a given character, are produced in equal numbers.

Selectivity, sē′lekt-iv″i-ti, *n.* *Wireless Tel.* property of a receiving apparatus which allows it to be adjusted so as to respond to waves of any selected frequency.

Self-determination, self-dē-ter′min-ā″-shon, *n.* Of small nations, right to choose national policy, free from interference by external governments.

Semi, sem′i, *n.* [L. *semi*, half. DEMY.] A student in the second year of Aberdeen University; the Franco-Scottish terms being *bajan* (which see), *semi*, *tertian*, *magistrand* (which see).

Sennet, sen′et, *n.* [L. *signum*.] A trumpet call or flourish, as a stage direction in Shakespearian plays.

Series, sēr′is, *n.* *Elect.* an end-to-end arrangement of the conductors in an electric circuit, such that the current passes through each of them in turn. The conductors are said to be *in series*.

Shell, shel, *n.* A long, slender rowboat used for racing.

Short circuit. *Elect.* connection, generally accidental, between two conductors, whereby the current takes a short cut.

Shunt, shunt, *n.* *Elect.* an electrical conductor or conducting path connected in PARALLEL with a dynamo, galvanometer, or other machine or instrument, so as to divert part of the current from the path through the dynamo, &c.

Side-chain. *Organic Chem.* a branch chain of atoms attached to the main chain or ring in the molecule of a compound. Complex molecules are supposed to react with one another through their side-chains, and the German bacteriologist *Ehrlich* has based on this property a theory of the facts of immunity.

Silencer, sīl′ens-ėr, *n.* A device on any form of engine or machine, for reducing the noise of escaping gases. In a motor-car, it usually consists of a series of baffles in the exhaust pipe.

Silicon steel. Steel containing silicon. Structural steel contains 0.4 per cent silicon, transformer steel 3 per cent, and acid-resisting steel 15 per cent. Silico-manganese steel is used for springs.

Simple harmonic motion. *Phys.* a vibratory motion in a straight line about a fixed mean position, the restoring force on the moving particle being directly proportional to the displacement from the mean position. The period of such a motion depends only on the factor of proportionality, and is independent of the magnitude of the maximum displacement.

Slot, slot, *n.* An aperture in an automatic machine for the insertion of the coin to start the apparatus inside.

Solo, sō′lō, *n.* [L. *solus*, alone.] A card game similar to whist, the chief distinction being that a single player often opposes the other three.

Sorbite, sorb′īt, *n.* [L. *sorbus*, service tree.] A sugary, crystalline substance extracted from the berries of the mountain ash; it is stereo-isomeric with MANNITE.

Soviet, sov′i-et, *n.* [Russian.] The method of government in Russia since the Revolution, local soviets (elected councils) sending delegates to larger bodies, and these, in their turn, to the Supreme Congress, which elects the Supreme Council.

Spark plug. In internal combustion engines, a plug screwed into the cylinder head, carrying the insulated secondary or high tension wire from the magneto to one end of the spark gap within the cylinder.

Spark spectrum. See ENHANCED SPECTRAL LINES.

Spectral series. *Phys.* a group selected from the lines in the spectrum of an element, with frequencies given by a simple algebraical formula, e.g. the Balmer, Lyman, and Paschen series of hydrogen.

Spencerian, spen-sēr′i-an, *a.* Of or belonging to the Synthetic Philosophy of Herbert Spencer.

Spherical aberration. Failure of rays of light diverging from a single point-source to converge to a definite focus after reflection at a mirror or passage through a lens, the failure being due to the spherical form of the mirror or lens.

Spout, *n.* An inclined slope formerly used in a pawnbroker's shop for shooting the pledges into a receptacle.—*Up the spout*, in pawn. (*Slang*.)

Standard deviation. In statistics, a number measuring the average divergence of a series of numbers from their arithmetic mean, being the square root of the average of the squares of the differences from the mean.

Statistical mechanics. A branch of mechanics which deals with systems comprising a very large number of individuals, and deduces properties which hold, not for single individuals, but on the average. The Kinetic Theory of Gases is an example.

Steinmetz' law, stīn′metz. The law that the loss of energy due to HYSTERESIS in magnetic material subjected to alternating magnetic force is proportional to the power 1.6 of the maximum magnetic induction.

Stimy, stī′mi, *n.* The position in golf when the opponent's ball lies on the putting-green between the player's and the hole.

Stunt, stunt, *n.* The act of making an airplane follow an irregular flight-path. The performance of a difficult feat exhibiting unusual skill, strength, or courage.

Sublimation, sub′lim-ā″shon, *n.* *Psych.* transfer of psychic energy from lower to higher levels of endeavour.

Superheat, sūp′er-hēt, *n.* The number of degrees (Fahr. or Cent.) by which the temperature of steam, or other gas, exceeds the saturation temperature corresponding to its pressure.

Sylvite, sil'vit, *n.* A mineral consisting of potassium chloride, first found in Stassfurt, Germany, and used as a fertilizer.

Synchronous, sin'kron-us, *a. Phys.* of vibrators, or alternating phenomena, having the same period; having the same period and phase.—**Synchronous motor**. An electric motor in which the period of revolution of the rotating system is fixed by the frequency of the alternating current supply, and the number of poles.

Syntonizing, sin-ton-īz'ing, *n. Wireless Tel.* bringing into tune.—**Syntony**, sin'-ton-i, *n.* Property of two circuits in tune with each other.

Trimetric, trī-met'rik, *a.* [*Tri-*, and Gr. *metron*, measure.] ORTHORHOMBIC.

Tropophyte, trop'ō-fīt, *n.* [Gr. *trepō*, I turn, *phyton*, a plant.] *Bot.* a plant (e.g. a deciduous tree) that undergoes seasonal changes with regard to its behaviour towards water.

Trypsin, trips'in, *n.* [Gr. *tripseis*, potted meat.] An enzyme in the gastric juice that converts proteins into PEPTONES (which see).

Tune, tūn, *v.t. Aviation*, to adjust an engine so that it yields its maximum horse-power

Upanishad, u-pan'i-shad, *n.* [Skr.] A division of the Vedas.

Virtual velocity. A small hypothetical displacement of the point of application of a force measured in the direction of the force; chiefly used in the name of the *principle of virtual velocities*, better known as the *principle of virtual work* or the *principle of work*.

Water-vascular system. In echinoderms, a set of tubes containing sea-water, concerned with breathing and locomotion.

Wing, *n.* In various sports, position to right or left of the center line, looking towards the opponent's goal.

Work, wėrk, *n.* When the point of application of a force moves, the force is said to do work, the measure of which is found by multiplying the force by the component displacement of the point in the direction of the force. See ERG; FOOT-POUND.

Xylidine, zī'li-din, *n.* A name for several coal-tar hydrocarbons resembling aniline, one of them yielding a fine red colour.

Yamen, Yamum, yä'men, yä'mum, *n.* [Chinese.] A Chinese government department or official residence; as, the Tsung li *Yamen* or department of foreign affairs.

Yapp, yap, *n.* [Name of inventor.] Bookbinding with projecting limp-leather cover.

Yellow peril, ye'lō per'il, *n.* The danger to which the white race is supposed to be exposed from the Chinese and Japanese races.—**Yellow Press**, *n.* Sensational or jingo press.

Yen, yen, *n.* The Japanese money unit, of the value of about 50 cents.

Yoga, yō'ga, *n.* [*Hindu*, union.] The Hindu ascetic doctrine of union of the believer's soul with the world-spirit.

Yogi, yō'gi, *n.* A Hindu devotee of the above doctrine.

Yulan, yū'lan, *n.* [Chinese.] A Chinese species of magnolia, with large white blossoms, now cultivated in Europe and America.

Zemstvo, zemst'vō, *n.* [Russian.] Local county council in Russia, under the Empire.

Zooecium, zō-ē'shi-um, *n.* [Gr. *zōon*, animal, *oikos*, house.] The chamber or receptacle in which resides one of the semi-independent animals of the polyzoa in company with others in similar chambers.

CYCLOPEDIA OF NATURE
The Pictorial
CYCLOPEDIA
OF NATURE

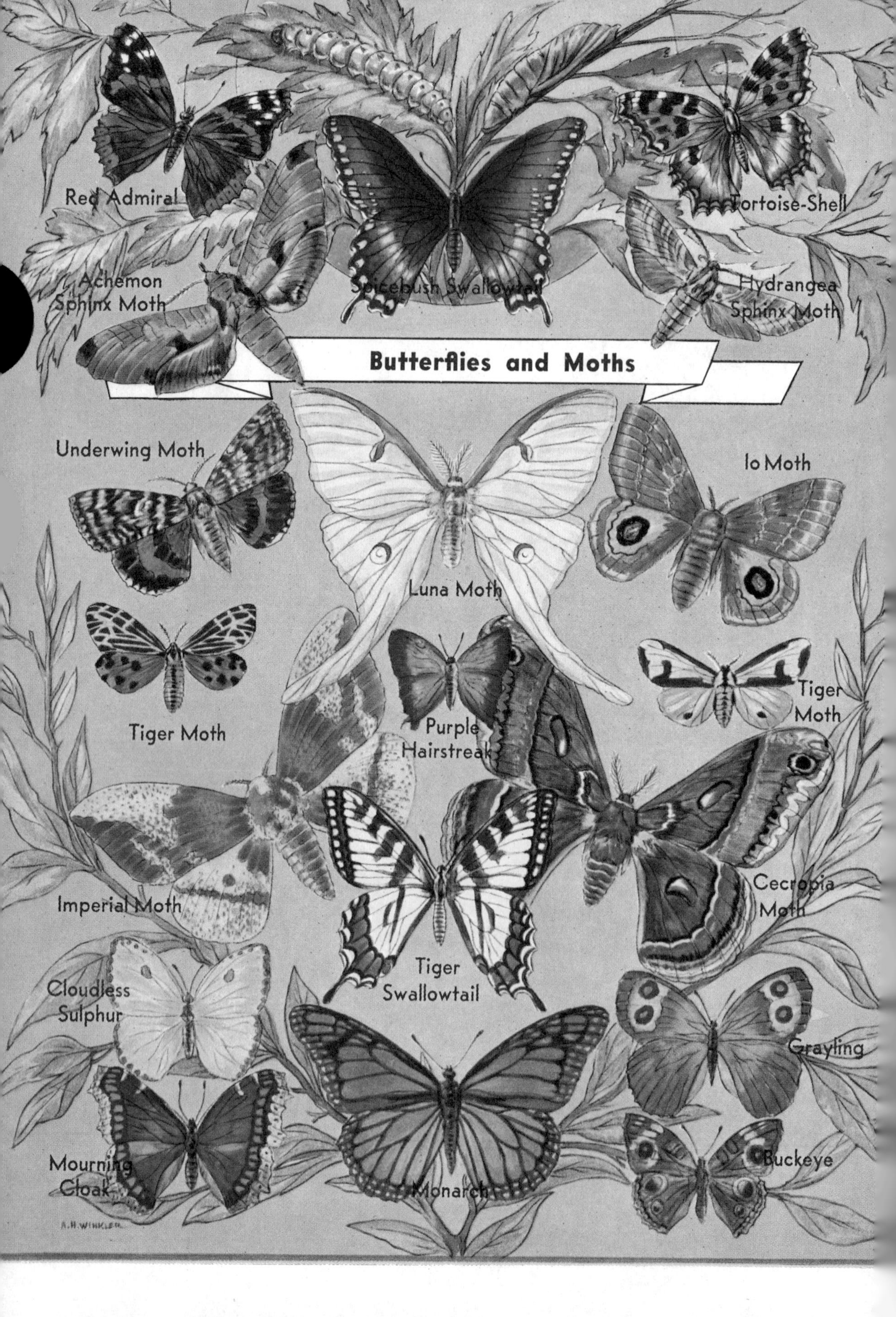
Butterflies and Moths
Red Admiral
Tortoise-Shell
Achemon Sphinx Moth
Spicebush Swallowtail
Hydrangea Sphinx Moth
Underwing Moth
Io Moth
Luna Moth
Tiger Moth
Purple Hairstreak
Tiger Moth
Imperial Moth
Cecropia Moth
Tiger Swallowtail
Cloudless Sulphur
Grayling
Mourning Cloak
Monarch
Buckeye
A. H. WINKLER

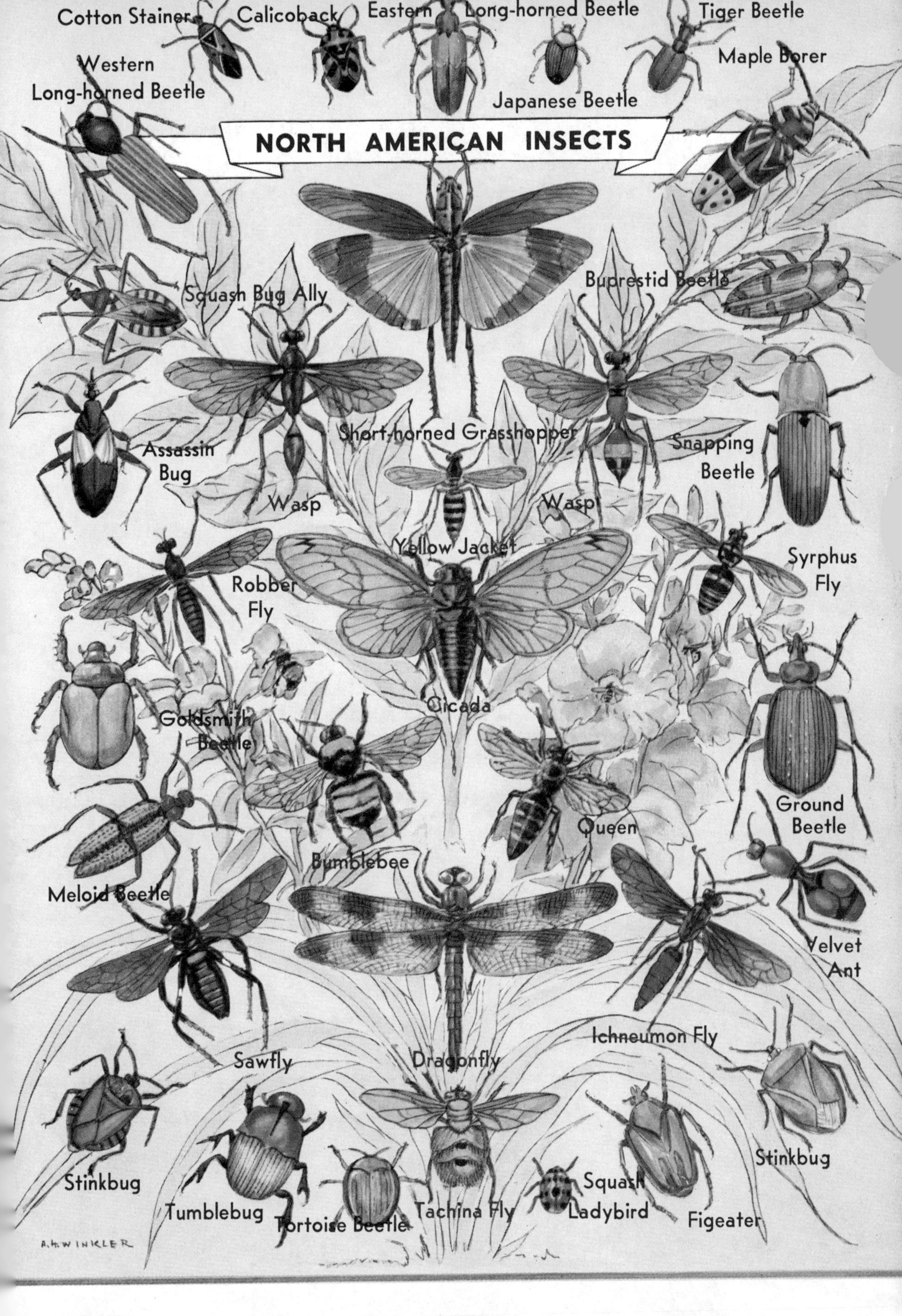

NORTH AMERICAN INSECTS
Cotton Stainer
Calicoback
Eastern Long-horned Beetle
Tiger Beetle
Western Long-horned Beetle
Maple Borer
Japanese Beetle
Squash Bug Ally
Buprestid Beetle
Assassin Bug
Wasp
Short-horned Grasshopper
Snapping Beetle
Wasp
Yellow Jacket
Robber Fly
Syrphus Fly
Cicada
Goldsmith Beetle
Queen
Ground Beetle
Bumblebee
Meloid Beetle
Velvet Ant
Ichneumon Fly
Sawfly
Dragonfly
Stinkbug
Stinkbug
Tumblebug
Tortoise Beetle
Tachina Fly
Squash Ladybird
Figeater
A. H. WINKLER

Landlocked Salmon
Smallmouthed Black Bass
Muskellunge
Lake Trout
Pickerel
Brook Trout
Sailfish
Yellow Perch
AMERICAN GAME FISH
Broadbill Swordfish
Yellowfin Tuna
Tarpon
Rose Coney
Thread Pompano

AMERICAN
GAME BIRDS
Ring-necked Pheasant
Wood Duck
Blue-winged
Teal
Canvasback
Gadwall
Mallard
Wilson's Snipe
Ruffed Grouse
Quail
White-fronted
Goose
Canada
Goose
Valley
Quail
Mountain Quail
Wild Turkey
Woodcock
Prairie Chicken

Herring Gull
California Condor
Road Runner
Osprey
Swallow-Tailed Kite
Rough-Legged Hawk
Great Horned Owl
Red-Tailed Hawk
Bald Eagle
CARRION BIRDS AND BIRDS OF PREY
Marsh Hawk
Turkey Buzzard
Raven
Kingfisher

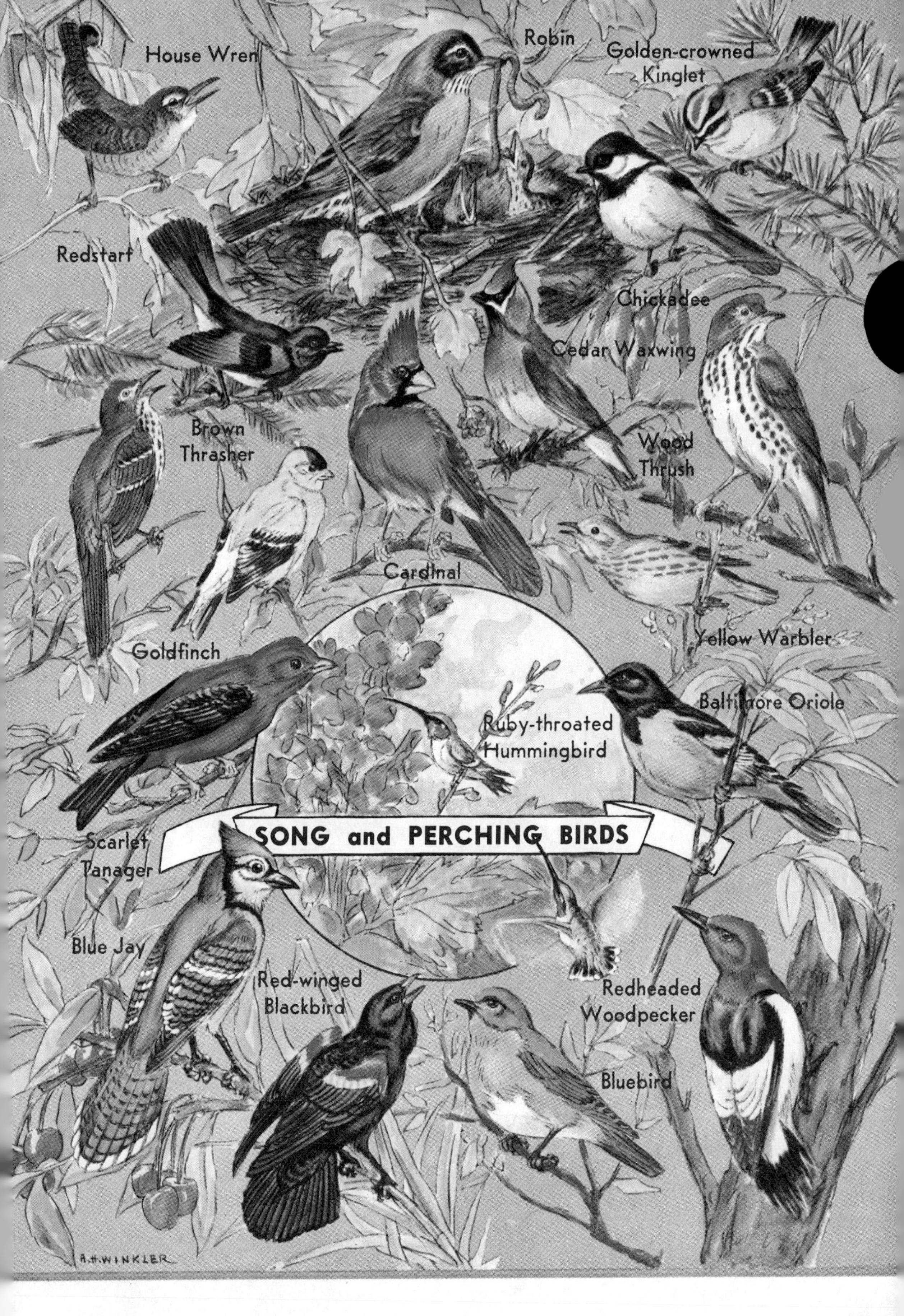
House Wren
Robin
Golden-crowned Kinglet
Redstart
Chickadee
Cedar Waxwing
Brown Thrasher
Wood Thrush
Cardinal
Yellow Warbler
Goldfinch
Baltimore Oriole
Ruby-throated Hummingbird
SONG and PERCHING BIRDS
Scarlet Tanager
Blue Jay
Red-winged Blackbird
Redheaded Woodpecker
Bluebird
A.H. WINKLER

AMERICAN
FUR-BEARING ANIMALS
Mink
Ermine
Pika
Fur Seal
Skunk
Gray
Squirrel
Silver Fox
Red Fox
Muskrat
Beaver
Black Bear
Raccoon
Mole

Rocky Mountain Goat
Virginia Deer
Wapiti
Moose
Coyote
Rocky Mountain Sheep
Lynx
WILD ANIMALS OF NORTH AMERICA
Pronghorned Antelope
Puma
Bison
Grizzly Bear
Timber Wolf
A. H. WINKLER

American Yew,
or Ground Hemlock
Common Juniper
Arbor
Vitae
White
Cedar
Red Cedar
Hemlock
AMERICAN CONIFERS
Giant Sequoia
Balsam Fir
Alpine Fir
Colorado Blue Spruce
White Spruce

Mock Orange
Bridal Wreath
FLOWERING TREES AND SHRUBS
Lilac
Forsythia
Magnolia
Flowering Crab
Flowering Cherry
Rhododendron
Dogwood
Honeysuckle

AMERICAN WILDFLOWERS
Wild Iris
American Senna
Lotus
Moccasin Flower
Lupine
Rose Mallow
Wild Geranium
Greater Bindweed
Fringed Gentian
Jacob's Ladder
Tuberous Water Lily
Pitcher Plant
Sneezeweed
Black-eyed Susan
Bee Balm
Yellow Pond Lily
Meadow Lily
Red Trillium
Swamp Milkweed
Butterfly Weed
H. H. WINKLER

GARDEN FLOWERS
Zinnia
Hardy Aster
Columbine
Campanula
Regal Lily
Veronica
Darwin and
Cottage Tulips
Phlox
Gladiolus
Peony
Delphinium
Hybrid
Tea Rose
China Aster
Chrysanthemum
Dahlia
Snapdragon
Japanese
Iris
Bearded Iris
Pansy
Trollius
A.H. WINKLER

Boletus
Field Mushroom
Little Wheel Mushroom
Garlic Mushroom
Fairy-Ring Mushroom
Gemmed Puffball
Morel
Oyster Mushroom
Glistening Coprinus
Pear-Shaped Puffball
Inky Coprinus
MUSHROOMS
WARNING: Many of these edible native mushrooms very closely resemble deadly poisonous varieties.
Equestrian Tricholoma
Orange-Milk Lactar
Skull Puffball
Caesar's Agaric
Early Pholiota
Gypsy Mushroom
Velvet-Stemmed Collybia

Mexican Rose
Beavertail Cactus
Giant Cactus
Soapweed Tree
Organ Pipe Cactus
Barrel Cactus
Candlewood
Grizzly Bear Cactus
Barrel Cactus
Sitting Cactus
Torch Cactus
Spanish Bayonet
Century Plant
Long Mamma
AMERICAN DESERT PLANTS
Silver Cholla
Nipple Cactus
Clock Face Cactus
Devil's Pincushion
Prickly Pear Cactus
Living Rock

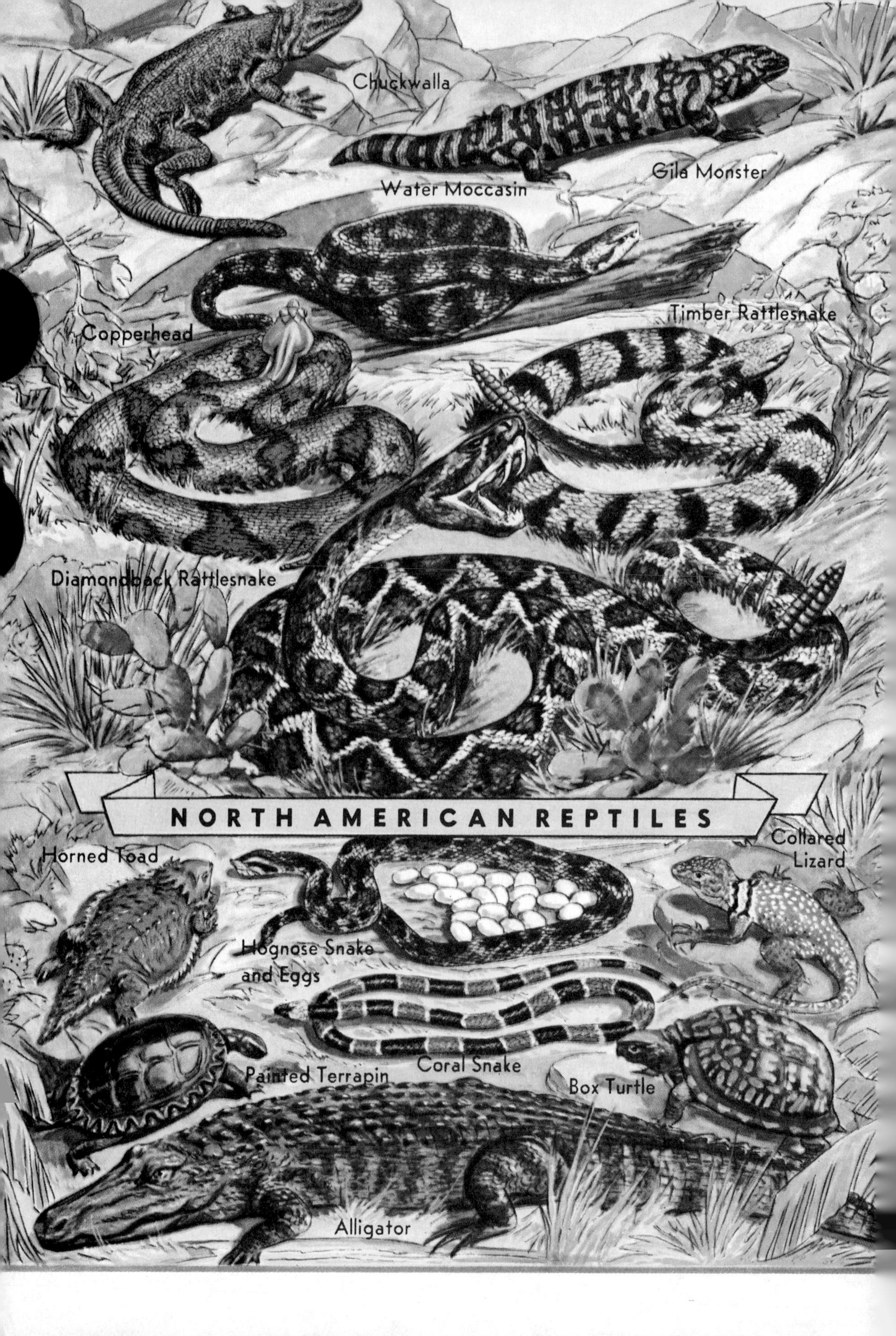

Chuckwalla
Gila Monster
Water Moccasin
Timber Rattlesnake
Copperhead
Diamondback Rattlesnake
NORTH AMERICAN REPTILES
Horned Toad
Collared Lizard
Hognose Snake and Eggs
Painted Terrapin
Coral Snake
Box Turtle
Alligator

A Dictionary of
SYNONYMS AND ANTONYMS

A treasury of words of similar *and* contrasted *meaning*

Abaft, aft, sternward, behind.
Ant.—Forward, ahead, afore, before.

Abandon, forsake, leave, desert, renounce, relinquish, resign, quit, forego, let go, waive, abjure, abdicate.
Ant.—Retain, hold, maintain, support, uphold, defend, keep, cherish, undertake, assert.

Abandoned, dissolute, wicked, reprobate, profligate, flagitious, corrupt, depraved, vicious, bad, sinful, unchaste.
Ant.—Worthy, virtuous, upright, good, chaste.

Abandonment, leaving, desertion, dereliction, renunciation, defection.
Ant.—Protection, maintenance, support.

Abase, lower, humble, humiliate, degrade, depress, disgrace, dishonor, bring down.
Ant. — Exalt, elevate, honor, raise, promote.

Abasement, degradation, fall, degeneracy, humiliation, abjection, debasement, servility.
Ant. — Exaltation, promotion, elevation, dignity, honor.

Abash, bewilder, disconcert, discompose, confound, confuse, shame.
Ant.—Encourage, cheer, animate, embolden, incite.

Abate, lessen, diminish, bate, reduce, decrease, remove, suppress, lower, moderate.
Ant.—Increase, extend, amplify, continue, enlarge.

Abbreviate, abridge, shorten, condense, contract, curtail, reduce, epitomize.
Ant.—Lengthen, extend, prolong, produce, expand, enlarge, amplify.

Abbreviation, abridgment, contraction, condensation, compression.
Ant. — Extension, expansion, enlargement, amplification.

Abdicate, give up, forsake, relinquish, quit, forego, surrender, vacate, resign, renounce.
Ant.—Occupy, retain, maintain.

Abet, help, encourage, instigate, incite, stimulate, aid, assist.
Ant.—Resist, oppose, hinder.

Abettor, accessory, accomplice, assistant, promoter, instigator, coadjutor, associate, companion, confederate.
Ant.—Foe, antagonist, opponent, counteractor, baffler, adversary.

Abhor, dislike intensely, view with horror, hate, detest, abominate, loathe, nauseate.
Ant.—Love, like, adore.

Abide, stay, dwell, live with, tarry, remain, await, wait, sojourn, tolerate.
Ant.—Depart, migrate, move, proceed, avoid, shun.

Abiding. (See Lasting.)

Ability, capacity, capability, talent, faculty, qualification, aptitude, skill, efficiency, power, dexterity, aptness.
Ant.—Inability, incapacity, incapability, imbecility, unreadiness, stupidity, incompetency, inefficiency.

Abject, degraded, groveling, low, mean, base, ignoble, despicable, vile, servile, contemptible, wretched.
Ant.—Dignified, worthy, noble, independent, honorable, haughty, arrogant.

Abjure, recant, recall, revoke, retract, forswear, disclaim, renounce, repudiate.
Ant.—Claim, assert, profess, vindicate, retain, maintain, hold.

Able, strong, powerful, vigorous, robust, brawny, skillful, competent, efficient, capable, telling.
Ant. — Inefficient, incapable, unable, weak, ineffective.

Abnegation, denial, abstinence, stint.
Ant. — Indulgence, assertion, license.

Abnormal, unnatural, anomalous, irregular, eccentric, unusual.
Ant.—Normal, natural, ordinary, customary, usual, regular.

Abode, residence, habitation, dwelling, domicile, home, quarters, lodging, (with the idea of permanence.)
Ant.—(With the idea of transience) — Halt, perch, tent, vestry, place.

Abolish, revoke, abrogate, annul, cancel, annihilate, extinguish, vitiate, invalidate, nullify, destroy.
Ant. — Establish, enforce, institute, restore, repair, erect, continue, sustain, support.

Abominable, hateful, detestable, odious, vile, execrable, foul.
Ant. — Delectable, desirable, admirable, enjoyable, pure, lovable, amiable, gracious, delightful, pleasing.

Abominate. (See Hate.)

Abortive, fruitless, ineffectual, idle, inoperative, vain, futile.
Ant. — Successful, fruitful, complete, perfect.

About, nearly, approximately, generally, concerning, regarding, relative to, with regard to, as to, respecting, with respect to, referring to, around.
Ant. — Precisely, exactly, away, away from, irrelevant.

Abridge. (See Abbreviate.)

Abridgment, epitome, summary, synopsis, compendium, abstract.
Ant. — Amplification, expansion, expatiation, dilation.

Abroad, away, apart, adrift.
Ant.—At home, near, close by.

Abrupt, sudden, unexpected, sharp, harsh, rough, rugged, steep, craggy, precipitous, hasty.
Ant.—Expected, slow, smooth, easy, undulating, courteous, polished.

Abscond, decamp, bolt, run off, steal away.
Ant.—Appear. emerge, show, stay, remain.
Absent, *a.* departed, inattentive, abstracted. not attending to, listless, dreamy.
Ant. — Present, attentive, evident, imminent, existent.
Absolute, unconditional. unqualified, entire. complete, unrestricted, despotic, arbitrary, tyrannous, imperative, authoritative, imperious.
Ant.—Conditioned, conditional, incomplete, imperfect, relative, dependent, accountable, contingent.
Absolve. (See Acquit.)
Absorb, swallow up, engulf, imbibe, consume, engross, merge, monopolize.
Ant.—Exude, emit, eject, dispense, dissipate
Abstain. (See Refrain.)
Abstemious. (See Temperate.)
Abstract. (See Abridgment.)
Abstract, *v.* draw from, steal, purloin, remove, part, separate.
Ant.—Add, unite, return, adduce, restore.
Abstruse, recondite, profound, hidden, occult.
Ant.—Easy, clear, plain, obvious, patent, trite.
Absurd, preposterous, ridiculous, irrational, silly, foolish, unreasonable, nonsensical, inconsistent.
Ant.—Sagacious, sensible, rational, reasonable, wise, consistent, sound.
Abundance, plenty, competency, sufficiency, more than enough.
Ant.—Scarcity, paucity, scantiness, deficiency, dearth, less than enough.
Abundant, plentiful, plenteous, teeming, copious, ample.
Ant.—Deficient, scarce, insufficient, scant, exhausted.
Abuse, *v.* asperse, revile, vilify, calumniate, defame, scandalize, malign, traduce, disparage, ill-use.
Ant.—Praise, laud, extol, protect, respect, cherish.
Abuse, *n.* invective, scurrility, ribaldry, contumely, obloquy, opprobrium, vituperation.
Ant. — Praise, commendation, eulogy, applause.
Accede, consent, assent to, acquiesce, comply with, concur, coincide, submit.
Ant.—Dissent, refuse, decline, withdraw, demur, protest, oppose.
Accelerate, quicken, hasten, hurry, expedite, forward, dispatch.
Ant. — Retard, hinder, delay, obstruct, clog, drag, block.
Accept, take, receive, admit, acknowledge.
Ant. — Refuse, decline, reject, disown.
Acceptable, agreeable, pleasing, pleasurable, gratifying, grateful, welcome, desirable.
Ant. — Unpleasant, disagreeable, unwelcome, objectionable.
Access, admission, approach, avenue, admittance.
Ant.—Exclusion, repulse, rejection, departure.
Accession, increase, augmentation, enlargement, addition, reinforcement
Ant.—Decrease loss, subtraction, weakening.
Accident, contingency, chance, fortuity, casualty, mishap, disorder.
Ant. — Law, purpose, ordainment, provision, preparation.
Acclamation, applause, plaudit, exultation, shouting, cheering, jubilation, outcry
Ant.—Obloquy, execration, silence, censure.
Acclivity, ascent, rise, incline.
Ant.—Declivity, descent.
Accommodate, adapt, adjust, fit, suit, serve, supply, furnish.
Ant. — Inconvenience, disoblige, distant, incommode.
Accompany, attend, go with, escort, convey
Ant. — Leave, avoid, desert, abandon, quit.
Accomplice. Confederate, accessory, abettor, coadjutor, assistant, ally, associate.
Ant. — Adversary, opponent, enemy.
Accomplish, do, effect, finish, execute, achieve, complete, perfect, consummate, perform, attain.
Ant — Fail, defeat, frustrate, disconcert, baffle, mar, ruin, spoil.
Accomplishment, attainment, qualification, acquirement.
Ant.—Defect, disability.
Accord, agree, consent, grant, allow, admit, concede.
Ant. — Differ, disagree, withhold, refuse, deny.
Accordant, compatible, harmonious, consonant, consistent, consenting, acquiescent.
Ant.—Different, incompatible, inharmonious, inconsistent.
Accost, address, speak to, stop, salute, greet, hail.
Ant. — Shun, pass, elude, ignore, avoid.
Account, narrative, description, narration, relation, detail, recital—monies, reckoning, bill, charge.
Ant.—Misrepresentation, confusion, distortion, caricature.
Accountable, punishable, answerable, amenable, responsible, liable.
Ant. — Absolute, supreme, irresponsible, independent.
Accredited, authorized, commissioned, empowered, entrusted.
Ant. — Unauthorized, uncommissioned.
Accumulate, collect, bring together, amass, gather, heap, increase.
Ant.—Dissipate, disperse diminish, scatter, waste.
Accumulation, collection, store, mass, concentration.
Ant. — Dissipation, dispersion, diminution
Accurate, correct, exact, precise, nice, truthful.
Ant.—Inaccurate, inexact, incorrect, faulty, defective.
Accuse, arraign, charge, incriminate, tax with.
Ant.—Acquit, absolve, exonerate, release, vindicate, discharge.
Accustom, use, inure, habituate, familiarize.
Ant.—Disaccustom, dishabituate, wean, estrange.
Acerbity, asperity, sharpness acrimony, roughness, acidity
Ant. — Sweetness, mildness, softness, gentleness.
Achieve, do, accomplish, effect, fulfil, execute, gain, win.
Ant.—Fail, lose, miss.
Achievement, feat, exploit, accomplishment, attainment, performance, acquirement, gain.
Ant.—Failure, loss, abortion.
Acknowledge, admit, confess, own, avow, grant, recognize, allow, concede, indorse.
Ant.—Repudiate, disown, disclaim, disavow, deny.
Acme, summit, apex, climax, end, culmination.
Ant.—Base, depth, foot, nadir
Acquaint, inform, tell, enlighten, apprise, make aware, make known, notify, communicate.
Ant. — Ignore, deceive, misguide, mislead, hoodwink.
Acquaintance, knowledge, familiarity, intimacy, cognizance, fellowship, companionship.
Ant. — Ignorance, unfamiliarity, inexperience.
Acquiesce, assent, agree, accede, consent, coincide with, concur.
Ant.—Dissent, demur, object, protest, resist, oppose.
Acquire, get, obtain, attain gain, procure, win, earn, reap, secure.
Ant. — Lose, forfeit, forego, miss, surrender.
Acquirement, acquisition, accomplishment, attainment, qualification.

Ant. — Intuition, inspiration, revelation.

Acquit, absolve, pardon, forgive, discharge, set free, clear.

Ant. — Condemn, accuse, charge, constrain, brief, compel.

Acrimonious, sharp, acrid, stinging, harsh, pungent, piquant, poignant, sour, acid.

Ant.—Amiable, smooth, bland, mild, friendly, pleasant.

Act, do, operate, make, perform, play, enact.

Action, deed, achievement, feat, exploit, accomplishment, battle, engagement, agency, instrumentality, movement.

Ant. — Inaction, rest, repose, quiet, cessation, quiescence.

Active, lively, sprightly, alert, agile, nimble, brisk, quick, supple, prompt, vigilant, laborious, industrious.

Ant.—Lazy, passive, indolent, inactive, slow, heavy, clumsy.

Actual, real, positive, genuine, certain.

Ant.—Fictitious, imaginary.

Actuate, instigate, move, impel, induce, prompt, persuade.

Ant. — Dissuade, prevent, deter, hinder, discourage.

Acute, sharp, shrewd, keen, intelligent, penetrating, piercing, severe.

Ant. — Dull, obtuse, stupid, blunt, heavy, chronic.

Adage, maxim, aphorism, proverb, apophthegm, by-word, saw.

Ant. — Discourse, harrangue, yarn, inquisition.

Adapt, accommodate, suit, fit, conform, adjust.

Ant.—Misfit, misconform, misapply.

Addicted, devoted, wedded, attached, given up to, dedicated, prone, inclined, disposed.

Ant. — Unaddicted, unaccustomed, indisposed, disinclined, free from, detached, untrammeled.

Addition, increase, accession, augmentation, reinforcement.

Ant.—Subtraction, abstraction, decrease, decline, separation.

Address, *n.* tact, skill, ability, dexterity, deportment, demeanor.

Ant.—Awkwardness, unmannerliness, clumsiness.

Address, *v.* accost, greet, speak to, approach.

Ant.—(See Accost.)

Adherent, follower, partisan, pupil, disciple.

Ant.—Opponent, enemy, antagonist, adversary.

Adhesion, adherence, attachment, fidelity, devotion.

Ant. — Desertion, opposition, treason, unfaithfulness, aversion, antipathy, alienation, aloofness.

Adieu, good-by, *au revoir*, farewell, leave-taking, valediction.

Ant.—Welcome, greeting, recognition, salutation.

Adjacent, near to, adjoining, contiguous, conterminous, bordering, neighboring.

Ant.—Remote, distant.

Adjourn, postpone, defer, prorogue, delay.

Ant. — Conclude, complete, consummate, dispatch, terminate, continue.

Adjunct, appendage, appurtenance, dependency, help, auxiliary.

Ant.—Essence, body, clog, impediment, drawback, hindrance, autonomy.

Adjust, right, fit, accommodate, adapt, arrange, settle, regulate, organize, reconcile.

Ant. — Dislocate, disarrange, derange, disturb, disorder, confuse, disorganize.

Administer, award, accord, give, serve, supply, afford, contribute, dispense, execute, perform.

Ant. — Withhold, retain, refuse, withdraw, divert, mismanage.

Admirable, striking, surprising, wonderful, astonishing.

Ant.—Detestable, abominable, horrible, hideous.

Admire, wonder, approve, appreciate, affect.

Ant.—Abhor, abominate, dislike, despise, disapprove.

Admit, receive, allow, grant, permit, acknowledge, tolerate.

Ant. — Exclude, debar, reject, repudiate, disavow, deny, prohibit.

Admonition, warning, notice, caution, censure, advice, rebuke, dissuasion.

Ant. — Encouragement, countenance, applause, aid, instigation.

Adopt, take, select, assume, appropriate, choose.

Ant. — Reject, discard, renounce, repudiate, abandon.

Adorn, beautify, decorate, embellish, ornament, deck.

Ant.—Mar, spoil, deform, deface, despoil.

Adroit, skillful, clever, dexterous, expert, apt.

Ant. — Awkward, clumsy, unskillful, inexpert, lubberly.

Adulation. (See Flattery.)

Advance, adduce, assign, allege, bring forward; promote, progress.

Ant. — Hinder, retard, withhold, degrade, oppose, decrease.

Advancement, preferment, promotion, progress.

Ant.—Degradation, hindrance, opposition, retrogression.

Advantage, benefit, good, profit, avail, utility, service.

Ant.—Disadvantage, unprofitableness, uselessness, harmfulness.

Advantageous, beneficial, profitable, salutary.

Ant. — Disadvantageous, unprofitable, useless, harmful, hurtful, noxious.

Adventure, incident, occurrence, casualty, contingency, accident, event.

Ant.—Matter of fact, matter of course, routine, rut.

Adventurous, bold, daring, enterprising, chivalrous, rash, precipitate, foolhardy.

Ant. — Unadventurous, timid, cautious, hesitating.

Adversary, opponent, antagonist, enemy, foe, rival, opposer.

Ant. — Friend, ally, assistant, accomplice, abettor, accessory.

Adverse, opposed, contrary, opposite, counteractive, hostile, repugnant.

Ant. — Favorable, propitious, fortunate, amicable, lucky.

Adversity, misfortune, sorrow, affliction, unfortunate, unfavorable, antagonistic, calamity, disaster.

Ant. — Prosperity, happiness, success.

Advert. (See Notice.)

Advertise, publish, announce, proclaim, promulgate.

Ant.—Conceal, suppress, hush, hoodwink.

Advice, warning, counsel, instruction, information, deliberation, consultation, reflection, consideration.

Ant.—Remonstrance, prohibition, dissuasion, expostulation.

Advise, acquaint, inform, communicate, notify, tell, persuade, prompt, incite.

Ant.—Misinform, deceive, delude, dissuade, deter, prohibit, remonstrate.

Advocate, counsel, defender, upholder.

Ant.—Accuser, impugner, adversary.

Aerial, airy, light, volatile, ethereal, empyreal.

Affability, courteousness, courtesy, urbanity, politeness, suavity.

Ant. — Haughtiness, contemptuousness, gruffness, discourtesy, superciliousness.

Affair, business, matter, question, subject, concern.

Ant.—Detail, item, point, circumstance.

Affect, influence, act upon, feign, pretend, assume.

Ant. — Eschew, shun, dislike, repudiate.

Affecting. (See Pathetic.)

Affection, fondness, attachment, kindness, love, tenderness, endearment, condition, state, inclination.

Ant. — Insensibility, indifference, repugnance, repulsion, aversion, distaste, hatred.

Affectionate, fond, kind.

Ant.—Harsh, cold, unfeeling.

Affinity, relationship, alliance, union, kin, kindred, relation, analogy, sympathy.

Ant.—Antipathy, dissimilarity, disconnection, unlikeness, antagonism.

Affirm, assert, asseverate, declare, aver, swear, protest, state, maintain.

Ant. — Deny, contradict, dispute, demur, doubt, oppose.

Affix. (See Attach.)

Afflict, grieve, give pain, distress, trouble, torment, agonize.

Ant. — Console, relieve, assuage.

Affluence. (See Wealth.)

Afford, produce, bestow, grant, give, impart, communicate, confer, spare.

Ant. — Withhold, stint, withdraw, retain, grudge.

Affray, brawl, fray, quarrel, contention, altercation, wrangle, contest, strife, fracas.

Ant. — Order, tranquillity, pacification.

Affright. (See Frighten.)

Affront, injury, wrong, insult, offense, outrage.

Ant.—Amends, homage, apology, salutation.

Afraid, fearful, timid, timorous, faint-hearted.

Ant.—Bold, courageous, heroic, fearless, audacious, venturesome.

Afterward, hereafter, subsequently, ultimately.

Ant. — Previously, hitherto, heretofore.

Age, period, time, date, generation, era, epoch, antiquity, senility.

Ant. — Moment, instant, infancy, youth, childhood.

Aged, old, elderly, senile, anile, ancient, antiquated.

Ant.—Young, youthful, recent, fresh, juvenile.

Agency, instrumentality, influence, operation, management.

Ant. — Counteraction, opposition, neutralization, interference.

Aggrandize, exalt, promote, prefer, advance, elevate.

Ant. — Debase, degrade, disgrace, dishonor, depress.

Aggravate, tantalize, irritate, inflame, provoke, chafe, nettle, embitter, exasperate, increase, enhance, heighten, make worse, magnify.

Ant.—Soothe, soften, palliate, attenuate, alleviate, mitigate, diminish.

Aggregate, *n.* total, entire, complete, the whole.

Ant.—Unit, part, element, ingredient.

Aggregate, *v.* heap up, amass, accumulate, get together.

Ant.—Separate, dissipate, disperse, divide, segregate.

Aggression, encroachment, assault, attack, offense, invasion.

Ant. — Resistance, repulsion, retreat, withdrawal.

Aggrieve. (See Trouble.)

Agile, lively, sprightly, nimble, brisk, quick, supple, alert, wide-awake.

Ant.—Slow, heavy, awkward, ponderous, inert.

Agitate, convulse, disturb, stir, move, shake, oscillate, upheave.

Ant. — Calm, soothe, allay, compose, smooth, pacify.

Agonize, distress, rack, torture, writhe, excruciate, pain.

Ant. — Soothe, relieve, ease, compose, comfort.

Agony, anguish, pain, distress, suffering, woe, torture.

Ant.—Peace, enjoyment, comfort, composure, relief.

Agree, consent, assent, accede, acquiesce, comply, coincide, tally.

Ant.—Disagree, differ, dissent, demur, decline.

Agreeable, gratifying, pleasant, pleasing, amiable, pleasurable, welcome, acceptable, suitable, jocular, smiling, charming.

Ant.—Disagreeable, offensive, unpleasant, obnoxious, unwelcome, rude, curt, gruff.

Agreement, concurrence, coincidence, concord, compact, contract, bargain, covenant, stipulation, accordance, harmony, unison.

Ant. — Disagreement, discord, promise, parole.

Aid, help, assist, cooperate, relieve, succor, further, forward, contribute, conduce, tend, facilitate, abet.

Ant. — Oppose, retard, resist, deter, baffle, withstand.

Ailing, unwell, sickly, diseased, ill.

Ant. — Well, healthy, sound, strong.

Aim. (See Purpose.)

Alacrity, readiness, willingness, agility, quickness, activity, promptitude.

Ant. — Slowness, repugnance, reluctance, unwillingness.

Alarm, terror, fright, affright, dismay, consternation, disquietude.

Ant. — Security, quiet, confidence, peace.

Alert. (See Agile.)

Alienate, estrange, withdraw from, transfer, assign, convey.

Ant. — Conciliate, retain, endear, secure.

Allay. (See Soothe.)

Allege, affirm, declare, maintain, adduce, advance, assign.

Ant. — Contradict, deny, disprove, refute, gainsay.

Allegory, parable, metaphor, fable.

Ant.—Fact, history.

Alleviate, assuage, mitigate, soothe, solace, relieve, abate, diminish, extenuate, soften.

Ant. — Aggravate, increase, augment, embitter.

Alliance, affinity, union, connection, relation, confederacy, combination, coalition, league, confederation.

Ant. — Antagonism, enmity, divorce, discord, hostility, separation, disruption.

Allot, apportion, appropriate, appoint, distribute, assign.

Ant.—Withhold, retain, unappropriate, refuse.

Allow, let, permit, admit, concede, yield, grant, give, tolerate, suffer, sanction, authorize.

Ant.—Disallow, refuse, resist, object, deny, withhold, protest.

Allude, refer, hint, insinuate, imply, intimate, suggest.

Ant.—State, demonstrate, declare, mention, specify.

Allure, entice, attract, decoy, tempt, seduce.

Ant.—Warn, scare, alarm, deter.

Alteration, change, variation, transition, changeableness, mutability.

Ant. — Fixity, permanence, stability, conservation, changelessness, identity.

Altercation. (See Quarrel.)

Alternating, intermittent, interrupted.

Ant.—Continual, constant.

Altitude, height, elevation, tallness, loftiness.

Ant.—Depth, lowness, depression, shortness, declination.

Altogether, wholly, totally, entirely, perfectly, completely, utterly.

Ant. — Partly, partially, separately, individually, imperfectly.

Always. (See Ever.)

Amalgamate, join, compound, mix, fuse, unite, consolidate.

Ant. — Separate, decompose, disintegrate, disunite.

Amass. (See Accumulate.)

Amazing, astonishing, wondrous, surprising, marvelous, stupendous, astounding.

Ant. — Commonplace, trivial, usual, ordinary, familiar, customary.

Ambassador, envoy, plenipotentiary, minister.

Ambiguous, equivocal, uncertain, vague, dubious, enigmatical.
Ant. — Plain, clear, obvious, unmistakable, indisputable, unequivocal, unambiguous.

Ameliorate, improve, amend, better.
Ant.—Injure, spoil, mar, debase, deteriorate.

Amenable, responsible, accountable, answerable for, liable, subject, dependent.
Ant.—Unamenable, independent, irresponsible, autocratic.

Amend, improve, correct, better, mend. (See Ameliorate.)
Ant.—Impair, injure.

Amends, compensation, recompense, restoration, reparation, atónement, restitution.
Ant. — Offense, injury, fault, insult.

Amiable, loving, pleasing, engaging, good, kind.
Ant. — Hateful, abominable, churlish, disagreeable, ill-natured.

Amicable. (See Friendly.)

Ample, complete, full, wide, spacious, capacious, extensive, liberal, expansive, diffusive.
Ant. — Scanty, insufficient, mean, narrow, stingy.

Amplification, enlargement, exegesis, expansion, development.
Ant. — Abbreviation, curtailment, epitome, retrenchment.

Amusement. (See Recreation.)

Analogy, similarity, affinity, purity, resemblance.
Ant.—Dissimilarity, inaffinity, inequality, incongruity, disproportion.

Ancient. (See Aged.)

Anger, *v.* vex, exasperate, enrage, inflame, irritate, kindle, provoke, imbitter, incense.
Ant. — Please, amuse, gratify, soothe, pacify.

Anger, *n.* wrath, passion, rage, fury, indignation, ire, choler, bile, exasperation, irritation, resentment, pique.
Ant. — Peace, peacefulness, peaceableness, appeasement, good nature, poise, self-control, forbearance, good will, conciliativeness, good temper.

Angry, passionate, irascible, choleric, hasty, sullen, moody, incensed, irritated, enraged, provoked, nettled, piqued, exasperated, wrathful.
Ant. — Peaceful, calm, good-tempered, forgiving, forbearing.

Anguish. (See Agony.)

Animate, cheer, enliven inspire, encourage, embolden, inspirit, instigate, urge.
Ant. — Dishearten, deter, depress, discourage.

Animation, life, vivacity, spirit, buoyancy, elasticity, activity, alacrity.
Ant. — Deadness, dullness, inertness, spiritlessness.

Animosity, enmity, malignity, hostility, antagonism, hatred, antipathy, aversion.
Ant. — Concord, alliance, friendship, companionship, unanimity, harmony, regard.

Annals, chronicles, records, registers, historical accounts.
Ant.—Traditions, legends, romance.

Annex. (See Attach.)

Annihilate, destroy, annul, extinguish, nullify, obliterate, efface.
Ant. — Perpetuate, keep, preserve, conserve, foster, protect.

Announce, declare, make known, publish, advertise, proclaim, report, notify, give out.
Ant.—Conceal, hush, suppress, withhold, stifle, bury.

Annoy, vex, tease, chafe, molest, incommode, inconvenience.
Ant. — Accommodate, please, quiet, gratify, regard.

Annul, revoke, abolish, abrogate, repeal, cancel, destroy, extinguish, quash, nullify.
Ant. — Exact, establish, institute, confirm, maintain.

Anomalous, irregular, abnormal, eccentric.
Ant.—Regular, ordinary, normal.

Antagonism. (See Animosity.)

Antagonist. (See Adversary.)

Antagonistic. (See Adverse.)

Anterior, prior, preceding, antecedent, previous, foregoing, former.
Ant.—Posterior, later, subsequent, succeeding.

Anticipate, forestall, foretaste, prejudge, prearrange, obviate.
Ant. — Misapprehend, recall, undo.

Antipathy, dislike, aversion, repugnance, contrariety, opposition, hatred, antagonism, hostility, feeling against.
Ant.—Affinity, amity, sympathy, attraction, fellow-feeling, harmony.

Antithesis, contrast, opposition.
Ant. — Equivalent, alike, synonymous, equal.

Anxiety, care, solicitude, attention, eagerness, trouble.
Ant.—Contentment, confidence, peace, apathy, nonchalance, contendedness.

Apathy. (See Indifference.)

Aphorism, adage, maxim, saying.
Ant. — Lecture, exhortation, speech, disquisition.

Apocryphal, uncertain, unauthentic, legendary, doubtful, spurious.
Ant.—Authentic, genuine, verified, attested, undisputed.

Appal. (See Dismay.)

Apparent, easily seen, visible, palpable, clear, plain, transparent, evident, unmistakable, unambiguous, manifest, distinct, self-evident.
Ant. — Inapparent, uncertain, dubious, unobservable, unseen, indistinguishable, mistakable, ambiguous, apocryphal, indistinct.

Appeal, refer, invoke, invocate, call upon.
Ant.—Deprecate, protest, disavow, disclaim.

Appearance, air, look, aspect, manner, mien — advent, apparition.
Ant.—Disappearance, non-appearance, concealment.

Appease. (See Soothe.)

Appellation, name, denomination, cognomen, title, designation.
Ant.—Anonymousness, namelessness.

Applaud, praise, extol, commend, approve.
Ant. — Disapprove, denounce, decry, execrate.

Applause. (See Acclamation.)

Appoint, assign, allot, ordain, depute, order, prescribe, constitute, settle, determine.
Ant.—Recall, cancel, suspend, withdraw, withhold.

Apportion. (See Allot.)

Apposite. (See Suitable.)

Appreciate, value, reckon, prize, esteem.
Ant. — Undervalue, misjudge, ignore, misappreciate.

Apprehend, think, feel, conceive, imagine, take, arrest, seize, fancy, anticipate, fear dread, understand.
Ant.—Misapprehend, misconceive, lose, miss, ignore.

Approbation, approval, concurrence, assent, consent.
Ant. — Disapprobation, disapproval, censure, dissatisfaction, refusal, denial, disclaimer.

Appropriate, *v.* (See Assume.) Ascribe, arrogate, usurp.
Ant. — Yield, render, surrender.

Appropriate, *a.* peculiar, particular, exclusive, apt.
Ant. — Inappropriate, unsuitable.

Approval. (See Approbation.)

Arbitrary, despotic, imperious, domineering, tyrannous.
Ant. — Limited, considerate, lenient, modest, mild.

Arbitrator, arbiter, judge, umpire, referee.

Ant.—Appellant, claimant, litigant, disputant.

Ardent, eager, fervid, hot, fiery, glowing, passionate.

Ant. — Cool, cold, indifferent, apathetic, passionless, phlegmatic.

Argue, discuss, dispute, debate, reason upon.

Ant. — Dictate, assent, command, propound.

Arise, flow, emanate, spring, proceed, rise, issue.

Ant.—Sink, fall.

Arouse, stir up, awaken, vivify, excite, stimulate.

Ant. — Allay, compose, quiet, assuage, pacify, deaden.

Arrange, put in order, place, assort, classify, regulate, dispose, adjust.

Ant. — Derange, disarrange, confuse, disturb, jumble, disorder.

Arrant, notorious, flagrant, heinous, flagitious, atrocious, monstrous.

Ant.—Slight, moderate, small.

Array, *n.* rank, order, disposal, disposition, arrangement.

Ant. — Confusion, disorder, rout.

Array, *v.* range, place, draw up, marshal, dress, deck out.

Ant. — Disarray, derange, displace.

Arrest, stop, apprehend, withhold, keep back, restrain, seize.

Ant. — Liberate, free, discharge, dismiss.

Arrogance, assumption, haughtiness, pride, loftiness.

Ant.—Humility, modesty, servility, bashfulness, diffidence, politeness.

Art, skill, tact, aptitude, adroitness, expertness, cunning, subtlety.

Ant. — Inexpertness, unskillfulness.

Artful, disingenuous, sly, tricky, insincere.

Ant.—Candid, frank, straightforward, sincere.

Artifice, trick, strategem, machination, deception, cheat, imposture, delusion, finesse.

Ant. — Openness, simplicity, fairness, candor, honesty.

Ascend, climb, mount, rise, soar, tower, scale.

Ant.—Descend, fall, sink.

Ascendency, superiority, influence, authority, sway, mastery.

Ant. — Subjection, inferiority, disadvantage, subordination.

Ascent. (See Acclivity.)

Ask, request, entreat, solicit, beg, claim, demand, invite, question.

Ant.—Command, order, insist, dictate, exact.

Aspect, light, view, appearance, complexion, feature, air, look, mien, countenance.

Ant.—Back, obverse, rear.

Asperity, acrimony, acerbity, harshness, smartness, pungency, poignancy, tartness, roughness.

Ant. — Mildness, softness, sweetness, gentleness, pleasantness.

Asperse, accuse falsely, malign, slander, traduce, defame, scandalize, disparage, depreciate, vilify.

Ant. — Eulogize, laud, extol, praise, defen uphold.

Assault, *v.* assail, attack, invade, encounter, storm.

Ant.—Defend, protect, repulse, retaliate.

Assemble, congregate, collect, gather, muster, bring together.

Ant. — Disperse, disrupt, adjourn, depart.

Assembly, assemblage, collection, group, company, muster, congregation, convention, congress, diet, council, convocation, conclave, synod, meeting, auditory, audience.

Ant. — Dispersion, disunion, adjournment, individual.

Assent, *v.* consent, accede, acquiesce, comply, concur.

Ant.—Dissent, disagree, differ, disclaim, protest.

Assert. (See Affirm.)

Assign, adduce, allege, advance, bring forward, appoint, allot, appropriate, apportion.

Ant.—Refuse, withhold, withdraw, retain.

Assist. (See Aid.)

Assistant, auxiliary, helping, conducive, furthering, instrumental.

Ant. — Opponent, enemy, foe, antagonist, rival, obstructionist, hinderer.

Associate, colleague, ally, partner, coadjutor, comrade, companion, consort.

Ant.—Rival, foe, alien.

Association, company, society, confederacy, union, partnership, fellowship, companionship, connection, alliance, combination.

Ant. — Disunion, separation, independence, solitude, individuality.

Assuage, compose, calm, pacify, allay, soothe, conciliate, appease, tranquillize, mitigate, alleviate, palliate, mollify.

Ant. — Excite, aggravate, increase, provoke, inflame, incite, stimulate.

Assume, pretend to, arrogate, usurp, appropriate, affect, wear, suppose.

Ant.—Abandon, concede, render, surrender, grant, allow, doff, prove, demonstrate.

Assurance, confidençe, certainty, consciousness, conviction, effrontery, impudence.

Ant. — Bashfulness, reserve, unobtrusiveness, decency.

Astonishing. (See Amazing.)

Athletic, stalwart, powerful, brawny, muscular, robust, able-bodied.

Ant. — Weak, sickly, puny, slight, unmuscular.

Atrocious, flagitious, heinous, enormous, flagrant, villainous, monstrous, inhuman, nefarious.

Ant. — Laudable, honorable, noble, admirable.

Attach, affix, append, annex, adjoin, connect, stick, conciliate, attract, win.

Ant. — Detach, unattach, unfasten, untie, disconnect, alienate, repel, estrange.

Attachment. (See Attach.)

Attack, *v.* assail, assault, impugn, encounter.

Ant. — Defend, resist, repulse, aid, repel, shield, shelter, support, protect.

Attempt, effort, exertion, endeavor, essay, trial, experiment.

Ant. — Neglect, laziness, inaction, abandonment.

Attend, go with, accompany, escort, wait on, listen, hearken heed.

Ant. — Leave, forsake, abandon, wander, disregard.

Attentive, careful, intent, wistful, vigilant, studious, considerate.

Ant.—Inattention, indifferent careless, abstracted, absent, distracted, remiss.

Attest, testify, witness, prove, vouch, confirm, establish, evidence.

Ant. — Contradict, refute, disprove, oppugn, deny.

Attire, *n.* dress, apparel, garments, clothes, habiliments, robes, vestment, costume.

Ant.—Nudity, bareness, *dishabille*, disarray, exposure.

Attitude, posture, position, pose.

Ant. — Movement, gesture, gesticulation, exercise, deportment, bearing, action.

Attract, draw to, allure, entice, charm, wheedle.

Ant. — Repel, repulse, deter, estrange, alienate.

Attractive, winning, charming, captivating, fascinating, bewitching, enchanting, agreeable.

Ant. — Unattractive, uninteresting, repulsive, unpleasant, disagreeable, forbidding.

Attribute, quality, property, mark, characteristic, accomplishment, attainment.

Ant. — Essence, nature, substance.

Audacious. (See Bold.)

Audacity, boldness, effrontery, hardihood.
Ant.—Meekness, humility.

Augment, increase, enlarge, extend, stretch out, spread out.
Ant. — Reduce, diminish, deduct, reserve, impoverish.

August, majestic, noble, dignified, stately, gorgeous, exalted.
Ant.—Mean, common, vulgar, despicable, paltry, undignified.

Auspicious, fortunate, favorable, propitious, prosperous, lucky, happy.
Ant. — Inconspicuous, unpropitious, unlucky, unhappy, discouraging, hopeless.

Austere, rigid, severe, rigorous, stern, harsh, hard, strict.
Ant. — Indulgent, genial, easy, luxurious, mild, tender, kindly, dissolute, dissipated.

Authoritative, powerful conclusive, potent, commanding, swaying, imperative, imperious.
Ant. — Weak, inconclusive, vague, indeterminate, indefinite.

Authorized, accredited, empowered, commissioned.
Ant. — Unauthorized, uncommissioned, unempowered, self-appointed, self-assumed.

Authority, weight, force, power, domination, supremacy, ground, justification.
Ant.—Spuriousness, weakness, usurpation wrong, groundlessness.

Auxiliary, assistant, helping, conducive, furthering, instrumental.
Ant.—Hindrance, opposing, retarding, obstructive, cumbersome.

Avail, advantage, profit, use, benefit, service, utility.
Ant.—Disadvantage, loss, injury.

Available, profitable, advantageous, useful, beneficial.
Ant.—Unavailable, useless, inoperative, unprocurable, inconducive, irrelevant.

Avarice, covetousness, cupidity, greed, rapacity.
Ant. — Generosity, liberality, profuseness, extravagance, unselfishness, waste.

Avaricious, niggardly, miserly, parsimonious.
Ant.—Generous, free-handed.

Aversion. (See Antipathy.) Dislike, hatred, repugnance.
Ant.—Affection.

Avocation, business, occupation, employment, calling, office, engagement, function, profession, trade.
Ant. — Idleness, leisure, holiday.

Avow. (See Declare.)

Awaken, arouse, excite, stir up, vivify.
Ant. — Stupefy, soothe, quiet, pacify, compose.

Award, adjudge, adjudicate, judge, determine, allot.
Ant. — Retain, withhold, refuse, misapportion.

Aware, sensible, conscious, cognizant.
Ant.—Unaware, ignorant, uninformed, unconscious.

Awe, dread, fear, reverence.
Ant.—Familiarity.

Awkward, clumsy, unpolished, rough, untoward.
Ant.—Graceful, elegant, neat, polished, dexterous, skillful, adroit, handy.

Awry, crooked, wry, bent, curved, oblique.
Ant.—Straight, right, true, direct.

Axiom, adage, aphorism, apothegm, by-word, maxim, proverb, saying, saw.
Ant.—Fallacy, babble, chatter, prattle, prate.

B

Bad, evil, wicked, unsound, unwholesome, baneful, deleterious, pernicious, noisome, noxious, sinful.
Ant. — Good, wholesome, sound, virtuous, suitable, reputable, honorable, excellent.

Baffle, defeat, discomfort, bewilder, frustrate, foil, balk, confound, disconcert.
Ant. — Aid, help, assist, encourage, promote, abet.

Balance, weigh, poise, neutralize, counteract, equalize, adjust.
Ant.—Overbalance, upset, tilt.

Balk. (See Baffle.)

Balmy, fragrant, sweet-scented, odoriferous, odorous, perfumed.
Ant.—Harsh, rough, mal-odorous, nasty, unpleasant, sour.

Baneful. (See Bad.)

Banquet, feast, fete, entertainment, festival.
Ant.—Fast, abstinence, starvation.

Banter, mockery, derision, raillery, irony, teasing.
Ant.—Argument, discussion.

Barbarous, savage, brutal, cruel, inhuman, ruthless, merciless, remorseless, unrelenting, uncivilized, rude.
Ant.—Polite, civilized, refined, humane.

Bargain, agreement, convention, compact, stipulation, covenant, contract, transaction.
Ant.—Loss, failure, cheat.

Base, bad, low, mean, sordid, groveling, ignoble, ignominious, dishonorable, vile, counterfeit, deep.
Ant.—Lofty, exalted, refined, pure, noble, esteemed, honored, shrill, worthy.

Battle, combat, engagement, action, conflict, contest, fight.
Ant. — Peace, truce, council, armistice, mediation, arbitrament.

Bear, hold, sustain, support, endure, carry, maintain, convey, transport, waft, suffer, tolerate, undergo, put up with.
Ant. — Drop, eject, reject, decline, resign, refuse.

Bearing, manner, deportment, demeanor, behavior, conduct.
Ant.—Attitude, pose, gesture, appearance.

Beastly, brutal, brutish, sensual.
Ant.—Human, refined, gentle, lofty, pure, kindly.

Beat, strike, knock, hit, belabor, thump, dash, vanquish, overpower, conquer, defeat, overthrow, rout.
Ant.—Caress, pat, stroke, defend, shield, fail, surrender.

Beautiful, elegant, beauteous, handsome, fair, pretty, fine.
Ant.—Ugly, homely, foul, hideous, disagreeable, deformed, unattractive, unsightly.

Beautify. (See Adorn.)

Becoming, befitting, comely, decent, fit, proper, suitable, seemly.
Ant.—Unbecoming, unseemly, indecent, ungrateful, incongruous, improper.

Beg, ask, beseech, implore, entreat, crave, solicit, supplicate.
Ant. — Demand, extort, exact, require, give, confer, donate.

Beginning, commencement, outset, opening, inception, start, origin.
Ant.—End, close, termination, conclusion, completion, consummation.

Beguile. (See Deceive.)

Behavior. (See Conduct.) Carriage, conduct, deportment, demeanor.

Behold, see, look, discern, view, descry, observe.
Ant.—Ignore, disregard, overlook, miss.

Belief, faith, credence, credit, trust, confidence, reliance, conviction, persuasion, avowal.
Ant.—Unbelief, disbelief, distrust, denial, heresy, doubt.

Below, beneath, under, underneath, lower, inferior, subordinate.
Ant.—Above, over, aloft, top, overhead, superior.

Bend, lean, incline, distort, stoop, descend, condescend, yield, submit.
Ant.—Stiffen, break, advance, resist.

Benediction, blessing, commendation, approval.

Ant.—Malediction, curse, disapproval, censure, execration.

Benefaction, gift, donation, alms, charity.
Ant. — Confiscation, deprivation, reservation.

Beneficent, benevolent, bountiful, bounteous, munificent, liberal, generous.
Ant.—Cruel, hard, oppressive, griping, stern, grinding, covetous, miserly. (See Avaricious.)

Benefit, advantage, good, profit, service, ability, avail, use, favor, kindness, civility.
Ant.—Injury, loss, evil, disadvantage, detriment, harm.

Benevolence, beneficence, benignity, kindness, generosity, humanity, tenderness.
Ant — Maleficence, unkindness, cruelty, harshness, churlishness, malevolence, malignity, brutality, inhumanity

Bent, tendency, bias, inclination, disposition, prepossession, propensity, predilection, proneness.
Ant.—Disinclination, indisposition, aversion.

Bereave, deprive, strip, dispossess, disarm, divest.
Ant. — Replenish, benefit, enrich, give, compensate, satisfy.

Beseech. (See Supplicate.)

Beset, surround, encompass, embarrass, hem, beleaguer.
Ant.—Liberate, abandon, free.

Betimes, early, soon, shortly, ere long.
Ant.—Late, slowly, sluggishly, behindhand.

Betoken forebode, bode, portend, augur, presage, prognostication, signify, foreshadow.
Ant.—Belie, hide, mask, mislead, misindicate.

Betray. (See Deceive.)

Better. (See Amend.)

Bewail. (See Lament.)

Bewilder. (See Perplex.)

Bewitch. (See Captivate.)

Bias. (See Bent.)

Bicker, wrangle, dispute, dissent, strife, contend, jar.
Ant.—Agree, converse, chat.

Bid, offer, proffer, tender, propose, call, invite, summon.
Ant.—Forbid, deter, prohibit, restrain.

Bide, wait, stay, remain, tarry, endure, await.
Ant.—Quit, depart, move, migrate, resist, adjourn.

Bigoted, illiberal, prejudiced, narrow, limited, intolerant.
Ant. — Liberal, tolerant, unprejudiced, broad.

Bind, tie, restrain, restrict, connect, link, engage, oblige.
Ant. — Unbind, untie, loose, loosen, unfasten, liberate, free, acquit.

Binding, astringent, costive, valid, obligatory, stringent, constraining.
Ant. — Loosening, purgative, freeing.

Bitter, harsh, pungent, poignant, stinging, sharp, tart, intense.
Ant —Sweet, mellow, pleasant, affable, kindly.

Black, dark, murky, pitchy, inky, cimmerian.
Ant. — White, light, radiant, shining, glorious.

Blacken, defame, calumniate, slander, scandalize, asperse.
Ant.—Whiten, eulogize, vindicate, clear.

Blamable. (See Blame.)

Blame, reprove, reprehend, censure, condemn, reprobate, reproach, chide, upbraid.
Ant.—Praise, approve, exonerate, exculpate, laud, eulogize.

Blameless, inculpable, guiltless, sinless, innocent, immaculate, unsullied, unblemished, spotless, pure.
Ant. — Guilty, blameworthy, faulty, answerable, criminated, culpable.

Bland, soft, gentle, mild, kind, gracious, benign, benignant.
Ant. — Harsh, abrupt, rough, disagreeable, unpleasant.

Blank, confused, confounded, dumfounded, abashed, nonplussed, disconcerted, empty, unfilled.
Ant.—Filled, modified, qualified, mitigated.

Blast, blight, wither, shrivel, destroy.
Ant.—Nurture, cherish, save, shield, protect.

Blatant, noisy, clamorous, braying, bellowing vociferous.
Ant. — Soft, noiseless, quiet, reserved, refined.

Blemish, *v.* stain, blur, sully, spot, obscure, dim, ruin, spoil, mar.
Ant. — Improve, clarify, cleanse, renovate, renew, purify, ornament.

Blemish, *n.* flaw, speck, defect, imperfection, fault.
Ant. — Adornment, embellishment, purity, unsulliedness.

Blend, mix, amalgamate mingle, commingle, compound, fuse.
Ant.—Divide, dissociate, separate, disintegrate.

Blessedness, bliss, happiness, felicity, beatitude.
Ant.—Wretchedness, unhappiness, sorrowfulness.

Blind, sightless, eyeless, unseeing, ignorant, prejudiced, heedless.
Ant.—Clear-sighted, keen, farsighted, aware, conscious, prudent.

Bliss, ecstacy, felicity, blessedness, blissfulness.
Ant. — Woe, misery, suffering, wretchedness.

Blithe, gay, blithesome, cheerful, merry, sprightly, vivacious.
Ant. — Heavy, dull, dejected, sullen, cheerless, gloomy, sorrowful.

Blockhead, dunce, dolt, dullard, numskull, jolthead, loggerhead, ignoramus.
Ant.—Sage, adept, *savant*, philosopher, master.

Bloodshed, carnage, slaughter, butchery, massacre.
Ant.—Peace, amity, festival.

Bloom, blossom, bud, sprout, germinate, shoot forth.
Ant.—Decay, blight, blast, wither.

Blot, speck, flaw, stain, blur, blemish, defect, cancel, efface, expunge, erase, obliterate, eradicate.
Ant. — Perfection, blamelessness, clearness.

Bluff, blustering, burly, swaggering, hectoring, bullying.
Ant. — Courteous, polished, graceful, reserved, elegant.

Blunder, mistake, error, delusion, hallucination, fault, oversight.
Ant. — Correctness, accuracy, exactness, truthfulness, foresight, correction.

Blunt, pointless, obtuse, edgeless, impolite, rough, rude.
Ant. — Sharp, keen, pointed, acute, polished, courteous, refined.

Blustering. (See Swaggering.)

Boast, glory, triumph, vaunt, brag.
Ant. — Deprecate, cringe, whine, whimper, to be modest.

Bodily, corporal, corporeal, material, physical, wholly, collectively, unitedly.
Ant.—Spiritually, ghostly, partially, piecemeal, fragmentarily.

Boisterous, violent, furious, impassioned, impetuous, vehement, stormy, turbulent.
Ant. — Peaceful, calm, serene, self-possessed.

Bold, fearless, undaunted, dauntless, brave, daring, adventurous, intrepid, audacious, impudent, contumacious.
Ant.—Timid, fearful, shy, inadventurous, bashful, retiring.

Bondage, slavery, thraldom, vassalage, servitude, serfdom, captivity, imprisonment, confinement.
Ant.—Freedom, liberty, independence, liberation, manumission.

Booty, plunder, loot, pillage,

Ant.—Restitution, confiscation, forfeiture, penalty.

Border, edge, brim, rim, verge, brink, margin, confine, boundary, frontier.
Ant. — Center, interior, space, substance.

Bound, *v.* limit, circumscribe, confine, restrict, restrain, terminate.
Ant. — Open, free, unconfine, liberate.

Boundless, unbounded, infinite, unlimited, interminable.
Ant.—Bounded, limited, finite.

Bounty, munificence, liberality, generosity, benevolence, beneficence, charity, benignity, humanity.
Ant. — Illiberality, closeness, miserliness, stinginess, churlishness.

Brag. (See Boast.)

Brand, mark, stigmatize, denounce.
Ant. — Honor, decorate, eulogize.

Brave, courageous, gallant, chivalrous, daring, dare, defy, adventurous, valorous, heroic, valiant, bold, dauntless, intrepid, magnanimous, fearless.
Ant.—Cowardly, fearful, timorous, weak-kneed, traitorous, ungallant, timid, weak, craven, cringe, cower.

Bravery, courage, valor.
Ant.—Cowardice.

Brawny. (See Athletic.)

Break, fracture, shatter, burst, rend, rack, violate, infringe, transgress, demolish, destroy, crush, pound, squeeze.
Ant.—Join, conjoin, heal, repair, readjust, renovate, restore, mend.

Breed, beget, engender, generate, hatch, brood, incubate, produce.
Ant. — Extirpate, destroy, eradicate, stifle.

Breeze, blast, gale, gust, hurricane, storm, tempest.

Brevity, shortness, conciseness, succinctness.
Ant.—Prolixity, diffusiveness, protraction, length, elongation.

Brief, short, concise, compendious, succinct, summary.
Ant.—Long, prolix, interminable, protracted.

Bright, clear, lucid, transparent, limpid, lustrous, translucent, shining, brilliant, luminous, radiant, gleaming, clever, witty.
Ant. — Dull, dim, cheerless, dead, murky, muddy, opaque, sullen, dejected, imbecile, foolish, stupid, muggy.

Brisk, active, agile, nimble, lively, quick, sprightly, prompt, alert, assiduous, vigorous, vigilant.
Ant.—Slow, sluggish, indolent, dully, heavy, inactive, stagnant.

Brittle, fragile, frangible, frail, breakable.
Ant. — Elastic, tough, strong, solid.

Broad, wide, large, ample, expanded, extensive, liberal, indelicate, coarse, generic.
Ant.—Narrow, restricted, limited, confined, illiberal, bigoted, refined, delicate, specific, pointed.

Broil. (See Affray.)

Brook, suffer, bear, endure, submit to.
Ant. — Resist, resent, reject, combat.

Bruise, break, crush, squeeze, pulverize, triturate.
Ant. — Heal, soothe, comfort, repair, renovate, strengthen.

Brutality. (See Brutal.)

Brutal, cruel, inhuman, merciless, ferocious, remorseless, ruthless, barbarous, savage, irrational, sensual.
Ant.—Humane, civilized, tender, kind, gentle, polished, generous.

Bud, sprout, germinate, blossom, shoot forth.
Ant. — Seed, flower, wither, die.

Build, erect, raise, construct, found.
Ant.—Overthrow, undermine, lower, tear down, raze, destroy.

Bulk, size, dimension, magnitude, greatness, bulkiness, bigness, largeness, massiveness.
Ant.—Portion, particle, atom, smallness, diminution.

Bullying. (See Swaggering.)

Buoyancy, floatableness, lightness, elasticity, animation, spirit, vivacity.
Ant.—Heaviness, sinkableness, depression, dejection, moodiness.

Burden, *v.* load, encumber, embarrass, oppress, afflict.
Ant.—Unburden, ease, alleviate, assuage, lighten, liberate, console, mitigate.

Burial, interment, sepulture.
Ant.—Resurrection.

Burning, glowing, ardent, fervid, impassioned, fervent, fiery, hot, blazing.
Ant.—Cool, extinguishing, smoldering, latent, sluggish.

Burst, break, crack, split, rend.
Ant. — Cohere, hold, stand, join, repair.

Bury, inter, inhume, entomb, immure.
Ant. — Disinter, exhume, excavate, expose, aggravate.

Business, vocation, employment, engagement, occupation, art, profession, trade.
Ant.—Avocation.

Bustle, stir, tumult, fuss.
Ant.—Quiet, repose.

Buy, purchase, gain, get, obtain, bribe.
Ant. — Sell, vend, hawk, dispose of.

By and By, anon, shortly, ere long, soon.
Ant. — Now, immediately, at once.

C

Cabal, combination, intrigue, faction, conspiracy, plot.
Ant. — Legislation, council, parliament, government.

Cajole, coax, wheedle, flatter, fawn, lure.
Ant. — Scold, warn, chide, blame, antagonize,, displease.

Calamitous, disastrous, unfortunate, unlucky, hapless, fatal, luckless, ill-fated, ill-starred.
Ant. — Felicitous, fortunate, auspicious, propitious, advantageous.

Calamity, disaster, misfortune, mischance, mishap.
Ant.—Good fortune, windfall, luck.

Calculate, compute, estimate, count, consider, reckon, suppose.
Ant. — Miscalculate, risk, chance, guess, conjecture.

Called, termed, designated, denominated, ycleped, named.
Ant.—Miscalled, misnamed.

Calling. (See Employment.)

Callous, hard, obdurate, impenitent, unfeeling, insensible, insensitive, unsusceptible.
Ant. — Sensitive, susceptible, soft, tender.

Calm, *v.* (See Soothe.)

Calm, *a.* quiet, undisturbed, serene, placid, composed, collected, imperturbable, tranquil, pacific, unruffled, still.
Ant.—Disturbance, noise, riot, agitation, excitement, stormy, unsettled.

Calumniate, vilify, revile, accuse falsely, asperse, malign, traduce, slander, defame, scandalize, disparage.
Ant. — Eulogize, vindicate, clear.

Calumny, slander, false accusation, aspersion, defamation.
Ant.—Eulogy, panegyric, vindication, clearance.

Cancel, blot out, obliterate, expunge, efface, wipe out, rub out, erase, quash, abolish, annul, repeal, abrogate, revoke, destroy, invalidate, nullify.
Ant.—Enact, enforce, re-enact, perpetuate, confirm.

Candid, fair, honest, open, artless, ingenuous, frank, sincere, plain.
Ant.—Unfair, unjust, disingenuous, insincere.

Canvass, discuss. contest. controvert. sift, examine. dispute. solicit. apply for.
Ant.—Ignore, disregard, admit, pass.

Capable, able, qualified, competent. efficient, fitted, susceptible, clever. skillful
Ant.—Incapable, dull. unqualified, inefficient, unfitted, stupid, awkward, shiftless. incompetent, inadequate.

Capacious, roomy, ample, spacious, extensive.
Ant.—Limited, shallow, restricted, narrow, petty.

Capacity, capability, skill, ability, faculty, power. talent, efficiency, caliber, size.
Ant. — Incapacity, inability. stupidity, insufficiency, narrowness, contractedness.

Caprice, freak, whim. humor, crotchet, fancy.
Ant.—Plan, reason, determination, decision, deliberation.

Captious, touchy, testy, cross, petulant, peevish, fretful, carping, censorious.
Ant. — Approving, appreciative, encouraging, commendatory, equable, well-balanced.

Captivate, charm, enchant, fascinate, enrapture, bewitch, entrance, enchain, enamor, confine, imprison.
Ant.—Liberate, free, unconfine, release, disenchant.

Captivity, imprisonment, confinement, bondage, slavery, thraldom, servitude. serfdom.
Ant.—Freedom, emancipation, liberty.

Capture, catch, seize, grasp, arrest, apprehend.
Ant.—Release, let go, miss, free, liberate, acquit.

Care, anxiety, solicitude, concern, attention, regard, circumspection, caution, foresight, prudence, heed, attention.
Ant.—Carelessness, disregard, neglect, indifference, temerity, improvidence, heedlessness, negligence.

Career, history, course, race, passage, life.
Ant.—Incident, fact.

Careful. (See Care.)

Careless. (See Care.)

Caress, fondle, hug, embrace, kiss.
Ant.—Persecute, annoy, tease, vex, spurn, buffet, rebuff.

Carnage, slaughter, butchery, massacre.

Carnal, fleshly sensual, voluptuous, luxurious, secular. worldly.
Ant.—Spiritual, ethereal, exalted, refined, pure, temperate.

Carnival, revel, rout. masquerade, festivity.
Ant.—Fast. mortification. Lent.

Carriage. walk, bearing. deportment. gait, manner. behavior demeanor, vehicle, conveyance.
Ant. — Miscarriage. misconduct. misconveyance.

Carry, bear, sustain. convey, transport.
Ant.—Set down, drop, abandon. surrender.

Case, condition, state, circumstance plight. predicament, suit, process, cause
Ant. — Theory. supposition, conjecture. fancy, hypothesis.

Cast down. downcast, dejected, depressed, discouraged, melancholy.
Ant. — Raised, elevated, encouraged, excited, animated, impressed.

Cast off. (See Abandon.)

Casualty, accident, contingency, incident, occurrence. event, adventure.
Ant. — Appointment. enactment, assignment. provision.

Catalogue, list, roll, record. inventory, index.
Ant.—Individual. unit, fact.

Catch, overtake, lay hold of, grasp, seize, capture. grip, clutch, snatch, arrest. apprehend.
Ant.—Lose, miss, escape, release, liberate, misapprehend.

Catching. (See Contagious.)

Cause, *n.* source, origin. agent. producer. creator, motive, reason, incentive. inducement, incitement. impulse. effort, work, operation.
Ant.—Effect, result. end, issue, production, accomplishment, consequence.

Cause, *v.* occasion. make, induce, originate, give rise to, evoke, provoke, incite.
Ant.—Effect, prosecute, conduct, apply.

Caution, care, vigilance, circumspection, admonition. warning, notice.
Ant. — Heedlessness, recklessness, temerity, indifference, carelessness.

Cavity, gap. hollow, aperture, chasm, opening.
Ant.—Surface, level, projection plain, abrasion.

Cease, leave off, desist, discontinue, pause, end.
Ant.—Continue, begin, start, prosecute.

Cede, give up, surrender, relinquish, quit, forego.
Ant.—Claim, adhere to, hold, take, accept.

Celebrate, commend, applaud, laud, extol, magnify, glorify.
Ant.—Decry, disgrace, hiss. shame. blame, condemn.

Celebrated, famous. renowned. far-famed, illustrious, glorious
Ant.—Unknown, obscure, undistinguished, mean, disgraced.

Celerity. rapidity, velocity, swiftness. quickness, speed, fleetness.
Ant.—Slowness, sluggishness, inertness. tardiness.

Celestial, heavenly, divine. godlike, seraphic. angelic, radiant.
Ant. — Terrestrial, earthly mortal, human, infernal.

Censure, *v.* blame, reprove. reprehend, reprobate, condemn, upbraid, animadvert. criticize.
Ant.—Praise, approve, encourage. commend, eulogize.

Ceremonial, official, imposing. service
Ant.—Ordinary, private, unostentatious.

Certain, sure, indubitable, unquestionable, unfailing, secure real, actual, positive, assured, true.
Ant.—Uncertain, dubious, exceptional. doubtful, undecided. irregular. occasional, casual hesitating.

Certify, testify, vouch, declare, avow, prove, evidence.
Ant.—Disprove, disavow, misinform.

Cessation, intermission, rest, pause. discontinuance, abeyance. suppression, stop.
Ant. — Continuance, incessancy

Chafe, fret, irritate, gall, vex, chagrin, worry, annoy.
Ant.—Soothe, smooth, calm, console.

Champion, leader, chieftain, head, hero.
Ant.—Private, renegade, traitor, miscreant, poltroon. coward.

Chance, accident fortune, casualty. hazard, luck, fate.
Ant — Law rule, sequence causation. purpose, design, plan

Change, *v* alter, vary, transform, exchange, barter, modify, qualify, shift, veer, substitute.
Ant.—Retain, conserve, stabilitate, hold, fix, clinch.

Change, *n.* variety, alteration, alternation, vicissitude.
Ant. — Stability, fixity, unchangeableness, monotony uniformity.

Changeable, variable, undecided, hesitating, unsteady, vacillating, fluctuating, wavering, inconstant, unsteadfast, unstable, versatile. restless, fickle, fitful, capricious. mutable.

Ant.—Regular, settled, steady, stationary, consistent, uniform, immutable, unchangeable, unmovable, steadfast, dependable.

Character, cast, turn, tone, description, nature, disposition, reputation, class, order, sort, kind, mature, repute, standing.
Ant.—Vagueness, anonymousness, non-descriptive.

Characteristic, peculiar to, sign of, distinctive, specific.
Ant.—Common, general, ordinary generic, indistinctive.

Characterize, name, designate, denominate, describe, particularize, style.
Ant.—Suggest, hint, insinuate.

Charge, *v.* accuse, impeach, arraign, inculpate, attack, assault, carry.
Ant.—Acquit, discharge, clear, free, liberate, defend.

Charge, *n.* care, custody, ward, trust, management, cost, price, expense, account, fee, bill, assault, shock, onset, attack, accusation, impeachment, imputation.
Ant.—(See *v.*)

Charity, kindness, benignity, beneficence, benevolence, tenderness.
Ant. — Uncharitableness, harshness, cruelty, inhumanity.

Charm. (See Captivate.) Enchant, enrapture, fascinate.
Ant.—Repel, disgust.

Chary, wary, cautious, prudent, careful, sparing, reluctant.
Ant.—Liberal, lavish, profuse, eager.

Chastise, correct, castigate, punish.
Ant.—Indulge, pamper, spoil, demoralize, degrade.

Chastity, purity, continence, virtue.
Ant.—Lewdness, immorality,

Cheap, inexpensive, inferior, common.
Ant.—Dear, expensive, costly.

Cheat, *v.* defraud, trick, beguile, deceive, gull, dupe, delude, hood-wink.
Ant.—Deal fairly with, guide, undeceive, compensate, remunerate.

Cheat, *n.* deception, imposture, fraud, delusion, artifice, deceit, trick, imposition, imposter, rogue, trickster.
Ant.—Honesty, openness, exposure, artlessness, genuineness, dupe, gull, victim.

Check, curb, restrain, repress, control, counteract, chide, reprimand, reprove, rebuke.
Ant.—Loose, liberate, instigate accelerate, indulge, abet.

Cheer, *v* exhilarate, animate, inspirit, inspire, enliven, gladden, comfort, solace.
Ant. — Depress, sadden, dispirit, dishearten.

Cheerful, gay, merry, sprightly
Ant.—Mournful, sad, doleful.

Cheerfulness, gayety, sprightliness, merriment, mirth, liveliness, vivacity, joviality
Ant. — Depression, sorrow, tearfulness, dumbness.

Cheerless, disconsolate, brokenhearted, comfortless, inconsolable, desolate, forlorn.
Ant.—Cheerful, lively, gay happy, bonny, blithe, pleasant.

Cherish, nourish, nurture, nurse, foster, sustain, value.
Ant.—Dislike, hate, despise, stifle, abandon, discard.

Chief, principal, main, supreme, paramount, leader, head, chieftain, champion, cardinal.
Ant. — Inferior, subordinate, minor, unimportant, lower, defective, mean.

Choice, option, preference, election, selection, rare, select, precious, valuable.
Ant. — Necessity, rejection, compulsion, refusal, common, ordinary, inferior, cheap, valueless.

Choose, prefer, select, elect, call, pick.
Ant.—Refuse, leave, dismiss, reject, decline, ignore.

Circuitous, roundabout, tortuous, flexuous, tiresome.
Ant.—Straight, direct, linear.

Circulate, spread, diffuse, disseminate, propagate.
Ant.—Suppress, hush, avert, cease, stagnate.

Circumlocution, verbosity, ambiguousness.
Ant. — Terseness, conciseness, directness, coherence, simplicity.

Circumspection, watchfulness, vigilance, caution, deliberation, thoughtfulness, wariness.
Ant.—Heedlessness, recklessness, thoughtlessness, carelessness.

Circumstance, situation, condition, position, fact, incident, happening.
Ant.—Transaction, deed, case, occurrence.

Cite, quote, adduce, summon, call.
Ant.—Discredit, dispute, contradict, dishonor.

Civil, polite, complaisant, affable, courteous, obliging, urbane, well-bred.
Ant. — Disobliging, boorish, clownish, churlish, uncivil.

Civilize, polish, humanize, cultivate, refine.
Ant. — Demoralize, debase, vitiate, spoil, depress, injure.

Claim, *v.* ask, demand, challenge, call for, plead, insist.
Ant.—Disclaim, waive, forego, abandon, concede, surrender, repudiate.

Clamor, outcry, fuss, noise, hubbub, uproar
Ant. — Silence, acquiescence, quiet, reticence.

Clandestine, hidden, secret, private, furtive, surreptitious.
Ant. — Open, public, advertised, announced, unconcealed.

Class, order, rank, degree, grade, category, caste, tribe.
Ant.—Individuality singularity, specialty, isolation alienation, division.

Clause, stipulation, proviso, term, article, portion, section.
Ant.—Document, instrument, paper.

Clean, cleanse, clarify, purify.
Ant.—Dirty, vitiate, befoul, deteriorate, stain.

Clear, *v.* absolve, acquit, liberate, deliver, release, set free, unbind, clarify, disentangle, extricate.
Ant.—Involve, implicate, contaminate, befoul, polute, encumber, embarrass.

Clear, *a.* apparent, palpable, visible, obvious, plain, evident, manifest, unmistakable, distinct, intelligible, transparent, limpid, bright, lucid, vivid.
Ant.—Indistinct, thick, muddy, opaque, turbid, foul, unintelligible, dubious, entangled, confused.

Clemency. (See Mercy.)

Clever, skillful, expert, dexterous, adroit.
Ant.—Dull, stupid, slow, awkward, bungling clumsy, botched, unskilled.

Climax, summit, height, consummation, acme, culmination.
Ant. — Anti-climax, depth, base, floor

Climb, get up, scale, mount, soar, tower, ascend.
Ant.—Descend, drop, fall, slip, tumble.

Cling, hold, stick, adhere, attach, cleave, hang, embrace.
Ant. — Relax, forego, drop, abandon, let go.

Cloak, mask, veil, cover, blind, disguise, screen.
Ant.—Revelation, exposition, showing, exposure.

Clog, encumber, burden, hinder, impede, obstruct, embarrass, trammel, fetter.
Ant.—Aid, assist, help, release, encourage, instigate.

Close, *v.* conclude, shut, end, terminate, finish, stop.
Ant.—Open, initiate, protract, conduct.

Close, *a.* compact, solid, firm, dense, shut, fast.
Ant.—Wide, open, spacious, ample, airy, unconfined, public, liberal, frank.

Clothed, clad, dressed.
Ant.—Naked, disrobe, undress.

Clothes, garments, vestments, dress, habiliments, apparel, attire, array, raiment, vesture, drapery.
Ant.—Nudity, nakedness, nature, disarray.

Cloudy, dim, obscure, dark, dusky, murky, indistinct, shadowy, mysterious.
Ant.—Clear, bright, distinct, palpable, open, limpid.

Clumsy, awkward, unpolished, uncourtly, ponderous.
Ant. — Adroit, dexterous, clever, skillful, adept, handy.

Clutch, grasp, lay hold of, catch, seize, grip.
Ant.—Liberate, let go, release, emancipate.

Coagulate, thicken, curdle, mix, blend.
Ant.—Rarefy, expand, dissipate, subtilize, discombine.

Coalition, alliance, union, confederacy, league, combination.
Ant.—Dissociation, disruption, disagreement.

Coarse, rough, rude, rugged, gruff, harsh, vulgar, immodest, unpolished.
Ant.—Fine, delicate, choice, refined, polished, well-bred, high-minded.

Coax, cajole, wheedle, flatter, fawn.
Ant.—Coerce, intimidate, impel, instigate, drive.

Cogent, forcible, strong, valid, irresistible, resistless.
Ant. — Weak, feeble, powerless, ineffectual.

Coincidence, concurrence, correspondence, agreement.
Ant.—Design, purpose, adaptation, variation, difference.

Cold, frigid, wintry, unfeeling, stoical.
Ant.—Hot, fiery, impetuous, impulsive.

Colleague, fellow, compeer, companion, partner, assistant.
Ant. — Competitor, opponent, rival, antagonist.

Collect, gather, assemble, muster, congregate, accumulate, board.
Ant.—Distribute, dispense, divide, sort, dispose, deal.

Collected, composed, placid, calm, serene, cool, attentive.
Ant.—Distracted, excited, bewildered, dazed, scared.

Collision, clash, clashing, striking together, encounter, conflict.
Ant.—Divergence, shave, opposition, escape.

Color, hue, tint, tinge, complexion, dye, stain.
Ant.—Achromatism, paleness, nakedness, transparency.

Colorable, ostensible, plausible, specious.

Colossal. (See Enormous.)

Combat, *n.* engagement, conflict, contest, fight, action, battle.
Ant.—Peace, surrender, submission, truce, arbitration, mediation, reconcilliation.

Combat, *v.* oppose, resist, withstand, thwart.
Ant.—Help, aid, assist, reconcile.

Combination, alliance, union, league, confederacy, coalition, conspiracy, synthesis, cabal, plot.
Ant. — Disunion, dissolution, division, opposition, analysis.

Comely, becoming, decent, seemly, agreeable, graceful, shapely.
Ant. — Unseemly, ungraceful, unshapely, homely.

Comfort, solace, console, encourage, revive.
Ant.—Discomfort, trouble, annoy, grieve, wound.

Comfortless, cheerless, forlorn, disconsolate, inconsolable, desolate, wretched.
Ant. — Comfortable, cheerful, happy, bright, gay, easy, pleasant.

Comic, funny, laughable, ludicrous, droll.
Ant.—Pathetic, tearful, sad, melancholy, doleful.

Command, order, decree, injunction, mandate, precept, behest.
Ant.—Entreaty, supplication, petition, prayer, wish, intimation.

Commence, begin, enter upon, initiate, inaugurate.
Ant.—Terminate, end, finish, complete, conclude.

Commend, praise, applaud, extol, eulogize, recommend.
Ant. — Blame, censure, condemn, denounce, disapprove.

Comment, note, observe, criticize, expatiate, explain, illustrate.
Ant.—Confuse, obscure, misinterpret, mystify, misconceive.

Commerce, dealing, trade, traffic, intercourse, interchange, reciprocity, business, barter.
Ant.—Stagnation, dullness, inactivity, interdict, embargo.

Commit, perpetrate, do, intrust, confide, consign.
Ant.—Omit, miscommit, misconsign, misentrust, fail.

Commodity, goods, merchandise, ware.

Common, vulgar, low, mean, frequent, ordinary, usual, general, universal.
Ant.—Refined, excellent, unusual, rare, scarce, uncommon, exceptional, extraordinary.

Communicate, make known, divulge, disclose, reveal, impart, tell, adjoin, attach.
Ant.—Secrete, suppress, conceal, reserve, withhold, disjoin.

Communion, fellowship, converse, share, association, participation, Lord's supper, eucharist, sacrament.
Ant.—Exclusion, deprivation, non-participation, alienation.

Community, society, commonwealth, social state, aggregation, association, order, nationality, fraternity.
Ant.—Segregation, secession, independence, individuality, rivalry, hostility, animosity.

Commute, substitute, change, alter, exchange, barter.
Ant.—Perpetuate, disallow, misappropriate.

Companion, comrade, coadjutor, partner, ally, associate, confederate, fellow, colleague.
Ant.—Rival, foe, antagonist, adversary.

Company, association, society, assembly, assemblage, audience, auditory, corporation, troop, horde, crew.
Ant. — Individual, separation, rivalry, opposition, antagonism.

Comparison, simile, similitude, illustration.
Ant. — Contrast, opposition, dissociation.

Compass, encircle, environ, encompass, invest, enclose, surround, beset, bring about, realize.
Ant.—Expand, unfold, amplify, display, fail, bungle, botch.

Compassion, pity, commiseration, sympathy, condolence, clemency.
Ant. — Cruelty, hard-heartedness, unforgiveness, vindictiveness, severity.

Compassionate, kind, merciful, clement, benign, gracious, benignant.
Ant. — Uncompassionate, unkind, hard, cruel, severe, vindictive. relentless.

Compatible, consistent, consonant, accordant, harmonious.
Ant.—Incompatible, inconsistent, discordant, hostile, antagonistic, incongruous.

Compel, force, constrain, coerce, enforce, oblige, necessitate.
Ant. — Persuade, convince,

coax, allure, induce, tempt, seduce, lead.

Compendious, brief, short, succinct, concise, condensed.

Ant.—Diffuse, vague, prolix, cumbrous.

Compendium, compend, abridgment, abstract.

Ant.—Enlargement.

Compensate, recompense, make amends, remunerate, requite.

Ant.—Injure, damage, cheat, dissatisfy, defraud.

Compensation, amends, recompense, remuneration, requital, reward.

Ant.—Injury, loss.

Competent, able, capable, efficient, qualified, fitted, clever, skillful, sufficient, adequate.

Ant. — Incompetent, weak, inadequate, unqualified, unfit.

Competitor, candidate, rival, aspirant, antagonist.

Ant. — Colleague, assistant, partner, auxiliary.

Complain, murmur, lament, regret, repine.

Ant.—Rejoice, approve, applaud, exult.

Complaint, malady, disease, distemper, disorder.

Ant. — Health, sanity, soundness.

Complete, accomplish, fulfill, realize, execute effect, achieve, conclude, finish, end, fill up, terminate.

Ant. — Begin, commence, inaugurate, incomplete, disappoint.

Complex, compound, complicated, involved, intricate.

Ant.—Simple, obvious, plain, direct.

Complicated. (See Complex.)

Compliment, praise, flatter, adulate, applaud.

Ant. — Insult, wound, condemn, blame.

Comply. (See Accede.) Conform, submit, yield.

Ant.—Refuse, reject, oppose.

Compose, construct, form, compound, put together, constitute, soothe, calm, quiet, lull, hush, frame, indite.

Ant.—Dissect, analyze, pull apart, destroy, imitate, excite, annoy

Composed, serene, placid, calm, collected.

Ant. — Decomposed, excited, bewildered, imitated, vexed, angry

Compound (See Complex.)

Ant.—Simple, unmixed.

Comprehend, comprise, take in, embrace, contain, embody, include, conceive, imagine, apprehend, understand, grasp, perceive.

Ant.—Exclude, except, misunderstand, mistake.

Comprehension, capacity, capability knowledge, intelligence, understanding.

Ant.—Misunderstanding, misconception.

Comprehensive, extensive, broad, wide, inclusive.

Ant.—Exclusive, narrow, restricted, shallow.

Compress, condense, press, squeeze, abridge.

Ant.—Expand, dilute, diffuse.

Comprise, embrace, contain, include, comprehend, embody.

Ant.—Exclude, except, omit, reject.

Compromise, arbitrate, adjust, concede, implicate, involve, entangle, embarrass.

Ant.—Aggravate, perpetuate, extricate, exonerate, disentangle.

Compulsion, constraint, force, coercion.

Ant. — Persuasion, coaxing, inducement, temptation, seduction.

Compute. (See Calculate.)

Comrade. (See Companion.)

Conceal, hide, secrete, disguise, dissemble, suppress.

Ant.—Reveal, exhibit, expose, publish, divulge, confess, avow, uncover.

Concede. (See Allow.)

Conceited, proud, vain, egotistical, affected.

Ant.—Humble, natural, simple, unaffected, honest.

Conceive, think of, imagine, suppose, comprehend, understand, design, believe.

Ant. — Misconceive, execute, express, produce.

Concern. (See Affair.)

Concerning, respecting, with regard to, regarding, with reference to, with respect to, relative to, in relation to, about.

Ant.—Omitting, disregarding.

Concert, contrive, devise, design, manage.

Ant.—Oppose, disregard, mismanage.

Concise. (See Brief.)

Conclude. (See Close.)

Conclusion. (See Close.) Inference, deduction.

Concord, concert, chorus, harmony, unity.

Ant. — Discord, disagreement, variance, animosity.

Concourse, crowd, confluence, conflux, assembly, mob.

Ant. — Solitude, dispersion, conclave, desertion, cabal.

Concur. (See Agree.)

Condemn, blame, reprobate, reprove, reproach, upbraid, censure, reprehend, doom, sentence, disapprove.

Ant. — Acquit, absolve, exonerate, pardon, approve, justify.

Condense. (See Compress.)

Condition, state, plight, case, predicament, category, stipulation, covenant, article, term.

Ant. — Relation, dependence, situation, circumstance, concession, fulfillment, adaptation.

Condolence, sympathy, commiseration, compassion.

Ant.—Congratulation, exultation, indifference.

Conduce, contribute, subserve, lead, tend, incline, avail, aid, converge.

Ant. — Indispose, counteract, deject, neutralize.

Conduct, guide, lead, direct, manage, bring, control, govern, regulate.

Ant. — Misconduct, mislead, miscarry, mismanage.

Confederate. (See Abettor.)

Confer, bestow, give, discourse, converse, consult.

Ant. — Withdraw, withhold, contrast, conjecture, disassociate.

Confess. (See Avow.)

Confide, trust, repose, depend, rely, believe.

Ant. — Doubt, distrust, disbelieve.

Confidence, assurance, trust, faith, reliance, hope.

Ant. — Doubt, distrust, disbelief, misgiving.

Confident, dogmatic, positive, absolute, bold, presumptuous, sanguine.

Ant.—Doubtful, fearful, weak, cowardly.

Confine, limit, bound, circumscribe, restrict, restrain, shut up.

Ant.—Expand, extend, widen, loosen, liberate.

Confirm, ratify, establish, substantiate, corroborate, settle, strengthen, approve, attest.

Ant. — Cancel, annul, repeal, abrogate, refute, weaken, upset, contradict, combat.

Conflict, combat, contest, contention, struggle.

Ant.—Peace, quiet.

Conflicting, jarring, discordant, irreconcilable.

Ant.—Congruous, harmonious, consistent.

Conform, agree with, comply with, act according to, harmonize, adapt, suit.

Ant.—Unconform, dissent, disagree, secede, vary.

Confound, confuse, disconcert, bewilder, stun, astound, absorb.

Ant. — Elucidate, unravel, arrange, classify, enlighten.

Confused, muddled, mixed, promiscuous, indistinct, deranged, disordered, disorganized, bewildered.

Ant.—Clear, simple, plain, obvious, transparent, elucidated.

Confusion, disorder, derangement, disorganization, chaos, anarchy, misrule.
Ant.—Order, simplicity, charity, arrangement.

Confute, disprove, refute, impeach.
Ant.—Approve, second.

Congregate, assemble, collect, gather, muster, convene, convoke, bring together.
Ant.—Separate, disperse, depart, go away.

Conjecture, guess, surmise, supposition, hypothesis.
Ant. — Inference, deduction, proof, fact, calculation.

Conjure, adjure, beseech, entreat, implore.
Ant. — Deprecate, protest, remonstrate, expostulate.

Connect, join, link, bind.
Ant. — Disconnect, separate, unbind, break apart, disassociate.

Connected, joined, related, akin, kindred, relative, cognate, congenial.
Ant. — Unconnected, foreign, unrelated, opposed.

Connection. (See Alliance.)

Conquer, vanquish, subdue, overcome, subjugate, surmount, defeat, master.
Ant.—Succumb, surrender, resign, lose, fail, fall, cede, fly, retire, yield.

Conscious, cognizant, aware, sensible.
Ant. — Unconscious, unaware, unsensible.

Consecrate, sanctify, hallow, devote, dedicate.
Ant. — Desecrate, secularize, profane, pollute.

Consent. (See Assent.)

Consequence, effect, result, event, issue, sequence.
Ant.—Cause, antecedence, origin, causation.

Consider, reflect, regard, weigh, ponder, deliberate, think, observe, investigate.
Ant. — Guess, hazard, conjecture, disregard, ignore, forget.

Considerate, thoughtful, reflective, deliberate, prudent, provident, careful, judicious, cautious.
Ant.—Inconsiderate, thoughtless, careless, rude, selfish.

Consistent, accordant, constant, compatible.
Ant. — Inconsistent, shifting, self-contradictory.

Console, soothe, comfort, solace.
Ant.—Harrow, worry, harass.

Consort. (See Associate.)

Conspicuous, distinguished, noted, marked, prominent, eminent, preeminent, illustrious, famed.
Ant. — Inconspicuous, unknown, unimportant, unnoticeable.

Conspiracy, plot, treachery, intrigue.
Ant. — Legislation, congress, parliament, revolution.

Constancy, stability, firmness, steadiness.
Ant.—Fickleness, flightiness.

Constantly, ever, always, continually, perpetually, incessantly, everlastingly.
Ant. — Never, seldom, irregularly, occasionally, accidentally.

Constitute, make, form, compose, mold.
Ant. — Decompose, dissolve, destroy, abrogate, disorganize, annul.

Constitutional, legal, regulated, organized, radical, rooted, fundamental.
Ant.—Unconstitutional, tyrannous, revolutionary, accidental.

Constrain. (See Compel.)

Construct, build, make, erect, compile, constitute.
Ant. — Destroy, demolish, derange, overthrow

Construction, interpretation, version, explanation, view, reading, meaning.
Ant.—Misconstruction, misinterpretation, misunderstanding.

Consult, advise with, take counsel, deliberate, debate.
Ant. — Dictate, explain, expound, direct, order, command.

Consume, burn, absorb, spend, swallow, imbibe, engulf, devour, use, appropriate, utilize, employ.
Ant.—Construct, discard, disuse, reject.

Consumption. (See Consume.)

Contagious, infectious, pestilential, miasmatic, catching.
Ant. — Preventive, sporadic, endemic.

Contain, comprise, comprehend, include, embrace, hold, incorporate, embody.
Ant. — Drop, exclude, emit, discharge, afford, yield.

Contaminate, corrupt, defile, pollute, taint.
Ant.—Purify, ennoble.

Contemn, despise, disdain, scorn, scout.
Ant.—Respect, revere, venerate, regard, esteem, honor.

Contemplate, meditate, muse, think, observe, behold, ponder.
Ant.—Ignore, overlook, waive, abandon.

Contemporary, contemporaneous, coeval, simultaneous.
Ant.—Incontemporaneous, past, future, asynchronous.

Contemptible, despicable, paltry, pitiful, vile, mean.
Ant.—Noble, worthy.

Contemptuous, disdainful, scornful, supercilious, insolent.
Ant. — Humble, affable, courteous, respectable, modest, bashful.

Contend, contest, debate, argue, dispute, cope, strive, vie, wrangle, struggle, combat.
Ant. — Relinquish, surrender, concede, allow, waive, resign, succumb.

Contest. *n.* (See Contend.)

Contest. *v.* (See Contend.)

Contiguous. (See Adjacent.)

Contingency, casualty, accident, incident, occurrence, adventure, event.
Ant. — Purpose, design, order, cause.

Continual, unceasing, incessant, continuous, perpetual, uninterrupted, unremitting, endless, everlasting, constant.
Ant.—Occasional, rare, fitful, casual, interrupted, intermittent.

Continually, always, ever, constantly, incessantly, unceasingly, uninterruptedly, perpetually.
Ant.—Sometimes, occasionally, rarely, fitfully, interruptedly.

Continuance. (See Continuation.)

Continuation, continuance, endurance, duration, sequence, prolongation.
Ant.—Interruption, cessation, break, gap, discontinuance, pause.

Continue, persist, persevere, pursue, prosecute.
Ant.—Cease, stop, halt.

Contortion, distortion, twisting, writhing, wrestling, wrenching.
Ant. — Symmetry, uniformity, contour, configuration.

Contract, *v.* abbreviate, curtail, shorten, condense, abridge, retrench, reduce, agree.
Ant.—Expand, dilate, amplify, elongate, concede.

Contract, *n.* agreement, compact, bargain, stipulation, covenant.
Ant.—Release, dissolution.

Contradict, deny, gainsay, oppose.
Ant.—Confirm, strengthen.

Contrary. (See Adverse.)

Contribute, give to, cooperate, conspire, supply.
Ant.—Refuse, withhold, misapply.

Contrition, repentance, penitence, remorse.
Ant. — Impenitence, callousness, obduracy, reprobation.

Contrivance, plan, device, scheme, design, invention.

Ant. — Chance, venture, hazard.

Control. (See Govern.)

Controversy, debate, contest, discussion, disquisition, dispute.

Ant.—Agreement, unanimity, coincidence.

Convene, call together, bring together, convoke, assemble, congregate, muster

Ant. — Disperse, dismiss, disband.

Convenient, commodious, suitable, adapted, handy, timely

Ant.—Inconvenient, awkward, useless, unseasonable, untimely.

Convention. (See Assembly.)

Conventional, usual, ordinary, fashionable.

Ant. — Natural, unusual, immutable, invariable, compulsory, unfashionable.

Conversation, dialogue, conference, talk, parley, colloquy, chat.

Ant. — Speech, oration, harangue, soliloquy, monologue, silence.

Convert, change, turn, transform, apply

Ant. — Divert, conserve, perpetuate, clinch, alienate.

Convey. (See Carry.)

Convivial, joyous, festal, social, sociable, hospitable

Ant. — Churlish, unsociable, ascetic, inhospitable, austere.

Convocation. (See Assembly.)

Convulse, upheave, upturn, shake, agitate.

Ant. — Soothe, compose, assuage.

Cool, cold, frigid, dispassionate, unimpassioned, calm, undisturbed, composed, collected, tranquil.

Ant.—Warm, disturbed, heated, irritated, excited, inflamed.

Cooperate, assist, abet, conspire, conduce, contribute.

Ant. — Oppose, thwart, rival, counteract, antagonize.

Copious. (See Abundant.)

Copy, model, pattern, imitation, exemplar, transcript, facsimile, illustration, duplicate.

Ant.—Original, prototype, example.

Corporal. (See Bodily.)

Corpulent. (See Stout.)

Correct, *v.* right, mend, amend, rectify, better, reform, improve, chasten.

Ant.—Corrupt, falsify, spare.

Correct, *a.* accurate, exact, precise, proper, faultless, strict, rectify, reform.

Ant.—Incorrect, false, untrue, faulty, wrong, muddle.

Correspond, fit, tally, answer, suit, agree, match.

Ant. — Differ, disagree, jar, clash, vary.

Correspondence, letters, intercourse, communication, commerce, coincidence, concurrence.

Ant.—Conversation, colloquy, difference, reservation, withdrawal.

Corrupt, *v.* contaminate, defile, taint, pollute, infect, adulterate, demoralize, deprave, spoil.

Ant. — Purify, cleanse, ameliorate, better, mend, repair.

Corrupt, *a.* depraved, debased, vitiated, demoralized, profligate

Ant. — Incorrupt, pure, undefiled, good, honest.

Corruption, defilement, contamination, pollution, infection, adulteration, vice, depravity, corruptness.

Ant. — Purity, honesty, goodness, amelioration.

Cost, price, charge, expense, outlay.

Ant.—Receipt, profit, revenue, income, emolument.

Council. (See Assembly.)

Counsel. (See Advice.)

Count, calculate, compute, reckon, number, sum, estimate, rate.

Ant. — Underestimate, guess, hazard, conjecture.

Countenance, encourage, patronize, support, confirm, sanction.

Ant — Discountenance, discourage, oppose, confront.

Counterfeit, spurious, forged, imitated, supposititious, false, cheat, fraud, pretense, ruse.

Ant.—Truth, fact, verity, reality, detection, exposure.

Countless, innumerable, numberless, incalculable, unnumbered.

Ant.—Few, scant, sparse, numbered, limited.

Courage, resolution, fearlessness, prowess, bravery, fortitude, chivalry, intrepidity, boldness, firmness.

Ant. — Timidity, cowardice, pusillanimity, poltroonery.

Course, way, road, route, passage, race, career, series, process, succession.

Ant.—Disorder, deviation, error, caprice.

Courteous, affable, conciliating, kind, urbane.

Ant. — Rude, churlish, arrogant, uncivil, ungracious.

Courteousness. (See Affability.)

Covenant. (See Contract.)

Cover, shelter, screen, hide, overspread, overshadow, cloak, conceal, secrete.

Ant.—Expose, reveal, betray, exhibit, produce.

Covert, secret, clandestine, hidden, latent, concealed, cabalistic, mysterious.

Ant.—Open, exposed, exhibited, revealed.

Covet, desire, wish for, long for, aspire to.

Ant.—Dislike, despise, undervalue.

Covetousness, avarice, cupidity.

Ant.—Beneficence.

Cowardice, fear, timidity, pusillanimity.

Ant.—Courage, intrepidity.

Cozen, cheat, gull, dupe, defraud, impose upon, deceive, wheedle.

Ant. — Undeceive, disabuse, enlighten.

Crafty, cunning, artful, sly, subtle, wily, tricky.

Ant. — Honest, open, frank, candid, straightforward, artless, sincere.

Crave, beg, entreat, solicit, beseech, implore, supplicate.

Ant.—Demand, insist, require, seize.

Crazy, imbecile, foolish, crackbrained, brainless, idiotic.

Ant. — Sound, robust, clever, vigorous, talented, learned.

Create, make, form, cause, produce, generate, engender, invent.

Ant.—Destroy, annihilate, demolish.

Credence, belief, faith, confidence.

Ant. — Disbelief, distrust, denial.

Credential, missive, diploma, title, testament, seal, warrant, letter, introduction.

Ant. — Autocracy, self-appointment, self-constitution.

Credit, belief, trustworthiness, reputation, security, honor.

Ant.—Disbelief, distrust, censure, disgrace, shame.

Credulity, gullibility, simplicity.

Ant.—Incredulity, scepticism, suspiciousness, shrewdness.

Crest, top, summit, apex, head, crown.

Ant.—Base, foot, bottom, sole.

Crime, offense, misdeed, misdemeanor, felony, sin, vice.

Ant.—Good-deed, well-doing, duty, obligation, exploit, virtue, rectitude.

Criminal, illegal, felonious, vicious, iniquitous, sinful, guilty, nefarious, immoral, convict, culprit, felon, malefactor.

Ant.—Lawful, right, just, virtuous, moral, meritorious, benefactor.

Cripple, weaken, impair, curtail, cramp.

Ant. — Strengthen, renovate, augment, ease.

Criterion, test, touchstone, proof, standard.

Ant. — Glance, conjecture, scan haphazard.

Critical, nice, exact, fastidious, precarious, ticklish, crucial, important, hazardous.
Ant. — Uncritical, loose, easy, indiscriminately, inexact, safe, decided, settled.

Criticize, examine, scan, analyze, discuss, anatomize.
Ant. — Overlook, survey, slur, skim.

Crook, bend, curve, swindler, shepherd's staff.
Ant. — Straight, direct, upright.

Cross, ill-tempered, fretful, ill-humored, crusty, peevish, fractious.
Ant. — Amiable, genial, good-humored, good-tempered.

Crude, raw, undigested, unconsidered, half-studied, harsh, unshaped, unfinished, unrefined, ill-prepared.
Ant. — Refined, finished, ripe, well-prepared, well-digested, well-considered, elaborate.

Cruel, savage, barbarous, inhuman, malignant, brutal.
Ant. — Humane, forbearing, merciful, benevolent, generous, kind, gentle.

Cupidity. (See Avarice.)

Cultivate, promote, foster, improve, cherish.
Ant. — Neglect, discourage, blight, blast, uproot, eradicate.

Cultivation, culture, refinement.
Ant.—Barbarism, boorishness.

Curb, restrain, hold, check, moderate.
Ant. — Loosen, release, liberate, instigate, incite, impel.

Curiosity, inquisitiveness, interest, rarity, celebrity, oddity.
Ant. — Abstraction, indifference, heedlessness, disregard, bagatelle, song, cipher.

Curious, inquiring, inquisitive, searching, interrogative, prying, peeping, peering, rare, odd.
Ant. — Indifferent, incurious, uninterested, trite, common.

Curse, malediction, anathema, bane, blight.
Ant. — Blessing, benediction, joy, crown, glory.

Cursory, summary, rapid, superficial, desultory, hasty, slight.
Ant.—Minute, elaborate, profound, thorough, painstaking.

Custody, keeping, guardianship, conservation, care.
Ant.—Neglect, exposure, abandonment, liberation, discharge.

Custom, manner, habit, use, prescription, fashion, practice.
Ant. — Law, regulation, command, rule, disuse, unconventionality.

Cut, sever, slice, sunder, avoid.
Ant.—Unite, splice, accost, approach, address, salute.

Cutting, sharp, biting, trenchant, piercing, bitter, sarcastic.
Ant.—Mild, soothing, conciliatory, indulgent, consoling.

Cynical, sarcastic, snarling, sneering, cross-grained.
Ant. — Lenient, tolerant, genial, complaisant, urbane.

D

Dainty, choice, luxurious, rare, refined, tasteful, exquisite, epicurean, fastidious.
Ant.—Coarse, common, dirty, nasty, gluttonous.

Damage, injure, hurt, loss, impair.
Ant. — Benefit, repair, bless, compensate, enhance, improve.

Danger, peril, hazard, risk, jeopardy.
Ant. — Security, safety, precaution, custody, defense.

Dare, venture, face, brave, hazard, risk, defy.
Ant. — Shun, dread, fear, shrink, cower.

Dark, black, dusky, sable, swarthy, opaque, obscure, abstruse, unintelligible, blind, ignorant, dim, shadowy, somber, joyless, mournful, sorrowful, dismal.
Ant.—Light, fair, white, bright, radiant, transparent, lucid, intelligible, plain, festive, luminous, clear.

Dash, hurl, cast, throw, drive, rush, send, fly, speed, course.
Ant. — Raise, erect, creep, crawl, lay.

Date, facts, grounds, postulates.
Ant. — Assumption, conjectures, inferences.

Dauntless, valiant, gallant, fearless, intrepid.
Ant. — Timid, cautious, cowardly.

Dawn, gleam, begin, rise, open, break.
Ant. — Wane, set, sink, close, depart, end.

Dead, defunct, deceased, departed, gone, inanimate, lifeless, insensible, heavy, unconscious, dull, spiritless.
Ant. — Living, alive, animate, vivacious, stirring, bustling.

Deadly, fatal, destructive, mortal.
Ant.—Life-giving, immortal.

Deaf, insensible, disinclined, averse, inexorable.
Ant. — Attentive, alive, acute, interested, sensible, willing.

Dear, beloved, precious, costly, expensive.
Ant.—Despised, cheap.

Death, departure, demise, decease, dissolution, mortality, expiration.
Ant.—Birth, growth, rise, life, spirit, vigor, activity, action, vitality, inauguration.

Debase, degrade, lower, depress, deprave, deteriorate, corrupt, alloy.
Ant. — Enhance, exact, raise, purify, improve, promote.

Debate. (See Argue.)

Debatable, dubious, doubtful, uncertain, problematical, unsettled.
Ant.—Indisputable, incontestible, certain, sure.

Debility, weakness, feebleness, lassitude, languor.
Ant.—Strength, energy, vigor, nerve, robustness.

Debt, obligation, liability, default.
Ant. — Credit, assets, gift, gratuity, trust, favor.

Decay, decline, wane, dwindle, waste, ebb, decrease, consumption.
Ant. — Flourish, luxuriate, grow, increase, rise, growth.

Decayed, rotten, corrupt, unsound, decomposed, faded, unprosperous, impoverished.
Ant. — Sound, flourishing, wholesome, fresh, healthful.

Deceit, cheat, imposition, trick, delusion, guile, beguilement, treachery, sham.
Ant.—Truthfulness, sincerity, candor.

Deceive, cheat, delude, impose upon, over-reach, gull, dupe.
Ant.—Enlighten, inform.

Decide, determine, settle, adjudicate, terminate, resolve.
Ant. — Waver, suspend, moot, brood over, cogitate, doubt, misjudge, vacillate.

Decipher, interpret, read, spell, solve.
Ant.—Vacillation.

Decision, determination, conclusion, resolution, firmness.
Ant.—Indecision, uncertainty, irresolution, weakness.

Declaim, speak, debate, harangue, recite.
Ant.—Read, study, write, compose.

Declamation, oratory, elocution, harangue, effusion, debate.

Declaration, avowal, statement, manifestation, profession.
Ant. — Denial, concealment, suppression.

Declivity, descent, fall, slope, incline.
Ant. — Ascent, rise, mountain, verticality.

Decorum, seemliness, propriety, dignity, order.
Ant. — Disorder, impropriety, disturbance.

Decrease, diminish, lessen, wane, decline, retrench, curtail, reduce.
Ant. — Increase, amplify, ex-

pand, extend, grow, augment, wax.

Decree, decision, determination, law, edict, order, manifesto, rule, verdict.
Ant. — Request, hint, intimation, suggestion.

Decrepit. (See Infirm.)

Dedicate, devote, consecrate, offer, set, apportion, assign.
Ant.—Misuse, alienate, misapply, misappropriate.

Deed, act, action, achievement, commission, instrument, document, muniment.
Ant.—Non-performance, omission, failure, invalidation, reversion.

Deem, judge, estimate, consider, think, suppose, conceive.

Deep, profound, subterranean, submerged, designing, abstruse, learned.
Ant.—Shallow, superficial, familiar, artless, undesigning, easy, plain.

Deface, injure, mar, spoil, disfigure.
Ant.—Beautify, improve.

Default, lapse, forfeit, omission, absence, want, failure, neglect.
Ant. — Maintenance, appearance, presence, place, satisfaction, attention, effort, assiduity, diligence.

Defeat, conquer, overcome, worst, rout, frustrate, baffle.
Ant.—Succumb to, surrender, foil, aid, advance, establish.

Defect, imperfection, flaw, fault, blemish.
Ant. — Supply, sufficiency, compensation, ornament, beauty, perfection.

Defend, guard, protect, justify.
Ant. — Abandon, betray, defeat, accuse, charge, retreat.

Defense, excuse, plea, vindication, bulwark, rampart.
Ant. — Desertion, abandonment, surrender, exposure, accusation, charge.

Defer, delay, postpone, put off, prorogue, adjourn.
Ant. — Hasten, press, urge, hurry, expedite.

Deference. (See Honor.)

Deficient, short, wanting, inadequate, scanty, incomplete.
Ant. — Complete, sufficient, full, correct, satisfactory, adequate.

Defile, pollute, corrupt, sully, contaminate, spoil, stain.
Ant.—Cleanse, purify, ameliorate, better, hallow, sanctify.

Define, fix, settle, determine, limit, circumscribe.
Ant.—Confuse, obscure, mystify, misstate, confound, dilate, distend.

Definite, precise, exact, correct, fixed, determined.
Ant. — Indefinite, vague, obscure, undefined, confused.

Deformity, ugliness, disfigurement, hideousness, monstrosity.
Ant.—Regularity, grace, beauty, ornament.

Defray, meet, liquidate, pay, discharge, quit.
Ant. — Repudiate, dishonor, dissatisfy, misappropriate.

Degenerate, debased, fallen, impaired.
Ant.—Regenerated, advanced, improved.

Degree, grade, extent, measure, mark, range, quantity, amount, limit.
Ant.—Space, mass, magnitude, size.

Dejected. (See Melancholy.)

Deliberate, *v.* consider, meditate, consult, ponder, debate.
Ant.—Hazard, risk, chance.

Deliberate, *a.* purposed, intentional, designed, determined.
Ant. — Irresolute, playful, hasty, quick, dictated, suggested, rash, ill-considered.

Delicacy, nicety, daintiness, refinement, tact, softness, modesty.
Ant. — Coarseness, indelicacy, roughness, rudeness, vigor, robustness, boorishness, indecency.

Delicate, tender, fragile, dainty, refined.
Ant.—Coarse, rough, clownish.

Delicious, sweet, palatable.
Ant.—Nauseous.

Delight, enjoyment, pleasure, happiness, transport, ecstacy, gladness, rapture, bliss.
Ant.—Pain, suffering, sorrow, trouble, misery, discomfort, dejection, disappointment, depression, distress, melancholy, annoyance.

Deliver, liberate, free, rescue, pronounce, hand to, give.
Ant. — Confine, hold, take, capture, retain, appropriate.

Demand, claim, insist.
Ant.—Disclaim, waive, petition, request, supplicate.

Demonstrate. (See Prove.) Show, exhibit, illustrate.
Ant.—Hide, conceal, obscure.

Denominate, name, call, designate, denote.
Ant.—Misname, miscall, describe, suggest.

Denude, strip, divest, lay bare.
Ant.—Invest, clothe, drape, ornament, enrich.

Deny. (See Refuse.)

Depart. (See Leave.) Quit, decamp, retire, withdraw, vanish, levant.
Ant.—Remain, abide, stay.

Department, section, division, office, branch, province.
Ant. — Institution, establishment, state, whole, body.

Deprive, strip, bereave, despoil, rob, divest.
Ant.—Supply, invest, endow, compensate, present, donate, bestow.

Depute, appoint, commission, charge, entrust, delegate, authorize, accredit.
Ant. — Recall, dismiss, discharge, supersede.

Deputy, vicegerent, lieutenant, representative, agent, commissioner, delegate, proxy, substitute.
Ant.—Principal, master, chief, head, ruler, sovereign.

Derision, scorn, contempt, contumely, disrespect.
Ant. — Respect, regard, admiration, deference.

Derivation, origin, source, beginning, cause, etymology, root, spring, analysis.
Ant.—Result, issue, application, use.

Describe, draw, delineate, portray, explain, illustrate, define, picture.
Ant.—Confuse, caricature, distrust, suggest.

Desecrate. (See Defile.) Profane, secularize, misuse, abuse, pollute.
Ant. — Sanctify, consecrate, dedicate, employ, devote, purify, solemnize.

Desert, wild, waste, wilderness, solitude, void.
Ant.—Garden, oasis, pasture, field.

Deserve, merit, earn, justify, win.
Ant.—Undeserve, forfeit, lose.

Design, delineation, sketch, drawing, cunning, contrivance, artfulness.
Ant. — Structure, execution, performance, result, issue, candor, fairness, sincerity, chance, accident.

Desirable, expedient, advisable, valuable, acceptable, proper, judicious, beneficial, profitable, good.
Ant. — Undesirable, unadvisable, unprofitable, evil, detestable, obnoxious.

Desire, longing, affection, craving.
Ant.—Loathing, aversion, hate, repugnance, abomination.

Desist, cease, stop, discontinue, drop, abstain, forbear.
Ant.—Persist, continue, proceed, persevere.

Desolate, bereaved, forlorn, forsaken, deserted, wild, waste, bare, bleak, lonely.
Ant.—Cheerful, attended, consoled, cultivated, sheltered, fertile, frequented, gay, contented, happy.

Despair, hopelessness, despondency, desperation.
Ant.—Hope, confidence, elation, sanguineness, anticipation.

Desperate, wild, daring, audacious, determined, reckless.
Ant. — Hopeful, remediable, cautious, timid, propitious, calm, unmoved.

Despised, degraded, worthless.
Ant.—Admired.

Destine, purpose, intend, design, devote
Ant.—Divert, alienate, misapply

Destination, purpose, intention, design, consignment, object, end, fate, doom, use, scope, goal, aim.
Ant.—Project, effort, operation, tendency, exercise

Destiny, fate. decree, doom, end
Ant.—Will, freedom, volition, choice.

Destroy. (See Annihilate.)

Destructive. (See Hurtful.) Detrimental, noxious, injurious, deleterious, baleful, baneful, subversive.
Ant.—Creative.

Desuetude, disuse, discontinuance.
Ant.—Continuance.

Desultory, rambling, discursive, loose, unmethodical, superficial, unsettled, erratic, fitful, spasmodic.
Ant. — Consecutive, continuous, methodical, systematic, periodical, diligent, serious, thorough, painstaking.

Detail, *n.* particular, specification, minutiae.
Ant.—Generalities.

Detail, *v.* particularize, enumerate, specify.
Ant. — Generalize, abstract, condense, sketch, amalgamate.

Detect. (See Discover.)

Deter, warn, stop, dissuade, dispirit, discourage, dishearten, terrify, scare.
Ant.—Prompt, tempt, encourage, incite, persuade.

Detest. (See Hate.)

Destitute. (See Devoid.)

Detract, lessen, deteriorate, depreciate, diminish.
Ant.—Enhance, raise, increase, augment.

Detriment. (See Harm.) Loss, injury, deterioration.
Ant.—Benefit, help.

Detrimental. (See Hurtful.)

Develop, amplify, expand, enlarge, enunciate, unfold.
Ant. — Envelop, compress, restrict, contract, involve, stunt, dwarf, stultify.

Device, artifice, expedient, contrivance.
Ant.—Openness, fortune, luck, hazard.

Devious, tortuous, circuitous, round-about, distorted.
Ant.—Direct, plain, straightforward, frequented

Devoid, void, wanting, destitute, unendowed, unprovided.
Ant. — Provided, supplied, furnished, replete, full, complete.

Devolve, impose, place, charge, commission, befall, fall on
Ant.—Deprive, withhold, cancel, alienate, lapse

Devoted. (See Fond.) Attached, absorbed, dedicated
Ant.—Indifferent.

Devotion, piety, devoutness, religiousness, dedication, love, attachment
Ant. — Aversion, indifference, antipathy, alienation, apathy.

Devour, eat, consume, gorge, swallow, bolt
Ant.—Disgorge, vomit, emit.

Dictate, prompt, suggest, enjoin, order, command.
Ant. — Follow, obey, echo, answer, repeat.

Dictatorial, imperative, imperious, domineering, arbitrary, tyrannical, overbearing, commanding.
Ant. — Persuasive, humble, subservient, submissive, meek.

Die, expire, depart, perish, decline, languish, wane, sink, fade, decay.
Ant.—Live, begin, originate, grow strong, flourish, luxuriate.

Diet, food, nourishment, nutriment, sustenance, victuals, fare, cheer, regimen.
Ant.—Abstinence, starvation, fasting, gluttony.

Difference, separation, discord, dissent, disagreement, estrangement, variety
Ant. — Similarity, likeness, agreement, sympathy, uniformity, identity, consonance, harmony

Different, various, manifold, diverse, unlike, separate, distinct.
Ant.—Similar, like, congruous.

Difficult, hard, intricate, involved, perplexing, obscure, unmanageable
Ant. — Easy, plain, simple, lucid, tractable, favorable, clear.

Diffuse, discursive, prolix, diluted, copious.
Ant.—Terse, laconic, epigrammatic, condensed, concise.

Dignify, aggrandize, elevate, invest, exalt, advance, promote, honor.
Ant.—Degrade, disgrace, humiliate, dishonor.

Dilapidation, ruin, decay, disintegration, crumbling, demolition.
Ant.—Solidity, freshness, integrity, roundness, reparation, structure.

Dilate, stretch, widen, expand, swell, distend , enlarge, descant, expatiate.
Ant.—Contract, narrow, restrict, constrict, concentrate, epitomize, condense, shrink

Dilatory, tardy, procrastinating, behind-hand, lagging, dawdling, lingering, slack
Ant. — Prompt, alert, eager, quick, beforehand, vigilant, nimble, quick, precipitate, swift, headlong

Diligence, care, assiduity, attention, heed, industry
Ant. — Indifference, carelessness, heedlessness, idleness, negligence.

Dimension, measurement, size, configuration, delineation.
Ant. — Segment, part, sector, fragment, mismeasurement

Diminish, decrease, lessen, reduce, contract, curtail, retrench.
Ant.—Increase.

Dingy, dim, dull, dusky, rusty, colorless, obscure, dead, somber.
Ant.—Bright, radiant, lustrous, shiny, glossy, gleaming.

Diplomatic, judicious, knowing, wise, prudent, sagacious.
Ant. — Undiplomatic, injudicious, awkward, bungling, ill-managed.

Disability, unfitness, incapacity.
Ant.—Ability, fitness, qualification, merit, power.

Discern, descry, observe, recognize, see, discriminate, separate, perceive.
Ant. — Overlook, confound, omit, undiscern, confuse, blend, mingle, involve.

Discernible, visible, conspicuous, manifest, palpable.
Ant.—Indiscernible, invisible, impalpable, obscure, minute.

Discernment, discrimination, far-sightedness, clearsightedness, penetration, observation, sagacity.
Ant. — Dullness, stupidity, blindness, heedlessness.

Discipline, order, strictness, training, coercion, punishment, organization.
Ant.—Disorder, confusion, rebellion, disorganization, encouragement, demoralization.

Disclose. (See Reveal.)

Discomfort, disquiet, vexation, annoyance, trouble.
Ant.—Comfort, ease, pleasure, agreeableness.

Disconcert, abash, confuse, confound, upset, baffle, derange, discompose, frustrate, discomfit.
Ant.—Rally, aid, untangle, encourage, arrange, order.

Disconsolate, sad, forlorn, melancholy, unhappy, desolate, woeful.

Ant.—Cheerful, joyous, blithe, merry, happy.

Discover, make known, find, invent, contrive, expose, reveal, detect.
Ant.—Conceal, suppress, mask, screen, cover, lose, secrete, miss.

Discredit, *v.* disbelieve, distrust, disgrace, dishonor.
Ant.—Credit, believe, trust.

Discredit, *n.* disgrace, disrepute, dishonor.
Ant. — Credit, honor, trust, faith, belief.

Discreditable, shameful, disgraceful, scandalous, disreputable.
Ant. — Honorable, favorable, worthy, confident, trusty, creditable.

Discreet, cautious, prudent, wary, judicious, considerate, politic, provident.
Ant.—Indiscreet, foolish, impudent, reckless, silly, thoughtless, unwary.

Discrepancy, difference, disagreement, variance.
Ant.—Agreement, consonance, similarity.

Discrimination, judgment, acuteness, discernment, caution.
Ant.—Obtuseness, gullibility.

Discuss. (See Argue.)

Disdain. (See Scorn.)

Disease, complaint, malady, disorder, ailment, sickness.
Ant.—Health, wholesomeness.

Disgrace, *n.* disrepute, reproach, dishonor, shame, odium.
Ant.—Honor, favor, confidence, trust.

Disgrace, *v.* (See Dishonor.) Debase, degrade, defame, discredit.
Ant.—Exalt.

Disgust, dislike, distaste, loathing, abomination, abhorrence.
Ant.—Fondness, partiality, liking, desire, avidity, relish, admiration.

Dishonest, unjust, fraudulent, unfair, deceitful, cheating, deceptive, wrongful.
Ant.—Honest, just, honorable, equitable, right, upright.

Dishonor, disgrace, shame, degrade, ravish, pollute.
Ant.—Honor, justify, improve, enhance, raise, better.

Dislike. (See Antipathy.)

Dismal, dreary, gloomy, lonesome, dull, melancholy, sad, pitiable, cheerless.
Ant.—Cheerful, gay, propitious, joyous, lively.

Dismay, *v.* terrify, frighten, scare, daunt, appal, dishearten.
Ant.—Inspirit, encourage, allure.

Dismay, *n.* **(See** *v.***)** Terror, dread, fear, fright.
Ant.—Assurance, confidence.

Dismiss, send off, discharge, discard, banish.
Ant.—Recall, retain, detain, keep.

Disorder, disease, malady, complaint, confusion, derangement.
Ant.—Order, health, sanity, arrangement, method, system.

Disorderly, irregular, confused, lawless, unruly.
Ant.—Orderly, regular, systematized, lawful, governable, amenable, pure.

Disown. (See Renounce.)

Dispel. (See Scatter.) Drive away, disperse, dissipate.
Ant.—Collect, gather.

Disperse. (See Distribute.)

Display, show, spread out, exhibit, expose.
Ant.—Hide, conceal.

Displease, offend, vex, anger, provoke, irritate.
Ant.—Please, amuse, gratify.

Dispose, arrange, array, place, order.
Ant.—Confuse, disarrange.

Dispute, *v.* argue, contest, contend, question, impugn.
Ant.—Waive, concede, allow, forego, assent.

Dispute, *n.* argument, debate, controversy, quarrel, disagreement.
Ant. — Agreement, decision, council, harmony.

Disregard, slight, neglect, despise, disparage.
Ant.—Regard, honor, exalt, listen, attend, hear.

Dissent, disagree, differ, vary.
Ant.—Assent.

Dissolve. (See Melt.)

Distance, interval, remoteness, space.
Ant.—Nearness, proximity, adjacency, contact, presence.

Distinct, clear, plain, obvious, different, separate.
Ant.—Dim, obscure.

Distinguish, perceive, discern, mark out, divide, discriminate.
Ant. — Miss, overlook, confound, confuse.

Distinguished, famous, glorious, far-famed, noted, illustrious, eminent, celebrated.
Ant.—Undistinguished, dishonored, disgraced, unknown, obscure, ordinary.

Distract, disturb, perplex, bewilder.
Ant.—Calm, soothe, reassure.

Distress, trouble, pain, afflict, grieve, take, seize, distrain.
Ant.—Soothe, compose, console, comfort, please, gratify.

Distribute, allot, share, dispense, apportion, deal.
Ant.—Receive, retain, withhold, restrict, keep, collect.

Disturb, derange, discompose, agitate, rouse, interrupt, confuse, annoy, trouble, vex, worry, perplex.
Ant.—Soothe, pacify, compose, quiet, order, arrange.

Disuse, discontinuance, abolition, desuetude.
Ant.—Use.

Divert, please, gratify, amuse, entertain, alter, change, deflect.
Ant.—Annoy, disturb, distress, prolong, continue, confine.

Divide, part, separate, sever, deal out, distribute, sunder.
Ant.—Unite, join, gather, convene, classify, combine, associate.

Divine, Godlike, holy, heavenly, sacred—a parson, clergyman, minister.
Ant.—Profane, unholy, devilish, satanic, layman, fiendish, diabolical.

Do, effect, make, perform, accomplish, finish, transact.
Ant.—Undo, omit, neglect.

Docile, tractable, teachable, compliant, tame.
Ant.—Stubborn, obstinate, intractable, mulish, unruly, pig-headed.

Doctrine, tenet, articles of belief, creed, dogma, teaching.
Ant.—Practice, conduct, action, duty, deed, performance.

Doleful, dolorous, woebegone, rueful, dismal, piteous.
Ant.—Joyous, happy, cheerful, merry.

Domicile. (See Abode.)

Doom, sentence, verdict, judgment, fate, lot, destiny.
Ant.—Pardon, liberation, respite, acquittal, salvation.

Doubt, uncertainty, suspense, hesitation, scruple, ambiguity.
Ant.—Certainty, precision, decision, conviction, determination, clearness, satisfaction, belief, faith.

Draw, pull, haul, attract, inhale, sketch, drag.
Ant.—Push, carry, propel, repel, impel, throw, thrust, describe, exhale.

Dread, fear, horror, terror, alarm, dismay, awe.
Ant.—Courage, confidence, assurance, boldness.

Dreadful, fearful, frightful, shocking, awful, horrible, horrid, terrific.
Ant.—Hopeful, inspiriting, encouraging, promising, attractive, pleasing, desirable.

Dress, clothing, attire, apparel, garments, costume, garb, livery.
Ant.—Nudity, nakedness, undress, disarrangement.

Drift, purpose, meaning, scope, aim, tendency, direction.
Ant.—Aimlessness, vagueness, indefiniteness, pointlessness.

Drill, train, teach, discipline, perforate, bore.

Ant.—Disorder, confuse, disarrange.

Drive, force, urge, press, compel, guide, direct.
Ant.—Draw, pull, hinder, obstruct, discourage.

Droll, funny, laughable, comic, whimsical, queer, amusing.
Ant. — Sad, lugubrious, funereal, tragic, solemn, grave, mirthless.

Drown, inundate, swamp, submerge, overwhelm, engulf.
Ant.—Dry, drain, expose, air, ventilate, resuscitate, emerge.

Drowsy, sleepy, heavy, dozy.
Ant.—Awake, alive, alert, vigilant.

Dry, arid, parched, lifeless, dull, tedious, uninteresting, meager, tiresome.
Ant.—Wet, moist, juicy, fresh, lively, entertaining, damp.

Due, owing to, attributable to, just, fair, proper, right.
Ant.—Undue, irrelative, independent, unfair, improper, deficient, exorbitant, unjust.

Dull, stupid, blunt, gloomy, sad, dismal, commonplace, opaque, cloudy.
Ant.—Sharp, clever, lively, animated, bright, brilliant, clear, interesting, entertaining.

Dunce, simpleton, fool, ninny, idiot.
Ant.—Sage, philosopher.

Dupe. (See Cheat.)

Durable, lasting, permanent, abiding, continuing.
Ant. — Perishable, unstable, transient, evanescent, ephemeral, perishable.

Dutiful. (See Obedient.)

Dwell, stay, stop, abide, sojourn, linger, tarry.
Ant.—Move, travel, wander, roam, migrate, flit, stray.

Dwindle, pine, waste, diminish, decrease, fall off.
Ant.—Enlarge, increase, flourish, develop, augment, grow.

E

Eager, hot, ardent, impassioned, forward, impatient.
Ant.—Listless, cool, indifferent, sluggish, diffident, detached.

Early, soon, by and by, shortly, ere long, anon, betimes.
Ant.—Late, backward, tardy, belated.

Earn, acquire, obtain, win, gain, achieve.
Ant.—Steal, lose, spend, waste, forfeit, forego.

Earnest, *a.* ardent, serious, grave, solemn, warm, pledge.
Ant.—Playful, flippant, idle, irresolute, indifferent, trifling, frivolous.

Earnest, *n.* pledge, pawn.

Ease, *n.* comfort, rest.
Ant.—Worry, discomfort, unrest.

Ease, calm, alleviate, allay, mitigate, appease, assuage, pacify, disburden, rid.
Ant.—Trouble, annoy, vex, incommode, excite, worry, disturb.

Easy, light, comfortable, unconstrained.
Ant.—Difficult, hard.

Eccentric, irregular, anomalous, singular, odd, abnormal, wayward, particular, strange, fussy, meticulous.
Ant.—Regular, ordinary, customary, normal, usual.

Eclipse, shade, overcast, cloud, overshadow.
Ant. — Brighten, enhance, heighten.

Economical, sparing, saving, provident, thrifty, frugal, careful, niggardly.
Ant. — Extravagant, wasteful, improvident, generous, loose, open-handed, prodigal, lavish.

Edge, border, brink, rim, brim, margin, verge.
Ant.—Middle, center.

Efface, blot out, expunge, obliterate, wipe out, cancel, erase.
Ant.—Restore, revive, portray, delineate, preserve, insert.

Effect, *n.* consequence, result, issue, event, execution, operation.
Ant.—Cause, origin, source, antecedent, purpose, reason, motive.

Effect, *v.* accomplish, fulfil, realize, achieve, execute, operate, complete.
Ant.—Prevent, obviate, mar, frustrate, fail, fall short, yield.

Effective, efficient, operative, serviceable.
Ant.—Weak, ineffective, futile, inoperative, vain, ineffectual, footless.

Effects. (See Property.)

Effectual. (See Effective.)

Efficacy, efficiency, energy, agency, instrumentality.
Ant.—Inefficiency, uselessness, futility.

Efficient, effectual, effective, competent, capable, able, fitted.
Ant.—Inefficient, useless, unable, unfitted, incompetent, futile, feckless.

Eject, thrust out, cast out, expel, oust, dislodge, throw out, dispossess.
Ant.—Receive, retain, accept, accommodate, lodge, welcome, admit, inject, introduce.

Elaborate, labored, studied.
Ant.—Simple, plain, unstudied.

Elapse, lapse, guide, pass.
Ant.—Wait, abide, hold, continue.

Elastic, ductile, flexible.
Ant.—Inelastic, rigid, inflexible, tough.

Elementary, primary, rudimentary, physical, material, natural, component, constituent, ultimate.
Ant. — Enveloped, organized, immaterial, incorporeal.

Eligible, fit, desirable.
Ant. — Ineligible, unfit, unworthy, worthless.

Eliminate, drive out, expel, thrust out, eject, cast out, dislodge, banish, proscribe, oust.
Ant.—Add, import, foist, involve, invite, welcome.

Eloquence, oratory, rhetoric, declamation.

Elucidate, make plain, explain, clear up, illustrate.
Ant.—Mystify, obscure, confuse, muddle, perplex.

Elude, evade, escape, avoid, shun.
Ant.—Meet, confront, encounter, defy.

Embarrass, perplexed, entangle, abash, distress, trouble.
Ant.—Assist, help.

Embellish, adorn, decorate, bedeck, beautify, deck.
Ant.—Disfigure, deface, mar.

Embolden, encourage, inspirit, animate, cheer, urge, impel, stimulate.
Ant.—Discourage, dishearten, deter.

Embrace, clasp, hug, comprise, comprehend, contain, include, embody, incorporate.
Ant.—Exclude, reject, except.

Eminent, illustrious, distinguished, signal, conspicuous, noted, prominent, elevated, renowned, famous, glorious.
Ant.—Low, obscure, unknown, unimportant.

Emit, discharge, give out, throw out, exhale, vent.
Ant.—Admit, inhale.

Emotion, perturbation, agitation, trepidation, tremor, mental conflict.
Ant. — Insensibility, indifference, impressiveness, stoicism, poise, repose, calm.

Employ, occupy, busy, take up with, engross, use, apply.
Ant.—Dismiss, discard, misuse, discharge.

Employment, business, avocation, engagement, office, function, trade, profession, occupation, calling, vocation.
Ant. — Idleness, slothfulness, leisure.

Empty, *v.* evacuate, exhaust, drain, draw out.
Ant.—Fill, supply, replenish, glut, swell, increase.

Empty, *a.* void, devoid, hollow, unfilled, unoccupied, unfurnished.
Ant.—Full, supplied, occupied, inhabited.

Enchanted, charmed, captivat-

ed, fascinated, spell-bound, transported, enchained, entranced, electrified, wrapt.
Ant.—Disenchanted, disgusted, repelled, horrified.

Encircle. (See Encompass.)

Enclose, fence in, confine, circumscribe.
Ant.—Expose, open, disclose, develop.

Encompass, encircle, surround, environ, beset, begird, invest.
Ant.—Open, disinclose, disencircle, avoid, withdraw.

Encounter, attack, conflict, combat, assault, onset, engagement, battle, action.
Ant.—Escape, retreat, surrender, defeat, plight.

Encourage, countenance, support, foster, cherish, sanction, inspirit, embolden, animate, cheer, incite, urge, impel, stimulate.
Ant. — Discourage, dissuade, deter, dispirit, daunt, deject, depress.

End, *n.* aim, terminate, object, purpose, result, conclusion, upshot, close, expiration, termination, extremity, sequel,
Ant.—Beginning, commencement, introduction, incipiency.

Endanger. (See Imperil.)

Endeavor, try, attempt, essay, strive, aim.
Ant.—Relax, shirk.

Endless, everlasting, perpetual, deathless, undying, imperishable, infinite, interminable.
Ant. — Terminable, limited, transient, brief, periodic, finite.

Endorse. (See ratify.)

Endue, invest, endow, enrich, store.
Ant.—Denude, strip, deprive, divest, spoiliate.

Endurance, fortitude, patience, resignation.
Ant.—Weakness, cowardice.

Endure, last, continue, support, bear, sustain, suffer, brook, submit to, undergo.
Ant.—Perish, succumb, stop, give way, fail, wane.

Enemy, adversary, foe, antagonist, opponent.
Ant.—Friend, comrade.

Energetic, effectual, efficacious, powerful, binding, stringent, forcible, nervous, active, industrious.
Ant.—Lazy, slothful, ineffectual, weak, slow, idle, indolent, passive, sluggish, slothful.

Energy, force, vigor, efficacy, potency, strength.
Ant. — Laziness, weakness, slowness.

Engage, employ, busy, occupy, attract, invite, allure, entertain, engross, take up, enlist.
Ant.—Refuse, dismiss, discard, disengage, withdraw.

Engagement, word, promise, battle, action, combat, conflict.
Ant.—Declination, refusal, dismissal, skirmish, retreat.

Engross, absorb, engulf, take up, occupy, engage, monopolize.

Engulf, swallow, absorb, imbibe, drown, submerge, bury, entomb, overwhelm.
Ant.—Cast out, disgorge, disperse, dissipate, eject, emit, exude.

Enjoin, order, ordain, appoint, prescribe.
Ant.—Release, recall, dispense, dissuade, accept, follow, obey, yield, submit.

Enjoyment, pleasure, gratification.
Ant.—Pain, sorrow, sadness.

Enlarge, increase, extend, augment, broaden, swell.
Ant.—Diminish, contract.

Enlighten, illumine, illuminate, instruct, inform.
Ant.—Obscure, perplex, confuse.

Enliven, animate, cheer, vivify, stir-up, inspire, exhilarate.
Ant.—Deaden, benumb, dispirit.

Enmity, invidiousness, animosity, hatred, hostility, ill-will, malignity, maliciousness.
Ant.—Love, affection, esteem, cordiality, friendliness, good will.

Enormous, gigantic, colossal, huge, vast, immense, prodigious.
Ant. — Diminutive, insignificant, trivial, ordinary, venial, little, small, petty.

Enough, sufficient, plenty abundance.
Ant.—Bare, scant, inadequate, insufficient, want, lack, paucity, poverty.

Enraged, infuriated, raging, wrathful, maddened .
Ant.—Soothed, quieted, tamed, pacified, pacific, mollified.

Enrapture, captivate, enchant, fascinate, charm, bewitch.
Ant.—Repel, revolt.

Enroll, enlist, list, register, record.
Ant.—Disrate, disqualify.

Entangle, embarrass, inveigle, implicate, involve, compromise, ensnare, entrap.
Ant. — Disentangle, unravel, extricate.

Enterprise, adventure, undertaking, effort, endeavor, attempt.
Ant.—Matter of fact, indifference.

Entertainment. (See Amusement.)

Enthusiasm, zeal, ardor, fervor, warmth, fervency, earnestness, devotion, intensity, vehemence.
Ant. — Indifference, coldness, callousness, repugnance, contempt, ennui, caution, wariness.

Enthusiast, fanatic, visionary.
Ant.—Indifferentist.

Entice. (See Allure.)

Entire, whole, complete, perfect, total.
Ant. — Partial, incomplete, broken, impaired.

Entitled, named, designated, denominated, styled, characterized, qualified, fit.
Ant.—Unentitled, unfit, disqualified, disabled.

Entrance, entry, inlet, ingress, porch, portal.
Ant.—Exit, egress, departure.

Entreat, beg, crave, solicit, beseech, implore, supplicate.
Ant.—Command, insist, order, bid, enjoin.

Enumerate, tell, relate, narrate, recount, specify, detail, reckon.
Ant.—Lump, mass, miscount, confound.

Envy, invidiousness, jealousy, suspicion, grudging.
Ant.—Satisfaction, generosity, gratification.

Epitome, abridgment, compendium, abstract, summary, digest.
Ant. — Amplification, expansion, enlargement, whole.

Equal, *n.* fellow, colleague, companion, peer, compeer.
Ant.—Inferior, superior, enemy, opponent.

Equal, *a.* equable, even, uniform, alike, adequate, sufficient, compensating, equivalent, impartial, same, like.
Ant.—Unequal, uneven, ununiform, unlike, inadequate, insufficient, disparate, dissimilar, different.

Equitable. (See Just.)

Era. (See Age.)

Eradicate, root out, extirpate, exterminate, annihilate.
Ant.—Implant, inculcate, instill.

Erase, scratch out, blot out, expunge, efface, cancel.
Ant.—Insert, mark, add, write, delineate.

Erect, set up, raise, elevate, construct, establish, institute, found.
Ant.—Lower, depress, overthrow, demolish, remove, destroy.

Erroneous, incorrect, inaccurate, faulty, inexact.
Ant.—Exact, correct.

Error, mistake, fallacy, blunder, fault.
Ant.—Correct, true, proper, honest, accuracy, precision.

Escape, elude, evade.
Ant. — Confront, encounter, meet, incur.

Escort. (See Accompany.)

Especially, particularly, specially, mainly, principally, chiefly.
Ant.—Generally, universally, commonly.

Essay, attempt, dissertation, tract, treatise.

Essential, necessary, indispensable, requisite, vital.
Ant.—Accidental, unnecessary, superfluous, redundant.

Establish, institute, found, organize, confirm, settle, fix, build up, strengthen.
Ant. — Overthrow, demolish, destroy, disestablish, unsettle, upset, refute, suppose, guess.

Estate, domain, demesne, lands, property, possessions.
Ant.—Waste, chattels, comity, goods, effects.

Esteem, prize, value, appreciate, respect, regard, reverence, venerate, revere, deference.
Ant.—Dislike, decry, undervalue, depreciate, contempt, scorn.

Estimate, calculate, appraise, compute, rate.

Estrangement, abstraction, alienation.
Ant.—Reconciliation.

Eternal, everlasting, endless, infinite, perpetual, deathless, immortal, undying, imperishable.
Ant. — Temporal, finite, transient, ephemeral, limited.

Evade, elude, equivocate, prevaricate, baffle.
Ant.—Confront, meet, encounter.

Evasion, shift, subterfuge, prevarication, quibble, equivocation.
Ant. — Honesty, uprightness, frankness, straightforwardness.

Even, equal, equable, smooth, plain, level, uniform.
Ant.—Uneven, unequal, variable, inclined, abrupt, rough, jagged.

Event, incident, occurrence, accident, adventure, issue, result, consequence.
Ant.—Cause, antecedent, operation, inducement, tendency.

Ever, always, eternally, everlastingly, evermore, aye, perpetual, continually, incessantly, endless, infinite.
Ant. — Never, momentarily, transiently.

Everlasting. (See Ever.)

Evidence, *n.* testimony, deposition, declaration.
Ant. — Surmise, conjecture, concealment, refutation.

Evidence, *v.* manifest, evince, demonstrate, exemplify.
Ant.—Conceal, surmise, hide, conjecture.

Evident. (See Apparent.)

Evil, ill, wicked, bad, unfair, mischievous, harmful, misfortune.
Ant.—Good, wholesome, beneficial, felicitous.

Evince, show, argue, prove, evidence, manifest, demonstrate.
Ant.—Conceal, suppress, negative.

Evoke, call out, invite, summon, challenge, provoke, elicit, produce.
Ant.—Silence, seal, prevent, stop, allay, stifle.

Exact, accurate, nice, particular, punctual.
Ant.—Careless, slip-shod.

Exaggerate, overstated, heightened, amplified, enlarged.
Ant.—Understated, mitigated, modified, qualified, palliated.

Exalt, raise, elevate, erect, lift up, dignify, ennoble.
Ant.—Debase, lower, depress, dishonor, defame, humble, degrade.

Examination, search, inquiry, research, scrutiny, investigation.
Ant. — Conjecture, hazard, guess.

Example, pattern, sample, model, specimen, copy, instance.
Ant.—Principle, law, rule, system, material, substance.

Exasperate. (See Irritate.)

Exceed, surpass, excel, outdo, transcend.
Ant.—Fall short.

Except, unless, save, saving, but.
Ant. — Counting, including, reckoning, admitting.

Exceptional, uncommon, rare, extraordinary.
Ant.—Usual, commonplace.

Excess, superfluity, redundance, redundancy.
Ant.—Deficiency, shortcoming, failure, temperance.

Excessive, exorbitant, extortionate, unreasonable, immoderate, inordinate, extravagant.
Ant.—Insufficient, scant, inadequate.

Exchange. (See Change.)

Excitable, irritable, susceptible.
Ant. — Insensible, composed, quiet, cool, self-possessed.

Excite, incite, arouse, awaken, stir up, disquiet, disturb, agitate, provoke, irritate, rouse.
Ant.—Allay, calm, quiet, pacify, quell, lull, soothe.

Exclaim, call out, shout, cry, ejaculate.
Ant.—Write, whisper, sign, intimate, draw.

Exclude, shut out, debar, preclude, seclude.
Ant.—Admit, include, open, retain, conserve.

Exclusive, sole, only, alone.
Ant.—Comprehensive, inclusive, comity.

Excursion, trip, ramble, tour, jaunt.
Ant.—Rest, peace, quiet, home.

Excusable, pardonable, venial.
Ant.—Inexcusable, unpardonable.

Excuse, palliate, mitigate, acquit, justify, absolve, dispense, exempt.
Ant. — Exact, charge, compel, condemn, accuse.

Execrable, abominable, detestable, hateful, accursed, cursed.
Ant.—Laudable, desirable, eligible, respectable.

Execute, accomplish, effect, fulfill, release, achieve, complete, finish, perform.
Ant.—Neglect, omit, drop, nullify, mar, frustrate, defeat.

Exempt, free, cleared.
Ant.—Subject, inculpated, incriminated.

Exemption, freedom, immunity, privilege.
Ant.—Liability, responsibility, amenableness.

Exercise, exert, practice, pursue, carry on.
Ant.—Rest, ease, relax, respite.

Exhale, emit, give out, smoke, steam.
Ant.—Absorb, inhale.

Exhaust, spend, drain, empty, deliberate.
Ant.—Fill, replenish, augment, invigorate, refresh.

Exhaustive, thorough, complete.
Ant.—Cursory, superficial.

Exhibition, show, sight, spectacle, pageant, representation.
Ant. — Concealment, mark, suppression, secretion.

Exigency, emergency.

Exile, banishment, deportation, expatriation, expulsion, proscription.
Ant.—Reinstate, recall, welcome, domesticate.

Exonerate, clear, acquit, absolve, discharge, justify.
Ant.—Charge, accuse, condemn.

Exorbitant. (See Excessive.)

Expand, spread, diffuse, dilate, extend, enlarge, amplify, unfold, develop.
Ant. — Contract, curtail, restrict, condense.

Expectation, expectancy, waiting for, hope, anticipation, confidence, trust.
Ant.—Realization, verification, exhibition.

Expedient, fit, necessary, essential, requisite.
Ant.—Inexpedient, disadvantageous, unfit.

Expedite, accelerate, quicken, hasten, facilitate, forward, advance.
Ant.—Hinder, retard, delay, obstruct, restrain.

Expel. (See Eject.)

Expend. (See Spend.)

Expensive, costly, dear, valuable, sumptuous.
Ant.—Cheap, poor, worthless, economical.

Experience, experiment, trial, proof, test.
Ant.—Conjecture, theory, hazard, hypothesis, intuition.

Experiment, proof, trial, test.

Expert. (See Adroit.)

Expiration. (See Termination.)

Expire. (See Die.)

Explain, expound, interpret, elucidate, clear up, illustrate.
Ant.—Mystify, obscure, confound, confuse, muddle, perplex, misinterpret.

Explanation. (See Explain.)

Explicit, express, plain, definitive, positive, determinate.
Ant.—Implicit, implied, suggested, limited, obscure.

Exploit. (See Achievement.)

Expound. (See Explain.)

Express, *a.* explicit, plain, positive, definitive, determinate, categorical.
Ant.—General, vague, undefined, loose.

Express, *v.* declare, enunciate, pronounce, articulate, denote, utter, signify, testify, intimate, tell.
Ant.—Hint, conceal, mystify, obscure, retain.

Expressive. (See Significant.)

Expunge. (See Erase.)

Exquisite, pre-eminent, superlative, consummate.
Ant. — Common, coarse, ordinary.

Extend, increase, stretch, elongate.
Ant. — Abridge, abbreviate, shorten.

Extensive, comprehensive, wide, large, expansive, diffusive.
Ant.—Contracted, limited, restricted, narrow.

Exterior, outward, outer, external.
Ant.—Interior, heart, core.

Exterminate, eradicate, root out, annihilate, extinguish.
Ant.—Propagate, populate, increase, augment.

Extinguish, abolish, destroy, extirpate, eradicate, kill.
Ant. — Establish, propagate, promote, fan, encourage, aid, replenish.

Extort, exact, wrest, wring, draw from.
Ant.—Coax, wheedle, cajole, cheat.

Extract, draw out, elicit, pump.
Ant.—Restore, resist, replace, incorporate.

Extraordinary, remarkable, signal, eminent, uncommon, peculiar, marvelous.
Ant.—Ordinary, usual, common, frequent.

Extravagant, prodigal, lavish, profuse, excessive, wild, absurd.
Ant. — Frugal, economical, sound, parsimonious, niggardly.

careful, rational, consistent,

Extreme, utmost, farthest, most distant, last, extravagant.
Ant.—Initial, primal, beginning, moderate, judicious.

Extricate, free, disengage, disentangle, disembarrass, liberate.
Ant.—Involve, enmesh, encompass, encircle.

Exuberant, plenteous, plentiful, luxuriant, abundant, rich.
Ant.—Scant, deficient, sparse, mean.

Exultation, transport, joy, triumph, elation.
Ant. — Depression, sorrow, grief, mournfulness.

F

Fable, apologue, novel, romance, tale.

Fabric, edifice, structure, pile, web, texture.
Ant.—Destruction, fragment, wreck, ruin, rage.

Fabricate, invent, frame, feign, forge, coin, make, construct.
Ant.—Narrate, copy, represent, portray, repeat, demolish, spoil.

Face, *n.* visage, countenance.

Face, *v.* front, confront, encounter.
Ant. — Avoid, escape, shun, elude.

Facetious, jocose, jocular, pleasant, witty.
Ant.—Grave, serious, dull, lugubrious.

Facile, easy, pliable, flexible, docile, manageable.
Ant.—Obstinate, determined, inflexible, self-willed.

Fact, reality, incident, circumstance, truth, deed.
Ant.—Fiction, falsehood, lie, delusion, invention, romance, supposition, theory.

Factor, agent.

Fail, to fall short, be deficient, decline, become bankrupt, waste away.
Ant.—Succeed, accomplish.

Failing, imperfection, weakness, frailty, foible, miscarriage, mishap.
Ant. — Virtue, power, vigor, strength.

Failure, omission, neglect, default.
Ant.—Success, achievement.

Faint, languid, weak, low, timid, dim, pale, feeble.
Ant.—Strong, vigorous, fresh, prominent, conspicuous, glaring, forcible.

Fair, clear.
Ant.—Stormy.

Fair, clear, bright, just, honest, equitable, impartial, reasonable.
Ant.—Lowering, dull cloudy, gloomy, foul, ugly, unfair, fraudulent, dishonorable, dishonest.

Faith, belief, creed, orthodoxy.
Ant.—Disbelief, infidelity, heterodoxy.

Faithful, true, loyal, constant.
Ant.—Faithless, treacherous, perfidious.

Faithless, unfaithful, false-hearted, treacherous.
Ant. — Faithful, true, firm, loyal, exact, accurate, close.

Fall, drop, sink, droop, decline, tumble.
Ant.—Rise, ascend, mount, climb, soar.

False, untrue, mendacious.
Ant.—True, correct, real, genuine, sound, authentic.

Falsehood, untruth, story, lie, fabrication, fib, falsity.
Ant.—Truth, fact, verity, reality, honesty.

Falter, halt, stammer, stutter, hesitate.
Ant.—Persevere, revolve, proceed, speed, discourse.

Fame, reputation, glory, renown, celebrity, honor, credit.
Ant.—Silence, disgrace, dishonor, hush, ignominy.

Familiar, free, frank, affable, conversant, intimate.
Ant.—Unfamiliar, new, unacquainted, rare, strange, uncommon.

Family, household, house, lineage, ancestry, race.
Ant.—Strangers, foreigners.

Famous, fame, celebrated, renowned, illustrious.
Ant.—Obscure, unknown, inconspicuous.

Fanciful, imaginative, ideal, fantastical, whimsical, capricious, grotesque, erratic.
Ant.—Natural, regular, sober, orderly, truthful, literal, practical, unimaginative.

Fancy, imagination, notion, conceit, vagary, frolic, inclination, liking, humor, thought.
Ant.—Reality, fact, law, truth, verity, aversion, honor, common sense.

Farewell, good-bye, adieu, leave-taking.
Ant.—Welcome, hail.

Farther. (See Promote.)

Farthest, most distant, extreme, remotest, utmost, uttermost.
Ant.—Nearest, adjacent, next, adjoining, neighboring.

Fascinate. (See Captivate.)

Fashion, custom, manner, mode, practice, form, usage.
Ant.—Eccentricity, strangeness, shapelessness, work, dress.

Fast, firm, solid, constant, steadfast, stanch, stable, steady, unyielding, inflexible, unswerving, wild dissipated,

gay, rapid, quick, fleet, expeditious.
Ant.—Loose, insecure, slow, tardy, virtuous, respectable, sluggish.

Fasten, fix, tie, link, stick, hold, affix, attach, annex.
Ant.—Unfasten, loose, undo, relax, detach, remove.

Fat, obese, corpulent, pursy, unctuous, rich.
Ant.—Lean, slender, barren, poor, scant.

Fatal, deadly, mortal, lethal, inevitable.
Ant.—Beneficial, wholesome, nutritious, salubrious, harmless.

Fatigue, weariness, lassitude, lanquor, enervation, exhaustion.
Ant.—Freshness, vigor, activity, vivacity.

Fault, blemish, imperfection, vice, failure, defect, omission.
Ant.—Perfection, correctness, completeness.

Favor, benefit, kindness, civility, grace, gift, boon.
Ant. — Disfavor, disapproval, refusal, denial, prohibition.

Fear, fright, terror, dismay, alarm, dread, trepidation, timidity, timorousness, consternation, apprehension.
Ant.—Boldness, confidence, courage, trust, assurance, bravery.

Fearless. (See Courageous.)

Fearful, afraid, timid, nervous, timorous, terrific, dreadful, awful, frightful, horrible, distressing, shocking.
Ant. — Fearless, bold, audacious, confident, hopeful, alluring, attractive.

Fee, charge, bill, account, reckoning.
Ant.—Favor, gift.

Feeble, weak, infirm, nerveless, forceless, failing, frail, enfeebled, debilitated, enervated, impotent, paralyzed, palsied.
Ant.— Strong, robust, active, effective, successful.

Feeling, emotion, sentiment, impression, sensation, consciousness, sensibility, susceptibility.
Ant.—Insensibility, coldness, callousness, imperturbability.

Feign. (See Pretend.)

Felicity, happiness, bliss, blessedness, beatitude, blissfulness.
Ant. — Unhappiness, sadness, gloominess, wretchedness.

Fell, cruel, inhuman, barbarous, merciless, ruthless, pitiless, remorseless, relentless, savage, ferocious, brutal.
Ant. — Generous, chivalrous, humane, lenient, propitious.

Fellow, comrade, equal, companion, colleague, mate.
Ant.—Foe, stranger, opponent, opposite, antagonist.

Fellowship, brotherhood, society, companionship, acquaintance, familiarity, intimacy.
Ant.—Severance, enmity, vendetta, disconnection.

Ferocious, fierce, savage, ravenous, voracious, cruel, inhuman, fell, barbarous, furious, wild.
Ant.—Gentle, docile, tame, harmless, calm, mild.

Fertile, fruitful, prolific, teeming, pregnant, productive, rich, luxuriant, plenteous.
Ant.—Sterile, barren, unfruitful, unproductive, unimaginative.

Fervid, glowing, ardent, impassioned, fervent, warm.
Ant.—Passionless, cool, apathetic, indifferent, phlegmatic.

Festal, festive, convivial, joyous, gay.
Ant.—Gloomy, deserted, solitary, sad, ascetic.

Festivity. (See Festal.)

Feud, fray, affray, boil, quarrel, dispute, enmity, strife.
Ant. — Friendliness, clanship, sympathy, reconciliation.

Fickle, unstable, inconstant, restless, fitful, variable, changeable.
Ant. — Reliable, stable, unchangeable, steady, trustworthy, uniform.

Fiction, romance, invention, falsehood, fabrication.
Ant.—Fact, truth, verity, reality.

Fictitious. (See Fiction.)

Fidelity, faithfulness, honesty, integrity, exaction.
Ant. — Treachery, disloyalty, untruthfulness, infidelity, inaccuracy.

Fiendish, diabolic, demoniacal, devilish.
Ant.—Angelic, divine, celestial.

Fierce. (See Furious.)

Fiery, hot, glowing, ardent, fervid, impassioned, passionate, impassionate, fervent, vehement.
Ant.—Cold, icy, tame, passionless, mild, quenched.

Fight, battle, action, engagement, combat, conflict, contest, encounter, contention, struggle.
Ant.—Pacification, reconciliation, truce, retreat.

Figure, image, allegory, emblem, type, symbol, form, shape, metaphor, picture.
Ant.—Misrepresentation, disfigurement, deformity.

Fill, satisfy, content, store, replenish, glut, gorge, stuff.
Ant. — Empty, drain, exhaust, diminish, subside, ebb.

Filthy, dirty, dingy, unclean, gross.
Ant.—Pure, sweet, clean.

Final, ending, ultimate, last, latest, conclusive, decisive.
Ant. — Inaugural, incipient, rudimentary, progressive, current.

Finale. (See End.)

Find, descry, discover, espy.
Ant.—Lose, overlook.

Fine, refined, delicate, pure, nice, handsome, pretty, beautiful, elegant, showy, subtle, minute.
Ant. — Coarse, large, rough, blunt, rude, illiberal, paltry, unaffected.

Fine, forfeit, forfeiture, mulct, penalty.
Ant.—Gift, donation.

Finite, limited, bounded, terminable.
Ant. — Infinite, unlimited, eternal, boundless.

Fire, glow, heat, warmth.
Ant.—Cold.

Firm, strong, robust, sturdy, fast, steadfast, stable, solid, constant, fixed.
Ant. — Loose, insecure, weak, irresolute, indulgent, wavering, unreliable, yielding.

First, primary, primitive, pristine, primeval, original, foremost, chief, earliest, paramount.
Ant.—Last, subordinate, subsequent, hindmost.

Fit, *v.* suit, adapt, adjust, equip, prepare, qualify, accommodate.
Ant.—Misfit, unsuit, misadjust, disqualify.

Fit, *a.* apt, suitable, meet, befitting, becoming, decent, decorous, expedient.
Ant.—Unfit, unsuitable, inadequate, inappropriate, inexpedient, unbecoming.

Fitful, fickle, unstable, unsteadfast, inconstant, mutable, versatile, restless.
Ant.—Regular, systematic, orderly, sober, equable.

Fix, *v.* fasten, tie, link, enlink, attach, stick, settle, establish, determine, define, limit.
Ant. — Unfix, displace, unfasten, untie, unsettle, disarrange, remove, disturb, change, transfer.

Flagitious, disgraceful, scandalous, heinous, monstrous.
Ant. — Honorable, creditable, meritorious, pardonable, excusable.

Flame, blaze, flare, flash, glare.

Flashy, showy, ostentatious, gaudy, pompous, tawdry.
Ant.—Subdued, dull, colorless, dim.

Flat, level, horizontal, even, insipid, mawkish, dull, spiritless, tasteless, lifeless.
Ant. — Hilly, rolling, uneven,

mountainous, exciting, thrilling, rugged.
Flattery, adulation, servility, cajolery.
Ant.—Insult, rebuke, reprimand, satire, censure.
Flavor, taste, relish, savor.
Ant.—Tastelessness, insipidity.
Flaw. (See Defect.)
Fleeting, temporary, transient, transitory, short-lived, ephemeral.
Ant. — Lasting, permanent, long-lived, eternal.
Fleetness, quickness, celerity, swiftness, speed, rapidity, velocity.
Ant.—Slowness, tardiness, inertness, sluggishness, laziness.
Flicker, flutter, quiver, waver, glimmer.
Ant. — Blaze, gleam, shine, stream.
Flexible, pliant, lithe, supple, ductile, pliable.
Ant.—Rigid, inflexible, hard, tough, inelastic, stiff, unbending.
Flightiness, levity, lightness, giddiness.
Ant.—Gravity, heaviness, sobriety.
Flimsy, light weak, superficial, shallow.
Ant. — Solid, sound, substantial, cogent, strong.
Fling, cast, throw, hurl, toss.
Ant. — Hold, keep, retain, grasp, snatch, arrest.
Flippancy, pertness, sauciness, lightness.
Ant.—Respect, gravity, sobriety, flattery, obsequiousness.
Flock, throng, crowd, swarm, shoal, congregate, assemble.
Ant.—Separate, disperse, scatter.
Flood, deluge, inundation, overflow, submersion, drowning.
Ant.—Drought, scarcity, drain, ebb, subsidence.
Flourish, thrive, prosper, wave, brandish.
Ant. — Decay, decline, fade, arrest, sheath, ground, degenerate.
Flowery, florid, ornate, embellished.
Ant. — Bare, nude, sober, chaste.
Fluctuate, waver, hesitate, oscillate, scruple, change.
Ant. — Persist, abide, stay, stick, adhere.
Fluctuating, wavering, hesitating, oscillating, vacillating, changing.
Ant.—Firm, steadfast, decided, resolute, stable.
Fluent, flowing, glib, voluble, unembarrassed, ready.
Ant.—Labored, strained, dribbling, difficult, unready, hesitating, halting.
Fly, soar, mount, tower.
Ant. — Crawl, sink, decline, descend.
Foe. (See Adversary.)
Foil, balk, defeat, frustrate, baffle.
Ant.—Aid, abet, assist, promote, advance, encourage.
Fold, wrap, envelop.
Ant.—Unfold, disengage, expose.
Folks, persons, people, individuals.
Follow, succeed, ensue, imitate, copy, pursue.
Ant.—Lead, precede, disobey, avoid, elude, cause, originate, create.
Follower, partisan, disciple, retainer, pursuer, successor, adherent.
Ant.—Leader, teacher, rival, antagonist, predecessor, superior.
Folly, silliness, foolishness, imbecility, weakness.
Ant. — Wisdom, prudence, sense, judgment, sanity, reasonableness.
Fond, enamored, attached, affectionate, loving, tender, devoted.
Ant. — Distant, irresponsive, unloving, averse, austere, sensible.
Fondness, affection, attachment, kindness, love.
Ant.—Aversion, dislike, hate.
Food, meal, repast, victuals, meat, viands, diet.
Ant.—Drink, want, starvation, hunger.
Fool, idiot, buffoon, zany, clown.
Ant. — Philosopher, student, scholar.
Foolery. (See Folly.)
Foolhardy, venturesome, incautious, hasty. adventurous, rash.
Ant.—Cautious, careful, provident.
Foolish, simple, silly, irrational, brainless, imbecile, crazy, absurd, preposterous, ridiculous, nonsensical.
Ant. — Sensible, wise, sane, sagacious, prudent, judicious, advisable, discreet.
Fop, dandy, dude, beau, coxcomb, puppy, jackanapes.
Ant.—Gentleman.
Foppish, dandified, dressy.
Ant.—Modest, dowdy, slovenly, unaffected.
Forage, spoil, pillage, depredate, plunder.
Ant.—Purchase, buy, protect, shield.
Forbear, abstain, refrain, withhold.
Ant.—Indulge, seek.
Force, *v.* compel, coerce, oblige, necessitate.
Ant.—Persuade, ask, coax.
Force, *n.* strength, vigor, dint, might, energy, power, violence, army, host.
Ant. — Weakness, feebleness, inefficiency, debility.
Forcible, strong, vigorous, energetic, effective, operative, powerful, cogent, irresistible.
Ant.—Weak, feeble, inefficient, disabled, ineffective, tame.
Forebode, presage, portend, augur.
Ant.—Doubt, confess, consult, admit.
Forecast, forethought, foresight, premeditation, prognostication.
Ant.—Result, effect, end, record, afterthought.
Forego, abandon, quit, relinquish, let go, waive.
Ant.—Insist.
Foregoing, antecedent, anterior, preceding, previous, prior, former.
Ant.—Subsequent, succeeding, latter, following.
Forerunner, herald, harbinger, precursor, omen.
Ant.—Successor, follower, issue, result.
Foresight, forethought, forecast, premeditation.
Ant.—Result, record, guess, hazard, issue.
Foretell. (See Predict.)
Forge, coin, invent, frame, feign, fabricate, counterfeit, falsify.
Ant.—Detect, expose, shatter, batter, shiver, blast, verify.
Forget, lose, overlook.
Ant. — Remember, recollect, retain, treasure, learn.
Forgive, pardon, condone, remit, absolve, acquit, excuse, except.
Ant. — Condemn, accuse, punish.
Forlorn, forsaken, abandoned, deserted, desolate, lone, lonesome.
Ant.—Cherished, beloved.
Form, *n.* ceremony, solemnity, observance, rite, figure, shape, conformation, fashion, appearance, representation, semblance.
Ant. — Informality, illegality, mockery, distortion, vagueness.
Form, *v.* make, create, produce, constitute, arrange, fashion, mold, shape, frame.
Ant. — Deform, derange, dislocate, distort, dissipate, analyze, destroy, demolish.
Formal, ceremonious, precise, exact, stiff, methodical, affected, regular, correct.
Ant.—Informal, easy, unceremonious, incomplete, incorrect, natural, unconventional, careless.
Former, antecedent, anterior, previous, prior, preceding, foregoing.

Ant.—Latter, succeeding, subsequent, posterior, future.

Formidable, terrible, dreadful, fearful, shocking, horrible.
Ant.—Contemptible, despicable, weak, trivial.

Forsake. (See Abandon.)

Forsaken, abandoned, forlorn, deserted, desolate, lone, lonesome.
Ant. — Cherished, protected, defended, pursued, supported, upheld.

Forthwith, immediately, directly, instantly, instantaneously.
Ant.—Soon, presently, by and by, hereafter, anon.

Fortify, strengthen, garrison, reinforce, intrench.
Ant.—Weaken, invalidate, dismantle.

Fortitude, endurance, resolution, fearlessness, dauntlessness, strength, courage.
Ant.—Timidity, faintness, delicacy, effeminacy, weakness.

Fortunate, lucky, happy, auspicious, prosperous, successful.
Ant. — Unfortunate, unlucky, unhappy, luckless.

Fortune, chance, fate, luck, doom, destiny, property, possession, riches.
Ant.—Misfortune, poverty.

Forward, cross, untoward, captious, fractious, perverse, peevish.
Ant. — Agreeable, obedient, docile, amenable.

Forward, *a.* onward, progressive, confident, presumptuous, bold, imprudent.
Ant.—Backward, slow, tardy, indifferent, retiring, modest.

Forward, *v.* further, advance, promote, prefer.
Ant. — Deter, retard, retain, hinder, obstruct.

Foster, cherish, nurse, tend, harbor, nurture.
Ant.—Neglect, disregard.

Foul, dirty, impure, nasty, filthy, unclean, defiled.
Ant.—Pure, clean.

Found, ground, base, rest, build, institute, establish, set up.
Ant. — Uproot, disestablish, subvert, overthrow, demolish.

Foundation, ground, basis, groundwork, establishment.
Ant. — Superstructure, building, disestablishment.

Fractious, cross, petulant, touchy, captious, testy, peevish, fretful, splenetic.
Ant. — Good-humored, agreeable, genial, blithesome, tractable, submissive, pliant.

Fragile, brittle, frail, delicate, feeble.
Ant. — Tough, hardy, stout, strong, sturdy, solid.

Fragment, piece, scrap, chip, remains, remnant, leaving.
Ant.—Bulk, body, mass, whole, solid, entity.

Fragrant, spicy, sweet-scented, balmy, perfumed.
Ant. — Malodorous, stinking, fetid, scentless.

Frailty, weakness, failing, foible, imperfection, fault, blemish.
Ant.—Strength, perfection.

Frame, form, construct, invent, coin, fabricate, forge, mold, feign, make, compose.
Ant. — Sunder, destroy, dissolve, rend.

Franchise, right, exemption, immunity, privilege, suffrage, freedom.
Ant.—Obligation, disqualification, disability, jurisdiction.

Frank, artless, candid, sincere, free, easy, familiar, open, ingenuous, plain.
Ant.—Disingenuous, close, reserved, taciturn, tricky, insincere, wily, shifty.

Frantic, distracted, mad, furious, raving, frenzied.
Ant.—Sane, sober, calm, collected, composed, unruffled, quiet, subdued, peaceful, normal.

Fraternize, cooperate, consort, associate with.
Ant.—Oppose, renounce, abjure, foreswear.

Fraud, deception, deceit, duplicity, guile, cheat, imposition.
Ant. — Honesty, straightforwardness, fairness.

Fray. (See Affray.)

Freak, fancy, humor, vagary, whim, caprice, crotchet.
Ant. — Purpose, resolution, consistency.

Free, *a.* liberal, generous, bountiful, bounteous, munificent, frank, artless, candid, familiar, open, unconfirmed, unreserved, unrestricted, exempt, clear, loose, easy, careless, independent, unconfined.
Ant.—Illiberal, biased, bound, shackled, restricted, clogged, impeded, subject, liable, amenable, qualified, slavish, stingy, artful.

Free, *v.* release, set free, deliver, rescue, liberate, enfranchise, emancipate, exempt, affranchise.
Ant. — Bind, shackle, restrict, clog, hinder, enslave, disenfranchise, confine, imprison.

Freedom, liberty, independence, unrestraint, familiarity, license, franchise, exemption, privilege.
Ant.—Slavery, bondage, serfdom.

Frequent, often, common, usual, general.
Ant. — Rare, few, solitary, scanty, casual, infrequent, unique, exceptional.

Fresh, new, novel, recent, modern, blooming, ruddy.
Ant.—Stale, old, weary, stagnant, faded, decayed, pallid, sickly, musty, putrid, former.

Fret, gall, chafe, agitate, irritate, vex.
Ant.—Soothe, console, please, appease.

Fretful. (See Fractious.)

Friendly, amicable, social, sociable, kindly.
Ant.—Hostile, inimical, adverse, antagonistic, distant, reserved, cool.

Fright. (See Alarm.)

Frighten, scare, affright, dismay, appal, terrify, daunt.
Ant.—Compose, reassure, allay, soothe, rally, embolden.

Frightful, fearful, dreadful, dire, direful, terrific, awful, horrible, horrid.
Ant.—Pleasing, attractive, fair, beautiful, lovely, gentle.

Frivolous, trifling, trivial, petty, silly.
Ant. — Serious, earnest, grave, important.

Frolic, gambol, play, game, sport, prank, spree, lark.
Ant.—Occupation, work, business, study, purpose.

Front. (See Face.)

Frugal, provident, economical, saving, temperate.
Ant. — Intemperate, profuse, extravagant, self-indulgent, wasteful, prodigal.

Fruitful, fertile, prolific, productive, abundant, plentiful, plenteous.
Ant. — Unfruitful, barren, sterile, useless, fruitless.

Fruitless, vain, useless, idle, abortive, bootless, unavailing, without avail.
Ant. — Fruitful, profitable, valuable, successful.

Frustrate, defeat, foil, disappoint, balk.
Ant.—Aid, abet, forward, push, incite, instigate, encourage, assist, help, satisfy.

Fulfill, accomplish, complete, effect.
Ant.—Neglect, ignore, disappoint, falsify, bungle, fail.

Fullness. (See Abundance.)

Fully, completely, abundantly, perfectly.
Ant.—Partially, partly.

Fulsome, coarse, gross, sickening, offensive, rank.
Ant.—Chaste, sober, nice, delicate, moderate.

Fun. (See Humor.)

Funereal, dismal, dark, mournful.
Ant.—Festive, joyous, lively.

Furious, violent, boisterous, vehement, dashing, sweeping, rolling, impetuous, frantic,

distracted, stormy, angry, raging, fierce.
Ant.—Calm, sober, quiet, composed, sane, dull, unruffled, unrestrained, placid.

Furniture. (See Effects.)

Further. (See Advance.)

Fury. (See Anger.)

Futile, trifling, trivial, frivolous, useless.
Ant.—Effective, powerful, cogent, useful, solid, capable.

G

Gaiety, merriment, jollity, mirth, hilarity.
Ant.—Sadness, sorrow, melancholy, gravity.

Gain, *n.* profit, emolument, advantage, benefit, winnings, earnings.
Ant.—Loss, forfeiture, disadvantage, failure.

Gain, *v.* get, acquire, obtain, attain, procure, earn, win, achieve, reap, release, reach, realize.
Ant.—Lose, forfeit, suffer, fail.

Gainsay, contradict, deny, dispute.
Ant.—Affirm, verify, conform, attest, witness.

Gallant, brave, bold, courageous, gay, fine, showy, intrepid, fearless, heroic.
Ant.—Cowardly, churlish, discourteous, rude, coarse, timid, shrinking, fearful, timorous.

Gallantry, prowess, courage, bravery, valor, heroism, boldness, fearlessness, politeness.
Ant. — Cowardice, timidity, rudeness, barbarity.

Galling, irritating, chafing, vexing.
Ant.—Soothing.

Gambol, frisk, prank, play, spree, caper.
Ant.—Droop, flag, tire, wean, work, study.

Game, play, pastime, diversion, sport, amusement.
Ant. — Toil, work, business, duty, study, labor, drudgery.

Gang, company, band, horde, mob, troop, crew.
Ant.—Individual.

Gap, breach, chasm, hollow, cavity, cleft, crevice, rift, chink.
Ant.—Contrivance, connection, sequence.

Garble, mutilate, misquote, distort, pervert, falsify.
Ant.—Quote, cite, extract, recite.

Garnish, embellish, adorn, beautify, deck, decorate.
Ant. — Denude, strip, dismantle, spoil, mark, pollute, deface, defile.

Gather, collect, pick, cull, assemble, muster, infer.
Ant.—Scatter, disperse.

Gaudy, showy, tawdry, gay, glittering, bespangled, flashy.
Ant.—Rich, simple, handsome, chaste, somber, dark, plain.

Gaunt, emaciated, scraggy, meager, lank, attenuated, spare, lean, thin, skinny.
Ant. — Sleek, fat, well-fed, unctuous, plump, stout.

Gawky. (See Awkward.)

Gay, cheerful, merry, lively, jolly, sprightly, blithe.
Ant.—Sad, melancholy, grave, heavy, somber, dull, solemn, funereal, doleful, dismal.

Generate, make, form, beget, produce.

Generation, formation, race, breed, stock, kind, age, era.
Ant. — Eternity, immortality, perpetuity.

Generous, beneficent, noble, honorable, bountiful, liberal, free.
Ant. — Stingy, mean, selfish, illiberal, ignoble, niggardly, close, parsimonious, miserly.

Genial, cordial, hearty, festive, joyous, warm.
Ant.—Ungenial, cold, distant, harsh, deadly.

Genius, talent, taste, nature, character, cleverness, intellect, invention, adept.
Ant. — Stupidity, imbecility, stolidity, inanity, dullness.

Genteel, refined, polished, fashionable, polite, well-bred.
Ant.—Boorish, clownish, rude, uncultivated.

Gentle, placid, mild, meek, tame, bland, docile.
Ant. — Rough, rude, harsh, coarse, fierce, savage, uncouth, boisterous, obstreperous.

Genuine, real, true, unaffected, sincere, authentic, veritable.
Ant. — Spurious, fictitious, adulterated, false, deceptive.

Germane, relative, allied, related, pertinent.
Ant.—Foreign, alien, irrelevant, unconnected.

Gesture, attitude, action, posture.

Get, obtain, earn, gain, attain, procure, achieve.
Ant.—Lose, forfeit, surrender, forego, fail.

Ghastly, pallid, wan, hideous, grim, shocking.
Ant.—Ruddy, blooming, fresh, comely, buxom, florid, high-colored, hectic, radiant.

Ghost, specter, sprite, apparition, shade, phantom.
Ant.—Substance, body, animal, organism.

Gibe, scoff, sneer, flout, jeer, mock, taunt, deride.
Ant. — Salute, compliment, hail, welcome, greet, cheer, encourage, applaud, approve.

Giddy, unsteady, flighty, thoughtless, lofty.
Ant. — Steady, stationary, wary, composed, slow, ponderous, thankful, low, reliable, poised, well-balanced, dependable.

Gift, donation, benefaction, grant, alms, gratuity, boon, present, faculty, talent
Ant. — Earnings, purchase, compensation, remuneration, forfeit, surrender, stupidity, inanity.

Gigantic, enormous, colossal, huge, vast, prodigious, immense.
Ant.—Diminutive, little, tiny, small, wee.

Gild. (See Adorn.)

Gird, belt, encircle, enclose, engird.
Ant.—Open, expand, ungird, disclose.

Give, grant, bestow, confer, yield, impart.
Ant.—Withhold, retain, refuse, deny, withdraw, take, absorb.

Glad, pleased, cheerful, joyful, gladsome, gratified, cheering.
Ant.—Sorry, unhappy, dismal, despondent, sad, melancholy, depressed.

Glare, flare, glisten, glitter, dazzle, gleam.
Ant. — Flicker, glimmer, sparkle, scintillate.

Gleam, glare, glimmer, glance, glitter, shine, flash.

Glee, gaiety, merriment, mirth, joviality, joy, hilarity.
Ant. — Sorrow, despondency, sadness.

Glib, voluble, fluent, flowing, ready, flippant.
Ant.—Stammering, slow, hesitating, abrupt, rough.

Glide, slip, slide, run, roll on.
Ant.—Jump, skip, hop, tumble, stumble, soar, fall.

Glimmer, flicker, gleam, glitter.

Glimpse, glance, look, glint.
Ant. — Scrutiny, analysis, investigation, inspection, exposure.

Glitter, flicker, gleam, shine, glisten, glister, radiate.

Gloom, cloud, darkness, dimness, blackness, dullness, sadness.
Ant.—Light, brightness, radiance, clearness, joy.

Gloomy, lowering, lurid, dim, dusky, sad, glum.
Ant. — Bright, clear, gay, merry

Glorify, magnify, celebrate, adore, exalt, elevate, honor.
Ant.—Debase, degrade, decry, defame, censure, abuse, overthrow, ruin, dishonor, disgrace.

Glorious, famous, renowned, celebrated, illustrious, distinguished, conspicuous, noble, exalted, grand.
Ant. — Degraded, infamous,

unknown, debased, dishonored.

Glory, honor, fame, renown, splendor, grandeur.
Ant. — Ignominy, dishonor, degradation, obscurity, infamy, shame, disgrace.

Glowing. (See Hot.)

Glut, gorge, stuff, cram, cloy, satiate, block up, fill to repletion, inundate.
Ant.—Empty, drain, draw off, starve.

Go, depart, proceed, move, budge, stir.
Ant.—Come, stand, stay, abide, remain, persist, endure.

God, Creator, Lord, Almighty, Jehovah, Omnipotence, Providence.
Ant. — Beelzebub, Lucifer, Satan, the devil.

Godly, righteous, devout, holy, pious, religious.
Ant. — Wicked, godless, impious.

Good, *n.* benefit, weal, advantage, profit, boon.
Ant.—Hurt, evil, injury, detriment, disadvantage, calamity, infliction, mischief, harm, loss.

Good, *a.* virtuous, righteous, upright, just, true, pious, efficient, reputable.
Ant.—Bad, evil, wrong, mean, disgraceful, imperfect, vicious, invalid, fictitious, wicked.

Goodly, comely, pleasant, graceful, desirable, considerable.
Ant. — Unpleasant, undesirable, inconsiderable, small.

Gorge, glut, fill, cram, stuff, satiate.
Ant.—Empty, starve.

Gorgeous, superb, grand, magnificent, splendid.
Ant. — Dowdy, dingy, bare, cheap, poor, mean, squalid.

Govern, rule, manage, command, direct, mold, sway.
Ant. — Misgovern, misrule, misdirect, tyrannize, comply, obey, submit, yield.

Government, rule, administration, cabinet, constitution, state, control, sway.
Ant.—Anarchy, revolution, rebellion.

Graceful, becoming, elegant, beautiful, comely.
Ant. — Ungraceful, awkward, deformed, gawky, ungainly, clumsy.

Gracious, merciful, beneficent, courteous, civil, kindly.
Ant. — Haughty, ungracious, churlish, disdainful, curt.

Gradual, slow, progressive.
Ant. — Sudden, instantaneous, intermittent, broken, periodic.

Grand, majestic, stately, dignified, lofty, elevated, exalted, splendid, gorgeous, superb, magnificent, sublime, pompous.
Ant. — Small, little, inferior, common, paltry, insignificant, undignified, petty, unimposing, shabby, poor, mean.

Grant, *v.* bestow, impart, give, yield, cede, allow, confer, invest.
Ant.—Withhold, deny, withdraw, reserve, absorb, take, assume, engross.

Grant, *n.* gift, boon, donation.

Graphic, forcible, pictorial, telling, picturesque, vivid.
Ant. — Weak, unpicturesque, undescriptive, vague, maundering, illusive.

Grasp, catch, seize, gripe, clasp, grapple.
Ant.—Loose, lose, abandon, relinquish, release, surrender, let go.

Grasping, greedy, avaricious, covetous, miserly.
Ant. — Generous, benevolent, philanthropic.

Grateful, agreeable, pleasing, welcome, thankful.
Ant. — Ungrateful, unacceptable, disagreeable, unpleasant, harsh, thankless.

Gratification, enjoyment, pleasure, delight, reward.
Ant.—Abstinence, abnegation, stinting, pain, dislike, disappointment.

Grave, *a.* serious, sedate, thoughtful, solemn, sober, important, weighty, pressing, heavy.
Ant.—Joyous, merry, frivolous, facetious, light, trivial, giddy, flighty.

Grave, *n.* tomb, sepulchre, vault.

Gravity, weight, heaviness, importance, moment, seriousness.
Ant. — Lightness, buoyancy, smallness, frivolity, triviality.

Great, big, huge, large, majestic, vast, grand, noble, august.
Ant. — Little, narrow, puny, few, scanty, short, mean, ignoble, weak, small, petty, unimportant.

Greediness, avidity, eagerness, voracity.
Ant.—Abstinence, temperance, indifference, content, generosity.

Grief, sorrow, affliction, trial, woe, tribulation.
Ant.—Joy, gladness, mirth, pleasure.

Grieve, mourn, lament, sorrow, pain, hurt, wound, bewail.
Ant. — Exult, rejoice, ease, console, soothe.

Grievous, painful, afflicting, heavy, baneful, unhappy, disastrous, calamitous, baleful.
Ant.—Joyous, pleasant, glad, acceptable, light, delightful, enjoyable.

Grind, crush, oppress, grate, harass, afflict.
Ant.—Bless, help.

Gripe, catch, seize, clutch, grasp, press, squeeze, pinch.
Ant.—Abandon, relax, soothe, ease, relieve.

Grisly, ghastly, terrible, hideous, grim, dreadful.
Ant.—Pleasing, beautiful.

Gross, coarse, outrageous, unseemly, shameful, indelicate, entire, whole.
Ant.—Pure, refined, partial, net, delicate, fine.

Ground. (See Establish.)

Groundless, unfounded, baseless, ungrounded, gratuitous.
Ant.—Well-founded, authoritative, authentic, substantial.

Group, assembly, cluster, collection, clump, order, class.

Grovel, crawl, cringe, fawn, sneak.
Ant. — Soar, aspire, mount, rise.

Grow, increase, vegetate, expand, advance.
Ant.—Diminish, contract, die, wane, fail, decay, decrease, shrink.

Growl, grumble, snarl, murmur, complain, croak, find fault, repine.
Ant. — Chuckle, cackle, grin, acquiesce, purr, approve, applaud, rejoice.

Grudge, malice, rancor, spite, pique, hatred, aversion.
Ant.—Welcome, liking, affection, attachment.

Gruff, rough, rugged, blunt, rude, harsh, surly, bearish.
Ant. — Affable, courteous, smooth, mild, pleasant, agreeable, amiable, polite.

Grumble. (See Growl.)

Guard *v.* (See Protect.)

Guard *n.* (See Protection.)

Guess. (See Surmise.)

Guide, lead, conduct, direct, regulate, manage, superintend.
Ant. — Mislead, misconduct, betray, deceive.

Guile, deceit, fraud, artifice, trickery.
Ant.—Honesty, candor, sincerity, frankness.

Guilt, crime, offense, sin.
Ant.—Honesty, truth, frankness, straightforwardness, virtue.

Guiltless, harmless, innocent.
Ant.—Guilty, harmful, sinful, criminal, noxious.

Guise, manner, aspect, mien, habit, dress.
Ant.—Individual, life, mind, soul, self.

Gull. (See Cheat.)

Gush, stream, flow, rush, spout.

Ant. — Drip, drop, dribble, trickle, ooze, filter
Gust, breeze, blast, gale, squall.
Ant.—Calm, quiet.

H

Habiliments. (See Dress.)
Habit, custom, practice.
Habitation. (See Abode.)
Habitual, usual, customary, accustomed, wonted, regular, ordinary
Ant.—Unusual, rare, exceptional, occasional, extraordinary
Hail, greet, salute, welcome, accost, call, address.
Ant.—Ignore, pass, cut, avoid
Hale. (See Healthy.)
Hallow, consecrate, sanctify, venerate, dedicate, enshrine
Ant. — Desecrate, profane, abominate, execrate.
Halt, rest, pause, falter, limp, hop, hobble
Ant.—Advance, speed, proceed, progress.
Handle. manage, use, wield, feel
Ant.—Drop, mismanage, bungle, abstain
Handsome, pretty, elegant, graceful, ample, beautiful, fine
Ant. — Uncomely, ugly, ill-looking, coarse.
Handy, near, convenient, ready, dexterous.
Ant. — Remote, inconvenient, unhandy, awkward, unwieldy
Hapless. (See Luckless.)
Happen, betide, befall, occur.
Ant.—Ordain, ordered, caused.
Happiness, felicity, bliss, prosperity, wellbeing, welfare, beatitude, blessedness.
Ant. — Unhappiness, sorrow, grief, despair, misery, sadness.
Happy, prosperous, successful, lucky, fortunate, glad
Ant. — Unhappy, sorrowful, miserable, dull, sorry, disconsolate
Harass. (See Perplex.)
Harbor, *n* port, haven, asylum, refuge.
Ant.—Exposure, peril, toil, labor, voyage.
Harbor, *v.* shelter, indulge, foster, cherish, entertain.
Ant.—Exclude, eject, expel, banish, dismiss.
Hard, firm, solid, flinty, unfeeling, harsh, cruel, difficult, arduous.
Ant.—Soft, fluid, liquid, elastic, brittle, easy, mild, lenient, tender, simple, yielding.
Hardened. (See Hard.)
Hardihood. (See Audacity.)
Hardy, manly, masculine, vigorous, courageous, brave, heroic, intrepid, stout, strong, firm.
Ant.—Weak, fragile, delicate, effeminate, enervated.
Harm, evil, ill, misfortune, mischief, mishap, injury, hurt, detriment, wrong, infliction.
Ant.—Benefit, boon, improvement, compensation, reparation, favor, kindness.
Harmless, safe, innocuous, innocent.
Ant.—Hurtful, noxious, poisonous.
Harmonious, symphonious, accordant, amicable.
Ant. — Discordant, incongruous, harsh, grating, riotous.
Harsh, rough, severe, rigorous, gruff, rugged, blunt, grating, jarring, sour, morose.
Ant.—Smooth, soft, melodious, suave, kindly, gentle, mild.
Hasten, push on, press on, accelerate, quicken, expedite, hurry, dispatch, speed.
Ant. — Retard, impede, obstruct, hesitate, halt, delay, hinder
Hasty, quick, precipitate, rash, excitable, hot, fiery, passionate, angry, cursory, slight, hurried, ill-advised.
Ant.—Slow, careful, close, reflective, thoughtful, deliberate.
Hate, detest, abominate, abhor, loathe, dislike.
Ant.—Love, cherish, like, approve
Hateful, odious, detestable, execrable, abominable, loathsome, repulsive.
Ant.—Lovable, desirable, delightful, attractive, pleasant.
Hatred, enmity, ill-will, rancor.
Ant.—Friendship, love
Haughtiness, arrogance, pride.
Ant.—Modesty, meekness, humility
Haughty, arrogant, disdainful, supercilious, proud.
Ant.—Meek, humble.
Haunt. (See Frequent.)
Havoc, destruction, desolation, devastation.
Ant. — Prosperity, conservation, augmentation, enrichment.
Hazard, peril, imperil, jeopardize, risk, dare, conjecture, venture, chance, contingency, fortuity.
Ant.—Insure, protect, guard, think, know, determine, certainty, safety, assurance, security.
Haze, fog, mist, rime.
Ant.—Clearness, transparency, brightness.
Head. (See Chief.)
Headstrong. (See Obstinate.)
Heal, cure, remedy, reconcile.
Ant. — Hurt, wound, harm, pierce.
Healthy, hearty, hale, sound, strong, wholesome, salubrious, salutary.
Ant. — Unhealthy, unsound, delicate, sick, weak, noxious, injurious.
Heap, accumulate, amass, pile up.
Ant.—Disperse, scatter.
Hear, hearken, overhear, listen.
Ant.—Ignore, disregard, refuse.
Hearty, healthy, cordial, sincere, warm.
Ant.—Insincere, cool.
Heavenly, celestial, divine, seraphic, angelic.
Ant. — Hellish, diabolical, devilish.
Heaviness, dullness, gloom, lethargy, torpor.
Ant. — Lightness, buoyancy, joyousness, animation.
Heavy, weighty, massive, dull, drowsy, insipid, oppressive, inert, slow, burdensome, ponderous.
Ant. — Light, agile, active, quick, brisk, animated, joyous.
Heed, mind, attend to, regard, notice, care, attention.
Ant.—Disregard, slight, ignore, heedlessness, unconcern.
Height, top, crisis, acme, apex, climax, zenith.
Ant.—Depth, base, lowness, depression, abasement.
Heighten, amplify, exaggerate, raise, enhance, increase, exalt, elevate.
Ant.—Lower, depress, debase, diminish, tone, modify.
Heinous, atrocious, flagitious, flagrant.
Ant.—Venial, trifling.
Help, aid, assist, relieve, succor.
Ant.—Hinder, block, check, counteract, embarrass, impede, retard.
Heretic, sectary, sectarian, schismatic, dissenter, nonconformist.
Heroic, courageous, brave, bold, intrepid, fearless, gallant.
Ant. — Cowardly, cravenly, dastardly, timidly.
Hesitate, falter, pause, demur, scruple, stammer, stutter.
Ant.—Resolve, decide, determine, proceed.
Hew, cut, fell, hack, chop.
Ant. — Mold, model, form, carve.
Hidden, secret, occult, mysterious.
Ant.—Open, exposed, revealed, understood, apparent, evident.
Hide, *v.* conceal, disguise, secrete, cover, screen.
Ant. — Expose, exhibit, discover, betray, show.
Hide. *n.* (See Skin.)

Hideous, ghastly, grim, grisly, frightful, horrible, ugly.
Ant. — Attractive, beautiful, graceful, lovely, entrancing.

High, tall, lofty, elevated, proud, conceited.
Ant.—Low, depressed, stunted, mean, base, affable, deep.

Hilarity, mirth, glee, jollity, merriment, joviality.
Ant.—Despair, grief, sorrow, mournfulness, depression.

Hinder, thwart, retard, stop, prevent, impede, obstruct.
Ant. — Expedite, promote, facilitate, accelerate, air, assist, relieve, succor.

Hint, suggest, allude, refer, intimate, insinuate.

Hire, pay, allowance, salary, wages, stipend.
Ant.—Gratuity, present.

Hit, strike, dash, beat, thump.
Ant.—Miss, mischance, fail, err.

Hoard, heap up, treasure, lay up, store.
Ant.—Waste, squander, dissipate.

Hoax. (See Trick.)

Hoist. (See Lift.)

Hold, have, possess, keep, detain, retain.
Ant.—Drop, abandon, release, forego, vacate, surrender, fail, let go.

Hollow, vacant, empty, void.
Ant.—Solid, full, strong, firm, genuine, sound

Holiness, sanctity, piety, sacredness.
Ant.—Wickedness, impiety

Holy, sacred, pious, devout, religious, divine, saintly, blessed.
Ant.—Unholy, profane, evil, impure, cursed, polluted, abominable, worldly

Homage, respect, deference, honor, veneration.
Ant.—Defiance, treason, rebellion, disaffection.

Home. (See Abode.)

Homely, plain, ugly, coarse.
Ant.—Beautiful.

Honest, upright, honorable, conscientious, virtuous.
Ant.—Dishonest, tricky, deceitful, fraudulent, guileful.

Honesty, integrity, purity, probity, sincerity, veracity, virtue, justice, uprightness.
Ant.—Dishonesty, fraud, deceit, deception, guile.

Honor, *n.* homage, dignity, grandeur, deference, respect, regard, reverence, esteem.
Ant.—Disrespect, irreverence, abasement, dishonor, ignominy.

Honor, *v.* reverence, revere, venerate, respect, dignify, exalt.
Ant.—Disrespect, despise, obscure, dishonor.

Hope, expectation, expectancy, trust, confidence, anticipation.
Ant.—Despair, despondency, disbelief.

Hopeless, desperate, pessimistic.
Ant.—Buoyant, hopeful, optimistic.

Horrible, fearful, dreadful, dire, direful, frightful, terrible, terrific, horrid.
Ant.—Lovely, desirable, enjoyable, beautiful, fair, amiable.

Hostile. (See Adverse.)

Hostility. (See Enmity.)

Hot, ardent, fervent, fiery, burning, glowing, intense, passionate.
Ant.—Cold, cool, slow, indifferent, passionless.

House. (See Abode.)

However, nevertheless, notwithstanding, yet.

Huge, (See Enormous.)

Humanity, kindness, benevolence, philanthropy, tenderness, sensibility.
Ant. — Inhumanity, cruelty, unkindness, bestiality.

Humble, *v.* lower, debase, degrade, disgrace, humiliate, mortify, abase.
Ant.—Raise, enhance, honor, elevate, exalt, promote.

Humble, *a.* lowly, modest, submissive, unpretending, unassuming, plain, unostentatious, simple.
Ant.—Eminent, proud, boastful, arrogant, pretentious, haughty, overbearing, supercilious.

Humiliation. (See Degradation.)

Humor, satire, wit, jocularity, temper, mood, frame, fun.
Ant. — Seriousness, gravity, sorrow, grief, nature.

Hunt, seek, chase.

Hurl. (See Fling.)

Hurricane. (See Gale.)

Hurry, *v.* hasten, speed, expedite, precipitate.
Ant.—Hinder, retard, restrain, obstruct, dally, tarry.

Hurt, annoy, grieve, vex, wound.
Ant. — Heal, soothe, repair, console, benefit, compensate.

Hurtful, pernicious, baneful, deleterious, noxious, detrimental, prejudicial, destructive.
Ant. — Advantageous, useful, beneficial, healthy, wholesome.

Husbandry, cultivation, tillage.

Hush, lull, calm, still. quiet, silence.
Ant.—Noise, riot, gale, disturbance, boisterousness.

Hypocrisy, deceit, pretense, cant.
Ant.—Honesty, candor, openness, virtue, fanaticism.

Hypocrite, dissembler, imposter, canter.

Hypothesis, theory, supposition.

I

Idea, imagination, conception, notion, thought, sentiment, impression.
Ant.—Object, form, subject, thing, reality.

Ideal, imaginary, imaginative, fancied.
Ant.—Physical, material, real, actual, palpable, visible, tangible.

Identical, same, self-same, particular.
Ant.—Different, distinct, contrary, opposed, separate.

Idiot. (See Fool.)

Idle, lazy, indolent, inactive, unemployed.
Ant.—Busy, employed, occupied, industrious, filled, populated.

Ignominious, shameful, scandalous, infamous.
Ant. — Creditable, reputable, honorable, noble.

Ignominy, shame, disgrace, obloquy, infamy, reproach.
Ant.—(See Honor.)

Ignorant, unlearned, illiterate, unlettered, uninformed, uneducated.
Ant.—Learned, wise, informed, educated, cultured, cultivated, erudite.

Ill, *n.* evil, wickedness, misfortune, mischief, harm.
Ant.—Good, blessing.

Ill, *a.* sick, indisposed, unwell, diseased.
Ant. — Well, healthy, sound, hearty.

Ill-tempered. (See Surly.)

Ill-will. (See Hatred.)

Illegal, unlawful, illicit, contraband, illegitimate.
Ant. — Lawful, legal, legitimate, honest.

Illimitable, infinite, boundless, immeasurable, unlimited.
Ant.—Limited, finite.

Illiterate, ignorant, unlettered, unlearned, untaught, uninstructed.
Ant.—Learned, educated.

Illness, sickness, indisposition, disease, disorder, malady, ailment.
Ant.—Health, vigor, soundness, activity.

Ill-tempered, crabbed, sour, surly, acrimonious.
Ant.—Good-natured, amiable.

Illusion, deception, phantasm, fallacy.
Ant. — Reality, body, substance.

Illusory, imaginary, chimerical, visionary.
Ant.—Real, actual, tenable.

Illustrate, explain, elucidate, clear.
Ant.—Obscure, confuse, mystify, darken.
Ant.—(See Elucidate.)

Illustrious, celebrated, glorious, noble, eminent, distinguished, famous, renowned.
Ant.—Infamous, disreputable, ignominious, disgraceful, obscure, unknown.

Ill-will, enmity, hatred, antipathy.
Ant.—Good-will, benevolence.

Image, likeness, picture, representation, effigy.
Ant. — Original, substance, subject, reality, truth, verity.

Imaginary, ideal, fanciful, illusory.
Ant.—Real, true, substantial, satisfactory, solid, actual, tangible.

Imagine, conceive, fancy, apprehend, think, presume.
Ant.—Prove, demonstrate, depict, exhibit, substantiate.

Imbecility, silliness, senility, dotage.
Ant. — Wisdom, shrewdness, sagacity, cleverness.

Imbibe. (See Absorb.)

Imbolden. (See Encourage.)

Imitate, copy, ape, mimic, mock, counterfeit.
Ant.—Alter, distort, caricature, modify, misrepresent, vary, originate, invent.

Immaculate, unspotted, spotless, unsullied, stainless.
Ant. — Defiled, impure, corrupt, sinful, contaminated, polluted, soiled, spotted, bedraggled.

Immediate, pressing, instant, next, proximate, contiguous.
Ant.—Distant, far, future, remote.

Immediately, instantly, forthwith, directly, instanter, presently, straightway.
Ant.—By and by, distantly, remotely.

Immense, enormous, vast, huge, prodigious, monstrous.
Ant.—Tiny, diminutive.

Immerse, dip, plunge, douse, souse.
Ant.—Dry, drain, air, ventilate, hoist out.

Immigration, colonization, settlement.
Ant.—Emigration, exodus.

Immunity, privilege, prerogative, exemption.
Ant. — Liability, obligation, impost, jurisdiction, responsibility.

Immure, confine, shut up, imprison.
Ant.—Release, dismiss, acquit, escape.

Impair, injure, diminish, decrease.
Ant.—Enhance, improve, augment, repair, increase, build up, perfect.

Impart, give, reveal, divulge, disclose, discover, bestow, afford.

Impartial, just, equitable, unbiased.
Ant.—Partial, prejudiced, interested.

Impassioned, passionate, glowing, burning, fiery, vehement, intense, impetuous.
Ant.—Cool, impassive, indifferent, unresponsive.

Impeach, accuse, charge, arraign, censure.
Ant.—Acquit, absolve, vindicate, condone, discharge, excuse, forgive, overlook, pardon, release.

Impede, obstruct, hinder, retard, prevent.
Ant.—Help, aid, assist.

Impediment, obstacle, obstruction, hindrance, barrier.
Ant.—Aid, assistance.

Impel, encourage, animate, induce, incite, instigate, embolden.
Ant.—Retard, check.

Impending, imminent, threatening.
Ant.—Distant, remote.

Imperative, commanding, dictatorial, authoritative, despotic, peremptory, dogmatic, domineering, overbearing.
Ant. — Indulgent, lenient, mild, supplicatory, optional, discretional, complaisant, compliant, docile, mild, submissive, yielding.

Imperfection, blemish, fault, defect, vice.
Ant.—Beauty, perfection.

Imperil, peril, endanger, hazard, jeopardize.
Ant.—Defend, secure, protect, shield, rescue, save, deliver

Imperious, dictatorial, commanding, authoritative, imperative, lordly, domineering, overbearing.
Ant.—(See Imperative.)

Impertinent, intrusive, meddling, officious, rude, saucy, impudent, insolent.
Ant.—Pertinent, related, appropriate, fit, proper, applicable, courteous, suave, polite.

Impervious, impassable, inaccessible, impenetrable.
Ant.—Penetrable, explorable, traversable.

Impetuous, violent, boisterous, furious, vehement, rapid, impulsive, hasty.
Ant.—Slow, thoughtful, deliberate, leisurely, calm.

Impious, profane, irreligious, godless.
Ant.—Pious, sacred, godly, religious, reverent.

Implicate, involve, entangle, embarrass, compromise.
Ant.—Extricate, acquit, disconnect, exonerate, clear, exculpate.

Implore. (See Entreat.)

Imply, involve, comprise, infold, import, denote, signify.
Ant.—Express, state, declare, pronounce.

Importance, signification, significance, avail, consequence, weight, gravity, moment.
Ant. — Unimportance, irrelevance, triviality, meanness, insignificance, pettiness.

Important, pressing, momentous, material, weighty, grave.
Ant. — Unimportant, insignificant, trivial, irrelevant, petty, mean.

Impose, put, place, set, fix, lay.
Ant.—Remove, unburden.

Imposing, impressive, striking, majestic, august, noble, grand.
Ant.—Ineffective, undignified, petty, insignificant, trivial.

Imposition. (See Cheat.)

Impost, tax, duty, custom, excise, tribute, toll.
Ant. — Exemption, immunity, proceeds, revenue.

Impostor. (See Cheat.)

Imposture. (See Cheat.)

Impotence weakness, incapacity, infirmity, frailty, feebleness
Ant.—Power, strength, vigor

Impotent, weak, feeble, helpless, enfeebled, nerveless, infirm.
Ant.—Strong, capable, effectual.

Impregnate. (See Saturate.)

Impression, feeling, sentiment, sensation, susceptibility, stamp, edition.
Ant. — Apathy, insensibility, evenness.

Impressive stirring, forcible, exciting, affecting, moving.
Ant.—Unimpressive, ordinary, common, laughable, ludicrous, ineffective, undignified, petty, insignificant.

Imprison, confine, incarcerate, shut up, immure.
Ant.—Liberate, set free.

Imprisonment, incarceration, captivity, durance, confinement.
Ant. — Freedom, release, acquittal, liberty.

Improve, amend, better, mend, reform, rectify, ameliorate, apply, use, employ.
Ant.—Debase, lower, disgrace, abase, drag down, make worse, deteriorate, aggravate, corrupt, impair, injure, mar.

Improvement, progress, proficiency, amendment, correction, advancement.

Ant.—Debasement, retrogression, blemish, fault.

Improvident, prodigal, careless, incautious, imprudent, wasteful, reckless, rash.

Ant.—Thrifty, careful, prudent, provident.

Impudence, assurance, impertinence, confidence, insolence, rudeness.

Ant.—Courtesy, attention, flattery, compliment, good breeding, politeness.

Impudent, impudence, saucy, brazen, bold, impertinent, forward, rude, insolent, immodest, shameless, aggressive.

Ant.—Gentle, polite, decorous.

Impugn, gainsay, oppose, attack, assail.

Ant.—Confirm, prove, establish, evidence.

Impulse, motive, incentive, incitement, instigation.

Impulsive, rash, hasty, forcible, violent.

Ant. — Deliberate, thoughtful, cool, quiet, self-restrained.

Impure, mixed, adulterated, tainted, foul.

Ant. — Pure, good, unadulterated, honest.

Imputation, blame, censure, reproach, charge, accusation.

Ant.—Withdrawal, retraction, acquittal.

Inability, weakness, impotence, incapacity, incapability.

Ant.—Ability, power, strength, capacity, capability.

Inactive, inert, lazy, slothful, sluggish, idle, indolent.

Ant.—Active, smart, energetic, alert.

Inadvertency, error, oversight, blunder, inattention, carelessness, negligence.

Inanimate, lifeless, dead, defunct, inert, extinct.

Ant.—Animate, alive, sensible, active, lively.

Incapable, unable, inadequate, incompetent, insufficient, unfit.

Ant.—Able, competent, fitted.

Incentive, motive, inducement, impulse.

Ant.—Deterrent.

Incessantly, always, unceasingly, continually, perpetually.

Ant. — Occasionally, periodically, intermittently, never.

Incident. (See Circumstance.)

Incidental, accidental, casual, contingent, occasional.

Ant. — Essential, invariable, regular, irrelative, uniform, inherent.

Incite, urge, instigate, excite, provoke, stimulate, encourage, impel.

Ant.—Deter, dishearten, discourage.

Inclemency, harshness, rigor, intensity, severity.

Ant.—Clemency, mercifulness, mildness, geniality.

Inclination, incline, leaning, slope, disposition, tendency, bent, bias, affection, attachment, wish, liking, desire.

Ant.—Aversion, distaste, dislike, repugnance.

Incline, slope, lean, slant, tend, bend, turn, bias, dispose.

Ant.—Diverge, ascend, rise, trend, indispose, disincline, deter.

Inclose, surround, shut in, fence in, cover, wrap.

Ant.—Exclude, debar, eject.

Include, comprehend, comprise, contain, embrace, take in, hold.

Ant.—Exclude, except, shut out, enclose.

Incoherent, loose, unconnected, incongruous, inconsistent, incompatible.

Ant.—Coherent, clear, continuous, intelligible.

Incommode, annoy, plague, molest, disturb, inconvenience, trouble.

Ant. — Accommodate, oblige, supply, reconcile, fit.

Incompetent, incapable, unable, inadequate, insufficient.

Ant. — Competent, capable, effective.

Incomplete, imperfect, defective, unexecuted.

Ant.—Complete, perfect, finished.

Inconstant, changeable, unsteadfast, unstable, fickle, restless, fitful, variable.

Ant. — Constant, faithful, changeless, stable, firm, steady.

Inconvenience. (See Incommode.)

Increase, *v.* extend, enlarge, augment, dilate, expand, amplify, raise, enhance, aggravate, magnify, grow.

Ant. — Decrease, diminish, modify, contract, narrow, lessen, dwindle, shrink.

Increase, *n.* augmentation, accession, addition, enlargement, extension.

Ant. — Decrease, diminution, shrinkage.

Inculcate, impress, infuse, instil, implant.

Ant.—Insinuate, suggest, disavow, abjure, denounce.

Incumbent, obligatory.

Incursion, inroad, invasion, irruption, aggression.

Ant. — Retreat, retirement, withdrawal, settlement, abode.

Indefinite, vague, uncertain, unsettled, loose, lax.

Ant.—Definite, exact, bounded, settled, fixed, unalterable, precise.

Indicate, point out, show, mark, declare.

Ant. — Conceal, contradict, falsify, misindicate.

Indication, mark, sign, note, symptom, token.

Ant. — Silence, misdirection, surmise, guess.

Indifference, apathy, carelessness, listlessness, insensibility, interest, eagerness, gravity, ardor, affection, importance, significance, application, assiduity.

Indigence, want, penury, poverty, destitution, privation, neediness.

Ant. — Abundance, wealth, richness, affluence, plenty.

Indignation, anger, wrath, ire. resentment.

Indignity, insult, affront, outrage, obloquy, opprobrium, reproach, ignominy.

Ant.—Deference, compliment, homage, respect, honor.

Indiscriminate, promiscuous, chance, indistinct, confused.

Ant. — Careful, discerning, sorted, select, chosen, picked.

Indispensable, essential, necessary, requisite, expedient.

Ant. — Dispensable, unnecessary, useless, inexpedient, supernumerary.

Indisputable, undeniable, undoubted, incontestable, indubitable, unquestionable, sure, infallible.

Ant. — Disputable, debatable, doubtful, contestible, fallible, uncertain, questionable, erroneous, mistaken.

Indistinct, uncertain, indiscriminate, confused, ambiguous, disputable, questionable, doubtful.

Ant.—Distinct, certain, exact, clear, plain, intelligible, indisputable, sure.

Indite, compose, couch, frame.

Ant.—Write, transcribe, pen, speak, say.

Indolent. (See Lazy.)

Indorse, ratify, confirm, superscribe.

Ant. — Repudiate, abandon, abjure.

Induce. (See Instigate.)

Inducement. (See Motive.)

Indulge, cherish, foster, fondle.

Ant.—Deny, refuse.

Industrious. (See Diligent.)

Ineffectual, useless, vain, unavailing, fruitless, abortive, inoperative.

Ant.—Effective.

Inequality, disparity, disproportion, unevenness, dissimilarity.

Ant.—Equality, justice, fairness, evenness, purity, similarity.

Inestimable, invaluable, priceless.
Ant. — Estimable, worthless, cheap, mean, poor.

Inevitable, unavoidable, not to be avoided, certain.
Ant. — Avoidable, uncertain, indeterminate, doubtful, unlikely.

Infamous, scandalous, shameful, ignominious, opprobrious, disgraceful.
Ant.—Famous, honorable, reputable, celebrated, renowned, noble.

Infect, pollute, contaminate, taint, defile, corrupt.
Ant.—Purify, disinfect.

Infectious. (See Contagious.)

Inference, deduction, corollary, conclusion, consequence.
Ant.—Premise, argument, statement, guess, assumption.

Inferior, secondary, subaltern, subordinate.
Ant.—Superior, better, greater, higher.

Infernal, diabolical, fiendish, devilish, hellish.
Ant.—Celestial, godly, heavenly, saintly.

Infest, annoy, plague, harass, disturb, haunt, beset.
Ant.—Regale, refresh, gratify, comfort.

Infidelity, unbelief, distrust, incredulity, disbelief.
Ant. — Faith, belief, trust, orthodoxy.

Infinite, boundless, unbounded, illimitable, unlimited.
Ant.—Limited, bounded, narrow, confined.

Infirm, weak, feeble, enfeebled, decrepit.
Ant. — Firm, strong, sound, forcible, active, cogent, robust, sturdy, vigorous.

Inflame, anger, irritate, enrage, incense, nettle, aggravate, embitter, exasperate, chafe.
Ant. — Cool, quench, extinguish, allay, pacify, quiet, soothe.

Inflict, lay on, impose.
Ant.—Remove, alleviate, suspend, spare.

Influence, *v.* bias, sway, prejudice, prepossess.

Influence, *n.* credit, favor, reputation, character, weight, authority, sway, ascendency.
Ant. — Neutrality, inefficacy, weakness, powerlessness, inefficiency.

Inform, communicate, tell, report, acquaint, apprise, notify, disclose, reveal, divulge.
Ant.—Be silent, conceal, retain, mislead, deceive.

Infraction, infringement, encroachment, invasion, intrusion.
Ant. — Observance, respect, maintenance, integrity.

Infringe, invade, intrude, contravene, break, transgress, violate.

Infuse, instil, ingraft, implant, inspire, breathe into, impart.
Ant.—Dry, drain, retract, divert, suck, withdraw.

Ingenuous, artless, candid, generous, open, frank, plain, sincere.
Ant.—Disingenuous, sly, reserved, mean, insincere, crafty, cunning.

Ingratitude, unthankfulness, thanklessness.
Ant.—Gratitude, thankfulness.

Ingress, entry, entrance, inlet.
Ant.—Egress, exit, outlet.

Inhabit, dwell in, reside in, occupy.
Ant.—Abandon, forsake, migrate.

Inherit, enjoy, possess, obtain, occupy.
Ant.—Acquire, earn, bequeath, devise.

Inhuman, cruel, brutal, savage, barbarous, ruthless, merciless, ferocious.
Ant.—Human, merciful, civilized, kind, gentle.

Iniquity, injustice, wrong, grievance.
Ant.—Justice, integrity, virtue, holiness.

Injunction. (See Order.)

Injure, damage, hurt, deteriorate, wrong, aggrieve, harm, spoil, mar, sully.
Ant.—Benefit, profit, repair, ameliorate, enhance, help.

Injurious, hurtful, baneful, pernicious, deleterious, noxious, prejudicial, wrongful, damaging.
Ant.—Beneficial, helpful.

Injustice, wrong, iniquity, grievance.
Ant. — Justice, right, law, probity, righteousness.

Inlet. (See Ingress.)

Innocent, guiltless, sinless, harmless, inoffensive, innoxious.
Ant.—Guilty, responsible, sinful, corrupt, bad, impure.

Innocuous, harmless, safe, innocent.
Ant.—Hurtful, injurious.

Innovation, alteration, novelty.
Ant. — Conservation, maintenance, archaism.

Inoffensive, harmless, innocent, innoxious, unoffending.
Ant. — Offensive, obnoxious, pernicious, harmful.

Inordinate, intemperate, irregular, disorderly, excessive, immoderate.
Ant.—Moderate, just, regular, temperate, orderly.

Inquisitive, prying, peeping, curious, peering.
Ant.—Indifferent, careless, incurious, dull, blind.

Inquiry, investigation, examination, research, scrutiny, disquisition, question, query, interrogation.
Ant.—Conjecture, guess, assumption, supposition, hypothesis.

Insane, mad, deranged, delirious, demented.
Ant.—Sane, healthy, sound, normal, rational.

Insanity, lunacy, madness, mental aberration, delirium.
Ant.—Sanity.

Inscribe, dedicate, devote, impress, engrave.
Ant.—Erase, expunge, obliterate, efface, deface.

Inside, interior, within, inland.
Ant.—Without, outside, extraneously, externally.

Insidious, sly, treacherous, crafty, artful, wily.
Ant.—Sincere, straightforward, undesigning.

Insight. (See Discernment.)

Insinuate, hint, intimate, suggest, infuse, ingratiate, introduce.
Ant.—State, affirm, propound, announce, withdraw, retract, extract.

Insipid, dull, flat, mawkish, tasteless, vapid, inanimate, lifeless.
Ant.—Racy, intense, strong, full-flavored, bright, sparkling.

Insist, persist, persevere, urge.
Ant.—Waive, yield, concede, surrender, forego.

Insolent, rude, saucy, pert, impertinent, abusive, scurrilous, opprobrious, insulting, offensive, outrageous.
Ant.—Deferential, polite, modest, respectful, considerate, courteous.

Inspect, examine, investigate, overhaul, supervise.
Ant.—Glance, overlook, connive, dismiss.

Inspire, animate, exhilarate, enliven, cheer, breathe, inhale.
Ant.—Depress, discourage, dispirit, deter.

Instability, mutability, fickleness, mutableness, wavering.
Ant.—Stability, durability, firmness, strength.

Install, induct, inaugurate, invest.
Ant.—Eject, degrade, dismiss, deprive.

Instance. (See Example.)

Instantaneous, direct, immediate, momentary, quick.
Ant. — Enduring, continuing, periodic, long, eternal.

Instantly, immediately, forthwith, straightway, directly, instanter.

Ant.—Soon, by and by, sometime.

Instigate, stir up, persuade, animate, incite, urge, stimulate, encourage, induce.
Ant. — Discourage, deter, dispirit, hinder, obstruct, abstain, depress, dishearten.

Instil, implant, inculcate, infuse, insinuate.
Ant.—Drain, extract, remove, eliminate, strain, deter, uproot, deaden, dull.

Institute, establish, found, erect, begin, form, organize, prescribe.
Ant.—Disestablish, overthrow, bankrupt, complete, finish, subvert.

Instruct, inform, teach, educate, enlighten, initiate.
Ant.—Misinform, misinstruct, misguide, mislead, deceive, barbarize, brutalize.

Instruction. (See Instruct.)

Instrument, tool, implement, utensil, medium, channel, agent.
Ant. — Bar, preventive, obstruction, hindrance, counteragent, opponent.

Instrumental, conducive, assistant, helping, ministerial.
Ant.—Non-instrumental, foreign, opposed, hindrance, hindering, impedimental.

Insufficiency, inadequacy, incompetency, incapability, deficiency, lack.
Ant. — Sufficient, enough, plenty, abundance, richness.

Insult, affront, outrage, indignity, blasphemy.
Ant.—Respect, honor, praise, flattery, compliment, esteem.

Insulting, insolent, rude, saucy, impertinent, abusive.
Ant. — Polite, well-mannered, gentle.

Insurrection, rebellion, mutiny, revolt, sedition.
Ant.—Law, peace, order, government, submission, subjection, obedience, bondage, servitude, pacification.

Integrity, uprightness, honesty, probity, entirety, entireness, completeness, rectitude, purity.
Ant. — Dishonesty, roguery, rascality, fraud, duplicity, meanness, chicanery.

Intellect, understanding, sense, brains, mind, intelligence, ability, talent, genius.
Ant.—Matter, force, passion, body, mechanism, organism, brute force, sense.

Intellectual, mental, ideal metaphysical, learned.
Ant. — Unintellectual, bodily, physical, ignorant, stupid, real, actual.

Intelligence, advice, information, instruction, notice, intellect, spirit, report, news.
Ant.—Stupidity, dullness, ignorance, misunderstanding, concealment, silence, misguidance.

Intelligent, understanding, enlightened, instructed, knowing.
Ant. — Unintelligent, stupid, foolish, ignorant.

Intelligible, clear, obvious, plain, distinct.
Ant. — Unintelligible, obscure, dull, indistinct, incoherent, abstruse.

Intemperate, immoderate, excessive, drunken, nimious, inordinate.
Ant. — Temperate, moderate, self-restrained, ascetic, austere, severe.

Intend. (See Purpose.)

Intense, ardent, earnest, glowing, fervid, burning, vehement, strained, forced, excessive, extreme.
Ant. — Indifferent, apathetic, cool, dispassioned, phlegmatic, cold, inert, uninterested.

Intent, purpose, design, intention, drift, view, aim, purport, meaning.

Intentional, designed, intended, contemplated, premeditated, studied.
Ant. — Unintentional, fortuitious, accidental, casual.

Inter, bury, entomb, inhume.
Ant. — Disinter, exhume, ressurrect.

Intercede, interpose, interfere, mediate, advocate.
Ant.—Inculpate, accuse, abandon, incriminate.

Intercourse, commerce, connection, intimacy, acquaintance.
Ant. — Reticence, cessation, suspension, opposition, isolation, separation, aloofness, detachment.

Interdict, forbid, prohibit, inhibit, proscribe, debar, restrain from.
Ant. — Grant, allow, indulge, concede, permit.

Interfere, interpose, meddle, intermeddle.
Ant.—Avoid, retire, stand off, withdraw.

Interior, inward, inner, inside, internal, intrinsic, inherent, innate.
Ant.—Exterior, outside, adjacent, external.

Intermediate, intervening, interjacent, between.
Ant. — Surrounding, outside, extreme, enclosing.

Interminable, endless, infinite, unlimited, illimitable, boundless, limitless, interminate.
Ant.—Terminable, brief, moderate, curt, short, concise, limited.

Intermission, cessation, pause, rest, stop, stoppage, interruption.
Ant. — Continuity, perpetuity, permanence, uninterruptedness.

Internal. (See Interior.)

Interpose, intercede, arbitrate, mediate, interfere, meddle.
Ant.—Retire, recede, remove, hold aloof, withdraw, retract. (See Interfere.)

Interpret, elucidate, explain, expound, unfold, decipher, translate, declare.
Ant. — Misinterpret, falsify, distort, mistake, misrepresent.

Interpretation, version, rendering, sense, construction, explanation.
Ant. — Misinterpretation, distortion, mistake, error, falsification, confuse, involve, perplex

Interrupt, disturb, hinder, break, divide.
Ant.—Continue, prosecute, expedite.

Interval, interlapse, space, period, gap.
Ant.—Continuity, simultaneousness.

Intervention, agency, interposition, mediation.
Ant. — Non-intervention, continuity, opposition, encouragement, instigation.

Intimate, hint, suggest, insinuate, express, signify, impart, tell.
Ant.—Conceal, retain, withhold, reserve.

Intimidate, frighten, dishearten, alarm, affright, scare, appal, daunt, cow, quail, browbeat.
Ant.—Encourage, inspirit, animate, reassure, cheer, countenance, embolden, inspire, promote.

Intolerable, insufferable, insupportable, unendurable, unbearable.
Ant. — Tolerable, allowable, endurable, supportable, bearable.

Intoxicated, drunk, tipsy, inebriated, fuddled, muddled.
Ant.—Sober, sane, depressed, melancholy, clearheaded.

Intrepid, bold, brave, daring, fearless, dauntless, undaunted, courageous, valorous, valiant, heroic, gallant, chivalrous, doughty.
Ant.—Cowardly, faint-hearted.

Intricacy, difficulty, complexity, complication, involution, perplexity.
Ant. — Simplicity, directness, obviousness, clearness.

Intrigue, plot, conspiracy, combination, artifice, ruse, cabal, amour.

Ant.—Rebellion, insurrection, candor, openness, honesty, probity.

Intrinsic, genuine, sterling, native, real, true, natural.

Ant. — Extrinsic, acquired, borrowed, added, assumed, pretended.

Introduce, present, usher, bring in, begin.

Ant. — Estrange, eject, conclude, terminate, end.

Introduction, preface, prelude, exordium, prologue, preamble.

Ant.—Conclusion, completion, end.

Intrude, force in, obtrude, trench, infringe, invade, interfere.

Ant.—Withdraw, hold back, retire, restrain, withhold.

Intrust. (See Commit.)

Inundate, drown, overflow, deluge, flood, submerge, overwhelm.

Ant.—Drain, dry, parch, burn.

Inure. (See Accustom.)

Invade, attack, assail, infringe, encroach, trench, intrude, violate.

Ant.—Vacate, abandon, evacuate, relinquish.

Invalid. (See Weak.)

Invalidate, quash, cancel, overthrow, vacate, nullify, annul.

Ant. — Confirm, sustain, strengthen.

Invasion, invade, incursion, irruption, inroad, aggression, raid, fray.

Invective, abuse, reproach, railing, censure, sarcasm, satire.

Ant.—Commendation, eulogy, panegyric, laudation, praise, encouragement.

Invent, devise, contrive, frame, fabricate, discover, design, find out.

Ant. — Imitate, copy, reproduce. (See Discover.)

Invert, upset, overturn, overthrow, subvert, reverse.

Ant.—Erect, fix, conserve establish, ground.

Invest, surround, besiege, endue, clothe.

Investigation, examination, search, inquiry, research, scrutiny.

Inveterate, confirmed, chronic, malignant.

Ant. — Incipient, unformed, undeveloped, inchoate.

Invidious, unfair, partial, envious, hateful, odious, malignant.

Ant.—Fair, impartial, considerate, due, just, benevolent, charitable, generous, kindly, humane.

Invigorate, brace, harden, nerve, strengthen, fortify.

Ant.—Enervate, depress, sadden, frighten, weaken, enfeeble.

Invincible, unconquerable, impregnable, insuperable, insurmountable.

Ant.—Weak, powerless, spiritless, puny, vulnerable.

Invisible, unseen, imperceptible, impalpable, unperceivable.

Ant.—Visible, seen, perceptible, palpable, tangible, evident, actual.

Invite, summon, challenge, ask, call, bid, request, allure, attract, solicit.

Ant. — Forbid, exclude, expel, discard, repel, cut, ignore.

Invoke, invocate, call upon, appeal, refer, implore, beseech.

Ant.—Ignore, defy, warn, inhibit, deprecate, avoid, dodge, elude, shun.

Involuntary, compulsory, exacted, coercive.

Ant.—Voluntary, spontaneous, free, deliberate, optional.

Involve, implicate, entangle, compromise, envelop.

Ant.—Separate, extricate, disconnect, disentangle, remove.

Inward, interior, internal, inner.

Ant.—Outward, exterior, external.

Ire. (See Anger.)

Irksome, tedious, wearisome, tiresome, annoying.

Ant.—Pleasant, delightful.

Irony, sarcasm, satire, ridicule, raillery.

Ant. — Compliment, seriousness, honesty

Irrational, foolish, silly, imbecile, brutish, unreasonable, absurd, preposterous, ridiculous.

Ant.—Rational, right, correct, learned, cultivated, reasonable, logical, sensible, sane, sound.

Irregular, eccentric, anomalous, inordinate, intemperate

Ant.—Regular, ordinary, common, temperate, established, fixed, formal, methodical.

Irreligious, profane, godless, impious, sacrilegious, desecrating.

Ant.—Religious, pious, orthodox, sacred, holy, saintly, godly.

Irreproachable, blameless, spotless, irreprovable, unblemished.

Ant. — Reproachable, blamable, censurable, reprovable, blame-worthy, culpable, faulty.

Irresistible, resistless, opposeless, irrepressible

Ant. — Resistible, defensible, repressible. (See Imperative.)

Irresolute, wavering, undetermined, undecided, vacillating.

Ant. — Resolute, determined, bold, decided, firm, persistent.

Irritable, excitable, irascible, susceptible, sensitive, hasty.

Ant. — Calm, good-tempered, cool, quiet, composed, placid.

Irritate, aggravate, worry, provoke, embitter, madden, exasperate, displease.

Ant.—Soothe, mollify, pacify, caress, comfort.

Issue, *v.* emerge, rise, proceed, flow, spring, emanate.

Ant.—Cause, originate, commence, order

Issue, *n.* end, upshot, effect, result, offspring, progeny.

J

Jade, harass, weary, tire, worry.

Ant.—Refresh, recruit, invigorate, inspirit, cheer, relieve, soothe, help.

Jangle, wrangle, conflict, disagree.

Ant.—Agree, debate, discourse, quiet, assuage.

Jarring, discordant, conflicting, inconsonant, inconsistent.

Ant.—Harmonious, consistent.

Jaunt, ramble, excursion, trip.

Jealousy, suspicion, envy, invidiousness, covetousness.

Ant. — Liberality, indulgence, toleration, indifference, confidence, trust.

Jeer, sneer, scoff, mock, deride, banter

Ant. — Flatter, fawn, compliment, eulogize.

Jeopard, hazard, peril, endanger.

Ant.—Safeguard, protect.

Jeopardy, risk, peril, hazard, danger, chance, venture.

Ant. — Safety, security, provision, insurance.

Jest, joke, sport, diversion.

Ant.—Gravity, seriousness, sobriety

Jocose, jocular, jolly, facetious, witty, pleasant.

Ant.—Serious, earnest, melancholy, grave, lugubrious.

Jocund, light-hearted, lively, sprightly, vivacious, sportive, merry, mirthful, blithesome.

Ant.—Melancholy, dull, grave, mournful, cheerless, sorrowful.

Join, accompany, go with, add, unite, append, adjoin, combine, confederate, league.

Ant. — Separate, leave, subtract, disconnect, oppose.

Jolly, merry, gay, mirthful, genial, joyous.

Ant.—Sad, mournful, cheerless, morose, gloomy.

Journey, tour, travel, passage.

Joviality. (See Merriment.)

Joy, delight, gladness, charm, pleasure, ecstacy, rapture, transport, mirth.

Ant.—Sorrow, pain, trouble,

misery, melancholy, grief, affliction, despondency, sadness.
Joyful, glad, rejoicing, exultant.
Ant. — Mournful, sorrowful, despondent.
Judge, justice, referee, arbitrator.
Judgment, discernment, discrimination, sagacity, intelligence, sentence, decision, order, award, understanding.
Ant.—Insagacity, inquiry, argument, speculation, proposition, investigation.
Judicious, wise, sage, thoughtful, discerning, just.
Ant.—Unwise, foolish, imprudent, injudicious, indiscreet, rash, blind, impolitic, unjust.
Juicy, succulent, bibulous, spongy.
Ant.—Dry, parched, wizened.
Jump, leap, bound, spring.
Ant.—Fall, crawl, glide, walk, run.
Junction, union, alliance, connection, confederacy, combination.
Ant.—Separation, disunion, dispersion, division, segregation, divergence.
Juncture, contact, touch, conjuncture, crisis.
Ant.—Course, arrangement, provision, preparation.
Just, right, proper, fair, equitable, impartial, honest, sound, reasonable, lawful.
Ant.—Unjust, unfair, partial, inexact, dishonorable, unsound.
Justice, right, equity, law (justice is right as established by law; equity according to the circumstances of each particular case.)
Ant.—Injustice, wrong, partiality, unfairness, illegality.
Justify, excuse, clear, exonerate, defend, absolve.
Ant.—Condemn, censure, convict, protest, accuse, inculpate.
Justness, accuracy, correctness.
Ant.—Error, fallacy.
Juvenile, young, youthful, boyish, infantile, childish.
Ant.—Mature, aged, manly, womanly, adult, elderly.

K

Keen, sharp, acute, penetrating, cutting, biting, stinging, sarcastic, satirical.
Ant.—Blunt, dull, blind, indifferent, languid.
Keep, retain, hold, detain, preserve, maintain, sustain, hinder, obey, continue, celebrate, save.
Ant.—Release, liberate, send, dismiss, betray, neglect, divulge, abandon, discard, disobey, forsake, desert, disregard.
Key. (See Solution.)
Kill, murder, assassinate, slay, massacre, butcher.
Ant.—Vivify, resuscitate, animate, save, protect.
Kind, *a.* thoughtful, affable, gentle, meek, tender, good, gracious, compassionate, indulgent, forbearing.
Ant.—Unkind, harsh, severe, cruel, hard.
Kind, *n.* species, sort, class, genus, nature, character.
Ant.—Inaffinity, irrelation.
Kindle, ignite, enkindle, awaken, arouse, stir up, excite.
Ant.—Extinguish, quench, suppress, allay.
Kindred, affinity, relatives, kinsfolk, related, connected, akin, consanguinity, relationship.
Ant. — Strangers, foreigners, disconnection, unrelated, alien, foreign.
Kingly. (See Regal.)
Kinsfolk. (See Kindred.)
Knave, rogue, scoundred, rascal.
Ant.—Gentleman, dupe, simpleton, innocent.
Knavish, roguish, dishonest, fraudulent.
Ant.—Honest, square, fair.
Knowledge, learning, scholarship, acquirements, attainments, information, understanding, erudition, science.
Ant.—Ignorance, inexperience, illiteracy, incomprehension, stupidity, folly.

L

Laborious, hard-working, industrious, diligent, assiduous, active, toilsome, wearisome.
Ant.—Idle, lazy, indolent, easy, light, simple.
Labor, work, task, toil, exertion, effort, drudgery.
Ant.—Indolence, ease, inactivity, rest, recreation, facility, skill, idleness, leisure.
Laborer. (See Workman.)
Lack, want, need, require, deficiency, scarcity, insufficiency.
Ant.—Supply, satisfy, plenty, abundance.
Laconic, short, brief, concise, curt.
Ant.—Prolix, garrulous, loquacious, prosy, long.
Lag, tarry, linger, loiter, saunter.
Ant. — Hasten, hurry, rush, press, speed.
Lame, limp, halt, hobble, hop, weak, hesitating.
Ant.—Agile, robust, efficient, telling, effective.
Lament, grieve, mourn, regret, bewail, deplore, bemoan, weep.
Ant.—Welcome, hail, rejoice, exult, triumph.
Language, speech, tongue, dialect, phraseology, idiom.
Ant.—Muteness, jargon, gibberish, cry, whine, howl.
Languid, weak, faint, drooping.
Ant.—Strong, healthy, robust, active.
Lank, lean, thin, skinny, meager, scraggy.
Ant.—Plump, rounded, short, full.
Lapse, elapse, glide, pass, roll.
Ant.—Fix, stay, stand, arrest, stop, retain.
Large, big, great, huge, vast, extensive, wide, liberal.
Ant. — Small, mean, narrow, contracted, scanty, petty, illiberal, bigoted.
Lascivious, loose, unchaste, lustful, lewd, lecherous.
Ant.—Chaste, modest.
Lash, scourge, whip, flog, beat, fasten.
Ant.—Anoint, smooth, rub, unfasten.
Lassitude, weariness, fatigue, languor.
Ant.—Health, strength, activity, freshness.
Last, latest, hindmost, utmost, extreme, final, ultimate.
Ant.—First, initiatory, opening, foremost, highest, next, nearest.
Lasting, durable, abiding, permanent, perpetual, continuing.
Ant. — Ending, transient, ephemeral.
Latent, hidden, secret, occult, inscrutable.
Ant.—Visible, apparent, manifest, conspicuous, explicit.
Laud. (See Praise.)
Laudable, commendable, praiseworthy.
Ant.—Blamable.
Laughable, ridiculous, comical, droll, ludicrous.
Ant.—Serious, grave.
Lavish, profuse, extravagant, prodigal.
Ant. — Chary, sparing, close, niggardly, mean, economical.
Lawful, legal, legitimate, rightful, constitutional, licit.
Ant.—Unlawful, illegal, wrong, lawless, unfair, ungovernable, inequitable.
Lax, loose, vague, dissolute, licentious, remiss.
Ant.—Concise, coherent, compact, strict, rigid, severe, conscientious.
Lazy, idle, indolent, slothful, sluggish, inactive.
Ant. — Industrious, energetic, laborious, active, alert.
Lead, conduct, guide, direct, induce, persuade, influence.
Ant.—Mislead, dissuade, follow, abandon, leave, misguide.
Leader. (See Chief.)
Leading, principal, chief, governing, ruling, important.
Ant. — Unimportant, subordi-

nate, inferior, lower, succeeding, following.

League, alliance, confederacy, combination, coalition, union.
Ant.—Dissolution, neutrality, secession, disunion, alienation.

Lean, *a.* thin, scraggy, lank, skinny, meager.
Ant. — Fat, stout, brawny, plump.

Lean, *v.* incline, tend, bend, slope, rest, repose, confide.
Ant.—Erect, raise, rise, straighten, stabilitate.

Leap. (See Jump.)

Learned, erudite, scholarly.
Ant.—Ignorant.

Learning, knowledge, scholarship, erudition, lore.
Ant.—Ignorance, illiteracy, intuition, revelation, inspiration.

Leave, *n.* liberty, license, permission.
Ant.—Prohibition, prevention, refusal, restriction.

Leave, *v.* quit, relinquish, renounce, give up, retire, depart, go, withdraw, abandon.
Ant.—Pursue, prosecute, seek, court, hold, keep, support, occupy, cherish, shelter, nurture, harbor, foster, entertain.

Legal. (See Lawful.)

Legend, fable, myth, memoir, chronicle.
Ant.—Fact, history, transaction, substantiation.

Legitimate, legal, lawful, genuine, fair.
Ant.—Illegitimate, illicit, unallowable, unfair, bastard.

Leisure, vacation, recess, freedom, convenience, ease.
Ant. — Toil, labor, business, employment, occupation, engagement.

Lengthen, extend, elongate, protract, prolong.
Ant. — Condense, abbreviate, shorten, contract.

Lessen, abate, diminish, decrease, lower, subside.
Ant.—Lengthen, increase, extend, elongate.

Let. (See Allow.)

Letter, epistle, note, communication.
Ant.—Word, speech, conversation.

Level, even, plain, smooth, flat.
Ant.—Uneven, unequal, rough, rolling, inclined.

Levity, giddiness, lightness, flightiness.
Ant. — Gravity, earnestness, seriousness.

Liable, exposed to, subject to, amenable.
Ant.—Independent, autocratic.

Libel, lampoon, pasquinade, defamation, calumny.
Ant.—Eulogy, panegyric, puff, encomium, apology, vindication.

Liberal, generous, bountiful, bounteous, munificent, plentiful.
Ant.—Illiberal, mean, ungenerous, bigoted, prejudiced.

Liberate, set free, free, deliver, discharge, release, let go.
Ant.—Confine, immure, imprison, restrict, bind, enslave.

Liberty, leave, permission, freedom, independence.
Ant.—Slavery, servitude, dependence, submission, constraint.

Licentious, loose, lax, dissolute, rakish, unbridled, debauched.
Ant.—Temperate, strict, sober, ascetic, rigid.

Lie, untruth, falsehood, falsity, fabrication, fiction, invention, story.
Ant.—Truth, fact, verity.

Life, animation, vivacity, buoyancy, spirit, history, career, existence.
Ant.—Death, decease, lethargy, torpor, dullness.

Lifeless, dead, inanimate, inert, sluggish.
Ant.—Vigorous, lively, animated.

Lift, raise, elevate, erect, exalt, hoist.
Ant.—Sink, depress, degrade, lower, cast, hurl.

Light, illuminate, illumine, enlighten, lighten, clear, bright.
Ant.—Darken, obscure, dim, shade, mystify, misinterpret, dark.

Lightness, levity, flightiness, volatility, giddiness, inconstancy, frivolity.
Ant.—Darkness, gravity, seriousness.

Likeness, picture, image, effigy, resemblance, similarity, representation, similitude.
Ant.—Original, unlikeness, dissimilarity, inequality, disparity, difference, variation.

Likelihood. (See Probability.)

Likewise, also, too, as well.
Ant.—Nor, otherwise.

Limit, *n.* extent, boundary, bound, border.
Ant.—Extension, infinity.

Limit, *v.* bound, circumscribe, restrict, confine.
Ant.—Extend, prolong, unconfine, loosen.

Limpid. (See Clear.)

Lineage, descent, family, house, generation.
Ant.—Source, origin, ancestry.

Linger, tarry, loiter, wait, lag, saunter.
Ant. — Hasten, speed, press, push, expedite, urge, quicken.

Link, tie, bind, join, chain.
Ant.—Disjoin, break, untie, unbind.

Liquid, fluid, juicy, watery, fluent, limpid.
Ant.—Solid, hard, congealed, dry, harsh, discordant.

List. (See Catalogue.)

Listen, list, hearken, heed, attend to.
Ant.—Ignore, disregard, refuse, repudiate.

Listless, indifferent, indolent, careless, languid.
Ant.—Eager, attentive, active, earnest, awake, interested.

Literal, actual, real, positive, true.
Ant.—General, metaphorical, figurative, free.

Little, small, diminutive, dwarf, tiny, short, scanty, brief, slight, weak, petty, paltry.
Ant.—Big, bulky, large, enormous, huge, long, full, much, important, liberal, generous, noble, great.

Live, exist, subsist, dwell, act.
Ant.—Die, perish, wither, vanish, fade, fail, depart.

Livelihood, living, support, sustenance, subsistence, maintenance.
Ant.—Want, starvation, beggary.

Lively, active, brisk, quick, sprightly, prompt, buoyant, racy, vivacious, jocund, merry, sportive, sprightly.
Ant.—Lifeless, listless, dull, indifferent, torpid, insensible, slow, languid, sluggish.

Loath, *a.* reluctant, backward, unwilling.
Ant. — Eager, willing, alert, anxious.

Loathe. (See Abhor.)

Lofty, high, tall, elevated, exalted.
Ant.—Low, depressed, stunted, undignified.

Logical, sound, argumentative, conclusive.
Ant. — Illogical, inconclusive, fallacious.

Loiter, wait, linger, tarry, saunter, lag.
Ant.—Hasten, hurry, speed, rush.

Lone. (See Solitary.)

Long, extended, extensive.
Ant.—Short, brief, concise.

Look, see, witness, view, eye, inspect, appear, seem, behold, scan, survey, watch, regard.
Ant.—Overlook, hide, avert, miss, lurk.

Loose, vague, indefinite, lax, slack, dissolute, licentious, rakish, wanton.
Ant.—Tied, fast, bound, tight, compact, accurate, exact, logical, conscientious.

Lose, miss, forfeit.
Ant. — Gain, obtain, secure, achieve.

Loss, damage, detriment, waste, deprivation.
Ant.—Gain, advantage, satisfaction, recovery, economy, profit.

Lot, destiny, future, doom.

Ant.—Law, provision, design, purpose, portion.

Loud, noisy, clamorous, vociferous, blustering, riotous, turbulent, tumultuous.

Ant.—Soft, quiet, gentle, subdued, dulcet, inaudible, low.

Love, endearment, affection, attachment, fondness.

Ant.—Hatred, dislike, coldness, indifference, repugnance, malice.

Lovely, charming, amiable, delightful.

Ant.—Homely, unlovely, unattractive, hideous, plain.

Lover, suitor, sweetheart, wooer.

Ant.—Rival, foe, opponent.

Low, humble, lowly, base, mean, filthy, foul, gentle, abject.

Ant. — High, tall, elevated, raised, loud, eminent, lofty, noble.

Lower, reduce, humble, humiliate, degrade, debase.

Ant.—Hoist, raise, heighten, increase, elevate.

Luck. (See Chance.)

Luckless. (See Hapless.)

Lucre, gain, profit, emolument, money.

Ant. — Loss, poverty, dross, failure, privation.

Ludicrous. (See Ridiculous.)

Lull, quiet, hush, still, calm.

Ant.—Storm, tempest, tumult, excitement.

Luminous. (See Light.)

Lunacy, derangement, madness, insanity, aberration, mania.

Ant.—Sanity, reason, intelligence, lucidity.

Lurid, gloomy, murky, lowering.

Ant.—Bright, luminous.

Luscious, honeyed, sweet, mellifluous.

Ant.—Sour, sharp, tart, bitter.

Luster, splendor, brightness, brilliancy, effulgence, refulgence.

Ant.—Dimness, dullness, darkness, cloudiness, gloom.

Lusty, stout, strong, able-bodied, stalwart, robust, muscular.

Ant.—Infirm, weak, disabled, effete, listless.

Luxuriant, overflowing, exuberant, redundant, abundant.

Ant. — Poor, mean, small, sparse, meager.

Luxury, plenty, profuseness, voluptuousness.

Ant.—Asceticism, self-denial, hardship, poverty.

M

Machination, strategem, imposture, fraud, cheat, trick, plot, intrigue, cabal, conspiracy.

Ant.—Detection, baffling, defeat, exposure, overthrow, artlessness, directness, candor.

Mad, wild, frantic, distracted, furious, rabid, insane, crazy, delirious, violent.

Ant. — Sane, sensible, composed, sober, rational, quiet.

Madden, irritate, enrage, exasperate.

Ant.—Calm, soothe, pacify, assuage.

Madness, mental aberration, insanity, lunacy, mania, frenzy, rage, fury.

Ant. — Sanity, sense, composure, sobriety, rationality.

Magisterial, august, dignified, majestic, pompous, stately.

Ant.—Pitiful, wretched.

Magnanimous, generous, august, dignified, noble, exalted, lofty.

Ant. — Mean, petty, paltry, spiteful.

Magnificence, splendor, grandeur, gorgeousness, pomp.

Ant.—Tameness, tawdryness, pettiness, smallness.

Magnify, enlarge, extol, applaud, laud, amplify.

Ant.—Diminish, contract, curtail, extenuate, decry.

Magnitude. (See Size.)

Maim, mutilate, mangle, cripple, lame.

Ant.—Mend, strengthen, restore.

Main, chief, principal, leading, first.

Ant.—Portion, inferior, subordinate.

Maintain. (See Support.)

Majestic, dignified, noble, stately, pompous, grand.

Ant.—Mean, small, undignified, petty.

Majesty, grandeur, dignity.

Ant.—Meanness, debasement, degradation.

Make, create, form, produce, mold, shape, construct, gain, fashion, cause, constitute, establish, execute, frame.

Ant.—Destroy, demolish, annihilate, dismember, undo, defeat, miss, lose, mar, break.

Malady, ailment, disease, distemper, disorder, sickness.

Ant.—Health, vigor, soundness.

Malediction, curse, imprecation, denunciation, anathema, execration.

Ant. — Benediction, eulogy, compliment, blessing.

Malefactor. (See Criminal.)

Malevolent, malicious, virulent, malignant.

Ant.—Benevolent, kindly.

Malice, spite, rancor, ill-feeling, grudge, pique, animosity, ill-will.

Ant.—Charity, toleration, love, kindness, affection, benignity, good-will.

Malicious, virulent, malignant, wicked, malevolent.

Ant.—Kind, lovable, affectionate, charitable, good.

Manacle, chain, shackle, fetter.

Ant.—Free, liberate.

Manage, contrive, concert, direct, handle, control, regulate.

Ant.—Mismanage, misconduct, upset, derange, govern.

Management, direction, superintendence, care, economy.

Ant.—Maltreatment, mismanagement, misconduct, neglect, remissness.

Mangle, maim, tear, lacerate, mutilate, cripple, rend.

Ant.—Heal, mend, secure, unite, weld.

Mania, madness, insanity, lunacy.

Ant.—Sanity.

Manifest, *v.* exhibit, clear, plain, evident, open, apparent, visible.

Ant.—Hidden, occult.

Manifest, *a.* (See Evident.)

Manifold, several, sundry, various, divers, complex, many, numerous.

Ant.—Limited, few, scant, rare, homogeneous, plain, simple, uncombined, uniform.

Manly, masculine, hardy, vigorous, courageous, brave, heroic.

Ant.—Effeminate, childish, unmanly, dastardly, weak, boyish, timid, feminine.

Manner, habit, custom, way, air, look, appearance, mode, style, fashion.

Ant. — Design, performance, life, action, appearance, being.

Manners, morals, habits, behavior, carriage.

Ant.—Misbehavior, awkwardness, misdemeanor.

Many, numerous, several, sundry, divers, various, manifold.

Ant.—Few, scarce, rare, infrequent.

Mar, injure, spoil, ruin, disfigure.

Ant.—Ameliorate, improve.

March, tramp, tread, walk, step, pace.

Ant.—Halt, stop, stand, rest, crawl, creep, jump, skip, run.

Margin, edge, rim, border, brink, verge.

Ant.—Center, space, figure, restriction, middle.

Marine, maritime, nautical, naval.

Ant.—Territorial, land, earthly.

Mark, *n.* sign, note, symptom, token, indication, trace, vestige, track, badge, brand.

Ant.—Erasure, effacement, obliteration, plainness, avoidance, neglect.

Mark, *v.* impress, print, stamp, engrave, note, notice, remark, show, indicate, designate.

Ant.—Ignore, overlook, omit, misindicate.

Marked. (See Remarkable.)
Marriage, wedding, nuptials, matrimony, wedlock.
Ant.—Celibacy, virginity, divorce.
Marsh. (See Swamp.)
Martial, military, warlike, soldierlike.
Ant.—Peaceful, civil.
Marvel, wonder, miracle, prodigy.
Marvelous, wonderful, wondrous, amazing, miraculous.
Ant.—Commonplace, usual.
Masculine. (See Manly.)
Mask, visor, cloak, veil, blind.
Ant.—Truth, exposure, detection, openness, candor.
Massacre, carnage, slaughter, butchery.
Ant.—Deliverance, quarter, ransom.
Massive, bulky, heavy, weighty, ponderous, solid, substantial.
Ant.—Slight, frail, light, slender, flimsy.
Master, possessor, proprietor, head, owner.
Ant.—Servant, slave, subject, property, pupil.
Masterly, skillful, clever, expert, dexterous, adroit.
Ant.—Clumsy, rude, unskilled.
Mastery, dominion, rule, sway, ascendancy, supremacy, authority, victory.
Ant. — Submission, tutelage, guidance, obedience, failure, defeat, surrender.
Matchless, unrivaled, unequaled, unparalleled, peerless, incomparable, inimitable, surpassing, unique.
Ant.—Common, ordinary, commonplace, usual.
Material, corporeal, bodily, physical, temporal, momentous, essential, important.
Ant. — Immaterial, spiritual, metaphysical, ideal, nonessential, ethereal.
Matrimony. (See Marriage.)
Matter. (See Substance; see also Affair.)
Mature. (See Ripe.)
Mawkish, insipid, flat, spiritless, vapid.
Ant.—Savory, sound, pungent, palatable.
Maxim, adage, apophthegm, proverb, saying, by-word, saw, apothegm, truism, dictum.
Ant.—Enigma, sophism, quibble, absurdity, paradox, demonstration.
Meager, poor, lank, emaciated, barren, dry, uninteresting.
Ant.—Stout, fat, brawny, fertile, copious, rich, abundant, fruitful.
Mean, *a.* stingy, niggardly, low, abject, vile, ignoble, degraded, contemptible, vulgar, despicable.
Ant.—Generous, openhanded, extravagant, noble, lofty, dignified, exalted, extreme, excessive.
Mean, *v.* design, purpose, intend, contemplate, signify, denote, indicate.
Ant.—Say, state, enunciate, do, perform.
Meaning, signification, import, acceptation, sense, purport, drift.
Ant.—Statement, saying, speech, proposition, passage.
Means, way, manner, method, mode, resources, instrument.
Ant.—End, purpose, object.
Mechanic. (See Workman.)
Meddlesome, officious, intermeddling, interfering.
Ant.—Helpful, unofficious, inobtrusive.
Mediate, intercede, interpose, interfere, arbitrate.
Ant.—Combat, excite, irritate.
Mediocrity, commonplace, mean, Average.
Ant.—Superiority, excellence, distinction.
Meditate, think, reflect, muse, plan.
Ant. — Execute, enact, complete, consummate.
Medium, means, organ, channel, instrument.
Medley, mixture, variety, diversity, miscellany, confusion, hodge-podge.
Ant.—Classification, order, arrangement, assortment, grouping.
Meek, unassuming, mild, gentle, yielding.
Ant.—Bold, arrogant, proud, high-spirited, haughty.
Meet, apt, fit, suitable, expedient, proper.
Ant.—Unsuitable, unfit, unmeet.
Meeting. (See Assembly.)
Melancholy, low-spirited, dispirited, dreamy, sad, dejected.
Ant.—Merry, lively, sprightly, blithesome, cheerful, happy, jolly, buoyant.
Mellow, ripe, mature, soft.
Ant. —Unripe, sour, harsh, crabbed, dry, immature.
Melodious, musical, tuneful, silver, dulcet, sweet.
Ant.—Discordant, grating, harsh.
Melt, liquefy, fuse, dissolve, moisten.
Ant.—Consolidate, freeze, congeal, crystallize.
Memoir, narrative, chronicle, legent, life, history.
Ant. — Myth, tradition, romance.
Memorable, signal, distinguished, marked, famous, remarkable, extraordinary.
Ant.—Ordinary, insignificant, petty, trivial, unimportant.
Memorial, monument, memento, commemoration, annals, archives.
Ant. — Obliteration, erasure, effacement.
Memory, remembrance, recollection, fame.
Ant.—Forgetfulness, oblivion.
Menace, threat.
Mend, amend, correct, better, ameliorate, improve, rectify, repair.
Ant.—Impair, damage, mar, corrupt, spoil, prevent.
Menial, servant, domestic, drudge.
Ant.—Master, lord, sovereign, autocrat.
Mention, tell, name, communicate, impart, divulge, reveal, disclose, inform, acquaint.
Ant.—Conceal, retain, withhold, suppress, omit, forget.
Mercenary, sordid, selfish, avaricious.
Ant.—Generous, prodigal, liberal, unselfish.
Merchant, trader, tradesman, dealer.
Ant.—Salesman, peddler, jobber, employee.
Merciful, compassionate, lenient, clement, tender, gracious, kind.
Ant.—Merciless, cruel, unmerciful, pitiless, remorseless, brutal, unfeeling.
Merciless, hard-hearted, cruel, unmerciful, pitiless, remorseless, unrelenting.
Ant.—(See Preceding.)
Mercy, lenient, mildness, clemency, compassion, pity.
Ant.—Vengeance, cruelty, harshness, execution.
Merit, worth, desert, excellence.
Ant.—Badness, demerit, imperfection, defect, fault, failing.
Merited, deserved, condign, suitable, adequate, proper.
Ant.—Unmerited, undeserved, improper.
Merriment, mirth, joviality, jollity, hilarity.
Ant. — Soberness, sobriety, gravity, moroseness, lugubriousness, sorrow, sadness, melancholy.
Merry, cheerful, mirthful, joyous, gay, lively, sprightly, blithe, blithesome, jovial, sportive, jolly, hilarious.
Ant.—Melancholy, dispirited, sad, gloomy, sober, grave, mournful, morose.
Metaphorical, figurative, allegorical, symbolical, tropical.
Ant.—Literal, exact, actual.
Method, way, manner, mode, process, order, rule, system, regularity.
Ant. — Disorder, assumption, hazard, guess-work, conjecture, chaos, confusion, irregularity.

Mien, air, behavior, look, manner, aspect, appearance.
Mighty, powerful, potent.
Ant.—Weak, impotent, feeble, infirm.
Migratory, roving, strolling, wandering, vagrant.
Ant.—Settled, sedate, permanent, fixed, stationary.
Mild, soft, meek, gentle, kind, calm, moderate.
Ant. — Violent, wild, fierce, savage, strong, severe, harsh, bitter.
Military, soldierlike, martial, warlike.
Ant.—Unmilitary, peaceful, civil, civilian, unmartial.
Mimic, imitate, ape, mock.
Ant.—Change, distort, transform, vary.
Mind, *v.* heed, advert to, regard.
Ant.—Disregard, ignore, overlook, miss.
Mind, *n.* sentiment, opinion, idea, notion, intellect, understanding.
Ant.—Body, limbs, action, conduct, object, aversion.
Mindful, observant, attentive, heedful, thoughtful, careful.
Ant.—Regardless, inattentive, mindless, oblivious, heedless, careless.
Mingle, mix, blend, compound, amalgamate.
Ant.—Separate, sift, sort, analyze, eliminate, unravel.
Minister, *n.* official, divine, clergyman, ecclesiastic, parson, curate, incumbent.
Ant. — Government, nation, master, head, layman.
Minister, *v.* administer, contribute, supply.
Ant.—Rule, command, exact.
Minute, particular, specific, circumstantial, microscopic.
Ant.—Big, huge, enormous, superficial, general, comprehension.
Mirth, joy, merriment, gladness, festivity, joviality, hilarity, cheerfulness, vivacity, gaiety, fun, jollity.
Ant.—Sadness, sorrow, trouble, gravity, sobriety, melancholy.
Miscellaneous, promiscuous, indiscriminate, mixed.
Ant.—Selected, classified, orderly, systematized, homogeneous.
Miscellany, medley, diversity, variety, mixture.
Ant.—System, order, group, collection, classification.
Mischance, calamity, disaster, misfortune, mishap, misadventure.
Ant.—Chance, design, purpose, predestination, law.
Mischief, injury, harm, damage, hurt, evil, ill.
Ant. — Compensation, benefit, favor, good, advantage, blessing, boon, remedy, service.
Misconception, misapprehension, misunderstanding, mistake.
Ant.—Conception, understanding, truth, verity.
Miscreant, rogue, caitiff, villain, ruffian.
Ant.—Benefactor, philanthropist.
Miserable, unhappy, wretched, distressed, afflicted.
Ant.—Happy, contented, comfortable, respectable, worthy, gay.
Miserly, stingy, niggardly, avaricious, griping.
Ant. — Prodigal, extravagant, generous, liberal, open handed.
Misery, wretchedness, woe, destitution, penury, privation, beggary.
Ant.—Happiness, comfort, content, respect, worth, luxury, ease, good fortune.
Misfortune, disaster, calamity, mishap, catastrophe.
Ant.—Good luck, windfall.
Misguide, mislead, dazzle, beguile, deceive.
Ant.—Guide, lead, show, conduct, aid, help, encourage.
Mislead. (See Misguide.)
Misrule, anarchy, confusion.
Ant.—Rule, order, stability, government, peace.
Miss, omit, lose, fail, miscarry.
Ant.—Meet, spy, accost, address, conduct, grasp, accomplish, understand.
Mission, commission, legation, embassy, errand.
Ant.—Assumption, usurpation, self-appointment, relaxation, pleasure.
Mistake, *n.* (See Error.)
Mistake, *v.* err, fail, misconceive, misapprehend.
Ant.—Apprehend, affirm, know, recognize.
Misty, murky, dark, dim, obscure, cloudy, shadowy, dusky.
Ant.—Bright, clear, lucid.
Misunderstand. (See Mistake.)
Mitigate, alleviate, relieve, abate, diminish.
Ant.—Aggravate, enhance, enlarge, increase, extend.
Mix. (See Mingle.)
Mixture. (See Variety.)
Mob, crowd, concourse, multitude, throng, bevy.
Ant.—Individual, meeting, congregation.
Mock, mimic, imitate, ape, deride, ridicule.
Ant.—Salute, respect, admire, compliment, copy.
Mode. (See Method.)
Model, copy, pattern, specimen, example, standard, type.
Ant.—Imitation, copy, execution, production, work.
Moderate, temperate, abstemious, sober, abstinent.
Ant.—Excessive, extravagant, intemperate, violent, immoderate, reckless.
Moderation, temperance, sobriety, abstemiousness.
Ant. — Excess, intemperance, extravagance.
Modern, novel, new, recent, present.
Ant.—By-gone, ancient, past, olden, antiquated.
Modest, chaste, virtuous, bashful, reserved, meek.
Ant.—Immodest, bold, vulgar, coarse, forward, pushing, assertive, impudent.
Moist, wet, damp, dank, humid, fertile, marshy, swampy.
Ant.—Arid, dry, parched.
Molest, annoy, incommode, discommode, incommodate, vex, tease, disturb.
Ant.—Soothe, caress, pacify, mollify.
Moment, consequence, weight, importance, instant, trice.
Ant.—Triviality, unimportance, insignificance, age, period.
Monotonous, unvaried, dull, tiresome, undiversified.
Ant.—Varied, diversified, different, relieved, diverse.
Monster, ruffian, villain, brute, prodigy.
Ant.—Beauty, gem, jewel, angel.
Monstrous, shocking, dreadful, horrible, prodigious, portentous, marvelous, abnormal, flagrant, huge, immense.
Ant.—Fair, comely, shapely, beautiful, ordinary, familiar, reasonable, just, excellent, superior, transcendent.
Monument, memorial, record, remembrancer, cenotaph.
Mood, humor, vein, temper, disposition, nature, character.
Moral, regular, strict, virtuous, ethical.
Ant.—Immoral, vicious, bad, physical, material.
Morass. (See Swamp.)
Morbid, sick, ailing, sickly, diseased, corrupted.
Ant.—Healthy, sound, wholesome, normal.
Morning, daybreak, morn, dawn, sunrise, forenoon, a. m.
Ant.—Evening, afternoon, night, sunset, p. m.
Morose, gloomy, sullen, surly, fretful, crabbed, crusty.
Ant.—Genial, kindly, gentle, indulgent, joyous, merry, gay.
Mortal, human, deadly, fatal, destructive.
Ant.—Divine, immortal, celestial, life-giving, eternal, everlasting.
Mortify, vex, chagrin, grieve, hurt, afflict, annoy, rot, putrefy.
Ant.—Please, gratify, delight,

indulge, pamper, heal, recover.

Motion, proposition, proposal, movement, change, action.
Ant.—Rest, equilibrium, stability, fixity, inaction, quiescence, quiet, repose, stillness.

Motionless, still, stationary, torpid, stagnant.
Ant.—Active, unstable, nervous, moving.

Motive, cause, reason, principle, inducement, incentive, impulse, spur, stimulus.
Ant.—Result, end, action, effort, deed, attempt.

Motley, heterogeneous, diversified, mixed.
Ant.—Uniform, homogeneous, alike.

Mottled, dappled, dotted, spotted, flecked, speckled.
Ant. — Uniform, unspotted, clear.

Mount, ascend, arise, rise, soar, tower, climb, scale.
Ant.—Descend, fall.

Mournful, sad, sorrowful, lugubrious, grievous, doleful, heavy.
Ant.—Happy, joyous, hilarious.

Move, actuate, impel, induce, prompt, instigate, persuade, stir, agitate, propel, push.
Ant.—Stand, stop, rest, stay, allay, deter, prevent, arrest, halt.

Moving, affecting touching, pathetic, melting.
Ant. — Laughing, ridiculous, absurd, ineffective.

Much, ample, plenteous, copious.
Ant.—Little, scant, short, near.

Muffle, deaden, disguise, conceal, cover, shroud.
Ant.—Unfold, exhibit, reveal.

Multitude, crowd, throng, host, mob, swarm.
Ant.—Paucity, scarcity, sprinkling, few, handful.

Munificent, bounteous, bountiful, generous, liberal.
Ant.—Niggardly, mean, beggarly, miserly.

Murder, kill, assassinate, slay, massacre, dispatch.
Ant. — Resuscitate, revivify, protect, shield, guard.

Murderous. (See Savage.)

Murky, dark, dusky, dim, cloudy, misty, shadowy.
Ant.—Clear, light, pleasant, bright.

Muse, meditate, contemplate, think, reflect, cogitate, ponder.
Ant.—Stir, act, move, perform.

Music, harmony, melody, symphony.
Ant.—Discord, babel, harshness, noise.

Musical, tuneful, melodious, harmonious, dulcet, sweet.
Ant.—Discordant, harsh, inharmonious, unmelodious, noisy.

Muster, collect, rally, assemble, congregate.
Ant.—Dismiss, disperse, disband, relegate.

Musty, stale, sour, fetid.
Ant.—Fresh, odorous, aromatic, fragrant, sweet.

Mutable, inconstant, unsteadfast, unstable, fickle, alterable, restless, fitful, variable, changeable, unsteady.
Ant.—Immutable, permanent, changeless, eternal.

Mute, dumb, silent, speechless.
Ant. — Voluble, garrulous, loquacious, talkative.

Mutilate, maim, cripple, disable, disfigure.

Mutinous, insurgent, seditious, tumultuous, turbulent, riotous.
Ant.—Orderly, obedient, quiet, pacific.

Mutual, reciprocal, interchanged, correlative.
Ant.—Disconnected, separate, unrequited, unshared.

Mysterious, dark, obscure, hidden, secret, dim, mystic, enigmatical, unaccountable.
Ant. — Clear, plain, obvious, simple, explained, understood, open.

Mystify, confuse, perplex, puzzle.
Ant.—Enlighten, inform, guide, elucidate, clear, explain.

Myth, fable, legend, fiction, parable.
Ant.—Fact, history, narration truth.

N

Naked, nude, bare, uncovered, unclothed, rough, rude, simple.
Ant.—Dressed, robed, clothed, protected, veiled, shrouded, covered, clad.

Name, *v.* denominate, style, designate, term, call, christen, specify, entitle.
Ant.—Misname, miscall, hint, suggest.

Name, *n.* appellation, designation, denomination, title, cognomen, reputation, character, fame, credit, repute.
Ant. — Misnomer, anonymity, pseudonym.

Narrate, tell, relate, detail, recount, describe, enumerate, rehearse, recite.
Ant.—Suppress, conceal, hide, retain, withhold, misrepresent, deny, hush up.

Narrow, bigoted, illiberal, contracted, confined, circumscribed, straightened, limited.
Ant.—Liberal, tolerant, generous, wide, broad, ample, easy.

Nasty, filthy, foul, dirty, unclean, impure, indecent, gross, vile.
Ant. — Nice, pure, agreeable, pleasant, good, proper.

Nation, people, community, realm, state.
Ant. — Individuals, subjects, dependents, colonists.

Native, real, genuine, indigenous, vernacular, mother, inborn.
Ant.—Foreign, alien, imported, acquired, artificial, assumed, affected.

Natural, original, regular, normal, bastard, spontaneous.
Ant. — Unnatural, abnormal, adventitious, fictitious, affected, forced.

Nausea, qualm, sea-sickness, disgust, loathing, aversion.
Ant.—Relish, enjoyment, taste, health.

Nautical. (See Marine.)

Near, nigh, neighboring, close, adjacent, contiguous, intimate.
Ant.—Far, distant, remote, off, foreign, removed.

Neat, nice, spruce, trim, precise, pure.
Ant.—Slovenly, careless, dirty, unclean, nasty.

Necessary, needful, expedient, essential, requisite, indispensable.
Ant. — Unnecessary, contingent, unessential, accidental, casual, optional, discretional, abortive, bootless, futile, ineffectual, nugatory, vain, valueless, worthless.

Necessitate, compel, force, oblige.
Ant.—Ask, suggest, hint, supplicate, beg, dissuade, hinder, impede, inhibit, prevent, restrain.

Necessity, need, occasion, exigency, emergency, urgency, want, poverty, requisite.
Ant.—Uncertainty, uselessness, superfluity, competence, casualty, contingency, freedom, choice, fortuity, option, possibility, uncertainty.

Need, *n.* necessity, distress, poverty, indigence, want, penury.

Need, *v.* require, want, lack, necessity.

Needful. (See Necessary.)

Neglect, *v.* disregard, slight, omit, overlook.
Ant.—Respect, consider, notice, observe, attend, regard, foster, cherish, nourish.

Neglect, *n.* omission, failure, default, negligence, remissness, carelessness, slight.
Ant.—Care, watchfulness.

Neighborhood, vicinity, nearness, adjacency, proximity, environs.
Ant.—Remoteness, distance.

Nerve, fiber, sinew, tendon, force, pluck, courage.
Ant. — Timidity, cowardice, hesitation.

Nerveless, feeble, impuissant, weak, forceless, enfeebled, debilitated, enervated, impotent, paralyzed, palsied.
Ant.—Strong, healthy, sound, active, bold, fearless.

Nervous, timid, timorous, shaky.
Ant.—Cool, collected, calm, confident, brave.

Nettle. (See Aggravate.)

Neutralize, counterbalance, counteract.
Ant.—Aggregate, enhance, intensify.

New, fresh, recent, novel, modern.
Ant.—Old, ancient, antique, antiquated, obsolete, trite, worn-out.

News, tidings, intelligence, information.
Ant.—Antiquity, oldness, staleness.

Nice, good, fine, delicate, exact, accurate, particular, precise, fastidious.
Ant. — Coarse, rude, rough, nasty, unscrupulous, inexact, inaccurate, careless, unpleasant.

Niggardly. (See Miserly.)

Nigh. (See Near.)

Nimble, active, brisk, lively, alert, quick, agile, prompt.
Ant.—Clumsy, dilatory, heavy, inert, sluggish, unready.

Nobility, aristocracy, greatness, grandeur, peerage.
Ant. — Obscurity, plebeian, meanness, commonality, smallness.

Noble, exalted, elevated, dignified, illustrious, great, grand, stately, lofty.
Ant.—Ignoble, mean, plebeian, paltry, small, low, vile.

Nocturnal, nightly, gloomy, dark.
Ant. — Diurnal, light, daily, brilliant, solar.

Noise, cry, outcry, clamor, row, din, uproar, tumult.
Ant.—Stillness, hush, silence, music, note, melody, quiet.

Nominate, name, entitle, appoint, invest, present.
Ant.—Suggest, indicate, recall, deprive, cancel, withdraw.

Nonsensical, silly, irrational, absurd, foolish.
Ant.—Sensible, rational, sane.

Notable, remarkable, plain, evident, signal, striking, rare.
Ant.—Obscure, insignificant.

Note, mark, token, symbol, sign, indication, remark, comment.

Noted, remarkable, distinguished, renowned, eminent.
Ant.—Obscure, unknown.

Notice, *n.* advice, notification, intelligence, information, warning.
Ant.—Neglect, oversight, disregard, slight, omission, ignore, overlook.

Notice, *v.* mark, note, observe, attend to, regard, heed.

Noticeable. (See Remarkable.)

Notification. (See Notice.)

Notify, publish, acquaint, communicate, inform, declare, apprise.
Ant.—Suppress, withhold, conceal, bury, hide.

Notion, conception, idea, belief, opinion, sentiment, impression.
Ant. — Misconception, misapprehension, falsification.

Notorious, noted, well-known, renowned, infamous, open, obvious, ill-famed.
Ant. — Suspected, reported, famous, mysterious, secret, unknown.

Nourish, nurture, cherish, foster, supply.
Ant.—Starve, blight, destroy, wither, kill, famish.

Nourishment, diet, food, sustenance, nutrition.

Novel, new, modern, fresh, recent, unused, strange, rare.
Ant.—Old, ancient, old-fashioned.

Noxious, hurtful, deadly, poisonous, deleterious, baneful.
Ant. — Wholesome, healthy, useful, beneficial, helpful, advantageous.

Nugatory, ineffectual, futile, useless, null, void.
Ant.—Potent, serious, important, efficacious, successful.

Nullify, annul, vacate, invalidate, repeal, quash, cancel.
Ant.—Confirm, establish.

Number. (See Count.)

Numerous, many, sundry, various, several.
Ant.—Few, sparse, scant.

Nuptials. (See Marriage.)

Nurture. (See Nourish.)

Nutrition, food, diet, nutriment, nourishment.
Ant.—Exhaustion, starvation, inanition.

O

Obdurate, hard, callous, hardened, unbending, graceless, unfeeling, insensible, unsusceptible.
Ant.—Tender, softened, flexible, yielding, amenable, docile, tractable.

Obedient, compliant, submissive, dutiful, respectful.
Ant.—Disobedient, rebellious, mutinous, antagonistic, obstinate, stubborn.

Obese, fat, corpulent, fleshy.
Ant.—Attenuated, thin, slender.

Obey, conform, comply, submit, yield.
Ant. — Resist, rebel, violate, transgress, disobey.

Object, *n.* aim, end, purpose, design, mark, butt.
Ant. — Idea, notion, subject, proposal, heedlessness, neglect, negligence, oversight.

Object, *v.* oppose, except to, contravene, impeach, deprecate.
Ant. — Agree, comply, aid, help, abet, encourage, assent, uphold.

Obligation, duty, favor, engagement, contract, bond.
Ant. — Promise, word, choice, freedom, intention, exemption.

Oblige, compel, bind, engage, concuss, coerce, constrain. force, impel, accommodate, gratify.
Ant.—Release, acquit, induce, persuade, annoy, disobey.

Obliging, accommodating, civil, courteous, considerate.
Ant.—Discourteous, rude, perverse, disobliging.

Obliterate, erase, blot out, expunge, efface.
Ant. — Insert, mark, note, introduce.

Obloquy, odium, reproach, censure, abuse, scurrility, opprobrium, shame.
Ant. — Praise, encomium, encouragement, congratulation.

Obnoxious, hateful, offensive, liable, exposed, unpopular, objectionable.
Ant. — Pleasant, wholesome, salutary, beneficial, popular, agreeable.

Obscene, lewd, foul, filthy, indecent, indelicate, shameless.
Ant.—Pure, modest, virtuous, decent.

Obscure, *a.* dim, misty, cloudy, shadowy, dusky, dark, gloomy, indistinct, unknown, humble, unintelligible, undistinguished.
Ant. — Plain, distinct, lucid, bright, luminous, prominent, eminent, distinguished.

Obscure, *v.* shade, dim, cloud, darken.
Ant. — Lighten, brighten, unveil, expose.

Observance, form, etiquette, ceremony, solemnity, rite, celebration, usage, custom.
Ant. — Disuse, omission, informality, disrespect, unmindful, unconventionality.

Observant, watchful, mindful, attentive, heedful.
Ant. — Unobservant, heedless, careless, neglectful, unmindful.

Observation, remark, comment, notice.
Ant. — Inattention, oversight, inadvertence, disregard.

Observe, keep, fulfill, heed, obey, perform, notice, remark, watch.
Ant.—Omit, miss, ignore, fail, disregard.

Obsolete, disused, antiquated, old-fashioned, ancient, old.
Ant. — Current, extant, modern, fashionable.

Obstacle, difficulty, impediment, stumbling-block, barrier, hindrance, obstruction.
Ant.—Aid, incentive, encouragement, help, course.

Obstinate, firm, dogged, pertinacious, perverse, intractable, stubborn, headstrong, contumacious, obdurate.
Ant. — Docile, complaisant, amenable, yielding, irresolute.

Obstruct, hinder, prevent, impede, bar, clog, barricade, choke, interrupt.
Ant. — Clear, open, facilitate, expedite, aid, help, advance, promote.

Obtain. (See Acquire.)

Obtuse, stolid, heavy-headed, dull, stupid, unintelligent.
Ant. — Acute, sharp, clever, intelligent.

Obviate, prevent, preclude, hinder, provide against.
Ant.—Necessitate, compel, order.

Obvious. (See Apparent.)

Occasion, *n.* necessity, need, event, opening, ground, reason, opportunity.
Ant. — Untimeliness, unseasonableness.

Occasion, *v.* cause, make, create, induce, generate.
Ant.—Frustrate, hinder, mar.

Occasional, accidental, casual, incidental.
Ant.—Frequent, often, always, permanent, continual.

Occult, secret, hidden, unknown, invisible, dark, mysterious.
Ant. — Plain, clear, open, familiar, exposed.

Occupation, occupancy, profession, holding, tenure, business, trade, avocation, calling, engagement, office, pursuit.
Ant. — Idleness, indolence, rest, enjoyment, leisure, resignation, abandonment.

Occupy. (See Hold.)

Occur, happen, take place, appear, offer, present itself.
Ant.—Pass, threaten, impend.

Odd, singular, eccentric, strange, extraordinary, whimsical, comical, droll, uneven.
Ant.—Usual, regular, normal, common, balanced, aggregate, matched, even.

Odious, hateful, loathsome, execrable, detestable, abominable, digusting, repulsive.
Ant. — Pleasant, pleasing, acceptable, delectable.

Odor. (See Smell.)

Offense, affront, insult, outrage, indignity, misdeed, trespass, transgression, wrong, misdemeanor,, injustice.
Ant. — Defense, innocence, gentleness, favor, right. (See Antonyms of Umbrage.)

Offend, displease, vex, nettle, irritate, shock, transgress, err.
Ant. — Conciliate, gratify, please.

Offensive, insulting, rude, saucy, impertinent, distasteful, obnoxious, opprobrious, insolent, abusive.
Ant. — Defensive, grateful, pleasant, agreeable, savory, admirable, beautiful, sweet, charming, worthy.

Offer, present, bid, tender, proffer, extend, propose, volunteer.
Ant — Withdraw, retract, retain, withhold, divert.

Office, business, post, situation, duty, charge, benefit, service, counting-house, function, place.
Ant.—Leisure, vacancy, sinecure, home.

Officer, functionary, official, commandant.
Ant.—Private, civilian, member, servant, subordinate.

Officious, busy, obtrusive, interfering, meddling.
Ant. — Modest, retiring, unofficious, negligent.

Offspring, issue, progeny, descendants, children.
Ant.—Ancestry, paternity.

Often, frequently, recurrently, repeatedly, many times.
Ant. — Seldom, infrequently, never.

Old, aged, superannuated, ancient, antique, antiquated, obsolete, old-fashioned.
Ant.—Young, new, modern.

Omen, presage, prognostic.

Omission, oversight, failure, neglect, default.
Ant. — Attention, insertion, notice, performance.

Omit, leave out, miss, overlook.
Ant.—Insert, notice, perform, do.

One, common, united, single, individual, undivided.
Ant. — Plurality, multitude, variety, diversity.

Onerous, burdensome, heavy, laborious, responsible, oppressive, toilsome.
Ant. — Light, easy, trivial, slight.

Onset. (See Attack.)

Onward, forward, ahead, progressive.
Ant.—Backward, back, retrograde.

Ooze, exude, drop, percolate, filter.
Ant.—Pour, rush, flow, strean..

Opaque, dull, dark, cloudy.
Ant. — Transparent, clear, bright.

Open, *a.* candid, frank, unreserved, free, ingenuous, sincere, clear, fair, unaffected, genuine, undisguised, unfolded.
Ant. — Close, shut, reserved, unavailable, settled, hidden, dark.

Open, *v.* unclose, unlock, unseal, exhibit, dissolve, spread, expand, begin.
Ant.—Close, shut, cover, conceal, inclose, mystify.

Opening, breach, aperture, gap, rent, hollow, chasm, cleft, crevice, cranny, fissure, chink, chance.
Ant. — Obstruction, enclosure, close, end, conclusion.

Operate, act, do, make, work, labor.
Ant.—Cease, rest, fail, stop.

Operation, action, agency, instrumentality, force, effort, enterprise.
Ant.—Cessation, inaction, rest, inefficacy.

Operative, stringent, effective, serviceable, binding.
Ant. — Inoperative, inefficacious.

Opinion, view, idea, sentiment, feeling, notion, impression, conviction, theory, judgment, belief.
Ant.—Knowledge, verity, fact.

Opinionated, conceited, egotistical.
Ant. — Decorous, modest, unassuming, unpretentious.

Opponent. (See Adversary.)

Opportune, seasonable, timely, fit, well-timed, proper.
Ant.—Inopportune, untimely, unseasonable, infelicitous.

Opportunity, occasion, chance, opening.
Ant.—Unseasonableness, lapse, omission.

Oppose, combat, bar, hinder, resist, withstand, contradict, thwart.
Ant.—Aid, abet, help, support, expedite, sustain, give way, yield, succumb.

Opposing, conflicting, jarring, neutralizing.
Ant. — Agreeing, supporting, aiding, helping.

Opposite, adverse, diverse, contrary, hostile, antagonistic, repugnant, incompatible, paradoxical, facing.
Ant. — Agreeing, coincident, neighboring.

Oppress, overburden, overbear, overtask, persecute, abuse.
Ant.—Encourage, support, assist, befriend.

Oppressive. (See Oppress.)

Opprobrious, abusive, scurrilous, insulting, offensive, outrageous, shameful.

Ant.—Eulogistic, panegyrical, flattering, pleasing, honorable.

Opprobrium, disgrace, odium, infamy, ignominy, obloquy.
Ant. — Honor, respect, glory, praise.

Option, choice, preference, election, discretion.
Ant. — Obligation, necessity, compulsion.

Opulent. (See Rich.)

Oral, verbal, spoken, parole.
Ant.—Written, documentary.

Oration, address, speech, harangue, discourse.
Ant.—Essay, letter.

Ordain, order, consecrate, prescribe, enjoin, institute.
Ant. — Revoke, cancel, annul, subvert, disestablish.

Order, *n.* succession, series, method, rule, class, rank, degree, fit condition, law, injunction, precept, command, system, regularity.
Ant.—Disorder, confusion, inversion, execution, disarrangement, misrule, anarchy.

Order, *v.* appoint, prescribe, enjoin, command, direct, arrange, range, dispose, regulate, organize, adjust, classify.
Ant. — Disorder, revoke, cancel, confuse, invert, execute.

Orderly, regular, systematic, methodical, quiet, peaceable.
Ant. — Disorderly, irregular, riotous.

Ordinance, decree, law, statute, edict, regulation.
Ant. — Custom, usage, prescription.

Ordinary, common, vulgar, plain, customary, settled, wonted, conventional, habitual, usual.
Ant.—Extraordinary, uncommon, strange, marvelous, remarkable, unconventional, unusual.

Organic, fundamental, radical, rooted, elemental.
Ant. — Accidental, unimportant, inorganic, vegetal.

Organize, dispose, arrange, regulate, adjust.
Ant.—Disband, break up, disorganize, dismember, distort, adjourn.

Organization, structure, form, instrumentality, construction.
Ant. — Disruption, disorganization, dismemberment, adjournment.

Orifice, aperture, opening.
Ant.—Stopper, plug, obstruction.

Origin, commencement, original, beginning, rise, source, spring, cause, occasion.
Ant. — Termination, conclusion, extinction, end.

Original, first, primary, pristine, primeval, peculiar, odd.
Ant. — Derived, subsequent, terminal, later, modern, plagiarized.

Originate, create, form, spring, ooze, issue, proceed, begin.
Ant.—Prosecute, conduct, apply.

Ornament, adorn, beautify, deck, embellish, emblazon.
Ant. — Disfigure, disgrace, brand, spoil, mar

Ostensible, manifest, visible, outward, colorable, professed.
Ant. — Real, genuine, concealed, actual, veritable.

Ostentation, display, pomp, show, parade, vaunting, boasting.
Ant.—Reserve, modesty, diffidence, unobtrusiveness.

Oust, remove, eject, expel, dislodge, evict.
Ant. — Install, restore, reinstate.

Outcast. (See Vagrant.)

Outcry, cry, clamor, noise, scream, yell.
Ant.—Quiet, silence, acclamation, plaudit.

Outdo. (See Excel.)

Outer. (See Exterior.)

Outlandish, strange, foreign, alien, barbarous, clownish.
Ant.—Regular, modish, fashionable, native.

Outline, sketch, plan, draft, contour.
Ant.—Form, substance, figure, ground, space.

Outlive, survive.

Outrage, affront, abuse, injury, insult, offense, indignity.
Ant.—Favor, moderation, self-control, coolness, calmness.

Outrageous, monstrous, flagrant, violent, furious, wild.
Ant. — Moderate, reasonable, justifiable.

Outset, commencement, start, beginning, opening.
Ant.—Close, termination, end, conclusion.

Outskirts, suburbs, environs, precincts.
Ant.—Interior, center, heart.

Outward, outer, external, exterior, extrinsic, extraneous, outside.
Ant. — Inward, internal, intrinsic, toward, homeward, inner, interior.

Over, above.
Ant.—Under, beneath.

Overbalance, outweigh, preponderate.

Overbear, bear down, overwhelm, overpower, subdue.

Overbearing, haughty, proud, arrogant.
Ant.—Gentle.

Overcharge. (See Oppress.)

Overcome. (See Defeat.)

Overflow, inundate, submerge, deluge, flood, inundation.
Ant. — Subsidence, deficiency, exhaustion.

Overlook, inspect, survey, excuse, forgive, pardon, neglect, miss.
Ant.—Visit, scrutinize, investigate, mark.

Overreach. (See Cheat.)

Overrule, supersede, suppress.

Oversight, inadvertence, inattention, neglect, mistake, error, omission, inspection, superintendence.
Ant. — Scrutiny, correction, emendation, attention, mark, notice, overspread, overrun.

Overt, open, public, notorious, manifest, patent.
Ant.—Covert, secret, clandestine.

Overthrow, prostrate, demolish, overturn, destroy, ruin, upset, beat, defeat, discomfit, rout.
Ant. — Restore, reinstate, regenerate, revive, construct, build.

Overture, proposal, offer, invitation, resolution.
Ant.—Inaction, quiescence.

Overturn, overthrow, invert, reverse, subvert.
Ant.—Establish, fortify.

Overwhelm, drown, overbear, oppress, overpower, subdue, crush, defeat, vanquish.
Ant.—Raise, re-establish, rescue, extricate, maintain, restore, support, uphold.

Owe, indebted, beholden.
Ant. — Repay, liquidate, defray.

Own, acknowledge, admit, confess, recognize, have, possess.
Ant. — Disown, abjure, disavow, forfeit, lose, alienate.

Owner, proprietor, possessor, master, holder.
Ant. — Servant, subordinate, lessee.

P

Pacific, peaceful, peaceable, mild, gentle, calm, quiet.
Ant. — Warlike, tumultuous, harsh, quarrelsome, exasperating.

Pacify, appease, calm, quiet, still, soothe.
Ant.—Excite, exasperate, irritate, provoke, rouse.

Pagan, Gentile, heathen, idolator.
Ant.—Believer, Christian.

Pageantry, pomp, splendor, show, magnificence.
Ant. — Illusion, mockery, disorder, turbulence.

Pain, *n.* anguish, agony, distress, suffering, pang, grief, qualm.
Ant. — Pleasure, joy, felicity, enjoyment, delight, ease,

amusement, comfort, happiness.

Pain, *v.* agonize, rack, torment, torture, trouble, annoy.
Ant. — Relieve, ease, refresh, please, gratify.

Paint, color, represent, portray, delineate, depict.
Ant. — Daub, caricature, misrepresent, misdepict, describe.

Palatable, tasteful, savory, appetizing.
Ant. — Unpalatable, disagreeable, sour, unsavory.

Pale, pallid, wan, whitish, sallow, faint.
Ant. — Ruddy, deep, high-colored, conspicuous.

Palliate, extenuate, varnish, cover, allay, soothe, soften.
Ant. — Expose, denounce, exaggerate, aggravate.

Pallid, pale, wan.
Ant. — Florid, rubicund, flushed.

Palpable. (See Apparent.)

Palpitate, flutter, pant, throb, pulsate.
Ant.—Pause, stop, cease.

Paltry, contemptible, pitiful, mean, sorry, despicable, shabby, beggarly.
Ant.—Admirable, magnificent, candid, straightforward, estimable.

Panegyric, eulogy, encomium, eulogium, praise.
Ant. — Satire, sarcasm, invective, tirade.

Pang, throe, twinge, agony, anguish, pain, distress.
Ant. — Delight, glow, enjoyment, pleasure, gratification.

Pant. (See Palpitate.)

Parable, fable, allegory, simile, similitude.
Ant.—History, fact, narrative.

Parade, show, ostentation, vainglory, procession, spectacle.
Ant.—Concealment, modesty, humility, plainness, retirement.

Parallel, equal, parity, analogous, like, similar.
Ant. — Divergent, different, opposed, incongruous.

Paralyze. (See Enervate.)

Paramount, supreme, principal, chief.
Ant. — Minor, inferior, subordinate.

Parasite, flatterer, sycophant, toady.
Ant.—Friend, antagonist, traducer, calumniator.

Pardon, forgive, absolve, overlook, excuse, remit, acquit, discharge, set free, clear, liberate.
Ant.—Condemn, punish, visit, accuse.

Parent, author, origin, source, cause.
Ant. — Offspring, child, issue, effect, progeny.

Parity. (See Equality.)

Parsimonious. (See Miserly.)

Parson, clergyman, incumbent, curate, minister.
Ant.—Layman, member, sinner.

Part, separate, divide, sever, dissever, disunite, break, division, portion, share, fraction.
Ant.—Join, annex, compound, add, unite, aggregate, amount, entirety, mass, sum, total, whole.

Partake, participate, share.
Ant.—Forfeit, relinquish.

Partial, biased, prejudiced, limited, incomplete.
Ant. — Impartial, just, fair, equitable, total, universal, whole.

Participate. (See Partake.)

Particular, singular, exact, nice, punctual, minute, careful, distinct, odd, strange.
Ant. — General, universal, comprehensive, rough, coarse.

Particularly, primarily, especially, chiefly.
Ant. — On the whole, generally.

Partisan. (See Adherent.)

Partition, part, divide, apportion, distribute.
Ant.—Unite, coalesce, include, collect, incorporate.

Partner, colleague, coadjutor, associate, sharer, confederate, spouse.
Ant. — Rival, opponent, competitor, antagonist.

Partnership, union, connection, firm, house, association, company, companionship, society.
Ant.—Dissolution, separation, disunion.

Party, faction, confederacy, combination, detachment, clique, league.
Ant. — Individual, nation, state.

Passage, journey, course, road, route, avenue, channel, clause, sentence.
Ant. — Halt, rest, stop, discourse, essay.

Pass, elapse, glide, slip, slide.
Ant. — Stay, remain, stand, wait.

Passion, anger, rage, fury, vehemence, impetuosity, love, affection.
Ant. — Apathy, indifference, coolness, frigidity.

Passionate, angry, excitable, fiery, vehement, impetuous, glowing, burning, ardent, hot, hasty, irritable.
Ant.—Impassionate, cool, deliberate, apathetic, quiet.

Passive, unresisting, unopposing, submissive, enduring, patient.
Ant. — Active, alert, positive, vehement.

Pastime, sport, play, recreation, amusement, diversion.
Ant. — Business, study, labor, task, work.

Paternal. (See Parent.)

Path. (See Road.)

Pathetic, moving, touching, affecting, melting, tender.
Ant. — Ludicrous, funny, unaffecting, farcical.

Patience, resignation, endurance, fortitude.
Ant.—Resistance, impatience, rebellion, inconstancy.

Patient, passive, submissive, meek.
Ant.—Hasty, irascible.

Patronize, befriend, favor, countenance, support.
Ant.—Discountenance, oppose, oppress, disfavor.

Pattern. (See Model.)

Pauperism. (See Poverty.)

Pause, demur, hesitate, deliberate—interval, suspense.
Ant. — Continue, proceed, advance, persist, persevere.

Pay, *n.* wages, salary, hire, stipend, recompense.
Ant.—Present, gratuity, gift.

Pay, *v.* liquidate, lessen, discharge, extinguish, cash, reward.
Ant. — Defraud, repudiate, hoard, retain, deprive.

Peace, quiet, calm, tranquillity, repose, amity.
Ant.—War, noise, tumult, disorder, strife, discord, riot, trouble, turbulence.

Peaceable, pacific, peaceful, quiet.
Ant.—Troublesome, riotous.

Peaceful, tranquil, quiet, still, pacific, undisturbed, calm, placid, serene, mild, gentle.
Ant. — Warlike, pugnacious, savage, hostile, fierce, violent.

Peasant, countryman, rustic, bumpkin, clodpole, swain.
Ant.—Citizen, townsman, autocrat, lord.

Peculator. (See Thief.)

Peculiar, particular, exclusive, remarkable, signal, special, singular, uncommon.
Ant. — General, universal, ordinary, common, public.

Pedantic, priggish, pedagogical, learned.
Ant.—Modest, unaffected.

Peel, skin, rind, husk.
Ant.—Heart, core.

Peerless, unequaled, unmatched, matchless, unique.
Ant.—Ordinary, commonplace, mediocre.

Peevish, ill-natured, touchy, testy, captious, fractious, cross, fretful, petulant, cynical, irascible.
Ant. — Genial, good-natured, good-tempered, complaisant.

Pellucid. (See Clear.)

Penal, punitive, retributive, corrective.
Ant. — Honorary, remunerative, reparatory.

Penalty, fine, amercement, mulct, forfeiture.
Ant. — Reward, wages, premium, prize, compensation, remuneration.

Penetrate, pierce, perforate, bore, fathom, reach, enter, stab, transfix.
Ant.—Withdraw, fail, depart, leave, issue, vacate.

Penetration, insight, sharpness, acuteness, sagacity, discernment, discrimination.
Ant. — Dullness, shallowness, obtuseness, ignorance, stupidity.

Penitence, contrition, repentance, remorse.
Ant. —Obduracy, congratulation, approval, hard-heartedness.

Pensive, thoughtful, meditative, dreamy, melancholy, dejected, depressed, cheerless, drooping.
Ant.—Vacant, careless, thoughtless, joyous, unreflective.

Penurious. (See Miserly.)

Penury, poverty, indigence, beggary, destitution, want, need, privation.
Ant. — Competence, wealth, affluence.

People, commonalty, populace, mob, nation, tribe, race, clan.
Ant.—Ruler, government, nobility, aristocracy.

Perceive, see, discern, distinguish, observe, understand, know, comprehend, note.
Ant.—Overlook, miss, misconceive, misobserve, ignore, lose, misapprehend.

Perception, seeing, sense, perceptibility, sensibility, susceptibility, sensation, apprehension, conviction, conception, notion, idea.
Ant. — Insensibility, ignorance, misapprehension.

Peremptory, absolute, positive, arbitrary, despotic, decisive, imperative.
Ant. — Suggestive, entreative, mild, gentle.

Perennial, imperishable, undying, immortal, deathless, enduring, perpetual.
Ant. — Occasional, periodical, uncertain, deficient.

Perfect, complete, whole, entire, finished, unbroken, thorough, mature, ripe, absolute.
Ant.—Imperfect, faulty, deficient, objective, scant, fallible, blemished, spoiled.

Perfidious, faithless, treacherous, insidious, unfaithful.
Ant.—True, staunch, faithful, honorable.

Perforate. (See Penetrate.)

Perform. (See Accomplish.)

Performance. (See Act.)

Performer, actor, player, comedian, tragedian.
Ant. — Spectator, looker-on, audience.

Perfume, odor, scent, fragrance, aroma, smell, incense.
Ant. — Stench, stink, fetor, reek.

Perhaps, perchance, possibly, peradventure.
Ant. — Certainly, inevitably, without doubt.

Peril, danger, hazard, jeopardy, risk, venture, insecurity, pitfall, snare.
Ant. — Security, safety, certainty.

Period. (See Age.)

Periodically, statedly, spasmodically, fitfully.
Ant.—Regularly, continually.

Perish. (See Die.)

Permanent, durable, abiding, enduring, lasting, fixed, stable.
Ant. — Transient, ephemeral, fleeting, frail, transitory.

Permission, permit, leave, liberty, license.
Ant.—Prohibition, denial, refusal, prevention, hindrance.

Permit, allow, tolerate.
Ant.—Forbid, interdict.

Pernicious. (See Hurt.)

Perpetual, constant, continual, continuous, endless, eternal, lasting, incessant, ceaseless, unceasing, uninterrupted.
Ant. — Occasional, transient, periodic, momentary, accidental, casual.

Perplex, embarrass, harass, confuse, bewilder, entangle, involve, puzzle.
Ant.—Clear, enlighten, elucidate, simplify, explicate.

Persecute, oppress, harrow, afflict, worry, annoy.
Ant. — Encourage, inspirit, abet, support.

Persevere, continue, persist, pursue, proceed.
Ant. — Lag, fail, rest, withdraw, refrain, abstain.

Persons, men, people, folks, individuals.
Ant. — Collection, assembly, nation, state.

Perspicuous, clear, plain, distinct, unequivocal, unmistakable, intelligible.
Ant.—Obscure, confused, unintelligible.

Persuade, exhort, urge, allure, incite, influence, entice, prevail upon.
Ant. — Deter, disincline, dissuade, coerce, compel, order, discourage, restrain.

Persuasion. (See Persuade.)

Pert, forward, flippant, saucy, impertinent, impudent.
Ant. — Modest, bashful, demure, staid.

Pertinacious, obstinate, inflexible, stubborn, determined.
Ant. — Inconstant, irresolute, volatile, unreliable.

Pertinent, fit, relevant, proper, appropriate, applicable, related.
Ant.—Alien, discordant, unrelated, unconnected, repugnant.

Perturb. (See Vex.)

Pervade, diffuse, spread, permeate, overspread, fill.
Ant.—Affect, touch.

Perverse, awkward, cross, untoward, petulant, peevish, crooked, froward, wayward, stubborn.
Ant. — Docile, complaisant, obliging, amenable, gentle.

Pest, bane, plague, ruin, pestilence, taint.
Ant.—Benefit, blessing, good, acquisition.

Pestilential, contagious, infectious, epidemical mischievous, pernicious, noxious, baneful, destructive.
Ant. — Innocuous, genial, wholesome, salubrious, salutary, pure, nutritive, healthy.

Petition, prayer, supplication, entreaty, request, suit, appeal.
Ant. — Protest, command, injunction, demand, exaction, requirement.

Petty, trifling, trivial, frivolous, insignificant, small, little.
Ant. — Large, liberal, broad, noble, generous.

Petulant. (See Peevish.)

Phantom. (See Ghost.)

Philanthropic, charitable, kind, benevolent, gracious.
Ant.—Selfish, egotistical, misanthropic, morose.

Philosophy, science, knowledge.
Ant.—Ignorance, stupidity.

Phlegmatic, frigid, cold, heavy, unfeeling, apathetic.
Ant. — Passionate, active, energetic, interested, alert.

Physical, material, corporeal, tangible, natural, bodily.
Ant. — Spiritual, mental, immaterial, moral, intangible.

Pick, pluck, choose, cull, select, gather.
Ant.—Reject, discard, repudiate, relegate, bunch, grasp.

Picturesque, graphic, imaginative.
Ant. — Unpicturesque, tame, desolate, cheerless, homely.

Picture, likeness, painting, image, resemblance, drawing, representation, effigy, engraving, print, illustration.
Ant. — Original, landscape, scene, body, nature.

Pierce, penetrate, perforate, bore, broach, tap.

Ant. — Blunt, soothe, allay, lull, compose.

Piercing. (See Pierce.)

Piety, religion, sanctity, holiness, devotion, grace, godliness.

Ant. — Impiety, ungodliness, profanity, hypocrisy.

Pile, *v.* heap, accumulate, hoard, amass, collect.

Ant. — Demolish, scatter, upset, overthrow, disperse, separate.

Pile, *n.* building, edifice, structure, thread, fiber.

Ant. — Heap, ruin, material, finish.

Pilfer, filch, steal, purloin.

Ant. — Pillage, rifle, plunder, restore, refrain.

Pillage. (See Plunder.)

Pillar, column, shaft, post, support.

Ant. — Base, capitol, arch, wall.

Pilot, guide, steer, direct, conduct.

Ant. — Mislead, betray, lose, misdirect.

Pinch. (See Squeeze.)

Pine. (See Languish.)

Pious, holy, godly, saintly, devout, religious.

Ant. — Impious, ungodly, sinful, hypocritical, bad.

Piquant, pungent, acrid, smart, keen, biting, harsh, stinging, cutting, racy.

Ant.—Tame dull, flat, insipid.

Pique. (See Spite.)

Pitch, fling, cast, launch, throw.

Ant. — Draw, pull, hold, restrain, push.

Piteous, doleful, pitiable, mournful, sad, deplorable, woeful, rueful.

Ant. — Joyous, pleasant, comfortable, desirable, delectable, cheerful, gay, genial, happy, merry, mirthful.

Pith, gist, kernel, cream, strength, marrow.

Ant.—Dressing, surroundings, verbiage.

Pithy, terse, concise, forcible, strong.

Ant.—Fruitless, vapid, weak, diluted, insipid.

Pitiful. (See Mean.)

Pitiless. (See Merciless.)

Pity, *n.* compassion, sympathy, condolence, mercy.

Ant. — Cruelty, pitilessness, hard-heartedness, relentlessness, brutality.

Place, *n.* position, spot, site, post, situation, station.

Place, *v.* put, set, lay, dispose, order, organize, array, marshal, arrange.

Ant.—Disturb, remove, disarrange, misplace, uproot, transport, confuse, derange, mislay, perturb, unsettle.

Placid, serene, calm, peaceful, tranquil, unruffled, mild.

Ant. — Ruffled, troubled, stormy, excited, agitated, disturbed.

Plague, annoy, molest, vex, tease, trouble, harass, torment.

Ant. — Please, gratify, amuse, soothe, comfort, allay.

Plain, even, level, flat, smooth, apparent, visible, clear, obvious, intelligible, certain, evident, manifest, distinct, palpable, open, candid, frank, sincere, free, ingenuous, overt.

Ant. — Uneven, undulatory, rough, broken, abrupt, confused, obstructed, uncertain, dubious, ambiguous, enigmatical, fair, beautiful, artful, secret, hidden.

Plaintive, doleful, sad, mournful, melancholy.

Ant. — Joyous, exultant, glad, cheerful, cheering.

Plan. (See Design.)

Plastic, pliant, ductile, tractile.

Ant. — Stubborn, unyielding, unmalleable, inflexible.

Plaudit. (See Acclamation.)

Plausible, colorable, specious, ostensible, feasible.

Ant.—Unmistakable, genuine, sterling, true.

Play, game, sport, pastime, amusement, gambol, drama.

Ant.—Occupation, labor, business, work, idleness, toil, drudgery.

Playful, sportive, lively, jocund, merry, gay, sprightly, vivacious, racy, buoyant.

Ant. — Inert, slow, sluggish, sad, melancholy.

Plea, excuse, apology, defense, vindication, entreaty.

Ant.—Charge, accusation, impeachment, action.

Plead, defend, vindicate, exonerate, justify, exculpate, excuse.

Ant. — Charge, accuse, impeach, condemn.

Pleasant. (See Agreeable.)

Please, gratify, satisfy, content, delight, fascinate, indulge, pacify.

Ant. — Displease, dissatisfy, annoy, trouble, vex, irritate.

Pleasure, comfort, enjoyment, gratification, joy, delight, rapture, charm, wish.

Ant. — Pain, suffering, affliction, trouble, asceticism.

Plebeian, ignoble, vulgar, lowborn.

Ant.—Patrician, noble, aristocratic, high-born, high-bred.

Pledge, pawn, earnest, security, surety, guaranty.

Ant. — Word, promise, parole, assurance.

Plentiful, abundant, ample, copious, plenteous.

Ant.—Rare, scanty, scarce.

Plenty, enough, sufficiency, abundance, fullness.

Ant. — Scantiness, insufficiency.

Pliable, pliant, flexible, lithe, supple, yielding, docile.

Ant. — Stiff, brittle, stubborn, unbending, unmanageable.

Plight. (See Pledge.)

Plot, *n.* strategem, conspiracy, combination, confederacy, scheme, plan.

Ant.—Action, execution, deed, resolution, law.

Plot, *v.* concoct, hatch, frame, contrive, conspire.

Ant. — Resolve, consult, debate, discover, defeat.

Pluck, courage, mettle, spirit, nerve.

Ant.—Timidity, cowardice.

Plump, fleshy, round, fat, full, chubby.

Ant. — Lean, thin, wizened, shriveled, emaciated, lank, weak.

Plunder, pillage, booty, loot, spoil, robbery, depredation.

Ant.—Wages, desert, gratuity, present.

Plunge, dive, dip, douse, sink.

Ant.—Emerge, issue, rise, extricate.

Ply. (See Urge.)

Poetical, metrical, versified, imaginative, dreamy, fictitious.

Ant. — Prosaic, unmetrical, commonplace, historical, mathematical, logical, sober.

Poignant, sharp, keen, biting, severe, deep, intense, stinging.

Ant.—Blunt, dull, gentle, shallow.

Pointed, aim, level, direct, sharpen, show, punctuate.

Ant.—Suggest, intimate, hint.

Point, peaked, sharp, marked, keen, severe.

Ant. — Pointless, aimless, feeble, inexpressive.

Poise, balance, equilibrium, equipoise.

Ant.—Instability.

Poison, bane, pest, venom, virus, infection.

Ant. — Purification, disinfectant, antidote.

Policy, plan, device, strategem, management.

Ant. — Conjecture, hazard, mismanagement.

Polish, brighten, burnish, glaze, civilize, cultivate, refine.

Ant.—Dull, scratch, mar, spoil, dim, barbarize.

Polite, refined, genteel, civil, accomplished, well-bred.

Ant. — Awkward, rude, uncouth, ill-bred, discourteous, boorish.

Politeness. (See Affability.)

Politic, wise, political, civil, judicious, prudential.

Ant.—Imprudent, unwise, improvident, impolitic.

Pollute, contaminate, soil, defile, taint, infect, corrupt, deprave, demoralize.

Ant. — Purify, clarify, disinfect, filter.

Pomp, parade, display, gorgeousness, splendor, grandeur, pageantry, show, state.

Ant. — Quiet, simplicity, privacy, plainness, unceremoniousness.

Pompous, majestic, stately, grand, august, dignified, lofty, inflated, bombastic.

Ant. — Unassuming, modest, unobtrusive.

Ponder. (See Reflect.)

Ponderous, heavy, weighty, massive, bulky.

Ant.—Light, trifling, airy, volatile, subtle.

Poor, indigent, needy, penniless, necessitous, deficient, scanty.

Ant.—Rich, wealthy, affluent, abundant, liberal, ample, moneyed, sufficient.

Populace, people, commonalty, vulgar, mob.

Ant. — Nobility, aristocracy, government, individual.

Popular, common, general, prevailing, favorite.

Ant. — Exclusive, restricted, scientific, unpopular, odious.

Port, harbor, haven, entrance, portal.

Ant.—Sea, ocean, coast.

Portal. See Gate.)

Portend, foreshow, auger, presage, forebode, betoken, threaten.

Ant.—Avert, contradict, nullify, negative, preclude.

Portion, part, division, share, piece, bit, section, fragment, parcel.

Ant.—Whole, substance, bulk, mass.

Portly, majestic, stately, grand, dignified, burly, stout.

Ant. — Thin, undignified, unimposing, mean.

Portray, draw, sketch, paint, depict, delineate, represent, describe.

Ant. — Caricature, misrepresent, misportray, suggest.

Position, place, locality, situation, spot, site, action, gesture, posture, attitude.

Ant.—Displacement, absence.

Positive, actual, true, real, certain, sure, definitive, fixed, confident, dogmatic, absolute, peremptory, decided, certain.

Ant.—Negative, fictitious, imaginary, contingent, dependent, conditional, implied, dubious, uncertain, doubtful.

Possess, have, own, hold, occupy.

Ant. — Abandon, renounce, surrender, lose, forfeit, resign.

Possessor, owner, proprietor.

Possible, practicable, likely, feasible, practical.

Ant.—Impossible, impracticable, visionary.

Possibly, perhaps, peradventure, perchance, haply.

Ant.—Certain, without doubt, positively, never.

Post. (See Position; also Mail, Stake, Pillar.)

Poverty, penury, indigence, need, want.

Ant. — Wealth, plenty, abundance, riches, affluence.

Power, authority, force, strength, dominion.

Ant.—Weakness, futility.

Powerful, mighty, potent.

Ant. — Futile, trivial, useless, weak.

Practical, serviceable, useful, experienced, skillful.

Ant.—Impracticable, theoretical, unserviceable, awkward.

Practice, custom, habit, manner, use, usage, exercise.

Ant. — Theory, speculation, disuse, inexperience, idleness.

Praise, *n.* approval, eulogy, commendation, applause, exaltation, honor, commend, extol, laud.

Ant. — Blame, censure, disapproval.

Praise, *v.* commend, extol, eulogize, panegyrize, laud, applaud, glorify.

Ant.—Condemn, reprove, disapprove, censure, blame.

Praiseworthy, laudable, honorable, commendable, meritorious, worthy.

Ant. — Blamable, censurable, reprehensible.

Prate, tattle, babble, chat, chatter, prattle, gossip.

Ant. — Orate, speak, debate, discuss.

Pray. (See Supplicate.)

Prayer, petition, entreaty, request, suit.

Preamble, preface, introduction.

Ant.—Perorative, finale, conclusion, essay, body.

Precarious, doubtful, dubious, uncertain, insecure, unsettled.

Ant. — Safe, certain, assured, systematic, immutable.

Precaution, care, forethought.

Ant.—Improvidence, carelessness, thoughtlessness.

Precede, lead, go before, herald.

Ant.—Succeed, follow.

Precedence, priority, pre-eminence, preference, antecedence.

Ant. — Inferiority, sequence, posteriority.

Precept, command, injunction, mandate, direction, order, rule, law, maxim, doctrine, principle.

Ant. — Suggestion, hint, prompting, impulse.

Preceptor, teacher, tutor, instructor, schoolmaster.

Ant.—Pupil, scholar, student.

Precincts, borders, limits, bounds, confines, districts.

Ant.—Heart, center, nucleus.

Precious, valuable, costly, dear, estimable.

Ant.—Worthless, valueless, unvalued.

Precipitate, *v.* hurry, hasten, cast down, expedite.

Ant.—Hinder, restrain, retard, deter, obstruct.

Precipitate, *a.* hasty, hurried, rash, premature.

Ant.—Deliberate, slow, shallow, inclined, undulating, level.

Precise, accurate, correct, particular, exact, nice, punctilious.

Ant.—Indefinite, vague, inexact, rough, loose, inaccurate, unceremonious.

Precision. (See Precise.)

Preclude, prevent, obviate, hinder, debar.

Ant.—Admit, promote, further, advance.

Precursory, preceding, anterior, prefatory.

Ant.—Subsequent, consequent, eventual, posterior.

Predecessor, ancestor, forefather, progenitor, forerunner.

Ant.—Successor, junior, posterity.

Predict, foretell, prognosticate, prophesy, foreshadow.

Ant.—Tell, narrate, recount, recall, report.

Predilection, preference, partiality, bias, prejudice.

Ant.—Aversion, antipathy, disinclination, apathy.

Predominant, prevailing, prevalent, ascendant, overruling.

Ant.—Subordinate, inferior.

Pre-eminence, priority, precedence, antecedence, superiority.

Ant.—Inferiority, equality.

Preface. (See Preamble.)

Prefer, choose, fancy, select, raise, exalt, promote, further.

Ant.—Reject, postpone, defer, withhold, degrade, debase.

Pregnant, prolific, teeming, replete, enceinte.

Ant.—Sterile, barren, void, meaningless.

Prejudice, prepossession, bias, partiality, detriment, harm.

Ant. — Impartiality, fairness, judgment, advantage.

Preliminary, prefatory, introductory, previous, antecedent.

Ant. — Subsequent, following, succeeding.

Prelude, introduction, preface, prologue.
Ant.—Sequel, conclusion.
Premature, precipitate, rash, hasty, untimely, early.
Ant.—Timely, seasonable, opportune.
Premeditation, forethought, forecast.
Ant.—Hazard, impromptu, extemporization.
Premium, recompense, reward, bonus, bribe.
Ant.—Penalty, fine, forfeit, depreciation.
Prepare, fit, equip, qualify, make ready, furnish, adapt, adjust, arrange.
Ant.—Derange, demolish, subvert, misfit.
Preponderate, predominate, prevail, overbalance, outweigh, outbalance.
Ant.—Fail, sink, succumb.
Prepossessing, charming, engaging, taking, attractive, winning.
Ant. — Repulsive, unprepossessing, disagreeable.
Preposterous, irrational, foolish, absurd, ridiculous.
Ant.—Reasonable, fair, just, moderate, sound, right.
Prerogative, privilege, immunity, right, exemption.
Ant.—Disqualification, disfranchisement.
Presage, foresee, predict, portend, augur, forebode, prognosticate, betoken, threaten.
Ant.—Fulfill, occur, recall, report, announce.
Prescribe, appoint, ordain, dictate, decree, enjoin, impose, order.
Ant. — Prohibit, discountenance, suggest.
Present, *a.* existing, subsistent, nigh, immediate, instant, current.
Ant.—Absent, distant, remote, separate.
Present. (See Gift.)
Present, *v.* offer, exhibit, give, introduce.
Ant. — Accept, take, receive, retain, withhold.
Presentiment, foreboding, foretaste, anticipation, forethought.
Ant.—Surprise, miscalculation, accident, fore-knowledge.
Preserve, keep, save, secure, defend, uphold, embalm, protect, guard, spare.
Ant.—Damage, impair, abandon, injure.
Press, compress, crush, squeeze, oppress, gall, urge, enforce, impress, crowd, harass.
Ant.—Relax, ease, free, relieve, liberate, entice, allure.
Pressure, urgency, exigency, hurry, crushing, squeezing.
Ant.—Relief, ease, liberty.
Presume, suppose, think, infer, believe, conjecture, apprehend.
Ant.—Deduce, prove, argue, hesitate, distrust.
Presumptuous, presuming, overconfident, forward, arrogant, bold, rash, foolhardy.
Ant.—Modest, diffident, bashful, hesitating.
Pretense, cloak, mask, garb, pretext, excuse, plea, subterfuge.
Ant.—Reality, truth, candor, fact, actuality, openness.
Pretend, feign, affect, simulate, profess.
Ant.—Substantiate, test, verify, detect, refute.
Pretext. (See Pretence.)
Pretty. (See Beautiful.)
Prevalence, influence, custom, power, operation, preponderance.
Ant.—Disuse, decay, obsoleteness, disappearance, abolition.
Prevail, predominate, obtain, succeed.
Ant. — Fail, sink, succumb, abolish, disappear.
Prevailing, proper, prevalent, ruling, ascendant, predominant, general.
Ant.—Mitigated, diminishing, subordinate, powerless, isolated, sporadic.
Prevaricate, quibble, cavil, shuffle, equivocate.
Ant.—Affirm, maintain, prove, substantiate.
Prevent, impede, thwart, obviate, hinder, obstruct, bar, neutralize, preclude.
Ant.—Promote, aid, expedite, encourage, advance, cause.
Previous, preceding, foregoing, antecedent, anterior, prior, introductory, preparatory, preliminary.
Ant.—Subsequent, succeeding, following, later.
Prey, food, victim, sacrifice, spoil, booty, ravage.
Ant.—Rights, earnings, wages, due.
Price, cost, charge, expense, figure, value, worth.
Ant.—Discount, allowance, donation, gift.
Priceless, invaluable, inestimable.
Ant.—Cheap, valueless.
Pride, arrogance, haughtiness, vanity, self-esteem, lordliness, conceit, loftiness, vainglory.
Ant.—Meekness, modesty, humility, lowliness.
Priggish, dandified, foppish, affected, coxcombical.
Ant. — Sensible, unaffected, plain, honest.
Prim, precise, demure, formal, starched, stiff, priggish.
Ant.—Informal, easy, genial, natural.
Primary, first, earliest, primitive, pristine, original, primeval.
Ant.—Secondary, subordinate, inferior, subsequent, later.
Prime, primal, first, capital, first-rate, perfect, excellent.
Ant.—Inferior, impaired, deteriorated, defective.
Primitive, old-fashioned, first, pristine, ancient, antiquated, primeval.
Ant.—Modern, modish, civilized, sophisticated.
Princely, royal, regal, stately, august, noble, munificent.
Ant.—Lowly, beggarly, mean.
Principal, chief, leading, first, highest, supreme, main, essential.
Ant.—Subordinate, secondary, subject, auxiliary, minor.
Principally, chiefly, essentially, mainly.
Ant.—Secondarily, subsequently.
Principle, ground, reason, motive, impulse, maxim, rule, rectitude, integrity.
Ant.—Action, issue, exercise, application. (See Doctrine.)
Print, mark, impress, stamp, imprint.
Ant.—Write, speak, engrave.
Prior. (See Previous.)
Pristine. (See Primary.)
Privacy, solitude, retirement, seclusion, retreat, secrecy, concealment.
Ant.—Publicity, exposure, notoriety.
Privation, loss, bereavement, destitution, poverty, want.
Ant. — Supply, benefaction, compensation, recovery, restitution.
Privilege, immunity, advantage, favor, prerogative, exemption, right, claim.
Ant.—Prohibition, inhibition, exclusion, disqualification, damage, detriment, drawback, loss, obstacle, obstruction.
Prize, *n.* seizure, capture, booty, spoil, loot, plunder, trophy, palm.
Ant.—Loss, forfeiture, penalty, sacrifice, failure, infamy.
Prize, *v.* esteem, rate, appraise, assess, value.
Ant.—Dislike, abhor, condemn, despise.
Probability, chance, likelihood, appearance, presumption.
Ant.—Improbability, unlikelihood.
Probity, honesty, integrity, uprightness, sincerity, soundness, rectitude.
Ant. — Dishonesty, rascality, vice, fraud, deceit.
Problematical, uncertain, doubtful, dubious, questionable, disputable, suspicious.
Ant.—Certain, sure, undoubted, proven.
Procedure. (See Proceeding.)

Proceed, move, pass, advance, arise, issue, emanate.
Ant.—Recede, retreat, stand, stop, stay, discontinue.

Proceeding, transaction, measure, step, procedure, process, course, form, progress, progression, suit, trial, case.
Ant.—Inaction, abandonment, desistence, deviation.

Procession, train, march, caravan, retinue, cavalcade, cortege.
Ant.—Rabble, mob, confusion, rout.

Proclaim, advertise, announce, publish, declare, promulgate, report.
Ant.—Conceal, suppress, secrete, contain.

Proclamation. (See Proclaim.)

Proclivity, propensity, tendency, bias, bent, proneness, aptitude.
Ant.—Aversion, indisposition, disinclination.

Procrastinate, delay, defer, adjourn, postpone, put off, dally.
Ant.—Hurry, complete, finish.

Procure, obtain, acquire, gain, get, reap, win, earn.
Ant.—Miss, lose, forfeit.

Prodigal, extravagant, improvident, lavish, profuse, wasteful.
Ant.—Frugal, economical, close, saving, miserly.

Prodigious, enormous, huge, vast, amazing, astonishing, remarkable, astounding, surprising, wonderful.
Ant.—Insignificant, small.

Prodigy, wonder, miracle, marvel, monster.
Ant. — Imposture, individual, nature.

Produce, yield, give, generate, occasion, realize, show, lengthen.
Ant. — Retain, withhold, destroy, contract, reduce.

Profane, impious, irreligious, unhallowed, secular, unholy, ungodly, godless.
Ant.—Pious, sacred, holy, devout, reverend.

Profess, affect, pretend, feign, own.
Ant.—Renounce, repudiate, abjure.

Profession, occupation, business, trade, vocation, office, employment, engagement, avowal.

Proffer, volunteer, offer, propose, tender.
Ant. — Withhold, detain, refrain, obey, submit, yield.

Proficiency, advancement, progress, improvement, skill, dexterity.
Ant.—Failure, backwardness, awkwardness.

Proficient, adept, master, expert.
Ant.—Tyro, amateur, novice, dunce.

Profit, gain, emolument, advantage, benefit, service, avail, use.
Ant. — Loss, detriment, damage, waste

Profligate, abandoned dissolute, depraved, vicious, degenerate, corrupt, demoralized.
Ant.—Virtuous, honest, principled, conscientious, good, upright, honorable.

Profound, deep, penetrating, solemn, abstruse, recondite, fathomless.
Ant. — Shallow, superficial, slight.

Profuse, extravagant, prodigal, lavish, improvident, excessive, copious, plentiful.
Ant.—Scanty, sparing, parsimonious, poor, miserly, niggardly, economical.

Progeny, children, descendants, race, offspring, issue.
Ant.—Stock, parentage, ancestry.

Prognosticate. (See Predict.)

Progress, advancement, growth, progression, movement, march, improvement.
Ant.—Delay, stoppage, retrogression, failure, relapse.

Prohibit, hinder, debar, prevent, forbid, interdict, inhibit.
Ant. — Permit, grant, allow, sanction.

Project, *n.* design, plan, scheme, contrivance, device.
Ant.—Hazard, chance, venture.

Project, *v.* shoot, discharge, throw, hurl, jut, protrude, bulge.
Ant. — Withdraw, draw, pull, attract, recoil, retain.

Prolific, fertile, productive, generative, fruitful, teeming.
Ant.—Barren, sterile.

Prolix, diffuse, long, prolonged, tedious, tiresome, wordy, verbose, prosaic.
Ant.—Concise, brief, succinct.

Prolong. (See Lengthen.)

Prominent, eminent, conspicuous, jutting, important, leading, marked.
Ant. — Inconspicuous, minor, unimportant, receding, indented, engraved, obscure.

Promiscuous, mixed, unarranged, mingled, indiscriminate, heterogeneous.
Ant.—Sorted, select, arranged, reserved, exclusive, nice, choice.

Promise. (See Pledge.)

Promote, encourage, aid, further, advance, forward.
Ant. — Repress, hinder, discourage, check, allay, dishonor, abase.

Prompt, *v.* incite, animate, urge, impel. (See Punctual.)
Ant.—Tardy, late, backward, sluggish, inactive.

Prompt, *a.* expeditious, quick, alert, agile, active, brisk, ready.
Ant. — Tardy, late, sluggish, behind-hand.

Promptitude, readiness, promptness, quickness, alacrity, activity, briskness.
Ant. — Unreadiness, tardiness, hesitation, inaction.

Promulgate, publish, announce, advertise, proclaim, declare, spread.
Ant.—Suppress, conceal, stifle, hush, discountenance.

Prone, inclining, prostrate, flat, tending, apt.
Ant.—Averse, disinclined, indisposed.

Pronounce, articulate, speak, utter, deliver, express, enunciate, declare, affirm.
Ant.—Mispronounce, suppress, stifle, silence, mumble.

Proof, demonstration, evidence, testimony, experience, trial, experiment, test, assay.
Ant.—Disproof, failure, fallacy, invalidity.

Prop, bolster, brace, buttress, maintain, sustain, support, stay.

Propagate, spread, circulate, diffuse, disseminate, extend, breed, increase, generate.
Ant. — Extinguish, contract, suppress, reduce, diminish, fail, die, decrease.

Propensity, inclination, disposition, bias, proneness, tendency, bent, predilection, proclivity.
Ant.—Aversion, disinclination, indisposition.

Proper, legitimate, right, just, fair, equitable, honest, suitable, fit, befitting, decent, pertinent, appropriate, meet, becoming, benefiting, adapted.
Ant.—Improper, wrong, unsuitable, common, indecent, unbecoming, unseemly.

Property, goods, possessions, wealth, estate, peculiarity, quality, attribute, effects.
Ant. — Poverty, want, failure, penury, aspect, essence.

Prophesy, foretell, predict, prognosticate.
Ant.—Recount, tell, relate.

Propitiate, conciliate, reconcile.
Ant.—Alienate, estrange, exasperate.

Propitious, fortunate, promising, favorable, auspicious, timely.
Ant. — Unpropitious, hostile, untimely, unfavorable.

Proportion, rate, ratio, degree.
Ant. — Misproportion, misadjudgment.

Proposal, offer, tender, overture, proposition.
Ant. — Withdrawal, order,

command, warning, prohibition.

Propose, purpose, intend, mean, move, propound, design, offer, proffer, bid, tender.
Ant.—Chance, risk, venture, revoke.

Proprietor, possessor, owner, master.
Ant. — Lessee, servant, subordinate.

Propriety, expediency, fitness, justness, decorum, correctness.
Ant.—Impropriety, indecorum, unconventionality.

Prorogue, adjourn, postpone, delay, defer.
Ant.—Convene, call, assemble, prolong.

Prosecute, continue, pursue, persevere, persist, arraign.
Ant. — Discontinue, abandon, exonerate, acquit.

Prospect, view, survey, landscape, perspective, vista, scene, promise, hope.
Ant. — Obscurity, darkness, cloud, hopelessness, improbability.

Prosper, succeed, flourish, grow rich, thrive, advance.
Ant.—Fail, lose.

Prosperity, welfare, well-being, weal, happiness, good luck.
Ant.—Poverty, failure.

Prostrate, oppressed, trampled on, abject, paralyzed.
Ant.—Erect, upright, restored, vertical, revived.

Protect. (See Defend.)

Protection, shield, defense, preservation, guard, shelter.
Ant.—Betrayal, abandonment, exposure.

Protest, assert, affirm, declare, predicate, aver, assure, denounce.
Ant.—Sanction, endorse, acquiesce, agree.

Protract. (See Prolong.)

Protrude, jut, project, bulge, shoot out, suspend.
Ant.—Recede, indent, incline.

Proud, stately, vain, lofty, arrogant, conceited, boastful, grand, assuming, haughty, vain-glorious.
Ant. — Humble, meek, lowly, affable, deferential.

Prove, examine, assay, evince, demonstrate, establish, confirm, manifest, argue, attest, verify.
Ant. — Disprove, refute, contradict.

Proverb, adage, maxim, aphorism, saying, byword, saw.
Ant.—Essay, dissertation, oration, yarn.

Provide, procure, prepare, furnish, supply, arrange, get.
Ant.—Neglect, overlook, withhold, retain, refuse, appropriate.

Provident, careful, cautious, thrifty, prudent, economical.
Ant. — Improvident, reckless, careless.

Provision, food, supplies, clause, duty, function.
Ant. — Neglect, oversight, want, destitution, pittance.

Provoke. (See Irritate.)

Prowess. (See Bravery.)

Proximity, nearness, vicinity, neighborhood.
Ant. — Distance, remoteness, separation.

Proxy, deputy, agent, representative, substitute, delegate.

Prudence, carefulness, judgment, discretion, wisdom.
Ant. — Impudence, rashness, indiscretion, silliness, recklessness, heedlessness.

Prurient, itching, craving, hankering, longing.
Ant.—Pure-minded.

Pry, scrutinize, peep, peer, look into, search.
Ant. — Disregard, overlook, connive.

Public, common, general, open, notorious.
Ant.—Private, personal, secret, secluded.

Publish, proclaim, advertise, announce, declare, divulge, disclose, reveal, issue, bring out, print.
Ant.—Suppress, reserve, conceal, whisper, deny.

Puerile, youthful, juvenile, boyish, childish, infantile, trifling, weak, silly.
Ant.—Manly, vigorous, powerful, cogent, strong, mature

Pull, draw, haul, gather, drag, tug.
Ant.—Push, eject, propel.

Punctilious, nice, particular, formal, precise.
Ant.—Unceremonious, unconventional, unscrupulous, negligent, careless.

Punctual, exact, precise, nice, particular, prompt, timely.
Ant.—Late, tardy, dilatory, unpunctual.

Pungent, acrid, acrimonious, piquant, smart, keen, stinging.
Ant. — Soothing, mellow, luscious, unctuous.

Punish, chastise, castigate, correct, chasten, scourge, whip.
Ant. — Reward, remunerate, approve, indemnify.

Puny. (See Weak.)

Pupil, scholar, disciple, learner, student, ward, tyro.
Ant.—Teacher, master, adept, guardian.

Purchase. (See Buy.)

Pure, unmixed, unspotted, unsullied, real, unadulterated, genuine, unblemished, spotless, immaculate, absolute.
Ant. — Impure, foul, corrupt, stained, defiled, sullied, tarnished, guilty.

Purify, clarify, clear, cleanse.
Ant.—Blacken, befoul, corrupt, stain, defile, sully.

Purloin. (See Steal.)

Purport, tenor, sense, meaning, import, drift, spirit, intent, signification.
Ant. — Statement, assertion, declaration, proposition.

Purpose, *n.* object, design, intention, view, aim, drift, end.
Ant. — Chance, fate, hazard, lot, accident.

Purpose, *v.* (See Propose.)

Pursue, chase, hunt, track, follow, prosecute.
Ant.—Catch, hold, stop, withdraw, retire, abandon.

Push, thrust, impel, urge, press, drive.
Ant.—Pull, draw, drag.

Putative, supposed, reputed, credited, deemed, reported.
Ant.—Real, veritable, authenticated, actual.

Putrefy, rot, decompose, corrupt, decay.
Ant.—Purify, preserve, freshen, disinfect, embalm.

Puzzle, perplex, confound, embarrass, bewilder, confuse, pose, mystify.
Ant. — Enlighten, instruct, illumine, clear, solve, explain, clarify.

Q

Quack, impostor, pretender, charlatan, empiric, mountebank, fakir.
Ant.—Dupe, gull, victim, authority, adept, expert, master, savant.

Quail, cow, daunt, dismay, intimidate, flinch, quake, tremble.
Ant.—Stand, defy, face, endure.

Quaint, artful, curious, far-fetched, fanciful, odd, singular.
Ant.—Commonplace, ordinary, common, modern, dowdy, conventional, customary.

Quake, quail, shake, tremble, shudder, quiver.
Ant.—Stand, rest, calm.

Qualification, capacity, fitness, capability.
Ant. — Disqualification, incapacity, unfitness.

Qualified, competent, fitted, adapted.
Ant.—Incompetent, ineligible.

Qualify, fit, adapt, suit, abate, modify, soften.
Ant.—Disqualify, unfit, absolve, incapacitate.

Quality, property, attribute, peculiarity, rank, fashion, distinction, character, station.
Ant.—Nondescript, incapacity, indistinctiveness, negation,

being, essence, nature, substance.

Quantity, amount, sum, deal, portion, part, division, share.
Ant. — Deficiency, insufficiency, loss, diminution.

Quarrel, altercation, brawl, broil, tumult, feud, affray, disagreement, wrangle.
Ant.—Peace, agreement, harmony, friendliness, amity, reconciliation.

Quarrelsome, irritable, hot, fiery, irascible.
Ant.—Peaceable, mild, meek, conciliatory, genial.

Quash. (See Annul.)

Queer, quaint, whimsical, odd, strange, eccentric, singular.
Ant. — Ordinary, familiar, common, usual.

Quell. (See Subdue.)

Quench. (See Extinguish.)

Querulous, complaining, repining, doubting, fretting.
Ant. — Contented, satisfied, genial, cheerful, long-suffering, patient, resigned.

Query. (See Question.)

Question, ask, interrogate, subject, point, doubt, dispute, query, inquiry, interrogatory.
Ant. — Answer, state, assert, dictate, concede, endorse, allow, reply.

Questionable, doubtful, uncertain, disputable, suspicious.
Ant.—Certain, evident, obvious, indisputable.

Quibble, cavil, evade, equivocate, prevaricate, shuffle.

Quick, lively, ready, prompt, alert, nimble, agile, active, brisk, expeditious, adroit, fleet, rapid, swift, impetuous, sweeping, dashing, clever, sharp.
Ant. — Slow, tardy, sluggish, inert, inactive, dull, deliberate.

Quicken, accelerate, hasten, expedite, dispatch, animate, revive, vivify.
Ant. — Retard, delay, clog, sway, detain, discourage.

Quickness, speed, velocity, celerity, swiftness, fleetness.

Quiescence, quiet, quietude, rest, repose, tranquillity, dormancy, abeyance, stillness, silence.
Ant.—Agitation, unrest, motion, noise, disturbance, excitement, tumult.

Quiet, *v.* calm, still, hush, lull, pacify, soothe.
Ant.—Rouse, excite, disturb, urge, agitate.

Quiet, *n.* (See Quiescence.)

Quit, relinquish, abandon, leave, forego, give up, resign, cede, surrender.
Ant. — Hold, seek, occupy, bind, enforce, enter.

Quite, altogether, completely, wholly, entirely, totally.
Ant.—Barely, hardly, partially, imperfectly.

Quiver. (See Quake.)

Quixotic, romantic, wild, freakish.
Ant. — Rational, reasonable, humdrum.

Quote, note, repeat, cite, adduce.
Ant. — Misquote, contradict, disprove, retort, refute.

R

Rabid, mad, furious, raging, frantic.
Ant. — Rational, sane, sober, reasonable.

Race, ancestry, course, match, pursuit, career, family, clan, house, lineage, pedigree.

Rack, torture, agonize, wring, excruciate, distress, harass.
Ant. — Soothe, comfort, console.

Racy, spicy, pungent, smart, spirited, lively, vivacious.
Ant.—Dull, insipid.

Radiance, splendor, brightness, brilliance, luster, glare, brilliancy.
Ant. — Dullness, darkness, gloom, obscurity.

Radiate, shine, gleam, glitter, glisten, sparkle, coruscate.
Ant.—Darken, dull, converge.

Radical, organic, innate, fundamental, original, constitutional, inherent, complete, entire, uncompromising.
Ant. — Adventitious, superficial, partial, derived, extraneous, unimportant, conservative, moderate.

Rage, *n.* anger, indignation, choler, fury, passion, frenzy, fashion.
Ant. — Reason, moderation, temperance, calm, mildness, softness.

Rage, *v.* storm, rave, fret, chafe, fume.
Ant.—Calm, assuage, cool.

Rail, censure, bluster, scold.
Ant. — Flatter, compliment, approve.

Raiment, clothes, vestments, garments, attire, garb, dress, apparel.
Ant.—Nudity, nakedness, nature.

Raise, hoist, lift, exalt, heave, heighten, aggregate, elevate, erect, levy.
Ant.—Lay, cast, depress, lower, depreciate, lull, quiet, calm, compose, destroy.

Rally, assemble, congregate, recall, inspirit, animate.
Ant. — Demoralize, disperse, disband.

Ramble, *n.* excursion, tour, jaunt.
Ant. — Rest, quiet, business, ride.

Ramble, *v.* wander, stroll, roam, rove, range, expatiate, stray.
Ant. — Hasten, speed, drive, run.

Rambling. (See Discursive.)

Rampant, prevalent, overruling, imperious, domineering, luxuriant, frisky, headstrong.
Ant.—Curbed, controlled, disciplined, demure.

Rampart, bulwark, defense, fence, security, guard, fortification, fort.
Ant.—Exposure, vulnerability.

Rancid, fetid, rank, stinking, sour, tainted, reasty.
Ant.—Sweet, pure, fresh, fragrant.

Rancor, malignity, hatred, hostility, antipathy, animosity, enmity, ill-will, spite.
Ant.—Forgiveness, gentleness, mildness, clemency.

Range. (See Arrange.)

Rank, order, degree, dignity, consideration, distinction, nobility.
Ant. — Disorder, confusion, commonalty.

Ransack, rummage, pillage, overhaul, explore, plunder.
Ant.—Skim, survey, overlook, leave, omit.

Ransom, emancipate, free, unfetter.
Ant.—Prosecute, hold, detain, indict, fine, forfeit, imprison, chain, fetter.

Rant, bombast, fustain, cant.
Ant.—Eloquence, rhetoric, reason, argument, sincerity, truth.

Rapacious, ravenous, voracious, greedy, grasping.
Ant. — Frugal, contented, liberal, bountiful, generous.

Rapidity, quickness, swiftness, speed, velocity, celerity, fleetness, activity, expedition, dispatch.
Ant. — Slowness, delay, tardiness.

Rapine. (See Pillage.)

Rapt, ecstatic, transported, ravished, entranced, spellbound, charmed, enchanted, delighted.
Ant. — Agonized, tortured, pained, indifferent, distracted.

Rapture, ecstasy, transport, delight, bliss.
Ant.—Agony, torture, pain, ennui, dejection, despair.

Rare, scarce, singular, uncommon, incomparable, unusual, unique.
Ant. — Common, frequent, abundant, numerous, usual, mean, dense, cheap, worthless, ordinary.

Rascal, rogue, scoundrel, knave, vagabond, scamp.

Rash, hasty, precipitate, foolhardy, venturesome, adventurous, thoughtless, heedless, reckless, careless.
***Ant.* — Wary, cautious, timid,**

discreet, deliberate, reluctant, reasoned.

Rashness. (See Rash.)

Rate, value, compute, appraise, estimate, chide, abuse.

Ratify, confirm, establish, substantiate, sanction, endorse.
Ant.—Reject, repudiate, abrogate, annul, nullify, protest, oppose.

Rational, reasonable, sagacious, judicious, wise, intellectual, sensible, sane, sound.
Ant.—Irrational, insane, weak, silly, absurd, injudicious, unreasonable, mad.

Ravage, overrun, overspread, desolate, devastate, despoil, destroy, swoop.
Ant.—Spare, preserve, protect, shield, indemnify, beautify, improve, build up.

Ravenous. (See Rapacious.)

Raving, distracted, frantic, mad, furious, angry, violent.
Ant.—Quiet, calm, reasonable, sane.

Ravish, entrance, enrapture, transport, enchant, charm, delight, violate, abuse, captivate.
Ant.—Disgust, displease, annoy, shield, protect, honor, disenchant, nauseate, repel.

Raze, demolish, destroy, overthrow, ruin, dismantle.
Ant. — Raise, erect, build, restore, strengthen.

Reach, touch, stretch, attain, gain, arrive at.
Ant.—Fail, miss, cease, rebate, stop, fall short.

Readiness. (See Ready.)

Ready, prepared, ripe, apt, prompt, adroit, dexterous, handy.
Ant. — Slow, tardy, late, reluctant, awkward, clumsy, unprepared, unwilling, constrained, dilatory.

Real, actual, literal, positive, certain, genuine, true, veritable, practical.
Ant.—Fictitious, unreal, imaginary, false, untrue, spurious, artificial, assumed, pretended, mythical.

Realize, accomplish, achieve, effect, gain, get, acquire, comprehend.
Ant. — Fail, lose, miss, dissipate, falsify, misrepresent. (See Accomplish.)

Reap, gain, get acquire, obtain.
Ant.—Sow, plant, waste, lose, squander, scatter.

Rear, lift, elevate, erect, breed, raise, train.
Ant.—Kill, destroy, demolish, stifle.

Reason, *n.* motive, design, end, argument, proof, cause, purpose, ground.
Ant. — Pretext, fallacy, folly, aimlessness.

Reason, *v.* deduce, draw from, trace, infer, conclude.

Reasonable, rational, wise, honest, fair, right, just.
Ant. — Unreasonable, foolish, perverse.

Rebellion, conspiracy, insurrection, revolt, anarchy.
Ant.—Support, adherence, law, order, authority, control, domination, government, organization, rule, sovereignty.

Rebuff, repell, repulse, rebuke, reprimand, reprove, check.
Ant.—Welcome, hail, encourage.

Recall, revoke, reclaim, call back, annul, cancel.
Ant.—Send, appoint, delegate, forget.

Recant, abjure, retract, revoke, recall.
Ant.—Propound, assert, maintain, declare, hold.

Recapitulate, repeat, recite, rehearse, enumerate.
Ant.—State, say, deliver, pronounce.

Recede, retire, retreat, withdraw, ebb.
Ant. — Advance, proceed, approach, flow, uphold.

Receive, accept, take, admit, entertain, hold.
Ant. — Give, impart, reject, discharge, emit, bestow.

Recent, fresh, late, new, novel, modern.
Ant. — Ancient, antiquated, archaic.

Reception, levee, receipt, admission, receiving.
Ant.—Dismissal, denial, protest, rejection, repudiation, egress, exclusion, exit, repulse.

Recess, retreat, depth, niche, vacation, alcove, intermission.
Ant.—Projection, promontory, protrusion, publicity, work, advancement.

Reciprocal, mutual, alternate, interchangeable.
Ant.—One-sided, unreciprocal.

Recite, relate, tell, repeat, rehearse, recapitulate.
Ant.—Write, read, hear, misquote, misrepresent.

Reckless, heedless, regardless, careless, indifferent, unmindful, headstrong, imprudent, wild.
Ant. — Careful, heedful, cautious, timid, considerate, wary.

Reckon. (See Calculate.)

Reckoning. (See Reckon.)

Reclaim, recall, reform, regain, recover.
Ant.—Vitiate, corrupt, debase.

Recline, lean, rest, repose, lie.
Ant.—Erect, raise, rise, stand.

Recognize, acknowledge, own, confess, avow, concede, remember.
Ant. — Ignore, overlook, cut, disown, repudiate, forget.

Recollect, bear in mind, remember, think of, recall.
Ant.—Forget, lose, disown.

Recompense, *v.* indemnify, compensate, repay, redeem, remunerate, reimburse, requite.
Ant.—Ignore, hurt, dissatisfy.

Reconcilable, placable, forgiving, consistent.
Ant.—Irreconcilable, inconsistent, incompatible.

Reconcile, conciliate, pacify, propitiate, harmonize.
Ant.—Estrange, alienate, separate, sever.

Record, *v.* enroll, note, register, minute, chronicle.
Ant. — Suppress, obliterate, erase, withhold.

Record, *n.* chronicle, register, note, trace, minute, memorandum.
Ant.—Oblivion, obliteration.

Recount, relate, rehearse, narrate, detail, describe, enumerate, state.
Ant.—Falsify, hear, listen.

Recover, regain, repossess, retrieve, repair, restore, rally.
Ant.—Lose, forget, miss, impair, decay, decline, relapse.

Recreant, cowardly, base, dastardly, craven, fearful, timid.
Ant.—Faithful, true, loyal, gallant.

Recreation, sport, pastime, play, amusement, game, fun.
Ant. — Weariness, toil, work, labor, fatigue, vocation.

Recruit, repair, replenish, renew, refresh, restore, replace, invigorate.
Ant.—Waste, lose, impair, relapse, decay.

Rectify. (See Correct.)

Rectitude. (See Integrity.)

Recumbent, leaning, lying, resting, reposing.
Ant.—Erect, vertical, standing.

Redeem, ransom, get back, recover, atone for, recompense, make amends, rescue, deliver, save, free.
Ant.—Profit, lose, abandon, betray, surrender, condemn.

Redolent, odorous, aromatic, fragrant, odoriferous.
Ant.—Fetid, ill-savored, stinking.

Redound, tend, conduce, contribute, add.
Ant.—Fail, miss, defeat, frustrate.

Redress, remedy, repair, abatement, relieve, mitigate, remission, relief, cure.
Ant.—Wrong, impair, aggravate, intensify, confirm, perpetuate, oppression, injury.

Reduce, abate, lessen, decrease, diminish, lower, abridge, shorten, conquer, curtail.
Ant.—Enlarge, increase, augment, extend, broaden, ex-

pand, invigorate, restore, liberate, transform, amplify, lengthen.

Redundant, superfluous, unnecessary, excessive, luxuriant.
Ant. — Defective, requisite, necessary.

Reel, stagger, totter, falter, roll.
Ant.—Walk, stand, run.

Refer, appeal, allude, revert, relate, belong.
Ant. — Disconnect, separate, alienate, misapply.

Referee, umpire, judge, arbitrator, arbiter
Ant.—Litigant, opponent, adversary.

Reference. (See Refer.)

Refined, polite, courtly, polished, genteel, purified, cultured.
Ant. — Coarse, vulgar, gross, rude, blunt, unsophisticated, uncultivated, boorish, ill-bred, bourgeois.

Reflect, consider, think, ponder, muse, censure, reprove, cogitate.
Ant. — Disregard, overlook, dream, wander, divert, dissipate. (See antonyms of Consider.)

Reform, amend, correct, mend, better, restore, ameliorate, improve, reclaim.
Ant.—Corrupt, deform, impair, vitiate, debase.

Reformation, reform, improvement, amendment.
Ant.—Corruption, ruin.

Refractory. (See Obstinate.)

Refrain, abstain, keep from, restrain, govern, forbear, desist from, refuse.
Ant.—Persist, continue, indulge, venture.

Refresh, revive, enliven, cheer, renew, vivify, regale, feast.
Ant. — Oppress, weary, tire, fatigue, exhaust, enervate.

Refuge, asylum, protection, sanctuary, shelter, retreat, harbor.
Ant.—Exposure, peril, snare.

Refund, reimburse, pay back, repay, return, restore.
Ant. — Expend, embezzle, appropriate, steal, divert, withhold.

Refuse, *v.* deny, reject, repudiate, decline, withhold.
Ant. — Grant, concede, afford, yield, comply, accept, avow, acknowledge.

Refuse, *n.* dregs, dross, scum, rubbish, leavings, remains.
Ant.—Cream, flower, prime.

Refute, disprove, falsify, negative.
Ant. — Prove, confirm, establish, affirm, accept.

Regain. (See Recover.)

Regale, feast, entertain, delight, refresh, gratify.
Ant. — Starve, stint, refuse, tantalize.

Regard, attend to, advert, mind, heed, notice, behold, view, consider, respect, reverence, revere.
Ant.—Disregard, miss, overlook, despise, hate, misjudge, slight.

Regarding. (See Referring.)

Regardless, indifferent, careless, heedless, unmindful, reckless, inconsiderate, disregarding.
Ant.—Careful, attentive, prudent, cautious, scrupulous, mindful.

Register. (See Record.)

Regret, grief, sorrow, lamentation, repentance, remorse.
Ant.—Indifference, exultation, callousness, satisfaction, complacency, delight.

Regular, orderly, methodic, systematical, uniform, unvaried, customary, ordinary, stated, periodical.
Ant. — Irregular, exceptional, abnormal, erratic, uncertain, rare, disorderly, confused.

Regulate, arrange, adjust, organize, govern, rule, methodize.
Ant.—Disorder, confuse, misrule.

Rehearse, narrate, repeat, recite, recount, tell, relate.
Ant. — Exhibit, perform, misrepresent.

Reimburse, refund, repay, satisfy, indemnify.
Ant. — Embezzle, defraud, retain, appropriate.

Rein, restrain, moderate, govern, control, check.
Ant.—Indulge, loose, vent.

Reiterate, repeat, reproduce, renew.
Ant.—Retract, reverse, contradict, cancel.

Reject, repel, renounce, decline, refuse, repudiate.
Ant.—Hail, welcome, accept, choose, select, admit.

Rejoice, delight, joy, gladden, exult, revel.
Ant.—Mourn, grieve, lament, weep.

Rejoinder, retort, parry, reply, answer, replication.
Ant.—Attack, hit, sally, sarcasm, silence.

Relate. (See Tell.)

Related, cognate, connected, kindred, akin.
Ant.—Separated, disconnected, opposed, different.

Relation, narration, narrative, account, recital, detail, affinity, kinsman.
Ant. — Irrelative, disconnection, dissociation, irrelevancy.

Relax, abate, slacken, loosen, soften, relent.
Ant. — Tighten, intensify, stretch, bend, brace, grow.

Release, free, extricate, disengage, liberate, loosen.
Ant.—Bind, constrain, confine, fetter, imprison.

Relent. (See Relax.)

Relevant, fit, proper, suitable, appropriate, pertinent, apt.
Ant.—Irrelevant, impertinent, inappropriate.

Reliance, trust, hope, dependence, confidence.
Ant. — Distrust, misgiving, suspicion, diffidence, doubt.

Relief, succor, aid, help, redress, alleviation.
Ant.—Oppression, trouble, exhaustion, weariness, injury, hurt, harm.

Religious, pious, godly, holy, devout, sacred.
Ant.—Irreligious, profane, ungodly, sceptic, impious.

Relinquish, forsake, give up, resign, surrender, quit, leave, forego.
Ant.—Retain.

Relish, taste, flavor, piquancy, gusto.
Ant. — Insipidity, drawback, disrelish.

Reluctant, unwilling, averse, loth, disinclined.
Ant. — Eager, active, ready, forward, willing, prompt.

Remain, stop, tarry, halt, abide, stay, continue, sojourn, wait.
Ant.—Fly, vanish, go, disappear, hasten, depart.

Remark, note, heed, comment, observe.
Ant. — Disregard, overlook, miss.

Remarkable, unusual, rare, noteworthy, noticeable, extraordinary, observable, striking.
Ant. — Ordinary, common, everyday, commonplace.

Remedial, healing, curative, mitigating.
Ant. — Noxious, hurtful, deleterious, unhealthy, unwholesome.

Remedy, help, relief, redress, cure, specific, reparation.
Ant. — Evil, ill, disease, hurt, plague, provocation, embarrassment, hindrance, interference, obstruction, opposition.

Remember, recall, recollect, mind.
Ant.—Forget, overlook, disregard.

Remiss. (See Careless.)

Remnant. (See Remainder.)

Remonstrate, object, protest, expostulate.
Ant.—Acquiesce, submit, coincide.

Remorse, self-condemnation, anguish, penitence.
Ant. — Indifference, complacency, self-approval.

Remorseless, pitiless, relentless,

cruel, ruthless, merciless, barbarous.
Ant.—Compassionate, humane, gentle, lenient, merciful.
Remote, distant, far, secluded, indirect.
Ant.—Near, close, immediate, proximate, present, urgent, adjacent, approximate.
Remove, displace, dislodge, withdraw, suppress, eject, oust.
Rend, tear, disunite, split, lacerate.
Ant. — Repair, unite, piece, patch, perpetuate.
Render, present, restore, return, requite, give.
Ant.—Keep, retain, withhold, appropriate.
Renew. (See Refresh.)
Renounce, reject, abjure, quit, forego, abandon, forsake, resign, relinquish, disown.
Ant.—Acknowledge, recognize, maintain, assert, own, avow, profess, defend.
Renown, distinction, reputation, fame, glory, celebrity.
Ant.—Infamy, disgrace, dishonor, disrepute, ignominy, oblivion.
Repair, mend, retrieve, recover, restore.
Ant. — Impair, injure, waste, deteriorate.
Repay, reimburse, reward, refund, return, requite
Ant. — Defraud, embezzle, cheat, extort, confiscate.
Repeal. (See Abolish.)
Repeat, recite, relate, reproduce, recapitulate, rehearse.
Ant.—Discontinue, drop, stop, ignore, suppress, conceal, misquote.
Repeatedly, again and again, frequently, often.
Ant. — Occasionally, infrequently.
Repel, reject, refuse, deter, repulse, beat back.
Ant.—Propel, advance, encourage, promote, attack, charge.
Repentance, self-reproach, penitence, contrition, remorse.
Ant.—Impenitence, obduracy, self-approval.
Replace, reinstate, refund, restore.
Ant.—Move, remove, derange, deprive.
Report, announce, notify, tell, communicate, relate.
Ant.—Silence, hush, suppress, conceal.
Repose, *n.* quiet, quietude, peace, ease, rest, sleep.
Ant. — Unrest, agitation, disturbance, commotion, tumult.
Repose, *v.* rest, recline, lie, settle, confide.
Ant. — Rise, move, labor, remove.
Reprehend. (See Censure.)
Represent. (See Portray.)
Representative. (See Agent.)
Repress, quell, crush, subdue, check, curb, restrain.
Ant. — Raise, rouse, excite, agitate, encourage, incite, stimulate, fan.
Reprieve, pardon, acquittal, respite.
Ant. — Conviction, condemnation.
Reprimand. (See Reprove.)
Reproach. (See Reprove.)
Reprobate, villain, ruffian, miscreant, castaway.
Ant. — Example, paragon, model, pattern.
Reproduce, propagate, imitate, represent, copy.
Ant.—Stifle, extinguish, exterminate, misrepresent.
Reprove, chide, rebuke, reprimand, scold.
Ant.—Praise, approve, commend, extol.
Repudiate, disavow, disown, discard, denounce, disclaim.
Ant. — Acknowledge, avow, admit.
Repugnant, antagonistic, averse, adverse, hostile, unwilling, distasteful.
Ant. — Friendly, harmonious, agreeable, consistent, congruous, acceptable.
Repulsive, odious, forbidding, ugly, disagreeable, revolting.
Ant.—Attractive, charming.
Reputable. (See Honorable.)
Request, desire, beg, ask, beseech, entreat.
Ant.—Command, order, insist, dictate, enjoin, exact.
Requite. (See Repay.)
Rescind. (See Cancel.)
Rescue, save, preserve, recover, recapture, retake.
Ant.—Endanger, expose, imperil, abandon, surrender.
Research, inquiry, examination, lore, learning, investigation.
Ant. — Oversight, ignorance, superficiality.
Resemblance, similarity, semblance, likeness, image.
Ant. — Unlikeness, difference, dissimilarity.
Resent, resist, oppose, repel, rebel.
Ant. — Overlook, submit, pardon.
Resentment, ire, indignation, anger, umbrage, animosity.
Ant.—Endurance, forgiveness, mildness, calmness.
Reserve, shyness, modesty, coyness, reservation.
Ant. — Frankness, candor, openness, forwardness, pertness.
Reside. (See Dwell.)
Resident. (See Inhabitant.)
Residue. (See Remainder.)
Resign, relinquish, leave, abandon, abdicate, forego.
Ant. — Retain, grasp, claim, appropriate, hold.
Resist, withstand, oppose, check, thwart, hinder.
Ant. — Encourage, promote, aid, help, submit, suffer, tolerate, permit.
Resolute, determined, steadfast, decided, steady, constant, persevering, dogged, unshaken, unflinching.
Ant.—Irresolute, weak, undecided, inconstant, vacillating.
Resolution, determination, resolve, decision, motion, courage, fortitude, firmness, conversion.
Ant.—Indecision, inconstancy, composition, union, synthesis.
Resort, fly to, retreat, repair, retire, go.
Ant.—Shun, ignore, avoid, discard.
Resound, echo, re-echo, ring, respond, reverberate.
Ant.—Whisper, murmur, mutter, die.
Resources, means, materials, devices, expedients, wealth, riches.
Ant. — Destitution, poverty, want, exhaustion.
Respect, regard, prefer, venerate, defer.
Ant.—Despise, condemn, disregard, dishonor.
Respectable, good, worthy, laudable, esteemed, reputable, decent, fair.
Ant.—Disreputable, bad, unworthy, mean.
Respite, reprieve, interval, stop.
Ant.—Completion, consummation, execution, performance.
Respond, reply, answer, rejoin, correspond, tally, accord.
Ant.—Ignore, overlook, disregard, disagree, differ.
Rest, repose, slumber, quiet, cessation, peace, tranquillity, interval, remainder, residue.
Ant.—Motion, commotion, tumult, noise.
Restive, obstinate, stubborn, impatient, uneasy.
Ant.—Docile, tractable, manageable.
Restoration, renewal, renovation, return, recovery, revival, reparation.
Ant. — Loss, lapse, forfeiture, abandonment, waste, seizure.
Restore, replace, refund, repair, refresh, heal, cure.
Ant. — Remove, displace, appropriate, deprive, demolish, injure.
Restrain, repress, check, stop, limit, hinder, withhold.
Ant.—Promote advance, urge, incite, aid, loosen, amplify, enlarge, extend.
Result, end, termination, conclusion, effect, issue, consequence.
Ant.—Beginning, cause, origin,

rise, operation, antecedent.
Resume, recommence, begin again, renew.
Ant.—Drop, interrupt, discontinue.
Retain, keep, hold, restrain, retard, detain, engage, hire.
Ant. — Abandon, forfeit, surrender, give up.
Retaliate, repay, revenge, requite, retort.
Ant. — Pardon, condone, forgive.
Retard. (See Impede.)
Retire. (See Depart.)
Retort. (See Reply.)
Retract. (See Recall.)
Retreat, departure, retirement, withdrawal, asylum, shelter, refuge.
Ant. — Advance, approach, publicity, exposure, prominence.
Retrench, reduce, abbreviate, diminish, curtail, contract, lessen, economize.
Ant. — Increase, extend, enlarge, augment, amplify.
Retribution, penalty, punishment, requital.
Ant.—Pardon, reprieve, escape.
Retrieve, recover, rescue, regain, restore, repair.
Ant. — Lose, forfeit, impair, surrender.
Retrospect, review, reminiscence, survey.
Return, reappear, recur, revert, repay, requite, yield.
Ant.—Depart, leave, go, vanish, disappear, appropriate, withhold.
Reveal, disclose, show, divulge, expose, publish.
Ant.—Hide, obscure, conceal, cover, cloak.
Revel, feast, carouse, luxuriate, banquet, wallow.
Ant.—Fast, abstain.
Revenge, vengeance, retaliation, requital, retribution.
Ant. — Pardon, comparison, remission, forgiveness.
Revengeful, unforgiving, spiteful, resentful, vindictive.
Ant. — Forgiving, generous, compassionate.
Revenue, produce, income, fruits, proceeds, wealth, assets.
Ant. — Expenditure, expense, waste, liabilities, debts, outgo.
Reverence, honor, respect, awe, veneration, deference, worship, homage.
Ant. — Irreverence, dishonor, contempt, contumely, execration.
Reverse, repeal, revoke, invert, overturn, overthrow, subvert.
Ant. — Order, arrange, place, ordain, affirm.
Revert. (See Recur.)
Review, retrospect, retrospection, survey, revision, criticism.
Ant.—Glance, look, establishment.
Revile, vilify, calumniate, asperse, slander, reproach, abuse, scandalize.
Ant. — Flatter, compliment, eulogize.
Revise, review, reconsider.
Ant.—Overlook, skim, dismiss, reject, turn down.
Revive, refresh, renew, renovate, animate, resuscitate, vivify, cheer, comfort.
Ant. — Extinguish, kill, depress, exhaust, droop, wither, dishearten.
Revoke. (See Repeal.)
Revolt, rebel, resist, shock.
Ant.—Obey, submit, acquiesce.
Revolting, shocking, disgusting, frightful, horrible.
Ant. — Attractive, pleasing, charming, genial.
Revolve, turn, circulate, whirl, twirl, wheel, rotate.
Ant. — Stand, proceed, fly, walk.
Reward, recompense, compensation, remuneration, requital, bounty, premium.
Ant. — Punishment, wages, earnings.
Rich, wealthy, affluent, opulent, copious, ample, abundant, exuberant, plentiful, fertile, fruitful, gorgeous, superb.
Ant. — Poor, needy, indigent, barren, sterile, unfruitful, destitute.
Ridicule, laugh at, deride, mock, lampoon, rally, chaff.
Ant.—Venerate, respect, salute, honor.
Ridiculous, ludicrous, droll, absurd, preposterous, grotesque, comical, laughable.
Ant.—Serious, grave, sober, important, weighty, majestic.
Rifle. (See Pillage.)
Right, *a.* lawful, correct, true, straight, direct, just, proper, fit, suitable.
Ant.—Wrong, unjust, untrue, incorrect, crooked, dishonest, bad, vile.
Right, *n.* claim, privilege, equity, justice.
Ant.—Wrong, injustice, falsehood, emptiness, encroachment, violence.
Righteous, godly, upright, just, fair, honest, virtuous.
Rigid, rigorous, austere, unyielding, stern, harsh, severe, unmitigated, firm, stringent.
Ant.—Pliant, docile, flexible, yielding, mild.
Riot, commotion, tumult, uproar, row, disturbance, confusion.
Ant.—Peace, order, law.
Ripe, ready, mellow, complete, mature.
Ant.—Raw, green, crude, immature, imperfect, unfit.
Rise, *v.* (See Ascend.)
Rise, *n.* origin, source, spring, fountain-head, beginning, acclivity, ascent, increase.
Ant.—End, subsidence, sinking, termination, disappearance, conclusion.
Risk. (See Venture.)
Rite. (See Ceremony.)
Rival, competitor, antagonist, opponent.
Ant.—Accomplice, ally, friend, helper, supporter.
Road, way, highway, route, course, path, pathway, anchorage.
Roam, ramble, rove, wander, stray, stroll.
Ant.—Hurry, speed, fly, hasten, abide, remain.
Roar, thunder, peal, howl, yell, vociferate.
Ant.—Silence, hush, whisper, breathe.
Robbery, theft, plunder, pillage, larceny, depredation.
Ant.—Restoration, protection.
Robust, strong, lusty, vigorous, sinewy, stout, sturdy, stalwart, able-bodied.
Ant.—Weak, frail, delicate, fragile, sickly, puny.
Rogue, scamp, knave, rascal, villain, scoundrel, cheat, swindler, sharper, miscreant.
Ant.—Gentleman, citizen, victim.
Roll. (See Catalogue.)
Romantic, sentimental, poetic, sensitive, fictitious, ideal.
Ant.—Practical, prosaic, literal, unvarnished.
Room, hall, chamber, apartment, space.
Ant.—Infinity, meadow, field, atmosphere.
Rough, craggy, uneven, shaggy, rugged, blunt, rude, gruff, harsh.
Ant.—Smooth, even, level, sleek, calm, tranquil, refined, courteous, finished.
Round, circular, entire, spherical, complete, plump.
Ant.—Square, oblong, convex, lean.
Rouse. (See Arouse.)
Rout, defeat, discomfit, beat, overthrow, scatter.
Ant.—(See antonyms of Conquer.)
Route, road, course, march, way, journey, path, direction.
Ant.—Ramble, wandering, hazard, chance.
Rove. (See Roam.)
Row, tumult, commotion, riot, disturbance, uproar, broil, affray.
Ant.—Peace, quiet, order.
Rubbish, fragments, debris, litter, wreck, dross, refuse, trash.

Ant.—Valuables, trinkets, property.

Rude, rugged, rough, uncouth, unpolished, harsh, gruff, impertinent, saucy, flippant, impudent, insolent, churlish.
Ant.—Refined, modest, bashful, civil, courteous, polished, elegant, gentle, calm, peaceful, serene, polite, well-bred.

Rugged. (See Rough.)

Ruin, destruction, wreck, havoc, desolation, ravage, defeat, overthrow.
Ant.—Success, rise, prosperity, completeness, integrity, regeneration, organization.

Rule, sway, method, system, law, maxim, precept, guide, formula, regulation, government, standard, test.
Ant. — Irregularity, chance, hazard, exception, deviation.

Ruling, prevalent, predominant, ascendant, dominant.
Ant.—Unimportant, unessential, minor, subordinate.

Rumor, hearsay, talk, fame, report, bruit.
Ant.—Verification, fact, proof, evidence.

Rumple, wrinkle, crumple, pucker, crease.
Ant.—Smooth, flatten, arrange.

Run, flee, scamper, fly, hasten, go, flow.
Ant.—Walk, saunter, lounge, stay, stop, halt, hold, fail, drop, hesitate.

Rupture, fracture, breach, burst, disruption, hostility.
Ant.—Union, coalition, fusion, junction.

Ruse. (See Trick.)

Rush, stream, sweep, dash, press, roll.
Ant.—March, halt, lag, hesitate.

Rustic, rural, countrified, rude, coarse, simple.
Ant.—Urbane, elegant, refined, polished.

Ruthless, cruel, savage, barbarous, inhuman, merciless, remorseless, relentless, unrelenting.
Ant.—Forbearing, careful, tender, gentle, lenient, compassionate, considerate, kind.

S

Sacred, holy, hallowed, divine, consecrated, devoted, dedicated.
Ant.—Profane, unholy, common, secular.

Sad, sorrowful, mournful, dull, dismal, downcast, lugubrious, dejected, gloomy, cheerless.
Ant.—Joyous, gay, cheerful, glad, happy, blithe.

Safe, sure, secure, certain, substantial, trustworthy, reliable, harmless.
Ant.—Unsafe, insecure, dangerous, hazardous, perilous.

Sagacious, shrewd, discerning, sage, wise, prudent, acute, discriminating, intelligent.
Ant.—Dull, obtuse, stolid, unintelligent.

Salary, wages, allowance, pay, stipend, hire, remuneration.
Ant.—Gift, gratuity, reward.

Salient, striking, remarkable, prominent, projecting, jutting.
Ant.—Minor, inconsiderable, retreating, retiring.

Salutation, greeting, address, welcome, congratulation.
Ant.—Disregard, scorn, affront, cut.

Sample, specimen, model, pattern, example, illustration.
Ant.—Exception, nondescript, variety, phenomenon.

Sanative. (See Salubrious.)

Sanction, confirm, countenance, encourage, support, ratify, authorize.
Ant.—Discountenance, disallow, prohibit, nullify, disapprove, oppose.

Sane, sober, lucid, sound, rational.
Ant.—Crazy, mad, insane.

Sanguine, hopeful, confident.
Ant.—Desponding, distrustful, suspicious, misgiving.

Sapient. (See Wise.)

Sarcasm, satire, irony, chaff, ridicule, mockery.
Ant.—Eulogy, compliment, panegyric.

Satiate, glut, gorge, satisfy, surfeit.
Ant.—Stint, starve.

Satire. (See Sarcasm.)

Satisfaction, gratification, compensation, amends, recompense, remuneration, contentment, complacency, payment.
Ant.—Discontent, dissatisfaction, grievance, vexation, annoyance, fraud, wrong, demand, claim, offense.

Satisfy, please, gratify, convince, satiate, glut, gorge.
Ant.—Dissatisfy, displease, annoy, stint, starve, puzzle, tantilize.

Saturate, steep, soak, imbue, impregnate.
Ant. — Drain, empty, dry, wrong.

Saucy, impertinent, rude, impudent, insolent, flippant, froward.
Ant.—Civil, deferential, obsequious, servile, modest, respectful, polite.

Saunter. (See Ramble.)

Savage. (See Barbarous.)

Save, rescue, deliver, keep, hold, husband, redeem, spare, retrench, economize.
Ant.—Lose, betray, abandon, destroy, surrender, impose, promote, induce, cause, endanger, risk, lavish, waste.

Savory, tasty, piquant, tasteful, palatable.
Ant.—Dry, flavorless, distasteful, nauseous.

Scandalize, shock, disgust, offend, calumniate, vilify, revile, malign, traduce, defame, slander.
Ant.—Praise, respect, honor, please, commend one's self.

Scanty, bare, pinched, insufficient, slender, meager.
Ant. — Ample, full, liberal, bountiful, generous, sufficiency, adequate.

Scarce, rare, singular, uncommon, unique, wanting, unusual.
Ant. — Common, frequent, abundant, plentiful, thick, valueless.

Scarcity, dearth, famine, lack, want.
Ant.—Plenty, abundance, frequency.

Scare. *v.* (See Frighten.)

Scatter, strew, spread, fling around, disseminate, disperse, dissipate, dispel.
Ant.—Collect, gather, heap, save, accumulate, unite.

Scheme, design, plan, project, theory, intrigue, plot.
Ant.—Blunder, miscontrivance, chance.

Scholar, disciple, pupil, student, savant.
Ant.—Teacher, master, professor, dunce.

Science, knowledge, learning, scholarship.
Ant. — Ignorance, inexperience.

Scoff, jibe, jeer, sneer, deride, taunt, twit.
Ant.—Salute, respect, compliment, honor.

Scope, range, purpose, intention, drift, aim, tendency, design, view, tenor, purport.
Ant. — Aimlessness, accident, deviation.

Scorn, contempt, disdain, mockery, sneer.
Ant.—Esteem, regard, honor, respect.

Scraggy. (See Lean.)

Scrap. (See Fragment.)

Screen. (See Conceal.)

Scruple, hesitate, doubt, waver.
Ant.—Proceed, decide, determine, act.

Scrupulous, strict, nice, conscientious, precise.
Ant.—Reckless, unscrupulous, confident, self-complacent.

Scrutinize, examine, sift, investigate, inquire into.
Ant. — Overlook, disregard, miss, glance.

Scurrilous. (See Offensive.)

Search, exploration, scrutiny, inquiry, investigation,

examination, research, quest, pursuit.
Ant. — Abandonment, withdrawal, stoppage.

Season, time, period, occasion, term, spell.
Ant.—Untimeliness, unseasonableness.

Seasonable, timely, fit, opportune, convenient, suitable.
Ant. — Unseasonable, unsuitable, unexpected, inopportune.

Seclusion. (See Privacy.)

Secondary, second, inferior, under, subordinate, minor, unimportant.
Ant.—Primary, leading, prominent, important.

Secrecy. (See Privacy.)

Secret, concealed, hidden, clandestine, sly, underhand, private, latent.
Ant.—Public, open, exposed, known, notorious, disclosed.

Secular, worldly, temporal, civil, lay, profane.
Ant.—Religious, clerical, monastic, spiritual.

Secure. (See Safe.)

Security. (See Protection.)

Sedate, settled, grave, composed, calm, quiet, serene, staid.
Ant.—Flighty, ruffled, frolicsome, indiscrete, playful.

Sedition, insurrection, rebellion, revolt, mutiny, tumult, riot.
Ant.—Union, allegiance, fealty, quiet, obedience, order.

Seditious, factious, tumultuous, tubulent, insurgent, mutinous, rebellious, incendiary.
Ant.—Obedient, orderly, quiet, calm, peaceful.

Seduce, allure, attract, decoy, entice, abduct, inveigle, deprave.
Ant. — Force, compel, command, overpower, save, convert.

Sedulous, assiduous, diligent, industrious, indefatigable, constant, persevering.
Ant.—Idle, inconstant, wandering, distracted.

See, behold, view, witness, eye, spy, descry, discern, perceive, understand, observe, note, mark, discover.
Ant.—Miss, overlook, disregard, misunderstand, ignore.

Seek, look for, search, explore, examine, find out, discover, detect, ask.
Ant.—Avoid, shun, elude, discard, abandon, ignore.

Seem, look, appear.
Ant.—Belie, misrepresent, differ.

Seemly, fit, suitable, becoming, decent, decorous, comely.
Ant.—Unseemly, unbecoming, unfit, unsuitable, improper, indecent, incongruous.

Seize, capture, catch, grasp, clutch, snatch, take, arrest, apprehend, bind, fasten.
Ant.—Loose, dismiss, liberate, abandon, drop, unfasten.

Seldom, rarely, unfrequently.
Ant.—Often, frequently, invariably.

Select, elect, prefer, choose, pick, cull.
Ant.—Lump, sweep, take.

Selfish, egotistical, self-seeking, earthly, sordid, mercenary, venal, greedy.
Ant.—Unselfish, disinterested, generous, liberal, magnanimous, considerate.

Sell, vend, dispose of, hawk, retail.
Ant.—Give, bestow, present.

Send, transmit, forward, dispatch.
Ant.—Detain, withhold, deny, recall.

Seniority, eldership, superiority, priority.
Ant. — Juniority, inferiority, subordination.

Sensation, perception, apprehension, feeling, impression.
Ant.—Apathy, insensibility.

Sense, discernment, appreciation, view, opinion, feeling, perception, sensibility, susceptibility, thought, judgment, signification, import, significance, meaning, purport, wisdom.
Ant.—Ignorance, folly, nonsense, insensibility, stolidity, misconception, misinterpretation, thoughtlessness.

Senseless, foolish, imbecile, brainless, absurd, nonsensical, unmeaning, silly.
Ant.—Sensible, wise, practical.

Sensible, wise, intelligent, reasonable, sober, sound, conscious, aware.
Ant.—Insensible, ignorant, intangible, invisible, impalpable, foolish, stupid, senseless.

Sensual, carnal, fleshly, voluptuous, animal.
Ant. — Spiritual, intellectual, abstemious, ascetic.

Sentiment, thought, feeling, notion, sensation, apprehension, opinion, impression, conviction.
Ant.—Vacuity, nonsense, ignorance, conjecture, assumption, prejudice.

Separate, distinct, different, unconnected, disconnected, detached, disjoined, severed.
Ant. — United, joined, tied, wedded, linked, consolidated, connected, fused, collected.

Sequel, end, close, termination, conclusion.
Ant.—Original, beginning, opening.

Serene. (See Calm.)

Series. (See Order.)

Serious. (See Grave.)

Serve. (See Aid.)

Service. (See Benefit.)

Servile, mean, low, abject, sneaking.
Ant.—Independent, refractory, stubborn, defiant, rebellion.

Set, put, place, lay, arrange, locate, settle.
Ant. — Remove, lift, raise, transfer, loosen, detach.

Settle, arrange, adjust, regulate, organize, conclude, determine, fix, ratify, confirm.
Ant.—Unsettle, remove, disturb, disorder, misplace, disarrange, upset.

Sever, break, disconnect, dissever, separate, detach.
Ant.—Unite, connect, include, join.

Several, sundry, divers, various, many.
Ant.—One, same, identical, united, total, analogous, homogeneous, similar.

Severe, harsh, stern, stringent, unmitigated, rough, unyielding.
Ant. — Gentle, considerate, lenient, kind, genial, indulgent, gay, cheerful, joyous, mild.

Shade, shadow, dim, obscure cloud.
Ant.—Light, illuminate, shine, glare, expose.

Shadowy. (See Dim.)

Shake, tremble, shudder, shiver, quake, quiver.
Ant. — Secure, fix, fasten, strengthen, stand, calm, compose, pacify, quiet, soothe.

Shallow, superficial, flimsy, slight.
Ant.—Deep, thorough.

Shame, disgrace, dishonor, immodesty, indecency.
Ant.—Honor, glory, renown, credit.

Shameful, shame, degrading, scandalous, disgraceful, outrageous.
Ant.—Honorable, noble, upright.

Shameless, shame, immodest, impudent, indecent, indelicate, brazen.
Ant.—Becoming, seemly, fitting.

Shape, form, fashion, mold, model.
Ant.—Distort, derange, pervert, caricature.

Share, portion, lot, division, quantity, quota, contingent.
Ant.—Whole, mass, aggregate, entirety. (See antonyms of Part.)

Sharp, pointed, biting, pungent, acute, keen, shrewd, clever, witty, penetrating, piercing, shrill.
Ant.—Blunt, dull, obtuse,

rounded, hollow, light, trivial, mild, gentle, tender, indifferent, careless.

Shatter, shiver, derange, disorder.
Ant.—Construct, organize, compose.

Shed, pour, effuse, spread, spill, diffuse.
Ant.—Absorb, collect, assume, retain.

Shelter, *n.* asylum, refuge, retreat, cover, haven, security.
Ant.—Exposure, betrayal.

Shelter, *v.* cover, screen, lodge, protect.
Ant.—Expose, endanger, imperil, betray.

Shift, *v.* transpose, contrive, change, alter, veer.
Ant.—Locate, fasten, fix, plant.

Shift, *n.* evasion, expedient, resource, alternative.
Ant. — Location, permanence, fixity.

Shine, glow, gleam, glisten, glitter, radiate, sparkle, glare.
Ant.—Fade, wane, glimmer, gleam.

Shiver, shatter, break, quake, shudder, quiver, tremble.
Ant.—Steady, stiffen, stand.

Shock, offend, disgust, appall, dismay, scare, stun, terrify.
Ant.—Gratify, please, delight, amuse.

Shocking, disgusting, revolting, dreadful, terrible.
Ant.—Pleasing, charming, delightful, creditable, attractive.

Short, brief, concise, curt, compendious, succinct, summary.
Ant.—Long, protracted, extended, unlimited, ample, abundant, complete, diffuse.

Shorten. (See Abbreviate.)

Show, exhibition, sight, representation, spectacle, scene, pageant, ostentation, indicate, mark, point out, exhibit, display.
Ant.—Secrecy, disguise, concealment, suppression, disappearance, hide, conceal.

Showy, pompous, gorgeous, fine, gay, grand.
Ant.—Quiet, subdued, unnoticeable.

Shrewd. (See Sagacious.)

Shroud. (See Cover.)

Shudder. (See Tremble.)

Shun. (See Avoid.).

Shut, close, preclude.
Ant.—Open, expand, unfasten, unclose.

Shy, timid, reserved, coy.
Ant.—Bold, impudent, forward, audacious.

Sick, ill, diseased, disordered, distempered, indisposed, unwell, ailing, sickly, unhealthy, morbid.
Ant.—Well, whole, healthy, strong, robust, normal, sound.

Sickness, illness, indisposition, disease, disorder.
Ant.—Health, soundness.

Side, edge, verge, margin, border, party, cause, interest, policy.
Ant.—Center, core, body, interior, neutrality, opposition.

Sight, seeing, perception, view, vision, spectacle, show.
Ant. — Blindness, invisibility, disappearance, oversight.

Sign, token, proof, indication, symbol, emblem, type, symptom, mark, omen, signal, badge.
Ant.—Misjudication, falsification, misrepresentation.

Signal, remarkable, noted, notable, extraordinary, eminent, conspicuous, memorable, important.
Ant.—Ordinary, common, unimportant, unnoticeable.

Significant, expressive, indicative, momentous, material, important.
Ant.—Insignificant, meaningless, unindicative, mute, slight, negligible.

Signification, import, sense, meaning.

Signify, express, declare, intimate, imply, denote, mean, betake.
Ant.—Conceal, suppress, nullify, refute, neutralize.

Silence, stillness, quiet, calm, secrecy, speechlessness, dumbness.
Ant.—Noise, clamor, din, tumult, roar, agitation, publicity, celebrity, loquacity, outcry.

Silent, dumb, mute, speechless.
Ant.—Talkative, noisy.

Silly, simple, imbecile, foolish, witless, unwise, indiscreet, nonsensical.
Ant. — Sagacious, intelligent, astute, wise, discreet, prudent, rational, sound.

Similar, resembling, alike, corresponding.
Ant.—Different, unlike, dissimilar, alien, incongruous.

Simile, comparison, similitude.

Similitude. (See Similar.)

Simple, silly, imbecile, foolish, elementary, unmixed, mere, plain, frank, open, shallow, single, uncompounded, artless.
Ant.—Complex, double, mixed, various, compound, elaborate, complicated, sagacious, wise, abstruse.

Simulate, dissimulate, dissemble, pretend.
Ant.—Exhibit, expose, manifest, proclaim, show, vaunt.

Sin, wrong, wickedness, iniquity, crime, ungodliness, evil.
Ant. — Goodness, virtue, righteousness, purity, holiness.

Sincere, unvarnished, genuine, honest, unaffected, upright, true, plain, frank, candid, cordial, hearty, pure, real.
Ant.—Insincere, false, feigned, pretended, dishonest, affected.

Single, sole, unmarried, singular, particular, individual, only.
Ant.—Plural, many, collective, double, numerous, frequent, married.

Singular, particular, odd, curious, eccentric, queer, strange, rare, scarce.
Ant. — Common, frequent, ordinary, usual, customary, general.

Sinister, unfair, disingenuous, dishonest, bad, evil, left.
Ant. — Honest, right, fair, lucky, fortunate, attractive.

Sink, droop, descend, suppress, conceal, submerge.
Ant. — Rise, ascend, mount, soar, swell, increase.

Situation, condition, plight, predicament, state, position.

Size, greatness, bulk, magnitude, largeness, dimension, bigness, extent.
Ant. — Smallness, littleness, minuteness, pettiness

Sketch. (See Portray.)

Skillful. (See Adroit.)

Skill. (See Aptitude.)

Skulk, sneak, hide, cover, sink, shroud, shelter, veil.
Ant.—Show, parade, issue.

Slack, loose, remiss, careless, negligent, backward, weak, slow.
Ant.—Tight, tense, diligent, alert, active, eager.

Slacken, loosen, unbind, relax, abate, flag, moderate.
Ant.—Tighten, increase, freshen.

Slander, *v.* defame, asperse, calumniate, traduce, detract, scandalize, revile, vilify, abuse, malign, vilipend.
Ant. — Vindicate, commend, praise, honor, extol, eulogize, flatter, glorify.

Slander, *n.* calumny, libel, vilification, defamation.
Ant. — Praise, commendation, applause.

Slaughter, bloodshed, carnage, butchery.
Ant.—Peace, order, arbitration.

Slavery, servitude, enthrallment, thralldom.
Ant.—Freedom, liberty.

Slavish. (See Servile.)

Slay. (See Kill.)

Sleek, glossy, shiny, velvety, silken.
Ant.—Rough, bristly, hairy.

Sleep, doze, drowse, nap, slumber.
Ant.—Toil, wake, watch, work.
Sleepy, sluggish, lazy, somnolent, slumbrous, drowsy, lethargic.
Ant.—Wakeful, vigilant, alert, awake, active.
Slender, slim, thin, small, trivial, slight, fragile.
Ant. — Stout, robust, thick, massive.
Slight, *a.* (See Slender.)
Slippery, smooth, glossy, unsafe, deceptive, evasive.
Ant.—Rough, firm, securely, safe, stable, trustworthy.
Slothful. (See Idle.)
Slovenly, loose, negligent, disorderly, tidy.
Ant.—Trim, neat, tidy, orderly, careful.
Slow, dilatory, tardy, sluggish, tedious, dull, lazy.
Ant.—Quick, fast, rapid, alert, active, ready, prompt.
Sluggish. (See Slothful.)
Sly, cunning, astute, crafty, artful, subtle, wily, underhand.
Ant. — Open, frank, artless, undesigning.
Small, little, diminutive, minute, slight, trivial.
Ant.—Great, large, big, bulky, ample, stout, spacious, strong, important, liberal.
Smart, quick, keen, brisk, sharp, caustic, severe, clever, witty, showy, spruce.
Ant. — Dull, heavy, slow, stupid, sluggish, dowdy, shabby, clownish.
Smartness. (See Smart.)
Smear, daub, besmear, begrime, varnish, spatter.
Ant.—Polish, scour, scrape.
Smell, odor, scent.
Smite, beat, strike, slay, kill, afflict, chasten, punish.
Ant.—Soothe, caress, console, repel.
Smoke, fumes, vapor, nothing, moonshine, triviality.
Ant.—Substance, reality, flame, importance.
Smooth, *a.* suave, bland, even, level, plain, polished, flat, mild.
Ant.—Rough, uneven, rugged, harsh, blunt.
Smooth, *v.* level, flatten, ease, calm, allay, mollify.
Ant.—Roughen, smear, dent, groove, excite, aggravate.
Smother, gag, strangle, alloy, stifle, conceal, choke, suffocate.
Ant.—Fan, ventilate, resuscitate, foster, cherish, publish.
Snare. (See Trap.)
Snatch, pluck, pull, twitch, catch, clutch, grasp, grip.
Ant. — Restore, release, unhand.
Sneak. (See Crouch.)
Sneer, scoff, taunt, jibe, mock.
Ant. — Compliment, eulogy, deference.
Snub. (See Rebuke.)
Snug, close, compact, concealed, comfortable.
Ant.—Exposed, loose, uncomfortable, bare.
Soak, wet, moisten, steep, drench, saturate, macerate, imbrue.
Ant.—Dry, air, wring, bleach, desiccate, drain.
Soar, rise, mount, tower, ascend, aspire.
Ant. — Drop, sink, descend, alight.
Sober, moderate, abstemious, abstinent, sedate, temperate, cool, calm, dispassionate, reasonable, self-possessed.
Ant.—Intemperate, drunk, intoxicated, excited, impassioned, agitated, furious, extravagant, eccentric.
Sociable, social, convivial, conversable, familiar, companionable, genial, friendly.
Ant. — Unsociable, ungenial, morose, retiring, bashful.
Social, civil, civic, sociable, convivial, friendly, hospitable, communicative.
Ant. — Individual, personal, solitary, physical, hostile, inimical, unkind, unsocial.
Society, association, company, corporation, companionship, community, fellowship, fraternity.
Ant. — Individuality, personality, separation, privacy.
Soft, supple, flexible, yielding, docile, tractable, manageable, mild, gentle, meek, tender, mellow, sleek, glossy.
Ant.—Hard, tough, rigid, unyielding, coarse, harsh, rough, unkind, stern, sharp, ascetic, resolute, cruel, exacting, flinty, hardened, obdurate.
Soften, civilize, mollify, mitigate.
Ant.—Harden, barbarize, excite, infuriate.
Soil, *v.* stain, sully, tarnish, begrime, defile, doleful, dirty.
Ant.—Cleanse, purity, bleach.
Sojourn, *v.* (See Dwell.)
Solace. (See Comfort.)
Sole, only, solitary, single, alone, individual, exclusive.
Ant.—Plural, numerous, collective.
Solemn. (See Grave.)
Solemnity, ceremony, rite, observance, form, celebration, sanctity, sacredness, impressiveness.
Ant. — Gaiety, profanity, triviality, desecration, vulgarity.
Solicit, ask, crave, beg, urge, pray, entreat, beseech, implore, supplicate, importune, invite.
Ant.—Demand, require, exact, claim.
Solicitude. (See Anxiety.)
Solid, hard, firm, stable, substantial, compact, dense, strong, valid.
Ant.—Hollow, soft, yielding, frail, brittle, elastic, weak, invalid, unsound.
Solitary, alone, sole, only, single.
Ant. — Manifold, multitudinous, many, numerous.
Solution, explanation, answer, key, disconnection.
Ant. — Union, combination, connection, complication, mystification, obscurity.
Solve. (See Explain.)
Sombre, dull, grave, gloomy, cloudy, murky, dusky, sable, dark, mournful, funereal, lugubrious.
Ant.—Bright, gay, sunny, joyous.
Song, ballad, carol, ditty, lay, strain, poem, hymn, anthem.
Ant.—Speech, prose, sermon.
Soothe, soften, allay, appease, relieve, assuage, compose, calm, quiet, still, hush, lull, pacify, mitigate.
Ant.—Rouse, excite, ruffle, irritate, agitate, aggravate, annoy, infuriate.
Sordid, earthly, selfish, mean, covetous, niggardly, greedy, close, dirty, foul, gross, vile, base.
Ant. — Pure, generous, unselfish, honorable, profuse, lavish, prodigal, extravagant.
Sorrow, affliction, distress, grief, trouble, sadness, mourning.
Ant.—Joy, gladness, rejoicing
Sorry, grieved, pained, hurt, afflicted, vexed, shabby, paltry, worthless, vile, sorrowful, sad, poor, insignificant.
Ant.—Glad, pleased, delighted, gratified, fine, respectable
Sort, species, kind, quality, class, genus, nature, character.
Ant.—Unlikeness, eccentricity, phenomenon, uniqueness.
Soul, spirit, life, reason, intellect, vitality, energy, courage, feeling, person, animation, vivacity, mind, spirit.
Ant. — Materiality, body, organism, physiology, soul is opposed to body, mind to matter.
Sound, *a.* healthy, orthodox, unbroken, unimpaired, firm, weighty, valid, sane.
Ant. — Unsound, imperfect, partial, broken, impaired, unhealthy, weak, frail, fragile, diseased, rotten.
Sound, *n.* tone, noise.
Ant.—Silence.
Sound, *v.* ring, peal, clash, clang, investigate, gauge.

Ant.—Silence, hush, overlook, disregard.
Sour, acid, sharp, tart, rancid, harsh, pungent, piquant, crabbed, morose, peevish.
Ant.—Sweet, wholesome, mellow, genial, kindly.
Source, origin, spring, fount, cause, rise, original, beginning, commencement.
Ant.—Mouth, end, exit, issue, result, effect.
Sovereign, regal, royal, imperial, principal, chief, predominant, paramount, effectual.
Ant.—Inferior, subject, subordinate, subservient, weak, inefficient.
Space, room, interval, extent, expanse, field, place, site, station.
Ant. — Limitation, restriction, confinement, proximity.
Spacious, ample, roomy, capacious, extensive, large, wide.
Ant.—Narrow, limited, cramped, confined.
Spare, *v.* afford, give, husband, store, forbear.
Ant.—Spend, squander, lavish, scatter, indulge.
Spare, *a.* meager, scanty, frugal, stinted, lean, thin.
Ant.—Ample, plentiful, abundant, profuse, liberal, generous, bountiful, available.
Sparkle, shine, flash, gleam, twinkle, glitter, glisten, glare, bubble, effervesce.
Ant.—Smoulder, stagnate, expire.
Sparse, scanty, thin.
Ant.—Luxuriant, abundant.
Speak, converse, say, tell, talk, discourse, utter, express, confer.
Ant.—Hush, sing, write, chant, conceal.
Special, exceptional, peculiar, particular, distinctive, specific.
Ant. — General, universal, common, generic.
Specify, particularize, state, designate, mention.
Ant.—Generalize, lump, combine, confound.
Specimen, model, sample, illustration, example, instance.
Ant. — Exception, anomaly, non-descript, freak.
Specious, colorable, plausible, showy.
Ant.—Absurd, ridiculous, inadmissible, unreasonable.
Spectacle, show, display, slight, scene, exhibition, representation, pageant.
Ant.—Fizzle, non-celebration.
Spectator. (See Observer.)
Speculation, contemplation, consideration, view, theory, scheme, conjecture.
Ant.—Realization, proof, fact, verification, certainty.

Speedy, early, quick, fast, rapid, swift, fleet.
Ant.—Late, slow, tardy, loitering, lingering.
Spend, expend, disburse, exhaust, squander, lavish, waste, consume, dissipate.
Ant.—Retain, save, hoard, accumulate, economize.
Spirit, breath, life, essence, soul, specter, apparition, ghost, courage, zeal, mood, temper, principle.
Ant.—Body, substance, flesh, frame, embodiment, torpor, deadness, timidity, dejection.
Spirited. (See Animated.)
Spiritual, divine, religious, incorporeal, immaterial, ecclesiastical, ghostly.
Ant.—Material, carnal, fleshly.
Spite, rancor, spleen, malice, malevolence, ill will, grudge, pique, vindictiveness.
Ant. — Good will, kindliness, benevolence.
Spleen. (See Spite.)
Splendid, magnificent, grand, brilliant, showy, superb, sumptuous, pompous, glorious, illustrious, signal.
Ant.—Tame, somber, dull, obscure, unimposing, mean, poor, ordinary, ineffective.
Split, cleave, break, burst, crack, divide, separate.
Ant.—Unite, cohere, coalesce, combine, agree, consolidate.
Spoil, destroy, mar, impair, injure, plunder.
Ant.—Preserve, improve, better, enrich, endow.
Spontaneous, voluntary, willing, gratuitous.
Ant. — Involuntary, compulsory, necessitated.
Sporadic, isolated, rare.
Ant.—General, prevalent.
Sport, amusement, diversion, recreation, pastime, game, play, frolic.
Ant.—Work, business, earnestness.
Spread, extend, disperse, expand, diffuse, distribute, circulate, propagate, disseminate, unfurl, scatter.
Ant.—Contract, gather, furl, fold, close, shut, secrete, suppress, restrict, hush, conceal, check, condense, confine, restrain.
Sprightly. (See Gay.)
Spring, rise, proceed, issue, flow, emerge, leap, bound, jump, fountain, source.
Ant.—Alight, land, drop, arrive, issue, end, terminate.
Sprout, bud, germinate, shoot forth, spring.
Ant.—Blight, wither, decay.
Spruce. (See Neat.)
Spur, goad, incite, urge, stimulate.
Ant.—Hold, discourage, rein, check, restrain, deter.

Spurious, counterfeit, fictitious, unauthentic, false, unsound.
Ant.—Genuine, true, veritable, legitimate, authentic.
Spurn. (See Scorn.)
Squalid, foul, filthy, dirty, unclean, poverty-stricken.
Ant. — Cleanly, wholesome, trim, neat, tidy.
Squander, waste, consume, dissipate.
Ant. — Save, retain, hoard, hold, acquire, get.
Squeeze. (See Press.)
Stable, firm, established, solid, substantial, constant, staunch, steadfast, steady, fast, standing, permanent, perpetual.
Ant.—Unstable, weak, infirm, insecure, precarious, frail, transient, evanescent.
Staff, prop, support, stay.
Stagger, reel, totter.
Stagnant, motionless, lifeless, tideless, standing.
Ant. — Brisk, flowing, rapid, lively, seething, restless.
Staid, steady, sober, demure, grave, sedate.
Ant. — Unsteady, flighty, indiscreet, eccentric, agitated.
Stain, color, dye, blot, befoul, soil, tarnish, sully, pollute, mar, injure, spoil, discolor, spot.
Ant.—Purify, cleanse, waste, decorate, honor, blemish.
Stalwart. (See Powerful.)
Stammer. (See Hesitate.)
Stamp, mark, impress, impression, print, genus, kind, description, make, mold, type.
Ant. — Formlessness, non-description.
Stand, stop, rest, stagnate, endure, halt.
Ant.—Move, proceed, advance, progress, yield, fall, fail, run, vanish, depart.
Standard, criterion, measure, gauge, test, rule.
Ant. — Mismeasurement, misconformity, misfit.
Standing, status, ground, station, rank, position.
Ant. — Insecurity, precariousness.
Starved, famished, lean, ill-fed, emaciated.
Ant.—Fat, well-fed, plump.
State, *n.* condition, commonwealth, realm.
State, *v.* specify, particularize, say, declare, propound, avow, narrate, recite.
Ant.—Suppress, conceal, suppose, imply, deny, retract, contradict, hear.
Stately. (See Dignified.)
Station, standing, position, post, office, situation, state, rank, location.
Ant. — Removal, departure, ejectment.
Stationary, immovable, fixed, motionless.

Ant. — Movable, changeable, migratory, alterable, unfixed.
Staunch. (See Sincere.)
Stay, remain, abide, continue, await; wait for, dwell, support, sustain, hold, stop, restrain, arrest, hinder.
Ant.—Go, leave, depart, move, proceed, hasten, speed, send, expedite, free, oppress, burden, fail.
Steadfast, constant, staunch, firm, resolved.
Ant. — Wavering, capricious, uncertain, dubious, irresolute.
Steady, firm, fixed, constant, regular.
Ant. — Unsteady, variable, changeable, inconstant.
Steal, purloin, pilfer, filch, embezzle.
Ant.—Buy, restore, renew, pillage.
Steep. precipitous, abrupt, hilly, craggy.
Ant.—Easy, level, gradual, accessible.
Sterile, unfruitful, barren, waste, unproductive.
Ant.—Fertile, fruitful, productive, luxuriant, cultivated.
Sterling, genuine, pure, unalloyed, unadulterated, sound, substantial.
Ant. — False, fictitious, specious, pretentious, unreliable.
Stern, harsh, severe, austere, rigid, rigorous, strict.
Ant. —Lenient, kindly, easy, genial.
Stick. (See Adhere.)
Stifle, extinguish, choke, suffocate, smother.
Stigma, mark, brand, infamy, disgrace, blot, stain.
Ant.—Decoration, laurels, credit, renown.
Still. (See Motionless.)
Stimulate. (See Encourage.)
Stingy, close, mean, niggardly, sparingly.
Ant. —Liberal, generous, lavish, bountiful.
Stint, limit, stop, restrict.
Ant.—Lavish, pour, heap, squander.
Stipend. (See Remuneration.)
Stipulate, bargain, contract, agree on, engage, covenant.
Ant.—Retract, decline, refuse, withdraw, disagree, protest.
Stir, budge, move, agitate, disturb, excite, arouse.
Ant. — Still, quiet, pacify, soothe, repress.
Stock. (See Store.)
Stolid, obtuse, heavy-headed; doltish, dull, senseless.
Ant. — Acute, quick, clever; bright, sensitive.
Stoop, bend, yield, condescend.
Ant.—Rise, erect, stand.
Stop, close, plug, cork, seal, arrest, check, hinder, impede, bar, terminate.
Ant. — Open, clear, unseal, promote, speed, hasten, proceed.
Store, stock, fund, supply, hoard, provision, treasury.
Ant.—Emptiness, lack, want, consumption, exhaustion.
Stormy, tempestuous, boisterous, blustering, roaring, raving, rough.
Ant.—Calm, quiet, peaceful, tranquil.
Stout, robust, athletic, vigorous, stalwart, corpulent, strong, lusty.
Ant. — Lean, thin, slender, weak, frail, feeble, timid.
Straight, right, direct, undeviating.
Ant. — Crooked, winding, curved, circuitous.
Strain, stretch, tighten, exert, filter.
Ant.—Loosen, relax, slacken.
Strait, narrow, confined.
Ant.—Broad.
Strange, odd, surprising, singular, eccentric, rare, uncommon, unusual.
Ant.—Familiar, usual, ordinary, common, regular, general.
Stranger. foreigner, alien.
Ant. — Neighbor, friend, acquaintance, countryman, comrade, associate.
Strategem, artifice, trick, deception, cheat, imposture, delusion, deceit, plot, plan, device.
Ant.—Attack, openness, frankness, blunder, defect.
Stray, rove, ramble, err, digress, deviate, wander.
Ant.—Adhere, abide, stick, return.
Strength, power, might, authority, force, vigor.
Ant. — Weakness, feebleness, infirmity, frailty, softness, insecurity, invalidity.
Strengthen, fortify, reinforce, invigorate, consolidate, establish, substantiate, confirm.
Ant.—Weaken, loosen, shake, undermine, diminish, abrogate, annul, cancel, destroy.
Strenuous, vigorous, zealous, vehement, bold, ardent, strong, resolute.
Ant.—Weak, feeble, irresolute.
Stress, emphasis, force, accent, strain, weight, pressure.
Ant.—Lightness, touch, triviality, unimportance.
Stretch, spread, expand, extend, lengthen, elongate.
Ant. — Contract, shorten, shrink, curtail.
Strict, close, accurate, correct, exact, nice, stringent, rigorous, severe.
Ant. — Loose, lax, indulgent, lenient, inaccurate.
Stricture. (See Censure.)
Strife, struggle, quarrel, contention, discord, disagreement, bickering, wrangle.
Ant.—Peace, amity, friendship, reconciliation, good will.
Strike, hit, beat, smite, touch.
Ant.—Avoid, graze, miss, escape, pass.
Striking. (See Marvelous.)
Strip, denude, divest, bare, despoil, rob, rifle.
Ant.—Clothe, invest, endow, enrich, compensate.
Strive, labor, struggle, aim, contend, vie, contest, endeavor.
Ant.—Submit, succumb, yield, withdraw.
Strong. forcible, cogent, powerful, fortified, potent, sturdy. stalwart, hale, robust, sinewy, athletic, hardy, firm.
Ant —Weak, frail, powerless, defenseless, feeble, sickly, infirm, calm, gentle, delicate, impotent, moderate, brittle, tender.
Struggle. (See Strive.)
Stubborn. (See Obstinate.)
Studious. (See Diligent.)
Study, thought, consideration, care, attention, application.
Ant.—Idleness, ease, carelessness. negligence.
Stupendous, astounding, amazing, marvelous, wondrous.
Ant. — Ordinary, unimposing, small.
Stupid, stolid, dull, obtuse, foolish, witless.
Ant.—Bright, quick, clever, sagacious, sensible, intelligent.
Sturdy. (See Strong.)
Suavity. (See Affability.)
Subdue. conquer, overpower, vanquish, subjugate, overcome, tame, quell.
Ant.—Exalt, aggrandize, strengthen, fortify, liberate.
Subject, *a.* exposed to, liable, obnoxious.
Ant.—Exempt, immune.
Subject, *n.* inferior, subordinate.
Ant.—Superior.
Sublime, grand, noble, raised, exalted, lofty, elevated, eminent, high.
Ant.—Low, mean, base. ignoble, inglorious, ordinary.
Submerge, inundate, drown, deluge, flood, sink.
Ant.—Raise, extricate, dry, save.
Submissive. (See Obedient.)
Submit, succumb, comply, yield, surrender.
Ant.—Resist, oppose, object, withdraw, resume, recover, retain, hold, keep.
Subsequent, later, posterior, following, succeeding.
Ant.—Prior, former, earlier, anterior, previous, preceding, antecedent.
Subsist. (See Exist.)

Substantial, real, true, solid, substantive, tangible, responsible, durable.
Ant.— Unreal, imaginary, fictitious, visionary, immaterial, weak, frail, ghostly, unsubstantial, flimsy.

Substitute. (See Deputy.)

Subterfuge, evasion, shift, quirk, subtlety, artifice, dodge.
Ant. — Candor, openness, frankness, honesty, challenge, assertion, exhibition.

Subtile, fine, thin, rare, delicate, nice, acute, refined.
Ant. — Coarse, thick, gross, dense.

Subtle, cunning, crafty, astute, sly, wily, artful, shrewd.
Ant. — Simple, artless, open, frank, rough, undiscerning.

Subtract, deduct, subduct, withdraw, remove, take.
Ant. — Add, import, give, bring.

Succeed, flourish, thrive, prosper, follow.
Ant.—Fail, lose, miss, precede, anticipate.

Successful, fortunate, lucky, happy.
Ant. — Unsuccessful, unfortunate, unlucky.

Succession, order, series, rotation, lineage, race.
Ant. — Irregularity, disorder, failure, intermission, break, gap.

Succinct, brief, short, concise.
Ant. — Prolix, diffuse, discursive, long.

Succor. (See Aid.)

Succumb. (See Submit.)

Sudden, abrupt, quick, unexpected, unlooked for, unanticipated.
Ant. — Gradual, expected, anticipated, slow.

Suffer, bear, endure, tolerate, admit, allow, let, permit.
Ant.—Resist, repel, reject, forbid, ignore.

Suffocate. (See Smother.)

Suggest, hint, allude, refer, intimate, insinuate, propose.
Ant.—Declare, insist, demand, dictate, enunciate.

Suit, serve, adapt, agree, answer, fit, please, harmonize, accord.
Ant. — Differ, disagree, misfit, vary.

Suitable, seemly, fit, apt, becoming, expedient, convenient, eligible, opposite.
Ant. — Unsuitable, unfitting, unbecoming, discordant.

Sulky, sullen, gloomy, morose, fretful.
Ant.—Genial, kindly, obliging.

Sully, stain, tarnish, soil, spoil, blemish, mar, disgrace, dishonor.
Ant.—Purify, cleanse, glorify, ennoble, dignify.

Sum, amount, quantity, total, whole, problem, aggregate.
Ant.—Part, portion, item, imperfection.

Summary, *n,* abstract, epitome, digest, abridgment, compendium.
Ant. — Expansion, dilution, explanation.

Summary, *a.* short, brief, concise, compendious, succinct.
Ant. — Tedious, protracted, circuitous, formal, slow.

Summit, top, height, culmination, acme, apex, zenith.
Ant. — Bottom, depth, base, foot, nadir.

Summon, call, fetch, cite, bid, challenge, convoke.
Ant. — Send, discharge, remit, disband, dissolve, dismiss.

Sumptuous, costly, expensive, dear, valuable, princely, superb.
Ant. — Poor, mean, inexpensive, sordid, beggarly, frugal.

Sunder. (See Separate.)

Sundry. (See Different.)

Superb, princely, grand, splendid, magnificent.
Ant. — Mean, commonplace, shabby.

Supercilious, haughty, arrogant, insolent.
Ant. — Affable, courteous, modest.

Superficial, shallow, flimsy, slight, imperfect, external, outer, untrustworthy.
Ant. — Deep, profound, abstruse, accurate, exact, thorough.

Superfluous, needless, excessive, useless, unnecessary.
Ant.—Essential, necessary, required, scant, deficient.

Superintend, supervise, overlook, control, direct, manage.
Ant.—Obey, submit, do.

Superior, higher, upper, noble, head, better, excellent.
Ant. — Inferior, lower, worse, subordinate, ordinary.

Superlative, highest, greatest, extreme, supreme, exquisite.
Ant. — Lowest, common, ordinary.

Supernatural, miraculous, preternatural.
Ant. — Natural, physical, human.

Supersede, overrule, annul, set aside, suspend, supplant.
Ant. — Confirm, perpetuate, continue, supply.

Supine, indolent, sluggish, lazy, listless, dull, apathetic, torpid, inactive, careless.
Ant. — Active, energetic, diligent, indefatigable.

Supple, lithe, flexible, pliant, bending, yielding, compliant.
Ant.—Firm, stiff, stubborn, inflexible, unbending, independent.

Supplicate, pray, beg, solicit, beseech, importune, entreat, implore, crave.
Ant. — Order, command, insist, demand.

Supply, furnish, give, grant, afford, provide, minister, contribute, yield.
Ant. — Expand, use, consume, absorb, demand, withhold.

Support, sustain, prop, uphold, maintain, help, befriend, assist, countenance, patronize, favor, second, further, forward, promote, nurture, nourish, foster.
Ant. — Drop, abandon, betray, surrender, discontinue, oppose, discourage, weaken, exhaust, subvert, suppress.

Suppose, presume, conceive, apprehend, imagine, think, assume, believe, deem.
Ant. — Prove, demonstrate, deny, negative.

Supposition. (See Conjecture.)

Suppositious, spurious, false, theoretical, speculative.
Ant.—Genuine, true, real.

Suppress, repress, crush, quell, restrain, put down, stifle, overwhelm, smother, check, stop.
Ant.—Raise, support, fan, excite, incite, instigate, aggravate, publish, spread, disseminate.

Supreme, paramount, highest, greatest, principal.
Ant. — Inferior, subordinate, subject, lower.

Sure, infallible, certain, indisputable, unmistakable, doubtless, firm, safe, secure, confident, positive, assured.
Ant. — Uncertain, ignorant, dubious, doubtful, weak, precarious, insecure, transient, fallible.

Surfeit, glut, gorge, cloy, pall, satiate.
Ant.—Stint, deprive, starve.

Surly, gloomy, morose, sulky, sullen, splenetic, ill-natured, rough, gruff.
Ant.—Genial, kindly, pleasant, happy.

Surmise, presume, conjecture, guess, suppose, suspect.
Ant.—Prove, establish, verify, state.

Surmount, overcome, subdue, vanquish, conquer, surpass, exceed.
Ant. — Succumb, fail, miss, submit, lose.

Surpass, excel, exceed, outdo, outstrip, surmount.
Ant.—Fail, foil, miss, equal.

Surplus, remainder, overplus, residue, excess, balance.
Ant.—Deficiency, deficit.

Surprise, astonish, amaze, startle, alarm.
Ant.—Forewarn, prepare, premonish.

Surrender, cede, give up, de-

liver, yield, relinquish, resign, abandon.
Ant.—Resist, defeat, retain, vindicate, withhold.

Surreptitious, underhand, furtive, stealthy, clandestine.
Ant.—Open, frank, honest, ingenuous.

Surround, environ, encompass, encircle, invest, besiege, inclose, embrace.
Ant.—Open, expose, liberate, free, exclude, shut out.

Survey, examine, scrutinize, review, view, inspect, reconnoiter.
Ant.—Overlook, ignore, miss, disregard.

Susceptible, sensitive, excitable, tender, sensible.
Ant. — Insusceptible, insensitive, impassive, cold.

Suspect, fear, surmise, guess, conjecture.
Ant.—Trust, credit, confide.

Suspense, doubt, uncertainty, anxiety, solicitude, respite, rest, pause.
Ant. — Settlement, decision, determination.

Suspicion, misgiving, jealousy, distrust, mistrust.
Ant.—Belief, trust, confidence.

Suspicious, doubtful, questionable, mistrustful.
Ant.—Trusting, confident.

Sustain, support, maintain.

Sustenance, support, living, livelihood, subsistence, maintenance, sustentation.
Ant.—Starvation, exhaustion, inanition.

Swallow, absorb, imbibe, engulf, engross, consume, devour.
Ant.—Vomit, disgorge, discharge.

Swamp, bog, fen, morass, marsh, quagmire.
Ant.—Field, meadow, river, lake, pond, hill.

Sway, influence, government, authority, dominion, supremacy, ascendancy, rule.
Ant. — Meekness, obedience, subservience, subjection.

Swear, declare, depose, testify, curse, blaspheme.
Ant.—Guess, surmise, conjecture, hesitate.

Sweet, sugary, luscious, delicious, pleasing, mild, gentle, winning.
Ant.—Sour, bitter, offensive, nasty, discordant, repulsive, unwholesome, tainted.

Swell, heave, rise, enlarge, enhance, heighten, dilate, expand, augment.
Ant.—Contract, lessen, diminish, reduce, condense, narrow.

Swift, quick, fleet, speedy, rapid, prompt, ready, eager.
Ant.—Slow, tardy, lazy, loitering, sluggish.

Swindler. (See Cheat.)

Sycophant, flatterer, parasite, adulator, toady, hanger-on.
Ant.—Friend, rival, opponent.

Symmetry, proportion.
Ant. — Deformity, disproportion, shapelessness.

Sympathy, commiseration, condolence, pity, compassion, agreement, fellow-feeling, union, concert.
Ant.—Antipathy, unkindness, harshness, maleficence, cruelty, churlishness, malignity, brutality, inhumanity, malevolence.

Symptom, token, sign, note, mark, suggestion.
Ant.—Misindication, mistake.

Synonymous. (See Equivalent.)

Synopsis, epitome, syllabus.
Ant.—Oration, essay, dilation, expansion.

System, method, arrangement, regularity, order, rule, plan, scheme.
Ant. — Disorder, confusion, chance, fortuity.

Systematic, orderly, regular, methodical.
Ant.—Chaotic, confused.

T

Tacit, silent, implied, understood, implicit.
Ant.—Open, avowed, declared, expressed.

Tact, address, adroitness, expertness, skill, nicety, discrimination, dexterity.
Ant.—Indiscretion, ignorance, awkwardness, mistake.

Tactics, strategy, policy, diplomacy.
Ant.—Blunder, mistake.

Taint, contaminate, defile, pollute, corrupt, infect, vitiate, disgrace.
Ant.—Purify, cleanse, disinfect, efface.

Take, accept, receive, catch, seize, remove, abstract.
Ant.—Drop, reject, abandon, lose, miss, repel, give.

Talent, ability, faculty, genius, cleverness, gift, endowment.
Ant. — Imbecility, stupidity, incompetence.

Talk, conversation, chat, gossip, dialogue, discourse, report, rumor.
Ant. — Writing, correspondence, literature.

Talkative, garrulous, loquacious, prating, chattering, chatty, communicative.
Ant. — Taciturn, silent, reserved, close, mute, reticent.

Tall. (See High.)

Tally, match, suit, correspond, agree, accord, harmonize.
Ant.—Differ, disagree.

Tame, gentle, domesticated, mild, docile, tedious, dull.
Ant.—Wild, savage, undomesticated, fierce, spirited, animated, exciting, lively.

Tangible, palpable, solid, substantial, material, perceptible.
Ant.—Intangible, impalpable, spiritual, incomprehensible.

Tantalize, aggravate, provoke, irritate, tease, vex, frustrate.
Ant.—Gratify, soothe, satisfy.

Tantamount, equivalent, synonymous, equal to.
Ant.—Unequivalent, unequal.

Tardy. (See Slow.)

Tarnish. (See Taint.)

Tarry, await, stay, remain, lag, loiter, abide, lodge, dwell.
Ant. — Press, push, speed, haste.

Tart, sour, sharp, keen, acrid, bitter, acrimonious.
Ant. — Mellow, sweet, mild, genial, kindly, oily, polite, courteous.

Task, business, work, labor, toil, lesson.
Ant. — Relaxation, leisure, amusement, hobby.

Taste, judgment, discernment, perception, sensibility, relish, gusto, zest, nicety, elegance, refinement, flavor, relish, savor.
Ant.—Indiscrimination, indiscernment, indelicacy, insipidity, coarseness, tastelessness.

Tasteless, flat, insipid, mawkish, vapid, dead, stale.
Ant. — Savory, toothsome, palatable, elegant, refined.

Taunt, gibe, jeer, sneer, scoff, twit, deride, reproach.
Ant. — Compliment, eulogy, panegyric.

Tax, toll, duty, rate, assessment, impost, contribution, custom, excise.
Ant.—Gift, wages, reward, remuneration.

Teach, instruct, inform, educate, inculcate, train, direct, guide, counsel, advise.
Ant. — Mislead, misinform, misguide, withhold, brutalize.

Teacher, schoolmaster, professor, preceptor, instructor, tutor.
Ant.—Pupil, student, scholar.

Tear, rend, break, lacerate, sever, sunder.
Ant.—Mend, unite.

Tease, vex, plague, torment, irritate, disturb, provoke, taunt, tantalize.
Ant.—Soothe, gratify, please, delight, fascinate, comfort.

Tedious, slow, dilatory tardy, wearisome, irksome, dreary, tiresome, prosy, sluggish.
Ant.—Quick, exciting, interesting, amusing, delightful.

Teeming, prolific, fertile, pregnant, fruitful, full, fraught, replete, swarming.
Ant.—Barren, scant, sparse, few.

Tell, number, enumerate, count, state, mention, communicate, apprise, impart, reveal, inform, ascertain, signify, acquaint, notify, intimate, report.
Ant. — Hear, listen, repress, suppress, misrecount, misnarrate, misjudge.

Temerity, foolhardiness, audacity, rashness, heedlessness.
Ant.—Timidity, caution, calculation.

Temperate, abstinent, moderate, sober, abstemious, calm, cool, sedate, frugal.
Ant.—Intemperate, immoderate, self-indulgent, torrid, frigid.

Tempest. (See Storm.)

Temporal, worldly, terrestrial, mundane, secular, transient.
Ant.—Religious, spiritual, eternal, sacerdotal.

Temporary, present, immediate, transient, partial, fleeting, transitory.
Ant.—Perpetual, lasting, complete, perfect, permanent, final, stable.

Temporize, fence, maneuver, procrastinate.
Ant.—Act, decide, determine, confirm.

Tempt, allure, try, test, draw, attract, decoy, entice, seduce.
Ant.—Dissuade, deter, warn, frighten, repel.

Tenable, defensible, sound, reasonable.
Ant.—Indefensible, weak, fallacious, irrational, absurd.

Tenacious, cohesive, pertinacious, retentive.
Ant. — (See Antonyms of Strong.)

Tend, keep, watch, guard, manage, incline, nurture.
Ant.—Betray, desert, abandon.

Tendency, inclination, leaning, propensity, proclivity, proneness, predisposition, scope, drift, aim, bias.
Ant.—Disinclination, aversion, deviation, tangency.

Tender, *v.* offer, proffer, produce, bid.
Ant.—Withhold, withdraw, retain.

Tender, *a.* mild, kind, bland, indulgent, compassionate, gentle.
Ant.—Strong, sturdy, hardy, tough, cruel, careless, liberal, rough, rude, unfeeling.

Tenet, opinion, position, view, conviction, belief.

Tenor, meaning, drift, intent, sense, purport.
Ant. — Incoherence, irrelevance, variance.

Tension, strain, force, tone, stretch, tightness.
Ant.—Looseness, laxity, slackness.

Term, designate, boundary, limit, period, time.

Terminate, close, end, conclude, complete, finish, stop.
Ant.—Begin, commence, initiate, establish, progress.

Terrestrial, worldly, earthly, mundane, sublunary.
Ant.—Celestial, infernal.

Terrible, awful, terrific, tremendous, fearful, dreadful, shocking, frightful, horrible.
Ant. — Ordinary, common, pleasant.

Terrify. (See Frighten.)

Territory, dominion, domain.

Terror. (See Alarm.)

Terse, neat, smooth, compact, concise, succinct, pithy, forcible, energetic.
Ant.—Coarse, rough, rude, inconcise, diffuse, prolix.

Test, criterion, standard, ordeal, experience, experiment, trial, proof.
Ant. — Misindication, error, misproof.

Testify, depose, declare, swear, attest, witness, prove, certify.
Ant.—Falsify, misaffirm, silence.

Testimony, witness, confirmation, attestation, proof, evidence.
Ant. — Refutation, contradiction, disproof, argument.

Testy. (See Irritable.)

Thankful, grateful, obliged.
Ant.—(See Thankless.)

Thankless, ungracious, profitless, ungrateful, unthankful.
Ant.—Thankful, profitable, reciprocative.

Thaw, melt, dissolve, liquefy.
Ant.—Freeze, congeal.

Theatrical, dramatic, showy, ceremonious, meretricious.
Ant.—Simple, quiet, subdued, plain, unaffected.

Theft, robbery, depredation, spoliation.

Theme, subject, topic, text, essay.

Theory, speculation, scheme, plea, hypothesis, conjecture.
Ant.—Fact, proof, verity, practice.

Therefore, accordingly, consequently, hence.

Thick, dense, close, compact, solid, coagulated, muddy, turbid, misty, foggy, vaporous.
Ant.—Thin, rare, fine, sparse, strained, pure, limpid, slight, clear, distinct.

Thin, slim, slender, slight, flimsy, lean, attenuated, scraggy, emaciated, diluted, gaunt, meager.
Ant. — Thick, dense, solid, close, bulky, deep, confused, fat, obese, rotund.

Think, cogitate, consider, reflect, ponder, contemplate, meditate, muse, conceive, fancy, imagine, apprehend, hold, esteem, reckon, consider, deem, believe, opine, regard.
Ant.—Guess, hazard, conjecture, trifle, doubt.

Thorough, accurate, correct, trustworthy, reliable, complete.
Ant.—Superficial, inaccurate.

Thought, idea, conception, imagination, fancy, conceit, notion, supposition, care, provision, consideration, opinion, view, sentiment, reflection, deliberation.
Ant.—Vacuity, dream, hallucination, aberration, misconception.

Thoughtful, considerate, careful, cautious, heedful, diligent, contemplative, reflective, provident, pensive, dreamy.
Ant.—Thoughtless, insonsiderate, rash, precipitate, heedless.

Thoughtless, inconsiderate, rash, improvident, precipitate, heedless.

Thralldom, slavery, enslavement, servitude, bondage, vassalage, captivity.
Ant.—Liberty, freedom, independence.

Threat, menace, intimidation.
Ant.—Promise, encouragement, allurement.

Threatening, imminent, impending, menacing, intimidating, foreboding.
Ant.—Encouraging, promising, reassuring, enticing.

Thrifty, sparing, careful, prudent, economical, frugal, saving, provident.
Ant.—Prodigal, wasteful, extravagant.

Thrive, flourish, prosper, increase, succeed, grow, fatten.
Ant.—Decay, fade, wither, waste, languish, droop.

Throng. (See Crowd.)

Throw, propel, cast, hurl, fling.
Ant.—Retain, revoke, hold, restrain, draw, haul.

Thrust, push, drive, force, impel, urge.
Ant.—Draw, retract, snatch.

Thwart. (See Frustrate.)

Tickle, amuse, titillate, gratify.
Ant.—Irritate, hurt, annoy, vex.

Tide, current, stream, course, influx.
Ant. — Stagnation, stoppage, cessation, subsidence.

Tidings. (See News.)

Tidy, orderly, neat, spruce, clean, cleanly.
Ant.—Untidy, dirty, unclean, slovenly.

Tie, *v.* bind, restrain, restrict, oblige, secure, unite, join.
Ant. — Untie, unbind, sever, separate, release, free, loose.

Tie, *n.* band, ligament, ligature.
Tight, tense, stretched, not slack, small.
Ant.—Loose, slack, open, lax, large.
Time, duration, season, period, era, age, date, span, spell.
Ant.—Eternity, indetermination, space.
Timely, seasonable, opportune, early, judicious.
Ant.—Untimely, late, inopportune, unseasonable.
Timid, timorous, fearful, afraid, pusillanimous, cowardly, dastardly, faint-hearted.
Ant.—Bold, daring, courageous, rash, venturesome, audacious.
Tinge, flavor, taste, color, dye.
Ant.—Disinfect, erase.
Tint, shade, tinge, hue, color, stain, dye, complexion.
Ant.—Pallor, bleaching, achromatism.
Tiny, small, little, diminutive, wee, lilliputian.
Ant.—Huge, large, gigantic, bulky.
Tip. (See End.)
Tipsy. (See Intoxicated.)
Tire, exhaust, fatigue, bore, weary, jade, harass, dispirit.
Ant.—Enliven, refresh, animate, amuse, excite.
Title, denomination, designation, name, appellation, style, dignity, epithet, right.
Ant.—Indistinction, nondescript, indenomination.
Tittle. (See Atom.)
Toil, work, task, travail, pain, labor, drudgery.
Ant.—Ease, relaxation, rest, amusement, pleasure.
Token. (See Sign.)
Tolerable, passable, ordinary, middling.
Ant.—Intolerable, unbearable, insupportable, insufferable.
Tolerate, allow, admit, receive, suffer, permit, let, endure, abide.
Ant.—Repel, prohibit, reject, resist, disallow, forbid, refuse.
Tomb. (See Grave.)
Tone, style, manner, mode, sound, intonation, pitch.
Ant.—Laxity, silence, hush.
Top, summit, apex, head, crown, surface.
Ant.—Foot, bottom, base, foundation.
Topic. (See Subject.)
Torment, torture, tease, worry, persecute, pain, offend, tantalize, plague.
Ant.—Soothe, gratify, please, delight, amuse.
Torpid, benumbed, numb, dull, stupid, sluggish, inert.
Ant.—Lively, animated, gay, nimble, brisk, active.
Torrid, burning, hot, parching, scorching, sultry.
Ant.—Frigid, arctic, cold, cool, fresh, temperate, icy, freezing.
Torturous, twisted, winding, crooked, indirect.
Ant.—Straight, direct.
Torture, torment, anguish, agony.
Ant.—Ecstacy, rapture, bliss, delight, relieve, ease, refresh, please, gratify.
Toss. (See Pitch.)
Total, sum, gross, whole, aggregate, entire, complete.
Ant.—Part, item, portion.
Totally, entirely, quite, altogether, fully, wholly.
Ant.—Partly, partially, incompletely.
Totter, falter, reel, rock, tremble, shake, stagger.
Ant.—Steady, stand, stay.
Touch. (See Move.)
Touching, tender, affecting, moving, pathetic.
Ant.—Amusing, ridiculous, indifferent, joyous, pleasant, comfortable, desirable, delectable, cheerful, gay, genial, happy, merry, mirthful.
Touchy. (See Irritable.)
Tough, strong, hard, firm, leathery, difficult.
Ant.—Soft, yielding, tender, fragile, brittle.
Tour. (See Excursion.)
Trace, derive, deduce, follow, pursue, track.
Ant.—Miss, lose, stop, retreat, fail.
Track. (See Road.)
Tract. (See District.)
Tractable, docile, manageable, amenable.
Ant.—Refractory, unmanageable, unamenable, obstinate, stubborn.
Trade, traffic, commerce, dealing, occupation, employment, office.
Ant.—Profession, idleness, leisure, relaxation.
Traditional, oral, uncertain, transmitted, apocryphal, legendary, unverified.
Ant.—Written, documentary, certainty, fact, history, truth, verity.
Traduce. (See Calumniate.)
Traffic, trade, exchange, commerce, intercourse.
Tragedy, disaster, calamity, affliction, catastrophe.
Ant.—Joy, delight, boon, prosperity, comedy.
Tragic, fatal, calamitous, mournful, sorrowful.
Ant.—Comical, joyous, gay, light.
Train, educate, instruct, discipline, drill, inure.
Ant.—Force, break, disqualify, miseducate.
Trait. (See Characteristic.)
Trammel, fetter, shackle, clog, bond, chain, impediment, hindrance.
Ant.—Freedom, liberation, extrication.
Tranquil, still, unruffled, peaceful, quiet, hushed.
Ant.—Agitated, disturbed, anxious, excited, restless, uneasy, noisy, boisterous.
Tranquilize. (See Soothe.)
Transact, perform, conduct, manage, negotiate, treat.
Ant.—Mismanage, misconduct, fail.
Transaction, negotiation, occurrence, proceeding, affair.
Ant.—Non-performance, mismanagement, suspension.
Transcend, surmount, overstep, exceed, surpass, excel, eclipse.
Ant.—Fail, fall, foil.
Transcendent, consummate, surpassing, unrivaled, unexampled, matchless, incomparable.
Ant.—Ordinary, attainable, common, average.
Transfer, make over, convey, remove, copy, transmit.
Ant.—Retain, keep, withhold, fix, appropriate, receive.
Transform, change, metamorphose, transfigure, transmute.
Ant.—Perpetuate, conserve, arrest.
Transgress, pass, exceed, violate, infringe, offend, trespass.
Ant.—Observe, keep, obey, fulfill, respect.
Transient, fleeting, passing, transitory, temporary, short-lived.
Ant.—Permanent, lasting, abiding, perpetual, enduring.
Transition, change, shifting, variation, transmutation.
Ant.—Stability, permanence, perpetuity.
Transmit, remit, dispatch, convey, send, forward.
Ant.—Retain, keep, withhold.
Transparent, clear, limpid, lucid, obvious.
Ant.—Opaque, thick, turbid, mysterious, questionable.
Transport, *n.* bliss, ecstacy, rapture, carriage, conveyance.
Ant.—Agony, distress, annoyance, vexation.
Transport, *v.* ravish, delight, enrapture, bear, carry, convey, remove, banish.
Ant.—Vex, displease, annoy, stop, hold, retain.
Transpose, change, reverse, shift.
Ant.—Retain, fix, keep.
Trap, snare, ambush, stratagem, pitfall.
Ant.—Warning, beacon, lighthouse, premonition.
Trappings, gear, ornaments, tackle, harness, paraphernalia.
Ant.—Nudity, nakedness, dismantlement.
Trash, nonsense, twaddle, trifles, dross.

Ant. — Sense, wisdom, usefulness, goods, property.
Travel, trip, ramble, excursion, journey, tour, voyage, peregrination.
Ant. — Rest, halt, stop, settlement.
Traverse, cross, pass, thwart, obstruct.
Ant. — Pass, omit, sanction, overlook, elude, avoid.
Treacherous, traitorous, disloyal, treasonable, faithless, false-hearted, perfidious, sly, false.
Ant. — True, faithful, open, honest, chivalric, trustworthy.
Treason, treachery, disloyalty, disaffection.
Ant.—Openness, fidelity, honor, chivalry.
Treasure, riches, wealth, stock, store, reserve.
Ant. — Trash, offal, refuse, dregs, scum.
Treat, negotiate, bargain, entertain, feast.
Ant.—Drop, abandon, decline, maltreat, mismanage, misarrange, trifle.
Treaty, convention, negotiation, agreement, contract.
Ant. — Neutrality, non-interference.
Tremble, quake, shake, quiver, shudder, totter.
Ant. — Steady, settle, still, calm.
Tremendous, awful, fearful, frightful, terrible.
Ant. — Unimposing, unappalling, inconsiderable.
Tremulous, trembling, jarring, quivering, vibrating, shaking.
Ant. — Motionless, smooth, equable.
Trenchant, cutting, sharp, severe, sarcastic.
Ant. — Weak, impotent, unavailing.
Trend, incline, diverge, bend, tend, stretch.
Ant. — Continue, proceed, advance.
Trepidation. (See Fear.)
Trial, experiment, test, gauge, proof, ordeal, essay, trouble, temptation, affliction, cause, action, suit.
Ant. — Hazard, conjecture, guess, theory, relief, refreshment, oversight, disregard.
Tribulation, affliction, grief, distress, trouble, misery, woe.
Ant.—Joy, rejoicing, gladness, rest, delight.
Tribute, tax, impost, subsidy, duty, charge, custom, offering, contribution
Ant.—Gift, wage , reward, remuneration.
Trick, fraud, cheat, artifice, stratagem, guile, deception, imposition, freak, antic, vagary, hoax.
Ant. — Exposure, artlessness, honesty, fairness, candor, openness.
Trifle, *n.* bauble, toy, gewgaw, bagatelle, wanton.
Ant.—Treasure, portent, phenomenon, crisis, importance, urgency, necessity.
Trifle, *v.* toy, play, dally.
Ant. — Treat, cope, tackle, grapple, deal.
Trifling, slight, silly, trivial, petty, unimportant, light.
Ant. — Important, grave, serious.
Trim, compact, snug, neat, nice, tidy, clean, spruce.
Ant.—Slovenly, untidy, loose, negligent.
Trip, mistake, error, blunder, excursion, tour, ramble, jaunt.
Ant. — Stand, speed, prosper, succeed.
Trite, stale, old, ordinary, commonplace, hackneyed.
Ant. — Original, novel, startling, unusual.
Triumph, achievement, ovation, victory, conquest, jubilation.
Ant.—Defeat, failure, discomfiture, disappointment.
Triumphant, elated, victorious, exultant.
Ant. — Unsuccessful, beaten, baffled, worsted, humiliated.
Trivial, trifling, petty, small, frivolous, unimportant, insignificant.
Ant.—Important, weighty.
Troop, assemblage, multitude, gang, band, horde, company.
Ant. — Scarcity, few, individual, bevy, squad.
Trouble, *v.* afflict, distress, agitate, annoy, tease, harass, perplex, disturb, grieve, oppress, aggrieve.
Ant. — Soothe, calm, allay, please, delight, gratify, refresh, entertain.
Trouble, *n.* affliction, distress, grief, tribulation, adversity, calamity, disaster, misfortune, anxiety, sorrow, misery, plague, torment.
Ant.—Happiness, pleasure, delight, joy, gladness, amusement.
Troublesome, tiresome, irksome, sore, grievous, arduous.
Ant.—Easy, pleasant, amusing, light.
Truant, idling, loitering, vagabond, shirking, vagrant.
Ant. — Diligent, industrious, domestic, loyal, faithful.
Truckling. (See Servile.)
True, genuine, actual, sincere, honest, upright, veritable, real, veracious, authentic, exact, accurate, correct, truehearted, unaffected.
Ant.—False, untrue, fictitious, erroneous, spurious, counterfeit, faithless, fickle, unfounded, dubious.
Trumpery, trivial, worthless, tawdry.
Ant.—Valuable, costly, good.
Trunk, stem, stalk, body, proboscis, chest, box.
Ant.—Head, limb, bag, satchel.
Trust, believe, credit, hope, expect.
Ant. — Distrust, suspect, discredit, doubt, disbelieve, resume, withdraw.
Trusty. (See (Trust.)
Truth. (See True.)
Try, attempt, endeavor, strive, struggle, test, examine, prove.
Ant.—Ignore, reject, abandon, decline, withdraw.
Tug. (See Draw.)
Tumble. (See Fall.)
Tumult, ferment, outbreak, brawl, fray, turbulence, uproar, commotion, hubbub, disturbance, riot.
Ant. — Peace, quiet, order, tranquillity, subsidence.
Tumultuous, turbulent, riotous, disorderly, disturbed, confused, unruly.
Ant.—Peaceful, orderly, quiet, tranquil, reposeful.
Tune, tone, air, melody, strain.
Turbid, foul, thick, muddy, impure, unsettled.
Ant. — Clear, crystal, crystalline, transparent, limpid, pure.
Turbulent. (See Tumultuous.)
Turmoil. (See Tumult.)
Turn *v.* revolve, circulate, whirl, twirl, wheel, incline, inflect, deviate.
Ant.—Fix, stand, stop, arrest, continue, proceed, perpetuate.
Turn, *n.* spiral, maze, labyrinth, cast, bent, tendency, character, tone, manner, round, bout, form.
Ant. — Straightness, stability, fixity, immobility, uniformity.
Turpitude, depravity, vileness, baseness, wickedness, sin.
Ant.—Goodness, nobility, virtue, excellence.
Tutor. (See Teacher.)
Twine, twist, wind, embrace, entwine.
Ant. — Untwine, untwist, unwind, detach, disengage, separate, sever, disunite.
Twirl. (See Turn.)
Twit. (See Mock.)
Type, emblem, symbol, figure, sign, kind, sort, letter.
Ant.—Caricature, monstrosity, deviation, eccentricity.
Tyrannical, cruel, severe, absolute, arbitrary, despotic.
Ant.—Humane, kindly, liberal, generous, just.
Tyrant, oppressor, despot, autocrat, persecutor.
Ant.—Philanthropist, judge.
Tyro, novice, beginner, learner.
Ant. — Adept, expert, master, professor.

U

Ugly, unsightly, ill-favored, hideous, plain, homely.

Ant.—Attractive, fair, beautiful, handsome, seemly.
Ulterior, further, more distant, beyond, succeeding.
Ant. — Immediate, present, prior, hither.
Ultimate, furthest, last, latest, final, eventual.
Ant.—Proximate, preliminary, prior, intermediate.
Umbrage, offense, dissatisfaction, displeasure, resentment.
Ant. — Complacency, satisfaction, gratification.
Umpire, referee, arbitrator, judge, arbiter.
Ant.—Litigant, disputant.
Unanimity, accord, agreement, unity, concord.
Ant. — Variance, discord, dissent, disagreement.
Unanimous, agreeing, likeminded.
Ant.—Dissentient, disagreeing.
Unaffected. (See Genuine.)
Unalterable. (See Changeless.)
Unanswerable, indisputable, unquestionable, undeniable.
Ant.—Questionable, doubtful, disputable.
Unbind, loosen, untie, unfasten, set free.
Ant.—Bind, tie, hold, fasten.
Unbounded, boundless, excessive, infinite, unsparing, unstinted, interminable.
Ant. — Finite, bounded, restricted, narrow.
Unbridled, wanton, licentious, dissolute, loose, lax.
Ant.—Austere, severe, ascetic, virtuous, self-controlled, restrained.
Unceasing. (See Eternal.)
Uncertain, doubtful, dubious, questionable, fitful, equivocal, ambiguous, indistinct, variable, fluctuating.
Ant.—Certain, dependable.
Uncivil, rude, discourteous, disrespectful, disobliging.
Ant. — Civil, well-behaved, courteous.
Unclean, dirty, foul, filthy, sullied.
Ant.—Clean, immaculate, spotless.
Uncommon, rare, strange, scarce, singular, unique, unusual, choice.
Ant.—Common, ordinary, average, usual.
Unconcerned, indifferent, careless, apathetic.
Ant.—Anxious.
Uncouth, strange, odd, clumsy, ungainly.
Ant.—Polite, neat, trim, courtly, graceful, polished, refined, well-bred.
Uncover, reveal, strip, expose, lay bare, divest.
Ant. — Cover, clothe, conceal, suppress, hide.
Under, below, underneath, beneath, subordinate, lower, inferior.
Ant.—Over, above, superior.
Undergo. (See Suffer.)
Understand, know, comprehend, apprehend.
Ant. — Misunderstand, ignore, declare, state, express.
Understanding, knowledge, intellect, intelligence, faculty, comprehension, mind, reason.
Ant. — Ignorance, misunderstanding, misapprehension, body, material, matter, substance.
Undertake, engage in, embark in, agree, promise.
Ant.—Abandon, drop, decline, discontinue, desist, dismiss, neglect, omit.
Undisturbed, quiet, still, tranquil, placid, peaceful.
Ant.—Disturbed, annoyed, irritated, troubled, vexed.
Undo, annul, frustrate, untie, unfasten, destroy.
Ant.—Unite, bind.
Uneasy, restless, disturbed, unquiet, stiff, awkward.
Ant.—Calm, easy, quiet, peaceful, unembarrassed, composed, equable.
Unequal, uneven, not alike, irregular, insufficient.
Ant. — Equal, alike, similar, even.
Unequaled, matchless, unique, novel, new, unheard of.
Ant.—Common, habitual, normal.
Unfair, wrongful, dishonest, unjust.
Ant.—Fair, just, equable, rational, honest, right, equitable.
Unfit, *a.* improper, unsuitable, untimely, incompetent, inconsistent.
Ant.—Fit, able, capable, ready, timely, qualified, competent, seemly, proper.
Unfit, *v.* disable, disqualify, incapacitate.
Ant.—Fit, enable, qualify.
Unfold, unravel, disclose, unbosom, divulge, display, reveal, declare, develop, explain.
Ant. — Fold, conceal, suppress, hide.
Unfortunate, calamitous, illfated, unlucky, wretched, unhappy, miserable.
Ant.—Fortunate, happy, lucky, cheerful, gay, joyous.
Unfriendly, inhospitable, ungenial, unkind, disobliging.
Ant. — Friendly, hospitable, amicable, kindly.
Ungainly, awkward, clumsy, lumbering, uncouth.
Ant.—Pretty, graceful.
Unhappiness, misery, wretchedness, distress, woe.
Ant.—Happiness, pleasure, delight, joy.
Unhappy, miserable, wretched, distressed, afflicted, painful, disastrous, dreary, dismal, drear.
Ant. — Happy, joyous, gay, merry, pleased, delighted, fortunate.
Uniform, regular, symmetrical, equal, even, alike, unvaried.
Ant. — Variable, varying, diverse, heterogeneous, irregular, bizarre, eccentric, varied, unlike.
Uninterrupted, incessant, continuous, perpetual, unceasing, endless.
Ant.—Intermittent, recurrent.
Union, junction, combination, alliance, confederacy, league, coalition, agreement, concert.
Ant. — Separation, disunion, divorce, secession, discord, disagreement, division.
Unique, unequaled, uncommon, rare; choice, matchless, unequal.
Ant.—Ordinary, commonplace, common.
Unison, harmony, concord, agreement, union.
Ant.—Discord, disunion, variance.
Unite, join, conjoin, combine, connect, add, attach, incorporate, embody, clench, merge, concert.
Ant.—Separate, sever, divide, part, sunder, disintegrate, disrupt.
Unity, oneness, concord, uniformity, agreement.
Ant. — Plurality, multitude, complexity, discord, variety, diversity.
Universal, general, all, entire, total, catholic.
Ant.—Special, particular, partial, local, exclusive, exceptional, sectional, limited.
Unlimited, infinite, absolute, boundless, undefined.
Ant.—Limited, finite.
Unreasonable, foolish, silly, absurd, preposterous, ridiculous, immoderate.
Ant. — Reasonable, rational, sensible, certain, logical, sagacious, undeniable, wise.
Unrivaled, unequaled, unique, unexampled, incomparable, matchless.
Ant. — Equaled, common, ordinary, average, mediocre.
Unroll, unfold, open, discover.
Ant.—Conceal, suppress, mask, screen, cover, lose, secrete, miss.
Unruly, ungovernable, unmanageable, refractory.
Ant. — Gentle, governable, manageable, tractable, docile.
Unseemly, unbecoming, indecorous, unsuitable, unfit, unbefitting.
Ant. — Decorous, polite, respectful, obedient, refined.
Unsettle. (See Disturb.)
Unsteady, wavering, unstable, variable, fickle, restless, fitful,

Ant. — Steady, fixed, firm, stable.

Untruth. (See Lie.)

Unusual, rare, singular, uncommon, remarkable, strange, extraordinary, unwonted.

Ant.—Usual, common, average, ordinary.

Upbraid. (See Blame.)

Uphold, maintain, defend, sustain, support, vindicate.

Ant.—Drop, betray, abandon, oppose, attack, abjure, renounce, desert.

Upright, vertical, perpendicular, erect, just, equitable, fair, pure, honorable.

Ant.—Inclined, horizontal, inverted, dishonest, corrupt, prone, iniquitous.

Uprightness, honesty, integrity, fairness, goodness, probity, honor, virtue.

Ant.—Dishonesty, vice.

Uproar, tumult, row, riot, disturbance, brawl, noise, clamor.

Ant.—Peace, quiet, order, silence.

Uproot, eradicate, exterminate, weed out.

Ant.—Sow, implant, cultivate, nurture, foster.

Urbanity. (See Affability.)

Urge, incite, impel, push, drive, instigate, stimulate, press, induce, solicit.

Ant. — Hold, restrain, retain, prohibit, retard, hinder, obstruct, impede, hold back, discourage.

Urgent, pressing, important, imperative, immediate, serious, cogent, wanted.

Ant.—Unimportant, trivial, insignificant, feeble, inconclusive, powerless, weak.

Usage, custom, fashion, practice, prescription.

Ant.—Anomaly, exception.

Use, *n.* usage, practice, habit, custom, advantage, utility, benefit, application, avail.

Ant. — Dissue, obscurity, neglect, desuetude.

Use, *v.* employ, exercise, occupy, practice, accustom, inure.

Ant. — Discard, suspend, ignore, avoid, abuse.

Useful, advantageous, serviceable, available, helpful, beneficial, good.

Ant.—Useless, fruitless, ineffectual, unavailable, unprofitable, bootless, futile, null, unavailing, unserviceable, vain, worthless.

Useless, unserviceable, fruitless, idle, profitless, vain, ineffectual.

Ant. — Useful, advantageous, helpful, beneficial. (See Above.)

Usual, ordinary, common, accustomed, habitual, wonted, customary, general.

Ant.—Unusual, common, rare, exceptional, extraordinary, abnormal, irregular.

Usurp, arrogate, seize, appropriate, assume.

Ant.—Receive, inherit, accept, yield, render, surrender.

Utility. (See Use.)

Utmost, farthest, remotest, uttermost, greatest.

Ant.—Nearest, next.

Utter, *a.* extreme, excessive, sheer, mere, pure.

Ant. — Moderate, palliative, partial, superficial.

Utter, *v.* speak, articulate, pronounce, express, issue.

Ant. — Reveal, suppress, repress, hush, stifle, retain, hear, conceal, hide.

Utterly, totally, completely, wholly, quite, entirely altogether.

Ant. — Partly, partially, in a measure, incompletely.

V

Vacant, empty, unfilled, unoccupied, thoughtless, unthinking.

Ant. — Full, filled, employed, engaged, occupied, thoughtful, tenanted.

Vacation, holiday, recreation.

Ant.—Term, business.

Vagrant, wanderer, beggar, tramp, vagabond, rogue.

Ant. — Workman, gentleman, laborer.

Vague, unsettled, undetermined, uncertain, indefinite, pointless.

Ant. — Definite, specific, limited, determined, strict, precise.

Vain, useless, fruitless, empty, worthless, inflated, proud, unreal, unavailing, conceited, vapid.

Ant.—Solid, real, substantial, sound, efficient, effectual, potent, modest, humble.

Valiant, brave, bold, valorous, courageous, gallant.

Ant.—Timid, cowardly craven, cringing, timorous.

Valid, weighty, strong, powerful, sound, binding, efficient.

Ant. — Invalid, weak, powerless, unsound, false, insufficient, void.

Valor, courage, gallantry, boldness, bravery, heroism.

Ant.—Cowardice.

Valuable, precious, costly, dear, expensive, inestimable.

Ant. — Valueless, cheap, poor, worthless, mean.

Value, appraise, assess, reckon, appreciate, estimate, price, esteem, treasure.

Ant.—Despise, underrate, under-value, disregard, dislike, scorn, contemn.

Vanish, disappear, melt, fade, dissolve.

Ant.—Appear, approach, loom, emerge.

Vanity, emptiness, conceit, self-conceit, affectedess.

Ant.—Substance, reality, truth, simplicity, modesty, humility, fullness.

Vanquish. (See Conquer.)

Vapid, dull, flat, insipid, stale, tame.

Ant.—Spirited, animated, pungent, pithy, sparkling, brilliant.

Vapor, fume, smoke, mist, fog, steam.

Ant.—Water, substance, fluid.

Variable, changeable, unsteady, inconstant, shifting, wavering, fickle, restless, fitful.

Ant. — Invariable, firm, constant, true, unchangeable, staunch, inimitable, changeless, stable.

Variance, disagreement, dissension, jarring, quarrel.

Ant. — Unity, reconciliation, harmony, peace, consent.

Variation, change, diversity, deviation, discrepancy, difference.

Ant.—Continuance, fixity, law, rule, uniformity, harmony.

Variety, difference, diversity, change, diversification, mixture, medley, miscellany.

Ant. — Uniformity, species, type, specimen, sameness, monotony.

Vary, change, alter, modify, diversify, variegate, differ, disagree.

Ant. — Perpetuate, strengthen, conform, harmonize.

Vast, enormous, spacious, boundless, mighty, immense, colossal, gigantic, huge, prodigious.

Ant.—Confined, limited.

Vaunt, boast, puff, hawk, advertise, flourish, parade, brag, display, flaunt.

Ant. — Suppress, conceal, disparage, decry, detract, cover, entomb, overwhelm.

Vehement, furious, ardent, fervid, burning, raging, eager, impetuous, forcible, vigorous.

Ant. — Mild, feeble, subdued, cold, passionless, weak.

Veil, screen, hide, intercept, mask, conceal, cover, disguise.

Ant.—Unveil, expose, strip, denude, exaggerate.

Velocity, swiftness, quickness, fleetness, celerity, speed, rapidity.

Ant.—Slowness, languor, inactivity, sluggishness.

Vend. (See Sell.)

Venerable, grave, sage, wise, old, reverend.

Ant. — Contemptible, despicable, young, foolish, frivolous, flighty.

Venial, pardonable, excusable, justifiable.

Ant. — Unpardonable, mortal, inexcusable, grave, serious.

Venom, poison, virus, spite, malice, malignity.
Ant. — Antidote, cure, corrective, remedy.

Venture, *n.* speculation, chance, peril, stake.
Ant. — Caution, calculation, law, method, insure, protect, guard, think, know, determine, certainty, safety, assurance, security.

Venture, *v.* dare, risk, jeopardize, adventure, hazard.
Ant.—Calculate, reserve.

Veracity, truth, truthfulness, credibility, accuracy.
Ant.—Falsehood, deceit, imagination, fiction, fraud, lie, untruth.

Verbal, oral, spoken, literal, unwritten, parole.
Ant. — Written, documentary, recorded.

Verdict, judgment, finding, decision, answer.
Ant.—Indecision, indetermination.

Verge. (See Border.)

Versatile, unsteady, changeable, unfixed, wavering, vacillating, oscillating, fluctuating, inconstant, fickle, restless, manifold.
Ant.—Immovable, fixed, one-sided, uniform, narrow, limited, stolid, immobile.

Versed, skilled, practiced, conversant, clever, proficient.
Ant. — Awkward, unskilled, ignorant, strange, unfamiliar.

Vex. (See Irritate.)

Vexation, chagrin, mortification.
Ant.—Pleasure, gratification.

Vibrate, oscillate, swing, sway, wave, undulate, thrill.
Ant.—Stand, remain, proceed, advance.

Vice, corruption, depravity, pollution, immorality, wickedness, guilt, iniquity, crime, fault, defect, blemish, vileness.
Ant. — Virtue, purity, perfection, goodness, holiness, integrity, morality.

Vicious, corrupt, depraved, debased, bad, contrary, unruly, demoralized, profligate, faulty, malicious.
Ant. — Pure, sound, perfect, virtuous, good.

Victim, sacrifice, food, prey, sufferer, dupe, gull.
Ant. — Sacrificer, seducer, attacker, fraud, cheat.

Victuals, viands, bread, meat, repast, provisions, fare, food.

View, *n.* thought, notion, sentiment, opinion, perspective, landscape, purpose, intention, design, light, aspect, end.
Ant.—Darkness, blindness, deception, error, delusion, misconception.

View, *v.* look, see, behold, eye, observe, scan, regard, prospect, survey.
Ant.—Ignore, overlook, disregard, miss, misjudge, oversight.

Vigilant, watchful, wakeful, observant, cautious, careful.
Ant. — Careless, inattentive, indifferent.

Vigorous, healthy, strong, powerful, energetic, stalwart, robust, hardy, firm, spirited, determined.
Ant. — Weak, feeble, powerless, debilitated, inactive, indolent, irresolute.

Vile, ignoble, base, low, worthless, abject, sordid, mean, dishonorable, sinful, wicked, vicious.
Ant. — Good, noble, exalted, pure, honorable, costly, rare, precious.

Vilify, debase, degrade, slander, decry, defame, scandalize, upbraid, brand, stigmatize, denounce.
Ant. — Purify, refine, exalt, raise, improve, praise, laud.

Villainous. (See Vile.)

Vindicate, justify, assert, uphold, support, defend.
Ant. — Fail, abandon, surrender, forego, nullify, destroy, subvert, vitiate, condemn.

Vindictive, spiteful, resentful, revengeful, unforgiving.
Ant. — Forgiving, generous, merciful, forbearing.

Violate, infringe, transgress, disobey, injure, hurt, ravish.
Ant.—Respect, foster, cherish, protect, regard, preserve, obey.

Violence, passion, rage, fury, vehemence, outrage, injustice.
Ant.—Mildness, self-restraint, gentleness, forbearance, self-control, obedience, protection.

Violent, forcible, raving, raging, passionate, furious, rapid, dashing, sweeping, rolling, boisterous, impetuous, vehement.
Ant.—Mild, feeble, calm, soft, gentle, quiet.

Virtuous, just, upright, moral, chaste, pure, honest.
Ant. — Vicious, bad, corrupt, debased, impure, immoral.

Visible. (See Apparent.)

Vision, apparition, dream, ghost, phantom, specter.
Ant.—Fact, reality, realization, verity.

Vital, living, necessary, essential, indispensable.
Ant. — Mortal, lifeless, unnecessary, unimportant, immaterial.

Vivacious, lively, brisk, gay, merry, racy, sprightly.
Ant.—Dead, lifeless, dull, stolid, moody, heavy, sullen, torpid, sluggish.

Vivid, lively, clear, lucid, bright, sunny, glowing, graphic.
Ant. — Dull, opaque, obscure, somber, dim, dusky, cloudy, pale, wan.

Vocation, profession, calling, trade, business, employment, office, mission.
Ant.—Leisure, incapacity.

Vogue, usage, way, custom, fashion, use, practice.
Ant.—Disuse, disrepute, abolition.

Void, null, invalid, unfilled, empty, hollow, useless, nugatory.
Ant. — Occupied, full, solid, valid, efficacious, sound.

Volume, book, scroll, bulk, size, capacity.
Ant. — Pamphlet, sheet, minuteness, smallness.

Voluntary, free, spontaneous, unconstrained, deliberate.
Ant. — Compulsory, involuntary, coercive.

Voluptuary, epicure, sensualist.
Ant.—Stoic, moralist.

Voracious, ravenous, rapacious, greedy.
Ant.—Generous.

Voracity, greediness.

Vote, suffrage, voice.

Vouch, certify, affirm, asseverate, aver, assure.
Ant.—Deny.

Vulgar, common, general, popular, ordinary, rude, coarse, low.
Ant. — Scientific, philosophic, restricted, technical, select, choice, refined, polite, well-bred.

Vulnerable, assailable, weak, exposed, tender.
Ant. — Invulnerable, impregnable, unassailable.

W

Waft, transport, bear, convey.
Ant.—Push, pull, drag, draw.

Wag, humorist, jester, joker, wit.
Ant.—Dullard, butt.

Wage, make, carry on, engage in, undertake.
Ant.—Desist, stop, abandon.

Wages, salary, hire, allowance, stipend, pay, remuneration, earnings, compensation.
Ant.—Gratuity, gift, premium, grace, bonus.

Wait, await, abide, bide, stay, remain, tarry, expect, look for, wait for.
Ant. — Speed, hasten, press, abandon, avoid, reject, shun.

Waive, forego, relinquish, let go.
Ant. — Press, urge, claim, arrest, enforce.

Wake, waken, awaken, arouse, stir up, excite, kindle, provoke.
Ant. — Soothe, allay, hush, quiet, tranquilize.

Wakeful, sleepless, vigilant, wary, watchful.
Ant.—Drowsy, dreamy, sleepy, somnolent.
Wander, stroll, ramble, gad, rove, roam, range, stray, err, deviate, swerve.
Ant.—Rest, stop, halt, lie, anchor, alight, moor, pause, repose.
Wandering, vagrant, roving, strolling, discursive.
Ant. — Stationary, fixed, immovable, permanent.
Want, *v.* need, lack, require, desire, wish, crave for.
Ant. — Supply, offer, demand, give, afford, furnish.
Want, *n.* poverty, penury, indigence, destitution, privation, necessity, need, lack, scarcity.
Ant. — Supply, sufficiency, provision, abundance, production, adequacy, plenty.
Wanton, licentious, libertine, unrestrained, unbridled, uncurbed, dissolute, loose, lax.
Ant. — Staid, sober, demure, austere, formal, deliberate.
Ward, avert, parry, fend, repel, turn aside, guard, defend.
Ant.—Attack, betray, surrender.
Warlike, bellicose, hostile, inimical, military.
Ant.—Friendly, peaceful.
Warm, fervid, affectionate, attached, devoted, ardent, fervent, glowing.
Ant. — Frigid, cold, tepid, starved, indifferent, passionless.
Warmth, ardor, fervency, fervor, cordiality, vehemence, heat, fervidness, glow.
Ant. — Frigidity, frost, coldness, calmness, indifference, apathy, slowness.
Warning... (See Admonition.)
Warrant, guarantee, insure, assure, secure, justify.
Ant. — Imperial, endanger, nullify, invalidate, repudiate.
Wary, careful, cautious, circumspect, guarded, watchful, heedful, prudent, vigilant.
Ant. — Unwary, unsuspecting, heedless, unguarded, foolhardy, reckless, intrepid.
Wash, clean, rinse, wet, moisten, tint, stain.
Ant. — Soil, foul, contaminate, dirty, stain.
Waste, *v.* squander, dissipate, lavish, destroy, decay, dwindle, wither.
Ant. — Restore, repair, preserve, protect, husband, economize, hoard, accumulate, multiply, develop, save.
Waste, *a.* desolate, stripped, bare, dreary, unproductive, wild, uncultivated.
Ant.—Fertile, productive, cultivated.
Wasteful, extravagant, profligate.
Ant.—Economical, frugal.
Watchful, alert, vigilant, attentive, cautious, heedful, observant, circumspect, wakeful.
Ant. — Heedless, careless, drowsy, incautious, unwary, distracted.
Wave, breaker, billow, surge.
Waver, *v.* hesitate, scruple, fluctuate, vacillate, flicker, quiver, flutter.
Ant.—Determine, decide, settle, rest, repose, abide, hold fast, stay, stick.
Wavering, unsteady, unsettled, fluctuating, changeable, inconstant, variable.
Ant.—Steady, constant, fixed, immovable, changeless.
Way, method, plan, system, means, manner, mode, form, fashion, course, process, road, route, track, path, habit, practice.
Ant.—Chance, hazard, conjecture, luck.
Wayward, forward, obstinate, stubborn, unruly, perverse.
Ant. — Docile, manageable, amenable.
Weak, feeble, infirm, enfeebled, debilitated, powerless, helpless, emaciated, prostrate, thin, watery, diluted, flimsy, slight, poor, silly, defenseless.
Ant.—Strong, vigorous, robust, muscular, powerful, tough, stout, sturdy, hard, potent, efficient, spirited, animated, sound, judicious, determined, forcible, able.
Weaken, enfeeble, debilitate, unnerve, paralyze, emaciate, attentuate, dilute, enervate, invalidate.
Ant. — Strengthen, empower, invigorate, confirm.
Weakness, feebleness, infirmity, frailty, silliness, imbecility, prostration, defect, failing, foible.
Ant.—Strength, power, nerve, spirit, vigor, activity, efficiency.
Wealth, riches, opulence, affluence, plenty, mammon, abundance.
Ant. — Poverty, indigence, scarcity, impecuniosity.
Wear, bear, carry, last, consume.
Ant. — Doff, abandon, renew, renovate, augment.
Weariness, exhaustion, languor, lassitude, fatigue.
Ant.—Buoyancy, vigor.
Wearisome, tedious, tiresome.
Ant. — Interesting, entertaining.
Weary, tired, fatigued, exhausted, worn, faint, harass, jade, tire, fatigue.
Ant. — Fresh, vigorous, renovated, hearty, refresh, inspire.
Wedding, marriage, nuptials, espousal.
Ant. — Divorce, celibacy, singleness.
Weep. (See Grieve.)
Weight, heaviness, pressure, oppression, burden, load, value, gravity.
Ant. — Lightness, weakness, levity, triviality, worthlessness.
Welcome, acceptable, agreeable, pleasing, grateful, pleasureable, gratifying, pleasant, satisfying.
Ant.—Unwelcome, ungrateful, distasteful, unpleasant, disagreeable, disappointing, distressing, hateful, melancholy, mournful, painful, woeful, wretched.
Welfare, good fortune, prosperity, happiness, success.
Ant.—Adversity, reverse, failure, ill luck, unhappiness, harm, hurt.
Well-being, happiness, prosperity, welfare.
Ant.—Adversity, poverty.
Wheedle. (See Coax.)
Whet, sharpen, incite, excite, provoke, stimulate.
Ant.—Blunt, pall, deaden, satiate, nauseate.
Whimsical, odd, singular, capricious, fanciful, fantastic, fantastical.
Ant. — Staid, serious, sober, sedate, orderly.
Whirl. (See Turn.)
White, snowy, pure, spotless, unspotted, unblemished, stainless, clean.
Ant. — Black, impure, stained, dirty, foul.
Whole, sound, healthy, well, total, all, entire, perfect, complete, integral, aggregate, undivided.
Ant. — Sick, unsound, impaired, partial, imperfect, incomplete, part.
Wholesome, nutritious, healthy, salubrious, healing, salutary.
Ant. — Unwholesome, unhealthy, deleterious, detrimental.
Wholly, entirely, totally, altogether, quite, perfectly, completely, utterly.
Ant.—Partially, in part, mostly.
Wicked, bad, ill, unjust, irreligious, ungodly, godless, profane, impious, unhallowed, black, dark, foul, atrocious, villainous, enormous, monstrous, outrageous, profligate, abandoned, iniquitous, nefarious.
Ant. — Good, virtuous, just, moral, upright, honest, pure, stainless, sinless, incorrupt, spotless, honorable, esteemed, immaculate.
Wickedness, evil, sin, crime, criminality, guilt, iniquity,

offense, vileness, turpitude, corruption, vice, pollution.
Ant.—Goodness, virtue, order, law, honor, purity.

Wide, broad, ample, large, expanded, diffuse, extensive
Ant. — Narrow, contracted, limited.

Wild, savage, uncivilized, loose, irregular, disorderly, untamed, undomesticated, unruly.
Ant. — Tame, civilized, cultivated, inhabited, regular, peaceful, domesticated, docile, gentle, mild, regulated, sane, coherent, sensible, calm.

Wilful, perverse, stubborn, self-willed, headstrong, obstinate.
Ant.—Thoughtful, considerate, amenable, docile, manageable, accidental, unintentional.

Will, determination, resolution, volition, wish, desire.

Willingly, voluntarily, spontaneously, gratuitously.
Ant. — Unwillingly, involuntarily, grudgingly.

Win, get, obtain, gain, procure, effect, accomplish, achieve, realize.
Ant.—Lose, fail, miss, forfeit, alienate.

Wind, coil, twine, wreath, turn, bend, curve, twist.
Ant. — Unwind, untwist, uncoil, straighten.

Wing. (See Fly.)

Winning, attractive, charming, captivating, fascinating, bewitching, enchanting, dazzling, brilliant.
Ant.—Repulsive, unattractive, displeasing, disagreeable, hateful, unlovely.

Wisdom, sense, knowledge, learning, prudence, judgment, intelligence, sagacity, information, foresight, far-sightedness.
Ant. — Ignorance, impudence, folly, foolishness, improvidence.

Wise, intelligent, learned, skilled, judicious, rational, discreet, prudent.
Ant. — Ignorant, foolish, stupid, imprudent, indiscreet.

Wish. (See Desire.)

Wit, mind, intellect, understanding, genius, imagination, humor, satire, irony, mirth, fun, raillery.
Ant.—Dullness, vapidity, stupidity, platitude, commonplace, solemnity, stolidity.

Withdraw, retreat, retire, go back, recede, recall, regress, retrograde, take back.
Ant. — Offer, proffer, produce, afford, confirm, reiterate, repeat.

Withhold, keep back, restrain, arrest, hinder, abstain, refrain, keep from, desist from, refuse, retain, reserve.
Ant. — Grant, furnish, afford, provide, allow, give, permit, encourage, incite, aid, help, abet.

Withstand, oppose, resist, thwart, confront.
Ant. — Yield, submit, surrender, support, encourage, aid.

Witness, attest, testify, evidence, prove, certify, vouch, see, behold, view, observe.
Ant.—Refute, invalidate.

Wizard, juggler, magician, conjurer, necromancer, sorcerer.
Ant.—Dupe, dolt, ignoramus.

Woe, distress, sorrow, affliction, disaster, trouble.
Ant. — Joy, gladness, comfort, happiness, prosperity, blessing.

Wonder, *n.* amazement, surprise, astonishment, admiration, miracle, marvel, prodigy, curiosity.
Ant. — Indifference, apathy, expectation, familiarity, triviality, anticipation, commonplace, truism.

Wonder, *v.* admire, amaze, astonish, surprise.

Wonderful, marvelous, wondrous, amazing, astonishing, striking, surprising, admirable.
Ant. — Common, regular, normal, usual, customary, expected, anticipated, calculated, natural.

Wondrous. (See Wonderful.)

Word, term, expression, accent, promise, engagement, account, tidings, message, order, command.
Ant.—Idea, conception, assurance, pledge, contract, agreement.

Work, *n.* employment, business, occupation, performance, production, toil, task, labor, achievement, action, drudgery.
Ant.—Rest, non-performance, leisure, holiday, ease, idleness, play, recreation, repose.

Work, *v.* labor, toil, drudge, strive, exert, ply.
Ant. — Rest, sleep, play, refresh, amuse, enjoy.

Workman, artisan, mechanic, craftsman, artificer, journeyman, operative.
Ant. — Idler, tramp, vagrant, vagabond.

Worldly, terrestrial, mundane, temporal, secular, carnal, earthly.
Ant. — Unworldly, spiritual, religious, moral.

Worry, plague, tease, torment, vex, annoy, irritate, fret.
Ant. — Soothe, calm, gratify, please, amuse, quiet.

Worship, adore, revere, venerate, reverence, deify, idolize, honor, respect.
Ant. — Despise, blaspheme, rail, jeer, loathe, abominate, curse, execrate.

Worth, price, value, desert, merit, virtue, excellence.
Ant.—Worthlessness, demerit, cheapness.

Worthless, useless, valueless, frivolous, corrupt, dissolute, abject, base, cheap, degraded, ignoble, low, mean, vile.
Ant. — Valuable, worthy, rich, rare, costly, estimable, excellent, noble, precious, admirable, virtuous, esteemed, exalted, honorable, honored, pure.

Worthy, excellent, deserving, eligible, preferable, meritorious, estimable, commendable, laudable, praiseworthy.
Ant. — Worthless, useless, valueless.

Wrap, muffle, envelop, fold, encase.
Ant. — Unwind, unfold, unwrap, develop, expose, show.

Wrath. (See Anger.)

Wrathful, angry, ireful, enraged, infuriated, exasperated.
Ant.—Calm, pleased, quiet.

Wreck, debris, ruins, havoc, rubbish.
Ant. — Perfection, substance, completeness.

Wretched, deplorable, miserable, unhappy, distressed, afflicted, unfortunate, afflicting, disastrous, calamitous, dreary, dismal.
Ant.—Prosperous, happy, admirable, noble, worthy, elated.

Wretchedness, misery, woe, distress, misfortune, calamity, disaster, affliction, unhappiness.
Ant. — Happiness, prosperity, pleasure, joy.

Writer, scribe, penman, author, scribbler, amanuensis, clerk, secretary.
Ant.—Speaker, orator, reader.

Writhe, distort, contort, twist, wrest, wrench, wring.
Ant.—Quiet, soothe, calm, rest.

Written, penned, inscribed, transcribed.
Ant.—Traditional, verbal.

Wrong, bad, evil, incorrect, erroneous, unsuitable, improper, unjust, dishonesty, injustice, injury, partiality, unfairness, untruth.
Ant. — Right, fit, proper, suitable, correct, accurate, just, fair, moral, beneficial, equity, fairness, integrity, law, justice, rectitude, truth, virtue.

Wry, twisted, distorted, awry, crooked, askew.
Ant.—Straight, right, fit, just, proper, comely, true.

Y

Yawn, gape, open wide.
Ant.—Close, snap.
Yearn, hanker after, long for, desire, crave.
Ant. — Despise, loathe, recoil, dislike, avoid, turn from.
Yearly, annually, year by year, per annum.
Ant.—Momentarily, eternally, weekly, daily, monthly.
Yell, bellow, cry out, scream.
Yellow, golden, saffron-like.
Yelp, bark, sharp cry, howl.
Yeoman, farmer, freeholder, commoner.
Ant.—Esquire, gentleman.
Yet, besides, nevertheless, however, ultimately, notwithstanding, still, at last, so far, thus far.
Yield, bear, give, afford, impart, bestow, abdicate, resign, cede, surrender, relinquish, relax, forego, let go, waive, comply, accede, acquiesce, succumb, submit, communicate, confer, quit, give up, assent.
Ant. — Withdraw, withhold, retain, deny, refuse, assert, claim, disallow, resist, dissent, protest, struggle, strive, decline, demur, object, oppose.
Yielding, supple, pliant, bending, compliant, submissive, unresisting.
Ant. — Unyielding, stubborn, dogged, persevering, obstinate, resolute.
Yoke, couple, link, connect, associate, join, unite.
Ant.—Unyoke, unhitch, sever, disconnect, separate, liberate, release, divorce, alienate, detach, disjoin, divide, part.
Yore, long ago, long since.
Ant.—Now.
Young, juvenile, inexperienced, ignorant, youthful.
Ant.—Old, ancient, tried.
Youth, boy, lad, minority, adolescence, juvenility.
Ant.—Man, maid, woman, maturity, majority, senility, age.
Youthful, young, juvenile, boyish, girlish, puerile.
Ant. — Old, aged, senile, mature.

Z

Zeal, fervor, ardor, earnestness, enthusiasm, energy, eagerness.
Ant. — Apathy, indifference, torpor, coldness, detachment.
Zealot, bigot, partisan, fanatic.
Ant. — Renegade, traitor, deserter.
Zealous, warm, ardent, fervent, enthusiastic, anxious.
Ant. — Careless, indifferent, unconcerned.
Zenith, top, apex, summit, pinnacle, climax.
Ant.—Bottom, nadir.
Zest, relish, gusto, flavor, recommendation.
Ant.—Distaste, disrelish, detriment, indifference, apathy, disgust, dislike.

HOUGHTS are as many-colored and swift-changing as the sunset. They soar up into new realms. They are as endless and various as life itself. Words, by contrast, are pedestrian and limited in number; they plod along in pursuit. Yet if ideas are to be expressed and communicated to others, the right words must be found, the words whose meanings are most suitable. As an aid in this search a dictionary of synonyms and antonyms is of great value. The meanings of synonyms are similar but not identical. Consider the nice shades of meaning presented by the synonyms of DELIGHT*—enjoyment, pleasure, happiness, transport, ecstasy, gladness, rapture, bliss;* ECSTACY *carries an overtone of excitement;* BLISS *suggests tranquil, perfect contentment;* RAPTURE *lies somewhere between;* TRANSPORT *suggests a joy so great as to lift a person out of himself;* GLADNESS *sounds a more social, hearty, human note;* PLEASURE *describes the qualities of a simple sensation; and so on. No two words are identical in thought-content; if they were, there would be no need for two. The writer cannot pull one out of a sentence and push in another, like a mason laying bricks of like size, weight, and color. The writer instead must select with care. Usually this selection comes naturally, but when it does not, the writer must search for the correct word—the right word used in the right place and at the right moment to render a new thought imperishable.*

Office Worker's Guide and Manual of Information

Notes on English Usage, including grammar, punctuation, abbreviation, and capitalization; Letter Writing, Typing, Shorthand, Filing, Business Routine and Etiquette; Postal Information, and Public Speaking

MODERN ENGLISH USAGE

This section is designed to point out some of the basic grammatical terms necessary for correct speech and writing. In addition, rules are given for the proper use of those forms of pronouns and verbs which are usually most troublesome.

The Parts of Speech

All words belong to one of eight categories, called the parts of speech. Every good dictionary indicates to which of these categories a word belongs. The parts of speech are the following:

NOUN. The name of a *person, place, thing,* or *idea.* Nouns may be classified as follows:

(a) Common: the name used to identify any object in general, such as *man, flower, dog, house,* etc.

(b) Proper: the name of a specific person, place, or thing, such as *Washington, Walt Whitman, Statue of Liberty.*

(c) Abstract: the name of that which is perceived through the intellect, such as *virtue, justice, morality.*

(d) Concrete: the name of that which has a physical existence and is perceived through the senses, such as *man, desk, machine,* etc.

(e) Collective: the name of a class composed of many individual parts, such as *government, company, crowd, congress, faculty, jury,* etc.

PRONOUN. A word that takes the place of a noun. Pronouns may be classified as follows:

(a) Personal: *I, thou, you, he, she, it, we, ye, you, they.*

(b) Demonstrative: *this, that, these, those.*

(c) Relative: *who, whose, whom, which, that.*

(d) Indefinite: *anyone, each, both, someone, either,* etc.

(e) Interrogative: *who, whose, whom, what, which.*

(f) Reflexive: *myself, yourself, himself, herself, itself,* etc.

(g) Intensive: *myself, yourself, himself, herself,* etc. The reflexive and intensive pronouns have the same forms; the distinction in function is determined by their position in the sentence. Thus, in the sentence "I wash *myself,*" *myself* is a reflexive pronoun; whereas, in the sentence "I *myself* do the washing," *myself* is an intensive pronoun.

(h) Reciprocal: *each other, one another.*

VERB. A word that indicates an action or state of being. Verbs permit of the following classification:

(a) Transitive verbs have their meaning completed by a direct object. In the sentence, "He threw the ball," *threw* is a transitive verb, and *ball* the direct object.

(b) Intransitive verbs cannot take a direct object. In the sentence, "The man walks slowly," *walks* is an intransitive verb, and *slowly* is an adverb.

(c) Copulative verbs (linking verbs) link a subject with a predicate noun or adjective, are usually restricted to a form of the verb *to be,* and are sometimes classified as intransitive verbs because they cannot take an object. In "Art *is* life," "Men *are* mortal," the copulas are *is* and *are* respectively, because they link *art* to *life,* and *men* to *mortal.*

Verbs show the following characteristics:

(a) Mood indicates the manner in which the action takes place. Moods can be classified as:

(1) Indicative: expresses a simple fact, declarative or interrogative.

It is cold.

Are you going?

(2) Imperative: expresses a command or request.

Sit down.
Please don't go.

(3) Subjunctive: expresses doubt, exhortation, wish, permission, supposition, expectation, possibility, condition contrary to fact, intention.

If I *were* you, I should do it.
Would that it *were* so.
He *may* go to the theatre tonight, but I doubt that he will.

(4) Conditional: expresses contingency, the verbal phrases being formed with *should* and *would*. This mood is sometimes regarded as a function of the subjunctive.

(b) Tense indicates the time of an action. The *simple* tenses, present, past, and future, merely indicate the time of an action; the *compound* tenses, present perfect, past perfect, and future perfect, indicate the extent to which an action was completed. The *emphatic* forms occur only in the simple present and past tenses, and are used to give emphasis to a statement. The *progressive* forms occur in all simple and compound tenses to show continuity of action at the time of reference.

(c) Voice indicates the manner in which the action of the verb is related to the subject. When the subject is acting, the voice is *active;* when the subject is acted upon, the voice is *passive*.

(d) Number indicates whether the subject of the verb refers to one person or thing, *singular*, or more than one, *plural*.

(e) Person, *first, second, third,* is indicated by the inflectional ending of the verb.

Verbals are verb forms which have the function of a noun or adjective. In the sentence, "*To walk* is pleasant," the infinitive *to walk* has the function of a noun, and is the subject of the verb *is*. In the sentence, "*Walking* is pleasant," the gerund *walking* has the function of a noun, and is the subject of the verb *is*. In the sentence, "*Seizing* the opportunity, he rode to popularity," the participle *seizing* has the function of an adjective, modifying *he*.

ADVERB. A word that modifies a verb, adjective, or another adverb. Adverbs may be classified as follows:

(a) Time: answers the question *when?* In the sentence, "It rained *yesterday*," *yesterday* is an adverb of time.

(b) Place: answers the question *where?* In the sentence, "The men marched *forward*," *forward* is an adverb of place.

(c) Manner: answers the question *how?* In the sentence, "It rained *hard*," *hard* is an adverb of manner.

ADJECTIVE. A word that modifies a noun or pronoun. Adjectives may be classified as:

(a) Limiting: the definite article *the*, and the indefinite articles *a, an.*

(b) Descriptive: denotes condition or quality, as a *red* building, a *good* deed, an *upright* man, etc.

(c) Pronominal: derived from pronouns.

(1) Possessive: *my, his, her, its, our, your, their.*
(2) Demonstrative: *this, that, these, those.*
(3) Interrogative: *what, which, whose.*
(4) Relative: *which, whose.*
(5) Indefinite; *neither, some, every, each, other,* etc.

(d) Numeral

(1) Cardinal: *one, two, three,* etc.
(2) Ordinal: *first, second, third,* etc.

PREPOSITION. A word that expresses the relation of a noun or pronoun to some other word in the sentence. The noun or pronoun governed by the preposition is always in the objective case. Hence, it is wrong to say "Between you and *I*," because *I* is a nominative form; the correct form is the objective *me*, because the pronoun is the object of the preposition *between*. The preposition and its object constitute a *prepositional phrase*. Prepositional phrases may be used as adjectives or adverbs. In the sentence, "He has a pot *of gold*," the prepositional phrase *of gold* is used as an adjective to modify the noun *pot;* in the sentence, "The book *lies on the table*," the prepositional phrase *on the table* is used as an abverb to modify the verb *lies*.

CONJUNCTION. A word that connects words, phrases, or clauses. Conjunctions may be classified as:

(a) Coordinating: connects words, phrases, or independent clauses.

(1) Pure conjunctions: *and, but, or, for.*
(2) Correlatives: *either . . . or, neither . . . nor, not only . . . but also, both . . . and,* etc.
(3) Conjunctive adverbs: *hence, consequently, besides, moreover, therefore, nevertheless,* etc.

(b) Subordinating: introduces a subordinate clause, and connects it with the main clause.

(1) Those that introduce adjectival clauses: *who, which, that.*
(2) Those that introduce adverbial clauses: *although, because, since, though, if, as if,* etc.
(3) Those that introduce noun clauses: *that.*

INTERJECTION. An exclamatory word that expresses strong or sudden feeling, having no grammatical function in the construction of a sentence: *ah, alas, oh, bah, pshaw,* etc.

OFFICE GUIDE SOCIAL SEC.

Sentence Structure

A *simple sentence* is the expression of a single thought. It may also be defined as an independent clause. (A clause is a group of words containing a subject and a predicate).

> The first reports came at eleven o'clock.

A *compound sentence* is formed by joining two or more simple sentences, or at least two independent clauses.

> We waited all evening, but the first reports did not come until eleven.

A *complex sentence* consists of one independent clause and one or more dependent clauses. (Dependent clauses do not make complete statements; they do the work of an adverb, adjective, or noun).

> Although we waited all evening, we did not receive a report until eleven o'clock. (The clause introduced by *although* is adverbial).

The *compound-complex sentence.*

> The men who were chosen were excellent players; they had had a great deal of experience, and they worked well together.

In the above sentence there are three independent clauses, and one dependent, *who were chosen,* which is an adjective clause.

Writers without much experience often use a compound sentence when a complex would be more effective, that is, when one of the parts of the sentence is really subordinate to the other in thought. For example: "I was very tired, and so I went to bed early," might be written "Because I was very tired, I went to bed early." Good writers vary the sentence structure to gain emphasis and to avoid monotony.

Sentence Analysis

Every clause consists of a *subject* (the thing talked about), a *verb* or *predicate* (which makes a statement about the subject), and when the verb is not complete, an *object* (with a transitive verb) or a *predicate noun* or *adjective* (with a linking verb). The remaining words in the clause are modifiers of one of these elements.

> The old house which we purchased from Mr. Jones has been a constant source of expense.

This is a complex sentence. The independent or main clause is *The old house has been a constant expense.* The dependent clause is *which we purchased from Mr. Jones.*

In the independent clause *house* is the subject. It is modified by the adjectives *the* and *old* and by the adjective clause *"which we purchased from Mr. Jones. Has been* is the verb. *Source* is the predicate noun and it is modified by the adjectives *a* and *constant.*

In the adjective clause, *we* is the subject; *purchased* is a transitive verb modified by the prepositional phrase (used like an adverb) *from Mr. Jones; which* is the direct object.

> They promised us that the boat would be ready, and having done business with them before, we accepted their promise.

This is a compound-complex sentence, consisting of two independent clauses connected by *and,* and one dependent clause, *that the boat would be ready.*

In the first independent clause, *they* is the subject; *promised* is the transitive verb; the noun clause *that the boat would be ready* is the direct object; *us* is the indirect object.

In the second independent clause, *we* is the subject, modified by the adjective-participial phrase *having done business with them before; accepted* is the verb; *promise* is the object, modified by the possessive pronominal adjective, *their.*

In the dependent noun clause, *boat* is the subject, modified by *the; would be* is the linking verb; *ready* is the predicate adjective; *that* is used only to introduce the clause.

In the participial phrase, the verbal *having done* has an object, *business,* and an adverbial modifier, the phrase *with them.*

It is possible, then, to account for the use of every word in any sentence.

Declension of the Noun

	Singular	Plural
NOMINATIVE	dog	dogs
POSSESSIVE	dog's	dogs'
OBJECTIVE	dog	dogs
NOMINATIVE	man	men
POSSESSIVE	man's	men's
OBJECTIVE	man	men

The Correct Use of Pronouns

Because pronouns have different forms for each of the three cases in the English inflectional system, they offer more difficulty than perhaps any other part of speech. People are often puzzled about the use of *who* and *whom;* they are uncertain whether *everyone* is singular or plural. It is to meet these questions that the following rules are given.

Cases of Pronouns

NOMINATIVE CASE	Used for the subject or predicate nominative.
POSSESSIVE CASE	Used to indicate ownership.
OBJECTIVE CASE	Used for the objects of verbs and prepositions.

Declension of the Pronoun

Personal

First Person, Masculine and Feminine

	Singular	Plural
NOMINATIVE	I	we
POSSESSIVE	*my, mine	*our, ours
OBJECTIVE	me	us

Second Person, Masculine and Feminine

	Singular	Plural
NOMINATIVE	you	you
POSSESSIVE	*your, yours	*your, yours
OBJECTIVE	you	you

*These forms are pronominal adjectives.

Third Person, Masc., Fem., Neuter

	Singular			Plural
NOMINATIVE	he	she	it	they
POSSESSIVE	his	*her, hers	its	*their, theirs
OBJECTIVE	him	her	it	them

*These forms are pronominal adjectives.

Relative

	Singular	Plural
NOMINATIVE	who	who
POSSESSIVE	whose	whose
OBJECTIVE	whom	whom

RULES FOR USE OF PRONOUNS

1. Use the Nominative Case as the subject of a finite verb.

"He is taller than *I.*" *I* is the subject of *am* (understood).
"Explain the situation to *whoever* comes first." *Whoever* is the subject of *comes,* not the object of the preposition *to.*
"He is the man *who* we believe should be elected. *Who* is the subject of *should be elected,* not the object of *believe.*

2. Use the Nominative Case after the various forms of the linking verb *be (was, were, is, are, have been,* etc.)

"It was *he* who called."
"The leaders were Walter and *I.*"
"We are certain it is *they.*"

3. Use the Possessive Case to modify a gerund.

"We objected to *his* leaving."
"*Dick's* losing the ball stopped the game."
"I am certain of *their* having been there."

4. Use the Objective Case for the object of a verb.

"I invited Mary and *him.*"
"She likes John better than *me.*" *Me* is the object of *she likes,* (understood).
"*Whom* did you see?" *Whom* is the object of *did see.*
"Give the book to *whomever* you see." *Whomever* is the object of *see.*

5. Use the Objective Case for the object of a preposition.

"She gave the book to Helen and *me.*"
"They were all there except *him.*"
"Three of *us* boys went camping."

PRONOUNS—NUMBER

Use a *singular* pronoun to refer to the indefinite words *anyone, either, everyone, each, every, nobody.*

"*Everyone* should have *his* own book."
"*Each one* of the girls read *her* essay."
"If *anyone* wishes help, *he* must ask for it."
"*Neither* of the boys could express *his* ideas."

AGREEMENT OF SUBJECT AND VERB

1. Use a singular verb with a singular subject.

"Mary *doesn't* like to work." *Don't* would be wrong in this sentence. Do not say *he don't, she don't, it don't,* because these are contractions of *he do not, she do not, it do not.*
"Each of the boys *is* capable in his own way." *Each* is singular.
"Neither Tom nor Peter is eligible." When the two parts of the subject are joined by *nor, or, but,* the verb agrees in number with the word nearest to it.
"Every member of the committee *agrees* to the proposal."
"John, together with his companion, *is* here." *John,* alone, is the subject.

2. Use a plural verb with a plural subject.

"There *are* several varieties of apples in the basket." *Varieties* is the subject of *are.*
"Applause and flattery *are* the breath of his existence." A compound subject, i.e., two words joined by *and,* requires a plural verb unless the two words designate the same person or thing, as in the sentence: "His guide and protector *is* Mr. Collins."

3. Collective nouns (words like *group, crowd, committee, choir, faculty, congress)* may take either a singular or plural verb according to the meaning intended.

"The *company* has been ordered to the coast." *Company* is here thought of as a unit.
"The *company* are not all willing to take the risk." Here *company* is considered as plural because several individuals are meant.

CONJUGATION OF THE VERB "TO CALL":

ACTIVE VOICE

Indicative Mood

Singular	Plural
Present Tense	
Simple	
1. I call	we call
2. you call	you call
3. he calls	they call
Emphatic	
1. I do call	we do call
2. you do call	you do call
3. he does call	they do call
Progressive	
1. I am calling	we are calling
2. you are calling	you are calling
3. he is calling	they are calling
Past Tense	
Simple	
1. I called	we called
2. you called	you called
3. he called	they called
Emphatic	
1. I did call	we did call
2. you did call	you did call
3. he did call	they did call
Progressive	
1. I was calling	we were calling
2. you were calling	you were calling
3. he was calling	they were calling

Future Tense

Simple

1. I shall call	we shall call
2. you will call	you will call
3. he will call	they will call

Emphatic

1. I will call	we will call
2. you shall call	you shall call
3. he shall call	they shall call

Progressive

1. I shall be calling	we shall be calling
2. you will be calling	you will be calling
3. he will be calling	they will be calling

Present Perfect

Simple

1. I have called	we have called
2. you have called	you have called
3. he has called	they have called

Progressive

1. I have been calling	we have been calling
2. you have been calling	you have been calling
3. he has been calling	they have been calling

Past Perfect

Simple

1. I had called	we had called
2. you had called	you had called
3. he had called	they had called

Progressive

1. I had been calling	we had been calling
2. you had been calling	you had been calling
3. he had been calling	they had been calling

Future Perfect

Simple

1. I shall have called	we shall have called
2. you will have called	you will have called
3. he will have called	they will have called

Progressive

1. I shall have been calling	we shall have been calling
2. you will have been calling	you will have been calling
3. he will have been calling	they will have been calling

Subjunctive Mood

Singular	Plural

Present Tense

Simple

1. if I call	if we call
2. if you call	if you call
3. if he call	if they call

Emphatic

1. if I do call	if we do call
2. if you do call	if you do call
3. if he do call	if they do call

Progressive

1. if I be calling	if we be calling
2. if you be calling	if you be calling
3. if he be calling	if they be calling

Past Tense

Simple

1. if I called	if we called
2. if you called	if you called
3. if he called	if they called

Emphatic

Singular	Plural
1. if I did call	if we did call
2. if you did call	if you did call
3. if he did call	if they did call

Progressive

1. if I were calling	if we were calling
2. if you were calling	if you were calling
3. if he were calling	if they were calling

Present Perfect

Simple

1. if I have called	if we have called
2. if you have called	if you have called
3. if he has called	if they have called

Progressive

1. if I have been calling	if we have been calling
2. if you have been calling	if you have been calling
3. if he has been calling	if they have been calling

Past Perfect

Simple

1. if I had called	if we had called
2. if you had called	if you had called
3. if he had called	if they had called

Progressive

1. if I had been calling	if we had been calling
2. if you had been calling	if you had been calling
3. if he had been calling	if they had been calling

Conditional Mood

Singular	Plural

Present Tense

Simple

1. I should call	we should call
2. you would call	you would call
3. he would call	they would call

Emphatic

1. I would call	we would call
2. you should call	you should call
3. he should call	they should call

Progressive

1. I should be calling	we should be calling
2. you would be calling	you would be calling
3. he would be calling	they would be calling

Perfect

Simple

1. I should have called	we should have called
2. you would have called	you would have called
3. he would have called	they would have called

Progressive

1. I should have been calling	we should have been calling
2. you would have been calling	you would have been calling
3. he would have been calling	they would have been calling

Imperative Mood

SIMPLE: call
EMPHATIC: do call
PROGRESSIVE: be calling

Present Infinitive

SIMPLE: to call
PROGRESSIVE: to be calling
GERUND: calling

Perfect Infinitive

SIMPLE: to have called
PROGRESSIVE: to have been calling
GERUND: having called

Participles

PRESENT: calling
PAST: (lacking)
PERFECT SIMPLE: having called

PASSIVE VOICE

Indicative Mood

Singular	Plural
Present Tense	
1. I am called	we are called
2. you are called	you are called
3. he is called	they are called
Past Tense	
1. I was called	we were called
2. you were called	you were called
3. he was called	they were called
Future Tense	
1. I shall be called	we shall be called
2. you will be called	you will be called
3. he will be called	they will be called
Present Perfect	
1. I have been called	we have been called
2. you have been called	you have been called
3. he has been called	they have been called
Past Perfect	
1. I had been called	we had been called
2. you had been called	you had been called
3. he had been called	they had been called
Future Perfect	
1. I shall have been called	we shall have been called
2. you will have been called	you will have been called
3. he will have been called	they will have been called

Subjunctive Mood

Singular	Plural
Present Tense	
1. if I be called	if we be called
2. if you be called	if you be called
3. if he be called	if they be called
Past Tense	
1. if I were called	if we were called
2. if you were called	if you were called
3. if he were called	if they were called
Present Perfect	
1. if I have been called	if we have been called
2. if you have been called	if you have been called
3. if he has been called	if they have been called
Past Perfect	
1. if I had been called	if we had been called
2. if you had been called	if you had been called
3. if he had been called	if they had been called

Conditional Mood

Singular	Plural
Present	
1. I should be called	we should be called
2. you would be called	you would be called
3. he would be called	they would be called
Perfect	
1. I should have been called	we should have been called
2. you would have been called	you would have been called
3. he would have been called	they would have been called

Imperative Mood

SIMPLE: be called

Present Infinitive

SIMPLE: to be called
GERUND: being called

Perfect Infinitive

SIMPLE: to have been called
GERUND: have been called

Participles

PRESENT: being called
PAST: called
PERFECT: having been called

Capitalization

Capital letters are employed to give emphasis to particular words, namely proper nouns and proper adjectives. The difficulty in this principle lies in determining when a noun or adjective is proper, and when a noun or adjective is common. It would be difficult, if not impossible, to list here an exhaustive set of rules to cover every instance. The following rules, however, will be found helpful insofar as they do apply to problems in capitalization met daily.

1. Capitalize the first word (a) of a sentence, (b) of a direct quotation, (c) of a line of poetry, or (d) of a formally introduced series of items or phrases following a colon.

(a) The room was uncomfortably warm.

(b) Turning quickly she said, "Please go now."

(c) Then I felt like some watcher of the skies,
  When a new planet swims into his ken:
Or like stout Cortez when with eagle eyes
  He stared at the Pacific—and all his men
Look'd at each other with wild surmise—
  Silent, upon a peak in Darien.

(d) The analysis revealed the following: Carbon, six parts; hydrogen, twelve parts; oxygen, six parts.

The first word of a fragmentary quotation is not capitalized.

He thought the play "was good, but amateurish."

The first word following a colon is not capitalized if that which follows merely expands, qualifies, or makes clearer the sense of that which precedes the colon.

Intelligence cannot be acquired or increased: it is native.
History shows that wars settle nothing: they merely unsettle things.

2. Capitalize the interjection O, but none of the other interjections.

O powerful western fallen star!

O shades of night—O moody, tearful night!

O great star disappear'd — O the black murk that hides the star!

O cruel hands that hold me powerless — O helpless soul of me!

O harsh surrounding cloud that will not free my soul.

3. Capitalize all proper nouns.

Bohemia	Louis Pasteur
China	King Philip of Macedon
America	John Macadam

4. Words derived from proper nouns, and retaining a proper meaning are capitalized.

Bohemian (of Bohemia)
American (of America)
Venetian (of Venice)
Moroccan (of Morocco)

a. Do not capitalize words derived from proper nouns for which a common or specialized meaning has been developed.

china	anglicize
morocco	pasteurize
venetian blinds	philippic
plaster of paris	macadam

5. Capitalize common nouns and adjectives which form an essential part of a proper name, as of streets, parks, specific buildings, geographical names, etc.

Chestnut Street	Delaware River
Franklin Parkway	Blair County
Michigan Avenue	Mount Everest
Cermak Road	Gulf of Mexico
Fairmount Park	Panama Canal
Elverson Building	Chesapeake Bay

a. Do not capitalize descriptive place references:

the valley of the Nile
the river Seine
the gorge of the Colorado

b. The following are never capitalized:

aqueduct	lock
breakwater	pier
buoy	slip
dike	spillway
ditch	tunnel
drydock	watershed
floodway	weir
levee	wharf

c. The following are always capitalized when they follow a proper name:

Archipelago	Harbor
Bay	Highway
Bayou	Hill
Bight	Hook
Borough	Inlet
Canal (for ships)	Island
Canyon	Isle
Cape	Lake
Channel	Mount
County	Mountain
Creek	Narrows
Desert	Peninsula
Falls	Plateau
Forest	River
Fork (stream)	Sea
Fort	Sound
Gap	Spring
Glacier	Valley
Gulch	Woods
Gulf	

6. Capitalize the *d', da, della, van,* and *von* when not preceded by a title or forename.

De Maupassant, but Guy de Maupassant
Van Gogh, but Vincent van Gogh
Von Tirpitz, but Alfred von Tirpitz
Della Robbia, but Luca della Robbia

a. In American and British names these particles are usually capitalized without regard to the above rule, but individual usage should be followed.

William De Morgan

Thomas De Quincey

Lucretia Van Zandt

Henry van Dyke (his usage)

7. Capitalize the names of organized bodies and their members to distinguish them from the common meaning.

Republican Party, a Republican; but, a republican (one who believes in a republican form of government.)
Democratic Party, a Democrat; but, a democrat (one who believes in democracy.)
an Elk; but, an elk (an animal.)

8. Capitalize *territory, state, nation, union, empire,* etc. only when these words refer to a particular political division.

the United States: the Republic, the Nation, the Union; *but* a republic, a nation, a union.
the British Empire: the Empire; *but* an empire.
Cook County: the County; *but* a county.

9. Capitalize descriptive terms used to designate a definite geographical region or feature.

the Middle Atlantic States
the Far East; the Near East
the Continental Divide
the North Pole; the South Pole
the Western Hemisphere; the Eastern Hemisphere

10. Capitalize names of months and days of the year.

January	Sunday
February	Monday
March, etc.	Tuesday, etc.

11. Capitalize names of historic events and eras, holidays, and ecclesiastical feast and fast days.

World War	Renaissance
Mexican War	Fourth of July
Middle Ages	Shrove Tuesday

12. Capitalize personification in figures of speech.

For Nature is neither kind nor cruel, merciless nor merciful; she follows inexorably her immutable laws.
The Chair introduced the guest speaker.

13. Capitalize all nouns and adjectives denoting the Deity, and all pronouns referring to the same.

the Holy Ghost	Jehovah
the Lord	Yahweh
the Almighty	Allah
Son of Man	the Virgin

14. Capitalize all names of creeds, religious bodies and their adherents.

Nicene Creed	Methodist Church
Augsburg Confession	Protestant
Christian	Buddhist

15. Capitalize all names for the Bible, books of the Bible, and all other sacred books.

Holy Writ	the Koran
Scriptures	the Vedas
Exodus	the Upanishads
Septuagint	the Talmud

a. Do not capitalize adjectives derived from such nouns.

apocryphal	scriptural
koranic	biblical

16. Capitalize all titles preceding a name.

Doctor Smith	King George
Professor Gibbs	General Butler
President Roosevelt	Justice Roberts

a. Capitalize a title in the second or third person.

Your Honor	Mr. President
Your Grace	Mr. Chairman
His Holiness	His Excellency

17. Capitalize the first word and every important word in the English title of a book, poem, play, article, essay, work of art, piece of music, report, publication, legal case, and historic document.

The Dawn of Civilization (book)
Caliban in the Coal Mines (poem)
Pillars of Society (drama)
Old Lamps for New (essay)
Essays of Elia (book)
Dinner for Threshers (painting)
Death and Transfiguration (music)

Punctuation

The purpose of punctuation is to aid the reader in assimilating the thought expressed through the written word.

Although very little conscious thought is given to punctuation in the actual reading of printed or written matter — the mind automatically stopping at periods, pausing for commas, and preparing for a change of thought at dashes — a thorough knowledge of the fundamental rules governing the correct use of punctuation marks is indispensible to the writer who wishes to express his thoughts, ideas, and feelings clearly, accurately, and logically.

The following rules will be found to embrace all cases arising in the course of ordinary formal and informal writing.

1. When reading, notice all punctuation closely and try to reason out why the marks encountered are used.

2. When writing, first organize in your mind what you want to say and then use only sufficient punctuation to insure the accurate conveyance of your thoughts.

3. Never use any mark of punctuation without a definite reason for so doing.

4. Give particular attention to the use of the comma as ignorance of the rules governing this mark is the major cause of punctuation trouble.

The Comma

The function of the comma is to break up the sentence into separate thoughts in the interest of clarity and ease of reading.

1. Use a comma between each element of pairs and series unless the pairs are connected by a coordinating conjunction.

The ride was long, exhausting.
The ride was long, hot, exhausting.
The ride was long and exhausting.

2. Use a comma before the *and* in a series having the form of *a*, *b*, and *c*.

We brought ham, pickles, and eggs.

3. Use a comma before any one of the conjunctions (*and*, *but*, *for*, *or*, *neither*, *nor*) when it joins a pair of main clauses.

He said he would be there, and I do not doubt his word.
Many are called, but few are chosen.
He read the book quickly, for he was late.
She will be there, or I am mistaken.

4. Use a comma to introduce a short, direct quotation in the form of a complete sentence and also at the end of a quotation if it is followed by explanatory, unquoted remarks. (Introducing a

direct quotation with a colon is permissible if the quoted sentence is long.)

The cynic replied, "Diplomacy is the art of lying."
"Diplomacy is the art of lying," replied the cynic.
"Diplomacy," replied the cynic, "is the art of lying."

5. Use a comma before and after such elements as *for example, to be sure, in fact, however, nevertheless,* and *therefore,* when they are used parenthetically.

We do not, for example, favor a moratorium.
He was, in fact, unequal to the work.
She will go, therefore, at six o'clock.

6. Use commas to enclose a geographical name explaining a preceding geographical name.

They lived in Chicago, Illinois, for many years.

7. Use commas to enclose a date explaining a preceding date.

In April, 1918, his regiment moved to the front.
On April 24, 1918, his regiment moved to the front.
Early in the morning of Monday, April 24, his regiment moved to the front.

8. Use commas to enclose any element taken from its natural position and placed elsewhere.

Their new car, when running at top speed, will go 90 miles an hour.

9. Use a comma between the parts of a name or phrase when they are written in reverse order.

Buchanan, James B.
Psychology, History of
Nouns, Use of
Chemistry, Organic

10. Enclose appositives with commas.

U. S. Grant, the great Civil War general, was short in stature.

11. Enclose absolute phrases with commas.

It is my belief, conditions being what they are, that war is inevitable.

12. Use a comma to separate two words or figures that might otherwise be confusing.

To Henry, Scott was a hero.
In 1939, 40 ships were lost.
January 24, 1939.
Instead of 10, 25 men answered the call for volunteers.

13. Use a comma to indicate the omission of a word.

He is tall; she, short.
The former illustrates the use of a semicolon; the latter, a comma.

14. Use a comma after a phrase or subordinate clause that precedes a main clause.

Caught on a reef, the vessel foundered.
Although a severe winter had been anticipated, we were pleasantly surprised by its mildness.

a. Do not use a comma after a main clause if the following adverbial clause is its logical completion.

This testimony is inadmissible because it is prejudicial.
The project can be completed only if all cooperate.

15. Use a comma between two of the same or similar words to avoid confusion.

That which is, is neither good nor bad.
That which was, is no more.
What will be, will be.

16. Use a comma before the abbreviations or degrees *Jr., Sr., M.A., M.D., Ph.D.,* etc.

Charles H. Leiter, Jr.
Anthony Ennis, M.D.
D. S. Platon, Ph.D.

17. Use a comma to separate thousands, millions, billions, etc. in numbers of four or more digits.

3,197 3,284,962
52,012 653,039,253

a. Do not use a comma in figures of four or more digits in telephone numbers, serial numbers, dates, and radio wave lengths.

Murray Hill 9912
A.D. 1925
No. F87831084 A
1170 kilocycles; 820 meters

18. Use a comma after a title or phrase in direct address.

Sir, the end is not yet.
Mr. President, the gentleman is out of order.
Gentlemen, we shall now proceed to the order of the day.

19. Use a comma between title and name of organization where *of* or *of the* has been omitted.

Commander, Fourth Army Corps
President, University of Chicago
Superintendent, Board of Health

The Dash

The dash may often be substituted for the comma, semicolon, colon, or parenthesis mark. It is used to enclose or introduce short elements and has great force. It should be used only in extreme cases, when other forms of punctuation are inadequate—and only then.

1. Substitute a dash for a semicolon when more effective grouping is desired.

The shouting ceased—all was quiet; evidently the mob had dispersed.

2. The dash may be used to call attention to a word or group of words following it.

He works hard—too hard, in fact.
The American character may be described in one word—courage.

3. The dash is useful at the end of a long series to introduce material concerning that series.

> With careful study, with diligent practice, with the desire for improvement—with all these, one should be able to succeed.

4. Use dashes to enclose parenthetical elements where commas would be weak or parentheses undesirable.

> Ruth—the best hitter in the league—has powerful shoulders.
> He thinks—and rightly—that the disease can be eradicated if properly controlled.

5. Use the dash to indicate an interruption or an unfinished sentence.

> He goes on to say that —. But never mind; it's of no importance.
> "This thing has be—."

6. Use a dash to link letters, figures, or letters and figures.

DO—X	1938—40
RZ—1	January—March
$5—$10	Monday—Thursday

7. Use a dash when there is repetition for additional or especial emphasis.

> We are now faced with a new problem—the problem of isolating the germ.

8. Use a dash for summarizing.

> Washington, Jefferson, Jackson—all had the same idea.

THE SEMICOLON

This mark is used to coordinate main clauses.

1. Use the semicolon between pairs of main clauses not coordinated by a coordinating conjunction (*and, but, for, or, neither, nor*).

> You may help him; I will not.

2. Use the semicolon between pairs of main clauses not connected by a coordinating conjunction especially when a conjunctive adverb (*therefore, nevertheless, however, otherwise,* etc.) is present.

> You may help him; however, I will not.

3. Use the semicolon between pairs of main clauses where a coordinating conjunction is present if such clauses are long, contain commas within themselves, or if emphasis is desired.

> It is most unusual; and it should not be tolerated.
> It is not just to the people, the state, or the country; and although difficult, a proper decision must be made.

4. Use the semicolon to separate statements so closely related that a comma would be too weak and a period too strong.

> It was so in the past; it is so in the present; and if the past and the present may be taken as a valid indication of the future, it will always remain so.

THE COLON

The colon is a mark of punctuation used to introduce a clause or phrase that amplifies a preceding clause.

1. Use the colon to introduce a clause that supplements or explains the preceding clause.

> Everett's speech was soon forgotten: he was too much occupied with form rather than substance.
> We live on a planet, not on a star: a star is a sun.

2. Use the colon to introduce formally a direct, lengthly quotation, or any other formal matter.

> These are his principal qualifications: attention to detail; many years of experience; and an instinctive ability to sell merchandise.
> He said: "I do not accept as valid the proposition that time goes. It would not be difficult to demonstrate that time is ageless; and it would also be easy to demonstrate that human beings are not ageless. No, it is we who go, not time."

3. Use the colon to express time.

> 8:30 A.M.
> 12:25 P.M.

4. Use the colon after the salutation of a letter.

Dear Sir:	Gentlemen:
My dear Sir:	Dear Madam:

5. Use the colon in biblical and other citations.

> Luke 4:7
> N. Y. Times, Nov. 20, 21:7

6. Use the colon in proportions.

> 1:3::3:9
> The ratio was 16:1.

PARENTHESES

1. Use parentheses to enclose that part of a sentence intended to be read as a side remark provided the removal of such part would not destroy the sense of the context. Also, use parentheses to enclose complete sentences intended as side remarks.

> Robert was playing great football (for the thrill of it; not merely to win) and several times staved off defeat.
> We hurried home the next day. (It was only too true that the river had risen. We were ruined.) But with characteristic vigor we began building anew.

2. Use parentheses to enclose an independent clause inserted in a sentence.

> The work (he was preeminently fitted for it) absorbed his attention for weeks.

3. Enclose with parentheses references to tables, diagrams, etc.

> The cost of living (See Chart II) has risen slowly but surely.

4. Use parentheses to inclose figures or letters used in enumerations.

> The immediate results were these: (1) a cornering of the market, (2) a decrease in available material, (3) an advance in prices.

BRACKETS

Brackets are used to enclose an explanatory remark in a quoted passage. They are rarely, if ever, used in a business letter. For all practical purposes the secretary can attain the same ends with parentheses.

"The rise of absolutism [Fascism, Hitlerism, etc.] has its roots in post-war conditions," the speaker pointed out.

QUOTATION MARKS

1. Use quotation marks to enclose all direct quotations.

Patrick Henry said, "Give me liberty, or give me death."

2. Use single quotation marks to mark a quotation within a quotation.

The coach said: "I heard one of our men say, 'It was the hardest game of the season.'"

3. When a quotation consists of more than one paragraph, use quotation marks before each paragraph, but at the end of only the last one.

"____.

"____."

4. When quoting poetry consisting of more than one stanza, use quotation marks before each stanza, but at the end of only the last stanza.

"Under the wide and starry sky,
Dig the grave and let me die.
Glad did I live and gladly die,
And I laid me down with a will.
"This be the verse you grave for me:
Here he lies where he longed to be;
Home is the sailor, home from sea,
And the hunter home from the hill."
—ROBERT LOUIS STEVENSON.

5. Enclose slang expressions, colloquialisms, technical words, or a word used in a humorous or ironical way, in quotation marks when such expressions are not in keeping with the style of writing in which they occur.

His wife is undoubtedly "Lord High Chancellor of the Exchequer" in their household.

He got himself "all balled up."

6. The comma and period are always placed inside the quotation marks.

"I shall come," she said, "if it does not rain."

The semicolon, exclamation mark, colon, question mark, and dash are all placed outside the quotation marks except when they form part of the quoted passage or when the quotation is not accompanied by such expressions as *he said, she replied,* etc.

Did she say, "I have lost my book"?
"May I come in now?" he asked.
"They're off!"
"Where?"
"At Latonia."

7. Dialogue should be written in separate paragraphs.

"Come in," she said, "and get warm."
"Thank you," he replied, "it is very cold tonight."

8. Enclose definitions requiring explanation with single quotation marks; for translations use double quotation marks.

Facetious means 'humorous' or 'jocular.'
Verboten means "forbidden."

9. Since there are no italics on a typewriter, quote the names of ships, of musical compositions, of art works, and the titles of books and pictures, or indicate italics by underlining:

The U. S. S. "Pennsylvania"
DaVinci's "The Last Supper"
Theodore Dreiser's <u>An American Tragedy</u>
George Gershwin's <u>Rhapsody in Blue</u>

THE PERIOD

1. Use the period at the end of a declarative sentence.

The soft rays of the morning sun illuminated the gold in the ripening wheat.

As the sun began to slip away the mountain underwent a slow progression in color, from warmer to cooler, from green through blue to purple, until a mere outline was left against a dusky sky which finally melted into the darkness of night.

2. Use the period at the end of an imperative sentence.

Hang up your coat.
Come to the fair.
Be there on time.

3. Use the period at the end of an indirect question.

Tell me what he said.
I should like to know how you do it.
I asked him what time it was.

4. Use the period after an abbreviation.

viz.	D. C.
N. Y.	q.v.
etc.	SW.

a. Do not use a period after the symbols for chemical elements.

Ag (silver)	K (potassium)
Au (gold)	O (oxygen)
Fe (iron)	S (sulphur)

b. Do not mistake a contraction for an abbreviation: a contraction is not followed by a period.

ass'n	assn.	sup't	supt.
m'g'r	mgr.	Penn.	Penn'a

5. Do not use a period after Roman numerals except in enumeration used in an outline.

George VI
Haakon VII
Gustavus V
I. The Colonial Period
II. The Ante-Bellum Period
III. The Post-Bellum Period
IV. The Twentieth Century

6. Do not use a period after *per cent, MS, MSS,* or after the French *Mlle* or *Mme.*

 the Cotton MS (manuscript)
 Mlle de Maupin
 Mme Bovary
 25 per cent

7. Always put the period within quotation marks.

 I have read "Leaves of Grass."
 He did not see the performance of "Mourning Becomes Electra."

THE EXCLAMATION POINT

This mark is used at the end of a declarative sentence or after an exclamation within the sentence to convey the idea of strong feeling, surprise, or irony.

 Here, get down from there!
 What! the only one we have! and I'm not to use it!
 Voting in a totalitarian state is an expression of popular sentiment? Popular sentiment, indeed!

THE QUESTION MARK

1. Use the question mark at the end of every sentence that asks a question.

 How fast are we going?
 "How fast are we going?" he asked.
 Can there not be such a thing as an absolute event quite independent of cause?

2. Use the question mark within the sentence when it is desirable to emphasize each element separately.

 Where now is his love of country? his political integrity? his unblemished record?

3. Use the question mark within parentheses to indicate doubt or uncertainty as to the correctness of the word or fact preceding it.

 Charles I, born in 1660 (?), was king of Sicily.

THE APOSTROPHE

The apostrophe is used to indicate the omission of one or more letters from a word or to form the possessive of certain nouns as indicated in the rules following.

1. Use the apostrophe to indicate the omission of one or more letters from a word, or figures from a number.

 I can't do it now.
 He wouldn't do it then.
 The class of '98 met in Chicago.

2. Use the apostrophe and *s* to form the possessive of singular nouns of more than one syllable including those which end in *s*.

 Fred's, James's, Mr. Jones's.

Some writers still use only the apostrophe for the possessive of singular nouns ending in *s*; but the *'s* is preferable.

3. Use the apostrophe alone when forming the possessive of plural nouns ending in *s*, or nouns ending in *s* and consisting of more than one syllable; add *s* with the apostrophe in the case of plural nouns which do not end in *s*.

 The Smiths' house.
 Girls', soldiers', children's, men's.
 The *New Testament* contains Jesus' parables.

4. Use the apostrophe and *s* to indicate joint possession.

 George and Mary's book.
 Chase and Sanborn's coffee.

5. Use the apostrophe and *s* to form the possessive of indefinite pronouns.

 One's, other's, another's, either's.
 Somebody else's coat.

The above rule does not apply to *its, hers, his, ours, yours, theirs, whose.*

6. Use the apostrophe and *s* to form the plural of a letter, a figure, or of a word used as a noun.

 There are two *f's* in *affect.*
 Your *8's* are not legible.
 He uses too many *if's* and *but's.*

Faulty Expressions

The following glossary of faulty expressions, while by no means exhaustive, is representative of the most common forms of incorrect usage. The secretary should avoid, in business correspondence, obsolete and archaic words, slang and vulgarisms. Although provincialisms and colloquialisms are permissible in conversation, their usage in a business letter detracts from its dignity and effectiveness. Too, the type of English frequently used in newspapers, written in a loose, racy, smart, or sensational style, should not be employed in business correspondence. The English may not be incorrect, but it lacks the character and dignity in keeping with the tone of a business letter, and is, therefore, to be avoided. The expressions listed here are those which are avoided by persons of good training. The secretary will do well to study them carefully, in order to avoid these common errors.

A.D. *In the year of our Lord.* The A.D. should precede the date and never be used with *in,* since that would be superfluous. Nor should the A.D. be used when speaking of a century.

 Wrong: He died in 1865 A.D.
 Right: He died A.D. 1865.
 Wrong: We live in the 20th century A.D.
 Right: We live in the 20th century of the Christian Era.

ACCEPT, EXCEPT. These words should not be confused. Accept means *to* receive, as *I accept your kind offer.* Except means *to exclude, The law excepts no one.*

AD. Colloquialism for advertisement. Although acceptable in speech it should be avoided in formal writing.

 Colloq.: Your ad was placed in the Sunday News.
 Preferable: Your advertisement was inserted in the Sunday News.

ADAPT, ADEPT. These words are carelessly confused. Adapt is a verb and means *to adjust,* as *He adapted the idea to his own needs.* Adept is an adjective and means *skilled,* as *He is adept at figures.*

ADVISE. Means *to offer an opinion* but is frequently used in business correspondence to mean *inform* or *tell.* In this sense, *inform* or *tell* is preferable to *advise.*

Permissible: Please be advised that the merchandise has been shipped.

Preferable: We wish to inform you that the merchandise has been shipped.

AFFECT, EFFECT. *Affect* is always a verb and means *to influence,* as *A high tariff will affect our cotton exports. Effect,* as a verb, means *to cause,* as *I want to effect a settlement;* as a noun it means *result,* as *Some believe that for every effect there is a cause.*

AFTER. This should not be used with a past participle, but may be used with the present participle.

Wrong: After having read the poem, I could appreciate it.

Right: Having read the poem, I could appreciate it.

Or also: After reading the poem, I could appreciate it.

AGGRAVATE. This means *to make an already bad condition worse* and, though sanctioned by popular usage, should not be used in the sense of *irritate, annoy,* or *provoke.*

Popular: His petty behavior aggravated me.

Preferable: His petty behavior irritated me.

AGREE TO, AGREE WITH. These are idiomatic expressions with different meanings. *Agree to* means *to give assent to,* as *I did not agree to pay that sum of money. Agree with* means *to be in accord with,* as *I agree with him in principle, but differ as to method.*

AIN'T. This word has been the subject of much controversy but most authorities agree that it should never be used except in written colloquial dialogue. In its place should be used *is it not?, am I not?* (but never the British-Hollywood vulgarism *aren't I?*), *are we not?* etc.

ALL OF. The *of* is superfluous.

Bad: He gave all of his property to charity.

Better: He gave all his property to charity.

ALL THE FARTHER, HIGHER, FASTER. These are frequently used incorrectly for *as far as, as high as, as fast as. All the* is correct when used in the sense of *just so much.*

Right: Disregarding the warning, we climbed all the higher.

Right: That day we climbed as high as 5,000 feet.

Wrong: Is this all the farther we are going?

ALLOW. The word means *to permit, to approve.* The provincial meaning *to think* or *believe* should be avoided.

Provincial: I allow that's so.

Preferable: I think that is so.

ALLUDE, DELUDE, ELUDE. *Allude* means *to refer to indirectly,* as *He alluded to unethical practitioners in the profession. Delude* means *to deceive,* as *He was deluded by the man's apparent honesty.* Elude means *to escape,* as *The gist of the story eludes me.*

ALLUSION, ILLUSION. *Allusion* has the meaning of *a casual reference,* as *There were many humorous allusions to human foibles in the drama. Illusion* has the meaning of a *false* or *deceptive appearance,* as *He lulled himself into a feeling of false security by an illusion of wealth.*

ALREADY, ALL READY. Both of these are correct, but each one has a different meaning. *Already* has the meaning of *beforehand* or *by now,* as *The merchandise has already arrived. All ready* has the meaning of *everything* or *everybody ready,* as *They are all ready.*

ALRIGHT, ALL RIGHT. There is no such word as the former; the latter is the correct spelling and should not be overworked in the sense of *very well.*

ALTAR, ALTER. The former is a noun and means *a shrine,* the latter is a verb and means *to change.*

ALTOGETHER, ALL TOGETHER. Both expressions are correct but have different meanings. The former means *wholly, totally;* the latter, *everybody* or *everything together.*

ALUMNUS, ALUMNI; ALUMNA, ALUMNAE. The first two are the masculine singular and plural forms respectively; the last two are the feminine singular and plural forms respectively.

AMONG, BETWEEN. The former is used of more than two persons, things, or groups, as, *You are among friends.* The latter is used where there are only two, as *This is between you and me.*

AND ETC. The *and* is unnecessary since *etc.* is the abbreviation of *et cetera* which means *and the rest.*

ANY. Do not use for *at all* as *He has not played any this game.* When comparing an object with another in the same class, use *any other:* "I like roast beef better than *any other* meat."

ANYHOW. Anyway is to be preferred as an adverb.

ANYPLACE, EVERY PLACE, NO PLACE, SOMEPLACE. These are colloquial expressions and should not be used for *anywhere, everywhere, nowhere,* and *somewhere.*

APT, LIABLE, LIKELY. Care should be exercised in the use of these words. *Apt* means *suitable; liable* implies *damage, danger, expense; likely* means *probable, suitable.*

Wrong: He is liable to go.

Right: He is likely to go.

Or: It is likely that he will go.

ANXIOUS, EAGER. While both words imply *interest,* the former carries the added implication of *worry,* as *He is anxious about your health;* but *He is eager to learn new things.*

APPROPRIATE. To appropriate means *to set apart for a special purpose.* Do not use *for take.*

AROUND. Do not use for *about* in the sense of *nearly.*

AS . . . AS, SO . . . AS. Use the latter in negative comparisons: "Jane is not *so* tall *as* Mary."

ASCENT, ASSENT. The former means *an upward slope, a climb;* the latter, *consent.*

AT. Vulgar in *Where do you work at? Where* means *at what place.*

AUTO. A colloquialism for automobile and should not be used in formal writing.

AWFUL, AWFULLY. Used only to express profound fear or reverence. Never use in the sense of *very.*

BAD, BADLY. The former is an adjective and is properly used with verbs relating to the senses of seeing, feeling, smelling, etc.; the latter is an adverb. Thus, *I feel bad,* means I feel ill; but as an adverb, *He limped badly.*

BALANCE. Do not use to indicate *remainder* except in a financial sense.

BEING AS, BEING THAT. Do not use for *since, because.*

BELONG TO BE. Do not use for *should be, ought to be.*

BESIDE, BESIDES. Modern usage confines the former to giving the idea of *by the side of* and the latter to *in addition to, moreover.*

BIANNUAL, BIENNIAL. The former means *twice a year;* the latter, *once in two years.*

BLAME IT ON. Do not use for *blame (some one) for.*

BOGUS. Slang. Say *counterfeit,* or *false.*

BOTH ALIKE. Omit *both, "They are alike."*

BRAINY. A colloquialism for *intelligent.*

BUNCH. Colloquial for *a group of people.*

BUSINESS. Do not use for *right,* as "He has no *right* (not *business*) to go there."

BUT THAT, BUT WHAT. *But that* means *except that:* "I have no doubt *that* I will go (not *but that*)." *But what* is a colloquialism for *that* or *but that.* Correctly used in a sentence such as "I will do nothing *but what* I want to do," since *but what* mean *except what.*

CALCULATE. Use only in a mathematical sense and not in the sense of *think* or *suppose.*

CAN, MAY. The former carries the idea of *ability;* the latter of *permission.*

CANNOT HELP BUT. Two idioms are confused, *can but* and *cannot help. Help* should be followed by a gerund: "He cannot help *liking* them."

CAN'T HARDLY. Do not use for *can hardly.*

CAN'T SEEM TO. Do not use for *seem not to* or *seem unable to.*

CAPACITY. Do not use for *ability.*

CAPITAL, CAPITOL. The former refers to the city, the latter to the building.

CASE. Commonly used indiscriminately in place of *instance, condition, situation, contingency,* etc. Better usage often dictates the choice of the more specific word.

CENSER, CENSOR, CENSURE. The first refers to a *vessel for burning incense,* the second refers to a person who approves or withholds, and the third to *condemnation.*

CHARACTERISTIC. Frequently used vaguely. It means *that which pertains to or indicates the character,* as "Dignity is one of the *characteristics* of a well-bred person."

CLAIM. Should not be used in the sense of *say, assert, maintain.* Its specific meaning is *to demand as a right* (usually in a legal sense).
Loose: He claims he saw it happen.
Better: He says that he saw it happen.

CLEVER. Commonly used for *agreeable, good-natured, witty.* Use the more specific word.

COINCIDENCE. Means *the occurring of two events at the same time.* Do not use of a single event.

COMMON, MUTUAL. The former means *belonging to two or more persons;* the latter means *reciprocal* or *interchangeable.* Do not confuse.

COMPLEMENT, COMPLIMENT. The former means *that which completes a thing* or *that which is complete;* the latter, *an expression of praise or delicate flattery.* Do not confuse.

COMPARE TO, WITH. Use the former to imply *rivaling,* the latter, and more formal expression, to liken two objects of real or supposed resemblance. Thus, one would say, *"Compared to* the sun the earth is small, but some of the other planets *compare* favorably in size *with* the sun."

CONSCIOUS, CONSCIENCE. Sometimes confused. The former means *aware;* the latter refers to moral sensibility. Thus, one may be *conscious* of the distinction between good and evil, but it is one's *conscience* that decides whether he shall do good or evil.

CONSIDERABLE. Sometimes incorrectly used for *considerably,* for *much,* or for *a great deal of.*

CONTINUAL, CONTINUOUS. Frequently confused. The former means *in rapid succession;* the latter, *without cessation.*

CONTRARY. Should not be used for *perverse.*

CONTRAST FROM. Incorrectly used for *contrast to* or *contrast with.*

CORRESPOND TO, WITH. The former means *to be in accord or harmony,* as "The part that I have *corresponds to* the part that you have. The latter means *to exchange* letters as "I *correspond* regularly *with* Mr. Jones."

CORPORAL, CORPOREAL. The former means *relating to the body as opposed to the mind;* the latter, *pertaining to matter or a material body.*

COULD OF. A vulgar corruption that should never be used for *could have.* This applies also to *had of, may of, might of, should of,* etc.

COUNCIL, COUNSEL, CONSUL. The first, *a deliberative body,* the second, *advice,* or *to give advice,* the third, *a commercial representative of a foreign government.*

COUPLE. Use only to indicate two persons or objects connected or linked in some way.

CREDIBLE, CREDITABLE. The former means *believable;* the latter, *praiseworthy.*

CROWD. Sanctioned by colloquial usage in the sense of a *social group* or *clique,* but should be avoided in formal writing.

CUNNING. Means *crafty, sly, designing.* Do not use for *attractive, pleasing.*

CURRANT, CURRENT. The former, *a berry;* the latter, *that which is passing.*

CUSTOM, HABIT. Communities, social groups, and institutions have customs, but individuals have habits. Thus, "It is the *custom* of this academy to make an annual award for outstanding research in chemistry"; but "I am in the *habit* of brushing my teeth twice daily."

DATA. The plural of *datum.* Say "data are."

DATE. Colloquially acceptable for an *appoint-*

ment or *social engagement*, but should not be used to indicate the person dated.

DEAL. A colloquialism for *transaction, bargain.*

DEFINITELY, DEFINITIVELY. The former means *precisely, with assurance;* the latter, *finally, conclusively, with exactness.*

DELIVER. It is better to say "He *gave* a lecture," "He *made* an oration."

DEMISE. Do not use for *death.* The word means *the passing of some authority, distinction, or privilege to another, perhaps by death*

DEPOT Means *warehouse, storage place.* May be used to indicate a freight warehouse but not a building for railway passengers. Say *station.*

DEPRECATORY, DEPRECIATORY. The former means *apologetic;* the latter, *tending to depreciate.* Do not confuse.

DETRACT, DISTRACT. The former means *to take away from;* the latter, *to bewilder, harass mentally.*

DIALECTAL, DIALECTICAL. The former means *characteristic of a dialect;* the latter, *pertaining to dialectics.*

DIE. Say *die of* not *die with.*
Wrong: He died with a heart attack.
Right: He died of a heart attack.

DIFFER FROM, WITH. Use the former to express *unlikeness*, as "These two objects *differ from* each other only in color." The latter indicates a *disagreement of opinion*, as "I *differ with* you on that point."

DISEASED, DECEASED. The former, *afflicted with a disease;* the latter, *dead.*

DISINTERESTED. Frequently misused for *uninterested. Distinterested* means *without self-interest; uninterested means lacking interest.*

DISTINCTLY, DISTINCTIVELY. The former means *plainly;* the latter, *in a way to distinguish one thing from another.*

DOESN'T, DON'T. The former is the contraction of *does not;* the latter is the contraction of *do not.* Say "*He doesn't*" not "*He don't*"; "*They don't,*" not "*They doesn't.*"

DONE. Never use for *did.* "He *did the work,*" not "He *done* the work."

DOUBT. This word is always followed by *whether* when uncertainty of choice is to be indicated, as "I doubt *whether* he did that." It is followed by *that* when a strong negative probability is to be expressed, as "I doubt *that* he did it."

DOVE. *Dived*, not *dove*, should be used as the past tense of *dive.*

DUAL, DUEL. The former, *composed of two;* the latter, *a combat between two persons.*

DUE TO. This is an adjective phrase and should not be used to modify a verb, as in, "I was late *due* to the heavy snow." Say, "I was late *because* of the heavy snow."

ECONOMIC, ECONOMICAL. The former refers to *the science of economics;* the latter to *saving, frugality.*

EACH OTHER, ONE ANOTHER. Use the former when referring to two; the latter when referring to more than two.

EFFICACY, EFFICIENCY. The former means *power to produce effects;* the latter, *dispatch with which such effects are produced.* Thus, "Because of their belief in the *efficacy* of prayer Roman legions always sought the blessings of the gods before entering a battle, but it was upon the superior discipline and general *efficiency* of their troops that the Romans relied for victory."

EITHER, BOTH, EACH. *Either* should be used only to indicate one or the other of two; *both* means *the one and the other, two together; each* refers to one of a number considered individually.

EGOISM, EGOTISM. These terms are alike in implying self-interest, but the latter suggests offensive exaltation of self.

ELEGANT. Means notable for *neatness, propriety,* and *refinement.* It should not be used for *good, enjoyable, pleasant.*

ELEMENT, FACTOR, PHASE. Frequently used vaguely. *Element* means *a constituent principle, essential part; factor* means *an agency that contributes to a result; phase* means *one stage in the development of a thing* or *one aspect of it.*

EMIGRATE, IMMIGRATE. The former means *to go out of a country or place;* the latter, *to go into a country or place.*

EMINENT, IMMANENT, IMMINENT. The first, *distinguished*, the second, *indwelling*, the third, *impending.*

ENTHUSE. A vulgarism for the phrases, *to become enthusiastic, to rouse enthusiasm*, etc.

EUPHEMISM, EUPHUISM. The former applies to a delicate word or expression substituted for an indelicate or offensive word or expression; the latter refers to an affected use of words or language.

EXPECT. Incorrectly used for *suppose, imagine, suspect.* It means *to look forward to.*
Wrong: I *expect* so.
Right: I *imagine* so.
Right: I *expect* to go to Florida in February.

EXTANT, EXTENT. The former means *not destroyed or lost;* the latter, *measure.*

EXTRA. Incorrectly used for *unusually.*
Wrong: This flour is ground *extra* fine.
Right: This flour is ground unusually fine.

FAKER, FAKIR. The former means *a swindler, one who fakes;* the latter, *a Mohammedan ascetic or mendicant priest.*

FARTHER, FURTHER. Use *farther* to indicate *greater distance or remoteness* and *further* to express *moreover, in addition to.*

FELLOW. Colloquial for *man, person, sweetheart.*

FEWER, LESS. In modern usage *fewer* is used with reference to *number; less* is used with reference to *quantity* or *degree.* Say "*fewer* people," not "*less* people."

FIRSTLY. Prefer *first* with reference to items in a series. *Secondly, thirdly*, etc., are acceptable but *second, third*, etc., are rapidly displacing the longer terms.

FIX. This word means *to make fast, secure, set or place firmly.* Do not use in the sense of *repair, mend.* The word is also used colloquially in the sense of *condition, predicament, situation.*
Colloq.: He is in a *bad fix.*

Better: He is in a *serious predicament.*

FOREGO, FORGO. The former means *to go before, precede;* the latter, *to abstain from.*

FORMER, LATTER. Used with reference to two (no more) persons or things previously mentioned.

FORMERLY, FORMALLY. The first means *at a former time;* the second, *in a formal manner.*

FUNNY. Means *laugh-provoking, droll, comical.* Do not use in the sense of *queer, odd, remarkable.*

GENTLEMAN, LADY. Use to describe only persons of good breeding.

GET. Do not use for *be, be able to, may, come, become.*

GOOD, WELL. *Good* is an adjective. Do not use as an adverb: "He plays the piano *well* (not *good*)."

GOT. Means *obtained, secured.* Unnecessary in the sense of having: "Have you a bicycle? (not *got*)." In the sense of *must* it is colloquial.

Colloq.: I *have got* to go.

Better: I *must* go.

GOTTEN. An older form of the past participle of *get.*

GUERRILLA, GORILLA. The former refers to *irregular warfare* or one who participates in it; the latter, *an ape.*

GUESS. Means *conjecture, hit upon at random.* Do not use in the sense of *think, suppose.*

HAD HAVE. A vulgarism for *had:* "I wish I *had* gone (not *had have*)."

HAD OUGHT. Never use in speech or writing.

Wrong: I *had ought* to do that.

Right: I *ought* to have done that.

Or: I *ought* to do that.

HEALTHY, HEALTHFUL. Frequently confused. *Healthy* means *possessed of health; healthful* means *health giving.* Thus, "He has a *healthy* appearance," but "This city has a *healthful* climate."

HEAP, HEAPS. Do not use for *much, a great deal, many.*

HONORABLE, REVEREND. Both should be written in full, preceded by *the* and followed by the full name: "The Honorable George Smith"; "The Reverend Thomas Matthews," but "The Reverend Mr. Matthews."

HOME, TO HOME. Say "He was not *at* home (not *home,* or *to home*)."

HOMEY. A provincialism for *homelike.*

HOW COME? A vulgarism for *why.*

HUNG. One form of the past tense of *hang.* When speaking of the death penalty use *hanged* in preference to *hung.*

HYPOCRITICAL, HYPERCRITICAL. The former means *deceitful;* the latter, *excessively critical.*

IF. *Whether* is preferred after verbs of *seeing, learning, doubting, asking,* etc.

Right: I doubt *if* I shall go.

Preferable: I doubt *whether* I shall go.

IN, INTO. *In* means *within; into* refers to the act of entering or motion toward, as "He was *in* the room," but "He walked *into* the room."

ILLEGIBLE, UNREADABLE. The former means *difficult to read;* the latter, *not suitable for reading.*

IN BACK OF. Do not use for *behind, at the back of.*

INCREDIBLE, INCREDULOUS. The former has the meaning of *unbelievable;* the latter, *skeptical.*

INDICT, INDITE. The first means *charge with a crime;* the second, *to write.*

INFER, IMPLY. Frequently confused. *Infer* means *to derive by induction or deduction; imply* means *to express indirectly, insinuate.*

INFERIOR. Say *inferior to* and not *inferior than.*

INGENIOUS, INGENUOUS. The former means *having skill, intelligent;* the latter, *frank, candid,* or (sometimes) *naive.*

INSIDE OF. The *of* is unnecessary.

INTERSTATE, INTRASTATE. The former means *between states;* the latter, *within a state.*

INVITE. This is a verb and should never be used as a noun.

IT'S, ITS. The former is the contraction of *it is;* the latter expresses possession.

KIND OF A, SORT OF A. Omit *a. Kind of, sort of* is also used colloquially in the sense of *rather, somewhat, somehow.*

Colloq.: His wit is *sort of* dull.

Preferable: Hit wit is *rather* dull.

LAST, LATEST. Use *last* to indicate *definite finality* and *latest* to indicate *most recent but not necessarily final.*

LATER, LATTER. The former means *after something else in point of time;* the latter means *the second of two things previously mentioned.*

LAUNDERED. Not *laundried.*

LAY, LIE. *Lie* is an intransitive verb and means *to recline; lay* is a transitive verb and means *to put down.* The principal parts of these verbs are:

lie lay lain.

lay laid laid.

Right: *Lie* down and rest a bit.

Right: *Lay* the book on the table.

LEAVE, LET. Do not use *leave* for *let* as in the sentence "*Let* (not *leave*) them go."

LIKE, AS. *Like* should not introduce a subject and verb. Say "He acted *as if* (not *like*) he had never heard of the subject."

LIKE TO HAVE. Do not use in the sense of *almost, come near to.*

LOAN. Except when referring to a financial transaction do not use as a verb: "*Lend* (not *loan*) me the book."

LUXURIANT, LUXURIOUS. The former means *superabundant in growth, profuse;* the latter, *costly indulgence in pleasures of the senses.*

LOSE, LOOSE. Frequently confused. *Lose* means *cease to have in possession; loose* means *not tight, to release.*

LOSE OUT, WIN OUT. Used in sports columns of newspapers, but should be avoided in all other writing.

LOT, LOTS OF. Do not use for *many* or *much.*

LOVELY. Has the meaning of *inspiring with love, lovable,* and should not be used loosely in the sense of *pleasant, delightful, interesting,* etc.

MAD. Frequently misused for *angry.* The word means *insane.*

MAGNIFICENT. Overworked as a substitute for *excellent, good,* etc.

MATTER. Used vaguely for *subject, question,*

trouble, request. Choose the more specific word.

MAY BE, MAYBE. The former is a verb; the latter, an adverb, meaning *perhaps.*

MEAN. Do not use for *irritable, vicious, ill-tempered, unkind.*

MIGHT OF. A vulgar corruption of *might have.*

MESSRS., MISS, MR., MRS. These titles should never be used alone but must always be followed by the surname.

MIGHTY. Do not use in the sense of *very.*

MOST, ALMOST. Do not use the former, which is the superlative of *much* or *many,* for the latter which is an adverb. "We went there *almost* (not *most*) every day."

NICE. Means *fastidious, precise, delicate.* Do not use for *pleasant, kind, admirable.*

NOHOW. A vulgarism. Say *anyhow, by no means.*

NOT A ONE. A colloquialism for *no one, not one.*

NOWHERE NEAR. Prefer *not nearly.*

NOWHERES. Preferable without the *s.*

OFF OF, OFF FROM. The *of* and *from* are superfluous.

OBSERVANCE, OBSERVATION. The former means *performance of rites;* the latter, *the act of observing.*

ON. Superfluous in such expressions as *continue on, later on,* etc.

OR. Should not be used with *neither.* Use *nor.*

ORAL, VERBAL. *Oral* means *by mouth;* verbal means *by word.*

ORDNANCE, ORDINANCE. The first means *artillery;* the second, *law* or *statute.*

OUT. Superfluous in such expressions as *lose out, win out,* etc.

OUT LOUD. Do not use for *aloud.*

OUTSIDE OF. Do not use for *except* or *aside from.*

OVER WITH. The *with* is superfluous
Wrong: The contest is *over with.*
Right: The contest is *over.*

PAIR, SET. These are singulars, not plurals.
Right: One *pair* of shoes.
Wrong: Two *pair* of shoes.
Right: Two *pairs* of shoes.

PARTY, PERSON, INDIVIDUAL. *Party* refers to a group and, except in a purely legal sense, should never be used to designate a single person. *Individual* refers to a particular being. In all other cases use *person, man, woman,* etc.

PECUNIARY, FINANCIAL. The former refers to money; the latter, to scientific management of monetary affairs.

PEEVE. Do not use for *annoy, vex,* or *irritate.* The word means *to make resentful.*

PER CENT, PERCENTAGE. The former should be used only after a numeral. The latter, a noun, should be used to indicate a specified quantity.

PERSECUTE, PROSECUTE. The first means *to harass vengefully;* the second, *bring suit against at law.*

PHENOMENA. The plural of *phenomenon.* Do not use for *events, facts, occurrences.*

PHENOMENAL. Do not use for *remarkable.*

PHONE. Colloquial for *telephone.* Should be avoided.

PIECE. Do not use in the sense of *distance* as "He lives up the road *a piece.*"

PLAN ON GOING. Say *plan to go.*

POORLY. Do not use for *ill.*

PRACTICAL, PRACTICABLE. The former means *useful;* the latter, *feasible, possible.*

PRINCIPAL, PRINCIPLE. The former means *occupying first place or rank;* the latter, *fundamental truth or law.*

PROPHECY, PROPHESY. The former means *a prediction;* the latter, *to predict.*

PROPOSE, PURPOSE. The former means *to bring forward* or *offer for consideration;* the latter, *design, end, to have an intention.*

PROPOSAL, PROPOSITION. The former refers to *that which is brought forward for consideration;* the latter, *to an offer of terms.*

PROVEN. Use *proved* as the past participle of *prove.*

PUT IN, PUT OVER, PUT ACROSS. Colloquial expressions, the first having the meaning of *devote, spend;* the last two, the meaning to *succeed despite opposition.* These colloquialisms should be avoided.

QUALITY. Frequently used vaguely. The word means *attribute, peculiar power or property.*

QUITE. Do not use in the sense of *almost.* The word means *wholly, completely.*

QUITE A FEW. Colloquial for *a good many.*
Colloq.: He has *quite a few* friends.
Preferred: He has *a good many* friends.

RAISE, RISE. The former is a transitive verb and means *to cause to rise;* the latter is an intransitive verb and means *to ascend.* The principal parts of these verbs are:
raise raised raised.
rise rose risen.
Right: I *raise* the window.
Right: I *rise* at six o'clock.
Raise in the sense of *to rear, to bring up children* is a colloquialism, and should be avoided.

RARELY EVER. Use *rarely* alone or *hardly ever.*

REACTION. Do not use for *response, opinion, attitude.*

REAL. Do not use for *very.*

REASON IS BECAUSE. Use *that* instead of *because.*

RECKON. Means to *compute, count.* Do not use for *think, suppose.*

REMEMBER OF. *Of* is superfluous.

REPEAT AGAIN. *Again* is superfluous.

RESEARCH. Means *investigation.* Do not say *"research* work."

RESPECTFULLY, RESPECTIVELY. The former means *with respect;* the latter refers to a particular person or thing.

RIGHT. Colloquial Southern usage for *very. Right along, right away, right off* are colloquial for *continuously, immediately, at once.*

ROUT, ROUTE. The first means *put to flight, scoop out;* the second, *to send by a certain way.*

RUN. Do not use in the sense of *conduct, amount to.*
Wrong: He *runs* a men's shop.
Right: He *operates* a men's shop.
Wrong: What's the bill *run to?*
Right: How much does the bill *amount to?*

SAME, SAID, SUCH. Avoid the use of these words as pronouns. Prefer *it, this, that.*

SATISFIED. Do not use in the sense of *convinced, sure.*

SCARCELY. Never follow with *than* or a negative.

SELF-CONFESS. The word *self* is superfluous. Obviously our misdeeds cannot be confessed by another.

SENSUOUS, SENSUAL. The first means *appealing to the senses;* the second, *pertaining to the grosser senses.*

SET, SIT. The former is a transitive verb and means *to place* or *put in position;* the latter is an intransitive verb and refers to the act of being in a sitting position. The principal parts of these verbs are:

set set set.
sit sat sat.

Right: The maid *set* the table.
Right: I *sat* in the balcony.

SEVERAL. Means *more than two* but not *many.*

SELDOM EVER. Say *seldom if ever, seldom or never.*

SHAPE. Do not use for *condition, state, manner.*

SHALL, WILL. To express simple futurity use *shall* for the first person and *will* for the second or third. To express determination or promise use *will* for the first person and *shall* for the second or third.

SHOULD OF. A vulgar corruption of *should have.*

SHOW. Do not use for *opportunity.* Also a colloquialism for a *movie, drama, performance,* etc.

SICK, ILL. The former connotes *nausea.* Use the latter except in this sense.

SIGHT. Do not use for *much, a great many.*

SIMPLY. Means *in a simple manner.* Do not use for *really, very.*

SIZE UP. Slang for *estimate.*

SMART. Do not use for *intelligent.*

SOME. Do not use as an adverb. Say *somewhat.*

SOMEWAY. Prefer *somehow.*

SPECIE, SPECIES. The former refers to money; the latter means *kind* or *class* and is both singular and plural.

STATIONARY, STATIONERY. Frequently confused. The former means *fixed, not moving;* the latter refers to writing materials and their accessories.

Right: The star Polaris is *stationary.*
Right: We buy our letterheads at the *stationery* shop.

STATUE, STATURE, STATUTE. A *statue* is a *sculptured figure; stature* means *height; statute* means *law.*

STOP. Use *stay:* "Where did you *stay* (not *stop*) in Philadelphia?"

STRATA. Plural of *stratum* and should be used only with plural form of the verb.

SUPERIOR THAN. Say *superior to.*

SUPERIOR, BETTER. Do not confuse. The former means *higher or above in place, rank, excellence,* etc.; the latter, *having good qualities in greater degree.*

SURE AND, TRY AND. Say *sure to, try to.*

SURVIVE. Do not use for *live,* or *persist.*

SUSPICION. This is a noun and should never be used as a verb.

Wrong: I *suspicion* him of the theft.
Right: I suspect him of the theft.
Or: I place him under *suspicion* of theft.

TASTE OF. *Of* is superfluous in such expressions as "She tasted of it."

TASTY. Colloquial for *agreeable, attractive, of good taste, palatable.*

TERMED AS. *As* is superfluous.

TERRIBLE, TERRIBLY. These words imply *fear, awe, terror.* Do not use for *extremely, very.*

THAT WAY. Say *in that way:* "You must do it *in that way.*"

THIS HERE, THAT THERE, THESE HERE, THOSE THERE. The usage of *here* and *there* with these demonstratives is vulgar.

Vulgar: *This here* book is good.
Right: *This* book is good.
Vulgar: *That there* boy.
Right: *That* boy.

THROUGH. In the sense of *finished* it should be avoided.

Wrong: He is *through* with his music practice for today.
Right: He has *finished* his music practice for today.

TO MY KNOWLEDGE. Do not use for *in my opinion.*

TRANSPIRE. Means *to become known.* Do not use for *happen, occur.*

TWO FIRST, TWO LAST. Illogical expressions. Say first two, last two.

TYPE. Overworked for *kind, sort, variety.*

UGLY. Means *offensive to the eye.* Do not use for *ill-tempered, vicious.*

UMPIRE, EMPIRE. The first means *an arbiter;* the second, *a realm governed by an emperor.*

UNIQUE. Means *sole, unequaled.* Do not use for *odd, rare, unusual.*

UNMORAL, IMMORAL. *Unmoral* means *not involving morality; immoral* means *not moral.*

UP. Do not use with *divide, end, finish, fold, open, rest, settle, or write.* Correctly used with *dig, double, lay, plow, wake, hang,* etc.

UP-TO-DATE. Correct as an adverb. Prefer *modern* as an adjective.

VENAL, VENIAL. The former means *mercenary;* the latter, *pardonable.*

VOCATION, AVOCATION. The first means *preferred for a profession or calling;* the second, *preferred for a secondary interest.*

VULGAR. Do not use for *immodest,* or *indecent.* The word means both *common* and *unrefined* but has no relation to indecency.

WAIT ON. Means *to serve.* Do not use for *wait for.*

WAYS. Say *way:* "He lives a short *way* up the road."

WEIRD. Means *uncanny.* Do not use for *odd, strange.*

WHERE. Do not use for *that:* "I saw in the evening paper *that* you were chosen."

WHICH. Use *who* or *that* when referring to persons, *which* when referring to animals or inanimate objects.

WHIP. The word means *to beat with a whip.* Do not use for *chastise,* or *defeat.*

WHOSE. This is the possessive case of *who*, not of *which*.
WILL, SHALL. See SHALL, WILL.
WIRE. A colloquialism for *telegraph*, *telegram*.
WITHOUT. Do not use for *unless*.
WOODS. Say *a wood*.
WORST KIND, SORT, WAY. Do not use for *very much*.
WOULD BETTER. Prefer *had better*.
WOULD OF. A vulgar corruption of *would have*.
WOULD RATHER. Say *had rather*.
WRITE UP. Slang for a *report, description, account*.
WRITER, THE WRITER. Affectation for *I*.
YOU WAS. Say *you were*.

Representation of Numbers

1. Spell out every number of less than three digits when used in ordinary text matter.

The price was two dollars.
There were eighty-two boys and eighteen girls.

2. Where similar numbers occur in groups, do not use figures for some and spell out others. If the largest contains three or more digits, use figures for all.

The number of bushels produced during June, July, and August was 42, 89, and 127 respectively.

3. Use figures to express dimensions, degrees, distances, weights, measures, sums of money, etc., in mathematical or statistical text.

92 pounds	22 miles
45 caliber	16 feet
$1,000	32°F

4. Compound numerals of less than one hundred should be hyphenated.

eighty-four but fifteen hundred

5. Spell out round numbers of even units (100, 1,000, 10,000, etc.).

There were about five hundred present.
There were 550 present.

6. Do not begin a sentence with figures, even if similar figures are used elsewhere.

Two hundred and eighteen ships, 417 flags, and 86 uniforms.

7. Spell out numbers representing the time of day except when used with A.M., or P.M.

He left at eight.
The race starts at half-past two.
At 4:00 P.M. (omit *o'clock*).

8. Spell out the age of persons, places, or things.

She was twenty-six years old.
This vase is one hundred and fifty-six years old.
Chicago is more than one hundred years old.

9. Do not use *st, nd, rd, th* with the day of the month.

January 15, 1935 not January 15th, 1935.

Diction

Diction is the choice of words for the accurate, effective, and varied expression of thought and feeling in speech and writing.

While accepted usage varies from occasion to occasion, from one class of people to another, and according to differences in locality, yet logic and good taste demand the observance and practice of certain standards of good usage in formal writing and speech.

The following rules and suggestions were formulated in accordance with these standards:

1. Do not use *archaic* or *obsolete* words.

Archaic words are those peculiar to remote periods of time such as *thou* for *you*, *forsooth* for *indeed*, etc.
Obsolete words are those which have completely gone out of use. Most authorities do not condemn as obsolete any word used in a major literary work written since the Restoration (1660).

2. Do not use *provincialisms* in formal speech or writing. Such expressions, however, are permissible in conversation or informal writing.

Provincialisms are words or expressions current in one section of a country but unknown or not used in the same sense elsewhere.
Examples: *Varmint* for *vermin*, *cayuse* for *horse*, *calculate* for *think*, *plumb* for *completely*.

3. Never use *vulgarisms*.

Vulgarisms are words or expressions characteristic of illiteracy.
Examples: *Them flowers, where does he live at, to enthuse.*

4. Avoid *improprieties*.

Improprieties are words or expressions correct in themselves but used either in an incorrect sense or in an incorrect function.

5. Do not use *colloquialisms* in formal speech or writing.

Colloquialisms are words or expressions permissible in ordinary conversation or writing but not used in formal speech or writing.
Examples: *Taxi, isn't, pal, backbone* for *taxicab, is not, friend, courage*.

6. Guard against affected or flowery language, too rigid adherence to bookish correctness, and a straining for accuracy which sometimes causes awkwardness.

7. Guard against *redundancy* and *tautology*.

Redundancy is the use of grammatically superfluous words or phrases.
Example: Come down off of the fence.
Tautology is the repetition of synonymous words or expressions. in close succession.
Example: The day dawned clear and bright, *without a cloud in the sky.*

8. *Idiomatic* words and expressions are accepted as good form.

An idiomatic word or expression is one which is peculiar to a language and sanctioned by long usage, although sometimes in violation of the rules of grammar.

Examples: *Plan to go, at home, different from, as regards.*

9. Use words that express the exact thought or feeling you wish to convey.

In addition to their literal meaning *(denotation)* many words are possessed of color, atmosphere, and tone, all of which give to them fine shades of meaning and powers of suggestion (*connotation)* beyond those of other words having the same literal definition.

Consult your dictionary for the literal meaning of the word you wish to use. If the meaning of that particular word does not completely express your thought, or if it is weak, trite, or overworked, look it up in your thesaurus and choose from its synonyms the one most suitable to your subject, the occasion, reader, or auditor.

10. Choose words having easy and pleasant combinations of sounds.

The following suggestions will be found helpful: (a) avoid placing in close succession words that rhyme; (b) avoid the use of a too regular meter (singsong effect); (c) avoid like sounds in close succession, especially sibilants.

Remember, finally, that the monotonous repetition of certain words and phrases, the habitual use of slang, and deliberate smartness in writing or speaking are usually indicative of a lazy mind!

Every effort made toward better diction will aid mental alertness, outline ideas more sharply, and freshen and strengthen the powers of expression—all of which makes utilization of one's intelligence a keen delight.

Spelling

Misspelling is often due to mispronunciation. Learn carefully how to pronounce words and, generally speaking, the correct spelling of them will be easy.

Never write a word of which you are not certain of the spelling. Use your dictionary constantly.

General Spelling Rules

The following rules are intended to provide a general guide to correct spelling and, though there are exceptions to them, they will be found adequate in most cases.

Suffixes

A suffix is a letter or a syllable added at the end of a word to serve a derivative, formative, or inflectional function.

1. Words of one syllable and those accented on the last syllable if ending in one consonant preceded by one vowel, generally double the consonant when a suffix beginning with a vowel is added.

mad madder
prefer preferred

When the accent is given to a syllable other than the last, the doubling does not occur.

visit visited

When the addition of a suffix causes a shifting of the accent to a syllable other than the last, the consonant is not doubled.

prefer preference

2. In words ending with silent *e*, drop the *e* when adding a suffix beginning with a vowel.

glide gliding

When adding a suffix beginning with *a* or *o* to words ending in *ce* or *ge* retain the *e* to preserve the soft sound of the *c* or *g*.

service serviceable
courage courageous

3. In spelling words containing *ei* or *ie* remember the jingle:

Write *i* before *e*
Except after c
Or when sounded as *a*
As in *neighbor* and *weigh*.

relieve freight receive

4. When adding a suffix to a word ending in *y* preceded by a consonant, change the *y* to *i*.

lazy laziness

Verbs ending in *y* retain it when *ing* is added.

play playing

The rule for changing *y* to *i* also applies to the forming of plurals except when the *y* is preceded by a vowel.

fly flies
play plays

Prefixes

A prefix is a letter or syllable placed at the beginning of a word to modify its significance.

1. Words beginning with a consonant do not double that consonant when a prefix ending in a vowel is attached.

proficient not profficient

2. When a prefix ending with a consonant is added to a word beginning with a vowel, the consonant is not doubled.

disappoint not dissappoint

3. Prefixes ending with a consonant retain it when followed by a word beginning with a consonant.

addition not adition

Plurals

1. Nouns which do not end in *s* or *es* form their plurals by adding *s*.

bees cows
trains bricks

2. Nouns ending with a sibilant *(s, sh, x, z)* form their plurals by adding *es*.

dresses taxes
fishes blazes

3. Nouns ending with *y* preceded by a consonant form their plurals by changing the *y* to *i* and adding *es.*

armies studies
factories follies

4. Nouns ending with *y* preceded by a vowel form their plurals by retaining the *y* and adding *s.*

plays jays
donkeys keys

5. Nouns ending in *o* preceded by a vowel form their plurals by adding *s.*

portfolios cameos
radios folios

6. Nouns ending with *o* preceded by a consonant add *s* or *es* to form the plural.

potatoes dynamos
Negroes solos

7. The following are examples of surviving Old English irregular plurals:

geese swine
oxen sheep

8. Foreign words commonly used in the English language usually form their plurals in accordance with the language from which they were borrowed. The present tendency, however, is to anglicize the pronunciation of the plural of such words.

alumna (feminine)
alumnae (pronounced a-lum'ne)
alumnus (masculine)
alumni (pronounced a-lum'ni)
basis
bases (pronounced ba'ses)
focus
foci (pronounced fo'si)

9. Compound nouns usually form their plurals by adding *s* or *es* to the governing word in the compound.

runners-up
daughters-in-law
courts-martial

If the compounded words are so closely associated as to form one word, the *s* or *es* is added to the end of the word.

bucketfuls
spoonfuls
basketfuls

COMPOUND WORDS

1. Adjectives formed of two or more words and preceding the noun which they modify should be hyphenated.

well-known author half-dead victim

Adjectives or adverbs in combined form should *not* be hyphenated when used *after* the word modified.

The new encyclopedia is strictly up to date.

2. When such words as *book, house, mill,* etc., are prefixed by a noun of one syllable, they form one word.

textbook sawmill
smokehouse

When the prefixed noun contains two syllables, use the hyphen.

sample-book lumber-mill
power-house

When the prefixed noun contains three or more syllables the two words are written separately.

policy book chocolate mill
business house

3. Compound numerals of less than a hundred and more than twenty, when used as adjectives, should be hyphenated.

forty-seven twenty-five
thirty-nine

When fractions are used as nouns, however, the hyphen is not used.

One sixth of the cotton was burned.

4. Words to which prefixes are attached are hyphenated only when such words begin with *w, y,* or the same vowel in which the prefix ends.

coeducation intra-yearly
co-operation tri-weekly
anti-idealist pro-oceanic

5. Compound words retain the hyphen when absence of it might cause difficulty in reading or interpretation.

re-creation recreation
twenty five-dollar bills twenty-five dollar bills

6. The following words and phrases are written separately:

all right good night
any one some one
any time some day
by and by some way
every one per cent

SHORTHAND AND TYPING

The modern business concern desires its office workers to be versatile, and frequently encourages versatility by shifting individuals from one kind of work to another, thus making it easier to handle emergency situations and also preparing the individual worker for promotion. A good working knowledge of shorthand and typing is always a valuable asset, even in a position which does not directly involve secretarial or stenographic duties. It cannot be too strongly emphasized, therefore, that the time taken in learning shorthand and typing is well spent and will repay the student many times over. Even a little knowledge of the fundamentals is better than none at all.

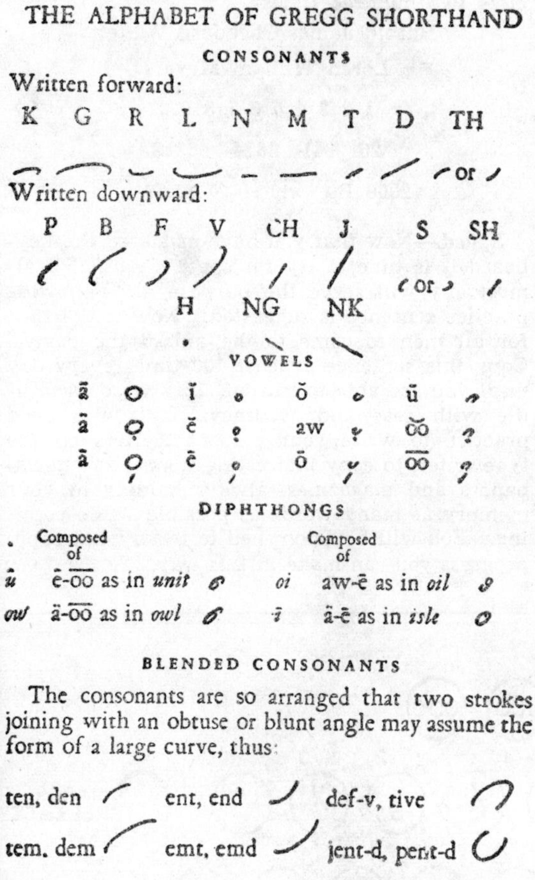

THE ALPHABET OF GREGG SHORTHAND

CONSONANTS

Written forward:

K G R L N M T D TH (or)

Written downward:

P B F V CH J S (or) SH

H NG NK

VOWELS

ă	ĭ	ŏ	ŭ
ä	ĕ	aw	ŏŏ
ā	ē	ō	ōō

DIPHTHONGS

	Composed of		Composed of
ū	ē-ōō as in *unit*	oi	aw-ē as in *oil*
ow	ä-ōō as in *owl*	ī	ä-ē as in *isle*

BLENDED CONSONANTS

The consonants are so arranged that two strokes joining with an obtuse or blunt angle may assume the form of a large curve, thus:

ten, den — ent, end — def-v, tive

tem, dem — emt, emd — jent-d, pent-d

Without knowing it, most office workers make use of a kind of simplified shorthand. That is, they learn to use abbreviations in noting down memorandums and making outlines for their own personal use. A few letters are made to stand for a word, and unessential words are eliminated. Shorthand carries this process a great deal further, by using an alphabet of marks, in which curving lines stand for syllables and words, and in which the particular curve and slant of each line and the position of each dot has a meaning. The accompanying illustration shows the characteristic shorthand alphabet. It is included through the courtesy of the Gregg Publishing Company. It is beyond the scope of this section to attempt a course of instruction on the subject of shorthand; that belongs to the schools and colleges of business.

Typing

With typing the situation is somewhat different. Today the typewriter has become an instrument of general use, neither confined to the office, nor requiring a highly skilled operator. This is because it is fairly easy for anyone to attain moderate proficiency in handling the machine. Of course, very speedy, accurate typing can only be accomplished by use of the "touch" system, which requires a rather long period of instruction. But very speedy typing is usually needed only for copy work. The demands of the average person are satisfied if he learns to type with sufficient speed to keep up with the words and sentences formulated in his mind. This is generally not difficult.

It is possible to attain a satisfactory degree of efficiency on the typewriter by the "sight" system without losing the time or going to the expense of mastering the elaborate touch system. In fact, any intelligent person in a few weeks can acquire such skill as would require many months by the touch system. With a typewriter in every office and in many homes, there is a real need for the simple exercises included in the following paragraphs. Sight typewriting is the system universally used by so-called one finger artists. In our system, however, we recommend right from the beginning the use of two fingers, the first and second on each hand. Later on as your skill increases you may bring into use the third and fourth digits.

The keyboards of all standard typewriters are identical and when you have mastered one you have mastered all. All keys to the right-hand side of the keyboard are struck with either the first or second finger of the right hand; all the keys to the left-hand side of the keyboard with the first and second fingers of the left hand. The space bar should always be operated with the thumb, and the shift keys, back spacer or tabulating keys with the little fingers, thus leaving the first two fingers free for the actual typing.

Exercise 1.—Fill one whole page with the word "them."

"t" is struck with the first finger of the left hand.

"h" is struck with the first finger of the right hand.

"e" is struck with the second finger of the left hand.

"m" is struck with the first finger of the right hand.

This exercise is put here for two reasons. In the first place the first three letters, "the" are used more than any other word in the English language. Secondly, it will introduce that important principle of typewriting, the alternate hand movement.

Exercise 2.—Copy each of the following words 300 times: then, these, theme, there, those, think.

This exercise introduces the principle of using one finger to strike two or three times in succession (se and ese).

Exercise 3.—Copy "they" three hundred times, and "that" three hundred times. Then fill up an entire page with the words, "they think that," and another whole page with the words "they think that those think." Be sure to strike the space bar with the thumb after each word.

Exercise 4.—Write the first three letters of the alphabet "a b c" one hundred times. Then add the next letter "a b c d" and write the combination 100 times. Keep adding one letter in this manner until you have written the entire alphabet one hundred times. This exercise will definitely locate in your mind every letter on the keyboard.

Exercise 5.—The following sentence contains all the letters of the alphabet:

"The big brown fox jumped quickly over the lazy dog."

Write the first word 100 times, the first two words 100 times, the first three words 100 times and so on until you have written the whole sentence 100 times.

Exercise 6.—Here is another sentence that contains every letter of the alphabet:

"Wafting zephyrs quickly vexed Jumbo."

Copy this sentence the same as in exercise 5.

Capitals, Figures, Punctuation Marks, and Symbols.—Capital letters are made by pushing down the shift key with the little finger and then striking the letter required with one of the other fingers. The standard keyboard provides a special row of keys for all the figures except 1, which is formed by the small "l" or by the capital 'I'. Punctuation marks and symbols, with the exception of commas and periods, are also made on most machines by depressing the shift key. Care must be used to release the shift key before striking the next letter.

Exercise 7.—Copy each of the following exercises two hundred times:

Harold James Theodore Walter

Loren William Meyers

1 2 3 4 5 6 7 8 9 0

26 341 8674 95216

2000 Bu. wheat @ $1.57⅜

Speed.—Now that you have mastered the keyboard it is time to try for speed. Although almost any will serve the purpose, the following practice sentence is suggested: "Now is the time for all men to come to the aid of the party." Copy this sentence at least 100 times every day until you are able to run off sixty words a minute with ease and accuracy. It is also good practice to write your personal letters on the typewriter, to copy interesting items from newspapers and magazines, always holding in your memory as many words as possible while copying. You will be astonished to learn what rapid progress you can make in this way.

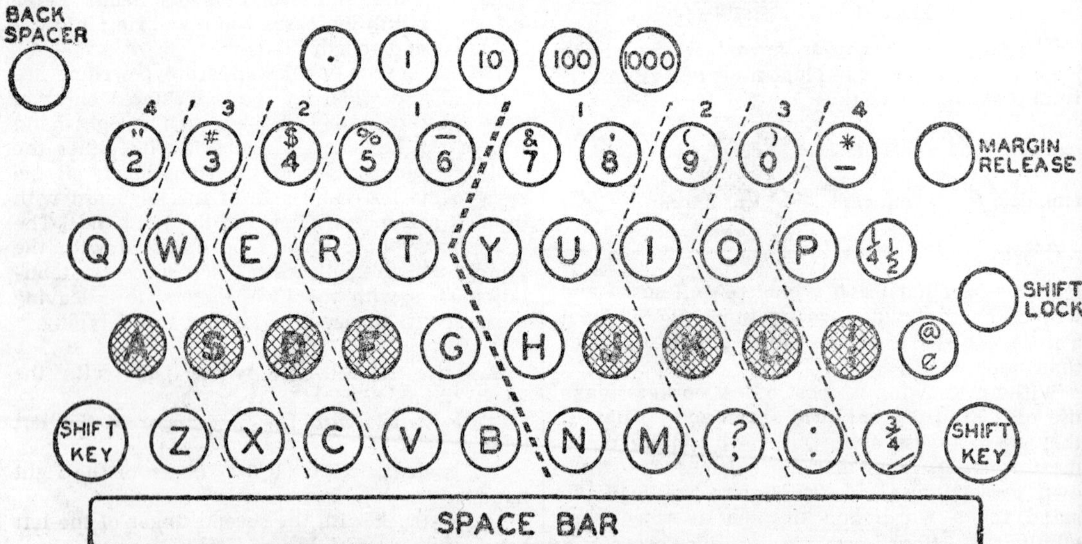

STANDARD TYPEWRITER KEYBOARD

ABBREVIATIONS

Discrimination must be exercised in the use of abbreviations. Under normal circumstances do not abbreviate a word if the abbreviated form is difficult or puzzling to read. The following rules will be found to govern all ordinary cases.

1. Capitalize an abbreviation only if the unabbreviated word would be capitalized.

2. Titles preceding personal names should be spelled out except the following:
   (a) Mr., Messrs., Mrs. before a name
   (b) Esq., Sr., Jr., after a name
   (c) Rev. and Hon., except in formal invitations and announcements when they are spelled out and preceded by *The*
      The Reverend Elwood Harbridge
      The Honorable Martin Franklin

3. Christian names should be spelled out except where they are abbreviated in a signature or from the author's choice.
   George C. Armstrong
   Geo. C. Armstrong

4. Do not abbreviate parts of geographic names except in tabular matter where space will not permit full spelling. In such cases it is permissible to abbreviate the first part of such names.
   Port Arthur
   Pt. Arthur

Note: *Saint* or *Saints* are always abbreviated when used before a name:
   St. Joseph
   St. Mary's Church
   SS. Peter and Paul

5. Abbreviate designations of weights and measures and symbols of measurements when these are preceded by a number.

3 yds.	6 gals.
4 hrs.	10 min.

Common Abbreviations

A

A, Angstrom units.
A., answer; academy; amateur.
a., about; acre; afternoon.
AA, antiaircraft.
A.A.A., Amateur Athletic Association; American Automobile Association.
A.&M., Agricultural and Mechanical.
A.A.O.N.M.S, Ancient Arabic Order of Nobles of the Mystic Shrine.
A.A.S., Academiae Americanae Socius (L., Fellow of the American Academy).
A.A.S.S., Americanae Antiquarianae Societatis Socius (L., Fellow of the American Antiquarian Society).
A.A.U., Amateur Athletic Union.
A.A.U.W., American Association of University Women.
A.B., Bachelor of Arts.
a.b., able-bodied seaman.
abb., abbess; abbey; abbot.
abbr., abbreviated; -tion.
ABC American Broadcasting Company.
Abp., Archbishop.
abr., abridged; -ment.
abs., absol., absolute.
abs., abstr., abstract.
a.c., ac, alternating current.
a/c, account; account current.
acc., acceptance; according; account; accusative.
A.C.S., American College of Surgeons.
act., active.
A.D., Anno Domini.
ad., adverb; advertisement.
A.D.S., American Dental Society.
ad inf., ad infinitum (L., to infinity).
adj., adjective; adjourned.
Adjt., adjutant.
ad lib., ad libitum (L., at pleasure).
Adm., Admiral; -ty; administrator.
adv., advent; adverb; advertisement; advice; advocate.
advt., advertisement.
A.E.F., American Expeditionary Forces.
AF, A.F., a.f., audio-frequency.
aff., affectionate; affirmative.
afft., affadavit.
A F of L, American Federation of Labor.
agcy., agency.
agr., agric., agriculture; -al.
agt., agent; agreement.
a-h., a.h., ampere-hour.
A.H.M.S., American Home Missionary Society.
A.I.A., American Institute of Architects.
A.I.C., American Institute of Chemists.
A.L.A., American Library Association.
alc, alcohol.
alg., algebra.
alt., alternate; -ion; altitude; alto.
Am., America; American.
A.M., Artium Magister (L., Master of Arts).
A.M., am., ante meridiem.
A.M.A., American Medical Association; American Missionary Association.
Amb., Ambassador.
A.M.E., African Methodist Episcopal.
Amer., America; American.
amp., ampere; amperage.
amt., amount.
anal., analogy; analysis.
anat., anatomical; -y.
anc., ancient; -ly.
ann., annual; annuity.
anon., anonymous.
ans., answer; -ed.
ant., antonym.
anthrop., anthropol., anthropology; -ical.
A.O.S.S., Americanae Orientalis Societatis Socius (L., Member of the American Oriental Society).
Ap., Apostle.
AP, Associated Press.
Apoc., Apocalypse; Apocrypha.
app., apparatus; appended; appendix; appointed.
appar., apparent; -ly.
approx., approximate; -ly.
Apr., April.
A.P.S., American Philatelic Society; American Physical Society.
aq., water.
A.R.A., American Railway Association.
A.R.C., ARC, American Red Cross.
arch., archaic; archery; archipelago; architecture.
archaeol., archaeology.
arith., arithmetic.
arm., armature.
arr., arrange; arrive.
art., article; artificial; artillery; artist.
A.R.V., American Standard Revised Version (Bible).
AS, A.-S., A.S., Anglo-Saxon.
A.S., Academy of Science; Air Service, Assistant Secretary.
A.S.A., American Statistical Association.
Assn., Association.
assoc., associate; -ion.
Asst., Assistant.
A.S.S.U., American Sunday School Union.
astrol., astrologer; -ical; -y.
astron., astronomer; -ical; -y.
asym., asymm., asymmetric.
at., atomic.
athl., athletics.
atm., atmosphere.
at, no.. atomic number.
att., atty., attorney.
Atty. Gen., Attorney General.
at. vol., atomic volume.
at. wt., atomic weight.
aud., auditor.
Aug., August.
auth., authentic; author; -ized.

Auth. Ver., A.V., Authorized Version.
auto., automatic; automotive.
aux., auxil., auxiliary.
a.v., A/V, ad valorum.
avdp., avoirdupois.
ave., avenue.
avg., average.
A.W.O.L., Absent Without Leave

B

B., Bible; British.
b., bachelor; bass; battery; book; born, brother.
B.A., Baccalaureus Artium (L., Bachelor of Arts); British Academy.
bact., bacteriology.
bal., balance.
bank., banking.
Bap., Bapt., Baptist.
bap., bapt., baptized.
Bar., Baruch.
bar., barometer; -ric; barrel.
barr., barrister.
Bart., Baronet.
bat., batt., battalion; battery.
BB, Bureau of the Budget.
BBC, British Broadcasting Corporation.
bbl., barrel; barrels.
B.C., Before Christ.
bd., band; board; bond; bound.
bd. ft., board foot.
B.E., Bank of England; Board of Education.
b.e., bill of exchange.
B.E.F., British Expeditionary Forces.
Bess., Bessemer.
bf, boldface.
bhp, brake horsepower.
Bib., Bibl., Bible; Biblical.
bibl., bibliotheca (library).
bibliog., bibliography; -er.; -ical.
biog., biography; -er; -ical.
biol., biology; -ical; -ist.
B.I.S., Bank for International Settlements.
bk., bank; block; book.
bkg., banking.
bkpg., bookkeeping.
bkpt., bankrupt.
B.L., Bachelor of Letters.
B/L, b.l., bill of lading.
bl., bale; barrel; black.
bldg., building.
B.L.E., Brotherhood of Locomotive Engineers.
B. Lit.(t)., Bachelor of Literature.
blk., black; block; bulk.
blvd., boulevard.
B.M., Bachelor of Music; British Museum.
B.O.T., Board of Trade.
bot., botanical; -ist; bottle.
bp., birthplace; bishop.
b.p., boiling point.
B.P.O.E., Benevolent and Protective Order of Elks.
Brig., Brigadier.
Brig. Gen., Brigadier General.
Brit. Mus., British Museum.
bro., brother.
B.S., Bachelor of Science.
B.T.U., Btu, British Thermal Unit.
bu., bureau; bushel.
bul., bull., bulletin.
B.V.M., Blessed Virgin Mary.
bx., box.

C

C., Catholic; centigrade; consul; court.
c., carat; carbon; cent; century; chapter; child; church; copyright; currency.
C., cent., Centum (L., a hundred); century.
c., ca., circa (L., about).
C.A., Chief Accountant; Coast Artillery; Consular Agent; Controller of Accounts; Court of Appeals.
C.A.A., Civil Aeronautics Authority.
cal., calendar; caliber; calorie.
canc., cancel; cancellation.
cap., capital; -ize; capacity.
C.A.P., Civil Air Patrol.
caps., capital letters.
Capt., Captain.
car., carat.
Card., Cardinal.
Cash., Cashier.
cat., catal., catalogue.
Cath., cathedral; Catholic.
cav., cavalry.
CBS Columbia Broadcasting System.
c.c., carbon copy; cashier's check; chief clerk; circuit court; county clerk; county commissioner; county court.
cc., cubic centimeter.
C.C.A., Circuit Court of Appeals; County Court of Appeals.
C.E., Chemical Engineer; Christian Endeavor; Church of England; Civil Engineer; Corps of Engineers.
cent., centum; central; century.
cert., certificate; certify.
cf., confer (L., compare).
C.G., Coast Guard; Commanding General; Consul General.
c.g., center of gravity.
c.g.s., cgs, centimeter-gram-second.
Ch., ch., chapter; chief; child; children; church.
c.h., court house; custom house.
Chanc., Chancellor; chancery.
chap., chaplain; chapter.
Chem. E., Chemical Engineer.
chem., chemical; -ist; -stry.
chg., charge.
Ch. J., Chief Justice.
chm., chmn., chairman.
Chr., Christ; Christian.
Chron., Chronicles.
chron., chronol., chronological.
Cie, Compagnie (Company)
C.I.D., Criminal Investigation Department.
CIO, Congress of Industrial Organization.
cir., circa.; circular.
cit., citation; citizen.
civ., civil; civilian.
C.J., Chief Justice.
ck., cask; check.
cl., class; clause; clearance; clerk.
C.L., Civil Law; Common Law.
class., classic; classification.
clin., clinical.
clk., clerk.
cm., centimeter.
C.M., Court Martial.
c/o., care of; carried over.
C.O., Colonial Office; Commanding Officer.
Co., company; county.
coad., coadjutor.
cod., codex.
C.O.D., Cash or collect on delivery.
C.O.F., Catholic Order of Foresters.
C. of E., Church of England.
C. of S., Chief of Staff.
Col., Colonel; Colossians.
col., collector; colony; column.
coll., colleague; collections; college; colloquial.
collab., collaboration; -or.
colloq., colloquial.
com., comedy; comma.
Comdt., Commandant.
comm., commander; commentary; commerce; commission; committee; commonwealth; communication.
comp., compare; compensating; composer; compositor; compound.
compar., comparative; comparison.
Comr., Commissioner.
con., consul, contra.
conc., concerning; concentrate.
conf., conference.
Confed., Confederate.
Cong., Congress; Congressional; Congregational.
conj., conjugation; conjunction.
cons., consecrated; consigned; consolidated; consonant; consulting.
con. sec., conic section.
consol., colsolidated.
Const., constable; constitution.
cont., contents; contract; contrary; control.
contd., continued.
contemp., contemporary.
contr., contract; contralto; contrary.
contrib., contributor.
conv., convent; convention; converter.
co-op., co-operative.
cop., copyright.
Cor., Corinthians.
cor., corner; coroner; correct; correspondent.
corp., corporal.

Corp., Corporation.
corr., correspond; corrected; corrupt.
Cor. Sec., Corresponding Secretary.
Corr. Mem., Cor. Mem., Corresponding Member.
cos, cosine.
Cos., companies; counties.
c.p., candle power; chemically pure; court of probate.
C.P.A., Certified Public Accountant.
C.P.O., Chief Petty Officer.
cr., credit; -or.
cres., cresc., crescendo.
crim., criminal.
crs., credits; creditors.
cryst., crystalline; -ized.
C. S., Christian Science; Civil Service.
c.s., capital stock.
C/S, cs., cases.
C.S.A., Confederate States of America.
CSC, Civil Service Commission.
C.S.D., Doctor of Christian Science.
ct., cent; count; court.
ctn., cotangent.
ctr., center.
cu., cub., cubic.
cu. cm., cubic centimeter.
cur., current; currency.
curr., currency.
C.V., Common Version (Bible).
cwt., hundredweight.
cy., capacity; cycle.
cyc., cyclo., cyclopedia.
cyl., cylinder.

D

D., Democrat; God; Lord.
d., date; daughter; dead; density; diameter; died; dividend.
D.A., District Attorney.
Dan., Daniel.
D.A.R., Daughters of the American Revolution.
dat., dative.
dau., daughter.
db., decibel.
D.B., Domesday Book.
D.&B., Dun and Bradstreet.
D. Bib., Douay Bible.
dbl., double.
D.C., da capo.
d.c., direct current.
D.D., Divinitatis Doctor (L., Doctor of Divinity).
D.D.S., Doctor of Dental Surgery.
DDT, dichlorodiphenyltrichloroethane.
Dea., Deacon.
Dec., December.
dec., deceased; declaration; decrease.
def., defense; deferred; deficit; definition.
deg., degree.
del., delegate; deliver.
Dem., Democrat; -ic.
dent., dental; dentistry.
Dep., Deputy.
dep., depart; department; deposit; depot; deputy.
der., derived; derivation.
desc., descendent.
Deut., Deuteronomy.
dft., defendent; draft.
D.G., Deo Gratia.
diag., diagr., diagram.
dial., dialect; dialectic.
diam., diameter.
dict., dictation; dictator; dictionary.
diff., difference; different; differential.
dim., dimension; diminutive; diminuendo.
dipl., diplomat; -ic.
dir., director.
disc., discount; discover.
disch., discharged.
dist., district; distance.
Dist. Atty., District Attorney.
distr., distributed; -or.
Div., Divinity.
div., divide; dividend; division; divorced.
D. Litt., Doctor of Literature.
D.L.O., Dead Letter Office.
DNB., *Dictionary of National Biography* (British).
D.O., District Officer.
do., ditto.
doc., document.
dol., dollar.
dom., dominion.
dom., domestic.
dom. econ., domestic economy.
doz., dozen; -s.
D.P., Displaced Person.
dpt., department; deponent.
Dr., Doctor.
dr., debit; debtor; dram; drawn.
d.r., dead reckoning.
dram. pers., dramatis personae.
D.S.C., Distinguished Service Cross.
D.S.M., Distinguished Service Medal.
D.S.T., Daylight Saving Time.
d.t., delirium tremens; double time.
D. Th., D. Theol., Doctor of Theology.
dupl., duplicate.
D.V., Deo Volente (L., God Willing); Douay Version (Bible).
D.V.M., Doctor of Veterinary Medicine.
d.w., dead weight.
dwt., pennyweight
dyn., dynamics.

E

E., east; engineer; English.
ea., each.
eccl., ecclec., ecclesiastic.
Eccles., Eccl., Ecclesiastes.
Ecclus., Ecclesiasticus.
ecol., ecology; -ical.
econ., economic; -y.
ed., edited; edition; editor.
educ., educated; -ion; -ional.
EE, Early English.
E.E., Electrical Engineer; errors excepted.
e.g., exempli gratia (L., for example).
elec., electric; -ity.
electrichem., electrochemistry.
electrophys., electrophysics.
elem., elementary; elements.
Elij., Elijah.
emb., embargo.
embryol., embryology.
E. Long., East Longitude.
emf., electromotive force.
Emp., Emperor; Empress.
e.m.u., electromagnetic units.
enc., encyc., encycl; ency., encyclopedia.
enc., encl., enclosure.
ENE, east-northeast.
eng., engine.
engr., engineer; engrave; -ing.
enl., enlarged; enlisted.
Ens., Ensign.
entom., entomology; -ical.
ep., epistle.
Eph., Ephesians.
Epiph., Epiphany.
Epis., Episc., Episcopal.
epit., epitaph; epitome.
eq., equal; -ize; equation; equipment.
equiv., equivalent.
erron., erroneous.
E.R.V., English Revised Version (Bible).
Esd., Esdras.
ESE, east-southeast.
esp., espec., especially.
Esq., Esquire.
est., established; estate; estimated.
Esth., Esther.
E.T., English Translation.
et al., et alibi; et alii (L., and others; and other things).
etc., et cetera (L., and so forth).
ethnol., ethnological; -y.
et seq., et sequens (L., the following).
etym., etymological.
E.U., Evangelical Union.
E.V., English Version.
ex., example; exchange; executed; executive; extra.
exam., examine; examination.
exc., excellent; except; excuse.
exch., exchange; exchequer.
Ex. Com., Executive Committee.
exec., executive; executor.
ex. lib., ex libris (L., from the books).
Exod., Exodus.
exp., expense; expiration; export; express.
ext., extension; external; extinct; extra; extract.
Ezek., Ezekiel.
Ez., Ezra.

F

F., Fahrenheit; Fellow.
f., father; fathom; female; folio; following; formula.

F.A., Field Artillery.
Fahr., Fahrenheit.
fam., familiar; family.
fasc., fascicle.
fath., fathom.
FBI, Federal Bureau of Investigation.
FCC, Federal Communications Commission.
Feb., February.
Fed., Federal.
fem., feminine.
ff., folios; following; fortissimo.
FHA, Federal Housing Administration.
fig., figurative; -ly; figure.
fin., financial; finish.
fl., flourished; flower; fluid.
fl. oz., fluid ounce.
FM, Frequency Modulation.
F.M., Field Marshal.
fm., fathom; from.
f. m. d., foot-and-mouth disease.
F.O., Field Officer; Foreign Office.
f.o.b., free on board.
F.O.E., Fraternal Order of Eagles.
fol., folio.
for., foreign; forestry.
fort., fortification; fortify.
Fr., Father; French; Friday.
fr., franc; from.
F.R.B., Federal Reserve Bank.
FRC., Federal Radio Commission.
Fri., Friday.
front., frontispiece.
frt., freight.
fs., facsimile.
ft., feet; flat; foot; fort.
FTC., Federal Trade Commission.
ft-lb, foot pound.
fut., future.
f.v., folio verso (L., on back of the page).

G

g., gauge; general; gold; good; gram; gravity.
G.A., General Assembly.
Gal., Galatians.
gal., gallon.
GAR, Grand Army of the Republic.
g.c.m., greatest common measure.
G. Com., Grand Commander.
gds., goods.
Gen., General; Genesis.
gen., gender; genus; generator; genitive.
geneal., genealogy.
Gen. Hosp., General Hospital.
gent., gentleman; gentlemen.
geod., geodesy; geodesic.
geog., geography; -er; -ical.
geol., geology; -ical; -ist.
geom., geometry;- ricial.
ger., gerund.
G.H.Q., General Headquarters.
G.I., Government Issue.
gloss., glossary.
gm.; gram.
G.O., General Order.
G.O.P., Grand Old Party (Republican).
Goth., Gothic.
Gov., gov., governor; -ment.
Gov. Gen., Governor General.
Govt., govt., government.
G.P., general practitioner. Glory to the Father.
G.P.O., General Post Office; Government Printing Office.
gr., grade; grain; gravity; great; gross.
gram., grammar; grammatical.
gro., gross.
G.S., General Security; General Staff.
G.T.M., General Traffic Manager.
guar., guaranteed.
gynecol., gynecological; -ist.

H

H., Headquarters.
h., harbor; height; high; hour; hundred; husband.
h.a., hoc anno (L., this year).
Hab., Habakkuk.
hab., habitat.
hab. corp., habeas corpus.
Hag., Haggai.
H.C., House of Commons.
h.c.l., high cost of living.
hdkf., handkerchief.
hdqrs., headquarters.
H. E., His (Her) Excellency; His Eminence.
h.e., hic est (L., that is).
Heb., Hebr., Hebrew.
hex., hexachord; hexagon.
hf., half.
h.f., high frequency.
H.H., His (Her) Highness; His Holiness.
Hipp., Hippocrates.
hist.. historian; -ical; -y.
H.J.S., His Jacet Sepultus (L., here lies buried).
H.L., House of Lords.
H.M., His (Her) Majesty.
H.M.S., His (Her) Majesty's Service, Ship, Steamer.
Hon., Honorable.
hon., honorably; honorary.
hor., horizon; horology.
hort., horticulture.
Hos., Hosea.
Hosp., Hospital.
H.P. hp, h.p., high pressure; horse power.
Hq., HQ., Headquarters.
H.R., House of Representatives.
hr., hour; hours.
H.R.E., Holy Roman Empire.
H.R.H., His (Her) Royal Highness.
ht., heat; height.
hund., hundred; hundreds.
H.W.M., High Water Mark.
hydraul., hydraulics.
hydrog., hydrographer; -y.
hyp., hypoth., hypothesis; hypothetical.

I

I, Inertia.
I., Imperator; independence; island.
I, and R., Initiative and Referendum.
ib., ibid., ibidem (L., in the same place).
I.C.C., Interstate Commerce Commission.
ich., ichth., ichthyology.
icon., iconography; -ic.
id., idem (L., the same).
i.e., id est (L., that is).
I.G., Inspector General.
I.H.S., Jesus Hominum Salvator; (G., Jesus the Saviour of man).
ill., illus., illustrated; -ion.
ILO, International Labor Organization.
imp., imperative; imperial; implement; import; imprimatur.
imperf., impf., imperfect.
in., inch; inches.
inc., incomel; included; incorporated.
incl., inclusive.
incr., increased; increasing.
I.N.D., in Nomine Dei (L., in the name of God).
ind., independent; index; indicative; indigo; industrial.
indic., indicative; indicator.
indiv., individual.
inf., inferior; infantry; infinitive; information.
infra, below.
init., initial.
in loc cit., in loco citati (L., in the place named).
in mem., in memoriam (L., in memory of).
INS, International News Service.
ins., inches; inspector; insulated; insurance.
inscr., inscription.
Inst., institute; institution.
inst., installment; institute; instant; instrument.
instr., instructor; instrument.
int., interest; interim; interior; internal; intermediate.
interj., interjection.
interrog., interrogation; -ive.
Int. Rev., Internal Revenue.
intro., introduction.
inv., invented; -or; investment; invoice.
IOF, Independent Order of Foresters.
IOOF, Independent Order of Odd Fellows.
IOU, I owe you.
I.Q., Intelligence Quotient.
I.R.O., Internal Revenue Officer.
irr., irreg., irregular; -ly.
Is., Isa., Isaiah.
is., isl., island; isle.

I.S.C., i.s.c., Interstate Commerce.
ital., italic.
I.V.A., Independent Voters' Association.

J

J., Judge; justice.
J.A., Judge Advocate.
Jan., January.
Jas., James.
J.C., Jesus Christ.
jct., junction.
J.D., *Jurum Doctor* (Doctor of Laws).
Je., June.
Jer., Jeremiah; Jeremy.
j.g., junior grade (Navy).
Jl., Joel; July.
Josh; Joshua.
jour., journal; journeyman.
J.P., Justice of the Peace.
J. Prob., Judge of Probate.
Jr., juror; junior.
Ju., June.
Jud., Judith.
jud., judicial.
Judg., Judges.
Jul., July.
Jun., June; Junior.
jurisp., jurisprudence.
juv., juvenile.
J.W.V., Jewish War Veterans of the United States.
Jy., July.

K

K., Kelvin; king; knight.
k., kilogram; kegs; karats; knot.
K.B., Knight of the Bath.
KC, Knights of Columbus.
kc., kilocycle.
kg., keg; kilogram.
kilo., kilogram; kilometer.
km., kilometer; kingdom.
K.O., knockout.
K. of C., Knights of Columbus.
K of L, Knights of Labor.
K of P, Knights of Pythias.
K.P., Kitchen Police.
K.T., Knight Templer.
kt., karat; knight.
kw., kilowatt.
kw-h., killowatt-hour.

L

L., lady; Latin; Linnaeus; Lord.
l., lake; land; latitude; league; left length; line.
Lam., Lamentations.
lam., laminated.
lang., language.
Lat., Latin.
lat., latitude.
lb., pound.
lbr., lumber.
L.C., Library of Congress.
l.c., left center; lower case.
l.c.d., lcd, lowest common denominator.
l.c.m., lcm., least common multiple.
L.D.S., Latter Day Saint.
led., ledger.
leg., legal; legate; legato; legend; legislation.
Leg., Legis., Legislature.
lex., lexicon.
L.H.D., Litterarum Humaniorum (L., Doctor of Humanities.)
lib., liber (L., book); library.
Lieut., Lieutenant.
lin., lineal; linear.
liq., liquid; liqueur.
lit., literal; literature.
Litt. D., Doctor of Literature.
lith., lithog., lithography.
ll., leaves; lines.
LL. D., Doctor of Laws.
loc. cit., loco citato (L., in the place cited).
log., logarithm.
lon., long., longitude.
l.p., low pressure.
L. R., Lloyd's Register.
lr., lira; lire.
Lt., Lieutenant.
L.T., Long Ton.
Ltd., ltd., limited.
Luth., Lutheran.

M

M., Monday; Monsieur, thousand.
m., male; mark; married; martyr; noon; mass; meter; minute; mountain.
M.A., Master of Arts; Military Academy.
Mac., Macc., Maccabees.
mach., machine; machinery.
mag., magazine; magnet; magnitude.
Maj., Major.
Mal., Malachi.
Man., Manasses.
manuf., manufacture; -er; -ing.
Mar., March.
mar., maritime.
marg., margin; -al.
masc., masculine.
math., mathematics; -ical.
Matt., Matthew.
max., maximum.
M.B.S., Mutual Broadcasting System.
M.C., Master of Ceremonies; Member of Congress.
M.D., Doctor of Medicine.
M.E., Methodist Episcopal; Military, mechanical, mining engineer.
mech., mechanical; -ics; -ism.
med., medical; medicine; medieval; medium.
mem., member; memoir; memorial.
memo., memorandum.
mer., meridian.
Messrs., Messieurs.
met., metaphor; metaphysics.
metal., metallurgy.
meteor., meteorology.
Meth., Methodist.
mfd., manufactured.
mfg., manufacturing.
mg., milligram.
mgr., manager; monsignor.
M.I., Military Intelligence.
mi., mile; mill; minor.
mid., middle; midshipman.
mil., military; militia.
min., mineral; -ogy; minimum; mining; minor; minute.
Min. Plen., Minister Plenipotentiary.
misc., miscellaneous.
miss., mission; missionary.
ml., milliliter.
MLD, minimum lethal dose.
Mlle., Mademoiselle.
mm., millimeter.
Mme, Madam.
mo., month.
m.o., mail order; money order.
Mon., Monday; Monsignor.
M.P., Member of Parliament; Military Police.
m.p., mp, melting point.
mph, miles per hour.
Mr., Mister.
Mrs., Mistress.
ms., manuscript.
M. Sc., Master of Science.
mt., mountain.
mus., museum; music; musician.
mut., mutual.
myth., mythol., mythological; -gy.

N

N., Nationalist; Navy; North.
n., name; born; net; noon; neuter; note; noun; number.
N.A., North America.
N.A.C.A., National Advisory Committee on Aeronautics.
N.A.M., National Association of Manufacturers.
N.A.S., National Academy of Science.
Nat., National.
nat., native; natural.
naut., nautical.
nav., naval; navigation.
n.b., nota bene (L., note well).
NBC, National Broadcasting Company.
N.C.O., Noncommissioned officer.
n.d., no date.
N.E.A., National Education Association.
neg., negative.
Neh., Nehemiah.
neut., neuter.
New Test., N.T., New Testament.
N/F, no funds.
N.G., National Guard; no good.
N.L., N. Lat., North Latitude.
NNE, north-northeast.
NNW, north-northwest.
No., no., number.
nol. pros., nolle prosequi (L., unwilling to prosecute).

nom., nomenclature; nominal; nominative.
noncom., noncommissioned officer.
non pros., non prosequitur (L., he does not prosecute).
non seq., non sequitur (L., it does not follow).
nor., north; northern.
Nov., November.
N.P., Notary Public.
N.S., National Society., (new style of dating after 1752).
N.S.F., not sufficient funds.
N.T., New Testament; New Translation.
nt. wt., net weight.
num., number; numeral.
Num., Numb., Numbers.
N.V., New Version (Bible).
NW, northwest.

O

O., Ocean; old.
o., octavo; only; order
Obad., Obadiah.
ob., obit.
obdt., obedient.
obj., object; -ion.
obs., observation; obsolete.
Oc., oc., ocean.
Oct., October.
O.D., Officer of the Day: Ordnance Department.
OE, Old English.
O.E.D., Oxford English Dictionary.
off., office; officer; -ial.
Old Test., O. T., Old Testament.
oleo., oleomargarine.
op., opera; operation; opposite; opus.
op. cit., opere citato (L., in the work cited).
opp., opposed; opposite.
opt., optics; option.
orch., orchestra.
ord., ordained; order; ordinance; ordinary; ordnance.
org., organic; organization.
orig., origin; original.
OS, Old Saxon.
O.S., Old Style (dating before 1752).
O.T.C., Officers' Training Camp.
oz., ounce.

P

P, pawn (chess) power (elect); pressure (physics).
P., past; port; president; prince.
p., party; page; participle; pastor; penny; per; period; pint; pope; population; pressure; post.
P/A, Power of Attorney.
paleon., paleontology.
pam., pamph., pamphlet.
par., paragraph; parallel; parish.
paren., parenthesis.
parl., parliament; -ary.
part., participle; participating; particular.
pass., passenger; passive.
pat., patent; pattern.
path., pathology.
Pat. Off., Patent Office.
payt., payment.
P.C., Privy Council.
P/C, p/c. Pct., per centum (L., by the hundred).
P.D., Police Department.
pd., paid; passed.
P.E., Protestant Episcopal.
Pen., pen., peninsula; penitentiary.
per an., per annum (L., by the year).
perf., perfect; perforated.
Pet., Peter.
P.H., Public Health.
Ph.B., *Philosophical Baccalaureus* (L., Bachelor of Philosophy).
Phar., pharmaceutical; pharmacopoeia; pharmacy; pharmacist.
pharmacol., pharmacology.
Phil., Philippians; philosophy.
Philem., Philemon.
philos., philosophy; -er; -ical.
phot., photog., photography; -y.
PHS., Public Health Service.
phys., physical; physician; physics.
pk., peck.
P.L., Poet Laureate.
pl., place; plate; plural.
pltf., plff., plaintiff.
plup; pluperf., pluperfect.
plur., plural.
P.M., Paymaster; Postmaster.
P.M., p.m., post meridian.
p.m., post mortem (L., after death).
P.O., p.o, Post Office; Postal order.
poet., poetic; poetry.
pol., political; politics.
pop., popular; -ly; population.
poss., possession; possessive.
p.p., parcel post; past participle; personal property; postpaid.
pp., pages; pianissimo.
ppd., prepaid.
ppm., p.p.m., parts per million.
pr., pair, power; present; price; prior; pronoun; province.
p.r.. prize ring.
pred., predicate.
pref., preface; preference; preferred; prefix.
prem., premium.
prep., preparation; preparatory; preposition.
Pres., President.
pres., present.
Presb., Presbyterian.
press., pressure.
prim., primary; primitive.
prin., principal; principle.
proc., proceedings; process.
Prof., Professor.
pron., pronoun; pronunciation.
prop., property; proposition.
Prot., Protestant.
pro tem., pro tempore (L., for the time being).
Prov., Proverbs.
prov., proverbial; province; provisional.
P.S., p.s., post scriptum.
Ps., Psa., Psalms.
ps., pseud., pseudonym.
psych., psychol., psychological; psychology.
pt., part; payment; pint; point; port.
P.T.A., Parent-Teachers' Association.
pub., public; publisher.
pvt., private.
P.O.W., Prisoner of War.
pwt., pennyweight.
PX, Post Exchange.

Q

Q., Queen; question.
q., quart; quarterly; quasi; query; question.
q.e., quod est (L., which is).
Q.E.D., q.e.d., quod erat demonstrandum (L., which was to be demonstrated).
q.l., q.lib., quantum libet (L., as much as you please).
Q.M.C., QMC, Quartermaster Corps.
qq., questions.
qt., quantity; quart.
q. t., quiet (slang).
qtr, quar., quarter; quarterly.
qu., queen; question.
ques., question.
quot., quotation.
q.v., *quod vide* (L., which see).
qy., query.

R

R., range; Réamur; recipe; registered; queen; king; river.
r., rabbi; radium dosage; railroad; rare; received; registered; residence; retired; right; road; rule; rod.
R.A., Rear Admiral; Regular Army.
R.A.F., Royal Air Force.
R.C., Red Cross; Reserve Corps; Roman Catholic.
R.C.M.P., Royal Canadian Mounted Police.
rct., receipt.
Rd., road.
R.E., Reformed Episcopal.
Réaum., Réaumer.
rec., receipt; recipe; record.
recd., received.
Rec. Sec., recording secretary.
rect., receipt.
ref., referee; reference; refining; reformed.
Ref. Ch., Reformed Church.
refl., reflection; reflex; -ive.
refrig., refrigeration.
reg., regent; region; register; regular; regulator.

Reg. Prof., Regius Professor.
rel., relative; released; religion.
rep., report; reporter; representative; republic.
Repub., Republican.
req., require; requisition.
res., research; reserve; residence; residue; resistance; resolution.
resp., respective; respiration; respondent.
ret., retired; retain; returned.
Rev., Revelations; Reverend.
rev., revenue; reverse; review; revise; revolve.
rf, **r.f.**, range finder; radio frequency; rapid fire.
R. F. D., Rural Free Delivery.
r.h., right hand.
R.I.P., Requiescat in pace (L., rest in peace).
Rm., reichsmark.
R.N., Registered Nurse.
Rom., Romans.
R.O.T.C., Reserve Officers' Training Corps or Camp.
R.P., Regius Professor; Reformed Presbyterian.
r.p.m., **rpm**, revolutions per minute.
R.P.O., Railway Post Office.
R.R., railroad; Right Reverend.
Rs., rupees.
R.S.V.P., **r.s.v.p.**, Répondez s'il vous plâis (F., please reply).
rte., route.
rt., right.
Rt. Hon., Right Honorable.
Rt. Rev., Right Reverend.
R.V., Reformed Version; Revised Version (Bible).
rw., **rwy.**, **ry.**, railway.

S

S., Sabbath; Saint; Saturday; science; senate; south; society.
s., school; see; second; section; shilling; silver; singular; socialist; son; soprano; southern; steamer; steel; stock; series; sun; surplus.
S.A., Salvation Army.
Sab., Sabbath.
Sam., Samaritan; Samuel.
Sat., Saturday.
S.C., Sanitary Corp; Signal Corps; Supreme Court.
sc., scale; scene; science; screw; scruple.
s.c., **s. cap.**, small capitals.
sci., science; scientific.
Script., Scripture; –al.
sculp., **sculpt.**, sculptor; –ure.
SE, **S.E.**, southeast.
sec., second; –ary; secretary; section; security.
sect., section.
sel., selected; selections.
Sen., **sen.**, Senate; senator; senior.
Sep., Septuagint.
Sept., September.
ser., series; sermon.
Sgt., sergeant.
shpt., shipment.
Sig., **sig.**, signature.
sin, sine.
sing., singular.
S.J., Society of Jesus.
S. Lat., south latitude.
S.M., Master of Science; short meter; state militia.
sociol., sociology.
sol., soluble; solution.
Song of Sol., Song of Solomon.
sp., special; specific; species; specimen; spelling.
SPARS, Women's Coast Guard Reserves.
S.P.C.A., Society for Prevention of Cruelty to Animals.
S.P.C.C., Society for Prevention of Cruelty to Children.
spec., special; specifications.
sp. gr., specific gravity.
sp. ht., specific heat.
sp. vol., specific volume.
sq., square; sequence.
Sr., Senior; Senor.
S.R.O., Standing Room Only.
SS, Saints; steamship.
SSE, south–southeast.
SSW, south–southwest.
St., saint; state; street.
st., stet; stone (weight).
S.T., short ton.
Sta., Santa; Station.
std., standard.
subj., subject; subjunctive.
suf., **suff.**, suffix.
Sun., Sunday.
sup., superior; supply.
Sup. C., **Sup. Ct.**, Supreme Court.
superl., superlative.
supp., **suppl.**, supplement.
Supt., **supt.**, superintendent.
surg., surgeon; surgery.
Surg. Gen., Surgeon General.
Sus., Susanna.
sym., symbol; symphony.
syn., synonym; synonymous.

T

T., Testament; township.
t., target; temperature; terminal; territory; time; ton; town; transitive.
tan., tangent.
t.b., trial balance; tubercle bacillus; tuberculosis.
tbsp., tablespoon.
T.D., Treasury Department.
tech., technical.
technol., technology.
tel., telegram; –graph; –phone.
temp., temperance; temperature; temporary.
term., terminal; termination.
terr., territory.
Test., Testament.
Th., Thursday.
theol., theology; –ian; –ical.
therm., thermometer.
Thess., Thessalonians.
Thurs., Thursday.
Tim., Timothy.
TNT., trinitrotoluene.
tonn., tonnage.
topog., topography; –ical.
tp., township.
tox., **toxicol.**, toxicology.
tr., trace; train; transitive; translation; transpose; treasurer; trustee.
trag., tragedy; tragic.
trans., transaction; transferred; transitive; transportation; transposed.
transf., transfer; transferred.
transl., translated; translation.
treas., treasurer; treasury.
trig., trigon; trigonometry.
Trin., Trinity.
trs., transpose.
Tues., Tuesday.
tsp., teaspoon.
typo., **typog.**, typographic; typography.

U

U., Union.
u., uncle; university.
U. B., United Brethren.
U. K., United Kingdom.
ult., *ultimo* (last).
ult., ultimate; ultimately.
U. N., United Nations.
Unit., Unitarian.
Univ., Universalist.
univ., universal; university.
U.P., United Presbyterian.
U.S.A., United States of America; United States Army.
U.S.C.G., United States Coast Guard.
U.S.G.A., United States Golf Association.
U.S.M., United States Mail; United States Marine.
U.S.M.A., United States Military Academy.
U.S.M.C., United States Marine Corps.
U.S.N., United States Navy.
U.S.N.A., United States Naval Academy.
U.S.N.G., United States National Guard.
U.S.P., **U. S. Phar.**, United States Pharmacopoeia.
U.S.P.H.S., United States Public Health Service.
U.S.S., United States Senate; United States Ship, Steamer.
usw., *and so weiter* (G., and so forth).

V

v, volt.
V., Venerable; Virgin; Vicar; Viscount.
v., valve; verb; verse; version; versus; vice–; violin; voice; verso.
V.A., Veterans' Administration.
v.a., verbal adjective.
Vat., Vatican.
v. aux., verb auxiliary.
vb., verb.

V.C., Vice Chairman; Vice Chancellor; Vice Consul.
v.d., vapor density; venereal disease.
Ven., Venerable.
vert., vertebrate; vertical.
vet., veteran; veterinary.
V.F.W., Veterans of Foreign Wars (of U.S.).
v.i., verb intransitive.
Vic., vicar.
Visc., Visct., Viscount.
viz., videlicet (L., namely).
vm., voltmeter.
v.n., verb neuter.
voc., vocative.
vocab., vocabulary.
vol., volunteer; volume.
volc., volcanic; volcano.
vox pop., vox populi (L., voice of the people).
V.P., Vice President.
vs., verse.; versus.
VSS., versions.
v.t., verb transitive.
Vulg., Vul., Vulgate.
vulg., vulgar.

W

W., Warden; Wednesday; Week; west.
w., watt; weight; width; wife; wide; with; word; work.
WAC, Women's Army Corps.
WAF, Women in the Air Force.
WAVES, Women Accepted for Volunteer Emergency Service.
W.B., Weather Bureau.
W.C.T.U., Women's Christian Temperance Union.
Wed., Wednesday.
wf, wrong font.
Wisd., Wisdom, Book of.
wk., week; work.
w.l., wave length.
W. Long., west longitude.
WNW, west-northwest.
WSW, west-southwest.
W.R.N.S., WRENS, Women's Royal Naval Service.
wt., warrant; weight.

X

X, Christ; Christian.
X, an unknown quantity.

Y

Y.B., Yearbook.
yd., yard; yards.
Y.M.C.A., Young Men's Christian Association.
Y.P.S.C.E., Young People's Society of Christian Endeavor.
yr., year; younger; your.
Y.W.C.A., Young Women's Christian Association.

Z

z., zone; zero.
Zech., Zechariah.
Zeph., Zephaniah.
zoochem., zoochemistry.
zool., zoology; -ical.
Z.S., Zoological Society.

SYMBOLS OF CHEMICAL ELEMENTS

The symbols listed below are not abbreviations, and should not be followed by periods.

Actinium	Ac
Aluminum	Al
Americium	Am
Antimony, stibium	Sb
Argon	A
Arsenic	As
Astatine	At
Barium	Ba
Berkelium	Bk
Beryllium, glucinum	Be
Bismuth	Bi
Boron	B
Bromine	Br
Cadmium	Cd
Calcium	Ca
Californium	Cf
Carbon	C
Cassiopeium, see Lutetium	
Cerium	Ce
Cesium	Cs
Chlorine	Cl
Chromium	Cr
Cobalt	Co
Columbium, see Niobium	
Copper	Cu
Curium	Cm
Dysprosium	Dy
Erbium	Er
Europium	Eu
Fluorine	F
Francium	Fr
Gadolinium	Gd
Gallium	Ga
Germanium	Ge
Gold, aurum	Au
Hafnium, celtium	Hf
Helium	He
Holmium	Ho
Hydrogen	H
Indium	In
Iodine	I
Iridium	Ir
Iron, ferrum	Fe
Krypton	Kr
Lanthanum	La
Lead, plumbum	Pb
Lithium	Li
Lutetium	Lu
Magnesium	Mg
Manganese	Mn
Mercury, hydrargyrum	Hg
Molybdenum	Mo
Neodymium	Nd
Neon	Ne
Neptunium	Np
Nickel	Ni
Niobium, columbium	Nb
Nitrogen	N
Osmium	Os
Oxygen	O
Palladium	Pd
Phosphorus	P
Platinum	Pt
Plutonium	Pu
Polonium	Po
Potassium, kalium	K
Praseodymium	Pr
Promethium	Pm
Protoactinium	Pa
Radium	Ra
Radon, niton	Rn
Rhenium	Re
Rhodium	Rh
Rubidium	Rb
Ruthenium	Ru
Samarium	Sm, Sa
Scandium	Sc
Selenium	Se
Silicon	Si
Silver, argentum	Ag
Sodium, natrium	Na
Strontium	Sr
Sulfur	S
Tantalum	Ta
Technetium	Tc
Tellurium	Te
Terbium	Tb
Thallium	Tl
Thorium	Th
Thulium	Tm
Tin, stannum	Sn
Titanium	Ti
Tungsten, see Wolfram	
Uranium	U
Vanadium	V
Wolfram, tungsten	W
Xenon	Xe
Ytterbium	Yb
Yttrium	Y
Zinc	Zn
Zirconium	Zr
#99	Unnamed
#100	Unnamed

Abbreviations of Geographical Names

The names of the states and territories of the United States are listed below. Names which should not be abbreviated are indicated.

Alabama	Ala.
Alaska	No abbreviation
Arizona	Ariz.
Arkansas	Ark.
California	Calif.
Canal Zone	C. Z.
Colorado	Colo.
Connecticut	Conn.
Delaware	Del.
District of Columbia	D. C.
Florida	Fla.
Georgia	Ga.
Guam	No abbreviation
Hawaii	T. H.
Idaho	No abbreviation
Illinois	Ill.
Indiana	Ind.
Iowa	No abbreviation
Kansas	Kan.
Kentucky	Ky.
Louisiana	La.
Maine	Me.
Maryland	Md.
Massachusetts	Mass.
Michigan	Mich.
Minnesota	Minn.
Mississippi	Miss.
Missouri	Mo.
Montana	Mont.
Nebraska	Neb.
Nevada	Nev.
New Hampshire	N. H.
New Jersey	N. J.
New Mexico	N. M.
New York	N. Y.
North Carolina	N. C.
North Dakota	N. D
Ohio	No abbreviation
Oklahoma	Okla.
Oregon	Ore.
Pennsylvania	Pa.
Philippine Islands	P. I.
Puerto Rico	P. R.
Rhode Island	R. I.
Samoa	No abbreviation
South Carolina	S. C.
South Dakota	S. D.
Tennessee	Tenn.
Texas	Tex.
Utah	No abbreviation
Vermont	Vt.
Virginia	Va.
Virgin Islands	V. I.
Washington	Wash.
West Virginia	W. Va.
Wisconsin	Wis.
Wyoming	Wyo.

Abbreviations of Geographical Names

Abbreviations for Canadian provinces and territories are listed below.

Alberta	Alta.
British Columbia	B.C.
Manitoba	Man.
New Brunswick	N.B.
Newfoundland	Newf.
Nova Scotia	N.S.
Northwest Territories	N. W. T.
Ontario	Ont.
Prince Edward Island	P.E.I.
Province of Quebec	P. Q.
Saskatchewan	Sask.
Yukon Territory	Y. T.

Abbreviations of Other Geographical Names

Afghanistan	Afgh.
Africa	Afr.
Albania	Alb.
Algeria	Alg.
Argentina	Arg.
Australia	Aust.
Bahama Islands	Ba. Is.
Belgium	Belg.
Belgian Congo	Belg. Cong.
Bolivia	Bol.
Brazil	Braz.
British West Indies	B. W. I.
Bulgaria	Bulg.
Burma	Bur.
Canada	Can.
Central America	C. A., Cen. Am.
Ceylon	Cey.
Chile	Chl.
China	Ch.
Colombia	Colom.
Czechoslovakia	Czech.
Denmark	Den.
Dominican Republic	Dom. Rep.
Ecuador	Ecua.
Egypt	Egp.
England	Eng.
Ethiopia	Eth.
Europe	Eur.
Finland	Fin.
France	Fr.
French Indochina	Fr. Ind. Ch.
Germany	Ger.
Great Britain	Gr. Br., Gr. Brit.
Greece	Gr.
Greenland	Grnld.
Guatemala	Guat.
Honduras	Hond.
Hungary	Hung.
Iceland	Ice.
Indonesia	Indon.
Ireland	Ire.
Israel	Isr.
Italy	It.
Japan	Jap.
Luxembourg	Lux.
Malay States	Mal. St.
Mexico	Mex.
Mongolia	Mong.
Morocco	Mor.
Nepal	Nep.
Netherlands	Neth.
Nicaragua	Nicar.
Norway	Nor.
North America	N. Am.
New Zealand	N. Z.
Pakistan	Pak.
Paraguay	Para.
Poland	Pol.
Portugal	Port.
Rumania	Rum.
Saudi Arabia	Sau. Ar.
Scotland	Scot.
South America	S. Am.
Spain	Sp.
Sweden	Swe.
Switzerland	Switz.
Syria	Syr.
Tibet	Tib.
Transjordan	Transj.
Turkey	Turk.
Union of South Africa	U. of So. Afr.
Union of Soviet Socialist Republics	U.S.S.R.
United Kingdom	U. K.
Uruguay	Uru.
Venezuela	Venez.
West Indies	W. I.
Yucatan	Yuc.
Yugoslavia	Yugo.

Abbreviations of Specialized United Nations Agencies

United Nations agencies which are designated by name are listed.

Food and Agriculture Organization of the United Nations	FAO
Inter-Governmental Maritime Consultative Organization	IMCO
International Bank for Reconstruction and Development	Bank
International Civil Aviation Organization	ICAO
International Monetary Fund	Fund
International Telecommunication Union	ITU
International Trade Organization	ITO
United Nations Educational, Scientific and Cultural Organization	UNESCO
United Postal Union	UPU
World Health Organization	WHO

FILING BY ALPHABET

Alphabetizing is the basis of the filing systems used in all business offices. Although the systems in ordinary use differ in details, all are based upon the same general rules. These rules are given below. It is important to remember that occasionally offices have developed systems which depart from standard practice in some respects.

Alphabetical Arrangement

Arrange words, or proper names, according to the order of their first, second, third letters, etc., carrying the process far enough to place the words in correct alphabetical order. For example:

Not Arranged	Alphabetically Arranged
Smithers	Smith
Smythe	Smithers
Smith	Smythe

and:

Not Arranged	Alphabetically Arranged
Abrams	Abarbanell
Abrahams	Abrahams
Abarbanell	Abrams
Bankhead	Bangs
Bangs	Bankhead
Davisson	Davidson
Davidson	Davisson
Slotkowsky	Slotkowski
Slotkowski	Slotkowsky
Schultz	Schmidt
Schulze	Schultz
Schmidt	Schulze
Winters	Stone
Witherspoon	Wallace
Wallace	Winters
Stone	Witherspoon

File the names of persons according to (1) surname, (2) given name, (3) middle names or middle initials. For example:

Edward H. Bangs should be filed as *Bangs, Edward H.*

Alternative Spellings

When the same name is spelled in more than one way, enter each spelling in the file and cross-refer each spelling to its alternatives.

Miller; *see also* Mueller, Muller.
Mueller; *see also* Miller, Muller.
Muller; *see also* Miller, Mueller.

Titles and Degrees

Professional titles and *academic degrees* are placed last, in parentheses ( ), and are not considered in alphabetizing.

Not Arranged	Alphabetically Arranged
Col. John Quincy Jefferson	Edwards, Anthony (Prof.)
Rev. Edward Holmes	Holmes, Edward (Rev.)
Prof. Anthony Edwards	Jefferson, John Quincy (Col.)
C. Arbuthnot McGuire, Ph.D.	McGuire, C. Arbuthnot (Ph.D.)

Titles of nobility are usually treated as part of the person's name.

Incorrect	Correct
Astor, Nancy (Lady)	Astor, Lady Nancy
Nordenskjöld, Nils (Baron)	Nordenskjöld, Baron Nils

When the title of nobility differs from the person's name, it is usually necessary to cross-refer to a listing by titles.

Buchan, John; *see* Tweedsmuir, Baron
Baldwin, Stanley; *see* Baldwin of Bewdley, Earl of
Disraeli, Benjamin; *see* Beaconsfield, Earl of
Wellesley, Arthur; *see* Wellington, Duke of

When several individuals have the same surname, and first names beginning with the same letter, the names of those individuals whose first names are represented by initials are listed first, followed by the spelled-out names in alphabetical order.

Not Arranged	Alphabetically Arranged
Herman Hitchens	Hitchens, H.
Herbert Hitchens	Hitchens, H. M.
H. McDougal Hitchens	Hitchens, H. McDougal
Henry Hitchens	Hitchens, Harold Montessori
H. Hitchens	Hitchens, Henry
H. M. Hitchens	Hitchens, Herbert
Harold Montessori Hitchens	Hitchens, Herman

In general, such prefixes as *da, de, von, van, Mac, Mc, O'*, etc., are treated as the first syllable of the surname, and apostrophes are not considered. This rule is observed in English, but it does not obtain in many other languages. In doubtful cases, usage must be the guide; and cross-references are often necessary.

Not Arranged	Alphabetically Arranged
Alfred von Tirpitz	D'Artagnan, Raoul
Jan van Rebeck	De Forest, Lee
Bernardo O'Higgins	De Grey, Lord
Marie de MacMahon	de MacMahon, Marie
Raoul D'Artagnan	de Saavedra, Angelo
Lee De Forest	O'Higgins, Bernardo
Lord De Grey	van Rebeck, Jan
Angelo de Saavedra	von Tirpitz, Alfred

Classify compound or hyphenated names by the first part of the compound.

Not Arranged	Alphabetically Arranged
Sir Johnston Forbes-Robertson	Byng-Enfield, Stephen
Stephen Byng-Enfield	Forbes-Robertson, Sir Johnston
Nikolai Rimsky-Korsakov	Rimsky-Korsakov, Nikolai
Ernestine Schumann-Heink	Schumann-Heink, Ernestine

Names of Organizations

In general, the names of businesses, societies, etc., are alphabetized as printed. Be sure the name used is correct, as set forth in the charter of incorporation. There are many exceptions to the rule for institutional names, the most important of which are given below. If confusion is likely to arise, cross-references should be used.

Not Arranged	**Alphabetically Arranged**
Smith and Wesson	American Tobacco Company
Oppenheimer Casing Company	Crown-Zellerbach Paper Company
General Cigar Company	General Cigar Company
American Tobacco Company	Lake Superior Piling Company
Crown-Zellerbach Paper Company	Northwestern Foundry Company
Lake Superior Piling Company	Oppenheimer Casing Company
West Virginia Pulp and Paper Company	Smith and Wesson
Northwestern Foundry Company	West Virginia Pulp and Paper Company

Ampersands (that is, the figure "&"), when correctly a part of the name, should not be written out.

Brown & Jones should not be written as *Brown and Jones.*

When *and* is spelled out in the name, the ampersand should not be used.

Jones and Brown should not be written as *Jones & Brown.*

Note that when such words as *American, Northwestern, Lake,* and *West* occur in corporate or institutional names, they are considered in alphabetizing. Compound words which are sometimes written as two words (northwestern —north western), are always arranged as though written in the compounded form.

When the name of an institution contains the name of an individual, the individual's name determines the classification.

Not Arranged	**Alphabetically Arranged**
Barron G. Collier Corporation	Collier, Barron G., Corporation
George E. Davies Foundation	Davies, George E., Foundation
L. C. Smith and Corona Typewriters, Inc.	Smith, L. C., and Corona Typewriters, Inc.

The, when it occurs at the beginning of a corporate or institutional name, is placed in parentheses at the end of the name. When it occurs elsewhere in the name it is disregarded entirely.

The *Bussert-Koffler and Leiber Company of Detroit* should be classified as:

Bussert-Koffler and Leiber Company of Detroit, (The)

And is similarly ignored. The instance above is properly classified as though it read:

Bussert-Koffler . . . . Leiber Company . . . . Detroit.

Notice that the hyphenated form *Bussert-Koffler* is treated as one word. Compounds not formed of the names of persons are treated in the same manner.

Not Arranged	**Alphabetically Arranged**
Smart and Daniels	Eat-and-Drink, Inc.
While-U-Wait Pressers	Express-Safety Trucking Company, (The)
The Express-Safety Trucking Company	Small Arms Manufacturing Company, (The)
Eat-and-Drink, Inc.	Smart-Cut Clothiers, Inc.
Smart-Cut Clothiers, Inc.	Smart and Daniels
Whitman and Kane	While-U-Wait Pressers
The Small Arms Manufacturing Company	Whitman and Kane

The suffix, *'s,* attached to the name of an individual within an institutional name, is sometimes ignored. When it is ignored, this type of classification results:

Foster's American Shoe Company
Foster, Lee and Company
Foster, Mark, Corp.
Foster's Shoe Store
Foster's Tailor Shop
Foster and Young, Inc.

Some organizations prefer to group the possessive forms separately, after the group of names without apostrophes. In such cases, this type of arrangement results:

Goldberg and Company
Goldberg, Max, and Company
Goldberg and Nathan, Inc.
Goldberg's Market
Goldberg's Meat Market
Goldberg's Shoe Store

The numbers in a name should be treated as though they were spelled out.

Not Arranged	**Alphabetically Arranged**
4-Deuces Club	Eighteenth National Bank
2222 Elm Street Building Corporation	Four-Deuces Club
18th National Bank	Twenty-two twenty-two Elm Street Building Corporation

When several organizations have the same name, arrange them alphabetically by their locations, considering the town first:

Economy Chevrolet Company, Fostoria, Ohio
Economy Chevrolet Company, Newmarket, Indiana
Economy Chevrolet Company, Newmarket, Wyoming
Economy Chevrolet Company, Seattle, Washington

Names of Government Agencies

The names of government subdivisions and officials are alphabetized under the customary English name of the government.

"Sverige," the official name in Swedish for Sweden, would be "Sweden" in an American file or index.

Where it is necessary to refer to a subdivision within the government or to an individual officer, the subdivisions are detailed in descending order, beginning with the most important.

The *Chief of the Bureau of Public Roads of the U. S. Department of Agriculture* should be filed as:

United States Government
Agriculture, Department of,
Public Roads, Bureau of,
.........................., Chief.

United States Government is the customary heading for agencies of the U. S. Government. Other examples:

U. S. Agricultural Marketing Service should be filed as:

United States Government
Agriculture, Department of,
Agricultural Marketing Service.

U. S. Employment Service should be filed as:

United States Government
Labor, Department of,
Employment Service.

The *Canadian Bureau of Parks and Forests* should be filed as:

Dominion of Canada
Mines and Resources, Department of,
Parks and Forests, Bureau of.

The *Wisconsin Power Commission* should be filed as:

Wisconsin, State of,
Power Commission.

The *Bureau of Transportation of the City of Chicago* should be filed as:

Chicago, City of,
Public Service, Department of,
Transportation, Bureau of.

LETTER WRITING

The Importance of Good Business Letters

Few secretarial tasks are so important or consume so much time as the writing of business letters. Some secretaries are expected merely to transcribe the letters dictated to them, with due attention to correctness and appearance; others have the additional responsibility of determining the wording of letters. Since secretaries are judged largely by the quality of their letters, they should become thoroughly familiar both with the effective use of English, and with correct business-letter usage in the arrangement of parts, spelling, punctuation, and related subjects treated in this office manual.

Secretaries will sense the importance of this phase of their work when they realize that every letter reveals the character and personality of the organization which sends it. If the letter is intelligently composed and carefully typewritten it adds to the recipient's respect for the organization, and in the long run to the esteem upon which a company's reputation and good will are based. The business letter thus has a role much like that of a firm's personal representative, who may impart either very favorable or extremely unfavorable impressions of his organization. The successful representative takes pains both to dress well and to approach his clients in a correctly trained manner. It rests with the secretary to see that the letter produces the proper effect by being suitably worded and neatly written.

The importance of excellent business letters is increased by the permanence of the impression they produce. In modern business establishments all correspondence is kept on file, at least until it becomes certain that it will no longer be needed. In this way a letter may serve for a long time as a point of contact between organizations and individuals. Every time the executive reviews a file of correspondence, he experiences again the pleasant or unpleasant impressions which the letters produced when first received. Time expended in the careful preparation of letters is therefore time well invested.

As suggested, the duties of the secretary in the writing of letters vary widely according to the individual situation. Some executives make a practice of indicating the gist of the letter in a few general sentences, and require the secretary to clothe their ideas in appropriate words. The secretary should have a practical knowledge of writing methods to perform such a task successfully; and the person who has this ability is an indispensable and highly valued assistant. Other executives dictate the letter in full. Some resent the change of a word or a punctuation mark as unwarranted presumption, and expect the secretary only to typewrite the letter exactly as dictated, putting the parts in proper order and spacing the materials correctly on the page. But with either method of work the secretary who is perfectly informed in letter-writing usages will achieve the most satisfactory results.

The Language of Business Letters

Letters are of two main kinds: business letters and social letters. The letters which a secretary in a business office prepares are nearly all of the first kind. In social correspondence between friends a good deal of latitude is permitted in the choice of words and the arrangements of parts, but in the business letter it is necessary to follow conventional usage with much greater strictness. The body of the business letter, however, sometimes offers scope for individuality of treatment, but business letters may not use slang and the freedom of treatment which are acceptable in letters between friends. Both business and social letters require the observance of good grammar and correct punctuation at all times.

In general terms, the most effective business letters are those which succeed best in combining cordiality with dignity. Such letters convey to the reader a sense of the sincerity and friendliness of the writer, and promote the objectives with which the letter is sent. Cordiality in business letters, however, degenerates into effusiveness if used to excess, sounding hollow and defeating its purpose of making the recipient desirous of cooperating with the writer.

The tone which business letters strive to achieve naturally varies according to the nature of the correspondence, and the social relationship between the writer and the reader. Courtesy and correctness are essential in all business correspondence, but the general tone will vary somewhat with the type of letter, depending upon whether an order for merchandise, a recommendation, a letter of information, an adjustment, or a sales letter is being written. An application for employment or a communication to an important governmental official is necessarily more formal and respectful than the ordinary business letter. Each sort of letter has a particular objective, and each should use the language and arrangement best suited for its attainment. Correspondence between people who have had a long business association in which an element of friendship may have entered usually is not as dignified and formal as correspondence between people who are communicating for the first time.

Trite Expressions

The message of the letter should be expressed in simple and natural terms. There are dozens of conventional phrases which have become so hackneyed that they have ceased to have any meaning, while others are unduly brief. Both types should be avoided entirely, since they destroy the clarity of the letter and make it seem old-fashioned. A business letter should resemble neither a telegram nor an engraved invitation to tea. Hence it should not contain telescoped expressions like "the 15th inst." and "in re," or effusions of pretended gratitude such as "your esteemed favor" and "thanking you in advance." Instead, brevity should be the result of clear thinking and avoidance of repetition. Courtesy should pervade the message as a whole, rather than being injected here and there by the use of a trite phrase.

Below are listed some of the trite and objectionable phrases which modern business letters should avoid in the interest of concise and unaffected expression. Beside the ones listed, there are many others of a similar character which the alert person will learn to detect and avoid.

ADVISE. Should not be used in the sense of *tell,* or *inform.*

AND OBLIGE. Not in good taste.

APPRECIATE. Means *to judge* or *estimate correctly.* Should not be used for *like, thank you for, feel kindly toward you for,* etc.

AS PER. A correct phrase is *according to.*

AT HAND. Trite.

ATTACHED FIND. If it is attached to the letter it will be found. It is better to say *attached is.*

ATTACHED HERETO. *Hereto* is superfluous.

BEG, OR BEG LEAVE. Trite, overworked, and useless.

BEG TO STATE, ADVISE, INFORM, ACKNOWLEDGE. To *beg* means to ask something for nothing. These expressions should be avoided.

CONTENTS CAREFULLY NOTED. One is expected to notice the contents of letters carefully. It is a waste of time to tell the correspondent that this has been done.

DICTATED BUT NOT READ. The letter of a correspondent who uses this expression ought to be returned with the notation "Received but not read."

ESTEEMED FAVOR. Only people are *esteemed* and a *favor* is a kindness.

FURTHER COMMANDS. This term is hackneyed.

HAND YOU. How can anything be handed to another in a letter? *Send you* is preferable.

HEREWITH. Superfluous. *Enclose* means as mucn as *enclose herewith.*

HOPING TO HEAR FROM YOU. This is usually taken for granted.

I HAVE BEFORE ME YOUR LETTER. The correspondent doesn't care where his letter is if it is given proper attention.

IN DUE COURSE. This is too indefinite.

IN RE. A Latin term meaning "concerning," or "in the matter of." Should not be used except in legal writing.

IN REPLY WISH TO STATE. This statement is a waste of time.

INST. An antiquated term for *this month.*

KIND, KINDLY. Overworked and trite.

PERMIT ME TO SAY. This is a needless prefix to an expression of opinion.

PROPOSITION. Business slang. It is better to say *proposal,* or *undertaking.*

PROX. The proper term is *next month.*

RECENT DATE. Letter should be referred to either by the exact date or the subject or by both.

SAME. Should not be used as a pronoun except in legal documents.

THANKING YOU IN ADVANCE. It is presumptuous to assume a request will be granted.

THE WRITER. The pronoun *I* is better because more direct.

THIS IS IN REPLY TO. Perfectly obvious from the contents of the letter.

ULT. A poor way of saying *last month.*

WISH TO SAY. Overworked, meaningless, and trite.

Five Essentials of Business-Letter English

The language used in every business letter, regardless of type, must contain five qualities which are indispensable in effective correspondence. These are:

1. Clearness
2. Conciseness
3. Completeness
4. Courtesy
5. Correctness

The writer who keeps these "Five C's" constantly in mind while composing the letter will find his task greatly simplified. Also, in reviewing the letter after it is drafted, he can estimate the value of his work according to the presence or absence of these qualities. The "Five C's" are the hallmarks of good modern correspondence, for their use distinguishes progressive letter-writing of the present from that of the past.

Clearness

A letter is first of all a message to a reader. If the reader does not grasp this message easily and thoroughly, the letter has failed in its purpose, no matter how correct its form or how attractive its appearance may be. Consequently the writer must make sure that the letter conveys a message in unmistakable terms.

Clarity in letters can be achieved by following a very simple yet important procedure. Before beginning the composition of the letter the writer must determine definitely what he wishes to say — whether or not he will order the materials, supply the information, give the recommendation, or do whatever else the reader has requested. If one waits until the actual writing of the letter to make these decisions, ambiguity and indecisiveness are almost certain to result. Although such a caution may appear obvious and needless, many letters are begun before the writers know what they are going to say.

After this first step, which is a matter of individual consideration for each case at hand, the writer must find the best words for expressing the message determined upon. Clearness in the actual writing is attained by care in the selection of words, and in the punctuation, the length and arrangement of sentences, and the paragraphing. It is important to avoid vague words or those subject to misinterpretation. Sentences should be as direct as possible, not weighed down by a burden of parenthetical expressions, subordinate clauses, or participial phrases. In addition sentences in a business letter should be reasonably brief, though too many very short sentences in succession give an undesirably staccato effect. Both vocabulary and sentence structure must be adapted to the intelligence and education of the reader: greater simplicity is obviously required in a letter to a farmer or a housewife than in one to an editor or an instructor. The principles of good paragraphing must also be observed, so that each topic or group of related topics occupies a paragraph by itself.

Conciseness

The man of business has so many claims on his limited time that he welcomes methods which conserve his working hours and energy. The best business letters, therefore, are those which enable him to grasp their message with the greatest ease and rapidity. Clearness in words and grammatical structure is one means to this end; another is conciseness. Conciseness in writing consists in the omission of unessential matter, and the avoidance of repetition and of unduly lengthy modes of expression. It should be noted, however, that concise writing need not be incomplete or discourteous writing. Really essential facts must not be overlooked, and the brusqueness which would result from the deletion of all expressions of cordiality and good will is undesirable. Without the usual pronouns and articles the language becomes clipped and telegraphic, as in the following instance, "Received yours of 29th ult."

The letter writer can find no better way to train himself in conciseness than to review his completed letters and note the number of phrases, words, and even whole sentences which could be left out without impairing the meaning of the whole.

Completeness

The completeness of the message should never be sacrificed in an exaggerated effort to achieve brevity of expression. Every item which is essential must find its place in the letter, for omission of important details is likely to cause confusion. The writer's best way of working to avoid this difficulty is to check over the items he intends to mention before the letter is begun, making sure that he has in mind all the needed details and no more. The letter should be read through after it is written, to see if it complies with the requirements of completeness. If something has been forgotten, the letter should probably be rewritten, since details tacked on in a postscript are an admission that the letter was inexpertly drafted in the first place.

Courtesy

Every successful business organization shows great courtesy in personal contacts with individuals and other companies, for much of its success depends on the esteem of its clients and associates. Courtesy in business letters is no less essential, especially in view of the permanence of written words.

There is a great difference, however, between true courtesy, which consistently takes into account the problems, needs, and feelings of the reader, and sham courtesy. The latter expresses itself in resounding phrases which do not truly represent the sentiments of the writer. Furthermore, exaggerated expressions of thanks and esteem are in poor taste, even if they are sincere.

Courtesy depends in part on a properly chosen salutation and complimentary close, but to a much greater degree on the language in the body of the letter. True consideration rests in the acts of the individual or company, but whether these favor or disfavor the reader's interests, they must be communicated in courteous terms. With skill even collection letters or refusals to grant charge accounts can be stated with a minimum of chagrin to the reader. Business letters of this type should show respect for the dignity and character of the recipient, and should avoid imputing bad faith to him. Sarcasm and abuse should never appear in business letters of any kind, since they brand the writer as ill-bred, and antagonize the reader.

Correctness

Correctness in the business letter is a requirement so absolute that without it the time spent in drafting a clear, well-phrased, and courteous message is hardly worth while, for a letter which contains errors in formal details furnishes but a sorry impression of the intelligence and character of the individual or firm which sends it. A carefully worded but carelessly transcribed letter is as ineffectual as a well-informed speaker with a severe stammer: neither the letter nor the speaker can win the favorable attention which the quality of their message deserves.

After the letter is composed, but before it is typewritten, it should be checked for its correctness in the following particulars: (1) grammar, (2) spelling, (3) capitalization, (4) punctuation, (5) the form of numerical expressions, (6) abbreviations. When it is ascertained that the letter is correct in these usages, it should be typewritten with care, that errors of fact do not creep in, and in accordance with the rules for spacing and the order of parts found in the following pages.

The Form of Business Letters

The letter's neat and pleasing appearance, like its correctness in details, enhances the value of skillful phrasing and offsets to some degree the bad effects of clumsy expression. Furthermore, clear-cut paragraph separations and proper spacing of the materials on the page permit quicker assimilation of the contents. Likewise, paper of good quality and a well-designed letterhead reflect credit on the writer.

The sheets of paper most commonly used in commercial correspondence, and those which best accommodate the business letter of average length are approximately 8½" x 11", though smaller sizes are used for some purposes. Most business stationery has an engraved or printed letterhead at the top of the sheet, bearing the name and address of the company. This letterhead should be well proportioned and should use faces of type which combine well. The typewriter ribbon should be black and must be fresh enough to make a clear imprint.

Carelessness in making erasures may produce smudges on the page which are hard to remove. These smudges can be avoided by use of a celluloid cutout which exposes only the letter or word to be erased. Typographical errors should not be struck over with the correct letter; instead the error should be carefully erased and the proper symbol typed in its place. Since it is difficult to insert the correction in exactly the right spot when the page has been removed from the typewriter and then replaced, it is best to read the letter over for errors before taking it out of the machine.

Few business letters run longer than one page. When they do, however, the bottom of the first sheet must not be crowded. The typist should never crowd a page to avoid using a second. The second sheet should bear the name of the reader, the page number, and the date, thus:

Mr. Ralph C. Roberts   Page 2   June 30, 19—

Letterhead stationery is preferably not used for any pages after the first. Instead, plain paper should be used, of the same color and quality as the first page.

Carbon copies should be made of all letters, as a matter of course, and promptly filed. This practice makes the review of correspondence an easy matter, and is therefore essential in the smooth running of the office.

Spacing

Proper spacing of the materials on the page has a great effect on the letter's legibility and attractiveness. The letter should be approximately centered on the page, but with the upper and left-hand margins slightly wider than the lower and right-hand margins. If the letter occupies a full page or more, the upper and left-hand margins should be not less than 1½ inches wide, and the lower and right-hand margins not less than 1 inch wide. A shorter letter will require wider margins, but these should maintain the same proportions. The length of the lines also varies according to the length of the letter. A letter of 100 words or less presents the best appearance if the lines are about 40 characters long (counting both letters and the spaces between words). A letter containing from 100 to 150 words should have 50-character lines; one of more than 150 words should have 60-character lines. If the typewriter used has "elite" type (that is, type which measures 12 characters to the inch), letters exceeding 200 words in length should have 70-character lines; but if the typewriter has larger type than this, a line of 70 characters will be too long for the minimum margins of 1½ inch and 1 inch. Before the transcription of the letter is begun the typist should make an approximate estimate of its length and set the typewriter's margin guides accordingly.

The length of the letter determines not only the preferable width of the lines, but also the vertical spacing. If the letter is a very brief one, it is likely to appear lost in a sea of white paper. This may be avoided by increasing the number of blank lines between the various parts of the letter, so as to expand it vertically on the page. The area which the letter covers on the page may also be increased by double-spacing the body of the letter (consult the section BODY).

BLOCK AND INDENTED STYLES

The left-hand margins of the various parts of the letter may follow either of two styles, known as block style and indented style. In block style, which is perhaps the more common in modern usage, each line of the address or the heading is flush on the left with the lines above and below. The following is an example of block style as applied to address and heading:

501 Shelby Street
Northfield, Vermont
June 30, 19—

Mr. Ralph C. Roberts
831 North Stacy Place
Jonesborough, Texas

In indented style each line begins a little more to the right than the line above it, thus:

501 Shelby Street
  Northfield, Vermont
    June 30, 19—

Mr. Ralph C. Roberts
  831 North Stacy Place
    Jonesborough, Texas

The application of block and indented styles to the paragraphs of the letter, and to the signature are explained in the sections BODY and SIGNATURE, below.

OPEN AND CLOSED PUNCTUATION

Two styles of punctuation are also acceptable. These are "open punctuation" and "closed punctuation." The first of these is much used at the present time. It uses no punctuation marks at the ends of lines except to indicate that a word is abbreviated. In "closed punctuation" the suitable punctuation marks close each line. It should be noted, however, that these distinctions of style do not apply to the body of the letter, which is always punctuated according to the rules applying to other types of writing. Furthermore, even in open punctuation it is customary to follow the salutation with a colon, and the complimentary close with a comma.

The foregoing examples of block and indented style have "open punctuation." The following is an example of "closed punctuation" applied to heading, address, salutation, and complimentary close:

501 North Shelby Street,
  Northfield, Vermont,
    June 30, 19—.

Mr. Ralph C Roberts,
  831 North Stacy Place,
    Jonesborough, Texas.

Dear Mr. Roberts:

(Body of the letter)

Very truly yours,

Whichever method of punctuation and indention is used must be applied consistently throughout the entire letter except the body. If the heading is in indented style with closed punctuation, the address and the complimentary close must follow the same form. The addresses on the envelope must also be uniform in treatment with the letter inside.

The Parts of Business Letters

Besides the envelope, the business letter consists of six main parts, usually found in the following order: (1) heading, (2) the inside address or introduction, (3) the salutation, (4) the body, (5) the complimentary close, (6) the signature.

HEADING

The heading consists of the name and address of the individual or organization, and the date. Most companies use letterhead stationery which has the name and the address at the top of the sheet. To complete the heading the date must be added. It may be placed either at the top beneath the letterhead, or, according to more conservative practice, a little below the letterhead but to the right, so that it is even with the right-hand margin of the body of the letter to follow. If letterhead stationery is not used, the entire heading should be typed in the upper right-hand corner, and should contain street address, city, state, and date in the order given.

Figures should not be used for the month or two digits for the year. No letters such as "st," "rd," or "th," should follow the day of the month. Correct and incorrect forms of the date line are illustrated as follows:

Incorrect—
April 17, '55
12/11/55
January 6th, 1955
September 23rd, 1955

Correct—
April 17, 1955
December 11, 1955
January 6, 1955
September 23, 1955

Correct methods for date lines on letterhead stationery:

(Printed Letterhead)

August 3, 19—

or

(Printed Letterhead)

August 3, 19—

Heading typewritten on plain stationery, extending to right-hand margin of letter:

119 Falk Street
Oak Center, Ohio
January 23, 19—

Inside Address

The inside address or introduction of the letter follows the same form as the address on the envelope. It should contain the name, street address, city, and state of the person to whom the letter is sent. Usually the name occupies the first line, the street address the second, and the city and state the third. If the name of the company is given to which the individual addressed belongs, this occupies the second line, all succeeding lines being pushed down. Sometimes the company itself is addressed, in which case the company name forms the first line. The name of a well-known office building or hotel sometimes supplements or replaces the street address.

The business title of the individual, indicating the position he holds in an organization, always follows the name, either on the same line or on the line below. The only words which precede the name are such terms of respect as "Mr.," "Mrs.," or "Miss," and the titles showing professional standing, like "Dr.," "Professor," and "The Reverend." Exceptions to this practice which may occur in addressing people of elevated position are listed under Forms of Address for Government and Ecclesiastical Officials, below. The term "Esq.," which is used for lawyers in England, and occasionally used in a general sense in the United States, always follows the name. In this case no title precedes the name. Two titles are not used for a single name.

The following examples illustrate correct and incorrect forms for the name line of the inside address:

Incorrect—
Treasurer Richard Wilts
Dr. Harold Coombs, M.D.
Mr. Samuel Slaughter, Esq.
or
Mr. Samuel Slaughter, Attorney
Bursar James McCabe

Correct—
Mr. Richard Wilts, Treasurer
Dr. Harold Coombs
or
Harold Coombs, M.D.
Mr. Samuel Slaughter
or
Samuel Slaughter, Esq.
or
Samuel Slaughter, Attorney
Mr. James McCabe, Bursar

The following are the various acceptable forms for the complete inside address, using both open and closed punctuation, and indented and block style in margins:

Mr. Roscoe Blair, Registrar
Municipal College of Fine Arts
1711 North Main Street
Pikesville, Tennessee
or
Mr. Roscoe Blair
Registrar, Municipal College of Fine Arts
1711 North Main Street
Pikesville, Tennessee

Economy Fuel Company
1181 Cross Street
Birmingham, Alabama

Mr. Harrison J. Watts, Vice President,
Economy Fuel Company,
1181 Cross Street,
Birmingham, Alabama
or
Mr. Harrison J. Watts,
Vice President, Economy Fuel Company,
1181 Cross Street,
Birmingham, Alabama.

Clarence Morton, Esq.,
1216 King's Place,
Manchester, England.

Miss Clair Bellingham,
Fulton Hotel,
1200 Broadway,
New York, N. Y.

The Reverend Albert Thwing, Secretary
Universal Gospel Society
Terminals Building
Washburn, Ohio

The preceding examples show the variety of ways in which the inside address may be treated. In friendly correspondence it is usually omitted entirely, so that the salutation directly follows the heading. In government correspondence and some very formal letters the inside address is frequently placed below the signature, at the lower left-half corner of the page. The usual practice, however, is one of those indicated above.

Salutation

The salutation marks the formal opening of the letter after the sender's and reader's addresses have been written. It begins at the left-hand margin, usually two spaces below the inside address, from which it is thus separated. It is followed by a colon, or in friendly letters by a comma. Users of the open punctuation system sometimes use no punctuation mark after the salutation, but the use of the colon is more general.

The choice of the salutation depends on the relationship between the writer and the reader of the letter. In ordinary business correspondence, moderately dignified salutations are desirable, unless the relationship has developed into a warmly personal one, when considerable informality is permissible. Special forms of address are used in writing to government officials; these are listed in FORMS OF ADDRESS FOR GOVERNMENT AND ECCLESIASTICAL OFFICIALS, below.

The salutations suitable for various situations are as follows:

For addressing a company—
  Gentlemen: (formal or informal)
For addressing a group of women—
  Ladies: (formal or informal)
  Mesdames: (formal)
For addressing an individual—
  My dear Mr. O'Hara: (formal)
  My dear Miss Foster: (formal)
  Dear Sir: (moderately informal)
  Dear Madam: (moderately informal)
  Dear Mr. O'Hara: (moderately informal)
  Dear Miss Foster: (moderately informal)
For addressing close acquaintances, and rarely used in business correspondence—
  Dear Tom, (:) (very informal)
  Dear Beatrice, (:) (very informal)
  Dear O'Hara, (:) (very informal)

The writer should observe that the word "dear" in a salutation is capitalized only if it is the first word in the phrase. All other words used in salutations are capitalized wherever they occur. The only abbreviations used in salutations are "Mr.," "Mrs.," "Dr.," and "Rev."

A letter addressed directly to an organization as such should use the salutation "Gentlemen." However, if the writer wishes the matter to receive the attention of a particular individual in the firm, this is accomplished by the phrase "Attention of Mr.——," written either on the same line as the salutation, or else below it to the right, thus:

Simmons and Tate, Inc.
803 Clinton Court
New York, N. Y.

Gentlemen: Attention of Mr. John Harris

or thus:

Simmons and Tate, Inc.
803 Clinton Court
New York, N. Y.

Gentlemen:
  Attention of Mr. John Harris

BODY

The body of the letter is the portion which contains the message. It begins one or two lines below the salutation.

There are two methods of typing the body: double-spaced and single-spaced. The choice of one or the other depends on the preference of the individual or firm, as well as on the amount of material in the letter, which affects the spacing. Materials intended to be printed, however, should always be double-spaced, to facilitate the work of the editor and the compositor.

If the body is double-spaced, the beginning of each paragraph must be indented so as to be clearly marked off from neighboring paragraphs. Paragraph divisions are made still more evident by leaving one or two blank lines between paragraphs, in addition to the indention at the beginning. However, the use of blank lines is optional in double-spaced matter.

If the body of the letter is single-spaced, paragraphs may begin flush with the left-hand margin, or indentions may be used if preferred. In either case the paragraphs must be separated from one another by one or more blank lines between them.

The block style of paragraphing is particularly suitable when the heading and the inside address are blocked. But when these parts of the letter are put in indented style, indented paragraph beginnings achieve a desirable effect of uniformity.

Regardless of the method of punctuation employed in the heading and inside address, the body of the letter must be punctuated in conformity with the punctuation rules in this book.

Double-spaced indented paragraphs with no blank lines between them:

Double-spaced indented paragraphs with blank line between them:

Single-spaced indented paragraphs with blank line between them:

Single-spaced paragraphs in block style, with blank line between them:

If the body of the letter contains an address for the information of the reader, it is helpful to make this stand out prominently for convenience in reference. This may be accomplished by putting it in the same form as the inside address of the letter, but centered on the page, as in this example:

> For additional details we advise you to communicate with America's foremost authority in this field:
>
> Dr. Franz A. Heiden
> 193 Wall Street
> New York, N. Y.
>
> We feel confident he can furnish the information you require.

Complimentary Close

The complimentary close is a formal expression of regard with which the writer takes leave of the reader. It follows the body of the letter, occupying a line by itself, two or more lines below the last line of the body. It should begin at the middle of the page, or slightly to the right of the middle.

The use of a particular phrase for the complimentary close, like the salutation, depends on the relationship between the sender and the receiver. The complimentary close should be consistent with the salutation in the degree of its formality.

The most frequently encountered complimentary closes for business correspondence are as follows:

Respectfully yours, (very formal, and used principally for government officials and people in superior positions)
Very truly yours, (moderately formal)
Yours very truly, (moderately formal)
Yours truly, (moderately formal)
Sincerely yours, (informal; most used in business correspondence between well-acquainted persons)

The complimentary closes of friendly letters are less subject to rule than those of business letters, many being devised by the writer. In some friendly letters the complimentary close is omitted.

The complimentary close should have only its first letter capitalized, and should contain no abbreviations. It should not be attached to the preceding sentence or follow such stereotyped expressions as "I beg to remain," "Believe me to be," and "Hoping for a prompt reply I am . . ." It is usually followed by a comma, even when open punctuation is used, though it is sometimes omitted in the latter case.

Cordially yours, (informal; most used in business correspondence between well-acquainted persons)

Signature

The signature of the business letter contains the name of the individual, the name of the organization, or both. Sometimes the position of the individual in the organization is also included.

The signature is typewritten from two to several lines below the complimentary close, the number of blank lines depending on the need of compressing or expanding the materials on the page. If the inside address follows block style, the one or more lines of the signature are lined up evenly under the complimentary close; but if the inside address follows indented style, it is preferable to begin the signature a little to the right of the complimentary close, with additional indentions for each succeeding line.

Complimentary close and signature in block style:

Very truly yours,

ECONOMY FUEL COMPANY
(Signature)
Harrison J. Watts, Vice President

Complimentary close and signature in indented style:

Very truly yours,

ECONOMY FUEL COMPANY
  (Signature)
    Harrison J. Watts, Vice President

If the signer of the letter wishes to indicate that he is writing as an individual, his name should precede the firm name; but if he is writing merely as a representative of the firm, the firm name should precede.

When letterhead paper is used the firm name is often omitted from the signature. The firm name in the signature, when included, is sometimes written in capital letters to give it prominence.

Skeleton Envelope Form

(Printed Letterhead
or
Typewritten Return Address)

(Room or Suite No. if any)

Skeleton Business Letter Form

(Single-spaced and in indented style, with closed punctuation)

TYPEWRITTEN HEADING

INSIDE ADDRESS

SALUTATION

BODY

COMPLIMENTARY CLOSE

SIGNATURE

—/—

IDENTIFICATION LETTERS
NOTICE OF ENCL.

SKELETON BUSINESS LETTER FORM

(Single-spaced and in block style with open punctuation)

LETTERHEAD

DATELINE

INSIDE ADDRESS

SALUTATION

BODY

COMPLIMENTARY CLOSE

SIGNATURE

IDENTIFICATION INITIALS

SKELETON ENVELOPE FORM

(Printed Letterhead
or
Typewritten Return Address)

("Attention of" Statement if any)

It is necessary that the reader should know the exact name of the individual writing the letter, so that his reply may reach the proper person. Since the scrawl with which names are sometimes written in signatures is confusing, it is courteous to have the name of the person typewritten below the handwritten signature. It is also helpful to the reader to know the writer's position in the firm. This may be added after the typewritten personal name, either on the same line or on the next line below. The statement of position should not be added to the handwritten signature, however.

Alternative methods of indicating official position:

(Handwritten signature)

Roscoe J. Blair, Registrar

or

(Handwritten signature)

Roscoe J. Blair

Registrar

An individual should always sign his name the same way in all business correspondence. The first and middle names may be either written in full or written as initials only. A woman may wish to indicate whether she is married or single. If she is single, the word "Miss" may precede her signature; if she is married the word "Mrs." in parentheses may precede the signature, or her married name may be typewritten beneath the signature:

(Miss) Francis K. Graham

(Mrs.) Alice C. White

or

Alice C. White

(Mrs. John White)

Neither the handwritten nor the typewritten portions of the signature should contain personal titles such as "Mr.," "Rev.," "Dr.," or "Professor"; or academic degrees such as "M.A.," "Ph.D.," or "LL.D." The only exception to this rule is the use in parentheses of a title indicating the marital status of a woman, as noted in the previous paragraph.

Three additional letter parts which require consideration, though they do not appear in all business letters, are the postscript, the identification letters, and the notice of enclosure.

Postscript

Postscripts are seldom used in well-written business letters, since their use is an evidence of confused thinking on the part of the composer of the letter, who only remembered to include an essential detail after the letter was typewritten. If the postscript is necessary, however, it should be added several lines below the signature, preceded by the letters "P.S."

Identification Letters

The identification letters are the initials of the writer of the letter, and those of the secretary who transcribed it. The initials of the writer always come first. Identification letters are placed in the lower left-hand corner of the page, on one line or on two, and in any of the following forms:

RJMcM/EMP   MDE
GF   AK,SED   PEQ:ls

Notice of Enclosure

The notice of enclosure informs the reader that something additional to the text of the letter is enclosed within the envelope, and must be looked for. The words "Encl." or "Enclosure" are written in the lower left-hand corner, just below the identification letters. If there is more than one enclosure, the number should be stated, as:

RJMcM/EMP
Enclosures (3)

Envelope

The envelope should be clean, carefully typed, and well spaced, because it comes first to the attention of the reader and may give him a favorable or unfavorable impression of the contents.

For business letters both the sender's and the receiver's addresses should appear on the face of the envelope, though in writing friendly letters the return address is sometimes placed on the back flap. Most business letters use letterhead envelopes with the sender's return address in the upper left-hand corner; on plain envelopes this information is typewritten in the same location.

The address to which the letter is being sent (also called the superscription), should begin about halfway down the envelope, and slightly to the left of the middle. It should usually contain the same information as the inside address, with which it should be uniform in using the block or indented style. The name of the county may be added after the name of the community if the latter is small or little-known. Abbreviations should be avoided whenever possible, since "Va." and "Pa.," and "Mass.," "Miss.," and "Minn." are easily confused.

If the address is in an office building or hotel, the number of the room or suite may be placed in the lower left-hand corner of the envelope, as:

Room 1271   Suite 37

When the letter is addressed directly to an organization, but the writer wishes it to be received by a particular individual, his name may be placed in the lower left-hand corner in the following form:

Attention of Mr. Jerome W. Pick

Forms of Address for Government and Ecclesiastical Officials

Letters addressed to people in high positions in governmental or religious organizations require the use of special forms for the address, the salutation, or the complimentary close; or sometimes for all three. Various expressions with different degrees of formality are possible in some cases, as indicated in the list below.

The inside address in a letter to a government official may be placed either before the salutation, as in most business letters, or in the lower left-hand corner of the page below the level of the signature.

Two terms which should be used with special care are "the Honorable" and "the Reverend." Since they are adjectives rather than titles, they must be followed by the first name, the initials, or the appropriate title, rather than by the surname alone. They are usually abbreviated to "Hon." and "Rev." if the word "the" is omitted.

Examples:

The Honorable Henry Robinson
The Honorable H. F. Robinson
The Honorable Mr. Robinson
not
The Honorable Robinson

Hon. H. F. Robinson
not
Hon. Robinson

The Reverend Matthew Watts
The Reverend M. Z. Watts
The Reverend Dr. Watts
not
The Reverend Watts

Rev. Matthew Watts
not
Rev. Watts

Officials in the United States

THE PRESIDENT

Address:
The President
The White House
Washington, D.C.
or
The President of the United States
The White House
Washington, D.C.

Salutation:
Sir:
or
Mr. President:
or
To the President:

Complimentary Close:
Respectfully yours,
or
Yours very truly,
or
Sincerely yours,

THE VICE PRESIDENT

Address:
The Vice President
The United States Senate
Washington, D.C.
or
The Honorable ——— ———
Vice President of the United States
Washington, D.C.

Salutation:
My dear Mr. Vice President:
or
Sir:

Complimentary Close:
Respectfully yours,

CABINET OFFICERS

Address:
The Secretary of State (of Commerce, etc.)
Washington, D.C.
or
The Honorable ——— ———
Secretary of State (of Commerce, etc.)
Washington, D.C.

Salutation:
Sir:
or
Dear Mr. Secretary:
(Mr. Attorney General, etc.)

Complimentary Close:
Very truly yours,

JUSTICE OF THE SUPREME COURT

Address:
The Honorable ———
Chief (or Associate) Justice of the Supreme Court
Washington, D.C.
or
Mr. Justice ———
Washington, D.C.

Salutation:
Mr. Justice:
or
Dear Mr. Justice:
or
Dear Justice ———: (informal)

Complimentary Close:
Very truly yours,

UNITED STATES SENATOR

Address:
The Honorable ——— ———
United States Senate
Washington, D.C.

Salutation:
Sir:
or
My dear Mr. Senator:
or
Dear Mr. ———: (informal)

Complimentary Close:
Very truly yours,

UNITED STATES CONGRESSMAN

Address:
The Honorable ——— ——— (full name must be given)
House of Representatives
Washington, D.C.

Salutation:
Sir:
or
Dear Sir:
or
Dear Mr ————: (informal)
Complimentary Close:
Very truly yours,

GOVERNOR OF A STATE

Address:
The Honorable ———— ————
Executive Mansion
State Capitol, State
or
The Honorable ———— ————
Governor of ————
State Capitol, State
Salutation:
Dear Sir:
or
Dear Governor ————: (informal)
Complimentary Close:
Very truly yours,

STATE OFFICIAL

Address:
The Secretary of State,
State Capitol, State
Salutation:
Dear Mr. Secretary:
Complimentary Close:
Very truly yours,

MAYOR

Address:
The Honorable ———— ————
Mayor's Office
City, State
Salutation:
Dear Sir:
or
Dear Mr. Mayor:
or
Dear Mr. ————:
Complimentary Close:
Very truly yours,
or
Respectfully yours,

JUDGE

Address:
The Honorable ———— ————
County Courthouse
State, City
Salutation:
Dear Sir:
or
Dear Judge ————:
Complimentary Close:
Very truly yours,

DIPLOMATIC OFFICIALS

UNITED STATES AMBASSADOR

Address:
His Excellency
The American Ambassador
(City and country where stationed)
or
The Honorable ———— ————
American Ambassador
(City and country where stationed)
Salutation:
Sir:
or
Your Excellency:
or
Dear Mr. Ambassador:
Complimentary Close:
Respectfully yours,
or
Very truly yours,

CONSUL

Address:
(Consular customs differ. Check with the nearest consulate.)
Salutation:
Dear Mr. Consul:
Complimentary Close:
Very truly yours,

PRESIDENT OF A UNIVERSITY

Address:
President ———— ————
University of ————
City, State
Salutation:
Dear Sir:
or
Dear President ————:
Complimentary Close:
Very truly yours,

ROMAN CATHOLIC CHURCH OFFICIALS

THE POPE

Address:
His Holiness, Pope Pius X——
The Vatican
Vatican City, Italy
Salutation:
Your Holiness:
Complimentary Close:
Sincerely yours,
or
(if the writer is a Catholic)
Sincerely yours in Christ,

CARDINAL

Address:
His Eminence Cardinal ————
or
His Eminence Francis, Cardinal ————
Archbishop of ————
City, State.
Salutation:
Your Eminence:
Complimentary Close:
Respectfully yours,
or
(if the writer is a Catholic)
Sincerely yours in Christ,

ARCHBISHOP

Address:
The Most Reverend ———— ————, D.D.
Archbishop of ————
City, State

Salutation:
Most Reverend Archbishop:
or
Your Excellency:
or
Dear Archbishop ————: (informal)
Complimentary Close:
Respectfully yours,
or
(if the writer is a Catholic)
Sincerely yours in Christ,

BISHOP
Address:
The Most Reverend ————,
Bishop of ————
City, State.
Salutation:
Your Excellency:
or
Dear Bishop ————: (informal)
Complimentary Close:
Respectfully yours,
or
(if the writer is a Catholic)
Sincerely yours in Christ.

MONSIGNOR
Address:
The Right Reverend Monsignor ————
City, State.
Salutation:
Right Reverend and dear Monsignor:
Complimentary Close:
Respectfully yours,

PRIEST (Secular)
Address:
The Reverend —— (followed by initials of degree)
City, State.
Salutation:
Reverend and dear Father:
or
Dear Reverend Father:
or
Dear Father ————: (informal)
Complimentary Close:
Respectfully yours,

PROTESTANT AND JEWISH ECCLESIASTICAL OFFICIALS

HEADS OF ECCLESIASTICAL INSTITUTIONS
Address:
Very Reverend ———— ————, D. D.
———— Seminary, etc.
City, State.
Salutation:
Very Reverend and dear Father (or Doctor)
Complimentary Close:
Respectfully yours,
or
Sincerely yours,

PROTESTANT EPISCOPAL BISHOP
Address:
The Right Reverend ————, Bishop of ————
City, State.
Salutation:
Dear Bishop ————:

Complimentary Close:
Sincerely yours,
or
Very truly yours,

METHODIST BISHOP
Address:
Bishop ———— ————
City, State
Salutation:
Dear Bishop ————
Complimentary Close:
Very truly yours,
or
Sincerely yours,

DEAN
Address:
The Very Reverend ————
St. ————'s Church,
City, State.
Salutation:
Dear Dean ————:
or
Very Reverend Sir:
Complimentary Close:
Very truly yours,
or
Sincerely yours,

ARCHDEACON
Address:
The Venerable ———— ————
St. ————'s Church
City, State.
Salutation:
Dear Archdeacon ————
Complimentary Close:
Very truly yours,
or
Sincerely yours,

PROTESTANT CLERGYMAN
Address:
Reverend ———— ————
or (if a Doctor of Divinity)
Rev. Dr. ———— ————
City, State.
Salutation:
Dear Sir:
or
Reverend Sir:
or
Dear Mr. (*or* Doctor) ————
Complimentary Close:
Respectfully yours,
or
Sincerely yours,

RABBI
Address:
Rabbi ———— ————
City, State.
Salutation:
Dear Rabbi ————: (informal)
Complimentary Close:
Respectfully yours,
or
Sincerely yours,

OFFICE ROUTINE

An effective office routine is based on common sense. It is no different from the routine used by a clear thinking and efficient individual in his personal affairs, except that it has greater scope and is adapted to the needs of a business and the workers who compose it. An orderly individual makes memoranda of approaching tasks and appointments, keeps a careful watch on bills, money orders, and bank statements, files away important letters, documents, and receipts in such a fashion that he can find them again easily, makes careful plans before traveling, and in general tries to dispatch the business of life with a minimum of bother and error. The same is true of an efficient office. Time is a precious commodity, and hours saved from routine can be devoted effectually to more important efforts.

This does not mean that all office routines are perfect. In some there is considerable hampering red tape and "system for system's sake." In others carelessness and laxity are conspicuous. It does mean, however, that an effective routine is intelligible to anyone who has common sense and is acquainted with the business in question. If things are done in a certain way, there is usually a sound reason. If certain rules are enforced and precautions taken, they are usually necessary. If a person wishes to understand any phase of office routine, he should try to determine the reason for it. Naturally a new worker will have to follow some routines blindly until he gets a chance to think them out. In the long run common-sense understanding makes for a better worker than does automatic, unreasoned obedience. This is especially true for the secretary, from whom a considerable degree of initiative is frequently expected.

There is, of course, considerable variation in method from office to office. Each business has its own individual problems, and each executive his own ideas about efficiency. Nevertheless, business organizations have many general principles of operation in common. They are all part of the same economic order, and the laws of common sense hold true for all of them.

The Secretary's Work

The secretary is an important figure in modern business. She performs a variety of duties, many of them demanding independent thought and decision. Her treatment of callers and handling of business letters help to establish the tone of a firm. She is to a large degree responsible for the smooth functioning of the executive or executives to whom she may be specially assigned. Her position is that of an important minor hub, around which the wheels of office routine revolve.

The secretary, although she must usually be a good stenographer, is much more than that. The stenographer takes dictation in shorthand and transcribes it on the typewriter into the characters of the alphabet; to be able to do this, she must in addition be an expert typist. She is judged by her reliability, accuracy, and speed. Her work, though essential, is decidedly limited when compared to that of the secretary.

The term secretary is a flexible one. It is applied to the general stenographic assistant and receptionist of the individual executive or professional man—in short, the private secretary. Such a secretary may sometimes be shared between two or more executives, performing like services for each. In committees, institutions, clubs, and other non-business organizations the term secretary is frequently applied to an important individual who performs all the actual work attendant on executing orders and decrees. This is in some ways similar to the secretary in the small office, who may be responsible for all office routine, or to the general secretary of a large office, who may have some of the duties of an office manager.

There are certain types of work which the business-office secretary will almost certainly be called upon to perform. These are (1) the opening and sorting of incoming mail; (2) the taking of dictation; (3) the transcription of shorthand; (4) the dispatch of outgoing mail; (5) the filing of letters and other materials; (6) the making of appointments; (7) the handling of callers and of telephone calls; (8) running errands. But there are many other types of work which the secretary may be called upon to learn and execute, among them the following: (1) the arrangement, in part, of her employer's schedule; (2) reading mail and drafting replies to routine letters; (3) organization and management of one or more filing systems and indexes; (4) clipping newspapers; (5) interviewing callers; (6) planning itineraries; (7) ordering office supplies; (8) handling petty cash, stamps, etc.; (9) making bank deposits; (10) writing checks and paying bills; (11) checking bank statements.

Few secretaries have to perform all these duties. Some, on the other hand, may be expected to handle these and more. There is no listing all possible duties, since each business may have special ones attached to it. The secretary attempting to master her job and improve her efficiency has three reliable guides: the instructions of her employer, her experience, and her common sense. This section is intended as an introduction to those secretarial duties which are common to many offices. For a general discussion of the personality qualifications of the secretary, the reader is referred to the sections THE SUCCESSFUL SECRETARY and ETIQUETTE FOR BUSINESS MEN AND WOMEN.

Adjusting to a New Job

When the secretary is acquainting herself with the routine of a new position, it is a good idea for her to make a list of all tasks required, with memoranda of detailed procedures involved in the more important work. Just as her employer has a daily schedule, which it may become her duty to arrange, so she ought to keep a similar daily schedule for herself, with reminders of future work, etc. She should also make a list of essential telephone numbers, and of the names of individuals and firms with which her employer comes in contact. Naturally many of these things will soon become a part of her memory, but lists are very helpful in the beginning.

Good work cannot be done in unpleasant or uncomfortable surroundings. The responsibility for such matters lies chiefly with the employer. Nevertheless, the new secretary should keep her desk neat and clean, try to obtain a swivel chair and adjust it to the most comfortable height, seek to avoid stuffy atmosphere and draughts, and do whatever else she is able in order to improve her working conditions. Her employer should appreciate this, since it increases her efficiency.

The following outline of the duties of the secretary is arranged for convenience in the order in which the tasks might ordinarily occur during the day.

The Executive's Schedule

The working hours of the modern executive must be apportioned carefully if he is to discharge his duties efficiently and advance the interests of his firm. For this purpose a series of written memoranda, entered on a desk pad or file cards, is much more reliable than memory. Many secretaries are responsible for such memoranda, and all secretaries should become familiar with the system their employer uses.

The executive's schedule contains two types of entries: (1) reminders of daily appointments and other important non-routine business; (2) "ticklers" or reminders that preparations should be made for matters that are coming up shortly, such as taxes or bills requiring payment, conferences at which a report or set of suggestions will have to be produced, or interviews necessitating special preparation. A "tickler" — so-called because it is intended to jog or "tickle" the memory—is entered on the schedule a suitable number of days before the coming event to which it refers. If it is taken care of, it is crossed off the schedule. If not, a similar entry is made for the following day, and so on until it is taken care of. Naturally reminders and ticklers are usually both entered on the same schedule, since they are closely related.

Whether such entries are made on desk pads, index cards, or in folders depends on their number and complexity. In any case the executive almost always keeps a desk pad, frequently divided into sections for each hour of the working day, on which both he and the secretary enter his daily appointments. Such a pad is handy to use, allowing appointments to be entered at the moment they are made. Tickler entries may also be made on the desk pad, but are usually kept on a separate pad or set of cards.

Too often the sheets of desk pads are torn off and discarded. As these sheets are a valuable record, some form of desk pad should be used which allows the sheets to be turned under or to one side from day to day.

The secretary often finds it advisable to keep a desk pad of her own, on which are entered those things she has been delegated to do and the things of which she is to remind her employer. The competent secretary has the knack of writing entries in a form which is clear and concise. It is unnecessary, for example, to preface each entry with the phrase "Remember to . . ." But no entry should be so brief as to be puzzling when referred to again after a few hours or days.

A tickler file consists of a set of cards, usually about thirty in number, one for each day of the month. At the end of each day, the card for that day is taken out and filed elsewhere, after the entries have either been crossed off or transferred to the card for the following day. At the same time a new card is added at the end of the file, thus keeping the number of cards in the file constant.

Another type of tickler file consists of a set of folders, again one for each day. Each folder contains notations of coming events and the documents such as tax bills, inventory forms, letters, etc., which bear on them. This is a convenient system for the executive, permitting him to lay his hands on the pertinent documents without delay, whenever he has a spare moment in which he can cast his thoughts ahead.

Handling Incoming Mail

In a small organization one person may open and sort all the mail. In a large organization mail for executives may be handled only by their secretaries. In either case, it is essential the mail be opened in such a way that there is little chance of tearing the contents or of throwing away enclosures with the envelopes. When the contents have been shaken away from the end to be opened, the envelope is slit with a paper knife. After the contents have been removed, the envelope may be cut on three sides and the interior examined to prevent the loss of enclosures, which should be clipped to the covering letter, if that has not already been done by the sender.

An entire delivery of mail should be opened at one time. When the letters have been opened, the next task is to sort them according to the nature of their contents. The custom of the office will determine the precise method of sorting, just as it will decide whether the secretary is to open letters marked "personal" or "confidential." As a rule advertisements and circulars are grouped together, orders are collected into another group, and routine correspondence is placed in a category by itself. Personal mail and letters requiring special handling are segregated from all other groups.

In a small office the secretary who opens the mail ordinarily distributes it among the individuals concerned. In a large office where the secretary is serving one executive, all the mail is placed on his desk, arranged according to the order of its importance, with the most urgent business at the top. Ordinarily the circulars and advertisements, being least important, would be placed at the bottom.

Some secretaries may be required to read incoming mail carefully, underline important matters to bring them to the executive's attention, and answer routine letters.

Taking Dictation

Success in taking dictation depends on a thorough knowledge of shorthand and English, but the ability of the stenographer and the person giving dictation to work together smoothly is also of vital importance. The stenographer—or secretary doing stenographic work—should behave in a manner that is tactful, thoughtful, courteous, and businesslike. She should sit facing the person giving dictation, her notebook supported on the desk or some other firm surface. Most business men do not like to dictate to a person whose attention seems to be concentrated elsewhere. Neither do they like to have their flow of thought interrupted by a person who habitually anticipates words or constantly interrupts. The competent stenographer shows an intelligent interest in the executive's words. In taking fast dictation she learns to concentrate separately on each word spoken, waiting for a pause before reviewing their meaning.

The secretary prepares to take dictation as soon as she has finished opening and sorting the mail. Notebooks and sharpened pencils should always be kept in the same, readily accessible place, so that there will be no delay in reporting for dictation. Several pencils should be taken into the executive's office, so that the breaking of a pencil point cannot cause loss of time. Filled pages in the notebook should be fastened together with a rubber band, so that the proper beginning page can be found immediately. Notes and notebooks should always be conspicuously dated, in order that quick reference can be made to past dictation—something the executive may frequently desire to do. Most offices require all stenographers to keep a file of their filled notebooks for at least one year. Even when this is not an office rule, it is a good practice, since stenographers' notebooks are a valuable record of past business transactions.

If, when taking dictation, the stenographer misses words or finds them confused, she may call attention to the matter by repeating the last word or phrase spoken. Or she may mark uncertain portions of her notes, and ask questions about them when the piece of dictation is finished. Pauses during dictation may be utilized in adding to and completing note, and in reading through those which have been taken. Such readings help to fix the meaning of the notes and make the task of transcription easier. If a visitor enters the room and the executive breaks off dictating, it is customary for the stenographer to leave, unless specifically requested to remain.

Special attention should be given during dictation to dates, numbers, and unfamiliar names. Accuracy being essential, the person giving dictation should allow the stenographer time to write these out in full.

If the dictation is too rapid, it is perfectly permissible for the secretary to request a more moderate pace. Most executives prefer such requests and questions about wording to the alternative presented by spoiled stationary and time wasted through enforced retyping.

Transcribing Shorthand

No system of shorthand is infallible in practice. Therefore shorthand notes cannot be transcribed automatically. Constant exercise of thought and judgment is necessary. It is a good idea to read each letter quickly before beginning to type it, in order to get a general idea of the contents. Then each sentence should be read for meaning and consistency before being typed out. This avoids erasures. It is wise to check dates and names against either enclosures or previous correspondence. Meaningless or ridiculous sentences should not be written in, but questioned; otherwise retyping will obviously be necessary. Doubtful material should be questioned, or at least indicated by a light-penciled question mark in the margin. The extent to which the stenographer may correct or improve wording depends entirely on the office and executive. In any case, she should watch out for excessive verbiage and words awkwardly repeated, since many dictators when groping for words tend to throw in unnecessary phrases.

In doing transcription, immediate attention should be given to telegrams, special instructions, and the like. Such notes should be prominently marked to distinguish them from the others. Telegrams should be transcribed and sent before letters are transcribed.

The transcriber should not hesitate to consult the dictionary and other authoritative works when in doubt. It is essential that the letter be cast in a proper form and effectively arranged on the page, and that the rules of proper spelling and good English be followed. For information on the form, arrangement, style, and content of business letters, the reader is referred to the section LETTER WRITING; for grammar and construction, to the section MODERN ENGLISH USAGE.

Unless otherwise instructed, the transcriber should always make at least one carbon copy of each letter, usually for filing with correspondence. Sometimes additional carbon copies will be needed, especially in the case of orders, instructions, etc. If more than four carbon copies are to be made, a typewriter with a hard platen should be used; otherwise the lower carbons will not be legible.

Before submitting letters for signature, the transcriber should assure herself that they are true copies of the shorthand notes, and that the typing is mechanically correct. The work of a good typist differs radically from that of an amateur. In addition to speed, it shows accuracy, uniformity of impression (all the characters being struck with equal force, so that they are alike in degree of blackness), and a pleasing arrangement of lines and margins.

Copy Typing

It is always possible to make mistakes when transcribing shorthand notes or in interpreting the words of a person giving dictation, but in copying materials already typed or printed the secretary is expected to do a perfect job. There is no excuse for mistaking definite words and characters.

Since such copies are usually of documents, contracts, letters received, and the like, absolute accuracy is essential. Copies should always be headed by the word "Copy" in parentheses, and any signatures should be preceded by "signed," also in parentheses. Unless the secretary is instructed otherwise, all apparent errors in the original should be copied faithfully. It is a common practice, however, to place an asterisk (*) after such errors and, at the bottom of the page, another asterisk, followed by a footnote explaining that the error occurs in the original. In the most strict variety of this work, such as that performed in legal offices, it may be necessary to copy line for line and page for page. All copy typing should be proofread against the original for errors.

Typing clean copies of rough drafts made by someone in the firm is quite a different matter, and the secretary is usually permitted to make corrections in spelling and grammar. If the meaning of some phrase cannot be determined, she should not hesitate to consult the writer.

Drafting Letters

In some offices it is part of the secretary's job to prepare replies to routine letters. She should learn to decide quickly which letters are routine and which are not. Her answers should be clearly reasoned and to the point. The general instructions contained in the section Letter Writing should be followed. According to the common procedure, she submits her replies to her employer for reading or signature at the same time that she shows him the incoming letters. This arrangement saves time.

Handling Outgoing Mail

Presuming that the letter has been typed and read, and the envelope typed, there are still certain precautions that the secretary should automatically take. She should make sure that the address on the envelope is identical with that given in the heading of the letter. She should assure herself that the letter has been signed. Finally, she should glance through the letter to ascertain what enclosures there are supposed to be, and then check the enclosures accordingly.

The letter should be neatly folded in such a way that it occupies most of the envelope but leaves ample space for opening the letter without danger of tearing the contents. Small supplementary folds made at the last minute have an ugly and untidy appearance. There is no excuse for them. The secretary should determine beforehand the most graceful way of folding all sizes of paper used in her office. Enclosures should usually be clipped to the letter, in order to avoid being lost. If pressure must be applied in sealing an envelope, it is advisable to place a sheet of paper over the flap, in order to avoid smudges. The stamp should be affixed securely, after it is checked for correct value.

To expedite business transactions, it is important that letters be mailed promptly. The accomplished secretary knows the times at which letters are collected from the box used by her office, and plans the mailing of batches of letters accordingly. If speed is essential letters may be sent straight to the main postoffice, and letters or packages may be sent direct to local destinations by messenger.

Detailed information on postal regulations, methods, and rates is contained in the section Postal Information, to which the reader is referred.

Filing Systems

In an efficient office, all materials pertaining to business transactions are made readily available for reference by a suitable filing system. The backbone of the system is almost always a correspondence file, consisting of folders, one for each separate firm or individual with whom there are business dealings — customers, creditors, manufacturers, advertising agencies, etc. Each folder contains letters received from the firm in question, carbon copies of letters sent in reply, and other pertinent documents, such as advertising matter and reports on interviews and conferences. The contents of each folder are arranged in the order of their dates, and therefore tell a complete, coherent story of vital importance to a business man wishing to review for one purpose or another the stages in a set of transactions.

The secretary may be responsible for keeping such a file in order and up to date. In any case it will be necessary for her to file carbon copies of the letters which she has written for her employer. She may frequently be called upon to find material in the files.

The arrangement of items (folders, in the case of the correspondence file) is almost always alphabetical. There is a detailed discussion of this method in the section Filing by Alphabet. Other arrangements include the geographical, in which firms are grouped by regions, a method convenient for sales campaigns and distributions; the numerical; and the Dewey Decimal Classification, familiar in libraries. The two latter methods are seldom used in business offices.

Cardboard guides are used to separate the folders in a file. These guides bear identification tabs, facilitating the locating of material. It is more convenient to file material in front of the guide referring to it, but the system of filing **behind** the guides is still used in many offices.

A large file is generally accompanied by a card index, in which each folder is represented by a corresponding card bearing the name of the firm or individual. If a firm is known by several different names, or different forms of the same name, there are cross reference cards; as, for example, "Corrugated Box and Fiberboard, Inc. Look under: Midwestern Corrugated Box and Fiberboard" or "Antiquarian Society of America. See American Antiquarian Society." Similar cross-reference cards would be used if the correspondence for two related firms happened to be filed in the same folder. Use of an index does away with time wasted in long searches through the bulkier files. For a small file, however, an index is seldom worth the time taken in maintaining it.

There are many supplementary files and indexes used in business offices. These may include mailing lists, lists of customers and prospective customers, files of newspapers and magazine clippings, legal documents, receipts, orders, employee records, indexes of references to books, and the like. In large offices each executive maintains an individual file of matters pertaining to his special province, and this file is usually kept in order by his private secretary.

A mailing list of any size is best kept on a series of cards, one for each firm or individual, rather than on typewritten sheets. Then names can be added to or dropped from the list without the need for a lengthy retyping and without disturbing the convenient alphabetical order. For similar reasons, card indexes of the names of customers and "prospects" are advisable. These may also be classified according to the item in which the customer is most interested, cards of a different color being used for this purpose; for example, a firm dealing in hardware might list purchasers of kitchen utensils on green cards, purchasers of tools on yellow cards, general purchasers on white cards, etc. Then if a special sales campaign for one type of product were undertaken, the appropriate cards could quickly be removed from the file.

There are certain general suggestions as to efficient filing:

(1) A file or index is only valuable if kept up to date. Otherwise it is a source of error and confusion. When a firm changes its name or address, a new card should be made out immediately, and correspondence transferred to a new folder.

(2) Care should be taken to list firms according to their complete, official name.

(3) If there is doubt as to where an item should most properly be filed, the quickest thing to do is to file it arbitrarily in one place and then make out a number of cross-reference cards.

(4) Preliminary to being filed, material may be kept in a general "suspense folder." However, the contents of the suspense folder should be filed at the earliest possible date; otherwise it will quickly become larger than the file itself. Instead of a single suspense folder, several may be used, one for each type of material, thus allowing for a certain amount of preliminary filing.

(5) In a large firm it is generally advisable for employees taking material from the files to sign a note to that effect, thus guarding against the loss of folders and making it easy to locate materials temporarily out of the files. If a folder is to be kept out for some time, it should be replaced with an "out card" the same size as the folder, thus quickly indicating to another searcher that the material has not been lost or filed elsewhere.

(6) Letters and other related papers are less bulky if stapled rather than clipped together.

(7) Bulky material, such as catalogues, samples, and pamphlets, should be kept in a separate file or case, with cross-reference cards indicating the location.

(8) The drawers of a filing cabinet should be kept closed when not in immediate use, and locked when the office is empty.

(9) The materials most frequently referred to should be kept where most easily reached, usually in the upper file-drawers rather than in those next to the floor.

(10) If several different folder files are in use in an office, it is well to mark the folders constituting each file with tabs of the same color, thus preventing folders from being returned to the wrong file.

The Treatment of Callers

It is the secretary's duty to learn the nature of the caller's business. Having learned it, she must decide on the basis of her past experience whether it is such as to be of interest to her employer and whether to send the caller in at once or make an appointment for him to see her employer at some other time. In many cases she may have to consult with her employer before arriving at a decision.

Many employers wish their secretaries to act as buffers between them and callers they are unable or unwilling to see. Secretaries in this rather uncomfortable position are required to exercise a good deal of tact and patience. A secretary who can perform such a difficult task well and who in addition can transact business with routine callers without referring them to her employer at all, is a very great asset to a business. There is a further discussion of these problems in the section ETIQUETTE FOR BUSINESS MEN AND WOMEN.

Many offices keep a daily list of callers, each entry ordinarily including the name of the caller, his business connections, and the errand on which he called. The lists are usually filed and retained as a semi-permanent record. Even when office rules do not require such a list to be kept, some secretaries make them because they are of value as records of transactions and because they serve to acquaint the secretary with the people who frequent the office.

The handling of telephone calls is essentially the same as the handling of callers. In both cases the secretary's duty is to learn the caller's business in as brief and courteous a way as possible, and then to refer the call in the manner determined by her experience. A cheerful voice creates a good impression. If a call must be kept waiting for some time before being answered by the person to whom it is referred, it is a good idea for the secretary to make occasional reassuring remarks so that the caller will not feel he has been forgotten or slighted. It is a good practice to keep a list of telephone calls similar to the list of those who call in person.

Appointments and Itineraries

In addition to scheduling her employer's day at the office, the secretary may be required to make arrangements for his time spent outside the office—visits to other firms, extended trips for the purpose of sales and conferences, and the like. For this purpose it is desirable that she have a good working knowledge of local transportation facilities, general traveling conditions, and her employer's personal preferences in such matters. Naturally she should consult him when in doubt, but if she performs her task sensibly and efficiently, he may come to rely greatly on her judgment.

In making appointments, courtesy and the dignity of her firm are important considerations. Where possible, appointments should be definite rather than tentative, and arranged by one phone call rather than several. This makes for efficient routine. It often proves advisable to combine business and social dates, as by having the meeting include a luncheon. There are certain hours of the working day during which an executive can best afford to be absent from the office; such hours, often those of the afternoon, are most suitable for outside appointments. Before leaving for his appointment he will usually want to refresh his mind by going over recent correspondence with the person he is going to meet. Therefore the appropriate folder should be on hand, together with notes on plans or proposals which he may wish to discuss. It is often a part of the secretary's duties to bring such matters to his attention.

The preparing of an itinerary for an extended trip is a more complicated task, usually involving the purchase of railroad or airway tickets, making hotel reservations, and making appointments in advance by letter or telegram. The secretary will need to rely to a considerable extent on the advice of travel bureaus, though she should always adopt an arrangement suited to her employer's preferences and convenience. It is wise for her to have time tables on hand, though great care should be taken to renew these whenever there is a change of schedules; otherwise they will prove a source of error. In general, all arrangements should be checked on by telephone or letter. Hotel reservations may be made by letter. The accomplished secretary familiarizes herself with the travel and hotel facilities in those regions to which her employer's business interests are apt to carry him.

In planning itineraries economy of time and movement is essential. If several cities are to be visited, appointments should be made in such an order as to involve the least amount of traveling; here a knowledge of the geography of the locality is essential.

After the itinerary has been planned, it should be drawn up on paper. A brief one may indicate only the hours of arrival and departure for each day, along with information as to the name of the railroad line, the station, and number of the car in which reservation has been made. Railroads and airways will furnish such an itinerary made out in full. A more complete itinerary indicates hotel reservations, time and place of appointments, names of individuals to be met, notes on matters to be discussed, plans and suggestions, subsidiary matters to be taken up if there is time available, local transportation arrangements, etc. Such an itinerary is chiefly for the convenience of the traveler, but copies should always be kept at the home office. Then it will be possible to get in touch with the traveler if any important instructions or periodic reports are to be forwarded to him.

The secretary may pack for the traveler a special folder containing such office supplies as blank letterhead paper, plain paper, notebooks, pencils, etc., if there will be occasion to use them.

Care of Office Equipment

Secretaries are not usually mechanics, and they are not expected to repair their own typewriters. They are, however, supposed to clean and oil them in accordance with the manufacturer's instructions. The ability of the secretary to turn out good work depends on her remembering to change the ribbon of her machine and to clean its type whenever necessary. The care of office equipment involves covering typewriters, adding machines, etc., at the end of the working day, and dusting desks and office equipment at regular intervals. The interior portions of typewriters may be dusted effectively with a narrow, long-handled brush.

The secretary is often, among other things, her employer's business housekeeper. In many offices the appearance of his desk is as much her responsibility as is the taking of his dictation. However, she should never rearrange his desk without determining whether that is agreeable to him.

Ordering Supplies

It may be part of the secretary's duties to order minor office supplies from an outside dealer. These usually include: paper bearing the firm's letterhead; blank sheets of the same size, color, and quality, for the pages of letters following the first; carbon paper; second sheets for carbon copies; envelopes, both blank and with the firm's name and address; stamps; postcards; stenographic notebooks; memorandum pads; index cards; file folders; labels; tabs; bank deposit slips; pencils; pens; erasers for pencil, ink, and typewriter; clips; staples; pins; typewriter ribbons; oil for typewriter; paste; transparent mending tape; etc.

The secretary may also have the responsibility of holding the petty cash box and keeping the petty cash account. In a large office she is more often required to requisition supplies from another department of the organization. In either case, it is her business to see that the quantities on hand are always adequate. Supplies should never be ordered in such quantities, however, that they deteriorate before use. Most typewriter ribbons rot, and certain kinds of white paper turn yellow with age. These items in particular should not be ordered unless there is reasonable certainty of their being used within a fairly short time. The secretary should keep a list of all supplies being used and note down impending shortages. All supplies should be orderly arranged in the proper cabinets.

Bank Accounts

The handling of a bank account involves three chief operations: (1) making deposits; (2) writing checks and paying bills; (3) checking bank statements.

The bank book should always be taken to the bank when a deposit is to be made. If for some reason it is necessary to leave the bank book in the office, a duplicate deposit slip should be made out by the secretary and initialed by the teller. This slip should be preserved by the secretary until it is possible to have the deposit entered in the bank book. All deposits should be entered in the stub of the check book so that the office may always know the approximate bank balance.

One method of endorsing checks should be adopted and maintained. This is the rule in almost all business offices.

When possible, bills should be paid by check. When this is impossible, a receipt should be obtained for the cash disbursed. All offices have a procedure of verifying bills before paying them. These procedures always embrace verification of quantity, quality, and specifications; the checking of credit allowances and discounts; and the checking of the arithmetic of the bill.

When, on or shortly after the first of the month, the canceled checks for the previous month are returned, the secretary should go over them carefully. The checking of a bank statement involves these processes:

(1) The checks as returned should be checked against the stubs in the book. This is an elementary precaution against forgery.

(2) The deposit items on the bank statement should be checked against the deposit items in the bank book. Bank book and bank statement should agree.

(3) The canceled checks should agree with the withdrawal items on the bank statement.

(4) By subtracting the total of the checks from the total of the deposit items, a figure is arrived at which should equal the current bank balance.

(5) Checks issued in one month and not presented until after the first of the following month are always a nuisance to bookkeepers and cashiers. It is perfectly permissible to ask that checks outstanding for a long time be deposited.

The Large Office

The routine of a large office has certain special characteristics setting it off from that of a small office. As a result of the difference in size, the number of tasks are multiplied. The proper carrying out of such a complex routine is far beyond the powers of one secretary of general ability, or even several. Specialization is essential, each employee concentrating on a few steps in a highly complicated process. Even the work of the private secretary is usually limited to that entailed in serving one executive.

This specialization, though inescapable, brings up certain difficulties seldom found in small offices. Greater dependence must be placed on a carefully-thought-out and foolproof routine. It becomes impossible for one person to oversee and coordinate everything. Yet the specialized office worker performing only one task has difficulty in understanding the function of his work and seeing it in the proper perspective, and when tasks are performed by many individuals instead of one or two, there is a correspondingly greater chance for misunderstanding, error, and confusion.

To offset this advantage, many large offices make a practice of shifting workers from one task to another, so that they will gain a greater understanding of the whole routine and be better able to detect errors. Some workers resent being assigned to new tasks, disliking the added mental effort involved and thinking it merely a matter of whim. Actually they should welcome such opportunities and look upon them as training for promotion. This is even more true when individuals are shifted from department to department, spending a certain amount of time in production work, advertising, merchandising, sales work, and distribution. Such varied training is a frequent preliminary to advancement.

It must always be remembered that the large modern office should be an adjusting mechanism between the other departments, which have a less flexible sort of work and must struggle with external factors — the production department with machines and materials, the distribution department with transportation facilities, the sales department with general business conditions and consumers' demands. Unfortunately some office administrations consider that their job is to exercise authority and direct the activities of all other departments. This mistaken authoritarianism is largely an inheritance from the days of smaller businesses, when one or a few individuals personally supervised all activities. The efficient modern office administration coordinates activities, smooths out difficulties, avoids inter-departmental difficulties, and in all ways acts as an adjusting mechanism. Therefore the more flexible the individual worker is and the better he is acquainted with other jobs besides his own, the better he will be able to serve his employer and himself.

POSTAL INFORMATION

Through its 37,000 post offices and thousands of rural routes the U.S. Postal Department handles billions of pieces of mail a year. A far greater percentage of losses on postage and value of mail contents occur because of careless affixing of stamps, insecure wrapping, and incorrect addressing. It is unnecessary to point out that delays and losses cause inconvenience, business misunderstandings, and incomplete financial transactions.

The Chicago Dead Letter Office alone receives approximately 1,225,000 dead letters each year, which require special examination and readdressing before delivery. This division returns all it can, but carelessness which misdirects a letter usually forgets a return address, with result that thousands of dollars' worth of unclaimed property has to be sold at auction annually. To avoid these losses keep in mind the following suggestions:

a. Remember return address.
b. Write "General Delivery" on mail for persons not permanently located in city addressed.
c. Write full name of addressee, street name and number, zone number, post office box or rural route number. If state has towns of similar name, add county.
d. Affix necessary postage, seal letters, wrap parcels securely, attach required labels.

First Class

To this class belongs all personal mail, wholly or partly handwritten. Mail sealed is treated as first class matter, unless printed labels giving permission for inspection of contents are affixed. Rates are:

(1) Written sealed matter for local and other than local delivery, 4c an oz., or fraction thereof.
(2) Postal cards, government, 3c each.
(3) Private post cards (3⁹⁄₁₆x5⁹⁄₁₆), 3c each.
(4) Business reply cards and envelopes, 2c each in addition to regular postage collected on delivery; by air mail 2c each extra.

First class matter prepaid at less than rate will be delivered collect to addressee.

Second Class

Includes newspapers and periodicals and must bear label "SECOND CLASS." For publishers' rate, consult local postmaster. Transient rate, 2c for first 2 oz., 1c for each additional oz., or 4th class rate, if cheaper.

Third Class

To this class belong merchandise and miscellaneous printed matter, photographs, books and catalogs of 24 pages or more, seeds, cuttings, roots, bulbs, scions, and plants. Weight is limited to but does not include 16 oz. The rate is 3c for the first 2 oz., and 1½c for each additional oz. or fraction thereof.

Bulk third class rate allows not less than 20 pounds or 200 separately addressed identical pieces to be shipped at 16c per pound, or less, but not less than 2c per piece which is increased to 2½c per piece in July, 1960. For merchandise and miscellaneous printed matter, circulars, books or catalogues of 24 pages or more, seeds, etc., the rate is 10c per pound or less but not less than 2c per piece increased to 2½c per piece in July, 1960. Minimum charge for pieces of odd shape or form is 6c per piece.

Certain nonprofit organizations, religious, educational, scientific, philanthropic, agricultural, labor, veteran's, or fraternal in nature, may use the special third-class mail rate of 1c for each ounce or fraction thereof, or the bulk rate of 1c per piece. In order to qualify for the mailing privilege the organization must submit, to the Assistant Postmaster General in Washington, D.C., through the local postmaster, a statement as to the type of organization it is, and whether it is organized for profit. The statement must be accompanied by the organization's charter, by-laws, constitution, and must indicate whether the organization is exempt from taxation by the Internal Revenue Department, the reason for the exemption, and the date of exemption.

Fourth Class or Parcel Post

Fourth class, or parcel post includes merchandise, books, printed matter and all other matter not included in first and second class mail. Size limit is 84 inches in length and girth combined; weight limit is over 16 ounces and not exceeding 40 pounds in the local, first and second zones, and 20 pounds in the third to eighth zone, at first class post offices, for delivery to other first class post offices.

However, parcels up to 70 pounds and 100 inches in combined length and girth are acceptable if they are

(1) Mailed at any post office, rural or star route, to a second, third or fourth class post office or rural station, to be delivered on a rural or star route.
(2) Mailed at a second, third or fourth class post office or on a rural or star route.
(3) If they contain baby fowl (1 day old), plants, trees, or agricultural commodities. Agricultural commodities include products grown or produced in connection with agriculture, such as fruits, vegetables, seeds, nuts, honey, eggs, etc. Parcels must be endorsed to show the nature of the product, and must be suitably wrapped.
(4) Books.
(5) Parcels mailed in the United States for delivery to any Army or Fleet post office, or any territorial post office, or post office located in any United States possession, or parcels mailed at an Army or Fleet post office, a territorial post office located in a possession of the United States for delivery in the United States.

Parcels which exceed 84 inches in length and girth combined, even though weighing less than 10 pounds, are charged the 10 pound rate of postage for the particular zone to which they are mailed.

The length of a parcel is determined by measuring in a straight line between the ends, but not around the parcel. The girth is the distance around the parcel at the thickest part.

Postage on parcel post mail must be fully prepaid, and fractions of pounds will be charged the full pound rate.

Third and fourth class parcels (except those containing circular or miscellaneous printed matter) may be sealed when bearing printed label "CONTENTS MERCHANDISE: Postmaster, this parcel may be opened for postal inspection if necessary." Undeliverable third and fourth and transient second class mail will be returned to the sender when the words "RETURN POSTAGE GUARANTEED" are printed under return address. New addresses will be furnished senders of third and fourth class mail, when known, if the following notice is printed in lower left hand corner of address side: "POSTMASTER: If addressee has moved, and new address is known, notify sender on FORM 3547, postage for which is guaranteed."

Fourth Class or Parcel Post Rates

W't. in Lbs.	Local	Zones 1-2 Up to 150 miles	3 150 to 300 miles	4 300 to 600 miles	5 600 to 1,000 miles	6 1,000 to 1,400 miles	7 1,400 to 1,800 miles	8 Over 1,800 miles
1...	$0.18	$0.23	$0.23	$0.24	$0.26	$0.28	$0.30	$0.32
2...	.20	.27	.29	.31	.36	.40	.46	.51
3...	.21	.31	.34	.38	.45	.52	.61	.69
4...	.23	.35	.39	.45	.54	.64	.76	.87
5...	.24	.39	.44	.52	.63	.76	.91	1.05
6...	.26	.43	.49	.59	.73	.88	1.06	1.23
7...	.27	.47	.54	.66	.82	1.00	1.22	1.41
8...	.29	.51	.60	.73	.91	1.12	1.37	1.59
9...	.30	.55	.65	.80	1.00	1.24	1.52	1.77
10*..	.32	.59	.70	.87	1.10	1.36	1.67	1.95
11...	.33	.63	.75	.93	1.19	1.48	1.82	2.13
12...	.34	.67	.80	1.00	1.28	1.60	1.98	2.31
13...	.36	.71	.85	1.07	1.37	1.72	2.13	2.49
14...	.37	.75	.90	1.14	1.47	1.84	2.28	2.67
15...	.39	.79	.96	1.21	1.56	1.96	2.43	2.85
16...	.40	.83	1.01	1.28	1.65	2.08	2.58	3.03
17...	.42	.87	1.06	1.35	1.74	2.20	2.74	3.21
18...	.43	.91	1.11	1.42	1.84	2.32	2.89	3.39
19...	.45	.95	1.16	1.49	1.93	2.44	3.04	3.57
20...	.46	.99	1.21	1.56	2.02	2.56	3.19	3.75
21...	.47	1.02	1.26	1.62	2.11	2.67	3.34	3.93
22...	.49	1.06	1.32	1.69	2.21	2.79	3.50	4.12
23...	.50	1.10	1.37	1.76	2.30	2.91	3.65	4.30
24...	.52	1.14	1.42	1.83	2.39	3.03	3.80	4.48
25...	.53	1.18	1.47	1.90	2.48	3.15	3.95	4.66
26...	.55	1.22	1.52	1.97	2.58	3.27	4.10	4.84
27...	.56	1.26	1.57	2.04	2.67	3.39	4.26	5.02
28...	.58	1.30	1.63	2.11	2.76	3.51	4.41	5.20
29...	.59	1.34	1.68	2.18	2.85	3.63	4.56	5.38
30...	.61	1.38	1.73	2.25	2.95	3.75	4.71	5.56
31...	.62	1.42	1.78	2.31	3.04	3.87	4.86	5.74
32...	.63	1.46	1.83	2.38	3.13	3.99	5.02	5.92
33...	.65	1.50	1.88	2.45	3.22	4.11	5.17	6.10
34...	.66	1.54	1.93	2.52	3.32	4.23	5.32	6.28
35...	.68	1.58	1.99	2.59	3.41	4.35	5.47	6.46
36...	.69	1.62	2.04	2.66	3.50	4.47	5.62	6.64
37...	.71	1.66	2.09	2.73	3.59	4.59	5.78	6.82
38...	.72	1.70	2.14	2.80	3.69	4.71	5.93	7.00
39...	.74	1.74	2.19	2.87	3.78	4.83	6.08	7.18
40...	.75	1.78	2.24	2.94	3.87	4.95	6.23	7.36
41...	.76	1.81	2.29	3.00	3.96	5.06	6.38	7.54
42...	.78	1.85	2.35	3.07	4.06	5.18	6.54	7.73
43...	.79	1.89	2.40	3.14	4.15	5.30	6.69	7.91
44...	.81	1.93	2.45	3.21	4.24	5.42	6.84	8.09
45...	.82	1.97	2.50	3.28	4.33	5.54	6.99	8.27
46...	.84	2.01	2.55	3.35	4.43	5.66	7.14	8.45
47...	.85	2.05	2.60	3.42	4.52	5.78	7.30	8.63
48...	.87	2.09	2.66	3.49	4.61	5.90	7.45	8.81
49...	.88	2.13	2.71	3.56	4.70	6.02	7.60	8.99
50...	.90	2.17	2.76	3.63	4.80	6.14	7.75	9.17
51...	.91	2.21	2.81	3.69	4.89	6.26	7.90	9.35
52...	.92	2.25	2.86	3.76	4.98	6.38	8.06	9.53
53...	.94	2.29	2.91	3.83	5.07	6.50	8.21	9.71
54...	.95	2.33	2.96	3.90	5.17	6.62	8.36	9.89
55...	.97	2.37	3.02	3.97	5.26	6.74	8.51	10.07
56...	.98	2.41	3.07	4.04	5.35	6.86	8.66	10.25
57...	1.00	2.45	3.12	4.11	5.44	6.98	8.82	10.43
58...	1.01	2.49	3.17	4.18	5.54	7.10	8.97	10.61
59...	1.03	2.53	3.22	4.25	5.63	7.22	9.12	10.79
60...	1.04	2.57	3.27	4.32	5.72	7.34	9.27	10.97
61...	1.05	2.60	3.32	4.38	5.81	7.45	9.42	11.15
62...	1.07	2.64	3.38	4.45	5.91	7.57	9.58	11.34
63...	1.08	2.68	3.43	4.52	6.00	7.69	9.73	11.52
64...	1.10	2.72	3.48	4.59	6.09	7.81	9.88	11.70
65...	1.11	2.76	3.53	4.66	6.18	7.93	10.03	11.88
66...	1.13	2.80	3.58	4.73	6.28	8.05	10.18	12.06
67...	1.14	2.84	3.63	4.80	6.37	8.17	10.34	12.24
68...	1.16	2.88	3.69	4.87	6.46	8.29	10.49	12.42
69...	1.17	2.92	3.74	4.94	6.55	8.41	10.64	12.60
70...	1.19	2.96	3.79	5.01	6.65	8.53	10.79	12.78

*Parcels Over 84 Inches—On parcels measuring more than 84 inches, but not more than 100 inches in length and girth combined, the minimum postage charge shall be the zone charge applicable to a 10-pound parcel.

Preparation, Packing and Wrapping

Fourth class mail must be wrapped so the contents may be easily examined by postal officials. It must be securely packed and wrapped so it can be transported without injuring mail bags, contents, or handlers. Postal regulations cover the packing of harmful articles, such as sharp pointed instruments, or pieces of machinery. Certain conditions govern the mailing of liquids, oils and inflammable substances.

Parcels requiring handling outside of mail bags must bear the black and red OUTSIDE MAIL label. Some objects sent by outside mail are parcels weighing over 35 pounds, fragile phonograph records, eggs, berries or cut flowers, mirrors or cut glass, small, exceptionally heavy parcels, etc.

Fragile and perishable articles must be so indicated.

Matter of a harmful nature is unmailable. Classified as harmful are poisons, explosives, corrosives, matches, except safety matches, live animals, fowl, except day-old poultry, insects, reptiles, articles with offensive odors, and intoxicating liquors. There is a severe legal penalty for mailing any of these articles

For further information on mailing harmful objects, liquids, oils, inflammable substances, perishable and fragile articles, consult the local postmaster.

Book Rate

Rate of 9c per lb., plus 5c for each lb. added, up to 70 lbs., is applicable to permanently bound books (for library books, 4c for first lb., 1c for each added lb.). They may be registered, insured, C.O.D., and Special Delivery, on payment of extra fees. The classification excludes advertising in book form or furthering commercial interests of a group, such as banking reports, or trade annuals. Rates on individually addressed catalogues and similar advertising matter in bound form, consisting of 24 or more pages, weighing 8 oz. to 10 lbs., are 12c to $1.28 according to zone and weight.

Special Delivery

To insure earlier delivery of mail than provided by postman, send Special Delivery. Such matter will be delivered by special messenger if received at post office of destination between 7 a.m. and 9 p.m. (6 p.m. Sunday). It should bear, in addition to regular postage, a Special Delivery stamp and the words "SPECIAL DELIVERY" written above the address. Special Delivery parcels of all classes receive immediate delivery. Rates for first class are: to 2 lbs., 30c; 2 to 10 lbs., 45c; over 10 lbs., 60c. For second, third, and fourth classes, rates are: to 2 lbs., 45c; 2 to 10 lbs., 55c; over 10 lbs., 70c. Register valuables if sent by Special Delivery.

Special Handling

Parcel post containing perishables will receive speediest handling practicable on payment of a special fee (charge does not include Special Delivery). Parcel must bear endorsement "SPECIAL HANDLING." Rates (in addition to regular postage): to 2 lbs., 25c; 2 to 10 lbs., 35c; over 10 lbs., 50c.

Registered Mail

First, second, and third class matter (and parcel post which is sealed and mailed at first class rates) may be registered. Money, valuable papers, articles of unusual value, articles for which a return receipt showing delivery is requested, letters to be delivered to addressee in person, should for safety be registered. Fees (in addition to regular postage) are:

Up to $10	.50c
$10.01 to $100	.75c
$100.01 to $200	$1.00
$200.01 to $400	$1.25
$400.01 to $600	$1.50
$600.01 to $800	$1.75
$800.01 to $1000	$2.00

The value of all mail which is to be registered must be declared by the mailer.

The Post Office suggests the following declaration of values on representative items presented for registry.

Currency: full value.

Negotiable securities: The market value quoted on the day of registration.

Jewelry and precious stones: full value.

Merchandise: full value.

Internal Revenue Documentary Stamps and Postage Stamps: full value. (When stamps of value to philatelists are mailed, the stamps should be registered according to the cost of replacement.)

Papers such as checks, drafts, deeds, wills, etc., have no registry value, and can be duplicated without expense.

Non-negotiable securities such as certificates of stock and warehouse receipts have no intrinsic value, but if registration is desired, the sender may pay a fee higher than the minimum in order to indemnify himself against the cost of duplication of the registered items in case of loss or destruction.

Receipts for registered mail should be held until sender is certain the mail has been received. If not delivered in reasonable time request at the post office to trace it.

Certified Mail

Any mail having no intrinsic value that is posted by 1st class or air mail rates may be certified. For a fee of 20c, in addition to postage, a receipt is furnished at the time of mailing and evidence may be obtained showing to whom and when the article was delivered. Restricted delivery (delivery made to addressee only), special delivery, and return receipts (showing address where article was delivered, date of delivery, and name of recipient) may be obtained for additional fees. Return receipts for certified, insured, or registered mail are available upon payment of 10c.

Insurance

Third and fourth class mail only may be insured. Fees (in addition to regular postage) are:

$ 0.01 to $ 10.00	$0.10
10.01 to 50.00	.20
50.01 to 100.00	.30
100.01 to 200.00	.40

The Post Office recently amended the Postal Laws to read that no liability is assumed for shellac or wax phonograph records sent as C.O.D. mail or contained in parcels accepted for insurance. However, records must be wrapped in accordance with packing regulations.

Collect-on-Delivery

First, third, and fourth class domestic mail may be sent, sealed and unsealed, C.O.D., and collection made through the Post Office Department, if shipment is based on bona fide agreement between sender and addressee. Not more than $200 may be collected on one C.O.D. parcel. Postage on all classes is at the first class rate. Fees include insurance and registration. For C.O.D. registered mail the fees on the amount to be collected are:

$ 0.01 to $ 5.00	$0.80
5.01 to 10.00	.90
10.01 to 25.00	1.35
25.01 to 50.00	1.45
50.01 to 100.00	1.55
100.01 to 150.00	1.90
150.01 to 200.00	2.00

When indemnity in excess of $200 is desired, fees, in addition to postage, surcharges, or other fees, are $2.25 to $3.00, on amounts up to $1,000.

For C.O.D. insured third and fourth class matter, the fees on amount to be collected are:

$ 0.01 to $ 5.00	$0.40
5.01 to 10.00	.50
10.01 to 25.00	.80
25.01 to 50.00	.90
50.01 to 100.00	1.10
100.01 to 150.00	1.30
150.01 to 200.00	1.40

C.O.D. mail held at office of address over 15 days is subject to demurrage charge of 5c a day. Request for alteration of charges on delivery of C.O.D. article, other than to addressee, must be accompanied by 10c. Request must be filed at MAILING OFFICE, and should in addition to above charge include local rate postage for second delivery attempt. If undeliverable, 5c shall be collected when notifying sender.

Money Orders

To prevent loss or theft of money in mailing, use money orders in amounts up to $100. Domestic fees are 15c for up to $5, 20c up to $10, and 30c up to $100. For sending money abroad, fees are 30c for up to $5, 40c up to $10, and 60c up to $100. Keep money order receipts until orders are cashed.

Air Mail

First class mail may be sent by air and may be registered, insured, C.O.D., or Special Delivery, for additional fees. It must be marked "AIRMAIL" and may be deposited in U.S. mailboxes. Ordinary postage stamps and envelopes may be used but government air mail stamps and red-white-and-blue-bordered air mail envelopes are desirable. Rates on first class matter are: within the U.S. and Alaska, to and from the continental U.S. including Alaska, Hawaii, Puerto Rico, Virgin Islands, Canton Island, Canal Zone and Guam, and to points within or between the territories where the United States air mail service operates. The rates also apply to members of the Armed Forces stationed outside the United States who have Army Post Office numbers or Fleet Post Office designations, and to civilian personnel authorized to receive mail through the Army or Navy post offices.

The limit on air mail is 8 ounces, at the rate of 7c per ounce or fraction thereof, and 5c for post cards.

Air Parcel Post

Zone rates prescribed for parcels carried by air shall apply to mailable matter of any class weighing over 8 oz. but not more than 70 lbs. not exceeding 100 inches in length and girth combined, including written or other matter of the first class, sealed or unsealed.

The air-zone rates provided shall be based on the eight postal zones applicable to fourth-class (parcel post) mail.

A fraction of a pound is chargeable as a full pound.

Parcels containing other first class matter, not inflammable or freezable, over 8 oz. in weight are classed as air parcel post. Rates are 7c an oz. for all domestic air mail up to and including 8 oz. regardless of zone; over 8 oz. the rates are from 60c to $50.43 in the first 7 zones. Parcels to the 8th postal zone (between any point in the continental U. S.; to, within, and from the U. S. territories and possessions, such as Guam, U. S. Virgin Islands, etc., and to APO's and to Navy and Marine units through Fleet Post Offices) including surface delivery, the rate is from 80c (8 oz. to 1 lb.) to $56 (to 70 lbs.).

Parcels weighing less than 10 lbs., but exceeding 84 inches in length and girth combined, require postage at the 10 lb. rate.

First class letters, with proper postage, may be affixed to second, third, and fourth class matter. Parcels MUST bear sender's name and address. They can be sent Special Delivery for surface delivery. Fees for registration, insurance, Special Delivery, and C.O.D. must be prepaid in addition to and according to zone postage.

International Postal Service

Articles of regular mail are handled through the International Postal Union.

Postage on letter and letter packages to Canada and Mexico is 4c per ounce. The weight limit on letter packages to Canada is 60 pounds. Postal cards may be sent to these two countries at 3c per single card and 6c for reply paid cards. Postal rates for letters and letter packages to all other countries is 8c for the first ounce and 5c for each additional ounce. Post cards, single, are 4c each and 8c, reply paid. The weight limit on letter packages to all countries, excepting Canada, is 4 pounds, 6 ounces.

The length, breadth and thickness combined, of letter packages, must not exceed 36 inches, and the length may not exceed 24 inches. The package, when sent as a roll, the maximum length is 32 inches, or are limited to 4 pounds 6 ounces, and small packets 40 inches. In some cases, however (inquire at the post office), when the object is indivisible, the length may go to 40 inches, and the length plus twice the diameter, may total 48 inches. Merchandise is not acceptable in letter packages in all countries, and information on foreign mails may be had at the local post office.

General printed matter is handled at a charge of 4c for the first 2 ounces and 2c for every additional 2 ounces. Weight limit varies from 6 pounds 9 ounces to 60 pounds, and this, also, should be checked with the post office. The book rate to most countries of the world is 8c per pound, with a weight limit of 60 pounds. Samples may be sent at the rate of 4c for the first 2 ounces and 3c for each additional 2 ounces. The weight limit is 18 ounces. Raised print for the blind is sent at 1 cent per pound, limited to 15 pounds 6 ounces. Commercial papers (minimum, 10c) are limited to 4 pounds 6 ounces, and small packets (minimum, 20c), are limited to 2 pounds 3 ounces. Small packets are not serviced in all countries, and information should be obtained from the post office.

10-cent Air Letters

An air letter sheet can be purchased at all post offices for 10c, and may be used for all foreign countries. The sheet folds into an envelope with a printed stamp and air mail markings. No enclosures can be made, the letter cannot be sealed with tape, and address labels cannot be applied. The sheets may be registered. Consult the local post office for rates for regular letters and letter packages.

International Air Parcel Post

Air parcel post service is now in effect in various parts of the world. The rates vary according to the rates of the individual countries. Packages may be sent registered, insured, or C.O.D. The same postal form (custom declarations, dispatch note, parcel post stickers, etc.) required for surface parcels, must be prepared for air parcels and the blue "Par Avion" label must be attached to the address side of the package and to the dispatch note if that is required.

Air parcels are subject to the same size and weight limitations as regular international parcel post. Inquire at the local post office for rates, weight and size limitations.

When the parcel arrives in the country of destination, it is sent to the recipient by surface transportation, except in the case of Colombia, Curacao and Venezuela. Air transportation is available in these countries, and parcels are so handled, if delivery can be expedited by air.

SOCIAL SECURITY INFORMATION

What is Social Security?

Social Security is the popular name for the program of economic benefits established by law under the United States Social Security Act of 1935. The program is administered by the Bureau of Old-Age and Survivors Insurance. The Bureau under the Commissioner of Social Security, operates as an agency of the Department of Health, Education and Welfare.

Social Security aims at guaranteeing certain minimum benefits to all eligible individuals. It provides insurance for the worker and his family, based on earnings from work covered by the Social Security law, by paying qualified persons a basic income in old age and by providing the survivors of a deceased worker with a basic income to replace funds lost by retirement or death.

The worker, employed or self-employed, contributes to his Social Security fund during his working years. If employed, he and his employer share the tax, each paying one half. The employer deducts the worker's contribution from wages each pay day and sends it, along with his matching contribution, to the Director of Internal Revenue, using Form 941 (commercial and industrial form) or 942 (simplified envelope return for domestic and household use). The self-employed person must report his earnings and pay his tax along with his yearly income tax, using Schedule C of Form 1040. Since January, 1959, the sum of $4,800 earned either in employment or self-employment is taxable.

The tax began in 1937 at 1 per cent and is scheduled to rise to 4½ per cent by 1969. The self-employment tax, which became effective January 1, 1951, through revision of the Social Security law, began at 2¼ per cent and will rise to 6¾ per cent by 1969. The rising tax rate is planned to meet growing obligations as an increasing number of people become insured and present claims, and to make the program financially self-supporting. See Table 1 for scheduled increases in tax rates.

Table 1

Year	Contributions*		
	Employer	Employee	Self-employed
1959	*2½	2½	3¾
1960–62	3	3	4½
1963–65	3½	3½	5½
1966–68	4	4	6
1969 on	4½	4½	6¾

*Percentage figures

All taxes collected by the Bureau of Internal Revenue are deposited in Federal Trust Funds, held by the U. S. Treasury. The Treasury Department, when advised by the Commissioner of Social Security as to the amount of benefits due entitled persons, pays all claims. Additionally, it pays all administrative costs of the Bureau out of tax funds. The residue of the trust fund is invested in U. S. government securities bearing interest.

Qualification for Benefits

The benefits obtained from Social Security can be placed in the following four general categories: payments to retired workers and their dependents; payments to the survivors of deceased workers; payments to disabled workers and their dependents.

The worker who retires must be 65 years of age if a man or 62 years of age if a woman, must apply for the benefits, must not earn, after retirement, more than $100 a month, and must be fully insured. When the worker reaches the age of 72, he receives his benefits regardless of his earnings. The benefits due his dependents or survivors depend on his insured status, and it is vitally important that the worker be aware of his status.

Full insurance for the worker depends upon the date retirement age is reached, or the date of death or disability before retirement age is reached. See Table 2. A minimum of six quarters is required. Forty quarters of coverage fully insures the worker for life.

A worker is currently insured if he earns 6 quarters of coverage out of 13 calendar quarters ending with the quarter in which he dies, is disabled, or becomes eligible for benefits.

Coverage is based on three-month calendar quarters beginning January 1, April 1, July 1, and October 1, each year. A quarter of coverage is earned if the worker is paid $50 as an employee, or earns $100 from self-employment in the three-month period. A calendar quarter may be counted only once in estimating coverage. If in a quarter a person is paid $50, and receives $100 in self-employment, he earns but one quarter of coverage.

A self-employed person with a yearly *net* income of $400 or more in covered self-employment earns four quarters of coverage. Self-employment earnings of less than $400 annually do not count toward benefit payments or apply toward quarters of coverage.

Quarters accumulated as an employee after 1936, and earned in self-employment after 1950, count toward meeting the insurance requirements. The worker who reaches retirement age who has insufficient coverage may earn the necessary quarters as an employee or in self-employment after he reaches such retirement age.

From 1937 through 1950, if yearly wages totaled $3,000 or more, the worker was credited with a quarter of coverage for the first quarter in the year in which he was paid $50 or more, and for each subsequent quarter of the year. Beginning January 1, 1959, credit for four quarters of coverage was given in each year in which income from wages, self-employment, or both totaled $4,800 or more.

The closer the worker is to retirement age the less coverage is needed. See Table 2.

Table 2

Year	Jan.-June	July-Dec.
1953 or earlier	6	6
1954	6	7
1955	8	9
1956	10	11
1957	12	13
1958	14	15
1959	16	17
1960	18	19
1961	20	21
1962	22	23
1963	24	25
1964	26	27
1965	28	29
1966	30	31
1967	32	33
1968	34	35
1969	36	37
1970	38	39
1971, thereafter	40	40

The center column lists coverage requirements for individuals who reach retirement age in the months of January through June, and the last column lists requirements for those who reach retirement age in the latter half of the year.

It is necessary, as we have said, for the worker to be fully insured in order to collect retirement payments on behalf of himself and his dependents. However, in some cases, currently insured status will provide his survivors with a source of income. Insurance requirements for all retirement and survivors payments are listed below. See Table 3.

Table 3

Monthly retirement payments will be made to:	*If the worker's insured status is:*
Retired worker, age 62 for women, 65 for men	Fully insured
Wife, 62 or over	Fully insured
Child, under 18, or disabled	Fully insured
Wife, regardless of age if caring for dependent child	Fully insured
Dependent husband, age 65	*Both* fully and currently insured
Monthly survivors payments will be made to:	*If the worker's insured status at death was:*
Widow, age 62	Fully insured
Widow or dependent divorced wife, regardless of age, if caring for dependent child	Fully or currently insured
*Child under 18, or disabled	Fully or currently insured
Dependent widower, age 65	*Both* fully and currently insured
Dependent parent (mother 62 or father 65)	Fully insured
*Lump sum death benefit paid to widow, widower or the person paying burial expenses	Currently or fully insured
Monthly disability payments will be made to:	*If the disabled worker's status is:*
Disabled worker, age 50-65, if totally disabled for work	Both fully and currently insured and has 20 quarters of coverage in the 40 calendar quarters before the beginning date of the disability

*One and one-half years of work or six quarters of coverage in the last three years of the worker's life will provide for the lump sum death benefit and for monthly payments to minor children and their widowed mothers.

If the worker becomes disabled after working long enough under the law, monthly payments can be received at age 50. The disabled worker's dependents will also receive benefits. Eligibility requires 5 years, or 20 calendar quarters, of work under social security. The work must be performed during the 10-year period ending with the calendar quarter in which the worker became disabled. If disability occurs after June 30, 1961, more than 5 years of work may be required as full insurance is necessary. The disability must be so severe that in the words of the law, it makes the worker unable to "engage in any substantial gainful activity." It must be a physical or mental condition which is expected to continue indefinitely or to result in death, and one which will show up in medical examinations and tests.

Disabled workers under 50 years of age can protect rights to future benefits for themselves and their families by applying to have their Social Security records "frozen." The "freeze" will prevent the worker's benefits (at age 50 or retirement age) from being lowered or forfeited.

Eligibility for disability insurance benefits or for the freezing of Social Security records requires that the disability must have lasted for 6 months or more and must have begun at least 6 months before the worker reached retirement age. The amount of monthly disability insurance payments will depend on the worker's average monthly earnings and will be the same as the amount of old-age insurance benefit the worker would receive if already of retirement age. The disability insurance benefits are changed automatically to old-age insurance benefits at retirement age. Social Security disability payments may be paid in addition to any State workmen's compensation benefit or Federal benefit.

All disabled people who apply under the provisions of the Social Security law will have their names referred to their State vocational rehabilitation agencies. Where practicable, these agencies will provide these disabled persons with help in overcoming their handicaps and in becoming self-supporting.

People found eligible for disability insurance benefits will not be paid those benefits if, without good cause, they refuse rehabilitation services offered to them by their State vocational rehabilitation agencies.

Benefits

Benefits do not begin automatically when the individual reaches retirement age, becomes disabled, or upon death. He or his survivors must file an application at the nearest Social Security district office, where assistance in making out the papers is given, gratis. Benefits may be lost if claims are not filed immediately. In any case, monthly back payments cannot be collected for more than twelve months preceding the filing of the application. In order to receive the lump sum death benefit, the claimant must file his application within two years after the death of the insured person.

The minimum monthly payment to the retired worker is $33, and the maximum payment is $127.

Table 4

Payment to:	*Part of monthly benefit:*
Wife, age 65*	One half
Child (when worker retires)	One half
Dependent husband, age 65	One half
Widow, age 62	Three fourths
Child (upon worker's death)	One half (plus an additional one fourth divided equally among all children)
Dependent widower, age 65	Three fourths
Dependent parents (father, age 65; mother, age 65 or age 62 at reduced rates)	Three fourths
Lump sum death benefit to widow, widower, or person paying burial expenses	Three times the amount of the monthly benefit

*A wife may be entitled to benefits in a reduced amount at age 62.

Payments to the family or survivors of the worker are determined by the sum of his monthly payments. The total payments to them cannot exceed $254. When any payment is not a multiple of 10 cents, the figure is raised to the next highest multiple of 10 cents. When family payments are higher than the maximum amount, individual payments to each dependent are reduced to bring the benefit down to the maximum amount.

If the survivor or dependent becomes eligible for benefits based on the account of more than one worker (for instance, the wife and mother, over 62, of deceased workers), the monthly amount paid will be no more than the largest of the benefits.

Benefits are awarded with certain qualifications. A child or children must be under 18, dependent, and unmarried. The dependent husband of 65 must be living with his wife and must be dependent on her for at least half of his support. The mother who cares for the dependent child under 18 must be living with the retired worker. Survivors (husbands or wives) must have been living with the deceased at the time of death. However, the widow or divorced wife of a worker, caring for his minor children, may collect benefits for the children until they each become 18. Dependent parents receive the survivor's benefits even if he or she was survived by a widow, widower, or child, if they were receiving at least one half of their support from the worker.

Estimating Benefits

Table 5

Examples of Monthly Payments Beginning After 1958

(For this table all amounts are rounded down to the next lower whole dollar figure)

If average monthly earnings after 1950 are:[1]	$50 or less	$150	$250	$350[2]	$400[3]
For retirement at 65	$33	$73	$95	$116	$127
For disability at 50	33	73	95	116	127
For retired woman worker starting at age 62[4]	26	58	76	92	101
For widow, or surviving child, or dependent widower, or parent	33	54	71	87	95
For retired couple, wife starting at age 62[4]	45	100	130	159	174
For retired couple, wife starting at age 65 or widow and 1 child or 2 dependent parents	49	109	142	174	190
For retired couple, and 1 child or widow and 2 children	53	120	190	232	254
Maximum family benefit	53	120	202	254	254
Single lump-sum death payment	99	219	255	255	255

[1]In figuring your average, you may omit up to 5 years of lowest earnings, and any period your record was frozen because you were disabled.

[2]Average monthly earnings over $350 will not be possible before 1960 in most cases.

[3]A $400 monthly average will generally not be possible for anyone who has reached the age of 27 before 1959.

[4]Retirement payments to women are permanently reduced if started before age 65.

The insured worker can estimate, with reasonable accuracy, what his retirement payments will be, although the exact figure is determined by the Social Security Administration. The average monthly wage can be figured from 1937 or from 1951, whichever will give the higher rate of payment. Monthly wage determination beginning with 1951 is only possible if the insured person has at least six quarters of coverage since that date. This is advantageous, since most average monthly wages are higher than they were in 1937 and in the immediately following years. If the wage earner was 22 years of age after 1950 the average monthly wage must be determined from 1951. See Table 5 for examples of monthly payments.

When applications are made for payments, the Social Security Administration will figure the benefit in all ways and will pay the highest possible benefit.

To determine the average monthly wage, not more than $3,600 a year from 1951 through 1954, $4,200 a year from 1955 through 1958, and $4,800 a year from 1959 and later can be counted. Up to five calendar years after 1950 in which earnings were lowest can be dropped. In dropping low years, ordinarily two years on which to base an average must be kept. For some people this will mean dropping fewer than the five years allowed. After the dropout of low years (and of any period during which earning records were frozen because of disability) the average monthly earning is figured by dividing the total earnings in the remaining period by the number of months in that period; however, if fewer than 18 months are left, the divisor must still be 18.

Self Employment

In 1950 the Social Security law was amended to cover a great many individuals having a yearly net earning of $400 or more from self-employment. For example, coverage was extended to business and trade people, either owners or partners. The 1954 amendment extended Social Security coverage to self-employed architects, professional engineers, accountants (including certified, registered or licensed, and full-time public accountants), funeral directors, and farm operators. The 1956 amendment included self-employed lawyers, dentists, doctors of osteopathy, veterinarians, chiropractors, naturopaths, and optometrists. Ordained, commissioned, or licensed ministers performing services in the exercise of their ministry, Christian Science practitioners, and members of religious orders who have not taken vows of poverty can also secure Social Security coverage. The only groups not covered are self-employed doctors of medicine and public officials.

Income from stocks and bonds is not counted for Social Security purposes unless the individual is a dealer in securities. Investment earnings from real estate are not counted unless the individual is a real-estate dealer. Interest from loans are not counted unless the individual is engaged in the business of lending money. Income from insurance policies and from pensions are not counted.

Self-employment income is reported along with the yearly income tax on Schedule C of Form 1040. The Director of Internal Revenue handles the funds in exactly the same way as the funds sent to him by employers.

The self-employed person reports net earnings only, the gross income less allowable business deductions derived from all sources of income coming under the Social Security law. Money from other sources *cannot* be reported.

The quarter of coverage applies to the self-employed individual. He receives credit for one quarter for every three-month calendar period beginning January 1, April 1, July 1, and September 1, for each full year in which his self-employment earnings total $400 or more. If yearly earnings are less than $400, he does not receive credit for any quarter. The self-employed person is eligible for benefits when he reaches 50, and is disabled, reaches retirement age (62 for women or 65 for men), and retires, or when he reaches 72, whether or not he has retired. The self-employed person, as also the wage earner, must continue to pay the Social Security tax regardless of age, and even though receiving Social Security benefits, as long as he is gainfully employed. Regulations governing payment of survivor benefits are the same as those for the wage earner.

If the individual is a wage earner who is also engaged in self-employment, both sources of income count toward the accumulation of Social Security credits up to $4,800 yearly from the combined sources. Wages are counted first, and the remainder is made up from self-employment contributions. Thus, a machinist who earns $3,000 and, with a partner, operates a business netting $5,000, of which each takes half, has his wages reported by his employer as $3,000. At the end of the year the machinist files his income tax, showing his self-employment earnings to be $2,500. His total yearly earnings are $5,500, of which only $4,800 is subject to Social Security taxation. He thus pays a Social Security tax on only $1,800 on self-employment and receives credit from both sources of income, for the maximum amount of $4,800.

If a man and wife operate a business as a genuine partnership, they each report their share of net earnings and each receives Social Security credit. This is done even if a joint income tax return is filed. The amount of net earnings each reports depends on the terms of the partnership. A father and son may likewise conduct such a partnership. If one merely assists the other, the owner alone reports the net profit and receives credit.

Domestic Employment

This classification includes maids, cooks, gardeners, laundresses, nursemaids, practical nurses, chauffeurs, baby-sitters, and all others employed in any capacity in private households.

A domestic worker's cash wages (including carfare if paid in cash) from an employer for work in a private household are covered by the law if they amount to $50 or more in a calendar quarter from any one employer regardless of the number of days on which the employee worked in that quarter. Room and board do not count in the wage minimum.

A person employed to do industrial work at home—piecework, quilting, needlework products, etc.—is covered by the law if the cash wages paid by his employer amount to $50 or more in a calendar quarter.

The domestic's employer is responsible for payment of the contribution. The employer writes to the Social Security Administration for an application card which she mails to the Director of Internal Revenue. She receives in return Form 942, which she completes and mails to the Internal Revenue office each quarter, together with her own tax and the domestic's contribution. However, if the employer as the owner of a business files social security reports on Form 941, the domestic help may be added to that form, dispensing with Form 942.

Agricultural Work

Net earnings from self-employment as the operator of a farm count toward benefits if they amount to $400 or more in a year. For taxable years ending on or after December 31, 1956, if the farmer's gross income from farming was $1,800 or less, he may count as his net earnings from farming either actual net earnings or two thirds of his gross farm income; if the gross farm income was more than $1,800 and the net farm earnings less than $1,200, he may count as net earnings from farming either actual net earnings or $1,200; if the gross farm income was more than $1,800 and the net farm earnings were $1,200 or more, the actual amount of net earnings must be used. These calculations can be used if either the actual net earnings or two thirds of the gross farm income was $400 or more. In the latter case, the income may be reported for Social Security purposes even if the actual net earnings were under $400 or the farmer suffered a loss.

Soil bank payments to farm operators under the "acreage reserve" and the "conservation reserve" programs count as net earnings from farming. These payments should be included in farm earnings for Social Security purposes.

The cash or crop shares a farm owner receives from a tenant or share-farmer will count for Social Security purposes if under the arrangements with the tenant or share-farmer the farm owner "participates materially" in the production of the crops or livestock or in the management of the production. In order to "participate materially" the farm owner must take an important part in the management decisions or in the actual production. The farm owner does not need, thus, to live on the property to get Social Security credit as a self-employed farmer.

If the share-farmer, one who farms land owned by someone else, divides between himself and the landlord crops or livestock under an ordinary crop-sharing arrangement, with shares dependent on the total amount produced, he is considered self-employed for Social Security purposes.

The farm worker who worked for a farmer or ranch operator in 1955 or 1956 is entitled to Social Security credit if the farmer paid him $100 or more in cash wages in the calendar year. Beginning with 1957 the farm worker's cash wages count toward Social Security benefits if his employer paid him $150 or more in cash during the year for his farm work, or if he did farm work for an employer on 20 or more days during a year for cash wages figured on a time basis. In the latter case, the total amount of cash wages does not matter.

Household workers employed on a farm or ranch operated for profit are covered under the same rules as other farm employees.

Agricultural work performed by foreign workers admitted to the United States on a temporary basis from any foreign country to do agricultural work is not covered by the law.

Work Abroad

United States citizens employed by American employers in foreign countries or aboard vessels or aircraft of foreign registry are covered by Social Security. (Seamen and airmen employed on American vessels or aircraft are ordinarily covered regardless of citizenship.)

United States citizens working abroad for a foreign subsidiary of a United States corporation may be covered by the law if the parent corporation makes an agreement with the Secretary of the Treasury to see that Social Security taxes are paid for all United States citizens employed abroad by the foreign subsidiary.

Military Service

Men and women who saw service in any branch of the armed forces after September 15, 1940, and through December 31, 1956, and were discharged under any condition other than dishonorable, received wage credits of $160 monthly for each month of active service. At least 90 days of active service is required, unless the individual was discharged or released because of disability or injury sustained in the line of duty. These wage credits may be granted to those who died in service as well as to those who died after discharge.

In general, Social Security wage credits were not given for one of these periods if monthly payments based in whole or in part on the same period were payable by the military organization or by another Federal agency (except the Veterans' Administration). The World War II period and the post-World War II period are treated separately. However, if the serviceman has active military service after 1956, he will receive wage credits for any active service after 1950 and before 1957 even though he received retirement pay from his service department based on that service.

Wage credits of $160 a month are also provided for certain American citizens who, before December 9, 1941, entered the military service of a foreign country which was, on September 16, 1940, at war with a country that became an enemy of the United States during World War II.

Credits for military service before January 1, 1957, count the same as wages in civilian employment. These credits are not actually listed on Social Security earnings records until application for retirement, disability, or survivor's benefits are made. At that time proof of military service will be needed.

The performance of active duty or active duty for training as a member of the uniformed services of the United States after 1956 counts toward Social Security. Base pay is credited to the Social Security record. The Social Security tax for old-age, survivor's, and disability insurance protection is deducted from military base pay just as the Social Security tax of a civilian employee is deducted from his wages.

Federal, State, and Local Government Employees

Before 1951, employment in State or local government was not covered by social security. Beginning 1951, the law provided for covering State and local government employees under voluntary agreements between the individual State and the Federal Government. However, before 1955, employees in positions covered by a State or local retirement system were excluded. Beginning January 1, 1955, employees who are under a State or local retirement system can be covered under social security if a referendum is held among the members of the system and a majority of the members eligible to vote in the referendum vote in favor of old-age and survivors insurance coverage. Most employees of the Federal Government not covered by another retirement system are covered by social security.

The Social Security Act provides for the coverage of certain State and local government employees, including policemen and firemen, under special provisions which apply only to certain States.

The law states it is the policy of Congress, in making coverage available to retirement system members, that coverage under old-age and survivor's insurance shall not impair the protection of members and beneficiaries under the existing retirement system.

Railroad Employees

A retired worker who has at least 120 months of railroad service and who has also done enough work under Social Security to qualify for Social Security payments may receive retirement benefits under both the railroad retirement and old-age and survivor's insurance systems. When a railroad worker retires with fewer than 120 months of railroad service, no railroad retirement annuity is payable and his railroad earnings after 1936 are considered in determining his disability or old-age payments under Social Security.

Survivors of a worker can be entitled under one system only, either railroad retirement or old-age and survivor's insurance, even though the worker may have been entitled during his lifetime under both. Regardless of which program pays, records of the deceased worker's railroad earnings after 1936 and his earnings under Social Security will be combined to determine whether he is insured and the amount of any payments to survivors.

If the worker was receiving a railroad retirement pension or annuity at the time of his death, any payment to his survivor is ordinarily made by the Railroad Retirement Board. Also, the Railroad Retirement Board usually makes payment to the survivor if the deceased railroad worker had 120 months or more of railroad service and no substantial amount of regular employment after his last 12 months of railroad service.

If the deceased worker did not have as many as 120 months of railroad service, and under certain other circumstances, the Social Security Administration makes payment to the survivor.

Employees of Nonprofit Organizations

Since 1951, employees of certain nonprofit organizations can be covered by social security under specified conditions. Eligible organizations are corporations, funds, and foundations operated solely for religious, charitable, scientific, literary, or educational purposes, or for the prevention of cruelty to children or animals. No part of the net profit may be paid to a private shareholder or individual, and no substantial part of the activity can be spent in propagandizing, lobbying, or trying to influence legislation.

The organization must file with the Director of Internal Revenue a certificate of waiver of its exemption from paying Social Security tax. At least two thirds of the employees, earning in a calendar quarter a minimum of $50, must indicate their desire to participate in the program by signing a form accompanying the certificate of waiver. Those who do not sign will not receive coverage, but anyone employed after the quarter in which the certificate of waiver is filed is automatically covered. Those employees who are in the organization's employ in the calendar quarter in which the certificate is filed and who fail to elect coverage may be brought in at any time within 27 months after the calendar quarter in which the certificate is filed.

Non-profit organizations which elect coverage after 1959 may make the coverage retroactive for a period not exceeding four calendar quarters before the quarter in which the certificate is filed. Non-profit organizations which elected coverage after 1955 and prior to 1960 may cover employees retroactively as far back as January 1, 1956.

Employees of a non-profit organization who are covered or are eligible to become covered by a State or local retirement system are treated as a separate group for Social Security purposes.

Family Employment

Individuals employed by sons, daughters, or spouses, and a child under 21, employed by his father or mother, are not covered by Social Security.

Loss of Benefits

Benefits are lost principally because money problems force the retired worker or his dependents and/or survivors to earn more than the allowed $100 monthly minimum in covered employment. If a retired man between the ages of 65 and 72 earns wages of or renders substantial services in self-employment equivalent to wages of more than $100 a month he will not receive his monthly payment. Regardless of his yearly income, benefit payments will be withheld only for months in which $100 or more is earned. Theoretically it is possible for a man between 65 and 72 years of age to earn $1,200 in one month. He would only lose one month's payment—the month in which he rendered substantial service and made over $100. When a retired or disabled worker is not due a benefit check for a certain month, no checks are payable for that month to his dependents whose benefits are based on his account. The earnings of a person who is receiving benefits as a dependent or as a survivor affect only his own benefits and will not stop payments to other members of his family.

Earnings from work of any kind, whether or not it is covered by the Social Security law, must be counted in deciding the number of monthly benefit checks due a beneficiary for a year. Total wages (not just take-home pay) and any net earnings from self-employment must ordinarily be added together in figuring up earnings for the year. However, income from savings, investments, pensions, and insurance does not affect old-age or survivor's insurance benefits and should not be counted in with earnings. The insured individual can, upon reaching age 72, earn as much as possible in covered employment and neither he nor his beneficiaries will suffer loss of benefits.

There are other events which end payments. If a person receiving monthly benefit payments as a dependent or as a survivor marries a person who is not also a beneficiary, his or her right to payments stops. Payments to a wife or dependent husband are ended if a divorce is granted, except in the case of a wife who has in her care a child entitled to benefits. Payments to a wife or widow under 62, or the divorced wife of an insured person, will stop when she no longer has in her care a child who is also entitled to monthly payments. Payments to a child under 18 stop when the child marries. When a child entitled to benefits reaches 18, his payments are stopped unless he is disabled. When the child of a deceased insured person is adopted, his payments end unless the adopting person is the child's step parent, grandparent, aunt, or uncle. When any person receiving monthly benefits dies, his or her payments are ended. If a person receiving disability benefits recovers or returns to work, his payments (and any payments to his dependents) will stop. If a person is convicted of treason, espionage, sabotage, sedition, or other subversive activities, the court may revoke his right to any old-age, survivor's, or disability insurance benefits based on earnings before the conviction. Benefits to his dependents and survivors are not affected. If a person receiving payments is deported from the United States, his benefits are stopped. Benefits to his dependents and survivors who are citizens of the United States or who are in the United States are not affected.

Double Taxation

Double taxation occurs when an individual changes jobs or works for more than one employer at the same time, and earns more than $4,800 in a calendar year. If tax was paid on income over $4,800, the excess may be claimed as credit on the income tax.

General Action

The individual covered by social security is given a numbered card, which he keeps all his life. The number on the card is used to identify his earning record and to distinguish his account from the accounts of other people of the same name. Both the name and the account number are needed to make sure the worker gets full credit for his earnings. The worker's employer uses the name and number exactly as they appear on the card when he sends in tax contributions.

If the card is lost or misplaced, the local social security office will issue a duplicate. If there is no local office, the post office will furnish an application blank to be used in obtaining the duplicate card. If a name has been changed, the worker must ask the social security office for a new card showing the same account number and the new name.

Each employer is required by law to give the worker a receipt for the taxes he has deducted from wages at the end of the year, or when employment ceases. The receipts help the worker check his account, because they show the amount deducted and the wages paid.

The account should be checked every three years, because there is a limit to the period in which adjustments of errors can be made. Addressed post cards for use in requesting wage information are available at the local office. If an error has been made, the local office will assist in having it corrected.

Certain documents are required as proof of claim. The worker should keep, and let his family know the location of, proof of his birth, birth of his wife, of each dependent child, dependent parent, and dependent husband. Personal records of employers, dates of employment, earnings, social security taxes paid, should be kept, as well as proof of marriage and military discharge papers.

At 65 (62 for women), the worker should contact the Social Security Administration concerning his account. If his earnings from work of any kind, whether or not it is covered by the Social Security law, are not more than $100 a month, he may be eligible for immediate benefit.

When the worker applies for payment, he receives a postal card to use in reporting anything which might affect his right to the monthly benefit. This report *must* be made.

The individual of 72 should contact the local social security office.

Upon the death of a covered individual, a member of the family should inquire at once at the nearest social security office concerning survivors benefits. If a worker becomes disabled before 65, he should get in touch with the social security office in order to have his earnings account frozen to protect his benefit rights. If he is between 50 and 65, he may be eligible for disability insurance benefits.

The address of the local office can be found in the telephone directory under U. S. Government, Department of Health, Education and Welfare.

Right of Appeal

Dissatisfied claimants can appeal their claim. They can request that the Bureau of Old Age and Survivors Insurance reconsider the case, or they can request a review by a referee of an appeals council. The local office will assist in filing the appeal, free of charge. If the individual is dissatisfied with the referee's decision, he may ask for a review by the Appeals Council of the Social Security Administration, and may go from there to a Federal Court.

Location

There are over 550 field offices which will assist in filing applications, estimate earning records, develop evidence of rights and determine the eligibility of the claimants and the amounts due. Six area offices review the decisions of the district offices and certify to the Treasury Department the eligibility of the applicants and the amounts due.

Considering future trends, the Bureau also studies actuarial, economic, fiscal, and administrative factors that affect the number of covered individuals and the amount of earnings and the effect of earning history on insurance trends, and check the trends in claims and the extent to which the program fulfills the purpose for which it was intended.

All tables courtesy of the Social Security Administration.

Table for Determining Primary Insurance Amount and Maximum Family Benefits According to 1958

I PIB Not more than	II Former PIA Not more than	III AMW Not more than	IV 1958 PIA	V Maximum Family Benefits	I PIB Not more than	II Former PIA Not more than	III AMW Not more than	IV 1958 PIA	V Maximum Family Benefits
$10.00	$ 30.00	$ 54.00	$ 33.00	$ 53.00	$36.40	$ 76.10	$188.00	$ 81.00	$150.40
10.48	31.00	56.00	34.00	54.00	37.08	77.10	193.00	82.00	154.40
11.00	32.00	58.00	35.00	55.00	37.60	78.00	197.00	83.00	157.60
11.48	33.00	60.00	36.00	56.00	38.20	78.90	202.00	84.00	161.60
12.00	34.00	61.00	37.00	57.00	39.12	79.90	207.00	85.00	165.60
12.48	35.00	63.00	38.00	58.00	39.68	80.80	211.00	86.00	168.80
13.00	36.00	65.00	39.00	59.00	40.33	81.70	216.00	87.00	172.80
13.48	37.00	67.00	40.00	60.00	41.12	82.70	221.00	88.00	176.80
14.00	38.00	69.00	41.00	61.50	41.76	83.60	225.00	89.00	180.00
14.48	39.00	70.00	42.00	63.00	42.44	84.50	230.00	90.00	184.00
15.00	40.00	72.00	43.00	64.50	43.20	85.50	235.00	91.00	188.00
15.60	41.00	74.00	44.00	66.00	43.76	86.40	239.00	92.00	191.20
16.20	42.00	76.00	45.00	67.50	44.44	87.30	244.00	93.00	195.20
16.84	43.00	78.00	46.00	69.00	44.88	88.30	249.00	94.00	199.20
17.60	44.00	80.00	47.00	70.50	45.60	89.20	253.00	95.00	202.40
18.40	45.00	81.00	48.00	72.00		90.10	258.00	96.00	206.40
19.24	46.00	83.00	49.00	73.50		91.10	263.00	97.00	210.40
20.00	47.00	85.00	50.00	75.00		92.00	267.00	98.00	213.60
20.64	48.00	87.00	51.00	76.50		92.90	272.00	99.00	217.60
21.28	49.00	89.00	52.00	78.00		93.90	277.00	100.00	221.60
21.88	50.00	90.00	53.00	79.50		94.80	281.00	101.00	224.80
22.28	50.90	92.00	54.00	81.00		95.80	286.00	102.00	228.80
22.68	51.80	94.00	55.00	82.50		96.70	291.00	103.00	232.80
23.08	52.80	96.00	56.00	84.00		97.60	295.00	104.00	236.00
23.44	53.70	97.00	57.00	85.50		98.60	300.00	105.00	240.00
23.76	54.60	99.00	58.00	87.00		99.50	305.00	106.00	244.00
24.20	55.60	101.00	59.00	88.50		100.40	309.00	107.00	247.20
24.60	56.50	102.00	60.00	90.00		101.40	314.00	108.00	251.20
25.00	57.40	104.00	61.00	91.50		102.30	319.00	109.00	254.00
25.48	58.40	106.00	62.00	93.00		103.20	323.00	110.00	254.00
25.92	59.30	107.00	63.00	94.50		104.20	328.00	111.00	254.00
26.40	60.20	109.00	64.00	96.00		105.10	333.00	112.00	254.00
26.94	61.20	113.00	65.00	97.50		106.00	337.00	113.00	254.00
27.46	62.10	118.00	66.00	99.00		107.00	342.00	114.00	254.00
28.00	63.00	122.00	67.00	100.50		107.90	347.00	115.00	254.00
28.68	64.00	127.00	68.00	102.00		108.50	351.00	116.00	254.00
29.25	64.90	132.00	69.00	105.60			356.00	117.00	254.00
29.68	65.80	136.00	70.00	108.80			361.00	118.00	254.00
30.36	66.80	141.00	71.00	112.80			365.00	119.00	254.00
30.92	67.70	146.00	72.00	116.80			370.00	120.00	254.00
31.36	68.60	150.00	73.00	120.00			375.00	121.00	254.00
32.00	69.60	155.00	74.00	124.00			379.00	122.00	254.00
32.60	70.50	160.00	75.00	128.00			384.00	123.00	254.00
33.20	71.40	164.00	76.00	131.20			389.00	124.00	254.00
33.88	72.40	169.00	77.00	135.20			393.00	125.00	254.00
34.50	73.30	174.00	78.00	139.20			398.00	126.00	254.00
35.00	74.20	178.00	79.00	142.40			400.00	127.00	254.00
35.80	75.20	183.00	80.00	146.40					

INSTRUCTIONS FOR USE OF TABLE

CAUTION: These instructions apply only to the majority of cases, but there are important exceptions. For more detailed instructions and explanation of savings clauses refer to the Summary of the 1958 Amendments.

ENTITLEMENT OR DEATH PRIOR TO 1959—Ascertain PIA under 1954 Act and locate in column II. The 1958 PIA is on the same line in column IV.

ENTITLEMENT OR DEATH AFTER 1958—

(a) OLD-START—Compute PIB and locate in column I. The 1958 PIA is on the same line in column IV.

(b) NEW-START—Compute AMW. Locate AMW in column III. The 1958 PIA is on the same line in column IV.

AUXILIARIES' BENEFITS—Ascertain the 1958 PIA and apply the appropriate fraction to determine the auxiliary's benefit. If necessary, adjust for the maximum family benefit shown in column V.

A Cyclopedia of Business and Finance

Money and Banking, Credits and Collections, Information for Shippers, Bookkeeping, and Business Arithmetic

MONEY AND BANKING

Under a banking system such as that in the United States where hundreds of millions of dollars change hands every day, it is only natural that huge losses occur. Some of them are direct—actual monetary losses in dollars and cents. Others are indirect, resulting in the loss of reputation, the lowering of credit standings, or the inability to grasp an opportunity when it presents itself. Most of them could be prevented.

Banking Losses

Banking losses are of two kinds: those due to carelessness and those resulting from ignorance of ordinary banking laws and customs. If every individual were as careful about money matters as he should be, and if he knew and understood the fundamental principles of money and banking, losses would be much smaller than they are.

Losses Due to Carelessness

Let us consider first of all the careless things people do in connection with their banking business. How do they write checks, how do they endorse them? How do they handle canceled vouchers? What about overdrafts? Why is it that some people have no bank account whatever? These and countless other questions must be considered if we are to avoid unnecessary loss.

Every banker knows that at least 50% of the checks passing through his hands could be raised or altered by the clumsiest amateur. The only reason that more of them are not changed is because there are not more dishonest people in the world.

Liability

Many persons believe that after making out a check payable to a firm or individual, writing in the amount, and affixing the signature, their responsibility ceases. But such is not the law. One of the decisions of the Supreme Court of the United States reads: "Your bank is responsible for the signature on your check, but not for what is written in the body of the check, and money paid in good faith and without negligence on an altered check, cannot be recovered by the maker thereof." Espey vs Cinni Bank, 18 Wall, U. S. 118.

How Checks Are Altered

There are several methods by which a dishonest man can alter a check to his personal advantage. In the first place there are simple pen changes, which include many combinations that can be made by a careful study of the handwriting. For example, one to eight—one to eighty — one hundred to eight hundred — one thousand to eight thousand, etc. The employees of a bank are not mind readers and will consequently pay the check if there is no evidence of fraud.

It is a comparatively simple matter to apply an acid and wipe off every written word or figure except the signature on a common white check. On colored checks the fine lines of the signature are covered up until after the acid bath, leaving the check perfectly white. Any convenient name and amount may then be written in. Even when safety paper (so called) is used, checks are altered every day. The professional check raiser has considerable knowledge of chemicals enabling him to alter checks, drafts, letters of credit and registered bonds. He is also something of an artist. For instance, if the payee's name on a safety check is to be changed, he delicately traces out the name with his acid, and then with a fine camel's hair brush he can restore the most delicate tints, leaving a perfect safety check for his own purposes. Thus no bank safety paper is a protection against him.

The largest percentage of loss from altered checks occurs from changing the payee's name. Large checks are seldom raised, but the payee's name is changed to "bearer" or "cash." Many names permit of changing by adding a letter or a syllable, or a few pen strokes. Thus, F. C. Ahrens is changed to F. C. Ahrenson by simply adding the letters "on."

Check Protectors

The first mechanical device for protecting the amount of checks was one which crimped the paper over the numerical amount of the check. This was followed by a machine which punched the numerical amount of the check through the paper. Next came the machine stamping the words "Not over $000 dollars." Check-protecting manufacturers then produced a great variety of machines which wrote or stamped the amount in words in colored ink, as well as machines which stamped the amount in numerals. Such machines were generally accepted as insurance against alteration, and are still so considered by many people.

The skill of the criminal, however, kept pace with the inventive genius of the manufacturer. He soon learned that it was a simple matter to iron out the crimped surface of the check and to paste on little discs of paper or apply tinted chalk when the check was perforated. In the case of machines which stamped the words "Not more than $000" in indelible ink he discovered a means of erasing the indelible ink and stamping in a greater amount by the aid of a similar device. With the invention of an instrument which broke up and disturbed the surface of the paper the criminal was forced to seek another method of fraud and he found it in the practice of changing the payee's name to bearer or to cash. Because of the fact that these check protectors do not permit of writing a large amount, the professional also devised the scheme of taking a small check reading:

THIRTY-FOUR DOLLARS FIFTY CENTS

and writing a larger amount above these words on a similar machine so that the check reads:

ONE THOUSAND NINE HUNDRED AND
THIRTY-FOUR DOLLARS FIFTY CENTS

The paying teller can see at a glance that it would be impossible to write the whole amount on one line so he pays the check without questioning it.

The modern check protector accomplishes three things. First, it macerates the amount line and prints the amount in indelible ink into this broken paper surface. In the second place, it prints the words at such an angle that the very largest amounts can all be written on one line and in the proper place. And finally, it so macerates the payee's name when once written that it can not be successfully altered.

Rules for Writing Checks

a. A check should be made payable "to the order of" a specific person, never to bearer.

b. Write figures plainly with ink, never with pencil.

c. Be sure that the amount in figures corresponds with the written amount. The bank will always pay the written amount.

d. Write the amount of the check as far to the left as possible so that no additional words or figures can be inserted.

e. Fill in the space remaining with a heavy black line so that nothing can be added.

f. Exercise the utmost care in writing and handing out checks. The person who carelessly draws a check must stand any loss which may occur through its alteration.

g. Remember that a check is your order to the bank TO PAY OUT MONEY, and that it is necessary for the bank to know WITHOUT QUESTION when, to whom, and how much it shall pay.

h. Use the best known mechanical methods of protecting your check against alteration.

The habit of endorsing checks in blank should be discouraged for more than one reason. If you endorse a check by simply signing your name across the back of it, that endorsement has the effect of making the check payable to any holder, or to the bearer. If it is lost or stolen it is as valuable to the finder or thief as the actual currency would be. Many business men make a practice of endorsing their checks in blank and carrying them to the bank for deposit. Suppose there is a hold-up or that in the excitement of an accident or a fire on the way to the bank, the checks disappear. The unfortunate owner has little chance of getting the money back. Again by endorsing a check you vouch for its genuineness in every respect. Thus, if you endorse in blank and permit the check to come into the hands of a forger who afterward raises the amount, you have made yourself liable for the larger amount. Always endorse a check payable to some specific person or firm. If the checks are intended for deposit, write across the back the words: "For Deposit in First National Bank" or "For Deposit Only" and sign your name.

Keeping Records

When a man puts money into a bank, his deposits and withdrawals are all carefully recorded by an efficient system of modern bookkeeping. However, the individual does not always exercise the same great care in keeping his own accounts. As a result he allows his account to be overdrawn, injuring his credit with the bank, or he issues checks when he has no money in the bank thus lowering his credit standing with his creditors. One check coming back marked "Not sufficient funds" will do more damage to a man's credit than a dozen past due accounts and may destroy a commercial reputation it has taken years to establish.

A depositor should call at the bank for his statement and vouchers every month. He should also check the bank statement with his own check book in order to avoid errors, detect strange checks, and save confusion and loss of time.

The following practices should be observed:

a. Always keep a correct record, on the stubs of your check book, of all deposits and checks.

b. See that you receive all checks charged to you on the bank statement, and arrange them in order.

c. Check off stubs for all checks returned with your statement, also verify deposits shown in your pass book with those shown on the statement.

d. To the balance shown on the last stub used on which this statement is balanced, ADD the amounts of all checks shown on the *unchecked stubs,* that is the amount of outstanding or unpaid checks.

e. The total should agree with the balance shown by the bank. Report any differences immediately.

The Value of a Bank Account

Although the number of bank accounts in the United States averages more than one for every person in the country yet there are thousands of people who do not take advantage of the convenience and safety which banks offer for the handling of money. There are four distinct ways in which the man who has no bank account is likely to lose. In the first place, when a check, a pass book, a certificate of deposit, or a bank draft is lost or stolen the owner has some chance to recover, but when the cash is gone, it is usually gone forever. Secondly, the lack of a bank account naturally leads to a lack of credit. The man without enough money to warrant a bank account has a decided limit placed on his buying power. Thirdly, the man who has no banking acquaintance is always subject to inconvenience and delay when he wishes to cash a check or a bank draft sent to him from another person. And in the last place it very often happens that a young man going into business is denied the financial help he needs from the bank for the single reason that he is unable to show any satisfactory savings balance or other visible evidence of his character and habits. Thus the man who has no bank account runs the grave risk of losing money, credit, time, and opportunity.

The holder of a check should present it for payment within a reasonable time after he receives it. He may keep it as long as he pleases, but if in the meantime the bank fails, he cannot demand payment again from the maker. The law provides that the check should be presented at the bank for payment or forwarded by mail for collection on the same day it is received or not later than the day following. Again, a man's death automatically stops payment on all his outstanding checks. In other words, if a man dies before you have deposited his check, the bank will refuse to cash it and you will be obliged to wait for your money until his estate is settled. It is a matter of safety, therefore, to deposit all checks, or enter them for collection without any unreasonable delay.

It is sometimes desirable for two persons to deposit money in their joint names, payable to either or both signatures. A joint account of man and wife subject to withdrawals by either during their lifetime, and by the survivor in event of the death of the other, is often a very wise arrangement. But in those states having an inheritance tax it may not be generally known that if one party to a joint account dies, the other is not permitted to draw out the money until the state treasurer or other authority has been notified of the death, and given his consent to the withdrawal. The same laws govern the actions of a bank or trust company having in its possession a safety deposit box of a deceased person. This box may not be removed or opened by friends or relatives until the proper state official has checked its contents and given his release. Thus it frequently happens that at a time when ready funds are most needed, the cumbersome processes of the law cause uncertainty and delay.

The Functions of a Bank

To many individuals, a bank is nothing more than an elaborately furnished building with a lot of dignified individuals sitting around at mahogany desks, trying to look wise, and an immense safety vault filled with gold and currency. To many others, a bank is merely a convenient place in which to a gét a check cashed. Few really understand the internal organization of a bank, or know its real functions. As a result of this lack of understanding, the banks are unable to perform the services they otherwise might. Here briefly are the real functions of a bank:

a. To provide a safe place for the custody of money and other valuables.

b. To lend money for legitimate business purposes.

c. To facilitate the transmission of funds by drafts, or bills of exchange.

d. To encourage thrift.

e. To act in an advisory capacity with its patrons on all matters of an economic or financial nature.

A banker primarily is a dealer in money. He borrows of one party and lends to another. The difference between the terms at which he borrows and those at which he lends, forms the source of his profit. By this means he draws into active operation those small sums of money which were previously unproductive in the hands of private individuals, and at the same time furnishes accommodation to those in need of additional capital for carrying on their commercial transactions. Anything that the banker can do to encourage thrift and improve methods of business among his customers, automatically increases his deposits and swells his profits. In banking, therefore, as in any other business, real service means success, not only for the bank individually, but for the community it serves.

A bank, therefore, means a place where you can leave your money in safety; a place in which to borrow money if you need it for some legitimate purpose; a place where you can purchase a draft or bill of exchange that will be legal tender in every country in the world; a place to learn the advantages of saving; and a place to turn to when you are in need of information, advice, or assistance in your business affairs.

The Federal Reserve System

The Federal Reserve System consists of twelve regional Federal Reserve banks. All national banks are required to become members of the system; state banks may, if eligible. The member banks form the capital stock of their district Reserve bank by subscribing six per cent of their capital, three per cent of which is paid in; they receive a six per cent dividend on the stock which they hold in the Federal Reserve Bank. The system is controlled by a Federal Reserve Board with supervisory powers, and by boards of directors for the regional banks.

The chief purpose of the Federal Reserve System is to accumulate a reserve that can be used as a basis for loans in time of temporary or seasonal need. Each member bank deposits a part of its deposits in its district Reserve Bank, and can borrow from the Reserve Bank to satisfy changes in currency and credit demand. Loans made by member banks may be discounted and sent to the Federal Reserve Bank, where they are rediscounted on the basis of the member bank's collateral notes. The notes may not be lent for investment purposes or for trading in any securities other than those of the United States government. By raising or lowering the rediscount rate, the district bank attempts to regulate the flow of credit. The Reserve Banks also attempt to regulate credit by purchases and sales of government securities and other paper in the open market.

Bank Statements

Many people who have no knowledge of accounting, feel that they can not understand a bank statement, and therefore pay no attention to it. This is a mistake. Every person who has money on deposit, either in a savings or checking account ought to know the condition of his bank, and how its condition compares with that of other banks. Below is a simple statement of a moderate-sized national bank, together with an analysis of the various items:

Resources

Cash on Hand and Due from Banks	$201,563.71
Loans and Discounts	964,393.37
Bonds and Other Securities	500,050.00
Banking House	50,000.00
Stock in Federal Reserve Bank	7,500.00
	$1,724,512.08

Liabilities

Capital Stock	$200,000.00
Surplus	50,000.00
Undivided Profits	22,197.25
Demand and Time Deposits	1,224,179.21
Rediscounts and Money Borrowed	225,000.00
Reserve for Taxes and Interest	2,135.62
	$1,724,512.08

By resources is meant what the bank owns. Let us consider each resource as it appears:

Cash on Hand and Due From Banks

This item represents the actual cash on hand in the bank, the money which the bank has on deposit with the Federal Reserve or correspondent banks, and checks deposited for collection which are drawn on other banks. Banks usually keep a considerable sum on deposit with other banks, in order that they may draw drafts against that money, when necessary.

Loans and Discounts

This represents the value of the promissory notes of the firms or individuals who have borrowed money from the bank. The interest from the loans constitutes the main source of the bank's income. When you apply for a loan your request is passed on by the officers of the bank or a discount committee appointed for that purpose, whose business it is to see that the bank is properly safeguarded in giving you the money.

Bonds and Other Securities

This sum represents the value of such bonds or other securities as the bank has invested in. High grade bonds make a very desirable investment for surplus funds because of their safety and because they can be sold advantageously on short notice, at a price quoted every day. Bonds of the United States government, and state and municipal securities are also held, in varying amounts.

Banking House

Under this head there is included the cost of the ground, building, furniture and fixtures used by the bank in carrying on its transactions. This is valuable property owned by the bank.

Stock in Federal Reserve Bank

All member banks in the Federal Reserve System must own a block of stock in their district reserve bank, equal to 6% of their combined capital and surplus.

Liabilities

By liabilities we mean the things that the bank owes. Every dollar paid into the bank immediately becomes a liability. The earnings belong to the stockholders, hence are liabilities. A deposit of money is recorded as a resource, but it really belongs to the depositor and must be included among the liabilities. In this particular statement the liabilities are shown under six different headings:

Capital Stock

When a bank is organized the stockholders pay in a certain amount of money to protect the depositors. This is called the capital or the capital stock of the bank. It is shown as a liability, because the bank is indebted to the stockholders for what money they pay in. In other words, the stockholders are the owners of the bank. If, however, the bank fails or is unable to pay its depositors, the capital may be used. In addition the stockholders in national banks and in some state banks are personally liable for an equal amount, if it is needed to pay the debts. Deposits are now insured up to a certain amount by the Federal Deposit Insurance Corporation.

Surplus

A national bank is required by law to accumulate from its profits a fund which will equal 20% of its capital. This is called the surplus fund. Many banks of course accumulate a fund much larger than 20% of their capital. The surplus is also a liability because it belongs to the shareholders, but it remains in the bank as part of the working capital.

Undivided Profits

The undivided profits account represents earnings which have neither been added to the surplus nor paid out in dividends. The size of this account varies with the earnings and when it is large enough, it is transferred to the surplus account. A well managed bank never pays out all its profits in dividends.

Demand and Time Deposits

Money deposited with a bank in a checking account is a demand deposit. The savings accounts on which interest is paid are time deposits. The bank owes its patrons for all these deposits and must be prepared to meet their demands.

Rediscounts and Money Borrowed

It frequently happens that a bank must borrow money from other banks in order to accommodate its customers. This is done by putting up good security as collateral for the loan, or in the case of a member bank in the Federal Reserve System, by rediscounting commercial paper as explained above. These loans being debts owed by the bank must be shown as direct or contingent liabilities.

Reserve for Taxes and Interest

Instead of carrying a large sum of money as undivided profits, most banks set up a reserve fund for the payment of taxes, interest, bad debts and other necessary expenditures. As the payments are made, they are charged against this account. Thus the bank avoids creating a wrong impression in the published statements it is required by law to make.

The law requires banks to submit statements to the proper authorities and to publish them regularly in local newspapers. This is in addition to the official examination to which all banks are subject by national or state bank examiners, clearing house officials, or reserve bank examiners. The published statements, if fully understood, will give depositors an accurate idea of the standing of their bank. By learning to read between the lines you will soon discover that what at first appears to be only a formidable and uninteresting column of figures, is in reality a very simple and instructive picture of the progress and condition of your bank.

CREDITS AND COLLECTIONS

Most businesses find it essential to do their customers the convenience and courtesy of extending them credit. However, the question of when and how to extend credit and how and when to collect overdue accounts, presents some difficulties. The firm that is haphazard, thoughtless, and over-generous in extending credit finds itself overwhelmed by bad debts. Suspiciousness, reluctance, and stinginess, on the other hand, offend reputable customers and break down good will.

The aim of every business man should be to keep his losses as near the zero point as possible without needlessly limiting sales. In order to accomplish this result, a person of good judgment must be in charge of and responsible for credits. In large concerns there is a credit man. In the vast majority of cases, however, this duty falls on the shoulders of the proprietor himself, or on one of the officers of the corporation. Slipshod methods of extending credit should never be permitted. They sap the very life blood of the business.

Sources of Credit Information

Where the trade is local the man in charge of credits needs to know all there is to know about the character, habits, and financial condition of the purchasers. Theoretically the same thing ought to be true when a house sells its goods over an extended territory, but for practical purposes he must content himself with such general information as is available, coupled with an exact knowledge of the general financial situation in the territory covered. Every possible effort should be made to learn the particular hazards and peculiarities of the customer's business. On the other hand the credit man must be thoroughly familiar with stock on hand, production costs, and all the operative details of his own business. In addition to all these other considerations, a familiarity with the laws of finance, collection, exemption, bankruptcy, and commercial paper is absolutely essential.

How is the credit man to obtain all this vital information? Government reports show up the light and dark spots in the general financial condition of different parts of the country. And as for the reputation, habits, and financial standing of individual customers, the credit man has four different sources of information open to him, namely: the mercantile agencies, local banks, trade reports, and salesmen's reports.

The mercantile agencies attempt to show the net worth and the credit standing of every corporation, partnership, or individual doing business. While their reports are not always accurate and must be qualified by past experience and other available information, they nevertheless are an invaluable source of credit information, and give business men a great inducement to keep their commercial records clean. It must always be remembered, however, that changes in personnel, location, and credit standing, change in these listings at the rate of well over 50% every year.

Many business houses prefer to get their credit information from local sources, such as the bankers or the attorneys in the customer's city. These are always valuable to verify the reports of the mercantile agencies, but as sources of original information they are not always reliable. Delay, partiality, enmity, inaccuracy, or indifference in answering the requests for information, result far too frequently. Most banks refuse to give out credit ratings unless the individual happens to be one of its own customers.

Credit men in the same or allied lines of business often exchange credit information. Manufacturers of certain products sometimes form an association to maintain prices, and co-operate in the manufacture and sale of their goods. The members of such an organization are always glad to exchange credit information. Some of these even go so far as to maintain what is known as a black list containing the name and address of firms which are not reliable, and every credit man has a copy of that list.

Firms which employ salesmen to sell their products are in a position to get definite and reliable information on their customers. The salesman makes frequent visits, becomes acquainted with the customer, knows his reputation, observes his method of transacting business and is able to supply first hand reports not only on the customers, but on the general condition of the trade in the city and surrounding country. It does not pay to depend altogether on his reports, however, because his zeal for increased commissions might lead him to ignore the usual danger signals.

Methods of Collecting Accounts

The granting of credit automatically gives rise to the problem of collecting overdue accounts. Even though every reasonable effort is made to secure accurate credit ratings, there will be slow or doubtful accounts. In a vigorous, forward-looking business this is inevitable, since customers are trusted and given the benefit of the doubt wherever possible.

When an account is not paid, it is unwise to resort to law—often a tedious and expensive process—or to forceful, unfriendly methods of dunning, except as a last resource. Every possible concession must be made to avoid litigation, if there seems to be any possibility of a friendly settlement and continued business relations. Non-payment of accounts is by no means evidence of intent to defraud on the part of the debtor. All sorts of everyday reasons may be responsible—temporary financial reverses, lost or misplaced letters, misunderstanding, inaccuracy on the part of a salesman, forgetfulness, or merely a kind of laziness in business matters. This should be taken into consideration. Tact and consideration turn many doubtful accounts into reliable and valuable ones.

The statement should be sent when the account becomes due and payable, not on the 1st and 15th of the month. It should be enclosed in a friendly letter calling attention to the maturity of the bill and making it clear that a remittance is expected. Many customers must be educated to the fact that payments must be met promptly at maturity in order to maintain a good commercial rating. After allowing a week or ten days for a reply, a second collection letter should be sent, courteously calling to the attention of the debtor his failure to pay. As many as four such letters may be sent. The latter may be given a more forceful tone, but all should be short and friendly, though not temporizing. They should convince the debtor of the writer's sincerity, get under his skin without being offensive. Threats are inadvisable.

If several collection letters do not induce a reply, there is little hope of a friendly adjustment.

It is at this point that a sight draft is valuable. Formerly when a merchant refused to honor a sight draft, he found that such action lowered his credit standing. This is not always true today because many firms make it a positive rule never to pay sight drafts. The presentation of such a draft, particularly in a small town, where everybody knows all about the affairs of everybody else, is likely to bring some results. If possible it is always more satisfactory to draw the draft through the debtor's own bank.

After the sight draft has been drawn and refused it may be advisable to send the collection to a Justice of the Peace, or to the debtor's local bank, either of whose charges will not exceed 10%. On the other hand an attorney may be able to effect a prompt settlement, his charge depending on the amount of the claim. Collection agencies using a series of letters threatening suit or attachment proceedings, or public advertisement, are often effective, but it must be understood that such a system does away with the last hope of future business.

In order to begin suit to enforce a civil debt a complaint is filed stating the facts upon which the action is founded. The court then summons the debtor to appear and answer the charges, and the case is tried upon its merits. If judgment is rendered in favor of the creditor, the sheriff attaches, seizes, and sells enough of the debtor's property to satisfy the judgment. Either before or after the judgment is actually rendered, the creditor may cause to be issued a writ of garnishment or a writ of attachment. The former attaches money or property of the debtor in the possession of a third party while the latter authorizes the sheriff to seize the debtor's property in case he is about to leave the State, abscond, or is a non-resident. Bond is necessary in both cases to indemnify the debtor against loss caused by a wrongful suit.

Recourse to law is seldom advisable unless the account is a large one, and all other efforts have failed. Proper care in extending credit, and a good collection system are worth more to a business than a hundred judgments.

INFORMATION FOR SHIPPERS

The carelessness and ignorance of the shippers and receivers of freight are responsible for a great annual loss of time and money.

In shipping freight one should comply with the following instructions:

a. See that each item is carefully checked in packing.
b. Use the utmost care in nailing, sealing, or tying the shipping case.
c. Mark the case plainly, showing name and address of both shipper and consignee.
d. Make out a uniform bill of lading in clear, legible form, and deliver to the transportation company.

Great care must be taken in accepting freight, in order that there may be no misunderstanding.

a. Remove freight promptly to avoid congestion and storage charges.
b. Examine all freight before giving a receipt to the company.
c. In case of any visible damage or loss, the agent should note it on the freight bill.
d. In case of invisible damage or loss, notify the carrier's agent to come immediately and verify your claim.
e. Notify the freight agent in writing if you intend to store the cases without checking until some later date.
f. If merchandise does not check with invoice, or if it is received in damaged condition, file a claim immediately.

Filing a Freight Claim

The law allows six months after date of delivery in which to file a claim on damaged merchandise, and four months for non-delivery of shipments after a reasonable time has elapsed. The documents required are:

a. The original paid freight bill.
b. The original invoice or certified copy.
c. The original bill of lading or memo.

On shipments damaged beyond repair or entirely lost, full invoice value plus freight should be claimed. An effort should be made to dispose of the damaged merchandise and allow credit for it on the claim. This in no way invalidates the claim. All correspondence should be answered promptly, quoting the file reference and furnishing all available information. The carrier's investigation may take from thirty to ninety days. In tracing claims, patience is essential. In making a claim against an express company, the procedure is practically the same. The invoice or copy thereof, and copy of original express receipt are the necessary documents. The Postal Department has a standard form to be filled in and signed when making claim for lost or damaged parcel post packages.

Rates and Classifications

It is very important for a shipper to consult the published rate. He cannot always depend on the statement of the carrier's agents. If the agent quotes an incorrect rate, the shipper is liable for the published rate. According to law the published rates are common documents, and carriers cannot charge any other rate. Ignorance of this law leads to many losses. A manufacturer may put in a bid on a certain order, and agree to pay all transportation charges. He may get the order, but in making shipment discover that he is compelled to pay a higher rate, which will wipe out his expected profit. On the other hand, he may figure the cost too high, and the order will go to his competitor, who makes it his business to consult the legal published rate.

Months or even years afterwards a shipper may learn to his sorrow that his merchandise has been moving under a wrong rate and be compelled to pay the difference.

According to law, a shipper must make it his business to know the correct freight classifications. He should do so for financial reasons as well. It is the duty of the traffic man to know the principal classifications, and the cheapest rate under each for his goods. He should describe the shipment in the exact language of the shipment, avoiding the use of trade names. Frequently there are chances to lower freight costs by finding the best designation in each classification. Thus the rates differ for goods crated and uncrated, in packages or in bulk, set up or shipped flat, the saving running as high as 50 or 75% in many instances.

LOSSES TO BE AVOIDED

When goods are improperly routed or sent to a wrong destination owing to the shipper's error in making out the shipping ticket or bill of lading, the shipper must pay the excess freight. This is always true when the bill of lading is made out incorrectly and usually so when there is an error in shipping ticket, because of the fact that the carrier relies on the accuracy of the shipping ticket to expedite the shipment. Because of such mistakes, shipments are frequently billed to another town of the same name in another state or in an entirely different section of the country, and the difference in the cost of freight is a considerable item.

A railroad allows forty-eight hours after official notice of arrival of cars in which to unload. An unloaded car standing longer than this is subject to a demurrage charge, listed in the published rates. No charge is made for Sundays, holidays, or days on which it rains to any extent. The charge is a just one, and the receivers of freight should empty cars promptly for two reasons: first to avoid paying the demurrage charge; and second, to release cars, enabling the carrier to reduce his fixed charges, and thus ultimately reduce the cost of transportation.

The following certificate must appear on shipping orders and bills of lading when goods are shipped in fiber boxes:

> "The fiber boxes used for this shipment conform to the specifications set forth in the boxmaker's certificate thereon, and all other requirements of Rule 41 of the Consolidated Freight Classifications."

Failure to do this may cost the shipper or his customer 20% more in freight charges.

BOOKKEEPING

Bookkeeping is the art of recording business transactions in a regular and systematic manner; in a sense it is a branch of mathematics based on certain accepted rules and principles. A set of books properly kept tells a story of profits and losses, a story essential to the successful functioning of any business firm. Systems of bookkeeping differ greatly. In a small business the system may be very simple and readily learned. In a large business it is exceedingly complex. Years can be spent at high schools, business and commercial schools, colleges and universities in detailed study of the art of bookkeeping and the more general field of accounting. This does not mean that there is anything mysterious about the art, but only that it has many ramifications. Like other business methods, it is based on common sense. Naturally, it is beyond the scope of this article to do more than give the reader a general picture and acquaint him with some of the more important concepts.

There are two fundamental systems of bookkeeping: single entry and double entry. The distinction between them is based on the idea that every business transaction may be viewed from two aspects. From one aspect it is a gain; from the other, a loss. For example, when a sale is made, money is received and goods are lost. Similarly, when a purchase is made, goods are received and money is paid out. In single-entry bookkeeping, only one of these aspects is taken account of, and only one entry is made for each transaction; this system is analogous to that of a simple cash book, in which the only entries are those for money received and money paid out. In double-entry bookkeeping, on the other hand, two entries, identical in value, are made for each transaction, the one a debit, the other a credit. Debit entries are made when assets are increased, or when liabilities or proprietorship is decreased. Credit entries are made when assets are decreased, or when liability or proprietorship is increased. Further explanation of these terms will be found in the section BOOKKEEPING TERMS.

Single-entry bookkeeping involves less clerical work and is sometimes suitable for small businesses. But double-entry bookkeeping provides an invaluable check against errors, since the sum of the debits should always equal the sum of the credits; in other words, the books should balance.

There are three principal kinds of books used in double-entry bookkeeping: the books of first entry or journals; the ledger or ledgers; and the auxiliary books or subsidiary ledgers. Books of first entry include the day book or journal, cash book, sales book, and voucher register. Transactions are first recorded in these books and later transferred to the ledger. The latter operation is known as posting. The ledger is the most important and essential of all the books.

The auxiliary books, or subsidiary ledgers, are used to facilitate the grouping of related accounts, such as accounts receivable, in a separate book in order to relieve the general ledger of a mass of detail. The most important of the auxiliary books are the accounts-receivable ledger, the accounts-payable ledger, and the inventory record.

Intelligent, accurate bookkeeping is obviously essential to the success of a firm. It serves many purposes besides the main one of recording the status of a business and analyzing the reasons for its success or failure. It makes it possible for a firm to obtain credit, since when credit is desired a correct statement of financial condition must be furnished. It may be of great service as evidence in legal disputes. Finally, it enables a firm to meet competition intelligently by showing what merchandise costs, what selling and overhead expenses are, and what percentage must be added to make sales profitable.

Bookkeeping Terms

The following terms, arranged alphabetically, consist chiefly of types of accounts and types of entries. Particular attention is given to the question of where and how various entries are made.

Accounts Payable

These are accounts owed others. Credit the general ledger account under that title with the total of all such accounts, and debit or charge it with all that has been paid on them during the month. The balance must agree with the sum of the individual balances or the accounts owed.

Accounts Receivable

These are accounts of persons or individuals in debt to the firm in question. Debit the general ledger account under that heading with the total of all charges against these accounts during the month, and credit it with all payments and allowances made on said accounts. The balance must agree with the sum of the balance of the individual accounts and represents an asset.

Accrued Expenses

Accrued expenses, such as interest payable, salaries or wages payable, etc., should be charged to these respective accounts at the end of the accounting period, in order to show correctly the amount of unpaid earnings at this time, and credited when paid.

Accrued Interest Receivable

Where interest has accrued but is not yet payable on notes and other commercial paper, due from others, charge this account with the amount, and credit the interest account. When the interest is received it is credited to "accrued interest receivable."

Allowances

Discount taken contrary to terms, but allowed, returned merchandise, etc., are debited to the terms account, and credited to the account of the firm in question.

Assets or Resourses

A resource or asset is anything of value owned by the firm from which cash can be realized. A few assets are cash, merchandise, buildings, real estate, store fixtures and furniture, notes receivable, accounts receivable, etc.

Balance Sheet

This is a statement showing the financial condition of a business at a particular time. The assets or resources are arranged in one group; and the liabilities in another. The difference between the totals of the two groups gives the net worth of the business. The title of the statement should be clearly stated and include the name of the business enterprise and the date on which the statement was made.

Cash

This is a title used to designate money. Under it is included currency, bank drafts, checks, express and postal money orders. Cash is debited when received and credited when paid out. The difference shows the cash on hand which is an asset.

Cash Book

This book is used for recording all cash transactions. One section is usually set aside to record cash received, and the other to record cash paid out. If the business is large separate books are kept for receipts and disbursements. The footings in these books are posted to the general ledger accounts at the end of the month or other accounting period.

Day Book and Journal

Formerly these two books were kept separately and entries made in the day book were arranged by debits and credits in the journal before posting to the ledger. Now the two books are consolidated into one, preferably called a "journal," and the entries arranged for posting by debits and credits, followed by a short explanation of the transaction. The ordinary two-column journal may be used, with the left hand column for the debit and the right hand column for the credit, but in order to save time and work in posting, special journals of four, six, eight and more columns are often prepared.

Deferred Charges

Insurance and other similar expense items paid ahead or beyond the date of closing the books are entitled to a credit for that portion of the premium on the unexpired time. This credit is entered on the credit side of insurance accounts and the difference charged to profit and loss. After closing the books this account will be brought forward to the debit side as an asset and appears as such in the financial statement. Office supplies, packing material on hand, etc., also come under this head.

DEPRECIATION

Property such as buildings, machinery, tools, store and office fixtures, depreciates from year to year by reason of wear and tear and obsolescence. In the course of time it becomes entirely worthless and must be replaced. Provision is made for such replacement by setting up a reserve-for-depreciation account. The percentage or amount to be charged off each year depends upon the estimated life or length of usefulness of the asset. Accounts and bills receivable are also subject to shrinkage in value when some of them are found worthless and uncollectable, and a reserve must be provided for bad debts. The amount of reserve is based on the past experience of the company.

EQUIPMENT

Store, office, and delivery equipment represent an investment. Charge store equipment with such items as counters, shelving, scales, measures, etc.; office equipment with such office furniture as desks, safes, letter files, etc.; delivery equipment with trucks, wagons, horses, harness, etc. Repairs for these should not be charged to any of these accounts; they are an expense. A reasonable amount should always be charged off annually for the depreciation of equipment.

EXPENSES

Under this title are generally included such items as rent, salaries, office supplies, fuel, light, postage, etc. If it is desired to show these items in detail, separate accounts may be opened for each one in the ledger. Expense accounts are finally included in the profit and loss account.

LEDGER

The ledger is the book of final entry, collecting and classifying from the books of original entry, all debits and credits having the same name under the one heading, called an account, by a process termed posting. In large business several ledgers or divisions of ledgers are used, viz.: general ledger, purchase ledger, and sales ledger, the latter two carrying controlling accounts on the general ledger. In a small business only one ledger is used. It may, however, be divided into three sections: (1) general accounts, (2) accounts receivable, (3) accounts payable. With the present loose-leaf ledger method this division can be easily made, and by arranging the accounts under each division in alphabetical order, the necessity for a separate index is avoided.

LIABILITIES

A liability is an obligation owed by the firm in question, such as notes payable or any personal account.

LOSSES AND GAINS

An account shows a loss if the thing it represents has cost more than it has produced; a gain if it has produced more than it cost.

MERCHANDISE

This is the general term for all goods and wares dealt in or carried in stock by an active business concern. A merchandise account may be opened and debited with all goods bought and credited with all the proceeds from goods sold. The value of goods on hand unsold added to the proceeds from sales, less the cost, shows the profit on the goods sold. However, if the cost exceeds the other two items, the goods were sold at a loss. The inventory of goods on hand is always an asset. Sometimes, for the purpose of showing profits and losses in greater detail, separate accounts are opened with such commodities as "flour," "potatoes," "apples," "corn," etc., instead of including all under one general title as "merchandise."

MONTHLY SUMMARY OF BUSINESS

A monthly summary of purchases, sales, expenses, and ratios is often useful. It may be arranged with columns for these various headings with the figures taken from the ledger. Each month the figures for that month should be recorded so that the record will give the total for each month from the first of the year to date. The sum of these monthly totals will be the record of totals for the year.

NOTES PAYABLE

These are notes, or written obligations, which others hold, for which the firm must pay a certain amount when due. Credit this account with all notes given to trade creditors, or trade acceptances and time drafts accepted in their favor, and charge the account as they are paid. The balance of the account shows obligations outstanding, which is a liability.

NOTES RECEIVABLE

These are other persons' notes or written obligations, for which, when due, the payment of a specific sum is expected. Charge this account with all notes, time drafts, and trade acceptances held against others, and credit it when paid or otherwise disposed of. The balance will show the sum of the unpaid items, which is an asset.

PERSONAL ACCOUNTS

Persons are debited when they get into debt to the firm, and when the firm gets out of their debt. Persons are credited when the firm gets into their debt, and when they get out of debt to the firm.

Profit and Loss Statement

This financial statement is second in importance only to the balance sheet. Its main difference is that it reflects the results of operations between two particular dates as distinguished from the financial condition at a particular time. The accounts used in making up this statement are the sales, purchases, and expense accounts. In other words, all accounts which cannot be classified as assets, liabilities, or net worth are used in the profit and loss statement.

Property

Property is debited under such titles as merchandise, real estate, cash, etc., when it comes into the firm's possession. It is credited when it goes out of the firm's possession.

Proprietorship

This account, occasionally called the proprietor's capital account, represents the proprietor's net capital. The account is debited for his liabilities assumed by the business, for all amounts drawn by him from the business, for his private use, and for his net loss if any. It is credited for the amount of his investment on commencing business, for all later investments, and for his net gain, if any. The balance of the account is his net capital at the time of closing.

Purchases Account

Modern practice is introducing the purchases account in place of the debit to merchandise. All merchandise purchased is debited or charged to purchase account. If accounts for freight, drayage, expressage, etc., on merchandise are kept separately, their totals should finally be charged into this account also. Credit the account with any merchandise returned to the seller or any discounts or allowances for defects, etc. The balance of the account is transferred to the debit of a "trading account."

Reserves

Part of the profits of a concern may be retained in the business to provide funds for certain future needs as for the payment of fixed debts or business extensions, depreciation, bad debts, income taxes, etc. The sum set aside for such purposes is taken out of and charged to the surplus account, and credited to the reserve set up for that special purpose.

Resources and Liabilities

An account shows a resource, if it represents property on hand or a debt owed to the firm; a liability, if it represents a debt owed by the firm. The excess in an account showing either a resource or a loss will always be on the debit side and the excess showing either a liability or a gain on the credit side.

Sales Account

Credit it with the total sales of all merchandise as shown by the sales book, sales tickets, or whatever method is used for recording sales. Merchandise returned by customers, whether for cash or credit, should be charged or debited at selling price to this account. The difference in the account, the net sales, is transferred to the credit of "trading account."

Sales Book

This is a book in which all the merchandise sales are recorded. The personal accounts charged therein should be posted daily and the total sales may be carried forward until the end of the month and then posted in one entry to the credit of a sales account in the ledger. Where sales and credit tickets are used instead of a sales book, they may be sorted at the close of the day, charging the total cash receipts to cash, crediting sales to the accounts of their respective customers, and crediting the total sales to the sales account. When goods are returned, sales accounts must be charged with them and the customer's account credited.

Trading Account

This account shows the inventory of merchandise at the opening of business, is charged with purchases and sales allowances and credited with sales. The inventory at closing is then credited and the balance shows the gross profit on trading. This gross profit is then transferred as a credit to the profit and loss account, and the inventory brought down for a new balance.

Trial Balance

The trial balance is taken to ascertain the equality of the debits and credits as posted in the ledger. It is nothing more nor less than a copy of the accounts or their balances, and if the footings of the debits and credits do not agree there is an error in posting. The trial balance is not an absolute proof of the correctness of the work, but if the footings are equal the work is generally regarded as correct.

Locating Errors in Double-Entry Bookkeeping

When trial balance totals do not agree it is certain that one or more errors have been made somewhere, but there is no single rule or combination of rules with which such errors can at once be located outside of a careful review of the entire work. However, the following hints and suggestions may be of service and help in locating them.

A large difference between the debit and credit totals of a trial balance usually indicates an omission of some item or account. See if all the accounts or balances of accounts have been included in the trial balance. If an amount has been omitted in posting, the trial balance also will be out of balance by that much. Look for such an unchecked amount in the books from which postings were made.

An amount posted to the wrong side of the ledger will throw the trial balance just twice that amount out of balance. If the difference is divisible by 2, look for half of that amount on the side with the smaller totals in the books from which postings were made and see if such an amount was posted to the other side of the ledger account. The cash and accounts-receivable balance can never be on the credit side, nor the accounts-payable balance on the debit side of the account.

If the difference between the debit and credit totals be 1, or in round numbers, as 10, 100, 1,000, the error very likely results from wrong addition or subtraction. Check the additions of the trial balance and if the error is not found there, check those of the ledger also. Where ledger balances only are entered in the trial balance an error may have been made in finding the difference between the two sides of an account. If an error is in the cents column only, the columns to the left need not be re-added.

If the difference is divisible by 9 the error may rest in a transposition of figures, as for instance 57 posted as 75 causing a difference of 18, or 735 posted as 537 causing a difference of 198, both of which are divisible by 9. Errors of transposition are difficult to find; however, if the difference consists of less than three figures such as 9, 18, 27, etc., a one-column transposition may have caused the error. Divide this difference by 9; if the quotient is 1, the difference between the two transposed figures is also 1; if 2 or 3 the difference between the transposed figures is likewise 2 or 3. When the difference lies between 99 and 1,000, the error may be due to a two-column transposition. Here the middle figure of the error is always a 9, as for instance 981 written as 189 results in an error of 792. Dividing the two outside figures of the difference (72) by 9, the quotient 8 is also the difference between the two transposed figures (9 and 1).

Another common type of error results from a transplacement or "slide." Figures are transplaced when some or all of the digits of a number are moved one or more places to the right or left without any change in their order; for instance 327 written as 32.70 or 3.27. The first is a one-column, the second a two-column slide. The error caused by a one-column slide is always divisible by nine, a two-column by 99, a three-column by 999, etc. Such division, disregarding decimals, always gives the figures whose transplacement has caused the error. The error caused by writing 327 as 32.70 is 294.30 which divided by 9 produces 327; or 327 written as 3.27 causes a difference of 323.73 which divided by 99 produces 327.

Legal Points in Bookkeeping

Occasions may sometimes arise in which the books of a firm become of importance in courts of law. Only records of original entry are accepted as evidence in court, especially the day book and journal, as evidence of sale and delivery of goods or work done. For this reason, as well as for many others, the time to make an entry or charge against the purchaser of goods or for work done is when the goods are ready for delivery, or the work has been completed. Entries to be admissable as evidence, should be made by the proper person, and without erasure, alterations, or interlineations. Mistakes should be corrected by marking the wrong entry void, and then making a correct entry. All accounts must be itemized and no general charge can be considered as evidence, unless it lists the separate items.

If A guarantees that he will see that B will pay a certain bill of goods, then the goods must be charged to A and not to B in order to hold A responsible; but if A guarantees the account of B, if the account is for some date of the past, then such a guarantee must be in writing.

To collect a debt on the evidence of book accounts from a person in a distant place, a copy of the account should be made out and accompanied by an affidavit, setting forth that the account is correctly taken from the book or records of original entries; that the charges were made at or about the same time of their respective dates; that the goods were sold and delivered at or about the time the charges were made; that the charges are correct and the accounts just; and that the person named is not entitled to any credit not mentioned in the account. The affidavit should be sworn to before a magistrate, commissioner or notary public. This obviates the trouble of producing or sending the books.

BUSINESS ARITHMETIC

This section is hardly intended to be an exhaustive study of business arithmetic; nor does it attempt to touch upon the theoretical abstractions of arithmetic. The inclusion of material has been guided by the practical needs of everyday business problems: problems involving fractions, decimals, percentage, interest, discounts and measurements. The principles of these arithmetical processes will be given, as well as such other aids as will be helpful.

The Four Fundamental Operations

The four fundamental operations of arithmetic — addition, subtraction, multiplication, and division — are familiar to everyone. The underlying principle of these operations is that *only similar quantities* can be added, subtracted, multiplied or divided. Thus, one can add *5 hats* and *3 hats*, for instance, and get *8 hats;* but one cannot add *5 hats* and *3 oranges*, because they are dissimilar quantities.

Addition

Addition is the process of uniting two or more numbers in one total called a *sum.* The sign used to indicate this process is called *plus* (+): $6 + 3 = 9$. To add rapidly it is best to group mentally the numbers in a column of figures, so that they total 8, 9, 10, 12, or some other convenient sum.

6	2	82
3	5	31
8	3	25
2	6	49
9	4	36
1	1	12
6	3	60
9	8	89
44	32	384

Accuracy is more important than speed in arithmetic. Of the various methods by which the correctness of an addition may be checked these two are the simplest: (1) If the column of figures has been added from top to bottom, then re-add starting at the bottom and going upward; if the results obtained by both methods are the same, the answer is probably correct. (2) Re-add the column of figures, omitting the top row of figures from the addition, and subtract this sum from the first result obtained; if the difference between these two sums is equal to the top row of figures omitted from the second addition, then the answer is probably correct. By applying this method to the above column, for instance, omitting the *82*, one obtains the sum of *302*, which when subtracted from *384* leaves *82*.

Subtraction

Subtraction is the operation of finding the difference between two numbers. The larger number, or the one from which the subtraction is being made, is called the *minuend*, the smaller number is called the *subtrahend* and the result is called the *remainder*. The sign used to indicate this process is called *minus* (—). In subtraction, the smaller number is always taken from the larger one, but the reverse is impossible except algebraically. Thus 6 can be subtracted from 10, but 10 cannot be subtracted from 6. To check the correctness of a result in subtraction, add the remainder to the subtrahend, and if the sum is equal to the minuend the answer is correct. Thus:

		Check
Selling Price	$831.50	$207.35
Cost	624.15	624.15
Profit	$207.35	$831.50

Multiplication

Multiplication is the process by which any given number or quantity may be augmented any number of times by a short method of addition. The number to be multiplied is called the *multiplicand*, the number by which it is multiplied is called the *multiplier*, and the result is called the *product*. The sign used to indicate multiplication is called *times* (×).

Of the many short cuts in this process, the multiplication table, which should be learned by heart, is one of the most helpful. Another short method is multiplying by 10, 100, 1000, etc. simply by adding the ciphers to the multiplicand. Thus, in 100×15, add the two zeros to the 15, and the product is 1500; in 1000×24, add the three zeros to the 24 and the product is 24,000, etc. If the number to the left of the ciphers in the multiplier is something other than 1 (as 40, 1600, 23,000) then multiply by that number and add the ciphers to the product.

23000	82
12	1600
46	492
23	82
276000	131200

If the multiplier is 9, 99, 999, etc., multiply by 10, or 100, or 1000 and subtract the multiplicand from the product. Thus, in 48×99 take 48 times 100, or 4800, and subtract 48:

$$48 \times 100 = 4800 - 48 = 4752.$$

If the multiplier is 11, 101, 1001, etc., multiply by 10, 100, or 1000 and add the multiplicand to the product. Thus in 16×101 take 16 times 100, or 1600, add 16:

$$16 \times 100 = 1600 + 16 = 1616.$$

To check the results of multiplication, divide the product by the multiplier, and if the quotient is equal to the multiplicand, then the answer is probably correct. The following will serve as an illustration of a multiplication and check:

```
   82              82
   16          16/ 1312
  ----             128
  492              ---
  82                32
  ----              32
  1312              --
```

DIVISION

Division is the process of determining the number of times one number is contained in another. The number to be divided is called the *dividend*, the number by which it is divided is the *divisor*, and the result is the *quotient*. If the solution does not come out to an even number the fractional part left over is called the *remainder*. The sign used to indicate division is ÷ .

In general, there are two methods of division: (1) *short* division, where the steps in the process are done mentally (usually with a divisor of 10 or less); (2) *long* division, where all steps in the process are written out. Thus 6432 ÷ 8 = 804 is an illustration of short division. Long division is illustrated by the following:

```
          815 67/85
     ----------
     85/ 69342
         680
         ---
          134
           85
          ---
          492
          425
          ---
           67
```

To check, multiply the quotient by the divisor (adding the remainder, if any, to the product), and if the product equals the dividend, the result is correct.

For numbers which are a power of 10, (100, 1000, 10,000) this short method is helpful: beginning at the right, cross out as many figures in the dividend as there are zeros in the divisor; the figures in the dividend, other than crossed out zeros, constitute the remainder.

$$16\emptyset \div 1\emptyset = 16$$

$$62\not{8}\not{5}\not{1} \div 1\emptyset\emptyset\emptyset = 62\frac{851}{1000}.$$

For numbers which are a multiple of 10 (30, 50, 200, etc.) proceed as above, dividing what is left by the remaining figure in the divisor.

$$15\emptyset \div 3\emptyset = \frac{15}{3} = 5$$

$$860\not{1}\not{3} \div 2\emptyset\emptyset = \frac{860}{2} + \frac{13}{200} = 430\frac{13}{200}.$$

Fractions

Fractions are parts of a whole expressed numerically. The number in a fraction written below the line is the *denominator;* the one written above the line is the *numerator;* both together are called the *terms* of a fraction. If the numerator of a fraction is less than the denominator, as $\frac{4}{5}, \frac{3}{10}, \frac{7}{8}$, it is a *proper* fraction. If the numerator is equal to, or exceeds, the denominator, as $\frac{4}{4}, \frac{6}{4}, \frac{7}{2}$, it is an *improper* fraction. If the fraction expresses a whole number and a fractional part, as $1\frac{3}{4}, 2\frac{5}{7}, 3\frac{3}{5}$, it is a *mixed number*.

Fractions are capable of being added, subtracted, multiplied and divided. It is frequently expedient, and a time saver, to reduce fractions to their lowest terms or to find their least common denominator before starting any one of these processes. For this a knowledge of factoring and cancellation is necessary. *Factoring* is the process of finding the smallest numbers (prime numbers) which are the divisors of a larger number. Thus 2 and 3 are the *prime factors* of 6 because they are the smallest numbers which, when multiplied together, equal 6; 2 and 2 and 2 are the prime factors of 8; 4 and 3 the prime factors of 12, etc. The following rules will be found helpful in factoring:

Two will divide evenly any even number.

Three will divide evenly any number the sum of whose digits is divisible by 3. Thus 3 will divide evenly 813 because 12, the sum of 8 + 1 + 3, is evenly divisible by 3.

Four will divide evenly any number whose last two digits on the right form a figure divisible by 4. Thus, 4 will evenly divide 69,816 because 16, the last two digits, is evenly divisible by 4.

Five will divide evenly any number ending in 0 or 5.

Six will divide evenly any even number the sum of whose digits is divisible by 3. Thus 6 will divide evenly 2616 because 15, the sum of 2 + 6 + 1 + 6, is divisible by 3.

Eight will divide evenly any number whose last three digits on the right make a figure divisible by 8. Thus, 8 will divide evenly 23,624 because 624, the last three digits, is evenly divisible by 8.

Nine will divide evenly any number the sum of whose digits is divisible by 9. Thus 9 will divide evenly 32,193 because 18, the sum of 3 + 2 + 1 + 9 + 3, is evenly divisible by 9.

Ten will divide evenly any number ending in 0.

Cancellation is the process of eliminating a common factor in both the numerator and denominator of a fraction. It is most useful in multiplying and dividing fractions, and in reducing a fraction to its lowest terms. For instance, the result

$$\frac{\overset{26}{\not{52}} \times \overset{3}{\not{18}}}{\underset{2}{\not{12}}} = 78$$

is obtained by determining that 6, a common factor of 12 and 18, divides into those numbers 2 and 3 times respectively. Two, a factor of 52, divides into this number 26 times. Multiplying 26 by 3, 78 is obtained.

An improper fraction can be changed to a whole number or mixed number by dividing the numerator by the denominator. Thus, the improper fraction $\frac{6}{2}$ is converted to the whole number 3 simply by dividing 6 by 2: likewise, $\frac{7}{2}$ is converted to the mixed number 3½ by dividing 7 by 2. To change 3½ (a mixed number) back to $\frac{7}{2}$ (an improper fraction) multiply 3 (the whole number) by 2 (the denominator of the fraction ½) and add 1 (the numerator of the fraction ½) to the product, retaining 2 as the denominator of the newly created fraction. Thus, $\frac{3 \times 2 + 1}{2} = \frac{7}{2}$

Addition of Fractions and Mixed Numbers

If the fractions to be added have the same denominator, add the numerators, write this sum over the denominator, and reduce to lowest terms, if necessary. Thus, $\frac{1}{5} + \frac{2}{5} = \frac{3}{5}$; similarly, $\frac{1}{6} + \frac{5}{6} = \frac{6}{6} = 1$

If the fractions to be added do not have the same denominator find the least common denominator, divide it by the denominator of each fraction, multiply the results by the respective numerators and write the new figures over the common denominator; add the numerators, and reduce to lowest terms if necessary.

$$\begin{array}{c|l} \frac{1}{2} & \frac{8}{16} \\ \frac{3}{4} & \frac{12}{16} \\ \frac{7}{8} & \frac{14}{16} \\ \hline & \frac{34}{16} = 2\frac{2}{16} = 2\frac{1}{8} \end{array}$$

The least common denominator, 16, is divided by 2, and the result, 8, multiplied by one. Similarly, it is divided by 4, and the result, 4, multiplied by 3, producing 12; and by 8 with the result 2, multiplied by 7, producing 14. Adding these newly obtained numerators, one arrives at $\frac{34}{16}$, which reduces to $2\frac{2}{16}$, which further reduces to $2\frac{1}{8}$.

If mixed numbers are to be added, add the fractions first, then the whole numbers, and finally combine the two sums.

$$\begin{array}{l|l} 1\frac{5}{8} & \frac{15}{24} \\ 2\frac{3}{4} & \frac{18}{24} \\ 6\frac{2}{3} & \frac{16}{24} \\ \hline 9 & \frac{49}{24} = 2\frac{1}{24} \\ 2\frac{1}{24} & \\ \hline 11\frac{1}{24} & \end{array}$$

The fractional part is done as in the example, so that $\frac{49}{24}$, which reduces to $2\frac{1}{24}$, is obtained. Adding the whole numbers, 9 is obtained, to which is added $2\frac{1}{24}$, producing the final result of $11\frac{1}{24}$.

Subtraction of Fractions and Mixed Numbers

If the fractions to be subtracted have the same denominator, subtract the numerators, write this remainder over the denominator, and reduce to lowest terms, if necessary. Thus, $\frac{2}{6} - \frac{1}{6} = \frac{1}{6}$; similarly, $\frac{5}{6} - \frac{1}{6} = \frac{4}{6} = \frac{2}{3}$.

If the fractions to be subtracted do not have the same denominator, the steps followed are the same as in addition except that the new numerators are subtracted instead of added.

$$\begin{array}{c|l} \frac{3}{6} & \frac{6}{12} \\ \frac{1}{4} & \frac{3}{12} \\ \hline & \frac{3}{12} = \frac{1}{4} \end{array}$$

If mixed numbers are to be subtracted, first subtract the fractions, borrowing 1 from the whole number if necessary, then subtract the whole numbers, and finally combine the two.

$$\begin{array}{l|l} 4\frac{3}{4} & \frac{12}{16} \\ 1\frac{5}{8} & \frac{10}{16} \\ \hline 3\frac{1}{8} & \frac{2}{16} = \frac{1}{8} \end{array}$$

The least common denominator, 16, when divided by 4 and multiplied by 3 produces 12; similarly, when divided by 8 and multiplied by 5, it produces 10. Subtracting, $\frac{2}{16}$ is obtained, which reduced to its lowest terms is $\frac{1}{8}$. Subtracting the whole numbers, 3 is obtained which is combined with $\frac{1}{8}$, giving the final result of $3\frac{1}{8}$.

$$\begin{array}{l|l} \overset{3}{4}\frac{2}{3} & \frac{8}{12} + \frac{12}{12} = \frac{20}{12} \\ 1\frac{3}{4} & \frac{9}{12} \\ \hline \frac{11}{12} & \frac{11}{12} \end{array}$$

The solution is the same as in the preceding problem, except that 9 could not be subtracted from 8, a smaller number. Hence, 1, or $\frac{12}{12}$, was borrowed from the whole number 4, and added to $\frac{8}{12}$, giving $\frac{20}{12}$, from which $\frac{9}{12}$ is subtracted. Then 1 from 3 is subtracted, giving 2, which is combined with $\frac{11}{12}$.

Multiplication of Fractions and Whole Numbers

If fractions are to be multiplied, cancel where possible, then write the product of the numerators over the product of the denominators, and reduce to lowest terms if necessary.

Thus, $\frac{2}{3} \times \frac{1}{6} = \frac{1}{9}$; similarly, $\frac{1}{3} \times \frac{2}{5} = \frac{2}{15}$.

If mixed numbers are to be multiplied, change the mixed numbers to improper fractions, cancel where possible, then write the product of the numerators over the product of the denominators, and reduce to lowest terms if necessary.

Thus, $8\frac{3}{5} \times 6\frac{1}{4} = \frac{43}{5} \times \frac{25}{4} = \frac{215}{4} = 53\frac{3}{4}$;

similarly, $4\frac{9}{10} \times 5\frac{3}{7} = \frac{49}{10} \times \frac{38}{7} = \frac{133}{5} = 26\frac{3}{5}$.

If a whole number and a fraction are to be multiplied, cancel where possible, multiply the whole number by the numerator, and divide by the denominator. Thus, $343 \times \frac{3}{7} = 147$;

similarly, $250 \times \frac{3}{4} = \frac{375}{2} = 187\frac{1}{2}$.

DIVISION OF FRACTIONS AND MIXED NUMBERS

If fractions are to be divided, invert the divisor, cancel where possible, and proceed as in multiplication. Thus, $\frac{5}{6} \div \frac{3}{4} = \frac{5}{6} \times \frac{4}{3} = \frac{10}{9} = 1\frac{1}{9}$;

similarly, $\frac{2}{3} \div \frac{1}{3} = \frac{2}{3} \times \frac{3}{1} = 2$.

If mixed numbers are to be divided, change these to improper fractions, invert the divisor, cancel where possible, and proceed as in multiplication.

Thus, $3\frac{5}{7} \div 8\frac{2}{5} = \frac{26}{7} \div \frac{42}{5} = \frac{26}{7} \times \frac{5}{42} = \frac{65}{147}$;

similarly, $6\frac{1}{2} \div 5\frac{1}{5} = \frac{13}{2} \div \frac{26}{5} = \frac{13}{2} \times \frac{5}{26} = \frac{5}{4} = 1\frac{1}{4}$.

If a whole number and a fraction are to be divided, invert the divisor, cancel where possible, and proceed, as in multiplication.

Thus, $69816 \div \frac{4}{5} = 69816 \times \frac{5}{4} = 87270$;

similarly, $840 \div 5\frac{3}{5} = 840 \div \frac{28}{5} = 840 \times \frac{5}{28} = 150$.

DECIMALS

A fraction can be written in one of two ways: As a common fraction, or as a decimal (also called decimal fraction). Thus, the common fraction $\frac{7}{10}$ can also be expressed decimally as .7 (to avoid confusion a zero is sometimes placed to the left of the decimal point, as 0.7); the common fraction $\frac{7}{100}$ can also be expressed decimally as .07; $\frac{7}{1000}$ as .007; $\frac{7}{10{,}000}$ as .0007, etc. From this it can be seen that in a common fraction the denominator is always written, whereas in a decimal the denominator is represented by a period or decimal point, which is placed to the left of the numerator ($\frac{7}{10} = .7$). The size of the denominator in a decimal fraction is always determined by the number of figures to the right of the decimal point. Thus, one decimal place represents tenths; two decimal places represent hundredths; three decimal places represent thousandths; four decimal places represent ten-thousandths, five decimal places represent hundred-thousandths, etc.

To change a fraction to a decimal. Divide the numerator by the denominator, placing a decimal to the right of the numerator and adding as many zeros as necessary to bring out the division evenly or approximately. Thus, $\frac{1}{4}$, for instance, is converted to a decimal in the following manner:

$$\frac{1}{4} = 4\overline{)1.00}\ (.25);\ \text{similarly,}\ \frac{2}{3} = 3\overline{)2.00}\ (.66\tfrac{2}{3}).$$

To change a decimal to a fraction, drop the decimal point, write in a denominator with as many zeros as there are figures to the right of the decimal, and reduce to lowest terms. Thus .875, for instance, is converted to a fraction as follows:

$$.875 = \frac{875}{1000} = \frac{7}{8};$$

$$\text{similarly, } .66\frac{2}{3} = \frac{66\frac{2}{3}}{100} = \frac{200}{300} = \frac{2}{3}.$$

(The $\frac{200}{300}$ is obtained by multiplying the numerator and denominator by 3.)

ADDITION OF DECIMALS

To add a column of decimals, arrange the figures so that the decimal points are placed one directly under the other, and proceed as in ordinary addition.

\$69.20	84.691
17.84	7.02
5.31	35.1
23.65	0.0921
14.78	3.1416
\$130.78	130.0447

Subtraction of Decimals

To subtract decimals arrange the figures so that the decimal points are placed one directly under another, and proceed as in ordinary subtraction.

```
$16.95        16.83
  3.22        12.0914
------        -------
$13.73         4.7386
```

(In subtracting 12.0914 from 16.83, zeros were added mentally so that it became 16.8300. This can be done because the addition of zeros to the last number of a decimal does not alter its value.)

Multiplication of Decimals

To multiply decimals, proceed as in ordinary multiplication, count the number of decimal places in the multiplier and multiplicand, and point off as many in the product, starting at the right and moving toward the left.

```
  4.56        3.1416
   8.3           .05
  ----      --------
  1368      0.157080
 3648
------
37.848
```

Division of Decimals

To divide a decimal by a whole number, place the decimal point on the quotient line, directly above the decimal point in the dividend, and proceed as in ordinary division. If the answer is not even, carry out to at least two decimal places.

```
    .46          30.12
  -----        -------
15/6.90       23/692.76
   60            69
   --            --
    90             27
    90             23
    --             --
                    46
                    46
                    --
```

To divide a decimal by a decimal, move the decimal point in the divisor to the extreme right, move it as many places to the right in the dividend as it was moved in the divisor, and proceed as in ordinary division. For example, to divide 8.5116 by 2.46, the decimal point must first be moved two places to the right in the dividend, changing that number from 2.46 to the whole number 246; then it must be moved an equal number of places in the dividend, changing that number from 8.5116 to 851.16.

```
          3.46
       -------
    246/851.16
        738
        ---
        1131
         984
        ----
        1476
        1476
        ----
```

To divide a whole number by a decimal, move the decimal point in the divisor to the extreme right, add as many zeros to the dividend as the decimal point was moved places in the divisor, putting a decimal point after the last of these zeros, and proceed as in ordinary division, carrying out to two decimal places if the answer is not even. For example, to divide 6248 by 1.25 the decimal point must first be moved two places to the right in the divisor, changing that number from 1.25 to the whole number 125. The decimal point having been moved two places in the divisor, two zeros must now be added to the dividend, changing that number from 6248 to 624800.

```
       4998.4
    ----------
    125/624800.0
        500
        ---
        1248
        1125
        ----
        1230
        1125
        ----
         1050
         1000
         ----
           500
           500
           ---
```

Since the result 4998 still left a fractional part, the latter was eliminated by carrying out to one more decimal place, giving the even answer 4998.4.

Percentage

Percentage is the expression of numbers in terms of hundredths. The sign used to indicate this process is called *per cent* (%). The number upon which the per cent is calculated is the *base;* the amount of the per cent is the *rate;* and the result of the calculation made with the base and the rate is called the *percentage.* For example, in 2% of \$125 = \$2.50, 2% is the rate, \$125 is the base, and \$2.50 the percentage.

If the base and the rate are known, divide the rate by 100 and then multiply the one by the other to find the percentage. Thus to find 8% of \$240 multiply one hundredth part of the rate (.08) by the base (\$240).

```
  $240   (base)
   .08   (rate)
------
$19.20   (percentage).
```

To find the rate when the base and percentage are known, divide the percentage by the base. Thus, if \$100 yielded a return of \$4.00, what was the rate of return?

$$\frac{\text{(percentage) } \$4.00}{\text{(base) } \$100} = .04 \text{ or } 4\% \text{ (rate).}$$

To find the base when the percentage and rate are known, divide the percentage by one hundredth part of the rate. Thus, if 4% yielded a return of \$4.00, how much money was invested?

$$\frac{\text{(percentage) } \$4.00}{\text{(rate) } .04} = \$100 \text{ (base).}$$

Where b = base, r = rate, and % = percentage, these three principles may be expressed with the following formulas:

(1) $b \times \frac{r}{100} = \%$

(2) $\frac{\%}{b} = \frac{r}{100}$

(3) $\frac{\%}{\frac{r}{100}} = b$

The following table of percentages and their fractional equivalents, because of their frequent use, should be memorized.

$12\frac{1}{2}\% = \frac{1}{8}$	$16\frac{2}{3}\% = \frac{1}{6}$
$25\% = \frac{1}{4}$	$33\frac{1}{3}\% = \frac{1}{3}$
$37\frac{1}{2}\% = \frac{3}{8}$	$66\frac{2}{3}\% = \frac{2}{3}$
$50\% = \frac{1}{2}$	$83\frac{1}{3}\% = \frac{5}{6}$
$62\frac{1}{2}\% = \frac{5}{8}$	$20\% = \frac{1}{5}$
$75\% = \frac{3}{4}$	$40\% = \frac{2}{5}$
$87\frac{1}{2}\% = \frac{7}{8}$	$60\% = \frac{3}{5}$
$8\frac{1}{3}\% = \frac{1}{12}$	$80\% = \frac{4}{5}$

Interest

Interest is the amount of money earned by, or paid for, the use of a sum of money called the *principal*. The *rate* is the per cent of interest charged or paid for the use of the money. In the calculation of simple interest a year consists of 360 days, or of 12 months of 30 days each. Unless otherwise specified, interest is always calculated on the basis of one year. Where I stands for interest, P for principal, R for rate, and T for time, the method of finding the interest on any principal can be expressed by the following formula:

$$I = P \times \frac{R}{100} \times T$$

This formula will always work, whether the time be expressed in terms of years, months, or days. The following examples will serve as illustration of usual and alternate methods of solution.

(1) Find the interest on $835 at 6% for 3 years.

(1)
```
 $835    (P)
  .06    (R)
 ------
 $50.10  (int. for 1 yr.)
    3    (T)
 ------
 $150.30 (int. for 3 yrs.)
```

(2)
```
  $835
   .18
  ----
  6680
  835
 -------
 $150.30
```

In this solution, since 6% for 3 yrs. amounts to 18%, the principal is multiplied by .18.

(2) Find the interest on $276 at 6% for 5 months.

(1)
```
 $276   (P)
  .06   (R)
 ------
 $16.56 (int.
         for
         1 yr.)
```

(2) $\frac{\overset{23}{\cancel{\$276}} \times .06 \times 5}{\cancel{12}} = \$6.90$

(3) $\frac{\overset{.23}{\cancel{\$2.76}} \times 6 \times 5}{\cancel{12}} = \$6.90$

(T) $\frac{5}{12} \times \overset{1.38}{\cancel{16.56}} = \$6.90$ (int. for 5 mos.).

In solution 3, by dividing $276 by 100, yielding $2.76, the .06 immediately changes to the whole number 6.

(3) **Find the interest on $496 at 8% for 45 days.**

(1)
```
 $496   (P)
  .08   (R)
 ------
 $39.68 (int.
         for
         1 yr.)
```

(2) $\frac{\overset{62}{\cancel{\$496}} \times .08 \times \cancel{45}}{\underset{8}{\cancel{360}}} = \$4.96$

(3) $\frac{\overset{.62}{\cancel{\$4.96}} \times 8 \times \cancel{45}}{\underset{8}{\cancel{360}}} = \$4.96$

(T) $\frac{\cancel{45}}{\cancel{360}} \times \overset{4.96}{\cancel{39.68}} = \$4.96$ (int. for 45 days).

Shorter Methods for Computing Simple Interest

To find the interest at 6% for 60 days, point off two places from the right on the principal. For example, the interest on $635 at 6% for 60 days is $6.35. By bearing this principle in mind the interest at 6% for any number of days can be quickly found.

(1) Find the interest on $345 at 6% for 45 days.

$345 = $3.45 (int. for 60 days)

$\frac{\overset{3}{\cancel{45}}}{\underset{4}{\cancel{60}}} \times \$3.45 = \frac{10.35}{4} = \$2.5875$

or $2.59 (int. for 45 days).

Since the interest was for a period of less than 60 days, the fractional part of 60 or $\frac{45}{60}$, had to be multiplied by $3.45 in order to find the interest for 45 days, resulting in $2.5875 or $2.59. If an interest problem does not come out even after the second decimal, carry it out to two more decimal places, and if the third number after the decimal point in the answer is 5 or more, add 1 to the result.

(2) Find the interest on $725 at 6% for 75 days.

$725 = $7.25 (int. for 60 days)

$\frac{\overset{5}{\cancel{75}}}{\underset{4}{\cancel{60}}} \times 7.25 = \frac{\$36.25}{4} = \$9.0625$

or $9.06 (int. for 75 days).

To find the interest for 60 days at a rate other than 6%, the following rules will be found helpful.

At 2%, since this is $\frac{1}{3}$ of 6, take $\frac{1}{3}$ of the int. at 6%.

At 3%, since this is $\frac{1}{2}$ of 6, take $\frac{1}{2}$ of the interest at 6%.

At 4%, since this is $\frac{1}{3}$ less than 6, subtract $\frac{1}{3}$ of the interest at 6%.

At 5%, since this is $\frac{1}{6}$ less than 6, subtract $\frac{1}{6}$ of the int. at 6%.

At 7%, since this is $\frac{1}{6}$ more than 6, add $\frac{1}{6}$ of the interest at 6%.

At 8%, since this is $\frac{1}{3}$ more than 6 add $\frac{1}{3}$ of the interest at 6%.

At 9%, since this is $\frac{1}{2}$ more than 6%, add $\frac{1}{2}$ of the interest at 6%.

At 10%, since this is 4% more than 6%, add 4% to that at 6%.

Banker's interest is the same as simple interest except that the exact number of days must be counted instead of using a 30-day month. For example, what would be the banker's interest on $858 at 6% from March 1 to May 9?

Days in March	31
Days in April	30
Days in May	9
	70

$858 = $8.58 (int. for 60 days)

$\frac{70}{60} \times \$8.58 = \$10.01$ (int. for 70 days). [1.43 written over the fraction; zeros cancelled]

Exact interest is the same as simple interest except that 365 (366, leap year) is used as the annual base instead of 360 days.

Compound Interest

Compound interest differs from simple interest in that the interest at the end of the year is added to the principal, and each succeeding year's interest calculated on the basis of interest plus principal. For example, what is the compound interest on $2500 for 3 years at 4%?

$2500	$2600	$2704
.04	.04	.04
$100.00 (int. for 1 yr.)	$104.00 (int. for 2nd yr.)	$108.16 (int. for 3rd yr.)
$2500	$2600	$2704.00
100	104	108.16
$2600 (int. plus prin. for 1 yr.)	$2704 (int. plus prin. for 2nd yr.)	$2812.16 (int. plus prin. for 3rd yr.)

Discount

Discount is the interest paid to a bank for converting commercial papers such as drafts, promissory notes, etc., into cash before their date of maturity. This is often called a *bank discount.* The *face* of a note or draft is the value of the paper (*i.e.*, the total amount of money involved) minus interest. The *value,* or *amount,* of a note or draft is what the paper is worth at the date of maturity. The *proceeds* of a note or draft are the value, less all charges. The *discount period* is the time (figured in days) between the date of discount and the date of maturity.

The bank discount and proceeds of a commercial paper are found by determining the value of the paper and the bank discount, and subtracting the bank discount from the value. For example, What are the proceeds of a note for $8200 dated May 3, due in 3 months, and discounted by the bank on June 2 at 5%?

Note due August 3

30–2 = 28 days in June	Face of note	= $8200.00
31 days in July	Bank discount	
3 days in Aug.	on $8200 for	
—	62 days	= 70.61
62 days = discount period at 5%		
	Proceeds	= $8129.39

Measurements

In business, the two measurements most frequently used are that of area or surface, a two-dimensional product expressed in terms of square inches, square feet, or square yards; and that of volume, a three-dimensional product expressed in terms of cubic inches, cubic feet, or cubic yards.

To find the area of a square or rectangle multiply the length by the width. For instance, How much linoleum is needed to cover a floor 15 feet long and 18 feet wide? Multiplying 18 by 15, one finds that 270 square feet are needed.

To find the area of a triangle, divide the product of the base and the height or altitude by $\frac{1}{2}$. (The altitude of a triangle is a perpendicular dropped from the vertex to the base.) For instance, what is the area of a triangle with an altitude of 5 feet 3 inches and a base of 9 feet 4 inches?

$$\frac{5\frac{1}{4} \times 9\frac{1}{3}}{2} = \frac{\frac{21}{4} \times \frac{28}{3}}{2} = \frac{49}{2} = 24\tfrac{1}{2} \text{ sq. ft.}$$

(It is best to work with a uniform unit of measurement. Hence, since $\frac{3}{12} = \frac{1}{4}$ of a foot, and $\frac{4}{12} = \frac{1}{3}$ of a foot, 5 feet 3 inches is changed to $5\frac{1}{4}$ feet and 9 feet 4 inches to $9\frac{1}{3}$ feet.)

To find the area of a circle, divide the product of the circumference and diameter by 4. The circumference of a circle is obtained by multiplying the diameter by *pi* which equals 3.14159 or about $3\frac{1}{7}$. For example, what is the area of a circle having a diameter of 5 feet?

3.14159 (pi)
5 (diameter)
15.70795 = circumference

$$\frac{15.70795 \times 5}{4} = \frac{78.53975}{4} = 19.635 \text{ sq. ft.} = \text{area}$$

To find the volume of a solid, multiply the length by the width by the height. For example, what is the volume of air in a room 12 feet high, 10 feet wide, and 14 feet long?

$12 \times 10 \times 14 = 1680$ cubic feet.

To find the number of board feet in lumber, multiply the length by the width by the thickness If the board is less than 1 inch thick, consider it as a full inch; if more than 1 inch thick, use exact dimensions. For example, how many board feet are in a piece of wood 20 feet long, 3 feet wide, and $\frac{3}{4}$ of an inch thick?

$20 \times 3 \times 1 = 60$ board feet.

A Law Dictionary

***Acknowledgments**, Affidavits, Agency, Bailment, Bankruptcy, Bonds, Brokerage, Carriers, Chattels, Citizenship, Contracts, Copyright, Corporations, Criminal Law, Deeds, Dower, Equity, Guarantee, Husband and Wife, Insurance, International Law, Licenses, Liens, Leases, Legal Remedies, Mortgages, Negotiable Instruments, Notaries, Parent and Child, Parliamentary Law, Partnership, Passports, Patents, Prescriptive Rights, Shipping, Statutes of Limitation, Trademarks, Wills*

Introduction

According to an old adage, the man who attempts to be his own lawyer has a fool for his client. There is, no doubt, a great deal of truth in that statement, and it is not the purpose of this book to enable a man to act as his own lawyer. In order to conduct his business intelligently, however, it is necessary for the layman to understand some of the principles of the laws which govern his rights and duties toward those with whom he deals. Never has this been more true than at present. In the course of his daily living, the average citizen is constantly coming into contact with the law and with legal problems.

It is to meet this need of a practical knowledge of the law on the part of the individual that this section is intended. BUSINESS LAW FOR THE LAYMAN contains up-to-date information on practically every branch of the law and covers all recent legislation with reference to bankruptcy, wages and hours, and the relationship of employer to employee. It also includes a complete set of the most commonly used legal forms.

In brief, this section contains an accurate, concise statement of the law, as it affects the average layman and business man, and should prove invaluable as a ready reference handbook and guide.

Explanation of Terms

1. Definition of Terms.—Statute refers to the laws passed by Congress and the several State Legislatures. The term **common law** refers to that body of law and jurisprudence which was originated, developed, and formulated in England prior to the time of the Colonial settlements in North America, and which has become the law in most of the United States, except where it has been abrogated by statute. An **action** is a suit or case which one party brings against another in court.

2. Common Law. — In a large measure the common law establishes the rules and regulations under which we live. Legal decisions are precedents which must be followed in other cases of the same general nature. The lower courts must follow the findings of the higher courts. The Federal Courts in a particular state must follow the decisions of the Supreme and Appellate Courts of that state, except in cases involving the interpretation of the constitution and laws of the United States. The courts in one state are not bound by the decisions of a court in another state. Of course, the common-law decision may be set aside by statute or modified when it no longer applies to present conditions.

3. Law and Equity.—These two terms appear frequently in the following pages and are quite generally misunderstood. The word **law** signifies a rule of action either written or unwritten. **Equity** rather looks to the substance than to the form. When an act is **equitable** it may be just, even though it has no foundation in the law. Formerly separate courts existed to try cases in equity. The modern tendency is to combine law and equity and to give judges the power to try both law and equity cases. (See Legal Remedies and Equitable Remedies)

4. Civil Law and Criminal Law.—The difference between civil and criminal law is not always understood. Criminal law may be defined as the law dealing with offenses against the people. The acts that are crimes are clearly defined by statute and the cases are prosecuted by public officers. Civil law takes in all law not criminal in nature. Wrongful acts may be subject to both criminal and civil actions. If a man steals an automobile, he has committed a crime against the State, and at the same time the person robbed has a civil action against him for the loss. (See Torts.)

5. Classes of Courts.—There are four main classes of courts in each of the states. The first are the courts which have jurisdiction over petty criminal offenses and in which minor suits are brought. Second, there are the courts of general jurisdiction, in which more important suits are brought. Next are the Appellate Courts, and finally, there is the Supreme Court, or court of last resort, which reviews the decisions of the lower courts.

Of course the judicial system varies widely in the different states. For example, the Illinois law provides for Justice of the Peace Courts in which minor cases are tried. Next comes the County Court, one in each county. Then there is the Circuit Court, comprised of three judges who can sit in any of the courts in their circuit. Following the Circuit Court comes the State Appellate Court, and at the top, the State Supreme Court. Besides these courts, the larger counties have special courts to hear probate cases and the like. Cities with a population of 50,000 or more have municipal courts with jurisdiction over cases confined to the city.

6. Federal Courts.—There are three classes of Federal Courts. The lowest is called the District Court, taking its name from the fact that the country as a whole is divided into districts with one court for each district. Next is the Circuit Court of Appeals, to which appeals from the District Court are taken. And finally, there is the United States Supreme Court, in which appeals may be sought from decisions of the Courts of Appeal and from the Supreme Courts of the several states and in certain criminal cases direct from the Federal District Courts. Upon application made in proper form this court decides whether or not it will review a particular case.

7. Basis of Appeals.—No court will review the decision of a lower court unless the application is founded on errors in the former proceedings. Thus the proof of wrongful admission of or refusal to admit proper evidence in the former trial would be sufficient to obtain a rehearing.

8. Evidence.—Evidence includes all means and ways by which the truth of an alleged fact is established or disproved. **Direct evidence** is the testimony of a witness or written documents and records, which are competent, relevant, and material to the issues joined and which, if believed, prove the existence of the fact in issue without any inference. **Circumstantial evidence** is a chain of facts or circumstances, all tending, when connected up, to establish a logical inference or conclusion that such fact does exist.

Acknowledgment of Deeds, Mortgages and Releases

All deeds, mortgages, releases, and other documents relating to or affecting real estate must be acknowledged before an officer authorized by law to take acknowledgments. Chattel mortgages must also be so acknowledged. Notaries public, justices of the peace, masters in chancery, and judges and clerks of courts of record having a seal are authorized to take acknowledgments in most cases.

The laws of some states require the acknowledgment to show, in cases where an instrument is signed by both husband and wife, that the wife signed out of the presence of her husband. Many states also require that where an acknowledgment is taken before a Notary Public, the date of the expiration of his commission must be shown.

Form 1, for Chattel Mortgages

STATE OF ILLINOIS,)
KANE COUNTY) ss.

I, John Richard, a Justice of the Peace in the Town of Dundee, in and for the said County, do hereby certify that this mortgage was duly acknowledged before me by the above named ...., the grantor therein named, and entered by me this 17th day of July, 19............

Witness my hand and seal.

(Seal)

JOHN RICHARD,
Justice of the Peace.

Form 2, for Releases

STATE OF ILLINOIS,)
COUNTY OF DU PAGE) ss.

I, John Smith, a Notary Public in and for said County, and in the State aforesaid do hereby certify that James Y. Scammon, who is personally known to me to be the same person whose name is subscribed to the foregoing instrument, appeared before me this day in person and acknowledged that he signed, sealed, and delivered the said instrument as his free and voluntary act for the uses and purposes therein set forth.

Given under my hand and Notarial Seal this 13th day of May, 19............

(Notarial Seal)

JOHN SMITH,
Notary Public.

Form 3, for Mortgages and Deeds

STATE OF ILLINOIS,)
COUNTY OF DU PAGE) ss.

I, John Smith, a Notary Public in and for said County in the State aforesaid, do hereby certify that Samuel P. Smith and Sarah E. Smith, his wife, who are personally known to me to be the same persons whose names are subscribed to the foregoing instruments, appeared before me this day in person and acknowledged that they signed, sealed, and delivered said instrument as their free and voluntary act for the uses and purposes therein set forth, including a release and waiver of all rights under and by virtue of the homestead exemption laws of this State.

Given under my hand and Notarial Seal this first day of January, A.D. 19............

(Notarial Seal)

JOHN SMITH,
Notary Public.

Form 4, General and Short Form

STATE OF..)
COUNTY OF..) ss.

On the ....day of .... in the year one thousand nine hundred and .... before me personally came (names of both parties), who are known to me to be the individuals described in and who executed, the foregoing instrument, and acknowledged that they executed the same.

(Signature.)

Affidavits

1. Definition.—An affidavit is a voluntary statement reduced to writing and sworn to o affirmed before an officer legally empowered to administer it. Affidavits are not testimony in courts of law, because the makers cannot be cross-examined; but a person who makes a false affidavit may be punished for perjury.

2. Form.—The following is a common form, and with certain modifications can be made to apply to most cases.

Common Form of Affidavit

STATE OF ILLINOIS,)
COUNTY OF HENRY) ss.
ss.

John Jones being duly sworn on his oath states that he is well acquainted with the handwriting of Daniel Seitz, one of the subscribing witnesses to the deed hereto attached; that affiant has frequently seen him write and knows his signature; that he believes that the name of the said Daniel Seitz, signed in the said deed, is in the handwriting of the said Daniel Seitz, and further affiant says not.

(Signed)
JOHN JONES.

Subscribed and sworn to before me this 28th day of February, A.D. 19............

E. M. SCHWARTZ,
Notary Public.

Agency

1. Definitions.—Agency is the relation between two or more persons by which one person (the agent) represents another (the principal) in the transaction of lawful acts or business. Agents are of two kinds, general and special. A **General Agent** is authorized to represent the principal in all of his business, or in all business of a particular kind. A **Special Agent** is authorized to do a specific thing, as sell a farm, buy a house, or transact some special business for the principal.

2. Who May Act as Principal and Agent.—Any person who is able to act for himself, may act as principal. This excludes a lunatic, an alien enemy, or any other person incapable of contracting. On the other hand any person who is competent to act in his own right, and who is of sound mind and understanding, may act as an agent. Husband and wife may act for each other, except where prevented by the statutes of the particular state. A person unable to contract on his own account, such as a person under age, may sometimes act as an agent. Anyone except a lunatic, imbecile, or infant of tender years may be an agent. Corporations often act as agents.

3. Authority, How Given.—The authority of an agent may be constituted in three ways: By deed under seal, by writing, or by mere word. Express authority is given to an agent by what is called a power of attorney. If the authority is to execute a writing under seal and acknowledged, the power of attorney must be likewise under seal and acknowledged. In a few states, however, this rule has been changed by statute. An agent to sell land, or to do any important business, where he is required to make contracts, draw or sign notes, drafts, or checks, should be appointed by a carefully drawn legal document. The general rule with respect to the liability of a principal for unauthorized acts of his agent is that the principal is liable to third persons for any acts done by the agent for the principal in the course of his duties and within the actual or apparent scope of his agency. Agency may be implied from previous dealings and transactions between the parties. If the principal has held a person out as an agent he will be bound by his acts, even though as a matter of fact the agent had no express authority to represent him. The acts or contracts of an agent made beyond the scope of his authority may be ratified by the principal and when so ratified are binding on the latter.

4. Agent's Responsibility.—An agent concealing his principal is himself responsible, and if acting fraudulently or deceitfully is himself responsible to third parties. He cannot appoint a substitute or delegate his authority to another, without consent of his principal. If an agent embezzles his principal's property it may be reclaimed if it can be identified or distinctly traced. An agent employed to sell property cannot buy it himself, or if employed to purchase property, cannot buy from himself.

5. Principal's Liability.—The principal is liable to the third person for the negligence or unskillfulness of the agent, when he is acting in the fulfillment of the agency business. The principal is liable for all acts of his agent within the scope of his agency, but money paid by an agent can be recovered by the principal, if it has been paid by mistake. The knowledge of the agent relating to the business of the agency is binding upon the principal, and notice to an agent as to matters relating to the agency is notice to the principal.

6. Authority May Be Revoked.—The authority of an agent may be terminated: First, by the express revocation thereof by the principal. Second, by renunciation of such power by the agent. Third, by the death of the principal. Fourth, by the expiration of the time within which the agent was to perform the acts which were to be done by him, or by his having completed and fully performed the commission and closed the business which he was to transact. Fifth, by the sale of the subject matter of the agency. Sixth, by the insanity of either principal or agent. Seventh, by the bankruptcy of the principal or the agent. A revocation of authority takes effect, so far as the agent is concerned, when he receives notice thereof; so far as the third persons are concerned, when they receive notice of such revocation. Personal notice or its equivalent is required, and is sufficient, to those who have dealt with the agent. Advertising the fact would be sufficient as to all others. Without a sufficient notice of the revocation, a contract made in good faith with the agent after revocation will bind the principal the same as before.

7. Special Rules of Agency.—An agent cannot delegate his powers to another without the consent of the principal, unless the act to be done is a minor service, or one requiring no personal ability or skill. Both principal and agent are liable if the persons with whom the agent is transacting business do not know of the agency relationship. An agent can receive no personal profit from a transaction.

8. Caution.—Persons dealing with agents who are strangers should be very careful to ascertain that the agent has authority to transact business in hand. In all transactions in regard to real estate the authority of the agent should be in writing, signed by the owner of the property, in order to be binding upon him. In all cases of doubt as to the authority of an agent or the extent of his authority, it would be wise to require of the agent a written proof of his agency and the extent of his authority.

9. Power of Attorney.—Whenever it becomes necessary to delegate to an agent the power to sign notes checks, or other legal documents, it is advisable to grant such powers in a written document. Such document is usually called a Power of Attorney. It should be signed by the principal and witnessed, and should set forth exactly and explicitly what the attorney or agent has power to do, and if the agent is to deal in real estate, it is sometimes required by law, and, in any event always advisable, that such Power of Attorney be under seal.

Power of Attorney, General Form

KNOW ALL MEN BY THESE PRESENTS, That I, James L. Binton, of Naperville, County of Du Page, and State of Illinois, have made, constituted and appointed, and BY THESE PRESENTS do make, constitute and appoint, Chas. A. Lerch true and lawful attorney for me and in my name, place and stead, (here state the purpose for which the power is given), giving and granting unto my said attorney full power and authority to do and perform all and every act and thing whatsoever, requisite and necessary to be done in and about the premises, as fully, to all intents and purposes, as I might or could do if personally present, with all power of substitution and revocation, hereby ratifying and confirming all that my said attorney or his substitute shall lawfully do or cause to be done by virtue thereof.

IN WITNESS WHEREOF, I have hereunto set my hand and seal the 2nd day of January, one thousand nine hundred ....

Signed, Sealed and Delivered
in Presence of

....

JAMES L. BINTON. (Seal.)

To be properly acknowledged before an officer, the same as a deed according to the law of the State.

Proxy or Power of Attorney to Vote

Know all men by these presents: That I, David E. Hughes, do hereby constitute and appoint C. A. Brown my true and lawful attorney, for me and in my name, place and stead, to vote as my proxy and representative at the .... meeting of the stockholders of the ...., a corporation, and at any adjournment of said meeting, all of the ....shares of the capital stock of said corporation standing in my name on the books of said corporation, as fully and amply as I could or might do were I personally present; with full power of substitution and revocation.

Witness my hand and seal at Aurora, Illinois, this 26th day of June, A.D. 19............

E. R. ZEMMER. ((Seal.)

Revocation of Power of Attorney

Whereas, I, Sylvester Jones of Aurora, County of Kane, and State of Illinois, did on the tenth day of June, 19............, by my letter or power of attorney appoint John C. Cook of Chicago my true and lawful attorney, for me and in my name to (here state in precise language what he was authorized to do) as by the said power of attorney, reference thereunto being had, will fully appear;

Therefore, know all men by these presents, That I, Sylvester Jones, aforesaid, have revoked and recalled the said power of attorney, and by these presents do revoke and recall all power and authority thereby given to the said John C. Cook.

Given this tenth day of October, 19............

Signed and sealed in presence of ....

SYLVESTER JONES. (Seal.)

Agreement to Purchase Land

1. Must be in Writing.—An agreement to purchase real estate must be in writing, and should be signed by both buyer and seller. The writing need not mention the amount to be paid for the land. It should be signed in ink, but is not invalid if signed with a lead pencil or even with a rubber stamp. The entire contract need not be on the same sheet of paper, and it sometimes happens that two or more sheets of paper constitute the contract, as in cases where the agreement to purchase land is completed through correspondence between the two parties.

2. Exceptions.—There are some exceptions to the rule that an agreement to purchase real estate is not enforceable unless in writing. For example, if A sells a piece of property to B and receives the purchase price, and without a written agreement allows B to take possession of the property, and if B makes valuable and lasting improvements on the property, the courts will compel A to give B a deed to the property.

3. A Common Misunderstanding.—It is quite generally believed that, if a purchaser makes an oral agreement to purchase land and pays part of the purchase price, he can compel the seller to give him a deed to the real estate. This is not the law. The purchaser, however, can compel the seller to return the money he has paid.

4. Options.—An option is a contract by which the owner of property agrees with the other party that he shall have the right to purchase the property at a fixed price within a certain time. For example A agrees to sell a piece of property to B at a certain price within a certain period of time, for which B gives A a valuable consideration. B must either exercise his option and purchase the property within the time limit, or forfeit his consideration. All options must be in writing. If no time limit is fixed in the agreement, the option must be exercised within a reasonable time.

5. Transferring of Title.—In most real estate contracts the seller agrees to furnish the buyer with a good and merchantable title. He also agrees to transfer title to the property by a Warranty Deed, which warrants the title in him and the buyer against any loss which might be occasioned by defects in the title. A purchaser should always insist that the contract provide that the seller is to furnish and deliver a merchantable title. The contract generally requires the seller to furnish, also, evidence that he has good title. This is done by producing either an Abstract, Guaranty Policy, or Torrens Certificate, showing good title in the seller.

6. Abstract of Title.—An abstract is a statement in substance of what appears in the public records affecting the title to the land in question from the time it was owned by the government down to date. The public records are searched and the matters shown therein. An abstract will show all transfers, mortgages, judgments, tax sales, liens of all kinds, court proceedings and everything in fact of record affecting the title to the property. These abstracts are prepared by private concerns or individuals known as abstract companies or abstracters. To determine whether or not the seller's title is good, the purchaser should have the abstract examined by an attorney competent to pass upon the law of real property. This examination by an attorney will reveal the validity or merchantability of the title. The objections to a clear title may be simple or exceedingly complex, and require the services of a competent attorney in that field. Usually the seller pays all of the expenses incidental to bringing the abstract down to date and getting the title acceptable to the purchaser's attorney. The purchaser generally pays the examination fee.

7. Title Insurance or Guaranty Policy.—Under this system the title company issues a policy guaranteeing the holder of the policy against any loss he might sustain by reason of any defect in the title, whether of record or otherwise, existing before or at the time of the issuance of the policy. This system is necessarily becoming more and more popular and in use in the cities because of the demand for facilities to expedite real estate transactions and also because of the protective feature.

8. Torrens System.—The Torrens System is a system providing for the registration of land titles in such a manner that, when the title is once registered, a certificate of the registrar of titles will show the exact condition of the title. In order to register a title under this system, it is necessary that a court proceeding be had first in which the decree of the court settles and establishes the title. After this has been done, the registrar of titles will issue an official certificate which will show who has title to the land, and what defects, if any, appear in his title. After the title to a particular parcel of property has been so registered, all subsequent transactions affecting the title to that property must be filed with the registrar of titles, and are noted upon the certificate of title. This enables a purchaser to determine the true state of the title by merely examining the certificate of the registrar. The purpose of the system is to simplify the transfer of real estate, and it is now in force in a number of states.

Agreement for Sale of Land

This agreement, made and entered into this .... day of ....by and between ...., party of the first part, and ...., party of the second part, witnesseth:

1. The said party of the first part, for and in consideration of the sum of $.............................. to be paid as hereinafter provided, hereby agrees to sell unto the party of the second part the following described tract of land:

(Description)

2. The said party of the second part hereby agrees to purchase said premises at said consideration of $.............................., and to pay the same as follows: (set out terms of payment).

3. The said party of the first part, upon receiving the final payment mentioned above, shall execute and deliver to the said party of the second part, or to his assigns, a duly acknowledged Warranty Deed, conveying to him or them the fee simple title to said premises, free and clear from all incumbrance.

In witness whereof the said parties have hereunto set their hands and seals the day and year first above written.

Form of Option

For and in consideration of the sum of .... dollars to me in hand paid, the receipt whereof is hereby acknowledged, I hereby grant unto .... an option for .... days from the .... day of .... 19..........., to purchase for the sum of ....dollars, the following described lands situated in the County of .... and State of ....:

(Insert description of property),

upon the following terms and conditions: (insert terms of sale), said .... to signify his intention to take or reject the same by due notice in writing within the time above specified, and a failure to serve such notice within the time specified shall terminate this option without further action, time being the essence of this agreement.

In case said notice shall be served in due time, then thirty days shall be given in which to examine abstract or other evidence of title, and close the sale.

Auctioneer

1. Definition.—An auctioneer is a person employed to sell property to the highest bidder at public sale.

2. Agent for Both Buyer and Seller.—An auctioneer is the exclusive agent of the owner until he accepts the purchaser's bid and knocks down the property to him. On accepting the bid the auctioneer becomes the agent of the purchaser also, and thus represents both parties.

3. Completion of the Sale.—A sale by auction is completed when the auctioneer announces its completion by the fall of the hammer, or in any other customary manner. Until such announcement is made, the auctioneer may withdraw the property from sale unless the sale has been advertised to be without reserve. Any bidder may also withdraw his bid at any time before the fall of the hammer.

4. Responsibility of Auctioneer.—Authority to sell property does not imply power to sell at auction. Thus a purchaser buying goods from an auctioneer, when he knows the auctioneer has no authority to sell them, acquires no title to the property thus purchased. The seller or owner is not bound by any statements by the auctioneer. An auctioneer must accept the most favorable bid. He cannot refuse to accept legitimate bids. He is justified, however, in rejecting the bids of insane or drunken persons, minors, trustees of the property, and persons who refuse to comply with the terms of the sale.

5. Things an Auctioneer Cannot Do.—An auctioneer is not permitted to delegate his duties to another, except minor or incidental duties. He cannot act contrary to the wishes and instructions of the owners in any matters relating to the details of the sale. He may not permit a bidder to withdraw his bid after its acceptance, without the consent of the owner. He cannot sell the property to himself, or employ another to bid it in for him. He is not permitted to sell at private sale contrary to the owner's instructions.

Automobile

1. The Right to Use the Highways.—The public has a right to use the public roads to travel and transport property. Drivers of automobiles have an equal right on the highways with other vehicles, but they do not have any greater right. All have the same rights and the same restrictions. The courts hold that all travelers have equal right to use the highways. Thus, a pedestrian has the same right as the driver of an automobile. The state cannot exclude nonresidents from the public roads, or place greater restrictions or burdens on non-resident motorists than those imposed on its own citizens.

2. Parking.—In the absence of any city ordinance or statutory regulation an automobile may be left at the side of the road after shutting off the engine and setting the brakes. However, an automobile so left after dark must be properly lighted.

3. License.—The several states issue licenses to the owners of automobiles, motorcycles, and trucks, permitting them to use the public highways. Most cities require a municipal license. Such a license is neither a contract nor a tax. It is simply a privilege, and as such does not pass to a purchaser of the vehicle and may be revoked for any good reason.

4. The Law With Reference to Rented Vehicles.—Suppose A rents his automobile to B for a certain consideration. The law will not hold A responsible for the negligent acts of B even if B is an unskilled driver. On the other hand if A knew when he rented the car that B was an immature child or of low mentality, or under the influence of alcohol, the courts would hold him responsible. If the owner lends his car with a chauffeur, he will be held liable for the negligent acts of the chauffeur. In case of damage to the rented car, the renter is liable only if it can be proved that he did not exercise ordinary prudence and care. Should the renter sell the car without the owner's authority, the owner can recover even from an innocent purchaser. The owner of an automobile is entitled to a fair compensation for its use, even if no definite sum is agreed upon, and he can collect a reasonable hire if his automobile is used by another without his knowledge or consent. Criminal liability also is attached to the unlawful use of another's automobile.

5. The Speed of Automobiles along a public road is regulated by law. Some state laws prescribe the maximum rates of speed for the business district, residence district, and country. A municipality has the right to modify the speed laws in accordance with local requirements. Courts of most states hold that it is the duty of a driver on a public highway to have his car under control and to operate it at a reasonable rate of speed, having regard to the traffic and other conditions. He must so operate it as to avoid endangering the life or limb of any person or the safety of anyone's property.

6. The Laws of the Road are intended to prevent collisions and accidents. 1. Vehicles approaching each other from opposite directions are required to pass each other on the right. If, therefore, two automobiles collide in a street which is wide enough for safe passage, the driver on the wrong side of the road is responsible for the other driver's injury, provided, of course, the other was not himself guilty of negligence. 2. Each driver must pass on his right side of the center of the traveled road. This applies even when the road is covered with snow, to side roads, and to roads under construction. 3. It is the duty of every driver to exercise reasonable care in avoiding accidents or injuries to others. This rule applies just as strongly when the driver's car is on the right side of the road. 4. At street intersections it is customary to allow the right of way to the vehicle approaching from the right and, in many states and municipalities, this rule has been embodied in the statutes and ordinances. 5. It is the duty of the driver to keep his car under control at all times. 6. If one willfully or negligently drives a car on a street or road at an unlawful speed, thereby killing another, he may be guilty of homicide. 7. The driver of a car may be charged with negligence if, without warning to others, he suddenly changes the course of his direction or backs his car.

7. The Fitness of the Driver.—The driver of an automobile should be physically and mentally fit. A man who is subject to fainting spells or epileptic attacks has no right to drive a car upon the public highway. The same rule applies to one with defective eyesight, but it has been held that proper eyeglasses may restore the competency of the driver. No person should ever attempt to drive an automobile while intoxicated, thereby endangering the lives of others.

8. The Chauffeur's Liability.— As a general rule the owner is liable for the acts of his chauffeur, provided the chauffeur is acting within the scope of the owner's business. However, should the chauffeur use the car without the consent or knowledge of the owner, or should he be using it for his own business and with the owner's consent, the owner is not liable for the driver's acts. The same rule applies when the owner's son uses the parent's car without his knowledge or consent. If the car is run with his knowledge by a member of his family, or for the convenience of other members of the family, the parent may be liable for the negligent acts of the driver. Most states require a chauffeur to take out a license.

9. Minor.—The statutes of most states forbid children under a certain age to drive automobiles. The ages vary in different states. The owner of a car, therefore, who allows a child to operate it, may be held responsible for accident or injury resulting from the child's negligence.

10. The Chauffeur's Rights.—A chauffeur may recover damages from his employer for injury received while operating the car, provided that the employer is in some way responsible for the injury. On the other hand, if his injury was due to a defective part, he could not recover from his employer, unless it so happened that the employer knew of the defect and the chauffeur did not. If a chauffeur should be injured while riding in a car driven by the owner, the chauffeur could recover for injuries sustained due to the owner's negligence.

11. The Owner's Injury.—If the owner of a car be injured in any way through the wrongful acts or negligence of his chauffeur, the chauffeur may be held liable.

12. Garage Keeper.—A garage keeper is bound to exercise reasonable care with reference to vehicles entrusted to him. The owner of a car is not liable to third parties for the negligence of the garage keeper or his employees in the care and operation of his automobile. If a garage keeper or his employee operates an automobile the garage keeper is liable for any damage done to the car or to third persons. A public garage, while not considered a public nuisance, is subject to public regulations as to location, odors, noise and fire hazards. A garage keeper is entitled to a reasonable compensation for storage of a car or for repairs which he has been instructed to make. He is not liable for fire damage to the automobile, unless the fire is caused by his own negligence or that of his employees. He is liable for theft, if he failed to use reasonable precautions to guard against it.

13. Used Automobiles.—There are two points to keep in mind when purchasing a second-hand automobile. Such automobiles are usually sold "as is" and the motorist often complains when he finds the car is not in perfect running order. If the cylinders prove to be scored or the bearings are loose, the purchaser has no redress at law. The law presumes that if any warranty was made, it would have been reduced to writing in the form of a contract.

14. Bill of Sale.—Statutes in most states require that a bill of sale be given, and the purchaser should be careful to see that the statute is complied with. The bill of sale should be drawn in accordance with the laws of the state where the purchase is made. The following form will answer the purpose in most of the states:

Bill of Sale

Know all men by these presents, that I (here insert name and address of party selling the car) in the county of ...., state of ...., in consideration of (here insert amount of money to be paid party selling by party buying) dollars this day to me in hand paid, do hereby grant, sell, transfer and deliver unto the said (here insert name of party buying) the following goods and chattels, to-wit: (Then insert name of automobile, its model, the engine number and the car number, also the type of car, its color, together with any other information which will help to identify it); to have and to hold said goods and chattels to the said (name of purchaser), his executors, administrators and assigns to their use forever.

I hereby covenant with the said grantee that I am the lawful owner of the said goods and chattels; that they are free and clear from all incumbrances; that I have good right to sell the same and that I will warrant and defend the same against the lawful claims and demands of all persons.

In witness whereof, I, the said (name of party selling) hereunto set my hand and seal the .... day of ...., 19..........

Signature of party selling .... Seal

15. In Case of Accidents.—Accidents will happen in spite of the most careful driving. If you happen to be in an accident, here are a few things to remember:

a. Do not drive away without reporting the facts to the police or nearest police station, or without giving your name, address, and license number to the other party involved. Leaving the scene of an accident may constitute a crime punishable by fine or imprisonment.

b. Be sure to get the name and address of the other party, or if he drives away, his license number.

c. Get the names and addresses of all persons who witnessed the accident, or saw the results of it, including all injured persons.

d. Try to visualize just how it happened, remember your own position and that of the other party, both before and after the accident, and note carefully the wheel marks on the road or pavement.

e. Be calm and courteous. Do not admit that you are in the wrong or accuse the other party.

f. Do not make immediate settlement or offer to do so, or incur any expense except for necessary medical relief.

Bailment

1. Definitions.—A Bailment is a delivery of a thing in trust for some special object or purpose, with the understanding, expressed or implied, that the person receiving it shall return it when that purpose has been fulfilled. **A Bailor** is one who makes a bailment or delivers goods to a bailee. A **Bailee** is a person who receives goods of another to hold according to the purpose of delivery.

2. Bailor and Bailee.—To create this relation the property must be delivered to the bailee. Thus if A takes his car to a public garage to remain over night, the garage owner becomes a bailee for hire. The contract of bailment also exists when a man takes a suit of clothes to a tailor shop to be altered, or when a farmer takes a load of oats to a mill to be ground.

3. The Law with Reference to Lost Property.—The finder of lost property is entitled to keep it until the owner is found, and the general rule is that the finder has good title to it against everyone but the true owner Usually the law provides the necessary steps to be taken in the case of lost property. The finder must make an honest effort to locate the owner. Failing in this, he may retain the property and maintain his rights as against all others. Should the true owner appear, the finder has no lien on the property, unless a reward has been offered for its return.

The finder does not always take title to the article found. The article must actually have been lost, not merely laid down or aside voluntarily, and forgotten. Thus, if a woman lay down a package in a department store, the owner of the store is the proper custodian, rather than the finder.

4. The Bailee's Responsibility.—A bailee can, provided the limitation is not in violation of law or public policy, and does not excuse him from negligence or fraud on his part, limit his liability by agreement. He becomes the custodian of the goods and is generally required to exert reasonable care against accident or loss. As a rule he cannot be held responsible for loss resulting from the nature of the goods stored. For example if a truck load of fruit arrives at a cold storage plant, the owner is not responsible for any loss due to the condition of the fruit when it arrived. On the other hand, if an employee of the storage company negligently allows the goods to spoil, the owner of the fruit can recover from the storage company.

Suppose your bank grants you the privilege of keeping a strongbox in the bank building without making any charge therefor. The bank, of course, is not bound to exercise as much care as a regular safety deposit company, but it is required to take reasonable precaution, as much care as it uses to protect its own property. Suppose the cashier steals the box. Would the bank be liable to you for the loss? If the bank exercised reasonable care, and if the cashier was a long-trusted employee against whom there was no cause for suspicion, the bank would not be responsible for the loss.

5. The Bailee's Duty.—The bailee is usually a keeper only. However, if he is keeping livestock, he must supply the food necessary to the animals' good condition. Milch cows must be properly milked; and in case of sickness animals must be given proper medical care and attention. In every case the bailee is required to exercise reasonable care for the goods in the bailment.

Bankruptcy

1. The Bankruptcy Act.—The Constitution of the United States grants to Congress the power to make uniform laws on the subject of bankruptcy. The Bankruptcy Act of 1938, popularly known as the Chandler Act, now contains the law on this subject.

2. Courts.—The Act gives jurisdiction in bankruptcy cases to the district courts of the United States and of the territories and possessions to which the Act applies, and to the District Court of the United States for the District of Columbia.

3. Bankrupts.—Bankrupts are of two classes, voluntary and involuntary. Voluntary bankrupts are those who are declared bankrupt upon their own petitions. Under the new Act, any person (or corporation) owing debts, except a municipal, railroad, insurance, or banking corporation or a building and loan association, is entitled to the benefits of the Act as a voluntary bankrupt. Involuntary bankrupts are those who are declared bankrupt by the proper courts, and who have committed one or more of the acts of bankruptcy hereinafter specified. Any natural person, except a building and loan association, a municipal, railroad, insurance, or banking corporation, owing debts to the amount of $1,000 or over, may be adjudged an involuntary bankrupt.

4. Acts of Bankruptcy.—As stated in the preceding paragraph, before a person can become an involuntary bankrupt, it is necessary for the petitioning creditors to show that he has committed an act of bankruptcy. The Bankruptcy Act specifically defines what constitutes an act of bankruptcy. A person has committed an act of bankruptcy when he has:

a. Conveyed, transferred, concealed, removed, or permitted to be concealed or removed any part of his property, with intent to hinder, delay, or defraud his creditors or any of them; or

b. Transferred, while insolvent, any portion of his property to one or more of his creditors with intent to prefer such creditor over his other creditors; or

c. Suffered or permitted, while insolvent, any creditor to obtain a lien upon any of his property through legal proceedings, and not having vacated or discharged such lien within thirty days from the date thereof or at least five days before the date set for any sale or other disposition of such property; or

d. Made a general assignment for the benefit of his creditors; or

e. While insolvent or unable to pay his debts as they mature, procured, permitted, or suffered voluntarily or involuntarily the appointment of a receiver or trustee to take charge of his property; or

f. Admitted in writing his inability to pay his debts and his willingness to be adjudged a bankrupt.

5. Filing a Voluntary Petition.—Any person who is entitled to the benefits of the Bankruptcy Act and wishes to avail himself of the same should file his petition, in duplicate, with the clerk of the court in the district where he has had his principal place of business, or resided, or has had his domicile for the preceding six months, or for a longer portion of the preceding six months than in any other jurisdiction. He must also file, with the petition, a schedule, under oath and in triplicate, setting forth: the names of his creditors and their residences if known, the amount due each, and what security they hold, if any; a description of the petitioner's property, showing its nature, location and value; and his claim for legal exemptions, if any. The judge then hears the petition, and either adjudicates the petitioner bankrupt or dismisses the petition.

6. Filing an Involuntary Petition. — Where a person owing debts to the amount of $1,000 has committed one or more of the acts of bankruptcy enumerated above and does not belong to one of the classes excluded by the Act (as wage earners and farmers), a petition to have such person adjudged a bankrupt may be filed by three or more creditors who have provable claims against him, fixed as to liability and liquidated as to amount, which amount in the aggregate, in excess of the value of securities held by them, to $500 or over; or if all of the creditors of such person are less than twelve in number, then the petition may be filed by one of such creditors whose claims equal such amount. The petition must be filed in triplicate with the clerk of the court and must include the following information and allegations: the name of the alleged bankrupt; that he has had his principal place of business within the district for a longer portion of the six months immediately preceding the filing of the petition than in any other judicial district; that he owes debts to the amount of $1,000 and is not a wage earner or a farmer; the names and addresses of the petitioning creditors; that they have provable claims against said alleged bankrupt, fixed as to liability and liquidated as to amount, amounting in the aggregate, in excess of securities held by them, to $500 or over; the nature and amount of petitioners' claims; that within four months next preceding the filing of the petition, the alleged bankrupt committed an act of bankruptcy; and a statement as to what acts on his part are alleged to have constituted said act of bankruptcy. The petition must also be duly signed and verified. Upon the filing of the petition, together with a filing fee of $30, the clerk will issue a subpoena to the alleged bankrupt, returnable within ten days. When the alleged bankrupt has been served with the subpoena and a copy of the petition, he is required to file his answer within five days after the return day. If it is necessary, the court may appoint a receiver to take charge of the alleged bankrupt's property to prevent loss.

7. Hearing in Involuntary Proceedings.—If the alleged bankrupt fails to appear and plead within the time allowed, the court will either adjudicate him bankrupt or dismiss the petition. If the alleged bankrupt wishes to deny any of the matters set out in the petition, he may do so by filing his sworn answer within the time allowed by law. The matter will then be set down for hearing, and on the day set the petitioners must either prove the allegations in their petition or the court will dismiss it on motion of the alleged bankrupt. If they do prove them, the court will proceed to enter the order of adjudication. Within five days after the order adjudging him bankrupt, the bankrupt is required to file schedules of his creditors and property similar to those filed by a voluntary bankrupt.

8. Statement of Affairs. — The law also requires a bankrupt to file in triplicate with the court at least five days prior to the first meeting of his creditors, a statement of his affairs in such form as may be prescribed by the Supreme Court. The purpose of this provision is to furnish helpful information to the creditors and trustee to assist them in administering the bankrupt's affairs as well as in their examination of the bankrupt.

9. First Meeting of Creditors.—After adjudication, that is, the order of court finding a person to be bankrupt, the procedure with reference to voluntary and involuntary bankrupts is the same. The court causes the first meeting of creditors to be held not less than ten nor more than thirty days after adjudication. The meeting is held at the county seat of the county in which the bankrupt had his principal place of business, resided, or had his domicile; or if that place would be manifestly inconvenient, the court may designate a more convenient place for the meeting. The judge or referee presides. He may allow or disallow claims presented there, and is required publicly to examine the bankrupt. He may also permit the creditors to examine him. At this meeting the creditors appoint a trustee, who is to act as their representative and take charge of the bankrupt's property. Relatives of the bankrupt, and, where the bankrupt is a corporation, its stockholders, officers, and members of its board of directors, are not allowed to vote. The new Act provides that the creditors may also appoint a committee of three or more creditors, which committee may consult and advise the trustee in connection with the administration of the estate. The bankrupt must be present at the first meeting of creditors.

10. Subsequent Meetings.—The law provides that the court shall call a meeting of creditors whenever one-fourth or more in number of those who have proved their claims shall file a written request for a meeting. Whenever the affairs of the bankrupt's estate are ready to be closed, the court orders a final meeting of creditors. A case in which there are no assets may be closed without such final meeting.

11. Voting at Meetings.—Matters submitted to creditors at their meetings are passed upon by majority vote in number and amount of claims of all creditors whose claims have been allowed and who are present. However, creditors holding claims which are secured or have priority are not entitled to vote in respect to such claims, and such claims are not counted in computing either the number of creditors or the amount of their claims, except in cases where the amounts of such claims exceed the values of such securities and priorities, and then only for such excess. The new Act also provides that claims of $50 or less shall not be counted in computing the number of creditors voting or present at meetings, but shall be counted in computing the amount.

12. Proof of Claims.—In order to share in any dividends which may be paid to creditors out of the property of the bankrupt, it is necessary for a creditor to file his claim in court or with the referee within six months after the first date set for the first meeting of creditors, to prove it and have it allowed by the court. The law requires that a proof of claim be filed, consisting of a statement under oath in writing and signed by the creditor, setting forth the claim; the consideration therefor; whether any, and if so, what securities are held therefor; whether any, and if so, what payments have been made thereon; and that the claim is justly owing from the bankrupt to the creditor. If the claim is founded upon an instrument in writing, such as a promissory note, such instrument, unless lost or stolen, shall be filed with the proof of claim. If such instrument has been lost or stolen, a sworn statement of such fact and the circumstances of such loss or destruction must be filed with the claim. After the claim has been allowed, such instrument may be withdrawn by permission of court upon substitution of copies.

Claims so properly presented, if liquidated claims, are allowed unless objected to by parties in interest or by the court. If objected to, they are set down for hearing before the court or referee.

Only fixed and liquidated claims and claims provable in law or equity are provable in bankruptcy. Contingent claims are not provable.

13. Discharge of Bankrupt.—Under the present Bankruptcy Act, it is not necessary for an individual who has been adjudged bankrupt to make application for his discharge in bankruptcy. The new act provides that the adjudication shall operate as an application for discharge. This is not true with reference to corporations, however. A bankrupt corporation may file an application for discharge within six months after its adjudication. In the case of individuals, the law now provides that after the bankrupt has been examined, either at the first meeting of creditors or at a meeting specially called for that purpose, the court shall enter an order fixing the time for the filing of objections to the bankrupt's discharge, that notice of said order shall be given to all parties in interest, and that at the expiration of the time fixed, if no objection has been filed, the court shall discharge the bankrupt. The effect of a discharge in bankruptcy is to release the bankrupt from all of his provable debts except the following (1) taxes; (2) liabilities for obtaining money by false pretenses, or for willful and malicious injuries to the person or property of another, or for alimony due or to become due, or for maintenance or support of wife or child, or for seduction, or for breach of promise of marriage accompanied by seduction, or for criminal conversation; (3) debts not scheduled in time for proof and allowance, with the name of the creditor, if known to the bankrupt, unless such creditor had notiee or actual knowledge of the proceedings in bankruptcy; (4) liabilities created by his fraud, embezzlement, misappropriation or defalcation while acting as an officer or in any fiduciary capacity; (5) wages earned within three months before the date of commencement of the proceedings in bankruptcy due to workmen, servants, clerks, or traveling or city salesmen, on salary or commission basis, whole or part time, whether or not selling exclusively for the bankrupt; (6) debts for moneys of an employee received or retained by his employer to secure the faithful performance by the employee of the terms of a contract of employment.

14. Compositions.—After a bankrupt has filed the schedule of his property and list of his creditors and has been examined in open court or at a meeting of creditors, he may, if he desires, offer terms of composition. That is, he offers to make immediate payment of a certain proportion of each claim provided the creditor will release him from the balance. This is, of course, precisely what happens by operation of law if the bankruptcy proceeding is carried to a conclusion, but a composition is often more desirable because it can be carried out at once, thus dispensing with a good many of the costs of longer proceedings, and preserving the estate in cases where the property is of a nature that will deteriorate or accumulate expense during a delay. Then, too, if the composition is confirmed by the court the debtor is spared some of the ignominy of having gone through bankruptcy and received a discharge. Before being filed in court the composition must have been accepted in writing by a majority in number of all creditors whose claims have been allowed, which number must also represent a majority in amount of such claims. When the application for confirmation of the composition is filed in court, the money necessary to carry the composition into effect, together with that necessary to pay all debts which have priority, and to pay the costs of the proceedings which have already taken place, must be deposited in such place as shall be designated by and subject to the order of the judge. If the judge is then satisfied at a hearing that the composition is for the best interests of the creditors and is offered by the bankrupt in good faith, he will confirm it and dismiss the case after each creditor has received his share of the money set aside by the bankrupt as a consideration for the composition. The confirmation of a composition has the same effect as a discharge in that it releases all debts of the bankrupt that would be released by a discharge in regular form.

Bonds

1. Definition.—A bond is defined to be an obligation in writing under seal. It is a form of contract which is almost infinite in variety. The parties to the bond are the obligor and the obligee, the former being the one who makes the promise and the latter the person to whom the promise is made.

2. A Simple Bond is an instrument promising payment of money at a certain time, and generally bears interest at the rate specified in the bond. Nearly all corporate and municipal bonds are of this character and contain no condition except for the payment of the amount of the bond at a certain time and place with a certain specified rate of interest. Frequently interest coupons are attached to the original bond, providing for the payment of the several installments of interest as they come due.

The following is the form commonly in use for such bonds:

UNITED STATES OF AMERICA.
JEFFERSON CITY, STATE OF MISSOURI.
RENEWAL SCHOOL BOND.
INTEREST 6 PER CENT, PAYABLE SEMI-ANNUALLY

The Board of Education of the City of Jefferson, County of Cole, and State of Missouri, being legally organized under and pursuant to an act of the General Assembly of the State of Missouri entitled "An act to revise and amend the Laws in relation to Public Schools in Cities, Towns and Villages," approved April 26th, 19............, for value received promise to pay to the bearer ten years after the date hereof ONE THOUSAND DOLLARS at the St. Louis National Bank, in the City of St. Louis, Missouri, together with interest thereon at the rate of Six per centum per annum from the date hereof, which interest shall be payable semi-annually at said St. Louis National Bank in the City of St. Louis, Missouri, on the surrender of the proper interest coupons hereto attached. This bond shall be redeemable at the pleasure of the said Board of Education of the City of Jefferson at any time after the expiration of Five years from the date hereof, and is issued under and pursuant to an act of the General Assembly of the State of Missouri, entitled "An Act to authorize Board of Education to issue renewal funding School Bonds to be sold or exchanged for the purpose of meeting and paying matured or maturing bonded indebtedness of school districts and for levying special tax to pay the bonded indebtedness of school districts," approved April 11th, 19............

In Testimony Whereof: the said Board of Education has caused this bond to be signed by the President, countersigned by the Secretary, authenticated by the seal of said Board of Education and attested by the Clerk of the County Court of said County of Cole, with the seal of said Court affixed this First day of July, 19............

JOHN JONES, President.
WM. SMITH, Secretary.
GEO. SMILEY, Clerk County Court.

3. Bonds of Public Officials conditioned for the faithful performance of their duties are of almost infinite variety and in common use. All state, county, town and city officers having in their hands moneys or funds of any character belonging to such corporation are required to give bonds for the proper performance of the duties of their office. The following form of a bond of city treasurer can be used with a few slight changes for almost any office:

KNOW ALL MEN BY THESE PRESENTS, That we, John Jones, Henry Smith, and Charles Marshall of the City of Naperville, County of Du Page, and State of Illinois, are held and firmly bound unto the City of Naperville in the penal sum of Twenty Thousand ($20,000) Dollars, for the payment of which, well and truly to be made, we bind ourselves, our heirs, executors, and administrators jointly and firmly by these presents.

Witness our hands and seals this 14th day of July, 19............

The condition of the above obligation is such that whereas the said John Jones has been duly elected to the office of City Treasurer of the City of Naperville; Now if the said John Jones shall faithfully perform all the duties of said office and shall account for and pay over all moneys that may come into his hands as such Treasurer, according to law and the ordinances of said City and the order and direction of the city council of said City, then this obligation to be void, otherwise to remain in full force and effect.

JOHN JONES, (Seal.)
HENRY SMITH, (Seal.)
CHARLES MARSHALL. (Seal.)

4. Officers of Corporation are often required to give bonds for the faithful performance of their duties. The following form can be used for nearly all such bonds:

KNOW ALL MEN BY THESE PRESENTS, That we, James Lord, John Williams, and Charles Smith, are held and firmly bound unto the Naperville Manufacturing Company, a corporation duly organized under the laws of the State of Illinois, in the penal sum of Ten Thousand ($10,000) Dollars, good and lawful money of the United States, for the payment of which, well and truly to be made to said corporation or its assigns, we bind ourselves jointly and severally by these presents.

Witness our hands and seals this 14th day of July, 19............

The condition of the above obligation is such that whereas the said James Lord has been elected President of the Naperville Manufacturing Company; Now Therefore, if the said James Lord shall well and truly perform the duties of his said office and shall account for and pay over all moneys that shall come into his hands as such President, and do all required of him by the bylaws of said corporation now in force or hereafter enacted, and obey all orders given him by the board of directors of said corporation, then this obligation shall be void, otherwise to remain in full force and effect.

JAMES LORD. (Seal.)
JOHN WILLIAMS. (Seal.)
CHARLES SMITH. (Seal.)

5. Indemnifying Bonds.—Bonds are also frequently given to indemnify persons who incur liability for another in nearly all walks of life. The following form may be used:

KNOW ALL MEN BY THESE PRESENTS, That William Marsh, Principal, and John Henry, Surety, are held and firmly bound unto John Jones in the penal sum of One Hundred ($100) Dollars, lawful money of the United States, for the payment of which, well and truly to be made, we bind ourselves, our heirs, executors, and administrators, jointly, severally and firmly by these presents.

Witness our hands and seals this 1st day of June, A.D. 19............

The condition of the above obligation is such that whereas the said John Jones has been surety for the above William Marsh on his note for One Thousand Dollars ($1000) payable to the order of Charles William, due in one year from the date hereof, with interest at the rate of 6 per cent per annum.

Now, Therefore, if the said William Marsh shall well and truly pay the said note with all interest thereon when the same comes due and shall from time to time and at all times hereafter save, keep harmless and indemnify the said John Jones of and from all actions, suits, costs, charges, damages, and expenses whatsoever, including attorney's fees, which shall or may at any time hereafter happen or come to him for any reason, by reason of his becoming surety on said note, then this obligation to be void, otherwise to remain in full force and effect.

WILLIAM MARSH, (Seal.)
JOHN HENRY. (Seal.)

6. Executor's Bond.—Executors, administrators, guardians, and conservators are required to enter into bonds to be approved by the proper court before they are allowed to enter upon their duties as such. The forms for such bonds, however, vary in the different states.

Broker

1. Definitions.—A broker is a person who transacts business for another, commonly in stocks, bills, notes, shipping, insurance, real estate, pawned goods, merchandise, etc., using the name of the principal. He does not have custody of the property. Brokerage is the fee charged by a broker for transacting business.

2. Why Brokers Are Employed.—Brokers are often employed to transact business or to negotiate bargains between different individuals. By specializing in a single line or a limited number of lines of business, they acquire a knowledge and skill that an average merchant does not possess. It is often advantageous for large firms to employ brokers to buy their raw material. In large cities brokers are extensively employed. The business of brokerage is regulated largely by the customs of the trade.

3. A Broker's Liability.—A broker usually has no special property in the goods he sells. If he does not disclose the principal's name he is liable to the same extent as other agents. He must serve faithfully and cannot act for both parties in the same transaction without the consent and knowledge of both. Neither can he delegate his powers without the principal's assent. He is bound to obey the express instructions of his principal, and to keep accurate accounts of his transactions.

4. A Broker's Compensation.—Usually a broker's compensation is a commission or percentage of the value of the thing sold or exchanged. If the amount of the compensation is not fixed, the custom of the trade rules. A broker is entitled to a reasonable compensation for his services.

5. A Real Estate Broker must act for his principal alone. He is employed to negotiate sales and exchanges of land, and often has such additional duties as renting real estate, collecting rent, and procuring loans. To gain his commission on the sale he must produce a customer who is ready, able and willing to accept and live up to the terms of the sale. A property owner cannot avoid paying the commission or brokerage by selling the property himself, or at a lower price than he listed with the broker.

6. Pawnbrokers. — The business of a pawnbroker, the rate of interest he may charge, and the sale of pawned goods are usually regulated by law. A license is usually required and the business is always subject to regulation and control. Suppose A takes a watch to a pawnbroker who advances him $20.00. A, or his assignee, or the purchaser of the pawn ticket, may redeem it within the fixed time, or even beyond that time, if the pawnbroker has not exercised his right to sell the watch. A pawner has the right to assign or sell his interest in the watch. If A fails to redeem the watch, the pawnbroker can usually hold him for any deficiency after the watch is sold.

Carriers

1. Definitions.—A carrier is a person or company that undertakes, or whose business it is, to carry persons or merchandise for hire. Carriers are of two kinds, private and common. A **Private Carrier** is one who carries only occasionally, and not as a public business. Such a carrier need not serve all who wish to employ him, but is liable for negligence in transporting the goods he accepts. A **Common Carrier** is one whose regular business it is to carry goods or passengers from place to place for all persons who elect to employ and pay him.

2. Examples.—A private carrier is usually an individual who, without being engaged in such business as a public employment, carries merchandise from one point to another for a consideration. He is bound to exercise such care of the property as a man of ordinary intelligence would of his own property. Examples of common carriers are railroad companies, steamship companies, streetcar companies, taxicab companies, truckmen, and express companies, who hold themselves out to carry goods or passengers from one place to another, for all persons who offer to employ them.

3. Responsibility.—Common carriers are generally responsible for all loss and damage caused by transportation from whatever cause, except the act of God or of the public enemy, and they are bound to carry all goods which are offered them, provided such goods come within the class of articles they hold themselves out to carry. The carrier is not responsible for losses occurring from natural causes, such as frosts, fermentation, or natural decay of perishable articles, or the necessary and natural wear in the course of transportation, provided it exercises all reasonable care to have the loss or deterioration as little as practical.

4. Act of God.—The term "Act of God" is generally held to mean such casualties as occur without human intervention. Great floods, electrical storms, tornadoes, and earthquakes have been held to come within this classification.

5. Loss by Fire.—The carrier is liable for any and all loss occasioned by accidental fire.

6. Perishable Goods.—Carriers are not responsible for loss to fruits that decay in their possession through no fault of theirs or for goods shipped in defective boxes, such as glassware not properly packed and other articles that are easily broken. Goods must be properly packed in order to make the carrier responsible.

7. Bill of Lading.—Bill of lading is the receipt given by the common carrier to the owner of the goods desiring to have the same shipped, and should contain a description of the quantity, the marks on the merchandise, the name of the shipper or the person sending the goods, and the consignee, the name of the person to whom the goods are shipped, place of departure and place of discharge of the goods and the price of freight, and also weight of the separate packages and the number of the car in which the same were shipped.

8. Equal Liability. — Railroad Companies and other carriers who allow express companies to carry parcels and packages on their cars or other vehicles are liable as the common carriers for all damages which occur, without regard to the contract between them and such express company. On July 1, 1918, the Government took over the control of the principal express companies, operating them as one unit under the name of the American Railway Express Company. The government control is now at an end, but the individual companies still act as one unit under the same name.

9. Baggage.—In the transportation of the baggage of passengers the liability of the carrier for loss to the same is the same as in case of transportation of goods for hire, and in case of loss the carrier must make it good.

10. When Liability Begins and Ends.—The responsibility of the common carrier begins upon the delivery of the goods for immediate transportation. A delivery at the usual place of receiving freight or to the employee of the company in the usual course of business is sufficient. The responsibility of the carrier as such terminates after the arrival of the goods at their destination and sufficient time has elapsed thereafter for the owner to have received them during business hours. After the expiration of such time the responsibility of the carrier is simply that of a warehouseman and he is required only to keep the goods with ordinary care.

11. Limitation of Liability.—A carrier can limit his liability by contract, unless forbidden by statute. Thus a bill of lading given as a receipt for a freight or express shipment, or a receipt given a passenger limiting the amount of the carrier's liability on his baggage is considered binding by the courts, and relieves the carrier of additional liability. The general rule is that a carrier may relieve himself from all liability except for loss or damage caused by his own negligence.

12. The Passenger's Rights.—The law requires common carriers to carry all passengers who pay the required fare, and who are in a sufficiently intelligent condition to travel. The carrier must exercise great care in transporting passengers and is liable for injury due to the carrier's negligence. If the passenger was himself negligent and contributed to his own injury, he cannot as a rule hold the carrier liable. Although a sleeping-car company is not a common carrier, it is liable for negligence in failing to protect the passengers from theft.

13. Different Lines.—Where goods are accepted for shipment to points beyond the line of the carrier to whom they are first delivered, such carrier is responsible for the delivery of the goods at their destination. The law now provides under such circumstances the carrier shall be liable for any loss or injury occurring during the shipment whether on its own line or that of the connecting carrier.

14. Demurrage is the sum charged by transportation companies for the non-removal of goods from their cars within the time fixed by the rules of the companies. The rules of a large number of railroad companies require that the car be unloaded within twenty-four hours after its arrival at the destination and a fixed rate of demurrage for each twenty-four hours of delay after the expiration of the usual time for unloading is imposed on the persons to whom goods are shipped.

15. The Carrier's Rights.—The carrier is entitled to a reasonable compensation for his services, and may demand payment in advance. The shipper is liable for freight, unless the carrier agrees to look exclusively to some other party; or after delivery the carrier may recover the amount of freight from the consignee. But freight may be collected only for the goods actually delivered, unless the delivery be prevented by the owner, or it be agreed that freight shall be payable regardless of losses by the way. The carrier also has a lien on the goods for his freight and advances on such goods, and may refuse to deliver until such charges be paid. This lien has priority over the owner's right of stoppage in transit, and the claims of the general creditors of the owner or consignee. A carrier by water also has a lien for salvage, and for customs duties advanced on imported goods.

16. Telegraph and Telephone Companies are not common carriers and may therefore establish reasonable regulation for the transmission of messages. Like common carriers, however, they are required to serve all who apply and offer to pay the charges, and are liable for damages when messages are not sent promptly and accurately. They come within the classification of public service corporations, and are subject to legislative regulation and control.

Chattel Mortgage

1. Definition.—A chattel mortgage is an instrument by which the owner conveys conditional title to personal property to secure the payment of a debt or the performance of a contract or other obligation. It is a pledge that the debt will be paid. Any personal property that may be sold may be mortgaged, such as livestock, machinery, farm implements, life-insurance policies, corporation stock, and crops. The **mortgagor** is the person who conveys the property. The **mortgagee** is the person to whom the transfer is made.

2. Form of Mortgage.—The usual form of a chattel mortgage is a bill of sale with the conditional clause stating the terms of the loan, and that on the mortgagor's failure to pay, the mortgagee may take possession of the property. Any person competent to make a contract, or his agent, may make a chattel mortgage. Partners or joint tenants may mortgage jointly on their individual interests. A corporation may also mortgage its personal property.

Chattel mortgages are usually given to secure notes in the same way in which real estate mortgages are given to secure notes. Greater strictness, however, is required in the acknowledgment, docketing, and recording of chattel mortgages than in the case of real estate mortgages. A chattel mortgage must be acknowledged before a justice of the peace or some other person authorized by law to take acknowledgments.

3. Describing the Property.—The property mortgaged must be described clearly enough to enable third persons to identify it, but this is determined largely by the nature of the chattels. "All" articles in a stated place is generally a valid description.

4. Foreclosure.—When the mortgagor fails to pay his debt, the right of the mortgagee to proceed in taking the property is regulated by law. In most chattel mortgages a clause is included permitting the mortgagee to seize and sell the property should the mortgagor fail to make payment.

5. General Principles.—A chattel mortgage remains in effect as between the parties themselves until it is released or becomes barred by what is known as the statute of limitations. However, in order to preserve its validity as against creditors of the mortgagor and subsequent purchasers, it must be refiled or renewed periodically. The periods vary in different states. They are generally from one to three years. To sell property covered by a chattel mortgage for a valuable consideration without notifying the purchaser of the existence of the mortgage is a criminal offense. Statutes in a few states provide that notes secured by chattel mortgages must show on their face that they are secured by chattel mortgages, or they are absolutely void; and that defense which the maker of the note secured by chattel mortgage could make against the original payee, is good against the note in the hands of an indorsee, even though indorsed before maturity. In other states, chattel mortgages on household goods must be signed by both the mortgagor and his wife. (See MORTGAGE.)

Chattel Mortgage with Power of Sale

Know all men by these presents, that I, A. B., in consideration of the sum of $.................... paid by C. D., have bargained and sold, and by these presents do hereby sell and convey to said C. D., the following goods and chattels, to wit: (describe the articles mortgaged, or refer to them as the goods and chattels mentioned in the schedule hereto annexed), and which are now in my possession.

Whereas, the said A. B. is justly indebted to C. D. in the sum of $...................., payable on the ....day of ...., 19.........., with interest at six per cent from the ....day of ...., 19.........., (upon a promissory note of even date herewith, or for goods sold and delivered).

Now the condition of the above obligation is such that if the said A. B. shall well and truly pay said C. D. said sum of money and interest when the same shall become due, then this conveyance shall be void, otherwise to remain in full force and effect. It is also agreed that said A. B. may retain possession of the said mortgaged property until said debt become due. But if default be made in the payment of said sum or any part thereof, the said C. D. and his assigns are hereby authorized to sell said goods and chattels, or so much thereof as will be necessary to satisfy the amount then due, together with the cost and expenses incurred by reason of said default.

(Signed) A. B.

In the presence of E. F.

Mortgage on Goods and Chattels, Another Form

Know all men by these presents, that A. B., residing at ...., of the first part, for securing the payment of the ...., hereinafter mentioned, and in consideration of the sum of $1, to ....in hand paid, at or before the execution and delivery of these presents, by C. D., of the second part, the receipt whereof is hereby acknowledged. has (have) granted, bargained, sold, and assigned, and by these presents does (do) grant, bargain, sell, and assign unto the said party (parties) of the second part, all ....now remaining and being ....

To have and to hold, all and singular, the goods and chattels above bargained and sold, or intended so to be, unto the said party (parties) of the second part, ...executors, administrators, and assigns forever. And the said party (parties) of the first part, for ....heirs, executors, and administrators, all and singular, the said goods and chattels above bargained and sold unto the said party (parties) of the second part, ...executors, administrators, and assigns, against the said party (parties) of the first part, and against all and every person or persons whomsoever shall and will warrant, and by these presents forever defend.

Upon condition, that if the said party (parties) of the first part shall and does (do) well and truly pay, or cause to be paid, unto the said party (parties) of the second part, ...executors, administrators, or assigns, the sum of ...., then these presents and everything herein contained shall cease and be void. And the said party (parties) of the first part, for ....executors, administrators, and assigns, does (do) covenant and agree to and with the said party (parties) of the second part, ... executors, administrators, and assigns, to make punctual payment of the money hereby secured .... And in case default shall be made in payment of the said sum above mentioned, or in case the said party (parties) of the second part shall sooner choose to demand the said goods and chattels, it shall and may be lawful for, and the said party (parties) of the first part does (do) hereby authorize and empower the said party (parties) of the second part, ...executors, administrators, and assigns, with the aid and assistance of any person or persons, to enter and come into and upon the dwelling-house and premises of the said party (parties) of the first part, and in such other place or places as the said goods and chattels are or may be held or placed, and take and carry away the said goods and chattels to sell and dispose of the same

for the best price they can obtain, at either public or private sale, and out of the money to retain and pay the said sum above mentioned, with the interest and all expenses and charges thereon, rendering the overplus (if any) unto the said party (parties) of the first part, ...executors, administrators, and assigns. And until default be made in the payment of the aforesaid sum of money, the said party (parties) of the first part to remain and continue in quiet and peaceable possession of the said goods and chattels, and the full and free enjoyment of the same, unless the said party (parties) of the second part, ...executors, administrators, or assigns, shall sooner choose to demand the same; and until such demand be made, the possession of the said party (parties) of the first part shall be deemed the possession of an agent or servant, for the sole benefit and advantage of his principal, the said party (parties) of the second part.

In witness whereof, the said party (parties) of the first part, has (have) hereunto set ....hand (s) and seal (s) this .... day of ...., 19......

Sealed and delivered in the presence of ....

.........................County of ....ss.:

On this ....day of ...., 19........, before me came ...., to me known to be the person(s) described in and who executed the foregoing instrument, and ....acknowledged that he (they) executed the same.

Notice of Sale Under Chattel Mortgage

Notice is hereby given that by virtue of a chattel mortgage, dated on the ....day of ...., 19.........., and duly filed in the office of the county clerk of ....county, ... on the ....day of ...., 19.........., in book ...., of ...., on page ...., and executed by A. B. to C. D. to secure the payment of the sum of $.........................., and upon which there is now due the sum of $........................ Default having been made in the payment of said sum, and no suit or other proceeding at law having been instituted to recover said debt or any part thereof, therefore, I will sell the property therein described, viz: (here describe the articles substantially as in the mortgage) at public auction to the highest bidder, for cash, at ...., in the (city, town, or precinct) of ...., in ....county, on the ....day of ...., at one o'clock P.M. of said date.

C. D.
Mortgagee.

Dated ...., 19..............

Assignment of Mortgage

This instrument, made this ....day of.........., 19.........., between ...., of the first part, and ...., of the second part, witnesseth: That the party (parties) of the first part, for a good and valuable consideration, to ....in hand paid by the party (parties) of the second part, has (have) sold, assigned, transferred, and conveyed, and does (do) hereby sell, assign, transfer, and convey to the party (parties) of the second part, a certain mortgage bearing date the ....day of ...., 19.........., made by ...., recorded in the clerk's office of ....county in book ....of mortgages, at page ...., on the ....day of ...., 19.........., at ....o'clock ....m., together with the bond accompanying said mortgage, and therein referred to, and all sums of money due and to grow due thereon. And the party (parties) of the first part hereby covenant that there is .... due on the said bond and mortgage the sum of ....

In witness whereof, the party (parties) of the first part has (have) hereunto set ....hand (s) and seal (s) the day and year first above written.

(Assignment clause.)

Citizenship

1. Definition.—A citizen is a member of a state or nation who enjoys political rights and is entitled to public protection. Citizenship, therefore, carries with it the duty of allegiance to the government and the right of protection from it.

2. General Principles.—A citizen residing in any of the several states owes an allegiance both to the United States and to the state, and may demand protection from each government. A citizen residing in the District of Columbia or Alaska is a citizen of the United States only. A citizen's ordinary rights are protected by the state government. All persons born or naturalized in the United States and subject to its jurisdiction are citizens of the United States. Formerly a woman took the citizenship of her husband upon marriage. Now marriage does not affect the citizenship of the wife unless her husband is ineligible for naturalization. Neither does naturalization of the husband operate to confer citizenship upon the wife.

3. Naturalization.—In order to be naturalized, an alien must follow the forms prescribed by law. His entry into the country must have been lawful, and he must furnish a certificate showing the time, place, and manner of his arrival. He must declare on oath, before the clerk of an authorized court in the district in which he resides, his intention of becoming a citizen of the United States and of residing here permanently, and he must renounce all allegiance to any foreign power. Not less than two nor more than seven years after he has made such declaration of intention, he must file his petition for admission to citizenship. He must declare on oath in open court that he will support and defend the Constitution of the United States, and renounce allegiance to any foreign power. The law also requires that no alien shall be admitted to citizenship unless immediately preceding the date of his petition he has resided continuously within the United States for at least five years, and within the county where he resided when he filed his petition for at least six months. Naturalization of the parent confers citizenship on his minor children if they reside in the United States at the time or subsequently begin to reside here permanently.

4. Aliens' Rights.—Aliens have the right to hold and transfer title to real estate. At common law they are entitled to purchase, own, and sell personal property, engage in business and to make contracts or wills. In return they must obey the laws of the land in which they reside.

Contracts

1. Definitions.—A contract is a mutual agreement between two competent parties for a valuable consideration to do or not to do a particular thing. A **Simple Contract** may or may not be in writing and requires no seal. A **Specialty** is a contract in writing which does require a seal to the signatures. An **Executed Contract** is completed, an **Executory Contract** is one still to be executed or completed. An **Express Contract** is a contract actually made between two or more parties; an **Implied Contract,** as the name suggests, is one in which some of the provisions or the entire agreement must be implied from previous agreements, from existing customs, or from the acts of the parties.

2. Requirements.—A contract must have:

a. Two or more competent parties,
b. Legal subject matter,
c. Consideration, and
d. Assent of the parties. There cannot be a contract when any of these are wanting.

The Form of the Contract

3. In many written contracts the parties are referred to as "party of the first part," "party of the second part," according to the order in which their names first appear. It does not matter which name is written first.

4. A written contract begins with a statement of the date, the names of the parties, and their places of residence. Then appears a statement of the consideration, followed by a full statement of all that the first party agrees to do, and all that the second party agrees to do.

5. Next appears a statement of the penalties or forfeitures in case either party does not faithfully and fully perform, or offer to perform, his part of the agreement.

6. The contract ends with the signatures of the parties and their seals and the signatures of witnesses. (A seal is simply the mark of a pen around the word "seal," written after the signature, or the word "seal" in parentheses printed or typewritten on the form.)

7. Competent lawyers should be employed in the drafting of a contract.

8. Errors in grammar or spelling do not affect the legality of the agreement.

9. If the language should be obscure on certain points, the court will try to determine the intent of the parties when they entered into the agreemen, providing the intent can be gathered from the terms of the instrument itself. It is of the utmost importance that the terms of the contract be specifically and explicitly stated. Competent attorneys should be employed.

10. When an agreement is written it must all be in writing. It cannot be partly written and partly oral.

The Vital Part of a Contract — Consideration

11. Definition.—A consideration is the thing which induces a party to make a contract. It is the substantial cause or reason inducing the parties to enter into an agreement.

12. A Sufficient Consideration.—The law does not require that the consideration should be a good or bad bargain. As long as something is done or suffered by either party, always providing it is not illegal, the consideration is good. The smallest consideration is sufficient to make it legal. The value of the consideration is generally unimportant.

13. A Valuable Consideration. — A valuable consideration is one which is equal to money or may be translated into monetary terms. It is sometimes defined as "money or its equivalent."

14. A Good Consideration.—A good consideration is one which is based upon love, gratitude or esteem, or blood relationship. A good consideration is not sufficient unless the agreement has to be performed by one or both parties.

15. Immoral Consideration. — All considerations which are immoral are consequently illegal, and contracts based upon them are generally void.

The Law Governing All Kinds of Contracts

16. An intentional alteration of a contract in a material part, by one party without the consent of the other, after its execution, discharges the other party from his obligations under the contract.

17. A contract made by a minor is not binding upon him, yet he can hold the party with whom he contracts, to all the conditions of the contract.

18. A fraudulent contract may be binding on the party guilty of fraud, although not laying any obligation on the part of the party acting in good faith.

19. A contract for the sale or purchase of personal property over a certain amount—ranging from $30 to $500 in the different states—must be in writing.

20. A contract which cannot be performed within a year must be in writing.

21. If no time of payment is stated in the contract, payment must be made on the delivery of the goods.

22. A contract totally restraining the exercise of a man's trade or profession is void, but one restraining him in any particular place is not void.

23. An offer or proposal, which includes the essential parts of a contract, becomes a contract as soon as accepted. Generally the acceptance must be at the time of receiving the offer. The offer may be withdrawn at any time before it has been accepted. Offers may be made and accepted within a reasonable time by word of mouth, telephone, telegraph, or mail.

24. A contract required by law to be in writing cannot be changed by verbal agreement.

25. A contract cannot be rescinded except by consent of both parties.

26. A contract binding in the place where it is made is binding everywhere, but courts of one state will not enforce contracts made in another state where to do so would be in violation of the statutes or public policy of their own state.

27. Each party to an agreement or contract should retain a signed copy.

28. While signatures or contracts written with a pencil are valid in law, it is always safer to write them in ink.

Contracts That Are Not Lawful

29. A contract to commit a breach of peace.

30. An agreement for immoral purposes.

31. An agreement procured by threats, violence, or fraud.

32. Wagers or bets (cannot be collected by law).

33. Interest at rates higher than the maximum rate fixed by law cannot be collected.

34. A contract with an intoxicated person, lunatic, or minor (cannot be enforced by the other party).

35. A contract in violation of a statute in the state in which it is made.

36. An agreement to prevent competition on a sale under an execution.

37. An agreement to prohibit the carrying on of a trade throughout the state.

38. Where consent to an agreement is given by mistake, such agreement cannot be enforced.

39. The right to vote or hold a public office cannot be sold by contract.

40. A contract without a consideration, such as a promise to make a gift, cannot be enforced.

41. Two or more persons cannot intentionally make a contract to willfully injure a third person.

42. Contracts for concealing felony or violating public trust, for bribery and extortion, are prohibited.

43. Useless things cannot become the subject of a contract, such as agreeing not to go out of the house for a month.

44. A verbal release without payment or satisfaction for the debt is not good. Release must be under seal, unless made for some new consideration.

45. If two parts of a contract are in direct conflict with each other, the former part holds good in preference to the latter.

46. Contracts in which there is misrepresentation or concealment of material facts cannot be enforced by the party guilty of such misrepresentation or concealment.

47. If a thing contracted for is not in existence at the time of making the contract (as in a case where parties contract for the purchase and sale of a horse not knowing that the horse is dead at the time) the contract is not valid.

48. If a person agrees to serve as a laborer or clerk, he cannot be compelled to fulfill his agreement; damages, however, can be recovered for a failure to perform.

49. An agreement with a thief to drop a criminal prosecution, in consideration of his bringing back the goods and paying all damages, is not good, and will be no bar to a future prosecution.

50. Guardians, trustees, executors, administrators, or attorneys cannot take advantage of those for whom they act by becoming parties to contracts in which the persons for whom they are acting are interested.

51. Quasi Contracts.—A quasi contract may be defined as almost a contract or partly a contract. It is a legal obligation resulting from some direct or indirect benefit accruing to one party from the other without any express agreement on the part of the first. The law, nevertheless, compels him to pay. For example:

a. One who has reason to believe that payment for goods tendered is expected, must not accept them unless he intends to pay for them. If he accepts the goods, he can be compelled to pay for them.
b. A man employed under the promise of good wages or division of profits is entitled to fair treatment, even though such an arrangement is no contract at all.
c. Money paid on an illegal contract or on one which is void because of non-existence of the property, may be recovered.
d. If an express company delivers valuable goods to the wrong party, the company can recover from the person who wrongfully accepted them.
e. If, on account of a mistake, a man pays his grocery bill twice for the same period, he can recover.
f. Action to recover can be brought against a man who sells property not his own, or which proves to be worthless.
g. All these questions hinge on the presence or absence of consideration in the agreement.
h. A liability of this kind cannot be imposed upon a person without his act or consent, either express or implied.

52. Statute of Frauds.—In every state there is a statute called the statute of frauds which provides that certain contracts must be in writing to bind the parties. Thus:

a. Agreements for the sale of real estate are unenforceable unless they are in writing.
b. A contract for the sale of goods for more than a certain amount, which amount varies in different states, must be in writing or there must be actual delivery and acceptance of the goods or part payment therefor.
c. A contract must be in writing to charge the defendant upon any special promise to answer for the debt, default, or miscarriage of another person.
d. A written contract is necessary to charge any person upon any agreement made upon consideration of marriage, or upon any agreement that is not to be performed within the space of one year from the making thereof.

Damages for Violation of Contract

53. A statute which provides no penalties for the lawbreaker is merely the expression of a wish, or the giving of advice. Similarly the contract must be binding on both parties. This element of mutual obligation is the very essence of a contract.

54. Where no actual loss has been sustained by the violation of a contract, the plaintiff is entitled to nominal damages only. Thus, A contracted to drill a well for B and to complete same within a specified time or forfeit $1000.00, said amount being intended not as an assessment of the damages which would probably be actually sustained, but to secure the performance of the contract by the imposition of a penalty. The courts will not compel A to pay the $1000.00 damages unless his failure to complete the well has actually meant a loss of $1000.00 to B. They will, however, permit B to recover from A such damages as he actually sustained as a result of A's failure to complete the well within the specified time.

55. Expected profits on speculations in real property cannot be recovered in case of a violation of contract.

56. Failure on the part of the seller to convey real estate or deliver personal property according to agreement entitles the plaintiff to recover damages or to sue for specific performance of the contract.

57. In case of loss of goods by a common carrier the plaintiff is entitled to the value of the goods where they were to be delivered, less the freight on such goods.

58. If a party contracts to employ another for a certain time, at a specified compensation, and discharges him, without cause, before the expiration of the time, the employee can obtain judgment for the full amount of wages for the entire unexpired balance of the time, provided he is unable to secure employment in the same line of work, after making an earnest effort to do so. Should he obtain work at a lower wage he can collect the difference.

59. To prevent lawsuits and disputes the amount of damages for the violation of contracts is sometimes fixed by the parties themselves by inserting in the contract some such provision as the following:

> AND IT IS FURTHER AGREED that the party that shall fail to perform this agreement on his part shall pay to the other the full sum of (here state amount), as liquidated damages.

General Form of Agreement

This agreement, made and entered into this .... day of ...., 19.........., by and between Clarence Ranck of Aurora, County of Kane, State of Illinois, party of the first part, and Charles Vandersall of Columbus, Ohio, party of the second part, witnesseth:

In consideration of (insert consideration), it is agreed between the parties hereto as follows:

Said party of the first part agrees (insert agreement of party of the first part).

Said party of the second part agrees (insert agreement of the party of the second part).

In witness whereof the said parties have hereunto set their hands and seals the day and year first above written.

CLARENCE RANCK (Seal)
CHARLES VANDERSALL (Seal)

Copyright

1. Definition.—A copyright is the exclusive right to reproduce, publish, and sell a literary or artistic work. Under the United States Copyright Law, a copyright may be granted for the following classes of material:

(a) Books, including collections, anthologies, and encyclopedias;
(b) Magazines and newspapers;
(c) Lectures, sermons, or other addresses for oral delivery;
(d) Dramatic and musical-dramatic compositions;
(e) Musical compositions;
(f) Maps;
(g) Works of art, including models and designs;
(h) Reproductions of works of art;
(i) Scientific or technical drawings or plastic work;
(j) Photographs;
(k) Prints and pictorial illustrations;
(l) Motion-picture photoplays;
(m) Other motion pictures.

Copyrights can also be secured on compilations, abridgments, arrangements, or adaptations, whether of non-copyrightable material or, with the permission of the copyright holder, of material that has been copyrighted already. Republished works that include new material are also copyrightable.

2. How to Obtain.—To secure a copyright on a work which is to be reproduced for sale or public distribution, the work should be published with a copyright notice, which may be in the following form:

Copyright, 1940, by
Jones, Smith, and Company

On maps, photographs, pictures, and other works where it is difficult to place a complete copyright notice, the letter C enclosed in a circle, ©, is used; it must be accompanied by a symbol or mark of the owner of the copyright, and his name must appear elsewhere on the work. After publication of the work, two copies of the best edition (or one copy in the case of a work by a foreign citizen and published first in another country) should be sent to the Copyright Office, Washington, D. C., with an application for registration. Books by American citizens or permanent residents of the United States must be accompanied by an affidavit stating that the typesetting, printing, and binding were done in the United States. Forms for the affidavit and application are supplied by the Copyright Office upon request.

3. Fees.—The fee for registration of a published work is $2; payment of this sum also entitles one to a certificate under seal of the Copyright Office. Registration of a published photograph costs $1 if a certificate is not desired. The cost of renewing a copyright is $1. Copyrights may be assigned to other persons; the fee for recording an assignment is $2 for each page or fraction larger than one-half page in the Copyright Office record book.

4. How to Obtain Copyright for Other Articles.—A copyright may also be obtained on certain works not published or reproduced for sale by filing an application for registration; the fee is $1. It should be accompanied by one manuscript of the work, if it is a lecture, sermon, address, or dramatic or musical composition; by one print, for copyright of a photograph not intended for general circulation; and by a photograph or reproduction in the case of works of art and scientific or technical drawings or plastic works. To obtain a copyright on a motion-picture photoplay not published or for sale, the application for registration must be accompanied by the title, description, and a print from each scene or act. An application for registration of another type of motion picture must be accompanied by the title, description, and at least two prints taken from different sections of the complete picture.

5. Duration of Copyright. — A copyright is valid for 28 years and may be renewed for the same length of time; provided application for renewal is made and registered within one year prior to the expiration of the original term of copyright. It cannot be renewed again. If an author is not living, his copyright may be renewed by the widow or widower, or his children. If none of these are living the executors have the right of renewal; and if there is no will the copyright may be renewed by the next of kin. The person to whom a copyright has been assigned may also renew it, at the expiration of the original 28-year period.

6. Prints and Labels. — Copyrights may be taken out on prints and labels for advertising purposes. They must be published first with a notice of copyright. Application for registration should then be filed by the owner or author. These copyrights are also effective for 28 years and may be renewed for a similar period.

7. Foreign Copyrights. — American citizens may secure copyrights in the following foreign countries with which the United States has copyright relations by Presidential proclamation: Argentina, Belgium, Chile, Colombia, Costa Rica, Czecho-Slovakia, Cuba, Denmark, Finland, France, Germany, Great Britain and all British possessions, Greece, Irish Free State, Italy, Luxemburg, Mexico, Netherlands and possessions, Norway, Palestine, Poland, Portugal, Rumania, Siam, South Africa, Spain, Sweden, Switzerland, Tunis. Citizens of these countries are allowed to obtain copyrights in the United States.

Proclamations have established agreements covering copyright control of mechanical reproduction of music with the following countries: Argentina, Australia, Belgium, Canada, Chile, Cuba, Denmark, Finland, France, Germany, Great Britain, Irish Free State, Italy, Luxemburg, Netherlands, New Zealand, Norway, South Africa, Spain, Sweden, and Switzerland. Similar copyright protection is included in the proclamations regarding Czecho-Slovakia, Greece, Poland, and Rumania, and in the convention with Hungary. The United States also has copyright treaties with China and Japan.

Although the United States is not a member of the International Copyright Union, it ratified the Copyright Convention of Mexico of 1902 and the Pan-American Copyright Convention, proclaimed in 1914. The latter agreement controls United States copyright relations with Bolivia, Brazil, Colombia, Costa Rica, Dominican Republic, Ecuador, Guatemala, Haiti, Honduras, Nicaragua, Panama, Paraguay, Peru, and Uruguay.

Corporations

1. Definition.—A corporation is a group of persons empowered to act as a single individual, and treated by the law as such in many respects.

2. Kinds of Corporations. — Corporations known as **Business Corporations** are the most common. **Public Corporations** are agencies of the government. Railroad corporations, and other public service corporations, though performing a public service, are nevertheless **Private Corporations.** Then there are **Religious, Charitable** and **Beneficial Corporations,** usually organized for beneficial purposes, not for profit. **Quasi Corporations,** such as school districts, resemble corporations in some ways. They can own and manage real estate, make contracts, sue and be sued like any other corporation. A **Close Corporation** is one where the capital stock or ownership is confined to one family or distinct group of individuals.

3. Formation of Corporation.—The formation of a corporation involves numerous legal questions, and should never be attempted without the services of a competent corporation lawyer. In most states the first step after having a certain amount of stock subscribed and paid for is to file with the Secretary of the state a statement giving name, object, amount of capital stock, amount of stock paid for, location of office, and duration of the proposed corporation. The charter is then issued and a meeting of stockholders is called to elect directors. State laws vary, but usually three or more individuals may form a corporation. Corporations created in one state may transact any lawful business in another state, and they can acquire and transfer property as individuals, provided they comply with the law of the state in which they do business and obtain a license to do business there.

4. Life of a Corporation.—A corporation exists until the expiration of its charter unless it fails or is discontinued for other good reasons. Most charters are now perpetual. The stockholder's rights may pass from one to another by sale or by inheritance.

5. Capital Stock. — Corporations generally have assets composed of money, real estate, buildings, machinery, patents, copyrights, etc. Capital stock is divided into parts called shares, and the owners of the shares are called stockholders. By this method of promotion the necessary money for the enterprise may be collected from many different sources, and unlike a partnership the individual stockholders are not personally liable for the debts of the corporation. In large measure these facts account for the great popularity of the corporate form of organization. Corporations may increase or decrease the amount of their capital stock, provided the change is made in good faith, without intent to defraud.

6. Who May Subscribe for Stock. — Anyone capable of making a contract may subscribe for the stock of a corporation. Minors are excluded. Where fictitious subscriptions are used to induce others to buy, the purchaser may refuse to pay his subscription. If already paid for he may recover the money, or he may keep the stock and sue for damages. The selling of subscriptions to stock is now very strictly regulated by statute.

7. The Stock Certificate is a written statement of the number and par value of the shares to which the holder is entitled. In other words, it is the evidence of ownership. A stockholder may prove ownership even though a certificate has never been issued him. When the capital stock of a corporation is increased each shareholder usually has the right to purchase a portion of the new stock before it can be offered for sale to outsiders.

8. Preferred Stock.—This kind of stock takes preference over the ordinary or common stock of a corporation. The holders of preferred stock are entitled to a stated percentage annually out of the net earnings of the corporation before a dividend can be declared on the common stock, or to some other preference set out in the certificate. Preference, rather than actual payment, is guaranteed. Holders of preferred stock usually have the right to vote at any stockholders' meeting on the same basis as the holders of common stock. In some states the law requires that each share of stock have equal voting rights with every other share.

9. Common Stock is the ordinary stock of a corporation. The holders are entitled to all the rights incident to their ownership.

10. Transfer of Stock.—This is provided for by statute. Usually the seller must assign the certificate to the transferee, execute a power of attorney, and deliver the certificate to the company for cancellation. The transfer agent then issues a new certificate to the purchaser.

11. A Subscription for Stock is a Contract and must be in writing. An agent cannot refuse to receive a subscription from a competent person, nor can he release a subscriber or alter the terms of the contract. The subscriber must inform himself as to his obligations and cannot evade payment unless he can prove fraud.

12. The Shareholder's Liability. — As stated previously, a corporation differs from a partnership in that the shareholders in a corporation are liable only for the amount of stock they own. Each member of a partnership is liable for all the debts of the firm. However, in the case of National Banks the shareholders are liable for double the amount of their holdings in case the bank fails, if that much more is required to pay the debts. The amount of a stockholder's liability is fixed by statute. A stockholder in any corporation is liable for the full amount of his stock, whether paid in full or not.

13. Receivership.—When a corporation fails a receiver is sometimes appointed by the court to take charge of its affairs. The receiver has the power to convert the property into cash, levy and collect assessments from the shareholders, where authorized by law, and pay dividends to the creditors, as in the case of bankruptcy proceedings. The receiver may be an individual, a group of individuals, or a trust company.

14. Management. — The power of a corporation rests in its members or individual stockholders—except as restricted or limited by law. Unless the charter or state laws alter the case, policies are determined by a majority vote; usually a shareholder has as many votes as he has shares in the corporation. The right to vote in a stockholders' meeting is determined by the stock record of ownership as of the date of meeting, or on the date the books are closed prior to the meeting. The bylaws of the corporation generally fix the time for the closing of the books. A stockholder has the right to vote even if no certificate has been issued to him. He may vote in person or by proxy. An executor or trustee may vote the stock of the estate.

15. Meetings.—The statutes or the bylaws of a corporation usually prescribe the manner in which meetings are to be called, and the bylaws fix the time and place of meetings. Should the proper officer fail to call a meeting at the required time, the meeting may lawfully be held later, and if he should refuse to issue the proper notice, he may be compelled by mandamus proceedings to do so. **Regular Meetings** are held in the manner set forth by the charter or bylaws, and the object of the meeting need not be stated in the notice. On the other hand, special meetings may be called at any time on proper authority, but the notice must state the object of the meeting, and no other business may be there transacted. Any authorized meeting may be adjourned from time to time or from day to day, and the adjournments must be considered as the same meeting. Even if a meeting is illegally called it becomes a valid meeting by ratification of the proper official or by the shareholders. Notice of meeting is sent to whoever has the right to vote the stock.

16. Directors. — Management of a corporation is vested in the directors. Most corporations delegate managerial powers to directors who are elected either by a majority vote of the shareholders, or by a cumulative system of voting in states in which such system is used. Their powers are established by statute, charter, or bylaws. As a rule they have general supervision over the business of the corporation. Their authority may be delegated to committees, corporate officials, or individuals. Thus the president, the secretary, the treasurer, and other officers and committees of the corporation are chosen by the board of directors to act in the capacity of agents, in administering its affairs. A director may not act for the corporation individually, but his unauthorized acts would bind the corporation if subsequently ratified. A director may not act both for the corporation and for himself in the same transaction. Unless otherwise provided, directors are not entitled to compensation for their services.

17. The Directors' Liability.—The directors of a company are liable to the company and to shareholders and outsiders for negligence, fraud, or for acts committed outside the scope of their authority. These are questions of fact to be determined by the courts. The directors of a corporation are personally liable for its debts if it can be proved that they incurred the obligations knowing that the corporation was insolvent. They have been held personally, jointly, and severally liable as partners, for debts of the corporation contracted in a state in which the company was found to have been doing business without having taken out a license.

18. The Officers of a corporation are usually the president, vice-president, secretary, and treasurer chosen by, and often from, the board of directors. The ordinary rules of agency govern their powers and duties.

The president is the chief executive officer and usually presides at meetings of the Board of Directors.

The vice-president takes over the duties of the president when, for any reason, the latter is unable to perform them. Quite frequently there are numerous vice-presidents assigned to different duties.

The secretary is the keeper of the records and the chief clerk of the corporation. He usually has the custody of the corporate seal.

The treasurer has charge of the corporation's finances. He is usually under bond for the faithful performance of his duties.

19. Dividends. A dividend is a payment to the shareholders out of the net profits of the corporation. It may be in actual cash, in property or in additional stock. When stock is selling above par on the exchange, corporations sometimes grant shareholders the right to purchase additional stock at par instead of declaring a cash stock dividend. The law will not permit the payment of dividends out of capital, or from borrowed money, without the consent of the stockholders, and the directors would be liable for such a fraudulent payment. Furthermore, illegally paid dividends may be recovered for the benefit of creditors. The net profit of a corporation is an asset, and not secure against creditors unless, or until, the money has been declared as a dividend. When the dividend has been legally declared payable, no action can be brought by creditors to stop its payment. The directors must act in good faith, but they cannot be compelled to pay dividends when they do not deem it advisable to do so. The courts hold that dividends must be general on all stock of the same class, so that each shareholder in that class will receive his just share, and that the dividends shall be paid to the owner as determined by the books of the company. According to income-tax rulings, a dividend in cash is considered as income, one in stock as capital.

20. Liabilities of a Corporation.—Through its agents or servants a corporation can be guilty of slander, libel, false representation, trespass, or negligence, and can be sued accordingly.

21. The Shareholder's Rights.—A shareholder has the right to inspect the company's books at any reasonable time for any proper purpose. Furthermore, he may employ an expert accountant to go through the records if he has reason to believe that the affairs of the company are not being handled properly.

General Proxy

Know all men by these presents, that I, ..., the undersigned, do hereby constitute and appoint ....my attorney and agent (with power of substitution for me and in my name, place and stead) to vote as my proxy for the election of directors and upon all matters that may be considered at the annual meeting of the stockholders of the ....company, to be held at its office at the city of ...., of the county of ...., state of ...., on the ....day of ...., 19.........., at ....o'clock ....M., or any adjournment thereof, according to the number of votes I should be entitled to vote if I were personally present at said meeting, hereby revoking all former proxies by me made and given.

In witness whereof, I have hereunto set my hand and seal this ....day of ...., 19..........

Witness:

.. (Signature)

Revocation of Proxy

Know all men by these presents, that I, the undersigned, do hereby revoke and annul a certain proxy by me given to .... (or, any and all proxies or powers of attorney heretofore given by me) authorizing and empowering the said .... to represent me and to vote in my name and stead and to act for me in any way whatsoever at any meeting or meetings of the stockholders of the .... company.

In witness whereof, I have hereunto set my hand and seal this .... day of ...., 19..........

(Witnessed.) (Signed.)

Criminal Law and Procedure

1. Definition.—A crime is an act in violation of some existing prohibitory statute and the common morality of the country. An individual cannot compromise a criminal wrong, for crime is a matter for the State to settle. Crimes may be classified as felonies, or more serious offenses; and misdemeanors, or less serious offenses; but the distinction is largely an arbitrary one.

2. Burden of Proof.—The burden of proof is upon the State. In other words a person accused of a crime is presumed to be innocent until the contrary is proved. The verdict of the jury must be unanimous to convict. If any doubt remains in the minds of the jury, after hearing all the evidence, it is its duty to acquit the defendant, and once acquitted, a prisoner cannot be brought to trial a second time for the same offense.

3. Defenses. — Two defenses which are often raised are the defense of insanity and that of self-defense. A person who cannot distinguish right from wrong is insane and cannot be held responsible for his acts, but the insanity must be proved. Also, a person may defend his person, family, or property and may use such force as is necessary. If he can show that the act was committed in self-defense, he is guilty of no crime.

4. Confession. — A legal confession must be voluntary and free from all compulsion, either physical or mental. Third-degree methods are unlawful, and a confession procured by the use of threats or violence has no standing in court.

5. Trial by Jury. — A person accused of a crime is guaranteed the right to a fair and impartial trial by a jury of twelve, and the right to be represented by a competent lawyer. The trial must occur in the county where the crime was committed unless a "change of venue" is granted. The defendant is entitled to a change of venue if it can be proved that on account of prejudice on the part of the judge or jury the accused could not there receive a fair trial.

6. Habeas Corpus. — A writ of habeas corpus is sometimes issued by the court to prevent people from being unlawfully deprived of their liberty. The prisoner is brought before the court and is released unless cause can be shown for his detention. This is a fundamental right under the Constitution.

7. Criminal Procedure. — The first step in criminal procedure is generally the issuing of a warrant by a justice of the peace or other judicial officer. When arrested the accused is either placed in custody, or, if he can furnish a satisfactory bond, he is released on bail awaiting trial. If the offense is a misdemeanor the case is usually tried and settled before the justice. If it is a felony, the justice holds a preliminary trial, certifying his findings to the grand jury. Acting in an investigating capacity, the grand jury may indict the accused, and the case is tried on its merits in the regular criminal court. If the grand jury fails to indict, the charge may be dropped on account of insufficient evidence.

Criminal Law in Brief

8. Adultery.—In many of the states, it is a crime for any married man and woman not married to each other to live together openly as man and wife.

9. Accessory to the Crime. — Any person assisting another to commit a crime or to escape from the scene of the crime is equally guilty with the principal.

10. Assault and Battery. — A person who threatens, or attempts to strike, another person is guilty of assault, even though the threat is not followed by actual battery. Assault becomes battery when injury is actually done. The slightest unlawful touching may be battery.

11. Bribery consists in the offering or giving of money or other valuable consideration to a public officer or one performing a public duty, as an inducement for him to commit an unlawful act. The giver and the receiver of the bribe are equally guilty.

12. Bigamy.—A person having more than one husband or wife at one time is guilty of the crime of bigamy.

13. Burglary consists in the unlawful breaking into and entering of the building of another with the intent to commit a crime.

14. Bail means the sureties who bind themselves to have the accused present in court when required for trial.

15. Contempt of Court.—Any attempt to obstruct justice or to injure the dignity of the court is punishable by the action of the court.

16. Conspiracy.—When two or more persons agree to do an unlawful act, the agreement is called a conspiracy, and is in itself a crime.

17. Embezzlement is the wrongful appropriation and use of the personal property of another person by one to whom it has been voluntarily turned over for some lawful use.

18. Extortion is the asking and accepting of unlawful fees by a public officer.

19. False Pretense.—It is a criminal offense to obtain money or other things of value by the false or fraudulent representation of a past or existing fact.

20. Fornication is illicit sexual intercourse other than adultery, as that between unmarried persons. It is punishable in some states.

21. Forgery is the false making, or the material alteration, of a written instrument, contract, or legal paper with intent to defraud.

22. Larceny is the unlawful appropriation and use of a person's property. It differs from embezzlement in that the original taking is unlawful.

23. Manslaughter is the unlawful killing of a human being without malice or premeditation.

24. Mayhem is the act of maiming, disfiguring, or cutting away any part of the human body.

25. Murder is the unlawful taking of a human life with malice and premeditation.

26. Malicious Mischief is a crime which consists of the willful and intentional injury of another's property.

27. Offenses on the high seas are tried by the country under whose flag the ship is sailing.

28. Perjury is the false swearing of a person under oath. A person inducing another to perjure himself is equally guilty.

29. Rape.—It is a felony to have sexual intercourse with a girl or woman without her consent.

30. Robbery is stealing property from another by force and intimidation. It is a felony punishable by imprisonment in the penitentiary.

31. Seduction. — To have intercourse with a woman of chaste reputation through false promises of marriage is a crime.

32. Stolen Property.—It is a crime to buy, receive, or conceal stolen property with the intent not to return it to the rightful owner. When buying property, demand proof of the ownership.

33. Treason. — It is treason to make war against, or to assist the enemies of, the existing government. It is punishable by death. A foreigner, owing no allegiance to the government, cannot be guilty of treason.

34. Unlawful Assembly.—It is a criminal offense for two or more persons to assemble in contemplation of some unlawful act.

Deeds

1. Definitions.—A deed is a written document, under seal, conveying real estate. There are two kinds of deeds in general use: warranty deeds and quitclaim deeds. Any person of legal age, competent to transact business and owning real estate, may convey it by deed. The seller is called the **grantor**, the buyer the **grantee**.

2. A Warranty Deed is one in which the seller or grantor warrants the title to be good, and agrees to defend the same against all parties. Such a deed usually provides:

(a) That the seller has a right to convey the real estate; (b) that he is the owner of the land mentioned in the deed; (c) that the land is free and clear from all former and other grants, bargains, sales, liens, taxes, assessments, and encumbrances of any kind; (d) and that the purchaser will have quiet enjoyment of the real estate; that is, that he will not be put out of possession by anyone having superior title. If it afterwards develops that the grantor did not have the right to sell, or if the grantee discovers an encumbrance on the land, or if he has any trouble about the title, the purchaser has a good cause of action against the seller.

3. A Quitclaim Deed conveys only what interest the grantor may have in the property. This form of deed is often given by one whose title to the real estate may be defective. The seller conveys only whatever interest he may have. A quitclaim deed contains no warranties.

4. General Principles.—

- **a.** Deeds must be written, typewritten, or printed.
- **b.** The names of the parties and places of residence are generally written first.
- **c.** The property must be fully described. The description should be by bounds, or by divisions of United States surveys, or by subdivisions into blocks and lots, as shown on the records in the county recorder's office.
- **d.** The deed must express a consideration, and be signed and sealed by the grantor or grantors. A deed without consideration is void.
- **e.** Numbers should always be written in words followed by figures in parentheses, thus, Two Hundred Dollars ($200.00).
- **f.** If the grantor is married both he and his wife should join in the deed, and it should be executed and acknowledged by both.
- **g.** The acknowledgment of a deed can be made only before persons authorized by law to take the same, such as justices of the peace, notaries, masters in chancery, and judges and clerks of the courts.
- **h.** The deed takes effect upon its delivery to the person authorized to receive it, and should be recorded at once.
- **i.** After the signing and acknowledgment of a deed the parties have no right to make the slightest alteration.
- **j.** Never purchase real estate without a careful examination of the title by a trusted attorney.
- **k.** Always procure an abstract of title or guaranty policy before advancing money or signing a contract for purchase of land or lots.
- **l.** A deed in which a mistake has been made can be corrected in all cases of fraud or accident.
- **m.** In investigating the title to real estate, the attorney is bound to make a careful examination of the records and report the facts and his conclusions with respect to the condition of the title, and is liable for any injury resulting from his negligence.
- **n.** A deed is considered recorded as soon as it reaches the recording officer, who generally notes upon it the day, hour, and minute when it was received by him.
- **o.** If the land is a gift and no price is paid for it, it is customary to insert "in consideration of one dollar and other good and valuable considerations."

Form of Warranty Deed

Know all men by these presents, that we.................... and ...., husband and wife, in consideration of the sum of $................ in hand paid, do hereby grant, bargain, sell and convey to ...., of ....county, ..., the following described real estate situated in the county of ...., and state of .... to wit: (describe premises), to have and to hold to his heirs and assigns forever. Together with all of the tenements, hereditaments, and appurtenances thereto belonging. And we hereby covenant with said .... that we are lawfully seized of said premises; that they are free from incumbrances; that we have good right and lawful authority to sell the same, and we covenant to warrant and defend the same against the lawful claims of all persons whosoever. And the said ...., hereby relinquishes her right of dower in said premises.

In witness whereof we have hereunto set our hands and seals this ....day of ...., 19.........
In presence of ....(Seal)
....(Seal)

State of..............................
..............................County.

....
....

On this ....day of ...., 19..........
before me, a notary public in and for said county, personally came the above named ....and.................., his wife, who are known to me to be the identical persons whose names are affixed to the above deed as grantors, and severally acknowledge the instrument to be their voluntary act, and deed.

In witness whereof I have hereunto set my hand the day and year above written.

....
Notary Public

N. B. Statutes in many states provide for a short form which may be used in place of the above and has the same effect.

Form of Quitclaim Deed

The grantor (here insert name or names of grantor or grantors and place or places of residence), of the city of ...., for the consideration of (here insert consideration), convey and quitclaim to (here insert name or names of grantee or grantees) all interest in the following described real estate (here in-

sert description), situated in the county of .... in the state of ....
Dated this ....day of ...., A.D., 19 ....

....(Seal)

N. B. Use same form of acknowledgment as that shown for warranty deeds above.

Dower

1. Definition.—Dower is the provision which the law makes for the support of a widow out of her deceased husband's estate. Unless modified by statute this interest consists of the use for life of one-third of her husband's land after his death. During the husband's life, the law protects the wife's interest by prohibiting the sale of real estate unless she joins with him in signing the deed. If the property is sold and she does not sign the deed, she still has her dower right in the property. The interest which a husband acquires in the land belonging to his wife after her death is called **curtesy.** In some states the term "curtesy" has been abolished and the word "dower" is substituted, so that the latter term applies to the interest of either the husband or the wife in the land of the deceased spouse.

2. General Principles.—a. The dower right is regulated by widely differing statutes in the several states. **b.** If the land is subject to a mortgage which was signed by the wife along with her husband, or a prior lien, the wife cannot get possession until the encumbrance has been removed. **c.** A woman may release her dower right by signing with her husband a deed for the conveyance of the real estate. **d.** A husband can will his wife a certain amount in place of her dower, but the wife can claim the dower instead if she prefers it. **e.** The widow is usually entitled to administer the estate of her deceased husband. **f.** Dower exists in growing crops and trees, and also in mines and quarries opened during the husband's lifetime. **g.** The widow of a partner is entitled to her dower in partnership land after payment of all debts of the partnership. **h.** A legal marriage is necessary to sustain a dower estate. An absolute divorce divests the wife of her dower if the divorce was granted to the husband by reason of the wife's misconduct. **i.** Dower is assigned to the widow either by direction of the court or by agreement. **j.** Dower may be barred by a marriage settlement or agreement made before marriage.

Drunkenness

1. Both the civil and criminal courts are frequently called upon to rule on cases in which one of the parties involved was intoxicated.

2. In Civil Cases the courts have recognized cases in which intoxication was an excuse for repudiating a contract. The mental condition must be taken into consideration, especially where a man has become utterly incompetent or insane as a result of his intemperate habits. As we have seen before, such a man cannot make a contract. If one is visibly intoxicated the contract could be declared void on the ground that the other party must have realized his condition. The element of fraud enters if one party deliberately induced the condition of the other. However, if the intoxicated party ratifies the agreement when sober, or fails to repudiate it, he would be legally bound by it.

3. In Criminal Cases the courts hold that one who voluntarily becomes intoxicated cannot claim his intoxication as an excuse for his criminal acts. Yet in all such cases the facts must show intent to commit the crime before there can be any conviction. This aspect has been brought up in many cases where the defendant was so drunk that he entered the wrong house, or carried off the property of others, or slandered the reputation of another.

4. General Principles.—(a) It is the duty of those who deal with an intoxicated person to take his condition into consideration. (b) A sober party must exercise a reasonable degree of care to avoid injury to a drunken individual. (c) A railroad company is also bound to take into account the helpless condition of its passenger, and to exercise reasonable care in keeping him out of danger. (d) Drunkenness is not a legal excuse for the commission of a crime, but sometimes it is evidence of the absence of malice.

Employer and Employee

1. Explanation.—The term employee refers to a person who is hired by a **contract of service** to perform certain duties for another person called the **employer.**

2. Kinds of Contracts. — There are two types of general employment contracts. a. Contracts to do some particular thing such as to buy and sell stocks or provisions, or collect accounts. **b.** Contracts to do whatever the employer may direct. Farm hands, domestic servants, and clerks belong to this class. Such contracts are frequently verbal, or even only implied, rather than written.

3. Compensation.—If no agreement has been made beforehand the employee is entitled to the wages usually paid for such service. If the employee leaves because of insufficient food, ill-treatment, or disabling sickness, he is entitled to pay for the time he worked.

4. Duties of Employee.—The employee is expected to perform faithfully the services for which he contracted for the entire term or period of service. In many cases, as in those of workers employed by the day or hour, this period of service may be very short. Courts frequently hold that if he leaves before expiration of time, he can claim no pay for the work done. Some judges have held, however, that even in this case the employee is entitled to pay for work done, less what the employer lost by necessity of paying higher wages to the employee's successor, or what he lost by the employee's failing to perform his contract. The employee is bound to take reasonable care of the property in his care, and is liable for any loss or injury to it when due to his negligence.

5. Discharge. — An employee may be discharged at the end of his contract without any cause or previous notice. If he is discharged without good cause before the termination of his agreement, however, he is entitled to pay for the whole period, provided he has first made an earnest attempt to secure other employment in the same kind of work. If he gets work at lower wages he is entitled to the difference. If his pay is equal to, or higher than, the former rate, he can not collect. If, however, the discharge is on account of incapacity, dishonesty, or misconduct, he is not entitled to any pay for the unexpired period. Frequently a person is hired for a month, or for a year, at the termination of which the work continues. In such cases the law presumes a new contract on the same terms.

6. Liability of Employer.—An employer's liability is of two kinds: **a.** liability for the acts of his employees, and **b.** liability for the injury or death of his employees.

7. Liability for Acts of Employee.—The employer is liable for the wrongful acts of his employee producing injury to others, provided the acts are done in the course of the ordinary employment. Thus a railroad company is liable to passengers for negligence of conductors and engineers while running trains on the road.

8. Workmen's Compensation. — Workmen's compensation acts have largely provided new remedies to take the place of the employee's right to sue his employer for injuries incurred in the course of his employment. Under these acts liability is generally imposed upon the employer without regard to the question as to whether or not the employer was at fault, and payments are made as insurance compensation rather than as damages.

9. Who is Entitled to Compensation. — Any person employed by a contract of service who is under the control of the employer while at work at the machine or other device from which the injury arose is entitled to compensation. Previous physical condition is not considered in determining the amount.

10. Who is Excluded. — The workmen's compensation acts differ in the several states. The Federal act protects persons employed by the United States and workmen engaged in Interstate Commerce. While it is difficult to give a general rule, the following are excluded from the benefits in most states, and in others the compensation is optional:

a. Minors and apprentices.
b. Farm laborers.
c. Domestic servants.
d. Casual employees.
e. Independent contractors.
f. Public officers.

11. Dependents.—The law also provides that the compensation be paid to dependents in case of death. Payments may be made only to actual dependents or to partial dependents in accordance with the degree of dependency. These include widows, children, step-children, illegitimate children, adopted children, or a dependent parent. Payments cannot be made to any other classes of relatives.

12. Payments. — The compensation acts provide for payments to the injured or his dependents in case of partial incapacity, permanent incapacity, or death, in amounts depending on the earning power of the injured at the time of the accident. Maximum and minimum amounts are usually specified.

13. Insurance. — The compensation laws are rigidly enforced, and to protect themselves, employers often take out liability insurance on the life and health of each employee. Then, when an accident occurs, the insurance company assumes all liability and relieves the employer of any claims which might be made under the workmen's compensation law. This method of limiting liability is provided for in the laws of all the states. The cost of such insurance is based on the size of the payroll and the nature of the employment. It ranges from a purely nominal figure for office work to a rather high rate for the more hazardous occupations.

14. Variations. — It is impossible in a brief space to attempt an explanation of the workmen's compensation laws in the different states. In some states deductions are made for contributory negligence, and in others awards are fixed for specific injuries, and in almost every state there can be found numerous variations.

15. Sources of Information. — Copies of the compensation and liability statutes may be secured free of charge by writing to the Secretary of State of the state for which information is desired. He should be addressed at the state capital. Owing to the technical nature of the subject, however, it is always a good plan to ask an insurance adviser to explain the duties and obligations under the law.

Assignment of Wages

For a valuable consideration to me in hand paid by ....of ....the receipt whereof is hereby acknowledged, I do hereby transfer, assign and set over to the said ...., his heirs, executors, administrators, or assigns, all salary or wages, and claims for salary or wages, due or to become due from ....& Company, or from any other person or persons, firm, copartnership, company, corporation, organization or official by whom I am now or may hereafter become employed, at any time before the expiration of .... years from the date hereof.

I do hereby constitute irrevocably the said ...., his heirs, executors, administrators or assigns, my attorney, in my name to take all legal measures which may be proper or necessary for the complete recovery and employment of the claim hereby assigned, and I hereby authorize, empower and direct the said ....& Company, or any one by whom I may be employed as above, to pay the said demand and claim for wages or salary to the said ...., his executors, administrators or assigns, and hereby authorize and empower him or them to receipt for the same in my name.

Dated at ....this ....day, 19..........

16. The Fair Labor Standards Act. — In 1938 Congress enacted the Fair Labor Standards Act which set a minimum wage and maximum work week for employees engaged in interstate commerce or in the production of goods for commerce. Because of the broad interpretation by the Supreme Court of the Federal Government's constitutional power to regulate interstate commerce, this act has a widespread effect on employment. It provides that employees shall be paid not less than 25 cents per hour during the first year of the operation of the law, not less than 30 cents during the next six years, and not less than 40 cents thereafter. The maximum work week for the first year of the operation of the law is 44 hours, 42 for the second year, and 40 thereafter. If the employee works more than the maximum number of hours he must receive one and one-half times the regular rate for the excess hours. Some occupations are exempted by the Act, such as farm laborers and domestic servants, and lower rates may be prescribed for apprentices, messengers, and persons whose earning capacity is impaired by physical or mental disability.

There are also provisions in the Act restricting the employment of children. Children under eighteen years of age may not engage in hazardous occupations. Children under sixteen years may work for their parents in non-mining or non-manufacturing occupations. Children between the ages of fourteen and sixteen years may work at non-mining and non-manufacturing occupations after school hours and under conditions which will not affect their health or well-being.

The Fair Labor Standards Act is administered by the Wage and Hour Division of the United States Department of Labor at Washington, D.C. Many of the states have similar legislation affecting employment conditions among employees working in business wholly within the state.

17. The National Labor Relations Act. — The National Labor Relations Act, known as "The Wagner Act," has given employees the legal **right** to organize and bargain collectively with their employer without interference or coercion by the employer. The National Labor Relations Board enforces the Act and may, upon request of the employer or employees, hold an election to determine the union which shall act as bargaining agent. The Board may prohibit the employer from using unfair labor practices and may, after proper hearing, compel the reinstatement of a former employee discharged because of union activities. Some states have legislation patterned after the Wagner Act.

18. The Norris - La Guardia Act. — Another Federal act affecting employer-employee relationships is the Norris-La Guardia Act which restricts the power of the Federal Courts to issue injunctions in labor disputes, and prohibits them from enforcing "yellow dog" contracts. A "yellow dog" contract is one by which the employee, as a condition of his employment, agrees to withdraw from, or refrain from joining, a labor organization. Some states have similar laws affecting their own courts.

19. The Social Security Act.—The two phases of the Social Security Act that are most important to employer and employee are: (1) that which sets up a permanent system of old-age benefits, and (2) that which promotes the enactment of permanent unemployment insurance systems by the states. The old-age benefit system is administered by the Federal Government, and to support the plan, employer and employee pay an equal tax based on the size of the employee's wage, which the employer must remit to the Federal treasury. When the employee reaches 65, his monthly benefit payments begin and their amount is calculated with reference to the total tax he has paid over his years of work. These benefit provisions apply to all classes of persons within the Act, and should not be confused with old-age pensions to needy persons.

The Act attempts to induce the states to enact and administer unemployment insurance systems. The employer who has eight or more employees must pay a 3 per cent tax on his total payroll into the Federal treasury. If the state has an unemployment insurance act which meets the standards set up by Congress, the Federal Government will grant money to the state to help pay the cost of the insurance. The employer may also deduct up to 90 per cent of the Federal tax to pay the state unemployment insurance tax.

Large classes of employees such as farm laborers, domestic servants, and casual workers are excepted from both the old-age benefit and unemployment insurance plans. Other sections of the Social Security Act provide for Federal grants to the states for maternal and child welfare, for public health work, and for aid to the blind, the needy aged, and dependent children.

Equitable Remedies

1. Definitions.—A **remedy** is the legal means employed to enforce a right or redress an injury. Suppose A has purchased an automobile from B who refused to deliver it. In a court of equity A could compel B to deliver the car and this would be an **equitable remedy.** In a court of law A could recover damages for the loss he had sustained through B's refusal to deliver the automobile, and this would be a **legal remedy.**

2. The Common Remedy.—Relief in equity is often sought to compel a person to execute a contract which he has made. It quite frequently happens that a seller regrets his action after the contract has been made. The court of equity will compel him to deliver the property, provided that the law gives the purchaser no adequate remedy. When an article has a peculiar sentimental value, when it is of rare value like an heirloom, or when it is an article which cannot be easily purchased in the open market, the one party can compel the other to fulfill his contract. Ordinarily, the buyer of articles like cattle, lumber, dry goods, hardware, etc., has only the legal remedy to recover damages.

3. Equity Will Enforce Agreements or Grant Relief:—

a. When legal remedies (or damages) would be inadequate.

b. When the seller of a business agrees not to enter into competition with the buyer.
c. When an employee agrees not to disclose the trade secrets of his employer.
d. When a tenant threatens or attempts to injure the real estate of the landlord.
e. When an established patent has been infringed.
f. In many other similar cases which would be too numerous to mention here.

4. Equity Will Not Enforce Agreements or Grant Relief:—

a. When the law has an adequate remedy.
b. When the goods contracted for can be readily purchased in the open market.
c. To force a person to perform his contract to render personal services.
d. When the contract in question is one where one party agrees to lend money to the other.
e. When there is a contract to form a partnership.
f. When such agreement would be in restraint of trade, would create a monopoly, or would be illegal for any other reason.

5. Injunctions.—Relief in equity is often brought about by the means of an injunction. An **injunction** is a restraining order issued by a court of equity on petition of the injured party. If the need is great the court will immediately issue a temporary injunction which orders the injuring party to do, or not to do, certain things, and fixes the time for a hearing. At this hearing, which is fixed within a reasonable time, and which is conducted like any ordinary trial, the court decides whether the injunction will be dissolved or whether it will be made permanent. Injunctions came into especial prominence through their use against labor unions during strikes. Injunctions were issued and upheld enjoining the members of labor unions from picketing, or otherwise preventing other workers from taking their places. Recent legislation has curbed the use of injunctions against labor groups.

Exemptions

1. Definitions.—A homestead is the abode or dwelling house of a family landowner and includes a specific amount of the adjacent land, varying in the different states. Exemption laws are defined as laws for the purpose of protecting those who are unable to pay their debts without causing distress to themselves and their families.

2. General Principles.—(a) The laws in some states provide that a person can waive his exemption rights in a promissory note or other written contract. (b) The laws of other states provide that exemptions cannot be waived. In nearly all the states an exemption in wages cannot be waived. A legal homestead is generally in one piece, but it may be divided by a road and in some states may consist of several distinct pieces. (c) A homestead is exempt from all debts except taxes, although in some states it is not exempt from pre-existing liens, fines for public offenses, and similar debts. (d) A person who is the head of a family, within the legal meaning of the term, is generally entitled to homestead exemption. This right survives to the husband or the wife in case of death, or to the surviving children until they come of age. (e) In divorce cases the wife ceases to be a member of the family and thus loses her homestead right unless reserved in the decree. (f) Desertion of the husband by the wife does not destroy his homestead right but does destroy hers. (g) A homestead may be sold or mortgaged regardless of the claims of creditors.

Guaranty

1. A guaranty is a written promise that a person will perform some duty or contract, or answer for the payment of some debt, in case of the failure of another person.

2. The person who guarantees the faithfulness of another is called the guarantor.

3. The guarantee or creditor is the person to whom the pledge is made.

4. A guaranty must be in writing.

5. A guaranty, to be binding, must be for a consideration.

6. A guaranty must be accepted in order for it to become a contract, and the guarantor must have notice of its acceptance within a reasonable time.

7. A guarantor, after paying the debt, can become the legally recognized creditor

Forms of Guaranty

Guaranty on Back of a Note

Fort Scott, Kansas, Oct. 12, 19......

For value received, I hereby guarantee the payment of the within note.

JAMES GLOVER.

Guaranty for Payment of a Bill

Dayton, Ohio, Aug. 30, 19............

W. Reinke, Esq.
Dear Sir:

I hereby guarantee the payment of any bill or bills of merchandise Mr. John A. Dahlem may purchase from you, the amount of this guaranty not to exceed five hundred dollars ($500), and to expire at the end of three months from date.

CHAS. ADAMS.

Guaranty of a Debt Already Incurred

St. Louis, Mo., July 10, 19.........

Messrs. H. E. Bechtel & Co., West Salem.
Gentlemen:

In consideration of one dollar and other good and valuable considerations paid me by yourselves, the receipt of which I hereby acknowledge, I guarantee that the debt of four hundred dollars ($400) now owing to you by Ira J Ferry shall be paid at maturity.

W A. PIPER.

Husband and Wife

1. Marriage is a civil contract. Marriage licenses are required by all the states, and many restrictions have been thrown around the issuing of such licenses within recent years. Marriages between whites and Negroes, between whites and Indians, and between whites and Chinese, are forbidden in various states. Unlike other contracts, marriage cannot be terminated by the consent of both parties.

2. Contract to Marry in the Future.—Mutual promise by a man and a woman to marry at some future day constitutes a valid contract in some states.

3. A Marriage Contract.—A marriage is a civil contract, and is entered into by the consent of the parties. If a man says to a woman, "Will you marry me?" or words to that effect, and she says "Yes," or words that imply an affirmative answer, it is, by law, an agreement or promise of marriage, and both parties are legally held to carry out in good faith the promise thus made.

4. Breach of Promise.—If either party refuses to carry out the contract, he or she is guilty of breach of promise, and in some states the other party may recover damages. It is not very often that the man sues the woman, though he has an equal right to do so if she fails to make good her promise. In several states, however, suits for breach of promise are now outlawed.

5. Necessary Proof.—Generally in case of a lawsuit for breach of promise, there are no direct witnesses, as people usually become engaged without the presence of a third party. The engagement may be implied from the conduct of the party sued.

6. Implied Evidence.—In states where suit for breach of promise is recognized, a promise of marriage may be implied from circumstances such as constant visits, presents, or open declaration of the parties, their reception by the parents or friends as an engaged couple, without any objections from the party being sued.

7. Excuses for Breaking the Promise.—A refusal to marry may be justified on the ground of the bad character or conduct of the other party; poor health of either party is sometimes a good excuse, but not generally. If the woman were a widow, or a divorcee, and concealed this fact from the man, this justifies a refusal on his part to marry.

8. Time of Marriage.—When a man promises to marry a woman without stating any special time, the law may hold him guilty of breach of promise unless he is ready to fulfill his engagement within a reasonable time; five years was held in one instance to be an unreasonable time.

9. When a Promise is Not Binding.—If either party is underage, he or she is not bound by promise to marry and the law will excuse the party underage.

10. Seduction.—Seduction of a woman under promise of marriage, and subsequent refusal on the man's part to marry subjects him to damages in a civil action and often to criminal liability as well.

11. Separation.—The law allows agreements between husband and wife in which they agree to live separately. This does not in any way abolish her rights in his estate unless the contract so specifies.

12. Divorce. — Divorces are of two kinds: namely, **(a)** absolute divorces, and **(b)** judicial separation. The word as now commonly used has the former meaning. In the case of an absolute divorce the marriage is ended, and the parties become single. A judicial separation is a limited divorce in which the court gives one party the right to live separately from the other. The decree of divorce usually makes provision for the payment of alimony, for the custody and support of the children, if there are any, and for the settlement of property rights between the parties. The divorce laws of the several states vary, although most states recognize and respect the laws of the other states. It is possible, however, to be legally married in one state but considered an adulterer in another; for children to be regarded as legitimate in one state and illegitimate in another.

13. Authority of Wife Living Apart from Husband to Bind Him.—Whether or not the person who supplies a wife with necessaries has knowledge at the time of her husband's provision for her support, the presumption of a wife's authority to pledge her husband's credit is negatived by the fact of their living apart, and the tradesman who supplies her under such circumstances upon the credit of her husband, and without his express sanction or approval, does so at his own peril. In order to charge her husband with the cost of supplies furnished her he must show that they were not only of the kind usually regarded as "necessaries," but that in consequence of the inadequacy of the husband's provision, they were actually required for the wife's proper support, commensurate with his means and her station in the community.

14. Property Rights of Married Women.—One of the marked evidences of the growth of true civilization in the United States is the enactment by nearly all the states of legislative provisions for the benefit of married women. These laws vary greatly in the different states, and there are frequent changes, but all tend toward the releasing of woman from her former condition of absolute dependence upon her husband. By the old common law a married woman had few rights. She was subject to the authority of her husband, and he could rule over her. This condition has now been changed, however, and the rights of married women are recognized by every court. All property owned by the wife before marriage, or received after marriage and held as her separate property, can be sold and transferred without the consent of her husband except his rights of dower or curtesy in her real estate. If a husband fails to make provision for the support of his wife, the law will compel him to furnish her proper support if he has sufficient means.

15. General Principles Regarding the Marriage Contract.—**(a)** There must be a serious agreement or mutual assent of both parties. **(b)** A marriage may be declared void because of fraud, incompetence of one of the parties, or the fact that one of the parties is underage. **(c)** The minimum age at which marriage can legally be contracted varies from state to state. With consent of parents or guardians, the minimum age in several states is 18 for men and 16 for women, in states under common law the ages are 14 and 12, respectively. Without such consent, the minimum age is frequently 21 for men and 18 for women, although there are numerous exceptions. **(d)** A marriage is not void simply because it has been improperly performed or licensed, but the officials responsible are liable. **(e)** At common law a wife is solely responsible for her crimes unless they were committed in her husband's presence, in which case coercion on the part of the husband is presumed. In many states this law has been changed so that the husband is responsible only when he participated in the crime, unless coercion is proved. **(f)** A married man can sue for the alienation of his wife's affections. In some states the wife has a similar right. Suits for alienation of affections are now prohibited by the laws of a number of states. **(g)** Either husband or wife may act as the agent for the other party. **(h)** The husband is not responsible for the debts or wrongs of his wife unless, of course, the debts are necessary for the support of the family. **(i)** The husband must provide a home, and support and protect his wife and children. His duty to protect his family carries with it all the rights of "self-defense." **(j)** He must maintain law and order in his household, and may use force in preventing a member of his family from committing a crime. **(k)** A wife is required to care for the house and family. She cannot be forced to go into business or enter any gainful occupation. **(l)** The husband must support his wife, and she can pledge his credit for articles necessary to sustain life and maintain her social position.

Innkeeper

1. Definition.—An innkeeper is one who keeps a public house for the reception and entertainment of travelers.

2. Gaining Admission to An Inn or Hotel.—An innkeeper is required to accommodate all comers with the following exceptions which vary in different states:

(a) He may exclude anyone if he has no accommodations.

(b) He may exclude those who do not come at a suitable time or in a proper manner.

(c) He must exclude certain persons such as criminals and thieves.

(d) He may refuse admission to those he believes would disturb the peace and safety of his guests.

(e) He can expel any guest who does disturb the peace and safety of his other guests.

If he refuses to provide reasonable and proper accommodations he is liable. He need not provide any particular room. If he operates a garage or stable in connection with the inn, he is under the same obligation to receive and care for the automobiles or horses of his guests.

3. The Innkeeper's Liability.—The law fixes the liability and responsibility of an innkeeper:

(a) An innkeeper is responsible for the loss or damage to a guest's baggage committed to his care unless such loss is caused by an act of God, a public enemy, or neglect or fault of the owner of the baggage.

(b) In most states innkeepers are relieved from liability for loss by fire unless the fire is caused by the negligence of the innkeeper or his servants.

(c) An innkeeper is liable for goods of a guest if they were stolen by the innkeeper's servants, by another guest, or by an outsider. However, he is not liable if the loss was due to the negligence of the owner.

(d) The innkeeper is bound to secure honest and trustworthy employees.

(e) If two guests occupy the same room, the innkeeper can be held responsible if a theft is committed by one against the other.

4. Liens.—An innkeeper has a lien on a guest's baggage or other property left in his care, to secure the payment for the accommodations.

5. Regulations.—An innkeeper may make regulations for the observance of his guests in order to protect their property. Thus he may limit his liability somewhat by notifying the guests that he is not responsible for the loss of valuable articles unless they are deposited with him. Such regulations will bind the guest if brought to his notice.

6. Lodging and Boarding Houses.—The keepers of lodging or boarding houses do not come under the same head as innkeepers as far as the law is concerned. They are not required to accommodate all who may apply. They are not liable for refusing to accommodate all comers.

Insurance

A. Fire Insurance

1. Definition.—Fire insurance is indemnity against loss by fire. It is now generally furnished by large stock companies or by mutual companies.

2. Mutual Companies are generally established by statute and provide for the payment of losses by pro rata assessment upon the policyholders, who constitute the stockholders, and who manage the affairs of the company. Some of these mutual companies require a small premium paid in advance, which, unless unusual losses occur, is enough to pay all the losses for the year. Others simply require a small fee to pay for the expense of making the survey and issuing the policy. All of them, however, in case of loss, make an assessment pro rata upon the policyholders to pay the same. Such companies are not common in cities, but operate mostly in the rural districts.

3. Stock Insurance Companies.—The insurance business of private corporations is carried on for profit.

4. Underwriters' Association.—The stock fire insurance companies all submit complete underwriting and loss figures to the National Board of Underwriters, which, in addition to acting as a clearing house and as statisticians for such information, also supervises common services to the public such as fire protection, information, and grading. There are also local agents' boards and state associations operating to promote uniformity of service and contract. Fire insurance rates are usually established by rating bureaus which are administered and paid for by a majority of companies doing business in the state or locality. Rates are usually adhered to by all agents either by common agreement or as directed by state law. Specific rates are published for mercantile houses, warehouses, business and manufacturing buildings. Rates by classes are used for dwellings, small apartment houses, farms, and similar property.

5. The Purpose of Fire Insurance. — Fire insurance is a means of distributing the cost of damages caused by fire. A fund is supplied by the payment of premiums, from which the insurance company agrees to pay the loss in case of fire.

6. Classification.—In order that each person thus protected from loss may contribute the proper amount to this fund, a system of classification has been worked out, whereby the premium rate has been established. This classification is based on the probability of fire. The National Board of Fire Underwriters, having the reports of the various insurance companies, knows the probable number of fires and the value of the property involved. Statistics show that a certain percentage of residences, barns, schools, merchandise, etc., will be burned each year. Also that buildings of one type of construction are more likely to burn than those of some other type of construction. Population, water pressure, fire department, building contents, and many other elements are taken into consideration by the rating bureau in determining the rate each person must pay for insurance on his property.

7. Reducing the Rate.—When you pay your premium, you can judge, by the rate you pay, what the experience of the insurance companies has been with regard to similar property, with similar conditions. If the rate is high, find out just what factors make it high. Then you may be able to make such changes or take such precautions that your rate will be reduced.

8. Who Has An Insurable Interest.—In order to be indemnified against loss the insured must have an interest in the property or goods insured, both at the time the insurance is issued and at the time of the loss. Thus the following may be insured:

a. A bailee (one who receives goods of another to hold).
b. A consignee (one to whom property is consigned or shipped).
c. A mortgagee (one who holds a mortgage on real or personal property).
d. An assignee (one to whom property is assigned).
e. A warehouseman.
f. An executor or an administrator.
g. A landlord.
h. A tenant.
i. The holder of a lien on property.
j. An agent who has the custody or care of the principal's property.

All these as well as many others, have what is called an insurable interest. If all insurable interests in a property are not noted on the policy at the time of loss, the company is not liable to the party having an interest which is not so noted.

9. An Insurance Policy is a Contract between the insurance company and the insured, by which the first party insures the property of the second party against loss by fire. The consideration, or premium, is usually paid when the policy is issued, although it may be charged on account or paid by check or note. The contract becomes binding and valid when the policy is properly executed. Actual delivery of the policy to the insured is not necessary. Thus if a loss occurs after the duly executed policy is in the hands of the insurance company's agent, but before it has been delivered to the insured, the company must pay the loss. A preliminary contract is sometimes made, in which case the risk begins immediately upon the signing, even though such contract be dated several days before the policy is actually issued. Most local agents have authority to protect an applicant for insurance against loss for a period of 5 to 30 days preceding acceptance of the risk by the company.

10. Cancellation.—A fire insurance contract, like any other contract, may be canceled by mutual agreement, but unless otherwise stated in the policy the company cannot cancel the contract without the consent of the policyholder.

11. General Principles.—

a. The property insured, and the terms of the contract, must be clearly defined.
b. If the written part of the policy contradicts the printed sections, the written part will hold.
c. Clerical or typographical errors may usually be corrected when discovered.
d. The insurance on the building covers those things which have become a part of it, but does not include fixtures or surrounding sheds or buildings.
e. Misrepresentation or fraud on the part of the insured renders the insurance policy null and void.
f. If a policyholder secures additional fire insurance on his property without the consent of the insurance company, his former policy becomes void. Most policies today, however, consent to the writing of additional insurance on the property by other companies and in case of loss the liability is pro-rated.
g. In addition to the actual fire loss most policies cover damage by water used to put out the fire, damage to goods while being removed to avoid fire, and damage from an explosion caused by fire.
h. An insurance company is not responsible for goods stolen while they are being removed during a fire.
i. An ordinary policy of insurance does not usually insure against lightning, but lightning clauses will be attached to nearly all policies if requested at the time of issue.
j. The insurance company is not relieved from liability by the carelessness of the policy-

holder, yet the insured is bound to take reasonable care to prevent fire.

k. In a total loss the insurance company is liable for the full value of the property, provided that this value does not exceed the amount of the insurance. In a partial loss the company is liable only for the actual loss.

l. In an open policy the amount of the insurer's liability is not fixed until after the loss. In a valued policy the maximum liability for a total loss is fixed.

m. In order to calculate the approximate loss on merchandise in case of fire, the value of the following items should be ascertained: the most recent inventory; invoices for goods bought subsequent to that inventory; freight and dray bills on same; credit memorandums for merchandise returned; production department payrolls; appreciation in value of goods since purchase. These items should be added together and from their sum should be subtracted the sum of the following items: outgoing charges, representing goods sold since the last inventory; depreciation in value of goods since purchase; salvage, or market value of goods not destroyed. The remainder gives the approximate value of goods destroyed, for which insurance compensation can be obtained.

B. Life Insurance

12. Definition. — Life insurance is a contract whereby the insurer agrees, on the payment of a fixed premium, to pay a certain sum of money to the insured when he reaches a certain age, or to his beneficiaries at his death. Thus it is possible for a man to insure his productive ability for the amount of money it would be worth to him if he were to survive his expected time. (See table of expectancy below.)

American Experience Table of Mortality

13.—The approximate number of years the average person may expect to live at different ages is shown in the following table:

Age years	Expectation of Life years	Age years	Expectation of Life years
10	48.7	27	37.4
11	48.0	28	36.7
12	47.4	29	36.0
13	46.8	30	35.3
14	46.1	31	34.6
15	45.5	32	33.9
16	44.8	33	33.2
17	44.1	34	32.5
18	43.5	35	31.7
19	42.8	36	31.0
20	42.2	37	30.3
21	41.5	38	29.6
22	40.8	39	28.9
23	40.1	40	28.1
24	39.4	41	27.4
25	38.8	42	26.7
26	38.1	43	26.0
44	25.2	70	8.4
45	24.5	71	8.0
46	23.8	72	7.5
47	23.0	73	7.1
48	22.3	74	6.6
49	21.6	75	6.2
50	20.9	76	5.8
51	20.2	77	5.4
52	19.4	78	5.1
53	18.7	79	4.7
54	18.0	80	4.3
55	17.4	81	4.0
56	16.7	82	3.7
57	16.0	83	3.3
58	15.3	84	3.0
59	14.7	85	2.7
60	14.1	86	2.4
61	13.4	87	2.1
62	12.8	88	1.9
63	12.2	89	1.6
64	11.6	90	1.4
65	11.1	91	1.1
66	10.5	92	.9
67	10.0	93	.8
68	9.4	94	.6
69	8.9	95	.5

14. Applications.—Nearly all companies require applications for life insurance to be in writing, and they are usually accompanied by the report of a medical examination made by the local medical examiner of the company. These applications are forwarded to the home office, and if they pass the head medical examiner the policy is issued to the insured and the application is made a part of the policy. Any false statement contained therein which is material to the risk will vitiate the policy, and applicants for insurance should be careful to see that all questions are fully and truthfully answered. The moral hazard involved is also carefully considered by the insuring company. Most life insurance policies provide that the insurance shall not be in force until the first premium is paid, and most policies are now incontestable after the payment of a certain number of premiums. By the laws of all states, in case default is made in the payment of premium after a certain number of full premiums have been paid, the policyholder may have the option to select any one of the following nonforfeiture provisions:

a. Cash surrender value.

b. Reduced paid-up insurance.

c. Term insurance for the full face amount.

15. The Policy.—The usual clauses contained in life insurance policies are these: That the insurance ceases unless the premiums are promptly paid; that the company shall be exempt if, within two years after the issuance of the policy, the insured commits suicide whether sane or insane, or if death shall come by the hands of justice for a violation of law; that agents are not authorized to alter or discharge any part of the contract; that assignments of the policy shall not take effect until notice thereof shall be received by the company at its home office; that after two years the policy will be incontestable except for fraud or non-payment of premium. All policies also provide for a 30 or 31 day period of grace after the due date for payment of premiums.

16. Insurable Interest.—In order to be valid an insurance policy must have as its beneficiary any person who would suffer loss, financial or otherwise, through the death of a second person, and who has a so-called insurable interest in the life of that second person. Companies hesitate to approve applications for life insurance where the named beneficiary has no such interest. The relationship of uncle or aunt and nephew or niece, or that of cousins is generally not sufficient.

17. Kinds of Policies.—There are many kinds of life insurance policies. Among the more common are the following:

a. **Ordinary Life Policy** in which premiums are paid during life and in which the face value of the policy is payable at death. This is the simplest and lowest-premium form of life insurance.
b. **Limited Payment Plan.**—The face value of the policy is payable only at death, and premiums are payable only for a limited period of years, or until death if it occurs within that period.
c. **Endowment Policy.**—The insurance company agrees to pay a fixed sum at the end of a fixed term of years, or at death, if it occur before the expiration of the term, provided a fixed premium is paid during the entire term.
d. **Convertible Term Policy** insures against death for a limited term of years, and may be converted into any other form of insurance, without medical examination, within a stated period.
e. **Income Agreements** may be issued on any of the other plans, with a provision that the face value of the policy is to be paid in monthly installments instead of in a lump sum.

18. General Principles:

a. Unless forbidden by statute, a life insurance policy may be assigned to one having an insurable interest, or to a person without such an interest, provided that the assignment is made in good faith. An assignment is often made for the benefit of creditors, or as security for the payment of a debt.
b. A contract for insurance does not take effect until it has been approved by the company, and the insured has paid the first premium.
c. A general agent can bind his principal even against the express terms of the policy provided that the insured was not negligent in failing to advise himself concerning the terms.
d. A life insurance contract may be void on account of a mistake in issuing it, on account of violation of statute, on account of fraud by either party, or if the policy is contrary to public policy.
e. Words or figures written or printed on the margin or on the back of the policy, or on a slip attached to the policy, must be considered as part of the agreement.
f. The payment of premiums to an agent will bind the company, unless the insured has received notice to the contrary.
g. A policy may be canceled by mutual agreement and the insured is then entitled to the surrender value of the policy or any other non-forfeiture option contained therein.

C. Other Forms of Insurance

19. Accident Insurance may be secured against all kinds of accidents. Upon payment of small premiums, policies may be had insuring against accident from one day to ten years, for any reasonable amount. The rates generally depend upon the occupation of the insured.

20. Marine Insurance. — Marine insurance is governed largely by the same rules that control fire insurance. This form of insurance may include all casualties resulting from unusual or violent actions of the elements, foundering at sea, grounding, collision, fire, perils of war, rests and restraints, jettison, and any other perils, losses, or misfortunes of the sea.

21. Fraternal Insurance.—This is one of the oldest forms of insurance, originating with the ancient secret societies. Originally the societies assumed an obligation to pay sick and death benefits to their members. Today there are numerous societies that issue standard life insurance policies, with a fixed premium rate and a limited amount of insurance payable at death.

22. Industrial Insurance.—Many large business organizations issue this form of insurance for the benefit of their employees. The amounts are usually small and the weekly or monthly payments are deducted from the wages of the insured.

23. Other Kinds of Insurance include employers' liability, public liability, tornado, explosion, automobile, burglary, fraud, insolvency, and loss through bad debts. Almost every kind of risk imaginable may be covered by insurance.

Assignment of Policy of Insurance

Know all men by these presents, that I, ... of the village of ...., for and in consideration of ...., to me in hand paid by .... of the same place, the receipt whereof is hereby acknowledged, have sold, assigned, transferred, and set over, and by these presents do sell, assign, transfer, and set over, unto the said .... the policy of insurance known as policy No. ....of the .... Insurance Company, and all sum and sums of money, interest, benefit, and advantage whatsoever, now due, or hereafter to arise, or to be had or made by virtue thereof, to have and to hold the same unto the said ....and his assigns forever.

In witness whereof, I have hereto affixed my hand this 20th day of June, 19..........

(Acknowledgment.) (Name)

International Law

1. Definitions.—International law is the body of rules designed to govern the conduct of nations toward one another. It includes customs and usages that have grown up among nations and have become generally accepted by them; and the enactments contained in treaties and conventions. International law is intended to do for nations what the domestic law does for individuals.

2. Treaties. — Much international law is embodied in treaties. A treaty is an agreement between two or more nations to adjust differences or to govern future conduct. Treaties are sometimes made for a limited period of years, but a treaty made by one administration is binding upon the following administration.

3. Representatives. — Ambassadors are the authorized diplomatic representatives of nations. They are immune from civil or criminal liability, but may be tried for crime by their home governments. A consul is a commercial representative sent by one nation to another to aid in the establishment and maintenance of trade relations between the nations, and to look after the interests of the citizens or subjects of his country. He is personally liable for his actions.

4. General Principles. There are certain well established principles of international law, which provide as follows:

a. One nation cannot interfere with the internal affairs of another.

b. Crimes committed on the high seas are under the jurisdiction of the nation under whose flag the ship sails.

c. The property of alien enemies is subject to confiscation.

d. A neutral country must be fair and impartial in its relations with warring nations.

e. It is a violation of international law for a warring nation to fight on, or cross the territory of, a neutral power.

f. It is also a violation of international law to carry the necessary finished goods or materials of warfare to a combatant nation.

g. A fugitive criminal cannot be brought back from another nation unless the terms of the treaty between the two nations so provide.

h. Confiscation is the penalty for attempting to violate a blockade in time of war.

5. Passports. — A passport is a document granted by the government to a citizen, enabling him to travel to other countries. (See PASSPORTS.)

Lease

1. Definitions.—The phrase **landlord and tenant** is used to denote the relationship which exists by virtue of a contract expressed or implied between two or more persons for the possession or occupancy of lands or tenements either for a definite period or at will. The **landlord** or **lessor** is the person who lets the land or premises. The **tenant** or **lessee** is the one who occupies the land or premises. The **lease** is the contract between the two.

2. Leases Should be in Writing.—Leases which are to run for more than a year or which are not to be performed within a year must be in writing, or they are invalid. Leases for a year or less and which can be performed within a year are valid even if not in writing. To avoid misunderstandings, disputes, and possible litigation it is always best, however, that the lease be in writing and signed by both parties, regardless of the length of the term.

3. Leases for life are those which are terminated by death either of the lessee or of some other person living at the date of the lease. Unless such leases contain covenants to the contrary, the life tenant or the lessee is required to pay all taxes on the premises and keep the same in repair.

4. Leases for Years.—The lessor, unless it is otherwise expressly provided in the lease, is under obligation to see that his tenant's possession is not disturbed by any title paramount to the landlord's. He is not required to make repairs unless he agrees to do so in the lease, nor is there an implied contract on his part that the premises are fit for the purpose for which they are let. He must pay all the taxes regularly levied and assessed against said premises and keep the buildings on said premises insured at his own expense if he desires to carry insurance.

5. Implied Agreement by Tenant. — Where there is no agreement to the contrary, the tenant is bound to take possession of the premises, take ordinary care of the same, keep them in a tenantable condition, and make repairs made necessary by his negligence, but he need not make repairs made necessary by ordinary wear and tear or inevitable accident.

If the premises leased be a farm, he is also required to cultivate the same in the manner required of good husbandry. He must not commit waste, alter buildings or fences, and must surrender up the premises at the end of his term in as good condition as when entered upon originally, ordinary wear and tear excepted. He is not required to pay taxes or keep buildings insured, but must pay the stipulated rent at the time it becomes due by the terms of his lease. If no time is specified in his lease, then the rent is due at the end of the term. He may sublet the premises or assign the lease unless it contains provisions to the contrary.

If he places permanent improvements upon the premises which are so attached to the buildings or land that they cannot be removed without injury to the buildings or land, he has no right to remove the same unless his lease so provides. He may remove trade fixtures, provided they are removed from the premises before the expiration of his lease.

6. Common Provisions of a Lease.—Most leases provide for the yielding up of the possession of the premises at the end of the term without notice, in as good condition as when they were entered upon by the lessee, loss by fire, inevitable accident, and ordinary wear expected. There is frequently a provision against subletting or assigning the lease, and a clause stating that in case of non-payment of rent, or failure to perform any of the covenants of the lease, the lessor shall have the right to terminate the lease and recover possession of the premises.

Farm leases usually provide, in addition to the

stipulations mentioned above, that the tenant shall keep the fruit and ornamental trees, vines, and shrubbery free from injury by stock, plowing, or otherwise; that the lessee will draw out the manure and spread it on the premises; that no straw shall be sold or removed from the premises during the term or at its termination; that the tenant will keep the buildings and fences in repair, the landlord to furnish necessary material; that the landlord may do fall plowing on the stubble ground after the grain has been removed therefrom, and that he may enter for the purpose of making repairs, viewing the premises, and sowing timothy seed. Sometimes the landlord covenants to make all new fences, to furnish water, and to carry out other provisions which may be inserted in the lease.

7. Termination of Lease. — Under the strict rules of the common law the landlord might terminate the lease for non-payment of rent, but in order to do so it was necessary for him to go upon the premises and make a demand for the exact amount of rent due upon the very day that the rent came due, and a failure to do this waived the right to obtain forfeiture. This strict rule of the common law has been modified in nearly all the states so that it is no longer necessary to make a demand for the rent on the day the rent comes due. Instead of this most of the states provide that before the landlord shall declare a forfeiture a demand in writing, for the amount of rent due, shall be served upon the tenant, and he be notified that in case he fails to pay the rent within a fixed time, generally five or ten days, the landlord will elect to terminate his lease. In such cases the tenant has until the end of the last day fixed in the notice to pay the rent and prevent the forfeiture. The statutes of the various states also provide that in case of breaches of other agreements contained in the lease, notice of such breaches and intention of the landlord to terminate the lease shall be served upon the tenant.

8. Termination of Tenancy from Year to Year and Month to Month.—Where a tenant has a lease for a year, and at the end of his term remains in possession of the property without a new agreement, the law construes this to be a leasing from year to year, and such tenancy at common law could be terminated only by either party's giving the other six months' notice prior to the end of any year. This notice has been changed by a statute in Illinois to sixty days prior to the end of any year, and a shorter time has been fixed in other states. A tenant who has a lease on property for one or more months and who remains on the property after the termination of his lease, is termed a tenant from month to month, and such tenancy can be terminated only by either party's giving the other party thirty days' notice.

9. Demand.—It is a general rule, subject to few exceptions, that in order to get possession of property where the original occupancy by the tenant was lawful, either a notice to quit or a demand for possession is necessary on the part of the owner before commencing proceedings to get possession.

10. Securing Possession. — When a lease has been terminated either by its term or by notice, and the landlord is entitled to possession, the most common method of recovering possession is to commence an action of forcible entry and detainer against the tenant for the possession of the premises. This may be done by filing a complaint before a justice of the peace and having a summons issued. If the possession of the tenant was lawful at the time of its beginning, the landlord has no right to dispossess him forcibly, and if he does so it is at his peril. Taking possession by force may subject the landlord to an action for damages. Leases sometimes contain clauses stating that where a forfeiture has taken place the landlord shall have the right to take possession of the premises leased, by force if necessary. Such provisions, however, cannot be enforced and do not justify the landlord in using force. The only legal course for the landlord is to begin an action, obtain a judgment for possession, and have the constable or sheriff put him in legal possession.

11. Distress for Rent.—An effective method of collecting rent is by distress warrant. This is a warrant issued by the landlord to some third person, authorizing and empowering such third person to levy said warrant upon any personal property of the tenant for the satisfaction of the rent. A very important advantage of this remedy is that it enables the landlord to seize the personal property of the tenant without delay. This process is of very ancient origin. As used here the term personal property means property other than real estate. The statutes of most of the states provide for this remedy, and the mode of procedure is generally prescribed by the statute. In general, it is the duty of the officer, as soon as the levy is made, to file with a justice of the peace or with the clerk of the court an inventory of the property levied upon, together with a copy of his warrant, and usually a summons is issued.

12. Time of Levy.—Under the common law the tenant had all of the day on which the rent came due to make payment, and a distress warrant could not be levied until the day after the rent came due. In some states, however, in case the tenant sells or attempts to dispose of the crop grown upon the premises, thereby endangering the landlord's lien for his rent, a distress warrant may be levied before the rent comes due. The person making the levy should be careful not to levy on more property than is necessary in order to satisfy the rent due, otherwise he may be liable to the tenant for making an excessive levy.

13. Landlord's Lien.—Under the common law the landlord had no lien upon the property of the tenant until a distress warrant was actually levied upon the property of the tenant. Most of the states, however, now provide that the landlord shall have a lien upon all the crops grown upon the leased premises until the rent for the year in which said crop was grown has been paid, and this lien is ahead of all other liens, even though another legal claim may have been levied upon such crops. The landlord's lien is paramount until the rent is satisfied. The usual method of enforcing the lien of the landlord is by distress warrant.

The Courts Have Held:—

(a) Unless the tenant makes a specific agreement relieving himself, he is liable for the rent of the building on the land leased, after the building has burned down, just as if he were still occupying it.

(b) When the terms of a lease are in doubt, the courts endeavor to ascertain the intention of the parties from the lease itself and from the circumstances under which it was made.

(c) The term of a lease expiring on a specified day continues through the whole of that day.

(d) When the tenant continues to occupy the premises without the consent of the landlord after the expiration of the lease, the landlord may treat him either as a trespasser or as a tenant for another term.

(e) A lease may be made to take effect at some future date.

(f) A lease must clearly define the property, but no special form or wording is necessary.

(g) Valid leases may be made by minors, married women, corporations, executors, administrators, or trustees, subject to certain restrictions. However, there is always uncertainty in a contract with a minor.

(h) A lease for an unlawful purpose is generally held to be void.

(i) As in other contracts, if the printed and the written parts of a lease do not agree, the written part will usually hold.

(j) The lease of a private house is not a warranty that it is fit to be occupied.

(k) When a landlord agrees to keep the building in repair and fails to do so, the tenant's remedy is to sue for damages. He may not continue to occupy the premises and refuse to pay rent.

(l) When a tenant is evicted he is excused from the payment of rent for any time after his eviction. Any act by the landlord which renders the property unfit for, or impossible of, occupancy is an eviction.

(m) If land is rented on shares the relation of landlord and tenant usually exists even if the rent is to be paid in produce instead of cash.

(n) The landlord is liable for injuries caused by defective stairways, open elevator shafts, or other dangerous conditions which exist in the parts of a rented building which are under his control.

Short Form of Lease

THIS INDENTURE, made this sixth day of April, 19......, between JOHN PARKS, as lessor, and J. B. MOULTON, as lessee, WITNESSETH: That the lessor has this day leased to the lessee the premises known as number 142 Archer Street, in the City of Chicago and State of Illinois, to be occupied by the lessee as a residence (or insert any other purpose for which building is leased) only, for and during the term commencing on the first day of May, 19......, and ending on the thirtieth day of April, 19......, upon the terms and conditions hereinafter set forth; and in consideration of said demise and the covenants and agreements hereinafter set forth, it is covenanted and agreed as follows:

FIRST.—The lessee shall pay to the lessor at the office of the lessor as rent for said leased premises for said term the sum of Six Hundred Dollars ($600.00) payable in advance in equal monthly installments upon the first day of each and every month during the term hereof.

SECOND.—The lessee has examined said premises prior to and as a condition precedent to his acceptance and the execution hereof and is satisfied with the physical condition thereof, and the lessee's taking possession thereof shall be conclusive evidence of the lessee's receipt thereof in good order and repair, except as otherwise specified herein, and the lessee agrees to keep said premises and the appurtenances thereto in a clean, sightly, and healthy condition and in good repair, and to yield back said premises to the lessor upon the termination of this lease, whether such termination shall occur by expiration of the term hereof or in any other manner whatever, in the same condition of cleanliness, sightliness and repair as at the date of the execution hereof, loss by fire or other casualty, and ordinary wear and tear excepted.

THIRD.—The lessee agrees to pay the water tax charged against said premises when due.

FOURTH.—The lessee agrees to allow the lessor free access to the leased premises for the purpose of examining or exhibiting the same, or making any needful repairs or alterations of said premises which the lessor may see fit to make: also to allow to be placed upon said premises at all times during the term hereof "For Sale" and "To Rent" signs and not to interfere with the same.

FIFTH.—The lessee agrees not to assign this lease, nor sublet said leased premises, or any part thereof, without the written consent of the lessor endorsed hereon.

SIXTH.—In case said leased premises shall be vacated during said term the lessor may take immediate possession thereof for the remainder of the term and in his discretion relet the same and apply the proceeds upon this lease, the lessee to remain liable for the unpaid balance of the rent.

SEVENTH.—The failure of the lessee to perform the foregoing covenants, or any of them, shall constitute a forfeiture of all of the lessee's rights under this lease and the further occupancy by the lessee of said leased premises after such forfeiture shall be deemed and taken as a forcible detainer of such premises by the lessee, and the lessor may, without notice, re-enter and take possession thereof, with or without force, and with or without legal process, evict and dispossess the lessee from and of said leased premises.

EIGHTH.—The foregoing covenants, and the terms and conditions of this lease, shall inure to the benefit of and be binding upon the respective heirs, devisees, personal representatives, successors, and assigns of the parties hereto, except as herein otherwise provided.

Witness the hands and seals of the parties hereto, the day and the year first above written.

JOHN PARKS (SEAL)

....
Lessor

J. B. MOULTON (SEAL)

....
Lessee

Legal Remedies

1. Definition. — As we have already seen, a **remedy** is a legal means employed to enforce a right or redress an injury. For example, suppose A and B enter into a binding contract for the purchase and sale of land. If A, the seller, refuses to live up to his contract, B can sue A for the damages he sustained through A's refusal to sell the land. This would be a **legal remedy.** In a court of equity B could compel A to sell him the land and that would be an **equitable remedy.**

2. Steps Necessary to Secure a Legal Remedy.—When one party to a contract has a legal cause of action against the other, he brings suit as follows:

1. B files a complaint against A, stating the agreement and giving the facts of A's failure to fulfill his contract, and the loss resulting to B from such violation of contract.
2. A is summoned to appear in court to answer the charge and the court is asked to render judgment against A for the damage resulting from A's refusal to fulfill the contract, and also for the costs.
3. The case is then tried, and if judgment is rendered against A, the court empowers the sheriff to levy on any property A may have above statutory exemptions, sell it, and turn the proceeds over to B for the damages awarded, returning any surplus to A.

3. Various Kinds of Actions. — The common-law forms of action have been abolished in most states, but similar actions are allowed by the codes which have supplanted the common-law forms of action. The following is a list of actions, for the most part designated and defined as they were at common law:

(a) **Assumpsit** is the action used for the breaking of an agreement or contract, either oral or written, but not under seal.

(b) **Complaint** is the general name used in many states for any legal action.

(c) **Covenant** is the form of action used to secure a legal remedy for the breaking of a contract under seal.

(d) **Ejectment** is a form of action to determine the title to land and right of possession.

(e) **Habeas Corpus** is an action or writ used to recover a person's liberty from illegal restraint.

(f) **Libel** is an action brought to collect damages for any malicious writing tending to injure the business or reputation of the plaintiff.

(g) **Mandamus** is an action to compel someone to do some specific thing pertaining to his office or duty.

(h) **Quo warranto** is a writ used to recover an office or a franchise from the person or corporation in possession of it.

(i) **Replevin** is a form of action for the recovery of the possession of specific personal property.

(j) **Slander** is an action to collect damages for malicious defamation by word of mouth.

(k) **Tort** is an action to recover damages for a private or civil wrong or injury arising independent of any contract.

(l) **Trespass on the case** is an action to recover damages for an indirect injury.

(m) **Trover** is an action to recover damages from one who has, without right, converted to his own use the goods of another.

License

1. Definitions.—A license is a right or permission granted by competent authority to a person, giving him the right to do something which otherwise he would not have the right to do. The **licensor** is the one who grants the license. The **licensee** is the one to whom the license is issued.

2. Kinds of Licenses.—Licenses are of almost infinite variety and are issued not only by the Federal government, but by states, counties, cities, towns, and villages. They may be issued to manufacturers or dealers in certain articles, such as tobacco or liquor, to proprietors of amusement places, peddlers, transportation companies, chauffeurs, automobile owners, itinerant merchants, and cab drivers. Such licenses are issued under what is known as the police power of the state.

3. Illegal Licenses.—Cities sometimes require the payment of a local license by salesmen or canvassers who are taking orders for goods to be shipped from another state at some future time. The supreme court has held such a license requirement as in restraint of interstate commerce, and therefore, illegal.

4. Marriage Licenses.—All states require a marriage license. The person who performs the ceremony is required by law to note the fact of the marriage on the face of the license, and to return it to the county recorder for record.

Lien

1. A Lien is a legal claim upon property for the payment of a debt. It is the right to hold possession of property until some claim against the owner has been satisfied.

2. Possession is always necessary to create a lien, except in case of mortgages and judgments and statutory liens such as mechanic's liens. The lien simply permits the holding of the property in question until the debt is satisfied. The property cannot be sold without the consent of the owner, except by order of the court.

3. Law.—The existence of a lien does not prevent the party entitled to it from collecting the debt or claim by taking it into court.

4. Parties Entitled to Liens. — Warehousemen, carpenters, tailors, dyers, millers, printers, etc., or any persons who perform labor or advance money on property or goods of another, usually have a lien on that property or those goods until all charges are paid.

5. Hotel Keepers have a lien on the baggage of the guests whom they have accommodated.

6. Common Carriers have a lien on goods carried for transportation charges.

7. Agents have a lien on goods of their principals for money advanced.

8. How to Hold the Lien.—Do not give up possession of the property until the debt is paid.

9. Real Property.—If the debt is on a house, barn or other real property, file a lien on the whole property, and have it recorded in the county recorder's office. The claim then partakes of the nature of a mortgage.

10. Mechanic's Lien.—Nearly all the states permit liens designed to protect certain classes of individuals, who furnish material and labor for the erection, construction, repair, and improvement of buildings. The method of securing these liens and enforcing them varies so widely in the different states that it is almost impossible to give such a statement as will cover all states. The courts have construed such laws very strictly, and in order to entitle a person to such lien the provisions of the law granting the same must be strictly complied with. Individuals desiring to avail themselves of these statutes should consult a lawyer and have him prepare the necessary papers. The following form is the one commonly in use in the State of Illinois:

Form of Mechanic's Lien

STATE OF ILLINOIS)
) SS.
COUNTY OF DU PAGE)

IN THE OFFICE OF THE CLERK
OF THE
CIRCUIT COURT, DU PAGE COUNTY, ILLINOIS

Julius Warren)
vs.) Claim for Lien
Martin Smith)

The Claimant, JULIUS WARREN, of the City of Wheaton, County of Du Page, State of Illinois, hereby files a Claim for Lien against Martin Smith of Du Page County, Illinois, and states:

That on the first day of October, 19........., said Martin Smith was the owner of the following described land, to wit: Lot two (2) in Block three (3) of the original town of Hinsdale, in the County of Du Page and State of Illinois.

That on the first day of October, 19......, the Claimant made a contract with said owner to furnish labor and materials for the building to be erected on said land for the sum of Seven Hundred Fifty Dollars ($750.00), and on the 23rd day of October, 19......, completed all work required to be done by said contract.

That said owner is entitled to credits on account thereof totaling $250.00, leaving due, unpaid and owing to the Claimant on account thereof, after allowing all credits, the balance of Five Hundred Dollars ($500.00), for which, with interest, the Claimant claims a lien on said land and improvements.

Julius Warren

STATE OF ILLINOIS)
) SS.
COUNTY OF DU PAGE)

Julius Warren, being first duly sworn, on oath deposes and says, That he is the above named Claimant, that he has read the foregoing Claim for Lien, knows the contents thereof, and that all the statements therein contained are true.

Julius Warren

Subscribed and sworn to before me
this 1st day of November, 19..........

GEORGE JOHNSON

....
Notary Public

(Seal)

Mortgage

1. Definition.—A mortgage is a conveyance of property, either real or personal, given to secure the payment of a debt. When the debt is paid the mortgage becomes void and is released. The person who mortgages his property is called the **mortgagor.** The person to whom the mortgage is given is the **mortgagee.**

2. Requirements. — All real estate mortgages must be in writing, and under seal unless the seal has been abolished by statute. The instrument must clearly state the amount of the debt and the day on which it falls due. The property must be clearly described. The mortgage must then be acknowledged before the proper public official and properly recorded in the county records. The mortgagor usually gives a bond or note as evidence of the indebtedness, stating on its face that it is secured by a mortgage of the same date.

3. Possession of the Property generally remains with the mortgagor. The mortgagor also receives all rents and profits from the property, and pays all taxes and other expenses.

4. Improvements to the Property.—If a mortgagor erects buildings on mortgaged land and the mortgage is foreclosed, the mortgagee in taking possession gets all these additions. If the mortgagee erects buildings and the mortgagor thereafter redeems his land, he gets the buildings without paying for them.

5. Assignment. — A mortgagee can transfer, sell, or assign his mortgage at any time regardless of the wishes of the mortgagor. On the other hand, if the mortgagor wishes to sell his real estate he must sell subject to the mortgage. In other words, he can do nothing to invalidate the mortgagee's security.

6. Insurance. — The property may be insured by both parties. In case of loss by fire the holder of the mortgage can collect the insurance which he had on the property and can also proceed to collect the debt from the mortgagor. Practically all mortgages now contain provisions requiring the mortgagor to keep the property properly insured. The insurance policy contains a clause showing the name of the mortgagee or trustee and providing for his protection in case of loss by fire; and the policy itself is usually held by the mortgagee.

7. Foreclosure.—A foreclosure is a legal proceeding to sell the property mortgaged to satisfy the debt. If the property is sold to satisfy the debt, the mortgagor has a right to purchase it. The following steps are necessary for a foreclosure:

(a) Application to a court.
(b) A hearing by the court.
(c) Referring to a master in chancery or a referee.
(d) Advertising the property.
(e) Public sale to the highest bidder.
(f) Deeding the property to the purchaser.
(g) Paying the money due to the mortgagee.
(h) Returning any surplus to the mortgagor.

8. Redemption.—Formerly, a mortgagor could **redeem his land only before or when the debt**

became due, but further time is now given. This right to redeem is called a right in equity to redeem, or an equity of redemption. The redemption period varies in different states according to statutes. This right to redeem is considered of so much importance that no party is permitted to lose it even by his own agreement. Even though the mortgagor agrees in the most positive terms to forfeit his equity of redemption, the law disregards such agreement and gives the debtor full time to redeem his property.

9. General Principles:—

a. A mortgage may be made to cover future advances.

b. As the county records are public and may be examined by anyone, the injured party alone is responsible if he buys, or lends money on, a piece of property without first making certain that there are no encumbrances on it.

c. The law assumes that the mortgage contract covers all the agreements concerning the payment of the debt and the return of the property. The courts, therefore, ignore other agreements made at the same time. Later agreements, however, will hold if based on valid consideration.

d. Several mortgages may be made on the same piece of real estate. The one recorded first has the first lien.

e. A creditor cannot compel payment of the mortgage before it is due. Neither can the debtor compel the creditor to accept the payment before it is due.

f. If after a foreclosure there is any deficit due the mortgagee, the mortgagor is still liable. (See CHATTEL MORTGAGE.)

g. A trust deed serves the same purpose as a real estate mortgage but conveys the property to a third party as trustee to hold title for the mortgagee, instead of conveying title direct to the mortgagee himself.

Assignment of Mortgage by Endorsement

KNOW ALL MEN BY THESE PRESENTS, That I, Henry Betzoid, the within named Mortgagee, for a consideration of eight hundred dollars ($800.00), hereby sell, assign, transfer, and set over unto E. B. Newman, his heirs and assigns, the within named instrument of mortgage, and all the real estate, with appurtenances therein mentioned and described, and the promissory note, debts, and claims thereby secured, to have and to hold the same forever, subject to the conditions therein contained.

In witness whereof the party of the first part has hereunto set his hand and seal this third day of March, in the year of our Lord nineteen hundred and ....

Sealed and delivered in the presence of

E. E. Hawthorne

(Most states no longer require this attestation.)

HENRY BETZOID. (Seal)

Form of Release

KNOW ALL MEN BY THESE PRESENTS, That I, James Y. Scammon, of the County of Cook, and State of Illinois, for and in consideration of one dollar, to me in hand paid, and for other good and valuable considerations, the receipt whereof is hereby confessed, do hereby grant, bargain, remise, convey, release, and quitclaim unto Samuel P. Smith and Sarah E. Smith, of the County of Du Page and State of Illinois, all the right, title, interest, claim, or demand whatsoever I may have acquired in, through or by a certain indenture or mortgage deed, bearing date the first day of January, A. D. 19......, and recorded in the recorder's office of Du Page County, Illinois, in book 25 of mortgages, page 100, in and to the premises situated in the .... of ...., in said county of .... and in said mortgage deed described as follows, to wit: (description) and which said deed was made to secure two certain promissory notes, bearing even date with said deed, for the sum of twenty-five hundred dollars.

Witness my hand and seal this 28th day of February, A. D. 19.......

JAMES Y. SCAMMON. (Seal)

10. A Trust Deed is a deed to a piece of real estate held by a third party in trust as security for a note. This deed is very extensively used because it takes the place of a mortgage deed and renders the note negotiable. States frequently have statutory forms for trust deeds, and where such forms exist it is advisable to use them.

Form of Trust Deed

This deed, made this .... day of ...., 19......., between .... of ...., county of ....and state of ...., of the one part, and .... of ...., and .... of.................. of the other part, witnesseth, that the party of the first part doth grant unto the parties of the second part the following property, to wit:

(Insert description of property).

in trust, to secure to .... of ...., in the state of .... the payment of .... dollars in .... years from this date, with interest at .... per cent per annum thereon, according to a promissory note made by the party of the first part to said .... for said sum.

In event that default shall be made in the payment of the above-mentioned sum as it becomes due and payable, then the trustees, or either of them, on being required so to do by ...., his executors, administrators, or assigns, shall sell the property hereby conveyed. And it is covenanted and agreed between the parties aforesaid that in case of a sale the same shall be made after first advertising the time, place, and terms thereof for .... days in some newspaper published in the said county of ...., and upon the following terms, to wit: for cash as to so much of the proceeds as may be necessary to defray the expenses of executing this trust, the fees for drawing and recording this deed, if then unpaid, and to discharge the amount of money then payable upon said note; and if there be any residue of such purchase money, the same shall be made payable at such time, and be secured in such manner, as ...., his executors, administrators, or assigns, shall prescribe and direct, or in case of his or their failure to give such direction, at such time and in such manner as the trustees, or either of them, shall think fit. The party of the first part covenants to pay all taxes, assessments, dues, and charges upon the said property hereby conveyed so long as he or his heirs or assigns shall hold the same, and hereby waives the benefit of all homestead exemptions as to the debt secured by this deed.

If no default shall be made in the payment of the above-mentioned debt, then, upon the request of the party of the first part, a good and sufficient deed of release shall be executed to him at his own proper costs.

Witness, the hand .... and seal .... of said Grantor this .... day of ...., A.D., 19........

....(Seal)

....(Seal)

Municipal Corporations

1. Definition. — A municipal corporation is a corporation formed to carry on the work of government in a town or city. Its charter is granted by the State and it possesses only such powers as the State confers upon it, and no others.

2. Powers. — A city government is usually given the power:

a. to make its own laws or ordinances with reference to matters over which its charter gives it jurisdiction,
b. to enforce its laws,
c. to control all matters and things within its corporate boundaries within the limits fixed by its charter,
d. to issue bonds.

3. Officers of a Municipal Corporation. — The mayor is usually the chief executive, the Board of Aldermen the lawmaking body, of a municipality. The titles of these officers vary widely, however, in the different states. Under the commission form of government the above offices are held by a commission of three or five men, who have complete charge of the business of city government. The judicial power is usually vested in the police magistrate's court, or in larger cities in the municipal court. These are courts of limited jurisdiction only, however, and their jurisdiction does not supersede or conflict with that of the courts of the county in which they are situated.

4. Wrongful Acts of Officers.—The city is not responsible for damage for injuries to persons or property caused in the execution of a governmental duty. But what is considered a governmental duty is a question that has been the source of much litigation. The city is not liable for false arrest, false imprisonment, or assaults by police officers. If any wrongful act is committed by an officer while acting in his official capacity, he is liable personally.

5. The City's Duty.—It is the duty of the city government to provide and maintain safe and passable streets and highways, maintain police and fire protection, and provide for the general safety and welfare of its citizens.

6. Liability.—If the city fails to maintain safe and passable streets, the city is liable for damages resulting to those rightfully upon the streets, provided the city had notice that the streets were unsafe and not passable, and failed to exercise reasonable care to make the streets safe. It is almost universally held that a city is not liable for loss or injury resulting from failure to maintain proper police and fire protection.

7. Police Power of Cities.—The police power of a city extends to the city limits and a reasonable distance beyond the city limits in certain instances. The police magistrate, sometimes called the recorder, sits in a court having jurisdiction equal to that of a justice of the peace. The police magistrate and the police officers are bound to enforce the laws of the city, called ordinances. An officer may arrest a person:

a. When a wrongful act is committed in his presence.
b. Upon a valid warrant.
c. Upon suspicion, when well grounded and in good faith, no warrant then being necessary.

8. Schools.—The schools of a city are usually controlled by a board of education. This board has control and supervision over teachers, students, and buildings.

9. Public Service Corporations.—Any corporation furnishing the public as a whole a service or commodity, is called a public service corporation. Its activities are as a rule controlled and supervised by a public service commission having the power to fix prices and regulate the activities of the corporations.

Negotiable Instruments

1. Definition.—A **negotiable instrument** is any paper that may be transferred by endorsement or delivery in such a way as to give the person receiving it the right to bring a suit thereon in his own name. The person who promises to pay is called the **maker** or **drawer**, and the one to whom he promises is called the **payee** or **drawee.**

2. Kinds of Negotiable Instruments. — Almost every written contract or agreement to pay money is negotiable, in the sense that the owner can sell it to a third person who can enforce it against the maker. However, in the more strict sense of the word there are three common forms of negotiable paper, namely, checks, notes, and bills of exchange or drafts.

3. Form of Negotiable Instruments.—The law does not require negotiable instruments to be in any prescribed form. However, certain things are necessary in all checks, notes, or bills of exchange to make them negotiable:

a. The instrument must be in writing.
b. It must be signed by the maker or drawer.
c. It must contain a promise or order to pay.
d. The promise or order must be unconditional.
e. The promise or order must be a promise or order to pay a certain sum in money.
f. The instrument must be payable on demand or at a fixed or determinable time in the future.
g. The instrument must be payable to the order of some person, or to bearer.
h. If the instrument is addressed to a drawee, as would be the case if it were a bill of exchange or draft, the drawee must be named or otherwise indicated in the instrument with reasonable certainty.

4. Consideration. — While it is not always necessary to express any consideration in negotiable paper, it is safer to do so. When an instrument is in the hands of an innocent third party, the law assumes a valuable consideration. The words "for value received" usually appear on promissory notes.

5. Protest.—A protest of a note, check, or draft is a formal statement by a notary public that the paper was presented for payment and was refused. The costs are added to the instrument.

6. Negotiability.—The words "to bearer," or "to the order of," or words of like effect, render a paper negotiable. Any person capable of making a contract is capable of making a negotiable instrument. A person who receives a negotiable instrument under the conditions hereinafter mentioned becomes what is known as a "holder in due course," and certain defenses which might have been raised against the original holder cannot be raised against him. He must have taken the instrument under the following conditions: (1) The instrument must be complete and regular on its face. (2) It must not have been overdue, and the holder must not have known it was previously dishonored if such were the fact. (3) He must have taken it in good faith and paid value for it. (4) At the time he took it he must have had no notice of any infirmity in the instrument or defect in the title of the person negotiating it to him.

A. Notes

7. Definitions. — **A note** is a simple written promise to pay a certain sum at a certain time to a person named therein. An **individual promissory note** is a note in which one party promises to pay another a certain sum of money at a specified time. A **joint promissory note** is the same as an individual note except that it is signed by two or more parties, all of whom are liable jointly but not severally. In a **joint and several promissory note** two or more parties severally and separately agree to pay a certain sum at a specified time, and each signer is responsible for the whole amount. Statutes in many states provide that all joint obligations shall be held to be joint and several.

8. Transferring Notes. — The following rules govern the transferring of notes:

a. Instruments payable to bearer may be transferred by delivery, payable to order by endorsement.
b. An endorser is a person who writes his name on the back of a note or other instrument.
c. Endorsement in blank is an endorsement which does not mention the name of the person in whose favor it is made.
d. The endorser is liable for the payment of a note if the maker fails to meet it and the endorser is properly notified.
e. An endorser who is compelled to pay a note has a claim against the maker and against each endorser whose name appears above his own.
f. An endorser to whose order a note is drawn or endorsed, can transfer it without becoming liable for its payment by writing the words "without recourse" over his signature on the back.

9. Collecting Notes.—

a. A note destroyed by mistake or accident can be collected upon proof of loss.
b. Money paid by mistake must be refunded.
c. If no time is specified the note is payable on demand.
d. The day of maturity is the day on which a note becomes legally due.
e. In finding the day of maturity, actual days must be counted if the note falls due a specific number of days after the day on which it was drawn, but months are counted when the note falls due a specific number of months after the day on which it was drawn.
f. Negotiable paper to bearer or endorsed in blank, which has been lost or stolen, cannot be collected by the finder or thief, but a holder who innocently receives it in good faith before maturity for value received, can hold it against the owner's claims.
g. A note made in one state, payable in another, must be governed by the laws of that state in which it is to be paid.
h. Demand for payment of a note must be made upon the day of maturity and at the place named. If no place is specified, it is payable at the maker's place of business or at his residence. In most of the states, when a note falls due on a Sunday or legal holiday, by statute the maker is given until the following day to pay the same.
i. An extension of the time of a note by the holder, releases sureties and endorsers, unless consent to such extension has been given by the endorsers or sureties.
j. Upon presentment for payment and refusal by the maker at maturity, in order to hold the endorser, notice of default must be given to the endorser immediately.

10. Payment of Notes. — All the parties who have endorsed a note are liable for the full amount, but only one satisfaction can be recovered. In certain cases notes are unenforceable, especially when held by the original payee. Among such cases are the following.

a. A note given by one who is not of age, unless the minor ratified it after becoming of age.
b. A note made by an intoxicated person.
c. A note given by one who cannot write, and not witnessed at the time.
d. A note obtained by duress, by putting the maker in fear of illegal imprisonment, or by threats that would lead an ordinary person to fear injury to his person, his reputation, or his property.
e. A note obtained by fraud.
f. A note given for illegal consideration.
g. One who receives a note knowing it to have defects, has no better right to collect it than the one from whom he received it had.
h. If a person at the time of taking a note has notice that it is void because of fraud or for any other reason, he cannot collect it.

Forms of Note

Negotiable by Endorsement

$375.00 Naperville, Ill., Oct. 7, 19......

For value received, one year after date I promise to pay to the order of J. L. Nichols the sum of Three Hundred and Seventy-five Dollars with interest at six per cent from date until paid.

J. R. PRICE.

Negotiable without Endorsement

$100.00 Cleveland, O., Aug. 1, 19.......

Ninety days after date I promise to pay to bearer, One Hundred Dollars, value received.

E. M. KECK.

Not Negotiable

$100.00 Chicago, Ill., Dec. 10, 19.......

Sixty days after date I promise to pay Geo. C. Dixon One Hundred Dollars, value received.

EUGENE LANSING.

A Corporation Note

$200.00 Augusta, Me., Mar. 18, 19.......

Nine months after date, the Granite Stone Company, a corporation, promises to pay S. A. Chilton, or order, Two Hundred Dollars, with interest at six per cent. Value received.

Attest: I. K. Dawes, Secretary.

GRANITE STONE COMPANY.
O. R. Phillips, President

N.B.—If corporation notes are drawn and signed in the above manner, the officers are not personally liable.

Collateral Note

$500.00 Mendota, Tex., Sept. 25, 19.......

Sixty days after date, for value received, I promise to pay to the order of T. J. Boyd, the sum of Five Hundred Dollars, with interest at the rate of six per cent per annum after date, having deposited United States Bonds of the face value of Six Hundred Dollars, which I authorize the holder of this Note, upon the non-performance of this promise at maturity, to sell, at public or private sale, without further notice, and to apply proceeds, or as much thereof as may be necessary to the payment of this Note, and all necessary expenses and charges, holding myself responsible for any deficiency

W. W. STRATTON.

Judgment Note

$2,000.00 Philadelphia, Pa., Jan. 4, 19......

Six months after date, for value received, I promise to pay to the order of J. W. Krasley Two Thousand Dollars, with interest at the rate of 6 per cent per annum, after maturity, until paid.

And to secure the payment of said amount I hereby authorize any attorney of any court of record to appear for me in such court, in term time or vacation, at any time after maturity, to waive a jury trial and confess judgment, without process, in favor of the holder of the note, for such amount as may appear to be paid thereon, together with costs and five per centum attorney's fees, and to waive and release all errors which may intervene on any such proceedings, and consent to immediate execution upon such judgment; hereby ratifying and confirming all my said attorney may do by virtue hereof.

GEORGE W. BAIRD.

Payable at Bank

$440.00 Chicago, Ill., Oct. 10, 19.......

Two years after date, for value received, I promise to pay T. M. Culver, or order, Four Hundred Forty Dollars at Second National Bank, with interest at six per cent per annum.

CHARLES HEARN.

On Demand

$25.67 Kansas City Mo., Oct. 12, 19.......

On demand I promise to pay to the order of J. T. Connor, Twenty-five 67-100 Dollars. Value received, with interest at six per cent.

A. H. SIMPSON.

N.B.—This note answers the same purpose as a note written one day after date.

Joint Note

$200.00 Lisle, Ill., Jan. 1, 19.......

One year from date, we promise to pay D. F. Shaw, or order, Two Hundred Dollars. Value received. Interest at six per cent.

J. LEWIS BEAN.
B. A. WHITE.

Joint and Several Note

$2,000.00 Ottawa, Ont., Nov. 25, 19.......

Ten months after date, we, or either of us, promise to pay Maggie Patterson Two Thousand Dollars, value received. Interest at five per cent.

J. C. HARDY.
R. E. WOOD.

Principal and Surety Note

New York, N. Y., Sept. 21, 19.......

For value received, on or before July 27, 19........, I promise to pay to the order of John Jackson, Six Hundred Dollars. Interest at five per cent.

W. J. SHAW, Principal.
THOS. RODDEN, Surety.

N.B.—The general form of a principal and surety note is for the principal to properly sign the note and the surety to endorse it.

A Note by One Who Cannot Write

$49.50 Cleveland, Ohio, Mar 20, 19.......

One year after date, I promise to pay N. Bowker, or order, Forty-nine 50-100 Dollars, with interest at five per cent. Value received.

H. A. Starr. Witness.

his
JOHN x ROURKE.
mark

N.B.—A note made by a person who cannot write should always be witnessed by a disinterested person.

My Own Order

New Orleans, La., July 20, 19.......

For value received, I promise to pay, sixty days after date, to my own order, Two Hundred Dollars, with interest at eight per cent.

A. S. BARNARD.

N.B.—A note may be drawn to the maker's own order, with his endorsement in favor of the creditor.

Note Secured by a Mortgage

$1,000.00 Chicago, Ill., April 15, 19.......

Six months after date I promise to pay to John Williams $1,000.00 with interest at six per cent.

This note is secured by a mortgage of even date herewith from Robert Jones to John Williams.

ROBERT JONES.

B. Checks

11. Definitions.—A check is an order drawn upon a bank, payable on demand. The person who writes the check is the **drawer**, the bank on which the check is drawn is called the **drawee**, the person to whom the check is made payable is called the **payee.**

12. Signature. — A check must be properly signed by the drawer or his duly authorized agent. A signature made on behalf of the drawer by another person is valid if authorized. It should, of course, be written in ink, but a signature made with a pencil or rubber stamp is valid if intended as a signature.

13. Presentation.—A check must be presented for payment within a reasonable time after its issue, or the drawer will be discharged from liability thereon to the extent of the loss caused by the delay; and it is generally held that one day after the receipt of the check is a reasonable time to present or forward the same for presentation

14. The Agreement to Pay is between the bank and the depositor. For this reason a check, of itself, does not operate as an assignment of any part of the funds to the credit of the drawer with the bank. Consequently, should the bank refuse to pay the check, the holder cannot bring action against the bank, unless or until the bank has accepted or certified the check. On the other hand, if the bank fails to fulfill its contract with the depositor he has a just cause of action against the bank. Should the bank refuse to honor a customer's check owing to an employee's mistake in bookkeeping, the bank could be held responsible for any loss resulting therefrom.

15. Certifying a Check. — A certification of a check by the bank is equivalent to an acceptance, and discharges the drawer and all the endorsers preceding the holder who secures the certification. When a check is presented to a bank for this purpose, the bank charges the drawer's account with the amount, so that as far as the drawer and the bank are concerned the check has actually been paid. Therefore, if a certified check is not presented at his bank for payment and is returned to the drawer, it should not be destroyed but should be redeposited as cash.

16. Stopping Payment. — The drawer of the check may order the bank to stop payment on a check before it is presented. The bank is required to follow these instructions and is liable for any loss resulting from failure to do so.

17. Forged Checks.—The law insists that the banker exercise the greatest care in paying the checks of customers. If the signature has been forged or the amount of the check altered, the bank is liable for any improper payment. The drawer of the check must also use every precaution to prevent alterations. He should write in a way to avoid confusing the banker who is to pay the check. The bank is not responsible for any loss caused by negligence on the part of the drawer in making out the check.

18. Vital Points on Checks. — A check is not due until presented. It is negotiable. It has no days of grace. Giving a check is not payment of an indebtedness, unless the check is paid, or unless it is accepted as payment. The death of the maker of the check before it is presented to the bank renders the check null and void. The amount of the check should always be written out in words as well as in figures. If a raised check is paid by the bank, the bank can charge the depositor only the amount for which he drew the check, unless the raising of the check was made possible by the carelessness of the maker. In that case the maker would be responsible for the loss.

If you write a check for a stranger who needs identification at your bank, have him endorse the check in your presence and under his indorsement write "Endorsement above guaranteed," signing your name. He can then usually cash the check without further identification, by signing his name again in the presence of the banker.

C. Drafts

19. Definition.—A **draft** is a written order by one person on another for the payment of a specified sum of money to a designated third person. The one who writes the draft is called the **drawer,** the one on whom it is written, the **drawee,** and the one to whom it is to be paid, the **payee.**

20. Kinds of Drafts. — Drafts may be made payable at sight, on demand, at a certain time after date, or after sight. A **sight draft** or **demand draft** is drawn by one person on another and is payable when presented. **Time drafts** are similar to sight drafts, but are payable a certain number of days after presentation. A **Bill of Exchange** is an unconditional order in writing addressed by one person to another, signed by the person giving it, requiring the person to whom it is addressed to pay on demand or at a fixed or determinable future time a certain sum of money to order or to bearer. The term includes drafts and checks.

21. Acceptance.—Sight and demand drafts are presented for payment only. Time drafts require acceptance by the party against whom they are drawn in order to bind him. The usual method of acceptance is to write across the face of the draft in red ink the word "accepted," followed by the date and the signature of the drawee. Should the person on whom the draft is drawn die before it was accepted, it should be presented to his legal representative for acceptance.

22. General Principles:—

a. When either acceptance or payment is refused, the draft may be protested like any note or check.
b. Drafts are negotiable both before and after acceptance.

Forms of Draft

Bank Draft

$100. State of Illinois, May 10, 19......

The First National Bank of Naperville. Pay to the order of F. A. Lueben, One Hundred Dollars.

To Union National Bank, W. L. HETZ, Cashier.
Chicago, Ill.

Demand Draft

$100. Troy Grove, Ill., Aug. 1, 19......

On demand pay to the order of Frank Myers at the Mendota First National Bank, One Hundred Dollars.

Value received.

To Charles Lerch, A. S. HUDSON.
Mendota, Ill.

Sight Draft

$500. Naperville, Tenn., July 10, 19.......

At sight pay to the order of C. Parman, Five Hundred Dollars, and charge to the account of

To Jessee Lerch, H. H. ZEMMER.
Meriden, Ill.

Time Draft

$450.30 Ottawa, Fla., July 5, 19.......

Ten days from date pay to J. L. Nichols, or order, Four Hundred Fifty 30-100 Dollars. Value received.

To Alvin Brown, C. E. LAMALE.
Ottawa, Fla.

D. Endorsements

23. Definition.—An endorsement is a writing on the back of a negotiable instrument for the purpose of transferring the title or ownership from one person to another. The writing may be in pen or pencil upon any part of the instrument or upon a paper attached thereto. It consists ordinarily of the payee's signature and that of other holders, if any.

24. How to Endorse.—Write across the back of the paper (not lengthwise) near the left end. Always endorse a check or note exactly as your name appears on the face. If the check is payable to F. Black, do not write Frank Black. If your name is misspelled, endorse first as it appears on the face and then write your correct signature underneath; no written explanation is necessary; banks are familiar with this practice. The same rules govern the endorsement of notes, drafts, and other written instruments. A check or other instrument may be endorsed and title thereby transferred many times. Each endorser is liable to those who endorse after him.

25. Kinds of Endorsement:—

An **endorsement in blank** is made when the payee simply signs his name in the proper place (across the left end of the reverse) without any statement of conditions. Such a note or check is negotiable without further endorsement. Endorsement in blank is commonly used when a check is deposited or cashed at a bank. It should not be used when there is danger of the check's being lost or stolen.

An **endorsement in full** or **special endorsement** consists of writing the name of the person to whom, or to whose order, the money is to be paid, followed by the payee's signature. For example: "Pay to F. Black or order, J. Jones"; when endorsed in this form, the check cannot be cashed until F. Black endorses it.

In a **qualified endorsement** the endorser relieves himself of any liability in connection with the instrument, by writing above his signature the words "Without recourse"; thus, "Without recourse, J. Jones."

A **restrictive endorsement** limits the payment of the note, bill, or check. The endorser writes "pay to F. Black only," or "for deposit in the First National Bank," signing his name underneath. A check or other instrument so endorsed cannot be further negotiated by the person or bank receiving it. Restrictive endorsement is a wise precaution when there is danger of a negotiable instrument's being lost or stolen after endorsement.

A **conditional endorsement** is one directing payment only upon the performance of a certain condition. The endorser's liability is thereby limited. For example, "Pay to the order of F. Black unless he previously receives the amount from my agent, J. Jones." Neither the original character of the note nor its negotiability is affected by such an endorsement. It may affect, however, the title of the one to whom it is transferred.

Endorsement by an agent is made in the following form: "J. Jones, by H. Smith, his agent." In this manner the agent endorses for his principal.

In a **guaranteed endorsement** one party guarantees payment on a note for another party. He writes above his signature "I hereby guarantee payment of this note," or words of like effect. He is then absolutely liable for the amount due by the terms of the note in case the maker fails to pay.

E. "IOU"

26. An IOU is not a promissory note, and is not negotiable. It is evidence of a debt due by virtue of a previous contract. The following is an example:

Chicago, Ill., June 4, 1940

Mr. A. O. Rogers,
IOU Sixty Dollars ($60.00).

W. G. ALLEN.

F. Due Bills

27. A due bill is not payable to order, nor is it assignable by mere endorsement. It is simply the acknowledgment of a debt; yet it may be transferred. It may be payable in money, in merchandise, or in services.

Due bills do not draw interest unless so specified.

$125.00 Chicago, Aug. 14, 19.......

Due Henry Harrington, for value received, One Hundred and Twenty-five dollars with interest at six per cent. Q. YINZER.

On Demand

$250.00 Naperville, Ill., July 1, 19.......

Due E. E. Miller, on demand, Two Hundred Fifty Dollars in goods from my store, for value received.

A. T. HANSON.

In Merchandise

$1,000.00 Lincoln, Neb., Nov. 1, 19.......

Due R. William, One Thousand Dollars, payable in wheat at market price, on the first day of January, 19.....

CHARLES SCHUERER.

G. Receipts

28. A receipt is an acknowledgment in writing that a certain sum of money or thing has been received by the party giving and signing the same.

29. A complete receipt requires the following

statements: that a payment has been received; the date of the payment; the amount of article received; from whom received, and if for another, on whose behalf payment is made; to what debt or purpose it is to be applied; the signature of the person receiving the property, and if for another, on whose behalf it was received.

30. If the giving and taking of receipts were more generally practiced in business transactions, less trouble, fewer lawsuits, and the saving of thousands of dollars would result.

31. If payment is made upon account, upon a special debt, or in full, it should be so stated in the receipt.

32. When an agent signs a receipt, he should sign his principal's name and then write his name underneath as agent.

33. It is not necessary to take a receipt on paying a note, draft, or other instrument indorsed by the payee, because the instrument itself becomes a receipt.

34. If a receipt is obtained through fraud, or given under error or mistake, it is void.

Receipt for Payment on Account

$250.00 Naperville, Ill., July 6, 19......

Received of J. L. Nichols, Two Hundred and Fifty Dollars on account.

J. K. ROHMER.

Receipt for Settlement of an Account

Joliet, Ill., March 20, 19......

Received of Thomas Rourke, Two Hundred and Twenty 14-100 Dollars, in full settlement of account to date. C. S. SELBY.

Receipt in Full of All Demands

Meriden, Conn., Jan. 14, 19......

Received of C. F. Hetche, One Thousand Dollars, in full of all demands to date.

O. N. OBRIGHT.

Receipt for a Particular Bill

Brooklyn, N. Y., Aug. 1, 19......

Received of Morris Cliggitt, Four Hundred Dollars, in payment for a bill of Merchandise.

R. ZACHMAN.

Receipt for Rent

Snyder, Tex., Mar. 20, 19......

Received of L. Heininger, Forty Dollars in full for one month's rent, for month ending April 20, 19......, for residence at 44 Olive Street.

J. LEWIS BEAN.

Receipt for a Note

Received, Buffalo, March 6, 19......, from Messrs. Taylor & Co., their note of this date, at three months, our favor, for Twelve Hundred and Twenty Dollars; which, when paid, will be in full of account rendered to 1st instant.

$1,220.00. C. H. OLIVER.

Receipt for Services

Lemont, Ill., July 23, 19......

Received of Samuel Lynn, Forty-four Dollars, in full for services to date.

$44.00. DANIEL FURBUSH.

Receipt for Money Advanced on a Contract

$500.00 Chicago, Ill., May 10, 19......

Received of Arthur Kahl the sum of Five Hundred Dollars, part payment on contract to build for him a house at No. 1439 Perry St., Chicago.

CARL DIENST.

Receipt for Interest Due on a Mortgage

$75.00 Chicago, August 1, 19......

Received of G. A. Caton, Seventy-five Dollars, in full of six months' interest due this day, on his note to me dated August 1st, 19......, for Two Thousand Five Hundred Dollars, secured by mortgage on property at 1430 Maple Street, Chicago.

EDWARD TRONT.

Notaries Public

1. The Office and Its Functions.—The office of notary public as it exists in the several states today is the outgrowth of various practices traceable to the Roman Empire. Anciently merely a scribe, the power and duties of the notary have been amplified by legislative enactments to meet the needs of changing conditions and a growing civilization. His commission is granted upon representation of his capacity and integrity. In accepting office the notary contracts the obligation to fill it intelligently and honestly.

2. Definition. — A notary public is a state officer whose function is to attest and certify, by his hand and official seal, various documents, in order to give them authenticity in other jurisdictions, to take acknowledgments of deeds and other conveyances and instruments, and to certify the same; and to perform other official acts, the power to do which is conferred by statutory enactment.

3. Classification of Functions. — As a general rule the functions of a notary are ministerial, not judicial. They are confined to the civil, as distinguished from the criminal, branch of the law, and consist for the most part in protesting inland and foreign bills of exchange and promissory notes, authenticating their dishonor by the refusal of the drawee or payee to accept or pay them on presentation or when due; the authentication of transfers or conveyances of property, and other documents required by the law to be authenticated; administering oaths and affirmations as to correctness of accounts; the taking of depositions under the rules and instructions of the courts when cases are pending; and the taking of affidavits as to the truth of statements made in legal papers for use in proceedings before courts of civil or maritime jurisdiction.

4. Definition of Functions.—The term **"protest"** as applied to commercial paper means the taking of such steps as are required to charge or fix liability upon one secondarily liable, such as an endorser. As applied to the notarial act it means a declaration made in writing by a notary public after doing the acts certified, that the bill or note to which it relates was, on the day it became due, presented for payment, and that payment was refused. To **"authenticate"** a document means for a notary to certify under his hand and seal of office with a notice of the date and in most states the expiration of his commission, such facts as the law requires to give the document operative effect. A **"deposition"** is the testimony of a witness taken down in writing, under oath or affirmation before a notary public, and usually subscribed by the witness, pursuant to special authority granted by a court after notice to the adverse party. It is authenticated by the notary. An **"affidavit"** is a voluntary ex parte statement, formally reduced to writing and sworn to or affirmed and subscribed before a notary public. An **"acknowledgment"** is an oral declaration or admission made by one who has executed a document, made before a notary public or other officer authorized by law to take acknowledgments, to the effect that the execution is his act and deed.

The written certificate endorsed on the document by the officer taking the acknowledgment, certifying to the facts of the same, is sometimes referred to as "an acknowledgment." The function of an acknowledgment is two-fold—to authorize the document to be given in evidence without further proof of its execution, and to entitle it to be recorded. A notary's **certificate of acknowledgment** is not part of its execution, but only evidence of it. At least six essential facts must appear in a certificate of acknowledgment: (1) the designation of the officer making the certificate; (2) the name of the person making the acknowledgment, and that he or she personally appeared before the officer; (3) that there was an acknowledgment; (4) that the person who made the acknowledgment was identified as the one who executed the instrument; (5) that such identity was personally known or proved by the officer taking the acknowledgment; (6) the day and year when the acknowledgment was made. An **"oath"** is an outward pledge, given by the person taking it, that his attestation or promise is made under an immediate sense of his responsibility to God.

5. Form and Manner of Administering Oaths, Affidavits, and Affirmations.—The customary and approved manner of administering an oath or taking an affidavit is to have the person making the same raise his hand and swear by the ever-living God. There should be at least some manifestation that the officer and the person taking the oath understand the nature of their undertaking; a mere mental process is not sufficient. In many states the form and manner of taking an oath are prescribed by law.

Any person who desires may in lieu of an oath or affidavit take and subscribe or assent to an affirmation, which is administered by the officer repeating the words, "You do solemnly, sincerely and truly declare and affirm that," etc., "and so you do affirm." It is not unusual to ask the question, "Do you swear or affirm" rather than to wait for the deponent to express his desire. A strict and solemn compliance with these forms is important. Any person who willfully and falsely swears or affirms to any material matter is guilty of perjury. The average citizen is inclined to attach only such importance and solemnity to these acts as the officer administering them shows. To perform these acts in a perfunctory manner is to deprive them of their intended value, and in some instances to encourage perjury.

6. Form of Affidavit or Affirmation:—

State of Pennsylvania,)
) SS.
County of Philadelphia.)

Allen B. White, being duly sworn (or affirmed), according to law, deposes and says (or in case of affirmation, in lieu of "deposes and says" insert "affirms and declares") that he is the person who executed the foregoing instrument (or if by an officer or agent of a corporation, insert in lieu of "he is the person," etc., the following: "he is the [name of office] of the [name of corporation] above named, that he has authority from it to make this affidavit [or affirmation] in its behalf); and that the facts therein set forth are true to the best of his (add "and its" where made by officer or agent for corporation) knowledge, information and belief.

Sworn (or affirmed) and subscribed before me this 22nd day of November, A. D. 19......

Allen B. White.

(Seal) C. D. Black.
Stamp com. expires.

7. Form of Acknowledgment Recommended by American Bar Association—By Single Person or by Husband and Wife:—

STATE OF ....)
SS.
COUNTY OF ....)

On this .... day of ...., 19......, before me, the subscriber (here insert title of officer), personally appeared A. B. (and C. B., his wife, if so), to me known to be the person (or persons) described in and who executed the foregoing instrument, and acknowledged that he (she or they) executed the same as his (her or their) free act and deed.

(Seal) (Signature and title), etc.

Parent and Child

1. Ancient Authority. — In the past ages the father was by custom considered an absolute monarch of the home. In the oriental countries of today the same custom still prevails; modern progress and modern ideas, however, have changed old customs, and the authority of the parent in civilized countries has been considerably limited by law.

2. Rights of Parents.—The parent has the right of control over his child, and has all reasonable authority to enforce obedience. As long as the parent treats his child properly, no one has a right to interfere with his authority, or take the child away and retain him against the wishes of the parent.

3. A Runaway Child.—A child has no right to leave home without permission of the parent, and should a child run away he can be brought back by force. If relatives or other parties keep him and refuse to give him up, the parent by legal process can obtain possession of his child, unless it can be shown that the father is brutal, or is not a fit person, on account of drunkenness or other causes, to take proper care of his child.

4. Punishment of Children. — A parent has a right to punish his minor child, provided he is not guilty of cruelty or brutality, which are crimes punishable by severe legal penalties. The parent must be reasonable in his punishment, and in no way injure the health of the child.

5. Rights to Earnings—A parent is entitled to all the earnings of his minor child. If the child should refuse to turn over his earnings to the parent, the employer of the child may be notified, and be compelled to pay the parent only.

6. Special Rights.—The parent may, however, make free his child from all obligations to himself and allow the child to collect his own wages for himself. When a parent thus makes public such a declaration, he cannot thereafter collect the child's wages.

7. The Property of the Child.—A parent may control the earnings of the child, yet he has no control of the property belonging to the child, acquired either by gift or by legacy, or in any other way. If a parent should appropriate his child's property, it would be just as criminal in the eyes of the law as stealing.

8. Parent's Obligation to Support. — Parents are legally held for the support of their minor children. The fact that a child has property does not relieve the parent from the support of his child; he, however, can apply to court and get permission to use a part, or all, of the income of the property for the child's support.

9. Illegitimate Children.—It is a parent's duty to support an illegitimate child. Such a child has legally no father, but his putative father, as he is called, may be compelled to furnish the child with reasonable support, so that it shall not become a burden upon the community. All children born in wedlock are legitimate, unless it is proved that the husband could not possibly be the father. The adultery of the wife cannot affect the legitimacy of the child. It is presumed to be that of the husband. It makes no difference how soon after marriage the child is born. A child born the same day as the marriage, if subsequent to the ceremony, is legitimate unless there is reason for believing that the husband is not the father.

10. Effect of Illegitimacy.—The only important legal effect of illegitimacy is that the child cannot generally inherit property from his father. He may, of course, take a legacy given to him by his putative father's will, but if there is no will he generally cannot inherit. An illegitimate child usually inherits from his mother even though there are legitimate children.

11. Children's Obligations.—Where the parents or grandparents are unable to support themselves, in many states the child is legally held for their support and care.

12. Crimes — A parent cannot be held for crimes committed by his minor child. If a child commits a premeditated crime, he is personally liable.

13. Guardian.—If a child has no parents living, a guardian may be appointed, or if he has arrived at a certain age, varying in different states, he may petition the court for the appointment of his own guardian, who will in a legal sense exercise the prerogative of a parent.

14. Contracts with a Minor.—A contract made by a minor is valid if it is for necessities. Just what constitutes a necessity depends on the circumstances and is a matter for the jury to decide. If a minor contracts for other things, the contract is not always void, but may be avoided by the minor. Even though a minor fraudulently represents himself to be of age and makes a contract for goods, the seller cannot recover on the contract. His only remedy is an action of deceit. A minor who has a parent or guardian cannot make a contract even for necessities. But if the minor receives and retains such articles with the permission of the parent or guardian, the parent or guardian will be deemed to have ratified the contract and will be held personally liable. If the parent or guardian is unwilling to provide the necessities he can be compelled to do so by the courts.

Parliamentary Law

1. Parliamentary Rules.—In every community it is necessary to hold public meetings from time to time, and in order to expedite the proceedings of such meetings, as well as to settle matters of dispute, it is necessary that rules of procedure be adopted. In order to be able to take an intelligent interest and part in such meeting, it is essential that young and old be informed on the most important points of parliamentary rules.

2. Rules of Parliamentary Law.—The following rules and suggestions will be found helpful in conducting public meetings:

a. The chairman selected should be a person of maturity and one held in respect and confidence.

b. To address the meeting permission must be obtained from the chairman by rising and saying: "Mr. President" or "Mr. Chairman."

c. No speaker should be interrupted unless his remarks are out of order, when he should be called to order by the chair. If the chairman fails to call him to order, any member may do so.

d. The proper way to make a motion is to say: "Mr. Chairman, I move that (here state motion)."

e. When a motion is presented to the meeting and seconded, it should be stated or read by the secretary or chairman, and remarks called for.

f. After debate, the motion should be put to the meeting, the chairman announcing the result.

g. A speaker is "out of order" when he is speaking of matters and things foreign to the issue before the house.

h. Any violation of rules must be recognized and checked by the presiding officer.

i. When a member is called to order by the president, he should take his seat, unless he is permitted to explain.

j. Any ruling of the chairman may be appealed and decided by a vote of the house.
k. It is the privilege of any member to call for the yeas and nays and thus put on record the vote of every member.
l. The chairman is the servant, not the master, of the house. To get rid of an undesirable chairman, the house may refuse to do any business, or may adjourn.
m. A motion to adjourn is always in order and is not debatable.

3. Over Three Hundred Points of Order. — Trace up each reference at the right, and then look up the corresponding numbers below, which give information bearing on the point in question.

Forms in which questions may be put	28, 29, 30, 31, 32
Questions of precedence of questions	19, 20, 21, 22, 23, 24, 25, 26, 27
Motion to withdraw a motion	1, 5, 7, 9, 13, 14, 16
To take up a question out of its proper order	1, 5, 7, 9, 12, 14, 16
Motion to take from the table	1, 5, 7, 11, 12, 14, 16
Motion to suspend the rules	3, 5, 8, 10, 13, 14, 16
To substitute in the nature of an amendment	3, 5, 8, 9, 13, 14, 16
Motion to make subject a special order	3, 5, 8, 9, 12, 14, 16
Question whether subject shall be discussed	1, 5, 7, 9, 12, 15, 17
Motion that committee do not rise	1, 5, 7, 10, 13, 14, 16
Motion to refer a question	3, 6, 8, 10, 13, 14, 16
Motion to reconsider an undebatable question	1, 5, 7, 10, 13, 14, 18
Motion to reconsider a debatable question	3, 6, 7, 10, 13, 14, 16
Reading Papers	1, 5, 7, 9, 13, 14, 16
Questions of privilege	3, 5, 8, 9, 13, 14, 16
Questions touching priority of business	1, 5, 8, 9, 13, 14, 16
Motion for previous question	1, 5, 7, 9, 13, 14, 16
Motion to postpone indefinitely	3, 6, 7, 9, 13, 14, 16
Motion to postpone to a definite time	4, 5, 8, 9, 13, 14, 16
Motion for the orders of the day	1, 5, 7, 9, 13, 15, 17
Objection to consideration of question	1, 5, 7, 9, 12, 15, 17
Motion to limit debate on question	1, 5, 8, 9, 12, 14, 16
Motion to lay on the table	1, 5, 7, 11, 13, 14, 16
Leave to continue speaking after indecorum	1, 5, 7, 9, 13, 14, 16
Motion to extend limits of debate on question	1, 5, 8, 9, 13, 14, 16
Motion to commit	3, 6, 8, 9, 13, 14, 16
Motion to close debate on question	1, 5, 8, 9, 12, 14, 16
Call to order	1, 5, 7, 9, 13, 15, 17
Motion to appeal from Speaker's decision generally	3, 5, 7, 9, 13, 14, 17
Motion to appeal from Speaker's decision re indecorum	1, 5, 8, 9, 13, 14, 17
Motion to amend the rules	3, 5, 8, 9, 12, 14, 16
Motion to amend an amendment	3, 5, 7, 9, 13, 14, 16
Motion to amend	3, 5, 8, 9, 13, 14, 16
Motion to determine time to which to adjourn	2, 5, 8, 9, 13, 14, 16
Motion to adjourn	1, 5, 7, 10, 13, 14, 16

Points of Order

1. Question undebatable; sometimes remarks tacitly allowed.
2. Undebatable if another question is before the assembly.
3. Debatable question.
4. Limited debate only on propriety of postponement.
5. Does not allow reference to main question.
6. Opens the main question to debate.
7. Cannot be amended.
8. May be amended.
9. Can be reconsidered.
10. Cannot be reconsidered.
11. An affirmative vote on this question cannot be reconsidered.
12. Requires two-thirds vote, unless special rules have been enacted.
13. Simple majority suffices to determine the question.
14. Motion must be seconded.
15. Does not require to be seconded.
16. Not in order when another has the floor.
17. Always in order though another may have the floor.
18. May be moved and entered on the record when another has the floor, but the business then before the assembly may not be put aside. The motion must be made by one who voted with the prevailing side, and on the same day the original vote was taken.
19. Fixing the time to which an adjournment may be made; ranks first.
20. To adjourn without limitation; second.
21. Motion for the Orders of the Day; third.
22. Motion to lay on the table; fourth.
23. Motion for the previous question; fifth.
24. Motion to postpone definitely; sixth.
25. Motion to commit; seventh.
26. Motion to amend; eighth.
27. Motion to postpone indefinitely; ninth.
28. On motion to strike out words, "Shall the words stand as part of the motion?" unless a majority sustains the words they are struck out.
29. On motion for previous question the form to be observed is: "Shall the main question be now put?" This, if carried, ends debate.
30. On an appeal from the chair's decision, "Shall the decision be sustained as the ruling of the house?" the chair is usually sustained.
31. A motion for Orders of the Day is put in the following form: "Will the house now proceed to the Orders of the Day?" This, if carried, supersedes intervening motions.
32. When an objection is raised to considering question, "Shall the question be considered?" objection may be made by any member before debate has commenced, but not subsequently.

Partnership

1. Definition. — The Uniform Partnership Act defines a partnership as "an association of two or more persons to carry on as co-owners a business for profit."

2. Kinds of Partnership.—A **general partnership** is one in which the partners agree to enter into a certain business without limitation or condition. There may also be a partnership in a single transaction, such as to buy and sell a single oil lease. An **implied partnership** is one in which one party acts in such a way as to lead outsiders to believe that partnership actually exists. In a **special** or **limited** partnership there may be general partners with unlimited liability and special partners with limited liability.

3. Kinds of Partner.—A **general partner** is one who is generally known as a partner and whose liability is not limited. A **secret partner** is one who is not openly declared as a partner. A **silent**

partner takes no active part in the business but shares in the profits, losses, and liabilities. A **nominal partner** is held out as a partner without sharing in the profits or losses of the business.

4. Forming a Partnership.—A partnership is formed by an agreement, usually in writing, though it may be oral. Any persons competent to transact business in their own names may become partners. Partners often have separate fields of endeavor, each doing the work for which he is best fitted. The article of agreement should specify the division of profits and losses and should be very carefully drawn. In the absence of any written agreement the law assumes that the partners share profits and losses equally. A partnership may hold both real and personal property.

5. Liability.—Each partner is a general asset and has full authority to act for the partnership. Not only common property, but also all the private property of each partner may be taken to satisfy the debts of the firm. A partner cannot make the firm responsible for his separate or private debt, nor bind the firm by entering into engagements unconnected with, or foreign to, the partnership. The authority of a partner usually extends to the making or endorsing of negotiable paper, and to all transactions fairly connected with the business. A person who, after due care, lends money to one of a partnership firm for the firm, can hold the firm liable, although the money is fraudulently appropriated by the partner to his own use. An illegal contract made by one partner will not bind the partnership.

6. How to Avoid Liability.—In order to avoid individual liability in transacting business, the partners may form a corporation or a limited liability partnership. The latter consists of two or more general partners and also special partners, whose contribution and liability are made known to the public. These special partners are liable only for the amount of capital they advanced.

7. Dissolution.—There are numerous ways in which a partnership may be dissolved:

a. Any partner, upon due notice to others, may withdraw at any time provided no specific date for the dissolution of the partnership is mentioned in the articles of agreement. There is some authority, however, to the effect that the power to withdraw should be exercised in a good faith so as not to prejudice the other partners. The retiring partner should notify the public of his retirement in order to relieve himself from future liability.

b. The partnership may be dissolved by mutual consent.

c. The death of one of the partners automatically dissolves the partnership.

d. The taking in of a new partner constitutes a new partnership. This is usually a matter of reorganization and the new partnership may or may not assume liabilities of the old firm.

e. The insanity or bankruptcy of one of the partners ends the partnership.

f. A court may dissolve a partnership for any good reason such as incapacity, drunkenness, or fraud.

g. The expiration of the time specified in the articles of partnership acts as a dissolution.

8. Liquidation.—In case of failure the assets of the partnership must be used to pay the debts of the partnership, the assets of the partners to pay their personal debts. If in either case any property remains, the partnership property is applied on the personal debts, and the partners' personal property must go towards the partnership debts. The affairs of the insolvent partnership are usually placed in the hands of one of the partners, subject to control of the court, or turned over to a receiver appointed by the court, either of whom has the right to liquidate the affairs of the partnership.

Articles of Co-Partnership

ARTICLES OF AGREEMENT, made ...., 19........, between .... and ....

The said parties hereby agree to become co-partners, under the firm name of ...., and as such partners to carry on together the business of buying and selling all sorts of dry goods, at .... street, in the city of ....

The said .... agrees to contribute two thousand dollars ($2,000) to the capital of said firm; and the said .... agrees to contribute one thousand dollars ($1,000) to the same; the sum of $2.500 of said capital to be expended in the purchase of a stock in trade.

The said .... shall have exclusive charge of all the buying for the firm.

All the net profits arising out of the business shall be divided in the following proportions, two-thirds to the said .... and one-third to the said ....

Each partner shall devote all his time, attention, and efforts to the said business.

Neither partner shall, without the consent of the other in writing, sign any bond, bill or note as surety, or otherwise become obligated as security for any other person.

Witness the hands and seals of the parties hereto, this .... day of .... A. D., 19........

....(Seal)
....(Seal)

Agreement to Dissolve Partnership

We, the undersigned, do mutually agree that the within mentioned partnership be, and the same is, hereby dissolved, except for the purpose of final liquidation and settlement of the business thereof, and upon such settlement wholly to cease and determine.

Witness our hands and seals this .... day of .... nineteen hundred and ....

Signed, Sealed and Delivered
in Presence of

....
....

(Most states do not require this attestation)

....(Seal)
....(Seal)

Passports

1. An application for a passport must be executed before a clerk of a Federal court or a state court authorized by law to naturalize aliens, or before an agent of the Department of State. An application executed before any other official will not be accepted. Passport Agents of the Department of State are located in New York (Subtreasury Bldg., also at Rockefeller Center, International Bldg.); Boston (U. S. Post Office and Courthouse); Chicago (New Post Office Bldg.); San Francisco (Federal Office Bldg.).

2. When a person makes application for a passport it is necessary to present:

a. Documentary proof of citizenship.
b. An identifying witness.
c. Previous passport if issued since January 2, 1918.
d. Photographs.
e. Fees, $10 ($9 must accompany the application to Washington and should be in the form of a postal money order made payable to the Secretary of State, Washington, D.C., and $1 paid to the clerk or agent before whom the application is executed).

Necessary Proof to Establish American Citizenship

All documents, such as birth certificates, baptismal certificates, certified copies of records, affidavits, etc., submitted as evidence of the American citizenship of an applicant for a passport must give the place and date of birth, and bear the seal of the office and signature of the officer before whom such documents were executed, or by whom they were issued. Birth and baptismal certificates to be acceptable must show that the birth or baptism was recorded shortly after birth.

Unless evidence of American citizenship was submitted with a previous application for a passport, an applicant must submit such evidence.

3. A native American citizen must submit with his application for a passport, a birth certificate, or, if such a certificate is not obtainable, a baptismal certificate or a certified copy of the record of baptism. If either of these certificates is not obtainable, the applicant should submit in lieu thereof an affidavit executed by a parent, brother, sister, or other relative, preferably an older person, or the physician who attended the birth, setting forth the date and place of birth of the applicant. If an affidavit of a relative or physician cannot be obtained, an affidavit of some other reputable person having knowledge of facts which enable him to testify as to the place and date of birth, should be submitted. In the affidavit a brief statement should be made showing how and through what source knowledge of the place and date of birth was acquired.

4. A person who claims American citizenship through birth abroad of a native or naturalized American father or mother should prove the parent's birth in the United States or naturalization as a citizen of this country by documentary evidence.

5. a. An American woman who was married to a native American citizen prior to September 22, 1922, may submit evidence of either her own or her husband's American citizenship. One married to a naturalized American citizen prior to September 22, 1922, must submit evidence of her husband's naturalization.

b. An American woman who lost American citizenship by marriage to an alien, but who alleges that after the termination of the marital relation and prior to September 22, 1922, she resumed American citizenship, must submit evidence that she was an American citizen at the time of marriage. If the marital relation is alleged to have been terminated by divorce, a certified copy of the decree of court granting the absolute divorce should be submitted. A legal separation or an interlocutory decree of divorce does not terminate marriage.

c. An American woman who was married to an American citizen or to an alien on or after September 22, 1922, must submit evidence of her own citizenship.

d. An alien woman eligible to naturalization who was married to an American citizen prior to September 22, 1922, must submit evidence of her husband's American citizenship.

6. A person who claims American citizenship by naturalization must submit with his application a certificate of naturalization.

7. A person who claims citizenship by the naturalization of husband or parent must submit with application for a passport the naturalization certificate of the husband or parent.

8. An applicant who holds an expired or unexpired passport issued since January 2, 1918, should submit the old passport for cancellation. Such document will be accepted as evidence of citizenship if proper documentary evidence of American nationality was submitted with the previous application. If a previous passport, issued since January 2, 1918, which has definitely expired cannot be presented for surrender or cancellation, it is necessary to state briefly in the new application the disposition of the previous passport. However, if the previous passport has not definitely expired it is necessary to submit under oath a separate statement setting forth in circumstantial detail the disposition of the valid passport.

Photographs

9. Two recently taken photographs (duplicates) must be submitted of each person named in application, one affixed to the application, the other, signed by the applicant, must accompany the application unattached. A group photograph should be used when a wife, or wife and children, are included in one application. Photographs must be full face, on thin paper, with a light background, and not over 3x3 inches nor less than 2½ by 2½ inches in size. Photographs printed on photographic paper the back of which is glazed, will not adhere to passports and therefore will not be accepted.

Identifying Witness

10. The identifying witness must appear in person with the applicant and fill in and sign the affidavit (on the application form) before a clerk of court or an agent of the Department of State. The identifying witness should be an American citizen (man or woman), who is able to state under oath that he has known the applicant for at least two years; that the applicant is the person he represents himself to be; and that the facts stated in the application are true to the best of the witness' knowledge and belief. An expired American passport bearing a signed photograph may be used as identification in lieu of an identifying witness. In cases of persons who have not previously obtained passports, the applicant or the witness must be known to the clerk of court or the Passport Agent, or the applicant or the witness must be able to establish his identity beyond reasonable doubt, by documentary evidence which should be listed on the application. If the applicant or the witness is not known to the clerk of court or Passport Agent and conclusive documentary evidence of the identity of either cannot be presented, the applicant will be required to obtain as a witness to his application an American citizen established in a recognized profession or business and having his office or place of business within the jurisdiction of the court or passport agency. However, if a clerk of court or a Passport Agent considers that an applicant has not been satisfactorily identified, he may forward the application to the Department of State with a statement of the facts in the case and give the names of two or more persons with whom the Department may communicate in order to satisfy itself on the identity and citizenship of the applicant.

Validity and Renewal of Passports

11. Under the act of May 16, 1932, a passport is valid for 2 years from date of issue unless limited to a shorter period. It may be renewed for a period of 2 years upon payment of a fee of $5, but the final date of expiration shall not be more than 4 years from the original date of issue. A passport which was issued within the period of 4 years prior to the time when application for renewal is made may be renewed.

Requests for renewal may be made by personal application or letter addressed to the Department of State, a Passport Agent, a diplomatic or consular officer of the United States, the United States High Commissioner to the Philippine Islands, or the chief executives of Hawaii, Puerto Rico, the Virgin Islands, Guam, or American Samoa, and the fee, in currency or postal money order, should accompany each request. Drafts or checks will not be accepted. Each request for renewal should be accompanied by the passport the renewal of which is desired.

Additional Notes

12. The holder of an expired passport who desires a new passport must submit a new application, accompanied by the usual fee.

13. Neither a passport, nor any travel document in lieu thereof, can be issued by the Department of State to an alien who has not completed his naturalization.

14. If the applicant signs by mark, two attesting witnesses thereto are required.

Patents

1. Definition.—As here used the word patent is defined to mean the granting by the United States to inventors for a limited time the exclusive right to the use, manufacture, and sale of their own inventions. The instrument by which this privilege is confirmed to the inventor is called the "letters patent" and is issued in the name of the United States of America under the seal of the Patent Office and is signed by the Secretary of the Interior, and countersigned by the Commissioner of Patents.

2. Items Patentable. — The law provides that "Any person who has invented or discovered any new and useful art, machine, manufacture, or composition of matter, or any new and useful improvement thereof, or who has invented or discovered and asexually reproduced any distinct and new variety of plant, other than a tuber-propagated plant, not known or used by others in this country before his invention or discovery thereof, and not patented or described in any printed publication in this or any foreign country before his invention or discovery thereof, for more than one year prior to his application, and not patented in a country foreign to the United States . . . more than twelve months before his application, and not in public use or on sale in the United States for more than one year prior to his application, unless the same is proved to have been abandoned, may, upon payment of the fees required by law, and other due proceedings had, obtain a patent."

3. Foreign Patent Not a Bar.—A person is not debarred from receiving a patent for his invention or discovery by reason of its first having been patented in a foreign country unless his application for the foreign patent was filed more than twelve months prior to his filing of the application in the United States. In the case of patenting designs, the interval is limited to six months.

4. Duration of Patent. — A patent is good for seventeen years, but now cannot be extended except by act of Congress. Inventions previously patented in a foreign country must expire at the same time that the foreign patent expires, but in no case shall they be extended more than seventeen years.

5. How Secured. — The method of securing patents is by petition, which must be in writing addressed to the Commissioner of Patents, and must state the name and residence of the petitioner requesting the granting of a patent, designate by title the invention sought to be patented, and contain a reference to the specifications of the invention. It must be signed by the applicant and attested by two witnesses. An alien may obtain a patent on the same terms as a citizen.

6. Specifications.—The specifications above referred to are a written description of the invention or discovery, and the manner of making, constructing, composing, and using the same, and they are required to be in such full, clear, concise, and exact terms as to enable any person skilled in the art or science to which the invention or discovery appertains, to make, construct, compose, and use the same. The inventor or discoverer must point out in particular how his invention or discovery is different from others in the same line.

The specifications and claims should be written on but one side of the paper and signed by the applicant. All interlineations and erasures should be avoided.

7. The Oath.—The applicant for a patent must make oath or affirmation that he verily believes himself to be the first and original discoverer of the art, machine, manufacture, composition, other article, or improvement for which he solicits a patent; that he does not know and does not believe that the same was ever before known or used. In addition he should state of what country he is a citizen and where he resides, and whether he is a sole or joint inventor.

The oath should be sworn to before a notary public or some other officer authorized to administer oaths and having an official seal.

8. Drawings.—The applicant for patent is required also to furnish drawing of his invention whenever the nature of the case admits. Drawings must be signed by the inventor and must be attested by two witnesses; they must show every feature of the invention covered by the claims. When the invention is an improvement on some old machine, a drawing must exhibit in one or more views the invention itself disconnected from the old structure, and also in another view so much of the old structure as will suffice to show the connection of the invention therewith.

9. Material. — Drawings must be made upon pure white, calendered, smooth, bristol board of three-sheet thickness. India ink alone must be used. Sheets must be exactly ten by fifteen inches in size. Drawings must be made with pen only, and must be absolutely black. Drawings must be made with the fewest lines possible consistent with clearness.

The scale to which a drawing is made must be large enough to show the mechanism without crowding.

10. Signature of the inventor should be placed at the lower right-hand corner of each sheet of drawing and two attesting witnesses should sign at the lower left-hand corner. Drawings should be rolled for transmission to the patent office. The drawings must never be folded.

11. Model.—A model must be furnished when required by the commissioner.

12. Specimens must be furnished when required by the commissioner.

13. Attorneys.—The practice of the Patent Office allows the applicant to retain an attorney and when the petition is prosecuted by an attorney a power of attorney should be included in the petition. In ordinary cases it is always best to retain some experienced patent attorney to prosecute the application.

14. Caveats.—Formerly an inventor could file a caveat setting forth the object and distinguishing characteristics of his invention and asking protection for his right until he had finished his invention. This operated for one year. This law was repealed in 1910 so that the only way an inventor can secure any form of federal protection on his patent is by applying for letters patent.

15. Fees.—The schedule of fees and prices of publications can be had on application to the Commissioner of Patents, Washington, D. C. The fee for filing applications ranges from $10 to $30. For any other information concerning patents an inquiry should be addressed to the Commissioner of Patents.

16. Preliminary Examinations.—An applicant for a patent may often save considerable expense by having a preliminary examination made of the patents allowed by the Patent Office, to determine whether or not the invention has been patented by somebody else. This examination cannot be made by the Commissioner or any one of his office, but patent attorneys will make the examination for a small fee.

17. Assignments.—Patents may be assigned in whole or in part, and the right to manufacture, sell, and use the patent in any county, state, township, or other district may be granted by the holder of the patent. All such assignments or transfers should be in writing, and are void unless recorded in the Patent Office within three months from their date.

18. Foreign Patents. — Contrasted with most foreign countries the cost of a patent is very low in the United States and the law is liberal in allowing the inventor to exploit it. The patent will remain protected even though the invention is not manufactured at all. Some European countries will protect patents only as long as the articles are actually manufactured within their own borders, and as long as the taxes are paid. In the United States foreigners can have their inventions patented without manufacturing them here, and without any taxes whatever.

Payment

1. Legal Tender.—In all agreements the payment is to be made in cash unless otherwise stipulated. Since 1933 all coins and currencies of the United States, including Federal Reserve notes, are legal tender for all debts. The United States, however, has ordered that gold coins and certificates payable in gold be exchanged at the Treasury for silver and silver certificates. Any provision in an obligation which calls for payment in gold is against public policy and may be discharged by payment in legal tender.

2. Checks.—In modern times checks are given and received in payment of debts. Legally, however, a check is not payment until it is cashed. In other words, a check is a conditional payment and if the check is not honored, the creditor can sue on the check. He can also sue any of the endorsers whose names appear on the check. But if the holder of the check does not present it for payment within a reasonable time and the bank on which it is drawn fails, he must suffer the loss caused by the delay.

3. Notes.—A note given in payment for a debt, may or may not cancel the debt. If the parties intended the note as actual payment the debtor cannot sue on the original debt; he must sue to recover on the note itself. This is a question of the facts in the case, to be determined by the court.

4. Applying Payment When There is More Than One Debt.—If a debtor owes more than one debt to the same creditor, he can apply his payments in any way he sees fit. If he fails to do so the creditor can make the application, and if neither does so, the law applies the payment first to interest due and the balance to the oldest debt. A signer on a note may insist that payment be applied first to the debt on which he is surety.

5. Receipts.—A receipt for a debt is regarded on its face as evidence of payment. This evidence, however, is not conclusive and can sometimes be contradicted by other evidence. For example, suppose "A" gave "B" a receipt for $20.00 and afterwards discovered that the bill "B" had given him was a counterfeit. "A" could introduce evidence to prove fraud and thus invalidate the receipt. A contract embodied in a receipt without seal or consideration is not binding, but if there is a valuable consideration, or if the instrument is under seal, such a contract would be as lawful as any other.

Prescriptive Rights

1. Definition.—A prescriptive right is a right acquired by use and time and allowed by law.

2. A Right of Way.—A person may acquire a permanent right of way over another's land by passing over that land to his own land for a period of time fixed by law. This right of way cannot be acquired against a minor or against any one who is incapable of defending his possessions. A person attempting to establish such a right of way can be stopped by appropriate legal action.

3. A Way of Necessity.—Sometimes a person sells a part of his farm which is not located on the road. The law allows the purchaser the right to enter and leave the premises, and such a right is called "a way of necessity." He must exercise reasonable care in selecting his road to the main road, and this road ultimately becomes part of the title to the property.

4. Restrictions. — The law prescribes restrictions on the use of a right of way or a way of necessity. Thus the purchaser of the farm away from the road could not subdivide it and transfer his right of way to others without permission of the real owner of the way. However, more than one person can claim a right of way. A tenant can never acquire a right of way beyond the duration of his lease.

5. Building Rights.—

a. The owner of a building has no action against one who cuts off his light, air, or view by erecting a building on adjacent land, unless the right has been expressly acquired. The right to light, air, and unobstructed view may sometimes be acquired by deed or by presumption. If the owner has acquired such a right he loses it by tearing down the building and erecting a new one.

b. A person has the right to the lateral support of his land. If, therefore, a neighbor excavates in an unreasonable manner and his building consequently falls down, the owner has an action against the neighbor and any excavator hired by him.

6. Water Rights.—

a. The water which runs through a person's land may legally be held back for a short time to furnish water power, or it may be used for any other reasonable purpose.

b. Neither a person nor a municipality may dump impurities or sewage into a stream, making the water unfit for use below.

c. As a general rule ditches or obstructions may not be dug either to hinder or to hasten the flow of water from one person's land to another in other than the natural way.

d. A riparian owner has the right to cut and sell ice which forms over the portion of the bed of the stream which he owns, provided he does not interfere with the rights of other owners.

e. A person digging a well cannot be held for cutting off his neighbor's water supply, unless it can be proved that he acted maliciously.

Professional Men

1. Doctors.—A doctor or physician is a person who has (1) been educated in the science of medicine and surgery, (2) been graduated from a medical college, (3) passed the state medical examination, and (4) been licensed by the state to practice his profession.

2. Confidential Disclosures. — It frequently happens that a doctor is called upon to give expert testimony in a civil or criminal case. He is not, however, required or permitted to divulge on the witness stand any confidential statement or information obtained in his professional relationship with his patient.

3. Liability.—A doctor is not legally liable for the success or failure of his treatment in the absence of an express contract. He is required to exercise the greatest care, diligence, and skill in his work, and can be held criminally liable only for carelessness and gross inefficiency. The crime of malpractice consists of any injurious or improper treatment.

4. Lawyers. — A lawyer is a person who has (1) been educated in the science of law, (2) been graduated from a law school (in some states), and (3) passed the state bar examination. Every man is entitled by law to have a lawyer represent him in his trial, but the court will furnish the services of a lawyer only in criminal cases.

5. Confidential Disclosures.—What has already been said about the confidential relationship existing between doctors and patients, applies even more strongly to attorneys and their clients. The matters spoken of between them are confidential and no law can force the lawyer to divulge them on the witness stand.

6. Liens.—An attorney has a lien for the payment of his fee on all documents, moneys and other things coming into his possession.

7. Liability.—A lawyer cannot be held liable for the failure of his case unless he did not exercise reasonable care and judgment.

Sale and Transfer of Property

1. Definition.—A sale is the exchange of property for a consideration called the **price**, which is either to be paid at once or at some future date. An agreement to sell at a future date is called an **executory sale.** A present sale is called an **executed sale.** A sale may be made either in writing or orally.

2. What Constitutes a Sale.—

a. Sales are based on mutual agreement.

b. Either the thing sold must exist at the time of the sale or there must be reason to believe that it will be in existence and in possession of the seller. For example: If a man sold a horse for $100 and the horse died before the actual time of the sale the transaction would not be a sale.

c. Grain or other produce not yet sowed or planted can be sold because the seller may reasonably expect a crop. Machinery or other manufactured goods may be sold before they are made and the seller can be held to perform his part of the contract as though the articles actually existed at the time of the sale.

d. The thing sold must be specified and set apart as the property of the buyer in order to complete the sale.

e. When nothing is said as to the time of payment when the sale is made the law presumes that the property must be paid for before the purchaser can secure possession. If credit is agreed upon the buyer is entitled to immediate possession.

f. When goods are sold "on sale or return" the title passes to the purchaser immediately, but may go back to the seller if the goods are returned within the time specified in the agreement.

g. If goods are sold on approval the title passes to the buyer when he signifies his approval or when he keeps them beyond the time set for their return.

h. When no price is fixed in the agreement the purchaser must pay a reasonable price.

i. Goods are often sold and shipped subject to bill of lading, that is, payment is not made until the goods are delivered. Thus the seller controls the property until it is paid for, although the title may pass to the buyer.

3. Statute of Frauds.—The Uniform Sales Act provides that a contract to sell $500.00 worth of goods or more, cannot be enforced:

a. unless the purchaser advances a sum of money to bind the bargain, or

b. unless the purchaser accepts a part of the goods, or

c. unless the contract is in writing.

This rule, of course, does not apply when the goods sold are to be manufactured especially for the buyer and would not be readily salable to others.

4. Relieving the Buyer. — The buyer's obligation is limited in various ways. For instance, the contract may be voided:

a. if the goods purchased have been damaged or destroyed before delivery;

b. if in his own opinion the goods are not satisfactory.

5. Warranties.—When goods are sold there are certain warranties by the seller which may be either expressed or implied. Any statement made by the seller tending to induce the buyer to purchase is an express warranty. In every sale there are implied warranties, (1) that the seller has the title to the property, and (2) that the goods will correspond with the description or sample. Any defects which can be seen in property when sold do not relieve the buyer from meeting his contract though he claims that he did not see the defects. The law does not furnish eyes for the purchaser of property. But defects in property which cannot be seen and of which the seller makes no statement, but recommends as good or sound, release the buyer from his contract.

6. The Bulk Sales Law is a part of the law of many states. It provides that when a stock of goods or merchandise is sold, transferred or consigned in bulk, the seller's creditors must be notified in writing a certain number of days before the sale is completed. Thus when a merchant sells his merchandise in bulk, the buyer should keep the following considerations in mind: First, he should demand a bill of sale. Second, he should either demand an affidavit from the seller that he has notified the creditors, or secure a sworn list of the creditors and notify them himself. This law applies to corporations, partnerships, and individuals; and any attempt to evade its provisions carries with it a penalty of a fine, a year's imprisonment, or both. If the creditors are not properly notified they can hold the purchaser liable for the debts.

7. Stock Market Speculation. — Trading in stocks, grains, and cotton, together with the buying and selling of futures, is now largely regulated by statute. A contract of this kind which involves the actual delivery of property is perfectly legal, even if at the time the sale was made, the seller did not own the property sold. However, when no exchange of property is ever contemplated and the parties merely propose to effect a settlement based on the market changes, the contract is not legal.

Form of Bill of Sale

KNOW ALL MEN BY THESE PRESENTS, That I, ... of ...., County ...., in consideration of six hundred ($600) dollars to me in hand paid by .... of the same place, the receipt of which is hereby acknowledged, do hereby grant, sell, assign, transfer, and deliver unto the said ...., his heirs and assigns, the following goods and chattels, to wit:

Four Yearling Heifers, at $50.00 each..................$200.00
30 head of Sheep, at $4.00 each 120.00
Five sets of Harness, at $20.00 each...................... 100.00
Two Farm Wagons, at $35.00 each.......................... 70.00
One Corn Planter, at $20.00................................. 20.00
Six Plows, at $15.00 each..................................... 90.00

To have and to hold all of the said goods and chattels to the said ...., his heirs and assigns forever. And I do hereby covenant to and with the said .... that I am the legal owner of said goods and chattels; that they are free and clear from all other and prior sales and incumbrances; that I have good right to sell and convey the same as aforesaid, and that in the peaceable possession of the said .... I will forever warrant and defend the same against the lawful claims and demands of all persons whomsoever.

In witness whereof I have hereunto set my hand and seal this 29th day of June, A.D. 19.........

In the presence of

....

....

(Signed) ....(Seal)

Note: In selling or buying automobiles, especially used cars, it is always wise to insert the name of the machine, its model, the engine number, the car number, also the type of car, its color, and any other information which will help to identify it.

Shipping

1. Registration. — The law requires all ships flying the United States flag to be registered. A ship engaged in foreign trade must be **registered** with the collector of customs in the district in which her home port is situated. This formality is called **enrollment** in the case of large ships engaged in coastwise or internal commerce, and **license** for smaller ships.

2. Ownership.—Vessels may be owned by individuals, partnerships, or corporations, and the ownership may be acquired either by purchase or construction. If several individuals own a ship they are tenants in common where there is no other relation between the part owners of a vessel than that arising out of joint ownership. Each part owner has his share of the profits and expenses, and no one individual can bind the others except for the necessary maintenance of the ship. When a partnership or corporation owns a vessel, the ordinary rules of corporations and partnership apply.

3. Sale.—The owner of a ship can sell or mortgage his interest at any time, but in order to effect a good title against third parties the contract should be in writing. If a ship is sold while it is at sea, the buyer takes it subject to all contracts made by the master before learning of the sale. In all other cases the buyer is not liable for repairs made or supplies furnished previous to the sale.

4. Maritime Loans.—In cases of great emergency, for example when a ship is in a foreign port without funds to purchase necessary supplies, a master can secure a maritime loan, in which the vessel is put up as security. If the vessel fails to reach home the lender loses his money, but in the event of a safe arrival, he has the boat as security and can hold the master personally. Such a contract calls for a high rate of interest but is perfectly legal. The technical name for the contract is "contract of bottomry."

5. The Master of a vessel is the chief officer. The law gives him authority to bind the owners for necessary repairs or supplies. He must render accurate accounts of his actions and money received, but his first duty is to the passengers and the crew. He has the power to regulate their actions in any manner which is necessary to their safety, comfort, and good order. If on account of illness, insanity, or other reason, the master is unable to perform his duties, they pass to the lower officers in the order of their rank.

6. The Seamen. — Statutes and maritime law generally require the execution of shipping papers between the master and the seamen before starting on a voyage to a foreign country or from one state to another. These articles must specify:

a. the exact nature of the voyage.
b. the destination.
c. the duration.
d. the amount of wages to be paid each seaman.

If shipping articles are not properly executed, or if the master violates the contract, the seaman can leave the ship and recover the highest rate of wages, his expenses home, and damages. On the other hand a seaman may be discharged for reasons which show him to be unfit for the service or to be trusted in the vessel, such as:

a. long continued disobedience.
b. drunkenness.
c. incapacity (due to his own conduct).

7. Courts of Admiralty have jurisdiction over all maritime contracts, torts, injuries, or offenses.

Statutes of Limitation

1. Definition.—A statute of limitation is a law which specifies the time in which debts are outlawed. All states have such laws providing different periods of time, varying from one to twenty years, within which legal actions must be brought, before the courts are closed to them.

2. The Time Begins to Run as soon as the debt is incurred or, in accounts, from the date of the last purchase. The debt may be renewed by a partial payment of principal or interest, or by a written acknowledgment in a note or paper, with an expressed willingness to pay indicated.

Torts or Wrongs

1. Definition.—A tort is a private or civil wrong or injury arising independent of contract. The proper remedy is an action for damages.

2. Torts and Crimes.—There is a distinction between torts and crimes. If a wrongful act violates a private right it is a tort; if it violates a public right it is a crime. Very frequently the wrongful act is in violation of both private and public rights. In such cases, even if the wrong-doer make personal restitution or settlement with the person wronged, the state still has the right to punish the wrong-doer for the crime. Suppose A steals $500 from B who finds it out and succeeds in getting A to return the money. "A" has still committed a crime against the public and can be punished as the law provides.

3. Violation of Contract.—Contracts frequently contain clauses fixing the amount of damages for breach of the contract. Such a clause is called a "liquidated damages" clause. If the clause is reasonable and does not amount to a penalty, it will be upheld by the courts.

4. Assault and Battery.—A person who intentionally invades the person of another by physical contact (or puts him in apprehension of an invasion of his person by threat of immediate physical contact) without such person's consent, and not in reasonable defense of person or other interest, and not in the performance of some duty imposed by law, or the exercise of some privilege by reason of the relation of the parties, is liable in damages. A successful assault becomes a battery when the injury is actually done.

a. Every person is entitled by law to liberty, security of life, and security of his property.

b. Mere words do not constitute an assault.

c. The wrong consists not so much in the actual striking of the person as in the manner and spirit of the act.

d. Accidental injury is not a battery.

e. A blow unlawfully aimed at one person but striking another is a battery.

f. Reasonable methods of self defense may be employed in resisting a battery and in defending a member of one's family, or property.

g. A school teacher has the right to require obedience to reasonable rules, and proper attention to his authority, and to inflict punishment for disobedience. Hence, reasonable punishment, having in mind the age, size, and physical condition of the pupil, is not a battery.

5. Defamation.—A defamation is a false and malicious imputation of bad character or reputation either by slander or by libel.

a. Every person has a right to his good reputation.

b. Every person is assumed to have a good reputation until the contrary is proved.

c. Slander is oral defamation.

d. Libel is defamation in writing or printing.

6. Slander.—In simple words this tort consists of speaking words in another's hearing which injure a third person's reputation. The United States Supreme Court has classified slanderous words which are objectionable:

a. Words falsely spoken of a person which impute to the party the commission of some criminal offense involving moral turpitude for which the party, if the charge is true, may be indicted and punished.

b. Words falsely spoken of a person which impute that the party is infected with some infectious disease, which, if the charge is true, would exclude the party from society.

c. Defamatory words spoken of a party which impute to the party unfitness to perform the duties of an office or employment for profit, or the want of integrity in the discharge of the duties of such an office or employment.

d. Defamatory words falsely spoken of a party which prejudice such party in his or her profession or trade.

e. Defamatory words falsely spoken of a person, which, though not in themselves actionable, occasion the party special damage.

7. Libel.—It is even more dangerous to defame a person's character in writing. Many words when written or printed are libelous, which if spoken would not be slanderous without proof of special injury.

a. The owners of books and newspapers generally are liable for the publication of libelous matter, though made without their knowledge and even against their orders.

b. Newsdealers are immune from any liability for selling or displaying newspapers or magazines which contain libelous matter, providing such dealers have no knowledge of the libelous matter.

c. In order to hold the editor or proprietor of the printing plant it must be proved that the libelous matter could be recognized by an intelligent person as libel.

8. The Defenses are given below:

a. The truth of the charge generally is a complete defense against an action for damages. Statutes, however, sometimes require that not only must the words be true, but they must be uttered in good faith.

b. A privileged communication, such as what is said or written in a judicial proceeding or in a legitimate newspaper report thereof, is not held to be libelous matter. This privilege extends to the heads of the executive departments of government. Statements rendered by mercantile agencies, and the reports of many semi-public societies are also conditionally privileged.

c. Fair comment is still another defense. The conduct of public men is held to be a proper matter for public discussion, so long as the writer keeps within the bounds of an honest intention to discharge a duty to the public, and does not make the occasion a mere cover for false allegations. The same rule applies to newspaper reports of literary or artistic productions offered to the public.

9. False Imprisonment is a crime and the person unlawfully imprisoned has a civil action for damages. The defense may be that the officer was clothed with the proper authority, and in the case of parent and child, guardian and ward, or teacher and pupil it may be shown that the alleged wrongdoer was acting within his duty.

10. Malicious Prosecution is another wrong. This is the malicious instituting of suit without probable cause, and both the malice and the lack of probable cause must be proved. A suit to recover for this wrong cannot be commenced before the alleged malicious prosecution has come to an end. That the party acted on the advice of his attorney after a full and fair disclosure of the facts is a good defense.

11. Conspiracy.—A conspiracy is a combination of two or more persons to accomplish an unlawful end which is injurious to another. Thus a trade union may lawfully agree that they will stop work, or that they will not work with certain other laborers, but they commit a wrong as soon as they interfere with the liberty of others. Employers combined to use unlawful methods to exclude a certain class of workmen, are also guilty of a wrong. An agreement among manufacturers that they will all operate as the majority agree may be a conspiracy in restraint of trade.

12. Religious Liberty is guaranteed to every man by the constitution. The law does not interfere with religious societies unless they wrongfully expel a member or otherwise break the laws.

13. Search and Seizure.—It is unlawful to search private premises unless a search warrant has been issued by proper authority. It is a criminal offense to open another's letters, or to retain or pry into them. The Federal and state constitutions protect persons against unreasonable searches and seizures.

14. Nuisances.—A nuisance is anything wrongfully done or permitted which injures or annoys another in the enjoyment of his legal rights. Below is a list of some of the common nuisances subject to an action in tort:

a. To remove or weaken the lateral support of the adjoining land.

b. To mine or tunnel under another's land without providing suitable support.

c. To extend buildings over another's land.

d. To allow filthy deposits to accumulate on one's property.

e. To deposit refuse in a stream of water.

f. To erect a dam, backing up the water to injure the land of another.

g. To use or care for explosives, loaded weapons, or dangerous machines in a negligent manner.

h. To conduct a place of business or amusement, or engage in any activity, in a way that will materially interfere with the ordinary physical comfort of others.

i. To allow poisonous or offensive materials to remain in a place where they may cause injury to others.

j. To put or allow a heavy article or substance where it is likely to fall and injure persons or property.

k. To erect, operate, and maintain electrical appliances without reasonable care in proportion to their danger.

l. For a state, county, or municipality to allow defects in streets, highways, or sidewalks which result in injury to persons or property.

Trade-Marks

1. Definition.—A trade-mark is an emblem or symbol to designate the goods of a merchant or manufacturer.

2. Registration.—The owner of a trade-mark may have it registered in the Copyright Office and thus acquire the right to keep others from using it.

3. Steps Necessary to Secure Registration.—The first step is to file or sign an application addressed to the Commissioner of Patents. This must include:

a. the name, domicile, location, and citizenship of applicant.

b. description of the goods for which trade-mark is used.

c. method of affixing trade-mark.

d. length of time the trade-mark has been used.

e. description of trade-mark.

f. drawing and specimens of the trade-mark.

The next step is the payment of the sum of $15.00 for registration.

4. Length of Time A Trade-Mark is Protected.—A certificate of registration remains in force for twenty years. The life of a trade-mark previously registered in a foreign country may be cut short of the twenty-year period if it ceases to be protected in that country. If application is made not more than six months prior to the expiration of the period, the certificate may be renewed upon payment of the regular fee of $15.00.

5. Restrictions.—The law has placed certain restrictions on the registration of trade-marks. For example, it is impossible to register a trade-mark:

a. if it is immoral or scandalous.

b. if it consists of or includes the flag or other insignia of the United States, any state, or any foreign country.

c. if it consists of the emblem of any fraternal society or club.

d. if it is similar to one used by another manufacturer who manufactures similar goods.

e. if it consists merely of the name of the individual, firm, corporation, or association, not set forth in any unusual way.

f. when it consists merely of words or devices.

g. if it consists of the photograph of an individual without his consent in writing.

h. if it consists of a mark used in unlawful business, or upon any injurious article.

6. Infringement.—The registration of a trade-mark is evidence of ownership. In case of infringement the owner can bring an action either in law or in equity. Thus:

a. he may have an injunction issued compelling the wrongdoer to cease, and

b. he may bring an action for the damages he has sustained by the wrongful use of his trade-mark.

7. State Registrations.—At moderate costs a person may secure registration in all states in which he does or intends to do business. This is important, as the Federal Registration Act protects a trade-mark only in interstate or foreign commerce. It gives a person no recourse when others use his trade-mark wholly within the borders of a state. Some firms rely altogether on permanent state protection because of the fact that most of the states are liberal in their registration requirements.

8. Foreign Trade-marks.—In foreign countries the first person to register a trade-mark can prove his ownership. Thus protection should be secured as soon as possible, even though foreign trade is not contemplated at the time.

9. Expert Assistance.—To be on the safe side, secure the advice of an expert in protecting new brands or trade-marks.

Vicious Animals

1. The Owner's Responsibility.—The owners of vicious animals are responsible for any injuries they may cause while running at large. If a dog annoys travelers on a public road by scaring horses or frightening children, the owner is responsible in damages to the injured party. The owner of a vicious bull or stallion is required to exercise the greatest care in protecting the public from injury. If a person on a social or business errand is injured by a savage animal on the premises of the owner, the owner is responsible.

2. Trespassers.—These rules do not apply to trespassers who know the dangerous nature of the animal.

3. Domestic Animals.—The owner of domestic animals is responsible in case injury results because of his own negligence. On the other hand, if the animals trespass on a neighbor's land they cannot be injured or killed by the neighbor. He has a legal remedy, however, and can collect damages.

4. Fence Laws.—In certain sections of the country there are open lands where cattle and other animals are allowed to graze at will. The owners of cultivated land are there required to provide their own protection against the animals. Most states, however, have stock laws providing that animals must be kept within an enclosure, and if damage results the owner of the animals is responsible.

Will

1. Definitions. — A **will** or **testament** is generally a written instrument making disposition of a person's property, to take effect after his death. A **testator** is the maker of a will when the same is made by a male person; if a female, the maker is called a **testatrix.** A **codicil** is an addition or alteration of a part of an executed will. A **legacy** is a gift or bequest of money or personal property by will. The person to whom it is given is called a **legatee,** and if the gift consists of the remainder of the property after paying all debts and other legacies he is called the **residuary legatee.** A person to whom real estate is given is called a **devisee.** An **executor** is a male person named in the will to whom is entrusted the duty of administrating the estate of the testator according to the provisions of the will. If the will names a female person, she is called the **executrix.** An **administrator** is the male person appointed by the court to administer the estate of a deceased person who did not have a will or if the party named in the will is incompetent or refuses to act. If the party appointed by the court is a female person, she is called the **administratrix.**

2. Who May Make a Will.—All persons are competent to make a will except infants, persons of unsound mind, and idiots. In like manner any person who is competent to make a will can appoint his own executor. If the person so appointed is legally competent to transact business, the court will confirm the appointment if he lives within the jurisdiction of the court.

3. Kinds of Wills.—There are two kinds of wills, written and unwritten. An unwritten will is called **nuncupative.** Such a will might be made by a soldier in active service or a sailor at sea, and depends upon proof of the persons hearing it.

4. Requirements:—

a. A will should be written.

b. A will should be dated.

c. Testator should sign his name in full, by mark if necessary.

d. It should be witnessed by two or more disinterested parties, the number of witnesses varying according to statutes.

e. It is not necessary that the witnesses should know the contents of the will. It is generally necessary that the testator acknowledge to them that it is his will, sign it in their presence, and request them to sign as witnesses in his presence and in the presence of each other.

f. The wishes of the testator should be fully and clearly expressed in the will.

g. No exact form of words is necessary to make a will.

h. In writing wills simple language should be used. Statements concerning every provision or condition of the will should be fully and plainly made.

i. A will is valid even if written with a lead pencil.

j. A will to be effective in matters pertaining to real estate must be executed according to the laws of the state in which the real estate is located. This requirement is generally in regard to the number of witnesses to a will. Care should be exercised to dispose of all the property belonging to the person making a will. In order to accomplish this a will should have a clause, "all the rest, residue, and remainder of my estate, I give" etc., or "all the rest, residue, and remainder of my estate shall be divided into the following parts, 1/3 to ...., 1/6 to ....," etc.

k. Personal property may be conveyed in accordance with the law of the state in which the testator resides.

l. If trust provisions or limited estates are to be provided for in a will, it is best to have the will drawn by a competent lawyer, as these provisions are very technical, and may result in much litigation if not carefully drawn.

m. Generally a person does not need to give his property or any part of it to his children, but mention of the names of all the children is evidence of the testator's competency.

5. Codicils.—The same principles apply to a codicil as to a will. It must be signed in the presence of witnesses.

6. Married Women.—A wife is entitled to a certain portion of her husband's property called the **dower.** If the will does not provide that amount for her she can have it set aside and claim her dower right.

7. When is a Will Set Aside?—

a. When it can be proved that the testator was feeble-minded or lacking in mental capacity.

b. When the testator revokes it before death. It is usually destroyed.

c. When the property devised has been disposed of during the testator's lifetime.

8. General Principles:—

a. Any person may be a devisee or a legatee, including married women, minors, or corporations.

b. Testator's property is primarily liable for testator's debts and funeral expenses, which must be paid before any part of it can be distributed to legatees.

c. A will has no force or effect until after testator's death.

d. The last will annuls all former wills.

e. A will takes effect from the day of the testator's death.

f. All matters pertaining to wills and inheritances are handled by the court having probate jurisdiction.

Form of Will

A will to be valid must be in writing and signed at the end by the testator in the presence of at least two witnesses (in some jurisdictions the requirement is three witnesses), who must all be present when the testator signs his name to the will, and the witnesses must also sign their names as such witnesses in the presence of each other and in the presence of the testator. If the will is written on more than one single sheet it is a wise precaution for the testator and the witnesses to sign their names on the margin of each sheet.

Will Form

I, ..., residing in ...., in the County of ...., and State of ...., being of sound mind and disposing memory do make, ordain, publish, and declare this to be my Last Will and Testament, hereby revoking all former Wills and Codicils by me made.

(Here insert all bequests and instructions)

Lastly, I make, constitute, and appoint .... to be the executor (trix) of this my Last Will and Testament.

IN WITNESS WHEREOF, I have hereunto subscribed my name and affixed my seal the .... day of ...., in the year of Our Lord, One Thousand Nine Hundred and ....

.........................(Seal)

Testator's Signature.

This instrument was on the day of the date hereof, signed, published, and declared by the said testator .... to be his (her) Last Will and Testament in the presence of us who at his (her) request have subscribed our names hereto as witnesses, in his (her) presence, and in the presence of each other.

(Witnesses' names and addresses)

Information for Executors and Administrators

An executor is named in a will to execute that will and settle the estate. If the will does not name an executor, or if named, he will not or cannot act, the Probate Court (in some states called the Surrogate, in others Orphans', Court) appoints an "administrator with the will annexed." If a person dies without leaving a will the court appoints an administrator, whose duty is the same as that of an executor, except that he, having no will of the deceased, distributes the property as the law directs.

The duties of an executor are: First: To see that the deceased is suitably buried, avoiding unreasonable expense if the estate is insolvent. Second: To offer the will for probate, or proving; to conform to the laws of his state and rules of the court, the clerk of which will give full instructions. Third: To make and return to the court within required time an inventory of the property. Real estate lying in another state need not be inventoried, for that must be administered upon in the state where it lies; but personal property situated in another state should be inventoried. If the real estate is encumbered, it should be described. Fourth: To collect the property, pay the debts and dispose of the remainder as the law and will, or either, directs. Generally the debts should be paid as follows: 1. Funeral expenses. 2. Expenses of last sickness. 3. Debts due the United States. 4. Debts due the state. 5. Claims of creditors. Fifth: To render the accounts as directed by the court.

The law provides that the widow of the intestate shall be the first entitled to act as administrator; next, the nearest of kin who are competent; next, any creditor who will accept the trust; and lastly, any other suitable person.

Executors and administrators are required to take an official oath; also to give bond, which is usually for double the amount of the estate.

Generally speaking, any l lanks for probate may be secured from the clerk of the court having probate jurisdiction.

Student's and Author's
MANUAL OF INFORMATION

A Dictionary of Careers, Writing to Sell, Musical Signs and Abbreviations, Sizes of Type, Proofreading, Weights and Measures, Christian Names of Men and Women, Foreign Words and Phrases, Dictionary of Mythology, and a Reference-Work Bibliography

CHOOSING A CAREER

"What shall I do with my life? Of the many careers open to me, which one shall I choose?" The question is a natural and healthy one; but the young man or woman cannot be given an absolute answer which will solve all difficulties at one stroke. It is no more possible to say "You must choose this career and no other," than it is for a fortune-teller to predict future events accurately and consistently.

For centuries people have sought for some magic and infallible method of guiding their lives. They have turned to astrology and palmistry, under the belief that their futures could be mapped out by study of the lines in the palm or investigation of the position of sun, moon, and planets on a certain date. They have put their faith in the pseudo-science of physiognomy, which purports to read character in the shape of the chin, nose, mouth, and other features; and in the pseudo-science of phrenology, which attaches great significance to the precise shape of the skull, its "bumps" and "hollows."

Today the claims of magic and pseudo-science have been thoroughly exploded, although they continue to impose on a credulous minority. However, the desire for some magic test of vocational aptitude is not dead. Many individuals have transferred their faith from the fortune-teller to the psychologist. They have formed the belief that modern psychology has perfected certain tests which will determine a person's ability and vocation as surely as a yardstick will measure his height. Scientific psychologists are quick to point out the falsity of this belief. It is true that certain psychological tests have been devised and standardized. A great deal of attention and careful work, for example, has been given to the development of intelligence tests, measuring the individual's "I.Q."—intelligence quotient. But intelligence, or mental capacity, is a general quality, not a special talent. Intelligence tests are useful for pedagogical purposes in gaging the general ability of students, but at the most they reveal a capacity for intellectual work. They cannot reveal special talents or point out the way to the right career. Another and very different type of test which has received widespread attention is the interest test, designed to determine the subjects or fields of activity to which an individual is most attracted. But they are still in an experimental stage and cannot in any case serve as a reliable index of ability or special talent.

There are a few tests whose purpose is to determine the fitness of an individual to enter a special field. Of these, the ones devoted to engineering have proved the most successful. But even the engineering tests cannot show whether an individual has a special talent for engineering, but only whether he lacks certain qualities necessary for the competent engineer.

Broadly speaking, psychological tests cannot give a positive and unqualified answer to the question "Which career shall I choose?" Man is too complex for accurate and complete analysis. His mind is no simple set of compartments or boxes—one for each trait, from "pugnaciousness" to "intellectual judgment"—as pictured on the phrenologist's chart of the brain. The human being has a long period of infancy, during which his nervous system slowly matures under the influence of the surrounding environment. Even after growth is completed, his mind continues to develop and he is able to adapt himself readily to new situations and perform a large number of unfamiliar activities. The average person is surprisingly versatile. His personality is not ready-made. It is a thing that grows as he grows, a product of the interaction of heredity and environment.

Because of the complexity of the human personality, the choice of a career is no easy matter. While each individual has a specific hereditary equipment, scientists do not know enough about this equipment to use it as a sure basis for determining careers. Mental and emotional hereditary equipment are particularly difficult to study, yet they are of prime importance. Moreover, mere-

STUDENT'S & WRITER'S GUIDE

ly to prove that an individual is capable of doing a certain type of work does not mean that he will be happy doing it. For the choice of a career depends on many factors, not the least of which are the individual's likes and dislikes.

Ultimately each individual must choose his own career. No one can make the choice for him, although financial and social pressure may drive him into a certain field of activity. In need of money for self or family, he may be forced to accept the first job offered. But necessity seldom smothers all possibility of free choice. Having been forced to take a certain job, he can still work his way by slow degrees into a more congenial occupation.

As the individual must ultimately choose his own career, everything possible should be done to make that choice an intelligent one, based on fact and not on fancy. To begin with, he should try to get a clear idea of what various fields of work are like. He should talk with individuals who have had experience in the field he is contemplating. He should visit stores, factories, offices, to see at first hand what the work is like. Stories and articles alone cannot always be trusted to give an accurate picture of such things, since they may create an atmosphere of false glamour. There is no substitute for first-hand experience.

The individual in search of a career should attempt to visualize, honestly and accurately, what his life would be like in a certain field of work. It may be that he desires the prestige, the social and financial rewards that go with a certain position—but does not in the least like the work involved. He should give careful thought to his own tastes: whether he like a settled life or a roving one; an indoor life or an outdoor one; whether he like best to deal with persons or with things, with thoughts or with objects.

He should carefully study the practical requirements of any contemplated career. Specialized education or independent capital may be required. In some occupations it is possible to earn a fair wage from the beginning. In others there is a long period of non-remunerative apprenticeship. In some cases a person must support himself while studying and preparing for a career; it may be possible for him to make the temporary job more than a stop-gap. Obviously all these matters deserve careful thought.

He should avail himself as much as possible of genuine psychological tests. They may give him a better understanding of his own likes and dislikes. They may reveal deficiencies which would make the choice of a certain career unwise.

Young men and young women seeking careers are usually given a great deal of advice. Parents and relatives, besides attempting to choose careers for them, are apt to say such things as, "John can't concentrate." "Joan is not industrious." "Jack has no patience." "Jean is very slow." Observations of this sort often have considerable influence on children, and may sometimes do harm. Traits like patience and concentration are not easy to measure. Most important of all, an individual's good qualities may become apparent only after he finds the right job. Under the influence of the right job his energy and capacity may increase, his thoughts develop more rapidly, his intellectual grasp become stronger. The job acts as a stimulant, arousing the latent powers of the individual. For this reason an individual should be cautious in appraising his own powers, cautious against deciding that he has a deficiency of one trait and a superabundance of another. There is no magic test.

In short, the question "Which career shall I choose?" is one that may take several years to solve. Of course, there are many cases in which an individual fixes on the right career from the very start; his parents happen to make a lucky choice or he shows in early childhood unmistakable signs of a very great talent. But in the majority of cases the choice comes more slowly. Instead of making a sudden decision, the individual slowly grows into a certain career, his powers maturing during the process. That is as it should be, for an individual's career is his life—and the question of how an individual should live his life cannot be solved without serious thought and the help of experience.

The following dictionary of careers gives a bird's-eye view of about fifty large vocational fields. Its purpose is to orient the individual with respect to certain broad divisions of human activity; to outline briefly the essential features of certain careers; and to suggest certain interesting possibilities which the individual can later study at first hand. These vocational fields necessarily overlap to a certain extent. Many of them contain a large variety of jobs. But each field has its individual characteristics, its special atmosphere.

A DICTIONARY OF CAREERS

Accountancy, the recording, analysis, and interpretation of financial facts; the devising and installing of systems of accounts for business firms, and the audit and examination of such accounts; in short, the art of bookkeeping in its widest aspects. In order to become a Certified Public Accountant, an individual must pass a state examination. Not all accountants, however, need be certified. An accountant may serve a large number of firms, auditing accounts, winding up companies, etc. Or his work may be more settled. Mathematical ability, mental accuracy, a sense for detail, and the power of concentration are desirable. General business judgment is a valuable trait. The truly competent accountant is able to see beyond his figures and make constructive suggestions. A specialized education is desirable and a specialized training is necessary.

Advertising, the application of the force of organized publicity to business. It includes the study of markets; the writing of advertising copy, slogans, and the like; the preparation and placing of printed advertisements; the organizing of prize contests and other publicity schemes; and the handling of such modern advertising media as radio and skywriting. Many phases of advertising involve art work. An understanding of business trends, a flair for the up-to-the-minute, and insight into the psychology of the average man, particularly with regard to his motivations and desires, are advantageous. The successful advertising man is original, adaptable, and dynamic.

Agriculture, broadly speaking, the production of plants and animals for the use of man. It includes the arts of cultivating and conserving the fertility of the soil, the planting of seed, the care and harvesting of crops, and the raising of livestock; also the scientific study of farming problems. The life of a farmer is outdoor and settled. He is more independent than the city worker, but must be satisfied with a modest income if he desires security. He needs physical stamina, persistence, deliberate judgment, and liking for a semi-solitary life. The farmer is a jack-of-all-trades; manual ability is necessary. The scientific student of agriculture needs specialized training; his work is somewhat less arduous and settled than that of the "dirt farmer."

Aircraft, the industry based on the science of aerial navigation. It includes the designing and manufacture of aircraft, the piloting of planes, the application of radio and other findings of scientific research to the problems of aviation. It is one of the great transport industries, and offers opportunities to the individual interested in transportation problems as well as aviation proper. The aviator should have rapid mental coordination, manual accuracy and dexterity, and the ability to come through in an emergency; his work is preeminently outdoor and roving, appealing to adventurous types. In its wider aspects the industry offers an endless variety of work. Since it is a relatively new field, adaptability and originality are at a premium.

Architecture, the art of building according to certain well-defined principles of proportion and symmetry, so that an edifice, when completed, will not only suit the purpose for which it is erected, but at the same time form a harmonious whole, externally and internally. The life of the architect is both indoor and outdoor, settled and roving. He must have artistic and technical ability, but also an understanding of requirements of the individuals and industries which use his buildings; he must adjust himself to his employers, deal with them diplomatically. Love of beauty, patience, mental accuracy, sense for both detail and mass, and a broad experience of men and the conditions of life are valuable. A general college training and several years of specialized education are necessary. Study abroad is very beneficial.

Art, the creation of painting, sculpture, and other forms of design, such as the woodcut, engraving, etching, lithograph, pen drawing, and pencil sketch. The life of the young artist is apt to be a roving and uncertain one, income insecure. Creativeness, love of beauty, manual dexterity, sense of color and line, and independence are necessary qualities. The commercial artist produces all types of artistic works for purposes of advertising, promotion and improvement of form and color of manufactured products. He must be able to adjust his work to the needs of the business employing him; an instinct for advertising and showmanship is valuable. The cartoonist should have a mature understanding of social and political situations. The creator of comic strips must either have the ability to tell a story and write dialogue, or be able to collaborate with a writer.

Automobile, the industry based on the manufacture and sale of self-propelled, trackless vehicles, generally powered by gasoline engines. There is opportunity for many kinds of talent, since the industry includes design, research, organization, manufacture, selling, advertising, distribution, and other phases. For many positions mechanical aptitude is required or advantageous. Saleswork is apt to be the most remunerative. Since the automobile industry is highly advertised and competitive, a dynamic personality is helpful, coupled with adaptability and a ready appreciation of new conditions and trends. A specialized education is not essential, but often valuable.

Banking, the practical science of handling money. It involves the lending of funds, the guaranteeing of credit, the safeguarding of savings, the exchanging of moneys, the buying and selling of securities, and the collecting of bills. Since banking touches on all fields of economic endeavor, the successful banker is generally a man of comprehensive business judgment. Discretion, deliberateness, the ability to concentrate, and a logical, accurate mind are also valuable qualities. Banking offers best opportunities to the individual who desires a settled, indoor life, and is not irritated by routine. Both a general and a specialized education are advisable.

Civil Service, the body of appointed public officials charged with conducting the civil administration of the United States, the individual states, municipalities, and localities. The U. S. Civil Service includes the Departmental, Custom House, Post Office, Internal Revenue, and Government Printing Services; there are important branches in the Department of Agriculture, the Interstate Commerce Commission, and the Department of Commerce and Labor; eligibility for appointment is determined by public competitive examinations, open to any citizen fulfilling certain requirements of knowledge and experience. There are opportunities for individuals interested in personal service, human relations, and administrative and clerical work. There is greater security than in private business and beginning salaries are higher, but there are no large financial rewards.

Clothing, the industry based on the production of garments of all kinds for men, women, and children: their manufacture, merchandising, distribution, and sale. Less specialized ability is required than in many other industries, at least in regard to highly technical knowledge. An individual may move more readily from one branch of the profession to another. Originality, adaptability, and understanding of trends in public taste are desirable. The retail selling of clothing constitutes a career for the individual who is a good manager and has a flair for advertising. Costume designing provides interesting opportunities, particularly for the woman with a sense of beauty and design, and a feeling for that almost unpredictable commodity—fashion.

Cosmetics, the industry based on the manufacture, promotion, and distribution of all preparations used for beautifying the skin and hair. Skin preparations in general comprise face and talcum powders, rouges, lip salves, creams, and lotions. There are opportunities, especially for women, in many phases of the industry: buying, business and department managing, selling, operating, demonstrating, instructing, advertising, editorial work, physical education, merchandising, and art work. A knowledge of chemistry and a feeling for form and color are helpful. Adaptability, originality, and self-assurance are valuable traits. The industry offers opportunities for roving as well as settled employment.

Diplomatic Service, the body of officials representing the United States in foreign countries for the purpose of fostering friendly relations, protecting the rights of citizens abroad, and expanding foreign commerce. Closely related is the Consular Service, in which the business function is emphasized—the gathering of information for the guidance of trade and commerce. Together they form the Foreign Service of the United States. Salaries are fairly generous but limited. Candidates are required to pass an examination, and are afterwards given special training. Knowledge of a foreign language, practical law, arithmetic, and the political and commercial history of the United States is necessary. The life of a diplomatic agent is apt to be a roving one. Tact, willingness to take responsibility, and ability to deal with people are desirable traits.

Editing, the selection and preparation of written matter for publication. The individual who corrects and revises manuscripts before they are sent to the printer, and who determines the form in which they will be printed, is an editor. Thorough knowledge of language and rules of grammar and punctuation, ability to handle detail carefully, and power of concentration are desirable. The term editor is applied also to the individual who determines the policy and supervises the making of a newspaper, magazine, or other publication. The editor deals with authors, reads manuscripts of stories and articles to determine which shall be bought and published. He should have a love of reading, an understanding of public taste, adaptability, and originality. Newspaper experience provides valuable training.

Education, the art of imparting knowledge and understanding to individuals, particularly to the young and the adolescent, but to adults as well. The educational profession includes classroom teaching; conference with individual students; the practical management of schools, teachers, and students; and the study of education itself and of educational methods. Special requirements vary according to locality. In some rural districts the teacher need have only a grammar or high-school education; for many positions, however, college or normal-school degrees and special courses in education are necessary. The educator should be able to adjust himself to other individuals, deal with them successfully. Patience, humor, love of teaching, regard for truth, and a liking for routine are valuable qualities for the classroom teacher.

Engineering, the practical science of executing public or other works demanding a knowledge of machines and the principles of mechanics. It includes such diverse fields as aeronautics, industrial chemistry, city planning, traffic control, the building of military works, irrigation, sanitary science, surveying, and the making of tools and machines. Constructiveness, rapid mental and manual coordination, adaptability, mathematical ability, and originality are valuable qualities. Since almost every field of human activity has an engineering aspect, there is opportunity for satisfying all kinds of interests. There is a broad field for the individual who prefers a roving, outdoor, independent life; but settled, highly specialized activity also is possible. A specialized education is required.

Foreign Trade, the handling of business and commercial dealings with foreign countries; includes the selling and buying of products, their transport, the setting up of factories and other production units in foreign lands, and various incidental services, such as those involved in dealing with legal problems. A groundwork in some phase of domestic business is a valuable preliminary. Knowledge of a foreign language is desirable, particularly Spanish, because of the large field for trade presented by Latin America. Cosmopolitan viewpoint, adaptability to the customs and business methods of foreign countries, aggressiveness, and tact are helpful traits. There are wide opportunities for persons with a love of adventure, a liking for other lands, and a willingness to lead a roving life.

Home Economics, the combined phases of the household arts. It includes matters relating to food, clothing, shelter, and the financial management of the home; also research in special problems, and the teaching of home economics itself. The woman who is a homemaker practices home economics. As a career outside the home, it offers opportunities in dietetics, restaurant management, interior decoration, budget management, etc. Directive ability, mental accuracy, and business sense are desirable. The work may be of a semi-settled character. Home economics is a broad and ever-widening field; the versatile, original person is at an advantage. Special education is required.

Industrial Relations, a field of endeavor which includes all work involved in the adjustment of industry and industrial environment with the needs and well-being of workers. It may involve personnel or welfare work in a business or industrial firm; employment in a labor organization as organizer, editor, speaker, investigator, educator, etc.; or employment in a governmental or private agency handling industrial problems. It includes more than the arbitration and settling of labor disputes; the prevention of such disputes is equally important. Ability to deal with people, adaptability, dynamic personality, and rapid mental coordination are valuable traits. Love of humanity, desire to improve working conditions, and willingness to meet difficult problems are desirable.

Insurance, the business of making contracts whereby, for a stipulated consideration, one party undertakes to indemnify or guarantee another against loss by a specified contingency or peril, called a risk. Risks include fire, marine disaster, accidents of various types, and death. Life insurance includes many different kinds of work: legal, medical, sales, promotion, investigation, management, and actuarial work (the scientific study of statistics, determination of rates of mortality, the calculation of insurance premiums, etc.). Actuarial work requires mathematical ability and special training. General insurance work requires competence in dealing with people, accuracy, and self-confidence. The work of the salesman is roving, and must often be carried on in the evenings.

Interior Decorating, the art which aims to harmonize in the interior of a building the requirements of utility and of beauty; it is similar in spirit and purpose to architecture but does not require the same extended specialized education, although some training in a school of fine and applied arts is valuable. Adaptability, sympathy, and patience in dealing with people are helpful traits; the interior decorator must often tactfully educate the individuals with whom he deals as to what furnishings are suitable and in good taste. The work of an interior decorator is of a non-routine sort. Nevertheless, he or she must have an infinite capacity for dealing with detail, as well as a sense of the beautiful and the tasteful.

Journalism, the business of gathering and publishing current news for periodicals in general and daily newspapers in particular. The work of a reporter is of an extremely roving sort, with no fixed hours, carrying with it little or no financial remuneration for the beginner. Perseverance, ingenuity, aggressiveness, and rapid mental coordination are desirable traits. The good reporter has an instinct for news, is quick to scent the possibility of a story that will interest the public, and knows the quickest ways of getting at current facts; he is able to write simple, straightforward, forceful English. An early apprenticeship with a small newspaper is advantageous. Executive jobs in a newspaper office are generally given to individuals who have had experience as reporters. The newspaper's business office offers a more settled type of work.

Law, the general code of rules for action habitually enforced by the authority of the government. A lawyer is a person who has been trained in the principles and practice of the law of the land, and licensed by the government or under its authority to conduct legal proceedings for others. As a member of a profession, his conduct is restricted; for example, he may not advertise. He is an officer of the court and must pass a bar examination before he is allowed to practice. A specialized education is necessary. The lawyer must have a clear mind, capable of analyzing and organizing confused sets of facts. He should have imagination and courage and, if he be a trial lawyer, powers of oratory and persuasion. His life is apt to be an unsettled one; during the first years of practice, his income is likely to be small.

Librarianship, the management of libraries, including the classification, cataloguing, and shelf arrangement of books; their selection and purchase; and the conduct of the loan and reference departments. The work may be in a public library, or in the library of a public or private educational institution, or in that of an individual or business firm. For some positions certification by the state is required. A specialized education is very desirable, in the form of a college graduate course, undergraduate or summer-school work, or apprenticeship combined with study. Mental accuracy, liking for books, concentration, attention to detail, and deliberateness are helpful qualities. There are interesting opportunities for the individual who desires work of a settled, precise, indoor sort.

Manufacturing, the business of making articles and wares of all sorts, usually with the use of machinery and by means of the cooperation of a large body of workers. This field is such an all-embracing one that it offers a vast variety of employment. For many positions manual accuracy and mechanical ability are advantageous. Manufacturing offers the most interesting opportunities to those individuals who have a liking for the work of production and construction, a knack for dealing with things as well as persons.

Medicine, the science and art of relieving human physical suffering, and of restoring and maintaining health; the diagnosis and treatment of disease and injurious conditions. A lengthy specialized training is required, including two years of premedical college work, four years of medical school, and at least one year of interneship at a hospital. The work is arduous and exacting, making continual and unpredictable calls on the practitioner's time. The income is usually ample but not overly large. Mental accuracy, rapid mental coordination, manual dexterity, powers of observation, sense of responsibility, self-control, and a sympathetic nature are desirable. Medicine is a profession suitable for the individual who likes to relieve suffering and desires a stimulating and varied sort of work.

Military, the armed forces of a nation; the army and navy considered as a career. Commissioned officers in the army are men who have risen from the ranks, or have been appointed from civil life, or have been graduated from the United States Military Academy (for the navy the corresponding school is the United States Naval Academy). The majority of officers are graduates of the Military Academy. Position and pay are secure, with generous provision in case of retirement. Promotion is by seniority. The life is roving but disciplined; the military man must obey orders. Desirable personal qualities are patriotism, manliness, liking for a strenuous life outdoors, sense of responsibility, manual and mental accuracy. The officer must instruct, care for, and mold the personalities of the men whom he commands.

Ministry, the service of God in conducting worship, caring for the spiritual and physical wants of a congregation, and managing the church; essentially, the interpreting of God's word to men. The minister should have a secure faith in God, deliberateness, sympathy, and an ability to deal with individuals. Educational requirements vary according to the church and the type of ministry intended. College education and specialized training at a religious seminary are usually required of the ordained preacher. The minister cannot advance his career in the same way as the business man; usually he must wait for appointments and promotion. Financial reimbursement is generally modest but certain. Missionary work offers more opportunity for an adventurous and roving life.

Motion Pictures, one of the youngest of large-scale industries. It involves the production, distribution, and exhibition of motion pictures. The work of production, which centers largely in and around Los Angeles, California, includes that of the scenario writer, director, art director, costume designer, actor, electrician, scenic designer, cameraman, property man, script clerk, etc. Some of these workers receive large salaries, but the competition is very great. Most motion-picture actors have had previous work on the professional legitimate stage. Most scenario writers have established their reputations in other fields of writing. Adaptability, dynamic personality, salesmanship, and ability to visualize scenes as they would appear when photographed, are valuable traits. Work in the fields of distribution and exhibition offers larger opportunities.

Music, the art of combining tones and rhythms in a manner pleasing to the ear; it includes the arts both of composition and of performance or interpretation. A long period of study is necessary for the composer or concert performer (seven years is recommended for the opera singer). Early musical training is desirable. Unquestionable talent is necessary; music demands a skill and technical proficiency more definite and tangible than perhaps any other art. The particular type of skill required varies. A pianist needs finger dexterity and manual accuracy; the concert singer, a good vocal equipment. The composer must have creative ability, persistence, studiousness. The writer or performer of light, popular music has a greater need for dramatic personality, salesmanship, and flair for catching the ear of the public.

Nursing, the practical art of caring for the sick and incapacitated, under the direction of a physician, in hospitals, private homes, clinics, institutions, etc. It is largely a woman's profession, although there are successful male nurses. A two- or three-year course of training in a school of nursing is required; this includes classroom instruction and a large amount of actual nursing experience in a hospital, the latter serving as pay for the nurse's education. In general, the work is of a roving, indoor sort. Patience, manual accuracy, and stamina are necessary; the working hours of a nurse are often very long. The nurse should have a genuine sympathetic interest in others and a desire to relieve suffering.

Personal and Domestic Service, the occupation of caring for the private needs of others. Personal service refers to those activities which directly serve the persons of other individuals; in this category are included barbers, beauty-shop operators, valets, masseurs, etc., as well as the performers of certain occasional services: blood doners and the like. The field of personal service provides considerable opportunity for individuals of agreeable and adaptable personality. While the field of domestic service is not conducive to great financial success, it sometimes offers unusual opportunities for security and pleasant environment.

Politics, the work of government, especially as carried on by the elected and appointed officials of the nation, exclusive of workers in the Civil Service. Broadly speaking, a politician should identify himself with a community or locality whose interests he desires to represent; he should become acquainted with as large a number of individuals as possible; he should have a knowledge of political science, economics, sociology, current events, and the history of the nation and of his home region. Since a politician's career as an office-holder may be terminated when his party goes out of power, he should have another source of income—a second career. The working hours of a politician are irregular and often very long. Independence, courage, and civic interest are valuable qualities.

Public Relations, the practical science of controlling public opinion in the interests of a certain client, which may be a business firm, an industry, an institution, a political party, an individual, etc. The public relations counsel differs from the advertising man in that his chief work consists in explaining his client's actions to the public and in avoiding adverse criticism. To this end he makes use of all facilities of publicity—newspapers, radio, magazines. A knowledge of sociology and psychology and a ready command of language are valuable. Helpful traits include judgment, tact, discretion, persuasiveness, and a wide understanding of human nature. Many public relations workers have had previous training as newspaper reporters or press agents. The hours of work are apt to be long and irregular.

Public Utilities, business organizations which provide essential and fundamental services for the public, especially the supplying of light, heat, and power, and are subject to a high degree of governmental regulation. Constituting a wide field, public utilities offer opportunities for careers to the organizer and salesman, the engineer and construction worker, the research expert and the individual of adventurous and roving bent, and many others. Efficient service is the keynote of the work. There is a greater degree of security than in many other businesses. Desirable personal traits include a sense of responsibility, efficiency, and an understanding of people and their wants.

Publishing, the production of printed books. The work of a publishing house has three chief phases: editorial—the selection and preparation of manuscripts for printing; manufacturing—the styling and printing of books; and sales and promotion. Taste, adaptability, deliberateness, judgment, and far-sightedness are helpful personal qualities. The publisher must be able to deal successfully with authors, agents, and booksellers. Valuable prerequisites are a deep liking for books, a wide knowledge of popular current literature, and practical experience in the printing and sale of books.

Radio, the broadcasting industry and all allied activities, including the manufacture and sale of radio receiving sets. A broadcasting station discovers or creates programs, seeks to sell them to sponsors for the purpose of advertising commercial products. Programs are heard by millions of persons, must have wide appeal. The individual who selects radio as a career should have a feeling for what is dramatic, novel, and popular. He may often need to make his own opportunities, as by creating a program that will interest a station or sponsor. Originality, resourcefulness, persistence, and adaptability are helpful personal traits. The technical aspects of radio provide a wide field for mechanical work, scientific research, and invention.

Railroading, the industry based on steam and electric traffic by rail. A wide field, it employs a great variety of workers: engineers, shopmen, enginemen and trainmen, yard forces, station agents, telegraphers, salesmen, accountants, purchasers, stewards and other personal service workers, rate experts, architects, research men, and office personnel. Railroading is no longer in its pioneering stages; economic and efficient operation has become the most important problem. But it is still an industry which has many opportunities for a person who desires an adventurous and roving life. Railroad work is comparatively secure; the factor of seniority is of considerable weight in determining promotions and assignments.

Real Estate, the business of buying, selling, and managing land and buildings. Since it deals with a basic and essential commodity, it touches on many fields of human endeavor. Specialized real-estate activities include those of broker, builder, building manager, operator, and dealer in mortgages and bonds. Salesmanship is a prime qualification for success, and in order to be a good salesman a real-estate worker must understand his product; therefore a knowledge of real-estate law, among other things, is valuable. Specialized education is helpful but not necessary. Energy, dynamic personality, and an ability to deal with people are useful traits. The hours of work are often irregular. Many of the activities of a real-estate man are partially outdoor and roving.

Restaurant Management, the business of organizing and maintaining an eating establishment. It involves the hiring and training of employees; the purchase of supplies and equipment; the determination of menus, prices, food portions, and standards of quality; the creation of attractive and comfortable surroundings for patrons; the business of advertising; and the handling of such matters as correspondence and complaints. Requisite personal qualities include tact, patience, business judgment, and attention to detail. The competent restaurant manager is an artist and exercises imagination and ingenuity in pleasing his patrons. The hours of work are irregular. Training in home economics is helpful. Actual experience of the work performed by each type of employee is invaluable.

Retail Merchandising, the sale of commodities to individual purchasers; the operation and management of a retail store, whether it be a large department store or a shop owned and operated by no more than one individual. The opening of a small retail store is a hazardous undertaking; a large percentage of such stores fail yearly in the United States. Nevertheless, it continues to provide an attractive career for the individual who has a bent for business and salesmanship and who wishes to work independently. The large department store offers a wide range of opportunities. Selling ability, attention to detail, adaptability, and knowledge of public taste are apt to be valuable qualities.

Scientific Research, the investigation of natural processes. It may be divided into work in applied science (research which has as its immediate aim the solving of industrial problems and improvement of technological processes) and work in pure science (research intended to increase the sum of human knowledge, but having no immediate practical aims); the line of demarcation between the two is not, however, very clear. Workers in pure science must have independent means or else obtain college positions which will allow them to devote time to research. Mental accuracy, concentration, deliberateness, originality, and patience are valuable traits. The general field is as broad as all science and allows of the satisfaction of many kinds of interests. It may be of a settled or roving sort.

Secretarial Work, the handling of office routine, particularly in regard to stenography. The secretary may be the personal assistant of an executive, relieving him of many routine duties and sometimes performing work of an executive nature. A knowledge of shorthand and typing is essential. Routine may include typing, taking dictation, filing, opening and sorting mail, taking telephone calls, making itineraries, writing checks, paying bills, checking bank statements, answering letters, interviewing callers, etc. Tactfulness, pleasing personality, sense of responsibility, feeling for detail, mental and manual accuracy, and a good memory are valuable qualities. The social secretary does work of a considerably different sort: answering social letters, planning parties and other entertainments, writing invitations, etc.

Social Service, the scientific study and practical treatment of social ills, including alleviation of poverty, furthering of clinical medicine and social hygiene, care and protection of children, the study of criminals and of crime prevention, and the coordination of beneficial social forces. Social service work is generally of a roving sort, involving the making of many new contacts. A relatively new field, it offers neither large salaries nor great security. The social service worker should have a serious, objective, sympathetic interest in human problems. Adaptability, accurate observation, energy, and a feeling for practical values are useful traits. A college education and specialized study at a school of social work are desirable.

Stage, the theatrical industry, including all the activities attendant on producing plays: organizing a company, financing, casting, designing scenery and costumes, determining the proper system of lighting, directing, acting, and finally the advertising and selling of the finished product. Adaptability, originality, a vital personality, and a flair for showmanship are desirable qualities. The kind of life involved is indoor but roving. Routine and security are generally at a minimum. Artistic ability is required in many of the jobs connected with the stage. The actor should have fiery ambition and an interest in human nature, which he interprets; singing and dancing ability, and a good speaking voice are valuable equipment.

Stock Breeding, the improvement of livestock by judicious mating; the creation of new breeds and strains of cattle, horses, sheep, and swine for sale to raisers of livestock. The stock breeder works with various ends in view; for example, he may specialize in beef cattle or dairy cattle. Practical experience and study at an agricultural college are advisable prerequisites. The independent stock breeder must have capital and be willing to devote years to the development of his business. Friendliness, salesmanship, patience, self-reliance, and liking for animals are advantageous traits.

Styling Merchandise, the business of coordinating the activities of the manufacturer, designer, and buyer in such a way that their products appeal to the largest market. The stylist studies trends in public taste, notes the success or failure of the latest fashions, and uses this information to advantage. He or she may, for example, act as a mediator between producer and designer, suggesting new patterns for old materials or new materials for old products. The department store is an ideal field of activity for the stylist, who generally acts in an advisory capacity for the buyer. Adaptability, flair for what is tasteful, sense of form and color, aesthetic judgment, imagination, and knowledge of practical values and consumer psychology are desirable traits. An apprenticeship in saleswork and buying is valuable.

Transportation, the general field of which the aircraft, automobile, and railroad industries form special branches, along with marine transport, urban transport, etc. This large field offers a great variety of employment, with interesting opportunities for those who like a roving sort of life. Efficiency and service are important concepts in transportation. Rapid mental coordination and adaptability are valuable traits.

Writing, the profession of authorship and art of literary creation, including the production of novels, short stories, verse, drama, motion-picture scenarios, articles, essays, editorials, long works of nonfiction, etc. The life of a free-lance writer is an independent one, may be either settled or roving. Financial returns are uncertain and insecure, particularly during the years of apprenticeship; knowledge of markets for written material is valuable. The ability to use language in a clear and effective manner is naturally one of the prime essentials. Self-discipline, observation, and originality are needed.

WRITING TO SELL

Markets

Writing is a business like any other. The professional writer is his own employer, office force, and efficiency expert. He is familiar with the various markets for written material, since in order to achieve success he must sell to those markets. Roughly, they may be divided into the book publishers, the smooth-paper magazines, the pulp-paper magazines, the newspapers and syndicates, the trade journals and house organs.

Book publishers form a very distinct class. They are looking for material of suitable length for publication in book form. They seldom constitute a profitable market for the beginner, who usually finds it wiser in the long run to concentrate on shorter pieces of writing, any one of which does not represent a great investment of time. Later he may work up to the novel and the long nonfiction work.

The magazines published on smooth paper are termed "slicks" by the writers. They include *The Saturday Evening Post, Red Book, Harper's*, etc. They print chiefly the work of established fiction authors and prominent writers of nonfiction. The pay is very good, but the volume and quality of competition leave little opportunity for the beginner. Nevertheless, since some of these magazines are found on every newsstand and in many homes, they receive a very large number of manuscripts from unknowns—manuscripts which would have a much better chance in less prominent markets.

The magazines printed on pulp paper—"pulps" in writers' parlance—publish fiction almost exclusively. They buy love stories and detective stories, tales of mystery and adventure, particularly in its "western" variety. But each "pulp" publishes only one kind of story. A magazine may be wholly devoted to adventure stories about aviators, or tales based on future scientific developments—"science fiction." Pay ranges approximately from ½ to 1½ cents a word (1940). A rapid-fire style, easy to read, with shrewd, terse characterizations is desired.

The newspapers pay relatively low rates to unknown outsiders. Most of their material is gathered and written by paid employees. Nevertheless they will sometimes accept interesting items from outsiders. Small newspapers particularly may be developed into a valuable market by the enterprising writer. The syndicates furnish material for newspapers and magazines. Some of them use only established authors. But others, which supply stories and articles to rural newspapers and small periodicals, are willing to accept material from unknowns. True, the pay is small—about five dollars for one short story—but the competition is not so keen and a matured style is not essential.

Trade journals are periodicals devoted to a single business or profession. Much of their material is written on contract. Still they should not be neglected by the author who has or is willing to gain the necessary specialized knowledge. House organs are the publications of single business firms, intended for circulation among employees and agents. Because they are little known, they sometimes offer interesting opportunities. It must be remembered that even the large newsstand does not give a true picture of writers' markets. Tiny periodicals and amateur magazines never appear on the newsstand. Many of these latter do not pay for the material they publish, but they should not therefore be invariably shunned by the writer. Merely to have a story or article published is a heartening achievement, psychologically valuable to the beginner.

In view of the confusing multiplicity of markets and the burdensome amount of work involved in selling, the writer can sometimes profitably avail himself of the services of an agent. An agent is a professional salesman of written material. He accepts stories and articles from a writer and receives from the writer a commission (almost invariably ten per cent) on anything he sells. A good agent has a wide knowledge of markets and, more important, he knows the condition of markets from month to month—which ones are actively buying, the sort of material for which there is a special call, the top price that can be asked and obtained for a certain manuscript in a certain market, etc. He is also personally acquainted with a number of editors, though this does not mean that an editor will buy everything an agent recommends. He understands publishers' contracts and is able to protect an author's rights effectively. Since his business office is usually located in New York, the chief publishing center, he can rapidly submit manuscripts to a large number of buyers. Unquestionably there are certain classes of writers for whom an agent's services are very valuable; among them may be mentioned the established author who wishes to be relieved of business responsibilities, the writer who dislikes and shirks the task of selling, and the beginner who is personally acquainted with an energetic agent. But certain possible disadvantages must be noted. An agent may not push the work of a beginner as energetically as might the writer himself. An agent may not be interested in sending material to the cheapest markets, since his commission would be trifling. Finally, an agent may be a considerable expense. In this connection it should be remembered that a good agent seldom charges a fee for reading a manuscript; he tries to make money *with* rather than *out of* a writer; he does not engage in the conduct of correspondence courses in writing; he is a salesman, not a teacher—although he is often able to give valuable advice to the authors whom he sponsors. Beyond this, the question of whether or not to employ an agent is one which each individual author must decide for himself.

Specific information about markets, the names and addresses of periodicals, etc., can be obtained in publishers' directories and in the magazines published especially for writers.

Study markets carefully and shrewdly. Write to fit the needs of markets, or at least try to find the markets in which your style of product has the best chance. A thorough search frequently will reveal a possible market for material that seems at first glance impossible to sell.

Fiction

The story that will sell is a story people like to read. Most people do not like to read about unpleasant subjects. Since they identify themselves with the hero or heroine, they do not like to read stories in which those characters come to grief or end up in a state of bafflement or bewilderment. This is not to say that the reader dislikes reading about struggles, difficulties, clashes of will and character. On the contrary, those are the very things he delights to read about. But he also wants things to come out well—or at least definitely—in the end. He demands a clean-cut finish. The story of failure and disillusionment has its place in literature, but the success story is easier to sell. Like it or not, the writer usually must cater to the daydreams and hidden ambitions of his readers.

The story that will sell is a story people can believe—at least while they are reading it. It need not be consistently realistic, but no single event in the story should strain the reader's credulity. Fantastic and improbable things may happen, but the reader's credulity must first be aroused by the proper suggestions and atmospheric touches. The motivation of the characters is especially important. Their problems must be easy to grasp, their reactions natural. The reader must be able to put himself in their place and feel that their emotions are genuine, their actions necessary.

Most stories can be reduced to a very simple formula: A. one or more characters want to attain a certain goal; B. obstacles arise which seem to make the attainment of the goal impossible; C. the obstacles are overcome (usually by the direct efforts of the characters involved) and the goal reached. For example, a young man falls in love with his employer's daughter; the employer makes their marriage contingent on the young man's selling a large insurance policy to a miserly millionaire; the young man manages to sell the policy and he and the girl are united. This particular plot is trite and outworn. Nevertheless it illustrates the essential elements. Obviously its story-interest would depend largely on the cleverness of the device by which the young man sold the policy. He might rescue the millionaire's grandchild from drowning. He might learn that the millionaire was a stamp-collector and find a rare stamp for him. He might make a bet with the millionaire. Or the girl might solve the problem instead of the young man. There is no end to the possible variations.

This basic plot-structure (goal-obstacle-success) can be applied to stories of all types. In the detective story it takes the form of: A. problem as to who committed a murder; B. false clues and misleading evidence; C. discovery of who committed the murder. In the outdoors story it is a man's struggle with and overcoming of the forces of nature. The formula fits the tale of two thwarted lovers and the story of a man's struggle to become reconciled with his God.

It must be remembered, however, that most successful stories do not use the simplest form of the A.B.C. formula. There are usually several obstacles, one giving rise to another. The obstacle may often take the form of an individual—the villain. One of the obstacles may come as a sudden surprise when the goal is almost in sight; a new character may enter the story, giving the plot a radical turn. This surprise element is especially useful and almost essential in lifting the reader's interest midway in the narrative. Or one of the characters may be a doubtful quantity, so that the reader does not know until the end whether he is an ally of the hero or an obstacle. In general, the most interesting struggles are those which depend on the clash of personalities. Readers like interesting, human characters with failings as well as good points.

All of which boils down to one essential consideration: the writer must keep the reader constantly in mind when he creates his story. He must keep the reader interested all the way.

Nonfiction

The writer of nonfiction has certain definite advantages over the fictionist. His market is, if anything, larger, and interesting subject matter can compensate to a considerable degree for defects in style. His work is based solidly on fact. If he comes across certain facts which he thinks make a story worth telling, there is a good chance that editors and readers will be of the same opinion. Human interest is his keynote. True-life happenings, the experiences of people who pursue unusual occupations or have been in out-of-the-way places—these are his stock in trade. Unless he has special aptitudes or advantages, he should avoid the more abstract and controversial subjects, such as politics, economics, and the like. He can find his subject matter within the range of his own experience. And he can readily expand the scope of his experience by making more acquaintances, seeing more of the city or district in which he lives, following up unusual stories which he hears at second hand—in short, imitating the practices of the competent free-lance reporter.

This does not mean that the nonfiction writer should neglect to read periodicals and books. On the contrary, he should make every effort to gauge the needs of the publications to which he is attempting to sell, and to keep up with and ahead of public taste. Moreover, reading may provide him with valuable clues and hints. Material supplied by newspapers and national publications may be reslanted to fit the needs of a lesser market. Dry scientific and scholarly articles may hide a good story. The writer should attempt to capitalize on his own interests and hobbies, develop them into specialties.

Although subject matter is the chief concern of the nonfiction writer, an interesting narrative style will add greatly to the marketability of his articles. Clarity is paramount. Obscure statements and hazy explanations should be avoided. The reader should be led along by easy stages. Each paragraph should satisfy a part of his curiosity and at the same time arouse his interest further. The first sentence should not tell the whole story. The writer should canvass the main points of interest in his subject and then space them out evenly through his article, neither packed at the beginning nor delayed until the end. If this practice is followed, the whole article gains in effectiveness.

Many poorly-written articles are published merely because the subject matter is interesting. If the writer combines interesting subject matter with an effective terse style of narration, he will find a market.

Important Points

Adapt your style and material to the market to which you are attempting to sell. Read the previous publications of that market; they are your blueprints. Study the information given in the writers' magazines. Become familiar with the editors' likes and dislikes. Learn which subjects are favored and which tabooed. The magazine market is roughly divided into groups of magazines of similar policy. A story rejected by one magazine can usually be offered for sale to half a dozen others with some hope of acceptance. Watch for new markets opening up. They will need more material and will be more likely to take the work of unknown authors.

Keep ahead of public taste. Don't just rewrite the stories which appeared in last month's magazines. They are dead wood. Strive for novelty. This does not mean that an editor will accept material violating the policy and special taboos of his publication. It does mean that editors are looking for new angles and new variants on old themes.

Take particular pains to make the beginnings of your stories or articles interesting. If the first paragraph sets a problem and suggests fascinating possibilities, the reader will be eager to go on. If the first paragraph is dull, even though later material is very exciting, the reader may go no further. A good story or article may fail because the writer did not give sufficient thought to catching the reader's interest. A story in the modern style begins with action, not with a long description of the characters and background.

If possible, type your manuscripts on regular typing paper (8½ by 11 inches). Double space the lines. Type only on one side of the paper. Leave wide margins. Do not crowd the pages. Most magazines will not return unwanted manuscripts unless they are accompanied by a self-addressed envelope with the required amount of postage already affixed. Manuscripts of any size are best sent flat in a large envelope. Small manuscripts may be folded and sent in a business-size envelope. They should not be rolled. Bulky manuscripts may be sent more economically by express, with enclosed directions that they be returned to you by express, collect. Do not address manuscripts to "The Editor"; it will not procure them additional attention. It is usually unnecessary to write an explanatory letter. Manuscripts whose form violates these rules are at a disadvantage, although they may still be read.

Above all, keep on writing! Don't be worried by rejection slips. Most successful authors spend five to ten years receiving nothing much else. There are a hundred reasons because of which a good story or article may be rejected. It may accidentally duplicate material already purchased. It may be submitted at a time when the market is slack, the editor buying little or nothing. Most magazines can buy only six or eight stories a month—a tiny fraction of the total material submitted. So don't let feelings of despondency interfere with your writing. An author is a poor judge of the quality of his own product. He may do some of his best work when he feels he is doing his worst. Inspiration is a rather rare commodity. You cannot depend on it. Set yourself definite working hours and keep them, whether or not inspiration comes. If you really want to write for a living, the effort will be worth while.

MUSICAL SIGNS AND ABBREVIATIONS

Musical signs or notes are written on a stave of 11 lines and 10 spaces, starting at G and finishing at F, sometimes called the Great Stave. This is supposed to cover the range of the human voice. For convenience, however, music is usually written in staves of 5 lines each, the top 5 being the Treble and the bottom 5 the Bass. The "normal C," which usually can be sounded by all voices, is one line below the stave in the Treble and one line above the stave in the Bass. The following diagram shows which 5 lines of the Grand Stave are used for the Treble, Alto, Tenor and Bass clefs respectively.

Signs denoting time or relative value of sound:

Breve. Semi-breve. Minim. Crotchet. Quaver. Semi-quaver. Demisemi-quaver.

Each of these notes represents twice the duration of sound of that which comes next in order. The sign to the right of each note indicates a rest or silence equal to its sound duration.

6 In time the figure above a line drawn thus across the stave denotes the length of the pause in bars.

Accel. Accelerando. Gradually increasing the speed.

Adg° or *Ad°*. Adagio. Slow; also name given to a slow movement or piece.

Ad lib. Ad libitum. Passages so marked may be rendered at the will of the performer.

And. Andante. Moderately slow: graceful; sometimes used as the name of a movement or separate piece.

Anim°. Animato. Animated: with soul.

A tem. A tempo. In time.

Bar. Double Bars.

Bar. A line drawn perpendicularly across the stave, separating the notes into measures of equal length; also the music comprised within two such lines.

⌒ ⌐¬ Bind or tie. Placed over two or more notes in the same position on the stave, to show they are to be played as one.

* ∧ ' Breath-marks. In vocal music, signs used to show where breath should be taken.

C ¢ Denoting common time: the former indicating four crochets to the bar, the latter two minims to the bar.

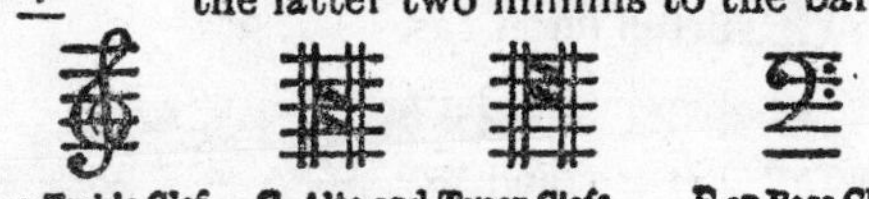

G or Treble Clef. C. Alto and Tenor Clefs. F or Bass Clef.

Clef. The sign placed at the beginning of a stave denotes the position of the middle C of the Grand Stave in the 5 lines being used.

< Crescendo. Gradual increase of tone.

(ˈ) Dash. When placed over or under a note, implies a very detached (*staccato*) style.

D.C. Da capo. From the beginning: indicating that the performer must return to the beginning of the movement, and conclude at the double bar marked *Fine.*

> Decrescendo. Gradually softer.

Dim. Diminuendo. Gradual decrease of tone.

(·) Dot. When added to a note or rest, lengthens it by one-half. When placed over or under a note, means that its duration should be cut short.

♭ Flat. The sign which lowers the pitch of a note one semitone.

f. Forte. Loudly: strongly.

ff. Fortissimo. Very loud.

f.z. Sforzando. As loud as possible.

f.p. Forte-piano. Loud, then soft.

Leg. Legato. In a smooth and gliding manner.

mf. or *mff.* Mezzo-forte. Moderately loud.

mp. Mezzo-piano. Moderately soft.

Marc. Marcato. In a marked manner, emphasized.

M.M. Maelzel's metronome.

M.M. ♩= 80. { Denoting that the beat of a crochet is equal to the pulse of the pendulum of Maelzel's metronome, with the weight set at 80.

♮ Natural. Restores a note, which has been raised by the sharp or lowered by the flat, to its original pitch.

Ott., O^{va}, 8va = Ottava. An octave—as 8va *alta* = *ottava alta*, (to be played) an octave higher; 8va *bas* = *ottava bassa*, an octave lower.

p. Piano. Softly.

P.F. or *pf.* Piano-forte. Soft, then loud.

pp. Pianissimo. Very soft.

ppp. Pianississimo. As softly as possible.

𝄐 Pause or *Corona.* When placed over a note or rest, indicates that it must be held longer than its natural length. When over a double bar, indicates where the piece is to be concluded after a repeat.

Pizz. Pizzicato. A direction to violinists to twang the string with the finger instead of using the bow.

Quintuplet. A group of five notes played in the time of four.

Rall. Rallentando. Becoming gradually slower.

Repeat when placed at the beginning and end of a passage or movement indicates that the portion so marked is to be played over again.

𝄋 Segno. The sign—as *Al Segno*, to the sign; *Dal Segno*, from the sign.

∧ ∨ > Sforzando. Denoting emphasis applied to a particular note or notes. Abbreviated *sf.*, *rf.*, *rfz.*

> Sforzato-piano. A sudden *forte* followed by a *diminuendo* or *piano.* Abbreviated *sfp.*, *sfz.p.*

♯ Sharp. The sign which raises the pitch of a note one semitone.

× Double Sharp. Used before a note already sharp, raising the pitch by a semitone. It is corrected by a natural and a sharp.

⌒ Slur. Showing that the notes over which it is placed must be played in a smooth (*legato*) manner.

Sos., *Sost.* Sostenuto. Sustained: prolonging the tone for the full duration of time indicated.

Trem. Tremolando. With trembling or wavering; a note or chord played with great rapidity, so as to produce such an effect.

3°. Trio.

SIZES OF TYPE

The following are the sizes of type in ordinary use for books, newspapers, magazines, pamphlets, etc. The sizes of type used in headings and advertisements are often very much greater than those given below. These large types, known as display types, sometimes are available in sizes as large as 72 point — six times the size of the largest type on this page. Type larger than 72 point is cast for special purposes only.

5 point

KNOWLEDGE IS OF TWO KINDS. WE KNOW A SUBJECT OURselves or we know where we can find information about it. The importance of reference books as an aid to knowledge and the enrichment of life is emphasized by this famous quotation from the writings of Samuel Johnson.

6 point

KNOWLEDGE IS OF TWO KINDS. WE KNOW A SUBject ourselves or we know where we can find information about it. The importance of reference books as an aid to knowledge and the enrichment of life is emphasized by this famous quotation from the writings of

8 point

KNOWLEDGE IS OF TWO KINDS. WE KNOW a subject ourselves or we know where we can find information about it. The importance of reference books as an aid to knowledge and the enrichment of life is emphasized by this famous

10 point

KNOWLEDGE IS OF TWO KINDS. WE know a subject ourselves or we know where we can find information about it. The importance of reference books as an

12 point

KNOWLEDGE IS OF TWO KINDS. We know a subject ourselves or we know where we can find information about it. The importance of reference

PROOFREADER'S MARKS

Courtesy, *A Manual of Style*, The University of Chicago Press.

- Delete
- Delete and close up
- Reverse
- Close up
- # Insert space
- ¶ Paragraph
- □ Indent one em
- Move to left
- Move to right
- Lower
- Elevate
- ^ Insert marginal addition
- Even space
- × Broken letter
- Push down space
- Straighten line
- ‖ Align type
- Insert comma
- Insert apostrophe
- Insert quotes
- =/ Hyphen
- em Em dash
- en En dash
- ;/ Insert semicolon
- Insert colon and en quad
- Insert period and en quad
- ?/ Insert interrogation point
- (?) Query to author
- Use ligature
- (sp) Spell out
- tr Transpose
- wf Wrong font
- bf Set in bold face type
- rom Set in roman type
- ital Set in italic type
- caps Set in CAPITALS
- sc Set in SMALL CAPITALS
- lc Set in lower case
- Lower-case letter
- stet Let it stand
- no ¶ Run in same paragraph
- ld> Insert lead between lines
- hr# Hair space between letters

HOW TO CORRECT PRINTERS' PROOFS

We therefore, the representatives of the United states of
America, in General Congress assembled, appealing to the
Supreme Iudge of the world for the rectitude of our inpten-
tions do, in the name and by authority of the good people
of these Colonies, solemnly publish and declare, that these
United Coloniesare, and of right ought to be,
independent and free States that they are absolved from all
allegiiance to the British Crown and that all political connection between them and the State of Great Britain is, and ought
to be totally dissolved; and that as free and independent States
they have full power to levy war, conclude peace, contract
alliances, establish commerce, and to do all other acts and
things whichindependent States may of right do And for
the support of this Declaration with a firm reliance on the
protection of Divine Providence, we mutually pledge to
each other our lives, our fortunes, and our sacred honour.

The following shows how the preceding printers' proof (the last paragraph of the DECLARATION OF INDEPENDENCE*) reads after the corrections have been made.*

We, therefore, the representatives of the United States of America, in General Congress assembled, appealing to the Supreme Judge of the world for the rectitude of our intentions, do, in the name and by authority of the good people of these colonies, solemnly publish and declare, That these United Colonies are, and of right ought to be, free and independent States; that they are absolved from all allegiance to the British Crown, and that all political connection between them and the State of Great Britain is, and ought to be, totally dissolved; and that as free and independent States, they have full power to levy war, conclude peace, contract alliances, establish commerce, and to do all other acts and things which independent States may of right do. And for the support of this declaration, with a firm reliance on the protection of Divine Providence, we mutually pledge to each other our lives, our fortunes, and our sacred honor

TABLE OF WEIGHTS AND MEASURES

Avoirdupois Weight

(Used in the United States, Great Britain and other English-speaking countries for weighing goods other than such small items as drugs, rare metals, precious stones, etc.)

27 11/32 grains (gr.)=1 dram
16 drams=1 ounce (oz.)
16 ounces, or 7,000 grains=1 pound (lb.)
25 pounds (in U. S.)=1 quarter (qr.)
28 pounds (in Great Britain)=1 quarter
4 quarters of 25 pounds=1 short, or U. S., hundredweight (cwt.)
4 quarters of 28 pounds=1 long, or British hundredweight (cwt.)
20 short hundredweights (2,000 pounds)=1 short ton
20 long hundredweights (2,240 pounds)=1 long ton

Linear Measure

12 lines=1 inch (in.)
12 inches=1 foot (ft).
3 feet=1 yard (yd.)
5½ yards or 16½ feet= 1 rod (rd.)
40 rods=1 furlong (fur.)
8 furlongs, or 5,280 feet=1 land or statute mile

Square Measure

144 square inches (sq. in.)=1 square foot (sq. ft.)
9 square feet=1 square yard (sq. yd.)
30¼ square yards, or 272¼ square feet=1 square rod (sq. rd).
160 square rods, or 43,560 square feet=1 acre (a.)
640 acres=1 square mile (sq. mi.)

In the United States, a square mile of public land is known legally as a *section.* 36 sections, when arranged in a square 6 miles by 6 miles, form a *township.* In some states and counties the *township* is an administrative or taxing division.

Cubic Measure

1,728 cubic inches (cu. in.)=1 cubic foot (cu. ft.)
27 cubic feet=1 cubic yard (cu. yd.)

Liquid Measure

4 gills (gi.)=1 pint (pt.)
2 pints=1 quart (qt.)
4 quarts=1 gallon (gal.)
31½ gallons=1 barrel (bbl.)
2 barrels=1 hogshead (hhd.)

The U. S. gallon is equal to .833 imperial gallon or British gallon.

Dry Measure

2 pints (pt.)=1 quart (qt.)
4 quarts=1 gallon (gal.)
2 gallons or 8 quarts=1 peck (pk.)
4 pecks=1 bushel (bu.)
8 bushels=1 quarter (qr.)

The Metric System

The metric system was developed in France, but it is now used everywhere for scientific purposes. It is the prevailing commercial system in most of the countries of continental Europe and has been officially adopted in Latin America. The basic units of the system are the *gram,* a measure of weight, the *meter,* a measure of distance, and the *liter,* a measure of volume. By combining these basic units with the following prefixes, fractional and multiple units are obtained.

milli-=one thousandth (.001)
centi-=one hundredth (.01)
deci-=one tenth (.1)
deca-=ten
hecto-=one hundred
kilo-=one thousand
myria-=ten thousand

Weight

The gram is the fundamental unit of weight, and is defined as one one-thousandth of the weight of a certain platinum-iridium bar kept at the International Bureau of Weights and Measures at Sèvres.

10 milligrams (mg.)=1 centigram (cg.)
10 centigrams=1 decigram (dg.)
10 decigrams=1 gram (gr.)
10 grams=1 decagram (dcg.)
10 decagrams=1 hectogram (hg.)
10 hectograms=1 kilogram (kg.)
10 kilograms=1 myriagram (myg.)
10 myriagrams=1 quintal (q.)
10 quintals=1 metric ton (1,000,000 grams)

Linear Measure

10 millimeters (mm.)=1 centimeter (cm.)
10 centimeters (cm.)=1 decimeter (dm.)
10 decimeters=1 meter (m.)
10 meters=1 decameter (dcm.)
10 decameters=1 hectometer (hm.)
10 hectometers=1 kilometer (km.)
10 kilometers=1 myriameter (10,000 meters)

Area or Surface Measure

100 square millimeters (mm^2 or sq. mm.)=1 square centimeter (cm^2 or sq. cm.)
100 square centimeters=1 square decimeter (dm^2, or sq. dm.)
100 square decimeters=1 square meter (sq. m., or m^2)
100 square meters=1 square decameter (dcm^2, or sq. dcm.)
100 square decameters=1 square hectometer (hm^2, or sq. hm.), or hectare
100 square hectares=1 square kilometer (km^2, or sq. km.) or myriare
100 square kilometers=1 square myriameter (sq. mym., or mym^2)

Volume or Liquid Measure

1,000 cubic millimeters (mm^3 or cu. mm.)=1 cubic centimeter (cm^3, or cu. cm.)
1,000 cubic centimeters=1 cubic decimeter (dm^3, or cu. dm.)
1,000 cubic decimeters=1 cubic meter (m^3, or cu. m.), or 1 stere
1,000 cubic meters=1 cubic decameter (dcm^3, or cu. dcm.)
1,000 cubic decameters=1 cubic hectometer (hm^3, or cu. hm.)
1,000 cubic hectometers=1 cubic kilometer (km^3, or cu. km.)
1,000 cubic kilometers=1 cubic myriameter (mym^3, or cu. mym.)

Capacity Measure

10 millileters (ml.)=1 centileter (cl.)
10 centileters=1 decileter (dl.)
10 decileters=1 liter (l.)
10 liters=1 decaliter (dcl.)
10 decaliters=1 hectoliter (hl.)
10 hectoliters=1 kiloliter (kl.)
10 kiloliters=1 myraliter (myl.)

Equivalents

1 meter=39.37 inches
1 kilometer=3,280.83 feet, or .62137 mile
1 cubic centimeter=.06102 cubic inch
1 liter=1.0567 U. S. liquid quarts, or .908 U. S. dry quart
1 gram=15.432 grains
1 decagram=.3527 ounce avoirdupois
1 kilogram=2.2046 pounds avoirdupois
907.18 kilograms=1 short ton
1,016.05 kilograms=1 long ton
1 foot=30.48 centimeters; 1 surveyors' chain=20.117 meters; 1 engineers' chain=30.48 meters.
1 square foot=929.03 square centimeters; 1 acre=4,046.87 square meters; 1 square mile=2.59 square kilometers.

Apothecaries' Weight

(Used in weighing drugs and medicines.)
20 grains (gr.)=1 scruple (℈)
3 scruples=1 dram (ʒ)
8 drams=1 ounce (℥)
12 ounces, or 5,760 grains=1 pound (lb.)

Apothecaries' Liquid Measure

(Used in the United States in measuring liquid drugs and medicines.)
60 minims (m.)=1 fluid dram (fʒ)
8 fluid drams=1 fluid ounce (f℥)
16 fluid ounces=1 pint (O.)
8 pints=1 gallon (Cong. or C.)

Angular Measure

(Used in measuring distances on the circumference of a circle or sphere.)
60 seconds (″)=1 minute (′)
60 minutes=1 degree (°)
90 degrees=1 quadrant, or right angle
360 degrees=1 circumference

Land Measure

9 square feet (sq. ft.)=1 square yard (sq. yd.)
30¼ square yards, or 272¼ square feet=1 square rod (sq. rd.)
40 square rods=1 rood (r.)
4 roods, or 160 square rods=1 acre (a.)
640 acres=1 square mile (sq. mi.)

Surveyors' Measure

7.92 inches=1 link (li.)
100 links, or 66 feet=1 surveyor's or Gunter's chain
80 chains=1 mile

or

12 inches=1 link (li.)
100 links (or feet)=1 engineers' or Ramsden's chain

Nautical Measure

(Used in measuring distances and depths at sea.)
6 feet=1 fathom
100 fathoms, or 120 fathoms=1 cable-length
1,000 fathoms=1 nautical mile

The length given above for the nautical mile is commonly used, but it is not the official length. In the United States the nautical mile is officially 6,080.27 feet, or one minute of a great circle on the earth. In Great Britain the nautical mile is officially 6,080 feet.

CHRISTIAN NAMES OF MEN AND WOMEN

A.-S. ...... Anglo-Saxon
Ar. ...... Arabic
Celt. ...... Celtic
D. ...... Danish
Eng. ...... English
Fr. ...... French
Ger. ...... German
Gr. ...... Greek
Teut. ...... Teutonic
Heb. ...... Hebrew
Ital. ...... Italian
Lat. ...... Latin
O.G. ...... Old German
O.H.G. ...... Old High German
Per. ...... Persian
Pg. ...... Portuguese
Russ. ...... Russian
Scand. ...... Scandinavian
Sp. ...... Spanish
Syr. ...... Syrian

* Of uncertain origin

NAMES OF MEN

A

Aaron. (Heb.) Possibly, mountain high or the enlightened.
Abel. (Heb.) Breath; vanity.
Abiel. (Heb.) The Lord is my father.
Abner. (Heb.) Father of light.
Abraham. (Heb.) Father of a multitude.—Dim. Abe.
Abram. (Heb.) Probably, exalted father.—Dim. Abe.
Adalbert. See **Ethelbert.**
Adam. (Heb.) Possibly, man; earth-man; red earth.—Dim. Ad.
Adolph, Adolphus. (O. H. G.) Noble wolf, i.e., noble hero.—Dim. Dolph.
Adoniram. (Heb.) My Lord is exalted.
Alan. (Lat.) *
Alaric. (O.H.G.) Ruler of all.
Albert. (O.H.G.) Illustrious through nobility.—Dim. Bert, Bertie.
Albion. (Celt.) Possibly, white-cliffed land. Albion was an ancient name for England.
Alexander. (Gr.) A defender of men. — Dim. Aleck, Ellick, Sandy, Sawney.
Alexis. (Br.) Help; defense.
Alfred. (O.H.G.) Elf in council, i.e., good counselor.—Dim. Alf.
Alfonso. See **Alphonso.**
Algernon. (Fr.) Bearded.*
Alonzo. (O.G.) The same as **Alphonso,** q.v.
Alphonso. (O.H.G.) Noble and ready.
Alvah, Alvan. (Heb.) Iniquity. *
Alvin, Alwin. (O.H.G.) Friend of nobility.
Amadeus. (Lat.) Lover of God.
Amasa. (Heb.) A burden.
Ambrose. (Gr.) Immortal; divine.
Amos. (Heb.) Borne by God.
Anastasius. (Gr.) Of the Resurrection.
Andrew. (Gr.) Strong; manly. —Dim. Andy.
Anselm. (O.H.G.) Under divine protection.
Anthony, Antony. (Lat.) * —Dim. Tony.
Archibald. (Ger.) Nobly bold. —Dim. Archie.
Armand, Armin. See **Herman.**
Arnold. (O.H.G.) Strong as an eagle.
Artemas. (Gr.) Gift of Artemi. (Diana).
Arthur. (Celt.)*—Dim. Art.
Asa. (Heb.) Healer; physician.
Asahel. (Heb.) Made by God.
Asaph. (Heb.) A collector.
Asher. (Heb.) Happy.
Ashur. (Heb.) Man of Horus.
Athelstan. (A.-S.) Noble stone.
Aubrey. (O.H.G.) Ruler of elves.
Augustin, Augustine, Austin. (Lat.) Belonging to Augustus.
Augustus. (Lat.) Exalted; majestic.—Dim. Gus.
Aurelius. (Lat.) Golden.
Azariah. (Heb.) Helped by the Lord.

B

Baldwin. (O.H.G.) Bold friend.
Baptist. (Gr.) A baptizer; purifier.
Barnabas, Barnaby. (Aramaic.) Son of exhortation.
Bartholomew. (Heb.) Son of Talmai.—Dim. Bat, Bart.
Basil. (Gr.) Kingly; royal.
Benedict. (Lat.) Blessed.
Benjamin. (Heb.) Son of the right hand (signifying fortunate).—Dim. Ben.
Bernard, Barnard. (O.H.G.) Bear-strong.
Bertram, Bertrand. (O. H. G.) Bright raven.—Dim. Bert, Bertie.
Bezaleel. (Heb.) In the shadow (protection) of God.
Boniface. (Lat.) A benefactor.
Brian. (Celt.)*
Bruno. (O.H.G.) Brown.

C

Caesar. (Lat.)*
Caleb. (Heb.) A dog (probably signifying faithfulness). — Dim. Cale.
Calvin. (Lat.) Bald.
Casper. See Jasper.
Cecil. (Lat.) Dim-sighted.
Cephas. (Aramaic.) A stone.
Charles. (O.H.G.) Strong; manly.—Dim. Charlie, or Charley.
Christian. (Lat.) Belonging to Christ; a believer in Christ. —Dim. Christie.
Christopher. (Gr.) Bearing Christ. — Dim. Kester, Kit, Chris, Christie.
Clarence. (Lat.) Illustrious.—Dim. Clarry.
Claude, Claudius. (Lat.) Lame.
Clement. (Lat.) Mild-tempered, merciful.—Dim. Clem.
Conrad. (O.H.G.) Of able counsel.
Constant. (Lat.) Firm; faithful.
Constantine. (Lat.) Firm; faithful.
Cornelius. (Lat.) * — Dim. Corny.
Crispin, Crispus. (Lat.) Having curly hair.
Cuthbert. (A.-S.) Noted splendor.
Cyprian. (Lat.) A man from Cyprus.
Cyril. (Gr.) Lordly.
Cyrus. (Per.) The sun.—Dim. Cy.

D

Daniel. (Heb.) God is my judge.—Dim. Dan.
Darius. (Per.) Possessing wealth.
David. (Heb.) Beloved.—Dim. Davy, Dave.
Demetrius. (Gr.) Belonging to Demeter (Ceres).
Dénis, Dennis. Same as **Dionysius.**
Derrik, Diedrik, Dietrich. See **Theodoric.**
Dexter. (Lat.) Dextrous; fortunate.
Dionysius. (Gr.) Belonging to Dionysus (Bacchus), the god of wine and dramatic poetry.
Donald. (Celt.) World ruler.—Dim. Don.
Duncan. (Celt.) Brown chief.—Dim. Dunc.

E

Eben. (Heb.) Rock or stone.—Dim. Eb.
Ebenezer. (Heb.) The rock of help.
Edgar. (A.-S.) Protector of property.
Edmund. (A.-S.) Defender of property. — Dim. Ed, Ned (a contraction of "mine Ed").

Edward. (A.-S.) Guardian of property.—Dim. Ed, Eddy, Ned, Neddy.
Edwin. (A.-S.) Gainer of property.—Dim. Ed, Eddy.
Egbert. (A.-S.) Bright sword; famous with the sword. —Dim. Bert.
Elbert. See **Albert.**
Eldred. (A.-S.) Of mature counsel.
Eleazer. (Heb.) God has helped.
Elfonzo. See **Alphonso.**
Eli. (Heb.) High.
Elias. See **Elijah.**
Elihu. (Heb.) God the Lord.
Elijah. (Heb.) Jehovah is my God.—Dim. 'Lije.
Eliphalet. (Heb.) God is my salvation.—Dim. 'Liph.
Elisha. (Heb.) God is salvation.
Elizur. (Heb.) God is my rock.
Ellis. (Heb.) A variation of Elias.
Elmer. (A.-S.) Noble; famous. (A contraction of **Ethelmer**).
Elnathan. (Heb.) God gave.
Emmanuel. (Heb.) God with us.
Emery, }
Emmery, } (A.-S.) Industrious,
Emory. } rich.
Enoch. (Heb.) Consecrated; dedicated.
Enos. (Heb.) Man.
Ephraim. (Heb.) Very fruitful. —Dim. Eph.
Erasmus. (Gr.) Lovely; worthy of love.
Erastus. (Gr.) Beloved.—Dim. 'Ras.
Eric. (Scand.) Rich; brave; powerful.
Ernest. (Ger.) Earnest.
Ethan. (Heb.) Firmness; strength.
Ethelbert. (A.-S.) Nobly bright. —Dim. Bert.
Eugene. (Gr.) Wellborn; noble. —Dim. 'Gene.
Eustace. (Gr.) Healthy; strong; steadfast.
Evan. (Celt.) Young warrior.
Ezekiel. (Heb.) Strength of God.—Dim. Zeke.
Ezra. (Heb.) Help.—Dim. Ez.

F

Felix. (Lat.) Happy; lucky.
Ferdinand. (Teut.) Bold; valiant.—Dim. Ferd.
Fernando. Same as **Ferdinand.**
Francis. (O.H.G.) Free.—Dim. Frank.
Franklin. (Teut.) A freeman or freeholder.
Frederic, } (Teut.) Peaceful.—
Frederick. } Dim. Fred, Freddy.

G

Gabriel. (Heb.) Man of God.—Dim. Gabe.
Gamaliel. (Heb.) Recompense of God.
Garret. See **Gerald,** or **Gerard.**
Geoffrey. See **Godfrey.**
George. (Gr.) Tiller of the soil; husbandman.—Dim. Georgie, Geordie.
Gerald, } (O.H.G.) Spear
Gerard. } wielder.—Dim. Jerry.
Gershom. (Heb.) An exile.
Gideon. (Heb.) A destroyer.
Gilbert. (O.H.G.) Bright; famous.—Dim. Bert.
Giles. (Fr. from L. Aegidius). A kid.
Given. (Eng.) Gift of God.
Goddard. (O.H.G.) Pious; virtuous.
Godfrey. (O.H.G.) At peace with God.
Godwin. (A.-S.) Friend of God.
Gregory. (Gr.) Watchful; vigilant.—Dim. Greg.
Griffith. (Celt.) Having great faith.
Gustave, } (Teut.) Staff of the
Gustavus. } Goths.
Guy. (Fr.) A leader.

H

Hannibal. (Punic.) Grace of Baal.
Harold. (A.-S.) Army commander.—Dim. Harry.
Heman. (Heb.) Faithful.
Henry. (O.H.G.) Head of the house; the ruler of private property. — Dim. Hal, Harry (by assimilation of consonant sound), Hen, Hank.
Herbert. (A.-S.) Glory of the army.—Dim. Bert, Bertie.
Herman. (O.H.G.) A warrior.
Hezekiah. (Heb.) Strengthened by the Lord.—Dim. Hez.
Hilary. (Gr.) Cheerful; merry.
Hiram. (Heb. from Phoenician.) Most noble.—Dim. Hi.
Horace. See **Horatio.**
Horatio. (Lat.) *—Dim. Harry.
Hosea. (Heb.) Salvation.
Howard. (Teut.) Chief warden or guardian.
Howell. (Celt.) Sound; whole.
Hubert. (O.H.G.) Bright in spirit; soul-bright. — Dim. Bert.
Hugh, } (D.) Mind; spirit;
Hugo. } soul.
Humphrey. (A.-S.) Protector of the home. — Dim. Hump. Humph.

I

Ichabod. (Heb.) Inglorious.
Ignatius. (Gr.) *
Immanuel. See **Emmanuel.**
Ingram. (Teut.) (Ram signifies raven.)
Inigo. (Sp. from Lat. Ennecus.)*
Ira. (Heb.) Watchful.
Isaac. (Heb.) Laughter. —Dim. Ike, Ikey.
Isaiah. (Heb.) Salvation of the Lord.
Israel. (Heb.) Contender with God.—Dim. Izzy.
Ivan. (Russ.) See **John.**

J

Jabez. (Heb.) He will cause pain.
Jacob. (Heb.) A supplanter.—Dim. Jake.
Jairus. (Heb.) He will enlighten.
James. (Heb.) See **Jacob.** —Dim Jeames, Jem, Jim, Jemmy, Jimmy.
Japheth. (Heb.) Enlargement.
Jared. (Heb.) Descent.
Jason. (Gr.) A Healer.
Jasper. (Fr.)*
Jedidiah. (Heb.) Beloved of the Lord.—Dim. Jed.
Jeffrey. (O.H.G.) See **Godfrey.** —Dim. Jeff., Geoff.
Jeremiah, }
Jeremias, } (Heb.) Exalted of
Jeremy. } the Lord.
Jerome. (Gr.) The holy-named. —Dim. Jerry.
Jesse. (Heb.) Wealth.
Joab. (Heb.) Jehovah is his father.
Job. (Heb.) Afflicted, persecuted.
Joel. (Heb.) The Lord is God.
John. (Heb.) God is gracious.—Dim. Johnny, Jack, Jock.
Jonah, }
Jonas. } (Heb.) A dove.
Jonathan. (Heb.) Gift of Jehovah.
Joseph. (Heb.) He shall add.—Dim. Joe.
Joshua. (Heb.) Jehovah is deliverance.—Dim. Josh.
Josiah, } (Heb.) Jehovah sup-
Josias. } ports.
Jotham. (Heb.) The Lord is perfect.
Judah, }
Jude. } (Heb.) Praised.
Julian. (Lat.) Sprung from, or belonging to, Julius. — Dim. Jule.
Julius. (Lat.) *—Dim. Jule.
Justin, }
Justus. } (Lat.) Just.

K

Kenelm. (A.-S.) Bold helmet.
Kenneth. (A-S Cynath).*

L

Laban. (Heb.) White.
Lambert. (O.H.G.) Illustrious with landed possessions.
Lancelot. (Fr.) A little lance or warrior; or a servant.
Laurence, } (Lat.) Of or be-
Lawrence. } longing to Laurentum, a town in Latium. Cf. **Laurus,** a laurel. — Dim. Larry, (Lawrie, Laurie, Scot; Larry, Irish).
Lazarus. (Heb.) Destitute of help.
Leander. (Gr.) Lion-man.*
Lemuel. (Heb.) Consecrated to God.—Dim. Lem.

Leo, } (Gr.) Lion.
Leon.
Leonard. (Ger.) Strong or brave as a lion.
Leonidas. (Gr.) Lion-like.
Leopold. (O.H.G.) Bold for the people.
Levi. (Heb.) Joining.
Lewis. (O.H.G.) Famous warrior.—Dim. Lou or Lew.
Linus. (Gr.) Flaxen-haired.
Lionel. (Gr.) Young lion.
Llewellyn. (Celt.) Lightning.
Lorenzo. (Lat.) See **Laurence.**
Lot. (Heb.) An envelope; a covering.
Louis. (Fr. form of **Lewis.**)
Lucian, } (Lat.) Belonging to, or sprung from, Lucius.
Lucien.
Lucius. (Lat.) Cf. Lat. *lux,* light.
Ludovic. (O. H. G. form of **Lewis.**)
Ludwig. (Ger. form of **Lewis.**)
Luke. (Gr.)*
Luther. (Ger.) Illustrious warrior.

M

Madoc. (Celt.) Good.
Malachi. (Heb.) Messenger.
Manasseh, (Heb.) Causing to forget.
Marcellus. (Lat.) Dim. of **Marcus.**
Marcius. (Lat.) See **Marcus.**
Marcus, } (Lat.) Probably derived from Mars, the god of war.
Mark.
Marmaduke. (A.-S.) A mighty noble.—Dim. 'Duke.
Martin. (Lat.) Of Mars; warlike.
Matthew. (Heb.) Gift of Jehovah.—Dim. Mat.
Matthias. See **Matthew.**
Maurice. (Lat.) Moorish; dark-colored.
Maximilian. (Lat., from Maximus+Aemilianus) The greatest Aemilianus.—Dim. Max.
Micah. (Heb.) Who is like God?
Michael. (Heb.) Who is like God?—Dim. Mike.
Miles. (O.G. Milo.)*
Moses. (Perhaps Egypt.) Child. —Dim. Mose.

N

Nahum. (Heb.) Comforter.
Napoleon. (Ital.)*—Dim. Nap.
Nathan. (Heb.) A gift.
Nathanael, } (Heb.) The gift of God.—Dim. Nat.
Nathaniel.
Neal, } (Celt.) Courageous chief.
Neil.
Nehemiah. (Heb.) Comfort of the Lord.
Nicholas, } (Gr.) Victory for the people. — Dim. Nick.
Nicolas.
Nicodemus. (Gr.) Possibly, conqueror of the people.
Noah. (Heb.) Rest; comfort.
Noel. (Fr.) Christmas.
Norman. (Scand.) A Northman; a native of Normandy.

O

Obadiah. (Heb.) Servant of the Lord.
Obed. (Heb.) Serving.
Octavius, } (Lat.) The eighth-born.
Octavus.
Oliver. (Fr.) *—Dim. Noll.
Orestes. (Gr.) A mountaineer.
Orlando. (Ital. form of Roland.)
Oscar. Cf. **Oswald.**
Osmund. (Teut.) Protection of God.
Oswald. (O.H.G.) Power of God.
Otho, } (Ger.) A giant.*
Otto.
Owen. (Celt.) Lamb; otherwise, young warrior.

P

Patrick. (Lat.) Noble; patrician. —Dim. Pat, Paddy.
Paul, } (Lat.) Little.
Paulus.
Peregrine. (Lat.) A stranger.
Peter. (Gr.) A rock. — Dim. Pete.
Philander. (Gr.) A lover of men.
Philemon. (Gr.) Loving.
Philip. (Gr.) A lover of horses. —Dim. Phil, Pip.
Phineas, } (Heb.) Mouth of brass.
Phinehas.
Pius. (Lat.) Pious; dutiful.
Pliny. (Lat.)*
Pompey. (Lat.)*

Q

Quentin, } (Lat.) The fifth-born.
Quintin.

R

Ralph. (O.H.G.) See **Rodolphus.**
Raphael. (Heb.) God has healed.
Raymond. (Teut.) Wise protection.
Reginald. (Teut.) Strong ruler. —Dim. Reg., Reggie.
Reuben. (Heb.) Behold, a son.
Reuel. (Heb.) God is his friend.
Reynold. (O.H.G.) Same as Reginald.
Richard. (O.H.G.) Strong like a ruler; powerful.—Dim. Dick.
Robert. (O.H.G.) Bright in fame.—Dim. Bob, Rob, Robin.
Roderic, } (O.H.G.) Rich in fame.—Dim. Rurik.
Roderick.
Rodolph, } (O.H.G.) Famous wolf, i.e., famous hero.
Rodolphus.
Roger. (O.H.G.) Famous with the spear. — Dim. Hodge, Hodgkin.
Roland, } (Teut.) Fame of the land.
Rowland.
Rudolph, } (O.H.G.) Variants of Rodolph.
Rudolphus.
Rufus. (Lat.) Red; red-haired. —Dim. Rufe.
Rupert. (O.H.G.) See **Robert.**
Rurik. See **Roderick.**

S

Samson, } (Heb.) The sun's man.
Sampson.
Samuel. (Heb.) His name is God.—Dim. Sam, Sammy.
Saul. (Heb.) Asked for.
Seba. (Heb.) Eminent.
Sebastian. (Gr.) Venerable; reverend.
Sereno, } (Lat.) Calm; peaceful.
Serenus.
Seth. (Heb.) Appointed.
Sigismund, } (O. H. G.) Conquering protection.—Dim. Sig.
Sigmund.
Silas. (Lat.) A contraction of **Silvanus.**
Silvanus. (Lat.) Living in the forest.
Silvester. (Lat.) Bred in the country; rustic.
Simeon, } (Heb.) Hearing. — Dim. Sim.
Simon.
Solomon. (Heb.) Peaceable.— Dim. Sol.
Stanley. (Old Eng.) Dweller at the stony lea, or (Slavonic) glory of the camp.
Stephen. (Gr.) A crown or garland.—Dim. Steve.
Sylvan, } See **Silvanus.**
Sylvanus.
Sylvester. See **Silvester.**

T

Thaddeus. (Syr.) The wise. — Dim. Thad.
Theobald. (Teut.) Bold for the people.—Dim. Theo.
Theodore. (Gr.) The gift of God.—Dim. Teddy.
Theodoric. (Teut.) Ruler of the people.
Theophilus. (Gr.) Dear to God.
Theron. (Gr.) A hunter.
Thomas. (Heb.) A twin.—Dim. Tom, Tommy.
Timothy. (Gr.) Honoring God. —Dim. Tim.
Titus. (Lat.)*
Tobiah, } (Heb.) The Lord is (my) good. — Dim. Toby.
Tobias.
Tristan, } (Celt.)*
Tristram.

U

Ulysses. (Lat., from Gr. Odysseus) A hater.—Dim. 'Lyss.
Urban. (Lat.) A man of the city; courteous; polished.
Uriah. (Heb.) My light is God.
Uriel. (Heb.) My light is God.

V

Valentine. (Lat.) Strong; healthy; powerful.—Dim. Val.
Victor. (Lat.) A conqueror. — Dim. Vic.

Vincent. (Lat.) Conquering; victorious.
Vivian. (Perhaps Celt.)*

W

Walter. (O.H.G.) Ruler of the army.—Dim. Wat, Walt.
Wilbert. (A.-S.) Wellborn. i.e., resolute protector.
William. (O. H. G.) Resolute helmet, i.e., resolute protector. —Dim. Will, Wylli, and (by interchange of convertible letters) Bill, Billy.
Winfred. (A.-S.) Peace winner.

Z

Zabdiel. (Heb.) Gift of God.
Zaccheus. (Heb.) Innocent; pure.
Zachariah, / **Zachary.** (Heb.) Remembered by the Lord.—Dim. Zack.
Zebadiah, / **Zebedee.** (Heb.) Gift of the Lord.
Zechariah. (Heb.) The same as Zachariah.
Zedekiah. (Heb.) Justice of the Lord.
Zenas. (Gr.) Gift of Jupiter.
Zephaniah. (Heb.) Hidden or treasured by the Lord.—Dim. Zeph.

NAMES OF WOMEN

A

Abigail. (Heb.) My father's joy.—Dim. Abby, Abbie.
Ada. (Heb.)*
Adaline. See **Adeline.**
Adela. See **Adeline.**
Adelaide. (Teut.) Of noble rank.
Adelia. A variant of **Adela.**
Adelina, / **Adeline.** (Teut.) Of noble birth.—Dim. Addie.
Agatha. (Gr.) Good; kind.
Agnes. (Gr.) Chaste; pure.
Alberta. (O.H.G.) Feminine of **Albert.**
Alethea. (Gr.) Truth.
Alexandra, / **Alexandrina.** (Gr.) Feminine of **Alexander.**
Alice, / **Alicia.** (Gr.) Truth.
Almira. (Ar.) Lofty; a princess.
Amabel. (Lat.) Lovable.
Amanda. (Lat.) Worthy to be loved.
Amelia. (Teut.) Busy; energetic.
Amy. (Fr.) Beloved.
Angelica, / **Angelina.** (Gr.) Lovely; angelic.
Ann, / **Anna,** / **Anne,** / **Annette.** (Heb.) Grace.—Dim. Annie, Nanny, Nancy, Nan, Nina.
Antoinette. (Lat.) Diminutive of **Antonia.** — Dim. Toinette, Nettie.
Antonia. (Lat.) Feminine of **Anthony.**
Ariana. (Gr.) A corruption of **Ariadne.**
Augusta. (Lat.) Feminine of **Augustus.** — Dim. 'Gusta, Gussie.
Aurelia. (Lat.) Feminine of **Aurelius.**
Aurora. (Lat.) The dawn; fresh; brilliant.

B

Barbara. (Gr.) Foreign; strange.—Dim. Bab.
Beatrice, / **Beatrix.** (Lat.) Happy; blessed.
Belinda. *
Berenice, / **Bernice.** (Gr.) Cf. *Nike*, victory.
Bertha. (Teut.) Bright.—Dim. Bertie.
Beulah. (Heb.) Married.
Bianca. (It.) White.
Blanch, / **Blanche.** (Teut.) White.
Brenda. (Teut.) Sword or firebrand. Feminine of **Brand.**
Bridget, / **Brigit.** (Celt.) Lofty; august; bright. — Dim. Biddy.

C

Camilla. (Lat.) A maiden of unblemished birth and character; an attendant at a sacrifice.
Caroline. Feminine of **Carolus,** the Latin for **Charles.**
Catharina, / **Catharine,** / **Catherine.** (Gr.) Cf. *katharos*, pure. — Dim. Cassie, Kate, Katy, Kit, Kitty.
Catalina. See **Catherine.**
Cecilia, / **Cecily.** (Lat.) Feminine of **Cecil.**—Dim. Sisley, Sis, Cis.
Celestine. (Lat.) Heavenly.
Celia. (Lat.) Heavenly.
Charlotte. (O.H.G.) Feminine of **Charles.**—Dim. Lottie.
Chloë. (Gr.) A green herb; a young shoot.
Christiana, / **Christina.** (Gr.) Feminine of **Christian.** — Dim. Chrissie, Tina.
Cicely. (Lat.) A corruption of **Cecilia.**
Clara. (Lat.) Bright; illustrious. —Dim. Clare, Cad.
Claribel. (Lat.) Brightly fair.
Clarice, / **Clarissa.** (Lat.) Variants of **Clara.**—Dim. Clare.
Claudia. (Lat.) Feminine of **Claudius.**
Clementina, / **Clementine.** (Lat.) Feminine of **Clement.** — Dim. Tina.
Cobina. Source not known.
Constance. (Lat.) Firm; constant.—Dim. Connie.
Cora, / **Corinne.** (Gr.) Maiden.
Cornelia. (Lat.) Feminine of **Cornelius.** — Dim. Cornie, Nellie.
Cynthia. (Gr.) Of or from Mt. Cynthus in the island of Delos.

D

Deborah. (Heb.) A bee.—Dim. Debby, Deb.
Delia. (Gr.) Of or from the island of Delos.
Diana. (Lat.) Goddess. (The name is evidently related to several words connoting brightness. Diana was the moon-goddess.)
Dinah. (Heb.) Judged.
Dolores. (Lat.) Sorrowful. Cf. Mater Dolorosa.
Dora. See **Dorothea, Eudora,** and **Theodora.**
Dorcas. (Gr.) A gazelle.
Dorinda. (Gr.) See **Dorothea.**
Doris. (Gr.) In Greek mythology, a sea goddess and mother of the sea nymphs.
Dorothea, / **Dorothy.** (Gr.) The gift of God. — Dim. Dora, Dol, Dolly (the **r** being etymologically convertible).
Drusilla. (Lat.) Lat. *Drusus.*

E

Edith. (A.-S.) Happiness; otherwise, rich gift.
Edna. (Heb.) Rejuvenation.
Eleanor, / **Elinor.** (Gr.) Light.*—Dim. Ella, Nell, Nellie, Nora.
Elisabeth, / **Elizabeth,** / **Eliza.** (Heb.) Consecrated to God.—Dim. Bess, Bessie, Betsy, Betty, Lizzy, Libby, Lisa, Liza.
Ellen. Cf. **Helen.**
Elsa. (Ger.)*
Elvira. (Sp.)*
Emeline, / **Emmeline.** (Teut.) See **Amelia.**
Emily. (Lat.) From Aemilia, feminine of Aemilius.*
Emma. (Ger.)* — Dim. Em, Emmie.
Enid. (Celt.) Soul or spirit.
Ernestine. (Ger.) Feminine dim. of **Ernest.**—Dim. Tina.
Esther. (Per.) Star.—Dim. Tess, Tessie, Ess, Essie.
Ethel. (A.-S.) Noble.
Ethelind, / **Ethelinda.** (A.-S.) Ethel, signifies noble.
Eudora. (Gr.) Generous.
Eugenia, / **Eugenie.** (Gr.) Feminine of **Eugene.**
Eulalia. (Gr.) Fair speech.
Eunice. (Gr.) Happy victory.
Euphemia. (Gr.) Of good report.—Dim. Effie.
Eva. (Heb.) Life.
Evangeline. (Gr.) Bringing glad news.
Eve. (Heb.) The same as **Eva.**
Evelina, / **Eveline.** (Heb.) Diminutive of **Eva.**

F

Faustina. (Lat.) Lucky; favorable.

Fay. (Fr.) Fairy, or (Lat.) a diminutive of **Faith.**
Felicia, / **Felice.** (Lat.) Happiness.
Fidelia. (Lat.) Faithful.
Flora. (Lat.) (The name of the goddess of flowers.)—Dim. Flo, Flossie.
Florence. (Lat.) Blooming; flourishing. — Dim. Florrie, Flossie.
Frances. (Ger.) Feminine of **Francis.**—Dim. Fannie, Frank.
Frederica. (O.H.G.) Feminine of **Frederic.**—Dim. Freddie, Frieda.

G

Georgiana, / **Georgina.** (Gr.) Feminine of **George.** — Dim. Georgie.
Geraldine. Feminine of **Gerald.**
Gertrude. (O.H.G.) Spear-maiden.—Dim. Gertie, Trudy.
Grace, / **Gratia.** (Lat.) Grace, favor.
Griselda. (Teut.) (Name is probably related to war.) — Dim. Grissel.

H

Hannah. (Heb.) See **Anna.**
Harriet, / **Harriot.** (O.H.G.) Feminine diminutive of **Henry.** —Dim. Hattie.
Helen, / **Helena.** (Gr.) * — Dim. Nell, Nellie, Lena.
Henrietta. (O.H.G.) Feminine diminutive of **Henry.**—Dim. Etta, Hetty.
Hephzibah. (Heb.) My delight is in her.—Dim. Hepsy.
Hester, / **Hesther.** (Per.) Variants of **Esther.**
Hilaria. (Gr.) Feminine of **Hilary.**
Honora, / **Honoria.** (Lat.) Honorable.
Hortense, / **Hortensia.** (Lat.) A lady gardener.
Huldah. (Heb.) A weasel.

I

Ida. (Teut.)*
Idabell. (Teut.) Godlike and fair.*
Inez. (Gr.) Old Sp. and Pg. forms of **Agnes.**
Inga. (Teut.) Daughter.
Ingrid. (Teut.) Daughter.
Irene. (Gr.) Peace. — Dim. Renie.
Isabel. / **Isabella.** (Heb.) The same as **Elizabeth.** — Dim. Belle, Bella.

J

Jacqueline. (Heb.) Feminine of **James.**
Jane, / **Janet.** (Heb.) Feminine of **John.**
Jean, / **Jeanne,** / **Jeannette.** (Heb.) The same as **Jane** or **Joan.**
Jemima. (Heb.) A dove.
Jerusha. (Heb.) Possessed; married.
Jessica. (Heb.) Wealth.
Joan, / **Joanna.** (Heb.) Feminine of **John.**
Josepha, / **Josephine.** (Heb.) Feminine of **Joseph.**—Dim. Josie, Jo, Phenie.
Joyce. (Lat.) Sportive.
Judith. (Heb.) Praised.—Dim. Judy, Ju.
Julia. (Lat.) Feminine of **Julius.**—Dim. Julie.
Juliana. (Lat.) Feminine of **Julian.**
Juliette. (Lat.) Diminutive of **Julia.**
Justina. (Lat.) Feminine of Justin.

K

Kate. Dim. of **Catherine.**
Katharine, / **Katherine,** / **Kathleen.** (Gr.) See **Catherine.**
Keturah. (Heb.) Incense.
Keziah. (Heb.) Cassia.

L

Laura. (Lat.) Perhaps for *laurea*, a laurel.
Lavinia. (Lat.) A woman of Lavinium, city in Latium.
Lena. (Gr.) Dim of **Helen.**
Leonora. Same as **Eleanor.**
Letitia. (Lat.) Happiness; joy. —Dim. Lettie, Lettice.
Lillian, / **Lilly.** (Lat.) Lily. — Dim. Lil.
Lois. (Gr.)*
Louisa, / **Louise.** (O.H.G.) Feminine of **Louis.** — Dim. Louie, Lou.
Lucia. (Lat.) Feminine of **Lucius.**
Lucile. (Lat.) See **Lucia.**
Lucinda. (Lat.) See **Lucia.**
Lucretia. (Lat.) Feminine of **Lucretius.***
Lucy. (Lat.) See **Lucia.**
Lydia. (Gr.) A native of Lydia, in Asia Minor.

M

Mabel. (Lat.) See **Amabel.**
Madeline. (Heb.) Another form of **Magdalene.**
Magdalene. (Heb.) Belonging to Magdala, on the Sea of Galilee.—Dim. Maud, Maudlin, Lena.
Marcella. (Lat.) Feminine of **Marcellus.**
Marcia. Feminine of **Marcius.** —Dim. Marsh.
Margaret. (Gr.) A pearl.—Dim. Greta, Mag, Madge, Maggie, Margie, Marjory, Meg, Meta, Peg, Peggy.
Maria. (Heb.) See **Mary.**
Marianne. (Heb.) A compound of **Mary** and **Anne.**
Marion. (Heb.) A French form of **Mary.**
Martha. (Heb.) Lady; ruler of the house.—Dim. Mat, Mattie, Pat, Pattie.
Mary. (Heb.) * — Dim. Moll, Mollie, Polly, May.
Mathilda, / **Matilda.** (O.H.G.) Mighty battle-maid; heroine.—Dim. Mat, Matty, Maud, Pattie.
May. A contraction of **Mary.**
Mehetabel, / **Mehitable.** (Heb.) Benefited by God. — Dim. Hetty.
Melicent. (Teut.) * — Dim. Millie.
Melissa. (Gr.) A bee.
Mildred. (Ger.) Of mild strength.—Dim. Millie.
Miranda. (Lat.) Worthy of admiration.
Miriam. (Heb.)* Cf. **Mary.**
Myra. (Gr.) She who weeps or laments.

N

Nancy. A familiar form of **Anne.** — Dim. Nan, Nance, Nina.
Nellie. Dim. of **Ellen, Helen,** or **Eleanor.**
Nora. A contraction of **Honora.**

O

Octavia. (Lat.) Feminine of **Octavius.**—Dim. Tavie.
Olga. (Teut.) Holy.
Olive, / **Olivia.** (Lat.) An olive; perhaps olive-complexioned.—Dim. Livie.
Olympia. (Gr.) Heavenly.
Ophelia. (Gr.) Help.*

P

Paula. (Lat.) Feminine of **Paul.**
Paulina, / **Pauline.** (Lat.) Dim. of **Paula.**
Penelope. (Gr.) A weaver.—Dim. Pen, Penny.
Persis. (Gr.) A Persian woman.
Phebe. (Gr.) The same as **Phoebe.**
Philippa. (Gr.) Feminine of **Philip.**
Phoebe. (Gr.) Pure; radiant.
Phyllis. (Gr.) A green bough.
Polly. (Eng.) Dim. of Mary.
Priscilla. (Gr. or Lat.) Cf. Lat. *priscus*, ancient.—Dim. Prissie.

R

Rachel. (Heb.) A ewe.
Ramona. (Teut.) Wise protectress. Feminine of **Raymond.**
Rebecca, / **Rebekah.** (Heb.) * — Dim. Becky.
Rhoda. (Gr.) A rose.
Roberta. (O.H.G.) Feminine of **Robert.**
Rosa. (Lat.) A rose. — Dim. Rosie.
Rosabel, / **Rosabella.** (Lat.) A fair rose.
Rosalia. (Ital.) Rose.

Rosalie. (Ger.) Rose.
Rosalind. (Sp.) Pretty rose.—Dim. Rose, Linda.
Rosamond. (Teut.)*
Roxana. (Per.) Dawn of day.
Ruth. (Heb.) Beauty.

S

Sabina. (Lat.) A Sabine woman.
Salome. (Heb.) Peaceful.
Sara, / **Sarah.** (Heb.) A princess. — Dim. Sadie, Sal, Sally.
Serena. (Lat.) Feminine of **Serenus** or **Sereno.**
Sibyl, / **Sibylla.** (Gr.) A prophetess.
Silvia. See **Sylvia.**
Sophia. (Gr.) Wisdom.—Dim. Sophie, Soph.
Sophronia. (Gr.) Common sense.
Stella. (Lat.) A star.
Stephana. (Gr.) Feminine of **Stephen.**
Sue, / **Susan,** / **Susanna,** / **Susannah,** / **Susette.** (Heb.) A lily.—Dim. Suke, Suky, Susie.
Sylvia. (Lat.) See **Sylvanus.**

T

Tabitha. (Syr.) A gazelle. —Dim. Tabby.
Theodora. (Gr.) Feminine of **Theodore.**—Dim. Dora, Theo.
Theodosia. (Gr.) The gift of God.
Theresa, / **Therese.** (Lat.)*—Dim, Tessie, Tess.

U

Ulrica. (Teut.) Rich.
Urania. (Gr.) Heavenly. (The name of the muse of astronomy.)
Ursula. (Lat.) Little she-bear.

V

Valeria. (Lat.) Feminine of **Valerius.**
Veronica. (Lat.) (Perhaps derived from **Berenice.**)
Vera. (Lat.) True.
Victoria. (Lat.) Victory. feminine of **Victor.**
Vida. (Heb.) Feminine of **David.**
Viola. (Lat.) A violet.—Dim. Vi.
Virginia. (Lat.) Virgin; pure.—Dim. Virgie, Jennie.
Vivian. (Perhaps Celt.)*—Dim. Vivie.

W

Wilhelmina. (O.H.G.) Feminine of **Wilhelm,** German of **William.** — Dim. Wilmett, Wilmot, Mina, Minella, Billie.
Willa. (A.-S.) The desired.
Winifred. (A.-S.) Feminine of **Winfred.**—Dim. Winnie.

Z

Zenobia. (Gr.) Having life from Jupiter.
Zoe. (Gr.) Life.

FOREIGN WORDS AND PHRASES

English is one of the richest languages in the world. Its ancestor, Anglo-Saxon, was augmented at the time of the Norman Conquest by a veritable wealth of Old French words, themselves derived from Latin, and during the Renaissance received a large influx of pure Greek and Latin words. Since that time many other foreign words have been adopted, being fitted more smoothly into the English language by changes in spelling and pronunciation. But there are other foreign words which, although used by writers of English, have retained their original form intact; the student or author should know them, since for one reason or another they have proved extremely useful. Some of these foreign phrases express a certain idea more concisely than could any combination of English words—"The Greeks had a word for it," as the saying goes. Others have a historical flavor and significance that would be lost if they were Anglicized. Phrases such as *coup d'état, tour de force, bête noire, vox populi, status quo,* and *raison d'être* are in common use today. Latin and Greek phrases also appear frequently as mottoes and inscriptions, such as *semper fidelis, requiescat in pace, labor omnia vincit, mens sana in corpore sano,* and *nemo me impune lacessit.* The following dictionary of foreign words and phrases is intended to enrich the appreciation of the student and general reader, and to provide a ready answer for many oft-recurring questions.

à bas. [Fr.] Down, down with.
Ab extra. [L.] From without.
Ab initio. [L.] From the beginning.
Ab intra. [L.] From within.
à bon chat, bon rat. [Fr.] Tit for tat.
à bon marché. [Fr.] Cheap; a good bargain.
Ab origine [L.] From the origin.
Ab ovo. [L.] From the egg; from the beginning.
Ab ovo usque ad mala [L.] From the egg to the apples (as in Roman banquets); equivalent to 'From the soup to the savoury'; from beginning to end.
Absente reo. [L.] The accused being absent.
Absit invidia. [L.] Let there be no ill-will; envy apart.
Absit omen. [L.] May the omen be averted.
Ab uno disce omnes. [L.] From one specimen judge of all the rest.
Ab urbe conditâ. [L.] From the building of the city; *i.e.*, Rome.
à cheval. [Fr.] On horseback.
Ad aperturam (libri). [L.] At the opening of the book; wherever the book opens.
Ad arbitrium. [L.] At pleasure.
Ad calendas Græcas. [L.] At the Greek calends; *i.e.*, never, as the Greeks had no calends in their mode of reckoning.
Ad captandum vulgus. [L.] To attract or please the rabble.
à deux mains. [Fr.] For two hands; two-handed; having a double office.
Ad finem. [L.] To the end.
Ad hoc. [L.] For this special object or duty.
Ad infinitum. [L.] To infinity.
Ad interim. [L.] In the meanwhile.
à discrétion. [Fr.] At discretion; unrestricted.
Ad libitum. [L.] At pleasure.
Ad nauseam. [L.] To disgust or satiety.
Ad referendum. [L.] For consideration.
Ad rem. [L.] To the purpose; to the point.
Adscriptus glebæ. [L.] Attached to the soil.
Adsum. [L.] I am present; here!
Ad unguem. [L.] To the nail; to a nicety; exactly; perfectly.
Ad unum omnes. [L.] All to a man.
Ad utrumque paratus. [L.] Prepared for either case.
Ad valorem. [L.] According to the value.

Ad vitam aut culpam. [L.] For life or fault; *i.e.*, till some misconduct be proved.
Ægrescitque medendo. [L.] He becomes more ill through remedies.
Æquo animo. [L.] With an equable mind; with equanimity.
Ære perennius. [L.] More lasting than brass.
Affaire d'amour. [Fr.] A love affair.
Affaire d'honneur. [Fr.] An affair of honour; a duel.
Affaire du cœur. [Fr.] An affair of the heart.
A fortiori. [L.] With stronger reason.
Age quod agis. [L.] Attend to what you are about.
à grands frais. [Fr.] At great expense.
à haute voix. [Fr.] Aloud.
Aide toi, et le Ciel t'aidera. [Fr.] Help yourself, and Heaven will help you.
à la belle étoile. [Fr.] Under the stars; in the open air.
à la bonne heure. [Fr.] In good time; very well.
à l'abri. [Fr.] Under shelter.
à la dérobée. [Fr.] By stealth.
à la Française. [Fr.] After the French mode.
à la mode. [Fr.] According to the custom or fashion.
à l'envi. [F.] Emulously; so as to vie.
Al fresco. [It.] In the open air; cool.
Allez-vous-en. [Fr.] Away with you.
Allons. [Fr.] Let us go; come on; come.
Alter ego. [L.] Another self.
Alter idem. [L.] Another exactly similar.
Amantium iræ amoris integratio est. [L.] Lovers' quarrels are a renewal of love.
Amende honorable. [Fr.] Satisfactory apology; reparation.
A mensa et toro. [L.] From bed and board.
à merveille. [Fr.] To a wonder; marvellously.
Amicus humani generis. [L.] A friend of the human race.
Amor patriæ. [L.] Love of country.
Amour propre. [Fr.] Self-love; vanity.
Ancien régime. [Fr.] The ancient or former order of things.
Anno ætatis suæ. [L.] In the year of his or her age.
Anno Christi. [L.] In the year of Christ.
Anno Domini. [L.] In the year of our Lord.
Anno mundi. [L.] In the year of the world.
Anno urbis conditæ. [L.] In the year from the time the city (Rome) was built.
Annus mirabilis. [L.] Year of wonder.
Ante meridiem. [L.] Before noon.
à outrance. [Fr.] To a finish.
Aperçu. [Fr.] A general sketch or survey.
à perte de vue. [Fr.] Till beyond one's view.
à peu près. [Fr.] Nearly.
à pied. [Fr.] On foot.
A posteriori. [L.] From the effect to the cause.
Après nous le déluge. [Fr.] After us the deluge.
à propos de bottes. [Fr.] Apropos of boots; foreign to the subject or matter in hand.
à propos de rien. [Fr.] Apropos of nothing; without a motive.
Arbiter elegantiarum. [L.] A judge or supreme authority in matters of taste.
Arcades ambo. [L.] Arcadians both; fellows of the same stamp.
Arcana imperii. [L.] State secrets.
Ardentia verba. [L.] Glowing language.
Argent comptant. [Fr.] Ready money.
Argumentum ad crumenam. [L.] An argument to the purse.
Argumentum ad hominem. [L.] An argument to the individual man; *i.e.* to his interests and prejudices.
Argumentum ad ignorantiam. [L.] An argument founded on a person's ignorance.
Argumentum ad judicium. [L.] Argument appealing to the judgment.
Argumentum ad verecundiam. [L.] Argument appealing to modesty.
Argumentum baculinum. [L.] An argument by stick; an appeal to force.
Ariston metron. [Gr.] Moderation is best.
Arrière pensée. [Fr.] Mental reservation.
Ars est celare artem. [L.] It is true art to conceal art.
Ars longa, vita brevis. [L.] Art is long, life is short.
Artium magister. [L.] Master of Arts.
Assem habeas, assem valeas. [L.] If you have a penny, you are worth a penny.
à tort et à travers. [Fr.] At random; without consideration.
Au contraire. [Fr.] On the contrary.
Au courant. [Fr.] Fully acquainted with matters.
Au désespoir. [Fr.] In despair.
Audi alteram partem. [L.] Hear the other side.
Au fait. [Fr.] Well acquainted with; expert.
Au fond. [Fr.] At bottom.
Auf Wiedersehen. [Ger.] Au revoir.
Aurea mediocritas. [L.] The golden or happy mean.
Au reste. [Fr.] As for the rest.
Au revoir. [Fr.] Adieu until we meet again.
Aussitôt dit, aussitôt fait. [Fr.] No sooner said than done.
Autant d'hommes, autant d'avis. [Fr.] So many men, so many minds.
Aut Cæsar aut nullus. [L.] Either Cæsar or nobody.
Aut vincere aut mori. [L.] Either to conquer or to die; death or victory.
Aux armes! [Fr.] To arms!
Avant propos. [Fr.] Preliminary matter; preface.
A vostra salute. [It.] } To your health.
à votre santé. [Fr.] } To your health.

Bas bleu. [Fr.] A blue-stocking; a literary woman.
Beatæ memoriæ [L.] Of blessed memory.
Beaux esprits [Fr.] Men of wit.
Beaux yeux [Fr.] Fine eyes; good looks.
Bel esprit. [Fr.] A person of wit or genius; a brilliant mind.
Bella! horrida bella! [L.] Wars! horrid wars!
Ben trovato. [It.] Well invented.
Bête noire. [Fr.] A black beast; a bugbear.
Bis dat qui cito dat. [L.] He gives twice who gives quickly.
Bon ami [Fr.] Good friend.
Bon gré, mal gré. [Fr.] With good or ill grace; willing or unwilling.
Bon jour. [Fr.] Good day; good morning.
Bonne et belle. [Fr.] Good and handsome.
Bonne foi. [Fr.] Good faith.
Bon soir. [Fr.] Good evening.
Breveté. [Fr.] Patented.
Brevi manu. [L.] With a short hand; extemporaneously.
Brutum fulmen. [L.] A harmless thunderbolt.

Cacoethes scribendi. [L.] An itch for writing.
Cadit quæstio. [L.] The question falls; there is no further discussion.
Cæca est invidia. [L.] Envy is blind.
Cæsar non supra grammaticos. [L.] Cæsar is not over the grammarians.
Cætera desunt. [L.] The rest is wanting.
Cæteris paribus. [L.] Other things being equal.
Campo santo. [It.] A burying-ground.
Carpe diem. [L.] Enjoy the present day; improve the time.
Casus belli. [L.] That which causes or justifies war.
Causa sine quâ non. [L.] An indispensable cause or condition.
Cause célèbre. [Fr.] A famous case.
Caveat emptor. [L.] Let the buyer beware.
Cedant arma togæ. [L.] Let arms yield to the gown; that is, military authority to the civil power.
Cela va sans dire. [Fr.] That goes without saying; that is a matter of course.
Ce n'est que le premier pas qui coûte. [Fr.] It is only the first step that is difficult.
C'est-à-dire. [Fr.] That is to say.
C'est plus qu'un crime; c'est une faute. [Fr.] It is worse than a crime; it is a blunder.
C'est une autre chose. [Fr.] That's quite another thing.
Ceteris paribus. [L.] See *Cæteris*.
Chacun à son goût. [Fr.] Every one to his taste.
Châteaux en Espagne. [Fr.] Castles in the air.
Chemin de fer. [Fr.] Iron road; a railway.
Cherchez la femme. [Fr.] Look for the woman.
Chère amie. [Fr.] A dear (female) friend.
Che sarà, sarà. [It.] What will be, will be.
Chi tace confessa. [It.] He who keeps silence confesses.
Ci git. [Fr.] Here lies.
Civis Romanus sum. [L.] I am a Roman citizen.
Clarum et venerabile nomen. [L.] An illustrious and venerable name.
Cogito, ergo sum. [L.] I think, therefore I exist.
Comitas inter gentes. [L.] Politeness between nations.
Comme il faut. [Fr.] As it should be.
Commune bonum. [L.] A common good.
Communibus annis. [L.] On the annual average.
Communi consensu. [L.] By common consent.
Compagnon de voyage. [Fr.] A travelling companion.
Compos mentis. [L.] Sound of mind.
Compte rendu. [Fr.] An account rendered; a report.
Con amore. [It.] With love; very earnestly.
Conditio sine quâ non. [L.] A necessary condition.
Conjunctis viribus. [L.] With united powers.
Conseil d'état. [Fr.] A council of state; a privy-council.
Consensus facit legem. [L.] Consent makes the law.
Consilio et prudentia. [L.] By wisdom and prudence.
Constantia et virtute. [L.] By constancy and virtue (or bravery).
Contra bonos mores. [L.] Against good manners.
Copia verborum. [L.] Rich supply of words.
Coram nobis. [L.] Before us; in our presence.
Cordon sanitaire. [Fr.] A line of guards to prevent the spreading of contagion or pestilence.
Coup. [Fr.] A stroke.—*Coup d'essai*, a first attempt.—*Coup d'état*, a sudden decisive blow in politics; a stroke of policy.—*Coup de grâce*, a finishing stroke.—*Coup de main*, a sudden attack or enterprise.—*Coup de maître*, a master stroke.—*Coup d'œil*, a rapid glance of the eye.—*Coup de pied*, a kick.—*Coup de soleil*, sunstroke.—*Coup de théâtre*, a theatrical effect.
Coûte qu'il coûte. [Fr.] Cost what it may.
Crambe repetita. [L.] Cabbage served up again.
Credat Judæus Apella non ego. [L.] Let Apella, the Jew, believe it; I won't; tell that to the Horse-Marines.
Credo quia absurdum. [L.] I believe because it is absurd.
Crux criticorum. [L.] The puzzle of critics.
Cucullus non facit monachum. [L.] The cowl does not make the friar.
Cui bono? [L.] For whose advantage? to what end?
Cum grano salis. [L.] With a grain of salt.
Cum privilegio. [L.] With privilege.
Curiosa felicitas. [L.] Nice felicity of expression.
Currente calamo. [L.] With a running or rapid pen.

Dame d'honneur. [Fr.] Maid of honour.
De bon augure. [Fr.] Of good augury or omen.
De bonne grâce. [Fr.] With a good grace.
Decies repetita placebit. [L.] When ten times repeated it will please.
De die in diem. [L.] From day to day.
De facto. [L.] In fact; actually.
Dégagé. [Fr.] Free; easy; unconstrained.
De gustibus non est disputandum. [L.] There is no disputing about tastes.
Dei gratiâ. [L.] By the grace of God.
De haut en bas. [Fr.] Contemptuously.
De jure. [L.] From the law; by right.
Delenda est Carthago. [L.] Carthage must be destroyed.
De minimis non curat lex. [L.] The law does not concern itself about trifles.
De mortuis nil nisi bonum. [L.] Say nothing but good of the dead.
De non apparentibus et non existentibus est eadem ratio. [L.] As to things which do not appear, the conclusion is the same as to things which do not exist.
De novo. [L.] Anew.
Deo adjuvante. [L.] God assisting.
Deo favente. [L.] God favouring.
Deo gratias. [L.] Thanks to God.
Deo juvante. [L.] With God's help.
Deo volente. [L.] God willing; by God's will.
De profundis. [L.] Out of the depths.
Dernier cri. [Fr.] The latest fad of fashion.
Dernier ressort. [Fr.] A last resource.
Désagrément. [Fr.] An annoyance.
Desipere in loco. [L.] To jest or be jolly at the proper time.
Desunt cætera. [L.] The rest is wanting.
Deus ex machina. [L.] A god from some mechanical device.
Dictum sapienti sat est. [L.] A word to the wise is enough.
Dies irae. [L.] Day of wrath.
Dieu et mon droit. [Fr.] God and my right.
Dieu vous garde. [Fr.] God protect you.
Dignus vindice nodus. [L.] A difficulty worthy of powerful intervention.
Dii penates. [L.] Household gods.
Dis aliter visum. [L.] It is otherwise decreed by the gods.
Disjecta membra. [L.] Scattered remains.
Divide et impera. [L.] Divide and rule.
Dolce far niente. [It.] Sweet idleness.
Dominus vobiscum. [L.] The Lord be with you.
Dramatis personæ. [L.] The persons or characters in a drama.
Dulce et decorum est pro patriâ mori. [L.] It is sweet and glorious to die for one's country.
Dum spiro, spero. [L.] While I breathe I hope.
Dum vivimus, vivamus. [L.] While we live, let us live.
Durante vitâ. [L.] During life.
Du sublime au ridicule il n'y a qu'un pas. [Fr.] From the sublime to the ridiculous is only one step.

Eadem sunt omnia semper. [L.] All things are always the same.
Ecce homo. [L.] Behold the man!
Ecce signum. [L.] Behold the sign!
Edition de luxe. [Fr.] A splendid and expensive edition of a book.
Editio princeps. [L.] The first printed edition of a book.
Ego et rex meus. [L.] I and my king.
Eheu! fugaces labuntur anni. [L.] Alas! the fleeting years glide by.
Emeritus. [L.] Retired or superannuated after long service.
En ami. [Fr.] As a friend.
En arrière. [Fr.] In the rear; behind; back.
En attendant. [Fr.] In the meantime.
En avant. [Fr.] Forward.
En déshabillé. [Fr.] In undress.
En effet. [Fr.] In effect; substantially; really.
En famille. [Fr.] With one's family; in a domestic state.
Enfant gâté. [Fr.] A spoiled child.
Enfants perdus. [Fr.] Lost children; a group of men forming a forlorn hope.

Enfant terrible. [Fr.] A child who is always making inopportune and embarrassing remarks.
Enfant trouvé. [Fr.] A foundling.
Enfin. [Fr.] In short; at last; finally.
En grande tenue. [Fr.] In full dress.
En plein jour. [Fr.] In broad day.
En rapport. [Fr.] In harmony; in agreement.
En règle. [Fr.] According to rules; in order.
En revanche. [Fr.] In requital; in return.
En route. [Fr.] On the way.
En suite. [Fr.] In company; in a set.
Entente cordiale. [Fr.] Cordial understanding, especially between two states.
Entourage. [Fr.] Surroundings; adjuncts.
Entre nous. [Fr.] Between ourselves.
En vérité. [Fr.] In truth; verily.
Eo animo. [L.] With that design.
Eo nomine. [L.] By that name.
E pluribus unum. [L.] One out of many; one composed of many.
Eppur si muove. [It.] Yet it does move.
E re natâ. [L.] According to the exigency.
Esprit de corps. [Fr.] The animating spirit of a collective body, as a regiment.
Esse quam videri. [L.] To be rather than to seem.
Est modus in rebus. [L.] There is a medium in all things.
Et cætera (or *Et cetera*). [L.] And the rest.
Et hoc (or *Et id*) *genus omne.* [L.] And everything of the sort.
Et sequentes, Et sequentia, [L.] And those that follow.
Et sic de cæteris. [L.] And so of the rest.
Et sic de similibus. [L.] And so of the like.
Et tu, Brute! [L.] And thou also, Brutus!
Ex adverso. [L.] From the opposite side.
Ex animo. [L.] Heartily; sincerely.
Ex cathedra. [L.] From the chair. (Since 1870 the Pope has claimed to be infallible when speaking *ex cathedra.*)
Exceptio probat regulam. [L.] The exception proves (or tests) the rule.
Exceptis excipiendis. [L.] The due exceptions being made.
Ex dono. [L.] By the gift.
Exempli gratiâ. [L.] By way of example.
Ex merâ gratiâ. [L.] Through mere favour.
Ex necessitate rei. [L.] From the necessity of the case.
Ex nihilo nihil fit. [L.] Out of nothing, nothing comes.
Ex officio. [L.] By virtue of office.
Ex parte. [L.] From one side only.
Ex pede Herculem. [L.] From the foot we recognize a Hercules; we judge of the whole from the specimen.
Experientia docet stultos. [L.] Experience instructs fools.
Experimentum crucis. [L.] An experiment of a most searching nature.
Experto crede. [L.] Trust one who has had experience.
Ex post facto. [L.] After the deed is done; retrospective.
Expressis verbis. [L.] In express terms.
Extra muros. [L.] Beyond the walls.
Ex uno disce omnes. [L.] From one judge of the rest.

Facile princeps. [L.] Easily pre-eminent; indisputably the first.
Facilis descensus Averni (or *Averno*). [L.] The descent to Avernus (or hell) is easy.
Façon de parler. [Fr.] Manner of speaking.
Fæx populi. [L.] The dregs of the people.
Faire bonne mine. [Fr.] To put a good face upon the matter.
Fait accompli. [Fr.] A thing already done.
Fallentis semita vitae. [L.] The pathway of life which escapes observation.
Fama clamosa. [L.] A current scandal.
Far niente. [It.] The doing of nothing.
Fas est et ab hoste doceri. [L.] It is right to be taught even by an enemy.
Fata obstant. [L.] The Fates oppose it.
Feræ naturæ. [L.] Of a wild nature; undomesticated (animals).
Festina lente. [L.] Hasten slowly.
Fiat justitia, ruat cœlum. [L.] Let justice be done though the heavens should fall.
Fiat experimentum in corpore vili. [L.] Let the experiment be made on a worthless body.
Fiat lux. [L.] Let there be light.
Fide et amore. [L.] By faith and love.
Fide et fiduciâ. [L.] By fidelity and confidence.
Fidei defensor. [L.] Defender of the faith.
Fide non armis. [L.] By faith, not by arms.
Fides Punica. [L.] Punic or Carthaginian faith; treachery.
Fidus Achates. [L.] Faithful Achates; a true friend.
Filius nullius. [L.] A son of nobody.
Filius terræ. [L.] A son of the earth; one of low birth.
Fille de joie. [Fr.] A prostitute.
Finem respice. [L.] Look to the end.
Finis coronat opus. [L.] The end crowns the work.
Flagrante bello. [L.] During hostilities.
Flagrante delicto. [L.] In the commission of the crime.
Flecti, non frangi. [L.] To be bent, not broken.
Fons et origo. [L.] The source and origin.
Forsan et hæc olim meminisse juvabit. [L.] Perhaps it will one day cause us pleasure to remember even these things.
Fortiter in re. [L.] With firmness in acting.
Fortuna favet fortibus. [L.] Fortune favours the bold.
Fronti nulla fides. [L.] There is no trusting to outward features.
Fruges consumere nati. [L.] Born to consume fruits; born only to eat.
Fugit irreparabile tempus. [L.] Irrecoverable time flies on.
Fuimus Troes. [L.] We were once Trojans.
Fuit Ilium. [L.] Troy has been.
Fulmen brutum. [L.] A harmless thunderbolt.
Fumum et opes strepitumque Romæ. [L.] The smoke and wealth and noise of Rome.
Functus officio. [L.] Having performed one's office or duty; hence, out of office.
Furor arma ministrat. [L.] Rage provides arms.
Furor loquendi. [L.] A rage for speaking.
Furor poeticus. [L.] Poetical fire.

Gaieté de cœur. [Fr.] Gaiety of heart.
Galeatum sero duelli pœnitet. [L.] It is too late to repent of having to fight when your helmet is on.
Gallicè. [L.] In French.
Garçon. [Fr.] A boy; a waiter.
Garde du corps. [Fr.] A body-guard.
Garde mobile. [Fr.] A guard liable to general service.
Gardez bien. [Fr.] Take good care.
Gardez la foi. [Fr.] Keep the faith.
Gaudeamus igitur. [L.] So let us be joyful.
Genius loci. [L.] The pervading spirit.
Gens d'armes. [Fr.] Men at arms.
Gens de guerre. [Fr.] Military men.
Gens de lettres. [Fr.] Literary men.
Gentilhomme. [Fr.] A gentleman.
Germanicè. [L.] In German.
Gloria in excelsis. [L.] Glory (to God) in the highest.
Gloria patri. [L.] Glory be to the Father.
Gnothi seauton. [Gr.] Know thyself.
Grace à Dieu. [Fr.] Thanks to God.
Grammatici certant. [L.] The grammarians disagree; doctors differ.
Grande parure. / *Grande toilette.* [Fr.] Full dress.
Grand merci. [Fr.] Many thanks.
Guerra al cuchillo. [Sp.] War to the knife.
Guerre à mort. [Fr.] War to the death.
Guerre à outrance. [Fr.] War to the uttermost.

Habent sua fata libelli. [L.] Books have their own fates.
Haud longis intervallis. [L.] At brief intervals.
Haud passibus æquis. [L.] Not with equal steps.
Haut goût. [Fr.] High flavour; elegant taste.
Helluo librorum. [L.] A devourer of books; a book-worm.
Hiatus valde deflendus. [L.] A chasm or deficiency much to be regretted.
Hibernicis ipsis Hibernior. [L.] More Irish than the Irish themselves.
Hic et ubique. [L.] Here and everywhere.
Hic labor, hoc opus est. [L.] This is labour, this is toil.
Hinc illæ lacrimæ. [L.] Hence these tears.
Hoc erat in votis. [L.] This was in my prayers.
Hoc volo sic iubeo. [L.] I desire this, thus I command.
Hodie mihi, cras tibi. [L.] Mine to-day, yours to-morrow.
Hoi polloi. [Gr.] The many; the vulgar; the rabble.
Homme d'affaires. [Fr.] A man of business.
Homme d'esprit. [Fr.] A man of wit or genius.
Homo sum; humani nihil a me alienum puto. [L.] I am a man; I count nothing human indifferent to me.
Homo unius libri. [L.] A man of one book.
Honi soit qui mal y pense. [O.Fr.] Evil to him who evil thinks.
Honores mutant mores. [L.] Honours change men's manners.
Horæ subsecivæ. [L.] Leisure hours.
Horresco referens. [L.] I shudder as I relate.
Hors de combat. [Fr.] Disabled; put out of the fight.
Hors de la loi. [Fr.] In the condition of an outlaw.
Hors de propos. [Fr.] Not to the point or purpose.
Hors-d'œuvre. [Fr.] A dish served at the commencement of a meal; an appetizer. (Lit., Outside of work.)
Hos ego versiculos feci: tulit alter honores. [L.] I wrote these lines; another got the credit for them.
Humanum est errare. [L.] To err is human.
Ibidem. [L.] At the same place (in a book).
Ich dien. [Ger.] I serve.
Id est. [L.] That is: often contracted *i.e.*
Id genus omne. [L.] All of that sort or description.
Ignorantio elenchi. [L.] Ignorance of the point in question.
Ignotum per ignotius. [L.] The unknown (explained) by the still more unknown.
Il a le diable au corps. [Fr.] The devil is in him.
Il penseroso. [It.] The pensive man.
Imo pectore. [L.] From the bottom of the heart.
Impari Marte. [L.] With unequal military strength.
Impedimenta. [L.] Luggage or baggage.
Imperium in imperio. [L.] A state within a state.
In æternum. [L.] For ever.
In articulo mortis. [L.] At the point of death; in the last struggle.
In bianco. [It.] In blank; in white.
In capite. [L.] In chief.
Incredulus odi. [L.] Being incredulous I cannot endure it.
In curiâ. [L.] In court.
Index expurgatorius. [L.] A list of books which may be read after correction or alteration.
Index librorum prohibitorum. [L.] A list of prohibited books.
In dubio. [L.] In doubt.
In equilibrio. [L.] In equilibrium; equally balanced.
In esse. [L.] In being; in actuality.
In extenso. [L.] At full length.
In extremis. [L.] At the point of death.
In formâ pauperis. [L.] As a poor man.
Infra dignitatem. [L.] Below one's dignity.
In futuro. [L.] In future; henceforth.
In hoc signo vinces. [L.] In this sign thou shalt conquer.
In hoc statu. [L.] In this state of things.
In limine. [L.] At the threshold.
In loco. [L.] In the place; in the natural or proper place.
In loco parentis. [L.] In the place of a parent.
In medias res. [L.] Into the midst of things.
In memoriam. [L.] To the memory of; in memory.
In nomine. [L.] In the name of.
In nubibus. [L.] In the clouds.
In nuce. [L.] In a nut-shell.
In omnia paratus. [L.] Prepared for all things.
Inopem me copia fecit. [L.] Plenty has made me poor.
In partibus infidelium. [L.] In parts belonging to infidels, or countries not adhering to the Roman Catholic faith.
In perpetuum. [L.] For ever.
In petto. [It.] Within the breast; in reserve.
In posse. [L.] In possible existence; in possibility.
In præsenti. [L.] At the present moment.
In propriâ personâ. [L.] In one's own person.
In puris naturalibus. [L.] Quite naked.
In re. [L.] In the matter of.
In rerum naturâ. [L.] In the nature of things.
In sæcula sæculorum. [L.] For ever and ever.
In situ. [L.] In its original situation.
In statu pupillari. [L.] In the state of a pupil (or ward).
In statu quo. [L.] In the former state.
Inter alia. [L.] Among other things.
Inter nos. [L.] Between ourselves.
In terrorem. [L.] As a means of terrifying; by way of warning.
Inter se. [L.] Among themselves.
In toto. [L.] In the whole; entirely.
Intra muros. [L.] Within the walls.
In transitu. [L.] On the passage.
In vacuo. [L.] In empty space; in a vacuum.
In vino veritas. [L.] There is truth in wine; truth is told under the influence of liquor.
Invitâ Minervâ. [L.] Against the will of Minerva; without genius or natural abilities.
Ipse dixit. [L.] He himself said it; a dogmatic saying or assertion.
Ipsissima verba. [L.] The very words.
Ipso facto. [L.] By the fact itself.
Ira furor brevis est. [L.] Anger is a short madness.
Italicè. [L.] In Italian.

Jacta est alea. [L.] The die is cast.
Je ne sais quoi. [Fr.] I know not what; a something or other.
Je suis prêt. [Fr.] I am ready.
Jet d'eau. [Fr.] A jet of water; a fountain.
Jeu de mots. [Fr.] A play on words; a pun.
Jeu d'esprit. [Fr.] A display of wit; a witticism.
Joci causâ. [L.] For the sake of a joke.
Jubilate Deo. [L.] Rejoice in God; be joyful in the Lord.
Judex damnatur ubi nocens absolvitur. [L.] The judge is condemned when the guilty is acquitted.
Judicium Dei. [L.] The judgment of God.
Jure divino. [L.] By divine law.
Jure humano. [L.] By human law.
Juris peritus. [L.] One learned in the law.

Juris utriusque doctor. [L.] Doctor of both the civil and canon law.
Jus canonicum. [L.] The canon law.
Jus civile. [L.] The civil law.
Jus divinum. [L.] The divine law.
Jus et norma loquendi. [L.] The law and rule of speech.
Jus gentium. [L.] The law of nations.
Jus gladii. [L.] The right of the sword.
Juste milieu. [Fr.] The golden mean.

Labor ipse voluptas. [L.] Labour itself is a pleasure.
Labor omnia vincit. [L.] Labour conquers everything.
Laborum dulce lenimen. [L.] The sweet solace of our labours.
La fortune passe partout. [Fr.] Fortune passes everywhere; all are liable to vicissitudes.
L'allegro. [It.] The merry man.
Lapis philosophorum. [L.] The philosopher's stone.
Lapsus calami. [L.] A slip of the pen.
Lapsus linguæ. [L.] A slip of the tongue.
Lapsus memoriæ. [L.] A slip of the memory.
Lares et penates. [L.] Household gods.
L'art pour l'art. [Fr.] Art for art's sake.
Latet anguis in herbâ. [L.] A snake lies hid in the grass.
Latinè dictum. [L.] Spoken in Latin.
Laudari a viro laudato. [L.] To be praised by one who is himself praised.
Laudator temporis acti se puero. [L.] One who praises the times when he was a boy.
Laus Deo. [L.] Praise to God.
L'avenir. [Fr.] The future.
Le beau monde. [Fr.] The fashionable world.
Lector benevole. [L.] Kind or gentle reader.
Legatus a latere. [L.] A papal ambassador.
Le grand monarque. [Fr.] The great monarch: Louis XIV of France.
Le jeu n'en vaut pas la chandelle. [Fr.] The game is not worth the candle; the object is not worth the trouble.
Le pas. [Fr.] Precedence in place or rank.
Le roi est mort; vive le roi! [Fr.] The king is dead; long live the king!
Les absents ont toujours tort. [Fr.] The absent are always in the wrong.
Lèse-majesté. [Fr.] High-treason.
Le style est l'homme même. [Fr.] The style is the man himself.
L'état, c'est moi. [Fr.] I am the state.
Le tout ensemble. [Fr.] The whole together.
Lettre de cachet. [Fr.] A sealed letter containing private orders; a royal warrant.
Lex loci. [L.] The law or custom of the place.
Lex non scripta. [L.] Unwritten law; common law.
Lex scripta. [L.] Statute law.
Lex talionis. [L.] The law of retaliation.
L'homme propose, et Dieu dispose. [Fr.] Man proposes, and God disposes.
Limæ labor et mora. [L.] The labour and delay of the file; the slow and laborious polishing of a literary composition
L'inconnu. [Fr.] The unknown.
Lite pendente. [L.] During the trial.
Litera scripta manet. [L.] The written letter remains.
Loco citato. [L.] In the place cited.
Locus classicus. [L.] A standard passage (i.e. the principal place from which knowledge of a word or subject is derived).
Locus sigilli. [L.] The place of the seal.
Longo intervallo. [L.] By or at a long interval.
Lucri bonus est odor ex re qualibet. [L.] Gain from any source has a sweet savour.
Lucus a non lucendo. [L.] Used as typical of an absurd derivation—*lucus*, a grove, having been derived by an old grammarian from *luceo*, to shine—'from not shining'.
Lupus in fabulâ. [L.] The wolf in the fable; speak of the devil, etc.
Lusus naturæ. [L.] A sport or freak of nature.

Ma chère. [Fr.] My dear (fem.).
Ma foi. [Fr.] Upon my faith.
Magna est veritas, et prevalebit. [L.] Truth is mighty, and will prevail.
Magna otia cæli. [L.] There is very little to do in heaven.
Magni nominis umbra. [L.] The shadow of a great name.
Magnum bonum. [L.] A great good.
Magnum opus. [L.] A great work.
Maison de santé. [Fr.] A private asylum or hospital.
Maître d'hôtel. [Fr.] A house-steward.
Maladie du pays. [Fr.] Home-sickness.
Mala fide. [L.] With bad faith; treacherously.
Mal de dents. [Fr.] Toothache.
Mal de mer. [Fr.] Sea-sickness.
Mal de tête. [Fr.] Headache.
Malgré nous. [Fr.] In spite of us.
Malum in se. [L.] Evil or an evil in itself.
Malum prohibitum. [L.] A evil prohibited.
Manibus pedibusque. [L.] With hands and feet.
Manu propriâ. [L.] With one's own hand.
Mardi gras. [Fr.] Shrove-Tuesday.
Mare clausum. [L.] A closed sea; a bay.
Mariage de convenance. [Fr.] Marriage from motives of interest rather than of love.
Mariage de la main gauche. [Fr.] Left-handed marriage; morganatic marriage.
Mauvaise honte. [Fr.] False modesty.
Mauvais goût. [Fr.] Bad taste.
Mauvais sujet. [Fr.] A bad subject; a worthless scamp.
Medio tutissimus ibis. [L.] In the middle you will be safest.
Mega biblion, mega kakon. [Gr.] A great book is a great evil.
Me judice. [L.] I being judge; in my opinion.
Memento mori. [L.] Remember death.
Mens sana in corpore sano. [L.] A sound mind in a sound body.
Mens sibi conscia recti. [L.] A mind conscious of rectitude.
Meo periculo. [L.] At my own risk.
Meo voto. [L.] According to my wish.
Meum et tuum. [L.] Mine and thine.
Mirabile dictu. [L.] Wonderful to relate.
Mirabile visu. [L.] Wonderful to see.
Mise en scène. [Fr.] The getting up for the stage, or the putting on the stage.
Modus operandi. [L.] Manner of working.
Mon ami. [Fr.] My friend (masc.).
Mon cher. [Fr.] My dear (masc.).
Monumentum ære perennius. [L.] A monument more lasting than brass.
More majorum. [L.] After the manner of our ancestors.
More suo. [L.] In his own way.
Mors omnibus communis. [L.] Death is common to all.
Motu proprio. [L.] Of his own accord.
Multis utile bellum. [L.] War advantageous to many.
Multum in parvo. [L.] Much in little.
Mutatis mutandis. [L.] With the necessary changes.

Natale solum. [L.] Natal soil.
Natura abhorret vacuum. [L.] Nature abhors a vacuum.
Naturam expelles furcâ tamen usque recurret. [L.] You may drive out nature with a pitchfork, but she will return again.
Necessitas non habet legem. [L.] Necessity has no law.
Nec te quæsiveris ultra. [L.] Nor seek (to judge) beyond yourself.
Née. [Fr.] Born; as an unmarried woman.
Nemine contradicente. [L.] No one speaking in opposition; without opposition.
Nemine dissentiente. [L.] No one dissenting; without a dissenting voice.
Nemo me impune lacessit. [L.] No one assails me with impunity.
Nemo mortalium omnibus horis sapit. [L.] No one is wise at all times.
Nemo repente fuit turpissimus. [L.] No one ever became a villain in an instant.
Ne plus ultra. [L.] Nothing further; the uttermost point; perfection.
Ne sutor supra crepidam. [L.] Let not the shoemaker go beyond his last; let no one meddle with what lies beyond his range.
Nihil ad rem. [L.] Nothing to the point.
Nihil quod tetigit non ornavit. [L.] He touched nothing without embellishing it.
Nihil simul inventum est et perfectum. [L.] Nothing is invented and perfected at the same time.
Nil admirari. [L.] To be astonished at nothing.
Nil desperandum. [L.] There is no reason for despair.
Ni l'un ni l'autre. [Fr.] Neither the one nor the other.
Nimium ne crede colori. [L.] Trust not too much to looks.
N'importe. [Fr.] It matters not.
Nisi Dominus frustra. [L.] Unless God be with us all is in vain.
Nobilitas sola est atque unica virtus. [L.] Virtue is the true and only nobility; 'tis only noble to be good'.
Noblesse oblige. [Fr.] Rank imposes obligations.
Nolens volens. [L.] Willing or unwilling.
Noli me tangere. [L.] Touch me not.
Nolle prosequi. [L.] To be unwilling to prosecute.
Nolo episcopari. [L.] I do not wish to be made a bishop.
Nom de guerre. [Fr.] A war name; a pseudonym; a pen name: often, incorrectly, *nom de plume*.
Non compos mentis. [L.] Not of sound mind.
Non est inventus. [L.] He has not been found.
Non libet. [L.] It does not please me.
Non liquet. [L.] The case is not clear; not proven.
Non omnia possumus omnes. [L.] We cannot, all of us, do everything.
Non possumus. [L.] We cannot (comply).
Non sequitur. [L.] It does not follow.
Nosce teipsum. [L.] Know thyself.
Noscitur a sociis. [L.] He is known by his companions.
Nota bene. [L.] Mark well.
Nous avons changé tout cela. [Fr.] We have changed all that.
Nous verrons. [Fr.] We shall see.
Novus homo. [L.] A new man; one who has raised himself from obscurity.
Nudis verbis. [L.] In plain words.
Nulla dies sine lineâ. [L.] Not a day without a line; no day without something done.
Nulli secundus. [L.] Second to none.
Nullum est iam dictum, quod non sit dictum prius. [L.] There is no saying now which has not been said before.
Nunquam non paratus. [L.] Never unprepared; always ready.

Obiit. [L.] He, or she, died.
Obiter dictum. [L.] A thing said by the way.
Obscurum per obscurius. [L.] An obscurity (explained) by something more obscure still.
Oderint dum metuant. [L.] Let them hate provided they fear.
Odi et amo. [L.] I hate and love.
Odi profanum vulgus. [L.] I loathe the profane rabble.
Odium theologicum. [L.] The hatred of theologians for one another; the bitterness of theological controversy.
Œil de bœuf. [Fr.] A bull's-eye, oval window.
Œuvres. [Fr.] Works.
O liberté! que de crimes on commet dans ton nom! [Fr.] O Liberty! how many crimes are committed in thy name!
Omne ignotum pro magnifico. [L.] Whatever is unknown is held to be magnificent.
Omne solum forti patria. [L.] Every soil is a brave man's country.
Omnia vincit amor. [L.] Love conquers all things.
Omnia vincit labor. [L.] Labour overcomes all things.
Operæ pretium est. [L.] It is worth while.
Operose nihil agunt. [L.] They laboriously do nothing.
Ora et labora. [L.] Pray and work.
Ora pro nobis. [L.] Pray for us.
Ore rotundo. [L.] With round full voice.
Origo mali. [L.] Origin of the evil.
O sancta simplicitas! [L.] O holy simplicity.
O! si sic omnia. [L.] O! if all things so; O! if he had always so spoken or acted.
O tempora! O mores! [L.] O the times! O the manners!
Otium cum dignitate. [L.] Ease with dignity.

Pace. [L.] By leave of; not to give offence to.—*Pace tua*, with your consent.
Palmam qui meruit ferat. [L.] Let him who has won the palm wear it.
Par excellence. [Fr.] By way of eminence.
Pari passu. [L.] With equal pace; step for step.
Par nobile fratrum. [L.] A noble pair of brothers; two just alike.
Parole d'honneur. [Fr.] Word of honour.
Pars pro toto. [L.] Part for the whole.
Particeps criminis. [L.] An accomplice in crime.
Parturiunt montes; nascetur ridiculus mus. [L.] The mountains are in labour; an absurd mouse will be born.
Parvis componere magna. [L.] To compare great things with small.
Passim. [L.] Everywhere; all through.
Pâté de foie gras. [Fr.] Goose-liver pie.
Pater patriæ. [L.] Father of his country.
Patres conscripti. [L.] Conscript fathers; Roman senators.
Pax vobiscum. [L.] Peace be with you.
Peccavi. [L.] I have sinned; I admit my mistake.
Peine forte et dure. [Fr.] Strong and severe punishment; a kind of judicial torture.
Pensée. [Fr.] A thought.
Per. [L.] For; through; by.—*Per contra.* Contrariwise.—*Per annum.* By the year; annually. *Per capita.* For each person.—*Per centum.* By the hundred.—*Per diem.* By the day; daily.—*Per saltum.* By a leap or jump.—*Per se.* By or in itself.
Per ardua ad astra. [L.] Through difficulties to the stars; to achieve fame in spite of obstacles.
Pereant qui ante nos nostra dixerunt. [L.] May those perish who have said our good things before us.
Perfervidum ingenium Scotorum. [L.] The intense earnestness of Scotsmen.
Persona grata. [L.] A person who is held in special favour.
Petitio principii. [L.] A begging of the question.
Peu à peu. [Fr.] Little by little.
Pied-à-terre. [Fr.] A resting-place; a temporary lodging; an occasional abode.
Pis aller. [Fr.] The worst or last shift.
Place aux dames. [Fr.] Make way for the ladies.
Poco à poco. [It.] Little by little.
Poeta nascitur, non fit. [L.] The poet is born, not made.
Point d'appui. [Fr.] Point of support.
Pons asinorum. [L.] The ass's bridge; a name for the fifth proposition of the first book of Euclid.

Populus vult decipi; decipiatur. [L.] The people wish to be deceived; let them be deceived.
Possunt, quia posse videntur. [L.] They can, because they think they can.
Post hoc; ergo propter hoc. [L.] After this; therefore on account of this.
Pour faire rire. [Fr.] To excite laughter.
Pour passer le temps. [Fr.] To pass the time.
Pour prendre congé. [Fr.] To take leave.
Præmonitus, præmunitus. [L.] Forewarned, forearmed.
Preux chevalier. [Fr.] A brave knight.
Primo. [L.] In the first place.
Primum mobile. [L.] The source of motion; the mainspring.
Principiis obsta. [L.] Resist the first beginnings.
Pro aris et focis. [L.] For our altars and our hearths.
Pro bono publico. [L.] For the good of the public.
Pro et contra. [L.] For and against.
Profanum vulgus. [L.] The profane vulgar.
Pro formâ. [L.] For the sake of form.
Proh pudor. [L.] O, for shame!
Propaganda fide. [L.] For extending the faith.
Pro patria. [L.] For our country.
Pro rege, lege, et grege. [L.] For the king, the law, and the people.
Pro re nata. [L.] For some special circumstance which has arisen.
Prudens futuri. [L.] Thoughtful of the future.
Punica fides. [L.] Punic or Carthaginian faith; treachery.

Quandoque bonus dormitat Homerus. [L.] Sometimes the good Homer nods.
Quantum libet. [L.] As much as you please.
Quantum meruit. [L.] As much as he deserved.
Quantum mutatus ab illo. [L.] How changed from what he once was.
Quantum sufficit. [L.] As much as suffices.
Que diable allait-il faire dans cette galère? [Fr.] What the devil was he doing in this galley?
Quelque chose. [Fr.] Something; a trifle.
Quem Deus vult perdere, prius dementat. [L.] Whom God wishes to destroy, he first makes mad.
Quid pro quo. [L.] Something in return; an equivalent.
Qui facit per alium facit per se. [L.] He who does a thing by another's agency does it himself.
Quis custodiet ipsos custodes? [L.] Who shall keep the keepers themselves?
Qui s'excuse s'accuse. [Fr.] He who excuses himself accuses himself.
Qui va là? [Fr.] Who goes there?
Quoad hoc. [L.] To this extent.
Quocunque modo. [L.] In whatever way.
Quod avertat Deus! [L.] Which may God avert!
Quod erat demonstrandum. [L.] Which was to be proved or demonstrated.
Quod erat faciendum. [L.] Which was to be done.
Quod vide. [L.] Which see.
Quorum pars magna fui. [L.] Of whom, or which, I was an important part.
Quot homines, tot sententiæ. [L.] Many men, many minds.

Raison d'état. [Fr.] A reason of state.
Raison d'être. [Fr.] The reason for a thing's existence.
Rara avis in terris, nigroque simillima cygno. [L.] A rare bird on earth, and very like a black swan (formerly believed to be nonexistent).
Reductio ad absurdum. [L.] The reducing of a position to an absurdity.
Re infecta. [L.] The business being unfinished.
Rem acu tetigisti. [L.] You have touched the matter with a needle; you have hit the thing exactly.
Requiescat in pace. [L.] May he (or she) rest in peace.
Res angusta domi. [L.] Narrow circumstances at home.
Res gestæ. [L.] Things done; exploits.
Res judicata. [L.] A case or suit already settled.
Respice finem. [L.] Look to the end.
Resurgam. [L.] I shall rise again.
Revenons à nos moutons. [Fr.] Let us return to our sheep; let us return to our subject.
Robe de chambre. [Fr.] A morning-gown or dressing-gown.
Ruat cœlum. [L.] Let the heavens fall.
Rus in urbe. [L.] The country in town.

Sal Atticum. [L.] Attic salt; *i.e.* wit.
Salus populi suprema est lex. [L.] The safety of the people is the highest law.
Salvo jure. [L.] The right being safe.
Salvo pudore. [L.] Without offence to modesty.
Sans peur et sans reproche. [Fr.] Without fear and without reproach.
Sans souci. [Fr.] Without care.
Sapere aude. [L.] Dare to be wise.
Sartor resartus. [L.] The botcher repatched; the tailor patched or mended.
Satis quod sufficit. [L.] What suffices is enough.
Satis superque. [L.] Enough, and more than enough.
Satis verborum. [L.] Enough of words; no more need be said.
Sauve qui peut. [Fr.] Let him save himself who can.
Savoir faire. [Fr.] The knowing how to act; tact.
Savoir vivre. [Fr.] Good-breeding; refined manners.
Secundum artem. [L.] According to art or rule; scientifically.
Selon les règles. [Fr.] According to rule.
Semper fidelis. [L.] Always faithful.
Semper idem. [L.] Always the same.
Semper paratus. [L.] Always ready.
Se non è vero, è ben trovato. [It.] If not true it is cleverly invented.
Sic itur ad astra. [L.] Such is the way to the stars, or to immortality.
Sic passim. [L.] So here and there throughout; so everywhere.
Sic semper tyrannis. [L.] Ever so to tyrants.
Sic transit gloria mundi. [L.] Thus passes away the glory of this world.
Sicut ante. [L.] As before.
Sic vos non vobis mellificatis apes; nidificatis aves; vellera fertis oves. [L.] So not for yourselves do you bees make honey; birds build nests; sheep wear fleeces.
Similia similibus curantur. [L.] Like things are cured by like.
Si monumentum requiris, circumspice. [L.] If you seek his monument, look around you.
Simplex munditiis. [L.] Plain in her adornments.
Sine curâ. [L.] Without charge or care.
Sine die. [L.] Without a day being appointed.
Sine dubio. [L.] Without doubt.
Sine morâ. [L.] Without delay.
Sine qua non. [L.] Without which, not; something indispensable.
Sint ut sunt aut non sint. [L.] Let them be as they are, or not be at all.
Si parva licet componere magnis. [L.] If small things may be compared with great.
Siste, viator. [L.] Stop, traveller.
Sit tibi terra levis. [L.] Light lie the earth upon thee.
Si vis me flere dolendum est primum ipse tibi. [L.] If you wish me to weep, you must first feel grief yourself.
Si vis pacem, para bellum. [L.] If you wish for peace, prepare for war.
Sola nobilitas virtus. [L.] Virtue the only nobility.
Spero meliora. [L.] I hope for better things.
Splendide mendax. [L.] Nobly untruthful; untrue for a good object.
Sponte suâ. [L.] Of one's (or its) own accord.
Stat magni nominis umbra. [L.] He stands the shadow of a mighty name.
Statu quo ante bellum. [L.] In the state in which things were before the war.
Status quo. [L.] The state in which.
Stavo ben, ma, per star meglio, sto qui. [It.] I was well, but, wishing to be better, here I am.
Stultum facit Fortuna quem vult perdere. [L.] When Fortune wishes to ruin a man she makes him a fool.
Sua cuique voluptas. [L.] Every man has his own pleasures.
Suaviter in modo, fortiter in re. [L.] Gentle in manner, resolute in execution.
Sub judice. [L.] Under consideration.
Sub pœna. [L.] Under a penalty.
Sub prætexto juris. (L.) Under the pretext of justice.
Sub rosa. [L.] Under the rose; privately.
Sub silentio. [L.] In silence.
Sub voce. [L.] Under such or such a word.
Suggestio falsi. [L.] Suggesting of falsehood.
Sui generis. [L.] Of its own peculiar kind.
Summum bonum. [L.] The chief good.
Summum jus, summa injuria. [L.] The rigour of the law is the height of oppression.
Suppressio veri. [L.] A suppression of the truth.
Supra vires. [L.] Beyond one's strength.
Sur le tapis. [Fr.] On the cloth; under discussion.
Suum cuique. [L.] Let every one have his own.
Suus cuique mos. [L.] Every one has his particular habit.

Tabula rasa. [L.] A smooth or blank tablet.
Tædium vitæ. [L.] Weariness of life.
Tantæne animis cœlestibus iræ? [L.] Can such anger dwell in heavenly minds?
Tant mieux. [Fr.] So much the better.
Tant pis. [Fr.] So much the worse.
Te judice. [L.] You being the judge.
Tempora mutantur, nos et mutamur in illis. [L.] The times are changing and we with them.
Tempus edax rerum. [L.] Time the devourer of all things.
Tempus fugit. [L.] Time flies.
Tenax propositi. [L.] Tenacious of purpose.
Terminus ad quem. [L.] The term or limit to which.
Terminus a quo. [L.] The term or limit from which.
Terra incognita. [L.] An unknown land.
Tertium quid. [L.] A third something; a nondescript.
Toga virilis. [L.] The manly toga; the dress of manhood.
To kalon. [Gr.] The beautiful; the chief good.
Tot homines, quot sententiæ. [L.] So many men, so many minds.
Totidem verbis. [L.] In just so many words.
Totis viribus. [L.] With all his might.
Toto cœlo. [L.] By the whole heavens; diametrically opposite.
Toujours perdrix. [Fr.] Always partridge; always the same thing over again.
Toujours prêt. [Fr.] Always ready.
Tour de force. [Fr.] A feat of strength or skill.
Tout à fait. [Fr.] Wholly; entirely.
Tout à l'heure. [Fr.] Instantly.
Tout au contraire. [Fr.] On the contrary.
Tout à vous. [Fr.] Wholly yours.
Tout de suite. [Fr.] Immediately.
Tout ensemble. [Fr.] The whole taken together.
Tria juncta in uno. [L.] Three joined in one.
Tu quoque. [L.] Thou also.

Ubi bene, ibi patria. [L.] Where it is well there is one's country.
Ubi supra. [L.] Where above mentioned.
Ultimus Romanorum. [L.] The last of the Romans.
Ultra vires. [L.] Beyond one's power.
Una voce. [L.] With one voice; unanimously.
Uno animo. [L.] With one mind; unanimously.
Usque ad nauseam. [L] To disgust.
Usus loquendi. [L.] Usage in speaking.
Utile dulci. [L.] The useful with the pleasant.
Ut infra. [L.] As below.
Uti possidetis. [L.] As you hold in possession.
Ut supra. [L.] As above.

Væ victis. [L.] Woe to the vanquished.
Valeat quantum valere potest. [L.] Let it pass for what it is worth.
Variæ lectiones. [L.] Various readings.
Varium et mutabile semper fœmina. [L.] Woman is ever changeful and capricious.
Venienti occurrite morbo [L.] Go to meet an approaching disease.
Veni, vidi, vici. [L.] I came, I saw, I conquered. [Cæsar's message home when he conquered Pharnaces, king of Pontus].
Ventre à terre. [Fr.] At full gallop.
Verbatim et literatim. [L.] Word for word and letter for letter.
Verbum sat sapienti. [L.] A word is enough for a wise man.
Veritas prevalebit. [L.] Truth will prevail.
Veritas vincit. [L.] Truth conquers.
Vérité sans peur. [Fr.] Truth without fear.
Vers de société. [Fr.] Society verses; light amusing poems written for people of some culture and position.
Vestigia nulla retrorsum. [L.] No returning footsteps; no traces backward.
Vexata quæstio. [L.] A disputed question.
Via media. [L.] A middle course.
Vide et crede. [L.] See and believe.
Video meliora proboque, deteriora sequor. [L.] I see and approve the better course, I follow the worse.
Vide ut supra. [L.] See what is stated above.
Vi et armis. [L.] By force and arms; by main force.
Vincit omnia veritas. [L.] Truth conquers all things.
Vires acquirit eundo. [L.] As it goes it acquires strength.
Virginibus puerisque canto. [L.] I sing to maids and to boys.
Vir sapit qui pauca loquitur. [L.] He is a wise man who says but little.
Virtute et fide. [L.] By or with virtue and faith.
Virtute et labore. [L.] By virtue and labour.
Virtute securus. [L.] Secure through virtue.
Vis comica. [L.] Comic power or talent.
Vis inertiæ. [L.] The power of inertness.
Vis medicatrix naturæ. [L.] The healing power of nature.
Vita brevis, ars longa. [L.] Life is short, art is long.
Vitæ via virtus. [L.] Virtue the way of life.
Vitaque mancipio nulli datur, omnibus usu. [L.] Life is given to no one absolutely, but everyone has the usufruct of it.
Vive la bagatelle. [Fr.] Long live trifling.
Voilà. [Fr.] Behold; there is; there are.
Voilà tout. [Fr.] That's all.
Voilà une autre chose. [Fr.] That's another thing; that is quite a different matter.
Volenti non fit injuria. [L.] No injustice is done to the consenting person.
Vox et præterea nihil. [L.] A voice and nothing more; sound but no sense.
Vox populi, vox Dei. [L.] The voice of the people is the voice of God.
Vulgò. [L.] Commonly

DICTIONARY OF CLASSICAL MYTHOLOGY

A knowledge of the classics and an acquaintance with the imaginary characters, places, and incidents of ancient mythology which have been such an inspiring influence to writers of all ages add greatly to one's enjoyment of literature, art, and conversation. Few people outside literary and educational pursuits have sufficient opportunity or leisure to acquire or keep up a knowledge of this particular branch of learning. It is important, therefore, to present in dictionary form the stories of gods, goddesses, heroes, and heroines of the old Grecian and Roman literature. It will help to a better understanding of the countless references which are made from time to time in the literature of the day to classic subjects. It is a great wonderland of poesy and romance, and forms a realm all its own.

Abderus, armor-bearer to Hercules. He was torn to pieces by the mares of Diomedes.

Absyrtus, a son of Aeetes, king of Colchis, who was murdered by his sister Medea when she fled with Jason.

Acamas, son of Theseus and Phaedra, who went with Diomedes to demand Helen from the Trojans and afterward took part in the Trojan War.

Acantha, a nymph, loved by Apollo and transformed into the acanthus.

Acarnas and **Amphoterus**, sons of Alcmaeon and Callirrhoe.

Acestes, king of Drepanum, who assisted Priam at Troy and after the war entertained Aeneas during his stay at Drepanum.

Achaei, the descendants of Achaeus, who constituted one of the chief divisions of the ancient Greeks.

Achaemenides, son of Adramastus, who was abandoned by Ulysses on the coast of Sicily and was later found by Aeneas.

Achates, a friend of Aeneas, known for his fidelity; whence the term *fidus Achates*.

Acheloides, the Sirens, daughters of Achelous.

Achelous, son of Oceanus and Tethys, god of the river Achelous in Epirus. Contending with Hercules for Dejanira, he changed himself into a serpent. Later, after Achelous had turned himself into an ox, Hercules broke one of his horns and defeated him.

Acheron, a son of Ceres, who was changed into a river in Tartarus for supplying the Titans with water in their battle with the gods. Over this river Charon ferried the souls of the dead.

Acherusia, a lake near Memphis, said to have been connected with the lower world. Across this lake the bodies of the dead were ferried by Charon.

Achilles, most famous of the Greek heroes that fought at Troy, son of Peleus and Thetis. When an infant, he was plunged by his mother into the Styx and made invulnerable except in the heel, by which she held him. During the Trojan War he quarreled with Agamemnon about Briseis and for a time refrained from fighting. But when his friend Patroclus was killed, he rejoined his comrades and slew Hector at the Scaean Gate. Ultimately Achilles himself was slain, wounded by an arrow in his vulnerable heel.

Achillides, Pyrrhus, son of Achilles.

Acis, a Sicilian shepherd, son of Faunus and Simaethis, who fell in love with the sea-nymph Galatea. Jealous of her love, the Cyclops Polyphemus crushed Acis to death with a rock. He was changed by Galatea into a stream on Mount Aetna.

Aconteus, a hunter, changed into stone at the sight of Medusa's head during the nuptials of Perseus and Andromeda.

Acrisius, son of Abas and Ocalea and father of Danae.

Actaeon, son of Aristaeus and Autonoe, who, because he watched Diana bathing, was changed into a stag and devoured by his own dogs.

Admeta, daughter of Eurystheus and priestess of Juno's temple at Argos. To obtain for Admeta the girdle of the queen of the Amazons was the ninth labor imposed upon Hercules by Eurystheus.

Admetus, king of Thessaly and husband of Alcestis. Apollo, who served him for a time as shepherd, urged the Fates to spare Admetus' life if some other person should be willing to die for him. Alcestis offered herself as substitute. Admetus was one of the Argonauts and was present at the hunt of the Calydonian boar.

Adonis, son of Cinyras and Myrrha and beloved by Venus. While hunting, he was killed by a wild boar and was transformed by Venus into the anemone. The gods of the underworld allowed him to spend six months of every year on earth with Venus.

Adrastus, king of Sicyon and leader of the Seven against Thebes, of whom he alone survived. Ten years later he led the Epigoni, sons of the Seven, to destroy Thebes.

Aeacus, son of Jupiter and Aegina. After the inhabitants of Aegina had been destroyed by pestilence, Jupiter transformed ants into human beings, whom Aeacus called *Myrmidons*. Aeacus with Minos and Rhadamanthus became a judge in the lower world.

Aeetes, king of Colchis and father of Medea, Absyrtus, and Chalciope. It was to his court that Phryxus fled on the back of a ram. After the ram had been sacrificed, its golden fleece was given to Aeetes.

Aegeus, king of Athens and father of Theseus. While at the court of Pittheus in Troezen, he married the king's daughter Aethra. Departing before the birth of his son, Aegeus told her to send Theseus to him as soon as he could lift the stone under which he had concealed his sword. Years later, when the young man arrived in Athens, his life was threatened by Medea, who meanwhile had married his father. Theseus soon sailed to Crete, where he destroyed the Minotaur. On his return voyage he forgot to hoist white sails—the pre-arranged signal of success—and Aegeus, concluding that his son was dead, threw himself from a high rock into the sea, which was named after him the Aegean.

Aegis, the shield of Jupiter, in the center of which was represented the Gorgon's head.

Aegisthus, king of Argos, son of Thyestes and Pelopea. He murdered Atreus to avenge the crime perpetrated against his father and ascended the throne of Mycenae, banishing Agamemnon and Menelaus. But Aegisthus at length became reconciled to the Atridae and during Agamemnon's absence at Troy was made guardian of his wife Clytemnestra. He fell in love with her, and the two murdered Agamemnon on his return from the Trojan War. Subsequently they themselves were killed by Orestes, son of Agamemnon.

Aeneades, descendants of Aeneas.

Aeneas, a Trojan prince, son of Venus and Anchises. At Troy he fought bravely against Diomedes and Achilles. After the storming of the city he rescued his father, his son, and the household gods and fled from the flaming ruins. With a number of companions he built twenty ships and set out for the Thracian Chersonesus; from there he sailed to Delos, the Strophades, Crete, and Epirus; thence to Drepanum, in Sicily, where he buried his father. On the voyage to Italy, the ships were driven upon the African coast near Carthage. In this city he was entertained by Queen Dido, whose unrequited love for him led her to commit suicide. Aeneas sailed back to Sicily, thence to Cumae, where the Sibyl conducted him to the lower world. After a voyage of seven years and the loss of thirteen ships he reached the Tiber. Latinus, king of Latinum, promised him his daughter Lavinia, already betrothed to Turnus. War ensued, and in a combat with Aeneas Turnus was killed. Aeneas later married Lavinia, in whose honor he built the town of Lavinium, and succeeded Latinus as king of Latium. After a short reign he died, either killed in war with the Etruscans or drowned in the river Numicus. The Caesars traced their origin to him, and his wanderings form the subject of Vergil's *Aeneid*.

Aeolus, son of Hippotes and god of the winds, who lived in the island of Aeolia. He presented Ulysses, on his return to Ithaca, with all the adverse winds tied in bags; but his companions from curiosity opened them, and so Ulysses was driven out of his course.

Aerope, wife of Atreus and mother of Agamemnon, Menelaus, and Anaxibia.

Aesacus, son of Priam by Alexirrhoe or by Arisba. Falling passionately in love with Hesperia, he pursued her till she despaired of escape; she flung herself into the sea and was transformed into a bird. At the same time Aesacus was changed into a cormorant.

Aesculapius, the god of healing and son of Apollo. He was killed by Jove's thunderbolt for restoring men to life.

Aeson, father of Jason and brother of Pelias, who succeeded his father as king in Iolchus but was deposed by Pelias. In his old age Aeson was restored to youth through Medea's magic powers.

Agamemnon, king of Mycenae and Argos, brother of Menelaus, and son of Atreus. On the death of Atreus, Thyestes seized Argos, and Agamemnon with Menelaus was forced to leave the city. The brothers fled to Tyndareus, king of Sparta, who gave them his daughters in marriage: Clytemnestra to Agamemnon, and Helen to Menelaus. Later Tyndareus helped them to recover their father's kingdom; Agamemnon established himself at Mycenae, and Menelaus succeeded Tyndareus at Sparta. When Paris ran off with Helen, Agamemnon assumed command of the forces against Troy and fought with great valor. After the war Cassandra foretold his murder by Clytemnestra, but he nevertheless returned to Argos, where, as he was leaving the bath, Clytemnestra and Aegisthus murdered him.

Agenor, king of Phoenicia, son of Neptune and Libya, father of Cadmus, Phoenix, Cilix, and Europa. He was an ancestor of Dido, queen of Carthage.

Aglaia, one of the Graces, daughter of Jupiter and Eurynome.

Ahenobarbus, an ancestor of Nero's, so named because his beard was changed to bronze by Castor and Pollux for refusing to believe in the victory at Lake Regillus.

Ajax, son of Telamon and next to Achilles the most famous Greek warrior. He sought to gain possession of the arms of Achilles after the latter's death. Informed that they had been awarded to Ulysses, he lost his mind and slaughtered a flock of sheep which he mistook for the sons of Atreus; then he stabbed himself, and where the blood from his wound sank into the earth appeared the hyacinth. The lesser Ajax was the son of Oileus and was swiftest of the Greeks after Achilles. On his return from Troy he was shipwrecked by Athena. He was rescued, but later for boasting of his escape he was killed by lightning.

Albion, Neptune's son by Amphitrite, who introduced astronomy and shipbulding.

Alcathous, son of Pelops and king of Megara. Accused of slaying his brother Chrysippus, he escaped to Megara, killed a lion that had destroyed the king's son, and succeeded to the throne.

Alcestis, daughter of Pelias and Anaxibia and wife of Admetus. She willingly sacrificed her life to save Admetus from death. Through Hercules' efforts, however, she was brought back from the lower world and returned to her husband.

Alcimede, mother of Jason by Aeson.

Alcinous, son of Nausithous and Periboea, king of Phaeacia. He married his niece, Arete, by whom he had a daughter, Nausicaa.

Alcithoe, daughter of Minyas, king of Thessaly. Her spindle was changed into a vine, her yarn into ivy, and she herself into a bat because she ridiculed Bacchus.

Alcmaeon, son of Amphiaraus and Eriphyle. He was driven to madness by the thought of having killed his mother. He fled from home and after a time married Arsinoe. But because he left her to marry Callirrhoe, her brothers killed him.

Alcmene, daughter of Electryon, who was promised in marriage to Amphitryon on condition that he avenge the death of her brothers. In Amphitryon's absence, however, Jupiter assumed his form and became the father of Alcmene's son Hercules.

Alectryon, a youth placed on guard in order to warn Mars of the approach of Phoebus while the god of war was visiting Venus. Alectryon was transformed into a cock for falling asleep.

Alpheus, the god of the river Alpheus in Arcadia. He fell in love with Arethusa, who was transformed by Diana into a fountain in the small island of Ortygia, near Syracuse. The Alpheus was said to flow under the sea and come to the surface in Ortygia.

Althaea, wife of Oeneus and mother of Meleager.

Amalthaea, daughter of King Melissus of Crete. She fed the infant Jupiter with goat's milk.

Amata, wife of King Latinus, who betrothed her daughter Lavinia to Turnus before Aeneas' arrival. When Amata learned that Aeneas had killed Turnus, she committed suicide.

Amazons, a race of warlike women dwelling in Asia Minor, who came to the help of Troy during the Trojan War.

Ambrosia, the food of the gods, which preserved for them their immortality.

Ammon, an ancient Egyptian divinity, identified with Jupiter and frequently referred to as Jupiter Ammon. The god was sometimes represented as a ram. One of his temples, renowned for its oracle, was in an oasis of the Libyan Desert, nine days' journey from Alexandria.

Amphiaraus, son of Oicles and Hypermnestra. He took part in the hunt of the Calydonian boar and in the Argonautic expedition. He was a great prophet; and though he foresaw the fatal end, he was persuaded by his wife Eriphyle to join the expedition of Adrastus against Thebes, where the earth swallowed him up before his enemies could kill him.

Amphion, a famous musician, the twin brother of Zethus, born to Jupiter by Antiope on Mount Cithaeron, where she had fled to avoid the wrath of Dirce. A shepherd succored the infants and when they had grown to manhood, they besieged Lycus, their granduncle, in Thebes, murdered him, and tied his wife Dirce to a wild bull, which dragged her to her death. Amphion became king of Thebes. While building the wall about the city, he played on his lyre, and the stones moved into position of their own accord. Niobe, daughter of Tantalus, was his wife.

Amphitrite, the daughter of Oceanus and Tethys and mother of Triton by Neptune.

Amphitryon, king of Thebes, who, because he avenged the deaths of the sons of Electryon, was appointed his successor and given his daughter Alcmene in marriage. While Amphitryon was absent, Jupiter appeared to Alcmene in the form of her husband and became the father of her child.

Amycus, son of Neptune, who became king of Melia. He was a skillful boxer but was killed by Pollux during a match.

Amyntor, king of Argos, who blinded his son Phoenix for insulting Clytia, his concubine.

Amyone, daughter of Danaus and Europa, who married Enceladus and killed him on the marriage night. Of the fifty Danaids she alone was absolved from the task of filling the leaky vessel in Hades because she had supplied Argos with water during a drought.

Anaxibia, sister of Agamemnon and wife of Nestor.

Ancaeus, an Argonaut killed at the Calydonian hunt.

Anchises, father of Aeneas and son of Capys and Themis. His surpassing beauty attracted Venus, herself the goddess of beauty, who fell in love with him and bore him Aeneas. After the fall of Troy Anchises was carried out of the city on the shoulders of his son. He accompanied Aeneas on his subsequent wanderings but died before reaching Italy.

Anchurus, the son of Midas, who sacrificed his life by leaping into a fissure in the earth. An oracle had declared that this chasm would not cease to swallow whatever appeared above it until Midas had thrown in, what was most dear to him.

Androcles, a slave who was thrown to the wild animals in the Roman arena but was spared by a lion from whose foot he had once extracted a thorn in an African cave. Amazed at the lion's behavior, the Roman officials pardoned Androcles and presented him with the lion.

Androgynae, a race of hermaphrodites, who lived in the region of Africa beyond the Nasamones.

Andromache, wife of Hector and mother of Astyanax. The passage in Homer's *Iliad* describing her farewell to Hector as he is about to leave for battle, is one of the best-known passages in the poem. After her husband's death and the fall of Troy, Andromache became the prize of Pyrrhus. Pyrrhus died, and she married Helenus, a fellow-captive.

Andromeda, wife of Perseus and daughter of Cepheus, king of Aethiopia. Her mother was Cassiopeia, who boasted that she was more beautiful than the Nereids. Out of revenge for this insult to the sea nymphs, Neptune inundated the land and sent a sea monster to ravage the shore. To appease the god of the sea, Cepheus was commanded by the oracle of Ammon to chain his daughter to a rock out in the sea. Perseus came to the rescue, however, by turning the monster to stone with the magic head of Medusa. Andromeda was saved and became the wife of Perseus.

Antaeus, a Libyan giant and wrestler, son of Terra and Neptune, who was vanquished by Hercules. Realizing that Antaeus' strength depended upon contact with his mother Earth, Hercules lifted him from the ground and crushed the life out of him.

Antigone, daughter of Oedipus by Jocasta, who defied the order of Creon, king of Thebes, that the body of her brother Polynices remain unburied. Condemned to be buried alive, Antigone killed herself.

Antilochus, son of Nestor and Eurydice, killed at Troy by Memnon.

Antiope, daughter of Nycteus, king of Thebes, who was wooed by Jupiter. To escape her father's anger, she fled to Mount Cithaeron, where her twin sons Amphion and Zethus were born.

Antiphus, son of Priam, who was killed by Agamemnon.

Aon, son of Neptune and king of Boeotia, after whom the Boeotians were called Aones, and the country Aonia.

Aphrodite, the goddess of love and beauty, identified with Venus by the Romans.

Apollo, god of light and prophecy and patron of the arts. He was the son of Jupiter and Latona and was born on Delos, which before had been a floating island, but was now anchored with chains to the bottom of the sea. Apollo became a renowned physician and himself instructed his son Aesculapius in medicine. When the latter was killed by Jupiter's thunderbolt for having restored the dead to life, Apollo took vengeance on the Cyclopes, who had forged the bolt. For this rash act he was ordered to shepherd the flocks of Admetus. Thereafter he aided Neptune in building the walls of Troy; however, because the king, Laomedon, refused him the promised reward, he sent a pestilence upon the inhabitants. Apollo's oracles were at Delphi—famed throughout the ancient world—Delos, Claros, Tenedos, Cyrrha, and Patara. The epithets most frequently applied to him were *Pythius*, *Phoebus*, *Cynthius*, and *Lycius*.

Arachne, daughter of Idmon of Colophon, who was so expert in weaving that she challenged Minerva. She chose for designs scenes which depicted the foibles of the gods. Angered by such insults, Minerva tore up the web. Arachne hanged herself in despair and was transformed into a spider—which hangs by the thread it spins.

Arcas, son of Jupiter and Callisto, who ruled over Pelasgia, which was called Arcadia after him.

Ares, the Greek god of war, identified with Mars.

Arethusa, a nymph who was pursued by the river-god Alpheus and changed by Diana into a fountain.

Argia, daughter of Adrastus, who married Polynices and was put to death by Creon for burying her husband against Creon's orders.

Argiphontes, a name meaning "slayer of Argus," which was given to Mercury because he killed the hundred-eyed Argus.

Argo, the ship used by Jason and his companions in their search for the Golden Fleece.

Argonauts, the companions of Jason on the *Argo*, among whom were Hercules, Theseus, Aesculapius, Nestor, Orpheus, Castor and Pollux.

Argus, a giant possessed of a hundred eyes, of which only two were asleep at a time. He was ordered by Juno to keep watch on Io, but Jupiter sent Mercury to kill him; afterward his eyes were put on the tail of Juno's sacred peacock.

Ariadne, the daughter of Minos of Crete. Having fallen in love with Theseus, she gave him some thread by means of which he was able to find his way out of the labyrinth. After Theseus had killed the Minotaur, he married Ariadne but deserted her later at Naxos. Bacchus gave her a crown of seven stars, which was turned into a constellation.

Arion, a famous musician, who, when returning from Sicily to Corinth with rich prizes, was threatened with death by the sailors. He leapt into the sea, and a dolphin, charmed by his playing, carried him safely to land.

Aristaeus, a Libyan shepherd, son of Apollo and Cyrene, who was reared by the Seasons and nourished with nectar and ambrosia. He married Autonoe, by whom he had a son Actaeon. He was indirectly responsible for the death of Eurydice, for in fleeing from his advances, she stepped on a snake and died of its bite. He was the first to teach men the art of keeping bees.

Arne, daughter of Aeolus, wooed by Neptune in the form of a bull.

Artemis, a Greek goddess, the guardian of forests and wild animals, who was identified with Diana.

Aruntius, a Roman intoxicated by Bacchus for ridiculing his rites and killed by his daughter Medullina, whom he had insulted.

Ascalaphus, son of Acheron, who, having been appointed by Pluto to watch Proserpina in the Elysian Fields, testified that the goddess had eaten pomegranates. For his spying Proserpina changed him into an owl.

Ascanius, son of Aeneas and Creusa and founder of Alba Longa.

Astarte, a Syrian goddess, corresponding to the Greek Aphrodite.

Asteria, daughter of Coeus, the Titan, and mother of Hecate. Courted by Zeus in the form of an eagle, she threw herself into the sea, where she was changed into an island, which was later called Delos.

Astraea, daughter of Astraeus and goddess of justice during the Golden Age. Disgusted with the wickedness of mortals, she returned to heaven and was transformed into the constellation Virgo. She is represented as holding a pair of scales in one hand and a sword in the other.

Astyanax, son of Hector and Andromache, who was thrown from the walls of Troy by the victorious Greeks.

Atalanta, the name of two mythological characters. The daughter of Jasus, the Arcadian, was a huntress, who took part in the hunt for the Calydonian boar and shared with Meleager in the prize of victory. The daughter of Schoeneus, of Boeotia, was also a huntress, but she is known best for her ability in foot-racing. Refusing to marry anyone who could not outrun her, she insisted that all her suitors run a race with her in which the penalty of defeat was death. At last Hippomenes (or Milanion, according to others) defeated her. From Venus he had obtained three golden apples and, as he ran, he threw them down, one after another. Atalanta, fascinated by them, stopped to pick them up, and thus Hippomenes won the race and married Atalanta.

Ate, the goddess of infatuation, who led men into rash actions.

Athamas, king of Orchomenos and son of Aeolus. He married Nephele, who bore him Phryxus and Helle. Later he divorced her and married Ino, by whom he had Learchus and Melicerta. Ino was jealous of Nephele's children and persuaded an oracle to predict that a pestilence then raging could only by their sacrifice be arrested. On being led to the altar Phryxus and Helle fled to Colchis through the air on a golden ram, whose fleece was later sought by Jason. During the voyage Helle fell off into the sea, hence called the Hellespont. Juno dispatched the Fury Tisiphone to torture Athamas to madness. In this condition he killed Learchus, whereupon Ino threw herself into the sea and was changed into a sea-goddess.

Athena, a Greek goddess, corresponding to the Roman Minerva.

Atlantides, the seven daughters of Atlas: Maia, Electra, Taygeta, Sterope, Merope, Alcyone, and Celaeno.

Atlantis, an island said to have existed in the Atlantic, west of Gibralter. It was once rich and powerful and blessed with every beauty but was later swallowed up by the ocean owing to the increasing wickedness of its inhabitants.

Atlas, son of Iapetus and Clymene and father of the Hesperides, Hyades, and Pleiades. He lived in northern Africa and carried the heavens on his shoulders. Perseus, after vanquishing the Gorgons, sought refuge with him. Because assistance was denied him, Perseus produced Medusa's head and changed Atlas into a mountain.

Atreus, son of Pelops by Hippodamia and king of Mycenae. Suspected of the murder of his half brother Chrysippus, he fled to Argos and succeeded Eurystheus as king, marrying his daughter Aerope, who bore him Agamemnon and Menelaus. Thyestes, the brother of Atreus, who had been banished for seducing Aerope, sent Plisthenes, Atreus' eldest son by a former wife, to murder his own father. But Plisthenes was killed by Atreus. On learning that he had slain his own son, Atreus murdered the two sons of Thyestes and served them up to their father at a banquet. For this crime Atreus and his house were cursed by the gods, and he himself was finally killed by Aegisthus.

Atrides, any one of the descendants of Atreus, but especially Agamemnon or Menelaus.

Atropos, one of the Fates, the goddess that cut the thread of life.

Attis, or **Atys**, a Phrygian god of fertility, who died and came to life again. He was loved by Cybele and was represented as a beautiful youth.

Augeas, king of Elis, owner of 3,000 oxen, whose enormous stables had not been cleaned for thirty years. The job of cleaning out the stalls was one of the twelve labors imposed on Hercules; for this work Augeas promised him a tenth of his herd. When Hercules diverted the waters of the Alpheus to send them through the stables, Augeas regarded this as a trick and refused to give him the reward. Hercules, therefore, conquered Elis and killed Augeas.

Aurora, daughter of Hyperion and Thea and goddess of the dawn, who rose from the couch of her husband Tithonus before the break of day. She is depicted as a veiled figure riding in a rose-colored chariot drawn by white horses and opening the gates of day.

Auster, the south wind, that brought rain and fog in winter and hot, dry air in summer.

Autolycus, son of Mercury, an Argonaut, and a notorious cattle thief. He was able to deceive the owners by changing the marks on the cattle, but Sisyphus, son of Aeolus, got the better of him by putting his marks under the feet of his oxen.

Automedon, son of Dioreus, charioteer to Achilles and afterward to Pyrrhus.

Avernus, a lake between Cumae and Puteoli, the waters of which were so fatal that no birds could live near it. It was one of the entrances to Tartarus.

B

Bacchanalia, a Roman festival in honor of Bacchus, marked by wild revelry.

Bacchantes, devotees of Bacchus, who danced and threw themselves about in barbaric abandonment at the Bacchanalia.

Bacchus, the god of wine, son of Jupiter and Semele. He was saved by Jupiter from Juno's jealous wrath, which compassed his mother's death, and was intrusted to Ino. While living on Mount Nysa Bacchus discovered how to make wine from grapes and afterward traveled to many foreign lands to teach the art of cultivating the vine, tilling the soil, and collecting honey. He is generally represented as crowned with vine and ivy-leaves. He married Ariadne after she was deserted by Theseus at Naxos.

Baucis, the wife of Philemon, who lived with her husband in a small cottage in Phrygia, where they were visited by Jupiter and Mercury in disguise. As a reward for the hospitality extended to them, Jupiter transformed the cottage into a splendid temple. Baucis and Philemon lived to a ripe old age and at death were changed into trees before the temple's doors.

Bellerophon, the son of Glaucus, who was sent by Iobates, king of Lycia, to attack the Chimaera, a fire-breathing monster. This action had been urged upon the king by his son-in-law, Proteus, whose wife accused Bellerophon of seducing her. Aided by Minerva, Bellerophon succeeded in destroying the Chimaera. Thereafter he tried to fly to heaven on his winged horse Pegasus, but Jupiter sent a gadfly to sting the horse and Bellerophon was thrown to earth. He wandered about, lame and blind, for the rest of his life.

Bellona, the goddess of war, daughter of Phorcys and Ceto, and companion or sister of Mars. Her priests, called Bellonarii, inflicted wounds on themselves when offering sacrifices.

Bergion, a giant, son of Neptune, who was killed with stones thrown from heaven, when he opposed Hercules.

Beroe, the nurse of Semele, whose form Juno assumed when she appeared before Semele. Juno persuaded Semele to obtain proof as to whether it was actually Jupiter who was visiting her.

Bomonicae, the youths who were whipped at the altar of Diana Orthia during her festivals. The one who cried out the least was awarded the prize.

Bona Dea, Roman goddess of fecundity. At her festival, celebrated on the 1st of May, no male was permitted to be present.

Boreas, the north or northeast wind, who carried away Orithyia to Mount Haemus in Thrace. According to one version he was the son of Astraeus and Aurora. He possessed twelve mares of such fleetness that they could cross the sea without getting their feet wet.

Branchus, son of Smicrus of Miletus, to whom Apollo gave the power of prophecy.

Briareus, son of Coelus and Terra, a giant with a hundred arms and fifty heads, who helped the Olympians against the Titans.

Briseis, a beautiful woman who was part of the spoils appropriated by Achilles after the conquest of Lyrnessus. Later Agamemnon claimed her, causing Achilles to withdraw from the Trojan War. After the death of Patroclus she was given back to Achilles.

Bucephalus, favorite horse of Alexander the Great, which died in India.

Busiris, king of Egypt and son of Neptune and Libya. When Hercules was in Egypt, Busiris had him bound hand and foot and carried to the altar. Hercules freed himself, however, and slew both Busiris and his courtiers.

C

Cacus, a giant, son of Vulcan and Medusa, who lived in a cave on the Aventine Hill. He stole some of the cattle of Hercules and dragged them by the tails into his cave. Hercules heard them low, however, and attacked and strangled Cacus.

Cadmus, son of Agenor, who, unable to find his sister Europa and not wishing to return home without her, consulted the Delphic oracle as to where he should settle. The oracle told him to follow a certain cow and to found a city where the cow should lie down. He killed a dragon, which lived near the spot where the cow lay down, and sowed its teeth in the ground. The armed men who sprang from the dragon's teeth formed the original population of Thebes. Cadmus later married Harmonia, who was the daughter of Venus.

Caduceus, the magic wand of Mercury, with which he conducted the souls of mortals across the Styx and raised the dead to life.

Caeneus, a girl transformed by Neptune into a man, who took part in the Calydonian hunt. Later he was transformed into a bird, but in Elysium he became a girl again.

Calchas, the Greek soothsayer and high priest who was chosen to accompany the Greeks to Troy. He declared that the fleet could not sail until Iphigenia was sacrificed; that the plague could not be stopped till Chryseis was restored to her father; and that Troy could not be taken without Achilles' aid, nor without a ten years' siege.

Calliope, the Muse of epic poetry, daughter of Jupiter and Mnemosyne. She was the mother of Orpheus by Apollo.

Callirrhoe, daughter of Scamander, who married Tros and became the mother of Ganymede and Assaracus. Coresus fell in love with her, but she scorned him. This angered Bacchus, whose priest Coresus was, and the god sent a pestilence; whereupon the oracle demanded that

Callirrhoe should be sacrificed. Coresus, compelled to lead the nymph to the altar, stabbed himself. Callirrhoe fled to Attica and there on the brink of a fountain killed herself.

Callisto, one of Diana's attendants and a daughter of King Lycaon, of Arcadia, who was changed into a bear and placed in the sky among the stars.

Calydon, a city of Aetolia, which was devastated by a boar sent by Diana in revenge for the neglect of her rites. This disaster gave rise to the famous hunt for the Calydonian boar, in which many heroes took part. Meleager succeeded in slaying the animal and presented its head to Atalanta.

Calypso, a sea nymph and queen of Ogygia. She offered Ulysses hospitality on his being shipwrecked, fell in love with him, and detained him seven years.

Camenae, fountain nymphs and goddesses of prophecy, who were identified with the Greek Muses.

Camilla, a warlike Volscian heroine, who was killed in the war between Aeneas and Turnus.

Capaneus, one of the Seven against Thebes, son of Hipponous and Astinome, and husband of Evadne. Having vowed to take Thebes in spite of Jupiter, he was killed with a stroke of lightning. On hearing the news Evadne committed suicide.

Cassandra, daughter of Priam and Hecuba, to whom Apollo granted the gift of prophecy. When she resisted him, however, he ordered that no one should believe her. After the fall of Troy she became the captive of Agamemnon, who took her to Mycenae, where Clytemnestra put her to death.

Cassiopeia, mother of Andromeda and wife of Cepheus.

Castalia, a fountain on Mount Parnassus, sacred to Apollo and the Muses.

Castor, twin brother of Pollux and noted for his skill in taming horses. The two brothers joined in the Calydonian hunt and Argonautic expedition. In the struggle with Idas and Lynceus, Castor was slain and after the death of Pollux the brothers were placed among the stars as the Gemini.

Cecrops, founder and first king of Athens.

Celaeno, a daughter of Atlas; also one of the Harpies.

Centaurs, a race of creatures half horse, half human, who inhabited Mount Pelion. They engaged in the famous contest with the Lapithae. Later the greater number of them were killed by Hercules, and the rest driven to Mount Pindus.

Cerberus, the three-headed dog which kept watch over the gates of Hades. It was one of the labors of Hercules to bring Cerberus to the upper world.

Ceres, the Roman goddess of the earth's produce, especially of grain, who was identified with Demeter. When her daughter Proserpina was carried away by Pluto, Ceres in her anger caused the earth to withhold its fruits and was appeased only when Proserpina was brought back. But since she had eaten a pomegranate seed in Hades, Proserpina had to spend half of each year in the lower world.

Chaos, the unfathomable abyss from which the earth, its first occupants, and all else gradually proceeded.

Charon, son of Erebus, whose duty it was to ferry the souls of the dead over the waters of the Styx and the Acheron to the infernal regions, receiving an obolus for each passenger; hence the ancient Roman custom of putting an obolus into the mouth of a corpse before interment.

Charybdis, a whirlpool in the Strait of Messina, exceedingly perilous to ships, which in avoiding Charybdis often ran aground on Scylla.

Chimaera, a monster shaped like a lion in front, a dragon behind, and a goat in the middle, which devastated Lycia until it was killed by Bellerophon.

Chiron, the most famous of the centaurs, killed by an arrow from the bow of Hercules.

Chryseis, a daughter of a priest of Apollo, taken prisoner by the Greeks and given to Agamemnon. Her father, Chryses, asked for her release, but Agamemnon refused; whereupon Apollo sent a plague upon the Greeks. To free them from this curse, Agamemnon had to surrender Chryseis.

Circe, daughter of Helios and Perseis and famous as a sorceress. After murdering her husband, she was banished to the island of Aeaea, to which Ulysses and his companions were later driven. Receiving them into her palace, she served them a magic concoction, touched them with her wand, and turned them into swine. Ulysses himself, who was saved by partaking of a herb that made the magic potion powerless, forced Circe to turn his companions back into men.

Clio, the Muse of history.

Clotho, one of the Fates, the goddess that spun the thread of life.

Clytemnestra, daughter of Tyndareus and Leda; sister of Castor, Pollux, and Helen; and wife of Agamemnon. While her husband was at Troy, she lived with Aegisthus in adultery. On Agamemnon's return she murdered him; later she herself was slain by her son Orestes.

Clytie, a water nymph, who fell in love with Apollo. She was transformed by him into a sunflower, so that she might always be turned toward him in his daily journey across the sky.

Comus, the god of revelry and feasting.

Coriolanus, a Roman patrician, exiled because of his haughty bearing toward the people. He joined the Volscians and led them against Rome but was finally persuaded by his mother and wife to retreat without attacking the city.

Cornucopia, the horn of plenty, presented by Jupiter to Amalthaea in return for her having fed him while young with goat's milk.

Creon, king of Thebes, whose decree condemning Antigone to be buried alive was the cause of her suicide, as well as that of her lover, Haemon, who was Creon's own son.

Cronus, one of the Titans, son of Uranus and Gaea, and father of Jupiter, Neptune, Pluto, Juno, Ceres, and Vesta. He was identified with Saturn by the Romans.

Cupid, son of Venus and god of love, who pierced the hearts of gods and men with arrows of desire. He was identified with Eros.

Cybele, a Phrygian goddess, worshiped as mother of the gods. She was identified with the Greek goddess Rhea and the Roman Magna Mater.

Cyclopes, a race of shepherds of gigantic stature with only one eye, which was in the middle of the forehead. They lived near Mount Aetna and assisted Vulcan at his forges.

D

Daedalus, a cunning craftsman, who flew from Crete to Italy with his son Icarus by means of wings fastened to their shoulders with wax. Daedalus arrived safely, but Icarus, flying too near the sun, which melted the wax, fell into the sea.

Danaë, daughter of Acrisius, king of Argos, and mother of Perseus. An oracle predicted that some day her son would kill his grandfather, Acrisius. To prevent such a calamity, the king had his daughter imprisoned in a dungeon so that no one might marry her. But she was visited by Jupiter, who distilled himself into a shower of gold. After the birth of Perseus she and the child were put in a chest and thrown into the sea, but they drifted to the shore of Seriphus and were saved. The oracle's prediction came true, for Acrisius was accidentally killed by a quoit thrown by Perseus.

Danaus, son of Belus and twin brother of Aegyptus. Aegyptus had fifty sons, Danaus had fifty daughters. To escape his brother and his nephews, Danaus fled with his daughters to Argos and there became king. Hearing of their uncle's success, the sons of Aegyptus betook themselves to Argos and demanded his daughters for wives. On the wedding night each wife killed her husband with a dagger provided by Danaus. Only one escaped, Lynceus, who killed Danaus.

Daphne, a nymph who was loved by Apollo but did not return his love. She fled, pursued by the god, and when she could run no more, she was changed into a laurel. Thereafter the laurel was Apollo's favorite tree.

Daphnis, a Sicilian shepherd, famous as a flutist. He was struck with blindness for faithlessness to a naiad.

Dardanus, son of Jupiter and Electra, who was the founder of Troy and the ancestor of the Trojans.

Dejanira, wife of Hercules and sister of Meleager, for whose love Achelous fought a fierce battle with Hercules. Afterward, jealous of her husband's attentions toward Iole, Dejanira steeped one of his robes in the poisonous blood of Nessus. The poison entered his body, and as he tried to pull off the garment, which clung to his skin, he tore away huge layers of flesh.

Delphi, a city in central Greece, famous for the temple and oracle of Apollo.

Demeter, Mother Earth, identified with the Roman goddess, Ceres.

Deucalion, son of Prometheus and husband of Pyrrha. Deucalion and Pyrrha were the only persons that survived the deluge sent by Jupiter to destroy the inhabitants of the earth. In order to repeople the earth, they were ordered to throw behind them the bones of their mother; therefore, picking up some stones from Mother Earth, they flung these behind them. The stones cast by Deucalion were transformed into men, and those by Pyrrha into women.

Diana, goddess of hunting, daughter of Jupiter and Latona, and twin sister of Apollo. She was also goddess of the moon. Two of her famous temples were at Ephesus and Taurus.

Dido, queen of Carthage, who fled from Tyre with a large number of friends and followers and established a colony on the coast of Africa opposite Sicily. She assisted Aeneas after he had been shipwrecked and fell in love with him. When he left her to sail on to Italy, she killed herself.

Diomedes, son Tydeus and king of Argos, who was a prominent Greek chieftain in the Trojan War. He fought with Mars in single combat, wounding him so severely that the god of war retired from the battle.

Dionysus, the god of wine and vegetation, who was identified with Bacchus.

Dioscuri, a name applied to Castor and Pollux, twin sons of Tyndareus and Leda. They rescued their sister Helen from Theseus, took part in the Argonautic expedition, and performed many other great deeds while on earth. Pollux was famed for his skill in boxing, Castor for his ability to manage horses. The Dioscuri were regarded as the patrons of seafarers. At the request of Pollux, Jupiter allowed them to share alternate days in the upper and the lower world.

Dirce, wife of Lycus, who herself suffered the torture which she planned to inflict upon Antiope: to be tied behind a wild bull and dragged to her death.

Dryads, wood nymphs; the spirits or souls of trees. They were not immortal; each Dryad came to life and died with her tree.

E

Echo, a mountain nymph who diverted the attention of Juno while Jupiter made love to other nymphs. When Juno discovered the deception, she transformed her into an echo, depriving her of the power of speaking except when spoken to. Echo pined away with love for Narcissus, until only her answering voice remained.

Electra, daughter of Agamemnon, who sent her brother Orestes to King Strophius in Phocis in order to protect him from Clytemnestra, her mother. After Orestes had avenged his father's death by killing his mother, Electra married her brother's good friend Pylades.

Elysium, the abode of the spirits of the blessed.

Endymion, a shepherd on Mount Latmos, a beautiful youth loved by Selene, who chose perpetual sleep in preference to death. He sleeps in a cave in Caria, where Selene visits him by night.

Erato, the Muse of love poetry.

Erebus, son of Chaos, who is one of the deities of the lower world. He is a personification of that dread darkness through which departing souls pass to Hades.

Eros, the Greek god of love, identified with Cupid.

Eteocles, a son of Oedipus and Jocasta. After his father's death he and his brother Polynices agreed to reign in alternate years, Eteocles taking the first turn. At the end of his year, however, he refused to relinquish the throne. Polynices, therefore, appealed to Adrastus, king of Argos, whose daughter he had married. Adrastus sent an army and seven of his bravest generals (the Seven against Thebes) to his son-in-law's aid, and a severe conflict ensued. In the end the two brothers agreed to settle their differences by single combat, and both were slain.

Eumenides, avenging spirits, known also as Furies (*q.v.*).

Euphrosyne, one of the Graces, daughter of Jupiter and Eurynome.

Europa, daughter of Agenor, king of Phoenicia. She was loved by Jupiter, who assumed the form of a white bull and carried her off to

Crete, where she became the mother of Minos, Sarpedon, and Rhadamanthus.

Eurydice, wife of Orpheus, who was granted permission to leave Hades and accompany her husband to the world above on condition that he should not turn around to look at her until they had reached the upper world. But Orpheus, unable to resist the temptation, turned around. Eurydice had disappeared.

Eurystheus, king of Mycenae, who imposed on Hercules the "twelve labors."

Euterpe, the Muse of lyric poetry.

Evander, son of Mercury, who was leader of a group of Arcadian colonists that settled in Italy. He joined Aeneas in the war against Turnus.

F

Fates, three daughters of Jupiter and Themis, who controlled the actions and destinies of man: Clotho, Lachesis, and Atropos.

Faunus, an old Italian divinity, protector of agriculture and shepherds. He was identified with the Greek Pan.

Flora, the goddess of flowers.

Furies, three hideous, winged females, sprung from the blood of the mutilated Uranus: Alecto, Tisiphone, and Megaera. They were avenging deities, who pursued and punished the guilty.

G

Galatea, the name of two mythological characters. The sea nymph of this name, who fell in love with Acis (*q.v.*), was the daughter of Nereus and Doris. The other Galatea was the girl whom Aphrodite brought to life when she transformed Pygmalion's statue of a maiden into a living form.

Ganymede, cupbearer to the gods, a mortal youth of such grace and beauty that Jupiter had him carried off to Olympus on the back of an eagle.

Genius Loci, the special divinity assigned to a particular place or region.

Glaucus, the name of several mythological characters, of whom two deserve to be identified: Glaucus, the father of Bellerophon (*q.v.*); and Glaucus, the Boeotian fisherman, who was changed by Oceanus into a divinity of the sea and granted the gift of prophecy by Apollo.

Golden Fleece, the hide of the golden ram, intrusted by Phryxus to Aeetes (*q.v.*) and guarded by Argus, the hundred-eyed dragon. It was for the purpose of obtaining this fleece that Jason (*q.v.*) fitted out the Argonautic expedition.

Gorgons, three hideous wenches, whose heads were covered with snakes instead of hair. The one most frequently mentioned is Medusa.

Graces, three daughters of Jupiter—Euphrosyne, Aglaia, and Thalia—who represented the perfection of grace in body and mind. They are known also as the Charites and are usually shown as attendants of Venus.

H

Hades, a name applied both to the ruler and to the regions of the underworld. The ruler, known also as Pluto, was the son of Saturn and the brother of Jupiter and Neptune. His wife was Proserpina. Hades is often represented as seated on a throne, with Cerberus lying at his feet.

Haemon, son of Creon and lover of Antigone. On hearing that his sweetheart had committed suicide, he too killed himself.

Hamadryads, tree nymphs, usually called Dryads (*q.v.*).

Harpies, greedy monsters with female heads, long claws, and wings, sent by the gods to torment mortals.

Hebe, cupbearer to the gods and daughter of Jupiter and Juno. She was represented as the goddess of youth and was called Juventas by the Romans.

Hecate, goddess of sorcery and witchcraft, often represented with three heads, who personified the darkness and terror of night. She was identified both with Diana and with Proserpina. Her domain extended over heaven, earth, and hell. She particularly haunted cross-roads and was associated with the howling of dogs.

Hector, son of Priam and Hecuba and husband of Andromache, who was the leader of the Trojan forces and the most valiant of them all. After killing Patroclus in battle, he was himself slain by Achilles, whom he had provoked to fight again. Hector's body was dragged in triumph three times around the walls of Troy. Jupiter then interposed and ordered the body to be given up to Priam for burial.

Hecuba, wife of Priam and queen of Troy, who saw her husband and her sons killed by the Greeks. After the capture of Troy she fell to the lot of Ulysses and accompanied the conquerors on their voyage back to Greece. While in the Thracian Chersonesus, after trying to avenge the murder of her son Polydorus, she cast herself into the sea.

Helen, daughter of Jupiter and Leda, famed for her beauty. In her youth she was carried off to Attica by Theseus and Pirithous but was rescued by her brothers, Castor and Pollux. She became the wife of Menelaus, king of Sparta, but later Paris, son of Priam, persuaded her to forsake her husband and accompany him to Troy. To avenge this insult, Menelaus urged the Greek princes to attack Troy. When Paris was killed, in the ninth year of the war, Helen married Deiphobus. Shortly afterward she betrayed him in order to regain the favor of Menelaus. She went back to Menelaus and lived with him until his death.

Helenus, son of Priam and Hecuba, famous for his prophetic powers, who settled in Epirus after the Trojan War and married Andromache.

Helicon, a mountain in Boeotia, sacred to Apollo and the Muses.

Helios, or Sol, the god of the sun, who daily drove his four-horsed chariot across the sky.

Helle, daughter of Nephele and Athamas (*q.v.*), who during her flight on the golden ram fell into the strait separating Europe from Asia, the strait later named the Hellespont in her honor.

Hephaestus, the Greek god of fire, identified with Vulcan.

Hera, wife of Zeus, identified with Juno.

Heracles or Hercules, son of Jupiter and Alcmene, renowned for his strength. While yet in his cradle he strangled two serpents which Juno had sent to destroy him. Before reaching manhood he killed the lion of Mount Cithaeron. Afterward, having been driven mad by Juno, he killed his own children and those of his brother. On recovering he was so stricken with grief that he exiled himself and went to consult the oracle of Apollo at Delphi. He was commanded to serve Eurystheus for twelve years, during which period he performed twelve labors. The gods assisted him in his tasks, and he carried them out successfully. His first labor was to kill the lion of Nemea, which he choked to death; the second, to destroy the nine-headed Lernaean hydra, which he killed with his club; the third was to capture the Arcadian stag, which he caught in a trap; the fourth, to kill the wild boar of Erymanthus; the fifth, to clean the Augean stables; the sixth, to kill the carnivorous birds of Stymphalis; the seventh, to capture the wild bull of Crete; the eighth, to capture the mares of Diomedes; the ninth, to obtain the girdle of the queen of the Amazons; the tenth, to capture the oxen of Geryon; the eleventh to obtain the golden apples from the garden of the Hesperides; and the twelfth, to bring Cerberus, the three-headed dog of Hades, to the upper world. Hercules was now free from service to Eurystheus and returned to Thebes. He married Dejanira, daughter of Oeneus of Calydon. When Nessus, a centaur, tried to abduct her, Hercules shot him with a poisoned arrow. The dying Nessus told Dejanira to keep his blood, as it would always preserve her husband's love. Later, fearing that she was being supplanted by Iole, Dejanira sent Hercules a garment soaked in the blood of Nessus, which poisoned him. After his death he was taken to Olympus and endowed with immortality.

Hermes, messenger of the gods, identified with Mercury.

Hero, the sweetheart of Leander (*q.v.*), who killed herself when she learned that her lover had been drowned.

Hesperides, the three daughters of Atlas and Hesperis, appointed to guard the golden apples which Earth gave Juno at her marriage to Jupiter. The dragon, Ladon, which was always on guard at the foot of the tree, was slain by Hercules when he seized the apples.

Hesperus, the evening star, king of the Western Lands.

Hippocrene, a fountain at the foot of Mount Helicon, dedicated to the Muses. It began to flow when the ground was struck by the hoofs of the winged horse, Pegasus.

Hippolytus, son of Theseus, who, having spurned the advances made by Phaedra, his stepmother, was accused by her of attempting to dishonor her.

Horatius Cocles, a Roman soldier, who with two comrades held off the Etruscan army from the bridge across the Tiber, while his fellow-soldiers were cutting down the bridge. When the bridge was destroyed, he leaped into the river and swam safely to the Roman shore.

Hyacinthus, a beautiful youth, accidentally killed by Apollo while playing quoits. From his blood sprang the hyacinth.

Hydra, a many-headed monster. The Lernaean hydra, which Hercules slew, was a water serpent with nine heads, one of which was immortal. For each head cut off, two would grow in its place unless the wound was cauterized. Hercules succeeded in burning away eight of its heads and buried the ninth under a rock.

Hygeia, goddess of health, daughter of Aesculapius.

Hylas, a beautiful youth loved by Hercules, who accompanied him on board the Argo. While Hylas was drawing water at a spring, a nymph drew him into the water and drowned him.

Hymen, or Hymenaeus, the god of marriage, represented as a youth bearing a bridal torch.

Hyperion, one of the Titans, son of Uranus and Gaea. He was the father by Thea of Helios, the sun-god; of Selene, the moon-goddess; and of Eos, goddess of the dawn.

I

Icarus, son of Daedalus (*q.v.*), who fell into the sea, named after him the Icarian Sea.

Io, princess of Argos and daughter of Inachus. She was loved by Jupiter, who, to allay the suspicions of Juno, transformed her into a heifer. But Juno was aware of the change and put Argus to watch her. When Argus was killed by Mercury, Juno tormented Io with a gadfly, which drove her from place to place until she reached the Nile, where she recovered her form and bore a son to Jupiter.

Iphigenia, daughter of Agamemnon and Clytemnestra, who was offered as a sacrifice to Artemis. At the outbreak of the Trojan War a priest of Apollo declared that the wrath of the gods, which had been aroused by Agamemnon's killing of a sacred stag, could not be appeased except by the sacrifice of Iphigenia; and furthermore, that contrary winds would detain the fleet until this was done. As the priest, raising his knife, was about to perform the sacrifice, Artemis carried Iphigenia off to Tauris and substituted a hind. The Greeks proceeded against Troy. Afterward Iphigenia, who meanwhile had become a priestess, was instrumental in saving the life of her brother Orestes when he was about to be sacrificed.

Iris, goddess of the rainbow, who was often sent as a messenger by the gods.

Ixion, king of Thessaly, who had promised his father-in-law, Deioneus, a valuable gift but being unable to obtain it, put him to death in order to be released from his promise. After a long period of expiation he was summoned by Jupiter to Mount Olympus and placed at the table of the gods. But Ixion, ill requiting the hospitality of his host, began to make love to Juno. As a punishment Ixion was sent to Hades and there tied to a fiery wheel, that never ceased to revolve.

J

Janus, an old Italian divinity, represented with two faces, turned in opposite directions. He was the god of beginnings and entrances; wherefore, the first month of the year was named after him, and gates and doorways were under his protection. His temple at Rome was open in time of war and closed in time of peace.

Jason, son of Aeson and leader of the Argonautic expedition. When his father was driven from the throne by Pelias, Jason was rescued and brought up by the centaur Chiron. Grown to manhood, he demanded the restitution of his father's kingdom, a request which Pelias promised to satisfy if Jason would bring him the Golden Fleece, kept by Aeetes in the custody of a dragon. Accordingly, Jason had a ship built, which was named the *Argo.* He assembled a crew and set out for Colchis. King Aeetes agreed to part with the fleece if Jason would perform several seemingly impossible deeds, such as yoking the fire-breathing oxen and sowing the dragon's teeth. He accomplished these tasks with the help of Medea, Aeetes' daughter, who had fallen in love with him. Shortly thereafter Jason returned home with the fleece, taking Medea with him. After several years he deserted her for another woman. Medea was driven mad with jealousy and in revenge killed her children by Jason. Years later Jason was killed by a beam that fell from his ship, the *Argo*.

Juno, daughter of Cronus and Rhea, sister and wife of Jupiter, and queen of heaven. She was an exacting and jealous wife, taking severe vengeance upon the numerous mortal maidens of whom Jupiter became enamored, as well as upon their offspring. She was the mother of Mars, Vulcan, and Hebe. In the Trojan War she was on the side of the Greeks.

Jupiter, son of Cronus and Rhea, father of gods and men, and lord of Olympus. He was brought up in a cave on Mount Ida so that he might be safe from his father, who had eaten all his other children. With the help of the Cyclopes he defeated Cronus and the other Titans and thus became master of the world. He gave the sea to Neptune, the infernal regions to Pluto, reserving heaven for himself. He is usually depicted as seated on a throne, with thunderbolts in one hand and a scepter of cypress in the other, wearing a wreath of olive or myrtle.

L

Lachesis, one of the Fates, the goddess that measured the thread of life.

Laertes, king of Ithaca, and father of Ulysses.

Laocoön, brother of Anchises, priest of Apollo and later of Neptune, who warned the Trojans against bringing the wooden horse into Troy. While the people hesitated whether to accept or reject his advice, two giant serpents emerged from the sea and attacked his sons. Rushing to their rescue, Laocoön himself was attacked, and all three persons were strangled.

Laodamia, wife of Protesilaus, in answer to whose prayers her husband was restored to life for three hours. When he died a second time, Laodamia died with him.

Laomedon, father of Priam and king of Troy, for whom Neptune built the walls of Troy. When Laomedon refused to give the promised reward, Neptune sent a monster to plague the city. The king was prepared to sacrifice his daughter to the beast, but Hercules appeared, rescued her, and slew the monster. Because Laomedon again broke his promise, Hercules attacked the city and killed him.

Lapithae, a people of Thessaly, who engaged in battle with the centaurs at the marriage feast of Hippodamia and Pirithous, their king.

Lares, ancient Roman divinities, the deified spirits of ancestors, who shielded their descendants against harm.

Latona, or Leto, daughter of Coeus and Phoebe and mother by Jupiter of Apollo and Diana. Persecuted by Juno, she wandered from place to place until Jupiter gave her a refuge on Delos, where she gave birth to her children.

Leander, a youth of Abydos, who swam nightly across the Hellespont to visit his sweetheart, Hero, living in Sestos. He was guided by a lamp which she hung out from a tower, but one stormy night the light was blown out, and Leander, losing his way, was drowned. On seeing his body washed up by the waves, Hero threw herself into the sea and was drowned.

Leda, wife of Tyndareus, king of Sparta, who was loved and approached by Jupiter in the form of a swan. She brought forth two eggs, from one of which sprang Helen and from the other Castor and Pollux.

M

Mars, the god of war, son of Jupiter and Juno, and lover of Venus.

Medea, a sorceress, wife of Jason *(q.v.)*, who murdered her own children to take vengeance upon her husband.

Medusa, one of the Gorgons, a terrible monster with hissing serpents for hair, whose face turned the beholder into stone. She was killed by Perseus, who, while observing her image in a mirror, cut off her head with his sword.

Meleager, son of Oeneus and Althaea, who took part in the Argonautic expedition and led the chase for the Calydonian boar. It had been decreed by the Fates that he should live only so long as a certain firebrand should remain unconsumed. Accordingly, his mother snatched the brand from the fire and jealously guarded it. When Althaea heard of Meleager's slaying of the boar, she went to the temple to return thanks. On the way, however, she came upon the bodies of her brothers, who had been slain by Meleager because they protested against the skin's being given to Atalanta. This so incensed Althaea that she cast the fatal brand into the fire, and when the brand was consumed, Meleager was dead.

Melpomene, the Muse of tragedy.

Menelaus, son of Atreus, brother of Agamemnon, and king of Sparta, who was one of the prominent Greek generals in the Trojan War. The abduction of his wife, Helen, was the cause of that war.

Mentor, friend of Ulysses and tutor of Telemachus, to whom was intrusted the care and education of the son of Ulysses during the latter's absence at Troy. The word "mentor" has become proverbial for a wise and faithful counselor.

Mercury, son of Jupiter and Maia, messenger of the gods, god of commerce, and patron of travelers, shepherds, traders, and robbers. Many of his exploits turn upon thievery or mischief. He wore a winged cap and had wings attached to his ankles that he might transport himself from place to place with the speed of the wind.

Midas, king of Phrygia, who, having done Bacchus a service, was permitted to choose his reward. Accordingly, he asked that whatever he touched be turned into gold. His prayer was granted. But when the food he touched, the clothes he wore, the water he washed in, turned into gold, he soon asked that the gift be revoked. On another occasion, because Midas ventured to remark that Pan made better music than Apollo, he was given ass's ears. At first, his barber was the only man to find out. Midas could not keep the secret to himself, however, and whispered it into a hole in the earth. Later, in this place, reeds grew up and as they were shaken by the wind they murmured and thus revealed the secret.

Minerva, goddess of wisdom, arts, and defensive warfare, who sprang full-grown from Jupiter's head. She was impervious to the passion of love and is depicted as wearing a helmet and carrying a shield. She was patron goddess of Athens, which was awarded to her as the result of a contest with Neptune, in which the city was to fall to the one who should present the more useful gift. Neptune produced the horse, and Minerva the olive.

Minos, the name of two kings of Crete. The one was a famous lawgiver, son of Jupiter and Europa, who became a judge in the lower world. The other was a grandson of the above-mentioned king, whose wife, Pasiphae, gave birth to a monster, the Minotaur *(q.v.)*. Minos had refused to sacrifice a white bull sent him by Neptune in answer to his prayer. As punishment for the king's perfidy Neptune drove his queen mad with love for the bull. To confine the offspring of this vile love affair, Minos commissioned Daedalus to construct a prison, known as the labyrinth.

Minotaur, the half-bull, half-human creature, offspring of Pasiphae and a bull, which was confined in the Cretan labyrinth by Minos. Every year the monster devoured seven youths and seven maidens sent as tribute by the Athenians. Finally, with Ariadne's help the Minotaur was slain by Theseus.

Morpheus, son of Somnus, who was the god of sleep and dreams. He is generally represented as a chubby, winged child, holding poppies in his hand.

Muses, daughters of Jupiter and Mnemosyne, nine divinities who presided over the arts. Their names and the arts assigned to them were: Clio, history; Euterpe, lyric poetry; Thalia, comedy; Melpomene, tragedy; Terpsichore, choral dance and song; Erato, erotic poetry; Polyhymnia, religious poetry and song; Urania, astronomy; Calliope, epic poetry.

N

Naiads, water nymphs, the daughters of Jupiter.

Narcissus, a beautiful youth, son of the river-god Cephissus, with whom the nymph Echo fell in love. But Narcissus did not return her love. To avenge what she regarded as a rebuke to herself, Venus, the goddess of love, caused him to become enamored of his own reflection in the waters of a stream. Unable to embrace or kiss the image, he pined away until he was changed into a flower, the narcissus.

Nemesis, goddess of vengeance and daughter of Night, who relentlessly meted out punishment to evildoers and lawbreakers.

Neoptolemus, or **Pyrrhus**, son of Achilles, who fought at Troy and later settled in Epirus, where he was killed by Orestes.

Nephele, wife of Athamas *(q.v.)* and mother of Phryxus and Helle.

Neptune, son of Saturn and Rhea and brother of Jupiter and Pluto, who was god of the sea. He made love to Amphitrite by assuming the form of a dolphin. His greatest gift to mankind was the horse. He is usually represented as seated in a chariot, drawn across the sea by brazen-hoofed horses, attended by Tritons and nymphs, and holding a trident in his hand.

Nereus, a sea divinity, son of Oceanus and Terra, and husband of Doris, by whom he had fifty daughters, called the Nereids. He was gifted with prophecy and lived in the Aegean Sea.

Nessus, a centaur slain by Hercules *(q.v.)*.

Nestor, king of Pylos, the oldest of the Greek commanders in the Trojan War, who was known for his wise counsel.

Niobe, daughter of Tantalus and wife of Amphion, whose intense pride in her children was the cause of their destruction. Because she had seven sons and seven daughters, she sneered at the goddess Latona, who had only two children, Apollo and Diana. Latona roused her children to take revenge for this insult. Apollo killed all Niobe's sons, while Diana killed all her daughters. Niobe herself was transformed by Jupiter into stone, from which streamed incessant tears.

Nisus, king of Megara, whose lock of purple hair (on which his life and fortune depended) was snipped off by his daughter Scylla and presented to King Minos, with whom she had fallen deeply in love. Nisus was transformed into a sea-eagle, and his daughter into a monster of barking dogs and hissing serpents.

Notus, the south wind, called also Auster.

Nymphs, female divinities that inhabited certain objects or places in nature. There were (1) Oceanids and Nereids, who were sea nymphs; (2) Naiads, fresh-water nymphs; (3) Dryads and Hamadryads, tree nymphs; and (4) Oreads, mountain nymphs.

O

Oceanus, son of Uranus and Gaea, brother of Cronus, and husband of Tethys, who was god of the sea and father of all river-gods and water nymphs.

Odysseus, the hero of the Odyssey, commonly called Ulysses *(q.v.)*.

Oedipus, king of Thebes, son of Laius and Jocasta, who unwittingly murdered his father and married his mother. An oracle had foretold that the son of Laius, if he should reach manhood, would be the slayer of his father. Therefore, as soon as the boy was born, he was ordered to be put to death, but Jocasta gave the child to a servant, who carried him to Mount Cithaeron. There he was discovered by a shepherd and brought up as his own child. After he had grown to manhood, he chanced to meet his father one day, who was driving along in his chariot. The road being narrow, the king ordered the stranger to make way for him. Oedipus refused, and in the encounter that ensued Laius was slain by his own son, as the oracle had predicted. Proceeding to Thebes, Oedipus found the population of the city threatened with destruction by the Sphinx, a monster sent by Juno, which proposed to all passers-by a riddle and destroyed those who failed to solve it. The kingdom and the hand of the queen were offered to whoever might find the solution and thereby free the people from the monster. Oedipus guessed the riddle. He became king and married his own mother, thus fulfilling the prophecy. Later, Thebes was visited by a plague, and an oracle declared that the epidemic would not cease until the murderer of Laius was discovered. Eventually, Oedipus became aware of his identity. Jocasta hanged herself, and Oedipus put out his eyes. Afterward he left Thebes, accompanied by his daughter Antigone, and died at Colonus, near Athens.

Oenomaus, a son of Mars by Sterope, the daughter of Atlas. He was king of Elis and father of Hippodamia.

Oenone, a nymph whom Paris married and later abandoned for Helen. On account of the indignities which she had suffered, she refused to heal the wound received by him in the battle before Troy. But when his injury proved fatal, she was overcome with remorse and hanged herself.

Olympus, a lofty mountain on the border between Macedonia and Thessaly, which was the abode of the gods.

Omphale, daughter of Jardanus and queen of Lydia, whom Hercules was forced to serve as slave for having murdered his friend Iphitus. She fell in love with him and freed him from slavery.

Oreads, the nymphs that inhabited mountains and caves.

Orestes, son of Agamemnon and Clytemnestra, who killed his mother and her paramour, Aegisthus, to avenge his father's death. Thereafter he was haunted by the Furies and fled from country to country. Afterward, by Apollo's command, he submitted to trial before the Areopagus at Athens and, being acquitted, returned to Argos and ascended the throne.

Orion, a famous giant and hunter, who asked for the hand of Merope, daughter of Oenopion, king of Chios. As the price of betrothal Oenopion set him the task of clearing the island of wild beasts. This deed Orion quickly accomplished. Instead of receiving his reward, however, he was made drunk and had his eyes put out by the king. Afterward, having recovered his eyesight by facing the rising sun, he took revenge on the king. Orion, after his death, was placed in the sky, where a constellation bears his name.

Orpheus, a famous lyrist, son of Apollo and Calliope, and husband of Eurydice, who received his lyre from Apollo and played upon it so exquisitely that all things, inanimate as well as animate, were charmed. He was one of the heroes of the Argonautic expedition and on his return married Eurydice. After Eurydice had died from the sting of a serpent, Orpheus followed her to Hades and begged Pluto to allow her to accompany him back to earth. His request would be granted, he was told, if he would not look at Eurydice until the borders of Hades had been passed. The temptation was too great however. He looked—and lost her forever. In grief for her he spurned the Thracian women, who became incensed and tore him to pieces during the celebration of the Bacchanalia.

Ossa, a mountain in Thessaly, on which the Giants piled Mount Pelion in order to climb to the heavens.

P

Palamedes, the ambassador sent by the Greek chieftains to urge Ulysses to join the expedition against Troy. Ulysses, pretending to be insane, yoked an ass and an ox to the plow and began to sow his land with salt. In order to test him, Palamedes placed Ulysses' son in the furrow before the plow. He was convinced that Ulysses was sane when he turned the plow aside to avoid striking his son.

Palladium, an image of Pallas Athene at Troy, on which the safety of the city depended; it was stolen by Ulysses and Diomedes.

Pallas, or Pallas Athene, the Greek goddess identified with Minerva.

Pan, the god of woods, fields, and shepherds, son of Mercury and a wood nymph. He is represented as having two small horns, a flat nose, and the lower limbs of a goat. He was very fond of music and enjoyed dancing with the nymphs. But he was also mischievous and frightened people who walked through the forests at night.

Pandora, the first woman ever to have been created, who was intended by Jupiter as a curse for mankind. (Till that time the human race, in some mysterious manner, had survived without the aid of woman.) Because Prometheus had stolen fire from heaven, Jupiter decided to punish man: He created woman. Since to this new work of creation all the gods and goddesses contributed something, it was called Pandora, "The gift of all the gods." Pandora married Epimetheus and presented him with a box given to her by the gods. Although she was forbidden to open it, she nevertheless lifted the cover, and there escaped every kind of human ill and plague, which quickly spread throughout the world. "Hope" alone remained in the box.

Parcae, the goddesses that shaped the destinies of gods and men. They are usually referred to as the Fates and are three in number: Clotho, Lachesis, and Atropos.

Paris, son of Priam, whose abduction of Helen, wife of Menelaus, was the cause of the Trojan War. He was brought up as a shepherd and married Oenone, a nymph of Mount Ida. At the marriage of Peleus and Thetis the goddess of discord, Eris, threw a golden apple, inscribed "For the fairest," among the assembled guests. Juno, Venus, and Minerva each claimed the apple, and so Jupiter thought it best to let Paris pass judgment. He decided in favor of Venus, who had promised him the most beautiful woman for a wife. The fairest of women proved to be Helen, the wife of Menelaus. Paris fell in love with her and took her with him to Troy. The Trojan War was the result. After Paris was wounded, he returned to Oenone. But she refused to heal the wound, and Paris died.

Parnassus, a mountain in Phocis, dedicated to the Muses and to Apollo and Bacchus.

Pasiphae, daughter of Helios, wife of Minos, and mother of Ariadne and the Minotaur.

Pasithea, or Aglaia, one of the Graces.

Patroclus, friend of Achilles, who was killed in battle by Hector. When Achilles refused to fight, Patroclus, wearing the armor of his friend, led the Greeks into battle. He fought bravely, but was slain. The desire to avenge his death brought Achilles back into the field.

Pax, the Roman goddess of peace.

Pegasus, the winged horse, which sprang from the blood of the slain Medusa. Mounted on this horse, Bellerophon soared through the air to conquer the Chimaera. Thereafter he wanted to scale the heavens on the back of Pegasus, but the horse threw him and flew up to Olympus alone.

Peleus, son of Aeacus and father of Achilles, who married the Nereid Thetis.

Pelias, father of Alcestis and uncle of Jason, who, having received the crown from his brother during the minority of Jason, refused later to surrender his authority. To prevent Jason from seizing the throne, he sent him in search of the Golden Fleece. When Pelias had grown old, his daughters requested Medea to rejuvenate their father. Medea consented, realizing that this would be the means of getting revenge. As a preliminary act in rejuvenation, she persuaded them, it was necessary for them to kill their father. But instead of restoring the old man to youth, she fled the country.

Pelion, a mountain of Thessaly. In their wars against the gods, the Giants placed Pelion on Mount Ossa to scale the heavens with greater ease.

Pelops, son of Tantalus, who was slaughtered by his father and served up to the gods. He was later restored to life, while Tantalus was sent to Tartarus. He won Hippodamia as his bride by defeating her father, Oenomaus, in a chariot race, in which death awaited the loser. The son of Pelops and Hippodamia was Atreus.

Penelope, wife of Ulysses, who was besieged by more than a hundred suitors during her husband's absence at Troy. She firmly believed that Ulysses would return and therefore delayed a decision as long as possible. Finally she promised to make a choice when she had completed a certain robe which she was then weaving. By undoing at night what she had woven during the day, she was able to put off the suitors until Ulysses returned.

Pentheus, king of Thebes, who was killed by his mother, Agave, and her sisters during a celebration in honor of Bacchus.

Penthesilea, queen of the Amazons, killed at Troy by Achilles.

Persephone, the Greek form of Proserpina *(q.v.)*.

Perseus, son of Jupiter and Danae and husband of Andromeda *(q.v.)*, who was sent by Polydectes to kill the monster Medusa. Obtaining winged shoes and Pluto's helmet, which rendered him invisible, he flew to the land of the Gorgons. He found them asleep, cut off Medusa's head, and flew away with it to Seriphus. There, by means of the magic Gorgon's head, he turned Polydectes and his court into stone.

Phaedra, daughter of Minos, who married Theseus after he had deserted her sister Ariadne. She fell in love with Hippolytus, the son of Theseus by Antiope, but was rejected by him.

Phaethon, son of Apollo, who was killed while driving his father's chariot across the sky.

Philemon, husband of Baucis *(q.v.)*, who was changed into a tree.

Phoebus, an epithet applied to Apollo.

Phryxus, son of Athamas *(q.v.)* and Nephele, who with his sister Helle rode through the air on the back of the golden ram.

Pleiades, daughters of Atlas, who, being pursued by Orion, appealed to the gods for help. Jupiter transformed them into doves and placed them among the stars.

Pluto, son of Cronus and Rhea and brother of Jupiter, to whom was assigned the kingdom of the lower world. His queen was Proserpina, the daughter of Ceres, whom he seized and carried off to the world below. Pluto is known also as Hades *(q.v.)*.

Pollux, son of Jupiter and Leda and twin brother of Castor, who was known for his skill in boxing.

Polyhymnia, the Muse of sacred poetry and song.

Polyphemus, son of Neptune and the most renowned of the Cyclopes, who was the rival of Acis *(q.v.)* for the affections of Galatea. When Ulysses with twelve of his companions entered his cave, Polyphemus devoured six of the men. Later, while Polyphemus was asleep, Ulysses put out his eye—the lone, huge eye in the middle of his forehead.

Poseidon, the Greek god of the sea, identified with Neptune.

Priam, king of Troy, husband of Hecuba, and father of Hector and Paris. In the fighting before Troy, he was killed by Neoptolemus.

Priapus, a Roman god of fertility.

Prometheus, a Titan, who stole fire from heaven for the benefit of mankind. For his crime he was chained by Jupiter to a rock on Mount Caucasus, where an eagle kept tearing at his liver until he was rescued by Hercules.

Proserpina, daughter of Ceres, wife of Pluto, and queen of the nether world. One day as she was playing with her companions, Pluto saw her and took her with him to the realm of the dead.

Proteus, a soothsayer who lived in a cave on the island of Pharos. He could be made to utter his prophecies only while asleep, since at other times he had the power of changing his shape so that he could not be recognized.

Psyche, a nymph whom Cupid married and visited nightly, concealing his features from her and leaving before dawn. She contrived to see him one night, however. Lighting her lamp, she was enraptured with his beauty. He was awakened by a drop of oil which fell on his face, and he fled immediately. Thereafter she wandered in search of him, incurring the hatred of Venus, who tried to thwart the lovers. Psyche ultimately joined Cupid in heaven and was endowed with immortality.

Pygmalion, a sculptor who carved an ivory statue of a woman and, falling in love with it, appealed to Venus to breathe life into it. The statue came to life and the woman, who was named Galatea, loved and married Pygmalion.

Pylades, friend of Orestes and husband of Electra.

Pyrrhus, another name for Neoptolemus *(q.v.)*.

Pyrrha, wife of Deucalion *(q.v.)*.

Python, the famous serpent of the caves of Mount Parnassus, which was slain by Apollo. It was born of the mud left by the Deluge.

R

Remus, twin brother of Romulus *(q.v.)*.

Rhadamanthus, son of Jupiter and Europa, who at his death was appointed one of the three judges in Hades, Minos and Aeacus being the other two.

Rhea, goddess of the earth, wife of Saturn, and mother of Jupiter.

Romulus, twin brother of Remus, son of the vestal virgin Sylvia. His mother was condemned to be buried alive. The children, set adrift on the Tiber, were rescued and suckled by a she-wolf. Afterward Romulus and Remus founded a city, named Rome in honor of Romulus.

S

Saturn, the god of agriculture, identified with the Greek Cronos, a son of Uranus and Terra, who usurped his father's kingdom, his brothers assenting on condition that he would not bring up any male children. Saturn, therefore, devoured his sons as soon as they were born, but his wife, Rhea, concealed from her husband her sons Jupiter, Neptune, and Pluto and gave him large stones to swallow instead of her male offspring. It was this that led to the Titans' making war upon Saturn and his ultimate overthrow by his son Jupiter.

Satyrs, rustic divinities addicted to sensual pleasure and associated with the worship of Bacchus.

Scylla, a rock near the Italian coast in the Strait of Messina, dangerous to mariners. In avoiding this peril, a boat was often drawn into Charybdis, a whirlpool near the opposite shore.

Selene, goddess of the moon.

Semele, daughter of Cadmus and mother of Bacchus. Hera, jealous of Jupiter's love, persuaded Semele to ask him to come to her in his true form. By the lightning, in which he came, Semele was killed, but she gave birth to Bacchus, whom Jupiter kept alive by enclosing him in his thigh till it was time for the child to be born.

Sibyls, women with the gift of prophecy, one of whom compiled the Sibylline Books, which were kept in Rome.

Silenus, a jovial old Satyr, companion of Bacchus.

Sirens, sea nymphs who by their song lured all who heard them to their death.

Sisyphus, son of Aeolus, who was punished in the underworld by having to roll uphill a huge rock, which, as soon as it reached the top, always rolled down again.

Sol, the sun-god.

Somnus, god of sleep and father of **Morpheus.**

Styx, the chief river of the underworld.

T

Tantalus, a son of Jupiter, who, for revealing his father's secrets, was punished in Tartarus with a raging thirst. Water and fruits that he saw close at hand always receded from his grasp.

Tartarus, the depths of Hades.

Telemachus, son of Ulysses and Penelope.

Tereus, a Thracian king, who married Procne, daughter of Pandion of Athens, and later abandoned her to marry her sister Philomela, whose tongue he cut out. But the sisters communicated with each other; and Procne killed her son Itys and served up his flesh to Tereus. The sisters fled, pursued by Tereus. They were changed by the gods into birds: Procne became a swallow, Philomela a nightingale, and Tereus a hawk.

Terpsichore, the Muse of choral song and dance.

Tethys, daughter of Uranus and wife of Oceanus.

Thalia, the Muse of Comedy; also one of the Graces.

Themis, one of the Titans, goddess of law and justice, who was mother by Jupiter of the Fates and the Hours.

Theseus, son of Aegeus, king of Athens, and legendary hero of Attica. His most famous exploit was the slaying of the Minotaur. He went to Crete as one of the youths whom the Athenians sent annually to Minos. Ariadne, daughter of Minos, fell in love with him, and with her help he slew the Minotaur and escaped from the labyrinth. He took Ariadne away with him but deserted her in the island of Naxos. Among his other adventures were the battle with the Amazons, whose queen he seized, and the carrying off of Helen from Sparta to Athens, whence she was rescued by Castor and Pollux. His friendship with Pirithous was proverbial.

Thetis. (See Peleus.)

Thisbe, the sweetheart of Pyramus, whose parents objected to her love affair. The lovers, consequently, arranged to meet secretly one day at the tomb of Ninus. As Thisbe reached the place, she saw a lion and fled, letting fall her cloak. When Pyramus arrived and found the torn garment, he thought she had been murdered; and therefore he killed himself. Thereafter Thisbe returned and, at the sight of her dead lover, put an end to her life also.

Tiresias, a Theban, whom the gods blinded and in compensation for the loss of his sight, gave the power of prophecy.

Titans, a race of giants, who waged ten years' war with Jupiter and were ultimately conquered and imprisoned in a cavern near Tartarus.

Tithonus, son of Laomedon and brother of Priam, for whom his wife, Aurora, secured immortality, but not eternal youth. In consequence, he gradually shriveled up.

Triton, a divinity of the sea, son of Neptune, who calmed the waves by blowing his trumpet.

Turnus, an Italian prince, who opposed Aeneas' settlement in Italy and was killed by him in battle.

Tyndareus, husband of Leda.

U

Ulysses, son of Laertes, husband of Penelope, and king of Ithaca. The wiliest of the Greek leaders at Troy, he was the inventor of the wooden horse. His wanderings home from Troy, which form the subject of Homer's *Odyssey*, lasted twenty years. Finally he reached home and killed the suitors by whom Penelope had been surrounded during his absence.

Uranus, god of the heavens, husband of Earth, who was dethroned by his son Saturn.

V

Venus, goddess of love and daughter of Jupiter and Dione. According to later legend she was born of the foam of the sea. She received the beauty prize in the judgment of Paris. Cupid was her son.

Vesta, the goddess of the hearth.

Vulcan, god of fire and son of Jupiter and Juno, who made the armor of the gods and had his workshops in volcanic mountains.

Z

Zephyrus, the west wind.

Zeus, the Greek name for Jupiter.

REFERENCE WORKS

Samuel Johnson, famous English lexicographer, once said, "Knowledge is of two kinds. We know a subject ourselves, or we know where we can find information upon it." This distinction is especially pertinent today, when the world's store of knowledge is so vast that no individual can hope to possess it. Our best guides to the fields of knowledge unfamiliar to us are reference works; with them we should be as familiar as a mariner is with compass and sextant.

Almost all libraries have the more important reference works, which are usually kept separate from other books. Probably the best way to learn about a subject is to consult several general encyclopedias. The encyclopedia article gives a valuable, general, comprehensive outline of the subject, and usually provides a preliminary bibliography. More specialized reference works may then be consulted; these in turn will list books and articles in the special field being investigated. It should be remembered that reference works, although valuable guides, usually deal only in a general way with a subject, and should not be regarded as final authorities. For more detailed, and probably more authoritative information, students should consult works which deal with the specific questions they are investigating.

The student should also become acquainted with the reference works which treat of language and its use. A familiarity with these books enriches one's knowledge of the language.

In various specialized fields there are also valuable reference works which the student should consult. Some of the most important of these have been selected.

ENCYCLOPEDIAS

- *American Peoples Encyclopedia*
- *Chambers's Encyclopaedia* (British)
- *Encyclopedia Americana*
- *Encyclopaedia Britannica*
- *Everyman's Encyclopaedia*
- *Der Grosse Brockhaus* (German)
- *Larousse du Siècle* (French)
- *Meyers Lexikon* (German)
- *Universal World Reference Encyclopedia*
- *Winkler Prins* (Dutch)

DICTIONARIES

General

- *Funk and Wagnall's New Standard Dictionary*
- *New Century Dictionary*
- *Oxford English Dictionary*
- *Wegster's New International* (2d ed.)

Desk

- *American College Dictionary*
- *Fowler's Concise Oxford English Dictionary*
- *Funk and Wagnall's New College Standard*
- *Shorter Oxford Dictionary*
- *Webster's New Collegiate Dictionary*
- *Webster's New World Dictionary of the American Language*

Special

- *Craigie's Dictionary of American English*
- Duffy, C., et al. *Dictionary of Literary Terms*
- Fowler's *Dictionary of Modern English Usage*
- Greet, W. C. *World Words, recommended pronunciation*
- Horwell's *Dictionary of Modern American Usage*
- Murray's *New English Dictionary on Historical Principles*
- Partridge's *Dictionary of Abbreviations*
- Partridge's *Dictionary of Slang and Unconventional English*
- Roget's *International Thesaurus of English Words*
- Taylor's *Language of World War II*

BIOGRAPHICAL DICTIONARIES

- Appleton's *Cyclopedia of American Biography*
- *Century Cyclopedia of Names*
- *Current Biography*
- *Dictionary of American Biography*
- *Dictionary of National Biography* (British)
- *International Who's Who*
- Preston, W. *American Biographies*
- *Webster's Biographical Dictionary*
- *Who's Who* (British)
- *Who's Who in America*
- *Who Was Who in America*

YEARBOOKS AND REFERENCES FOR CURRENT EVENTS

- *American Peoples Encyclopedia Yearbook*
- *Americana Annual*
- *Britannica Book of the Year*
- *Congressional Record*
- *New York Times Index*
- *Statesman's Yearbook* (British)
- *Times* (London) *Official Index* (British)
- *U. S. Government Organization Manual*
- *World Almanac*

PERIODICAL INDEXES

- *Canadian Periodical Index*
- Poole's *Index to Periodical Literature*
- *Reader's Guide to Periodical Literature*
- *Subject Index to Periodical Literature* (British)
- Special subject indexes, e.g., Biography, Agriculture, Education, Industrial Arts, Public Affairs Information Services, etc.

MAPS AND ATLASES

- *Encyclopaedia Brittanica World Atlas*
- *Hammond's World Atlas*
- *International Encyclopedic World Atlas*
- *New Pictorial Atlas of the World*
- Philip's *Historical Atlas, Ancient, Medieval and Modern*
- Rand McNally's *World Atlas*
- U. S. atlases: a list of national, state, county, city, and regional atlases in the Library of Congress

SPECIAL REFERENCE WORKS

- Bailey, L. H. *Cyclopedia of American Agriculture*
- Bartlett, J. *Familiar Quotations*
- Benet, S. V. *Reader's Encyclopedia*
- *Book Review Digest*
- Brewer, E. C. *Dictionary of Phrase and Fable*
- *Cambridge History of American Literature*
- *Cambridge History of English Literature*
- *Cambridge Ancient History*
- *Cambridge Medieval History*
- *Cambridge Modern History*
- *Catholic Encyclopedia*
- *Encyclopedia of Religion and Ethics*
- *Encyclopedia of the Social Sciences*
- *Grove's Dictionary of Music and Musicians*
- *Guide to Historical Literature*
- *Jewish Encyclopedia*
- Logasa, H. *Biography in Collections*
- *Oxford History of Music*
- Strong, J. *Exhaustive Concordance of the Bible*
- *U. S. Dept. of Agriculture Yearbook*
- *U. S. Official Postal Guide*

A MEDICAL DICTIONARY

A Compendium of Medical Terms

NOTE: *This dictionary is not intended as a guide to self-diagnosis or self-treatment of disease, nor does it in any way take the place of the skilled services of a physician. It can serve as a guide to the knowledge of biology and physiology which should form a part of everyone's education.*

Abdomen. The belly; that part of the body which lies between the chest and the pelvis, and contains the digestive organs (stomach, intestines, liver, gallbladder, and pancreas), the spleen, and the kidneys. It is separated from the chest by a dome-shaped muscle called the diaphragm.

Abiogenesis. Spontaneous generation.

Abortion. Expulsion of the unborn child from the uterus before the baby is capable of independent existence. In medicine the term abortion is usually restricted to expulsion early in pregnancy. Later expulsion before the infant is viable is called miscarriage. The induction of abortion, except for the purpose of saving the mother's life or as a protection against serious illness, is an illegal act, and even in skilled hands poses considerable risk to the life of the mother. Common causes of abortion in the early months of pregnancy may be inflammation or displacement of the uterus and abnormality of the embryo.

Abrasion. That type of injury resulting when an area of skin or mucous membrane is rubbed away by friction or any other force. Since the skin is the body's first line of defense against infection, an abrasion forms a breach through which disease-producing germs may invade the body. To prevent infection abrasions should be washed with soap and water, painted with an antiseptic solution, and covered with a sterile bandage.

Abscess. A collection of pus within any tissue of the body. Although the cells composing the organs and members of the body are frequently invaded by pathogenic micro-organisms, either through a wound or by way of the blood stream, they only very rarely succumb to the infection. The germs multiply in the tissues and attack the cells with which they come in contact; but some cells have the capacity to destroy germs, and to their assistance is mobilized a defensive army, consisting mainly of the white corpuscles of the blood, which surround the invaders and limit the area of the battlefield. This battlefield, or abscess, is strewn with dead or dying tissue cells, germs, and blood corpuscles; and together these constitute the thick yellowish fluid known as pus. When a tissue is attacked by germs, it acts to localize the infection and prevent the spread of organisms to other parts of the body. An abscess represents just such a localization of infection. Treatment has been virtually revolutionized by introduction of the various antibiotics, of which penicillin is used most commonly. This, with aureomycin and streptomycin, may be given by injection; other antibiotics may be applied locally.

Abstinence. Refraining from the use of food or stimulants, or from the indulgence of a desire. The term withdrawal syndrome is given to the state of overexcitement or intense depression that occasionally follows abstinence from an accustomed stimulant.

Acetanilid, also called Antifebrin, is a drug that relieves pain and reduces fever. Because even a moderate dose may produce harmful effects in some people, it should never be used except by prescription.

Acetone. A colorless pleasant-smelling liquid having the formula CH_3COCH_3. It occurs in the urine of persons suffering from diabetes, fever, cancer, or severe and prolonged vomiting, and sometimes in that of normal persons whose diet contains too much fat and too little sugar or starch.

Acetylcholine. An acetic acid ester usually present in many parts of the body. It has important physiological functions. Some of its salts are used to relax peripheral blood vessels.

Acidity. The quality of being acid or sour. The term is commonly applied to a condition associated with heartburn, belching, and a feeling of discomfort in the stomach.

Acidosis. A condition occurring when the alkali reserves of the blood are diminished. The normal reaction of blood plasma is generally slightly alkaline, that is, the acids and bases contained in the blood maintain an equilibrium. If the acid concentration of the blood becomes too high, coma occurs; if the alkaline concentration is too great, tetany results.

Acne. A chronic, inflammatory disease of the skin involving the sebaceous glands and hair follicles, commonly those of the face, back and chest. The eruption is varied in character, blackheads, pimples, pustules, and nodules forming the chief components. Acne is mainly a disease of adolescence. Occasionally, however, cases are met with in young children and in persons past middle age. Although the etiology of acne has not been definitely established, constipation, a sedentary indoor life, and a poor diet, especially one containing an excess of sweets and starchy food, seem to be predisposing causes. Some mild cases may be cured simply by correcting dietetic errors, training the bowel to empty itself regularly, and persuading the patient to take sufficient exercise outdoors. Severer cases are treated by a variety of methods which include administering preparations of yeast, vitamins, and sulphur internally, injecting vaccines prepared from various organisms, and exposing the affected parts to ultraviolet and x-ray irradiation.

Acromegaly. This is a chronic disease which results in abnormal growth. The bones of the head, face, hands, and feet become greatly enlarged and out of proportion with the rest of the body. The lower jaw becomes enlarged and projects forward; the teeth become separated; the lips, nose and ears thicken; the skin becomes coarse and greasy; and the hands and feet may become enormous. Acromegaly is due to excessive secretion of the growth hormone by the pituitary gland.

ACTH is an abbreviation for adrenocorticotropic hormone. This hormone is one of many secreted by the pituitary gland. Its principal function appears to be stimulation of the adrenal cortex to secrete cortisone. It has been used successfully to treat a great variety of diseases.

Actinomycin. An antibiotic particularly effective against fungus infections and the tubercle bacillus. Its great toxicity unfortunately renders it unsuitable for human use.

Actinomycosis. A chronic disease characterized by the formation of multiple abscesses caused by infection with ray fungi. In many cases, the infection takes place through the mucous membrane of the mouth, pharynx, or larynx. The involved areas are hard at first but eventually break down and discharge a yellowish pus through numerous openings. Treatment usually includes surgical intervention and administration of a combination of the sulfa drugs or penicillin with iodides.

Actinotherapy. The treatment of disease by exposing the body, in whole or in part, to light rays, especially to actinic or invisible ultraviolet rays.

Addiction. The state of being given up to a habit; for example, the habit of taking certain drugs. The drug addict must be clearly distinguished from the person who occasionally, under medical supervision, takes drugs for a specific and useful purpose—as, for example, the relief of severe pain. The addict takes drugs because he has an irresistible craving for them; starting perhaps to take morphine, cocaine, or heroin, to name three of the commonest drugs of addiction, for the escape they offer from an intolerable mental strain, or simply to enjoy a new and pleasant sensation, he finds, as time goes on, that he needs larger and larger doses of the drug to produce the desired effect, and ultimately that he must take it simply to relieve the intense depression by which he is possessed when not under its influence. The treatment of drug addiction consists of gradual withdrawal of the drug with milder and milder substances being given to relieve the abstinence crises. This procedure is carried out in special hospitals. Increased emphasis is now being placed on the importance of psychological counseling and psychiatric care as essential not only to correct the habit but also to insure that the former addict does not return to it.

Addison's Disease is a complex of symptoms characterized by general weakness and fatigue, low blood pressure, digestive disturbances, and browning or discoloration of the skin. It is due to destruction of the cortices of the adrenal glands, often by tuberculosis. It occurs chiefly among middle-aged persons. Treatment consists of administration of adrenal cortical hormone and a diet high in salt and low in potassium. Without treatment the disease is usually fatal.

Adenitis. Inflammation of a gland.

Adenoid, or pharyngeal tonsil, is an overgrowth of the glandlike tissues that ordinarily line the cavity behind the nose and mouth. This cavity is known as the pharynx, and it is in the upper part, designated as the nasopharynx, that adenoid growths tend to appear. Owing to the obstruction produced by the overgrown tissues, the patients become mouth breathers, acquire a thick manner of speech, and snore in sleep. Chronically inflamed tonsils and adenoids may serve as a focus for infection to spread to the tube communicating between the nasopharynx and the ear, and thus may produce deafness, earache and a dangerous infection behind the ear drum. Surgical removal of the enlarged tonsils and adenoids is the most effective treatment.

Adenoma. A tumor having a glandlike structure, closely resembling that of the organ from which it arises. Any glandular organ may become the seat of an adenomatous growth; for example, the breast, intestine, or thyroid gland. Unlike cancer, an adenoma is benign, causes no deterioration of health, and can endanger life only if it develops in or presses upon some vital organ. The growth, moreover, seldom tends to recur after it has been surgically removed.

Adhesion. An abnormal union between two surfaces of the body; any band or patch by which such abnormal union is effected. Adhesions may form between different portions of the gut, as a result of operation or disease, and occasionally require corrective surgery.

Adipose. Of a fatty nature; fat. The term adipose tissue is applied to the fat-containing structures of the body.

Adrenal Glands. Two small glandular organs situated just above the kidneys. Each consists of an outer layer or cortex and an inner layer or medulla. The medulla manufactures a substance called adrenalin and secretes it into the blood in small quantities. A gland that secretes its product directly into the blood is called an endocrine or ductless gland, and the product an internal secretion or hormone. Adrenalin, then, is a hormone secreted into the blood stream by the adrenal glands. Such secretion is believed to occur particularly in association with anger, excitement and fear, and through its influence the body is prepared for fight or flight. The heart beats at a faster rate; the blood pressure is raised; the skin becomes pale; the hairs stand on end; the pupils dilate; and the muscles become tense and ready for action. It has been found experimentally that the adrenal medulla is not necessary for life. On the other hand, the adrenal cortex is a vital endocrine organ. Its removal in animals experimentally and its destruction in humans, as a result of disease processes, produces the syndrome of Addison's Disease.

Adrenalin. (See *Adrenal Glands* and *Epinephrine.*)

Aeremia The presence of air in blood vessels.

Aerobe. A micro-organism that lives and grows best in the presence of free oxygen.

Aero-otitis Media, a traumatic inflammation of the middle ear caused by differences in pressure inside the ear cavity and that of the atmosphere. Changes in altitude such as are met with in air flights or mountain ascents are causative factors. Symptoms are a fullness and ringing in the ears and dizziness. Relief may be obtained by swallowing, chewing gum, or holding the nose closed tightly and blowing through the mouth.

Aerophagy. Air swallowing; this habit is a common cause of flatulence and belching. In most cases it is preceded by a sensation of discomfort in the stomach, which the patient erroneously attributes to the presence of gas, and tries to relieve accordingly. The only result of his efforts is that he gulps down a large volume of air, which eventually is brought up by belching. There may then be a few minutes of respite, after which the whole process begins over again. The condition is usually treated by explaining to the patient exactly what it is he does, for only rarely does he suspect that the gas he has been at such pains to get rid of has accumulated as a result of his efforts to bring up gas that was not there. Aerophagy is common among hysterical patients.

Afebrile. Without symptoms of fever.

Afterbirth. The structure, consisting of membranes, placenta, and umbilical cord, that has united the unborn infant with the mother, expelled from the womb after the birth has taken place.

Afterpains. Pains due to contraction of the womb, sometimes felt during the few days immediately following delivery.

Agoraphobia. A morbid fear of open spaces. Some writers use the term to denote a fear of being in crowds.

Agraphia. A condition produced by disease of the brain whereby the patient becomes unable to express his thoughts in writing. Commonly associated with it is aphasia, also a symptom of brain disease, as a result of which the patient, while retaining unimpaired intelligence, loses the power of expressing thought by speech.

Ague. Recurrent attacks of fever accompanied by shivering and chills. (See *Malaria.*)

Air Swallowing. (See *Aerophagy.*)

Albinism. A congenital deficiency of pigment in the skin, hair and eyes, that may affect even persons belonging to dark races. Albinos, as those suffering from this disorder are known, have an exceptionally white skin, white hair, and pink eyes, and usually tend to avoid strong light.

Albumin. A class of simple proteins containing the elements carbon, hydrogen, nitrogen, oxygen, and sulphur. They are transparent, viscous substances present in living protoplasm.

Albuminoids or scleroproteins. Organic compounds containing nitrogen, chemically related to proteins, but differing from them and from one another in various ways.

Albuminuria. A term denoting the presence of albumin in urine. It may be detected by heating the acidified urine, which thereupon becomes cloudy owing to the presence within it of coagulated albumin. Albuminuria, it should be realized, is not a disease; it is a symptom which accompanies a great variety of diseases, and may sometimes be found in persons enjoying perfect health. Bright's disease, fevers, infections and tumors of the kidney, diseases of the circulation, and inflammation of the bladder, are among the many causes of albuminuria. The condition may be found, on the other hand, in the urine of athletes who have just undergone a great exertion. There is thus no single remedy for albuminuria. In each case the treatment depends on and is directed toward removing the cause.

Alcohol. A colorless, volatile liquid, of aromatic odor. It may be formed synthetically from its elements, but industrially is often produced by fermentation of sugar-containing solutions. Alcohol is used in medicine chiefly as an antiseptic, disinfectant, solvent, tissue preservative, and anesthetic. It also forms the intoxicating constituent of wines, beer, and spirits.

Alcoholism, a chronic addiction to alcoholic beverages. Taken in small amounts by healthy persons, alcohol produces its characteristic effects by inhibiting or depressing the higher mental faculties, and thus allowing freer play to impulses that are normally held in check by self-consciousness. Although it gives the effect of a mental stimulant it is, in fact, a depressant, careful experiment having shown that mental and physical work demanding fine judgment, speed and co-ordination, suffer in quality even if only a small amount of alcohol is taken. Chronic alcoholism, the state that results from the long-continued consumption of large quantities of alcoholic liquor, is marked by physical and mental deterioration. Disease occurs in the stomach, liver, kidneys, heart, blood vessels and nerves. The patient sleeps badly and becomes incapable of sustained mental effort. He is overcome by moods of deep depression from which he seeks relief in larger doses of strong spirits. His appetite fails and usually he vomits as soon as he rises from bed. Many of the symptoms and much of the pathology of chronic alcoholism have been shown to be due to dietary deficiencies incurred by the substitution of drink for food. Moderate intoxication requires little treatment other than complete cessation of intake. The use of certain drugs in connection with psychologic or psychiatric treatment has been highly successful in preventing hopeless addiction.

Alimentary Tract. The passage from the mouth to the anus, by way of the pharynx, esophagus, stomach, and intestines, in which nutrient materials are acted upon and transformed by the digestive juices, and along which the indigestible residue of food and other waste matters passes on its way to the exterior. Opening into this tract and pouring their juices into it are the salivary glands, the liver and the pancreas; but besides these there are numerous glands in the walls of the tract itself. Imbedded in the lining membrane of the stomach, for example, are glands that secrete pepsin and hydrochloric acid and other chemical substances, by whose action the proteins and other constituents of food are broken down to simpler compounds. In the intestine the process of digestion begun in the mouth and continued in the stomach is brought to completion by the joint action of the juices secreted by the glands in the wall of the intestine, the bile, and the pancreatic juice. Absorption of digested foods takes place in the small intestine.

Alkaloid. One of a group of organic, alkaline, physiologically active compounds found in plants. Well-known alkaloids are morphine, nicotine, caffeine and strychnine—all capable of producing profound effects on the body. Most alkaloids are poisonous, even in small doses, though in still smaller doses they may serve as valuable drugs. Morphine, for example, administered medicinally may save life; in large amounts it is rapidly fatal.

Alkalosis. A condition of the human body characterized by an abnormal increase in the relative alkali reserve. (See *Acidosis.*)

Allergy. A general term used to denote any sensitization reaction in man. Any condition in which symptoms of a disease appear after the use of a substance which, in similar amounts, has proved to be harmless to people of normal constitution is called an allergy. Minute amounts of any substance may produce violent reactions in a sensitized person. Among the most common substances producing symptoms of allergy are the proteins. A person unduly sensitive to egg protein may, on eating a seemingly trifling amount, have a severe attack of asthma, a typical allergic disorder. Rashes resulting from overindulgence of strawberries are also manifestations of allergy. The tendency to these allergic reactions runs in families and is transmitted by heredity, but members of an affected family may not all suffer from the same agent nor through the same allergic manifestations. Tracing the causative factor of an allergy is not always easy since practically any substance could be involved. However, by inoculating a person with minute amounts of suspected materials and watching reactions carefully, the sensitizing substance may be determined. When the agent has been discovered, a desensitization program may be instituted which may control evidence of the allergy, but it may not be possible to cure the allergy or to prevent its reappearance in another form against another agent. Since allergy appears to be connected with the secretion of a substance called histamine, the symptoms can often be relieved by drugs which counteract it. (See *Histamine and Antihistamine.*)

Alopecia. (See *Baldness.*)

Altitude Sickness. A condition occurring at high altitudes such as are reached in an airplane or high in the mountains. Elevations above 12,000 feet may cause symptoms. A diminishing of the pressure of oxygen in the body is the causative factor. An increase in breathing, elevation of pulse rate, headache, lassitude, and sometimes vomiting are the symptoms. Oxygen inhalation is used for treatment.

Amaurosis. Blindness. The term is applied especially to cases of blindness in which the eye itself is apparently unaffected, the underlying cause being in the optic nerve or in the brain.

Amblyopia. Dullness of sight due to imperfect reception by the retina of visual stimuli.

Amenorrhea. Absence or abnormal interruption of the menstrual flow.

Amentia. Mental deficiency; defect of the mind manifesting itself as idiocy, imbecility, feeblemindedness or moral delinquency. This disorder in most cases is transmitted by heredity, but some cases are due to injury at the time of birth or disease of the brain acquired in early life. The diagnosis of amentia is made by means of special intelligence tests, whereby a "mental age" may be assigned to the person under examination. If, thus, the patient can pass tests that come within the competence of a child of two, but not those of a child of three, his mental age is said to be two years. Adults below two in mental age are idiots; those between three and seven are imbeciles; and those above seven but below twelve are morons.

Amputation. The surgical removal of a limb or other part of the body.

Amylase. Any one of a series of enzymes that convert starch into sugar.

Amyloid. Starchlike; a white starchy substance deposited in various organs as a result of wasting disease or chronic infection.

Anabolism. The upbuilding, constructive process whereby the body cells transform food or other materials into more complex forms, and ultimately into living matter itself. Side by side with this process there takes place what is known as katabolism, a continuous breaking down of living tissues, in the course of which they are transformed to simpler chemical substances and ultimately expelled from the body as waste products. The sum of all the chemical and physical changes whereby living tissue is built up (anabolism) and broken down with the liberation of energy (katabolism) is known as metabolism.

Anaerobe. A germ that can thrive in the absence of air.

Analgesics. Drugs which are used to relieve pain. They inhibit pain perception by depressing regions of the central nervous system.

Anatomy. The science of the structure of the body as learned by dissection.

Anemia. A disturbance of health characterized by a deficiency of blood pigment or hemoglobin. The blood of the average healthy adult contains about 5,000,000 red corpuscles and about 6,000 white corpuscles in each cubic millimeter. Hemoglobin, the blood pigment, is a purple-colored iron compound, which combines with oxygen in the lungs and as it circulates through the body, gives up its oxygen to the tissues—a process on the efficient performance of which the health of every single cell of the body must ultimately depend. If there is a deficient number of red cells or a deficient amount of hemoglobin in each cell, the tissues will receive less than their normal requirement of oxygen, and will fail in consequence in their various functions. It is to this cause that the symptoms of anemia are due. The patient's skin is pale or even waxy. He then may feel weak, and become breathless on slight exertion, and is troubled by palpitation of the heart. He is overcome by attacks of dizziness, and may faint. Whether the anemia is the result of hemorrhage, or of a disease that destroys the red corpuscles, or of a chronic infection that interferes with the formation of red cells, these symptoms will appear. Pernicious anemia is marked by a striking diminution in the number of red corpuscles, which may fall to as low as half a million per cubic millimeter. All treatment of anemia is aimed at increasing the amount of circulating hemoglobin and varies according to etiology. If hemorrhage is the causative factor and a great blood loss has been sustained, transfusion of whole blood is indicated, supplemented perhaps by treatment with iron, liver, or liver extract. Nutritional studies have shown that folic acid and vitamin B_{12} are even more effective than liver extract or liver as stimulants for new red blood cell formation. Often the disease is cured simply by general improvement of nutrition and physical activity, preferably outdoors.

Anesthetic. A drug which produces loss of sensation and is used in surgery to prevent pain. Anesthetics are of two kinds: those which, like chloroform, ether, or nitrous oxide, make the patient unconscious; and those which, without putting the patient to sleep, temporarily abolish sensation in the part upon which the operation is performed. Most drugs of the former type are given in the form of vapor, which the patient inhales; some, however, are injected as fluids into the rectum or into the veins; ether may be given in any of these ways. Drugs of the second type, known as local anesthetics, may be sprayed over the area to be incised, rendering it white, frozen and insensitive to pain; or, by means of a hypodermic syringe, they may be injected into and around this area; or they may be injected into the sensory nerve trunks connected with it, and thus block the path between the site of operation and the brain. Finally, some local anesthetics, novocaine for example, may be injected into the cerebrospinal fluid in the canal of the spinal cord, thereby producing complete anesthesia of the body below the level of the injection.

Aneurism. A sac, containing blood or a blood clot, formed by a dilatation of the walls of an artery. As, at each heartbeat, the blood is pumped through the blood vessels, their elastic walls expand slightly under its pressure, recoiling again between the beats. If, however, any part of the artery is weaker than the rest, whether as a result of injury or disease, it is liable to give way under the pressure, and gradually to expand, forming a swelling along the course of the artery. Such a swelling is an aneurism. Two types of disease make the development of such dilatations possible: first, disease that attacks the blood vessels, weakening parts of their walls; secondly, diseases or habits of life that produce a high blood pressure and then an increased strain on the vessels along which the blood is pumped. Syphilis and the lodgment of infected clots in the vessel walls belong to the first type; kidney disease, arteriosclerosis, and hypertension to the second. In whatever part of the body the aneurism may be situated, it forms a pulsating, blood-filled tumor, which is liable to rupture or to become inflamed, with serious or even fatal results. Spontaneous healing seldom occurs. The kind of treatment adopted depends on the site of the aneurism. If it is situated along the course of a limb, surgical methods may be applicable; but in the case of one of the most common and serious aneurisms, that affecting the aorta, the tumor forms inside the chest or abdomen, and only medical treatment, by rest, diet, and the administration of anodynes, is feasible. A small proportion of abdominal aneurisms may be suitable for surgical treatment, but usually the disease process is generalized and new aneurisms arise in other parts of the blood vessel.

Angina Pectoris. A serious illness marked by sudden attacks of pain in the chest accompanied by feelings of suffocation and faintness. It is caused by spasm or constriction of the coronary arteries of the heart resulting in a failure of the blood supply to that vital organ. Relief is obtained by administration of nitroglycerin and PETN which dilate the coronary vessels.

Ankylosis. Immobility of a joint, partial or complete, resulting from injury or inflammation, or deliberately produced by surgical operation.

Anodyne. A drug or combination of drugs given for the relief of pain.

Anorexia. Lack of appetite. Such a condition developing in a previously healthy person may have no particular significance; it may, on the other hand, be the first symptom of serious illness; for example, of anemia, tuberculosis, or cancer of the stomach. The cause in any particular case can be determined only by careful medical examination.

Anoxia. An oxygen deficiency resulting from the failure of the cells to get enough oxygen.

Antabuse. A drug used in the treatment of alcoholism. When given by mouth it causes headache, increased heart and respiration rates, and giddiness when followed by ingestion of alcohol. The drug must be used only under careful medical supervision.

Anthrax. A serious disease due to infection by *Bacillus anthracis*, a germ that attacks many animals and may be transferred from them to man either directly or indirectly by exposure to the animals or animal products. The lesion of the disease is a peculiar carbuncle-like formation, but without pus. Penicillin, the sulfonamides, aureomycin, and terramycin have been used with favorable results.

Antibiotics are substances produced through an antagonistic relationship between certain fungi, molds, yeasts, and bacteria. These substances act upon other organisms to inhibit their growth or to kill them. Some antibiotics are used against disease-producing organisms. (See *Actinomycin, Aureomycin, Gramicidin, Neomycin, Penicillin, Streptomycin,* and *Terramycin.*)

Antibodies. Complex substances that work against bacteria or other foreign substances that would be harmful. They are produced in the body in response to invading antigens.

Antidote. A remedy given to counteract a poison. Some antidotes act chemically by changing the poison into a comparatively harmless substance; some act mechanically by preventing the absorption of the poison; and some physiologically by producing in the vital organs effects contrary to those produced by the poisons against which they are given. Much can be done to prevent death from poisoning even if the nature of the poison is not known. In all instances in which poison is suspected, a doctor should be called at once. If help is not immediately available the patient should be given a quart or more of warm water by mouth to dilute the poison. Soapsuds or bicarbonate of soda mixed in the water will aid in producing vomiting. Placing the fingers far back in the throat will cause vomiting in most individuals. Additional water should be given and vomiting induced again until the vomitus comes back clear. If a caustic substance such as lye or ammonia has been taken, lemon juice or vinegar should be added to the water in place of the bicarbonate of soda, and pieces of ice placed in the mouth will relieve the pain and reduce the local action of the poison. If breathing stops, artificial respiration should be started at once and continued until the patient is revived or until a doctor can be summoned. If the patient is unconscious but breathing he should be made to inhale aromatic spirits of ammonia and the limbs should be vigorously rubbed in the direction of the body. When consciousness is restored, copious quantities of warm water should be given and vomiting induced as previously described. The patient should be kept warm at all times.

After vomiting has removed most of the poison from the stomach, raw whites of eggs and milk can be given to prevent digestion of the eroded mucous membrane by gastric juices. Enemas will further aid in the elimination of poisons from the system.

If an overdose of a sedative drug has been taken every effort should be made to keep the patient active. Stimulants in the form of strong black coffee may be given. This treatment may be used in cases of alcoholic poisoning also. If a stimulating drug has been taken, every effort should be made to keep the person absolutely quiet. A doctor should be called at once.

Snake-bite poisoning can be prevented by prompt first-aid measures applied immediately after one is bitten by a poisonous snake. A tourniquet should be applied between the wound and the rest of the body so as to prevent the spread of the poison. Deep cuts should then be made into the wounds to cause bleeding which will carry away the poison. Crystals of potassium permanganate placed in the wound will destroy the poison and cauterize the tissues. Medical treatment should be sought without delay.

Carbon-monoxide poisoning occurs from the inhalation of poisonous carbon monoxide gas. This gas is colorless, odorless, and tasteless, and is present in the exhaust gases of automobile engines, and is also produced by ordinary furnaces. The gas gives no warning of its presence and causes sudden paralysis, stupor and loss of consciousness. Victims are usually found in closed garages with the automobile engine running and in overheated houses and apartments with leaky flues. Treatment should be begun without delay. The victim should be immediately removed to the outside air and revived with spirits of ammonia held under the nose, and vigorous massage of the limbs. If breathing stops artificial respiration must be begun at once and must be continued until a doctor can arrive. The patient should be kept warm at all times.

Antigen. A micro-organism or other substance that stimulates antibody production when introduced into the body. Antigens include bacteria and other micro-organisms, in addition to the toxins and ferments produced by them.

Antipyretic. Any agent that reduces the heat production of the body.

Antiseptic and **Disinfectant.** Substances which destroy or prevent the growth and development of germs. Carbolic acid, iodine, iodoform, alcohol, bichloride of mercury, potassium permanganate, and Lysol are a few of the antiseptics most generally used in medical and surgical practice. The antiseptic method of surgery was introduced by Lord Lister with the object of preventing the development of germs in surgical wounds. This was a revolution in practice, comparable in its effects with the discovery of general anesthesia. Infected, festering wounds, and a high mortality from even small operations, till then the general rule, became and have remained the exception. Today the surgeon expects the wounds he makes in the course of an operation to heal cleanly; before Lister's time, festering of operation wounds was regarded as inevitable. The technique practiced by Lister has been slightly modified, asepsis, sterilization of all instruments, gloves, dressings, etc., that come in contact with the wound, having become the fundamental rule of operative technique; but the principles underlying present-day practice are in every respect the same as those that were formulated by Lister and formed the basis of his great discovery.

Antispasmodic. A drug that relieves or prevents involuntary spasms of smooth or striated muscle and thus prevents the pain or discomfort usually accompanying such reactions. Some of these drugs exert their effect through general sedation, whereas others have a direct effect on specific areas, or block nervous impulses causing the spasm.

Antitoxin. A substance in the blood serum that combines with and neutralizes a toxin, the term applied to the poison secreted by germs. Each antitoxin is antagonistic to one toxin, and one only: diptheria antitoxin to diphtheria toxin, tetanus antitoxin to tetanus toxin, and so forth. Antitoxin forms in response to the presence of toxin in the blood, resulting from invasion of the tissues by toxin-producing germs or the injection of such germs into the system. (See *Immunity.*)

Anuria. Inability to pass urine.

Anus. The outlet of the bowel.

Aorta. The great arterial trunk which rises from the left ventricle of the heart and gives off branches through which oxygen-carrying blood is distributed to every organ and tissue of the body.

Aphasia. (See *Agraphia.*)

Aphrodisiac. A drug that excites sexual impulses.

Apoplexy. A condition, commonly called stroke, caused by hemorrhage into the brain, cerebral embolism, or cerebral thrombosis. Clinical signs include nausea, convulsions, and often either local or generalized paralysis depending on the location of the lesion. Eventual recovery is usual when the area of damage is limited. (See *Embolism* and *Thrombosis.*)

Appendicitis. Inflammation of the appendix, a wormlike, tubular organ continuous with the pouch-shaped swellings in the course of the bowel known as the cecum. The condition is due to an invasion of the appendix by disease-producing germs, but chronic constipation, failure of blood supply to the appendix, and dietary indiscretion seem to be predisposing factors. In most cases the earliest symptom is a sharp pain in the abdomen which is usually most severe low in the right side. The patient is feverish and constipated, and may vomit without relief of the pain. A physician should be consulted as soon as possible, and ice packs applied to the abdomen until he arrives. Cathartics should never be given in an attempt to relieve abdominal pain. Surgical removal of an inflamed appendix offers the only cure.

Arteriosclerosis. Hardening of the arteries. The arteries are the vessels through which the blood is pumped from the heart to the various parts of the body. They have a wall that consists of three layers, all of which contain a certain amount of elastic tissue. As, at each heartbeat, blood is forced into the circulation, the arteries, by virtue of their elasticity, expand slightly, and thus create a wider channel for the blood to flow through. If however, they are attacked by arteriosclerosis, they lose their elasticity and become rigid. Greater force then becomes necessary to maintain the circulation; the heart must pump with greater force and the blood pressure rises. It is to this extra strain on the heart and the increased blood pressure that the symptoms of arteriosclerosis are due. Among the many causes of this condition are Bright's disease, hypertension, Raynaud's disease, Buerger's disease, chronic alcoholism and many other diseases. Headaches, giddiness, shortness of breath, buzzing noises in the ears, and insomnia are the commonest symptoms.

Artery. The terms artery, capillary and vein may conveniently be considered together. For a description of the heart's action the reader is referred to the section on the circulation, but here the point to note is that three kinds of tubes, or, as they are called, blood vessels, serve to carry the blood through the body. Arteries are thick-walled tubes, composed largely of elastic and muscular tissues, in which the blood is conveyed from the heart to all parts of the body. In their course, these tubes give off branches, meanwhile becoming narrower and narrower, until at last their caliber becomes very minute indeed and they lead into and become continuous with the most minute blood vessels of all, known as the capillaries. The capillaries, cylindrical tubes having an average diameter of about 1/2000 of an inch, form a network within the body, and through their thin walls, which consist of but a single layer of flattened cells, the tissue exchanges that have been described as "the essential business of life" take place. Here the tissues give up their waste to the circulating blood and receive nutriment and oxygen in exchange. The blood then passes into the veins, tubes which at their beginning are only slightly larger than capillaries, but by coalescing, much in the same way as do the tiny tributaries of a river, form bigger and bigger vessels within which the blood is eventually returned to the heart. Briefly, arteries are vessels in which blood is conveyed from the heart to the tissues; capillaries are the network of fine vessels that join the arteries with the veins; and veins are vessels within which blood is conveyed from the tissues back to the heart.

Arthritis. Inflammation of one or more joints. A widespread acute arthritis, affecting several joints at one time, and sometimes passing from joint to joint, occurs most commonly in the course of rhumatic fever; but it may develop also as a complication of pneumonia, influenza, scarlet fever, the venereal diseases, and many other infections. Very occasionally, the condition known as rheumatoid arthritis, or chronic rheumatism, or rheumatic gout, has a sudden onset, especially when it occurs in young people. But generally the condition develops insidiously, producing pain, stiffness and weakening of one or more joints. Chronic infection, derived from some such focus as inflamed tonsils or pyorrhea, is believed to be the chief cause in many cases. Hereditary predisposition seems to play an important part; and persons living in a cold, damp climate are especially liable to be attacked. The treatment of rheumatoid arthritis depends upon its source. If a focus of infection is present it is removed. A well-balanced diet high in vitamins and rich in fruits and vegetables is indicated. Treatment is varied because of the variety of causative factors. Salicylates, iron and gold salts are sometimes used. Certain patients have responded favorably to the steroid drugs, ACTH and cortisone. Local measures such as massage, exercise and dry heat are used effectively. The specific value of any treatment in chronic arthritis is not really known.

Artificial Respiration. Maintaining respiration by artificial means. The back-pressure arm-lift method permits greater exchanges of air in the lungs than the Schafer prone-pressure method, is less fatiguing to the operator, can be performed by a small person on a heavy victim, and is relatively easy to teach. In the back-pressure arm-left method, the victim is placed prone with the arms bent and the hands one upon the other; the head is turned slightly so the cheek rests on the hands. To start the cycle, the operator kneels on either knee, places his hands on the victim's back with the thumbs touching and the heels of the hands just below a line running between the victim's armpits. The operator rocks forward slowly, elbows straight, until his arms are almost vertical. The operator rocks backward slowly sliding his hands to the victim's arms which are raised until resistance is felt in the victim's shoulders; the arms are then dropped. This completes the full cycle which should be repeated 12 times a minute at a steady, uniform rate.

Ascites. An accumulation of serous fluid in the abdominal cavity. The condition may result from inflammation of the membrane that lines the walls of the abdomen, or from disease of the heart, liver or kidneys.

Asphyxia. Suffocation: the condition that arises from interference with the act of breathing. Among the causes of asphyxia are the presence of an obstruction within the air passages; pressure on the windpipe from without, as in cases of strangling or garrotting, or of tumors of the neck or chest; replacement of air in the lungs by water, as in cases of drowning, or by poisonous gas; and the closure of the glottis as a result of swelling or spasms. Surgical treatment varies with the cause. In asphyxia of sudden onset artificial respiration should be started at once, care being taken to see that the air passages are free from obstruction.

Asthma. A constitutional disorder marked by paroxysms of breathlessness, cough, and wheezing, that may last from a few minutes to several days. The immediate cause of an attack is spasm and swelling of the lining membrane of the smaller bronchial tubes, but these changes occur only in constitutionally predisposed persons in response to the appropriate stimulus. In many cases this stimulus is a protein substance to which the patient has an abnormal reaction. Thus, a patient sensitized to the protein of feathers may excite an attack by sleeping on an ordinary pillow; in some patients a meal in which eggs, strawberries or oysters are included may have a similar effect. Such cases belong to what is known as the allergic type and should be treated accordingly. (See *Allergy.*) Some asthmatics, however, have no abnormal reaction to proteins. Their paroxysms seem to be brought on by irritation, associated often with an infective process, which causes the bronchial tubes to go into a state of spasm. By direct experiment, it has been shown that stimulation of the membrane lining the nose will cause such a spasm, and to this and similar causes may be attributed the cases of asthma that arise in association with infections situated in the nose, throat and intestines. Some cases of asthma are caused by heart disease, as a result of circulatory stagnation in the lungs. The successful treatment of asthma demands careful attention to many small details. No one remedy is effective in all cases. Even in allergic cases desensitization of the patient is not always effective in bringing about a cure. The constitutional predisposition remains unaffected and the patient, desensitized to one protein, may become sensitized to another. Immediate, though temporary, relief from bronchial spasm is often attained by administration of epinephrine, ephedrine, cortisone, or cortisone derivatives. Hormone preparations, vaccines, and X-rays are but a few of the remedies that have been successful in the treatment of some cases.

Astigmatism. A defect of the eye that causes blurred vision. It may be due to irregularities in the curved surface of the cornea or lens, or both.

Aura. The sensation that immediately precedes an epileptic attack.

Aureomycin. An antibiotic produced by a soil mold. It has been used effectively in treating many bacterial infections.

Auscultation. The act of listening for sounds within the body. The hollow instrument interposed between the practitioner's ears and the patient's body for the purpose of magnifying these sounds is called a stethoscope.

Avitaminosis. Any disease due to deficiency of vitamins in the diet. (See *Vitamins.*)

B

Bacillus. A rod-shaped germ.

Bacitracin. An antibiotic produced in shallow culture by *Bacillus subtili.* It is used against active Gram-positive bacteria and as a growth factor for chickens, turkeys, and hogs.

Backache. Sometimes the sign of fatigue or general weakness or a result of faulty posture, backache may be a disease symptom.

Bacteria. Germs, microscopic single-cell organisms, which multiply by splitting into two parts. Bacteria exist in the following forms: (1) spherical (cocci); (2) rods (bacilli); (3) twisted rods (spirilliform). For certain bacteria (aerobes) free oxygen is a necessary condition for growth. For others (anaerobes) the presence of free oxygen is directly injurious. Many forms of bacteria are capable of motion. Many diseases are now known to be due to bacteria which invade the body and multiply within the tissues; but most kinds of bacteria are harmless to man.

Baldness, or Alopecia, is a temporary or permanent, partial or complete, loss of hair from the scalp.

Bang's Disease. (See *Brucellosis.*)

Banthine. A drug used in the treatment of peptic ulcer. Its beneficial effects are due to the reduction of hydrochloric acid secretion in the gastric juice, reduction of the spontaneous movement of the gastrointestinal tract, and delay of gastric emptying.

Barbital, or Veronal. A long-acting, habit-forming drug used as a sedative or hypnotic. Untoward reactions are not uncommon.

Barbiturates. Narcotics which are widely used as sleeping powders. In small doses they induce sleep; in large doses they induce deep narcosis, or stupor. They are habit-forming.

Basal Metabolism. A term used to designate the heat production, due to chemical changes, in the tissues that supply energy for the vital activities of the body when it is at rest. The Basal Metabolic Rate (B.M.R.) may be measured by special instruments and is sometimes an important factor in diagnosis.

Bedsore. Sores which develop at any point where unrelieved pressure has been maintained so long that the tissues have lost vitality. Scrupulous cleanliness, thorough drying, and frequent position changes are preventive measures.

Benadryl. An antihistamine used in the treatment of some allergic conditions. It is sometimes used in the treatment of epilepsy.

Bends, Caisson Disease, or Decompression Sickness. A condition which results from the sudden reduction in pressure of the atmosphere. Caisson workers, tunnel workers, deep-sea divers, and aviators are susceptible.

Benzedrine or Amphetamine. A synthetically produced chemical which acts as a stimulant and vasoconstrictor.

Beriberi. A nutritional disease caused by a deficiency of Vitamin B_1.

Bile. A bitter, greenish-brown fluid manufactured by the liver and poured into the bowel, where it acts as an antiseptic and helps to bring about the digestion of fats.

Biopsy. The removal, usually for microscopic examination, of tissues from the body for the purpose of diagnosis.

Biotin or Vitamin H. Found in minute amounts in every living cell. The richest sources are liver, kidney, pancreas, yeast, and milk.

Birth and Labor. The process by which the baby (fetus) is expelled from the womb (uterus) is called labor. There are three stages: the first begins with pains caused by rhythmic contractions of the uterus which press the baby against the mouth of the uterus causing the opening to widen to allow the baby to pass through. In the second stage, the baby passes from the uterus through the vaginal canal and is born. In the final stage, the uterus again contracts to expel the afterbirth and constricts into a round, hard mass.

Birthmark. A reddish patch or swelling of the skin formed by a network of distended blood vessels bound together by a little connective tissue.

Bladder. The hollow organ in the pelvic cavity that serves as a reservoir for the urine. Its walls are perforated obliquely by the ureters, the ducts along which the urine passes down from the kidneys, and at the center of its base it becomes continuous with the urethra, the canal through which the urine and, in the male, the semen are discharged from the body.

Blood. The fluid and cells that circulate through the heart, arteries, veins and capillaries, carrying oxygen and food to the tissues, and waste matters to the kidneys and lungs, through which they are expelled. In each cubic millimeter of plasma, the colorless liquid part of the blood, there are about 5,000,000 red corpuscles, about 6,000 white cells of different kinds, and from 200,000 to 500,000 platelets. The color of the blood is due to hemoglobin, the iron-containing pigment of the red corpuscles. (See *Anemia.*)

Blood Pressure. The circulation of the blood, upon which the maintenance of life and health depends, is rendered possible by the existence of pressures in the circulatory system that are highest in the ventricles of the heart at the instant of their contraction, diminish progressively through the arteries and capillaries, and become least in the veins. If by its contraction, the heart failed to make the pressure of the blood in the ventricles higher than that in the arteries, then blood could not flow from the former to the latter. For a similar reason the pressure of the blood must be greater in the arteries than in the capillaries, greater in the capillaries than in the veins, and so through the circulatory system. The force responsible for giving the greatest impetus to the blood is the contraction of the ventricular muscle, which at each beat forces blood into the large arteries communicating directly with the heart. The walls of these arteries contain a great amount of elastic tissue which by its recoil helps to transmit the circulating blood along the arterial system. Just before the point at which the arteries become continuous with the capillaries, the very narrow vessels, called arterioles, act as a partial dam to the flow of blood, with the result that in the capillary network the blood pressure is considerably lower than it is in the arteries. This, however, is only one of the effects of the partial dam, or, to give it its technical name, the "peripheral resistance," set up by the arterioles. Experiment has shown that increased resistance at this point, such as might be produced by a constriction of the arterioles, results in a raised blood pressure within the arteries; similarly, dilation of the arterioles is followed by a fall of blood pressure in the arterial system. The chief forces then that serve to maintain the blood pressure are the contraction of the heart muscle, the elastic recoil of the arteries, and the peripheral resistance set up by the arterioles. In a normal healthy young adult at rest the blood pressure in the arteries of the arm, as measured by an instrument called a sphygmomanometer, is equal—when the heart is actually contracting—to that exerted by a column of mercury 120 millimeters high, and a column 70 millimeters high when the heart is at rest. But with the passing of the years the arteries lose their elasticity, the peripheral resistance tends to become greater, the heart muscle has to pump with greater force to circulate the blood through the body, and, as a consequence, the blood pressure gradually rises. Such a state of affairs occurs all the more readily if the arterial system undergoes degeneration as a result of chronic disease—arteriosclerosis, chronic Bright's disease, and certain forms of aortic disease being among the conditions that are characterized by a high blood pressure. Low blood pressure occurs in conditions in which the heart action is feeble or the arterioles are dilated—in pulmonary tuberculosis, Addison's disease, wasting fevers, and conditions of shock and collapse. Exercise and excitement tend to raise the blood pressure only temporarily. High blood pressure is a symptom, not a disease. It may well be that the pressure is higher because it would otherwise be insufficient to overcome the peripheral resistance, and in such a case reduction of the blood pressure may, by making the circulation too sluggish, have a very serious effect on the patient's health. (See *Aorta, Artery, Circulation,* and *Heart.*)

Blue Baby. A child born with a defect which prevents the blood from getting enough oxygen.

Boil. A deep red, tender, cone-shaped swelling that results from infection of a hair follicle or one of the skin glands by a variety of germs called staphylococci. When a boil comes to a head, a whitish spot appears at its most prominent point, and through this are discharged its contents, consisting of pus and a mass of gangrenous tissue called the core. Although a boil is but a local inflammation, its original cause may be constitutional, and the proper treatment depends, therefore, on the result of a general examination of the patient. Treatment consists of immobilization of the affected part and the application of hot moist dressings until localization is complete. Incision and drainage, if necessary, enable the healing process to begin. Because of the danger of systemic infection boils should be treated by a physician.

Bradycardia. An abnormally slow heart action.

Brain. The portion of the central nervous system contained within the cranial cavity. The brain in man is a very complicated structure, the essential components of which are masses of nervous tissue known as the gray and the white matter. The former consists mainly of nerve cells, the latter of nerve fibers. Continuous with the brain is the spinal cord with its nerve cells and tracts, the central nervous system being so constructed that some of the tracts lead from the spinal cord to the brain, and others to the spinal cord from the brain. It is usual to describe the brain as a kind of enormous telephone exchange, and this analogy, as long as it is not pressed too far, serves very well. Messages, known technically as "impulses," are constantly being transmitted to the brain along the tracts that lead to it from the spinal cord, and along various other paths as well; sensations of touch, heat, cold, pressure and pain, sensations from the organs and muscles, impulses that travel along the nerves and up the spinal cord to the brain, yet never become "conscious," are passing up all the time, and in the brain—the great telephone exchange—they are received, sifted, co-ordinated, and interpreted. For instance, the smell of good cooking assails the nostrils; an impulse is transmitted to the brain along the nerves of smell and is there correctly interpreted; in consciousness appears the sensation of hunger, while along the nerves to the digestive glands fresh messages are transmitted from the brain; the mouth starts to water, digestive juices are passed into the stomach in preparation for the forthcoming meal, and the whole body makes a move toward the dining room. Only a very small part of the brain is concerned with "thinking." The great bulk of the exchange is conducted without the intervention at any point of so-called "awareness." Consciousness, emotion, imagination, volition—all these are believed to be associated with activity of the brain, but there exist large areas of the brain which are not concerned with such "mental" operations.

The brain is divided anatomically into the cerebrum, the primary center of nervous activity, and lesser centers, the cerebellum, pons, and medulla oblongata, all of which are essential to physiological processes of the individual.

Bright's Disease or Nephritis. This is a general term used for a number of diseases of the kidney. The causative factors for these diseases are not definitely known but such infections as tonsillitis and scarlet fever may be complicated or followed by nephritis. Edema is a common symptom. Treatment consists of bed rest, dietary restrictions, and restriction of salt.

Bromide. A salt of bromine, which is a nonmetallic element. It has a general quieting effect; however, it does not compel sleep as do the barbiturates and other sleeping powders.

Bromidrosis. Offensive perspiration, a condition affecting chiefly the feet and armpits. Bathing the affected parts with boric acid lotion and dusting boric acid powder over the affected parts is in most cases an effective treatment.

Bronchi and Bronchial Tubes. The windpipe, or trachea, branches into the right and left bronchi, one for each lung. Each of these bronchus divides and redivides into smaller and smaller tubes; the final branches form clusters of blind air sacs in whose walls the exchange of oxygen and carbon dioxide takes place.

Bronchiectasis. A condition in which one or both of the bronchial tubes becomes dilated. The patient usually has a chronic cough and spits up large amounts of foul sputum; however, definite diagnosis can be made only through x-ray.

Bronchitis. Inflammation of the bronchial tubes, a condition that may occur as part of a common cold, in which case it is accompanied by inflammation of the lining membrane of the nose and throat; or as the result of irritation of the air passages by fog, dust or pungent vapors; or as a complication of a local infection elsewhere in the body, as, for example, chronic tonsillitis, or of a general infection, such as influenza or allergic factors may be significant as in bronchial asthma. Most important feature of treatment is bed rest. Steam inhalations, cough mixtures, and fluids are given. Antibiotics such as penicillin, aureomycin, and terramycin are sometimes given.

Brucellosis. An infectious disease transmitted to man generally by domestic animals, especially cattle, hogs, and goats. This disease is also known as Undulant Fever and Malta Fever. It is cused by the same genus of bacteria (*Brucella*) responsible for infectious abortion (Bang's Disease) in cattle and swine. Weakness, fatigue, and exhaustion, and an intermittent fever are some of the symptoms. Diagnosis may be made with certainty only on the basis of laboratory tests.

Bruise. An injury to tissue which does not result in breaking the tissue. The capillaries in the tissue are generally ruptured and cause the discoloration usually associated with this type of injury.

Burns. Burns and scalds are wounds of varying seriousness, extent and depth, brought about by the action of physical and chemical agents. Thus, in addition to burns caused by excess heat, there are burns caused by chemicals and certain kinds of irradiation.

Burns are classified as first, second, and third degree, according to the extent to which the tissues are injured, thus a third-degree burn, the most serious type, may extend through the skin and subcutaneous tissues even to bone and viscera. The seriousness of burns is determined also by the area involved—a burn extending over more than one-third the surface of the body is generally fatal.

The pathological effects of burns are due to three important reactions: (1) the local tissue destruction at the site of the burn and the loss of body fluids from the wound; (2) the shock or collapse; and in some severe burns (3) systemic effects such as the formation of duodenal ulcers, etc. The treatment of burns is directed toward combating the pathological effects, and insofar as is possible to relieve pain and clean the burned area. Severely burned patients are prone to tetanus infection and should receive prophylactic tetanus antitoxin.

The chief difficulty of treating burns is usually due to contamination of the wound, with subsequent pus formation and greater loss of tissue. For this reason every effort should be made to keep the wound clean. In all burns nothing should be applied to the wound except a clean dressing to prevent exposure. The wound and surrounding tissues should be thoroughly cleaned with soap and water (the patient should be anesthetized if necessary), and all necrotic tissue and foreign material removed under aseptic conditions. When the wound is thus cleaned it should be dressed with sterile moist dressings and allowed to heal. In some burns it may be desirable to apply dilute tannic acid and gentian violet, or some such preparation to coagulate the raw tissue surfaces and prevent extensive fluid loss. If the burns are extensive, blood transfusions may be required to prevent secondary shock from loss of fluids from the burned area. Deep burns heal by the formation of connective or scar tissue which is easily infected, easily torn, unsightly, and contracts with age, producing deformities and crippling limitation of movement of the affected parts. For these reasons it is often advisable to remove the scar and graft or transplant normal skin obtained from some other part of the body to the site of the burn.

Bursa. A saclike fluid-containing cavity situated in the tissues covering bony prominences or other sites at which friction is likely to develop. Thus, there are bursas in front of the kneejoint, at the point of the elbow, and around the shoulder joint.

Bursitis. An inflammation of a bursa which makes movement painful.

C

Calculus. Any stonelike matter formed in an organ of the body by mineral salt deposits. Most common sites for such deposits are the gallbladder and the kidney. Through the use of x-rays and special dyes, the stones may be visualized.

Cancer. A malignant growth composed mainly of cells derived from covering tissues, such as the skin, for example, or the membranes lining internal organs. In its beginning, cancer is invariably a strictly localized disease, which can, if it forms at a site accessible to surgical treatment or to the action of cancer-destroying radiations, whether from x-rays or radium, be completely extirpated or destroyed. Beyond the early stages, however, cancer not only spreads by direct extension in such ways as may make local treatment ineffective, but isolated cells may break off and be carried through the blood and lymph to organs and tissues far removed from the original focus. It is therefore vitally important to diagnose cancer very early, when radical cure is still possible. A delay of even a few weeks sometimes turns a curable into an incurable case. Cancerous growths may arise in any part of the body but are frequently found in the uterus, breast, stomach, prostate gland, and the mouth. The one cause that has been proved definitely to predispose to cancer is tissue irritation, local or general. The removal of sources of such irritation is therefore the most important preventive measure available. The greater incidence of cancer in certain industries indicates that other possible cancerigenic substances are some coal tar derivatives, undue x-ray exposure, and overexposure to other unusual radiations such as ultraviolet light. The early signs of cancer may be comparatively harmless conditions such as warts; indigestion and loss of weight and appetite in a person who has hitherto had no such troubles; hoarseness that does not clear up within a few days; or irregular losses of blood in the intervals between monthly periods. The earliest sign of a possible cancer of the breast is a small, hard, and usually painless lump in the glandular tissues. In every such case cancer is a possible cause, and except by a thorough examination there is no way of deciding if it is present or not. The treatment of cancer is varied, and several methods of combating this disease may be employed conjointly, depending on the site and extent of the tumor. Surgical removal is the method of choice when irradiation has proved ineffective and the growth is so situated as to make its excision simple and complete. Irradiation of the tumor with x-rays, radium, cobalt-60, and cesium-137, which destroy cancer cells, is effective in other cases. Radioactive isotopes are widely used when the tumor is confined to an organ that has great affinity for a particular chemical. This may be illustrated by the utilization of radioactive iodine in the treatment of cancer of the thyroid or radioactive phosphorus in connection with leukemia. Hormone therapy is often employed when a hormone overproduction or imbalance is believed to be related to the cancer. Most important in the treatment of any cancer is prompt and efficient investigation of any irregularity by a qualified medical practitioner. To stop the growth before it has spread to other organs is of prime importance.

Capillary. (See *Artery.*)

Carbuncle. A severe infection of the tissues immediately underlying the skin due to invasion by pus-producing germs, notably *Staphylococcus aureus*. The condition starts as a hard painful swelling over which the skin is red and tight. Later, as this swelling extends, the skin becomes thin, and perforations appear in it through which pus is discharged. Heat must be applied to prevent further spread of the infection and the entire carbuncle surgically excised; or as an alternative treatment, it is incised, the necrotic tissue is removed and the wound is allowed to heal from below upward.

Cardiac. Relating to the heart. Thus cardiac failure means simply heart failure; cardiac disease, heart disease.

Caries. Literally this term means rottenness. It is applied particularly to an inflammation of bone in the course of which the tissue is decalcified and undergoes decay. When such a process occurs in the teeth, it is known as dental caries, a condition in which the enamel and dentine are gradually disintegrated. It has been shown by careful experiment that dental caries may generally be prevented by a diet rich in vitamin D; for this substance, by ensuring the proper assimilation of calcium and phosphorus, provides the teeth with the elements that give them firmness, and at the same time opposes the action of any caries-producing bacteria that may live in the mouth.

Carminative. A medicine given for the purpose of relieving flatulence. Familiar examples are ginger, cardamom, cajuput, peppermint, and dill.

Carotene. The yellow pigment found chiefly in carrots, green vegetables, milk, fat, animal fats and egg yolk. Its importance lies in the fact that it is converted into vitamin A in the body and therefore is the supply of this vitamin in the diet.

Carrier. A person who harbors disease-producing germs in his body and is thus likely to distribute infection to others, though himself showing no symptoms of the disease he is carrying.

Catalepsy. A condition marked by loss of the power to move the muscles voluntarily. The muscles become rigid, the skin becomes cold and pale, and the pulse rate slow. Attacks of catalepsy, which occur in the course of certain nervous and mental diseases, or may be induced artificially by hypnotism, last from a few moments to days at a time.

Cataract. An opacity of the lens of the eye that is sufficient to cause dimness of vision. The condition is very occasionally present at birth. It may be acquired as a result of accident or disease, diabetes notably having cataract as one of its complications; or it may develop gradually with the passing of the years as one of the changes of senility. Surgical removal is the only effective treatment.

Catarrh. This term means a "flowing down," and is applied to the free discharge of mucus that accompanies inflammation of the membranes lining any of the body canals or cavities that communicate with the outer air. Thus, nasal catarrh is such an inflammation of the membrane lining the nose; gastric catarrh, of the membrane lining the stomach; and bronchial catarrh, of the membrane lining the bronchial tubes. The disorder generally known as a cold in the head is a catarrhal inflammation of the lining membranes of the nose, throat and eyes, which may spread by way of the larynx to the windpipe and bronchial tubes. Various kinds of organisms are held to be responsible for this condition; but predisposing causes are dampness, sudden changes in temperature, exposure to drafts, and a state of fatigue or poor general health. Bed rest, fruit juices, and plenty of water are beneficial in most cases.

Cathartic. A medicine that brings about emptying of the bowel; a purgative.

Cauterization. The application of heat to the tissues by means of oxidizing substances or hot metals. The process is used for controlling bleeding from vessels that cannot be easily reached in other ways, and for dividing tissues without loss of blood. Many surgical operations which, carried out in the ordinary way, using a knife, would be followed by severe bleeding, can be completed bloodlessly by cauterization.

Cerebellum. The part of the brain that is situated

between the cerebrum and the pons and contains the nerve centers that govern the co-ordination of muscular movements. It comprises a central and two lateral lobes which are connected with the rest of the brain by means of stemlike processes called peduncles, of which the upper pair is joined with the cerebrum, the middle pair with the pons, and the lower pair with the medulla oblongata. Definitions of all these technical terms are given under the appropriate headings. (See also *Brain.*)

Cerebral Cortex. (See *Brain.*)

Cerebral Hemorrhage. A hemorrhage occuring within the cranium or into the cerebrum.

Cerebral Palsy. A group of disorders caused by injury to the motor centers of the brain. The most common forms of cerebral palsy, of which the "spastic" is one, are those which affect body movement, and especially the muscles of the arms, legs and hands. At least half of all affected persons also suffer a speech handicap, and hearing or sight may also be affected. Only a minority of palsied persons are mentally retarded. The condition is not hereditary and not contagious. It seldom affects the lifespan.

Cerebrospinal Fluid. A fluid containing protein which flows through the spinal canal and over parts of the brain through special channels.

Cerebrum. The front and larger part of the brain. This highly complex mass of nervous tissue is composed of two practically equal portions called cerebral hemispheres, which are connected by a dense bundle of white matter called the corpus callosum. The gray matter covering the surface of the cerebrum has been proved by physiological experiment and other methods of study to be the seat of such mental processes as volition and sensation. Its area has, furthermore, been carefully mapped out, definite portions of cerebral cortex—as this outer layer of gray matter is called—having been found to govern a separate group of physiological activities. Thus the nerve center concerned with voluntary movement of the left foot is known to be situated at the top of the right motor area in front of the central fissure; similar centers have been localized in relation to taste, smell, hearing, speech activity, sight, tactile sensation, and so forth. (See *Brain.*)

Cesarean Section. Delivery of a baby by way of a surgical opening through the abdomen and the wall of the uterus.

Chancre. The sore that appears in the first stage of syphilis, one of the venereal diseases.

Change of Life. The disturbances, mental and physical, that attend the final cessation of the menses. The period at which the change occurs is also known as the menopause or climacteric. In some women it occurs comparatively early, even before the age of forty; in others it is delayed past fifty. Usually those who started menstruating early finish late, and vice versa. Common symptoms at the menopause are hot flushes, depression, anxieties, and a tendency to either gain or lose weight. In some women the change comes abruptly; but in the majority it is spread over a year or even longer.

Chickenpox. An acute contagious disease, chiefly of young children, marked by an eruption of small blisters which appear in crops and usually heal completely. It is believed to be caused by a virus. The disease is very contagious, runs a mild course with very little fever, and is usually over in about a week. One attack seems to confer protection, a second attack in the same person being very rare. Isolation of the patient is essential to prevent spread of the infection. Treatment is essentially palliative, but complications may require additional therapeutic measures.

Chilblains. Painful inflamed swellings that develop in the fingers, toes or ears as a result of exposure to cold. The condition appears chiefly in people with poor circulation. In the earliest stage, the affected part becomes white and numb, but shortly after, the overlying skin becomes red, hot, shiny and itching. A swelling forms beneath the skin, and a blister may develop and burst. The best preventive measures are to keep the hands and feet warm and exercise to improve the circulation.

Chloramphenicol or Chloromycetin **is an antibiotic** effective against certain bacteria that are not at all affected by penicillin and unsatisfactorily controlled by streptomycin.

Chlorophyll. A chemical constituent of plant life necessary to the process of carbohydrate manufacture in green plants.

Cholera. An acute infectious disease marked by copious watery discharges from the bowel, vomiting, and great prostration. Epidemics of this dangerous disease occur frequently in India and other Asiatic countries. Cholera is subject to foreign quarantine. The causative organism, the *Vibrio comma,* was described by Robert Koch in 1883. A vaccine made from the germ affords partial immunity lasting only a few months.

Chorea. St. Vitus's Dance; a nervous disorder marked by irregular jerking bodily movements over which the patient has no control. It occurs chiefly in children, in girls more than in boys, and most cases are held to be due to an acute rheumatic infection. Adult cases usually occur in connection with pregnancy, but even among these many of the patients have suffered from rheumatic fever in childhood. Although recovery within three months is the rule, relapses are common, and a tendency for spasm to occur in one group of muscles may persist when all other signs of the disease have disappeared. Rheumatic heart disease may accompany the acute stage or may develop some time thereafter as a complication. Prolonged bed rest is necessary to prevent serious and permanent damage to the heart.

Chronic. A term applied to diseases that run a prolonged course. (See *Acute.*)

Chyme. The thick, pulpy mass into which food is changed by digestion in the stomach.

Cicatrix. A scar; the permanent mark left at the site of an ulcer or a wound when these have finally healed.

Circulation of the Blood. The constant movement of the blood in the living body whereby it passes from the heart into the arteries and, having traversed the capillaries, returns to the heart by way of the veins. This movement goes on without a pause so long as life persists. Day in, day out, the heart at each beat pumps blood into the arteries, and this intermittent movement is made continuous by the elastic recoil of the arterial walls, which keeps the blood moving forward even during the intervals between beats when the heart is resting. To understand the cause of the circulation, it is necessary to know the bare facts about the structure of the heart and the blood vessels described in the sections entitled *Aorta, Artery,* and *Heart.* From these it will be gathered that the heart is a complicated muscular organ consisting of four chambers, two of which, called auricles, act as reservoirs into which blood is poured from the veins, and two, called ventricles, as pumps from which blood is forced into the arteries. When the muscle composing the ventricular wall contracts, the oxygen-containing blood contained within this chamber is driven first into the aorta, and then from this great arterial trunk, into the arteries and distributed to the head, neck, trunk, abdomen, limbs, and other organs and members of the body. The blood flows slowly through the intricate capillary network, when, having given up oxygen and nutriment to the tissues and received tissue waste products in exchange, it passes into the veins, which gather the deoxygenated blood from all parts of the body into two great vessels that pour their contents straight into the right auricle of the heart. In short, oxygen-carrying blood is pumped through the body from the left ventricle, and returns, deprived of its oxygen, to the right auricle. From the right auricle the blood passes into the right ventricle, which forces it into a large artery called the pulmonary artery. The branches of this great vessel are distributed to the lungs and lead to the capillary network through the walls of which fresh oxygen, derived from inspired air, reaches the blood, and carbon dioxide, one of the products of tissue waste, is passed from the blood into the external air. The blood, ready once more to be pumped through the body, now passes from the pulmonary capillaries to the pulmonary veins, and from these by way of the left auricle back to the left ventricle. Thus the blood in its circulation traverses two distinct paths; first, from the left ventricle of the heart, oxygen-carrying blood is distributed to all the tissues of the body, and returns, deprived of its oxygen, to the right auricle; secondly, deoxygenated blood is pumped from the right ventricle into the lungs, and having here been recharged with oxygen, makes its way through the pulmonary veins and left auricle back to the left ventricle again. The former of these paths is known as the "systemic circulation;" the latter, as the "pulmonary circulation." About one minute is required for the blood to complete the circulatory course that has been described.

Circumcision. An operation to remove the foreskin of the penis of a male for the sake of sanitation. In the female, circumcision provides for the freeing of tissue adhering to the clitoris.

Cirrhosis. A disease of the liver characterized by replacement of the liver cells with fibrous tissue. It is caused by any condition or disease in which toxic substances, circulating in the blood, destroy liver cells. Chronic alcoholism is one of the outstanding causes of cirrhosis. The liver enlarges, mainly as a result of the formation within it of fibrous bands, which gradually replace the liver cells, and, by their contraction, press on the blood vessels passing through the liver, thereby impeding circulation.

Claustrophobia. A morbid fear of being shut up in a confined space. People with claustrophobia have a horror, for example, of traveling in elevators or of sitting in the middle of a row in the theater, or of being in any place from which they feel there would be difficulty in getting out.

Cleft Palate. A rare defect whereby a back-to-front slit is present at birth in the roof of the mouth, allowing an abnormal passage to exist between the mouth and the nose. A child with this deformity has very limited power of suction and needs to be carefully spoon-fed. It is liable, moreover, to develop a chronic and unpleasant infection of the nose, and is never able to pronounce words distinctly. The condition can be corrected by operation, usually undertaken when the child is two or three years old.

Climacteric. (See *Change of Life.*)

Clubfoot. Any deformity in which the foot is twisted out of shape.

Cocaine. A bitter alkaloid obtained from the coca plant. It is used as a narcotic. Addiction to the pure drug is rare, a mixture with the opiates being preferred. Apprehension, hallucinations, and delusions are characteristic reactions to large doses of the drug.

Cold. An inflammation of the upper respiratory tract for which the causative agent is as yet unknown. Congestion in the nose, sneezing, coughing, running eyes and nose, and a general malaise may all be symptoms. Treatment is based mainly on alleviation of symptoms.

Colic. An acute pain in the belly. The term is used more widely for any attack of pain brought about by the stretching of a hollow organ. Thus, when a stone is passed from the gallbladder into one of the ducts leading to the bowel, this duct is stretched, and the spasms of pain then suffered by the patient are called biliary colic. Similary, the pain felt when a stone passing from the kidney to the bladder stretches the walls of the canal joining these organs, is called renal colic.

Colitis. Inflammation of the large intestine. In its less serious form, called catarrhal colitis, the condition shows itself by pain, swelling and tenderness of the abdomen, and frequent bowel movements containing mucus and sometimes blood. Ulcerative colitis, the more serious form, has very similar symptoms, but the stools contain pus as well as mucus, and bright red blood is commonly passed from the bowel. The patients, moreover, feel far worse than those with catarrhal colitis, suffer from fever, and become very thin and weak. In both types of disease careful and prolonged medical treatment and nursing are essential. An ulcerative inflammation of the bowel occurs in the course of typhoid fever, tuberculosis of the intestine, and certain other diseases. In such cases treatment is directed to curing the underlying conditions.

Colon. The large intestine; that part of the bowel which extends from the cecum, a dilated pouch in the course of the intestinal tract, to the rectum. In the majority of persons the cecum is situated in the right lower part of the abdomen, the direction of the colon being first straight upward toward the right under surface of the liver, then across the upper part of the abdomen from right to left, and finally downward into the left side of the pelvis. When in the course of digestion, the intestinal contents reach the cecum, they are liquid; but so much fluid is absorbed from them in the colon that by the time they have reached the rectum their consistency is firm and semisolid.

Coma. A state of complete loss of consciousness from which even great and sustained efforts fail to rouse the patient. Apoplexy or stroke, a condition due to hemorrhage into the brain, is one of the common causes of coma; but other diseases of the brain, for example, meningitis, abscess, or tumor; certain severe illnesses, notably typhoid fever, nephritis and diabetes; opium and alcoholic poisoning; and epilepsy and hysteria, may in certain cases have coma as one of their symptoms.

Communicable Disease. Any disease which may be transmitted from one person to another.

Concussion of the Brain. Stunning; a condition of giddiness, confusion of thought, or even, in serious cases, of total loss of consciousness, resulting from a violent blow on the head. The patient suffering from concussion is pale and clammy; his pulse is weak and respiration rate slow. Symptoms of intercranial hemorrhage must be watched for during the patient's recovery. Bed rest is essential.

Congenital. Existing at or before birth. Thus a congenital disease may be transmitted by heredity, or it may be acquired by the infant while it is yet in the womb, or when it passes through the maternal passages.

Congestion. This term, in its strict sense, means the excessive accumulation of blood in any part of the body. It is used popularly to denote the feeling of stuffiness that accompanies catarrh of certain organs; thus catarrh of the bronchial tubes is sometimes called, incorrectly, congestion of the lungs; and nasal catarrh, especially when the mucus makes breathing difficult, is equally incorrectly called congestion of the nose. True congestion of a part is the result either of some obstruction that will not allow the blood to escape from it, or of an infection that causes an extra amount of blood to flow into it.

Conjunctivitis. Inflammation of the delicate membrane that lines the eyelids and the eyeball. A discharge exudes from the eye and clings to the lashes, and the surface of the eye becomes red, hot, swollen and painful. Several kinds of conjunctivitis are known, and each requires a more or less distinct type of treatment. Anesthetics can be instilled into the eye to alleviate the pain, and antiseptic ointments applied to combat the infection. Silver nitrate (1%) is required by law in many states to be placed in the eyes of newborn infants as a means of preventing blindness due to congenital gonorrheal conjunctivitis.

Constipation. A condition in which the stools or feces are excessively solid, causing difficult bowel movements. Proper consistency of the stool is essential; but the frequency of the bowel movements has little significance. Although most individuals have one bowel movement daily, it is entirely normal for others to have two movements daily, and still others normally move their bowels every other day. Regularity of bowel movements is also essential to well being, but irregularity should not be followed by the use of cathartics. A vicious circle can easily be established by the use of cathartics, since evacuation of the bowel stimulated by these agents is likely to be so complete as to require an extra interval of time for a stool to form anew. This fact is generally overlooked by the patient and an additional dose of laxative is taken in order to obtain a movement. Drugs should be taken only on a doctor's prescription. Self-medication with laxative pills and other preparations often makes the condition worse, and ultimately may bring the patient to a state in which he cannot have a bowel movement except by taking increasingly large quantities of drastic purgatives. Irritation of the delicate lining of the bowel thus induced may lead to colitis, a serious inflammation of the bowel.

Consumption. (See *Tuberculosis.*)

Contagion. Spread of disease by contact either with the patient or with articles that have been infected by him, or through contact with another individual, as, for example, when an adult who has been in contact with a case of whooping cough conveys the infection to susceptible children, though himself remaining free of the infection.

Convulsions. Violent spasms or series of spasms of the muscles. Children often have convulsions in the course of severe disease. Among the illnesses in which convulsions may occur are infectious fevers, brain diseases, rickets, paroxysms of whooping cough, and worms. Teething is a very rare cause. Sedative drugs such as chloral and potassium bromide are most commonly prescribed. Once the immediate danger has been removed, treatment should be directed to the cure of the disease of which the convulsions are but a symptom.

Corns. Localized thickenings of the skin that occur most commonly on parts of the foot and toes that are subjected to pressure. At the center of each corn is a horny plug that extends deep below the surface of the skin and, by pressing on the underlying tissues, produces a feeling of pain. This pain is especially intense if inflammation occurs below the plug, with the formation of pus. Infection may result from attempted removal of corns unless proper precautions are observed. Properly fitting shoes will aid in preventing a recurrence.

Coronary Arteries are branches of the ascending aorta which encircle the heart and supply it with blood.

Coronary Disease. Any disease of the coronary arteries of the heart and heart muscles in which lesions, interfering with the coronary blood flow, prevent adequate supplies of blood from reaching the heart muscle. Three conditions that may affect the coronary arteries are coronary spasm, coronary thrombosis, and coronary embolism. Coronary disease may occur in any of the coronary arteries. If one of the main arteries is affected, however, the outcome is usually fatal.

Cortisone. One of the hormones secreted by the adrenal cortex. It has a complex chemical structure, but is produced commercially by various methods.

Cough. A sudden, noisy expulsion of air from the lungs. The most important fact about cough is that it is a symptom, not a disease. It may be caused by comparatively trivial complaints, a cold in the head, for example, or by serious and even dangerous illnesses, such as tuberculosis and syphilitic aneurism. Medicines designed to ease cough may or may not be useful. Thus they may prevent exhaustion of the patient by inhibiting a cough known to be of little pathological significance, or they may aid in the expulsion of mucus and secretions from the lungs in certain diseases by stimulating coughing; on the other hand, should coughing be stimulated in the former case and suppressed in the latter, exactly the opposite will obtain, to the detriment of the patient. Soothing medicines may be dangerous in yet another way; by relieving the cough they may create in the patient's mind the illusion that he is better, though, in fact, the underlying disease may actually be getting worse. Thus, it is sometimes very easy by means of certain drugs to stop the cough of early tuberculosis; but the tuberculosis goes on, and if it is not treated gets worse and eventually incurable. Regular winter cough, cough persisting into the summer months, coughing up phlegm streaked with blood, are all danger signals. Examination may show that they are the result of a comparatively harmless condition; it may, on the other hand, prove them to be symptoms of tuberculosis or some other serious illness that demands instant skilled treatment. In the great majority of cases, blood coughed up in the sputum comes from the lungs and is a symptom of pulmonary tuberculosis.

Cretinism. A symptom of the deficiency or complete lack of thyroid hormone during fetal life or early infancy. This condition is evidenced by slow growth, dwarfism, stupidity of expression, and mental deficiency.

Crisis. The turning point in a disease, whether for better or for worse. Such a change occurs notably in lobar pneumonia, in which usually on the sixth or eight day, when the illness is apparently as severe as it can be, the patient may suddenly take a turn for the better and within about 12 hours have a nearly normal temperature, pulse, and respiration rate.

Cyanosis. Blueness of the skin, due commonly to such conditions as heart disease or disease of the lungs that prevent a sufficient supply of oxygen from reaching the blood. Cyanosis of parts of the body may result from inadequate circulation of blood in the areas involved.

Cyst. Any sac, normal or abnormal, distended with fluid or semifluid material.

Cystitis. Inflammation of the urinary bladder. The patient, during an acute attack of this disease, suffers pain and tenderness in the lower part of the belly; his bladder is irritable and he makes frequent painful efforts to pass urine, though he passes very little at a time; usually he is very feverish. The urine may contain blood, pus and bacteria. Cystitis is always due to an invasion of the bladder walls by bacteria. Some predisposing local disturbance—for example, stone in the bladder, enlargement of the prostate gland preventing the free flow of urine, or spinal injury resulting in paralysis of the bladder muscle—is found in most cases to have caused a retention of urine, thereby affording an excellent culture medium within the bladder for the growth of bacteria. Acute cystitis unaccompanied by any other local disease is treated by bed rest, a high fluid intake, and the use of urinary antiseptics such as urotropin. Reversal of the acid-base reaction of the urine is also effective. In chronic cases, cure can be brought about only by treating the predisposing cause—removing the large prostate or the stone, or doing whatever else may be necessary.

D

Dactylitis. Inflammation of a finger or toe, a condition due in some cases to tuberculosis or syphilis of the affected part.

Dakin's Solution. An antiseptic solution of 0.5 per cent sodium chloride in water, which is used for cleansing wounds.

Dandruff. The formation of dry loose scales round the hair follicles. The cause of dandruff has not been discovered, but in certain cases it may be brought about by infection of the horny layer of the skin by a yeastlike fungus called the Pityrosporum. The condition can be controlled by various preparations containing small amounts of some germicide and fungicide such as bichloride of mercury, salicylic acid, etc.

Deafness. Partial or complete loss of the sense of hearing. Deaf-mutism is the name given to the state of being both deaf and dumb, persons thus affected being known as deaf mutes. Deafness may be due to disease affecting the nervous mechanism of hearing, or to any condition that prevents stimulation of the nervous mechanism. A tumor pressing on the auditory nerve or auditory centers in the brain will cause deafness of the former type, or perception deafness. Occlusion of the auditory canal by wax or a foreign body, or fixation or destruction of the tiny bones of the middle-ear cavity will cause the latter type, conduction deafness. Paradoxic deafness is a form of deafness in which the deaf person can hear better in the presence of noise than can normal individuals. Electric hearing devices employing the principle of the microphone are designed for each type of deafness, air conduction for conduction deafness, and bone conduction for nerve deafness.

Death Rate. The number of persons who die in a year compared with the total number of the population. Thus, if of every thousand persons in a given community a dozen die in the year, the death rate is recorded as 12 per 1000. In recent years the death rate both of infants and of the whole population has fallen fairly steadily, owing largely to improved hygiene and better medical care of the people. But so much has the birth rate fallen in the same period that a great change has been and is continually being effected in what is called the age-distribution of the community. The proportion of old to young people is increasing, and there are now relatively more people at the ages at which death may be expected to occur than ever before. For this reason a higher death rate is likely to ensue in the future.

Debility. Lack or loss of strength. Debility, it must be realized, is not a disease; it is a symptom that may appear in the course of many diseases. In children the condition may be due to improper feeding and a resulting malnutrition and vitamin deficiency. In adults it may follow such an illness as influenza or be an early sign of anemia, tuberculosis, or some other malady that demands skilled diagnosis and treatment. The practice of self-medication with tonics may produce harmful results. Debility should be treated by removing its underlying cause, not by masking its effects.

Decompression Sickness. A condition that results when the barometric pressure drops so suddenly that gases dissolved in the blood and tissue fluids are released as bubbles. All of the symptoms are the result of these bubbles interfering with the normal bodily processes. (See *Bends.*)

Defecation. The act of emptying the bowel. The undigested matter thus passed is called feces.

Defense Mechanism. In psychology, a reaction whereby a person unknowingly justifies his actions by constructing reasons and excuses for what he does.

Deficiency Disease. Any disease due to the lack of some essential constituent of the diet. The term is discussed more fully in the section on vitamins, for it is to diseases known to be caused by a deficiency of these food factors that the term is especially applied. (See also *Beriberi, Pellagra, Rickets,* and *Scurvy.*)

Deglutition. The act of swallowing.

Delirium. A mental disturbance occurring in the course of some forms of insanity, or in sane patients as a result of fever or brain injury, wherein for a few minutes, or even hours at a time, the person affected becomes excited and intensely restless and incoherent, and at the same time suffers from illusions, hallucinations and delusions. The condition called low delirium that occurs in the course of some severe fevers, notably enteric, appears rather as a confused muttering than as excitement. Persons overcome by delirium tremens, a condition resulting from alcoholic poisoning, show terrific excitement, tremble, and are troubled by hallucinations. Their chief need is to be nursed very carefully, for if they are not constantly watched they may, in their excitement, do themselves injury. Measures to produce sleep and to secure an effective bowel movement also help to bring an attack to an end.

Delusion. A false belief that persists in spite of the most striking evidence to the contrary. Patients suffering from certain forms of mental illness are given to such beliefs. They may, for example, though poor and of humble birth, claim to possess great riches or noble titles; they are said then to be suffering from delusions of grandeur. Or they may believe themselves to be the victims of a conspiracy in which all around them are concerned, suffering in such case from delusions of persecution. These abnormal mental states must not be confused with illusions or hallucinations. Illusions are false impressions of things actually present to the senses. Thus, if a person going into a dark room mistakes a curtain for a ghost, that is an illusion. Hallucinations, on the other hand, are visions or other sense impressions of objects that actually are not present. The strange animals seen by persons suffering from delirium tremens are hallucinations. It is useless arguing with a person under the influence of delusions in the hope that eventually he will "see reason." Delusions are impervious to reason; no one can be talked or bullied out of them.

Dementia. A form of insanity, marked by great impairment of intellect, will and memory.

Demulcent. Substances which soothe mucous membranes and other exposed surfaces. They include glycerin, lanolin, tragacanth, and flaxseed.

Denatured Alcohol. Alcohol which is not fit for human consumption.

Dengue. Breakbone fever; an infectious tropical disease marked by severe pains in the bones, head, eyeballs and joints, and a rash that appears on or about the fifth day of illness. The causative organism, a filtrable virus, is carried by *Aedes aegypti*, a tropical species of mosquito, and the disease is transmitted by bites from the insect.

Dental Caries. (See *Caries.*)

Dentrifice. A paste, powder, or liquid used for cleaning the teeth.

Dentine. The main substance of a tooth which surrounds the tooth pulp and is covered by enamel on the exposed surface and by cementum on the portion embedded in the jaw.

Deodorant. Any chemical or aromatic substance used to neutralize or disguise unpleasant odors.

Depilation. The process of removing hair. Substances used for this purpose, such as quicklime, calcium sulphate and arsenic, are called depilatories. These remove hair only temporarily. Electrolysis, by means of which each hair is removed separately, produces permanent results, but is liable, unless applied by a skilled person, to leave unsightly scarring.

Dermatitis. Inflammation of the skin. Such an inflammation may be due to infection with germs, fungi, viruses or animal parasites; to the action of drugs, either taken internally or applied externally; to exposure to heat, the rays of the sun, or x-rays; to scratching and other direct injuries; or the presence of toxins in the blood.

Diabetes Insipidus. A disease characterized by a disturbance of water metabolism in which an excess of urine is passed. The kidneys cannot concentrate the urine because of malfunction of the pituitary gland. The disease can be controlled by pituitary extracts.

Diabetes Mellitus. A disease affecting carbohydrate metabolism in the body and characterized by abnormal amounts of sugar in the blood and in the urine. This is the disease usually referred to simply as "diabetes." It may occur at any age, but usually occurs between the ages of 40 and 60, and is more common in women than in men. The exact cause of diabetes can not be determined in the majority of cases. There seem to be many contributing factors. Among these are the endocrine glands about which much is not known. Because there are few physical symptoms in uncomplicated diabetes, the first indication may occur in a routine urinalysis when excessive sugar is found in the urine. Patients usually pass large amounts of urine, are inordinately thirsty, and frequently have increased appetites but fail to gain either weight or strength. Complications of diabetes are acidosis and coma, arteriosclerosis, eye disorders, boils, and skin infections. At the present time, diabetes mellitus is looked upon as a chronic and incurable disease, although it must be remembered that there have been occasions when a cure has been effected. In the treatment of diabetes the aim is to maintain health and normal nutrition on a regimen that will keep the patient in an almost sugar-free state. In accordance with these aims, a dietary regimen, with or without insulin, is established and the patient is educated so that he will understand his disease, prepare and regulate his diet, test his urine, administer his insulin, and recognize complications which may occur. The diabetic person may lead an almost normal life, but he must ever be on the alert and may never forget that he is a diabetic, for laxity in attention to diet or tests may result in serious complications.

Diagnosis. The science and art of distinguishing diseases from each other.

Diaphragm. The sheath of muscles and tendons that separates the chest cavity from the abdominal cavity.

Diarrhea. Looseness of the bowels; a condition in which the stools are more liquid and are passed with greater frequency than the normal. Such a condition may arise from many causes: food poisoning, overeating, or taking a diet which contains an excessive amount of irritating matter; emotional causes, especially fear; infections of the bowel, as, for example, in typhoid fever, intestinal tuberculosis, colitis and dysentery; and the habit of taking purgatives to excess. The treatment of diarrhea is directed toward removing the cause.

Diastole. The phase of relaxation in the heartbeat; the brief interval in which the heart relaxes and rests between its contractions.

Diathermy. A therapeutic measure whereby heat is created in the body tissues by their resistance to the flow of high-frequency electrical waves.

Diathesis. Constitution; the total bodily and mental make-up of a person by virtue of which he has a tendency to suffer from or to resist diseases.

Dick Test. A method devised by George, and Gladys Dick of Chicago for discovering if any given person is susceptible to or immune from scarlet fever. The test is carrid out by injecting a very small measured quantity of a vaccine prepared from scarlet fever germs into the skin of the person under investigation. If redness develops at the site of injection it shows that he is susceptible and would contract the disease if exposed to infection.

Diet. The food prescribed by a physician, or the day-to-day allowance of food taken by any person. As far as healthy persons are concerned, the most important dietetic rules are that food should be partaken of unhurriedly at regular intervals; that the ingredients should be sufficiently varied and balanced to include all the essential food components — proteins, fats, starches, vitamins, minerals and water—in suitable relative amounts; that, other things being equal, fresh should be preferred to preserved foods; that no more should be taken at a meal than is needed to satisfy the appetite; and at all times meals should be skillfully cooked and served in an appetizing manner in order that they may by their appearance and fragrance excite the flow of the juices that are required for their digestion. A generous diet suits youth, but not age. In sickness, the diet prescribed will depend on the patient's condition. In pernicious anemia, Bright's disease, gastric ulcer and many other illnesses, the prescription of an appropriate diet forms the most important part of the treatment.

Dipsomania. An uncontrollable craving for alcoholic or intoxicating beverages.

Diphtheria. An acute infectious disease commonly affecting the mucous membranes of the mouth, nose and throat, in the course of which these structures and the air passages become covered by a closely adherent membrane composed of fibrin, mucus, blood, and dead tissue cells. The patient is subject to two distinct dangers: first, that this membrane, by impeding his breathing, may produce suffocation; secondly, that the deadly poison liberated by the diphtheria bacilli, the cause of the disease, may produce a fatal paralysis or heart failure. A sore throat covered with patches of white membrane, fever, great weakness and a feeble pulse, are among the commoner symptoms of diphtheria; but to these, when the glottis is affected, must be added hoarseness, a brassy cough, distressed breathing and asphyxia. Treatment is essentially preventive. Therefore prompt administration of antitoxin is vital. The antitoxin will not dissolve the membrane, destroy the bacteria, or neutralize toxin already implanted in tissue. Its advantage lies in protecting tissue from toxins and allowing the mechanisms of recovery to work freely. Once destructive forces of the toxin are firmly implanted it is ineffectual. It has been found possible to protect susceptible children against diphtheria by inoculating them with a vaccine made from diphtheria toxins and antitoxins; and this preventive treatment has been extended to doctors and nurses whose work brings them into dangerous contact with cases of the disease. In 1921, Bela Schick, a New York doctor, devised a test for susceptibility which is now widely used. A small measured dose of toxin is injected into the skin of the person under investigation and if, in 24 hours, a red patch develops at the site of injection it shows that he is susceptible and should be inoculated with a toxin-antitoxin vaccine.

Disinfectant. (See *Antiseptic.*)

Dislocation. A deformity that results when the bones of a joint are displaced from their normal position. Such a condition may be present at birth, the bones of the hip joint being most commonly affected, or it may be produced by disease or injury.

Diuretic. Any substance that stimulates the secretion of urine from the kidneys.

Diverticulitis. An inflammatory condition of pouchlike formations of the bowel. The cause for these formations is not known. They are rarely found in children, not common in young adults, but their incidence increases with age. They are most usually found in the lower sections of the big bowel. Only a small fraction of patients with diverticula develop diverticulitis. Cramping pains and rigidity of the lower left side of the abdomen may be symptoms. X-ray examination will show a peculiar sawtooth formation of the bowel. Treatment consists of rest in bed with hot applications to the abdomen and mineral oil may be given. Rarely does this condition demand surgery.

Dramamine. A proprietary drug useful in preventing various forms of motion sickness.

Drop Foot. Paralysis of the toes and foot resulting usually from alcoholic neuritis, but sometimes caused by pressure of tight casts on the feet of bedridden patients.

Dropsy. The abnormal accumulation of fluid in any of the tissues or cavities of the body. Such a condition may arise in the course of many diseases, notably of the heart, liver, kidneys, and blood. If the dropsy is widespread through the body it is called anasarca; dropsy of the abdomen is called ascites; of the chest, hydrothorax; of the skin, edma; of the brain, hydrocephalus. Although in all cass of dropsy measures are taken to reduce the amount of fluid abnormally distributed in the tissues, the essential tratment is directed to improving or curing the disease of which the dropsy is but a symptom.

Duodenum. The first part of the small intestine. It is about a foot in length and extends from the pylorus of the stomach to the jejunum, the second portion of the small intestine. It is an important part of the digestive tract, as here the acid contents of the stomach are neutralized and converted to an alkaline medium by the contents of the small intestine. Two ducts are usually present by which the pancreas and the liver pour their secretions into the intestine.

Dysentery. A term applied, when used in its strict sense, to two diseases, both of which are marked by inflammation of the bowel, pain in the abdomen, and frequent passing of stools containing blood and mucus. Bacillary dysentery, one of these diseases, is caused by the germ *Shigella dysenteriae;* the other, amebic dysentery, by the organism *Endamoeba histolytica.* These germs gain entry into the human body through the gastrointestinal tract by way of contaminated food and water. Wherever large groups of people gather together and sanitation is inadequate or defective, dysentery is likely to occur. In tropical climates, the disease is spread through flies and other arthropods and may often reach epidemic proportions. In the temperate climates, the disease occurs more frequently in the warm weather, but almost never reaches epidemic proportions. The onset of dysentery is usually abrupt, with fever and abdominal cramps the first complaints. Diarrhea follows within a short time. Headache, lassitude, and prostration may occur. Complete bed rest with heat particularly to the abdominal area and strict attention to sanitation are indicated. The sulfonamide drugs are often given. Antiserums do not seem to be practical. Prevention of the disease is most important. Strict attention to sanitation, as well as detection, isolation and treatment of both sufferers from the disease and asymptomatic carriers are indicated. Public health measures such as adequate sewage disposal, fly control, and safeguarding of food and water supplies are prophylactic measures.

Dyspepsia. Indigestion. This common condition may arise acutely as a result of overeating or of taking an ill-balanced meal, the symptoms in either case being discomfort and pain in the upper part of the abdomen, headache, palpitation of the heart, and sometimes vomiting. Chronic dyspepsia may be best regarded as a series of symptoms—pain after eating, heartburn, flatulence, sickness, foul breath, constipation, and headache—that occur in the course of any disease that interferes with the normal action of the stomach and the upper part of the intestine. It may thus be associated with such a diversity of conditions as chronic gastritis, gastric ulcer, cancer of the stomach, gall stones, appendicitis, constipation, fever, pregnancy, and Bright's disease. If the condition persists despite dietary precautions, a thorough examination is indicated to determine the cause of the symptoms.

Dyspnea. Difficult or labored breathing, a condition that occurs in healthy people as a result of exercise, but in sick people, especially those with certain forms of heart, lung, and kidney disease, may be present even when at rest.

Dysuria. Pain occasioned when passing urine.

E

Earache. This occurs commonly in children, especially those suffering from tonsillitis, adenoids, a cold in the head, measles, or scarlet fever—all conditions liable to be complicated by acute inflammation of the middle ear, and thus by earache and deafness. The secretions formed by the inflammation may press on the ear drum with sufficient force to rupture the drum membrane. As this is an extremely painful process it is preferable to anesthetize and incise the drum membrane before rupture can occur, and drain the pus from the middle-ear cavity, thereby affording immediate relief. Complications of earache may result if inadequate treatment is given and the disease process spreads to nearby structures. Treatment with sulfonamides or antibiotics has reduced the incidence of such complications as mastoiditis.

Eclampsia. Any sudden attack of convulsions. It may occur in a woman during pregnancy. This dangerous condition is believed to result from the presence of toxic substances in the blood of pregnant women and caused by some metabolic disturbance of pregnancy. Fortunately, it occurs in only a small percentage of pregnancies and can be recognized before the onset of convulsions. This is but one of many reasons for the need of frequent examinations during pregnancy.

Eczema. An inflammatory condition of the skin that begins with the formation of red patches and then of blisters, but later—owing to the bursting and "weeping" of the blisters—crusts and scales become more conspicuous than these; and at any stage, moreover, owing to scratching and rubbing by the patient, the inflamed areas may become thickened and pustular. The agents that may produce eczema in sensitized persons are almost without number, and range from food constituents and germs to heat and cold winds. Occupational eczema occurs in susceptible persons whose work necessitates their handling such eczema-producing irritants.

Electrocardiograph. A machine that records the potentials generated by heart muscle activity. The records provide valuable information in diagnosing and treating conditions of the heart.

Elephantiasis. A chronic disease, chiefly of the tropics, marked by overgrowth of the skin and connective tissues of the part affected, caused by obstruction of the lymphatic channels of the areas involved.

Embolism. The presence of clots or other obstructions in the arteries or veins. Among the conditions that may be complicated by emboli are inflammation of a vein, some forms of heart disease, and various parasitic diseases. The obstructing plug is called an embolus, and its effects depend partly on its nature; for example, whether or not it is infected, and the site of the body in which it ultimately lodges. Organs most commonly affected by embolism are the brain, lung, spleen, kidney, liver and intestine, as capillary networks in these organs prevent emboli from passing through into the general circulation. Air bubbles and fat globules can also act as emboli.

Embryology. The science that treats of the development of the embryo or fetus of animals.

Emetic. A preparation that causes vomiting. A reliable emetic is apomorphine which is given by injection. Copper sulfate, zinc sulfate, mustard and water, and ipecac are also reliable.

Emphysema. A disease in which the air spaces of the lungs are abnormally distended, with the result that the lungs themselves lose their elasticity and the network of blood vessels in the walls of the air spaces is gradually destroyed. In most cases of emphysema the cause is chronic bronchitis, the cough and obstruction of the tubes tending to bring about a state in which air can be more easily drawn into the lungs than expelled from them. Shortness of breath and a bluish tint of the skin, especially of the lips, are the chief symptoms, but in most cases the symptoms of bronchitis are present as well. The appearance of the patient is characteristic: he has a broad, deep, barrel-shaped chest, raised shoulders, crowded upper ribs, and lower ribs farther apart than normal—the total effect to the inexperienced eye being one of fine, healthy development. It is impossible to cure emphysema, but much can be done to relieve the symptoms.

Empyema. An accumulation of pus in the chest—a condition that may occur in connection with severe cases of pneumonia, blood-poisoning, scarlet fever, tuberculosis and abscess of the lung, suppuration in the abdomen, and perforating wounds of the chest. The chief symptoms are cough, shortness of breath, wasting, fever, and copious sweats; but the diagnosis is confirmed by introducing a hollow needle into the chest and examining the fluid.

Encephalitis. Inflammation of the brain. *Encephalitis lethargica*, a form of sleeping sickness, is a rare malady the chief symptoms of which are drowsiness, apathy and lethargy, muscular weakness and paralysis. Mental impairment, defective vision, and other difficulties may follow encephalitis.

Endemic Disease. A disease which is peculiar to a particular area or region.

Endocarditis. An inflammation of the membranes lining the heart and the heart valves. The causative factors may be of bacterial origin or some debilitating disease. Congenital lesions of the heart and such diseases as rheumatic fever are predisposing factors. The onset of the disease is insidious and often the symptoms are attributed to other causes such as "grippe." Significant heart murmurs are usually present, but signs of actual heart damage are not common until late in the disease. General supportive measures are used as treatment and the antibiotics, either singly or in combination, have been used.

Endocrine. Glands that secrete their products directly into the blood stream are called ductless or endocrine glands. These products, known as internal secretion or hormones, circulate through the body and produce striking physiological effects by stimulating various organs to activity. Examples of endocrine glands are the thyroid gland, the pancreas, and the suprarenal glands, which secrete thyroxin, insulin and adrenalin, respectively.

Endometritis. Inflammation of the lining membrane of the uterus.

Enema. A liquid injected into the rectum.

Enteric. (See *Typhoid Fever.*)

Enteritis. Inflammation of the lining membrane of the intestine, a malady marked by diarrhea, abdominal pain, and sometimes vomiting.

Enuresis. Involuntary discharge of the urine. Bed-wetting that occurs during sleep is called nocturnal enuresis, and affects chiefly nervous young children. In many cases the condition can be remedied by removing some source of physical irritation; in others the cause is psychological rather than physical, and treatment is correspondingly more difficult.

Ephedrine. A drug which stimulates the sympathetic nerve terminations. It is more stable than adrenalin and is often used instead of it.

Epidemic. A disease that attacks many people in one region at one time and spreads quickly from place to place.

Epidermis. The cuticle; the outermost layer of the skin. This forms a protective covering for the true skin or corium.

Epiglottis. The lidlike structure at the root of the tongue that partly covers the opening of the larynx.

Epilepsy. Epilepsy is a convulsive state manifested by the impairment of psychic factors such as consciousness, and involuntary movements of the muscles. Heredity seems to be a predisposing factor, however brain pathology developing after birth, certain diseases, and convulsant drugs may result in these seizures. Seizures may be so slight and transient as to be barely recognizable or be intense, prolonged convulsions. About half the patients have premonitions (aura) of a seizure. Two forms of the disease are called "grand mal" and "petit mal." The first is evidenced by its convulsive seizure and after-symptoms, the second by its abrupt onset and termination, lasting but a few seconds, and complete lack of after-symptoms.

Epistaxis. Nosebleed. Hemorrhage from the nose is caused by rupture of delicate blood vessels in the membranes lining this organ. It is caused by trauma, inflammation, or infection and generally runs a self-limited course. Severe bleeding from the nose can be stopped by the application of cold compresses and packing of the nostrils. Astringents are usually effective. A medical examination should be made to determine the cause of recurrent epistaxis.

Epithelioma. A malignant tumor derived from the skin or from the surface of a lining membrane.

Epithelium. The tissue, containing one or more layers of cells, which covers the exposed surfaces of the body and lines the cavities.

Epsom Salts. A mineral salt which, when taken internally, acts as a cathartic.

Ergosterol. This chemical substance, which occurs in small quantities in animals and plants and most plentifully in yeast, is believed to be the precursor of vitamin D; for although it has no antirachitic properties, it acquires all the properties of vitamin D on being exposed to ultraviolet radiation. The curative effect of ultraviolet baths on rickets can be explained by the fact that these baths convert the ergosterol contained in the skin to vitamin D which is absorbed into the general circulation.

Erysipelas. An acute contagious disease of the skin due to invasion of the surface lymphatic vessels by a virulent micro-organism, *Streptococcus erysipelatis*. The eruption appears as a spreading, rose-red patch that is slightly raised, owing to swelling of the underlying tissues. The patient feels very feverish and ill and suffers a burning pain and itching in the affected parts. In mild cases the redness and swelling begin to subside on about the fourth day and the patient is convalescent in a week. But in debilitated persons and in very old and very young patients the disease may take a more dangerous course. It may be attended by serious complications involving the kidneys, brain, or lungs. The disease is highly contagious, hence isolation is essential. Patients are kept at rest in bed and aspirin or other mild pain-killing drugs are given for pain. Cold packs are sometimes applied to the involved areas to alleviate pain. Copious quantities of fluids are given. The sulfa drugs and penicillin have proved effective in the treatment of erysipelas.

Erythema. Redness of the skin due to congestion of its blood vessels.

Estrogens. Phenolic compounds of biological or synthetic origin. When taken internally they may produce a variety of effects and the presence of more than the normal amount produces unnatural or toxic reactions.

Eugenics. The science of race improvement; the application of knowledge derived from all relevant fields—from genetics, medicine, sociology, and psychology—for the purpose of eliminating undesirable stocks from the human race and raising the general physical, mental and moral level of future generations.

Exanthema. Any eruptive disease; any fever accompanied by a rash.

Expectorant. Any medicine given for the purpose of promoting the ejection of phlegm from the lungs and bronchial tubes.

Extrasystole. A contraction of the heart, independent of the normal beat, which does not originate in the sino-auricular node.

F

Fainting. Temporary loss of consciousness due to anemia of the brain. The condition is treated by placing the patient in a recumbent position, lowering his head, loosening his clothing, sprinkling his face with cold water, and applying some stimulant to the nostrils, such as smelling salts or alcohol.

Favus. An infection of the skin and hair follicles by a parasitic fungus called *Achorion Schönleinii.* The eruption consists of round, cup-shaped crusts which form most frequently on the scalp, causing baldness, but may affect any part of the body. As the disease spreads, the indented crusts become continuous with each other and present a honeycomb appearance. The disease is difficult to cure, but by removing the crusts and exposing the skin to x-rays, good results are obtained in many cases.

Feces. Excrement; the waste matter that forms in and is discharged from the bowel.

Fetus. An unborn child during the last five or six months before birth.

Fever. Abnormally high body temperature; any disease of which such a temperature is a characteristic symptom.

Fibrinogen. A protein constituent of blood plasma essential in the coagulation of blood.

Fibroid. This term is usually applied to benign tumors of the uterus composed of fibrous and muscular tissue and separated from normal uterine tissue by a clearly defined capsule. The condition occurs most often in childless women over thirty, but many women who have borne children are also affected. Surgical removal is resorted to only if the fibroid is growing rapidly, or causing undesirable symptoms.

Fibroma. A benign tumor consisting mainly of fibrous tissue.

Fistula. An abnormal channel joining two hollow organs or a hollow organ and the surface of the body. If it has formed as a result of inflammation, a fistula is in effect a long, narrow, sinuous ulcer leading from one organ to another or from an organ to the skin. Thus a rectovesical fistula is an abnormal passage between the rectum and the bladder; and anal fistula is strictly speaking a passage joining the skin of the buttocks with the anus or rectum, but the term is applied loosely to any pus-containing tract formed in this region. Surgical repair by excision or cautery is the most effective treatment.

Fit. A convulsion or paroxysm such as occurs in epilepsy, apoplexy, brain diseases, etc. (See *Convulsions.*)

Flatfoot. This condition, characterized by flattening out of one or more of the arches of the foot, affects chiefly young persons whose work forces them to stand about a great deal or to carry heavy loads, and elderly individuals in whom the leg muscles have become weak. The arches of the feet are to a great extent supported by the muscles of the legs which send tendons down into the feet to support the bony structure. When this support is withdrawn the weight of the body rests upon small ligaments of the feet which hold the bones in alignment. Stretching of these ligaments under undue stress causes sagging and eventually flattening of the arches. Little can be done to correct the condition once it has developed; however, much can be done to alleviate pain and discomfort. The wearing of shoes that hold the arches to their former alignment, corrective exercises, and massage are most widely used.

Flatulence. Wind; distention of the stomach or intestines with air or gas. (See *Aerophagy.*)

Fluoroscope. An x-ray device used for diagnostic purposes, or for the location and identification of foreign bodies.

Focal Infection. A term applied to persistent infection which manifests its results elsewhere.

Folic Acid. One of the B-complex vitamins found in liver, yeast, and spinach. It has been effective in treating the leukopenia and anemia resulting from the administration of some drugs, but not in treating iron-deficiency anemias.

Fracture. A break or rupture of a bone, resulting most often from external violence, but occasionally from a sudden vigorous muscular contraction. Fractures may be classified in three groups: simple fractures, in which the bone is broken but no external wound is formed at the site of injury; compound fractures, in which, owing to laceration of the skin, a communication is established between the broken bone and the outer air; and comminuted fractures, in which the bone is broken in more than two pieces. Whatever the type of fracture, unskilled treatment or moving the patient unnecessarily may do more harm than good, and may turn a simple into a compound fracture. If, however, moving the patient before the doctor's arrival cannot be avoided, then care should be taken to prevent further injury to the patient by gently fixing a firm support to the affected limb so that motion between the parts cannot occur.

Frostbite. A condition due to the freezing of tissues when the cells are injured by formation of minute ice crystals. Cheeks, nose, ears, fingers, and toes are most usually involved. A sharp, prickling sensation in these areas is often the first sign. Abundant warm clothing, scrupulous dryness of clothing and skin, and liberal greasing of exposed areas help guard against frostbite. Frostbitten skin should not be rubbed with snow or warmed too rapidly. A sensitivity of the affected parts to cold may remain.

G

Gallbladder. The pear-shaped sac that acts as a reservoir for the bile secreted by the liver.

Gallstones. (See *Calculus.*)

Ganglion. A cystlike swelling formed in connection with a joint or the sheath of a tendon. The most usual site of ganglion is the back of the wrist where it forms a round elastic tumor containing a gelatinous semisolid substance. Surgical excision is usually necessary to correct the condition.

Gangrene. The death and degeneration of a tissue brought about by interference with its blood supply and a subsequent invasion by saprophytic organisms.

Gastric. Pertaining to the stomach. Thus, gastric ulcer means ulcer of the stomach.

Gastritis. Inflammation of the stomach, a condition which may arise acutely as a result of eating indigestible or decomposing food, or chronically as a result of excessive drinking of alcoholic beverages, or infection of the lining membrane of the stomach by pathogenic micro-organisms. The common symptoms are pain, vomiting, flatulence, and loss of appetite. (See *Dyspepsia.*)

Gastroenteritis. Inflammation of the stomach and intestines, sometimes caused by the consumption of trichinous pork.

Gastroscope. An instrument that enables the user to see the interior of the stomach in living patients. It consists of a slender metal tube fitted with a system of mirrors and lenses, and is lowered into position through the esophagus. It has greatly simplified the diagnosis of digestive pathology.

Geriatrics. A branch of medicine which deals with the problems of the aged. It is divided into two main categories: the medical problems associated with the normal aging process, and those associated with the effects of disease in older persons, insofar as they differ from those in younger people.

Gestation. The period of time in which the embryo develops in the uterus, covering the time from conception until birth.

Gingivitis. Inflammation of the gums, a common but serious condition which may be recognized by the swollen and red appearance of the gum margin and the fact that slight pressure causes bleeding. Gingivitis is far more easily prevented than cured. Regular brushing of the teeth ordinarily aids in maintaining healthy gums, but if overdone or if too stiff a brush is used, inflammation is likely to occur. Gingivitis may also result from mouth infections and vitamin deficiencies.

Gland. This term is used in several senses, but mainly to denote an organ that manufactures a physiologically active fluid. Thus, the salivary gland manufactures saliva, which helps to digest starch; the breast manufactures milk; the liver, bile; the thyroid gland, thyroxin. Glands which pour their products into the blood stream are called glands of internal secretion or endocrine glands; glands supplied with a duct through which their products pass to some other organ are called glands of external secretion. The name gland is also given to such organs as the spleen which do not seem to manufacture any secretions, but are glandular in structure.

Glaucoma. A disease of the eye marked by great increase of pressure within the eyeball. Symptoms suggesting the onset of glaucoma are pain in the eye, dilatation of the pupils, intense headache, dimness of vision, and a sensation of haloes about distant lights. An immediate operation is essential to save the eyesight in acute cases, but medical treatment is available for less severe and chronic cases.

Goiter. A noninflammatory enlargement of the thyroid body, a ductless gland situated in front of and on either side of the windpipe. There are different kinds of thyroid disease, each producing characteristic symptoms. In simple goiter, the swelling and consequent pressure on neighboring structures are the only symptoms. Surgical removal may be required to relieve the pressure or for cosmetic reasons. In exophthalmic goiter, or hyperthyroidism, symptoms result from an excessive secretion of the thyroid gland. Retraction of the eyelids producing the characteristic bulging of the eyes, irritability, rapid pulse, and muscular tremors are all evidence of an overactive thyroid. In both diseases, iodine deficiency is a contributing factor. Hypothyroidism is the result of either the deficiency or complete lack of the thyroid hormone. It may start at any time, even before birth. Thyroid tablets which contain standardized amounts of thyroid and iodine are used in treatment.

Gonorrhea. A venereal disease caused by the gonococcus *Neisseria gonorrhoeae.* This organism causes acute inflammation of the lining of the genito-urinary tract with attendant symptoms of pain and discharge. The disease is usually spread through sexual intercourse. Frequent complications involving the heart and joints, as well as the genito-urinary organs, make gonorrhea a crippling disease. In females it often produces sterility. Local treatment consists of the application of germicidal preparations. Chronic cases are treated by diathermy or by other means of inducing artificial fever. Sulfanilamide has proved to be a valuable therapeutic agent in the treatment of gonorrhea, often eradicating the infection within a week. Penicillin and streptomycin have also been used effectively.

Gout. A disease characterized by an excess of uric acid in the blood, the formation of chalky deposits in the joints and elsewhere in the body, and attacks of acute and very painful arthritis. Painful swelling of the large toe is usually the first sign of gout. Treatment is largely dietary, uric-acid-forming foods and drinks, especially red meat, sweetbreads, liver, tea, coffee, cocoa, malt liquors and strong wines being eliminated from the diet. Certain drugs, notably colchicum, cinchophen, and neocinchophen, are useful for preventing and relieving attacks, but these must be administered by a physician because of the dangers associated with their use.

Gramicidin. An antibiotic effective against Gram-positive cocci and Gram-negative bacilli. It is not suitable for systemic administration because of its toxic effects.

Granulation. A process of healing which involves formation of small conical projections on the surface of an open wound or on the base of an ulcer during the process of repair.

Gynecology. That branch of medicine that is concerned with the diseases peculiar to women, especially of the female genital tract and the structures and glands connected with it.

H

Halitosis. A condition of offensive breath. The most common causes are atrophic rhinitis, pyorrhea, dental caries, follicular tonsillitis, and adenoids.

Hallucination. (See *Delusion.*)

Hammer Toe. A clawlike deformity of the toe as a result of which the first joint sticks up, pressing against the upper leather of the shoe, while the tip of the toe or even the nail points downward. In this condition abnormal pressure is exerted upon the toe, causing pain and crippling. The condition can be corrected by surgery.

Harelip. A congenital cleft in one or both lips, usually in the upper lip only. Surgery is the only effective treatment.

Hay Fever. A form of allergy affecting the respiratory system.

Headache. This, like so many other common disorders, should not be regarded as a single disease for all cases of which the treatment is more or less the same, but as a symptom that may appear in the course of many diseases, some very severe, others trivial and of short duration. Digestive disturbances of all kinds, including gastritis and constipation, eyestrain, anemia, the circulation in the blood of toxins derived from some focus of infection, fever, working under conditions of poor lighting and ventilation, diseases of the brain—these among many other conditions, are causes of headaches. If headaches are frequent and severe a thorough examination should be undertaken to determine their causes. Permanent relief can be obtained in most cases by treating the fundamental disorder which is accompanied by headache; temporary relief can be had by resorting to the use of an analgesic drug. The latter procedure is advisable when headaches are mild and infrequent but should not be substituted for an attempt to find the primary pathology in severe headaches.

Heart. The muscular organ which is situated in the chest between the lungs, is the great pump by the action of which the blood is circulated throughout the body. It consists of four chambers, known respectively as the right auricle, the right ventricle, the left auricle, and the left ventricle. The walls of the auricles are comparatively thin, those of the ventricles are thick, especially those of the left ventricle, which is the largest of the chambers. The chambers of the right side are completely shut off from those of the left by a partition, so that it is impossible, except in certain abnormal conditions, for blood to pass directly from one side of the heart to the other. Each auricle communicates freely with its corresponding ventricle, but between the two a system of valves is disposed in such a manner that blood can flow only from the auricle to the ventricle, and not in the opposite direction. Leading into the right auricle are the two great veins, called the superior and inferior vena cava, through which blood is poured into the heart from all parts of the body. The right ventricle communicates with the pulmonary artery, from which, in turn, blood is conveyed to the great capillary networks that permeate the lungs. Blood is forced into this artery from the right ventricle at each heartbeat. The left auricle communicates with the pulmonary veins, through which blood, having been oxygenated, is returned from the lungs to the heart. The left ventricle leads directly to the aorta, the great arterial trunk along which oxygen-carrying blood is pumped to every organ, member and tissue of the body. Valves at the base of the pulmonary artery and the aorta prevent blood from flowing back into the heart, once it has been forced out into these vessels by contraction of the ventricles. The sequence of events at each heartbeat is as follows. First the two auricles contract together, this phase of heart action being known as auricular systole. As a result of their contraction blood is forced from the right auricle into the right ventricle, and from the left auricle into the left ventricle. Now follows the phase of ventricular systole, when both the ventricles contract, the right ventricle forcing blood into the pulmonary artery and the left into the aorta. The disposition of the valves between the auricles and the ventricles prevents the return of blood to the auricles during this phase of the heartbeat. Ventricular systole is followed by a relaxation of the heart, a phase of diastole in which the heart rests before going through the whole cycle of contractions all over again. This process—auricular systole, ventricular systole, diastole—is repeated incessantly so long as life persists. In a normal adult at rest it completes itself on an average of 72 times a minute, each cycle of changes occupying about four-fifths of a second. (See *Aorta, Artery, Blood Pressure, Diastole, Systole,* and *Circulation.*

Heartburn. A burning sensation in the lower part of the esophagus due to regurgitation of acid stomach contents.

Heart Disease. Disease processes may attack any part of the heart. The chief causes of heart disease are rheumatic fever, syphilis, arteriosclerosis, and hypertension. Infection may begin in the lining membrane, the heart muscle, or in the pericardial sac in which the heart is contained. Most frequently, microscopic organisms lodge in the delicate tissues of the heart valves and cause anatomic changes which interfere with the function of these structures. The mitral valve, which separates the left auricle and left ventricle, and aortic valve, between the left ventricle and the aorta, are the parts most often involved. As a result of disease processes the valves become incompetent and blood regurgitates or "leaks" back against the direction of flow of the general circulation. As a result the chamber into which this leakage occurs becomes enlarged with the additional blood and general circulation is slowed. To compensate for this deficiency the heart rate accelerates and the leaking chamber contracts with greater force in an attempt to maintain the circulation. In this way the heart may completely compensate for the defect and the patient may be unaware of the disorder except on exertion. Such individuals may lead normal lives unless the process is progressive. Disease processes may attack the coronary blood vessels, that supply the heart muscle with blood. These small vessels may become narrowed and occluded, producing the symptoms of angina pectoris and acute heart failure. In all forms of heart disease rest is the basic treatment. Much can be done to alleviate symptoms of circulatory failure and prevent further damage to the heart in the early stages of heart disease.

Heart Failure. The symptoms that result when from any cause—for example, weakness of the muscle, of incompetence of the valves—the heart becomes incapable of carrying out its task of maintaining the circulation of the blood. Shortness of breath on slight exertion and swelling of the ankles are usually the earliest signs, but as the failure of the heart progresses, symptoms due to congestion of the lungs, liver and kidneys make their appearance. In its popular sense, the term heart failure denotes sudden and fatal cessation of the heart's action.

Heat Stroke. A condition caused by exposure to excessive heat. Two forms are recognized: sunstroke, which, as a rule, comes on suddenly, and is accompanied by a rapid rise of temperature; and heat exhaustion, the principal symptoms of which are dizziness, excessive sweating, and a feeling of weakness.

Heliotherapy. The treatment of disease by exposing the body, wholly or in part, to the sun's rays. These rays, by virtue of their invisible ultraviolet component, excite chemical changes as a result of which vitamin D is generated in the skin, and the blood becomes richer in calcium and phosphorus, and more capable than it was before of destroying disease-producing germs. Heliotherapy is used extensively for the treatment of surgical tuberculosis, especially of the bones, glands, joints and abdomen, and of rickets, a disease caused by lack of vitamin D, in which the blood is grossly deficient in calcium and phosphorus.

Hematemesis. Vomiting of blood, a symptom that may appear in the course of a number of diseases, including gastric ulcer, cancer of the stomach, cirrhosis of the liver, and certain blood diseases.

Hematoma. A localized swelling containing fluid or clotted blood.

Hematuria. The presence of blood in the urine. This may appear in the course of a number of diseases of the urinary tract, including inflammations, tumors and stone of the bladder or kidneys, enlargement of the prostate gland, and irritation of the membranes by certain drugs. Among the general diseases of which hematuria is an occasional symptom may be mentioned heart disease, anemia and blood diseases. Treatment must be directed to removing the underlying cause.

Hemiplegia. Paralysis of one side of the body.

Hemoglobin. (See *Anemia.*)

Hemophilia. (See *Bleeder.*)

Hemoptysis. Spitting of blood. This is often an outstanding symptom of pulmonary pathology, as in the majority of cases the blood comes from the lungs and is usually the result of pulmonary tuberculosis. Gastric ulcer, cancer of the stomach, cirrhosis of the liver, and many other diseases may also cause hemoptysis. Because of the serious condition that it may signify, hemoptysis, no matter how slight, should always warrant a complete medical examination.

Hemorrhage. Bleeding; a discharge of blood from the blood vessels.

Hemorrhoids. (See *Piles.*)

Hepatic. Pertaining to the liver.

Hepatitis. Inflammation of the liver.

Heredity. The transmission of qualities from parents or ancestors to their offspring.

Hernia. A rupture; the protrusion of an organ or of a portion of an organ through a breach in the wall of the cavity of tissue in which it is contained. The most common type is abdominal hernia, in which a loop of intestine bulges outward through a weak point in the abdominal wall. The usual sites are the inguinal regions and the area around the navel. Hernias occur also internally, through the diaphragm and elsewhere. Hernias result from a weakness in structure subjected to a sudden stress, usually unexpected. Lifting heavy objects is the most frequent cause of hernia. Abdominal hernia causes local discomfort and general fatigue, and limits physical activity. Some hernias can be controlled by means of a mechanical support or truss, but permanent cure in adults is available only through surgical repair of the tissues involved. Hernias often cause acute abdominal conditions when they become strangulated, with consequent obstruction of the intestine and death of the tissue from failure of the blood supply. Operation is then imperative.

Heroin. An artificial derivative of morphine. It is a powerful respiratory depressant. Its dangerous addiction liability led to the prohibition of its importation and manufacture in the United States by an Act of Congress.

Herpes. Shingles; an acute and extremely painful skin disease marked by an eruption of blisters, usually along the course of one of the nerves of the skin. It is caused by an inflammatory process involving the nerve root where it leaves the spinal cord.

Histamine and Antihistamine. Histamines are the decomposition products of histidine, and are normally found in the tissues of animals and vegetables. Antihistamines are drugs which counteract the action of these histamines. The most widely known are benadryl, particularly useful in the treatment of hives, and pyrebenzamine, successful in counteracting many allergies.

Hives. A skin condition which is characterized by the appearance of whitish areas, or wheals which itch severely.

Hodgkin's Disease. (See *Lymphadenoma.*)

Hormone. (See *Gland.*)

Hormones. Secretions of the endocrine glands. The complete action of these substances is not yet known, but they affect the activity of the glands which produce them and also are carried through the body and act upon other organs.

Hydrocephalus. A condition in which the fluid circulating through brain and spinal cord is increased in amount and thus exerts an abnormal pressure on the brain substance and the cranium. The disease is marked by enlargement of the head, atrophy of the brain matter, mental disorders and convulsions.

Hydrophobia. Rabies; an infectious disease caused by a virus present in the saliva of infected animals, usually dogs, and transmitted by the bite of these animals to man. The incubation period varies considerably, the average being fifty to sixty days. Fever, restlessness, insomnia, and melancholy are first to appear but are shortly followed by typical convulsive seizures, vicelike contractions of the throat muscles, and respiratory difficulties. Death usually occurs in two or three days. A paralytic type occurs also and is evidenced by a high fever, pain in the region of the bite, and finally a general paralysis and death. Once the symptoms of either type have become evident, death is inevitable. Treatment consists of destruction of the virus at the time of injury, and immunization. Any animal should be considered rabid until proved otherwise. The biting animal should not be killed but should be kept under observation so that diagnosis of rabies can be confirmed or excluded. Suppressive measures such as the destruction of all ownerless dogs and restraint of dogs by owners have been helpful in lowering the incidence of this disease.

I

Icterus. (See *Jaundice.*)

Ileum. (See *Intestine.*)

Immunity. The power of the living organism to resist and overcome disease. Every living creature is subject to stresses and strains, to the action of poisons and parasites, of chemical and physical agents, which, unresisted, would inevitably destroy it. Living organisms have necessarily developed all kinds of expedients for defeating their enemies and overcoming attacks on their health and vitality; immunity is essentially this ability to combat disease. Immunity may be congenital or acquired, partial or complete, active or passive. Some races and persons are born with a resistance to certain diseases; subjected to influences which would produce these diseases in susceptible persons, they remain unaffected; they have a *congenital* immunity. Where, however, this desirable state is lacking, an immunity can still be acquired. Persons who have suffered from certain infectious diseases appear to be insusceptible to a further attack; similarly, persons who have been inoculated with vaccines do not contract the diseases from the germs of which these vaccines have been made. They have, in short, an acquired immunity. When immunity exists or is developed in the organism's own cells, tissues or tissue fluids, it is called active; when it depends not on these natural defenses but upon the injection of a serum obtained from an immune animal or person, it is called passive. Examples of active immunity are the protection afforded by one attack of measles against further attacks of the same disease, or by vaccination against smallpox; serum treatment of diphtheria or for prevention of lockjaw, on the other hand, are examples of passive immunity.

Impetigo. A superficial inflammation of the skin marked by the eruption of isolated pustules and blisters. It is contagious.

Indigestion. (See *Dyspepsia* and *Gastric Ulcer.*)

Infantile Paralysis. (See *Poliomyelitis.*)

Infection. Invasion of the body by disease-producing organisms.

Inflammation. The changes that occur within living tissues when they are irritated by micro-organisms, heat, cold, poisons, or any other chemical or physical agents. Inflammation should be regarded as one of the processes by which the living body mobilizes its forces for the purpose of meeting and overcoming potential infection. The redness and heat are due to the increased amount of blood supplied to the irritated area; swelling occurs when blood fluid and cells leave the vessels and accumulate in the tissues, and pain results from the pressure exerted by the fluid and cells upon the nerves. As a result of these changes the irritating organisms are walled off from normal tissue and are destroyed by tissue cells. New tissue grows in to replace that destroyed by the inflammatory process and eventually healing is complete. If the invading organisms are numerous and powerful or if the resistance of the host is low, suppuration and even gangrene may ensue. Constitutional symptoms such as fever, wasting, loss of appetite, indigestion, constipation, and occasionally exhaustion and collapse, usually accompany severe inflammation.

Influenza. An acute infectious disease marked by fever, inflammation of the respiratory tract, and sometimes of the stomach and intestines, pains in the limbs, intense headache, prostration and depression. Influenza is believed to be caused by a filtrable virus, an ultramicroscopic micro-organism; but there is some evidence that a bacillus, *Haemophilus influenzae*, may also play a role in producing the disease. Influenza, or grippe as it is sometimes called, is highly contagious and occurs frequently in epidemic form. It is often complicated by pneumonia and infections of the ear. Heat, rest, antipyretic drugs, and fluids are the basis of treatment.

Inoculation. (See *Immunity.*)

Insomnia. The physiology of sleep is not thoroughly understood but much has been learned that is of practical value in the treatment of insomnia. Habit is perhaps the most important factor in obtaining normal sleep. Irregularity in the retiring hour soon destroys the sleep habit. Second, there must be a need for sleep. Daily physical activity should be sufficient to create a desire for sleep at the end of each day. Third, the immediate environment must be conducive to sleep and free from disturbing influences. Quietude, darkness, comfortable sleeping quarters and clothing, all contribute to undisturbed sleep. Fourth, mental as well as physical relaxation is essential to normal sleep: subjective factors such as worry, anxiety, tenseness, etc., must be completely suppressed. The majority of cases of insomnia will respond favorably to treatment aimed at fulfilling the foregoing conditions. Others obtain relief by taking warm drinks at bedtime. When insomnia has existed for a long period of time soporific drugs may be used to advantage in re-establishing the sleep habit. Because of serious reactions that sometimes occur, and the danger of becoming addicted to the use of these drugs, they should be used only when prescribed by a physician. A medical examination should always be made to determine the cause of persistent insomnia before recourse is had to this method of obtaining sleep.

Insulin. The internal secretion or hormone of the pancreas. It is commercially prepared from slaughter-house animals for use in the treatment of diabetes mellitus. Injected daily into diabetic patients it lowers the level of the blood sugar and promotes normal metabolism of fats and carbohydrates. (See *Diabetes.*)

Intestine. The bowel; that part of the alimentary tract which extends from the stomach to the anus. In a normal human adult the intestine is a long tube of which the first portion, known as the small intestine, is narrow and about twenty feet long, and the second, known as the large intestine, is wider but only about five feet long. The small intestine is further subdivided into the duodenum, the jejunum, and the ileum; and the large intestine into the cecum, the colon, and the rectum. In their minute structure the different parts of the intestine differ from each other in important respects; certain glands are found only in the membrane lining the inside of the duodenum, certain agglomerations of lymphatic tissue only in the inner lining membrane of the ileum. These differences of structure correspond with differences of function, each subdivision of the intestine playing its own part in the process of digestion.

Iritis. Inflammation of the iris, the circular muscle surrounding the pupil and forming the colored part of the eye. Injury, rheumatism, the venereal diseases, tuberculosis and other infections, are capable of producing this condition, of which the chief symptoms are pain, congestion of the affected region, contraction of the pupil, and abnormal intolerance to light.

Irradiation. Treatment by x-rays, ultraviolet rays, radium, or any other form of biologically active radiation. (See *Actinotherapy*, *Heliotherapy*, *X-rays* and *Radium.*)

Itch. (See *Scabies.*)

J

Jaundice. Yellowness of the skin, eyes, mucous membranes and bodily secretions, due to the presence of bile pigments in the blood. Such a condition may be brought about in three ways; by the excessive destruction of red blood cells, such as occurs, for example, in pernicious anemia, and results in the presence of bile pigments in the blood serum; by the destruction of liver cells, whether produced by chemical or bacterial poisons; and by obstruction from any cause of the flow of bile from the liver. Besides the characteristic jaundiced appearance, to which is given the name icterus, other symptoms due to excess of bile pigments in the blood are a slow pulse, itching, constipation, and the passage of highly colored urine. Treatment varies according to the cause of the condition.

Jejunum. (See *Intestine.*)

K

Katabolism. (See *Anabolism.*)

Keratitis. Inflammation of the cornea, the transparent horny structure that forms the anterior covering of the eyeball.

Kidney Stones. Hard, round or irregular bodies usually formed in the pelvis of the kidney. They are formed from ordinary urinary constituents which under normal conditions remain in solution. Minute, smooth stones may be passed without symptoms, but when a stone obstructs the urinary passage, the excruciating pain of renal colic occurs. The stones may pass spontaneously or special urologic and surgical procedures may be necessary.

Kidneys. Two glandular organs situated on either side of the spinal column and beneath the lowermost ribs. In a man of average size each kidney is about four inches long, two inches wide and one inch thick; it weighs about 4½ ounces. On the side facing the spinal column is a notch called the hilum, communicating with which are the urinary duct (known as the ureter), and the arteries, veins and nerves of the kidney. The structure of the kidney is very complicated: under the microscope it is seen to consist of large numbers of capillary blood vessels that come into intimate relationship with long twisted glands known as uriniferous tubules. The latter separate waste products and water from arterial blood that is pumped through the kidneys by the action of the heart; and the urine thus formed trickles into the ureter, by way of which it reaches the bladder.

Kyphosis. Humpback; a condition in which the backbone sticks out prominently, usually in its upper part, the common causes being rickets, poor posture, especially among rapidly growing children, occupations that necessitate carrying heavy weights or continually bending over a desk or bench, and certain general and local diseases and injuries of the spine.

L

Labor. Childbirth; the process of bringing forth a child. (See *Birth.*)

Lactation. Suckling; the secretion of milk by the breast. Normally this secretion begins on the second or third day after labor, the quantity of milk gradually increasing as the days go by and being maintained at a sufficiently high level to meet the infant's needs during the following six to nine months.

Lanugo. The fine, soft hair covering the body of the fetus.

Laryngitis. Inflammation of the larynx or organ of voice, a condition marked by hoarseness, cough, a dry and sore throat, and pain on swallowing. In its acute form, laryngitis usually arises from infections of the mouth, nose, and throat. It appears also as a complication of diphtheria, measles, and sometimes of other infectious fevers. Chronic laryngitis is in some cases a sequel to the acute form of the disease. It occurs also from prolonged overuse of the voice. Complete loss of voice sometimes occurs as a result of laryngitis but the function of speech usually returns when the inflammation recedes. Abstinence from speech is an essential part of the treatment of the acute inflammation.

Leprosy. Also known as Hansen's Disease. This is a chronic communicable disease affecting the skin and nerves. Its incidence is world-wide, but it occurs most often in tropical and subtropical countries. It is not considered to be either hereditary or congenital. The onset of the disease is usually insidious and early symptoms are variable. The appearance of nodules accentuating the natural folds of the skin and gradually transforming them into masses of thickened folds is typical. When this nodular tissue breaks down, great deformity and mutilation result. The sulfone drugs have become the drugs of choice.

Lesion. Any wound, injury, or degeneration in an organ or tissue.

Leucoplakia. This name is given to white, thickened, horny patches that appear on the tongue as a result of chronic irritation, such as may be produced by excessive smoking. These areas sometimes become malignant.

Leucorrhea. A white sticky discharge from the uterus and vagina, resulting from infection in these parts.

Leukemia. A rare disease in which there is an enormous increase in the number of white cells in the blood, together with a swelling and multiplication of lymph cells in the spleen, lymph glands, and bone marrow. As the disease progresses, hemorrhages occur in all parts of the body, and the patient becomes more and more anemic and exhausted. Roentgen therapy, radioactive phosphorus, urethane, blood transfusions, antibiotics, and ACTH and cortisone may be used as therapeutic measures, but no definite cure has been discovered.

Leukocytosis. An increase in the number of white cells in the blood. Such a condition occurs normally during digestion, the number of white cells in each cubic millimeter of blood being greater after than before meals. It is significant in that it develops also in the course of various fevers, diseases, inflammation, and in certain types of blood disease.

Ligaments. Bands of tissue which connect bones or support organs. The stretching or tearing of a ligament is called a strain or a sprain.

Liniments. Preparations for external application in which the active principle is usually a counterirritant.

Lipoma. A benign tumor made up of fat cells.

Liver. A large glandular organ, dark red in color, situated in the upper part of the abdomen, mainly on the right side. Its upper surface is dome-shaped and fits up against the diaphragm. Emerging from its under surface are two ducts by way of which bile manufactured in the liver can pass into the gallbladder and into the intestine. The gallbladder is closely applied to the under surface and serves as a reservoir for bile. The liver receives a supply of blood from two sources: ordinary oxygen-carrying blood direct from the heart by way of a vessel called the hepatic artery; and blood carrying the products of digestion from the intestine by way of a vessel called the portal vein. All its blood, however, is returned to the heart by way of the hepatic veins. Within the liver occur many of the processes that are essential to health and life; bile is manufactured, sugars are stored up in the form of glycogen, urea is separated from the products of protein digestion, and certain tissue poisons are destroyed.

Lockjaw. Tetanus; an acute disease of the nervous system caused by a toxin liberated by the tetanus bacillus, a germ that exists in soil, manure, garden mold and road dirt, and finds its way into wounds contaminated by these materials. The earliest symptom is stiffness of the jaw and of muscles in the throat and neck. Soon after, the jaw muscles become fixed and the patient is no longer able to open his mouth. The muscles of the back, chest, and abdomen are the next to become rigid, and violent spasms of the muscles begin, which eventually prevent respiration so that death from asphyxia results. The disease can be prevented by the injection of tetanus antitoxin shortly after a wound likely to be contaminated with tetanus bacilli has been incurred. An active immunization may be achieved by a series of injections with tetanus toxoid and it is urged that children, farmers, and artisans be thus protected.

Lordosis. Abnormal curvature of the spine with a convexity toward the front of the body.

Lungs. The organs of respiration, two large spongy organs that fill the greater part of the chest. They are made up of numerous very small air cells that are surrounded by a network of capillaries and communicate directly or indirectly with branches of the bronchial tubes. Air passing into the air sacs by way of these tubes conveys oxygen to the blood circulating through the capillaries and from it receives the carbon dioxide that has formed in the tissues as a waste product. The effect of inspiration, therefore, is to charge the blood circulating through the lungs with a fresh supply of oxygen; the effect of expiration is to expel unwanted carbon dioxide from the system. Each lung is enveloped by a saclike membrane called the pleura, the layers of which are in contact with each other, but covered with just enough lubricating fluid to enable the movements of expansion and retraction to be carried out freely and without pain. The right lung is made up of three lobes, the left of two. These lobes in their turn are formed from smaller structures called lobules, each of which consists of a collection of air sacs surrounded by capillaries, lymphatic vessels, nerves, and connective tissue, and communicates directly with a branch of a bronchial tube.

Lymphadenoma, or Hodgkin's Disease. A comparatively common disease in which there is a painless progressive enlargement of the lymph nodes. Often the spleen is enlarged and lymphatic tissue throughout the body is involved. Anemia may occur in the late stages. The cause of the disease is unknown and the prognosis unfavorable. Nitrogen mustard and x-ray therapy are the usual choice of treatment. Cortisone and ACTH may reduce the size of the spleen and lymph nodes. Blood transfusions may be given as a supportive treatment.

M

Malaria. A febrile disease caused by a parasite which is conveyed to the body by the bite of an infected mosquito. Only female mosquitoes of the genus *Anopheles* transmit the disease. The fever recurs periodically every day, every other day, or every third day, according to the nature of the infecting parasite. The first symptom of a typical malarial attack is chill, this being followed by a stage of high fever and finally of sweating. If this sequence of events takes place every day, the disease is called quotidian; if every other day, it is called tertian; and if every third day, quartan. Malaria is further classified into two main varieties, a benign and a malignant—the former rarely fatal, the latter having a fairly high mortality. All types of malaria respond to quinine and quinine substitutes, such as atabrine. The drugs chloroquine and pentaquine have been found very effective.

Marijuana. A narcotic drug obtained from the leaves of the hemp plant and often used illegally in cigarettes.

Mastitis. Inflammation of the breast. Like other inflammations, this condition may be acute or chronic, the former occurring most commonly in recently confined women, probably as a result of an invasion of the breast by germs that made their way through a cracked nipple, the latter in women at all ages, but especially in those at or near the change of life. The condition is very painful and requires surgical incision and drainage. The chronic forms may predispose to malignant growths in the breast.

Measles. A contagious disease marked by fever, an eruption of pink spots, catarrh of the respiratory tract and inflammation of the eyes. It occurs in epidemics, attacking chiefly young persons, though very rarely infants under six months old. One attack seems to confer a lasting immunity, a fact which suggests that persons who have had measles possess in their blood substances that are able to neutralize the virus to which the disease is due. An injection of blood taken from a convalescent patient will cut short an attack and reduce the likelihood of dangerous complications. This expedient has also been used for preventing measles in children who have been exposed; but by waiting until the disease has developed and then injecting the serum, it is possible to ensure both a mild attack and active immunity, rendering the child insusceptible to a second attack of the disease. (See *Immunity.*)

Medulla Oblongata. The cone-shaped portion of the central nervous system that is continuous with the spinal cord below and the pons above. The nerve centers that determine and control the movements of the heart, lungs, and the walls of blood vessels, and such physiologically important acts as swallowing, vomiting, and glandular secretion are all situated within or closely connected with this small nervous structure, which regulates the essential functions of life. (See *Pons* and *Spinal Column.*)

Meningitis. Inflammation of the membranes that envelop the brain and spinal cord. The acute form of this serious disease, which may be due to tuberculosis or infection by other disease-producing organisms, especially such organisms as may reach the brain by extension from an inflamed ear or other neighboring organ, is marked by high fever, chills, intense headache, vomiting, delirium, abnormal intolerance to light, and such symptoms as spasm and paralysis of groups of muscles, due to irritation of the nerve cells on the surface of the brain. Epidemic cerebrospinal meningitis, known commonly as spotted fever, occurs in epidemics and seems to be transmitted to susceptible persons by healthy carriers. (See *Carriers.*) The sulfa drugs, penicillin, and streptomycin are given, the choice of drug depending on the type of infecting organism.

Menopause. (See *Change of Life.*)

Menorrhagia. Excessive bleeding. It may be caused by a number of conditions including inflammation of the lining membrane of the uterus, a fibroid growth, and an abnormality in the internal secretions manufactured by the ovaries. The cause of menorrhagia should be determined without delay as serious pathology may be present.

Menstruation. The monthly discharge from the uterus that begins at puberty and terminates with the change of life.

Metabolism. (See *Anabolism.*)

Miscarriage. (See *Abortion.*)

Morphine. The chief active ingredient of opium. It is a powerful pain killer, but its use is limited by danger of addiction.

Motion Sickness. Illness resulting from the motion peculiar to riding. Examples are car, train, sea, and air sickness. Dramamine has been effective as a preventive.

Mucous Membrane. A thin layer of tissue lining those tracts and cavities of the body that communicate with the external air—for example, the respiratory tract, the stomach, the bowel, and the urinary tract—and secreting a sticky fluid called mucus that serves to protect it.

Multiple Sclerosis. (See *Sclerosis.*)

Mumps. A contagious disease marked by swelling of the large salivary glands in the mouth, the testes, and the breasts. While it lasts the condition is extremely painful, but fortunately the symptoms subside after a few days and gradually disappear. One attack confers immunity.

Myocarditis. Inflammation of the heart muscle, a condition that occurs acutely in the course of rheumatic fever, and in a chronic form, leading to progressive degeneration of the muscular tissue, as a result of alcoholism, syphilis, Bright's disease, high blood pressure, chronic bronchitis and emphysema. (See *Heart Failure.*)

Myxedema. One of the conditions due to degeneration of the thyroid gland and deficiency of its internal secretion, thyroxin, in the blood. In adults this deficiency produces myxedema; in infants, cretinism. Myxedema is commonest in middle-aged persons. The patient's skin becomes thickened, puffy and dry; his hands and feet become broad and "spadelike"; his hair falls out; mentally he becomes dull and apathetic, and his movements become sluggish and languid. The regular administration of dried thyroid gland or thyroid extract produces striking disappearance of these symptoms. (See *Cretinism.*)

N

Narcolepsy. A rare condition in which the patient is seized at intervals with an uncontrollable desire for sleep. Its cause is unknown and it is treated by the administration of stimulating drugs.

Narcotic. Any drug or treatment given to induce sleep or stupor and to relieve pain.

Necrosis. The death of a limited portion of tissue, such as occurs, for example, when an organ or a part of an organ is deprived of its blood supply. The term has a very wide application and covers conditions in which the death of tissue results from infections, heat and cold, poisoning, and the action of other biological, chemical, and physical agents.

Negativism. This term is applied to the mental state of persons who feel a compulsion to do just the opposite of what is asked or expected of them. In its extreme form it leads to the patient's resisting even his own desires, denying himself food, for example, or refusing, despite great discomfort, to empty his bowel. Children against whom authority often has been harshly or inconsistently exercised often develop negativistic traits.

Neomycin. An antibiotic proposed for use in the treatment of tuberculosis and other mixed infections.

Neoplasm. Any abnormal new growth or formation of tissue. Thus, cancer is a neoplasm, and so is an adenoma; the former is malignant; the latter, benign.

Nephritis. Inflammation of the kidney. The acute form of this disease is described in the section on Bright's Disease. A chronic form, called chronic interstitial nephritis, occurs in persons who have at some time been attacked by the acute disease or poisoned by alcohol or lead, or have suffered from gout. Weakness, headaches, shortness of breath, dizziness and diarrhea, and the passage of copious amounts of light-colored urine are the predominant symptoms. The need to empty the bladder arouses the patient from his sleep once, twice, or even more often every night. In all cases, the arteries degenerate, the blood pressure is raised above the normal level, and the heart enlarges. Skilled medical treatment and a hygienic mode of life can do much to mitigate the symptoms of chronic interstitial nephritis, but the damage to renal tissue is permanent.

Nerve. A connective tissue, cordlike in structure, conveying impulses from one part of the body to another. The nervous system consists of two parts—the central nervous system made up of the brain and the spinal cord, and the peripheral nervous system made up of the nerves. The latter are cordlike structures that convey impulses to and from the central nervous system. Nerves that carry impulses toward the nerve centers are called "afferent" nerves; those that carry impulses from the nerve centers are called "efferent."

Neuralgia. Pain felt along the course of a nerve, the term being applied somewhat loosely to any severe throbbing pain for which no organic cause can be found. Organic disease, however, is frequently the source of neuralgia as, for example, an abscessed tooth may cause a facial neuralgia; similarly, in neuralgia of the chest the cause sometimes lies in inflammation in or near the spine exerting pressure on the nerves as they emerge from the spinal cord.

Neuritis. Inflammation of a nerve or of nerves, a condition marked by pain and tenderness along the course of the nerve trunks, paralysis and wasting of muscles, and numbness, tingling and other disturbances of sensation. Diabetes, diphtheria, gout, alcoholism, and poisoning by arsenic or lead are among the conditions that may in some cases give rise to neuritis. Treatment is directed to removing the underlying cause, but massage, electrical stimulation, exercise, splinting, and pain-relieving drugs are prescribed for the purpose of mitigating the symptoms and the effects of neuritis.

Neurosis. A functional nervous disorder.

Nevus. A pigmented place on the skin.

Niacin or nicotinic acid. A vitamin used for the prevention and treatment of pellagra.

Night Blindness. Subnormal or lack of vision in dim light. It is caused by the slow regeneration or lack of visual purple in the retinal rods after exposure to light. Night blindness is usually traced to vitamin A deficiency, although hereditary factors may be involved. Treatment consists of correction of the cause of deficiency and vitamin administration.

Nullipara. A woman who has never given birth to a child.

Nystagmus. Involuntary jerking movements of the eyes that occur occasionally in association with some organic disease of the nervous system. The condition appears in coal miners and other persons who do long stretches of fatiguing work in insufficient light. The movements may be slow or fast, sideways or rotatory, coarse or fine.

O

Obesity. Excessive fatness. Physiologically speaking, fatness is excessive if it interferes with the normal functioning of the body; if it causes lethargy, shortness of breath and palpitation, reduces the resistance to infections, or predisposes to diabetes. Much harm can be done by excessive obesity, for this condition places a great burden upon the vital organs. On the other hand, once obesity is present, serious damage may be done by various methods of losing weight. Thus dieting may cause vitamin deficiencies, degenerative changes in the digestive organs, and predisposition to various diseases. Some cases of obesity moreover, are little affected by a low diet, the cause of the condition lying in an abnormality of one or more of the internal secretions of the body, usually those of the thyroid, pituitary or sexual glands. Just as some people with enormous appetites remain thin despite what would seem to be overeating, others remain fat, no matter how rigidly they diet. The treatment of obesity must in every case be preceded by medical diagnosis. If the cause is dietetic, then alteration in the diet will cure it; but if the fault lies in the internal secretions, then only treatment that is directed to regulating them can possibly be effective.

Obstetrics. Midwifery; the branch of medicine that deals with the management of pregnancy and childbearing.

Opium. One of the oldest of the narcotic drugs. It is obtained from the juice of the unripe capsules of the white poppy. It is habit forming.

Orchitis. Inflammation of a testicle, a condition that may arise as a result of injury, or in the course of mumps, typhoid or other fevers, or by an extension of a gonorrheal or tuberculous infection from other parts of the genito-urinary tract.

Orthopedics. The branch of surgery that deals with the prevention and correction of deformities and the treatment of diseases and injuries of the bones and joints.

Osteomalacia. A rare disease marked by softening, bending and fracture of the bones, rheumatic pains, progressive weakness, and ultimately death from exhaustion. The condition occurs more frequently in women than in men, pregnancy being a common antecedent. Vitamin D and calcium-containing foods are employed in the treatment.

Osteomyelitis. Inflammation of the bone marrow and of the bone surrounding it, a disease of childhood and youth caused by infection by pus-producing organisms, chiefly staphylococci. Fever and severe pain are always present. Injury is one of the most common factors in the development of the disease. The symptoms are tenderness and swelling in the affected region. Penicillin is used as the drug of choice in acute osteomyelitis, but surgical intervention is often necessary in the chronic form of the disease.

Otitis. Inflammation of the ear, called otitis externa, media, or interna, according to whether the outer, middle, or inner ear is the part affected. The outer-ear infection is comparatively unimportant. It includes such conditions as eczema, boils and other inflammations which give little trouble if treated promptly. Otitis media, inflammation of the middle ear, is both common and dangerous. It affects chiefly young children, appearing in most cases as a complication of a common cold or of tonsillitis, measles and scarlet fever. Earache and deafness, the most prominent symptoms, should be regarded as urgent danger signals. Medical treatment applied without delay may cause the otitis to subside completely, without any need for operative measures, but neglect increases the danger of perforation of the ear-drum membrane and spread of the infection from the middle ear to the mastoid bone or to the brain, producing dangerous complications that cannot be dealt with except by a major surgical operation. It is frequently necessary to incise the drum membrane to relieve the pain and drain pus away from the danger area. Inflammation of the inner ear, a condition that usually arises from the extension of a middle-ear infection, produces characteristic symptoms, of which the most prominent are dizziness, a tendency of the patient to fall toward the affected side, vomiting, and jerky movements of the eyeballs. (See *Earache.*)

Ovaries. Female sex glands. They produce the reproductive cells, the ova, and the hormones, estrogen and progesterone. There are two ovaries, one on either side of the pelvic cavity.

Oviducts. Tubular passages for extrusion of the reproductive cells liberated by the ovaries.

Ovulation. The period which occurs with rhythmical precision during which the reproductive cell, the ovum, is discharged from the ovary.

P

Pediatrics. The branch of medicine which is concerned with the diseases of children.

Palpitation. Rapid action of the heart. Exertion, excitement, fever, Graves' disease and anemia are a few of the conditions that may cause this symptom.

Palsy. (See *Paralysis.*)

Pancreatitis. Inflammation of the pancreas, a gland that secretes digestive ferments into the bowel, and a hormone called insulin that enables the tissues of the body to utilize sugar and starchy foods. (See also *Endocrine* and *Insulin.*) Pancreatitis, a serious condition, is attended by severe pain, distention of the abdomen, and vomiting.

Pandemic. A widely spread epidemic. (See *Epidemic.*)

Papilloma. Any nonmalignant growth of the skin or mucous membranes in which the lining cells cover nipple-shaped elevations or ridges of the underlying tissues. Thus, a wart is a papilloma of the skin, and polypi are papillomatous growths of mucous membranes and internal organs.

Para-aminobenzoic Acid. An important factor in nutrition, as it is part of the vitamin B complex. It has been found useful in the treatment of rickettsial diseases such as typhus and spotted fever. Its effects have been found to be nullified by sulfa drugs.

Papule. A pimple; a solid elevation of the skin.

Paralysis. Loss of the power of motion, or of feeling in any part of the body. Such a condition may be due to a disease of the body—for example, of the nerves or muscles—or to a disease of the mind. In the former case the paralysis is called organic; in the latter, functional. Organic paralysis may arise from disease of the brain, spinal cord, nerve trunks or muscles. In all these cases either the muscle itself is so injured that it loses the power of movement, or the nerve-connections are so interfered with that messages from those parts of the brain that control movement are unable to pass. By examination and simple tests, it is possible to discover the exact site of the underlying trouble, whether it is in the brain itself, or in the spinal cord, or the nerve trunks, or the muscles. Functional paralysis occurs in hysteria and other nonorganic nervous disorders. In such cases there is no bodily disease or injury to account for the loss of power or of feeling, but a careful examination of the patient's mind, a kind of mental analysis, often reveals some unconscious wish or wishes that have found their gratification in this inconvenient way. Thus, shell-shock is often complicated by a functional paralysis, the effect of which was to get the sufferer out of the firing line. The soldier had, so to speak, successfully fought down the wish to be back in some place of safety, but the repressed wish had lost none of its force; it had realized its purpose by making the soldier unfit for service. Psychological treatment is often effective in curing a functional paralysis; organic paralysis may or may not be curable; it depends on the underlying cause, and for this reason a careful diagnosis must precede treatment in every case.

Paraplegia. Paralysis of the legs and the lower part of the body. This condition, which is marked both by loss of sensation and of power of motion in the region affected, may result from disease and injury of the spine, locomotor ataxia, neuritis due to chronic alcoholism, disease of the brain and many other conditions.

Parathyroid Glands. Although, as their name denotes, these small glands are situated very close to and sometimes embedded in the thyroid gland tissue, they have entirely different functions. It is true that like the thyroid, they are glands of internal secretion, that is to say, they manufacture a physiologically active chemical substance that is secreted into the blood stream; but this chemical substance—parathyroid hormone—differs entirely from thyroxin, the chemical secreted by the thyroid gland. Parathyroid hormone is responsible for maintaining the calcium in the blood at a constant normal level and thus plays an important role in the growth and development of bone. If the parathyroid glands are extirpated by operation the blood calcium falls; if, on the other hand an extract of the parathyroid gland is injected, the amount of calcium in the blood is increased. A marked fall in the blood calcium is generally fatal, death being preceded by tremor, cramps, and convulsions.

Paronychia. Infection or abscess of the tissues at the base of a nail. In the early stages hot moist dressings should be applied until the infection is completely localized. A small incision is then made to drain the pus so that healing can begin.

Parotitis. Inflammation of the parotid gland, a large salivary gland near the ear. (See *Mumps.*)

Parturition. The act of giving birth to a child.

Pasteurization. A method of arresting fermentation in beer, milk and other fluids by heating gradually to a temperature of 140° F. for about half an hour.

Pathology. The branch of medicine that deals with the essential nature of disease, especially with the changes of structure and function that occur in disease.

Pediculosis. Lousiness; a skin disease produced by lice.

Pellagra. A serious disease, occurring in Southern Europe and in central and southern parts of the United States, which is marked by the appearance of a severe rash, shedding of the skin, weakness, pain, convulsions, and grave mental disorders. It appears only in persons who have lived for long periods on a diet deficient in Vitamin B, and for this reason is classed with rickets, beriberi and scurvy, as a deficiency disease. (See *Vitamin.*)

Pelvis. The hip bones; the large basin-shaped bony ring that is situated at the lower end of the abdomen and supports the spinal column. Connected with the pelvis on each side and forming the hip joints are the thigh-bones, and contained within it are the organs of reproduction, the urinary bladder, a portion of the large intestine, and the rectum.

Pemphigus. A skin disease marked by the formation of large watery blisters. It occurs in many different forms and with varying degrees of severity. Treatment with ACTH, cortisone, and aureomycin has been found helpful.

Penicillin. An antibiotic discovered by Alexander Fleming in 1928. It has been found to be effective against a number of germs, especially the staphylococcus, streptococcus, and pneumococcus.

Peptic Ulcer. An ulcer of the lining of the stomach or duodenum caused by the digestive action of the acid gastric juice. The cause of this condition is not yet thoroughly understood, but it is known that chronic irritation of the stomach lining by highly seasoned foods and prolonged physical and nervous strain predispose to the formation of peptic ulcers. Unfortunately, the early symptoms are vague and indefinite. Only when the lesion has extended into the deeper layers of stomach tissue does pain become perceptible. This gradually becomes more noticeable and soon the patient notices that the pain appears in definite relation to his eating habits. Thus, in gastric ulcer the pain occurs about one hour after each meal and gradually subsides between meals. In duodenal ulcer, on the other hand, the taking of food eases the pain. The condition may become acute if the stomach or duodenal wall is eaten away, the resulting perforation causing a generalized peritonitis. Rarely the inflamed tissue within the ulcer undergoes malignant change with the formation of a carcinoma. In other cases the attempted healing of the ulcer by connective-tissue formation causes a large obstructive growth with narrowing of the channel, and symptoms of obstruction may be present. Peptic ulcer can be detected with the aid of certain laboratory procedures including aspiration of the stomach contents after a test meal, X-ray of the stomach after a solution containing barium sulphate has been swallowed, and direct inspection of the stomach through the gastroscope. Treatment consists of a bland diet, rest, and supportive measures. In many cases, surgical repair of the ulcer and gastro-enterostomy, the establishment of a new passageway between stomach and intestine that minimizes the exposure of the ulcer to digestive juices, have been successful.

Pericarditis. Inflammation of the pericardium, the thin sac that contains the heart. This disease, which may arise as a complication of rheumatic fever, pneumonia, tuberculosis and other infections is marked by pain in the region of the heart, fever, cough, and shortness of breath. Fluid accumulates in the pericardium and may create a pressure great enough to prevent the return of venous blood to the heart, a rapidly fatal condition known as cardiac tamponade.

Perineum. The region between the anus and the genital organs.

Periostitis. Inflammation of the periosteum, the tough network of cells and fibers that forms the outer lining of bone. In its acute form, periostitis, which is invariably due to infection, is marked by great pain and tenderness, high fever, and the formation of pus along the surface of the affected bone. The symptoms of chronic periostitis, a more common disease, are swelling of the bone and thus of the overlying tissues, and persistent aching pain.

Peristalsis. Wavelike contractions along a tubular organ as, for example, the contractions that pass along the stomach and bowel whereby their contents are propelled toward the rectum.

Peritonitis. Inflammation of the peritoneum, which is the name given to the strong, smooth, colorless membrane that lines the inner walls of the abdomen and covers, more or less completely, the organs therein contained. The symptoms of such an inflammation are severe abdominal pain and tenderness, constipation, vomiting and fever; its causes are many and include infections derived from the alimentary canal, as, for example, from an inflamed appendix, invasion by the tubercle bacillus, gonococcus, pneumococcus, or other organisms and perforating, infected wounds of the abdomen. Peritonitis is a serious complication of many abdominal conditions. Modern medical knowledge has greatly reduced the mortality rate of peritonitis, which formerly was almost invariably fatal.

Pernicous Anemia. (See *Anemia.*)

Pertussis. (See *Whooping Cough.*)

Petit Mal. (See *Epilepsy.*)

Pharmacopeia. A book contaning a description of products used in medicine, with details of how these should be identified, prepared, and compounded in prescriptions, and of the doses in which they may be administered to patients. The United States Pharmacopeia is the authoritative work in this country and is revised every ten years.

Pharyngitis. Inflammation of the pharynx, the cavity lying behind the nose and the mouth and forming the upper part of the esophagus. Acute pharyngitis sometimes occurs in the course of a common cold and is marked by fever, pain in the throat, especially on swallowing, a feeling of dryness, and sometimes an irritating cough. The condition may become chronic as a result of frequently repeated acute attacks; or may be of tuberculous or syphilitic origin.

Phlebitis. Inflammation of a vein, a condition that may arise as a complication of varicose veins, gout or rheumatism; or as a result of infection of the surrounding tissues; or from an invasion by bacteria such as may occur following childbirth or the period of convalescence from a surgical operation. It is marked by the formation of a blood clot in the vein, and pain, redness, swelling and sometimes a "knotty" feeling of the overlying tissues. Very careful treatment is required, and the affected part must be kept at complete rest to prevent separation of the clot. (See *Embolism.*)

Photophobia. An abnormal intolerance of light; inability to keep the eyes open except in darkness or a dim light.

Phthisis. Wasting of the body; more commonly, a term applied to tuberculosis of the lungs, a disease in which such wasting is a prominent symptom. (See *Tuberculosis.*)

Physiology. The science which treats of the functions of the living organism and of its organs, and tissues, and cells.

Piles. These swellings, known also as hemorrhoids, consist of distended, varicose veins in the lower part of the rectum and surrounding the region of the anus. Any condition that hinders the return of blood from these parts, pressure on the veins, for example, will predispose to the formation of piles. The condition frequently results from constipation and pregnancy. Obstruction to the flow of blood through the liver also is a common cause of piles, as blood from the perirectal tissues returns to the heart by way of the liver. The symptoms are itching, pain, and a sensation of weight in the rectum, followed by bleeding. Treatment varies with the cause and severity of the condition, surgical removal and cauterization being the most widely used.

Pituitary Body. A small rounded glandular organ situated at and connected with the base of the brain and fitting into a depression in the floor of the skull. It is often called the "master gland" of the body as its many hormones influence the activity of all other endocrine glands; yet this important structure is no larger than a garden pea. It consists of two distinct lobes, anterior and posterior, and a small intermediate portion. The most important hormones of the anterior lobe are those which stimulate bodily growth and the development of secondary sex characteristics. The hormones of the posterior lobe cause contraction of the muscles of blood-vessel walls and of the intestine and uterus. Overproduction of the hormones regulating growth produces the condition of acromegaly; removal of the lobe that manufactures these hormones causes stunted growth and arrest of sexual development. Pituitrin, an extract of the posterior lobe, is used in obstetrics to promote contraction of the uterus, and in medical and surgical practice to stimulate the bowel.

Pityriasis. A name applied to various skin diseases which, though differing from each other in origin and course, are all marked by the formation of branny scales.

Placenta. The structure by means of which transfer of metabolic products takes place between the circulatory system of the mother and that of the unborn infant. It is firmly adherent to the uterine wall during pregnancy and is connected to the fetus by the umbilical cord. It constitutes the major part of the afterbirth.

Plague. Pestilence: a term formerly applied to any severe epidemic, but now confined to a serious and usually fatal disease caused by the *Bacillus pestis.* Outbreaks of plague occur not only among human beings but among rats and reptiles, the disease being spread in part by the bites of fleas that have acquired the germ from plague-infested rats. Apart from high fever, intense headache, and great prostration, the chief characteristic of plague is in the formation of swellings, called buboes, of the lymphatic glands; and from these it derives the name by which it is now generally known—bubonic plague. The systematic extermination of rats, and the inoculation, by means of a vaccine, of populations in plague-ridden areas, and isolation of infected patients, are the most effective methods of combating the disease.

Plasma. The fluid portion of the blood. It is composed of water, mineral salts, and soluble proteins, and various organic compounds. Plasma is widely used in transfusions. While it does not replace lost blood cells, it helps maintain circulation by replacing plasma proteins.

Pleurisy. Inflammation of the pleura, the tough, smooth, serous membrane that covers the lungs and the inner wall of the chest. Pleurisy is almost invariably the result of organic infection in the chest and usually accompanies infection by the tubercle bacillus. Often inflammation of the pleura complicates other diseases, notably pneumonia, measles, rheumatic fever, scarlet fever, pulmonary tuberculosis, influenza and Bright's disease; but whatever its cause, it seems to start invariably as "dry pleurisy," passing from this to a condition known as "pleurisy with effusion." The early symptoms are sharp pain in the chest, cough, and fever. The pain is alleviated as the surfaces of the pleura are separated from each other by the liquid effusion.

Pneumonia. Inflammation of the lungs, a condition of which there are two typical forms: lobar pneumonia, an infection involving large portions of lung at a time, and bronchopneumonia, in which small infected patches are surrounded by areas of more or less healthy lung. Lobar pneumonia is a specific infection; it has a definite cause—namely, infection of the lung by the pneumococcus. In practically all cases, the disease starts with a chill, attended or followed by a sharp rise of temperature, pain in the side, shortness of breath with an increase in the rate of breathing, cough, and the expectoration of rusty-colored phlegm. After a few days, during which these symptoms remain unchanged or increase in severity, the crisis usually occurs; in the course of a few hours the temperature, pulse rate and rate of breathing fall to nearly normal, and the patient, who has been very ill and perhaps delirious, suddenly feels almost well again. In fatal cases fever increases about this time, the breathing becomes even more labored and the patient passes into a state of coma.

Unlike lobar pneumonia, which affects mainly young adults, bronchopneumonia is essentially a disease of very young children and of aged persons. Moreover, it is an illness that has a variety of causes, of which invasion of the lung by the pneumococcus is a comparatively uncommon one. In most cases it appears as a complication of measles, whooping cough, influenza, bronchitis, or scarlet fever, especially when these diseases attack young, debilitated, undernourished children. In elderly persons bronchopneumonia is liable to occur at the end of any long-continued wasting illness, and in such cases it is usually fatal. Whether it occurs in infants or the aged, this disease does not have the definite course that characterizes lobar pneumonia. It may last for a week or for a month; recovery may be rapid or gradual and prolonged; there may be remissions before recovery is complete. One of the greatest dangers attending many forms of pneumonia is the possibility of effusion of blood and serum into the lung. The fluids solidify, creating a smaller breathing space, and this decreases the amount of oxygen entering the blood. Penicillin, the sulfonamides, and the tetracycline drugs are administered singly or in combination in the treatment of pneumonia. In addition to chemotherapy, oxygen therapy and general supportive measures, including complete bed rest, are instituted.

Pneumothorax. An accumulation of air or other gas in the pleural cavity. Such a condition may arise as a result of disease of the lung, as, for example, the rupture of superficial air cells, or as a complication of a chest wound; or it may be induced deliberately, being then called artificial pneumothorax, as part of the treatment of lung disease, especially of pulmonary tuberculosis. By collapsing and inactivating the diseased lung, pneumothorax favors the healing process.

Poliomyelitis. Inflammation of the gray matter of the spinal cord. Acute anterior poliomyelitis—or, as it is commonly called, infantile paralysis—derives its name from the fact that it is a disease of sudden onset due to an infection of the anterior portion of the spinal gray matter. The infecting agent belongs to the class of organisms known as filtrable viruses, microorganisms so small that they pass readily through the pores of a porcelain filter. The affected gray matter is composed mainly of nerves that transmit impulses to muscles.

Poliomyelitis is an epidemic disease spread by contact, and children seem to be more susceptible than adults. In temperate climates, the disease occurs late in summer or early in fall. The majority of polio cases go unnoticed because of the mildness of clinical signs. When the disease is present in its more virulent form, fever, vomiting, and paralysis of groups of muscles are manifested. No specific treatment has yet been made available. Complete bed rest and isolation are essential. Relief of pain may be attained by strapping the chest, by hot packs, or hot baths. The advent of the Salk vaccine has practically eliminated the disease in its epidemic form.

Polyarthritis. Inflammation of several joints at the same time.

Polycythemia. Excess in the number of red corpuscles in the blood. Such a condition may be quite normal, as in persons living at a high altitude, or it may result from any disease of the heart or lungs that causes oxygen want; in such cases, polycythemia, by increasing the number of hemoglobin carriers, compensates for the inability of the heart and lungs to supply sufficient oxygen to the tissues. (See *Blood.*) Very rarely, polycythemia is due to a primary disease of the blood-forming organs.

Polyp. A growth arising from the surface of a mucous membrane and attached to it by a narrow stalk-like process of this membrane. Polyps may be true tumors or they may be simply outgrowths of mucous membrane formed as a result of inflammation.

Polyuria. Excessive secretion and discharge of urine, a condition met with in several diseases.

Pons. The part of the central nervous system which serves as a bridge connecting the cerebrum, cerebellum, and medulla oblongata.

Pregnancy. The condition of being with child, or with young.

Primipara. A woman who has given or is giving birth to her first child.

Prognosis. The forecast of the probable result of an illness.

Prolapse. The falling down or sinking of some organ of the body from the position that it usually occupies. Prolapse of the uterus is the most common condition of this kind.

Prophylaxis. The prevention of disease; the term is applied to preventive treatment in general. Measures and remedies adopted to this end are called prophylactics.

Prostate. The gland which in the male is situated at the base of the bladder, and surrounds the upper portion of the duct, called the urethra, through which urine and seminal fluid are passed out of the body.

Pruritus. Intense itching. Pruritus is not in itself a disease; it is a symptom that may appear in the course of many diseases.

Psoriasis. A chronic skin disease marked by the formation of extensive red scaly patches chiefly on the back of the arms, the front of the legs, the back, chest, and abdomen. The treatment varies with the cause of the condition, internal and external medication being usually required.

Psychiatry. The diagnosis and treatment of mental disorders.

Psychoanalysis. This term, which is applied indiscriminately and totally incorrectly to all forms of mental treatment, should be confined strictly to the system of ideas and the method of treatment discovered and practiced by Sigmund Freud and his followers. It is believed that by psychoanalysis, that is to say, by a technique designed to make conscious the ideas and feelings repressed into the unconscious, it is possible to bring about a cure in many cases of hysteria and other mental disorders.

Psychosis. A class of mental diseases, generally referred to as insanity.

Psychosomatic Medicine. A field combining medicine and psychiatry, which deals with the cause, nature, and treatment of disturbances in bodily functions that occur when a person is subjected to emotional and environmental stresses.

Ptomaine. A term applied to any poisonous substance formed in food during putrefaction. In its strict sense the term refers to a group of amines, which are formed in food by the disintegration of amino-acids. Ptomaines lower the blood pressure and sometimes produce severe toxic symptoms.

Puerperium. The period of confinement. The word "puerperal" means relating to childbirth; thus, puerperal fever is the name given to an infectious disease which is peculiar to recently confined women.

Pulmonary. Pertaining to the lungs; thus, pulmonary tuberculosis means infection of the lungs by the tubercle bacillus.

Pulse. The movement of expansion and contraction in the arteries that corresponds with the heartbeat and may be visible on the surface of the body or felt with the finger, the usual site selected for this purpose being the radial artery in the wrist.

Purgative. A medicine that causes evacuation of the bowel. (See *Constipation.*)

Purpura. A condition in which hemorrhages occur under the skin and mucous membranes producing an eruption of purple-colored spots. Purpura is a manifestation of disease rather than a distinct disease in itself. Thus, the eruptions of measles, scarlet fever, spotted fever, and a number of other specific infections, are purpuric and similar hemorrhages occur in the course of scurvy, hemophilia, cirrhosis of the liver, Bright's disease, and heart disease. Certain types of purpura seem to occur in the absence of any other disease; they are called primary purpuras, and are due in some cases to a blood disease and in others to vitamin K deficiency and allergy. (See *Allergy.*)

Pustule. A small pus-containing pimple.

Pyelitis. Inflammation of the pelvis of the kidney, the structure that communicates with the ureter, or urinary duct. This condition, which is marked by pain, tenderness, and swelling in the loin, the frequent passage of blood- or pus-containing urine, fever and disturbances of the stomach and bowels, sometimes appears as a complication of stone in the kidney or of inflammation elsewhere in the urinary tract—in the bladder, for example. But many cases are due to stagnation of urine, such as might be produced by the impaction of a stone in the ureter, or ascending infection from urine retained in the bladder in prostatic hypertrophy, or by the pressure on the ureter by a pregnant uterus. The treatment in every case depends on the cause. Medical measures, which include the administration of drugs that act as urinary antiseptics, may be curative in some cases; but very often surgical treatment must be employed.

Pyemia. Invasion of the blood stream by pus-forming germs. These are carried round in the circulation and, becoming impacted in the smaller blood vessels, form multiple abscesses in different parts of the body. Pyemia is marked by the occurrence of severe attacks of shivering, irregular fever, and profuse sweating. It is a serious condition but can be combated by the administration of salicylates, sulfanilamide, sulfapyridine, and sulfamethylthiozol, various other drugs, and specific antiserums, all depending upon the type of organism present.

Pyorrhea Alveolaris. A purulent discharge from the gums due to infection of the membrane that lies between the teeth and their sockets in the jaw. It is accompanied by retraction of the gums, destruction of the sockets themselves and looseness of the teeth. The condition is unsightly, as the teeth become crooked and pockets of pus are in many cases visible along the gum margin; it is a prominent cause of offensive breath; and it leads to serious and sometimes incurable disturbances of general health. The infection in the mouth becomes a focal point for the dissemination of virulent organisms to other parts of the body. Pyorrhea can be prevented by a mixed diet rich in foodstuffs containing vitamins C and D, regular cleaning habits, and periodic inspection of the teeth by a competent dentist. Treatment may include topically applied anti-inflammatory agents and surgical removal of the diseased tissue.

Pyrexia. Fever; an abnormally high temperature of the body.

Pyrosis. Water brash; a burning sensation in the stomach and gullet with belching up of a sour-tasting liquid. It is one of the symptoms of dyspepsia.

Pyuria. The presence of pus in the urine, a condition that may be due to infection of any part of the urinary tract.

Q

Quarantine. The forcible detention of ships or persons coming from infected ports in order to ensure that if by any chance they are harboring an infection they will not transmit it to persons or animals on shore. The term is applied also to the isolation of persons, houses, or districts that might otherwise become the source of an epidemic disease.

Quinine. An alkaloid of cinchona bark. It is used to suppress febrile malarial attacks. An eight-gram dose is toxic and sufficient to cause death by respiratory failure.

Quinsy. Suppuration and the formation of an abscess in or around a tonsil. This condition, which is an occasional complication of ordinary acute tonsillitis, is marked by swelling of the affected area, difficulty in swallowing, a high temperature, and severe pain. The abscess must be drained before healing can take place, but care is essential to prevent spread of the infection to other parts of the body.

R

Rabies. (See *Hydrophobia.*)

Radium. A rare element which gives off three distinct kinds of chemically and biologically active rays—known respectively as alpha, beta, and gamma, rays—that have proved of value in the treatment of disease. Experience has shown that these rays—especially the gamma-rays—are able to penetrate the body, and thus act upon deep-lying tissues which otherwise could be reached only by the knife; it appears, moreover, that the gamma-rays attack and destroy abnormal cells, for example, the cells of cancerous growths, far more easily than they do the ordinary cells of the body; and these facts together have led to the development of radium therapy, a method of treating disease by irradiating the tissues with gamma-rays. So far the method has had its greatest successes in the treatment of cancer of the uterus, breast, tongue and larynx. In other sites of the body, cancers seem more radio-resistant, which means that they can be destroyed only by an application of radium that is sufficient to destroy the surrounding healthy tissues as well. Radium therapy is effective only if the growths to which it is applied are strictly local; once the disease has become disseminated through the body, radium treatment is useless. It is worth recalling, moreover, that the earlier the diagnosis, the better the chances of cure; that even localized growths in the most favorable regions may still fail to respond to treatment, once they have become too big. Radium can destroy a growth only if the gamma-rays can penetrate to all its cells; this obviously is more possible in the case of small growths than of big ones. Surgical excision is still the chief weapon in the war against cancer; radium therapy is a useful adjunct.

Rectum. The lower part of the large intestine, extending from the end of the colon to the anus; its length is about six inches. It is lined by mucous membrane gathered into folds and is usually empty and collapsed. Filling of the rectum initiates reflex defecation. (See *Colon.*)

Relapse. The return of a disease after the patient's apparent recovery.

Relapsing Fever. An acute infectious disease in which periods of fever alternate with periods of normal temperature, each lasting about a week. There are several varieties of relapsing fever, all caused by spirochetes of the genus *Borrelia*.

Renal. Pertaining to the kidney. Thus, renal calculus means stone of the kidney, and renal tuberculosis, tuberculosis of that organ.

Resistance. The power to combat and overcome disease. (See *Immunity.*)

Resolution. The restoration of an inflamed tissue to its normal state. The most striking example of resolution occurs in the lungs during the crisis of lobar pneumonia. (See *Inflammation.*)

Respiration. The act of breathing. In healthy adults at rest, respiration occurs about 16 times a minute, and at each inspiration about 500 c.c. of air are drawn into the lungs. In deep breathing this amount may be increased to 1500 c.c. During exercise and as a result of fever the respiration rate is increased, and such an increase is specially marked in diseases such as pneumonia, in which portions of the lung are inactive. Essentially, respiration is the exchange of oxygen and carbon dioxide.

Retinitis. Inflammation of the retina. The retina is the innermost coating of the eye; it is formed by a fine network of nerve cells, and nerve fibers from the optic nerve and acts as the visual receiving apparatus, resembling in this respect the sensitive film of a camera. Inflammation of this delicate structure occurs in kidney disease, diabetes, arteriosclerosis, syphilis, diseases of the blood, and poisoning.

Rh Factor. A property of human blood cells. It is transmitted as a Mendelian recessive trait, and is found in the majority of people. Those who possess it are Rh positive, while those who do not are Rh negative. Transfusions of blood with the positive factor to persons whose blood possesses the negative factor, or vice versa, can have serious or even fatal reactions.

Rheumatic Fever. An infectious disease characterized by pain which spreads among the joints, chiefly of the hand, wrist, elbow, and knee. It occurs most prevalently in children and young adults. Nutritional deficiencies and poor living conditions are predisposing factors. The disease is probably caused by a streptococcus and is often preceded by an upper respiratory infection. Signs of this disorder include fever, arthritic and abdominal pain, and often cardiac manifestations such as breathlessness, palpitation, and heart murmur. Joint injury is transient, whereas permanent heart damage may occur. Treatment consists of absolute bed rest, administration of penicillin, cortisone or its derivatives, salicylates for relief of pain, and oxygen therapy. Care must be taken to avoid overexertion in order to prevent recurrences of the disease.

Rheumatism. This term is used to denote practically any disease of which pain or inflammation of joints or muscles is an outstanding symptom; but there has been in recent years a tendency to limit its use to the clearly defined disease that is known technically as chronic rheumatoid arthritis. This disease, like many of the other conditions that have been at some time called "rheumatism," is marked by inflammation of the joints, but it has certain peculiarities that mark it off from the rest. In the first place, it occurs chiefly in women; secondly, it tends to involve the small joints, such as those of the fingers, rather than the bigger joints of the body; furthermore, it seems to select for attack the muscles and connective tissues around the joints rather than the bones themselves. Although the exact etiology is uncertain, predisposing conditions include infections, endocrine or metabolic disturbances, and neural diseases. If the disorder progresses untreated, there may be cartilage destruction and stiffening and fixation of the joints. Treatment includes medication with salicylates, cortisone, and gold salts. Local application of heat is a therapeutic measure and brings relief from pain. Rest and physical therapy are important for rehabilitation. Even with adequate medical care, there may be spontaneous recurrences of joint and muscular pain.

Rhinitis. Inflammation of the lining membrane of the nose.

Rickets. Rachitis; a disease of children characterized by softening and curvature of the bones, growth failure, weakness of the abdominal wall, and convulsions. Essentially rickets is a disease in which the body is lacking in calcium and phosphorus, the chief mineral constituents of bone, and is caused by a deficiency of vitamin D in the child's body, for in the absence of this vitamin calcium and phosphorous needed for healthy growth and development cannot be absorbed. Rickets is thus a deficiency disease, and may be classed with scurvy, beriberi, and pellagra, all of which are also known to be due to lack of one or the other vitamins. It may, moroever, like the other deficiency diseases, be prevented or cured by introducing a sufficient amount of the appropriate vitamin into the diet. For this reason cod-liver oil, which is rich in vitamin D, is commonly included in the diet of even healthy infants. It has been found that sunlight has the capacity to produce vitamin D from its precursor, carotene, a pigment normally present in the skin and in many foods. Thus rickets can be prevented or cured by simple exposure of the patient to sunlight or by irradiating the patient's food. Although little can be done with deformities already present, a diet rich in calcium, phosphorus, and vitamin D prevents further damage to the skeletal system and relieves all other symptoms of the disease.

Rigor. A chill; an attack of shivering in the course of a feverish illness. The onset of many fevers, pneumonia, for example, is marked by a rigor, and rigor is a characteristic symptom of malaria and pyemia.

Ringworm. A contagious disease of the skin marked by the appearance of round scaly patches. It is caused by an invasion of the skin by certain fungi, and the site of the disease is determined by the nature of the infecting fungus. Various parts of the body may be attacked, including the scalp, fingers and toes. The application of ointments containing fungicides is effective in most cases; rarely, x-ray may be necessary to eradicate the disease.

Roentgen Rays (See *X-rays.*)

Rubella. German measles; an acute fever which resembles a mild attack of measles. The patient suffers from catarrh, sore throat, and pains in the body; a rash appears on the first day of the illness, and the glands of the neck and behind the ears are usually swollen. The temperature may be slightly elevated. The disease usually disappears within a week.

Rupture. (See *Hernia.*)

S

St. Anthony's Fire. (See *Erysipelas.*)

St. Vitus's Dance. (See *Chorea.*)

Salicylates. Pain-relieving and fever-reducing agents which act on the heat-regulating centers of the brain. They include simple salts of salicylic acid such as sodium salicylate, esters such as acetylsalicylic acid (aspirin), and methyl salicylate or synthetic oil of wintergreen.

Saliva. Spittle; the juice that is secreted into the mouth by the salivary glands and serves to lubricate the food and to initiate the digestion of starch.

Salpingitis. Inflamation of the Fallopian tubes, the slender channels along which the female egg cells pass on their way from the ovaries to the uterus. The condition may occur as a complication of childbed fever or of gonorrhea; more rarely it results from tubercular infection or from contact with an inflamed appendix. If medical treatment is ineffective, surgical removal of the tubes is indicated, as their function is usually destroyed by the inflammatory process.

Sarcoma. A malignant tumor derived from connective tissues and, in its structure, resembling these tissues as they are in their rudimentary state. (See *Cancer.*)

Scabies. Acariasis, a disease of the skin caused by a small insect-like parasite belonging to the family of mites. The female parasite burrows under the skin, laying her eggs as she does so. In the tunnel thus formed, these eggs are rapidly incubated, and the most mature find their way to the surface, where they are hatched. The invasion of the skin produces a more or less severe local irritation which the patient very naturally tries to relieve by scratching. As a result the burrows become still further infected, pus forms in them and the surrounding skin becomes inflamed. Sulphur ointment applied to the affected parts, and disinfection of clothing are effective measures in treating the disease.

Scalds. Burns caused by hot liquids or vapor. (See *Burns.*)

Scarlatina. Scarlet fever; an acute infectious fever marked by the appearance on the second day of a bright red rash consisting of close-set red spots. The disease is ushered in by a painful sore throat and a high fever, followed by chills and vomiting. On the third or fourth day the rash fades and in favorable cases the temperature falls and the patient feels better. By the end of a week the rash has usually disappeared, and as it fades the skin is shed in fine scales or in large flakes. Convalescence begins usually in the third week, and complete recovery may be expected within the following month. The complications of scarlatina are very serious, the commonest being inflammation of the ear (otitis) caused by an extension of inflammation from the throat, and acute Bright's disease, which may appear three or four weeks after the beginning of the illness, when the patient is apparently well along toward recovery. Scarlet fever is essentially a disease of children and young persons; second attacks are rare. The measures adopted for the prevention of scarlet fever include isolation of patients and the application whenever necessary of the Dick test, (See *Dick Test*) a means of determining susceptibility to the disease. Immunity can be conferred by graded injections of scarlatina toxin. Scarlatina antitoxin or whole blood from a person who has recovered from the disease greatly reduces the severity of the disease and the likelihood of complications.

Sciatica. A painful affection of the sciatic nerve, a thick nerve trunk that extends down the back of the leg. The pain may be very severe and sometimes is accompanied by wasting of the calf muscles. Sciatica should be regarded not as a disease in itself, but as a symptom of some underlying condition the exact nature of which can be discovered only by a skilled investigation. In sciatica caused by inflammation, medical treatment and physiotherapy may be effective; in other forms, surgery may be required.

Sclerosis. A hardening that results from inflammation or from deposition of connective tissue. The term is applied especially to such hardening of the arteries, and of the central nervous system—for example, of the spinal cord. The disease of the nervous system known as multiple sclerosis is marked by the appearance of hard patches throughout the brain and cord. Its outstanding symptoms are weakness, muscular inco-ordination, jerky movements of the eyeballs, paralysis, and a curious, deliberate way of speaking, known commonly as scanning speech. The condition has periodic remissions, and on the whole tends to become worse, but is seldom an immediate threat to life.

Scoliosis. Abnormal lateral curvature of the spinal column.

Scorbutic. Pertaining to scurvy. The term antiscorbutic is applied to any food or drug that is effective in preventing or curing scurvy. (See *Scurvy.*)

Scurvy. A disease caused by deficiency in vitamin C in the diet, and marked by anemia, softening of and bleeding from the gums, and hemorrhages under the skin and mucous membranes. The condition affects undernourished infants and was formerly common among sailors and explorers who lived for long periods of time on a diet deficient in fresh fruits and vegetables. The juice of oranges, lemons, limes and tomatoes is rich in vitamin C, and its inclusion in the diet serves as both a preventive and cure of scurvy.

Seasickness. Nausea and vomiting caused by the motion of a ship, or any moving vehicle.

Sebaceous Cyst. A firm, rounded, elastic swelling containing a thick, semisolid substance, that may occur anywhere on the surface of the body but most commonly on the scalp, chest or back. It is due to obstruction of the duct of a sebaceous gland, a gland of the skin that secretes a fatty lubricating substance. Surgical excision can be performed under local anesthesia with little inconvenience to the patient.

Seborrhea. A chronic disease of the sebaceous glands marked by excessive discharge of sebum, a lubricating substance which, on the surface of the body, forms solid plugs and greasy scales. Itching is a common symptom.

Sedative. A medicine given for the purpose of allaying excitement and producing mental and physical rest.

Sepsis. Poisoning by bacteria or their products.

Septicemia. A serious disorder due to the presence in the blood of disease-producing bacteria and the poisons they generate. It is marked by irregular fever, chills, sweating and weakness.

Serum. The clear fluid that separates from the blood when it coagulates. The term is also applied to the blood serum of animals that have been inoculated with bacteria or their poisonous products. (See *Immunity.*)

Shingles. (See *Herpes.*)

Silicosis. A disease of the lungs due to inhalation of minute particles of stone, flint or sand, such as may occur in persons whose occupation necessitates their working in an atmosphere laden with these substances. It is also called grinder's rot. It is an incapacitating disease and predisposes to the development of pulmonary tuberculosis.

Sinusitis. Inflammation of one or more of the air cavities situated in the cranial bones that communicate with the nose. The condition occurs not uncommonly as a complication of influenza or of a severe cold. The symptoms include pain and tenderness in the affected region, headache, facial neuralgia, and nasal obstruction. Treatment may include application of astringents to reduce swelling and reduction of infection with the use of sulfa drugs and antibiotics. If the attack is very severe and proceeds to suppuration, surgery may become necessary to open up the affected sinus in order to drain the pus.

Skin. The skin is the external covering of the body and has many important functions. It is that part of the body which contacts the environment. It is quite as important, for example, as the kidneys and the lungs, two organs with which it co-operates very closely in maintaining body health. Its most obvious function is that of protection. The unbroken skin serves as an indispensable first line of defense against germs and other noxious influences which would certainly, but for its presence, invade and overwhelm the internal cells of the body. It is for this reason that cuts, abrasions and other injuries of the skin must be properly treated. They form a breach in the defenses which must be closed at once by some germ-destroying substance, for example, tincture of iodine. By virtue of its content of ergosterol, and the action upon this substance of sunlight or of ultraviolet rays from some artificial source, the skin serves to keep the system supplied with vitamin D, and thus to maintain the amounts of calcium and phosphorous in the blood at a level consistent with good health. The skin, moreover, is an essential part of the temperature-regulating mechanism of the body. By means of its sweat secretion, which goes on incessantly though for the most part invisibly, it helps to keep the temperature of the body practically constant, an important factor in the maintenance of health. Through this sweat secretion toxic substances may be eliminated as well as water, and advantage is taken of this excretory function of the skin in the treatment of kidney diseases, wherein, by measures designed to increase the flow of sweat, some of the burden is taken off the diseased and inefficient organs. Another secretion of the skin is called sebum, an oily product of the sebaceous glands that serves to keep the skin supple and the hair glossy. That branch of medicine which treats of diseases of the skin is known as dermatology.

Sleeping Sickness. A serious chronic disease of the tropics prevalent chiefly among Negroes living in the Congo and caused by an invasion of the body by a tiny germlike parasite known as a trypanosome. When this parasite attacks the nervous system the patient becomes lethargic and depressed, and sleeps practically all the time. Death usually follows as a result of fever and starvation.

Smallpox. Variola; an acute infectious disease marked by fever, pains, vomiting, and the formation of an eruption that appears first in the form of red pimples, then of blisters, and finally of pustules. These pustules ultimately dry up, forming crusts which fall off and leave the typical pitted scars known as pockmarks. The disease seems to have two distinct forms—malignant smallpox, responsible for deadly epidemics in the past and still prevalent in certain parts of the world, and varioloid, a relatively mild disease that causes but little discomfort to the patient, rarely produces disfigurement, and is seldom fatal. Vaccination protects against both forms of smallpox.

Sore Throat. (See *Laryngitis, Pharyngitis,* and *Quinsy.*)

Spasmophilia. A tendency to spasms; a condition, mainly of infants, in which the patient is abnormally sensitive to external stimuli, and suffers from spasms of the muscles and convulsions. The condition is usually associated with rickets and is probably a manifestation of that disease. (See *Rickets.*)

Spinal Cord. The cordlike column of nerve tissue contained in the spinal canal and extending from the brain to a cone-shaped termination near the level of the second lumbar vertebra. Together with the brain it forms the central nervous system to and from which all nervous impulses are conducted; and like the brain it is made up of two kinds of matter, a gray and a white. The gray matter consists of nerve cells and fibers, of which those in the ventral part of the cord conduct impulses to the organs and members of the body, and those in the dorsal part conduct impulses in the opposite direction. Each nerve fiber conducts impulses in only one direction. The white matter of the cord consists of nerve fibers which are assembled in bundles called nerve tracts. These also are of two kinds—namely, ascending tracts which convey impulses from the periphery to nerve centers in the cord or the brain, and descending tracts which convey impulses from these centers to the periphery.

Spleen. A deep-red-colored glandular organ situated in the abdomen immediately to the left of the stomach and under cover of the lower ribs. Examined under the microscope, sections of the spleen may be seen to contain a considerable amount of lymphoid tissue, which contributes to the production of varieties of white blood corpuscles called lymphocytes. The spleen serves, furthermore, as a kind of dump for worn-out red blood corpuscles; here they are finally scrapped, and their hemoglobin is made available to the liver for conversion into bile pigment. Enlargement of the spleen occurs in the course of many diseases: in typhoid fever, blood poisoning, Hodgkin's disease, malaria, cirrhosis of the liver, pernicious anemia, leukemia, and a number of others.

Sprain. An injury of a joint marked by tearing or stretching of its capsule and other attachments, but not so severe as to lead to a dislocation of the bones. The signs of sprain are well known, for it is a type of injury that occurs very commonly in the ankle. The joint is swollen, hot, very painful, and tender. A medical examination is available in all severe sprains to rule out the possibility of dislocation and fracture. The application of alternate hot and cold compresses, together with tight bandaging and rest of the injured part, usually brings about a complete recovery.

Sprue. A chronic disease of the tropics caused by invasion of the body by a minute parasitic fungus. The patient becomes very thin, anemic and weak. He suffers from a sore tongue, sickness and diarrhea, with the production of large, pale, frothy stools. Treatment by means of liver or liver extract has been found to be very effective.

Sterilization. This term has two distinct meanings. It is applied to the process of rendering the hands, instruments, clothes, or any other materials surgically clean—that is to say, completely free of germs. But it also refers to the process whereby an individual is rendered infertile, or, in other words, incapable of producing children.

Stillbirth. The birth of a dead infant.

Stomach. This term is commonly used as a synonym for abdomen, but the stomach proper is that portion of the alimentary canal situated between the esophagus and the duodenum. It is located high in the left side of the abdomen, but in normal adults is very mobile, frequently moving far down in the abdomen during digestive activity. The stomach is a strong muscular pouch lined by mucous membrane from which minute glands secrete the substances that constitute gastric juice. The rhythmic muscular contractions of the stomach churn the food into a semiliquid consistency, bringing it into intimate contact with the digestive juice which contains dilute hydrochloric acid and enzymes that break down the large food molecules. Pepsin, the principal enzyme of gastric juice, partially digests protein foods, and rennin acts similarly on milk. Carbohydrate foods are also partially digested, but fats are essentially unchanged in the stomach. When the stomach has completed its work, it discharges its contents into the duodenum, the first part of the small intestine, where the process of digestion is continued.

Stomatitis. Inflammation of the mouth, a condition that is usually attended by pain, excessive secretion of saliva, and offensive breath.

Stone. (See *Calculus.*)

Streptomysin. An antibiotic extracted from a fungus-like substance in the soil. It is used in treating meningitis, pneumonia, and tuberculosis.

Stricture. The narrowing of any of the ducts, canals or passages of the body. This condition may have any of three distinct causes. It may follow an inflammation of the part of the body concerned that results in the formation within its walls of scar tissue, which ultimately contracts, as scar tissue invariably does. Or it may be caused by the pressure of some abnormal tissue, a growth, for example, on the affected part. Or it may result from the actual deposition of such abnormal tissue within the duct, canal or passage affected. Temporary stricture may be functional; it may result, in other words, from a muscle spasm for which no organic cause can be discovered.

Stridor. Harsh, high-pitched, noisy breathing that accompanies spasm and other abnormalities of the respiratory passages.

Stroke. (See *Apoplexy.*)

Sty. Inflammation of a sebaceous gland of the eyelid, forming a painful swelling of the lid margin. It is also known as hordeolum. (See *Sebaceous Gland.*)

Sulfamethylthiozol. A synthetic drug similar in composition to sulfanilamide and sulfapyridine. It has been found to be a highly effective therapeutic agent in the treatment of infections and diseases caused by the staphylococcus.

Sulfanilamide. A synthetic drug and dye derivative widely used in modern medical practice. It is almost specific in its action against infection or disease caused by the beta-hemolytic streptococcus and is effective against many other pathogenic organisms of the cocci group. In blood-stream invasion by the hemolytic streptococcus, a condition that formerly followed a rapidly fatal course, sulfanilamide often brings about an equally rapid recovery. Gonorrhea is susceptible to the new chemical, even chronic infections caused by the gonococcus are frequently cleared up within a relatively short time by sulfanilamide. Scarlet fever, erysipelas, and pneumonia are also vulnerable to sulfanilamide. In other diseases, notably rheumatic fever, the drug is without therapeutic value. If used in excess, symptoms of toxicity appear, including cyanosis, skin eruptions, high fever, and various subjective sensations. Destruction of both red and white blood cells constitutes the most serious disadvantage, but with judicious administration of the drug no harm results from these reactions and the therapeutic action is not lessened. Sulfanilamide is administered either orally or intravenously.

Sulfapyridine. A synthetic drug similar in composition to sulfanilamide. It is the drug of choice in the treatment of pneumonia caused by the pneumococcus. Sulfapyridine has greatly reduced the mortality rate of pneumonia and is effective in practically all infections and diseases caused by the pneumococcus. It is administered by mouth and, if given in excess, causes toxic effects similar to those produced by sulfanilamide.

Sunstroke. Fever, convulsions, nausea, vomiting and giddiness that may culminate in complete loss of consciousness, brought about by excessive exposure to strong sunlight. The condition is especially liable to attack persons who are suffering from or are in the convalescent stage of an illness, but alcoholism and fatigue are also important predisposing causes. The most useful first-aid measures are to remove the patient to a cool place, loosen his clothing and dash cold water on his face and neck. A physician should always be summoned, as sunstroke is a serious condition and is often fatal.

Suppository, a medicated solid usually in the form of a cone, especially designed for introduction into the rectum, vagina, or urethra. Cocoa-butter and glycerine are used as bases.

Sycosis. (See *Barber's Itch.*)

Syncope. (See *Fainting.*)

Syndrome. A set of symptoms that occur together;

any group of symptoms the concurrence of which is characteristic of a known disease.

Synovitis. Inflammation of a synovial membrane, the smooth tissue that lines the cavities of joints and bursas, and the sheaths of tendons, and secretes a lubricant fluid called the synovia. The condition is marked by the formation of a tense, painful swelling due to the presence of a fluid effusion within the synovial cavity. Injury, cold, sepsis, rheumatism, and infection by the organisms of gonorrhea, syphilis and tuberculosis are among the causes of synovitis, which is usually treated by resting the affected part, applying warm moist dressings, and, if necessary, draining off the fluid by means of a syringe. Later, massage and exercise aid in restoring the function of the tissue.

Syphilis. A disease caused by invasion of the body by a micro-organism, the *Spirochaeta pallida.* Syphilis is a highly contagious venereal disease transmitted usually by direct contact from an infected individual, most frequently through the agency of sexual intercourse. An indurated, elevated, slowly healing sore or chancre develops at the site of entrance of the organisms, but this may be absent or may heal completely, thereby giving the infected person a false sense of security. Symptoms may not appear until several years later when the effects of serious damage to the vital organs of the body become apparent. On the other hand many patients develop a generalized skin eruption within six to twenty-four months after exposure. Syphilus attacks the entire body, but tends to strike the vascular system and the nervous system in particular, producing syphilitic heart disease and aortitis in the former, and paresis and tabes dorsalis in the latter.

The damage caused by syphilis can be prevented by early diagnosis and treatment. The Wassermann and Kahn tests provide a simple method of detecting syphilitic infection. The antibiotic penicillin is very effective in treatment of syphilis.

Systole. The phase of contraction in the heart beat; the period during which the ventricles expel their contents into the aorta and the pulmonary artery. In the average healthy adult at rest the heart beats 72 times in a minute; in other words, each beat is completed in four-fifths of a second. The time occupied by systole is about three-tenths of a second. (See also *Circulation*, *Diastole*, and *Heart.*)

T

Tabes Dorsalis. Locomotor ataxia; a disease due to syphilitic infection of certain nerve tracts in the spinal column and of the sensory nerve trunks emerging from it. The disease usually occurs several years after the syphilitic infection was originally contracted. It is marked by disturbances of sensation, paroxysms of intense pain, incoordination, wasting of the body, a curious, uncertain, staggering gait, the development of sores which do not heal, destruction of joints, loss of control over the bladder, and other evidence of nervous pathology.

Tachycardia. Excessively rapid action of the heart. In normal adult persons at rest the heart beats at a rate of about 72 to the minute. In persons with tachycardia the rate may be 130 and over. In paroxysmal tachycardia, attacks of such rapid heart action come on abruptly, last for a few minutes, hours, or even days, and then pass off as abruptly as they came. Tachycardia is a symptom of disease, not a disease in itself.

Talipes. Clubfoot; a deformity of the foot in which it is twisted from the normal shape or position.

Tapeworm. A parasitic worm composed of many segments united in a long ribbon or tapelike form, often found in the intestines of man and various animals. The larval forms or undeveloped worms are present in the tissues of infested fish and animals and are transmitted to man by ingestion. The worms become firmly fixed high in the intestinal tract and grow at the expense of their victim, causing malnutrition, severe anemia, and general debility. Frequently segments become detached and can be seen in the stools. Treatment consists of the administration of drugs, which narcotize the worms, and purgatives which flush them from the bowel. The worm head by which the worm attaches itself to the intestinal wall must be eliminated or the worm will regenerate from this part. Larval forms may penetrate the digestive tract and invade the tissues, forming small cysts. These may also cause symptoms.

Teeth. The temporary or milk teeth begin to erupt usually when the infant is about six months old. In all there are twenty such teeth, ten in each jaw. Taking each jaw separately and working from the center outward, there are two central incisors, two lateral incisors, two canines and four molars. Usually the lower central incisors are the first to appear; these are followed by the upper central incisors and then in order by the lateral incisors, the first molars, the canines, and the second molars. This order is by no means followed in every case, nor is there anything necessarily wrong with an infant in whom the process begins rather late. But if by the ninth month there is no sign of teething, a medical examination is indicated in order to determine the cause. The permanent teeth, of which there are thirty-two, sixteen in each jaw, begin to appear when the child is about six. Each set consists, beginning from the middle and working outward, of four incisors, two canines, four bicuspids and six molars. The outermost molars are called the wisdom teeth. If the milk teeth are allowed to decay, if caries in them are not arrested or properly treated, the permanent teeth are likely to be defective. A diet containing large amounts of calcium and phosphorus, and vitamins C and D, together with good dental hygiene, will ensure sound teeth in most individuals.

Terramycin. An antibiotic generally administered orally. It has been used in the treatment of all types of pneumonia, acute gonorrhea, infections due to Gram-negative organisms, and certain virus infections.

Tetanus. (See *Lockjaw.*)

Tetany. A condition characterized by painful spasm of the muscles, especially those of the limbs. It occurs in calcium- and vitamin-D deficiencies and is seen in rickets and following surgical removal of the parathyroid glands Tetany also occurs as a result of alkalosis Treatment varies according to the cause.

Therapeutics. The science and art of healing; the sum of measures adopted for the treatment of disease.

Thorax. The chest; the part of the body between the neck and the abdomen, and separated from the latter by the diaphragm. It contains the heart and the great blood vessels leading into and from it, the lungs, the trachea and its ramifications, the esophagus, and the thymus gland or its remains.

Thrombosis. The formation of a clot inside a blood vessel. It may result from injury or inflammation of the vessel walls, or by increased coagulability of the blood from any cause, most commonly the presence within it of bacteria or their toxins, or a diminished rate of blood flow such as may occur when the heart action has been weakened by disease. The clot itself is called a thrombus. One of the dangers of thrombosis is that the clot may separate and be carried in the blood stream till it becomes lodged within some vessel, causing obstruction to the blood flow therein. (See *Embolism.*)

Thrush. A disease of infants due to a fungus infection of the membrane lining the mouth. It is characterized by the formation of white spots and sometimes of ulcers. Digestive disturbances and fever accompany the disease.

Thymus. A gland situated in the chest just behind the upper part of the sternum. It is far larger in children than in adults, tending to shrink and practically disappear after childhood. Abnormal persistence of the thymus, which seems to be associated with overgrowth of the thyroid gland and of lymphoid tissues throughout the body, is known as status lmyphaticus.

Thyroid. (See *Goiter, Myxedema,* and *Cretinism.*)

Tic. Involuntary spasmodic twitching of a group of muscles—*e.g.* as of the face. The condition is also called habit spasm and is liable to occur in young persons of the neurotic type. Tic douloureux or trigeminal neuralgia is an excruciatingly painful spasmodic neuralgia of the face that has been found to result from irritation or inflammation of the fifth cranial nerve.

Tinnitus. Ringing, buzzing, or clicking sounds in the ears. They are usually heard by patients suffering from chronic middle-ear disease or an affection of the auditory nerve.

Tonsillitis. Inflammation of the tonsils, small almond-shaped masses situated in the folds of membrane that form pillar-like structures on either side of the arched passage between the mouth and the pharynx. Tonsils which tend to become chronically inflamed should be excised.

Torticollis. Wryneck; an abnormal rotation and bending of the head caused by contraction of the muscles of the neck. The condition is sometimes congenital, but it may be acquired as a result of disease or injury of the muscles concerned, or of the nerves supplying them. Some cases are functional, occurring in the absence of any recognizable organic lesion and are believed to be symptomatic of hysteria or some other mental disturbance.

Toxemia. A disturbance of health due to the absorption of bacterial poisons from some focus of infection, as from the intestine, the tonsils, or a decayed tooth.

Toxin. A poisonous product of bacterial action. The name is also applied to certain substances, for instance, snake venom, that have a toxin-like action. (See *Immunity.*)

Trachea. The windpipe; the tube extending from the larynx to the bronchi.

Trachoma. A highly contagious disease marked by the development of small inflammatory swellings, and later of scar tissue, on the inner side of the eyelids, and ultimately by deformity of the lids when this scar tissue contracts. Complications during the long course of the disease frequently impair or destroy vision. The condition is commonest in Egypt and the Far East but also occurs in Occidental countries.

Transfusion. The process by which blood is transferred from one person into the circulatory system of another. Before performing transfusion the surgeon must determine that the blood of the donor is compatible with that of the recipient. There are, it has been discovered, four blood groups, to one or other of which everybody belongs. Persons in the first group are called universal recipients, for they can receive blood from members of any group; persons in the second and third groups can give blood only to persons belonging to their own group and to the universal recipients; and the fourth group consists of universal donors, for they can give blood to members of any group, though they can receive it safely only from members of their own. Transfusion of blood to a recipient whose blood is incompatible with that of the donor may lead to disaster, the red blood corpuscles of the donor then forming clumps in the plasma of the recipient. But properly carried out, transfusion has proved itself again and again a means of saving lives. In cases of serious hemorrhage, in certain anemias, in septic conditions, and in all serious chronic diseases, transfusion may offer to the patient his one chance of recovery.

Trauma. A wound or injury. The name psychic trauma is given to any emotional experience that produces a lasting effect on the mind.

Trephine. A round saw designed for opening up the skull by removing from it a round disc of bone. The term also means to operate with such a saw.

Tuberculin. A preparation obtained from attenuated cultures of tubercle bacilli. Tuberculin is used chiefly in the diagnosis of tuberculosis or in determining susceptibility to that disease, by means of an intradermal reaction that follows injection of the preparation into the skin. Tuberculin has been used also in the treatment of tuberculosis.

Tuberculosis. An infectious disease caused by invasion of the body by the tubercle bacillus, and characterized by the formation of numerous small nodules or tubercles in the tissues involved. Tuberculosis is practically a universal disease among civilized peoples, affecting most individuals at some time during their life. It is transmitted by direct and indirect contact and by droplet infection through the respiratory passages, as from coughing and sneezing. The disease is sometimes spread through milk and dairy products from tuberculous cattle. It is highly probable that nearly every adult living in a modern city has at some time been infected with tubercle bacilli; but only a small proportion of persons thus infected actually contract tuberculosis and show manifestations of the disease. The severity of the infection depends on several factors, principally the number and virulence of the organisms and the resistance of the patient. Frequent repeated small exposures to tubercle bacilli may confer some degree of immunity against a subsequent major infection; on the other hand, a single exposure may sensitize the individual and thereby cause a severe reaction at a later time to even minimal exposure. That some degree of racial immunity to tuberculosis is present, is shown by the rapidly fatal course of the disease in aboriginal peoples, who are generally without previous exposure to the disease. Predisposing factors in the incidence of tuberculosis are overwork, malnutrition, poor hygiene, and crowded living conditions.

The unit lesion of tuberculosis is the tubercle. This consists of tubercle bacilli surrounded by necrotic tissue destroyed by the organisms, and fibrous tissue deposited by the body in an effort to localize the infection. The tubercle may be microscopic or may attain sufficient size to be visible to the unaided eye. Tuberculosis usually affects the lungs but not uncommonly also may involve the bones, lymphatic system, nervous system, gastrointestinal tract, and genitourinary tract. Few symptoms are exhibited in the early stages of pulmonary tuberculosis. As the disease progresses to the stage where actual lesions may be seen on x-ray, signs of fever, weakness, and loss of weight appear. The coughing up of blood, attended by severe chest pain, is often the first symptom of this disease.

Pulmonary tuberculosis is diagnosed on evidence of lung pathology seen by x-ray or finding of the tubercle bacilli in the sputum. Guinea pigs are used in establishing an otherwise doubtful diagnosis of tuberculosis. They die within a few weeks after the inoculation with bacilli-laden sputum.

Chemotherapy of tuberculosis consists of long-term treatment with streptomycins, isoniazid, and PAS. Surgical intervention is often necessary. A pneumothorax may be considered beneficial to afford rest to the tubercular lung, while hindering the spread of the disease to the healthy lung. This operative procedure introduces air into the pleural cavity, effectively reducing the respiratory movements of the lung and thus promoting rapid healing. Complete rest and general supportive measures are required in all forms of tuberculosis. Prophylactic measures include maintenance of general health, periodic chest x-rays, avoidance of exposure to the disease, and, when this is impossible, vaccination with BCG.

Tumor. A swelling; the term is applied more particularly to a swelling due to a growth of new tissue. Tumors are classified in two groups; benign and malignant. Benign tumors are strictly localized and do not grow into other tissues; they simply push them aside. They do not undermine the general health, and when removed they have no tendency to recur. Malignant tumors are localized at first, but sooner or later produce secondary growths elsewhere in the body; they grow into adjacent tissues, disturb the general health, and recur, if incompletely removed.

Typhoid Fever. An infectious fever caused by an invasion of the body by the *Bacillus typhosus*. It is marked by inflammation and ulceration of the small intestine, especially of patches of lymphoid tissue that are distributed along its inner lining membrane. The first symptoms are somewhat indefinite; they may point to any of a number of different infectious disorders. The patient has a headache, pains in the back, tenderness of the abdomen and a fever. The temperature is characteristic; it climbs upward gradually despite daily remissions and becomes constant at a high level. About the sixth or seventh day of the illness a rose-colored rash appears on the chest, abdomen and the flanks, and at this time the patient begins to suffer from diarrhea. After a week or two, under favorable conditions, the fever gradually subsides and with it there is a lessening of diarrhea and other symptoms. Convalescence may be very slow and relapses are not uncommon. In grave cases the patient becomes delirious, and is in a state of complete coma and muscular prostration. The most serious complications are perforation of an intestinal ulcer, peritonitis, pneumonia, pleurisy, otitis, kidney disease, and the formation of clots in the blood vessels. Closely resembling typhoid fever, and caused by germs very like the *Bacillus typhosus*, are two acute infectious fevers known as paratyphoid fever A and paratyphoid fever B. Troops in the field and other persons liable to be attacked by typhoid fever can be protected by means of a vaccine made from the germs of typhoid, paratyphoid A and paratyphoid B. Persons who have had a typhoid infection may continue to excrete the germs of this disease in their urine and feces for many years, and so act as "carriers," transmitting the infection to persons about them. Many outbreaks of typhoid fever have been traced to such carriers. (See *Carrier*.)

Typhus. An infectious fever the causal organism of which is transmitted by the bites of body lice. It is endemic in many countries and occasionally assumes epidemic proportions. Filth and overcrowding favor its occurrence, armies in the field and prisoners in jail being particularly susceptible to attack. The patient at the onset of the disease suffers from intense headache, a feeling of illness, chills, pains all over the body and great weakness. A high fever is always present. On the fifth day the rash appears as a mottling of the skin, together with numerous pink spots. Meanwhile the prostration increases, delirium develops, and the patient passes into a state of coma. The fever lasts in all for about two to three weeks, at the end of which, in favorable cases, the temperature falls quickly to normal and the patient makes rapid progress. Convalescence, however, is prolonged and may last several months. The disease has a high mortality, especially when epidemic in distribution.

Typing of Blood. Determination of the type of isoagglutination of the donor and the patient prior to a blood transfusion. The purpose of this is to select a donor whose blood is of the same type as the patient's in order to prevent agglutination or hemolysis. The blood of man can be divided into four main groups, the difference between them being constitutional and hereditary.

U

Ulcer. An open wound or sore resulting from destruction of the surface tissues. It may arise from injury, infection, or the spreading or breaking down of tumors. The treatment varies with the cause and site. In uncomplicated ulcers of accessible sites the obvious measures are to remove the cause, if this is still operating, and to protect the injured surface from mechanical irritation and germ infection. It is usual to keep the ulcerated part at rest, covering it meanwhile with some antiseptic dressing. So-called indolent ulcers—chronic lesions that tend grad ually to extend in area and depth—may require more drastic treatment. They occur most commonly on the legs of aged persons and are usually associated with varicose veins. Measures for improving the circulation in the affected limb, and high vitamin diets are employed. (See *Peptic Ulcer.*)

Ultraviolet Rays. (See *Actinotherapy* and *Heliotherapy.*)

Umbilicus. The navel; the abdominal scar at the site of the umbilical cord.

Uremia. A grave disorder caused by an accumulation of urinary waste products in the blood. A common antecedent is Bright's disease, but uremia may arise from any disease of which suppression or deficient secretion of urine is a symptom. It is marked by headaches, nausea, vomiting, dimness of vision, a rise in the blood pressure, convulsions, and coma.

Ureter. The duct along which urine is conveyed from the kidney to the bladder.

Urethra. The duct along which urine is discharged from the bladder. In the male this same duct serves also to convey the semen.

Urethritis. Inflammation of the urethra, a condition due commonly to a gonorrheal infection, but sometimes to gout.

Urine. The secretion of the kidneys that is stored in the bladder and from it periodically discharged by way of the urethra. The healthy adult passes urine three or four times in the day and not at all, or only very rarely, at night. The average total quantity in twenty-four hours is about one and a half pints. By way of the urine are discharged various waste products that are formed as a result of the ingestion of food, and the building up and breaking down of the body tissues. Chief among these are urea, uric acid, common salt, certain phosphates, sulphates, and oxalates, and the urinary pigments. (See also *Albuminuria* and *Hematuria.*)

Urticaria. Nettle rash or hives; a skin disease marked by the eruption of firm, elevated patches, pinkish in color, though sometimes having a white center, and each surrounded by an area of redness. The condition, which usually subsides in a day or two but sometimes lasts longer, is attended by intense itching. Urticaria occurs in persons who have been sensitized to some chemical substance—a food constituent, for example, or the poison from an insect bite—and these persons are liable to suffer an attack every time this constituent is present in their food, or this poison is injected into their system. Shellfish, pork, eggs, and strawberries are among the foods that may provoke an attack in susceptible persons. Many drugs have a similar action, and in some cases the responsible agent seems to be the poison liberated by germs or parasites that the patient happens to be harboring in his body. The treatment of urticaria aims at relieving the immediate symptoms and preventing the recurrence of attacks; thus adrenalin usually is administered to control the immediate ailment and an investigation is begun to determine the cause of the condition. (See *Allergy.*)

Uterus. The womb; the hollow muscular organ in which the embryo develops during pregnancy.

Uvula. The soft, fleshy, conical mass that hangs from the back of the palate over the base of the tongue.

V

Vaccination. The process of conferring protection against smallpox by inoculating lymph containing the virus of cowpox. The term is applied more widely to include protection similarly conferred against any disease by means of an emulsion of the germs or virus believed to be responsible for its occurrence. True vaccination was first carried out by Edward Jenner in 1796. He had observed that milkmaids and others who had accidentally contracted cowpox were subsequently immune to smallpox, and conceived the idea of inducing cowpox deliberately as a protection against the far more serious disease. Vaccination has since become the most effective means of controlling smallpox and many other diseases. (See *Vaccination* and *Immunity.*)

Varicose. Permanently dilated or enlarged. The term is applied chiefly to veins, the dilated vessel being called a varix. Piles, variocele and dilated veins of the leg are all examples of varicose veins. The treatment of this condition depends on its site and the exact state of the vein or veins affected. Palliative treatment of varicose veins of the legs consists in application of an elastic bandage; but in many cases operative treatment of one kind or another is advisable. It is possible to obliterate varicose veins by injecting into them a sclerosing solution, but not all cases are suitable for such treatment.

Variola. (See *Smallpox.*)

Vasomotor. This term refers to the expansion and contraction of blood vessels, and is applied to the nerves, hormones, and other agents by which these changes are effected.

Vein. (See *Artery.*)

Ventricle. (See *Heart.*)

Vertebra. A bone of the spinal column. There are in all thirty-three such bones; seven cervical, twelve thoracic, five lumbar, five sacral, and four coccygeal, those in the last two groups, however, being fused to form the sacrum and the coccyx, respectively.

Vertigo. Dizziness; a condition that may arise from disorders of the heart, stomach or eyes, from middle-ear disease, anemia, high blood pressure, brain tumors, or wax in the eardrum. The causes include serious and trivial conditions and diagnosis should not be delayed.

Vitamin. One of a class of substances present in minute quantities in certain foodstuffs, and serving as "accessory food factors" the presence of which in the diet is essential for the promotion of normal growth and nutrition and for the prevention of a group of diseases which, because they appear only in animals and persons who have been fed on a diet lacking in one or more vitamins, are called "deficiency diseases." Vitamin A is essential for growth, particularly of the epithelial and glandular tissues. The liver stores this vitamin, and cod-liver and halibut-liver oils are especially good natural sources. A deficiency of vitamin A results in a decrease in acuity of vision in dim light. The vitamin B complex is a group of substances having common distribution in plant and animal foodstuffs. Some of its components are: Thiamine, vitamin B_1, which stimulates appetite, promotes growth, and is used to prevent beriberi; Riboflavin, vitamin B_2, improves growth, promotes health, and acts as an antipellagric vitamin. (See *Pellagra.*) It is found abundantly in yeast. Vitamin C is also known as the antiscorbutic factor; its distribution is described in the entry on *Scurvy.* The vitamins of the D group are the "sunshine" vitamins. Vitamin D is present in cod-liver oil and can be manufactured by exposing a substance called ergosterol to ultraviolet radiations. The action of vitamin D is described in detail in the sections on Rickets and Spasmophilia. Vitamin E is found in wheat germ and in green vegetables. Not very much is yet known about this vitamin except the fact that its absence from the diet of some animals produces sterility. Vitamin K is the antihemorrhagic or coagulation vitamin.

W

Wart. An elevation or excrescence of the skin or mucous membrane due to overgrowth of a papilla or a group of papillae. (See *Papilloma.*)

White Leg. Swelling of the leg due to the formation of a clot in one of the large veins through which blood in normal circumstances is returned from the leg to the heart. It is a condition that occurs occasionally as a complication of the lying-in period or of typhoid fever.

Whooping Cough. Pertussis; an acute infectious disease caused by the *Bacillus pertussis,* and marked by catarrh of the respiratory tract and paroxysms of cough that end in a prolonged high-pitched inspiration called a "whoop." The paroxysms are characteristic; the patient draws a deep breath and then emits a long series of short coughs during which his face becomes livid, and his eyes become bloodshot; at the end of it he takes in a long breath, which is usually accompanied by the "whooping" sound. Vomiting is often present. The illness passes through three fairly well-defined stages; the first, called the catarrhal stage, lasts about a week, during which the patient has what are in effect the symptoms of an ordinary cold—a running nose, a slight cough, and some fever: the stage of paroxysms follows, and may continue for about a month, and this is succeeded by the final stage—the stage of decline, in which all the symptoms gradually subside and ultimately disappear. The complications and sequels of whooping cough may be very serious. They include convulsions, bronchopneumonia, hemorrhage in the brain and other tissues. Second attacks are extremely rare, infection by the germ responsible for whooping cough having almost the invariable effect of making the patient immune for the rest of his life. Children, as is well known, are affected far more commonly than adults. The treatment resolves itself mainly into checking the number and the severity of the paroxysms, and bed rest. Whooping cough can be prevented by vaccination.

Wryneck. (See *Torticollis.*)

X

X-ray. Electromagnetic radiations generated by passing an electric current through a vacuum. They are used in medical and surgical practice for making photographs, called radiograms, of various parts of the body, including deep-lying organs and tissues, and thus to reveal the presence of foreign bodies, fractures, or the changes characteristic of disease. They are used, moreover, for the treatment of certain diseases—for example, cancer, eczema, ringworm, and Hodgkin's disease—experience having shown that in such cases the x-rays are able to destroy or otherwise disorganize the diseased part without seriously injuring the healthy tissue surrounding it.

Y

Yellow Fever. An acute infectious fever caused by a virus, occurring chiefly in West Africa and other tropical districts, and marked by fever, jaundice, albuminuria, black vomit and great weakness. It is transmitted by a mosquito called *Aedes aegypti,* by the bite of which the virus is transferred from infected to uninfected persons. The mortality rate is high. There is no specific treatment. Control of the disease includes vaccination and elimination of the mosquito.

Z

Zymotic. Pertaining to zymosis, a name applied to any infectious or contagious disease.

THERMOMETER COMPARISONS

The Fahrenheit thermometer, in general use throughout the United States and the British Empire, was introduced in 1714, and is an adaptation of the thermometer invented by Sir Isaac Newton, and described by him in the *Philosophical Transactions* for 1701. Newton's lowest point was that of freezing, his highest that of boiling water, his starting point, however, being the temperature of the human body, which he called by the round number 12, the duodecimal system being then in use; that is, he divided the space between the freezing point and the temperature of the body into twelve parts. When Fahrenheit took the thermometer in hand he divided each of Newton's degrees into two parts, so getting a more minute record, while he got lower temperatures than freezing by using a mixture of ice and salt for his zero. Newton used linseed oil as the fluid within the thermometer, but mercury came into general use as it was more convenient. The boiling point of a Fahrenheit thermometer is 212°, the freezing point 32°.

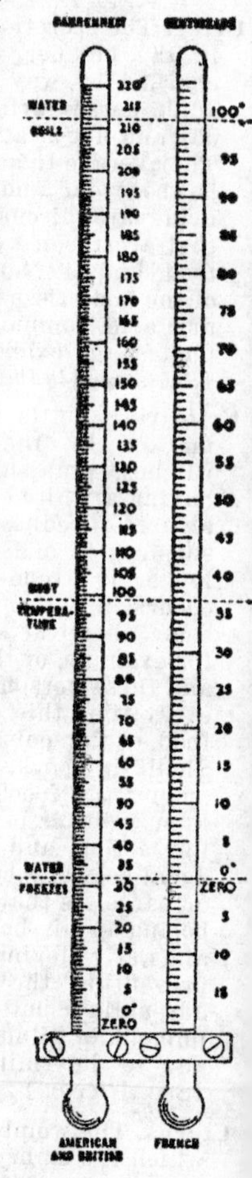

The centigrade thermometer, in general use in France and Latin America, has 0° for its freezing point and 100° for boiling point. The temperatures below freezing point are indicated by a minus sign— prefixed to the degree number. To convert a reading on the Fahrenheit scale to Centigrade temperature subtract 32 and multiply by 5/9. To convert Centigrade to Fahrenheit multiply by 9/5 and add 32.

A Dictionary of GENERAL INFORMATION

A digest of essentials in the fields of Art, Architecture, Literature, Music, History, Science, Biology, Anthropology, Anatomy, Geology, Navigation, Invention, Economics, Commerce, and Industry

Abacus, the upper portion of the capital of a column; also a contrivance for adding figures, still used in some countries.

Abaddon, the angel of the bottomless pit—Apollyon, Satan.

Abattis, a military term signifying an entrenchment of trees placed side by side with the branches outward.

Abbeys, monasteries or convents governed by an abbot or an abbess—were among the earliest of Christian institutions, and were adopted in western Europe under the Benedictines in the 6th and 7th centuries; by 1415 no fewer than fifteen thousand and seventy abbeys had been established by this order alone.

Abdication. The term refers usually to the act of a sovereign who relinquishes the supreme power in a state. There have been only two instances of the abdication of an English monarch; that of James II in 1688 and Edward VIII in 1936. Among continental European nations there have been many. In France we have those of Napoleon I, Charles X, and Louis Philippe. The Emperor William of Germany and the Emperor Carl of Austria both abdicated on the defeat of the Central Empires in the Great War in 1918.

Abduction is the taking away of any person. It is either a civil or criminal offense. It is used chiefly for the taking away of a wife from a husband, a child from a parent, or a ward from her guardian and is an offense that is severely punished as felony.

Abiogenesis, a term invented by Thomas H. Huxley to indicate the origin of living from nonliving matter. The abiogenesis theory supports that of evolution by tracing the organic from the non-organic.

Aborigines is a term first applied to an ancient Latin race, but now signifies the original inhabitants of any country. The Maoris of New Zealand and the Indians of North America represent two prominent examples.

Absinthe, an aromatic liquor formerly much consumed in France, and made from a distillation of wormwood and other roots steeped in alcohol. The manufacture is prohibited in France and Switzerland. Absinthe drinking is a great evil, destroying the brain and ultimately producing paralysis. Zola's novel *L'Assommoir* is a scathing indictment of the absinthe habit.

Absolution, an ecclesiastical term denoting the liberation of a person guilty of sin from its consequences by the act or intercession of religious authority. Now confined in its strict form chiefly to the Roman Catholic and Greek Churches, although a modified form is occasionally used in certain churches of the Anglican Communion.

Academy is a Greek term, originally applied to the groves where Plato taught, but subsequently adopted to indicate higher educational institutions of a special kind. The word is also applied to high schools. Academies of science are numerous in all parts of the world, and in addition there are what may be called literary academies of which the French Academy, established in 1635, is a notable example. There are also academies of history, of medicine, of music, and of art. The London Royal Academy of Arts was founded in 1768. The National Academy of Design, organized in the United States in 1826, is composed of American painters, sculptors, and engravers. In 1904 the American Academy of Arts and Letters was established in New York to further the interests in fine arts.

Acclimatization expresses the process by which animals or plants are gradually inured to a climate other than that of their origin.

Acetic Acid, an organic acid obtained by the destructive distillation of wood, or from the leaves of certain plants. Is used in medicine, as a condiment, in vinegar, as a mordant, and in the preparation of varnishes, artificial silk, etc.

Acetylene, a gas compounded of hydrogen and carbon, produced by the action of water on calcium carbide. It is used in welding and as an illuminant.

Acids are compound substances which combine chemically with an alkali or base and result in a new body that has neither acid nor alkaline properties. These resultant bodies are termed salts, and as many salts can be produced as there are basic substances to be neutralized. Acids are classified as organic acids and inorganic or mineral acids. The chief mineral acids, sulphuric, hydrochloric, and nitric, are utilized for an immense variety of commercial purposes.

Acolyte, one who assists the priest in the Roman Catholic service by lighting the candles and performing other minor duties.

Acoustics, the science of sound as related to the sense of hearing certain vibrations in the air or other matter in contact with the organs of hearing. In ordinary cases of hearing the vibrating medium is air, but fishes hear under water, and all substances capable of vibrating may be employed to propagate and convey sound. Accurate propagation and reproduction of sound in large auditoriums, radio stations, theaters, and the like, can be attained through the use of properly designed surfaces covered or lined with suitable materials that absorb sound vibrations to such a degree as to prevent distortion, confusing overtones, echoes, and areas of unequal sound density. The use of public address or amplifying systems with speaker units placed at strategic points has greatly overcome many of the difficulties formerly encountered when clarity had to be sacrificed for volume. The analysis of sound waves for acoustic purposes has been greatly facilitated by the development of the oscillograph, an instrument that projects an instantaneous graphic picture of sound waves of all kinds, including those beyond the normal audible range, thus making accurate study possible.

Acrobats were originally rope dancers, and among the ancient Greeks and Romans this kind of performance was very popular. In modern days the term has had a much extended meaning, and includes performers in a variety of feats of strength and dexterity which were not practiced by the ancients; thus, in the general term acrobats are included men and women who perform on the trapeze, the horizontal bar, etc.

Acropolis, the high part of any ancient Greek city, usually an eminence overlooking the city, and frequently its citadel. Most notable among such citadels was the Acropolis of Athens, to which the name is now chiefly applied. The Acropolis of Athens was the original city of Athens, later the upper city, as distinguished from the lower, and was built upon a separate spur of Mt. Hymettus. The hill rises out of the plain, a mass of rock about 300 feet high, with precipitous sides, save a narrow access at the western end where there was a zigzag road for chariots. The summit of this rock forms an uneven plain 500 by 1,150 feet at the maximum breadth and length. Within this area were built, chiefly in the days of Pericles, remarkable specimens of architectural art. The buildings were grouped around two principal temples, the Parthenon and the Erechtheum. The largest building of the Acropolis is the imposing gateway, the Propylaea, beside which stands the exquisite little temple of Athena Nike. About the steep sides were lesser temples, statues, theaters, fanes, and odea ("music halls"). Among the famous buildings on the south side of the Acropolis are the Dionysiac theater, and the Odeum of Pericles and the Odeum built by Herodes Atticus in honor of his wife Regilla.

Acrostic, a kind of verse which has afforded amusement to ingenious individuals from very ancient times, and consists of a composition so arranged that the initial letters of the lines, read consecutively, form certain names or words.

Actinic Rays are light rays that cause chemical reaction. The fading of colors, the bleaching of linen, the rotting of fabrics, and the exposure of photographic plates are common effects of the action of actinic rays.

Actinozoa, a group of marine animals of the Sea-Anemone class.

Acts of Parliament comprise public acts which are binding on all British citizens, and private acts which refer to particular persons or places. Although the Magna Charta may be said to have initiated the English Statute Book, it was not until the time of Edward I that Acts of Parliament came to be in any sense general. Acts of Parliament were not printed until the reign of Richard III, and they were not printed in English until the fourth year of Henry VII. The first authorized edition of English Acts of Parliament was published between 1810 and 1824. Scottish Acts date back to 1292 and Irish Acts to 1310.

Adder, or viper, a small, common, poisonous snake widely distributed through Europe and Asia. The scientific name of the adder is *Vipera berus*. Its color is yellowish-brown or olive, with a double series of black spots along the back. The sides are a little paler and are also spotted with black. The adder has a broad, triangular head and a short tail. It rarely exceeds two feet in length.

Adipocere, a chemical substance resembling wax or spermaceti. It is formed when the bodies of men or animals buried in soil of a certain kind are subjected to the action of water or otherwise brought in contact with moisture. In such circumstances the soft parts of the corpses, instead of decaying, may become transformed into adipocere.

Adobe, a kind of clay, the unburned brick made therefrom, and buildings constructed with such brick; common in the southwestern United States and in Latin America. Adobe houses are fireproof, warm in winter and cool in summer.

Adulteration is the act of mixing an inferior substance with a superior one for the sake of greater profit. Adulteration of food, drink, and drugs is prohibited by law.

Advent, a period devoted to religious preparation for the coming celebration of the Nativity (Christmas). It comprises four Sundays. Advent was not observed before the fourth century.

Advertising. "The printed, written, spoken, or pictured representation of a person, product, service, or movement, openly sponsored by the advertiser and at his expense for the purpose of influencing sales, use, votes, or endorsement". This definition of advertising was selected by the judges of a contest conducted in 1932 by *Advertising Age*, a trade paper.

The use of advertising dates back to ancient Greece and Rome, notices painted in black and red having been found by archaelogists on the walls of Pompeii and Herculaneum. In the Middle Ages some merchants employed public criers who walked the streets ringing bells and crying the wares of their clients. The first printed advertisement in the English language appeared in *The Impartial Intelligencer*, London, in 1648; in America the first newspaper advertisement appeared in *The Boston News Letter*, 1704.

At the present time the principal advertising media in the United States and Canada are newspapers, magazines, radio, television, billboards, and direct mail. There is no way of estimating the circulation of the form letters, mail order catalogues, etc., used in direct mail advertising, but it is known that their distribution is enormous. The major part of the expenditure is made by the many small advertisers —retail stores, specialty shops, realtors, auto dealers, and even by individuals. In a country of great distances and a large population, advertising is considered to be a necessary sales and distribution tool. It informs people quickly about goods and the brand names of products and helps them to buy efficiently. To sell the same volume of goods with personal salesmen and no advertising would greatly increase the selling expense. This would add to the ultimate cost to the consumer. While all marketing expense including advertising must be included in the sales price, selling without advertising almost always costs more than selling with the aid of advertising. Moreover, by increasing the sales of a product, advertising often enables the manufacturer to lower the cost of production per unit and to sell articles more cheaply. The costs of advertising on most established items are less than a cent per item.

Because human beings do not act on a simple statement of fact, but rather when desires and emotions are aroused, advertising must be attractively presented with fundamental emotional appeal. So long as it is consistent with truth and is not misleading, such appeal is considered to be proper.

Aerated Bread is made by a special process in which carbonic acid gas is used instead of yeast.

Aerial Navigation. Modern aerial navigation makes extensive use of communication between ship and ground stations via radio. Radio beams projected along the principal airways inform the pilot by means of a signal system of his position with relation to the course he should be flying. Radio beacons are employed in determining directions. The growing use of radar by commercial airlines has provided a new and important navigational device, allowing pilots to find clear paths through stormy areas and giving warning of unseen obstructions at night or in foggy weather.

An important development in navigation is the automatic or "robot" pilot which is a device consisting of two enclosed gyroscopes, one set controlling the rudder and ailerons, the other set controlling the elevators. Should the ship turn off its course, dip, rise, or slip sidewise, the gyroscopes establish contact with an electric motor which operates the controls to right the ship. A more complex system, called inertial guidance, can continuously provide the exact location and height.

The automatic pilot is used extensively in transoceanic and transcontinental service and has been perfected to the point where it can be made to follow a radio beam automatically and land the ship if necessary (as in fog, heavy snow, etc.), using a ground-controlled radar guidance system.

Aerial Photography, photography from the air. As with other phases of aeronautics, aerial photography received its great impetus in the World War period when its importance as a mapping device was made clear. Following that time aerial photography has been put to wide usage, notably in surveying and topographical work. It is also used to make studies of timber growth, the location of archaeological remains, city planning, and in the discovery and location of schools of fish and seal herds. Modern aerial cameras are so constructed as to permit photographing wide areas on a single film.

During the Second World War aerial photography reached a higher degree of perfection. The taking of pictures at high plane speed even at extremely low altitudes was achieved. Cameras were attached to the fastest fighter planes, minus guns to accommodate heavy photo equipment, and these high-speed cameras snapped wide-angled, detailed photographs of the terrain within enemy lines. Color photography was made practicable for aerial use through fast new films and processes.

Aerial Transportation. In the early days of air transportation only mail was carried, but with phenomenal rapidity the service was extended to accommodate passengers and freight. In 1919, which may be said to mark the beginnings of air transportation, the world routes totaled only 3,200 miles. By 1933 the airlines, previously interested only in carrying the mail and willing, but not anxious, to carry passengers, began to seek passenger service with the introduction of the first relatively modern-appearing aircraft. These twin-engine airplanes, having streamlined bodies and engines faired into the wings, included the Boeing 247, the Lockheed Electra, and the Douglas DC-2. When the Civil Aeronautics Act was passed in 1938, those airlines that had managed to weather the depression (principally through government mail contracts) had largely converted to the Douglas DC-3, made famous during World War II as the C-47, the workhorse of the air. Despite a top speed of about 220 miles per hour, their dependability, and their ability to take off from short airfields kept them on local service airlines into the late 1950's.

The airlines did an incredible job of transporting people and goods during World War II, despite the loss of many aircraft, pilots, and crews to the services. By the end of the war, the people of the United States had become airminded, and the airlines rushed to convert to the four-engine aircraft, developed during the war, that would serve them through the 1950's; the Lockheed Constellation, the Douglas DC-6 with its later modification, the DC-7, and the Boeing Stratocruiser, a huge airliner developed as a modification of the B-29 Superfortress bomber. These new aircraft had pressurized cabins to maintain comfortable air pressures even at great heights, engines with such an excess of power that the planes could take off and climb on any two engines of the four, and height and range capability to take them over or around bad weather and on nonstop transoceanic and transcontinental flights. All could cruise at over 300 miles per hour, and all had adjustable-pitch propellers to allow the engines to operate more efficiently and to aid the wheel brakes in slowing these aircraft.

During this period, also, two-place, four-place, and larger light planes came into ever increasing use by business houses and individuals to carry executives around the country in their work. These planes had one or two engines or, more recently, small jet engines that frequently carried them at speeds above 200 miles per hour over great distances.

The first flight of the Boeing 707 on July 15, 1954, inaugurated the use of four-jet passenger planes designed to cruise at speeds over 500 miles an hour in the United States. Other four-jet passenger aircraft included the Douglas DC-8 and the Convair 880.

Aerial Warfare. It was not long after the airplane had been developed to the point where sustained flights of reasonable duration could be made that it was realized that planes could be usefully adapted to military and naval operations. The first uncertain warplanes, flown in 1914, were used solely for spotting artillery targets and enemy troop concentrations. The beginnings of aerial warfare occurred when enemy observation planes began taking pot shots at each other, first with pistols and rifles, later with swiveling machine guns, and finally with fixed machine guns synchronized to fire through the whirling propeller blades. These aircraft developed into fighter planes that sought out and tried to shoot down enemy airplanes wherever they could find them, often with the result that spectacular dogfights were fought between opposing pilots. Multi-engined bombing planes also were developed, and World War I saw the development of strategic bombing, aerial mapping and photography, ground support tactics, antisubmarine patrolling, tactical naval aviation, and antiaircraft artillery. The outbreak of World War II, 30 years later, found airplanes playing a dominant role in the German march across most of Europe and the subsequent Allied march into Germany and Japan. Pearl Harbor and later Pacific battles clearly demonstrated that air power, properly applied, could destroy sea power and immobilize land power.

The end of World War II saw the beginning of atomic bombs and of the jet aircraft that were eventually to be able to deliver an atomic or hydrogen bomb on any target in the world. World War II had also seen the first use of rockets fired from aircraft and the first ballistic missile, the V-2; these were later to evolve into tactical guided missiles and intercontinental ballistic missiles.

The Korean War was the first in which jet aircraft met in combat. The Communist Chinese, North Korean, and, it is believed, some Russian pilots flew the fast and maneuverable Mig-15, made in the U.S.S.R., while the most important United Nations plane, flown principally by U. S. pilots, was the F-86 Saber. The air victory went to the U. N. primarily because of the better training and tactics of the U. S. pilots.

Many warplanes of the post-Korean period had top speeds in excess of 1,000 miles per hour and utilized both guided and unguided rocket missiles in place of both bombs and bullets. The guided missiles actually seek out and destroy the enemy.

Aerodynamics, in physics, that branch of dynamics which deals with the motion of gases and the force exerted by them. More commonly the term is used to describe the science of the mechanical principles involved in the construction and flight of airplanes and airships. An outstanding development is the wind tunnel by means of which the force exerted by air against the wings and fuselage of an airplane or the resistance offered by these, may be studied.

Aerolite, the name given to meteoric stones which sometimes fall from the sky to the earth. These substances usually contain a large proportion of iron, and many have been of great weight and dimensions.

Aesthetics concerns itself with the beautiful, and is applied not only in the field of art, but in connection with metaphysics and science. From the days of ancient Greece there have been ardent followers of aesthetics, and many systems have been evolved.

Affidavit is a written or printed statement of facts to which a deponent makes formal oath before a judicially qualified person.

Affirmation is a declaration made in lieu of an oath by persons objecting to be sworn because of religious or other scruples.

Afrikander, a name usually given to the South African Dutch, but rightly applied to all African-born whites.

Afterdamp is a mixture of carbon monoxide and carbon dioxide that is formed in a mine after an explosion and causes suffocation. It is also called "choke-damp."

Agape, a "love-feast" held by the early Christians, in commemoration of the Lord's Supper. Condemned by the Council of Carthage, 397, but revived in recent times in a modified form by Moravians and some Methodists.

Agar-agar, a vegetable gum obtained from seaweeds, and largely employed in the Orient in making soups and jellies.

Agate, a variegated stone composed of nearly pure silica. Germany, Brazil, and India furnish the main supplies, and Scotland has a species of agate called Scotch pebble.

Agave, the American aloe, which sometimes does not attain to flowering maturity under sixty or seventy years, and then dies.

Age is a term of wide application, variously used at different periods. In classical mythology five successive ages or races were defined—the golden or primitive, when people enjoyed unalloyed happiness without labor, and lived on the fruits of the earth; the silver, when the worship of the gods was neglected; the brazen, which was warlike and violent; the heroic when the gods and semi-gods held sway; and the iron, representing the lowest point of human degradation. Hesiod and Ovid both retain this classification. It is common to call the ages after some pre-eminent, dominating personality or characteristic; thus, we have the Age of Pericles, the Augustan Age, the Elizabethan Age, the Dark Ages, the Middle Ages, the Steam Age, and so forth. Then there are the geological ages—classifying the ages according to the evidences of the various strata. Archaeologists divide the prehistoric periods into the Stone, Bronze, and Iron Ages. As regards individual life, age has its four main divisions of infancy, youth, manhood, and old age. Shakespeare gave us his "Seven Ages"; Keats adopted the four seasons classification.

Agnosticism, a term first used by Huxley in 1869 to denote the theory that beyond our personal knowledge of phenomena all is uncertainty. This was his own attitude toward spiritual things. Agnosticism neither denies nor affirms the existence of God.

Agnus Dei (Lamb of God), the name of a Roman Catholic prayer.

Ahriman, the Zoroastrian spirit of destruction.

Air is a mixture of gases forming the atmosphere we breathe. The normal constituents of air are, nitrogen 78.1 per cent, oxygen 21.0 per cent, and argon 0.9 per cent, together with varying amounts of water vapor and carbon dioxide, and traces of neon, helium, hydrogen, krypton, and xenon. Beyond these are found varying traces of nitric acid, ammonia, and particles of solid matter. The height of the atmosphere is supposed to be about 40 miles. It is the oxygen of the air that maintains animal life.

Airbrush, a device for the application of paint, varnish, shellac, enamel, or some other protective fluid to a surface by means of compressed air. The atomizing powers of compressed air when applied to liquids were first investigated many years ago, but it is only during the last thirty years that commercially successful airbrushes have been manufactured.

The first practical airbrushes were used for photographic retouching and the hairline work in newspaper display advertising and show-card writing. Later, adaptations and enlargements of this brush became common in mass-production industry, and in recent years portable airbrush machines have been used for such outdoor work as house and bridge painting.

Aircraft Carrier. An important development of the use of aircraft at sea is the aircraft carrier, an armed ship designed and constructed as a landing field, hangar and repair shop for airplanes. Toward the end of World War I the advantage of a "floating base" became apparent, and the carrier was designed. Its top deck is flat, with superstructure contained in an "island" to allow aircraft enough space for landing and taking off. Lower decks contain hangar space, repair shops, and quarters for personnel. Carriers in World War II increased by many miles the range of fighting power. Faster but less heavily armed than battleships, their planes are their best protection; they provide air cover for landings, convoys, task forces.

Air Gun, a gun which propels bullets by the expansive power of compressed air. The modern air gun is primarily a toy rather than a weapon. It is operated by means of an air chamber attached to the gun into which compressed air is introduced by a pumping device. When the trigger is pulled a valve releases the compressed air behind the bullet, firing the gun. Air guns have been known in some form for more than 200 years, but have never been satisfactorily used in warfare.

Air Lock, a transitional chamber between the outer air and those parts of a pneumatic caisson which contain compressed air. Pneumatic caissons are often used in river-bed and off-shore construction work. It is impossible for men to pass directly from them to regions of normal pressure without running grave risk of incurring "the bends," a painful and sometimes fatal condition caused by sudden and extreme reductions in air pressure. By entering the air lock when it is under high pressure and sitting in it until the pressure has been reduced to that of the outer air, workmen minimize the risk of incurring "the bends".

Airplane, a man-carrying device propelled by some form of internal-combustion engine and supported in the air by one (usually) or more fixed wings.

It was not until 1809 that the first practical and original contribution was made to aeronautics as a science. In that year, and again in 1810, Sir George Cayley, an Englishman, published a record of experiments with large model gliders and even calculated the energy necessary for propulsion by an engine. The first model actually to fly was built by John Stringfellow.

Experiments with gliders continued to be made by Lilienthal, Chanute, and the Wright brothers, the last-named progressing so far as to design a model in which they installed a 16-horsepower four-cylinder engine; and on Dec. 17, 1903, at Kitty Hawk, North Carolina, made a successful flight lasting 59 seconds and covering a distance of 859 feet. This marked the first instance in which a person had been carried from the ground in actual flight by mechanical means.

General use of the airplane began in World War I, when the airplane, of necessity, began to acquire the vitally essential qualities of speed, reliability, and great strength for a minimum of weight. The years following the war saw a slow but steady increase in the numbers and uses of airplanes. American and British fliers made long-distance flights, while the barnstorming ex-military pilots flying open cockpit planes around the country familiarized people with airplanes and their possibilities. Commercial aviation and air-mail flying also began to develop during this period, particularly after Charles Lindbergh's 1927 nonstop flight from New York to Paris brought new popularity to the airplane and a new appreciation of what it could do. By the middle of the 1930's, regular air service had been established in nearly all civilized parts of the world.

Mechanically, the principal changes in airplanes during these years were increases in size and power and the development of more efficient airfoils and engines. The monoplane with enclosed cabin or cockpits replaced the open-cockpit biplane in general acceptance, and the trend was toward multiengined aircraft, particularly for transports and bombers.

During the six years of World War II, 1939-1945, the development of airplanes was greatly accelerated by the military needs of the warring nations. Among the more important developments of this period were the development of reversible-pitch propellers, to shorten landing runs, jet-assisted take-off (JATO) rockets to shorten take-off runs, more powerful engines, and pressurized cabins for high-altitude flying. Perhaps the most notable advance of this period, however, was the introduction of the first operational jet plane, the German Messerschmitt ME 262 Sturmvogel (Stormbird), in early 1944. Fortunately for Allied bombers, which this jet fighter could destroy almost at will, only 1,294 Sturmvogels were built by the end of the war.

Following the war, government-sponsored airplane research in the U. S. was continued, spurred on by the Korean conflict and the Cold War. The experimental rocket-powered aircraft, the Bell X-1, was the first airplane to exceed the speed of sound when, on Oct. 14, 1947, it attained 967 miles per hour at 70,140 feet altitude. The X-1 later flew 1,652 miles per hour and could reach an altitude of 90,000 feet. Its successor, the Bell X-2, was able to fly 1,900 miles an hour and reach an altitude of 125,000 feet.

The first operational U. S. jet airplane, the Lockheed F-80 Shooting Star, was also the first U. S. jet airplane to engage an enemy jet, the superior Russian Mig-15, during the Korean War. Rapid airplane development continued, and speeds continuously increased. As speeds increased above the speed of sound, speeds began to be measured in Mach numbers, multiples of the speed of sound. By the late 1950's, operational jet military aircraft were able to fly continuously at speeds above Mach 2, twice the speed of sound (about 1,400 miles per hour). These included the Convair B-58 Hustler, a bomber, and the Lockheed F-104 Starfighter, capable of approaching Mach 3.

Airpocket, the variation in wind velocity which causes aircraft to ride unevenly, called by pilots gusts or bumps.

Air Pump, an instrument for withdrawing air from a closed space (a vacuum pump) or a similar instrument for compressing air. A simple type of vacuum pump consists of a closed chamber from which the air is to be exhausted, connected with a cylinder, in which there is a piston. In the piston and between the chamber and cylinder are valves opening toward the outside atmosphere. When the piston is drawn up, atmospheric pressure closes its valve, and air is drawn from the chamber. When it is pushed down, pressure from the cylinder opens its valve, while keeping the valve leading to the chamber closed. Successive strokes of the piston produce a partial vacuum in the chamber. Air pumps of this type were constructed by Otto von Guericke (1601-1686), earliest experimenter on vacua. A pump for compressing air would be similar in structure, except that the valves would open away from the outside atmosphere, thus confining air in the chamber except when pressure in the cylinder was greater.

Airship. The airship is an outgrowth of the balloon and is distinguished from it in that it is cigar-shaped instead of globular, but it is similar in that a lighter-than-air gas, hydrogen or helium, is used for lifting power. It is mechanically propelled and may be non-rigid, semi-rigid, or rigid in form.

The non-rigid type is held in shape by the internal pressure of its gas content and is known as a blimp; the semi-rigid type has a keel running lengthwise along its bottom, and the rigid design, commonly known as the *dirigible*, consists of a framework of aluminum or duralumin divided into compartments which contain the gas cells, the whole being covered by fabric. Motive power is supplied by gasoline engines which drive propellers jutting on arms from the sides. Built into the lower front of the framework and protruding from it is the gondola which contains accommodations for crew, passengers, freight, observation and control rooms.

To Guyot of France must go the credit of conceiving the airship when in 1784 he published a proposal to build an egg-shaped balloon the length of which should exceed its height. General Meusnier, also of France, was the first to introduce small bags or balloonets in the envelope, forerunners of the modern gas cells.

To Count Zeppelin goes the credit for constructing the first airship having a rigid framework. It was 420 ft. long, 38 ft. in diameter and had a capacity of 400,000 cu. ft. The frame was of aluminum covered with specially treated linen and silk; the hydrogen used for lifting power was contained in bags in special compartments. Two 16-horsepower engines were mounted in separate cars. He flew this ship successfully on Oct. 21, 1906, and achieved a speed of almost 20 miles per hour.

In England, the rigid airship was not developed to any appreciable degree until after the World War, although a small craft, the R9, was completed in 1917. In 1916 a German dirigible was brought down in good condition, and the British ship, R-34, was designed from it and made the first trans-Atlantic dirigible flight (1919).

In the United States, airship development paralleled that in England, the first domestically built ship, the Shenandoah, being completed by the Navy in 1923. After a few flights she was destroyed by a storm in 1925. Meanwhile an Italian-made ship, the Roma, had been purchased but she, too, crashed (1922), carrying 34 men to death. Another foreign-built ship, the German ZR-3, later the Los Angeles, was delivered to the government (1924) as part of war reparations, and for ten years served as a training and experimental ship, ultimately living out her days secured to a mooring mast and used to accumulate mooring data. Two ships of new design, the Akron and the Macon, were commissioned; but the former crashed in 1933 and the latter went down in the Pacific, 1935. These disasters mark the end of rigid airship construction in the United States.

Akka, a race of pigmies inhabiting the territory between the rivers Aruwimi and Nepoko, in Central Africa.

Alabama Claims. The *Alabama,* a Confederate cruiser which destroyed Northern shipping during the American Civil War, was a bark-rigged steamer of 1,040 tons, built at Birkenhead, England. The purpose of the building of the ship was known to the United States minister, but before orders for her detention were finally obtained she had departed (July 31, 1862). At the Azores she was equipped and manned by an English crew, under the command of Capt. Raphael Semmes of Maryland. In less than two years the *Alabama* captured or sank between sixty-five and seventy Northern vessels with cargoes valued at about $5,000,000. In June, 1864, she was intercepted outside Cherbourg by the Federal corvette, *Kearsarge,* and was surrendered after an hour's battle.

In 1871, after fruitless negotiation, the United States made a series of claims against the British government for damages done to American shipping by the *Alabama* and other Confederate raiders built in England in violation of international law. By the Treaty of Washington the two governments referred the question to an arbitration tribunal which met in 1872. The tribunal decided that the British government was not responsible for the acts of six of the vessels, but awarded damages of $15,500,000 for the depredations of the *Alabama* and two others. Claims for indirect damages, such as decrease of trade and prolongation of the war were rejected. The award was paid promptly, and the incident was significant as being the first formal use of arbitration to settle disputes between major powers, defining the responsibilities of a neutral toward nations at war.

Alabaster, a soft, crystalline form of sulphate of lime, or granulated gypsum, easily worked for statuary and other ornamental articles, and capable of being highly polished. Solterra, in Tuscany, yields the finest; that in highest ancient repute came from Alabastron, in Egypt, near the modern Antinoë.

Alamo, The, a Franciscan mission in what is now San Antonio, Texas, and the site of a gallant defense during the Texan War for Independence. It was built about 1722 and consisted of a chapel, convent yard, convent and hospital building, and a plaza, all surrounded by a stout wall. After the disappearance of the Indians from the locality, the mission was abandoned, although after 1793 it was used occasionally as a fort.

Al Araf, the mid-heaven of the Koran, where those whose deeds have been neither decidedly good nor very bad spend their afterlife.

Albatross, a large white ocean bird whose wings measure from ten to twelve feet when outstretched.

Albigenses, a small religious sect who in the 12th century, at Albi, in France, opposed the papal rule, but were ultimately put down by Innocent III.

Albino, a term first applied to designate certain white Negroes whom the Portuguese navigators met with in Africa. It is now used to describe plants and animals which lack normal pigmentation. Albino animals have white skin and hair and pink eyes. Albinos cannot see well in the sunlight; it is only in semi-darkness that they discern objects clearly.

Al Borak, a winged being on which Mohammed was credited with having traveled through the heavens.

Album, a term now used for a book of photographs, autographs, or other collections, but originally applied to the tablets on which public decrees, edicts, etc., were inscribed in ancient Rome. In Medieval times the word was used to designate lists of various kinds.

Albumin, protein common to most animal and vegetable tissues. It coagulates under heat, or by the action of acid or alcohol, and is further capable of soluble or insoluble modifications.

Alcalde, a Spanish mayor, judge or magistrate, or in Portugal a justice of the peace: not to be confounded with the similar word "alcaide" which signifies the keeper of a castle or prison along both shores of the Mediterranean. The latter is a military term, the former signifies always a civil functionary, but both are from the same Arabic root.

Alcazar, the famous palace at Seville, in ancient days the residence of the Moorish kings.

Alchemy was from the 12th to the 17th century regarded by many philosophers and enthusiasts as a science capable of demonstration in the production of one or other of three supposed chemical combinations—the philosopher's stone, which was to transmute the baser metals into gold; the elixir of life, that was to prolong existence indefinitely; and the alkahest, or universal solvent. Men of great attainments, monarchs, ecclesiastics, and all classes of people dabbled in alchemy; lives were given up entirely to it, fortunes were wasted upon it. Gerber, Roger Bacon, Albertus Magnus, Paracelsus, and many other men of note were devoted alchemists. The experiments of the alchemists, however, in spite of their being directed toward an impossible end, resulted in many discoveries that were of value to the real science of chemistry.

Alco, a dog, native to tropical America. It is long-haired and has pendulous ears; sometimes domesticated. The colors most prominent are yellow and white, and the animal is tractable and held in considerable esteem.

Alcohol, a chemical combination of carbon, hydrogen, and oxygen, produced by the distillation of fermented liquors. Various alcohols are used in the manufacture of numerous products, such as chloroform, ether, perfumes, etc. The most general use, however, is in imparting a stimulative action to liquors. Methyl alcohol or wood alcohol is poisonous.

Aldebaran, a star of the first magnitude, commonly known as the Bull's Eye, being in the constellation of Taurus.

Aldehyde, the generic term for a class of chemical bodies, of which the best-known is acetaldehyde. They are produced by oxidation of primary alcohols and many are used in the manufacture of synthetic resins.

Alderman, a title first instituted by the Saxons and given to governors, magistrates, etc. Afterward adopted to designate a member of the legislative branch of a city government.

Aldine Editions, the books printed by Aldus Manutius and his family, in Venice, 1490-1597. They comprise the first printing of many Greek and Roman classics; others contain corrected texts of modern classic writers, as of Petrarch, Dante, or Boccaccio, carefully collated with the MSS. All of them are distinguished for the remarkable correctness of the texts. The editions published by Aldus Manutius (1450-1515), the father, form an epoch in the annals of printing. In all he created 9 new type faces for the printing of Greek, and 14 new type faces for the printing of Latin. It is to him, or rather to the engraver, Francesco of Bologna, that we owe the types called by the Italians *Corsivi*, and known to us as italics, which he used for the first time in the octavo editions of ancient and modern classics, commencing with Vergil (1501).

Alexandrian Library, a remarkable collection of books, the largest of the ancient world, was founded by Ptolemy I of Egypt and fostered by his son. During its most flourishing period, under the direction of Zenodotus, Aristarchus of Byzantium, Callimachus, Apollonius Rhodius, and others, it is said to have contained 490,000, or, according to another authority, including all duplicates, as many as 700,000 volumes. The greater part of the library, which embraced the collected literature of Greece, India, and Egypt, was contained in the famous Museum, in the quarter of Alexandria called the Brucheion. During Julius Caesar's occupation of Alexandria, this part of the library was destroyed by fire.

Alexandrines are stanzas each line of which contains twelve syllables—six measures.

Algae, a variety of aquatic flowerless plants of which seaweed is a leading example. There are two main divisions—marine and fresh-water algae.

Algebra, a branch of mathematics in which symbols are used in place of numbers. Sir Isaac Newton styled it the "universal arithmetic".

Algol, a double star of the Perseus constellation situated in the head of Medusa.

Alhambra, the ancient palace of the Moorish kings near Granada, built in the 14th century, and remarkable for its architectural grace and beauty.

Alias, a Latin term signifying "otherwise," and used in legal proceedings to indicate the assumption of a false name or names.

Alibi, signifying "elsewhere" is the plea of a person who desires to prove that he was at some place away from that he is charged with having been at when a particular offense was committed.

Alien, any person residing in a country of which he is not a citizen. By the laws of the United States all those born in the U. S., and the children of its male citizens born abroad are held to be American citizens; but all other foreign-born individuals are aliens until made citizens by naturalization. In the United States aliens are nominally prohibited from acquiring title to real estate, but in practice they may own lands subject to proceedings by the state to determine the fact of alienage; and, moreover, in nearly all the states there are special provisions removing such restrictions from resident aliens who are in the course of naturalization. The rights of aliens to hold personal property and carry on trade are the same as those of citizens.

Alimony, in law, the allowance awarded out of her husband's estate, to which a wife is entitled on separation or divorce. Jurisdiction in this matter in England rested with the ecclesiastical court until 1857, when it was conferred upon a court of divorce. In the United States it is vested in the courts of equity. Alimony may be granted by the court during litigation, in which case it is known as *pendente lite* (during the suit); or at the conclusion of the suit, when it is called permanent. The former enables the wife to pursue the litigation, whether proceedings have been brought by or against her. The amount granted lies within the discretion of the court. Permanent alimony is a periodical allowance, awarded to the wife if the termination of the suit is favorable to her. By a writ of *ne exeat* (let him not depart), the court can prevent the husband from leaving the State if he has not provided sufficient security to cover the payments awarded to his wife.

Alizarin, the chief coloring matter of madder; now produced synthetically from coal tar.

Alkali, the general name given to a number of substances which are the opposite of acids in their chemical action. The term is commonly applied to soluble alkaline bodies, the principal of which are potash, soda, lithia, aqueous ammonia, lime, baryta, and strontia. The action of the solutions of these bodies is caustic on animal and vegetable substances, and they are extensively used in industrial processes.

Allegiance, the duty owing from a citizen to the state or community which affords him protection. Natural or implied allegiance is the obedience which every native citizen owes to the state or community in which he lives. By enjoying the benefits of a society he comes under an implied obligation to defend it. Express allegiance is the obligation arising from a promise or an oath, as in the case of naturalized citizens. Local or temporary allegiance is the obedience which a foreigner owes to the laws of the country in which he lives. In the United States, allegiance is due first and principally to the federal constitution and government, and second to the state constitution and government in and under which a citizen resides. When children of citizens of the United States are born in a foreign land, they still owe allegiance to the United States.

Allegory, a narrative or discourse couched in figurative language and extended to point a moral; a good example is Bunyan's *Pilgrim's Progress*.

Allergy, the reaction exhibited by susceptible persons to substances which produce no ill effects in the majority of people. The term "allergy" was coined in 1906 by von Pirquet, who described the "altered reactivity" of certain individuals to foreign substances. Hay fever is probably the most widespread of allergic disturbances; while hives, affecting the skin, and bronchial asthma, affecting the bronchial tubes, also occur frequently. It is estimated that these ailments and other less easily recognized forms of allergic reaction afflict about one out of ten inhabitants of the United States. More than a million Americans are believed to suffer severely from asthma, and from two to three millions from hay fever alone.

Alligator, the lizardlike reptile common in the lower Mississippi and adjacent lakes and marshes.

Alliteration, a succession of words in which the accented syllables begin with the same letter. This device was widely used in Old German, Norse, and Anglo-Saxon verse before the introduction of rhyme. Alliteration has, at different times, had varying degrees of popularity. In the early part of the seventeenth century its usage was fashionable not only in poetry but also in prose. Since then it has suffered an eclipse in prose, though it still lingers in such daily expressions as "kith and kin," "house and home," "life and limb." In poetry, however, it has been retained to produce certain desired effects.

Gray, in his *Elegy Written in a Country Churchyard*, attained a neat effect by means of alliteration:

The curfew tolls the knell of parting day,
The lowing herd winds slowly o'er the lea,
The ploughman homeward plods his weary way,
And leaves the world to darkness and to me.

Alloys are combinations of metals. The alloys best known are brass, composed of copper and zinc; German silver, of copper, zinc and nickel; pewter, of tin and lead; bell-metal, of copper and tin. An alloy containing mercury is termed an amalgam.

All Saints' Day, Nov. 1, is common to both the Episcopal and Roman Catholic churches, and is in commemoration of the saints generally, or such as have no special day set apart for them. Instituted by Pope Boniface IV early in the 7th century, this ecclesiastical festival was formerly called "All Hallows".

All Souls' Day, Nov. 2, is a festival of the Roman Catholic Church, intended for the mitigation by prayer of the sufferings of souls in purgatory. The commemoration was enjoined by Abbot Odilo of Cluny during the 11th century upon the monastic order over which he presided, and was afterward adopted generally throughout the Roman Communion.

Allspice, a flavoring obtained from a West Indian tree of the myrtle order. The essential oil of its unripe fruit is a powerful irritant, and the bruised berries are carminative.

Alluvium, accumulations of sand, mud, gravel, etc. washed down by rivers and forming deposits.

Almanac, an annual compilation, based on the calendar, embracing information pertinent to the various days of the year, the seasons, etc., with astronomical calculations and miscellaneous information more or less detailed, according to the special purpose for which it is prepared. Before the invention of printing there was no satisfactory method of distributing to the public systematically arranged information about the calendar for the year and the forthcoming astronomical phenomena; but different devices were employed by the people. One of these was the so-called clog almanac, a block of wood, upon which the Sundays and other fixed days were notched, and characters inscribed to distinguish them. It is supposed to have originated with the Danes and was still in use in rural households in the northern portion of England at the end of the 17th century.

The oldest printed almanac is attributed to Georg von Purbach, of Vienna, in the middle of the 15th century, and entitled Pro Annis Pluribus. Yearly almanacs were printed elsewhere in Europe in the course of the 16th century. In the 17th century all sorts of astrological and meteorological information and other kinds of news were published in the almanacs and took the place, in a measure, of the newspaper of today.

The first American almanac was that of William Pierce of Cambridge, published in 1639. The most famous of American almanacs were *Poor Richard's*, published in Philadelphia by Benjamin Franklin, from 1733 to 1757, under the pseudonym of Richard Saunders. These almanacs contained many pleasant and witty verses, jests, and sayings.

Some of the almanacs that are regularly published every year are extremely useful and are indeed almost indispensable to men engaged in official, mercantile, literary, or professional business. Several of the largest newspapers in the United States now issue almanacs, which are compilations of vital statistics, and year-books of current events.

Almond, the fruit of the *Amygdalus communis*, indigenous to Persia, Asia Minor, and parts of North Africa. There are sweet and bitter almonds, the former being a favorite edible, the latter containing prussic acid.

Almoner was a monastery official charged with the distribution of alms.

Aloe, a large plant of the lily-wort family, growing naturally only in warm climates, and yielding by evaporation a purgative substance of great bitterness. It flowers every eight years.

Alopecias, a genus of fishes of the shark family, one of the most notable varieties of which is the thresher, or fox-shark.

Alpaca, a South American ruminant whose wool is woven into a soft fabric known by the same name.

Alpha and Omega, an expression incorporating the first and last letters of the Greek alphabet and used to convey the idea of the beginning and end of anything—the whole of it.

Alphabet (so called from the first two letters of the Greek alphabet—alpha, beta) is the term applied to the collection of letters from which the words of a language are made up. The Semites are credited with the invention of the first alphabet. The Chinese have no alphabet, but signs which convey ideas. The Sanskrit alphabet has 40 letters.

Altar, originally a table or elevated place upon which sacrifices were offered up, and still symbolically the place of sacrifice in Roman Catholic churches. In most Protestant churches the communion table is the altar.

Altimeter, an instrument designed for the compilation or measurement of altitudes.

Altitude, an astronomical term, signifying the angular elevation of a heavenly body above the horizon, true or apparent—that is, as it appears to the eye, or as the result of calculation. The observation may be made with quadrant or sextant.

Alto-Relievo, a term applied to sculptured designs which are depicted in prominent relief on a flat surface, technically signifying that the projection exceeds one-half of the true proportions of the objects represented. Basso-relievo is carving kept lower than one-half such proportionate projection.

Altruism, a term invented by Comte to denote devotion to the welfare of others, the opposite of egoism.

Alum, a compound salt used in various industrial processes, especially dyeing, its constituents being sulphuric acid, alumina, an alkali, and water. The nature of the alkali introduced gives it its distinctive character, so that there are potash alum, soda alum, and ammonia alum.

Alumina, is the oxide of aluminum and is used as a basis for fine pottery.

Aluminum, a metallic element having properties of light weight, pliability, and great strength. It resists the action of the air, is impervious to nitric acid, and its conductivity is about one-third that of silver. It forms alloys with most metals.

Amalgam, the term applied to any alloy of which mercury forms a part.

Amazons, the women of an Indian tribe on the banks of the Maranon, in South America, who assisted their husbands in resisting Spanish invasion; also the female warriors of any land, such as the Amazons attached to the army of the king of Dahomey. The Amazons were a mythological race supposed by the ancients to have inhabited some region of Asia and to have been ruled by warlike women. According to Pliny they were in the habit of cutting off the right breast, to be able to use the right arm freely in war.

Amber, a brittle resinous substance of vegetable origin, obtained mostly from the Baltic coasts and used for ornaments, pipe mouth-pieces, etc.

Amblyopsis, a species of fish, practically sightless, with inoperative organs of hearing and feeling, that inhabits the Mammoth Cave of Kentucky — a remarkable illustration of the failure of senses not brought into use.

Ambulance, an ambulating hospital, for affording surgical aid to persons wounded in battle; the term is also applied to vehicles for conveying injured or sick persons to hospitals. An Ambulance Corps is part of a regular army equipment. The French were the first to adopt ambulances.

Ambuscade, a military maneuver by which troops are ambushed for a surprise attack upon an enemy.

America's Cup, a prize trophy first offered in 1851 by the Royal Yacht Squadron and open to yachts of all nations. It was won in the first year by the *America*, a New York yacht, and has remained in the United States ever since, despite attempts to recapture it by Lord Dunraven, Sir Thomas Lipton, Mr. T. O. M. Sopwith, and others.

Amethyst, a variety of precious stone of violet-blue or purple color, occurring in crystals and greenstone rocks, and fairly abundant in Brazil, Russia and India.

Amianthium, a plant of the bunchflower family, called "Fall Poison" because of the notion that cattle feeding on its foliage in autumn will suffer ill effects.

Amice, a linen vestment worn about the neck by Roman Catholic and many Episcopal priests under the alb when officiating at Mass or Holy Eucharist. Formerly it was worn on the head by priests and pilgrims.

Amiens, Treaty of, signed by England, France, Spain, and Holland in 1802. Fresh cause of quarrel was soon found, however, and Napoleon resumed the warfare, which ended only with Waterloo.

Ammonia, a colorless gaseous compound comprising three atoms of hydrogen to one of nitrogen. It is obtained from various sources but formerly was made by heating the horns and hoofs of deer, thus acquiring the name of spirits of hartshorn. The ammonia of commerce is now produced by coal decomposition in the course of gas-making and by direct synthesis.

Ammonites, extinct snail-like animals which inhabited coiled shells of beautiful design. Their fossils are found in the secondary system of rocks.

Ammonium, the basic radical of ammonium salts, a compound of hydrogen and nitrogen.

Amnesty, an act of grace by which a ruler or governing power pardons a group of political offenders. It is usually absolute, but it may be partial, as when it excepts certain specified persons from its operation.

Amoeba, a minute form of life, gelatinous, without rudiments, of the lowest organization, and only discernible through the microscope. It is found in fresh and stagnant waters.

Amorphism, a term used to indicate the absence of crystalline form in any body or substance.

Ampere, the recognized unit of measure for electric currents.

Amphibia, a class of vertebrate animals possessing structural peculiarities common to both reptiles and fish, enabling them to live either in water or on land. The most familiar examples of the class are frogs, newts, and toads.

Amphitheater, a double theater. The ancient theaters were nearly semi-circular in shape. The place where the exhibitions were given was called the arena (Lat. "sand"), because it was covered with sand or sawdust. The part next the arena was called the podium, and was assigned to the emperor, the senators, and the ambassadors of foreign nations. It was separated from the arena by an iron railing and by a canal. Behind it rose tiers of seats, the first 14, which were cushioned, being occupied by the equites, and the rest which were of bare stone, being given over to the common people. Except when it rained or was exceedingly hot, the amphitheater was uncovered. Among the sights were combats of gladiators and of wild beasts. The Romans built amphitheaters wherever they went. Remains are still to be found in various parts of Europe but the most splendid ruins are those of the Colosseum at Rome, which was said to have held 87,000 people. The term is applied in modern usage to the oval stadia devoted to open-air concerts and sports. The Chicago stadium has a capacity of 125,000; Franklin Field, Philadelphia, 83,000; the Yale Bowl at New Haven, 80,000; the stadium at Baltimore 78,000; and the Municipal Stadium at Los Angeles has held 105,000.

Amphora, a large clay vessel used by the Romans for preserving wine, fruit, oil, etc.

Amulet, a necklace or other ornament worn as a charm against evil.

Anabaptists, a sect that came into prominence during the Reformation period. John of Leyden was one of their leaders, but Munzer was their chief prophet. They committed many acts of violence under the cloak of religious zeal, but their operations were mainly confined to Germany. They are not to be identified in any way with the Baptists.

Anabasis, Xenophon's narrative of the exploits of Cyrus the Younger against his brother Artaxerxes of Persia, 401 B. C. It is the title also of Arrian's history of Alexander the Great's expedition to Asia.

Anachronism, a confusion of time and events; alluding to something as belonging to a period to which it does not properly belong. To represent persons of the 18th century riding in railway trains would be an obvious anachronism.

Anaconda, a large and powerful South American snake.

Anagram, a literary exercise which consists of using the letters in a given word or phrase to form a different word or phrase.

Analogy, a method of argument whereby an inference is drawn from one set of facts and applied to another to which it has some resemblance.

Analysis, the process by which a substance is reduced or broken up into its original elements. Qualitative analysis reveals the presence of certain materials; quantitative analysis shows those materials in their respective proportions. Analysis as applied to grammar, mathematics, and logic resolves phrases, propositions, and arguments into their separate parts.

Anarchism, a political and social theory advocating a state of society in which authority is at a minimum, and organized authoritarian government nonexistent. According to anarchism, the structure of the ideal society would derive from cooperation and agreements between groups of workers of varying occupation, and not from any formalized rule imposed from above; centralized authority, as well as capitalism and private property, would no longer exist. Anarchistic tendencies first became notably influential as a phase of thought toward the middle of the 19th century, when they were developed under an increasing sense of the misery of the oppressed masses of humanity. The founder of modern anarchism was Peter Joseph Proudhon (1809-1865). The labor agitations that began in the middle of the 19th century were accompanied by a development of the anarchist party, chiefly under the influence of Russian thinkers. The founder of this party was Michael Bakunin (1814-1876). He followed Proudhon in advocating the free development of the powers of the individual in groups and societies of workers, resting upon a sense of solidarity. Unlike Proudhon, however, he advocated revolution as the means to the end. One of the most eminent representatives of anarchistic doctrines was the Russian Prince Kropotkin (1842-1921). Kropotkin advocated a system of communistic anarchy based upon the idea of free production and consumption, with a free development of industrial powers in groups and societies. According to this theory, everybody would share as he pleased in production and also in the enjoyment of the fruits of collective effort. False relations would not exist, since everyone, following a higher morality, would give his best efforts to a participation in collective production.

Anathema, the Greek term for things accursed by the gods. Anathematization in the Catholic Church is the extreme form of excommunication.

Ancestor Worship, the religious regard of ancestors, real or imagined. The worship of ancestors may be of three kinds: family worship of immediate ancestors; clan worship of a lost chief; national worship of an ancient ruler or rulers. The custom of the ancient Romans, whose ancestral deities were made into images set up in the home and appeased with offerings, is one of the best examples of ancestor worship among European peoples. Ancestor worship seems to have been the earliest form of religious emotional expression. The Egyptians embalmed with great care the bodies of the dead and held them in veneration. The Chinese and the Japanese, to the present day, have followed detailed burial rituals in reverence for the departed souls, even to the extent of offering food and drink and of reading prayers every day. The general idea in the minds of those who followed the belief of ancestor worship can be summed up in the thought that the souls of the dead were spirits which have the power of aiding or doing evil to the living. Consequently, the living did not wish to displease the spirits, but rather to please them through the worship of souls.

Anchor, a mechanism for mooring ships. Great improvements have been introduced in recent years; stockless anchors are now chiefly used, consisting of a shank and a loose fluke. Many anchors are now made of cast steel.

Anchovy, a fish, the *Engraulis encrasicholus* of Fleming; the *Engraulis vulgaris* of Cuvier. It belongs to the Clupeidae, or herring family. In general, its length is from 4 to 5 inches; but specimens have been found 7½ inches long. It is common in the Mediterranean and parts of the ocean. Shoals of anchovies annually enter the Mediterranean, and various fisheries exist along its northern shores, the most celebrated being at Gorgona, a small island W. of Leghorn. Sometimes another species, the *Engraulis maletta,* is either mixed with, or substituted for, the genuine fish. Anchovies are used fresh, canned, and pickled. Spiced and salted, they are prepared as fillets or as anchovy paste, both of which are esteemed as hors d'oeuvres.

Anemometer, a wind-measuring instrument, now in general use at all meteorological stations, and in its more recent developments capable of recording the force and variations of the wind with accuracy.

Aneroid, the name given to a barometer based on a different principle from the mercurial barometer; it consists of a metallic box, exhausted of air, having a fluted lid upon which the atmosphere presses; the pressure acts upon levers, which indicate on a dial every atmospheric movement.

Angels, divine messengers or agents communicating with or guarding human beings, a conception which is included in the Christian and other doctrines; in former times, particularly in the Catholic Church, special functions were accorded to certain angels and archangels, and their intercession was constantly appealed to.

Angelus, a church bell rung in Roman Catholic countries at morning, noon, and sunset, to remind Catholics to say their Angelic Salutation.

Angle, a term used to denote the inclination to each other of two straight or curvilinear lines. Angles are measured by the degrees in the circumference of a circle (which is divided into 360 equal parts); for example, the angle formed by two lines radiating from the center of a circle is measured by the degrees in the circumference which the lines intercept. A right angle is one of 90°.

Angles, a Germanic tribe which originally settled in Schleswig and later joined the Saxons in invading Britain.

Anglican Communion, a religious denomination which comprises all the churches affiliated with the English Episcopal Church, including the Protestant Episcopal Church of the United States. British colonial churches are now free from state control, except that the appointment of colonial bishops still remains with the heads of the mother church.

Anglo-Saxon Language, the parent of modern English; it is a member of the Teutonic group of languages and belongs to the Low German, as distinguished from the High German and Scandinavian branches. It was not called Anglo-Saxon by the people who spoke it, but English *(Englisc).*

Anglo-Saxon Law, the body of laws which grew up among the Anglo-Saxons from the time of their conquest of Britain, during the 5th and 6th centuries, until the invasion of the Normans in 1066. The earliest written record of these laws dates back to the 6th century, although the principal sources of information about them are the sketchy and incomplete records of laws promulgated by the various Anglo-Saxon kings. On the whole, the laws were an outgrowth of the Teutonic folk customs, known as folk laws, which the Anglo-Saxons brought with them from the continent.

Angora Goats, the animals bred in the vicinity of Angora (Ankara), Turkey; they are famous for their fine, long silky hair, from which mohair fabrics are made.

Aniline, a well-known product obtained from coal tar. In some of its reactions it yields brilliant colors. In 1858 Sir W. H. Perkin succeeded in producing from aniline a dyestuff to which the name of mauve was given. From that time aniline dyes came into wide adoption, and at the present time aniline can be utilized for every color desired. For the dyeing of fabrics aniline colors are universally employed; also for tinting pulps and for making cosmetics, colored inks and soaps, etc. Most aniline products were obtained from Germany before 1914.

Animal Heat arises from the oxidation of food within the tissues. It has been estimated that an adult man produces in twenty-four hours enough heat to boil five or six pints of water. The temperature of the atmosphere has little appreciable effect upon the body's heat when a person is healthy. Cold-blooded animals—reptiles, fishes, amphibians, and invertebrate creatures—have the temperature of their surroundings; they may be frozen and after being thawed out may continue to live.

Animal Kingdom comprises all living beings, but in some of the lowest organisms it is difficult to discriminate between what is vegetable and what is animal. The two main divisions of the animal world are the *Vertebrates* (those possessing a backbone) and the *Invertebrates* (which are without a backbone). There are five classes of *Vertebrates: Mammalia,* such as suckle their young; *Aves,* birds; *Reptilia,* reptiles; *Amphibia,* animals living on land or water at will; and *Pisces,* fishes. The *Invertebrates* include *Protozoa,* the lowest forms of animal life, *Coelenterata,* of which the hydra and the sea-anemone are examples; *Annuloida,* star-fishes, etc.; *Annulosa,* comprising insects; and *Mollusca,* including snails, oysters, etc.

Animalcule, a term used to designate one of the minute animal creatures which are too small to be seen except by the aid of the microscope. These organisms exist in such vast multitudes that in a single drop of water the microscope reveals enormous numbers.

Anime, a transparent resinous substance exuded from the courbaril tree, which receives its name from its being alive with insects in its natural state. It is used in perfumery and varnish making and has also medicinal properties.

Animism, the tendency, common among primitive peoples, to explain natural phenomena as due to direct spiritual agencies rather than to mechanical forces, and to endow animate and inanimate objects with feelings, personality, and consciousness. Certain scholars use the term animism only when referring to belief in a human apparitional soul, and employ the term animatism in describing other expressions of the primitive tendency to personalize objects.

Anise, an umbelliferous plant growing mostly in warm climates and valued for its fruit, aniseed, which possesses certain medicinal properties and yields a volatile oil. The fruit is highly aromatic and is used as a condiment for pickles and soups.

Annals, historical records, such as those kept by the Romans from an early period. In modern times the term is used to designate any general record of events arranged according to years.

Annealing, the process of slowly cooling glass and metal substances, as a result of which their brittleness is removed and they become capable of resisting breakage. Some large castings are gradually cooled over a period of two or three months.

Annunciation, Feast of the, a church festival (March 25) commemorating the announcement by the angel Gabriel to the Virgin Mary of the incarnation of Christ.

Anodyne, a term covering any application for the relief of pain, and includes the various opiates, quinine, salicylates, and barbiturates.

Anointing, the pouring of consecrated oil upon the body as a mark of supreme honor. In England it is a ceremony restricted chiefly to the ceremony of the monarch's coronation. In the Roman Catholic Church anointing represents the sacrament of extreme unction.

Anomaly, a term used in astronomy for the angle measured at the sun between a planet in any point of its orbit and the last perihelion.

Anonymous, a term meaning without name and indicating that a book or article was published without the author's name being divulged.

Anser, a genus of swimming birds, the most familiar example of which is the goose.

Ant, an insect of the same order as bees and wasps (Hymenopters). Ants live in communities under a well-defined system and comprise males, females, and neuters. When the male and the female, which are winged, leave their nest and pair, the male dies, while the female sheds her wings and is made queen of a new community. The neuters comprise a working and a defending body, as well as a band of slave ants captured from another species. As in the case of the bees, the work of the ants consists in the storing up of provisions for the future, and their anthills contain a regular series of passages and storehouses. They feed on both animal and vegetable matter and upon a kind of milk exuded by plant lice.

Antacids, in medicine, agents designed to diminish acidity in the human system by increasing its alkalinity.

Antarctic Zone, the region lying between the Antarctic Circle (parallel to the Equator and about 23½° from the Pole) and the South Pole. Captain Scott, who returned from his discovery voyage in 1904, penetrated 300 miles farther than any previous explorer. In 1911 two parties attempted to reach the Pole, one led by Captain Scott and the other by the Norwegian Roald Amundsen. Amundsen and four companions, using 52 dogs of which 12 came back, made a fast and fortunate trip. They reached the Pole on December 14, 1911, after a journey of 55 days, returning in 38 days. Scott's party arrived at the Pole on January 18, 1912, after a trip of 69 days, during which they man-hauled their sledge for the last five hundred miles, only to find Amundsen had been ahead of them. On the return journey they all perished from cold, hunger, scurvy and exhaustion, their bodies and records being found the next year.

In 1928 Sir Hubert Wilkins made a successful flight over the two main islands of the Antarctic Archipelago, North and South Graham, finding the latter separated from the mainland by a strait about forty miles wide. In the same year Byrd established "Little America," a base at the eastern end of the Ross Barrier. On November 28 and 29, 1929, he and three companions made a successful flight to the Pole, landing once to refuel at a gasoline-depot laid by a party using dog teams. Flights east of Little America resulted in the discovery of Rockefeller Mountains and Marie Byrd Land, while the geological party under Lawrence Gould did notable work. Byrd's second expedition (1933-35) also based at Little America and continued explorations in detail. Byrd himself remained alone at an advance base 95 miles inland during the winter of 1934 to make meteorological observations and almost died from carbon monoxide poisoning. A party using a tractor came to his relief from Little America, making a remarkable journey through the Antarctic night. On this expedition transportation by gasoline-powered vehicles, in the past only employed experimentally, was proved to be definitely practicable. Various misfortunes balked Lincoln Ellsworth's attempts to explore the Antarctic in 1933 and 1934. Late in 1935 he and Herbert Hollick-Kenyon flew from Dundee Island in the Archipelago to Ross Sea, a distance of 2,100 miles in about 13 days, their airplane being forced down on several occasions by blizzards. They found food and shelter at deserted Little America, and were eventually rescued. In June, 1939, the United States Congress established the Antarctic Service, a new government bureau, headed by Rear Admiral Byrd, and voted $340,000 for a project to lay official claim to certain sections of Antarctica. Subsequent explorations showed that the Antarctic was only one continent with no strait between Weddell Sea and Ross Sea. Fossils of plants and animals indicate a milder climate in geologic time.

Anteater, a mammal found in South America and South Africa, with a long cylindrical tongue coated with a viscid secretion. This tongue it thrusts into ant-hills and draws it forth covered with ants, which it devours. The American species is toothless; the African has molar teeth.

Antediluvian, a term which applies to fossil evidences belonging to a period prior to human record; it is commonly regarded as indicating a time prior to the Deluge.

Antelope, a large genus of Mammalia, mainly deer-like animals, fleet of foot, with lustrous eyes.

Antennae, feelers of insects and crustaceans, usually two in number, though in the case of certain wingless insects, four or six. Their precise functions are unknown, but it is probable that they serve some purpose additional to that of tactility.

Anthem, a choral composition with or without instrumental accompaniment. The words are from the Scriptures, and the composition may be either for solo voices, full choir, or both.

Anthology, the figurative term used to describe a selection or collection of literary compositions, usually poems or hymns. The *Greek Anthology*, comprising the choicest pieces by Greek classical poets, was compiled by Meleager about 90 B. C. The *Latin Anthology* of verse from the age of Ennius to about A. D. 1000 was made by Peter Burmann the Younger.

Anthracite, a hard kind of coal which burns without flame and contains upward of 90 per cent of carbon. Pennsylvania is the largest known anthracite coal region. The next-largest field is in South Wales.

Anthropoid, meaning "resembling man," is the term employed to designate the order of apes whose structure has similarity to that of man. The gorilla, orangoutang, and chimpanzee are of this order and, in number and general form of limbs, bear a closer resemblance to human beings than any other creatures. On this fact much of the theory of evolution has been built.

Anthropology, the study of man with respect to origins, races and cultures. The interest in anthropology was greatly stimulated by the development of the study of biology in the 19th century, resulting largely from the enthusiasm created by the theories of Darwin and others relating to the origin of species and the descent of man. The ancient Greeks had discussed these same problems as early as Anaximander (610-546 B. C.) and had outlined a theory of development that anticipated the theory of evolution. The work of archaeologists in Egypt, Babylonia, Asia Minor, and elsewhere, along with the research carried on among the aboriginal peoples of Africa, Java, Borneo, Tasmania, and other areas opened up new fields of interest and provided much valuable material for the scientific study of man. Environment plays an important part in the evolution of man. Fertile lands, mountains, rivers, have control over food supply, transportation and commerce and consequently intercourse with other peoples and development of culture. The anthropologists, observing certain physical characteristics, have distinguished many different types of men. Their habitats, languages, customs, art, religions, and morals, are the sources of increasing researches that are constantly throwing more light on the origin of man, his nature, his adaptation to the world, and his chances for surviving in the struggle against nature and other men. Anthropology has many practical sides and is proving very valuable in individual and group conduct. It is important to those nations that have large colonial possessions, as it furnishes the ruling peoples with much accurate information about their subjects. In some colonies the ruling nations have put professional anthropologists to work. These experts live with the people, generally away from the governmental headquarters so as to allay the suspicions of the peoples and thus obtain a more complete knowledge of them. This research is valuable not only for administrative purposes but for science in general.

Anthropometry, the system of human measurement invented by M. Bertillon, of the French Criminal Department, for the purposes of establishing identity. The evidence of finger prints has been introduced successfully in criminal cases.

Anthropomorphism, the application to a deity of the attributes of man, a form of belief which belongs more or less to all religions, for the reason that man is incapable of imagining beings of a higher form than his own.

Antichrist, the name given to the enemy of Christ, as mentioned by St. John, and long anticipated by the early Christians.

Anticlimax, the reverse of climax, introducing the strong point of a story or argument before the close instead of reserving it for the end.

Antimony, a crystalline metal of great brittleness. On being burned, it gives off dense fumes of oxide of antimony. By itself it is not of special utility; but as an alloy for hardening other metals, it is much used. As an alloy with lead for type-metal, and with tin and copper or zinc for Britannia-metal, it is of great value. All antimoniacal compounds are poisonous.

Antiphony, in the singing of psalms, the alternation of parts by two different sets of voices of a choir or congregation.

Antipodes, the parts of the earth exactly opposite to each other, having seasons, etc., at exactly opposite times. Thus the North Pole is the antipode of the South Pole.

Anti-Semitism, a form of agitation against the Jews. The term is used only in reference to the Jews, whose ancestors were members of the Semitic branch of the Caucasian race, although by intermarriage they have long since ceased to be a racial entity, partaking to a large extent of the blood of the peoples among whom they live. Modern anti-semitism originated as a political and social movement against Jews, but in the course of the agitation it took on religious significance as well. Adolf Hitler, as leader of the Nazi party, revived the anti-semitic agitation in Germany which ultimately resulted in the exclusion of Jews from all commercial, religious, educational, and political positions. In November 1939 Hitler announced his intention to establish a "pale of settlement" solely for Jews in that part of Poland which had been occupied by Germany.

Antiseptics, the term applied to substances which destroy or weaken microbes, bacteria, or germs, and often arrest the spread of diseases caused by those minute putrefying agents. Among the chief antiseptic substances are carbolic acid, corrosive sublimate, or chloride of mercury, iodine, and peroxide of hydrogen.

Antitoxin, a substance produced in the body, in response to stimulation by certain toxins (poisons), which neutralizes or destroys the toxin exciting its production; i.e., the antitoxin produced is specific in its action against the toxin which stimulated its production regardless of what animal body produces it. Certain diseases of man, such as diphtheria and tetanus (lockjaw), can be successfully treated or prevented by injecting the specific antitoxin which has been manufactured in some animal.

Aorta, the main trunk of the arterial system, in direct communication with the heart.

Apaches, a tribe of Indians, formerly spread over the middle-western part of the United States.

Aphasia, in neurology and psychiatry, a symptom of certain conditions of the nervous system, in which the patient loses the power of expressing ideas by means of words, or loses the appropriate use of words, the vocal organs the while remaining intact and the intelligence sound.

Aphelion, the point in the orbit of a planet farthest from the sun, where the motion is slowest.

Aphids, plant lice, a numerous species of destructive parasites living on roots, leaves, and plants.

Apis, the sacred bull worshiped by the ancient Egyptians; also the scientific name for the bee.

Apocalyptic Writing, that which deals with revelation and prophecy, more especially the Revelation of St. John.

Apocrypha, the title given to the Jewish writings, not regarded as canonical by the Jews, but accepted by the Roman Catholic Church. Regarded as only historical records by the Protestant churches. The term applies mainly to the additional Old Testament books, but there are also some Christian writings of the same character. The Apocryphal books include 1 and 2 Esdras, Tobit, Judith, Esther x-xvi, Wisdom, Ecclesiasticus, Baruch, Song of the Three Holy Children, Bel and the Dragon, the Prayer of Manasses, and 1 and 2 Maccabees.

Apoplexy, or stroke, a sudden loss of consciousness that may be attended with convulsions, paralysis, or fever. The condition is recognized as being due to hemorrhage in the higher nervous centers or in the spinal cord and may be caused by any disease that weakens the blood vessels, especially those in the regions indicated. Hence, it is usually associated with degenerative changes and loss of elasticity of the blood vessels in old age, a condition in which high blood pressure is also present and likely to cause vascular ruptures.

Apostasy, a revolt, by an individual or party, from one form of opinion or doctrine to another.

Apostolic Council, held at Jerusalem, A.D. 52, presided over by James, to decide what the obligations of Christians were to the Mosaic law.

Apostolic Fathers, the immediate disciples or followers of the Apostles, especially those who left writings, including Barnabas, Clement, Hermas, Ignatius, Polycarp, etc.

Apostolic Succession, the derivation of holy orders by an unbroken chain from the Apostles, and the succession of the ministry to the powers and privileges of the Apostles.

Apotheosis, the Greek term for the deification of a mortal. Divine honors were accorded to Julius Caesar and Augustus.

Apparitions, supposed supernatural appearances, once much believed in. There are many who still have faith in spiritual manifestations, but science looks askance at these claims.

Appian Way, the oldest Roman road, originally laid by Appius Claudius from Rome to Capua, and afterward extended to Brundisium.

April, the fourth month of the year, so called from *aperire*, to open—the period when vegetation opens.

Apse, a semicircular recess at the east end of the choir or chancel of early churches, and vaulted over.

Apteryx, a large, wingless, New Zealand bird of the ostrich order, valued for its skin.

Aquarium, a container for keeping aquatic plants or animals in captivity. The term is also applied to establishments where such aquatic collections are maintained. Aquariums have been kept for hundreds of years, both the ancient Romans and the Chinese having kept fish as pets or ornamental specimens in private tanks. The first public aquarium, however, was not established until 1853, when a small one was built in Regent's Park, London. Since that time other public exhibits of aquatic life have been created, among which those of Amsterdam, Naples, New York and San Francisco are notable. The John G. Shedd Aquarium, built in Grant Park, was presented to the city of Chicago in 1931. One of the most remarkable aquariums in existence is that at Marineland, near St. Augustine, Florida, opened in 1938. It consists of two immense salt-water pools constructed at the edge of the Atlantic, which provides an inexhaustible supply of sea water. The pool contains many varieties of marine life, including fish, sharks, and porpoises which carry on the struggle for existence here as much as they would in the open sea. Glass ports outside the tanks and below the level of the water permit observation of the processes of oceanic life.

Aquatint is a method of etching on copper, by which imitations of drawings in water-colors, India ink, bister, and sepia are produced.

Aqueduct, an artificial channel or conduit for the conveyance of water from one place to another; more particularly applied to structures for supplying large cities with water from distant sources. The most famous system was that of the Roman aqueducts, of which the first was the joint work of Appius Claudius Caecus and Caius Plautius Venox, censors in 312 B. C. In all, nine different aqueducts were built to bring water to Rome, the longest being about forty miles. The Romans also constructed important aqueducts for cities throughout the empire. One built for Carthage A. D. 120 brought water by arched bridges of stone from a distance of about 60 miles. Today it is still used to supply Tunis with water. Modern aqueducts use pressure conduits in closed channels constructed of iron or steel, concrete, wood, stone, or tunnels. The capacity is enormous compared to Rome's 130 million gallons a day. In 1925 Los Angeles began work on a $220,000,000 project to build a 250-mile aqueduct designed to bring more than a billion gallons of water a day from the Colorado River, in order to supplement an aqueduct recently completed. San Francisco's new aqueduct is capable of drawing 400 million gallons of water from Yosemite Park, 156 miles away. New York's greatest aqueduct is in the Catskills, 120 miles away, providing the city with 650 million gallons of water per day.

Arabesque, the term applied to the elaborate decorations introduced into Europe by the Moors. The arabesques of the Vatican galleries, by Raphael, are a splendid example.

Arabian Nights, a collection of fascinating tales of the Orient, of mixed Indian, Persian, Arabic and Egyptian origin, and first made known in Europe by Antoine Galland, a French Oriental scholar whose original translation was called *The Thousand and One Nights*.

Arabic Numerals, the system introduced into Europe by the Arabs in the 8th century, consisting of the digits 1, 2, 3, 4, 5, 6, 7, 8, 9, and 0. By displacing the Roman numerals they gave impetus to the development of arithmetic as a science.

Arachnida, name given by Lamarck to a class which includes spiders, scorpions, mites and ticks without antennae or wings.

Aragonite, a mineral consisting of carbonate of lime in a crystalline form, sometimes found pure and sometimes mixed with other metals in minute quantities. Crumbles to powder under heat. First discovered in Aragon.

Aramaic, the language of the Aramaeians or Syrians, which was the common dialect of the trading people of the Near East in the 1st century of the Christian era.

Arbitration, an adjudication by private persons, called arbitrators, appointed to decide a matter or matters in controversy, either by written or oral submission, by agreement of the disputants. It differs from a reference in that it is not made by the order of a court of law. The proceeding generally is called a submission to arbitration; the parties appointed to decide are termed arbitrators, not referees; and their adjudication is called an award. This mode of settling disputes has been approved by legislatures at various times, and there are statutes in a number of states regulating the proceeding. International arbitration has been employed in matters of dispute between nations more than a hundred times. Arbitration has been used between the United States and Great Britain to settle the San Juan boundary question, the Alabama question and the Bering Sea sealing controversy. The first general treaty of arbitration ever drawn between nations was signed Jan. 11, 1897, in Washington by Richard Olney, Secretary of State for the United States and Sir Julian Pauncefote, Ambassador of Great Britain to the United States, for Great Britain. This treaty was placed before the United States Senate, Jan. 11, 1897, accompanied by a special message from President Cleveland, but the Senate refused to ratify it. International arbitration occurs when two disputing nations air their differences before a selected person or persons, the dispute to be adjudged the basis of civilized law. By the creation of the League of Nations a new advance in international relations was made. Members were required to bring disputes before the League Council and abide by its decisions. The League, however, failed to act when Japan invaded Manchuria. In 1935 the sanctions voted by the League against Italy could not be effectively enforced, and Ethiopia was overrun. When Germany invaded Czecho-Slovakia and Poland it became clear that the League of Nations was incapable of arbitrating a serious international dispute.

Arblest, a steel crossbow set in a shaft of wood and worked with a trigger, introduced by the Normans.

Arbor Day, a day devoted to the planting of trees. First adopted in Nebraska, the movement has spread to all parts of the United States, Canada, New Zealand, and South Australia.

Arbor Vitae, the name given to the tree-like appearance of the cerebellum when it is cut through, due to the arrangement of the white and gray nerve matter. Also the name of a cone-bearing plant of the cypress order possessing medicinal properties.

Arcadia, a district of the Peloponnesus, the southern peninsula of Greece, whose inhabitants in the days of the Pelasgi were of extreme simplicity; the term has ever since been used to denote an idealized country of primitive, simple habits.

Arch, introduced into architecture by the Romans, and thereafter widely adopted to relieve the straight-line methods of Greece.

Archaeology, a science dealing with the relics of ancient times, constructing historical deductions, and ascertaining the manners and customs of past periods.

Archaeopteryx, a bird which is supposed to be the connecting link between reptiles and birds, its fossilized remains revealing some of the characteristics of both orders.

Archaism, a term denoting a style of composition or discourse of an obsolete or antiquated kind, admissible in poems and other writings of a highly idealized or allegorical form, but otherwise out of place.

Archbishop, a chief bishop. In the early days of Christianity, the pastors of the various churches were called bishops. After a time the bishops of the larger cities, surrounded as they were by many smaller churches, were called archbishops by way of distinction. The bishop of Alexandria was one of the first, if not the first, to claim the title. In the United States the Roman Catholic and Greek Catholic Churches are the only ones that have dignitaries of this rank.

Architecture, or the art of building, is of three main classes—military, naval, and civil—the general application of the term being to the last-named. The five leading orders of architecture are the *Doric*, the oldest, of which the best examples were shown in the Greek temples; the *Ionic*, another Greek variety, lighter and more decorative, as shown in the Erechtheum at Athens; the *Corinthian*, introduced in the time of Alexander the Great, well known by its graceful columns and enrichments; the *Tuscan*, which the Romans invented—a solidified *Doric*; and the *Composite*, which combined the leading features of the Ionic and Corinthian. The name "Gothic architecture" has been applied to the architectural styles gradually developed in Western Europe from the thirteenth through the sixteenth centuries. The principles of the concentration of strain and balanced thrusts were the structural basis of the Gothic style. The ribbed vaulting and the pointed arch were the characteristic results of the application of these principles. The Renaissance saw a revival of the ancient Roman and Greek style of architecture. It was not in great buildings, such as cathedrals and palaces, but in smaller works such as gateways, chapels, tombs, and fountains that the architects of the Early Renaissance did their finest work. With the advent of the steel-cage form of construction, building tended upward instead of outward, and the skyscraper came into existence. Skyscrapers are built with the idea of utilizing the upper spaces and thus economizing upon ground area as much as possible. The best modern architects strive to design buildings according to the ideal of functionalism, a term signifying the adaptation of form to purpose, and to the nature of the materials used. From the functional standpoint any architectural feature which serves no purpose but that of ornamentation is to be avoided. Well designed buildings of the present, both in Europe and America, have façades tending toward simplicity or extreme plainness, ornamented only by the placing of the windows; their rectangular, monolithic masses are interrupted, in the case of skyscrapers, by setbacks. Beauty is secured by harmonious proportions of masses rather than by the way in which ornamental details are applied.

Arctic Exploration dates from a very remote period, but it was not until the 16th century that men began to make serious attempts to discover either a northwest or northeast passage to the Orient. Sir Hugh Willoughby, Davis, Chancellor, Baffin, Frobisher, and Henry Hudson were the most famous early explorers. Dr. Nansen's crossing of Greenland in 1888, and his subsequent journey with the *Fram* in 1893-1896, were memorable events. Nansen and Lieutenant Johansen, with two kayaks and a number of dogs, reached 86° 14′ N., 200 miles nearer to the Pole than had been reached before. The Duke of the Abruzzi's expedition, under Captain Cagni, in 1899 reached 86° 33′, 22 miles farther north than Nansen. In 1906 Peary got within 201 miles of the Pole, the American thus approaching nearer by 35 miles to the objective than Nansen. In September, 1909, the world was startled by the news that Dr. Cook, an American explorer, had actually reached the Pole, but later evidence did not substantiate this. This was followed closely by the announcement that Peary had also planted the Stars and Stripes at the Pole. Peary then published a full description of his discovery. Several attempts to explore the Polar regions have been made by air. Rear-Admiral Richard E. Byrd flew to the North Pole in 1926. The Italian dirigible *Italia* was lost in an attempt in 1928, and Sir Hubert Wilkins flew over the North Pole about the same time. Captain Amundsen set out in a seaplane in June 1928, to try to find the "Italia," and was never heard of again.

Argon, a chemical element in air discovered by Lord Rayleigh in 1894.

Aricine, an alkaloid contained in the bark of arica, and also in *Cinchona ovata*.

Aries, the Ram, the first of the signs of the Zodiac.

Arion, in Greek mythology, the horse of Adrastus, which was said to have the gift of utterance and of prophecy, and figured in the Theban War.

Arithmetic, the science of numbers, did not flourish to any great extent until the adoption of the Arabic numerals. It is supposed to have originated as a science in India. The system of the Greeks and Romans was complicated and it was not until the 16th century that the science reached any great development.

Ark of the Covenant, the sacred chest, overlaid with gold, which occupied the inner sanctum of the Temple, and symbolized God's covenant with his people.

Armada, Spanish, the naval expedition fitted out by Philip II of Spain in 1588 against England, commanded by the Duke of Medina Sidonia. It comprised 129 ships, was manned by 8,000 sailors and carried 10,000 soldiers and more than 2,000 cannon, with food for 40,000 men for six months. Against this formidable force, Queen Elizabeth had only 80 ships manned by 9,000 sailors, under Lord Howard of Effingham, under whom served Drake, Hawkins, and Frobisher. The British fleet awaited the Armada off Plymouth. At Tilbury was a considerable defensive land force under the command of the Earl of Leicester. On July 19 the ships of the Armada were sighted off the Lizard, disposed in a crescent seven miles long from horn to horn. The excellent maneuvering of the English, their fire-ships, and a gale from the northwest combined so effectively to cripple the Spanish ships that the Armada was scattered in confusion, a very small remnant contriving to reach home.

Armadillo, a genus of animals found in South America, having a hard bony covering over the back, under which the animal can completely conceal itself when attacked, rolling itself up like a hedgehog.

Armageddon, according to the Revelation of St. John, the great battle in which the last conflict between good and evil is to be fought.

Armature, the portion of an electrical dynamo consisting of wire coils so arranged as to give an increased flow of electrical energy when rotated.

Armistice, a temporary truce or a complete cessation of hostilities by agreement of both sides. Armistice Day, Nov. 11, 1918, commemorates the cessation of hostilities in the Great War, and the signing of the Armistice between the Allies and Germany.

Armor, protective covering worn formerly by those engaged in military pursuits, and consisting of a great variety of pieces and material, from hauberks of mail to a complete panoply of plate.

Arms, Coat of, or Armorial Bearings, a collective name for the devices borne on shields, banners, etc., as marks of dignity, and distinction and, in the case of family and feudal arms, descending from father to son. They were first employed by the Crusaders and became hereditary in some European families at the close of the 12th century. They took their rise from the knights painting their banners or shields each with a figure or figures proper to himself, to enable him to be distinguished in battle when clad in armor.

Army, an organized equipment of land forces for carrying on the work of war. Egypt possibly had such an organization under Sesostis, 1600 B.C. The Persians later on were similarly equipped, but it was the Romans who brought into operation an immense regular army in which every citizen between 17 and 45 could be compelled to serve.

The Turkish Janizaries, the earliest standing army in Europe, were fully organized in 1632; but the formation of standing armies among Western Powers dates from the establishment of *compagnies d'ordonnance* by Charles VII of France, nearly a century later. Frederick the Great, in the next century, introduced a most rigid and exact system of tactics and drill. He greatly improved the calvary tactics and restored to this arm a reliance on the effect of a rapid charge, while the introduction of horse artillery added to its power. The French Revolution effected almost as great changes in the military as in the political organization of Europe. The struggle from which France emerged victorious in 1797 had exhausted even the enormous levies which had fed her armies for the previous five years; and in 1798 a law was passed establishing compulsory military service. Every citizen was liable to five years' service, and all between the ages of 20 and 25 were enrolled. The immense advantage which this terrible power gave Napoleon compelled other nations to follow the example of France, and in continental Europe voluntary enlistment has disappeared. Now, in most nations, will be found an army of reserve, intended to augment the standing army from a peace to a war strength, and consisting of two classes—those waiting an immediate call to arms, if required, and those constituting the militia—the entire effective military power of the state. It may be interesting here to mention certain distinctions in the application of the word army. A covering army is encamped for the protection of the various passes or roads which lead to the town or other place to be protected. A siege army is ranged around or in front of a fortified place, to capture it by a regular process of besieging. A blockading army, either independent of, or auxiliary to, a siege army, is intended to prevent all ingress and egress at the streets or gates of a besieged place. An army of observation takes up an advanced position, and by celerity of movement keeps a close watch on all the maneuvers of the enemy. The army of reconnaissance has a more special duty: at a particular time and place to ascertain the strength and position of the enemy's forces. A flying column is a small army carrying all its supplies with it, so as to be able to operate quickly and in any direction independently of its original base of operations.

World War I brought about many changes in the armies of both belligerents and neutrals. The draft system of compulsory military service was generally used by both sides. Radical changes in the type of fighting brought about equally revolutionary changes in the equipment and fighting forces. Important features were trench warfare, rapid-fire arms—machine guns and artillery—, poison gas, tanks, and use of airplanes and dirigibles.

In World War II the tactics of the *blitzkrieg* (lightning war) called for highly mobile armies with the use of tank columns, dive bombers, and heavy bombing of supply and communications areas. With the increased use of motorized equipment for rapid mobility of the armed forces, there was a great increase in the importance of logistics. There was a greatly increased demand for gasoline, ammunition, food, and many other materials, and the destruction of the enemy's production facilities became a decisive factor. These war aims combined led to the development of air power—parachute troops, long-range bombers, and the atomic bomb—rockets, and amphibious warfare, combining land, sea, and air power.

As a result of experiences in World War II there developed a tendency to combine army, navy, and air forces. With the advent of the hydrogen bomb and intercontinental ballistic missiles, the organization of armies underwent critical examination. Other important influences were the Korean War, the Cold War, and colonial struggles for self-determination.

Arnica, the name of a genus of plants of which the dandelion is a leading example.

Arnotto, a reddish-yellow dye obtained from the seeds of the *Bixa orellana*, a South American plant. It is employed for coloring cheese and butter, also in chocolates and soups; and a preparation of the pigments imparts an orange tint to certain varnishes.

Arpeggio, in music, indicates the striking of a chord or notes in rapid succession, instead of simultaneously.

Arrowroot, obtained from the rhizomes of the tropical maranta, also from the potato and the arum. It provides a pure starch food, suitable for invalids.

Arsenals are repositories for storing, or workshops for making, arms, guns, accoutrements, stores, etc.

Arsenic, a chemical element, regarded by some as a metal, of a crystalline and brittle nature, usually met with as a constituent of other minerals, but sometimes by itself. One of the most virulent of poisons.

Artesian Wells, so called because of their first being discovered at Artois, are borings made through strata which water cannot permeate to others of a porous kind which are full of water. The fountains in Trafalgar Square, London, are fed by artesian wells sunk through the clay into the chalk about 400 ft. At Passy, near Paris, there is an artesian well 1,923 ft. deep, and at St. Louis, Missouri, there is one 3,843 ft. deep; and one in Queensland, Australia, reaches the depth of 7,009 ft.

Artificial Silk, a textile made of cellulose, such as rayon. It is a substitute for real silk. Its production is very cheap, and the finer sorts are with difficulty distinguishable from natural silk.

Artillery, all sorts of great guns, cannon, or ordnance, mortars, howitzers, machine-guns, etc., together with all the apparatus and stores thereto belonging, which are taken into the field, or used for besieging and defending fortified places. It is often divided into (1) coast artillery; (2) field artillery; and (3) siege artillery. Field artillery is artillery designed to be taken with an army to the field of battle; a park of artillery is artillery with the carriages, tractors, and stores of all kinds necessary for its effective use; siege artillery is artillery of heavy metal designed to be employed in breaching fortification; a train of artillery is a certain number of pieces of cannon mounted on carriages, with all their furniture fit for marching.

Arundel Marbles, a collection of ancient sculpture formed by Thomas Howard, Earl of Arundel, in the 17th century and presented to Oxford University.

Aryan is a term used to denote the lingual and ethnological groups otherwise known as Indo-European or Indo-Germanic. Comprises two branches, Western or European, and Eastern or Armenian. The Aryan languages show common origin by their vocabulary, syntax, and inflexions. The nearest to the parent tongue is Sanskrit, and the chief divisions in Europe are the Teutonic, Romance, Slav and Celtic. The Turks, Magyars, Basques, and Finns are non-Aryan. The common ancestors of the Aryan groups dwelt among the Pamirs at a period of remote antiquity.

Asafoetida, a well-known drug made from the juice of plants of the Umbelliferae order, including celery, parsnip, etc. Has a very offensive odor.

Asbestos designates a peculiar form of mineral, occurring in crystals in pyroxene; massed together it is fireproof. The finest comes from Savoy; it is abundant in Canada and Tasmania.

Ascension Day, or **Holy Thursday**, is the 40th day after Easter.

Asceticism was originally the term applied to the training practiced by Greek athletes. The Stoics and others used it to express the mastering of the passions. The idea passed into Christianity, and from celibacy and abstinence was carried to terrible lengths in the way of self-mutilation, torture, and human sacrifice. The chief manifestations of asceticism in modern times have been monasticism and the various forms of personal humiliation, fasting, penance, pilgrimage, etc., but the principle survives nowadays only in a very mild form.

Asgard, the heaven of the Scandinavian mythology.

Ash, a familiar tree of the olive family, remarkable for its thick foliage and height of growth, often attaining from 100 to 150 feet. Is a valuable timber tree, tough and elastic, and largely used for wheels. In Scandinavian mythology the first man and woman were the ash and the elm, and the court of the gods was held under an ash.

Ash Wednesday, first day of Lent, on which ashes were sprinkled on the head as sign of penitence under an injunction of Pope Gregory the Great in the 6th century.

Asmodeus, a demon whose story appears in the apocryphal book of Tobit, and figures frequently in Jewish traditions. Asmodeus is the super-natural figure in Le Sage's *Le Diable Boiteux.*

Asp, a small poisonous snake, often mentioned in ancient literature and traditionally supposed to have been used by Cleopatra in killing herself. It belongs to the cobra de capello genus.

Asparagus was a favorite vegetable with the ancient Romans, and is much prized today. Possesses a perennial root and yields edible stalks every spring.

Asphalt, or mineral pitch, is a bituminous substance, the result of decayed vegetable matter, containing 80 per cent of carbon, with hydrogen, nitrogen, and oxygen. Is largely used, mixed with sand, chalk, etc., for making road surfaces in dry climates, such as the United States, France, Italy, Germany, and to a considerable extent also in England, though the English climate is too humid for its general adoption, it becoming slippery with moisture. The ancient Egyptians used it for embalming, and the Babylonians made wells of it. Trinidad, the Rhone Valley, the Dead Sea, and many other places yield asphalt.

Assassins were first heard of in Persia about 1090. They were a secret religious sect, at the bidding of whose chief they murdered persons as an act of duty. Similar bodies were formed in various connections in later times, but the term assassination is now used to specify the slaying only of some public personage, and does not necessarily imply plot or collusion, although the majority of assassinations in recent times have been connected with political or anarchist movements. Among the most notorious instances of assassination may be mentioned the following: —Julius Caesar, 44 B. C.; James I of Scotland, 1437; Rizzio, 1566; Henry IV of France, 1610; Marat, 1793; Lincoln, 1865; Garfield, 1881; Alexander II of Russia, 1881; President Carnot, 1894; the Empress of Austria, 1898; King Humbert, 1900; President McKinley, 1901; Grand Duke Sergius of Russia, 1905; Carlos I, King of Portugal, and Crown Prince Luiz, 1908; Archduke Francis Ferdinand of Austria and his wife, 1914; French President Paul Doumer, 1932; King Alexander of Yugoslavia, Chancellor Dollfuss of Austria, and M. Louis Barthou of France, 1934; Huey P. Long, senator from Louisiana, 1935; Leon Trotsky near Mexico City, 1940; Mohandas K. Gandhi in New Delhi, India, 1948; Count Folke Bernadotte in Jerusalem, 1948; King Abdullah Ibn Ul-Hussein of Jordan in Jerusalem, 1951.

Assaying, the estimation of the amount of pure metal, and especially of the precious metals in an ore or alloy. In the case of silver, the assay is either by the dry or by the wet process. The dry process is called cupellation, from the use of a small and very porous cup, called a cupel.

Association of Ideas, a term used in psychology to comprise the conditions under which one idea is able to recall another to consciousness. Recently psychologists have been disposed to classify these conditions under two general heads; the law of contiguity and the law of resemblance. The first states the fact that mental states of any sort—actions, sensations, emotions and ideas—which have occurred together or in close succession, tend to suggest each other when any one of them is afterward presented to the mind. The second indicates that present actions, sensations, emotions, or ideas tend to recall their like from among previous experiences.

Astarte, a bivalve mollusc, of which there are many widely distributed fossil species, but only some twenty living species inhabiting the Arctic and North Atlantic oceans.

Asteroids were unknown until the discovery of Ceres by Piazzi in 1801; at present more than 500 are catalogued, the application of photography being responsible for the great majority. Most of the minor planets are mere celestial footballs, some having a diameter of only five miles. Their orbits lie between those of Mars and Jupiter. Whether these bodies are the fragments of a large planet is a question that is not yet determined.

Astrakhan, the curled wool of a species of black sheep native to the Russian province of Astrakhan.

Astrology, the so-called science of the stars, was a serious study at one time; monarchs and other illustrious personages were frequent consulters of the astrologists, and had their horoscopes cast. The Chaldeans are supposed to have invented astrology, which is an abstruse and involved systematization. Astrologers divide the heavens into twelve equal parts called *houses*, and endow the planets with certain influences and base their predictions on the positions occupied by the heavenly bodies at a person's birth or at any critical period. For a horoscope it is important to discover in which sign of the Zodiac the sun was at the time of a person's birth, also the position of the moon and which sign was rising.

Astronomy, the oldest and one of the most fascinating of sciences, was in early times associated with astrology, but by a long series of observations and mathematical calculations a gradual knowledge of the movements of the heavenly bodies grew up, and it now ranks as one of the positive sciences. Pythagoras (520 B. C.) believed that the earth revolved upon its axis, but it was not until two thousand years later that his theory gained general acceptance, when first Copernicus and then Tycho Brahe and Galileo demonstrated the truth of the Pythagorean theory. With the setting forth of the Copernican system, astronomy was placed on a sure foundation, and the movements of the planets began to be more clearly comprehended. Naturally there was much that was crude and imperfectly defined in the system of Copernicus, but it was a working basis, and the studies of Kepler and Galileo, making their observations with the telescope, resulted in an immense increase of astronomical knowledge. Newton, to whom we owe the discovery of the law of gravitation, the improvement of the telescope, and many other discoveries, placed physical astronomy on well-defined lines. Halley, Laplace, Herschel, and other eminent astronomers also added to the further comprehension of the science, and in our own day a vast accumulation of knowledge on this interesting subject has resulted from the improved scientific apparatus and equipment now available.

Atavism, the "breeding back" to remote ancestral characteristics, observed in all forms of animal life.

Atheism is the denial of the divine, and assumes three forms—denial of the existence of God, denial that God has been *proved* to exist, and denial of the possibility of knowing of divine existence.

Atherine, a little fish found in the Mediterranean and along the south coast of Britain. The latter variety is familiarly styled the sand-smelt.

Athletics of all kinds are more generally indulged in today than at any former period. In ancient Greek and Roman times wrestling and running were regular sports in which the contestants were chiefly trained professional men, and great honor was paid to the winners. Euthymus, Milo and Hipposthenes were among the more celebrated "classical" athletes, while Plato, Pythagoras, and Cleanthes were amateur contestants of ability. The Isthmian Games at Corinth, and the Olympian Games on the banks of the Alpheus in the Peloponnesus, were immensely popular. The same kind of games continued to be practiced more or less in all countries, from century to century. The developments in athletics during the 19th and 20th centuries were surprising. In high schools, colleges, and universities, at industrial establishments, athletic clubs were formed, while every town, village, and hamlet had its athletic clubs in sufficiently large numbers to afford youths and young men everywhere the opportunity of becoming members. The whole country became interested in athletic sports, and baseball in the summer and football in the autumn have their adherents in every locality.

Athos, Mount, a famous mountain of Macedonian Greece, on a peninsula projecting into the Aegean Sea. It rises abruptly from the water to a height of 6,349 feet above sea level and in its lower parts is covered with forests of pine, oak, chestnut, etc., above which towers a bare conical peak. Athos has been famous both in ancient and modern times. Herodotus states that the fleet of Mardonius, the Persian general, in attempting to double this mountain, was reported to have lost more than 300 ships and 20,000 men. When Xerxes invaded Greece he determined to guard against the recurrence of a similar disaster by cutting a canal across the peninsula of such dimensions as to admit of two triremes passing abreast; of this great work the traces still remain. In modern times Athos has been occupied for an extended period by a number of monks of the Greek Church, who live in a sort of fortified monasteries, in number about 20, of different degrees of magnitude and importance. These, with the farms attached to them, occupy the whole peninsula; hence it has derived its modern name of the "Holy Mountain."

Atlantic Cable Telegraph. Trans-oceanic telegraphy was talked of for some years before an attempt was made to accomplish the feat of laying a cable. Morse suggested the idea as early as 1845, but it was not until 1858 that it assumed a practical shape, Sir Charles Bright succeeding in that year in laying the first cable between Valentia, in Ireland, and Newfoundland. It was 2,500 miles long. For a variety of reasons however, this first cable did not work successfully. A second cable was laid in 1865, the famous *Great Eastern* steamship being utilized on the occasion, but the cable broke in mid-ocean, and for the second time failure had to be written in respect to the scheme for connecting England and America by telegraph. The following year, however, a further attempt was made with complete success, a new cable was laid, and the one of the previous year was picked up and spliced, thus two Atlantic cables were finished at the same time. There are more than 16 cables across the North Atlantic. In Oct., 1924, a new cable was completed between New York and the Azores, capable of transmitting 1,700 letters a minute. Cable telegraphy is now being superseded by wireless telegraphy.

Atlantis, or Atlantica, an island, said by Plato and others to have once existed in the ocean immediately beyond the Straits of Gades; that is, in what is now called the Atlantic Ocean, a short distance W. of the Straits of Gibraltar. Homer, Horace, and some others made two Atlanticas, distinguished as the Hesperides and the Elysian Fields, and believed to be the abodes of the blessed. Plato states that an easy passage existed from the one Atlantis into other islands, which lay near a continent exceeding in size all Europe and Asia. Some have thought this America. Atlantis is represented as having ultimately sunk beneath the waves, leaving only isolated rocks and shoals in its place. Geologists have discovered that the coast-line of Western Europe did once run farther in the direction of America than now; but its submergence seems to have taken place long before historic times, so that the whole ancient story about Atlantis was probably founded on erroneous information, or arose from a clever guess put forth by a man of lively imagination.

Atom, the smallest unit of a chemical element retaining the characteristic chemical properties of that element. An atom is almost incredibly tiny, far below the range of the most powerful microscope. For example, a volume of gas equal to a cube with sides only four-hundredths of an inch long may contain more than one hundred quadrillion atoms.

The atom is not usually, however, the smallest unit of an element existing as an independent body. Such a body is called a molecule. The molecules of most elements consist of two atoms closely bound together.

According to a widely accepted theory, supported by experimental evidence, all atoms are made up of even smaller units: protons, bearing a constant charge of positive electricity; electrons, bearing a constant charge of negative electricity equal in amount to the proton's positive charge, and having only 1/1850 the mass of the proton; and neutrons, bearing no electrical charge but equal in mass to the proton. Protons and neutrons (sometimes with electrons in addition) form the atom's minute nucleus, which bears a positive charge equal to the number of protons in excess of any electrons in the nucleus itself. This number is known as the atomic number. The nucleus of a helium atom, for example, contains two protons and two neutrons, and therefore has a positive charge of two. The first nuclear chain reaction was achieved in 1942, the first atomic bomb was exploded in 1945, first hydrogen bomb in 1952.

Atrium was the central court of a Roman house, uncovered in the center, usually with a marble tank (impluvium) beneath the opening to receive the water from the gutters of the surrounding roofs.

Attar of Roses (oil of roses), an essential oil obtained from the petals of three species of roses; *Rosa centifolia, moschata* and *damascena.* The rose gardens at Ghazipur, in India, have long been famed for the production of this precious liquid. These gardens are large fields, planted with rows of small rose bushes. The blossoms, which unfold in the morning, are all gathered before noon, and their petals are at once transferred to clay stills and distilled with twice their weight of water. The rose water which comes over is placed in shallow vessels covered with moist muslin to exclude dust and exposed all night to the cool air. In the morning the thin film of oil which has collected on the top is carefully swept off with a feather and transferred to a small vial. This process is repeated morning after morning, till nearly the whole of the oil is separated from the water. Heber says that about 20,000 roses are required to yield a rupee weight (170 grains) of attar. Attar is also imported from Smyrna and Istanbul; but it rarely, if ever, reaches the consumer in a pure state. It is commonly adulterated with spermaceti and a volatile oil, which appears to be derived from one or more species of *andropogon,* and which is called oil of ginger-grass, or oil of geranium.

August, the month named after the Emperor Augustus.

Auk is the name given to a genus of swimming birds now extinct. It lived in the temperate region of the North Atlantic, and bred largely on St. Kilda. The female laid only one egg a year.

Aurora Borealis, a luminous meteorologic phenomenon appearing in the North, most frequently in high latitudes, the corresponding phenomenon in the southern hemisphere being called aurora australis, and both being also called polar light, streamers, etc. The northern aurora has been far the most observed and studied. It usually manifests itself by streams of light ascending toward the zenith from a dusky line of cloud or haze a few degrees above the horizon, and stretching from the N. toward the W. and E., so as to form an arc with its ends on the horizon, and its different parts and rays constantly in motion. Sometimes it appears in detached places; at other times it covers almost the whole sky. It assumes many shapes and a variety of colors, from a pale red or yellow to a deep red or blood color; and in the northern latitudes serves to illuminate the earth and cheer the gloom of the long winter nights. The aurora borealis is believed to be associated with static electrical phenomena.

Austerlitz, Battle of, was fought near Brünn, in Moravia, on December 2, 1805, when Napoleon, with 70,000 men, defeated the forces of Russia and Austria, numbering 95,000.

Autogiro, a type of aircraft designed for a practically vertical take-off which, instead of fixed wings, has freely rotating blades revolving horizontally about a vertical axis. The ship itself relies upon the customary gasoline engine and propeller for power. It was invented by de la Cierva and was first successfully demonstrated in England, 1925. The advantages of the autogiro are that it can take off and land in a very limited space, travel safely at very low speed, and in the event of engine failure can parachute to the ground by means of the rotating blades. In flight, turning movements are slow because of the gyroscopic influence of the revolving wings.

Automata are self-moving machines worked by invisible mechanism, and have existed since ancient times when Archytas of Tarentum built an automatic pigeon. The most perfect constructor of modern automata was Vaucanson, who, about 1740, invented a flute-player and a duck that could eat, drink, and quack. Kemton's chess-player was a celebrated automaton that attracted much attention in the early part of the 19th century. In toyland, automatic contrivances of a very ingenious kind are common. One of the newer forms of automata is the robót, or mechanical man.

Automatic Writing, the term used by spiritualists to describe the writing done by the subject of a seance presumably under the direction of the spirit of a deceased person. It may be done in a trance, in somnambulism, under the power of suggestion, or under abnormal nervous conditions. The planchette and ouija board are commonly used as instruments. Although discredited in the sense described above, automatic writing is widely used by psychologists and psychoanalysts to explore the sub-conscious mental and emotional processes.

Autonomy denotes the right of self-government, and was first used in reference to the municipalities of ancient Greece, where the right of self-government was exercised by the city-states.

Autoplasty, a mode of surgical treatment which consists in replacing a diseased part by means of healthy tissue from another part of the same body. The most familiar instance is the rhinoplastic, or taliacotian operation, for supplying a new nose from the skin of the forehead. It is more popularly known as skin-grafting.

Autumn, the third season of the year, begins with the autumnal equinox about September 22, and ends on December 21, but the term is generally understood as covering the period between Labor Day and Thanksgiving.

Avalanches are of four kinds: (1) Powdery avalanches consisting of snow which has become loose and dry. (2) Creeping avalanches, which are loosened in spring, but being on a gentle slope, creep down slowly by the force of their own weight. (3) Glacier avalanches, masses of ice which split off in summer with a great noise, and go tearing down a precipice to be smashed to pieces at the bottom. (4) The real avalanches are huge accumulations of snow, which are hurled over almost perpendicular walls of rock into the valleys beneath.

Aventine, one of the seven hills of **Rome.**

Avernus, a lake in Italy whose vapors were supposed to be fatal to birds, and whose sides were so steep that it was deemed the entrance to Hades.

Avesta, the title of the sacred books of the Parsees or Zoroastrians.

Avocado, a West Indian fruit, called also avocado pear, alligator pear, subaltern's butter tree, avigato, and sabacca. It belongs to the order Lauraceae (laurels) and is the *Persea gratissima.* It is found in tropical America. The fruit is about the size and shape of a large pear. A considerable part of it is believed to consist of a fixed oil. The fruit itself is very insipid, on which account it is generally eaten with the juice of lemons and sugar to give it poignancy.

Avoirdupois *(avoir du pois,* "to have weight") is the scale of weights used in the United States for weighing everything except precious metals, gems, and drugs.

Axe, one of the first tools devised by primitive man in all parts of the world. Axes of stone, bronze, and rough iron have been found in the geological strata.

Axiom, a statement of general truth which admits of no dispute.

Aztecs, a race of people who settled in Mexico early in the 14th century, ultimately extended their dominion over a large territory, and were still extending their supremacy at the time of the arrival of the Spaniards. Their political organization, termed by the Spanish writers an absolute monarchy, appears to have consisted of a military chief exercising important, but not unlimited, power in civil affairs, in which the council of chiefs and periodic assemblies of the judges had also a voice. On the arrival of Cortez in 1519 the Aztec throne was occupied by Montezuma, who had made successful war on the powerful and highly civilized neighboring state of Tlascalta, and on Nicaragua and Honduras. As oracles had foretold the fall of the Aztecs, Montezuma, when he heard of the landing of Cortez, sent a propitiatory embassy. But the Spanish captain with a handful of men advanced from St. Juan de Ulloa to Mexico and subdued the Aztecs.

Slavery and polygamy were both legitimate, but the children of slaves were regarded as free. Although ignorant of the horse, ox, etc., the Aztecs had a considerable knowledge of agriculture, maize and the agave being the chief produce. Silver, lead, tin, and copper were obtained from mines, and gold from the surface and river beds, but iron was unknown to them, their tools being of bronze and obsidian. In metal work, feather work, weaving, and pottery they possessed a high degree of skill. To record events they used an unsolved hieroglyphic writing, and their lunar calendars were of unusual accuracy. They believed in one supreme invisible creator of all things, the ruler of the universe, named Taotl. Under this supreme being stood 13 chiefs and 200 inferior divinities. At their head was the patron god of the Aztecs, Huitzilopochtli, the Mexican Mars. Quetzalcoatl, the beneficent god of light and air, with whom at first the Aztecs were disposed to identify Cortez, also claimed their reverence. Their temples, with large, terraced, pyramidal bases, were in charge of an exceedingly large priesthood, who were responsible for the education of the young. Descendants of the Aztecs are still found in Central America.

Azurite, a blue-colored carbonate of copper, sometimes called chessylite because of its abundance in beautiful crystals at Chessy, near Lyons, France.

B

Baal, the god of the sun, was worshiped by the ancient Chaldeans, Phoenicians, and Assyrians.

Babel, Tower of, described in Gen. xi. 9., the erection of which was given as the cause for the confusion of tongues.

Baboon, a species of monkey, ranking next to the apes, with short tails and large heads. The common baboon is a native of Guinea.

Babylonian Captivity, of the Jews captured by Nebuchadnezzar at the taking of Jerusalem in 586 B. C., lasted upward of 50 years, until Babylon was in turn taken by Cyrus.

Bacchanalia, or Dionysia, feasts in honor of Bacchus, or Dionysus, characterized by licentiousness and revelry and celebrated in ancient Athens. In the processions were bands of Bacchantes of both sexes, who, inspired by real or feigned intoxication, wandered about rioting and dancing. They were clothed in fawn skins, crowned with ivy, and bore in their hands *thyrsi,* that is, spears entwined with ivy and having a pine cone stuck on the point. These feasts passed from the Greeks to the Romans, who celebrated them until the Senate abolished them in 187 B. C.

Baccharis, an oil-yielding plant, of many species, widely distributed over the western hemisphere. Plowman's spikenard is perhaps the best-known variety in this large genus, and the resinous product of local species is used medicinally in Brazil for febrile and rheumatic disorders.

Bachelor, an ancient word of obscure origin and varied meaning. Was early in use in connection with university degrees. Pope Gregory IX introduced the term to denote the passing of the first grade in the academic course in the University of Paris in the 13th century. Later it was applied to single men generally.

Bacillus, the leading division of the group of minute plants named bacteria, and including the *tubercle bacillus,* the cause of tuberculosis. Other bacilli are the *bacillus diphtheriae,* causing diphtheria; *bacillus pestis,* causing the plague; and many others.

Baconian Philosophy, the inductive philosophy of which many maintain that Lord Bacon was the founder; in another sense "Baconian" means anything pertaining to Francis Bacon.

Bacteriology is the science of bacteria, founded by Pasteur, and comprising what is called the "germ theory" of disease. Dr. Koch has been another eminent worker in the same field, and the discoveries resulting from scientific effort in this direction are of the utmost importance. Bacteria are the causes of fermentation and putrefaction, and in time, as far as disease is concerned, may be exterminated. To experiments in the science of bacteriology we owe our fuller knowledge of sanitary principles and of preventive hygiene as well as of the active principles of agriculture, brewing, etc.

Bactris, a genus of palms common in the marshy places of the tropics and certain parts of America. The long slender stems are largely converted into canes. The Tobagocane is a bactris exported from Jamaica.

Badger, a carnivorous animal of the otter family, but very easily tamed. Of nocturnal and burrowing habit. Badger-hunting is an exciting sport.

Badges are a part of heraldry, and in early times usually bore some allusion to the wearer's name or office, or some incident in his career. Distinctive badges are worn by officers of every rank in the Army and Navy.

Bad Lands, tracts of land in the N. W. part of the United States. The absence of vegetation enables the rains to wash clean the old lake beds and in many instances to disclose remarkable fossils of extinct animals. They were first called Bad Lands *(mauvaises terres)* by the French explorers in the region of the Black Hills in South Dakota, on account of the ever changing irregularity of the surface, which the rain causes by the unconsolidated sediment moving into hills and ravines upon the solid strata.

Bagpipes, a musical wind instrument, chiefly played in Scotland and Ireland, and comprising bellows and pipes. In Assyria, India, and China a form of bagpipes was in use in ancient times, and in Italy and Greece they are common at the present day.

Bailiwick, an ancient legal term which originally denoted the limits of a bailiff's jurisdiction.

Balance, a form of lever supported in the center, and having scales at each end for ascertaining the weight of a substance. Stability and sensibility are the two chief requisites of a true balance; the first characteristic returning the balance to its original position after a weighing has occurred, the second showing a response to the slightest action.

Balcony, a projecting portion of a house, of stone, wood, or iron. Known to the Greeks and Romans, and a common feature of modern buildings.

Baldrick, an ornamental belt worn across the shoulder or round the waist, to support a bugle or sword.

Balearic Crane, the crowned crane of the Balearic Islands in the Mediterranean and the North African mainland, distinguished by its yellowish, black-tipped occipital tuft and by its trumpet note.

Ballad, a term used originally in regard to popular songs of war or romance, and now applied to folk compositions in narrative form. Scott, Lewis, Coleridge, Keats, and in later times Tennyson and Swinburne, have all produced effective pieces of the old ballad form. The term ballad is given to songs in general so long as they are simple in theme and construction.

Ballast is weighty matter placed in the bottom of a ship for balancing purposes, and varies in amount with the build, the size, and the cargo of a vessel. Water is now in general use for ballast.

Ballet was admitted into the old Greek religious exercises, and also formed part of the Roman pantomime, when a story was represented by ballet action. France adopted the ballet in the 16th century, and it was greatly patronized by Henry IV and Louis XIV. Ballets were highly popular in the early part of the 19th century in connection with operas. An active revival of the ballet has taken place in recent years, consequent mainly upon the style of dancing practiced by members of the Russian ballets, the late Anna Pavlova and Tamara Karsavina being among the chief exponents of this style of dancing, while Vera Zorina, Irina Baronova and others have won much fame for impersonation dancing in the United States.

Ballistic Curve, the actual course taken by any projectile upon discharge.

Ballot, a ball, ticket or paper by which a vote is registered. The word is also used to mean the total number of votes cast or recorded. French balla and Italian ballotta signified the little balls which were used in the Middle Ages in voting, as in the election of a pope by the College of Cardinals. In Greece similar balls are still used at elections. Paper ballots have almost universally taken the place of balls but the word "ballot" has been retained. Paper ballots were used in Europe in the 17th century, and the American colonists used them from the beginning. The paper ballots were supposed to insure secrecy; but some political organizations furnished an unlimited supply of printed ballots, any number of which could be marked and put in the box.

In 1851 Mr. Francis S. Dutton, of South Australia, proposed a ballot system which insures a secret vote if properly administered. The names of all the nominees are printed on the ballot with space for checking. The ballots are printed in a limited number by the government, and only one is given to each voter.

Balsam, the name of a genus of plants bearing handsome flowers. A term given also to certain liquids and substances used as ointments or unguents and mostly obtained from trees. Thus, the old Balm of Gilead was made from the bark of certain shrubs growing in Egypt and Arabia Felix.

Baltimore Bird, a lively black- and orange-plumaged starling of the oriole sub-family extending from Brazil to Canada; builds a well-constructed hanging nest.

Balusters are small pillars, short distances apart, made of metal, stone, or wood, used as supports for cornices, etc., or for enclosing stairs. A range of balusters and that which they support is called a balustrade.

Bambino, an image of the Infant Christ in the church of the Ara Coeli at Rome, and supposed to possess miraculous powers, is also a term applied in Italian art to images of the Infant Christ.

Bamboo, a genus of strong grasses, growing from 50 to 60 feet high, and much used by the Chinese for all kinds of purposes. The shoots of some species are tender and edible; the short canes are used as walking-sticks.

Ban or Bann, a proclamation or public notice whereby a thing is commanded or forbidden.

Banana *(Musa sapientum),* a large herbaceous plant cultivated in tropical and semi-tropical regions in great abundance, and one of the most productive plants known. The fruit of the banana is the staple food of the natives in many of the Pacific Islands.

Bandana, the name given to a red-spotted handkerchief usually made of cotton, but formerly only applied to silk handkerchiefs of that color and design.

Bandicoot, an Australian burrowing animal, of rat-like appearance, which carries its young in a pouch. The Indian *Mus giganteus,* as large as a rabbit, is also called a bandicoot. The oriental animal is a grain feeder, and the name signifies "pig-rat."

Banner, a flag indicating rank, office, or command, including the standard or national banner, regimental colors, a ship's flag, pendant, ensign, etc.

Bantu is the name of a group of African languages spoken by Zulus, Kaffirs, and others.

Baobab, or monkey-bread tree, is found in West Africa. Its trunk sometimes attains a girth of 70 feet, and there are specimens supposed to be thousands of years old. Yields a pulpy fruit from which a drink is made. The dried leaves are eaten.

Baptism is a rite practiced, either with infants or adults, by almost all Christian sects except Quakers, and is regarded as the act by which they are admitted "into the visible Church of Christ." The Baptists perform the rite only with adults and by the immersion of the entire body.

Baptistery, a building or portion of a building devoted to the rite of baptism.

Baptists came into prominence after the Reformation. For a time they suffered much persecution, but gradually made headway by their zeal and sincerity. Their distinctive tenet is that every member must make his own profession of personal faith and allegiance to Christ before baptism. Today this sect is spread over all parts of the Protestant world, though not always in large communities. They are strong in the United States. Throughout the world the Baptists have more than 11,500,000 communicants.

Barbarian, in the times of ancient Greece, meant anyone who could not speek Greek. Now the term is applied to savage or uncivilized people generally.

Barbary Ape is a small species found on the rock of Gibraltar, its ancestors having probably been brought from Barbary. It is the only kind of monkey existing in Europe.

Barbel, a European river fish, deriving its name from a sort of beard hanging from its jaw.

Barberry, a berry-producing shrub, belonging to the family Berberidaceae. Grows in a large compact bush and bears bright red berries growing in clusters.

Barcarole, a Venetian gondolier's song applied to instrumental as well as vocal compositions.

Bard, among the ancient Celts a poet or minstrel whose mission was to sing of heroic deeds. He was supposed to have the gift of prophecy, and was exempt from taxes and military service.

Barges are generally flat-bottomed boats, but the term is applied to most slow-moving river boats, such as ore-boats, house-boats, and sometimes to "lighters" and "keels" employed in canal and other waterway freight traffic.

Barium, a metal usually occurring as sulphate of barium and carbonate of barium. It is white, lustrous, heavy, and radio-opaque.

Bark, the external covering of trees, comprises the cuticle or *epidermis*, the outer bark or *cortex*, and the inner bark or *phloem*. It has many uses, and numerous kinds, rich in tannin, are utilized for tanning purposes. Various species of oak bark are most commonly used in Europe; whereas the bark of the hemlock spruce is used in North America. Many barks are used as medicines.

Bark, a three-masted vessel without a mizzen topsail. The term however, is often applied to almost any small ship.

Barlow Lens, a modification of the object-glass of the telescope, increasing its magnifying power without the loss of light which would ensue from the use of an eye-piece of shorter focus. Named after Peter Barlow, at one time a professor of mathematics at Woolwich, England.

Barnacle is a kind of crustacean, often found in large numbers attached to the bottoms of ships, rocks, or timbers, under water. There is also a species of goose called the barnacle.

Barometer, an instrument for measuring the weight or pressure of the atmosphere, was invented at Florence by Torricelli, pupil of Galileo, in 1644. Ordinarily, it is a glass tube 3 ft. long, filled with mercury, and inverted into a vessel also containing mercury, this causing the liquid in the tube to descend a few inches, leaving a *vacuum* at the top. The pressure at all points in the same horizontal plane of a liquid being equal, the level of the mercury in the tube must rise when the air gets heavier and fall when the air gets lighter. Gay-Lussac's barometer is siphon-shaped, with two scales graduating in opposite directions to a zero point; Bunter's is a slight improvement on this.

Barracks are buildings for the lodging and accommodation of soldiers, officers and men, and exist in all places where bodies of troops are stationed. It was not until toward the end of the 18th century that barracks began to be erected, and even down to the close of the Napoleonic Wars in 1815 the provision in this respect was very defective.

Barrel Organ, a musical instrument in which the music is made by a barrel or cylinder, set with pins and staples, which rotate so as to open the valves for admitting the wind to the pipes. Now almost, if not entirely, superseded by other musical instruments.

Barricades are temporary street fortifications usually erected at times of revolution. The most notable have been those of Paris. In 1830, 1848, and during the Commune disturbances of 1871 they were much resorted to, and were the scenes of many sanguinary conflicts.

Basalt Rocks are dark-colored and of igneous origin, and occur either as lava currents or as intrusive sheets.

Basanite, a smooth black siliceous mineral, or flinty jasper; a crypto-crystalline quartz, sometimes styled the Lydian Stone. An alloyed metal being rubbed across basanite, the mark of color left will indicate the nature and depth of the alloy, hence it obtains its name, which signifies, in Greek, "a touchstone."

Base, a chemical term denoting that which combines with an acid to form a salt. It is always a compound body, and the oxide of either a metal or of an elementary group possessing the power of a metal.

Basel, Council of, was the last of the three great councils held in 1431-1449.

Bashi-Bazouks, irregular Turkish troops, consisting of a rough but brave class of men from the Asiatic provinces.

Basilisk is a lizard of aquatic habits, with an elevated crest (which it can erect or depress at will) down the center of its back.

Basques are an old race living in the Pyrenees, with a language of their own, different from all other languages.

Bas-Relief ("low relief"), a term used in sculpture to denote a class of sculptures the figures of which are only slightly raised from the surface of the stone or clay upon which the design is wrought.

Bass, a genus of fish with spiny fins, of the perch family, found in the sea only in Europe, but inhabiting fresh waters in America.

Bassoon, a musical wind instrument of three octaves, the bass of the reed band. Invented by an Italian canon in 1539.

Bastille, a term originally used to denote any old French castle, but now generally referring to the state prison of Paris, destroyed by the people on the outbreak of the Revolution in 1789.

Bastinado, a beating, administered on the soles of the feet, formerly inflicted with cruel frequency in China, Turkey, and elsewhere in the Orient.

Bat, an order of mammals, with fore limbs held together by a membrane that serves the purpose of a wing. It has small eyes and large ears, and is of nocturnal habits, only emerging from its concealment at the approach of darkness. Bats are mostly insectivorous. The vampire-bat, which sucks the blood of sleeping animals, occurs only in South America.

Bathos is an unconscious lapse from the sublime to the trivial, and is often the result of over-eagerness to be impressive.

Batrachia, an order of amphibians, of which frogs and toads are typical representatives. The young of these animals are tadpoles, and grow from eggs or spawn, at first living entirely in the water. The subsequent developments, including the substitution of lungs for gills, are rapid.

Battering Ram, a medieval military apparatus composed of a heavy, iron-bound beam, which was impelled with great force upon the walls of a besieged place.

Battlement, a raised wall running along the top of a building, with embrasures through which an enemy could be fired upon. At first solely for military purposes, it was later used frequently as an architectural ornamentation.

Battles involving immense slaughter have been fought in past wars, but recent records reveal a far more serious carnage. In the wars of the French Revolution and those of Napoleon, which surged backward and forward over Europe from 1793 to 1815, it is estimated that the French lost two millions in killed alone. In nine of the battles in which Napoleon himself took part, the losses were as follows:—

Battle		Men engaged. (thousands)	Killed and Wounded. (thousands)
Austerlitz	1805	148	25
Jena	1806	98	17
Eylau	1807	133	42
Friedland	1807	142	34
Eckmuhl	1809	145	15
Wagram	1809	370	44
Borodino	1812	263	75
Leipzig	1813	440	92
Waterloo	1815	170	42

In the Peninsular War England left fifty thousand dead, and the French a quarter of a million behind them in Spain. At Salamanca the British lost 15 per cent of their troops, and at Albuera 65 per cent. In the Crimea the total losses of Russia and the Allies were put at 480,000. The American Civil War involved a loss of six hundred thousand men. In the seven months of the Franco-German War, 1870-71, the killed and disabled numbered 371,751. A million Germans and 710,000 Frenchmen took the field, and the following were the casualties:—

	French	Germans	Total
Killed	41,000	19,782	60,782
Died of wounds	36,000	10,710	46,710
Died of sickness	45,000	14,259	59,259
Disabled	116,000	89,000	205,000
Totals	238,000	133,751	371,751

In four of the principal battles the following were the results in killed and wounded:—

	French (thousands)	Germans (thousands)	Total (thousands)
Woerth	32	11	43
Mars-la-Tour	26	16	42
Gravelotte	28	20	48
Paris	30	13	43

In the Russo-Turkish War of 1877-78, with its total loss of nearly 200,000, the only notable battle was before Plevna, when in the course of a protracted siege there fell in a single day 18,000 out of 80,000 Russians engaged. In the Russo-Japanese War many of the battles were of the most deadly character. At the battle of Liau-yang the Russian losses in killed were nearly 20,000 and the Japanese losses about 18,000. At Sha-ho, the Russian casualties were estimated at 60,000, the Japanese at 16,000; and the battle of Mukden, in which nearly a million soldiers were engaged, was even more sanguinary. Battles during World War I lasted usually several days and the losses were enormous. During the first three months of the war the German drive for the Channel Ports cost the French in killed, wounded, and prisoners 854,000 men; the British 85,000; and the Germans 677,000. In the first three weeks alone—to the victory of the Marne—the French lost 330,000 killed and prisoners and 280,000 wounded, and most of these casualties occurred from Aug. 21 to 24 and Sept. 5 to 9, that is to say, in a period of eight days' fighting. The principle battles of World War II included the Battle of Stalingrad, the Battle of the Coral Sea, the Battle for Leyte Gulf, the Normandy invasion, the Ardennes Bulge, the invasion of Iwo Jima, and the invasion of Okinawa. Dead and wounded in the U. S. Armed Forces numbered over a million.

Bauxite, a mineral consisting mainly of the oxides of iron and aluminum.

Bayonet, a weapon taking its name from Bayonne, where it was first made about 1660. It was originally fitted into the gun-barrel, but General Makay, in 1689, introduced the socket-bayonet, which allows the gun to be fired with the bayonet fixed.

Bay-window, a structure projecting from the main part of the building; it is usually semi-octagonal or semi-hexagonal in plan; a bow-window forms the segment of a circle.

Beads have been used as personal ornaments from very early times, valuable specimens having been found in the tombs of the ancient Egyptians. They are made of various materials, from precious stones to glass. They have been and are much used as objects of barter in dealing with uncivilized races.

Beans, the seeds of certain food-plants of many varieties, including the common bean, the

French bean, and the kidney bean. India and South America yield special species. All beans possess a high proportion of nutritive qualities, the common bean excelling wheat in this respect. The Greeks and Romans used white and black beans in balloting for magistrates, the black meaning an adverse vote.

Bear, a genus of mammals of the order Carnivora, which use the entire sole of the foot in walking. They are found in most parts of the globe except Australia. The common brown bear was once spread over the whole of Europe including England but now is confined to the northern forests of Europe and Asia. The black bear of America is nearly allied to the brown species. America has also a larger kind, the grizzly. In the Arctic regions the polar bear forms a distinctive species, and differs from the rest in being exclusively carnivorous. The other bears feed mostly on roots, fruits, honey, etc.

Beard, one of the distinctive signs of manhood; it was regarded as a sacred possession by ancient races. The Jews were proud of their beards and wore them during the days of their Egyptian bondage, even though the Egyptians shaved. The Greeks and Romans of ancient times generally shaved, and the term barbarous (beard-wearing) was applied for a long period to peoples who were considered outside the pale of civilization. Nevertheless, beards were worn even by the Greeks and Romans and came to be associated with wisdom. Alexander the Great prohibited beards among his soldiery. Beards have been taxed occasionally, as in Russia by Peter the Great, and at an earlier date in England.

Beau-ideal, a conception of some perfect object free from all shortcomings.

Beaver, a genus of mammals of the Rodentia order, with short, scaly ears and webbed hind feet; it attains a length of from 2½ to 3 feet. Beavers live in communities and construct dams and habitations for themselves.

Bedouins, the Arabs who inhabit parts of northern Africa and western Asia. They are divided into independent tribes, each governed by its own sheikh.

Beds. The form of beds as used in ancient Egypt, Greece, and Rome has remained much the same. The Anglo-Saxons had wooden beds in recesses, the bedding being of straw. The "four-poster," which remained the model for many centuries, was introduced in the 16th century, and many handsome specimens of carved and heavily draped beds of this kind are still preserved. At the Victoria and Albert Museum in London is shown the Great Bed of Ware, capable of accommodating a dozen people and said to have belonged to Warwick, "the King-maker." It is of oak and bears the date of 1463.

Bee, a family of insects of the order Hymenoptera. Aristotle and Vergil in ancient times and Maeterlinck in recent times have described their industrial queendoms and forms of government. The hives are tenanted by the queen bee, the working bees (or neuters, which are imperfectly developed females), and the drones or males. The workers do all the honey gathering and storing and the constructing of the cells, which are divided into store cells and egg cells. The queen—and there is but one queen to a hive—lays eggs and governs, obtaining complete obedience from the workers. The drones form less than one-tenth of the population of the hive, and their lives are over in about three months. At the proper time, and then only, the queen quits the hive followed by the drones, which gather round her in the air. After impregnation she returns to the hive and begins to fulfil her mission of egg-laying, depositing egg after egg at the rate of some 200 a day in the cells prepared for them. The process of hatching a bee takes about 21 days. When new queens arise among the newcomers, the old queen tries to destroy her rivals; and also among young queens enmity exists. In apiculture they have to be separately guarded and liberated singly at wide intervals. Each queen thus attracts a swarm of her own, and other bee colonies are formed in fresh hives.

Beech, one of the finest of trees, with massive trunk and smooth shiny bark. Its horizontal branches, covered with close foliage, make a deep shade. Its wood is rather brittle but capable of being utilized in the manufacture of many industrial articles.

Bee-eater, a bird of the genus *Merops*, common in North Africa. It has a black-bordered yellow patch on the throat but the plumage is mainly brownish-red, with blue markings on the head, and with long greenish tail-feathers.

Beef-eater, the name given to the Yeomen of the Guard, who originally formed part of the guard of Henry VII of England. The word is a corruption of *buffetier*, i. e., one who attends the buffet. Their dress dates from Henry VIII, who, it is said, made them dress in thick costumes so that they would look as stout as he himself.

Beelzebub, a corruption of Baal or Bel, whom the Philistines worshiped at Ekron.

Beer, a liquor made by fermentation from malted barley and hops. A similar drink was known in Egypt long before the Christian era. Beer contains from 2 to 5 per cent of alcohol. Ale, small beer, and bitter beer are varieties differing from one another in strength and in proportion of hops. Porter and stout are prepared like beer, but owe their peculiar flavor to the use of a proportion of malt heated so as to convert part of the sugar to caramel.

Beeswax, the secretion of the bee, used for the formation of the cells or honeycomb of the hive; when melted it is what is commercially known as yellow wax, white wax being made by bleaching. Being impervious to water, beeswax acts as a good resistant and is an article of much utility.

Beet, a genus of plants of the order Chenopodiaceae, and a native of the shores of the Mediterranean. The leaves of the white beet are used like spinach. The red variety has a thick root, and it is estimated that 12 per cent of its weight is sugar.

Beetle, an order of coleopterous (or sheath-winged) insects, comprising more than 150,000 species. They possess two pairs of wings, the hinder ones being but rarely used for flight. Beetles remain concealed during the day; they are found on plants, among stones, in the ground, in wood, and on water. They feed on animal and vegetable matter and are valuable in destroying noxious insects and putrefying substances.

Beg or Bey, a Tartar and Turkish title (equivalent to prince or chief) given to superior military officers and distinguished foreigners. The latter form of the word is commonly met with in Tunis and other parts of northern Africa.

Behemoth, the name of a large four-footed beast referred to in the Book of Job; it is probably the hippopotamus, but by others it is thought to be the elephant, and by still others the rhinoceros.

Belfry, in early times a movable tower used for defense during a siege. Later the term was applied to any watchtower or alarmbell tower and finally to any tower in which a bell was hung.

Belgae, the name given by the Romans to the Teutonic and Celtic tribes inhabiting certain parts of Gaul.

Bell, a hollow body of metal used for making sounds. Bells are usually made of bell metal, or alloy of copper and tin, but small bells used for interior functions are often made of silver, gold, or brass. Ordinary hand bells are generally of brass. The largest bell in the world is the Great Bell of Moscow, which weighs about 180 tons and is 19 feet high and 60 feet round the rim. Cast in 1733, it cracked while still in the furnace. Emperor Nicholas caused it to be placed on a platform, to form the dome of a chapel. The largest bell in use is another in Moscow, which weighs 128 tons. Other gigantic bells are the Great Bell at Peking (53 tons); Nanking (22 tons); Cologne Cathedral (25 tons); Big Ben, Westminster, London (13½ tons). The number of changes that can be rung on a peal of bells is the *factorial* of the number of bells. Thus four bells allow 24, and eight bells 40,320. For private houses, hotels, etc. electric bells are now generally in use.

Belladonna (deadly nightshade), a well-known poisonous wild plant found in southern Europe and western Asia. The poisonous alkaloid atropine which it contains is valuable in medicine.

Belles-Lettres, a term embracing the various branches of literature—rhetoric, poetry, history, criticism, philology, etc.

Benedictines, the followers of St. Benedict, who at different times belonged to various religious orders, such as the Cistercians, the Silvestrines, the Celestines, the Praemonstratensians, and the Grandmontensians. They were introduced into England at the beginning of the 7th century and were called the Black Monks (not to be confounded with the Black Friars, who belonged to the Dominican Order) because of the color of their dress.

Benedictus, a canticle used in church services, deriving its name from the first word of the Latin version, *benedictus,* meaning blessed.

Bengal Light, a blue signal-light, used at sea in time of shipwreck. It is of niter, sulphur, and the black sulphide of antimony, in proportions of 6, 2, and 1 respectively.

Benthamism, the philosophy of Jeremy Bentham, the essential principles of which were that the end and aim of human life is happiness. Communities and individuals, it taught, should strive after the greatest happiness of the greatest number, the effort to achieve the greatest good for the greatest number being accounted in itself the highest morality.

Benzene, a compound of carbon and hydrogen, discovered by Faraday, and the chief constituent in the production of aniline dyes.

Benzoin, a gum resin used in perfume making, and obtained from an East Indian tree *(Styrax benzoin).* It has numerous commercial uses, and is employed medicinally in chronic lung complaints.

Berbers, the inhabitants of the mountainous parts of Barbary and the northern portion of the Sahara; they are supposed to be the descendants of the aborigines of northern Africa. They live mostly in the fastnesses of the Atlas Mountains, and number about 4,000,000.

Bering Sea Arbitration, an agreement between Great Britain and the United States in regard to the seal fisheries, made in 1893 in Paris and resulting in the sea being declared open beyond the territorial limits.

Berlin Congress, held at the conclusion of the Russo-Turkish War of 1878. All the European Powers were represented, and the Treaty of Berlin was the result.

Beryl, a mineral, of which the emerald is a variety. It is yellowish, greenish-yellow, or blue; it is found in veins which traverse granite or gneiss, is sometimes embedded in granite and sometimes in alluvial soil formed from such rocks. Transparent specimens are found in Brazil.

Bethlehem, the traditional birthplace of Jesus and of King David, about six miles south of Jerusalem. It is famous for its Church of the Nativity, built in the form of a cross. Below the church is a crypt where Jesus is said to have been born.

Bhang, a hemp plant containing highly narcotic and intoxicating properties and yielding the drug called hashish. The natives of India chew the leaves and seeds of this plant.

Bible, the name applied to the Christian Scriptures, which contain both the Old Testament and the New Testament. The Old Testament, written originally in Hebrew, consists of 39 books and may be divided into three parts: the Law, the Prophets, and miscellaneous writings. The Hebrew text as now printed is called the Massoretic. The apocryphal books, excluded from the Bible used by Protestants, are accepted by Roman Catholics. The books of the New Testament were written in Greek and are believed to be the work of the Apostles or their contemporaries. The whole Bible was translated into Latin (Vulgate) about A. D. 400. Portions were translated into Anglo-Saxon in the 8th century, and the Venerable Bede put the greater part of St. John's gospel into English, but it was not until 1535 that a complete, printed English version appeared—the Coverdale Translation. The Authorized Version dates from the reign of James I.

Bible Society, an association founded specifically with the object of translating, printing, and circulating the Scriptures. In 1710 Baron Hildebrand von Canstein founded at Halle, in Saxony, the institute which was perhaps the earliest Bible society in the specific sense, the Canstein Institute. The British and Foreign Bible Society was founded in 1804, the American Bible Society in 1816, and the National Bible Society of Scotland in 1861.

Bibles with Nicknames. Among the earlier versions of the Bible were many with curious misprints, nicknamed from their errors. The Vinegar Bible derived its appellation from the misprinting of the word "vinegar" for "vineyard." The Breeches Bible, also known as the Geneva Bible issued in 1560, owed its name to the translation of Gen. iii, 7: "Making themselves breeches out of fig-leaves." The Bishop's or Treacle Bible was printed by Richard Jugge in 1572, and Jeremiah viii, 22, runs, "Is there not tryacle at Gilead; is there no phisition there?" And this volume has the variorum rendering, Judges ix, 53, of "All to break his head" as "All to break his brayne panne." In another edition the rendering is, "But a certaine woman cast a piece of millstone upon Abimelech's head and brake his braine pan." In one Bible the word "rosine" was used where "balm" now occurs, with a note "For at Gilead did grow most souveraign balme for wounds." Of Bibles which are rare, that of 1551 is said to be the scarcest. In 1661 was published what has been styled the "Wicked Bible," receiving the name from its having the word "not" omitted from the Seventh Commandment. A similar error occurs in a small pearl Bible of 1653, in which St. Paul is represented as asking "Know ye not that the unrighteous shall inherit the Kingdom of God?"

Bibliomancy, divination by turning at random to pages, lines, or verses of the Bible, frequently resorted to in olden times.

Bicycle, a two-wheeled vehicle, the successor to the velocipede of three wheels, which came into vogue about 1880. It consisted of one high wheel driven by pedals, and a small connecting wheel behind. In its present form, with two wheels of even circumference, pneumatic tires and effective gearing, it has become very popular.

Bill, the horny, lipless, and toothless jaw of a bird, the upper and lower portions being generally equal, except in birds of prey, when the upper is longer. The bill is used for seizing and dividing food, for fighting, nest-building, etc.

Bill of Rights, one of the great instruments of the British constitution. It was formulated in 1689, being based upon the Declaration of Right of the previous year. The Bill of Rights did not introduce any new concepts, but reasserted the "ancient rights and liberties" of Parliament, which had been taken away by James II and earlier Stuart kings. It prohibited the sovereign from executing or suspending laws, from levying money, from creating special courts of law, and from raising an army, unless these acts were performed with Parliamentary consent. It declared against royal interference in elections to Parliament or in any Parliamentary proceedings, and against the requirement of excessive bail or the imposition of cruel or unusual punishments. Many of the most important provisions of this portion of the Bill of Rights were later embodied in the Constitution of the United States, and in the constitutions of the several states. Besides dealing with these general matters, the Bill of Rights contained provisions for the accession to the throne of the Prince and Princess of Orange, afterward William and Mary. It also excluded Roman Catholics from the English throne.

Billeting, a system of feeding and lodging soldiers by quartering them on the inhabitants of a town.

Binnacle, a table or box on which the compass of a ship is placed. It stands in front of the steering apparatus and steersman.

Biology deals with the phenomena of living matter, describing its properties, growth, changes and conditions. Starting with the protoplasm, it traces the operations of life through the various classifications, the metamorphoses undergone in plant and animal life, and their development, distribution, organism, and functions.

Birch, a genus of forest trees of the order Betulaceae, and only found in northern regions. In America the birch grows to goodly proportions, and forms one of the most graceful of trees, with its drooping branches and egg-shaped leaves. It has a white bark, which is used for tanning, steeping nets, sails, etc. The Indians used to make canoes of it.

Birdlime, an adhesive substance placed on twigs of trees, walls, wire netting, or elsewhere, to trap birds. It is prepared from the middle bark of the holly, mistletoe, or distaff thistle. It is also made from flour admixed with other adhesives.

Bird of Paradise, a bird allied to the crows, found almost exclusively in New Guinea, the males having a beautiful plumage of long branching feathers.

Birds, or Aves, are, next to mammals, the highest order of animal life. They are vertebrate, warm-blooded, oviparous, are covered with feathers, and possess wings. In construction they vary greatly, according to their classification and their conditions of life. Birds are of three distinct classifications—*Carinatae*, possessing keeled breastbones and having power of flight; *Ratitae*, having raft-like breastbones, and incapable of flight; and *Saururae*, a lizard-tailed genus, of which only one species is known —the extinct archaeopteryx.

Biretta, a four-cornered head-covering worn by ecclesiastics of the Roman Catholic and Episcopal Churches and varying in color according to the rank of the wearer. A cardinal's biretta is red, a bishop's purple, a priest's black.

Bismuth, one of the elements, with atomic number 83, atomic weight 209, and the chemical symbol Bi. In its pure state it is a brittle, silvery white metal, with a tinge of red. It has a specific gravity of about 9.8, and a melting point of 507° F. Bismuth, both pure and in ores, is found widely distributed, the most important sources being Saxony, Bohemia, California, Australia, Ontario, Cornwall, and Bolivia. Bismuth has numerous uses both in industry and in medicine. Certain bismuth alloys have very low melting points and are consequently used in fire-extinguishing systems in buildings. Since bismuth expands on solidification it is useful in making type metal, preventing the type from shrinking as it cools. Bismuth subnitrate is a fine white powder which has long been used as a face powder. Various bismuth salts are much used in medicine, especially as mild astringents in inflammatory conditions of the digestive tract. A more recent use consists in intramuscular injections of the salts of bismuth or of suspensions of the pure metal, to supplement mercury or arsphenamine preparations in the treatment of syphilis.

Bison, a ruminant animal, comprising the European and American bison. The former is found in Lithuania and the Ural and Caucasus Mountains. The American bison, commonly called buffalo, is practically extinct in its wild state.

Bittern, a bird of the heron genus, with long, loose plumage on the front and sides of the neck. It is a solitary bird inhabiting marshes.

Bitumen, a combustible mineral substance, the term embracing various mineral oils and resins, such as naphtha, petroleum, and mineral pitch.

Bivalves, a term applied to shell-fish whose shell consists of two valves, lying one on each side of the body, such as mussels, oysters, and cockles.

Blackbird, or Merle, a familiar songbird in parts of northern Africa and Europe.

Black Death, an epidemic or plague, which carried off thousands all over Europe in the 14th century, one-third of the population of England dying from it. Its appalling virulence may have been attributable to unsanitary conditions.

Black Hole of Calcutta, the place where 146 Englishmen were confined in 1756 by order of Suraj-ul-Dowlah. The men were driven into a room 20 feet square, and only 23 were found alive the next morning.

Black Lead, graphite or plumbago, a mineral found in the United States, Canada, Norway, Siberia, Spain, and Ceylon.

Black Letter, the Old English or Gothic type first used in printing blocks.

Blasting, a method of loosening or breaking masses of solid matter by means of explosives.

Bleaching, the art of whitening textiles. The old method was to bleach by exposure to the sun; but chemical bleaching is now general, chloride of lime being used for the purpose. Sun-bleached linen has advantages in durability not possessed by chemically bleached fabrics.

Blight, a noxious influence exerted upon vegetation by inauspicious atmospheric conditions, or by attacks of parasitic fungi or injurious insect life.

Blindworm, or slowworm, a reptile of the lizard order; found in most parts of Europe; non-venomous. Its principal food is the slug.

Blockade, an operation for capturing a town or fortress, preventing the besieged from receiving supplies. A naval blockade hinders the entrance or egress of the enemy's ships from a port.

Blockhouses, an important feature of guerilla warfare. The houses are of logs or corrugated iron, covered in with earth to render them fire- and bomb-proof, and loopholes are made for firing through.

Block System, on railroads, a method of signaling to prevent the distance between two signal boxes from being occupied on the same line of rails by more than one train at a time.

Blood, the life-sustaining circulating fluid of animals. In animals having a backbone it is red; in the lower animals it is colorless. Blood is either arterial or venous; that is, either contained in the arteries which carry the fluid from the heart to the tissues, or in the veins through which it is returned to the heart to be repurified. Under the microscope, blood reveals a composition of nearly colorless liquid and a large number of corpuscles, some red, some white. The red corpuscles distribute the oxygen from the lungs.

Bloodhound, a dog celebrated for its keen scent and deriving its name from its power of following a trail. Bloodhounds are sometimes used for hunting and for tracking fugitive criminals.

Bloodstone, a variety of green quartz, spotted with jasper, like blood-drops. A kind of hematite iron ore used for burnishing is also called bloodstone.

Blowpipe, an instrument used for driving a blast of air or gas into a flame to increase its temperature. Used in soldering metals and in analytical chemistry and mineralogy for ascertaining the nature of a substance under great heat.

Bluebird, a North American bird, deriving its name from its deep blue plumage. It is one of the few songbirds of America and familiar in the woods from early spring to November.

Blue-breast, a name sometimes given to the blue-throated warbler *(Phoenicura suecica)*.

Blue Monday, the Monday immediately preceding Lent, when in the 16th century many churches were bedecked internally with hangings of blue.

Blue Ribbon, a term in general use to express the highest order of English knighthood, the Garter, which has for the chief part of its insignia a garter of blue velvet.

Blue Vitriol, sulphate of copper, used for dyeing, principally for aftertreating certain dyed colors to render them fast.

Blunderbuss, a short, bell-mouthed musket with wide bore, capable of firing many balls at once. It was common in the 17th century.

Boa, a term applied to a family of snakes of large size, some attaining a length of 30 feet. They are not poisonous but kill their prey by crushing—constriction; hence the name "boa constrictor," They occur in both the Old World and the New.

Boar, or wild hog, an animal largely distributed over the forest regions of Europe, Asia, Africa, and South America. It has a longer snout and shorter ears than its descendant, the domestic hog, and is provided with tusks. Having to forage for itself, it is a more active and intelligent animal than the pig of the sty and offers good sport to the hunter.

Bobierrite, a colorless mineral, found in Peruvian guano in the form of six-sided prisms; a tribasic phosphate of magnesia. It is named after Bobierre, who first described it in 1868.

Bode's Law, an astronomical law discovered by Bode in 1778, which indicates the relative distances of the planets from the sun. By adding 4 to each of the doubled numbers in the series, 0, 3, 6, 12, 24, 48, 96, one arrives at the numbers 4, 7, 10, 16, 28, 52, 100; these totals being, approximately, the distances between the principal planets and the sun, the real distances being: Mercury 3.9; Venus, 7.2; Earth, 10; Mars, 15.2; Jupiter, 52.9; Saturn, 95.4. The apparent failure in the 28 is accounted for by the orbits of the asteroids.

Bodleian Library, connected with Oxford University and named for Sir Thomas Bodley, who in 1598 restored and added greatly to its treasures. A copy of every book published in the United Kingdom has to be sent free to this library.

Boer War, lasted from October 11, 1899, when the Boers invaded Natal, to May 31, 1902, when the peace treaty was signed at Pretoria.

Bog Oak, oak found buried in peat bogs. It is of a deep black color throughout.

Boiling Point, the temperature at which the pressure of the vapor is equal to the pressure of the atmosphere. Under increased pressure the boiling point is higher and under reduced pressure as on the top of a mountain, it is lower. As represented on the centigrade scale the boiling point of water is 100°; alcohol, 78.4°; and ether, 35.6°. On the Fahrenheit scale, the boiling point of distilled water is 212°.

Bolshevism, the revolutionary majority which under Lenin took over the government of Russia in 1917, establishing a communistic, centralized control of economic production and distribution on the basis of a federal government.

Bombs, metal containers charged with explosive material and fired by clockwork, a time fuse, or some other mechanism.

Book of the Dead, a book of ancient Egyptian prayers, copies of which have been found in tombs.

Books. At first, collected writings were produced in the form of rolls; and when the art of printing spread, they began to be issued in bindings upon the principle still in use. The earlier books were massively bound, with metal clasps and bands, and samples centuries old survive to show their durability and workmanship. Books are technically described, according to their sizes, as 4to, 8vo (quarto, octavo), and so on, the names indicating the number of folds in a sheet. Thus when a book is printed on a sheet folded in half, it is known as *folio* and consists of 4 pages; doubled in half again, it consists of 8 pages and is *quarto* size; doubled once more it is *octavo* and consists of 16 pages; and by a further doubling we get 16mo; while other methods of folding give 12mo, 18mo, 24mo, 36mo, etc.

Boomerang, a weapon used by the Australian aborigines, made of wood, in the form of a parabola, one side flat, the other round. When thrown forward into the air, it whirls round and rebounds behind the point from which it was projected. Used both as a missile of war and for killing game.

Borax, the tetraborate of sodium, found in California, Peru, Tibet, and elsewhere; it acts as a mild alkali upon the alimentary canal and makes a useful gargle in inflammation of the throat and mouth membranes.

Botany, the science of the plant kingdom, its broad classifications consisting of structural botany physiological botany, systematic botany, and economic botany—terms which explain themselves. Plants consist of an axis or main shaft (which bears the branches, leaves and flowers) and the root by which the nourishing substances necessary to the plant's life are obtained from the earth. The stem is the leaf-bearing part of the plant, when soft, herbaceous. Branches are shoots from the stem, and of the same structure; leaves grow from the branches, and are of various forms. A leaf comprises two parts, the stalk and the blade. The flower is a clusterous modification of leaves which becomes the medium of the plant's reproduction. Plants are flowering or nonflowering.

Boulevard, in its original significance, the rampart of a fortified city; later, any important, wide thoroughfare.

Box, a plant of two varieties: a shrub that grows from 8 to 10 feet high, and a dwarf variety used for garden edging that grows to a height of only a few inches. Boxwood is the best medium for wood engraving.

Boxers, members of a secret society in China, who in 1896 rose against foreigners and were guilty of many massacres and atrocities directed especially against missionaries. A combined European force was sent out against the Boxers in 1900. The rising was suppressed and large indemnities were demanded and conceded.

Boycott, a term used in connection with a person with whom the general body of people, a party, or society refuse to have dealings; originally used when Captain Boycott was refused recognition by the Irish Land League.

Brahmanism, the chief religion of the Hindus, is an adaptation rather than an adoption of the doctrine set forth in the sacred books of *Vedas*, and was built on the system of caste. In Brahmanism there is a supreme God, with a divine triad consisting of Brahma Vishnu, and Siva. There are four castes: the Brahmins, or priests; the Kshatryas, kings and soldiers; the Vaisyas, who are traders; and the Sudras, or the artisan classes. Many other divisions and subdivisions of caste have been developed from these four, and the preservation of caste is regarded as a Hindu's foremost duty.

Braille, an alphabet for the blind, a raised-dot system of notation applied to both writing and music; invented by a Frenchman called Braille about 1830, and now in world-wide use by the blind.

Brandy, obtained by distilling wine, is prepared chiefly in France, the Cognac variety being the best.

Brandywine, Battle of, fought between the British and the Americans in 1777, resulting in victory for the former.

Brass, an alloy or compound metal, two-thirds copper and one-third zinc; and though harder than copper, it is more easily worked.

Brazil Nut, the seed of a large myrtle common in Brazil. The seed clusters have from fifteen to fifty nuts, enclosed in huge woody coverings.

Breadfruit Tree, native to the South Sea Islands, supplies the natives with a wholesome food. The fruit is the size of a melon and contains a white pulpy substance, which is roasted before being eaten. The plant has been successfully acclimatized in the West Indies.

Breakwaters, artificial structures of stone or concrete built across the entrances to harbors, to stay the force of the sea and to leave the inner portion calm and safe for ships.

Breeding, in one of its senses, implies the art of improving animals by selection or by treatment intended to produce certain special qualities in their progeny. It is an art that has been practiced with highly successful results in the case of horses, sheep, cattle, fowl, cage birds, and fish—some of the results amounting almost to the production of new species.

Brevet, a special commission entitling an officer to a rank in the army higher than that which he actually holds in his own regiment, without increase of pay.

Breviary (meaning abridgment), the short service book of the Roman Catholic Church, fixed in its present form by Pope Pius V in 1568.

Brewing, the art of preparing a fermented beverage, chiefly beer and ale, from an infusion of grain. Intoxicating drinks have been brewed in all ages and countries from the most remote times.

Bricks, uniformly shaped and sized portions of baked clay, used for building. All ancient nations made bricks, at first baking them in the sun, and afterward in fire. The Israelites were employed in brickmaking during their captivity in Egypt. The Romans used bricks for all ordinary building purposes and introduced them into England. In these days brickmaking is done mainly by machinery under methods which greatly increase the scale of production and improve the quality of the bricks.

Bridges, structures for continuing roads across streams, rivers, ravines, or above other roads. Until the 18th century the art of bridge-building was in its infancy; it has only been since road traffic assumed large proportions that the art has come to be practiced on a great scale along scientific lines. Wood was the first material used; then came stone; toward the end of the 18th century iron was brought into use; and now steel has largely superseded iron. Some famous bridges are the Brooklyn (suspension); the London Tower Bridge (suspension); the Tay Bridge in Scotland, 10,300 feet long; the Zambesi Bridge, 12,064 feet long; the Triborough Bridge, New York; the San Francisco Bay Bridge; the Golden Gate Bridge, San Francisco, having the longest single span in the world; the Straits of Mackinac Bridge, the longest suspension bridge from anchorage to anchorage; and Lake Pontchartrain Causeway.

Britannia Metal, a silvery-white alloy composed of tin, copper, zinc, antimony, bismuth, and occasionally lead, capable of taking a high polish, and used for various kinds of metal ware.

British Museum, opened in London at Montagu House in 1759, was founded with Sir Hans Sloane's collection, which the British Government acquired for approximately $100,000. In 1823 the present building in Great Russell Street was started, and completed in 1847, from designs by Sir R. Smirke. The library, to which copies of all books published in Great Britain have to be sent free, is a great treasure house of books, ancient and modern. George III's library of 70,000 volumes, valued at approximately $1,000,000, was added to it by a gift of that monarch's successor in 1823, and many other valuable private collections have been derived in a similar way. The museum proper contains invaluable collections of sculptures, antiquities, bronzes, jewels, geological specimens, rare manuscripts, and books. The Natural History Department is now separately housed at South Kensington. The Science Department (Kensington) is replete with working models of all kinds of machinery. The British Museum is supported by Parliamentary grants.

Brocade, a special kind of cloth in which the design or pattern is woven in relief on the surface of the material.

Bronze, an alloy of copper and tin, sometimes with zinc, iron or lead added.

Brownies, according to old superstition, nocturnal household fairies who performed various domestic duties for the good people who had won their favor.

Bucephalus, Alexander the Great's celebrated war horse, to whose memory the king built a town bearing the animal's name.

Buddhism, a religious system supposed to have originated in India about the 6th century B. C., the founder being a native prince named Siddhartha Gautama. Around this personality many strange myths gathered, Buddha representing the highest mystic state of human existence, beyond which there is no recognition of a God. In Buddhism nirvana represents the perfecting of knowledge and the attainment of the most complete oblivion to reality, and involves the realization of developing conditions tending to the highest blessing. There is no caste in Buddhism. In its more modern phases Buddhism remains, in its purity, a philosophical system in which selflessness and universal charity are leading elements. Buddhism, driven out of India by the Brahmins, is now one of the important religions of the people of China, Japan, Ceylon, Siam, Burma, and Nepal—some 450,000,000 in all

Buffalo, a species of wild ox, still existing in large numbers in the wilds of Africa. The name buffalo is commonly applied to the American bison.

C

Cabala, a mysterious Hebrew theosophy, which had its rise in the 10th century and was announced as a special revelation, enabling Rabbis to explain the hidden meanings of the sacred writings. This was carried to great excess by later cabalists, who pretended to read signs and evidences in letters, forms, and numbers contained in the Scripture.

Cabinet, the principal members of the executive branch of the government. The cabinet of the President of the United States is composed of the heads of the several administrative departments of the government. They are Secretary of State, Secretary of the Treasury, Secretary of Defense, Attorney General, Postmaster General, Secretary of the Interior, Secretary of Agriculture, Secretary of Commerce, Secretary of Labor, and Secretary of Health, Education and Welfare. Although members of the cabinet are appointed by the President, they must be confirmed by the Senate, but can be removed by the President at any time. Contrary to foreign systems, the United States cabinet members do not have seats in Congress; there is no premier; and the President, not the cabinet members, is responsible for the acts of the government. The salary of members of the cabinet is $25,000 a year. In Great Britain the cabinet is the body of ministers who carry on the government. It is the executive organ of Parliament; while subject to considerations of use and custom, its action can be suited to the exigencies of time and circumstance. Members of the cabinet are chosen by the Prime Minister for about 20 cabinet posts. Since the cabinet is fully responsible to the Parliament, the leader of the majority party in the House of Commons becomes prime minister, and he chooses the cabinet members from his own party. If Parliament votes against the cabinet on an important issue, the cabinet must resign as a body. On the other hand, the cabinet may dissolve Parliament and call an election. Because of this power, the cabinet may in fact be the government.

Cable, the rope or chain that is attached to a ship's anchor. Chain cables are now in general use except for very deep waters. A cable's length is 100 fathoms, 200 yards. Submarine telegraph cables are composed of copper wires.

Cacao, a tree, from 16 to 40 feet high, growing abundantly in tropical America, the West Indies, and Ceylon, and yielding a nutritive fruit, from which cocoa and chocolate are manufactured.

Cachalot, a cetacean inhabiting chiefly the northern seas; called also the spermaceti whale. The Mexican and South Sea sperm whales, allied species, are found in warmer waters; all swim in schools.

Cachet, Lettre de, a private letter of state signed by the king, much in use in France up to the time of the Revolution, for consigning obnoxious or troublesome people to prison without trial.

Cactus, a prickly plant of exogenous nature and of varied form and size, fleshy and succulent, often leafless, and of very abnormal shape. The

"Indian fig" cacti have sessile flowers, which bloom at night and quickly die.

Caduceus, the name of the wand of authority borne by Hermes, or Mercury, being a plain rod, the fillets of which are in the form of snakes, surmounted by a couple of wings. A herald's staff of office is also styled a caduceus.

Caffeine, a highly stimulative alkaloid found in coffee and tea having a bitter flavor.

Cainozoic, a geological term used to indicate all the strata which lie above the chalk—that is, the "most recent" strata. Tertiary is an alternative and equivalent term.

Calcium, a widely diffused metal of light yellow color, burning vividly at red heat. It is not found in a free state, but occurs in combination with most of the native silicates. Calcite, limestone, marble and chalk are calcium carbonates.

Calc-spar (Calcite) is one of the commonest minerals, and occurs in a wide variety of crystalline forms of the hexagonal system. It possesses the property of perfect cleavage, and easily splits up into rhombs.

Calculating Machines. Many kinds have been devised from time to time. They are mostly adding, subtracting, multiplying or dividing machines. The first to attract special notice was that of Babbage, which was intended to calculate even algebraical problems, but it was never completed. Tide-predicting machines, machines for integrating differential equations, logical machines, calculating scales, etc., are all of the same class.

Calendar, a collection of tables showing the days and months of the year, the astronomical recurrences, chronological references, etc. The Julian Calendar, introduced by Julius Caesar, fixed the average length of the year at 365¼ days. Under this arrangement of the year, there was a loss of 11 minutes and 10 seconds per annum. The shortcoming was rectified by the Gregorian Calendar, introduced in Italy in 1582, but not adopted in England before 1752, when 11 days were dropped out of the calendar. The Gregorian year is 365 days, 5 hours, 49 minutes, and 12 seconds.

Caliph, the name given to the heads of the Moslem faith and meaning successor—that is, successor to Mohammed. At first the title could be borne only by direct descendants of the Prophet. Only four so-called "perfect" caliphs, however, reigned after Mohammed at Medina. Then others of the Prophet's tribe succeeded. There were 13 caliphs at Damascus between 661 and 750, and 37 at Bagdad between 750 and 1258. When the Turks overthrew the Ottoman dynasty in 1922, they abolished the caliphate. There is no official caliph now.

Calumet, a sacred, decorated, reed tobacco pipe used as a symbol of peace or war by the Indians of North America, the bowl being composed of soapstone, and the long tube being decked with feathers. To accept the calumet when offered was to be friendly, to reject it was to proclaim enmity. There was also a distinctive calumet of war used only on a declaration of war between tribes.

Cambrian Group, in geology strata belonging to the Silurian series, and so named because of its abundant development in Wales. These strata are the lowest and oldest, containing fossil remains which include zoophytes, mollusks, crinoids, worms, and crustacea.

Cambridge University, probably founded in the reign of Henry III, although the town was mentioned in 916 as a seat of learning, when certain privileges were confirmed. The principal colleges, with the dates of founding are: St. Catharine's, 1473; Christ's, 1505; Clare, 1326; Corpus Cristi, 1352; Downing, 1800; Emmanueal, 1584; Gonville and Caius, 1348; Jesus, 1496; King's, 1441; Magdalene, 1542; Pembroke, 1347; Peterhouse, 1284; Queens', 1448; Sidney Sussex, 1596; St. John's, 1511; Trinity, 1546; Trinity Hall, 1350; Selwyn, 1882.

Camel, a large, ruminant quadruped, inhabiting Asia and Africa, where it is largely used as a beast of burden. There are two species: the Arabian camel or dromedary, with only one hump; and the Bactrian, or double-humped camel.

Cameo, the name given to a precious stone upon which some design has been carved in relief. There is an agate cameo at the Sainte Chapelle, Paris which measures 11 by 13 inches, and depicts the apotheosis of Augustus. Shell cameos are common.

Cameras, instruments by which a convex lens is made to reflect and depict the image of an external object upon a screen. It is constructed in the form of a box, in two compartments, and is, in fact, like the human eye, a camera obscura. Photographic cameras are made in many shapes and sizes and specialized as landscape cameras, copying cameras, portrait cameras, snapshot cameras, and so forth. (*See* Photography.)

Camlet, the name of a very fine dress fabric, made from silk and camels' hair. In modern days there are many cheaper kinds of camlets, in the construction of which wool and goats' hair play an important part.

Camomile, a low, close, creeping, composite perennial plant, cultivated for its flowers, which are white with a yellow center. Camomile flowers are of an exceedingly bitter taste.

Camorra, an Italian secret party largely composed of criminals, which at one time influenced politics considerably by their terrorizing action. Naples was the birthplace of the movement. In 1911 the ringleaders were brought to trial and sentenced to long terms of imprisonment.

Campaniles, bell-towers, usually but not always, detached from their parent churches. The most famous, which are in Italy, are lofty and elaborate structures. That by Giotto at Florence, in connection with the cathedral of Santa Maria del Fiore, is architecturally the finest in the world. Other famous campaniles are in Cremona (395 feet high) and in Pisa (the Leaning Tower). The pointed campanile of St. Mark's, Venice, which fell and was later rebuilt, is very much admired.

Campus Martius, a large plain used by the ancient Romans as a military camping ground. It was situated between the Quirinal and Capitoline Hills. Today it is entirely built over and forms the heart of modern Rome.

Canoe, a kind of light boat employed by many peoples in primitive times, made originally of a hollowed tree trunk, or of bark or skins stretched over a rude framework, and generally propelled by paddles. Large canoes were used by the islanders of the South Seas and elsewhere for war purposes. Canoes employed in civilized lands for pleasure purposes are very light boats, narrow in the beam, and are constructed from strong thin wood, waterproofed canvas, or other suitable material.

Canon, a term applied to signify a recognized rule or guide for conduct in matters legal, ecclesiastical, and artistic, or an authoritative ordinance;

thus we have Canonical Scriptures, Canon Law, etc. A canon is also a dignitary of the church, usually a member of a cathedral chapter in the Anglican Communion, or in the Roman Catholic Church a member of an order standing between regular monks and secular clergy.

Canonization, the entering of the name of a person, who has been dead over fifty years, on the list of saints of the Roman Catholic Church, after establishing proof of the performance of miracles and of purity and sanctity in life. This having been done, a day is named for the keeping of the anniversary of the saint's death, which thenceforward appears in the Church Calendar.

Capet, the family name of a line of French kings, founded by Hugh Capet in 987. The houses of Valois (1328) and Bourbon (1589) were of the same blood; and Louis XVI was tried and sentenced under the name of Louis Capet.

Capital Punishment, the punishment of crime by death. In the United States treason, murder, and kidnapping are punishable in this manner. The manner of inflicting the death penalty varies in different countries. In the United States twenty-three states and the District of Columbia put criminals to death by electrocution, seven states by hanging, and eleven states by the use of lethal gas. In Utah the condemned person has a choice of being hanged or shot. Six states have abolished the death penalty: Maine, Michigan, Minnesota, North Dakota, Rhode Island, and Wisconsin. A number of European countries and most Central and South American nations have done away with capital punishment. In Great Britain the court before which the trial of a prisoner is held not only hands down the sentence but directs the execution of it. In the courts of the United States there is a like authority; but in the laws of many of the states there is a provision that the execution shall not take place except by a warrant from the governor. Capital punishment is not inflicted on persons who are insane or on women who are pregnant, until these conditions are past. Juveniles are also generally excluded from capital punishment—the term "juvenile" denoting various age limits in different countries and in different states of the United States.

Capitol, a term that was first applied to the Temple of Jupiter on the Capitoline Hill, Rome, completed in 507 B. C. It was several times destroyed by fire and rebuilt. In each of the chief cities of the ancient Roman Empire there was a capitol or town hall. In the United States the building occupied by Congress at Washington bears the name Capitol, and the halls of the legislative assemblies of the different states are so named.

Capricorn, a zodiacal constellation between Sagittarius and Aquarius, imagined in ancient times as a figure with its fore part like a goat and its hind part like a fish.

Capstan, an apparatus on ships for raising anchors and performing other heavy work. It is of upright form, is made of wood or iron, turns on a vertical axis, and is moved by poles fitted into sockets in its upper part.

Capuchins, members of a mendicant order of Franciscans, founded in the 16th century, and named from the capuche or cowl worn by them. They still form a numerous order, though freed from any restrictions applied to them in earlier times.

Carbohydrates, the name of a group of organic bodies containing carbon atoms allied with hydrogen and oxygen atoms, the last two in the proportion in which they form water. Starch, sugar, glucose, and cellulose are of this group.

Carbolic Acid, derived from the distillation of coal tar, is composed of carbon, hydrogen, and oxygen. It is valuable as an antiseptic, but poisonous in large doses. Treated with certain acids and alkalies, it becomes valuable in the manufacture of dyestuffs.

Carbon, a non-metallic element occurring in diamonds, graphite, and in the amorphous form of charcoal, coke, lampblack, soot, etc. Its distribution extends throughout the whole of the animal and vegetable kingdom, and the number of its components is beyond enumeration.

Carbonari, members of a secret Italian society, numerous in the first half of the 19th century, whose chief aim was to free Italy from foreign rule. Their name was adopted from the charcoal burners (carbonari), and their passwords, signs, etc. were all in the phraseology of that fraternity.

Carbon Dioxide, a gaseous compound consisting of 12 parts of carbon and 32 of oxygen, colorless and odorless, and resulting when a substance containing carbon is burnt with a free current of air. It is used as the effervescing element in carbonized beverages, champagnes, bottled beer, etc. It is largely evolved from fissures in the earth and is a constituent of the afterdamp that so often causes explosions in mines, though not itself inflammable.

Carbonic Oxide, or **Carbon Monoxide**, a colorless, odorless, very poisonous substance formed of 12 parts of carbon and 16 parts of oxygen. It is produced when any substance largely composed of carbon is consumed with only a small supply of air.

Carboniferous System, in geology, the term used to designate the strata from which coal is obtained. It consists of three groups: the coal measures, the millstone grit, and the mountain limestone.

Cardamon, the seeds of various zingiberaceous plants, mainly indigenous to Malabar, useful medicinally in purgative compounds and carminatives.

Cardinal, a Roman Catholic ecclesiastical dignitary of high rank. The distribution of the 70 cardinals is as follows: 6 cardinal bishops, 50 cardinal priests, and 14 cardinal deacons. They are appointed by the pope and are associated with him in the government of the church. A cardinal's dress consists of a red cassock, a rochet, a short purple mantle, and a low-crowned red hat with cords and tassels.

Cardinal Sins, according to medieval classification, were seven in number: pride, vanity, indolence, avarice, gluttony, envy, and anger.

Caribs, a tribe of American Indians, now mainly confined to South America but originally from the islands in the Caribbean Sea.

Carlovingians, the second dynasty of French kings (established 753), which included such notable rulers as Charles Martel and Charlemagne. The family was succeeded by the Capet dynasty in 987.

Carmelites, a body of mendicant friars taking their name from Mount Carmel, in Syria, where the order was established in 1156. Persecuted by the Saracens, they made their way to Europe, founding monasteries and convents in various countries.

Carnival, the festival celebrated in Roman Catholic countries, and especially in Rome and Naples, with great mirth and freedom during the week preceding Lent. In the United States carnivals are annually celebrated in New Orleans, St. Louis, and Memphis. That at New Orleans, known as the Mardi Gras, is especially spectacular, the festivities lasting three days.

Carp, a fresh-water fish, found in most American and European waters and sometimes reaching a length of 4 feet. The goldfish belongs to this family.

Carpets, thick fabrics used for covering floors, were first made in Oriental countries—Egypt, Persia, India, etc.—and were introduced into Europe in the Middle Ages. A carpet factory was established in France in the time of Henry IV, and one was set up at Mortlake, in England, in the reign of James I. It was the custom in early times to use single carpets for covering beds, couches, tables, etc.

Carthusians, an order of monks founded in 1086 by St. Bruno at the Grande Chartreuse, near Grenoble, and introduced into England about a century later. Their habit includes a haircloth shirt and cowl. The liqueur *Chartreuse* was invented by this order and is still their secret. For many years they have derived large revenues from the sale of the cordial.

Cartridge, a case of metal, paper, or pasteboard, containing the exact charge of gunpowder or other explosive required for a rifle or a gun.

Casein, a phosphoprotein, the chief protein of milk, which forms the basis of curd when in contact with rennet or dilute acids.

Cassowary, a large bird of the ostrich family, inhabiting the Molucca Islands, New Guinea, and northern Australia. It has black plumage, three toes, and a horny crest upon its head. In fleetness it can outstrip the horse.

Castanets, spoon-shaped shells of hardwood or ivory, attached by a cord to the thumb, and struck together by the middle finger, making a crisp sound. Castanets, of Moorish origin, are used by Spanish dancers as time-beating accompaniments.

Caste, a term used to specify the different social classes into which the laws of Brahmanism divide the Hindus. The four leading castes are: (1) the Brahmans or priests; (2) the military caste; (3) the Vaisyas or traders; (4) the Sudras or laborers. Caste is a term applied also in other countries to class distinction.

Castor-Oil Plant, native to India, but now widely distributed in all tropical regions. It grows to a considerable height, has broad palmate leaves, and bears a spiny fruit containing seeds which when pressed yield the well-known castor oil. A larger, but less valuable, quantity of oil results from heating.

Cat, the general name for all quadrupeds of the family Felidae of the carnivorous order, from the lion down to the domestic cat. The latter is supposed to be descended from the wild cat. The Egyptians are credited with having been the first to domesticate the cat. The finest varieties are the Angora (or Persian), the Maltese, and the Manx.

Catacombs, subterranean places of interment. The most famous are those of Rome, constructed by the early Christians, where in times of persecution they concealed themselves. They are very extensive, consisting of a labyrinth of vaulted galleries, 4 to 5 feet wide, built at different levels. In some modern cemeteries there are churches or mausoleums containing in their walls, chambers of stone or brick, which are called catacombs.

Catapult, a military engine used in ancient times for shooting arrows. It was constructed of wood, and by means of a freed spring let fly the arrows with great force into the ranks of an enemy. The balista was an adaptation of this.

Catechism, an elementary book of principles in any science or art, but more particularly in religion, in the form of questions and answers. Among the well-known catechisms are the Catholic, the Lutheran (prepared by Luther in 1529), Calvin's Geneva (1536), and the Anglican (in the Book of Common Prayer).

Caterpillar, the larva of a lepidopterous insect, wormlike in its segmented body, often curiously marked and colored, and frequently more or less hairy.

Cathedral, the chief church of a diocese so called from its containing a bishop's seat, or episcopal chair. The finest cathedral in the world is that of St. Peter's at Rome, founded in 1450. Other celebrated cathedrals are Notre Dame of Paris, the cathedrals of Cologne and Milan, and St. Paul's in London.

Caucus, in the political nomenclature of the United States, a gathering preliminary to a public meeting of citizens for election or for other purposes, generally political; a private conclave designed to influence the general body of the citizens. Also a secret preliminary meeting of the leaders of a political party to determine on a course of action, the conclusions of the caucus being binding on all the members.

Cavalier, a name applied to the supporters of Charles I of England and to the Royalist party during the civil wars of the 17th century. It is also used generally in reference to a gallant, or imperious person.

Cavalry, a portion of the army in which soldiers are trained to fight on horseback. Cavalry was used by the ancient Egyptians and formed an important part of both Greek and Roman tactics. Until the advent of modern trench warfare this branch of the army was the spearhead of every offense. After the first months of the World War I, however, the fighting on the western front revealed that its usefulness had decreased. By the final days of the war cavalry had been supplanted by mechanized units except in the areas of open fighting along the eastern front and in Palestine. Used as mechanized cavalry and armored forces prior to and during World War II, the cavalry was abolished as a separate arm after the war and merged with the Armored Cavalry, becoming Armor in 1950.

Cave, an opening produced by nature within the solid crust of the earth by the chemical and mechanical action of water, volcanic action, or earthquakes. One of the most remarkable caves in the world is Fingal's Cave in Staffa, one of the Western Islands of Scotland; its sides are formed of ranges of basaltic columns, which are almost as regular as hewn stone. The most famous in the United States are Madison's and Luray Caves in Virginia; Mammoth Cave in Kentucky, which incloses about 40 miles of subterranean windings; Carlsbad Caverns in New Mexico, the Nickojack Cave in Georgia; and the cave at Hannibal, Missouri, made famous through *The Adventures of Tom Sawyer* by Mark Twain.

Caviar, a Russian preparation made from the salted roe of certain fish, such as sturgeon, sterlet, and sevruga.

Cedar, a dark-leaved, cone-bearing, horizontal-branched evergreen tree that grows to a considerable height and girth.

Celluloid, a compound of guncotton, camphor, and other ingredients, closely resembling ivory, or, when colored, numerous decorative objects, such as coral, amber, tortoise shell, etc.

Cellulose, a carbohydrate and a constituent of nearly all plants and vegetable structures. By being treated with strong acids and boiled with water, glucose is obtained. Cellulose occurs in an almost pure state in the fibers of linen and cotton.

Celts, an ancient race of western Europe, originally settled in what is now France, and afterward spread over other parts of Europe, including Britain. The two chief divisions of Celtic Britons were the Gaels of Ireland and northern Scotland and the Cymri of Wales. The descendants of these races still retain many of their ancient characteristics, and considerable interest is manifested in their language and literature.

Cement, a name applied to various substances, such as glue, sealing wax, paste, putty, and other adhesives, but the main class consists of substances for binding together brick or stone, and comprises mortar, Portland cement, Roman cement, and plaster of Paris.

Censor, the title of two Roman magistrates originally appointed for the purpose of taking the census, or register, of the number and property of the citizens. But their powers were much increased subsequently when they had the inspection of public morals entrusted to them, with authority to degrade senators and knights from their respective orders, and remove other citizens from their tribes, depriving them of all their privileges except liberty. The office of censor was abolished under the emperors, who, however, exercised the greater part of its functions. In modern usage it denotes one whose duty it is to inspect and examine books, plays, magazines, and newspapers before they are published, to insure that they contain nothing to offend against public morality or decency. The censor is also an official appointed in time of war, at military headquarters, to supervise and endorse all press dispatches.

Census, the name given in ancient Rome to a register of citizens, with full particulars as to their family, children, slaves, and so forth. The term is now used in regard to the general enumeration of population that has been taken in the United States every ten years since the first census in 1790.

Center of Gravity, the point through which the entire weight of a body seems to act by the force of gravity. This center may be found either by experiment, such as suspending a body by a string, when the true vertical position will be marked, or by the rules of geometry. The center of gravity of a straight bar is at the middle point; of a disk, at the geometrical center.

Cerium, a metallic element, discovered in 1803, highly malleable and ductile. Salts of cerium mixed with salts of thorium are used in the manufacture of gas mantles.

Cestus, a girdle worn by Greek and Roman women giving them the power to excite love. It was also the name of the gauntlet, loaded with lead, worn by boxers in the Roman arena.

Cetacea, the order of mammals comprising the whale, the dolphin, and the porpoise, which, though strictly aquatic, breathe air, suckle their young, and are warm-blooded.

Chain Armor, composed of links of hammered iron, was worn over garments by soldiers in the 12th and 13th centuries. These garments were called coats of mail and were superseded by armor made of metal plates.

Chalk, a white, soft mineral consisting of calcium carbonate only slightly consolidated. It is made into lime by burning and becomes whiting when purified. Chalk was formed during the Cretaceous period, and fossil remains reveal mollusks, sponges, and sea urchins.

Chalybeate Waters, waters containing iron in solution. Chalybeate springs are numerous in many parts of the world, and have therapeutic value.

Chama, a genus of large bivalves of the mollusk family, found in tropical waters, especially among coral reefs. *Chama gigas* weighs sometimes as much as 300 pounds.

Chameleon, a family of lizards of which there are numerous species. The common chameleon is a native of Africa and is about 12 inches long, including tail. It is remarkable for its power of changing color to resemble its surroundings —a power that is due to the presence of pigment-bearing cells beneath the skin. It is slow in movement and insectivorous.

Chamois, a species of antelope, native to western Europe and Asia. It is not much larger than a goat, lives in mountainous regions, and possesses wonderful leaping power. The chamois skin is commercially valuable.

Champagne, a sparkling wine made chiefly in the department of the Marne, the former province of Champagne, France.

Chancellor, in ancient times, a petty officer stationed at the fence of bars or lattice work in a law court, to introduce such functionaries as were entitled to pass inside. The lord chancellor of England was originally the king's chief secretary, to whom petitions were referred. He is now the highest judicial functionary in the kingdom and the keeper of the great seal. Writs for the assembling of parliament are issued in his name. The term is also used as the title of the head of a university or other educational institution. In the ecclesiastical sense, the chancellor of a cathedral is an official who superintends arrangements for religious ceremonies and services.

Charcoal, a term applied to wood that has been subjected to a process of slow combustion. It refers generally to the carbonaceous remains of vegetable, animal, or combustible mineral substances submitted to a similar process. Charcoal is employed as fuel, as an ingredient in the making of gunpowder, as a disinfectant, and as a filter. It is practically insoluble except when reduced to a fine powder.

Chasuble, a sleeveless vestment worn by ecclesiastics over the alb during the celebration of the mass. It is supposed to symbolize the seamless coat of Christ.

Chauvinism, a term applied to exaggerated devotion to a cause, more particularly to exaggerated, noisy patriotism. The word is derived from Nicholas Chauvin, whose extravagant devotion to Napoleon I made him a laughingstock among his comrades.

Cheese, an article of food made from the curd of milk, which is separated from the whey and pressed in moulds and gradually dried. There are many varieties of cheese. Among the best-known are Swiss, Parmesan, Dutch, Gorgonzola, Roquefort, and Gruyere. The soft cheeses, such as Limburger, Camembert, Brie, and cream, keep for only a short time.

Cheetah, the large spotted cat of Africa and southern Asia, often called the "hunting leopard" because of its employment in the chase. It is long-legged with non-retractile claws.

Chemistry, the science which analyzes and describes the properties and composition of various natural substances. It had its rise in alchemy, and has gradually developed into a science of vast magnitude and importance.

Cherokees, a large tribe of American Indians who formerly occupied the Carolinas, Georgia, Alabama, and Tennessee.

Chiaroscuro, a term used in painting to denote the arrangement of light and shade in a picture. On the proper handling of chiaroscuro depends the fidelity of depiction of objects and distances.

Chimpanzee, a large anthropoid ape, native to tropical western Africa, having the body covered with shining black hair, arms reaching to the knee, large ears, and a general organization resembling that of man. It possesses considerable intelligence, can walk erect with ease, and when full grown is about four feet tall.

Chinchilla, a South American rodent, valuable for its beautiful fur.

Chipmunk, a squirrel-like animal of the genus *Tamias*, common in the United States.

Chippendale Furniture, introduced in the reign of George I by Thomas Chippendale, a Worcestershire cabinetmaker who migrated to London. He was fonder of making designs for furniture than of manufacturing it, and in 1752 published a book of patterns.

Chlorine, a gaseous element of the halogen family, obtained by the action of manganese dioxide on hydrochloric acid, It is valuable as a bleaching agent and as a disinfectant.

Chloroform, a volatile colorless liquid, prepared for commercial purposes by distilling a mixture of chloride of lime, alcohol, and water. For medical use it is made from chloral, which yields a purer distillation. When chloroform is inhaled it produces unconsciousness. It owes its discovery to Liebig, and its first application for medical purposes to Sir James Young Simpson.

Chocolate, a paste made from the kernels or beans of the cacao tree and flavored with sugar, vanilla, or other substance. Chocolate beverage is made by dissolving chocolate in boiling water or milk. It was thus used by the Mexicans as far back as the time of Montezuma.

Christianity, the religion proclaimed by Jesus Christ. Its principles are set forth in the New Testament, and its churches abound all over the world. About one-third of the inhabitants of the globe are Christians.

Christian Science, the religion or interpretation of the Christian religion, as propounded by Mary Baker Eddy. It was defined by Mrs. Eddy as "The law of God, the law of good, interpreting and demonstrating the divine principle and rule of universal harmony."

Christmas Cards. The first Christmas card was sent in 1844, and it is believed that the sender was W. E. Dobson, an Englishman. He had a friend, from whom he received certain courtesies, for which he desired to show some special appreciation. He made a sketch symbolizing the spirit of the festive season and mailed it to his friend. The sketch was done on a piece of Bristol board about twice the size of the modern postal card. It depicted a family group toasting absent friends.

Chromascope, an instrument for demonstrating the three optical effects of colors: the reflection of mirrors, the transmission of light through transparency, and the refraction of lenses and prisms.

Chromatics, the science which investigates and explains the properties of colors, forming a branch of optics.

Chromium, a yellow metal obtained from chrome ironstone, a mineral compound of chromic, ferric and ferrous oxides, extensively used for plating the bright parts of automobiles.

Chronology, the science of computing periods of time by orderly division, and of assigning to events their proper relative dates.

Chrysoberyl, a mineral found in rolled pebbles in Brazil and Ceylon, in fine crystals in the Ural, and in granite in the United States. It is of a yellowish-green color, and when opalescent makes an attractive gem.

Cid, The, a famous Spanish hero of the 11th century, Don Rodrigo Diaz, who, before he was twenty, led a Spanish force against the Moors and drove them out of Spain. He is celebrated in poem, play and romance.

Cinchona, an evergreen tree common in the warmer portions of South America, growing at a high altitude and famous for its bark, from which quinine is derived.

Cinnamon, the dried bark of a tree common in the East Indies, producing an aromatic spice.

Cistercians, an order of monks and nuns taking their name from Cisteaux, near Dijon, where their first convent was established in 1098. The monks wear white cassocks, the nuns white dresses.

Clay, a term used to designate certain plastic earthy compounds composed of hydrated silicates of alumina. China clay, from which porcelain is made, is the purest clay and is obtained by the natural crumbling of feldspar, which is well distributed in China, Japan, and the United States. Other varieties are pipe clay, fire clay, potter's clay, and brick clay.

Cliff-Dwellers, aboriginal tribes who had their homes in recesses of the rocky cliffs of New Mexico and elsewhere in the southwestern regions of what is now the United States. Also the title of a book by Henry B. Fuller, and the name of an exclusive club in Chicago whose membership is limited to the arts.

Clock, a horological contrivance, usually having a motive spring or weight and geared train, with a pulsative device to govern the rate at which the mechanism moves; also commonly having a figured dial and index hands. One of the earliest inventions for keeping time was the sundial, upon which the clepsydra, or water clock, followed. Archimedes knew how to set wheels going by springs and weights, but who first regulated their speed and applied their controlled motion to a pointer traversing a dial has not been ascertained. About A. D. 1000 a student at Cordova University added the escapement to a pendulum clock.

Clog, a wooden shoe worn by the peasantry of numerous Continental nations. Clog dancing is a performance in which the dancer wears wooden footwear to provide a loud accompaniment as he beats out a clattering rhythm.

Cloisonné, a kind of fine pottery with enameled surface, decorated with elaborate designs, the outlines of which are formed by small bands or fillets of metal.

Cloisters, arched, covered walks attached to monastic and ecclesiastical buildings and usually consisting of a series of vaulted arcades surrounding a quadrangle. They were intended mainly as places of exercise and relaxation for the monks.

Clouds, collections of visible vapor suspended in the upper atmosphere at a height of from two to three miles. When similar vapors gather close to the earth they form fog. Clouds are the result of a process of evaporation that is continuous over sea and land. They are usually classified as follows: the cirrus cloud, feathery or resembling locks of hair; the cumulus cloud, dense, hill-like masses, called summer clouds; the stratus or night cloud, which forms in level streaky sheets; the cirrostratus cloud, a collection of small, round dappled clouds, usual in hot weather; the cumulo-stratus cloud, and the nimbus, or rain cloud.

Clover, various plants of the genus *Trifolium* of which there are about 200 species. The best-known are white clover, a common pasturage product in nearly all parts of the world; and red clover, the most widely cultivated of all, used as fodder for cattle.

Cloves, the dried flower buds of a species of myrtle, grown principally in the East Indies.

Coal, a carbonaceous mineral substance, commonly dull or shiny black and easily breakable. It is inflammable, and consequently employed as fuel in most civilized lands. It is composed of chemically altered vegetable matter, chiefly of the long extinct lycopodiaceous trees. The best coal for fuel purposes is that belonging to the Carboniferous series of the Paleozoic era. Anthracite and the more highly bituminous coals are extensively employed in manufacturing industries. A ton of coal will yield from 10,000 to 15,000 cubic feet of gas, 8 to 12 gallons of tar, half a ton of coke and about 20 gallons of ammoniacal liquor, varying according to the class of coal used.

Coast Guard, a division of the United States Treasury Department, formed in 1915 by combining the Revenue Cutter Service and the Lifesaving Service. Prior to this time the duties of the two had been overlapping, since the Revenue Cutter Service was often called upon to do at sea what the Lifesaving Service was doing from shore. The Coast Guard Service operates from eight divisions: the North Pacific, the South Pacific, the Eastern, the New York, the Norfolk, the Gulf, the Lakes, and the Bering Sea fleet which is drawn from the Pacific division. In Great Britain the Coast Guard was introduced shortly after the Napoleonic wars to prevent smuggling and since 1856 has been under the command of the admiralty.

Cobalt, a steel-gray, malleable metal, resembling nickel, found in combination with arsenic and sulphur. It is of great value in the arts as a coloring medium, its protoxide yielding a brilliant blue, largely utilized for coloring glass and porcelain, as well as for painting.

Cobra, the hooded snake of India, Ceylon, and Africa, and one of the most venomous of the vipers. It grows to a length of 4 or 5 feet and possesses the power of dilating its neck and head to a hoodlike shape when disturbed.

Coca, a South American shrub, which yields three crops a year of leaves and flowers. The leaves are chewed by the natives and act as a strong stimulant, enabling them to withstand hunger and fatigue to an astonishing degree. It is used in medicine as a tonic, and yields the alkaloid cocaine.

Cochineal, a dyestuff consisting of the dried bodies of the females of a class of insects of the genus *Coccus*. These insects, which exist in countless myriads in tropical America, Java, etc., feed on special cacti which are cultivated for them, and are gathered twice a year. The coloring principle contained in the insects is carminic acid and is a brilliant crimson. It takes 70,000 insects to make a pound of the dye stuff.

Cockades, badges or rosettes worn on the hat, which came into general use when the House of Hanover succeeded to the throne of Great Britain. In later times the cockade became a badge of servitude.

Cockatoo, a white-plumaged bird of the parrot family with a movable crest, usually of some shade of yellow. Cockatoos are found chiefly in Australia and the Malay Archipelago and are much in favor as pets.

Cockroach, sometimes called the black beetle, a genus of insects distributed over many countries, though native to Asia. It is of nocturnal habits, infests kitchens, pantries, etc., and is often difficult to exterminate.

Cocktail, any of several kinds of small alcoholic drinks. They are made of alcoholic liquors such as whisky, gin, or rum, to which liqueurs, bitters, fruit juices, or other flavoring agents are added.

Coconut Palms, tropical trees which grow to a height of from 50 to 100 feet and have their tops surrounded by feather-like curving leaves. The fruit of this tree is the ordinary coconut and grows in bunches of from 12 to 20. The fiber of the husk is used for a variety of purposes, such as making drinking cups, spoons, brushes, matting, and cordage. The trunk of the tree is utilized in the manufacture of various fancy articles.

Cod, found in abundance off the coasts of New England and Newfoundland. Their capture and preparation for the market and the extraction of the oil they yield, form important industries.

Code, a term used to designate a system of properly classified laws. Codes were made by the Gothic tribes as well as by the Romans, who formulated several codes of historic importance including the Theodosian code, summarizing the Roman laws from the time of Constantine to 483; the Papian code, devised for the Roman subjects of the Burgundians, 517-523; the Justinian code, 527-565 (the most important of the Roman codes); and the Gregorian code, another collection of Roman laws. The most important of modern codes is the Code of Napoleon, compiled between 1803 and 1810, which is still in force in France.

Codex, a name referring to the manuscripts of the classics and the Bible. The Scriptural codices comprise the Sinaitic codex of the 4th century, the Vatican codex of the same period, the Alexandrian codex of the 5th century, and others. The British Museum, in 1933, purchased "Codex Sinaiticus" from the Soviet Government for about $500,000.

Coffee, a shrub found originally in Arabia and Abyssinia, but now extensively grown in the West Indies, Brazil, India, and Central America.

It yields a seed or berry which, after undergoing the necessary preparation, is ground and used in most countries as a popular beverage. The best coffee is the Mocha, an Arabian variety. The beverage was introduced into Europe in the 16th century.

Coke, a substance formed from coal by heating it in a kiln without air. It burns without emitting smoke or flame, thus it is largely used for smelting and heating purposes where the presence of smoke would be objectionable or injurious.

Cola Nut, the name of a seed obtained from the cola tree of tropical Africa, Brazil, and the West Indies. It has strong stimulative qualities and contains two or three times as much caffeine as coffee.

Colonel, the title of a military officer ranking next above a lieutenant-colonel and below a brigadier-general.

Colony, a settlement of people who have migrated from their native land to some possession of the mother country. The earliest colonists were the Phoenicians, who established themselves in various lands bordering on the Mediterranean. Later the Greeks did considerable colonizing but were eventually displaced by the greatest colonizers of ancient times, the Romans. Colonization, in its more modern significance, was the result of important geographical discoveries made in the Western World in the 15th century by the Spaniards, Portuguese, Dutch, and French. From about the beginning of the 17th century England developed a colonizing spirit which resulted in an empire of immensely greater extent than that of any other country. Modifications of the colonial system after World War I and particularly after World War II led to the promotion of self-government in some areas and to violent struggles for independence in others.

Color Blindness, a defect of vision causing inability to recognize certain colors. This defect shows itself in from two to six per cent of males, while fewer than one per cent of females suffer from it. Color blindness is sometimes total, but in the majority of cases only partial, the most common form being red-green color blindness.

Colossus, the name which the ancients gave to any statue of gigantic size. The Colossus at Rhodes, which was a bronze statue of Apollo, was the most famous and was reckoned among the seven wonders of the world. It was 70 cubits high and stood astride the mouth of the harbor, so that ships could sail between its legs. It was destroyed during an earthquake in 224 B. C.

Comets, celestial bodies which move around the sun in elliptical or parabolic orbits. Usually these starlike bodies are accompanied by a long stream or tail of light. The parabolic comets are seen once only and do not reappear; the elliptical comets are periodic, and their recurrence can be calculated with accuracy. Comets are of enormous magnitude, sometimes covering millions of miles, but their light is feeble in comparison with that of a star. The great comet years, so far as recorded, have been 1456, 1680, 1811, 1843, 1858 (Donati's), 1861, 1874, and 1881.

Commander-in-Chief. This term is commonly used to describe the principal military officer of an army or fighting force. In the United States the President is, by virtue of the Constitution, commander-in-chief of the armed forces. The first commander-in-chief was George Washington, who was so designated during the American Revolution.

Commodore, in some navies the lowest flag rank, coming below a rear-admiral but above a captain. The grade has been extinct in the United States Navy since 1899. In the British service the title is applied to a senior captain temporarily in command of more than one ship. The title is applied also to the senior officer of a yacht club.

Common Law, in the United States and Great Britain, the unwritten law established by custom, usage, and precedent, and not by statute. Both statute laws and equity overrule common law when courts are called upon to decide between them.

Commune, a municipal administrative division in France, Italy, and Belgium, generally presided over by a mayor and a municipal council.

Commune of Paris, originally the Paris Revolutionary Committee, established in 1789 but superseded by the Convention of 1794. The second Paris Commune was that of 1871, which took possession of Paris after the withdrawal of the German troops and destroyed the Tuileries, the Vendôme Column, the Hôtel de Ville, and other public buildings, but was ultimately suppressed by the National troops.

Communism, a political system which seeks the absorption of all property and means of production by the state for the common good. It also claims the right of the state to control production, distribution, and consumption and to determine an equitable division of labor.

Compass (or **Mariner's Compass**), an instrument by which the magnetic north is indicated, and, in the liquid compass, consists of a horizontal bowl containing alcohol and water, a card upon which the 32 points of the compass are marked, and the steel needles which always point to the magnetic north. The dry compass consists of a very light aluminum frame carrying several light compass needles supported on a pivot. The origin of the mariner's compass is unknown, but it is supposed to have come from China.

Complex, a term used in psychology to denote a group of impressions or ideas which is the result of suppressed thought, instinct, or desire, and which reacts upon the subject without revealing its real nature or cause to conscious reason. Complexes produce abnormal mental and physical states and irrational actions. Psychoanalysts in their treatments endeavor to resolve their patients' complexes.

Concordat, an agreement or convention between the pope and a secular government regarding ecclesiastical matters. The Concordat of Worms in 1122 between Calixtus II and the Emperor Henry V was famous as deciding a long struggle in regard to investiture. In 1801 Napoleon concluded a concordat with Pius VII, defining the restored relations between the head of the Church and the French Roman Catholics. The concordat known as the Lateran Treaty, negotiated in 1929 between Pius XI and Mussolini, settled the dispute between the papacy and the Italian government and made the popes sovereigns of Vatican City.

Concrete, a substance formed by uniting in coagulated masses various hard materials, such as crushed stone, sand, gravel, and lime, or Portland cement. It is much used for floors, foundations, sea-walls, etc. In recent years reinforced concrete, that is, concrete combined with steel, has come into wide use in construction work.

Congregationalists, the Christian denomination in which each church has complete control of its own affairs. The sect had its origin in Elizabethan England; subsequently persecution forced some of its members to flee to the Netherlands. Under Cromwell they extended their ministrations and became a powerful body. Charles II's Act of Uniformity drove them forth again, but they regained full liberty of worship under William III. Congregationalism began in the United States with the landing of John Robinson's congregation from the *Mayflower* at Plymouth in 1620. In 1957, the General Council of the Congregational Christian Churches joined with the Evangelical and Reformed Church to form the United Church of Christ. Status of local churches was not changed by this union.

Congress of the United States, the legislative branch of the Federal Government, deriving its powers from the Constitution and consisting of a Senate and a House of Representatives. The powers of Congress are enumerated in Article I, section 8 of the Constitution, and all powers not granted to Congress are reserved to the states or to the people. The Senate is composed of two members from each state; the members of the House are apportioned on the basis of population. Bills that have passed both Houses are sent to the President, who may either sign or veto them or do neither; in the latter case the bill becomes a law after 10 days unless Congress has previously adjourned. A bill vetoed by the President may become a law only after it has been passed by two-thirds of the membership of each house. A regular annual meeting of Congress is required by the Constitution. Previously the day of convening was specified as the first Monday in December; the 20th Amendment, adopted in 1933, sets the date as Jan. 3. Each house conducts its affairs under its own rules. The real work of legislation is done by committees, of which there are about 45 in the House and 35 in the Senate. The Vice President is the presiding officer of the Senate. He has no vote except in case of a tie. The House elects from its own membership a presiding officer, called the Speaker. The Senate has power to ratify or reject all treaties and to confirm or reject appointments submitted by the President of cabinet members, federal judges, and officers of the army and navy. A senator is elected for a term of six years; the terms of one-third of the senators expire every two years. Representatives are chosen for two-year terms.

Conic Sections, a division of geometry, dealing with such curved lines as can be produced by the intersections of a plane with a right circular cone. Five sections can be found: triangle, parabola, hyperbola, circle, and ellipse.

Coniferae, cone-bearing trees, including firs, pines, cedars, cypresses, junipers, yews, etc.

Conscientious Objector, a pacifist, a man who refuses to do military service for moral or religious reasons.

Conscription, a system of compulsory military service by lot or enrollment. France, Germany, and most other European nations have compulsory service, rendering all able-bodied males liable to a term of military duty. In the United States the system was adopted during the Civil War and was again used in both World Wars.

Constable, an officer of high rank in medieval times. Before the introduction of the police system in England every parish had its constables upon whom devolved the duty of keeping the peace. In the United States the village constable still functions in many rural communities.

Constitution of the United States, the document embodying the fundamental law of the land. The Constitution of the United States was the product of a few great minds assembled in convention in 1787. The convention was composed of 55 members; the Constitution was signed by 39, including Washington. The Constitution had failed to provide for the safeguarding of private rights, and in June, 1789, Madison introduced a series of amendments of which 10 were ultimately ratified by the states, known as the "Bill of Rights." The 11th Amendment was adopted in 1798 to prevent a citizen of one state from suing another state in the Federal courts. The 12th Amendment was ratified in 1804 as the result of the tie presidential vote between Jefferson and Burr. The Civil War fostered 3 new amendments; the 13th (1865) prohibiting slavery; the 14th (1868) defining citizenship and further protecting private rights; and the 15th (1870) guaranteeing suffrage. In 1913 the 16th Amendment was passed to clarify Federal powers of taxation. The same year the 17th Amendment provided for direct popular election of senators. The 18th Amendment, outlawing the liquor traffic, became part of the Constitution in June, 1919, effective June 1st, 1920. The 19th Amendment provided for woman suffrage and became effective in 1920. The 20th Amendment provided for the beginning of the terms of President and Vice President on Jan. 20 and those of senators and representatives on Jan. 3, effective in 1933. The 21st Amendment repealed the 18th, effective Dec. 5, 1933. The 22nd Amendment limited presidential terms of office to two, effective Feb. 26, 1951.

Consul, the title borne by the two chief magistrates of the Roman Republic. Three consuls were appointed for France after the dissolution of the Directory in 1799, Napoleon becoming first consul and holding the office until 1804, when he was made emperor. At the present day official, commercial representatives of the United States and other governments are styled consuls.

Copper, one of the most familiar of metals, used as an alloy with tin to produce bronze. Copper ores are most abundant in North America. Spain, Chile, Australia, and Prussia also yield large quantities. All copper compounds are poisonous. Copper sulphate is largely used in calico printing and in the production of blue and green pigments. The annual copper production of the world is normally over 2,000,000 tons. The United States is by far the most important producer. Other important producers are; Canada, Chile, Russia, Japan, and the Belgian Congo. The annual copper production of the United States is worth more than $100,000,000.

Copts, descendants of the ancient Egyptians professing a modified form of Christianity, the head of their system being a patriarch. They do not marry out of their own race.

Copyright, the right of publishers and authors to prevent the issue of unauthorized editions of their works. In the United States the publishing rights of any book remain the property of the author, his heirs, or assignees for a term of twenty-eight years from the date of copyright and can be renewed once for a like term. The Berne Convention to protect copyright in all countries was agreed to in 1872 and was signed by representatives of all the great countries except the United States. However, the United States, through special copyright conventions, is in copyright relations with most civilized nations throughout the world.

Coral, a hard calcareous substance, the exoskeleton of various anthozoans, which provides them habitation and support. They vary in color and texture, some being red or pink and some white, some compact and smooth, and some rough and porous. Coral secretions assume a variety of forms, being fan-like, tree-like, mushroom-shaped and so forth. Red coral is obtained mainly from the Mediterranean. The coral reefs of the Pacific and Indian Oceans and the Red Sea are often many miles in extent.

Cordite, a smokeless explosive adopted for small arms and heavy artillery by the defense forces of most countries, is composed of 58 parts of nitroglycerine, 37 of gun cotton, and 5 of vaseline. It is a jelly or plastic dough and is used in the form of sticks or tubes.

Cork, the bark of a species of oak grown largely in southern Europe and northern Africa. The cork tree yields bark every eight or ten years and grows to a height of from 20 to 60 feet.

Cormorant, a large swimming and diving bird, of which there are over 20 species. It lives mostly on fish and is famed for its voracity. It is found in Europe, Asia, and America.

Corn, a term used to designate such cereal products as are used for food, but more especially applied to maize in the United States, wheat in England, and oats in Scotland. Maize was domesticated by the Indians, who taught its use to the first settlers in America. The Corn Belt stretches from Ohio into Kansas.

Coroner, an officer whose duty it is to hold inquests on the bodies of people who are suspected of having died from other than natural causes. He is usually an elected official of the county and as such may impanel juries over which he presides during the course of the inquiry.

Corporation, a body of persons authorized by law to carry out specific acts, to hold property, or to accept responsibilities as if it were an individual. In the United States, each state has its own corporation law. There are three kinds of corporations: municipal, corporations for profit, and corporations not for profit.

Cortes, the name of the parliamentary assemblies of Spain and Portugal.

Cotton, the vegetable fiber from which most clothing, surgical dressings, and industrial fabrics are made. Because of its low price the uses of cotton are constantly increasing. Of the numerous species, three are commercially important: (1) Indian cotton; (2) American cotton; and (3) Sea Island, or Egyptian cotton. All three varieties have been cultivated since remote antiquity. The manufacture of cotton textiles was first developed in India. At the time of the discovery of the New World cotton cloth was scarce and expensive in Europe. The development of spinning and weaving machinery in the latter part of the 18th century increased the demand for cotton enormously and revolutionized agriculture in the "Cotton Belt" of the United States.

Cottonseed Oil, an extract from the seed of the cotton plant, commercially valuable as a substitute for olive oil.

County, originally the territory of a count or earl. In the United States a county is an administrative subdivision of a state. There are more than 3,000 counties in the United States.

Coup d'Etat, a sudden revolutionary act carried out by force. The best-known examples in modern times were the overturning of the Directory by Napoleon in 1799 and of the French National Assembly by Louis Napoleon in 1852, whereby he became emperor.

Courier, a servant accompanying a person or party on a journey, to make and superintend the arrangements as to conveyance and accommodation; formerly the term implied a messenger dispatched on any mission of importance necessitating speed and circumspection.

Crabs, crustaceans, breathing through gills, and provided with ten external limbs or claws, the side and smaller limbs being used for walking and the two front claws for grasping.

Crape, a light fabric made of silk, the natural gum causing the crisp, wavy character of the material. A courser kind of crape is made from cotton.

Creed, a brief statement of a particular belief or religion. The Apostles' Creed is adapted from I Corinthians, xv, 3-8. The Nicene Creed, which proclaims the Godhead of Christ, was promulgated at Nicaea in 325. The Athanasian Creed, which expounds the doctrine of the Trinity, dates from the 5th century.

Cremation, the ancient custom, revived in modern times, of burning the dead. Many scientific men commend the practice on hygienic grounds, and numerous eminent people have in recent years been cremated in accordance with instructions given by will.

Creole, a West Indian and Spanish American term applied to a native of foreign race. The word has a variety of local meanings and in some regions is used to describe mixed-bloods.

Creosote, a substance obtained from coal tar by fractional distillation. It is a valuable antiseptic, prevents decay in wood, and is used to flavor whisky.

Cretaceous System, the term given to the uppermost strata of rocks of the Mesozoic period. It has the following subdivisions: Maestricht beds, chalk with flints, chalk devoid of flints, chalk marl, upper greensand, and gault.

Cricket, a genus of insects of the grasshopper order, which move by leaps. The male produces a chirping noise by the action of its wings.

Crimean War was begun in the spring of 1854 and lasted until March, 1856. Great Britain, France, Sardinia, and Turkey were engaged against Russia.

Crocodile, the name of the largest existing reptile and classed with the alligator and the gavial. The crocodile inhabits the Nile region, the alligator the lower Mississippi, and the gavial the waters of the Ganges.

Cross-word Puzzle, a pattern or design in which a number of blank spaces have to be filled with letters which will form words that can be read both horizontally and vertically. These words must correspond to clues provided with the puzzle. Many newspapers provide cross-word puzzles some very difficult, for their readers.

Crow, a genus of well-known birds, including the common crow, the rook, the raven, and the jackdaw. It lives on flesh, garbage, and insects and builds its nest in trees. Its plumage is black.

Crusades, military expeditions undertaken by some of the Christian nations of Europe with the object of wresting Jerusalem from the Mohammedans. Peter the Hermit started the agitation in 1095, and from that date to 1271 various crusades were undertaken. Millions of lives and an enormous amount of treasure were sacrificed in these enterprises, and when all was done, Jerusalem remained in the possession of the Mohammedans.

Cryolite, a mineral found in extensive beds in Greenland; and one of the main sources of aluminum. It is also used, with silica and zinc oxide, for making a creamy white glass.

Crypt, a vaulted, subterranean portion of an abbey, cathedral, or church, used for burials.

Cryptogamia, the twenty-fourth and final order of the botanical system of Linnaeus, including the Fungi, Algae, Filices, and Musci.

Cuckoo, a well-known migratory bird, which has a very characteristic note, uttered by the male during the mating season. It lays its eggs in the nests of other birds, but only one egg in each nest.

Cuneiform, the term applied to the writing or to the arrow-headed characters used in ancient Assyria, Persia, and Mesopotamia.

Cupola, the inner portion of a dome. Famous cupolas are those in the Roman Pantheon, the Mosque of St. Sophia at Istanbul, St. Peter's at Rome, and St. Paul's in London. In the United States the word is applied colloquially to any small structure built on top of a house or farm building. They are common on barns and country houses of the late 19th century.

Curfew, the custom of requiring the extinguishment of fires and the retirement of people from the streets at a fixed hour every evening. The hour of curfew was usually signaled by a bell. The custom of curfew was observed in parts of medieval Europe.

Curlew, a wading bird of which there are several species. It frequents marshy places, feeds on worms and insects, and possesses a very long curved bill.

Cyanogen, a compound of nitrogen and carbon, obtained from heated dry mercury cyanide, and highly poisonous. It combines to form numerous cyanides and is of great use in producing, in combination with iron, various deep-blue pigments, including Prussian blue, Chinese blue, etc.

Cyclone, a storm spirally revolving in a counter-clockwise direction from an area of higher pressure toward an area of lower pressure. Extra-tropical cyclones are constantly traveling over the surface of the earth, usually accompanied by cloudiness, precipitation, and changes in temperature. Tropical cyclones have their origin in the doldrums, on the western sides of the oceans, and are much more violent. The tornadoes of the Mississippi watershed, which are locally known as cyclones, are similar to tropical cyclones but are even smaller and more violent. The center of a tornado may be no more than a few feet in diameter; the wind velocity in the area surrounding the center may be as great as 500 miles per hour.

Cynics, adherents of a philosophy founded by Antisthenes, the pupil of Socrates. Holding that virtue was the only good, they condemned arts, sciences, pleasures, and riches. Diogenes was the most famed of the Cynics.

Czar, the title of the emperors of Russia. The word is derived from Caesar. The first czar was Ivan IV, crowned in 1547. The title was in use until the downfall of the Russian monarchy.

Czechs, a branch of the Slavonic race inhabiting Czechoslovakia and numbering together with their kinsmen, the Slovaks, ten millions.

D

Dachshund, the German badger-hound, remarkable for its short legs and long body.

Dacite consists of plagioclase and quartz, together with minerals of the hornblende and pyroxene families. It occurs mostly in Transylvania and the Cordilleran districts of the United States.

Dactyl, a measure in versification, each foot consisting of three syllables: the first long, and the second and third short, as *lovingly, verily.*

Dado, a term denoting the portion of a pedestal between the base and the cornice; also applied to the lower part of the walls of a room when decorated differently from the upper part.

Dagger, a stiletto or sharp-pointed instrument for stabbing, used in medieval times as a private weapon, and still occasionally carried on the person in Italy and Spain.

Daguerreotype, a photographic process invented in Paris by Daguerre during the years 1824-1839, resulting in the employment of the camera for the exposure of a silver plate, sensitized by iodine fumes in a dark chamber.

Dail Eireann, the name of the elected legislature of Eire.

Dairies are properly places where milk is stored and converted into butter and cheese, but in large cities the term is applied to bottling plants from which milk is distributed. Great improvements have been made in recent years in the construction and management of dairies, and hand processes in the making of butter and cheese and in the filling of bottles have been largely superseded by mechanical power.

Dais, an elevated part of a floor or a platform in a large room or hall. It usually has a seat or seats upon it, and is covered with a canopy. It is a place of honor occupied by the most distinguished personages.

Damask, a figured textile, made in various forms, originally woven in the city of Damascus; it may be a combination of silk and wool or cotton; it may be of linen for use in table-cloths, etc.; or it may be of cotton.

Damaskeening, the art of inlaying one metal upon another, largely practiced in the East in medieval times, especially in the decoration of sword blades.

Dancing, a form of art or exercise, generally performed to a musical accompaniment. It was originally a religious observance and was gradually developed, with the advance of music, into an art. In modern times dancing has been cultivated professionally in the form of the ballet, and in private life it is much indulged in, balls and dances forming a leading social diversion. Among the different styles step dances performed by one person—such as the jig and hornpipe—are among the oldest, while dances executed in pairs, including the waltz, fox-trot, one-step, etc. are more modern. Of so-called square dances, the country dance takes precedence in point of time; others of this class are the quadrille, the reel, the mazurka, etc. Minuets, gavottes, and cotillions belong to the stately period of the 17th and 18th centuries. Bands playing dance music are now provided at many restaurants and other popular resorts.

Date Palm, a tree native to northern Africa. It grows also in southern Europe and western Asia. It attains a height of from 60 to 80 feet, and its fruit is of great value as food. From the leaves the Africans build roofs for their huts; ropes are made from the fibrous parts of the stalks; and the sap furnishes an alcoholic beverage.

Dauphin, the title borne by the eldest son of the king of France from 1349 to the Revolution of 1830.

Davenport, a small ornamental writing desk much in vogue in the 19th century. The word is applied also to a couch or sofa.

Day, Sidereal, the interval between two successive transits of the same star across the same meridian. The earth rotates on its axis 365¼ times a year, giving a length to the sidereal day equal to 23 hours, 56 minutes, and 4.091 seconds. The Babylonians counted their day from sunrise to sunrise, the Hebrews and Athenians from sunset to sunset, and the Romans from midnight to midnight.

Day Nurseries are modern institutions, the result of a movement for the protection of the young children of working people, where infants are nursed and cared for while their mothers are at work. They originated in France.

Deacon, an ecclesiastical official who assists in some of the smaller ministerial duties in a church or chapel.

Dean, a church dignitary ranking next below a bishop and head of the chapter of a cathedral. The name is also applied to those senior officials of colleges and universities who have charge of students.

Debenture, a document or certificate signed by a public officer, corporation, or company, acknowledging indebtedness for money lent and guaranteeing repayment with interest. In the United States debentures are popularly equivalent to bonds not secured by a mortgage.

Decade, a group of 10, generally a period of 10 years.

Decalogue, the Ten Commandments, which, according to the Book of Exodus, were given to Moses on Mount Sinai and were inscribed on two stone tablets.

December, the twelfth month of the year and the tenth of the old Latin calendar. The Anglo-Saxons called it the Yule month.

Deciduous Trees are such as shed their leaves at maturity or at certain seasons, as distinguished from evergreens or permanently foliaged trees or shrubs.

Decimal System, based on a unit of 10, is the basis of the monetary system of the United States, Canada, France, Mexico, and many other countries. The metric system of weights and measures is based upon the decimal system.

Deck, the floor of a ship, which in large vessels includes the first or lower deck; the middle deck; and the main deck, which is the uppermost, except for the reserved, elevated part known as the quarter-deck.

Declaration of Independence, a document drawn up by a committee of the Second Continental Congress consisting of Thomas Jefferson of Virginia, John Adams of Massachusetts, Roger Sherman of Connecticut, Robert R. Livingston of New York, and Benjamin Franklin of Pennsylvania. A draft was reported by this committee on June 28, 1776. On July 2 a resolution was adopted declaring the colonies free and independent states. And on July 4 the Declaration of Independence was agreed to, engrossed on paper, and signed by John Hancock, president. It was afterward engrossed on parchment and signed by the representatives of the states. The independence of the United States was acknowledged by France Jan. 16, 1778, and by Holland April 19, 1782; and provisional articles of peace were signed by England Sept. 3, 1782.

Decomposition, the act of separating the elements of any compound substance. Oxygen and hydrogen are obtained by the decomposition of water.

Decree, a special edict or regulation issued by a supreme or governing power. The judgment of a superior court is also called a decree.

Dedication, the consecration to sacred purposes of any building or ground, or the setting apart of any building, institution, or enterprise for a special use. The term also applies to the author's inscription in a book.

Deer, hoofed or antlered ruminants very widely distributed and including many species. No true deer are found in South Africa or Australia.

Deism, the philosophy which upholds the belief that there is a God but rejects revelation and the Christian doctrines.

Delawares, a tribe of Indians once very numerous in Pennsylvania, who lived along the banks of the Delaware River, from which they took their name.

Deliquescence, the process of liquefaction or dissolving by the absorption of moisture from the atmosphere. For instance, chromic acid crystals on exposure to the air quickly deliquesce.

Delta, a triangular tract of land lying at the mouth of a river between its diverging branches, so called from its general resemblance to the Greek letter *delta*. The best-known examples are the deltas of the Nile, the Ganges, the Niger, and the Mississippi.

Deluge, a flood; a term commonly applied to the flood mentioned in the Bible, in which Noah and the Ark figure. A similar tradition lingers in the mythologies of all ancient nations.

Democracy, a form of government in which the sovereign power is in the hands of the people collectively and is exercised by them either directly or through elected representatives. Direct democracy, under which the citizens themselves assemble for the purpose of making laws, reached its highest development in Athens and other Greek city-states during the 5th century before Christ. Representative democracy, in which the functions of government are carried out through representatives of the people, was practiced as early as the 3rd century B. C. in the Achaean League, a confederation of Greek city-states. A democracy in which the executive power is vested in a president, as in the United States, Switzerland, or France, is a republic.

Density, a term by which the quantity of matter in any given bulk is assessed; the quantity of matter per unit of space. The density of gold is 19.3, silver 10.5, copper 8.9, earth 5.6, diamond 3.5, air 0.0013.

Deodar, a coniferous tree of the cedar order.

Department, a division of a government; applied in France to the provinces, or chief administrative territories, which again are subdivided into arrondisements. In the United States the members of the President's cabinet administer the government departments. Similar divisions prevail in the governments of the several states and territories.

Derby, the leading English horse race, run on the Epsom course on the last Wednesday in May or the first Wednesday in June. Originated in 1780 by the twelfth Earl of Derby, the race now carries a stake of about $30,000 and attracts the best English three-year-olds. In the United States the name is applied to many races, the most important of which is the Kentucky Derby, which has been run at Louisville every year since 1875.

Derrick, a special jib crane for lifting and moving heavy weights.

Dervish, a Mohammedan mendicant monk, of which there are more than 30 orders, including howling and whirling dervishes.

Descloizite, a rare olive-green mineral (scientifically described as a vanadate of lead and zinc), found in Argentina and other parts of South America and named after Des Cloizeaux, a French mineralogist.

Deserts, large, barren sparsely settled tracts of country, chiefly in hot climates. The most famous are the Sahara, the Arabian Desert, and the Steppes of Central Asia.

Desmidiaceae, microscopic, fresh-water algae, unicellular, and often assuming beautiful chain-like forms.

Destiny, a foreordained end, an overmastering force that supposedly impels the current of events to a final climax. In ancient times the belief in fate, or destiny, was common.

Detectives, investigators, either private or governmental, employed in collecting evidence or effecting the capture of offenders in cases of more than ordinary difficulty. There are numerous detective agencies in the chief cities of the world.

Detonating Powders, chemical compositions which explode when heated or when given a sudden blow. Ammonia with silver or gold, the chloride and iodile of nitrogen, and the fulminates of silver and mercury are among the best-known detonating compounds.

Deuteronomy, the fifth book of the Pentateuch, containing the statement of the law; believed to have been written by Moses but regarded by many modern critics as of a much later period.

Deviation of the Compass, caused by the counter-attraction of the iron of a ship, is generally corrected by putting magnets near the compass and by careful watching and calculation.

Devil, the spirit of evil, Satan, Beelzebub, the enemy of God and of good, to whom a varied personality has been ascribed by different religious systems in different ages.

Devil-worship, a belief in the efficacy of incantations to propitiate evil spirits. This kind of worship is confined to certain primitive races of Asia and Africa and to a few Indians of North America.

Devioscope, an apparatus by which the relation between "the angular velocity of the earth and that of a horizon around the vertical of any place whatever" can be ascertained.

Devitrification, the process of rendering glass soft and pliable and incidentally of depriving it of transparency.

Devonian System, in geology, refers to the strata between the Silurian and the Carboniferous formations; it is also termed the Old Red Sandstone Formation.

Dew, the moisture which collects in small drops on the surfaces of substances by atmospheric condensation, chiefly in the night time. It is most abundant in hot climates and gathers freely on bodies that are not good conductors of heat, such as grasses, etc.

Dextrin, a white, odorless, viscid substance of the same composition as starch, from which it is obtained. It is used as gum, being the material put on the backs of postage stamps and on other articles which need to be made adhesive. It is utilized also in calico printing.

Diaeresis, the sign (¨) placed over the second of two adjacent vowels, indicating that the two vowels are not to be pronounced as a diphthong but that each is to be pronounced separately, as in the word coöperate. The sign is also employed to indicate that vowels, ordinarily silent, are to receive pronunciation: Oh, cursëd, spite; my belovëd.

Diagometer, a form of electroscope for measuring the conducting power of various bodies, having a magnetized needle for an indicator. The diagometer was invented by Rousseau.

Dialect, a form of speech special to a locality or district and differing from the general literary language of the country. There are many dialects of English, in all of which some survivals of ancient speech may be found. The works of Chaucer, Spenser, Shakespeare, and even later writers contain many words which have become obsolete in the general literary language but which are still familiar in certain of the dialects. The dialects which exerted the greatest influence on modern literature were the Scottish, the Negro, the lower Mississippi, and the Appalachian Mountain dialects. The American Dialect Society has contributed greatly to the understanding of the force and meaning of dialects.

Diamagnetism, the phenomena revealed in certain substances which, when suspended and under magnetic influence, assume a position showing the longer axis at right angles to the magnetic lines of force.

Diameter, a straight line passing through the center of a circle or other figure, and terminating at both ends in the circumference. In architecture the diameter of the lower bed of a column, divided into 60 parts, constitutes the scale whereby all the parts of a classical order are measured.

Diamond, a mineral of pure carbon, the most valued of precious stones, though, before the art of cutting was perfected, diamonds were considered inferior to the ruby and the emerald. India was in former times the chief diamond country. At the present day, South Africa yields the largest quantities, between 3 and 4 million metric carats being mined yearly, more than 126,000 men being employed in South African diamond mining. In Brazil and Australia there are many rich diamond mines. Diamonds mostly occur in alluvial deposits.

They form the hardest known substance and have a high refractive power. The largest diamond ever found is the Cullinan Diamond, which was discovered in the Premier diamond mine, near Pretoria, South Africa, in January, 1905. It weighed 3,030 carats and was valued at $75,000,000. It was three times as large as the largest of the other big diamonds in history. A number of small stones have been cut from it. Other large diamonds found are:—

	Place of discovery	Weight in carats
"Excelsior"	South Africa	971 (uncut)
"Great Mogul"	India	280 (cut)
"Jonker"	South Africa	726 (uncut)
"Regent"	India	410 (uncut)
"Orloff"	India	900 (uncut)
"Koh-i-noor"	India	103 (cut)

"Excelsior" was found by Captain Ed. Jorgansen. In its natural state it was valued at $5,000,000, but purchasers of such gems are not plentiful, and so in 1904 it was cut into nine smaller gems. The "Great Mogul" is another famous diamond; it weighed 280 carats after being cut and in size and shape resembled one-half of an ordinary chicken's egg. Its history is romantic. It was seen at the court of Aurungzebe in 1665 by a French jeweler, stolen at the sacking of Delhi in 1739, and broken up. The largest cut diamond up to the cutting of the Cullinan was the "Orloff," which formerly adorned the Czar's sceptre. It was stolen from an Indian idol's eye and sold to Catherine of Russia. It weighed about 200 carats. The famous "Koh-i-noor", an Indian stone, is the property of the British government. It weighed nearly 900 carats uncut, but by bad cutting was brought down in weight to 103 carats. Other famous diamonds are the "Pitt" (136 carats), the "Florentine" (133 carats), and the "Star of the South" (124 carats).

Diapason, the concord of the first and last tones of an octave, and the fixed rule by which organ pipes and other instruments are arranged to proper pitch.

Diaphoretics, medicines used to induce perspiration and thereby increase the action of the digestive organs.

Diaspore, an infusible hydrate of aluminum, almost colorless, occurring in crystals and foliated masses. A small portion placed in a flame instantly disperses.

Diathermy, the application of heat in the treatment of various diseases.

Diatonic Scale represents the use of musical tones, intervals, and harmonies without chromatic variation.

Dice, small cubes, usually made of bone or a synthetic plastic, which are used in playing games. The sides of each cube are numbered from 1 to 6 and are so arranged that the sum of the opposite sides always equals 7. Dice are of very ancient origin, cubes similar to modern dice having been found among Babylonian and Egyptian remains.

Dictaphone, a dictating machine used in offices, which records the dictator's voice on a wax cylinder. The voice is then reproduced by placing the cylinder in a transcribing machine, and the typist types the words as she hears them. This eliminates the taking of shorthand notes. The wax cylinder can be shaved and used repeatedly.

Dictator, the title given by the ancient Romans to their supreme magistrates under the republic, in times of great exigency. The dictatorship was limited to six months, but while it lasted the dictator's rule was absolute. Another class of dictator was the Greek tyrant, and many despotic rulers of more recent times have in effect, if not in name, been dictators. In Paraguay and other South American countries the title of dictator has been borne by numerous rulers. Although the title is avoided in modern Europe, the rulers of the Fascist and Communist states, Mussolini, Hitler, and Stalin, were dictators.

Dictionary, an alphabetical list of words, giving their meaning, pronunciation, and etymological significance. The earliest English dictionaries of any pretensions to accuracy and completeness were those of Bullokar (1616) and Cockeran (1625). Dr. Johnson's famous dictionary was published about the middle of the 18th century. Of the 19th- and 20th-century dictionaries there are the Standard, the Century, Webster's, Ogilvie's, Chambers', Nuttal's, Skeat's, and numerous others, and from the 50,000 words of Johnson's day we now have from 400,000 to 500,000 words. In addition to word dictionaries there are dictionaries of many other kinds, such as dictionaries of music, biography, etc.

Diet, an assembly of dignitaries or delegates called together to debate upon and decide important political or ecclesiastical questions. The most famous diets in history were those of Worms in 1495 and 1521 and the Diet of Augsburg in 1530, all of which dealt with matters of religious controversy awakened by the Reformation movement.

Diffusion, the process of spreading or mixing two fluids or gases by contact. Liquids diffuse much more slowly than gases. According to Graham's law, the rate of diffusion of different gases is in inverse proportion to the square roots of their relative densities.

Digit, a finger or toe; in arithmetic, any number of one figure. The Arabic numerals from 1 to 9 inclusive are digits.

Dilemma, in logic, an argument which resolves itself into two alternative conclusions each of which amounts to a denial of the proposition maintained; hence the term the "horns of a dilemma". The oft-quoted example of a dilemma from Gellinus may be repeated: "Every woman is fair or ugly; it is not good to marry a fair wife, because she will flirt; it is not good to marry an ugly wife, because she will not be attractive; therefore, it is not good to marry at all".

Dilettante, a term applied to amateurs in any of the arts or sciences. The word is usually used in a patronizing sense.

Dimensions are measured magnitudes and involve the qualities of length, breadth, and thickness. A line has only one dimension: length; a plane surface two: length and breadth; and a solid three: length, breadth, and thickness.

Diminutives, words denoting smallness or littleness, as illustrated in the suffixes, *kin, ler,* and *ling.*

Dimorphism, the quality of assuming two distinct forms not derivable from each other. For instance, carbon, which is graphite in one form, is the diamond in another. Pasteur demonstrated that dimorphism most commonly occurs when the two forms are close to the limit of their respective systems.

Dingo, the wild wolflike dog of Australia. It is of a reddish color, has a bushy tail, and is very destructive to sheep.

Dinosauria, the name of a group of extinct reptiles of the Mesozoic period, some of which were of immense size—much larger than crocodiles.

Dinotherium, an extinct quadruped of enormous size, fossil remains of which were discovered in the Tertiary strata along the Rhine and elsewhere. It has tusks and a trunk like the elephant's. It was about 18 feet long.

Diocese, a territory under the pastoral authority of a bishop. The term originated in the time of the Roman Empire and at that time represented a civil rather than an ecclesiastical administrative territory.

Dioptase, a rare copper ore occurring in prismatic emerald green crystals and composed of silicate of copper; found in Russia, and sometimes styled emerald-malachite.

Diorama, a series of spectacular paintings exhibited in a darkened room with the light thrown onto the pictures in such a manner as to produce optical effects that give the appearance of reality. These effects can be varied so as to represent night or day scenes, or scenes of cloud or sunshine. The diorama was the invention of Daguerre and Bouton in 1822.

Diorite, a rock of crystalline structure composed of feldspar and hornblende, and occurring in association with magnetite and apatite. It used to be classed as greenstone.

Diphthong, the conjunction of two vowels pronounced in one syllable. What is called a proper diphthong combines the sound of both vowels, as in "boy," "noise," and "out," while the improper diphthong represents the sound of only one of the vowels, as in "pail," "breach," "juice," etc. Belonging to the latter class are the diphthongs "ae" and "oe", but these are confined to words from the Latin or Greek.

Diplodocus, a class of extinct mammoth reptiles belonging to Mesozoic times. Fossil remains of it have been discovered in Colorado and Wyoming. The height of the spines of the dorsal vertebrae was nearly 14 feet. Four thousand centuries are supposed to have elapsed since it lived.

Diploma, a certificate of authority signed by the heads of universities, colleges, or other learned bodies, conferring upon the recipient some honor, degree, or privilege, and usually affording evidence of graduation.

Diplomacy, the practice of official intercourse between nations, as carried on by ambassadors and other agents of states and governments.

Directory, a term applied to the group of five men who held authority during the French Revolution from October, 1795, until Nov. 9th, 1799, when Napoleon overthrew it and established the Consulate. The term, as generally used, signifies a book in which names of residents, traders, etc. in any particular locality or sphere are recorded.

Dirge, a hymn or song of mourning and lamentation, consisting usually of a combination of music and words.

Dirk, an ancient Scottish stabbing weapon, shaped like a dagger but much longer and heavier. It was usually worn in a scabbard.

Discus, a flat, circular piece of metal or stone about 12 inches in diameter, used in athletic contests by the ancient Greeks and Romans. Throwing the discus was a favorite sport; a famous statue of the 5th century B. C., the "Discobolus", represents an athlete in the act of throwing a discus. In modern times the art has been revived and is now a feature of track meets and of the Olympic Games.

Disk, a flat, circular plate; in astronomy the seemingly flat surface of celestial bodies.

Dissenters, in English history, those who dissented from the beliefs of the Church of England.

Distaff, the staff of a spinning wheel, being a cleft stick on which wool, cotton, or flax was wound for spinning on the spindle. It was held between the left arm and the side.

Distance, the space between two objects or between two points of time. Accessible distances can be measured by ordinary linear measure; inaccessible distances are calculated by triangulation. The mean distance between a planet and the sun is an arithmetical mean between the greatest and least distances.

Distich, a term used in poetry to indicate a couplet, i.e., two lines or verses constituting a complete idea.

Distillation, the process of separating one substance from another by evaporation and condensation. First the original substance is heated in a still; then the liquid, after it has become volatilized, passes through a condenser and emerges again in liquid form. Thus volatile liquids are separated from non-volatile and solid matters. Distillation is used in the production of alcoholic liquors and essences.

Distinguished Service Cross, in the United States, a bronze cross awarded by Congress since 1918 for extraordinary heroism in war. In Great Britain it is a silver cross awarded since 1915 to naval officers below the rank of lieutenant-commander for conspicuous bravery in action.

Diving Bells, bell-shaped mechanical contrivances in which a diver can sit and be lowered into a body of water, fresh air being supplied through a communicating flexible pipe. Another diving apparatus commonly used is the diving helmet, which fits over the head and renders the diver free to move about at the bottom of the water in comparative safety.

Divorce, a legal dissolution of the marriage tie. In the United States the authority to legislate on divorce is within the province of the states. Each state has its own statute on divorce, and the provisions of the laws differ widely. Adultery, desertion, cruelty, habitual drunkenness, and incurable insanity are the most common grounds. Jurisdiction in divorce cases usually lies with the courts of equity.

Docket, a summary copy of any decree; a brief list, or label. The word is derived from dock, *to curtail.*

Docks, enclosed water spaces wherein ships rest while being loaded or unloaded or while waiting for cargo. The wet dock is for loading and unloading; the dry dock, or graving dock, is for overhauling and repairing vessels and is so constructed that, after a ship has been docked, the water can be drawn off; the floating dock is a rectangular structure which is sunk beneath a ship to raise it. The largest series of docks in the world are those on the Thames, which extend for many miles.

Doctor, a term of wide application, applying not only to those that practice medicine, but also to holders of a doctor's degree in any department of learning; thus there are doctors in divinity, doctors of music, doctors of science, etc.

Dodo, an extinct bird of the island of Mauritius which is known to have existed as late as the end of the 17th century. It was a clumsy, short-legged bird; unable to fly, it died out because of its inability to protect itself against the animals imported into the island by settlers. Certain paintings of the dodo, made by Dutch artists who actually saw it, give us a very fair idea of this curious bird.

Doge, the chief magistrate of the Venetian Republic, whose office existed from the 8th century to 1797. Till the 16th century he was elected for life; thereafter the term of office was curtailed to two years.

Dogfish, a well-known genus of fishes of the shark family, but considerably smaller, being seldom more than three feet in length.

Dogs, a species of the genus *Canis*, descended probably from one or more wild species, such as the wolf, fox, jackal. There are six classifications of domestic dogs: wolf-dogs, including Borzoi, Eskimo, Newfoundland, St. Bernard, sheep-dog, etc.; cattle and watch-dogs, comprising the German boar-hound, the deerhound, the Danish dog, etc.; greyhounds; hounds, such as the staghound, the bloodhound, the pointer, etc.; curs, terriers, etc.; and the mastiff breeds, including the bulldog, the pug, etc. The subdivisions of these classifications—which are by no means arbitrary—are numerous and fanciful. Dogs do not reach full growth until two years old. They do not perspire but expel heat through the tongue. A litter of puppies is usually from six to eight, and the period of gestation is 63 days.

Doily, a small napkin or mat, used as a table covering on which to place glasses or earthenware; it is also the name of a species of woolen fabric.

Dole, an apportionment of money, food, or other charitable gifts, distributed according to the terms of the charity. In medieval Europe doles were often associated with monasteries and churches.

Dollar, the monetary unit of the United States and Canada. Dollars are in circulation in many other countries, especially in the republics of South America. The word is derived from the German word *Thaler*.

Dolphin, an ocean mammal of the whale family, from 6 to 8 feet long, with a long sharp snout. Dolphins abound in most temperate seas and swim in shoals.

Dome, a large cupola, hemispherical in form, rising over the main building of a cathedral or other prominent structure. The finest dome, that of the Pantheon at Rome, is also the oldest, dating from the time of the emperor Augustus. It is 143 feet high, and 142½ feet wide. The dome of St. Peter's in the same city is 330 feet high, but its diameter is 3½ feet less than that of the Pantheon. The dome of the cathedral at Florence is 310 feet high and 139 feet in diameter; and the dimensions of St. Paul's, London, are 215 feet high and 112 feet in diameter.

Dominicans, an order of mendicant friars, established in 1216 in Languedoc by Dominic de Guzman. They formed a powerful body, being, next to the Franciscans, the most noted. The order is still important in many parts of the Christian world.

Dormer, the name of a special kind of window projecting from a sloping roof. Such windows were common in edifices of the Netherlands, northern France, and Belgium after the 14th century. They were a common feature of American architecture, though not so popular now.

Dower, the share allowed by law to a widow out of the real estate of her deceased husband, in case he died without having made other disposition in her favor. Dower is of common-law origin, but in the United States it has been regulated by statute in many states.

Drachm or **Drachma**, the name of the chief silver coin used by the ancient Greeks and worth about twenty cents in American money. It is the basic monetary unit of modern Greece.

Dragon, a fabulous monster common to the folklore of most countries; it is generally represented as a winged reptile, with fiery eyes and breath of flame. In the New Testament there is a reference to "the dragon, that old serpent, which is the devil." Medieval legend abounds in dragons, and they have also a conspicuous place in heraldry. The imperial emblem of China was the dragon.

Dragon Fly, the common name of a well-known class of insects having two pairs of membranous wings. They are often of very brilliant color, swift of flight, and may be seen hovering over sheets of water in the sunshine all through the summer.

Dragoons, a mounted military force in many armies of the 18th and 19th centuries. The word survives in the names of some European cavalry regiments.

Drama, a composition in verse or prose, or both, with characters and a succession of scenes representing some story of human or supernatural action. Thespis and his car give us the first crude form of the drama; then we have the virile developments shown in the Greek drama, with its two distinctive branches, tragedy and comedy. After the classic era of Greece and Rome, the drama lost much of its power, and in the miracle and the morality plays of the Middle Ages is found little of real dramatic force. In the 16th century came the splendid dramatic revival under Shakespeare, Marlowe, and other famous Elizabethans. The subsequent dramatic periods in English literature are the Restoration, noted for its licentiousness, and the Georgian, in which Goldsmith, Colman, Sheridan, and others took part. In more recent times the drama has undergone notable developments, passing from the poetic drama to opera bouffe, from opera bouffe to light opera and musical comedy.

Drawbridge, a bridge that can be lifted so that no passage can be made across it. It was a usual feature of a fortified castle in the Middle Ages; it was raised or lowered by chains and levers. It spanned the fosse, or moat, and on the approach of an attacking party the bridge was raised, forming a special barricade to the gate. Modern drawbridges are raised to allow the passage of boats up and down a river.

Dreams, subjective phenomena dependent on the psychic life of the individual which present themselves to the mind during sleep. The principal characteristic is the absence of voluntary control over the current of thought, so that the principle of suggestion has unlimited sway. The utter want of coherency in the images that appear before the mental eye of the dreamer excites no surprise in him. All reflex actions are lowered; breathing and the action of the heart become slower, and the other organic functions are diminished. Among the peoples of antiquity dreams were regarded as direct messages from the spiritual world, of either divine or diabolical origin; dream interpretation was elevated to the rank of science. At the royal court of Babylon the interpretation of dreams was a part of the duties of soothsayers. The Bible stories of the dreams of Joseph, Jacob, and Pharaoh are well known. Modern psychoanalysis is removing the veil of mystery from dreams and is studying them as purely mental phenomena. The analytic approach to the interpretation of dreams has as a basis the psychic life of the particular person concerned. It is possible that important facts concerning the attributes of the human mind may be ascertained through the study of dreams. Thus a great service to mental healing may be rendered.

Dredging Machine, an apparatus employed in collecting mud and silt from the bottoms of harbors, rivers, canals, etc. They are usually flat-bottomed, carrying a crane and an endless chain of buckets. The buckets descend into the water, collect the mud, bring it up, and discharge it into the flat alongside the machine. Steam dredges, of which there are many kinds, are now generally used.

Dress, costume or attire for the body. The attire of primitive peoples and peasants exhibits many local variations, and in some parts of the world interesting costumes of ancient origin are still in use. Costumology, the study of the attire of man at different periods of history, is a minor branch of historical research.

Drought, a period of dry weather. It is a normal and recurring condition in many regions and is frequently provided against by irrigation. In 1936 a severe drought caused great damage in the mid-western United States and in the prairie provinces of Canada.

Drum, a percussion instrument having a hollow, cylindrical body of wood or metal, the ends of which are closed with tightly-stretched pieces of membrane. Drums, which emit more or less vibrant sounds when struck with sticks, are of three kinds: the bass drum, held horizontally and beaten at both ends; the side drum, or snare drum, slung to the side and played on the upper surface with a pair of wooden drumsticks; and the kettle-drum, or timpano, the shell of which is of copper or brass, and the head of parchment.

Dry-rot is caused in timber by a fungoid growth and occurs chiefly in damp climates. The most effective treatment is saturation with creosote. Dry wood always escapes dry-rot.

Dualism, a term used both in religion and in philosophy. In religion it involves the doctrine of two distinct principles, one good, the other evil, as the controlling influences; in philosophy it differs from materialism and idealism in that it insists that spirit and matter are separate substances.

Duchess, the wife or widow of a duke, or the lady who has, in her own right, control or sovereignty in a duchy.

Duck, a bird of the family Anatidae, widespread and of many species, the mallard or wild duck being regarded as the common ancestor.

Duckbill, a fur-covered mammal inhabiting Australia and Tasmania, possessing a bill like that of a duck and a body resembling that of an otter. It lays eggs and suckles its young. It is called also the duck-mole and the duckbilled platypus. Adults are about 20 inches long.

Duck Hawk, the common name of the peregrine falcon in the United States and Canada.

Ducking-Stool or Cucking-Stool, an old instrument of punishment, consisting of a chair suspended on a pole over a sheet of water. It was used for "common scolds," who were tied in the chair and dipped in the water.

Ductility, a property possessed by most metals, which renders them capable of being stretched without breaking. Gold is the most, and lead the least, ductile of metals; the order being gold, silver, platinum, iron, copper, palladium, aluminum, zinc, tin, lead.

Dueling originated during the feudal period. It existed in England through medieval times and down to the days of George III. In the German army and among German students there are frequent duels of a kind; but in no country at the present time are such encounters indulged in, except on rare occasions, with intent to kill. In the United States and in Great Britain duels are now looked upon as childish or foolish methods of settling disputes, and are an offense against the law.

Duet, a musical composition for two voices or two players, which, in the case of the piano, can be performed on one instrument.

Duke, the highest rank in the peerage next to that of a royal prince. Edward, the Black Prince, eldest son of Edward III, was the first English duke. He was created Duke of Cornwall in 1337, a title which since that time has been held by every heir to the throne.

Dulse, a crimson-colored seaweed, eaten as food in some nothern countries.

Duma, the Russian national parliament, established in 1906, reconstructed in 1907, and abolished by the Bolsheviks in 1917.

Dunes, hills of loose sand, which form on the shores of seas or lakes. In some places they have aggregated at the mouth of an estuary and, remaining fixed, have caused the estuary to be blocked against the tide.

Duodecimo, a sheet of paper folded into twelve leaves, usually written "12 mo."

Duodenum, the first portion of the small intestine, connecting with the stomach and receiving the hepatic and pancreatic secretions.

Dwarfs, persons of very diminutive size, of which many notable examples are recorded in history. Stanley reported a tribe of dwarfs in central Africa. The smallest of modern dwarfs were "General Mite," 21 inches tall, and "Tom Thumb," 31 inches.

Dyestuffs are of various kinds and the number has been greatly increased in modern times by chemical discoveries. They include cochineal, indigo, logwood, madder, fustic, and the various aniline derivatives.

Dyke, the term applied to masses of igneous rock which have flowed into grooves of strata or have become infused therewith; the word also signifies a sea wall or an open drain.

Dynamics, the science dealing with natural forces either in motion or at rest, describing their positions, velocities, and constitution.

Dynamism, Leibnitz's doctrine that all substances in nature involve force.

Dynamite, a powerful explosive whose chief element is nitroglycerine. It has a disruptive force of about eight times that of gunpowder. Nobel discovered it in 1867.

Dynamo, a machine consisting of electro-magnets, between the poles of which there is an armature of coils of insulated copper wire, which is made to revolve by mechanical power, thus producing an electric current.

Dynasty, a succession of monarchs of the same family, such as the Carlovingian, the Bourbon, the Plantagenet, etc.

E

Eagle, a large diurnal, raptorial bird of the family Falconidae, having about ten species, including the golden, the Russian, the imperial, and the bald eagles. Eagles are fairly common in Europe, Asia, and Africa, but only the golden eagle is found in America.

Ear, the organ of hearing, which in mammals comprises the external ear, containing the pinna and auditory meatus; the middle ear, containing the ossicles and the drum membrane, or tympanum; and the internal ear, through which the sound vibrations are transformed to nervous impulses and transmitted to the brain.

Earl, a British title of nobility of the third rank, duke and marquis coming first and second. The title dates from Saxon times and until 1337 ranked highest in the peerage.

Earring, a personal adornment of ancient origin, worn attached to the ear lobe. The custom of wearing earrings is almost universal; in the Occident they are worn only by women, but in the Orient they are worn by men and women alike. Among some Eastern peoples they are used as insignia of rank. Some earrings have had religious or ritualistic significance for their wearers; other have been used as amulets.

Earth, our habitable globe, the third of the planets in order from the sun. It makes one revolution upon its axis in one sidereal day, the whole earth revolving around the sun in an ellipse in one year. The distance of the earth from the sun is 93,000,000 miles. The shape of the earth is that of an oblate spheroid, its axis measuring 7,926 and 7,899 miles respectively. Two-thirds of the earth's surface is covered with water. It has only one satellite, the moon.

Earthenware, a term comprising objects or utensils made from baked or fired clay. Earthenware may be either unglazed or enameled. The word is frequently employed to designate only the coarser kinds of pottery.

Earthquake, a violent disturbance of the earth's surface. Earthquakes are frequent in some countries, especially in certain countries of South America. Occasionally they occur in unexpected places, though only in a mild form. An earthquake causes an undulating motion, varying in duration, sometimes lasting only a few seconds, at other times continuing in a series of shocks for a considerable time. The most serious earthquake of modern times was that of Lisbon in 1755, in which 50,000 people lost their lives. There was a destructive earthquake and fire in San Francisco in 1906. In 1907 Jamaica, particularly the capital Kingston, suffered severely. Earthquakes also occurred in north and central Italy (1920), Japan (1923 and 1935), New Zealand and Nicaragua (1931), California (1933), and India (1934 and 1935). In December 1939 a series of very severe earthquakes occurred in Turkey.

Earthworm, an animal having a cylindrical body, tapering at both ends, and segmented into rings. It moves by contraction of its rings, aided by retractive bristles; it is eyeless but has a mouth, gullet, and stomach. Earthworms exist in immense numbers and perform an important part in the scheme of nature by loosening the soil and rendering it more amenable to tillage. They also form a valuable food for birds and for certain mammals.

Easement, a legal term applied to a privilege which one person may exercise over another's property, the most familiar example being the right of way.

Easter, the annual festival in commemoration of the resurrection of Christ. The name is derived from Eostre, the goddess of spring. The date cannot fall earlier than March 22 or later than April 25.

Eau de Cologne, a popular distilled perfume first manufactured at Cologne in the 18th century by Johann Maria Farina, an Italian, and now made in large quantities in Cologne and elsewhere.

Eavesdropper, one who secretly listens to the private conversation of others. Offenders of this kind were often severely punished in medieval times.

Ebony, a name applied to various hard, black woods, the best of which are grown in Mauritius and Ceylon. There are also Indian and American varieties. Only the inner portion of the tree, the heart-wood, is of the desired hardness and blackness. Ebony is largely used in ornamental cabinet work and for piano keys, canes, etc.

Ecclesiastes, a book of the Old Testament, the word signifying "the preacher." It is supposed to contain the reflections of Solomon, though many critics dissent from this view.

Ecclesiasticus, the title of one of the books of the Apocrypha, dating from about 180 B. C. Its alternative title is "The Wisdom of Jesus, the Son of Sirach."

Echo, a repercussion or the repetition of a sound caused by some obstructing object, which throws the sound waves back to their starting point. Woods, rocky defiles, valleys, mountains, and walls all act as echo-producers under favoring conditions.

Eclipse, an obscuration of the light of the sun, moon, or other heavenly body by the passing of another body either between it and the observer or between it and the source of its light. The sun is eclipsed by the moon's intervening between it and the earth; the moon by the earth's passing between it and the sun. Eclipses vary in number from year to year. During 1933 there were two eclipses of the sun but none of the moon, in 1934 two eclipses of the moon and two of the sun, in 1935 five eclipses of the sun and two of the moon, and in 1940 two eclipses, both of the sun.

Ecliptic, the circle describing the course of the earth around the sun. Its position at a given date is styled the fixed ecliptic; the position of the fixed ecliptic in relation to the equinox is the mean ecliptic; and the true ecliptic is the mean ecliptic as affected by inclination. The obliquity of the ecliptic signifies the angle of inclination of the ecliptic of the equinox.

Edda, the book of the mythological lore of Scandinavia, compiled by Snorri Sturluson in the 13th century.

Education. Education was to the ancients a process of developing the powers of the body and mind by proper instruction and training. Youths were taught to absorb knowledge, to acquire skill in action and discipline in conduct. Herbert Spencer (1820-1903), an English philosopher and educator, gave a very brief but comprehensive definition of the purpose of education: "To prepare us for complete living is the function which education has to discharge." Certain leaders of the past looked upon education as the means of training the young for their particular stations in life. This view of education distinguished different types of instruction for different groups. It tended to preserve the social order as it was. Other leaders looked upon education as a means of leading the youth out from fixed stations into a broader interpretation of life. A few outstanding thinkers regarded education as an attempt to move forward by means of experiment, investigation, and creative activity into larger realms of thought and action.

Educational training may be obtained in the following types of schools: (1) grade schools (grades 1-6) for children 6-12 years old; (2) junior high schools (grades 7, 8, & 9) for children 13-15 years old; (3) senior high schools (grades 10, 11, & 12); (4) colleges or universities: four years' work giving the degrees of B.A., B.S., etc.; (5) professional schools: medicine, law, theology, engineering, etc. The courses in the professional schools lead to specialized degrees and generally take three or four years. In the United States there are also parochial, or denominational, schools. Most of the parochial grade schools are under Roman Catholic, a considerable number under Lutheran, auspices. In addition there are colleges and universities belonging to these and other denominations. The school budget of an American city is normally the largest item of municipal expenditure. The public schools are maintained by direct taxation, while the parochial schools are maintained by their respective churches.

Eels, soft-finned, serpentine fish, almost without scales, abundant in many parts of the world. Generally they do not exceed three feet in length, the females being larger than the males. Young female eels make their way from salt to fresh water and at maturity return to the sea for breeding purposes. The conger (marine) eel grows to more than twice the size of the fresh-water eel. The electric eel of South America is an interesting variety, possessing the power to produce electric shocks.

Eggplant, an egg-shaped plant cultivated for its fruit, varying in color from dark purple to white. The fruit is used as a vegetable in the United States and Canada.

Egret, a bird of the heron family, of pure white plumage, famed for its beautiful, silky tufts, which appear during the breeding season. There are two varieties: the larger kind is found in eastern Europe, northern Africa, and America; the smaller is confined to eastern Europe and to Asia.

Egyptian Vulture, a species common in Eastern countries, valuable for the scavenging duties it performs. In certain countries it is considered a moral offense to kill one of these birds.

Eider Duck, a genus of large ducks, of which there are five species. It is an inhabitant of northern latitudes and supplies the beautiful soft down called eider down. These birds line their nests with down which they pluck from their breasts. It is this particular down that is so highly prized; the down plucked from other parts of the duck is of much less value. Eider down is so elastic that a pound or two of it will fill an ordinary bed covering.

Eland, a species of antelopes, native to Africa; it has large, pointed horns, stands five feet high at the withers, and weighs several hundred pounds. It is a fleshy animal and greatly valued as food.

Elasticity implies a power of expansion under strain and reversion to the original form when the strain is withdrawn. Perfect elasticity is illustrated by gases and liquids; solid bodies vary in elasticity according to their composition. Of solids, rubber, tempered steel, ivory, and glass possess the greatest amount of elasticity; lead and clay, the least.

Elder, a small tree of the genus *Sambucus* of the honeysuckle family, with pinnate leaves and clusters of small purple-black berries. The black elder, the best known, is common in most parts of Europe. A wine is made from its berries. The juice is used also as an aperient.

El Dorado, "the golden land," believed by the early Spanish explorers to exist somewhere on the South American continent. Many expeditions were fitted out to discover a country abounding in gold and precious stones. Sir Walter Raleigh went forth on such a quest. The term is still used to allude to a place of rich promise.

Election, in politics, the selection, by voting, of a person or persons to occupy some post or office. The most important elections are those for the executive and for members of the supreme legislative assemblies in the various countries. In such elections voting by ballot is now general. The jurisdiction of election laws of the United States extends to such officers of the Federal government as are elective; namely, the President, the vice president, and members of the Congress of the United States. The election of officers of the state governments is regulated by the several state codes. The President and vice president are elected by a college of electors, which college is composed of as many electors as there are senators and representatives in Congress at the time of the election of such electors. The people vote directly for these electors. Members of Congress are elected as follows: Each state is entitled to two senators in Congress, who are elected by the people of the several states as provided for by the 17th Amendment to the Constitution, which went into effect May 31, 1913. Previously, senators were elected by the state legislatures. In general, it may be said that all citizens of the United States are entitled to vote except those residing in the District of Columbia. In 1870 Negroes were given the right to vote.

The several states have enacted laws for the regulation and management of elections for the officers of state, city, and county. The constitutions of the several states secure to citizens the right of suffrage. The laws of each state provide the means of effecting the ends of the constitution and prescribe the qualifications of voters, which vary somewhat in the different states. The length of residence in the state previous to an election is fixed by state law and varies in the different states. Many states have a literacy test for voters. Registration must precede voting and in cities is generally required in each election year.

Electra, in astronomy, one of the Pleiades; the term is applied also to an asteroid, discovered in 1873 by Peters.

Electricity, the name given to certain phenomena of attraction and repulsion, the true nature of which is still incompletely understood. It is customary to treat of two forms of electricity: frictional, and voltaic or current. Frictional electricity was discovered in the 6th century B. C. by rubbing amber with silk. Further experiments were made by rubbing together other substances. In the utilization of frictional electricity, its distribution over the surface of a conductor has to be provided for, and electrical machines are employed for developing quantities of electricity. In voltaic or current electricity, the electricity is produced by a battery, a coil of wire, or a dynamo.

Electric Light, the light produced by electricity: the arc-light and the incandescent light. The former is produced if a strong current passes between two carbon electrodes, first brought together, then slightly separated, leaving the current to continue, but setting up a resistance that causes the carbon points and air between them to assume a white heat, which gives forth an intense light. The incandescent light is obtained by passing the current through a thin metallic wire or other strong resisting substance until it is heated to the point of incandescence.

Electric Power, although largely utilized in manufacturing plants and in certain mines and irrigation projects, is still in its infancy. Modern industry and social life are depending more and more on this source of power. The limitations placed upon its further extension are imposed because of our lack of experience. The four most important practical difficulties are: to maintain perfect insulation; to secure protection from lightning discharges, etc.; to eliminate loss due to brush discharges from high-tension conductors; and to prevent deterioration of the high-tension conductors. The solution of these problems can be effected only by experience. The Tennessee Valley Authority (TVA) is the largest producer and transmitter of electric power in the United States.

Electric Telegraph may be said to date from 1837, when Morse invented his famous recording instrument. The first electric cable was laid between Dover and France in 1850. The first Atlantic cable was laid in 1858; the second in 1866. It was in 1899 that the first Marconi wireless telegraph messages were sent between England and France.

Electrolysis, the condition established when an electric current passes through a conducting liquid and between electrodes connected with the poles of a battery, thus resulting in the decomposition and separation of the compound. Water is decomposed into hydrogen and oxygen.

Electrometer, an instrument for measuring the amount of an electric discharge.

Electronic Theory asserts that matter when analyzed into its ultimate components consists of electricity. Many leading physicists accept the theory, which, it is claimed, forms a working hypothesis capable of accounting for all the known phenomena of electricity.

Electroplating, the process of coating metals or other substances with a metallic film, applied in a bath of the solution of the coating material by the action of an electric current.

Elements, according to ancient interpretation, comprised earth, air, fire, and water. In chemistry, an element is a substance which cannot be reduced to any simpler form. There are ninety-two of these elements, the most recent discoveries being illinium, virginium, and alabamine. Elements are classed as metallic or non-metallic.

Elephant, a proboscidian mammal of which only two species exist—the Asiatic (in India) and the African. No other animals possess a trunk. Both males and females have large ivory tusks of considerable commercial value. A full-sized elephant weighs about 7,000 pounds and stands three yards high at the shoulders. Elephants are the largest existing quadrupeds. Several fossils of still larger bulk have been discovered, including the mammoth and the mastodon. The Indian elephant is domesticated and is used as a beast of burden.

Elevation, rising ground, such as a hill; also a military expression being the angle to which the barrel of a gun is raised to throw a projectile the required distance.

Elf, a fairy of playful disposition, supposed to interfere in human affairs with mischievous intent.

Elk, the largest animal of the deer family, possessing enormous antlers. Mature elks attain a height of about seven feet. The American moose is of the same family.

Ellipse, in geometry, a compressed circle or oval, forming a curve so marked out that the sums of the distances of each point in its periphery from two fixed points are the same.

Elm, a large, wide-spreading tree having a dozen species, and common to Europe, India, China, and North America. It makes valuable timber, its wood being hard and durable; and for shade and ornament the elm is unsurpassed.

Elongation, an astronomical term for the angular distance from an interior planet to the sun.

Embalming, the process by which dead bodies are preserved from decay by means of spices and drugs. The art reached its highest development in ancient Egypt, as is shown by the mummies which have been found there. In modern times many new methods of embalming have been developed.

Embossing, the art of stamping in relief letters or designs upon pliant substances.

Embryology, the science of embryos, which treats of their development from the fertilized germ or seed to its maturity. The science includes all sections of the animal and vegetable kingdoms.

Emerald, a variety of beryl of a clear, transparent, green color. It is highly valued as a gem. The finest come from Colombia and Peru.

Emery, a granular substance of the corundum order, generally mixed with other metallic substances, and ground into a powder for polishing and grinding purposes. Emery stone is found chiefly in Asia Minor and the Greek Archipelago.

Eminence, a title of honor, conferred on cardinals of the Roman Catholic church. It was introduced by Pope Urban VIII in the year 1630.

Emir, a title signifying head or chief, applied in Mohammedan countries to princes, chiefs, and rulers. The direct descendants of Mohammed's daughter Fatima were also called emirs. Chiefs of various tribes in Africa and the East have also assumed the title.

Emu, a large bird of the family Struthionidae, inhabiting central Australia, and resembling the cassowary. It is unable to fly but is very fleet of foot; and it is frequently hunted.

Enamel, a vitrified substance applied as a coating to pottery and porcelain. The art of enameling, practiced by the Assyrians and the Egyptians, was introduced into Europe by way of Greece. Enamels are either transparent or opaque and are susceptible to an immense variety of coloring, according to the metallic oxides introduced.

Encyclical Letters, a term used in reference to letters addressed by the pope to his bishops upon matters of doctrine or discipline.

Encyclopedists, a term first applied to the eminent writers who collaborated in preparing the French *Encyclopédie* (1751-65). These writers were Diderot, D'Alembert, Voltaire, Helvetius, and others; and their writings generally were sceptical as to religion, revolutionary in politics, and had great influence in popularizing the social ideas which afterward resulted in the French Revolution.

Endive, a plant of the chicory family, a hardy annual with a profusion of leaves. It is generally used for salad.

Endogens, the name applied to a large family of flowering plants, of which lilies, orchids, arums, grasses, and sedges are prominent examples. The leaves are usually parallel-veined. It is estimated that there are more than 20,000 species of endogens, which include 5,000 orchid species.

Energy is of two kinds: kinetic, such as a body attains by virtue of its motion; and potential, which is the energy conserved. It is generally believed that energy can be neither created nor destroyed; that a definite amount exists, which does not diminish even though its form may be changed. Heat is the energy of the universe emanating from the sun.

English Language, an Anglo-Saxon language to the development of which Norman French, Scandinavian, Dutch, Greek, Latin, and Celtic elements have contributed. The result is a strong, expressive, composite language now spoken by all people of English descent, by many non-English subjects in the various dependencies of the British Empire, and by numerous others throughout the world.

Engraving, the art of cutting or otherwise forming pictures or designs on wood, stone, or metal for reproduction by some method of printing. Wood-engraving was the earliest, dating from the 15th century. Later, with engraving on steel and copper plates, came the mezzotint, lithograph, stipple, aquatint, etc. With the development of photography and an increased knowledge of the use of acids, many readier methods of engraving were adopted, such as "process" engraving, etc.

Enlistment, the act of volunteering for military or naval service. The term of enlistment in the Armed Forces of the United States varies among the services and is subject to change by legislative action.

Ensign, the lowest rank of commissioned officer in the United States Navy. The title was formerly applied also to commissioned officers of the lowest rank in infantry regiments.

Ensilage, a method of storing and preserving fodder, vegetables, etc. either in silos or in pits dug in the ground from which air or light have been excluded.

Entomology, the study of insects. The three main groups of insects are the *Ametabola,* which are wingless and undergo no metamorphosis; the *Hemimetabola,* which experience metamorphosis in three very similar stages; and the *Holometabola,* which go through the same metamorphosis, each stage being markedly different from the other.

Envelopes, as wrappers for enclosing letters, were not in general use in the United States until after the introduction of the postal system in the 19th century. They were known in France, however, as early as the 17th century.

Envoy, a special diplomatic agent delegated to represent a government or to perform a special service, such as the negotiation of a treaty.

Eocent, a geological term applied to the lower division of Tertiary strata, in which have been found fossils indicating the beginnings of existing species.

Epic, a heroic narrative poem dealing with mythological, legendary, or historical events and including supernatural features; the most famous examples are Homer's *Iliad and Odyssey,* Vergil's *Aeneid,* Ariosto's *Orlando Furioso,* Tasso's *Jerusalem Delivered,* and Milton's *Paradise Lost.*

Epidemiology, the science of epidemics, an important branch of medical study.

Epigram, a term used originally to mean an inscription engraved on a monument; afterward it was applied to a concise verse which often contained a bitter and cutting remark; in later times it was applied to short, witty expressions in prose as well as in verse.

Epilogue, an address, in prose or verse, delivered at the end of a play; it was the usual accompaniment to the dramatic works of the 16th, 17th, and 18th centuries.

Epiphany, a church festival celebrated on January 6.

Epoch, a period of time of such importance that succeeding years and events are reckoned from it; an era is a succession of time but an epoch is a point of time. Among various epochs may be mentioned the birth of Christ, the Reformation, the French Revolution, and the European War. There are also the geological epochs and the epochs in art, science, and invention.

Equation of Time refers to the difference between clock-time and sundial time. This difference is greatest in November, when the sun is sixteen minutes behind. The only days on which there is perfect accord between the two times are April 15, June 15, August 31, and December 24.

Equator, the imaginary great circle of the earth, every point of which is 90 degrees from the earth's poles. From this circle, which divides the Northern from the Southern Hemisphere, the latitude of places north and south is reckoned.

Equinox, the time when the sun crosses the plane of the earth's equator, making day and night of equal length; this occurs about March 21st and September 22nd, the beginning of spring and autumn respectively.

Equity, a term used to express a modification of the severer form of law in order to insure equal justice. It is the principle of fairness applied to general rule. All American courts of record administer equity. All remedies dealing with property rights belong to courts of equity.

Era, a succession of time associated with some remarkable historical event or person. The Christian era, dating from the birth of Christ, was adopted for reckoning time in the 8th century. The Jewish era dates from 3700 B. C.; the Julian era from the alteration of the calendar by Julius Caesar, 45 B. C.; the Mohammedan era from A. D. 622.

Ermine, a small animal found in northern latitudes and abundant in Arctic America. Its coat becomes a lovely white in winter, only the tip of the tail remaining black. Its fur is highly prized.

Error, Writ of, a process issued when a palpable error has been made in court proceedings, authorizing review in a higher court.

Erse, the old Gaelic dialect of Ireland, and afterward of the Scottish lowlands.

Escalator, a mechanically moving staircase which carries people up or down. It is frequently used in subways, large stores, factories, etc.

Escapement, the contrivance by which the pressure of the wheels in a watch or other timepiece is accommodated to the vibratory action of the pendulum or balance-wheel, providing the regulating power which maintains an even impulse in spite of irregularities caused by friction or air resistance.

Escarpement, the face of an abrupt cliff or hill; also a portion of fortified ground whose edge is cut away almost vertically to prevent the enemy from occupying the position.

Escurial or Escorial, a magnificent palace built in the 16th century by Philip II of Spain at a village 26 miles northwest of Madrid. In addition to a palatial residence it has a fine Doric church, a valuable library, and the royal mausoleum, the burial place of the kings of Spain.

Escutcheon, a shield-shaped surface called a field, upon which a man's armorial bearings are represented. A woman's escutcheon is lozenge-shaped.

Eskimos, the people of the Arctic regions. They dwell in skin tents in summer and in closed huts in winter and live by hunting and fishing.

Eskimo Dog, a very hardy animal used by the inhabitants of the Arctic region as sledge-drawers. In appearance it suggests the Pomeranian or Spitz dog but is of a larger breed.

Esoteric, a term which had its origin in the teachings of Aristotle and later was applied to such doctrines as were intended only for privileged students or for those of the inner circle.

Esparto Grass, a plant growing in great abundance in Spain and North Africa, the pulp of which is used mainly for paper-making.

Esperanto, an artificial, international, universal language, invented by Dr. Zamenhoff of Warsaw and based on phonetic principles. Many Esperanto societies exist in various countries.

Esquire, in England, a distinctive title applied formerly to the otherwise untitled sons of nobles, knights, officers, officials, and professional men; now used occasionally, also in the United States as a courtesy title.

Essential Oils, oils derived from plants by distillation or expression. They are used in perfumery and, to some extent, in medicine.

Etching, a process of engraving, usually on copper, the design being drawn with a steel needle, and the lines being produced by the action of an acid or mordant. Etchings are of two kinds: line and texture.

Ether, a volatile liquid consisting of carbon, oxygen, and hydrogen. It is a valuable anesthetic and can be obtained by heating alcohol and sulphuric acid.

Ethics, the science of moral conduct and duty, a study founded on psychology and intended to determine what is right and what is wrong, according to circumstances, conditions, natural powers, and obligations. Aristotle, Plato, Kant, Bacon, Hobbes, Paley, Whewell, Hume, Bentham, Locke, Mill, and Herbert Spencer have all contributed to the development of ethics.

Ethnography and Ethnology, kindred sciences which treat of mankind, the former classifying and describing various racial differences, the latter inquiring into "the mental and physical differences of mankind and the organic laws upon which they depend." Both sciences are included in anthropology. Ethnologists divide mankind into three classes: Mongols, with sallow skins, straight black hair, flat faces, and receding foreheads; Negroes, with black or brown skins, flat noses, projecting jaws, and dark woolly hair; and Caucasians, with white skins, straight foreheads, prominent noses, and hair usually brown. These characteristics are not an absolute criterion, however; the Hindus, who have dark skins, belong to the Caucasian race. In general, the Mongols are native to Asia, America, and Polynesia; the Negroes to Africa; and the Caucasians to Europe and western Asia.

Etymology, that part of the science of philology which treats of the origin and derivation of words.

Eucalyptus, an Australian tree that grows to a great height. It exudes a valuable gum, has a fibrous bark, and its leaves yield an oil which is of great use in bronchial diseases.

Eugenics, the science of racial progress as affected by heredity and environment. One of the pioneers in eugenics was Sir Francis Galton.

Euphemism, substitution of a pleasant for an unpleasant, a refined for a vulgar word, in speech or writing.

Euphuism, an affected literary style, which originated in the 16th century and derived its name from Euphues, the chief character in John Lyly's *Anatomy of Wit*, a work of forced elegance and bombast.

Eurasian, a half-caste, one of whose parents is European and the other Asiatic.

Eurhythmics, the art of rhythmic movement or dancing accompanied by music; introduced by Emile Jaques-Dalcroze. It has been an aid in the appreciation of music and dancing.

Evaporation, the process by which a liquid or a solid is transformed into vapor through heat. It is a process that is going on continually, especially on the surface of seas and other bodies of water. The vapor, being lighter than the air, rises and forms clouds, which afterward return to earth again as rain. The same process is constantly going on over smaller surfaces, the rate of evaporation being dependent on the general atmospheric conditions.

Evolution, the theory, as laid down by Darwin, that all existing species, genera, and classes of animals and plants have descended from a few simple forms, the process being controlled by natural selection. In the words of Huxley evolution is "a general name for the history of the steps by which any living being has acquired the morphological and the physiological characters which distinguish it."

Excommunication, exclusion from the rights and privileges of the church. It is of two kinds—the greater, which means a total cutting off; and the lesser, which excludes only from participation in the Eucharist. In the Middle Ages greater excommunications were often launched against rulers and leaders.

Executions, the carrying out of the sentence of death. In the United States hanging and electrocution are the usual forms of execution; in some European countries the guillotine or headman's axe are used.

Executor, a person named by will to administer a testator's estate.

Exoteric, the opposite of esoteric, a term applied to doctrines openly expounded.

Exotics, plants of tropical origin not fully acclimatized.

Explosives, substances by the combustion of which gas is generated in such volume as to induce explosion. Gunpowder is the best-known example and has been in use for many centuries. Recent years have seen great developments in explosives, many powerful preparations having been introduced, including nitroglycerine, dynamite, guncotton, cordite, forcite, lyddite, etc.

Extract, an essence or tincture drawn from a substance by chemical processes; the agent of evaporation is water, alcohol, or ether, or a combination of these, according to the substance to be treated.

Extradition, the surrender of a criminal by one nation or state to another. Between nations the terms and conditions of extradition are usually established by treaty. As a rule, political offenders cannot be extradited. Between states of the United States extradition is required by the Constitution.

Extreme Unction, the final sacrament of the Roman Catholic and Orthodox churches, administered to a dying person after confession and absolution, and consisting of the anointing with holy oil.

Eye, the organ of vision, which in infusorians is very rudimentary but in the higher animals extremely complex and delicate. In man, it is a hollow ball of globular shape, consisting of an opaque membrane, the *Sclerotic*, forming the outer covering of the eyeball with the cornea in front, a horny, transparent structure; the *Choroid*, intersected with blood vessels and nerves, and including the iris and muscle of accommodation; and the *Retina*, the innermost coating of the eye-ball. The optic nerve transmits to the brain the visual images received on the light-sensitive retina. The eyeball is filled with fluid refractive media, and the crystalline lens in the axis of vision brings the rays of light to a focus on the retina. The movements of the eye are controlled by six muscles extending from the back of the orbit to the front of the eyeball. The lachrymal gland is at the outer corner of each eye and secretes the watery fluid called tears. Protective functions are performed by the eyelids, eyelashes, and eyebrows.

Eye-teeth, the two canine teeth of the upper jaw, next to the grinders.

Eyra, a small American cat, about the size of a domestic cat, but remarkable for the elongation of the body, which resembles that of a weasel, and for the uniform, reddish, unspotted coloration. It attacks domestic fowls. It inhabits the eastern region of South America, and northward to Texas.

F

Fables, fictitious narratives intended for some moral precept. They may be either in prose or in verse and may deal with personified animals and objects or with human beings. Aesop in ancient times, Hans Christian Andersen and the Brothers Grimm in recent times wrote fables. Mention must also be made of La Fontaine's and Krylov's fables.

Faction, a name given originally to the contending parties in ancient Roman chariot races. The contestants, who were distinguished by different-colored garments, and their supporters were drawn into fierce conflict outside the arena. In modern times the term is used generally to designate the various groups within a political party or organization.

Factory, an establishment in which a group of people produce manufactured articles through division of labor. The factory system differs from the domestic system in that the various operations are performed in a single establishment, with automatic machinery. The development of the factory system received its first great impetus with the invention of automatic spinners and looms. The first factory in the United States was established in 1790. Machinery called for a concentration of capital and required greater space than the home afforded. Now, industry could be concentrated in large centers only with adequate transportation facilities; and the railroads filled this need. The factory system brought about profound social changes. When work was done in the home, many workers lived in rural areas, but with the concentration of labor in factories the cities grew in population, and serious slum conditions resulted. The early factories employed men, women, and children at extremely inadequate wages, causing evils that have not yet been entirely corrected. Symptomatic of the conflict which evolved between the owners and the laborers is the strike.

Faïence, a kind of glazed, decorated earthenware invented in Faenza, Italy, about the end of the 13th century. Wedgwood ware is a notable example of modern faïence.

Fairies, imaginary creatures supposed to be invested with supernatural powers. At one time a general belief in them was prevalent, especially among the peasantry, and uncivilized races still cling to similar ideas. It was fancied that the world of fairyland was composed of good and evil spirits, variously embodied, always contending for supremacy, and exercising good and bad influence over mankind. If a person was lucky, it was the work of the good fairy; if unfortunate, the evil fairy was the cause. Early literature is filled with fairies, elves, fays, sylphs, sprites, gnomes, goblins, genii, and so forth. Among fairies of the domestic order were Robin Goodfellow; the Banshee, with its warning apparition; and the Brownie, who rendered nocturnal help in household affairs. In oriental literature, particularly in the *Arabian Nights*, the fairyland is a wonderfully vivid and active realm.

Fairs were established in medieval times as a means of bringing traders and customers together at stated periods and formed the chief means of distribution. The great English fairs of early times were those of Winchester and Stourbridge, to which came merchants and traders from all parts of England and even from foreign countries, everything being sold at these gatherings from precious stones to herrings, from costly silks to homely buckram. The typical American fair differs from the European fair in being not a market but an exhibition of the products of a region or an industry. State and county fairs are very common in the United States. They usually combine the exhibition of products with such entertainments as horse racing, baseball games, etc. Industrial fairs, held annually by trade associations, are sometimes very extensively advertised. They may be either national or regional in scope.

Fakirs, Mohammedan or Hindu mendicants who are held in great regard in India. There are two classes: those called dervishes, who are strict devotees of Islam; and those who are unattached to any religious order and are simply wandering beggars or so-called "holy men." Some of the more fanatical fakirs commit self-mutilation and pride themselves upon their wretchedness.

Falcon, a diurnal bird of prey of the family Falconidae, feeding on birds and small mammals, which it captures alive. It has a short bent bill, sharp-hooked claws, and a keen eye. The gerfalcon, which inhabits northern latitudes, is the most powerful of the falcon family. It was the peregrine falcon that was mostly used in the sport of falconry in medieval Europe. These birds were difficult to train, and the office of falconer was an honorable and important one. When the quarry was sighted, the bird was unhooded and set free, and after mounting high into the air would dart down swiftly and strike its prey. The heron was the usual victim.

Falsetto, in music, refers to the tones of a voice higher than the natural tones. It is more common in males than in females and is seldom used in choir singing except by male altos.

Fantail, a variety of domestic pigeon; also a genus of Australian birds of the family Muscicapidae.

Fantasia, a musical composition which does not conform to any regular style or series of movements.

Farce, comedy in its broadest form, admitting of free and exaggerated treatment calculated to arouse laughter.

Fasces, symbols of authority in ancient Rome, consisting of a bundle of rods with an axe-head protruding from them. They were carried by lictors before certain Rome magistrates on public occasions.

Fascism, a political movement instituted in Italy in 1918 under the auspices of Mussolini to counteract the influence of socialism. The movement was authoritarian and extremely nationalistic. Members of the Fascist party were distinguished by "black shirts" and had a special salute. The intensive nationalistic policy of the Fascists greatly affected Italian political life and had serious reverberations in other European states.

Fatalism, the theory that events are foreordained and are destined to happen. Fatalism is quite generally accepted in the Orient. Among prominent fatalists of the Occident were Napoleon I and Napoleon III.

Fathers of the Church, certain early writers who laid the foundations of Christian ritual and doctrine. Their writings include important controversial works, legal codes, histories, topographies, and speculations of a scientific and philosophical nature. The earliest were the Apostolic Fathers, some of whom were contemporary with the Apostles. The next were the Primitive Fathers of the 2nd and 3rd centuries, including Justin Martyr, Clement of Alexandria, and Tertullian. The later Fathers were of the 4th and 5th centuries, among them being Athanasius, Basil, John Chrysostom, and St. Augustine.

Fathom, a measure of depth, used in sea soundings. One fathom equals six feet.

Fats, oily substances forming the chief adipose tissue of animals. Among the solid neutral fats are spermaceti, lard, and suet, which are composed of carbon, hydrogen, and oxygen. Stearin, palmitin, and olein are common forms of fats. Fats are converted into soaps by combination with alkalies.

Fault, a geological term designating a breakage or displacement in the continuity of rock strata. The breakage amounts sometimes to thousands of feet, but ordinarily to not more than a few feet.

Feathers, the covering forming the plumage of birds. A feather comprises a main stem or shaft, a supplementary stem or after-shaft, and a series of lateral webs, each of which contains numerous small branches termed barbs. A bird has several classes of feathers, the two main divisions being the quill feathers of the wings and tail, and the clothing feathers of the body. Feathers are of every variety of color and of many shapes, the more beautiful of them being extensively utilized in millinery and for other adornments.

February, the second month of the year, comprising ordinarily 28 days, but in leap years 29 days. It is said that when February was first introduced into the Roman calendar by Numa about 713 B. C., it was made the last month of the year and preceded January; and that it was not until 450 B. C. that it was made the second month.

Fee, a payment for services; originally the granting of land in exchange for services under feudal law. The etymological meaning is property The term is used in property law; *e.g.*, to own property in fee-simple is to hold an estate which can be willed freely by the owner.

Felidae, the scientific name of all mammals of the order Carnivora which walk upon the tips of their toes, and embracing the members of the cat family.

Felony, in law, any crime of a more serious nature than a misdemeanor. In former times such an offense was punishable by death, but at present most felonies are punishable by prison sentences.

Feldspar, the name given to a group of minerals known also as silicates of aluminum. It is formed in granite and other rocks of ancient formation and is much used in the manufacture of porcelain. Moonstone is a variety of feldspar.

Felt, unwoven wool, hair, and fur matted together by moisture and heat, the fiber becoming so closely intertwined that a compact cloth surface is formed. Roofing felt is produced by mixing the material with coal-tar or asphalt.

Fenians, an Irish organization founded about 1855 with the object of establishing a republic in Ireland. The movement spread to the United States. In 1864 numerous arrests of Fenians were made in Dublin, and in the following year the American Fenians issued a manifesto that American officers were proceeding to Ireland to organize an army of 200,000 men. A considerable fund was raised in America, and in 1866 an attempt to invade Canada was made by a band of Fenians, but it was suppressed. The organization continued until about 1887, when dissensions within the brotherhood brought it to an end.

Ferret, a carnivorous animal of the polecat family, with a pointed head and long sinuous body; well adapted for following rabbits and game into their burrows and hiding places. It is a native of Spain and Africa.

Fetishism, the worshiping of a fetish, *i. e.*, any object supposed to be invested with supernatural powers, such as a serpent, a bear, a tooth, etc. It has been practiced more or less by all primitive races.

Feudal System, the social, political, and economic system that existed in Europe from about the 11th until almost the 19th century. It was a military and political organization based on land tenure, the land being divided into feuds or fiefs and held on condition that certain military duties were performed. In default of these performances the land reverted to the superior lord. Feudal tenures were abolished by statute in England in 1660, although after 1495 they had been practically inoperative. The system was abolished in Scotland in 1747, but not in France until the Revolution of 1789. The Japanese feudal system prevailed until 1871.

Fiasco, an Italian word signifying a flask but applied both in Italy and elsewhere to a complete breakdown or failure in any enterprise, especially in regard to musical or dramatic performances.

Fiber, a thread-like filament, such as that constituting the tissues of animals and plants.

Fibrin, a nitrogenous compound of the proteid class, present in animal and vegetable tissues. It is a white substance insoluble in water but dissolves in solutions of certain neutral salts. When extracted it tends to form fiber-like filaments.

Fibrolite, a white or light gray mineral of a fibrous structure; a sub-silicate of aluminum.

Field Marshal, the highest rank in many European armies. The grade does not exist in the United States Army.

Field Officer, a term applied to any military officer ranking between a captain and a general, namely major, lieutenant-colonel, and colonel.

Fife, a small flute with a compass of about two octaves.

Figaro, a well-known comic character in drama and opera, originated by Beaumarchais and adapted by Rossini and Mozart.

Figurehead, the figure, bust, or statue attached to a ship's prow immediately under the bowsprit. Since the advent of steamships this fashion has disappeared.

Filibuster, a name first given to pirates and buccaneers in the 17th century, who took possession of small islands or lonely coast lands and there maintained themselves apart from any governing authority. In later times the term was used to specify men taking part in expeditions whose object was to inaugurate or aid revolutions in foreign countries, in disregard of international law. The most notable expeditions of this kind in modern times were those of Narcisco Lopez against Cuba in 1850-51 and of William Walker against Nicaragua in 1855. In recent years the term filibuster has been applied to the obstructionist tactics of minorities in legislative bodies, when an orator speaks indefinitely merely to consume time.

Filigree, the name given to a kind of ornamental work done with threads of gold or silver, or with fine wire, and frequently attached to apparel or decorative objects. Work of this sort was done by the ancient Greeks, and in the Middle Ages it was greatly in vogue and reached a high standard of artistic beauty. This art is still practiced in certain parts of Italy.

Filter, an apparatus used for clarifying liquids and constructed in many different forms. The filtering substances that are used range from sand, charcoal, and sponges to porous stones and fabrics.

Filtration, the process of separating suspended solid matter from a liquid. This is effected by passing the liquid through a filtering medium such as cloth, paper, carbon, or sand; the suspended matter is retained by the medium. In the purification of water for domestic purposes, filter beds made up of fine and coarse sand, fine and coarse gravel, and large stones are used.

Fir, a cone-bearing tree with small evergreen needles. It is of considerable use as timber. There are four leading varieties—the silver fir, the Norway spruce, the larch, and the Lebanon cedar. All these firs attain a considerable height, and all yield turpentine or other resinous material.

Firefly, a small winged insect which is able to throw out a strong phosphorescent light in the dark. There are some remarkable specimens in tropical countries.

Fireship, the name given to a vessel stored with inflammable and explosive material and floated into the midst of an opposing fleet to cause destruction and alarm. They were used in naval warfare until the advent of steam.

Fixed Stars, those which are supposed to maintain a fixed position (relative to each other) in the firmament; thus they are contradistinguished from the planets, or wandering stars.

Flagellants, a fanatical sect which became prominent in the 13th century during a time of plague. They held processions, walked naked about the streets, and flogged themselves until they bled. They declared that sins could not be remitted without such practices. The sect continued down to the 16th century, in spite of their being declared heretics by Pope Clement VI. Flagellant sects existed in various parts of Mexico and South America until quite recent times.

Flageolet, a sweet-toned musical instrument, made of wood, with a mouthpiece, and a tube in which finger-holes and keys are placed. It is said to have been invented in 1581. There is also a double flageolet, having only one mouthpiece but producing double notes.

Flag Officer, a naval officer who enjoys the right of flying a flag at the masthead of his ship. He is of the rank of admiral, vice-admiral, or rear-admiral.

Flagship, the naval vessel that flies the admiral's flag and from which all orders proceed.

Flamingo, a bird of dominant bright-red or rose color, with long slender legs, long sinuous neck, and a huge curved bill. They are picturesque birds, live on worms and mollusks, and are found in Florida, South America, and Egypt.

Flat, a sign in musical notation (b) indicating that the note in front of which it appears is to be played or sung a semi-tone lower than its natural sound.

Flax, a textile fiber obtained from the flax plant, an annual largely cultivated for commercial purposes in Russia, Germany, Italy, Holland, the United States and Northern Ireland. After undergoing various preparatory processes, the flax is spun into yarn and woven into linen fabrics.

Flea, a genus of parasitic insects possessing a suctorial mouth, from which protrudes a lancet-shaped proboscis, with which it can pierce the skin of animals and draw blood. It is said that the *Pulex irritans* can leap 200 times its own length.

Flemings, a people of Flanders, whose ancestors in medieval times excelled in the textile arts.

Fleur-de-lis, the former national emblem of France ("the flower of the lily"). It was superseded by the tricolor in 1789, but it is still venerated by French monarchists.

Flint, a kind of silica of light gray color and excessive hardness, used in the formation of cutting implements in prehistoric times. Before the invention of matches, flint was used along with steel for striking fire.

Flint Implements, found in geological strata, often bear evidence of the condition and life of men in prehistoric ages. The implements include knives, clubs, arrowheads, scrapers, etc., and were used as weapons, tools, and possibly as surgical instruments and symbols in religious ceremonies. At the end of the Neolithic Period and at the beginning of the Bronze Age a people using a new type of stone axe appeared in Europe, advancing toward the southern and central regions. They are supposed by many to have been the ancestors of the present Europeans. Similar to prehistoric tools are the flint and obsidian implements of some modern savages, *e. g.* the Maori of New Zealand. Ritual weapons and sacrificial knives continued to be made of stone long after the introduction of metals.

Florist, one who cultivates, or is concerned with the cultivation and sale of, flowering plants.

Flour, the finely ground meal of any kind of grain, but more particularly applied to that of wheat.

Fluorine, a chemical element, found in combination with calcium as fluor spar and occurring in minute quantities in certain other minerals. First obtained by Moissan in 1886, it possesses extraordinary corrosive properties.

Fluor Spar, a compound of calcium and fluorine, occurring chiefly in silver, tin, lead, and cobalt ores. It is used in fusing refractory minerals.

Flute, a musical instrument of high pitch played by blowing across a mouth-piece and by manipulating finger-holes and keys. Familiar to the ancients, it was greatly improved by German and French instrument makers in the 17th and 18th centuries. It has a range of about three octaves.

Flux, any substance used in assisting the fusion of metals. The most common fluxes for large operations are limestone and fluor spar, for smaller purposes, alkalies, borax, etc. Black flux, obtained from cream of tartar, is used mainly for analytical operations, while white flux, obtained from carbonates of sodium and potassium in equal portions, is used for decomposing minerals.

Fly, the name for a large number of insects having a proboscis terminating in a sucker through which fluids can be drawn up. The best-known species are the common house-fly, the blue-bottle, and the blow-fly. In the larval form, flies are maggots and feed upon decaying substances, such as putrefying animal flesh. Flies are able to walk on ceilings or upright surfaces because they have suckers on the soles of their feet.

Fly-catcher, a family of birds, of which there are nearly 300 species. They feed on insects which they catch in the air.

Flying Dutchman, a mythical mariner who, in expiation for his crimes, was doomed ever to strive to reach harbor but never to succeed. Wagner composed an opera on this subject.

Flying Fish, frequently seen in southern waters, are capable of flying through the air for considerable distances without touching the water. They can be caught in nets while in flight.

Flying Fox, an animal of the bat family, but of much larger size, found chiefly in Africa and Asia. Its habits resemble those of the common bat, except that it feeds entirely on fruits.

Flying Lemur, a family of mammals (of which there are only two species) inhabiting Java, Sumatra, and Borneo. They live on insects, fruits, and birds and are provided with a parachute-like membrane, which covers them from neck to tail and is used in regulating their flight.

Flying Lizard, a kind of Asiatic lizard, possessing wing-like projections on each side of the body which enable it to make flying leaps through the air.

Flying Squirrel, an animal of which there are several species in Europe and in America. It possesses a parachute-like fold of skin by means of which it glides through the air. It is of the true squirrel type.

Focus, a word designating the point at which heat or light is concentrated by refraction or reflection.

Fog, the aqueous vapor or the minute globules of water in the atmosphere near the earth's surface, caused by the cooling of the air below the dew-point. According to Huxley, "a fog is a cloud resting on the earth; a cloud is a fog floating high in the air."

Foil, an extremely thin layer of rolled metal, such as gold, tin, or lead. Jewelers use it as a background to increase the color or luster of inferior precious stones. Any thin substance which is used for throwing other objects into relief is termed foil. Tin-foil, as its name implies, is tin rolled into thin sheets.

Foliation, a geological term applied to rocks whose component minerals are arranged in parallel layers as the result of strong metamorphic action.

Folio, a paper and printing term for paper which is folded only once, a half sheet constituting a leaf.

Folklore, a term denoting the beliefs, traditions, legends, customs, and superstitions of a nation or race.

Foot, a lineal measure of 12 inches, originally adopted from the average length of the human foot. In prosody the foot, which is the unit of the line or verse, consists of a number of syllables. By dividing a verse into feet, the more or less regular succession of stressed and unstressed syllables becomes apparent.

Force, a term in physics, signifying an influence or exertion which, when made to act upon a body, tends to move it if at rest, or to stop its progress if it be already in motion. Gravity, traction, and repulsive energy are all physical forces.

Foreign Legion, a name applied to the *régiments étrangers* in the French army, which consist chiefly of men of foreign nationality.

Forestry, the science that comprises the principles under which forests are managed with a view to their continued use and the preservation of their effects on mankind. In a narrower sense, it is the art of utilizing, reproducing, and improving in productive efficiency natural forests, or of establishing and maintaining new forests. Forests are valuable as a source of lumber, timber products (such as telephone poles and railroad ties), numerous by-products (such as turpentine and tannin), and the materials for a number of manufactured products, including paper and rayon. They play a vital part in the preservation of soil, in the regulation of stream-flow, and in the prevention of erosion and floods. Forests are the natural home of many of the game birds and animals, and provide important recreational opportunities for the people. The effect of forest cover on climate has been determined only recently. It was long known that forests furnished valuable shading and windbreaking qualities. Now it is also known that the tendency of a forest cover is to reduce the extremes of temperature. Forests tend to keep the air within them, and to some extent the air above them, more humid and, according to some scientists, to induce precipitation of moisture-bearing currents passing over them. By acting as a windbreak and adding moisture to winds, they reduce the evaporation from the soil and lessen frosts. The forestry problem has long been dealt with by European nations. In Germany intensive forest management has been practiced for many years. France has made outstanding contributions in reclamation projects in some of its mountainous areas and in the vicinity of the Bay of Biscay. The results of uncontrolled forest exploitation in past centuries are evident in Spain and China where forest growth, once abundant, has largely disappeared.

Forgery, the fraudulent imitation of another's signature or writing with intent to do injury or to deceive. Forgery is a felony in every state of the United States.

Formic Acid, an acid obtained from a colorless fluid secreted by ants and other insects as well as plants. It is a strong irritant. It is obtained artificially from oxalic acid.

Formula, a prescribed or special form of words in which anything is stated or declared.

Forte, a musical term signifying "loud," and represented by the letter "f"; the letters "ff" (fortissimo) mean "very loud."

Forum, in ancient Rome, a public meeting place, market, or exchange. Forums were used for commercial purposes, religious observances, and political speeches. Forums like those of Rome were built in the provincial cities of the empire and thus contributed to that fundamental similarity which even today can be observed in all the European cities which had their origin in the days of the Roman Empire.

Fossils, petrified substances of organic origin found in the various strata of the earth's crust. They are of both animal and vegetable origin and have been a means of obtaining knowledge of prehistoric periods.

Fox, a carnivorous animal of the vulpine family, found in considerable numbers in most parts of the world. The red fox of North America and the common fox of Europe are burrowing animals of nocturnal habits, living upon birds, rabbits, and domestic poultry. The fur of platinum and silver foxes is of great value. Notable species are the Arctic fox and the red fox of North America.

Franchise, the enjoyment of civil rights, more particularly, the right to vote. Originally the word meant exemption from feudal burdens; as such exemptions became the rule rather than the exception, the word changed its meaning.

Frankincense, an incense used in certain religious services and obtained from olibanum, an Eastern shrub. Another kind, a resinous exudation derived from firs and pines, is used in pharmacy.

Freehold, a legal term signifying an estate held either in fee simple or for life.

Freemasonry, a secret organization, having lodges for social enjoyment and mutual assistance. Masonic secret societies exist in many countries, but there is no international organization. Freemasonry dates back to medieval times, if not to a more remote period. The movement was established in America in 1733, and has numbered among its members George Washington and many other distinguished Americans. In the United States the Anti-Masons, a political party which opposed Masonry, had a brief career. The Order of the Eastern Star is a secret sisterhood to which only Freemasons and certain women relatives may belong; it is not a Masonic order.

Fresco, a painting executed upon plaster walls or ceilings, extensively used for churches and public buildings in former times. The work is done with prepared pigments.

Friars, members of certain mendicant orders of the Roman Catholic Church. The four chief orders are the Franciscans or Gray Friars, the Dominicans or Black Friars, the Carmelites or White Friars, and the Augustinians (Austin Friars).

Friday, the 6th day of the week, named after Frigga, the wife of Odin. It is the Mohammedan sabbath and is a general fast day of the Roman Catholic Church. According to popular superstition Friday is an unlucky day.

Frigate, a small, swift war-vessel, generally with two decks, and carrying a number of guns, usually from 30 to 60. It was the cruiser of navies of sailing-ship days.

Fringillidae, a family of birds of the order Passeres, including finches, sparrows, linnets, grosbeaks, weaver-birds, etc.

Frog, an amphibian which breathes through gills during the earlier (tadpole) period of its existence, and through lungs later. It remains three months in the tadpole stage. The frog hibernates in winter at the bottom of ponds, lakes, etc.

Fugue, a kind of polyphonal musical composition of a contrapuntal form, in which a theme is enunciated, followed by one or more countersubjects, and then the whole interwoven with varying elaborations. Fugues are of several kinds, named in relation to the character of the theme, as diatonic, chromatic, doric, etc. Bach was perhaps the greatest of fugue composers; Handel was also highly effective in fugue writing.

Fuller's Earth, a special kind of clay, possessing highly absorbent qualities and used from ancient times in the "fulling," that is, the cleansing and felting, of cloth.

Fur, the hairy protective coating of numerous animals, especially of those in the colder regions, utilized by mankind for winter clothing. The fur most highly prized is probably the sable, the best coming from Siberia. The sable is a small animal (about 18 inches long) wearing a lustrous coat of amber-brown hair. To avoid spoiling the fur, hunters catch the sable in traps or by throwing nets over its hole. There are numerous other animals—the lynx, the beaver, the fox, the squirrel, the seal, and the bear—which contribute to our stock of furs. The northwest portion of the American continent is prolific in fur-bearing animals, and there the Hudson Bay Company, founded in 1670, has carried on a most profitable enterprise in pelt capture. The founder of the Astor fortune was a fur trader in Oregon. London, New York, St. Louis, Leipzig, and Nijni Novgorod are the chief fur marts of the world, the fairs at the two last-named places being very important.

Fusel Oil, a resultant of alcohol, being the residue left after the separation of ordinary alcohol from the raw spirit by fermentation. It has a strong odor and a fiery taste, and its consumption is injurious to the brain.

Fusible Plug, a safety-plug placed in the metal plate of a steam-boiler. When a dangerously high temperature is attained, the plug melts and allows the contents of the boiler to escape.

Fustian, the name given at various times to different kinds of textile fabrics. Originally the term was applied to linen and cotton; later to wool; and in recent times, to a twilled cotton material with a nap surface.

Fustic, a kind of dyewood yielding various shades of yellow according to the mordants used. The tree grows in India, tropical America, and the West Indies.

G

Gabardine, in medieval Europe, a loose outer garment which in some countries was the prescribed clothing of the Jews. In modern times the word is applied to a twilled cloth of cotton woof and woolen warp, used in raincoats and light overcoats.

Gable, the triangular end of a building, between cornice and apex. The end wall of a sloping-roofed house is called the gable-end; and a gable-window is a window situated in the gable or constructed in gable form.

Gaelic, relating to the Gaels and their language, a term now applied only to the Celtic people inhabiting the Highlands of Scotland, but formerly also to the Celts of Ireland and the Isle of Man.

Galena, sulphide of lead—one of the commonest of minerals. One variety carries silver.

Gall, a vegetable growth, the result of an egg-deposit on leaves or bark by certain insects. Galls on oaks are called oak-apples. They are nearly spherical in form, inodorous, bitter, and from blue to deep olive and black in color. They yield an acid useful for dyeing, tanning, and other commercial purposes.

Galleon, the name given to the old three-decked Spanish treasure vessels employed in conveying precious minerals from the American colonies to Spain.

Galley, an oar-propelled boat, used by the ancient Greeks and Romans for transport purposes and manned by slaves. Boats of a similar class were used by the French down to the middle of the 18th century; they were manned by convicts.

Gallic Acid, obtained from gall nuts, sumach, tea, coffee, and the seeds of the mango, is used in the manufacture of inks and as an astringent in medicine. It is odorless, has a bitter taste, and is mostly of a pale yellow color.

Gallows, a wooden structure consisting of two posts surmounted by a cross-beam, used for hanging criminals. Sometimes it takes the form of a single projecting beam, which serves to carry the rope.

Galvanism, the branch of electricity which deals with electric currents produced by chemical action; it is named after its discoverer, Aloysius Galvani.

Galvanized Iron, iron coated with zinc or other substances.

Game Laws, laws relating to the killing of certain wild animals pursued for sport, and called game. Formerly in Great Britain certain qualifications of rank or property were required of those who killed game, but in 1831 gaming laws were modified to permit anyone to hunt, if licensed. In Canada and the United States the chief restrictions are in regard to killing wild animals during the breeding season. In the United States the game laws are designed to preserve wild life from ruthless slaughter. The Federal government is considered to have ownership of migratory birds; the states, of other game and fish. Land owners have no property rights in transitory game on their lands. They may, however, fish and hunt there to the exclusion of other hunters, whose intrusion is considered trespassing. Essentially the laws proclaim "open" and "closed" seasons, state permitted methods of trapping, limit the number of the kill, and require the purchase of a license.

Game, Preservation of. The threatened extinction of many kinds of wild game in the United States led to the establishment of government preserves as well as of many private parks where these animals can be cared for. Of the former, the national parks of the Yosemite and the Yellowstone are well maintained, such large game as buffalo, elk, and moose being especially protected. Yellowstone National Park was established in 1872 and has 2,142,720 acres; Yosemite National Park, established in 1890, has 719,622 acres. Of private parks for this purpose, the first to be established in the United States was that of Judge J. D. Caton at Ottawa, Ill., in 1860, where many varieties of game animals were brought together. In 1889 Austin Corbin enclosed the large preserve known as Blue Mountain Forest, which is situated near Newport, N. H. and covers about 27,000 acres. Numerous states have their own game preserves, such as New York's Adirondack State Park, covering 2,030 square miles. In 1914 George Vanderbilt bequeathed most of his estate at Biltmore, N. C., to the government. Attention has also been given to bird preservation by federal and state authority, as well as by private individuals.

Games and Sports, amusement or recreation, of either physical or mental nature, usually involving a contest, the goal of which is often honor or satisfaction rather than a more tangible objective. As to the reasons why men indulge in sports or games, psychologists differ. Some speak of the play instinct, others recognize at least that the tendency to play is inherent in all the higher animals. Some believe that play is as important as sleep as a means of relaxation; others consider it an outlet for surplus energy. Regardless of the propelling force, all of the higher animals indulge in it. Kittens and puppies spit and growl at imaginary enemies, and small children spend most of their waking hours in play. From very early times, games and sports have had a part in social intercourse. The famed Olympic games of ancient Greece, the chariot races and gladiatorial contests of the Romans, the jousts and tournaments of medieval times, and the present-day prevalence of athletics and amusements of all kinds are indications of the importance of games and sports in man's existence.

Gannet, the name of a genus of birds of the pelican family. Gannets are found in large numbers on the islands of the North Atlantic.

Gargantua, the hero of Rabelais' satire, a giant with an immense capacity for eating and drinking.

Gargoyle, a projecting spout for carrying off water from the roof gutter of a building. Gargoyles are found only on old structures, modern waterpipe systems having rendered them unnecessary. In Gothic architecture they were turned to decorative account and made to take various grotesque forms—grinning goblins, hideous monsters, dragons, etc.

Garlic, a bulbous plant of the onion family, possessing a very strong odor. It is used in salad dressings, sausages, etc.

Garnet, a precious stone, varying in color, but usually red. The finest garnets are blood-red and transparent.

Garnishee, to serve warning upon a person to hold moneys or property in his possession belonging to the defendant in a suit for recovery of debt or damages.

Garrison, a body of troops stationed in a fortified place; also a fort, manned with troops, guns, etc.

Gas, in chemistry, a substance possessing the quality of perfect fluid elasticity and presenting under constant pressure a uniform rate of expansion, and when reaching its maximum density behaving as a vapor. Of the 92 chemical elements, those which are gases at ordinary temperatures are: Hydrogen, oxygen, nitrogen, chlorine, fluorine, and the so-called rare gases, neon, argon, krypton, xenon, and helium. There are, however, many other compound gases. All gases have the property of diffusion so that, if two containers with two different gases in them are joined, in a short time the gases will mingle until there is a uniformity of composition in both vessels.

Gasoline Engine, an internal-combustion engine in which the fuel, usually gasoline or light oil, is atomized and exploded, the explosion pushing a piston down to do useful work. In the ordinary internal-combustion engine spark plugs enter the combustion chambers and ignite the fuel. Although such engines are sometimes air-cooled, as in the case of the radial airplane engine, most automobile engines are cooled by water passed through jackets surrounding the cylinders.

Ordinary gasoline engines are of the four-cycle type, *i.e.*, four strokes of a piston are required for a single operation. The comparison between firing a cannon and operating a four-cycle gas engine is often used to make the operations more understandable. First, the downstroke of the piston of an engine draws a mixture of fuel and air into the compression chamber. This is the intake stroke and corresponds to loading the cannon. Second, the upward stroke of the piston compresses the mixture of fuel and air. This is the compression stroke and corresponds to ramming the charge in the cannon. The spark now ignites the mixture in the cylinder just as a match ignites the cannon. The third stroke of the piston is the power stroke which moves the piston downward just as the cannon moves the ball outward. It is on this stroke that the work of turning the crankshaft is done. The final stroke clears the chamber of burned gases. This is the exhaust stroke and corresponds to the clearing of the cannon barrel by the ramrod. The four-cycle engine was invented by N. A. Otto of Cologne, Germany.

Gauchos, Argentine cattlemen, noted for their skill in the saddle, and for their lasso throwing.

Gauge, a standard dimension or measurement, applied to various articles and structures. Thus, the standard railway gauge is 4 feet 8½ inches in the United States, Great Britain, Canada, France, Germany, Austria, Holland, Egypt, Belgium, Denmark, Italy, Hungary, Sweden, Switzerland, and Turkey. In India, Ceylon, and Spain the gauge is 5 feet 6 inches. Narrow-gauge railways are in use on very steep inclines in various countries. Other gauges were established for building, gun-boring, etc.

Gauls, the inhabitants of ancient Gaul, who dwelt in what is now France, Belgium, and parts of the Netherlands, Switzerland, and Germany.

Gauze, a thin, transparent material, plain or figured, made of silk combined with cotton, linen, or hemp. There are also gauzes of flannel, lace, ribbon, and wire.

Gazelle, an animal of the antelope family, of small and delicate shape, with large eyes and short cylindrical horns. It is fawn-colored, native to North Africa, and easily domesticated.

Geissler Tubes, used for producing light by means of an electric discharge through rarefied gases. The tube is sealed, and the electric spark is transmitted through platinum connections at each end.

Gelatine, a transparent, tasteless, organic substance obtained by boiling animal membranes, bones, and tendons in water. It is of various kinds, according to the substances used in making it. Isinglass, the purest form, is made from air-bladders and other membranes of fish; the coarser kind, glue, is made from hoofs, skins, hides, etc. The constituents of gelatine are carbon, hydrogen, oxygen, and nitrogen. It is of great utility and is applied to a large number of purposes, from the making of food jellies to preparations for photography.

Gemini, one of the signs of the zodiac, lying east of Taurus and containing numerous stars, only two of which—Castor, the upper and brighter one, and Pollux, the lower one—are visible to the naked eye. The stars are named after the twin divinities, Castor and Pollux.

Gems, precious stones cut and polished and worn as jewelry.

Gender, one of the classes into which words are divided by grammarians. In English nouns and pronouns are classified as to gender, which may be masculine (male), feminine (female), and neuter (no sex). The French language has only masculine and feminine genders, rendering gender classification difficult and complicated. In modern Persian there is no gender distinction.

Genealogy, the study of family descent, treating of ancestors and their descendants in various branches in the natural order of succession.

General, the highest grade of commissioned officer in the United States Army. Ranking below full general are lieutenant-general, major-general, and brigadier-general.

Genesis, the first book of the Bible, which carries the scriptural narrative from the Creation to the death of Joseph.

Geneva Convention, the document signed at a conference of representatives of the leading nations in 1864, whereby the neutrality of ambulances, hospitals, sanitary officers, chaplains, and others engaged in succoring the sick and wounded was guaranteed. All persons employed in such service are required to wear a Geneva cross—a red cross on a white background—as a badge of office. The organization of the Red Cross dates from the Geneva Convention.

Genre, a term used to describe a style of painting which deals with subjects of homely life; in France the word is applied also to other kinds of painting, such as *genre du paysage* ("landscape painting"), *genre historique* ("historical painting"), etc.

Gens, a term derived from Latin designating any particular group, the members of which have a common ancestor. The modern word clan most nearly corresponds to *gens*.

Gentian Root, the dried root of the *Gentiana lutea*, used in pharmacy as a tonic. The plant bears clusters of blue flowers. The most valuable species commercially are those of central and southern Europe.

Gentile, a term used in the Scriptures to designate any person not a Jew.

Genus, a term used in biology to designate a group, or class of species.

Geodesy, the art of calculating the configuration and extent of the earth's surface and of determining exact geographical positions and directions, with variations of gravity, etc. Formerly the term geodesy was applied to land surveying in general.

Geognosy, the science of the origin and structure of the earth.

Geography, the science which describes the earth's surface, its physical peculiarities, and the distribution of the various animals and plants upon it. It is usual to divide the subject into two main branches: physical geography, which deals with the composition of the earth's surface; and political geography, which deals with the peoples and governments of the earth.

Geology, the science which deals with the development and the structure of the earth and with the evidences of ancient forms of life. The various geological periods are the Primary or Palaeozoic, the Secondary or Mesozoic, the Tertiary or Cainozoic, and the Post-tertiary.

Geometrical Progression, a term used to indicate numbers which increase or decrease at an equal ratio, as 3, 9, 27; or 27, 9, 3.

German Silver, an alloy of copper, zinc, and nickel, used in the manufacture of tableware.

Germ Theory, the biological doctrine which holds that living matter cannot be generated from non-living matter but must spring from germs, or seeds. In medicine it maintains that zymotic diseases are due to the presence of bacterial germs.

Gestation, the carrying of young during pregnancy. The period varies considerably with different mammals. In the case of elephants, the period is 21 months; camels, 12 months; cats, 8 weeks; horses, 48 weeks; dogs, 9 weeks; and pigs, 16 weeks.

Gethsemane, a garden at the foot of the Mount of Olives, to which Jesus went shortly before his crucifixion.

Geysers, hot springs of volcanic origin and action, remarkable for the fact that they spout huge streams of boiling water. The geysers of Iceland number over a hundred, the principal one having an opening 70 feet in diameter and discharging a column of water to a height of 200 feet. There are large and famous geysers also in Yellowstone National Park and in New Zealand.

Ghetto, the name given to the Jewish quarter in a city or town. The word was applied originally to such quarters in Italy.

Gibbon, the name of a long-armed tail-less ape, inhabiting the East Indian Archipelago. It can move very rapidly among the trees of the forest.

Ginger, a condiment obtained from the root of a reed-like perennial plant which grows in tropical countries. There are two varieties, black ginger and gray ginger.

Gingham, a kind of cotton fabric, plain, dyed, or figured, which received its name from being manufactured originally in Guingamp, Brittany.

Giraffe, the tallest of existing animals, attaining a height of from 18 to 20 feet. Its sloping back and elongated neck seem to be the evolutionary result of an animal that feeds on the branches of trees. It is a native of Africa, is of a light fawn color marked with darker spots, and has a prehensile tongue.

Girl Scouts, an organization founded in the United States in 1912 by Mrs. Juliette Low. It is patterned after the Girl Guides of Great Britain, and its organization and rules are similar to those of the Boy Scouts. As a national, incorporated, non-sectarian movement, its purpose is to promote a contented, wholesome life among American girls through activities in small, self-governing groups. Girl Scouts range in age from seven through high school age and are Brownie Scouts, Intermediate Girl Scouts, or Senior Girl Scouts. They are organized in patrols of 8, led by a member elected from the group. Two or more patrols, usually 4, make up a troop, headed by a captain. Girl Scout training includes instruction and examination in cooking, home nursing, sewing, child-care, self-help, and resourcefulness. The governing body, known as the national executive board, is located in New York.

Girondists, one of the prominent parties of the early period of the French Revolution. They were moderates, and until 1792 were a strong party. Their first leaders come from the department of Gironde, hence their name. With the beginning of the Reign of Terror their influence came to an end and Robespierre and his party overthrew them.

Glacial Epoch, the period when a large part of North America and Europe was covered with a perennial sheet of ice. Geological evidence of the extent of glaciation during the epoch is found in the many fossil remains which have been discovered, in the Tertiary formation, of animals such as exist today only in arctic regions. The topography of many temperate parts of the United States and Canada also proves that these regions were once covered by great glaciers.

Glaciers, huge masses of ice and snow which form in arctic countries and high mountain ranges and are gradually impelled by their own force down the mountain sides until they reach a point where the temperature causes them to melt and run off in streams. Some of the glaciers of the Himalayas are forty miles long. The Muir in Alaska is of enormous magnitude; the glacier of Justeldals Brae in Norway is the largest in Europe.

Glands, secretory organs whereby certain natural fluids, such as urine, milk, bile, saliva, sweat, tears, etc., are drawn from or distributed into the body. Glands of internal secretion pour their products into the blood stream and are important parts of the body mechanism. Glands are composed of numberless minute secreting cells, arranged in simple or compound vesicles.

Glass, a more or less transparent substance obtained from the fusion of a combination of silica with various bases. There are numerous kinds of glass, but they group themselves under one or other of the following classifications:—flint glass or crystal, whose components are potash, silica, and oxide of lead; window glass, made from soda, lime, and silica; Bohemian glass, containing potash, lime, and silica; and bottle glass, composed of soda, lime, alumina, silica, and oxide of iron. Glass was made by the Phoenicians, and was known in ancient Egypt. The Egyptians introduced it into Rome. In the Middle Ages Venice was famed for its glass manufactures, but after the 17th century Bohemia acquired pre-eminence in the industry. Window glass was not used until about the 7th century.

Glee, a musical composition for three or more voices without accompaniment. It is an essentially English type of composition and was much in vogue during the 18th and the first half of the 19th century.

Globigerina, an oceanic unicellular animalcule with a perforated shell, which occurs in certain parts of the Atlantic in such vast numbers as to form a bed of chalk ooze with its empty shells. The English chalk cliffs are survivals of prehistoric beds of globigerina ooze.

Glucose is the name given to a group of sugars produced from cane sugar, dextrine, starch, cellulose, etc., by the action of reagents. It also occurs in many plants, fruits, and honey. For brewing purposes glucose is prepared by the conversion of starch into sugar by sulphuric acid.

Glue, a gelatinous substance obtained by boiling and chemically treating hides, hoofs, etc.

Gluten, the insoluble nitrogenous element in flour or wheat and other grains. It is a proteid substance and is a mixture of gluten casein, gluten fibrin, mucin, and gliadin.

Glycerine, a tri-hydric alcohol which occurs in natural fats combined with fatty acids, and is obtained by decomposing those substances with alkalies or by superheated steam. It is colorless and sweet, and is put to a variety of commercial uses, being widely utilized for medicaments, for lubricating purposes, and in the manufacture of nitro-glycerine.

Gnomes, dwarf supernatural beings, popularly supposed to exercise protective powers over mines and minerals.

Gnu, an animal of the antelope family, combining the characteristics of the buffalo in its head and horns, the ass in its neck and mane, and the horse in its long and bushy tail. There are two species, the common and the brindled, and they are about the size of an ass. They abound in Africa and congregate in herds.

Goats, horned ruminant quadrupeds, indigenous to the Eastern Hemisphere, but now domesticated in all parts of the world. Though allied to the sheep, they are much hardier and more active animals. The male has a tuft of hair under the chin. Many species, including those of Cashmere and Angora, are valuable for their hair, which is used for fine textile fabrics. The milk of the goat is nutritive and medicinal; goat-skins are converted into soft and pliable leathers.

God, the term by which the concept of a supreme being is expressed. The idea of God varies with different religions and has changed frequently during the development of mankind. Originally applied to the members of the ancient pantheons, the long association of the term with the central figure in the great monotheistic religions—Christianity, Mohammedanism, and Judaism—has caused God to be defined generally in accordance with the tenets of those creeds. Among philosophers the idea of God sometimes differs markedly from the orthodox religious concepts. By most theists God is regarded as an infinite being, the author and ruler of the universe, although many theists would not express their belief in anthropomorphic terms. On the other hand, the school of agnosticism refuses, in the absence of definite proof, either to affirm or deny His existence. Deists believe in an impersonal God, while atheists deny the existence of God.

Gold, one of the precious metals, found in many parts of the world. We have evidence of its use from the days of the Phoenicians. Because it has always been a universal medium of exchange, it has been to man the strongest of all allurements. The most remarkable discovery of gold occurred in California in 1848. The next in importance was the discovery of the Australian gold fields in 1851. Among the more recently developed gold fields are those of Colorado, the Klondike, and South Africa. The largest gold nugget was found in Australia. It weighed more than 184 lbs. and was worth when melted about $50,000.

Goldbeater's Skin is the outside membrane of the large intestine of the ox, specially prepared and used by goldbeaters for placing between the leaves of gold while they beat them. This membrane is of great tenacity, and is beaten to such extreme thinness that it is used on cuts and bruises.

Golden Rose, the Pope's rose of wrought gold blessed and sent from time to time to the church or community his Holiness selects to honor.

Gondola, the type of boat common on the canals of Venice, propelled with one oar by a gondolier who stands at the stern, his passengers being accommodated in a covered space in the center.

Gorilla, the largest of the anthropoid apes, found in the forests of equatorial Africa, and at maturity standing from 4 to 5 feet high.

Gospels, those portions of the New Testament which deal with the life, death, resurrection, and teachings of Christ. They are the books of Matthew, Mark, Luke, and John; the first three are called the *synoptic gospels* because of their general unity of narrative. That of John is of somewhat wider scope and gives in addition to the story of the Passion, an account of the ministry in Judea. Numerous other versions of the life of Christ have been prepared but they are regarded as apocryphal.

Goths, a Teutonic people whose descent on Central Europe from the Baltic and conquest of the greater part of the Continent occurred in the 4th and 5th centuries. Under the leadership of Alaric, and known as the Visigoths, they conquered both Greece and Rome in 410, but by the 8th century had been merged in the Spanish race.

Gram, the unit of weight in the metric system, or one one-thousandth part of the weight of a certain piece of platinum called the "kilogramme des archives," preserved at Sèvres, near Paris. It is equal to 15.432 grains Troy.

Gramophone, an apparatus on the disk principle for recording and reproducing vocal sounds, invented by E. Berliner. It was at one time the most popular of the talking machines.

Grampus, a cetacean of the dolphin family, frequent in temperate waters, and at maturity over 20 feet long.

Graphite, or **Plumbago,** commonly called blacklead, is a form of carbon occurring in foliated masses in limestone, granite, etc. It is soft, will make black marks on paper or other plain surfaces, and is used for lead pencils. The best graphite comes from Siberia.

Graphophone, a disk sound-recording and reproducing machine, different in construction from the phonograph, but producing results of a similar kind.

Graphotype, a type of block used in printing, the drawings for which are made on a chalk surface with a silicious ink. The soft parts are brushed away after the surface is dry, and a block is made from what remains in relief.

Grass-Cloth, a fabric made from China grass, the fiber of certain plants of the nettle order.

Grasses form the general verdurous covering or herbage of the fields, and include a wide variety of plants. Ordinarily the term is applied to pasturage plants on which cattle and other animals feed, but in its broader application it includes the various cereal plants, such as wheat, barley, oats, rice, etc.

Grasshopper, an insect whose third or hind pair of legs are so constructed as to enable it to progress by leaps. There are many species, most of which are of the locust order. The male grasshopper makes a shrill sound as he leaps. The most familiar American grasshopper is the red-legged one, common to the East.

Gravitation, the natural attraction of bodies to to the center of the earth or to other bodies; the principle was first formulated by Sir Isaac Newton.

Grease, animal fat in a soft condition, used for lubricating purposes and as an unguent. Also semi-solid mineral lubricants.

Great War, or World War I as it has been called since World War II, began with an Austrian ultimatum to Serbia protesting the assassination of Archduke Ferdinand of Austria at Sarajevo and demanding a large indemnity under conditions which it was impossible to accept, thus making it virtually a declaration of war. This involved the Russian Government, which was bound by promises to protect the interest of Serbia. In the meanwhile tension between France and Germany had become acute, and German troops occupied Belgium in August in defiance of the Treaty guaranteeing the neutrality of Belgium, signed by France, England, and Prussia in 1830. War was declared on Germany by Great Britain on Aug. 4, 1914. The war involved Italy, Rumania, Japan and ultimately the United States as allies of Great Britain and France, while Turkey and Bulgaria participated on the German-Austrian side. The war areas included eastern France, Poland, Transylvania, the Balkans and northern Italy. Other complications resulted in fighting in Mesopotamia, Syria, Africa and on the high seas, the chief naval theater being the North Sea. The decisive engagements include: the Battles of the Marne (1914), which checked the advance of German troops on Paris; Neuve Chapelle, Ypres in the British offensive of 1915; German offensive, Verdun, 1916; naval battle of Jutland, May, 1916; the Franco-British offensives on the Somme, in 1916, and Vimy Ridge, Passchendaele Ridge, etc., 1917; German offensive on Western front, March, 1918; Rheims, Amiens, Cambrai, etc. A treaty was concluded between Germany and Russia in 1917 at Brest-Litovsk. Mutiny in the navy and the breaking down of the morale of the German army, the exhaustion of the working masses and their political leaders culminated in a revolution and induced Germany to sign an armistice on Nov. 11, 1918.

Greek Church, those churches in accord with the Greek patriarchal see of Constantinople and not subject to the authority of the Pope. In 1054, when Pope Leo IX excommunicated the Patriarch, the churches comprised in the Greek, Greco-Roman, Russian, and certain Oriental groups remained faithful to the patriarchal cause. Although the Orthodox church has no formal organization, many of these groups now recognize the authority of the Patriarch of Constantinople. The Greek Church accepts the doctrine of transubstantiation, believes in the intercession of the Virgin and saints, and the power of priestly absolution; but rejects purgatory, Papal supremacy, and allows its priests to marry. It has more than 144,000,000 adherents, nearly two-thirds being Russians.

Gregorian Song, a name applied to the ritual music established by Pope Gregory I. Gregorian music requires a more rigid harmony than can be given in the modern system, and is peculiarly appropriate for church use.

Grenade, an explosive shell thrown by hand, or from a specially-constructed rifle. The first grenades were made of wood, glass, gun-metal, bronze, etc., and were in use in the 17th century. Modern grenades are of spherical shape and are usually cased in cast iron.

Greyhound, one of the oldest known varieties of dog, bred for the chase, and of great fleetness. It is used in the popular sport of coursing and for dog-racing. Among its sub-varieties are the Scotch deerhound, the Irish boar-hound, and the Russian wolf-hound.

Griffin, an imaginary monster, half eagle, half lion; it is familiar in heraldry, legend, and architectural decoration.

Grindstone, a wheel of sandstone, employed in smoothing surfaces and grinding and sharpening tools; it may be worked by treadle or machinery. The millstones used for grinding corn are also called grindstones.

Grotto, a natural or artificial cave. The most famous are those of Capri and Antiparos. The latter is covered with stalactite formations of singular picturesqueness.

Gruyère, a type of cheese invented in the small town of that name in the canton of Freiburg, Switzerland, but now made in other parts of Switzerland and in France. It is of a pale yellow color, and contains air passages and bubbles which give it a honeycombed appearance.

Guano, the excrement of sea-birds, found in the largest quantities on the rocky islands off the western coasts of South America. It has been used as a fertilizer for more than 700 years. Beds of guano of from 50 to 60 feet in thickness are not uncommon. Fish guano and bat guano from caves in South America and the Bahamas are also used as fertilizers.

Guardian, one who has the care of the person or property of another.

Guelphs, the name of a powerful German family of the Middle Ages, for a long time in conflict with the Ghibellines. The Guelphs were founders of the royal houses of Brunswick and Hanover. The present royal family of England, formerly known as the Guelphs, assumed the name of Windsor during the World War.

Guilds, associations for fostering and protecting various trades. They were organized in Europe during the early Middle Ages, and from the 12th to the 16th centuries exercised great influence and enjoyed many privileges. There were trade guilds and craftsmen's guilds, and in all large cities and towns there was a guildhall. Their successes in the Middle Ages led to many monopolistic abuses, and in the end it became necessary to free commerce from their restrictive power. In some European countries they still exist, but only as ceremonial organizations.

Guillotine, an instrument of execution used in France and several other European countries. It consists of an oblique-edged knife, fixed between two grooved posts, and which being heavily weighted, falls forcibly on the neck of the victim, severing head from body. The machine, which is a modification of a beheading machine used in various countries in the Middle Ages, was named after Doctor Guillotine, on whose motion in the French National Assembly of 1789, such a method of execution was adopted. Dr. Guillotine was not the actual inventor of the machine nor did he, himself, as is popularly supposed, suffer death by its agency.

Guinea Pig, a small animal of the cavy order, a native of South America, of various colors and very prolific. It is often kept as a pet, but does not display much intelligence. How it got its popular name is a mystery, since it did not come from Guinea, nor is it a pig.

Guitar, a six-stringed musical instrument of the lute order. Spain seems to have been its country of origin, and it is still popular there, in Italy and in France. It is sometimes used by vaudeville entertainers for playing accompaniments.

Gull, a web-footed sea bird of numerous species, inhabiting the sea coasts of all parts of the world. They are mostly of a soft grayish-white plumage, and are voracious feeders, living on fish, eggs, small birds, worms, etc.

Gulliver, the hero of Swift's satire, *Gulliver's Travels*, who, in Lilliput and Brobdingnag, passed through a series of adventures which were so contrived as to reflect the humors, follies, and shortcomings of Swift's day.

Gums, glutinous compounds obtained from vegetable sources, soluble in cold or hot water but not in alcohol. There are innumerable varieties. Gum Arabic is exuded from a species of acacia grown in Senegal, the Sudan, Arabia, India and other countries, and is a valuable commercial product, used in dyeing, ink-making, as a mucilage, and in medicine. Rubber is an elastic gum. Gums are also made from starch, potatoes, wheat, etc., from seeds, bark, roots, and weeds. Many so-called gums are resins.

Guncotton, a powerful explosive formed by subjecting a prepared cotton to the prolonged action of a mixture of three parts sulphuric acid and one part nitric acid. When ignited, it merely burns; a detonator such as fulminate of mercury is necessary to explode it.

Gunny, a coarse cloth made in India from jute and hemp, used chiefly for bags and sacking, though sometimes also for clothing by the very poor.

Gunpowder, the oldest of explosive mixtures. It is a compound of potassium nitrate, sulphur, and charcoal thoroughly mixed and reduced to fine powder. The proportion of the ingredients is varied according to the uses for which it is destined. In recent years a smokeless gunpowder has been employed, an oxidizing agent being used to prevent smoke.

Gutta Percha, the juice of an evergreen tree common in the Malay Peninsula. After being subjected to high temperatures it becomes pliant. It is used for covering electric wires, being a non-conductor; and in hose, golf balls, belting, and other flexible goods. When combined with the more elastic caoutchouc it is easily vulcanized.

Gymnasium, a term given by the Greeks to public buildings where young men trained for athletic contests; they later became educational and cultural centers as well. The term is now applied to a type of college-preparatory school in Germany (similar to an American junior college); and to enclosed places or buildings for athletic exercises, exhibitions, and contests.

Gymnastics, exercises for the express purpose of developing the body.

Gypsoplast, a cast taken in white lime or plaster of Paris.

Gypsum, a whitish mineral consisting of sulphate of calcium and two molecules of water. Some varieties are of a brown-red tint. Ground to a powder, it forms a fertilizer; heated to 400° F., it resolves itself into plaster of Paris. The finest gypsum is alabaster.

Gyroscope, an instrument consisting in its simplest form of a rapidly rotating flywheel, the axis of which is so mounted that it can turn freely in any direction. Its peculiar characteristic is that in apparent contradiction of the laws of gravitation it cannot be made to lose its balance. This is due to the tendency of the flywheel to maintain its plane of rotation, and to its resistance to any force tending to tip it out of that plane. The spinning top operates on the same principle of physics. The gyroscope was first put into practical application in 1774, being used to create an artificial horizon for seamen. In 1896 it was used by Obry to guide the self-propelled torpedo.

Another practical application of the gyroscopic principle was made by Elmer A. Sperry, an American engineer, who perfected the gyrocompass, which has been of great service to mariners. This compass obtains its directive force from the rotation of the earth, and always points to the true or geographic north. It is invaluable in iron and steel ships, where the deviation of the old magnetic compass caused considerable trouble. Sperry also achieved considerable success with auto-stabilizing devices for ships and airplanes. The tendency of a ship to roll causes the gyros to shift their position so as to counteract that tendency and keep the ship on relatively even keel. The Sperry airplane stabilizer utilizes a gyroscope whose spinning wheel is operated by current from a generator on the shaft of the engine; it works a pilot valve which operates the horizontal rudders against any tendency of the plane to tip about its horizontal axis, and another feature prevents the speed from falling below the critical point. The Sperry Gyropilot, weighing only 60 pounds, permits a plane to be piloted automatically once it is clear of the airport.

H

Habeas Corpus, the name of a writ ordering a person under restraint or imprisonment to be brought into court.

Habendum, the name applied to the special clause of a deed of conveyance which specifically sets forth the estate or interest which the grantee is "to have and to hold."

Haddock, a fish common in northern seas and averaging about 4 lbs. in weight. Smoked haddock is sold as "finnan haddie."

Hadji, a title given to any Mohammedan who has made the pilgrimage to Mecca and is therefore entitled to wear a green turban.

Hafiz, the name of a famous Persian poet, and also a title conferred upon anyone who has committed the whole of the Koran to memory.

Hagiographa, the holy writings of the Jewish Scriptures, comprising the Chronicles, the Psalms, Proverbs, Song of Solomon, Ecclesiastes, Job, Ruth, Lamentations, Esther, Daniel, Ezra, and Nehemiah.

Hagiology, the branch of literature devoted to the history of the saints and the telling of the stories and legends associated with their names.

Hail, frozen raindrops or hailstones, which are composed of ice and snow, and vary in shape according to the producing conditions, although they are usually conical. It is on record that hailstones weighing half a pound have occasionally fallen. Hail is often an accompaniment of a thunderstorm. Hailstorms do much damage to vines, fruits and other agricultural produce.

Hair, fine capillary covering on the skin of animals, in many instances covering the entire body, but in human beings having its chief development on the head. Human hair grows longest on the heads of women. Ordinarily, the structure of a hair comprises a root, a stem or shaft, and a point. The root, which is bulbous, is enclosed in a skin follicle, connected with which are sebaceous glands whose secretion imparts gloss to the hair. Hair bears a coloring pigment, black, brown, flaxen, or red, and when the supply of it begins to diminish, the hair loses its color and turns gray.

Halibut, one of the largest of the flat fishes, averaging when full grown from 4 to 6 feet in length, and highly esteemed for the table. Specimens of still larger size occasionally occur. It is widely distributed. Its two eyes are on the right side of the head.

Halo, a lustrous circle surrounding the sun or moon, and caused by the refraction of light by ice crystals in the higher atmosphere. Small halos are termed coronae. Solar halos are rainbow-hued; lunar halos are usually colorless.

Halogen, a general term applied to the four combinable nonmetallic elements, chlorine, bromine, iodine, and fluorine.

Hand, a measure of four inches, the average size of the palm; used in reckoning the height of horses.

Handicap, in horse racing or other contests, an equalizing of the chances of the contestants by putting extra weight on proved superior horses or men, or by conceding privileges, in shortened distances, or otherwise, to inferiors. The aim is to give all competitors an even chance.

Hanseatic League, a formidable trading confederation established in 1241 for purposes of mutual protection in carrying on international commerce. The Hanse towns numbered over one hundred when the League was at the height of its power. The League exercised great influence, concluding treaties and possessing almost supreme authority within its own limits. The League safeguarded the seas from pirates, the land from robbers, and coerced opposing governments. The Hanseatic League existed until the middle of the 17th century. Hamburg, Lubeck, and Bremen are today the only cities which, as free ports, still by commercial courtesy retain the name of Hanse towns.

Hara-kiri, the custom of suicide by compulsion, or "happy dispatch," still occasionally practiced in Japan. The condemned person gives himself the first cut, and if his courage then fails him the fatal blow is dealt by a friend.

Hare, the commonest member of the genus *Lepus*. Noted for having four upper front teeth, one pair behind the other, long ears, short tufted tail, and a cleft upper lip. It is a very swift animal, and intelligent in eluding pursuit.

Harem, the portion of old-fashioned Mohammedan houses set apart for the female members of the family, and forbidden ground to visitors. In India the harem is called the *Zenana*.

Harmonics, the science of musical sounds; the term is specially applied to the class of sounds which can be given on a musical instrument in addition to the primary sounds. These are produced by skilled manipulation, causing the instrument played upon to emit its overtones.

Harmonium, a keyed musical wind instrument, invented by Debain in 1840, the air being supplied from bellows operated by the feet and driven through metallic reeds. The old-fashioned "parlor-organ" is a kind of harmonium.

Harp, one of the most ancient of stringed instruments, in its simpler form much used in Gaelic lands, in early times. The modern harp is a greatly improved instrument, the present double-action harp being capable of producing music in any key. It forms a part of most large orchestras.

Harpoon, a kind of barb-headed spear used for attacking whales. These used to be thrown by hand, but the modern harpoon is fired from a gun.

Harp-seal, the ordinary Greenland seal, which has a dark harp-shaped marking on its back, hence its name. It is common from Newfoundland north toward the Arctic.

Harpsichord, the prototype of the piano. Its keyboard was from 4 to 6½ octaves, and the notes, which were thin, were produced by a plucking operation, not by striking as in the piano. The harpsichord is now a rare instrument.

Harpy Eagle, a native of South America, one of the most powerful birds of prey in existence. It is of gray plumage, and has a large crest. It attacks sheep, calves, and deer, and is very destructive.

Harrow, an agricultural implement for breaking up, pulverizing, and leveling the soil. Some harrows have curved or straight teeth; others consist of series of discs.

Hartebeest, a species of common African antelope, of a gray-brown color, with knotted horns bending backward and tapering to sharp points; it is gregarious, of large size, and capable of domestication. Its flesh is not unlike beef in flavor.

Harvest Moon, the full moon that occurs nearest to the autumn equinox, in September. It rises for several nights running about the same time, and yields an unusually brilliant series of moonlight nights.

Hashish, a narcotic drug prepared from the gum extracted from Indian hemp, used for smoking by the Arabs, and made into a beverage called *bhang* in India; it has much the same effect as opium.

Hatchways, places or openings in the center of a ship's decks, through which goods are lowered to or lifted from the hold.

Hawk, a diurnal bird of prey of many species; including buzzards, falcons, kites, ospreys, kestrels, etc. The name hawk is properly applied only to the smaller kinds, such as the goshawks and sparrow hawks, which swoop down on their prey from a height. Many species of hawks are common in the United States.

Heart, the organ for circulating blood in men and animals, dilating, contracting, and pulsating with the regular action of a force-pump. Its position in men is behind the breast bone, between the two lungs, and its beating is most apparent below the left nipple, between the fifth and sixth ribs. The male heart weighs 10 to 12 ounces, the female 8 to 10 ounces. Its average size is about 5 inches long, 3½ inches wide, and 3½ inches in greatest depth.

Heat, according to the modern definition, is not a material substance, but molecular energy. This molecular motion consists, in the case of a liquid, of the irregular movements of its molecules; in a solid the movements are oscillatory; and with gas the motions are rectilinear, with swift alterations of velocity and direction as the molecules approach each other. Cessation of motion results only at absolute zero. As to the transmission of heat, Lord Kelvin laid it down that "in the strictest modern scientific language, the word *heat* is used to denote something communicable from one body or piece of matter to another." The transmission of heat may be effected in three ways; by convection, by conduction or by radiation.

Heath, a hardy plant of the genus *Erica*, very widely distributed over uncultivated spaces of Europe and Africa.

Hebrews, Epistle to the, one of the books of the New Testament, thought by many critics to have been written by Origen. Its chief purpose was to proclaim Christianity as the continuation and fulfillment of the older Jewish faith.

Hedgehog, a common insectivorous animal covered with sharp spines which it can, when on its defense, project in every direction by rolling itself up into a ball. It is a hibernating animal.

Hegira, an Arab term signifying departure or flight, and used more particularly in reference to Mohammed's departure from Mecca for Medina, A.D. 622, from which date the Mohammedan era is reckoned.

Heliograph, an apparatus, used for sun-signaling, consisting of a movable mirror fixed on a tripod. The mirror flashes light reflections to a distant station according to a pre-arranged code, on the dot and dash system, forming an effective means of communication. Heliograph signaling can be carried on at very long distances—up to 50 miles in ordinary weather—without the aid of field glasses.

Heliometer, an instrument for measuring the angular distance between fixed stars, consisting of a telescope which has had its objective cut through the optical axis, admitting of both halves being conjointly utilized, one directed on one star while the other brings another into coincidence.

Heliostat, an instrument consisting of a mirror operated by clockwork which reflects the sun's rays in a fixed direction.

Heliotherapy, an ancient method of healing by the sun practiced by the Egyptians and the Greeks, as shown in various papyri and documents; it was rediscovered by medical men in the 19th century, and is now used mainly in the treatment of surgical tuberculosis, skin diseases and war wounds. Artificial sunlight is also used with the same object. Arc-lamps and mercury vapor lamps are installed in many hospitals and other institutions for treatments of this type.

Heliotrope, a favorite sweet-scented flowering plant in tropical and subtropical countries.

Heliotype, a method of printing from photograph negatives by the use of a chemically treated gelatine surface as from a lithograph stone.

Helium, a gaseous element discovered in 1895 by Sir William Ramsay in cleveite, uranite, and other kindred minerals associated with argon and nitrogen. It is found also in the gas given off by radium. Texas is a leading producer of helium.

Hell, in the tradition of most religions, a place of punishment. The three basic concepts of hell are: (1) a vague notion of a future life to be spent in misery, with little or no idea of moral retribution; (2) a place of torment for those who have offended the gods, but limited in duration; and (3) an important factor in the moral government of the universe, a place where evil deeds are rigorously punished. Hell, as the place of woe, is mentioned in the New Testament as Gehenna, from the Hebrew Gehinnom.

Helmet, a soldier's, athlete's, or miner's protective head covering. In medieval times helmets were usually of metal and varied in shape. Roman gladiators wore helmets that covered the face entirely; the helmets worn at tournaments in the 15th and 16th centuries were so closed in that the wearers could see only through the perforations of the visor. The stiff hats sometimes worn by soldiers, policemen, and firemen are called helmets.

Helvetii, an ancient Celtic race which inhabited the western part of modern Switzerland.

Hemisphere, half of the terrestrial or celestial globe. Taking the equator as the dividing line, the Northern Hemisphere is above that line and the Southern Hemisphere below it. In the geographical division of the earth into the Eastern and Western Hemispheres, the former consists of Europe, Asia, Africa, Australia, and their outlying islands; the latter includes North and South America.

Hemlock, a plant of the family Umbelliferae containing a strong alkaline poison. This alkaline substance is a powerful sedative when prepared as a medicine. According to Pliny, hemlock was the poison used by the Athenians in putting criminals to death.

Hemp, a plant of the nettle family, growing abundantly in tropical countries, where it is cultivated for the valuable fiber contained in its bark. This fiber, which is obtained by maceration, is tough and strong, and is used for rope-making and manufacturing coarse fabrics. It contains a resinous substance from which the hashish smoked by the Arabs is made. The seed yields a valuable oil; it is also used as bird food.

Henna, an Egyptian plant bearing small white flowers; Mohammed's "chief of flowers." The leaves yield a dye with which it is the practice of Eastern women to stain their nails, eyelids, and hair.

Heptarchy, the name applied to the seven kingdoms into which England was divided after the Anglo-Saxon invasion. The country was divided from 457 to 827, when Egbert became king of all England.

Herald, in the Middle Ages, an officer of state empowered to make formal proclamations and deliver messages. The herald was also charged with the recording of armorial bearings.

Heraldry, the art of genealogy and armorial bearings, was a medieval invention. "Heraldry," says Stubbs, "became a handmaid of chivalry, and the marshaling of badges, crests, coat-armor, pennons, helmets, and other devices of distinction, grew into an important branch of knowledge." The *shield* or *escutcheon* is the ground upon which armorial signs are traced, the color of the shield being called the *tincture*, the signs recorded the *charges*. There are seven *tinctures: or, argent* (silver), *gules* (red), *azure* (blue), *vert* (green), *purpure* (purple), and *sable* (black).

The *charges* are classed as "Honorable" and "Subordinate" ordinaries, comprising lines and geometrical forms; and "Common" ordinaries, which latter include all representations of natural objects. There is also a system of external signs, such as crowns, coronets, miters, helmets, mantlings, wreaths, and crests.

Herbarium, a systematically classified collection of plants.

Herbivora, animals, especially mammals, which subsist upon grass, herbs, or other plants.

Herbs, all plants with succulent, non-wood producing stems, whose leaves or flowers, and sometimes roots, die on the approach of winter.

Heredity, the transmission of physical or mental characteristics from parent to offspring.

Hereford Cattle, a breed having a dark red body, with a white face and breast, and sometimes a long line of white upon the back. They are hardy grazing animals, excellent beef cattle, but are not useful for dairying purposes.

Heretics, a term applied to those who adopt a religious belief opposed to the popular belief, or to that imposed for by the state.

Hermaphrodite, human beings, animals, or plants possessing both male and female generative characteristics. True hermaphrodites very rarely occur among animals.

Hermit, one who retires into seclusion for the purpose of religious contemplation or because of a desire to live apart from the world. Hermits were regarded with reverence in the Middle Ages and were free to wander about. Peter the Hermit instigated the first Crusade.

Hermit Crab, a kind of crab having a soft fleshy body, without shell protection. It possesses itself of the empty shell of some mollusk, into which it backs itself, and this usurped shell it carries about with it thenceforward, or until it has outgrown its dimensions, when it seeks a larger one.

Heron, a large wading bird with a long curved neck and pointed bill, a member of the family Ardeidae, of which there are many species. Egrets and bitterns are members of this family. Herons are to be met with in marsh lands and near rivers and lakes, where they feed on fish and frogs. They nest in trees in large numbers, these colonies being called heronries.

Herring, a sea fish common in northern seas. The fishing season proper lasts from May to October, the enormous shoals being followed as they move from place to place. The spawning season is about the end of August. One female herring will yield from 20,000 to 50,000 eggs.

Hexagon, a figure consisting of six sides and six angles, called a regular hexagon when all the sides and angles are equal.

Hexameter, a measure of verse consisting of six feet, the first four of which may be either spondees or dactyls, and while the fifth is normally a dactyl, the sixth must be a spondee.

Hexateuch, the title given to the first six books of the Old Testament, comprising the Book of Joshua in addition to the five books of the Pentateuch.

Hibernation, the dormant condition in which numerous mammals, reptiles, amphibians, insects, plants, etc. pass the winter. In the case of animals hibernation is a period of deep sleep, due more probably to the winter being the period when natural food is unobtainable than to cold. Before hibernation sets in, the animals fatten themselves up, but in spite of this preparation they usually lose considerable weight during their sleep. Animals of the torrid regions pass through an analogous period during the hot season, when the sources of food are dried up.

Hickory, an American tree of the walnut family, remarkable for its very hard, solid, heavy wood, and bearing an edible, four-lobed nut.

Hierarchy, a term applied to ecclesiastical or church government, involving a graded organization with a supreme head.

Hieroglyphics, the earliest form of pictured symbolic expression, supposed to have been invented by the ancient Egyptians. They are conventionalized drawings of animals, plants, signs, and objects, and in their later examples express, in abridged form, ideas and records from which significant historical information has been gleaned. The key to the Egyptian hieroglyphics was discovered more than a century ago, and most of the ancient writings have been deciphered. The Mexican and Central American picture writings are still largely unsolved.

Hinduism, the system of religious belief held by the Hindus, as distinguished from those of the Indian aborigines and the Mohammedan and Christian invaders. Hinduism is frequently called Brahmanism, but this name is more properly applied to Indian religious beliefs during the post-Vedic period. Hinduism embraces the mythological teachings of the sacred books of the Brahmans. Its great variety of traditions, beliefs, and rituals derives from a people differing in historical background and social status. The literary works, the *Upanishads* and the *Brahmanas*, illustrate the development of the Vedic religion into Brahmanism proper, which occurred between about 1000 and 500 B.C. From about 500 B.C. to A.D. 500, the use of Buddhism in the North and Jainism in the South threatened to supplant Brahmanism. Brahmanism persisted, however, but its strict, formal ritual and difficult teachings were greatly modified. The new conception of the legends and traditions was caused by the appearance of the great epics, the *Mahabharata* and the *Ramayana*, and the *Laws of Manu*. Eventually, the personal god, Brahma, became a supreme being, a universal spirit, the creative power; Vishnu became the preserver and Siva the destroyer. Brahma in modern India is too abstract to be grasped by the Indian masses, although Vishnu and Siva are still held in great reverence. The British rule in India and the advent of Western influence had an effect upon Hinduism. Child marriages became less common and the rigid taboo against the untouchables is slowly changing. Pilgrimages to the sacred cities of Puri, Benares, Allahabad, and the Ganges and Narbuda rivers are still rigidly observed.

Histology, that part of anatomical science which deals with those details of the tissue structure which can be investigated only with the aid of the microscope.

Historiography, the study and criticism of history as a branch of knowledge.

Hittites, an ancient race of northern Syria, referred to in the Old Testament.

Hobbies, subjects apart from daily business duties in which a person interests himself. Hobbies are of many forms, of which making collections is one. Many people earn their livelihoods by capitalizing on their hobbies. Some sports and avocations are loosely referred to as hobbies, such as yachting, flying, dramatics, art, music, and dancing. There are many other avocations, such as the construction of models, etc. Photography is a hobby occupying the attention of many. Some of the chief articles collected as hobbies are coins, stamps, books, canes, dolls, antique furniture, autographs, firearms and other weapons, crockery, pottery, glassware, relics, old shoes, cigar bands, gems, minerals, manuscripts, maps, laces, linens, china, porcelain, boxes, pitchers, and lamps.

Hobson's Choice, a term meaning the compulsory acceptance of the thing offered, is a proverbial phrase which had its origin in the method of renting horses practiced by an innkeeper named Hobson, of Cambridge, England, who compelled each customer to take the horse which stood nearest the stable door.

Hog, the common name of animals of the family Suidae, including the wild boar, pig, and sow. The wild boar, *Sus scrofa*, is the common ancestor. The skin of the hog is covered with bristles, the snout truncated, and each foot has four toes. Hogs are omnivorous feeders.

Holly, a hardy evergreen shrub. Its wood is white and hard, valued for carved work; its bark yields a gummy substance which can be converted into birdlime. Because of its bright red berries and dark green leaves it is used as a Christmas decoration.

Holograph, a letter, manuscript, or document written entirely in the hand of its author.

Holy Alliance, the league entered into after the battle of Waterloo by Russia, Austria, Prussia, and the other European powers except England, for the mutual protection of their dynasties and the prevention of any member of the Bonaparte family from occupying a European throne.

Holy Grail, the cup from which Christ drank at the Last Supper, supposed to have been preserved by Joseph of Arimathea. Many poets and romancers have made the "Quest of the Holy Grail" the subject of their imaginings. Tennyson made use of it in his *Idylls of the King*.

Holy Rood, an annual Roman Catholic festival, on September 14th, to celebrate the recovery by the Emperor Heraclius in 615 of a portion of the original Cross, after it had been lost for nearly 300 years and had fallen into the hands of the Persians.

Holy Water, water blessed by a priest and kept in small fonts at the entrance to Roman Catholic churches, used by worshipers and by priests in sprinkling.

Holy Week, or Passion Week, is the week preceding Easter Sunday, and includes the days of the Sufferings of Christ, ending on Good Friday.

Homeopathy, a medical system developed by the German physician, Hahnemann, early in the nineteenth century, and founded on the principle that "like cures like." The homeopathic theory is that diseased conditions are curable by the administration of such drugs as would, if the conditions were healthy, produce symptoms similar to the disease itself. Homeopathic medicines are given in infinitesimal doses with the idea that the minute subdivision of a drug adds to its power. Homeopathy has still many professors and adherents, but it can hardly be said to have realized the expectations of its earlier exponents.

Home Rule, the control of its own affairs by a people or state; in British politics, the phrase long meant self-government for Ireland. The leading object of the Irish Home Rule party was the establishment of a native Parliament in Ireland to enact local and internal legislation, leaving the general government of the British Empire to an imperial Parliament. In 1893 a Home Rule bill was passed by the Commons but defeated by the Lords. In 1898, however, an act passed both houses of Parliament, providing for a system of local self-government in Ireland. It followed the main lines of the legislation adopted for England and Scotland, accompanied only by such variations as were necessary because of the special circumstances of Ireland.

In May, 1914, the royal assent was given to what was officially known as the "Government of Ireland Bill" and popularly as the "Home Rule Bill," which had passed the House of Commons in three successive sessions and had been twice rejected by the House of Lords. As this act was not accepted by Ulster, an amending bill was introduced in the House of Lords and passed in September, 1914, but another act was passed at the same time, suspending the operation of the Home Rule Bill until after the close of the war. It was repealed, and a new act was passed in 1920, establishing one parliament in northern Ireland and another in southern Ireland. This act went into effect in Northern Ireland but it was disregarded in the south of Ireland when the Irish Free State was established. Northern Ireland is still governed, as regards imperial affairs, by the English Parliament, but it has a Parliament of its own for local affairs.

Homicide (the killing of a human being) has three classifications: *justifiable*, as when the killing is an act of necessity, or performed in the execution of justice; *excusable*, when done in self-defense or by accident, as manslaughter; and *felonious*, when done of deliberate intent, as murder and suicide.

Honey, the sweet substance gathered by the honeybee and some other insects from flowers, and deposited by them in honeycombed cells as food storage. It is of a yellow-white color, and is composed largely of water, dextrose, and levulose. Honey ferments when exposed to the air.

Honeysucker, an Australian bird, of which there are many species, provided with a long curved bill and tufted tongue. It lives by sucking the nectar from flowers.

Honors of War, privileges sometimes conceded to a defeated force, as of marching out of a place surrendered, with colors flying and drums beating.

Hookah, or **Narghile**, an oriental pipe or apparatus for tobacco-smoking, the smoke being drawn through the water of a glass goblet by means of a long flexible tube.

Hop, a twining plant, cultivated for its female flowers, which are used for flavoring malt liquors. Hop vines are trained upon poles; in the autumn the flowers are picked by hand.

Horizon, the limit of vision, the line where sea and sky, or land and sky, apparently meet. This is termed the *sensible* or visible horizon. The astronomical horizon is a plane which, perpendicular to gravity at any point, divides the celestial sphere into two equal portions, upper and lower halves. There is also an artificial horizon, consisting of a surface of mercury or other fluid, whereby the altitude of any particular star can be reckoned. An ordinary person at a height of 5 feet can see for approximately 3 miles; at 20 feet, 6 miles; at 50 feet, 9½ miles; and at 1,000 feet, 42 miles.

Horn, a musical wind instrument, usually of brass and of varying size, shape, and musical power, ranging from the long coaching horn to the small hunting horn. The French horn is formed of a continuous twisted tube, and is furnished with a movable mouthpiece.

Hornbill, a large bird, remarkable for having an immense horned helmet growing over its beak. It inhabits tropical regions and feeds on fruits. When the female has laid her eggs in the hollow of a tree, the male bird stops up the entrance, and keeps her imprisoned until the hatching is completed and the young ones are ready to fly.

Hornblende, a hard common mineral, a silicate of calcium, magnesium, iron and aluminum, of a dark green color. It is a constituent of numerous rocks, including diorite, syenite, and hornblende schist.

Hornets, insects of the wasp family that live in communities, generally nesting in hollows of trees. The hornet's sting is very painful.

Hornpipe, an old English single-step dance, which used to be executed to the music of a hornpipe.

Horology, the science of measuring time, including the construction and management of clocks, watches, etc. Instruments of this kind are not known to have existed before the 12th century; until the introduction of the pendulum in the 17th century, clocks were ill-regulated and inaccurate. The time-recording mechanisms of the present day include (*a*) the *clock*, which shows the hours and minutes by hands, and strikes the hours, and sometimes quarters; (*b*) the *timepiece*, which is usually not a fixture and shows the time, but does not strike; (*c*) the *watch*, which is a pocket timekeeper; and (*d*) the *chronometer*, which indicates the minutest portions of time.

Horoscope, the pseudo-science of reading the signs of the planetary bodies, according to the methods of astrologers, at the date of a personal nativity, or other given date. In ancient times to many royal courts astrologers were attached whose "castings" and predictions had many believers.

Horse, a large, solid-hoofed quadruped, long domesticated, and employed as a beast of burden and for carrying a rider. How, when, or where its first domestication occurred is uncertain, but it is known to have taken place in prehistoric times. With one exception, the wild horses of the present day can be traced from domestic breeds which have broken from restraint, such as the wild horses of the South American pampas and of central Asia. The two leading types are the Arabian, whose strain is apparent in the race horse and other animals in which speed is the most pronounced characteristic, and the powerful Flemish horse which has contributed the elements of strength and endurance to the many breeds of draught horses.

Hospice, a place of refuge and rest for travelers and pilgrims. The most famous is that of the St. Bernard Pass, in Switzerland, where dogs are kept for the succor and help of belated wayfarers.

Hospitals. The earliest hospital is supposed to have been opened at Caesarea in the 4th century. In the 7th century the Hôtel Dieu was founded in Paris; in the 9th century there were 24 hospitals in Rome. Modern private hospitals are largely dependent on voluntary contributions and on paying patients. There are excellently equipped medical schools attached to some general hospitals, where expert research workers are engaged in the investigation of diseases.

Hottentots, an African race of herdsmen and hunters, numbering some 200,000 individuals.

Hounds, dogs that were originally bred and trained for hunting, such as the greyhound, foxhound, bloodhound, wolfhound, deerhound, beagle, harrier, etc., but are now often kept as domestic dogs. The greyhound, deerhound, and wolfhound hunt by sight, the others, with the bloodhound first in order, track by scent.

Hourglass, a glass instrument tapering in the middle to a narrow orifice, through which the flow of sand marks the passing of an hour of time. When the sand has run through from one end, the instrument can be reversed and made to count the hour in the opposite direction. The same kind of glass with smaller supplies of sand will indicate shorter periods, as an egg-glass which runs its course in three minutes, the time usually required to boil an egg.

Houseboat, a boat fitted up with living, sleeping, and cooking apartments, and serving for temporary occupation by families or pleasure parties in making river excursions. In Eastern countries, houseboats that are permanent habitations are common on the big rivers.

Hovas, the dominant tribe in Madagascar until the French took possession of the island in 1895.

Howdah, a railed, canopied seat fitted to the back of an elephant. The name is given also to a somewhat similar contrivance for the backs of camels.

Howitzer, an artillery piece having a shorter tube than a gun of the same caliber, a more curved trajectory, and a higher muzzle velocity.

Huguenots, the French Protestants of the 16th and 17th centuries. Under Francis I and later monarchs they were subjected to many persecutions, and at times were in active conflict with the Catholics. Ten thousand of them were put to death in the massacre of St. Bartholomew's Day, 1572. Henry of Navarre, by the Edict of Nantes in 1598, granted them religious freedom. In 1685 they were further persecuted when the Edict of Nantes was revoked by Louis XIV, hundreds of thousands leaving the country never to return. A large proportion of them took refuge in England and Germany, where they greatly helped in the development of many industries.

Humanism, originally a movement to combat the intellectual and spiritual dominance of the ecclesiastical and scholastic bodies which had controlled European thought during the Middle Ages. The traditional, formalized learning of medieval times was in the 15th century superseded by a direct approach to the ancient classics and a determination on the part of students to regard learning as a means of understanding man and his affairs rather than as a prescribed unchangeable body of accepted fact and theory. The term has lately been applied to European and American schools of thought founded on pragmatic conceptions of human values.

Humming Birds are so called because of the humming sound made by the vibration of their wings in flying. They are of radiant plumage, and in size they are among the smallest birds. There are from four to five hundred species, confined wholly to North and South America; they are most numerous in the tropical latitudes.

Hundred Days, the period between Napoleon's arrival in France after his escape from Elba and his final surrender after the battle of Waterloo.

Hundred Years' War, a term applied to the almost incessant contest between England and France, lasting from 1338 to 1453, including such famous battles as Crecy, Poitiers, and Agincourt, and engaging successively the English Kings Edward III, Henry V, and Henry VI.

Huns, a fierce people of unknown origin, who swept over eastern Europe in the 4th century and took possession of the country between the Volga and the Don; Attila was their most formidable leader. They defeated the Goths and forced the Romans to pay tribute. After their defeat at Chalons in 451, and the death of their leader in 453, they were soon driven back. It is doubtful whether any of the present races of eastern Europe are their direct descendants.

Hurricane, a tropical, cyclonic storm, common in the China seas and the East and West Indies.

Hussites, followers of John Huss, the Bohemian reformer, who was burned at the stake in 1415. After their leader's death the Hussites became a formidable body and took up arms on behalf of their faith. Their religion had a strong political tinge. They were subdued in 1434 and later were absorbed by other Protestant sects. In the United States, the teachings of Huss are now represented by the sects of the United Brethren.

Hyalograph, an instrument designed for tracing upon transparent surfaces.

Hybrid, an animal or plant produced by the union of two distinct species.

Hydrates, compounds formed by the combination of metallic oxides with water, or the union of water with salts. The most common hydrates are caustic soda, caustic potash, and slaked lime.

Hydraulics, the science of applied hydrodynamics, or water-machine engineering, including the design and use of pumps and marine engines.

Hydrocarbons, compounds of carbon and hydrogen, forming one of the principal groups of compounds and with their derivatives constituting the simplest compounds of organic chemistry. They are classed as gaseous, liquid, and solid, according to the proportions of hydrogen or carbon.

Hydrochloric Acid, a colorless gas, consisting of hydrogen and chlorine, and produced in considerable quantities as a by-product of soda-ash or salt-cake manufacture. Its solution forms the common hydrochloric or muriatic acid of commerce, which is largely utilized in dyeing, calico-printing, bleaching, and in the production of chlorine. Dilute hydrochloric acid is secreted by the stomach during digestion.

Hydrocyanic Acid, cyanide of hydrogen or prussic acid; very poisonous, and of the odor of bitter almonds. It was discovered by Scheele in 1782.

Hydrodynamics, the science of the application of the laws of dynamics to fluids, including both fluids in rest and fluids in motion.

Hydrofluoric Acid is obtained from a distillation of fluor spar with sulphuric acid, and is a compound of fluorine and hydrogen. Its action is highly corrosive, it is a valuable agent in etching on glass, and is a rapid decomposer of animal matter.

Hydrogen, a colorless element, the lightest of all substances, and the accepted standard unit for measurement of the specific gravity of gases. It is 14.4 times as light as air, and is found in a free state in volcanic regions and in the emanations of oil wells. It can be obtained by the action of metals on acids, and when burned in air combines with oxygen to form water.

Hydrography, the science of water measurement as applied to seas, rivers, lakes, currents, rocks, reefs, etc., and the basis of the art of navigation. It also treats of the contours of the ocean bed; the temperature, circulation, physical and chemical properties of sea water; the currents, tides, and waves; the composition and distribution of marine deposits; the aspects of biological oceanography, and the relations of man to the ocean.

Hydrometer, an instrument for measuring the specific gravity of water and fluids, used especially for ascertaining the strength of alcoholic liquors and solutions. It is usually in the form of a glass bulb, to the lower end of which a smaller bulb, containing mercury, is attached, which forces the instrument to sink into the liquid which it is to test. The larger bulb has a scale fixed to it and the indication on the scale of the sinking point shows the specific gravity. There are many types of hydrometers.

Hydropathy, the method of treating disease with water, by either bathing or drinking. Natural springs of special chemical and therapeutic properties, such as sulphur springs, have been used since prehistoric times for this purpose. It is probably one of the most ancient methods of cure.

Hydrophobia, rabies resulting usually from the bite of a mad dog; a contagious disease, the result of a specific poison, for which Pasteur's method of inoculation is the only antidote.

Hydrostatics, the science of the pressure and equilibrium of non-elastic liquids.

Hyena, a carnivorous quadruped of which there are three species: the striped, or laughing hyena, common to northern Africa, India, Syria, and Persia, and noted for the peculiar cry from which its name is derived; the brown hyena with long shaggy hair, a native of southern Africa; and the spotted hyena, also confined to Africa. They are scavengers of nocturnal habits.

Hygiene, the study of the preservation of bodily and mental health, both in the individual and in the community. The progress made in hygienic science during the last hundred years has led to many legislative enactments and preventive measures which have resulted in a great improvement in the general standard of public health.

Hygrometer, an instrument for measuring the moisture of the atmosphere. The hygrometer of Daniell is the best known, and consists of a bent glass tube with two bulbous ends, one of which is enclosed in a muslin covering while the other is of black glass with a thermometer and a quantity of ether inside. By dropping ether on the muslin bulb, a connecting evaporation is set up which enables the measurement to be taken.

Hyperbole, a rhetorical term implying extreme exaggeration for the sake of effect.

Hypnotism, the act of inducing by mesmeric influence a somnambulistic state of the body involving temporary loss of taste, touch, sight, and feeling. The operator controls the will of the hypnotic subject to a large extent; but the power of producing the hypnotic state, as well as the peculiar nervous condition necessary to its being induced, is not common. Hypnotism, however, has been surrounded by so much exaggeration and imposture that it is still far from being accurately defined or understood. There have been instances of surgical operations performed while patients have been hypnotized.

Hypotenuse, the name given in geometry to that side of a right-angled triangle which is opposite to or subtends the right angle.

Hypothesis, in the sciences, a principle tentatively set forth as an explanation of phenomena. When proved or verified it ranks as a theory.

I

Iambic Verse is characterized by alternate short and long syllables. It is the ordinary heroic measure when it rhymes in couplets; unrhymed, it is blank verse. Each line must consist of five feet, a foot having a short and a long syllable.

Ibis, an Egyptian bird usually found in lakes and swamps. It has white and black plumage and a long curved beak. One species is the sacred ibis of Egypt, which is held in great veneration by the people. There are 20 species.

Ice, water frozen to a solid condition; it is lighter than water in a liquid state. It is brittle and transparent, and has a specific gravity of nearly 0.92. Ordinarily ice is produced naturally in cold seasons, freezing beginning at 32 deg. F., but it is also obtained in enormous quantities by means of freezing machines designed for domestic, commercial and experimental purposes.

Iceboat, either a boat used for breaking a passage through ice, in which case it is usually steam-propelled; or a boat with masts and sails mounted on runners for sailing on the surface of the ice.

Ice-breakers, heavy bow-plated boats used for breaking up ice on navigable waters. On the Baltic and the St. Lawrence especially, they have the effect of considerably shortening the icebound period each winter.

Icefloe, a small ice-field or sheet of floating ice, which frequently freezes to other icefloes, imprisoning any ship enveloped.

Icelandic Literature, the largest body of Old Norse writings. They consist of metrical verse; the famous *Sagas*, which are narratives of discovery and warfare; and a few religious prose works which are among the oldest produced in northwestern Europe.

Ice Sheet, an extended glacier occupying large territories such as the Antarctic Continent or Greenland.

Ichthyology, the department of zoological science which concerns itself with the structure and variation of fishes, their habits and distribution.

Ichthyosaurus, a gigantic lizard of the Mesozoic age. The fossils are found mostly in the Lias formation. Some were not less than 30 feet in length, and are shown to have been amphibian.

Iconoclasts, originally an Eastern sect of the 8th and 9th centuries, whose object was to prevent the worship of, and to destroy, images used in religious rites. The term has been applied in modern times to all enemies of religion.

Idea, in Platonic philosophy, the archetype or pattern of which existent forms are imperfect copies. To Plato, ideas were the only basic realities. In most modern idealist philosophies ideas are acts of perception which thereby establish the reality of that which is perceived.

Idealism, the theory, according to Kant and other philosophers, that "objects are not there till they are thought." Idealism, however, has many aspects—the transcendental, as with Kant; the subjective, as with Fichte; and the absolute, as set forth by Hegel.

Idiom, expressions characteristic of a country, district, dialect or language, which sometimes give force or color to a phrase or sentence. The idioms of a language are its distinctive marks.

Idolatry, the worship of idols, images, inanimate objects, animals or symbols. Some kind of idolatry existed in all primitive communities; instances are numerous in the earliest records of mankind. In symbolic forms images have a considerable part in the rites of the Roman Catholic Church and other advanced religions.

Idols are images or effigies which are made objects of worship and are usually of wood or stone, but sometimes of ivory or more precious materials. They attain their symbolic significance after being put in the places destined to receive them, when they are made objects of veneration by some religious dedication.

Idyll, a poem or story of a simple or pastoral kind dealing with rural characters and events; sometimes used in a broader sense, notably in Tennyson's *Idylls of the King*, which are of a distinctly imaginative form.

Igneous Rocks are those which have been transformed by the action of great heat, or volcanic disturbance, and include two main groups, the volcanic or eruptive, and the plutonic or irruptive.

Iguana, a large South American lizard with a long tail, a scaly back and head, a thick fleshy tongue and a prominent dewlap in the throat. It averages from four to five feet in length, and lives mostly in trees. Its flesh is edible, somewhat resembling beef.

Iliad, the great epic poem of ancient Greece, thought by most modern scholars to have been written by Homer, though, according to some 19th-century critics, the work of many authors. The story is that of the siege of Troy, which had its origin in the attempt to recapture Helen who had been carried off from Sparta by Paris.

Imagination, the creative power or faculty which enables a person to picture to himself scenes, events, and persons of whom he may have heard or read.

Immigration, the entrance into a country of aliens with a view to settlement. The principal cause of immigration is desire for personal betterment, though famine, religious persecution, political unrest, and war are also important factors. The voluntary immigration of aliens into the United States has been a potent factor in increasing its population.

The United States statutes now prohibit the immigration of illiterates and provide simple but adequate tests of literacy. In 1882 the race-labor problem became so intense in California that Congress passed the Chinese Exclusion Act, which was designed to exclude Chinese coolies. In 1885, as a protection to American standards of living, organized labor sponsored the act excluding contract laborers. The Immigration Act of 1917 prohibited immigration from southwestern Asia. Conditions after World War I made a revision of U. S. immigration policy necessary. Legislation in 1924 restricted the number of immigrants from any country to 2 per cent of the number of their people living in the United States in 1890. Amendments to this law have since liberalized immigration, allowing for admission of certain Asiatics, displaced persons, and refugees.

Impact, in physics, the impingement of two bodies one against the other, a subject generally considered in relation to the resulting after-motion which comes within the field of kinetics. Direct impact is the collision of objects moving in the same direction; oblique impact is the collision of bodies moving in opposite directions.

Impeachment, the act of accusing or charging with a crime or misdemeanor; the arraignment, usually of a public officer, for maladministration or treason. The Constitution of the United States provides that the House of Representatives shall have the sole power of impeachment; and that the Senate shall have the sole power to try all impeachments. Section 4 of Article II provides that the President and Vice President and all civil officers of the United States shall be removed from office by impeachment upon conviction of treason, bribery, or other high crimes or misdemeanors.

The most noted case of impeachment in United States history was that of Andrew Johnson on March 4, 1868. The eleven articles charged the President with violation of the Tenure of Office Act, with violation of the Constitution, with conspiracy to prevent the execution of the Tenure of Office Act, with conduct and utterances tending "to bring the high office of President into contempt, ridicule, and disgrace," and with the public declaration in his speeches that the Thirty-ninth Congress was no constitutional legislature. The memorable trial lasted for nearly three months and the hottest of political passions were enlisted. Thirty-six votes were needed to convict. The Senate stood 35 for conviction to 19 for acquittal, impeachment thus failing by a single vote.

Impressionist, an artist or author who attempts in his work to convey by broad effects the impressions which a subject has stamped on his own imagination, apart from detail or form. The word is particularly applied to a group of late nineteenth-century French painters allied to the naturalists, who attempted to paint in terms of color, form, shadows and perspective.

Inca, the title borne by the ancient priest-kings of Peru.

Incandescent Light is produced in electric lamps by a thin metal filament which, when acted upon by the electric current, is raised to white heat; in gaslighting, incandescent illumination is obtained by a cone-like "mantle" made of inconsumable earths which is placed over the part where the flame plays.

Incarnation, in theology, designates the doctrine that the Divine Spirit, incarnated in human form in the person of Jesus Christ, has had actual existence on earth, subject to human limitation, yet without losing the Divine essence.

Incense, an aromatic resinous substance which, under combustion, gives off a pungent odor, and is used, mixed with fragrant perfumes, in the celebration of the Mass in Roman Catholic and certain other churches. Olibanum or frankincense is ordinarily the leading ingredient.

Incognito, the dropping of name, identity, or distinctive mark, so as to pass unknown.

Incubation, ordinarily the artificial hatching of eggs by means of an apparatus called an incubator; a term also applied to conditions of heating and feeding by which children prematurely born or exceptionally feeble are nurtured and developed.

Index Expurgatorius, an index, prepared under the authority of the Roman Catholic Church, of such books as may not be read by the faithful at all, and such as can be read only in part; that is, with what are considered objectionable passages expunged. The first Expurgatorial List was issued by Pope Paul IV in 1557; all later lists have been under direct papal authority.

India Ink, a pigment made from lampblack and gum or glue, originally prepared in China and Japan. It is used by artists for shading and lettering.

Indian File, marching forward in single file, as Indians progress through the woods.

Indictment, a formal document of accusation setting forth the criminal charge or charges upon which a person is to be tried before a proper tribunal. It represents the "finding" of the grand jury, and is framed on the "true bill" returned by that body.

Indigo, the substance obtained from certain plants of the order Indigofera, inhabitants of the tropical regions of Asia, Africa, and America, India being the chief producing country. The coloring matter is the result of the decomposition and fermentation of a glucoside contained in the plant. This is afterward dried and becomes the caked indigo of commerce. Many shades of indigo are formed by the admixture of other coloring substances. The discovery of Indigotin, obtained from coal tar, has in late years largely superseded the use of vegetable indigo in dyeing.

Individualism, a principle of government diametrically opposed to socialism and other collective forms and favoring freedom of action on the part of individuals without the interference of the state.

Indo-European, a term used to designate the Aryan family of languages, which includes the Indo-Aryan, Iranian, Celtic, Greek, Italic, Slavonic, and Teutonic subfamilies.

Induction, in logic, an inference in regard to an entire class of facts, based on actual demonstration as to individual facts comprised in the class. In physics it is a term applied to the action or effect produced by an electric or magnetic body upon a non-electric substance near to it but not in actual contact.

Induction Coil, a machine for producing electric currents by induction. It consists of a soft iron cylinder, or a mass of straight iron wires, around which is wound a primary coil of silk-covered copper wire, whose ends are attached to a galvanic cell, while around the primary coil, still another, the secondary coil, of finer copper wire and of considerably greater length, is coiled. One coil is carefully insulated from the other, and the different parts of the secondary coil are also insulated from each other. The current is generated in the secondary coil by induction every time the current starts or stops in the primary coil. A rapid series of alternating currents of a very high tension is thus set up.

Indulgence, a remission of penances or punishment for sins, formerly granted by the Pope in return for contributions in aid of religious purposes. The indiscriminate sale of indulgences by Tetzel and other papal agents in the 16th century was one of the grievances which led to the Reformation.

Industrial Revolution, a term usually applied to the social and economic changes which resulted in the modern industrial system. It is commonly used to refer to the latter part of the 18th century and the early part of the 19th century in English history. Many scholars have objected to the term, however, and have pointed out that the process was more gradual than the name indicates and that the changes in economic life between 1540 and 1640 were in many ways more profound than those of the 18th century. Whatever its exact time or characteristics, however, the Industrial Revolution apparently had its origin in the breakdown of feudal systems of manufacturing and in the tremendous expansion of English commerce that followed the great period of exploration. Extension of commerce and markets led to demands for more goods; as a result manufacturing methods were improved and new sources of power sought. Steam and water power were the first to be developed, and their use necessitated the centralization of labor and materials in factories. The increased industrial production which resulted led to even wider commerce and a demand for better transportation facilities. Roads, canals, and steam railroads were built to satisfy this need. The Industrial Revolution had important repercussions on agriculture also. It speeded up the enclosure movement and stimulated new and better methods of production to satisfy the needs of new city populations which grew up around the factories. The processes of the Industrial Revolution were repeated in other countries, although much later; it may be said to have begun in France in 1830, in Germany in 1850, and in the United States about 1860. As in England, the Industrial Revolution in these countries resulted in sweeping changes: the rise of a complex urban society; the development of the factory system; tremendous improvements in transportation and inter-communication; and a high degree of mechanization in agriculture.

Industrial Workers of the World, a revolutionary labor organization, started in 1904 by a group of labor leaders meeting in Chicago. It achieved prominence in the textile strikes at Lawrence, Mass. (1912), at Paterson, N. J. (1913), and again in 1917, when leaders of the organization instigated strikes in the western part of the United States. During World War I the I. W. W. was antimilitaristic and was accused of accepting German subsidies; many of its members were jailed. The I. W. W. stood for vertical industrial unions, all coordinated in "One Big Union," and advocated three methods of "direct attack," propaganda, the boycott, and the strike. After 1930 the membership of the I. W. W. rapidly declined, but the organization is important in the history of American labor.

Inertia, a property of matter, being the resistance of a body at rest to being moved; and of a moving body to any force operating to change its direction or speed.

Infallibility, the Roman Catholic doctrine that accords the Pope divine immunity from error when speaking *ex cathedra* on matters of faith and morals. It was first proclaimed as a dogma of the Church by the Vatican Council of 1870.

Infante, the title of any son but the eldest of the king of Spain or Portugal. *Infanta* was similarly the title of any daughter except the one who was expected to inherit the throne.

Infantry, the portion of an army which consists of foot soldiers equipped with small arms.

Inflection, in physics, the change or deviation experienced by light as it moves over the edges of an opaque body, causing the scattering of colored rays; in language, a word so modified as to indicate its relationship to the other words in the sentence of which it is a part.

Ink, a liquid pigment ordinarily made from an infusion of nut-galls, copperas and gum arabic. Sumac is substituted for nut-galls in inferior inks. An acid is sometimes added to prevent oxidation, and in blue-black inks a small quantity of an indigo solution is used for coloring. Copying ink contains glycerine or sugar, which keeps the ink moist. Lampblack is the leading ingredient in printer's ink. Marking ink is composed of a solution of nitrate of silver, gum, ammonia, and carbonate of soda. For red, blue and other colored inks, coloring solutions are used.

Innocents' Day, a festival day in Roman, Greek and Episcopal Churches in commemoration of the killing of the children of Bethlehem by Herod, December 28th.

Inquisition, or Congregation of the Holy Office, a Roman Catholic ecclesiastical court for dealing with charges of heresy, founded in the 13th century during the pontificate of Pope Innocent III. It was established in the various Catholic countries of Europe, obtaining semi-independence of the Papacy in Spain in the days of Ferdinand and Isabella, when Torquemada was Grand Inquisitor, or chief of the system of courts. In the 18th century its influence began to wane, and although the congregation of the Holy Office still exists at Rome, its jurisdiction is limited to the suppression of heretical literature.

Insectivora, animals which live almost exclusively on insects and worms; the term includes hedgehogs, moles, shrews, etc.

Insectivorous Plants, plants provided with a leaf or flower arrangement by which insects are attracted. A gummy secretion spreads over the surface, and when an insect becomes entangled the glandular hairs close over the victim rendering escape difficult; the plant then absorbs the captured insect by a process of digestion.

Insects, an extensive class of invertebrate creatures abounding in all parts of the world. Their bodies are usually segmented, and they have commonly four or more legs, in addition to a pair of antennae and a pair of mandibles. Flies of all kinds, fleas, bugs, butterflies, moths, bees, wasps, grasshoppers, crickets, beetles, lice, and thousands of other species make up this order.

Insolvency, the condition which marks a man's or a firm's inability to meet monetary obligations in full. When a person is in this condition, he can either call his creditors together and endeavor to come to some private arrangement with them, according to the nature of his assets, or he can institute bankruptcy proceedings, whereupon a court will administer the estate and distribute the assets for the benefit of the creditors.

Instinct, in psychology, usually used to describe an innate tendency, disposition or activating force arising from the vital needs of the organism and expressed in activity not based upon past experience of the individual.

Institute of France was formed in 1795 and after various modifications was organized on its present basis in 1832. Its five divisions are: French Language and Literature, Belles Lettres, Science, Fine Arts, Ethics and Politics. It is restricted to 40 members.

Insulation, material used as a non-conductor of electricity. Glass, shellac, ebonite, and gutta-percha are all non-conductors; wires are usually insulated by wrappings of cotton, silk, or rubber.

Insurrection, a rising against constituted authority by a body of persons aiming at the removal of a grievance or the upsetting of civil power. Less serious than a rebellion, it is more widespread than a mutiny and often develops into a revolt or revolution.

Interdict, a Roman Catholic ecclesiastical prohibition, directed either against a country, community or church, or against persons. When a parish is placed under an interdict no public church ceremonies may be held and the dead may not receive Christian burial.

Interest, in its commercial sense, payment made for the loan or use of money, and calculated according to a specified rate. Interest is either *simple* or *compound*. When simple interest is paid, the principal sum remains the same; in the case of compound interest, each year's interest is added to the principal, and succeeding interest calculations are on the increased amounts.

Interlude, any short stage piece, or brief musical composition, intended for performance between more important pieces. In one sense an interlude is an *instrumental* composition played between the acts of an opera or musical comedy.

Interval, in music, the difference in pitch between two sounds, it may be *melodic*, as when they are sounded successively, or *harmonic*, as when they are sounded together.

Invention of the Cross, a Roman Catholic festival, held on May 3rd each year to celebrate the finding of the Cross at Jerusalem by Heraclius in 615.

Invertebrata, the zoological term for animals without backbone or other internal bony framework.

Investiture, the ceremony of conferring honor, office, or possession.

Iodine, a substance formerly obtained exclusively from the extract of seaweed. After the salts have been removed by crystallization, there are left in solution iodide and bromide of sodium, potassium, and magnesium, and these heated with chemical agents yield iodine. Nearly all iodine now in use is derived from the purification of Chile saltpeter (sodium nitrate). Many combinations are effected with iodine, some of which are of considerable commercial value and of use in medicine.

Ionic Order, in architecture, one of the five classic orders, its leading characteristics being the volute of its capital, which has on each side distinctive curved or scrolled ends.

I O U, an informal written and signed acknowledgment of indebtedness, which, though not a promissory note, can be sued upon.

Iridescence, a glittering, rapidly changing glow of colors, showing different hues in different lights.

Glass, metals, and fabrics are rendered iridescent by chemical treatment.

Iridium, one of the heaviest of known metallic elements, found in alliance with platinum. It is silver-white in color, is of considerable commercial value as an alloy, and is in general use for the making of standard weights on account of its durability.

Iris, the typical genus of the botanical order Iridaceae, an order of herbs or under-shrubs of the Endogen family, with tuberous or fibrous roots and flag-like leaves. Many of the family have beautiful flowers.

Iron, an element extracted by smelting from hematite, magnetic iron, or spathic iron, coal or coke being now universally used in the smelting process. The kinds of iron produced are cast iron, wrought iron and steel. The total amount of pig iron produced throughout the world in 1938 amounted to about 79,300,000 long tons. About 64% of the total was produced by the United States, Germany, and Great Britain.

Iron Age, the period when primitive man made and used iron weapons and implements. It came after the Stone and the Bronze Ages.

Ironwood, the extremely hard and heavy timber of certain kinds of trees, native to the warmer regions of Asia and Africa, and mostly of the order Sapoteae.

Irony, a form of sarcastic speech or writing by which blame appears in the guise of praise and the real meaning is contradictory to the expression.

Iroquois, a confederacy of related tribes of North American Indians in what is now western New York. Originally called the Five Nations, it included the Seneca, Cayuga, Onandaga, Oneida, and Mohawk tribes. The Iroquois became the Six Nations in 1714, upon the admission of the Tuscarora.

Irrigation, a method of artificially providing water for the growth of vegetation on lands where the natural supply of water is deficient. It has made immense progress during the last fifty years, and has been the means of bringing into profitable cultivation in the western United States, India and Australia vast tracts of territory which had previously been arid wastes. The systems are various and are adapted to the special conditions of the land to be irrigated. Irrigated lands are often more productive than lands which receive the normal amount of moisture from the elements; the irrigation supply can be distributed and regulated exactly according to requirements.

Isinglass, a gelatinous substance manufactured from the air bladders of certain fish, the best kinds coming from Russia and Brazil. Some of the coarser sorts of isinglass are made from hides.

Islam, the Mohammedan religion; the word signifies devotion to God.

Isobaric Lines, the lines on maps which link together places of equal barometric pressure.

Isomerism, a chemical term indicating two compounds having the same formulae and the same molecular weight, but differing in chemical or physical properties. This arises from the difference in the arrangement of the atoms in the molecule.

Isothermal Lines, lines appearing on maps, showing the points on the earth's surface possessing an equal mean temperature.

Isthmian Games were held in alternate years by the ancient Greeks on the Isthmus of Corinth, in honor of Neptune, and were of the same class as the Olympian Games. Wreaths were the only prizes.

Ivory, the dentine substance of which the tusks of the elephant, hippopotamus, walrus, etc., are composed. The tusks of the African elephant sometimes weigh as much as 100 lbs., and reach a length of 8 or 9 feet.

Ivory Black, a species of bone black, made by the calcination of ivory scraps and turnings; it is used as a pigment in the manufacture of printer's ink, paint, etc.

Ivy, a climbing shrub, most varieties of which are evergreen. It furnishes a sudorific, and the berries also have emetic properties.

J

Jackal, a kind of wild dog or wolf, common in oriental countries, of nocturnal habits, a carrion feeder, and of strong odor. Jackals hunt in packs and make the night hideous with their discordant yells.

Jacobins, a French revolutionary club or party, formed in 1789. The name came from its habit of meeting at a Jacobin convent. It became a controlling force in the Revolution, especially in the movement which led to the Terror, Robespierre being its chief spokesman.

Jacobites, adherents of the Stuart cause after the abdication of James II. First James himself, then his son (the Old Pretender), and later his grandson (the Young Pretender) tried to organize rebellions in Scotland and Ireland, but after the defeat at Culloden in 1745 their cause was lost.

Jade, a hard transparent mineral found in China, America, and New Zealand, and used for making vases, bracelets, and other ornamental articles. There are many varieties, and there is evidence that the stone was in use in prehistoric times for weapons and utensils.

Jaggernaut, or **Juggernaut,** the name of the great Indian idol at Puri, which once a year is brought forth from its temple, placed on an enormous car, and conveyed at the head of a procession through the streets. Multitudes of pilgrims assemble on these occasions; it used to be the practice for fanatics to throw themselves beneath the wheels of the car and allow themselves to be crushed to death.

Jaguar, an American carnivorous animal of the leopard family, but much larger and more powerful. It is the most formidable beast of prey in the New World, and haunts the shores of the large rivers and lakes of Central and South America.

Jail, a place of confinement for persons charged with or convicted of criminal offenses.

Jam, the popular name for boiled, sweetened, and preserved fruit.

Jamb, one of the upright sides of a door, window, fireplace, or other aperture, which support the lintel and entablature, or mantel and shelf.

Janissaries, a band of Turkish foot soldiers who acted as the Sultan's bodyguard and were noted for their turbulence and cruelty. They existed from the 14th century until 1826, when they were finally disbanded after the people had risen against them.

January, the first month of the year, named after Janus, the two-faced god of the Romans. It was the *Wolf monath* and *Aefter Ule* of the Saxons.

Japanese Art is a development of the Chinese art and culture which was brought to Japan by Korean Buddhist missionaries in the sixth century. Japanese painting is done in Chinese ink or water colors on thin silk or soft paper. In recent years the traditional styles have been greatly modified through Western influences.

Japanning, the process of coating metal, wood, and other surfaces with hard, brilliant varnishes which produce a lacquered effect and are capable of receiving a high polish.

Jasmine, a graceful climbing plant, with odoriferous blossoms, now acclimatized in many varieties.

Jasper, a precious stone of the quartz variety, opaque, and colored red, brown, yellow or green. It was greatly esteemed by the ancients, the Bible containing numerous allusions to it.

Jay, a bird of the crow family, of many species, and having a wide distribution, ranging from Europe, where there are six species, to North and South America, where the varieties are numerous. In the United States the blue jay is very common.

Jazz, a syncopated music dependent for its effect upon instrumentation and its characteristic rhythm, which is the repetition of a double beat against the syncopation. Jazz developed in the United States from "ragtime"; many of its features can be traced to early Negro spirituals. It first emerged as a definite form of music in the waterfront districts of Memphis, New Orleans, and other river towns. In 1915 a jazz band was brought from the South to play in a Chicago cafe; the new music soon became popular, and within a short time was well known throughout the country. Based on ragtime, and employing many "blues" effects, jazz was in its early years characterized by much improvisation and a striking orchestral color achieved by the introduction of unusual and eccentric sound effects. Too crude and irregular for general ballroom dancing, jazz was gradually modified after 1920, when ballroom dancing became more general. The newer jazz was characterized by slower, more regular rhythms, sentimental melodies, and relatively full harmonies. This "sweet" dance music gained steadily in popularity until the free and barbaric tendencies of jazz had been almost obliterated. The rise of "swing" in 1934 saw a revival of interest in jazz, but like its predecessor "swing" waned in popularity because it was not suitable for general dancing purposes. The basic rhythmic foundation of jazz, as well as its accentuation of orchestral color, remain, however, as characteristics of both "swing" and "sweet music." Jazz has had some effect upon the development of American music; George Gershwin's *Rhapsody in Blue;* John Alden Carpenter's *Krazy Kat;* and Ferde Grofe's *Grand Canyon* and *Mississippi* suites are efforts to utilize it in more serious musical expression.

Jehovah, a modern reconstruction of one of the Hebrew names of the Deity. The English translators of the Old Testament rendered it "the Lord." The ancient Jews, however, regarded the word as too sacred for speech, and used the equivalents *Adonai* or *Elohim*.

Jellyfish, the common name for a wide variety of fishes of gelatinous structure, such as acalephs, sea bubblers, medusas, etc.

Jeremiad, any utterance or writing in which sorrow or complaint is the chief characteristic, so named as recalling the style of the "Lamentations of Jeremiah," in the Old Testament.

Jesuits, members of the Society of Jesus, the largest Catholic religious order, founded by St. Ignatius Loyola at Paris in 1534. It was organized with a sort of religio-military ideal to counteract the progress of the Protestant Reformation and was partially responsible for the Counter-Reformation of the latter half of the 16th century. The Jesuits are often called "The Soldiers of the Church."

The order was approved by Pope Paul III in 1540 and in the following year Ignatius was elected the first general. The constitution was based on the *Spiritual Exercises of Ignatius*. From 1773 until 1814, due largely to opposition within the church, the order was suppressed everywhere except in Russia and Prussia.

The offices of the order are to preach; teach the catechism; administer the sacraments; conduct preaching missions in parishes; organize confraternities; go to foreign fields as missionaries; write pamphlets, magazine articles, and books. Many Catholic schools, colleges, and universities are headed by Jesuits, and many Jesuits have been distinguished men of learning. The headquarters of the order are at Rome, where the Father General lives. The society has for its motto *Ad Majorem Dei Gloriam* ("for the greater glory of God").

Jet, a deep black fossil substance admitting of a high polish and much used in jewelry, ornaments, and trimming. It is found in the Tertiary and Secondary rocks.

Jetsam, in admiralty law, cargo thrown into the sea to lighten a ship in time of danger. The term applies particularly to goods which sink and remain under water, *flotsam* being floating goods thrown overboard for the same purpose.

Jetty, a construction of wood, masonry, or ironwork, projecting into the sea and serving as a wharf for shipping and merchandise or as a mole for harbor protection.

Jib, the front triangular sail of a ship, resting on a stay, and in large vessels, projecting from the end of the jib-boom. There may also be a flying jib outside this.

Jihad, a Mohammedan holy war. Fanatics attempted to set one on foot in India in 1877, and simultaneously another was proclaimed at Constantinople against the Russians.

Jingos, an English political term which came into vogue in 1877-78 during the Russo-Turkish War. The term is commonly applied to politicians favoring warlike measures and corresponds to chauvinism in France and one-hundred-percentism in the United States.

Jinrikisha, a hooded, two-wheeled vehicle drawn by one or two men; used in Japan, India, and other Eastern countries.

John Bull, the cartoonist's figure of an Englishman, bluff, big, and burly. Arbuthnot's *History of John Bull* is supposed to have originated the character.

Joiner, a carpenter who makes doors, lintels, and other small parts of buildings and ships with framings, glue, screws, nails, etc.

Joist, a horizontal timber standing on edge, employed in the support of floors and ceilings;

steel joists are used in the construction of larger buildings, particularly skyscrapers.

Joule, the electrical unit adopted by Siemens and representing the work accomplished in one second, "in maintaining a current of one ampere against a resistance of one ohm." The name commemorates that of Prof. J. P. Joule, the eminent scientist.

Jove, a classical name for Jupiter, chief of the Roman divinities.

Jubilee, the year following the seventh seven-year period; that is, the fiftieth year. In the Roman Catholic Church the Jubilee Year is every 25th year from Christmas to Christmas, during which time plenary indulgence is obtainable. Introduced by Boniface VIII, February 22, 1300. In recent years the word Jubilee has been applied to any form of 50th-year celebration.

Julian Calendar, named after Julius Caesar, who in 46 B.C., finding the Roman year 90 days in advance of the real time, readjusted the calendar to the solar year, the average length being fixed at 365¼ days. There was still an overplus of a few minutes every year; this was rectified by the Gregorian calendar, introduced by certain western nations during the 16th century and by England and the United States during the 18th century.

July, the seventh month of the year, named after Julius Caesar. It was the *Maed monath* (meadow-month) of the Saxons.

July Revolution, the French revolution of 1830 whereby Charles X was deposed and Louis Philippe made "Citizen King," the latter being himself deprived of kingship in the revolution of 1848.

Jumpers, religious sects or bodies who make jumping or dancing a part of their ceremony of worship. Certain Methodists of Wales, some Irvingites, the Shakers of America, and a Russian sect adopted the practice. The Holy Rollers are an American jumping sect.

Junco, the name given to a genus of snowbirds, confined to North America.

June, the sixth month of the year, containing 30 days. The name may possibly be derived from Juno. It was the *Sear* (dry) *monath* of the Saxons.

Jungle, a word of Hindu origin meaning a forest or dense tract of undergrowth.

Juniper, the Nova Scotian name of the American larch; also all the trees of the genus *Juniperus;* from the unripe fruit of some species is distilled the stimulant and diuretic oil of juniper.

Junk, a flat-bottomed Chinese sea-going boat, carrying large masts and employed on the coasts and seas of China and Japan.

Junkers, a name applied to the East Prussian aristocracy. It was extended to include other conservative German agrarians.

Junta, a Spanish word designating a council of state, a committee, or a legislative assembly entrusted with the passing of laws or the deciding of policy.

Jupiter, the largest body of the planetary system except the sun, from which it is 483,000,000 miles distant. It is 300 times as heavy as the earth and 1,300 times as large. It has nine satellites. In Roman mythology Jupiter was the supreme deity, identified with the Greek Zeus.

Jurassic Formation, a series of rocks (noticeable especially in the Jura Mountains) lying between the Cretaceous and Triassic groups and including the Oölite and the Lias. It is a formation rich in fossilized animal remains and extends through a great part of Europe and America.

Jury, a body of men chosen and sworn to hear and pass verdict upon evidence brought forward at a trial, inquest, or inquiry.

Jurymast, a word of doubtful origin, indicating an improvised mast put up in place of one lost.

Jute, a fibrous plant grown in India and other tropical countries, the fiber of which is used in the manufacture of coarse cloths, cordage, etc.

Jutes, a Low-German tribe who in the 5th century invaded the southeastern part of England, establishing themselves in Kent and making Canterbury their capital.

K

Kaaba, the inner shrine of the Great Mosque at Mecca, thrown open to the faithful only three times a year. It contains in its southeastern corner the famous and sacred "black stone," said to have fallen from heaven with Adam.

Kaffirs, a native race of southern Africa, which includes the Zulus and other powerful tribes. They were called Kaffirs, meaning "infidels," originally because of their refusal to adopt the Mohammedan religion.

Kaiser, the German form of the word Caesar, borne till 1918 by the monarchs of Germany and Austria-Hungary. Charlemagne was the first ruler to assume the title of Kaiser.

Kaleidoscope, an optical instrument, invented by Sir David Brewster, being a cylindrical tube containing two mirrors inclined toward each other at an angle to produce a symmetrical reflection of any transparent, colored substances placed between them. An endless variety of beautiful patterns is obtainable by revolving the cylinder.

Kalmucks, a branch of the Tartar or Mongol race who, in the 17th century, were expelled from Tibet and China and settled on the banks of the Volga. Many of them returned to China in 1771 and since then have wandered over many lands. Their religion is a modified Buddhism.

Kangaroo, a large marsupial or pouch-bearing animal confined entirely to Australasia. Captain Cook, in 1770, was the first European to observe the animal. There are 56 species. A male kangaroo stands from 6 to 7 feet high; the female, which carries her young in her abdominal pouch, is considerably smaller. These animals can move at an extremely rapid pace, progressing by tremendous leaps of from 10 to 20 feet.

Kantianism, the principles propounded by Immanuel Kant, the 18th-century German philosopher, who sought to limit philosophy to the consideration of matters of possible human experience. He formulated the theories of knowledge and ethics on which many subsequent philosophies have been based.

Kaolin, a fine clay used extensively in the manufacture of Oriental, Sèvres, and other fine pottery. It results from the decomposition of feldspar, and is found in China, Japan, at Limoges, France, and in certain parts of the United States.

Karma, the Buddhist theory that man's conduct not only governs his life but also determines the form of his successive reincarnations.

Katydid, a large green-winged insect of arboreal habits, common in the central and eastern portions of the United States; noted for its shrill note, which sounds like its name and is produced by stridulation of the wing-covers.

Kauri Pine, the tree which yields the kauri gum, used in varnish making. The tree is confined to New Zealand. The gum is found in a fossilized form on the sites of ancient kauri woods.

Kelp, the ash of burned seaweed, which yields carbonates, sulphates, and chlorides of soda, as well as small proportions of iodine and bromine in conjunction with sodium and magnesium; formerly used in the manufacture of soap and glass, but superseded for such purposes by barilla and other substances.

Kerosene, illuminating and heating oil distilled from petroleum and shale. It is sometimes used as fuel for tractors.

Ketch, a sailing vessel which is clear amidships and has two tall masts, fore and aft.

Key, a musical term indicating the central, dominating note that gives the melodic order in which the tones of a tune or composition are arranged. It is the starting-point, and different starting-points demand different scales. The natural key of C, for instance, requires no flats or sharps; all other keys require the use of sharps or flats to bring the notes of their scales into proper relation.

Keystone, the stone which occupies the center and highest point of an arch and is usually the last to be inserted.

Khan, a title formerly of importance in Eastern countries, which was given to princes and governors of states; it is now scarcely more than a courtesy designation.

Khedive, the title borne by the viceroys of Egypt from 1867, after Ismail Pasha's arrangements with the Sultan established hereditary succession in his family, until 1919, when Egypt became a kingdom.

Kilt, a short, pleated, plaid, skirt-like garment forming part of the Scottish Highland costume, and reaching from the waist to the knees. A similar garment is worn by many Balkan mountaineers.

Kilting, a dressmaking term denoting an arrangement of flat single pleats, placed side by side.

Kindergarten, a school, for children from four to six years old, of the type developed by Friedrich Froebel during the 19th century, intended to inculcate instruction by means of toys, games, singing, and other activities in which children naturally delight. The system is now well established in nearly all countries, having been highly developed in the United States in connection with the primary schools.

Kinematics, the science of pure motion, including conceptions of velocity and time but not of force. All the properties of a curve may be deduced from the kinematics of a point.

King Crab, a crustacean inhabiting the seacoasts of America and the Moluccas, carrying a shield-shaped shell, and having a long pointed spine projecting from its posterior. The body comprises three separate sections articulated together. These crabs—in the United States known commonly as the horseshoe crab because of their shape—are from 18 to 24 inches in length.

Kingfisher, a widely distributed family of brilliant-plumaged birds. The larger species are fish-eaters, the smaller, insect-eaters. All kingfishers have long bills. In the Malay Archipelago, New Guinea, the Moluccas, and Australia the varieties are very numerous, but Europe and North America have each only two species. The quaint laughing jackass of Australia is the largest of the kingfisher family.

Kiosk, a small open pavilion of light construction, used in Eastern countries as a place of shade and rest. Similar structures are commonly used in the streets of some cities as news and advertisement stands.

Kismet, an Arabic word signifying fate, destiny, or doom, frequently employed by Moslems as an ejaculation, and common in European literature and speech.

Kitchen Middens, certain large mounds, presumably the sites of prehistoric villages, distinctive features of which are stone hearths. These mounds often contain fossil remains of edible mollusks, bones of birds, animals, and fishes, fragments of implements, etc. They exist in the largest numbers on the east coast of Denmark, and here and there on the coasts of Scotland, Ireland, England, and North America.

Knapsack, a bag containing necessary articles which a soldier or camper carries strapped to his back. Formerly its contents consisted of food, but in recent times it has been utilized mainly as a receptacle of articles of clothing.

Knighthood, a degree of honor common in Europe since the Middle Ages, at first exclusively a military order. In great Britain the four main orders of knighthood are those of the Garter, the Bath, the Thistle, and St. Patrick. A knight is given the title *Sir*, which, not being hereditary, ranks below that of a baronet.

Knot, a unit of speed, the measure of the speed of ships. A ship making ten knots is traveling ten nautical miles per hour. A nautical mile is equal to about 1⅙ statute miles.

Knout, a whip of many thongs, used as an instrument of punishment upon Russian criminals since the 15th century. A hundred and twenty strokes were considered equivalent to a sentence of death, half that number sufficing to kill in many instances. Czar Nicholas I changed the form of the knout and made it a much milder instrument.

Know-Nothing, a member of a secret political society in the United States, organized for the purpose of obtaining restrictions on immigration. It was powerful during the early 1850's.

Kohlrabi, the turnip-rooted cabbage, the stem of which has a protuberance just above the ground line which is its most edible part.

Koodoo, a beautiful African antelope, the males being noted for spiral horns which when full grown are 4 ft. long. The animal is about 5 ft. high at the shoulder, and its gray-brown coat has white stripes. It affords good sport to the hunter, being one of the fleetest animals on the African continent.

Koran, the Bible of the Mohammedans, written by Mohammed in the 7th century and supposed to be a transcript of a series of divine messages revealed to the prophet at Mecca and Medina during a period of 23 years. It constitutes the law of life—civil, military, and religious—to Mohammedans. It recognizes Christ and Moses as prophets of God but gives the chief place to Mohammed. It was not until 1734 that the first English translation of the Koran, by George Sale, appeared. After the Bible the Koran is easily the most influential book in the world.

Kraal, a hut or collection of huts in an African village; also an enclosure for cattle.

Kremlin, in general, any Russian fortress or citadel of the feudal period; specifically, a large citadel in Moscow, containing the cathedral in which the czars were crowned, the former imperial palace, and important garrisons and arsenals. At the foot of the Ivan Tower rests the great Ivan Bell, weighing 200 tons. The Kremlin is now the headquarters of the Soviet Government.

Krypton, an atmospheric gas, one of the inert elements belonging to the helium group.

Ku Klux Klan, the name of two American secret societies. The first, organized in Tennessee in the summer of 1865, had as its purpose the reestablishment of the supremacy of the Southern whites over the Negroes and their carpetbagger and scalawag allies. At a meeting in Nashville in 1867 many of the Southern vigilante groups were merged into the Ku Klux Klan under the leadership of General Nathan Bedford Forrest, the famous Confederate cavalry leader. In 1869 Forrest resigned his leadership and ordered the dissolution of the Klan, apparently because he feared the uses to which its power would be put. In spite of his act, local units of the Klan lingered on for many years and were effective in gaining political control by ex-Confederates in many states.

The second Ku Klux Klan, not related to the first in any way except that it appropriated the name of the older organization, was founded in 1915 at Atlanta, Georgia, by William J. Simmons. To the anti-Negro attitude of the old Klan, Simmons' organization added a militant nativism and strong anti-Jewish, anti-Catholic, and anti-labor attitudes. These additions to its program made the new Klan popular in certain sections of the North as well as the South; for a time it was very powerful politically in Texas, Oklahoma, Indiana, Oregon, and Maine. The scandals in which certain of its leaders were involved and the decline of the militant chauvinism of the early post-World War I period lessened the influence of the Klan. There have been, however, partial revivals of its activities.

Kurds, a native race inhabiting Kurdistan; a wandering people, they profess the Mohammedan faith and speak an Iranian dialect.

Kymograph, an instrument used in physiology for graphically recording motion. It has a revolving cylinder containing a smoked paper on which the recording is made.

L

Laboratory, a department or room fitted with apparatus for prosecuting scientific investigations.

Labyrinth, or **Maze,** a combination of roads and passages so constructed as to render it difficult for anyone ignorant of the design to trace his way to the central part. The Egyptian labyrinth on Lake Moeris had 3,000 rooms, half of them subterranean and the remainder above ground. The Cretan labyrinth was said to have been constructed by Daedalus to house the Minotaur. There was one at Lemnos, renowned for its stalactite columns; and another at Clusium constructed by Porsenna, king of Etruria, about 520 B.C.

Lac, a resinous matter deposited on the branches of a number of tropical trees by the female of the lac insect, the exudation including eggs and a viscous covering for female, eggs, and young. The branches containing the insects are broken off and dried in the sun; this lac is termed *stick-lac.* From this, *seed-lac* is produced, by removing the extraneous accretions and dissolving the residue. *Shell-lac* is seedlac after it has been melted and otherwise prepared. This is the best-known of the lacs, being used in printing, in the manufacture of varnishes and sealing wax, and for other commercial purposes.

Lace, a delicate fabric of linen, silk, or cotton threads, made by hand or machinery in various ornamental designs. The kinds of lace are many, deriving their distinctive names either from the method in which the lace was made or from the place where a particular variety was produced. The best-known makes are bobbin lace, woven and plaited by hand; needlepoint lace, worked by the needle over a traced design; and machine lace, which dates from the latter part of the 18th century. Some of the famous laces are the following: *Alençon,* a needlepoint lace; *Brussels,* a very fine kind, with needlepoint sprigs and flowers; *Chantilly,* a silk variety with flowers and openwork; *Cluny,* a net lace with darned stitch; *Honiton,* a delicate kind with dainty sprigs and figures; *Mechlin,* generally made in one piece and with varied design; and *Valenciennes,* a bobbin lace of great durability, now manufactured mainly in Belgium.

Lacquer, a varnish made from shellac and certain coloring matters, used for imparting luster to surfaces of metal or wood. In China and Japan the production of lacquer ware of a decorative character has long been an important industry, bringing into use gold, coral, vermilion, sprinkled, and other lacquers.

Lacrosse, a ball game of Indian origin, popular in Canada and in the northern United States. The ball, which is of soft rubber, is carried or passed from player to player by means of the crosse, or racket. The field and the strategy are similar to hockey and soccer.

Lactic Acid, an organic acid, occurring in its commonest form in sour milk. It is found also in certain fermented vegetable juices and in putrefying animal matters.

Lactic Ethers, three ethers, containing the same monatonic radical derived from lactic acid: ethylic lactate, diethylic lactate, and monoethylic lactate.

Lactometer, a tube-shaped instrument for ascertaining the proportion of cream in a quantity of milk; called also a galactometer.

Ladybird, the common name of a class of beetles, the Coccinella, which is usually of a red or yellow color with small black spots. Ladybirds are of service to the gardener because they destroy plant lice. The beetles lay their eggs among the lice, and as the larvae come to life, they feed on them.

Lady Day, the day of the festival of the Annunciation of the Virgin Mary, March 25th.

Lake Dwellings, prehistoric habitations built on piles above the waters of lakes or rivers, evidences of which have been found in Switzerland, Britain, and other parts of the Old and New Worlds.

Lakes, bodies of water collected in depressions of the earth's surface. The most notable lakes are the Great Lakes of North America, including Superior, Michigan, Huron, Erie, and Ontario which empties into the St. Lawrence River,

Africa has an enormous area of lakes, including Albert Nyanza, Victoria Nyanza (forming the sources of the White Nile), Tanganyika, Nyassa, Tchad, etc. Smaller lakes are numerous in other countries, such as Switzerland, Germany, Italy, and great Britain.

Lamaism, the form of Buddhism prevalent in Tibet. It maintains a very exclusive sacerdotal organization of which the Grand Lama is head.

Lamination, a geological term designating the arrangement, in thin sheets or plates, of rocks such as slate or shale.

Lampblack, a carboniferous pigment now produced in specially constructed furnaces, in which bodies rich in carbon, such as tar, resin, and petroleum, are burned. The resulting soot is called lampblack, and is used in the manufacture of ink and paint.

Lance, a long spear used by mounted soldiers. The war lance of the Middle Ages was about 16 feet long; the lance still used in some cavalry regiments rarely exceeds 11 feet in length.

Land. The desire of individuals and social and political groups for the use and ownership of land is one of the greatest factors in human history. Primitive man wielded his big stick viciously to protect his cave and its surroundings. As he became family-conscious, his ideas of land became more definite. As head of a family, the patriarch controlled the land on which the family hunted game, herded its flocks, or raised its crops. As families united into a clan or tribe and chose a chief and combined their flocks and increased their lands, they had a sense of common ownership. In Italy in early times there was considerable private ownership by freemen, but gradually the land tended to get into the hands of a few. It was this concentration of ownership, with the consequent extinction of the yeoman class, that was, according to many historians, one of the causes of the decline of the Roman Empire. With the creation of the United States of America there came a new phase of land ownership, homesteading. Large tracts of land were opened up, and a grant of a certain number of acres was made to those who would live on the land for a required number of years. There were also "land rushes," when people lined up and at a certain moment were allowed to rush forward and stake a land claim on territory thrown open by the government for settlement.

There is nothing fixed absolutely in the tenure of land, since revolutions, exceptional taxation, and conquests are always changing its ownership. There was a redistribution of land in Mexico under President Cárdenas. The present land system of France dates back only to the Revolution. At the time of the formation of the Irish Free State, the British government coöperated by buying certain lands for distribution to the Irish people. In modern Palestine land purchased with Jewish National Fund moneys is purchased in the name of the Jewish People of the World and leased to coöperative groups or individual holders on long-term leases. This land may not be resold. Taxation has operated in many instances to cause large landowners to dispose of part of their estates. In many countries statesmen and economists have urged that large estates be taxed so heavily, especially if not in production, as to cause their sale or even that they be appropriated for distribution. Land is transferred outright by deed or is transferred for various periods of years by lease.

Land Crab, a family of crabs which live mainly on land, though, as a rule, they migrate to the sea to deposit their eggs. When their offspring have attained full development in the water, the mature crabs return to their inland quarters, taking their young ones with them.

Landslide, a breakage of a mass of soil or rocks away from a mountain, hill, or cliff, due to a variety of natural causes, such as the saturation of the earth by water or the decay or slipping of portions of the rock. Many serious landslides have occurred from time to time. In 1618 at Plurs, on Lake Como, many buildings were destroyed, and numerous lives were lost by an earthfall. In 1806 a portion of Rossberg, a mountain in Switzerland, slid into the valley below and buried many villages and hamlets and more than 800 people. At Lyme Regis, England, in 1839, a chalk cliff, from 100 to 150 feet high and three-quarters of a mile long, came crashing down, doing terrible damage. About 200 people were killed by the landslide in Nynee Tal, India, in 1880. And at Quebec, in 1889, Cape Diamond gave way, destroying many buildings and lives.

Language, the expresson of thoughts through words, signs, or symbols. The majority of languages spoken in Europe belong to the Indo-European group, which comprises the Germanic languages, including English, German, Dutch, Yiddish, Swedish, Norwegian, Danish and Icelandic; the Romance languages, including French, Spanish, Portuguese, Italian, Rumanian, and Romansh; the Balto-Slavonic languages, including Russian, Polish, Lettish, Lithuanian, Czech, Slovak, Serbo-Croat, and Bulgarian; Modern Greek; and Albanian. To the Finno-Ugrian group belong Finnish, Estonian, Magyar, and Turkish. Of the Indo-European languages, Lithuanian has undergone the least change in form. English is spoken by 240 millions, Russian by 165 millions, German by 100 millions, French by 70 millions, and Spanish by 65 millions.

Lapis-lazuli, an azure-blue mineral, found in limestone and granite, from which the ultramarine pigment is obtained.

Laplanders, the natives of northern Scandinavia.

Larboard, the old nautical term indicating the left-hand side of a ship, now more commonly called the portside. Starboard is the right-hand side.

Larch, a familiar coniferous tree in the mountain regions of northern Europe. It is one of the best turpentine-yielding trees; the bark is used for tanning.

Larceny, the fraudulent appropriation of the personal goods of another. Larceny is of two kinds: *simple larceny,* which is theft without accompanying aggravation; and *compound larceny,* which is theft with assault or forced entrance into an enclosed place, such as a house or store.

Lard, clarified pork fat, originally used almost exclusively for cooking, but now also for a variety of commercial purposes, such as the making of lubricating oil, the manufacture of candles, etc.

Lark, a family of birds, the Alaudidae, which includes about 100 species, some of which, notably the skylark, are famed for their marvelous singing and soaring. They build their nests on the ground in the open country. Africa has the greatest number of species. In North America the chief species is the horned lark; the meadow lark is not a true Alaudida.

Larkspur, the common name of the genus *Delphinium,* a favorite garden flower.

Larva, the undeveloped form of an animal which, before maturity, undergoes metamorphosis. The term was used formerly to designate only insects in the caterpillar stage, but it now includes the tadpole, which is the larval form of the frog, and numerous other animals in the early stages of their development.

Lateen, a triangular sail affixed to a tapering yard, used on light cargo vessels of the Mediterranean.

Latent Heat, the heat which is absorbed when a solid is converted into a liquid, or a liquid into a gas. Having no effect on the thermometer, it is described as latent.

Lateran Council, any of the five ecclesiastical conventions held in the Lateran Basilica at Rome to decide important questions of church doctrine and policy. The first, held in 1123 at the conclusion of the investiture controversy, forbade the marriage of clerics. At the second, which convened in 1139, clerical concubinage and marriage were prohibited and dangerous tournaments forbidden. The third Lateran council, in 1179, decreed that henceforth the pope was to be elected by the cardinals alone, a two-thirds vote being necessary. Among the legislation of the fourth council, held in 1215, were the commandment for annual confession and the arrangements for a new crusade. The fifth Lateran council, in 1512, prohibited the printing of books without the authority of the church.

Latitude, the extent of the earth or the heavens reckoned from the equator to the poles, first determined by Hipparchus of Nicaea, about 120 B.C.

Laughing Gas, nitrous oxide, a colorless, somewhat sweet-tasting gas, which received its name from the common after-effect of exhilaration. It was one of the earliest anesthetics and is used widely in dentistry and in minor surgical operations.

Laughingstock, a butt for ridicule, a person or an object provoking scornful hilarity.

Laundry, any room or building in which the work of washing and ironing clothes is carried on. Steam laundries have become common in recent times, and by the introduction of improved washing soaps and of electrical and other labor-saving contrivances laundry operations have been greatly simplified.

Laurentian System, a series of rocks in northeastern Canada, representing at some points a thickness of 30,000 feet. No fossils are found in this group, and the inference is that it is among the most ancient.

Lava, the molten fluid rock which is ejected from a volcano while in eruption.

Lawn, a very fine sun-bleached linen, called "cloth of Rheims" in the Middle Ages.

Lead, a soft malleable, metallic element occurring in numerous ores, most of which are easily smelted. It is found in its native form in small quantities in Sweden. On account of its pliability lead is used extensively in the making of service pipes, and as an alloy element it is used in the making of type metal, stereo metal, shot metal, pewter, and many other compounds. The lead output of the world now averages 1,700,000 metric tons annually. The principal producers are the United States, Mexico, Australia, Canada. Germany, and Burma.

League of Nations, a confederation of states formed in 1920 to promote international peace and security. The original members were signatories of the treaty of peace at Versailles. The membership of the League at one time included 53 nations, but the United States refused to join. The objects were international cooperation for world peace; just and honorable relations between nations; and preservation of peace by submitting disputes to the League before resorting to war, by waiting six months for a decision, and by allowing three more months to elapse. The Assembly met at Geneva annually. The Council met four times a year. The Permanent Court of International Justice sits at The Hague, in the Netherlands.

Leap Year, the year of 366 days, fixed by Julius Caesar, 45 B.C., the addition of one day in every four years making the calendar year even with the astronomical year, with three minutes per year over; this again is leveled by dropping leap year at stated intervals. Thus 1700, 1800, and 1900 were not leap years.

Leather, the tanned hides or skins of animals. It was made in ancient Egypt, Greece, and Rome and has played an important part in the service of man. Leather is classed according to the skins from which it is made or the system of preparation employed. The best-known kinds are morocco, kid, Russia, chamois, cordovan, grained, patent, russet, tan, calf, and Hungarian. Untanned skins are known as pelts.

Leech, an aquatic blood-sucking worm, found in fresh-water ponds. Each end of the body is provided with a sucker; at the head end it has jaws and teeth. The medicinal leech has three jaws. The leech attaches itself with avidity to animal bodies and sucks until glutted.

Leeward, a nautical term meaning the sheltered side of a vessel, that is, the opposite side to that from which the wind is blowing.

Legend, a story in which the marvelous, the supernatural, or the mythical is the leading feature.

Legion, a unit of the Roman army, the number of men varying at different periods. Under Marius a legion consisted of 6,200 soldiers; under Caesar, of from 3,000 to 5,000. Augustus' army was composed of 45 legions with the addition of 25,000 horses and 37,000 light-armed troops. A legion was divided into 10 cohorts, and every cohort into three companies.

Legion of Honor, the French order for distinguished service, military or civil, instituted by Napoleon I in 1802 and confirmed and modified under later rulers. There are five grades: *grand croix, grand officier, commandeur, officier,* and *chevalier.*

Legumin, a nitrogenous protein substance obtained from peas, beans, and similar plants. It is called also "vegetable casein."

Lemming, a small light-brown rodent with dark spots, abounding in Scandinavia and Siberia. There is an American species, found in the Hudson Bay region. The lemming is about 5 inches long and has a short tail.

Lemur, a mammal resembling the monkey, noted for having strong, pliant toes, which enable it to use its feet as hands, and well-developed thumbs on its hands. Lemurs have long, squirrel-like tails and fox-shaped heads and are distributed over the tropical parts of the Old World.

Lent, the 40-day period of fasting that precedes Easter; observed in the Catholic, Anglican and Lutheran Churches.

Leopard, a carnivorous spotted mammal inhabiting Africa and Asia. Its skin has a light tawny ground which is covered with dark brown spots.

Lettres de Cachet, sealed letters which the kings of France issued to their agents to secure the imprisonment of distrusted or disliked persons without trial. Lettres de Cachet were abolished in 1789.

Lever, a rod-like bar of metal or wood used for raising heavy bodies. The point at which the lever is supported is called the fulcrum.

Leyden Jar, an apparatus for storing static electricity, invented by Cuneus of Leyden in 1746. It is a jar coated inside and out with tinfoil for about two-thirds of its height, its inner coating being connected with the top by a brass knob and chain.

Libel, any writing, printed matter, picture, or illustration put forth with malicious intent for the purpose of bringing a person into public ridicule and contempt. An aggrieved person may proceed either by civil action or by criminal indictment. If the words complained of are true and if it is to the public advantage that they be made known, suit cannot be brought. A spoken libel is slander.

Libraries, before the invention of printing, were few and were collected at enormous cost. At Nineveh remains of libraries, consisting of tablets of baked clay, have been discovered. A public library existed in Athens in 540 B.C. The library at Alexandria, destroyed when Julius Caesar set fire to the city in 47 B.C., contained 400,000 valuable MS books. Among the great libraries of later times may be mentioned the Vatican Library at Rome, founded in 1588; the Bibliothèque Nationale at Paris (1350); the Astor Library, New York; the Bodleian Library, Oxford; and the Library of Congress.

Libyan, a group of languages spoken by tribes inhabiting the mountain and desert districts of northern Africa.

License, governmental permission to do or sell certain specified things. Licenses are required for keping motor vehicles and dogs, for shooting game, for peddling, for selling liquor and patent medicines, etc.

Licorice, a juicy substance obtained from the root of the *Glycyrrhiza glabra*, used in the making of sweetmeats and as a throat remedy.

Lien, a claim by one person upon the property of another for satisfaction of debt.

Lieutenant, a title implying the holding of an office under or for a superior. Thus, a lieutenant-general is next under a full general and takes his place in his absence. In the army a lieutenant ranks next to a captain and in the navy, next to a lieutenant-commander.

Light, a form of energy, the nature of which is not definitely known. It has a velocity of 186,000 miles a second, eight minutes sufficing for light to travel from the sun to the earth, a distance of 92,000,000 miles.

Lighthouses, to warn ships of dangerous places and to indicate coasts, points, and harbors, have existed since the building of the first Pharos, at Alexandria, in 285 B.C. In early lighthouses the lights were fires. A coal-fire light was shown at Tynemouth Castle Lighthouse in England in 1638. The whole problem of lighthouse building and lighting, invested though it has been with tremendous difficulties, may be said to have been mastered within the last century. Not only are the present structures impregnable against storm and tempest, but they are also supplied with light that is a thousand times more brilliant than were the lights produced by the older methods. The introduction of parabolic mirrors was a great improvement, providing a reflecting medium that carried to a great distance.

Lightning, an electric discharge from the clouds, usually forked or sheet. The former is the more dangerous.

Lightning Conductor, a metal rod, the upper part of which is of copper with a conical point; the lower portion is of iron and extends into the earth. Its effect is to gather to itself the surrounding electricity and discharge it into the earth, thus preventing its falling upon the building. In ships, lightning conductors are affixed to the masts and carried down through the ship's keel sheathing.

Lignite, an intermediate substance between peat and coal; it is, in fact, undeveloped coal, sometimes called brown coal.

Limburger, a strong cheese made originally in Limburg, a duchy which was later divided between Belgium and the Netherlands.

Lime, an alkaline earth obtained from kiln-heated limestone, used in making mortars and cements, as a manure for difficult soils, and in tanning.

Limestone, sedimentary rock consisting mainly or wholly of calcium carbonate. It is found in every geological formation and is highly fossiliferous. Marble is limestone of an especially hard kind.

Linseed, the seed of the flax plant, containing oily and nitrogenous matter from which linseed oil is obtained. The fibrous substance is converted into cattle food.

Lion, the chief representative of the Felidae and Carnivora, now found chiefly on the African continent. At one time it roamed over Europe, fossil lions having been discovered as far north as Britain. Its large square head, its flowing mane (in the males only), and its tufted tail distinguish it from other animals.

Liqueurs, essences combined with alcoholic liquors, named according to their flavorings, producers, or places of production, as Maraschino, Chartreuse, Curaçao, Benedictine, Noyau, Kümmel, etc.

Lithium, an element, the lightest metal known, obtained from an alkaline substance name lithia. It was discovered in 1817 by Arfvedson.

Lithography, the art of printing from stone or metal plates. Under the newer method a picture, writing, or design is produced on aluminum or zinc plates, and from these, ink-impressions are taken. Lithography was invented by Aloys Senefelder about 1796.

Litmus, a special kind of coloring matter produced from certain lichens by fermentation and ammoniacal treatment. The resulting color is violet, which can be converted into various blues and reds. It is turned red by acids and blue by alkalies.

Lizard, the name of a diversified family of reptiles, of which there are about 1,600 species.

Llama, a South American ruminant closely allied to the alpaca and of the same structure as the camel except for the hump. It is domesticated and used as a beast of burden as well as for its wool, though the latter is not so long as that of the alpaca.

Loam, soil composed of clay and sand in such proportions as to keep the ground porous.

Lobsters, marine crustacean animals existing in enormous numbers in the seas of America and Europe.

Lockout, a term applied to the stopping of work by employers, locking the doors against workers in order to force them to a settlement of a dispute, or to force them to strike.

Locust, an insect of the grasshopper family but much more powerful. Sometimes locusts make their appearance in enormous swarms, devastating all the vegetation that comes within their course. The locust-tree *(Ceratonia siliqua)* is supposed to have furnished food to St. John the Baptist in the wilderness, and its "beans" have accordingly been styled "St. John's Bread."

Log, a contrivance used for reckoning the speed at which a ship is traveling. It was first used in the 16th century. The log line is divided into spaces of 50 feet each, marked off by knots. The time is measured by a half-minute sand glass, bearing the same proportion to an hour as 50 feet bear to a mile.

Logarithms, a system of calculation invented by Napier in 1614 and developed by Henry Briggs a few years later. Logarithms are "the indexes of the ratio of numbers one to another."

Logwood, a dye-wood obtained from a tree abundant in the West Indies and in some parts of South America. It is red in color and is used for producing a series of shades from red to black.

Longitude, the distance of any place east or west of the prime meridian, which passes through Greenwich, England. The distances are expressed in degrees; 15 degrees represent a difference of one hour in time.

Lords, House of, the upper house of the British parliament, made up of the lords spiritual and temporal; that is, the archbishops and bishops of the established, or Anglican church, and all the adult temporal peers of Great Britain from the rank of baron upward, as well as certain Scottish and Irish representative peers.

Louvre, one of the world's most important museums of art and science, formerly one of the old royal palaces of Paris. Reconstruction of the original building into its present form was begun by Francis I and was completed by Louis XIV. Napoleon I turned it into a museum and enriched it with the plunder of many foreign art galleries. Much damage was done to the building by the communists in 1871. The great extension to the building begun under Napoleon I was completed under Napoleon III in 1857. Among its famous treasures are the "Venus de Milo" and Leonardo da Vinci's "Mona Lisa."

Lovebird, a small parrot belonging to the genus *Psittacula*, indigenous to South America, or to the genus *Agapornis*, indigenous to Africa. It has a delicate green plumage, with pink, red, and black markings at the neck.

Lunar Month, the period in which the moon makes its revolution around the earth—about 29¼ days.

Lupus, the constellation of the Wolf, in the southern heavens, on the east side of the Centaur. It contains no star of more than the third magnitude. In pathology, lupus, or king's evil, is a spreading inflammation caused by tuberculosis of the skin.

Lusiad, a famous Portuguese epic poem by Camoens, which celebrated the establishment of Portuguese sway in India; first published in 1571.

Lute, a pear-shaped, stringed instrument, introduced into Europe from the Orient in the 6th century.

Lye, a strong alkaline solution, especially sodium hydroxide, used in the soap, textile, tanning, refining, and canning industries.

Lynch Law, the meting out of summary punishment to offenders by private individuals without appeal to the law. It gets its name from one Charles Lynch, a Virginia planter and soldier of the Continental Army, who dealt out summary justice to Tory conspirators.

Lynx, a carnivorous mammal of the cat family, with tufted ears and spotted fur, inhabiting many parts of the world. It commits serious ravages among sheep and goats. The American species are the bobcat and Canada lynx.

Lyra, the constellation of the Harp, situated between Hercules and Cygnus, comprising twenty visible stars, the chief of which is Vega, one of the most brilliant of all the stars.

Lyre, an upright stringed instrument, similar to a harp, held in the hand while played. It was popular in ancient Greece and Rome.

Lyrebird, a genus of Australian birds, the males of which possess a beautiful lyre-shaped tail. The bird is not more than 15 inches long, but its tail is 23 inches in length.

M

Macadamizing, the system of road making invented by John McAdam in 1819. The roadbed is laid with crushed stones of nearly uniform size, which are bound together by a paste of stone dust and water. The stones are placed on the roadbed in thin layers; each layer is pressed into place by a multi-ton roller.

Macaque Monkey, a genus of long-tailed, large-shouldered, olive-brown, black-spotted, catarrhine monkey, common in the Malay Archipelago.

Macaw, a genus of large parrots, with brilliant scarlet and sky-blue plumage intermingled with green; native to South America and Cuba.

Maccabees, a Jewish family instrumental in regaining the independence of Judea from Syria and in maintaining it until the Roman conquest. The revolt of the Maccabeans in the 2nd century B.C., in which Judas Maccabeus captured Jerusalem and recovered the Temple, is the most famous exploit connected with this historic name. The feast of the Maccabees, known as Chanukah, is usually celebrated in December.

Machine Gun, a gun with an extremely rapid rate of fire, controlled by pressure on the trigger and reloading automatically by gas from expended cartridges or by recoil of parts. Bullets are held in belts or magazines; the barrel is air or water cooled. A light machine gun, firing small-arms ammunition, is handled by one man. Heavy machine guns are mounted on armored cars, tanks, or aircraft. They are also used for antiaircraft and antitank guns, firing .50 ammunition.

Mackerel, a sea fish common in the northern waters of both hemispheres; it is valuable as food.

Madrigal, an unaccompanied musical composition for three or more voices, developed in the Netherlands and in Italy in the 15th century.

Maelstrom, or Moskenström, a great whirlpool off the coast of Norway, between the islands of Moskenesö and Mosken in the Lofoten group.

Mafia, Sicilian secret terroristic society supposed to have had its origin in the disturbed period following the abolition of feudalism in Sicily. Efforts of the Italian government to suppress it led to the emigration of many members to the United States and South America. Mussolini finally destroyed the Mafia.

Magenta, an aniline dye discovered in 1859 by Sir W. H. Perkin; named after the great battle of that year between the French and the Austrians.

Maggot, the larva of an insect, a term usually applied to the larva of the common fly, which feeds upon putrid animal and vegetable substances.

Magi, a priestly caste of ancient Persia. Zoroaster, their great leader, lived about 600 B.C. and after him their religion is called Zoroastrianism. Small groups of Zoroastrians still exist in India and Persia. The Magi of the Bible were the three wise men who came from the East to adore the infant Jesus; they were the first to tell Herod of the birth.

Magic, the art of performing miracles, or of controlling the forces of nature by means of secret formulae. Magic has been practiced in all primitive communities and in all ages. Many rituals, including those of the most advanced religions, contain elements which seem to have been originally magical in intent. Among existent savages magic is severely practical; the purpose of a magic rite and the spell which is its climax is always to bring rain, to destroy an enemy, or to serve some similarly well defined end. The practice of magic as a serious study was continued in Europe during the Middle Ages in spite of the efforts of the church to uproot it. In time the pseudo-science came to be as carefully departmentalized as any of the rational disciplines. Thus, there was *black magic,* which communed with evil spirits; *white magic,* dealing with good spirits; and *natural magic,* the science of the occult; while *astrology* and *alchemy* were the more advanced outcome of these superstitions.

Magic Lantern, an apparatus for throwing pictures or images on a screen, invented by Kircher in the 17th century. Behind the light of the lantern is a reflector; in front is a tube carrying a condensing lens, this being supplemented by a double convex lens, which enlarges the object to be shown.

Magistrate, a title given various civil officers charged with either administrative or judicial functions. The first magistrate of a republic is the president.

Magna Carta, English charter of liberty, sealed by King John at Runnymede on June 15th, 1215, in obedience to the insistent demands of the barons, and confirmed thirty times by later monarchs. Its most important provisions have proved to be: that no free man should be imprisoned or lose his property except by the judgment of his peers in accordance with the law of the land; that there should be one system of weights and measures throughout the kingdom; that foreign merchants should have freedom of commerce; that no scutage or aid should be imposed except by consent of the council; and that ancient liberties generally should be preserved. Four copies were made, one of which is in the British Museum, one in Salisbury, another in Lincoln Cathedral, and another in the Library of Congress.

Magna Graecia, the collective name of the independent states established by Greek colonists in southern Italy before the rise of Rome. They included Syracuse, Tarentum, Heraclea, Thurii, Croton, Cumae, Naples, and Paestum. They allied themselves with Hannibal when he invaded Italy, 216 B. C., and his defeat involved their collapse as free states.

Magnesia, the oxide of the metal magnesium; it is a white powder.

Magnesium, a metallic element first found at Magnesia in Asia Minor, which as a constituent of dolomite and other mineral substances has a very wide distribution. It is obtained by electrolysis and burns with a brilliant white flame when heated to the proper point. The magnesium light is so rich in chemical rays that it is frequently used in photographing objects by night or in caverns or other dark places where photography would otherwise be impracticable. Magnesium lamps have been used for lighting up tunnels during construction.

Magnet, a body having the ability to attract, as the lodestone or a magnetized bar of steel. A single bar is called a simple magnet; several bars fastened together form a compound magnet. Electromagnets are very powerful, some being capable of attracting weights of more than a ton.

Magnetism, the property of attraction, possessed especially by the lodestone or magnet stone. Magnetism was known to the ancient Greeks, Chinese, and Arabians. Roger Bacon knew of the power of attraction possessed by the earth's magnetic poles, and it was this property that led to the invention of the magnetic needle and of the mariner's compass.

Magnolia, the typical genus of the family Magnolicae and the order Magnoliaceae, a deciduous tree or shrub with alternate leaves and large, terminal, odoriferous flowers; native to North America and Asia. *M. grandiflora,* or laurel bay, is a fine evergreen tree, which has large, beautiful, fragrant flowers. There are white, yellow, rose, and purple magnolias.

Magyars, the Hungarian race, of Finno-Ugrian stock, which settled in Hungary during the 9th century.

Mahogany, a fine hard wood distinguished for the beauty of its color and markings. The tree which produces this wood, the *Swietenia,* is native to the West Indies and tropical America.

Majolica, a kind of pottery carrying a highly colorful glaze or enamel, supposed to have been introduced into Europe by the Moors from Majorca in the 15th century. Raphael and other great artists have made designs for the ware. After the 16th century the production of majolica practically ceased, though in recent times skillful imitations of the old ware have been manufactured

Major, in the United States Army, the rank next below a lieutenant colonel. A major general ranks beneath a lieutenant general.

Malachite, a green copper ore, common in South America, Russia, and Australia; the finer specimens are capable of being polished and are used as gems.

Malays, a race of people with oblique eyes, high cheek bones, and brown skin; the dominant race in the Malay Archipelago, Polynesia, and the Philippines.

Malt, barley or other grain which has gone through a steeping and preparing process to render it suitable for brewing purposes.

Malta, Order of, or Knights Hospitalers, a military religious order founded in the time of the Crusades. Its chief function was to protect the Christians in the Near East against the Mohammedans. The headquarters were originally at Jerusalem, whence they were removed successively to Acre, to Rhodes, and to Cyprus. Pursued everywhere by the rising tide of Mohammedanism, the Knights finally settled at Malta, which Emperor Charles V ceded to them. There they remanied for three centuries until Napoleon, on his way to Egypt, dispersed them. Later Czar Paul of Russia protected them. In recent years the order has maintained headquarters at Rome, but its existence is hardly more than nominal.

Maltese Dog, one of the smallest of dogs, with long, silky white hair and pendulous ears; a common household pet.

Mamelukes, a bodyguard of Turkish and Circassian slaves in the service of the sultans of Egypt. It attained such influence that in 1250 it was strong enough to appoint one of its own members to the throne, and from 1250 to 1517 a succession of Mameluke sultans reigned in Egypt. When the Turks annexed Egypt, they took the Mamelukes into their service. For a time, after Napoleon's conquest of Egypt, the Mamelukes regained their power, but in 1811 they were virtually annihilated by Mohammed Ali.

Mammalia, a zoological term applied to a class of vertebrates the females of which are provided with mammary glands for suckling their young. Mammalia are warm-blooded and, except for the monotremes, are viviparous.

Mammoth, an extinct species of elephant of gigantic size. In 1799 an entire skeleton of the animal was found in Siberia in a block of ice. In prehistoric times the mammoth inhabited America, as well as Europe and Asia.

Mammoth Cave, a series of spacious limestone caverns in south central Kentucky, about 10 miles long and from 40 to 300 feet wide and at one point 300 feet high. Stalactites and stalagmites abound.

Mammoth Tree of California, the giant of the famous coniferous grove at Calaveras, 327 feet high and 90 feet in circumference, believed to be from 3,000 to 4,000 years old.

Manatee, an aquatic mammal of the genus *Manatus*, averaging when full-grown eleven feet in length, with shovel-shaped tail and with forelimbs and nails resembling arms and hands.

Manchus, the people inhabiting Manchuria (Manchukuo), which conquered China in the 17th century; they are Mongoloids and speak a language related to Mongolian and Turkish.

Mandarin, a Chinese official of the former imperial regime, either civil or military, whose rank was indicated by the wearing of a special kind of button.

Mandolin, an Italian fretted guitar, so called from its almond conformation.

Manganese, a hard, brittle, metallic element, which oxidizes rapidly when exposed to the air. It is found in combination in many minerals. As a commercial product, in its numerous oxides, it is of great value. Formerly included among the iron ores, it was isolated by Gahn in 1774.

Manichaeism, a religion founded by the prophet Mani in Persia about A. D. 260. Mani rejected the Old Testament and propounded a system of his own, based partly on Christianity and partly on Zoroastrianism. Manichaeism, which spread into Egypt, Arabia, and Europe, was second only to Christianity among the religions of the later Roman Empire; as Albigensianism it survived in Europe until the 14th century.

Manikin, a dwarf or pigmy; a woman employed to display gowns by wearing them; an artificial figure employed in anatomical demonstrations, made sometimes of papier-mâché.

Manna, a tree of the ash genus grown in southern Europe and in the Orient; it exudes a sweet substance which is gathered, boiled, and used as food.

Manslaughter, the unlawful killing of another without malice or premeditation. It is classed as voluntary, when it is done under a sudden provocation; involuntary, when it is the result of some unlawful act.

Manure, a natural or artificial substance spread upon land to aid cultivation. Natural manures include farmyard manure, sewage, leaves, etc.; artificial manures include bones, nitrate of sodium, guano, soot, and limes.

Manx, the now almost extinct language of the Celtic inhabitants of the Isle of Man; it is allied to Irish Gaelic and Scottish Gaelic.

Maoris, the native race of New Zealand. They speak a Malayo-Polynesian language and are believed to have arrived in their present home between A. D. 1200 and 1400. They are an intelligent, energetic people and have absorbed, to a large extent, the culture of the white New Zealanders. There are about 54,000 Maoris in New Zealand, but they are rapidly being absorbed in the general population.

Maple, a tree of the genus *Acer* containing about 75 species in the Northern Hemisphere. The sugar maple abounds in Canada and the eastern parts of the United States. The maple-leaf is the Canadian national emblem.

Maraschino, a liqueur distilled from cherries; Zora, in Italy, and Corsica are the chief centers of production.

Marble, limestone in its hardest and most crystalline form. There are many varieties, of which white marble is the purest and rarest. From about 568 B. C. white marble was used by Greek sculptors for statues. Rome was rich in marble buildings and monuments, and Palmyra was built mainly of white marble. Vermont, Massachusetts, and Tennessee are the chief marble-producing states. American marbles are mostly light gray.

March, the third month of the year and the first of the old Roman calendar. It was named after the god Mars and was the *hlyd* (storm) month of the Anglo-Saxons.

Mardi Gras, Shrove Tuesday, the day before Ash Wednesday. Mardi Gras, being the day before the beginning of Lent, is in many places a day of carnival; the New Orleans Mardi Gras is famous.

Mariolatry, the veneration of the Virgin Mary, begun in the 4th century and still a prominent part of Roman Catholic religious observances.

Marionette, a puppet moved by strings, which originated in the *Fantoccini* of the 15th century. These dramatic representations had great vogue in Italy and are still popular. Puppetry is now a minor form of the drama.

Marmoset, a small South American monkey, squirrel-like in appearance, with long bushy tail and thick woolly fur. They are often kept as pets.

Marquetry, a kind of inlaid work in which thin layers of colored woods are wrought into a design.

Mars, the planet coming next after the earth in order of distance from the sun, Mercury being first and Venus second. It is the planet that has been most closely studied because of its comparative nearness. It has two satellites.

Marseillaise, the French national anthem, written and composed by Rouget de L'Isle, an engineering officer, who was inspired to write it in 1792 to encourage the Strasbourg conscripts. It immediately became popular; its name comes from the fact that it was sung by a contingent of Marseilles troops while marching into Paris.

Marsupialia, animals having a marsupium or pouch; the young, at birth, are comparatively small and imperfectly developed and are transferred to the maternal pouch.

Marten, a carnivorous animal of the weasel family, with dark-brown fur. It feeds on birds and small mammals.

Mass, a Latin liturgy in celebration of the Eucharist in the Roman Catholic Church. It is high or low, i. e., performed with full choral service or by the recital of prayers without singing. The form of celebration has remained virtually unchanged since the sixth century.

Mast, a tall, tubular piece of timber, steel, or iron, placed directly above, and vertical to, the keel of a ship. To the mast are attached the various parts constituting the rigging. The lowest section of the mast, in the case of larger ships, is called the lower mast, the next higher section being the topmast, while above that may come the topgallant mast and the royal mast. There are also foremasts, mizzenmasts, trysail or spankermasts, and jiggermasts.

Mastic, a resinous substance obtained principally from the bark of *Pisticia lentiscus*, a tree which flourishes in the Greek Archipelago. It is used in the manufacture of varnish.

Mastiff, a large, massive dog, with pendulous ears; a formidable watch dog.

Mastodon, an extinct quadruped of the families Mammutidae and Bunomastidontidae, closely resembling the elephant. Abundant remains have been found in North America.

Materialism, in philosophy, the doctrine that "the psychic life is determined by the body and its physical relations." This point of view assumes that matter and motion are the fundamental realities. Materialistic doctrines were organized into a philosophic system as early as the 4th century B. C. by Democritus.

Materia Medica, the study of the different drugs used in the practice of medicine and of their constituents and effects.

Mathematics, the science of computation and measurement; it is defined as *pure* when treating of quantity in the abstract and *mixed* when dealing with material bodies and facts.

Matins, an early morning religious service. In the Roman Catholic Church it includes the Lord's Prayer, the Angelic Salutation, the Creed, and certain psalms.

Matriarchy, a social organization in which descent is reckoned in the female line. The system is common among primitive peoples and does not involve rule by the mother.

Mausoleum, a special place of burial, usually for the reception of the remains of members of a family of distinction. The name is derived from the tomb of King Mausolus at Halicarnassus, erected about 350 B. C., which was one of the seven wonders of the ancient world.

Mauve, a coloring matter, produced from lichens by Stenhouse in 1848; from aniline by Perkins in 1856. It was the first of the aniline dyes to be prepared on a large scale. The term *mauve* was used in France in the 18th century to designate a purple shade.

May, the fifth month of the year, said to have been named after Maia, the mother of Mercury, to whom sacrifices were offered on the first day of this month. May Day is the occasion of many festivities, including crowning of the May Queen, dancing round the Maypole, etc.

Mayflower, the name of the ship which in 1620 conveyed the Pilgrim Fathers, 102 in number, from England to America.

Mazdaism, the religion of the ancient Persians; another name for Zoroastrianism.

Mechanics, the science dealing with kinematics and dynamics and with forces and their influence upon matter.

Meerschaum, a white or yellowish-white, earthy mineral, a hydrous silicate of magnesium, found in Asia Minor, Greece, and other places. Its chief use is in making pipe-bowls.

Megaphone, a conical tube for carrying the sound of the voice.

Melon, a tropical fruit having numerous varieties, nearly all of which are used as food: muskmelon, cantaloupe, rock melon, watermelon, etc.

Mendel's Law, a principle of genetics, determining the ratio of variation of the characteristics in the offspring of different individuals and the classifications of characters discontinuously inherited. It was formulated by Gregor Johann Mendel, a monk of Brünn, Czechoslovakia. The results of his most important experiments—those dealing with the crossing of peas—were published in 1866 and showed that when two strains are crossed, the resultant hybrids will exhibit the dominant features of one parent; the offspring of the second generation will show those of both grandparents. This fact is explained by the transmission of germ cells, or gametes, bearing certain characters which may lie dormant in one generation, but which that generation can transmit to the next.

Mendicant Friars, members of certain religious orders—Franciscans, Dominicans, Augustinians, and Carmelites—who originally depended entirely on alms.

Mennonites, a pietist sect named for Menno Simons, 16th century Dutch Anabaptist leader. They accept civil authority but refuse to exercise it themselves and decline to take oaths or bear arms. The Church of God in Christ, the Mennonite Brethren, the Amish Brethren, and the Herrites are the largest American Mennonite bodies.

Mercator's Projection, a method of indicating meridians and parallels of latitude on maps, introduced by Mercator, a Flemish geographer in the 16th century. On such a map the parallels and meridians are straight lines, drawn at right angles to each other.

Mercury, one of the smaller planets, the orbit of which is nearest the sun. Its minimum distance from the sun is about 28½ million miles; its minimum distance from the earth, about 50 million miles. Mercury has no satellite. The chemical element mercury, or quicksilver, is the only element which is liquid at ordinary temperatures. It was one of the first elements to be discovered and is obtained from the sulphide cinnabar, which is found in Mexico, South America, China, and Japan. Pure mercury is not altered by exposure to the air. It is used in thermometers and barometers, is very valuable in medicine, and forms, in combination with other metals, various alloys called amalgams. In Roman mythology, Mercury was the god of commerce and the messenger for the other gods; he was identified with the Greek Hermes.

Meridian, an imaginary circle extending through the North and South Poles and any given place. When the sun is at its midday height at any place, it is "on the meridian."

Merovingians, the first dynasty of French kings, beginning with Clovis, 467, and ending with Chilperic, 753.

Mesmerism, the so-called science of animal magnetism developed by Friedrich Mesmer, an Austrian physician and astrologer, between 1766 and 1778.

Metallurgy, the science of obtaining metals from their ores and applying them to the uses of man.

Metamorphic Rocks, geological deposits which have undergone alterations of structure and composition. The most active agents in producing these metamorphic changes are heat, water, and pressure.

Meteorite, a solid substance which enters the earth's atmosphere from outside. The small meteors, which are appropriately called shooting stars, are very numerous. These are igneous rocks, usually containing iron, which are heated by air resistance until they become white hot and break into fragments. Larger meteors are known as fireballs. Some of these reach the earth and are then known as meteorites. In some meteorites iron is the predominant element. At Laigle, in France, in 1803 from 2000 to 3000 meteoritic stones fell; this fall is famous because it convinced scientists that meteorites really do come from outside our atmosphere. A meteorite weighing no less than 36½ tons was found in Greenland and is now in New York. On June 30, 1908, an enormous meteor fell in a sparsely inhabited region of Siberia. A hot blast destroyed all trees within a radius of about 20 miles. For the next few nights there was brilliant illumination in Europe's northern sky because of sunlight falling on clouds of dust at a great height. Whether this dust had accompanied the meteor in its journey through space like the tail of a comet or whether the dust had come from Siberia is unknown. When the place where the meteor fell was visited in 1927, some 200 craters were found, but no considerable meteorite was recovered.

Meteorograph, an instrument for recording continuous fluctuations in temperature, pressure, and humidity of the atmosphere.

Meteorology, the science which treats of the various atmospheric phenomena included in the term weather.

Meter, the unit of linear measure in the metric system, equivalent to 39.370432 English inches. A meter is the ten-millionth part of the distance from the equator to the North Pole.

Methodism, the religious movement which grew out of the life and teachings of John Wesley. In 1729, while a student at Oxford, Wesley began to meet regularly for religious exercises with his brother Charles, George Whitefield, and a few like-minded friends. From 1735 to 1737 Wesley served as a missionary in Georgia. He was an ordained minister of the Church of England; both he and his early followers subscribed to its creed. In spite of this acceptance, his relations with the established church, which regarded Wesley's revivals as undignified, were often strained. He and his followers were often denied access to church buildings; after his death in 1791 the Methodists formally withdrew from the Anglican Church and organized their own religious community. During Wesley's life many of his disciples came to America to preach. One of these, Francis Asbury, became after the Revolution the first Methodist bishop in the United States. The Methodist Church is distinguished from other Protestant bodies by the itinerant system, under which ministers are transferred from church to church at comparatively short intervals, and its adoption of an episcopal system of church government. Though often divided over slavery and questions of church government. Methodists have long constituted the second-largest single Protestant bloc in North America. In 1925 the Canadian Methodists united with the Presbyterians and Congregationalists to form the United Church of Canada. In 1939 the Methodist Episcopal Church, the Methodist Episcopal Church, South, and the Methodist Protestant Church were merged into the Methodist Church; this one body represents the overwhelming majority of Wesley's adherents in the United States. The combined Methodist bodies in the United States number over 11,000,000.

Metric System, a system of weights and measures adopted in France in 1793 and since officially adopted in many other nations, including all the republics of Latin America. It is now universally used in scientific work. The system is based upon the meter, a measure of length, and upon the decimal system of calculation.

Metrochrome, an instrument for the measurement of color, consisting of three hollow wedges of glass of identical capacity and angle so arranged between two screens that any portion of their tapering sides may be presented at will to an aperture through which a ray of light may be thrown.

Metronome, an instrument for beating time during the performance of a musical composition. It has a double pendulum and is wound up like a clock.

Mezzotint, an engraving from copper or steel plates which, burnished and scraped, yield an impression effectually graded in light and shade.

Mica, a translucent mineral which has great heat-resisting power and can be split into thin plates.

Micrometer, an instrument for measuring minute distances; usually attached to the eye-pieces of a miscroscope or telescope and consisting of two very fine hairs or wires stretched across the field of view, one fixed, the other movable. It was invented by William Gascoigne in the 17th century.

Microphone, an instrument invented by David Edward Huges, in 1878, for giving audibility to sounds which are otherwise imperceptible to the ear. It is used for telephone communications, in broadcasting, and in phonograph recording.

Microscope, an instrument which by a combination of lenses magnifies objects, making visible animalcules and other minute substances which cannot be seen by the naked eye. Microscopes are simple, compound, or binocular. The more powerful instruments have a magnifying capacity of 2,000 diameters. The microscope was invented about 1590 by Janssen and was improved by Galileo, Fontana, and others.

Middle Ages, a period of about 1,000 years, from approximately A. D. 500 to 1,500, during which feudalism was the prevailing politico-economic system of Europe.

Mikado, the hereditary male ruler of Japan. Since 1868 the mikado has been the real sovereign of the country; previously he was only the nominal and spiritual head, the shogun possessing the governing responsibility.

Milky Way, a broad track of small stars almost encircling the heavens. The ancients regarded it as a luminous streak. The name commemorates the mythological legend that Juno while suckling Mercury or Hercules scattered milk across the sky.

Millet, a nutritious cereal cultivated in nearly all warm climates; native to the East Indies.

Millimeter, a metric lineal measure, equivalent to a thousandth of a meter, or 0.03937 of an English inch.

Minim, a musical term denoting a note equal to two crochets, or half the value of the semibreve. It is the same as a half-note.

Minimizers, the name applied to certain writers of the 19th century who advocated the limitation of property. The group included John Stuart Mill, Herbert Spencer, and W. von Humboldt.

Minnesinger, one of a class of minstrel poets who, during the 12th and 13th centuries, composed and sang love ballads to amuse the nobility. One of the greatest of the minnesingers was Walther von der Vogelweide.

Minnow, a very small fresh-water fish of the carp family, abounding in all the waters of America and Europe. It has a mottled back and silvery belly and forms a popular bait for larger fish.

Minor, a musical term referring to intervals and scales; thus, a minor interval is a semi-tone less than the corresponding major interval.

Minstrels, originally a special class of instrumentalists and singers engaged by barons and manorial lords to amuse their tenants. Later, minstrels assumed nomadic habits, touring the houses of the great and the medieval fairs.

Miracle Plays, sacred dramas, representations of some Scriptural or saintly story. Performed usually in market places or church yards, they were immensely popular in medieval Europe. The form still survives in isolated peasant communities.

Mirage, an optical illusion often observed in desert regions when the objects on the surface of the earth appear as if reflected in a surface of water. Mirages are due to the unequal heating of the different parts of the atmosphere, which bends the light rays and so produces distorted images.

Mirrors, surfaces which can produce clear and exact images. In ancient times they were made of burnished metal, usually of brass. Silver mirrors were introduced by Praxiteles, 328 B. C. The Venetians were the first to make mirrors of glass in the 14th century.

Missal, in the Roman Catholic Church, a book containing directions and texts for the celebration of the Mass, first compiled about 495 by Pope Gelasius I and revised by Gregory I, 590-604. The present Roman missal was sanctioned by the Council of Trent, 1545-63. In the Episcopal Church the Book of Common Prayer superseded the missal in 1549.

Mistletoe, a parasitic plant that grows on trees, particularly the apple tree. The druids made it an object of reverence; as a decoration it is especially associated with Christmas.

Miter, an ecclesiastical headcovering worn originally by the Jewish high priest; later adopted by the Christian Church and now worn by bishops.

Mnemonics, the art of developing the memory. The earliest known system was invented by Simonides the Younger during the 5th century B. C.

Moabites, a people of Judea, said to have been descendants of Lot. They were often in conflict with the Israelites and were finally subdued by Jehoshaphat, 895 B. C.

Moabite Stone, a stone of the 9th century B. C. bearing the earliest known inscription in Phoenician characters; discovered at Dibon in 1868.

Mockingbird, an American bird of the thrush family, widely distributed over the Western Hemisphere, and well known for its ability to imitate the song of other birds.

Modoc Indians, a warlike tribe which formerly occupied extensive lands in northern California and southern Oregon. They were allotted other lands by the United States Government, but being dissatisfied with their new quarters, they returned to Oregon and defied the troops sent to expel them. After severe fighting the Modocs surrendered in 1873 and now are confined to the Klamath Indian Reservation.

Mohair, the wool of the Angora goat, used in the worsted trade for the manufacture of dress fabrics, upholstery, etc.

Mohammedanism, Islam, the religion of the Moslems as set forth by Mohammed and embodied in the Koran. The doctrine includes complete submission to the one God, the immortality of the soul, and a last judgment. It is professed by more than 400 million people, mainly in India, Iran, Africa, and the Near East. There are 12 million Mohammedans in Europe. Since the reforms of Mustafa Kemal the Mohammedans of Turkey are no longer orthodox, and the caliphate has been abolished.

Moire, a silk fabric called also watered silk because in the finishing process water marks are produced by wetting and pressing.

Molasses, sugarcane juice in its uncrystallizable form. The crystals which are separated from it in the manufacturing process are raw sugar.

Mole, a burrowing animal about the size of a small rat, with short legs and with forefeet armed with strong claws for digging in the earth. Moles build odd, subterranean dwellings, from which they emerge only for the purpose of making raids on mice, frogs, snails, etc.

Molecule, the smallest mass of any substance, whether element or compound, capable of independent existence while still retaining the properties of the substance.

Mollusks, the class of soft-bodied invertebrate animals, most of which are protected by a shell. These shells are either univalve (of one piece), as in the case of snails; bivalve, as in the case of oysters; or multivalve.

Molybdenum, a metallic element found in combination with sulphur. It forms an acid which, combined with metals, produces salts called molybdates. It is often found in granite and is very similar to graphite in appearance, though totally different in its properties.

Mongols, a nomadic yellow race of central Asia. In the 13th century under Jenghiz Khan they conquered large portions of Asia, including China, Persia, and India. During the next century Tamerlane, a descendant of Jenghiz Khan, extended the Mongol Empire by conquering Mesopotamia, Syria, Turkey, and the territory between the Volga and the Great Wall. The Mogul dynasty in India was founded in 1525 and remained in power until the end of the 18th century, when the country came under British control. Mongolia, the territory now occupied by the Mongols in northeast Asia, is divided into a Soviet-dominated republic and a Chinese province.

Monitor, a genus of water lizards noted for their great size, long beards, long tails, and scaly covering. They are supposed to signal the approach of the crocodile to their neighbors by a curious hissing sound. There are 18 species, inhabiting southern Asia, Australia, New Guinea, and Africa.

Monkey, a quadrumanous mammal of the order Primates, including all members of that order except man and the lemurs. Monkeys with short tails are usually called apes; those with long dog-like faces, baboons; small bushy-tailed monkeys, marmosets.

Monotheism, the doctrine that there exists but one God. The chief monotheistic religions are Christianity, Judaism, and Islam.

Monroe Doctrine, a policy of the United States, first definitely announced by President James Monroe. It was intended to prevent interference by European powers in the affairs of the several American states. President Monroe's annual message to Congress in 1823 contained the following sentences: "We owe it to candor and to the amicable relations existing between the United States and the allied powers, to declare that we should consider any attempt on their part to extend their system to any portion of this hemisphere as dangerous to our peace and safety. With the existing colonies or dependencies of any European power we have not interfered and shall not interfere; but with the governments which have declared their independence and maintained it, and whose independence we have, on great consideration and just principles, acknowledged, we could not view an interposition for oppressing them or controlling in any other manner their destiny, by any European power, in any other light than as a manifestation of an unfriendly disposition toward the United States . . . The American continents should no longer be subjects for any new European colonial settlement." As popularly understood, the Monroe Doctrine has long meant political protection and a guaranty of freedom from European interference to all states of North and South America.

Monsoons, certain winds which change their direction with the seasons. They sweep over warm latitudes, especially India, where the "wet monsoon" prevails from April to October.

Monstrance, an ornamental receptacle in which sacred relics of the Roman Catholic Church are held up for inspection.

Montessori System, a method of education originated and developed by Maria Montessori in the early 20th century. She began her work with defective children (aged 3-6) in the slum districts of Rome. Her results were so amazing that she experimented with normal children. Dr. Montessori invented apparatus for her pupils which stimulated interest and attention. Children in her schools learned to read, write, count, and do simple arithmetic before the age of 6. Her method revolutionized infant education and is being used in many countries.

Month, the 12th part of the calendar year. A *lunar month*, which is the period of one revolution of the moon around the earth, has a mean duration of 29 days, 12 hours, 44 minutes, 2.87 seconds. A *sidereal month* represents the time of the moon's course from a given star back to the same star: 27 days, 7 hours, 43 minutes, 11.5 seconds. A *solar month* covers the time the sun passes through one sign of the zodiac: 30 days, 10 hours, 29 minutes, 4.1 seconds.

Moon, the earth's satellite, a globe 2,160 miles in diameter, 238,000 miles distant from the earth. The period from one full moon to another is 29 days, 12 hours, and 44.4 minutes.

Moors, the name applied in modern times to the natives of Morocco. At one time they were a very powerful race; from 1237 to 1492 they held possession of the kingdom of Granada. They were expelled from Spain in the 17th century and established themselves in northern Africa.

Moravians, a religious sect, known also as United Brethren. They were called Bohemians at first and were a branch of the Hussites. When the Calixtines came to terms with the Council of Basel in 1433, the Moravians refused to subscribe to the articles of agreement and constituted themselves a distinct body. In 1522 they proposed closer cooperation with Luther, whose doctrines they accepted in part, but ultimately they adopted Calvinistic views as to the Lord's Supper. Their discipline was very strict. Though they never were numerous, yet in the latter part of the 18th and the beginning of the 19th century they had a larger proportion of their membership engaged in foreign missions than any other Christian denomination since Apostolic times.

Mormons, a religious sect, known also as Latter Day Saints, founded by Joseph Smith April 6, 1830, at Fayette, New York. According to Mormon belief the Book of Mormon is a record of certain Hebrews who came to America and were visited by Christ. Opponents claim it is based on "The Spaulding Romance," but this was disproved when a manuscript was discovered at Honolulu in 1884 by President James

H. Fairchild of Oberlin College, Ohio. After the death of Smith in 1844 the church, which numbered upward of 200,000, was scattered. The two largest factions today are the Reorganized Church and the Utah Church, of which Brigham Young assumed leadership in 1847. He introduced polygamy as a doctrine, but polygamy is now repudiated by the Mormons.

Morphology, the science which deals with the form, structure, and development of the different parts of animals and plants.

Morse Alphabet, a system of dots and dashes, intended to be used in combination with the indicator in telegraphy; but usually read by sound, the receiving operator writing down the words in the system as transmitted. Samuel F. B. Morse of Massachusetts was the inventor.

Mortar, a short gun with a large bore and close chamber for throwing bombs. Mortars are said to have been first used in the 15th century at Naples. They can throw shells of nearly 2,000 pounds a distance of over five miles.

Mosaic, a joining together of small pieces of colored glass, marble, or other materials in designs to imitate painting. The ancient Greeks and Romans were skilled in this art; it was revived in Italy in the Middle Ages with considerable success, many eminent painters designing subjects for mosaics. It still flourishes, and notable examples occur in some of the principal modern buildings.

Mosque, a Mohammedan church, the largest being St. Sophia at Istanbul, now converted into a museum of Byzantine art.

Moss, the name of numerous flowerless, close-growing plants, common to moist, hilly lands.

Motet, a sacred choral composition, of which many fine examples survive. Most of them were written in the 15th and 16th centuries.

Mule, the spinning machine invented by Crompton in 1779, so called from its combining the principles of Hargreaves' spinning jenny and Arkwright's cotton-spinning frame.

Mummies, embalmed bodies exceptionally well preserved. Many of those found in Egypt are the corpses of distinguished people who lived thousands of years ago. Mummies have been found also in Peru, Mexico, and Persia. The embalming process which enabled the bodies to be preserved can only be conjectured, though it is known that various aromatic substances were used after the viscera and other vital organs had been removed, the cavities being filled with absorbent dust, chippings, and cedar wood. A splendidly preserved and magnificently decorated mummy of Pharaoh Tutankhamen (B.C. 1350) was found in 1925.

Musk Deer, a small and interesting ruminant, which inhabits the mountain regions of central Asia. It is gray in color, slightly brindled, and carries a small pouch in its abdominal region, containing what is commercially known as musk, an article of great value in the manufacture of various perfumes.

Musk Ox, an animal partaking of the characteristics of both the sheep and the ox and having a musk odor. It is native to northern Canada.

Mussel, a well-known bivalve found in great abundance on the rocks of the seashores. There is also a fresh-water species plentiful in streams and ponds.

Mustang, the American wild horse, descended from the stock first introduced by the Spaniards.

Myriapoda, the class of invertebrate animals including centipedes, millipedes, and many others.

Myrrh, a resinous substance obtained from a tree of the order Amyridaceae, growing plentifully in Abyssinia and Arabia. Its use for medical, aromatic, and embalming purposes may be traced to very early times.

Mysteries, theatrical performances given by ecclesiastics in the Middle Ages, with the object of conveying moral lessons and presenting Scripture stories in more or less realistic form. The Oberammergau Passion Play is a survival of one of these ancient mysteries.

Mythology, the name given to any collection of traditions and fables concerning gods and goddesses.

N

Nadir, the point in the celestial sphere directly underfoot from the observer. It is the point opposite the zenith. A straight line drawn from the zenith through the point on the surface of the earth where the observer stands, will pass through the nadir.

Nahum Festival, a festival of the Roman Catholic Church, celebrated on December 1st, in commemoration of Nahum, the 7th of the 12 minor Hebrew prophets. Nahum flourished about 700 B. C. during the reign of Hezekiah and wrote his prophecies after Sennacherib's invasion.

Nantes, Edict of, a decree promulgated by Henry IV of France in 1598, giving full freedom of worship to the Protestants of the country. It was the revocation of this famous edict in 1685 by Louis XIV that drove thousands of French Huguenots to England and Germany.

Naphtha, a combustible liquid believed to have been one of the ingredients of "Greek fire" and called by the Greeks "oil of Media." Mineral naphtha consists chiefly of mixtures of the hydrocarbons paraffin and olefine. Other kinds are obtained from coal tar and from wood by distillation.

Naphthalene, a hydrocarbon procured from coal tar. Its derivatives are used in the manufacture of colors and explosives.

Narcotic, a substance which induces sleep or stupor and, if taken in large doses, causes insensibility or death. The best-known narcotic is opium.

Narcotine, an alkaloid obtained from opium; in its action less powerful than morphine.

Narghile, an oriental tobacco pipe so constructed that the smoke passes through water and up a long flexible tube before reaching the lips of the smoker.

Narwhal, a kind of dolphin, found only in northern seas, whalelike in form, and attaining a length of 16 feet. The male possesses a spiral ivory rod, projecting from its head.

Nasalis, a type of monkey with a long prominent nose. The proboscis monkey of Borneo belongs to this class.

National Assembly, the congress which convened in France on June 17, 1789. Three days later the king ordered the meeting place closed, but the assembly met at the Church of St. Louis and proceeded to perform acts of legislation. In 1792 the National Assembly became the National Convention.

Nativity, a festival in the Christian church, usually in commemoration of the birth of Christ; Christmas. In the Roman Catholic Church the natal days of the Virgin Mary (Sept. 8th) and of John the Baptist (June 24) are also celebrated.

Natural, a musical term signifying the production of sounds without flats or sharps. A composition is in the natural key when in the normal scale of C.

Natural Selection, the term employed by Darwin to describe the process by which the fittest survived, and the feeblest became extinct.

Nautilus, a term applied to a pearly-shelled mollusk, the sole surviving example of the four-gilled Cephalopoda, remarkable for its peculiar compartmented shell and its power to sink instantly. It is found only in the open seas.

Nave, the main, open portion of a cathedral or church, extending from the chief entrance to the choir, or chancel. In mechanics, a nave is the hub or central part of a wheel.

Navy, a fleet; the warships belonging to a country, taken collectively; the naval establishment of a country, including the ships, officers, men, armaments, and stores. Carthage, a Phoenician colony, rose to high rank among the nations of antiquity by virtue of its naval commerce. In the long struggle with Rome it was mainly the wealth acquired by commerce which enabled Carthage to maintain the conflict. A Carthaginian vessel which had been cast upon the coast of Italy is said to have furnished the model for the first Roman fleet, which consisted of 100 quinqueremes and 20 triremes. The Romans used grappling hooks by means of which Roman vessels could be firmly attached to those of the enemy, thus permitting close-range and hand-to-hand fighting. The first great naval battle between Rome and Carthage was fought off the Lipari Islands, 260 B. C., and resulted in a complete victory for the Roman fleet under the command of Duilius. The galley was the war vessel of the ancients. It was comparatively narrow and about 100 feet in length. The bow had a projecting iron beak which was designed to ram the side of an enemy ship. The famous Viking ships of the Norsemen were used in raiding expeditions and were met by the ships of England, Holland, and France. Attacks by the Danes on England in the 9th century were met by a navy built up by King Alfred. Henry VIII hurriedly organized a navy which was more fully developed in the reign of Queen Elizabeth. A strong Spanish fleet, the Spanish Armada, set out to attack England in 1588, but storms and the tactical maneuvers of the English commanders, which put the Spaniards at a disadvantage, destroyed the Armada. In the middle of the 13th century, the French navy was organized by Louis IX. Peter the Great built a navy for Russia, and in the 19th century strong navies were developed by Germany, Italy, and Japan. For nearly a century after the defeat of the Spanish Armada Holland was the most important naval power, but finally yielded to England.

The United States Navy had its beginnings in the appropriation of money by Congress in 1775 for the building of ships and the organization of an American fleet by Congress in 1775. The tiny American navy demoralized British commerce and won a number of important engagements, thus playing a large part in the ultimate gaining of independence. During the War of 1812 the United States Navy won a number of signal victories over the British. The Navy was reorganized in 1815 and continued to be of moderate strength until the Spanish-American War gave new impetus toward building it into a strong force. President Theodore Roosevelt brought the Navy to a high point of efficiency and ordered the cruise around the world in 1907-08 which gave it a prestige and morale never before attained in peacetime. At the outbreak of World War I the United States navy ranked fourth among navies of the world, but by the end of World War II it had far outstripped all others in size and strength. Many naval ships are now maintained in an inactive status in a "mothball fleet."

Nazarenes, a sect of Jewish Christians, flourishing in the 1st century, who accepted the divinity of Christ.

Nearctic Region, the territory comprising Greenland and that part of North America extending approximately to the Tropic of Cancer.

Nebulae, luminous celestial masses of gaseous matter, either spiral or chaotic in form, the latter being the earlier stage of the former. They are visible through the telescope beyond the limits of the solar system.

Nebular Hypothesis, the theory, developed by Kant, Swedenborg, Herschel, La Place, and others, that the solar system was formed by the condensation and cohesion of nebulae. This hypothesis was at one time generally accepted by astronomers.

Necromancy, magic, the pseudo art of foretelling the future by communicating with the dead. It is supposed by some that there is an occult power enabling certain people to converse with the spirits of the dead.

Negroes, members of the black-skinned, woolly-headed races, natives of tropical Africa or descendants from such natives. The people of the Sudan, Senegal, and the great lake regions are the truest types, though it is customary to call Kaffirs, Zulus, and other blacks Negroes. There are about 15,000,000 Negroes in the United States.

Neoplatonism, a philosophical system founded by Plotinus in the 3rd century and developed by Porphyry, Proclus, Hypatia, and others. Its essential doctrine is that the One, or Unity, pervades all, and that from this One *emanate* the souls of men and all matter in the universe. Neoplatonic thought seems to have influenced certain of the early Christian theologians and thus may have affected Christian doctrine.

Nepotism, the granting of patronage or other privileges to one's relatives.

Neptune, a planet, at a mean distance of about 2,790 millions of miles from the sun, requiring about 160 years to make one revolution around the sun.

Nestorians, followers of Nestorius, a patriarch of Constantinople in the 5th century. He taught that Christ was both human and divine, receiving His divinity from God and His human nature from Mary. There are still some Nestorian communities, principally in the Levant.

Nests, the habitations formed by birds for the reception of their eggs and the hatching and raising of their young. They are of the most varied character, some being mere resting places on the ground, others displaying a remarkable skill in construction. Thus, the bowerbird and certain other species show very distinctive peculiarities. The usual materials for birdnest building are leaves, twigs, moss, wool, feathers, mud and clay. Some birds burrow in sand hills. Certain mammals and fishes build nestlike structures in which to breed.

Neuroptera, an order of insects which includes dragonflies, caddis flies, may flies, and other four-winged species. The larvae have six-jointed legs.

New Year's Day, the first day of the year. In the Gregorian calendar it is January 1; in the Jewish calendar, the first day of Tishri (which falls between September 6 and October 4); in the Chinese calendar, between January 10 and February 19.

Nibelungenlied, the German epic of the 12th century comprising numerous mythical poems or sagas. These poems have been used with great effect as the themes for Wagner's famous series of operas, "The Ring of the Nibelung."

Nicene Creed, a summary of the principles of Christian faith, drawn up in 325 by the Council of Nicaea and revised in 381 by the Council of Constantinople.

Niche, a recess or nook for the statues of saints or for other ornaments.

Nickel, a white, ductile, metallic element forming useful alloys. It is extensively used in United States and Canadian coins, as well as in the manufacture of German silver.

Nihilism, in metaphysics, the doctrine which denies any objective basis for truth.

Nihilists, members of a political organization which found its most numerous supporters in Russia. They carried on their work in secret and had representatives in all classes of society. They were regarded as the moving spirits in many of the conspiracies and assassinations in Russia, their activity being greater than ever during the troubles subsequent to the Russo-Japanese War. The Nihilists were a powerful force against autocracy.

Nimbus, a circlet of light depicted around the heads of saints or divine persons in ancient and medieval art.

Nirvana, in Buddhism, the condition of supreme attainment, which involves the extinction of every form of desire, ambition, or unrest. It is the holy state.

Niter, a white crystalline substance known also as potassium nitrate or saltpeter. It is usually manufactured by the double decomposition of sodium nitrate and potassium chloride; it forms the explosive ingredient in gunpowder, matches, and detonating powders and is used in the manufacture of fertilizers. It is found in large quantities in certain parts of South America.

Nitric Acid, a compound of nitrogen, hydrogen, and oxygen, first separated by Raymond Lully, the alchemist, in the 13th century. It was not, however, until the end of the 18th century that Cavendish demonstrated its real nature. It oxidizes many metals.

Nitrogen, a non-combustible gaseous element devoid of taste or smell and constituting nearly four-fifths of the atmospheric air. In the 18th century Scheele separated the oxygen of the air from the nitrogen.

Nitroglycerin, an explosive yellow fluid produced by mixing small quantities of glycerin with a combination of one part of nitric acid and two parts of sulphuric acid. It was first employed as an explosive agent by Alfred Nobel in 1864. It is the main constituent of dynamite.

Nitrous Oxide, an anesthetic gas combining nitrogen and oxygen. It was discovered by Priestley in 1772.

Nobel Prizes, awards made from a fund of $9,200,000 bequeathed by Alfred B. Nobel, the interest of which is divided into five equal parts, to be distributed annually to the persons who during the year have contributed most to the advancement of mankind in 1) physics; 2) chemistry; 3) medicine and physiology; 4) literature; 5) world peace. The cash value of each prize is about $40,000. The prizes for physics and chemistry are awarded by the Swedish Academy of Science; that for physiological or medical work by the Stockholm Faculty of Medicine; the one for literature by the Swedish Academy in Stockholm; and the peace prize is awarded by a committee of five persons elected by the Norwegian Storting. One stipulation by the founder is that the nationality of the candidates have no bearing whatever on the awarding of the prize, although the nationality of each recipient is announced when the award is made. In 1940, 1941, and 1942 no prizes were announced.

Nocturne, a name applied by John Field to a certain kind of musical composition suggestive of night. Chopin used the term for his nocturnes for the piano, and Whistler for some of his famous night effects.

Nonconformists, the dissenters who do not conform to the doctrine of the Church of England. Up to the passing of the Act of Uniformity in 1662 they were called Puritans. At various times the noncorformists were rigorously persecuted, but later toleration was granted to them. The oldest bodies of nonconformists are the Presbyterians, Baptists, and Independents. The Quakers, Unitarians, and Methodists are later nonconformists.

Norfolk Islanders, descendants of the mutineers of the *Bounty* who established themselves on Pitcairn Island in 1789. The Pitcairn families, in the course of the next half century, became so numerous that the island was unable to support them all, and so in 1856 the British government removed them to Norfolk Island, which was stocked with sheep, cattle, and horses for their benefit. The Norfolk Islanders now number about 1,230, two-thirds of whom are descendants of the original mutineers.

Northmen, the early inhabitants of Scandinavia, famous as sea adventurers and pirates. Their attacks on Britain and other parts of northern Europe prior to the 11th century were often successful, and they established settlements in the islands off the Scottish coasts and in the north of France, where they founded the duchy of Normandy, from which the Normans who conquered England in the 11th century were descended.

Northwest Passage, a water route from the Atlantic to the Pacific through the Arctic Ocean. To discover this passage was a dream of adventurous navigators for centuries, and many were the expeditions which sailed at great sacrifice of life and money. The route is now known, but climatic conditions prevent its commercial use.

Notre Dame, the famous Paris cathedral, founded in 1163, one of the finest specimens of Gothic architecture in Europe. An excellent description of the building is given in Victor Hugo's *Nôtre Dame de Paris*.

November, the eleventh month of the year. At a very early period in Roman history the year began with March, and November was the ninth month, as its derivation from *novem*, meaning nine, indicates.

Nunc Dimittis ("Now lettest thou thy servant depart in peace"), a familiar hymn forming part of the evening service in many Christian churches. (Luke ii. 29.)

Nuncio, a papal envoy appointed to a foreign state.

Nunnery, a convent or residence for women who have taken religious vows. There are many Catholic nunneries in the United States and Canada.

O

Oasis, any fertile spot in a desert. Such spots are fairly numerous in the Sahara and Libyan deserts, and some of them are extensively peopled and successfully cultivated.

Oath, a solem affirmation or declaration made with an appeal to God for the truth of what is affirmed. By appealing to the Supreme Being, the person making an oath is understood to invoke His vengeance if that which is affirmed or declared is false; or, in case of a promissory oath, if the promise or obligation is willfully broken.

Oats, a cereal product, native probably to Asia but cultivated with considerable success for many centuries in most temperate regions. The United States produces yearly over a billion bushels of oats. Cakes and porridge of oatmeal are common articles of food in many countries.

Obelisk, a slender, four-sided shaft of stone, terminating in a pyramid; regarded by the ancient Egyptians as the symbol of God. It was customary to place these pillars before Egyptian temples, one on each side of the entrance. Twelve obelisks were transported from Egypt to Rome; there are others in New York, London, Paris, and Berlin.

Oberammergau, the Bavarian village where the Passion play is acted, depicting episodes in the suffering and crucifixion of Christ. These performances take place every ten years.

Obi, a colored sash commonly worn by Japanese women, which is tied in back with a large bow.

Oblation, a gift offered in worship, referring especially to the bread and wine given by the laity for the Eucharist.

Obscurantists, a term applied to persons who are adverse to the extension of knowledge and view with distrust all measures of reform and the opening up of new lines of thought.

Observatory, a building for the observation and study of astronomical phenomena. In ancient Babylon and Egypt observatories were often erected on towers and temples. The most famous Egyptian observatory was built at Alexandria by Ptolemy Soter in 300 B. C. Among important observatories built during the last few centuries were those at Nürnberg (1472), Padua, Paris (1667), and Greenwich (1675). In recent times such institutions have become numerous. At the Lick Observatory, California, the telescope has a 36-inch refractor; that at the Yerkes Observatory, of the University of Chicago, has a tube 75 feet long and an object glass 40 inches in diameter. Mount Wilson Observatory in California has a 100-inch reflector. The 200-inch reflecting telescope at the California Institute of Technology is the largest in the world.

Obsidian, a form of volcanic rock of vitreous structure; usually a silicate of aluminum, lime, magnesium, etc.

Ocarina, a kind of wind instrument made usually of terra cotta and having finger holes and a whistle-like mouthpiece.

Occultism, the practice or study of the supernatural sciences, including alchemy, astrology, magic, spiritualism, palmistry, etc.

Ocean, the sea, or the body of salt water. Properly speaking, there is but one ocean, since the bodies of salt water on the globe, with the exception of the Caspian Sea, the Sea of Aral, and the Dead Sea, are in communication with one another. Different portions of the ocean have received distinctive names: the Arctic, the Atlantic, the Indian, the Pacific, and the Antarctic. The unequal heating of portions of the vast expanse of water on the globe, the rotation of the earth, the winds, and other causes tend to keep the water in constant circulation and thus to prevent it from becoming stagnant and impure. The attractions of the moon and sun cause tides. The area of the ocean is about 155,000,000 square miles, or nearly three-fourths of the whole surface of the earth.

Ocean Currents, well-defined streams running through certain portions of the ocean and caused in various ways. Usually the currents run from the equator in the direction of the poles, and by a natural counteraction currents are set up in the opposite direction.

Oceanography, that branch of science which deals with the geology, geography, physical and chemical characteristics, and life of the seas. Oceanography as a science is about a century old; the early explorers added little to it except knowledge of a geographical nature. The physical and chemical properties of the oceans have been investigated by the Carnegie Institution of Washington during the many cruises of the non-magnetic yacht *Carnegie*. The results of these investigations form a series of valuable monographs. Ethyl fluid for treating gasoline and small quantities of gold are extracted from the sea in South Carolina. Chemicals, chiefly bromides and potash, are extracted also from the Dead Sea, and the manufacture of salt from sea water is an important industry in many countries where inland salt deposits are not available. Perhaps the most famous studies of undersea life are those made by Dr. William Beebe who made several descents in his bathysphere. At the Tortugas Laboratory of the Carnegie Institute, located on Loggerhead Key, one of the islands of the Dry Tortugas group, studies of undersea life are also carried on. The depths and the sea-bottom characteristics of most of the oceans have been determined by soundings and samples, and charts have been made indicating contours and depths.

Ocelot, usually called the leopard cat, common in the southern United States, Mexico, and Brazil. It is about 4 feet in length, including tail, and of a gray or tawny color and spotted. It is very destructive to weaker animals; it does not devour them but sucks their blood.

Ocher, the name of a number of natural earths impregnated with mineral colorings, chiefly silica and alumina; oxides of iron and lead. They include iron ocher, yellow ocher, and plumbic ocher and are used in the making of paints.

Octave, in music, a series of eight notes or an interval of seven tones.

October, the 10th month of the year. It was the 8th in the ancient Roman calendar and was sacred to Mars.

Octopus, an invertebrate fish of the Cephalopoda class, sometimes called "the devil fish." It has eight arms covered with suckers, a head with horny jaws, and large globular eyes. It is very common in the Mediterranean.

Ode, originally, a poem sung with musical accompaniment in honor of the gods by the ancient Greeks and Romans. Odes were divided into three sections; strophe, antistrophe, and epode. The most famous ancient odes were those of Anacreon, Pindar, and Horace. Among the best-known odes in English are those of Milton, Dryden, Collins, Gray, Wordsworth, and Keats.

Odontograph, in mechanics, an instrument which enables engineers to design and mark off the teeth of gear wheels.

Odyssey, Homer's famous epic poem about the wanderings of Ulysses on his way back to Ithaca after the siege of Troy.

OGPU, the secret political police of U.S.S.R. Prior to 1922 it was the Cheka; in 1934 it was absorbed by the NKVD; after World War II it became the MVD.

Ohm's Law, the rule, discovered by G. S. Ohm, a German physicist, by which the quantity of the electromotive force of the voltaic battery is determined. An ohm is the unit of resistance in electromagnetics.

Oil, a greasy, viscous fluid, insoluble in water. There are three classes of oils: fatty or fixed, volatile or essential, and mineral. Fatty oils are obtained from animal and vegetable matters; fixed oils are used in the manufacture of soap, for lubricating purposes, and for illumination. Volatile or essential oils are obtained by distillation and are used mainly for essences and coloring mediums; mineral oils are used mostly for producing artificial light and are largely utilized as oil fuel.

Oil Cake, an article of feed for cattle. It is made from linseed, rape, and cotton seed, after the oils have been extracted, and is very fattening.

Ojibway Indians, a tribe inhabiting the Great Lakes districts of Canada. At one time they were very warlike and troublesome, but in recent years they have become largely civilized and live in prosperous settlements.

Olefiant Gas, or ethylene, a hydrocarbon obtained by treating ethyl alcohol with concentrated sulphuric acid or phosphoric acid. It is present in coal gas to the extent of about 6 per cent. It is a useful anesthetic.

Olefines, a series of hydrocarbons, in which the hydrogen atoms are double the number of carbon atoms. The first member of the series is olefiant gas. Olefines differ from paraffins in that they combine directly with the halogens and the haloid acids.

Oleic Acid, a fatty acid found in fats and oils and obtained from olives, almonds, and similar fruits. It is an organic acid containing oxygen, carbon, and hydrogen and is much used in the manufacture of certain soaps.

Olein, a colorless oil obtained from animal and vegetable fatty oils. It is not found in a pure state; it is soluble in alcohol and ether, but not in water.

Oleograph, a reproduction of an oil painting, the colors of the original being more or less faithfully copied. The process is one that closely resembles chromolithography.

Oleomargarine, a solid fat of a yellowish color obtained from the leaf fat of cattle. This fat is submitted to certain patented processes and sold as margarine, a substitute for butter.

Oleometer, an instrument for ascertaining the specific gravity of oil.

Olive, the fruit of the olive tree, which grows abundantly in Italy and in recent years has been cultivated with considerable success in southern California and Australia. A stone fruit, in its unripe condition it is used extensively for pickling purposes. Olive oil is obtained from the pulp of the fruit and is the lightest of all fixed oils.

Olympiad, a period of four years, a measure of time used by the ancient Greeks. This method of computation began with the first olympiad in 776 B. C. and lasted until A. D. 440.

Olympic Games, athletic contests instituted by the Greeks in honor of Zeus and held every four years at Olympia in the Peloponnesus. These festivals continued, with intervals, from 776 B. C. to A. D. 390.

Omega, the last letter of the Greek alphabet; used widely, in the figurative sense, to indicate the end of anything.

Omen, a sign or presentiment of some coming event, often an evil event. In ancient times omens, portents, and signs were regarded seriously and were interpreted by priests or augurs, who were thought to be the recipients of the warnings of the gods.

Onyx, a kind of agate or quartz having its colors arranged in parallel layers. Onyx is easily cut and polished and is much used for cameos.

Opal, a gem of silica-like quartz of numerous varieties and colors ranging from white to brown and green. Some have a vitreous luster and transparency called "opalescence." The best opals come from Hungary and Australia.

Opera, a drama in which music is the dominating feature. The beginnings of this art can be traced as far back as 1240, when a French opera was performed. Italian opera came into being toward the end of the 15th century, and in 1600 an opera on the subject of Eurydice was given at Florence on the occasion of the marriage of Marie de' Medici and Henry IV of France. Louis XIV set up an opera in Paris in 1672. Scarlatti was the most prolific producer of operas during the 17th century. About 1684 a sort of opera was performed in London; in 1711 Handel's *Rinaldo* was produced there at the Haymarket. Gay's *The Beggar's Opera* was first given in 1727 and ran for 63 nights. The operas of Mozart had a marked influence upon the development of operatic music in the latter part of the 18th century. The leading composers of the 19th century were Beethoven, Rossini, Weber, Donizetti, Auber, Verdi, Meyerbeer, Gounod, and Wagner, the last named producing the most marked development that has hitherto occurred in the history of opera. Important operatic composers of the 20th century include: Richard Strauss, Humperdinck, Mascagni, Debussy, and Weinberger. Among the composers of light operas the names of Offenbach in France and Sir Arthur Sullivan in England rank high.

Opium, a narcotic obtained from the white poppy. The unripe "head," or seed capsule, of that flower yields a juice which when dried becomes opium. The poppy is extensively cultivated in India, Egypt, Persia, and Asia Minor for the sake of this juice, which yields various alkaloids, such as morphine, narcotine, and thebaine. Laudanum is tincture of opium. The Chinese were great smokers of opium. In 1906 the Chinese government proposed to the British government an arrangement by which the importation of Indian opium into China should cease within ten years, and at the same time measures were adopted for closing opium dens in China. The cultivation of opium is restricted in India to a government monopoly. The largest opium farms of Europe are in Macedonia, which produces sufficient opium for the medicinal needs of the whole world.

Opium War, the war which followed on the destruction in 1840 of a number of British vessels carrying opium into Chinese ports. The result was the establishing of the "Treaty Ports" of China and the cession of Hong Kong to England.

Opossum, a marsupial mammal found in the United States, South America, and Australia. It has a long, prehensile tail and is not much larger than a cat. The females possess a pouch in which they keep their young. The opossum is of nocturnal habits and is a good scavenger.

Opportunists, a term applied to those members of the Republican party in France, after the Franco-Prussian War, who held that the true political policy was not to force opinions upon the people, but to wait until circumstances favored their advocacy. Gambetta was the leader of this faction.

Optics, the science which investigates the nature and properties of light and the phenomena of color. Ptolemy wrote a treatise on optics in 120 B. C., and burning glasses were known to the ancient Greeks. Spectacles were invented in the 13th century; the camera obscura in the 16th century. Telescopes were not known until about 1571, and the microscope not before 1620.

Optimism, the theory that everything happens for the best, held by many Christians and by many philosophers from Plato to Rousseau. It is the opposite of pessimism.

Oracle, in Greek religion, a message inspired by a god and delivered through priests to those who wished to learn the future. The gods and the places where oracles were given were also called oracles. The most famous Greek oracles were at Delphi (Apollo) and Olympia (Zeus).

Orangemen, members of a society founded in Ireland in 1795 to uphold Protestantism. The society, called the Loyal Orange Institution, derived its name from having supported William III, Prince of Orange. The membership is strongest in the province of Ulster.

Orangutan, one of the largest of the anthropoid apes, found only in Borneo and Sumatra. When full-grown, it stands over four feet in height and has very long arms. It lives mostly in trees and exists on fruits, buds, etc.

Oratorio, a sacred musical drama, performed without scenery. It derived its name from the oratory built by St. Philip Neri, where concerts of sacred music were given. From about 1550 to the early part of the 18th century this class of composition was not known outside of Italy. In 1738 Handel's oratorio *Israel in Egypt* was performed; his *Messiah* was first produced in 1741. Other great oratorios are Haydn's *Creation,* Beethoven's *Mount of Olives,* and Mendelssohn's *Elijah.*

Orchestra, a group of instrumental musicians playing together. A full orchestra comprises stringed, brass, wood-wind, and percussion instruments. There are four principal types of orchestras: symphonic, operatic, theatrical, and dance.

Ordeal, a primitive method of trial to determine the innocence or guilt of an accused person. Law courts in the Middle Ages resorted to trials by fire and by water. In the trial by fire the victim was forced to walk through flames or to carry in his hand white-hot iron. If he escaped uninjured, he was judged innocent. A suspect was convicted of murder if upon touching the corpse of the victim blood flowed from the body. In the water ordeal the suspect was bound hand and foot and thrown into a river. If he floated, he was judged innocent.

Orders, Holy, classes of church officials. In the Roman Catholic Church there are seven, ranking from doorkeepers, exorcists, readers and acolytes to deacons, priests, and bishops. In the Episcopal church there are only three—deacons, priests, and bishops.

Ordination, the ceremony of installing a person in a clerical office. The custom has existed in the Christian church from earliest times. In the Catholic, Orthodox, Episcopal, and Methodist churches the rites of ordination are administered by bishops.

Ore, metalliferous rock from which, by the process of smelting, the metallic element is separated. Ores are found in layers, or beds, and are oxides, carbonates, sulphates, etc.

Organ, a musical instrument in which sound is produced by forcing air through pipes or across reeds. It is said to have been invented about 250 B. C. as an adaptation of the primitive Pandean pipe. The organ began to be used in Christian churches in the 7th century, and thereafter it became the most popular musical instrument for church services.

Orgy, originally, a secret celebration in honor of Bacchus which was noted for the license displayed by the celebrants.

Oriel, a bay window which projects from an upper story of a building. It may be rectangular, triangular, pentagonal, or curved and usually rests upon molded sills supported by corbels.

Origin of Species, the title of Darwin's famous work, published in 1859, by many considered to be the most important book of the 19th century.

Oriole, a family of birds of the order Passeres. The *golden oriole,* the most common in Europe, has bright yellow plumage, with black wings and tail. The North American orioles are members of the blackbird family; the *Baltimore oriole* is the best known.

Orion, a famous constellation, comprising nearly a hundred stars, all visible to the naked eye. It contains three stars of the second magnitude in a line; these are called "Orion's Belt."

Orleanists, a French political group, originating during the Revolution. They advocated a liberal monarchy; their leaders were members of the Orleans branch of the French royal family.

Ornithology, the branch of zoology which treats of the structure and habits of birds.

Osier, a species of willow growing in damp soils and yielding branches utilized in basket-making.

Osmium, a metallic element of the platinum order and one of the heaviest of known metals. It is obtained from the platinum of South America, California, Australia and Russia. The chief commercial purpose to which it is put is that of providing tips for gold pens.

Osprey, a bird of prey widely distributed over all northern latitudes. It is commonly known as the fish hawk, and feeds almost entirely on fish.

Osteopathy, a system of healing and health based on the theory that structural derangements are the chief cause of disease, and that lesions can be set right by manipulation of the spinal and other joints. Osteopaths also advocate exercise and sensible diet. The American School of Osteopathy was founded in 1892, since when osteopathy has spread considerably, and is regulated by law in the United States and parts of Canada. There are more than 7,000 osteopathic practitioners in the United States.

Ostracism, a method of proscription adopted by the ancient Greeks, whereby sentences of banishment for ten years were voted. The names of objectionable persons were written on small oyster shells by the people, and these were collected in an urn and presented to the Senate, when a scrutiny took place, and the one whose name appeared most often was sentenced; but no one could be ostracized unless at least 6,000 votes were recorded against him.

Ostrich, a large African bird which inhabits the sandy plains, and is highly valued for the rich feathers grown on its wings and tail. The neck and legs are naked. The wings are useless for flight, but the birds have a fleetness of foot exceeding that of the swiftest horse. An ostrich's egg weighs 3 lbs.

Ostrogoths, or Eastern Goths, a Germanic people who flourished in the 4th and 5th centuries. Under their famous leader, Theodoric, they founded a monarchy in Italy in 493, but were overthrown by the forces of the Eastern emperor in 553.

Otter, an aquatic carnivorous mammal widely distributed over North America and Europe. It averages about two feet in length, exclusive of tail, has webfeet, and is an expert swimmer. Otters like to slide down steep, slippery banks.

Oviparous, a zoological term applied to mammals, birds, reptiles, and fishes that bring forth eggs to be hatched outside the body of the parent.

Ovis, the zoological name for the typical genus of sheep.

Ovoviviparous, a zoological term applied to animals which produce eggs which are hatched in the body of the parent; the viper, the scorpion, and the earthworm are examples.

Owl, a raptorial nocturnal bird distributed over the greater part of the world. Owls have large heads and round piercing eyes surrounded by rings of feathers. They are voracious feeders and live on the smaller mammals, birds, insects, and fish.

Ox, the popular name of the bovine quadrupeds included in the genus *Bos*. They are hollow-horned hoofed ruminants, and include the various classes of domestic cattle as well as the different wild species. The adult male is called a bull, the female a cow, and the young a calf. The best-known breeds of domesticated cattle are the Shorthorn, Angus, Jersey, Ayrshire, Hereford, Holstein-Friesian, Guernsey, and Brown Swiss.

Oxalic Acid, an organic acid obtained from numerous plants, such as sorrel and rhubarb. It is produced artificially in many ways. It combines with metals to form oxalates.

Oxford University, the oldest English university. It was founded during the 12th century on the site of certain schools which were said to have been built by King Alfred in 872. Merton College was founded in 1264. Queen Elizabeth granted the University a charter of incorporation in 1570. The University has been greatly extended in modern times and has today between 3,000 and 4,000 undergraduates. It comprises the following colleges: University, Balliol, Merton, Exeter, Oriel, Queen's, New, Lincoln, All Souls, Magdalen, Brasenose, Corpus Christi, Christ Church, St. John's, Trinity, Jesus, Wadham, Pembroke, Worcester, Hertford, Keble, St. Edmund's Hall, as well as private halls and 5 women's societies.

Oxygen, the most abundant of all elements, a gas that forms one-third of the solid earth, one-fifth of the atmosphere, and eight-ninths by weight of all water. It is colorless, tasteless, and odorless, and forms the chief life-supporting element of animal and vegetable life.

Oyster, a bivalve mollusk of the genus *Ostreae*, having a very numerous species and abounding in nearly all seas. The shell is rough and irregular, and the body shows a very simple organization. Oysters are exceedingly prolific, spawning in May and June. The most important American oyster beds are in Chesapeake Bay and Long Island Sound.

Oyster Catcher, a wading bird of considerable size found in most parts of the world. It feeds on small oysters and other mullusks.

Ozone, an active modification of oxygen. It contains three atoms to the molecule, while oxygen contains only two. It is present only in extremely small quantities.

P

Pacifism, a movement opposed to war and the use of threats of war in international relations.

Pagans, adherents of pre-Christian pantheistic religions, or of the animist cults still professed by some primitive peoples. The word is from Latin, *paganus*, a countryman or an uncultivated person. In the Middle Ages the term was used largely to describe Mohammedans (Moors, Saracens, etc.).

Pagoda, the name given in China, India, and other Asiatic countries to a high pyramidal or octagonal tower.

Paleontology, the science which is devoted to the investigation of fossil evidence of life in earlier geologic periods. It is closely related to geology, and is divided into *paleobotany and paleozoology*.

Paleozoic, the third great era of geologic time. It was one in which the land was alternately submerged and then raised. The Paleozoic era is estimated to have lasted 350,000,000 years.

Palimpsests, ancient MSS or parchments which have been partly effaced and used for fresh writings. Many valuable MSS were thus lost, but sometimes the second writing has been washed out, enabling the original writings to be deciphered. Among such restorations are a dialogue of Cicero's, and a portion of a book of Livy.

Pallium, a vestment ornamentation of white wool presented by the Pope to archbishops on their appointment, and the sign of papal confirmation.

Palm, a large straight-trunked plant or tree common to tropical countries, and usually fruit-yielding. Many commodities useful to man are obtained from this tree.

Palmitic Acid is obtained from either palm oil or solid fats, and forms a white tasteless and odorless substance. In combination with glycerin it forms "palmitin."

Palm Sunday, the Sunday before Easter, upon which occasion it is customary to carry palms to the churches in some countries, in commemoration of Christ's entry into Jerusalem for the Feast of the Passover, when the people went forth to greet Him with palm branches.

Pampas Cat, the wild cat of the pampas of South America. It is of a yellow-gray color with striped sides, and exists in very large numbers.

Pampas Deer, a small, graceful deer that inhabits the South American pampas. The males possess large antlers.

Panama Canal. A waterway traversing the Isthmus of Panama and connecting the Caribbean Sea on the Atlantic Ocean with the Bay of Panama on the Pacific Ocean. As the Isthmus of Panama runs almost east and west at its narrowest point, the line of the canal extends more nearly north and south than east and west and its Atlantic terminus lies to the north and west of its Pacific end. The air-line distance across the Isthmus is about 30 miles, and the canal is 43.84 nautical miles in length from deep water to deep water. The channel is 300 to 1,000 feet wide and its minimum depth is 41 feet. The canal was first undertaken by the French in 1879, but the company went into the hands of receivers after an unsavory record of promotion and corruption. Meanwhile the people of the United States were becoming interested and when the New French Panama Canal Company offered to sell its interest in the project for $40,000,000, the acceptance of their proposal was authorized by Congress. In the meantime the United States had been negotiating with Colombia to gain the right to build a canal. After Colombia's rejection of the proposed treaty, Panama declared its independence and a treaty was negotiated with the new republic. By this treaty the United States gave Panama $10,000,000 and annual payments of $250,000 in return for the concession of all rights for the construction of the canal and a grant in perpetuity of a strip ten miles wide known as the Panama Canal Zone. By the Hay-Pauncefote treaty of 1901, Great Britain agreed that the United States had sole right to build the canal.

Starting on the Atlantic side the canal runs at sea level to Gatun, where there are three sets of locks to lift ships 85 feet to Gatun Lake. They cross this lake to Gamboa, go through the Gaillard or Culebra Cut to the single lock at Pedro Miguel, where they are lowered 31 feet to Miraflores Lake, and cross to the two Miraflores locks to be lowered to the level of the Pacific Ocean. The canal was opened in 1914, but minor slides necessitated closing it for short periods, and in 1915 a disastrous slide at the Gaillard Cut caused it to be closed for about seven months. During this time the channel was dredged and widened 300 feet for about a quarter mile. Since then constant dredging has made it possible to keep the canal open. Ships of all nations pass through the canal and pay toll according to their tonnage. The canal produces more than enough revenue to meet its operating costs. Harbors have been dredged to allow larger vessels to use the canal, and docks, warehouses, and facilities for repairing have been provided.

In 1935 a dam of concrete was finished on the Chagres River at Alhajuela to form Madden Lake. This provides storage for 22,000,000,000 cubic feet of water and prevents danger of water shortage which has sometimes threatened the canal. It also lessens danger of an overflow from the Chagres River during the rainy seasons. Most ships can pass through the Canal, two notable exceptions being the *Queen Mary* and the *Queen Elizabeth*, which are too long for the lock chambers. In 1955 a new treaty between the United States and Panama was signed, increasing the annual payment for use of the Canal, among other agreements.

Panda, a carnivorous quadruped of the genus *Ailurus*, found in the Himalayas and Tibet, belonging to the raccoon family, and whose fur is reddish-brown on the back and sides, and black on the underside and legs. The *Giant panda* is an animal of the genus *Ailuropoda*, and is related to and resembles the bear in form and disposition. Its fur is white except for black patches around the eyes, and a black collar, legs, and tail. It is easily domesticated.

Panslavism, a movement to form a close cultural alliance between the various Slavic peoples, advocated widely in the 19th century. In its origin, the movement was entirely non-political.

Pantheism, the doctrine of the identity of God and the universe. A kind of pantheism has found its way into many religious and philosophical systems; Buddhism and Hinduism partake of this doctrine. Spinoza was the leading philosophical exponent of Pantheism.

Pantheon, a famous temple in Rome, built in 27 B. C by Agrippa and consecrated to the gods. Its splendid dome and portico constitute one of the most interesting architectural monuments of ancient days. Since the 7th century it has been used as a Christian church. The Pantheon at Paris, built in 1764, is modeled after it.

Pantomimes, stage representations in which speech is not permitted, all the action being carried on by gesture and movement. The ancient Greeks and Romans favored them. Later on pantomime became popular throughout Europe, and in the 18th century, with clown, harlequin, and columbine, was adopted as a form of Christmas entertainment. In Europe the word pantomime is used to describe many kinds of entertainment, especially Christmas entertainments, but in the United States it still bears its original meaning.

Papacy, a term applied to the office of the pontiff of the Roman Catholic Church in Rome, or to his papal jurisdiction. The papacy derives its claims to ecclesiastical supremacy from its apostolic succession, based on the founding of the church by St. Peter, vicar of Christ on earth. The church in the early centuries grew rapidly, and as it spread, the power of the successive bishops of Rome increased in proportion. Other apostolic sees were founded in the East but they did not endure. The church, with its monasteries, was the great civilizing factor and the preserver of culture during the so-called Dark Ages. It therefore became the practice to submit political as well as controversial spiritual matters to the judgment of the pope. The early bishops of Rome claimed only spiritual authority, but Gregory VII, who became pope in 1048, stated that temporal matters were inferior to spiritual matters. His assertion, however, was not substantiated by succeeding pontiffs until the reigns of Boniface VIII (1294-1303) and John XXII (1316-1334). Papal jurisdiction reached its greatest power in the reign of Innocent III, but even then the pronouncements of the papacy were predicated on the validation of temporal rulers. There have been 262 pontiffs officially credited by the church. Of the more recent popes, three are notable in particular for their advocacy of humanitarian principles. Leo XIII (1878-1903) became noted especially for his famous encyclical, *Rerum novarum* (1891) which applied Christian principles to the relations between capital and labor. He thus earned the title "the workingman's pope." Benedict XV actively pleaded for peace during the World War. Pope Pius XI (1922-1939) substantiated the social doctrines of Leo XIII.

Papal infallibility, a dogma of the Roman Catholic Church, that the Pope is infallible when he speaks *ex cathedra* on matters of faith or morals. The ecumenical councils are likewise considered infallible as long as their canons do not disagree with the doctrines promulgated by the Papacy. The dogma was enunciated by the Vatican Council in 1870; Catholic theologians differ as to when a declaration of the Pope satisfies the conditions necessary to make it infallible.

Paper has been known in one form or another from very early times. The papyrus reeds of the Nile swamps served the ancient Egyptians for sheets upon which to inscribe their records. The Chinese and Japanese, centuries later, were using something more akin to modern paper in substance, an Asiatic paper-mulberry, yielding a smooth fibrous material. With the spread of learning in western Europe, there was increased demand for paper, and it came to be manufactured from pulped rags and other substances, though as to the precise period when this was accomplished, or by what country, there is no definite information. Paper was made in England in the reign of Elizabeth from linen and cotton rags, and down to a comparatively recent period these materials have constituted the chief components of paper. Other paper-making staples have been introduced in recent years, such as surat, a kind of bark brought from India; waste jute; esparto grass; and wood pulp. In modern mills logs are dissolved with sulphur and other solvents, and become pulp in three or four days. Then this is ground to finer consistency in a series of machines, and is ultimately run off through heated rollers in continuous sheets, sometimes miles in length. Sizing is introduced generally at the pulp stage. Blotting and filtering papers are unsized, and are rendered additionally absorbent by the use of wool. The machinery for cutting the paper into sheets as required is of very ingenious construction. "Hand-made" paper is formed exclusively of prepared rags.

Papier-mache, a composition of paper pulp and other substances, to which when molded into form, coatings of varnish, with gilt and colored inlayings, are added. Elegant and decorative objects are made of papier-mache. A ceramic papier-mache is very durable.

Papyrus, the ancient Egyptian paper-like material; made from a Nile reed.

Parachute, an apparatus in the shape of an umbrella, intended for the descent of passengers and crew from disabled aircraft.

Paradise, a Persian word used by the translators of the Old Testament to designate the Garden of Eden, and since meaning any place of happiness.

Paraffin, a mineral wax first obtained by distillation of coal, the process being discovered about 1830. About 1848, James Young procured it from mineral oil, and peat also yielded it. The main source of paraffin supply today is crude petroleum. It is used largely in the manufacture of candles, for waterproofing, and numerous other purposes.

Parchment, dried animal skin. It was formerly used in place of paper, most books being written on parchment until after the 8th century. Vellum is parchment made from the skins of young calves or lambs. Parchment is used today in book bindings, diplomas, lamp shades, drum heads, and for banjos and tambourines.

Pariah, a very low caste of Hindu, outside the pale of regular castes, and avoided as something unclean. Pariahs are among the lowest class of laborers, but are often employed as servants to European families.

Parliament, a legislative assembly, specifically that of Great Britain, which has its origin in early medieval times. The Icelandic parliament is the oldest parliament in the world. The name is derived from the French *parlement,* or discourse.

Parquetry, a style of flooring consisting of small pieces of wood laid down in geometrical design

Parrot, one of a widely distributed order of tropical birds, including the African gray parrot. the green parrot of South America—both familiar cage pets in this country—and the various parrakeets, cockatoos, macaws, lories, etc. Nearly all of these birds possess a remarkable gift of imitating sounds, especially the human voice.

Parsees, descendants of the Zoroastrians or fire-worshipers of Persia, are now more numerous in India than in their early home. They are born traders, and many of them not only possess great wealth but are renowned for their charities.

Parthenon, the famous temple of Athena on the Acropolis at Athens, erected about 442 B. C. under the supervision of Phidias, who therein placed his renowned statue of the Greek goddess. The Parthenon was 227 feet long by 101 feet broad, and was in the pure Doric style. The ruins still existing are of considerable extent.

Passover, the Jewish festival commemorating the departure from Egypt and the passing of the Angel of Death over the houses of the Israelites.

Passport, a warrant of protection and authority to travel abroad issued by a government to one of its citizens. In the United States, passports are issued by the State Department and must be signed by the Secretary of State or an officer acting under his instructions and must be countersigned by a consular agent of the country which the traveler intends to visit. The fee is $10; the life of a passport is two years; it is renewable for two years more at a charge of $5.

Pathology, the science of diseases, particularly their physiological and anatomical effects.

Peacock, a game bird of large size and beautiful plumage; it is a native of eastern Asia, and is a member of the pheasant family. There are two species. The plumage of the male is brightly colored.

Pearl, a gem stone produced by secretions of certain shelled mollusks, chiefly the oyster. The inner surface of the shell of the pearl oyster yields "mother-of-pearl," and distinct pearls are believed to be morbid secretions, caused by some external irritation. Many fine pearls are found in the actual body of the oyster. Madagascar, Ceylon, the northwest coast of Western Australia and the Gulf of Mexico are among the most productive pearl-fishing grounds. Western Australia has produced a 40-grain pearl, the finest in the world. The largest pearl ever found was the "Beresford-Hope Pearl," which weighed 1,800 grains, over six times as much as the oyster that produced it.

Peat, decayed vegetable matter found mostly in marshy places. Peat is the first stage in the development of coal. It is used as fuel in some parts of the world, especially Ireland.

Pedometer, an instrument for recording distances walked; it is capable only of registering the number of steps taken.

Pelican, a large, aquatic bird which has a long bill, with a pouch suspended beneath, enabling the bird to hold a number of fish in reserve for future consumption. It has immense wings and webbed feet.

Penance, a punishment prescribed or voluntarily accepted as an atonement for a sin or offense. Public penance was formerly exacted and in the Roman Catholic Church today penance appointed to the sin is imposed at confession.

Penguin, a genus of large birds with small wings and webbed feet, existing in enormous numbers in the Antarctic Ocean. They breed on the rocky coast, and in the season are to be seen in vast numbers standing erect over their eggs. They are facile swimmers, and live on fish.

Pentateuch, the first five books of the Old Testament: Genesis, Exodus, Leviticus, Numbers, and Deuteronomy.

Pentecost, in the Christian Church, the festival in commemoration of the descent of the Holy Ghost upon the apostles during the feast of the Pentecost; to the Jews it is a time of solemn celebration—"the feast of weeks," celebrated on the 50th day, or seven weeks after the Passover.

Pepsin, the principal enzyme of the gastric juice, which may be obtained from the mucous membrane of the stomach of suitable manniferous animals. It used as a remedy for indigestion and other medical purposes.

Pepys' Diary, the diary of Samuel Pepys, an English naval official of the Restoration period. It was first published in 1825, and gives a graphic picture of the social life of the time.

Perch, a family of small fresh-water fish, found in Europe, Asia, and North America. The flesh is edible.

Peripatetics, the followers of Aristotle, the name arising from the philosopher's habit of walking up and down while he expounded his theories. The Peripatetic school of philosophy occupied itself chiefly in preparing commentaries and interpretations of Aristotle.

Periscope, an optical instrument which enables the user to observe objects concealed by an intervening body or not in his direct line of vision. The periscope was used during World War I in trench warfare. Periscopes also enable submarines to retain surface visibility while submerged. When so used, they are constructed so that they may be turned to permit a view of the entire horizon.

Perjury, the offense of giving false evidence. The ancient Romans threw perjurers from the Tarpeian Rock, and after the Empire was Christianized, those who swore falsely upon the Gospel had their tongues cut out. The usual punishment in England from the 16th to the 19th century was the pillory, fine, and imprisonment. It is now punishable by imprisonment.

Permian Formation, a group of rocks lying between the Triassic and the Carboniferous strata. It has three subdivisions, Upper, Middle and Lower Permian, all of which are rich in fossil deposits.

Perpetual Motion, a problem that has engaged the ingenuity of many inventors, known and obscure, including George Stephenson and Richard Arkwright, both of whom struggled with the idea until convinced of its impracticability. There are even yet people who imagine that a machine that will possess within itself the power of supplying its own motion is among the inventive possibilities.

Peruke, the wig worn by men in the 17th and 18th centuries, and up to the end of the first decade of the 19th century. They were common in the United States in colonial times. Perukes did not make their appearance in England until about 1260, and during the Restoration period were of great length, falling upon the shoulders.

Pessimism, the belief in the dominance and necessity of pain in life and in the world. Its foremost exponent in philosophy was Schopenhauer, who held that pain conquers pleasure in all life, since to desire is painful, and to be satisfied causes boredom.

Petition of Right, a petition sent by Parliament to Charles I, in 1628. It declared that no freeman should be compelled to pay taxes except by consent of Parliament; that none should be illegally imprisoned; that soldiers and sailors should not be billeted on private property; and that martial law should not be declared in time of peace. It is important as a forerunner of both the English and the American Bills of Rights.

Petroleum, an oily mixture of hydro-carbons (a form of bitumen), found in the upper strata of the earth. It was of little importance until 1859, when an oil well was drilled in Pennsylvania. As a source of kerosene for lighting purposes, it became important, but had almost no other use until the development of the internal-combustion engine and its application in automobiles, trucks, tractors, airplanes, and motorboats. Petroleum has since become important in dyes and drugs and as fuel for locomotives and steamships. Petroleum is found in many parts of the world. Of the total production of crude petroleum, over 6 billion barrels per year, the United States supplies almost half. Other leading producers are the U.S.S.R., Venezuela, Kuwait, Saudi Arabia, and Iraq. The search for new deposits never ends.

Petty Officers in the navy correspond with non-commissioned officers in the army.

Pewter, an alloy of tin and lead, and sometimes of tin, copper, and antimony.

Phalanx, a formation of heavy infantry, used by the ancient Greeks. The troops were drawn up in close array, with overlapping spears, and eight, ten, or more rows deep. The Macedonians stood sixteen deep. A Macedonian phalanx consisted of 16,384 men.

Pharmacology, the science which deals with the action of drugs upon living tissues. The history of the various theories of the use of drugs goes back to the ancient Hindus, who believed that the plants banded together to help man combat animals. Thus the shape of the fruit of the plant might indicate the purpose for which it was to be used. For instance, the lemon, somewhat heart-shaped, was to be used as a remedy for heart disease. This belief persisted for some centuries. Hippocrates (born 460 B. C.) was one of the first to evolve a logical conception of drug treatment; he made many of his own medicines, using such things as poultices, gargles, pills, and ointments. The first real authority for the use of drugs was Galen, who lived in the second century of our era. His teachings were followed until about the 15th century, when allopathy (liberal use of strong drugs) and homeopathy (the opposite theory, which held that drugs were more effective in increasing dilutions) came into existence. Modern usage of drugs, or therapeutics, is an inductive science. The first experiment in pharmacology was performed by Robert Boyle, who found that the characteristic actions of drugs could be obtained by introducing them into the blood stream. Modern experimentation began with the work of Magendie on strychnine and Claude Bernard on curare. In the United States the first important work was done by Cushney and Abel. The actions of drugs may be due to several processes, and it is hard to say which is the fundamental one. Certain drugs, such as saline cathartics, act by drawing water out of the tissues into the intestine. Others act chemically, as baking soda, neutralizing the acid of the stomach. Still others act by a way that is not definitely known; probably neither chemical nor physical mechanisms are wholly responsible.

Pharmacopoeia, a book containing the prescriptions for the preparation of medicines recognized by the general body of practitioners. In the United States the first national pharmacopoeia was issued in 1820. The Food and Drug Act of 1906 made this the legal standard, and it is revised every ten years by a committee composed mainly of physicians and pharmacists.

Pharmacy, preparation of drugs according to medical prescription. It is an ancient art, and was for a long time in the hands of priests. During the 18th century pharmacy and medicine were separated. The American Pharmaceutical Association was founded in 1852. The necessity of considerable training for pharmacists was recognized with the standardizing of pharmacopoeias. Colleges of pharmacy were established in New York and Philadelphia toward the end of the 19th century, and in 1932 the university course for students of pharmacy was increased from three years to four.

Pharos, the name of the first lighthouse, built by Ptolemy I, 283 B. C., on the Isle of Pharos, at the entrance to the harbor of Alexandria. It was 460 feet high.

Pheasant, a familiar bird of the order Gallinae, allied to the jungle fowl and turkeys, and comprising some 15 species. Pheasants came from western Asia, are of beautiful plumage, and are bred for game.

Philippics, the orations delivered by Demosthenes, 352-341 B. C. against Philip of Macedon—remarkable for their acrimonious invective. Similar discourses have been styled philippics ever since.

Philology, the science of language.

Philosophy, the branch of knowledge which treats of the basic facts and principles of reality, human existence, and human conduct. To the ancient Greeks it meant "the love of wisdom" or the quest for truth, and the term was so interpreted except when it was appropriated to dignify the teachings of a particular philosopher. During the Middle Ages philosophy continued to include in its scope virtually all knowledge except manual and vocational skills. With the rise of specialization in speculation, many phases of learning became separated from philosophy; physics and psychology were among the most important. There remain, broadly speaking, five significant divisions in philosophy: logic, metaphysics, ethics, aesthetics, and epistemology (theory of knowledge).

Phoenix, a fabled bird worshiped in ancient Egypt. It was a symbol of renewed life.

Phonograph, an instrument for recording and reproducing sounds, invented by Thomas A. Edison in 1877. It consists of a mechanism for recording sound vibrations by means of grooves in the surface of a soft cylinder or disk, and the apparatus by which the sounds are reproduced. The term phonograph is now usually applied to the reproducing apparatus only, and is used to include all types of sound reproducers.

Phosphorus, an element discovered in urine by Brandt in 1667. It is found, more or less, in most animal and vegetable tissues, and in many minerals. It is an essential element of all plants and of the bones of animals, and is now chiefly obtained from bones. In combination with various metals it forms different phosphates, which are largely utilized as manures. The chief commercial use of phosphorus, however, is in the preparation of matches.

Photo-electric cell or Electric Eye, an instrument which registers light intensities. Its uses are numerous, and include measurement of stellar light, the density of photographic plates, and the conversion of light waves into sound waves as in sound motion pictures.

Photography, the process of reproducing images of objects on a sensitized material by means of the chemical action of light. The effect of light on a surface covered with a sensitive chemical was known to many experimenters before Thomas Wedgwood began making silhouettes by placing objects on such a surface and then exposing the whole to light. The invention of actual picture photography was in 1839 when Daguerre invented the camera and the daguerreotype. A few years later Talbot patented the calotype, which involved the first use of negatives. Important subsequent developments in photography included the *wet plate* process; improvements in camera and film which enabled amateurs to take pictures; color photographs; moving pictures, and 3-dimensional pictures.

Photometer, an instrument for measuring the intensity of light. Bunsen and Rumford photometers were improved by Lummer and Brodhun.

Phrenology, the theory that the human mind consists of independent faculties, each located in a definite brain-region, the size of which indicates the development of the particular faculty. It is not accepted by scientists.

Physiology, the science of the structure and functions of animal and plant life.

Piano, a musical instrument of the keyboard type. Its sounds are produced by taut wires which are struck by hammers connected to the keys. The wires, arranged chromatically, exert a combined stress upon the frame of about 25 tons. Foot pedals control the volume of the tones produced. The compass of the standard keyboard is 7 octaves. Invented about 1715 by Bartolommeo Cristofori, the piano stemmed from such earlier keyboard instruments as the clavichord, the virginal, the spinet, and the harpsichord. It was slow in attaining popularity and did not replace the harpsichord until the time of Beethoven. The name of the piano was originally *pianoforte*, from the fact that unlike the harpsichord its tones could be increased or diminished. At present there are three types of pianos: the grand piano, in which the strings are parallel to the keys; the square piano, in which they are stretched horizontally but at right angles to the keys; and the upright piano, in which the strings are stretched vertically.

Picts, a people who inhabited northern Great Britain and NE Ireland in pre-Roman times. They are held by some historians to be a branch of the people who lived in the islands before the arrival of the Celts. Their relationship to other peoples is uncertain. The Picts were conquered in 846 by Kenneth MacAlpin.

Pig, a young swine, popularly, any hog. A mature male hog is a boar. A mature female is a sow.

Pike, a large fresh-water game fish of Europe and North America. It sometimes attains a weight of from 20 to 30 lbs. It is extremely voracious, has long, powerful jaws, and has no front dorsal fin.

Pilchard, a fish of the herring family, but smaller and with a more rounded body.

Pilgrimages, journeys to a distant place or shrine to satisfy a religious vow or secure spiritual benefit. They have been made since the earliest recorded times. The first Christian pilgrimages began about 300. In the Middle Ages they became common, and were undertaken by monarchs and people of rank in all Christian countries. Mohammedans have been making pilgrimages to Mecca ever since the death of the Prophet. In recent years Roman Catholic pilgrimages to Lourdes, La Salette, and other places have drawn large numbers of the devout.

Pilgrims, the 74 men and 28 women, all English Puritans, who, after living some years in exile in Holland, to escape persecution in their own country, set sail from Southampton on Aug. 15, 1620, for America, landing at Plymouth Rock, Massachusetts, on Dec. 21. They founded the settlement of Plymouth, and are regarded as the pioneers of American colonization, although 13 years earlier a small Virginia colony had been established.

Pilgrim's Progress, John Bunyan's famous allegory, first published in 1678. It describes the journeys of Christian and his wife to the Celestial City. It is a masterpiece of style and characterization and has gone through hundreds of editions.

Pillory, a wooden instrument of punishment. It consisted of a pair of movable boards with holes through which the culprit's head and hands were put, and was usually erected on a scaffold. Persons convicted of forgery, perjury, or libel were often condemned to the pillory.

Pine, a coniferous tree of the Northern Hemisphere, important commercially. All species are valuable lumber trees, and many yield turpentine and tar.

Pins, were in existence in prehistoric times, and bone pins have been unearthed in Neolithic barrows. Brass pins were first made about 1540.

Pipe-fish, an eel-like fish with an elongated snout resembling a pipe. There is an American species. Pipe-fish belong to the same family as the "sea horse."

Pitcairn Islanders, descendants of the mutineers of the *Bounty*, who took possession of the island in 1790. The mutineers, under their leader, Fletcher Christian, settled down to a communal existence, married women from a neighboring island, and increased in numbers. Their descendants are still the only inhabitants of the island.

Pitchblende, a very scarce mineral which is the source of radium. Scientifically, it is an oxide of uranium, and is of black or brown color. It occurs in masses with ores of lead, silver and tin, in the latter connection being found in Cornwall. Saxony, Bohemia, and Hungary also yield it in lead. Large deposits of relatively pure pitchblende have been discovered in Canada.

Plaid, a woolen material checked and colored in distinctive markings for different Scottish clans and worn by women as well as men.

Planets, the celestial bodies that revolve around the sun in elliptical orbits. The name was first used by the Greeks to indicate the difference between the planets and the fixed stars. There are nine primary planets: Mercury, Venus, the Earth, Mars, Jupiter, Saturn, Uranus, Neptune, and Pluto. The asteroids or minor planets revolve between Mars and Jupiter.

Platinum, a scarce, white, metallic element generally allied with iridium, osmium, ruthenium, and paladium. It can be melted only in an oxyhydrogen flame or electric furnace, but can be rolled out into a film-like sheet, or drawn out to the finest wire.

Plebeians, in ancient Rome, the lower class of citizens as distinguished from the patricians. There were various restrictions upon the plebeians, intermarriage between the two classes being prohibited at one time. During the 4th century B. C. the differences between plebeians and patricians gradually disappeared.

Pleiades, the name applied to the seven stars of the Taurus constellation, which really consists of many thousands of stars.

Pluto, a planet, discovered by C. W. Tombaugh of the Lowell Observatory, Arizona, on January 21, 1930. It is similar to the earth in that it is a solid and cold body. At present it is estimated to be 3,680 million miles distant from the sun. Its discovery followed mathematical predictions of its existence.

Pointer, a sporting dog of Spanish origin, crossed with the foxhound to produce the English pointer. When it sees game it stands still and points with its nose.

Polecat, a European animal of a dark-brown color about 18 inches in length, exclusive of tail. It is carnivorous and belongs to the weasel family. Like the skunk, it emits an offensive odor.

Polestar, a bright star near the north celestial pole. It is Polaris, of the constellation Ursa Minor. It is in line with the two stars of the

Big Dipper farthest away from the handle and at a position five times the distance between. It is always visible in the northern hemisphere, and about one degree from true north. It is therefore an important guide in navigation.

Police, an organization operated by a government to enforce law and order and to maintain public health and morals. In Grecian times the citizen was authorized to act in a police capacity. In Rome police duties were delegated to officers. In 1828 England established her police system following the enactment of the Peel Act. In 1931 the English force totaled 58,080. The first police force in the United States was organized in 1841 in New York City. It consisted of two constables in each ward, 300 night watchmen, 100 marshals, 100 wardens, and sundry officers. In 1845 the organization was improved and the men were uniformed. Other cities followed the lead of New York until, at the beginning of the 20th century, local and state police were highly organized throughout the country. In 1931 New York City had approximately 20,000 patrolmen. In the larger cities, the police department is under the control of a commissioner, as in New York, Chicago and San Francisco. The popularity of the automobile has led to a high development within cities of the traffic patrol, and on highways, of the motorcycle patrol. Radio-equipped cars known as "squad" cars have supplemented the neighborhood patrolmen. A number of the states have state police organizations, first instituted in Pennsylvania in 1905. City police forces generally include their own detective organizations. Other types of police apart from metropolitan and state organizations are the Texas Rangers and, in Canada, the Royal Canadian Mounted, both of which patrol wide and open territories, especially in criminal pursuit. The Royal Canadian Mounted now employ automobiles in their work.

Polo, a game played on horseback, and of the same nature as hockey. The players are equipped with mallets, and the object of each team is to drive the ball through the opponents' goal. There are four players on a side; there are three on a side in indoor polo. In the 19th century the game became popular with British officers in India. It was introduced in England in 1869, and in America in 1876.

Polyandry, a type of marriage, in which the woman has more than one husband. It prevails only in a few primitive communities.

Polytheism, belief in more than one God.

Pontifex, the title assigned in ancient Rome to members of the chief college of priests, whose duties were of a general kind. The pontifex maximus was the chief religious official.

Pontoon, any temporary floating structure that supports a bridge across a river. Pontoons are in various forms, mostly cylindrical and hollow, but others take the shape of deck-boats locked together. Pontoon bridges capable of supporting railway trains are a feature of modern military equipment.

Poodle, a variety of domestic dog, of German or French origin. It has a thick curly coat which in France it is the custom to cut close on the lower part of the body. It is an exceptionally intelligent animal and can be taught many tricks.

Porcupine, a large rodent covered with long, sharp, barbed quills, which form a powerful means of defense. There are several species. The *Canada porcupine* is the most common in northern North America.

Porphyry, a form of crystalline rock of many varieties that in ancient Egypt was quarried and used for the decorative portions of buildings and vessels. The term is applied generally to the eruptive rocks of the porphyritic class.

Porpoise, a marine mammal of the dolphin family, a common inhabitant of northern seas. Porpoises travel in schools, their progression being marked by constant leapings and plungings. Their average length is from five to ten feet.

Port, a sweet wine, made in Portugal. Its name is derived from Oporto.

Portcullis, a strong, movable timber or iron grating let into the wall of the gateway to a feudal castle, and capable of being lowered or raised at will. It formed an effective protection before the days of firearms.

Portland Cement, a high-grade cement. It is a mixture of aluminates and silicates of calcium with lime or gypsum, obtained by heating clay, shale, or slag with limestone, chalk, or marl. It sets in water, and is much used in making piers for bridges.

Positivism, a system of philosophy propounded by Auguste Comte. It rejects all metaphysical conceptions, accepting only knowledge based on experience.

Postal System, a governmental agency for forwarding letters, newspapers and packages. The beginnings of a postal service in North America date from 1639, when the house of Richard Fairbanks in Boston was employed for the receipt and delivery of letters for or from beyond the seas. A deputy postmaster-general for America was appointed in 1692; and by act of Parliament in 1710 he was directed to keep his principal office in New York. The system was greatly improved after 1753, when Benjamin Franklin became postmaster-general. In 1789, the postoffice was transferred to the new federal government. The system of registering letters was introduced in 1855. In 1863 free delivery was extended to more than 50,000 inhabitants; rural free delivery was inaugurated in 1896. The Postal Union was formed in 1875; more than 100 countries have since become members, all of them guaranteeing freedom of transit to mail from other countries. An international system of parcel post was instituted in 1878. Following the example of England, the United States established in 1913 a domestic parcel post system. Since that time the development of air mail routes has greatly reduced the time of mail delivery. It is possible to send letters and certain types of packages by air to any part of the world. Issuance of money orders is another service of the post office.

Post-Impressionism, Cubism, and Futurism, three latter-day art movements. The Post-Impressionists regard drawing as secondary to beauty of paint, and leave the artist to scatter his colors as may best convey his impression. The Cubists and Futurists go still farther, and aim at realizing, by a series of chaotically-placed colors, the pictorial idea in the mind of the artist. While to the lay onlooker all three movements signify little that is understandable, to their devotees they indicate a healthy desire to break away from old conventions.

Potassium, a metallic element discovered by Sir Humphry Davy in 1807, and now generally obtained by the electrolysis of fused potassium hydroxide. It is a common constituent of numerous rocks, and is found in many soils and vegetable and animal tissues.

Pottery, utensils or decorative objects made from baked clay. The manufacture of pottery is one of the oldest and most widespread of man's activities. It was practiced by all ancient peoples, and reached a high degree of artistry among the Greeks. In the Middle Ages the Italians, Germans, Flemings and Dutch made great progress in pottery developments, bringing into use enamels and glazes. Delft, in Holland, introduced a class of earthenware in imitation of porcelain which was in great vogue throughout Europe for a considerable time. In France, Bernard Palissy produced the famous enameled ware which bore his name, and a little later the English Staffordshire potteries came into prominence, and attained great prosperity and high artistic merit under Wedgwood. Among the other great centers of pottery and porcelain production may be mentioned Dresden and Sevres. In the Far East the Japanese and Chinese have always been famed for their productions of beautiful ware.

Praetorian Guards, a personal bodyguard established by the Emperor Augustus, and employed by the Roman emperors until the time of Constantine. It was frequently of great influence in choosing a new emperor.

Prairie Dog, a rodent common in the western United states. It lives underground.

Predestination, the doctrine that from and to all eternity, God predestined everything to happen as it does and must happen, even to the fixing of the souls to be rewarded and punished. It was adopted by Calvin.

Pre-Raphaelites, a brotherhood of poets and painters formed about 1850. They attempted to avoid the academic in art, and included Millais, Rossetti, Holman Hunt, and others. Their motive was to use their art to bring about ideals of beauty among the people, by going back for inspiration to Italian Art before Raphael.

Presbyterian Church, the name applied to those Christian denominations which hold that there is no order in the Church superior to that of presbyters, or elders, and which vest church government in presbyteries, constituted of ministers and elders possessed of equal powers, and without superiority among themselves. Presbyterianism does not recognize the bishop as the superior of the presbytery, arguing that the two names or titles in the New Testament are used interchangeably. Presbyterian congregations elect their own ministers, elders, deacons, and trustees; the deacons take charge of the charities of the church and the trustees of its temporal or financial affairs. The session, consisting of the minister and elders, has the spiritual oversight of the church. The presbytery is constituted by ministers and elders in equal numbers. A synod consists of a number of presbyteries within defined boundaries. The general assembly is the highest court of the church and consists of representatives, ministers, and elders elected by the presbyteries, the number of each depending on the number of members of the churches in their respective presbyteries. There are several branches of the Presbyterian Church in the United States, each having its own theological seminaries, colleges, and publications. In 1958 the Presbyterian Church in the United States of America joined with the United Presbyterian Church of North America to form the United Presbyterian Church in the United States of America. The total membership of the churches holding the Presbyterian system is almost 4 million.

Printing, the art of producing an impression on paper or any other suitable material. There are three distinct classifications in printing according to the surface from which the impressions are made: 1) The process of making an impression from raised letters on the surface of the type, half-tone engravings, zinc etchings, woodcuts, or any other material with a relief printing surface, called letterpress or relief printing; 2) The making of an impression by a process based on the properties of a smooth surface and a greasy ink, called lithograph; 3) an impression made from sunken or deep-etched letters or pictures on copper, zinc, or steel plate, called intaglio, photo, or rotogravure printing. Modern printing is made up of a large number of different trades. In the branches of typesetting and presswork alone there are a dozen different trades which need so much knowledge and skill that they require special training and experience.

Privateers, ships of private individuals licensed in time of war to seize and plunder the ships of the enemy. Privateering was abolished by the Declaration of Paris in 1856.

Prohibition, meaning the prohibition of the manufacture and sale of alcoholic beverages, was in effect in the United States from 1920 until 1933, when the Prohibition Amendment to the Constitution was repealed.

Protestant, as a denominational term, was first applied to the Lutherans, who, in 1529, protested against the encroaching power of the papacy. The name is now applied to all non-Catholic Christians.

Protoplasm, the jelly-like basic substance of which all living things are made. Scientifically, protoplasm is defined as consisting of hydrogen, carbon, oxygen, and nitrogen in intricate combination. Attempts to make protoplasm synthetically have so far failed.

Prussic Acid, a compound of nitrogen, carbon and hydrogen, obtained by distillation of cyanide of potassium. It is probably the most poisonous of known compounds.

Psalms, Book of, a book of the Bible, containing 150 songs. Its age and authorship is uncertain, although many of the Psalms are ascribed to David.

Psychical Research, investigation of the nature of the mind and spirit, possible super-material powers, and survival after death. On the spiritualistic side the movement is a religious one, while other aspects of the study represent a desire for a rationalistic treatment. Rightly, most of these problems belong to the field of psychology on the one hand and to physiology and physics on the other.

Psychoanalysis, a therapeutic treatment of neuroses based on the theory of the unconscious mind, which retains the impressions which the conscious mind suppresses, thus setting up a series of complexes. Treatment consists mainly of bringing to light by a process of conference and free association the nature of these suppressions and suggesting the best method of dealing with them. The first to formulate and practice these methods, by means of the interpretation of dreams and the explanation of symbolism in dreams and subconscious ideas, was Sigmund Freud of Vienna. Later divergent schools, such as those of Jung and Adler, have considerably modified his theories.

Psychology, the science of the mind; scientific investigation of the phenomena of consciousness and individual behavior. The term was first used in the 17th century, but as a separate study and in its applications to medicine, education and sociology it has developed only since the beginning of the present century. There are many schools of psychology, among them structuralism, behaviorism, and functionalism in various forms.

Publican, in ancient Rome, a person holding a state monopoly in return for an annual rent. The publicans mentioned in the Gospels were tax-farmers, employees of the Roman holders of the tax concessions.

Puma, a carnivorous quadruped of North and South America, often called the mountain lion or cougar. It is the second largest American animal of the cat family, often attaining a length of eight feet. It preys on sheep, goats, deer, and cattle, but does not attack humans.

Pumice, a volcanic glass, utilized for cleaning purposes, for polishing, and for smoothing surfaces and edges of pasteboard and surfaces of wood, metal, and other material.

Punt, a small, flat-bottomed boat, used for fishing and ferrying, propelled by pushing a long pole against the bed of a stream.

Purgatory, in comparative religion, any place or state succeeding the present life and serving as means of moral purification. In Catholic theology, it is a place in which souls who depart this life in the grace of God suffer for a time, because they still need to be cleansed from venial sins or have still to pay the temporal punishment due to mortal sins, the guilt and eternal punishment of which have been remitted. The doctrine of purgatory is not held by most Protestants.

Puritan, the name given originally to those in the reign of the English Queen Elizabeth, who desired a simpler, and what they considered to be a purer, form of worship than the civil and ecclesiastical authorities sanctioned. The Puritan controversy commenced as early as 1550, when Bishop Hooper, appointed to the see of Gloucester, refused to be consecrated in the ecclesiastical vestments then in use. The name first given to those who objected to vestments and ceremonies was Nonconformists. It was not until after 1564 that the name Puritan came into use. When, toward the close of Queen Elizabeth's reign, many of the Anglican clergy began to lean toward Arminianism, the Puritans remained sternly Calvinistic. New England was settled very largely by the Puritans.

Puritanism, the system of political and religious doctrines to which the Puritans adhered. Theologically, they taught a doctrine similar to that of Calvin and Knox. They looked upon the world and man as essentially evil and taught that secular pleasure should not be over-emphasized. They taught the Calvinistic doctrine of predestination and held that they were the chosen people. Austerity, frugality and industry were considered essential virtues. They varied greatly in their church policy: the Presbyterians believed in a centralized church government, while the independents considered the individual congregation as the unit of church life. Politically, they reached the peak of their power in the reign of Charles I. The English Civil War followed and the Puritan Round Heads, being victorious, set up the Commonwealth with Oliver Cromwell as protector. In New England they set up a Puritan theocracy called the Holy Commonwealth but by the Charter of 1692 Massachusetts became a secular state. After the Restoration, Puritanism began to disappear as a separate movement, and its adherents began to enter the new reformed churches. Puritan attitudes and ethics continued to be of influence, however. The congregational democracy of their individual churches was carried into political life, and was a potent source in the rise of modern democracy.

Pyramid, a building with plane triangular sides that taper to a point. Those of ancient Egypt are the best known. They are vast masses of brick or stone with inner chambers and subterranean entrances, the first dating from about 3650 B. C. The largest was built by Cheops, an Egyptian king, for his tomb, and there he was buried. According to tradition, 100,000 men were employed for 20 years upon it. This is called the Great Pyramid, and had a height of 482 feet, and its base was 768 feet square. It is supposed to have been enclosed originally in a marble casing. The brother and successor of Cheops erected the second pyramid, and the third was built by Mycerinus, a son of Cheops. The second and third pyramids, though of vast proportions, are considerably inferior in size to the Great Pyramid.

Pythian Games, one of the four great Greek festivals of Apollo and Diana, when many contests were held and laurels distributed as prizes. These games took place every fourth year near the temple of Delphi.

Python, a large, non-poisonous snake which destroys its prey by crushing it. Some species average 30 feet in length, and prey upon deer and small mammals. It is found only in the Old World, and is harmless to man.

Q

Quack, a charlatan or pretender to skill, particularly medical. Although not so numerous now as in former times, quacks are still to be found in all countries. There is nothing to prevent a man's offering a remedy or a person's taking it; but if fraud can be proved, or a quack does injury by what he persuades people to buy, he is liable to prosecution.

Quadrant, an astronomical instrument for measuring altitudes, superseded in modern times by the sextant. It consists of a brass arc of a circle 90 degrees in length properly graduated.

Quadrille, a dance adapted from an old French country dance. It became fashionable throughout Europe and America in the early part of the 19th century.

Quadruped, the term applied to four-footed animals generally, irrespective of class or species.

Quaestor, an official of the public treasury elected annually in ancient Rome. At first two quaestors sufficed; then the number was increased to eight; and under Julius Caesar there were 40.

Quahog, a bivalve of the clam order valued highly as a food. It is found chiefly on the Atlantic coasts of North America.

Quail, a name applied to several game birds, including the bobwhite and the mountain partridge. Some species are found in North America and others in the Old World.

Quakers, the popular name for members of the Society of Friends, a religious sect founded by George Fox in the 17th century. In matters of belief they do not differ materially from other Protestant bodies; the chief difference is in worship, the Quakers having no prescribed formulas. They assemble in their meeting houses, and anyone in the congregation speaks when individually prompted, "as the Spirit moves him." Silent meetings are not infrequent. The sacraments of baptism and the Lord's Supper they reject. They object to swearing upon oath and were at one time persecuted on that account. Until recent times they practiced great simplicity of attire, and in addressing people used the second person singular, but they now conform to common usage. Many Friends have attained distinction both in public life and in business, and as a body they are highly respected for their honorable dealings. William Penn was one of the most prominent early Quakers, and introduced the sect in America. The term Quaker was first applied to the sect because of the founder's frequent use of the word "Tremble" in his exhortation.

Quartet, a musical composition in four parts, vocal or instrumental. String quartets, consisting of first and second violin, a viola, and a violoncello were most in vogue in the 18th century, and some of the finest instrumental music we possess was composed for these instruments.

Quarto, a sheet of paper folded to make four leaves, or eight pages, usually abbreviated to "4to".

Quartz, a common and usually colorless mineral, which occurs usually in crystallized masses. When pure its specific gravity is 2.66. It is one of the constituents of granite, gneiss, etc. Among the quartz varieties are *rock crystal* (colorless), *smoky quartz* (tinged, as *yellow topaz*, *amethyst*, and *sapphire*), ordinary or false, *milky quartz*, and *rose quartz*. Quartz veins in metamorphic rocks often yield rich deposits of gold. Mining for gold in the rock is termed quartz-mining.

Quaternary Deposits, or **Post Tertiary**, are the latest stratified rocks of the earth's crust, and include the Glacial, post-Glacial, and Recent systems.

Quaver, a note of music, equal to one-eighth of a semibreve and one-fourth of a minim. It is the same as an eighth note.

Queen, a female sovereign. The first queen of which there is historical record is said to have been Sebeknefrure, of the 12th Theban dynasty, who reigned in Egypt about 1650 B. C.

Quercitron, the bark of a species of American oak, from which a yellow coloring matter is obtained. It is also used in tanning.

Quince, a hardy orchard tree of the pear family, bearing fragrant, yellow, pear-shaped fruit, largely used for preserves.

Quinine, a vegetable alkaloid obtained from the bark of several trees of the genus *Cinchona*. It is extremely bitter and colorless. The drug, sulphate of quinine, is one of the most valuable medicines. It is antineuralgic and antipyretic, and a specific for malaria.

Quintet, a musical composition of five parts, for voices or strings.

Quirinal, one of the seven hills of Rome.

Quiscalus, a class of birds of black plumage belonging to the order Passeres, popularly known as boattails, because of the tail's being turned up. They are confined to the southern United States and Central and South America.

Quorum, the number of members of any body or company necessary to be present at any meeting before business can be transacted.

R

Rabbi, the title of a Jewish minister, also given to distinguished students and doctors of the law; the equivalent of priest or pastor.

Rabbit, a burrowing rodent, a native of Europe but now common in other countries where it has been introduced and multiplied enormously, especially Australia. In its wild state it has a brownish fur, while in its domesticated varieties it is of many colors—gray, white, and black. They breed rapidly, rearing several litters a year. The fur is utilized for clothing and other purposes, and the flesh is a popular food.

Raccoon, a plantigrade carnivorous mammal, common in North America. It is about two feet long, with a bushy ringed tail, and sharp snout. Its skin is valuable. The raccoon has the peculiar habit of dipping its food in water before eating it.

Rack, an ancient instrument of torture, consisting of a platform fitted with bars, one of which was movable. The feet of the victim were fastened to one bar and the hands to the other; then by means of the movable bar the limbs were stretched to great tension until the tortured one "confessed" or became senseless.

Radar, sound detecting device which transmits electromagnetic waves at a rate of 186,000 miles a second (the speed of light); these waves, striking a steel object, are reflected back into a receiver which translates the duration of their return into terms of distance. The instrument is used to detect and trace the movements of aircraft, naval vessels, etc.

Radiology, the science dealing with radiant energy. The word is also used to mean the application of radiant energy in medicine. Five kinds of radiation are known: (1) radiant heat, applied to thermotherapy; (2) light for heliotherapy; (3) ultraviolet rays for actinotherapy; (4) X rays for radiotherapy, and (5) gamma rays for radiumtherapy. All these radiations travel with the speed of light. Radiology has been successfully applied to the treatment of cancer and the removal of tumors.

Radiometer, an instrument invented by Sir William Crookes in 1876 for transforming radiant energy into mechanic force. It consists of four horizontal arms of fine glass, poised so as to revolve easily on a point, and is enclosed in a glass or metal cube almost exhausted of air. The arms move under the influence of light and heat, according to the strength of the rays.

Radium, a chemical element with an atomic weight of 225.95 and an atomic number of 88. Becquerel, a French chemist, in 1898 noticed streaks of light on a photographic plate that had been left in a drawer with a piece of uranium ore. He asked Marie and Pierre Curie to investigate the phenomenon and after a long series of chemical reactions they discovered polonium and radium. Radium in its pure state is a grayish-white metal which gives out three kinds of rays, called alpha, beta, and gamma. At the end of 1,690 years half of its energy will have been dissipated.

The discovery of radium gave physicians and chemists a key with which to unlock the mysteries of the nature of the chemical elements. It led to further investigations into the atomic theory proposed by Dalton many years before, and the era of modern atomic physics began with its discovery.

The ore from which the Curies isolated radium was pitchblende from Austria. Radium is always associated in nature with uranium; after its final energy has passed off it becomes lead. After the work of the Curies had given radium to the world it was found that carnotite deposits in Colorado contained radium. Subsequently the discovery of rich deposits in the Belgian Congo made it uneconomical to produce radium from Colorado ore.

The most recent discovery of radium-bearing ore was made at Great Bear Lake on the Arctic Circle in Canada. The three veins located there are the richest in the world. The ore is crushed at a mill on the lake and transported 4,000 miles to Port Hope, where a refinery has been erected by Eldorado Gold Mines, Ltd. Canadian production of radium has considerably lowered the price of radium, and the capacity of the refinery is being increased to meet the demands. Radium is used in the treatment of tumors, and since radium salts are easier to handle and just as effective, no pure metallic radium is produced. The salts produced in the Port Hope refinery are shipped to London for final preparation and shipment to all parts of the world.

Radius, in geometry, a straight line or the distance from the center to the circumference of a circle or curve.

Railroad, a means of transporting persons or property in cars or trains over a fixed track consisting of two metal rails which guide, as well as support, the wheels of the vehicles passing over them; these cars or trains are hauled by locomotives or other motive power units usually driven by steam or electricity. The development of railroads in the United States began in 1828. The germ of the railroad idea, however, and the basic inventions and discoveries that made railroads possible go back for a longer stretch of time in Europe, particularly in England.

The growth of railroads in the United States parallels the country's expansion westward and constitutes one of the most exciting periods of American history. By 1855 New York and Chicago were joined by rails, but it was not until after the Civil War that the railroad builders, pushing over mountains and prairies and through hostile Indian country, crossed the continent. In a historic ceremony at Promontory, Utah, on May 10, 1869, the rails of the Union Pacific met those of the Central Pacific, joining the East Coast and the West Coast of the United States.

Until well into the twentieth century, railroads carried most of the nation's freight; the advent of diesel-powered engines and refrigerator cars improving their service. But development of motor vehicles and airplanes has offered great competition in recent years, and railroads no longer monopolize freight and passenger transportation as they once did.

During World War II, by order of the president, all railroads were taken over by the army to prevent a strike; they were soon returned to private management.

Rain, water discharged from clouds in drops. It is formed of the aqueous vapor of the atmosphere, which is derived from the evaporation of water from both sea and land. Before it reaches the earth it is the purest form of water known. The heaviest rains occur in equatorial regions.

Rajah, the title of a Hindu prince, once equivalent to that of king, but now only implying chieftainship in the native states of India.

Rape, an herb of the same genus as cabbage, extensively grown in all parts of Europe and India. Rape oil or colza is made from the seed, and the leaves and refuse are used for fodder. Rape oil is a yellow, thick oil, of considerable commercial importance as a lubricant. It was at one time much used as an illuminant.

Rat, an order of rodent embracing many species. The *Norway rat* appeared in Europe in the early part of the 18th century, coming from the East and entering by way of Russia; now it is widespread in the Western world. The *house rat* which was the common rat before the arrival of the brown species, is a smaller animal and is now comparatively scarce. There are numerous other kinds, including the *wood rat* and *kangaroo rat*, found in America. In many places rats are so numerous as to constitute a pest. Attempts at rat extermination are common in most cities.

Rationalism, a system of thought which claims reason is the best means of obtaining ultimate human knowledge. It recognizes only what is demonstrable to the human intellect, thus rejecting the superior claims of faith. It does not, however, deny the existence of a God or the immortality of the soul.

Rattlesnake, a venomous snake which obtains its name from the possession of a rattle in the end of its tail, consisting of horny pieces so arranged that when vibrated they make a rattling sound. The rattlesnake is found only in North and South America.

Raven, a black-plumaged bird of the crow family, with raucous voice and massive bill. It is found in many parts of Europe, Asia and North America. Ravens are easily domesticated.

Ray, a marine fish belonging to the shark family. It has a very flat body and broad and fleshy pectoral fins. There are about 140 species.

Reaping Machine, an agricultural implement which cuts down standing grain and binds it in sheaves. It was invented by Cyrus McCormick.

Rebus, a kind of word-puzzle in which pictures of things are given in place of words and letters.

Recitative, a style of singing only slightly removed from ordinary speaking, and utilized for narrative portions of operas, oratorios, etc.

Rector, in some denominations a clergyman having charge of a parish.

Red Letter Day, a church festival day indicated in the Book of Common Prayer by red letter; now a popular term for any day of special significance.

Red Sandstone, the general name for red sandstone geological formations, chiefly produced by the disintegration of ordinary crystalline or metamorphic schists, oxide of iron forming the coloring matter.

Redwing, a bird of the thrush family. It is not as large as the common thrush, but it is very similar in its general coloring and structure.

Redwood, the name of various sorts of wood of a red color: an Indian dyewood, the product of *Lingorum santalinum; L. indicum*, or Andaman wood; *Soymida febrifuga* or rohan; wood of *Sequoia sempervirens*, a coniferous tree of California, the redwood of the timber trade;

that of *Soymida febrifuga*, of which the bark is used in India for fevers, and has been employed successfully in Europe for typhus.

Redwood, a tree found along the Pacific Coast of the United States from Oregon to California. It often attains a height of 300 feet and lives to a remarkable age, sometimes several thousand years. It has oblong cones and foliage resembling the hemlock. The available redwood is now confined to about 318 miles of coast. The annual product in this region is about 320,000,000 feet and it is estimated, at the present rate of consumption, that there is enough timber standing to last for 150 years. The redwood is the *Sequoia sempervirens* of botanists and is distinct from the *Sequoia gigantea* of the Sierras. The first is never found far from the sea, the latter always on the declivities of the Sierra Nevadas and seldom at an altitude lower than 4,000 feet, and in regions where the rainfall is never excessive. In size they are much alike. The few remaining groves of the *Sequoia gigantea* are in Mariposa and Calaveras counties, California, and some of the trees are 400 feet in height and of tremendous girth. The timber is inferior to that of the redwood, which is noted for endurance and strength. In addition to other fine qualities the wood takes on a beautiful polish.

Reed Instrument, any wind instrument of the oboe or clarinet class, the sound of which is produced by the vibrations of a tongue or plate of reed, wood, or metal in the mouthpiece, when air is blown through it.

Refectory, the name given to the eating room of a monastery or other institution where meals are regularly served.

Reformation, the great religious movement of the 16th century, which resulted in the establishment of Protestantism. In the previous century Wycliffe, Huss and others had sounded the warning note, and when later on Luther took up the cause in Germany, and Zwingli in Switzerland, adherents soon became numerous. The wholesale vending of indulgences by the Papal agents had incensed the people, and when Luther denounced these things he spoke to willing ears. After much controversy, the Reformers boldly propounded the principles of the new doctrine, and the struggle for religious supremacy grew bitter. They claimed justification by faith, and the use as well as the authority of the Scriptures, rejecting the doctrine of transubstantiation, the adoration of the Virgin and Saints, and the headship of the Pope. Luther was excommunicated, but the Reformation principles spread, and ultimately a great part of Germany, as well as Switzerland, the Low Countries, Scandinavia, England and Scotland, were won over to the new faith. In England, Henry VIII readily espoused the cause of the Reformation, his own personal quarrel with the Pope acting as a partial incentive. Under Mary there was a brief and sanguinary reaction, but Elizabeth completed the work her father had initiated.

Reform Bills, a term applied to certain acts of the British Parliament by which the parliamentary representation of the people was altered. The first was that of 1832, which in addition to a sweeping redistribution of seats, granted the franchise to borough householders paying a £10 rental, and in counties to those with a rental of £50. The Reform Bill of 1867 extended the franchise to nearly all male householders. The bill passed in 1884 added 2,000,000 electors and effected a large redistribution of seats. The Parliament Bill of 1911 may also be classed with Reform Bills, since it practically abolished the veto of the House of Lords, and paved the way for the reconstitution of the chamber. The Representation of the People (Equal Franchise) Act in 1928, gave women of 21 years of age the right to be registered as Parliamentary electors, thus adding several million names to the register.

Regatta, originally a gondola race held annually at Venice. The term is now applied to any important sailing or rowing race, in which a number of yachts or boats contend for prizes. The events may include sculling races and races for four-oared shells, motorboats, and power or sailing boats of almost every type and size. The regatta held on the Hudson River in 1837 was the first in America. Since that time numerous regattas have been held in various sections of the country. The annual Royal Henley Regatta in England is the most noted in the world. One of the best known in America is the annual Poughkeepsie Regatta, in which the leading eight-man crews of American universities compete to determine rowing supremacy.

Reichstag, the representative legislative body of Germany under the Weimar Constitution, adopted after World War I, and abolished in 1933 when Adolf Hitler became chancellor. During an election campaign in 1933 a fire partially destroyed the Reichstag building. Hitler denounced this as a Communist plot, persuaded President von Hindenburg to suspend many civil liberties, and thus helped the Nazi party rise to power.

Reign of Terror, a period of the French Revolution, conspicuous for its horrors and cruelties. It is generally considered to extend from Jan. 21, 1793, the date of the execution of Louis XIV, to July 28, 1794, when Robespierre and other sanguinary leaders were guillotined on the spot where their victims had been killed. During this time about 2,500 persons were beheaded by the guillotine.

Reindeer, a genus of horned deer occurring only in northerly regions. It has an average height of 4 feet 6 inches and is very fleet of foot. The Laplanders utilize it as a draft animal and as a source for meat and milk.

Relativity, a physical theory propounded by Prof. Albert Einstein in the 20th century and accepted by almost the entire scientific world. The theory is based on the hypothesis that the interval of space between two objects and the interval of time between two events are not absolute but relative, and have different values for different observers.

Relics, pieces of the True Cross, bones and garments of saints, etc., which are treasured in churches and shrines, and often attract large bodies of pilgrims. The Roman Catholic Church does not require belief in the authenticity of relics and teaches that they are to be revered only as memorials of saints.

Relief, sculptural works which project from their background. They are of three kinds: high relief (alto-relievo), in which the figures stand out to the extent of one-half of their natural proportions; low relief (bas-relief) in which the figures project but slightly; and middle relief (mezzo-relievo), when the projection is intermediate.

Religion, a systematized consciousness of a superhuman power. At the present time it is estimated there are throughout the world about 820,400,000 Christian adherents, including 484,000,000 Roman Catholics and 207,500,000 Protestants; 319,000,000 followers of Hinduism; 350,000,000 Confucians and Taoists; 416,000,000 Mohammedans; 150,000,000 Buddhists; and 11,908,000 Jews.

Renaissance, a term used to designate the period of transition between medieval and modern times. Usually applied to the years between 1350 and 1550, it is also used with reference to certain cultural, intellectual, political, and economic movements of the time. The notion of the Renaissance as the sunrise of liberty, the quest for knowledge and the ideal of beauty after the darkness of the Middle Ages is now abandoned by scholars. There were, however, certain important changes during the Renaissance. The expansion of commerce produced wealth which in many cases was used to support artists and scholars. The rise of the ideal of versatility, including knowledge of the classics, in the upper classes led to a greater appreciation of various forms of secular knowledge as well as a heightened popular interest in the writers and artists of Greece and Rome. There was a certain amount of scientific activity. Virtually every movement of the Renaissance was, however, a gradual development of elements already present in the Middle Ages. Although the pervasiveness of its influence and the novelty of its characteristics have been exaggerated, the Renaissance was of importance in furthering culture among the wealthy classes, and to some extent paved the way for the Reformation.

Reptilia, the class of vertebrate animals including tortoises, lizards, snakes, crocodiles, etc. They are in structural arrangement very similar to birds, and the theory of evolution indicates that birds are the descendants of the Reptilia.

Republic, a form of political organization in which the supreme power is vested, not in a hereditary ruler, but in the hands either of certain privileged members of the community or of the whole community. Theoretically, the purest and perfect form of a republic is a state in which all the members of the community meet in public assembly to enact laws, and transact all other national business. Such a system is, however, practicable only in very small states and has therefore given way in all modern republics to the representative system—one in which the supreme power is vested in rulers chosen periodically by and from the whole body of the people, or by their representatives assembled in a congress or national assembly. The United States and Switzerland are federal republics, composed of a number of separate states bound together by compact, subject to a central government for all national purposes, but having powers of self-government in matters affecting individual states.

Requiem, a Mass for the dead, musical settings for which have been written by many eminent composers. Among the best-known Requiems are those of Palestrina, Mozart, Verdi, and Brahms.

Respirator, a device for breathing, either to purify the air or to assist the lungs in the function of breathing. A respirator of the first type is a mask worn over the mouth, made of gauze or other medicated substance to filter the air. Of the second type the pulmotor may be mentioned. The pulmotor is attached by a tube to the mouth, and air is forced in and sucked out by the machine. The Drinker respirator, or "iron lung," works on a different principle, changing the air pressure on the respiratory system and thereby causing breathing. It enables a paralyzed person to breathe.

Rest, in music, a term denoting silence or cessation from playing for the period represented by the character of the rest. Thus there are minim, semibreve, quaver, and other rests, which represent the same lengths of silence as the notes themselves would represent in sound.

Retriever, a sporting dog used for bringing in game that has been shot. It is a water dog, usually black or brown.

Revolver, a pistol provided with a number of revolving chambers (six being the usual number), each of which can be fired in succession by the pulling of the trigger. A weapon of this kind existed in the 17th century, but it was not until 1851, when Colt's revolver was introduced, that a really serviceable small arm of this class was available.

Rhinoceros, a huge hoofed quadruped, of which there are nine existing species; it is native to the river and marsh regions of Africa, India, Borneo and Java. It is remarkable for its thick hide and upturned snout bearing one or two vertical horns. The white rhinoceros, which is scarce, is the biggest species, attaining a length of 10 to 12 feet and height of from 5 to 6 feet. The black rhinoceros is the best known.

Rhodium, a rare metallic element discovered by Wollaston in 1804 in platinum ores.

Rialto, a famous bridge that crosses the Grand Canal at Venice, and dates from 1591.

Ribbonfish, a deep-sea fish, deriving its name from the ribbon-like shape. Though many feet in length, it is only an inch or two thick. By reason of its keeping to the ocean depths, the ribbon fish is rarely met with.

Ribbon Seal, a kind of seal found in the North Pacific, remarkable for being ornamented with an almost white broad band along its back and around its neck.

Rice, a cereal grass. The only important species is the common rice (*O. sativa*), one of the most useful and extensively cultivated of all grains, supplying the principal food of nearly one-half of the human race. It is a native of the deltas of the great Asiatic rivers, but is now cultivated in all quarters of the globe and almost wherever conditions of warmth and moisture are suitable. It is adapted to tropical and subtropical climates and requires much moisture, rather in the soil than in the air. Rice is an annual, varying from two to six feet in height. The principal rice-producing countries are located in Asia and the nearby islands, where it is the most valuable and productive crop that can be grown, being the chief energy food of the people. In the United States, rice is grown in South Carolina, Texas, Louisiana, Arkansas, and California. In the higher lands, notably in Arkansas and Texas, rice irrigation is regulated by pumps. In Japan and China hillside pumps are occasionally operated by treadmills.

Rifle, a firearm with a long barrel which is grooved to give a spinning motion to the bullet. It was the chief weapon of the pioneers of eastern North America, and is the basic infantry arm today.

Rights of Man, part of the title of the declaration of the French National Assembly in 1798, proclaiming that all men have equal rights. It is also the title of a famous book by Thomas Paine, justifying the French Revolution.

Rinderpest, an infectious cattle disease. It spreads very quickly when once it breaks out, and causes enormous losses of cattle. The disease brings about a congestion of the mucous membranes and cessation of milk secretion.

Rockefeller Center, an establishment in New York City for amusement and commercial enterprises; begun by the Rockefeller interests in 1932. It will become the property of Columbia University in 2069. Its 15 buildings occupy several blocks along Fifth Avenue and contain business offices, shops, and eating places, in addition to radio and television studios and a large music hall. More than 34,000 people work there daily.

Rocket, a device propelled by an internal combustion engine that emits hot gases rapidly and that is unique in not needing oxygen from the air for combustion of the fuel. Because it needs no air, the rocket is the only possible means of propulsion in space, beyond the earth's atmosphere. Rockets must, however, carry an oxidizer to burn the fuel, replacing the oxygen from the air that is used for other types of internal combustion engines, such as jet engines. Because this oxidant usually weighs more than the fuel it burns, most of the average rocket's weight consists of propellant (fuel and oxidizer). The rocket, like the jet engine, forces gases at high velocity out the rear of the engine. The momentum of these gases rushing out causes the rocket to move forward with equal momentum. (Momentum is velocity times mass or, roughly, weight.) The rocket, therefore, does not "push against" the air and, in fact, operates most efficiently in empty space, where the hot gases may be pushed out most rapidly.

Rodentia, an order of mammals of the gnawing class, and including rats, mice, squirrels, etc.

Rodeo, originally an adjunct to the round-up, being contests of skill among cattle herders, at "bull-dogging," riding, roping, and shooting. Today a rodeo is an organized exhibition of cowboy feats, rather like a circus. There are three great Western rodeos—the Pendleton in Oregon, the Calgary in Alberta, and the Cheyenne in Wyoming. In the East rodeo shows travel about like circuses, and include only professional performers.

Rogation Week, the week beginning with Rogation Sunday, the Sunday before Ascension Day, when extra prayers and supplications are offered as a preparation for the Ascension.

Roman Catholic Church, the Christian church which acknowledges the spiritual supremacy of the pope as the bishop of Rome and the successor of St. Peter. It is the largest of the Christian denominations. From its place of origin in the Near East the Church spread rapidly throughout the Roman Empire. It survived the barbarian invasions which isolated for centuries many of the churches on the fringes of the Empire, and amid the welter of conflicting temporal powers, the Church at Rome came to be the dominant force in Western Christianity. Missions sent out by it between 400 and 1200 united all of Western Christendom under the Roman Catholic Church, and during the Middle Ages it was the most powerful institution in Europe. It controlled education, held vast amounts of property, and at times challenged the secular authority. The rise of widespread abuses within the Church led to demands for reform; in the 15th century these resulted in the Reformation, the first important revolt from the Church. Within a century most of northern Europe had become Protestant. This movement was checked and many abuses abolished during the Counter or Catholic Reformation, and Roman Catholicism remained the dominant religion in Southern Europe, Austria, southern Germany, Belgium, Poland, and Ireland. In succeeding centuries the Church was disestablished in most countries but expanded its work into the Americas, Asia, and Africa. The Church has seven sacraments, the chief being the Eucharist, in which (according to the doctrine of transubstantiation) bread and wine become the body and blood of Jesus Christ. For administrative purposes the Church is divided into parishes, dioceses, and archdioceses. In the United States there are about 34,600,000 Roman Catholics; throughout the entire world they number about 484,000,000.

Romanesque Architecture, a style in building that was dominant in Europe from about 1000 to 1150, although it was used both before and after. Its chief features were round arches and heavy masonry vaulting. Romanesque was superseded by Gothic architecture.

Roman Walls for defense against invasion were built by Agricola, Hadrian, and Septimius Severus on the northern borders of England as a protection against the Picts and Scots. The first wall was begun by Agricola in A. D. 79, and extended a distance of 80 miles from the Tyne to the Solway Firth: the second was built from the Firth of Forth to the Firth of Clyde, 36 miles. Agricola's wall was extended by Hadrian in 121, and by Septimius Severus in 208, and ran from Bowness to Wallsend-on-Tyne. Many parts of these walls remain.

Rondo, the name of a short musical composition with one prominent theme recurring.

Röntgen Ray, an invisible radiation discovered in 1895 by Wilhelm Röntgen. While experimenting with a Crookes vacuum tube, he found that a photographic plate, contained in a dark box and exposed to its rays, reflected metal objects, the box itself seeming transparent. Further experiments developed the idea, and now by the aid of Röntgen Rays photographs can be obtained of objects enclosed in solid bodies, enabling bullets and any solid bodies of metal, as well as bones, in the body to be perfectly located and investigated. As a diagnostic tool X rays have thus revolutionized modern surgical practice; they are also used therapeutically in treatment of skin diseases and tumors.

Rorqual, a marine mammal of the whale order, of which some specimens from 70 to 100 feet long have been found. They yield very little blubber, and therefore are not much hunted. Rorquals are found in all parts of the ocean.

Rosary, a circular chain of beads, used by Catholics when reciting a particular form of sustained prayer. Each bead represents an entire prayer, and the combined prayers constitute the rosary.

Rose, one of the most popular of flowering plants. There are both wild and cultivated species, and it is grown in many parts of the world. The finest rose-gardens in the world are those in Bulgaria, where plantations extend for more than 40 miles in the Valley of Maritza. Here nearly 6,000 lbs. of attar of roses are produced every year, requiring several thousand tons of picked petals.

Rose Beetle, an injurious insect, so-called because it feeds, wherever possible, on the juice of the rose. It is of a green color on the back, red underneath, and is not more than one inch in length.

Roses, Wars of the, a disastrous succession of conflicts between the rival houses of York and Lancaster, for the possession of the English crown. They began in the reign of Henry VI and ended with the death of Richard III on Bosworth Field. The emblem of the Lancastrians was the red rose, and of the Yorkists the white rose. All rivalry between the Roses ended with the marriage of Henry VIII, a Lancastrian, to the Princess Elizabeth, daughter of Edward IV, a Yorkist.

Rosetta Stone, a piece of black basalt, found in 1799 by the French at Rosetta in Egypt and subsequently placed in the British Museum. Written on it is a decree of Ptolemy Epiphanes, of about 195 B. C. in hieroglyphic, demotic, and Greek characters. The presence of the same inscription in three languages furnished the key for deciphering hieroglyphics.

Rosewood, the name given to the timber of various South American trees of the order Leguminosae. Its color is dark brown with red streakings.

Rosicrucians, members of an international society devoted to study of the mysteries of existence. The roots of the society go back at least as far as 1600. American Rosicrucians promulgate a form of theosophy.

Rotary Clubs, local clubs of business men. The first was organized in Chicago in 1905, to further business service, foster social relations, and encourage high ethical standards in business. Meetings take place at the headquarters of each club at luncheon, after which business matters are discussed. The movement has spread considerably. In 1912 the organization became an International Association, and Rotary clubs are now found in many countries of the world. The total membership is over 442,000.

Rouge, a powder form of ferric oxide, made by calcining ferrous sulphate. This form of rouge is utilized both for polishing purposes and as a pigment. The term rouge is applied also to a cosmetic used to add red coloring to the cheeks and lips.

Roulette, a gambling game played on a table carrying a revolving disk divided into 37 or 38 compartments, colored red and black respectively. The players stake their money on any compartment, color, or combination of numbers they please. The disk is whirled around and a ball is set rolling in the opposite direction, dropping finally into one of the compartments, thus deciding the winning number or color.

Round, a song in several parts, taken up by different participants at successive points, and effecting a harmonious combination throughout.

Roundheads, the Parliamentary party during the English Revolution. It was originally a term of derision applied by the Royalists.

Royal Society, an English institution for the advancement of the sciences, founded by Royal Charter in 1662, Viscount Brouncker being the first president. Its *Philosophical Transactions* dates from 1665. The meetings are held in Burlington House. Among the presidents have been Sir Christopher Wren, Samuel Pepys, Sir Isaac Newton, Sir Joseph Banks, Sir Humphry Davy, Thomas Huxley, Lord Rayleigh, Sir Archibald Geikie, Sir J. J. Thomson, Sir C. S. Sherrington, Lord Rutherford, and Sir William Henry Bragg.

Rubber, an elastic compound obtained from certain trees and shrubs of tropical countries. It is in such extensive demand for industrial purposes that rubber plantations have been established in almost every part of the world where rubber can be grown. The best kinds come from the Amazon Valley. Other regions which produce rubber include: the Malay Peninsula, India, the East Indies, Tropical Africa, and Central America. During World War II most sources of crude rubber were cut off from the United States, and synthetic rubber was developed for emergency use. There are several types of snythetic rubber now being used.

Rubicon, a small river falling into the Adriatic, which formed one of the Italian boundaries. Caesar crossed it in 49 B. C., thereby committing himself to war against the Roman senate. Thus the phrase "crossing the Rubicon" came into general use, denoting an act from which there is no withdrawal.

Rubidium, a scarce element first discovered in certain mineral waters in Bavaria in 1861 by Bunsen. It is always associated with lithium and frequently with potassium and sodium.

Ruby, a deep red kind of corundum, and one of the most valued of precious stones, the best examples being worth more than diamonds of the same size and quality. Burma yields some of the finest, and rubies of inferior color are found in Siam, Ceylon, South Africa, and Brazil.

Ruffed Grouse, a North American species of grouse of the same genus as the hazel grouse of Europe. It is named from the tufts of feathers on the sides of its neck, and frequents forests and thickets. The ruffed grouse is sometimes called pheasant or partridge.

Rum, an alcoholic beverage distilled from molasses, and containing from 40 to 50 per cent of alcohol. Most rum is produced in the West Indies, and caramel is usually added to it.

Rumba, a popular dance rhythm, with accents on the first, fourth and seventh notes of an eight-note measure in fast four-quarter time. The dance originated among the lower classes of Cuba and spread rapidly over the United States in 1930. It is interesting for exhibition dancing because of its strongly accented motions, but it has not become a common ballroom dance.

Runes, the alphabet of the ancient Germans. Runic MSS. have been found in England and Scandinavia, and in Sweden the use of runes persisted after the Middle Ages.

Rusa, a genus of deer inhabiting India, Ceylon, the Philippines, and the Malay Archipelago. It stands about 5 feet high, is of a dark brown hue, and of a somewhat sturdy build. Its antlers are long and powerful. The sambur is the most familiar species.

S

Sabbatarians, Christians who insist there is no Biblical authority for regarding the first day of the week as a holy day, and who believe that the seventh-day Sabbath of the Decalogue should still be observed. The principal groups of Sabbath-keeping Christians are Seventh-day Adventists and Seventh-day Baptists. The term sabbatarian is applied also to a person who upholds a strict observance of Sunday as the Sabbath.

Sabbath, the Bible name for the seventh day of the week, designated as the day of rest in the fourth commandment. It corresponds with Saturday in the modern calendar. The Christian "Sunday" is the first day of the week though this day is nowhere in the Scripture called the Sabbath.

Sabines, a people inhabiting the central part of Italy in early times. They were finally subdued by Rome in 290 B. C.

Sable, a furred mammal of the weasel family mainly inhabiting Siberia. It is bright brown in color, and has a long, bushy tail. There is also an American variety. It is hunted for its valuable fur.

Saccharin, a coal-tar product which in a pure form is 550 times as sweet as cane sugar. It is not used as a substitute for sugar, but simply as a sweetening agent when sugar is forbidden, as in certain diseases, or when there is a shortage, as, for instance, in wartime. It has no value as a food.

Sacrament, a type of religious ceremonial. Roman Catholics hold that sacraments are both vehicles and symbols of grace; Protestants believe that they are only the outward symbols of inward grace. In the Roman Catholic Church there are seven sacraments: baptism, confirmation, the Eucharist, holy orders, penance, matrimony, and extreme unction. Protestants recognize only baptism and the Eucharist as sacraments.

Safety Lamp, a lamp used by coal miners to prevent gas explosions. The first safety lamp was invented by Sir Humphry Davy in 1815, and was based on the principle that flame surrounded by fine wire-gauze cannot ignite inflammable gases. George Stephenson invented a safety lamp about the same time and much on the same principle. At present the safety lamp has been largely replaced by the electric light.

Sagittarius, in astronomy the ninth sign of the Zodiac. The name is also given to a constellation, sometimes called the Archer.

St. Bartholomew's Day, Massacre of, a massacre of French Protestants, which began in Paris, on the night of Aug. 23-24 (St. Bartholomew's day), 1572. The anti-Huguenot leaders were Charles XI, the queen-mother, Catherine de' Medici, and the Duke of Guise. It has been said that the queen-mother instigated the king to his fatal persecution of the Huguenots. Coligny was the first victim of the St. Bartholomew massacre. It spread over France and about 30,000 lives were lost.

St. Peter's, the cathedral of Rome, the largest and one of the most magnificent churches in Christendom. It is a cruciform building in the Italian style, surmounted by a lofty dome, and built on the legendary site of St. Peter's martyrdom. In 306 Constantine the Great erected on this spot a basilica of great magnificence. In the time of Nicholas V it threatened to fall into ruins, and he had it demolished. He ordered the construction of a new church, but it proceeded slowly until Julius II adopted a new plan for its completion. He laid the foundation stone of the new cathedral in 1506. It was completed in 1626. The interior diameter of the dome is 139 feet, the exterior diameter 195½ feet; its height from the pavement to the base of the lantern, 405 feet, and to the top of the cross outside, 448 feet. The length of the cathedral within the walls is 613½ feet. The circumference of the piers which support the dome is 253 feet. The floor of the cathedral covers nearly 5 acres, and its cost is estimated to have exceeded $50,000,000.

Salamander, a species of amphibian, of which there are several varieties; among the most common are the hellbender, mud puppy and mud eel. It is found chiefly in temperate regions. It was formerly thought that salamanders lived in fire.

Salic Law, a Germanic code of laws; it was the code of the Salian Franks. It contained a provison prohibiting female inheritance of property; this was probably the source of the use of the term Salic law for the rule which excludes women from succession to the throne. Actually there is no such provision in the Salic law.

Salicylic Acid, an organic acid obtained from the flowers of the meadowsweet, and from the oil of wintergreen. It is now usually prepared by the action of carbon dioxide on sodium under pressure. The acid is then prepared from the sodium salicylate. It is used both as an antiseptic and as a food preservative.

Salmon, marine food and game fish. It breeds in fresh waters, ascending the rivers every autumn for this purpose. It is found in both the Atlantic and the Pacific, the annual catch of Pacific salmon being more valuable than that of any other fish.

Salt, the most used of the condiments. It exists in many substances, and is sodium chloride, compounded of the non-metal chlorine and the metal sodium. It is obtained from deposits in the earth, from salt-water springs, and from seawater. There are salt mines in Galicia which have been worked for hundreds of years.

Salvage, compensation given for a ship or property saved from shipwreck, pirates, enemy capture, or fire. Salvage compensation varies with the value of the rescued property, and the effort and danger involved.

Salvation Army, an international philanthropic and religious organization, founded in London in 1865 by William Booth. In 1878 it adopted a quasi-military organization, with its general (Booth) as its commander-in-chief. The movement had for its object the promotion of religion among the masses. It preaches in 104 languages, and publishes 126 periodicals. Its operations extend to 95 countries and colonies. It supplies annually about thirteen million beds and more than thirty-four million meals. The General died in 1912, and was succeeded by Bramwell Booth, his eldest son. In 1929 he was succeeded by Commissioner Edward J. Higgins. Evangeline Booth became General in 1934 and remained in that position until her retirement in 1939. The organization performed valuable services in both World War I and World War II. The estimated world membership is several millions. In the United States there are 247,000 members.

Sanitation, the subject which deals with the preservation of health. It includes public and private hygiene, the former having regard to the healthy condition of persons in communities, in camps, barracks, and workhouses; the latter to the health of individuals.

Sanskrit, an ancient Indo-European language. As written in India at the present day the Sanskrit alphabet comprises 47 letters—14 vowels and 33 consonants. The language is still spoken in certain parts of India.

Sapphic Verse, a form of verse said to have been invented by Sappho, the lyric poetess of Mitylene, who flourished about 600 B. C. This verse consists of five trochees, the second of which is a spondee, and the third a dactyl.

Sapphire, a valuable deep-blue stone, next in hardness to the diamond, found mostly in Siam, Kashmir, Ceylon, Australia, and Montana.

Saracens, tribe of Bedouin Arabs, who in the early Middle Ages were employed with considerable success by the Emperor Valens against the Goths. In the 6th century they became Mohammedans, and in the 8th conquered Spain. Later, the term Saracen was used to indicate the non-Christian races generally against whom the Crusades were directed.

Sarcophagus, the name given to a stone coffin, such as was used by the ancient Egyptians, Greeks and Romans, for receiving the remains of their famous dead. These sarcophagi were often decorated with rich carvings and sculptures.

Sardines, a name given to several varieties of small fish adapted to preservation in oil, including young herring and young pilchards. They are found in many waters, chiefly in the Mediterranean, and off the Norwegian, Japanese, and American coasts.

Satellite, Artificial, a man-made device launched by rocket into a stable orbit about the earth's atmosphere and circling the earth fast enough to balance the earth's gravitational pull.

The first artificial earth satellite, the U.S.S.R. Sputnik I, was launched by a 3-stage rocket on Oct. 4, 1957, into an orbit inclined 65 degrees to the Equator and ranging from about 150 to 580 miles above the earth. It weighed 184 pounds, was 22.5 inches in diameter, and transmitted radio signals for about 2 weeks at 20.005 and 40.002 megacycles. It circled the earth every 96.2 minutes at about 18,000 miles an hour for about 3 months before disintegrating from friction with the earth's upper air. Sputnik II, launched Nov. 3, 1957, weighed 1,120 pounds and carried a live dog. The U. S. Explorer, a 30.8-pound satellite, was launched Jan. 31, 1958, by a 4-stage Jupiter-C rocket.

Satellites, small planetary bodies revolving around the larger ones. The moon is the earth's only satellite. Saturn has at least nine.

Satinwood, the timber of a tree plentiful in India and Ceylon, and valued for cabinet work. It is of fine grain and very hard. Varieties also exist in the West Indies, Florida and Tasmania.

Satrap, the name given in ancient times to a Persian provincial governor.

Saturday, the seventh day of the week (the Jewish Sabbath), derived its name from Saturn, or, as some hold, is called after the Saxon idol Saterne, which was worshiped on this day.

Saturn, a planet, the sixth from the sun, from which it is distant about 887 million miles, and around which it makes a revolution in 10,759 days. It is about 72,500 miles in mean diameter, and rotates on its axis in about ten and a quarter hours. It is surrounded by a series of rings apart from, but revolving around, the planet. It has at least nine satellites.

Saturnalia, festivals held in ancient Rome in honor of the god Saturn. They were occasions of much licentious merrymaking.

Sawfish, a tropical fish whose snout often attains a length of several feet, and is provided with sawlike projections. Contrary to popular belief, sawfish do not attack whales.

Saxons, a Germanic people who originally inhabited what is now northern Germany and Schleswig. Along with the Angles they formed an important element among the Teutonic tribes which settled in England before the 6th century.

Saxophone, a reed musical instrument invented by Adolphe Sax, about 1840. It is used principally in bands and dance orchestras. There are six sizes, most of them transposing instruments.

Scarab, a type of beetle widely distributed through Africa and Asia and southern Europe. It was the "Sacred Beetle" of the Egyptians and numerous representations of it are found on ancient monuments.

Scepter, the staff or rod constituting the symbol of supreme authority. Tarquin the Elder was the first Roman to assume the scepter, in 468 B. C. The French kings of the 5th century made a golden rod their scepter.

Schist, the geological name for certain rocks in closely parallel layers, the mica schist being the most important. Quartz is a main constituent.

Scholastic Philosophers, a group of philosophers who, in the Middle Ages, devoted themselves to the study and exposition of questions of religious inquiry, and attempted to reconcile the teaching of the Church to the dictates of human reason. The chief schoolmen were Archbishop Anselm, Albertus Magnus, Thomas Aquinas, Peter Lombard, Duns Scotus.

Schooner, a small vessel with fore and aft sails, rigged on two or more masts. Some also carry topsails. The schooner is a favorite sailing vessel because of its speed.

Scorpion, one of the arachnids, in structure not unlike a crayfish. It is found only in hot climates, and often attains a length of 6 or 7 inches. The tail is provided with a venomous sting, which, though seldom fatal, causes extreme pain.

Scotland Yard, the headquarters of the Metropolitan Police of London, England, from which all public orders are given to the police force. The original Scotland Yard was a street near Trafalgar Square, so called because a palace stood there, given by King Edgar in the 10th century to Kenneth II of Scotland. New Scotland Yard is on the Thames embankment, and the famous Criminal Investigation Department has its headquarters there.

Scruple, in apothecaries' weight, the equivalent of 20 grains, or the third of a dram. In ancient Rome a scruple was the 24th part of an ounce, and also indicated a surface and time measure.

Sea Elephant, a curious species of seal, the males of which possess a proboscis a foot or more in length. It is found on the coast of California, and in certain parts of the south Pacific; its blubber has a commercial value.

Sea Horse, a rather common seafish, very numerous in the tropics and comprising some 20 species. Its body is ringed and it has a prehensile tail. The head somewhat resembles a horse's head and it swims in a vertical position.

Seasons, the four natural divisions of the year. They are caused by the inclinations of the earth's axis to the plane of the ecliptic. The spring season is entered about March 21, autumn about Sept. 22. The summer and winter seasons are governed by the solstices, and begin respectively about June 21 and December 22.

Sea Urchin, an echinoderm which is encased in a calcareous globular shell, covered with spines which are used for both defense and locomotion.

Secretary Bird, an African bird of prey, so called because of the quill-like plumes about its ears. It is of considerable service as an exterminator of snakes. It is a large bird about 4 feet in height.

Sedan Chair, a type of chair first made at Sedan in France, in the 16th century, and introduced into England in the reign of James I. Sedan chairs were in general use in the 18th century, when they were the usual means of conveyance for ladies and gentlemen. They were slung from poles borne by two men, and accommodated only one person.

Selenium, a non-metallic element of a dark red color, and solid, found associated with sulphur, iron pyrites, etc., though only in small quantities. It possesses strong electrical resistance which varies according to whether the element is illuminated or not, and is valuable in the construction of electrical instruments.

Seminoles, a group of North American Indians originally located in Florida, but now for the most part living on reservations in Oklahoma.

Semitic Languages, an important language group, which includes Hebrew, Arabic, Syriac, and Assyrian.

Senate, the higher governing assembly of a bicameral legislature. The Senate of Rome originally comprised 100 members, all of whom were patricians. The number was increased from time to time, and under Julius Caesar reached 900. The French Senate dates from 1799; the United States Senate from the establishment of the Republic.

Seneschal, a high official of a royal or noble household. The title originated in France in the 10th century, and was afterward adopted in England and other parts of Europe.

Separatists, the name given to the more radical Puritans, who wished to establish a church separate from the Established church.

Sepia, a pigment prepared from a dark-brown secretion of the cuttle-fish. In the East it is used as a writing ink, but elsewhere is best known as a color, formed by its being treated with caustic lye.

Sepoys, native Indian troops under the command of British officers. The name dates back to the 16th century when the Prince of Sind had a bodyguard of natives dressed and armed like Europeans. In 1857 Sepoy troops, who made up four-fifths of the army, mutineed at Meerut and were suppressed with great difficulty.

September, the ninth month of the year, and the seventh of the old Roman calendar; hence the name, from Septimus. The designation was several times changed by the emperors, but none of the new names survived for long.

Septuagesima Sunday, the third Sunday before Lent.

Serfdom, a system of modified slavery, characteristic under feudalism. It is distinguished from slavery by the body of rights held by serfs according to law and recognized custom, and by the fact that serfs were bound as a class or group, not individually. Contrary to popular belief, serfs were not always bound to the soil. With the passing of feudalism, serfdom gradually melted away, and the serfs became tenants or independent owners. In Russia serfdom lasted until 1861, when by the Emancipation Act, 15,000,000 serfs were freed and provided with land.

Seven Churches in Asia, referred to in the Revelation of St. John, were those of Ephesus, Smyrna, Pergamos, Thyatira, Sardis, Philadelphia, and Laodicea.

Seven Sages (or Seven Wise Men of Greece), regarded as the chief philosophers of the age before Socrates, were, according to the best authorities: Solon of Athens; Thales of Miletus; Pittacus of Mitylene; Bias of Priene; Chilon of Sparta; Cleobulus of Lindus; and Periander of Corinth.

Seventh-Day Adventists, an evangelical, Protestant denomination which observes the seventh day of the week as the Christian Sabbath. They believe in the second coming of Christ. There are about 8,000 Seventh-Day Adventist Churches throughout the world, with a total membership of nearly half a million.

Seven Wonders of the World were: the Pyramid of Cheops; the tomb of Mausolus, king of Caria; the temple of Diana at Ephesus; the Hanging Gardens of Babylon; the Colossus of Rhodes; the statue of Zeus by Phidias; and the Pharos lighthouse at Alexandria.

Seven Years' War, the struggle of Frederick the Great and England against Austria, France and Russia, from 1756 to 1763. It resulted in the cession of Silesia to Prussia, of Canada to England, and in the strengthening of the British control in India.

Sewing Machine, a machine for stitching cloth or other materials, and operated by manual, steam, or electric power. Many attempts were made to produce such a machine between 1780 and 1840, but the first really practical invention of the kind was that of Elias Howe, an American, in 1841. Other sewing machines were afterward introduced, and many improvements have been effected.

Sextant, an instrument for measuring the altitude of the sun and other heavenly bodies. By determining the sun's angle of elevation at noon, and reference to tables in the nautical almanac, a ship's latitude can be ascertained. The sextant was invented by Thomas Godfrey and John Hadley about 1730.

Shad, a small fish of the herring family, found in the North Atlantic. It is an important food fish, caught usually in the spring as it ascends rivers to spawn.

Shake, a musical term, signifying a vibrant effect produced by the rapid trilling of two notes.

Shakers, members of a communistic religious group founded in England. They emigrated to America in 1774, and under the leadership of Ann Lee established themselves in a community at Watervliet, in New York State, from which they spread to other parts of the United States. They practiced celibacy and oral confession, held goods in common, and rejected baptism and the Lord's Supper.

Shamrock, a plant with a three-branched leaf, which is the national emblem of Ireland.

Shark, a large and powerful ocean fish, of which there are many species, very widely distributed, but most numerous in tropical seas. It has formidable teeth and is one of the most voracious of all fishes. It usually attains a large size, the white or man-eating shark being often of a length of 50 feet. Commercially, the shark yields shagreen from its skin, the fins are made into gelatin, and an oil is obtained from the liver.

Sheep, a well-known family of ruminants of great utility as wool-producers, and for food. Most modern domestic breeds originated in England. They include: Leicester, Cotswold, Southdown, Hampshire, Shropshire, and Cheviot. Of other breeds the most valued are Merino and Karakul. At the present day Australia, the United States, Argentina and New Zealand are the largest wool-producing countries in the world.

Shibboleth, the test word which Jephthah in the Old Testmaent, used to distinguish the Gileadites, his own men, from the Ephraimites as they passed the Jordan. Such as could not pronounce the word were refused passage. The term is now frequently used to designate any special watchword or party phrase.

Shield, a weapon of defense carried on the arm by soldiers before the invention of firearms, mostly made of metal, leather, or wood. In heraldry the term implies a shield-shaped escutcheon forming the ground on which arms are displayed.

Shilling, an English coin used from Saxon times. The present style of shilling dates from the time of Henry VII. It is the equivalent of 12 pence, or about 14 cents in American money.

Shoes, outer coverings for the human foot; they have been worn from the earliest times. They are referred to in the Bible, and early historical records. The shoes of the Jews were made of wood, rushes, linen, or leather. Pythagoras directed his followers to wear shoes made from the bark of trees. The Romans were the first to set the example of costly shoes, and introduced various decorative adornments of ivory and precious stones. In the Middle Ages fashion played some fantastic tricks with shoes, and about the middle of the 15th century, shoes with such long points were worn that they had to be tied to the knees for convenience in walking, the dandies using silver chains for the purpose. It was about 1733 when shoes of the present form were introduced, and in 1668 the buckle came into use as an ornament. These continued in vogue up to the 19th century, before which period shoes were not made "rights" and "lefts."

Shot, the name given to solid projectiles fired from guns. In the time of Henry V stone shot was used, later leaden shot, then iron shot, and finally steel shot, introduced by Sir Joseph Whitworth.

Shrike, the name of an extensive group of birds, inhabiting both the Eastern and Western Hemispheres. It is commonly called the "Butcher Bird," and is of sober plumage. It preys upon small animals and birds, and from the effective way in which it kills its victims gets its common name.

Shrimp, a marine crustacean of the genus *Crangon,* allied to lobster, crayfish, and prawn. Its form is elongated, tapering, and arched. The rostrum is very short and the claws small. The fixed finger is merely a small tooth, the movable finger unciform. The whole structure is delicate and subtranslucent, and of such hues that the species may readily escape observation, whether resting on a sandy bottom or moving through the water. When alarmed, shrimps bury themselves in the sand by a peculiar motion of the telson. The common shrimp *(C. vulgaris),* about two inches long, greenish-gray dotted with brown, is esteemed as an article of food.

Shrove Tuesday, the day before the first day of Lent. Its name is derived from the old custom of shriving, or making confession, on that day.

Sibyls, or **Sibyllae**, women reputed to be inspired, who flourished at different periods in various parts of the world. Pliny, Plato, Aelian and Varro mention some of these weird creatures; and the Cumaean sibyl, who offered books of destiny for a large sum to Tarquin II, is famous in classic history.

Sicilian Vespers, the massacre of the French population of Sicily in 1282. The French were then in occupation of the island, and had been guilty of many cruelties. On Easter Monday at Palermo in the year named, by a preconcerted signal, a general rising began on the stroke of the Vesper Bell, and spread through the whole island, 8,000 persons being killed in Palermo alone. The result was the supersession of French by Spanish rule.

Signals, for conveying information or warning, are used in both military and civilian activities. Radio signals for the guidance and identification of aircraft are in common use. Flags, hoisted on a ship or manipulated by hand on land, send messages visually. Wireless signals and flashing lights are other methods of signaling. Distress signals, especially at sea, are usually sent by rocket or flare. By day heliograph is sometimes used. Semaphores are the principal signals on railways, in connection with colored lamps. The block-signal system now in general use—which ensures the safety of a train within a given distance by not permitting another train to be on the same line of rails within that distance—has been of great service in preventing railway accidents. There are also electric, automatic, and pneumatic signals, and for times of fog explosives called fog-signals are placed on railway tracks.

Sikhs, a religious sect founded in the 15th century in India. Its members settled mainly in the Punjab, and developed an intensely military spirit. The Sikhs, under Pandit Singh, strongly opposed the British rule in the early part of the 19th century, and many fierce battles were fought before they were finally subdued and their country annexed in 1848.

Silicon, an important non-metallic element entering into the composition of many earths, minerals, and metallic oxides. Next to oxygen it is the most abundant constituent of the crust of the earth.

Silk, a soft glossy fabric manufactured from the fiber produced by the silkworm. It was known to and highly prized by the ancients, being at one time paid for, weight for weight, with gold. The manufacture of silk was carried on in Sicily in the 12th century, later spreading to Italy, Spain, and southern France. It was not manufactured in England before 1604; but when certain French refugees established themselves at Spitalfields in 1688, the industry was developed and became of importance. The culture of silkworms has never become an industry of economic importance in the United States.

Silkworm, the larva of a species of moth. It is native to China, and has been cultivated with success in India, Iran, Turkey, and Italy. The silkworm of commerce feeds on mulberry leaves, and produces a cocoon of silk varying in color from white to orange. The cocoon is the silken habitation constructed by the worm for its entrance upon the pupa stage, and to obtain the silk the pupa is killed by immersion in hot water.

Silver, a white precious metal, found in a free state, also in certain combinations, and in a variety of ores. The chief silver-producing regions are in the Western Hemisphere. Peru, Bolivia, and Mexico have yielded vast supplies of the metal since the 16th century, and Colorado and Nevada in the United States have also been very productive in silver yield.

Sinn Fein, the organization which supported the Irish Republican Party, through which Irish independence was achieved. During the World War it began a series of revolts as well as less violent manifestations of anti-British sentiment, which resulted in the withdrawal of British rule and the creation of the Irish Free State (now called Eire) in 1922.

Sioux, or **Dakota**, **Indians**, a once powerful confederation of North American Indians. Their number is estimated at 25,000; they are well advanced in civilization and are increasing in population. In the 18th century they migrated from the Great Lakes to the Black Hills region. There they were at peace with the whites until 1862, when they rose in revolt and massacred more than 800 soldiers and settlers in Minnesota. This uprising was put down, but the Sioux continued restless, and from 1868 to 1877 waged intermittent warfare against the whites. They inflicted defeats on several army detachments, notably at the Battle of the Little Big Horn in 1876, in which the Sioux wiped out General Custer and a large part of his command. Placed upon reservations in 1877, they staged a final outbreak in 1891; it was quelled by General Miles. The Sioux are now divided into small groups and located on several reservations, chiefly in North and South Dakota and Minnesota.

Sirius, the Dog Star, so called because of its situation in the mouth of the Dog (Canis Major); it is the brightest star and one of the nearest to the earth.

Sisal, or Grass Hemp, a species of plant yielding a valuable fiber. It is a native of Yucatan, and is cultivated in South and Central America, Africa, Asia, and tropical islands. It is grown in stony ground, and the leaves, from which the fiber is prepared, are from two to three feet long. The pulp is cleaned away from each side of the leaf and the remaining fiber is then washed and sun-dried. It has considerable commercial value in the manufacture of cordage and coarse cloth.

Sistine Chapel, the chapel of the pope in the Vatican, renowned for its marvelous frescoes by Michelangelo.

Skis, long, thin, wooden runners, for travel over smooth, packed snow. They were first used in Scandinavia. They are attached to the feet and used for rapid travel over snow; going downhill, high speed can be attained. Skiing is much in vogue as a winter sport in regions of suitable climate. Finnish troops on skis played an important part in resistance to the Russian invasion of 1939-40.

Skunk, a North American mammal of the weasel family, with short legs and long bushy tail, and of a black color, with a white patch on the back. It secretes and ejects for defense purposes a foul-smelling fluid. Anything tainted with this fluid retains the odor for days. The skunk is carnivorous and nocturnal.

Slavery, a system of human bondage, varying greatly in form. It is known to have been practiced since the earliest recorded times, and was originally connected with the subjection of one tribe to another as a result of warfare. Slavery was a characteristic of all the civilizations of the ancient world, but for the most part died out in the early Middle Ages, being replaced by serfdom. The opening up of the New World led to an increase in slave traffic, and slavery became a part of nearly every colonial economy. In 1772 it was declared illegal in the British Isles. Humanitarian sentiment against slavery began to grow; during the revolutions of the former Spanish possessions it was abolished in all Hispanic-American countries, and in 1833 the Emancipation Act abolished slavery in all British possessions. In the southern United States, however, it persisted as an important feature of the economic and social life, and was not abolished until after the Civil War, in 1865. Constant activity by the British Navy resulted in a sharp decline in the slave trade carried on along the west African coast. Slavery continued, however, in Asia and Africa, despite efforts of the great powers to eradicate it. At present slavery still exists in Central Asia, parts of China, Arabia, and in some sections of Africa.

Sling, a weapon for hurling stones. It is mentioned in the Old Testament, as the instrument with which David slew Goliath. There were bodies of slingers in the Carthaginian and Roman armies, and slings were used as late as the 17th century when it was necessary to save powder.

Sloop, a fore-and-aft-rigged, one-masted vessel, carrying jib, fore-staysail, mainsail and gaff-topsail. A sloop of war was a fast sailing vessel carrying from 12 to 18 guns, and used in navies till about 1850. It was in some ways analogous to the modern destroyer.

Sloth, a curious family of arboreal animals found only in South America. They dwell almost entirely in the trees, proceeding from branch to branch with their bodies hanging downward, and live upon leaves and fruit. When on the ground they move very slowly and with much difficulty, hence their name.

Smithsonian Institution, a scientific institution, organized at Washington, D. C., by Act of Congress in 1846, pursuant to the will of James Smithson. The management of the institution is in the hands of regents appointed by the United States government. Part of the income of the institution is devoted to scientific research and the production of works too costly for publication by private individuals. Under its direction are the National Museum, the National Gallery of Art, the National Collection of Fine Arts, the Freer Gallery of Art, the International Exchange Service, the Bureau of American Ethnology, the National Zoological Park, the Astrophysical Observatory, including the Division of Radiation and Organisms, the National Air Museum, and the Canal Zone Biological Area. The Museum of History and Technology is the newest building planned.

Snake, an important class of reptiles, having scaly, cylindrical bodies without limbs. Locomotion is accomplished by means of the extreme mobility of the ribs, which are very numerous. All snakes have teeth which serve only for seizing prey; the few poisonous varieties are furnished with poison fangs in the upper jaw. These fangs are perforated and the venom passes into them from glands in the skull. Snakes are found in both warm and cool climates, but are most common in tropical and sub-tropical regions.

Snow, frozen rain formed in the upper portion of the atmosphere and taking the form of light flakes, which fall at a much slower rate than rain. All snow assumes the form of crystals.

Soap, any of a large variety of combinations of salts of fatty acids with alkali which combine with water to make an emulsion for removing dirt. Hard soaps are made from tallow, mutton fat, palm kernel, coconut, cottonseed, soybean, and hydrogenated oils, by boiling with caustic soda and adding salt which converts the batch into a fibrous mass. The soap is then dried and hardened in frames and cut into bars with wire. Soft soaps are made from linseed, castor and other vegetable-seed and fish oils, to which tallow or rosin is sometimes added for stiffening, while potash lye is used as the saponifying ingredient. Toilet soaps are made of hard soap molded into the desired form and scented with mild oils. To obtain a transparent toilet soap, sugar, honey, or alcohol is added in the process of manufacture. Laundry soaps are made in the same fashion as hard soaps, but they do not contain as much water, and there is usually added sodium naphthenate or some other derivative of naphtha, which gives the soap an additional property of loosening grime and grease in textiles more readily than ordinary soap.

Sociology, the study of the origin, history, and constitution of human society. The term sociology was coined about 1838 by August Comte, the founder of sociology, who, in his book *The Positive Philosophy*, first placed sociology in the "hierarchy of sciences" (mathematics, astronomy, physics, chemistry, biology, and sociology), describing it as the science of the organic conception of human society.

Soda Ash, carbonate of soda, is now obtained mainly by certain processes of manufacture from common salt. It was formerly obtained from the ashes of plants permeated with sea salt. Bicarbonate of soda results from the action of carbonic acid gas upon soda crystals, and is a white powder much utilized for effervescent drinks, and for medicinal purposes.

Sodium, a metallic element first obtained by Sir Humphry Davy in 1807 from soda, by means of the electric battery. It is found in the various forms of salt, in combination with chlorine in many minerals, and in most vegetable and animal organisms.

Soil, the upper portion of the crust of the earth, the medium from which all vegetation springs. It consists of rocky decomposition and organic matter, and is always characteristic of the rock formation where it is found. It includes either sand or clay, and chalk or humus.

Solar System, a general term embracing the sun, the planets and their satellites, and all celestial bodies which revolve around the sun.

Solstice, an astronomical term indicating the point at which the sun is most distant from the equator, which occurs about June 21st, when the summer solstice is entered, and December 22nd, for the winter solstice.

Sonnet, a poem of 14 lines, with a definite rhyme scheme. Shakespeare, Milton, Wordsworth and Keats have especially excelled in it. It originated in Italy, and was probably a development of medieval songs.

Soot, a black substance deposited from the combustion of coal, wood, oil, or other fuel which contains a large amount of carbon. Excessive quantities of soot in the air diminish sunlight and help cause fog.

Sophists, the first Athenian teachers of philosophy, in the 5th century B. C., who were supposed to base their reasoning on false premises, sacrificing much to mere quibble of rhetoric. They were denounced by Socrates and avenged themselves upon that philosopher by plotting against him. Plato and Aristotle also railed against the Sophists, and the term "sophism" has in later times been applied to fallacious arguments.

Sounding, determination of the depth of water, for practical purposes of navigation or scientific research. The *lead and line* is a device traditionally used in sounding. Modern sounding for scientific purposes utilizes various instruments to record water pressure, which varies with depth. In echo sounding a noise is made at the surface and the time it takes to travel to the bottom and back again is measured. Since the exact speed of sound is known, the depth can then be ascertained.

South Sea Bubble, the financial speculation in England centered around the South Sea Company. Harley, Earl of Oxford, who was then in power, received the idea of utilizing this project for getting together a sufficient sum to pay off the national debt, then standing at about £10,000,000. The company contracted to redeem the whole debt in 26 years on condition that they were granted a monopoly of the South Sea trade. The idea fascinated the public, fabulous profits being dreamed of, and there was an immense demand for shares, which ran up in value from £100 to £1,000. All classes joined in the gamble, but by the wise policy of Sir Robert Walpole the fraud was exposed in 1720, and the whole scheme collapsed. Thousands of people were ruined financially.

Sovereign, a British gold coin worth *20s.* It was first coined in 1489, and has ever since remained the principal coin of the realm. Its weight was fixed at 123.27447 grains troy, and it consists of 22 parts of pure gold to 2 parts of alloy.

Spectator, The, a famous periodical of London, first issued on March 1st, 1711, the last issue being December 20th, 1714. Most of the sketches were contributed by Addison and Steele.

Spectroscope, an instrument for forming, investigating and ascertaining the composition of spectra of luminous bodies. It consists of a tube through which the light enters to a collimating lens, and then through a prism for investigation, a telescope serving the purpose of examination instrument.

Spectrum, the name applied to a colored band of light from the sun or other luminous body passed through a small hole or slit refracted by a prism, and resulting in an intermingling of various colors: red, orange, yellow, green, blue, indigo and violet. Newton was the first discoverer of the phenomenon, and in later times experiments have led to various chemical discoveries.

Speculum Metal, a white hard substance formed of one part of tin with two parts of copper. On account of its high polishing quality it is much used for the reflecting surfaces of telescopes.

Spermatozoa, the infinitesimal organisms constituting the generating element in male animals, and possessing the power of fertilizing the female ovum.

Spider, an arachnid without antennae or a true jaw. It has eight legs, breathes through pulmonary sacs, has usually eight eyes, and in most species spins webs composed of a viscid fluid.

Spinet, a keyed instrument of the 17th century, something like the harpsichord.

Spirituals, Negro melodies with religious inspiration, and which are still spontaneously created, but have also passed into formal music.

Sponge, a marine organism of a low order, comprising a series of aggregated amoeba-like animals. While the sponge lives a current of water circulates through the main apertures. It is the dead skeleton of this mass that forms the sponge of commerce.

Squirrel, a small rodent found in Europe, Africa, Asia, and the Americas. It is of arboreal habits, and feeds on vegetable substances.

Stalactites, calcium deposits formed on the roofs and sides of limestone caves, and in tunnels, under bridges, and in other places where the acid of rainwater percolates through and partly dissolves the limestone, resulting in the growth of icicle-like forms that often assume groupings. The water that drops from these and rests upon the ground accumulates and hardens into a series of sharp mounds or hillocks called stalagmites.

Starch, an organic compound occurring in granules in nearly all green plants, and especially in the seeds of dicotyledonous and cereal plants, potatoes, rice, etc. In its pure form starch is a tasteless, odorless white powder, and is a carbohydrate consisting of carbon, hydrogen, and oxygen. It enters largely into various kinds of foods.

Starling, a well-known European insectivorous bird. It nests in holes and crevices, and is a familiar object on roofs and chimneys. It was introduced into the United States, where it has multiplied so greatly as to become a nuisance.

Steam, the vapor which is derived from water heated to the boiling point, and of great service as a motive power, possessing great capacity to expand, enabling it to be applied to many industrial purposes.

Steam Engine, a machine which uses steam as an active agent in producing power. The leading types of steam engine are: *reciprocal,* in which steam expands in a cylinder, and acts upon a rod which is connected to a crankshaft; and *rotary,* or the steam turbine.

Steam Hammer, a tool invented by an Englishman, James Nasmyth, in 1839, which proved of great utility in the development of the iron industry. The hammer itself is fixed to the end of a piston-rod passing through a cylinder. Its action can be so accurately gauged that it can be made to crack the glass of a watch without actually breaking it, or brought down upon a mass of molten iron with a force representing many hundreds of tons.

Stearin, the portion of fatty matters and oils which remains solid at an ordinary temperature; it is a compound of stearic acid with glycerin. It is largely used in the manufacture of candles and for other commercial purposes.

Steel, a compound of iron, carbon, and small amounts of manganese, sulphur and phosphorus. The oldest method, and the one now generally adopted for the manufacture of steel, is that known as the cementation process, but the most important methods today are the Bessemer and open-hearth processes. In the Bessemer process air is blown through molten iron to oxidize the impurities in it. In the open-hearth process pig iron is mixed in a furnace with iron ore or scrap steel; the resulting chemical reaction reduces the carbon content and purifies the metal The United States, Great Britain and Germany are the leading countries in steel production.

Stencil, a wax sheet or metal plate, on which is cut a pattern or set of words. By placing the stencil on a sheet of paper or other substance and applying ink or paint to the cut-out pattern, a copy of the pattern is obtained on the paper. Modern business practice has proved the usefulness of stencils. Cut on wax sheets by a typewriter, a good stencil can produce several thousand copies or duplicates.

Stereoscope, an optical instrument that blends into one picture two plane representations of things seen by each eye separately, and has the effect of seeming to throw objects into relief. It was only after photography was utilized in connection with the stereoscope that it became of special significance.

Stereotype, a metal cast taken from movable type which has been set in the ordinary way. An impression of the type matter is first taken by means of a mold of prepared plaster of Paris or moistened sheets of specially prepared paper, and when the molten stereo metal is poured upon the mold and allowed to cool and harden, the stereo plate is formed, and can be printed from as a solid block for some time.

Stethoscope, an instrument by which the action of the heart and other organs of the chest can be heard and gauged. The form invented by Laennec, of Paris, in 1816, consists of a cylinder, one end having a funnel-shaped opening which is placed against the chest, while the other end is held to the listener's ear. The sort now in general use is the binaural stethoscope, which has two earpieces connected to the bell by rubber tubes.

Stocks, an instrument of punishment, consisting of a framework of wood, with holes through which the offender's feet were put: he was compelled to sit in that position for a prescribed time.

Stoics, the followers of Zeno, a Greek philosopher of the 5th century B. C. Zeno's doctrine was that happiness is attainable only by living agreeably to nature and reason, and that God is the soul of the world.

Stonehenge, a remarkable collection of huge stones arranged in two circles, and covering an area of 10,000 feet in circumference, situated on Salisbury Plain, in Wiltshire, England. There are numerous theories as to the origin of Stonehenge; it was probably an ancient burial ground.

Stork, a family of heron-like birds with long bills, widely distributed over Europe, Asia, and Africa, and inhabiting marshy regions.

Storting, the Norwegian legislative assembly. It dates from 1814.

Strontium, a metallic element existing chiefly as celestine and strontianite. The native carbonate of strontia was discovered at Strontian, in Argyllshire in 1787, and in 1808 Sir Humphry Davy first obtained from the metal strontium. It is much used in the preparation of fireworks.

Sublimation, the process by which solid substances are first turned into vapor by heating and then allowed to cool into solidity without passing through the liquid state, thus becoming freed from impurities.

Submarine, a vessel of war able to travel under water as well as on the surface. Although crude types had been used earlier, the first practical submarine was built by John P. Holland about 1875; the modern underseas vessel is a development of this craft. In tonnage submarines range from 29 tons (midget) to several thousand tons in the newest atomic-powered craft. Compressed air and water tanks are used to regulate depth, the water being blown out when the vessel is to come to the surface. Submarines not propelled by atomic power use diesel engines while on the surface and electric motors while submerged. During World War II the Germans developed the snorkel, an intake and exhaust tube which greatly increased the underwater range of submarines.

The main armament of the submarine is the torpedo, a cylindrical, self-propelled projectile, usually with a guiding mechanism, and filled with a powerful explosive. Most submarines carry 12 torpedoes. While under water, submarines sight surface ships by periscope or track them by sonar, an underwater sound detecting device comparable to radar.

Submarines were effective weapons during both World Wars, in offensive warfare and in destruction of merchant shipping.

Suez Canal, an artificial waterway between the Red Sea and the Mediterranean. It is about 100 m. long and traverses the narrow isthmus between Asia and Africa. There were various canals in ancient times which connected the two seas; the present canal was completed in 1869. Controlling interest in it was purchased by Great Britain in 1875, and since that time agitation against the British military occupation ended with withdrawal of British troops in 1956, 12 years before the canal was to revert to Egypt. Immediately Gamal Abdul Nasser, president of Egypt, seized the canal and declared that it would be operated by the Egyptian government. Egypt rejected all proposals for international control of the canal.

Sugar, an article of food obtained from the juices of the sugar cane, the sugar beet, the sugar maple, and certain grasses. These yield sugar in its crude form, after which it is refined.

Sulphur, an elementary brittle crystalline solid abounding in the vicinity of volcanoes. It occurs in combination with other elements, as sulphates and sulphides, and allied with oxygen, hydrogen, chlorine, etc., is of great commercial utility. Used in its pure state it constitutes one of the inflammable elements in gunpowder; it is also used for matches.

Sulphuric Acid, a compound of great commercial importance, used in a variety of manufactures. It is composed of sulphur, oxygen and hydrogen.

Sultan, the title of a Turkish ruler and first held by Angrolipez and Musgad in the 11th century. The last of the sultans, Mohammed VI, escaped to Malta in Nov. 1922, after the National Assembly declared a republic in Turkey on Oct. 29, 1922.

Sun, the center of the solar system, estimated to be distant from the earth about 93,000,000 miles, to have a diameter of 864,100 miles, and to possess a mass 332,000 times that of the earth. It has a seeming diurnal motion from east to west caused by the earth's rotation on its axis, and an apparent annual motion through the ecliptic. From these motions we get the variations of day and night, and the seasons. Large spots are observed on the sun—varying in size from 30,000 miles in diameter—which form and disappear at frequent intervals. Investigation of the solar system shows that in its atmosphere are present hydrogen, oxygen, calcium, radium, helium, sodium, magnesium, lead, uranium, aluminum, and other elements. The sun's temperature is such that it is estimated each square meter of the sun's surface radiates a sufficient quantity of heat per minute to raise 10,000 kilograms of water from freezing to the boiling point.

Sunday, the first day of the week. In ancient times it was the day on which the sun was worshiped. In the early days of the church Christians began to observe the first day of the week in honor of the Resurrection in addition to keeping the seventh-day Sabbath of the Decalogue. Gradually the seventh-day Sabbath was abandoned and the first day adopted, though without any Biblical authority, as the Christian rest day. The first Sunday law was that of Constantine the Great A. D. 321.

Sun Dial, an instrument which indicates the time of day by a shadow thrown on a marked surface. The dial, the first form of outdoor clock, was introduced into Europe from the East. It is made in various forms—horizontal, upright, or inclined.

Sword, an offensive weapon consisting of a one- or two-edged blade and a hilt. Swords vary in size from short piercing weapons to broadswords wielded with both hands.

Symphony, an orchestral composition of wide scope, and comprising from three to five different movements, in the latter case consisting of an introduction, allegro, andante, scherzo, and finale. The most famous composers of symphonies have been Beethoven, Handel, Haydn, Mozart, Schubert, Brahms, Schumann, Tschaikowsky, and Sibelius.

Syndicalism, a labor movement which demands that industries shall be controlled by those who work in them.

T

Taj Mahal, the white marble mausoleum built at Agra, India, by Shah Jehan in memory of his favorite wife. More than 20,000 men were occupied for twenty years in its construction.

Talc, a lustrous silvery mineral found in foliated and granular masses, soft to the touch, and used as a substitute for chalk. Soapstone is a variety of talc. It is the chief ingredient of talcum powders.

Tallow, the more solid portion of animal fat, prepared from beef, mutton and other fats by melting at a low temperature. Stearin is its chief constituent. It is used for making candles, soap, etc.

Talmud, the book containing the civil and canonical laws of the ancient Jews, comprising the Mishna, a compilation from oral tradition, and the Gemara, a collection of criticisms and comments on the Mishna by eminent Jewish rabbis. There are two Talmuds—the Jerusalem, compiled in the 4th or 6th century, and the Babylonish, in the 6th.

Tamarind, a leguminous evergreen tree, found in Asia and Africa. The wood makes good building timber, the bark has tonic properties, the leaves yield a valuable dye, and the fruit is used in the making of sauces and cooling drinks.

Tambourine, a light, small one-headed drum, formed of a ring or hoop of wood, or metal, with loose disks of metal let into the sides, which jingle when shaken. In ancient times this instrument was called the timbrel. It is much played in southern Europe as a dance accompaniment.

Tank, an armored motorcar, equipped with machine guns or artillery pieces, and moving on "caterpillar" bands enabling it to travel over the roughest ground. It was first used by the British as a complete surprise to the enemy in World War I in Sept. 1916. Tanks were also used in World War II. Tanks are usually classified as light (under 25 tons), medium (25 to 40 tons), and heavy (over 40 tons).

Tannin, a substance obtained from a variety of plants and trees, from oak-bark, and from gallnuts, and largely used in leather making.

Tanning, the process by which skins and hides are converted into leather. Tannin, tannic acid, is the chief ingredient used, and this is obtained mainly from the bark of oak, hemlock, birch, beech and other trees. The skins are steeped in baths or tanks of the tannic preparation for a considerable time, and in absorbing acid become gradually converted into leather.

Tantalum, a scarce metal occurring in very small quantities in combination with various rare minerals such as tantalite and columbite, associated with niobium.

Tapestry, a fabric largely used in former times for wall decoration and hangings. It was known to the ancient Greeks, but in its modern form came into prominence in the 15th and 16th centuries, when it was manufactured in a marked degree of excellence by the weavers of Flanders, especially those of Arras. Tapestry manufacture was introduced into England early in the 17th century, and was attended by considerable success. At the present day the term is applied to worsted cloths for furniture coverings, and there are also various kinds of tapestry carpets now made. The most famous tapestries of olden times were the Aubusson Tapestry, and the Savonnerie. The Gobelin Tapestry factory originated in Paris in the reign of Francis I is still a national establishment.

Tapioca, a starchy food obtained from the root of a tropical plant, the cassava.

Tapir, a hoofed quadruped of hog-like form, having a flexible proboscis. It is a vegetable eater, lives in the forest regions of South America, Sumatra and Borneo, and is of a dark brown color.

Tar, a dark viscid product obtained from the distillation of wood, coal, peat, etc. The woods mainly used are of the pine family. The product of the distillation of wood is acid; that of coal is alkaline. In the course of distillation they yield light oil consisting of benzene, and similar hydrocarbons; carbolic acid, aniline, naphthalene, etc.; and pitch, a leading ingredient in asphalts and black varnishes. From coaltar numerous dyes and other compounds are obtained.

Targums, certain Aramaic paraphrases of portions of the Old Testament, probably of the 1st century. The most valuable Targums are those on the Pentateuch.

Tarsus, the seven small bones constituting the ankle or instep, including the three metatarsal bones.

Tartan, a cloth of woolen or worsted plaid; each clan of the Scottish Highlanders has its own tartan.

Tartar, an Asiatic people, but also a term used to denote a person of irascible temper, a vixen or shrew; to "catch a tartar" was to encounter more than was bargained for.

Tartaric Acid is prepared from tartar deposited in wine vats during fermentation. The commercial kind is obtained from acid potassium tartrate, and used in dyeing, calico printing, and the manufacture of effervescing beverages.

Tea, *Thea sinensis*, a shrub or tree, the prepared leaves of which yield one of the world's most popular drinks. The plant, probably native to India and later introduced into China and Japan, reaches a height exceeding 30 feet, although leaf production under cultivation is increased by pruning the plant to a small, many-branched shrub. Black and green teas differ not in variety but in preparation, although certain species of tea are more easily prepared into black than green. Some tea has been cultivated in the southern part of the United States. Before the Civil War many Southerners raised their own crops. It has been mostly experimental, however.

China is the world's greatest tea-producing country, with Japan, India, Pakistan, Ceylon, Formosa, Indonesia, and Central Africa also producing important quantities. Oolong tea, more flavorful than green or black tea, comes mainly from Formosa. It is often scented with flowers such as jasmine, gardenia, or rose.

Teak, the wood of an East Indian and African tree of great hardness and durability, largely used in shipbuilding.

Teal, a popular name for the genus *Nettion* or *Querquedula*. They are the smallest of the ducks, and widely distributed over the world, generally frequenting rivers and lakes, and feeding, principally at night, on aquatic insects, worms, small mollusks, and vegetable matter.

Te Deum, the song of Praise ("Te Deum laudamus"—"We praise Thee, O God"). It is traditionally ascribed to St. Ambrose and dates from the 4th century. It is used in the services of the Roman Catholic and English churches.

Telegraph, the first practical telegraphic instruments were invented by Gauss and Weber, in 1833, and by Sir Charles Wheatstone in 1836, although the idea of using electricity for transmitting intelligible messages had been suggested toward the close of the 18th century. The telegraphic system now most widely used was invented by Samuel Morse, an American, about 1837. It operates by sending along a wire electrical impulses which are interrupted at intervals so as to be of long or short duration. These impulses are translated into sound or movement at the receiving end. The slight clinking sounds alone are sufficient to interpret the message, the letters being indicated by various combinations of dots and dashes. From 60 to 100 words per minute can be transmitted by this method. In some systems the impulses are automatically recorded on a moving tape. Of late years various systems of multiplex telegraphy have been devised, by means of which many messages can be transmitted over the line at the same time.

Telepathy, a word used to indicate communication between persons, without external means and independent of the ordinary action of the senses.

Telephone, an instrument for reproducing sound at a distance over a conducting wire or cord by the agency of electricity. It was invented by Alexander Graham Bell in 1876, although it is only within the 20th century that it has come into general use. It consists of a thin disk of iron vibrating in front of a magnet, surrounded by a coil of insulated copper wire which is connected with a similar coil at a distant station. By speaking into the mouthpiece of the telephone, currents of electricity are induced which are transmitted through the line, and thus sounds are reproduced.

Telescope, an optical instrument for viewing objects at a distance. The ordinary telescope consists of an object-glass and an eye-lens, with two intermediates to bring the object into an erect position. A lens brings it near, and the magnifier enlarges it for inspection. A refracting telescope gathers the rays near the eyepiece, and is necessarily limited as to size, but the reflecting telescope collects the rays on a larger mirror, and these are thrown back to the eyepiece. The object glass of a refractor rarely exceeds 40 inches in diameter, but "reflectors" are made up to 200 inches in diameter, and it is thought possible that in the future these may, by being built up of glass plates, reach 50 feet in diameter. Several large refractors are now erected in South Africa, but the largest reflectors are at the Mount Wilson Observatory in California with a 100-inch mirror; the Victoria, B. C., Observatory with a 72-inch mirror, and the observatory at Bloemfontein, South Africa, with a 60-inch reflector. Late in 1936 The Corning Glass Company of Corning, New York, manufactured the largest reflector ever produced, a disk of Pyrex measuring 200 inches in diameter. It was shipped across the United States on a slow-moving train (25 miles per hour) to Mount Palomar, California, for erection in the world's largest reflecting telescope. The origin of the telescope is doubtful. Roger Bacon is known to have used it, and probably invented it. Galileo constructed one in 1609, and was the first to use the telescope extensively in astronomy.

Television, the transmission of recognizable images of moving objects by electrical impulses, either by wires or over the air. The first television "talkie" was shown in London in March, 1930, and since that time great strides have been made in its development, including color and overseas transmission. It has great educational as well as entertainment value.

Tellurium, a rare element, found in minute quantities in its native state and in combination with gold, silver, and other metals. It is a crystalline, brittle substance, resembling sulphur and selenium.

Templars, soldier knights organized in the 12th century for the purpose of protecting pilgrims in their journeyings to and from Jerusalem. They obtained their name from a temple granted to them by Baldwin II for their accommodation. At first they were non-military, and wore neither crests nor helmets, but a wide mantle and a red cross on the left shoulder. They were established in England about 1180. During the Crusades they rendered valuable service, showing great bravery and devotion. In the 12th century they founded numerous religious houses in various parts of Europe and became possessed of considerable wealth. It was this that caused their downfall. Kings and popes alike grew jealous of their influence, they were subjected to much persecution, and Pope Clement V abolished the order in 1312. Edward II in 1308 seized all the property of the English Templars. The English possessions of the order were transferred to the Hospitalers of St. John, afterward called the Knights of Malta.

Temple, a building dedicated to the worship of a deity or deities. Those built by the ancient Greeks at Olympia, Athens, and Delphi were the most famous. The Temple of Diana at Ephesus was another. The Temple of Solomon, built in 1012 B. C. was destroyed by Titus, A. D. 70.

Tempo, a musical expression referring to the pace at which a composition is to be played, and generally used in combination with a qualifying word as "Tempo Ordinario" ordinary time.

Termites, insects of the order Isoptera, popularly called "white ants." They are common in hot countries and live in colonies, their habitations being built in wood, which they hollow out to make a labyrinth of galleries and chambers. A king and queen fulfill the reproductive needs of the colony. The other individuals are sexually immature rather than sexless, the males being soldiers and the females workers.

Terra cotta, a form of hard-baked pottery, mostly of red color, largely used for building and garden decoration.

Terrapin, a kind of tortoise, especially those in fresh water. They are common on the Atlantic coast of America.

Teutonic Knights, a military religious order, founded in Palestine at the end of the 12th century for succoring the wounded of the Christian army before Acre. They were important in the expansion of Germany eastward. The order lost most of its power in 1525, when it was secularized. It continued to exist until 1805, and was revived in 1834, chiefly as an honorary order.

Teutons, a Germanic people that came into prominence in the 4th century B. C., and later invaded Gaul, but were defeated by Marius in 102 B. C. The name Teutons was afterward applied to the German peoples generally.

Thallium, a rare metallic element discovered by Sir William Crookes in 1861 from the refuse left after the distillation of selenium. It is found in iron and copper pyrites, and is employed in the manufacture of glass.

Theodolite, an instrument, used by surveyors, for measuring horizontal angles upon a circle.

Theosophists. The Theosophical Society, which has its headquarters in Madras, was founded by Madame Blavatsky and Col. Olcott in 1873 in New York, and has now over 400 branches in different parts of the world. Its aims are: (1) to form a nucleus of the universal brotherhood of humanity; (2) to encourage the study of comparative religion, philosophy and science; (3) to investigate the unexplained laws of nature and the powers latent in man. Among other things, theosophy claims to "restore to the world the science of the spirit," while its bond of union is "not the profession of a common belief but a common search and aspiration for Truth."

Therapeutics, the science which treats of the healing of diseases and the laws of health.

Therm. The charges for gas for lighting and heating (formerly reckoned by the cubic foot) are now based on the calorific, or heat, value of the gas, and the unit is termed a therm. The gas therm is 100,000 British Thermal Units. This unit of measure is in general use in the United States and the British Empire.

Thermite, a mixture of granulated aluminum and oxide of iron in atomic proportions; it was developed by Dr. Johann Goldschmidt. It is used with success for welding railroad and streetcar rails. Thermite may be stirred with a red hot poker, thrown into the fire, or have melted cast iron poured over it without setting up any visible action; but, raised to a higher temperature, reaction ensues, and a heat a thousand degrees hotter than any furnace is generated.

Thermodynamics, a term first applied by Joule to designate that branch of physical science which treats of the relations of heat to work. What is called the first law of thermodynamics is thus stated by Clerk Maxwell: "When work is transformed into heat, or heat into work, the quantity of work is mechanically equivalent to the quantity of heat." The second law asserts that "the heat tends to flow from a body of hotter temperature to one that is colder, and will not naturally flow in any other way."

Thermoelectricity, the electrical current resulting from the heating or cooling of two or more dissimilar metals at the point of union.

Thermometer, an instrument for measuring temperature. It was invented by Galileo, and developed by his pupils in the early part of the 17th century. The commonest form of thermometer consists of a glass tube with a very small bore, containing in general, mercury or alcohol. This expands or contracts by variation in the temperature, and the pressure of the atmosphere, the body, liquid, or gas as the case may be. The temperature is indicated by a scale on the surface of the tube. Various forms of the thermometer are used for particular purposes.

Thorium, a rare metallic element of the nature of aluminum. It ignites below a red heat and burns with great brilliancy.

Thorough Bass, a musical notation, which consists of numbers over or under the note, showing the chord applicable to it.

Thrush, the name for any bird of the family Turdidae. Thrushes are universally distributed, except in New Zealand, and are very highly organized birds. Their omnivorous diet has made it possible for them to establish themselves on a number of remote islands. They differ widely in their habits and in their habitats; some are gregarious, others live solitarily or in pairs. The wood thrush *(Hylocichla mustelina)* is abundant in North America in summer as far N. as Hudson Bay and retires to tropical and subtropical regions in winter. It is smaller than the song thrush, and very similar to it. Several other species are found in North America. The American robin, *Turdis migratorius*, is the best-known of the New World thrushes. The type genus *Turdus* has several European species, but to only three of these is the name thrush applied. They are the song thrush, throstle, or mavis *(Turdus musicus)*, the missel thrush *(T. Viscivorus)*, and white thrush *(T. varius)*.

Thugs, a secret organization in India, of fanatical assassins. They strangled their victims, buried their bodies with a consecrated pickax, and set apart one-third of their plunder to the goddess Kali. These assassins were difficult to suppress, but vigorous measures ultimately secured their extermination about 1831.

Thumbscrew, an instrument of torture used in olden times to extort confessions from prisoners. It consisted of a frame of three upright bars, between which the thumb of the victim was inserted; then a screw was turned with sufficient force to give intense pain without jeopardizing life.

Thursday, the 5th day of the week, named after Thor, the Scandinavian deity. To the ancient Romans Thursday was *dies Jovis*, or Jupiter's day.

Tiara, originally a head ornament worn by the ancient Persians. The name was afterward applied to the papal triple crown. The tiara of the first French kings was a high round cap. At the present day any coronet or frontal head ornament is styled a tiara.

Tide, a distortion produced in the water of the earth by the gravitational attraction of the sun and moon. According to the laws of physics, gravity varies directly with the mass of an object and inversely with the square of the distance. The diameter of the moon is 2,160 miles and that of the sun 860,000; but the moon is only 240,000 miles from the earth, while the distance from the earth to the sun is 93,000,000 miles. Thus the tides produced by the moon are far greater than the solar tides. The strongest tides are the high tides, which alternate with low tides twice with each rotation of the earth. When a tide is coming in, it is known as the rising or flowing tide; when it flows out, it is the ebb tide. A very strong tide is produced when the sun and the moon are in a line on the same side of the earth and the tides are weakest when they are in opposite positions. These are the spring and neap tides, respectively. The vertical distance between the crest of a rising tide and trough of an ebbing tide is usually only two or three feet, but in certain broad open bays the difference between the tides may be very great, such as in Turnagain Arm of Cook Inlet, Alaska, where the difference is 54 feet. Rip tides are tides that have a choppy surface on the waves as they come in; another special type is the bore, which rushes in like a river over mud flats. Notable examples of the bore are in the Bay of Fundy, the Seine, and the Amazon.

Tiger, a powerful carnivorous animal of the cat family, which is found in India and certain other parts of Asia. Its skin is of a tawny yellow, relieved by black stripings of great beauty of formation. The tiger is hunted in India, and its ferocious disposition renders the sport both exciting and dangerous. The prey of the tiger includes buffalos, antelopes, and occasionally human beings, although the man-eating tiger is the exception rather than the rule. Some tigers attain a length of ten feet.

Tile, slabs of baked clay, used for covering floors, roofs, passages, etc., and for sewers, drains, and conduits. They were used in ancient times and were often made with enameled finishes. In modern times tile has been largely used for decorative purposes, especially in baths, fireplaces, hearths, swimming pools, and kitchens.

Tin, a metallic element generally found in veins of rock, and most plentiful in the East Indies, Bolivia, the Malay peninsula, and Cornwall, England. It is a white metal, susceptible of being rolled to an extreme fineness, and enters into several useful alloys, including solder, bronze, and pewter.

Tire, a circular continuous band of iron, steel, or fabricated rubber placed on the wheels of various vehicles either to reduce wear or, as in the case of the rubber type, to supplement spring action in decreasing vibration and road shock and to increase traction. Iron or steel tires are used on vehicles such as carriages, wagons, railroad locomotives, and cars. Such tires are heated to expand the diameter, fitted to the wheel and then quickly cooled to shrink them into place. Rubber tires are of two kinds: pneumatic, or air-filled; and solid. The pneumatic tire used on nearly all types of motor vehicles consists of a heavy outer casing enclosing a lighter tube which is equipped with a valve for the introduction or emission of air. The outer casing is built up of alternating layers of cotton cord and rubber which are vulcanized together. Solid rubber tires were formerly much used on the wheels of heavy-duty vehicles, but extra-large pneumatic tires are now supplanting them.

Titanium, a very rare metallic element, discovered by Gregor in 1789. Symbol Ti; at. wt. 47.90. It is never found in the metallic state, but may be obtained by heating the double fluoride of potassium and titanium with potassium in a covered crucible, or by mixing titanic oxide with one-sixth of its weight of charcoal and exposing to the strongest heat of an air furnace. It is a dark-green, heavy powder, having the color and luster of iron. The spectroscope shows that there is titanium in the sun. Titanium is used in making incandescent mantles and as a constituent of steel.

Tithe, an ecclesiastical tax consisting of a tenth part of the annual produce, known to the ancient Jews, and first imposed by Christian authorities in the 4th century, although not made compulsory in England before the 9th century. Tithes derived from land are termed "praedial," those derived from cattle being styled "mixed," while others are "personal." After the passing of the English Tithes' Commutation Act of 1836, tithes were gradually converted into rent charges, and today the old forms of tithes exist only to a small degree.

Toad, the common name of any species of the family Bufonidae, a species of tailless amphibia related to the frog. It is almost universally distributed, but it is rare in the Australian region. Two species are found in the British Isles: the common toad *(Bufo vulgaris)* and the natterjack *(B. calamita)*. The most common American species is *(B. lentiginosus*, which is more active than the European species, moving principally by leaping. The body is swollen and heavy-looking, covered with warty skin; the head is large, flat, and toothless, with a rounded, blunt muzzle. Some toads live chiefly on land, others in water.

Tobacco, a plant belonging to the natural order Atropaceae, or nightshade order, the leaves of which are used in the manufacture of cigars, cigarettes, pipe and chewing tobacco, and snuff. The name tobacco was probably derived from the term used in Haiti to designate the pipe, or from Tabaca in Santo Domingo, whence it was introduced into Spain and Portugal in 1559 by a Spaniard. It soon found its way to other European countries and was first used in the shape of snuff. Smoking is generally supposed to have been introduced into England by Sir Walter Raleigh. The most commonly cultivated tobacco plant *(Nicotiana tabacum)* is glutinous, and covered with a very short down; the stem is upright, four or five feet high, and branching; the leaves are lanceolate, from 6 to 18 inches long; the flowers are terminal and rose-colored. All the tobacco plants are natives of America, but they are now grown in many countries of the world. The chief tobacco-growing regions are Virginia and Kentucky. Tobacco was first cultivated in Holland early in the 17th century and soon extended to other countries, including Austria, Germany, Russia, the Balkan Peninsula, Turkey, France, British India, Cuba, Brazil, the Philippine Islands, Japan, and Australia. Cultivation in Great Britain was forbidden from an early date till 1866, when it was permitted under certain conditions. During the 1950's a great deal of research was carried on by the medical profession and by tobacco manufacturers to determine the relationship, if any, between smoking and lung cancer.

Toga, an outer robe worn by the ancient Romans, and corresponding to the pallium of the Greeks. It was made of wool, and worn over the tunic.

Toltecs, an ancient Mexican people of the Nahua race, who are supposed to have flourished from the 7th to the 11th centuries. They were completely obliterated by the Aztecs and Tezcucans, who held the country when the Spaniards first landed. The Toltecs present striking analogies to the Etruscans, and in a lesser degree to the Egyptians and Assyrians. They were great builders, and their religion included human sacrifice and worship of the sun.

Tomato, a plant of the nightshade family, the fruit of which is globular in shape and ranges in color from orange to deep red. Cultivated in Mexico and parts of South America for centuries before the arrival of Europeans, the tomato was until comparatively recent times considered only as decoratively useful. It now ranks high among the vegetable crops in the United States, is widely used as food in a variety of forms, and is easily grown in nearly every part of the United States. California ranks first in tomato production, followed by Indiana, Maryland, New Jersey, and Florida. New Jersey and Maryland process and can over one third of the nation's total tomato crop every year.

Tonsure, the practice of cutting some of the hair from the head of members of the clergy in some Christian churches. In the Roman Catholic church the usual practice is to shave a patch on the crown of the head; although different religious orders have different types of tonsures.

Topaz, a mineral gem. It is a silicate and fluoride of aluminum, and is found in many types of rocks. It is usually colorless or yellow.

Torpedo, a cylindrical, self-propelling, underwater projectile. The first modern type of torpedo was developed in 1866 by Robert Whitehead, a Scottish engineer. Present-day torpedoes are built on the same general lines, and are divided into four chambers. In the war-head, which is in the front part of the torpedo, is a heavy charge of explosive, usually TNT or wet guncotton. The rest of the torpedo contains a water chamber, an air chamber, and the machinery. The propulsion of one type of torpedo is steam; compressed air and alcohol are burned together to heat the water. The fire is ignited by a spark from a built-in battery. The battery current and valves which control the flow of water, alcohol, and air are all turned on by a lever which is tripped when the torpedo is sent into the water. The engine turns two propellers which drive the torpedo through the water at a speed of from 40 to 60 m.p.h. The steering machinery is extremely intricate, and is designed to keep the torpedo at a certain depth as well as on its set course. Torpedoes are fired from submarines, surface craft, or low-flying airplanes, and are ejected from tubes by air or gases. Torpedoes are usually about 21 feet long, 21 inches in diameter, and weigh about 3,000 pounds. Electric-powered torpedoes operate on about the same principle, but delicate mechanisms prevent their being fired from the air or surface. They are slower but leave no wake. Some torpedoes can travel 10 miles.

Tort, a wrong which can be remedied by civil action, except a breach of contract. Torts are classed as wrongful acts, such as trespass, libel, etc., and acts resulting in pecuniary loss, such as negligence, nuisance, etc.

Tortoises or Turtles, reptiles of the order Chelonia. They are encased in a strong shell protection, the shells of some species being of a beautiful horny substance, in much demand for combs, spectacle frames and ornamental work. Of the marine forms, the green turtle is the sort most valued as food.

Torture, the intentional infliction of pain to extract evidence from unwilling witnesses, to force confessions from accused persons, or to implement executions by making them more cruel. It has been practiced in all ages, although not always legally. Among the Greeks and Romans it was legal only upon slaves. During the early Middle Ages it was almost extinct as a legal aid; it was revived for the rising national governments and the Inquisition. It had been generally abandoned, as illegal, in England, by 1600; other European countries followed suit in the next two centuries. The use of torture in Oriental countries and among savage tribes lasted much longer; and it has never been wholly absent as an adjunct to the operations of thieves, robbers, and kidnappers. Although torture was used to some extent in early colonial times, its use in America has generally been restricted to lynchings.

Tournaments, contests between armed horsemen, frequent in the Middle Ages. They were military games, intended to simulate actual battle.

Tower of London, an ancient and famous structure in London, England. It was a royal palace from the time of William the Conqueror, who began the building of the White Tower in 1078. Later kings made considerable additions. From the 15th to the 18th centuries many princes and nobles were executed or imprisoned in the tower. The crown jewels are kept at the Tower, and in the armory a fine collection of armor of various dates is preserved.

Tractarianism, a term that came into use in about 1833 in reference to an English religious movement, headed by Pusey, Keble, Newman, and other Oxford High-churchmen, who published "Tracts for the Times," in which their views were set forth. Among other things, they advocated a higher degree of ceremonial in worship, and their enthusiasm put new activity into the Anglican Church, although the secession to the Catholic church of some of their more prominent members showed the tendency of the movement.

Trafalgar, Battle of, a fight off Cape Trafalgar on October 21, 1805, between the British and the combined French and Spanish fleets, the former, under Nelson's command, consisting of 27 vessels; the latter, under the command of Villeneuve, comprising 18 French and 15 Spanish men-of-war. The British destroyed, captured, or sank nineteen of the enemy's ships and gained a complete victory, though at the cost of Nelson's life.

Transcendentalism, a name for any philosophic doctrine that affirms belief in a realm of intuitive truth that is higher and more important than the truths of science and everyday life. The term has, however, a stricter meaning, given it by Kant, and it is also the distinguishing mark of an American school of letters and philosophy, most ably represented in the works of Emerson and Bronson Alcott. Further, transcendentalist doctrine was a characteristic of the Anglo-Catholic, or Oxford, movement led by Keble and Newman.

Transept, the portion of a church which extends across the interior between the nave and the choir. Some of the older churches have two transepts.

Transmigration of Souls, a doctrine expounded by Pythagoras, and which forms part of the Brahmin and Buddhist religions. The ancient Greeks termed it metempsychosis, and the theory is that after death the soul of a person passes into the body of a new-born infant, or an animal.

Transubstantiation, the conversion of the bread and wine of the Eucharist into the body and blood of Christ. It is a part of the doctrines of the Roman Catholic and Orthodox churches.

Trappists, an austere order of monks, a branch of the Cistercians, founded at La Trappe, in Normandy, in 1140. A new Order of Trappists was established by Rance in 1662, the members of which were enjoined to silence, prayer, worship, manual labor, and study. They were expelled from France in 1789, when the Revolution broke out, and settled in Worcestershire, but in 1815 they removed to Mount Melleray, in Ireland. There are today Trappists' monasteries in France, Belgium, Italy, Algeria, Ireland, Canada, and the United States.

Treadmill, a large cylindrical machine provided with a series of steps, and maintained in rotary motion by the weight of persons or animals treading on the steps of the periphery. A rail is fixed outside the wheel, and to this the workers of the treadmill hold by their hands, while their feet are kept continually in motion from step to step, the weight of their bodies keeping the machinery moving.

Treble, the highest register in music. It is usually sung by soprano voices, or played by the violin or other instrument of high pitch.

Trent, Council of, the 19th ecumenical council of the Roman Catholic church. It first sat in 1545, and completed its work in 1563. At this Council the general policy, principles, and dogmas of the Roman Catholic church were authoritatively settled, and the chief measures of church reform promulgated.

Triassic, a period in geologic time at the beginning of the Mesozoic Era. During this time the North American continent was emerging, and desert conditions prevailed. Thus most Triassic rocks are freshwater deposits of coarse red sediments, although volcanic rocks of this age are found from California to Alaska and from Virginia to Nova Scotia. Along the Pacific Coast were deposited some 4,000 feet of marine sediments. These deposits spread out over California, Nevada, and Oregon, and into Idaho. In British Columbia over 13,000 feet of Triassic formations are found, chiefly lavas and volcanic ashes.

Tribunes, Roman officials, elected to defend the rights of the plebeians. At first there were only two, then the number was raised to five, and finally to ten. They held the power of veto, and their persons were regarded as sacred.

Tricolor, the flag of the French Republic since 1789, consisting of three equal vertical bands of blue, white, and red.

Trigonometry, the mathematical science that deals with angles and their functions in every form. It is divided into two sections—plane trigonometry and spherical trigonometry.

Trinity, the term applied to the existence of God in three persons; usually thought of as Father, Son, and Holy Ghost. The doctrine of the Trinity has general acceptance among Christian communities, and has been explained in different ways. One of the earlier statements of it is the

Athanasian: "We worship one God in Trinity, and Trinity in unity: neither confounding the Persons, nor dividing the substance."

Triple Alliance, a name applied to several combinations of nations, among them: England, Sweden and the Netherlands against France in 1668; Great Britain, France, and the Netherlands in 1717 against Spain; and Germany, Austria, and Italy, from 1882 to 1915.

Tripolitan War, a war between the United States and Tripoli, 1801-1805. It was caused by the refusal of the United States to pay tribute for immunity from the depredations of the Tripolitan corsairs. After several conflicts between the pirates and American naval expeditions, Tripoli agreed to refrain from asking tribute and molesting American ships.

Trireme, an ancient war vessel, with three rows of oars. It was a long, narrow ship, propelled by 150 to 200 oars. The Romans copied it from the Greeks.

Triumvirate, a term used to denote a coalition of three persons in the exercise of supreme authority. The first Roman triumvirate was that of Pompey, Julius Caesar, and Crassus, 60 B. C.; the second was that of Mark Antony, Octavian, and Lepidus, 43 B. C.

Troglodyte, signifying a "cave dweller"—a term used by several classic writers in speaking of prehistoric races who lived in caverns and excavations where they could be safe from the attacks of wild animals.

Trombone, a brass wind instrument. It consists of two tubes, so constructed that one may slide in and out of the other and thus form one tube that can be lengthened at will to produce different tones. There are three kinds of trombones: alto, tenor, and bass. The alto trombone is now little used. The tenor trombone is the most generally used, although a bass trombone is occasionally employed in band and orchestra for playing extremely low parts. In an orchestra there are usually two or three tenor trombones, or two tenor trombones and a bass trombone. The tone of the trombone is mellow and majestic.

Troubadour, a medieval poet of the south of France. The songs of the troubadours were almost entirely devoted to romantic and amatory subjects and generally complicated in meter and rhyme. They flourished till the end of the 13th century. Troubadours frequently attached themselves to the courts of kings and nobles; but as a rule some lady was selected, and to her love songs, complaints, and other poems were addressed. The poems of the troubadours sometimes treated of the conditions of society, the evils of the times, the degeneracy of the clergy, and other subjects. The language was usually Provençal, a dialect which sprang up in France on the decline of literary Latin and lent itself to their purposes extremely well because of its rhyming facilities. The term troubadour has sometimes been applied to wandering minstrels of other regions.

Trouvere, a name given to a member of the class of ancient poets of northern France, corresponding to the troubadour of Provence. Their productions partake of a narrative or epic character and thus contrast broadly with the lyrical, amatory, and more polished effusions of their southern rivals.

Troy Weight, a system of weights used for gold, silver, platinum, and precious stones. The Troy pound contains 12 ounces, 240 pennyweights, and 5,760 grains, being thus less than the avoirdupois pound, which contains 7,000 grains. The old apothecary's weight, which had the same value of pound as the Troy, but was subdivided into 12 ounces, 96 drachms, and 288 scruples, was abolished in Great Britain, and the new apothecary's weight made the same as the avoirdupois. The name Troy was given to the standard pound in 1495.

Truffles, edible subterranean fungi; they have been considered a delicacy from ancient times. There are many species, found in considerable quantities in France, England, Italy, and other places. They are often found under birch or oak trees, and prefer calcareous soils, but there are no positive indications on the surface to show where they are, and they cannot be cultivated. Hogs, and sometimes dogs, are used to scent them out.

Trumpet, in music, a brass wind instrument of bright and penetrating tone. In its modern form it is a single brass tube, twice curved back upon itself, with a mouthpiece at one end, and a bell at the other. There are three valves. Most trumpets are pitched in B♭; they are consequently transposing instruments, sounding lower than the notes written.

Tuber, in botany, an underground fleshy stem or appendage to the root, usually oblong or round. It is composed chiefly of cellular tissue with a great quantity of starchy matter, intended for the development of the stems or branches which are to spring from it. Examples are the potato, the Jerusalem artichoke, and arrowroot. Tubers are distinguished, according to their forms, as didymous (in pairs), palmate (hand-like), fasciculate, globular, and oblong.

Tuberculosis, an infectious disease caused by the acid-fast-tubercle bacillus and characterized by tubercle formation. The tubercle bacillus, which is the causative agent of tuberculosis, was first demonstrated by Koch in 1882. It contains a fatty envelope that takes the acid stain, a protein, and a carbohydrate portion. Since 1900 there has been much evidence to show that the disease is rapidly declining in the United States. The most obvious explanations for this are the improved living conditions of the general population, the earlier diagnosis, and the better methods of treatment available.

Tudor, an English royal house, whose members ruled from 1485 to 1603. The first Tudor sovereign was Henry VII, descended from Owen Tudor; then followed Henry VIII, Edward VI, Mary, and Elizabeth, the last of the line.

Tuesday, the third day of the week, named after Tiw, a Germanic god of battle. To the Romans it was the day of Mars.

Tuileries, a French royal and imperial palace, dating from 1564. It was attacked by insurgents during the outbreaks of 1793, 1830, and 1848, and in 1871 was burned down by the Commune.

Tulle, a delicate kind of silk lace, originally made at Tulle in France. It was much used for the ornamentation of ladies' garments, hats, etc., and for veils.

Tuna, a large fish of the mackerel family, found in warm parts of oceans and seas. Various species differ greatly in size. The Atlantic tuna often weighs more than 1,000 lbs. while the Pacific tuna seldom weighs more than 300 lbs. It is a game fish and provides popular sport for fishermen. The leaping tuna, or blue fin, is found chiefly in the Atlantic, Pacific, and Mediterranean. The flesh of tuna fish is usually canned in America.

Tundras, the vast treeless plains of Northern Russia and Siberia. Small lakes and morasses are scattered over them, but they are almost devoid of vegetation. The tundras are a frozen desert for most of the year. There are smaller tundra regions in North America, Greenland, and Iceland.

Tungsten, a metallic element some of whose ores are known as *wolframite* and *scheelite*.

Turban, a head-dress worn by men in Oriental countries. It is a scarf wrapped round the tarboosh or cap. Turbans vary in material, color, and folds, according to the rank of the wearer.

Turbine, in mechanics a term formerly confined to horizontal water wheels, the revolution of which is due to the pressure derived from falling water, but now applied generally to any wheel driven by water, air, or steam escaping through small orifices subject to such pressure. The turbine was invented by Fourneyron in 1823, and the first one was made in 1827. In the original form the water enters at the center, and, diverging from it in every direction, then enters all the buckets simultaneously and passes off at the external circumference of the wheel. The pressure with which the water acts on the buckets of the revolving wheel is in proportion to the height of the fall of the water, which is conducted into these buckets by fixed curved girders secured upon a platform within the circle of the revolving part of the machine. The steam turbine was developed by C. A. Parsons in 1884. In it the force of a head of water, or nozzle-stream, as the case may be, is replaced by the force of expanding steam. The expansive force is turned into velocity by forcing the steam through nozzles, which direct it against the blades of the turbine wheel. Steam turbines can be used anywhere that power is needed and fuel is readily available. Their chief uses are in generating electricity, either as primary or supporting generators, and in propelling ships and shaft-driven machinery.

Turmeric, a yellow dye substance obtained from an East Indian plant of the ginger family, cultivated also in China. Turmeric, in its commercial form, comprises the root of the plant dried or powdered. It is used in curry powder, and as a medicine and dye.

Turpentine, a resinous substance obtained from a variety of mostly coniferous trees, the Pinus australis, of which there are large forests in North Carolina, being the most productive of the oily matter. The crude turpentine undergoes distillation, the oil being separated from the resin. It is colorless and has a pungent odor. It is largely utilized in making paints and varnishes, and has medicinal properties.

Turquoise, a blue, or greenish-blue precious stone, the earliest and best specimens of which came from Persia. It is a phosphate of aluminum, with small proportions of copper and iron. India, Tibet, and the Sinai peninsula yield turquoises; they are also found in New Mexico, Nevada, Arizona, and Colorado.

Turtledove, a bird widely distributed in the warmer parts of Europe; it is a summer visitant to the cooler latitudes. It is rust-colored with white markings and has a soft, mournful note. In America a similar bird is sometimes called the Carolina or mourning dove.

Tweed, a twilled fabric, consisting of two or more colors of yarn combined in the same cloth; it should be entirely of wool, though there are inferior kinds in which cotton has a part. The surface of the cloth is unfinished. Tweed was woven originally in the valley of the Tweed, hence its name, but is now manufactured in all cloth-producing centers.

Twelfth Day, the twelfth day after Christmas, on which is held the festival of Epiphany. On the eve of this day, called Twelfth Night, various social rites and ceremonies are observed in different countries.

Twilight, the light reflected in the atmosphere where the sun is below the horizon before sunrise or after sunset. The term is most usually understood to refer, however, to the evening light; the morning light we call dawn. The twilight varies in duration in different latitudes and at different seasons.

Tympanum, in architectural phraseology, the triangular space at the back of a pediment, or, any space in a similar position, as over a window or between the lintel and the arch of a doorway. In ecclesiastical edifices the tympanum is often utilized for sculptured ornamentation.

Typhoon, a cyclonic storm of great violence occurring in the autumn months in the China seas and India.

U

Ultramarine, a sky-blue pigment obtained from lapis lazuli, a stone found in Tibet, Persia, Siberia, and some other countries. A cheaper ultramarine is now produced by grinding and heating a mixture of clay, sulphur, carbonate of soda and resin.

Umbrella, a light frame covered with silk, cotton, or other fabric, and held above the head as a protection against sun or rain. The use of the umbrella originated in the East, where it is considered a symbol of royalty or dignity. It has a ceremonial significance among some African tribes. As protection from rain it was not generally used in the Occident till the middle of the 18th century.

Uncials, written characters of a form used in times prior to the 10th century; while smaller than capitals they were larger than the later minuscule. The term uncial was a misapplication of St. Jerome's literae unciales, "inch-high letters."

Uncle Sam, the jocular name of the United States Government, used as John Bull is with respect to England. It is an extension of the letters U. S. (United States), printed or stamped on Government property. It was first used in Troy, N. Y., in 1812, when certain goods purchased for the Government and branded U. S. were officially inspected by Samuel Wilson, whose local nickname was "Uncle Sam." The coincidence of initials suggested the application of the nickname in full to the Government.

Unction, the act of anointing with oil, a symbol of consecration practiced in the Roman Catholic, Greek, and other churches, but not in the Protestant. Extreme unction is the rite of anointing a dying person with holy oil.

Undulatory Theory, a theory which traces light to vibrations set up in an invisible medium termed the luminiferous ether, and from there transmitted and diffused through all space.

Unearned Increment, an increase in value of land, houses, etc., brought about by influences independent of the efforts or outlay of the owner.

Unionism, a comprehensive term denoting such activities as are designed to unite all those employed in a trade, industry, profession, shop, or locality into an organization for the raising of wages and the improvement of working conditions. Unionism is not restricted to manual labor or wage earners; there are substantial organizations of clerks, teachers, hospital workers, and other employees in most countries.

The two principal divisions of unionism are craft unionism and industrial unionism. The philosophy of American craft unionism was developed by Samuel Gompers, an English cigar-maker, who emigrated to the United States while a young man. A founder of the American Federation of Labor in 1881, he was its president for more than forty years. His theory was embodied in the organization of laborers according to their crafts, i.e., plumbing, bricklaying, electrical repair, die making, etc. William Green succeeded Gompers to the presidency of the Federation in 1924, with admittedly the same philosophy of trade unionism as his predecessor. Under Green's leadership, the Federation collaborated with governmental agencies to achieve union advances, and explicitly rejected the idea of basing a new political party on trade unions. The Congress of Industrial Organization (formerly the Committee for Industrial Organization) was formed in 1935, by leaders representing several large unions. Among them were John L. Lewis, head of the United Mine Workers of America; David Dubinsky, president of the International Ladies' Garment Workers; Sidney Hillman, chief of the Amalgamated Clothing Workers of America; and others. The C.I.O. advocated industrial or "vertical" unions, which include all workers in a factory or group of factories. In 1955 the American Federation of Labor and the Congress of Industrial Organization joined, choosing **George L. Meany** as the president.

Unitarianism, the doctrine which proclaims that God is one person and thus denies the doctrine of the Trinity. It was not until after the Reformation that Unitarianism developed to any particular extent in England. In the United States, Unitarianism has produced such eminent leaders as William Ellery Channing and Theodore Parker.

United Daughters of the Confederacy, an organization composed of the widows, wives, mothers, sisters and lineal female descendants of men who served honorably in the army and navy of the Confederate States, or who gave personal services to the Confederate cause. It was organized at Nashville, Tenn., Sept. 10, 1894.

United States Military Academy, an institution established by the Federal Government for the practical and theoretical training of young men for the military service, authorized by Congress in 1802, and located at West Point, New York. The Department of the Army supervises the academy; the Secretary of the Army has jurisdiction over appointment of instructors. Direct supervision of the academy is under the Assistant Chief of Staff, Operations, U. S. Army.

United States Naval Academy, conducted by the Department of the Navy for the training of men for the commissioned ranks of the navy and marine corps, is located at Annapolis, Md. It was founded in 1845, by George Bancroft, historian, educator, and Secretary of the Navy. It occupies the site of the former Fort Severn.

United States Naval Observatory, an astronomical observatory maintained by the Bureau of Navigation of the United States Navy Department. It is located at Georgetown Heights, Washington, D. C. Its principal object is to serve navigation by observing the heavenly bodies and testing, repairing, and supplying sextants, chronometers, compasses, and other navigation instruments used in vessels and aircraft.

Universal Time, in astronomy, a method of reckoning time for international purposes, agreed on by the International Conference, held at Washington, D. C., in 1883. Universal time is reckoned from mean noon at the meridian of Greenwich, the day commencing at midnight, and divided into 24 hours (instead of into two portions of 12 hours each). Since the earth is divided into 360° and the day into 24 hours, every 15° represents a difference of one hour.

University Extension, a method of extending university teaching to men and women who would otherwise be unable to avail themselves of university advantages. Under this scheme classes are opened and lectures given in the chief centers of population, and the higher education of the universities is thus brought within popular reach.

Unknown Soldier, Tomb of the, a tomb erected after World War I to commemorate the unknown dead. An unknown soldier was buried with military honors in or near the nation's capital. This was done in Great Britain, France, Belgium, Italy, and the United States. In the United States the Tomb of the Unknown Soldier is in Arlington National Cemetery in Virginia, near Washington, D. C. It was dedicated on Nov. 11, 1921, and the Unknown Soldier was awarded the first Congressional Medal of Honor. In 1958 two more unknown soldiers were interred there, commemorating unknown dead of World War II and the unknown dead of the Korea conflict.

Uranus, the seventh of the major planets in distance from the sun, from which it is removed about 1,800 millions of miles. It is nearly four times the diameter of the earth and has four satellites. Sir William Herschel discovered the planet in 1781.

Ursa Major, the Great Bear, "Charles' Wain," or the Big Dipper, a constellation familiar to all observers because of the brilliance of the seven stars forming its outline.

Ursa Minor, the Lesser Bear constellation. It has, like Ursa Major, seven prominent stars, of which the pole star is the brightest.

Utilitarianism, the theory that the greatest happiness for the greatest number constitutes the greatest good. The theory was brought forward particularly by Jeremy Bentham, and was advocated by John Stuart Mill also. Both Bentham and Mill identified happiness with pleasure. Bentham held that the value of a pleasure is determined by its intensity, duration, and the number of persons experiencing it. Mill, however, differentiated pleasures on the basis of quality.

Utopia, an ideal state, where perfect conditions of government and life exist. Although the name is taken from the fictitious land in Sir Thomas More's *Utopia*, the conception of such a state has existed since ancient times; Plato's *Timaeus* and *Republic* are notable examples. Among the most important Utopian works written since More's time are: Sir Francis Bacon's *The New Atlantis*, Campanella's *City of the Sun;* Samuel Butler's *Erewhon;* and Edward Bellamy's *Looking Backward.* The word *Utopian* is now used to describe a visionary or impractical scheme of reform. The Utopias of modern writers are frequently glorifications of the machine age.

Utrecht, Treaty of, the treaty which ended the War of the Spanish Succession. Its most important provisions were: renunciation by Louis XIV of the right of his grandson, Philip V of Spain, to the French throne; cession to England of the Hudson Bay territory, Acadia, St. Kitts, Newfoundland, Gibraltar, and Minorca; cession to Savoy of Sicily; and confirmation of the Empire's right to Naples, Milan, and the Spanish Netherlands.

V

Valentine, a letter or other missive sent by persons of both sexes to each other on February 14, or any missive of an amatory or satirical nature, sent on that day. Some valentines are highly ornamental and artistic, while others (commonly called "comic valentines") are caricatures, designed to reflect on the personal appearance, habits, and character of the persons to whom they are addressed. Valentines are named for St. Valentine, a Roman martyr who is considered the patron of lovers; his feast day is February 14. Valentine traditions are probably survivals of a pagan love festival on about the same date.

Valhalla, in Scandinavian mythology, the special paradise to which the souls of warriors slain in battle were transported.

Valkyries, in Norse and Germanic mythology, handmaidens of Odin, who ride through the air to battlefields and point out the heroes who are to fall. One of these Valkyries is the heroine of Wagner's opera *Die Walküre*.

Valley of Ten Thousand Smokes, a large area of recent volcanic activity, on the southern coast of Alaska. The valley was incorporated in the Katmai national monument by President Wilson, September 24, 1918. It has an area of 1,700 square miles, and includes Mt. Katmai, which in June, 1912, erupted violently covering most of Alaska with volcanic ash.

Vampire, or Werewolf, according to ancient superstition, a specter in human form which rose from its grave in the night and preyed upon the living as they slept, sucking their blood, and then returned to the grave.

Vampire Bat, a type of bat found in the warm regions of the Western Hemisphere. It wounds other animals and then sucks their blood.

Vanadium, a rare metallic element found in iron ores and certain minerals and clays. It forms oxides which develop salts of commercial value in dyeing and calico printing. Originally discovered by Sefstrom in 1830, it was found also in the copperbeds of Cheshire by Roscoe in 1865. It is now obtained chiefly from ores found in Peru and the western United States.

Vandals, a Germanic people who about the 3rd century were living in or near the Oder valley. At the beginning of the 5th century they began a series of migrations. They crossed Germany and Gaul, moved into Spain, and by 430 had crossed the Mediterranean to northern Africa. They conquered most of N. Africa, attained dominance in the Mediterranean, and in 455 attacked Rome. The Vandals were conquered by Belisarius in 533-34; their existence as an independent people was ended, and northern Africa restored to the Empire.

Vanilla, a climbing orchid of tropical America, found also in Asia; the dried fruit of certain species furnishes the agreeable aromatic vanilla of commerce.

Vase, a hollow vessel of a decorative character, with or without handles, and of various shapes and designs. One of the finest examples of a Greco-Roman vase is the famous Portland Vase.

Vatican City, an independent, sovereign state, the residence of the pope within the city of Rome. The Lateran Treaty, signed in 1929 by Mussolini, King Victor Emmanuel III, and Cardinal Gasparri (for Pius XI), ended the Roman Question, which since 1871 had kept the pope a voluntary prisoner in the Vatican in protest against Italian seizure of the papal states. In this concordat between Italy and the Holy See, Italy recognized the existence of the Vatican City as an independent, sovereign state and guaranteed it protection. The state covers an area of 108.7 acres and has a population of about 1,000.

Venue, in law, the place where an action is laid. In the United States, the county in which the trial of a particular cause takes place is said to be the venue of that trial. In local actions, as for damages for an actual trespass or for waste, affecting land, the plaintiff must lay his declaration or declare his injury to have happened in the very county and place where it really did happen; but in transitory actions, for injuries that might have happened anywhere, as debt, detinue, slander, and the like, the plaintiff may declare in what county he pleases, and then the trial must be had in that county in which the declaration is laid. To lay a venue is to allege or fix a place of trial. To pray a change of venue is to petition that a cause may be tried before another judge or in another place than the one first selected.

Venus, in astronomy, the second of the known planets in order from the sun. With the exception of the moon, Venus is nearest of all heavenly bodies to the earth, being at the time of inferior conjunction 25,702,000 miles away. When Venus is at its maximum of brightness, it can sometimes be seen with the naked eye in sunlight within an hour of noon. Its diameter is 7,575 miles. Its mean distance from the sun is 67,200,000 miles. Its periodic time is 224.7 mean solar days. Observation of the passage of the planet across the sun's disk is the best method of ascertaining the distance of the great luminary; this passage, known as the transit of Venus, was first observed by Horrocks in 1639 and subsequently by Halley; it has revealed that Venus has an atmosphere, but its composition is as yet uncertain. Venus has no known satellites.

Versailles, Treaty of. On June 28, 1919, at the close of World War I, Versailles was the scene of the signing of the treaty between the Allies and Germany. It became effective Jan. 10, 1920, and provided for a drastic reduction in Germany's military and naval forces, the restoration of Alsace-Lorraine to France, the confiscation of Germany's overseas colonies, and the payment by Germany of large reparations to various members of the Allies. It required a denunciation of the Bucharest and Brest-Litovsk treaties and the acceptance by Germany of full responsibility for the war. Incorporated in the treaty also were provisions for the establishment of the League of Nations, the Permanent Court of International Justice, and the International

Labor Office. The United States was not a party to this treaty.

Vertebrata, animals possessing a backbone or spinal column. Vertebrates include cyclostomes, shark-like fishes, bony fishes, amphibians, reptiles, birds, and mammals. Special sense organs tend to concentrate in the head along with the development of the brain, which is enclosed by a skull. The process of respiration is carried on by organs developed from the pharynx; and the closed circulatory system is composed of blood vessels and a muscular heart of at least two chambers. Reproduction in vertebrates is normally bi-sexual. The fertilized eggs develop externally in some vertebrates, while in other forms they develop in the body of the mother. With but few exceptions, there are only two pairs of appendages which are variously modified as organs of locomotion adapted to the organism's habitat.

Vigilantes, citizens organized for the purpose of administering justice in the absence of or failure of formal courts of law. In the United States the custom of organizing vigilance committees in times of public emergencies was typical of frontier regions. During the Revolutionary War such committees were formed to prevent English commodities from being brought into the country and to detect the activities of Tories. Before the Civil War the South organized such groups to discover the members of the Underground Railroad, and to stop abolitionists from circulating literature. After the war, vigilante groups were formed to frighten "scalawags" and "carpetbaggers." Many such groups were later merged in the Ku Klux Klan. In the West, during the gold rush, there was much lawlessness, which, because of lack of governmental courts and officers, could be suppressed only by the organization of law-abiding citizens into vigilantes. The practice of forming into unauthorized committees, self-appointed to administer justice, has occasionally been abused when lynching mobs have been organized to commit crimes of violence.

Vikings, the Norse sea-rovers who harried the coasts of Europe from about the 8th to about the 10th century, a period called the Viking Age. They were excellent shipbuilders and sailors. The earlier viking raids were for plunder; later, permanent settlements were made in England, Ireland, and Normandy. Russia was ruled by the vikings for several centuries. The Christianization of the vikings was the most important factor in ending their raids.

Vinegar, a sour liquid obtained by the fermentation of certain alcoholic liquids. It is primarily a diluted acetic acid. Vinegar has been used as a condiment from the days of the Romans, and is used in the preparation of pickles and many sauces.

Violin, a familiar stringed musical instrument, a smaller form of the more ancient viol. Instruments of the violin type have been used from remote times, and the form as now played upon is practically the same as that of the 16th century. In the following two centuries the families of Amati, Guarneri, and Stradivari perfected the violin.

Violoncello, a large, stringed instrument, tuned an octave lower than the viola, and held by the performer between his knees while playing. Commonly called *cello,* it is the bass of the violin family.

Virgo, the 6th constellation of the Zodiac, lying between Leo and Libra. It has seven prominent stars ranged in the form of the letter "Y". One of these stars, Spica, is of the first magnitude, the other six being of the third magnitude.

Vishnu, the second person of the Hindu Trinity, representing the principle of stability, or preservation.

Visigoths, a Germanic people, related to the Ostrogoths. They defeated Roman forces sent against them in 378, ravaged the Balkan peninsula, invaded Italy, and in 410 captured and sacked Rome. In 412 the Visigoths migrated to southern France and northern Spain. Gradually they were pushed by the Franks and Burgundians farther into Spain, where they established control, and set up a kingdom. Torn by conspiracies and revolts, the Visigothic kingdom fell before the Moors, who by 713 conquered all of Spain and ended the dominance of the Visigoths.

Vitriol, an old name for sulphuric acid, represented in its pure form by oil of vitriol. Sulphate of copper forms blue vitriol; sulphate of iron, green vitriol; and sulphate of zinc, white vitriol. Among other vitriols are nickel vitriol, red vitriol, and blue vitriol.

Volcano, a vent in the earth's crust through which molten rock, steam, and gases are discharged, either continuously or at intervals. The name is also applied to a hill or mountain built up by ejected material, around the vent. The most active volcanoes of modern times have been those of Etna, Vesuvius, and Stromboli, in Italy; Hekla in Iceland; and Mont Pelée in Martinique. The last named was in violent eruption in 1902, when the chief town of St. Pierre was completely destroyed, and many lives were lost. In Hawaii there are Mauna Loa, Mauna Kea, and Hualalai; others have recently been active in Japan and the West Indies.

Volt, a unit of potential electric power, named after the Italian physicist, Alessandro Volta. It is defined as the electromotive force (e.m.f.) required to send a current of one ampere through a conductor having a resistance of one ohm. The volt expresses the difference of potential between two points in a circuit, and is equal to 10^7 ergs or 1 joule per ampere second. A cell of standard electromotive force, consisting of cadmium and mercury in dilute sulphuric acid, is used as a unit of potential for the calibration of electrical instruments. A freshly prepared cadmium or Weston cell exerts an electromotive force of 1.0183 volts at 20°C.

Volunteers of America, a religious body organized from former members of the Salvation Army in March, 1896, by Commander and Mrs. Ballington Booth and consisting of 6 regiments, embracing 9 companies or central societies and nearly 100 self-supporting posts. The head officer is elected by the members as commander-in-chief, and by the directors as president. There are four branches of philanthropic work: (1) the sociological branch, which provides homes for destitute men; (2) the Home of Mercy branch for friendless young women; (3) the tenement work for the worthy poor; (4) the philanthropic branch, which works among unprotected children. The Prisoners' League is an important department of Volunteer activity.

Voting machine, a device for vote-recording and counting. The instrument consists of a switchboard which is unlocked when the voter enters and, by an automatic handle, draws a curtain around himself. The name of each candidate is in the column-listing of his party and has a separate lever which the voter presses. The machine is so arranged that the voter may cast only one vote for each office.

Vulcanite, a hard and non-elastic variety of vulcanized rubber, used for making combs, dental plates, and numerous other objects. It contains from 30 to 60 per cent more sulphur and is subjected to a higher and more prolonged heat in curing than ordinary vulcanized rubber. It is of a brownish-black color, is hard and tough, lustrous, and is not affected by water or any of the other caoutchouc solvents. It evolves a considerable amount of static electricity when rubbed and is hence much used in the construction of electric machines. In petrology, vulcanite is a name sometimes given to pyroxene.

Vulcanization, the treatment of rubber with some form of sulphur, in order to increase its durability and elasticity, and adapt it for various uses in industry and the arts. This was originally effected by dipping the rubber in melted sulphur and heating it to nearly 300°. Several other methods have been employed. The substance thus formed is elastic at all temperatures, cannot be dissolved by the ordinary solvents, and resists the effects of heat within a considerable range of temperature. Vulcanized rubber is used for waterproofing cloth, for boots, shoes, mats, toys, belting, buffers, wheel-tires, washers, valves, pipes, fire-hose, and medical and surgical appliances.

Vulture, a famous bird of prey of two distinctive groups: that of the Old World which has the nostrils divided by a mass of bone; and the New World vulture, which has no such division. Vultures feed on carrion and are the great scavengers of tropical regions. The European species are the griffon vulture and the Egyptian vulture. Vultures have no feathers on the head and neck.

W

Waikiki, a strip of beach at Honolulu, on Honolulu Bay, upon the Hawaiian island of Oahu. A famous winter playground, Waikiki Beach is especially noted for its surf-board riding. This sport is made possible here by the location of the protective coral reef, the contour of the ocean bottom, and the currents; these produce the "continuous rollers" necessary for surfing. The native Hawaiians, who are particularly adept at the sport, do all sorts of difficult maneuvers on the boards.

Wailing Wall, the remains of the western wall of the outer court of Solomon's temple in Jerusalem. It is situated within the bazaar of the Old Jerusalem next to the mosque of Omar built on Mount Moriah, the old Jewish temple site. The length of the wall is 156 feet and its height 59 feet. It is composed of nine rows of large stones, the lower five roughly hewn are thought to be of the earlier temple, and the upper four of the later Herodian temple. Eleven rows of much smaller stones were superimposed during the Arabic period. Recent excavations below the ground surface have revealed nineteen rows below similar to the nine rows above. The wall receives its name from the fact that Jews throughout the world have made it an object of pilgrimage and of mourning over the destruction of the temple.

Wake, the ancient custom of keeping watch over the dead. It is practiced among most primitive peoples and formed an important part of the tradition of the Gaelic inhabitants of Scotland and of the Welsh. Among civilized nations today, however, it is confined to Ireland and the newer Irish settlements in various parts of the world. In Anglo-Saxon countries, communities used to gather for an all-night solemn vigil in commemoration of some saint or an event. The only remnant of this practice is possibly the custom of watching the old year out.

Waldenses, the name given to a sect of Christians, who were followers of Peter de Waldo of Lyons. The Waldenses now have more than fifty places of worship in Piedmont and a membership of more than 15,000. They have had full freedom of worship since 1848.

Wall of China (The Great), begun in 214 B. C. and intended as a barrier against invasion. It is nearly 1,500 miles in length, stretching along the northwestern boundary of the country, and varying in height and thickness, being the strongest in the neighborhood of Peking.

Wall Street, in New York City, a narrow street leading from Broadway to the East River. It occupies the former site of a stockade wall built across the island of Manhattan by the burghers of New Amsterdam as a defense against the Indians. A number of banks and trust offices are situated on this street. The New York Stock Exchange has its own building at the corner of Broad and Wall streets. As the banking business, however, has outgrown the narrow accommodations of one short street, the term has been extended to include adjacent territory. In this larger sense Wall Street is applied to the entire financial district of New York City. It includes seven exchanges, the subtreasury, nearly forty banks, about thirty trust companies, and not less than five hundred railway, insurance, express, telegraph, mining and manufacturing offices that handle funds on a larger scale. Wall Street is one of the two greatest financial districts in the world, ranking in the magnitude of its operations with the corresponding financial district in London, which centers about the Bank of England.

Walpurgis Night, the night before the 1st of May, when witches and creatures of evil are supposed to have liberty to roam. It is named after St. Walpurgis, an English nun, who went on a mission to Germany in the 8th century. She was considered a protectress against magic, during the Middle Ages. There is a famous Walpurgis Night scene in Goethe's *Faust.*

Walrus, a large marine mammal having in the upper jaw two large curved tusks, which average in length from fifteen inches to two feet. It lives on fish and inhabits the North polar regions.

Wapiti, the American elk. Its range is now practically limited to the northern Rocky Mountains; there are large herds in Yellowstone Park. It is closely allied to, but considerably larger than the red deer. It is about 54 inches high at the shoulder; yellowish brown on the upper parts; is gray on the sides; has long coarse hair in front of the neck; and large antlers. It frequents low grounds, or woody tracts near savannahs or marshes. The venison is of little value, as it is coarse and dry; but the hide makes excellent leather. It is called also, but erroneously, the elk and gray moose.

War, a fight between nations (international war), or between groups within a nation (civil war). The basic aim in war is to secure the recognition by the enemy of certain demands or conditions, after his defeat. His defeat is attempted by means of efforts to destroy his armed forces or his property; the destruction of noncombatants also is an occasional accompaniment, sometimes accidental, sometimes intentional. Wars have been fought as far back as man's records extend; in many respects they are an extremely complex manifestation of the human struggle for existence. Most of the wars from ancient times to the Napoleonic Wars have involved only the rulers of nations, and relatively small bodies of professional soldiers. The modern war is much more of a "total war," utilizing large conscript armies and subordinating nearly every activity of the state and its individual members to its prosecution. As a result the objectives of war have broadened; they involve the destruction of civilian morale and efforts to throttle the economic life of the enemy as well as the defeat of his armed forces. Not all former wars were limited in their objectives, however; the Thirty Years War visited destruction upon the land and the people as well as upon the ranks of the opposing armies. Nor do all modern wars involve "total" warfare; fears of reprisal frequently cause a reluctance to go beyond the established bounds in attacking an enemy. Modern machines have greatly increased the destruction wrought during war, and have correspondingly led to radical changes in the strategy and tactics of war. In general, however, the destruction of the enemy's armed forces is still the basic aim of strategy; military means, however, are being increasingly supplemented by propaganda and economic warfare. The broad scope of modern war frequently makes the neutrals' position a difficult one.

War College, The National, a joint service school at Fort Lesley J. McNair, in Washington, D. C. Organized by the Joint Chiefs of Staff, it has the mission of preparing selected ground, air, and naval officers and officers of the State Department and other executive departments for joint staff and command duties on the highest level in behalf of the national security.

Warm-blooded Animals, the name given to mammals and birds, in contradistinction to fishes, amphibians, and reptiles, as lower vertebrata, and to all invertebrate animals. In the latter, the blood is only a degree or two warmer than the medium in which they live, while in mammals and birds the blood greatly exceeds the outer temperature in heat. The average mammalian temperature varies from 99° F. to 100° F., as in man and his nearest allies, to 103° F. in the whales. In birds, which are the most warm-blooded animals, the lowest temperature is about 104° F., and may range to 110° or 112° F. In hibernating animals the temperature falls considerably, as the tissue waste is reduced to its minimum. The production of heat depends on the union of oxygen in the blood with carbon and hydrogen in the tissues.

War of 1812, the second serious conflict between Great Britain and the United States. During the Napoleonic Wars, American vessels carried on extensive shipping with French and Spanish colonies and with Europe. Many British sailors joined the American merchant marine during this period to evade British naval service. As a result, Britain began stopping American ships and searching them for British deserters. When war was declared on June 18, 1812, the United States found itself unprepared. The liberal group in Congress, led by Calhoun and Cheves, found their hopes of conquering Canada shattered. In 1813 Britain won many decisive victories on the sea and preserved its naval supremacy. The famous victory of Perry's fleet on Lake Erie in October, 1813, gave the United States control of the entire Lake Erie region. Complications began to develop in 1814. Government funds were running low, and New England, unsympathetic with the war, threatened to secede. The possibility of Napoleon's defeat made it seem likely that Great Britain would soon devote its entire naval and military forces to the subjection of the United States. This crucial period in American history was made worse by the burning of the Capitol and the White House by a British expedition. But the British were checked at Fort McHenry, near Baltimore, and at Plattsburg. After these battles negotiations for peace were begun, and the Treaty of Ghent was signed on Dec. 24, 1814, and ratified Feb. 18, 1815. The most decisive battle of the war, the Battle of New Orleans, won by General Andrew Jackson and a handful of men against General Pakenham and veterans of the Peninsular War, occurred on Jan. 8, 1815—more than two weeks after peace was signed.

War of Independence, the Revolutionary War. It may be divided into three periods. The first ends with the Declaration of Independence. In May, 1776, the Second Continental Congress convened and John Hancock of Massachusetts was elected president. The session was one of great and permanent interest. The first resolution of this body on the subject of independence was introduced on June 7 by Richard Henry Lee, of Virginia, and on June 11 a committee was elected to draft a declaration according to the spirit of Lee's resolution. This committee reported a Declaration of Independence, which was adopted on July 4. By this instrument the thirteen American colonies declared themselves free and independent under the name of the United States of America. The issuance of this declaration changed the character of the war. Washington's army was now a national army. The Second Continental Congress could seek foreign assistance with the possibility of success. Those who remained loyal to the English were considered traitors to the colonists.

The second division of the war covered the time from the Declaration of Independence to the entrance of France into the struggle in February, 1778. The Battle of Saratoga during this period, in October, 1777, is considered one of the fifteen decisive battles of history. It was the turning point of the war; it improved the morale of the American soldiers; it hastened the alliance between the United States and France; it left the British without a plan of war; and it helped to bring Spain and Holland to the assistance of the Americans.

The third period closed with the signing of the treaty of peace at Paris, September 3, 1783—eight years after the Battle of Lexington which inaugurated the war. Benjamin Franklin, John Jay, and John Adams were the American envoys. The chief provisions of the treaty were as follows: 1) Great Britain was to recognize the independence of the United States; 2) the United States was to have a share in the Newfoundland fisheries; 3) the American Congress was to recommend the return of confiscated property to the Loyalists who had not fought against the rebelling colonies, and the payment of debts owed by Americans to English subjects; 4) the boundaries of the United States were defined.

Washing Machine, a machine for washing clothes, linen, and other fabrics with water and soap. There are numerous varieties, the common feature of all being that the clothes are agitated by artificial means in a vessel containing water and soap. Those used in public laundries are usually of the rotary type. Small machines for home use generally have a tub or cistern equipped with an agitator which moves up and down or back and forth so as to force the hot soapy water through the material being washed. The agitator is operated by an electric motor or a small gasoline engine. A wringer or a centrifugal container for the removal of excess water is usually attached to the washing machine. Some modern machines are equipped with electric mangles.

Washington Monument, a magnificent monument erected by the American people in honor of George Washington. It stands on the Banks of the Potomac, Washington, D. C. The cornerstone was laid by President Polk, July 4, 1848, and on Dec. 6, 1884, the capstone was set in position. The monument is made of blocks of marble two feet thick, and its height above the ground is 555 feet. The pyramidal top terminates in an aluminum tip, which is 9 inches high and weighs 100 ounces. The total weight, foundation and all, is nearly 81,000 tons. An immense iron framework supports the machinery of the elevator. At one side begin the stairs, of which there are 50 flights, containing 18 steps each. There are eight windows, at a height of 520 feet. The Washington Monument is the highest masonry monument in the world.

Watch and Time Regulations on Board Ship. A ship's crew is mustered in two divisions: the starboard (right side, looking forward) and the port (left). The day commences at noon and is divided thus:

Afternoon watch........noon to 4 p. m.
First dog watch........4 p. m. to 6 p. m.
Second dog watch......6 p. m. to 8 p. m.
First watch........8 p. m. to midnight.
Middle watch........12 p. m. to 4 a. m.
Morning watch........4 a. m. to 8 a. m.
Forenoon watch........8 a. m. to noon.

This makes seven watches, which the crew keeps alternately: the watch which is on duty in the forenoon one day has the afternoon the next day, and the men who have only four hours of rest one night have eight hours the next. This is the reason for dog watches, which are made by dividing the hours between 4 p. m. and 8 p. m. into two watches.

Time is kept by means of "bells." Two strokes of the clapper with an interval of a second, then an interval of two seconds, then two more strokes with an interval of a second, then a rest of two seconds, thus:

B (Bell). s. (second). B.2s. B.s. B.2s.

1 Bell is struck at 12:30 and again at 4:30, 6:30, 8:30 p. m., 12:30, 4:30, and 8:30 a. m.
2 Bells at 1 (struck with an interval of a second between them—B.s.B.), the same again at 5, 7, 9 p. m., 1, 5, and 9 a. m.
3 Bells at 1:30 (Bs.B. 2s. B.), 5:30, 7:30, 9:30 p. m., 1:30, 5:30, and 9:30 a. m.
4 Bells at 2 (B.s. B. 2s. B.s.B.), 6, 10 p. m., 2, 6, and 10 a. m.
5 Bells at 2:30 (B.s. B. 2s. B.s.B. 2s. B.), 10:30 p. m., 2:30, 6:30, and 10:30 a. m.
6 Bells at 3 (B.s. B. 2s. B.s.B. 2s. B.s.B.), 11 p. m., 3, 7, and 11 a. m.
7 Bells at 3:30 (B.s.B. 2s. B.s.B. 2s. B.s.B. 2s. B.), 11:30 p. m., 3:30, 7:30, and 11:30 a. m.
8 Bells (B.s.B. 2s. B.s.B. 2s. B.s.B. 2s. B.s.B.), at noon, 4, 8 p. m., midnight, 4, and 8 a. m.

Water Color, the art of painting with pigments mixed with water. Water-color work may be divided into several classes: aquarelle, encaustic fresco, true fresco, and tempera. Gum arabic, glue, wax, or white of egg may be used as a binder, which is mixed with dry color and dissolved in water. The art of water-color painting is very old. It was used in clear wash and in tempera form long before oil painting was discovered. A form of fresco was used on the walls of the caves of Atlanura and Perigord about 20,000 years ago. Colored plasters, with water as the solvent, were used for Egyptian wall paintings. The Greeks and Romans used the medium extensively. The paintings in the Palace of Knossus, executed in the Minoan Period, are good examples.

Water Gas, a colorless gas that burns with a hot, blue flame. Water in the form of steam is passed over red-hot coke, forming hydrogen and carbon monoxide. The hydrogen and carbon monoxide are then passed through a retort in which carbonaceous matter, such as resin, is undergoing decomposition, absorbing therefrom sufficient carbon to render it luminous when burned.

Waterloo, Battle of, the final battle of the Napoleonic Wars, fought on Sunday, June 18, 1815, at Waterloo, Belgium. Napoleon had 74,000 men and 246 guns; Wellington's army at the beginning of the battle comprised 67,600 men and 156 guns. The battle raged from 10 in the morning until 5 in the afternoon with alternating success, Wellington gradually gaining the mastery, however. When the Prussian forces under Blücher joined him late in the afternoon, the whole allied army moved forward and completely defeated Napoleon's army. The total losses of the allied army in killed, wounded, and missing were 22,976. The French lost about 32,000 men.

Waterproofing, a method of rendering cloths capable of resisting water. The first article of the kind was mackintosh, made mainly of India rubber, but later processes mingle the waterproofing with the threads of the fabric by the introduction of additional substances.

Water Spirit, a spirit supposed to reside in lakes, rivers, and the sea. Water spirits were believed to be the active agents in all cases of drowning and shipwreck and were said to avenge the rescue of drowning persons on their rescuers. Hence arose the widespread superstition that it was unlucky to save a shipwrecked person or one who had fallen into the water.

Waterspout, the funnel-shaped column of water in the center of a tornado over a lake or ocean. It consists of water drawn from the surface, condensed air, and water from the low cloud which forms the top of the column. The phenomenon lasts usually less than 30 minutes; frequently a number of waterspouts form and discharge simultaneously or in rapid succession.

Wax, the name applied to certain plant and animal substances or mixtures used in bleaching, in the making of wax candles, paper cups, polishes, artificial flowers, anatomical models, etc. Wax is used also in pharmacy for plasters, ointments, etc. The best-known natural wax is beeswax; others are spermaceti, obtained from the sperm whale, and Chinese wax, which is a ceryl cerotate.

Weather Bureau, a government organization sponsored in nearly every civilized country for the purpose of studying meteorological conditions, forecasting weather, and publishing this information. The United States Weather Bureau maintains 200 regular observatories, each representing about 15,000 square miles of territory. The work of accumulating data, forecasting, and making available the fruits of its researches led to the organization of the Climatological Service. The country is divided into 45 sections, and each collects and publishes data on temperature and precipitation from more than 5,000 co-operative stations. In 1870 Congress passed an act authorizing the Secretary of War to establish observation stations at military outposts and other points in the country in order to take observations of meteorological conditions and to give warnings of approaching storms on the Great Lakes and along the sea coasts. A year later a bill provided for taking data on the stages of water in the rivers of the country, and in 1872 provision was made for a code of signals to warn of the approach and probable force of storms for the benefit of agricultural and commercial interests. This work was transferred to the Department of Agriculture in 1890, and the scope of the Bureau was greatly enlarged. The Weather Bureau is now in charge of weather forecasting, the issuance of storm warnings, and the sending of weather and flood signals for the benefit of agriculture, commerce, and navigation.

Weaving, the art of making cloth on a loom. The principle of weaving is the same today as it was thousands of years ago: a warp extends lengthwise through the loom; the threads are held in separate, regular order by being passed through a reed while the weft is crossed through alternating threads of the warp by means of a shuttle which holds the weft. Thus the fabric is built up. Weaving was done by hand till the early part of the 19th century, when Cartwright's steampower loom was introduced.

Wednesday, the fourth day of the week, which derived its name from Woden or Odin, the Norse god of war.

Week, a period of seven days, approximately ¼ of the lunar month, and 1/52 of the tropical year. The ancient Greeks did not recognize any such unit of time as the week, nor did the Romans until the reign of Theodosius (4th century). The week originated among the Jews, Assyrians, and Egyptians, and it is probably from the Jews and Christians that the Romans derived it. The English names for the days of the week are the Anglo-Saxon equivalents of the Latin names, e.g., Dies solis, Dies lunae, etc. The Egyptians named the days after sun, moon, and five planets in the following order: Saturn, Jupiter, Mars, Sun, Venus, Mercury, Moon. Accordingly the cycle of days began every eighth, fifteenth, and twenty-second day.

Weevil, the popular name of an order of destructive beetles. They abound in all parts of the world and devour leaves, seeds, and grain.

Weights and Measures, are said to have been introduced by Pheidon, tyrant of Argos, in 895 B. C. At first, standards of weight were determined by objects in nature, such as a grain of wheat; the lowest unit of weight is still called a grain. The basis of ancient measure was the human body, the length of a joint of the thumb being taken as the lowest unit.

Welding, the joining of two or more pieces of metal. Usually the joint becomes as strong as the original pieces. One method employs an oxyacetylene flame. In the thermite process metallic aluminum and iron oxide are ignited and heat the two metals so quickly and to such a high temperature that they fuse. There are two types of electric welding: spot welding in which the natural resistance of metals to flow of electrical current produces heat and joins the metals at one particular spot; and electric arc welding, in which a rod of one metal is connected to one terminal of an electric generator and the metal to be welded to another terminal. When the two are brought together, the electric arc melts not only the metal of the plates but also the welding rod. The two molten metals flow together and produce the welded joint. When two flat plates are joined at right angles the operation is known as a fillet weld. The temperature reached in electric arc welding is about 7,000° F. (the melting point of steel is about 2,800°). Welding is sometimes used in construction work instead of riveting.

Western Empire, a portion of the Roman Empire —consisting of Italy, Illyricum, Spain, Gaul, Britain, and Africa—which Valentinian I reserved for himself when in 364 he appointed his brother Valens to rule the Eastern Empire—the eastern half of the Balkan Peninsula, Greece, Egypt, Syria, and Asia Minor. This partition of the Roman Empire became final in 395, when Theodosius the Great divided the Roman World between his two sons: Honorius, who became emperor of Rome and the West; and Arcadius, who became emperor of Constantinople and the East. The Western Empire fell in 476.

Whale, a marine animal averaging 50 feet in length when full-grown, the head comprising nearly one-third of the whole length. It inhabits the Arctic Ocean and is hunted for the sake of its blubber, a thick mass of fat which underlies its skin to a depth of from 8 to 16 inches. The blubber yields whale oil. Whalebone is derived from the baleen plates forming the structural portion of the mouth.

Wheat, the most valuable and, next to maize, or Indian corn, the most productive of all the cereal grasses. It was cultivated as early as the New Stone Age and has been a very important grain in western civilizations. The first wheat produced in the United States was planted in New England in 1602; and nine years later wheat was sown in Virginia.

About 60 per cent of American wheat is winter wheat. According to official standards in the United States, wheat is divided into five commercial classes: (1) hard red spring wheat, (2) durum wheat, (3) hard red winter wheat, (4) soft red winter wheat, and (5) white wheats.

With respect to nutritional value, wheat is an excellent source for carbohydrates and minerals, a good source for vitamin B, and a fair source for protein and vitamin A.

Whirlpool, a current of water revolving with great force. Small vessels may be drawn in and submerged, but larger ships are not endangered. Two of the most famous whirlpools are the Maelstrom and Charybdis.

Whisky, a spirit distilled from barley, wheat, rye, corn, or oats. There are four varieties: rye, corn (Bourbon), Irish, and Scotch. Genuine Irish whisky is made from barley, oats, and malt brewed in large pot stills. For the preparation of the wort, the grain is mashed and mixed with malt, and to this, yeast is added to hasten fermentation. The wort is then placed in a large kettle and heated over a peat or coal fire. The vapor is condensed in a pipe passing through cold water and finally falls into a receiver. It is distilled three times and consequently has a high alcoholic content. The smoke of the peat fire accounts for the distinctive taste of certain old Irish whiskies. Scotch is made of malt in the same way as Irish, except that as a rule only one distillation takes place. Corn whisky, manufactured chiefly in the southern part of the United States, and rye whisky, manufactured chiefly in Canada, are made from a mixture of their respective grains and malt, and are distilled several times. Less malt is used in corn and rye than in Scotch and Irish. In stills less primitive than the pot still the volatile part of the wort is extracted by steam. By means of successive chambers of varied temperature, the chambers at the top being cooler, the more alcoholic part of the condensed liquor (because of its lower boiling point) passes off into the receiver, while the less alcoholic part remains to be redistilled.

White Cross, an organization similar in many respects to the Red Cross, from which it differs chiefly in the fact that it is distinctly American. It was founded in 1898 by Mrs. Jane Creighton, of Portland, Ore., who became its first president. Its emblem was designed to represent the cross bandages of white on the blood-red field of war, encircled by the blue of the firmament, comprising the triple color of the Union. The motto of the organization is "Truth, Charity, and Philanthropy," and its purposes include not only the caring for wounded and sick American soldiers and sailors, but also the aiding of the widows and orphans of those who are killed in battle or die of disease or accident.

White Elephant, a term in common use to designate a gift that causes the recipient more trouble or cost than it is worth; derived from an old custom of the kings of Siam, who presented a white elephant to a courtier they desired to ruin.

White House, the official residence of the President of the United States, in Washington, D. C., so called because it is painted white. It is situated on Pennsylvania Avenue, a mile and a half from the Capitol. The original structure was begun in 1792, when the cornerstone was laid, and the building was completed in 1800. John Adams was the first President to occupy the mansion. The British captured Washington in 1814 and burned the White House together with the Capitol and other buildings, but its restoration was authorized by Congress the following year. In 1818 the new structure was ready to be occupied, and it has since been the official residence of the President. In 1947 President Truman had a second floor porch built into the south portico. In 1948 Congress authorized complete reconstruction of the building.

Wichita Indians, a tribe of North American Indians, remnants of which now reside in western Oklahoma on the Caddo Reservation. The most important of the several subtribes were the Tawakoni and Waco. They lived in conical grass houses and engaged chiefly in agriculture. They once occupied territory as far north as Kansas and were probably the people visited by Coronado in 1541. In 1834 they moved from a village on the Red River in Oklahoma to the vicinity of the modern Ft. Sill. After the Civil War they moved to Wichita, Kansas. In 1872 they ceded their lands to the United States government.

Will, a document legally executed containing directions as to the disposition of a person's property or possessions after his death. The person making a will must be of legal age, and the will must be signed in the presence of two witnesses, who must also sign their names to the document in the testator's presence.

Wilmot Proviso, a resolution introduced into the United States Congress by David Wilmot. On Aug. 8, 1846, pending the consideration in Congress of a bill placing $2,000,000 at the disposal of President Polk to negotiate a peace with Mexico, David Wilmot, a representative from Pennsylvania, offered the following amendment: "Provided that, as an express and fundamental condition to the acquisition of any territory from the republic of Mexico by the United States by virtue of any treaty which may be negotiated between them, and to the use by the Executive of the moneys therein appropriated, neither slavery nor involuntary servitude shall ever exist in any part of said territory, except for crime, whereof the party shall first be duly convicted." The resolution became the source of great agitation throughout the country. It was adopted in the House by a vote of 94 to 78 and was under debate in the Senate when the hour arrived for the adjournment of the session. At the next session, when Wilmot again introduced it, a fierce and angry contest commenced. The House remained firm in favor of the amendment, and passed it by a decided majority, but the Senate did not act on it.

Wind, air set in motion by special atmospheric conditions, ranging from a slight rustling breeze to a hurricane. Winds are constant, such as trade winds or antitrade winds; periodic, as monsoons and other wind visitations due to influences of the season; cyclonic and anticyclonic, when their motion is spiral; whirlwinds, hurricanes, and tornadoes, when high temperature and great density induce extreme agitation. Ordinarily, a wind is named for the point from which it blows. The sirocco, the mistral, and the simoon are local forms of winds of great velocity.

Windmill, a machine operated by the force of the wind. There were windmills in use in the East in ancient times, but in Europe, not much before the 13th century. Wind sawmills were invented by a Hollander in the 17th century. Great improvements have been made in recent years, especially in the United States, where, by the application of the wind-shaft principle, much space is saved, and the mills can be used for pumping water, grinding grain, and generating electricity.

Window, originally, an aperture in a building for the admission of the wind. Later, the opening was closed with a pane of glass and used only for the admission of light. Glass windows were used at Pompeii in Roman times.

Wine, the fermented juice of the grape. The varieties are innumerable, each obtaining its distinctive character from the kind and quality of the grapes used, the locality in which it is produced, or the amount of alcohol it contains. "Sparkling" wines, such as champagne, are bottled before fermentation is completed; "still" wines are noneffervescent. The alcohol in ports and sherries is from 16 to 25 per cent; in lighter wines, from 7 to 10 per cent.

Winnebago Indians, a tribe of North American Indians of the same linguistic stock as the Sioux. When the whites came to America, they first came into contact with the Winnebago Indians in the region of Winnebago Lake, Wisconsin, and in the country to the southwest. Territory adjacent to theirs was occupied by the Menominee, Ojibwa, Miami, Sauk, and Fox tribes, from whom the Winnebagoes acquired many of their customs. There was a great similarity between the culture of the Winnebagoes and that of the Menominees. The Winnebagoes used bark, skins, wood, and reed in the construction of their dwellings and, like the other Sioux tribes, were divided into clans. In addition to securing much of their food through hunting, fishing, and gathering wild rice, they were agriculturists to a certain extent. The first white man, as far as is known, to come in contact with the Winnebagoes was Jean Nicolet, in 1634.

Witchcraft, the art or practice of sorcery, generally accepted throughout the Middle Ages. In England laws against witchcraft existed down to 1736; the last executions of witches were in 1716. According to one authority, "the judicial murders for witchcraft in England in 200 years numbered 30,000." In the New England colonies witchhunting was at its worst in Salem, Mass., in 1692.

Wolverine, or Glutton, a carnivorous mammal of the weasel family inhabiting the more northerly parts of the United States. It is dark in color and somewhat resembles the polar bear in shape and structure.

Wood Pulp, a preparation made from wood; used in the manufacture of paper, rayon, plastics, and innumerable other products. The wood pulp for the manufacture of newsprint is generally produced by the groundwood, or mechanical, process. Logs, generally spruce, are ground by pressing them against large rotating stone rollers with an abundance of water flowing on the grinding surface, thus grinding the fibers from the logs. Enough chemically treated wood pulp is then added to provide requisite quality and cohesion. Groundwood pulp permits the utilization of the entire log without perceptible shrinkage or waste.

Wool, a sort of hair which grows on the backs of sheep and certain other animals. Wool differs from hair in that it has a wavy notched fiber, its curl being a notable characteristic, whereas hair has a smooth surface which is comparatively free from notches. Long wools are used mostly for worsted goods, and short wools, for woolen cloth. Improvements in machinery, however, have enabled manufacturers to utilize short wools to a great extent for dress fabrics as well as for woolens. The finest wools are obtained from the fleece of the Spanish merino sheep. Australia, New Zealand, and the Argentine are the greatest wool-producing countries.

Workmen's Compensation Acts, acts providing for the compensation of a workman by his employer in case of accident. The worker has a right to compensation for injuries received whether negligence on the part of the employer is proved or not. Compensation legislation falls into two classes: compulsory and voluntary. In most states only hazardous employments are directly subject to the act, but even in those states the employer not subject to the act can agree with the employees to accept its provisions. The statutes of each state must be examined to determine whether a particular type of employment is specifically exempted from operation of the act. Domestic, agricultural, and casual help, and those businesses having fewer than a stipulated number of employees are usually excepted.

World War II began in September, 1939, when Adolf Hitler's *blitzkrieg*, lightning war, struck in Poland. But the softening up of his enemies by economic and political infiltration had been going on for years, aided by the appeasement policy of Britain, France, and the U. S. By June, 1940, Germany and its ally, Italy, held all of western Europe, with only England left to conquer. One year later they had pushed back the British in Africa, taken the Balkans, and invaded Russia. But they had still not conquered England. The German invasion of Russia was bogging down when, on Dec. 7, 1941, Japan attacked the United States at Pearl Harbor, turning the hostilities into a global war. No part of the world remained untouched thereafter. Britain, the U. S., and their allies turned their power first to conquering the Axis in Europe. At great cost they invaded the French coast and the Italian coast, pushed back the Nazis and finally forced their surrender in May, 1945. Concentrating their power in the Pacific, and after dropping two atomic bombs on Japanese cities, the Allies forced Japan's surrender on Sept. 2, 1945.

Wrestling, an athletic contest in which each of the two participants attempts to overthrow the other for a chance to score. The methods employed in the sport consist of innumerable body, arm, leg, and head holds according to various rules. The first recorded wrestling match took place in 720 B. C. at the great Olympic Games. Wrestling was both a separate event and one of the five games of the pentathlon. One of the objects of the sport was to make every attack with elegance and grace under rules of a most intricate nature; the game was described by Plutarch as the hardest form of athletics. The beginnings of wrestling in Japan have been traced to the year 32 B. C. Of the two most important types of wrestling employed in that country, jujitsu is the more spectacular. The opponent is defeated by making him use his bulk and weight against himself. A small man who is expert in jujitsu can easily overcome a much larger person by employing skill rather than strength. In the other type of wrestling, known as sumo, more emphasis is placed upon weight, many wrestlers weighing 300 pounds or more. In sumo a fall is called if one of the wrestlers can make any part of his opponent's body, other than his feet, touch the ground.

Wyandot Indians, a tribe of North American Indians belonging to the Iroquois family. In Canada they are better known as Hurons, for at the beginning of the 17th century they were settled on the eastern shore of Lake Huron. In a tribal war in 1636 they were nearly exterminated, and the rest of the tribe settled at Lorette in lower Canada, where their descendants, about 400 in number, still remain. Other groups wandered westward, going from their early sanctuary on Manitoulin Island into Michigan. About 1750 they settled at Sandusky, Ohio, and near Detroit, Michigan. In the Revolutionary War and the War of 1812 they fought on the side of the English. They migrated to Wyandotte County, Kansas, in 1842 and to the Oklahoma reservation in 1867. They number approximately 600.

Wyclif's Bible, the first translation of the Bible into English completed about 1384. Collaborators on this work were Nicholas Hereford and John Purvey. Wyclif's Bible helped to standardize the English language.

X

X Rays, invisible radiations discovered by Wilhelm Röntgen in 1895; hence called also Röntgen rays. The rays proceed from a glass or porcelain bulb, termed a Geissler or Crookes tube, from which most of the air has been exhausted and through which an electric charge is conducted. The rays are produced whenever cathode rays encounter matter. The fascinating feature of these rays is their extraordinary ability to penetrate many opaque substances. The degree of penetration depends on the density of the matter; bone, for example, is penetrated more deeply than flesh. X rays affect a photographic plate or film. They cannot be refracted or reflected and are not bent by a magnetic or electric field; hence they do not carry an electric charge. The rays possess the property of ionizing or imparting temporary electrical conductivity to a gas, which ordinarily is a nearly perfect insulator. X rays are similar to light waves. The shorter the wave length, the more penetrating are the X rays.

Xylophone, a very ancient musical instrument which in its original form consisted of strips of resonant wood graduated in length and resting on belts attached to a frame. The frame was laid flat and the strips of wood beaten by a small hammer so as to give out musical notes, the long strips giving the deeper notes, and the short ones the higher notes. By grading the length of the wood strips carefully, the complete chromatic scale could be obtained. In the modern xylophone the strips are made of bronze, bell metal, or even of hollow glass; and an additional row of heavier strips is added at the back so that a bass can be played, while open metal tubes are hung below the strips to increase their resonance.

XYZ Affair, an incident in the relations between the United States and France during 1797 and 1798. The United States was both unable and unwilling to carry out its alliance with France, made in 1778, and the French became antagonistic because of the Jay Treaty between United States and England. Hostilities took the form of minor naval engagements and a refusal, on the part of the French government, to recognize Charles Pinckney, appointed United States minister to France. Finally John Marshall, Charles Pinckney, and Elbridge Gerry were sent to negotiate with French officials. Three French agents, represented in press reports as X, Y, and Z, demanded payment of a large bribe by the United States, but this was refused. Talleyrand, the chief French representative, would negotiate only with Gerry, who was pro-French. Reports of the XYZ incident caused great indignation in the United States, and led to widespread demands for war with France. However, Gerry and Logan established friendly relations with France, and in 1800 a treaty between the two countries was signed.

Y

Yacht, a decked pleasure vessel driven by sail, steam, or internal combustion engines. Racing yachts are built along very fine lines. Yacht racing as a sport dates from 1680, when a vessel of Charles II emerged victorious over the entries of the Dutch and the Duke of York respectively. The oldest British yacht club was the Water Club, founded in 1720 at Cork, Ireland. Almost a century later, in 1812, the Royal Yacht Club of England drew up its charter. The New York Yacht Club was established with nine members in 1844 as an outgrowth of a Hoboken sailboat club. The first international race for a cup was won by the *America* August 22, 1851 in world competition over a 60-mile course around the Isle of Wight during the London World's Fair. The trophy offered by the Royal Yacht Club was the Queen's Cup, valued at $2,500. The time for the *America* in the Queen's Cup race was 10 hours, 34 minutes Second place went to the British 47-ton cutter *Aurora*, which crossed the line 24 minutes later. In subsequent races American-owned ships successfully defended their prize. The trophy became known later as the *America's Cup*. Specifications for the vessels were revised from time to time. The conditions of the course and race were also changed. Later, the races were held in American waters, principally over the New York Yacht Club course off Sandy Hook. British efforts to gain the cup were unsuccessful. The late Sir Thomas Lipton took up the challenge in 1899 with the *Shamrock*, but failed. Repeated efforts in 1901, 1903, 1920, and 1930 with new yachts of the *Shamrock* class were also futile. In 1934 and again in 1937 Thomas Sopwith attempted to win back the cup in the *Endeavor* but was defeated by Harold Vanderbilt in the *Rainbow*.

Yankee Doodle, a song now regarded as one of the national airs of the United States. Many accounts have been given of its origin, but all are uncertain. It is quite probable that the tune is of English origin. The first known reference to the song was in the Boston *Journal of the Times* for September, 1768.

Yard, a standard measure of 36 inches, the word being derived from the Saxon *gyrd*, or rod. The yard was anciently regarded as the circumference of the body, but Henry I decreed it should be the length of his arm.

Yarn, any textile fiber prepared for weaving into cloth. Cotton yarn is numbered according to the number of hanks contained in a pound of 7,000 grains. Each hank, or skein, measures 840 yards. Worsted yarn has 560 yards to the skein; woolen yarn is wound upon reels and is made up into leas, hanks, and bundles. Flax and jute yarns are numbered according to the number of leas of 300 yards per pound.

Year, a unit of time marked by one complete revolution of the earth around the sun. The year is either astronomical or civil. The former is determined by astronomical observation and is of different lengths, according to the point of the heavens to which the revolution is referred.

When the earth's motion is referred to a fixed point in the heavens, as a fixed star, the time of revolution is the time that elapses from the moment when the star, the sun, and the earth are in a straight line, till they again occupy the same position; this is called a sidereal year. If the revolution is referred to one of the equinoctial points, the year is somewhat shorter than the sidereal year on account of the precession of the equinoxes, that is, the retrogression of the equinoctial points along the ecliptic; this is called the equinoctial, tropical, or solar year. The length of the sidereal year is 365.2422414 mean solar days, or 365 days, 5 hours, 48 minutes, 49.7 seconds. The difference between these two years is 19 minutes, 19.2 seconds mean solar time—the time required for the earth to advance in its orbit a distance of 50.1" of arc. The civil year is the year of the calendar.

Yearbook, an almanac or annual publication. Formerly yearbooks contained annual reports of legal cases; they were issued, in England, as far back as the 11th century and represent the first attempt to establish legal reports.

Yeast, a substance that sets up fermentation, discovered in 1836 to be a fungoid or vegetable cell. Yeast added, with warm water, to flour commences the process of fermentation that gives sponginess to bread. It is the potent agent in the production of alcohol from sugar.

Yoga, one of the leading systems of Hindu philosophy, which holds that the devotee, by means of certain postures, controlled breathing, and "the concentration of thought within," can liberate the soul from its body so that it may join the Universal Spirit.

Yuma Indians, a tribe of North American Indians, who for a long time previous to the invasion of the white man inhabited the Colorado and Gila River country. They lived in parts of southwestern Arizona, southeastern California, Sonora, and Lower California. The Yumas seem to represent a higher type of aborigine than most of the North American Indians and are believed to have been descendants of the prehistoric peoples who inhabited portions of Arizona and the adjacent territory. In 1833 the United States government established a reservation for them. The name Yuma has become generalized; the common linguistic stock bears the name and includes the Cocopa, Havasupai, the Maricopa, Mohave, Walapai, Diegueno, and the Mission Indians. Sometimes the Seri Indians are classed as Yuman.

Z

Zebra, an African quadruped of whitish-gray color, with regular black stripings, perhaps the most beautiful member of the equine family. Somewhat larger than an ass, and smaller than a horse, it has a tufted tail, is light in build, wild, and swift of foot.

Zebu, a species of light-gray oxen having a large hump on the shoulder, and short horns. In India and some parts of Africa zebus are domesticated and become very docile beasts of burden. Their flesh is good to eat; the Hindus, however, do not butcher them, for they regard them with much veneration.

Zend-Avesta, the name given to certain ancient, sacred books of the Zoroastrians or Parsees. They originally numbered 21, but only three are extant.

Zenith, the highest point in the heavens to an observer at any given place; the point from which, if the earth were absolutely spherical, a perpendicular let fall would pass through its center. It is 180° from, and directly opposite to, the nadir. Both zenith and nadir are 90° from the celestial horizon, which is a great circle midway between them. The zenith distance is the space measured by the angle between the zenith and any object in the heavens. The geocentric zenith is a point in the celestial sphere cut by a line through the center of the earth and the observer.

Zenith Sector, an astronomical instrument for ascertaining the zenith distance of a star. It is a telescope swinging upon pivots and has attached to it an arc graduated into degrees and minutes. From the upper end of the telescope hangs a fine silver wire, which terminates in a weight supported in water to keep it steady.

Zinc, a metallic element occurring in zinc sulphide, carbonate of zinc, and other substances. It is used to galvanize iron; to form the negative plate in electric cells; and to prepare alloys, such as brass, bronze, babbitt, and German silver. The United States is the greatest producer of zinc. The metal was known to the ancients, who used it in making brass.

Zinc White, a mineral pigment, zinc oxide, derived from oxidized ores of zinc. It is an amorphous, insoluble substance having a very high melting point (above 1,800° C.). The mineral oxide is ground to a fine white powder and mixed with oils in the manufacture of paints.

Zionism, a Jewish nationalist movement with the basic aim of establishing a national home for the Jews. The spiritual founder of the movement was Theodor Herzl, and the first Zionist congress was held in Basel, Switzerland, in 1897. In 1917 the Balfour Declaration stated that the British government viewed with favor the establishment of a national home for the Jewish people in Palestine. Through a worldwide organization the Zionists acquired land in Palestine for Jewish settlement. After World War II large-scale emigration from Europe to Palestine was resisted by the British, and fighting with the Zionists broke out. When the British withdrew from Palestine in 1948, the Jews established the state of Israel. World Zionist organizations continued to give political and economic support to the nation.

Zodiac, the imaginary belt of the firmament enclosing the circuit over which the principal planets travel. It is divided into 12 equal spaces of 30 degrees each, comprising the 12 signs of the Zodiac: Aries, Taurus, Gemini, Cancer, Leo, Virgo, Libra, Scorpio, Sagittarius, Capricornus, Pisces, Aquarius.

Zone, an imaginary geographical belt encircling the earth. There are five zones: the Torrid Zone, from tropic to tropic; two Temperate zones, from the tropics to the Polar circles; and two Frigid zones, from the Polar circles to the North and South Poles respectively.

Zoology, the science of animal biology, treating of the structure, classification, and distribution of the various members of the animal kingdom.

Zoophyte, the name given to a class of organisms combining the nature of both plants and animals, such as corals, sponges, sea anemones, etc.

Zouaves, a body of soldiers in the service of France. The Zouave regiments were organized in Algeria and consisted originally of Berber natives, but later chiefly of Frenchmen.

A Dictionary of BIOGRAPHY

***Important facts** and leading achievements in the lives of the most distinguished men and women of all ages and countries*

DICTIONARY OF BIOGRAPHY

Abbas II (1874-1923), khedive of Egypt; succeeded Tewfik Pasha, 1892; deposed Dec. 18, 1914.

Abbey, Edwin Austin (1852-1911), a famous American painter and illustrator, who settled in London in 1878, and from 1890 was a regular exhibitor at the Royal Academy.

Abdul-Hamid II (1842-1918), a sultan of Turkey who succeeded his brother, 1876; began his reign with proposals of reform, but after the Russo-Turkish War (1877-1878) assumed autocratic rule. He conceded a constitution in 1898, but was deposed in April, 1909.

Abelard, Peter (1079-1142), French scholar, philosopher, and theologian. The romantic attachment between him and Héloïse, mainly set forth in letters of the latter, has been more written about than perhaps any other love affair. Their remains now lie in one tomb in Père Lachaise, to which they were removed after the Revolution.

Abercrombie, Lascelles (1881-1938), English poet and critic; was professor of English literature at London University, 1929-35. In addition to several volumes of verse he has written: *Thomas Hardy: A Critical Study, The Theory of Poetry, Poetry: Its Meaning and Music.*

Abruzzi, Duke of, Prince Luigi Amadeo Giuseppe Maria Ferdinando Francesco (1873-1933), an Italian naval officer who distinguished himself by Arctic exploration. In 1899 he advanced nearer to the North Pole than any previous explorer had done, his expedition reaching 86 degrees 34 minutes N. latitude, or 20 minutes beyond Nansen's 1893-1896 achievement. Commander-in-chief Italian navy, 1915-17.

Acheson, Dean G. (b. 1893), U. S. public official born in Middleton, Conn., educated at Yale and Harvard. He was Undersecretary of the Treasury in 1933, Assistant Secretary of State in 1941, Undersecretary (1945-47) and in 1949 Secretary of State. He was the leading advocate of the North Atlantic Treaty and chief architect of the Truman foreign policy. In 1951 he reaffirmed the stand of the U.S. against appeasement of Communist aggression. Following the defeat of the Democratic party in November, he resigned as Secretary of State.

Adams, John (1735-1826), second President of the United States; born in Braintree, Mass. In 1774 he was chosen as a delegate to the first Continental Congress. He was on the committee which drafted the Declaration of Independence. He served on many important committees throughout the Revolutionary War, and aided in drafting the peace treaty with Great Britain. Adams was the first American envoy to Great Britain; in 1788 was elected the first Vice President under the Constitution; and in 1797 he succeeded Washington as President. He was defeated for re-election by Jefferson, and retired to his home in Quincy, where he spent the rest of his life.

Adams, John Quincy (1767-1848), sixth President of the U. S., and son of John Adams. He served as ambassador to the Netherlands, U. S. Senator from 1803 to 1806, and professor of rhetoric at Harvard, 1806-1809. He was later ambassador to Russia and a member of the commission which negotiated the treaty ending the War of 1812. From 1821 to 1825 he was Secretary of State under Monroe and then succeeded him in the Presidency, 1825-1829. He was elected to the House of Representatives in 1831 and was a member until his death. He was one of the outstanding leaders of the anti-slavery movement in Congress.

Adams, Maude (1872-1953), an American actress, born at Salt Lake City. At 16 years of age Miss Adams joined E. H. Sothern's company in *The Midnight Bell.* Thereafter she played in *The Little Minister* (1898), *Peter Pan* (1906), Rostand's *Chanticleer* (1911), and Barrie's *The Legend of Leonora* (1913).

Adams, Samuel (1722-1803), American statesman, known as the "American Cato," who worked all his life for American independence, and signed the declaration (1776). He organized the "Boston Tea Party."

Addams, Jane (1860-1935), famous American sociologist, who founded Hull House, Chicago, in 1889; was Chairman of the Women's International League for Peace and Freedom, 1915-35.

Addison, Joseph (1672-1719), the son of an English clergyman, who achieved fame both as a writer and a politician. In 1706 he was undersecretary of state, and from 1708 to his death was a member of Parliament. He is best known for his essays which appeared in the *Tatler* and the *Spectator*, along with those of his friend and associate, Steele.

Adeler, Max (1841-1915), American humorist who wrote, among other works, *Out of the Hurly Burly* (1874), and *Elbow Room* (1876).

Adler, Alfred (1870-1937), an Austrian physician and psychologist; was a pupil of Dr. Sigmund Freud until 1913; founded the school of Individual Psychology.

Aeschylus (525-456 B. C.), the father of the Greek tragic drama. Composed seventy plays and gained the prize for dramatic excellence thirteen times. *Seven Against Thebes* and *Agamemnon* are his best-known dramas.

Aesop (b. in Greece about 620, d. 544 B. C.), a Greek slave, whose fables are the most celebrated productions of their kind.

Agassiz, Louis Jean Rodolphe (1807-73), American naturalist and authority on ichthyology. He was the author of a five-volume work on *Researches on Fossil Fishes* (1833-43), and his scientific investigations into the movements of glaciers resulted in *Studies on Glaciers* (1840). His great work, *Contributions to the Natural History of the United States,* was left unfinished.

Agricola, Cnaeus Julius (A. D. 37-93), became Roman consul of Britain A. D. 78. He strengthened the power of the Romans in that country, corrected many abuses, and did much to encourage trade and industry.

Agrippa, Heinrich Cornelius (1486-1535), German soldier, diplomatist, and philosopher, who achieved great eminence under the German Emperors Maximilian and Charles V. As a theologian he incurred the violent hatred of the Dominican monks; as a student of the occult he acquired the reputation of a magician.

Agrippa, Marcus Vipsanius (63-12 B. C.), Roman soldier, the greatest military commander after Julius Caesar.

Agrippina (the Elder) (12 B. C.-A. D. 33), Roman noblewoman, daughter of Marcus Vipsanius Agrippa; wife of Germanicus; and mother of Caligula. She was one of the most virtuous and heroic women of her time, remarkable for her bold defiance of the tyrant Tiberius.

Agrippina (the Younger) (c. 15-59), daughter of the last named, and mother of Nero; notorious for her licentiousness and perfidy. Claudius made her his consort in A. D. 48. Her career was one long course of intrigue and infamy; she was ultimately put to death by the order of Nero.

Akbar the Great (1552-1605), Mogul Emperor from 1556 to 1605 and a monarch of great enlightenment and power.

Alaric I (376-410), the famous chief who led the Visigoths against the Romans, and afterwards invaded both Greece and Italy. He took Rome in 410, died the following year, and was buried with a vast treasure in the bed of the River Busento.

Alban, St., who flourished in the latter part of the 3rd century, was born at Verulamium (where St. Albans now stands) and served as a soldier under Diocletian at Rome. Later he was converted to Christianity, and was for a time a renowned preacher of that religion, finally suffering martyrdom. Offa, king of the Mercians, built a monastery to his memory near Verulamium, four or five hundred years later. St. Alban's Day in the calendar of the Roman Church is June 22nd, and in that of the Anglican Church June 17th.

Albani Gye, Dame Emma Cecile (1852-1930), an operatic soprano, b. at Chambly, near Montreal; better known by her stage name of Madame Albani. She made her first appearance in England at Covent Garden in 1872 and was for many years a leading prima donna, achieving great ce ebrity as Elsa in *Lohengrin.* Author of *Forty Years of Song* in 1911.

Alberoni, Giulio Cardinal (1664-1752), minister of Philip V of Spain, was an Italian of humble birth. For some years he exercised great influence. His object was to restore to Spain her ancient power, but plunging into war with Austria, he found himself confronted with the Quadruple Alliance—Austria, England, Holland and France—and his plans were defeated. He was banished from Spain and died in his native town of Piacenza.

Albert, King of the Belgians (1875-1934), son of the Count of Flanders, succeeding his uncle, Leopold II, Dec. 17, 1909. His brave part in the World War won him lasting fame; he was killed while mountaineering in the Ardennes.

Albert, Prince Francis Augustus Charles Emmanuel (1819-1861), consort of Queen Victoria of England. On his marriage with the queen in 1840 Parliament granted him an income of £30,000 a year. The prince adapted himself with considerable success to the difficulties of his position, and gradually secured the confidence and esteem of statesmen and public alike. He died of typhoid fever in December, 1861; the Albert Memorial forms a tribute to his memory.

Albertus Magnus, St. (c. 1206-80), was a distinguished German philosopher, and voluminous writer on the occult sciences; became bishop of Ratisbon in 1260. His dabblings in alchemy and astrology gained him wide notoriety.

Alcaeus, a Greek poet who flourished c. 600 B. C.

Alcibiades (c. 450-404 B. C.), Athenian statesman and general treacherously killed in battle at Melissa, Phrygia. He was a pupil and friend of Socrates.

Alcott, Louisa May (1832-88), a famous American author of the latter half of the 19th century. The charm and naturalness of her writings made her a favorite among children's authors, and her books are still read on both sides of the Atlantic. Her most famous book, *Little Women,* appeared in 1868; it is a children's classic, a film version of which was produced in Hollywood in 1933.

Alcuin (735-804), was an English ecclesiastic and writer.

Aldington, Richard (b. 1892), English poet of the Imagist school. Gained wide popularity by his war book, *Death of a Hero.*

Aldred (d. 1069), an English ecclesiastic of the 11th century in great favor with William the Conqueror, whom he crowned. He was bishop of Worcester (1044-60), and archbishop of York (1060-1069).

Alekhine, Alexander (1892-1946), Russian chess master; champion of the world from 1927 to 1935 and again from 1937 to 1946.

Alembert, Jean le Rond d' (1717-1783), a Parisian mathematician and philosopher who achieved great eminence by his numerous scientific works, including the *Theory of the Winds* and the *Precession of the Equinoxes.*

Alexander I (1888-1934), king of Yugoslavia 1921-34, assassinated Oct. 10, 1934.

Alexander I of Russia (1777-1825), succeeded his father, Paul I, and played an active part in the Napoleonic wars, joining the coalition against Napoleon in 1805 and again in 1812.

Alexander II of Russia (1818-1881), succeeded his father, the Emperor Nicholas I, in 1855. In 1861 he emancipated 23 million serfs. On March 13, 1881, he was assassinated by bombs thrown beneath his carriage in St. Petersburg by Nihilists.

Alexander I of Serbia (1876-1903), was the son of King Milan, and succeeded his father on the latter's abdication in 1889, the rule of the country being carried on under a regency until

1893. Alexander and his queen, Draga, were both assassinated by military revolutionaries in 1903.

Alexander the Great (356-323 B. C.), king of Macedon, succeeded his father Philip in 336 B.C., and from the first showed himself fitted for mighty military exploits. He conquered the Thebans and the Persian satraps, overthrew Darius, overran Syria and Phoenicia, possessed himself of all the cities along the Mediterranean, conquered Egypt, founded Alexandria, and finally retired to Babylon, where he died eleven days later.

Alexandra (1844-1926), a queen of England, daughter of Christian IX of Denmark, married to the Prince of Wales (afterwards Edward VII) on March 10, 1863. She was queen from 1901 to 1910.

Alfieri, Count Vittorio (1749-1803), Italian poet, was the author of twenty-one tragedies and six comedies.

Alfonso the Wise (1221-1284), a celebrated king of Leon and Castile, founder of the legal code which became the basis of Spanish jurisprudence, a liberal patron of literature and science, particularly of astronomy; dethroned by his son Sancho in 1282.

Alfonso XIII (1886-1941), king of Spain, acceded to the throne in May, 1886; deposed April 14, 1931.

Alfred the Great (849-901), king of the West Saxons; succeeded his father, Ethelwulf, at the age of twenty-two, and found himself in conflict with the Danes from the outset. After six years of unsuccessful effort he took refuge in the Isle of Athelney, but the following year defeated the Danes in great force at Edington (Ethandun). Later, the Danes again invaded the country, and the rest of Alfred's reign was occupied in conflict. He died at fifty-two, after a reign of thirty years, and was buried at Winchester.

Alger, Horatio (1834-99), an American writer of juvenile books, born at Revere, Mass. Graduated from Harvard in 1852, settled in New York in 1866, and became interested in the condition of self-supporting boys. These he described in his series of more than 50 books, including *Ragged Dick, Tattered Tom, Luck and Pluck,* which became very popular. He also wrote a series of juvenile biographies of Webster, Lincoln, Garfield, etc.; and *The Young Salesman* (1896). He died in Natick, Mass.

Allen, Ethan (1738-89), an American Revolutionary leader; born in Litchfield, Conn. He served in the French and Indian War at Fort William Henry in 1757, and in 1770 became leader of the Green Mountain Boys, organized to defend the New Hampshire land grants against the claims of New York. On May 10, 1775, he and the Green Mountain Boys captured Fort Ticonderoga. In 1778 he was made a lieutenant colonel by Washington, and later in the year was given command of the Vermont Militia with the rank of major general. In 1780 he became deeply involved in an attempt to arrange a treaty with Great Britain by which Vermont would have been made a British province. It is not known whether this was his real intention or whether he merely wanted to force the United States to recognize Vermont's claims. Allen wrote *A Narrative of Col. Ethan Allen's Captivity* and several other books, most of them dealing with the New Hampshire or Vermont claims against New York.

Allenby, Edmund, 1st Viscount (1861-1936), British army officer; commander of the Cavalry Expeditionary Force in 1914; distinguished himself on the Western Front, 1915-16; in 1917 carried through the Palestine campaign with success, capturing Jerusalem on Dec. 9, 1917; High Commissioner for Egypt, 1919-25.

Alleyne, Edward (1566-1626), a famous English actor, contemporary of Shakespeare, and founder of Dulwich College.

Alma-Tadema, Sir Lawrence (1836-1912), the son of a Netherlands notary, was educated at Antwerp, and came to England in 1869, where he soon made a name for himself as a painter of classical pictures of great beauty.

Amanullah (b. 1892), king of Afghanistan from 1919-29, toured Europe in 1928, and on his return endeavored to introduce great reforms in his kingdom, which were resented especially by the priesthood. Consequently he was forced to flee the country, settling in Italy in 1929.

Amherst, Jeffrey, Lord (1717-1797), a British officer. He entered the army as a page and by 1756 had attained the rank of lieutenant colonel. In 1758 Pitt promoted him major general, in command of the expedition against French Canada. By the capture of Louisburg and the reduction of Forts Ticonderoga, Duquesne, and Niagara, Amherst paved the way for the conquest of all Canada. In 1760 he was named governor-general of British North America. In 1773 Amherst was made commander-in-chief of the British forces and in 1776 he was raised to the peerage.

Ampère, André Marie (1775-1836), a celebrated French mathematician who devoted himself successfully to the study of electricity and magnetism, and was the first to propound the electro-dynamic theory.

Amundsen, Captain Roald (1872-1928), Norwegian explorer, in 1897 was a member of the Gerlache expedition. In 1906 he navigated the Northwest Passage. In 1911 he set out on a voyage to the Antarctic, and early in 1912 he succeeded in reaching the South Pole. In 1926 he endeavored to reach the North Pole in an airplane and was given up for lost, but returned after four weeks; later in the same year he flew over the North Pole. He lost his life in the Arctic in 1928, while attempting to assist in the rescue of the Nobile expedition.

Anacreon (c. 560-475 B. C.), the celebrated Greek poet whose odes hold a high place in poetic literature.

Anaxagoras (500-428 B. C.), Greek philosopher of the Ionic school, among whose pupils were Socrates, Pericles, and Euripides.

Anaximander (611-547 B. C.), a Greek philosopher. He is said to have been the first to note the obliquity of the ecliptic; he invented geographical maps, and laid down the theory that the moon shines with light from the sun.

Anaximenes, a Greek philosopher of the Ionian school, flourished 6th century B. C.; friend of Anaximander; regarded air as the chief element in nature.

Andersen, Hans Christian (1805-1875), a Danish author, and one of the most gifted writers of fairy tales that the world has known; his *Story of My Life* is as interesting as his fairy tales.

Anderson, Maxwell (b. 1888), American playwright, educated at the University of North Dakota and at Stanford. After some years as a journalist he collaborated with Lawrence

Stallings on the play *What Price Glory*, which established both of them in the forefront of American playwrights. His own plays include *Saturday's Children*, *Mary of Scotland*, *Winterset*, and *Knickerbocker Holiday*.

Anderson, Richard Henry (1821-1879), a Confederate army officer; born in South Carolina. He served in the Mexican War, and in May, 1861, after the outbreak of the Civil War, resigned from the United States service to become a brigadier general in the Confederate army. He served with distinction throughout the war, rising to the rank of lieutenant general. In 1864 he succeeded Longstreet as commander of the first corps of Lee's army, and served in this capacity until the end of the war.

Anderson, Robert (1805-1871), an American army officer; born in 1805 near Louisville, Ky. He served under General Scott in the Mexican War, and was commissioned major and in 1860 was appointed to command the forts in Charleston harbor. On April 14, 1861, the Confederate forces began the Civil War by shelling Fort Sumter. After a 36-hour bombardment had virtually destroyed the fort, Anderson was compelled to surrender. Later in the year he was promoted brigadier general and assigned to command the Department of Kentucky. Failing health caused him to be relieved from active duty, and in 1863 he was retired from the service and brevetted major general.

Anderson, Sherwood (1876-1941), novelist, born at Camden, Ohio; served in the Spanish-American War, later entering business. Becoming interested in social and labor problems, he resigned his position, went to Chicago and there produced his first novel, *Windy McPherson's Son* (1916). With *Winesburg, Ohio* (1919) came national recognition. Settling in Marion, Virginia, as editor of two newspapers, one Democratic and the other Republican, he continued to write. Among his outstanding novels are *Poor White*, *Dark Laughter*, *Tar*, *Hello Towns*, *Beyond Desire*, and two autobiographical works, *A Story Teller's Story* and *Sherwood Anderson's Notebook*.

Andrea del Sarto (1487-1531), Italian painter, son of a Florentine tailor, one of the great Italian artists of his time, known as the "faultless painter." Most of the famous galleries of the world contain examples of his magnificent fresco and other painting, dealing mainly with religious subjects.

Andrée, Salomon August (1854-1897), a Swedish explorer who attempted in 1897 to reach the North Pole by balloon. Except for a message despatched two days after his ascent, he was not heard of again. In August 1930, a Norwegian scientific expedition led by Dr. Gunnar Horn discovered the remains of the Andrée expedition on White Island. The discovery included a log book, sketch maps, and the diaries kept by Andrée. A translation of these was published in English in 1931.

Andreyev, Leonid Nikolayevich (1871-1919), Russian author and playwright; born at Orel. Andreyev studied law at both the St. Petersburg (now Leningrad) and Moscow universities, but his heavy drinking, extreme morbidity, and constant financial difficulties almost ruined his academic career. With the help of Maxim Gorky and Leo Tolstoy, Andreyev became a regular contributor to the leading Russian magazines. His plays were regularly produced in Moscow during the first ten years after the turn of the century. The best of them, *He Who Gets Slapped*, is well known in its English translation. Other works of Andreyev available in English include: *The Seven That Were Hanged*, *The Waltz of the Dogs*, *The Dear Departing*, and *The Sabine Women*. Soon after the outbreak of the Bolshevik Revolution Andreyev fled to Finland, where he died at Kuokkala.

Angelico, Fra (1387-1455), an Italian painter of religious subjects, mostly in the form of frescoes, of which the best examples are at Florence.

Angell, Sir Norman (b. 1874), a British journalist and economist. His works include *The Economic Chaos* and *The Peace Treaty* (1919), *The Great Illusion* (1910) and *The Money Game* (1928). He was awarded the Nobel Prize for peace for 1933.

Anglesey, 1st Marquess of (1768-1854), a celebrated British field marshal who led the cavalry at Waterloo; was twice lord lieutenant of Ireland.

Angstrom, Anders Jonas (1814-1874), Swedish physicist, whose life was devoted to the study of heat, magnetism, and spectroscopy; in all three he contributed greatly to scientific knowledge. The unit used for measuring the wave length of light was named the Angstrom unit in his honor.

Anne (1665-1714), queen of Great Britain and Ireland from 1702 to the time of her death, was a daughter of James II, and succeeded William III, her cousin. During her reign England, in alliance with Austria, Holland, Prussia, Savoy, and Portugal, entered upon the War of the Spanish Succession. She was the last of the Stuarts to occupy the British throne, and the first monarch to be styled Sovereign of Great Britain, the union between England and Scotland dating from 1707. Anne was married to Prince George of Denmark, and their progeny all died in childhood.

Anselm, St. (1033-1109), archbishop of Canterbury, was a native of Aosta, and succeeded Lanfranc as English primate. He was in serious conflict with William Rufus on the question of ecclesiastical rights, and for a time suffered exile. He died at Canterbury, and was canonized in 1494, his day being celebrated in the Roman Church on April 21st.

Anson, George, Baron (1697-1762), a British navigator, whose *Voyage Round the World* is still a popular book of adventure. He won many victories, obtained a peerage, rose to full admiral's rank in the navy, and served two terms as first lord of the admiralty.

Antoninus Pius (86-161), emperor of Rome from A. D. 138 to 161, successor of Hadrian, endeavored to govern more with an eye to the public well-being than his own personal pleasure. It was during his reign that the wall between the Firth of Forth and the Clyde in Scotland was built.

Antony, St. (or Anthony) (c. 251-356), was a native of Upper Egypt, and according to his own account spent much time in conflict with the devil. He is one of the best-known saints of the Roman calendar, and his festival is on January 17th. He was believed to give relief to those who appealed to him when suffering from erysipelas, from which tradition the name St. Anthony's fire is given to the disease.

Apelles, a Greek painter, flourished in the time of Alexander the Great, whose friendship he enjoyed. His "Aphrodite Anadyomene," painted for the temple of Aesculapius in Cos, has been regarded as the most perfect picture of antiquity.

Apponyi, Count Albert (1846-1933), Hungarian patriot and politician, known as the "Grand Old Man of Hungary."

Aquinas, St. Thomas (1225-1274), the "Father of Moral Philosophy," was a native of southern Italy and came of a noble family. In 1243 he joined the Dominicans, and the remainder of his life was spent in religious pilgrimages and disputations. In 1263 he visited London. He left behind him numerous theological and philosophical writings, the most important being the *Summa Theologica*. He was canonized in 1323.

Arabi (Ahmed) Pasha (1841-1911), was the leader of the Egyptian rebellion of 1881, and defended Alexandria against a British fleet. Later he suffered defeat and was captured at Tel-el-Kebir, was banished to Ceylon, but released in 1901.

Arago, Dominique François Jean (1786-1853), a French astronomer and natural philosopher of great eminence, whose researches added much to our knowledge of electricity and magnetism. His expositions of the polarization of light did much to advance that branch of science.

Archimedes (287-212 B. C.), a Greek geometrician and philosopher of remarkable power, to whom we are indebted for the discovery of the principles of the lever and of specific gravity, and for the invention of the famous Archimedean screw.

Argand, Aimé (1755-1803), Swiss physician, inventor of the lamp bearing his name, which for the first time introduced a current of air to permeate and increase the power of the flame, by using a chimney glass and circular wick.

Ariosto, Ludovico (1474-1533), the author of *Orlando Furioso,* was one of the most celebrated of the Italian poets. In addition to his famous epic he wrote many comedies, satires and poems.

Aristeides (or Aristides), a Greek writer, and founder of the school of prose romance; flourished in the 2nd century B. C. His *Milesian Tales* are among the most celebrated works of fiction.

Aristides (530-467 B. C.), Athenian general, was of noble descent, and first achieved fame at the battle of Marathon, 490 B.C. He was renowned no less for his valor than for his scrupulous honesty and a desire to do justice to others; hence he was surnamed "the Just."

Aristippus (c. 435-356 B. C.), founded the Cyrenaic school of philosophy, which taught that sensual pleasure was the only happiness. He was a native of Cyrene, in Africa, but became a pupil of Socrates, and settled in Athens.

Aristophanes (c. 444-385 B. C.), was one of the foremost Athenian play-writers and the greatest of the Greek comic poets. He is said to have composed fifty-four plays in all. Eleven of these only have survived. They are sharply satirical, and deal unsparingly with the people and institutions of his time.

Aristotle (384-322 B. C.), the most famous of the Greek philosophers. He was a disciple of Plato, after whose death he retired from Athens. Later he undertook the education of Alexander the Great. Subsequently at Athens he established the Lyceum and founded the Peripatetic school of philosophy, which had great influence upon the development of scientific thought. Among his most important works are his treatises on ***Logic, Ethics, Rhetoric, Poetics, Politics, Physics***, and *Metaphysics*. In the latter part of the 19th century his long-lost work the *Constitution of Athens* was discovered.

Arkwright, Sir Richard (1732-1792), an English inventor. Becoming interested in mechanical problems, he set himself the task of inventing an improved cotton-spinning machine. Arkwright experimented until, by adopting an arrangement of rollers that moved with different velocities, he succeeded in perfecting his "spinning-frame." He took out his first patent in 1769, and became a manufacturer on a large scale, in 1771 establishing the first spinning-mill worked by water-power. He was knighted in 1786.

Arliss, George (b. 1868), famous stage and film actor, who was starred in *Disraeli, Voltaire, The House of Rothschild* and other popular films.

Armstrong, William George, Baron (1810-1900), a British inventor. He devoted himself to the invention of the hydraulic crane and other machinery for the better utilization of water-power. During the Crimean War he studied the subject of guns, and produced the famous Armstrong gun, the most effective that had up to that time been constructed. He introduced many improvements in gun construction, and became a manufacturer of guns and ships of war. He was raised to the peerage in 1887.

Arne, Thomas Augustine (1710-1778), an English composer of great popularity in his day. He composed numerous ballad operas, and at Drury Lane, Covent Garden, and Vauxhall organized the chief performances for long periods. His best-known opera was *Artaxerxes*, and his most popular songs were "Rule, Britannia!" and "Where the Bee Sucks."

Arnold, Benedict (1741-1801), Revolutionary soldier, born in Norwich, Conn. He made a distinguished record in the early years of the war, participating in Montgomery's expedition to Canada, halting a British invasion by way of Lake Champlain, and exhibiting reckless courage that contributed to the American victory at Saratoga. Anger at Congress' slowness in promoting him, at being court-martialed for mishandling the affairs of Philadelphia when he was the city's commander, and indignation at the alliance with France led him to begin a treasonable correspondence with the British commander. Throughout 1779-1780 he sent important military information to the enemy. He was attempting to betray West Point when his treason was finally discovered. He escaped and served with the British army for the remainder of the war. After the war he lived in England and Canada.

Arnold, Sir Edwin (1832-1904), an English writer, educated at University College, Oxford, where he gained the Newdigate Prize in 1852; was at the Government Sanscrit College, Poona, India, for some years, and returning to England in 1861 became connected with the *Daily Telegraph's* editorial staff. He was the author of the *Light of Asia* and numerous other poems; and wrote several popular books of travel.

Arnold, Matthew (1822-1888), an English poet, literary critic, and educator. As the propounder of the principles of "sweetness and light," as well as by his graceful verse, he secured a high place amongst the literary men of the Victorian era. "Dover Beach," the elegy "Thyrsis," and "Sohrab and Rustum," an epic narrative, are among his most distinguished works.

Arrhenius, Svante August (1859-1927), Swedish chemist who became director of the physico-chemical department of the Nobel Institute in 1905. He did valuable work in the theory of ionization.

Artaxerxes, was the name borne by several ancient Persian kings, some of whom achieved great distinction. The first Artaxerxes was the son of Xerxes, and reigned from 465 B. C. for 40 years; he was succeeded by Darius II (424-405 B. C.), who in turn was followed by Artaxerxes II, who reigned 45 years. The last to bear the name of Artaxerxes was the founder of the Sassanid dynasty, A. D. 223.

Arthur, a famous British chieftain and supposed king, who is stated to have flourished in the 6th century, and around whose life many legends have been written, including Sir Thomas Malory's *Morte d'Arthur.*

Arthur, Chester Alan (1830-1886), 21st President of the United States, born in Fairfield, Vt., was the son of Scottish parents, his father being pastor of Baptist churches in Vermont and New York. He chose law as a profession and practiced in New York. As a politician he became a leader in the Republican Party. During the Civil War he was energetic as quartermaster general of New York in getting troops raised and equipped. He was afterward collector of customs for the port of New York In 1880 he was elected Vice President, succeeding as President on the death of James A. Garfield in 1881. He died in New York City, Nov. 18, 1886.

Arundel, Thomas, Archbishop of Canterbury (1353-1414), in the reigns of Richard II and Henry II; previously bishop of Ely and archbishop of York, and for a time lord chancellor. An active politician and bitter enemy of heresy.

Asbury, Francis (1745-1816), the first Methodist bishop consecrated in America, born at Handsworth, Staffordshire, England. When 16 years old he became an itinerant Wesleyan preacher, and in 1771 he was sent as a missionary to America, where he was consecrated in 1784. He ranks with Wesley, Whitefield, and Coke in the Methodist movement of his time. He died in Richmond, Va.

Aspasia, flourished about 440 B. C., the Athenian hetaera and mistress of Pericles; noted for her learning and beauty.

Asser, John, a Welsh monk of the 10th century, noted for having been tutor, friend and biographer of King Alfred. He was made bishop of Sherborne and died in 910.

Astor, John Jacob (1763-1848), American merchant. He was born in Germany, and emigrating to America, went out to the Northwest and began trading in furs; later invested a fortune in New York real estate, which rapidly increased in value.

Astor, Nancy Witcher, Viscountess (b. 1879), a British politician, born of American parents in Virginia. In 1906 she married W. W. Astor of England. She was the first woman ever to be elected to the House of Commons, and served for 26 years, from 1919 to 1945.

Ataturk, Kemal (1881-1938), president of Turkish Republic 1923-38. Was the Turkish Nationalist leader who drove the Greek army out of Asia Minor, Sept. 1922, and assumed virtual dictatorship.

Athanasius, St. (296-373), was bishop of Alexandria. He spent much of his time in bitter theological controversy, and was driven from Alexandria; taking refuge in the desert, he wrote numerous letters interpreting Christian doctrine, and under Julian was recalled to Alexandria. The Athanasian creed is supposed to reflect his beliefs.

Athelstan (895-940), grandson of Alfred the Great, was crowned king of England in 925, and was the first ruler of all England.

Attila (406-453), king of the Huns, was a warlike leader who achieved many conquests over the Romans, ravaging large areas. He marched through Germany and Gaul, and died while preparing a second invasion of Italy.

Attlee, Clement Richard (b. 1883), a British political figure, member of the second Labour Ministry (1929-31), and leader of the Labour party since 1935. Lord Privy Seal in Winston Churchill's World War II coalition cabinet, in 1945 he became the second member of his party to hold the office of Prime Minister. When the Labour party was defeated in 1951, Attlee became Opposition leader.

Auber, Daniel François Esprit (1782-1871), was a distinguished French composer of light operas, including *Masaniello, Fra Diavolo,* and *Le Domino noir.*

Audubon, John James (1780-1851), an American naturalist of French extraction, born near New Orleans; was educated in France and studied painting under David. In 1798 he settled in Pennsylvania, but, having a great love for ornithology, he set out in 1810 with his wife and child, descended the Ohio, and for many years roamed the forests drawing and painting the birds which he shot. In 1826 he went to England, exhibited his drawings in Liverpool, Manchester and Edinburgh, and finally published them in an unrivaled work of double-folio size, with 435 colored plates of birds the size of life, *(The Birds of America,* 4 vols., 1827-1839), with an accompanying text *(Ornithological Biography,* 5 vols., partly written by William MacGillivray). On his final return to the United States he labored with Dr. Bachman on an illustrated work entitled *The Quadrupeds of America* (1843-1850, 3 vols.). He died in New York City.

Auer, Leopold (1845-1930), famous Hungarian violinist and teacher of the violin, among his pupils being Mischa Elman and Jascha Heifetz. He was professor of the violin at the St. Petersburg Conservatory for nearly fifty years (1868-1917).

Augustine, St., of Hippo (354-430), was born at Tagaste in Africa of a pagan father and a Christian mother; went to Rome, and under the influence of St. Ambrose became deeply religious, writing much upon doctrinal subjects.

Augustine, St. (d.604?), missionary monk who was sent to Britain by Gregory the Great in 597. He succeeded in converting King Ethelbert, after which he won many converts among the people; became the first archbishop of Canterbury.

Augustus, Caius Octavianus (63 B. C.-A. D. 14), was the first emperor of Rome; succeeded Julius Caesar. After a triumvirate of twelve years, in which he was associated with Mark Antony and Lepidus, he became ruler, and for forty-five years exercised a beneficent and powerful sway.

Aurelius, Marcus Antoninus (121-180), emperor of Rome, a man of great intellectual power and a disciple of the Stoics.

Austen, Jane (1775-1817), one of the foremost English novelists, noted for her realism, humor, and skillful delineation of character. Author of *Pride and Prejudice.*

Austin, Stephen Fuller (1793-1836), an American pioneer, born in Austinville, Va.; a son of Moses Austin. The father, who was the real founder of the state of Texas, about 1820 obtained permission from the Mexican government to establish an American colony in Texas, but died before his plans were accomplished. Stephen took up the work, and located a thriving colony on the site of the present city of Austin in 1821. In 1835 he was a commissioner to the United States Government to secure the recognition of Texas as an independent state.

Autolycus, a Greek astronomer of the 4th century B. C., who wrote treatises on the fixed stars and the revolving sphere.

Averescu, Marshal Alexandre (1859-1938), Rumanian statesman and soldier, chief of the general staff in the war against Bulgaria; army commander in the World War, and three times premier of Rumania.

Averroes (Ibn Rosha) (c. 1130-98), an Arabian philosopher of Spain. He studied philosophy, theology, and jurisprudence, succeeded his father as a judge, and wrote his famous comments on Aristotle. His theory of "The Universal Soul" played a large part in medieval philosophy.

B

Babbage, Charles (1792-1871), a British mathematician; professor of mathematics at the University of Cambridge. He attracted much attention by inventing a calculating machine which partially realized its designer's aim.

Baber or Babar (Zahir ud-din-Mahomet) (1483-1530), a descendant of Tamerlane, and the founder of the Mogul dynasty which ruled northern India for three centuries.

Bach, Johann Sebastian (1685-1750), German composer, probably the greatest master of counterpoint and the art of polyphonic composition of all time. His major works include the *Mass in B Minor, St. Matthew Passion, The Art of the Fugue,* and *A Musical Offering.* He also wrote hundreds of chorale preludes, and preludes and fugues for both organ and clavichord.

Bacon, Francis, Lord Verulam, and Viscount St. Albans (1561-1626), one of the greatest of English philosophers and statesmen. He was attorney-general to Elizabeth, and under James I became lord chancellor. His political career was tarnished by certain acts of corruption, for which he was fined and forced to leave office. His writings were marked by keen insight, brilliancy of language, and a depth of thought which place them in the first rank of philosophical literature. His *Novum Organum* and his *Essays* are splendid monuments of learning and wisdom.

Bacon, Roger (1214-1294), an English philosopher and scientist, generally alluded to as "Friar" Bacon. The invention of gunpowder has been ascribed to him, and he is also said to have invented the air-pump, and was acquainted with the principle of the telescope. For a long time he was looked upon as an alchemist and sorcerer, and only in modern times have his discoveries been rightly appreciated.

Baden-Powell, Robert Stephenson Smyth, 1st Baron (1857-1941), soldier and founder of the Boy Scout movement; defender of Mafeking during the Boer War. After the war he organized the South African Constabulary. He founded the Boy Scouts in 1908; Chief Scout of the world since 1920.

Baer, Karl Ernst von (1792-1876), Russian zoologist, born in Estonia; studied in Germany. He was the founder of the science of comparative embryology, and was the discoverer of the human ovum.

Baez, Buenaventura (1810?-1884), a Dominican statesman, born in Haiti; aided in the establishment of the Dominican Republic; was its president, 1849-1853; was then expelled by Santana, and went to New York City; was recalled in 1856, on the expulsion of Santana, and again elected president; served additional terms in 1865 and 1868.

Baffin, William (1584-1622), British navigator and explorer who, in 1616, discovered the bay which separates the northeast coast of Canada from Greenland, and bears his name.

Bagehot, Walter (1826-77), English economist and journalist; editor of the *Economist,* 1860-77. He wrote three books of lasting importance, *The English Constitution,* 1867; *Physics and Politics,* 1872; and *Lombard Street,* a description of the money market, 1873.

Baker, Sir Benjamin (1840-1907), British civil engineer. He was consulting engineer to the Egyptian Government for the Assuan Dam, joint engineer with Sir John Fowler of the Forth Bridge, and engineer of the Central London Tube Railway.

Baker, Newton Diehl (1871-1937), American political leader, born in Martinsburg, W. Va. After a varied public career, he entered President Wilson's cabinet in March, 1916, as Secretary of War. In 1928 President Coolidge appointed him to the Court of International Justice at The Hague.

Baker, Ray Stannard (1870-1946), American author; educated at the University of Michigan; entered newspaper work, later turning to magazine writing, notably contributing to *McClure's Magazine* and to the *American Magazine,* of which he became editor. Under the pen name "David Grayson" he published many books of rural sketches and essays. A close friend of Woodrow Wilson, he was sent by the latter to Europe (1918) as a peace agent, and at the Versailles Peace Conference was director of the press bureau of the American Commission to Negotiate Peace. A prolific writer, he is recognized as a leading authority on Woodrow Wilson and in 1940 was awarded the Pulitzer prize for his biography *Woodrow Wilson: Life and Letters.*

Baker, Sir Samuel White (1821-1893) a British traveler and author. After a period in Ceylon he set out to explore Central Africa, and discovered Lake Albert Nyanza. The khedive of Egypt made him governor-general of the new territory for four years.

Balboa, Vasco Núñez de (1475-1517), Spanish explorer who was the first European to set eyes upon the Pacific Ocean.

Baldwin, Lord Stanley, 1st Earl Baldwin of Bewdley (1867-1947), a British Conservative statesman; Prime Minister and First Lord of the Treasury, 1923-24, 1935-37. Prime minister at the time King Edward abdicated, he was created Earl Baldwin in 1937.

Balfour, Arthur James Balfour, 1st Earl of (1848-1930). a British statesman; entered Parliament in 1874. He became president of the Local Government Board in 1885. In 1891 he became first lord of the Treasury. He was prime minister, 1902-1905. He took an active part in the peace conference after the World War. Among his published works are the *Defense of Philosophic Doubt* and *Foundations of Belief.*

Baliol, John de, an English nobleman, whose widow in 1269 founded the college at Oxford which bears his name. He died in exile in 1269.

Baliol, John de (1249-1315), king of Scotland, competed with Robert Bruce for the Scottish throne; Edward I decided in his favor. Only reigned four years, when Edward deposed him, committing him to the Tower, and finally banished him from the country. His son, Edward de Baliol, recovered his father's kingdom in 1332, and was upheld by Edward III.

Ball, Sir Robert Stawell (1840-1913), an English astronomer and mathematician; wrote many books on astronomical subjects and was a popular lecturer.

Baltimore, George Calvert, Lord (1580-1632), an English colonist, born in Yorkshire; was for some time secretary of state to James I, but this post he resigned in 1625 in consequence of having become a Roman Catholic. He retained the confidence of the king, who, in the same year, raised him to the Irish peerage. In 1632 he obtained a grant for territory in the New World, located north of the Potomac River, later known as Maryland. He died before the charter was completed, and it was granted to his son Cecilius, who governed the colony by deputies. The last deputy was his son Charles, who governed the colony from 1661 to 1689, when his power was broken by a Protestant revolt.

Balzac, Honoré de (1799-1850), one of the greatest of French novelists, and the author of over eighty novels to which he gave the covering title of "La Comédie humaine."

Bancroft, George (1800-1891), an American historian, born near Worcester, Mass. He was educated at Harvard and in Germany. In 1845 he was appointed Secretary of the Navy, and effected many reforms and improvements in that department. He was American Minister to England (1846-1849). He wrote ten volumes on the history of the formation of the Constitution of the United States (1882-1885).

Banks, Sir Joseph (1743-1820), an English naturalist, president of the Royal Society for upwards of forty years.

Banting, Sir Frederick Grant (1891-1941), physician, discoverer of insulin. Prof. of Medical Research, Toronto University, after 1923.

Barbusse, Henri (1874-1935), noted French author and writer of the famous war novel *Under Fire*, which is one of the most remarkable and realistic of all war books, and portrays in a starkly vivid way the experience of the common soldier.

Barham, Richard Harris (1788-1845), an English clergyman who gained a deserved reputation as a humorist by his *Ingoldsby Legends.*

Baring-Gould, Sabine (1834-1924), an English clergyman and folklorist, the author of numerous novels, including *John Herring, Court Royal*, and *Mehalah.*

Barkley, Alben William (1877-1956), U. S. political leader, born in Kentucky. Graduating from the University of Virginia Law School, he practiced law briefly before serving in the House of Representatives (1913-26) and the Senate (1927-48). He was Vice-President from 1948 to 1953, U. S. senator from 1955 to 1956.

Barnum, Phineas Taylor (1810-1891), was America's most famous showman, and originator of Barnum and Bailey's "Greatest Show on Earth."

Barr, Archibald (1855-1931), Scottish engineer and inventor; his numerous inventions include range-finders and the optophone for enabling the blind to read books by sound.

Barrie, Sir James Matthew (1860-1937), an English writer; after passing through Edinburgh University, entered journalism, and later published a series of essays and sketches which at once made him popular. He followed these up with some very clever novels, including *A Window in Thrums, The Little Minister, Sentimental Tommy*, etc., and in more recent years achieved considerable success as a dramatist, *Peter Pan* being among his most popular plays. Chancellor of Edinburgh University, 1930-1937.

Barrymore, John (1882-1942), **Lionel** (1878-1954), and **Ethel** (b. 1879), famous family of actors, won acclaim in all media of entertainment. High critical approval was given John for his interpretations of Shakesperian roles, particularly *Hamlet*. Lionel, perhaps better known for the many character roles he created so well in motion pictures, also starred on the stage and radio. Ethel made her Broadway debut at the age of 17 and, in 1933, made her first sound film, *Rasputin and the Empress*, which also featured her two brothers.

Bartolommeo, Fra (1469-1517), the distinguished Florentine painter and friend of Savonarola.

Batten, Jean Gardner (b. 1909), a famous New Zealand airwoman, and one of the world's greatest fliers; made aviation history by her record solo flight from England to Australia in 1936, and as being the first to fly from England to New Zealand, Oct. 1936; also held the record for a solo flight from Australia to England, Oct. 1937.

Baudelaire, Charles (1821-1867), a French poet, born in Paris. In his youth he traveled to India, and on his return to Paris he became a notable figure in the second group of romantic poets who carried on the movement begun by the Romanticists of 1830. Baudelaire translated into French many of the works of Edgar Allan Poe. His masterpiece is a volume of verse, *Flowers of Evil.*

Baum, Vicki (b. 1896), German novelist and scenario writer; author of *Grand Hotel.*

Bayard, Pierre du Terrail, Chevalier de (1475-1524), a French knight of exemplary conduct and remarkable for his chivalry.

Beaconsfield, Benjamin Disraeli, Earl of (1804-1881), a statesman and novelist. He was the son of Isaac D'Israeli; and after being privately educated, passed some time in a lawyer's office, and then took to authorship, meeting with but indifferent success until he published his *Vivian Grey*. Drifting into society he was made much of because of his brilliance, and after a few more essays in novel writing he entered Parliament in 1832 and not long afterwards became a prominent and picturesque figure in that assembly. He allied himself with the Tory party, and ultimately became one of its chief leaders. He was made premier in 1868 on the retirement of Lord Derby, and again in 1874, retaining office until 1880, dying the following year. He was raised to the peerage in 1876 for his services to the Empire.

Beard, Charles (1874-1948), American historian and political scientist, born in Knightstown, Ind. He was adviser to the Institute of Municipal Research, Tokyo, in 1922; president of the American Political Science Association in 1926; and president of the American Historical Association in 1933. His books include: *Introduction to English Historians* (1906); *Economic Interpretation of the Constitution* (1912); *Economic Origins of Jeffersonian Democracy* (1915); *Rise of American Civilization* (1927, 1936); *America in Mid-Passage* (1938).

Beard, Daniel Carter (1850-1941), author, naturalist and illustrator, born in Covington, Ky. His illustrations appeared in many magazines, including *Harper's*, *Scribner's* and *Century;* and at the request of Mark Twain he illustrated *A Yankee in King Arthur's Court.* In his enthusiasm for outdoor life, he founded the Boy Pioneers and Sons of Daniel Boone; afterwards he merged them with groups organized by Ernest Thompson Seton to form the Boy Scouts of America. His publications include: *American Boy's Book of Wild Animals;* and *Wisdom of the Woods.*

Beatty, David, 1st Earl (1871-1936), British admiral; from 1916-1919 admiral of the main British fleet. On Aug. 28, 1914, fought the German fleet in the Heligoland Bight; on May 31, 1916, Lord Beatty with his battle cruisers engaged in a great sea fight with the Germans off Jutland.

Beaumont, Francis (1584-1616), **and Fletcher, John** (1579-1625), English playwrights, joint authors of many plays, including *The Maides Tragedy* and *Philaster.* Fletcher is thought by some to be the author of some plays attributed to Shakespeare.

Beauregard, Pierre Gustave Toutant (1818-1893), an American military officer, born at St. Martin's Parish, La., was graduated at the United States Military Academy. He distinguished himself in the Mexican War (1846-1848). After the secession of Louisiana in 1861 he was appointed commander of the Confederate forces at Charleston, S. C., and there opened the hostilities of the Civil War by bombarding Fort Sumter, April 11. He commanded the Confederate forces in the Battle of Bull Run, July 21; was second in command at the battle of Shiloh, and in June, 1863, took charge of the defense of Charleston. He published *The Principles and Maxims of the Art of War* (1863), and was the last survivor of the full generals of the Confederacy. He died in New Orleans.

Beaverbrook, William Maxwell Aitken, Lord (b. 1879), an English newspaper proprietor, whose interests have embraced the London *Express, Evening Standard,* and important provincial papers. His vigorous and sometimes sensational methods changed the traditionally conservative character of British journalism. He held administrative posts during the First World War, and in the Second World War was Minister of War Production, retiring in 1942.

Becket, Thomas à (1118-1170), an English churchman; archbishop of Canterbury under Henry II. He was a powerful and ambitious prelate, who boldly supported the authority of the pope against the dictates of the king; was assassinated in Canterbury Cathedral December 29th, 1170, and was canonized two years later.

Bede, "The Venerable" (673-735), an English monk of great influence and ability. His historical works cover a great range, and are valuable in the study of medieval history.

Beecham, Sir Thomas (b. 1879), an English conductor, composer, and operatic impresario, founded the London Philharmonic Orchestra.

Beecher, Henry Ward (1813-1887), an eminent American preacher and lecturer, whose church at Brooklyn was for many years one of the most popular in the United States. Brother of Harriet Beecher Stowe, the author of *Uncle Tom's Cabin.*

Beecher, Lyman (1775-1863), an American clergyman, born in New Haven, Conn. Graduating from Yale in 1796 he entered the ministry, and in 1832 he became president of Lane Theological Seminary, near Cincinnati, Ohio. His influence throughout the country was very great, especially on the questions of temperance and of slavery. His sermon on the death of Alexander Hamilton, in 1804, and his *Remedy for Dueling* (1809), did much toward discouraging the practice of dueling in the United States. He died in Brooklyn, N. Y.

Beer, George Louis (1872-1920), American historian, born in Staten Island, N.Y., was educated at Columbia University, and after intensive study in English archives published a notable series of volumes on the British colonial system of the 18th century. He was chief consultant in the organization of mandates after the First World War.

Beerbohm, Max (1872-1956), English critic and caricaturist, educated at Charterhouse and Merton College, Oxford; has contributed largely to the *Saturday Review.*

Beethoven, Ludwig van (1770-1827), a German composer, born at Bonn, died in Vienna. His sonatas, overtures, and chamber music all reach the highest levels of musical imagination. His nine symphonies are generally considered to be his greatest compositions.

Behring, Emil von (1854-1917), a distinguished German scientist, discoverer of an anti-toxin for diphtheria, and claimant to a cure for phases of tuberculosis.

Belisarius (505-565), a famous Roman general under Justinian. His defeats of the Goths, the Vandals, and the Persians, were great achievements.

Bell, Alexander Graham (1847-1922), an English inventor, born in Edinburgh, Scotland, came to America in 1870. In 1876 he exhibited an invention which became the modern telephone. He also invented the photophone, and devoted much attention to the education of deaf-mutes.

Bell, Gertrude Margaret (1868-1926), an English writer and Orientalist; was a famous traveler in the East, especially in Arabia.

Bellini, Gentile (c. 1429-1507), a celebrated Venetian painter, whose "Preaching of St. Mark at Alexandria," in St. Mark's College, Venice, is one of the renowned pictures of the world.

Bellini, Giovanni (c. 1430-1516), a celebrated Venetian painter, brother of the last-named, famous for his many altarpieces, his "Doge Loredano," "St. Francis," etc.

Bellini, Vicenzo (1802-1835), an Italian operatic composer of great popularity during the first half of the 19th century. His *La Sonnambula, Norma* and *I Puritani* are still performed.

Belloc, Joseph Hilaire Pierre (1870-1953), British author and famous Catholic historian. He wrote biographical and historical studies of Danton, Robespierre, Richelieu, Charles II, and

Archbishop Laud. He has also written several novels and short stories, as well as essays, poems, and nonsense verse.

Benedict XV, Pope (1854-1922), born Giacomo della Chiesa. Elected pope Sept. 3, 1914, being at the time cardinal archbishop of Bologna.

Benedict, St. (480-544), Italian monk, built twelve monasteries, and founded the order of Benedictine monks, at Monte Cassino, near Naples.

Beneš, Eduard (1884-1948), Czech statesman, who was president of Czechoslovakia from Dec. 1935 to Oct. 1938, when he resigned after the signing of the Munich agreement. In 1939 he organized the provisional Czech government in exile. Returning in 1945, he founded a new government, of which he became president in 1946. He reluctantly endorsed the Communist regime of 1948 but he refused to sign the constitution and resigned a few months after the Red coup.

Benét, Stephen Vincent (1898-1943), American author, born in Bethlehem, Pa. His book-length poem, *John Brown's Body*, a dramatic narrative dealing with the Civil War, won the Pulitzer Prize for 1929. His writings, in verse, fiction, and essay, were noted for their blending of fantasy, drama, and social content. He was a passionate exponent of the American democratic tradition, expressed in his last, uncompleted, work, *Western Star* (1943); *Thirteen O'Clock* (1937); and plays for radio.

Benét, William Rose (1886-1950), American author, born in Fort Hamilton, N.Y. With Henry Seidel Canby and Christopher Morley, he founded the *Literary Review* and the *New York Evening Post*, which in 1924 developed into *The Saturday Review of Literature*. A poet who ranged from whimsy to ballads based on American history, he won the 1942 Pulitzer poetry prize for *The Dust Which Is God*, a book of autobiographical verse.

Benjamin, Judah Philip (1811-1884), an American lawyer, born at St Croix, West Indies. In 1861 he accepted the office of Attorney-General in the Cabinet of Jefferson Davis and afterward became successively Confederate Secretary of War and Secretary of State. After the war he went to London, England, where he was admitted to the bar in 1866. He gained a successful practice and in 1872 was made queen's counsel. He wrote *A Treatise on the Law of Sale of Personal Property* (1868). He died in Paris.

Bennett, Arnold (1867-1931), British author and journalist. His stories of the pottery-making towns, where he was brought up, are of high merit. *The Old Wives' Tale*, *Clayhanger*, and *Hilda Lessways* are among his most successful novels. He also wrote plays, including *Milestones*, *The Great Adventure* and *Mr. Prohack*.

Bennett, James Gordon (1795-1872), American journalist; born in Scotland. He emigrated to the United States in 1819, where he founded the *New York Herald* as an independent newspaper in 1835. He spared no effort and expense in securing news, and laid the foundation of its later enormous success. It was the first newspaper to publish stock quotations and a daily article on finance.

Bennett, James Gordon (1841-1918), American newspaper proprietor, son of the last-named and owner of the *New York Herald*. He sent out Stanley on the expedition which resulted in the finding of Livingston.

Bentham, Jeremy (1748-1832), an English philosopher, the founder of utilitarianism, the tenets of which were extended by John Stuart Mill. His *Government Usury* and *The Principles of Morals and Politics* expound the system with great lucidity.

Benton, Thomas Hart (1782-1858), an American statesman, born near Hillsboro, N. C.; settled in Tennessee, where he studied law, and was elected to the legislature. In 1812 he raised a regiment of volunteers, and also served on General Jackson's staff. On the admission of Missouri as a State, he was chosen United States Senator in 1820, and in this post, during 30 years' continuous service, took a leading part in public affairs. A determined opponent of Calhoun's nullification scheme, he afterward supported Jackson in his war on the Bank of the United States and earned the sobriquet of "Old Bullion" by his opposition to the paper currency. Although a slaveholder, Benton favored gradual emancipation and was a staunch upholder of the Union.

Benton, Thomas Hart (b. 1889), an American artist, grandson of the last-named, born in Neosho, Mo. Studied art in Chicago and Paris. The murals done for the Whitney Museum and New School for Social Research in New York City, and for the state legislatures of Indiana and Missouri are among his most famous works. In 1933 he was awarded the gold medal by the Architectural League.

Béranger, Jean Pierre de (1780-1857), was the most popular songwriter that France has produced. His songs were often written to serve some passing political purpose, and usually expressed popular sentiment.

Bergner, Elisabeth (b. 1898), Austrian actress, who appeared in a wide variety of plays, including German versions of Bernard Shaw's *St. Joan* and Margaret Kennedy's *The Constant Nymph*. She has also starred in the motion pictures *Catherine the Great*, *As You Like It*, *Escape Me Never*, and *Stolen Life*.

Bergson, Henri Louis (1859-1941), a French philosopher, exponent of the theory of vitalism; professor of philosophy at the Collège de France, 1900-21; author of *Matter and Memory*, *Creative Evolution*, etc.

Bering, Vitus (1681-1741), a Danish explorer who entered the Russian navy, and in 1728 discovered the strait now named after him. He was afterward wrecked on Bering Island, where he died.

Berkeley, Sir William (1608-77), English colonial governor. He was graduated from Oxford and in 1632 made a commissioner of Canada. In 1641 he was appointed governor of Virginia, which under his leadership remained loyal to the king during the English Civil War and during the first years of the Commonwealth. His failure to repress Indian incursions led in 1676 to Bacon's Rebellion, a revolt against the governor's arbitrary authority.

Berlin, Irving (b. 1888), American composer of popular songs, and a pioneer of both ragtime and jazz music; his "Alexander's Ragtime Band," "Always," and "What'll I do?" were among the first popular jazz songs.

Berlioz, Hector (1803-1869), was an eccentric but highly endowed French musical composer who studied in Paris and Rome, and afterwards settling in Paris, devoted himself to conducting and composing. His originality and his ardent romanticism fascinated such men as Paganini and Liszt, and he ranks as one of the musical geniuses of the 19th century. His *Damnation of Faust*, *Romeo and Juliet* symphony, and *Fantastic* symphony are his most inspired productions.

Bernadotte, Jean Baptiste (1764-1844), a French soldier of great distinction who served under Napoleon, and in 1810 was chosen heir to the throne of Sweden. In 1818 he succeeded as Charles XIV.

Bernard, St. (1091-1153), a French churchman, who took an active part in promoting the crusade of 1146, and founded the monastic order of the Bernardines.

Bernhardt, Sarah (1845-1923), a French actress, the most renowned tragedienne of her time; became a member of the Comédie Francaise after the Siege of Paris, and thereafter occupied a specially prominent position. Among her most conspicuous successes were Théodora, Fédora, and La Tosca; and she also appeared with distinction as Hamlet.

Bertillon, Alphonse (1853-1914), an ingenious Parisian police prefect, who invented the anthropometric method for the identification of criminals, particularly finger-printing.

Besant, Sir Walter (1836-1901), a prolific English author and novelist. His best-known works are *All Sorts and Conditions of Men* and *Dorothy Firster;* he also wrote a number of books on ancient London.

Bessemer, Sir Henry (1813-1898), an English inventor, discoverer of the Bessemer process for converting cast-iron direct into steel. The American William Kelly, working independently, also discovered the process.

Bethmann-Hollweg, Theobald von (1856-1921), chancellor of the German Empire, 1909 to July, 1917. It was he who called the treaty guaranteeing Belgium's neutrality a "scrap of paper." His efforts toward conciliation and attempts to restrict submarine warfare led to his overthrow by Ludendorff and Hindenburg.

Beveridge, Albert Jeremiah (1862-1927), an American politician and writer, born in Highland County, Ohio; was brought up on a farm; graduated at De Pauw University; and engaged in law practice in Indianapolis. In 1899 he was elected United States Senator from Indiana, and served in the United States Senate until 1911. He devoted the remainder of his life to writing biography, his most important works being *Life of John Marshall* in four volumes (1916-1919), and *Life of Abraham Lincoln* in two volumes (1928).

Bichat, Marie Francois Xavier (1771-1802), French physiologist who founded the study of general anatomy, on which he wrote several important works, showing the important connection between the brain, heart, and lungs.

Biddle, Nicholas (1786-1844), an American financier, born in Philadelphia; went to England as secretary to James Monroe, then as United States Minister. He was elected to the House of Representatives in 1810, appointed a director of the United States Bank in 1819, and in 1822 became president of the bank, managing it ably down to the expiration of its charter. Besides miscellaneous writings, he published a *Commercial Digest*, and *History of the Expedition of Captains Lewis and Clark.*

Bierce, Ambrose Gwinett (1842-1913?), an American author, born in Ohio. He served in the Union Army during the Civil War, then established himself as a newspaper man, first in San Francisco, and later in Washington, D. C. Bierce is important for his satirical and fantastic short stories. Among his works are *Nuggets and Dust, Cobwebs from an Empty Skull, Tales of Soldiers and Civilians,* and *The Monk and the Hangman's Daughter.* He disappeared in Mexico in 1913.

Binet, Alfred (1857-1911), a French psychologist educated at the Sorbonne, in 1894 becoming director of the psychological laboratory there. He is known for his research and innovation in testing and measuring human intelligence. The Binet-Simon tests were introduced into the United States by Goddard. Binet wrote *Les Alterations de la personalite* (1892), *L'Ame et le corps* (1905), *Etude experimentale de l'intelligence,* and, with Simon, *Mentally Defective Children.*

Birney, James Gillespie (1792-1857), an American statesman, born at Danville, Ky. Though a Southern planter, he emancipated his slaves and became a prominent anti-slavery leader, and proprietor of the journal, *The Philanthropist.* He constantly advocated political action to abolish slavery.

Bishop, Sir Henry Rowley (1786-1855), an English composer of many popular ballads, operas and songs. *Maid Marian, Guy Mannering* and *The Miller and His Men,* are his best-known operas. He was also a very successful glee-writer, and was the composer of "Home, Sweet Home."

Bismarck, Prince Otto Eduard Leopold von (1815-1898), the most prominent and capable of the German statesmen of the 19th century; entered the diplomatic service in 1851, and filled positions in succession at Vienna, Petrograd, and Paris. In 1862 he was appointed minister of foreign affairs, from which time dates the strong Bismarckian policy which resulted in the defeat of Denmark, Austria, and France, and the unification of Germany with her establishment as the dominant power of Central Europe. As imperial chancellor he directed the destinies of his country down to the death of the Emperor William in 1888, when Emperor William II began to assume a direct control. He presided at the famous Berlin Conference of 1878. In 1890 he was forced to resign, and retired to private life. His son, Count Herbert von Bismarck (1849), was appointed German foreign minister in 1885.

Bizet, Georges (1838-1875), a French composer, who wrote several operas, *Carmen* being the most popular. He also wrote much orchestral music, of which the *L'Arlesienne* suites are the best known.

Bjornson, Bjornstjerne (1832-1910), a Norwegian poet, dramatist and novelist, whose poems, plays, and stories are marked by a strong intellectuality and a rich imagination.

Blackmore, Richard Doddridge (1825-1900), English novelist who in 1869 made a great reputation with his romantic novel, *Lorna Doone.*

Blackstone, Sir William (1723-1780), an English jurist, whose great work, *Commentaries on the Laws of England,* became a cornerstone in the interpretation of the British common law.

Blaine, James Gillespie (1830-1893), an American statesman, born at West Brownsville, Pa. He was one of the founders of the Republican Party and in 1856 was a delegate to the first Republican National Convention. He was Speaker of the House of Representatives 1869-1875; member of the Senate from 1876 to 1881; and twice Secretary of State (1881-1882 and

1889-1892). He was defeated for the Presidency in 1884 by Grover Cleveland. Blaine wrote *Twenty Years in Congress* (2 vols., 1884-1886).

Blake, Robert (1599-1657), English admiral. By his defeat of the Royalist and the Portuguese fleets, he established British sea power in the Mediterranean. He twice defeated the Dutch fleet and in 1656, during the war with Spain, completely destroyed a Spanish fleet in Santa Cruz harbor, Teneriffe.

Blake, William (1757-1827), English painter, poet and mystic, whose *Songs of Innocence* and scriptural drawings reveal an intense spirituality.

Blasco-Ibáñez, Vicente (1867-1928), a Spanish man of letters who wrote *The Four Horsemen of the Apocalypse* and other novels which made him world-famous.

Bleriot, Louis (1872-1936), French airman; the first to fly the English Channel from Calais to Dover, July 25, 1909.

Blondin, Charles (Jean François Gravelet) (1824-1897), a famous French rope performer, who crossed Niagara Falls on a tight rope, and was for many years the most popular acrobat of his day, living mostly in England.

Blücher, Gebhard Leberecht von (1742-1819), a Prussian commander who, after a long and brilliant military career, joined forces with Wellington in the final campaign against Napoleon and helped win at Waterloo.

Blum, Léon (1872-1950), French statesman, of Jewish stock, noted for his part in defense of Dreyfus; Socialist premier of France 1936-38, 1946-47; prisoner of Vichy regime and German Nazis, 1942-45.

Boccaccio, Giovanni (1313-1375), an Italian author who has often been called "The Father of Novel-writing." He had a lively imagination and a graceful style, and his famous *Decameron* has been a fount of inspiration to poets and story-tellers.

Bohr, Niels Henrik David (b. 1885), Danish physicist, who received the 1922 Nobel prize in physics for his work with atomic structure. He served as consultant at the Los Alamos, N.M., atomic bomb laboratory during World War II, where he aided in making the first atomic bomb.

Boileau-Despréaux, Nicolas (1636-1711), a French poet contemporary with Molière; wrote many classical imitations.

Boldrewood, Rolf, pseudonym of Thomas Alexander Browne (1826-1915), Australian novelist, born in London. Went with his parents to Australia in 1830, becoming a squatter and sheep-farmer in New South Wales, where he wrote his famous tale of bush-ranging, *Robbery Under Arms.*

Boleyn, Anne (1507-1536), English queen and second wife of Henry VIII; mother of Queen Elizabeth. Anne was originally maid-in-waiting to Queen Catharine, who was divorced by Henry to make way for her. She is said to have championed Protestantism. After three years as queen she was beheaded on a charge of treason.

Bolívar, Simón (1783-1830), leader of the South American republics in their long struggle for independence from Spain. After their achievement of independence he became president of Colombia, which included the present-day countries of Venezuela and Ecuador. He wrote the Bolivian constitution, was dictator of Peru, and attempted to unite the countries of northern South America into a great confederation, like the United States. His plans were frustrated and he retired from public life in 1828. He is often called the Washington of South America.

Bonaventura, St. (1221-1274), a Franciscan monk born in Italy, of great learning and piety, and a leading Schoolman. He was called "the Seraphic Doctor."

Bonheur, Rosa (1822-1899), a native of Bordeaux, France, and one of the most noted animal painters of the 19th century. "The Horse Fair" is probably her most popular picture.

Boniface, St. (680-754), an English monk, who spent most of his life in Germany in Christianizing missions, and became the first archbishop of Mainz. He and a number of followers were massacred in Friesland.

Boone, Daniel (1734?-1820), American pioneer born in Bucks County, Pa. After service under Braddock in the French and Indian War, he explored a portion of Kentucky, and tried, unsuccessfully, to plant a colony of settlers there. In 1775 with a small band of followers he blazed the trail later known as the Wilderness Road and established a fort on the future site of Boonesboro. Following the settlement of the new territory, he became a captain of militia and held a number of political offices. One of his famous exploits was his escape from the Indians who held him captive, in 1778, just in time to warn and defend Boonesboro against attack. Later he moved to West Virginia, and to Missouri when the latter was still Spanish territory. There he died, in 1820.

Booth, Edwin (1833-1893), an American tragedian of great eminence; son of Junius Brutus Booth the English tragedian, and brother of John Wilkes Booth, who assassinated President Lincoln. As a Shakespearean actor Booth took high rank and is said to have played Hamlet oftener than any other actor.

Booth, Evangeline (1865-1950), daughter of the founder of the Salvation Army. She became "general" of the organization in Nov., 1934.

Booth, William (1829-1912), an English religious reformer. When a young man he became a Methodist preacher and a traveling evangelist. He founded the Salvation Army in 1878, which under his direction became an organization of world-wide influence.

Booth, William Bramwell (1856-1929), son of William Booth, and his successor as "general" of the Salvation Army from 1912 until deposed by the organization's high council in 1928.

Borah, William Edgar (1865-1940), a prominent American Senator from Idaho from 1907 to 1940, and a leading member of the Republican party for many years. He was a leader of the isolationist group which kept the United States from joining the League of Nations.

Borden, Sir Robert (1854-1937), premier of Canada from 1911 to 1926; leader of the Conservative party in the Canadian House of Commons 1901-1920.

Borgia, Caesar (1476-1507), the masterful and unscrupulous son of Pope Alexander VI, who paved his way to power by the murder of those who opposed him. Aided by Louis XII of France he became ruler of Romagna, the Marches, and Umbria. Pope Julius II banished him from Rome, and he was imprisoned in Spain, but escaped to find a soldier's death in the army of Navarre during the invasion of Castile.

Borgia, Lucrezia (1479-1519), an Italian noblewoman, the daughter of Pope Alexander VI, and sister of Caesar Borgia. Many of the latter's crimes have become attached to the name of his sister, but it is denied that she deserves her evil reputation. Dominated by her father and brother, she was married three times, the last time to the Duke of Ferrara, at whose court she became noted for her charities and her patronage of culture.

Borodin, Alexander Porfirevich (1834-1887), a Russian composer. He was a professor of chemistry at the Medico-Surgical Academy of St. Petersburg (now Leningrad) and was one of the first to encourage higher education, including that of medicine, for women. He wrote chamber music, two symphonies, and the unfinished opera *Prince Igor*, which was finished by Rimsky-Korsakov and Glazunov, and first presented in St. Petersburg in 1890.

Borrow, George Henry (1803-1881), an English traveler and writer. He was for many years traveling agent for the British and Foreign Bible Society, and in the course of his wanderings made a special study of gypsy life. His sojourns in Spain produced his best-known work, *The Bible in Spain; Lavengro* and *Romany Rye* are classics of gypsy life.

Boscawen, Edward (1711-1761), British admiral in command of the fleet that took Madras, India. In the operations at Cape Finisterre, Quebec, Louisburg, and Cape Breton, he rendered distinguished service.

Bose, Sir Jagadis Chandra (1858-1937), eminent Indian scientist. He published many works on plant physiology. For the study of plants he designed certain instruments, of which the best known is the crescograph, which can magnify movement 100,000 times.

Boswell, James (1740-1795), a Scotch writer and lawyer, famous for his *Life of Samuel Johnson*. He came to London from Scotland, and devoted himself assiduously to studying Johnson's character, spending some years in close intimacy with the great lexicographer.

Botha, Louis (1863-1919), South African general who succeeded Joubert in command of the Boer forces in the Boer War, 1899-1902. In 1910 he was made first premier of the South African Union.

Botticelli, Sandro (c. 1444-1510), Italian painter, an apprentice of Fra Filippo Lippi. Produced many notable pictures, and assisted in the decoration of the Sistine Chapel. His illustrations for Dante's *Divine Comedy* are world-famous.

Boucicault, Dion (1822-90), a playwright and actor, born in Dublin, Ireland. At twenty years of age he achieved success with his play *London Assurance*. Other popular plays, some of them dealing with Irish subjects, were *The Colleen Bawn, The Octoroon,* and *Arrah-na-Pogue*. Many years of his life were spent in the United States, where his plays were as popular as in Great Britain.

Bowdler, Thomas (1754-1825), a pious English physician, who issued expurgated editions of Shakespeare and Gibbon, eliminating all expressions he considered offensive to good taste. Hence the term "bowdlerize."

Bowers, Claude G. (b. 1878), American author and diplomat, born in Indiana. Besides doing editorial work for newspapers he wrote a number of noted and popular historical works, including *Jefferson and Hamilton* (1925), and *The Tragic Era* (1929). In 1928 he was the keynote speaker of the Democratic National Convention. He was appointed ambassador to Spain in 1933 and was recalled in March 1939, and soon after was appointed ambassador to Chile. His *Spanish Adventures of Washington Irving* was published in 1940.

Bowman, Isaiah (1878-1950), president of Johns Hopkins University and important American geographer; born in Waterloo, Ontario, Canada. He became president of Johns Hopkins University in February, 1935. His published works include: *The Andes of Southern Peru* (1916); *International Relations* (1930); and *Geography in Relation to the Social Sciences* (1933).

Boyd, Belle (1843-1900), a Confederate spy, born in Martinsburg, W. Va., who rendered invaluable aid to the Southern cause by detecting the Federal plans of campaign and revealing them to the Confederates.

Boyle, Kay, American author, born in St. Paul, Minn., 1903. Before she was seventeen she had written hundreds of stories, poems, and a novel. In 1922 she went to France and remained there. Her works include: *Short Stories, Wedding Day and Other Stories, Death of a Man,* and *White Horses of Vienna.*

Boyle, Robert (1627-1691), English chemist. He was the first to differentiate between chemical elements and chemical compounds; invented the air pump, and established Boyle's Law.

Braddock, Edward (1695?-1755), British general, born in Perthshire, Scotland. He entered the Coldstream Guards in 1710 and was appointed major general in 1754. Nine months later he sailed as commander against the French in America and with a force of 2,100 British and provincial troops reached the Monongahela on July 8, 1755. On the 9th he pushed forward with a smaller force to invest Fort Duquesne, on the present site of Pittsburgh, Pa. On the right bank of the river his advance guard was attacked by a party of about 900 French and Indians from the fort. Braddock was defeated and mortally wounded while vainly trying to rally his men; he died four days later, near Great Meadows, where he was buried.

Bradford, Gamaliel (1863-1932), an American author, born in Boston, educated at Harvard. He wrote a large number of brief "portrait biographies" of noted people. His works include *Lee, the American* (1912); *Portraits of American Women* (1919); *Damaged Souls* (1923), and *Saints and Sinners* (1932).

Bradford, Roark (1896-1948), American writer, educated at the University of California; served as first lieutenant in the artillery during World War I, and then began to write for newspapers. His *Ol' Man Adam an' His Chillun* won him widespread fame when it was dramatized by Marc Connelly as *The Green Pastures.* Among his other books are *Ol' King David, John Henry, Kingdom Coming,* and *Three-Headed Angel.*

Bradford, William (1588-1657), an American colonial governor and author, born in England. He was one of the signers of the celebrated Compact on the Mayflower. In 1621 on the death of the first governor of Plymouth colony, John Carver, he was elected to the same office, which he continued to fill until his death. His *Diary of Occurrences,* covering the first year of the colony, was published in 1622. He left a number of religious compositions in verse and historical prose writings of great value, the most important being his *History of Plymouth Plantation* from the formation of the society in England, in 1602, down to 1647.

Bradley, Omar Nelson (b. 1893), U. S. general, born at Clark, Mo.; graduated from West Point, 1915; commanded II Corps in North Africa in 1943; commanded U. S. ground forces in Europe (1943-45). He became U. S. Veterans Administrator (1945), chief of staff (1948), and chairman of the joint chiefs of staff (1949).

Bragg, Braxton (1817-1876), Confederate army officer; graduated from West Point and served in the Mexican War. He joined the Confederate service, and in 1862 became commander of the Army of the Tennessee. He invaded Kentucky, but withdrew after the drawn battle of Perryville. He won the Battle of Stone River in the same year, and in 1863 inflicted a severe defeat on the Union army at Chickamauga. Grant then forced him into Georgia, where he was relieved of his command and made nominal commander-in-chief of the Confederate armies.

Brahe, Tycho (1546-1601), a celebrated Danish astronomer, and fellow-worker of Kepler.

Brahms, Johannes (1833-1897), a German composer, one of the greatest of modern times. His compositions are of a varied order, mostly classical in form, and possess deep intensity of expression and poetic significance. His piano music covers a wide range. He wrote some 300 songs. His larger works include four symphonies and the *German Requiem.*

Braille, Louis (1809-52), French educator, who as teacher of the blind perfected a system of reading and writing for the blind. As the result of an accident he himself had become blind at the age of three years.

Brandeis, Louis Dembitz (1856-1941), U.S. Supreme Court justice and jurist. He was counsel in proceedings involving the constitutionality of women's ten-hour laws and minimum wage laws; in 1910 he acted as chairman of the arbitration board in the New York garment workers' strike. President Wilson appointed Brandeis associate justice of the Supreme Court in 1916. His many dissenting opinions gained him a wide reputation. Justice Brandeis wrote *Other People's Money; Business, a Profession;* and *The Curse of Bigness.* He retired from the Supreme Court in 1939.

Brandes, Georg (1842-1927), Danish literary critic. His classic work, *Main Currents in Nineteenth Century Literature,* was translated into many languages. From 1912 he was professor of aesthetics at Copenhagen University. He was the author of many fine critical works, the most noteworthy of which were his studies of Goethe and Shakespeare.

Brangwyn, Frank (1867-1956), English painter, etcher, and designer; one of the most important figures in contemporary British art.

Brant, Joseph (1742-1807), a Mohawk chief, born in Ohio. He aided the British in many campaigns and in 1774 became secretary to Col. Johnson, superintendent-general of Indian affairs. In 1786 he visited England, there published the *Book of Common Prayer* and the *Gospel of St. Mark* in Mohawk and English. He died in Canada.

Breasted, James Henry (1865-1936), American Orientalist and historian. In 1894 he became an instructor in Egyptology at the University of Chicago. Successively he was director of the Haskell Oriental Museum, director of the University of Chicago Egyptian Expedition (1905-1907), professor of Egyptology and Oriental History, and chairman of the department of Oriental Languages and Literature. In 1919 Breasted was appointed director of the Oriental Institute and headed its first expedition in Egypt and Western Asia. He directed several such expeditions in the "Fertile Crescent," from the Persian Gulf to the Nile Valley. Breasted was the author of some twenty books on ancient history, among them: *A History of Egypt, Ancient Times—A History of the Early World* (both of which were translated into several languages), and also a more popular volume, *The Dawn of Conscience.*

Brewster, Sir David (1781-1868), a Scottish physicist who edited the *Edinburgh Encyclopedia* in 1808, invented the kaleidoscope in 1816; was one of the founders of the British Association, and a voluminous writer on science. He made important discoveries respecting the polarization of light.

Briand, Aristide (1862-1932), a French statesman, who was 11 times prime minister, 16 times foreign minister, in addition to holding other important public offices. He was chiefly responsible for the Locarno and Kellogg-Briand pacts, and advocated a United States of Europe.

Bridger, James (1804-1881), an American frontiersman. He entered the service of William H. Ashley in 1822 and for the next 20 years led trapping expeditions into the mountains. He accompanied Jedediah Smith's expedition through South Pass in 1823 and in 1825 explored Great Salt Lake. In 1843 he built Fort Bridger on the Oregon Trail and in 1856 opened Bridger's cut-off. He guided Johnston's army in the invasion of Utah in 1857 and the Raynolds expedition to explore Yellowstone Park in 1858. He assisted Gen. G. M. Dodge in the surveys for the Union Pacific R. R. and measured the Bozeman Trail.

Bridges, Horace James (b. 1880), author, lecturer; born in London, England. With Stanton Coit, Mr. Bridges was associate leader of the London Ethical Society from 1905 to 1912, after which time he lived in the United States. He became leader of the Chicago Ethical Society in 1913, and president of Booth House (a social settlement), Chicago. He is author of *The Ethical Movement—Its Principles and Aims* (1911), *Signs of the Times in Religion* (1935), *The Emerging Faith* (1937), and other books.

Bridges, Robert (1844-1930), English poet laureate, 1913-30. He practiced medicine up to 1882 thereafter devoting himself mainly to literature. He published several volumes of poems and plays. His *Testament of Beauty* was published in 1930.

Bright, John (1811-1889), a British Radical Quaker statesman and orator, one of the chief promoters of the Reform movement which led to the introduction of Free Trade.

Brontë, Charlotte (1816-1855), an English romantic novelist, one of the most gifted of the 19th century. Her *Jane Eyre,* published in 1847, attracted widespread notice, and her other novels, *Shirley, Villette,* and *The Professor,* are all marked by the force of strong genius. Her sisters, Emily and Anne, also wrote novels and poems, Emily's *Wuthering Heights* and some of her verse showing exceptional power.

Brooke, Rupert (1887-1915), a British poet who died during the World War. His best-known poems are "The Great Lover," and the war sonnets "The Soldier" and "The Dead."

Brooks, Phillips (1835-1893), an American clergyman of the Episcopal church, born in Boston

He was rector of Protestant Episcopal churches first in Philadelphia and later in Boston; and was made bishop of Massachusetts in 1891. He was an impressive pulpit orator, had great spiritual force, and published many volumes of sermons and lectures, notably *Lectures on Preaching* (1887), and *Essays and Addresses* (1894).

Brooks, Van Wyck (b. 1886), American critic and author, born in Plainfield, N. J. He was associate editor of *The Freeman* (1920-24). Brooks' published works have earned a critical reputation, especially in the interpretation of the culture of New England. His most outstanding books are: *America's Coming-of-Age, The Ordeal of Mark Twain, The Pilgrimage of Henry James, The Life of Emerson*, and *The Flowering of New England.*

Brougham, Henry, 1st Lord (1778-1868), British statesman and lawyer; was an eloquent advocate of reform, and became lord chancellor in 1830.

Broun, Heywood (1888-1939), American newspaperman and author, and president of the Newspaper Guild. Broun worked for several New York dailies and was widely read for his column in the *World* (1921-28). Known as a left-wing liberal, Broun played an active role in the campaign to organize American newspapermen. His published books include *Pieces of Hate* (1921), *It Seems to Me—1925-1935* (1935).

Brown, Sir Arthur Whitten-(1886-1948), British aviator, the first to fly the Atlantic, together with Sir John Alcock, in 1919.

Brown, Benjamin Gratz (1826-1885), an American politician, born in Lexington, Ky.; graduated at Yale in 1847. He practiced law in Missouri and became leader of the Free-Soil movement in that state. From 1863 to 1867 he was United States Senator from Missouri and in 1871 was elected governor of his state.

Brown, John (1800-1859), American Abolitionist, whose action in inciting certain Negro slaves to rebel in 1859 struck the note of alarm which culminated in the outbreak of the Civil War. His attempt to take the U. S. arsenal at Harper's Ferry was defeated, and he was hanged, being afterward regarded as a martyr by the Abolitionists.

Browne, Charles Farrar (Artemus Ward) (1834-1867), one of the most whimsical and entertaining of American humorists. In addition to his books he wrote and delivered humorous lectures. He was making an English tour when he was seized with a fatal illness, and died at Southampton.

Browne, Hablot Knight (1815-1882), an English artist best known as "Phiz," the illustrator of Dickens' novels, from the period of *Pickwick Papers* down to *Little Dorrit.*

Browne, Sir Thomas (1605-1682), an English physician and author. He was a scholar of great learning, whose best-known works are essays on philosophical and religious subjects. *Religio Medici; Hydriotaphia, Urn Burial;* and *Pseudodoxia Epidemica*, are full of odd facts and erudite observations; their highly ornamented, imaginative prose ranks with the best in English.

Browning, Elizabeth Barrett (1806-1861), an English poet who, between 1830 and 1860, wrote many poems showing keen intellectual grasp and imaginative fervor. *Aurora Leigh*, a novel in poetic form, is, in portions, on a high level of poetic execution. She was married to Robert Browning in 1846, and afterwards lived mostly in Italy. Her greatest work is *Sonnets from the Portuguese*, inspired by her love for Browning, beautiful in sentiment and execution.

Browning, Robert (1812-1889), a British poet, one of the greatest of the later Victorian era. His earlier poems and dramas, though marked by singular insight and power, were far from popular, mainly because of a somewhat obscure and involved style from which he only occasionally freed himself. His *Strafford* and *The Blot on the 'Scutcheon* were both produced by Macready, and attained some measure of stage success; but Browning was essentially a poet to be read, rather than acted. Some of his dramatic characterizations are of striking power. From about 1840 he published many works and knew at last what it was to be an appreciated poet. His *Men and Women, Dramatis Personae*, and *The Ring and The Book* contain some of the finest poetry of modern times.

Brownlow, William Gannaway (1805-1877), an American politician, journalist, and author, born in Virginia. During his early career he was an itinerant preacher, editor, and lecturer. He was a Union champion during the Civil War and was banished from Tennessee in 1862. When Northern troops occupied eastern Tennessee, he organized pro-Union sentiment, was elected governor, and was re-elected in 1867. He was United States Senator from 1869 to 1875. Among his works are *The Great Iron Wheel Examined* (1858); and *Sketches of the Rise, Progress and Decline of Secession* (1862).

Brownson, Orestes Augustus (1803-1876), American clergyman and author. Originally a Presbyterian, he became a Universalist minister, then a Unitarian minister, a leader of the Transcendentalist movement, and in 1844 a Roman Catholic. He was a friend of Channing and Thoreau, and editor of various reviews. Among his books were *New Views of Christianity, Society, and the Church* (1836), and *The Convert* (1857).

Bruce, Charles Granville (1866-1939), soldier and mountaineer, who was leader of the Mt. Everest expeditions of 1922 and 1924.

Bruce, James (1730-1794), a celebrated Scotch traveler who successively explored Syria, the Nile Valley, and Abyssinia (now Italian East Africa), and reached the source of the Blue Nile.

Bruce, Robert (1274-1329), king of Scotland. He took part with Wallace in the revolt against Edward I, and at Bannockburn overthrew the English army and ultimately secured Scottish independence. He reigned twenty-two years as King Robert I.

Bruce, Stanley Melbourne (b. 1883), prime minister of Australia 1923-29; high commissioner for Australia, 1933-45; created viscount, 1947.

Bruckner, Anton (1824-1896), Austrian composer. His chief works are his nine symphonies, of which the fourth (the "Romantic") and the seventh are the best, and a *Te Deum.* Bruckner was profoundly religious in feeling, and his music has a mystical, sublime quality.

Brummell, George Bryan (1778-1840), "Beau Brummell," the fashion leader in English society when George IV was Prince of Wales; was a famous *bon vivant* and gamester.

Brunelleschi, Filippo (1379-1446), the great Italian architect and pioneer of Renaissance architecture, adapting the ideals of the classical period to the conditions of his day.

Bruno, Giordano (c. 1548-1600), Italian philosopher and martyr; entered the Dominican order at Naples in his 15th year. In 1592 he was arrested by the Inquisition, and after 7 years in prison was burned at the stake.

Brutus, Marcus Junius (85-42 B. C.), Roman statesman and provincial governor who, desiring the re-establishment of the Roman republic, assassinated Julius Caesar, then virtually a dictator.

Bryan, William Jennings (1860-1925), American politician, born in Salem, Ill. He moved to Nebraska in 1887, entered politics, and became a leader of the groups advocating free and unlimited coinage of silver. At the Democratic National Convention in 1896, his famous "Cross of Gold" speech was received so enthusiastically that he was nominated for the Presidency. He lost the election, however, to McKinley. Bryan was again defeated for the Presidency in 1900 and 1908. From 1913 to 1915 he was Secretary of State under Woodrow Wilson. An ardent reformer, Bryan was particularly interested in income tax laws, prohibition, woman suffrage, popular election of senators, and the promotion of international peace by arbitration treaties.

Bryant, William Cullen (1794-1878), an eminent American poet and editor. His poem "Thanatopsis," was welcomed both in his own country and in England as the work of a serious poetic mind.

Bryce, James, Viscount (1838-1922), British statesman and author, from 1907 to 1912 British ambassador to the United States. Among his historical and political writings *The American Commonwealth, The Holy Roman Empire*, and *Modern Democracies* hold high rank.

Buchanan, James (1791-1868), an American statesman, 15th President of the United States, was born near Mercersburg, Pa. In 1820 he was elected to Congress, serving successive terms by re-election for 10 years. In 1828 Andrew Jackson appointed him Minister to Russia; in 1834 he entered the United States Senate, serving there 12 years, where he declared against the right of the government to interfere with slavery in the states. He was appointed Secretary of State by President Polk. He was elected President in 1856; his Cabinet contained men who supported the secession of South Carolina and eventually joined the Confederacy. He denied the right of secession but said the Federal government could not prevent it by force, and this unwillingness to take decisive action enabled the seceding states to arm and prepare for war. He died in Lancaster, Pa.

Buchman, Frank Nathan Daniel (b. 1878), American clergyman, organizer of the Oxford Group, which emphasizes personal religion and national spiritual revival, and of Moral Re-Armament.

Buck, Pearl Sydenstricker (b. 1892), an American novelist, born of missionary parents in West Virginia. Many years spent in China gave her sympathetic insight into Chinese life and character, which she interpreted in a trilogy *The House of Earth;* its first volume, *The Good Earth*, was awarded the Pulitzer prize (1939). She received the Nobel prize for literature in 1938, a year before publication of *The Patriot*.

Buckle, Henry Thomas (1821-1862), an English historian, the author of *The History of Civilization in England*, one of the most enlightening productions of the 19th century.

Budge, Sir Ernest Alfred Wallis (1857-1934), an English archaeologist who conducted many excavations in Mesopotamia and Egypt; was keeper of Egyptian and Assyrian antiquities at the British Museum, 1893-1924.

Buell, Don Carlos (1818-1898), an American military officer, born in Ohio. He was graduated at West Point in 1841, and served in the Mexican War. When the Civil War broke out he was made a brigadier general of volunteers. In November, 1861, he succeeded Sherman in command of the Department of the Ohio, performing valuable services at Shiloh and Perryville. In 1862 he resigned his regular commission.

Buffon, George Louis Leclerc, Comte de (1707-1788), a French naturalist, devoted his life to the study of the animal kingdom. His famous work in thirty-five volumes gave a more elaborate description than had previously been published concerning the animal kingdom.

Bulfinch, Thomas (1796-1867), an American author, born in Boston; graduated from Harvard University in 1814. His best-known work is the famous Bulfinch's *Mythology*, consisting of *The Age of Fable* (1855); *Age of Chivalry* (1858); *Legends of Charlemagne* (1864).

Bülow, Bernhard Heinrich Martin, Prince von (1849-1929), German statesman. He entered the diplomatic service in 1873; he served as minister to Bucharest (1888-1893), ambassador to Rome (1893-1897), head of the foreign office (1897), chancellor (1900-1909), and ambassador to Rome (1914-1915). He defended his policy in a book entitled *Imperial Germany*.

Bulwer, Henry Lytton Earle (Lord Dalling) (1801-1872), an English author and diplomat, brother of Sir Edward Bulwer-Lytton. Among his works are *An Autumn in Greece; France, Social, Literary, and Political*, and *Life of Byron*.

Bulwer-Lytton, Edward, Lord Lytton (1803-1873), an English author, born in London. In 1847 and again in 1852 he sat in Parliament; and in 1858-1859 was colonial secretary, when he established British Columbia and Queensland as separate colonies. Altogether Bulwer's works number 110 volumes. His novels were very popular, and the contemporary estimate of his talents, particularly as a historical novelist was exaggerated. Among the best-known of his novels are *The Last Days of Pompeii; The Last of the Barons; Kenelm Chillingly; Harold, the Last of the Saxons;* and *Pelham*. His plays, particularly *Richelieu* (1838), were also very popular.

Bunche, Ralph Johnson (b. 1904), U. S. Negro official of United Nations; UN mediator in Palestine, 1946-49. Nobel Peace Prize, 1950.

Bunsen, Robert Wilhelm (1811-1899), noted German chemist, discoverer of the metals caesium and rubidium, and inventor of the Bunsen burner, battery, and pump. Made many important observations in spectrum analysis.

Bunyan, John (1628-1688), an English author; worked as a traveling tinker and fought with the Cromwellians. Joining a Baptist society in Bedford in 1655, he became imbued with religious enthusiasm and was for some years a popular preacher. After the Restoration he was imprisoned for twelve years, and there wrote his world-famous allegory of the Christian life, *Pilgrim's Progress*. Other works are *Grace Abounding to the Chief of Sinners* and *The Life and Death of Mr. Badman*.

Burbank, Luther (1849-1926), American plant-breeder, who devoted his life to the development of new and improved plant forms. At his nursery at Santa Rosa, California, he worked with hundreds of thousands of specimens of many species. By painstaking selection and hybridization he produced the Burbank potato, the Burbank plum, and many new varieties of fruits, flowers, and vegetables.

Burdett-Coutts, Angela Georgina, Baroness (1814-1906), an English philanthropist, granddaughter of Thomas Coutts, an English banker, whose vast fortune she inherited. Her philanthropies covered almost every department of charitable effort, and caused her elevation to the peerage.

Burghley, Cecil, Lord (1520-1598), an English statesman, secretary of state and lord treasurer in the reign of Queen Elizabeth. During his long public career he became one of the most influential personages of the kingdom.

Burke, Edmund (1729-1797), English statesman, born in Dublin of a Protestant father and a Catholic mother. He graduated from Trinity College, Dublin, in 1748, began to study law, and then turned to literary work. His *Philosophical Inquiry into . . . the Sublime and Beautiful* was published in 1756. He entered Parliament in 1766, and gained notice by defending the repeal of the Stamp Act and other measures hostile to Grenville. During North's administration, he protested against coercion of the American colonies, delivering the famous speeches, *American Taxation* (1774), *Conciliation with America* (1775), and *Letter to the Sheriffs of Bristol* (1777).

Burne-Jones, Sir Edward (1833-1898), an English painter of the Pre-Raphaelite group. A romantic mysticism dominated his pictures. His most famous works are "The Days of Creation," "The Mirror of Venus," "The Briar Rose," and "King Cophetua."

Burns, Robert (1759-1796), Scottish poet, born in Ayrshire. His first volume of poems was published in 1786, and attracted immediate attention. Among other poems it included "To a Louse," "To a Mountain Daisy," and "The Cotter's Saturday Night." Among his later poems were "Highland Mary," "Duncan Gray," "O Wert Thou in the Cauld Blast," and "Tam o' Shanter." His spontaneous humor and sympathetic understanding have made Burns one of the best-loved poets in the English language.

Burnside, Ambrose Everett (1824-1881), an American military officer, born in Liberty, Ind. He was graduated from the U. S. Military Academy at West Point in 1847; retired from the Army in 1853; returned as colonel of volunteers in 1861. For a time he commanded the Army of the Potomac, but was replaced after his disastrous defeat at Fredericksburg. In November, 1863, he successfully held Knoxville against a superior force, and in 1864 he led a corps under General Grant through the battles of the Wilderness and Cold Harbor. From 1867 to 1873 he was governor of Rhode Island, and from 1875 until his death in 1881 was U. S. Senator.

Burr, Aaron (1756-1836), an American political leader and third Vice President of the United States, born in Newark, N. J., Feb. 5, 1756. His father was the president of Princeton College and his mother the daughter of Jonathan Edwards. He entered Princeton College at the age of 12 and graduated at 16. In 1775 he joined the American army, under Washington at Cambridge. In 1789 he was made attorney-general of New York. From 1791 to 1797 he was a member of the United States Senate, where he was distinguished as a leader of the Jeffersonian party. In 1800 he was a candidate for the Presidency and received the same number of votes as Thomas Jefferson (79), and the choice was thus left to the decision of Congress, which on the 36th ballot elected Jefferson as President and Burr as Vice-President. In 1804 was fought the famous duel between Alexander Hamilton and Burr, in which the former was killed. In 1807 his suspicious southwestern colonization scheme led to his being charged with treason; he was, however, after a long trial acquitted. He resumed the practice of law, but lived in comparative obscurity until his death on Staten Island, Sept. 14, 1836.

Burton, Sir Richard Francis (1821-1890), English explorer, Orientalist, and diplomatist, who became famous after making a pilgrimage to Mecca in 1853, disguised as a Mohammedan. Later he did much exploring in Central Africa, and wrote popular books on that region. Perhaps his greatest work was the translation of the *Arabian Nights* in their entirety, in sixteen volumes.

Butler, Benjamin Franklin (1818-1893), an American politician and soldier, born in Deerfield, N. H. He studied law and was admitted to the bar in 1841. Though a Democrat, he was a strong Unionist, and in 1861 was made a major general of volunteers. As military governor of New Orleans, his rule, though effective, was severely critized. After the war he was a member of Congress. In his time he was considered an extreme radical, running for the Presidency for the Greenback and Anti-Monopolistic parties. His autobiography was published in 1892.

Butler, Joseph (1692-1752), an English divine who occupied an important place among eighteenth-century thinkers. In 1736 he published his *Analogy of Religion*, which was a reply to the deistic attacks on revealed religion.

Butler, Nicholas Murray (1862-1947), an American educator; president of Columbia University from 1902 to 1945; well-known publicist and internationalist, and one of the most honored and distinguished leaders in the world of education. He shared the Nobel peace prize with Jane Addams in 1931.

Butler, Samuel (1612-1680), English poet and satirist. His most famous work was the mock-heroic poem *Hudibras*, which ridiculed the Puritans.

Butler, Samuel (1835-1902), English author; born in Nottinghamshire, England. His family intended him for the ministry, but his opinions did not permit him to enter that calling, and he went to New Zealand where he became financially independent in five years. He returned to England, and, becoming deeply interested in art, music, biology, and literature, he exhibited at the Royal Academy, composed several cantatas after Handel, wrote a book on biology opposed to the teachings of his friend Darwin, and produced in 1872 *Erehwon* (an anagram for "Nowhere"). This work presented satirically a Utopia which resembles New Zealand in scene. The sequel, *Erehwon Revisited*, appeared in 1901. His novel, *The Way of All Flesh*, considered Butler's greatest work, and published posthumously, was based on his own personal experiences.

Butterick, Ebenezer (1826-1903), the inventor of standardized patterns for dressmaking, born in

Sterling, Mass. He collaborated with his wife in devising and marketing these patterns, which achieved a great success. In 1869 the Buttericks started a factory in Brooklyn, N. Y., and published a fashion magazine entitled *Delineator*.

Buxton, Sir Thomas Fowell (1786-1845), British reformer, who organized the Anti-Slavery Society, and whose efforts had much to do with the British abolition of slavery in 1833.

Byrd, Richard Evelyn (1888-1957), the American aviator and polar explorer; was in command of the Macmillan arctic expedition, 1925; flew over the North Pole, 1926; with three companions flew across the Atlantic, 1927; and in 1929 made the first flight over the South Pole. Discovered Edsel Ford Mountains and Marie Byrd Land on his first expedition to the Antarctic, 1928-30. On his second Antarctic expedition, 1933-1935, he spent several months alone at an advanced base. Byrd set out on his third expedition to the Antarctic in 1940.

Byrd, William (1542-1623), English composer. He was appointed organist of Lincoln Cathedral in 1563 and in 1570 was made member of the Chapel Royal where he held with Tallis, his teacher, the honorary position of organist. In 1575 the two men were licensed by Queen Elizabeth to print and sell exclusively all music and music-paper. Byrd is often called the "Father of English Music."

Byrd, William (1674-1744), American colonial planter and author, born at Belvidere, near the James River in Virginia. He was educated in England and returning in 1696 became one of the most brilliant members of the Virginia tidewater aristocracy. Living in splendid colonial style at Westover, he increased his inheritance of 26,231 acres to 179,000 acres. In 1728 he was one of the commissioners who established the North Carolina-Virginia boundary. In 1733 he founded Richmond, Va., on his own lands. A patron of art and science, he had a library of more than 4,000 books, the largest library in the colonies. His *Westover Manuscripts* were based on his diaries.

Byron, George Gordon, 6th Lord (1788-1824), English poet. Educated at Harrow and Cambridge, he published his *Hours of Idleness* at twenty, a volume which was violently attacked by the *Edinburgh Review*. Byron retaliated with *English Bards and Scotch Reviewers*, which caused a great sensation because of its unsparing criticisms of the writers of the day. His *Childe Harold's Pilgrimage*, the first two cantos of which were published in 1812, at once placed him in the front rank of poets, and thenceforward to the time of his death he continued to produce poems. The best are *Manfred*, a poetic drama; *Don Juan;* and *The Prisoner of Chillon*. He made an unhappy marriage in 1815 with the daughter of Sir Ralph Milbanke, from whom he parted after a year. He lived abroad, and died at Missolonghi, Greece.

C

Cabell, James Branch (1879-1958), noted author; born in Richmond, Va. He was educated privately, and later attended William and Mary College. Among Cabell's most notable works are: *The Eagle's Shadow, Gallantry, Chivalry, The Rivet in Grandfather's Neck, From the Hidden Way* (verse), *The Cream of the Jest, Beyond Life, Jurgen, Figures of Earth, The Silver Stallion, Something About Eve, The High Place, Domnei*, and *Hamlet's Uncle*.

Cable, George Washington (1844-1925), a well-known American author, born in New Orleans, the scene of many of his best works. He excelled in the writing of historical romances, and in the re-creation of the spirit of pre-Civil War Louisiana. Among his writings were *Old Creole Days* (1879), and *Strange Stories of Louisiana* (1889).

Cabot, John (1450-1497), a Venetian explorer, the discoverer of the mainland of North America. He settled as a merchant, about 1490, in Bristol, England. Under letters patent from Henry VII, he set sail from Bristol in 1497 with two ships, accompanied by his sons. On June 24 they sighted Cape Breton Island and Nova Scotia. A second expedition was undertaken in 1498, exploring the coasts of Greenland, Baffin Land, and Newfoundland, proceeding as far south as the 38th parallel. Failing to find the desired route to Asia, Cabot returned to England, where he died the same year.

Cabot, Sebastian (1474-1557), an English naval explorer and map-maker, son of John Cabot. He sailed on his father's second expedition; later he served Ferdinand V and Charles V of Spain, as well as Edward VI of England.

Cadbury, George (1839-1922), English manufacturer and social reformer. He founded the model industrial town of Bournville, and financed agitation for better labor conditions, old age pensions, and unemployment insurance.

Cade, John ("Jack"), an adventurous English rebel, who, in 1450, headed an insurrection, and entered London with 30,000 men, defeating the Royal forces at Sevenoaks. Cade was executed the same year near Heathfield, and his followers soon dispersed.

Cadman, Charles Wakefield (1881-1946), American composer; born in Johnstown, Pa. He was music critic on the *Pittsburgh Dispatch* and organist in several Pittsburgh churches. He published a collection of ballads in 1904 and made a collection of Indian music at the Omaha Indian Reservation. Cadman's compositions include *Four American Indian Songs*, and two operas: *Shanewis* and *A Witch of Salem*.

Cadman, Samuel Parkes (1864-1936), American clergyman, born in Wellington, Shropshire, England. From 1895-1901 he was pastor of the Metropolitan Temple, New York City, and became pastor of the Central Congregational Church, Brooklyn, in 1901. From 1924-1928 he was president of the Federated Council of Churches of Christ in America. Dr. Cadman was the author of many books dealing with religious questions: *Imagination and Religion, The Christ of God, The Parables of Jesus*, and *The Prophets of Israel*.

Cadorna, Marshal Count Luigi (1850-1928), Italian soldier. He was chief of general staff of the Italian army, and was in command when it was disastrously defeated in the Battle of Caporetto during the World War.

Cædmon (d. 680?), an Anglo-Saxon monk of Whitby, and the first British poet to write in the vernacular. He paraphrased the Scriptures with poetic effect.

Caesar, Caius Julius (100-44 B. C.), Roman soldier, dictator, and man of letters. He was appointed successively military tribune, quaestor, aedile in 65, and pontifex maximus in 63. A year later he was praetor and formed the first triumvirate. In his Gallic campaigns, Caesar displayed great military ability. He invaded Britain, in the civil war defeated Pompey, and in the Alexandrine war was brought into contact with Cleopatra, whose power over him did not cease till his death. On his return from Africa in 44 he was assassinated by Brutus, Cassius and others, who regarded his dictatorial powers as a hindrance to the restoration of the Republic.

Cagliostro, Alessandro, Count de (1743-1795), an Italian charlatan whose real name was Giuseppe Balsamo, who came to grief in connection with the Marie Antoinette diamond necklace scandal. For this he was imprisoned in the Bastille, but escaped.

Caillaux, Joseph (1863-1944), a prominent French politician, was premier 1911-12, and later Minister of Finance in several cabinets.

Caine, Sir Thomas Henry Hall (1853-1931), British novelist. After spending some years as a journalist he produced his first novel, *The Shadow of a Crime,* in 1886. He subsequently produced numerous novels, including *The Deemster, The Manxman, The Christian,* and in 1904 *The Prodigal Son,* and *The Woman Thou Gavest Me.* His *Life of Christ* was published posthumously in 1938.

Calderón de la Barca, Pedro (1600-1681), a Spanish dramatist of great eminence whose plays number nearly 200. He was writer of court plays for Philip IV. His most famous work is *La Vida es Sueño.*

Caldwell, Erskine (b. 1903), American author, born in White Oak, Georgia. He studied at the University of Virginia and the University of Pennsylvania. For a time he worked on the *Atlanta Journal.* His first story appeared in *The New Caravan* in 1929. His first two novels, *The Bastard,* and *Poor Fool,* were privately printed, and he did not win wide recognition until the publication of *Tobacco Road* (1932) and the attempted suppression of *God's Little Acre* in 1933. The dramatization of *Tobacco Road,* done by Caldwell and Jack Kirkland, made a notable record by the length of its Broadway run. His other books include *American Earth* (1931); *We Are the Living* (1933); *Journeyman* (1935); *Kneel to the Rising Sun* (1935); *Some American People* (1935); *Southways* (1935); and, with Margaret Bourke-White, whom he married in 1939, *You Have Seen Their Faces* and *North of the Danube* (1939). Caldwell's work is notable for its sharp realism, particularly in his delineation of life among the poorer classes in the South.

Calhoun, John Caldwell (1782-1850), American statesman; born in South Carolina. He was graduated from Yale in 1804, served two terms in the South Carolina Legislature, and in 1811 was elected to Congress. During the rest of his life he was in either Congress or the Cabinet. Calhoun became Secretary of War in 1817, and Vice-President in 1825 and 1829. He became the foremost defender of slavery, the basis of the economic life of the South, and as Secretary of State during the negotiations for the admission of Texas made protection of slavery the chief reason for its acquisition. Later Calhoun opposed the Wilmot Proviso and the admission of California with a constitution prohibiting slavery. In his *Disquisition on Government* and *Discourse on the Constitution* and *Government of the United States,* published after his death, Calhoun argued that the nation was a confederation of sovereign states, and that if the Federal Government ignored the rights of a minority of the states, this minority could secede through exercise of its sovereign rights, or could nullify Federal laws.

Caligula, Caius Caesar Augustus Germanicus (A. D. 12-41), was the third of the Roman emperors. At first mild and just, he developed into a bloodthirsty tyrant, killing and torturing thousands. He was murdered in A. D. 41, after having aroused the people with his monstrous acts.

Calvin, John (1509-1564), one of the leading religious reformers of the 16th century, born in Picardy. He attained great popularity as a preacher in Paris, but was expelled. He then lived at Geneva, where he continued to preach Protestant doctrines. The body of his teachings, called Calvinism, was distinguished from Lutheranism by its doctrine of predestination. Calvin's teachings became important in the beliefs of the Scotch Covenanters, the French Huguenots, and the English Puritans.

Camacho, Manuel Avila (1897-1955), Mexican political leader, born in Puebla. In 1914 he joined Madero's army and by 1929 had become a major general. He later served as Secretary of War, Navy, and National Defense. Supported by President Cárdenas, the Mexican labor federation, and the Party of Mexican Revolution, Camacho was elected President in July, 1940, and served until 1946.

Camden, William (1551-1623), an English antiquary and historian whose researches, especially in the field of topography, were of great value.

Cameron, Verney Lovett (1844-1894), an English explorer who was the first to cross the African continent from east to west. He explored Lake Tanganyika, and made many valuable geographical discoveries. In 1878-79 he explored Persia.

Camoens, Luiz Vaz de (1524-1580), the author of *The Lusiad,* the great epic poem of Portugal, which sets forth the adventures of the discoverers of India, and celebrates the achievements of the principal personages in Portuguese history.

Campbell, Alexander (1788-1866), an American clergyman, originator (with his father, Thomas Campbell) of the religious body known as the Disciples of Christ; born in the county of Antrim, Ireland. By his zeal in preaching, he gathered numerous followers, who began about 1827 to form themselves into a denomination. In 1840 he founded Bethany College at Bethany, W. Va. His published works include about sixty volumes, among them his *Christian System* and *Remission of Sin.*

Campbell, Sir Malcolm (1885-1949), British motorboat and automobile racer, and holder of world's records.

Campbell, Thomas (1777-1844), British poet who at twenty-two published *The Pleasures of Hope.* Many of his lyrics and songs take high rank, notably "Ye Mariners of England," "Hohenlinden," "The Battle of the Baltic," and "The Exile of Erin."

Campbell-Bannerman, Sir Henry (1836-1908), British statesman. He was secretary for war, 1886, 1892-1895; leader of the Liberal party from 1898; and prime minister from 1905 to his death.

Canby, Henry Seidel (b. 1878), American critic; born at Wilmington, Del.; studied and taught at Yale. He organized and edited *The Saturday Review of Literature* from 1924 to 1936 with Christopher Morley and William Rose Benét.

Classic Americans, *American Estimates*, and *Seven Years' Harvest* are noteworthy among his books.

Canning, George (1770-1827), English statesman. He entered Parliament in 1793; was foreign minister, 1807-09 and 1822-27; he opposed the intervention of the Holy Alliance in Spain, aided Greece in her struggle for independence, and recognized the independence of the Spanish American colonies. His suggestion to Richard Rush for a joint Anglo-American declaration to protect South America was the basis of the Monroe Doctrine.

Canova, Antonio (1757-1822), an Italian sculptor, leader of the Classic Revival. He is famed for his "Cupid and Psyche" groups and "Pauline Borghese," a representation of Napoleon's sister as Venus.

Canute (995-1035), a king of England, as well as of Norway and Denmark. He invaded England with a Danish force, and in 1013 succeeded in dethroning Ethelred the Unready, and setting up his own father, Sweyn, in Ethelred's stead. Sweyn dying in 1014, Canute claimed the crown, but it took him some years to establish himself firmly. Later he fell heir to Denmark, and conquered Norway, Sweden, and Scotland.

Capablanca, José Raoul (1888-1942), world's chess champion 1921-27; defeated by Alekhine.

Capek, Karel (1890-1938), Czech author and journalist. His *R. U. R.*, *The Life of the Insects*, and *Adam the Creator* are well-known satirical dramas.

Cárdenas, Lazaro (b. 1895), Mexican politician. He became Governor of Michoacan, and in 1930 was made president of the National Revolutionary party. Later he became Secretary of the Interior, Secretary of War, and in 1934 was elected President. He inaugurated his "Six-Year Plan" in December, 1934. It called for the splitting up of large estates to be distributed among the peons; socialization of several industries; and the transferring of all education from the hands of the Church to those of the state. In 1935 Cárdenas eliminated foreign ownership of Mexican oil lands, and nationalized additional properties. His term of office expired in 1940, and in 1942 he was appointed Minister of War, resigning in 1945.

Carlyle, Thomas (1795-1881), British author, born in Dumfriesshire. His first important work was *Sartor Resartus*, written in 1831. Later he wrote the *French Revolution*, *Heroes and Hero Worship*, *Oliver Cromwell's Letters*, and *Frederick the Great*. Carlyle emphasized the reality of spiritual rather than temporal things. Although he advocated social reforms, he distrusted democracy as a solution of all evils and preferred that humanity be guided by a class of heroes—the "great man" theory of history.

Carman, William Bliss (1861-1929), Canadian poet, worked as a journalist. He published many volumes of poetry, among them *Pipes of Pan*, *Ballads and Lyrics*, and *Far Horizon*.

Carmen Sylva, pen name of Elizabeth (1843-1916), queen of Rumania. She published several books including *Thoughts of a Queen*, *Whispered Words*, and several volumes of poetry.

Carmona, Antonio Oscar de Fragosa (1868-1951), a Portuguese general who became dictator of Portugal in 1926, and president, 1928-1951.

Carnegie, Andrew (1835-1919), an American manufacturer and philanthropist; born in Dunfermline, Scotland. In 1848, after his family had emigrated to America, he got a job as a bobbin boy in a cotton factory of Allegheny City, Pa. He became successively telegraph messenger boy, operator, railway employee of the Pennsylvania Company, and superintendent of the Pittsburgh division of the system. His fortune was begun through the Woodruff Sleeping-Car Company, and increased by land investments near Oil City, Pa. In 1868 he laid the foundation of his great steel industries, which were finally consolidated in 1899 as the Carnegie Steel Company. In 1901 he retired, and the company became the "billion dollar" United States Steel Corporation. After his retirement he distinguished himself by making large gifts of money for educational and philanthropic purposes, the total amount being $350,000,000. The most noteworthy of his gifts were for public libraries, the Carnegie Institute of Technology, the Carnegie Institution of Washington, and the Carnegie Endowment for International Peace.

Carnot, Lazare Nicolas Marguerite (1753-1823), French military engineer and statesman. He was a member of the Committee of Public Safety under Robespierre, and later minister of war and a member of the directory. He wrote several works on mathematics and military engineering; his masterpiece was *The Defense of Fortified Positions* (1810).

Carnot, Marie François Sadi (1837-1894), grandson of the last-named; was elected to the French National Assembly in 1879, and in 1887 became president of the Republic; was assassinated at Lyons in 1894.

Carol II (1893-1951), king of Rumania. He was married morganatically to Mme Zizi Lambrino but divorced her in 1921 to marry the Princess Helen of Greece. One child, the Crown Prince Michael, was born to them in 1921. Carol renounced the Rumanian throne in 1925 and left his country, going to Paris with Mme Magda Lupescu. In 1930 he returned to Rumania where he was warmly received, supplanting his son on the throne. The assassination of Premier Calinescu in September, 1939, led Carol to exact severe reprisals on the Fascist group known as the Iron Guard. However, the power of the succeeding premier, Antonescu, and a combination of intrigues, forced Carol to abdicate the throne in 1940; he and Mme Lupescu were married in 1947. He died in Portugal.

Carpenter, John Alden (1876-1951), American composer of modern tendencies, born in Park Ridge, Ill. His principal works include *Adventures in a Perambulator*, *Concertino*, *The Birthday of the Infanta*, *Skyscrapers*, *Patterns*, a string quintet, a piano quintet, and a violin concerto.

Carrel, Alexis (1873-1944), biologist and surgeon, born at Sainte Foy les Lyon, France. He was educated at the University of Lyon, came to the United States in 1904, and was appointed (1906) to the staff of the Rockefeller Institute for Medical Research. He received the Nobel prize in 1912 for physiology and medicine, in recognition of his accomplishments in transplantation of organs and in suturing blood vessels; and the Nordhoff-Jung cancer prize in 1930. He developed a method for treating wounds by irrigating them with an antiseptic solution prepared by H. D. Dakin. With Charles A. Lindbergh, he discovered a new method, using an "artificial heart," for cultivating entire organs outside the body. He wrote *Man, the Unknown* (1935).

Carroll, Charles (1737-1832), signer of the Declaration of Independence, born in Annapolis, Md. He studied at Paris, became a member of the Inner Temple at London, returned to his native country in 1764, and was elected to the Continental Congress in 1776.

Carroll, Lewis. (See *Dodgson, Charles Lutwidge.*)

Carson, Christopher (1809-1868), commonly called Kit, an American hunter and scout, born in Madison Co., Ky. When only a year old he was taken by his parents to the Missouri frontier, where in 1824-26 he was apprenticed to a saddler. He ran away to join a Santa Fe hunting party and in the following years accompanied other expeditions, learning much of the geography of the West. As guide to General Fremont on his exploring expeditions of 1842, 1843-44, and 1845-46, he became nationally famous. Carson fought in a number of battles in the Mexican War and in 1854-61 gave valuable service as Indian agent at Taos, N. M. In the Civil War he was brevetted brigadier general "for important services in New Mexico, Arizona, and the Indian Territory." He died at Fort Lyon, Colo.

Carter, Howard (1873-1939), British Egyptologist and archaeologist who was associated with the 5th Earl of Carnarvon in discovering the tomb of Tutankhamen in the Valley of Kings, Egypt.

Cartier, Jacques (1494-1557), French navigator, born at St. Malo, whose exploration of Canada, and especially of the St. Lawrence River, proved of great geographical importance.

Cartwright, Edmund (1743-1823), British clergyman who invented the power loom, and also a wool-combing machine. He worked with Robert Fulton in the development of the steamboat.

Cartwright, Peter (1785-1872), an American clergyman, born in Virginia; ordained in Kentucky in 1806, and in 1823 removed to Illinois, where he worked for nearly half a century. He sat in the state legislature there, and in 1846 was defeated by Abraham Lincoln in an election for congressman. Cartwright was one of the most famed of the Methodist circuit riders in the early days of the Middlewest.

Caruso, Enrico (1873-1921), Italian tenor, was born in Naples and made his first operatic appearance in his native city. Besides being a great singer, he was a man of many activities, among other things, a clever caricaturist.

Cass, Lewis (1782-1866), an American statesman, diplomat, and soldier; born in Exeter, N. H. Serving in the War of 1812, he was active in the campaign which ended with the British defeat at the Battle of the Thames. Later, as civil governor of Michigan (1813-1831), he led the party which explored the territory north of Illinois between Lake Michigan and the Mississippi river. He also negotiated 22 Indian treaties which ceded vast territories to the United States; prepared these regions for settlement by directing surveys, building roads and forts. He was appointed Secretary of War in 1831, and further distinguished himself in the Black Hawk War (1832). In 1845 he was elected to the Senate where he was outstanding as an expansionist, furthering the annexation of Texas and advocating adherence to the Oregon claims. He was defeated as the Democratic candidate for President in 1848 but was elected to a second term in the Senate (1849-1857). From 1857-1860 he served as Secretary of State. He died in Detroit.

Cassius (Caius Cassius Longinus), a Roman general who opposed the dictatorship of Julius Caesar, and took part in his murder. He died in 42 B. C., after being defeated by Mark Antony.

Castlereagh, Robert Stewart, 2nd Viscount (1769-1822), an English statesman. He represented England at the congresses of Chatillon and Vienna (1814-1815), at the Treaty of Paris in 1815, and at the Congress of Aix-la-Chapelle in 1818.

Cather, Willa Sibert (1876-1947), American author; born near Winchester, Va. She became an editor of *McClure's Magazine* in 1906 and served in that capacity until 1912, traveling extensively in Europe and the American Southwest. Giving up her position to devote all her time to writing, Miss Cather produced *O Pioneers!*, *The Song of the Lark*, *My Antonia*, *One of Ours* (awarded Pulitzer prize in 1922), *A Lost Lady*, *Death Comes for the Archbishop*, *Shadows on the Rock*, and *Not Under Forty.*

Catherine of Aragon (1485-1536), an English queen, the daughter of Ferdinand and Isabella of Spain; first wife of Henry VIII. She had previously been the wife of Arthur, Henry's elder brother, who died shortly after the marriage. Henry divorced her in 1526.

Catherine II, Empress of Russia (1729-1796), wife of Peter III, who was murdered; succeeding him, she proved herself a capable ruler, adding much territory to Russia, and introducing many reforms.

Catherine de' Medici (1519-1589), wife of Henry II of France. She was a woman of commanding power and influence, especially during her regency, which continued while her son, Charles IX, was in his minority. Her antagonism to the Protestants led to the Massacre of St. Bartholomew.

Cato, Marcus Porcius (234-149 B. C.), a Roman statesman, soldier, and writer, of strict virtue, simplicity and wisdom, who strongly condemned the luxury of his time. He was surnamed "the Censor."

Catullus, Caius Valerius (87-54 B. C.) Roman poet, whose lyric poetry is among the finest of its kind.

Cavell, Edith Louisa (1865-1915), a British nurse and patriot who assisted wounded British soldiers to escape over the Dutch frontier from Belgium during the World War. She was court-martialed and shot by the Germans.

Cavour, Count Camillo Benso (1810-1861), a distinguished Italian statesman, who, as premier to Victor Emmanuel II, did much for the unification of Italy.

Caxton, William (1422-1491), the first English printer. In 1475 he printed the first book in English.

Cecil of Chelwood, Edgar Algernon Robert, 1st Viscount (b. 1864). English statesman. During the World War he was under-secretary for foreign affairs. He took a prominent part in drafting the Covenant of the League of Nations. In 1924 he was awarded the $25,000 Prize of the Woodrow Wilson Foundation for meritorious services in the cause of international cooperation and peace. In 1937 he was awarded the Nobel Peace Prize.

Cellini, Benvenuto (1500-1571), Florentine sculptor, engraver, and goldsmith. Of a bold, honest and open character, but vain and quarrelsome, he was often entangled in disputes which frequently cost his antagonists their lives. He visited the court of Francis I of France. He afterwards returned to Florence, and under the patronage of Cosimo de' Medici made a bronze statue of "Perseus with the head of Medusa"; also a statue of Christ, in the chapel of the

Pitti Palace, besides many excellent dies for coins and medals. His *Autobiography* is a literary classic. He died in Florence. His works may be divided into two classes. The first comprises his smaller productions in metal, embossed decoration of shields, cups, salvers, ornamented sword and dagger hilts, clasps, medals and coins. The second includes his larger works as a sculptor, such as his "Nymph of Fontainebleau"; a colossal "Mars" for a fountain at Fontainebleau; and a lifesize "Jupiter" in silver.

Cerdic, a Saxon who invaded Wessex in the early part of the 6th century, and made himself ruler of that kingdom. He conquered the Isle of Wight in 530.

Cervantes Saavedra, Miguel de (1547-1616), a Spanish novelist, famous throughout the world as the author of *Don Quixote.* He had a most adventurous career, taking part in many military expeditions, and not turning to literature until his retirement. In spite of the great success of his work, he died in poverty.

Cézanne, Paul (1839-1906), a French painter. He attempted to combine the techniques of both classical art and impressionism. His painting is characterized by vivid coloring and a striving for depth.

Chaliapin, Feodor Ivanovich (1873-1938), a world-famous Russian opera singer, a bass who possessed great dramatic gifts.

Chamberlain, Arthur Neville (1869-1940), British prime minister; son of Joseph Chamberlain, and brother of Joseph Austen Chamberlain. He was educated at Rugby and at Mason College, Birmingham, England. He was chancellor of the exchequer in 1923-24 and again in 1931-1937. Upon the resignation of Stanley Baldwin in 1937 he became prime minister. His administration was marked by a policy of appeasement toward the totalitarian powers, culminating in the Munich Pact signed in September, 1938, by Hitler, Mussolini, Daladier, and Chamberlain. After Hitler violated this pact in March, 1939, seizing the remaining sections of Czechoslovakia, Chamberlain made a decisive change in attitude, instituting conscription in England, and joining France in a full military alliance with Poland. On September 3, 1939, two days after the German invasion of Poland, Britain entered the war. Chamberlain's policies lacked, however, both aggressiveness and foresight, and after the invasion of Norway and the Low Lands in the Spring of 1940 Chamberlain was forced out of office and was succeeded by Winston Churchill. Chamberlain served as Lord President of the Council until shortly before his death on November 9, 1940.

Chamberlain, Joseph (1836-1914), British statesman, born in London. Following a successful manufacturing career in Birmingham, he entered Parliament in 1876, and became a national political figure. In 1895 he accepted office as secretary of state for the colonies under Lord Salisbury and in that post won a great reputation.

Chamberlain, (Joseph) Austen (1863-1937), British statesman, the eldest son of Joseph Chamberlain. He was civil lord of the admiralty 1895-1900; financial secretary to the treasury 1900-02; chancellor of the exchequer 1903-06 and again 1919-21; secretary of state of India 1915-17; foreign secretary 1924-29; first lord of the admiralty 1931. He was awarded the Nobel Peace Prize, 1925.

Champlain, Samuel de (1567-1635), a French navigator who explored the St. Lawrence River in 1603, founded Quebec in 1608, and in the following year discovered the lake named for him.

Channing, William Ellery (1780-1842), American clergyman and author. In 1803 he was ordained pastor of the Federal St. Congregational Church in Boston and became a leader in the development of Unitarianism. He was a leader in the anti-slavery movement and, in his denunciation of war, treatment of labor questions, and advocacy of general education, was far in advance of his time.

Chantrey, Sir Francis Legatt, (1781-1842), an English sculptor who contributed many statues to Westminster Abbey and St. Paul's. He left a considerable fortune to the Royal Academy to be appropriated in the purchase of works of art for the encouragement of sculpture and painting.

Chaplin, Charles Spencer (b. 1889), film actor who in the early days of silent motion pictures won fame with his creation of a sadly funny tramp. Considered by many to be the classic clown, Chaplin managed to combine pathos and slapstick in such outstandingly successful films as *The Gold Rush, City Lights* (two films which won second place in a British best-films-of-all-time contest), *The Kid,* and others. In *The Great Dictator* Chaplin satirized Mussolini and Hitler, and in 1952 produced, directed, and wrote both score and scenario for his most controversial picture, *Limelight.* Although most of his life was spent in the United States, Chaplin never gave up his British citizenship, and in 1952 was barred from re-entry into the United States.

Chapman, George (1559-1634), an Elizabethan dramatist who acquired fame by his translation of Homer. Keats's sonnet on reading Chapman's "Homer" is a splendid tribute to him.

Chapman, John (1775-1847), known as "Johnny Appleseed," was a frontier hero who traveled for 40 years throughout the Middle West, planting orchards and urging the settlers to do likewise. He developed large nurseries. Many legends were told of his adventures, such as his saving Mansfield, Ohio, from an Indian attack during the War of 1812. Chapman is buried near Fort Wayne, Indiana.

Charlemagne, Charles the Great, King of the Franks, and subsequently Emperor of the West; born in 742, probably at Aix-la-Chapelle. His father was Pepin the Short, King of the Franks, son of Charles Martel. On the decease of his father in 768 he shared the kingdom of the Franks with his younger brother Carloman, at whose death in 771 Charlemagne made himself master of the whole empire by victorious campaigns against the Saxons, Bavarians, and Lombards. On Christmas Day 800 he was crowned and proclaimed Caesar and Augustus by Leo III. Charlemagne was a friend of learning. He attracted the most distinguished scholars to his court and established an academy in his palace at Aix-la-Chapelle. He invited teachers of language and mathematics from Italy to the principal cities of the empire and founded schools of theology and the liberal sciences in the monasteries. He died Jan. 28, 814, and was buried at Aix-la-Chapelle, his favorite residence. His son Louis succeeded him.

Charles Edward (Stuart) (1720-1788), the "Young Pretender" to the British throne, grandson of James II. He lived in exile after the Battle of

Culloden, and his later career was mainly one of dissipation. He died in Rome, Italy.

Charles I (1600-1649), succeeded his father James I as King of England in 1625, and early came into conflict with Parliament. His monetary demands and unjust taxation resulted in the violent opposition which led to the English Civil War. Charles was captured in 1646 by Parliamentary troops and beheaded on charges of treason in 1649.

Charles II (1630-1685), king of England, son of Charles I; was in command of the Royalist forces in the West during the English Civil War, and escaped to the Continent after the Battle of Naseby. Subsequently he became King at the Restoration, and following upon the sober quietude of the Commonwealth period, formed an acceptable change to the people at large. Later he incurred unpopularity by his secret treaty with France, whereby he promised to become a Catholic and wage war on Holland. By 1674 Charles was forced to abandon this policy. In 1681 he dissolved Parliament and ruled absolutely until his death in 1685. Charles had no children except illegitimate offspring by his numerous mistresses. He was succeeded by his brother, James II.

Charles V (1500-1558), Holy Roman Emperor and king of Spain, son of Philip I of Spain. In 1516 he became king of Spain, and in 1519 succeeded to the Hapsburg possessions and was elected emperor. Throughout his career he fought to defend Catholicism against the Reformation, and to preserve the authority and territories of the Empire, which was endangered by the rising spirit of nationalism. In 1554 Charles began making over his empire to his son and to his brother, Ferdinand; in 1556 he retired to a monastery; and in 1558, just before his death, he abdicated in favor of his brother. Despite his great power, Charles failed to halt either the Reformation or the rise of Nationalism, and by his numerous wars depleted Spain of capital and man-power.

Charles XII (1682-1718), king of Sweden, was a brave but impulsive monarch whose rule was distinguished by a fearless and often foolhardy policy of war, in the execution of which he sometimes sustained serious defeat. Peter the Great was victorious over him at Poltava, and he was killed at the siege of Frederikshall, Norway.

Chase, Salmon Portland (1808-1873), an American jurist. In 1846 he argued the Fugitive Slave Law with William H. Seward in a celebrated case, and his support of the anti-slavery cause soon made him a leader of the Liberty party and a leading spirit in the Free-Soil and Republican parties. In 1848 he was elected to the United States Senate; in 1855 he became Governor of Ohio; in 1860 he was a prominent candidate for the Republican presidential nomination. He was appointed Secretary of the Treasury by President Lincoln in 1861, and in 1864 became Chief Justice, in which office he presided at the impeachment trial of President Johnson.

Chateaubriand, François René, Vicomte de (1768-1848), French writer and statesman. In 1791 he came to the United States on a government expedition to discover the northwest passage. He lived in England until 1800; there he published his first book, *Essai historique, politique et moral sur les révolutions* (1797). After his return to France in 1801 he published *Atala* and in 1802 *Le Génie du Christianisme.* In 1811 he published *Itinéraire de Paris à Jérusalem.* On the restoration he was made a peer of France, was ambassador to England, and minister of foreign affairs. He spent the last years of his life writing *Mémoires d'outre-tombe.*

Chatham, William Pitt, Earl of (1708-1778), British statesman. He entered Parliament in 1727, and despite the King's objections to him, became leader of the House of Commons in 1756. Pitt's policies were largely responsible for the triumph of England and the downfall of French power in the Seven Years' War. He retired from the House of Commons in 1760, re-entered Parliament as a member of the House of Lords, and retired again in 1768. Known as the "Great Commoner," Pitt was not equaled as an orator, and will be remembered for his sound principles of colonial administration.

Chaucer, Geoffrey (c.1340-1400), English poet, who achieved lasting fame by his *Canterbury Tales,* which give a most graphic description of the life and characters of his time.

Chekhov, Anton (1860-1904), a Russian dramatist and short-story writer. Although his plays and stories have little of plot in them, they are virtually cross-sections of Russian life before the Revolution.

Chesterfield, Earl of (1694-1773), British statesman and author. He served as ambassador to Holland, Lord Lieutenant of Ireland and Secretary of State. His fame rests, however, upon his *Letters to His Son,* which for purity of style and grace of expression have seldom been excelled.

Chesterton, Gilbert Keith (1874-1936), British author. A convert to Roman Catholicism, Chesterton devoted many of his works to its advocacy and defense. Characterized by frequent use of paradox, they include studies of Dickens, Browning, Shaw, and Stevenson; *The Man Who Was Thursday; The Ballad of the White Horse; A Short History of England; New and Collected Poems;* and *Come and Get It.* He completed his autobiography two months before his death.

Chiang Kai-shek (b. 1887), Chinese soldier and politician, leader of the Kuomintang, the Chinese Nationalist party, and of the Nationalist government, which he established at Nanking in 1927 by conquest. During 1935, a year marking increasing political unrest, he became virtual dictator of China. He ruthlessly attacked Chinese communists and Kuomintang dissidents. He was kidnapped on Dec. 12, 1936, by the hostile troops of Marshal Chang Hsueh-liang, forced to make concessions to the communists and the others, and released after 13 days. When Japan invaded China in the summer of 1937, Chiang led a unified Chinese people in fighting the aggressor, but was finally driven into the interior. During the next eight years, Chiang directed Chinese resistance from the provisional capital at Chungking, assisted by his wife, the former Mai-ling Soong, and U. S. military officers. Postwar unrest enabled the communists to gain control of China by 1949, when Chiang moved the government of the Republic of China to Formosa.

Chippendale, Thomas (1718-1779), English cabinetmaker, whose designs became the basis of 18th-century English furniture. His catalogue, published in 1754, first brought him into general notice. His designs were followed by many American cabinetmakers of the colonial and early national periods.

Choate, Joseph Hodges (1832-1917), an American lawyer and diplomat. He was a nephew of Rufus Choate, and became a partner in the law firm of Evarts, Choate and Beaman. He was ambassador to Great Britain, 1899-1905; and first U. S. delegate to the International Peace Conference at The Hague, 1907, after which he practiced law in New York.

Choate, Rufus (1799-1859), American lawyer. He was admitted to the bar and began practice in Danvers, Mass., in 1823; was a member of Congress in 1830-34, was successor of Daniel Webster in the United States Senate, 1841-1845; returned to Boston in the latter year and resumed practice. After Webster's death Choate was acknowledged the leader of the Massachusetts bar. While a United States Senator, he made many political speeches, including those on the Oregon Boundary, the Smithsonian Institution, and the Annexation of Texas.

Chopin Frédéric François (1809-1849), Polish pianist and composer. His father was a Frenchman from Lorraine who had settled in Poland. In 1829 he went to Vienna where he won success as a pianist. He went to Paris in 1831 and, though he performed at concerts occasionally, spent the rest of his life in composing. In 1837 he became the lover of George Sand and from then until 1847, when they parted, he produced many of his major works. His works include 4 sonatas, 2 concertos, 20 nocturnes, 27 études, and 26 preludes.

Chou En-lai (b. 1896?), Chinese Communist leader, born in Kiangsu province. During the 1930's he directed Communist affairs in his home province, and he served as a liaison officer between the Communists and the Kuomintang during the war against Japan. When the Communists gained control of China in 1949, Chou became premier and foreign minister, but he gave up the latter post in 1958.

Chrysostom, St. John (347-407), a prominent father and saint of the Greek Church who was made archbishop of Constantinople and was famous for his eloquent preaching and persuasive writing.

Churchill, Lord Randolph (Henry Spencer) (1849-1895), British statesman. In 1885 he became secretary for India, and in the following year was chancellor of the Exchequer and leader of the House of Commons.

Churchill, Winston Leonard Spencer (b. 1874), English statesman and soldier, son of Lord Randolph Churchill. He was educated at Harrow and Sandhurst, entered the army in 1895, served in that year with the Spanish forces in Cuba, later with the British in India and Egypt, and in the South African War (1899-1902), being taken prisoner by the Boers. In 1900 he was elected Conservative member of Parliament for Oldham; was under-secretary for the colonies, 1905-1908; home secretary, 1910-1911; first lord of the admiralty, 1911-1915; minister of munitions, 1916; secretary of war and air, 1919-1921; chancellor of the Exchequer, 1924-29. From 1933 he sharply denounced the Nazi regime and opposed the appeasement policy. In 1939 Churchill became First Lord of the Admiralty and, in May, 1940, Prime Minister, with a coalition cabinet. He was chiefly responsible for the vigor of Britain's war effort, but his domestic policies found little favor with British voters, and in 1945 his Conservative party was badly defeated, failing by a narrow margin again in 1950. His party won a majority in 1951, and at 77 Churchill became the oldest British prime minister since Gladstone. He was knighted in 1953 and retired in 1955.

Ciano di Cortellazzo, Galeazzo, Count (1903-1944), Italian diplomat, son-in-law of Mussolini.

Cibber, Colley (1671-1757), an English actor and dramatist of great repute in his day. *The Careless Husband,* and *Love's Last Shift* are the best of his comedies. Poet Laureate, 1730-57.

Cicero, Marcus Tullius (106-43 B. C.), Roman orator and statesman, born at Arpinum, studied oratory under several famous teachers. He joined the party of Pompey, head of the nobility, and was elected consul for the year 63 B. C. After the civil war between Caesar and Pompey, Cicero retired to his country estates and occupied himself with writing philosophy, rhetoric, and poetry. His greatness as an author is founded not upon his orations alone but also upon his letters and philosophical writings. With his *Tusculan Disputations, Republic, Nature of the Gods, Moral Duties,* the essays on *Old Age* and on *Friendship,* Cicero made Greek philosophy accessible to the Romans and the scholars of the Middle Ages. After the assassination of Caesar (44 B. C.), Antony took Caesar's place; and as a last act Cicero delivered his famed *Philippics* against Antony. Before he could leave the country Antony's troops caught him and killed him.

Cid (El Campeador) (c. 1035-1099), the name given to the famous Spanish knight, Rodrigo Diaz, Count of Vivar, whose exploits in battle and adventure made him the national hero.

Cimabue, Giovanni (1240-1302), a Florentine painter, teacher of Giotto, and the leader of the precursors of the Florentine school.

Clarendon, Edward Hyde, Earl of (1609-1674), English statesman and historian. His *History of the Rebellion* is a valuable work, having the advantage of being written by one who was a witness of, and often an important figure in, the events described. His daughter Anne was the wife of the Duke of York, afterward James II, and it was her daughter who became Queen Anne. Clarendon died in exile at Rouen.

Clark, George Rogers (1752-1818), American frontiersman, Revolutionary hero, and later general, born in Virginia, 1752. At twenty he was surveying lands along the Ohio, and in 1774 was commissioned captain during Lord Dunmore's War against the Ohio Indians. Under Virginia's sovereignty, he assumed command of Kentucky's forces to repel attacks of British and Indians in that region. In 1778, with 175 men under his command, he captured Kaskaskia, Cahokia, and Vincennes, thus taking the old Northwest from British control and securing it for Virginia. Clark and his men kept up continual warfare against the British and Indians and built many forts along the western frontier.

Clark, William (1770-1838), explorer; brother of George Rogers Clark born in Virginia; emigrated with his family at the age of 14 to the falls of the Ohio, in Kentucky, on the present site of Louisville. In 1803 he was appointed in conjunction with Capt. Meriwether Lewis to the command of an expedition designed to explore the newly acquired Louisiana Territory and to travel to the Pacific Ocean. His journal and the account kept by him of the astronomical observations made by him and Captain Lewis have been published. He was appointed in 181[illegible] governor of the Missouri Territory and superintendent of Indian affairs, which offices he retained till 1821, when Missouri was created a state. Later he helped suppress the Winnebago and Blackhawk uprisings.

Clarkson, Thomas (1760-1846), English abolitionist. He spent his entire public life in agitation against the slave trade and slavery in the British colonies. With William Wilberforce, he was chiefly responsible for the abolition of these abuses in British territory. He wrote *History of the Rise, Progress, and Accomplishment of the Abolition of the African Slave Trade.*

Claude Lorraine (1600-1682), the most famous landscape painter of his century. His real name was Claude Gelée, was born at Chamange in the Vosges, and lived in Rome most of his life.

Claudius I, Tiberius Drusus Nero, surnamed Germanicus and Britannicus, the fourth Emperor of Rome; born in Lyons 10 B. C. After spending 50 years of his life in a private station, unhonored and little known, he was proclaimed Emperor, A. D. 41, by the soldiers and confirmed in the sovereignty by the Senate. Claudius went to Britain two years after his accession and made it a Roman province. He built the port of Ostia, the Claudian aqueduct, and executed other great works. He died A. D. 54, of poison administered by his fourth wife, Agrippina.

Clausewitz, Karl von (1780-1831), Prussian military officer and writer on strategy; born in Burg, June 1, 1780. He served with distinction in several campaigns in the Prussian and Russian services between 1793 and 1815. Of his works the best-known are his great book *Of War*, which was the basis of military strategy during the 19th century, and his life of Scharnhorst.

Clay, Henry (1777-1852), an American statesman; born in Hanover County, Va. Becoming a student of law in his 21st year, he was admitted to the bar and began practice at Lexington, Ky. In 1803 he entered politics and in 1806 became United States Senator for a single year, to fill an unexpired term. In 1811 he was elected to the House of Representatives and became speaker. In 1824 he was a candidate for the Presidency against J. Q. Adams, General Jackson, and W. H. Crawford, and no choice being obtained in the Electoral College, the election came before the House of Representatives. Clay and his friends voted for Adams, thereby securing his election. During the Adams administration, 1825-29, Clay was Secretary of State; in 1831 he returned to the Senate and became leader of the opposition to Jackson's administration. Through his influence the Compromise Bill was passed through Congress, which ended the Nullification controversy by a partial abandonment of the protective system. In 1832 he was again a candidate for the Presidency; in March 1842, he resigned his seat in the Senate and retired to private life until 1844, when he came forward a third time as candidate for the Presidential chair. In a highly-exciting campaign he was again defeated, but by a very small numerical majority. In 1849 he resumed his seat in the Senate, in view of the contest impending between the slave-holding party and its opponents, on the California and territorial questions. He was the author of the celebrated Compromise of 1850. Because of his active part in three great compromises which saved the Union, he has been called the "Great Pacificator."

Clayton, John Middleton (1796-1856), American statesman; born in Sussex County, Del., in 1796; became United States Senator in 1829 and held office till the close of 1836, when he resigned. He was then appointed chief justice of his native state and continued on the bench for three years. In 1845 he was again sent to the Senate, and remained there till March 1849, when he became Secretary of State under Gen. Taylor.

Cleaveland, Moses (1754-1806), American pioneer, born at Canterbury, Conn. and graduated from Yale in 1777. He served in Washington's army until 1781, when he retired and practiced law in his native city. In 1795 he joined the Connecticut Land Company, which had purchased $1,200,000 worth of land in Ohio, and was chosen a director. He surveyed the property with a party of 52 and at the mouth of the Cuyahoga River founded the city which bears his name. The spelling was changed to "Cleveland" in 1830.

Clemenceau, Georges Eugène (1841-1929), French statesman and editor. A leading exponent of French Radicalism, he sacrificed his independent position to become Premier and Minister of the Interior in October 1906-09, Prime Minister and Minister of War, 1917-20. He was a great orator, a sturdy defender of Dreyfus, and was partially responsible for the French success in the World War.

Clemens, Samuel Langhorne (Mark Twain) (1835-1910), American humorist; born in Florida, Mo. When he was four, his family moved to Hannibal, Mo., on the Mississippi River, where he grew up with little formal education, much in the manner of his own brain children, Tom Sawyer and Huck Finn. His associates—boat captains, Negro roustabouts, and river characters—furnished raw material for later tales of life on the Mississippi. He learned the printer's trade on the Hannibal Journal; as a printer he worked his way east to Philadelphia and New York before he was 19. In 1857, Clemens became a "cub" pilot under Horace Bixby, famous steamboat captain, and obtained his pilot's licence. Shortly after the outbreak of the Civil War, he headed west with Orion, who had been promised an appointment as lieutenant governor of Nevada. After some experience as a silver miner near Carson City, he went to work on the Virginia City, (Nev.) *Enterprise*, where he first used his *nom de plume* "Mark Twain." He soon moved to San Francisco, where he joined the circle of wits that gathered about the *Golden Era*. His associates included such men as Artemus Ward, Bret Harte, and Charles Warren Stoddard. Mark's most famous story, "The Celebrated Jumping Frog of Calaveras County," which first appeared in the New York *Saturday Press*, 1865, brought him immediate popular acclaim both in New York and London. He sailed on the *Quaker City* on a cruise to visit the Mediterranean lands. The result of this trip was his *Innocents Abroad*, which had so great popularity that he became the most widely read author in America. In 1870 he married Olivia Langdon, of Elmira, N. Y., and soon removed to Hartford, Conn., where he made his home for 30 years, his richest writing period. The failure of a publishing venture climaxed a series of bad investments and forced him to an international lecture tour which enabled him to pay off all obligations. In 1907, Oxford University honored Clemens with the degree Litt. D. His later years were spent at "Stormfield," his home at Redding, Conn., where he died April 21, 1910. His best-known works beside those already mentioned include, *Roughing It, The Prince and the Pauper, Life on the Mississippi, Tom Sawyer, Huckleberry Finn, A Connecticut Yankee in King Arthur's Court, Joan of Arc, Pudd'nhead Wilson,* and *Following the Equator.*

Cleopatra, Queen of Egypt, born 68 B. C. At the age of 17 she married her brother Ptolemy. Julius Caesar came to her support in a successful war against her brother for the throne of Egypt. Caesar remained in Egypt for some time and Cleopatra had a son Caesarion, by him. After the assassination of Caesar, the Roman province of Egypt was given to Mark Antony, who fell completely under the influence of Cleopatra. After a few years feeling grew so strong against Antony in Rome, that a war was brought against him led by Augustus Octavian, (32 B. C.). When Augustus was victorious at the battle of Actium (31 B. C.), Antony fell on his sword. Cleopatra committed suicide shortly after, poisoned by an asp. She died in 31 B. C. after a reign of 22 years.

Cleveland, Grover (1837-1908), American statesman, twice President of the United States; born in New Jersey. He went to Buffalo in 1855, was elected sheriff of Erie county in 1870, and mayor of Buffalo in 1881. With a reputation as a reformer, he became governor of New York in 1882, was nominated for the Presidency on the Democratic ticket in 1884, and elected, becoming the first Democratic President since 1861. During his first administration he advocated moderate tariff, civil service, and pension reforms. He was defeated for re-election in 1888, but renominated and elected in 1892. He stood firmly for the gold standard, and alienated the silver wing of his party by securing the repeal of the silver purchase clause of the Sherman Act. Upon the end of his second term, in 1897, Cleveland retired from political life.

Clinton, De Witt (1769-1828), American lawyer and statesman, born in Little Britain, N. Y., March 2, 1769. He was graduated from Columbia College in 1786 and was a member of the New York State Legislature from 1797 to 1802. Elected to the U. S. Senate in 1802, he resigned in 1803 to become mayor of New York. He was elected governor of N. Y. in 1817, was a promoter of the Canal, and broke the ground for it the same year. In his third term as governor (1825-1828) he formally opened the canal. He wrote *Antiquities of Western New York.*

Clinton, Sir Henry (1738?-1795), commander-in-chief of the British forces during the American Revolution, served in the French and Indian War; was sent in 1775 with the rank of major general to America, where he distinguished himself in the battle of Bunker Hill. He defeated the Americans at Long Island but was forced to evacuate Philadelphia to General Washington. In 1780 he captured Charleston; and in 1782 he returned to England. He died at Gibraltar.

Clive, Robert, Lord (1725-1774), went out to India as a clerk in the service of the East India Company when 17. In the war between England and France for control of India, he was given a command and displayed such remarkable military genius that he virtually became commander-in-chief. He succeeded in laying the foundation of the British Empire in India on a secure basis; on his return to England in 1760 he was raised to the peerage.

Clovis (c. 465-511), founder of the Merovingian line of Frankish kings. He was a convert to Christianity, and became its champion among the barbarians. He defeated the Burgundians and West Goths, and fixed his court at Paris.

Cobbett, William (1763-1835), British journalist and reformer. He was an ardent supporter of parliamentary and economic reform, and a leader of the working classes. In the discussion which preceded the passage of the Reform Bill of 1832 he took a prominent part. He spent the years 1792-1800 and 1817-1819 in the United States.

Cobden, Richard (1804-1865), English politician, the "apostle of free trade." He was born in Sussex June 3, 1804, and after a meager education, made a fortune as a merchant. As a member of Parliament, he long advocated free trade and parliamentary reform and took part in the successful struggle of repeal of the Corn Laws. His great work was the commercial treaty between England and France in 1860. He died in London.

Cody, William Frederick (1845-1917), better known as Buffalo Bill, an American plainsman of the early days of the West, born in Scott County, Iowa. Cody served the Union Army as a scout during the Civil War. During the construction of the Union Pacific Railroad he furnished more than 4,000 buffaloes for meat to the construction camps: hence the name "Buffalo Bill." He was engaged in many Indian fights. He had a cattle ranch at North Platte, Neb., where he raised buffalo. Later he organized a "Wild West" show with which he toured the U. S. and Europe.

Cohan, George Michael (1878-1943), actor and playwright, who became well known by his plays, *Get-Rich-Quick Wallingford, Seven Keys to Baldpate, Hello Broadway,* and others, in all of which he took the leading part. He played the leading part in the musical comedy, *Of Thee I Sing.*

Cohn, Ferdinand Julius (1828-1898), German bacteriologist, of which science he was the virtual founder.

Coke, Sir Edward (1551-1621), an English lawyer; in 1593 he was made attorney-general. In 1606 he became chief justice of the Court of Common Pleas. In 1620 he was elected to Parliament, where he framed the Petition of Rights. His principal works are *Reports, from 1600 to 1615; Institutes of the Laws of England,* in four parts, the first of which contains the celebrated commentary on Littleton's *Tenures, Coke upon Littleton; A Treatise of Bail and Mainprise;* and a *Complete Copyholder.*

Colbert, Claudette (b. 1905), French-American actress who came to the United States at the age of eight and first appeared on the stage in New York in 1923. Among the many plays in which she appeared were *The Ghost Train, The Barber,* and *See Naples and Die.* Commenced her film career in 1929 in *For the Love of Mike, The Sign of the Cross* and *Four Frightened People.* Later she appeared in *It Happened One Night, Bluebeard's Eighth Wife,* and *Tovarich.*

Colbert, Jean Baptiste (1619-1683), Marquis de Seignelay, French statesman; born in Rheims. Louis XIV appointed him controller general of finances in 1661. Under Colbert's administration order was restored in the finances, the revenue increased, and the royal treasury was soon enabled to furnish the means for foreign wars as well as for internal improvements. Because of the extravagance and high military expenses of Louis XIV, Colbert failed in his efforts to economize and reduce taxes.

Colden, Cadwallader (1688-1776), American scientist and colonial official; was born in Scotland. He was graduated from the University of Edinburgh and emigrated to the American colonies in 1708. He devoted himself to botany and astronomy and also to public affairs, becoming surveyor general of New York and in 1760 lieutenant-governor. He wrote *Cause of Gravitation* and *History of the Five Indian Nations.* He died on Long Island.

Cole, George Douglas Howard (b. 1889), English economist and author; has written many books on social and economic problems including *The Intelligent Man's Guide through World Chaos,* 1932.

Coleridge, Samuel Taylor (1772-1834), one of the great poets of the early part of the 19th century, whose *Ancient Mariner* and some other poems stand unsurpassed for poetic beauty and originality.

Coleridge-Taylor, Samuel (1875-1912), English musical composer. In 1911 he composed the music for Alfred Noyes's *Peace Poem.*

Colette, Sidonie Gabrielle Claudine (1873-1954), French author. Her fame as a French novelist largely rests on a series of studies beginning with *The Vagabond of Love.* Other works include *Claudine in Paris, The Innocent Wife,* and *Renée.* In 1935 she visited the United States to report the maiden voyage of the *Normandie* for a Paris periodical.

Colfax, Schuyler (1823-1885), American statesman; born in New York. He was elected to Congress in 1854 by the newly formed Republican party and was re-elected until 1869, being three times chosen Speaker. In 1868 he was elected Vice President of the United States, in Grant's first term. Implicated, unjustly, as he and his friends claimed, in the Crédit Mobilier charges of 1873, he spent the remainder of his life in political retirement.

Collins, Michael (1890-1922), was commander-in-chief, Irish Free State Forces; Minister of Finance, 1921-1922; Chairman of Provisional Government of Irish Free State, January-August 1922. Assassinated, Aug. 1922.

Collins, William Wilkie (1824-1889), English novelist, was for many years associated with Charles Dickens. He wrote *The Dead Secret, The Woman in White,* and *No Name.*

Colman, Ronald (1891-1958), English actor. First appeared on the stage in 1914, and in the United States in 1920. Made his film debut in 1923 as leading man to Lillian Gish in *The White Sister.* Achieved a reputation in *Beau Geste, Bulldog Drummond, Raffles,* and other films.

Colt, Samuel (1814-1862), of Hartford, Connecticut, invented the revolver and patented it in 1835. It was some time before its utility was recognized, but after being used with great effect in the Mexican War it was universally adopted.

Colum, Padraic (b. 1881), Irish author; born in County Longford, Ireland. He has produced verse, novels, plays, and children's fantasies, among which are *Broken Soil, Castle Conquer, Balloon,* and *The Girl Who Sat by the Ashes.* Colum was early associated with the National Theater movement; in 1911 he helped found and for two years (1912-13) edited *The Irish Review.* He published *Poems* in 1932, and *The Legend of Saint Columba* in 1935.

Columba, St. (521-597), the founder of the monastery of Iona, was a native of Ireland.

Columbus, Christopher (c. 1446-1506), Italian navigator, who prevailing upon Ferdinand and Isabella of Spain to bear the expense of an expedition of discovery, set out on his first voyage in 1492. He first discovered the Bahamas, Cuba, and other West Indian Islands, and, on his third voyage, in 1498, landed on the lowlands of South America. He died in Spain, and was buried in Santo Domingo.

Compton, Arthur Holly (b. 1892), American physicist, professor of physics at the University of Chicago, 1923-45, and chancellor of Washington University, 1945-53. He was awarded the Nobel Prize in physics in 1927 and other honors.

Compton, Karl (1887-1954), an American physicist, brother of Arthur Holly Compton; professor of physics at Princeton (1919-30) appointed president of Massachusetts Institute of Technology in 1930. He was awarded the Rumford Medal for his studies of spectroscopy and thermionic emission.

Comte, Auguste (1798-1857), a French philosopher, founder of the Positivist school of philosophy.

Confucius (c. 551-478 B. C.), Chinese philosopher and reformer, the founder of Chinese philosophy.

Congreve, William (1670-1729), Restoration dramatist whose comedies of manners brilliantly reflect the spirit of his age.

Conkling, Roscoe (1829-1888), American politician; born in Albany, N. Y.; was admitted to the bar in 1850; sat in Congress as a Republican in 1858-1862 and 1864-1866 and was elected to the United States Senate in 1867, 1873, and 1879. In 1876 and 1880 he was an unsuccessful candidate for the Republican nomination for the Presidency.

Connelly, Marc (b. 1890), an American playwright, born in McKeesport, Penn. He collaborated with George S. Kaufman in the plays: *Merton of the Movies; Beggar on Horseback;* and *The Butter and Egg Man.* He is most noted for his play, *Green Pastures,* suggested by the book, *Ol' Man Adam and his Chillun,* by Roark Bradford. In these tales Bradford sketched the native American Negro's conception of Paradise, half mystical, half humorous. This material when dramatized in *Green Pastures* won for Connelly the Pulitzer Prize.

Conrad, Joseph (1857-1924), Anglo-Polish novelist and short story writer who specialized in sea stories. His name was Josef Konrad Korzeniowski, but he adopted the pen name when he settled in England. His first novel of note was *Almayer's Folly,* 1895.

Constable, John R. A. (1776-1837), English landscape painter. He exerted a strong influence on the development of landscape art.

Constant, Jean Joseph Benjamin (1845-1902), French landscape and portrait painter, of Oriental subjects.

Constantine, the Great (c. 272-337), Emperor of Roman Empire from 306 to his death. Transferred the Capital of the Empire from Rome to Byzantium, thereafter called Constantinople.

Constantine I (1868-1923), King of Greece, 1913-17, and 1920-1922.

Cook, Captain James (1728-1779), British explorer and navigator, author of *Voyages Round the World.* He made many discoveries, including the Hawaiian Islands, where he was murdered by natives.

Cooke, Jay (1821-1905), an American financier; born in Sandusky, O. He founded in 1858 the house of Jay Cooke & Co., which financed the Civil War bond issues of the United States to the extent of $2,000,000,000. The house failed in 1873, causing widespread financial panic. In 1894 he re-established his fortune by investing in Western land and securities.

Coolidge, Calvin (1872-1933), was born in Plymouth, Vt., thirtieth President of the United States. He was graduated from Amherst College, in 1895 studied law in Northampton, Mass., and was admitted to the bar in 1897. Member and president of State Senate of Massachusetts, 1912-15; Lieutenant Governor, 1916-18, and Governor of Massachusetts, 1919-20. He was elected Vice President on the Republican ticket with Warren G. Harding in 1920; and on the death of President Harding in August, 1923, became President of the United States. He was re-elected in 1924.

Cooper, Alfred Duff (1890-1954), British statesman. He served in Parliament, 1924-29, 1931-45. He rose in the cabinet to secretary of state for war and then to first lord of the admiralty. Cooper was ambassador to France, 1944-47, and was created 1st viscount Norwich in 1952.

Cooper, Gary (b. 1901), American film actor; was educated in England, and first worked as a newspaper artist in the United States. Famous for his parts in such films as *Wings*, *A Farewell to Arms*, *Mr. Deeds Goes to Town*, etc.

Cooper, James Fenimore (1789-1851), American novelist, who from about 1820 to the time of his death produced a succession of stirring stories of adventure, which enjoyed much popularity, among them *The Spy*, *The Last of the Mohicans*, *The Pathfinder*, *The Deer Slayer*, etc.

Copernicus (Koppernick), Nicolaus (1473-1543), the Polish astronomer who propounded the astronomical system which bears his name.

Copley, John Singleton (1737-1815), American painter, born in Boston, Mass. When only 18 years old he painted a portrait of George Washington, and in 1774 he went to London where he was commissioned to execute the portraits of the king and queen. He was made a member of the Royal Academy. He is known for the originality and spirited execution of his works, which were generally on historical subjects.

Coppé François Edouard Joachim (1842-1908), one of the most popular of modern French writers.

Coquelin, Benoit Constant (1841-1909), eminent French actor ("Coquelin ainé") and **Coquelin,** Ernest ("Coquelin cadet") his youngest brother (1848-1909), were leading lights of the Théâtre Français.

Corelli, Marie (1864-1924), English novelist whose writings were very popular, among them: *Barrabas*, *The Sorrows of Satan*, *The Master Christian*, *The Treasure of Heaven.*

Corneille, Pierre (1606-1684), French tragic dramatist, whose *Cid*, *Polyeucte*, *Le Menteur*, and other plays marked a new era in French dramatic production.

Cornell, Katharine (b. 1898), American actress; born in Berlin, Germany, of American parents. In 1919 she joined Jessie Bonstelle's stock company. After a year of touring in *The Man Who Came Back*, she went to London in *Little Women*. She first attracted attention in New York in *A Bill of Divorcement*, later appearing in *Will Shakespeare*, *The Way Things Happen*, *Candida*, *The Green Hat*, *The Letter*, and *Dishonored Lady*. In 1931 she became her own manager and produced *The Barretts of Wimpole Street*. This met with great success and was followed by *Lucrece* and *The Alien Corn*. In 1936 she revived Shaw's *St. Joan* and appeared in Maxwell Anderson's *The Wingless Victory*. She was married in 1921 to Guthrie McClintic, who has produced and directed many of her plays.

Coronado, Francisco Vasquez de (1510-1554), Spanish explorer of the southwestern United States. In 1539 he was appointed to lead an expedition to expand the Spanish territory to the north of Mexico and to seek the supposed riches of the new land. With a thousand men Coronado crossed parts of Arizona and New Mexico. His followers were the first white men to see the Grand Canyon; the company wintered at Santa Fe, returning to Mexico the next autumn, disillusioned as to the riches of the northern territories.

Cornwallis, Marquess (1738-1805), commander of the British forces which surrendered to the Americans at Yorktown in 1781, thus ending the War of Independence; was twice Governor-General of India.

Corot, Jean Baptiste (1796-1875), a French landscape painter of great repute.

Coreggio, Antonio Allegri da (1494-1534), the great Italian painter of the Lombard School.

Cortes (or Cortez), Hernando (1485-1547), a Spanish adventurer who earned great renown by conquering Mexico for Spain.

Cortot, Alfred (b. 1877), Swiss pianist and conductor, studied at the Paris Conservatoire and became chorus director at Bayreuth. Conducted the first complete performance in Paris of Wagner's *Ring*.

Cosgrave, William Thomas (b. 1880), member of the Irish parliament, 1922-44; president of the Executive Council of the Irish Free State 1922-32, holding ministerial posts in 1923 and 1924.

Cotton, John (1585-1652), a Puritan clergyman; born in Derby, England, who came to America in 1633, and became a teacher of the first church in Boston. Cotton published nearly fifty books.

Coué, Émile (1857-1926), French psychotherapeutist, an authority on auto-suggestion.

Cousin, Victor (1792-1867), French philosopher who founded what is called the eclectic school of modern philosophy.

Cousins, Samuel, R. A. (1801-1887), the greatest mezzotint engraver of his day, who made plates after Reynolds, Millais, Landseer, and Hogarth.

Coverdale, Miles (1488-1568), English churchman and reformer collaborated with Tyndale in translating the Bible; the Psalms still used in the Prayer Book are from their translation.

Coward, Noel (b. 1899), English actor and author of the plays, *Fallen Angels*, *Bitter Sweet*, *Private Lives*, *Cavalcade*, *Tonight at 8:30*, *Blithe Spirit*, and *Nude with Violins*.

Cowper, William (1731-1800), English poet, whose *Task* is one of the great poems of the 18th century.

Crabbe, Rev. George (1754-1832), a poet of rural life and scenes, noted for his faithful pictures, characterization and soundness of his sentiments.

Craig, Edward Gordon (b. 1872), British writer on stagecraft. Has produced many plays in England and the United States.

Crane, Stephen (1871-1900) American novelist and poet, born in Newark, N. J. He was educated at Lafayette College and Syracuse University. After writing *The Red Badge of Courage,* a vivid story of the Civil War, he became a correspondent for the *New York Journal* during the Spanish American War. His works include *Maggie* and *Whilomville Stories.*

Cranmer, Thomas (1489-1556), Archbishop of Canterbury under Henry VIII and Edward VI; was executed for refusing to return to Catholicism.

Crawford, Francis Marion (1854-1909), American novelist, author of *A Roman Singer, Saracinesca,* and *Saint Ilario.*

Crawford, William Harris (1772-1834), American statesman; born in Amherst County, Va. In 1783 he settled in Columbia County, Ga.; was elected to the State Senate in 1807; appointed Minister to France in 1813. Two years later he was appointed Secretary of War and the next year became Secretary of the Treasury.

Cripps, Sir Richard Stafford (1889-1952), British Labour statesman, ambassador to the U.S.S.R., 1940-42, cabinet minister under Churchill and Attlee, rising to chancellor of the exchequer in 1947. He wrote *Why This Socialism?* (1934).

Crispi, Francesco (1819-1901), Italian statesman who aided Garibaldi. Was Premier 1887-91 and 1893-96.

Crittenden, John Jordan (1787-1863), American legislator; born in Woodford Co., Ky. In 1817 he was elected to the United States Senate. In 1848 he became governor of Kentucky, and was largely responsible for the Union loyalty of the state during the Civil War.

Croce, Benedetto (1866-1952), Italian philosopher and critic who made an international reputation by his writings on aesthetics and history. He was Minister of Education, 1920-21, and also served in the Italian cabinet after 1944.

Crockett, David (1786-1836), American pioneer, hunter, politician, and humorist; born in Limestone, Tenn. He was a member of Congress from Tennessee; served in the Texas War; and was one of the eccentric characters of the Southwest, about whom numerous stories were told. He wrote his *Autobiography* (1834); *Tour to the North and Down East* (1835); *Sketches and Eccentricities,* etc. He was killed during the siege of the Alamo, Texas, March 16, 1836.

Croesus (died *c.* 546 B. C.), the last king of Lydia (560-546 B.C.), who reigned fourteen years and acquired such immense wealth that his name has ever since been proverbial.

Croker, Richard (1843-1922), American politician; born in Black Rock, Ireland; came to the United States in early life. He was alderman of New York three times and was city chamberlain, 1889-1890. He was at the head of Tammany Hall for several years; and was long the Democratic dictator of New York State and City.

Cromer, Earl of (1841-1917), British diplomat and imperialist, Comptroller General of Egypt, 1883-1907. Under his rule Egypt was lifted from financial difficulty and internal disorder to a condition of prosperity. Author of *Modern Egypt* (1908), and *Ancient and Modern Imperialism* (1910).

Cromwell, Oliver (1599-1658), Lord Protector of England from 1653 to his death. At one time contemplated emigrating to America, but entering Parliament and becoming enthusiastic in the popular cause, obtained recognition as one of the Parliamentary leaders, and ultimately, on the outbreak of the Civil War, became General of the Roundheads, later being installed at the head of the Commonwealth.

Cromwell, Richard (1626-1712), son of the foregoing, and his successor in the Protectorate.

Cronin, Archibald Joseph (b. 1896), Scottish physician and novelist. Author of *Hatter's Castle* (1931), which was followed by other realistic studies of Scottish life, including the *Citadel.*

Crookes, Sir William (1832-1919), British scientist, whose discoveries in optics, chemistry, and electricity have been of the greatest importance. He was the discoverer of thallium and inventor of the radiometer.

Crowder, Enoch Herbert (1859-1932), American army officer; he was graduated from West Point in 1881 and fought in the Indian wars against Geronimo and Sitting Bull; drafted and administered the Selective Service Act during the World War, when he served as provost marshal general. He was appointed the first ambassador to Cuba in 1923, serving until 1927.

Cruickshank, George (1792-1878), British illustrator who for a time illustrated the works of Charles Dickens, and later illustrated numerous works of other novelists.

Cullen, Countee (1903-1946), American Negro poet, born in New York City. His best-known works are *Copper Sun* (1927); *The Ballad of the Brown Girl* (1928); and *One Way to Heaven* (1932), a novel.

Cummings, Bruce Frederick (1889-1919), English zoologist and man of letters. Author of the *Journal of a Disappointed Man.*

Cunninghame-Graham, Robert Bontine (1852-1936), British writer on Spanish-American life.

Curie, Eve (b. 1904), daughter of Pierre and Marie Curie. An ardent advocate of Free France, she wrote *Madame Curie* (1937) and *Journey Among Warriors* (1943).

Curie, Pierre (1859-1906), and **Curie, Marie** (1867-1934), the discoverers of radium. M. Curie was a Frenchman, but Mme. Curie was a Pole; they were both indefatigable scientific investigators. Shared the Nobel Prize for physics 1903, while their daughter, Mme. Irene Joliot-Curie, shared with her husband, M. Joliot, the 1935 Nobel Prize for chemistry, awarded for their researches in radio-activity.

Curzon of Kedleston, Marquess (1859-1925), British colonial administrator and statesman. Entered Parliament in 1886, and having filled numerous minor offices became Viceroy of India.

Cushing, Caleb (1800-1879), American statesman, born in Salisbury, Mass. He served in Congress from 1835 to 1843; was sent to China as a commissioner to secure a commercial treaty. Cushing served as Attorney General in Pierce's cabinet, and led the Democratic group that nominated Breckenridge. After the secession of the Confederate States he became a Republican and supported Lincoln.

Custer, George Armstrong (1839-1876), American army officer, born in New Rumley, Ohio. He was graduated from West Point in 1861; was on McClellan's staff during the Peninsular campaign and in 1863 led a brigade of Michigan cavalry. His brigade distinguished itself against Stuart at Gettysburg, and in 1863 he aided Sheridan in his raids. In 1864 he was made commander of the 3rd division of cavalry and won the battle of Woodstock. Custer took part in the Indian campaigns and in 1874 led the expedition to the Black Hills. The expedition discovered gold and stirred up hostility among the Sioux. In the ensuing campaign against the Indians Custer found an Indian encampment at Little Big Horn, Montana, and decided to attack. He had a force of 264 men and the Indians numbered about 4,000. Custer and his band were annihilated on June 25, 1876. He wrote *My Life on the Plains,* (1874).

Cuvier, Georges Léopold, Baron (1769-1832), a French naturalist who founded a system of classification in zoology, and originated the science of comparative anatomy.

Cuyp, Albert (1605-1691), a famous Dutch landscape painter.

Cymbeline (died *c.* A. D. 43), was the father of Caractacus and is remembered chiefly as the central figure of one of Shakespeare's plays.

Cyprian, St., ecclesiastic of the 3rd century, who wrote treatises on Christian doctrine.

Cyrus the Great (*c.* 600-529 B. C.), founded the Persian monarchy in the 5th century B.C., conquered Media, Assyria, Babylon, parts of India, Arabia, and Asia Minor, and was eventually slain in battle.

D

Daguerre, Louis Jacques Mandé (1789-1851), French artist who invented the earliest photographic process, and then devoted himself to scene-painting.

Daimler, Gottlieb (1834-1890), inventor with Otto of the Otto gas engine, and in his later years eminent as the developer of the automobile.

Daladier, Edouard (b. 1884), Premier of France from April 1938 to March 1940. Entered the Chamber of Deputies 1919, and held office in several ministries, including those of Herriot, Painlevé, and Chautemps and served under Chautemps as Minister for National Defense Jan.—April 1938, after which he became Premier of France for the third time.

Dalin, Olof von (1708-1763), a Swedish poet and historian; "father of modern Swedish literature." The influence of the study of the French classical drama is seen in his epic poem, *Sweden's Liberties*, his drama *Brynhilda* and his comedy, *The Jealous Man.* His *History of the Kingdom of Sweden* (4 vols.), to the death of Charles IX, is important.

Dalton, John (1766-1844), English chemist and mathematician who in 1810 published his *New System of Chemical Philosophy,* in which the atomic theory was first propounded.

Damien, Father (Joseph de Veuster) (1840-1889), Belgian missionary who took spiritual charge of the Hawaiian leper colony of Molokai and remained there until in 1889 he himself was stricken with leprosy and died.

Damocles, the flatterer and favorite of Dionysius of Syracuse. The legend related by Cicero concerning him is that one day he went to a banquet, where he found himself sitting beneath an unsheathed sword suspended by a single hair. Hence the familiar simile, "the sword of Damocles." The incident is referred to as of the first half of the 4th century B.C.

Dampier, William (1652-1712), an English navigator. During many years of active service in privateers and trading vessels he several times visited the South Seas; the results of his observations were published as *A Voyage Round the World.*

Damrosch, Walter Johannes (1862-1950), an American musician; born in Breslau, Germany. He succeeded his father as conductor of the New York Oratorio Society, which was founded by the elder Damrosch. Walter Damrosch himself founded the Wagnerian Opera Co; was elected conductor of the New York Philharmonic Society in 1902. His publications include two operas: *Cyrano,* and *The Scarlet Letter;* and a book, *My Musical Life,* (1923).

Dana, Richard Henry, Jr. (1815-1882), American lawyer and author; born in Cambridge, Mass. He entered Harvard College in 1832, but being compelled by an affection of the eyes to suspend his studies, he made a voyage to California. This voyage he described in *Two Years Before the Mast* (1840). He later completed his law course and was admitted to the Boston bar. In 1841 he published a book on seamanship, a useful dictionary of sea terms, and valuable information on maritime law. In 1859-1860 he made a voyage round the world. He was counsel for the United States in the proceedings against Jefferson Davis for treason, 1867-1868.

Daniels, Josephus (1862-1948), American statesman and editor; born in Washington, N. C. He was prominent in national and state politics as editor of the *Raleigh State Chronicle* (1885-1894) and the *News and Observer* since 1894. He was Secretary of the Navy under President Wilson (1913-1921) and was appointed Ambassador to Mexico in 1933 by President Roosevelt.

D'Annunzio, Gabriele (1863-1938), Italian poet, dramatist and novelist. In Sept. 1919 he led an unofficial raid on Fiume and seized the port and town. When the Treaty of Rapallo was signed in 1920, D'Annunzio refused to recognize it and declared war against Italy. Fiume was attacked and D'Annunzio, after a short resistance, surrendered.

Dante Alighieri (1265-1321), the greatest of Italian poets, whose *La Divina Comedia* has been translated into many languages.

Danton, Georges Jacques (1759-1794), a member of the National Convention at the period of the first French Revolution. Was made President of the Committee of Public Safety, but Robespierre attacked and supplanted him, Danton being consigned to the guillotine shortly afterward.

Darius was the name borne by three Persian kings. The first reigned from 521 to 485 B.C., and was defeated by the Greeks at Marathon. The second was a natural son of Artaxerxes Longimanus and, having obtained the crown by the murder of his brother, reigned from 424 to 405 B.C. The third Darius was the last of the namesakes, reigning only from 336 to 331 B.C., when Alexander the Great invaded his kingdom and defeated him in two great battles. Darius was soon afterward assassinated.

Darnley, Earl of (1545-1567), was married to Mary Queen of Scots—as her second husband—in 1565. Two years later, after Mary had entered into an intrigue with Bothwell, he was murdered.

Darrow, Clarence Seward (1857-1938), American lawyer. He practiced in Chicago for more than 50 years, and was the foremost criminal advocate in the United States for more than half that period. Appeared as counsel for the defense in a number of important cases, among them the Debs Strike Case (1895), the Macnamara Case at Los Angeles (1911), the Loeb-Leopold Case in Chicago, and the Dayton Monkey Trial (1925).

Darwin, Charles Robert (1809-1882), British scientist, whose *Origin of Species* first clearly formulated and elaborated the theory of evolution. His first work (1837) described a five years' cruise in the *Beagle*, which the British Government had sent out for scientific purposes. His *Origin of Species* appeared in 1859, and though defended and supported by the scientific thought of the time, was attacked by theologians. In 1871 Darwin issued his *Descent of Man*, a still further elaboration of the evolution theory. His other principal works were *The Expression of Emotion in Man and Animals* (1872), *Insectivorous Plants* (1875), *Different Forms of Flowers* (1877), and *Worms* (1881). He was buried in Westminster Abbey.

Darwin, Erasmus (1731-1802), grandfather of Charles Darwin; was a physician and a poet of considerable repute.

Daudet, Alphonse (1840-1897), French humorist and novelist, all of whose works have been translated into English.

Daumier, Honoré (1808-1879), French painter and caricaturist. He contributed cartoons to the magazine *Caricature* in which he ridiculed the bourgeois class and the corrupt practices of the government. Later he drew a long series of pictures making fun of the society and manners of his time. Daumier is also well known for his paintings, especially his landscapes.

David, Jacques Louis (1748-1825), a French painter of classic and historic subjects.

Davidson, Jo (1883-1952), American sculptor. Among his busts of prominent men—many of them of World War I fame—is one of Robert M. LaFollette, in the Rotunda of the National Capitol in Washington. His tablet in memory of John P. Mitchell is in Columbia University.

Davies, Arthur Bowen (1862-1928), American painter of portraits and landscapes, was one of the leaders of the American romantic school. The international art exhibition in New York in 1913 was due in large part to his efforts, when the United States gained its first introduction to the cubists, futurists, and post-impressionists. "Girdle of Ares", "Night Overture", "The Place of the Mother," and "Leda and the Dioscuri" are among his important works.

Davis, Jefferson (1808-1889), American statesman; born in Abbeville, Christian Co., Ky. He was graduated from the United States Military Academy in 1828 and was appointed a second lieutenant of infantry; served on the Northwestern frontier during the Black Hawk War of 1831-1832. In June, 1835, he resigned his commission and retired to a cotton plantation in Mississippi. In 1845 he was elected a Representative to Congress; served in the Mexican War, greatly distinguishing himself at Monterey and Buena Vista, being severely wounded in the latter battle. In 1847 he was chosen to fill a vacancy in the United States Senate and was re-elected in 1850. In 1853 he was appointed Secretary of War by President Pierce and in 1857 was again elected to the United States Senate, where he took a prominent place among the Southern leaders. The Confederate Congress, at Montgomery, Ala., chose him President, under the Provisional Constitution, on Feb. 9, 1861. Davis continued to be President of the Confederacy until his capture at Irwinsville, Ga., May 10, 1865. He was conveyed to Fort Monroe and indicted by the Grand Jury of the District of Columbia for treason; after two years' imprisonment he was released on bail at the instance of the government; but was included in the General Amnesty Act of Congress of Dec. 25, 1868. In 1871 he had a public reception at Atlanta, Ga., and made a speech in which he reaffirmed his adhesion to the doctrine of state sovereignty. The last years of his life were spent at Beauvoir, Miss.; he died in New Orleans, La. He wrote a narrative of the stirring events of 1861-1865 in *The Rise and Fall of the Confederate Government* (1881).

Davis, John (1550-1605), one of the great Elizabethan explorers and discoverer of Davis Strait, the channel between the Atlantic and Arctic Oceans on the west of Greenland. Invented the backstaff, or Davis' quadrant.

Davy, Sir Humphry (1778-1829), British chemist, the inventor of the safety-lamp. Was the first to employ the electric current in chemical decomposition and discovered nitrous oxide, or laughing gas.

Dawes, Charles Gates (1865-1951), United States Ambassador to Great Britain, 1929-32. Vice-President, United States, 1925-29. Originated the Dawes plan of Reparations. Member American Delegation to London Naval Conference, 1930.

Debs, Eugene Victor (1855-1926), American socialist; born in Terre Haute, Ind. He received a common school education and became a locomotive fireman. He was elected to the Indiana Legislature in 1885 and was later an official of the Brotherhood of Locomotive Firemen, and, from 1893 to 1897, president of the American Railway Union. He conducted the strike of 1893 in Chicago and was later jailed, although he pleaded innocence of any crime and requested a jury trial. He then became leader of the Socialist party, being nominated for President of the United States five times, twice polling more than a million votes. He was imprisoned at Atlanta for his pacifist speeches during the World War, but was pardoned by President Harding. He was the author of various books and pamphlets dealing with socialism and labor problems: e.g., *Liberty; Unionism and Socialism, a Plea for Both; The Children of the Poor.*

Debussy, Claude Achille (1862-1918), French composer, whose work marks an epoch in musical history.

Decamps, Alexandre Gabriel (1803-1860), French painter who produced numerous historical paintings.

Decatur, Stephen (1779-1820), an American naval officer; born in Sinnepuxent, Md. He was of French descent, and obtained a midshipman's warrant in 1798. He saw some service against the French and was commissioned lieutenant in the following year; and at the close of the French War in 1801 was one of the 36 lieutenants retained in the reduced strength of the navy. In the war with Tripoli (1801-1805) he gained great distinction. His brilliant achievement of boarding and burning the captured *Philadelphia* in the harbor of Tripoli and then escaping under the fire of 141 guns Nelson pronounced "the most daring act of the age." For this he received his commission as captain in 1804; in 1810 he was appointed commodore. In the war with England in 1812 he captured the frigate *Macedonian*, but in 1814 he was obliged to surrender, after a resistance that cost him a fourth of his crew, to four British frigates. In 1815 he chastised the Algerines for their piracy and compelled the Bey to declare the American flag inviolable. He obtained indemnities for violating treaty stipulations from the Bey of Tunis and the Pasha of Tripoli. He was appointed a Navy Commissioner in 1816, and was killed in a duel by Commodore James Barron near Bladensburg, Md., March 22, 1820.

Decius, Caius Messius Quintius Trajanus (201-251), Roman Emperor from 249 to 251, notorious for his cruel persecution of the Christians.

Deeping, George Warwick (1877-1950), British novelist, author of *Sorrell and Son* and others.

De Falla, Manuel (1876-1946), Spanish composer, best known in the United States for his enchanting ballet *The Three-Cornered Hat,* which was one of Diaghilev's greatest post-war successes.

Defoe, Daniel (1660-1731), English novelist. He became a political writer and novelist, obtaining world-wide fame by his *Robinson Crusoe,* written when he was nearly sixty years of age.

Delacroix, Ferdinand (1799-1863), a French painter, one of the leaders of the romantic school.

De la Mare, Walter John (1873-1956), English poet and story writer, author of *Songs of Childhood, The Listeners, Peacock Pie, Memoirs of a Midget,* and *The Burning Glass.*

Delaroche, Paul (Hippolyte) (1797-1856), an eminent French historical painter.

Delcassé, Théophile (1852-1923), French statesman, entered the Chamber in 1889, and in 1893 was Under Secretary for the Colonies. In 1898 was appointed to the Foreign Office, which position he filled with great success. In 1903 he accompanied President Loubet on a visit to England. Resigned in 1905 on the Morocco difficulty. Ambassador to Russia, 1913, and in 1914-15 was Foreign Minister again.

Delibes, Clément Philibert Léo (1836-1891), a French composer of much graceful and refined music, including two or three operas, numerous operettas, and some exquisite ballets.

Delius, Frederick, (1862-1934), was a prominent English composer.

Democritus (460-357 B. C.), the Greek philosopher to whom the conception of the atomic theory is attributed. His cheerful disposition led to his being styled "the laughing philosopher," and tradition tells that he put out his eyes in order to prevent distraction from his speculations.

De Morgan, William Frend (1839-1917), son of Augustus de Morgan (1806-71), was engaged in artistic pursuits until 1906, when he wrote *Joseph Vance.* His later novels include *Alice-for-Short* (1907), *Somehow Good* (1908), and *When Ghost Meets Ghost* (1914).

Demosthenes (385-322 B. C.), the famous Grecian orator, statesman and warrior. Sixty-one of his orations were preserved, and are regarded as perhaps the finest examples of their kind.

Denis, St., the patron saint of France, over whose grave the abbey of St. Denis was erected. He lived in the 3rd century.

De Quincey, Thomas (1785-1859), a British essayist and critic, the friend of Coleridge, Wordsworth, and Southey. His *Confessions of an Opium-eater* is an English classic.

De Reszke, Jean (1853-1925), and **De Reszke, Edouard** (1856-1917), Polish operatic singers, the first a tenor, the second a baritone, who achieved fame by their singing.

Descartes, René (1596-1650), the famous French philosopher, mathematician, and author, whose idealistic philosophy, the basis of which is summed up in the words "Cogito, ergo sum" ("I think, therefore I exist"), has been important in modern times.

Desmoulins, Lucie Simplice Camille Benoît (1760-1794), one of the fiercest of the French Revolutionary leaders, from the destruction of the Bastille to the early days of the Terror was unflagging in his onslaughts upon the aristocrats and the priesthood. He incurred the displeasure of Robespierre, however, and was sent to the guillotine along with Danton.

De Soto, Fernando (1499?-1542), discoverer of the Mississippi, assisted Pizarro in the conquest of Peru. Charles V then gave him permission to conquer Florida at his own expense and appointed him governor of Cuba; he anchored in the bay of Espiritu Santo (now Tampa Bay) on May 25, 1539, and for three years, harassed by hostile Indians, his ever decreasing company continued their toilsome march over a route that cannot now be clearly traced. In 1541 the Mississippi was reached and crossed, and the third winter was spent on the Washita River. Returning to the Mississippi in the spring, De Soto, worn out by disappointments, died of a fever on its banks, in June, 1542.

De Valera, Eamon (b. New York, 1882), Sinn Fein President of Ireland until establishment of the Irish Free State. President of Executive Council and minister for external affairs, 1932-38; prime minister, 1937-48, 1951-54, again in 1957.

Dewar, Sir James (1842-1923), Scottish chemist. In 1888, with Sir Frederick Abel, invented cordite. He performed many experiments with gases, and in 1891 succeeded in obtaining liquid oxygen. Introduced thermos flasks into science and industry.

Dewey, George (1837-1917), an American naval officer; born in Montpelier, Vt. After the Civil War he served both ashore and at sea, rising to the command of the Asiatic squadron in 1898. With orders to "capture or destroy the Spanish squadron," he entered Manila Bay. He sank, burned, or captured all the Spanish ships in the bay, silenced and destroyed three land batteries, and held the bay until the city was taken, May 1, 1898. In recognition of this feat he was made Admiral of the Navy, a rank created by act of Congress for the special purpose of honoring him.

Dewey, John D. (1859-1952), American philisopher, psychologist and educator, who after holding professorships at the Universities of Minnesota, Michigan and Chicago, where he was also director of the School of Education, was appointed professor of philosophy at Columbia University. A follower of William James, he became well known as an adherent of pragmatism. Author of *Psychology, How We Think, Democracy and Education, The School and Society, Reconstruction in Philosophy, Human Nature and Conduct,* etc.

Dewey, Thomas Edmund (b. 1902), American politician. Governor of New York for three terms beginning in 1942, he was twice (1944 and 1948) the Republican candidate for President.

Diaz, José de la Cruz Porfirio (1830-1915), Mexican soldier and statesman, was born in Oaxaca. After serving in the war with the United States (1847-48) he helped to overthrow Santa Anna (1857). During the French occupation he was a leader of the native opposition, and two days after the execution of Maximilian entered Mexico City, and proclaimed martial law, June 21, 1867, delivering the presidency to Juarez. A revolution in 1877 resulted in Diaz' election to the presidency, which office he held, except for a short interlude, until 1910, when he was forced to flee from the country. He died in Paris.

Dickens, Charles (1812-1870), the most popular British novelist of the 19th century. Possessed of incredible energy, Dickens at 24 wrote a humorous masterpiece, *The Pickwick Papers,* and for the rest of his life wrote a new novel almost every year, growing in ability, artistic stature, and popularity with each new book. Although severely criticized for his blatant melodrama and saccharine sentimentality, Dickens, through such novels as *Oliver Twist, Nicholas Nickelby,* and *Bleak House,* did much to bring about censure of social and economic conditions hitherto regarded as necessary evils, and immeasurably enriched literature through the creation of such characters as "Scrooge," "Micawber," "David Copperfield," "Little Nell," "Tiny Tim," "Fagin," and many others.

Dickinson, Emily (1830-1886), American poet, born in Amherst, Mass. A recluse, her poetry did not become known until after her death, when she acquired a critical following which has steadily increased. Among her works are, *The Single Hound,* and *Complete Poems.*

Dickinson, John (1732-1808), American political writer and statesman; born in Maryland. He was the author of *Letters from a Pennsylvania Farmer to the Inhabitants of the Colonies* (1767), and *Essay on Constitutional Power of Great Britain over the American Colonies.*

Diderot, Denis (1713-1784), the famous French philosopher and editor of the *Encyclopédie.*

Diefenbaker, John George (b. 1895), Canadian Progressive Conservative politician, entered Parliament (1940), became prime minister (1957).

Diesel, Rudolf (1858-1913), German engineer, inventor of the diesel engine.

Dietrich, Marlene (b. 1902), film actress. She began her career under Max Reinhardt in Berlin, and after coming to the United States became famous as a dramatic actress and film star.

Diocletian (A. D. 245-313), Roman Emperor from 284 to 305.

Diogenes (412-322 B.C.), Greek cynic philosopher.

Dionysius. Two of the tyrants of Syracuse bore this name. The first was a great soldier and statesman as well as a poet and philosopher, and lived from c. 430-367 B.C. The second Dionysius was his son and successor, but was of such a cruel disposition that he was driven from the throne and died in obscurity in 343.

Disney, Walter Elias ("Walt") (b. 1901), American cartoonist; creator of the Mickey Mouse cartoons, and the "Silly Symphonies," and producer of many famous juveniles, as *Snow White,* and *Pinocchio.*

Disraeli, Benjamin. *(See Beaconsfield.)*

D'Israeli, Isaac (1766-1848), the father of Benjamin Disraeli, wrote several volumes dealing with authors and their writings. His best-known work is his *Curiosities of Literature.*

Dobson, Henry Austin (1840-1921), British poet, was in the civil service from 1860 to 1901, and was the author of several volumes of society verse and some prose works, dealing with the 18th century.

Dodgson, Charles Lutwidge (1832-1898), British writer and professor of mathematics at Oxford, who under the pseudonym of Lewis Carroll, achieved lasting fame by his *Alice's Adventures in Wonderland,* one of the most delightful books for children ever written.

Dolci, Carlo (1616-1686), Florentine painter, examples of whose madonnas and saints are to be found in most public collections.

Dollfuss, Engelbert (1892-1934), Austrian statesman and chancellor. His regime was notable for its social reforms, diplomatic victories, and resistance to Nazi attempts at overthrowing the government and annexing Austria to the Reich. On July 25, 1934, a group of Nazis seized the Chancellery and assassinated Dollfuss.

Dominic, St. (1170-1221), founder of the Order of Dominicans.

Domitian (Titus Flavius Domitianus Augustus) (52-96), a Roman emperor who aroused the enmity of the people and was finally assassinated.

Donatello (Donato di Niccolò di Betto Bardi) (1386-1466), Italian sculptor of the early Renaissance period.

Donizetti, Gaetano (1798-1848), Italian composer who wrote the music for the operas *Lucia di Lammermoor, La Fille du Régiment, La Favorita,* and others.

Donne, John (1573-1631), a British clergyman and religious writer whose poems are among the best of the later Elizabethan period.

Doré, Gustave (1833-1883), French artist, famous for his scriptural paintings and his illustrations of the works of Dante, Milton, Rabelais, and others.

Dos Passos, John Roderigo (b. 1896), American novelist, born in Chicago. Known primarily as an experimenter with technique through such novels as *U.S.A.* (a trilogy), and *Manhattan Transfer,* Dos Passos is capable of a conventional narrative as is demonstrated by *Three Soldiers* and *Adventures of a Young Man.*

Dostoievsky, Feodor Mikhailovich (1821-1881), born in Russia. Regarded as one of the great writers of all time, Dostoievsky's novels are sprawling and crowded with characters but are at the same time tense and passionate with the religious and ethical issue Dostoievsky recognized as very real. An epileptic, Dostoievsky was arrested for treason just three years after his first book, *Poor Folk,* had made him famous. After his return from Siberia, he entered his most productive period with, among others, *Crime and Punishment, The Idiot,* and *The Brothers Karamazov,* his crowning achievement.

Douglas, Clifford Hugh (1879-1952), British consulting engineer and economist; propounder of the Douglas Social Credit Scheme for solving the problems of under-consumption and unemployment.

Douglas, Norman (1868-1952), English writer. He is best known for his *South Wind,* a tale of Capri. Among his other works are *Three of Them, Goodbye to Western Culture,* and *Looking Backward,* an autobiography.

Douglas, Stephen Arnold (1813-1861), American statesman; born in Brandon, Vt. After a career in Illinois state politics he served in the House of Representatives from 1843 to 1847, and in the Senate from 1847 until his death. In the Lower House he advocated the annexation of Texas, and of Oregon up to 54° 40′ N. lat., and favored the war with Mexico. On the question of slavery he maintained that the people of each territory should decide whether it should be a free state or a slave state; this was known as the doctrine of "popular sovereignty" or "squatter sovereignty." In 1857 he secured the passage of the Kansas-Nebraska Act, which repealed the Missouri Compromise. In 1860 he received the regular Democratic nomination for the Presidency. Douglas obtained 12 electoral and 1,357,-157 popular votes, as against 180 electoral and

1,866,352 popular votes cast for Lincoln. In the early days of the Civil War, he gave Lincoln his unfaltering support.

Douglass, Frederick (1817-1895), American lecturer and journalist; the son of a Negro slave. In 1845 he published his autobiography, and afterwards made a successful lecturing tour in England. In 1871 he was appointed secretary of the commission to Santo Domingo; and United States Minister to Haiti, 1890.

Doumer, Paul (1857-1932), president of the French Republic, 1931-32, assassinated by a Russian fanatic, May 6, 1932.

Doumergue, Gaston (1863-1937), President of the French Republic, 1924-1931; Premier from Feb. to Nov., 1934.

Dowie, John Alexander (1847-1907), founder of a religious cult. In 1896 he organized the Christian Catholic Church in Zion, placing himself at its head.

Doyle, Sir Arthur Conan (1859-1930), British novelist who reached the point of highest popularity in his detective stories, in which "Sherlock Holmes" was the central figure. Began life as a physician, turned to fiction, and in his later years became an advocate of Spiritualism, which he treated in his *History of Spiritualism.* Among his fictional works are *A Study in Scarlet* and *The White Company.*

D'Oyly Carte, Richard (1844-1901), English theatrical manager, associated with the production of the Gilbert and Sullivan comic operas. The D'Oyly Carte Opera Companies played Gilbert and Sullivan all over the world.

Drake, Sir Francis (c. 1540-1596), the great English admiral of Queen Elizabeth's time, who made many adventurous voyages, bent partly on discovery and partly on plunder. He was a leading figure under Lord Howard in the attack on and destruction of the Spanish Armada in 1588.

Draper, John William (1811-1882), American chemist, born in Liverpool, he emigrated to America in 1831, and in 1841 was one of the founders of the Medical School of New York University.

Dreiser, Theodore (1871-1945), American author, and one of the great writers of definitely American literature, whose novels of American life are written in vigorous prose. Among his better-known works are *Sister Carrie, Jenny Gerhardt,* and *An American Tragedy.*

Dressler, Marie (1869-1934), Canadian actress, her real name being Leila Koerber. She became famous as a portrayer of comedy and pathos on the screen and made many successful appearances.

Dreyfus, Lt. Col. Alfred (1859-1935), a French officer, condemned by a military secret tribunal on a charge of divulging secrets in 1894 to a foreign power, and condemned to imprisonment for life on Devil's Island in French Guiana. At a sensational new trial in 1899 he was again found guilty, and sentenced to a mitigated term of incarceration for ten years; but strenuous efforts on his behalf secured a pardon later. In 1906, at a third public trial, he was entirely exonerated and reinstated in the army, with the rank of major, and made a Chevalier of the Legion of Honor.

Drinkwater, John (1882-1937), British dramatist and poet. His plays *Abraham Lincoln* and *Oliver Cromwell* had great success.

Dryden, John (1631-1700), one of the most vigorous and prolific of English poets and writers, and a popular dramatist. His translation of Virgil ranks with Pope's translation of the *Iliad.* He became poet laureate in 1670.

Du Barry, Marie Jeanne Bécu, Comtesse (1746-1793), the favorite who exercised great influence over Louis XV, but after his death, and the outbreak of the Revolution, took refuge in England. On her return to Paris in 1793, she was arrested and guillotined.

Du Chaillu, Paul Belloni (1835-1903), a French explorer and writer who wrote many valuable books of African travels, his studies of the gorilla being especially interesting.

Dumas, Alexandre (1802-1870), the famous French novelist, and dramatist, who published more volumes than any other man of his time, the greater part of them of high merit. His thrilling story *Monte Cristo* is one of the great novels of the nineteenth century.

Du Maurier, George Louis Palmella Busson (1834-1896), author of the novels *Peter Ibbetson, Trilby,* and the *Martian.*

Dunbar, Paul Laurence (1872-1906), American author; born of Negro parents in Dayton, O. His works include *Oak and Ivy, Lyrics of Lowly Life* and *The Uncalled,* a novel.

Dunne, Finley Peter (1867-1936), American humorist. He was city editor successively for the *Chicago Times, Evening Post* and *Evening Journal* before he gained fame as a humorous columnist and critic of men and affairs as Martin Dooley of the *Times-Herald.* His series appeared in book form in several volumes.

Dunning, William Archibald (1857-1922), American historian. After studying in Berlin he returned to Columbia as professor of history and remained there the rest of his life. He is best known for his *History of Political Theories* (1920), *Essays on the Civil War and Reconstruction* (1898), and his *British Empire and the United States* (1914).

Duns Scotus, Johannes (c. 1265-1308), a famous scholastic, born at Duns, in Berwickshire, and became a Franciscan friar and theological professor at Oxford. He was the great doctrinal opponent of Thomas Aquinas.

Dunsany, Lord (1878-1957), Irish dramatist and author of a number of colorful, whimsical and deeply imaginative novels, as well as short stories, and many plays.

Du Pont, Eleuthère Irénée (1771-1834), an American manufacturer; a son of Pierre Samuel Du Pont de Nemours; born in Paris. He came to the United States in 1799, soon afterward erected his first powder works on the Brandywine River, near Wilmington, Del., the beginning of E. I. Du Pont de Nemours & Co. The firm is internationally known, and has supplied vast quantities of explosives to the government since the War of 1812; notably during the World War.

Du Pont de Nemours, Pierre Samuel (1739-1817), a French economist and statesman. In 1782 and 1783, with Dr. Hutton, the English agent, he negotiated the basis of the treaty by which the independence of the United States of America was acknowledged. Besides various political treatises he is likewise the author of a French translation of the first three cantos of the *Orlando Furioso.* He died near Wilmington, Del.

Dürer, Albrecht (1471-1528), the great German painter and engraver, and friend of Luther. Of Nuremberg birth, he may be regarded as the founder of the German school and the inventor of etching.

Duse, Eleonora (1859-1924), an Italian tragedienne of world-wide reputation.

Dvořák, Antonin (1841-1904), the eminent Czech composer. Combined with a striking originality, his compositions show fine musical qualities.

E

Eadmer (c. 1060-1124), was the name of an English monk and historian, who lived in the latter part of the 11th century.

Eakins, Thomas (1844-1916), American portrait painter and sculptor; studied painting at the Pennsylvania Academy of Fine Arts; studied further under the painters Gérôme and Léon Bonnat and the sculptor A. A. Dumont in Paris. He is known chiefly for his realistic paintings, notably the large canvas, "The Surgical Clinic of Professor Gross," at Jefferson Medical College in Philadelphia.

Earhart, Amelia (Mrs. G. P. Putman) (1898-1937), famous American airwoman. The first woman to fly the Atlantic from Newfoundland to Burryport, Wales, June 18, 1928. Left, with Capt. Noonan as navigator, Miami, Florida, on June 1st to fly round the world and after leaving Lae, New Guinea, on July 2nd, was not heard of again.

Eastman, George (1854-1932), American inventor of the roll photographic film and the Kodak camera. He amassed a vast fortune and during his lifetime gave $60,000,000 for educational endowments, especially to the University of Rochester, where he had been educated, and the Eastman School of Music.

Eastman, Max (b. 1883), American poet, author and editor, born in Canandaigua, N. Y., Jan. 4, 1883. He was educated at Williams College and taught later at Columbia. He was editor of *The Masses* from 1913 to 1917, and of *The Liberator* from 1918 to 1922. His works include poetry, essays, and a novel, including *Enjoyment of Poetry*, his first book (1913); and *Enjoyment of Laughter* (1936).

Ebert, Friedrich (1871-1925), leader of the German Social Democratic party from 1916; chancellor of Germany from Nov. 9, 1918, and president of the German Republic from 1919 until his death.

Eddington, Sir Arthur Stanley (1882-1944), became Plumian professor of astronomy, Cambridge, 1913; Director of the Cambridge Observatory since 1914. Author of *The Nature of the Physical World* and other scientific works.

Eddy, Mrs. Mary Baker (1821-1910), founder of the religion which she named Christian Science, and of the Church of Christ, Scientist. Author of the Christian Science textbook, *Science and Health with Key to the Scriptures* (1875).

Eden, Sir Robert Anthony (b. 1897), British statesman. Elected to Parliament in 1923, he served in various posts, becoming under secretary for foreign affairs (1931) and minister for League of Nations affairs (1935). Eden resigned his post of foreign secretary (1935-38) in opposition to the appeasement of Mussolini. In 1940 he was named secretary of war and then foreign secretary. With the return of the Conservatives to power in 1951, Eden again became foreign secretary, and upon Churchill's resignation in 1955, he became prime minister. Eden himself resigned in 1957 following the disastrous Suez Canal conflict during his ministry, and after a period of ill health.

Edison, Thomas Alva (1847-1931), American inventor. As a boy he interested himself in electrical problems. He established himself in New York in 1869 and invented an improved printing telegraph. In 1876 he set up an elaborate laboratory and factory at Menlo Park, New Jersey, where he made many startling inventions, including a system of duplex telegraphy, afterwards improved into quadruplex and sextuplex transmission, the phonograph, and a method of preparing carbon filaments for the electric lamp. Edison patented more than 1300 inventions.

Edward the Confessor (c. 1004-1066), Anglo-Saxon king of England, who immediately preceded, save for the brief reign of Harold, the Norman Conquest. He was a religious-minded mystic, and was canonized in 1161.

Edward I (1239-1307), was king of England from 1272 to 1307. Took part in the Crusades, completed the conquest of Wales and overcame Scottish opposition.

Edward III (1312-1377), was one of the ablest of English kings who, although much taken up with long and bitter wars with France and Scotland, did much for the commercial interests of the nation.

Edward IV (1442-1483), king of England, attempted unsuccessfully to regain the lost English possessions in France. He entered into trading treaties with the commercial nations of Europe which were of benefit to his people.

Edward VI (1537-1553), king of England, succeeded his father, Henry VIII, when in his tenth year and died in his sixteenth year. The Reformation, first under the Regency of Somerset and later of Northumberland, made considerable progress during his brief reign.

Edward VII (1841-1910), king of England from 1901 to 1910, succeeded to the throne on the death of Queen Victoria. Edward VII was a powerful factor in the preservation of the peace of Europe, his friendly intercourse with the heads of the French, German, and other nations earning for him the title of "Edward the Peacemaker."

Edward VIII (b. 1894), succeeded to the throne on the death of his father, George V, Jan. 20, 1936; Prince of Wales 1911-36. Abdicated in favor of his brother, the Duke of York, Dec. 10, 1936, and was created Duke of Windsor.

Edwards, Jonathan (1703-1758), American theologian; born in East Windsor, Conn. After taking his degree in 1720, Edwards remained nearly two years at Yale, preparing for the ministry. After more than 23 years in a Northampton church he accepted a call to serve as a missionary among the Indians at Stockbridge, Mass., where he remained six years. Here he composed his famous works on the *Freedom of the Will* and on *Original Sin*. In 1757 he was chosen president of the College of New Jersey, now Princeton University.

Eggleston, Edward (1837-1902), an American author. He chose the ministry as a profession, but his fame rests upon his novels. His best fiction was based upon life in southern Indiana in pioneer days, while as a historian he made a specialty of American subjects. His works include *The Hoosier Schoolmaster*, *The Circuit Rider*, *The Hoosier Schoolboy*, and *The Beginners of a Nation*.

Ehrlich, Paul (1854-1915), German scientist; studied at Breslau, Strassburg, Freiburg and

Leipzig. By experiments on animals he formulated theories which are the basis of modern knowledge of the nature of toxins and antitoxins. His researches on dyes revealed the potentialities of chemotherapy, the treatment of disease with specific chemicals, and led to his discovery of "606," an arsenical compound also known as salvarsan, the first effective and practical drug to be used in the treatment of syphilis. This was the 606th compound tested by Ehrlich in his laborious search for an antisyphilitic drug, hence its name.

Einstein, Albert (1879-1955), American physicist, born at Ulm, Germany, of Jewish parents. His family emigrated to Italy in 1894, and he went from there to Switzerland to attend the University of Zurich. His *Electrodynamics of Moving Bodies* set forth his special theory of relativity as a means to solve the paradoxes of the Michelson-Morley experiment of 1905, and in 1913 he was invited to lecture before the Prussian Academy of Science. In 1921 he received the Nobel Prize for physics. His *Toward a Unified Field Theory* aroused keen scientific interest in 1929. A refugee from the Hitler regime, he came to the United States in 1933, accepted a chair at Princeton's Institute for Advanced Study, and became a citizen in 1940. His "Unified Field Theory," published as an appendix to the third edition of his *Meaning of Relativity* in 1950, was hailed as a development of as great importance as his original theory of relativity.

Eisenhower, Dwight David (b. 1890), American military and political leader, the thirty-fourth president of the United States. Educated at West Point, he served in World War I and saw duty in the Philippines, 1935-40. Made a brigadier general in 1941, he rose rapidly during World War II, becoming Supreme Commander of the North African and Italian campaigns, and later of the Allied Expeditionary Force in Europe. He was made a five-star general in 1944. After service as Army chief of staff (1945-48), he became president of Columbia University. He returned to the army in 1950 as commander of the forces of the North Atlantic Treaty nations. In 1952 he resigned this post to become the Republican presidential candidate. He was inaugurated in January, 1953, and was reelected in 1956. He attended the Geneva summit conference in 1955.

Elgar, Sir Edward (1857-1934), British conductor and composer of *Dream of Gerontius, Pomp and Circumstance*, and *The Apostles*.

Eliot, Charles William (1834-1926), an American educator, was born in Boston. He graduated from Harvard in 1853. In 1869 he became president of Harvard, which from that time entered upon an unprecedented period of development, reconstructing its system and broadening its methods. The introduction of the elective system by President Eliot had marked influence on American education. He resigned Nov. 4, 1908. From 1914 to 1915 he was president of the American Association for the Advancement of Science. His publications include: *American Contributions to Civilization, and Other Essays* (1897); *Educational Reform* (1898); *The Durable Satisfactions of Life* (1910).

Eliot, George (1819-1880), the pen name of Mary Ann Evans, who produced some of the most memorable novels of the 19th century, including *Adam Bede, The Mill on the Floss, Silas Marner, Middlemarch*, and *Daniel Deronda*.

Eliot, Thomas Stearns (b. 1888), American poet and critic, born at St. Louis, Mo. He was graduated from Harvard in 1909 and studied at Oxford and the Sorbonne. In 1927 he became an English citizen. His *Poems* (1920) were considered among the best of the decade. His critical writings include *Homage to John Dryden* (1924); and *For Lancelot Andrewes* (1928). His play, *Murder in the Cathedral*, was presented and published in 1936.

Elizabeth (1533-1603), queen of England, came to the throne in 1558 at the age of twenty-five and reigned forty-five years. The defeat of the Spanish Armada, the execution of Mary Stuart, the naval supremacy of England, the extension of the British colonies, the glory of a great new literature of which Shakespeare was the brightest ornament, are features associated with her reign.

Elizabeth II (b. 1926), queen of Great Britain after the death of her father, King George VI, in 1952. She and her husband, the Duke of Edinburgh, have two children, Prince Charles, Duke of Cornwall (b. 1948), and Princess Anne (b. 1950).

Ellis, Havelock (1859-1939), English author. He wrote, *Studies in the Psychology of Sex, Sex in Relation to Society*, and *The Dance of Life*.

Elman, Mischa (b. 1891), one of the world's greatest violinists, born in Russia, who became a naturalized citizen of the United States in 1920.

Emerson, Ralph Waldo (1803-1882), American essayist and philosopher, was born in Boston. He entered Harvard in 1817, graduated in 1821, and taught for three years in his brother's school. Finding the work uncongenial, he entered the theological school at Cambridge, and became in 1829 pastor of the Old North Church, Boston. He was popular with his congregation, but decided in 1832 that he could no longer agree with its members about the validity of the sacrament, and left the pulpit. His first published essay, *Nature* (1836), contains the nucleus of his philosophy—his belief in the essential goodness of man, in the soundness of his intuition and instincts as guides to living, thinking, and feeling. Emerson became widely known as a lecturer. There clustered about him in Concord a group of men and women who called themselves "Transcendentalists"; Emerson, although he edited their periodical, *The Dial*, for two years, did not identify himself with them or with their experiment in communal living at Brook Farm. In 1847 he made a second trip to Europe, where he was cordially received by Carlyle and others. His best known books include: *Essays* (1840 and 1842); *Addresses and Lectures* (1849); *Representative Men* (1850); *English Traits* (1856); *The Conduct of Life* (1860); *Society and Solitude* (1870).

Emmet, Robert (1778-1803), the enthusiastic youth who led the rebellion in Ireland in 1803 and was tried and executed in the same year for treason. He is one of Ireland's patriot heroes.

Engels, Friedrich (1820-1895), German socialist; the son of a wealthy manufacturer. He wrote *The Working Classes in England*. He is best known as the friend, colleague, and disciple of Karl Marx, with whom he collaborated on *The Communist Manifesto*, and as the author of works on the family, and the development of socialism. After 1869 he lived mainly in London.

Ennius, Quintus (239-169 B. C.), the Roman epic poet and friend of Scipio Africanus the Elder.

Epictetus of Hierapolis (c. 100 A. D.), Stoic philosopher; a moral teacher of great repute and influence.

Epicurus (342-270 B. C.), founder of the Epicurean philosophy, which taught that virtue leads to happiness.

Epstein, Jacob (b. 1880), prominent sculptor, was born in New York of Russian-Polish parents. His work includes the "Hudson Memorial," "Rima," "Day," and "Night".

Erasmus, Desiderius (1466-1536), Dutch philosopher and scholar; at the Reformation he refused to abandon Catholicism. Author of *In Praise of Folly*, *The Manual of the Christian Knight*, etc.; publisher of the first complete edition of Aristotle.

Ericson, John (1803-1889), Swedish engineer who competed with George Stephenson in the first trial of locomotives. Later he settled in the United States and devoted himself with much success to marine engineering. He built the iron-clad "Monitor," used by the Union Navy during the Civil War.

Erskine, John (1879-1951), American author and educator, born in New York City. He was graduated in 1901 from Columbia University and in 1916 he was made a professor of English. He wrote several volumes of poetry and edited some of the classics. He is best known for his novels, such as *The Private Life of Helen of Troy* and *Adam and Eve*. His more serious works include *The Literary Discipline*, *Democracy and Ideals*, and *The Moral Obligation to Be Intelligent*.

Ervine, St. John Greer (b. 1883), British author, dramatist and critic; wrote the plays *Jane Clegg* and *The First Mrs. Fraser*. His most important critical work is *The Theatre in My Time*.

Essex, Robert Devereux, Earl of (1567-1601), became Queen Elizabeth's favorite after the death of Leicester, but offending the Queen by certain acts in Ireland, was committed to prison. He was later implicated in a rebellious movement, for which he was executed.

Eucken, Rudolf Christoph (1846-1926), a famous German philosopher and theologian.

Euclid, Greek mathematician, who lived in the 3rd century B. C., and whose elements of geometry have become classic.

Eugenie, Empress of the French (1826-1920), married Napoleon III in 1853, and for many years kept a brilliant court. After the collapse of the Second Empire Eugenie lived in England.

Euler, Leonard (1707-1783), Swiss mathematician, regarded as the founder of pure mathematics.

Euripides (480-406 B. C.), was the greatest of Greek tragic poets. He wrote seventy-five plays, eighteen of which have been preserved, the most famous being *Alcestis, Medea, Iphigenia,* and *Orestes*.

Eusebius (264-340), Greek ecclesiastical historian; his *Chronicon* is a history of the world down to his own time, while his *Ecclesiastical History* traces the career of the Christian Church.

Everett, Edward (1794-1865), American statesman and educator, born in Dorchester, Mass. After some years in Germany and England he was appointed professor of Greek literature at Harvard in 1815. From 1820 to 1824 he was editor of the *North American Review*. He was governor of Massachusetts from 1836 to 1840, and from 1841 to 1844 was American minister to England. He became president of Harvard in 1846, and in 1852 he became Secretary of State under Fillmore, succeeding Daniel Webster. Famed as an orator, he was invited to deliver the principal oration at the dedication of the national cemetery at Gettysburg. New York newspapers reported that Mr. Lincoln also spoke.

Eyck, Hubert van (c. 1366-1426), and **Eyck, Jan van** (c. 1386-1440), two of the greatest masters of the early Flemish school of painting.

F

Fabius Maximus (Cunctator) (d. 203 B. C.), Roman consul and dictator, saved Rome from conquest by Hannibal by strategic evasion of battle. The term "Fabian Policy" is derived from Fabius's tactics.

Fahrenheit, Gabriel Daniel (1686-1736), Dutch scientist who first used mercury in the construction of thermometers, and laid down the Fahrenheit thermometric scale now in use.

Fairbanks, Douglas (1883-1939), for many years one of the world's best-known film actors. He portrayed the roles of many romantic and legendary heroes; his son Douglas Fairbanks, Junior (b. 1908), is also an actor.

Fairfax, Thomas, 3rd Lord (1612-1671), British soldier and statesman, a prominent leader of the Parliamentary army during the Civil War.

Falkenhayn, Erich von (1861-1922), minister of war for Germany in 1915 and 1916; became chief of staff after the resignation of von Moltke.

Fall, Albert Bacon (1861-1944), American politician. Elected to the U.S. Senate in 1912, he was appointed Secretary of the Interior by President Harding in 1920. After resigning in 1923, he was convicted of conspiracy to defraud the government for his part in the oil scandals.

Faraday, Michael (1791-1867), British chemist, discoverer of electromagnetic induction and formulator of the laws of electrolysis. He was one of the first students of the transformation of mechanical into electrical energy.

Farman, Henri (1873-1934), Anglo-French pioneer in aviation. He was a famous designer and builder of airplanes.

Farnol, John Jeffery (1878-1952), well-known English author of historical romances.

Farragut, David Glasgow (1801-1870), American naval officer; was born in Campbell's Station, Tenn. Soon after the Civil War broke out, Farragut received the command of the Gulf squadron which engaged and passed the two strong forts of the Mississippi in April, 1862, bringing about the surrender of New Orleans on the 28th of the same month. Natchez was taken in May, and Farragut's fleet ascended as far as Vicksburg, which he bombarded until the fall of water compelled him to return to New Orleans. He was the first officer in the Navy to receive the rank of admiral, in 1862. He took the forts commanding the harbor of Mobile, in August, 1864, and Mobile surrendered April 12, 1865.

Faulkner, William (b. 1897), American novelist and winner of the 1949 Nobel prize for literature. His novels, concerned mainly with a fictional county in his native Mississippi, include *Soldiers' Pay, Sartoris, The Sound and the Fury, As I Lay Dying, Sanctuary, Light in August, Absalom, Absalom! A Fable, The Town.*

Fawkes, Guy (1570-1606), English conspirator,

who with Catesby and others planned the Gunpowder Plot, and was hanged.

Feisal, King of Iraq (1885-1933), son of the first King of the Hedjaz; succeeded by his son Emir Ghazi; was king of Iraq, 1921-33.

Fènelon, François de Salignac de la Mothe (1651-1715), archbishop of Cambrai and a writer of great distinction; his *Telemachus* is a French classic.

Ferber, Edna (b. 1887), American novelist. Among her many books are, *Show Boat* (1926), *Cimarron* (1929), and *So Big* (1924). With George S. Kaufman she wrote the plays, *Dinner at Eight, Minick*, and *Stage Door*.

Ferdinand V (1452-1516), married Isabella of Spain; with her expelled the Moors, equipped Columbus' ships, instituted the Inquisition.

Fermi, Enrico (1901-1954), Italian physicist, winner of the 1938 Nobel physics prize for work on radioactive substances. He came to the United States in 1939, and was a leader of the Chicago project which in 1952 first achieved atomic fission.

Fessenden, William Pitt (1806-69), U. S. statesman born at Boscawen, N. H. He entered the Senate as a Whig in 1855, was secretary of the treasury (1864-65), and served in the Senate again until his death.

Feuchtwanger, Lion (b. 1884), noted German author; has written plays, poems and novels. Like most German artists, he left Germany when the Nazis seized power.

Fichte, Johann Gottlieb (1762-1814); was professor of philosophy, first at Jena and then at Erlangen, and later rector of the University of Berlin. His idealist philosophy had great influence upon the thought of his time. His chief works are *The Destination of Man* and *The Way to the Blessed Life*.

Field, Cyrus West (1819-1892), American engineer, took a prominent part in the development of submarine cables. In 1856 he connected the United States with Newfoundland by cable, subsequently organizing the company which established the first successful Atlantic cable in 1866.

Field, Eugene (1850-1895), American journalist and poet; born in St. Louis, Mo. He worked on several newspapers in the West before coming to Chicago in 1883. His poems for and about children are admirable in their simplicity and in their sympathetic insight into the child's world of thought and feeling. His works include: *Love Songs of Childhood; A Little Book of Western Verse; The Love Affairs of a Bibliomaniac;* and *With Trumpet and Drum.* He wrote in collaboration with his brother Roswell Martin Field, verses in the tradition of Horace, including *Echoes from the Sabine Farm.* He was one of the early newspaper columnists, conducting a column in the *Chicago Daily News* called "Sharps and Flats."

Field, Marshall (1835-1906), American merchant, born near Conway, Mass. He organized the firm which later became known as Marshall Field and Company in 1865. Field became a noted philanthropist through his donations to the University of Chicago and the Field Museum.

Fielding, Henry (1707-1754), English novelist, the greatest of the eighteenth century. He wrote *Tom Jones, Joseph Andrews*, and *Jonathan Wilde*, as well as many plays.

Fillmore, Millard (1800-1874), American statesman, 13th President of the United States. He was elected to the New York state assembly (1829-31); to Congress in 1832; and to the office of Vice-President of the United States in 1848. On the sudden death of President Taylor in July, 1850, Fillmore succeeded him. While in this office he signed and tried to enforce the fugitive slave law; he served as President until 1853.

Fink, Mike (1770?-1822), king of the keelboatmen on the Ohio and Mississippi Rivers and hero of many legendary exploits. He served as Indian scout at Fort Pitt; piloted a keelboat on the Ohio during the early Westward movement; and later joined the first Ashley expedition up the Missouri and was fatally shot in a quarrel. The Mike Fink stories, collected by Walter Blair and Franklin J. Meine, form an important American saga.

Finsen, Niels Ryberg (1860-1904), Danish medical scientist who developed the light cure for lupus.

Firdausi (Abul Kasim Mansur) (c. 940-1020), was the great epic poet of Persia. His *Book of Kings* contains 60,000 verses, and professes to relate the history of Persia.

Fish, Hamilton (1808-1893), American statesman, was born in New York City. In 1851 he was elected to the United States Senate, where he joined the Republican party on its formation. He was Secretary of State under Grant from 1869 to 1877.

Fiske, John (1842-1901), an American philosopher and historian; was born in Hartford, Conn.; graduated at Harvard College in 1863, and in 1865 took his degree in law. He was for a while lecturer on philosophy at Harvard, and was author of *Myths and Myth-Makers, The Discovery of America, Old Virginia and her Neighbors,* and *The Dutch and Quaker Colonies in America.*

Fitch, William Clyde (1865-1909), American playwright. He was educated at Hartford, Conn., and Amherst College, Amherst, Mass. and wrote a number of successful plays, among them *A Modern Match, The Truth,* and *The City.*

Fitzgerald, Edward (1809-1883), English poet who gained world-wide fame by his translation of *The Rubaiyat of Omar Khayyam* into English.

Flammarion, Camille (1842-1925), French astronomer, famous for his observations on double stars, and star-drift. Founded the Astronomical Society of France in 1887.

Flamsteed, John (1646-1719), was the first English Astronomer Royal, and a close friend of Sir Isaac Newton, whom he aided in many of his experiments.

Fleming, Sir Alexander (1881-1954), British bacteriologist and discoverer, in 1928, of penicillin. For this and subsequent research he was knighted in 1944, and shared a Nobel prize in physiology and medicine in 1945. He also identified lysozome, substance in tears, saliva, and egg albumen that can destroy germs (1922).

Fletcher, John (1579-1625), the famous collaborator with Beaumont in numerous plays which were popular in their day and have taken a high position in dramatic literature.

Flotow, Friedrich, Baron von (1812-1883), German composer of opera whose *Stradella* and *Martha* enjoyed much popularity.

Foch, Marshal Ferdinand (1851-1929), Chief of the Allied Armies in France during the last years of the World War; previously commander-in-chief of the French armies.

Fokine, Michel (1880-1942), Russian dancer and director of Russian ballet. He wrote choreography for *Les Sylphides, Scheherazade, Prince Igor, The Dying Swan,* and *Cleopatra.*

Fokker, Anton Hermann Gerard (1890-1939), famous Dutch airman and aeronautical engineer; designer and builder of the well known Fokker military and commercial airplanes.

Fontanne, Lynn (b. 1889), American actress. With her husband, Alfred Lunt, she has achieved great success on the English and American stage, particularly in *Design for Living, Reunion in Vienna, The Guardsman, Idiot's Delight,* and *Amphitryon 38.*

Foraker, Joseph Benson (1846-1917), American politician; born in Ohio. Began law practice in Cincinnati in 1869; was judge of the Superior Court of Cincinnati in 1879-1882, governor of Ohio in 1885-1889, and was elected United States Senator in 1896 and 1903.

Forbes-Robertson, Sir Johnston (1853-1937), British actor-manager, was trained as an artist, but went on the stage; became a leading player with Henry Irving and later produced many of the plays of A. W. Pinero and Charles Rann Kennedy.

Ford, Ford Madox (Ford Madox Hueffer) (1873-1939), English novelist. With Joseph Conrad he wrote *The Inheritors* and *Romance.* In 1908 his magazine, *The English Review,* was founded and drew such contributors as Hardy, Conrad, William James, John Galsworthy, and John Masefield.

Ford, Henry (1863-1947), U. S. automobile manufacturer; born at Greenfield, Mich. After a district-school education he learned the machinist's trade and later worked as an engineer. In 1903 he organized the Ford Motor Company which, under his supervision, became one of the world's largest business organizations. On Jan. 5, 1914, he established a minimum wage of $5 per day, then the highest basic wage in the U. S. His industrial methods and decentralization of production laid the foundation for modern American mass production. He made large philanthropic contributions and the Ford Foundation, established by his son in 1936, carried on extensive philanthropies.

Forrest, Nathan Bedford (1821-1877), American soldier, distinguished as a cavalry commander in the Confederate service during the Civil War. As major general in November, 1864, he was given command of all the cavalry with the Army of the Tennessee. In 1865, he was placed in command of the cavalry in Alabama, Mississippi, and east Louisiana, and became a lieutenant general. Throughout the Civil War he was regarded as one of the most daring and skillful cavalry officers on either side.

Fortuny y Carbo, Mariano (1839-1874), a celebrated Spanish painter. "Choosing a Model," and "The Snake Charmers," are among his best-known paintings.

Fosdick, Harry Emerson (b. 1878), American clergyman. Was a baptist minister 1904-1915. Since then he has been professor of theology, Union Theological Seminary, New York, and since 1925, pastor of the Riverside, formerly the Park Avenue Baptist Church, New York. One of the best-known preachers in the United States.

Foster, Stephen Collins (1826-1864), American songwriter; born in Pittsburgh, Pa.; was educated at Athens Academy and Jefferson College, Pa. His musical talents were developed early and at the age of 16 he wrote his first published song, *Open Thy Lattice, Love.* He composed over 125 popular songs, among them the well-known *Old Folks at Home, Old Black Joe, My Old Kentucky Home, Massa's in de Cold, Cold Ground, Nelly Bly, Old Dog Tray, Swanee River,* and *Oh Susannah.*

Fouquet, Nicolas (1615-1680), French statesman; born in Paris. He was finance minister under Louis XIV of France.

Fourier, François Charles Marie (1772-1837), French Socialist who propounded a system of associative enterprise for giving everyone ample means on a system of communal industry. He made some attempts to carry out his Utopian ideas, but they did not succeed. He is best known by his *Traité de l'Association Domestique Agricole.*

Fox, Charles James (1749-1806), British statesman, entered Parliament at nineteen, and became a lord of the admiralty in 1770. Through the whole of Pitt's premiership he was that statesman's most formidable opponent. He favored American Independence; opposed the war with France; denounced the slave trade and advocated Parliamentary reform.

Fox, George (1624-1691), was the founder of the Society of Friends and one of the greatest religious leaders of his century. His *Journal* has appeared in many editions.

Foxe, John (1516-1587), the English martyrologist whose *Acts and Monuments,* or *Book of Martyrs,* is one of the best-known books in the language.

France, Anatole (Jacques Thibault) (1844-1924), French novelist and satirist, author of *The Crime of Sylvester Bonnard, The Kitchen of Queen Pédauque, Thaïs, Penguin Island,* and many short stories and critical studies. Most of his works are translated into English. He is generally regarded as the outstanding French writer of his age.

Francis I (1494-1547), was king of France from 1515 to his death. He was involved in many wars and was taken prisoner by Charles V of Germany at the Battle of Pavia. After friendly relations had been established between Francis and Henry VIII of England, the two met on the "Field of the Cloth of Gold."

Francis of Assisi, St. (1182-1226), founded the Franciscan Order of Monks and devoted himself to a holy life. He is a saint of the Roman Catholic Church, having been canonized by Pope Gregory IX, and is commemorated on October 4th.

Franck, César Auguste (1822-1890), modern French composer, noted for his magnificent organ music, his beautiful oratorio *Les Béatitudes,* and his one symphony.

Franco, Francisco (b. 1892), Spanish dictator, born in Galicia. He served in the army and became chief of staff in 1935. He led the insurgent forces in the Spanish Civil War (1936-39), and established a totalitarian state on the Hitler-Mussolini model. He proclaimed re-establishment of the monarchy, but did not permit enthronement of a king.

Frankfurter, Felix (b. 1882), American jurist, was born in Vienna, Austria; came to the United States when he was twelve years of age. In 1914 he was appointed to a chair at Harvard Law School, and also served as major and as judge advocate of the Officers' Reserve Corps, as assistant to the Secretary of Labor, and in 1918 as chairman of the War Labor Policies Board. Among his writings are, *The Case of Sacco and Vanzetti, Cases on Administrative*

Law, and *Mr. Justice Brandeis.* In 1939 President Roosevelt appointed Frankfurter to the Supreme Court.

Franklin, Benjamin (1706-1790), American statesman, scientist and publisher, was born in Boston. He learned the printer's trade and for a time managed his brother's newspaper, the *New England Courant.* When he was seventeen he moved to Philadelphia, where within a few years he owned and edited the *Pennsylvania Gazette* and *Poor Richard's Almanack,* two of the most popular publications in colonial America. Franklin had taught himself several languages and had read most of the scientific books of his day when, in 1748, he retired from business to devote himself to science. He invented a lightning rod, the type of stove which bears his name, and distinguished between positive and negative electricity. Becoming interested in Pennsylvania politics, he served in the colonial assembly and was joint deputy postmaster-general of the colonies, 1753-1774. In 1757-1762, and again in 1764-1775, he was Pennsylvania's agent in London, where he successfully pleaded the colonists' case against the colonial proprietors and fought the Stamp Act, for the repeal of which he was partially responsible. On his return to America he was elected to the Continental Congress; among the committees on which he served was that which drafted the Declaration of Independence. Late in 1776 he sailed for France; before his return nine years later he had secured French recognition for the United States, had negotiated loans from France and secured commercial treaties, and had served as one of the commissioners who had negotiated the peace with England. His last service to his country was as a member of the Constitutional Convention of 1787; although the Constitution as submitted differed from the draft he had proposed, he was instrumental in obtaining its adoption. Franklin was one of the outstanding men of the eighteenth century and the first American to be famous abroad.

Franklin, Sir John (1786-1847), British Arctic explorer, whose final expedition in command of the *Erebus* and *Terror* ended disastrously, all the members of the expedition perishing. Many attempts were made to rescue Franklin, but without obtaining anything save very fragmentary knowledge of his fate.

Frazer, Sir James George (1854-1941), anthropologist; author of *The Golden Bough* and numerous other works on his subject.

Frederick II (1712-1786), usually called Frederick the Great, was king of Prussia from 1740 to the time of his death, and by his masterful government and military successes greatly increased the power of his country. He was a scholarly potentate, and his published works extend to thirty volumes.

Frémont, John Charles (1813-1890), American soldier and explorer, born in Savannah, Ga. He entered the army as a lieutenant of topographical engineers and spent the years 1838-39 in exploring between the Missouri River and Canada. In 1845 he cleared northern California of Mexican troops and made a 3,500-mile journey of exploration which included the Sierra Nevada region, Alta California, and the San Joaquin and Sacramento valleys. He became a lieutenant colonel, the military commandant and civil governor of California. In 1856 he was the first Republican candidate for the Presidency. In 1861 he was put in command of the western Union Army, and later, 1878-1881, was governor of Arizona. In April, 1890, he was appointed major general and placed on the retired list.

Freud, Sigmund (1856-1939), was professor of neurology, Vienna University, 1902-38. The founder of psychoanalysis; author of many books on his subject; left Austria after the *Anschluss* to take up residence in England.

Frobisher, Sir Martin (1535-1594), was the first British navigator to attempt to find the northwest passage to India; his name is commemorated in Frobisher's Strait, to the south of Baffin Land.

Froebel, Friedrich Wilhelm August (1782-1852), was the founder of the Kindergarten system of education, the object of which is "to give children employment in harmony with their nature, to strengthen their bodies, to exercise their senses and lead them up to the original ground of all life, to the idea of unity with themselves."

Froissart, Jean (1337-1410), French writer who visited England and Scotland; the author of the famous *Chronicles,* which contain excellent accounts of the customs of medieval society.

Frost, Edwin Brant (1866-1935), American astronomer. From 1898-1905 he was professor of astrophysics at the University of Chicago, leaving there to become director of Yerkes Observatory. His observations have been concerned with thermal radiation of the sun and with sunspots. His publications include *A Photographic Atlas of Selected Regions of the Milky Way.*

Frost, Robert Lee (b. 1874), American poet, was born in San Francisco. While still a child he moved to New England, where he studied at Dartmouth, Harvard, and other colleges. In 1912 he visited England, where he published *A Boy's Will* (1913) and *North of Boston* (1914). The latter volume won him recognition as an outstanding interpreter of New England life. In 1916 he published *Mountain Interval; Collected Poems* appeared in 1930. He was professor of English at Amherst College 1916-20 and from 1923-25. He won the Pulitzer Prize for poetry in 1924, 1931, 1937, and 1943.

Fuad I, King Ahmed (1868-1936), became sultan of Egypt in Oct. 1917, educated in Italy and served in the Italian Army. Fuad was king of Egypt, 1922-36.

Fuller, Thomas (1608-1661), the author of *Worthies of England* and a *Church History of Britain,* two well-known historical works.

Fulton, Robert (1765-1815), American engineer and pioneer of steam navigation who in 1807 launched the *Clermont* on the Hudson, the first steamboat in the world.

Furtwaengler, Wilhelm (1886-1954), German musician and conductor, for many years conductor of the Berlin Philharmonic Orchestra.

G

Gable, Clark (b. 1901), American actor who, after a short career on the stage, made his film debut in 1930, scoring successes in the films *It Happened One Night, Mutiny on the Bounty, San Francisco, Gone with the Wind, The Hucksters.*

Gadsden, James (1788-1858), American diplomat; was born in Charleston, S. C. He was appointed minister to Mexico in 1853, and negotiated the *Gadsden Purchase,* which fixed a new boundary between Mexico and the United States.

Gainsborough, Thomas (1727-1788), one of the most popular English landscape and portrait painters. Revealing the influence of Watteau and Van Dyke, his portraits (more than 200) include "Mrs. Siddons," "The Baillie Family," and "The Duchess of Devonshire."

Gaitskell, Hugh Todd Naylor (b. 1906), English Labour politician, rose in the Attlee ministry to become chancellor of the exchequer. In 1955 he became leader of the Labour party when Attlee retired.

Gale, Zona (1874-1938), American writer, born in Portage, Wis. She worked on Milwaukee newspapers and the *New York World*. She wrote short stories collected in *Friendship Village*, and the novels *Miss Lulu Bett*, *Preface to a Life*, and *Borgia*. Her dramatization of *Miss Lulu Bett* was awarded a Pulitzer prize in 1921.

Galilei, Galileo (1564-1642), Italian astronomer, who while still a youth discovered the law of pendulum vibration by seeing a lamp swinging from the roof of the cathedral in Pisa. He also constructed the first telescope, with which he discovered the satellites of Jupiter and studied the surface of the moon. He was an early advocate of the Copernican astronomy.

Gallatin, Albert (1761-1849), American statesman and financier; was born in Geneva Switzerland. In 1780 he came to the United States, and from 1795 to 1801 he served in the House of Representatives; from 1801 to 1813 he was Secretary of the Treasury. In 1814 he took an important part in the negotiations for peace with England and signed the Treaty of Ghent. From 1815 to 1823 he was minister at Paris, and in 1826 he was sent to London as ambassador extraordinary. He was the first president of the Ethnological Society of America; and from 1843 to his death he was president of the New York Historical Society. Gallatin was an extremely able Secretary of the Treasury and was one of the most important leaders of Jefferson's party.

Galli-Curci, Amelita (b. 1890), world-famous Italian operatic soprano.

Galsworthy, John (1867-1938), British novelist, author of *The Forsyte Saga*, many other novels and several plays, awarded Nobel Prize for literature in 1932.

Galton, Sir Francis (1822-1911), British scientist, whose studies in hereditary transmission founded the science of eugenics, and whose expositions of the markings of fingertips resulted in the adoption of what is known as fingerprint identification.

Galvani, Luigi (1737-1798), Italian scientist whose experiments during a course of lectures on anatomy at Bologna discovered the principle of animal electricity; hence the term Galvanism.

Gama, Vasco da (c. 1460-1524), the Portuguese navigator who discovered the sea route to India in 1498 by rounding the Cape of Good Hope.

Gandhi, Mohandas Karamchand (1869-1948), Indian political leader; studied law in London and upon his return to India became an advocate of the Bombay High Court. In 1893 he inaugurated passive resistance in South Africa in protest against the inhumane conditions imposed upon his people in that country. He sought to foster home industries, himself weaving cloth by hand. As a result of his example of passive resistance, strikes and riots broke out. He was imprisoned (1922-24); later, upon his release, he became president of the Indian National Congress. His bestowal of his wealth upon the poor, his own life of asceticism, his deep religious fervor, his earnest endeavors for the uplifting of the oppressed classes, and his eloquent preaching won for him the surname "Mahatma" (Great Soul") and the reputation of a saint. He was assassinated in 1948 by a Nationalist fanatic. His writings include his autobiography and *Young India*.

Garbo, Greta (b. 1906), Swedish film actress. She studied at the Royal Dramatic Academy in Stockholm and gained her first successes in Sweden. Since coming to the United States she has appeared in *Grand Hotel*, *Anna Karenina*, *Queen Christina*, *Ninotchka*, etc.

Garfield, James Abram (1831-1881), American statesman, 20th President of the United States; was born in Orange, O. In 1859 he was elected to the Ohio senate. In 1861 he was commissioned lieutenant colonel of the 42nd regiment of Ohio Volunteers, and made a brigadier in a few months. In 1863 he left the army to enter Congress, where he remained for 16 years. In 1880 he was elected United States Senator from Ohio, and in June the Republican National Convention nominated him to the Presidency and he was elected in November. On July 2, 1881, when passing through the Baltimore and Ohio passenger station in Washington, in company with J. G. Blaine, Garfield was shot by Charles J. Guiteau, a disappointed office seeker, and died Sept 19.

Garibaldi, Giuseppe (1807-1882), Italian soldier and patriot. In 1848, he joined the Roman Republican movement, but was compelled to flee for his life, and emigrated to New York. In 1854 he returned to Italy; on the outbreak of war in 1859 had a command given to him and scored several victories against the Austrians. The next year found him at the head of a great volunteer army, intent upon liberating Italy. This tremendous task he successfully carried through, earning the admiration of the world for his generalship and patriotism.

Garland, Hamlin (1860-1940), American author, born in West Salem, Wis. A provincial author of the midwest, Garland's first book, *Main Traveled Roads* (1890), was followed by other stories, poems and autobiographical works dealing with that region. His early writings were characterized by realistic pictures of frontier farm life, but his later works treated the subject less severely. His books dealing with the Mississippi Valley include: *Main Traveled Roads*, the autobiographical *Son of the Middle Border*, *A Daughter of the Middle Border*, and *The Trail Makers*.

Garrick, David (1717-1779), British actor, the leading tragic actor of his time and a highly successful theatrical manager.

Garrison, William Lloyd (1805-1879), American editor and anti-slavery agitator; born in Newburyport, Mass. He started the *Liberator* (1831), published weekly. In 1832 appeared his *Thoughts on African Colonization*, and in the same year he established the American Anti-Slavery Society. He subsequently visited England, where he was welcomed by Wilberforce, Brougham, Buxton, and others. In 1835 he was saved with difficulty from a Boston mob; but his principles made steady progress till 1865, when the Anti-Slavery Society was dissolved with its work accomplished.

Gaskell, Mrs. Elizabeth Cleghorn (1810-1865), English novelist, whose *Mary Barton*, *Ruth*,

Cranford and other stories dealing largely with Lancashire life achieved great popularity. Her *Life of Charlotte Brontë* is valuable.

Gates, Horatio (c. 1729-1806), American soldier; born in England. He entered the British army, served through the French and Indian War, and retired in 1765. In 1772 he removed from England to Virginia, and in 1775 joined the Continental Army as a brigadier general. Promoted major general in 1776, he was given command of the Northern Department in 1777, and forced Burgoyne to surrender at Saratoga.

Gauguin, Paul (1848-1903), French painter of the post-impressionist school, was born in Paris. A pupil of Pissarro, he deserted a banking post to paint, distinguishing himself with his Breton landscapes. Later, in southern France, he painted his well-known self-portrait and his "Yellow Christ." In 1891 he went to Tahiti, where he painted the life of the South Seas.

Gaulle, Charles André Joseph Marie de (b. 1890), French soldier and head of the French government in exile. He served with distinction during the World War and the Polish campaign of 1920. In 1937 he became a colonel. From 1928 De Gaulle was a persistent advocate of mechanization and offensive tactics. His ideas were unheeded by the French, but in May 1940 he was promoted major general and later named chief war assistant to Premier Reynaud. He refused to accept the French surrender, established a provisional government in London, and organized forces to continue the fight against Germany. Many French colonies declared for him, and were banded together under a Council of Defense for the French Empire, with De Gaulle at its head.

Gautier, Théophile (1811-1872), French critic and novelist, one of the leaders of the Romantic school. His romance, *Mademoiselle de Maupin*, caused a great sensation.

Gay, John (1685-1732), the English poet who wrote *The Beggar's Opera*, and the well-known collection of poetic *Fables*.

Geddes, Norman Bel (b. 1893), an American artist and scenic designer; born in Adrian, Mich. educated at the Cleveland Art School and the Chicago Art Institute. His first scenic production was for Cadman's *Shanewis* in 1918. His most popular work was for *The Miracle*.

Genêt, Edmond Charles (1765-1834), French diplomat, was born at Versailles. He became minister to the United States at the outbreak of the French Revolution in 1792 and attempted to stir up public opinion to sympathize with the French cause against England. The United States demanded that the French government recall him in 1794, but he remained in the United States.

Genghis Khan, or Jenghis Khan (1162-1227), Mongol conqueror, born near the Onon river, Mongolia. He succeeded his father when only 14 years of age and made himself master of the neighboring tribes. After much warfare with various Tartar tribes Genghis was proclaimed Khan of the united Mongol and Tartar tribes. He professed to have a divine call to conquer the world, and the idea so animated the spirit of his soldiers that they were easily led on to new wars. Seven years in succession was the conqueror busy in the work of destruction, pillage, and subjugation, and extended his ravages to the banks of the Dnieper. At his death in Mongolia, in 1227, his immense dominions were divided among his four sons.

Genseric (c. 395-477), Vandal king of Spain in 419, after being driven into Africa by the Visigoths, subdued the Roman provinces of North Africa, and afterwards crossed to Italy and sacked and pillaged Rome, doing irreparable damage to public monuments and sculptures. Hence the term "vandalism."

Geoffrey of Anjou, Duke of Brittany (1158-1186), founder of the Angevin dynasty of England, was son-in-law of Henry I and father of Henry II, the first Angevin or Plantagenet king.

Geoffrey of Monmouth (1100-1154), was the author of the famous English chronicle which bears his name. He was born at Monmouth, and became bishop of St. Asaph in 1152. His *Historia Britonum* is a compilation from older authors, and is notable for containing the stories of King Arthur, King Lear, and Cymbeline.

George I (1660-1727), king of England, born in Hanover. On the death of Queen Anne in 1714 he was called to the throne of England, as the nearest heir in the Protestant line. He was thus the founder of the present British royal house. He was neutral in most of the Continental wars of his time, although he joined the Triple Alliance of 1717 and the Quadruple Alliance of 1718 against Spain. His popularity with his English subjects was greatly lessened by his inability to speak English. He died in Germany.

George II (1683-1760), king of England; son of George I; born in Hanover, Germany; succeeded his father in 1727. He retained as his prime minister Sir Robert Walpole. In the War of the Austrian Succession he declared himself on the side of the Empress Maria Theresa and against France. When war again broke out on the continent of Europe, 1755, England experienced fresh reverses in Germany and lost her Hanoverian dominions, but these losses were more than compensated by brilliant and valuable conquests in the East Indies and in America.

George III (1738-1820), king of England. He succeeded his grandfather George II, in 1760. In the early part of his reign he gained brilliant successes over France and Austria in the Seven Years' War and in 1763 concluded an advantageous peace. In 1764 Granville, the prime minister, began those measures which led to the American Revolution; the Stamp Act was passed the following year. The death of George's youngest child, the Princess Amelia, which happened toward the close of 1810, gave the king a shock from which he never recovered.

George IV (1762-1830), king of England; succeeded his father George III in 1820. Though he had at first declared for the Whigs, he gave himself up to Tory influence for a long time, and had as his prime ministers Lord Liverpool and the Duke of Wellington. During his regency occurred the final overthrow of Napoleon. He married in 1795 the Princess Caroline of Brunswick, whom he afterward caused to be tried on a charge of adultery.

George V (1865-1936), king of Great Britain and Ireland and Emperor of India, the second son of King Edward VII and Queen Alexandra. He became heir apparent to the throne on the death of the Duke of Clarence and Avondale, his elder brother, and succeeded to the throne May 6, 1910. During the World War the king renounced his German titles and in 1917, by royal decree, changed the name of the royal house from Saxe-Coburg to Windsor. During his reign Ireland secured home rule; a larger share in self-government was given to India and there was a great development of the British Commonwealth with the Crown as the chief link of the empire. In May, 1935, there was great celebration throughout the British Empire, on the silver anniversary of his accession. He died Jan. 20, 1936, and was succeeded by his eldest son, who became Edward VIII.

George VI (1895-1952), king of Great Britain and Ireland and Emperor of India. During World War I he served in the navy and was present at the Battle of Jutland. He married Lady Elizabeth Bowes-Lyon, a commoner, 1923. He succeeded his brother, Edward VIII, to the throne upon the latter's abdication, Dec. 10, 1936.

George, Henry (1839-1897), American political economist; born in Philadelphia. He went to California in 1857, where he did newspaper work. He moved to New York City in 1880. During these years he developed his political theory of the "single tax" on land which made him famous. He was nominated by the Labor party for mayor of New York in 1886, received 67,000 votes, but was defeated. In 1897 he ran again for the mayorship but died in the midst of a strenuous campaign. His publications include *Progress and Poverty, The Land Question, Property in Land*, and *Protection and Free Trade.*

Gérôme, Jean Léon (1824-1904), a French historical painter. Among his best-known paintings are "The Duel after the Ball" and "The Age of Augustus."

Geronimo (1829-1909), an American Indian, chief of the Apaches in Arizona, who led raiding parties against white settlements in Arizona and New Mexico which resulted in the killing of over 100 Americans between 1881 and 1886. When pursued, they hid in the Sierra Madre mountains of Mexico. General George Crook was ordered to capture the bandit chief in 1882, but he was unsuccessful and was replaced by General Nelson A. Miles. Geronimo ultimately surrendered, and with his warriors was sent to live first in Florida, then in Alabama, and ultimately in Fort Sill, Oklahoma, where Geronimo died.

Gerry, Elbridge (1744-1814), an American statesman; born in Marblehead, Mass. He was a member of the Continental Congress, 1776-1780 and 1783-1785; member of Congress from Massachusetts, 1789-1793; governor of Massachusetts in 1810-1812; and Vice-President of the United States in 1813-1814. During his governorship his political party attempted to maintain itself in power by re-arranging the electoral districts to its own advantage. This maneuver has since been known as "gerrymandering."

Gershwin, George (1898-1937), American composer. He developed jazz themes for orchestral arrangement. He was self-taught, but displayed remarkable talent in the composition of symphonic jazz music. Probably his best work is the *Rhapsody in Blue.* Other notable compositions are: *The King of Jazz, An American in Paris* and the score from the musical show, *Porgy and Bess*, which was produced in 1936.

Gesner, Konrad von (1516-1565), a scholarly Swiss naturalist, whose work helped to lay the foundations for biological classification.

Ghazi, King of Iraq (1912-1939), came to the throne upon the death of his father, King Feisal. Sept. 8, 1933.

Gibbon, Edward (1737-1794), British historian, author of the *Decline and Fall of the Roman Empire.*

Gibson, Charles Dana (1867-1944), American artist and illustrator; the creator of "The Gibson Girl," a type of female beauty that was much admired.

Gide, André Paul Guillaume (1869-1951), French man of letters, a novelist, dramatist, and poet. His works are characterized by acute psychological analysis and an absolute mastery of style. Among his novels are *The Counterfeiters* and *The Immoralist.*

Gilbert, Sir Humphrey (1539-1583), English mariner, was commissioned by Queen Elizabeth to undertake voyages of exploration and colonization. While seeking the Northwest Passage, he landed in Newfoundland and added it to the British possessions. He was drowned off the Azores.

Gilbert, Sir William Schwenk (1836-1911), an English poet and playwright. He attracted notice by *Bab Ballads*, a volume of satirical verse. A few years later he began his famous partnership with Sir Arthur Sullivan, supplying satirical librettos to which the latter supplied the music. This association continued for 25 years, during which a large number of very popular operas were produced, including *H.M.S. Pinafore, Patience, Iolanthe,* and *The Mikado.* Gilbert was knighted in 1907.

Gilder, Richard Watson (1844-1909), an American writer, who became editor of *Scribner's Magazine* and *Century Magazine;* he was also the author of several volumes of poems.

Gillette, William (1855-1937), an American actor and playwright; author of several successful plays, in many of which he assumed the leading parts. Among his best-known productions are: *The Professor* (1881), *Esmeralda* (1881), *Too Much Johnson* (1895), and *Secret Service* (1896).

Gillray, James (1757-1815), British caricaturist of the time of George III, who produced upwards of a thousand political cartoons, some of which were very popular.

Giolitti, Giovanni (1842-1928), an Italian statesman. In 1903 after filling several other government offices, he became the premier of Italy, holding this post almost uninterruptedly until 1914. He became premier again in 1920-21.

Giorgione, Giorgio Barbarelli (c. 1478-1510), an Italian painter; born in Castelfranco. The Museum of Paris contains four of his works: "Salome Receiving the Head of John the Baptist," "Jesus Sitting on His Mother's Knees," "The Rural Concert," and "Gaston de Foix." His masterpiece is a picture of "Christ Carrying His Cross," preserved at Venice. He died in Venice.

Giotto di Bondone (1266-1337), Italian painter, sculptor, and architect, whose beautiful tower at Florence and his many works of art in various churches there, as well as the churches themselves, form splendid monuments to his memory.

Gissing, George (1857-1903), English novelist. He made a remarkable study of the London masses, from the ranks of skilled labor to the most noisome human refuse of the slums, particularly in *The Nether World, New Grub Street, Demos* and *Sleeping Fires.*

Gladstone, William Ewart (1809-1898), British statesman. He was elected to Parliament as a Tory member in 1832; in 1834 was made a lord of the treasury under Peel, and in the following year became undersecretary for the colonies. In 1841 Peel made him vice-president of the Board of Trade, and in 1843 president with cabinet rank. After holding various other public offices, he became prime minister in 1868, the first of four periods in this office between 1868 and 1893. From 1874 until 1880 he was in retirement, but was re-elected as prime minister on the latter date as a result of his denunciation of the imperialism of Disraeli. In 1886 he introduced his first Home Rule Bill, on which he was defeated and resigned, and at the general election following, the Conservatives had a majority, and it was not until 1892 that Gladstone was again in power. In 1893 he brought in his second Home Rule Bill, which passed the House of Commons but was defeated in the House of Lords. After that he resigned and took no further part in Parliament.

Glass, Carter (1858-1946), American statesman; born at Lynchburg, Va. As a young man he did newspaper work and participated in Virginia politics, becoming a member of the United States House of Representatives. He was Secretary of the Treasury in President Wilson's cabinet, from Dec. 1918 to Feb. 1920, and resigned to return to the Senate, where he served again until 1943.

Glazunov, Alexander (1865-1936), a Russian composer; born at St. Petersburg, now Leningrad; studied music under Rimsky-Korsakov. His principal works are symphonies, five suites, four concert overtures, and a violin concerto.

Gluck, Christoph Willibald (1714-1787), one of the most eminent composers of opera of the 18th century. His *Orfeo* and *Iphigenie* are his best-known works.

Godwin, William (1756-1836), British radical political writer. His best-known works are a treatise on *Political Justice* and a philosophical novel, *Caleb Williams.* His first wife was Mary Wollstonecraft, a feminist writer, and mother of Mary Wollstonecraft Shelley.

Goebbels, Paul Joseph (1897-1945), minister for propaganda in the Hitler government of Germany, 1933-45; believed to have committed suicide with Hitler in Berlin air raid shelter as Russian troops entered the city.

Goering, Hermann (1893-1946), German Nazi leader. A flyer in World War I, he was credited with shooting down 36 enemy planes. He joined Hitler in 1922 and organized the Storm Troops, leading the abortive Munich putsch in 1923. Elected to the Reichstag, he became its president (1930) and entered Hitler's cabinet in 1933. He was made a field marshal (1938), head of the air force, and (1940) dictator of the German economy. He was convicted by an Allied court as a war criminal (1946), but committed suicide by poison two hours before his scheduled death by hanging.

Goethals, George Washington (1858-1928), American military engineer, born in Brooklyn, N. Y. He was appointed in 1907 chief engineer of the Panama Canal Commission. Under his direction the Canal was completed. In 1914 he became first civil governor of the Canal Zone. In 1919 he voluntarily retired from active service to set up a consulting engineering practice.

Goethe, Johann Wolfgang von (1749-1832), the most distinguished of German poets and writers. After producing the *Sorrows of Werther,* and various dramas he settled down at Weimar, received a ministerial appointment, and began his famous dramatic poem *Faust,* which is one of the world's greatest literary works.

Gogh, Vincent van (1853-1890), Dutch painter. In his painting he re-created scenes from peasant life, making use of somber browns. However, from 1886 on, he was influenced by the Impressionists and adopted the use of more vivid coloring. In the next two years he did most of his work painting in southern France. It consisted of still lifes, landscapes, figure studies, and portraits; he handled his light effects in expert fashion. Some of his best works are: "Autumn Landscape," "Prison Court," "The Restaurant on Montmartre," and "Mairie au 14 Juillet." He committed suicide in 1890.

Gogol, Nikolai (1809-1852), Russian novelist. He is the author of a novel entitled *Dead Souls,* and two collections of short tales illustrative of rural life in *Little Russia.* He spent some years abroad, returned to Russia in 1849, and died in Moscow.

Goldsmith, Oliver (1728-1774), an English author born in Ireland. After leading a wandering life he settled down to literary hack-work in London, but gradually acquired fame by his writing, entering into the most distinguished literary society of his day. His best-known works are *The Traveller* and *The Deserted Village* (poems); *The Vicar of Wakefield* (a novel); and *She Stoops to Conquer* (a play).

Gómez, Juan Vicente (1857?-1935), president of Venezuela. After taking part in the civil war he became president in 1908. From this time until his death he ruled the country as a dictator. He promoted an extensive program of internal improvements, especially in railroads and communications, and used foreign capital to develop oil fields and mines. Though he was generally popular, liberal elements opposed his harsh and repressive despotism; an attempted revolution failed, and its leaders were exiled or imprisoned. Gómez died in office in 1935.

Gompers, Samuel (1850-1924), American labor leader; born in London, England. He came to the United States in 1863, and worked as a cigar maker. In 1864 he joined the Cigar Makers' International Union, of which he became the leader. He served as president of the American Federation of Labor continuously (with the exception of one year) from 1882 until his death in 1924. Under his guidance the Federation acquired great power and prestige. Among Gompers' gains for the cause of labor were the 8-hour day for government workers and the establishment of Labor Day. He represented the American Federation of Labor at the Peace Conference in 1918 and 1919. He firmly believed that labor could secure its aims best through the existing economic order and directed the policy of the Federation toward that end. He was editor of the *American Federationist,* and wrote *Labor in Europe and America* and other books.

Goodyear, Charles (1800-1860), American inventor; born in New Haven, Conn. He failed as an iron manufacturer in 1830, but in 1834 turned his attention to the preparation of rubber, the uses of which were limited because of its alteration under extremes of temperature. By mixing rubber and sulphur in the process called vulcanization he overcame this difficulty. In all he secured 60 patents to cover his inventions. He lived to see rubber applied to a great diversity of uses, and become the basis of one of the world's most important industries.

Gorchakov, or **Gortchakoff, Prince Alexander Mikhailovich** (1798-1883), prominent Russian statesman; foreign minister during the Crimean War. In later years he became chancellor of the Russian Empire, and achieved many diplomatic victories. He resigned in 1882 and died the following year.

Gordon, Charles George (1833-1885), British soldier and administrator known as "Chinese Gordon." He saw active service in the Crimea, China, and India, and in 1873 was made governor of the Egyptian Sudan. After a period spent in Mauritius, he returned to the Sudan in 1844 to quell the revolt of the followers of the Mahdi. During a gallant defense of Khartoum, which was besieged by the rebels for ten months, he was killed.

Gorgas, William Crawford (1854-1920), an American surgeon. In 1880 he was made a United States Army surgeon and became famous for his work against yellow fever while stationed in Havana, Cuba, where he was chief sanitary officer during the years 1898-1902. He added to his fame by his establishment of sanitary conditions in the Panama Canal Zone, where he was chief sanitary officer from 1904-1913. He died in 1920.

Gorky, Maxim, pen name of Aleksey Maximovich Pyeshkov (1868-1936), Russian author, the foremost cultural figure of Soviet Russia. He became converted to Marxist doctrine, and participated in the Bolshevik revolution. His writing is noted for its realism and vigorous social content. His works include *Foma Gordeyev, A Confession,* and a play, *The Lower Depths.*

Gosse, Sir Edmund (1849-1928), British poet and critic who wrote lives of Gray, Congreve, and Dome; his *History of 18th-Century Literature* and *History of Modern English Literature* show great critical power and appreciation.

Gould Jay (1836-1892), American capitalist and financier, born in Roxbury, N. Y. After working as a surveyor he became interested in railroad stocks, and became a director of the Erie Railroad. He worked in close conjunction with Daniel Drew and James Fisk for manipulating stocks in their own interest. Their scheming precipitated the scandalous Black Friday panic of 1869. Being forced out of the Erie Railroad by popular indignation, Gould turned his attention to the Southwest, where his unscrupulous methods enabled him to gain monopolistic control of four railroads (the "Gould system"). He later acquired a controlling interest in the Western Union Telegraph Company, and in the elevated railroads of New York City. He died in 1892, leaving a fortune of $72,000,000.

Gounod, Charles François (1818-1893), French composer, whose *Faust,* produced in 1859, was one of the most successful operas of the 19th century. Other famous operas are *Roméo et Juliet* and *Le Médecin malgré lui.* He also composed much sacred music, including an oratorio, *The Redemption.*

Grady, Henry Woodfin (1850-1889), American publisher and orator. Part owner of the Atlanta Constitution from 1879 to 1889. Most famous oration was *The New South* in 1886.

Grahame, Kenneth (1859-1932), British writer, a popular writer of books for and about children, including *The Golden Age, Dream Days,* and *The Wind in the Willows.*

Grainger, Percy Aldridge (b. 1882), Australian pianist and composer; an authority on folk music, the influence of which is apparent in his compositions.

Grant, Ulysses Simpson (1822-1885), American general and 18th President of the United States; born in Point Pleasant, Ohio. He was graduated from West Point in 1843, entered the regular army, and served in the Mexican War. In 1854 he resigned from the army, and after engaging in a number of unsuccessful business ventures, was in Galena, Illinois, when the Civil War broke out. Made colonel and then brigadier general, he was put in command at Cairo, Ill., and early in 1862 invaded Kentucky. By a series of rapid movements he surrounded and then captured Forts Henry and Donelson; the loss of these strongholds forced the Confederates to abandon western Kentucky. In his next battle, however, at Shiloh, Grant was saved from defeat only by the arrival of reinforcements. In March, 1863, after a brilliant campaign, Grant surrounded Vicksburg, and in July the city was surrendered. Later in the year, in the Chattanooga campaign, he defeated Bragg at Lookout Mountain, and drove the Confederates out of eastern Tennessee. In March 1864 Lincoln made Grant lieutenant general and commander of all Union armies, and although in the Wilderness Campaign, at Spotsylvania, and at Cold Harbor he failed to outmaneuver or defeat Lee, his overwhelming strength enabled him to continue the assault. For months Grant besieged Lee at Petersburg, and in April, 1865, Lee was forced to evacuate the city and a few days later surrendered his army, Grant allowing his defeated enemy generous terms. In 1866 he was made a full general, and from 1869 to 1877 was President of the United States. Grant in many respects was an ineffective President, his reputation being tarnished by the actions of disreputable politicians and financiers with whom he associated. His *Personal Memoirs* have become a historical and military classic.

Granville-Barker, Harley (1877-1946), English dramatist, producer and actor. He introduced the plays of Ibsen and Shaw to the British public. His own plays are realistic in dialogue, and include *The Voysey Inheritance* and *Madras House.*

Grasse, François Joseph Paul, Comte de (1723-1788), a French naval officer, who aided the Americans during the Revolutionary War. In 1781 he commanded a French fleet, and by landing his troops and blockading the Virginia coast, aided in the defeat of Cornwallis. He also participated in naval engagements in the West Indies; captured Tobago, but was defeated by the English Admiral, Rodney.

Gray, Thomas (1716-1771), English poet, whose "Elegy Written in a Country Churchyard" is one of the most beautiful poems in the language. His other poems were not numerous, but included a fine "Ode on a Distant Prospect of Eton College" and a notable "Ode to Adversity."

Greco, El ("The Greek") (1542-1613), is the name by which the master painter, Domenico Theotocopuli is known. Born of Greek parents in Crete, he became a pupil of Titian; his works reveal the influence of Tintoretto and the Bassanos. His greatest paintings were done in Toledo, Spain. Among his passionate, imaginative, and deeply religious masterpieces are "The Adoration of the Shepherds," "The Resurrection," "The Coronation of the Virgin" and "The Assumption," in the Chicago Art Museum.

Greeley, Horace (1811-1872), an American journalist; born in Amherst, N. H. After working as a printer he entered journalism, moved to New York, and started *The New Yorker*, a weekly literary journal. In 1841 he commenced the publication of the *New York Tribune.* This newspaper, which was much above the journalistic standards of its day, served as a vehicle for Greeley's vigorous progressivism. In 1848 Greeley became a member of the 30th Congress. He zealously supported the causes of labor and feminism; was an ardent abolitionist; sustained the Union cause during the Civil War. In 1872 he was nominated by the Democratic party for the Presidency in opposition to General Grant, but he failed to be elected.

Greely, Adolphus Washington (1844-1935), an American Arctic explorer and scientist. He served in the Civil War. In 1881 he commanded an American meteorological expedition to Greenland and Smith Sound, north of Canada. A member of this party reached a point farther north than any predecessor. Greely was one of seven survivors of the expedition, which was rescued in 1883. As head of the U. S. Signal Corps and of the Weather Bureau, Greely directed the establishment of thousands of miles of cable and telegraph lines in the American territories. In 1906 he took charge at San Francisco after the earthquake and fire; in 1907 he put down a Ute uprising in Wyoming.

Green, Duff (1791-1875), American journalist and politician. He owned and edited the *St. Louis Enquirer*. In 1825 he purchased the *United States Telegraph* of Washington, D. C., and as a supporter of Jackson participated in the latter's "Kitchen Cabinet." In Tyler's administration Green served as an unofficial envoy in England; later he promoted the annexation of Texas. He started, in 1844, a New York paper which advocated free trade.

Green, Hetty Howland Robinson (1835-1916), an American capitalist, born in New Bedford, Mass. Through her personal administration of the vast fortune inherited from her father in 1865, she became known as America's richest woman and the greatest woman financier in the world.

Green, Paul (b. 1894), American playwright, born in North Carolina. He began teaching philosophy at the University of North Carolina in 1923. For *In Abraham's Bosom*, a play which feelingly depicted the Southern Negro's problem, he won the Pulitzer Prize in 1927. He wrote a number of other plays and short stories of the South, as well as a novel, *Laughing Pioneer*.

Green, William (1870-1952), American labor leader. A coal miner, he became a leader of the United Mine Workers of America. He served two terms in the Ohio senate; in 1912 he was a delegate to the Democratic National Convention. In 1924 Green became president of the American Federation of Labor, to which office he has been re-elected annually. With the establishment of the Congress of Industrial Organizations, Green became the outstanding opponent of John L. Lewis, its founder.

Greene, Nathanael (1742-1786), American soldier; born in Rhode Island. In 1775 he was chosen general of the contingents furnished by Rhode Island to the American army. He was made major general in the Continental Army in 1776; and played a creditable part in engagements at Trenton and Germantown. In 1778 he was appointed quartermaster general. After the defeat of General Gates (1780) at the battle of Camden, S. C., he was appointed to the command of the army in the South, and contributed much to its morale. In March, 1781, he was defeated by Lord Cornwallis in the hard-fought battle of Guilford Court House. Greene defeated the forces of Colonel Stewart at Eutaw Springs in September, 1781, and thereby put an end to the British power in South Carolina.

Gregory I, or **Gregory the Great** (540-604), first of the sixteen popes of that name, and next to Leo I, greatest of the ancient bishops of Rome. He was pope from 590 to his death. It was probably he who introduced Gregorian chant or plain song into church ritual.

Gregory XIII (1502-1585), the pope who introduced the Gregorian calendar.

Grenfell, Sir Wilfred Thomason (1865-1940), doctor, who began in 1892 his work as a medical missionary among the isolated Eskimos and fishermen of Labrador and Newfoundland. Through his efforts hospitals, nursing stations and hospital ships were furnished for their care. He wrote several books dealing with his life work, including *Vikings of Today* and *A Labrador Doctor*.

Grenville, Sir Richard (1541-1591), English seafighter, who with his one ship engaged a fleet of Spanish war-vessels off Flores, in 1591, was captured, and shortly after died on the Spanish flagship *San Pablo*, an exploit celebrated in Tennyson's ballad, "The Revenge."

Grey, Charles, 2nd Earl (1764-1845), English statesman who succeeded, as prime minister, in securing the passage of the Reform Bill of 1832, the bill abolishing slavery throughout the British Empire (1833), and the Poor Law Amendment Act, 1834.

Grey, Lady Jane (1537-1554), an English noblewoman; daughter of the Duke of Suffolk and great-granddaughter of Henry VII. On the death of Edward VI she was proclaimed queen, but reigned for only ten days, Queen Mary ousting her and maintaining the Tudor succession. Six months later Lady Jane and her husband, Lord Guilford Dudley, were executed.

Grey of Fallodon, Edward Grey, 1st Viscount (1863-1933), British statesman; under-secretary for foreign affairs, 1892; and foreign secretary 1905-1916. Though he managed the international problems preceding the World War, particularly those in the Balkans, with discretion, he was unable to avert the conflict. He resigned his office in 1916. Grey was the leader of the Liberal party in the House of Lords until 1924.

Grey, Zane (1875-1939), American writer of popular fiction, who gave up dental practice in New York for a novelist's career. *Riders of the Purple Sage, To the Last Man,* and *The Thundering Herd* (1934) are among his 42 books, several of which were made into moving pictures.

Grieg, Edvard Hagerup (1843-1907), a Norwegian composer, whose music, romantic and charged with melancholy, reflects the character of his country. Derived in large part from folk music, his compositions include songs, piano works, and the popular *Peer Gynt* suites.

Griffith, Arthur (1872-1922), was the first president of the Irish Free State in 1921; founder of the Sinn Fein movement.

Griffith, David Wark (1875-1948), an American motion picture director and producer, born in La Grange, Ky. The first notable film drama to win nationwide acclaim, *The Birth of a Nation,* was produced by him. Other successes were *Intolerance, Hearts of the World, Broken Blossoms,* and *Way Down East.* He introduced many new techniques into motion picture production, and pioneered in the use of the fade-out and the close-up.

Grimm, Jacob Ludwig Karl (1785-1863) and **Wilhelm Karl** (1786-1859), German philologists and folklorists, were born in Hanau. The brothers collaborated on a collection of old German folk tales which became famous as "Grimms' Fairy Tales." Jacob Grimm was one of the formulators of a theory of certain consonant changes in Indo-European languages; this theory became known as Grimm's Law.

Gropius, Walter (b. 1883), German architect; a leader in the "functional" movement of modern architecture, making extensive use of glass and other materials, with modern engineering methods, and striving for an integral architectural expression. After the advent of the Hitler government, Gropius emigrated to the United States.

Grouchy, Marshal Emmanuel, Marquis de (1766-1847), one of Napoleon's generals who, at Hohenlinden, Wagram, and in the retreat from Moscow, rendered signal service. After Waterloo he led the defeated army back to Paris.

Guggenheim, Meyer (1828-1905), American capitalist, born in Switzerland. After his immigration to this country, he became a successful merchant. Later he acquired mining property and set up smelters and refineries. With his fortune he established the Guggenheim Foundations for social welfare and the encouragement of the arts.

Guido Reni (1575-1642), eminent Italian painter of the Bolognese school. His "Michael Vanquishing Satan," "Magdalene," and "The Massacre of the Innocents" are among the world's great pictures.

Guitry, Sacha (1885-1957), French actor and dramatist. He has been a prolific writer since the age of 21, writing more than 60 plays, many of which compare well with Molière's comedies. Among his most successful dramas are *Béranger, Pasteur,* and *Le Blanc et le noir.* He won acclaim as an actor both in Europe and in the United States.

Gustavus II, or Gustavus Adolphus (1594-1632), king of Sweden. On the death of his father, Charles, Gustavus succeeded him. Gustavus, then in his 17th year, was in command of the army during the war with Denmark, which was concluded in 1613. Gustavus then took a personal share in a war with Russia, upon whose throne he tried unsuccessfully to place his brother, Charles Philip. He succeeded, however, in adding Estonia and Livonia to the Swedish dominions. The war with Russia was followed by a nine-years' war with Poland, concluded on advantageous terms for Gustavus in 1629. Under Gustavus' brilliant leadership Sweden then engaged in the struggles of the Thirty Years' War in Germany. His army defeated the forces of Tilly in a brilliant victory near Leipzig in 1630. Two years later Gustavus Adolphus defeated Wallenstein in the battle of Lützen, but was himself mortally wounded.

Gustavus V (1858-1950), Swedish king. He succeeded to the throne in 1907. He advocated expansion of the army, and was criticized for his part in the defeat of the Staaf ministry. A highly popular monarch, he succeeded in maintaining neutrality through two world wars.

Gutenberg, Johann (1397-1468), German printer generally credited with the invention of printing from movable type.

H

Haakon VII (1872-1957), king of Norway, son of Frederick VIII of Denmark. He was elected the Norwegian king after Norway's separation from Sweden (1905); succeeded by his son Olav V.

Haber, Fritz (1868-1934), German chemist. He was a professor of physical chemistry at Berlin, director of the Kaiser Wilhelm Institute and in 1918 was awarded the Nobel Prize. The Haber process is his notable contribution to chemistry. In it, ammonia is synthesized by the direct combination of nitrogen and hydrogen under 200 atmospheres of pressure at a temperature of 500° C.

Hadrian (76-138), Emperor of Rome in succession to his uncle Trajan, and one of the greatest of Roman rulers. He visited Britain, and in A. D. 121 built the wall between Newcastle and Carlisle for protection of his dominions against the Picts and Scots.

Haeckel, Ernst Heinrich (1834-1919), eminent German scientist and philosopher, and professor of zoology at Jena University. An earnest supporter of the evolution theory, his writings became popular throughout Europe.

Haggard, Sir Henry Rider (1856-1925), English author. He spent several years in South Africa in official positions in the seventies, and then returned to England where he wrote *Dawn, Allan Quartermain, Belshazzar, King Solomon's Mines, She, Jess,* and *Queen Sheba's Ring,* all novels. He also wrote *The Poor and the Land,* a study of colonization in South Africa.

Hahnemann, Samuel Christian Friedrich (1755-1843), founder of the system of homeopathy.

Haig, Douglas (1861-1928), British soldier. He succeeded Sir John French as Commander of the British Forces in France, in Dec., 1915.

Haile Selassie I (b. 1892), emperor of Ethiopia (Abyssinia), after April 1930.

Hakluyt, Richard (1553-1616), English maritime historian. By his *Divers Voyages Touching the Discovery of America,* and *Principal Navigations, Voyages, and Discoveries of the English Nation,* he did much to increase the colonizing spirit.

Haldane, John Burdon Sanderson (b. 1892), English biologist; professor of genetics, University College, London University, after 1933.

Hale, Edward Everett (1822-1909), American author and Unitarian clergyman; born in Boston, Mass. He was graduated at Harvard in 1839, studied theology, and was pastor of the Church of the Unity, Worcester, Mass., 1846-1856. In 1902 he was made chaplain of the United States Senate. He was an influential preacher, and a leader in religious and philanthropic work. As an author is best known by his short story, *The Man Without a Country.* Among his other works are: *Philip Nolan's Friends* (1876), *The Story of Massachusetts* (1891), and *A New England Boyhood* (1893).

Hale, Nathan (1755-1776), American patriot; born in Coventry, Conn. He rose to the rank of captain in the Continental Army, and, having volunteered to penetrate the British lines and procure intelligence for Washington, was detected and executed as a spy in New York City.

Halifax, Earl of. Edward Frederick Lindley Wood (b. 1881), British statesman. He was elected to Parliament in 1910, and served in France during the World War. He was Under-Secretary of State for the colonies, 1921-22; President of the Board of Education, 1922-24; Minister of Agriculture, 1924-25; and Viceroy of India, 1925-31. He served again as President of the Board of Education, 1932-35. From 1935 to 1941 Halifax was leader of the House of Lords, becoming in 1938 Foreign Secretary. In 1940 he was appointed ambassador to the United States, serving there until 1946.

Hallam, Henry (1777-1859), English historian. His *View of the State of Europe during the Middle Ages, Constitutional History of England,* and *Introduction to the Literature of Europe* are distinguished for their clearness of style and correctness of judgment.

Halleck, Henry Wager (1815-1872), American soldier; born in Westernville, N. Y. He was graduated at the United States Military Academy in 1839. In November, 1861, he was appointed Commander of the Department of the Missouri, where he displayed considerable ability. In July, 1862, he became General-in-Chief of the armies of the United States; and directed from Washington the movements of the generals in the field, till, in March, 1864, he was superseded by General Grant. Halleck was chief of staff till 1865, commanded the Military Division of the Pacific till 1869, and that of the South till his death. He wrote *Elements of Military Art and Science* and other works.

Halley, Edmund (1656-1742), English astronomer. He discovered what is known as Halley's comet.

Hals, Franz (1584-1666), a famous painter of the Dutch school.

Hamilton, Alexander (1757-1804), an American statesman; born in Nevis, W. I. In 1773 he entered King's College (now Columbia University). When the Revolution broke out he was appointed (1776) captain of artillery and in 1777 was made a member of Washington's staff. In 1781 he left the staff for more active service, and fought brilliantly at Yorktown. After the war Hamilton practiced law and served in Congress and the New York legislature. In 1787 he was a member of the Constitutional Convention, where he unsuccessfully advocated an extremely strong national government. As author of most of the *Federalist Papers,* however, he helped bring about the ratification of the Constitution. He was the first Secretary of the Treasury and placed the new government on a firm financial basis by his policies which included: payment of the national debt in full; assumption of the state debts; increased excise duties; and the establishment of a National Bank. Hamilton's policies made him a leader of the Federalists, and brought him into constant conflict with Jefferson, who favored a weak central government. In 1795 Hamilton resigned to re-enter private practice. In 1800 his influence defeated Aaron Burr, who was Jefferson's chief rival for the Presidency. In 1804 Hamilton again used his influence to defeat Burr, this time when he was seeking the governorship of New York. Burr challenged him to a duel, in which Hamilton was mortally wounded.

Hammerstein, Oscar (1847-1919), German-American impresario. He was influential in New York City's theatrical development. In 1888 he erected the Harlem Opera House; in 1892 the Manhattan Opera House. In the second building of this latter name (built 1906) he produced his outstanding successes, including *Pelléas and Mélisande, Elektra,* and *Louise.* He agreed with the Metropolitan Opera Company not to produce further operas in the United States for ten years and went abroad to manage his London Opera House. That failed, and in 1913 he returned to the United States.

Hampden, John (1594-1643), English patriot, who opposed Charles I's "Ship Money" tax, and by his resistance and eloquent advocacy of the people helped the Parliamentary cause.

Hampton, Wade (1818-1902), American soldier; born in Charlestown, S. C. At the outbreak of the Civil War he entered the Confederate army; was promoted major general in 1864, and in August of the same year appointed commander-in-chief of Confederate cavalry in Northern Virginia; lieutenant general in 1865. He distinguished himself in several actions, including the defeat of Sheridan's cavalry at Trevilians, Va. After the conclusion of peace he was a stanch advocate of conciliation between North and South; was elected governor of South Carolina in 1876 and 1878; held a seat in the United States Senate, 1879-1890.

Hamsun, Knut (1859-1952), Norwegian author. He wrote several novels including *Hunger, Growth of the Soil, Vagabonds, Mysteries,* and *Roads Lead On;* a trilogy of plays; and *The Wild Chorus,* a volume of lyrics.

Hancock, John (1737-1793), American Revolutionary patriot; born in Quincy, Mass. He was a wealthy colonial merchant, and at the inception of the revolutionary struggle was a leading spirit. Hancock was a member of the Continental Congress from 1775 to 1780, also from 1785 to 1786, serving as its president from 1775 to 1777. He served as governor of Massachusetts 12 years.

Hancock, Winfield Scott (1824-1886), soldier; born in Pennsylvania. He was graduated at the United States Military Academy in 1844, and served during the Mexican War. In 1861 he was appointed brigadier general of volunteers, and attached to the Army of the Potomac; at the battle of Fredericksburg, in December, 1862, he commanded a division of the 2d Corps, and for his services was promoted major general; he took part in the battle of Chancellorsville and at Gettysburg was largely responsible for the Confederate defeat. In 1880 he was the unsuccessful Democratic nominee for President.

Handel, George Frederick (1685-1759), German composer, who spent most of his life in England. He wrote 16 suites and 12 concertos for the harpsichord, organ concertos, various miscellaneous music, and about forty operas; but he is best known for his 25 oratorios, among them *Esther, Saul, Israel in Egypt, Samson,* and *The Messiah.*

Handy, William Christopher (b. 1874), American Negro composer; born in Memphis, Tenn. He was important in the rise of American jazz, and wrote *Memphis Blues, St. Louis Blues,* and *Beale Street Blues.*

Hanna, Marcus Alonzo (1837-1904), American politician; born in Ohio. He joined his father in the wholesale grocery business, became a coal and iron dealer, and by 1880 had acquired interests in coal and iron mines, a shipyard, a lake steamship line, a bank, a newspaper, an opera house, and the Cleveland traction system. He entered politics, attained virtual control of the Ohio Republican party, and was responsible for the rise of William McKinley. In 1896 he managed McKinley's campaign for the Presidency, and urged his election as a means of defending property rights against the radical doctrines of Bryan and the Democratic party. He was a member of the Senate from 1897 until his death.

Hannibal (247-183 B. C.), Carthaginian general, who led an army against Rome, and achieved many notable victories over superior numbers. He was at last defeated by Scipio at the Battle of Zama, suffered exile, and poisoned himself.

Hardie, James Keir (1856-1915), British socialist politician. He was one of the founders of the Labor party, and the first Socialist to be elected to Parliament.

Harding, Warren Gamaliel (1865-1923), 29th President of the United States; born in Ohio. He began his political service as a Republican state senator; after a term as lieutenant-governor he was chosen to nominate Taft in 1912, and in 1914 was elected to the United States Senate. He was nominated in 1920 for the Presidency and elected by a large majority. One accomplishment of the Harding administration was the Washington Conference for the Limitation of Armaments, held in 1921-22. The Teapot Dome and other scandals, involving two of his Cabinet members, Attorney-General Daugherty, and Secretary of the Interior Albert B. Fall, made the Harding administration one of the most corrupt in history. Harding died in San Francisco, Aug. 2, 1923, after a trip to Alaska.

Hardwicke, Sir Cedric Webster (b. 1893), English actor, well known on the stage and screen in the United States as well as in his own country.

Hardy, Thomas, (1840-1928), English writer, was educated as an architect, and practiced for some time, but became known as a novelist in 1871 with his story *Desperate Remedies.* In 1874 his *Far from the Madding Crowd* was published, which at once made him a name. Following that, at short intervals, came a long series of novels. Perhaps the most notable of his stories are *The Trumpet Major, The Mayor of Casterbridge, Tess of the D'Urbervilles,* and *Jude the Obscure.* In 1908 he completed a dramatic poem entitled *The Dynasts,* whose central figure is Napoleon. He later wrote several volumes of poetry and short stories.

Hargreaves, James (1720-1778), English carpenter and weaver, who invented the spinning jenny.

Harkness, Edward Stephen (1874-1940), American financier, and one of the nation's foremost philanthropists.

Harold II (1022-1066), last Saxon king of England. The son of Earl Godwin, he was crowned king in succession to Edward the Confessor in 1066. The coming of William the Conqueror, with his great army, put an end to the hopes of Harold and his followers; and the Battle of Hastings terminated at once his life and Saxon rule in Great Britain.

Haroun al-Raschid (766-809), the famous Caliph of Bagdad, familiar to all by the references to him in the Arabian Nights. He was a great patron of arts, letters, and science.

Harper, William Rainey (1856-1906), American educator; born in New Concord, O. He was graduated at Muskingum College in 1870; professor of Hebrew at the Baptist Union Theological Seminary, 1879-1886; of Semitic languages at Yale, 1886-1891; then first president of University of Chicago.

Harris, Joel Chandler (1848-1908), American journalist and author, famous as the creator of "Uncle Remus." The Negro humor of his stories brought him world-wide popularity among adults and children alike. He wrote many books depicting Southern life and relating Negro legends, among them *Uncle Remus, His Songs and Sayings; Daddy Jake, The Runaway; Mingo; Free Joe; History of Georgia.*

Harrison, Benjamin (1833-1901), American statesman, 23rd President of the United States; born in North Bend, O. He was a grandson of William Henry Harrison, 9th President of the United States. He was graduated at Miami University, and entered the Union Army in 1862. He served with conspicuous gallantry in the Atlanta campaign and at the close of the war was a brevet brigadier general. He was elected to the United States Senate in 1881; and as the Republican candidate, was elected President in 1888. His administration was marked by the amicable settlement of the dispute with Chile, and by the passage of the McKinley Tariff Bill. In 1892 he again received the Republican nomination, but was defeated by Cleveland. He retired and practiced law.

Harrison, Frederic (1831-1923), English jurist, sociologist, and historian; as leader of the English Positivists, he took a prominent part in philosophical discussions during the last quarter of the 19th century. In 1907 he published *The Creed of a Layman* and *The Philosophy of Common Sense,* and in 1919 *On Jurisprudence and the Conflict of the Laws.*

Harrison, William Henry (1773-1841) 9th President of the United States; born at Berkeley, Va. During the War of 1812 he distinguished himself at Tippecanoe and on the Thames against the Indians. He was sent to Congress in 1816 and served as U. S. minister to Colombia in 1828. He was nominated for the Presidency by the Whigs and elected (1840) on the slogan "Tippecanoe and Tyler too," in the famous "log cabin hard cider" campaign. Harrison died of pneumonia April 4, 1841, a month after his inauguration.

Hart, Albert Bushnell (1854-1943), historian, born in Clarksville, Pa., educated at Harvard and in Germany. He was made professor of government in 1910. He retired in 1926. He edited a number of important historical works, among them the "American Nation" series; *Epochs of American History; American History Told by Contemporaries;* and *Commonwealth History.* He edited the *American Historical Review* and was joint editor of *American History Leaflets,* and *Guide to the Study of American History.*

Harte, Francis Bret (1839-1902), American poet and author, famous for his stories of California mining life. Among his best-known works are his stories, *The Luck of Roaring Camp,* and *The Outcasts of Poker Flat,* and the poem, *The Heathen Chinee.* Harte was an American consul in Germany and Scotland from 1879 to 1885.

Harvard, John (1607-1638), American clergyman, and chief founder of Harvard College; born in England in 1607. He came to Massachusetts in 1637, and became the minister at Charlestown. He died in 1638, and bequeathed $3,700 and 320 volumes from his library to the new college, which honored him by taking his name.

Harvey, William (1578-1657), English physician, who discovered the circulation of the blood, in 1616.

Hastings, Warren (1732-1818), English statesman, the first governor-general of India. He was removed from office and impeached in Parliament on charges of corruption and excessive cruelty, but was ultimately acquitted.

Hauptmann, Gerhart (1862-1946), German poet, dramatist and novelist. Among his early plays, which dealt with social problems, were *The Weavers*, *Before Dawn*, and *The Red Cock*.

Hawkins, Sir John (1532-1595), British naval officer of the Elizabethan period, who did much sea fighting in many climes, and commanded the *Victory* in the defeat of the Spanish Armada.

Hawthorne, Nathaniel (1804-1864), American novelist; born in Salem, Mass., July 4, 1804. He was graduated at Bowdoin in 1825. In 1832 he published anonymously a romance, *Fanshawe*, and in 1837 *Twice-told Tales*, a collection of stories. His next work was *Mosses from an Old Manse*. He was surveyor of the port of Salem (1846-1849). In 1850 he published *The Scarlet Letter*, a romance of early New England life; this was followed by *The House of the Seven Gables*, *Marble Faun*, and *The Blithedale Romance*. In 1853 he was appointed American consul at Liverpool by his college friend, Franklin Pierce, then President of the United States. This office he held till 1857, when he went to travel on the Continent. Other works of his are *Transformation* (1860), *Our Old Home* (sketches of England and the English) and *The Snow Image*.

Hay, John (1838-1905), American statesman and author, born in Salem, Ind. He went to Washington in 1861 as one of Lincoln's private secretaries. He served from 1865-1870 in the legations at Paris, Vienna, and Madrid. Returning to the United States, he did editorial work on the *New York Tribune*. In 1897 he was appointed by President McKinley as ambassador to England, and from 1898 until his death he was Secretary of State. His writings include *Abraham Lincoln: A History*, *Pike County Ballads*, and *Castilian Days*.

Haydn, Franz Joseph (1732-1809), Austrian composer. Because of his work in developing the sonata form, he is sometimes called the "Father of the Symphony." Haydn wrote 118 symphonies; sonatas and concertos for piano; church music; much chamber music; and five oratorios, including *The Creation* and *The Seasons*.

Hayes, Helen (b. 1900), American actress. She played a number of juvenile roles before winning success in mature roles in *Caesar and Cleopatra*, *What Every Woman Knows*, and *Coquette*. Her greatest stage triumph was in *Victoria Regina*. She appeared in the motion pictures *The Sin of Madelon Claudet*, and *A Farewell to Arms*.

Hayes, Rutherford Birchard (1822-1893), 19th President of the United States; born in Delaware, Ohio. He attended Kenyon College and Harvard Law School. Upon the outbreak of the Civil War he was made a major in the 23rd Ohio Infantry. He served throughout the war, was wounded four times, and was mustered out as a major general of volunteers. He sat in Congress, 1865-1867, and served three terms as governor of Ohio. In 1876 he was the Republican candidate for President. The election results were disputed, and an Electoral Commission decided that Hayes had been elected, although his Democratic opponent, Tilden, had a popular majority. As President, Hayes proved wise and capable. His removal of the last Federal troops from the South was an important factor in reconciling the sections. Hayes was not interested in another term, and in 1881 retired to private life.

Hayne, Robert Young (1791-1839), American statesman: born in South Carolina. When Calhoun became Vice-President in 1825, Hayne took his place in the Senate. He was a constant opponent of the tariff. In 1830 occurred his famous debate with Webster. Begun over a resolution regarding the public lands, it ranged over all questions at issue between North and South. In the debate Hayne expounded the idea of nullification, which provoked Webster's famous defense of the Union. Hayne later served as governor of South Carolina.

Hazlitt, William (1778-1830), English essayist and critic. His essays were important contributions to study of the Elizabethan drama. He wrote: *Views of the English Stage*, *Lectures on the English Poets*, *Lectures on the English Comic Writers*, *Characters of Shakespeare's Plays*, and *Table Talk*.

Hearst, William Randolph (1863-1951), American newspaper publisher. Placed in control of the *San Francisco Examiner* by his father, he became a pioneer in popular journalism, and acquired a large chain of newspapers and magazines. Hearst was long an influential member of the Democratic party, but did not hesitate to criticize its policies when they came into conflict with his own opinions.

Hedin, Sven Anders (1865-1952), Swedish explorer, who led important scientific expeditions in Tibet, Turkestan, Mongolia, the Himalayas, and Central Asia. He wrote *My Life as an Explorer*, *Across the Gobi Desert*, *The Conquest of Tibet*, and many technical reports of particular explorations.

Hegel, Georg Wilhelm Friedrich (1770-1831), German philosopher. His philosophy was an absolute idealism, based on the idea of an active world soul, and included such concepts as *thesis*, *antithesis*, and *synthesis* in all social processes; the rationality of progress, both in nature and in society; the essential unity of mind and matter, which are merely different modes of one thing, the Absolute; the idea of history as a warfare of ideas; and the ability of man by means of philosophy to understand the Absolute, or the world process. His theory of the state advocated absolutism and thus became the basis of extreme monarchism in Germany. Hegelian dialectic was adopted to some extent by Karl Marx, and a form of Hegelianism became the basis of later Marxism, particularly in Russia.

Heidenstam, Carl Gustaf Werner von (1859-1940), Swedish author. He received the Nobel Prize for Literature, in 1916.

Heifetz, Jascha (b. 1901), Russian violinist who became (1925) a naturalized American. He studied with Auer in St. Petersburg, and at the age of ten made his first concert appearance. His world tour of 1926-27 established him as one of the most perfect technicians, and one of the greatest interpretative artists of his day.

Heine, Heinrich (1797-1856), German lyric poet who lived for the best part of his life in Paris, and produced from time to time poems of profound beauty and subtlety of thought. Cynical, satirical, and often bitter, many of his writings excited great conflict of opinion, and showed intense emotional power.

Helmholtz, Hermann Ludwig Ferdinand von (1821-94), German physicist and physiologist, immortalized by the Young-Helmholtz theory of the nature of light. He also did important work in the fields of conservation of energy, hydrodynamics, electrodynamics, meteorological physics and optics.

Heloïse (c. 1101-64), niece of Canon Fulbert of Notre Dame. She is famous for her romance with Abelard. Her love letters are literary classics.

Hemingway, Ernest (b. 1898), American novelist, author of *The Sun Also Rises, A Farewell to Arms, Death in the Afternoon, For Whom the Bell Tolls, The Old Man and the Sea.* He was awarded the Nobel prize in literature in 1954.

Henley, William Ernest (1849-1903), English poet and journalist, close friend of R. L. Stevenson.

Henry I (1068-1135), King of England. He was the youngest son of William the Conqueror, and reigned from 1100 to 1135.

Henry II (1133-1189), King of England from 1154 to 1189. He had serious conflicts with the Church. His reign was notable for administrative reforms, and establishment of the jury system and common law.

Henry III (1207-1272), King of England from 1216 to 1272.

Henry IV (1367-1413), King of England from 1399 to 1413.

Henry IV (Henry of Navarre) (1553-1610), King of France. Prior to becoming king he was the leader of the French Huguenots, and although going over to the Catholics on being crowned, remained in sympathy with the Protestants and protected them by the famous Edict of Nantes. Ravaillac, a religious fanatic, assassinated Henry.

Henry V (1387-1422), King of England, reigned from 1413 to 1422, and distinguished himself in the wars with France, the Battle of Agincourt being his greatest triumph.

Henry VI (1421-1471), King of England from 1422 to 1461 and 1470-1471.

Henry VII (1457-1509), King of England, the first of the Tudor line, reigned from 1485 to 1509, succeeding Richard III.

Henry VIII (1491-1547), King of England, reigned from 1509 to 1547. He was a luxury-loving monarch of great diplomatic gifts, unscrupulous to a high degree when his own personal desires were concerned. His quarrels with the Church resulted in the acceptance of the Reformation. His half-dozen matrimonial exploits, his deposition of Wolsey, and his suppression of the monasteries are familiar incidents of history.

Henry "the Navigator" (1395-1460), a Portuguese Prince, son of John I. He discovered Madeira and the Azores, and encouraged exploration and the science of navigation.

Henry, O. (1862-1910), the pen name of William Sidney Porter, an American author. During his early years he was a reporter and editor in Houston, Texas, and served as teller in an Austin, Texas, bank. For an unaccounted cash shortage he was sentenced to prison in 1896, where he began writing. After devoting some time to banana culture in Honduras he returned to Texas and worked in a drug store. In 1901 he went to New York and became very popular as a short-story writer. His tales are largely pictures of New York and Western life. *Cabbages and Kings* (1904) was based on his years in Honduras, *The Four Million* (1906), a collection of short stories, with themes of city life. He died in 1910. His "surprise" endings were an innovation that influenced a large number of later short-story writers.

Henry, Patrick (1736-1799), an American patriot; born in Hanover Co., Va. Henry was a delegate to the First Continental Congress, which met in Philadelphia, in 1774, and delivered the first speech in that assembly. In 1776 he carried the vote of the Virginia convention for independence; and in the same year he became governor of the new State. He was four times re-elected. In 1791 he retired from public life, and returned to his law practice; in 1795 he declined the Secretaryship of State offered him by Washington.

Hepplewhite, George (d. 1786), one of the four great English 18th-century cabinetmakers. He was a contemporary of Chippendale, Robert Adam and Sheraton. His name is identified with the style of furniture which followed the Chippendale period.

Heraclitus (576-480 B.C.), a famous Greek philosopher, who wrote numerous works on religion and politics. He lived at Ephesus.

Herbert, Alan Patrick (b. 1890), well-known English author and humorist and writer of comic operas.

Herbert, Victor (1859-1924), American composer, born in Dublin, Ireland. He studied at Stuttgart and came to America in 1886 as cello soloist in the Metropolitan Opera House, New York. He conducted the Pittsburgh Symphony Orchestra (1898-1904) after which he devoted all his time to composing. His works include the operas *Natoma* (1911) and *Madeleine* (1914). Among his 35 operettas are: *Babes in Toyland* (1903), *Mlle. Modiste* (1906), *Naughty Marietta* (1910), and *Princess Pat* (1915).

Hergesheimer, Joseph (1880-1954), American author. Once a painter, he turned to writing. In 1914 he published *The Lay Anthony,* his first novel to attract the reading public. Other well-known books include: *Three Black Pennys* (1917), *Swords and Roses* (1929), and *The Limestone Tree* (1931).

Herod the Great (c. 73-4 B. C.), tyrannical King of Judea, whose reign dated from 40 B. C. It is believed that it was during his reign that Christ was born.

Herodotus (c. 484-424 B. C.), great Greek historian, the "Father of History."

Herrick, Robert (1591-1674), English lyric poet. He is best known for his lyrics of rural life and love, among them "Night-Piece: to Julia," "Gather Ye Rosebuds While Ye May," and "Corinna's Maying." He also wrote a number of sacred poems, among them, "Litany to the Holy Spirit."

Herriot, Edouard (1872-1957), French statesman and scholar. He was professor of rhetoric at Nantes and later at Lyons. He became interested in politics and at the age of 33 was elected mayor of Lyons as a Progressive Democrat. While still mayor Herriot entered national politics as a Radical Socialist, and held the office of premier of France three times, in 1924, 1926, and 1932. Among Herriot's books the best known are *Action* (1917), *The Cry* (1919), *The United States of Europe* (1930), and *The Life and Times of Beethoven* (1935).

Herschel, Sir John Frederick William (1792-1871), English astronomer who did much to extend the power of the telescope.

Herschel, Sir William (1738-1822), Anglo-German astronomer, father of the last-named. He discovered the planet Uranus. His sister, Caroline Lucretia (1750-1848), was a zealous participator in his studies.

Hertz, Heinrich (1857-1894), German physicist who demonstrated the similarity between electro-magnetic light and heat waves, and worked on electric discharges in gases.

Hertzog, General, James Barry Munnik (1866-1943), Premier, 1924, and Minister of External Affairs of the Union of South Africa, 1929. At the outbreak of war in 1939 he was succeeded by General Jan Christian Smuts.

Herzl, Theodor (1860-1904), founded modern political Zionism.

Hess, Myra (b. 1890), English pianist. She made her debut in 1907, and won immediate success, showing herself to be a fine interpretative artist, especially of early modern composers.

Hewlett, Maurice Henry (1861-1923), a writer of romance. His novel, *The Stooping Lady*, was issued in 1907; *Mrs. Lancelot*, 1912; *Bendish*, 1913; *A Lover's Tale*, 1915.

Heyward, Du Bose (1885-1940), author and playwright. Forced by poverty to leave school at an early age, he worked first as a newsboy and later as a checker in a cotton warehouse on the Charleston wharves, where he observed the waterfront Negroes and acquired much of the background for his later works. After World War I, Heyward collaborated with Hervey Allen on a work, published in 1922, called *Carolina Chansons*. In 1925 *Porgy* was published with great success. He later dramatized it, and in 1927 the play was produced by the New York Theater Guild, winning the Pulitzer Prize. He later wrote *Mamba's Daughters*, and *Star-Spangled Virgin*.

Hichens, Robert S. (1864-1950), English novelist and playwright. As a novelist he succeeded best in tales of the Orient. *The Garden of Allah*, which was dramatized in 1920, and subsequently filmed, was his most popular work.

Hiero I and Hiero II, were two tyrants of Syracuse. The former reigned 478-467 B.C., and made his court the home of Aeschylus, Pindar, and other men of learning. The latter reigned 270-216 B. C.

Hill, Benjamin Harvey (1823-1882), an American legislator; born in Jasper Co., Ga. In 1861 he was elected a member of the provisional Confederate congress. Soon afterwards he was promoted to the Confederate senate. He was confined as a prisoner of war from May to July, 1865, in Fort Lafayette, New York harbor. In 1875 he was elected to the House of Representatives from the ninth district, and during the next year was given a seat in the Senate, which he held until his death. As an orator and constitutional lawyer his reputation was deservedly high.

Hill, James Jerome (1838-1916), an American railroad builder, born in Canada. In 1870 he organized the Red River Transportation Company, which opened communication between Winnipeg and St. Paul; and in 1873, the syndicate which obtained control of the St. Paul and Pacific Railroad. He re-organized this system as the St. Paul, Minneapolis and Manitoba Railroad, and finally became its president. In 1890 it was incorporated in the Great Northern system, which Hill had begun to develop in 1883. Of this system, and of the Northern Securities Company, which he had promoted, Hill became president.

Hindenburg, Field Marshal Paul von (1847-1934), was president of the German Reich, 1925-34. He played a great part in the World War and was chief of the German general staff, 1916-18.

Hippocrates, (460-357 B. C.)) the Father of Medicine. Was a native of Thessaly, and practiced and taught in Athens.

Hirohito, Emperor of Japan (b. 1901), acceded to the throne Dec. 1926.

Hitler, Adolf (1889-1945), German dictator from 1933 to 1945. Born in Austria, he fought in World War I, after which he organized the National Socialist party. He acquired a large following from various discontented groups and in 1933 forced himself into the Chancellorship, later assuming full dictatorial powers. His policy was marked by intense nationalism, anti-Semitism, opposition to the Versailles Treaty, and an aggressive foreign policy. He annexed Austria and Czechoslovakia, and in 1939 invaded Poland, precipitating World War II. Highly successful in the early years of the war, Hitler's failure to conquer England, the entry of the United States into the war, and the ill-advised invasion of Russia contributed to his ultimate failure. According to all available sources, Hitler and his wife committed suicide Apr. 30, 1945, and their bodies were cremated by the SS guard while Russian troops stormed their way into Berlin.

Hoare, Sir Samuel (b. 1880), British statesman. Elected to Parliament in 1910, he served as Air Secretary, 1922-24, and again 1924-29 and in 1940. He was Secretary of State for India from 1931 to June 1935, when he became Foreign Secretary. Opposition to his appeasement of Italy forced his resignation within six months. Hoare served as First Lord of the Admiralty, 1936-37; Home Secretary, 1937-39; Lord Privy Seal, 1939-40; and ambassador to Spain, 1940-45.

Hobbes, Thomas (1588-1679), an English philosopher, the father of psychology, and the first great English writer on the science of government. His principal works are the treatises, *On the Citizen*, *The Leviathan*, *Human Nature*, and *Behemoth*.

Hofer, Andreas, a Tyrolese patriot; born in St. Leonard, in the valley of Passeyr, in 1767. When the Tyrol, long a part of the Austrian dominions, was given by the treaty of Presburg to the king of Bavaria, then the ally of Napoleon, the Tyrolese revolted, and Hofer became their leader. He defeated French and Bavarian invasions three times, but during the fourth invasion was betrayed to his enemies, condemned by a court-martial at Mantua, and shot Feb. 20, 1810.

Hogarth, William (1697-1764), English engraver and painter. His "Harlot's Progress," of six engravings, was published in 1734 and gained him immediate fame. In 1735 he produced his equally celebrated "Rake's Progress," a series of eight engravings. These were followed by numerous others, including "Marriage a la mode," "Industry and Idleness," and "The March to Finchley."

Hogg, James (1770-1835), Scottish poet; born in Selkirkshire. After receiving a scanty education, he became a shepherd. His early rhymings brought him under the notice of Sir Walter Scott, by whose advice he published a volume of ballads under the title of *The Mountain Bard.* The appearance of the *Queen's Wake* in 1813 established Hogg's reputation as a poet.

Hokusai (1760-1849), a Japanese artist, born in Tokyo in 1760. At 13 he was apprenticed to an engraver. He was original in his drawings and depicted Japanese scenes accurately. Among his works are "Views of Famous Bridges," "Ten Thousand Sketches," and "Views of Lu-Chu Islands."

Holbein, Hans, the Elder (c. 1460-1524), a famous German painter, father of Hans Holbein.

Holbein, Hans, the Younger (1497-1543), was born at Augsburg and settled in London in 1530, where he won the favor of Henry VIII for whom he painted many portraits and produced the famous "Dance of Death."

Holbrooke, Josef Charles (b. 1878), composer of operas and orchestral works, and a successful conductor and teacher.

Holl, Francis Montague (1845-1888), a noted English painter. Among his best-known works are "No Tidings from the Sea," "Leaving Home," "Deserted," and "Ordered to the Front."

Holland, John (1841-1914), American inventor of submarines; born in Liscannor, Ireland, 1841. He had a mechanical turn of mind and in 1875 built his first submarine, followed in 1877 and 1881 by improved models. In 1898 *The Holland No. 9* was tested in New York bay and found satisfactory, and the United States Navy purchased a number of this type of underwater craft. Their design became the basis of later submarine construction.

Holmes, Oliver Wendell (1809-1894), American author; born in Cambridge, Mass. In 1847 he became professor of anatomy at Harvard. His best-known prose works are: *The Autocrat of the Breakfast-Table, The Professor of the Breakfast-Table,* and *The Poet at the Breakfast-Table.* Holmes wrote three novels: *Elsie Venner, The Guardian Angel,* and *A Mortal Antipathy.* His most famous poems are: "Old Ironsides," "The Chambered Nautilus" and "The Wonderful One-Hoss Shay."

Holmes, Oliver Wendell, Jr. (1841-1935), an American jurist; son of Oliver W. Holmes. After serving three years in the 20th Massachusetts Regiment during the Civil War, he took up the study of law. He became instructor of constitutional law at Harvard (1870-1871) and edited the *American Law Review,* 1870-1873. From 1873 to 1882 he practiced law, then served as associate justice of the U. S. Supreme Court from which he resigned in 1932. He was author of *Common Law* (1881), *Speeches* (1891, 1913), and an editor of *Kent's Commentaries* (1873).

Holst, Gustav Theodore (1874-1934), a British composer, born in Sweden, professor of music and music master at St. Paul's Girls' School, London, 1905-34. His most important work is *The Planets,* a suite of seven orchestral tone poems.

Holst, Hermann Eduard von (1841-1904), a German-American historian; born in Fellin, Livonia, Russia. He came to the United States in 1866 and engaged in literary work and lecturing; he returned to Europe, becoming professor in the University of Strassburg (1872) and Freiburg (1874); appointed professor in the University of Chicago (1892). He was author of *Constitutional and Political History of the United States;* lives of John C. Calhoun and John Brown; *Constitutional Law of the United States,* and *The French Revolution Tested by Mirabeau's Career.*

Homer (c. 850 B. C.), epic poet of ancient Greece, author of the *Iliad* and the *Odyssey.* His long epic poems, the earliest known works in European literature, have had a very significant influence on the literary tradition of the Western world.

Homer, Winslow (1836-1910), an American painter, born in Boston. His first oils, on the Civil War, brought him membership in the National Academy in 1865. But his greatest works, produced after 1884, were sea subjects. Among the paintings of this period are "The Maine Coast," "On a Lee Shore," and "Stowing the Sail." Homer, self-taught and free of foreign influence, has been called the most native of American painters.

Hood, John Bell (1831-1879), an American military officer; born in Kentucky. He was graduated at West Point in 1853. He entered the Confederate army in 1861, became a brigadier general, and was severely wounded at Gaines's Mill, at Gettysburg and at Chickamauga. He was made lieutenant general and succeeded Gen. J. E. Johnston in command of the Confederate forces around Atlanta. Although the plans of his campaign were sound, Hood was repulsed after severe fighting at the Battles of Peach Tree Creek and Atlanta, and was forced to evacuate the city on Sept. 1, 1864. He was later defeated by Thomas at Franklin and Nashville, Tenn., when he attempted to cut Sherman's communications.

Hood, Samuel, Viscount (1724-1816), British admiral, who commanded a squadron in the Revolutionary War. In 1793 he was put in command of the Mediterranean fleet, and showed great capacity in that post, taking and occupying Toulon and capturing Corsica among other exploits.

Hood, Thomas (1799-1845), an English poet and humorist. Of his serious verse, *The Song of the Shirt, The Dream of Eugene Aram,* and *The Bridge of Sighs* may be cited as the best examples.

Hooker, Joseph (1814-1879), Union general during the Civil War, was born in Hadley, Mass. He was graduated from West Point in 1837. During the Civil War he was nicknamed "Fighting Joe Hooker" by McClellan's men and in 1863 was made commander-in-chief of the Army of the Potomac. He resigned his command after losing the battle of Chancellorsville to the Confederates under Lee. His reputation was somewhat redeemed by his brilliance as a corps commander under Grant at the Battles of Lookout Mt. and Missionary Ridge. He retired in 1868.

Hooker, Richard (1554-1600), English churchman famed for his great book on *Ecclesiastical Polity.*

Hoover, Herbert Clark (b. 1874), 31st President of the United States, born in West Branch,

Iowa. At the outbreak of World War I, Hoover became chairman of the American Relief Commission. He served as Secretary of Commerce under Harding and Coolidge, and initiated the St. Lawrence Seaway and Hoover Dam projects. In 1928 he was elected President, and in October and November of the following year, 1929, the stock market crash occurred, followed by the great depression. He was defeated for re-election in 1932. After World War II he was an adviser to the government on problems of relief and reconstruction abroad. He was appointed by President Truman in 1947 to head a board of inquiry on the antiquated structure of government, which resulted in the famous "Hoover Report."

Hopkins, Johns (1795-1873), an American philanthropist. In 1873 he gave property worth $4,500,000 to found a free hospital, presented Baltimore with a public park, and also gave over $3,000,000 to found the Johns Hopkins University in Baltimore.

Horace (Quintus Horatius Flaccus) (65-8 **B. C.**), famous Roman satirist and poet, who was the friend of Virgil and attained immortal fame by his *Satires, Epodes.* and *Odes.*

Hore-Belisha, Lord Leslie (1893-1957), British Secretary of State for War from 1937 to 1940; Minister of Transport, 1934-37; Financial Secretary to the Treasury, 1932-34; Parly. Sec. to the Board of Trade. 1931-32.

Horthy de Nagybanya, Admiral Nicholas (1868-1957), regent of Hungary from 1920 to 1944.

Horton, Robert Forman (1855-1934), English Congregational minister and author. In 1927 he founded the Oxford Conference.

Houdini, Harry (1873-1926), famous American magician, who was originally a locksmith but went on the vaudeville stage as an expert in escaping from handcuffs, locked chambers, etc.

Houdon, Jean Antoine (1740-1828), a French sculptor. After studying in Italy, he returned to Paris and executed the busts of Voltaire, Rousseau, Molière, Franklin, Buffon, Catherine II, etc. In 1778 he became a member and a professor of the Academy of Fine Arts. He was invited to the United States and made the statue of Washington, now at the Virginia state capitol in Richmond.

House, Edward Mandell (1858-1938), an American statesman, born at Houston, Texas. In 1912 he helped win the presidential nomination for Woodrow Wilson. He was appointed a personal representative of the President, and during 1914 and 1915 gave his efforts to the attainment of peace. In 1918 he was named American delegate to draft the armistice. He was a member of the American Peace Commission at Paris, of the Peace Conference for the League of Nations, and of the Commission of Mandates, 1919. His valuable war notes, published as *The Intimate Papers of Col. House,* were widely read.

Housman, Alfred E. (1859-1936), English poet and classical scholar. As professor of Latin at the University of London, and Cambridge, he edited the works of several Roman authors. He is best known as the writer of *A Shropshire Lad* (1896) and *Last Poems* (1922), two small volumes of poems, characterized by simplicity of language and exquisite descriptions of the English countryside. His *Collected Poems* were published in 1940.

Housman, Laurence (b. 1865), English author; brother of A. E. Housman. Among his poems are *Green Arras* (1896) and *Spikenard* (1898); he also wrote a play, *Prunella;* and two play cycles: *Palace Plays,* and *Little Plays of St. Francis.*

Houston, Sam (1793-1863), American soldier and statesman; born in Rockbridge Co., Va. In 1823 and 1825 he was elected to Congress, and in 1827 governor of Tennessee. On removing to Texas in 1832 he was made a general of Texas troops. In 1836 he defeated the Mexicans in the battle of San Jacinto, which resulted in the independence of Texas, and was elected president of the new republic. In 1845 Texas entered the Union, and Houston was chosen United States Senator. He was elected governor of Texas in 1859, but was deposed for adherence to the Union in 1861.

Hovey, Richard (1864-1900), an American poet; born in Normal, Ill. He wrote *Launcelot and Guenevere* (1880-98), a series of poetic dramas; *Songs from Vagabondia* (1893-96), written with Bliss Carman; *Along the Trail* (1898); and *Taliesin: a Masque* (1900).

Howard, Bronson (1842-1908), an American playwright; born in Detroit, Mich. He was a reporter for several New York newspapers from 1867 to 1872. His greatest success came with *The Henrietta* (1887), a burlesque on American business, and *Shenandoah* (1888).

Howard, John (1726-1790), British reformer, who earned celebrity for his philanthropic efforts on behalf of prison reform.

Howard, Sidney Coe (1891-1939), dramatist. After ambulance and aviation service during World War I he became a staff member of various magazines. Among his plays, *They Knew What They Wanted* was awarded the Pulitzer Prize in 1925; *Alien Corn* (1933) won wide acclaim; *The Silver Cord* was produced in motion pictures after a successful stage run. In addition he has translated and adapted several European dramas.

Howard of Effingham, Lord (1536-1624), commander of the fleet which defeated the Spanish Armada, 1588, and took part in the capture of Cadiz, 1596.

Howe, Elias (1819-1876), an American inventor; born in Spencer, Mass. He constructed a sewing machine in 1846, and was for several years involved in lawsuits to establish his right to reap the benefits of his ingenuity.

Howe, Julia Ward (1819-1910), American philanthropist and poet, famous as the author of the *Battle Hymn of the Republic* (1861), a leader of the Woman Suffrage movement, and the first woman to be elected to the American Academy of Arts and Letters.

Howe, Richard, Earl (1726-1799), British admiral during Revolutionary War who in 1758 destroyed Cherbourg, and 1794 won the famous victory over the French off Brest.

Howells, William Dean (1837-1920), American novelist. While U. S. consul at Venice from 1861 to 1865 he collected material for *Venetian Life* and *Italian Journeys.* He joined the staff of the *Atlantic Monthly* in 1866 as assistant editor and became editor in 1872. His best stories, *A Modern Instance* and *The Rise of Silas Lapham* are realistic novels of American life.

Hrdlicka, Ales (1869-1943), American anthropologist, born in Bohemia. He made anthropological studies of the Southwest and Mexico for the American Museum of Natural History of New York. In 1910 he became curator of the U. S. National Museum at Washington. Among his published works are *Ancient Man in North America, Physical Anthropology* (American), and *Old Americans* (1925).

Hubbard, Elbert (1859-1915), American author, born in Bloomington, Ill. He established the Roycroft Press in 1895, for making de luxe editions of the classics and published a magazine, the *Philistine. Little Journeys*, a series on visits to the homes of great men, won great popularity. Among his best known essays is *A Message to Garcia*. He and his wife died with the sinking of the Lusitania.

Hudson, Henry (c. 1550-1611), famous English navigator who discovered the Hudson River, Hudson Strait and Bay.

Hudson, William Henry (1841-1922), English author and naturalist, who spent his early years in South America, memories of which influenced much of his work. His books include *The Purple Land* (1885), *Green Mansions* (1904), *Afoot in England* (1909) and *British Birds* (1895).

Hughes, Charles Evans (1862-1948), Chief Justice of the United States Supreme Court; born in Glens Falls, N. Y. He began to practice law in 1884, continuing till 1891, when he accepted a professorship at Cornell. In 1893 he resumed active law practice in New York, and eventually won fame, particularly in the gas and insurance investigations he conducted. In 1906 he was elected governor of New York, and from 1911 to 1916 was Associate Justice of the United States Supreme Court. From 1921 to 1925 he was United States Secretary of State, and from 1926 to 1930 he was a member of the Permanent Court of Arbitration at The Hague. In 1930 he was named Chief Justice of the United States Supreme Court. He retired in 1941.

Hughes, Rupert (1872-1956), an American author. He served in the Spanish-American War and in World War I and was raised to the rank of lieutenant colonel. Among his novels are *The Thirteenth Commandment* (1916); *The Unpardonable Sin* (1919); in 1927 his biography of George Washington appeared.

Hughes, Thomas (1822-1896), English author, educated at Rugby and at Oxford. His best-known work is *Tom Brown's Schooldays*.

Hugo, Victor Marie (1802-1885), great French poet, dramatist, and novelist, who headed the Romantic movement in France in the early part of the 19th century. His best-known dramas are *Hernani, Lucrèce Borgia, Ruy Blas*, and *Le Roi s'amuse*. Among his novels, *Notre Dame, Les Misérables, Les Travailleurs de la mer*, and *L'Homme qui rit* are the most important.

Hull, Cordell (1871-1955), American statesman and Secretary of State, born in Tennessee. He was admitted to the bar in 1891, and served in the Tennessee House of Representatives, 1893-1897. From 1903 to 1907 he was judge of the Fifth Judicial Circuit Court of Tennessee. Hull served in the U. S. House of Representatives from 1907 to 1921, and was elected to the U. S. Senate in 1931, but resigned in 1933 to take over the duties of Secretary of State. He resigned in 1944 because of ill health. He received the Nobel Peace Prize in 1945, for his work in organizing the United Nations.

Humboldt, Friedrich Heinrich Alexander von (1769-1859), German explorer and naturalist; his books described his travels and his various scientific discoveries—especially in geology and natural history.

Hume, David (1711-1776), Scottish historian and philosopher. He went to France, where he wrote his *Treatise of Human Nature* (1738). Hume's *Essays, Moral, Political, and Literary*, appeared in 1742 and 1752. In 1752 appeared his *Inquiry Concerning the Principles of Morals*. In 1754 he published the first volume of his *History of England*, which he did not complete till 1761. While this work was in progress he published *The Natural History of Religion*.

Humperdinck, Engelbert (1854-1921), a German composer. He was made head of the Berlin Meisterschule in 1900; before that time he had instructed at the Barcelona Conservatory and in Frankfurt. His most noteworthy operas are *Hänsel und Gretel* and *Die Königskinder*.

Hunt (James Henry) Leigh (1784-1859), an English poet, politician, and essayist. His literary fame rests chiefly on his essays. He was the author of "Abou ben Adhem."

Hunt, Wm. Holman (1827-1910), one of the three founders of the Pre-Raphaelite movement, and an artist who achieved distinction by several remarkable paintings.

Hurst, Fannie (b. 1889), an American novelist and story writer born in 1889. Among her works are *Five and Ten, Back Street, Great Laughter, Humoresque*, and *Vertical City*.

Huss, John (1369-1415), celebrated reformer, a native of Bohemia. Sentenced to death unless he recanted, he suffered martyrdom on June 7, 1415. His death caused a civil war which lasted for many years.

Hutchins, Robert Maynard (b. 1899), American educator, born at Brooklyn, N. Y. He was professor of law and dean of the Law School at Yale University. In 1929 he became president of the University of Chicago. In his book *The Higher Learning in America* (1936) and elsewhere Hutchins advanced his progressive theories of education. He became chancellor of the University of Chicago in 1945, and resigned (effective 1951) to assist Paul G. Hoffman, head of the Ford Foundation.

Huxley, Aldous Leonard (b. 1894), English novelist, poet, and essayist, author of *Crome Yellow, Jesting Pilate, Brave New World, Point Counter Point, After Many A Summer Dies the Swan*.

Huxley, Julian (b. 1887), English biologist and writer, brother of Aldous Huxley. Some of his later works are *Science and Social Needs* and *A Scientist Among the Soviets*. In 1935 he became president of the Zoological Society in London.

Huxley, Thomas Henry (1825-1895), British scientist and author. After the publication of Darwin's *Origin of Species*, Huxley became an ardent evolutionist. His biological work, *Man's Place in Nature*, and his numerous essays were marked by great vigor and clearness of thought and gave him a leading position. He held numerous important appointments and was president of the Royal Society in 1883.

Huygens, Christian (1629-1695), Dutch mathematician and astronomer. In pure geometry, Huygens gave the reason for the quadrature of the hyperbola, the ellipsis, and the circle; in mechanics he formulated the theory of the pendulum and its application to the clock; he announced the law of the motion of bodies revolving in circles, thereby anticipating the law of gravitation. In optics he laid the foundation of the theory of undulations.

Hyatt, John Wesley (1837-1920), an American inventor. He invented a lock-stitch sewing machine, a machine for squeezing the juice from sugar cane and devised a method of solidifying hard woods.

Hyde, Douglas (1860-1949), president of Eire, and well-known historian, poet and folklorist. His *Literary History of Ireland* (1899) was the first worthy attempt at writing a systematic and comprehensive account of Gaelic literature. He became president of the Gaelic League upon its foundation in 1893, of the Irish Texts Society, and of the Irish National Literary Society. Besides being the author of numerous works in Gaelic, he wrote plays, poems, and histories in English. He was professor of Modern Irish in National University, Ireland, from 1909 until 1932. He was elected to the presidency of Eire in 1938, serving until 1945.

I

Ibrahim Pasha (1789-1848), Egyptian statesman, general, and viceroy, who, adopted by Mohammed Ali as his son, contributed largely to the success of Egyptian policy. His conquest of Syria was a notable feat of generalship.

Ibsen, Henrik (1828-1906), Norwegian poet and dramatist. His first literary works were essays and poems. In 1862 he produced *Love's Comedy*, a satirical play which brought his name out of obscurity. A historical drama, *The Pretenders* (1864), was followed by the dramatic poems, *Brand* (1866), and *Peer Gynt* (1867). Moving to Germany in 1874, Ibsen produced a series of dramas in which he realistically set forth his views of the individual versus society. Among them were: *The Pillars of Society, A Doll's House, Ghosts, An Enemy of the People, The Wild Duck, The Lady from the Sea, Hedda Gabler, The Master Builder, Little Eyolf.*

Immermann, Karl Leberecht (1796-1840), German dramatic poet and writer of romance. He is most famous for short stories and satirical novels. Among his well-known works are *Münchhausen*, the poem *Tulifäntchen* (1827), and the epic *Tristan and Isolde.*

Indy, Vincent d' (1851-1931), French composer, pupil of César Franck. He was one of the founders of the Société Nationale de Musique and of the Schola Cantorum. In 1912 he was appointed to teach in the Paris Conservatory. Among his works are the drama *Fervaal* and the symphonic trilogy *Wallenstein*, besides various symphonic variations and orchestral, piano, and other instrumental compositions.

Inge, William Ralph (1860-1954), English cleric and author. From 1911 to 1934 he was dean of St. Paul's Cathedral. Because of a type of pessimism which he manifested, the term "the gloomy dean" became synonymous with his name. He became well known as a university lecturer. His many writings include *Personal Realism and Mysticism, Christian Ethics and Modern Problems, God and the Astronomer.*

Ingersoll, Robert Green (1833-99), American lawyer, writer, and lecturer. He was one of the world's greatest orators, and became known by reason of his lectures directed principally against Christianity.

Inness, George (1825-1894), an American painter, born in Newburgh, N. Y. His paintings show the influence of the Barbizon school and are noted for the accuracy with which they represent the American climate and the aspects of American scenery. His "American Sunset" was exhibited in the Paris Exposition of 1867. His other works include "Peace and Plenty," "A Vision of Faith," "A Passing Storm," "Twilight," "The Afterglow," "The Morning Sun," and "Delaware Water Gap."

Innocent III (1160-1216), one of the most powerful of the popes, who succeeded in bringing all the monarchs of Christendom under his sway.

Inonu, Ismet (b. 1884), president of Turkey from 1938 to 1950; minister for foreign affairs and prime minister in 1923; prime minister 1924-27 and 1927-37.

Irving, Sir Henry (1838-1905), English actor. His first success was in *The Two Roses*, followed by *The Bells, Eugene Aram*, and Shakespearean plays.

Irving, Washington (1783-1859), an American author, born in New York City. He was educated for the legal profession, but his tastes were in the direction of literature. He visited France, Italy, Switzerland, Holland, and England and in December, 1809, appeared his celebrated *History of New York by Diedrich Knickerbocker*. In 1815 he embarked for England where he began the series of papers entitled the *Sketch Book*, which contained *"Rip Van Winkle"* and *"The Legend of Sleepy Hollow."* During this period he wrote some of his most famous works, including *Bracebridge Hall, Tales of a Traveler*, and *The Alhambra.* Irving served as minister to Spain from 1842 to 1846. Among his later works were *Oliver Goldsmith*, and *Life of George Washington.*

Isaacs, Sir Isaac Alfred (1855-1948), Australian jurist and statesman. He was governor-general of Australia 1931-1936, being the first native-born Australian to occupy that position; and chief justice of the High Court of Australia, 1930-31.

Isabella I (1451-1504), reigned jointly with Ferdinand V, her husband. During their thirty years' sway Spain was united as a single monarchy and achieved the height of its greatness, the discovery of America, the conquest of Granada, and the expulsion of the Moors from Spain being among the events of their reign.

Ismail Pasha (1830-1895), khedive of Egypt, whose policy rendered Egypt practically independent of Turkey. Because of reckless extravagance he involved himself in difficulties, which caused the sale of his Suez Canal shares to England, the establishment of the dual control of England and France, and his own abdication in 1879.

Isocrates (436-338 B. C.), Greek orator and rhetorician, born in Athens. At an early age he showed great ability in public speaking and later opened a school of oratory. Of his compositions, rhetorical and epistolary, 121 are extant, among them the *Areopagiticus* and the *Panegyricus.*

Ito, Hirobumi, Prince (1841-1909), one of the most enlightened statesmen of Japan. The social changes which Japan experienced in the latter half of the 19th century owed much to his guidance and influence. He was four times premier.

Iturbi, Jose (b. 1895), Spanish pianist and conductor. He became head of the faculty in piano at the Paris Conservatory and from 1919 to 1923 was professor of piano at the Geneva Conservatory. In 1936 Iturbi was made conductor of the Rochester Symphony Orchestra.

Iturbide, Augustin de (1787-1824), Mexican soldier and emperor. On the outbreak of the struggle for Mexican independence, he joined the Royalist forces, and in 1815 rose to the chief command of the army. Later he went over to the rebel side and proclaimed himself emperor of Mexico in 1822. His reign was troublesome and came to an end in less than a year by his abdication. In 1824 he returned and made an attempt to recover the crown, but was arrested, and shot. His grandson was adopted as his heir by Emperor Maximilian.

Ivan III, the Great (1462-1505), grand duke of Russia. By conquest he added Great Novgorod, Viatka, Yaroslavl, and Rostov to his domain in 1478. Through autocratic government he effected laws to improve social conditions and the imperial courts.

Ivan IV, the Terrible (1530-1584), czar of Russia. He adopted the title of czar at his coronation in 1547, being the first Russian sovereign to take this title. He subdued Kazan and Astrakhan, and from his reign dates the first annexation of Siberia. He concluded a commercial treaty with Queen Elizabeth after the English had discovered the way to Archangel by sea. Ivan died of sorrow for his son, whom three years before he had slain in a fit of rage.

Ives, Frederick Eugene (1856-1937), an American inventor. His pioneering in orthochromatic and trichromatic photography and photoengraving led to the invention of the halftone process of photoengraving (1878), and the three color printing process in the typographic press (1886). He was director of the photographic laboratory at Cornell University from 1874 to 1878. His other inventions include the short-tube single objective binocular microscope, the parallax stereogram, and a process for recording motion pictures in natural colors.

J

Jacks, Lawrence Pearsall (1860-1955), English philosopher and Unitarian clergyman. Principal of Manchester College, Oxford, 1915-31 and professor of philosophy in that College, 1903-31. Editor of the *Hibbert Journal*, 1902, and author of numerous books.

Jackson, Andrew (1767-1845), an American statesman and general, 7th President of the United States, born probably in Waxhaw Settlement, S. C. Tennessee was admitted to the Union in 1796, and Jackson was sent as its Representative to Congress. He was elected to the Senate in 1797 but resigned his seat in 1798 to become judge of the Tennessee Supreme Court, where he served six years. When the War of 1812 broke out, he offered his services with 2,500 volunteers of Tennessee militia, of which he was commander-in-chief. In 1814 Jackson was made a major general and put in command of the Department of the South. He repulsed the enemy at Mobile, took Pensacola by storm, and then marched to New Orleans, where he fortified the city. His victory on Jan. 8, 1815, made Jackson the hero of the nation. When in 1819 the United States purchased Florida, Jackson was appointed governor, and in 1823 he was elected to the Senate. In 1824 he was nominated for the Presidency; but the election went to the House of Representatives, which chose John Quincy Adams. In 1828 Jackson was again nominated, defeating Adams by a large electoral and popular majority. He introduced the theory that "to the victors belong the spoils," and made wholesale removals of Federal officials to make room for his own appointees. He attacked the United States Bank, opposing the renewal of its charter, which would expire in 1836. He was reëlected in 1832, and opposed the South Carolina nullification movement. After his second term, Jackson lived in retirement at "The Hermitage" near Nashville.

Jackson, Helen Maria Fiske Hunt (1831-1885), an American author, born in Amherst, Mass. She went to Colorado and became actively interested in the treatment of the Indians by the government. In 1883, she was appointed a special commissioner to investigate the condition of the Mission Indians of California. Her published works include: *Verses, A Century of Dishonor*, and *Ramona*.

Jackson, Thomas Jonathan "Stonewall" (1824-1863), Confederate army officer, born in Virginia. He was graduated from West Point and served with distinction in the Mexican War. In 1861 he became a brigadier general in the Confederate forces. The firm stand of his brigade at Bull Run won him the nickname "Stonewall." Jackson's Shenandoah Valley Campaign of 1862 is one of the classics of military strategy. He defeated three separate Union armies and prevented the Western Federal army from reinforcing McClellan. Later in the same year Jackson aided Lee in the Seven Days' Battles, co-operated in the strategy that resulted in the brilliant Confederate victory of Second Bull Run, and captured Harper's Ferry. Jackson was accidentally shot by his own men after having executed a flank march which surprised Hooker and contributed to Lee's victory at Chancellorsville. Pneumonia set in, and his death resulted.

Jacquard, Joseph Marie (1752-1834), French mechanic, whose loom provided a new and effective method of weaving designs in textiles.

James I (1566-1625), king of England from 1603 to 1625, was the son of Mary Stuart. He succeeded to the English throne on the death of Elizabeth. Numerous plots were formed against him, including the Gunpowder Plot of 1605. He persecuted the Puritans, granted many monopolies, and increased the power of the Crown.

James II (1633-1701), king of England 1685-1688, succeeding his brother Charles II. The Declaration of Indulgence, the persecution of the bishops, and other high-handed proceedings disgusted his people, and he fled to France in December, 1688, making way for William III and his more popular rule.

James, Henry, (1843-1916), an American novelist who produced a number of notable stories, remarkable for their intellectual subtlety and careful characterizations. For the last thirty years of his life he resided mostly in England, and in 1915 became a British subject. His best-known novels are *The American, Daisy Miller, The Bostonian, The Portrait of a Lady* and *What Maisie Saw.* In 1907 he wrote *The American Scene* and later published *Finer Grain.*

James, Jesse Woodson (1847-1882), notorious American outlaw, born in Clay Co., Mo. The

Southern sympathies of his parents caused them much suffering in the Civil War and in 1862 young Jesse joined the band of guerilla fighters led by C. W. Quantrell. He soon distinguished himself as an unerring pistol shot and a man of courage, and in 1867 when Quantrell was killed Jesse and his brother Frank (1843-1915) took over the leadership of the outlawed band. When a $10,000 reward was offered for him, "dead or alive," two of his own followers shot him in the back.

James, William (1842-1910), an American psychologist and educator, born in New York City. He received degrees from Harvard and Princeton; and from 1872 to 1907 taught at Harvard University. He was an analytical psychologist of the school of Wundt and Ribot and his theory of knowledge, called Pragmatism, exercised a wide influence upon American and European thought. Among his published works are *Principles of Psychology, The Will To Believe and Other Essays in Public Philosophy,* and *The Varieties of Religious Experience.*

Janssens, Abraham (c. 1570-1632), Dutch painter. His most famous pictures are the "Entombment of Christ" and the "Adoration of the Magi." Because of his vigorous drawing and admirable coloring he ranks next to Rubens among the historical painters of the period.

Jay, John (1745-1829), an American statesman, born in New York City. He was elected to the First Continental Congress in 1774. In 1777 he drafted the constitution of New York State and was appointed chief justice of the state; was returned to Congress in 1778 and elected its president and in the following year was sent as minister to Spain. From 1784 to 1789 he was secretary for foreign affairs. On the drafting of the Constitution in 1787, he wrote in its favor in the *Federalist;* and after the organization of the Federal government, when he was offered his choice of offices by Washington, he selected that of chief justice of the Supreme Court. In 1794 he concluded with Lord Grenville the convention familiarly known as "Jay's treaty," which provided for reciprocity of inland trade between the United States and British North America. Jay was governor of New York from 1795 to 1801, and thereafter retired from public life.

Jefferson, Joseph (1829-1905), American actor, born in Philadelphia, Pa. In 1857 he made a hit as Doctor Pangloss in New York and in 1858 created the part of Asa Trenchard in *Our American Cousin.* In 1865 he visited London and at the Adelphi Theater played for the first time his world-famous part of Rip Van Winkle.

Jefferson, Thomas (1743-1826), American statesman, 3d President of the United States; born in Shadwell, Va. He was graduated from William and Mary College in 1764, and in 1769 was sent to the Virginia House of Burgesses, where he gained local fame by a speech supporting the emancipation of slaves. Elected in 1774 as a delegate to the Colonial Congress but unable to go, Jefferson sent a "Summary View of the Rights of British North America." Jefferson was a member of the second Congress, in 1775, and of the third, in 1776, and wrote most of the Declaration of Independence. In 1779 he was elected governor of Virginia. In 1783 he was returned to Congress, where he secured the adoption of the decimal system of coinage and assisted in other important measures. In 1784, with Franklin and Adams, he was instrumental in making important treaties with Prussia and Morocco, and in 1785 he was made minister to France, where he served during the stormiest period of the French Revolution. In 1789 he was made Secretary of State by Washington. Jefferson came to be recognized as the leader of the Republican party, the other members of the Cabinet and Washington himself being Federalists. In 1794 he retired to his estate and passed three years in study and leisure. In 1797 he was chosen Vice-President with Adams, and in 1801 was elected President; in 1805 he was re-elected. His administrations were marked by the war with Tripoli, the admission of Ohio to the Union, the purchase of Louisiana Territory, the Embargo Act, and the trial of Aaron Burr for treason. In 1809 he retired to private life, where he devoted himself to study and philanthropic enterprises, his chief undertaking being the establishment of the University of Virginia. Jefferson was steadily democratic in his views and a champion of the rights of the states, as against centralization in government. He died in Monticello, Va., July 4, 1826, on the day of John Adams' death, and the 50th anniversary of the famous Declaration.

Jellicoe, John Rushworth (1859-1935), British admiral. He served in Egypt in 1882, and in China from 1898 to 1901. In 1907 he was made rear admiral, and in 1914 he was given command of the Grand Fleet. He commanded the fleet in the Battle of Jutland in 1916. From 1919 to 1923 he was governor of New Zealand. He wrote *The Grand Fleet, 1914-16, Its Creation, Development, and Work* (1920), *The Crisis of the Naval War* (1920).

Jerome, Jerome Klapka (1859-1927), English writer, who made his first success with his humorous book, *Three Men in a Boat.* He also wrote a play, *The Passing of the Third Floor Back.*

Jerome, St. (340-420), a noted theologian of the 5th century, whose Latin translation of the Scriptures ("the Vulgate") made him famous. He died at Bethlehem.

Jesus Christ, the founder of Christianity. Jesus, his given name, is the Greek translation of the Hebrew *Joshua.* Christ is the Greek name for the Hebrew *Messiah,* the redeemer of the Jews who had been promised by many prophecies recorded in the Old Testament. So little is known about Jesus historically, despite his tremendous impact on history, that he cannot properly be discussed strictly as a historical character. In his human capacity, as the Son of Man, he was born in the town of Bethlehem, Palestine, three to five years before the Christian Era. His parents were Joseph, a carpenter of Nazareth, and Mary, of the house of David. Jesus was of royal blood, descended from a long line of Hebrew prophets and kings. However, Roman occupation of his native land had caused his family's position to be reduced to what might be considered "middle class." The history of his youth and early manhood is fragmentary. His parents escaped with him to Egypt at an early age, when King Herod ordered the slaughter of all babies. He is next heard of in the temple at Jerusalem at the age of twelve, amazing the wise men with his understanding. There is no further authentic report of him until he began to teach at the age of 30; and three years later he was crucified.

To the Christian world Jesus was the Son of God, whose life on earth was for the purpose of teaching mankind spiritual truths, and is now in Heaven, interceding for every member of the human race. Substantially all that is known of Jesus is recorded in the Gospels of Matthew, Mark, Luke and John, which comprise the first four books of the New Testament.

Joan of Arc (1412-1431), French peasant girl, whose heroism inspired the French to drive the English out of Orleans and enabled Charles to be proclaimed king at Rheims. She was burned as a heretic at Rouen, and canonized in 1919.

Joffre, Joseph Jacques Césaire (1852-1931), French soldier. He served in the artillery during the Franco-Prussian War. In 1911 he was appointed commander-in-chief of the French Army and held that post during the first half of World War I. Although he helped in defeating the Germans at the Battle of the Marne, he failed to recognize the changed conditions of warfare on the Western Front and insisted too strongly on siege warfare and offense. After Verdun, he was recalled and in 1917 visited the United States.

John (c. 1167-1216), king of England from 1199 to 1216. He made himself so unpopular that the barons determined to limit his power and establish their privileges. John consented to whatever the barons chose to dictate, and thus was obtained the basis of English constitutional freedom—the Magna Charta.

John III (John Sobieski) (1624-1696), king of Poland. He was the youngest son of James Sobieski, governor of Cracow. In 1665 he was made grand marshal and general of the Polish armies. In 1673 he gained the memorable battle of Choczim, near the Dniester, in which the Turks lost 28,000 men. On the death of Michael in the following year he was elected king of Poland and shortly afterward compelled the Turks to sue for peace.

John of Gaunt (1340-1399), duke of Lancaster, fourth son of Edward III. Toward the close of his aged father's reign John gradually became the most influential personage in the realm. Richard II reposed considerable confidence in John, made him duke of Aquitaine, and intrusted him with several embassies to France. After 1385, he gradually ceased to be a factor in English politics.

John, St., the Baptist (executed A.D. 28), the forerunner of Christ.

John Chrysostom, Saint (347-407), Greek churchman and orator, born in Antioch. He became bishop of Constantinople in 398 and was active in building hospitals and in reforming monasteries. Chrysostom was finally exiled in 407 by the emperor and died on the way to his place of banishment.

John, St., the Evangelist (d. c. A.D. 99), the son of Zebedee, retired to Patmos after the Crucifixion, but returned from exile to Ephesus later, and there died at a great age.

Johnson, Andrew (1808-1875), American statesman, 17th president of the United States; born in Raleigh, N. C. In 1826 he emigrated to Tennessee. In 1835 and in 1839 he was sent to the Tennessee legislature, and from 1843 to 1853 he served in Congress. In 1857 he was sent to the United States Senate, where he secured the passage of a homestead bill, which President Buchanan vetoed. He ardently advocated the Union cause, was made military governor of Tennessee by Lincoln in 1862, and gave vigorous support to the Federal government. In 1864 he was elected Vice-President, and on the assassination of Lincoln in April, 1865, became President. His administration was marked by constant dissension between himself and Congress, and he was impeached before that body for various alleged "high crimes and misdemeanors," although the real cause was his opposition to the severe Southern Reconstruction program of Congress. The trial was presided over by Chief Justice Salmon P. Chase. A two-thirds vote necessary to convict could not be secured; a change of one vote, however, would have carried conviction. When his term expired he retired to Tennessee. In 1875 he was again elected to the United States Senate.

Johnson, James Weldon (1871-1938), Negro author, born in Jacksonville, Florida. He was American consul from 1906 to 1912 in Puerto Cabello, Venezuela, and Corinto, Nicaragua. In 1916 he became secretary of the National Association for the advancement of Colored People, and in 1930 professor of creative literature in Fisk University. He is the author of many books and articles, including *Fifty Years and Other Poems, God's Trombone, Negro Sermons in Verse, Black Manhattan, Along This Way*. With his brother, Rosamond Johnson, he has written several light operas and compiled two books of Negro spirituals.

Johnson, Dr. Samuel (1709-1784), English lexicographer and author. His *Dictionary* was published in 1755. Other works include *Vanity of Human Wishes* and *Rasselas*. For two years he published the *Idler*, a collection of essays after the style of the *Spectator*. His *Lives of the Poets* appeared in 1781. The classic biography of Johnson was written by James Boswell.

Joliet, Louis (1645-1700), French-Canadian explorer, born in Quebec. He attended the Jesuit College of Quebec, became interested in exploration and trading, and spent many years with the Indians. In 1673, with Father Marquette, a Jesuit priest, and five others he explored the Fox, Wisconsin, and Mississippi Rivers. They prepared maps and charts of the region. Joliet also explored Labrador.

Jones, Jesse Holman (1874-1956), Federal Loan Administrator July, 1939, and Secretary of Commerce of the United States August, 1940, was born in Robertson County, Tennessee. At the age of 20 he went to Dallas, Texas, entered the lumber business, and was sent as general manager of his company to Houston in 1898. This city has been his home ever since, and he is largely credited with its rebuilding after the panic of 1907. During World War I he was assigned to military relief work for the American Red Cross in France. Later he became interested in politics, and in 1928 became chairman of the advisory finance committee of the Democratic Party. In 1932 he was appointed director of the Reconstruction Finance Corporation by President Hoover, and in 1933 he was appointed chairman of the RFC by President Roosevelt. He served as Federal Loan Administrator, 1939-1945, and as Secretary of Commerce, 1940-1945.

Jones, John Paul (1747-1792), American naval hero; born in Scotland. Early in life he took to sea, and during the Revolutionary War commanded various ships on behalf of the Colonists, and was most daring in his onslaughts upon British vessels. He died in Paris.

Jones, Robert Tyre (Bobby) (b. 1902), American golfer, by profession a lawyer, who in 1930 had the unique distinction of winning the Open and Amateur Championships of both England and America.

Jones, Sir William (1746-1794), English philologist and jurist, devoting himself to the study of languages, he became the most celebrated English linguist of his time, being familiar with both the dialects and literature of 27 languages. In India he further distinguished himself by his researches into Asiatic literature and archaeology. He translated many works from the Sanskrit, Persian, and other languages and had an important influence on the science of comparative philology.

Jonson, Ben (1573-1637), English dramatist. The characters in his plays are well-known types of the Elizabethan age. Among his best plays are *Every Man in His Humor*, and *The Alchemist*. Among Jonson's lyric poems are "Hymn to Diana," and "Drink to Me Only With Thine Eyes." He was an intimate friend of Shakespeare.

Jordan, David Starr (1851-1931), American educator, born in Gainesville, N. Y. He studied at Cornell and Harvard. From 1885 to 1891 he served as president of the University of Indiana. He was the first president of Leland Stanford University. He wrote numerous scientific books, especially on fishes.

Josephine (1763-1814), empress of France, the wife of Napoleon I, until he divorced her in 1809 and married Marie Louise. Josephine had previously been married to Vicomte Alexandre Beauharnais, by whom she had two children.

Josephus, Flavius (c. 37-c. 100), a Jewish historian whose *History of the Jewish War* and *Antiquities of the Jews* contained much valuable historical evidence bearing upon Biblical history.

Joule, James Prescott (1818-1889), English physicist. Among the results of his research were the discovery of the mechanical equivalent of heat and the formulation of Joule's Law.

Jowett, Benjamin (1817-1893), English classical scholar. His outstanding works include translations of the *Dialogues* of Plato and *History* of Thucydides.

Joyce, James (1882-1941), Irish author. His most famous works are *Dubliners*, the autobiographical *Portrait of the Artist as a Young Man*, *Ulysses*, and *Finnegan's Wake*.

Juarez, Benito (1806-1872), president of Mexico; born of Indian parents in Gueletao, Oaxaca. On the overthrow of the Liberal president by the Clerical party in 1858 Juarez assumed the executive position but was compelled to retire to Vera Cruz. His government was recognized by the United States in 1859, and in 1861 he was elected president for four years. From 1861 to 1864 he waged war against the French attempt to establish Maximilian as Emperor of Mexico. Juarez retreated gradually to the frontier and stayed for nearly a year at El Paso del Norte. He entered Mexico City again in July, 1867, Maximilian having been shot meanwhile by order of court-martial. Juarez was again elected president and died in office.

Jung, Carl Gustav (b. 1875), Swiss psychologist, founder of the school known as analytical psychology.

Junot, Androche, Duc d'Abrantes (1771-1813), one of Napoleon's great generals. He was brilliantly successful until defeated by Wellington at Vimiera.

Jusserand, Jean Jules (1855-1932), French historian and diplomat. He was chancellor of the French embassy in London (1887-1890), and became ambassador to the United States in 1903. In his literary work he made a specialty of the Elizabethan age and of the literature of England in the Middle Ages. His writings include *The English Theater from the Conquest to the Immediate Predecessors of Shakespeare*, *The Novel in the Time of Shakespeare*, and *A Literary History of the English People*.

Justinian I (Flavius Anicius Justinianus) (483-565), Roman emperor of the East, whose fame rests chiefly on his laws. His *Corpus Juris Civilis* remained the accepted textbook of Roman law to the end of the 19th century and is still one of the most important of all monuments of jurisprudence. He reigned from 527 to 565.

Juvenal (Decimus Junius Juvenalis) (60-140), Roman poet and rhetorician of the age of Trajan. His sixteen celebrated *Satires* are among the finest in classical literature.

K

Kagawa, Toyohiko (b. 1888), Japanese Christian philosopher and author. Kagawa has exerted a strong influence on the political, economic, social, and religious life of Japan. Although he was imprisoned in 1921 for organizing the first labor union in his country, he later became adviser of the government on labor questions. The rapid growth of consumer cooperatives in Japan was due in large measure to his efforts. Among Kagawa's works, which include novels, essays, poetry, and religious writings, are *Before the Dawn*, *A Shooter at the Sun*, *The Psychology of the Poor*.

Kalb, Johann (1721-1780), general in the American Revolution, born in Huttendorf, Germany. He is more generally known as Baron de Kalb. In 1776 he entered the Continental Army, and was appointed a major general. He fought gallantly in the war until 1780 when he fell mortally wounded at the Battle of Camden.

Kant, Immanuel (1724-1804), German philosopher, whose *Critique of Pure Reason*, published in 1781, had immense influence in shaping the philosophical thought of the 18th and 19th centuries.

Karolyi, Count Michael (1875-1955), Hungarian liberal statesman. He was made premier of Hungary in 1918 and became the first president of the republic in 1919. Upon the establishment of the communist dictatorship of Bela Kun in 1919, he fled and lived in exile. During World War II he led the Free Hungarian Movement.

Kauffmann, Angelica (1741-1807), Swiss painter. Her works are chiefly of religious and classical subjects.

Kaufman, George S. (b. 1889), American playwright. He wrote *The Butter and Egg Man* (1925) and is co-author with Edna Ferber, Marc Connelly and others of such stage successes as *Dulcy* (1921), *The Royal Family* (1927), *Of Thee I Sing*, *Stage Door*, *First Lady*, *I'd Rather Be Right*, *You Can't Take It With You*, and *The Man Who Came to Dinner*.

Kaulbach, Wilhelm von (1805-1874), German portrait painter.

Kautsky, Karl (1854-1938), German writer and Marxian socialist. With Haase he founded the

Independent Social Democratic party in 1917. Kautsky opposed any changes in Marxian socialism and severely denounced Lenin and Russian communism. He was the chief editor of the *Kautsky Documents* treating of the origin of the World War.

Kaye-Smith, Shelia (Mrs. Penrose Fry) (1888-1956), English author, known for her novels of village life.

Kean, Edmund (1787-1833), one of the greatest tragic actors in the history of the British stage.

Keats, John (1795-1821), English poet, who produced a number of poems which in richness of imagination and beauty of thought are not excelled by anything in the language. His "Odes," his two poems, "Isabella" and "The Eve of St. Agnes," are exquisite in form and expression.

Keller, Helen Adams (b. 1880), American writer, who, as the result of illness, became deaf and blind at the age of 19 months but was taught to read and write and graduated with honors from Radcliffe College. She has written several books, including *The Story of My Life* (1902), *The World I Live In* (1908) and *Mid-Stream* (1930).

Kellogg, Frank Billings (1856-1937), American statesman. He became U. S. Senator (1917-23), ambassador to Great Britain (1924-25), and secretary of state (1925-29). He was co-author of the Kellogg-Briand Pact, and for his effort to ban war he won the Nobel Peace Prize for 1929. In 1930, he became a judge of the Permanent Court of International Justice.

Kelvin, William Thomas, Lord (1824-1907), English scientist, who co-ordinated various theories of heat, and established firmly the law of conservation of energy. He made many discoveries and improvements in submarine telegraphy, and invented the minor galvanometer and the siphon recorder.

Kemble, Frances Ann ("Fanny") (1809-1893), English writer and actress. She married an American and lived on a Georgia plantation, but afterwards wrote against slavery.

Kemble, John Philip (1757-1823), English actor and for many years manager of Drury Lane Theater in London.

Kemmerer, Edwin Walter (1875-1945), American economist. In 1903 he was financial adviser to the U. S. Philippine Commission and head of the Islands' currency division. His work as economic adviser to the Carranza government in Mexico (1917) enhanced his reputation, and he became known as the "money doctor." He headed numerous advising commissions, including those to Guatemala (1919), Colombia (1923), Chile (1925), and Poland (1926). He was a consultant in the Dawes Reparations Commission (1925). He opposed the "commodity" dollar and Franklin D. Roosevelt's financial policies.

Kempis, Thomas à (1380-1471), name by which the German mystic and writer Thomas Hammerken was known. He was an Augustinian monk, whose life was mainly spent at a monastery near Zwolle. He was the author of *The Imitation of Christ*.

Kent, James (1763-1847), American jurist, born in Philippi, N. Y. He was the author of *Commentaries on the American Law* (4 vols. 1826-1830), which holds in the United States a position similar to that occupied by Blackstone's *Commentaries* in Great Britain. It treats of international law, the American Constitution, state laws, and legal rights of persons and property. Kent was chief justice of New York.

Kent, Rockwell (b. 1882), American painter and author. He has traveled to Alaska, Greenland and South America. Among his paintings, which are noted for their vigor and originality, are "Winter," "Mother and Child," and "Deer Season." His writings include *Wilderness, N by E*, and *Salamina*.

Kepler, Johann (1571-1630), a renowned German astronomer, who made numerous discoveries in regard to the motions of planets. The system he formulated is known as "Kepler's Laws."

Kerensky, Alexander Feodorovich (b. 1881), a Russian revolutionary leader, prime minister July to Nov., 1917, when he was ousted by the Bolshevists.

Kern, Jerome (1885-1945), American composer, born in New York City and best known for his light operas, among them *Very Good Eddie*, *Sunny* (1925), *Show Boat* with its song "Ol' Man River" (1929), *Roberta* (1933), and *I Dream Too Much* (1933).

Key, Francis Scott (1780-1843), American lawyer. While detained on one of the British ships during the bombardment of Fort McHenry, in 1814, he wrote the words of *The Star-Spangled Banner*.

Keynes, John Maynard (1883-1946), British economist. He wrote *Economic Consequences of the Peace*, *The End of Laissez-Faire*, and *Treatise on Money*.

Khrushchev, Nikita (b. 1894), Russian Communist leader, elected to the central committee of the party in 1934, became a member of the Supreme Soviet in 1937. After Stalin's death, he was instrumental in ousting Malenkov, Molotov, and Zhukov, and held the real power in the U.S.S.R.

Kidd, Captain William (c. 1645-1701), famous British pirate who engaged in numerous piratical expeditions under cover of the English flag. He was hanged after a sensational trial.

Kilmer, Joyce (1886-1917), American poet. He became prominent as a poet and literary critic prior to World War I and contributed to the *New York Times*. His best-known lyric is "Trees." He was killed in World War I.

King, Ernest Joseph (1878-1956), U.S. naval officer born at Lorain, O. He became a naval flyer at 49 and chief of the Bureau of Aeronautics in 1933. He commanded the Aircraft Battle Force (1938-40) and the Atlantic Fleet (1940-41). He served simultaneously as commander-in-chief of the U. S. fleet and chief of naval operations from 1941 and retired in 1946.

King, Rufus (1755-1827), American statesman. He served in the American Revolution, and was a member of the Constitutional Convention. He became a leader of the Federalists, sat in the Senate 1789-1796, and 1813-1825, and was minister to Great Britain, 1796-1803.

King, William Lyon Mackenzie (1874-1950), Canadian statesman. From 1900 to 1908 he was deputy minister of labor. He organized the Canadian Department of Labor, edited the *Labor Gazette*, and was appointed chairman of several government commissions. In 1919 he succeeded Sir Wilfrid Laurier as leader of the Federal Liberal Party of Canada, and in 1921 was made prime minister, a post which he retained, with only slight interruption, until 1930. In 1935 he resumed office as prime minister and resigned in 1949.

Kingsley, Charles (1819-1875), English clergyman

and novelist. He wrote *Hypatia, Westward Ho!* and *Hereward the Wake*. He was an influential leader of Christian Socialism.

Kipling, Rudyard (1865-1936), English author, born in Bombay. He was educated in England and in 1882 returned to India and joined the staff of the *Civil and Military Gazette*. From 1892 to 1896 he lived in Vermont. In 1907 he was awarded the Nobel Prize for literature. He was a prolific and versatile writer. His earliest works are considered by many to be his greatest. Among his important works are: *Plain Tales from the Hills, The Light that Failed, Barrack Room Ballads, Captains Courageous*, and *Kim*.

Kitchener, Horatio Herbert, Earl (1850-1916), British soldier. He entered the army in 1871, and had a brilliant career in Cyprus, Egypt, India, and South Africa. On the outbreak of war with Germany he was made secretary for war, and his work in building up the army won universal admiration. On his way to Russia in 1916, he was drowned when the *Hampshire* sank, probably after hitting a mine.

Knox, John (1505-1572), Scottish religious reformer and historian, who stirred Scotland to accept Protestantism in the reign of Mary Queen of Scots. He was the founder of Scottish Presbyterianism.

Knox, William Franklin (1874-1944), American political leader and newspaperman, born in Boston and educated at Alma (Mich.) College. In 1898 he served with the Rough Riders in the Spanish-American War; in the same year he entered newspaper work. In 1901 he began as a publisher, and continued in the newspaper business, becoming in 1931 editor and publisher of *The Chicago Daily News*. He served in the Army during the World War and was active in politics; in 1936 he was the Republican candidate for Vice President. Knox was appointed Secretary of the Navy in 1940.

Koch, Robert (1843-1910), German bacteriologist. He discovered the tubercle bacillus (1882), and the comma bacillus or cholera germ (1884). In 1885 he was appointed professor of hygiene at the University of Berlin, where he made researches in the causes and treatment of tuberculosis and malaria. Won Nobel Prize, 1905.

Kosciusko, Thaddeus, or Kosciuszko, Tadeusz (1746-1817), Polish patriot; born in Lithuania. He fought for the colonists in the American Revolution, and in 1792 became leader of the Polish forces fighting for independence. In 1794 he was made dictator; his defeat at Maciejowice in the same year ended Polish independence, and made him a prisoner. Two years later Emperor Paul restored him to liberty. He spent the remainder of his life chiefly in France and Switzerland.

Kossuth, Louis (1802-1894), Hungarian patriot and leader, who in the struggle for his country's freedom in 1849 was for a time successful, but ultimately had to acknowledge defeat, and fled first to Turkey and afterwards to England, where he lived for some years.

Kreisler, Fritz (b. 1875), Austrian violinist. At the age of seven, he entered the Vienna conservatory to study under Hellmesberger. In 1885, he began studying in Paris under Massart (violin) and Delibes (composition). He made several concert tours of the United States, and established a reputation as being one of the world's greatest violinists.

Kropotkin, Peter Alexeivich, Prince (1842-1921), anarchist, geographer and explorer, who, after a distinguished career in Russia, his native country, was imprisoned for favoring the political action of a workingmen's association. He escaped to England, and wrote many important books on socialistic and geographical subjects.

Kruger, Stephanus Johannes Paulus (1825-1904), South African Dutch statesman. He participated in the "Great Trek" across the Vaal River, helped form a stable Boer government, and in 1883 became president of the Transvaal. Under his administration difficulties with England over his rigid treatment of English settlers led to the Jameson Raid and his declaration of war upon England. Boer reverses led to his departure for Europe, where he died.

Krupp, Alfred (1812-1887), German engineer, who founded the great gun factories at Essen. By his introduction of the Bessemer plan of casting steel and the steam hammer into Germany, he brought about important developments in heavy breech-loading guns, and built up factories which employed 20,000 workmen.

Kublai Khan (1216-1294), a famous Mogul emperor and grandson of Jenghiz Khan. He greatly extended the Mogul empire by conquest, and was the founder of the Mongol dynasty in China.

Kun, Bela (b. 1886), Hungarian politician and journalist who led the Communist revolution in Hungary in 1919 and became chairman of the Council of People's Commissars during the short-lived Soviet regime. After its collapse he fled to the U.S.S.R., where he disappeared about 1937, supposedly a purge victim.

L

La Farge, John (1835-1910), American artist, born in New York City. He executed remarkable paintings, altar pieces, and decorations of interiors—notably of Trinity Church, Boston; and designed stained-glass windows for churches and many other buildings, in the new American manner, of which he was the originator, with Louis Tiffany.

Lafayette, Marie Joseph Paul Roch Yves Gilbert Motier, Marquis de (1757-1834), French soldier and statesman, born in the castle of Chavagnac, Auvergne. He entered the army, and upon hearing of the American Revolution, sailed for America, and was appointed a major general in the Continental Army. He fought at Brandywine, negotiated for French aid to the United States, and played an important part in the campaign which was ended at Yorktown. After the war he returned to France, where he became a liberal leader in the Revolution which began in 1789. He lived in retirement during the First Empire, but after the Restoration became a member of the Chamber of Deputies, where he was a member of the liberal group. By invitation of Congress he revisited the United States in 1824, and in the Revolution of 1830 he was a leader of the moderates.

La Follette, Robert Marion (1855-1925), American political leader: born in Wisconsin. As a regular Republican he served three terms in Congress, 1885-1891. From 1906 until his death he served in the Senate. He voted against the American declaration of war on Germany, and opposed the World Court and the League of Nations. In

1924 he ran for President on the Progressive ticket, but carried only his own state.

La Fontaine, Jean de (1621-1695), French poet and fabulist. His fables are satires of the society of his period, and are written in verse of great beauty and variety.

Lagerlöf, Selma (1858-1940), Swedish novelist who was awarded in 1909 the Nobel Prize for literature. She wrote a series of novels called *The Ring of the Löwenskölds*; and several collections of short stories, among them *The Adventures of Nils, The Girl from the Marsh Croft,* and *Men and Trolls.*

Lamarck, Jean Baptiste Pierre Antoine de Monnet, Chevalier de (1744-1829), French naturalist. His chief work was the *Histoire naturelle des animaux sans vertèbres.* His theory of evolution was based upon the inheritance of acquired characteristics.

Lamb, Charles (1775-1834), English author. His *Essays of Elia* are characterized by great felicity of expression and much genial humor. In some of his writings he was assisted by his sister, Mary Lamb, to whom he was devoted.

Landseer, Sir Edwin Henry (1802-1873), the most celebrated English animal painter of his time. He designed the lions for the base of the Nelson Monument in Trafalgar Square.

Lang, Andrew (1844-1912), Scottish author, born in Selkirk. He was a versatile writer, and published many volumes including *Ballads and Lyrics of Old France* (1872), *Custom and Myth, Books and Bookmen, Letters to Dead Authors, The Making of Religion,* and *The Red Book of Animals.* He edited several collections of stories, fairy tales, and poetry for children. His versatility is shown by his authoritative work in folklore and anthropology; Greek, French, and English literature; and his investigations in psychic phenomena.

Lang, Cosmo Gordon (1864-1945), archbishop of Canterbury, after 1928. He was archbishop of York from 1908-1928.

Langley, Samuel Pierpoint (1834-1906), American scientist. In 1867 he became director of the Allegheny Observatory, and in 1887 secretary of the Smithsonian Institution. He was the inventor of the bolometer, and one of the great pioneers of aviation.

Langmuir, Irving (1881-1957), American chemist. In 1909 he entered the research laboratory of the General Electric Company at Schenectady, N. Y. His accomplishments include the development of gas-filled tungsten lamps, electron discharge apparatus, a condensation high vacuum pump, and atomic hydrogen welding. He received the Nobel Prize in 1932 for work in surface chemistry.

Lansing, Robert (1864-1928), American statesman; born in Watertown, N. Y. He became Secretary of State in 1915. He was a member of the American commission to Negotiate Peace, at Paris, where he disagreed with President Wilson, who asked him to resign. Lansing resumed his law practice and was a counsel for Chile from 1923 to 1925. He wrote *The Peace Negotiations* and *the Big Four and Others of the Peace Conference.*

Lao-Tsze, one of the ancient philosophers of China, who flourished about 600 B. C. The work which his fame rests upon was entitled *The Path to Virtue.*

Laplace, Pierre Simon, Marquis de (1749-1827), French astronomer, who was the author of the nebular hypothesis.

La Salle, René Robert Cavelier, Sieur de (1643-1687), French explorer: born in Rouen. He was educated by the Jesuits, and in 1666 went to Canada, where he traveled much, learned Indian customs and languages, and established Fort Frontenac, which he later made a trading post. In 1679 he led an expedition which sailed the Great Lakes to Green Bay, and then crossed overland to the Illinois River. After despatching Michel Aco and Father Hennepin to explore the Upper Mississippi, La Salle returned to Fort Frontenac and Montreal for supplies. In 1682, at the head of a large party, he descended the Mississippi to its mouth, and claimed the whole of the valley for France. In the following year he sailed for France, where he was authorized to govern the region he had explored. In 1684 he set sail for the Gulf of Mexico, intending to plant a colony at the mouth of the Mississippi. After losing several vessels in a vain search for the mouth of the river, he landed and started for Canada to obtain supplies. On the way he was shot and killed by mutinous members of the expedition.

Lassalle, Ferdinand (1825-1864), German socialist. Although wealthy, he developed an interest in the working classes, and urged the substitution of cooperatives for the wage system. In 1863 he formed a society to secure political rights for workers; this developed into the Social Democratic Party. Lassalle's ideas laid the basis for German socialism, and were particularly of influence on Bismarck's program of state socialism.

Latimer, Hugh (1485?-1555), English reformer, who became bishop of Worcester under Henry VIII, but when Mary came to the throne was condemned as a heretic, and burned at the stake.

Lavoisier, Antoine Laurent (1743-1794), French chemist and physicist, who is often called the "father of modern chemistry," was born in Paris, and was the first to establish the fact that combustion is a form of chemical action.

Lawrence, David Herbert (1885-1930), English novelist and poet. His works deal largely with the psychology of sex relations. He wrote: *Women in Love, Lady Chatterley's Lover, The White Peacock, Sons and Lovers, The Plumed Serpent, The Woman Who Rode Away,* and *The Virgin and the Gypsy.*

Lawrence, Thomas Edward (1888-1935), English adventurer, soldier, and scholar. As an archaeologist, he became well acquainted with Arabia and the Near East, and upon the outbreak of World War I became a member of the British Intelligence Service in that region. He joined the Arabs, stirred them to revolt against the Turks, and led them in a campaign against Turkish communication lines. His daring raids, in which he utilized camels, horses, armored cars, and bombing planes, were an important factor in the destruction of Turkish power in Arabia and in the final success of the British forces under Allenby. Lawrence was a delegate to the Peace Conference, and after the war, because of his dislike of publicity, resigned his commission and enlisted as a private in the British army. He wrote *Seven Pillars of Wisdom* and *Revolt in the Desert,* both accounts of his Arabian adventures, and a translation of Homer's *Odyssey.*

Leacock, Stephen Butler (1869-1944), humorist and economist. He is head of the Dept. of Political Economy, McGill University, but is best known throughout the world as a humorous writer, author of many books, among them *Literary Lapses, Nonsense Novels, Beyond the Beyond.*

Lebrun, Albert (1871-1950), president of the French Republic after 1932. He was minister for Colonies, 1911-12; vice-president of the Chamber, 1913; president of the Senate, 1931-32.

Lecky, William Edward Hartpole (1838-1903), English historian. His best-known works are *Religious Tendencies of the Age; Declining Sense of the Miraculous; Democracy and Liberty; Spirit of Rationalism in Europe,* published in two volumes in 1865; the *History of European Morals from Augustus to Charlemagne,* published in two volumes in 1869; and the *History of England in the Eighteenth Century,* 1878-90.

Lee, Richard Henry (1732-1794), American statesman, born in Westmoreland Co., Va. He received part of his education in England, and after his return to Virginia was chosen a delegate to the House of Burgesses. He was sent as delegate to the First Continental Congress at Philadelphia (1774), and on June 7, 1776, introduced the motion breaking political connection with Great Britain. In 1784 he was unanimously elected president of the Congress, and when the federal Constitution was established he entered the Senate. In 1792 he retired to private life.

Lee, Robert Edward (1807-1870), American soldier; born in Westmoreland Co., Va. He was graduated from the United States Military Academy in 1829, saw service in the Mexican War, and was breveted colonel in 1847. In 1861 Lee was offered command of the Union army, but refused, and although opposed to slavery and secession, resigned his United States commission when Virginia seceded. He was made commander of the Virginia troops and in May, 1862, replaced Gen. J. E. Johnston in the command of the Army of Northern Virginia. In the campaign that ensued General Lee, aided by "Stonewall" Jackson, made a vigorous assault on McClellan's army, and forced it back from Richmond. In August, Lee defeated the Union army in the Second Battle of Bull Run, and invaded Maryland; he withdrew after the drawn battle of Antietam. In Dec., 1862, he inflicted a severe defeat on the Union army at Fredericksburg. Another northern advance was halted in May, 1863, when Lee's brilliant strategy resulted in the Confederate victory at Chancellorsville. In June he invaded Pennsylvania, and though victorious in the first day's battle at Gettysburg (July 1, 1863), met with disastrous repulse two days later, and retreated. On the defensive through 1864, Lee parried every Northern thrust, but on April 2, 1865 he was at last dislodged from his intrenchments by superior forces, compelled to retreat from Petersburg, and eventually to surrender his army to General Grant on April 9, 1865. General Lee was installed president of Washington College (now Washington and Lee University), Oct. 2, 1865.

Lee, Sir Sidney (1859-1926), English Shakespearean scholar and joint editor with Sir Leslie Stephen of the *Dictionary of National Biography.*

Leeuwenhoek, Anton van (1632-1723), a Dutch scientist and early experimenter with microscopes, born in Delft. He made over 247 microscopes, some capable of magnifying objects 270 times. He was the first man to see bacteria and protozoa and the first to give a complete description of red blood cells.

Lehar, Franz (1870-1948), Hungarian composer, chiefly of light operas of the "Viennese" type. Besides his famous *The Merry Widow,* which was first produced in 1905, and quickly gained world popularity, he has written *Gipsy Love, The Count of Luxembourg, Eva, Frasquita, The Land of Smiles* and *Giuditta.*

Leibnitz, Gottfried Wilhelm, Baron von (1646-1716), German writer and philosopher who propounded a new system of philosophy, in which he maintained that the ultimate elements of the universe are individual centers of force, or monads.

Leif Ericsson (c. 1000), discoverer of North America. He was a Norseman, born probably in Iceland. He was the son of Eric the Red. His early years were probably spent in Greenland, whence he went to Norway. He embraced Christianity and was sent as a missionary to Greenland. The *Hanksbók* sagas state that he was blown off his course on the voyage to Greenland and as a result discovered the eastern coast of North America. The *Flateyjarbók* saga states that he went first to Greenland, performed his work of conversion and then set out deliberately on a voyage of discovery. Scholars generally agree that Leif Ericsson landed on the North American coast but they are unable to determine the exact location of Vinland, some considering it as far south as Virginia, others, as far north as Nova Scotia.

Lenin, Nickolai (Vladimir Ilyich Ulyanov) (1870-1924), the founder of the U.S.S.R. He was an active worker for the Russian Revolution from 1893-1917 both "underground" in Russia and abroad. It was in this period that the revolutionary group known as the Bolsheviks developed, and Lenin was its leading spirit. He was banished to Siberia, but in April, 1917, returned to Russia. In the November Revolution of 1917 the Provisional Government was overthrown by the Bolsheviks and Lenin became president of the new government, the Council of People's Commissars—the Sovnarkom. From 1917 to his death, Lenin remained the active head of the Russian Soviet Government.

Leonardo da Vinci (1452-1519), one of the world's greatest universal geniuses. He was skilled in art, music, engineering, and science. His most famous paintings are two "Annunciations," "Madonna of the Rocks," "Last Supper," and "Mona Lisa." As a military engineer he designed a flying machine, an armored tank, and a breach-loading cannon. A restless experimenter, he recorded in his *Notebooks* observations, far advanced for his time, on anatomy, botany, mathematics, and geophysics.

Lesseps, Vicomte Ferdinand de (1805-1894), French diplomat and engineer who, while vice-consul at Alexandria, conceived the plan of the Suez Canal, which was completed in 1869. He afterwards projected the original Panama Canal which failed.

Lessing, Gotthold Ephraim (1729-1781), a noted German critic and dramatic poet, whose best-known works are *Laocoön,* and *Minna von Barnhelm.*

Leverrier, Urbain Jean Joseph (1811-1877), French astronomer, co-discoverer with John Couch Adams of the planet Neptune.

Lewis, John L. (b. 1880), American labor leader. In 1909 he became legislative agent of the United Mine Workers of America and in 1911 a representative of the American Federation of

Labor. He was a member of the Labor Advisory Board and of the National Labor Board of N.R.A. (1933), vice-president of the American Federation of Labor, and president of the United Mine Workers of America. Lewis was the leader of the group within the A. F. L. which advocated industrial unionism, or the formation of unions to embrace all workers within an industry regardless of trade or craft. He resigned as A. F. L. vice-president in 1935 and formed a Committee for Industrial Organization, with eight unions participating. This group later became the Congress of Industrial Organizations, with Lewis as president. He resigned in 1941 after Roosevelt, supported by the C. I. O., won a third term despite Lewis' personal opposition, and withdrew his U. M. W. In 1951 he effected an agreement with the soft coal industry which raised the basic daily wage of miners to $16.35.

Lewis, Meriwether (1774-1809), an American soldier and explorer, born near Charlottesville, Va. With George Rogers Clark, he was a leader of the expedition sent out by Jefferson to explore the Louisiana Territory, in 1803. Lewis was soon after made governor of the northern part of Louisiana Territory. On his way east to prepare the journal of the expedition, he died, probably by murder, at an inn on the Natchez Trace.

Lewis, Sinclair (1885-1951), an American author born at Sauk Center, Minn.; educated at Yale. He devoted several years to writing but was unsuccessful in selling his works. In 1910 he became editor and advertising manager for the George H. Doran Company but resigned in 1916 to devote himself exclusively to his own writing. Lewis's reputation as an author was made with the appearance of his *Main Street* (1920). He was the first American novelist to win the Nobel Prize in literature. In 1926 he refused the Pulitzer Prize because of the objectionable terms in which that prize was stated. *Babbitt*, *Arrowsmith*, and *Dodsworth* are among his best-known works.

Lie, Trygve (b. 1896), Norwegian statesman and United Nations official. An officer of the Norwegian Labor party 18 years, he served in the government from 1935 until 1945, four years as foreign minister. Chosen U. N. secretary general in 1946; re-elected 1950.

Liebermann, Max (1847-1935), German painter, played an important part in the development of modern art in Germany. He was president of the Prussian Academy of Art, 1920-32. Among his finest pictures are "The Flax Spinner," "The Women with Goats," and "The Net-Menders."

Lincoln, Abraham (1809-1865), American statesman and 16th President of the United States; born in Hardin County, Kentucky, on Feb. 12, 1809, the son of Thomas and Nancy Hanks Lincoln. His boyhood was spent on pioneer farms, in an environment of hardships and poverty. The constant labor of wrestling with the wilderness left him little time for formal schooling; in all he had less than a year, but eager for knowledge, he read and re-read every available book. Most of Lincoln's boyhood was spent in Indiana. In 1830 his family moved to Illinois, and in the following year he settled in New Salem, where he remained for six years. During this time he clerked in a store, managed a mill, split rails and did other odd jobs, was the village postmaster, studied law, and constantly strove to improve his education. By his sincerity, honesty, and great physical strength, he won popularity and respect. Lincoln was a volunteer captain during the Black Hawk War, and served in the state legislature, 1834-1841. At this time occurred the significant love affair with Ann Rutledge, who died in 1835. In 1837 Lincoln began to practice law, but continued his interest in politics and served in Congress from 1847 to 1849; he then retired to his law practice, but entered politics again in 1854, when agitation over slavery extension reached a dangerous height. Lincoln attacked the Kansas-Nebraska Bill, and any measure which would allow slavery to expand into the territories. In 1856 he joined the new Republican party, and in 1858 became its candidate for Senator from Illinois. In his speech accepting the nomination, Lincoln stoutly upheld the Union against Southern threats of secession, and declared that, "A house divided against itself cannot stand." The campaign was notable for a series of debates between Lincoln and his Democratic opponent, Stephen A. Douglas. In these debates, Lincoln defended the Union and the democratic ideal; he argued that slavery was an injustice and an evil, and opposed its extension. Although he lost the election, he had become a national figure, and in early 1860 made a number of speeches in the East. In May he was nominated as the Republican candidate for President; because of a split in the Democratic party he was elected in November, although he polled less than a majority of the popular vote. The South regarded Lincoln's election as a deadly threat to slavery, and by the date of his inauguration, seven states had seceded. War was imminent, but Lincoln refused any compromise which would allow further extension of slavery. Although exerting efforts toward conciliation, he was determined to preserve the Union, and when the Confederate attack on Fort Sumter opened hostilities between the sections, he issued an immediate call for volunteers to put down the rebellion. As war-President, Lincoln, despite his early vacillation and lack of military knowledge, proved his greatness amid a crisis that threatened the very existence of the nation. Beset on all sides by radicals and conservatives, by Southern sympathizers and unthinking abolitionists; hampered by early military reverses and differences among his advisers; Lincoln yet pursued, with unflagging energy and profound faith, the task of restoring and preserving the Union. Although this was at first his sole aim, the abolition of slavery was added in 1863, as a war measure. Amid the war weariness of 1864, the number of his enemies mounted and many of his own party deserted him; but Sherman's victories brought brighter days, and in November he was re-elected. As the war drew to a close, Lincoln continued to express the generous and conciliatory attitude of his famous Gettysburg Address, and in his Second Inaugural declared for a peace, "With malice toward none; with charity for all." The war ended on April 9, 1865; five days later Lincoln was shot by John Wilkes Booth, an actor.

Lind, Jenny (1820-1887), famous Swedish soprano.

Lindbergh, Charles Augustus (b. 1902), American aviator, born in Detroit, Mich. After two years of study in engineering at the University of Wisconsin he learned to fly, purchased a plane, did some "barnstorming" and entered the U. S. Air Service Reserve at Brooks Field, San Antonio, Texas. Commissioned a second lieutenant, he flew the air mail (1925-26) between Chicago and St. Louis. In 1927, in a monoplane of his own design, *The Spirit of St. Louis,* he crossed the Atlantic from New York to Paris alone in 33½ hours. He was received with enthusiastic acclaim in France, Belgium, England, and, on his return, in America; he was awarded many decorations and prizes, including the $25,000 Orteig prize. In 1927 and 1928 he toured Mexico and Latin America in a "good-will" flight. In 1928 he was employed by Transcontinental Air Transport, and also, in 1929, as technical adviser in aeronautics to the Department of Commerce. In the same year he married Anne Morrow, daughter of Dwight Morrow, United States ambassador to Mexico. The Lindberghs made several flying tours over most of the world. A first son, Charles Augustus Lindbergh, Jr., born in 1930, was kidnaped and killed in 1932. Lindbergh made flights of archæological interest over Mayan areas, and was associated with Dr. Alexis Carrel in biological experiments. Before the advent of the U. S. into the Second World War he strongly opposed American aid to the Allies, and was a frequent and favorite speaker before isolationist groups. During the War he served as research consultant at Ford aviation plants.

Linlithgow, 2nd Marquess of (1887-1952), civil lord of the admiralty, 1922-24; British commissioner on Indian agriculture, 1926-28; viceroy and governor general of India, 1936-43.

Linnaeus, Carl von Linne (1707-78), a tireless Swedish doctor and scientist who became one of the most distinguished of naturalists, and the founder of modern botany. His *Systema Naturae* was published in 1735, and other monumental works followed. He was the first to expound the true principles for defining genera and species.

Lippi, Fra Filippo (c. 1406-1469), commonly known as Lippo Lippi, a Florentine painter. He painted religious subjects, which he conceived and designed from a human standpoint. His greatest work was done on the choir walls of the cathedral of Prato—illustrations of the lives of John the Baptist and St. Stephen. He was executing a series of incidents from the life of the Virgin in the cathedral apse at Spoleto, when death overtook him. Besides these works he painted several Madonnas and altarpieces.

Lippmann, Gabriel (1845-1921), French physicist, whose more important work was in the field of color photography. His numerous inventions include the capillary-electrometer, which bears his name, and many other delicate instruments. He was awarded the Nobel Prize in physics in 1912.

Lippmann, Walter (b. 1889), American editorial writer, author and columnist. He received his education at Harvard, graduating in 1909, and was first associated with the *New Republic.* Later, he was a staff member of the *New York World,* and after 1931 was connected with the *New York Herald Tribune* as a special writer. His material was syndicated for use by other papers. Lippman also wrote magazine articles. Among his books are: *A Preface to Morals, Men of Destiny, Method of Freedom.*

Lister, Lord (1827-1912), English scientist, who achieved renown for his discovery of the antiseptic treatment which has accomplished much on behalf of surgery. He was president of the Royal Society, 1895-1900.

Liszt, Franz (1811-86), Hungarian pianist and composer. As a pianist he was unequalled for many years. His best-known compositions are his *Hungarian Rhapsodies,* and several symphonic poems, a form he invented.

Litvinov, Maxim Maximovich (1876-1951), Russian diplomat and statesman. Appointed the first Soviet representative to Great Britain, 1917, and instrumental in securing American recognition of Soviet Russia. He was commissar for foreign affairs 1930-1939.

Livingstone, David (1813-1873), Scottish explorer and missionary, whose discoveries in Africa greatly advanced geographical knowledge.

Livy (Titus Livius) (59 B. C.-A. D. 18), Roman historian of the Augustan Age. He wrote a *History of Rome* in 142 books, of which only 35 remain.

Lloyd George, David (1863-1945), an English liberal leader, born in Manchester. He entered Parliament in 1890, was appointed Chancellor of the Exchequer in 1908, and reorganized the financial system. During World War I he was made minister of munitions in 1915, and secretary of war to succeed Lord Kitchener in July, 1916. He became prime minister toward the close of the same year. After active participation in the Versailles Peace Treaty in 1919 he aided in establishing the Irish Free State in 1920, and left the ministry in 1922. He wrote six volumes of *War Memoirs* (1933-36), and *The Truth About the Peace Treaty* (1938).

Locke, John (1632-1704), English philosopher. Of his philosophical works his *Essay on the Human Understanding* is the best known. His arguments were strongly pragmatic, and he attempted to show that all ideas were derived through sensory experience. Locke asserted that moral judgment was the result of voluntary action, and he was a strong defender of individual liberty. In 1690 he wrote *Two Treatises of Government,* a defense of the sovereignty of the people. In *Some Thoughts Concerning Education* (1693) Locke advocated physical and moral development as opposed to the mere accumulation of knowledge. Locke's ideas directly affected Berkeley, Hume, Rousseau, and Voltaire.

Lockyer, Sir Norman (1836-1920), English scientist and astronomer.

Lodge, Sir Oliver Joseph (1851-1940), physicist, principal of Birmingham University, 1900-1919. A great scientist interested in psychical research, president British Association, 1912. Author of *Faith and Science,* etc.

London, John Griffith ("Jack") (1876-1916), American novelist who led an adventurous life on fishing and sealing vessels, in the Klondyke goldfields, and as a war correspondent in Japan, Korea and Manchuria, 1904, and Mexico, 1914. He wrote many popular novels and stirring books on adventure, among them: *The Call of the Wild, White Fang,* and *The Sea Wolf.*

Longfellow, Henry Wadsworth (1807-1882), an American poet, born in Portland, Maine. He was graduated at Bowdoin College. In 1839 he published *Hyperion,* a novel, and *Voices of the Night,* a series of poems. His best-known works are *The Belfry of Bruges, The Golden Legend, Hiawatha, The Courtship of Miles Standish,* and *Tales of a Wayside Inn.* He resigned his chair at Harvard in 1854; and received the honorary degrees of LL.D. and D.C.L. from the Universities of Cambridge and Oxford respectively. He died in Cambridge, Massachusetts.

Longstreet, James (1821-1904), an American military officer, born in South Carolina; Commander of the 1st Corps of Lee's army in the Confederacy. In the battle of the Wilderness (May 5, 6, 1864), General Longstreet was dangerously wounded, occasioning his retirement for some months from active service. After the fall of Richmond he surrendered and lived in comparative retirement for some months from active service. After the fall of Richmond he surrendered and lived in comparative retirement till 1869, when he was appointed collector of customs at New Orleans; later he was made minister to Turkey, and United States marshal for the District of Georgia.

Louis XIV (1638-1715), king of France from 1643 to his death. He was responsible for the persecution of the Huguenots, the repeal of the Edict of Nantes, and for the War of the Spanish Succession.

Louis XV (1710-74), king of France. He took little active interest in politics, and his attitudes were determined by his mistresses, of whom Pompadour and Du Barry were the chief. During his reign France lost the greater part of her colonial empire to England and suffered defeat by Frederick the Great of Prussia.

Louis XVI (1754-93), king of France, who married Marie Antoinette, allowed his country to be swayed by first one statesman and then another, until at last he saw himself divested of every shred of power by the Revolution. He and his queen were subsequently imprisoned and sent to the guillotine.

Lowell, Amy Lawrence (1874-1925), an American poet and critic, of the Imagist school; born in Brookline, Mass.; received her education by private tutoring and travel in England and on the Continent. She published her first volume of poems, *A Dome of Many-colored Glass*, in 1912. Other poetic works include *Men, Women and Ghosts*, *Pictures of the Floating World*, and *Legends*.

Lowell, James Russell (1819-91), an American author, born in Cambridge, Mass.; educated at Harvard; became an abolitionist and in his famous *Biglow Papers* and other writings did much to make the movement popular. In 1855 he was appointed successor to Longfellow as professor of literature in Harvard University. He was the first editor of the *Atlantic Monthly* and also one of the editors of the *North American Review*. At the outbreak of the Civil War the poet again attacked the slavery party in a series of *Biglow Papers*. Later he wrote two volumes of essays, *Among My Books* (1870), and *My Study Windows* (1871). He was a United States minister to Spain in 1877-1880 and to Great Britain in 1880-1885. His other works include: *The Vision of Sir Launfal* and *Poems* (1848), *Life of Keats* (1854), *Poetical Works* (2 vols. 1858), and *Democracy and other Addresses* (1887). He died in Cambridge, Mass.

Loyola, St. Ignatius of (1491-1556), was the founder of the Order of Jesuits.

Lucretius, (Titus Lucretius Carus) (95-52 B. C.), the Roman poet whose *De rerum natura* is noted for its exposition of the atomic theory of Leucippus.

Ludendorff, Erich von (1865-1937), a German soldier, who was chief of staff, and shared with Hindenburg the military leadership of Germany during the World War. He was largely responsible for the victory of Tannenberg and the overwhelming successes in 1915. However, his 1918 offensive on the Western Front was ineffective.

Ludwig, Emil (1881-1948), German writer, best known for his psychological studies: *Napoleon*, *Lincoln*, *Bismarck*, and *Wilhelm II*.

Luther, Martin (1483-1546), German leader of the Protestant Reformation, ordained a priest in 1507. He became professor of theology at the University of Wittenberg and until 1517 was an orthodox Roman Catholic. His first idea of revolt occurred when he saw indulgences being sold, a practice which he openly condemned. For this he was excommunicated; summoned before the Diet at Worms, he made a memorable defense. He then separated himself from the Roman Catholics, his doctrine being formulated in the Confession of Augsburg. He lived to see the principles of the Reformation established.

M

McAdam, John London (1756-1836), a Scottish engineer who invented the process of road building called "macadamizing" which consists of small pieces of hard stone bound together by a dressing of rock dust.

MacArthur, Douglas (b. 1880), American general, born in Little Rock, Ark. Graduated from West Point in 1903, he was commander of the District of Manila (1922-25) and of the Department of the Philippines (1928-30). Chief of staff of the U.S. Army (1930-35), he returned to the Philippines (1935-37) as military adviser to the commonwealth. He retired in 1937 but was recalled to active service in 1941 and received the Japanese surrender in 1945, becoming Supreme Commander of Allied Forces in Japan. In 1950 he was appointed U.S. commander in the Korean theater of war and United Nations' commander in Korea. In 1951 he came in conflict with the Truman administration on policy and was relieved of all commands by the president.

Macaulay, Thomas Babington (1800-1859), English historian of the Victorian Era. His fame was assured by his *Essays*, *Lays of Ancient Rome*, and his *History of England*. He sat in Parliament for some years, also serving for five years as a member of the Supreme Council of Calcutta. He, at different times, filled the offices of paymaster-general and secretary for war.

Macbeth (?-1057), according to Holinshed's *Chronicle*, was the usurping Scottish king who succeeded Duncan, whom he murdered. Macbeth was slain by Duncan's son Malcolm in 1057, after a reign of seventeen years. His history forms the subject of Shakespeare's celebrated tragedy.

McClellan, George Brinton (1826-1885), an American military officer; born in Philadelphia; was graduated from the United States Military Academy in 1846. In 1861 he was appointed major general of the Army, and given command of the Army of the Potomac. In the spring of 1862 he invaded Virginia, and advanced on Richmond, but was defeated in a series of battles in July, and compelled to retreat. After the defeat of General Pope in the Second Battle of Bull Run, 1862, he reorganized the forces before Washington, met the forces of General Lee at Antietam, and halted his invasion of the North. His failure to pursue Lee closely led to his replacement by Burnside. In 1864 he was Democratic candidate for the Presidency. He was elected governor of New Jersey in 1877.

McCormick, Cyrus Hall (1809-1884), inventor of the reaper; born in Rockbridge County, Va. In

1831 the reaper was tried out and found successful, and McCormick established a local business for its manufacture and sale. It was patented in 1834, after Obed Hussey had announced a similar invention. The McCormick factory in Chicago was established in 1847. Improving and perfecting his machine assiduously, McCormick soon drove many of his competitors from the field, and his business grew more and more prosperous.

MacDonald, Sir John Alexander (1815-1891), a Canadian statesman, the chief organizer of the Dominion of Canada, born in Glasgow, Scotland. His parents emigrated to Canada when he was five years old, and settled in Kingston. He entered political life in 1844, and in 1847 was given a cabinet position in the government. A conference in 1864 debating the union of portions of eastern Canada, by MacDonald's initiative and tact was merged in the larger question of the union of all the British American provinces, which resulted in the British North America Act of 1867. Of the new dominion thereby formed MacDonald became the first premier.

McDougall, William (1871-1938), American psychologist born in England. He was professor of psychology at Harvard University 1920-27, and at Duke University, 1927-38. He wrote many important works including *Body and Mind* (1911), *The Group Mind* (1920), *Outline of Psychology* (1923), and *World Chaos* (1931).

MacDowell, Edward Alexander (1861-1908), an American pianist and composer, born in New York City. He studied at the Paris Conservatory. He was head of the piano department of the Darmstadt Conservatory and from 1896 until his retirement in 1904 was professor of music in Columbia University. Among his works are four symphonic poems for orchestra and two orchestral suites, one of them, the *Indian Suite*, based on themes from Siouan music.

McGuffey, William Holmes (1800-1873), an American educator. He was president of Cincinnati College (1836-1844) and taught at the University of Virginia (1845-1873). He originated the *McGuffey Eclectic Readers*. *McGuffey's First Reader* was published in 1836 and was followed by consecutive readers until the *Sixth Reader*, the last in the series, was published in 1857. They were revised many times and reached a sale of 122,000,000 copies.

Machiavelli, Niccolò (1469-1527), a Florentine diplomat and historian, whose book *The Prince* has maintained its celebrity as a masterly exposition of the method of governing by artifice.

Mackensen, Field Marshal August von (1849-1945), a German general who entered the army in 1870, and served in the Franco-Prussian War. A great organizer and military authority, he was responsible for the conduct of the campaign against the Russians in 1915.

McKinley, William (1843-1901), an American statesman, 25th President of the United States, born in Niles, Ohio, Jan. 29. He fought in the Civil War, rising from private to major. In 1876 he was elected to Congress, where he remained for six successive terms. In Congress he drew up the tariff bill which bore his name. In the Presidential election of 1896 McKinley was the Republican candidate. The chief issue was free coinage of silver, which the Republican platform opposed. After an intensive campaign, McKinley was elected. The Spanish-American War occurred during his first administration. He was re-elected in 1900. He was shot during a public reception at the Pan-American Exposition in Buffalo, N. Y., Sept. 5, 1901, by Leon F. Czolgosz, and died nine days later.

MacLeish, Archibald (b. 1892), an American poet. *The Pot of Earth, Streets in the Moon, New Found Land*, and *Poems, 1924-1933*, are among his works. In 1932 his *Conquistador* was awarded the Pulitzer Prize. He was appointed Librarian of Congress in 1939.

MacMillan, Donald Baxter (b. 1874), an American explorer, born in Massachusetts. From 1910-1912 he studied the ethnology of the Eskimos in Labrador. He led an expedition which explored the coast of Greenland and several islands to the west. He led three expeditions to Greenland and Baffin Island (1926-29) and the Labrador Aerial Expedition (1931).

Macmillan, Harold (b. 1894), British statesman. He entered Parliament in 1924. When the Conservatives returned to power in 1951, he held a succession of cabinet posts, rising to foreign secretary and chancellor of the exchequer. In Feb. 1957 he succeeded Eden as prime minister, and in Sept. visited the United States.

Madariaga, Salvador de (b. 1886), a Spanish author and diplomat. In 1922 he headed the disarmament section of the League of Nations. He was subsequently ambassador to the United States, Spanish delegate to the Council of the League of Nations, and ambassador to France.

Madison, James (1751-1836), an American statesman, 4th President of the United States, born in Port Conway, Va., March 16. He studied law. In 1780 he entered the Continental Congress, where he served three years; in 1784 he was elected to the Virginia Legislature, where he advocated the abolition of the feudal system of entail and primogeniture, and the removal of the remaining hindrances to religious freedom. In 1785 he urged a meeting of the states by delegates to perfect a common government, and was a member of the Constitutional Convention of 1787, and one of the chief framers of the Constitution of the United States. He advocated the adoption of it in some of the ablest papers of *The Federalist*. In 1794 he married a brilliant society woman, Mrs. Todd, who became known as Dolly Madison. His writings to some extent produced the reaction against the Federalists that resulted in the election of Jefferson, who made him Secretary of State. He was elected to the Presidency in 1808. The principal events of his administrations were the War of 1812 with Great Britain and the concluding treaty. He filled the office for two terms.

Maeterlinck, Maurice (1862-1949), a distinguished Belgian poet and critical writer. His principal works are *Pelléas et Mélisande, The Life of the Bee*, and *The Blue Bird*.

Magellan, Ferdinand (c. 1480-1521), a famous Portuguese navigator, and commander of the first expedition (1519-1522) to sail round the world. He was killed by natives in the Philippines, but the circumnavigation was completed by 31 survivors of the original crews of the five vessels.

Mahan, Alfred Thayer (1840-1914), an American naval officer and writer. He was graduated from the United States Naval Academy in 1859; served in the Civil War; was president of the Naval War College, Newport, in 1886-1889 and 1890-1893. During the war with Spain he was a member of the Naval Board of Strategy. His chief work, *Influence of Sea Power upon History* (1890), with its continuation, *Influence of*

Sea Power upon the French Revolution and Empire (1892), gave him a world-wide reputation.

Malenkov, Georgi (b. 1901), Soviet leader after the death of Stalin in 1953; born in Orenburg (now Chkalov). He was made Stalin's personal secretary in 1925 and rose quickly in Soviet official hierarchy. He was appointed to the Central Committee of the Communist party (1939) and to the Politburo (1941). Stalin's death left the government in the hands of three men: Malenkov, Molotov, and Beria. In 1953 Malenkov was confirmed as premier and Beria was purged, but in 1955 Malenkov was replaced by Bulganin and two years later was ousted from the party.

Malthus, Thomas Robert (1766-1834), English clergyman and political economist, who in his essay on *The Principle of Population* maintained that poverty and distress are unavoidable because of the more rapid increase in population than in the means of subsistence.

Manet, Edouard (1833-1883), a French painter, founder of Impressionism, which was more fully developed by Claude Monet. Manet's "Spaniard Playing a Guitar" (exhibited 1861) created a furor in art circles. His best portraits include those of Henri Rochefort, Emile Zola, and Eva Gonzales. Among his other works are "The Funeral," "Boy with a Sword" and "Dead Toreador."

Mann, Horace (1796-1859), an American educator, born in Franklin, Mass. He attended Brown University, and was graduated with honors. Later he studied law and was admitted to the bar. Becoming secretary of the Massachusetts state board of education in 1837, he emphasized the importance of a good education in promoting social efficiency and good citizenship. Through his efforts the first normal school in the United States was started, and the schools of the state were organized into one system. He published, besides his educational lectures and voluminous controversial writings, *A Few Thoughts for a Young Man* (1850); *Slavery; Letters and Speeches* (1851); and *Powers and Duties of Women* (1853).

Mann, Thomas (1875-1955), German novelist, born at Lübeck. His novel *Buddenbrooks*, published in 1903, treated the affairs of an old family of Lübeck, and is thought to be in part autobiographical. His writings became popular and in 1929 he won the Nobel Prize. His writings include also *The Magic Mountain, Joseph and His Brothers, Young Joseph, Joseph in Egypt*, and *Joseph the Provider*. Exiled by the Nazis in 1933, he came to the U. S. in 1938 and became a citizen in 1944.

Mannerheim, Baron Carl Gustaf Emil (1877-1951), Finnish soldier. As head of the Finnish army he set up the Mannerheim Line, overrun by the Russians (1939-1940). He was appointed president in 1944 during the German Occupation of Finland but was forced to resign in 1946.

Manning, Henry Edward (1808-1892). An Anglican churchman up to 1851, he entered the Roman church and was created a cardinal in 1875.

Mansfield, Katherine (1890-1923), a British short-story writer, born in New Zealand. Her first story was published in 1911, and in 1913 she married John Murray, a literary critic and editor of *The Athenaeum*. Her stories are collected in *The Garden Party, The Dove's Nest*, and other books.

Mantegna, Andrea (1431-1506), an Italian painter born in Vicenza. About 1459 he went to Verona, where he painted a magnificent altarpiece in the Church of St. Zeno. At Mantua, where he was patronized by the Marquis Gonzaga, he opened a school and painted, among other important works, "*The Triumph of Julius Caesar*," "*Madonna della Vittoria*," "*Wisdom Vanquishing Vice*," "*Parnassus*" and others. Mantegna excelled in perspective, which was then a rare merit; he also introduced the art of engraving on copper into upper Italy.

Manutius, Aldus, or Aldo Manuzio (1447-1515), an Italian printer. In 1488 he established himself at Venice. He printed the works of most of the ancient Latin and Greek authors extant as well as many productions of his contemporaries and some treatises of his own composition. He was the inventor of italic type, and the first to use small capital letters. His business was continued by his son Pavlo Manuzio (1512-1574), a man distinguished as a classical scholar no less than as a printer.

Mao Tze-tung (b. 1893), Chinese Communist leader. He served with Sun Yat-sen's army in 1910, worked as librarian, teacher, and editor, and in 1921 took part in forming the Chinese Communist party. He organized a revolutionary army in 1927. He became chairman of the Central Executive Committee of the party in 1945 and president of a Communist republic in 1949.

Marat, Jean Paul (1743-1793), one of the leading revolutionists during the French Reign of Terror, killed by Charlotte Corday.

Marconi, Guglielmo (1874-1937), Italian scientist. In 1896 he invented an apparatus by which he succeeded in sending wireless messages. He succeeded in transmitting transoceanic messages in 1902; established a public wireless telegraph service across the Atlantic in 1907; and was awarded the Nobel Prize for physics in 1909. He was president of the Reale Accademia d'Italia from 1930 until his death.

Marco Polo (1256-1323), a famous Venetian traveler and explorer, who made journeys through China, India, and other eastern countries and published the record of his various wanderings, recounting the many wonders and marvels he had seen—a record which seemed for the most part beyond credence to his contemporaries but is now largely confirmed.

Marcus Antonius, popularly known as **Mark Antony** (c. 83-30 B. C.), celebrated Roman triumvir and general; a prominent adherent of Caesar; engaged in intrigues after the latter's death, and was opposed by Brutus and Cassius. His association with the Egyptian queen Cleopatra made him a prominent figure in historic romance.

Maria Theresa (1717-1780), empress of Austria, a woman of considerable strength of character and ability, regarded as one of the most capable of the Hapsburgs. Austria made social progress during her reign, but lost certain territories.

Marie Antoinette Josèphe Jeanne (1755-1793), a queen of France; daughter of the Emperor Francis I of Austria; wife of Louis XVI of France. In the events which followed the outbreak of the Revolution she was one of the chief sufferers, but met her death on the scaffold with unflinching courage.

Marie Louise (1791-1847), daughter of Francis I of Austria, became the second wife of Napoleon in 1810, and bore him a son. She deserted Napoleon when he was exiled to Elba, and remained outside of France thereafter.

Marius, Gaius (155-86 B. C.), was one of the most distinguished Roman generals, a tribune of the people, praetor, and seven times consul.

Marlborough, John Churchill, Duke of (1650-1722), English general, whose victories at Blenheim, Ramillies, Oudenarde, and Malplaquet prevented French domination of the Continent.

Marlowe, Christopher (1564-1593), one of the greatest of the Elizabethan dramatists. His principal plays are *Dr. Faustus*, *Tamburlaine the Great*, *Edward II*, and *The Jew of Malta*.

Marquette, Jacques (1637-1675), a French missionary and explorer; born in Laon, France. He became a Jesuit priest in 1666 and went to Canada as a missionary. In 1673 and 1674 he and the French explorer and trader Joliet explored the Mississippi River from its juncture with the Wisconsin as far south as the Arkansas. They were the first to establish the size and the importance of the Mississippi River as a highway from the Great Lakes to the Gulf of Mexico. After writing a journal of their discoveries, Marquette died in the wilderness.

Marshall, George Catlett (b. 1880), American general and statesman born at Uniontown, Pa. He entered the army in 1901 and rose to the post of chief of staff, with the rank of general, in 1939. He became a general of the army in 1944. He retired in 1945 and was named special ambassador to China in December of that year. In January, 1947, he was appointed secretary of state, the first soldier ever to hold that office. He resigned in 1949, and in 1950 was recalled to the Truman cabinet as secretary of defense.

Marshall, John (1755-1835), an American jurist, born in Germantown, Va. He was an officer in the Colonial army from 1775 to 1779. He was elected in 1788 to the Virginia Convention that ratified the United States Constitution, where he shared with James Madison the work of influencing its adoption. He went as an envoy to France in 1798. In 1799 he entered Congress, and in 1801 he was appointed Chief Justice of the United States by President John Adams. This office he held for 34 years, during which his decisions on constitutional questions established precedents in the interpretation of the Constitution which have been accepted ever since. He died in Philadelphia.

Martial (Marcus Valerius Martialis) (43-104), a Roman writer, born in Bilbilis in Spain. He spent the greater part of his life in Rome, where he acquired fame as a poet and epigrammatist.

Marx, Karl (1818-1883), German socialist, born in Trier. After a brief study of law he took over the editorship of the *Rheinische Zeitung* in 1842. The following year the paper was suppressed, and Marx moved to Paris, later to Brussels, and then to London. In collaboration with Friedrich Engels he wrote the *Communist Manifesto*. His chief work, however, is *Das Kapital*. Marx's writings and theories had tremendous influence on politico-economic thought in all countries, but particularly in Russia, where some of his doctrines were put into practice by Lenin after the Russian Revolution of 1917.

Mary I (1516-58), queen of England from 1553 to 1558, daughter of Henry VIII. Religious persecutions during her reign earned her the appellation of "Bloody Mary." In 1554 she was married to Philip of Spain, but died four years later.

Mary II (1662-94), queen of England, daughter of James II; came to the throne in 1689, having been married to her cousin, William of Orange, fifteen months previously. They reigned jointly, after assenting to the "Declaration of Rights," until her death.

Mary (1867-1953), consort of King George V and mother of King George VI of England.

Mary, Queen of Scots (1542-87), daughter of James V of Scotland. She was married to the dauphin of France at sixteen years of age, and lived at the French court. On the death of her husband in 1560 she returned to Scotland, and for a time was acknowledged queen of Scotland. In 1565 she married Lord Darnley. In 1567 Darnley was murdered, supposedly by Bothwell, who married Mary three months afterwards. The Scottish nobles, angered by these acts, rebelled against Mary. She was made a prisoner in Lochleven Castle, compelled to abandon Bothwell and to sign an Act of Abdication in favor of her son. Escaping to England, she sought the protection of Elizabeth, but the English queen refused to give her her freedom and imprisoned her for the next nineteen years in various castles and ultimately had her beheaded on a charge of conspiracy.

Masaryk, Thomas Garrigue (1850-1937), Czech statesman, and founder and first president of Czechoslovakia.

Mascagni, Pietro (1863-1945), an Italian composer, who attained sudden celebrity by his opera *Cavalleria Rusticana* in 1890.

Masefield, John (b. 1878), poet laureate of England, novelist and dramatist. He went to sea at 13 and began writing at 22. His books of verse include *Salt Water Ballads*, *Everlasting Mercy*, *Dauber*, and *Helen of Troy*.

Masters, Edgar Lee (1869-1950), American poet, born in Garnett, Kansas. At the age of 23 he went to Chicago, where he practiced law and worked for several newspapers. The famous *Spoon River Anthology* was published in 1915. Other works are *Lincoln the Man* (1931), *Vachel Lindsay* (1935), and *Across Spoon River* (1936).

Matisse, Henri (1869-1954), French painter, one of the leading representatives of the modern school of painting in France. His work is remarkable for its use of pure and brilliant color, and its reliance on color variations to express form and relief.

Maugham, William Somerset (b. 1874), English author and playwright, born in Paris. His best-known novel, *Of Human Bondage*, was published in 1915. *Cakes and Ale* aroused criticism because of the resemblance of certain characters to English authors. He also wrote novels based on his travels in the East.

Maupassant, Henri René Albert Guy de (1850-1893), a French author and writer of short stories; a friend of Flaubert, Zola, and Daudet; one of the world's greatest short-story writers. Among his best-known collections of short stories are *La Maison Tellier*, *Mademoiselle Fifi*, *Clair de lune*, *Yvette*, and *Le Horla*.

Mawson, Sir Douglas (b. 1882), a British explorer, born in England. He was the leader of the Australian Antarctic expedition of 1911-14 and of the British-Australian and New Zealand Antarctic expedition 1929-31. He was president of the Australian and New Zealand Association for the Advancement of Science in 1932-37.

Maximilian (1832-1867), emperor of Mexico, earlier known as Ferdinand Maximilian Joseph, archduke of Austria; born in Vienna. In 1857 he married Princess Charlotte, daughter of King Leopold I of Belgium. In 1863 he was offered the crown of Mexico by a deputation of notables who were puppets of the French. Conditionally renouncing his rights as an Austrian prince, he accepted the crown in 1864. When Napoleon III withdrew his forces from Mexico, partly because the United States disapproved of French influence in the Western Hemisphere, Maximilian stayed on in an attempt to maintain the empire. Betrayed by General Lopez in 1867, he was tried by court-martial and executed.

Maxwell, James Clerk (1831-79), Scotch physicist. In 1871 he became a professor of experimental physics at Cambridge University. His best-known work is his treatise on electricity and magnetism, published in 1873. He developed the electro-magnetic theory of light, and his electrical researches were invaluable for the later development of radio.

Mazarin, Jules (1602-61), an Italian cardinal who became chief minister of state under Louis XIV of France, and was for a number of years the real ruler of the nation, succeeding Richelieu.

Mazzini, Giuseppe (1805-72), an Italian patriot, who in his endeavors to secure the independence of Italy, incurred the disfavor of the authorities and was compelled to leave the country. He started an organization called *Young Italy* at Marseilles devoted to Italian liberation, and in 1837 moved to London and kept up his attacks upon existing governments. In 1848 he was back in Rome and was elected dictator of the Roman Republic. He was not allowed to hold this position long, however, for the French occupied Rome and Mazzini was again driven to England.

Meade, George Gordon (1815-72), an American military officer. During the Civil War he distinguished himself at Antietam and at Fredericksburg and was promoted major general in November, 1862. He was in command of the Army of the Potomac when Lee was defeated in the decisive Battle of Gettysburg.

Meany, George (b. 1894), American labor official. A business representative of a New York plumbers local (1922-34), he rose to the presidency of the AFL in 1952, and was chosen president of the combined AFL-CIO in 1955.

Medici, Lorenzo de' (1449-1492), an Italian poet, and virtual ruler of Florence; styled Lorenzo the Magnificent. In 1469 he succeeded his father, the illustrious Cosimo de' Medici, as head of the Florentine Republic. Literature, philosophy, and art engaged the attention of Lorenzo no less than political affairs; he patronized scholars and artists, and collected manuscripts at great expense. The quiet of his reign was interrupted in 1478 by the conspiracy of the Pazzi, to which Pope Sixtus IV was a party, and which had for its object the overthrow of the Medici. Lorenzo barely escaped death, and his brother was killed. The pope then excommunicated Lorenzo, allied himself with the king of Naples, and declared war against Florence. Peace was finally declared in 1484.

Melanchthon, Philipp (1497-1560), Luther's coworker in the Reformation; born in Bretten, in the Rhenish Palatinate. In 1512 he went to Tübingen and devoted himself to theology. In 1519 he came forward as a champion of Luther's opinions. The Augsburg confession carried his name throughout Europe and brought him an invitation from Francis I to visit France and assist at a conference for composing the religious differences of that country. His friendship with Luther continued until the latter's death.

Melchers, Gari (1860-1932), American artist, born in Detroit, Mich., in 1860. He studied in France and in Holland, and was distinguished particularly for his paintings of Dutch peasant life. He returned to America in 1914. Important works are "The Fencing Master," "The Supper at Emmaus," "The Ship Builder," and "The Vespers."

Melville, Herman (1819-91), an American author, born in New York. He went to sea in a merchant ship, where he suffered such ill treatment that he deserted, and escaped to the Marquesas Islands. There he lived happily with the natives for several months, describing them in his books *Typee* (1846) and *Omoo* (1847). He returned to the United States and settled down in a minor government position. *White Jacket*, which he published in 1850, described the hardships of life in the Navy, and helped to improve the lot of the sailor. *Moby Dick*, a story of whaling, is considered his masterpiece. Melville received scant recognition until after his death.

Mencken, Henry Louis (1880-1956), American editor, author, and critic, born in Baltimore, Md. He was co-editor of the magazine *Smart Set* from 1914 to 1923. In 1924 he became co-editor with George Jean Nathan of the *American Mercury;* he was sole editor from 1925 to 1933. His trenchant and satirical essays were published in a series entitled *Prejudices*. His *American Language* (1919) is an authoritative work in the field of philology.

Mendel, Gregory Johann (1822-84), Austrian botanist. He became a monk, and lectured in natural history in the Realschule at Brünn. His main interest, however, was the study of hereditary characteristics, and his elaborate observations of the common garden pea resulted in the famous law of heredity which today bears his name.

Mendelssohn-Bartholdy, Felix (1809-47), German-Jewish composer. He was director of concerts in Leipzig for a time, lived in Italy several years, and was a frequent visitor to England. He composed a large volume of delightful and enduring music, including chamber music, pianoforte music, a number of symphonies, the musical setting for *A Midsummer Night's Dream*, and two oratorios, *St. Paul*, and *Elijah*. He died at the age of 38.

Mendoza, Antonio de (1490?-1552), a Spanish statesman. He was appointed viceroy of Mexico in 1535, and made many reforms, especially in relieving the oppressed natives. He developed agriculture and mining; established the first Mexican mint; founded the first college; and introduced the first printing press. In 1551 he became viceroy of Peru, where he prepared a code of laws that has been the basis of the colonial and (to a large extent) of the present laws of the republic.

Menelik II (1844-1913), emperor of Abyssinia, succeeded to the throne in 1880, and proved a vigorous ruler.

Menuhin, Yehudi (b. 1917), Jewish violin virtuoso, born in New York City, he is one of the greatest musical prodigies of the 20th century.

Mercator, Gerardus (1512-1594), Flemish geographer. He made a celestial and a terrestrial globe, and he originated the type of map known as the Mercator Projection, which has meridians and parallels of latitude crossing each other at right angles, both being indicated by straight lines. This greatly simplified navigation.

Meredith, George (1828-1909), English novelist and poet. In 1859 he published his *Ordeal of Richard Feverel,* which was a brilliant and successful work. Among his other novels are *Evan Harrington, Rhoda Fleming, The Egoist, Diana of the Crossways,* and *The Amazing Marriage.*

Metternich, Clemens, Prince von (1773-1859), an Austrian statesman; born in Coblenz. In 1809 he was appointed chancellor of state; and for nearly 40 years he exercised the highest authority in the Austrian empire. He first attempted to bring about a marriage between Napoleon and an Austrian archduchess, but after the great French disasters in Russia, embroiled Austria in war with France. After Napoleon's defeat at Leipzig Metternich was raised to the dignity of a prince of the empire. In 1815 he presided over the Congress of Vienna. In 1848 he was compelled to flee from Vienna; he returned in 1851, but never again assumed office.

Meyerbeer, Giacomo (1791-1864), operatic composer, born in Germany. He spent most of his life in Paris, however, where he produced all his great operas, which include *Robert le Diable, Les Huguenots,* and *Le Prophète.*

Michelangelo (Michelagniolo Buonarroti) (1475-1564), the renowned Italian painter, sculptor, and architect. He was in some respects the greatest of the Italian sculptors; his large paintings, particularly "The Last Judgment" in the Sistine Chapel of the Vatican, are famous. His sculptures include those for the mausoleum of Pope Julius II and for the Medici chapel.

Michelson, Albert Abraham (1852-1931), an American physicist, born at Strelno, Prussia. In 1892 he became head of the department of physics at the University of Chicago. He is best known for his calculations of the speed of light, and for his experiments on the interference of light waves. In 1907 he won the Nobel Prize, the first American scientist so honored. He was president of the American Society for the Advancement of Science (1910); and of the National Academy of Science (1923-27).

Mill, John Stuart (1806-73), English philosopher and economist, a founder of utilitarianism and follower of Bentham. His principal works are: *Principles of Political Economy, Essay on Liberty, A System of Logic, Utilitarianism,* and his *Autobiography.*

Millais, Sir John Everett (1829-96), English painter, at one time the most prominent of the English Pre-Raphaelites. Among his numerous works are "The Eve of St. Agnes," "Autumn Leaves," "The Order of Release," "Effie Deans," and "Chill October."

Millay, Edna St. Vincent (1892-1950), American poet, born at Rockland, Maine. Her more important books are: *A Few Figs from Thistles, The Harp-Weaver and Other Poems, The Buck in the Snow, Fatal Interview,* and *Wine from These Grapes.* She has written a number of plays in verse, notably *The Lamp and the Bell, Aria da Capo,* and *The King's Henchman.* In 1922 she was awarded the Pulitzer Prize for poetry.

Millet, Jean Francis (1814-75), French painter of pastoral subjects; one of his best-known works is "The Angelus."

Millikan, Robert Andrews (1868-1954), American physicist. From 1896 to 1921 he was a member of the faculty of the University of Chicago. He became head of the governing council of the California Institute of Technology and of the Norman Bridge Laboratory in 1921. For his work in the isolation of the electron and the measurement of its charge, he was awarded the Nobel Prize in 1923; for his research in cosmic rays, he was awarded the Roosevelt Association Medal in 1932.

Milton, John (1608-1674), England's chief epic poet, a champion of personal freedom, whose *Paradise Lost* is the greatest religious epic in the English language. He supported the Presbyterians and the Commonwealth, although he took no part in the English Civil War. In 1652 he became totally blind. Other works include *L'Allegro, Il Penseroso, Comus,* and *Lycidas.*

Minot, George Richards (1885-1950), American physician; became professor of medicine at Harvard in 1928; famous for his researches in the pathology of the blood, and for his discovery of the curative properties of liver in pernicious anemia. Shared the Nobel Prize for medicine, 1934.

Mirabeau, Gabriel, Comte de (1749-91), French statesman and orator, a prominent figure during the early stages of the French Revolution; led opposition to the king, but favored a constitutional monarchy.

Mithridates (c. 131-63 B.C.), king of Pontus from 120 to 63 B.C.; showed great capacity as a commander, conquering a great part of Asia Minor and Greece, but was eventually conquered by the Romans.

Mohammed (570-632), the founder of the Mohammedan religion, born in Mecca, Arabia; fled to Medina in 622, which is reckoned the year 1 in the Mohammedan calendar. By his constant preaching and proclaiming of the one God he gathered round him a vast number of followers and was able to return to Mecca eight years later, an acknowledged conquerer. His religious revelations were partially based on Jewish and Christian tradition.

Molière (Jean Baptiste Poquelin) (1622-73), the greatest of French comic dramatists, who, once a poor strolling player, became the leading dramatist of his time. His greatest comedies were *Tartuffe, Le Misanthrope, Le Malade imaginaire* and *Le Médecin malgré lui.*

Molotov, Vyacheslav Mikhailovich (b. 1890), one of three leading Communists who inherited Joseph Stalin's power, he was a Communist from his youth and was imprisoned and exiled several times. He was Russian premier (1930-41), and became foreign minister in 1939. Active in founding the United Nations, he was ousted from the party by Khrushchev in 1957.

Moltke, Count Hellmuth von (1800-1891), German field marshal and chief of staff of Prussian army during Franco-Prussian War.

Mommsen, Theodor (1817-1903), a German historian, born in Schleswig. His great work is *Roman History* (1854-1856).

Monet, Claude (1840-1926), French painter, born in Paris. His early works were influenced by the Barbizon school and by Manet. Later he identified himself with the Impressionist school represented by Cézanne, Duranty, and Sisley. Monet painted landscapes and still life, using color and light to reproduce transitory effects; to him subject matter was of secondary importance. His best landscape works include "The Cathedrals" (17 studies of the Rouen Cathedral), "The Breakfast" and "Waterloo Bridge."

Monroe, James (1758-1831), an American statesman and 5th President of the United States; born in Westmoreland Co., Va., April 28. He was wounded at the battle of Trenton, took active part in the battles of Brandywine, Germantown, and Monmouth, rising to the rank of colonel. In 1782 he was elected to the Assembly of Virginia and in 1783 became a delegate to the Continental Congress. Washington appointed him minister to France in 1794. On his return in 1799, he was elected governor of Virginia. In 1802 he was sent to France as envoy extraordinary by Jefferson to negotiate the Louisiana Purchase. He was minister to Great Britain, 1803-1808. He was again elected governor in 1811 and in the same year appointed Secretary of War. In 1817 he succeeded Madison as President and was re-elected for a second term. The chief events in his administration were the purchase of Florida from Spain, the adoption of the Missouri Compromise, and the enunciation of the Monroe Doctrine. In 1825 he retired to private life in Virginia.

Montaigne, Michel, Seigneur de (1533-92), a French essayist of world-wide celebrity. His works, the first of which were published in 1580, are characterized by quiet wisdom and unaffected, familiar style.

Montcalm, General Louis Joseph, Marquis de (1712-59), commander of the French army in Canada in the final struggle for the possession of Canada between the French and English in 1756-59; defended Quebec against Wolfe until killed in the Battle of the Plains of Abraham.

Montesquieu, Charles Louis de Secondat (1689-1755), French philosopher and author. His most famous work was *On the Spirit of Laws.*

Montessori, Maria (1869-1952), Italian educator. The "Montessori" method she invented for infant education had wide influence on kindergartens and other child schools. It is based on early muscular training and early development of initiative.

Montezuma II (1480-1520), an emperor of Mexico and the last Aztec ruler of Mexico when Cortés invaded that country. He was slain by natives, while held a captive by Cortés.

Montfort, Simon de, Earl of Leicester (1203-65), English baron, with liberal views, and a hatred of kingly tyranny. It was his bold action that forced Henry III, his brother-in-law, to assemble the first English Parliament.

Montgolfier, Joseph Michel (1740-1810), and **Jacques Etienne** (1745-1799), French brothers who, during the last twenty years of the 18th century, demonstrated the practicability of a balloon inflated by heated air.

Moody, Dwight Lyman (1837-1899), an American evangelist, born in Northfield, Mass. In Chicago, in 1873 he began with Ira D. Sankey the evangelistic work which soon made him famous in both the United States and England. His publications include the *Second Coming of Christ* and *The Way to God and How to Find it.*

Moore, George (1852-1933), an Irish novelist; author of *Confessions of a Young Man, Esther Waters, Evelyn Innes,* etc. Among his later masterpieces were *The Brook Kerith* (1916), and *Heloise and Abelard* (1921). His best novels are noted for their brilliant style and mastery of detail. His last book, *Aphrodite in Aulis,* he himself thought his best.

Moore, Thomas (1779-1852), Irish poet, the author of *Irish Melodies, Lala Rookh, The Epicurean,* and many other works. He enjoyed immense popularity in both England and Ireland. He was the friend and biographer of Lord Byron

More, Sir Thomas (1478-1535), English author and statesman, who succeeded Wolsey as lord chancellor under Henry VIII, but fell into disgrace by refusing to take the oath of supremacy, and was ultimately executed. His *Utopia,* picturing an ideal state, is one of the world's most noted books.

Morley, Christopher (1890-1957), editor, writer, born at Haverford, Pennsylvania. Among his works are the fantasy, *Where the Blue Begins* (1922); the novel, *Thunder on the Left* (1925); *Swiss Family Manhattan* (1932); *Mandarin in Manhattan* (1933); *Human Beings* (1933); *The Trojan Horse* (1937) and *Kitty Foyle* (1939).

Morris, William (1834-1906), an English poet, author of *The Earthly Paradise, The Life and Death of Jason,* and other works of poetry and prose. He was also a socialist and an art designer who did much for the improvement of domestic decoration.

Morse, Samuel Finley Breese (1791-1872), an American inventor and artist, who invented the Morse system of telegraphy and the Morse code of signals.

Moses, Hebrew prophet and law giver, fl. about 15th century B. C. He led the Hebrews from Egypt, established the worship of Yahweh (Jehovah), and gave his people the basic Jewish law, including the Ten Commandments. The full story is told in the Bible, in Exodus.

Motley, John Lothrop (1814-1877), American historian, is best known for his *History of the Rise of the Dutch Republic,* published in 1856. He later served as U. S. minister to Austria and to Great Britain.

Mozart, Wolfgang Amadeus (1756-1791), Austrian composer, who showed musical talent while very young, and performed on the clavichord in various capitals of Europe when only eight years of age. At twenty-five he accepted the position of composer to the imperial court of Vienna, and then began to write operas, producing in succession *The Marriage of Figaro, Don Giovanni,* and *The Magic Flute.* He also wrote a great deal of other music, including symphonies, sonatas, string quartets, masses, and a *Requiem* of unsurpassed beauty.

Muller, Max (1823-1900), German philologist, born in Dessau. He popularized philology and mythology, prepared the standard edition of the *Rig-Veda,* and compiled translations of numerous other Oriental religious writings.

Mumford, Lewis (b. 1895), an American author and editor. He became associate editor of *Fortnightly Dial,* (1919). Among his best-known books are *Sticks and Stones, The Golden Day Technics and Civilization, The Culture of Cities,* and *Men Must Act.*

Münchhausen, Baron Hieronymus Karl Friedrich von (1720-1797), a German military officer, born in Hanover. He gained the reputation of being the greatest story-teller of his time. A compilation of his prodigious "yarns," said to have been based on the Baron's stories, was published in London in 1785, under the title of *Baron Münchhausen's Narrative of His Marvelous Travels and Campaigns in Russia.*

Murat, Joachim (1771-1815), a French soldier, and one of Napoleon's most famous marshals. He married Napoleon's sister, and was made king of Naples.

Murillo, Bartolomé Estéban (1617-1682), a Spanish painter. His chief works, religious and genre subjects, include "Moses striking the Rock," and "Vision of St. Anthony."

Murray, Philip (1886-1952), American labor leader who with John L. Lewis organized the C.I.O. He succeeded Lewis as president of that organization in 1940.

Mussolini, Benito (1883-1945), Italian dictator. He urged Italy's entry into World War I, and served in the army, 1915-1917. His Fascist Party seized the government by coup d'état in 1922, instituted a totalitarian regime featuring militant nationalism, and became an absolute dictator. He conquered Ethiopia (1936), and Albania (1939). In 1937-38 he and Hitler set up the Rome-Berlin Axis to which Japan later adhered. In June, 1940, he entered World War II. In July, 1943, after the invasion of Sicily, he was ousted by the Grand Council of the Fascist Party. In April, 1945, he was captured and executed by Italian guerrillas.

N

Nansen, Fridtjof (1861-1930), a Norwegian explorer, who after two or three expeditions across Greenland, in 1893 started out on a North Polar expedition, which occupied three years, and which he described in *Farthest North.* After the World War, he was active in Russian famine relief, relief of the Armenians, and the repatriation of war prisoners. He was awarded the Nobel Prize for peace, 1922.

Napoleon I or Napoleon Bonaparte (1769-1821), was born at Ajaccio in Corsica. He was sent to France to receive a military education and was a captain at the age of twenty. An expert artilleryman, he served in the French Revolutionary Army in Italy in 1794 with such distinction that he won a generalship, and next year was appointed commander-in-chief. A series of most brilliant successes followed. He defeated the Austrian forces in 1797, conducted an expedition to Syria and Egypt in 1798, returned in 1799 to find himself the most popular man in France and in November of that year he ended the Revolution by the coup d'état of the 18th Brumaire and proclaimed himself First Consul. In 1800 he was again in Italy and once more victorious. In 1804 he was made emperor, and the following year was in the field against England, Russia, and Austria, achieving a series of victories at Austerlitz and elsewhere, and practically became dictator of Europe, distributing kingships among his brothers in the most profuse manner. Joseph Bonaparte became king of Naples, Louis king of Holland, and Jerome king of Westphalia. Napoleon's invasion of Russia was disastrous, the Peninsular War went against him, and in 1814 the Allies entered Paris and forced him to abdicate. He was sent to Elba, but made his escape in the following year, gathered his old army about him and went forth to meet the English and Prussian armies. He was completely defeated at Waterloo on June 18, 1815, and exiled to St. Helena, where he died six years later.

Napoleon II (1811-32), was the son of Napoleon I and Marie Louise of Austria. He was born in Paris and proclaimed king of Rome. Napoleon I named his son as his successor when he abdicated in 1814, but his son never ruled. He was made a virtual prisoner in Vienna, where he died when only twenty-one, being known at the time of his death as the Duke of Reichstadt.

Napoleon III (1808-1873), known as Louis Napoleon, was the son of Louis Bonaparte, king of Holland, and of Hortense, daughter of Empress Josephine. According to the Napoleonic claims he became the heir to the throne of France on the death of the Duke of Reichstadt. He twice attempted the overthrow of Louis Philippe, in 1836 at Strasbourg and in 1840 at Boulogne. After the Revolution of 1848 he was elected to the French National Assembly and a few months later became president of the republic. In 1851 by a *coup d'état* he gained complete control of the government; the next year he restored the empire and became Napoleon III. His aggressive and ambitious foreign policy led in 1870 to the Franco-Prussian War, which ended the Second Empire and compelled Napoleon III to go into exile in England.

Nasser, Gamal Abdel (b. 1918), Egyptian politician. Beginning his military career as an infantry officer, he led the *coup d'état* that overthrew King Farouk in 1952; after a period as the real power behind President Mohammed Naguib, Nasser was elected president in 1956. He effected a union of Egypt and Syria in 1958.

Nebuchadnezzar (d. 562 B.C.), a king of Babylonia. He greatly extended the limits of his empire by wars of conquest, in the course of which he took Jerusalem and led some of the inhabitants captive to Babylon. When his vassal king of Judah, Jehoiachin, revolted, he deposed him and put an end to the kingdom of Judah. He next turned his arms against Tyre, which after an obstinate resistance of more than 12 years, he finally took.

Nehru, Jawaharlal (b. 1889), Indian statesman. He co-operated with Gandhi in working for Indian independence, became prime minister of India in 1947, and led a powerful Asian bloc in the United Nations in opposition to European colonialism.

Nelson, Horatio, Viscount (1758-1805), English naval commander, an important figure in the wars against the French Revolutionary forces and, later, against Napoleon. In 1793 he was captain of the *Agamemnon* and proved his capacity and daring against the French. In 1798 he achieved a great victory over the French in Aboukir Bay. He was victorious at Copenhagen in 1801. In 1805 he commanded the British fleet during the famous Battle of Trafalgar, in which the French fleet was destroyed and Nelson was killed.

Nero, Claudius Caesar (A.D. 37-68), Roman emperor, successor to Claudius. His reign of fourteen years, though notable for the rebuilding of Rome on a magnificent scale, was rendered infamous by his cruelty and licentiousness. Misrule and heavy taxes led to revolt in Gaul, Spain, and Italy. Nero committed suicide.

Newman, John Henry, Cardinal (1801-90), English churchman and writer, became a priest in the Church of England in 1824, but was converted to faith of the Roman Catholic church, which he entered in 1845. After a visit to Rome he settled at Edgbaston, Birmingham, England, as the head of a community of the Order of St. Philip Neri. In his *Apologia pro Vita Sua* he described the development of his religious thought. He also wrote the hymn "Lead, Kindly Light," and *The Dream of Gerontius.*

Newton, Sir Isaac (1642-1727), English physicist, mathematician, and philosopher, who laid the groundwork of modern physics. His discoveries include the law of gravitation and the differential calculus. His theory of motion and mechanics remained almost unquestioned until the 20th century.

Ney, Michel (1769-1815), a French soldier, one of Napoleon's most noteworthy generals. He shared in Napoleon's defeat at Waterloo, and was afterwards executed for treason.

Nicholas II (1868-1918), emperor of Russia, son of Alexander III; succeeded to the throne in 1894. He was unable to cope with the corruptness of the Russian bureaucracy and nobility, and with the changing economic conditions. Despite his peaceful intentions, Russia became embroiled in the Russo-Japanese War, which brought on the abortive revolution of 1905, and in World War I, during which he took over command of the army. As a result of the Revolution of 1917, Czar Nicholas was forced to abdicate. He and his family were later arrested and imprisoned at Tobolsk and finally executed at Ekaterinburg (Sverdlosk) by the Bolsheviks, July 16, 1918.

Nietzsche, Friedrich Wilhelm (1844-1900), German philosopher; attacked the traditional "morality of pity," and developed the stern and heroic doctrine of the "superman," or natural aristocrat; emphasized the importance of will; author of *Zarathustra*, *Beyond Good and Evil*, etc.

Nightingale, Florence (1820-1910), English hospital administrator, a noted figure in the Crimean War, where she organized a band of nurses which did great service in relieving the sufferings of the soldiers. Her system for nursing was adopted and developed in all parts of the world.

Nijinsky, Waslaw (1890-1950), Russian dancer, who was one of the famous company of dancers, which included Pavlova, Karsavina, and Fokine, brought by Diaghilev to Paris and London just before the World War. His sensational dancing in such ballets as *Les Sylphides*, *Spectre de la Rose* and *L'Aprés-midi d'un faune* won him a high place among male dancers. He afterwards suffered a mental breakdown.

Nixon, Richard M. (b. 1913), an American political leader born in Yorba Linda, Calif. A lawyer, he was elected a representative to Congress in 1946. In 1950 he became a senator, and in 1952 was elected Vice-President on the Republican ticket. He was reelected to that post in 1956.

Nobel, Alfred Bernhard (1833-96), a Swedish engineer and chemist, the inventor of dynamite, who amassed a large fortune, a great portion of which he set apart as a fund for annual prizes to such persons as during each year should have contributed most materially to the benefit of mankind. There are five of these prizes, given in the following fields; physics, chemistry, physiology or medicine, literature, and peace promotion.

Noguchi, Hideyo (1876-1928), Japanese bacteriologist and physician best known for his work on the syphilis spirochete and for his smallpox serum.

Noyes, Alfred (b. 1880), English poet, whose first book of verse, *The Loom of Years*, was published in 1902, followed almost annually by a long series of other volumes. Was visiting professor of English literature at Princeton University, 1914-23.

Noyes, Henry Drury (1832-1900), American ophthalmologist, born in New York City. From 1868 until his death he was professor of ophthalmology and otology in Bellevue Hospital Medical School. He was a founder of the American Ophthalmological Society.

O

Occam, William of (c. 1270-1347), English scholastic philosopher. He entered the order of the Cordeliers, and passed the latter part of his life on the Continent. In 1322 he attended a general assembly of Franciscans at Perouse, where he asserted the independence of princes in temporal affairs and denounced the vices of the pope.

O'Connell, Daniel (1775-1847), Irish orator and politician, a highly successful lawyer, known as "the Liberator." In Parliament he advocated the cause of Ireland with courage and audacity.

Oehlenschläger, Adam Gottlob (1779-1850), dramatic poet of Scandinavia, born in Vesterbro, near Copenhagen, Denmark. Among his greatest works are: *The Death of Balder*, *The Gods of the North*, and *Aladdin*.

Oersted, Hans Christian (1777-1851), Danish philosopher and scientist. He discovered the close relationships between magnetism and electricity. His work did much to make possible the invention of the telegraph and other electrical devices.

Offenbach, Jacques (1819-1880), a French operatic composer, born of Jewish parents in Cologne. He went to Paris and became orchestra leader in the Théâtre Français in 1848. Among his most notable operas are *Orpheus in Hades*, *Bluebeard*, and *The Tales of Hoffmann*.

Oglethorpe, James Edward (1696-1785), an English military officer and philanthropist. Through his efforts a colony was formed of insolvent debtors and persecuted Protestants, whom he brought to the United States and settled in Georgia in 1733. He remained in the United States till 1743, when he returned to England.

Ohm, Georg Simon (1787-1854), German physicist and mathematician, the discoverer of the law of electric current which is known as Ohm's Law.

Olaf I (995-1030), the first Christian king and patron saint of Norway.

Omar I (581-644), the second caliph of the Mohammedans and the first to be designated the Commander of the Faithful. He conquered Syria, Mesopotamia, Persia, and Egypt, reigned from 634-644, and died at the hands of a slave.

Omar Khayyam, Persian poet and mathematician, flourished in the 11th and 12th centuries. *The Rubaiyat*, known to us through the translation of Fitzgerald, is usually attributed to him.

O'Neill, Eugene, Gladstone (1888-1953), American dramatist. He engaged in many occupations in the United States, Central America, and South America, and sailed the seas for two years. Before he became a playwright, he was an actor and newspaperman. He won the Pulitzer prize four times. Among his plays are *Beyond the Horizon*, *Anna Christie*, *The Emperor Jones*, *Desire Under the Elms*, *Strange Interlude*, *Long Day's Journey into Night*.

Origen (185-254), a church father and one of the most learned ecclesiastical writers in the early Christian church, born in Alexandria. He went to Rome, where he began his famous *Hexapla*, an edition of the Hebrew Bible with five Greek versions. At the command of his bishop he returned to Alexandria and was ordained. Soon after this, he began his *Commentaries on the Scriptures*. His philosophical object was to reconcile Christianity with Greek thought. His great talents and popularity exposed him to the jealousy of the bishop, whose persecutions at length drove him from his native country and for a long period made him a wanderer.

Osler, Sir William (1849-1919), Canadian physician. At Oxford he became curator of the Bodleian Library and held the chair of medicine. His most important work was on the spleen and the blood, and in 1892 he published *The Principles and Practice of Medicine*, a classic in the field of medical literature.

Ovid (Publius Ovidius Naso) (43 B. C.-A. D. 17), Latin poet, whose *Metamorphoses* and *Art of Love* are among the best-known examples of Roman literature.

Owen, Robert (1771-1858), British social reformer and author. He early turned his attention to social questions, publishing in 1812 *New Views of Society; or, Essays upon the Formation of Human Character*, and *Book of the New Moral World*. He attempted to found semi-communistic societies in England, in New Harmony, Ind., and later also in Mexico.

Oxenstjerna, Axel, Count (1583-1654), a Swedish statesman. On the accession of Gustavus Adolphus in 1611, he was made chancellor. After the death of his king at Lützen (1632) he was recognized, at a congress assembled at Heilbronn, as the head of the Protestant League. In 1636 he returned to Sweden and took his seat as chancellor of the kingdom and one of the five guardians of the queen. In 1645 he assisted in the negotiations with Denmark at Brömsebro, and on his return was created a count by Queen Christina, whose determination to abdicate he unsuccessfully opposed.

P

Paderewski, Ignace Jan (1860-1941), Polish pianist, composer, and patriot, born in Russian Poland. Took an active part in advocating the cause of Poland during the World War; was premier of Poland from Jan. to Dec. 1919; first delegate from Poland to League of Nations, 1920.

Paine, Thomas (1737-1809), an American political writer and agitator for liberty born in Thetford, England. He was a devout Quaker and was persuaded by Benjamin Franklin to come to America. In January, 1776, the pamphlet *Common Sense* established him as one of the foremost advocates of liberty in the American colonies. The first number of *The Crisis* appeared in December, 1775, beginning with the famous sentence, "These are the times that try men's souls." In 1787 he went to England. There, in defense of the French Revolution, Paine wrote *The Rights of Man*, a work which had a profound effect on the French revolutionists. Going to France, he became a member of the committee which drafted the new French constitution. As an enemy of the Jacobins, he was imprisoned, but American influence eventually effected his release. In his *Age of Reason*, Paine presented his religious philosophy, condemning orthodox religions as hypocritical. He was a strong advocate of religious and political liberty. Paine returned to America in 1802 but was ostracized from society for his liberal views on personal religion.

Palestrina, Giovanni (1525-94), Italian composer, chiefly of church music; spent much of his life as a choirmaster at the Vatican.

Palgrave, Sir Francis (1788-1861), English historian and political economist, author of *The Rise and Progress of the English Commonwealth*, and *A History of the Anglo-Saxons*, and editor-in-chief of the *Dictionary of Political Economy*.

Palissy, Bernard (1510-89), French potter, discoverer of the art of producing white enamel.

Palladio, Andrea (1518-80), Italian architect, who introduced the style of architecture known as Palladian, based on his careful studies of ancient Roman buildings.

Palmerston, Viscount (1784-1865), English statesman, entered Parliament in 1807. Before the passing of the Reform Bill he was a Conservative, but afterwards joined the Liberals. In 1859 he became prime minister, and remained in that office until his death.

Papin, Denis (1647-1714), a French mathematician and scientist who invented the condensing pump and the safety valve. His discoveries in connection with steam power entitle him to be considered among the first to put that power to a practical test.

Paracelsus, Philippus Aureolus (1493-1541), Swiss physician and alchemist. He made numerous important discoveries, being the first to employ laudanum and antimony in pharmacy.

Parnell, Charles Stewart (1846-91), Irish statesman, who for ten years, from 1880, was leader of the Irish party in the British Parliament and made it more powerful than it had ever been before. He succeeded in winning Gladstone's confidence, and was largely responsible for the home rule policy which that statesman adopted towards the end of his parliamentary career.

Pascal, Blaise (1623-62), French philosopher whose *Provincial Letters* exhibit remarkable wit and genius. He was a distinguished mathematician and invented an ingenious adding machine, besides making many brilliant experiments in hydrostatics and pneumatics.

Pasteur, Louis (1822-95), French chemist and scientist, whose researches in connection with hydrophobia, bacteriology, and the specific germs of cholera and other diseases have been of immense benefit to mankind. He was elected a member of the Academy of France in 1882. In his later years the Pasteur Institute, founded by him in Paris, attained universal celebrity.

Pavlov, Ivan Petrovich (1849-1936), Russian physiologist, director of the Physiological Institute, a pioneer in the investigation of the conditioned reflex. In 1904 he was awarded the Nobel Prize.

Pavlova, Anna (1885-1931), Russian ballet dancer, who became world-renowned. Her most famous dance was Saint-Saëns' *Dying Swan*.

Payne, John Howard (1792-1852), an American dramatist. He wrote, translated, and adapted over 60 plays but is most famous as the author of "Home Sweet Home." He died in Tunis, April 10, 1852.

Peabody, George (1795-1869), an American merchant who lived for the greater part of his life in London, and acquiring a large fortune, bequeathed considerable sums for philanthropic purposes, such as the endowment fund for Peabody College for Teachers.

Peary, Robert Edwin (1856-1920), an American Arctic explorer who, in 1891-92, conducted a sledging expedition towards the North Pole. In 1893, 1895, and 1898 he was again in the Arctic regions. On April 6, 1909, he reached the Pole.

Peel, Sir Robert (1788-1850), a prominent British statesman. In 1834 Peel was prime minister for four months and in 1841 again occupied the same position. It was then that the anti-Corn Law agitation became formidable, and Peel abandoned his former Protectionist attitude and carried the repeal measure in 1846.

Penn, William (1644-1718), Quaker preacher, founder of the state of Pennsylvania, born in London. In his early years he was persecuted for preaching his faith, but in 1681 he took from the Crown the grant of a province in America in lieu of arrears due his father. With 100 emigrants Penn landed at New Castle, Del., 1682. After just and magnanimous dealings with the Indians, Penn established a truly democratic colony, with universal toleration, a charter of liberties, and humanitarian principles. Deprived of his colony due to an accusation of treason, Penn was later cleared and allowed to return to Pennsylvania.

Pepin (714-68), surnamed "the Short," first Carlovingian king of France, and father of Charlemagne.

Pepys, Samuel (1633-1703), an English diarist. He served for many years as an official in the Admiralty, but his chief claim to remembrance is his famous *Diary*, covering the years 1660-69.

Pericles (490-429 B. C.), Athenian statesman, general, and orator, who encouraged artistic creation and raised Athens to the point of its greatest prosperity. War with Sparta, however, destroyed most of his accomplishments.

Péron, Juan Domingo (b. 1895), Argentine political leader. As an army colonel he was back of a Fascist military junta which executed the coup d'état of 1943, and was the power behind a pro-Nazi, totalitarian regime first as Secretary of Labor and of War, and then as Vice-President. In 1946 he was elected President and in 1952 caused himself to be re-elected. He instituted many reforms in Argentina, but rigidly controlled freedom of speech and press. He was overthrown and exiled in 1955.

Perón, Maria Eva Duarte (1919-1952), wife of Juan Perón, was an actress until her marriage in 1945. She organized social welfare groups and was very active in politics.

Perry, Matthew Calbraith (1794-1858), American naval officer. He served in the War of 1812, and rose to the rank of commodore. In 1852 Perry was sent to Japan with a fleet, and he succeeded in opening that country to foreign trade.

Pershing, John Joseph (1860-1948), an American general, born in Missouri. After graduating from West Point in 1886 he served in several Indian campaigns. He served in Cuba and the Philippines until 1903. In 1906 he returned from Tokyo, where he was a military attaché, to the Philippines and successfully put down a Moro uprising. During the campaign he was promoted from captain to brigadier general. In 1916 Pershing commanded the expedition into Mexico against Villa. In 1917 he was sent overseas as commander-in-chief of the American Expeditionary Force. He was made a full general, the fourth to hold that rank since George Washington. In 1925 he was head of the Tacna-Arica plebiscite commission.

Pétain, Henri Philippe (1856-1951), French marshal, famous for holding back the Germans at Verdun during World War I. Between 1918 and 1939 he held various positions with the government, and in 1940 became premier and negotiated with the Germans, becoming the head of a French totalitarian government. He was sentenced to death in 1945, but the sentence was commuted to life imprisonment.

Peter the Great (1672-1725), czar of Russia, who devoted himself largely to reorganization of his army and navy. He spent some months in England studying shipbuilding. He founded St. Petersburg in 1703, and conquered Livonia, Finland, and Pomerania. Among the prisoners taken by him at the Battle of Pultowa was Catherine, the wife of a Swedish soldier who had been killed. He married her and she succeeded him to the throne.

Petrarch, Francesco (1304-74), Italian poet, whose odes and sonnets "To Laura" are of marvelous beauty and fervor, and have been translated into many languages.

Petronius, Gaius (better known as Petronius Arbiter) (d. A. D. 66?) Roman satirist and favorite of Nero's court. His *Satyricon* is a graphic realistic picture of the social life and manners of the time. Falsely accused of treason, Petronius committed suicide.

Phidias, one of the greatest Greek sculptors, flourished from about 490 to 432 B. C.; nothing now remains to attest his genius except the sculptures of the Parthenon attributed to him. These are in the British Museum, and are known as the "Elgin Marbles."

Philip II (382-336 B. C.), king of Macedonia, was trained in military arts in Greece; when he came to the throne he instilled martial ideas into his subjects, and entered upon a career of conquest that did not end until he had become master of Greece.

Philip II (1527-1598), king of Spain, succeeded his father, the Emperor Charles V, and was engaged in numerous wars, including his futile attempt to invade England with the Spanish Armada.

Philip V (1683-1746), king of Spain, founded the Bourbon dynasty in Spain, and was the son of the dauphin Louis of France. His uncle, Charles II of Spain, bequeathed the kingdom to him, and this led to the War of the Spanish Succession, which ultimately confirmed him as king.

Philip, Duke of Edinburgh (b. 1921), husband of Elizabeth II of England, born in Greece, the son of Prince Andrew of Greece. He was raised in England by his uncle, the Earl of Mountbatten, and was educated at the Royal Navy College, serving as an officer in World War II. He renounced his claim to the Greek throne, and, when he married Princess Elizabeth in 1947, he became the duke of Edinburgh. In 1957, he was created prince of the United Kingdom.

Phyfe, Duncan (1768-1854), an American cabinet-maker, born in Scotland; came to America about 1783.

Picasso, Pablo (b. 1881), a foremost 20th-century artist, born in Spain, settled in France after 1904. He initiated cubism and experimented with a variety of styles in painting. His major U. S. exhibition opened in 1957.

Pickering, Timothy (1745-1829), an American statesman; born in Salem, Mass., served under Washington in the American Revolution. He negotiated a treaty between the United States and the Six Nations in 1797, and a month later was appointed Postmaster-General. He was Secretary of State under Presidents Washington and Adams but was dismissed during the "X. Y. Z." papers dispute in 1800. He was elected to the United States Senate in 1804.

Pierce, Franklin (1804-1869), an American statesman, 14th President of the United States; born in Hillsboro, N. H. In 1837 he was elected to the United States Senate. In 1842 he resigned from the Senate and retired to private life. In 1846 he enlisted for the Mexican War, was appointed brigadier in the volunteer army, and led his brigade in the battles of Contreras and Cherubusco. In 1852 he was nominated for the Presidency on the 49th ballot by the Democratic National Convention and was elected over General Scott by an electoral majority of 254 to 42. During his administration the Missouri Compromise was repealed, a reciprocity treaty for trade with the British American colonies was made; a treaty with Japan was established; and the Mexican boundary disputes were settled.

Pilsudski, Joseph Clemens (1867-1935), a general and marshal of Poland; virtual dictator of the nation from 1920 until his death.

Pindar (522-433 B. C.), a lyric poet of ancient Greece, especially noted for determining the form of the Pindaric ode.

Pirandello, Luigi (1867-1936), Italian dramatist and novelist, author of *As You Desire Me*, *Six Characters in Search of an Author*, and others.

Pitt, William (1759-1806), an English statesman, second son of the Earl of Chatham; elected to Parliament in 1780. In 1783 he became prime minister; was active in the negotiations of peace with the United States, and was instrumental in the passage of many important measures. Retiring in 1801, he was recalled to office when the Peace of Amiens was broken and war with Napoleon recommenced. Through his public career he was noted as a parliamentary leader and orator.

Pius XI (1859-1939), an Italian named Achille Ratti; born near Milan. Successively named Archbishop of Milan and Cardinal Ratti, he was elected Pope Feb., 1922, on the death of Benedict XV.

Pius XII (b. 1876), the 262nd pope, and successor to Pius XI. He was born in Rome as Eugenio Pacelli, the descendant of an ancient Roman family. He was ordained in 1901 and soon entered the field of papal diplomacy. He was named papal nuncio to Munich in 1917, where he attempted to secure a hearing for Pope Benedict's plan for ending the World War. In 1924, having concluded a concordat with Bavaria, he was sent as papal nuncio to Berlin, where a concordat with Prussia was formed. He was then recalled to Rome, made a cardinal, and succeeded Cardinal Gasparri as papal secretary of state. Pope Pius XI died February 10, 1939, and Cardinal Pacelli was elected as his successor on March 2, 1939. President Roosevelt sent Myron C. Taylor as his personal representative to the Pope, in February, 1940.

Pizarro, Francisco (c. 1471-1541), Spanish explorer, who, after Columbus' discoveries in the New World, set out for South America, conquering Peru for the Emperor Charles V. Pizarro's career in Peru was characterized by excessive cruelty, and in the end he was killed by his own soldiers.

Planck, Max (1858-1947), German physicist, to whose investigations into the propagation of energy we mainly owe the quantum theory. He was awarded the Nobel Prize for physics, 1918.

Plato (429-347 B. C.), Greek philosopher. His *Dialogues* are among the greatest works of the ancients and embody a philosophical system which has provoked thought and discussion in all succeeding ages. He was Socrates' disciple and Aristotle's teacher.

Plautus, Titus Maccius (d. 184 B. C.), a Roman comic poet, born at Sarsina in Umbria. Twenty of his comedies are still extant. The best-known of his comedies are the *Captives*, the *Menaechmi*, the *Braggart Captain*, and the *Trinummus*.

Pliny the Elder (A. D. 23-79), a Roman naturalist of high reputation. Pliny the Younger, his nephew, achieved renown by a series of historical letters, and died A. D. 113.

Plutarch (c. 46-120), Greek biographer and essayist. His *Lives*, which are short biographies contrasting notable people of Greece and of Rome, form one of the world's most famous literary productions.

Poe, Edgar Allan (1809-1849), American poet and prose writer, born in Boston; spent much of his youth in Richmond, Virginia. In Boston he published his first book, *Tamerlane*. In 1831 his volume entitled *Poems*, among which are "Lenore" and "Israfel," was published in New York. These poems are hypnotic in their somber and sensuous beauty, and their euphony is striking. In 1835 he became editor of the *Southern Literary Messenger*, and married Virginia Clemm. In 1837 he again moved to the North, where he eked out a bare subsistence for himself and his young wife by doing hack writing. Poe later became literary critic, and formulated basic principles of criticism. In 1845 he published *The Raven and Other Poems*. His writings were much admired in France and influenced French poets and short-story writers. He originated the detective story and greatly influenced the development of the horror story.

Poincaré, Raymond (1860-1934), French statesman, who served as president, 1913-20; premier, 1912, 1922-24 and 1926-29; minister for foreign affairs, 1912 and 1922-24; and minister of finance 1894, 1906 and 1926-28.

Polk, James Knox (1795-1849), an American statesman, 11th President of the United States. In Congress he was consistently a Democrat, supporting unwaveringly the administrations of Jackson and Van Buren, and opposing that of Adams. In 1839 he was elected governor of Tennessee and in 1844 unexpectedly nominated as a compromise candidate of the National Democratic Convention for the Presidency, and elected over Henry Clay, the Whig candidate. During his administration Texas was annexed, the Mexican War fought, and the Oregon boundary determined by compromise with England. At the close of his single term Polk declined to stand for renomination and retired to private life.

Polk, Leonidas (1806-1864), an American military officer of the Confederacy; and an Episcopalian bishop. He served in the Civil War first as major general, and later as lieutenant general. At Belmont he repulsed Grant; at Shiloh he commanded the 1st corps; he conducted the retreat from Kentucky. He joined Johnston in opposing Sherman's march to Atlanta. He was killed while reconnoitering on Pine Mountain.

Polybius (204-122 B. C.), Greek historian, who wrote a history in over forty books; only the first five and certain fragments of the remainder have been preserved.

Pompadour, Jeanne Antoinette Poisson, Marquise **de,** otherwise known as Madame de Pompadour (1721-64), for a long time the favorite of Louis XV of France, over whom she exercised great influence.

Pompey (Gnaeus Pompeius) (106-48 B. C.), Roman soldier and politician, distinguished himself under Sulla while young, and ultimately became, with Caesar and Crassus, triumvir. He led the conservative opposition to Caesar, lost to him at the battle of Pharsalus, and was murdered in Egypt.

Ponce de León, Juan (1460-1521), a Spanish explorer, the discoverer of Florida. In 1510 he obtained the government of Puerto Rico, and had conquered the whole island by 1512, when he was deprived of his post. He then set out on a quest for a land of which he had heard, reputed to contain a "fountain of perpetual youth." On March 27, 1512, he reached Florida, landing a little north of where St. Augustine now stands. He secured the appointment of governor of the country, and returned in 1521 to conquer his new subjects; in this, however, he failed, and was killed while fighting the natives.

Pons, Lily (b. 1904), famous French operatic singer, who made her debut at the Metropolitan Opera House, New York, in 1931, and immediately established herself as one of the world's greatest sopranos.

Pope, Alexander (1688-1744), an English poet. In 1711 he published his *Essay on Criticism,* which was followed by *The Rape of the Lock,* the latter a polished and witty narrative poem founded on an incident of fashionable life. From 1713 to 1726 he was engaged on a poetical translation of Homer's works, the *Iliad* (completed in 1720) being wholly from his pen, the *Odyssey* only half. His *Essay on Man* was published anonymously in 1733.

Pope, John (1822-1892), an American military officer. He served in Florida (1842-1844), and in the Mexican War. After a few successes in the Civil War, he was put in command of the Army of Virginia. He opposed Lee in the second battle of Bull Run and was badly beaten.

Porter, David (1780-1843), American naval officer who, court-martialed for a diplomatic offense after a distinguished naval career, joined the Mexican navy as admiral, but returned later to become the American Minister to Turkey.

Porter, David Dixon (1831-1891), an admiral in the United States Navy, commanded the Union sloop-of-war *Powhatan* in the Civil War and distinguished himself in the capture of New Orleans and Vicksburg. Appointed rear admiral in 1862, he was given command of all naval forces on rivers west of New Orleans. He became superintendent of the United States Naval Academy at Annapolis and was raised to the rank of admiral in 1870.

Pound, Ezra Loomis (b. 1885), an American poet, one of the founders of the Imagist school of poetry, famous both for the beauty of his verse and for his excellent translations of Provençal, Latin, Chinese, French and Italian poets.

Prescott, William Hickling (1796-1859), an American historian, most famous for two works, *The Conquest of Mexico* and *The Conquest of Peru.*

Priestley, John Boynton (b. 1894), British novelist and literary critic, his novel *The Good Companions* achieving a great success.

Priestley, Joseph (1733-1804), an English scientist and minister; the discoverer of oxygen and other gases. Becoming unpopular because of his sympathy with the French Revolution, he emigrated to the United States.

Prior, Matthew (1664-1721), an English poet and diplomat, writer of epigrams and society verse.

Prokofiev, Sergei Sergeevich (1891-1953), Russian composer. He has written symphonies, concertos, operas, and orchestral suites, including *The Classical Symphony,* the opera *The Love for Three Oranges,* and his fairy tale for orchestra, *Peter and the Wolf.*

Protagoras (c. 480-411 B. C.), a Greek Sophist philosopher, who taught that truth is not absolute, but depends on the perceptions of the individual. He was banished in his old age for his religious agnosticism.

Proudhon, Pierre Joseph (1809-65), a French political economist. His theories influenced the syndicalist movement.

Proust, Marcel (1871-1922), a French psychological novelist; author of a series of 15 novels known under the title of *Remembrance of Things Past.* His work is notable for subtlety and subjectivity.

Ptolemy, an astronomer of Alexandria, who flourished between 139 and 161. He founded the Ptolemaic system, which taught that the earth was stationary and the heavenly bodies revolved around it.

Puccini, Giacomo (1858-1924), an Italian composer of operas, notably *La Bohéme, Madame Butterfly,* and *Manon Lescaut.*

Pulitzer, Joseph (1847-1911), an American journalist, born in Hungary. He came to the United States at the age of 17. In 1877 he became special European correspondent for the *New York Sun.* He bought the *St. Louis Dispatch* and the *Evening Post* in 1879 and united them under the name of the *Post-Dispatch.* In 1883 he purchased the *New York World.* He was noted for his gifts for educational purposes and for his establishment of the "Pulitzer Literary Awards," annual prizes in the fields of journalism and literature.

Pupin, Michael Idvorsky (1858-1935), an American scientist, famous for his work and discoveries in X ray and telephony. His autobiography *From Immigrant to Inventor* is well known.

Purcell, Henry (1658-95), the most gifted of English composers, and for many years organist of Westminster Abbey. He left a large volume of music of various sorts, best known being his admirable opera *Dido and Aeneas.*

Putnam, Israel (1718-1790), military leader in the American Revolution, was made a major general by the Continental Congress for his heroic activities during the battle of Bunker Hill. In 1777 he lost Forts Clinton and Montgomery to the British.

Pyrrhus (318-272 B. C.), king of Epirus, made war on the Romans, and in a desperate battle fought on the banks of the Syris, in Calabria, totally defeated the Roman army. The Romans at length triumphed, and Pyrrhus returned to Greece. In a subsequent war with the Argives, Pyrrhus was killed.

Pythagoras (c. 582-500 B. C.), a Greek philosopher, who taught the doctrine of the transmigration of souls, and also a system of astronomy similar to that of Copernicus.

Pytheas of Massilia, an explorer, contemporary with Alexander the Great. He probably explored Britain and the mouth of the Elbe. He was the first to determine latitude by the shadow cast by the sun.

Q

Quezon, Manuel (1878-1944), first president of the Philippine Commonwealth. He served with Filipino forces under Aguinaldo (1898-99), and as governor of Tayabas (1906-07). He was resident commissioner at Washington (1900-16) and president of the Philippine senate (1919-35).

Quiller-Couch, Sir Arthur Thomas (1863-1944), novelist and essayist, who as "Q" published many stories, including *Dead Man's Rock, Troy Town*, and *The Splendid Spur*.

Quincy, Joseph (1744-1775), an American lawyer, took part in the town meeting which resulted in the "Boston Tea Party"; and in 1774 went to England to speak in behalf of the colonists.

Quincy, Josiah (1772-1864), an American author and orator, entered Congress in 1805, where he distinguished himself by his opposition to the policy of Jefferson and Madison, and was one of the earliest American statesmen to denounce slavery.

Quisling, Vidkun (1887-1945), Norwegian traitor who aided the German invasion of Norway in 1940 and became puppet ruler. After the war he was executed for treason.

R

Rabelais, François (c. 1495-1553), French satirist, first adopted the career of a monk, then studied medicine, and settled at Lyons as a doctor. There he published *Gargantua and Pantagruel*, one of the greatest masterpieces of humor in any language.

Rachmaninov, Sergei Wassilievitch (1873-1943), Russian composer and pianist. His first important work, the opera *Aleko*, was produced at Moscow in 1893. He also composed two symphonies, the opera *Francesca da Rimini*, and many piano compositions.

Racine, Jean (1639-99), a French tragic dramatist, best known by his dramas in verse, including *Andromaque, Phèdre*, and *Athalie*.

Raleigh, Sir Walter (1552-1618), an English scholar, courtier, soldier, sailor, and statesman. In 1584 Queen Elizabeth granted him a patent for the discovery and settlement of unknown countries to the west of England. The colonization of Virginia followed. At one time he was in great favor at court, but quarreled with the queen, and was temporarily imprisoned. After James I came to the throne, Raleigh was kept a prisoner in the Tower of London for twelve years, and there he wrote his *History of the World*, and other works. In 1615 James set him at liberty in order to head an expedition to Guiana in the hope of finding gold, but being unsuccessful he was again imprisoned on his return, and finally beheaded.

Ramsay, Sir William (1852-1916), English physicist. In conjunction with Baron Rayleigh he discovered argon, hitherto an unknown constituent of the air, and later detected other new atmospheric gases, which he called neon, krypton, and xenon.

Randolph, Edmund Jennings (1753-1813), an American statesman. From 1786 to 1788 he was governor of Virginia and in 1787 a member of the convention which framed the Constitution of the United States. In 1794 he was made Secretary of State, but after the President's signing of the Jay Treaty (1795) he resigned.

Randolph, John (1773-1833), an American statesman, claimed descent from Pocahontas, the Indian princess. In 1799 he was elected to Congress, where he became the acknowledged leader of the administration party. His opposition to the War of 1812 caused his defeat in the following election; but he was re-elected to Congress in 1814, where he remained for several years.

Ranke, Leopold von (1795-1886), a German historian, one of the originators of the modern method of historical investigation.

Raphael Sanzio (1483-1520), Italian painter whose works excel in their beauty of expression and inspired treatment. He lived a considerable period in Rome, where he painted his famous frescoes for the Vatican and St. Peter's, and also the celebrated cartoons designed for the tapestries of the Papal chapel. His last painting was "The Transfiguration."

Rasputin, Grigori Yefimovich (1871-1916), a Russian monk, born of peasant stock. In 1907, through the influence of Feofan, the tsarina's confessor, he was introduced at court where, because of his beneficial influence on the health of the tsarevich, his influence became powerful. Finally his enemies banded together under the leadership of Grand Duke Dmitry Pavlovich and Prince Yussoupov, and murdered him.

Rathenau, Walter (1867-1922), German industrialist and statesman. He directed the supply of materials during World War I and, later, payment of reparations.

Ravel, Maurice (1875-1937), one of the foremost modern French composers, famous for his piano compositions, chamber music and orchestral compositions.

Rayleigh, John William Strutt, Baron (1842-1919), British physicist; an authority on sound vibrations; the co-discoverer of argon.

Reade, Charles (1814-84), English novelist of the Victorian era. His first story, *Peg Woffington*, was published in 1852. *It's Never too Late to Mend, Griffith Gaunt*, and *The Cloister and the Hearth*, are his best-known novels.

Réaumur, René Antoine Ferchault de (1683-1757), an eminent French chemist, who invented the thermometer which bears his name, the degrees of which are designated with the letter "R."

Reed, Walter (1851-1902), an American army surgeon and bacteriologist. He is best known for his research work in Havana during the yellow fever epidemic, and for his discovery of the method of transmission of yellow fever. Three months after he had discovered that the mosquito *Aëdes aegypti* was the carrier of the disease, the epidemic was brought under control.

Reid, Whitelaw (1837-1912), an American editor and diplomat, became in 1872 editor-in-chief of the *New York Tribune*. He was minister to France, 1889-1892; he became ambassador to England in 1905, a position he held until his death.

Reinhardt, Max (1873-1943), Austrian theatrical producer. After 1934 he became famous for production of Hollywood film spectacles.

Remarque, Erich Maria (b. 1897), German novelist. He served in World War I, afterward expressed his disillusionment by writing *All Quiet on the Western Front*.

Rembrandt Harmensoon van Rijn (1606-69), a painter of the Dutch school, who produced many remarkably successful portraits, as well as numerous figure subjects, all of them distinguished by their masterly qualities. He was an etcher of high ability.

Renan, Ernest (1823-92), a French author who wrote much upon religious subjects, and won special fame by his *Life of Jesus*, published in 1865.

Renoir, Pierre Auguste (1841-1919), a French artist, an impressionist, an associate of Monet, Cézanne, Pissarro, and Diaz. He used all the different types of subjects: still life, landscapes, portraits; but he was chiefly interested in the human figure.

Renwick, James (1818-1895), an American architect. Among the many buildings which he planned are Grace Church, New York City, completed in 1845; the Smithsonian Institution and the Corcoran Art Gallery, in Washington, D. C.

Reuter, Fritz (1810-1874), a German humorous writer. His greatest work is a series of prose tales, which stamped him as a master of the Low German dialect.

Reuter, Paul Julius (1821-99), a naturalized Englishman, the pioneer of telegraphic press services.

Reuther, Walter Philip (b. 1907), American labor leader. Active in union affairs when in school, by 1939 he had risen to a key position in the United Automobile Workers of America. He was elected vice-president of that organization in 1942 and president in 1952. The same year he was elected president of the CIO, and following its merger with the AFL in 1955, he became president of the CIO division.

Revere, Paul (1735-1818), an American patriot and silversmith, famous for his midnight ride from Boston to Lexington to arouse the Minute Men. He was the leader of a group of young men pledged to watch the movements of the British.

Reynolds, John Fulton (1820-1863), American military officer. At the beginning of the Civil War he was appointed a lieutenant colonel of volunteers; he led a brigade in the Seven Days' Battles. He was killed at Gettysburg.

Reynolds, Sir Joshua (1723-92), an English portrait painter, the first president of the Royal Academy. Possessed of a brilliant technique, he painted more than two thousand portraits. Especially famous is his "Mrs. Siddons as the Tragic Muse."

Rhodes, Cecil John (1853-1902), British colonial statesman and financier; went to Cape Colony in South Africa in 1871; entered a diamond-mining enterprise at Kimberly; by 1888 obtained virtual control of the diamond industry; became premier of the Cape colony in 1890, ruling as an autocrat. Determined to extend British power, he organized The British South Africa Company to exploit the territory which, in 1893, was finally acquired by war and named Rhodesia. He left the bulk of his fortune for the founding of Anglo-American scholarships at Oxford.

Ricardo, David (1772-1823), English political economist, whose *Principles of Political Economy* gained him a high place among the exponents of the science.

Rice, Alice Caldwell Hegan (1870-1942), American who became famous as the author of *Mrs. Wiggs of the Cabbage Patch* (1901).

Rice, Elmer (b. 1892), American playwright. His reputation is based on *Street Scene*, for which he won the Pulitzer Prize in 1929.

Richard I (1157-99), king of England from 1189 to his death. Known as "the Lionhearted," he participated in the Third Crusade. On his way back to England he was shipwrecked, captured by enemies, held for ransom and eventually released. He died while besieging the Castle of Chaluz in Normandy.

Richard II (1367-1400), English king. In 1399 he was deposed and succeeded by his cousin, the Duke of Hereford, who became Henry IV. Richard was murdered the following year.

Richard III (1452-85), last king of England from the house of York. He became regent for the boy-king, Edward V, and king in 1483 on the death of Edward, whom he was later accused of murdering. His claim to the throne was disputed by Henry Tudor, Earl of Richmond, and in the battle between their rival forces at Bosworth Field, Richard was slain.

Richelieu, Armand Jean du Plessis, Cardinal Duc de (1585-1642), French ecclesiast and statesman, who was minister of Louis XIII for eighteen years. He was practically master of France during most of his cardinalate.

Richthofen, Manfred, Baron von (1892-1918), German aviator, World War ace of the German forces; credited with 80 victories. He wrote *Red Battle Flyer* shortly before his death.

Rickenbacker, Edward Vernon (b. 1890), American aviator. In 1918 he became commander of the 94th Aero Pursuit Squadron of the A.E.F. As destroyer of 26 enemy planes he was the leading American "ace." In 1942 he spent three weeks on a liferaft at sea before rescue.

Rienzi, Cola di (1313-1354), an Italian leader of the people. During the seven months that he was permitted to exercise supreme power in Rome, he proved himself a true friend of the poor. Ultimately, however, his enemies proved too strong for him and he was imprisoned for three years at Avignon. Returning to Rome after gaining his freedom, he was murdered.

Riis, Jacob August (1849-1914), an American author. He wrote *How the Other Half Lives, The Children of the Poor, A Ten Years' War, The Making of an American;* and many magazine articles.

Riley, James Whitcomb (1853-1916), an American poet. His verses are characterized by both humor and pathos, and by their excellent pictures of rural life. Among other volumes of poetry he published *Old Swimmin' Hole, An Old Sweetheart of Mine, Rhymes of Childhood,* and *Raggedy Man.*

Rimsky-Korsakov, Nicholas Andreievich (1844-1908), Russian composer whose works include *Le coq d'or* (1910), *Scheherazade,* and many orchestral suites, overtures, songs and piano pieces.

Rinehart, Mary Roberts (b. 1876), American author. Among her numerous works are *The Altar of Freedom, The Haunted Stair, The Amazing Interlude,* and *My Story.*

Ripley, Robert Leroy (1893-1949), an author and traveler, creator of the "Believe It or Not" cartoons syndicated in newspapers throughout the world.

Rivera, Diego (1886-1958), Mexican painter with a social outlook. His murals depict Mexico's life and problems. He has painted murals in educational buildings and in palaces in Mexico. He did frescoes in San Francisco, in the Detroit Institute of Arts, and in the New School for Research in New York.

Rizzio, David (c. 1540-1566), Italian secretary of Mary Queen of Scots. Suspected of a too great attachment to Mary, he was murdered by

Darnley and some other Scottish nobles, in the Palace of Holyrood, after he had been dragged from the queen's presence in the supper chamber.

Roberts, Owen Josephus (1875-1955), American jurist. President Hoover appointed him Associate Justice of the United States Supreme Court in 1930 and retired in 1945. After World War II he headed a commission to investigate the Pearl Harbor attack of Dec. 7, 1941.

Robespierre, Maximilien François Marie Isidore de (1758-94), was a country advocate until the outbreak of the French Revolution, when he went to Paris, became an enthusiastic leader of the Jacobin party, and was made a member of the Assembly. With the support of the lower classes in general and the Paris Commune in particular, he became the chief power in France. As president of the Committee of Public Safety he sent many to the guillotine. His power was broken by the counter-revolution of Thermidor. He was denounced, shot, and guillotined.

Robinson, Edwin Arlington (1869-1935), an American poet. He won the Pulitzer Prize for poetry three times: for *Collected Poems*, in 1921; *The Man Who Died Twice*, in 1925; and for *Tristram*, in 1927.

Robinson, James Harvey (1863-1936), American historian and editor. Among his published works are *Introduction to the History of Western Europe* (1903), *The Mind in the Making* (1921), and *The Ordeal of Civilization* (1926).

Rob Roy (the traditional nickname of **Robert McGregor**, 1671-1734), a Scottish outlaw who levied blackmail on the farmers and rich people in return for certain protective services.

Rockefeller, John Davison (1839-1937), American capitalist. In 1870 he became president of the Standard Oil Company. By enlarging this enterprise, driving out and absorbing rival companies, and by establishing the Standard Oil Trust, he secured, by 1879, a virtual monopoly in the petroleum refining industry. By 1902 he had relinquished active control of his widespread financial interests. The fortune which he had accumulated at the time of his retirement was valued at over a billion dollars. In the years that followed he made large gifts for the promotion of science, religion, education, and medicine. The Rockefeller Foundation was created in 1913 by an endowment of $165,281,624.

Rockefeller, John Davison, Jr. (b. 1874), an American capitalist, became associated with his father's business and philanthropic activities. Under his guidance Rockefeller Center was established.

Rockefeller, Nelson Aldrich (b. 1908), Chairman of the board of Rockefeller Center since 1945, son of John D. Rockefeller, Jr. He was assistant secretary of state, 1944-45, treasurer of the Museum of Modern Art, 1939-41, and from 1946 forward.

Rodin, Auguste (1840-1917), a French sculptor, who possessed a bold and original genius. His numerous statues and his fine historic monuments, especially that for Calais commemorating the bravery of Eustache de Saint-Pierre, brought Rodin well-deserved fame. His best-known piece is perhaps "The Thinker."

Roebling, John Augustus (1806-1869), an American engineer. He surveyed and located three railroads from Harrisburg to Pittsburgh across the Allegheny Mountains. He constructed the suspension bridge over the gorge of the Niagara River, completed in 1855. His greatest work was the bridge over the East River connecting Manhattan and Brooklyn.

Rogers, Will (1879-1935), American humorist, actor, and author. Leaving the stage for moving pictures, he became one of the outstanding artists in that medium. He wrote several humorous books. Rogers died with Wiley Post when the latter's plane crashed, Aug. 15, 1935, near Point Barrow, Alaska.

Rolland, Romain (1866-1944), French author whose finest work, *Jean Christophe*, in ten volumes, gained him the Nobel Prize for literature, 1915.

Rolvaag, Ole Edvart (1876-1931), a writer, born in Rolvaag, Norway, came to the United States in 1892. His fame is based on his novels of Norwegian life, especially of the pioneering folk of the American Northwest. They include *Giants in the Earth*, *Peder Victorious*, and *Pure Gold*.

Romains, Jules (b. 1885), a French writer. His real name is Louis Farigoule, and he has become known as a playwright, poet, and novelist. His many novels include the triology *The Body's Rapture*. He is the author of *Men of Good Will*, a serial novel, depicting modern civilization with Paris as the focal point. The eighth volume, *Verdun*, appeared in 1940.

Römer, Ole (1644-1710), a Danish astronomer, noted for his discovery of the fact that time is required for light to travel through space. In his study of the eclipses of Jupiter's satellites he estimated the velocity of light.

Rommel, Erwin (1891-1944), German general who commanded the Afrika Corps (1941-43) and the German defense against the Normandy invasion (1944). He was reported to be involved in the 1944 plot to assassinate Adolf Hitler and to have been executed.

Romney, George (1734-1802), English portrait painter, especially noted for his handling of flesh tones.

Röntgen, Wilhelm Konrad (1845-1923), German scientist who discovered the Röntgen rays (X rays) in 1895. He made other important laboratory investigations, resulting in the solution of difficult chemical problems.

Roosevelt, Anna Eleanor (b. 1884), wife of the 32nd President of the United States, daughter of Elliott Roosevelt, who was the younger brother of President Theodore Roosevelt. She married Franklin Delano Roosevelt March 17, 1905. Mrs. Roosevelt has engaged in educational, philanthropic and political endeavors, is a newspaper columnist and is chairman (1946, re-elected 1950) of the U. N.'s Human Rights Commission.

Roosevelt, Franklin Delano (1882-1945), 32nd President of the United States. In 1905 he married Anna Eleanor Roosevelt, a niece of his fifth cousin, Theodore Roosevelt. When Wilson was elected President, Roosevelt was appointed Assistant Secretary of the Navy. In 1928 he was elected governor of New York, and was re-elected in 1930. Nominated for President on the Democratic ticket in 1932, Roosevelt was swept into office in the November elections by a plurality of over 7,000,000 votes. He carried 42 states, and his party gained control of both houses of Congress. The first year of the new President's term was marked by legislative activity unprecedented in nature and extent. First in order came a bank moratorium. There followed the repeal of the 18th Amendment and in June the passage of the National Industrial Recovery Act. A huge public works program designed to increase employment was also set up. The succeeding 73rd and 74th Congresses approved most of the Administration measures. President Roosevelt was re-elected in 1936 by an overwhelming majority. In his second term some of his proposals met with strong opposition. The crisis caused by the German victories in 1940 was thought to have prompted Roosevelt to run for a third term. He was elected, and in 1941 became the first man to serve more than two terms as President. He was elected for a fourth term in 1944, but served less than three months before his death from a cerebral hemorrhage April 12, 1945.

Roosevelt, Theodore (1858-1919), President of the United States from the death of McKinley in 1901, until 1909. He led the Rough Riders in the Spanish-American War, and was also a notable big-game hunter. Governor of New York 1898-1900; in 1900, when McKinley was elected President, he was elected Vice-President. On the assassination of McKinley in 1901 he succeeded to the Presidency, and in 1904 was re-elected to the position. His administration was characterized by an aggressive foreign policy, increase in the powers of the President's office, and attacks on big business trusts. For his efforts in promoting peace he was awarded the Nobel Prize in 1906. In the presidential elections of 1912 he ran on the Bull Moose ticket, splitting the Republican party.

Root, Elihu (1845-1937), American statesman. Secretary of War, 1899-1904; Secretary of State, 1905-1909. Awarded Nobel Peace Prize, 1912.

Rosa, Salvator (1615-73), Italian painter, who first attracted notice by selling pictures in the streets of Naples. Being encouraged by Lanfranco, he went from Naples to Rome, and quickly became one of the most noted artists of his time. His pictures were chiefly landscapes and battle scenes.

Rosenwald, Julius (1863-1932), an American capitalist and philanthropist, became president of Sears, Roebuck and Company. He gave much time and money to the promotion of Negro education, the establishment of a large science museum, and Jewish relief in the Near East.

Ross, Sir James Clark (1800-62), English explorer, achieved distinction in the Arctic, accompanying his uncle, Sir John Ross, and Captain Parry on their expeditions. He was commander of the expedition of 1839-43, and discovered the North Magnetic Pole in 1831.

Rossetti, Dante Gabriel (1828-82), an English poet and painter. He became one of the Pre-Raphaelite Brotherhood, formed in 1848. From about 1850 he produced a great number of pictures remarkable for their extreme beauty of drawing, splendor of coloring, and poetic force. He also distinguished himself as a poet; his two volumes, published in 1870 and 1881 respectively, reflect many of the characteristics of his paintings.

Rossini, Gioachino Antonio (1792-1868), Italian composer. His first opera, *Tancredi*, was produced at Venice when he was twenty-one. It was followed after a short interval by *Il Barbiere di Siviglia*, *La Ceneventola*, *Otello*, *La Donna del Lago*, and *Guillaume Tell*.

Rostand, Edmond (1868-1918), French dramatist and member of the French Academy, author of *Cyrano de Bergerac* (1898), one of the most popular plays of modern times.

Rothschild, Anselm Meyer (1743-1812), Jewish financier, the founder of the famous family, was born at Frankfort-on-the-Main, and, after some experience in a bank as clerk, set up for himself first as a moneylender, then as a banker. By his genius for finance he acquired a large fortune. His son, Nathan Meyer Rothschild (1777-1836), took charge of the London house, and conducted its affairs with great success. He was succeeded by his eldest son, Baron Lionel de Rothschild (1808-1879), who was the first Jewish member of the English House of Commons.

Rousseau, Jean Jacques (1712-1778), French philosopher and writer, was born at Geneva. He studied social questions with great ardor, and in 1759 published his romance *La Nouvelle Héloïse*, which was followed in 1762 by *Émile*. These two works contained so much that was at variance with convention, that the orthodox objected and Rousseau was obliged to leave France for a time. It was while in England that he wrote his remarkable *Confessions*, and his celebrated *Contrat social*.

Royce, Josiah (1855-1916), an American educator and philosopher, became professor of the history of philosophy at Harvard in 1892, a position he occupied until 1914, when he became Alford professor of natural religion. He was considered one of America's leading philosophers; his theories dealt with loyalty and individualism.

Rubens, Peter Paul (1577-1640), a Flemish painter. He became socially and politically prominent, acquired immense wealth and was twice married, the first time to Isabella Brant, and the second time, in 1631, to Helena Fourment; he painted many portraits of them as well as of himself. Other works include "The Adoration of the Magi," "Battle of the Amazons," and "Venus in the Smithy of Vulcan."

Runyan, (Alfred) Damon (1884-1946), American writer. He became a war correspondent and a feature writer for the Hearst Syndicate. He also contributed fiction to such magazines as *Cosmopolitan* and *Collier's*, and published collections of poems and short stories.

Rush, Benjamin (1745-1813), an American physician. Elected a member of the Continental Congress, he signed the Declaration of Independence (1776). In April, 1777, he became physician general of the Continental Army. In 1799 Rush was appointed treasurer of the United States Mint, which post he held till his death.

Ruskin, John (1819-1900), English art critic and philosopher, son of a wealthy London wine merchant. His *Modern Painters* exhibited his ability as a writer and critic. Meanwhile he had published *The Seven Lamps of Architecture* and *The Stones of Venice*, two memorable works which considerably enhanced the author's fame. Always taking a deep interest in economic questions, Ruskin delivered and published numerous lectures on a wide range of subjects.

Russell, Bertrand Arthur William (b. 1872), English philosopher. He studied mathematics, and in 1910-13 he published *Principia Mathematica* in conjunction with A. N. Whitehead. His works include *Scientific Method in Philosophy*, *The Analysis of Matter*, *The Analysis of Mind*, *Marriage and Morals*, and *Mysticism and Logic*.

Russell, George William (1867-1935), Irish poet who wrote under the pen name of "A. E."; widely known as a leader in co-operative enterprise and a pioneer of the Abbey Theater.

Russell, John, Earl (1792-1878), British statesman, was one of the principal leaders of the English liberals during a large part of the nineteenth century. Russell was largely responsible for the Reform Act of 1832, and for the nonrecognition of the Confederacy.

Ruth, George Herman "Babe" (1895-1948), American baseball player, famous for hitting home runs. He retired from baseball in 1935.

Rutherford of Nelson, Lord (1871-1937), was born in New Zealand. Won the Nobel Prize for physics in 1908; professor of physics, Cambridge University, 1919-1937.

S

Sachs, Hans (1494-1576), the German shoemaker poet, of Reformation times, was an earnest worker in the Protestant cause, and wrote over 5,000 different pieces, poetry and prose.

Saint-Gaudens, Augustus (1848-1907), an American sculptor; born in Dublin, Ireland. He was brought to the United States in infancy; studied art at Cooper Institute, New York City, in 1861; at the National Academy of Design in 1865-1866; and at Paris, where he attended the École des Beaux Arts in 1867. In 1871, while in Rome, he produced his first figure, *Hiawatha*, but returned to the United States in 1872. Among his works are the bas-relief, *Adoration of the Cross by Angels;* statues of Admiral D. G. Farragut, Robert R. Randall, and Lincoln; the Shaw monument in Boston; and the original Diana on the Madison Square Garden, New York.

Saint-Just, Antoine (1767-94), one of the later leaders of the French Revolution.

Saint-Pierre, Jacques Henri Bernardin de (1737-1814), French author; the romanticist who attained fame by his story, *Paul and Virginia.*

Saint-Simon, Claude Henri, Comte de (1760-1825), a French social philosopher, the founder of French socialism; born in Paris. After completing his education he entered the army, and in 1777 participated in an expedition sent by Louis XVI to assist the United States in its war with England. He retired from the army at the outbreak of the French Revolution and devoted himself to what he termed a "physico-political" reformation, for which purpose he entered into the study of all the physical sciences: mathematics, astronomy, general physics, and chemistry. His last efforts were directed toward the foundation of a new religion, which he called the New Christianity. His most important works were, *Introduction to the Scientific Labors of the Nineteenth Century, The Reorganization of European Society,* and *New Christianity.*

Sainte-Beuve, Charles Augustin (1804-1869), a French writer, one of the greatest of modern critics; born in Boulogne. He studied medicine at Paris, but abandoned that science in favor of literature, his first work of importance treating with French literature of the 16th century. His critical articles were later published in 28 volumes. *Port Royal,* a study of the Jansenists, marked his evolution toward Classicism, with which he tried to reconcile Romanticism. Sante-Beuve was a precursor of Taine in his use of documentary detail. He was elected to the Academy, 1844; Senate, 1865.

St. Laurent, Louis Stephen (b. 1882), Canadian Liberal political leader. A lawyer and professor of law, he became minister of justice and attorney general in 1941, and, in 1948, prime minister of Canada, serving until the Liberals were defeated in 1957.

Saint-Saëns, Charles Camille (1835-1921), a distinguished French composer whose works include the operas *Samson et Delilah* and *Henry VIII,* besides symphonic music.

Saintsbury, George Edward Bateman (1845-1933), English critic; professor of rhetoric and English literature, Edinburgh University, 1895-1915. Author of numerous critical works on literary subjects, on which he was a leading authority.

Saladin (c. 1137-1193), sultan of Egypt, a conquering general, and a deadly foe of Christianity. He swept over Syria and Macedonia, and captured Jerusalem after a great victory at Tiberias. It was against Saladin that the Third Crusade was undertaken, and after his defeat by Richard I, in 1191, his power was shattered.

Sand, George (1804-76), French novelist, real name, Amantine Lucile Aurore Dupin, Baroness Dudevant. Both as novelist and dramatist she achieved the highest success. A friend of men of such singular power as Alfred de Musset, Chopin, and Sandeau.

Sankey, Ira David (1840-1908), the celebrated American evangelist, singer, and composer, associated with Dwight L. Moody, the revivalist, in mission-work in the United States and Great Britain for many years.

Sappho (flourished 611-592 B. C.), lyric poetess of ancient Greece, of whose erotic poetry only a few samples survive.

Sardou, Victorien (1831-1908), French dramatist, began writing plays in 1854, but was at first unsuccessful. Later he obtained an introduction to Mlle. Déjazet, the famous actress, for whom he wrote some plays that proved highly popular and placed him at the head of French popular dramatists.

Sargent, John Singer (1856-1925), American portrait painter, was educated in France and spent much of his life in England. One of the great artists of his day, famous for his murals.

Sartre, Jean Paul (b. 1905), French writer and philosopher. He was one of the originators of French existential philosophy. He taught philosophy, then served in the French army during World War II. His writings include the novels *Age of Reason* and *The Reprieve*, and among his plays are *The Flies* and *No Exit*. His philosophic works include *Existentialism.*

Sassoon, Siegfried (b. 1886), English poet known for his works attacking war: *Counterattack,* etc.

Saunders, Sir Charles Edward (1867-1937), Canadian scientist who evolved special breed of wheat for the Canadian government.

Savonarola, Girolamo (1452-98), Florentine preacher and reformer, one of the most learned men of his time, who denounced the follies and luxuries of his time, especially within the Church. He was excommunicated and executed by the Florentine government. His works have been translated into many languages.

Scarlatti, Alessandro (1659-1725), Italian composer. He composed an immense number of operas, masses, cantatas, madrigals, etc.; much of his music is still performed.

Schelling, Friedrich Wilhelm Joseph von (1775-1854), a German metaphysician, who attracted much attention by his system of idealistic philosophy.

Schiller, Johann Christoph Friedrich (1759-1805), German dramatist and poet, born at Marbach in Württemberg. Though educated for military service, his literary bent was paramount. In 1782 he had his first play, *The Robbers*, successfully produced at the Mannheim Theater, to which he was subsequently appointed dramatic composer. He left Mannheim for Leipzig in 1785. Later he proceeded to Dresden, where he completed his *Don Carlos;* and in 1789 he was at the University of Jena as professor of history. While thus engaged he wrote his *History of the Thirty Years' War*, and made the acquaintance of Goethe, at whose suggestion he removed to Weimar, and during the next ten years produced his greatest works—*Wallenstein*, *Mary Stuart*, *The Maid of Orleans*, and *William Tell*. He died at the age of forty-six.

Schlegel, August Wilhelm von (1767-1845), a German critic who for a number of years held the post of professor of history in the University of Bonn. He is best known in the United States for translations of his *Lectures on Dramatic Art and Literature*, which are remarkable for their appreciation of Shakespeare and their scholarly handling of the drama.

Schley, Winfield Scott (1839-1911), an American naval officer, born in Frederick Co., Md. He graduated from the United States Naval Academy in 1860. In the Civil War he secured the first prize ship, the *General Parkhill*. At the beginning of the Spanish-American War he attained the rank of commodore, and was given command of a squadron. The American ships commanded by Schley destroyed the Spanish fleet in the Battle of Santiago. After being made a rear admiral Schley resigned from the Navy in 1901. At his request a court of inquiry investigated charges made against him of negligence and misconduct. Dewey's report praised Schley, but the majority of the court found him guilty; however, it was recommended that no action be taken. An appeal to the President failed to set aside the verdict. Schley died in New York City, Oct. 2, 1911.

Schliemann, Heinrich (1822-90), was a celebrated German traveler and archeologist, who excavated the site of Troy, and discovered a number of royal tombs at Athens and Mycenae.

Schnitzler, Arthur (1862-1931), Austrian writer. He was educated in medicine; his tendency to analyze his characters may be traced to this early training. His works are outstanding for psychological penetration and beauty of style. He wrote many novels, short stories, and dramas, among them *Anatol*, *Liebelei*, *Professor Bernhardi*, and *Bertha Garlan*.

Schofield, John McAllister (1831-1906), American soldier, was born in Gerry, N. Y. He graduated at the United States Military Academy in 1853. After service in the Civil War, he became Secretary of War, 1868-69; commanded the Army of the United States as senior major general; and was promoted to the rank of lieutenant general. He was the author of *Forty-six Years in the Army* (1897).

Schönberg, Arnold (1874-1951), Austrian composer whose style was atonal. He originated the 12-tone scale. He wrote a number of quartets and compositions for voice and instruments, including *Erwartung* and *Pierrot lunaire*.

Schopenhauer, Arthur (1788-1860), was a German philosopher notable for the pessimism of his general outlook. His mysticism partook somewhat of the higher Buddhism. His chief works are *The World as Will and Idea*, and *The Two Fundamental Problems of Ethics*.

Schreiner, Olive (1859-1920), South African novelist, noted for the veld scenery and Dutch character she reproduced so well in such books as *The Story of an African Farm* (1883).

Schubert, Franz Peter (1797-1828), one of the most eminent of Austrian composers, whose songs and symphonies are among the most inspired of musical compositions, full of melodic beauty and emotional power. He also wrote operas, masses, and cantatas, many of which reached a high level of merit.

Schumann, Robert Alexander (1810-56), a famous German composer and music critic, who did much for the advancement of German music. He was the author of numerous fantasias, songs, and orchestral compositions, and attained a prominent position among modern composers. His wife, Clara Schumann (1819-1896), was a noted pianist and interpreter of Chopin, and also a composer.

Schurz, Carl (1829-1906), an American statesman; born in Sibhar, near Cologne, Prussia. He came to the United States in 1852. After fighting in the Civil War for the Union forces, he was elected senator from Missouri. From 1877 to 1881 he was Secretary of the Interior, and from 1881 to 1884 was editor of the *New York Evening Post*. Schurz wrote several books, among them a *Life of Henry Clay*.

Schuschnigg, Kurt von (b. 1897), became chancellor of Austria shortly after the assassination of Dollfuss in 1934, continued in office until March 1938, when Austria was seized by Germany. The Nazi government kept him in prison after the Anschluss. He was freed by the Allies in 1945 and settled in the United States, as professor at St. Louis University, 1948.

Schweitzer, Albert (b. 1875) missionary in Lambarene, musical critic, authority on Bach's music, famous organist, and a noted scholar who became a doctor of medicine in order to devote his life to missionary work in equatorial Africa.

Scipio, Publius Cornelius (c. 232-183 B. C.), the greatest of the Scipios, known as Scipio Africanus the elder. A distinguished Roman general in the 2nd Punic War.

Scott, Cyril M. (b. 1879), English composer. He is best known for his songs, folk tunes, and pianoforte pieces. He also published several books of verse and an autobiography, *My Years of Indiscretion*.

Scott, Robert Falcon (1868-1912), British naval officer and Antarctic explorer. He entered the navy in 1882 and from 1901 to 1904 commanded the British Antarctic Expedition, on which he verified the findings of Ross, established a new record for southward journeys, found King Edward Land, and carried on considerable scientific work. In 1910 he left England in command of another Antarctic Expedition and reached the South Pole, Jan. 18, 1912. Scott and four of his companions were frozen to death on the return journey, and their bodies and records were found a year later.

Scott, Sir Walter (1771-1832) British novelist and poet. His *Minstrelsy of the Scottish Border* was published in 1802. This was followed by *The Lay of the Last Minstrel*, *Marmion*, *The Lady of the Lake*, *Rokeby*, and *The Lord of the Isles*. Scott's historical novels include *Waverley*, *Ivanhoe*, *Guy Mannering*, *The Antiquary*, *Old Mortality*, *Rob Roy*, and *The Heart of Midlothian*. Scott made large sums of money by his writings and was in the full tide of success when the failure of Ballantyne, his publisher, saddled him with enormous liabilities. Scott, who was then fifty-five, placed himself in the hands of trustees and before his death had satisfied all his obligations and purchased back his old estate.

Scott, Winfield (1786-1866), American soldier. He was educated at William and Mary College, and studied law. In 1808 he was appointed captain of light artillery in General Wilkinson's division, stationed at Baton Rouge, La.; and at the commencement of the War in 1812 he was appointed lieutenant colonel. In 1841 he was appointed commander-in-chief of the United States Army. During the Mexican War, Scott won the battles of Vera Cruz, Cerro Gordo, Jalapa, Perote, Puebla, Contreras, Churubusco, Molino del Rey and Chapultepec, and captured Mexico City in Sept. 1847. The same year he was brevetted lieutenant general. In 1852 Scott was the unsuccessful candidate of the Whig party for the Presidency.

Scribner, Charles (1821-1871), an American publisher, born in New York City, founder (1846) of the publishing house of Charles Scribner's Sons and (1870) of *Scribner's Monthly* (merged with *Hours at Home* and later called *Century Magazine).* His son Charles (1854-1930), born in New York City, became head in 1879.

Semmes, Raphael (1809-1877), an American naval officer. In 1828 he was appointed a midshipman on board the *Lexington;* he rose by successive steps to the rank of commander in 1855. In 1861, he joined the Confederate service, and was made commander of the war steamer *Sumter.* With this vessel he caused considerable damage to the United States merchant navy. In 1862 he took command of the *Alabama,* with which he captured more than 60 ships. The *Alabama* was sunk off Cherbourg, France, by the Union ship *Kearsarge,* but Semmes and a number of his crew were rescued by an English boat. Semmes returned to America, commanded a squadron on the James River, and, after receiving the rank of brigadier general, assisted in the defense of Danville, Va. After the war, he practiced law in Mobile, Ala.

Seneca, Lucius Annaeus (c. 4 B. C.-A. D. 65), Roman philosopher, statesman, and dramatist, who was tutor to Nero, and one of that emperor's most influential advisers. Having lost Nero's favor, Seneca was sentenced to end his own life. Among his works are *Epistolae ad Lucilium* several philosophical treatises, and a number of tragedies, the only Roman tragedies extant.

Service, Robert William (b. 1874), a Canadian poet and novelist who led a varied life in Canada, his poems reflecting the sterner aspects of the Northwest. His best-known works are *Songs of a Sourdough, Ballads of a Cheechako* and *Rhymes of a Rolling Stone.*

Severus, Lucius Septimius (146-211), Roman emperor from 193 to his death. After many victories in the East, he invaded Britain with an army, subjugated the Caledonians, and repaired and partly rebuilt Hadrian's wall. The triumphal arch of Severus still stands in Rome.

Seward, William Henry (1801-1872), an American statesman. In 1830 he was elected a member of the New York Senate. Displaying marked abilities as a politician, he was in 1838 and 1840 chosen governor, and in 1849 was elected to the United States Senate, where he distinguished himself by his firm resistance to the extension of slavery. In 1860 he was a candidate for the Presidency, but being defeated in the convention by Abraham Lincoln, he worked to secure Lincoln's election; Lincoln afterward appointed Seward Secretary of State. He was dangerously wounded in April, 1865, when President Lincoln was assassinated, but recovered and filled the same office under Lincoln's successor, Andrew Johnson. He resigned his post on the accession of President Grant in 1869.

Seymour, Horatio (1810-1886), an American statesman. After serving three terms, with marked ability, in the New York Legislature, he was elected governor on the Democratic ticket in 1852. During the Civil War he was decidedly in favor of the Union, and as governor a second time (1863-1865) showed conspicuous energy and ability in raising troops. In 1868 he was defeated for the Presidency by General Grant.

Shackleton, Sir Ernest (1874-1922), commander of the Nimrod Farthest South expedition of 1907-09, reached within 100 miles of the South Pole, and embarked on a new expedition in 1914. He died on a scientific voyage to the Antarctic.

Shakespeare, William (1564-1616) English dramatist and poet, born in Stratford-on-Avon, Warwickshire. Shakespeare was educated at the free grammar school of Stratford, and in his 19th year married Anne Hathaway, daughter of a yeoman of the neighboring hamlet of Shottery, and eight years older than himself. About 1586, Shakespeare went to London There he gained a reputation as an actor and playwright in the theater of Blackfriars, and afterward in that of the Globe; and enjoyed the favor and patronage of Queen Elizabeth, James I, the Earl of Southampton, and the warm friendship of Ben Jonson. The first collected edition of Shakespeare's plays was the folio of 1623. His poems *Venus and Adonis,* and *The Rape of Lucrece,* were published in 1593 and 1594, and were the only works which appeared with his name in his lifetime. Of the 36 plays (exclusive of *Pericles),* the dates of publication of only a few are known. The *Two Gentlemen of Verona,* and *Love's Labor's Lost;* were among the earliest; and *Tempest, Troilus and Cressida, Henry VIII, Coriolanus, Julius Caesar,* and *Antony and Cleopatra* among the latest. The *Midsummer Night's Dream, Merchant of Venice, Romeo and Juliet, Richard II, Richard III, Henry IV* and *King John* were all produced before 1598. A copy of *Hamlet* is extant, bearing the date 1602. *Twelfth Night* was produced in 1601; *King Lear* was printed in 1607; the *Tempest* was written in 1611. The second folio edition of the collected plays appeared in 1632, and two others subsequently. It is said that by 1830 not less than 82 editions had been published. Shakespeare's plays show an extraordinary knowledge of human nature, and for sheer poetic beauty they have never been equalled. Few would deny that he is the greatest of English writers. He was buried in the chancel of Trinity Church, Stratford.

Shaw, George Bernard (1856-1950), Irish writer, noted for his pungent wit and highly individual opinions, whether in musical criticism, socialist pamphlets or plays. His plays include *Man and Superman, Heartbreak House, Back to Methuselah,* and *The Apple Cart.* In 1925 Shaw was awarded the Nobel Prize for literature.

Shaw, Henry Wheeler (1818-1885), American humorist, born in Lanesborough, Mass. In 1858 he settled in Poughkeepsie, N. Y., as an auctioneer, soon began writing humorous pieces for newspapers, and became widely known under his pseudonym of Josh Billings. His grotesque phonetic spelling and homely philosophy gave an air of quaint originality to his work. His *Farmers' Allminax* (1870-1880) had a remarkable sale, and his other writings met with almost equal popularity.

Shays, Daniel (1747-1825), an American insurgent. He served as an ensign at the battle of Bunker Hill, and attained the rank of captain in the Continental Army. He took a leading part in the popular movement in western Massachusetts for the redress of alleged grievances, appearing before Springfield, Mass., at the head of 1,000 men to prevent the meeting of the Supreme Court at that place.

Shearer, Norma (b. 1904), Canadian film actress who early came to the United States and had a highly successful career on the screen. Among other motion pictures, she appeared in *The Barretts of Wimpole Street*, *Idiot's Delight*, *Marie Antoinette* and *The Women*.

Shelley, Percy Bysshe (1792-1822), English poet. His poems, most of which were written in the last five years of his life, include: *Alastor; Prometheus Unbound; Lines on the Euganean Hills; The Cenci*, a tragedy in verse; *Epipsychidion;* and *Adonais*, his famous elegy on the death of Keats. Shelley also wrote a prose essay, *The Defence of Poetry*. Much of his best poetry is in his shorter lyrics, among them "To a Skylark," and "Ode to the West Wind." Shelley is recognized as one of the greatest of the Romantic poets.

Sheraton, Thomas (1751-1806), was the last of the great English cabinetmakers of the 18th century. The Sheraton style which he introduced marks a reaction against the Chippendale.

Sheridan, Philip Henry (1831-1888), American general; born in Albany, N. Y. He was graduated from the United States Military Academy in 1853, and served in the army in Texas and Oregon. At the outbreak of the Civil War he was appointed quartermaster of the army in southwestern Missouri. In April, 1864, he was given command of the cavalry corps of the Army of the Potomac, and rendered valuable services during Grant's movements against Lee. In June he was made commander of the Army of the Shenandoah, and defeated Early in several engagements in the Valley. Sheridan's maneuvers were particularly responsible for the Confederate evacuation of Richmond and Petersburg, and the final surrender of Lee's army Sheridan commanded the U. S. Army from 1883 to 1888, being raised to the rank of general in the latter year.

Sheridan, Richard Brinsley (1751-1816), British dramatist. His first comedy, *The Rivals*, was produced in 1755, and was followed by *The Duenna*, *The School for Scandal*, and *The Critic*. Sheridan wrote no more plays until 1789, when *Pizarro* was produced. From 1780 to 1812 Sheridan was a member of Parliament.

Sherman, William Tecumseh (1820-1891), American soldier; born in Ohio. He was graduated from West Point in 1840, served in the Mexican War, became a banker in San Francisco in 1853, and in 1859 was appointed superintendent of the Louisiana State Military Institute. Upon the outbreak of the Civil War he resigned, was commissioned a colonel in the regular army and commanded a brigade at Bull Run. In April, 1862, he commanded a division at Shiloh, and in December was given command of the 15th Corps. In 1863 he became commander of the Army of the Tennessee, and in 1864 became the leading general in the west after Grant was made commander of all Union armies. Sherman immediately invaded Georgia, captured Atlanta after a series of battles, and began a "march to the sea," destroying all Confederate crops, supplies, and railroads which lay in his line of march. He captured Savannah in December, 1864, and in February, 1865, moved northward. In March he defeated Johnston's army at Goldsborough, and received its surrender in April, after the surrender of Lee's army to Grant. From 1869 to 1834 Sherman commanded the United States Army.

Shostakovich, Dmitri (b. 1906), Russian composer. He won repute when quite young with his first symphony (1925). He wrote nine symphonies, several ballets, an opera, and music for drama and films, as well as concertos and piano works.

Sibelius, Jean Julius Christian (1865-1957), Finnish composer of eight symphonies as well as an opera, a violin concerto, several suites, *Valse Triste*, and several symphonic poems, among them *En Saga*, *Finlandia*, and *The Swan of Tuonela*. With the exception of his first two symphonies, Sibelius's works are not based on folk or national themes.

Sidney, Sir Philip (1554-1586), British statesman, poet and soldier. He wrote *Arcadia*, a prose romance; *Apologie for Poetrie;* and *Astrophel and Stella*, a sonnet sequence. He was killed at the battle of Zutphen.

Sienkiewicz, Henry (1846-1916), Polish author well known for his work, *Quo Vadis*.

Simeon Stylites (390-459), a Syrian monk of the 5th century, who is said to have passed thirty years of his life on a pillar near Antioch, from which he preached daily to great crowds.

Simms, William Gilmore (1806-1870), American author; born in Charleston, S. C. His publications include *Atalantis: A Tale of the Sea*, the longest and most noted of his poems; *The Wigwam and the Cabin or Tales of the South: The Maroon, and Other Tales*, and *War Poetry of the South*.

Simon, Jules François (1814-1896), eminent French philosopher and statesman. His writings include a history of the Thiers Government and *Liberty of Conscience*.

Simonson, Lee (b. 1888), American scenic designer, studied at Harvard and in Paris. From 1912 to 1916 he was with the Washington Square Players as designer, and in 1919 became director of the Theater Guild.

Simpson, Sir James Young (1811-70), British scientist, the discoverer of the use of chloroform as an anesthetic. He was a native of Scotland, and one of the most accomplished experimental surgeons of the 19th century.

Sims, Admiral William Sowden (1858-1936). American naval officer. He commanded the American Fleet in European waters during the World War.

Sinclair, Upton (b. 1878), American novelist, whose fame as a writer was established when he published *The Jungle* in 1906.

Skinner, Cornelia Otis (b. 1901), American actress, known for her dramatic monologues. She is the daughter of Otis Skinner and has appeared in a series of original sketches, notably the *Wives of Henry VIII*.

Skinner, Otis (1858-1942), actor. Some of his outstanding performances were in *Kismet*, *The Merry Wives of Windsor*, *Merchant of Venice*, and *A Hundred Years Old*. He wrote two books on the theater.

Smetana, Friedrich (1824-1884), Czech composer. Besides symphonic poems, songs, and piano compositions, he wrote eight operas. His most popular opera is the *Bartered Bride*.

Smith, Adam (1723-90), British writer, the father of the science of economics. He was the author of *Theory of Moral Sentiments* and *Wealth of Nations*, the latter expounding the idea of laissez faire in economic relations.

Smith, Alfred Emanuel (1873-1944), American politician, was governor of New York for four terms, and in 1928 was nominated for President of the United States on the Democratic ticket, but was not elected.

Smith, Francis Hopkinson (1838-1915), American painter, writer, and civil engineer. He was educated as a mechanical engineer; built the wall around Governor's Island, the Race Rock lighthouse off New London, Conn., and the foundation for the Statue of Liberty in New York harbor. He won fame as a water-color artist, and as a lecturer on art. His literary works include *Book of the Tile Club* (1890), *Colonel Carter of Cartersville* (1891), *American Illustrators* (1892), *A Gentleman Vagabond* (1895), and *Gondola Days* (1897).

Smith, Captain John (1580-1631), British seafarer and adventurer who, in 1607, was a leading spirit in the colonization of Virginia, and founded Jamestown.

Smith, Joseph, (1805-44), founder of Mormonism. He was the son of a Vermont farmer. He claimed that *The Book of Mormon,* which became the bible of the sect, was derived by divine communication to him. Smith, who was murdered, was not a polygamist; Brigham Young, who succeeded him, was.

Smollett, Tobias George (1721-71), English novelist and humorist, whose *Roderick Random, Peregrine Pickle, Count Fathom* and *Humphrey Clinker* abound in fun and genial characterization, while their pictures of sea life are inimitable.

Smuts, Jan Christian (1870-1950), South African statesman; he was a British subject of Boer parentage. During the Boer War he became commander-in-chief of the Boer forces in Cape Colony. After the war, Smuts advocated reconciliation with Great Britain, and aided in the establishment of the Union of South Africa, under which he held several offices. During the World War, he led the conquest of German Southwest Africa and German East Africa, and in 1917 joined the British war cabinet. After making important contributions to the peace conference, Smuts returned to South Africa where he became prime minister (1919). Even after the defeat of his South African party in 1924 he continued to advocate conciliation in regard to native demands, and when the coalition government was established in 1933, he was made deputy prime minister. Among his publications is *Africa and Some World Problems* (1930). In 1939 Smuts again became prime minister and served until 1948.

Snell, Baron Henry (1865-1944), leader of the Labour party in the British House of Lords after 1935. The son of an agricultural laborer, he was educated at a village school, becoming successively a farm worker, a groom, a waiter, a clerk, and an insurance agent, and later acquired university education by his own effort.

Snowden, Philip, (1864-1937), English statesman. When the Independent Labour party was formed, he became a member and was president from 1903 to 1906 and from 1917 to 1920. In 1924, and from 1929 to 1931 he was Chancellor of the Exchequer; in 1931 he was made a viscount.

Snyders, Franz, or Frans, (1597-1657), great Flemish animal painter who was associated with Rubens, Jordaens, and other masters. He was also adept at flower- and fruit-painting, and skillful in landscape work.

Sobieski, John, *See* JOHN III.

Socinus, Laelius (1525-62), Italian Protestant thinker and anti-Trinitarian, founder with his nephew, Faustus Socinus (1539-1604), of the Socinian system of theology.

Socrates (469-399 B.C.) Greek philosopher, was the son of a sculptor, and for some time followed that calling himself, but, having other ambitions, joined the army, and fought in the battle of Potidaea, and also in the battle of Delium, saving the life of Alcibiades in the first, and of Xenophon in the second. Returning to Athens, he devoted himself to study and began to exhort the people on public questions and the conduct of life. In 406 B. C. he was made one of the Senate of Five Hundred, and had other honors accorded him, continuing his teaching alternately with his public duties. Not long afterwards Anytus charged him with impiety, and he was found guilty and sentenced to death. When the fatal day came he calmly drank the poison which ended his life. Socrates wrote nothing himself; his life and teachings were recorded by Plato, his pupil.

Solon (638-558 B. C.) was one of the Seven Sages of Greece, and became an eminent legislator, after having made a reputation as a poet. Solon's Laws, though severe, were highly esteemed, and were the basis of later Greek legislation.

Solyman (1490-1566), sultan of the Turkish Empire, known as "the Magnificent," He was famous as a conqueror, law-giver, administrator, and patron of learning.

Sophocles (495-406 B. C.), Athenian dramatist, who with Aeschylus and Euripides, was one of the three greatest Greek tragedians. Of his many plays only seven have survived.

Soult, Marshal Nicolas Jean de Dieu, Duke of Dalmatia (1769-1851), was one of Napoleon's favorite and most capable generals. He distinguished himself in the Swiss and Italian campaigns, and also in the Peninsular War.

Sousa, John Philip (1854-1932), American bandmaster and composer. In 1880 he became leader of the Marine Band in Washington, D. C. In 1892, he left that organization to form his own band. This band of 100 pieces became internationally famous. Sousa wrote more than 300 musical compositions, but he is most famous for his marches, of which he composed more than 100. The most popular are: *Semper Fidelis; El Capitan; Stars and Stripes Forever;* and *King Cotton.*

Southey, Robert (1774-1843), English poet. He was overshadowed by the greater genius of Byron and Shelley, but in prose he was eminently successful, his *Life of Nelson, The Doctor, Commonplace Book,* and *Life of Wesley* being masterpieces of prose writing.

Spartacus (d. 71 B. C.), a Thracian who became a Roman slave and gladiator in Capua, and headed an insurrection in Italy in 73 B. C. The slaves he raised routed several Roman armies, but he was eventually defeated and slain by Crassus in 71 B. C.

Spencer, Herbert (1820-1903), English philosopher. His chief works are *Social Statics, Principles of Psychology* and several volumes of his *Synthetic Philosophy.* Spencer attempted to apply the principle of evolution to all phases of life, including politics and society.

Spengler, Oswald (1880-1936), German philosopher. In 1918 he published *The Decline of the West* (Eng. trans., 1926-28) which won him world fame. This work was based on the theory that all civilizations pass through regular evolutionary phases and eventually die. He predicted that the occidental culture of Europe would become extinct within 300 years, and be supplanted by an oriental civilization. His other works include *Man and Technics* (1932), and *The Hour of Decision* (1934).

Spenser, Edmund (1552-99), English poet; born in London and educated at Cambridge. He wrote his *Shepheard's Calender* and the allegory, *The Faerie Queene* while employed in the government service in Ireland. Among his other works are *Epithalamion, Amoretti* and *Prothalamion.*

Spinoza, Baruch (1632-77), Dutch philosopher, born in Amsterdam of a Jewish family. Having expounded philosophical doctrines antagonistic to Judaism, he was excommunicated by the rabbis as a heretic. In 1663 he published his critical work on the Cartesian philosophy, and set forth his own system of Pantheism, which makes God the cause and substance of the Universe, abolishes free will, and establishes the necessity of the Divine Nature. His *Ethics* was not published until after his death.

Spyri, Johanna (1827-1901), Swiss author. She wrote many stories dealing with the life of children in Switzerland. The most popular is *Heidi.*

Staël, Madame de (Anne Louise Germaine Necker, Baronne de Staël-Holstein) (1766-1817), French author, the daughter of Necker, the famous finance minister under Louis XVI. She was married to Baron de Staël at twenty. Two years after her marriage she came into prominence with her *Letters on Bousseau*, and was regarded as in sympathy with the Revolution. Later on she fell into disfavor, first with the Revolutionary leaders, then with Napoleon, and was exiled by both. She made good use of her exile by writing *Corinne* and other works.

Stalin, Joseph (Djugashvili, Joseph Vissarionovich (1879-1953), Russian Communist leader. From 1913 to 1917 he was in exile in Siberia, but during 1919-1920 he led one of Lenin's armies, published the journal *Pravda,* and became commissar of nationalities. After the death of Lenin in 1924, he used his position as general secretary of the Communist party to increase his personal power. Trotsky was exiled in 1929; others were killed or rendered powerless. Stalin became the dictator of Communist Russia. Under his guidance a program of general industrialization and increased production was undertaken in the form of the two five-year plans of 1928 and of 1933. Agriculture was reorganized and partially collectivized, though at the cost of many peasant lives. Stalin continued to consolidate his power, beginning in 1936 a new series of purges of old revolutionaries, army leaders, and other unruly elements. Stalin gave Russia's foreign policy a new form, discarding in part the Trotzkyite plan for fomenting world revolution, and proposing that Communist Russia and the democracies should together resist the growing power of Fascism. Failure of this policy led to a nonaggression treaty with Germany in 1939, but in 1941 Germany attacked Russia and Stalin resumed a policy of co-operation with the West until 1946, when the rapid spread of Communism into other countries developed a wide breach between the Soviet bloc and the West. This break eventually led to the Korean war and the cold war of 1950-51.

Stallings, Laurence (b. 1894), American playwright and critic. In collaboration with Maxwell Anderson he wrote and produced *What Price Glory* in 1924. He followed it in 1925 with *Plumes* and *The Buccaneer*, and wrote the scenarios for *The Big Parade* and *Old Ironsides.* He was the coeditor of the *First World War,* a history in photographs.

Standish, Miles (1584-1656), American colonist; born in Lancashire, England. He became a soldier in Holland, and although not a member of the Leyden congregation, sailed with the *Mayflower* colonists to Massachusetts in 1620. Standish was the military head of the Plymouth colony, and was long its treasurer. Longfellow's *The Courtship of Miles Standish* is a fictional account.

Stanley, Sir Henry Morton (1841-1904), English explorer. In 1859 he went to the United States. He served with the Union forces during the Civil War, and after the war became a roving newspaper reporter. In 1871 he was sent by the *New York Herald* to Africa to search for the noted missionary-explorer, David Livingstone, who had not been heard from for several years. After an arduous eight months' journey Stanley found him, and together they explored Lake Tanganyika and the Ruiszi River. Stanley later discovered the source of the Nile, and from 1874 to 1877 explored the Congo Basin. He was largely responsible for the founding of the Congo Free State. Stanley wrote several books describing his African expeditions, including *In Darkest Africa* and *Through South Africa.*

Stanton, Edwin McMasters (1814-1869), American statesman; born in Ohio. In 1860 he was appointed Attorney-General by Buchanan. Although a Democrat and a believer in the constitutional rights of slaveholders, he opposed slavery, and later upheld the Union. In 1862 he was appointed Secretary of War by Lincoln, and proved able and forceful. Stanton remained in Johnson's cabinet, although he was a critic of the President's reconstruction policies. He resigned in 1868.

Stanton, Elizabeth Cady (1815-1902), American reformer, born in New York. With Lucrecia Mott and several others, she called the first woman's rights convention, in 1848. She was president of the Equal Rights Association, 1848-69, of the National Woman's Suffrage Association, 1869-89, and of the National American Woman Suffrage Association, 1889-92. She advocated legal, political, and industrial equality for women, and was the author of *The History of Woman Suffrage, Eighty Years and More, The Woman's Bible;* and other works.

Steele, Sir Richard (1672-1729), British essayist and playwright. Born in Dublin, he was a captain in the army when he began writing. At first he wrote poems and pieces for the stage, but his real success came when, in 1709, he began the publication of the *Tatler*, which made a great hit, Addison contributing many papers. Two years later he and Addison were associated in *The Spectator*. Steele's prose is rippling and spontaneous; it is best illustrated in the *Sir Roger de Coverley Papers.*

Stefansson, Vilhjalmur (b. 1879), Canadian explorer, born at Arnes, Manitoba. He was a member of expeditions to Iceland in 1904 and 1905, and in 1906-07 to the Mackenzie delta, where he studied the Eskimos. In 1909-17 he made three expeditions into the Arctic regions. In the Coronation Gulf region he discovered and lived for a year with a race of "blond" Eskimos, who had never before seen a white man. Their European-like characteristics led Stefansson to connect these people with an early colony which disappeared from Greenland between 1412 and 1585. After 1918 Stefansson gave his time to lecturing and writing. His books include *The Friendly Arctic* (1921), *The Adventure of Wrangell Island* (1925), and *The Standardization of Error* (1927).

Steffens, (Joseph) Lincoln (1866-1936), American editor, lecturer and author. He was managing editor of *McClure's Magazine*, 1902-06; and associate editor of the *American Magazine* and *Everybody's* (1906-11). He wrote sensational articles which exposed municipal graft and corruption in a number of the largest cities. His books include *The Shame of the Cities* (1904), *The Struggle for Self-Government* (1906), and his *Autobiography* (1931).

Stein, Gertrude (1874-1946), American writer. She was graduated from Radcliffe in 1897, and after 1903 lived chiefly in Paris. Her novel, *The Making of Americans* (1926), caused a controversy in the literary world over the quality of her work. The endless repetition of words impressed many as the manifestation of genius, while others considered her style a stupid striving for effect. Among her works are *Autobiography of Alice B. Toklas* (1933), *Four Saints in Three Acts* (1934), and *Lectures in America* (1935).

Stein, Heinrich Friedrich Karl, Baron von (1757-1831), Prussian statesman. In 1804 he became minister of finance and trade. In this capacity he laid the foundation of important social reforms; but, exciting the jealousy of Napoleon, he was exiled to Prague. In 1812 he went to St. Petersburg, where he rendered great services to the Russian government during the French invasion. Subsequently returning to his own country, he was largely responsible for the revival of Prussia after it had been removed from the yoke of Napoleon.

Steinach, Eugen (1861-1944), Austrian physiologist. His laboratory for the study of comparative physiology was the first of its kind in the German-speaking countries. His experiments with rats produced many extraordinary results. He later co-operated with Viennese surgeons in experiments on the rejuvenation of elderly men and animals through the transplantation of sex glands.

Steinmetz, Charles Proteus (1865-1923), American electrical engineer; born in Germany. At the age of 24 he came to the United States. From 1893 until his death he was a consulting engineer for the General Electric Company, serving also from 1902 to 1913 as professor of electrical engineering at Union University. He was intensely interested in socialism. Steinmetz made many important discoveries in electrical theory, among them the law of hysteresis which enabled accurate forecasting of losses of power due to magnetism. In 1921 he constructed a generator which produced artificial lighting. Among Steinmetz' books are *Radiation, Light, and Illumination* (1909), *America and the New Epoch* (1916), and *Theory and Calculation of Electric Circuits* (1917).

Stendhal (1783-1842), pen name of **Marie Henri Beyle**, a French writer. He was a follower of Napoleon, serving with him in the Prussian and Moscow campaigns. He settled in Milan after Napoleon's fall and devoted himself to Italian art and music. His novel, *Le Rouge et le noir*, published in 1831, met with little success, although it is now considered his masterpiece. His other major works were *Chartreuse de Parme*, and *La Vie D'Henri Brunard*. These novels were the forerunners of modern psychological and analytical fiction. Stendhal's works include lives of Haydn, Mozart, Napoleon, and Rossini.

Stephens, Alexander Hamilton (1812-1883), American statesman, vice-president of the Confederacy. He was a member of the Georgia legislature, 1836-42, and of Congress, 1843-59. He opposed the Mexican War, but upheld Southern interests on other questions. One of the ablest defenders of the constitutional rights of secession, he led the Southern opposition to the secession movement of 1860-61. When he was defeated, he accepted his state's decision, became a supporter of the Confederacy, and its vice-president. Throughout the Civil War he defended the rights of the states within the Confederacy, and opposed the exercise of arbitrary power by the Confederate government. After the war he was imprisoned for five months. He served in Congress, 1873-1882, being elected governor of Georgia in the latter year. Stephens' *Constitutional View of the Late War between the States* is an effective defense of state sovereignty and secession.

Stephens, James (1882-1950), Irish poet and novelist. His poems and stories are colorful, and filled with fanciful situations and characters. His first book was a satirical fantasy, *The Crock of Gold.* His other works include *The Rocky Road to Dublin*, a volume of poems; *In the Land of Youth*, and *Deirdre*, both derived from Gaelic legends; two volumes of short stories, *Here Are Ladies*, and *Etched in Moonlight;* and *Irish Fairy Tales.*

Stephenson, George (1781-1848), English engineer. He became interested in steam engines, and in 1814 invented one which could draw coal out of mines. In 1821 he became chief engineer for the Stockton and Darlington Railway, and induced its directors to adopt steam locomotion. Later he constructed the Liverpool-Manchester Railway, for which he built his famous locomotive, "The Rocket." Stephenson built other English railroads, and was consulted on the building of railroads in other countries.

Sterne, Laurence (1713-1768), British author; born in Ireland. He was educated at Cambridge, and entered the Anglican Church. He wrote *Tristram Shandy, Sermons of Mr. Yorick*, and *A Sentimental Journey*, among the most important early English novels.

Steuben, Frederick William, Baron von (1730-1794), American soldier; born in Prussia. He entered the Prussian army and served throughout the Seven Years' War, becoming in 1762 aid to Frederick the Great. In 1777 he was persuaded to come to America to assist the colonists. During the winter at Valley Forge, he re-organized and drilled Washington's army, and in May, 1778 was made inspector general. In 1780 he was placed in command of the district of Virginia, and in 1781 took part in the siege of Yorktown. He had spent his fortune in the service of the colonies, and after the war was pensioned by Congress, and settled in New York.

Stevens, Thaddeus (1792-1868) American statesman; born in Vermont. He practiced law in Pennsylvania, and in 1833 was elected to the legislature, where he successfully defended the state's common-school system against a bill to abolish it. He served in the House of Representatives, 1849-1853 and 1859-1868. He was a zealous abolitionist, opposed to the Fugitive Slave Law, and frequently defended runaway slaves in the courts. He helped found the Republican party, and became leader of its radical wing. In 1861 he became chairman of the Ways and Means Committee and was of great influence in the prosecution of the war. Stevens clashed with Lincoln over reconstruction policy, and, under Johnson, was responsible for the 14th Amendment and the placing of the South under military rule. He introduced the bill to impeach Johnson, and was chairman of the committee which prepared the charges against the President.

Stevenson, Adlai Ewing (b. 1900), American political leader, born in Los Angeles, Calif., and raised in Bloomington, Ill. Educated at Harvard and Princeton and graduated from Northwestern University's law school, he practiced law, then entered government service and served as a special assistant to the Secretary of the Navy and as a representative at the United Nations Conference in San Francisco. In 1948 he was elected governor of Illinois, and in 1952 and 1956 he was the Democratic presidential nominee, defeated in both elections by Dwight D. Eisenhower. In 1953 he visited Korea as part of a world-wide tour.

Stevenson, Robert Louis (1850-1894), British author. Plagued by poor health, he settled in Samoa in 1888. His best-known works are adventure stories such as *Treasure Island*, *The Master of Ballantrae*, and *Kidnapped*.

Stimson, Henry Lewis (1867-1950), American statesman. From 1911 to 1913 he was Secretary of War, and in 1927 was Governor-General of the Philippines. He served as Secretary of State under Hoover from 1929 to 1933. In 1940 he was appointed Secretary of War by President Roosevelt, resigning in 1945.

Stockton, Francis Richard (1834-1902), American author. He attained reputation as a writer of entertaining short stories, marked by quaintness of subject and dry humor. Of these were the *Rudder Grange stories*, *The Lady or the Tiger*, and *The Casting Away of Mrs. Lecks*.

Stone, Harlan Fiske (1872-1946), American jurist educated at Amherst and Columbia. He was dean of Columbia Law School from 1910 until 1924, when President Coolidge named him Attorney General of the United States. He was appointed to the U. S. Supreme Court in 1925 and served until his death.

Stone, Lucy (Blackwell) (1818-1893), an American reformer; born in West Brookfield, Mass. She was graduated from Oberlin College in 1847. In 1869 she helped organize the American Woman Suffrage Association, and in 1870 founded the *Woman's Journal*.

Story, Joseph (1779-1845), American jurist. From 1811 until his death he was an associate justice of the United States Supreme Court. He was important in defining the power of the Supreme Court over state courts and legislation. His works include *Commentaries on the Constitution of the United States*, *Commentaries on the Conflict of Laws*, and *Miscellaneous Writings*.

Stowe, Harriet Elizabeth Beecher (1811-96), American novelist. She was the author of *Uncle Tom's Cabin*. Written to expose the horrors of slavery, it did much to advance the cause of abolition. Mrs. Stowe wrote several other works, notably a volume of New England sketches, *Old Town Folks*.

Strachey, (Giles) Lytton (1880-1932), English biographer; his best-known books are *Queen Victoria*, *Eminent Victorians*, *Elizabeth and Essex*, and *Books and Characters*.

Stradivari, Antonio (1644-1737), Italian maker of violins. The instruments made by him have never been surpassed.

Strauss, Johann (1804-49), an Austrian composer and conductor, famous for his dance music, of which he produced some 250 pieces, many of them of a very high level. His son, Johann (1825-99), was even more distinguished in the same line as the composer of the *Blue Danube* waltz and nearly 400 other waltzes; while a younger son, Eduard (1835-1916), became conductor of the court balls at Vienna in 1870, and was responsible for more than 200 compositions; another son, Joseph Strauss (1827-1870), was also a prolific composer of dance music.

Strauss, Richard Georg (1864-1950), German composer. He served as a choirmaster and assistant conductor of several orchestras, and was later court conductor in Munich and Berlin. He wrote seven tone poems for orchestra: *Don Juan*, *Tod und Verklärung*, *Till Eulenspiegel*, *Also sprach Zarathustra*, *Don Quixote*, *Macbeth*, and *Ein Heldenleben;* ten operas, including *Salome*, *Elektra* and *Der Rosenkavalier;* three symphonies, including the *Sinfonia Domestica;* a ballet; choral works; and a number of songs. A master of orchestration, Strauss also had a magnificent power in portraiture in music. His compositions are full of dazzling colors and novel harmonies.

Stravinsky, Igor Fedorovich (b. 1882), Russian composer. He studied under Rimsky-Korsakov and became noted for his compositions, *Petrouchka*, *Le Sacre du printemps*, and *L'Oiseau du feu*. The last named was given by Diaghilev's Ballet Russe in Europe and the United States. In 1936, and again in 1940, Stravinsky toured the United States, conducting orchestras in many of the large cities.

Stresemann, Gustav (1878-1929), German statesman and leader of the National Liberal party until after the 1918 revolution.

Stuart, Gilbert Charles (1755-1828), American painter. He went to London in 1775 to study and two years later joined Benjamin West. In addition to painting portraits of many important Americans of Revolutionary times, Stuart did portraits of George III and the Prince of Wales. Stuart was a decided admirer of George Washington, and his life-size painting of the first President is considered a masterpiece in technique as well as in faithfulness of expression.

Stuyvesant, Peter (1602-1682), Dutch colonial governor. He served in the West Indies, and was director of the Dutch colony of Curaçao. In 1647 he was made director-general of the New Netherlands. In 1664, during the war between England and Holland, an English fleet appeared in the bay and compelled the surrender of New Amsterdam, after which its name was changed to New York.

Sudermann, Hermann (1857-1928), German dramatic poet and disciple of Ibsen.

Sue, Marie Joseph Eugène (1804-1857), French novelist. On his father's death in 1829, he inherited an immense fortune and having abandoned medicine, he devoted himself to literature. His first work was a sea novel entitled *Kernock the Pirate*, which was quickly followed by *Plick* *and Plock.* His most famous works are *The Mysteries of Paris* and *The Wandering Jew.*

Sullivan, Sir Arthur Seymour (1842-1900), British composer. He won the Mendelssohn Scholarship at the Royal Academy of Music in 1856, and after that studied at Leipzig. In 1862 his music to Shakespeare's *Tempest* was first performed. A musical version of *Box and Cox,* and *Trial by Jury,* with the libretto written by W. S. Gilbert, indicated a ready road to popularity, and from 1877, when *The Sorcerer* was produced, the Gilbert-Sullivan operas became the most profitable stage productions of the time. They comprised *H. M. S. Pinafore, Pirates of Penzance, Patience, Princess Ida, The Mikado, Ruddigore, The Yeomen of the Guard, The Gondoliers,* etc.

Sullivan, Louis Henry (1856-1924), American architect. At the age of 16 he was a student in the Massachusetts Institute of Technology and at 17 was a draftsman with a concern building houses in large quantities after the Chicago fire. For some time he studied at L'École des Beaux Arts in Paris but returned to Chicago where he formed a partnership with Denkmar Adler. One of their first buildings was the Auditorium in Chicago, the largest building ever to be set on a floating foundation. He departed radically from old romantic ideas and built skyscrapers in the modern style. His famous pupil and friend was Frank Lloyd Wright. Sullivan wrote one book, *The Autobiography of an Idea.*

Sully, Maximilien de Béthune, Duc de (1560-1641), French Protestant statesman, a friend and companion of Henry of Navarre. His *Memoirs* are an important source for knowledge of his period.

Sumner, Charles (1811-1874), American lawyer and statesman. In 1851 he was elected to the Senate of the United States and distinguished himself by his strong antipathy to slavery. At first, Sumner was a supporter of Lincoln, and in 1861 he became chairman of the Senate Committee on Foreign Relations. He was hostile to the policy of President Johnson and opposed the home and foreign policy of President Grant.

Sun Yat-sen (1867-1925), the founder and first president (1912) of the Chinese Republic, from which position he resigned almost immediately in favor of Yuan Shih-Kai. He founded in 1905 the China Revolutionary League in Europe and Japan, and played a large part in the revolution of 1911, being elected president of the southern provinces by the Nanking Convention in the following year.

Sutro, Alfred (1863-1933), author and dramatist. His most successful plays were *The Walls of Jericho* (1904), and *John Glayde's Honor* (1907). He published English translations of the works of Maeterlinck.

Swedenborg, Emanuel (1689-1772), Swedish philosopher, scientist, mystic. In later life he announced that divine authority had been given him to explain natural and spiritual evidences. He published in quick succession *Arcana Coelestia, The Apocalypse Revealed, Four Preliminary Doctrines,* and *The True Christian Religion.*

Swift, Jonathan (1667-1745), British satirist, was born at Dublin, educated at Trinity College at the expense of an uncle, and became secretary to Sir William Temple. Entering the Church, he was made Dean of St. Patrick's in 1713. Getting entangled in political controversy, and changing his views from the Whig to the Tory side, he lost favor with the popular party, but consoled himself by turning to creative writing. *Gulliver's Travels, The Tale of a Tub,* and *The Battle of the Books* are among his best-known works.

Swinburne, Algernon Charles (1837-1909), English poet, educated at Oxford, who in the early sixties of the last century gave to the world a number of poems of singular poetic beauty and musical charm. Swinburne's most famous productions include *Atalanta in Calydon, Songs Before Sunrise, Bothwell* and *Mary Stuart.* Perhaps the best of his prose writings is his essay on William Blake.

Symonds, John Addington (1840-93), English poet and critic, author of *The Renaissance Period in Italy.*

Szigeti, Joseph (b. 1892), famous Hungarian violinist, who made his debut in 1905, toured through Europe and settled for some years in England.

T

Tacitus, Publius Cornelius (c. 55-120), one of the ablest of Roman historians. Among his works are a life of *Agricola* and his *Annales,* which have formed the groundwork of much that has since been written on the early history of the Roman Empire.

Tacitus, Marcus Claudius (205-276), the Roman emperor who succeeded Aurelian in A. D. 275. His short reign was marked by moderation.

Taft, Lorado (1860-1936), American sculptor. As an instructor in the Art Institute of Chicago, he greatly influenced the style of sculpture in the Middle West. His principal works include the great statue of Black Hawk overlooking the Rock River near Oregon, Ill.; the "Fountain of the Great Lakes" and the "Fountain of Time," Chicago; "Columbus Memorial Fountain," Washington, D. C.; and a memorial to the "Pioneers of America" in the town of his birth, Elmwood, Ill.

Taft, Robert (1889-1953), American political leader. Son of President Taft, he was graduated from Harvard Law School in 1913, and began to practice law in Cincinnati. He served in both houses of the Ohio legislature, and in 1938 was elected United States Senator from Ohio, reelected in 1944 and 1950. He was an unsuccessful candidate for the Republican presidential nomination (1936, 1940, 1948, 1952).

Taft, William Howard (1857-1930), American statesman. Graduated from Yale in 1878, he served as judge of Ohio's Superior Court from 1887 to 1890. He was a Federal judge from 1892 to 1900, and governor of the Philippines, 1901-04. He was then made Secretary of War, and in 1908 was elected President, his candidacy having been supported by Theodore Roosevelt. He was an able President and continued many of Roosevelt's policies, but in 1911 Roosevelt decided to run again, and the split thus caused in the Republican party resulted in Taft's defeat by Wilson in 1912. For the next five years Taft was professor of law at Yale, and during 1918-19 served as chairman of the War Labor Conference Board. In 1921 he was appointed Chief Justice of the United States Supreme Court, and held that post until his retirement in 1930 because of ill health.

Tagore, Sir Rabindranath (1861-1941), Bengali poet; Nobel Prize for literature in 1913. Much of his later work is written in English.

Talleyrand-Périgord, Prince (1754-1838), French diplomat and prelate. After the Reign of Terror he became foreign minister under the Directory. He remained in that office, and greatly distinguished himself in it until 1807, when Napoleon deposed him.

Tamerlane, or Timur the Tartar (1335-1405), descendant of a follower of Jenghiz Khan, and founder of the Mogul dynasty in India. He succeeded as chief of the Berlas Turks in 1361, and in turn conquered Turkestan, Persia, and Syria. He was a masterful warrior, and the scourge of the East in his day. He died in India, while preparing an invasion of China. His familiar name is a corruption of Timurlenk—"Timur the Lame."

Taney, Roger Brooke (1777-1864), American statesman, born in Calvert Co., Maryland. During the War of 1812 he led the wing of the Federalist party that upheld the policy of the government. In 1816 he was sent to the state senate. He became attorney-general of Maryland in 1827 and in December, 1831, Attorney-General of the United States. He was appointed Secretary of the Treasury under President Jackson on Sept. 24, 1833, but was forced to resign the next year. However, he was nominated Chief Justice of the United States Supreme Court and was confirmed by the United States Senate on March 15, 1836. He held this office until his death, and rendered decisions on many important cases, notably those of Dred Scott and Sherman M. Booth, both bearing on the Fugitive Slave Law.

Tarbell, Ida Minerva (1857-1944), American writer. She was graduated from Allegheny College and studied in Paris, 1891-1894. From 1894 to 1906 she was associate editor of *McClure's Magazine*. Her works include *Life of Napoleon Bonaparte, Life of Madame Roland, Life of Abraham Lincoln, History of the Standard Oil Co.*, and *Life of Judge Gary*.

Tarkington, (Newton) Booth (1869-1946), leading American novelist, author of many books, of which the best known are *Monsieur Beaucaire, Penrod*, and *Seventeen*.

Tasman, Abel Janszoon (c. 1602-1659), famous Dutch navigator; in 1642 he discovered Tasmania and New Zealand.

Tasso, Torquato (1544-95), one of the great Italian poets of the 16th century.

Taylor, Deems (b. 1885), American composer and critic. He studied music with Oscar Coon (1908-11) and worked as a writer for several encyclopedias and newspapers. In 1921 he succeeded James Huneker as music critic of the *New York World*. His best-known musical compositions include a cantata, *The Chambered Nautilus*, an opera, with Edna St. Vincent Millay, *The King's Henchman*, an orchestral suite, *Through the Looking Glass* and another opera, *Peter Ibbetson*.

Taylor, Frederick Winslow (1856-1915), industrial engineer. He learned the machinists' trade and by 1881 was foreman at the Medvale Steel Co. During a labor crisis he became interested in wages and, after conducting many time-labor experiments, developed the Taylor system of scientific management. His best-known books include *The Adjustment of Wages and Efficiency, Shop Management*, and *Principles of Scientific Management*.

Taylor, Jeremy (1613-67), English religious writer of great influence. The most famous of his works was his *Holy Living and Holy Dying*.

Taylor, Zachary (1784-1850), 12th President of the United States, born in Orange Co., Va. The family removed to Kentucky in 1785. He served in the Black Hawk War of 1832, and in 1837 was given full command in Florida, where he defeated the Indians in the battle of Okeechobee, thereby ending the Indian War. In 1840 he was given command in the Southwest. In the Mexican War he won the battles of Palo Alto, Resaca de la Palma, and Buena Vista. In 1848 he was nominated by the Whig convention for the Presidency, and was elected. He was inaugurated on March 4, 1849, and died the following year.

Tell, William legendary Swiss patriot. The story of his having been compelled by Gessler to shoot an apple from the head of his boy, and his dramatic revenge, is a myth that had become a common Teutonic tradition before Tell's time. The hero of Uri played, however, a great part in the strenuous struggle for Swiss independence in the early 14th century.

Tempest, Dame Mary Susan (1866-1942), English actress who won many successes in light opera and comedy.

Teniers, David (the younger) (1610-94), Flemish painter born at Antwerp. He died at Brussels. His father, David Teniers the elder (1582-1649), was also one of the leading landscape painters of the time.

Tenniel, Sir John (1820-92), English cartoonist and caricaturist. Tenniel illustrated numerous books, including *Alice in Wonderland*.

Tennyson, Alfred, Lord (1820-92), English poet, one of the most famous literary men of his century. Born at Somersby in Lincolnshire, he evinced the poetic gift while quite young, and in 1827 joined his brother Charles in the publication of *Poems by Two Brothers*. In 1830 and 1832 he again appeared before the public, the two small volumes of those years being written entirely by himself. In 1847 he published *The Princess;* in 1850 *In Memoriam*, in which he enshrined his affection for the memory of his dead friend Arthur Hallam; and in 1855 *Maud* appeared. His other works included *The Idylls of the King, Enoch Arden, Queen Mary, Harold*, and *Becket*.

Terence, (Publius Terentius Afer) (c. 194-158 B. C.), a Roman poet and dramatist, who rose from the position of a slave to that of one of the most honored men in Rome.

Tertullian, Quintus (c. 150-c. 230), a Father, and writer, of the Latin Church. His chief work was his *Apologeticus*, a defense of Christianity.

Tesla, Nikola (1856-1943), electrician and inventor, born in Serbia; was for a time connected with the Telegraph Engineering Department of the Serbian government; later he was in Paris, engaged in electric-lighting experiments; and in 1882 he came to the United States and became associated with Edison for a time. He was an active promoter of electrical developments.

Tetzel, Johann (c. 1460-1519), German Dominican monk and Inquisitor, the scandal of whose sale of indulgences roused Luther to publish his memorable ninety-five theses at Wittenberg in 1517, an act which led to the Reformation.

Thackeray, William Makepeace (1811-63), British novelist, was one of the most popular writers of the nineteenth century. He studied art, and for a time worked as a newspaper artist. To *Fraser's Magazine* and to *Punch* he contributed a large number of burlesques, sketches, poems, etc., all full of spirit and fun; but it was not until later life that his greatest successes were won. *Vanity Fair*, which was issued in monthly parts between 1846 and 1848, proclaimed him a master in the realm of fiction. *Henry Esmond, The Newcomes, The Virginians, Philip*, and *Lovel the Widower* are his most important novels. He edited the *Cornhill Magazine* from the first number, January 1860, for a few years, contributing to it his *Roundabout Papers*. His *Yellowplush Papers* and *The Book of Snobs* were widely read and admired.

Thales of Miletus (c. 624-c. 548 B. C.), one of the seven wise men of ancient Greece. The earliest of the Ionian philosophers, he created a sensation by the precalculation and prediction of an eclipse of the sun, which took place in 585 B. C.; he looked upon water as the basic element.

Themistocles (c. 526-c. 460 B. C.), was chief archon of Athens. When Xerxes assailed Greece he commanded the Athenian fleet.

Theocritus (285-247 B. C.), one of the great Greek poets. Thirty "Idylls" and a number of "Epigrams" are still extant.

Theodoric the Great (455-526), king of the East Goths, was born in Pannonia. In medieval German romance he is known as "Dietrich von Bern," and had a reputation for good government, akin to that ascribed in England to King Alfred. He was founder of the Gothic kingdom of Italy.

Theodosius the Great (346-395), was Roman Emperor of the East for nearly twenty years. He gained victories over the Goths, and the year before his death became sole emperor. Noted in ecclesiastical history for his conversion to Christianity, and for his submission to the penance imposed by St. Ambrose.

Theophrastus (c. 372-287 B. C.), succeeded Aristotle as president of the Lyceum at Athens. His *History of Plants* and his *Moral Characters* are the best known of his writings.

Thierry, Jacques Nicolas Augustin (1795-1856), distinguished French historian known by his *History of the Norman Conquest*.

Thiers, Louis Adolphe (1797-1877) French statesman and man of letters, author of a *History of the French Revolution*.

Thomas, George Henry (1816-1870), American general, born in Southampton Co., Va. He was graduated from the United States Military Academy in 1836; took part in the Florida War in 1840-1842; and the war with Mexico in 1846-1848; participated in the Seminole campaign in 1849-1850. At the outbreak of the Civil War he was made a colonel of cavalry and took part in the operations in the Shenandoah valley in the summer of 1861. Later, as commander of a corps of the Army of the Cumberland, he engaged in the battles of Murfreesboro and Chickamauga, and in 1863, as commander of the Army of the Cumberland, he bore an important part in the battle of Missionary Ridge and in the Atlanta campaign under Sherman. In October, 1864, he was sent to Nashville to oppose the Confederates under Hood, whom he finally defeated before Nashville, Dec. 15, 1864. For his services he was made major general.

Thompson, Francis (1859-1907), English poet. His *Poems* appeared in 1893, containing "The Hound of Heaven," the poem for which he is best remembered. Two other publications were *Sister Songs* (1895) and *New Poems* (1897). Other works include essays and Catholic biographies, and some additional verse was published posthumously.

Thoreau, Henry David (1817-62), American writer and nature-lover. He was the friend of, and for a time lived with, Emerson, but in 1845 adopted a life of solitude and pursued those studies of nature which afterward made him famous. His *Walden, or Life in the Woods*, is an American classic.

Thorndike, Edward Lee (1874-1949), an American educator and psychologist. In 1906-23 he served as professor of educational psychology, and from 1923 as professor of education, at Columbia University. In 1921 he was appointed director of the psychology division of the Institute of Educational Research. Among his best-known works are *Educational Psychology, The Original Nature of Man, The Measurement of Intelligence*, and *Adult Learning*.

Thucydides (471-401 B. C.), a distinguished Greek historian.

Tiberius, Claudius (42 B. C.-A. D. 27), the second Emperor of Rome.

Tilden, Samuel Jones (1814-1886), American statesman. In 1845 he was elected to the state assembly. Tilden became leader of the Democratic party in New York State in 1868, and in that capacity strenuously opposed the corrupt administration of the Tweed faction. In 1876 he was nominated for the Presidency by the National Democratic Convention. In the election Hayes received 4,033,295 popular votes and Tilden 4,284,265. In 1877, on the finding of the Electoral Commission, the Presidency was awarded to the Republican candidate by an electoral vote of 185 to 184.

Tintoretto (Jacopo Robusti) (1518-94), Venetian painter, famous for his religious pictures. His real name was Jacopo Robusti, and he received the cognomen of Tintoret, or Tintoretto, from his father's vocation, that of a dyer.

Tirpitz, Adm. Alfred Peter Friedrich von (1849-1930), commanded the German fleet, 1914-16; he organized the German torpedo and submarine service.

Titian, or Tiziano Vecelli (1477-1576), one of the greatest of painters. He studied under the Bellinis, and made his first attempts at painting in conjunction with Giorgione, whom he soon surpassed. In 1511 he was at Padua, where he painted some notable frescoes; in 1512 he returned to Venice. From this time forward he was in great demand, and exercised his powers almost to the end of his life. He died of the plague at the age of ninety-nine.

Titus (A. D. 41-81), Roman emperor, and son of Vespasian, fought in the Jewish war which terminated in the capture and destruction of Jerusalem; he was deemed a profligate and a tyrant, but no sooner was he in power than he exerted himself to the utmost to please the people.

Tocqueville, Alexis Charles Henri Maurice Clérel, Count de (1805-59), French statesman and writer, author of the celebrated book *Democracy in America*.

Todd, David (1855-1939), noted American astronomer. In 1878, he became chief editor of the *U. S. Nautical Almanac*, and in 1882 he was placed in charge of the observations of the transit of Venus at Lick Observatory. He is noted for the thousands of photographs he took of the planet Mars and of the sun's corona.

Tolstoy, Count Leo Nikolayevich (1828-1910), Russian novelist, one of the most distinguished personalities in modern Russian literature.

Born of a noble family, he was for a time in the army, but was so greatly moved by the trials and sufferings of the people that he was impelled "to take up his pen and write." At twenty-four he published *Childhood*, and in 1854, while in camp in the Crimea, wrote his *Tales from Sebastopol*. He was a persistent advocate of progressive ideas, and before the Emancipation Act for freeing all Russian serfs was enforced he had given the serfs on his own estate their freedom. In 1862 he married and settled down to a quiet country life, shortly afterwards publishing his *War and Peace* and *Anna Karenina*. In later years Tolstoy developed a sort of religious mysticism. Among his later works are *The Power of Darkness*, *The Kreutzer Sonata*, *The Cossacks*, *Resurrection*, and *The End of the Age*.

Toombs, Robert (1810-1885), American statesman. A Whig member of Congress from Georgia 1845-1853; and a United States Senator 1853-1861, he was expelled from the Senate in 1861, and in the same year was elected to the Confederate Congress.

Torquemada, Tomás de (1420-98), the chief officer of the Spanish Inquisition.

Torricelli, Evangelista (1608-47), Galileo's pupil. He invented the barometer and improved both the microscope and the telescope.

Toscanini, Arturo (1867-1957), Italian conductor. After 1886, he conducted orchestras in the largest cities of Europe and North and South America. He conducted at New York City's Metropolitan Opera House from 1908 to 1915. In 1934-36 he was conductor at the Salzburg Festival. In 1937-38 he conducted radio concerts in the United States and organized the first symphony orchestra for radio.

Toulouse-Lautrec, Henri (Count Henri Marie Raymond de Toulouse-Lautrec Monfa) (1864-1901), French artist noted for his poster art. He was deformed by an accident and, rejected by society, he lived and worked in Paris' Bohemian society.

Toussaint L'Ouverture, François Dominique (1743-1803), Haitian patriot. Born a slave, he joined the Negro insurgents (1791) and became a French general. He expelled the British and Spanish and began an independence movement. Captured by a French naval force, he was imprisoned in France, where he died.

Toynbee, Arnold Joseph (b. 1889), English historian. He wrote a series of yearbooks, *A Survey of International Affairs* (1920-38), and books on Near Eastern history and civilization. His ambitious work, *A Study of History*, in which he investigated the development and decline of civilizations in broad cultural terms, brought him his greatest fame.

Trajan (c. 52-117), Roman emperor from 98 to his death. His rule was enlightened, and he was esteemed by the people.

Travis, William Barrett (1811-1836), American military officer. He was commanding the small garrison at the Alamo when the fort was taken after a heroic defense against overwhelming odds. Travis, one of six survivors, was shot by order of the Mexican General Santa Anna.

Trevelyan, George Macaulay (b. 1876), Regius Professor of Modern History at Cambridge University since 1927. An eminent historian, author of many works, including *A History of England*.

Trollope, Anthony (1815-82), British novelist. Author of *Barchester Towers*, *The Small House at Allington*. *The Last Chronicle of Barset*, etc.

Trotsky, Leon, name assumed by **Lev Davidovich Bronstein** (1877-1940), a leader of the 1917 Russian Revolution. War minister of the Bolshevik government, and its leading representative at the Brest-Litovsk conferences of 1917-18. Dismissed from office, 1925, he went eventually to Mexico, where he was assassinated. Author of a *History of the Russian Revolution*.

Truman, Harry S. (b. 1884), the 33rd President of the United States. He was born in Lamar, Mo., and worked his way through school. He served in World War I as a captain, and on returning entered politics in Missouri. He was elected a judge in Jackson County in 1922, and served in that position until 1934, when he was elected to the United States Senate, where he was a strong supporter of New Deal policies and as head of the Truman Committee investigated war contracts. At the Democratic Convention in 1944 he was nominated for vice-president, and took that office when Franklin Roosevelt was elected to his fourth term. Truman became President on April 12, 1945, after the death of President Roosevelt. He continued to support New Deal policies, and he initiated the Marshall Plan for aid to European nations, and the Point Four program to underdeveloped areas. He strongly supported the United Nations, and in 1950 led them in entering the Korean conflict. He succeeded himself as President, and in 1952 declined renomination.

Trumbull, John (1750-1831), American jurist and Revolutionary satirist. One of the Hartford Wits, he was a graduate of Yale, served as judge of the superior court, and then of the supreme court of errors of Connecticut. His principal work was *McFingal*, a satirical burlesque directed against the Tories.

Trumbull, John (1756-1843), American artist, grandson of the first Jonathan Trumbull. He was graduated from Harvard College in 1773 and studied painting in Boston. After having served in the Revolutionary War on the staffs of Generals Washington and Gates he went to England to become a pupil of Benjamin West. In 1786 he produced his first historical picture, the "Battle of Bunker Hill," which was soon followed by the "Death of Montgomery before Quebec." In 1817 he was employed by Congress to paint four pictures for the rotunda of the Capitol at Washington: "The Declaration of Independence," the "Surrender of Burgoyne," the "Surrender of Cornwallis," and the "Resignation of Washington at Annapolis."

Trumbull, Lyman (1813-1896), an American statesman. He became secretary of state for Illinois in 1841, and justice of the supreme court of the state in 1848. In 1854 he was elected to Congress as a Democrat, and in 1855 was chosen United States Senator. He joined the Republican party on the anti-slavery question in 1860 and supported Abraham Lincoln, whose friend he became. He was re-elected to the Senate and secured the passage of the Fourteenth Amendment.

Truxtun, Thomas (1755-1822), an American naval officer. In 1798, when the United States Navy was organized, he was selected as one of its six captains, and placed in command of the *Constellation*.

Tschaikovsky, Peter Ilyich (1840-93), Russian composer of orchestral music, one of the greatest musicians of the nineteenth century.

Tull, Jethro (1674-1741), English agriculturist, the inventor of the first practical seed-sowing machine.

Turner, Joseph Mallord William (1775-1851), English painter, who entered the Royal Academy in 1789. Of his larger pictures may be mentioned "The Sun Rising through Vapor," "Crossing the Brook," "Dido Building Carthage," "The Fighting Temeraire," and "Calais Pier." Ruskin, through his book on *Modern Painters*, brought about a fuller appreciation of Turner's genius.

Tussaud, Madame Marie (1760-1850), a Swiss woman who, after practicing the art of modeling wax in Paris at the time of the French Revolution, made her escape to England and set up a small exhibition of wax figures in the Strand, later carried on by her son, grandson and great-grandson.

Tut-ankh-amen (c. 1358 B. C.), an Egyptian Pharoah of the 18th dynasty whose tomb was discovered by Howard Carter in 1922, with the mummy intact. The magnificence of the coffins and ornaments together with large quantities of furniture, etc. caused world-wide interest.

Twain, Mark. *See* CLEMENS, SAMUEL L.

Tweedsmuir, John Buchan, Baron (1875-1940), British author, politician, and war correspondent. Governor general of Canada, 1937-1940.

Tyler, John (1790-1862), 10th President of the United States, born in Charles City, Va. In 1825 he was elected governor of Viginia and in 1827 Senator of the United States. He upheld the states' rights policy in Congress, voted against the so-called force bill empowering President Jackson to enforce the revenue laws in South Carolina, and for the resolutions censuring Jackson for removing government funds to state banks. In 1839 he was elected to the Virginia legislature and in 1840 was elected Vice-President on the Whig ticket with William H. Harrison. On April 4, just one month after entering upon the duties of this office, President Harrison died, and Tyler became President by succession. The most important acts of his administration were a treaty with China, and the annexation of Texas in 1845. In 1861 he joined the Confederacy and served in the Confederate congress till his death in Richmond, Va.

Tyler, Wat (d. 1381), British insurgent, the leader of the Peasants' Revolt, during the reign of Richard II, against the poll tax.

Tyndale, William (c. 1492-1536), English religious leader, educated at Oxford. He completed the translation of the New Testament at Wittenberg, where he was associated with Luther. This version was first published at Antwerp, and then found its way to England where it was publicly burned. Tyndale afterwards was associated with Miles Coverdale in a translation of the Old Testament but only completed the Pentateuch and the Book of Jonah. In 1535 he was arrested at Antwerp for heresy and put to death by strangling and burning.

U

Ulfilas, or Wulfila (311-383) Gothic bishop and translator of the Bible. He was sent to Constantinople, possibly as a hostage, and there adopted Christianity. Later he was appointed anagnost, and it was probably while holding this office, which in the Greek Church involves preaching as well as reading, that he translated the Scriptures into Gothic. Early in the year 341 he was consecrated bishop of the Goths, and immediately returned to his people across the Danube, for whose conversion to Christianity he was largely responsible.

Unamuno, Miguel de (1864-1936) Spanish author and scholar. After serving for a time as professor of Greek at the University of Salamanca he became rector of that institution (1901). Exiled for his hostility to the Rivera dictatorship, Unamuno returned to Spain when it collapsed. He led the successful movement to overthrow the monarchy and to establish the Spanish republic (1931). Unamuno was one of the greatest Spanish authors of the early years of the 20th century. His most famous work is *The Life of Don Quixote and Sancho Panza* (1905); he died mysteriously during the Spanish Civil War.

Undset, Sigrid (1882-1949), Norwegian novelist. She first became well known by the publication of *Jenny* in 1912. Her prominence as a writer became international when she published *Kristin Lavransdatter* in 1920-22, a historical novel of Norway in the Middle Ages, written as a trilogy. The Nobel Prize was awarded her in 1928. Another novel of historical importance is *The Master of Hestviken* (1928-29).

Untermeyer, Louis (b. 1885), American poet and anthologist. In 1923 he joined the editorial staff of *The Masses* and conducted a column in the *Chicago Evening Post* entitled "And Other Poems." He edited *Modern British Poetry, Modern American Poetry*, and *A Miscellany of American Poetry*. Among his works are *The Younger Quire*, a volume of burlesque; *First Love*, a sequence of lyrics; *Challenge; These Times;* and *Poems of Heinrich Heine*.

Updike, Daniel Berkeley (1860-1942), printer and publisher. His literary works, lectures, and creative work as a printer have greatly influenced the development of typographical art. Among his works are *Printing Types—Their History, Forms and Use* (1922), and *In the Day's Work* (1924).

Upton, Emory (1839-1881), American military officer. He participated in the Battle of Bull Run and in the Peninsular Campaign early in 1862. He originated a system of military tactics which was adopted by the government in 1867. His publications include *A New System of Infantry Tactics* (1867); *The Armies of Asia and Europe* (1878); and *The Military Policy of the United States.*

V

Valens, Flavius (328-378), Roman emperor of the East. The chief event of his reign was the war with the Goths, who received permission to settle on Roman territory. Being dissatisfied, the Goths took up arms, and in 378 killed Valens, and routed his army at Adrianople.

Valentino, Rudolph (1895-1926), Italo-American film actor; made his screen debut as Julio in *The Four Horsemen of the Apocalypse* in 1922. His romantic appeal made him the most admired screen personality of his day.

Vanbrugh, Sir John (1664-1726), prominent English architect as well as a successful dramatist: he designed Castle Blenheim; *The Relapse* was one of his most successful plays.

Van Buren, Martin (1782-1862), 8th President of the United States, born in Kinderhook, N. Y. In 1821 he entered the United States Senate, of which he was a member till his election in 1828 to the governorship of New York. In the same year he zealously supported Jackson for the Presidency, and in 1829 was rewarded by being made Secretary of State. He was elected Vice-President, and in 1836, President. Van Buren's four years of office were darkened by the gloom of financial panic, and he was defeated for President in 1840.

Vancouver, George (1758-1798), British navigator who served under Captain Cook, and later explored the Gulf of Georgia and the Straits of San Juan de Fuca in the American Northwest, and the shores of Vancouver Island.

Vanderbilt, Cornelius (1794-1877), American merchant and speculator, who accumulated a fortune of about 100 million dollars from his railroad and shipping operations. His son, William Henry Vanderbilt (1821-1885), carried on his father's business, and promoted many philanthropies.

Van Doren, Carl Clinton (1885-1950), American critic, editor. He taught English at Columbia University; was literary editor of the *Nation* (1919-1922), and of *Century Magazine* (1922-1925). Among his books are *Contemporary American Novelists, American Literature*, and *Other Provinces* and *Ninth Wave* (both fiction).

Van Doren, Mark (b. 1894), American poet and critic, brother of Carl Van Doren; author of critical studies of Dryden, Thoreau, and E. A. Robinson; and of the volumes of poems, *Spring, Thunder, Now the Sky*, and *Jonathan Gentry.*

Van Dyck, Anthony (1599-1641), Flemish artist. He was born at Antwerp, and after studying under Rubens went to Italy where he made a name as a portrait painter. In 1629 he went to England where he became court painter for King Charles I.

Van Dyke, Henry Jackson (1852-1933), American author; he was also a Presbyterian minister, and later was a teacher of English literature at Princeton University. He was appointed U. S. minister to Holland and Luxembourg in 1913. He wrote *The Reality of Religion, The Poetry of Tennyson, The Friendly Year, The Ruling Passion*, and many other books of essays, poetry, and short stories.

Van Loon, Hendrik Willem (1882-1944), Dutch-American historian, born in Rotterdam; came to the United States in 1903. In 1922 he published *The Story of Mankind*, a picture history-book originally intended for children. He also wrote on geographical, historical, and biographical subjects.

Van Rensselaer, Stephen 1764-1839), American military officer who founded Rensselaer Polytechnic Institute at Troy, N.Y. He was a member of the U.S. Congress, 1823-29.

Van Vechten, Carl (b. 1880), American author whose fame rests on his sophisticated novels, including *Peter Wiffle, Spider Boy*, and *Nigger Heaven.*

Vauban, Marshal Sébastien le Prestre de (1633-1707), renowned French military engineer, who introduced great improvements in methods of fortification, conducted fifty-three sieges, and took part in 140 battles.

Vedder, Elihu (1836-1923), American painter and illustrator. He studied at Paris and in Italy, where he ultimately made his residence. His pictures are mostly romantic and include "Death of Abel," "Cumean Sibyl," and "Nausicaa and Her Companions."

Velásquez, Diego (1465-1523), Spanish soldier and companion of Columbus, sent to conquer Cuba. Velásquez founded Santiago and Havana.

Velázquez, Diego Rodríguez de Silva y (1599-1660), the foremost of Spanish painters, and one of the greatest names in the history of art. He spent many years in Madrid at the court of Philip IV, with whom he was personally intimate. His paintings of the Spanish nobility and the royal family are numerous, and like all his paintings show a technique rarely equaled, and a fine insight into the character of his sitters. Among his best-known paintings are "The Topers," "The Forge of Vulcan," "Philip IV as a Youth," and "Pope Innocent X."

Venizelos, Eleutherios (1864-1936), Greek statesman, active in the liberation of Greece from Turkish control.

Verdi, Giuseppe (1813-1901), the most popular composer of Italian opera of the 19th century. His works include *Ernani, Rigoletto, Il Trovatore, La Traviata, Aida, Otello* and *Falstaff.*

Vergil (Publius Vergilius Maro) (70-19 B.C.), Roman epic poet, born near Mantua. He moved to Rome at thirty, where he became known to Octavian and Maecenas and wrote his *Eclogues* and *Georgics*. His most famous work, the *Aeneid*, comprised twelve books, dealing with the story of the wanderings of Aeneas after the destruction of Troy.

Vermeer, Jan, also known as **Vermeer of Delft** and **Jan van der Meer** (1632-75), a Dutch painter noted for his invention of his own method of applying paints which produced remarkable color effects. He received little recognition in his own time, but today is considered one of the great Dutch masters. His paintings include "View of Delft," "Milkmaid," and "Soldier and Laughing Girl."

Verne, Jules (1828-1905), French author; one of the most popular authors of stories of science and adventure. The best-known of his numerous works are *Twenty Thousand Leagues Under the Sea, The Mysterious Island, Around the World in Eighty Days*, and *Michael Strogoff.*

Vernier, Pierre (1580-1637), French scientist, who invented the mechanism of the *vernier* auxiliary scale, enabling lines and angles to be measured to a minute degree.

Veronese, Paul, or Paolo Cagliari (1528-88), Italian painter of religious subjects. His "Marriage Feast at Cana in Galilee," "The Feast in the House of Simon," and "The Presentation of the Family of Darius to Alexander," are paintings of world-wide celebrity.

Verrocchio, Andrea del (1435-1488), Italian sculptor and painter. First a goldsmith, he became a sculptor in marble and bronze. Only one extant picture can be attributed to him with certainty: "Baptism of Christ" in the Florentine Academy. Of his bronze statues, the "David" and the "Unbelieving Thomas" in Florence and the great equestrian statue of Bartolommeo Colleoni at Venice are among the most notable.

Vespasian (Titus Flavius Vespasianus) (9-79), was Roman emperor during the last nine years of his life. At one time he commanded the Roman army of occupation in Britain.

Vespucci, Amerigo (1451-1512), Italian navigator. In 1499 he reached America and explored the coast line for some hundreds of leagues, returning to Spain the same year. It was for him that the newly discovered continents were named.

Victor Emmanuel III (1869-1947), king of Italy, 1900-47, succeeded to the throne on the death of his father, Humbert I. The defeat of Fascist Italy in World War II discredited his reign and he abdicated in 1946 in an effort to save the monarchy for his son. Instead, the Italians voted to abolish the monarchy and set up a republic.

Victoria (1819-1901), queen of Great Britain and Ireland and empress of India. She was a daughter of the Duke of Kent, and came to the throne in 1837 on the death of her uncle, William IV. In 1840 she married Prince Albert of Saxe-Coburg-Gotha, who died in 1861. Victoria's reign was notable for the expansion of the British Empire in Asia and Africa, and the transformation of Great Britain into a democracy.

Villard, Oswald Garrison (1872-1950), American newspaper owner and writer, born in Wiesbaden, Germany. He was the son of Henry Villard and the grandson of William Lloyd Garrison. In 1897 he joined the *New York Evening Post*, which had been purchased and combined with the *Nation* by his father. He was managing owner and leading editorial writer of this newspaper until 1918, when he sold it, keeping the *Nation*, which he established as an outstanding liberal weekly. He retired from active newspaper management in 1935.

Vinson, Frederick Moore (1890-1953), chief justice of the U. S. Supreme Court, appointed in 1946. He had previously held several other judicial and administrative posts, was a member of Congress from Kentucky (1923-29, 1931-38), and secretary of the treasury (1945-46).

Volta, Alessandro, Count (1745-1827), professor of natural philosophy both at Como and at Pavia University. In the course of his studies on electricity he discovered the voltaic pile, giving his name thereto, and also to the electrical unit, the volt.

Voltaire, François Marie Arouet de (1694-1778), French philosopher and writer. Because his first essays offended the authorities, he fled to London where he lived for two years (1726-28), and there wrote some of his dramas. Returning to France, he published his *Philosophical Letters*, which aroused the enmity of the priesthood. The Marquise du Chatelet offered him the asylum of her castle of Cirey, and for the next fifteen years he made this his home, writing there his *Discourses on Man, Essay on the Morals and Spirit of Nations, Age of Louis XIV*, etc. From 1750-53 he lived in Berlin, on the invitation of Frederick the Great.

Voronoff, Dr. Serge (1867-1951), Russian physiologist and a leading authority on gland-grafting, his name being prominently associated with attempts to improve various physical conditions, including senility, by transplantation of animal glands.

W

Wade, Benjamin Franklin (1800-78), American statesman, anti-slavery leader and acting Vice-President under President Johnson.

Wadsworth, James Samuel (1807-1864), American military officer; born in Genesee, N. Y. He enlisted as a volunteer in the Union army early in 1861, and was appointed a brigadier general in August. He was engaged in the battles of Fredericksburg, Chancellorsville, Gettysburg, and the Wilderness as the commander of a division, and was killed in the last-named battle.

Wagner, Wilhelm Richard (1813-83), German composer born at Leipzig. He revolutionized operatic methods, and doing away with set ballads and choruses, endeavored to give the same unity of action to an opera as would be realized in a play without music. This continuity of musical thought and action was a long time in forcing itself into acceptance, but today is acknowledged as the only adequate interpretation of dramatic musical expression. Wagner's greatest work is his tetralogy, *The Nibelungen Ring*, which includes the operas *Das Rheingold, Siegfried, Die Walküre*, and *Die Götterdämmerung*. Three other operas also display Wagner's musical genius to a high degree: *Tristan und Isolde, Die Meistersinger*, and *Parsifal*. His earlier operas, among them *Rienzi, The Flying Dutchman, Tannhäuser*, and *Lohengrin*, are less significant musically.

Walker, William (1824-1860), American filibuster. In 1850 he went to California, where he practiced law and edited various newspapers. His filibustering attempt against Sonora and Lower California in 1853 failed. Two years later, with 58 followers, he went to Nicaragua, became commander-in-chief of the Liberal army, and defeated the Conservative forces and an invading Costa Rican army. Aided by increasing numbers of Americans, Walker became president and virtual dictator, re-establishing slavery, and parceling out land among his followers. An alliance of the Central American states, backed by Cornelius Vanderbilt, whose Transit Company Walker had seized, defeated Walker, who was saved from surrender by the U. S. Navy and taken back to the United States. In 1860 he was captured in a filibustering attempt in Honduras, and was executed.

Wallace, Alfred Russel (1823-1913), English naturalist. In 1853 he attracted notice by his book, *Travels on the Amazon*. In 1858, the idea of evolution occurred to him, and he drafted his first notes upon it and sent them to Darwin in England while the latter was on the eve of publishing his own exposition of the theory. The result was the reading of a joint paper on the subject to the Linnean Society. The coincidence was fully acknowledged by Darwin. There were differences, however, between the points of view of the two scientists. Wallace's *Darwinism* fully expressed his own views on the subject.

Wallace, Henry Agard (b. 1888), Vice President of the United States, born in Iowa, the son of Henry C. Wallace, Secretary of Agriculture 1921-24. President F. D. Roosevelt appointed him secretary of agriculture (1933), and he was the principal architect of the Roosevelt farm program. In 1940 he was elected Vice President, and in 1945 Truman named him secretary of commerce. He resigned in 1946 after a foreign policy dispute and formed the Progressive party, which made him its Presidential candidate in 1948. Wallace failed to carry any state. He broke with the party in 1950 when the party opposed the Korea campaign.

Wallace, Major General Lewis ("Lew") (1827-1905), American novelist. During the Civil

War, he served as a division commander in the Union Army. His historical romance, *Ben Hur: A Tale of the Christ*, made him famous.

Wallenstein, Albrecht Wenzel Eusebius von (1583-1634), German statesman and general. He led the Imperial army in the Thirty Years' War.

Walpole, Horace (1717-97), an English author and antiquarian; the younger son of Sir Robert Walpole. He filled a number of government positions, and was a member of the House of Commons. He retired in 1768 to his favorite house at Strawberry Hill, and devoted himself to the writing of books and the accumulation of works of art. He is best known for his Gothic romance, *The Castle of Otranto*, and for his letters and memoirs.

Walpole, Hugh (1884-1941), novelist, whose novels include *Fortitude, The Dark Forest*, and *Mr. Traill.*

Walpole, Sir Robert (1676-1745), a British statesman of the Whig party, who showed enlightened views on financial policy. He was prime minister for twenty-two years; he relieved from duty more than 100 export and 40 import articles, a policy which greatly extended the scope of British commerce.

Walton, Izaak (1593-1683), an English author, known as the "Father of Angling." At the age of fifty he retired from commerce in favor of writing and angling. Besides biographies of Donne, Wotton, Hooker, and Herbert he wrote *The Compleat Angler, or the Contemplative Man's Recreation.*

Ward, Artemus. *See* BROWNE, CHARLES FARRAR.

Ward, Mrs. Humphry (1851-1920), an English novelist. Her first successful novel was *Robert Elsmere* (1888); subsequently she wrote *Marcella, Fenwick's Career*, and *Missing.*

Warner, Charles Dudley (1829-1900), an American author, who practiced law for a time, then began editorial work for *Harper's Monthly Magazine.* With Mark Twain he wrote *The Gilded Age* (1873). His other works include *Backlog Studies, Life of Washington Irving;* and he also edited the "American Men of Letters" series.

Warren, Earl (b. 1891), American politician and chief justice of the Supreme Court. Beginning his career as a crusading district attorney in central California (1925-39), Warren was elected attorney general and then governor of that state in 1942, 1946, and 1950, resigning in 1950 when he was appointed chief justice. He handed down the court's unanimous school desegregation decision in 1954.

Warton, Thomas (1728-90), an English poet and critic, author of *History of English Poetry.* He was poet laureate for the last five years of his life.

Warwick, Richard Neville, Earl of (c. 1428-71), called "The Kingmaker"; leader of the York party in the Wars of the Roses.

Washington, Booker Taliaferro (1859?-1915), American Negro educator, born a slave in Hale's Ford, Va. After a period combining schooling and mining labor, he graduated from the Hampton Institute in 1875, and became a teacher. In 1881 he was chosen principal of the Tuskegee Normal and Industrial Institute for Negroes, in Alabama. This school he organized and built up. Besides lectures on educational and racial subjects he wrote *Sowing and Reaping* (1900), *Up from Slavery* (1901), *Character Building* (1902), *The Story of the Negro* (1909), and *My Larger Education* (1911).

Washington, George (1732-1799), the commander-in-chief of the American forces during the Revolutionary War, and the first President of the United States. He was born at Bridges Creek, Virginia, on February 22, 1732. In his youth he practiced surveying, and then entered military service as one of the leaders of the British forces during the French and Indian Wars. Returning to civilian life, he married Mrs. Martha Custis, a widow of wealth, in 1759, and settled down to the management of his estate at Mount Vernon in Virginia. Though a member of the Virginia House of Burgesses, he was not very active in politics before 1770, when he joined with other colonial leaders in opposition to the British policies toward the American colonies. In 1774 he became a delegate to the first Continental Congress. The following year he was chosen commander-in-chief of the American army. While his generalship was not always brilliant, his courage and good sense enabled the Americans to prosecute the war through every discouragement, until the surrender of Cornwallis at Yorktown and the evacuation of New York brought the conflict to an end in 1783. Washington then took leave of his command, and returned to Mount Vernon for the next four years. Believing the Articles of Confederation were insufficient to avert national disaster, he was one of the moving spirits in the formation of the Constitutional Convention of 1787, over which he presided. With the formation of the Union, he was unanimously elected to be its first president. He was re-elected for a second term in 1792, and set a precedent by refusing a third. He labored during his administration to consolidate the position of the new republic, weakening the power of the separatist elements in the country, and balancing region against region and party against party. In 1797 he retired to Mount Vernon, where he resumed the management of his property during the last two and a half years of his life. He died Dec. 14, 1799.

Watson, John Broadus (b. 1878), American psychologist who formulated the theory known as Behaviorism, of which he became the leading exponent. According to this theory the only data of value in the study of human psychology are responses, glandular or muscular.

Watson, Sir William (1858-1935), an English poet. In 1880 his *Prince's Quest* was published, followed in 1884 by *Epigrams of Art, Life, and Nature.* These, however, attracted less attention than *Wordsworth's Grave* (1890).

Watt, James (1736-1819), a Scotch engineer and inventor. His work as a mathematical-instrument maker led him to conceive the high pressure steam engine. Watt took out his first patent in 1769; the engine, however, was used only for mining operations until 1785, when it was applied to a cotton factory. Watt was greatly aided in his developments of the engine by the business ability of his partner, Matthew Boulton.

Watteau, Jean Antoine (1684-1721), a French painter. His shepherds and shepherdesses, rustic dance and fete scenes were noteworthy for their harmonious brilliancy of coloration. His most famous work is the "Embarkation for the Isle of Cythera" in the Louvre.

Watts, George Frederick (1817-1904), an English painter. His paintings, many of them symbolical, are numerous, and include "Love and Death," "Hope," and "The Angel of Death." His portraits of Swinburne, Carlyle, Cardinal Manning, Browning, and Tennyson are also notable.

Watts, Isaac (1674-1748), an English hymn-writer; author of the famous hymn beginning, "Oh God, our help in ages past."

Webster, Daniel (1782-1852), American statesman and orator, born in Salisbury, N. H., studied at Dartmouth College and entered the legal profession. In 1813 he was elected to Congress as a Federalist, but then set up a law practice in Boston, where his remarkable abilities won him great success in the next seven years. He was elected to the Massachusetts Constitutional Convention, and on Dec. 22, 1822, delivered a remarkable oration at Plymouth on the anniversary of the landing of the Pilgrims.

In 1822 he was elected to Congress from Boston. In 1826 he became a United States Senator; in 1841 he became Secretary of State under President Harrison; remained in the administration under Taylor till 1843; and became Fillmore's Secretary of State in 1850. On several occasions Webster had been an unsuccessful candidate for the Presidency.

Webster, Noah (1758-1843), an American lexicographer. After serving in the Revolutionary War he graduated from Yale. In 1788 he published three textbooks, which had an immense sale and greatly influenced American education: *Webster's Spelling Book, A Plain and Comprehensive Grammar*, and *An American Selection of Lessons in Reading and Speaking*. In 1806 he published an eight-volume English dictionary. His great work, *The American Dictionary of the English Language*, finished in 1828, was improved and enlarged as the *International Dictionary* after his death. His last great task was to revise the Bible and to correct errors in its translation and grammar.

Wedgwood, Josiah (1730-1795), the most famous of English potters. After an apprenticeship he set up a business of his own in 1759. In a few years he produced such an improved form of chinaware that it came into great demand, and led to a great extension of the Staffordshire earthenware industry. His works at Etruria were the most extensive of the kind in Great Britain.

Weismann, August (1834-1914), German biologist noted for his work on evolution, especially in the field of individual variability. He is remembered particularly for his theory that acquired characteristics cannot be transmitted.

Weizmann, Chaim (1874-1952), Jewish statesman and scientist. A renowned chemist in England during World War I, he became a leader of the World Zionist Organization and served as the first president of the state of Israel from its founding in 1948 until his death in 1952.

Wellington, Arthur Wellesley, 1st Duke of (1769-1852), the most famous British general of the 19th century. He distinguished himself in India and conducted successfully the Peninsular War. In 1814 he was made a duke, and became the British ambassador at Paris. The following year he commanded the allied forces which terminated Napoleon's career at the Battle of Waterloo. From 1828 to 1830 Wellington was prime minister; and from 1842 to his death he was commander-in-chief of the army.

Wells, Herbert George (1866-1946), English novelist whose work, whether romantic as in *Kipps* and *The History of Mr. Polly*, or scientific as in *The Outline of History*, gained him a world-wide reputation. Social, political and educational problems are treated with breadth of vision and are clearly analyzed in his books.

Wesley, Charles (1708-88), an English poet and preacher, brother of John Wesley, and the poet of Methodism. He wrote a large number of hymns of enduring merit.

Wesley, John (1703-91), the founder of Methodism. In 1735 he went to Georgia as a missionary and allied himself with the Moravians. Returning to England, he abandoned all ecclesiastical traditions, and established the Methodist sect. His organizing ability and strength of purpose enabled him to build it up as one of the most influential Protestant groups.

West, Benjamin (1738-1820), an artist who was born in America, but settled in England in 1763. He was a painter of religious and historical pictures, such as "Christ Healing the Sick," "Penn's Treaty with the Indians," "The Black Prince at Poitiers," and "The Death of General Wolfe."

West, Mae, an American stage and screen actress. She acted in several daring plays in New York City. In the 1930's she entered moving pictures, and played with success a number of alluring roles, for which she wrote part of the dialogue. *Diamond Lil* was one of her most popular pictures; she was starred in *My Little Chickadee* in 1940.

West, Rebecca (b. 1892), an English author of force and originality. Her critical works include *Henry James* (1916), *The Strange Necessity* (1928), and *Particular Graces* (1933). Among her novels are *The Return of the Soldier* (1918), *The Judge* (1922), and *Harriet Hume* (1924). Later works include *The Thinking Reed* (1934), and *The Harsh Voice* (1935).

Westinghouse, George (1846-1914), American engineer who built the dynamos for Niagara Falls. In 1865 he invented the brake known by his name, and developed a compressed-air system of railway signaling.

Wharton, Edith (Jones) (1862-1937), an American author. Her first novel, *The Valley of Decision*, was published in 1902. In 1911 appeared *Ethan Frome*, a brief and tragic New England love story. After 1906 she made her home in France. Among her books are *The Marne, The Age of Innocence, A Son at the Front*, and *Hudson River Bracketed*. Her autobiography, *A Backward Glance*, appeared in 1934.

Wheatstone, Sir Charles (1802-75), British scientist, whose experiments in association with W. F. Cooke resulted in the first application in England of the principle of the electric telegraph. The stereoscope was also one of his inventions.

Whistler, James Abbott McNeill (1834-1903), American artist and writer, who first went to Europe from the United States in 1857, and made a name as an etcher both in Paris and in London. The finest of his oil paintings are his portrait of his mother and that of Carlyle.

White, William Allen (1868-1944), an American author and journalist, born in Emporia, Kansas. In 1895 he became the owner and editor of the *Daily Gazette* in Emporia and stirred a great deal of comment by publishing editorials against the Populist party. He was an ardent supporter of Theodore Roosevelt in 1912, and later of Hoover and Landon. His novels of life in the Middle West include *A Certain Rich Man* and *In the Heart of a Fool*.

Whitefield, George (1714-70), an English evangelist. He was for a time associated with John

Wesley at Oxford in the propagation of Methodism, and attracted great attention by his gifts as a preacher. In 1741, differing from Wesley on a point of doctrine, he left the Methodists, and thenceforward simply preached as an evangelist, allying himself with no sect.

Whitehead, Albert North (1861-1947), English philosopher and mathematician who, with Bertrand Russell, brought modern mathematical analysis to philosophy. His writings include *Science and the Modern World* (1925) and *Process and Reality.*

Whitman, Walt (1819-92), an American poet, the first to make an extended use of free verse; a portrayer of democracy and the American scene. He served in the Civil War, and his vigorous humanity, as expressed in his writings, made him a distinguished personality. His works include *Leaves of Grass, Drum Taps,* and *Democratic Vistas.*

Whitney, Eli (1765-1825), American inventor; was graduated from Yale in 1792; later went to the South as a tutor. There he became interested in the problem of separating cotton from its seed, a laborious task when performed bv hand, and invented for the purpose the cotton gin. His model was stolen and reproduced; consequent litigation and confusion prevented him from realizing any profit from his device. In 1798 he secured a government patent for the manufacture of firearms. He made a fortune by this enterprise, being the first to introduce the principle of interchangeable parts into industry.

Whittier, John Greenleaf (1807-92), America's Quaker poet, was the son of a New England farmer, and for a time followed the trade of a shoemaker. After some experience in journalism, he published his first book of poems, *Legends of New England* (1831). His best-known volumes are: *Lays of My Home* (1843), *Voices of Freedom* (1846), *Songs of Labor* (1850), and *National Lyrics* (1865). Much of his writing was devoted to the Abolition cause, of which he was one of the leaders.

Whittington, Richard (c. 1358-1423), a mayor of London. He went up to be apprenticed in London, and there found fortune and fame as a merchant. He was four times mayor of London, and represented the city in Parliament.

Wiggin, Kate Douglas (1856-1923), an American author of quaint charm. Her works include *The Birds' Christmas Carol,* and *Rebecca of Sunnybrook Farm.*

Wilberforce, William (1759-1833), an English reformer; educated at Cambridge; entered Parliament in 1780. In 1789 he made the first of his many proposals in the House of Commons for the abolition of the slave trade, but it was not until 1807 that such an act was passed.

Wilde, Oscar Fingall O'Flahertie Wills (1856-1900), Irish author and dramatist. The son of Sir William Wilde, a well-known Dublin surgeon, he was the leader of a cult of aestheticism, of art for art's sake. His works included poems, fairy-tales, and short stories. He is best known, however, for his brilliantly witty comedies, *Lady Windermere's Fan, A Woman of No Importance, The Ideal Husband* and *The Importance of Being Earnest.*

Wilder, Thornton (b. 1897), American novelist and playwright. His first novel to gain renown was *The Bridge of San Luis Rey,* which won the Pulitzer Prize in 1927. Subsequent works include *The Woman of Andros, The Long Christmas Dinner, Heaven's My Destination,* and *Our Town.*

Wilkes, John (1727-1797), British statesman and popular leader. For a violent attack on the government in his paper *The North Briton,* he was committed to the Tower, but obtained release on the ground that he was a member of Parliament. Wilkes' popularity increased and he was eventually made mayor and chamberlain of London.

Wilkins, Sir Hubert (b. 1888), famous British Arctic explorer, who conducted the 1931 *Nautilus* expedition to the Arctic.

Willard, Frances Elizabeth (1839-1898), an American reformer. She began her active temperance work in 1874, and was made secretary of the National Woman's Christian Temperance Union; president in 1879. She was chosen president of the World's Woman's Christian Temperance Union in 1888.

William I (1027-87), king of England, better known as "William the Conqueror," was Duke of Normandy when he claimed the throne of England as legally appointed successor to Edward the Confessor. The claim was resisted by Harold II, but the battle of Hastings, in which Harold was slain and his army routed, gave the victory to William, who in due course was crowned in Westminster Abbey. The story of his life and reign is the story of the crushing of Saxon power, the parcelling out of the country among his Norman followers, and for the rest, a firm rule that made England an important nation.

William II (1056-1100), king of England, son of William the Conqueror, reigned from 1087 to his death. He was in constant conflict with his barons and oppressive to his subjects.

William III (1650-1702), king of England, son of William II of Orange. While stadtholder of the Netherlands, he married Mary, eldest daughter of the Duke of York (afterwards James II). In 1688, when James had abdicated and fled from England, William was invited to succeed him, he and Mary becoming joint sovereigns. Later he was at war with France, and suffered defeats, but ultimately effected peace by the Treaty of Ryswick in 1697.

William IV (1765-1837), king of England, the third son of George III ascended the throne in 1830 in succession to his brother, George IV. He showed little of kingly capacity, but was genial and pleasure-loving.

William I (1797-1888), emperor of Germany. He succeeded to the throne of Prussia in 1861, and it fell to him to have the control of his country during a period of transition and development, with Bismarck as his chief minister. The war with Austria which signalized the opening year of his reign rendered him highly popular, and when in 1870 the war with France was entered upon the whole German people rallied round him. After a series of brilliant achievements by his army he was proclaimed emperor on the 18th of January, 1871.

William II (1859-1941), emperor of Germany, deposed 1918. He succeeded his father, the Emperor Frederick, in 1888. His reign produced a few partial measures of social reform, and military and naval expansion. He was both headstrong and vacillating. Contrary to the popular belief, he apparently did not seek the outbreak of World War I as an opportunity for the enlargement of the German Empire. In November, 1918, when a revolution broke out in Germany and the Socialists proclaimed the establishment of a republic, he resigned the throne and fled to Holland. Here he was given sanctuary in a castle at Doorn, where he lived in seclusion, having promised to refrain from political activity.

William the Silent (1553-1584), the first leader in the Dutch war of independence. Under the emperor Charles V, he became governor of the provinces of Holland, Zealand, and Utrecht. When Philip II of Spain, Charles's son, attempted to subdue the Netherlands and institute the Inquisition under the Duke of Alva, William came forward and raised the standard of independence. After a long conflict, Holland was liberated by the relief of Leyden, which William effected by laying the whole country under water in 1574. He was elected stadtholder, and Calvinism became the established religion. In 1576 William united all the provinces in one confederation, but he found it impossible to heal internal causes of disunion, and the Spaniards were able to repossess the southern provinces, under the Duke of Parma. Philip set a price on William's head, and he was assassinated in 1584.

Williams, Roger (*c.* 1603-1683), clergyman, founder of Rhode Island. He was born in London and in 1631 went to Boston. In 1636 Williams founded Providence, on Narragansett Bay. In 1644 he obtained a charter for this and nearby settlements, all of which were characterized by his tenets of democratic government and religious liberty. They later became the state of Rhode Island.

Willkie, Wendell Lewis (1892-1944), American lawyer, business man, and political leader. In 1933 he became president of Commonwealth and Southern Corporation. Originally a Democrat, he was the Republican Presidential candidate in 1940. He was defeated in one of the closest of presidential elections. He then pledged his party to a loyal opposition, and in 1941 made a personal investigation of war conditions in Great Britain.

Wilmot, David (1814-1868), an American jurist. He became a member of Congress in 1845, and was the author in 1846 of the celebrated Wilmot Proviso, which would have prohibited slavery in territories acquired from Mexico.

Wilson, Thomas Woodrow (1856-1924), 28th President of the United States, born in Staunton, Virginia. He became the president of Princeton University in 1902. He was the successful Democratic nominee for governor of New Jersey in 1910, and was elected President of the United States in 1912. His first term resulted in the lowering of tariffs, the initiation of the Federal income tax, and the Clayton Anti-trust Act. After the outbreak of World War I in August, 1914, Wilson urged strict neutrality for Americans. He was reelected in 1916 on the campaign slogan, "He kept us out of war." Nevertheless, during his second term Wilson's attitude toward Germany was hardened by the German conduct of hostilities. War was declared by Congress in response to his request on April 6, 1917. He continued, however, in his efforts to secure a just "peace without victory." His celebrated program for peace called the "Fourteen Points" was expounded in January, 1918. Wilson himself was present at the ensuing peace conference, but in spite of his great influence he was unable to secure adoption by the victorious Allies of the Fourteen Points. Returning to the United States, he was unable to secure Congressional ratification of the Treaty of Versailles. While touring the country in an effort to win popular support for these measures, he suffered a nervous breakdown in September, 1919. He served out his term of office, but thereafter lived in seclusion.

Winthrop, John (1588-1649), first governor of Massachusetts. He came with the first colonists to Boston in 1630 as their governor, an office which he held for twelve terms. He left a journal of the proceedings of the colony which is a valuable contribution to the early history of Massachusetts.

Wise, Stephen Samuel (1874-1949), an American rabbi, founder of the Free Synagogue of New York, and one of the founders of the Zionist Organization of America. He has concerned himself with many social and political problems, both American and international. Among his books are *The Ethics of Solomon Ibn Gabiral, How to Face Life, Child Versus Parent*, and *The Great Betrayal.*

Wister, Owen (1860-1938), an American author, who was most successful in depicting frontier life in the West. His most successful book was *The Virginian.* His other works include: *U. S. Grant, Philosophy 4, Watch Your Thirst, When West was West*, and a biography of Theodore Roosevelt.

Wodehouse, Pelham Grenville (b. 1881), English humorist, author of many popular stories whose central character is Jeeves, the butler.

Woffington, Margaret (1714?-60), familiarly known as *Peg Woffington*, a bricklayer's daughter who became a celebrated English actress.

Wolfe, General James (1727-59), a British soldier, who commanded the British forces in Canada at the siege of Quebec, where he won a brilliant victory, but was fatally wounded.

Wollaston, William Hyde (1766-1828), English chemist and physicist. He discovered rhodium and palladium, the dark lines in the solar spectrum and the ultra-violet rays, invented the goniometer and the camera lucida, and carried out many important investigations in electricity and optics.

Wolsey, Thomas (1471-1530), an English statesman and cardinal, the son of an Ipswich butcher. He was educated at Oxford, and later entered the Church, where he gradually rose to a position of eminence, and was entrusted with several diplomatic missions. He secured rapid preferment under Henry VIII, being in turn bishop of Lincoln, archbishop of York, and cardinal, becoming Henry's chancellor. By his diplomacy he did much to strengthen the kingly power. But when Wolsey was unable to obtain the papal sanction for Henry's divorce of Katharine, he fell into disfavor, and declined rapidly from a position of great power. He died at Leicester Abbey, a broken and dejected man.

Wood, Leonard (1860-1927), an American military officer. He studied medicine, and was appointed 1st lieutenant and assistant surgeon in the United States Army in 1886. In the Spanish-American War he was made brigadier general of volunteers, and was a commander at the battle of San Juan Hill. He was military governor of Cuba from 1899 to 1902. He was governor of Moro Province, Philippine Islands, in 1903-1906; commanded the Military Division of the Philippines in 1906-1908, and the Department of the East in 1908-1909. During the first stages of the World War Wood insisted upon the establishment of civilian training camps. He was governor general of the Philippines from 1921 until his death.

Wood, Robert Williams (1868-1955), an American physicist and author. He devised the method now generally used of thawing frozen water mains and pipes by passing electric currents through them. After 1901 he was a professor of experimental physics at Johns Hopkins University. He was awarded the John Scott Legacy medal for his work in color photography; he also made contributions to the theory of light. He wrote fiction, including *The Man Who Rocked the Earth.*

Woodin, William Hartman (1868-1934), an American Cabinet officer and industrialist; president of the American Car and Foundry Company. He was appointed to President Roosevelt's Cabinet as Secretary of the Treasury in 1933 during the banking moratorium, and did much in the reorganization of the banking system. Illness compelled his retirement shortly before his death.

Woolf, Virginia (1882-1941), novelist; author of *To the Lighthouse, Mrs. Dalloway,* and other works.

Woolworth, Frank Winfield (1852-1919), an American merchant. In 1879 he opened a five-and ten-cent store in Lancaster, Pennsylvania. He expanded the business to 1,000 stores before his death and built the famous building in New York that bears his name.

Wordsworth, William (1770-1850), one of the greatest British poets, educated at Cambridge. In association with Coleridge he issued the volume, *Lyrical Ballads,* in 1798. He settled with his sister in the Lake Country, where he spent the rest of his life. There he wrote his poetry and carried out his creed of "plain living and high thinking." As an interpreter of Nature in her many moods he stands unrivaled. He succeeded to the poet laureateship on the death of Southey in 1843. His best-known long poems are *The Prelude* and *The Excursion.*

Wren, Sir Christopher (1632-1723), English architect. His greatest undertaking was the reconstruction of St. Paul's Cathedral after the Fire of London. Chelsea and Greenwich Hospitals and a number of London's finest churches were also his work.

Wright, Sir Almroth Edward (1861-1947), a British pathologist; the discoverer of antityphoid inoculation, of vaccinotherapy, and of methods of measuring protective substances in the human blood.

Wright, Carroll Davidson (1840-1909), an American statistician. As United States Commissioner of Labor from 1885 to 1905, he completed the Eleventh United States Census. He also taught economics, and became president of Clark University in 1902. His works include *Census of Massachusetts* (1876-77), *The Factory System of the United States* (1882), and reports of the United States Department of Labor, including *Industrial Depressions* (1886), and *Strikes and Lockouts* (1887).

Wright, Frank Lloyd (b. 1869), American architect. He began his career under the guidance of Louis Sullivan in Chicago. He developed a highly individual style, his residences being characterized by their broad eaves and their low horizontal construction. His home, "Talicsin," at Spring Green, Wis., the Midway Gardens in Chicago, and the Imperial Hotel at Tokyo, Japan, are good examples of his style. Wright became an architect of international importance, and his influence in Europe has been particularly great. His writings include *An Interpretation of Japanese Prints* (1912), *In the Cause of Architecture* (essays appearing in the *Architectural Forum,* 1909-1923), and an autobiography, *Frank Lloyd Wright* (1932).

Wright, Orville (1871-1948), and **Wilbur,** his brother (1867-1912), American inventors of the airplane. They began their famous gliding experiments on the sand dunes at Kitty Hawk, North Carolina, and by the end of 1902 had practically solved all the problems of airplane control. To the glider they built they added a gasoline engine, and on the 17th of Dec., 1903, they made four flights, the longest being 852 ft. These flights were the first in which a man had been carried from the ground in flight by a power-driven airplane. In 1908 the brothers went to France, and demonstrated in a remarkable series of flights that they had conquered the air. Their first machine flew for 59 seconds.

Wyatt, Sir Thomas (1503-42), English poet, was the first writer of English sonnets, and a poet who did much to develop the earlier forms of verse. He was also a distinguished diplomatist.

Wyatt, Sir Thomas ("the Younger") (c. 1520-54), an English conspirator who joined with the Duke of Suffolk in favor of Lady Jane Grey and against Queen Mary. He led the men of Kent in rebellion on London in 1554, but was captured and executed.

Wycherley, William (1640-1715), an English dramatist of the Restoration, for many years in high favor at court. His comedies have clever plots, adroit characterization, and witty dialogue, but are extremely coarse, in accordance with the taste of the period. They have often been revived. His plays include *The Country Wife, Love in a Wood,* and *The Plain Dealer.*

Wycliff, John (c. 1324-84), an English religious reformer. He adopted the principles of the Reformation, and brought down upon himself the bitter enmity of the Roman Catholic leaders, and would probably have been put to death but for the protection of John of Gaunt. While in comparative retirement as Rector of Lutterworth, in Leicestershire, he finished his translation of the Bible into English.

X

Xavier, St. Francis (1506-1552), a Jesuit missionary born in Spain; called "the Apostle of the Indies." He was the follower of Ignatius Loyola, and devoted his life to missionary work in India and Japan. He was canonized in 1621.

Xenocrates (396-314 B.C.), a Greek writer and philosopher; born in Chalcedon. In early youth he removed to Athens, where he joined Plato. He was for some years scholarch, or rector, of the Academy. His numerous writings, chiefly on metaphysics and ethics, laid special stress on the latter, and worked on Platonic lines. He is said to have first divided philosophy into physics, didactics, and ethics.

Xenophon (c. 430-357 B.C.), a Greek historian, philosopher and pupil of Socrates. Having joined the expedition against the king of Persia, Xenophon took part in the "Retreat of the Ten Thousand," described in his *Anabasis.* He attached himself to Agesilaus, king of Sparta, and fought against his native city in the battle of Coronea (394 B.C.). The Spartans rewarded him with an estate where he lived for about twenty years. His principal works are the *Anabasis, History of Greece*, the *Cyropaedia* (education of Cyrus the Elder), *Memorabilia* (reminiscences of Socrates), the *Symposium*, and the *Economics*.

Xerxes (c. 519-465 B.C.), king of Persia, the son of the first Darius. He undertook an expedition against Greece with a large army in 481 B.C., and defeated the Spartans at Thermopylae. His fleet was overcome at Salamis. Later he died by assassination.

Y

Yale, Elihu (1649?-1721), an Anglo-American merchant and philanthropist, born in Boston. He went to the East Indies as a trader, where he acquired great wealth. From 1678 to 1692 he was governor of Fort St. George, Madras. He gave to the Collegiate School at Saybrook, Conn., a donation worth about $4,500, which caused the college to be named for him after its removal to New Haven.

Yeats, William Butler (1865-1930), an Irish poet; one of the leaders of the Irish literary revival, and prominent in the Abbey Theater, at Dublin. He was awarded the Nobel Prize for literature in 1923 and was a member of the Irish senate, 1922-1929. Among his works are: *The Wanderings of Oisin, Kathleen ni Houlihan, Responsibilities, The Tower, Commentaries and Poems*, and *Dramatis Personae*.

Yoshihito (1879-1926), 123rd emperor of Japan. In 1889 he entered the army. In 1912 Yoshihito ascended the throne, but his health prevented his ruling after 1921, when his son, Hirohito, was made prince regent.

Young, Brigham (1801-77), American pioneer and Mormon leader. In 1844 he succeeded Joseph Smith as the head of the sect. He led the migration into Utah, and founded Salt Lake City. He served as governor after Utah was placed under U. S. control, but came into conflict with the Federal Government and was forced to resign.

Yuan Shi-Kai (1859-1916), president of the Chinese Republic, 1913-16. He was favored by the empress dowager and held important governmental posts prior to her death. In 1911, on the outbreak of the revolution he supported the Manchu dynasty. After the formation of the republic he was elected president.

Z

Zaharoff, Sir Basil (1849-1936), a European financier, and manufacturer and seller of munitions, known as the "Armaments King"; believed to have been born of Greek parents in Turkey. By sales of munitions he gained an international political influence and a large fortune. He was connected with the Vickers-Armstrong munitions works in England. His services to the Allies during World War I won him a British knighthood and decorations from the French government.

Zamenhof, Ludwig Lazarus (1859-1917), Polish linguist, an oculist by profession, who invented the "universal language," Esperanto.

Zangwill, Israel (1864-1926), a Jewish man of letters, born in London; a prominent leader in the Zionist Movement. His most famous novel depicting Jewish life, *Children of the Ghetto* (1892), was produced as a play in England and the United States in 1899. Other novels are *Ghetto Tragedies, Ghetto Comedies*, and *Dreamers of the Ghetto*. Among his plays are *The Melting Pot*, and *Plaster Saints*.

Zenger, John Peter (1680-1746), an American journalist and publisher; born in Germany. At the age of 20 he came to America, and after serving for some time as a printer's apprentice under William Bradford, began the publication of the *New York Weekly Journal* (1733). In 1734, during the controversy between Van Dam and Governor Cosby, Zenger's paper published several virulent criticisms of the government. Zenger was arrested, imprisoned, and tried for libel. Andrew Hamilton defended the publisher, and his subsequent acquittal was regarded as the acknowledgement of the American principle of the freedom of the press.

Zeno of Cyprus (c. 340-264 B.C.), Greek philosopher who founded the Stoic system.

Zeppelin, Ferdinand, Count von (1838-1917), inventor of the type of rigid dirigible airship bearing his name. His first long flight was in 1900. He organized a zeppelin service for the German army during World War I.

Ziegfeld, Florenz (1869-1932), American producer of musical comedies. He was the originator of the annual Ziegfeld Follies. His musical shows included *Rio Rita, Kid Boots*, and *Show Boat*.

Zinoviev (Grigory Evseyevich Apfelbaum) (1883-1936), a leading figure in Bolshevik Russia after the Revolution; president of the Communist International in 1919. He was expelled from the Communist party in 1926, but later was given a minor position. He was executed in 1936 for alleged plotting against the Soviet government.

Ziska, John (1360-1424), a Bohemian general, who led the Hussites in a series of military victories over the Catholic emperor, Sigismund.

Zog I (b. 1895), king of Albania from 1928 to 1939. He was president during the period when Albania was a republic. His regime as ruler of the kingdom was supported by the Italian government; nevertheless Italian forces invaded the kingdom in April, 1939, and Zog and his family were forced to flee from the country.

Zola Émile Edouard Charles Antoine (1840-1902), French novelist, noted for his naturalistic treatment of his materials. His works dealt largely with social, political, and psychological problems. He wrote a long series of novels dealing with a Second Empire family; the best of them are *L'Assomoir and Nana*. *Fecondité* too was a great success. Zola is remembered also for his courageous championship of the unfortunate officer Dreyfus, whose release from a French penal colony he helped to secure.

Zorn, Anders (1860-1920), noted Swedish painter, etcher, and sculptor.

Zwingli, Ulrich (1484-1531), one of the ablest of the Swiss Reformation leaders.

An International Atlas and Gazetteer of the World

Nine Maps in full color, with a geographic dictionary describing the principal countries of the world.

ADEN COLONY AND ADEN PROTECTORATE

Aden, built in the crater of an extinct volcano, is an important bunkering station on the seaway to the East, and the harbor and capital city of the British colony of Aden and protectorate of Aden, which lie along the southern end of the Arabian Peninsula in southwestern Asia. The region is one of the hottest places on earth, and British soldiers serving there are credited with double time. The area of the colony, which includes Perim Island and the Kuria Muria Islands, is 75 square miles; the protectorate, which includes the islands of Socotra, is 112,000 square miles. The population of the colony is made up principally of Arabs but includes Jews, Somalis, Indians, and some Europeans. The population is about 650,000. The people of the protectorate are principally Arabs who live in nomadic groups and are governed by hereditary sultans. Mohammedanism is the predominant religion, and several Arabic dialects are spoken. Although education is not widespread, there are a number of primary and secondary schools.

The colony is administered by a British governor, who is president of a legislative council and is also commander in chief. The protectorate, although not directly administered by the British government, is subject to the control of the governor of Aden Colony.

Industrial enterprises include the refining of salt and oil, the making of cigarettes, and the building of Arab vessels called dhows. The country is mostly barren volcanic rocks and sand, and its resources consist of crude salt (evaporated from sea water) and a little timber from which certain gums are produced. The natives take advantage of the infrequent fertile places to raise grains, tobacco, sugar, coffee, and livestock. Aden exports cigarettes, salt, gums, coffee, grain, sugar, and butter.

AFGHANISTAN

Long a jealously guarded land, which discouraged travelers with signs reading, "It is absolutely forbidden to cross this border into Afghan Territory," the kingdom of Afghanistan lies between Iran and Pakistan and has an area of some 250,000 square miles. The population is about 12,000,000. The main tribes are the Durani, or Afghans proper, the Pathans, the Ghilzai, the Tajik, the Hazara, and the Kaffirs. The most important cities are Kabul, the capital, Kandahar, and Herat, the western terminus of an ancient trade route to the Orient. Many of the people live in small nomad groups. They speak Persian, Pashto (Pushtu), or Turki and are predominantly Mohammedan, though the village of Balkh, now of minor importance, was once the center of the great religious movement founded by Zoroaster. Primary schools are fairly common, but secondary schools are found only in the capital and the provincial capitals. The king governs his people with the aid of a senate appointed by him for life and an elected national assembly. The country has a constitution.

Afghanistan has rich copper deposits, lead and iron ore, silver, gold, and the best lapis-lazuli in the world; however, such resources are not completely exploited. A few fertile places, some of which are irrigated, yield fruits, grains, and vegetables. Pasture land is plentiful.

The winter climate is cold and damp, and summer is hot and dry. Of the passes leading into the country, the most famous is the Khyber Pass connecting Kabul with Peshawar in Pakistan.

A few state-owned factories make matches, buttons, furniture, textiles, leather goods, and shoes. Timber, fruit, skins (especially karakul), raw wool, cotton, and carpets are exported.

ALASKA

Alaska, with a land area of 571,065 square miles and a total area of 586,400 square miles, is a territory of the United States but is pressing for statehood. Its own legislative acts are subject to veto by the Federal congress. The population is about 129,000. Military forces are numerous. Most of the inhabitants are white; the native Eskimos, Indians, and Aleuts number about 33,000. Many Eskimos speak English and profess Christianity as a result of intense missionary efforts. Education is carried on separately by churches and the Federal government. The territory administers and finances schools in the incorporated towns and in rural areas; native schools are operated by the Federal government through the Office of Indian Affairs. Higher education is provided in the University of Alaska, near Fairbanks.

In topography Alaska roughly resembles the western United States. It has mountains, plateaus, and lowlands. The climate is variable, the territory being cold and icebound most of the year in the extreme north, while the cities of Juneau and Sitka boast that their climate is similar to that of Washington, D. C. Agriculture is possible, principally in the Matanuska and the

Tanana valleys, where some grains, potatoes, and hardy vegetables and fruits are grown.

The most important cities of Alaska are Juneau, the capital, Ketchikan, Nome, Sitka, Anchorage, Fairbanks, Eastchester, and Mountain View. Anchorage, which quintupled in population from 1940 to 1950, is almost twice as large as any other city. The leading exports are fish and fish products, furs, and gold.

ALBANIA

The inhabitants of this south European country, independent since 1912, call their land Shqipenija, a name that means "land of eagles." The Ghegs of the north and the Tosks of the south are the chief groups of this nation. The population is about 1,380,000. Albania has an area of 10,629 square miles, approximately that of Vermont. There is no state religion, but about 70 percent of the people are Moslems; 20 percent, mainly in the south, are Orthodox Christians; and 10 percent, mainly in the north, are Roman Catholics. Bowing to Christian pressure, the state abolished polygamy in 1929. Primary education is nominally obligatory, but a shortage of schools makes it useless to enforce this law. The Albanian language is of indirect descent from the Illyrian tongue, now extinct, which was spoken by the ancient Thracians before the Golden Age of Greece.

Albania's mountains are relieved by green groves and glistening minarets. Mountain tops are still the hideouts of bandits, but quiet agrarian communities dot the green valleys. The Albanian climate is similar to that of Spain and Italy. As late as 1940 it was the only European country without a railroad, and there are still only a few miles of tracks on the Durres-Elbasan line. Most of the principal towns of Albania are accessible by motor vehicle, but in the mountain districts of the north, pack animals are the means of transportation.

The fine timber lands and rich mining sections and mineral deposits make Albania a country of natural wealth, but little advantage is taken of the resources. Most of the people are small farmers, raising excellent tobacco, livestock, grain, fruits, and vegetables. Fishing is an important occupation with fine opportunities, as the country lies at the lowest east entrance of the Adriatic Sea. The chief exports are crude petroleum, cattle, cheese, eggs, hides, furs, fish, and bitumen, while imports consist of cotton textiles, sugar, coffee, benzine, and gasoline.

ALGERIA

Algeria, a country in Northern Africa, is divided into two parts: Northern Algeria, the smaller area, consisting of the three prefectures of Algiers, Oran, and Constantine, is considered a part of metropolitan France; Southern Algeria, containing the four territories of Ain Sefra, Ghardaia, Touggourt, and the Saharan Oases, is a French colonial territory. Northern Algeria is in part subject to ministries in Paris and in part to the governor general of Algeria; Southern Algeria is administered by the governor general. Most of Algeria's 847,500 square miles is wasteland, either desert or mountain. The people consist of native Berbers, Moors, Arabs, Negroes, Turks, and mixtures, though approximately a million French and other Europeans live here for business or political reasons. French is the official language, but the mixture of peoples has brought confusion in native dialects. The religions most common are Mohammedan, Protestant, Catholic, and Jewish. There is a comprehensive though inadequate education system in Algeria, based on the French plan. The capital is Algiers. Other cities are Constantine, Oran, Bône, Philippeville, Tlemcen, Blida, and Sidi-bel-Abbès, headquarters for the world-famous Foreign Legion.

The climate of the country is fairly even, though high temperatures prevail and the daily range is great. There is little rainfall except near the coastal regions of high fertile plains. The rest is mountainous and wild or sandy and bare with unbelievable heat rising in waves from the baked desert. The principal agricultural area is near the coast and is owned and cultivated by the Europeans. Its chief crops are grains, flax, vegetables, tobacco, dates, and other fruits. The country is rich in natural resources, including timber, iron, zinc, lead, mercury, copper, salt, coal, marble, and onyx. The manufacture of olive oil, the refining of metals and minerals, and the cutting of lumber make up most of the industrial life. Major exports are wines, cereals, phosphate, iron ore, potatoes, and fresh vegetables.

ANDORRA

In a labyrinth of mountains and valleys of the eastern Pyrenees between France and Spain lies the tiny republic of Andorra, probably one, and the last to survive, of the independent states Charlemagne established as buffers to keep the Moors from overrunning France. The country has only about 191 square miles of territory, thus being approximately one-sixth the size of Rhode Island. The population is about 5,300. Most of Andorra's people live within the confines of the country's six scattered villages. The capital is Andorra-la-Vieja. The language of the Andorrans is Catalan, and the religion is Roman Catholic.

The Spanish and French frontiers are connected by a good road, which crosses Andorra. Although arable land is limited in the high and rough country, crops include barley, rye, tobacco, and vines. The principal wealth lies in the raising of livestock. Although iron and lead are found, the deposits are undeveloped because of transportation difficulties.

ANGOLA

This Portuguese province, with more than a thousand miles of coast line, is situated on the west coast of Africa, about midway between the Cape of Good Hope and the Equator. It has an area of 481,351 square miles, and its population is mostly made up of native Bushmen, Bantus, and Bakongo tribesmen. There are minorities of half-castes and also of Europeans, predominantly Portuguese and German. The natives were Christianized as early as the 17th century; Catholicism is the state religion, and missionary efforts are claiming many natives. The economic language is Portuguese, but even European traders must familiarize themselves with the many native dialects of the Kishi-Kongo, Kimbundu, and Umbundu tongues. Native schools are conducted both in Portuguese and in Kishi-Kongo, though no thorough-going attempt at universal education is made. The province is divided into 13 administrative districts and is under authority of a governor general; actual tribal organization is not distributed, but officials are predominantly Portuguese. The population is about 4,317,000.

Geographically, Angola has a flat and sterile coastal plain, a central plateau, and mountain chains running parallel to the coast. The climate is mostly unsuited to Europeans, though the higher regions seem fairly healthful. Malaria, sleeping sickness, and plagues infest the low, warm, and damp areas.

The resources of Angola include diamonds, copper, lignites, salt, and much useful timber and rubber trees. Coffee, corn, sugar, palm trees, cotton, wheat, tobacco, sisal, and cacao are raised, and livestock is plentiful in the plateau regions. Angola exports coffee, rubber, diamonds, wax, coconuts, and ivory.

ANTARCTIC REGIONS

The Antarctic regions differ widely from their northern counterpart, the Arctic. The Antarctic land area is estimated at 5,500,000 square miles, most of which is covered with a permanent coating of ice. Generally speaking, temperatures are about 5 degrees lower in the Antarctic than in the Arctic. Most of the Antarctic is a great, white, silent waste, which resists extensive exploration because of its extreme storminess. Heavy snows fall, and violent winds having a velocity of up to 200 miles per hour sweep across the rocky continent and the volcanic islands that surround it.

The South Polar plateau is about 10,000 feet high. Thick sea-ice and the ice barriers make approach to this plateau very hazardous. The Ross Ice Shelf alone is a great sheet of floating ice, 600 to 1,000 feet thick with an area larger than that of France. Mountains rising to heights of 15,000 feet have been discovered in Antarctica.

Few living things can endure the rigors of the Antarctic climate. However, whales are found in abundance in the waters around the continent, and those caught account for 90 percent of the whale products of the world. Other animals found in the region include penguins, petrels, seals, various fish, and insects; plants found include mosses, lichens, and algae. The resources of the region are as yet not fully known, but there is much evidence to indicate that the Antarctic, if it possesses mineral wealth under its coat of ice, is much too isolated and severe of climate to entice exploitation.

Territory in Antarctica is claimed by Australia, France, New Zealand, Argentina, Chile, and Great Britain, the last three nations having overlapping claims in the area of the Palmer Peninsula. Neither the United States nor the Soviet Union recognizes these claims or makes claims of its own, but both reserve the right to make future claims because of previous exploration and discovery.

ARCTIC REGIONS

Most of the region lying within the Arctic Circle is occupied by the Arctic Ocean, whose area is about 5,900,000 square miles. For the most part Arctic waters are deep—from 100 to more than 2,600 fathoms. The land area includes parts of the mainland of North America, Asia, and Europe; most of the great island of Greenland; and numerous other islands, among them the Spitsbergen Islands, Novaya Zemlya, the Sverdrup Islands, Ellesmere Island, most of Baffin Island, Victory Island, Banks Island, and the Parry Islands. The land area of the Arctic is about 4,000,000 square miles, but estimates of land and sea are apt to be in error because of the drifting pack ice. Approximately half the Arctic lands lie within the Soviet Union, which has given particular attention to the development of crops and minerals and other resources in the area. The region around the Pole is under water and capped with ice.

The principal inhabitants of the Arctic Regions are Eskimos, Lapps, Nentsi, and Evenki. Centers of importance within the Arctic Circle include (in the U.S.S.R.) Pechenga (formerly Petsamo); Murmansk, the terminus of the Northern Sea Route to the Pacific and the largest Arctic city; Igarka, a timber port; and Verkhoyansk, where −90° F. has been recorded. In Norway are Hammerfest, the northernmost city in the world and one frequently used as a base by Arctic explorers; Narvik, a port and the terminus of the Lapland railway; and Tromsö. Kiruna and Gallivare (Sweden) are the centers of a rich iron district. In Alaska are the small settlements of Point Barrow, northernmost center of Alaska; Fort Yukon, former Hudson's Bay Company post; and Umiat, an oil center. Aklavik and Coppermine in Canada are among the chief settlements of the Northwest Territories.

The Arctic has much to offer in the way of natural resources. Coal, oil, copper, gold, silver, and platinum are known to exist, and in sufficient quantities to be profitably mined. The land is covered with valuable timber, and enough vegetation exists in untimbered tracts to provide ample pasturage for large flocks of livestock. Grain crops are even possible. The waters, both fresh and salt, abound in fish, and the ocean provides profitable whaling grounds. There are also seals, polar bears, reindeer, and musk oxen.

ARGENTINA

Among the greatest stretches of unbroken agricultural and grazing land in the world are the fertile, nearly level pampas of Argentina, also known as the Argentine Republic. With its area of 1,073,700 square miles, it is the second largest country in South America, being exceeded only by Brazil. Because its temperate climate and its terrain are more favorable for settlement than the tropical lands to the north, it has attracted settlers from many European nations—principally Spanish, Portuguese, Italian, and German. Few other Latin-American countries have so high a proportion of white people as is found in Argentina. The population is about 19,470,000. Though Argentina has large colonies of Europeans not yet assimilated to the national pattern, the great majority of Argentines speak Spanish and adhere to the Roman Catholic religion. Education is free and is compulsory between the ages of 6 and 14 years.

Argentina is a wedge-shaped country, the base of the wedge being made up by the torrid forest land of the Chaco crossed by the Tropic of Capricorn, while the point of the wedge lies more than 2,200 miles to the south, where the bleak island of Tierra del Fuego caps the southernmost tip of the South American continent. In the northeast the Uruguay River and its continuation, the broad estuary of the Río de la Plata, separate Argentina from the smaller republic of Uruguay. South of the estuary, the Atlantic Ocean forms the eastern boundary of Argentina, providing a long coast with many indentations but few good harbors. From the coast westward the land, arid in some stretches, well watered in others, slopes gradually upward to the mighty and almost impassable range of the southern Andes, which separates Argentina from Chile.

Argentina's industry is largely limited to the processing of crops and livestock. Farming and ranching account for most of Argentina's national wealth. The leading crops include alfalfa, wheat, corn, flax, sugar, tobacco, and wine grapes. Some of the land under tillage must be irrigated, especially in the northwest and in Patagonia (the narrow southern part of the country), where the Andes interfere with rainfall. Second in importance only to farming is the raising of livestock, most notably of cattle and sheep. The country's chief exports are hides, wool, meat, wheat, and corn.

The greatest density of population lies in the mid-part of the country, between the hot Chaco region on the north and the sterile desolation of Patagonia on the south. After Buenos Aires, which is by far larger than any other Argentine community, the principal cities are Rosario, Córdoba, Tucumán, Santa Fé, Mendoza, and Paraná.

AUSTRALIA

The area of Australia, including Tasmania, which is itself a separate island, is about 2,974,581 square miles. Excluding Antarctica, Australia is the most sparsely settled continent. In addition to its European population, there are about 50,000 aborigines, or native tribesmen, most of whom continue their ancient customs, languages and dress, living in government-protected reserves in the north and northwestern sections of the country. The aborigines are dark skinned, rather short, and given to primitive methods of hunting and fishing. Clothing is worn mostly for decorative purposes, and they paint weird designs in white on their chocolate-colored skins. The bow and arrow are almost unknown to them, and their chief weapons are spears, hatchets, clubs, and the famous boomerang. With the exception of the aborigines, southern European immigrants, and a few thousand Chinese, the Australians are almost wholly British by descent, attitude, and tradition. Their religious life, their educational system, their language, their currency, their weights and measures, and their government are all British.

Australia has six states and two territories. The states are: New South Wales, capital city, Sydney; Victoria, capital city, Melbourne; Queensland, capital city, Brisbane; South Australia, capital city, Adelaide; Western Australia, capital city, Perth; and Tasmania, capital city, Hobart. The territories are called Northern Territory (chief city and port, Darwin) and the Australian Capital Territory, in which is located the federal capital, Canberra. The population of Australia is about 9,534,000.

The Commonwealth also administers the territory of New Guinea (under a United Nations trusteeship); Nauru (a United Nations trusteeship jointly governed by Australia, New Zealand and the United Kingdom); the territory of Papua; Norfolk Island; Ashmore and Cartier Islands; the Australian Antarctic Territory; Heard Island; the MacDonald Islands; and the Cocos (Keeling) Islands.

The western part of Australia is a great plateau section, and the eastern part is composed of lowlands and a coastal belt of highlands. There are few high mountains, and only 1/20 of Australia is more than 2,000 feet above sea level, but the flat lowlands lead with such suddenness to rocky uprisings along the coast that the contrast makes much of the land appear mountainous. The highest point is Mt. Kosciusko in the southeast. The northern third of Australia lies within the Torrid Zone, with a generally high temperature. Monsoonal rains there bring a yearly fall of over 80 inches in some areas. Regions in the interior are arid, receiving sometimes less than 5 inches of rainfall a year, and temperatures may range from over 100° F. in the day to freezing or below at night. Yet the average range of temperature for the whole continent is small, about 15 degrees. Snow falls infrequently, even in the southern coastal regions. Tasmania has a climate remarkably like that of England, mild and moist. The principal rivers are the Murray and its chief tributaries, the Darling and Murrumbidgee. Most of the rivers are in eastern Australia.

Australia is rich in natural resources, having salt, gypsum, gold, tin, silver, copper, zinc, iron, coal, uranium, and some precious stones such as opals and sapphires, timber, much fertile soil, and a favorable climate for agriculture.

Of great domestic importance to Australia is manufacturing. Near the large coastal cities are numerous factories for meat preserving, wool handling, furniture, bootmaking, and textiles. Foundries, steel mills, automobile factories, flour mills, sawmills, and sugar refineries, as well as butter and cheese factories are other enterprises.

Agriculture and pastoral industries, such as sheep and cattle raising, are of major importance for the export trade. The wool industry is especially important, for Australian wool is of the finest quality and is in demand throughout the world. The raising of grains (especially wheat), root crops, sugar cane, cotton, tobacco, and vines and fruits, dairying, and poultry and bee farming are growing in importance. Altrough Australia has extensive mineral deposits, mining is still relatively unexploited. However, World War II gave impetus to the discovery of uranium and new fields of coal, copper, tin, lead, and zinc. Lumbering and fishing play minor roles in the industrial development of Australia.

Wool, meats, hides and skins, leather, tallow, flour, dairy products, other food products, and concentrates and ores are the principal Australian exports.

AUSTRIA

Present-day Austria, lying to the east of Switzerland, and composed generally of the German-speaking lands of the old Austrian Empire, has an area of some 32,375 square miles. The population is about 6,974,000.

The Austrian people are predominantly of Alpine stock, and their language is German, except for the Slavic peoples on the southeastern frontier whose language, customs, and physical attributes are more closely allied to neighboring Slav states. About 90 percent of the population is Catholic, with 5 percent Protestant, and 1 percent Jewish. Education is generally compulsory and free for children between the ages of 6 and 14, though widespread exemption exists for those over 12.

The eastern stretches of the Alps cross Austria in two main parallel chains, and between them lie warm, fertile valleys. The variation in altitude gives the country great variety of climate. The Austrian Tyrol district has impressive winter and summer resorts, which are as famous as those in the Swiss Alps. In the warmer valleys are industrial and cultural centers such as Vienna, the capital, Graz, Linz, and Innsbruck, as well as agricultural districts. The production of grains, vegetables, fruits (especially grapes), and tobacco, and livestock raising are the chief occupations of the people. The chief industries are metallurgy and metal products; textile trades are important. Austria has mineral deposits of iron, petroleum, gypsum, magnesite, graphite, and salt. Timber, before the extensive cutting of the forests during and after World War II, led the export list, which also included textiles, paper, leathers, and metal work.

BAHAMA ISLANDS

One of these numerous coral islands lying off the southeastern coast of Florida was the first land touched by Columbus in his historic search for a western route to the Far East. As far as can be determined, it was San Salvador. The land area of the group is 4,404 square miles. Some 20 of the islands are inhabited. The population is about 98,500. About 85 percent of the people are Negro. In former days the islands were the resort of pirates, among whom was the infamous "Blackbeard," Edward Teach.

The Bahamas are a British crown colony under the authority of a governor, who, together with a legislative council of 9, an executive council of 8, and an elected representative assembly of 29, manages the affairs of the island group.

Nassau, the capital, is a popular center for a growing tourist trade. The waters of the Atlantic provide excellent deep-sea fishing grounds. The Bahamas have a most agreeable climate, a mean temperature of 80° F. in the warm season (June to September) and 70° F. in the coldest season (January to March). The average rainfall is about 50 inches, and the shallow soil that covers the coral formation is made fertile by the use of fertilizers. Tomatoes and other vegetables are the principal crops. Crawfish, salt, and tomatoes comprise the islands' chief exports. Sisal and sponges, formerly among the chief exports of the colony, have diminished in importance.

Primary education is compulsory and free for children between the ages of 6 and 14. Higher education is provided at denominational schools, mainly in Nassau. English is generally spoken throughout the island group.

BAHREIN ISLANDS

The Bahrein Islands, a group of 5 low islands and a number of islets in the Persian Gulf, some 20 miles from the Arabian shore, are known for pearl fisheries and, since 1932, for a large production of petroleum under American auspices. The Bahrein Islands are ruled by a sheik under British protection; they have a total area of 213 square miles. The islands' population is about evenly divided between adherents of the Sunni and the Shia sects of Islam; there are also small communities of wealthy Indians, Persians, and a few thousand Americans and British living in the country. The occupations include boatbuilding, weaving, the manufacture of reed mats, and the breeding of fine white donkeys. Dates and hay are the chief crops. Exports include petroleum and pearls. Petroleum is of prime importance, and the Bahrein Islands' income is derived mainly from oil royalties. The population is about 120,000.

BELGIAN CONGO

Formerly called the Congo Free State, this Belgian colony in Africa is rich in copper, diamonds, gold, tin, cobalt, iron, and uranium. The Katanga district is one of the principal sources of the world's supply of pitchblende, from which uranium and radium are extracted; the district also is rich in reserves of copper and coal.

Belgian Congo has an area of 904,757 square miles. The population is about 12,660,000. There are relatively few Belgians and other Europeans, and they are engaged in government or business. The natives, some of them pygmies, live in small villages, scattered in the forests and grasslands. They speak various Bantu tongues; Bangala, Kingwana, Kikongo, Kiluba, and Lomongo are the commercial languages. Aside from a few million Christian converts, most of the tribes practice fetishism. They are slowly being educated by the cooperative efforts of native chiefs, missionaries, and the government. Leopoldville is the seat of the governor general. Elizabethville, Jadotville, Stanleyville, and Coquilhatville are important towns. Matadi, Boma, and Banana are the chief ports.

Much of the land is low river basin territory and produces cotton, nuts, coffee, cacao, sugar, and palms. Cattle raising is of increasing importance, although only in the areas where the tsetse fly does not flourish. The mountainous territory of the east and west has fine timber in an inexhaustible supply and also jungle-like forests of rubber trees. Wild animals such as elephants, rhinoceros, lions, leopards, and monkeys infest both the equatorial forests and the savannas.

Copper, diamonds, uranium, other minerals, palm oil, rubber, cotton, and ivory are the main exports. Industry is limited to the exploitation of resources, such as mining and the processing of rubber and palm oil.

BELGIUM

Belgium, constitutional monarchy, is bordered by the Netherlands, France, and Germany and has an area of 11,775 square miles. The population is about 8,896,000. The Walloons in the south are mainly of Celtic origin; the Flemings in the north, Teutonic. The latter speak Flemish, a form of Dutch; the Walloons speak French, often local dialects. In Brussels both languages are used. Both are official. German is spoken in some districts. Full religious liberty prevails, and all denominations are partly state supported. The major religion is Roman Catholicism. Education is free and universal for children between the ages of 6 and 14, and the universities of Ghent, Liège, Brussels, and Louvain are famous. The principal cities of Belgium are Brussels, the capital and heart of the country, Antwerp, Ghent, Liège, and Mechelen.

The climate is generally temperate, and the topography is monotonously level. As in the Netherlands, some of the Belgian land must be protected by dikes. Areas of poor soil have been carefully fertilized and worked, although agriculture in Belgium is less important than industry. Crops include grains, sugar and fodder beets, potatoes, tobacco, fruits, and vegetables. Stock raising and dairying are important. Belgium must, however, import much of its foodstuffs.

The country's resources include coal, iron, zinc, lead, and timber. It exports mainly the products of its metallurgical, engineering, textile, and chemical industries. Rivers and canal networks connect all of Belgium with the outside world. In 1948 an economic union came into effect among Belgium, the Netherlands, and Luxembourg (Benelux). A great world's fair was held in Brussels in 1958.

BERMUDA ISLANDS

This Atlantic Ocean group of 360 tiny islands, only 20 of which are inhabited, is a British crown colony, which lies about 580 miles east of the North Carolina coast. The land area is about 21 square miles. The population is about 41,160. Somewhat less than half the people are white, engaged in the lucrative tourist trade or governmental affairs. Most of the natives are half castes (Negro and Spanish). The English language is spoken throughout the islands. Most of the population belongs to the Anglican Church. Education is nominally compulsory for children between 7 and 13 years of age, but instruction is not absolutely free; the government does make grants to the schools, however.

Hamilton, the chief city, is the seat of the British governor, who, together with an executive council of 7, a legislative council of 11, and an elected representative body of 36 members, manages the official affairs of the colony. In 1940 the United States leased air and naval bases on the islands from Great Britain.

The mild and healthful climate, plus interesting scenery, makes this British colony a famous winter and summer resort. The mean annual temperature is about 70° F. The relatively thin layer of soil covering the coral and limestone formations is very fertile, and garden vegetables, bananas, and flowers flourish. Lily bulbs, cut flowers, and potatoes are the chief exports.

BHUTAN

Bhutan, lying among the Eastern Himalayas north of Calcûtta, is more closely allied to Tibet in racial characteristics, language, and customs than it is to India. The area of the country is about 18,000 square miles. The original inhabitants were the Tephus, conquered in the 18th century by military invasion from Tibet. Other peoples are the Bhotiyas and the Nepalese. The population is about 700,000. Most of the people speak variations of the Tibetan language. The Bhutanese follow the Buddhism of Tibet, and there are numerous monasteries among the mountains in which the Buddhist priests pursue a life of contemplation and learning.

Bhutan is governed by a hereditary maharaja. Outside influence is negligible in internal affairs, but the maharaja accepts advice from the Indian government on external affairs and also receives an annual subsidy.

The lower altitudes are hot and steamy with some 200 inches of rain per year; the lofty, rugged mountains, which rise to heights of more than 24,000 feet in the north, are continually cold and bleak. The chief cities, such as Punakha, the capital, and Tashi Chho Dzong, are like fortresses or castles, naturally protected by towering crags and narrow passes. To travel between cities one must use pack horses or be carried over the mountain trails in chairs supported on poles carried by native porters. The chief industry is a primitive agriculture, the principal products being rice, corn, and millet. Lac and wax are obtained; some coarse textiles, muzzle-loading rifles, and steel swords are made.

BOLIVIA

Bolivia, an inland republic of South America, is hemmed in by Brazil, Peru, Chile, Argentina, and Paraguay. It has an area estimated at 416,040 square miles. The population is about 3,235,000. More than half the people are pure Indian, living mainly in the highlands. About a third are of mixed Indian and Spanish blood. The small minority of unmixed Spanish descent dominates business and government. Spanish is the language of the educated class, and the Indians speak Quechua or Aymará. Roman Catholicism is the state religion, and the church cooperates with municipalities to provide free and nominally compulsory primary education. However, school attendance is low, and over half the people are illiterate.

Sucre, named after the Bolivian patriot, is legally the capital and the seat of the judiciary, but La Paz is the actual executive and legislative center of the nation. Other important cities are Cochabamba, Oruro, Potosí, Santa Cruz, and Tarija.

Though Bolivia is wholly within the Torrid Zone, its climate varies from tropical to arctic characteristics. There are swamp forests, low-lying plains, high plateaus, and lofty Andes. The lowlands occupy about three-fourths of the area of Bolivia and are of little use, either for livestock or agriculture, though some areas above the flood level provide rich grazing land. The western part, which lies in the Andes, is one of the highest inhabited places of the world.

The mountain slopes and low forests are rich in timber, as yet unexploited. Deposits of silver, copper, gold, lead, zinc, antimony, important amounts of wolfram, and about 15 percent of the world's supply of tin make Bolivia a land of extraordinary resources. Petroleum and gas are extensive in the southeast. The mining industry flourishes, and small-scale stock raising is carried on. Agricultural areas produce potatoes, grains, sugar, rice, coffee, tobacco, and fruits, depending on location. Tin and other ores are the main exports.

BORNEO

The island of Borneo, part of the Malay Archipelago, is divided between Indonesian and British administration and has an area of 286,969 square miles and a population of about 4,000,000. The people are Malays, Dyaks, and Chinese; a considerable number of Europeans and Eurasians live in some areas. The native languages are nearly all some branch of the Malay tongue, and religious practices are either pagan rituals (though missionaries have made some converts to Christianity), Mohammedanism, or Buddhism. Education of the natives was first instituted by the Netherlands and Great Britain.

The climate of the island is equatorial and enervating. The temperatures are generally high, and there is much rainfall. Mountainous in character, Borneo's highest peak (13,455 feet) is Kinabalu, at the northern end of the island. The shores are usually sandy marshes and swamplike. The inland regions of Borneo are full of wild animals, and the fierceness of the native tribes has created legends of the Wild Men of Borneo.

Borneo is rich in resources, having petroleum, which made Borneo a rich prize for the Japanese during World War II, as well as diamonds, gold, copper, iron, antimony, sulfur, marble, coal, mercury, timber, and salt. Mining, ironwork, and agriculture are the chief industries. Rubber, gutta-percha, camphor, and cinnamon are the chief forest products. Sugar cane, vegetables, fruits, coffee, rice, and tobacco are the principal crops. Trade is carried on mainly in petroleum, timber, dried fish, and pepper and other spices.

Indonesian Borneo, formerly called Dutch Borneo, includes the largest part of the island, about 208,285 square miles. The capital is Bandjermasin. Tarakan and Balikpapan have famous oil fields. In 1950 the area became part of the new republic of Indonesia.

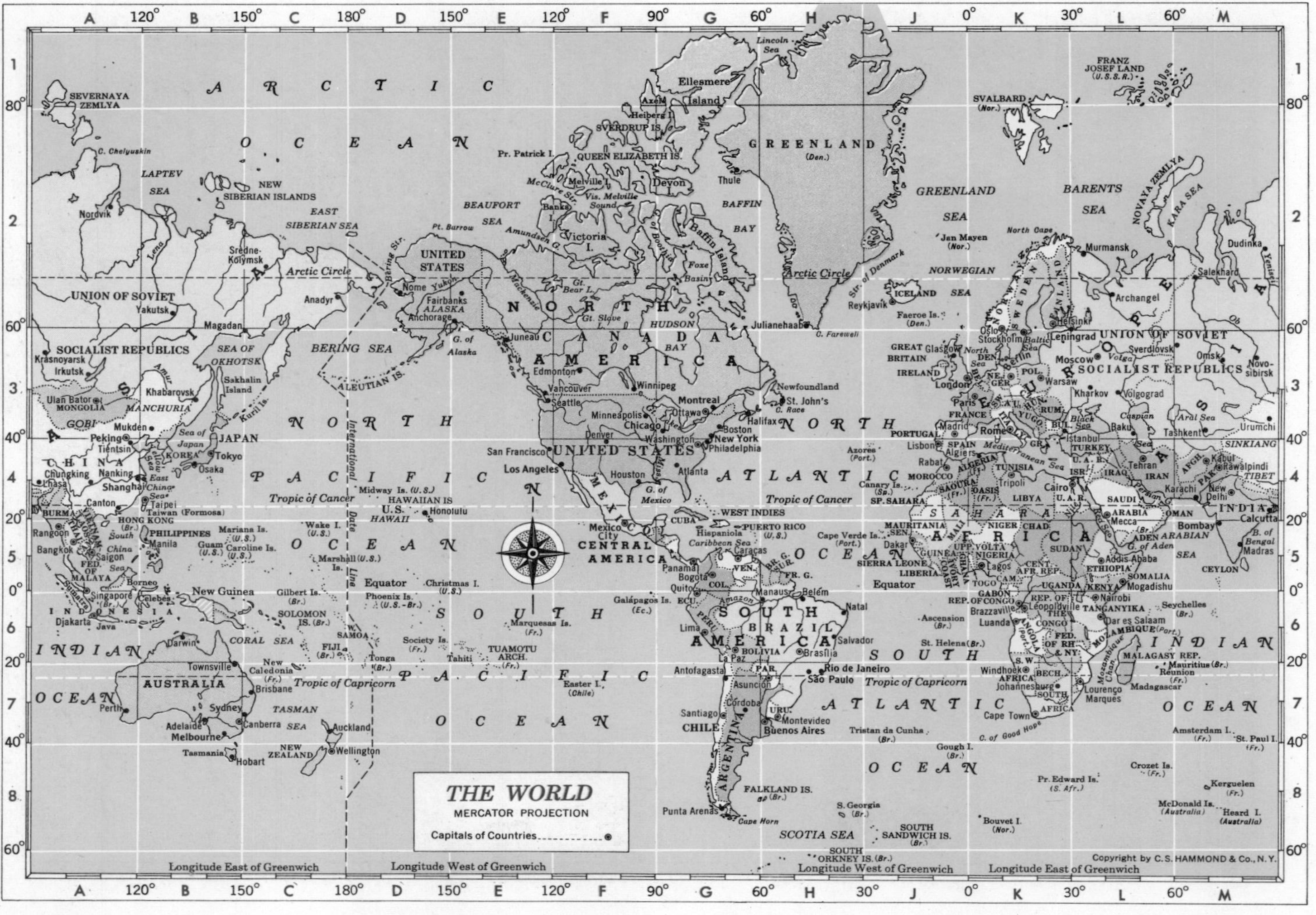
THE WORLD
MERCATOR PROJECTION
Capitals of Countries
Copyright by C. S. HAMMOND & Co., N. Y.
Longitude East of Greenwich
Longitude West of Greenwich
Longitude West of Greenwich
Longitude East of Greenwich
A 120° B 150° C 180° D 150° E 120° F 90° G 60° H 30° J 0° K 30° L 60° M
1 80° 2 60° 3 40° 4 20° 5 0° 6 20° 7 40° 8 60°
ARCTIC OCEAN
NORTH PACIFIC OCEAN
SOUTH PACIFIC OCEAN
NORTH ATLANTIC OCEAN
SOUTH ATLANTIC OCEAN
INDIAN OCEAN
Tropic of Cancer
Tropic of Capricorn
Equator
Arctic Circle
International Date Line
SEVERNAYA ZEMLYA
C. Chelyuskin
LAPTEV SEA
NEW SIBERIAN ISLANDS
EAST SIBERIAN SEA
Nordvik
Sredne-Kolymsk
Anadyr
Yakutsk
Magadan
UNION OF SOVIET SOCIALIST REPUBLICS
Krasnoyarsk
Irkutsk
SEA OF OKHOTSK
Sakhalin Island
Khabarovsk
Ulan Bator
MONGOLIA
MANCHURIA
GOBI
Mukden
Peking
Tientsin
KOREA
Sea of Japan
JAPAN
Tokyo
Osaka
CHINA
Chungking
Lhasa
Nanking
Shanghai
East China Sea
Taipei
Taiwan (Formosa)
Canton
HONG KONG (Br.)
BURMA
Rangoon
Bangkok
Saigon
PHILIPPINES
Manila
South China Sea
MALAYA
Singapore
Borneo
Celebes
INDONESIA
Djakarta
Java
Sumatra
New Guinea
Darwin
AUSTRALIA
Townsville
Brisbane
Sydney
Canberra
Adelaide
Melbourne
Perth
Tasmania
Hobart
CORAL SEA
TASMAN SEA
NEW ZEALAND
Auckland
Wellington
New Caledonia (Fr.)
FIJI (Br.)
W. SAMOA
Tonga (Br.)
SOLOMON IS. (Br.)
Gilbert Is. (Br.)
Marshall (U.S.) Is.
Wake I. (U.S.)
Mariana Is. (U.S.)
Guam (U.S.)
Caroline Is. (U.S.)
Midway Is. (U.S.)
HAWAIIAN IS
U.S.
HAWAII
Honolulu
Christmas I. (U.S.)
Phoenix Is. (U.S.-Br.)
Society Is. (Fr.)
Tahiti
Marquesas Is. (Fr.)
TUAMOTU ARCH. (Fr.)
Easter I. (Chile)
Galápagos Is. (Ec.)
BERING SEA
ALEUTIAN IS.
Bering Str.
Nome
Fairbanks
ALASKA
Anchorage
G. of Alaska
UNITED STATES
Pt. Barrow
BEAUFORT SEA
Pr. Patrick I.
QUEEN ELIZABETH IS.
SVERDRUP IS.
Ellesmere Island
Axel
Heibers I.
Melville I.
McClure Str.
Vis. Melville Sound
Banks I.
Victoria I.
Amundsen G.
Devon I.
G. of Boothia
Baffin Island
Foxe Basin
BAFFIN BAY
Thule
Lincoln Sea
GREENLAND (Den.)
Julianehaab
C. Farewell
Str. of Denmark
Gt. Bear L.
Gt. Slave L.
Mackenzie
NORTH AMERICA
CANADA
HUDSON BAY
Juneau
Edmonton
Vancouver
Seattle
Winnipeg
Montreal
Ottawa
Newfoundland
St. John's
C. Race
Halifax
Boston
New York
Philadelphia
Washington
Minneapolis
Chicago
Denver
San Francisco
Los Angeles
UNITED STATES
Houston
Atlanta
G. of Mexico
MEXICO
Mexico City
CENTRAL AMERICA
CUBA
WEST INDIES
Hispaniola
PUERTO RICO (U.S.)
Caribbean Sea
Caracas
Panama
Bogota
VEN.
BR. G.
SUR.
FR. G.
COL.
Quito
ECU.
PERU
Lima
Manaus
Amazon
Belém
SOUTH AMERICA
BRAZIL
Natal
Salvador
Brasília
BOLIVIA
La Paz
PAR.
Asunción
Antofagasta
Rio de Janeiro
São Paulo
Córdoba
URU.
Montevideo
Buenos Aires
Santiago
CHILE
ARGENTINA
FALKLAND IS. (Br.)
Punta Arenas
Cape Horn
SCOTIA SEA
S. Georgia (Br.)
SOUTH SANDWICH IS. (Br.)
SOUTH ORKNEY IS. (Br.)
Tristan da Cunha (Br.)
Gough I. (Br.)
St. Helena (Br.)
Ascension (Br.)
Bouvet I. (Nor.)
GREENLAND SEA
Jan Mayen (Nor.)
NORWEGIAN SEA
ICELAND
Reykjavik
Faeroe Is. (Den.)
SVALBARD (Nor.)
FRANZ JOSEF LAND (U.S.S.R.)
BARENTS SEA
NOVAYA ZEMLYA
KARA SEA
North Cape
Murmansk
Archangel
Dudinka
Salekhard
Yenisei
Ob
GREAT BRITAIN
Glasgow
IRELAND
London
North Sea
Oslo
Stockholm
SWEDEN
FINLAND
Helsinki
Leningrad
Baltic Sea
DEN.
Berlin
POL.
Warsaw
NE.
GER.
Paris
FRANCE
Madrid
SPAIN
PORTUGAL
Lisbon
Rome
HUN.
RUM.
YUGO.
BUL.
GR.
Black Sea
Istanbul
Mediterranean Sea
Moscow
Volga
Kharkov
Volgograd
Sverdlovsk
Omsk
Novosibirsk
Caspian Sea
Aral Sea
Tashkent
Urumchi
SINKIANG
TIBET
Baku
TURKEY
U.A.R.
ISR.
IRAQ
Tehran
IRAN
AFGH.
PAK.
Kabul
Rawalpindi
Karachi
New Delhi
INDIA
Calcutta
Bombay
B. of Bengal
Madras
CEYLON
ARABIAN SEA
SAUDI ARABIA
Mecca
ADEN
G. of Aden
OMAN
Red Sea
Azores (Port.)
Canary Is. (Sp.)
Rabat
MOROCCO
Algiers
ALGERIA
TUNISIA
Tripoli
LIBYA
Cairo
SAHARA
SP. SAHARA
MAURITANIA
MALI
NIGER
CHAD
SUDAN
SEN.
Dakar
Cape Verde Is. (Port.)
GUINEA
SIERRA LEONE
LIBERIA
IVORY COAST
GHANA
UPP. VOLTA
NIGERIA
Lagos
TOGO
CAM.
CENT. AFR. REP.
GABON
REP. OF CONGO
Brazzaville
Léopoldville
THE CONGO
AFRICA
ETHIOPIA
Addis Ababa
SOMALIA
Mogadishu
UGANDA
KENYA
Nairobi
TANGANYIKA
Dar es Salaam
Luanda
ANGOLA (Port.)
FED. OF RH. & NY.
MOZAMBIQUE (Port.)
Mozambique Chan.
MALAGASY REP.
Madagascar
Seychelles (Br.)
Mauritius (Br.)
Réunion (Fr.)
S. W. AFRICA
Windhoek
BECH.
Johannesburg
SOUTH AFRICA
Lourenço Marques
Cape Town
C. of Good Hope
Pr. Edward Is. (S. Afr.)
Crozet Is. (Fr.)
Amsterdam I. (Fr.)
St. Paul I. (Fr.)
Kerguelen (Fr.)
McDonald Is. (Australia)
Heard I. (Australia)

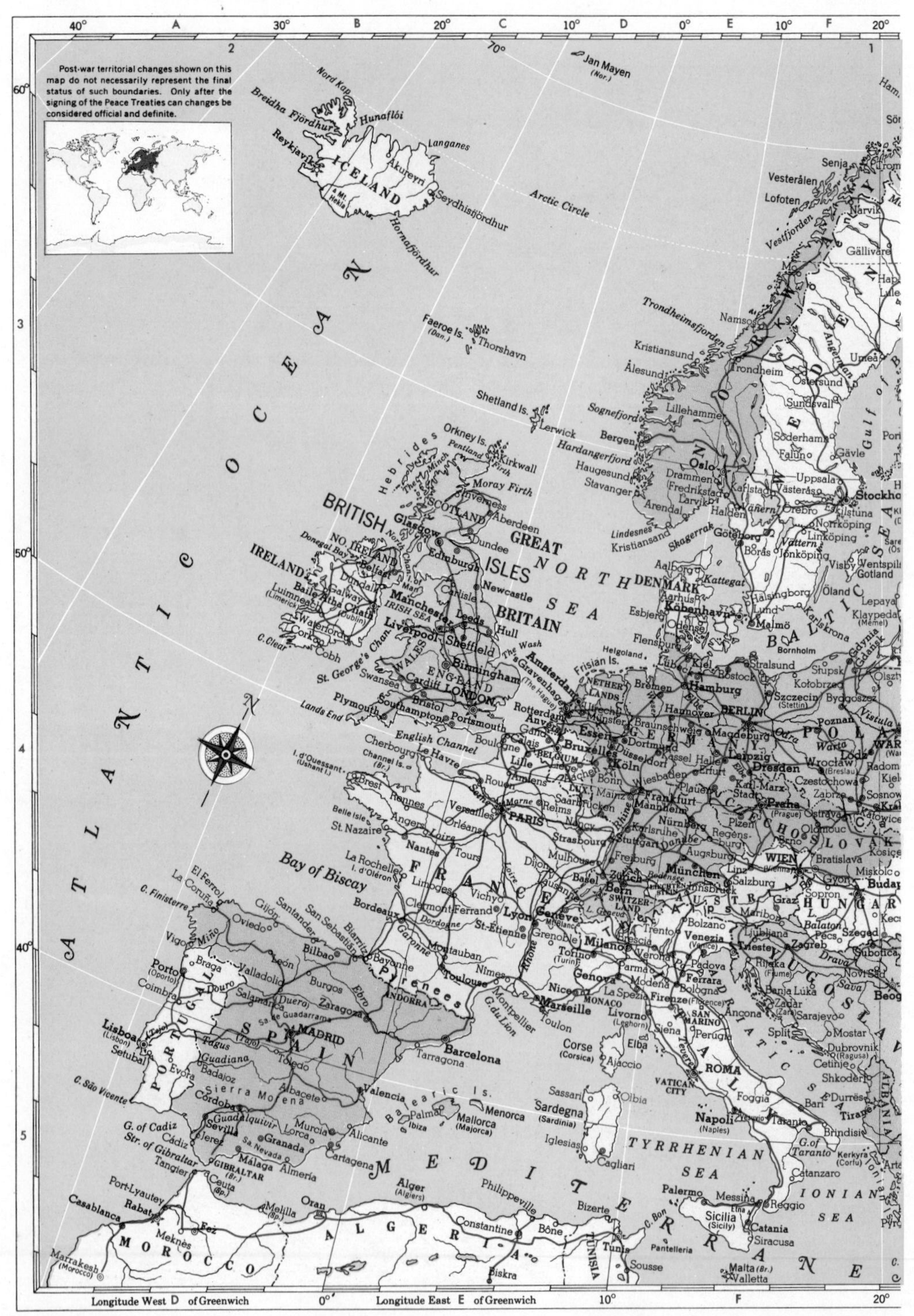

Post-war territorial changes shown on this map do not necessarily represent the final status of such boundaries. Only after the signing of the Peace Treaties can changes be considered official and definite.
40°
A
30°
B
20°
C
10°
D
0°
E
10°
F
20°
60°
50°
40°
70°
Jan Mayen (Nor.)
Nord Kap
Breidha Fjördhur
Hunaflói
Reykjavik
ICELAND
Akureyri
Langanes
Seydhisfjördhur
Hornafjördhur
Arctic Circle
ATLANTIC OCEAN
Faeroe Is. (Dan.)
Thorshavn
Shetland Is.
Lerwick
Orkney Is.
Kirkwall
Moray Firth
Hebrides
BRITISH ISLES
SCOTLAND
Inverness
Aberdeen
Glasgow
Edinburgh
Dundee
GREAT BRITAIN
NO. IRELAND
Belfast
IRELAND
Donegal Bay
Galway
Dundalk
Baile Átha Cliath (Dublin)
Luimneach (Limerick)
Waterford
Cork
Cobh
C. Clear
Newcastle
Carlisle
Manchester
Leeds
Hull
Liverpool
Sheffield
IRISH SEA
WALES
St. George's Chan.
Birmingham
ENGLAND
Swansea
Cardiff
LONDON
Bristol
Plymouth
Southampton
Portsmouth
Lands End
The Wash
NORTH SEA
English Channel
Channel Is. (Br.)
I. d'Ouessant (Ushant I.)
Cherbourg
Le Havre
Brest
Rennes
Belle Isle
St. Nazaire
Angers
Nantes
Loire
Tours
Orléans
Versailles
PARIS
Rouen
Amiens
Lille
Boulogne
Calais
Reims
Marne
Bay of Biscay
La Rochelle
I. d'Oléron
Limoges
Bordeaux
Dordogne
Garonne
Clermont Ferrand
Vichy
Lyon
St.-Étienne
Dijon
FRANCE
Grenoble
Montauban
Toulouse
Nîmes
Montpellier
Marseille
Toulon
Nice
MONACO
G. du Lion
Pyrenees
ANDORRA
Bayonne
Biarritz
San Sebastián
Bilbao
Santander
Gijón
Oviedo
La Coruña
El Ferrol
C. Finisterre
Vigo
Miño
León
Burgos
Ebro
Valladolid
Douro
Duero
Salamanca
Zaragoza
Guadarrama
MADRID
SPAIN
Tajo
Tagus
Toledo
Guadiana
Badajoz
Barcelona
Tarragona
Valencia
Albacete
Sierra Morena
Córdoba
Guadalquivir
Sevilla
Murcia
Lorca
Alicante
Cartagena
Granada
Sa. Nevada
Málaga
Almería
Jerez
Cádiz
G. of Cadiz
Str. of Gibraltar
GIBRALTAR (Br.)
Ceuta (Sp.)
Tangier
Porto (Oporto)
Braga
Coimbra
Lisboa (Lisbon)
Setúbal
Évora
PORTUGAL
C. São Vicente
Balearic Is.
Palma
Mallorca (Majorca)
Menorca
Ibiza
Port-Lyautey
Rabat
Casablanca
Fez
Meknès
Marrakesh (Morocco)
MOROCCO
Melilla (Sp.)
Oran
Alger (Algiers)
Philippeville
Constantine
Bône
Biskra
ALGERIA
Bizerte
Tunis
Sousse
TUNISIA
C. Bon
Pantelleria
MEDITERRANEAN
Corse (Corsica)
Ajaccio
Sardegna (Sardinia)
Sassari
Olbia
Iglesias
Cagliari
TYRRHENIAN SEA
Sicilia (Sicily)
Palermo
Messina
Catania
Siracusa
Reggio
Malta (Br.)
Valletta
IONIAN SEA
Napoli (Naples)
Foggia
Bari
Taranto
G. of Taranto
Brindisi
Catanzaro
ROMA
VATICAN CITY
Elba
Livorno (Leghorn)
Siena
Perugia
Firenze (Florence)
SAN MARINO
Bologna
Ancona
La Spezia
Genova
Torino (Turin)
Milano
Verona
Parma
Modena
Ferrara
Padova
Venezia (Venice)
Trieste
Bolzano
Trento
ITALY
ADRIATIC SEA
Genève
L. Geneva
Bern
Basel
Zürich
SWITZERLAND
Mulhouse
Strasbourg
Nancy
Saarbrücken
LUX.
Bruxelles
BELGIUM
Antwerpen
Gand
Rotterdam
The Hague
'sGravenhage
Amsterdam
NETHERLANDS
Utrecht
Frisian Is.
Helgoland
Essen
Dortmund
Düsseldorf
Köln
Bonn
Aachen
Wiesbaden
Mainz
Frankfurt
Mannheim
Karlsruhe
Stuttgart
Nürnberg
Regensburg
Augsburg
München
Freiburg
Danube
Rhine
Kassel
Erfurt
Münster
Bremen
Hamburg
Hannover
Braunschweig
Magdeburg
Leipzig
Halle
Dresden
Karl-Marx-Stadt
Plauen
BERLIN
Elbe
Oder
Lübeck
Kiel
Rostock
Stralsund
GERMANY
Salzburg
Innsbruck
Linz
WIEN
Graz
AUSTRIA
Maribor
Ljubljana
Zagreb
Rijeka (Fiume)
Zadar (Zara)
Split
Sarajevo
Mostar
Dubrovnik (Ragusa)
Cetinje
Shkodër
Durrës
Tirane
ALBANIA
Banja Luka
Novi Sad
Subotica
Beograd
Drava
Sava
YUGOSLAVIA
Pécs
Szeged
Balaton
Sopron
Gyor
Budapest
HUNGARY
Bratislava
Miskolc
Košice
Praha (Prague)
Plzeň
Brno
Olomouc
Ostrava
CZECHOSLOVAKIA
Katowice
Zabrze
Częstochowa
Wrocław (Breslau)
Łódź
Poznań
Bydgoszcz
Warta
Vistula
Szczecin (Stettin)
Kołobrzeg
Słupsk
Gdynia
Gdańsk
POLAND
Bornholm
BALTIC SEA
Klaypeda (Memel)
Lepaya
Ventspils
Visby
Gotland
Öland
Karlskrona
Malmö
Lund
Hälsingborg
København
Odense
Esbjerg
Aarhus
Aalborg
Flensburg
DENMARK
Kattegat
Skagerrak
Göteborg
Borås
Jönköping
Vättern
Linköping
Norrköping
Eskilstuna
Örebro
Västerås
Stockholm
Uppsala
Gävle
Falun
Söderhamn
Sundsvall
Östersund
Umeå
Lulea
Gällivare
Narvik
Ångerman
Gulf of Bothnia
Vänern
Karlstad
Halden
Arendal
Kristiansand
Lindesnes
Stavanger
Haugesund
Hardangerfjord
Bergen
Sognefjord
Lillehammer
Oslo
Drammen
Fredrikstad
Larvik
Ålesund
Kristiansund
Trondheim
Trondheimsfjorden
Namsos
Vestfjorden
Lofoten
Vesterålen
Senja
NORWAY
SWEDEN
Longitude West D of Greenwich
Longitude East E of Greenwich

EUROPE
LAMBERT AZIMUTHAL EQUAL-AREA PROJECTION
SCALE OF MILES
0 100 200 300 400 500
SCALE OF KILOMETRES
0 100 200 300 400 500
Capitals of Countries
International Boundaries
Canals
Railroads
Copyright by C.S. HAMMOND & CO., N.Y.
BARENTS SEA
BLACK SEA
CASPIAN SEA
UNION OF SOVIET SOCIALIST REPUBLICS
RUSSIAN SOVIET FEDERATED SOCIALIST REPUBLIC
TURKEY
MOSKVA (Moscow)
LENINGRAD
Kiev
Kharkov
Stockholm
Helsinki (Helsingfors)
WARSZAWA (Warsaw)
Bucuresti (Bucharest)
Istanbul (Constantinople)
Ankara (Angora)
Budapest
Beograd
Sofiya
Athenai
Tbilisi
Baku
Sverdlovsk
Kuibyshev (Samara)
Gorki
Volgograd (Stalingrad)

ATLANTIC OCEAN
GREENLAND
UNITED STATES
ALASKA
North Pole
ARCTIC OCEAN
BERING SEA
Aleutian Is.
PACIFIC OCEAN
Iceland
NORTH SEA
BARENTS SEA
KARA SEA
LAPTEVYKH SEA
SEA OF OKHOTSK
SEA OF JAPAN
BALTIC SEA
BLACK SEA
CASPIAN SEA
MEDITERRANEAN SEA
ADRIATIC SEA
RED SEA
UNION OF SOVIET SOCIALIST REPUBLICS
MONGOLIA
MANCHURIA
CHINA
TIBET
SINKIANG
INNER MONGOLIA
JAPAN
TURKEY
IRAQ
IRAN (PERSIA)
SAUDI ARABIA
AFGHANISTAN
PAKISTAN
KASHMIR
Arctic Circle
Tropic of Cancer
London
Paris
Berlin
Moskva
Leningrad
Warszawa
Wien
Budapest
Istanbul
Ankara
Tehran
Baghdad
Kabul
New Delhi
Lhasa
Peiping
Nanking
Shanghai
Seoul
Tokyo
Vladivostok
Irkutsk
Novosibirsk
Sverdlovsk
Tashkent
Ulan Bator
Kunlun Mountains
Trans-Himalaya
Ural Mts.
Caucasus
Stanovoi Mts.
Kamchatka
Sakhalin I.
Novaya Zemlya
Severnaya Zemlya
New Siberian Is.
Wrangel I.

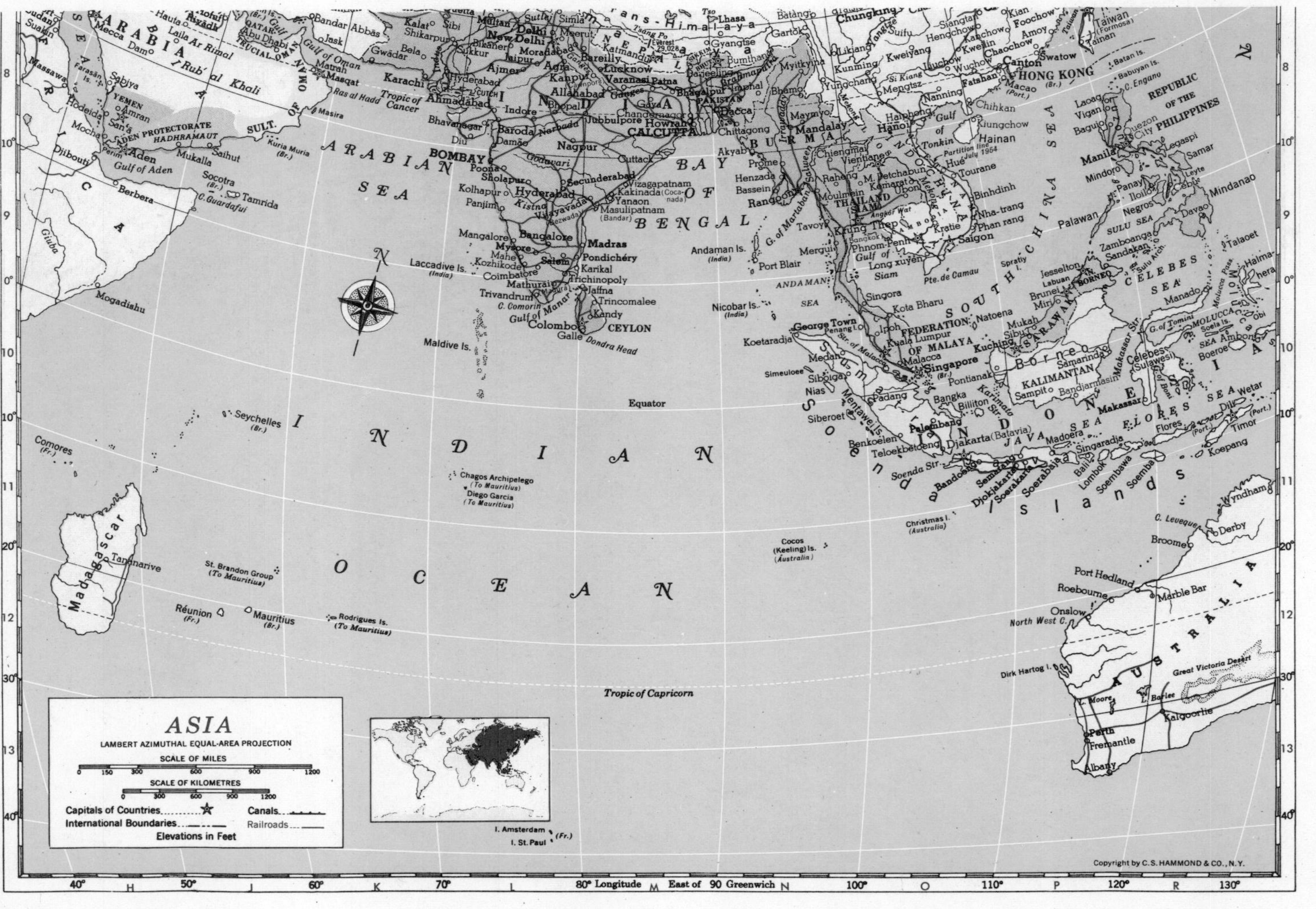
ASIA
LAMBERT AZIMUTHAL EQUAL-AREA PROJECTION
SCALE OF MILES
0 150 300 600 900 1200
SCALE OF KILOMETRES
0 300 600 900 1200
Capitals of Countries
International Boundaries
Elevations in Feet
Canals
Railroads
INDIAN OCEAN
ARABIAN SEA
BAY OF BENGAL
SOUTH CHINA SEA
INDONESIA
AUSTRALIA
BURMA
THAILAND
CEYLON
FEDERATION OF MALAYA
REPUBLIC OF THE PHILIPPINES
HONG KONG (Br.)
ADEN PROTECTORATE
YEMEN
SARAWAK
KALIMANTAN
Madagascar
Tropic of Cancer
Equator
Tropic of Capricorn
BOMBAY
CALCUTTA
Madras
New Delhi
Colombo
Singapore
Manila
Saigon
Rangoon
Djakarta (Batavia)
Perth
Seychelles (Br.)
Mauritius (Br.)
Réunion (Fr.)
Maldive Is.
Laccadive Is. (India)
Andaman Is. (India)
Nicobar Is. (India)
Chagos Archipelego (To Mauritius)
Cocos (Keeling) Is. (Australia)
Christmas I. (Australia)
I. Amsterdam (Fr.)
I. St. Paul
Copyright by C. S. HAMMOND & CO., N.Y.
40° 50° 60° 70° 80° Longitude East of 90 Greenwich 100° 110° 120° 130°

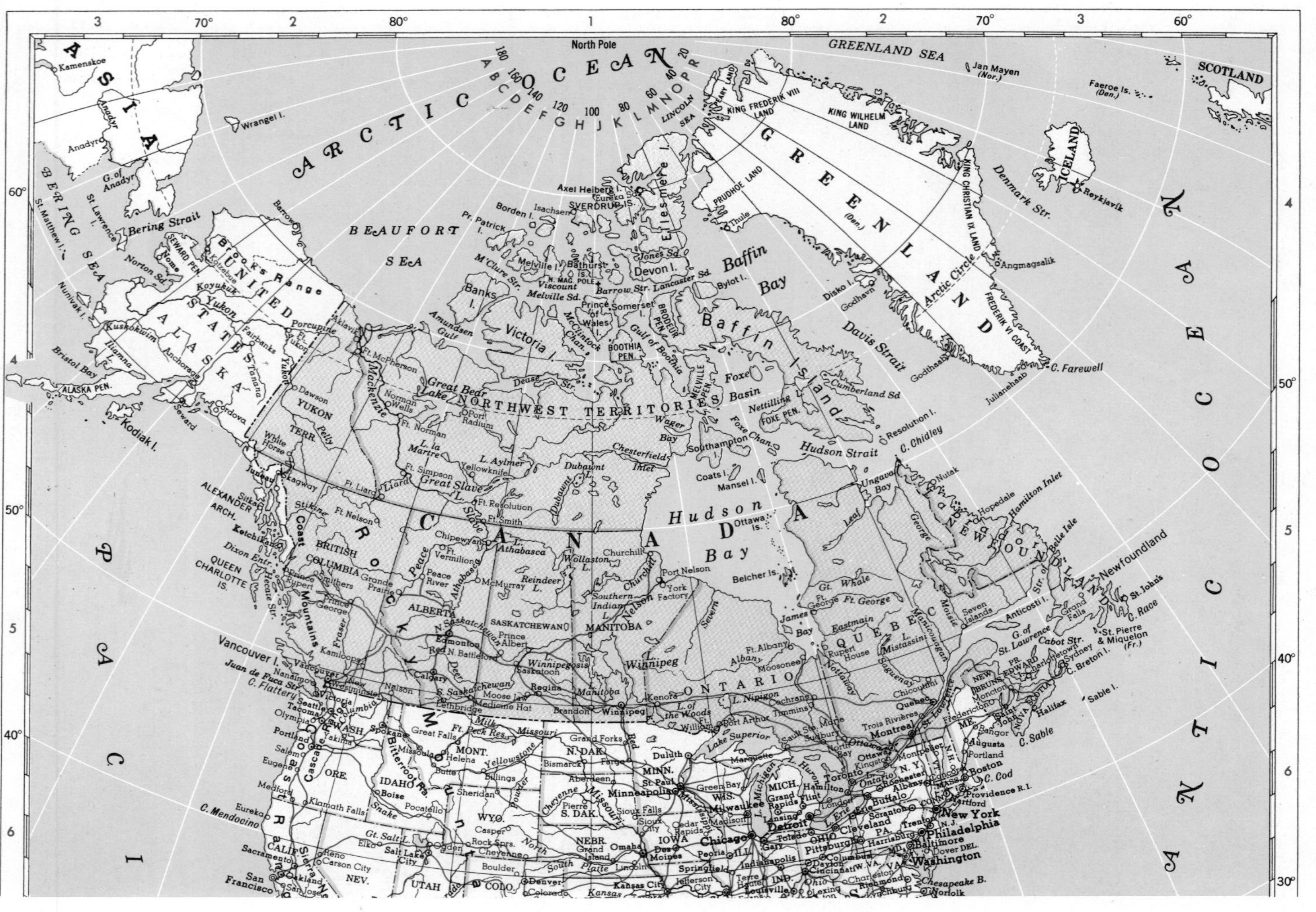

North Pole
ARCTIC OCEAN
GREENLAND SEA
BEAUFORT SEA
BERING SEA
ASIA
GREENLAND
(Den.)
ICELAND
Reykjavik
SCOTLAND
Faeroe Is. (Den.)
Jan Mayen (Nor.)
Denmark Str.
Davis Strait
Baffin Bay
Baffin Island
Hudson Strait
Hudson Bay
Foxe Basin
Ellesmere I.
Devon I.
Victoria I.
Banks I.
NORTHWEST TERRITORIES
YUKON TERR.
CANADA
ALASKA
UNITED STATES
Brooks Range
Bering Strait
Kodiak I.
Great Bear Lake
Great Slave L.
Mackenzie
BRITISH COLUMBIA
ALBERTA
SASKATCHEWAN
MANITOBA
ONTARIO
QUEBEC
Newfoundland
Arctic Circle
C. Farewell
C. Chidley
Hudson
Winnipeg
Montreal
Quebec
Halifax
Boston
New York
Philadelphia
Washington
Chicago
Detroit
Cleveland
Minneapolis
Denver
Vancouver I.
Seattle
San Francisco
QUEEN CHARLOTTE IS.
ALEXANDER ARCH.
Coast Mountains
ATLANTIC OCEAN
PACIFIC

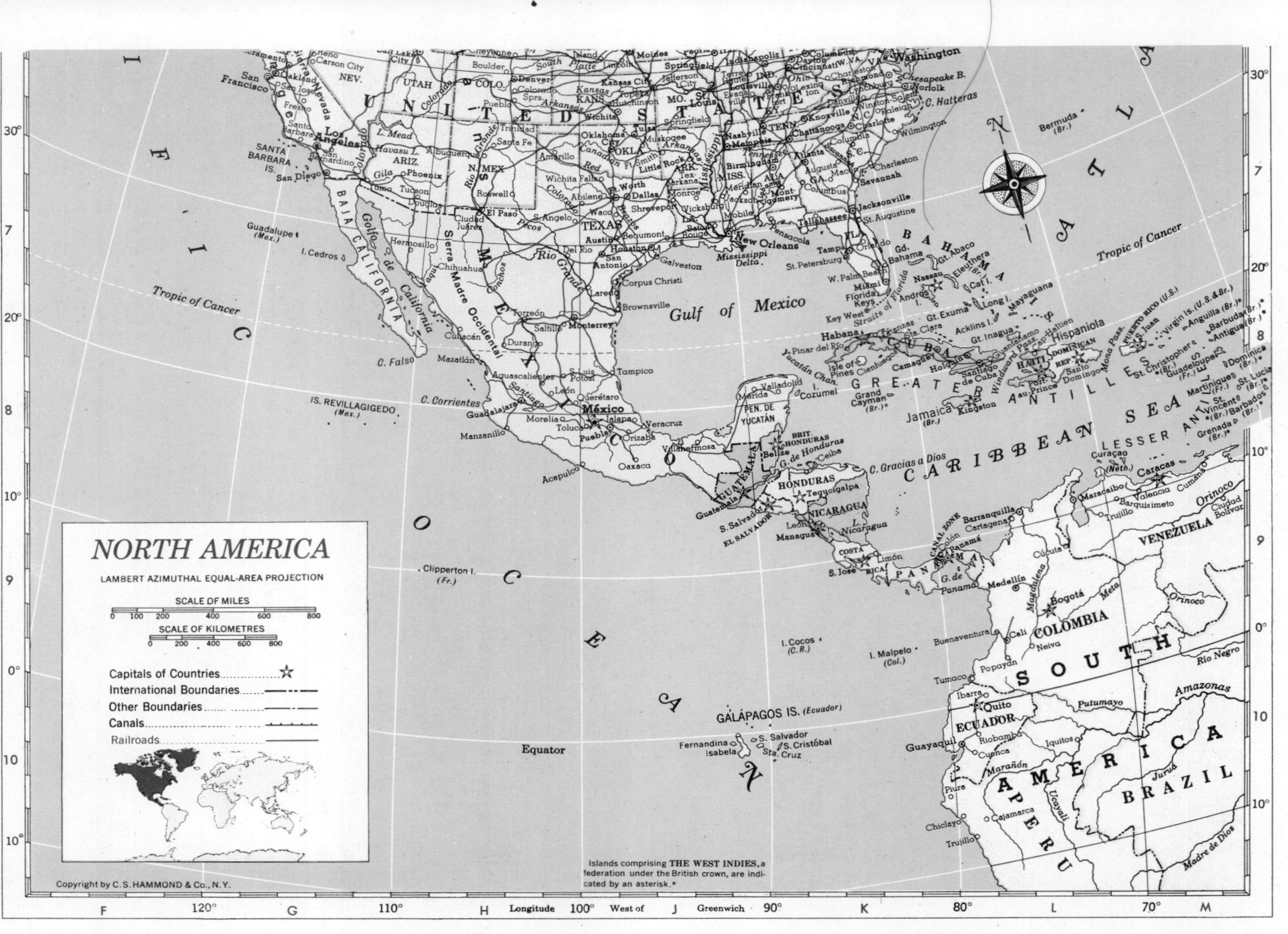

NORTH AMERICA
LAMBERT AZIMUTHAL EQUAL-AREA PROJECTION
SCALE OF MILES
0 100 200 400 600 800
SCALE OF KILOMETRES
0 200 400 600 800
Capitals of Countries
International Boundaries
Other Boundaries
Canals
Railroads
Islands comprising THE WEST INDIES, a federation under the British crown, are indicated by an asterisk.*
Copyright by C. S. HAMMOND & Co., N. Y.
Longitude West of Greenwich
F 120° G 110° H 100° J 90° K 80° L 70° M
UNITED STATES
MEXICO
Gulf of Mexico
CARIBBEAN SEA
GREATER ANTILLES
LESSER ANTILLES
PACIFIC OCEAN
SOUTH AMERICA
Tropic of Cancer
Equator
BAJA CALIFORNIA
Golfo de California
Sierra Madre Occidental
Washington
New Orleans
México
Habana
HONDURAS
NICARAGUA
COSTA RICA
PANAMA
GUATEMALA
EL SALVADOR
BRIT. HONDURAS
PEN. DE YUCATÁN
CANAL ZONE
COLOMBIA
VENEZUELA
ECUADOR
PERU
BRAZIL
Hispaniola
HAITI
DOMINICAN REP.
Jamaica (Br.)
BAHAMA IS.
Bermuda (Br.)
GALÁPAGOS IS. (Ecuador)
IS. REVILLAGIGEDO (Mex.)
Clipperton I. (Fr.)
I. Cocos (C.R.)
I. Malpelo (Col.)
Guadalupe I. (Mex.)
SANTA BARBARA IS.
Bogotá
Caracas
Quito
Amazonas
Orinoco
Rio Negro
Rio Grande

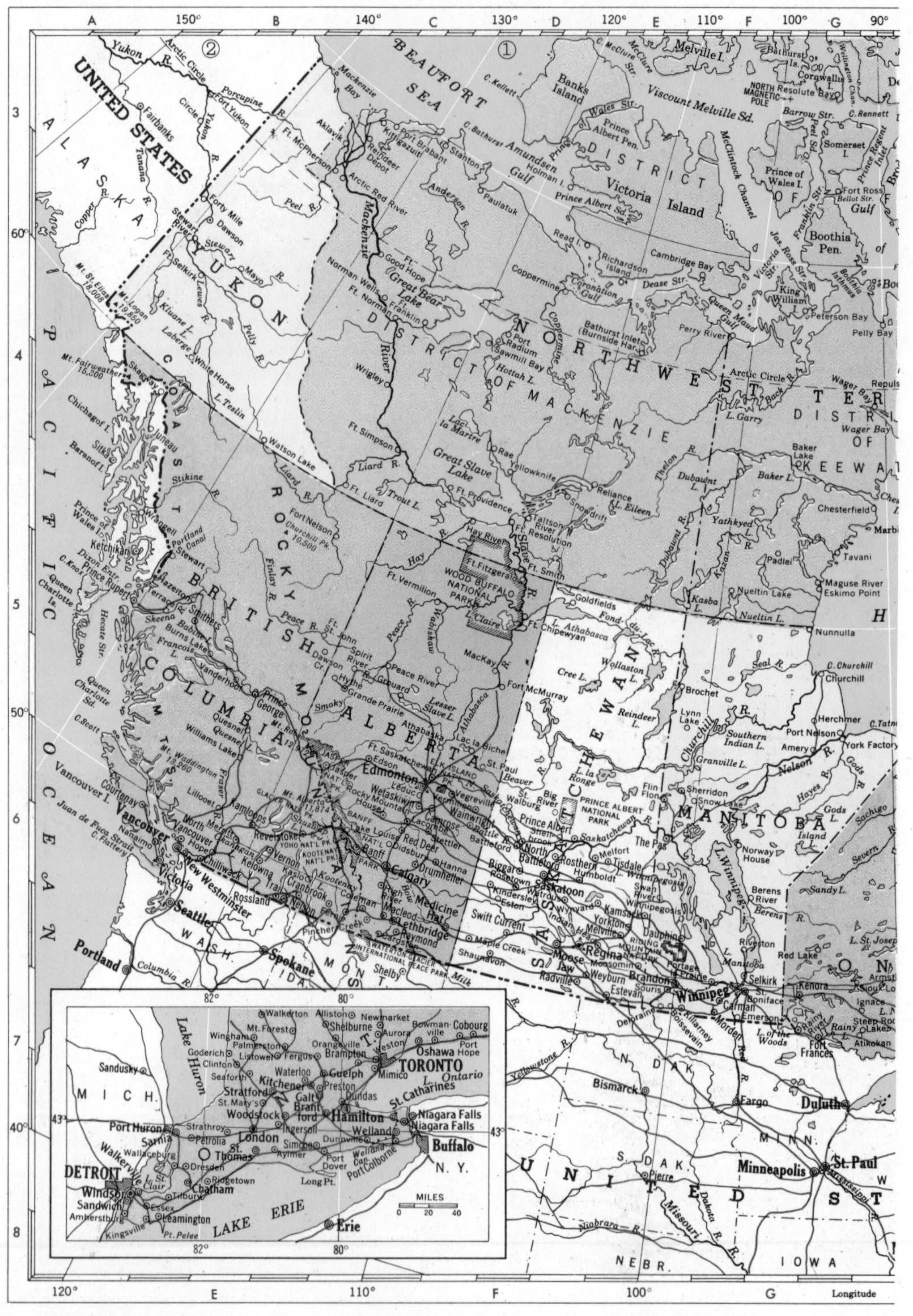

BEAUFORT SEA
UNITED STATES
ALASKA
YUKON
DISTRICT OF MACKENZIE
NORTHWEST TERRITORIES
DISTRICT OF FRANKLIN
DISTRICT OF KEEWATIN
BRITISH COLUMBIA
ALBERTA
SASKATCHEWAN
MANITOBA
PACIFIC OCEAN
Banks Island
Victoria Island
Great Bear Lake
Great Slave Lake
L. Athabasca
Lake Winnipeg
Edmonton
Calgary
Vancouver
Victoria
Seattle
Portland
Spokane
Regina
Saskatoon
Winnipeg
Fargo
Duluth
Minneapolis
St. Paul
Bismarck
Lake Huron
Lake Erie
L. Ontario
TORONTO
Hamilton
London
DETROIT
Windsor
Buffalo
Niagara Falls
MICH.
N.Y.
MILES
Longitude

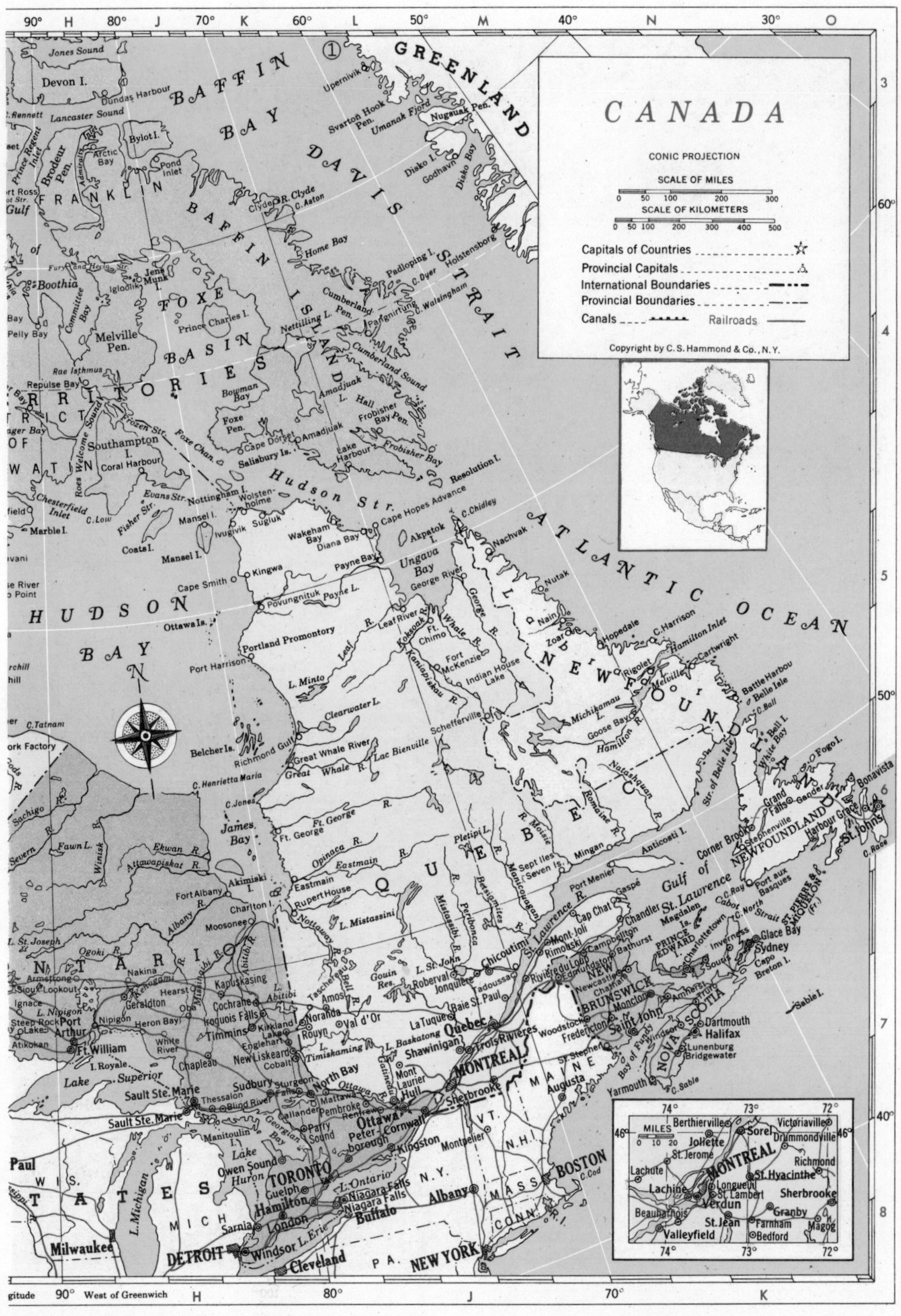
CANADA
CONIC PROJECTION
SCALE OF MILES
0 50 100 200 300
SCALE OF KILOMETERS
0 50 100 200 300 400 500
Capitals of Countries
Provincial Capitals
International Boundaries
Provincial Boundaries
Canals
Railroads
Copyright by C. S. Hammond & Co., N.Y.
90° H 80° J 70° K 60° L 50° M 40° N 30° O
3
4
5
6
7
8
60°
50°
40°
gitude 90° West of Greenwich H 100° 80° J 70° K
BAFFIN BAY
DAVIS STRAIT
GREENLAND
BAFFIN ISLAND
FOXE BASIN
HUDSON BAY
Hudson Str.
Ungava Bay
ATLANTIC OCEAN
NEWFOUNDLAND
QUEBEC
ONTARIO
NEW BRUNSWICK
NOVA SCOTIA
PRINCE EDWARD I.
Gulf of St. Lawrence
MAINE
VT.
N.H.
MASS.
CONN.
R.I.
N.Y.
PA.
MICH.
WIS.
Devon I.
Jones Sound
Lancaster Sound
Dundas Harbour
Bylot I.
Pond Inlet
Arctic Bay
Upernivik
Umanak Fjord
Nugsuak Pen.
Disko I.
Godhavn
Disko Bay
Holstensborg
Clyde
C. Aston
Home Bay
Padloping I.
C. Dyer
Cumberland Pen.
Pangnirtung
C. Walsingham
Cumberland Sound
Nettilling L.
Amadjuak L.
Hall
Frobisher Bay
Lake Harbour
Resolution I.
Cape Dorset
Amadjuak
Salisbury Is.
Nottingham I.
Southampton I.
Coral Harbour
Foxe Chan.
Melville Pen.
Boothia
Igloolik
Prince Charles I.
Repulse Bay
Rae Isthmus
Chesterfield Inlet
Marble I.
Mansel I.
Coats I.
Ivugivik
Sugluk
Wakeham Bay
Diana Bay
Cape Hopes Advance
Akpatok I.
C. Chidley
Payne Bay
Payne L.
Kingwa
Cape Smith
Povungnituk
George River
Leaf River
Ft. Chimo
Fort McKenzie
Nachvak
Nutak
Nain
Zoar
Hopedale
C. Harrison
Hamilton Inlet
Cartwright
Rigolet
L. Melville
Michikamau L.
Goose Bay
Battle Harbour
Belle Isle
Str. of Belle Isle
Ottawa Is.
Portland Promontory
Port Harrison
L. Minto
Clearwater L.
Indian House Lake
Schefferville
Belcher Is.
Richmond Gulf
Great Whale River
Lac Bienville
C. Henrietta Maria
James Bay
Ft. George
Akimiski I.
Fort Albany
Charlton I.
Moosonee
Eastmain
Rupert House
L. Mistassini
Natashquan
Mingan
Sept Iles
Seven Is.
Anticosti I.
Port Menier
Gaspé
Corner Brook
Stephenville
Grand Falls
Gander
Fogo I.
Bonavista
Harbour Grace
St. Johns
C. Race
Port aux Basques
ST. PIERRE & MIQUELON (Fr.)
Cabot Strait
C. North
C. Ray
Magdalen Is.
Glace Bay
Sydney
Cape Breton I.
Inverness
Sable I.
Charlottetown
Summerside
Chandler
Cap Chat
Mont-Joli
Rimouski
Campbellton
Bathurst
Newcastle
Chatham
Moncton
Amherst
Truro
Dartmouth
Halifax
Lunenburg
Bridgewater
Yarmouth
C. Sable
Bay of Fundy
Saint John
Fredericton
Woodstock
St. Stephen
Augusta
Chicoutimi
Jonquière
Roberval
Tadoussac
Baie St. Paul
Rivière du Loup
Quebec
La Tuque
Shawinigan
Trois Rivières
MONTREAL
Sherbrooke
Hull
Ottawa
Mont Laurier
Amos
Val d'Or
Noranda
Rouyn
Kirkland Lake
Timmins
Cochrane
Iroquois Falls
Kapuskasing
Hearst
Geraldton
Nakina
Port Arthur
Ft. William
L. Nipigon
Nipigon
I. Royale
Lake Superior
Sault Ste. Marie
Sudbury
North Bay
Cobalt
New Liskeard
Chapleau
Pembroke
Renfrew
Parry Sound
Manitoulin I.
Georgian Bay
Lake Huron
Owen Sound
TORONTO
Guelph
Hamilton
London
Sarnia
Windsor
DETROIT
L. Ontario
Niagara Falls
Buffalo
L. Erie
Cleveland
Kingston
Cornwall
Peterborough
Montpelier
Albany
BOSTON
C. Cod
NEW YORK
Milwaukee
L. Michigan
Paul
Berthierville
Sorel
Victoriaville
Drummondville
Joliette
St. Jerome
Lachute
St. Hyacinthe
Richmond
Lachine
Longueuil
St. Lambert
Verdun
Beauharnois
St. Jean
Granby
Farnham
Bedford
Magog
Valleyfield
74° 73° 72°
46°
MILES 0 10 20

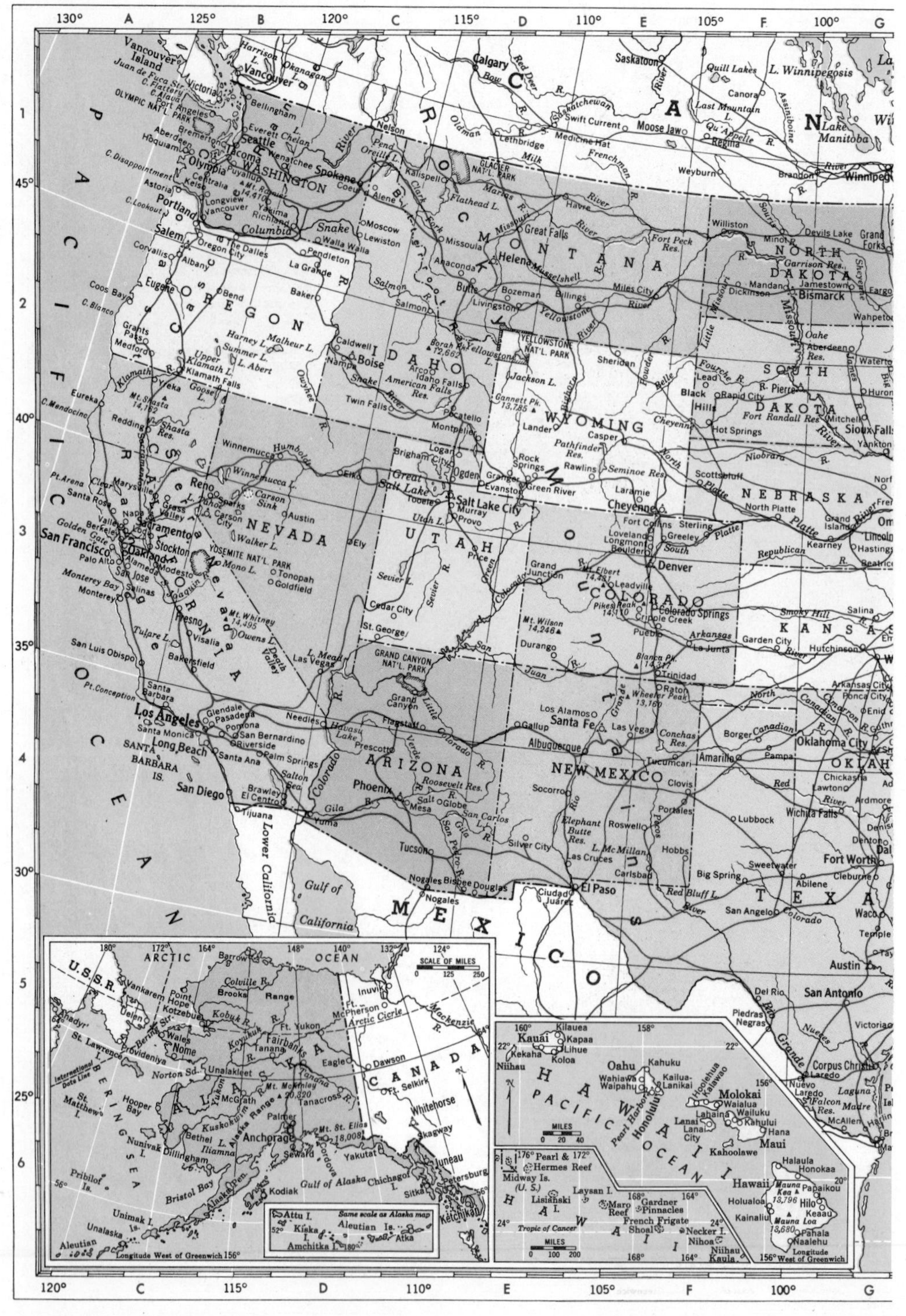

130° A 125° B 120° C 115° D 110° E 105° F 100° G
PACIFIC OCEAN
CANADA
ROCKY MOUNTAINS
WASHINGTON
OREGON
IDAHO
MONTANA
WYOMING
NORTH DAKOTA
SOUTH DAKOTA
NEBRASKA
NEVADA
UTAH
COLORADO
KANSAS
CALIFORNIA
Sierra Nevada
Cascade Range
Coast Range
ARIZONA
NEW MEXICO
TEXAS
MEXICO
Lower California
Gulf of California
Vancouver Island
Vancouver
Victoria
Seattle
Tacoma
Olympia
Spokane
Portland
Salem
Eugene
Boise
Salt Lake City
Ogden
Reno
Carson City
Sacramento
San Francisco
Oakland
San Jose
Fresno
Los Angeles
Long Beach
San Diego
Las Vegas
Phoenix
Tucson
El Paso
Albuquerque
Santa Fe
Denver
Cheyenne
Colorado Springs
Pueblo
Butte
Helena
Great Falls
Billings
Bismarck
Pierre
Calgary
Saskatoon
Regina
Moose Jaw
Winnipeg
Lubbock
Amarillo
Oklahoma City
Fort Worth
San Antonio
Austin
Corpus Christi
Mt. Rainier 14,410
Mt. Shasta 14,162
Mt. Whitney 14,495
Mt. Elbert 14,431
Pikes Peak 14,110
Gannett Pk. 13,785
Borah Pk. 12,662
Mt. Wilson 14,246
Blanca Pk. 14,317
Wheeler Peak 13,160
YELLOWSTONE NAT'L. PARK
GLACIER NAT'L. PARK
YOSEMITE NAT'L. PARK
GRAND CANYON NAT'L. PARK
OLYMPIC NAT'L. PARK
Great Salt Lake
Colorado R.
Snake R.
Columbia R.
Missouri R.
Rio Grande
120° C 115° D 110° E 105° F 100° G
ARCTIC OCEAN
U.S.S.R.
ALASKA
CANADA
BERING SEA
Gulf of Alaska
Brooks Range
Alaska Range
Mt. McKinley 20,320
Mt. St. Elias 18,008
Anchorage
Fairbanks
Juneau
Nome
Kodiak
Ketchikan
Aleutian Is.
Arctic Circle
SCALE OF MILES 0 125 250
Same scale as Alaska map
Longitude West of Greenwich 156°
HAWAII
PACIFIC OCEAN
Kauai
Niihau
Oahu
Honolulu
Pearl Harbor
Molokai
Lanai
Maui
Kahoolawe
Hawaii
Hilo
Mauna Kea 13,796
Mauna Loa 13,680
Midway Is. (U. S.)
Tropic of Cancer
MILES 0 20 40
MILES 0 100 200
156° West of Greenwich

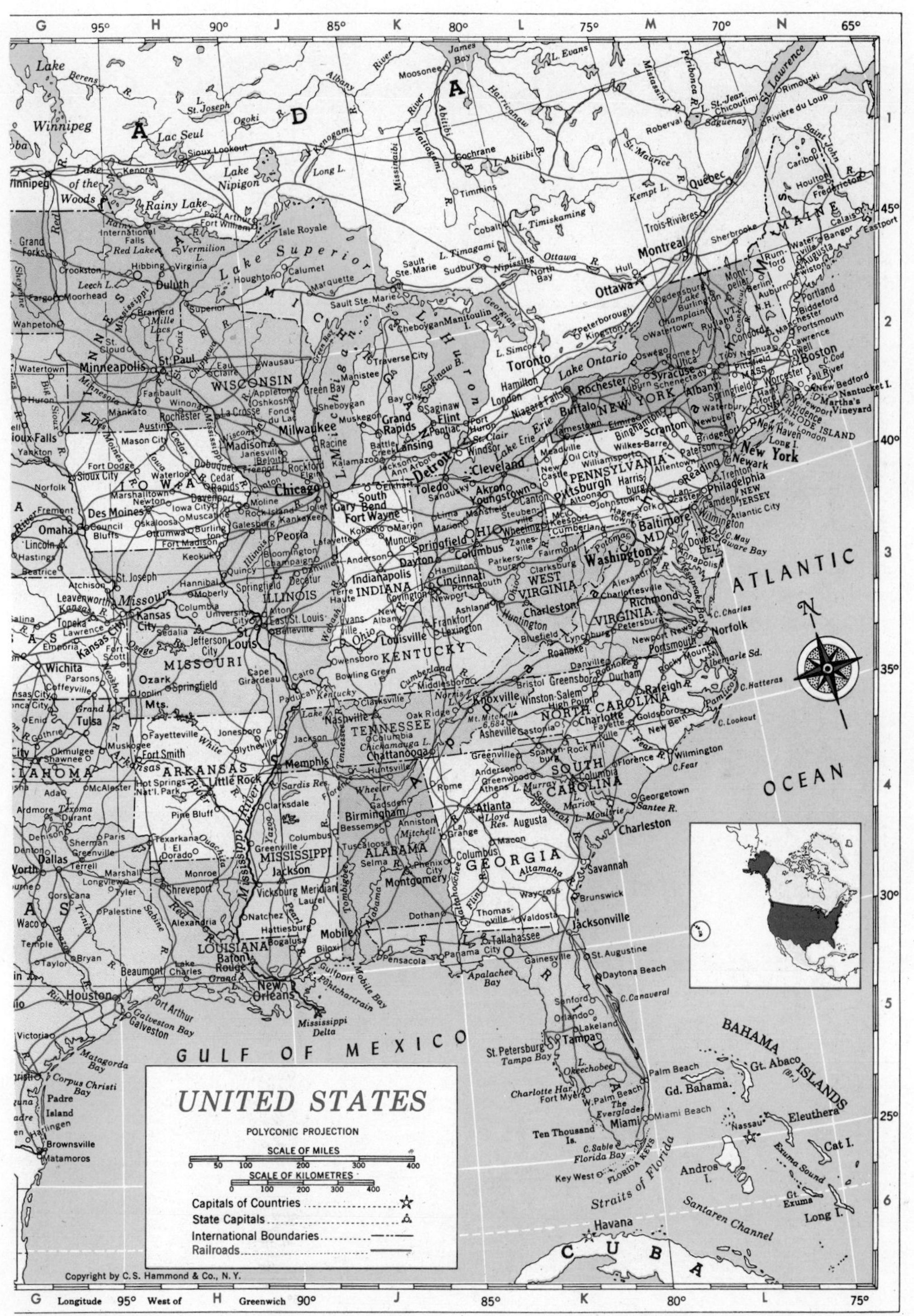
UNITED STATES
POLYCONIC PROJECTION
SCALE OF MILES
0 50 100 200 300 400
SCALE OF KILOMETRES
0 100 200 300 400
Capitals of Countries
State Capitals
International Boundaries
Railroads
Copyright by C. S. Hammond & Co., N. Y.
Longitude 95° West of Greenwich 90°
ATLANTIC OCEAN
GULF OF MEXICO
BAHAMA ISLANDS
CUBA

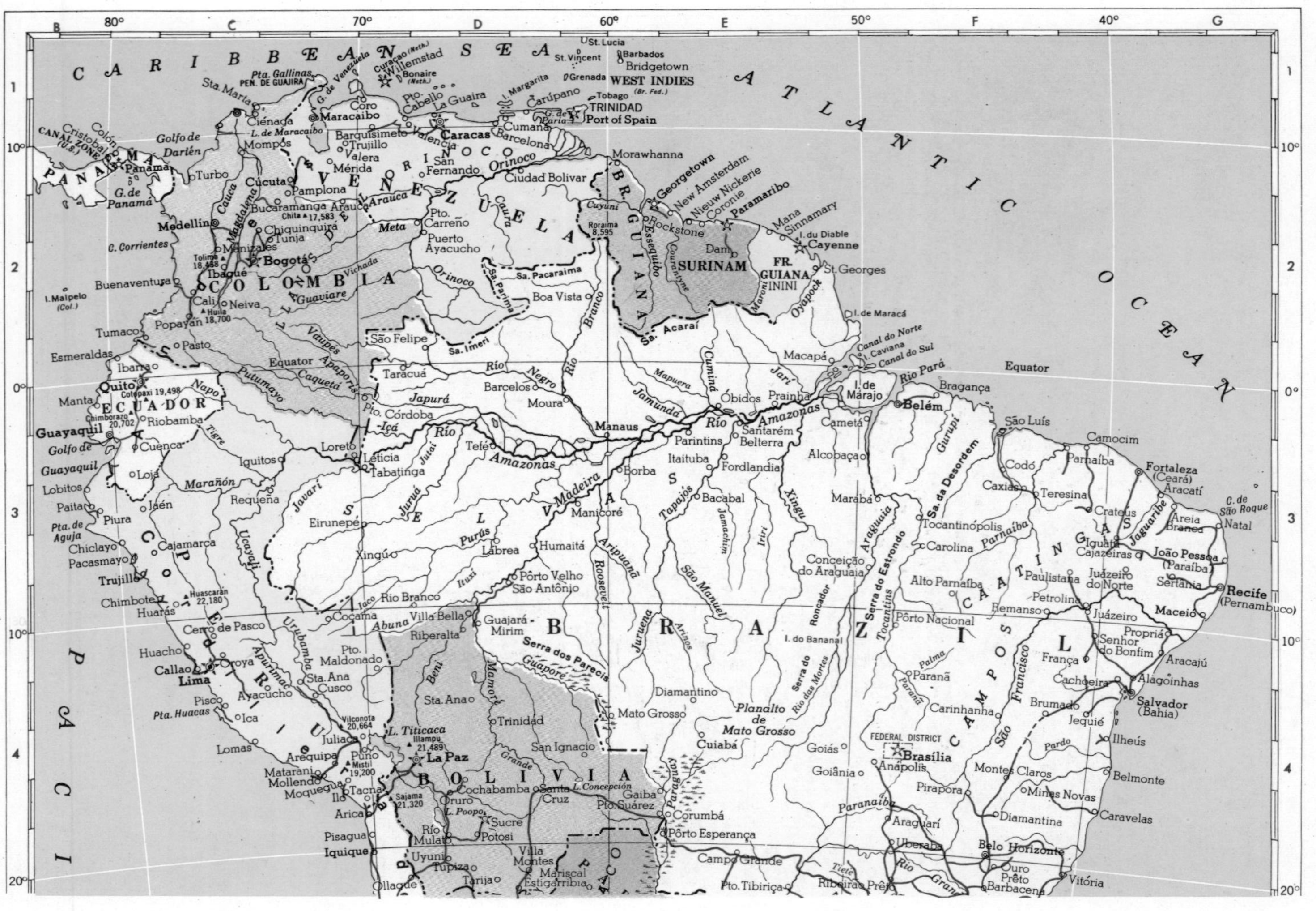

CARIBBEAN SEA
ATLANTIC OCEAN
PACI
Equator
WEST INDIES (Br. Fed.)
TRINIDAD
Port of Spain
VENEZUELA
Caracas
Maracaibo
Ciudad Bolívar
BR. GUIANA
Georgetown
SURINAM
Paramaribo
FR. GUIANA
Cayenne
COLOMBIA
Bogotá
PANAMA
CANAL ZONE (U.S.)
ECUADOR
Quito
Guayaquil
PERU
Lima
Callao
BOLIVIA
La Paz
L. Titicaca
BRAZIL
Manaus
Belém
Fortaleza (Ceará)
Recife (Pernambuco)
Salvador (Bahia)
Brasília
Belo Horizonte
Río Amazonas
Orinoco
Planalto de Mato Grosso
Serra dos Parecis
Serra do Estrondo
São Francisco
Tocantins
Xingu
Tapajós
Madeira
Río Negro

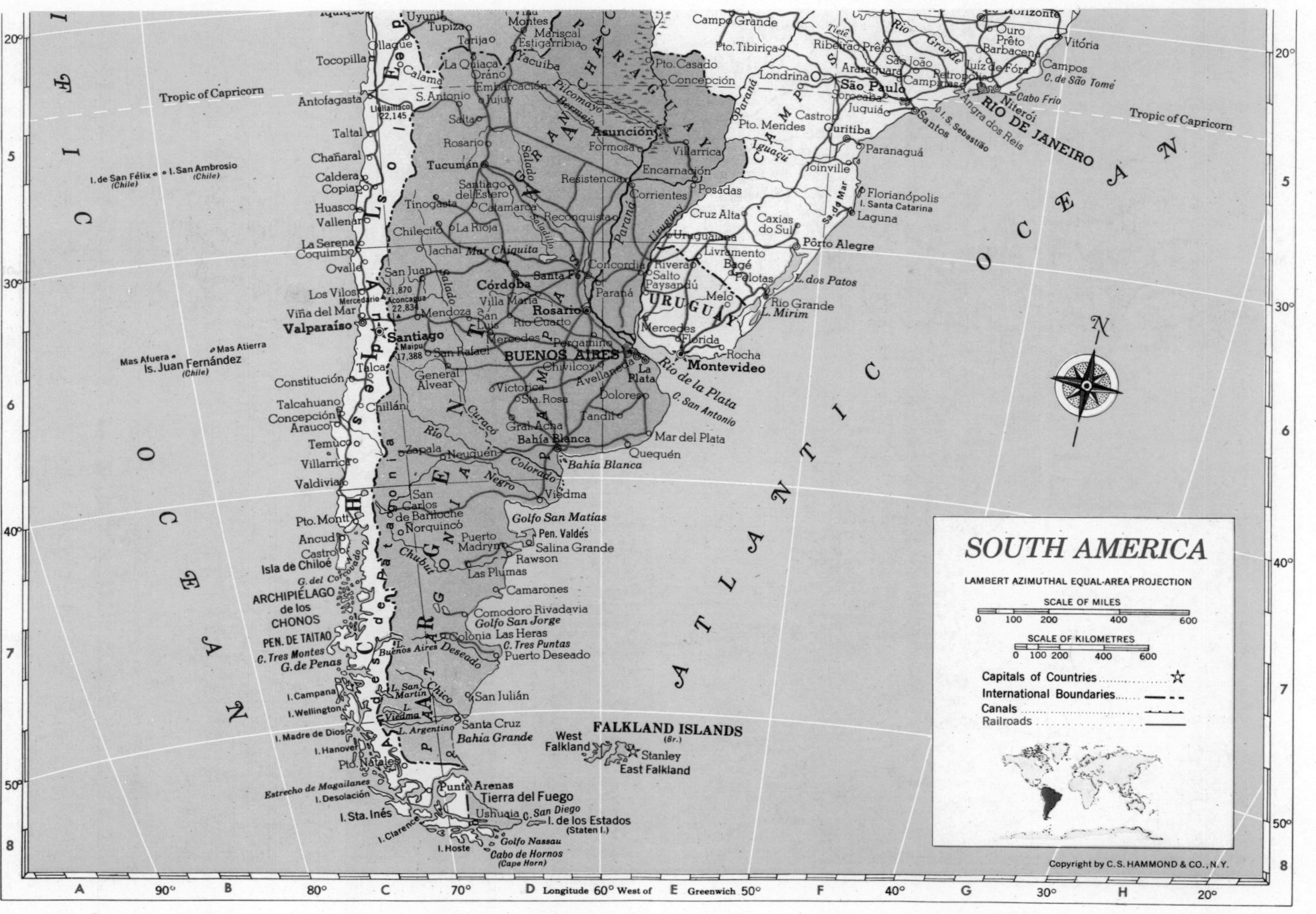
SOUTH AMERICA
LAMBERT AZIMUTHAL EQUAL-AREA PROJECTION
SCALE OF MILES
0 100 200 400 600
SCALE OF KILOMETRES
0 100 200 400 600
Capitals of Countries
International Boundaries
Canals
Railroads
Copyright by C. S. HAMMOND & CO., N.Y.
ATLANTIC OCEAN
Tropic of Capricorn
URUGUAY
FALKLAND ISLANDS (Br.)
West Falkland
East Falkland
Stanley
Tierra del Fuego
Cabo de Hornos (Cape Horn)
BUENOS AIRES
Montevideo
Santiago
Valparaíso
Asunción
RIO DE JANEIRO
São Paulo
Córdoba
Rosario
Rio de la Plata
Is. Juan Fernández (Chile)
I. de San Félix (Chile)
I. San Ambrosio (Chile)
ARCHIPIÉLAGO de los CHONOS
Isla de Chiloé
PEN. DE TAITAO
Estrecho de Magallanes
Golfo San Matías
Golfo San Jorge
Bahía Blanca
Punta Arenas
Ushuaia
I. de los Estados (Staten I.)
Longitude 60° West of Greenwich

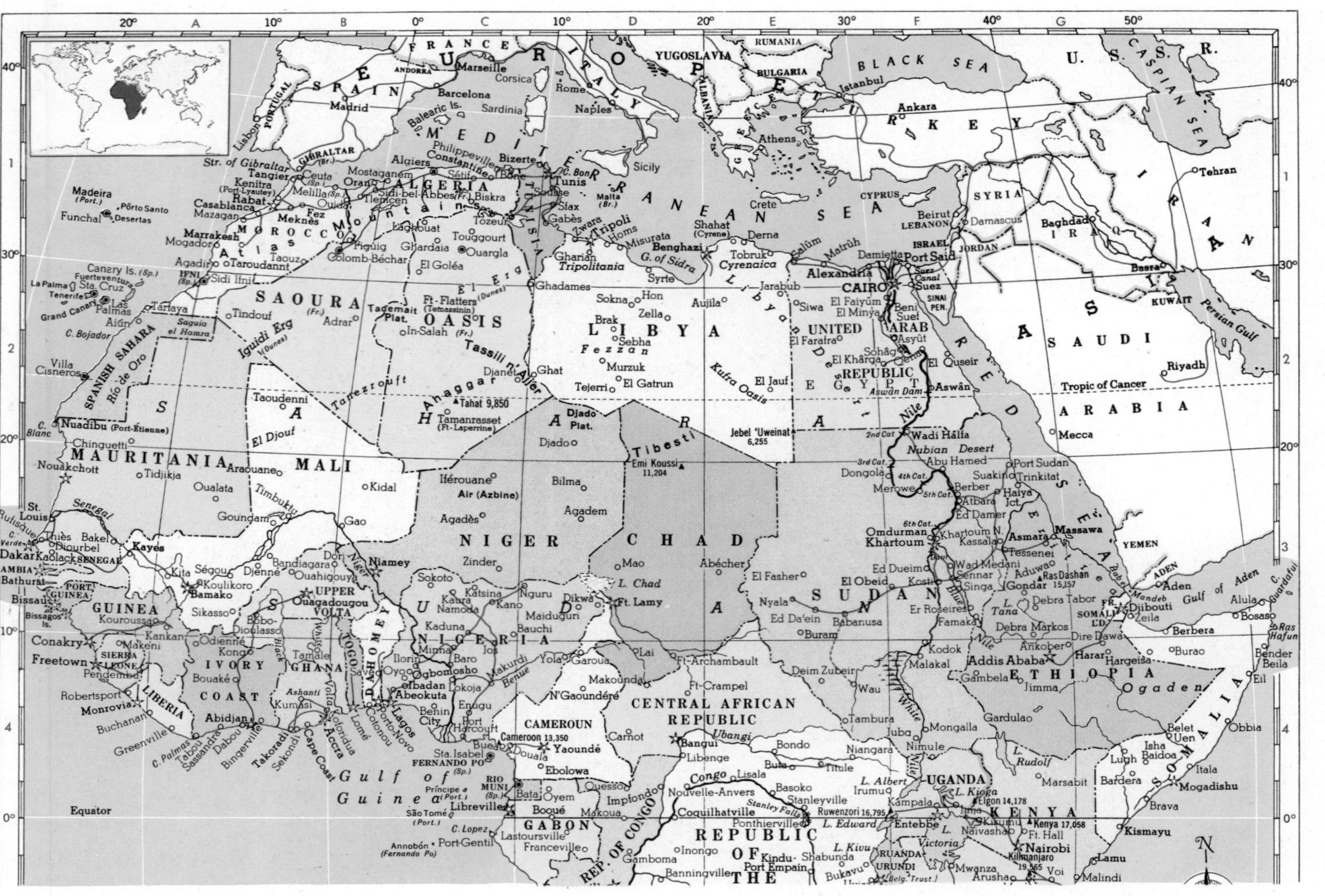

BLACK SEA
CASPIAN SEA
MEDITERRANEAN SEA
Persian Gulf
Gulf of Aden
Gulf of Guinea
Tropic of Cancer
Equator
U. S. S. R.
TURKEY
IRAN
IRAQ
SYRIA
CYPRUS
LEBANON
ISRAEL
JORDAN
KUWAIT
SAUDI ARABIA
YEMEN
ADEN
UNITED ARAB REPUBLIC
EGYPT
LIBYA
TUNISIA
ALGERIA
MOROCCO
SPANISH SAHARA
MAURITANIA
MALI
NIGER
CHAD
SUDAN
ETHIOPIA
SOMALIA
KENYA
UGANDA
RUANDA URUNDI
NIGERIA
CAMEROUN
CENTRAL AFRICAN REPUBLIC
GABON
REP. OF CONGO
REPUBLIC OF THE
GHANA
TOGO
DAHOMEY
UPPER VOLTA
IVORY COAST
LIBERIA
SIERRA LEONE
GUINEA
PORT. GUINEA
GAMBIA
SENEGAL
SPAIN
PORTUGAL
FRANCE
ITALY
YUGOSLAVIA
ALBANIA
GREECE
BULGARIA
RUMANIA
EUROPE
ASIA
SAHARA
Tehran
Baghdad
Riyadh
Mecca
Damascus
Beirut
Ankara
Istanbul
Athens
Rome
Naples
Madrid
Lisbon
Barcelona
Marseille
CAIRO
Alexandria
Port Said
Suez
Aswân
Wadi Halfa
Khartoum
Omdurman
Addis Ababa
Asmara
Massawa
Djibouti
Mogadishu
Nairobi
Kampala
Tripoli
Benghazi
Tunis
Algiers
Oran
Rabat
Casablanca
Marrakesh
Dakar
St. Louis
Bamako
Niamey
Ft. Lamy
Ouagadougou
Kano
Lagos
Ibadan
Accra
Abidjan
Monrovia
Freetown
Conakry
Yaoundé
Bangui
Libreville

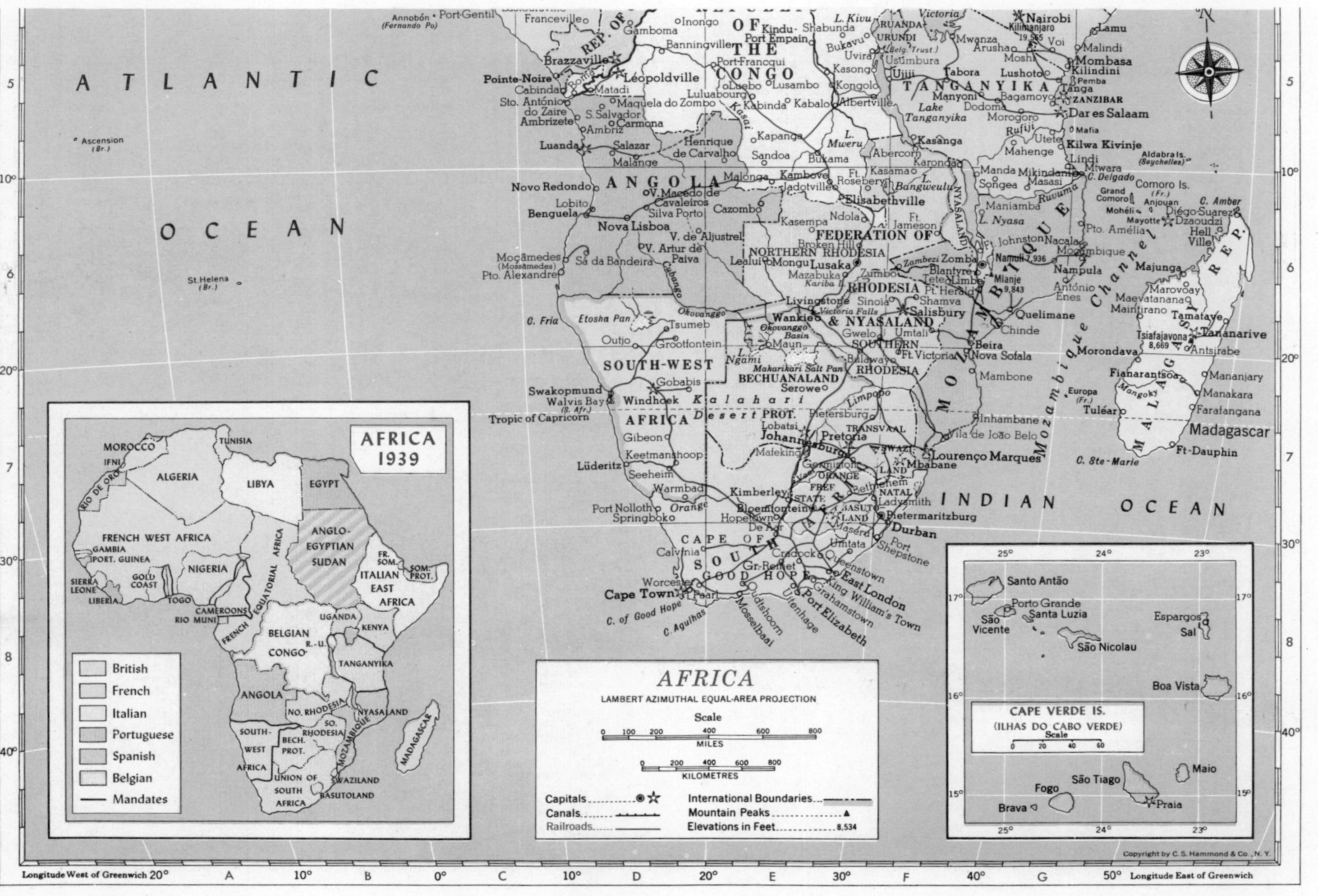
AFRICA
LAMBERT AZIMUTHAL EQUAL-AREA PROJECTION
Scale
MILES
KILOMETRES
Capitals
Canals
Railroads
International Boundaries
Mountain Peaks
Elevations in Feet 8,534
ATLANTIC OCEAN
INDIAN OCEAN
AFRICA 1939
British
French
Italian
Portuguese
Spanish
Belgian
Mandates
CAPE VERDE IS.
(ILHAS DO CABO VERDE)
Santo Antão
Porto Grande
Santa Luzia
São Vicente
São Nicolau
Espargos
Sal
Boa Vista
Maio
São Tiago
Praia
Fogo
Brava
Copyright by C. S. Hammond & Co., N. Y.
Longitude West of Greenwich
Longitude East of Greenwich

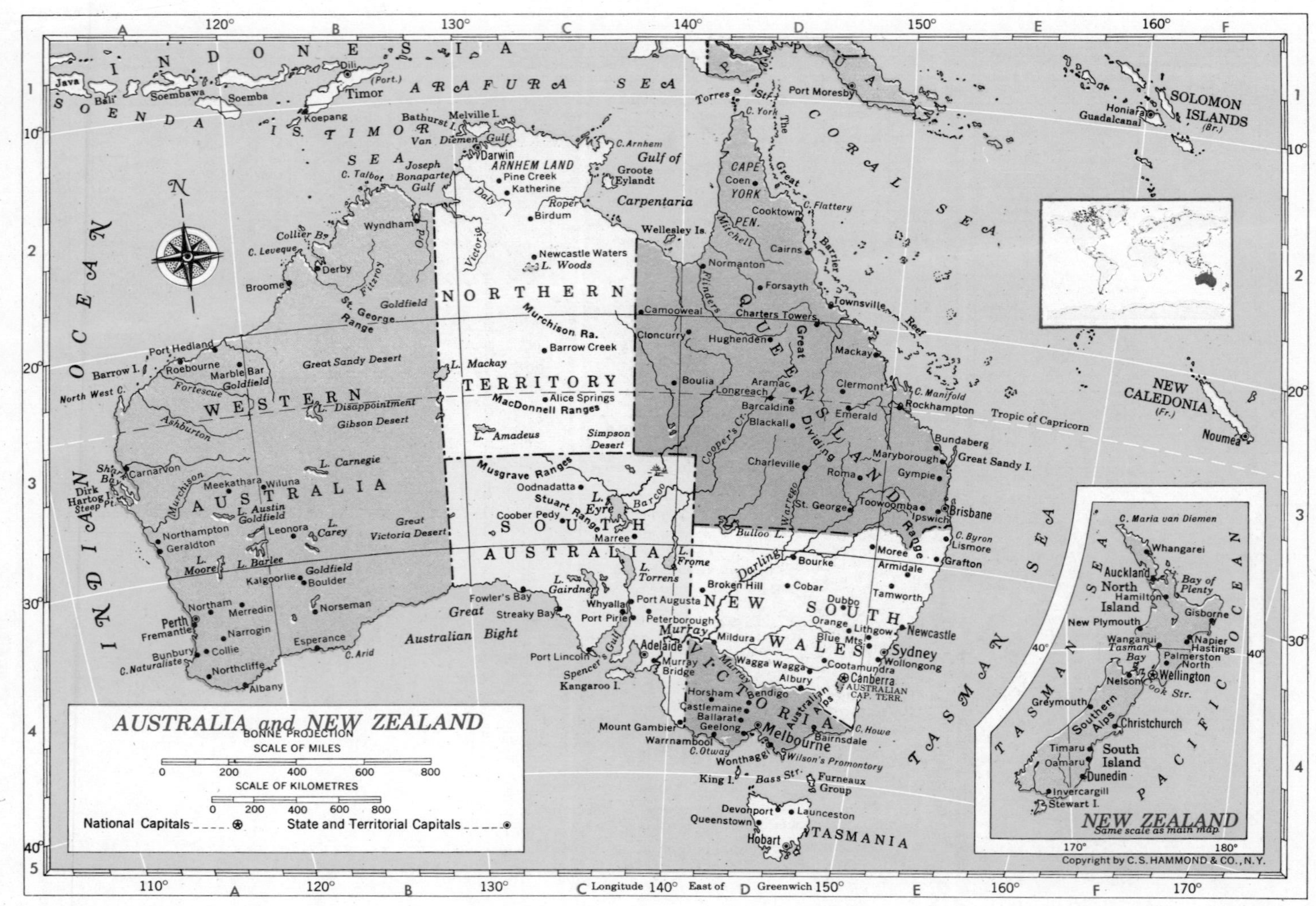
AUSTRALIA and NEW ZEALAND
BONNE PROJECTION
SCALE OF MILES
0 200 400 600 800
SCALE OF KILOMETRES
0 200 400 600 800
National Capitals
State and Territorial Capitals
INDONESIA
ARAFURA SEA
TIMOR SEA
CORAL SEA
TASMAN SEA
INDIAN OCEAN
SOENDA
Java
Bali
Soembawa
Soemba
Timor
(Port.)
Dili
Koepang
SOLOMON ISLANDS
(Br.)
Honiara
Guadalcanal
Port Moresby
Torres Str.
C. York
CAPE YORK PEN.
Coen
Cooktown
C. Flattery
Cairns
Great Barrier Reef
Townsville
Mackay
Clermont
C. Manifold
Rockhampton
Emerald
Tropic of Capricorn
Bundaberg
Great Sandy I.
Maryborough
Gympie
Brisbane
Ipswich
Toowoomba
C. Byron
Lismore
Grafton
NEW CALEDONIA
(Fr.)
Noumea
Bathurst I.
Melville I.
Van Diemen Gulf
Darwin
ARNHEM LAND
Pine Creek
Katherine
C. Arnhem
Gulf of Carpentaria
Groote Eylandt
Roper
Birdum
Wellesley Is.
Joseph Bonaparte Gulf
C. Talbot
Wyndham
Collier B.
C. Leveque
Derby
Broome
Fitzroy
Ord
Victoria
Daly
Mitchell
Flinders
Normanton
Forsayth
Charters Towers
Camooweal
Cloncurry
Hughenden
Boulia
Aramac
Longreach
Barcaldine
Blackall
Cooper's Cr.
Charleville
Roma
St. George
Warrego
Bulloo L.
Great Dividing Range
QUEENSLAND
NORTHERN TERRITORY
Newcastle Waters
L. Woods
Murchison Ra.
Barrow Creek
L. Mackay
Alice Springs
MacDonnell Ranges
L. Amadeus
Simpson Desert
Musgrave Ranges
Oodnadatta
Coober Pedy
Stuart Range
L. Eyre
Barcoo
Marree
SOUTH AUSTRALIA
L. Frome
L. Torrens
L. Gairdner
Port Augusta
Whyalla
Port Pirie
Peterborough
Murray
Adelaide
Murray Bridge
Port Lincoln
Spencer's Gulf
Kangaroo I.
Mount Gambier
Fowler's Bay
Streaky Bay
Great Australian Bight
WESTERN AUSTRALIA
Port Hedland
Roebourne
Marble Bar
Goldfield
Barrow I.
North West C.
Fortescue
Ashburton
Great Sandy Desert
St. George Range
L. Disappointment
Gibson Desert
L. Carnegie
Great Victoria Desert
Shark B.
Carnarvon
Dirk Hartog I.
Steep Pt.
Murchison
Meekathara
Wiluna
L. Austin
Leonora
L. Carey
Northampton
Geraldton
L. Moore
L. Barlee
Kalgoorlie
Boulder
Norseman
Northam
Merredin
Perth
Fremantle
Narrogin
Bunbury
Collie
C. Naturaliste
Northcliffe
Albany
Esperance
C. Arid
NEW SOUTH WALES
Darling
Bourke
Moree
Armidale
Broken Hill
Cobar
Dubbo
Tamworth
Mildura
Orange
Lithgow
Blue Mts.
Newcastle
Sydney
Wollongong
Wagga Wagga
Cootamundra
Albury
Canberra
AUSTRALIAN CAP. TERR.
VICTORIA
Horsham
Bendigo
Castlemaine
Ballarat
Geelong
Melbourne
Australian Alps
Bairnsdale
C. Howe
Warrnambool
C. Otway
Wonthaggi
Wilson's Promontory
King I.
Bass Str.
Furneaux Group
TASMANIA
Devonport
Launceston
Queenstown
Hobart
NEW ZEALAND
Same scale as main map
C. Maria van Diemen
Whangarei
Auckland
Bay of Plenty
North Island
Hamilton
Gisborne
New Plymouth
Wanganui
Napier
Hastings
Tasman Bay
Palmerston North
Nelson
Wellington
Cook Str.
Greymouth
Southern Alps
Christchurch
South Island
Timaru
Oamaru
Dunedin
Invercargill
Stewart I.
PACIFIC OCEAN
TASMAN SEA
Longitude 140° East of Greenwich
Copyright by C. S. HAMMOND & CO., N.Y.

Sarawak, a British crown colony, has an area of about 47,000 square miles. It is under the jurisdiction of a governor, assisted by a supreme council and a legislative council. The capital is Kuching. Rubber and timber are important resources.

British North Borneo, a crown colony, has an area of 29,387 square miles. It is administered by a governor, assisted by an executive and a legislative council. The capital is Jesselton. Rubber and timber are the chief exports.

Brunei, a British protectorate, is surrounded on the land sides by Sarawak. It has an area of 2,226 square miles. The supreme governmental authority lies in the Sultan in Council, a 12-member body presided over by the Sultan of Brunei. A British resident carries out the general administration. The capital is Brunei. Oil production is the chief industry.

BRAZIL

This largest South American republic, officially the United States of Brazil, has an area slightly larger than that of the United States, much of it unexplored and unsettled. Most of its area of 3,288,051 square miles lies within the tropics and has great river systems—including that of the Amazon—varied and colorful plant and animal life, and almost half the people of the continent. The population is about 61,000,000. An estimated 63 percent of the people are of European descent, 15 percent Negro, and 21 percent of mixed blood. Native Indians and Japanese form small minorities. Europeans are mainly Portuguese, Italian, Spanish, and German. The official language is Portuguese, but Italian and German are also used, especially in the southern areas of the country. Most of the inhabitants are Roman Catholic in religion. Education, which on the primary level is maintained chiefly by the state and local governments, is free and compulsory. But about half the population is still illiterate.

Rio de Janeiro and São Paulo are the largest cities. São Paulo is South America's largest industrial center. Other great cities are Recife, Salvador, Pôrto Alegre, and Belo Horizonte. A new city, Brasília, has been built in the country's interior to replace Rio de Janeiro as the national capital in 1960.

The topography of Brazil is dominated by the river systems: the Amazon and the Parnaíba in the north, the São Francisco in the east, and the Paraná-Paraguay in the south. Coastal areas are low, but the interior is a plateau with a general elevation of 1,000 to 3,000 feet. The mountains at the rim of the plateau have delayed the development of communications with the interior of the country. Rainfall is heavy in the north near the Equator; southern Brazil has a warm wet season and a cool dry season. In between the north and the south are areas of tropical savanna where temperatures are high, and there is a definite dry season; in some parts droughts occur frequently.

Coffee, cotton cacao, corn, tobacco, wheat, rice, sugar cane, and fruits are the principal crops. Livestock raising is especially important. Rubber, carnauba wax, tung oil, and yerba maté are other important products of the country. The forests are not exploited because of difficulties in working them and in transporting timber. Brazilian mines yield high grade iron ore, quartz crystal, industrial diamonds, chrome ore, mica, gold, manganese, and many other minerals. Petroleum and extensive deposits of low grade coal are found. Manufacturing is largely confined to the production of textiles and the processing of foodstuffs, although there are a growing iron and steel industry and small plants producing such things as clothing, chemicals, drugs, and furniture. Coffee, cotton, and cacao are the chief items of export.

BRITISH EAST AFRICA

British East Africa is a convenient term for certain areas in eastern Africa under varying degrees of British control: Kenya, Uganda, Tanganyika, and Zanzibar. These cover a land area of about 676,351 square miles and have a population of about 19,000,000. The population of British East Africa includes minorities of Europeans, Arabs, and Asiatics, the last principally from India. The rest are natives of many groups including Bantu, Bushmen, Baganda (for whom Uganda is named), Swahili, Somalis, Gallas, and Masai. The natives are pagans, Mohammedans, or Christians.

Lowlands generally front the 700 miles of coast, but the interior rapidly rises and is mountainous to the westernmost branch of the Great Rift Valley, a great fault extending from the Red Sea through Ethiopia to southern Tanganyika, which forms the western boundary of the area. In this valley are the great lakes of Nyasa, Tanganyika, Kivi, Edward, Albert, and Rudolph. Lake Victoria, a vast expanse of water abutting Tanganyika, Kenya, and Uganda, lies between the eastern and western branches of the Great Rift Valley and is relatively shallow; from it flows the headstream of the Nile. The two highest peaks are Kilimanjaro, Africa's highest, at 19,317 feet, and Kenya, 17,040 feet. The climate varies with height but is generally tropical.

Agriculture is the principal occupation, and the chief crops are cloves (Zanzibar), coffee, sisal hemp, corn, wheat, coconuts, sugar cane, rice, peanuts, and cotton. Cattle and sheep are also raised. There is some mining; the chief minerals found are gold, silver, tin, diamonds, mica, coal, tantalum, wolfram, and copper. The principal exports are coffee, cotton, tea, sisal hemp and other fibers, hides and skins, pyrethrum, gold, oil seeds, diamonds, copra, cloves, and ivory.

Kenya is a crown colony; Kenya Protectorate embraces a narrow coastal strip and some islands rented from the sultan of Zanzibar. The total land area is about 219,730 square miles. Nairobi is the capital. The administration is headed by a governor, assisted by a council of ministers, an executive council, and a legislative council. From 1952 to 1956 the Mau Mau, a secret Kikuyu society pledged to expel the white people, terrorized Kenya. In 1957 the first national election sent Negro members to the legislative council.

Uganda Protectorate is an interior land having 93,981 square miles. About one-fifth of the population is made up of Baganda, the most civilized and powerful people of the protectorate. The capital is Entebbe, and the chief commercial city is Kampala. Heading the administration is a British governor, who is assisted by a legislative council and an executive council. Four areas of Uganda are permitted a limited autonomy under native kings; the rest is under the governor's direct administration.

Zanzibar, including the islands of Zanzibar and Pemba, is a sultanate under British protection. The capital is the port of Zanzibar. The chief administrator is a British resident, who presides over the executive and legislative councils. The sultan, who initiates legislative decrees, presides over a privy council. The people are mainly

Bantu Swahili, Omani Arabs, and some Indians.

Tanganyika Territory, formerly a German possession, was mandated to the British after World War I; after World War II it continued under British administration as a United Nations' trust area. Tanganyika has 362,000 square miles and is peopled by Swahili and many other tribes, Indians, Europeans, and Arabs. A British governor heads the government, assisted by executive and legislative councils. Africans, Asians, and Europeans are equally represented in the latter.

BRITISH GUIANA

Ceded to Great Britain in 1814 by the Dutch, British Guiana lies east of Venezuela on the north coast of South America. Its area is approximately 83,000 square miles. Georgetown is the capital. The population is about 5,000,000. East Indians outnumber Negroes, and very little of the population is of European origin, chiefly Portuguese, Dutch, and English. Mixtures of Indian and European are common. The aborigines, dwindling in numbers, are of the Arawak and Carib tribes. Aside from native dialects, the common language is a kind of pidgin English—a mixture of Dutch, Portuguese, Indian, and English. Catholicism and the Anglican faith are the main creeds besides Hinduism. The churches cooperate with the government to provide educational facilities. Owing to Communist intrigues to take control of the colony, British Guiana's constitution was suspended in 1953. Under a new constitution, approved in 1956, administration is under the British governor and a legislative council of 28 members, half of them popularly elected.

Known resources of Guiana include rich timber, gold, diamonds, manganese, and huge deposits of bauxite. The dunes and low, sandy soils near the coast rise to high plateaus with wide savannas, then to hills and mountains on the west and south. Eastern Guiana is well forested. The climate is hot and damp. Coast rainfall is about 80 inches, lessening considerably inland.

The growth and processing of sugar cane is the chief industry of Guiana. Rice, coffee, coconuts, cacao, and fruits are other crops. The chief exports are sugar, molasses, rum, rice, timber, diamonds, gold, and bauxite.

BRITISH HONDURAS

Once a center of the Mayas, this Central American British crown colony of 8,867 square miles is now populated by an ever diminishing number of pure Indians, many Negroes, a few white people, and mulattoes from interbreeding during the days of slavery and buccaneers. The population is about 80,900. Languages spoken are English and Spanish and native mixtures. Catholicism and the Anglican Church are represented, though no particular form of religion is predominant. Government affairs are controlled by a governor, a legislative assembly (most members elected), and an executive council drawn therefrom. Belize is the capital and seaport. Primary education is provided by government funds, and secondary education is entirely denominational.

The climate is hot and damp, ranging between 60° F. and 90° F. Rainfall averages about 82 inches, increasing southward. Inland are low swamplike jungles and sandy ridges of mixed scrub, leading to mountains. A rich alluvial belt about a mile wide produces such crops as sugar cane, citrus fruits, coconuts, and bananas. Mahogany, pine, cedar, and other woods are obtained from the great forests, providing the colony's chief income. It exports mainly lumber, chicle, and citrus fruits.

BRITISH SOMALILAND

After the British captured Aden in 1839 in order to protect the southern entrance to the Red Sea (Strait Bab el Mandeb), they became interested for a like reason in the opposite African shore—an area that was part of Somaliland. However, it did not officially become a British protectorate until 1887. Behind the coastal lowlands, 10 to 60 miles wide, rise rugged heights reaching as high as 7,900 feet. The land is dry and stony, and the climate, hot and arid. British Somaliland has an area of some 68,000 square miles and a population of about 640,000. The Somalis are a nomadic people, holding their wealth in livestock—camels, sheep, and goats. Oil, coal, and other minerals have been found in the interior, but these resources have not been exploited. Dates are grown, and frankincense and myrrh collected. The chief exports are livestock, hides and skins, and ghee. The British governor is the sole legislative and executive authority. The capital is Hargeisa.

BRITISH SOUTH AFRICA

British South Africa is a convenient term to designate areas of South Africa under varying degrees of British control, but it does not include the Union of South Africa. These are Northern Rhodesia, Southern Rhodesia, Nyasaland, Bechuanaland, Basutoland, and Swaziland. Southern Rhodesia is a self-governing territory; Northern Rhodesia and Nyasaland are protectorates, as is Bechuanaland, and Basutoland and Swaziland are British possessions that are to a great extent native reserves. Population is over 11,000,000.

The Federation of Rhodesia and Nyasaland (Central African Federation), proclaimed in 1953, unites Northern and Southern Rhodesia and Nyasaland under a federal constitution. The federation's total land area measures 478,010 square miles. The federal capital is at Salisbury, Southern Rhodesia. The population is mainly African, with small minorities of European, Asiatic, or mixed ancestry. The Africans are Bantu people, mainly Shona, Nyanja, and Bemba. Most of the Negroes are unqualified to vote, and government is primarily in the hands of the European minority. The federal government, headed by a governor general, assisted by a cabinet and an assembly, is responsible for all education other than that of Africans.

Southern Rhodesia is a territory enjoying a liberal form of self-government, headed by a governor. Within the 150,333 square miles comprising the territory are native reserves. The capital is Salisbury. Bulawayo is another important town. The chief crops are tobacco, corn, and citrus and other fruits. Livestock is important. Gold, asbestos, chrome, coal, and other minerals are mined.

Northern Rhodesia is somewhat less developed than its neighbor. A protectorate, it is administered by a governor, assisted by an executive and a legislative council. Lusaka is the capital; other important towns are Broken Hill, Fort Jameson, and Livingstone. The area of Northern Rhodesia is 290,323 square miles. Copper and other minerals are the most important products. Corn, tobacco, cattle, and timber are also produced.

The Nyasaland Protectorate, situated along the western and southern shores of Lake Nyasa, has almost a colonial status. The land area of Nyasaland is 37,374 square miles. An overwhelming majority of the population is African. The capital is Zomba; other important towns are Blantyre and Limbe. Cattle, goats, and other livestock are raised.

Basutoland is a native area under a resident commissioner responsible to the British high commissioner for South Africa. The capital is Maseru. The area of Basutoland is 11,716 square miles. Practically the entire population consists of Africans, since settlement by Europeans is prohibited. The few Europeans are mainly government officials, missionaries, and traders. Thousands of Africans from Basutoland are recruited to labor in the mines and fields of the Union of South Africa. The chief products are wheat, corn, sorghums, barley, oats, beans, and peas.

Bechuanaland Protectorate is a vast area of some 275,000 square miles, much of which is a part of the Kalahari Desert and sparsely settled. The population consists mainly of Bantu tribes; there are few Europeans, Asiatics, and mixed bloods. There is a British resident commissioner responsible to the high commissioner for South Africa. Under him the chiefs have control of their people. The capital is Mafeking, just over the border in Cape Province in the Union of South Africa. Bechuanaland's chief products are cattle and dairy products, sheep, goats, and gold, silver, and asbestos.

Swaziland is a largely native area owned by the British, who maintain a resident commissioner there. Native affairs are nominally under a hereditary chief. The capital is Mbabane. Swaziland has high veld and middle veld, which are well watered and healthful, and a low veld, where malaria is prevalent. The climate is amenable except in the low veld during summer. Swaziland's area is 6,705 square miles; its population includes Swazis, Zulus, and a few Europeans, Asiatics, and colored. The chief products are cotton, tobacco, corn, sorghums, peanuts, cattle, sheep, goats, and pigs. Asbestos and tin are mined; coal, gold, and iron ore have been found.

BRITISH WEST AFRICA

British West Africa is a convenient term to designate certain areas in western Africa under British control: Nigeria, Gambia, Sierra Leone, and part of the former German area of the Cameroons, which was mandated by the League of Nations to France and Great Britain after World War I and now is administered by them as a United Nations trust. British Cameroons is administered by the government of Nigeria.

The Federation of Nigeria is a colony and protectorate with an area of 373,250 square miles. Nigeria is divided administratively into five regions. Each has its own legislature, executive council, premier, and governor. The people of Nigeria belong mainly to Hausa, Yoruba, Ibo, Fula, and Kanuri tribes. Islam, Christianity, and animism are practiced. The Nigerian coast lies along the Gulf of Guinea at the east of Africa's great bulge. The coastal region has lagoons and tropical forests; inland the surface rises to a plateau, the northern part of which is a dry, grassy plain. The rain is heavy, in coastal Cameroons totaling more than 350 inches a year, but the interior areas receive only about 25 inches per year. Products include palm oil, cotton, cacao, peanuts, hides and skins, bananas, rubber, sesame, lumber, gum arabic, tin, gold, coal, and iron. Chief exports are palm oil and kernels, coal, peanuts, cacao, and rubber. Lagos is the chief port.

Gambia is also a colony and protectorate, having areas of 29 square miles and 3,974 square miles, respectively. The native peoples are Negroes, chiefly Mandingo, Wolof, Fula, and Jola. The capital is Bathurst. Gambia is a narrow area on both sides of the Gambia River. Some 40 inches of rain fall annually. Gambia's chief exports are peanuts, palm kernels, wax, and hides.

Sierra Leone, a colony and protectorate, was chosen by the British in the 18th century as a place to land natives rescued from slave ships; it lies on the southwestern part of the Great African bulge, to the north of the American-sponsored Negro republic of Liberia. The colony, including those portions administered as a protectorate, has an area of about 2,500 square miles. Together, the colony and protectorate cover about 27,925 square miles. Most of the people are Negroes, with small minorities of Europeans and Asians. The capital is Freetown, also the chief port. The protectorate is divided into chiefdoms, which function as local governmental units; the assembly has advisory but no legislative power. Sierra Leone's agricultural products are palm kernels, palm oil, piassava, rice, cacao, coffee, peanuts, ginger, and cassava. Iron ore, diamonds, and chrome are the principal minerals.

Population of British West Africa is about 35,000,000.

BRITISH WEST INDIES

Geographically, the British West Indies consist of the Bahamas, Jamaica, the British Leeward Islands (including the British Virgin Islands), the British Windward Islands, Trinidad and Tobago, and Barbados. With the exception of the Bahamas and the Virgin Islands, these formerly separate colonies united in 1958 to form the Federation of the British West Indies, with the ultimate objective of attaining dominion status in the commonwealth. The federal capital is on Trinidad.

The British Leeward Islands—Antigua with Barbuda and Redonda, St. Kitts and Nevis with Anguilla and Sombrero, Montserrat, and the Virgin Islands—have an area of 422 square miles. The Windward Islands—Grenada, St. Vincent, the Grenadines, St. Lucia, and Dominica—total 829 square miles. Trinidad covers 1,864 square miles, Tobago 116, and Barbados 166. See separate articles for the Bahamas and Jamaica.

In general, sugar cane and sugar derivatives, especially rum, are the economic mainstays, although cotton, tropical fruits, cacao, and spices are important on certain islands. Trinidad has valuable petroleum and asphalt deposits. The people of the West Indies are predominantly Negro; the white population is gradually decreasing. The population is about 1,140,000.

The West Indies form a great curve, extending from the Bahamas to Trinidad. To the east lies the Atlantic Ocean; to the west lie the Gulf of Mexico and the Caribbean Sea. Average temperatures range from 75° to 80°F., making the West Indies a favorite winter resort area. The northeast trade winds blow all year and bring heavy rains on the windward sides of the mountainous islands. In late summer hurricanes often occur.

BULGARIA

Bulgaria is a Russian-dominated republic, and agriculture and its related activities are the most important economic activity of Bulgarians—sheep or cattle raising, general farming, or the cultivation of roses. The country grows much corn and wheat, and wine grapes and tobacco are raised in great quantities. While less than formerly, still much oil of roses is made from flowers that grow in the Bulgarian valleys.

Bulgaria lost two wars. After World War I Bulgaria lost her Thracian territories; following World War II, a 20-year treaty of cooperation and mutual assistance was signed with the U.S.S.R.

Bulgaria's 42,796 square miles are used for pasture, farming, or timberland. The Balkan Mountains run across the country in an east and west direction, and much valuable timber is in this region. Industry is not developed, although there are extensive woolen mills. The country is also rich in coal. Export figures show shipments of tobacco, attar of roses, corn, eggs, prunes, live animals, and wheat. The Bulgarians are Slavs of the Eastern Orthodox faith, but the 1,100,000 members of national minority groups include over 600,000 Moslems, as well as Catholics, Protestants, and Jews. The Bulgarian language is of Slavic origin, written in a modified Russian alphabet. Education is obligatory and free for all children between the ages of 7 and 15.

The principal towns of Bulgaria are Sofia, its capital, located in the western part of the country, and Plovdiv, Varna, Ruse, Burgas. Dimitrovo, Pleven, Stara Zagora, Sliven, and Tolbukhin. The population is about 7,630,000.

BURMA

Burma, long a British possession, received its independence on Jan. 4, 1948, as the Union of Burma. The Mongoloid Burmese, originally from Tibet, form most of the population; immigration of neighboring peoples has resulted in many racial and religious minorities. Burma's area, including the semi-independent Shan, Kachin, Karen, Kayah, and Chin states, is 261,789 square miles. The population is about 19,856,000. Buddhism is widespread, and its monasteries have done much in education. The government supports primary and secondary schools.

Though half of Burma is outside the Torrid Zone, it is all essentially tropical in climate. The average annual temperature is about 80°F. in the southern regions and slightly lower in the north. Near the Arakan mountains and on the west coast the annual rainfall is about 200 inches. The Arakan Yoma range (separating Burma from India), the Shan plateau, and the Central Basin lying between the mountains and the plateau are the chief topographical features. There are many short and turbulent streams in Burma, and three important rivers; the Irrawaddy, Salween, and Tenasserim. All are used extensively for transportation and in floating teakwood logs downstream to the lumber yards. In addition to valuable and extensive timber lands, Burma has deposits of tin, wolfram, salt, lead, silver, zinc, copper and gold. Petroleum is its most important mineral product. Amber, jade, and rubies also are found. Most Burmese engage in some form of agriculture. Rubber plantations are numerous, and the production of rice reaches the astonishing figure of one-half ton per capita. Millet, cotton, beans, peanuts, sugar, and tobacco are other crops. Water buffalo, humped oxen, and elephants are commonly used as beasts of burden. Oil refining, fish packing, metalworking, and weaving are major industries. Rice, teak, metals, and cotton are exported. Japanese forces invaded Burma in 1941 and occupied it until 1945. Since its independence, civil strife between the government and dissident ethnic and political groups has plagued the country continually.

CAMBODIA

Cambodia is a kingdom of about 69,900 square miles located in the south of the Indochinese peninsula, bounded on the west by the Gulf of Siam, on the north by Thailand and Laos, and on the south by Vietnam. The country forms a large, flat basin, drained by the Mekong. In the west is a large, elongated lake, the Tonle Sap, connected with the Mekong by a channel.

Cambodians form 85 percent of the population; there are minorities of Chinese, Vietnamese, Chams, Thai, and Europeans. Buddhism is the principal religion. The Cambodians are probably descendants of the Khmer, who formed a mighty empire in the peninsula from the 9th to the 15th centuries. In 1863 France made Cambodia a protectorate. It retained this status until 1940, when the invading Japanese proclaimed it independent. Following the return of Cambodia to France at the end of World War II, the country became an Associate State within the French Union (1949). By 1954 it was an independent constitutional monarchy with a National Assembly of 91 seats. In 1955 King Sihanouk abdicated in order to promote constitutional reforms, being succeeded by his father, King Norodom Suramarit.

The chief cities are Phnom-Penh (the capital), Battambang, Kampot, and Kompong-Cham. The ruins of the temple-city of Angkor bear witness to the advanced state of Khmer civilization. Principal products are rice (80 percent of cultivated land), fish, pepper, corn, kapok, sugar, and tobacco, all important exports. Cattle-breeding is extensive throughout the country. The population is about 5,000,000.

CANADA

Canada, the largest unit of the British Commonwealth of Nations, has often been called the "Good Neighbor" of the United States. Neither country patrols the common long boundary with armed guards.

The Canadian people are largely of British or French extraction; only about 1 percent are Indians, Eskimos, or half-breeds. The population is about 16,650,000. English and French are Canada's two official languages. The French-speaking people, living for the most part in the eastern stretches of Canada, are Roman Catholics. The United Church has the next highest percentage of adherents; this, the Anglicans, and various other Protestant faiths having about the same number of followers as Catholicism.

Canada's area, which totals 3,845,774 square miles, is larger than that of its neighbor, the United States. In topography they are strikingly similar. To the west, the Canadian Rockies are a continuation of the United States chain, and to the east of these, Canadian prairies and plains slope gradually down to Hudson Bay, which for the purposes of comparison may be likened to the Great Lakes. The St. Lawrence River runs through fertile and thickly populated valleys to its own gulf and the North Atlantic. Canada is richly endowed with numerous other rivers and thousands of lakes. The climate is very similar to that of the northern United States, but the winters are generally more severe.

The ten provinces of Canada, with their capital cities, are Alberta, Edmonton; British Columbia, Victoria; Manitoba, Winnipeg; New Brunswick, Fredericton; Nova Scotia, Halifax; Ontario, Toronto; Prince Edward Island, Charlottetown; Quebec, Quebec; Saskatchewan, Regina; and Newfoundland, St. John's. In addition there are the large, sparsely populated districts of Yukon and Northwest Territories, governed by an appointed commissioner and elected council for Yukon, and an appointed commissioner and a council (partly appointed and partly elected) for Northwest Territories. The national capital of Canada, located in Ontario, is Ottawa—the seat of the governor general (who is appointed by the British Government) and the Canadian legislature.

The natural resources of Canada are coal, gold, silver, copper, lead, zinc, petroleum, uranium, radium, iron ore, salt, asbestos, timber, nickel, and miscellaneous others. The chief occupations of the Canadian people are farming and stock raising, though lately the manufacturing and oil industries have given a greater return. The broad middle western prairies provide excellent pasturage, as well as fertile soil for such crops as wheat, other grains, tobacco, and garden vegetables. Forestry, fur farming, fishing, dairying, and fruit farming are other important industries. Manufacturing enterprises are largely concerned with conversion of natural resources and agricultural products. The manufacturing districts are in Quebec and Ontario, where factories for textiles, wood pulp and paper, minerals, chemicals, iron and steel, and public utilities are conveniently located with access to foreign markets and local outlets. The chief exports of Canada are newsprint, wheat, wood pulp, planks and boards, flour, aluminum, nickel, copper, asbestos, farm implements, grains other than wheat, and fish.

Canadian export trade was steadily growing in world importance when the outbreak of World War II disrupted international trade. Canada played an important role in achieving final victory over the Axis in 1945, particularly in the European Theater of Operations. The Alaskan Highway (built in cooperation with the United States, and opened in October, 1942), from Dawson Creek, British Columbia, to Fairbanks, Alaska, was a war project. Newfoundland (with Labrador), formerly a British colony, became Canada's tenth province in 1949. In 1954 the United States and Canada agreed to construct a radar system (DEW Line) in Arctic Canada for protection against possible transpolar air attack. Completion of the project to deepen the St. Lawrence Seaway, in 1959, opens the Great Lakes to large ocean vessels. Elizabeth II, as Queen of Canada, visited the country in 1957.

CEYLON

Ceylon, a dominion of the British Commonwealth of Nations, a tear-shaped island at the southeastern tip of India, has an area of about 25,332 square miles. The population is well over 8,589,000. The south and middle parts are mountainous, and covered with dense forests. The climate is warm, though relieved somewhat by the cool ocean air and the monsoons which bring rainfall, varying from 40 to 200 inches. Colombo (the capital), Galle, Jaffna, and Kandy are the chief towns. Anuradhapura, site of the ancient capital, contains interesting remains of what must once have been a beautiful city. Ceylon, a former British crown colony, on Feb. 4, 1948, became a self-governing dominion. More than half of the inhabitants are Sinhalese, and the remainder are Tamils and Moors. Sinhalese and Tamil are the predominant languages, but the aboriginal Veddahs, who live in rock caves, speak an obscure language of their own. Buddhism is predominant, but Hinduism, Islam, and Christianity have adherents. Education is free from the kindergarten through the university level.

Ceylon is noted for its satinwood and ebony trees. Its chief minerals are graphite, sapphires, rubies, and other gems. Pearl fishing is a growing enterprise. Agriculture occupies about two-thirds of the population, and rice, tea, coconuts, rubber, cacao, coffee, and tobacco are the principal crops. Industries are plywood, leather, shoes, cement, and tortoise-shell, earthenware and lacquer pieces, carving and weaving. Exports are tea, rubber, palm products, tobacco, cinnamon, citronella oil, graphite, and cacao.

CHILE

On the southwestern coast of South America is Chile—a long narrow republic squeezed into the Andes between the Pacific Ocean and Argentina. Chile has an area of 286,396 square miles. The population is about 6,941,000. Santiago is the capital city. Among the country's many seaports are Valparaiso, Antofagasta, San Antonio, Coquimbo, Tocopilla, Iquique and Arica. The north of Chile is about the driest region known. The rest of Chile has a temperature rather low and steady for its latitude. The Humboldt current washes the entire 2,600 mile coastline, and temperatures rarely rise above 85° or fall below 38°F. The mountainous regions show greater variation in climate.

Chile has a coast range to the west, the high, isolated Andean peaks on the east, and between the two is a narrow, fertile valley.

Large numbers of Germans, English, and Italians emigrated to Chile, as well as the original Spanish settlers; as a result the Chilean people are more northern European than any other Latin-American people. The native Indians are the nomadic Fuegians of Tierra del Fuego, the fiercely resistant Araucanians of southern Chile, living in practical isolation, and the Changos, living along the northern coast. The compulsory school age is from 7 to 15 years. Spanish is the country's official language, and Roman Catholicism is the principal religion.

Copper, nitrates, iron, coal, gold, silver, constitute most of the mineral wealth. Chile is one of the world's largest producers of copper. Wheat, barley, oats, and beans are the important agricultural products. Manufactures are largely food products, leather, and textiles, but there is some heavy industry. Principal exports are copper, nitrates, iron, and other minerals.

CHINA

The topography of China is extremely diversified. Mountains, deserts, wind-swept plains, and fertile river valleys characterize the country. The deserts and mountains are stormy, bleak and cold, and thinly populated. Near the coast, and in the river valleys the weather conditions are ideal. The marginal mountain regions have abundant rainfall and dense forests. Some of the central and northern regions are comparatively dry, and suffer extremes of heat and cold. The people are Mongoloid. While over 90 percent are Chinese, there are large minorities of Thai, Turki, Yi, Miao, and Mongols among the 44 recognized ethnic groups in China. The languages span four linguistic families and have hundreds of dialects. It is nominally compulsory for children 6 to 12 to attend school. Most of the people of China are adherents of Confucianism, Buddhism, or Taoism. There are also large minorities of Mohammedans, Roman Catholics, and Protestants.

The total area of China, including Tibet, is 3,800,000 square miles. The population is about

601,912,000. After World War II, China regained Manchuria and the Island of Formosa. The seat of the Communist government is Peking. Other important cities are Nanking, Shanghai, Canton, and Tientsin.

All farming is done on a small scale, almost entirely by hand labor. Rice, wheat, cereals, peas, beans, sugar, and tea are the principal crops. Silkworm culture, and the processing of silk, cotton and woolen mills, flour and rice mills, glass, match and metal factories lead industrial enterprises. The chief resources of China are coal, iron, tungsten, tin, antimony, copper, and gold. Exports are animal products, oils, textiles, fibers, metals, and tea. After the end of World War II and the Chinese civil war, the Communists proclaimed the "People's Republic of China," the Nationalist forces fleeing to Formosa.

COLOMBIA

Although Colombia is situated wholly within the Torrid Zone, the climate of its inhabited areas is temperate because of the altitude. The northern Andes, here a series of 3 ranges called the Eastern, Central, and Western Cordilleras, ridge the whole of the western section with bare peaks, timbered hills, and rich agricultural regions. The southeastern part of the country is a bare plain drained by tributaries of the Amazon. Land near the Caribbean is hot and low. Colombia occupies the northwest corner of South America and has an area of 439,553 square miles. The population is about 12,939,000. The people descended from Spanish settlers, Indians, and Negroes, but the racial proportions differ widely in various parts of the country. Spanish is the official language, although many Indian tongues are spoken by the tribes that inhabit Colombia's sparsely populated eastern lowlands. Roman Catholicism is the national religion. Primary education is free, but not compulsory, in numerous sectarian schools. The principal cities are Melellín, Barranquilla, Cali, Manizales, and Bogotá, the capital. A president is elected by popular vote.

Colombia yields much of the world's supply of platinum, generous amounts of silver, copper, gold, iron, coal, petroleum, lead, manganese, mercury and emeralds. Forest products are valuable timber and rubber. Agriculture, cattle raising and mining are the most important industries, and manufacturing enterprises are steadily growing. Plants for metallurgical industries, meat packing, textiles, cigars and cigarettes, and breweries are on the increase. The chief crops are coffee (the fine-flavored Colombian coffee is used for blending purposes), bananas, cotton, tobacco, plantains, sugar cane, corn, cacao, beans, rice, fruit, wheat, and other grains. The chief exports are coffee, petroleum, gold, platinum, hides, and tobacco.

COSTA RICA

Discovered and probably named the "Rich Coast" by Columbus on his fifth and last voyage to the New World, Costa Rica borders both the Pacific and the Caribbean. It has an area of about 19,690 square miles. The population is about 1 million. Most Costa Ricans are pure descendants of Spanish settlers, and minorities of mestizos and Negroes are small. San José is the capital. Other important towns are Alajuela, Cartago, Heredia, and Limón, the chief port. The republic is governed by a president, assisted by a cabinet of 9 members, and a single-chamber legislative body of 45 members. Formation of a national army is outlawed by the constitution. Spanish is the language, and most Costa Ricans are Roman Catholics. Primary education is free and compulsory, and the government provides secondary and vocational schools. Costa Rica is an elevated tableland whose volcanic mountains drop sharply to the coasts. Coastal temperatures are very warm, but the highlands are cool and refreshing. Agriculture with its related activity is the chief industry. Lumbering, with its rich resources of virgin timberland, containing many precious cabinet woods such as rosewood, mahogany, and cedar, as well as balsa, is growing in importance. Gold and silver are the most valuable mineral products. Coffee, bananas, cacao, corn, sugar cane, rice, potatoes, and tobacco are the chief crops. These, with lumber, and gold and silver constitute the export trade.

CUBA

Cuba, the large, plow-shaped island off the tip of Florida, has an area of 44,206 square miles. The population is about 5,832,000. Over half of the people are of Spanish descent; the rest are mulatto or Negro. English is often heard, but Spanish is official. Primary education is compulsory and free, and the University of Havana, whose students take such an active part in all political upheavals of the island, was founded in 1721. Since the days of Spanish domination in Cuba, Catholicism has been the main religion. The most important cities are Havana, the capital, Holgúin and Camagüey. The climate is uniformly warm, with only about 10° variation between the coolest and warmest months. The average annual temperature of Havana is 76°F., and precipitation is about 40 inches. The western section of Cuba is flat. Camagüey Province has rolling plains, and Oriente Province in the east has high mountains.

In 1898, as a result of the Spanish-American War, Spain relinquished its sovereignty over Cuba, and an independent republic state was established.

Fertile lands, dense forests, and deposits of iron, copper, manganese, salt and gold are the chief resources of Cuba. Crops are tobacco, sugar, coffee, cacao, cereals, potatoes, and fruits. Livestock raising is important, and cattle are the most numerous. The sugar industry is by far the most important, and Cuba ranks as the world's top sugar producing country. Manufacturing of cigars and cigarettes has long been famous. Sugar and sugar products constitute most of Cuba's exports.

CYPRUS

Cyprus is a British island colony in the eastern Mediterranean, some 40 miles south of Turkey. The area is 3,572 square miles. The population of about 527,000 is composed of Cypriots, mostly of Greek and Turkish descent. About 80 percent are Greek Orthodox in faith, and about 17 percent are Moslems. There is a small Armenian minority. Each religion has a separate educational system under government control. The chief towns are Nicosia, the capital, Limassol, and Famagusta. A British-appointed governor is the administrative head.

Two mountain ranges enclose a central plain, the chief agricultural area, which produces wheat and other cereals, carobs, grapes, raisins, potatoes, and cotton. The local industry processes these products. Sponge fishing and cattle raising also occupy the islanders. Iron ore is mined, and there are deposits of various other minerals such as asbestos, gypsum, and terra umbra.

CZECHOSLOVAKIA

Czechoslovakia, a republic, surrounded by Germany, Poland, the U.S.S.R., Hungary, and Austria, has an area of 49,381 square miles. The population is about 13,224,000. The inhabitants are Czechs, Slovaks, Germans, Hungarians, Russians, and Poles. The Czech language is a Slavic branch of the Indo-European group, and is widely used throughout the land. although German, Magyar, Russian, and Polish are used in certain localities. While about 75 percent of the population is Roman Catholic, there are minorities of Protestants, Greek Catholics, Jews, as well as persons who profess no religion. Czechoslovakia is a highly literate country. School is compulsory from 6 to 14. Prague, the capital, Brno, Ostrava, Olomouc, Bratislava, and Plzen are the chief cities. Prague is becoming increasingly important as a center of European trade. The climate is about like that of the state of Illinois, except that snowfall is heavier. The average annual temperature is about 48° F., and the precipitation about 25 inches. There are mountainous territories in the west and central portions, and the whole of the northwest area of the coast has a northwesterly slope.

One third of its area is covered with valuable timber, and resources of coal, iron, graphite, garnets, silver, copper, lead, rock salt, and uranium make it one of Europe's richest lands. The principal crops are grains, potatoes, sugar beets, corn, hops and fruit. Manufacturing enterprises are metallurgical plants, textile mills, glass and stone works, furniture, paper, shoes, chemical, and foodstuff factories. Wool and cotton textiles, glass, metals, leather, sugar, clothing, and shoes are the chief exports.

DENMARK

The kingdom of Denmark, the smallest of the Scandinavian countries, is only about one third the size of New York state and lies to the north of Germany, jutting up into the cleft between Norway and Sweden. Denmark has an area of 16,576 square miles. Ninety-seven percent of its population was born in the country, and the greater number of the remainder is either Swedish or Norwegian. The population is more than 4,439,000, the capital, Copenhagen, on the island of Sjaelland. Other important cities are Aarhus, Odense, Aalborg, Horsens, and Randers, all in Jutland, the peninsula directly west of Sjaelland. The Evangelical Lutheran Church is established in Denmark, but there is complete freedom of worship. Primary education has been compulsory since 1814. There are secondary schools and two universities. Denmark is a constitutional monarchy. Executive power is in the hands of the crown, acting through the state council responsible to a unicameral parliament, which was established under a constitution ratified in 1953.

Denmark is a rather flat country, deficient in ore deposits, has little timberland, and rural areas are cut up into small farms. The climate of Denmark is equable. Summer days are warm without being humid, and one can then eat with comfort in the terrace restaurants which are so numerous. The winters are long and dark. The snow is heavy, and often the temperature drops below zero, but rarely does it become too cold for winter sports. During June it does not get completely dark, though a deep twilight settles over the land between 11:00 P.M. and 4:00 A.M.

Dairying is a key part of the Danish economy, and a high percentage of all butter that enters international trade is produced in Denmark. Other dairy products exported in quantity are eggs and condensed milk. Many of the people including shopkeepers, understand and speak English, though the national tongue is Danish.

Manufactures are growing rapidly, but they deal for the most part with production for home use, or with artistic products of lace, textiles, porcelain, and silver. Surrounded on three sides by the waters of the North and Baltic Seas, Denmark is naturally a nation of fishermen. Aside from extensive dairying, Danish farmers raise mostly grains, potatoes, and fodder. Shipping is important.

DOMINICAN REPUBLIC

The Dominican Republic, occupying the eastern two thirds of the island of Hispaniola in the West Indies, has an area of 19,332 square miles. The population is about 2,608,000. The inhabitants are mainly a mixture of Spaniards, Indians, and Negroes, though there are small pure-blooded Spanish and Negro minorities. Spanish is the common tongue, though English and Haitian patois are also spoken. A considerable proportion of the adult population is still illiterate. Primary schooling is now free and compulsory. Roman Catholicism is the predominant religion. In 1844 this territory acquired its independence and set up a republican form of government. Frequent revolutions and financial troubles resulted in occupation by the U.S. Marines (1916-1924). Government consists of a president, a Senate, and a Chamber of Deputies, all serving terms of 5 years. The capital is Cuidad Trujillo; Santiago de los Caballeros and San Pedro de Macorís are other important cities.

The climate is generally warm, and rainfall is abundant except to the south of the mountains which run roughly through the middle of the island in a strip 80 miles wide and about 10,000 feet high. Much of the land is uninhabited mountainous forests. Resources of gold, copper, iron, petroleum, and coal are largely undeveloped. The chief crops are sugar, rice, coffee, cacao, corn, and tobacco. Agriculture and the processing of sugar are the most important industries. Exports are sugar, tobacco, coffee, cacao, and molasses.

ECUADOR

Situated in northwestern South America, Ecuador lies entirely within the tropics, crossed by two parallel ranges of the Andes. While the coast and eastern lowlands are hot, the highlands remain cool throughout the year. The Pacific coast is dry, and the eastern stretches of the country are vast uninhabited forests. The heart of the industrial and political life of the republic is in the inter-Andean plateaus which are ideally suited for raising rice, cereals, potatoes, fruits, vegetables, cacao, coffee, sugar, and cotton. Ecuador's area is about 104,500 square miles. The population is about 3,777,000. Most of the people are Indians or mestizos; persons of pure Spanish blood are a small minority. Quito is the capital; other important towns are Guayaquil, Cuenca, and Ambato. The administration is headed by a president, elected by direct vote for a four year term; there is a bicameral congress. The Galápagos Islands belong to Ecuador. All faiths are allowed; Catholicism is predominant. Spanish is the common language. Primary education is free and compulsory.

Ecuador's resources include wild rubber, timber, gold, silver, petroleum, copper, iron lead, coal, sulfur, and salt. Agriculture is the chief industry, but manufacturing of Panama hats, textile factories, breweries, flour mills, and sugar works have recently gained in importance. Exports are mainly cacao, bananas, coffee, petroleum, gold, straw hats, and balsa wood.

EGYPT

Bounded by the Mediterranean, the Red Sea, the Sudan, and Libya, the republic of Egypt has an area of 386,198 square miles. Its population is about 23,410,000. A British protectorate from 1914 to 1922, the hereditary sultan was proclaimed king then and Egypt became independent. In 1952 General Mohammed Naguib seized control and forced Farouk I to abdicate. Egypt became a republic the following year, with Naguib as its first president. In 1954 Naguib was ousted by Lieutenant Colonel Gamal Nasser, whose nationalization of the Suez Canal in 1956 provoked a military action by France, Great Britain, and Israel.

The Egyptian people, basically of Hamitic stock, include Arabs, Nubians, and various mixtures. They are chiefly Moslems, but some are Christians and Jews. Modern speech is largely Arabic, but because of the presence of many foreigners, English, French, Italian, and Greek are widely understood. Education, until recently wholly in the hands of Moslems, is compulsory between 6 and 12.

Egypt is a rich store of treasures and history for the archeologist. Extensive ruins—the Pyramids, which are burial vaults for the ancient Egyptian kings, the great temples at Karnak and Luxor—draw thousands of students and tourists every year. Except for the Nile valley and the shores of the Mediterranean, Egypt is largely desert. The valley itself, and the broad delta are rich, fertile plains. Near the Mediterranean there is plenty of rain, but elsewhere it is exceedingly dry. The winter temperature averages about 57° F., summer, 81° F., but in the desert the variation is greater.

Sixty-two percent of the population is engaged in agriculture. Fishing, public works such as construction and repair of dams and reservoirs, pottery, and textile trades are other important occupations. Principal crops are cotton, sugar cane, rice, corn and other grains, beans, lentils, and onions. The mineral resources of Egypt include phosphate rock, petroleum, gypsum, talc, building stone, ochres, and manganese. Egypt exports cotton and grains.

ETHIOPIA

One of the oldest of empires, Ethiopia has an area of 395,000 square miles, including Eritrea. The population is about 19,500,000. The dominant people are the Amhara, who inhabit the highlands. North of them live the Tigréans. These two groups, of Hamito-Semitic origin, speak Cushite languages and are Coptic Christians. Other Cushite peoples are the Galla (over half the population), the Somali, and the Afar or Danakil. Some of these peoples are Christians, some Moslems, and some pagans. In the west and south are Negroid tribes. A Jewish group, the Falasha, lives north of Lake Tana. The western half of Ethiopia is mountainous, often exceeding 10,000 feet. Eastward the country descends to a plateau and then the Somali Desert. Forests are rare except in the south. The climate is generally tropical, but the temperature range is wide, varying with the altitude. The capital is Addis Ababa; other cities are Dire Dawa, Harar, and Gondar. The emperor is assisted in governing by a council of ministers and parliament. The chief products are coffee, vegetables, hides, and cereals. Mineral resources, which include petroleum, gold, silver, iron, and marble, have been discovered but have been little developed.

Eritrea, formerly an Italian colony, lies on the African coast of the Red Sea and has an area of 45,000 square miles. Its population is about 1,080,000. Its natives are seminomadic shepherds of Arabic and Hamitic origin, most of whom are either Mohammedans or Christians (Coptic Rite). They speak Arabic and two dialects similar to Ethiopian speech. Eritrea is less suitable for European settlement than Ethiopia, because its lowlands are tropical and damp, with high temperatures prevailing. Inland, where the land is higher, the heat lessens, but the country is wild and uninteresting. The coastal plains are fertile; the higher interior contains deposits of gold, salt, and potash. Some natives carry on pearl fishing in the waters of the Red Sea. Grains, garden vegetables, and coffee are raised. Exports are salt, fish meal, skins, and palm nuts. Native industries are farming, raising livestock, mat and cotton weaving, and silver work.

Administered after World War II by a British military government, Eritrea was federated with Ethiopia in 1952. It has its own government, which is responsible for local affairs. Foreign affairs, general economic policy, and defense are in the hands of the imperial government. Asmara is the capital, and Massaua the chief port.

FINLAND

Finland, located on the eastern coast of the Gulf of Bothnia, between Sweden and Russia, was a part of the Swedish kingdom from 1145 to 1809, when it became an autonomous grand duchy united with Russia. At the time of the Russian revolution, Finland declared its independence (1917), and, in 1919, it became a republic. After its hostilities with the Soviet Union during World War II, it retained an area of 130,091 square miles. The population is about 4,288,000. The national church of Finland is Evangelical Lutheran, although complete religious liberty prevails. Literacy is high because of an established system of elementary, secondary, vocational and technical schools, and universities. In language and nationality 90 percent are Finnish and 10 percent Swedish. The capital is Helsinki; other important cities are Turku, Tampere, Pori, and Vaasa. The surface of Finland is a tableland, which rises in the north to 2,000 feet, with some peaks reaching a height of 3,000 feet. The southern part of the country is in the lake region, and there are many short, swift streams. Northern Finland is a part of Lapland, in which reindeer are the chief source of food and clothing. About 74 percent of the land area is forested. The climate is rigorous, the winters long and dark.

Lumbering is the chief industry; the manufactures include wood products, paper, textiles, iron products, and chemicals. A large percentage of the people are engaged in agriculture, producing oats, rye, wheat, barley, hay, and dairy products.

FORMOSA

The island of Formosa, or Taiwan, lies 90 miles off the south coast of China. It has an area of 13,890 square miles. The population is about 10,000,000. From 1683 until its cession to Japan in 1895, Formosa belonged to China. It reverted to China in 1945 upon Japan's surrender. After his defeat by the Communists in 1949 Chiang Kai-shek withdrew to Formosa with the Nationalist government, still claiming jurisdiction over the mainland. The government derives its powers from the popularly elected National Assembly, which elects the president and vice-president. Besides the national administration, Formosa has its own provincial governor and elected legislature. The chief towns are Taipei (the capital), Taichung, and the ports of Kaohsiung, Tainan, and Keelung. The western side of Formosa, on which are found almost all the large towns, farms, and railroads, is a plain. The eastern side is mountainous and forested. The climate is subtropical. Formosa's economy is mainly devoted to intensive agriculture to provide food for a population that rose 50 percent in the five years after 1948. Fishing is also a vital occupation. The exports include rice, sugar, tea, and tropical fruits. Resources include coal, sulfur, oil, natural gas, copper, gold, and silver. Formosa is the world's greatest producer of camphor.

FRANCE

France, on the Atlantic coast of western Europe, has an area of 212,659 square miles. The coastline is about 1,900 miles long. Most of the French mountains are near the frontiers. They include the Alps, the Jura and Vosges ranges, and the Pyrenees. Between these high areas stretch the great plains of France, broken by low plateaus, fertile valleys, and river basins.

The people are chiefly of Alpine or Celtic stock. The population is about 43,787,000. French derives from Vulgar Latin, as developed in Gaul. The predominant religion is Roman Catholicism, but church and state are separate. Education is compulsory between the ages of 6 and 14.

Since 1946 the country has been the chief member of the French Union, which is made up of metropolitan France and the overseas departments and territories. The president of the republic, who is elected by the legislature, is also the president of the French Union. The new constitution (1946) provides for a bicameral legislature. Metropolitan France is divided into 90 administrative departments.

Agriculture is a leading industry and occupies about 35 percent of the working population. The most important crops are potatoes, wheat, beets, oats, barley, rye, and numerous varieties of grapes. The greatest wine-producing country in the world, France has a yearly production of more than one billion gallons of wine and exports it in great quantities. Coal, iron ore, potash, and bauxite are found in France. The chief manufactures are iron and steel products, sugar, alcohol, textiles, chemicals, perfumes, and distilled liquors. The principal exports include these manufactured items and automobiles, wine, jewelry, clothing, porcelain and glassware, and leather goods.

The chief city is Paris, one of the world's best known capitals. Marseille, Lyon, Toulouse, Bordeaux, Nice, and Nantes are the next largest cities. The main seaports are Marseille, Bordeaux, and Le Havre.

FRENCH EQUATORIAL AFRICA

Gabun, Middle Congo, Ubangi-Shari, and Chad are the four territories that make up French Equatorial Africa, formerly called French Congo. The total area is 969,000 square miles, and the population is about 4,492,000. Most of the inhabitants are Negroes, many of whom have strains of Semitic or Berber blood. There are some pygmy tribes. Government and mission schools exist, but the educational facilities are limited. There are some Moslems and Christians, but most of the natives practice animism or fetish-worship. The government is headed by a governor general, who is assisted by a government council and a grand council. Representatives are sent to the government in Paris. Each territory has its own governor. Brazzaville is the administrative center; the chief towns are Libreville, Fort Lamy, Bangui, and Pointe-Noire.

The topography of French Equatorial Africa is varied. Most of the colony is lowland, covered with dense tropical forests. There are also swamps, savannas, mountainous regions, and, in Chad, great stretches of desert. The resources are mostly undeveloped. Vast forests contain valuable hardwoods, and mineral deposits include gold, lead, manganese, and diamonds. The principal native occupation is subsistence agriculture, with manioc, yams, plantains, corn, millet, and sesame among the main crops. Cotton, coffee, cacao, peanuts, and sisal are cultivated for export.

FRENCH GUIANA

This area on the northeast coast of South America fronting on the Atlantic was long famous as the penal colony of France. Several miles off the coast was the place of confinement of the more hardened criminals, Devil's Island. The penal settlements were closed during the 1940's and the convicts returned to France. The area of French Guiana is 35,135 square miles, and the population is about 28,000. The chief town and port is Cayenne. There is free primary education. In 1946 the status of French Guiana was changed to that of an overseas department. The government is headed by a prefect, who is assisted by an elected council general. Guiana is represented in the Paris government.

The land is low, covered with valuable forests and threaded by a number of streams, which furnish the chief means of transport. Guiana has been little developed, perhaps as a result of its former status and the moist heat. The most important occupation is gold mining. The chief crops are rice, corn, manioc, cacao, bananas, and sugar cane. The chief export is gold.

FRENCH SOMALILAND

This overseas territory of France lies on Africa's eastern coast at the south end of the Red Sea. It has an area of 9,071 square miles and a population of about 65,400. The majority of the people are Somalis, Arabs, and Danakils. The capital is Djibouti. Many of the native peoples are pagans. The territory is administered by a governor, who is assisted by a representative council, and it is represented in the Paris government. There are a number of primary schools. Salt production is the only industry of the country, and salt is the principal export. Deposits of gypsum, sulfur, mica, amethyst, and petroleum have been located but not exploited.

FRENCH WEST AFRICA

This French overseas territory occupies much of the great African bulge, more than 1,000,000 square miles of which is a part of the Sahara Desert. It is made up of the territories of Senegal, French Sudan, Mauritania, French Guinea, the Ivory Coast, Upper Volta, Dahomey, and Niger, each of which is under a governor. The area is 1,805,000 square miles, and the population is about 18,777,000. The people in the north are of Hamitic or Ethiopian stock with Mediterranean and Negro infusions. Others include the Ouolofs and Fulbés. The religions include paganism, Islam, and Christianity. There are a number of elementary, secondary, technical, and teacher-training schools, and higher education is offered at Dakar. The government is headed by a governor general, assisted by a governor in each of the territories. The capital is Dakar, and other important cities are St. Louis (Senegal), Conakry (Guinea), Abidjan (Ivory Coast), Porto Novo (Dahomey), Niamey (Niger), and Bamako (Sudan). The more mountainous areas are in Guinea and Niger. Most of the rest of the country except for the low coastlands is part of the great African plateau. The chief rivers, all important to transport, are the Niger, Senegal, Casamanca, Cavally, and Sassandra.

Little of the areas is developed. The principal occupations are stock raising and agriculture, and the chief crops are peanuts, millet, corn, rice, castor beans, coconuts, rubber, bananas, coffee, cotton, pineapples and other fruits, and cacao. Near the coastal area are forests with valuable woods. French West Africa produces some gold, bauxite, and iron ore. The main exports are fruits, oil and oil seeds, cacao, gold, timber, coffee, and gum.

FRENCH WEST INDIES

Lying in the southern portion of the string of islands that stretch between the coasts of Florida and Venezuela, the French West Indies consist of the islands of Martinique and Guadeloupe, with the smaller islands of Marie-Galante, Les Saintes, Désirade, St. Barthélemy, and two-thirds of St. Martin (of which the other part is Dutch). Since 1946 Martinque and Guadeloupe have each been overseas departments of France. Each has representatives in the Paris government. Negroes comprise the majority of the inhabitants. While French is the official language, the common spoken tongue is a French patois. The main economic activity is agriculture, with sugar and rum, coffee, cacao, bananas, and pineapples the chief products.

Martinique has an area of 425 square miles and a population of about 239,000. Its capital is Fort-de-France. The island is very mountainous, culminating in the volcano Mont Pelée. The mild climate has little temperature variation throughout the year.

Guadeloupe and its dependent islands cover 680 square miles and have a population of about 229,000. Basse-Terre is the capital, and Pointe-à-Pitre is the chief port. The Rivière Salée separates Guadeloupe into a mountainous western part, Basse-Terre, and a low-lying eastern part, Grande-Terre. Here, as in Martinique, hurricanes occur frequently during the late summer.

GERMANY

Germany, a country of central Europe, has been split into East and West Germany. The Germans have long been noted for their cultural and industrial progress, but they have not been politically united during most of their history. Not until 1871 did they become a united nation. In 1933 Adolf Hitler came into power, and under his Nazi dictatorship there was a drive toward expansion, leading to war in 1939. Eventually Germany was crushed by the combined might of the Allied forces. The war ended in May, 1945. The country was then divided into occupation zones for each of the Big Four, the United States, Soviet Russia, Great Britain, and France. The city of Berlin, lying within the Soviet zone, was also split into four sectors. The area of West Germany is 95,724 square miles, and the population is about 53,500,000. East Germany has an area of about 42,100 square miles and a population of about 18,000,000.

In appearance Germans show both Nordic and Alpine characteristics. Their language is gutteral and highly inflected. Nearly two-thirds of the people are Protestants and about one-third are Catholics. German universities are world famous. The chief cities are Berlin, Hamburg, Munich, Leipzig, Essen, Cologne, Frankfurt, Dortmund, Düsseldorf, Stuttgart, Dresden, Bremen, Hanover, and Duisburg.

Although the soil is rather poor, Germany is noted for its extensive forests and scientific forestry. Coal is one great natural resource. Lignite is widely distributed, and there are considerable potash and salt deposits. Other minerals are iron ore, copper, uranium, and petroleum, but resources in general are inadequate, requiring considerable imports for Germany's industry. Important industrial products are iron and steel, machinery, electrical equipment, chemicals, optical products, and dyes and varnishes. The Kiel Canal and the Rhine River are important commercial waterways, and the latter is also a scenic route for tourists.

GHANA

Ghana, on the Guinea coast of west Africa, is bounded on the west by the Ivory Coast and on the north by the Upper Volta, both of them parts of French West Africa; on the east lies Togoland, a United Nations protectorate that belonged to Germany before World War I. Ghana consists of the former British colony of the Gold Coast, with Ashanti and the Northern Territories, and includes part of Togoland. It has an area of 91,843 square miles and a coastline of 334 miles. The people are Fanti, Ashanti, and other West African Negroes. Of approximately 4,691,000 people, the majority are animists, but there are also many Christians and Moslems. Ghana achieved independence in March, 1957, though choosing to remain within the British Commonwealth of Nations. It is governed by a prime minister, cabinet, and a national assembly; a governor general represents the British sovereign.

The chief towns are Accra (the capital), Kumasi, Sekondi, Takoradi, and Cape Coast. Takoradi is the chief port. The coastline is generally low, with a few sharply rising heights; the great African plateau begins farther inland. Cacao is by far the country's chief crop and export. Ghana is the world's leading producer. The oil palm is widely distributed, and cotton and tobacco cultivation are increasing. Food crops include manioc, corn, millet, peanuts, plantains, yams, and rice. Besides cacao, the principal exports are gold, manganese, timber, diamonds, and palm kernels.

GIBRALTAR

Gibraltar, a British crown colony, lies to the south of the Spanish province of Cádiz near the point where Europe and Africa are closest. The British territory is about 2½ square miles in area, occupying a short, narrow peninsula. The population is about 24,900. As the town itself is a fortress, further settlement is frowned upon, and most of the Spanish have withdrawn to the cities of San Roque and La Linea de la Concepción, a short distance away. Spanish is the common language, though English is the official language and has come to be taught as a foreign language in the government schools. Roman Catholicism is the predominant religion. Matters of government are in the hands of the commander in chief of the garrison, who is assisted by an executive council and a legislative council. In climate it is similar to southern Spain. The rock itself shoots abruptly up from a low coast ledge to heights from 300 to 1,400 feet. It is about 2½ miles long. The chief peacetime value of Gibraltar is for coaling and repairing of passing vessels. Its strong fortifications and strategic position give Great Britain control of the western entrance to the Mediterranean.

GREAT BRITAIN

The United Kingdom of Great Britain and Northern Ireland includes England, Scotland, Wales, and the six counties of Northern Ireland. The Isle of Man and the Channel Islands are also subject to the British crown. The area of the United Kingdom is 94,279 square miles, and the population is about 51,208,000. Supreme legislative power is vested in the bicameral Parliament, consisting of the largely hereditary House of Lords and the elected House of Commons. Members of the latter are elected every five years, unless Parliament is dissolved, to represent county and borough constituencies. While the head of state is the monarch, executive power is wielded by a cabinet of ministers, headed by the prime minister, who is selected from the majority party in the House of Commons.

The British Isles are separated from Europe by the English Channel and the North Sea. Northern Ireland is separated from western Scotland by the North Channel, which connects the Irish Sea with the Atlantic Ocean. England occupies central and southern Britain; Wales, an extension on the southwest; and Scotland, the north. Scotland has a deeply indented shoreline and many outlying islands, including the Inner and Outer Hebrides, the Shetland, and the Orkney Islands. The Grampian Mountains divide Scotland's Highlands and Lowlands, and to the south, the Cheviot Hills form the border between England and Scotland. The Pennines, running southward, form the watershed for northern England.

Great Britain supports a large population in a small area because it is one of the most highly industrialized regions in the world. The home of the Industrial Revolution, the country has been a great importer of raw materials and exporter of manufactured goods. This economy is based on Britain's resources of coal and iron ore. The most important exports are iron and steel products, machinery, and textiles. To handle its commerce the country built a great merchant marine, which was formerly the largest in the world.

Since World War II Great Britain has lost her industrial supremacy. The older British factories are often less efficient than the newer foreign plants. Britain is at a disadvantage because she must import most of her raw materials, and the colonies from which these came are gradually slipping away from the control of the government in London. Finally, during the two world wars most of the British investments abroad were liquidated to meet the pressing military needs.

England. Smaller than the state of Florida, England is the heart of a vast commonwealth that contains more than a fifth of the earth's land surface and a fourth of the world's population. England has a population of about 41,840,000. London, one of the world's largest cities, is the capital. Birmingham, Liverpool, Manchester, Leeds, Sheffield, and Bristol are the next largest cities. The English language is a member of the Germanic branch of the Indo-European family.

England has a comprehensive educational system. Nursery schools, for the pre-school age child, are part of the general plan. On the secondary level, the best institutions are private schools, called "public schools" by the English. Oxford and Cambridge are among the oldest and best known European universities. The Established Church is the Anglican (Episcopal) communion, a Protestant denomination.

Scotland. The Gaelic influence is more pronounced in Scotland, which the Roman legions never penetrated and which the Teutonic tribes were not successful in conquering. Gaelic is still spoken in isolated parts of the Scottish Highlands, and Low Scots, a dialect of English, makes the speech of many Scotsmen almost unintelligible to English speakers. Standard English is, however, spoken by the majority of the Scots. Although there is an Anglican Church in Scotland, Presbyterianism is predominant. Edinburgh is the capital, but Glasgow, the famous shipbuilding center, is the largest city and the most important industrially. Other cities are Aberdeen and Dundee. The population is about 5,133,300.

The industrial and agricultural life of Scotland is similar to that of England, but on a smaller scale. Scotland is noted for its fine woolen goods and Scotch whisky. Hydroelectric power, made available by many rivers and lochs, has been increasingly developed in the Highlands since World War II.

Wales, technically a principality, is actually an integral part of the United Kingdom. The eldest son of the reigning British sovereign bears the title "Prince of Wales." The population is about 2,601,000. Approximately 25 percent of the Welsh speak Welsh, a Celtic language, but they also use English, and Welsh is gradually dying out. Wales is a beautiful mountainous country with a rocky and indented coast. Cardiff, Swansea, Rhondda, Newport, and Merthyr Tydfil are the principal cities.

The mineral resources include rich deposits of coal, iron, slate, lead, and zinc. Mining and manufacturing have been more important than agriculture.

Northern Ireland. The six counties in northwestern Ireland occupy most of the old province of Ulster. The population is about 1,394,000. The people of Northern Ireland are predominantly Protestant, one of the reasons why they chose to remain within the United Kingdom rather than join the Irish Republic in breaking with Britain. Northern Ireland has a separate Parliament of two houses, the Senate and the House of Commons, but is also represented in the British Parliament at London. The executive is the governor, appointed by the crown, and there is a ministry headed by the prime minister. Belfast is the capital and chief city.

Agriculture is the most important occupation; wheat, oats, barley, corn, potatoes, flax, turnips, and hay are grown. Cattle and sheep are raised. Mineral products include basalt and igneous rocks, chalk, clay, diatomite, fireclay, granite, limestone, and sand and gravel. Linen and ships are most important manufactures.

GREECE

Modern Greece, including Crete, the Dodecanese, and other islands, has an area of 51,246 square miles. Its population is about 8,031,000. Almost all the people speak modern Greek, which is closely related to the classical language. In religion the overwhelming majority belong to the Greek Orthodox Church, but there are small groups of Roman Catholics, Protestants, Mohammedans, and Jews. Athens, the famous center of antiquity, is the modern capital and principal city. Other important cities are Piraeus, the port of Athens, Salonika, Patras, Kavalla, and Larissa. Throughout the country are scattered the ruins of places that are famous in the history of ancient Greece. The climate is warm and pleasant. Only a fourth of the land is cultivable; the rest is barren and mountainous. Natural resources include iron, emery, copper, zinc, lead, silver, manganese, timber, and marble.

Manufacturing enterprises include the making of olive oil, wine, textiles, chemical products, and foodstuffs, but the predominant industry is agriculture, the chief products of which are grains, tobacco, cotton, grapes, currants, olives, citrus fruits, rice, milk, and cheese. Export trade consists of minerals, tobacco, currants, raisins, and sponges.

GREENLAND

Greenland, lying off the northeastern coast of Canada and largely within the Arctic Circle, belongs to Denmark and is represented in its Parliament. The administration is under a governor representing the Danish prime minister. The largest island in the world, Greenland has an area of about 840,000 square miles, nearly seven-eighths of which is covered with ice. The climate is too cold and bleak for European habitation. The coastline is indented with fiords, like that of Norway. Greenlanders are Eskimos with some Danish blood.

Livestock and vegetables are raised along the coasts, where the inhabitants have small villages. Fish, seal, and whale are abundant. The mineral resources include cryolite, iron, coal, and copper. Cryolite is the chief export. Greenland was discovered and colonized by Eric the Red about 982. This colony disappeared several centuries later. Greenland became a full member of the Danish Commonwealth under a new Danish constitution ratified in May, 1953.

GUATEMALA

The most populous and one of the largest Central American republics, Guatemala lies south of Mexico. It has an area of about 42,042 square miles. Its population is about 3,349,000. About 54 percent is pure Indian. The rest is mixed Spanish and Indian, or of European descent. Many native dialects are in use among the Indians, but most of the people also speak Spanish, the official language. In religion the inhabitants are overwhelmingly Roman Catholics. Aside from the regular primary and secondary schools, Guatemala has a university and schools of art and music. The capital is Guatemala City. Guatemala has been a republic since 1839. At the head of state is a president.

Though the climate is warm and damp, it is quite healthful. The Pacific coast area is low, but much of the rest of the land is hilly or mountainous, interspersed with high valleys, grassy plains, and forests. Timber, chrome, silver, gold, copper, iron, and lead are natural resources, but there is little mining.

Agriculture is the chief industry, including the raising of coffee, bananas, sugar, corn, beans, and rice. Industries are mainly agricultural processing and the making of pottery, which is sold to tourists in the market places of the towns. Important items of export are chicle (Guatemala being one of the largest producers of chicle, used in the making of chewing gum), coffee, bananas, cotton, essential oils (citronella and lemon grass), and lumber.

HAITI

The republic of Haiti occupies the western third of the island of Hispaniola. Its area is about 10,714 square miles. Its population is roughly 3,305,000. Port-au-Prince, the capital, is built on a large bay and has a good harbor. The inhabitants are mostly Negroes, but there are large numbers of mulatto Haitians, who are descendants of former French settlers. The common language is French, but it has been adulterated by native words and careless pronunciation. Catholicism is the principal religion, and the educational system is patterned after that of France. Voodooism, a kind of secret rite connected with magic, superstition, and sacrifices involving the use of human blood, was once prevalent in many of the West Indies, especially Haiti. It is less common today, but it has by no means been wiped out.

The Haitian climate is wholly tropical. Lying in the West Indies hurricane belt, it is often visited by severe storms. The land has high mountains descending abruptly to the shores, alluvial plains, rugged plateaus, and great valleys. Its resources are valuable forests, gold, silver, copper, iron, antimony, tin, sulfur, coal, limestone, and porphyry, but little development of these riches has occurred. The people are predominantly agricultural, and the chief products are coffee and sugar. Other crops grown are cacao, cotton, sisal, tobacco, and bananas. Coffee, lumber, cotton, sisal, sugar, and cacao are the chief exports.

HAWAII

After Queen Liliuokalani was deposed in 1893 the Hawaiian people formed a republic and asked for annexation by the United States. Congress granted the request in 1898, and in 1900 created the Territory of Hawaii. The governor is appointed by the president; the two-house legislature is elected by the people. Hawaii is represented in the U.S. House of Representatives by a popularly elected delegate.

The main islands in the group (which used to be called the Sandwich Islands) are about 2,400 miles southwest of San Francisco. They are the crossroads of the Pacific for both ships and planes. Hawaii, Maui, Lanai, Molokai, Oahu, Kauai and Niihau are the larger islands, and about 13 smaller ones stretch northwest across the Pacific for 1,600 miles. The total area is 6,420 square miles. The population is about 500,000. Honolulu, capital of the islands, is on the island of Oahu; Hilo is on Hawaii. The inhabitants are native Hawaiians, mixed groups including many Japanese, Americans, and Europeans. Most of the natives are Christians, some Protestant and some Catholic. The native tongue is dying out, and English is spoken generally and is taught in the schools.

Hawaii has luxurious forests and areas of valuable fertile soil. Sugar and pineapples are the chief crops and the most important commercially, but coffee, rice, and bananas are also grown. Agriculture, processing of various crops, canneries, and fertilizer factories are the main industries. The export list includes sugar, pineapples, molasses, coffee, hides, bananas, sisal hemp, cotton and wool.

HONDURAS

Bounded on the north and east by the Caribbean, and on the west by El Salvador and a short stretch of the Pacific, Honduras has an area of 43,227 square miles and has approximately 1,711,000 people. Tegucigalpa, an island city, is the capital of the republic, and its chief ports are Amapala on the Pacific and Puerto Cortés on the Gulf of Honduras. It is estimated that about 40 percent of the people are of unmixed Indian descent; the rest are chiefly mestizos. Other elements in the population are Negroes (along the Caribbean coast) and people of Spanish or other European ancestry. Spanish is the official language, and Roman Catholicism the predominant religion. Education between the ages of 7 and 15 is free and entirely secular, but much of the population is illiterate.

Honduras is an undulating land of valleys and hills. To the west rise sharp volcanic peaks. The climate in the highlands is delightful and warm, but the lowlands, especially along the east coast, are hot and moist. The industrial life of the republic consists of the manufacture of items for local use, large-scale banana culture, mining, and the raising of livestock. Coffee, tobacco, and coconuts are other agricultural products. The mining industry yields gold, silver, copper, lead, zinc, iron, antimony, and coal. Bananas are the most important export. The export trade also includes lumber, coffee, livestock, and silver.

HONG KONG

This British crown colony is an enclave within China, consisting of an island and islets near the coast and a mainland area, all totaling 391 square miles. The population, overwhelmingly Chinese, is about 2,600,000. The administration of the colony is in the hands of a British governor, who is assisted by an executive council and a legislative council. There are numerous schools and the University of Hong Kong. The Hong Kong harbor is one of the best in the world. The capital is Victoria, on the island, and Kowloon, on the mainland, is also important. The climate is subtropical. Hong Kong's great harbor has made it the chief distributing center for south China.

HUNGARY

Hungary has an area of 35,912 square miles and is situated in the Danubian Plain of south-central Europe. Most of the inhabitants are Magyars, an ethnic group of Asiatic origin. Its population is about 9,700,000. Roman Catholics are predominant. Topographical features include the extensive Hungarian plain and the great Danube River, one of the key waterways of Europe. The chief crops are grains, potatoes, beets, and grapes; natural resources consist of timber, petroleum, coal, and bauxite. Fishing in Lake Balaton and in the many rivers is an important occupation and source of food for the people. Manufacturing includes flour milling, distilling of wine, sugar refining, iron and steel foundries, and the processing of hemp and flax. Budapest is the capital; Miskolc and Debrecen are the other most important cities.

ICELAND

An island republic in the North Atlantic Ocean, its northern tip touching the Arctic Circle, it has an area of 39,758 square miles; its population is about 162,000. The people are almost entirely Icelandic. About one-fourth live in rural areas. The capital is Reykjavik, where homes are heated by water from nearby hot springs. The Evangelical Lutheran Church is state supported, but there is full religious tolerance. There is no illiteracy in the republic; higher education is offered at the university. The island is mountainous, and there are a number of volcanoes. The coast is much indented and the inhabited areas of the island are generally the coastal lowlands. Most of the interior surface is barren rock, which is here and there covered by glaciers. The climate, in spite of the northern position, is relatively mild because of the influence of the Gulf Stream. Reykjavik seldom has much snow. Agriculture is almost entirely devoted to raising hay for livestock, but some potatoes and turnips are grown. About one-fifth of the working population is engaged in fishing. The chief exports are fish and products, hides, and wool.

INDIA

An independent republic and member of the British Commonwealth of Nations, India occupies the vast peninsula jutting into the Indian Ocean, separated from Asia proper by the high Himalaya Mountains. It has an area of 1,269,640 square miles. Its population is about 381,690,000. The Indians are a dark-skinned people, largely Caucasoid in origin but mixed with other races. The chief religion is Hinduism, which developed the caste system now outlawed by the Indian government; other religions are Islam, Sikhism, Buddhism, Jainism, and Christianity, the latter having only about 8,000,000 adherents. The masses of the Indian people are largely illiterate, but with Indian independence great strides toward the elimination of illiteracy were made. There are a number of universities, among which are included a number of Christian schools. The capital is New Delhi, near the old Mogul capital of Delhi. Other important cities are Calcutta, Bombay, Madras, Hyderabad, Ahmedabad, Cawnpore, Lucknow, and Nagpur, all of which are of considerable size.

South of the great mountain barrier at the north of the country is a low fertile area contained in the Ganges and Brahmaputra river basins. To the south of the Ganges basin rises the great Deccan Plateau. Rajputana is largely desert; there are other parts somewhat less arid. Irrigation and power dams have been built throughout the country and a forward-looking policy calls for the building of more, so that India may become more self-sufficient in food supplies.

Agriculture is the chief occupation and supports a large percentage of India's population. Old systems of landlordism are being reformed. The chief crops are rice, wheat, sugar cane, tea, cotton, and jute; cattle, sheep, goats, and other animals are raised. Industries include weaving, metalworking, iron and steel, food preparation, leather, shipbuilding, and building materials. Principal minerals found are coal, iron ore, manganese, petroleum, salt, mica, copper, gold, saltpeter, chromite, and thorium. The principal exports are jute and jute products, cotton goods, tea, hides and skins, leather goods, oilseeds, spices, manganese ore, tobacco, lac, fruits and vegetables, oils, wool and woolen goods.

INDONESIA

The Republic of Indonesia is the independent country that came into existence in 1949 when the Dutch gave up their sovereignty over the rich Malay Archipelago. The new republic comprises all the islands of the former Netherlands East Indies, except Dutch New Guinea, which is still in dispute. Indonesia includes thousands of islands, chief of which are Java, Sumatra, Celebes, most of Borneo, part of Timor, the Moluccas, and the Lesser Sundra Islands. The total area of these islands is about 735,800 square miles, and the population is about 81,900,000. The Indonesians are Malays, a branch of the Mongoloid race. Some Negrito and Papuan peoples are found there also. More than 90 percent of the people are Moslems, and there are small minorities of Christians, Buddhists, Hindus, and pagan peoples. Only about 60 percent of the people are literate, but great efforts are being made to extend the educational facilities. The capital is Jakarta on Java, and other important cities are Jokjakarta, Surabaya, Bandung, Semarang, and Surakarta on Java, Palembang on Sumatra, Banjermasin on Borneo, and Macassar on Celebes.

The islands have irregular coastlines, mountains (some with active volcanoes), swamps, and thick jungles. The climate is tropical. Indonesia is rich in rubber, tin, petroleum, coal, gold, silver, manganese, bauxite, and phosphate. Self-sufficient in food supplies, the islands produce rice, sugar, coffee, tea, cinchona, tobacco, cacao, palm oil, copra, spices, and fine hardwoods. All of these are exported.

IRAN

Iran, called Persia generally until 1935, has an area of about 630,000 square miles and a population of about 18,945,000, much of which represents nomadic tribes. Besides the Iranians there are many minorities, including Turks, Kurds, Baluchis, Lurs, and Arabs. Islam is the prevailing religion. Iran is governed by a hereditary shah, a Senate and National Assembly, and a prime minister and cabinet. Almost half of the people are illiterate, but great strides have been made in education. Teheran is the capital; other large cities are Tabriz, Isfahan, and Meshed.

Iran's surface has vast portions of desert territory and numerous mountain ranges. On the south lie the Persian Gulf and the Arabian Sea. Dasht-I-Kavir, the great salt desert, lies between Iran's western mountains and the Afghan border. The Iranian oil field is one of the richest in the world. Iron, coal, copper, lead, manganese, nickel, and cobalt are also found. Agriculture is the chief occupation, and grains, fruits, cotton, tobacco, and wool are the principal products. The Persian hand-loomed carpets are famous. Important exports are petroleum, carpets, dried fruits, gums, skins, and furs.

IRAQ

This country, known anciently as Mesopotamia, was freed from the Turks during World War I, and for a while was mandated to Great Britain. It is now an independent state with a limited monarchy and a responsible ministry. The legislature consists of a Senate of nominated "elder statesmen" and a lower house elected by male suffrage. The area is about 172,000 square miles, and the population is about 4,842,000. In addition to the Iraqi (Arab) majority, there are Kurds, Turks, and Iranians. The nation is chiefly Moslem. The Arabic language is in common use and is taught in the government schools. Baghdad is the capital, Basra is the chief seaport, and Mosul is another large city.

The rich valleys of the Tigris and Euphrates rivers run the length of the country, and the soil is very fertile, though some of it must be irrigated. The southern borders are almost wholly desert, but mountains form the northern and eastern boundaries, beyond which lie Turkey and Iran. Iraq's resources are few in number but great in value. Iraq produces much petroleum and about 80 percent of the world's trade in dates. In 1952 Iraq forced the British-owned oil company to share equally in profits and to grant other concessions. In 1958 Iraq and Jordan announced the unification of their countries under the name "Arab Federation."

IRELAND

Ireland, or Eire, formerly the Irish Free State, an independent republic, occupies all of the island of Ireland except for the northeastern part (six counties), which is part of the United Kingdom. The republic has an area of 27,137 square miles. Its population is about 2,895,000. The president is elected for a term of seven years; the prime minister is the executive head. The capital is Dublin; other important towns are Cork, Limerick, and Waterford. English is spoken by all inhabitants, but the use of Gaelic is encouraged. The majority of the Irish are Roman Catholics, but there is no state church. Elementary education is free.

The island is not unlike a bowl, rimmed by hills of bold relief, which slope inland to low hills. The coastline is irregular; there are a great many bays, particularly along the west coast. The interior heights vary from 500 to 3,414 feet.

Ireland is generally a fertile agricultural and pastoral land, with most of the population supported by the soil. The principal crops are wheat, oats, potatoes, barley, turnips, sugar beets, and flax. There is much stock raising. The leading manufactures are beet sugar, agricultural implements, prepared seafoods, cheese, butter, margarine, alcoholic beverages, flour, and woodwork.

ISRAEL

Israel is an independent Jewish republic in former Palestine. The republic was declared on May 14, 1948, at the end of the term of British mandate over Palestine. The state was immediately subjected to invasion by Arab forces from neighboring states, but in the months of fighting that followed, Israeli arms were the more successful. The original area apportioned by the United Nations to Israel was considerably enlarged as a result of Israeli victories.

Lebanon lies to the north, Syria and Jordan to the east, Egypt to the southwest, and the Mediterranean to the west. Israel has an area of 8,048 square miles. The population is about 1,872,000. Israel's capital is the city of Jerusalem. Other cities are Tel Aviv-Jaffa and Haifa. Jerusalem, which is a holy city for Jews, Christians, and Moslems, is now divided; the old city is under Jordan while the new city is part of Israel. Hebrew and Arabic are official. Education is free and compulsory.

Israel is generally arid, but the littoral is warm and moist during the summer. Here there is sufficient rain for agriculture. Irrigation is practiced in some of the drier areas. The chief crops are citrus and other fruits, grains, olives, and vegetables. Stock raising is important. Citrus fruits and polished diamonds are the main exports. The attack on Egypt by Israel, France, and Great Britain over the Suez Canal seizure in October, 1956, was quickly ended under United Nations pressure.

ITALY

Since 1946 Italy has been a republic. Italy has an area of 116,224 square miles on the long peninsula that juts into the Mediterranean. The population is about 48,223,000. Roman Catholicism is the state religion. Elementary education is free and compulsory between the ages of 6 and 14. There are secondary and technical schools. Italy has many universities, that in Bologna being the oldest in Europe. The capital is Rome; other important cities are Milan, Naples, Genoa, Turin, Palermo, Florence, Venice, and Bologna.

The northern borders of the country are rimmed by the Alps; between them and the Apennines, which run the length of the Italian Peninsula as a kind of backbone, is the broad basin of the Po River. Italy has one of the warmest climates in Europe. Rural areas are given over to the production of grains, leguminous plants, vegetables, vines, olives, and forage for livestock. Italy's limited mineral resources include iron ore and pyrites, sulfur, zinc, mercury, and building stone. Mining is important in Sicily, Sardinia, Tuscany, and Lombardy; textiles, raw silk, sugar, cheese, and wine are products of other enterprises. Exports are mainly agricultural products, textiles, as well as motor vehicles and machinery.

JAMAICA

Discovered by Columbus in 1494, the island of Jamaica, which lies just south of the eastern end of Cuba, remained a Spanish possession until 1655 when it was taken by the English. With the Cayman Islands and the Turks and Caicos Islands, Jamaica has an area of 4,680 square miles. It is a member of the British West Indies Federation, which was formed in 1958. About three-fourths of the people are Negroes. The population is about 1,542,000. Kingston, the capital and chief port, is on the southern coast of the island.

Jamaica is famous mainly because of the fine rum produced there, but its exports of sugar, bananas, and bauxite are more important. Coffee, cacao, and allspice are also exported.

JAPAN

The Japanese nation consists of four main islands, Honshu, Hokkaido, Kyushu, and Shikoku. Most of the territory is mountainous and volcanic. Fujiyama, the sacred snow-capped volcano of Japan, is 12,395 feet high, and has been dormant since 1707. Occasionally sudden flows of lava from long inactive craters will do a great deal of damage and take many lives; however, the chief physical disturbance is an almost constant series of earthquakes, a few of which have been horrible national catastrophes. Summer is usually hot, humid, and short; winters are cold and long, though not severe. Japan's area is about 142,700 square miles. The population is about 90,000,000. Japanese, an agglutinative speech written in ideographs instead of letters, bears some resemblance to both Korean and Chinese. Shintoism and Buddhism are the principal religions. However, Christianity is slowly growing. Japan has established a comprehensive and modern educational system. All children must attend school up to the age of 15.

The emperor of Japan is called *tenshi* (Son of Heaven), or *tenno* (Heavenly King). The Diet consists of a House of Representatives whose members are elected for four years by universal suffrage and a House of Councilors also elected by the people. The executive power is in the hands of a prime minister and cabinet responsible to the Diet. Tokyo is the capital; other large cities are Osaka, Kyoto, Nagoya, and Yokohama.

Natural resources of coal, copper, gold, zinc, iron pyrites, petroleum, silver, sulfur, lead, and chromite are claimed to be inadequate for the industrial development, which has taken great strides in the 20th century. Agriculture—intensive production of rice, cereals, tobacco, tea, and fruits—mining, silk culture, fishing, and factory work, producing textiles, paper, vegetable oil, pottery, leather, matting, canned goods, and machinery, are the principal industries. Exports are various manufactured goods with textiles forming more than half the total.

JORDAN

The present Haskemite Kingdom of Jordan was formerly the British mandated territory of Trans-Jordan. Jordan's area is approximately 37,500 square miles and lies to the east of Israel. The population is about 1,500,000. Amman is the capital, Jerusalem and Bethlehem famous biblical cities. The people are predominantly Moslem and Arab-speaking. The chief river is the famous Jordan, which empties into the Dead Sea in a great depression 1,292 feet below sea level. East of the Jordan the country is mostly desert with few streams and towns.

Agriculture, greatly dependent on irrigation but Jordan's principal occupation, is largely carried on in the Jordan Valley. The chief crops are grapes, cereals, citrus and other fruits, and vegetables; large areas are used for grazing sheep, goats, and camels. Minerals exploited include phosphates, building stone, and potash (from the Dead Sea); other known deposits include copper and iron ore, and probably oil.

KOREA

Korea, a country of east Asia occupying a strategic position between China, the U.S.S.R., and Japan, has been divided between North and South Korea since 1945. It is a peninsula about 480 miles long and about 200 miles wide, and with its adjacent islands it has an area of about 85,266 square miles. The population is about 21,800,000. North Korea's area, after United Nations negotiations ended in 1954, was 46,814 square miles. South Korea's area totaled 38,452 square miles. The Korean people are related to the Chinese and Japanese but are mixed with other east Asian peoples; they often use Chinese ideographs in writing, but their language is quite different. Buddhism and Confucianism are the chief religions, but Christianity is growing. By Asiatic standards Korea has a good school system and a low illiteracy rate.

Korea is very mountainous but has much rich agricultural land. Farming is the chief occupation; products include rice, wheat, barley, beans, tobacco, and cotton. The country has one of the world's richest deposits of tungsten; other minerals are coal, iron ore, copper, zinc, lead, gold, and silver. In North Korea the Japanese developed hydroelectric power and built up many industries, which produce textiles, iron and steel, chemicals, and fertilizers. The chief exports are rice and minerals.

LAOS

This southeast Asian land, formerly part of French Indochina, was settled prior to the 14th century by Thai (Lao) immigrants from China. It was usually divided among rival kingdoms. After 1707 Laos consisted of two quarreling kingdoms, Luang Prabang and Vientiane, often at war with Siam. In 1893 France established a protectorate over them. The French were temporarily ousted by the Japanese in 1945. In 1947 the two kingdoms became a unified constitutional monarchy, which became an independent state within the French Union in 1949. In 1953 it was invaded by Vietminh forces supporting a local insurrectionist movement, the Pathet Lao. A truce was called in 1954, but hostilities did not cease until 1956. Laos has an area of 91,450 square miles and is largely mountainous and forested. The population is about 3,000,000. The people are mostly Lao, with minorities of other Thai groups and various Mon-Khmer, Indonesian, and Sino-Tibetan hill tribes. The chief religion is Buddhism. There are many primary, but fewer higher schools. Main towns are Luang Prabang and Vientiane, the administrative center. Rice, corn, fruit, tea, and tobacco are grown. Teak and other woods are exported.

LEBANON

A Near Eastern republic to the north of Israel and west of Syria, with the Mediterranean on the west, Lebanon was founded in 1941 from areas mandated to the French after World War I. The country has an area of about 4,000 square miles. The population is about 1,450,000. Christians slightly outnumber the Moslems, but each group is split into several sects. Arabic is the common and official language, but French, Greek, and other languages are also spoken. The state has established schools, and in addition there are Moslem and Christian mission schools. There are three universities in Beirut, Lebanese, American, and French. The capital is Beirut; other important towns are Tripoli, Zahle, Saida, and Tyre.

The republic has two mountain ranges, Lebanon and Anti-Lebanon; between these lies the fertile Bekaa plain. The climate is Mediterranean, and the rainfall varies from 15 to 45 inches a year. Agriculture is the principal occupation and the chief crops are citrus and other fruits, vegetables, nuts, olives, tobacco, cotton, wheat and other cereals. Donkeys, cattle, goats, and sheep are raised. Iron ore and lignite are mined. Lebanon manufactures textiles and cement. The chief exports are fruits, nuts, vegetables, wool, silk, livestock, and animal products.

LIBERIA

The efforts of several American philanthropic societies to make provision for freed American slaves resulted in the establishment of Liberia, an independent republic of Africa between British Sierra Leone and French Ivory Coast, in 1847. The capital, Monrovia, was named for James Monroe. Its area is 43,000 square miles. The population is about 2,750,000. Native African tribes constitute the bulk of the population, there being not more than 20,000 descendants of former slaves.

The resources of the land are undeveloped except for timber and rubber. The inhabitants are farmers, raising coffee, cassava, rice, sugar, and other foodstuffs. Liberia is a plateau country, densely forested, with perhaps the best supply of timber in all of West Africa. Its climate is equatorial, with a rainfall of more than 150 inches a year. Throughout its history Liberia has been under the protection of the United States.

LIBYA

The kingdom of Libya, occupying a great expanse of desertland in North Africa, has an area of about 679,000 square miles. The population is about 1,340,000. It has Arabs, Berbers, and Negroes, with minorities of Italians and Jews. Most of the people are Arabic-speaking Moslems. Tripoli and Bengazi are the chief cities. Libya has a climate similar to that of Sicily. The coastal strip raises grains, olives, fruits, tobacco, and figs. The grasslands make excellent pasturage for livestock. Aside from a little timber and some salt, the country is almost devoid of resources. Orchard products, such as olives, citrus fruits, dates, and figs are exported in large quantities. On Dec. 24, 1951, Libya became an independent state under United Nations sponsorship. There are two capitals, Tripoli and Bengazi.

LIECHTENSTEIN

Between Austria and Switzerland is the little hereditary principality of Liechtenstein with an area of 62 square miles. The population is about 14,750. Vaduz is the capital, residence of the prince, and the seat of the popularly elected Diet of 15 members. The principal products of the country are corn, wine, dairy cattle, and marble. Textiles, leather, and pottery trades flourish. The principality was founded in 1719 as part of the Holy Roman (German) Empire, but became independent in 1866. It uses Swiss currency and is within the Swiss customs union. Most of the people are Catholics of German descent.

LUXEMBOURG

An independent Grand Duchy between Belgium, Germany, and France, Luxembourg has an area of 999 square miles. The population is about 312,000. In the north it lies in the Ardennes plateau, rising to heights of 1,800 feet on the Belgian border. The southern part, a continuation of the Lorraine plateau, is a fertile agricultural section. The country is drained by the Alzette, Moselle, and Sauer Rivers. Lying between two great nations, Luxembourg has become a buffer state. Although it was legally a neutralized country it was occupied by Germany during both World Wars. After World War II Luxembourg joined the United Nations and the North Atlantic Treaty Organization and entered the Benelux customs union with Belgium and the Netherlands. The official language is French but the common speech is a German dialect. School attendance is compulsory between the ages of 6 and 13. Nearly all the people are Roman Catholics. The state is headed by a Grand Duchess, but the executive power is in the hands of a prime minister and cabinet, who are responsible to a popularly elected Chamber of Deputies.

Almost a third of the population is engaged in agriculture, the chief crops raised being oats, potatoes, rye, and wheat. Fruits are also cultivated. Mining and the manufacture of iron are the region's main industries. Factories for the production of cement, machinery, metalwares, chemicals, wines, leather, and brushes are important. The capital and largest city is Luxembourg. Esch-Alzette is an iron mining center.

MADAGASCAR

The natives of Madagascar, a French overseas territory in the Indian Ocean some 240 miles off the southeast coast of Africa, are Malagasy, similar to those found in the East Indies. The Island, separated from the mainland by Mozambique Channel, has an area of about 227,760 square miles (including the nearby French islands). The population is about 4,500,000. There is a small French minority. Some of the tribes have been Christianized, although many of the outlying people are pagan. From 6 to 14 education is compulsory for all children. Tananarive, the capital, Majunga, Tamatave, the chief seaport, and Fianarantsoa are the principal cities.

Natural resources are timber, semiprecious stones, graphite, mica, and other minerals. The chief crops are rice, millet, corn, manioc, sugar cane, coffee, cotton, tobacco, yams, and peanuts. Some livestock, chiefly cattle, is raised. There are textile and weaving mills, metal works, sugar refineries, and meat packers. Native industries include basketry, fiber cloth weaving, and straw hat making. Exports are confined to minerals, spices, raffia, and canned meats.

MALAYA, FEDERATION OF

The Malay Peninsula, beginning at the Isthmus of Kra, extends south from southeastern Asia to the Singapore Strait, with the Gulf of Siam and the South China Sea on the east, the Bay of Bengal and Strait of Malacca on the west. Lower Siam (Thailand) occupies about half of the peninsula's northern section; the southerly part is taken up by the nine sultanates of Perak, Selangor, Negri Sembilan, Pahang, Johore, Kelantan, Trengganu, Kedah, and Perlis, and the areas of Penang and Malacca, which make up the Malayan Federation. The area is 50,690 square miles, population about 6,252,000.

Chinese, Malays, and Indians form the bulk of the population. The languages spoken are Chinese and variations of the Malay and Indian tongues. Educational facilities are provided by government grants to native schools, mission schools, and actual government foundations. The Mohammedan, Hindu, and Buddhist religions are the most prevalent, though many of the interior tribes practice pagan rites.

The climate is very warm, with heavy and regular rainfall. The west coast region is especially uncomfortable for Europeans. Dense jungles (inhabited by wild animals and colorful birds) and highland forests provide many fine woods and valuable forest products. Comparatively little of the peninsula (except in Pahang) is suited for agriculture. The chief products are lumber, rubber, copra, coconuts, betel nuts, palm oil, tin, gold, coal, rice, tapioca, and pineapple, all of which are exported in some quantities. Rubber and tin are the most important in the world market. Rubber plantations and tin mines offer the greatest employment.

Chief cities are Kuala Trengganu, Kuala Lumpur, Taiping, Johore Bahru, Seremban, Alor Star, and Kota Bahru. Malaya was occupied by the Japanese in 1942 but recovered by the British in 1945. Since the end of the war the federation has been constantly troubled by Communist guerrillas and terrorists.

MALTA

Malta, a British island colony, important as a Mediterranean naval base, lies between Europe (Sicily) and Africa (Tunisia). The area, with Comino, Gozo, and other isles, is 122 square miles. The population is about 314,000. Malta is oval-shaped and very rocky, with a rugged coastline. The surface is composed of coral limestone, yellow sandstone, a blue clay abounding in fossils, and an excellent yellow-white limestone used for building. The island has no rivers or lakes, but there are numerous springs. The climate is mild and healthful. Valletta is the capital and chief port; other cities are Sliema, Hamrun, and Birkirkara.

The people are descendants of the island's many conquerors, and are called Maltese. The majority of them are Roman Catholics. They speak English and Maltese, a language akin to Arabic and having an Italian mixture. Good schools are provided by the government. The chief industries are farming, canning, fishing, and quarrying.

MAURITIUS

Mauritius, an island and British colony, lies in the Indian Ocean, 500 miles east of Madagascar. With other islands the area is 804 square miles; the population is about 569,000. A coastal plain lies in the north, and in the south mountains rise to heights of 2,710 feet. The rivers become torrents during the rainy season. There are thousands of acres of olive, coconut, bamboo, and other trees.

A densely populated area, Mauritius is inhabited by Indians, Negroes, Europeans, and mixed people. English and French are official languages; Hinduism and Roman Catholicism, the principal religions. Education is free, but not compulsory, in the state-supported primary and secondary schools. The largest towns are Port Louis, the capital and chief seaport, Curepipe, a mountain resort, Mahébourg, and Souillac.

The leading industry of the island is the cultivation of sugar cane and its refining. Other crops are corn, millet, yams, tobacco, rice, tea, aloe fiber, indigo, turmeric, and spices. Tropical fruits are also grown. Exports are sugar, copra, molasses, alcohol, tea, and tobacco.

MEXICO

The federal republic of Mexico lies between the United States and Central America with an area of 760,375 square miles. The population is about 30,538,000. Mexico is a series of high terraced plateaus, which extend southeast between two great mountain chains, with fertile coastal plains along the Pacific, the Gulf of Mexico, and the Caribbean Sea. The lowest point is the Yucatan Peninsula, a flat, dense jungle. In the eastern chain are the famous volcanic peaks, Orizaba (18,696 feet), Popocatepetl (17,883 feet), and Ixtaccihuatl (17,342 feet).

Mexico is the second most populous of the Latin-American states. Most of the people are mixed Indian and Spanish, but there are some of pure Spanish descent. Although Spanish is the common speech, many Indian languages are also used. The prevailing religion is Roman Catholic; the church, however, is subject to strict regulation. Primary education is compulsory up to the age of 15.

The chief cities are Mexico City, the capital, Guadalajara, Monterrey, Puebla, and Mérida. The country is divided into 29 states, 1 federal district, and 2 territories.

With resources of timber, oil, gold, silver, copper, lead, zinc, coal, and graphite, Mexico is one of the most richly endowed nations of the world. Only 8 per cent of the land is actually used for agricultural purposes, though three times as much is available. The chief crops are wheat, cotton, sugar, tomatoes, corn, rice, and henequen. Industries consist of petroleum and sugar refineries, iron foundries, tobacco, and textile factories. Petroleum and other minerals and agricultural products are the chief exports.

MONACO

The independent principality of Monaco, covering an area of 370 acres, is a rocky peninsula extending into the Mediterranean, surrounded on land by the French department of Alpes-Maritimes. The population is about 20,500.

Monaco's fame and revenue come from the gaming tables at the Monte Carlo Casino, established in 1856. Once a possession of the Grimaldi of Genoa, Monaco has been ruled since 1297 by a prince descended from that family, under the protection in turn of Spain, France, Sardinia, and again France. It became independent in the 19th century. The present ruler, Prince Rainier, became head of the principality in 1949 and in 1956 married Grace Kelly.

MONGOLIA

Bounded on the north by Siberia and on the south by China, Mongolia spans a plateau of steppe and the Gobi Desert. Extremes of temperature characterize the climate. Nomadic Mongol herdsmen trade their wool, fur, and horn produce in Ulan Bator (the capital) and other centers. Formerly the Chinese province of Outer Mongolia, the Mongolian People's Republic is now independent. It has an area of 580,150 square miles and a population of over 1,000,000. Gold and coal are mined.

MOROCCO

Morocco, lying at the northwest corner of Africa, has an area estimated at 172,104 square miles. The population is about 8,620,000. It is a sovereign independent monarchy whose king (formerly known as sultan) rules absolutely and is assisted by a cabinet and by the National Consultative Assembly.

Morocco was divided, from 1912 to 1956, into a French protectorate, a Spanish protectorate, and the international zone of Tangier. The region has been ruled successively by Phoenicians, Romans, Arabs, and European nations. Inhabitants are mainly Berbers, Arabs, and Jews. Arabic is the official language and is most common, although Spanish and French are also used.

The inland mountains, called the Atlas, lie between the coast regions and the Sahara, and rise to 13,665 feet. The interior high, desert-like plateau has extremes of heat and cold and scanty rainfall. The principal cities are Casablanca, Fez, Marrakech, Tetuan, Larache, Alcazarquivir, Tangier, Meknès, and Rabat, the capital.

Forests contain cork, cedar, oak, and conifer trees, and considerable supplies of phosphates, lead, manganese, cobalt, iron, coal, and zinc have been found. Farming and stock raising are the chief industries. Cereal grains, garden vegetables, linseed, hay, and canary seed are the important crops. Domestic animals raised are cattle, sheep, goats, pigs, horses, mules, and camels. There are food-processing and textile industries, and native craftsmen produce rugs and leatherwork.

MOZAMBIQUE

Mozambique, or Portuguese East Africa, opposite the island of Madagascar, on the southeast coast of Africa, was discovered by Vasco da Gama, a Portuguese explorer, in 1498. It has an area of 297,731 square miles. The population is about 6,050,000. This Portuguese province is governed by a governor general, assisted by an executive council and a government council. The province is divided into 9 districts; the capital is Lourenço-Marques. Other important cities are Beira, Mozambique, and Quelimane. The country is plateau-like, with mountains and a 1,700-mile coastline to the east, and forested hills on the north. Temperatures in the uplands are temperate and healthful. Rains fall almost steadily from December through March, when the lowlands are oppressive and disease ridden.

The people are mainly of various Bantu tribes and speak Bantu dialects. There are comparatively few Europeans. The colony has a number of church missions, including Roman Catholic and Methodist, but few of the natives have been converted to Christianity.

Mozambique has fine resources of gold, silver, coal, bauxite, mica, tin, diamonds, uranium, corundum, asbestos, and oil, as well as valuable mahogany, ebony, and sandalwood. The chief occupation is agriculture, rice, tea, sesame, peanuts, tobacco, sugar cane, corn, cotton, copra, and sisal being raised. There are a few European plantations which grow citrus fruits and bananas. Livestock raised are oxen, sheep, goats, and pigs. Manufactures are cement, brick and tile, tobacco, soap, paper, and oil. The main exports are sugar, copra, cotton, and sisal.

NEPAL

An independent kingdom lying in the Himalayas with an area of about 54,000 square miles. The population is about 8,400,000. Nepal has some of the world's highest peaks—Mt. Everest (29,028 feet), Kanchenjunga (28,146 feet), and Dhaulagiri (26,810 feet). A narrow fertile strip lies along the southern border. The Katmandu Valley somewhat protects Katmandu, the capital city, from the snows and winds which are common elsewhere.

The population is mainly made up of Mongolian stock with a mixture of Indian. Hinduism and Buddhism are the dominant religions, and the languages of the country are a variety of Tibetan and Hindu tongues. The chief towns, besides Katmandu, are Patan and Bhatgaon.

The chief occupations are farming and livestock raising. Rice, corn, and wheat are the chief crops. Cattle, sheep, and goats are raised. Mineral wealth of the country includes coal, quartz, salt, mica, and copper. There are valuable forests in the south, and in the north great quantities of medicinal herbs. The exports are hides and skins, opium, medicinal drugs, gums, resins, dyes, jute, wheat, rice, pulse, butter, timber, oil seeds, spices, and saltpeter.

NETHERLANDS

This maritime kingdom of northwestern Europe, commonly called Holland, has a low coastline of sandy dunes broken by deltas of the Maas and Rhine rivers. The interior of the country is flat, and almost half the total area (13,000 square miles) is actually below sea level. Tremendous dikes hold back the sea, and long pipes over the dikes are attached to pumps draining off marshy lands, which, when reclaimed, are very fertile. Much of the Zuider Zee, now called Ijsselmeer, has been drained.

The population is about 10,956,000. The people speak Dutch, which has developed from three Low German dialects. Although the ruling family and many of the rest of the inhabitants belong to the Reformed Church, liberty of worship is traditional in Holland, the refuge of religious and political nonconformists for centuries. The throne is hereditary; the present sovereign is a woman.

Amsterdam, the largest city, is officially the capital, but The Hague is actually the seat of the government. At The Hague is located also the Palace of Peace, now used by the International Court of Justice. Other large cities are Rotterdam, Utrecht, and Haarlem.

The Netherlands was occupied by German troops during World War II. In 1948 the country entered into an economic union (Benelux) with Belgium and Luxembourg. In 1949 the government voted to join the North Atlantic Treaty Organization.

The Netherlands is an agricultural and industrial country. Grains, peas, beans, potatoes, sugar beets, onions, flax, and flowers are grown, mainly on small truck farms. Dairy and beef cattle are raised. Among the industrial enterprises are textile mills, electrical goods factories, sugar refineries, meat, fish, fruit, and vegetable canneries, flour mills, and breweries. The raising of tulips and other bulb plants has grown to considerable importance. Coal, salt, and some petroleum are the chief natural resources. The North Sea provides herring, plaice, sole, haddock, cod, and whiting. From the rivers and the Zeeland beds come eels, anchovies, smelt, shrimp, lobsters, mussels, crabs, and oysters. The major exports are milk and dairy products, eggs, fabrics, fertilizers, chemicals, electrical machinery and equipment, flower seeds and bulbs.

NETHERLANDS OVERSEAS TERRITORIES

The Netherlands Overseas Territories are Netherlands Guiana, or Surinam, and Netherlands West Indies. In 1950 both territories were granted self-government as autonomous parts of the Netherlands Kingdom. Each is administered by a governor. Netherlands New Guinea is still under Dutch control, but its status is undecided.

Surinam lies on the north coast of South America between British and French Guiana; it has an area of 55,143 square miles. The population is about 250,000. It is mainly a low plateau, surrounded by sandy lowlands near the coast and mountainous forests to the south. Peaks of this section rise to heights of 4,200 feet. The climate is hot and oppressive; the rainfall is about 80 inches a year. Paramaribo is the capital and only city of importance.

The people of Surinam are descendants of Dutch settlers, Negroes (former slaves), natives of India and the East Indies, South American Indians, and Chinese. Dutch is the official language, but other languages are spoken. Various Christian faiths are represented, especially the Moravian Brethren, Roman Catholics, Dutch Reformed, and Lutherans; other religious groups are the Moslems and Hindus. The government provides primary and normal schools. Agriculture, timber cutting, balata gum gathering, and mining are the principal industries. Rice, sugar cane, cacao, corn, and citrus fruits are cultivated. Livestock raised are cattle, goats, and pigs. Exports are sugar, rum, molasses, rice, coffee, balata, bauxite, gold, and fruits.

The Netherlands West Indies are two groups of islands in the Caribbean Sea. Near the coast of Venezuela are Curaçao, Bonaire, and Aruba; about 500 miles to the northeast among the Leeward Islands are St. Martin (17 square miles comprising the Dutch portion of this French-Dutch island), St. Eustatius, and Saba. Their total area is 366 square miles. The population is about 184,000. All the islands have a tropical climate; the three larger ones are semiarid, but those in the Leeward group have abundant rainfall. Willemstad, Curaçao, is the capital.

More than 80 percent of the people are Negroes or mulattoes; among other groups are Dutch, British, and Americans. Dutch is the official language, but on the principal islands a mixed language called Papiamento is commonly used, while English is spoken in the Leeward group. Curaçao and Aruba are important industrially because of their oil refineries, which use petroleum imported from Venezuela. The other four islands are of little economic importance.

NEW GUINEA

New Guinea, world's second largest island, has three political divisions. Almost half the island's area of about 312,000 square miles belongs to the Netherlands and is administered by a Dutch governor. The other two sections are the Territory of New Guinea, administered by Australia under a United Nations trusteeship, and the Territory of Papua under Australian sovereignty. The population is about 2,475,000, white inhabitants constituting a minority. The native peoples of New Guinea are mostly Papuans, Melanesians, and Negritos; some of the interior tribes are head hunters. Protestant and Catholic missionaries operate mission schools. Tribes still live in primitive villages along the rivers, sometimes building their huts on piles sunk at the water's edge. The climate is tropical and oppressive. Temperature ranges from 70° to 90° F., and the long wet season brings about 100 inches of rain.

Oil, nickel, cobalt, gold, and manganese are found, but mine activities are limited because of the difficulty in transporting machinery. Small farms produce coffee, tobacco, papaya, sago, sweet potatoes, cucumbers, coconuts, and some grains. Coconuts, bananas, and other tropical fruits grow wild. Copra, gold, oil, forest produce, and coconut oil are the chief exports.

Netherlands New Guinea, area about 160,000 square miles including many offshore islands, is not yet fully explored. Its southern regions contain flat swamps and forests; the northern section of this western half of the island is high, rising to magnificent peaks in the extensive Snow Mountains. This territory was formerly part of the Netherlands Indies. Since Indonesia became independent in 1949 it has been demanding possession of the New Guinea territory, but the Dutch have refused to give up their sovereignty.

The Territory of Papua, area about 90,600 square miles including nearby islands, occupies the southeastern section of New Guinea. Annexed by Great Britain in 1888 and called British New Guinea, the territory came under Australia when the Dominion was established in 1901, and in 1906 it was renamed the Territory of Papua.

It is partly mountainous, the Bismarck Range running (with peaks rising to 13,000 feet) from the northwest corner to the southeast tip of the section, ending in the Owen Stanley Range. Along the southern shore the land is low and sandy. Port Moresby is the seat of administration. The Territory of New Guinea comprises North Eastern New Guinea, New Britain, New Ireland, and the Admiralty Islands in the Bismarck Archipelago, also Bougainville and Buka in the Solomon group. The total area is about 93,000 square miles, much of it mountainous.

NEW ZEALAND

About 1,200 miles southeast of Australia is the Dominion of New Zealand, comprised of three main islands, (North, South, and Stewart) and the Chatham Islands. The area is 103,736 square miles. The population is about 2,208,800. Two-thirds of the area is suitable for agriculture or grazing. Most of the people are of British descent. There is a small minority of Maoris. English is spoken. The British crown is represented by a governor general, but the real power is exercised by a prime minister and cabinet responsible to an elected House of Representatives. Protestantism is the main religious faith, and secular, compulsory, and free primary education is provided according to the English system.

New Zealand is mainly undulating plains and uplands, broken by middle ranges of mountains and foothills. Gold, silver, and coal are the principal resources; agriculture and animal products furnish the raw material for the chief manufacturing enterprises, which are dairy goods factories and meat preserving plants. Other industries are textiles, electrical supplies, sawmilling, and furniture.

Wellington is the capital, but Auckland is the largest city. Discovered by Abel Janszoon Tasman in 1642, New Zealand became a British colony in 1840, a self-governing dominion in 1907.

NICARAGUA

Nicaragua is one of the largest and most sparsely populated of the Central American republics. It has an area of 57,143 square miles. The population is about 1,245,000. Managua is the capital; other large cities are Matagalpa, León, Jinotega, and Granada. Most of the inhabitants are of mixed Indian and Spanish stock, but some are of pure Indian descent. Spanish is the common language, and Roman Catholicism is the chief religion. Primary education is free and compulsory for all children between the ages of 6 and 13. The president and Congress are elected for six years. The country has suffered from political instability and frequent revolutions.

Resources consist of vast timberlands, gold, silver, copper, and precious stones. Agriculture and livestock raising are the most important industries. Coffee, gold, tropical woods, and sesame are the leading exports.

Nicaragua lies between Honduras and Costa Rica, and has fine valleys between two coastal mountain chains. The Caribbean shore is low and swampy, and the Pacific Coast is rocky. Most of the people still live along the Pacific coast.

NORWAY

Norway was a part of Denmark from the 14th century until 1814, when it was turned over to Sweden. In 1905, after gradual political changes, the nation peacefully dissolved its union with Sweden and became a constitutional, hereditary monarchy, governed by the elected king and the bicameral Storting.

The area of Norway is about 125,182 square miles. Nearly one-fourth of the country is covered with forests, and only 4 percent is suitable for agriculture. Most farms are small, and they cling to the mountainsides. Rugged mountains and long, deep, narrow fiords, walled in by dark cliffs over which countless beautiful falls come rushing with incredible power, make Norway a haven for the tourist, but they do not provide a livelihood for its own people. It must import most of its land-grown food.

Almost 100,000 Norwegians are engaged in the fishing industry. Cod, whale, and herring constitute the bulk of the fish haul. The lumber industry vies with fishing in importance. Norway has few natural resources—limited deposits of pyrites, iron ore, copper, and zinc. Because of the lack of coal the country has to make extensive use of hydroelectric power for its industry. Norway's principal exports are wood pulp and paper, fish and fish products, fats and oils, non-ferrous metals and manufactures.

The capital is Oslo, a gay and beautiful "Paris of the North." Other important Norwegian cities are Bergen, an old Hanseatic merchant town on the west coast, now a fishing center, and Trondheim, the old capital. The population is about 3,470,000.

Norwegian speech differs in vocabulary and inflection from the other Scandinavian tongues, but it is also one of the Germanic languages. Education is quite advanced in state schools; education is compulsory from 7 to 14. Evangelical Lutheran is the established faith and is supported by the state.

PACIFIC ISLANDS TRUST TERRITORY

The Trust Territory of the Pacific includes some 2,000 islands in the western Pacific administered by the United States under United Nations trusteeship. It comprises the Marshall, Caroline, and Mariana Islands, except Guam, which is under American sovereignty. The Marshall Islands have been used for testing atom and hydrogen bombs. During World War I the islands were seized by Japan, and were placed under a Japanese mandate after the war. In defiance of the mandate terms, the islands were fortified and treated as Japanese territory. During World War II most of the islands were captured by American troops. By agreement with the U.N. the islands became a trusteeship in 1947. The combined area of these widely scattered islands is about 687 square miles, and the population is about 65,000. They have little economic value. Exports are phosphate and copra.

PAKISTAN

Pakistan, an independent republic in the British Commonwealth of Nations, came into being in 1947, when India was partitioned into the Moslem state of Pakistan and the Hindu state of India. Pakistan is divided into two parts, West Pakistan in the valley of the Indus River and East Pakistan in the Ganges-Brahmaputra delta, the two parts being separated by about 900 miles of Indian territory. The area covers 364,737 square miles. The population is about 83,603,000. Pakistan is the world's most populous Moslem nation. It has a governor general representing the British crown, but the real power is exercised by a prime minister and cabinet who are responsible to an elected unicameral legislature. The capital is Karachi in West Pakistan. Lahore and Dacca are other large cities. About 86 percent of the people are Moslems; other groups are Hindus, Sikhs, Parsees, and Christians.

East Pakistan has about 15 percent of the area but about 55 percent of the population. About four fifths of the people are engaged in agriculture. Wheat is the principal crop in West Pakistan, rice in East Pakistan. The most important resources are chrome, coal, and oil. The chief industries engage in the processing of farm crops. Exports are jute, cotton, tea, and wool. Since Pakistan gained its independence it has had to resettle millions of Moslem refugees from India. Another problem is the dispute over the state of Kashmir, claimed by both India and Pakistan.

PALESTINE

The Holy Land is a region of some 10,000 square miles located between the Jordan River and the eastern Mediterranean. It is the land of the Bible, and its capital, Jerusalem, is a holy city for Jews, Christians, and Moslems. During biblical times Palestine was inhabited by the Hebrews, or Jews, but later the Moslem Arabs became the dominant group. After World War I Palestine was taken from Turkey and put under a British mandate. Then came the immigration of Zionists seeking a Jewish national home in their ancestral land. Civil strife broke out between Arabs and Jews. In 1947 the United Nations General Assembly voted to partition the land between the two groups, with Jerusalem as an international zone. After the British gave up their mandate on May 14, 1948, war broke out between the Arabs and the new Jewish state of Israel. In the fighting the Israelis extended their territory somewhat beyond the U.N. recommendations. The result was the division of Palestine between Israel and the Hashemite Kingdom of Jordan.

PANAMA

Panama, the southernmost of the Central American republics, was part of Colombia until 1903. It has an elected one-house National Assembly and president, but political changes are often made by revolutionary means. Panama, the capital and largest city, lies near the Pacific end of the Panama Canal. The only other large city is Colón, which is on the Atlantic side.

About five-eighths of the land is uninhabited, much of it being too mountainous and rugged for settlement. Among the natural resources are valuable woods and many minerals, including iron ore, coal, gold, silver, manganese, mercury, and lead. Panama is one of the most healthful of all tropical countries, because of the sanitation and health service of American authorities located at the Canal Zone. The area of the republic is 28,576 square miles. The population is about 934,000. While Spanish is the common language, English is also used. Except in the Canal Zone the dominant religion is Roman Catholicism. Primary education is free and compulsory from 7 to 15.

Agriculture and government work with the Canal authorities are the chief occupations of the people. The principal crops grown include bananas, coconuts, coffee, sugar cane, tobacco, rice, cacao, corn, beans, and abacá (Manila hemp). Livestock raised are cattle, hogs, and chickens. Industries are food processing, meat packing, sugar refining, and there are a few small factories producing shoes and soap. Around the Pearl Islands are pearl fisheries. The chief exports are bananas, abacá, and cacao.

PANAMA CANAL ZONE

The Panama Canal Zone, a strip of land 10 miles wide across the Isthmus of Panama, was acquired by treaty in 1903 from the Republic of Panama. The United States gave $10,000,000 outright for this land, and from 1913 until 1939 paid $250,000 yearly. In 1939 the sum was increased to $430,000. The canal runs through the middle of the strip and was built at an approximate cost of $366,650,000.

Due to the position of the isthmus, the Pacific Ocean outlet of the canal is 22½ miles east of the Atlantic Ocean outlet. The channel is almost 51 miles long, nowhere less than 41 feet deep, and its six pairs of "double-barrelled" locks allow ships to pass in opposite directions simultaneously.

A treaty between Great Britain and the United States provides that "the Canal shall be . . . open to the vessels of commerce and of war of all nations . . ." A normal passage takes from seven to eight hours, and the canal's capacity is about 17,000 vessels a year.

The cities of Colón and Panama are not under the authority of the U.S.A. except in matters of sanitation and quarantine. The zone is really a government reservation, with strong fortifications and a number of military installations. Residence is restricted to the forces utilized in the operation and defense of the canal. The population is about 39,000. The area, with inland waters, is 559 square miles. The zone is administered by a governor appointed by the President of the U.S.A. Balboa Heights is the permanent administrative center.

PARAGUAY

Paraguay, an inland republic of South America, became independent of Spain in 1811. A constitution of 1940 provided for a president with extensive powers and a Diet of one chamber. Paraguay is an extension of the great Brazilian plateau, and its soil is dry, porous, and sandy, though fertile. The area of the country, since the settlement in 1938 of the Chaco dispute with Bolivia, is estimated at 157,047 square miles. The population is about 1,601,000. The people are of mixed Spanish and Indian descent, and they speak Spanish, though Guaraní, the language of now almost extinct Indian tribes, is still common. The state has made Roman Catholicism the established religion. An inadequate school system, in which primary education was free and nominally compulsory, is now being revised.

Resources of Paraguay are iron, copper, manganese, and extensive forests. Commercial products consist of hides, yerba maté, tobacco, timber, citrus fruits, sugar, corn, cotton, and petitgrain oil, derived from bitter-orange leaves and widely used in the manufacture of perfumes. The chief industries are packing plants, sugar refineries, lace factories, and oil distilleries. Exports include timber, yerba maté, hides, meat, and petitgrain oil. Asunción, the capital, Coronel Oviedo, and Villarrica are important towns.

PERU

From 1821 to 1824 Peru warred with Spain and finally obtained its freedom. Its present republican constitution (1933) provides for the election of a president, Senate, and a Chamber of Deputies.

Peru's area is 514,059 square miles. The population is about 9,651,000. Many of the inhabitants are Indians; Europeans (mostly Spanish), Negroes, and mixtures of these make up the rest of the population. Spanish and native tongues such as Quechua and Aymará are spoken. Some of the Indians retain ancient religious customs, but Roman Catholicism is the chief religion. The compulsory school age in Peru is 7 to 16.

The coastal strip of Peru is about 30 miles wide, and leads to uplands and the Andes mountains. East of the higher peaks is an extensive plateau. Most of the tributaries of the Amazon rise in Peruvian territory. Gold, most of the world's vanadium, copper, petroleum, salt, antimony, iron, coal, lead, cadmium, tungsten, bismuth, zinc, and dense forests of valuable timber make Peru a wealthy state. About 80 percent of the population is engaged in agriculture, the products of which are cotton, sugar, coffee, wool, hides, rice, tobacco, wines, wheat, cacao, and coca. Irrigation is widely used. Manufactured products are textiles, refined sugar, and petroleum. Exports include copper, lead, petroleum, cotton, and sugar. Coastal shipping is important, and many of the large towns, Callao, Trujillo, and Mollendo, are ports. Lima, the capital, Cuzco, Arequipa, and Ayacucho are inland cities.

PHILIPPINES, REPUBLIC OF THE

The Philippine Islands, ceded to the United States by Spain in 1898, were made an autonomous commonwealth in 1935 and became independent in 1946. The constitution provides for a president and a bicameral legislature. The islands were seized by Japan in 1942 and liberated by American forces in 1945. A Philippine-U.S. mutual defense treaty was signed in 1951.

The area of the Philippine Islands is 115,600 square miles; there are 7,100 islands, the largest of which are Luzon, with Quezon City, the capital; Mindanao; Samar; Negros; Palawan; and Panay. Important cities are Manila, Iloilo, Cebu, Zamboanga, and Davao. The population is about 22,265,300. Malay languages, Spanish, and English are spoken. The great majority of Filipinos are Roman Catholic. American influence in the islands has developed a general system of free, secular education, instruction being given in English and native languages; Tagalog has become the state language. The inhabitants are mixtures of Malay, Asiatic, and Spanish peoples.

The fertile volcanic and coral islands are quite mountainous, with narrow coastal plains and rich interior valleys. Earthquakes are common. Rich forests, gold, silver, manganese, chromite, and iron constitute the natural resources. Agricultural products are rice, Manila hemp, copra, coconut oil, sugar cane, corn, tobacco, bananas, and rubber. Sugar refineries, tobacco plants, lumber mills, and cement factories are the main industries. Exports are sugar, coconut oil, tobacco, hemp, and copra.

POLAND

Poland became an independent state in the 10th century, but in the 18th century was partitioned between Austria, Prussia, and Russia. It was occupied by Austro-German forces in World War I. In 1918 Marshal Pilsudski, a Polish national hero, took full executive powers. After dispute of the Polish Corridor, German forces in 1939 invaded Poland, at which Britain and France declared war on Germany. Partitioned in 1939 by Germany and Russia, Poland was occupied by the Nazis invading Russia from 1941 until released by the Russians in 1944. Warsaw is the capital; other important cities are Lodz, Krakow, Wroclaw, and Poznan. Poland's area is 120,355 square miles. The population is about 28,070,000. After World War II only a small percentage of the people were not Polish. There were White Russian, Jewish, German, Slovak, Czech, Lithuanian, and Gypsy minorities. The war brought great destruction and the displacement of Poland's former large minorities. The Nazis tried to destroy all Polish national life. When freed, Poland regained much of its former territory, except for Soviet-dominated regions in the east. It was given claim on about two-thirds of East Prussia, the former free city of Danzig (with the surrounding Danzig province of 750 square miles), and the East German government in 1950 recognized the Oder-Neisse line as the Polish-German boundary.

In the east central portions are great marshes, and the Carpathian Mountains lie to the south. Most of the land consists of plains and plateaus. Timber, petroleum, natural gas, salt, potassium, iron, zinc, and one of Europe's largest supplies of coal constitute the natural resources.

The majority of the Polish people are of Roman Catholic faith. Most of the people speak Polish, except isolated minorities. Education is free and compulsory up to the age of 14.

Though the industries of Poland were much damaged during World War II, textile looms, refineries and metallurgical factories have rapidly regained their importance. Agriculture is the chief occupation, the principal crops being grains, potatoes, sugar beets, flax, hemp, and hops. Exports include timber, coal and coke, and foodstuffs.

PORTUGAL

Portugal, independent since the 12th century, was a monarchy until 1910, when a republican form of government was established. The present constitution (1933) provides for an elected president and a one-chamber National Assembly. The area of Portugal, including the Azores and Madeira, is 35,466 square miles. The population is about 8,837,000.

The sharp, bleak heights of the Serra da Estrela give Portugal a mountainous character. Rising to about 6,500 feet, the mountains are a favorite sport and resort area. There are sand dunes on the coast, and inland between the mountains and moors are rich river valleys and medicinal warm springs. Lisbon, the capital, and Oporto are the chief towns and the principal ports.

Before the Roman conquest, Portugal was inhabited by Lusitanians, and later was occupied by Visigoths and Moors. The people are akin to the Spaniards. Portuguese, a Romance language, is quite different from Spanish. Roman Catholicism is the most common religion, but freedom of worship is a guaranteed right. Primary education is compulsory.

About one-fifth of Portugal is covered with forests of pine, cork oak, and other species. The valuable mineral deposits of coal, pyrites, lead, copper, tin, wolfram, kaolin, and sulfur are largely unworked but are being developed. The cultivable land is used for pasturage, vineyards, fruit trees, or for growing potatoes, wheat, and cereals. Portugal ranks fourth among olive-producing countries of the world. Cattle raising is carried on extensively in the northern part of the country; sheep, goats, hogs, and mules are raised in the central and southern parts. Industrial enterprises include resin and turpentine works, sardine canneries, distilleries, porcelain and tile kilns, and manufactures of cotton, silk, linen and woolen textiles, fine laces and embroideries, metalware, earthenware, cork products, and cigars and cigarettes. Exports are crude cork, sardines, wines, turpentine, pickled fish, laces, embroideries, textiles, and olive oil.

PORTUGUESE GUINEA

Portuguese Guinea is an upper West African territory on the Atlantic coast entirely surrounded on land by French territory. The area is 13,948 square miles, and the population is about 547,000. Discovered by the Portuguese about 1446, it is governed by a Portuguese governor. The land is a low-lying deltaic area, its interior swampy, with a very warm climate. In the southeast are forests of mahogany, ironwood, baobab, and acacia. The Geba River, the Rio Grande, and other streams form wide estuaries where they enter the ocean. At their mouths lie the Bijagós (Bissagos) Islands, an archipelago that includes the islands of Orange and Bolama. Bissau, the chief port, is the capital. In the interior are many varieties of wild animals and beautiful tropical birds. Sharks and crocodiles infest the rivers.

The inhabitants are, in addition to a few Portuguese, the Fulani, Biafer, and Mandina tribes. The people are Roman Catholics and Moslems. Education is provided by government and mission trade schools. Agriculture and stock raising are the chief industries. Major crops are rice, copra, palm kernels, and peanuts. Cattle are grazed in the hilly areas. Exports are rice, palm oil and kernels, and hides.

PUERTO RICO

The island of Puerto Rico, a commonwealth of the United States, is in the Caribbean Sea, just east of Hispaniola. The area, including small neighboring islands, is 3,435 square miles. The population is about 2,210,000. The island is one of the summits of a submerged mountain chain. In the waters to the north, soundings as great as 30,200 feet have been taken. The climate is warm and even the year round. Puerto Rico is in the hurricane storm belt, but often escapes the full force of the "blows." The population is composed of native whites, the descendants of early Spanish settlers, foreign whites, Negroes, and mulattoes. The native Indians have almost all disappeared. Spanish and English are generally spoken, and the main religion is Roman Catholicism. Primary education is free and compulsory. San Juan is the capital city, and other important towns are Ponce and Mayagüez.

The main occupations of the people are agriculture, fishing, and mining. Deposits of marble, china clay, gold, silver, iron, lead, copper, tin, bismuth, mercury, platinum, nickel, manganese, and salt are found. Important agricultural products are sugar, tobacco, coffee, pineapples, citrus fruits, and coconuts. Cigars, cigarettes, hats, and textiles are manufactured, and there are distilleries, sugar refineries, and manganese mills. The principal exports are tobacco, sugar, pineapples, rum, and molasses.

The Virgin Islands of the United States, just east of Puerto Rico, were purchased from Denmark in 1917 and are of strategic importance. Of some 50 islands and islets, only St. John, St. Croix, and St. Thomas are important. Charlotte Amalie, on St. Thomas, is the capital. The U.S. islands, lying southwest of the British Virgin Islands, have an area of 133 square miles. They have become a popular winter resort. Rum and bay rum are the chief exports. The people are mainly Negroes.

RUMANIA

Rumania, generally spoken of as part of the Balkans although too far north to be considered so geographically, is bounded on the east by the Black Sea and Soviet Russia, on the north by Russia, on the west by Hungary and Yugoslavia, and on the south by Bulgaria. It has an area of 91,584 square miles. The population is more than 17,490,000. Bucharest is the capital; important cities are Cluj, Iasi, and Ploesti. Over three-fourths of the people are Rumanian; there are minorities of Hungarians, Germans, Jews, Ukrainians, Gypsies, and several Slavic peoples. The Rumanian language developed from Vulgar Latin, with considerable Slavic influence. In faith Rumanians are largely Eastern Orthodox. Primary education is free and compulsory.

The northwest section of the country is separated from the fertile plateau of Transylvania and the Hungarian plains by a curved spur of the Carpathian Mountains. Between the Danube and the Black Sea are steppe regions. Principal resources are salt, coal, lignite, iron, copper, petroleum, natural gas, and valuable timberlands. Occupations are mostly agriculture and stock breeding, though steps toward industrialization of the country have been taken. Oil refineries, textile and flour mills are important enterprises. The generally fertile soil produces crops of grains, grapes, fruits, and tobacco. Exports are petroleum products, cereals, and wood.

SALVADOR, EL

El Salvador, on the Pacific coast between Guatemala and Honduras, has an area of 13,176 square miles. The population is about 2,268,000. Capital of this smallest, most densely populated Central American republic is San Salvador. Other important towns are Santa Ana, San Miguel, San Vincente, Ahuachapán, and Sonsonate. The natives of the country are Indians, but the bulk of the population is a mixture of Spanish and Indian blood. The common language is Spanish, and Roman Catholicism is the dominant religion. Primary education is both free and obligatory. El Salvador declared its independence in 1839, and is now governed by a president and a single-chamber legislature.

Coastal and inland mountain chains enclose rich river valleys and plateaus. The higher grounds are usually pleasant, but the coast region and valleys are hot, sultry, and often windless. El Salvador is occasionally visited by earthquakes. The largest rivers are the Lempa and the Río Grande de San Miguel.

Besides gold, silver, coal, copper, iron, lead, zinc, sulfur, and mercury, El Salvador has fine timberlands. Its balsam trees provide the world's richest supply of medicinal gums. The principal industry is agriculture (70 percent of the land is cultivated), but there are also small manufacturing plants such as sugar and vegetable-oil refineries, flour mills, distilleries, coffee-packing houses, and cotton-textile mills. Native industries produce woven reed baskets, fiber rugs, and straw hats. The principal crops grown are coffee, corn, cacao, tobacco, and sugar cane. Coffee constitutes

85 percent of the total export trade, which includes henequen and balsam as other important items.

SAN MARINO

Claiming to be the oldest independent state in Europe, San Marino was probably founded in the 4th century by a Dalmatian Christian named Marinus (Marino), A.D. 350. Lying wholly within the borders of Italy, it is governed by the Grand Council of 60 elected members, from whom two regents are chosen every six months to act as executives. The administration of justice is in the hands of Italian magistrates. San Marinans are like Italians in racial characteristics, language, education, and religion. The republic issues its own coins and postage stamps, the sale of which is lucrative. The area is about 23 square miles, and the population is about 14,000. The capital, San Marino, is situated on a towering crag called Mount Titano (2,382 feet), which overlooks the Adriatic Sea. San Marino is mainly an agrarian country. Wine, woolen goods, hides, cattle, and building stone are the only exports. Trade is chiefly with Italy.

SAUDI ARABIA

Though Saudi Arabia, comprising the greater part of western and central Arabia, is a single kingdom, it has two distinct parts, Hejaz and Nejd, with two capitals, Mecca and Riyadh. The founder and first king of Saudi Arabia, Ibn-Saud, acquired his kingdom by defeating the Turks and the Hashemite Arabs. The area is 600,000 square miles. The population is about 6,500,000. Nejd, with a short seacoast between Hejaz and Yemen, includes about two-thirds of the area and population. Great Britain formally recognized the independence of the kingdom in 1927. Saudi Arabia declared war on the Axis in 1945, and joined the Arab League in that year. The people are Arabs; some live in settled agrarian communities and others wander over the warm, arid, desert-like territory. About half of Nejd is wholly desert. There are few roads, but many established caravan routes. Aside from agriculture, the Hejaz people depend a great deal on the pilgrimage trade in and around Mecca. Countless numbers of Mohammedans each year come to Mecca, the holy city of Islam. Exports are oil (by far the most important), dates, hides, butter, and the famous Arabian horses.

SINGAPORE

Singapore is a British island colony lying in the South China Sea, off the southern end of the Malay Peninsula, from which it is separated by the Johore Strait, and from the Indonesian island of Batam by Singapore Strait. The area, including islets, is 224 square miles. The population is about 1,264,000. Low hills are distributed over the island, which is about 26 miles long by 14 miles wide. The climate is hot and humid. In suburban sections agriculture is the chief industry. Rubber trees, pineapples, tropical fruits, spices, indigo, peppers, gutta-percha, and garden vegetables are cultivated. Livestock raised are cattle, pigs, sheep, and goats.

SOMALILAND (ITALIAN)

This former Italian colony, now Somalia, is located in East Africa on the Gulf of Aden and the Indian Ocean, and is bordered by British Somaliland, Ethiopia, and Kenya. The area is about 200,000 square miles, and the population is about 1,225,000. The people are largely nomadic Somali (Moslem), with Bantu, Arab, and Italian minorities. The land is generally an arid plateau with elevations ranging from 1,000 to 2,000 feet, but near the coast it is low. The chief crops are sugar cane and bananas; goats, camels, cattle, and sheep are raised. The capital and chief port is Mogadiscio; Kismayu is another port. About half the world's incense comes from Somaliland. British troops took the colony during World War II (1941). In 1950 the United Nations voted to make it a trust territory under Italian administration. Somalia's independence is due in 1960.

SOUTH-WEST AFRICA

South-West Africa, mandate of the Union of South Africa, lies between Angola and Cape Province of the Union. The area is 317,725 square miles, and the population is about 447,000. Once a German colony, the country was seized by Union of South Africa forces during World War I. Since 1920 it has been administered by the Union under a League of Nations mandate, and the Union, since 1945, has refused to permit it to become a United Nations trusteeship. Seat of government is Windhoek. Walvis Bay is an important port. Most of the country lies on a high plateau, from which rise the Kaokoveld Mountains in the northeast, the Auaz Mountains in the center, and the Karas Mountains in the south. Brandberg (over 8,550 feet) is the highest peak. On the west coast between the Ugab and Orange rivers is the wide Namib Desert, adjoining the plateau. Besides the Europeans, there are Ovambos, Hereros, Bergdamaras, Hottentots, and Bushmen, the last the earliest inhabitants of the area.

Economic life centers around stock raising, especially karakul sheep, dairying, the processing of karakul pelts, and mining.

SPAIN

The Bourbon dynasty in Spain closed in 1931 when, following the overwhelming victory of Republicans in municipal elections, King Alfonso XIII went into exile. A republic was established that separated church and state, secularized education, divided the large estates among the peasants, and introduced other economic reforms. Dissatisfaction of military and other conservative elements broke out in civil war in 1936. In general terms, the contest raged between the Loyalists (Republicans) and the Rebels (Fascists). Madrid, the capital, was surrendered in March, 1939, after which General Francisco Franco became dictator of a totalitarian, one-party state. Catholicism was reestablished as the state religion, and the liberty of all non-Catholic religious groups was curtailed. Spain gave the Axis troops and supplies during World War II. It is barred from the U.N. Since 1951 the U. S. has given Spain military and economic aid in return for rights to build air and naval bases.

The land of Spain in general is a high plateau known as the Meseta, with the Cantabrian Mountains along the northern edge, the Pyrenees in the northeast, and the Sierra Morena in the south. The area is 194,232 square miles. The population is about 29,203,000. Seven-eighths of the border is seacoast; Portugal to the west and the Pyrenees on the northeast form the only land boundaries. The Mediterranean coast is bold and rocky and there are few harbors. Madrid, Barcelona, Valencia, Sevilla, Málaga, Zaragoza, Bilbao, Murcia, and Granada are the chief cities. Madrid is the nation's capital. The Spanish language has two main dialects—Castilian and Catalan. Primary education is free and compulsory, but one-seventh of the population still cannot read or write. Religious instruction has been brought back into the public schools.

Iron, copper, coal, zinc, nickel, lead, manganese, silver, mercury, sulfur, salt, graphite, and antimony comprise Spain's extensive natural resources. Pig iron, cement, wine, textiles, paper, and cigarettes are manufactured. Agriculture is the chief industry of Spain; crops produced are wheat, corn, barley, oats, rye, rice, and garden vegetables. Fruits cultivated are olives, grapes, peaches, oranges, lemons, dates, and limes, and there are extensive almond and cork-tree groves. Bulls, bred for the sport of ring fighting, dairy cattle, and Merino sheep, noted for their fine wool, are the most important livestock raised. Exports are foodstuffs, wines, minerals, timber, cotton, silk, and fine woolen textiles, almonds, cattle, and citrus fruits. The Guadalquivir is the most important river for navigation and is open to seagoing vessels as far as Sevilla.

SUDAN

The Sudan formerly Anglo-Egyptian Sudan, is an independent republic in northeastern Africa. A region of desert, fertile river land, and tropical forests, it is drained by the Nile River and its tributaries. Sudan has an area of 967,500 square miles. Most of the population are nomadic Arabs, Hamito-Semitic tribes, Nubians, and Sudanic Negroes. The population is about 10,000,000. The predominant religion is Islam, but paganism prevails among interior tribes. Khartoum is the capital, and the adjoining Omdurman is the largest city.

Most of the territory is fairly level, although near the Red Sea are mountains that reach heights of over 7,000 feet; in the west the land rises to over 4,000 feet; in the south and southwest are low hills. The regions near the Nile are very fertile; cotton, grains, vegetables, melons, and date palms are grown. Livestock is raised. Forests produce much fine mahogany and gum arabic. In the Red Sea Hills are gold deposits, along with copper, iron, and lignites. In the upper regions of the White Nile are vast quantities of papyrus.

SWEDEN

Sweden is the eastern neighbor of Norway. The two countries share a common frontier of about 1,030 miles, part of which runs along the Kjölen Mountains. Sweden has an area of 173,378 square miles. The population is about 7,341,000. Ten percent of the land is fit for farming, and one-half the country is covered with valuable timber. Lacking the tempering effect of the Gulf Stream, it has long cold winters, with much snow, and many ports are frozen over from early fall to late spring.

The government of Sweden is a democratic, limited monarchy. The reigning family is the Bernadotte, in direct line from Napoleon's marshal, Count Bernadotte, who was invited to be king in 1818. Parliament consists of two chambers elected by the people. The principal cities are Stockholm, the capital, Göteborg, and Malmö, all ports. The Swedish landscape is dotted with lakes and mountains, but it lacks the wild beauty of Norway's fiords and higher peaks, having instead a quiet, pastoral aspect. The recognized religion is Evangelical Lutheran; the church is supported by the state. Schooling has by law been compulsory and free for children between the ages of 7 and 14 since 1842.

Sweden is rich in natural resources, the chief being timber, iron ore, silver, copper, manganese, arsenic, and sulfur pyrites. She lacks coal, but recent harnessing and extensive use of her tremendous water power has overcome this disadvantage. Manufacturing is the leading economic activity, but agriculture, mining, fishing, and lumbering are also important. The industries include iron and steel works, wood and paper mills, flour and grist mills, and dairies. The principal exports are wood and wood products, machinery, iron ore, and other minerals and mineral products. In value, timber, wood pulp, and paper are the most important. Sweden's consumer and producer cooperatives have attained a high degree of excellence and stability.

SWITZERLAND

In 1815, Switzerland was guaranteed perpetual neutrality and inviolability by Austria, Great Britain, Portugal, France, Prussia, Russia, Spain, and Sweden. Since then, except for minor civil strife in 1847 and 1890, the Swiss have maintained peace within their borders, even during the days of the two world wars. The present federal republican constitution of Switzerland dates from 1874.

Switzerland is almost wholly mountainous, the ranges of the Alps running across the south, central, and eastern sections. The area is 15,944 square miles. The population is about 5,023,000. The cities of Switzerland are located on the rolling central plateau, and include Bern (the capital), Zürich, Basel, Geneva, Lausanne, and Lucerne. The magnificence of the scenery in Switzerland has made it a mecca for tourists.

For centuries the Swiss have intermarried with, obeyed the customs, and spoken the language of the peoples of the countries along their borders. In the 16 cantons of the central and northeastern areas the language and customs are German. In the southeast the inhabitants are more like the Italians, and along the west there is a definite French influence. All three of these languages are official. The ancient Romansch, a Romance language, is also official, being used especially in Graubünden. Slightly over half of the population adheres to Protestantism; most of the rest are of the Roman Catholic faith. Generally speaking, primary education is obligatory and free.

About 22 percent of the population is engaged in agriculture and cattle raising. Aside from dairy produce such as milk and cheese, the chief agricultural products are potatoes, wheat, rye, barley, and wine. Extensive forests and water power, plus salt deposits and iron and manganese ores, constitute the natural resources of the country. Manufacturing enterprises, such as watchmaking, textile trades, embroidery, expert woodcarving, and the production of fine scientific and musical instruments, occupy about 46 percent of the population.

SYRIA

Syria is situated at the northeastern end of the Mediterranean, wedged between Turkey, Iraq, Israel, Lebanon, and Jordan. The area is 72,234 square miles. The population is about 3,856,000.

Wars for the control of Syria were waged in the 12th and 13th centuries between Christian

Crusaders and the Moslem Mameluke sultans of Egypt. The latter won and ruled Syria until ousted in 1516 by the Ottoman Turks, who controlled the area until World War I. In 1920 Syria was awarded to France under a League of Nations mandate. Syrian self-government was promised by a 1936 treaty, but independence was delayed by World War II. Troops loyal to Vichy France occupied Syria until expelled in 1941 by the British and Free French, who then proclaimed Syria an independent republic. All foreign troops were gone by April, 1946. A constitution passed in 1950 provided for a popularly elected president and a Constituent Assembly, but internal disorder soon resulted in a series of military *coups d'état* and led to eventual establishment of a Communist-influenced government. Early in 1958 Syria merged with Egypt to form the United Arab Republic, with the capital at Cairo and Nasser of Egypt as its president.

From the Turkish border down western Syria are a narrow coastal strip and the swamps of the Orontes River, backed by the high Anti-Lebanon range, which tapers down to the Sea of Galilee in the southwest corner. Its highest peak is Mt. Hermon (9,282 feet). A large portion of Syria is covered by the arid Syrian Desert. Fertile spots are found in the oasis around Damascus, along the course of the Euphrates River in the east, and in the Hauran plain in the southwest. Northeast of the Hauran lies a high, rocky plateau, the Jebel ed Druz.

Damascus is the administrative seat of Syria. Other important towns are Aleppo, Homs, Hama, Latakia (which is the chief port), Deir-ez-Zor, and Meskene. The population is a mixture of Arabs, Turks, Circassians, Armenians, Persians, Jews, Maronites, Druses, and Yezidis. Arabic is the official language, but others are alsc widely spoken. Islam is the chief religion, although Christianity has been important since earliest times. Primary education is compulsory.

The principal resources are salt, bitumen, petroleum, building stone, lead, copper, gypsum, nickel, chrome, antimony, and phosphates, but commercially these deposits are of less importance than agriculture and livestock raising. Industries are on a small scale and include sponge fisheries, flour mills, olive-oil refineries, and factories that produce gold and silver threadstuffs, cashmere shawls, soap, glass, cement, cotton and silk textiles, beet sugar, earthenware, and leather goods. Exports are raw silk, wool, and cotton, grains, gum, hides, lamb skins, olive oil, tobacco, dates, figs, seeds, and sponges.

THAILAND (Siam)

Thailand, or Siam, is a limited monarchy with a unicameral parliament (the National Assembly) and a Council of Ministers. The Assembly, established by the Constitution of 1932, has half its members appointed by the king and the rest popularly elected. In area Thailand is 196,861 square miles. The population is approximately 20,686,000. Besides the native Thai people (90 percent), there are Chinese, Indian, Malay, Cambodian, Vietnamese, and Burmese minorities, as well as scattered hill tribes of Miao, Karen, and others. Buddhism is the major religion, followed by Islam and Christianity. Education is compulsory from 7 to 14 and is free in the many state elementary and secondary schools. Until fairly recently Bangkok, the capital and leading port, was built on pontoons or stationary piles along numerous canals that served as streets, but now it is a modern city. Throughout the state are many magnificent Buddhist temples with tiled roofs and gilded spires.

The outstanding physical feature of Thailand is the great central plain along the Chao Phraya (Menam) River, one of the richest agricultural sections of the world. Northern Thailand, between the Mekong and Salween rivers, is more mountainous, peaks of the region rising to 8,400 feet. Eastern Thailand, bordered by Cambodia and Laos, is called the Korat, a high plateau watered by the Chi and Mun, tributaries of the Mekong. Southernmost Thailand takes up about half the length of the Malay Peninsula, and is thickly forested.

In spite of mining for minerals, precious metals, and jewels such as rubies, sapphires, and zircons, and the intensive working of valuable teakwood forests, agriculture has retained first rank in importance. Its main products are rice, sugar, coconuts, tobacco, spices, cotton, and livestock. Rice, teak, rubber, tin, and wolfram constitute the bulk of exports.

TIBET

Tibet is a theocratic state of Asia, lying between India and China. It was invaded by the Chinese army in October, 1950, and eventually was made an autonomous region of China. It has an area of 470,000 square miles. The population is about 1,000,000. Tibetans are mostly Mongoloid people. The speech is a Tibeto-Burman language of the Indo-Chinese group. The religion is Lamaism, a form of Buddhism. The spiritual and temporal ruler is the Dalai Lama, supposedly a reincarnation of Tibet's patron saint. He is selected when a child to rule for life; during his childhood a lama (priest) is regent. The ministers and members of the National Assembly are generally lamas. The capital is Lhasa. Tibet is mountainous throughout. Several of the great Asiatic rivers have their sources in Tibet.

Tibet's farm and pastoral products are sufficient for the country's needs. Gold, iron, salt, soda, potash, and borax are found. The chief exports are religious statuary, medicinal herbs, yak tails, wool, hides, musk, salt, and borax.

TUNISIA

Tunisia, on the north coast of Africa, is a sovereign independent republic. Before 1881 it was under Turkish suzerainty. From 1881 until 1956 it was a French protectorate. The Assembly, elected by general adult franchise, abolished the monarchy in July, 1957. The population is about 3,783,000. Most of the inhabitants are Moslems and Jews; the Europeans are largely Catholic. The interior is practically empty as the population is almost entirely urban and coastal. Tunis, the capital, Sfax, and Bizerte are the chief towns. The ancient city of Carthage was located on the Tunisian coast opposite Sicily. European languages are widely spoken, but Arabic is official. Education, supervised by the state, is free at the primary level.

Tunisia is a warm country, and almost the whole southern half is an extension of the Sahara. The north is fairly fertile, but irregular rainfall makes agriculture an uncertain occupation. Olives, dates, citrus fruits, grains, and grapes are raised, as well as livestock. An important forest product is cork, and Tunisia has an almost inexhaustible supply of phosphates, iron ores, zinc, and lead. Agriculture, fishing, mining, and sponge fishing are important industries, and the natives weave textiles and mats and do beautiful leather tooling and embroidering. The chief exports are phosphate rock, esparto grass, and olive oil.

TURKEY

Until 1922, Turkey was a sultanate, and the center of the government was Constantinople, a city of mosques and palaces. The power of the sultan was defied finally by a group of nationalists, who were strongly opposed to any alliance with the Allies after Turkey had suffered such rigorous peace terms at the end of World War I. The leader, Mustafa Kemal Pasha, later Kemal Atatürk, proposed a constitutional amendment by which Turkey would become a republic. The country was formally made a republic, with Mustafa Kemal as its first president, in 1923. Thus came to an end the great Ottoman Empire which had held sway in Asia Minor since the 14th century. The ancient capital, Constantinople, is now called Istanbul. Other large cities are Izmir, Adana, Bursa, and Eskisehir. The capital is Ankara.

Turkey is mainly a high plateau, with wooded foothills and valleys. Eastern frontiers are broken and mountainous. The area is 296,500 square miles. The population is about 24,797,000. Islam is the religion of the great majority. Turkish, the official language, is spoken by most of the people. In the eastern provinces of Turkey the Moslem population includes over a million Kurds, a fierce, nomadic, pastoral people, who dwell in a tribal society. Resources include chrome, coal, oil, iron, lignite, manganese, and copper, but they are inadequately developed. Tobacco, cereals, figs, olives, nuts, cotton, and opium are the main agricultural products, most of which enter export trade. A plan of industrialization is under way, encouraging the growth of textile, mining, paper, glass, metallurgical, and chemical industries.

UNION OF SOUTH AFRICA

In 1910, the British colonies called Cape of Good Hope, Natal, Orange Free State and Transvaal (all in the lower tip of Africa) were united to form the Union of South Africa. Total area of the Union is 472,733 square miles. The population is about 13,915,000. The European minority is descended mostly from Dutch and British settlers; there are Indians and many native tribes, the Bantus, Hottentots, and Bushmen. Native languages are numerous. Afrikaans, a language developed from Dutch, and English, both are official and are widely spoken. Protestantism is the dominant faith, but Roman Catholicism, Judaism, Hinduism and Islam, as well as primitive paganism, are represented. Primary and secondary education are well developed, and there are nine excellent universities. Since World War II, the Union has experienced considerable racial tension. The National Party has held a rigid policy of white supremacy and enforced segregation.

The climate is healthful, the range of temperature small because the altitude increases as the latitude decreases. Physical characteristics are a high interior plateau, rimmed by mountainous regions and the coastal plain. The southern mountain ranges provide interesting scenery.

The Union is highly industrialized, and its commerce is handled through the large port towns. Johannesburg is the largest city. Pretoria (in the Transvaal) is the seat of government, and Capetown is the legislative center. The capital city of Natal is Pietermaritzburg, and of the Orange Free State, Bloemfontein. Industries are mining, agriculture, forestry, dairying, and manufacturing. There are public utilities and plants producing refined metals, chemicals, textiles, food and drink, leather, vehicles, and furniture.

Resources of the Union are gold, diamonds, copper, tin, silver, antimony, coal, and timber. The chief exports are gold, wool, diamonds, hides, and corn. Crops of grain, corn, potatoes, sugar cane, and tea are raised. The breeding of livestock, and production of cotton and tobacco are other important agricultural pursuits.

UNION OF SOVIET SOCIALIST REPUBLICS

One-sixth of the earth is included in territories called the Union of Soviet Socialist Republics, which makes the Union the world's largest nation. Its area of 8,500,000 square miles includes more than one-half of Europe, and one-third of Asia. The population is approximately 200,200,000. Within its official limits are the following 15 republics: Russian Soviet Federated Socialist Republic, spreading across eastern Europe from the northern Caucasus to the Arctic Ocean and across northern Asia from the Urals to the Pacific Ocean, over nearly four-fifths of the entire U.S.S.R.; the Ukraine, in southeast Europe along the shores of the Black and Azov seas; Belorussia (White Russia), in the west; Azerbaijan, Georgia, and Armenia, in Transcaucasia; the Turkmen, Uzbek, Tadzhik, Kazakh, and Kirghiz republics, occupying the arid region in central Asia east of the Caspian Sea; Moldavia, next to Rumania; and Estonia, Latvia, and Lithuania, along the Baltic shore. A number of autonomous regions and national areas lie within these republics.

Three-quarters of the population of the Union are Russian or Slavic peoples. Russian is the official tongue, and the languages of the national groups are also used in their sections. The government does not recognize any religion, but many Russians retain the Orthodox faith; Jewish as well as Protestant, Catholic, and Moslem churches are also tolerated. Primary education is free and compulsory from the age of 7. There are many universities and technical colleges as well as medical schools. Science and engineering courses are given precedence over the liberal arts. The chief administrative center of the Union is Moscow. Other important cities are Leningrad, Kiev, Kharkov, Baku, Gorky, Odessa, Tashkent, Tbilisi, Rostov, Riga, Dnepropetrovsk, Stalino, Stalingrad, Sverdlovsk, and Kazan.

European Russia, with a climate much like that of Poland, has vast plains stretching east to the Ural Mountains, which are usually considered to be the dividing line between Europe and northern Asia. Asiatic Russia has a more rigorous climate, and consists of lowlands, plateaus, arid steppes, and mountainous territory. In northern Siberia, where it is often 85°F. in summer, winter temperatures as low as -90°F. have been officially recorded. No ocean ports are open the year around, except at Murmansk. Vladivostok is kept open by ice breakers, and even Black Sea harbors are apt to be frozen over. This immense country has valuable natural resources—forests, iron ore, manganese, copper, apatite, coal, uranium, gold, and oil, all of which are being developed. Industrial organization of the U.S.S.R. is based for the most part on state ownership and control, administered by trusts and combines. These include mines, blast furnaces, iron and steel works, pipe-rolling mills, tractor, tank, turbine, and railway rolling-stock plants, aircraft factories, flour mills, and factories producing aluminum wares, chemicals and drugs, electrical and railway equipment, agricultural, building, and transportation machinery and tools, woodwork, rubber goods, silk, cotton, woolen and linen goods and textiles, cement, asbestos, sugar, leather goods, clothing, and boots and shoes. There are also large food-processing plants, and factories for producing textile fiber from glass.

The total area under cultivation, including owner farms, state farms, and collective farms, is about 400,000,000 acres. Seventy percent of the farm work is done by mechanical power. The principal crops are wheat and other cereal grains, potatoes, cotton, flax, hemp, rubber plants, sugar beets, tobacco, tea, rice, melons, and sunflower seed; fruits cultivated are grapes and citrus and orchard fruits. Livestock raised are horses, cattle, pigs, sheep, goats, and poultry. Bees and silkworms are also raised.

THE UNITED STATES OF AMERICA

The United States of America, a federal republic, occupies the central portion of the North American continent. It is bounded on the north by Canada, on the east by the Atlantic Ocean, on the south by the Gulf of Mexico and the republic of Mexico, and on the west by the Pacific Ocean. Its total area is 3,022,387 square miles. The United States extends 2,807 miles in its extreme points from the Atlantic to the Pacific coast, and it is 1,598 miles long at its greatest north-south extremities. The total coastline of the United States measures 11,936 miles. According to the official census of Apr. 1, 1950, the population of the United States was 150,697,361; by 1958 the official estimate of population surpassed 172,000,000.

The United States is composed of 48 states and the District of Columbia, in which Washington, the national capital, is located.

Government. The government of the United States has three co-ordinate branches. Executive authority rests with a president, popularly elected every four years, who chooses a cabinet composed of the secretaries of state, treasury, defense, interior, agriculture, commerce, labor, and health, education, and welfare, the attorney general, and the postmaster general. Each of these cabinet officials directs the operation of his administrative department.

The legislative branch is represented by the Congress of the United States, a bicameral body composed of the House of Representatives, whose members are elected to two-year terms on a proportional basis, and the Senate, to which each state sends two senators for six-year terms.

The federal judiciary is composed of a Supreme Court, with eight associate justices and a chief justice, and a system of federal district courts and courts of appeal.

History. After the American Revolution, also called the War of Independence, the United States fought Great Britain once more, in the War of 1812 (1812-1814) to bring an end to British violations of her rights on the seas.

In 1790 the United States covered an area of 888,811 square miles. The Louisiana Purchase (1803), negotiated with France, almost doubled the size of the country. In 1819 the U.S. acquired Florida from Spain by treaty and the payment of indemnity to Spanish citizens there. The historic doctrine of President James Monroe, read to Congress in 1823, announced the U.S. intention to prevent further colonization in the Western Hemisphere by European powers. Texas, having freed itself from Mexico, was annexed by the U.S. in 1845, and the U.S. claim to the Oregon country (Oregon, Washington, and Idaho) was recognized by Great Britain in 1846.

In the short Mexican War (1846-1848) the United States acquired title to a vast amount of land north of the Rio Grande, which, however, was already being settled by Americans. The Mexican cession of California in 1848 and the Gadsden Purchase in 1853 of the southern parts of Arizona and New Mexico from Mexico completed the addition of territory in the continental United States.

The great conflict over slavery and states rights that occupied the nation during the first half of the 19th century finally came to a head in the Civil War (1861-1865).

In the half century between the end of the Civil War and World War I, the United States industrialized rapidly. The sinking of the battleship *Maine* in the harbor of Havana, Cuba, in February, 1898, led to the Spanish-American War (1898), during which the United States also emerged as a world naval power. Further territory had been acquired by the purchase of Alaska in 1867; the annexation of the Hawaiian Islands took place upon petition of its citizens in 1898. Puerto Rico and Guam were acquired during the Spanish-American War. Receipt of title to American Samoa was obtained by convention with Germany in 1899; the U.S. gained a perpetual lease of the Panama Canal Zone in 1904 and purchased the Virgin Islands from Denmark in 1917.

The U.S. was able to stay out of World War I until 1917. Then, allied with Britain, France, Italy, Belgium, Russia, and Japan, the U.S. helped defeat Germany, Austria, Bulgaria, and Turkey, and took an active part in the peace settlement at Versailles. However, isolationist forces at home blocked the U.S. entry into the League of Nations.

Again, when World War II broke out in Europe in 1939, the U.S. remained neutral, although she sent lend-lease supplies to the Allies. Finally, the Japanese bombing of Pearl Harbor on Dec. 7, 1941, led the U.S. to declare war on Japan, Germany, Italy, and the other Axis powers. The war against Japan was ended after the U.S dropped the first two atomic bombs on Hiroshima and Nagasaki. The United States was instrumental in helping form the United Nations in April, 1945, and after the war took an active part in the U.N. and its many agencies. She also extended aid for postwar recovery to the nations of western Europe under the Marshall Plan and joined the West in the North Atlantic Treaty Organization. The United States was granted a trusteeship over the Marshall, Caroline, and Marianas Islands by the United Nations in 1947. The last three comprise the Pacific Islands Trust Territory. The U.S. also holds Midway, Wake, and other small Pacific islands.

Although the country is almost completely self-sufficient for its food, and agriculture is one of the principal occupations in many parts of the U.S., the gross national income is derived largely from manufactures and commerce.

Commerce. Owing to its self-sufficiency in many areas, the United States has an enormous volume of domestic trade, that is, trade among the various parts of the country. Nevertheless, the United States depends upon other countries for certain commodities. It depends upon them also as markets for its vast amount of manufactured and processed goods and farm produce. Principal U.S. exports include machinery, automobiles and parts, iron and steel products, coal and coke, wheat and wheat flour, raw cotton, tobacco and tobacco products, cotton manufactures, copper and copper products, rubber and rubber goods, animal fats and oils, fruits and nuts, sawmill and other wood products, meat products, oil cake and oil cake meal, naval stores and resins, and leather and leather manufactures.

URUGUAY

Uruguay has an area of 72,172 square miles. The population is about 2,615,000. Uruguayans are largely of European descent, speak Spanish, and are devout Roman Catholics. Primary education is compulsory and free, and secondary education may also be had without charge. The constitution now in effect provides for a legislature of two houses, consisting of a Senate and a House of Representatives, both elected by the people for four years. The office of president was replaced by a nine-man Federal Council in 1952.

Uruguay has an excellent temperate climate. The southern and eastern half of the land is a low, rolling prairie leading to plateaus in the north and west. Though there are small deposits of silver, lead, copper, manganese and coal, mining is of minor importance. Sixty percent of the land is given over entirely to raising of livestock, another 20 percent to mixed stock and dirt farms, and only 7 percent wholly to agriculture. Grains, grapes, and tobacco are the principal crops. Animals and animal products constitute 95 percent of the export trade. Several good harbors, such as Montevideo, which is the capital and one of the three best known South American cities, facilitate coastal trade.

VATICAN CITY

In 1929 the Lateran Treaty between the Italian government and the Vatican gave the papacy full sovereign powers over an area of 109 acres within the city of Rome, as an independent papal state. Within the area are the Vatican Palace, Vatican gardens, basilica of St. Peter, Vatican Library, and other structures on the lower, walled-in elevation overlooking the Tiber. The city has a radio transmitting station and issues postage stamps, coins, and an official journal. Vatican Palace is the official residence of the pope, the spiritual ruler of the Roman Catholics of the world, numbering some 484,000,000. It takes its name from the hill of Rome on which it is situated. The Vatican Hill first became prominent in Christian history from the wide-spread and authoritative tradition that the martyrdom of St. Peter took place there. The basilica, built on the site of Emperor Constantine's basilica, was begun in 1506 under Pope Julius II. Raphael and Michelangelo are only two of the great artists who helped to make the edifice majestic and beautiful. The population of Vatican City is about 1,000.

VENEZUELA

Amicably seceding from Colombia in 1830, Venezuela became an independent republic. Its climate is tropical except where the altitude modifies the heat, and it is generally healthful. The southern and western borders of the country are mountainous, but much of it is composed of low coastal plains and the Orinoco basin. The area is 352,143 square miles. The population is about 5,950,000. There are mestizos, Indians, whites, Negroes, and mulattoes in Venezuela. Catholicism and the Spanish language are evidences of Spain's former extensive influence. Education is free and compulsory for children from the age of seven until completing elementary grades. The president of the republic is elected for a five-year term, but the two-house legislature, composed of a Senate and a Chamber of Deputies, is elected for four years. Caracas is the capital city, and other important towns are Maracaibo and Barquisimeto.

Venezuela has a vast supply of minerals, especially petroleum, gold, copper, magnesite, coal, sulfur, phosphate rock, iron, manganese, asbestos, and nickel, as well as extensive limestone deposits. Its great forests have scarcely been touched. About two-fifths of the people are engaged in agriculture, the chief crops being coffee, cacao, sugar cane, rice, cotton, corn, and beans. In some sections, sweet and white potatoes, yams, okra, peanuts, and cassava are also grown. Fruits cultivated are oranges, lemons, limes, bananas, figs, grapes, coconuts, pineapples, strawberries, plums, breadfruit, and mangoes. Cattle, sheep, goats, mules, hogs, and some horses are raised. Industries include textile mills, brick and cement plants, oil refineries, and small factories that produce items such as shoes, clothing, and furniture for domestic use. There are fisheries and pearl beds around the offshore islands of Margarita, Coche, and Cubagua.

VIETNAM

Situated in southeast Asia, Vietnam is bounded by China, Laos, Cambodia, and the South China Sea. Formerly part of French Indochina, it was stirred by a desire for freedom from colonial rule during World War II. Resistance centered in two groups, nationalists and the Communist-led Vietminh. France instituted limited autonomy, but the Vietminh refused to recognize the new government. Civil war broke out (1946), and after severe fighting the country was divided at the 17th parallel into North and South Vietnam (1954). Vietnam presents geographic extremes. In the far south it is fractured by the Mekong River delta, and the resulting fertile swampland is largely planted in rice. Hill country north of the delta runs about 600 miles, where it gives way to a coastal plain that merges into the Red River delta. Some of the mountains west of the plain exceed 10,000 feet.

South Vietnam has an area of 65,750 square miles and a population swollen by refugees from the north. The majority are Vietnamese, with Chinese, Cambodian, and French minorities. The northern highlands are populated by primitive Mon-Khmer tribes. Major religions are Taoism, Buddhism, and certain indigenous sects. Products include rice and rubber in the lowlands and tea, coffee, quinine, dyes, bamboo, raw silk, and cinnamon from the plateaus. Fishing is important. There are light industries such as chemicals, sugar derivatives, tobacco, and soap. Saigon, the capital, is an important port, serving Cambodia and part of Thailand.

North Vietnam has an area of 63,384 square miles. The bulk of the Vietnamese majority and Chinese minority is squeezed into the Red River delta and the coastal plain. The mountains are inhabited by numerous Thai and Miao-Yao tribes. Chief products are rice, coal, tea, coffee, corn, and vegetables. Fishing is important. North Vietnam's capital is Hanoi, which is linked by railroad to Saigon and other important cities.

YEMEN

Yemen, abandoned by the Turks in 1918, was recognized by treaty with Great Britain and India in 1934 as an independent kingdom ruled by Imam Yahya. It is an absolute monarchy, today ruled by Saif Al Islam Ahmad, son of Yahya, and was admitted to the United Nations in 1947. The country, anciently known as Sheba, kingdom of the biblical queen, lies at the southwest corner of the Arabian peninsula. Its area is 75,000 square miles. It has a population of approximately 22,000,000.

Inland Yemen is mountainous; its highest peak rises to 10,561 feet. In the mountains are plateaus and fertile valleys, where grains and coffee are grown, and here are found hot springs, sulfur deposits, and large groves of frankincense and almond trees. The lower, desert region is called the Tihama and is barren except for occasional oases.

The people are Arabs, and the ruling class are called Zaidis (Saiyids), of the Shiite sect of Islam. In other parts of the country are the Qabils and Sunni Moslems. Schools for boys are maintained in the cities. The chief cities are San'a, the capital, a walled city, Mocha and Hodeida (ports), and Sada, Taiz, Yarim, Ibb, and Manakha. Agriculture and stock raising are the principal occupations of the tribes, and in the cities are a few industries such as textile, clothing, and leather-goods factories. An unusually handsome filigree work in silver and gold is done by native craftsmen in forms of jewelry and other ornaments. Crops raised in the fertile sections are alfalfa, wheat, barley, millet, coffee, potatoes, kat, melons, and garden vegetables; fruits include grapes, oranges, lemons, limes, bananas, dates, figs, coconuts, and papayas. Livestock raised are cattle, sheep, goats, camels, and the famed horses of Arabian strain.

YUGOSLAVIA

The first shots of World War I were those of Austrian guns bombarding Belgrade, the capital of what was then Serbia. After this war Yugoslavia, composed of parts of the Austro-Hungarian Empire, Montenegro, and Serbia, became an independent kingdom of the Serbs, Croats, and Slovenes, governed by a hereditary king and a two-house legislature. This form of government continued until outbreak of World War II and German invasion in 1941, when the boy king fled and set up a government-in-exile in London. After defeat of Germany in 1945, Yugoslavia became the Federal People's Republic, and a new constitution and Communistic government was set up under the dictator, Marshal Tito, with a parliament of two chambers, the Federal Council and the Council of Producers. The peace treaty of 1947 with Italy gave Yugoslavia the greater part of the Italian province of Venezia Giulia, the commune of Zara, and the island of Pelagosa. A 20-year treaty of alliance between Yugoslavia, Turkey, and Greece was signed in 1954. The area of Yugoslavia is 99,069 square miles. Its population is about 17,800,000.

Three languages are recognized as official, Serbo-Croat, Slovene, and Macedonian. Serbo-Croat is the commonest. The Croats and Slovenes print in the Latin alphabet, but the Serbs and Macedonians use the Cyrillic alphabet. The chief cities are the capital Belgrade, Zagreb, Ljubljana, Sarajevo, and Subotica. Though there is no state religion, there are adherents of the Orthodox faith, Protestantism, Roman Catholicism, and Islam. Elementary education is free and compulsory.

A western mountain belt and the Danubian plain with hill country and valleys give Yugoslavia a climate like that of Italy. There are dense forests, deposits of coal, iron, copper, gold, lead, chrome, antimony, lignite, and bauxite. Grains, grapes, and livestock are the chief agricultural products, and manufacturing—flour mills, cement works, distilleries, textile factories, pottery, iron and carpet works, meatpacking plants, and paper mills—has developed rapidly. Exports consist of timber, lead, copper, tobacco, and meat. Yugoslavia broke with the Communist-bloc nations in 1948 to pursue an independent course.

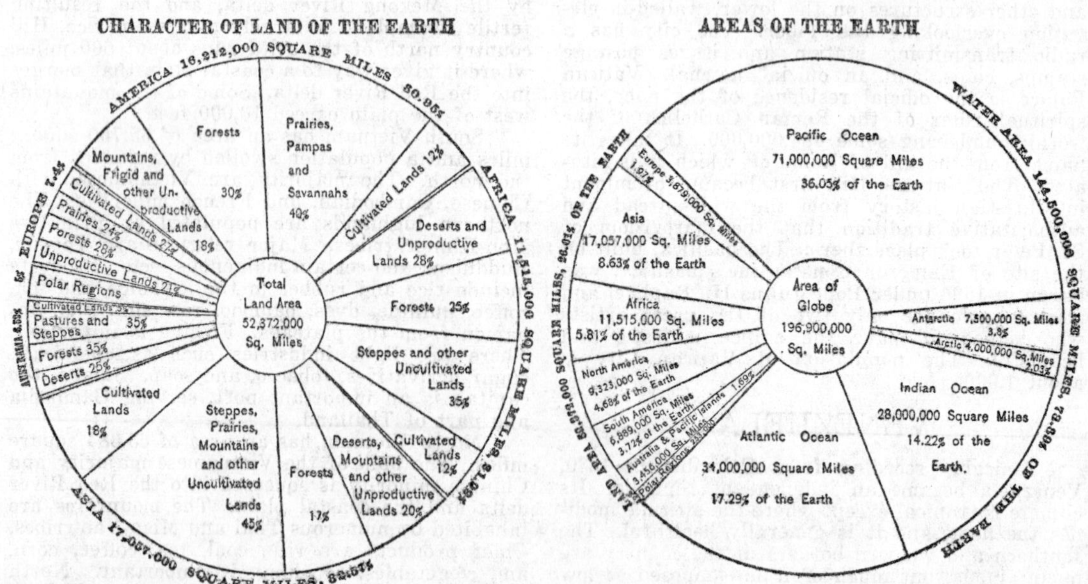

EARTH AND SOLAR SYSTEM

Elements of the Solar System

Planets	Distance from Sun in Miles Maximum	Distance from Sun in Miles Minimum	Period of Revolution in Days	Diameter in Miles	Density (Earth = 1)
Sun	—	—	—	864,392	0.26
Mercury	43,355,000	28,566,000	87.97	3,008	0.70
Venus	67,653,000	66,738,000	224.70	7,576	0.88
Earth	94,452,000	91,342,000	365.26	7,918	1.00
Mars	154,760,000	128,330,000	686.98	4,216	0.72
Jupiter	506,710,000	459,940,000	4,332.59	86,682	0.24
Saturn	935,570,000	836,700,000	10,759.20	72,332	0.13
Uranus	1,866,800,000	1,698,800,000	30,685.93	30,878	0.23
Neptune	2,817,400,000	2,769,600,000	60,187.64	32,932	0.29
Pluto	(average)	3,800,000,000	90,470.23	10,000	0.29

Dimensions of the Earth

Superficial area	196,950,000	sq. miles
Land surface	57,510,000	"
North America	8,500,000	"
South America	6,814,000	"
Europe	3,750,000	"
Asia	16,990,000	"
Africa	11,500,000	"
Australia	2,974,581	"
Water surface	139,440,000	"
Atlantic Ocean	31,505,000	"
Pacific Ocean	63,988,000	"
Indian Ocean	29,340,000	"
Arctic Ocean	5,541,600	"
Equatorial circumference	24,902	miles
Meridianal circumference	24,860	"
Polar circumference	24,859.76	"
Equatorial diameter	7,926.677	"
Polar diameter	7,899.988	"
Equatorial radius	3,963.34	"
Polar radius	3,949.99	"
Volume of the Earth	260,000,000,000	cubic miles
Mass, or weight	6,592,000,000,000,000,000,000	tons
Mean distance from the Sun	92,897,416	miles

The Moon, the only satellite of the Earth, from which her mean distance is 238,857 miles, occupies an average period in her revolution round the earth, of 29 days, 12 hours, 44 minutes, 5 seconds; her diameter is 2,160 miles, and her mean density 0.60.

TIME THROUGHOUT THE WORLD
AS COMPARED WITH TIME IN NEW YORK
A.M.
HONOLULU
A.M.
JUNEAU
A.M.
CHICAGO
A.M.
VALPARAISO
A.M.
DENVER
A.M.
SAN FRANCISCO
A.M.
MEXICO CITY
A.M.
BUENOS AIRES
A.M.
WINNIPEG
A.M.
WASHINGTON, D.C.
A.M.
WELLINGTON
P.M.
ROME
P.M.
MELBOURNE
A.M.
NEW YORK
P.M.
LONDON (Greenwich)
P.M.
CALCUTTA
P.M.
TOKYO
P.M.
MADRID
P.M.
ISTANBUL
P.M.
MOSCOW
P.M.
BOMBAY
P.M.
CAIRO
P.M.
CAPE TOWN
P.M.
PARIS
P.M.
BERLIN
P.M.
SHANGHAI
P.M.
MANILA
C.S.HAMMOND & Co. N.Y.

PAINTING ★ SCULPTURE ★ CHE
LITERATURE ★ ARCHITECTURE
KNOWLEDGE IS MAN
A. H. WINKLER